BIOGRAPHY AND GENEALOGY MASTER INDEX 1994

ISSN 0730-1316

Gale Biographical Index Series
Number 1

BIOGRAPHY AND GENEALOGY MASTER INDEX 1994

A consolidated index to more than 450,000 biographical sketches in over 95 current and retrospective biographical dictionaries

Barbara McNeil, Editor

Gale Research Inc. • DETROIT • WASHINGTON, D.C. • LONDON

Editor: Barbara McNeil
Contributing Editors: Miranda H. Ferrara, Amy L. Unterburger, Paula K. Woolverton
Associate Editors: Karen D. Kaus, Catherine A. Coulson, Terrance W. Peck
Assistant Editors: Aileen Collins, Julie K. Karmazin, Kelly L. Sprague
Senior Editor: Peter M. Gareffa

Manager, Technical Support Services: Theresa Rocklin
Programmer: Ida M. Wright

Data Entry Supervisor: Benita Spight
Data Entry Group Leader: Gwendolyn Tucker
Data Entry Associates: Nancy S. Jakubiak, Tara Yvette McKissack, Armenta Young

Production Director: Mary Beth Trimper
Production Assistant: Catherine Kemp

Art Director: Cynthia Baldwin
Desktop Publishers/Typesetters: C.J. Jonik, Nicholas Jakubiak

™ The paper used in this publication meets the minimum requirements of American National Standard for Information Sciences—Permanence Paper for Printed Library Materials. ANSI Z39.48-1984.

This book is printed on recycled paper that meets Environmental Protection Agency standards.

Library of Congress Catalog Number 82-15700
ISBN 0-8103-8002-1
ISSN 0730-1316

Printed in the United States of America

Published simultaneously in the United Kingdom
by Gale Research International Limited
(An affiliated company of Gale Research Inc.)

ITP™

The trademark **ITP** is used under license.

Advisory Board
For
Biography and Genealogy Master Index

The Gale Biographical Index Series

Biography and Genealogy Master Index
Second Edition, Supplements and Annual Volumes
(GBIS Number 1)

Children's Authors and Illustrators
Fourth Edition
(GBIS Number 2)

Author Biographies Master Index
Second Edition and Supplement
(GBIS Number 3)

Journalist Biographies Master Index
(GBIS Number 4)

Performing Arts Biography Master Index
Second Edition
(GBIS Number 5)

Writers for Young Adults: Biographies Master Index
Second Edition
(GBIS Number 6)

Historical Biographical Dictionaries Master Index
(GBIS Number 7)

Twentieth-Century Author Biographies Master Index
(GBIS Number 8)

Artist Biographies Master Index
(GBIS Number 9)

Business Biography Master Index
(GBIS Number 10)

Abridged Biography and Genealogy Master Index
(GBIS Number 11)

Contents

Introduction

Biography and Genealogy Master Index 1994 is the thirteenth in a series of annual updates to the *Biography and Genealogy Master Index (BGMI)* base volumes published in 1981. Containing more than 450,000 citations, *BGMI 1994* provides an index to 150 volumes and editions of over 95 biographical dictionaries, including new editions of sources previously indexed as well as new titles. With the publication of *BGMI 1994*, the total number of biographical sketches indexed by the *BGMI* base set and its thirteen updates exceeds 9,282,000. The chart at the conclusion of this introduction provides further details on *BGMI* publications already available and those planned for the future.

Concept and Scope

BGMI is a unique index that enables the user to determine which edition(s) of which publication to consult for biographical information. Almost as helpful, if there is no listing for a given individual in *BGMI* it reveals that there is no listing for that individual in any of the sources indexed. In cases where *BGMI* shows multiple listings for the same person, the user is able either to choose which source is the most convenient or to locate multiple sketches to compare and expand information furnished by a single listing.

Biographical sources indexed in *BGMI* are of several different types: 1) biographical dictionaries and who's whos, which supply information on a number of individuals; 2) subject encyclopedias, which include some biographical entries; 3) volumes of literary criticism, which may contain only a limited amount of biographical information but give critical surveys of a writer's works; and 4) indexes, which do not provide immediate information but refer the user to a body of information elsewhere. *BGMI* indexes only reference books containing multiple biographies; it does not index periodicals or books of biography about only one individual.

Sources indexed by *BGMI* cover both living and deceased persons from every field of activity and from all areas of the world. (Names from myth or legend and literary characters are not indexed.) The sources are predominantly current, readily available, "standard" reference books (for example, the Marquis Who's Who series); however, *BGMI* also includes important retrospective sources and general subject sources that cover both contemporary and noncontemporary people.

Although the majority of the sources indexed in *BGMI* covers individuals in the United States, this index also includes sources that cover individuals in foreign countries in such titles as *The Dictionary of National Biography* (Great Britain), *Dictionary of Canadian Biography,* and *Who's Who in the World.*

BGMI 1994, for example, indexes general works, both current and retrospective *(Biography Index, Contemporary Black Biography).* Also included are sources on special subject areas such as literature *(American Women Writers, Contemporary Authors, Spanish American Authors),* business *(Encyclopedia of American Business History and Biography; Standard and Poor's Register of Corporations, Directors and Executives),* music *(Baker's Biographical Dictionary of Musicians, Contemporary Musicians, Oxford Dictionary of Opera),* and law and politics *(Law & Business Directory of Corporate Counsel, Oxford Companion to the Supreme Court of the United States).* Other subject areas covered in *BGMI 1994* include art, anthropology and sociology, entertainment, ethnic and special interest groups, explorers, military, science, and sports.

How to Read a Citation

Each citation in *BGMI* gives the person's name followed by the years of birth and/or death as found in the source book. If a source has indicated that the dates may not be accurate, the questionable date(s) are preceded by a *c.* (circa) or followed by a question mark. When the source gives flourished dates rather than birth or death dates, this is indicated in *BGMI* by the abbreviation *fl.* Centuries are indicated with the

abbreviation *cent.* If there is no year of birth, the death date is preceded by a lower case *d.* The codes for the books indexed follow the dates.

Walsh, William 1512?-1577 *DcNaB*
Youll, Henry fl. c. 1600- *Baker 92*
Sokoine, Edward d1984 *NewYTBS 84*

References to names that are identical in spelling and dates have been consolidated under a single name and date entry, as in the example below for *Bernard Goodwin.* When a name appears in more than one edition or volume of an indexed work, the title code for the book is given only once and is followed by the various codes for the editions in which the name appears.

Goodwin, Bernard 1907- *IntMPA 81, -82, -84, WhoAm 80, -82, -84, WhoWor 82*

Another feature of the *BGMI* updates is the portrait indicator. If the source has a portrait or photograph of the person, this is indicated by the abbreviation *[port]* after the source code.

Daniel, C William 1925- *WhoCan 84 [port]*

A list of the works indexed in *BGMI 1994,* and the codes used to refer to them, is printed on the endsheets. Complete bibliographic citations to the titles indexed follow this introduction.

Editorial Practices

All names in an indexed work are included in *BGMI.* There is no need to consult the work itself if the name being researched is not found, since it is editorial policy to index every name in a particular book. Names that are not listed in the sources selected for indexing are not added to *BGMI.*

Many source books differ in their method of alphabetizing names; therefore, some names may have an alphabetic position in a source book different from their position in this index. Names are alphabetized in *BGMI* letter-by-letter.

John, Terry
Johncock, Gordon
John-Sandy, Rene Emanuel

Delasa, Jose M
De las Heras, Gonzalo
Delavigne, Casimir
De La Warr, Earl

Names appear in *BGMI* exactly as they are listed in the source books; no attempt has been made to determine whether names with similar spellings and dates refer to the same individual, or to add dates if they are known but are not listed in the source. With a file consisting of millions of names, it is not possible to edit each name thoroughly and still publish on a timely basis. Therefore, several listings for the same individual may sometimes be found:

Bellman, Richard 1920- *ConAu 12NR*
Bellman, Richard 1920-1984 *ConAu 112*
Bellman, Richard E 1920- *WhoAm 84*
Bellman, Richard Ernest 1920- *WhoFrS 84*

Despite the variations in the form of the name, it is apparent that the same person is referred to in the above citations. The existence of such variations can be of importance to anyone attempting to determine biographical details about an individual.

In a very few cases, extremely long names have been shortened because of typesetting limitations. For example: *Robertson, Alexander Thomas Parke Anthony Cecil* would be shortened to:

Robertson, Alexander Thomas Parke A

It is believed that such editing will not affect the usefulness of individual entries.

Research Aids

Researchers will need to look under all possible listings for a name, especially in the cases of:

1. Names with prefixes or suffixes:

   Angeles, Victoria De Los
   De Los Angeles, Victoria
   Los Angeles, Victoria De

2. Compound surnames which may be entered in sources under either part of the surname:

   Garcia Lorca, Federico
   Lorca, Federico Garcia

   Benary-Isbert, Margot
   Isbert, Margot Benary-

3. Chinese names which may be entered in sources in direct or inverted order:

   Chiang, Kai-Shek
   Kai-Shek, Chiang

   Or which may be listed by the Pinyin spelling:

   Hsiang, Chung-Hua
   Xiang, Zhonghua

4. Names transliterated in the sources from non-Roman alphabets:

   Amelko, Nikolai Nikolayevich
   Amelko, Nikolay Nikolayevich
   Amel'ko, Nikolay Nikolayevich

5. Pseudonyms, noms de plume, and stage names:

   Clemens, Samuel Langhorne
   Twain, Mark

   Crosby, Bing
   Crosby, Harry Lillis

6. Names which may be entered in the sources both under the full name and either initials or part of the name:

   Eliot, T S
   Eliot, Thomas Stearns

   Welles, George Orson
   Welles, Orson

To further aid research, cross-references are included in *BGMI* when significant biographical information on an individual is included within the biographical sketch of another person or group. For example, if information on Mike Love appears in a biographical dictionary under the entry for Brian Wilson, a cross-reference will appear in *BGMI:*

Love, Mike 1941- *See* Wilson, Brian 1942- *Baker 92*

In addition, all cross-references appearing in indexed publications have been retained in *BGMI* as regular citations, e.g., *Morris, Julian SEE West, Morris* would appear in *BGMI* as *Morris, Julian* followed by the source code.

Available in Electronic Formats

The data base used to create *BGMI* and its updates is also available in a microfiche edition called *Bio-Base,* on-line through DIALOG Information Services, Inc. as *Biography Master Index (BMI),* and on CD-ROM

as *BGMI CD-ROM*. The chart below outlines the relationships, in existing and future publications, between the *BGMI* hardcover annual updates and cumulations, and the microfiche, on-line, and CD-ROM formats. *BGMI* is also available for licensing on magnetic tape or diskette in a fielded format. Either the complete data base or a custom selection of entries may be ordered.

<table>
<tr><th>YEAR OF PUBLICATION</th><th colspan="2">HARDCOVER</th><th>MICROFICHE</th><th>ELECTRONIC</th></tr>
<tr><td>1980-81</td><td colspan="2">Biography and Genealogy Master Index, 2nd ed.</td><td rowspan="9"></td><td rowspan="15"><u>ON-LINE</u>
Entire data base is in DIALOG BMI File 287 (updated annually)

<u>CD-ROM</u>
Entire data base is available as BGMI CD-ROM (updated annually)</td></tr>
<tr><td>1982</td><td>BGMI 1981-82 Supplement</td><td rowspan="4">BGMI 1981-85 Cumulation</td></tr>
<tr><td>1983</td><td>BGMI 1983 Supplement</td></tr>
<tr><td>1984</td><td>BGMI 1984 Supplement</td></tr>
<tr><td>1985</td><td>BGMI 1985</td></tr>
<tr><td>1986</td><td>BGMI 1986</td><td rowspan="5">BGMI 1986-90 Cumulation</td></tr>
<tr><td>1987</td><td>BGMI 1987</td></tr>
<tr><td>1988</td><td>BGMI 1988</td></tr>
<tr><td>1989</td><td>BGMI 1989</td></tr>
<tr><td>1990</td><td>BGMI 1990</td><td>Bio-Base 1990 Master Cumulation (Supersedes all previous editions)</td></tr>
<tr><td>1991</td><td>BGMI 1991</td><td rowspan="5">BGMI 1991-95 Cumulation</td><td>Bio-Base 1991</td></tr>
<tr><td>1992</td><td>BGMI 1992</td><td>Bio-Base 1991-92</td></tr>
<tr><td>1993</td><td>BGMI 1993</td><td>Bio-Base 1991-93</td></tr>
<tr><td>1994</td><td>BGMI 1994</td><td>Bio-Base 1991-94</td></tr>
<tr><td>1995</td><td>BGMI 1995</td><td>Bio-Base 1995 Master Cumulation</td></tr>
</table>

Suggestions Are Welcome

Additional sources will be indexed in future publications as their availability and usefulness become known. The editor welcomes suggestions for additional works which could be indexed, or any other comments and suggestions.

Bibliographic Key to Source Codes

Code	Book Indexed
AfrAmBi	*African American Biographies.* Profiles of 558 current men and women. By Walter L. Hawkins. Jefferson, NC: McFarland & Co., 1992.
AmWomPl	*American Women Playwrights, 1900-1930.* A checklist. Compiled by Frances Diodato Bzowski. Bibliographies and Indexes in Women's Studies, no. 15. Westport, CT: Greenwood Press, 1992.
AmWomWr 92	*American Women Writers.* Diverse voices in prose since 1945. Edited by Eileen Barrett and Mary Cullinan. New York: St. Martin's Press, 1992. Use the Table of Contents to locate biographies.
AmWr S3	*American Writers.* A collection of literary biographies. Supplement III. Two parts. Edited by Lea Baechler and A. Walton Litz. New York: Charles Scribner's Sons, 1991.
AnObit 1991	*The Annual Obituary. 1991.* Edited by Deborah Andrews. Detroit: St. James Press, 1992. Use the "Alphabetical Index of Entrants" to locate biographies.
Au&Arts	*Authors & Artists for Young Adults.* Detroit: Gale Research, 1992-1993. ***Au&Arts 9*** Volume 9; 1992. ***Au&Arts 10*** Volume 10; 1993.
Baker 92	*Baker's Biographical Dictionary of Musicians.* Eighth edition. Revised by Nicolas Slonimsky. New York: Macmillan, 1992.
BiDAMSp 1989	*Biographical Dictionary of American Sports.* 1989-1992 supplement for baseball, football, basketball, and other sports. Edited by David L. Porter. Westport, CT: Greenwood Press, 1992. Use the Index to locate biographies.
BioIn 17	*Biography Index.* A cumulative index to biographical material in books and magazines. Volume 17: September 1990-August 1992. New York: H.W. Wilson, 1992.
BlkAmWO	*Black American Women in Olympic Track and Field.* A complete illustrated reference. By Michael D. Davis. Jefferson, NC: McFarland & Co., 1992.

BlkAuIl 92 — *Black Authors & Illustrators of Children's Books.* Second edition. By Barbara Rollock. Garland Reference Library of the Humanities, vol. 1316. New York: Garland Publishing, 1992.

BritWr S2 — *British Writers.* Supplement 2. George Stade, General Editor. New York: Charles Scribner's Sons, 1992.

ChlBIID — *Children's Book Illustration and Design.* Edited by Julie Cummins. Library of Applied Design. New York: PBC International, 1992. Distributed by Rizzoli International Publications, New York.

ChlFicS — *Children's Fiction Sourcebook.* A survey of children's books for 6-13 year olds. By Margaret Hobson, Jennifer Madden, and Ray Prytherch. Brookfield, VT: Ashgate Publishing Co., 1992.

ChlLR — *Children's Literature Review.* Excerpts from reviews, criticism, and commentary on books for children and young people. Detroit: Gale Research, 1992-1993.

ChlLR 27	Volume 27; 1992.
ChlLR 28	Volume 28; 1992.
ChlLR 29	Volume 29; 1993.

ClMLC — *Classical and Medieval Literature Criticism.* Excerpts from criticism of the works of world authors from classical antiquity through the fourteenth century, from the first appraisals to current evaluations. Detroit: Gale Research, 1993.

ClMLC 9	Volume 9.
ClMLC 10	Volume 10.

ColdWar — *The Cold War, 1945-1991.* Resources: chronology, history, concepts, events, organizations, bibliography, archives. Edited by Benjamin Frankel. Detroit: Gale Research, 1992.

ColdWar 1	Volume 1.
ColdWar 2	Volume 2.
ColdWar 3	Volume 3. Contains no biographies.

CmdGen 1991 — *Commanding Generals and Chiefs of Staff, 1775-1991.* Portraits & biographical sketches of the United States Army's Senior Officers. Revised edition, 1775-1991. By William Gardner Bell. Washington, DC: Center of Military History, United States Army, 1992.

Use the Index to locate biographies.

CngDr 91 — *Congressional Directory.* 102d Congress, 1991-1992. Washington, DC: United States Government Printing Office, 1991.

Use the "Name Index" beginning on page 1155 to locate biographies.

ConAu — *Contemporary Authors.* A bio-bibliographical guide to current writers in fiction, general nonfiction, poetry, journalism, drama, motion pictures, television, and other fields. Detroit: Gale Research, 1992-1993.

ConAu 136	Volume 136; 1992.
ConAu 137	Volume 137; 1992.
ConAu 138	Volume 138; 1993.
ConAu 139	Volume 139; 1993.

ConAu — *Contemporary Authors, Autobiography Series.* Detroit: Gale Research, 1992-1993.

ConAu 16AS	Volume 16; 1992.
ConAu 17AS	Volume 17; 1993.

ConAu *Contemporary Authors, New Revision Series.* A bio-bibliographical guide to current writers in fiction, general nonfiction, poetry, journalism, drama, motion pictures, television, and other fields. Detroit: Gale Research, 1992-1993.

ConAu 37NR	Volume 37; 1992.
ConAu 38NR	Volume 38; 1993.
ConAu 39NR	Volume 39; 1992.
ConAu 40NR	Volume 40; 1993.

ConBlB *Contemporary Black Biography.* Profiles from the international black community. Detroit: Gale Research, 1993.

ConBlB 3	Volume 3.
ConBlB 4	Volume 4.

ConEn *Contemporary Entrepreneurs.* Profiles of entrepreneurs and the businesses they started, representing 74 companies in 30 industries, including biographical information, the origin of the venture, revenues, how business growth was managed, business obstacles faced and how they were overcome, and personal perspectives on keys to success, future vision, and the lessons gleaned from experience. Edited by Craig E. Aronoff and John L. Ward. Detroit: Omnigraphics, 1992.

ConGAN *Contemporary Gay American Novelists.* A bio-bibliographical critical sourcebook. Edited by Emmanuel S. Nelson. Westport, CT: Greenwood Press, 1993.

ConHero 2 *Contemporary Heroes and Heroines.* Book II. Detroit: Gale Research, 1992.

ConLC *Contemporary Literary Criticism.* Excerpts from criticism of the works of today's novelists, poets, playwrights, short story writers, scriptwriters, and other creative writers. Detroit: Gale Research, 1992-1993.

ConLC 70	Volume 70: Yearbook 1991; 1992. Use the "Cumulative Author Index" to locate entries.
ConLC 71	Volume 71; 1992.
ConLC 72	Volume 72; 1992.
ConLC 73	Volume 73; 1993.
ConLC 74	Volume 74; 1993.
ConLC 75	Volume 75; 1993.

ConMus *Contemporary Musicians.* Profiles of the people in music. Detroit: Gale Research, 1993.

ConMus 8	Volume 8.
ConMus 9	Volume 9.

ConTFT 10 *Contemporary Theatre, Film, and Television.* A biographical guide featuring performers, directors, writers, producers, designers, managers, choreographers, technicians, composers, executives, dancers, and critics in the United States and Great Britain. Volume 10. Detroit: Gale Research, 1993.

CurBio 92 *Current Biography Yearbook. 1992.* Edited by Judith Graham. New York: H.W. Wilson Co., 1992.

CurBio 92N	Obituary section located in the back of the volume.

DcAmChF *Dictionary of American Children's Fiction.* Books of recognized merit. By Alethea K. Helbig and Agnes Regan Perkins. Westport, CT: Greenwood Press, 1986-1993.

DcAmChF 1960	*1960-1984* ; 1986.
DcAmChF 1985	*1985-1989* ; 1993.

DcChlFi — *Dictionary of Children's Fiction from Australia, Canada, India, New Zealand, and Selected African Countries.* Books of recognized merit. By Alethea K. Helbig and Agnes Regan Perkins. Westport, CT: Greenwood Press, 1992.

DcCPCAm — *The Dictionary of Contemporary Politics of Central America and the Caribbean.* Edited by Phil Gunson and Greg Chamberlain. New York: Simon & Schuster, 1991.

DcLB — *Dictionary of Literary Biography.* Detroit: Gale Research, 1992-1993.

DcLB 116	Volume 116: *British Romantic Novelists, 1789-1832.* Edited by Bradford K. Mudge; 1992.
DcLB 117	Volume 117: *Twentieth-Century Caribbean and Black African Writers.* First Series. Edited by Bernth Lindfors and Reinhard Sander; 1992.
DcLB 118	Volume 118: *Twentieth-Century German Dramatists, 1889-1918.* Edited by Wolfgang D. Elfe and James Hardin; 1992.
DcLB 119	Volume 119: *Nineteenth-Century French Fiction Writers: Romanticism and Realism, 1800-1860.* Edited by Catharine Savage Brosman; 1992.
DcLB 120	Volume 120: *American Poets since World War II.* Third Series. Edited by R.S. Gwynn; 1992.
DcLB 121	Volume 121: *Seventeenth-Century British Nondramatic Poets.* First Series. Edited by M. Thomas Hester; 1992.
DcLB 122	Volume 122: *Chicano Writers.* Second Series. Edited by Francisco A. Lomeli and Carl R. Shirley; 1992.
DcLB 123	Volume 123: *Nineteenth-Century French Fiction Writers: Naturalism and Beyond, 1860-1900.*; 1992.
DcLB 124	Volume 124: *Twentieth-Century German Dramatists, 1919-1992.* Edited by Wolfgang D. Elfe and James Hardin; 1992.
DcLB 125	Volume 125: *Twentieth-Century Caribbean and Black African Writers.* Second Series. Edited by Bernth Lindfors and Reinhard Sander; 1993.
DcLB 126	Volume 126: *Seventeenth-Century British Nondramatic Poets.* Second Series. Edited by M. Thomas Hester; 1993.
DcLB 127	Volume 127: *American Newspaper Publishers, 1950-1990.* Edited by Perry J. Ashley; 1993.
DcLB 128	Volume 128: *Twentieth-Century Italian Poets.* Second Series. Edited by Giovanna Wedel De Stasio, Glauco Cambon, and Antonio Illiano; 1993.

DcLB DS10 — *Dictionary of Literary Biography, Documentary Series.* An illustrated chronicle. Volume 10. Edited by Edward L. Bishop. Detroit: Gale Research, 1992.

Use the "Contents" to locate entries. This volume provides multiple essays for most of its subjects.

DcLB — *Dictionary of Literary Biography, Yearbook. 1992 Yearbook.* Edited by James W. Hipp. Detroit: Gale Research, 1993.

DcLB Y92	Use Table of Contents to locate entries.
DcLB Y92N	"Obituaries" section begins on page 286.

DcMexL — *Dictionary of Mexican Literature.* Edited by Eladio Cortes. Westport, CT: Greenwood Press, 1992.

DcTwHis *Dictionary of Twentieth-Century History, 1914-1990.* By Peter Teed. Oxford: Oxford University Press, 1992.

DrEEuF *Directory of Eastern European Film-Makers and Films, 1945-1991.* By Grzegorz Balski. Westport, CT: Greenwood Press, 1992.

DramC 3 *Drama Criticism.* Criticism of the most significant and widely studied dramatic works from all the world's literature. Volume 3. Detroit: Gale Research, 1993.

EncAACR *Encyclopedia of African-American Civil Rights.* From emancipation to the present. Edited by Charles D. Lowery and John F. Marszalek. Westport, CT: Greenwood Press, 1992.

EncABHB 8 *Encyclopedia of American Business History and Biography. The Airline Industry.* Edited by William M. Leary. New York: Facts on File, 1992.

Expl 93 *Explorers and Discoverers of the World.* First edition. Edited by Daniel B. Baker. Detroit: Gale Research, 1993.

Use the Table of Contents to locate biographies.

GayN *The Gay Nineties in America.* A cultural dictionary of the 1890s. By Robert L. Gale. Westport, CT: Greenwood Press, 1992.

HarEnMi *The Harper Encyclopedia of Military Biography.* First edition. By Trevor N. Dupuy, Curt Johnson, and David L. Bongard. New York: HarperCollins Publishers, 1992.

HispAmA *The Hispanic-American Almanac.* A reference work on Hispanics in the United States. By Nicolas Kanellos. Detroit: Gale Research, 1993.

Use the Index to locate biographies.

HolBB *Hollywood Baby Boomers.* By James Robert Parish and Don Stanke. New York: Garland Publishing, 1992.

IntDcAn *International Dictionary of Anthropologists.* Edited by Christopher Winters. Garland Reference Library of the Social Sciences, vol. 638. New York: Garland Publishing, 1991.

IntDcF 2-3 *International Dictionary of Films & Filmmakers.* Second edition. Volume 3: *Actors and Actresses.* Edited by Nicholas Thomas. Detroit: St. James Press, 1992.

IntDcOp *International Dictionary of Opera.* Two volumes. Edited by C. Steven LaRue. Detroit: St. James Press, 1993.

IntLitE *International Literature in English.* Essays on the major writers. Edited by Robert L. Ross. New York: Garland Publishing, 1991.

Use the Index to locate biographies.

IntvWPC 92 *Interviews with Writers of the Post-Colonial World.* Edited by Feroza Jussawalla and Reed Way Dasenbrock. Jackson, MS: University Press of Mississippi, 1992.

Use the Table of Contents to locate biographies.

JeAmFiW — *Jewish American Fiction Writers.* An annotated bibliography. By Gloria L. Cronin, Blaine H. Hall, and Connie Lamb. Garland Reference Library of the Humanities, vol. 972. New York: Garland Publishing, 1991.

JeAmHC — *Jewish-American History and Culture.* An encyclopedia. Edited by Jack Fischel and Sanford Pinkser. Garland Reference Library of the Social Sciences, vol. 429. New York: Garland Publishing, 1992.

JrnUS — *Journalists of the United States.* Biographical sketches of print and broadcast news shapers from the late 17th century to the present. By Robert B. Downs and Jane B. Downs. Jefferson, NC: McFarland & Co., 1991.

Law&B 92 — *Law & Business Directory of Corporate Counsel.* 1992-93 edition. Two volumes. Englewood Cliffs, NJ: Prentice Hall, Law & Business, 1992.

Use the "Corporate Individual Name Index," which begins on page I-95, to locate biographies.

LitC — *Literature Criticism from 1400 to 1800.* Excerpts from criticism of the works of fifteenth-, sixteenth-, seventeenth-, and eighteenth-century novelists, poets, playwrights, philosophers, and other creative writers, from the first published critical appraisals to current evaluations. Detroit: Gale Research, 1992-1993.

LitC 19	Volume 19; 1992.
LitC 20	Volume 20; 1993.
LitC 21	Volume 21; 1993.

MagSAmL — *Magill's Survey of American Literature.* Six volumes. Edited by Frank N. Magill. North Bellmore, NY: Marshall Cavendish, 1991.

MagSWL — *Magill's Survey of World Literature.* Six volumes. Edited by Frank N. Magill. North Bellmore, NY: Marshall Cavendish, 1993.

MajAI — *Major Authors and Illustrators for Children and Young Adults.* A selection of sketches from *Something about the Author.* Six volumes. Detroit: Gale Research, 1993.

MiSFD 9 — *Michael Singer's Film Directors.* A complete guide. Ninth international edition. Edited by Michael Singer. Los Angeles: Lone Eagle Publishing Co., 1992.

MiSFD 9N	The Obituary section begins on page 318.

ModArCr 3 — *Modern Arts Criticism.* A biographical and critical guide to painters, sculptors, photographers, and architects from the beginning of the modern era to the present. Volume 3. Detroit: Gale Research, 1993.

NewYTBS 92 — *New York Times Biographical Service.* A compilation of current biographical information of general interest. Volume 23, Numbers 1-12. Ann Arbor, MI: University Microfilms, 1992.

Use the annual Index to locate biographies.

News — *Newsmakers.* The people behind today's headlines. Detroit: Gale Research, 1992-1993.Issues prior to 1988, Issue 2, were published as *Contemporary Newsmakers.*

News 92	1992 Cumulation; 1992.
News 92-3	1992, Issue 3; 1992.
News 93-1	1993, Issue 1; 1993.
News 93-2	1993, Issue 2; 1993.

Use the "Cumulative Newsmaker Index" to locate entries. Biographies in each quarterly issue can also be located in the annual cumulation.

NinCLC *Nineteenth-Century Literature Criticism.* Excerpts from the criticism of the works of novelists, poets, playwrights, short story writers, philosophers, and other creative writers who died between 1800 and 1899, from the first published critical appraisals to current evaluations. Detroit: Gale Research, 1992-1993.

NinCLC 35	Volume 35; 1992.
NinCLC 36	Volume 36; 1992. Contains no biographies.
NinCLC 37	Volume 37; 1993.
NinCLC 38	Volume 38; 1993.
NinCLC 39	Volume 39; 1993.

NotHsAW 93 *Notable Hispanic American Women.* First edition. Detroit: Gale Research, 1993.

OxCSupC *The Oxford Companion to the Supreme Court of the United States.* Edited by Kermit L. Hall. New York: Oxford University Press, 1992.

OxDcByz *The Oxford Dictionary of Byzantium.* Three volumes. Edited by Alexander P. Kazhdan. New York: Oxford University Press, 1991.

OxDcOp *The Oxford Dictionary of Opera.* By John Warrack and Ewan West. Oxford: Oxford University Press, 1992.

PoeCrit *Poetry Criticism.* Excerpts from criticism of the works of the most significant and widely studied poets of world literature. Detroit: Gale Research, 1992-1993.

PoeCrit 5	Volume 5; 1992.
PoeCrit 6	Volume 6; 1993.

PolBiDi *Polish Biographical Dictionary.* Profiles of nearly 900 Poles who have made lasting contributions to world civilization. By Stanley S. Sokol and Sharon F. Mrotek Kissane. Wauconda, IL: Bolchazy-Carducci Publishers, 1992.

PolPar *Political Parties and Elections in the United States.* An encyclopedia. Two volumes. Edited by L. Sandy Maisel. Garland Reference Library of Social Science, vol. 498. New York: Garland Publishing, 1991.

QDrFCA 92 *Quinlan's Illustrated Directory of Film Comedy Actors.* By David Quinlan. New York: Henry Holt and Co., 1992.

ScF&FL 92 *Science Fiction & Fantasy Literature, 1975-1991.* A bibliography of science fiction, fantasy, and horror fiction books and nonfiction monographs. By Robert Reginald. Detroit: Gale Research, 1992.

ShSCr *Short Story Criticism.* Excerpts from criticism of the works of short fiction writers. Detroit: Gale Research, 1992.

ShSCr 10	Volume 10.
ShSCr 11	Volume 11.

SmATA *Something about the Author.* Facts and pictures about authors and illustrators of books for young people. Detroit: Gale Research, 1992-1993.

SmATA 69	Volume 69; 1992.
SmATA 70	Volume 70; 1993.
SmATA 71	Volume 71; 1993.
SmATA 72	Volume 72; 1993.
SmATA 73	Volume 73; 1993.

SmATA *Something about the Author, Autobiography Series.* Detroit: Gale Research, 1993.

SmATA 15AS	Volume 15.
SmATA 16AS	Volume 16.

SoulM *Soul Music A-Z.* By Hugh Gregory. London: Blandford, 1991. Distributed by Sterling Publishing Co., New York.

SpAmA *Spanish American Authors.* The twentieth century. By Angel Flores. New York: H.W. Wilson Co., 1992.

St&PR 93 *Standard & Poor's Register of Corporations, Directors & Executives.* 1993 edition. Volume 2: *Directors and Executives.* New York: Standard & Poor's Corp., 1993.

SweetSg *Sweethearts of the Sage.* Biographies and filmographies of 258 actresses appearing in Western movies. By Buck Rainey. Jefferson, NC: McFarland & Co., 1992.

SweetSg A	"The Pathfinders" section begins on page 2.
SweetSg B	"The Trailblazers" section begins on page 98.
SweetSg C	"The Pioneers" section begins on page 240.
SweetSg D	"The Homesteaders" section begins on page 466.

TwCLC *Twentieth-Century Literary Criticism.* Excerpts from criticism of the works of novelists, poets, playwrights, short story writers, and other creative writers who lived between 1900 and 1960, from the first published critical appraisals to current evaluations. Detroit: Gale Research, 1992-1993.

TwCLC 45	Volume 45; 1992.
TwCLC 46	Volume 46; 1992. Contains no biographies.
TwCLC 47	Volume 47; 1993.
TwCLC 48	Volume 48; 1993.

WhoAfr *Who's Who in Africa.* Leaders for the 1990s. By Alan Rake. Metuchen, NJ: Scarecrow Press, 1992.

Use the Index to locate biographies.

WhoAm 92 *Who's Who in America.* 47th edition, 1992-1993. Two volumes. New Providence, NJ: Marquis Who's Who, 1992.

WhoAmW 93 *Who's Who of American Women.* 18th edition, 1993-1994. New Providence, NJ: Marquis Who's Who, 1993.

WhoAsAP 91 *Who's Who in Asian and Australasian Politics.* First edition. London: Bowker-Saur, 1991.

WhoCanL 92 *Who's Who in Canadian Literature.* 1992-1993 edition. By Gordon Ripley and Anne Mercer. Teeswater, ON, Canada: Reference Press, 1992.

WhoE 93 *Who's Who in the East.* 24th edition, 1993-1994. New Providence, NJ: Marquis Who's Who, 1992.

WhoEmL 93 *Who's Who of Emerging Leaders.* Fourth edition, 1993-1994. New Providence, NJ: Marquis Who's Who, 1992.

WhoIns 93 *Who's Who in Insurance.* 1993 edition. Englewood, NJ: Underwriter Printing & Publishing Co., 1993.

WhoScE *Who's Who in Science in Europe.* A biographical guide in science, technology, agriculture, and medicine. Seventh edition. Essex, England: Longman Group UK, 1991. Distributed by Gale Research, Detroit.

- ***WhoScE 91-1*** Volume 1: *United Kingdom.*
- ***WhoScE 91-2*** Volume 2: *EC Countries A to F.*
- ***WhoScE 91-3*** Volume 3: *EC Countries G to Z.*
- ***WhoScE 91-4*** Volume 4: *Non-EC Countries.*

For volumes covering multiple countries, use the Table of Contents to locate appropriate section. This book often alphabetizes by titles of address, e.g., Dr., Mrs., and Sir.

WhoSSW 93 *Who's Who in the South and Southwest.* 23rd edition, 1993-1994. New Providence, NJ: Marquis Who's Who, 1993.

WhoUN 92 *Who's Who in the United Nations and Related Agencies.* Second edition. Edited by Stanley R. Greenfield. Detroit: Omnigraphics, 1992.

WhoWor 93 *Who's Who in the World.* 11th edition, 1993-1994. New Providence, NJ: Marquis Who's Who, 1992.

WhoWrEP 92 *Who's Who in Writers, Editors & Poets.* United States & Canada. Fourth edition, 1992-1993. Edited by Curt Johnson. Highland Park, IL: December Press, 1992.

WomChHR *Women Champions of Human Rights.* Eleven U.S. leaders of the twentieth century. By Moira Davison Reynolds. Jefferson, NC: McFarland & Co., 1991.

Use the Index to locate biographies.

WorLitC *World Literature Criticism.* 1500 to the present. A selection of major authors from Gale's Literary Criticism Series. Six volumes. Detroit: Gale Research, 1992.

BIOGRAPHY AND GENEALOGY MASTER INDEX 1994

A

2Pac
See Digital Underground *ConMus 9*
Aab, R.T. 1949- *St&PR 93*
Aaberg, Philip *BioIn 17*
Aaby, Andee Alesia 1955- *WhoEmL 93*
Aaby, Peter Emil Schepelern 1944- *WhoWor 93*
Aach, Allyn Jay 1933- *St&PR 93*
Aach-Feldman, Susan Regine 1951-1990 *BioIn 17*
Aadahl, Jorg 1937- *WhoAm 92*
Aadland, Donald Ingvald 1936- *WhoAm 92*
Aadland, Sophia Karla 1958- *WhoSSW 93*
Aagaard, George Nelson 1913- *WhoAm 92*
Aagard, Todd Allen 1961- *WhoEmL 93*
Aaker, David Allen *WhoAm 92*
Aaker, Mark *Law&B 92*
Aakhus, Patricia *ScF&FL 92*
Aakvaag, Asbjorn 1931- *WhoScE 91-4*
Aakvaag, T. *WhoScE 91-4*
Aalbersberg, W.I.J. *WhoScE 91-3*
Aall, Christian Bergengren 1955- *WhoWor 93*
Aalseth, Jack E. 1932- *St&PR 93*
Aalto, Alec M. 1942- *WhoUN 92*
Aalto, Alvar 1898-1976 *BioIn 17*
Aaltonen, Erkki 1910- *Baker 92*
Aalund, Ole 1930- *WhoScE 91-2*
Aamodt, Bjarne *WhoScE 91-4*
Aamodt, Donald *ScF&FL 92*
Aamodt, Nils-Godtfred 1926- *WhoScE 91-4*
Aamodt, Roger Louis 1941- *WhoAm 92*
Aamoth, William Lyle 1954- *WhoEmL 93*
Aanderud, Stephen Allen 1948- *St&PR 93*
Aanestad, Jonathan Robert 1954- *WhoWor 93*
Aanstoos, Christopher Michael 1952- *WhoSSW 93*
Aardal, Dan C. *Law&B 92*
Aardema, Verna *BioIn 17, ConAu 39NR*
Aardema, Verna 1911- *MajAI [port]*
Aarestad, James Harrison 1924- *WhoE 93*
Aario, Risto Tapani 1937- *WhoScE 91-4*
Aarland, Tor Leif 1957- *WhoWor 93*
Aarli, Johan A. 1936- *WhoScE 91-4*
Aarne, Els 1917- *Baker 92*
Aarnes, Halvor 1948- *WhoScE 91-4*
Aaron *BioIn 17, OxDcByz*
Aaron d1052 *Baker 92*
Aaron, Allen Harold 1932- *WhoAm 92*
Aaron, Anna 1931- *BioIn 17*
Aaron, Arthur Myron 1957- *WhoEmL 93*
Aaron, Benjamin 1915- *WhoAm 92*
Aaron, Betsy 1938- *ConAu 139, WhoAm 92*
Aaron, Bud 1927- *WhoWor 93*
Aaron, Chester 1923- *ConAu 38NR, MajAI [port], ScF&FL 92*
Aaron, Chloe Wellingham *WhoAm 92, WhoAmW 93*
Aaron, Christine Mary 1945- *WhoAmW 93*
Aaron, Daniel *BioIn 17*
Aaron, Debra M. *Law&B 92*
Aaron, Evalyn Wilhelmina *WhoE 93*
Aaron, Frank W., Jr. 1942- *WhoIns 93*
Aaron, Friedlieb Leslie 1936- *WhoAm 92*
Aaron, Gary Mel 1952- *WhoSSW 93*
Aaron, Hank 1934- *BioIn 17*
Aaron, Henry 1934- *WhoAm 92*
Aaron, Henry Jacob 1936- *WhoAm 92*
Aaron, Henry Louis 1934- *AfrAmBi*
Aaron, Herve *BioIn 17*
Aaron, Howard Berton 1939- *St&PR 93*
Aaron, Judith Glass 1951- *WhoE 93*
Aaron, M. Eugene 1944- *WhoE 93*
Aaron, M. Robert 1922- *WhoAm 92*
Aaron, Marcus, II 1929- *WhoAm 92*
Aaron, Neal C. 1940- *WhoIns 93*
Aaron, Patricia J. 1947- *St&PR 93*
Aaron, Paul *MiSFD 9, WhoAm 92*
Aaron, Pietro c. 1480-c. 1550 *Baker 92*
Aaron, Richard James 1930- *St&PR 93*
Aaron, Ronald 1935- *WhoE 93*
Aaron, Roy H. 1929- *St&PR 93*
Aaron, Roy Henry 1929- *WhoAm 92*
Aaron, Shirley Mae 1935- *WhoAmW 93*
Aaron, Truman Elwood 1930- *St&PR 93*
Aaronios *OxDcByz*
Aaronovitz, Ben *ScF&FL 92*
Aarons, Edward S. 1916-1975 *ScF&FL 92*
Aarons, Sherry A. *Law&B 92*
Aarons-Holder, Charmaine Michele 1959- *WhoEmL 93, WhoWor 93*
Aaronson, Allen G. 1926- *St&PR 93*
Aaronson, Arthur Lee 1946- *WhoEmL 93*
Aaronson, Howard Arnold, Jr. 1935- *St&PR 93*
Aaronson, Hubert Irving 1924- *WhoAm 92*
Aaronson, Lawrence 1941- *St&PR 93*
Aaronson, Paul R. *Law&B 92*
Aaronson, Robert H. 1955- *St&PR 93*
Aaronson, Robert Jay 1942- *WhoAm 92*
Aaronson, Stephen F. 1938- *St&PR 93*
Aaronson, Stuart J. 1944- *St&PR 93*
Aaronson, Victor Stephen 1941- *St&PR 93*
Aars, Harald 1930- *WhoScE 91-4*
Aars, Rallin James 1941- *WhoSSW 93*
Aarsleff, Hans *WhoAm 92*
Aartomaa, Tapani *BioIn 17*
Aarts, Christianus Josephus Maria 1919- *WhoWor 93*
Aarts, Joseph Evert Carolus Maria 1951- *WhoWor 93*
Aarvik, Egil 1912-1990 *BioIn 17*
Aase, Asbjorn *WhoScE 91-4*
Aase, Knut *WhoScE 91-4*
Aase, Mark Mitchell *Law&B 92*
Aasen, Lawrence Obert 1922- *WhoAm 92*
Aaseng, Nate *MajAI*
Aaseng, Nathan 1953- *MajAI [port]*
Aaslestad, Halvor Gunerius 1937- *WhoE 93*
Aastrup, Rondi Suzanne 1955- *WhoWrEP 92*
Aav, Evald 1900-1939 *Baker 92*
Aavik, Juhan 1884-1982 *Baker 92*
Abacha, Sanni *WhoWor 93*
Abaco, Evaristo Felice dall' 1675-1742 *Baker 92*
Abaco, Joseph Marie Clement dall' 1710?-1805 *Baker 92*
Abad, Diego Jose 1727-1779 *DcMexL*
Abad, Florencio B. 1954- *WhoAsAP 91*
Abad, Victoriano Alvin Santos 1964- *WhoWor 93*
Abad Granda, Gorky 1937- *WhoWor 93*
Abadi, Fritzie 1915- *WhoAm 92*
Abadie, Jean M. 1919- *WhoWor 93*
Abadie, Lloyd Joseph 1929- *St&PR 93, WhoAm 92*
Abadie-Brackin, Robelynn Hood 1950- *WhoEmL 93*
Abad-Rico, Juan Manuel 1945- *WhoWor 93*
Abady, Samuel Aaron 1954- *WhoEmL 93*
Abagi, Carole *Law&B 92*
Abahai 1592-1643 *HarEnMi*
Abair, C. Terry 1947- *St&PR 93*
Abajian, Henry Krikor 1909- *WhoWor 93*
Abajian, Vincent V. 1922- *St&PR 93*
Abajian, Wendy Elisse 1955- *WhoAmW 93*
Abakanowicz, Magdalena *BioIn 17*
Abakanowicz, Magdalena 1930- *NewYTBS 92 [port], PolBiDi, WhoWor 93*
Abal Khail, Muhammad-Ali 1935- *WhoWor 93*
Abany, Albert Charles 1921- *WhoE 93*
Abaray, Raymond F. 1932- *St&PR 93*
Abarbanel, Judith Edna 1956- *WhoAmW 93, WhoEmL 93*
Abarbanell, Gayola Havens 1939- *WhoAmW 93, WhoWor 93*
Abare, Bess Cox *Law&B 92*
Abas, Piet 1946- *WhoWor 93*
Abatai 1589-1646 *HarEnMi*
Abatay, Mehmet 1953- *WhoScE 91-4*
Abate, Abebe 1938- *WhoUN 92*
Abate, Andrew Anthony 1964- *St&PR 93*
Abate, Donna Jean 1956- *WhoAmW 93*
Abate, Edward J. 1949- *St&PR 93*
Abate, Joseph P. *Law&B 92*
Abatino, Elio 1933- *WhoScE 91-3*
Abaunza, Donald Richard 1945- *WhoSSW 93, WhoWor 93*
Abaya, Antonio M. 1934- *WhoAsAP 91*
Abaya, Gavino, Jr. 1935- *WhoUN 92*
Abazinge, Michael Dennis 1956- *WhoEmL 93*
Abbad, I d1042 *HarEnMi*
Abbad al-Mu'tadid, II d1069 *HarEnMi*
Abbad al-Mutamid, III d1095 *HarEnMi*
Abbadia, Natale 1792-1861 *Baker 92*
Abbado, Claudio 1933- *Baker 92, IntDcOp [port], OxDcOp, WhoAm 92, WhoWor 93*
Abbado, Marcello 1926- *Baker 92*
Abbagnaro, Louis Anthony 1942- *WhoAm 92*
Abbas *BioIn 17*
Abbas, II 1632?-1667 *HarEnMi*
Abbas, Abul *BioIn 17*
Abbas, Akmal Kamel *Law&B 92*
Abbas, Elizabeth Keutgen 1947- *WhoEmL 93*
Abbas, Ferhat 1899-1985 *BioIn 17*
Abbas, Syed Asghar 1946- *WhoWor 93*
Abbasi, Tariq Afzal 1946- *WhoWor 93*
Abbas Mirza 1783-1833 *HarEnMi*
Abbas the Great, I 1571-1629 *HarEnMi*
Abbatini, Antonio Maria c. 1597-c. 1679 *Baker 92*
Abbatini, Antonio Maria 1609?-1677? *OxDcOp*
Abbatucci, Jacques-Severin 1923- *WhoScE 91-2*
Abbe, Colman 1932- *WhoAm 92*
Abbe, Elfriede Martha *WhoAm 92*
Abbel, Robert Wilhelm 1933- *WhoWor 93*
Abbene, Michael 1936- *St&PR 93*
Abbensetts, Michael 1938- *ConAu 37NR*
Abberley, John J. 1916- *WhoAm 92*
Abbett, J. Conrad 1927- *St&PR 93*
Abbett, Rockford R. 1962- *St&PR 93*
Abbey, Edward 1927-1989 *BioIn 17, MagSAmL [port], ScF&FL 92*
Abbey, Edwin Austin 1852-1911 *BioIn 17*
Abbey, G. Marshall *Law&B 92*
Abbey, G. Marshall 1933- *St&PR 93*
Abbey, George Marshall 1933- *WhoAm 92*
Abbey, James Blades 1949- *WhoEmL 93*
Abbey, John 1785-1859 *Baker 92*
Abbey, Joseph Leo Seko 1940- *WhoAfr*
Abbey, Kirk Joseph 1949- *WhoSSW 93*
Abbey, Lloyd 1943- *ScF&FL 92, WhoCanL 92*
Abbey, Lynn 1948- *ScF&FL 92*
Abbey, Marilyn L. *ScF&FL 92*
Abbey, Richard S. 1950- *St&PR 93*
Abbey, Scott Gerson 1951- *WhoAm 92*
Abbink, F.J. *WhoScE 91-3*
Abbot, Anthony 1893-1952 *BioIn 17*
Abbot, Quincy Sewall 1932- *WhoAm 92*
Abbot, Willis J. 1863-1934 *JrnUS*
Abbott, Alfred Beaumont *BioIn 17*
Abbott, Alvin Arthur 1928- *WhoAm 92*
Abbott, Anthony John *WhoScE 91-1*
Abbott, Anthony John 1930-1991 *BioIn 17*
Abbott, Barry A. 1950- *WhoAm 92, WhoEmL 93*
Abbott, Bellamy Priest 1913- *WhoSSW 93*
Abbott, Benjamin Edward, Jr. 1928- *WhoWor 93*
Abbott, Berenice 1898-1991 *AnObit 1991, BioIn 17, ConAu 136, CurBio 92N*
Abbott, Betty Jane 1931- *WhoAm 92, WhoAmW 93*
Abbott, Bob 1932- *WhoAm 92*
Abbott, Bud *BioIn 17*
Abbott, Bud 1895-1974 *IntDcF 2-3 [port]*
Abbott, Bud 1895-1974 & Costello, Lou 1906-1959 *QDrFCA 92 [port]*
Abbott, Carl John 1944- *WhoAm 92*
Abbott, Charles Favour, Jr. 1937- *WhoWor 93*
Abbott, Charles Warren 1930- *WhoSSW 93*
Abbott, Christopher Cunningham 1956- *WhoE 93*
Abbott, David Henry 1936- *WhoAm 92*
Abbott, Douglas Eugene 1934- *WhoAm 92*
Abbott, Edith 1876-1957 *BioIn 17*
Abbott, Edward Leroy 1930- *St&PR 93, WhoAm 92*
Abbott, Eleanor Hallowell 1872-1958 *AmWomPl*
Abbott, Emma 1850-1891 *Baker 92, OxDcOp*
Abbott, Emory Reginald 1960- *WhoSSW 93*
Abbott, Ernest B. *Law&B 92*
Abbott, Ernest Monroe 1931- *WhoSSW 93*
Abbott, Ethelyn *AmWomPl*
Abbott, Forrest A. 1921- *St&PR 93*
Abbott, Frances Elizabeth Dowdle 1924- *WhoAmW 93*
Abbott, Frank Harry 1919- *WhoAm 92*
Abbott, Gayle Elizabeth 1954- *WhoEmL 93, WhoSSW 93*
Abbott, George *BioIn 17*
Abbott, George 1887- *MiSFD 9, WhoAm 92, WhoE 93*
Abbott, Gregory *SoulM*

Abbott, Gregory B. 1948- *St&PR 93*
Abbott, Henry Livermore 1842-1864 *BioIn 17*
Abbott, Herschel L., Jr. *Law&B 92*
Abbott, Ira Richmond, III 1950- *WhoE 93*
Abbott, Isabella Aiona 1919- *WhoAm 92*
Abbott, J. Carl 1946- *WhoAm 92*
Abbott, Jack Henry 1944- *BioIn 17*
Abbott, Jacquelyn M. *Law&B 92*
Abbott, Jacquelyn Meng 1951- *WhoEmL 93*
Abbott, James Anthony Jim 1967- *WhoAm 92*
Abbott, James Edward 1959- *WhoEmL 93*
Abbott, Jane Ludlow Drake 1881- *AmWomPl*
Abbott, Jim *BioIn 17, NewYTBS 92 [port]*
Abbott, Jim 1967- *ConHero 2 [port]*
Abbott, John B., Jr. 1956- *WhoWrEP 92*
Abbott, John Sheldon 1926- *WhoAm 92*
Abbott, Joseph 1937- *WhoE 93*
Abbott, Joseph C. 1929- *St&PR 93*
Abbott, Julian B. 1926-1990 *BioIn 17*
Abbott, Kathleen Marie *Law&B 92*
Abbott, Keith 1944- *ScF&FL 92*
Abbott, Keith George 1944- *WhoWrEP 92*
Abbott, Kenneth Wayne 1950- *WhoEmL 93, WhoSSW 93, WhoWrEP 92*
Abbott, Lee Kittredge 1947-1989 *WhoWrEP 92*
Abbott, Lyman 1835-1922 *BioIn 17*
Abbott, Manager Henry *MajAI*
Abbott, Mary Ann 1955- *WhoEmL 93*
Abbott, Mary Elaine 1922- *WhoAmW 93, WhoWor 93*
Abbott, Maxwell Todd 1946- *St&PR 93*
Abbott, Melanie Beth 1951- *WhoAmW 93*
Abbott, Michael Anthony 1952- *WhoSSW 93*
Abbott, Muriel Macpherson *WhoE 93*
Abbott, Philip *WhoAm 92*
Abbott, Preston H. *Law&B 92*
Abbott, Preston Sargent 1922- *WhoAm 92*
Abbott, R. Tucker 1919- *BioIn 17*
Abbott, R(obert) Tucker 1919- *ConAu 37NR*
Abbott, Ralph E. 1940- *St&PR 93*
Abbott, Rebecca Phillips 1950- *WhoAmW 93*
Abbott, Regina A. 1950- *WhoAmW 93*
Abbott, Richard C. 1946- *St&PR 93*
Abbott, Robert Alvin 1929- *WhoWrEP 92*
Abbott, Robert Carl 1955- *WhoEmL 93*
Abbott, Robert E. *BioIn 17*
Abbott, Robert Elliott 1946- *WhoEmL 93*
Abbott, Robert S. 1868-1940 *BioIn 17, EncAACR, JrnUS*
Abbott, Robert Tucker 1919- *BioIn 17, WhoAm 92, WhoWrEP 92*
Abbott, Rohn Dunseth 1943- *St&PR 93*
Abbott, Sarah *ConAu 38NR, MajAI*
Abbott, Scott 1949- *ConAu 138*
Abbott, Sharon S. 1957- *St&PR 93*
Abbott, Sharon Stoner *Law&B 92*
Abbott, Shirley *BioIn 17*
Abbott, Stanley Eugene 1942- *WhoAm 92*
Abbott, Steve 1943- *ConGAN*
Abbott, Steven R. 1947- *St&PR 93*
Abbott, Susan Alicia 1947- *WhoAmW 93, WhoEmL 93*
Abbott, Susan Marie 1956- *WhoAmW 93*
Abbott, Thomas Benjamin *WhoAm 92*
Abbott, Thomas Edward 1949- *WhoE 93*
Abbott, Vicky Lynn 1951- *WhoEmL 93*
Abbott, William Louis 1860-1936 *IntDcAn*
Abbott, William M. 1936- *WhoE 93*
Abbott, William Thomas 1938- *WhoSSW 93, WhoWor 93*
Abbott, Wilton Robert 1916- *WhoAm 92*
Abbott, Woodrow Acton 1919- *WhoAm 92, WhoWor 93*
Abbott, Zane Allen, Jr. 1964- *WhoEmL 93*
Abboud, A. Robert 1929- *St&PR 93*
Abboud, Alfred Robert 1929- *WhoAm 92, WhoSSW 93*
Abboud, Ann Creelman 1952- *WhoAm 92*
Abboud, Francois Mitry 1931- *WhoAm 92*
Abboud, G. Jason 1955- *WhoE 93, WhoEmL 93*
Abboud, Ibrahim 1900-1983 *DcTwHis*
Abboud, John Matthew 1942- *St&PR 93*
Abboud, Joseph 1950- *BioIn 17*
Abboud, Labeeb *Law&B 92*
Abboud, Margaret Mary 1963- *WhoAmW 93*
Abbrecht, Peter Herman 1930- *WhoAm 92, WhoE 93*
Abbrederis, Dale E. 1957- *St&PR 93*
Abbruzzese, Carlo 1944- *WhoScE 91-3*
Abbruzzese, Carlo Enrico 1923- *WhoWor 93*
Abbruzzese, Salvatore J. *Law&B 92*
'Abd al-'Aziz ibn Sa'ud 1880-1953 *BioIn 17, DcTwHis*
Abd al-Hadi, Awni 1889-1970 *DcTwHis*
Abdalian, Arbak Arshak 1920- *WhoAm 92*
Abd al-Ilah ibn Ali ibn Hussein 1913-1958 *DcTwHis*
Abd al-Krim 1881-1963 *DcTwHis*
Abdalla, Abdalla Ahmed 1933- *WhoWor 93*
Abdalla, Lawrence Hamadi 1954- *WhoEmL 93*
Abdallah 1882-1951 *BioIn 17*
Abdallah, John J. *Law&B 92*
Abdallah, Mahmoud M. 1948- *St&PR 93, WhoAm 92, WhoIns 93*
Abdallah, Michael Joseph 1952- *WhoIns 93*
Abd-Al-Malik 646-705 *HarEnMi, OxDcByz*
Abd-Al-Mu'min 1094-1163 *HarEnMi*
'Abd al-Qadir ibn Muhyi al-Din 1807?-1883 *BioIn 17*
Abdalyan, Ani M. *Law&B 92*
Abdela, Angelo Solomon 1942- *St&PR 93, WhoAm 92*
Abdel-Ghany, Mohamed 1940- *WhoAm 92*
Abd El-Hadi, Nabil Hussein 1935- *WhoUN 92*
Abdelhak, Sherif Samy 1946- *WhoAm 92*
Abdelhamid, Mohamed Salah 1944- *St&PR 93*
Abdel-Hamid, Tarek Kamal 1950- *WhoEmL 93*
Abdel Jaber, Tayseer M. 1940- *WhoUN 92*
Abd el-Kader 1807?-1883 *BioIn 17*
Abd-El-Kader 1808-1883 *HarEnMi*
Abdel-Khalik, Ahmed Rashad 1940- *WhoAm 92*
Abdel-Khalik, Said Ibrahim 1948- *WhoAm 92*
Abd-El-Krim 1881-1963 *HarEnMi*
Abdella, Joseph James 1935- *St&PR 93*
Abdella, Paul Albert 1943- *St&PR 93*
Abdellah, Faye Glenn 1919- *WhoAm 92, WhoAmW 93*
Abdel-Latif, Ata Abdel-hafez 1933- *WhoSSW 93*
Abdel Meguid, Ahmed Esmat 1923- *WhoWor 93*
Abdelmoneim, Mohamed Osman 1934- *WhoUN 92*
Abdelmoumene, M. *WhoScE 91-4*
Abdelmoumene, Mohamed 1937- *WhoUN 92*
Abdelnour, Ziad Khalil 1961- *WhoE 93, WhoEmL 93*
Abdel-Rahman, Aisha *WhoWor 93*
Abdelrahman, Talaat Ahmad Mohammad 1940- *WhoE 93, WhoWor 93*
Abdelsamad, Amin 1931- *WhoUN 92*
Abderholden, Susan 1954- *WhoEmL 93*
Abd Er-Rahman d732 *HarEnMi*
Abd-Er-Rahman, I 731-788 *HarEnMi*
Abd-Er-Rahman, II 788-852 *HarEnMi*
Abd-Er-Rahman, III 891-961 *HarEnMi*
Abd-Er-Rahman Khan 1844-1901 *HarEnMi*
Abdessalam, Belaid 1928- *WhoWor 93*
Abdi, Ali Issa 1945- *WhoUN 92*
Abdinaser, Abdalla 1932- *WhoUN 92*
'Abdisho' bar Berika d1318 *OxDcByz*
Abdnor, James 1923- *WhoAm 92*
Abdo, E.J. 1912- *St&PR 93*
Abdo, Joseph T. 1920- *St&PR 93*
Abdo, Lynda Lee 1955- *WhoEmL 93*
Abdo, Virginia Richie 1929- *WhoSSW 93*
Abdoo, Frederick F. 1919- *WhoIns 93*
Abdoo, Helen Theresa 1956- *WhoE 93*
Abdoo, Richard A. 1944- *St&PR 93, WhoAm 92*
Abdou, Ikram Escandar 1948- *WhoEmL 93*
Abdou, Moudi 1943- *WhoUN 92*
Abdou, Nabih I. 1934- *WhoAm 92*
Abdoulaye, Oiga 1945- *WhoUN 92*
Abdrasitov, Vadim 1945- *DrEEuF*
Abdul, Corinna Gay 1961- *WhoAmW 93, WhoWor 93*
Abdul, Paula *BioIn 17, WhoAm 92*
Abdul, Paula 1962- *WhoAmW 93*
Abdul, Raoul 1929- *BlkAuII 92*
Abdul Aziz bin Zakaria 1923- *BioIn 17*
Abdul Ghafar Bin Baba 1925- *WhoAsAP 91*
Abdul Ghaffar, Muhammad Abdulla 1949- *WhoUN 92*
Abdulghani, Sami M. R. 1955- *WhoWor 93*
Abdul Halim Mu'adzam Shah, Ibni Al-Marhu 1927- *WhoWor 93*
Abdul Halim Mu'adzam Shah Ibni Al-Marhum, Haji 1927- *WhoAsAP 91*
Abdul-Jabbar, Ahmed Khalil 1921- *WhoUN 92*
Abdul-Jabbar, Kareem 1947- *AfrAmBi, BioIn 17, ConAu 139, WhoAm 92*
Abdulla, Mohamed 1937- *WhoWor 93*
Abdullah, King of Jordan 1882-1951 *BioIn 17*
Abdullah, Gwen Harvey *BioIn 17*
Abdullah, Mohamed Ibrahim 1934- *WhoScE 91-4*
Abdullah, Mohammad Islam 1959- *WhoE 93*
Abdullah, Muhammad 1905-1982 *DcTwHis*
Abdullah, Syed Mohammad *WhoSSW 93*
Abdullah bin Ahmad, Dato' *WhoAsAP 91*
Abdullah Bin Mohd Salleh, Tan Sri 1926- *WhoWor 93*
Abdullah Et Taaisha 1846-1899 *HarEnMi*
Abdullah Fadzil bin Che Wan 1945- *WhoWor 93*
Abdullah ibn Hussein 1882-1951 *DcTwHis*
Abdullah Ibn-Zubayr d692 *HarEnMi*
Abdulla Khan d1598 *HarEnMi*
Abdul Latif, Ahmed Ali 1948- *WhoUN 92*
Abdul Malek Chua 1951- *WhoAsAP 91*
Abdul Qudus Ghurbandi, Comrade 1933- *WhoAsAP 91*
Abdul-Rahmad, Mahdi 1942- *BiDAMSp 1989*
Abdul Rahman 1903-1990 *BioIn 17*
Abdul Rahman, Sadiq 1936- *BioIn 17*
Abdul Rahman Bin Haji Sulaiman 1941- *WhoAsAP 91*
Abdulshafi, Osama A. 1950- *WhoAm 92*
Abdurazakov, Ubaydulla 1932- *WhoWor 93*
Abe, Akihiro 1934- *WhoWor 93*
Abe, Christopher Columbus 1954- *WhoAsAP 91*
Abe, Fumio 1922- *WhoAsAP 91*
Abe, Hiroaki 1889-1949 *HarEnMi*
Abe, Kazuhiko 1933- *WhoWor 93*
Abe, Kobo 1924- *BioIn 17, ScF&FL 92, WhoWor 93*
Abe, Komei 1911- *Baker 92*
Abe, Masahiko 1947- *WhoWor 93*
Abe, Masami 1932- *WhoWor 93*
Abe, Mikio 1919- *WhoAsAP 91*
Abe, Mitsuyuki 1932- *WhoWor 93*
Abe, Noruyuki 1875-1953 *HarEnMi*
Abe, Shintaro *BioIn 17*
Abe, Shintaro 1924- *WhoAsAP 91*
Abe, Shintaro 1924-1991 *AnObit 1991*
Abe, Shogo 1938- *WhoAsAP 91*
Abe, Yoshiaki 1939- *WhoUN 92*
Abe, Yoshihiro 1935- *WhoWor 93*
Abe, Youichi 1941- *WhoWor 93*
Abecassis, George 1913-1991 *AnObit 1991*
Abee, Rose Rooney 1959- *WhoSSW 93*
Abeel, John Nelson 1769-1812 *BioIn 17*
Abegg, Martin G. 1925- *WhoAm 92*
Abehassera, Jean Pierre 1947- *WhoWor 93*
Abeille, Johann Christian Ludwig 1761-1838 *Baker 92*
Abejo, Rosalina 1922- *Baker 92*
Abel *BioIn 17*
Abel, Andrew Bruce 1952- *WhoAm 92, WhoEmL 93*
Abel, Arend Jesse 1960- *WhoEmL 93*
Abel, Barbara *AmWomPl*
Abel, Brent Maxwell 1916- *WhoAm 92*
Abel, Carl Friedrich 1723-1787 *Baker 92*
Abel, Carlos Alberto 1930- *HispAmA, WhoAm 92*
Abel, Clarence John 1900-1964 *BiDAMSp 1989*
Abel, Corinne Prevost d1991 *BioIn 17*
Abel, Douglas Stewart *Law&B 92*
Abel, Edward William *WhoScE 91-1*
Abel, Elie 1920- *WhoAm 92*
Abel, Eric William *WhoScE 91-1*
Abel, Ernest Lawrence 1943- *WhoWrEP 92*
Abel, Florence Catherine Harris 1941- *WhoAmW 93*
Abel, Francis Lee 1931- *WhoAm 92*
Abel, Fred Herman 1936- *WhoE 93*
Abel, Gary V. 1953- *St&PR 93*
Abel, George H., II *Law&B 92*
Abel, Hans Heinrich 1928- *WhoScE 91-3*
Abel, Harold 1926- *WhoAm 92*
Abel, Hazel Hempel 1888-1966 *BioIn 17*
Abel, James Joseph 1946- *St&PR 93*
Abel, Mark Martin 1960- *St&PR 93*
Abel, Mary Ellen Kathryn 1949- *WhoAmW 93*
Abel, Mati 1942- *WhoWor 93*
Abel, Michael L. 1952- *WhoEmL 93, WhoWor 93*
Abel, Nancy S. 1933- *St&PR 93*
Abel, Paul E. *Law&B 92*
Abel, Paul Edward 1953- *WhoEmL 93*
Abel, Peter Mead *Law&B 92*
Abel, Reuben 1911- *WhoAm 92*
Abel, Robert Allen 1958- *WhoEmL 93*
Abel, Robert Berger 1926- *WhoAm 92*
Abel, Robert H(alsall) 1941- *ConAu 37NR*
Abel, Robert Halsall 1941- *WhoWrEP 92*
Abel, Robert J. 1937- *MiSFD 9*
Abel, Rudolf I. 1902-1971 *BioIn 17*
Abel, Rudolph 1936- *St&PR 93*
Abel, Sherry Goldman d1992 *BioIn 17, NewYTBS 92*
Abel, Ulrich Rainer 1952- *WhoWor 93*
Abel, Vernon T. *St&PR 93*
Abel, William Luther 1942- *St&PR 93*
Abel, Wolfgang Othenio 1932- *WhoScE 91-3*
Abelard, Peter 1079-1142 *BioIn 17*
Abel-Christian, Stacey Lynn 1960- *WhoEmL 93*
Abele, Homer E. 1916- *WhoAm 92*
Abele, Lawrence Gordon 1946- *WhoSSW 93*
Abele, Robert Christopher 1958- *WhoEmL 93*
Abeles, Charles Calvert 1929- *WhoAm 92*
Abeles, Daniel C. *Law&B 92*
Abeles, James David 1916- *WhoAm 92*
Abeles, Joseph 1907-1991 *BioIn 17*
Abeles, Joseph Charles 1915- *St&PR 93, WhoAm 92*
Abeles, Joseph Hy 1955- *WhoE 93*
Abeles, Kelly Ann 1961- *WhoEmL 93*
Abeles, Linda 1959- *WhoAmW 93, WhoSSW 93*
Abeles, Robert Heinz 1926- *WhoAm 92*
Abeles, Sigmund M. 1934- *WhoAm 92*
Abeles, Theodore Lillien 1934- *WhoAm 92*
Abel-Grippo, Julie Jacelyn 1961- *WhoAmW 93*
Abelite, Jahnis John 1950- *WhoEmL 93*
Abell, Arthur M. 1868-1958 *Baker 92*
Abell, Arunah 1806-1888 *JrnUS*
Abell, Arunah Shepherdson 1806-1888 *BioIn 17*
Abell, Creed W. 1934- *WhoAm 92*
Abell, David Robert 1934- *WhoAm 92*
Abell, Erwin Marshall 1962- *WhoEmL 93*
Abell, Jerrold J. 1934- *St&PR 93*
Abell, John 1652-1724 *Baker 92*
Abell, Lawrence Carlisle 1941- *WhoAm 92*
Abell, Millicent Demmin 1934- *WhoAm 92, WhoE 93*
Abell, Murray Richardson 1920- *WhoAm 92*
Abell, Paul Irving 1923- *WhoAm 92*
Abell, Richard Bender 1943- *WhoAm 92, WhoE 93, WhoSSW 93, WhoWor 93*
Abell, Richard Gurley 1904- *WhoE 93*
Abell, Richard S. 1935- *St&PR 93*
Abell, Steven 1945- *WhoAm 92*
Abell, Thomas Henry 1909- *WhoAm 92*
Abell, William F. *Law&B 92*
Abell, William Frederick 1947- *St&PR 93*
Abella, Alex 1950- *ScF&FL 92*
Abella, Jack M. *Law&B 92*
Abella, Maria Ligaya 1950- *WhoAmW 93*
Abella, Marisela Carlota 1943- *WhoAmW 93, WhoWor 93*
Abella, Remedios Claro 1950- *WhoWor 93*
Abella, Rosalie S. *BioIn 17*
Abellanas, Pedro 1914- *WhoWor 93*
Abelli, Luigi 1957- *WhoWor 93*
Abello, Anna *BioIn 17*
Abello, Juan *BioIn 17*
Abello-Virgili, Joaquim 1935- *WhoWor 93*
Abeln-Touhey, Maura J. *Law&B 92*
Abelov, Stephen L. 1923- *St&PR 93*
Abelov, Stephen Lawrence 1923- *WhoAm 92*
Abels, Bruce Arthur 1953- *WhoEmL 93*
Abels, Doris Holloway 1925- *WhoE 93*
Abels, Herbert 1941- *WhoWor 93*
Abels, Joann Carla 1952- *WhoEmL 93*
Abels, Paul M. d1992 *BioIn 17, NewYTBS 92 [port]*
Abelson, Alan 1925- *ConAu 136, WhoAm 92, WhoE 93*
Abelson, Elias 1932- *WhoE 93*
Abelson, Herbert Traub 1941- *WhoAm 92*
Abelson, Jack Irwin 1946- *St&PR 93*
Abelson, Jeffrey Allen 1949- *WhoEmL 93*
Abelson, Jeremy John *Law&B 92*
Abelson, Philip Hauge 1913- *WhoAm 92*
Abelson, Robert Paul 1928- *WhoAm 92*
Abelt, Ralph William 1929- *WhoAm 92*
Abely, Joseph F. 1929- *St&PR 93*
Abend, Martin *BioIn 17*
Abend, Renee Irene 1953- *WhoAmW 93*
Abend, Serge *Law&B 92*
Abend, Sheldon 1929- *WhoWrEP 92*
Abend, Stephen Neil 1939- *WhoAm 92*
Abendroth, Hermann 1883-1956 *Baker 92*
Abendroth, Walter 1896-1973 *Baker 92*
Abeng, Tanri *BioIn 17*
Aber, Adolf 1893-1960 *Baker 92*
Aber, John David 1949- *WhoEmL 93*
Aber, Marvin 1936- *St&PR 93*
Aber, Stanley Irwin 1939- *WhoE 93*
Aber, William Thomas 1935- *St&PR 93*
Aberbach, Joachim Jean d1992 *BioIn 17, NewYTBS 92*
Aberbach, Joel D(avid) 1940- *WhoWrEP 92*
Aberback, Darya *Law&B 92*

Aberconway, Charles Melville McLaren 1913- WhoWor 93
Abercrombie, James 1706-1781 HarEnMi
Abercrombie, Josephine BioIn 17
Abercrombie, Neil 1938- CngDr 91, WhoAm 92
Abercrombie, Nora 1960- ScF&FL 92
Abercrombie, Stanley 1935- WhoAm 92
Abercromby, Ralph 1734-1801 HarEnMi
Abercrumbie, P. Eric AfrAmBi
Abere, Andrew Evan 1961- WhoAm 92, WhoE 93, WhoEmL 93
Aberg, Hans E. 1934- WhoScE 91-4
Abergel, Frederic 1963- WhoWor 93
Aberhart, William 1878-1943 BioIn 17
Aberle, David Friend 1918- WhoAm 92
Abernathy, Barbara Eubanks 1963- WhoAmW 93, WhoSSW 93
Abernathy, Blair 1962- St&PR 93
Abernathy, Bobby Franklin 1933- St&PR 93
Abernathy, Charles C., Jr. 1934- St&PR 93
Abernathy, David M(yles) 1933- ConAu 37NR
Abernathy, David Paul Law&B 92
Abernathy, Donad Kendrick 1937- WhoSSW 93
Abernathy, Frederick H. 1930- WhoAm 92
Abernathy, Jack Harvey 1911- WhoAm 92, WhoWor 93
Abernathy, James Logan 1941- WhoAm 92, WhoWor 93
Abernathy, Joseph Duncan 1944- WhoAm 92
Abernathy, Lewis MiSFD 9
Abernathy, Ralph D. BioIn 17
Abernathy, Ralph David 1926-1990 AfrAmBi
Abernathy, Ralph David, Sr. 1926-1990 EncAACR
Abernathy, Robert L. 1931- St&PR 93
Abernathy, Robert Noel 1952- WhoEmL 93
Abernathy, Vicki Marie 1949- WhoEmL 93
Abernathy, William J(ackson) 1933-1983 ConAu 37NR
Abernathy, William R. 1925- St&PR 93
Abernethy, David Ford 1958- WhoEmL 93
Abernethy, Durant Stewart, III Law&B 92
Abernethy, George Lawrence 1910- WhoAm 92
Abernethy, Irene Margaret 1924- WhoAmW 93
Abernethy, James Arthur 1920- St&PR 93
Abernethy, Rita M. Law&B 92
Abernethy, Ronald Bruce 1948- St&PR 93
Abernethy, Thomas A. St&PR 93
Abernethy, Virginia Deane 1934- WhoSSW 93
Abers, Julia Ellen Law&B 92
Abersfeller, Heinz Andrew 1920- WhoAm 92
Aberson, Leslie Donald 1936- WhoAm 92
Abert, Anna Amalie 1906- Baker 92
Abert, Hermann 1871-1927 Baker 92
Abert, Johann Joseph 1832-1915 Baker 92
Abert, Karl J. Law&B 92
Abetti, Pier Antonio 1921- WhoAm 92
Abetz, Peter 1926- WhoScE 91-3
Abeyesundere, Nihal Anton Aelian 1932- WhoUN 92, WhoWor 93
Abeyratne, Ruwantissa Indranath Ramya 1951- WhoWor 93
Abeysundara, Urugamuwe Gamacharige Yasan 1964- WhoWor 93
Abeyta, Elizabeth 1954- BioIn 17
Abgarian, Robert 1928- St&PR 93
Abhau, William Conrad 1912- WhoAm 92
ab Hugh, Dafydd 1960- ScF&FL 92
Abhyankar, Shreeram S. 1930- WhoAm 92
Abicht, Walter 1934- WhoScE 91-3
Abidi, Syed Kazim Husain 1939- WhoWor 93
Abiko, Takashi 1941- WhoWor 93
Abikoff, William 1944- WhoE 93
Abildskov, J. A. 1923- WhoAm 92
Abilheira, Richard B. 1949- WhoEmL 93
Abines, Crisologo A. 1943- WhoAsAP 91
Abiodun, Adigun Ade 1939- WhoUN 92
Abiola, Moshood Kashimawo Olawale 1937- WhoAfr
Abiri, Mohammed 1933- WhoE 93
Abis, Bernardo Fajardo 1962- WhoWor 93
Abish, Cecile WhoAm 92
Abish, Walter 1931- ConAu 37NR, JeAmFiW
Abita, Jean-Pierre WhoScE 91-2
Abita, Jean-Pierre 1941- WhoScE 91-2
Abitanta, Frances Cerchiaro WhoAmW 93
Abitz, Kenneth G. 1952- St&PR 93
Abkarian, Edward 1951- WhoE 93
Abkowitz, Miles A. 1957- St&PR 93
Abkowitz, Stanley 1927- St&PR 93
Abla, Vern W. 1943- St&PR 93
Ablabius OxDcByz
Ablahat, Newton Andre 1914- St&PR 93
Ablan, Francis Adiarte 1928- WhoWor 93
Ablan, Roque R., Jr. 1932- WhoAsAP 91
Ablard, Charles David WhoAm 92
Able, Edward H. BioIn 17, WhoAm 92
Able, W. Walter 1932- St&PR 93
Able, Warren Walter 1932- WhoAm 92
Abler, David Gerard 1960- WhoEmL 93
Abler, Ronald Francis 1939- WhoAm 92
Ables, Clinton E. Law&B 92
Ables, Nancy Bumstead 1948- WhoAmW 93
Ablin, Richard Joel 1940- WhoAm 92
Ablon, Arnold Norman 1921- WhoSSW 93, WhoWor 93
Ablon, Carl S. 1918- St&PR 93
Ablon, R. Richard WhoAm 92
Ablon, R. Richard 1949- St&PR 93
Ablon, Ralph E. 1916- St&PR 93, WhoAm 92
Ablow, Joseph 1928- WhoE 93
Ablow, Keith Russell 1961- WhoEmL 93
Ablowitz, Enid M. 1948- WhoAmW 93
Abnee, A. Victor 1923- WhoAm 92
Abner, Ewart SoulM
Abney, Bill Hartley Law&B 92
Abney, Bobbie Jean 1933- WhoAmW 93
Abney, Frederick Sherwood 1919- WhoAm 92
Abney, Glenda May 1963- WhoAmW 93
Abney, Lucille Allen 1946- WhoAmW 93
Abney, Ray Chandler 1947- WhoE 93
Abo, Ronald Kent 1946- WhoEmL 93
Aboff, Sheldon Jay 1947- St&PR 93, WhoAm 92, WhoWor 93
Aboimov, Ivan Pavlovich 1936- WhoWor 93
Aboites, Vicente 1958- WhoWor 93
Abokhair, John K. Law&B 92
Abokor, Ali Ismail 1940- WhoAfr
Abolafia, Yossi 1944- BioIn 17
Abolins, Maris Arvids 1938- WhoAm 92
Abolins, Peter Law&B 92
Aboobaker-Labauge, Fawzia Hassam 1946- WhoUN 92
Abood, Leo George 1922- WhoAm 92
Abood, Robert George 1961- WhoEmL 93
Aboody, Albert Victor 1947- WhoAm 92
Aborn, Foster L. 1934- St&PR 93
Aborn, Foster Litchfield 1934- WhoAm 92
Abos, Girolamo 1715-1760 Baker 92, OxDcOp
Abotteen, Rasim Abdul-Hafiz 1950- WhoSSW 93
Abouaf, Luce 1940- WhoScE 91-2
Abouchakra, Ghazi 1936- WhoUN 92
Abouchar, John W. 1929- St&PR 93
Abou-Haidar, Nabil Ibrahim 1958- WhoWor 93
Abou Samra, Abdul Badi 1954- WhoScE 91-2
Abouseif, Ayman Adib 1960- WhoWor 93
Aboussie, Marilyn 1948- WhoEmL 93
Aboutalybov, Ramiz 1937- WhoUN 92
Abowd, Anthony Michael 1953- WhoEmL 93
Abowd, George T. 1932- St&PR 93
Abplanalp, Glen Harold 1914- WhoAm 92
Abragam, Anatole 1914- WhoWor 93
Abraha d570 HarEnMi
Abraha fl. 535-558 OxDcByz
Abraham BioIn 17
Abraham, Abram Kenneth 1951- WhoE 93
Abraham, Albert David 1924- WhoWor 93
Abraham, Andrew 1958- WhoEmL 93
Abraham, Carl Joel 1937- WhoE 93, WhoWor 93
Abraham, Claude 1931- WhoWor 93
Abraham, Eileen Mary 1949- WhoEmL 93
Abraham, F. Murray BioIn 17
Abraham, Fahrid Murray 1939- WhoAm 92
Abraham, George 1918- WhoAm 92
Abraham, George David, Jr. 1948- WhoSSW 93
Abraham, George G. 1906- WhoAm 92
Abraham, Gerald 1904-1988 Baker 92
Abraham, Harry J. 1938- St&PR 93
Abraham, Henry Julian 1921- WhoAm 92
Abraham, Herard 1940- DcCPCAm
Abraham, Irene 1946- WhoAm 92, WhoEmL 93
Abraham, Jacob A. 1948- WhoAm 92
Abraham, Jean 1929- WhoScE 91-2
Abraham, John 1956- WhoE 93
Abraham, John A. St&PR 93
Abraham, Joseph Paul Law&B 92
Abraham, Katharine Gail 1954- WhoEmL 93
Abraham, Kathy BioIn 17
Abraham, Kenneth Samuel 1946- WhoAm 92, WhoEmL 93
Abraham, Laurie 1957- WhoEmL 93
Abraham, Lawrence Dagger 1949- WhoEmL 93
Abraham, Marvin Meyer 1930- WhoSSW 93
Abraham, Max 1831-1900 Baker 92
Abraham, Nathan Samuel 1946- WhoEmL 93
Abraham, Nicholas Albert 1941- WhoAm 92, WhoE 93
Abraham, Otto 1872-1926 Baker 92
Abraham, Patricia Sisson 1954- WhoEmL 93, WhoSSW 93
Abraham, Paul 1892-1960 Baker 92, OxDcOp
Abraham, Raymond John WhoScE 91-1
Abraham, Richard Kenneth 1955- WhoEmL 93
Abraham, Rita Betty 1951- WhoEmL 93
Abraham, Robert 1938- St&PR 93
Abraham, Robert E. 1952- St&PR 93
Abraham, Ronald Maroni 1941- WhoWor 93
Abraham, S. Daniel BioIn 17
Abraham, S. Daniel 1924- WhoAm 92
Abraham, Samuel Victor 1899-1992 BioIn 17
Abraham, Seth Gabriel BioIn 17
Abraham, Sheldon Clifford 1956- WhoAm 92
Abraham, Willard B. 1916- WhoAm 92
Abrahami, Kenneth Josef Chayim 1930- St&PR 93
Abrahamian, Shahen 1945- WhoUN 92
Abrahams, Allen E. 1926- WhoAm 92
Abrahams, Athol Denis 1946- WhoAm 92
Abrahams, Clark Richard 1951- WhoSSW 93
Abrahams, Doris ScF&FL 92
Abrahams, Glen D. 1953- St&PR 93
Abrahams, Jim 1944- ConAu 138, MiSFD 9
Abrahams, John Hambleton 1913- St&PR 93, WhoAm 92, WhoIns 93
Abrahams, Karen L. Law&B 92
Abrahams, Karin Beth 1951- WhoAmW 93
Abrahams, Kees 1935- WhoWor 93
Abrahams, Lloyd Alan 1952- WhoEmL 93
Abrahams, Mick 1943- See Jethro Tull ConMus 8
Abrahams, Paul William 1935- WhoE 93
Abrahams, Peter 1919- BioIn 17
Abrahams, Peter (Henry) 1919- DcLB 117 [port]
Abrahams, Phillip S. Law&B 92
Abrahams, Richard L. 1929- St&PR 93
Abrahams, Robert David 1905- WhoAm 92
Abrahams, Ronald H. 1942- St&PR 93
Abrahams, Ruth Karen 1950- WhoAmW 93
Abrahams, William 1919- ScF&FL 92
Abrahams, William Miller 1919- WhoAm 92, WhoWor 93, WhoWrEP 92
Abrahamsen, Adele Arline 1946- WhoSSW 93
Abrahamsen, David 1903- WhoAm 92, WhoE 93
Abrahamsen, Egil 1923- WhoWor 93
Abrahamsen, Gunnar 1938- WhoScE 91-4
Abrahamsen, Hans 1952- Baker 92
Abrahamsen, Roger K. 1946- WhoScE 91-4
Abrahamsen, Samuel 1917- WhoAm 92
Abrahamson, A. Craig 1954- WhoEmL 93
Abrahamson, Barry 1933- WhoAm 92
Abrahamson, Bruce Arnold 1925- WhoAm 92
Abrahamson, Dale Raymond 1949- WhoEmL 93, WhoSSW 93
Abrahamson, H. Grant 1942- St&PR 93
Abrahamson, John E. 1961- St&PR 93
Abrahamson, Lark Anne 1952- WhoEmL 93
Abrahamson, Rebecca P. AmWomPl
Abrahamson, Ronald G. 1947- St&PR 93
Abrahamson, Shirley Schlanger 1933- WhoAm 92, WhoAmW 93
Abrahamson, Warren Gene, II 1947- WhoE 93
Abrahamsson, Sixten 1930- WhoScE 91-4
Abram, Alice Wilson 1945- WhoAmW 93
Abram, Marian Christine 1958- WhoEmL 93
Abram, Morris Berthold 1918- JeAmHC, WhoAm 92, WhoWor 93
Abram, Prudence Beatty 1942- WhoAm 92, WhoAmW 93
Abram, Ruth Jacobeth 1945- WhoE 93
Abramczuk, Tomasz 1954- WhoWor 93
Abramios, John fl. 1370-1390 OxDcByz
Abramoff, Peter 1927- WhoAm 92
Abramov, Aleksandr 1904-1985 ScF&FL 92
Abramov, Konstantin Ivanovich BioIn 17
Abramovic, Anthony Mark 1948- St&PR 93
Abramovitz, Max 1908- WhoAm 92, WhoE 93
Abramovitz, Moses 1912- WhoAm 92
Abramovsky, Abraham 1946- WhoEmL 93
Abramowicz, Alfred L. 1919- WhoAm 92
Abramowicz, Mark St&PR 93
Abramowitz, Ann Jacoff 1948- WhoAmW 93
Abramowitz, Ava J. 1948- WhoEmL 93
Abramowitz, Jerrold 1953- WhoEmL 93
Abramowitz, Jonathan 1947- WhoEmL 93, WhoSSW 93
Abramowitz, Mordecai 1952- WhoEmL 93
Abramowitz, Morton I. 1933- WhoAm 92, WhoWor 93
Abramow-Newerly, Jaroslaw 1933- WhoWor 93
Abramowski, Horst Otto 1940- WhoSSW 93
Abramowski, Robert John 1950- St&PR 93
Abrams, Alan M. Law&B 92
Abrams, Alan Michael 1936- St&PR 93
Abrams, Amy L. Law&B 92
Abrams, Barbara WhoAmW 93
Abrams, Barry S. Law&B 92
Abrams, Bell-Ann Law&B 92
Abrams, Bernard 1920- St&PR 93
Abrams, Bernard W. 1925- St&PR 93
Abrams, Bernard William 1925- WhoAm 92
Abrams, Burt Jay 1934- WhoAm 92
Abrams, Burton M. 1923- St&PR 93
Abrams, Charles L. 1932- St&PR 93
Abrams, Constance L. Law&B 92
Abrams, Creighton W., Jr. 1914-1974 CmdGen 1991 [port]
Abrams, Creighton Williams, Jr. 1914-1974 HarEnMi
Abrams, Diane Kobisher 1954- WhoAmW 93, WhoEmL 93
Abrams, Douglas Breen 1954- WhoEmL 93
Abrams, Edward M. 1927- St&PR 93
Abrams, Edward Marvin 1927- WhoAm 92
Abrams, Elliot 1947- WhoE 93
Abrams, Elliott BioIn 17
Abrams, Elliott 1948- WhoAm 92, WhoEmL 93
Abrams, Erwin Edward 1941- St&PR 93
Abrams, Floyd 1936- WhoAm 92
Abrams, Gary Michael 1955- WhoE 93
Abrams, Gerald David 1932- WhoAm 92
Abrams, Harold Eugene 1933- WhoAm 92
Abrams, Herbert BioIn 17
Abrams, Herbert Kerman 1913- WhoAm 92
Abrams, Herbert LeRoy 1920- WhoAm 92
Abrams, Irving 1928- WhoE 93
Abrams, James S. d1991 BioIn 17
Abrams, Jay Harrison 1948- St&PR 93
Abrams, Jerome Brian 1956- WhoEmL 93
Abrams, Joan D. d1991 BioIn 17
Abrams, Joseph 1936- St&PR 93
Abrams, Jules Clinton 1927- WhoAm 92
Abrams, Julie Marie 1962- WhoAmW 93, WhoSSW 93
Abrams, Karen 1960- WhoEmL 93
Abrams, Katherine S. Law&B 92
Abrams, Kenneth WhoAm 92
Abrams, Kenneth Theodore 1928- WhoE 93
Abrams, Leigh J. 1942- St&PR 93
Abrams, Leigh Jeffrey 1942- WhoAm 92
Abrams, Linda WhoAmW 93
Abrams, Linsey 1951- WhoWrEP 92
Abrams, Lloyd 1939- WhoE 93
Abrams, Lori 1959- WhoEmL 93
Abrams, M.H. 1912- BioIn 17
Abrams, Mark Alan 1957- WhoE 93
Abrams, Mary Louise 1934- WhoE 93
Abrams, Meyer Howard BioIn 17
Abrams, Meyer Howard 1912- WhoAm 92
Abrams, Muhal Richard 1930- WhoAm 92
Abrams, Neil A. Law&B 92
Abrams, Norman Law&B 92
Abrams, Norman 1933- WhoAm 92
Abrams, Paul Gordon 1948- WhoEmL 93
Abrams, R. Vaughan 1949- ScF&FL 92
Abrams, Richard Brill 1931- WhoAm 92
Abrams, Richard Lee 1941- WhoAm 92
Abrams, Robert 1938- WhoAm 92, WhoE 93
Abrams, Robert Allen 1937- WhoAm 92
Abrams, Robert Herman 1932- St&PR 93
Abrams, Roberta Busky 1937- WhoAm 92, WhoAmW 93
Abrams, Rosalie Silber 1916- WhoAmW 93
Abrams, Rubin 1921- St&PR 93
Abrams, Ruth Ida 1930- WhoAm 92, WhoAmW 93
Abrams, Samuel K. 1913- WhoAm 92
Abrams, Sharon E. Law&B 92

Abrams, Steven Leon 1958- *WhoEmL 93*
Abrams, Susan Elizabeth 1945- *WhoAm 92*
Abrams, Talbert 1895-1990 *BioIn 17*
Abrams, Tevia 1934- *WhoUN 92*
Abrams, Vincent David 1961- *WhoSSW 93*
Abrams, Warren Elliott 1928- *WhoAm 92*
Abrams, William Bernard 1922- *WhoAm 92, WhoWor 93*
Abrams, Zelda 1932- *St&PR 93*
Abramsky, Alexander 1898-1985 *Baker 92*
Abramson, Andrew Edward 1924- *St&PR 93*
Abramson, Arnold Ernest 1914- *WhoAm 92*
Abramson, Arthur Seymour 1925- *WhoAm 92*
Abramson, Barbara 1938- *WhoAmW 93*
Abramson, Bruce S. 1936- *WhoE 93*
Abramson, Carol R. *Law&B 92*
Abramson, Clarence A. 1932- *St&PR 93*
Abramson, Clarence Allen 1932- *WhoAm 92, WhoE 93*
Abramson, Daniel 1922- *WhoAm 92*
Abramson, David *Law&B 92*
Abramson, Earl 1934- *St&PR 93*
Abramson, Hanley Norman 1940- *WhoAm 92*
Abramson, Herb *SoulM*
Abramson, Hyman Norman 1926- *St&PR 93, WhoAm 92*
Abramson, Ira 1930- *St&PR 93*
Abramson, Irwin Barry 1939- *St&PR 93, WhoE 93*
Abramson, Jerry 1946- *WhoAm 92, WhoSSW 93*
Abramson, Joan 1932- *ConAu 37NR*
Abramson, Lawrence 1946- *St&PR 93*
Abramson, Lawrence B. 1951- *WhoEmL 93*
Abramson, Leonard *BioIn 17*
Abramson, Leonard 1932- *St&PR 93*
Abramson, Leonard 1938- *WhoE 93*
Abramson, Lowell E. 1928- *St&PR 93*
Abramson, Mark Chad 1956- *WhoEmL 93*
Abramson, Mark E. *Law&B 92*
Abramson, Mark Joseph 1949- *WhoEmL 93*
Abramson, Marsha A. 1950- *St&PR 93*
Abramson, Martin 1921- *WhoAm 92, WhoWrEP 92*
Abramson, Maxwell 1935-1991 *BioIn 17*
Abramson, Morrie K. 1934- *St&PR 93*
Abramson, Morrie Kaplan 1934- *WhoAm 92*
Abramson, Morris 1901-1990 *BioIn 17*
Abramson, Morris Barnet 1910- *WhoE 93*
Abramson, Nils Hugo 1931- *WhoWor 93*
Abramson, Norman 1932- *WhoAm 92*
Abramson, Norman 1939- *WhoAm 92*
Abramson, Norman S. 1944- *WhoE 93*
Abramson, Paul R(obert) 1937- *ConAu 37NR*
Abramson, Paul Robert 1937- *WhoAm 92*
Abramson, Robert M. *WhoE 93*
Abramson, Rochelle Susan 1953- *WhoAm 92, WhoAmW 93*
Abramson, Sara Jane 1945- *WhoAmW 93*
Abramson, Stephen Davis 1945- *St&PR 93*
Abramson, Warren Blake 1953- *WhoE 93*
Abramson, William Edward 1935- *WhoAm 92, WhoE 93*
Abrams Sacks, Julie Barnett 1960- *WhoEmL 93*
Abrantes, Paulo Manuel 1953- *WhoWor 93*
Abrantes Fernandez, Jose d1991 *BioIn 17*
Abranyi, Cornelius 1822-1903 *Baker 92*
Abranyi, Emil 1882-1970 *Baker 92, OxDcOp*
Abrash, Merritt 1930- *ScF&FL 92*
Abrashkin, Raymond 1911-1960 *ScF&FL 92*
Abrassart, Joanne Yocum 1950- *WhoEmL 93*
Abraszewski, Andrzej 1938- *WhoUN 92*
Abravanel, Allan Ray 1947- *WhoEmL 93*
Abravanel, Isaac 1437-1508 *BioIn 17*
Abravanel, Maurice 1903- *Baker 92, WhoAm 92*
Abreu, Elizabeth F. 1953- *WhoEmL 93, WhoSSW 93*
Abreu, Francisco A.T.V. 1944- *WhoScE 91-3*
Abreu, Jose G. 1954- *St&PR 93*
Abreu, Luis Alberto 1956- *WhoEmL 93*
Abreu, Lynn M. *Law&B 92*
Abreu, M. Albert 1927- *St&PR 93*
Abreu, Maria Manuela 1949- *WhoScE 91-3*
Abreu, Sue Hudson 1956- *WhoAmW 93*
Abreu de la Mota, Francisco Julio 1955- *WhoEmL 93*
Abreu Gomez, Ermilo 1894-1971 *DcMexL*
Abreu Rebello, Eduardo 1949- *Baker 92*
Abreu Rebello, Sergio 1948- *Baker 92*
Abrew, Frederick H. 1937- *WhoAm 92*
Abrial, Jean-Marie Charles 1879-1962 *HarEnMi*
Abrikosov, Aleksey Alekseyevich 1928- *WhoWor 93*
Abromaitis, Karin 1952- *WhoAmW 93*
Abroms, Edward *MiSFD 9*
Abromson, Ellen Jane *Law&B 92*
Abromson, I. Joel 1938- *St&PR 93*
Abron, Neal R. 1933- *St&PR 93*
Abronson, Charles *BioIn 17*
Abrous, Abdennour 1934- *WhoUN 92*
Abruzzese, Peter A. *Law&B 92*
Abs, Hermann J. 1901- *WhoWor 93*
Absalom *BioIn 17*
Absalon c. 1128-1201 *HarEnMi*
Abse, Leo 1917- *ConAu 137*
Absher, Howard Thomas 1948- *WhoSSW 93*
Absher, Janet S. 1955- *WhoEmL 93*
Abshier, H.A., Jr. 1931- *St&PR 93*
Abshire, David M. 1926- *ConAu 37NR*
Abshire, David Manker 1926- *WhoAm 92*
Abshire, Judith Lee 1952- *WhoAmW 93*
Abshire, Richard Brian 1952- *St&PR 93*
Abshire, Richard K. *ScF&FL 92*
Absi, Elie Michel 1928- *WhoScE 91-2*
Absil, Jean 1893-1974 *Baker 92*
Absolon, Karel B. 1926- *WhoWrEP 92*
Abston, Dunbar, Jr. 1931- *St&PR 93, WhoAm 92*
Abt, Clark C. 1929- *St&PR 93*
Abt, Clark C(laus) 1929- *WhoWrEP 92*
Abt, Clark Claus 1929- *WhoAm 92*
Abt, Francois 1921- *WhoScE 91-2*
Abt, Franz (Wilhelm) 1819-1885 *Baker 92*
Abt, Jacob J., Mrs. *AmWomPl*
Abt, Jeffrey 1949- *WhoAm 92*
Abt, John J. 1904-1991 *BioIn 17*
Abt, Klaus 1927- *WhoScE 91-3*
Abt, Ralph Edwin 1960- *WhoEmL 93*
Abt, Sylvia Hedy 1957- *WhoAmW 93, WhoEmL 93*
Abt, Walter L. 1917- *St&PR 93*
Abts, Gwyneth Hartmann 1923- *WhoAmW 93, WhoWor 93*
Abts, H.W. 1918- *St&PR 93*
Abts, Henry William 1918- *WhoAm 92*
Abu-Al-Abbas c. 721-754 *HarEnMi*
Abu Al-Fida' 1273-1331 *OxDcByz*
Abu al-Raghib, Ali *WhoWor 93*
Abu Bakar Bin Datu Bandar Abang Haji M., Datuk Abang 1941- *WhoAsAP 91*
Abu-Bakr 573-634 *HarEnMi*
Abu Bakr 570?-634 *OxDcByz*
Abu-Bakr Ibn-Umar d1088 *HarEnMi*
Abu-Bakr Malik al-Adil, I 1145-1218 *HarEnMi*
Abuchowski, Abraham 1948- *St&PR 93*
Abud, Ronaldo Leao 1956- *WhoWor 93*
Abudarham, Samuel *WhoScE 91-1*
Abu Firas 932-968 *OxDcByz*
Abu-Gazaly, Ramsey 1962- *St&PR 93*
Abu-Gharbieh, Walid Ibrahim 1935- *WhoWor 93*
Abu-Ghazaleh, Talal Tawfiq 1938- *WhoWor 93*
Abu-Haimid, Abdulrahman Ibrahim 1942- *WhoWor 93*
Abu Hassan Bin Omar 1940- *WhoWor 93*
Abuhoff, Daniel Mark 1954- *WhoAm 92*
Abu Jabir, Kamal 1932- *WhoWor 93*
Abuladze, Tengiz 1924- *DrEEuF, MiSFD 9*
Abularach, Rodolfo Marco Antonio 1933- *WhoAm 92*
Abul Enein, Fayez Rifat 1945- *WhoWor 93*
Abu-Lughod, Janet Lippman 1928- *WhoAm 92*
Abu-Lughod, Lila 1952- *WhoAmW 93*
Abumrad, Naji 1945- *WhoAm 92*
Abu Muslim 720-755 *HarEnMi*
Abu Nidal *BioIn 17*
Aburdene, Odeh Felix 1944- *WhoAm 92*
Aburdene, Patricia *BioIn 17*
Abu-Risha, Yahya Abdurrahman 1933- *WhoWor 93*
Abu Said 1424-1469 *HarEnMi*
Abu Saleem, Mohammad Ibrahim 1930- *WhoWor 93*
Abu-Saymeh, Sadi Abdel-Hadi 1940- *WhoWor 93*
Abushadi, Ahmed M. 1940- *WhoUN 92*
Abushadi, Mohamed Mahmoud 1913- *WhoWor 93*
Abusharif, Ibrahim Naseem 1958- *WhoWrEP 92*
Abu-Soud, Tawfiq Sufyan 1958- *WhoWor 93*
Abut, Charles C. 1944- *WhoAm 92*
Abuyahia Yarmorasen d1282 *HarEnMi*
Abu Zakariya c. 1203-1249 *HarEnMi*
Abu Zayyad, Ray S. *WhoAm 92*
Abuzinada, Abdulaziz Hamid 1940- *WhoWor 93*
Abu Zora Tarif fl. c. 700- *HarEnMi*
Abuzzahab, Faruk Said 1932- *WhoAm 92*
Abzug, Bella *BioIn 17*
Abzug, Bella S. 1920- *PolPar*
Abzug, Bella S(avitzky) 1920- *ConAu 137*
Abzug, Bella Savitzky 1920- *WhoAm 92*
Abzug, Jesse L. *Law&B 92*
Abzug, Martin d1986 *BioIn 17*
Abzug, Robert Henry 1945- *WhoWrEP 92*
Acamovic, Thomas 1952- *WhoWor 93*
Acampora, Anthony Salvator 1946- *WhoAm 92*
Acampora, Judith W. *Law&B 92*
Acampora, Louis V. 1913- *St&PR 93*
Acampora, Ralph Joseph 1941- *St&PR 93, WhoAm 92, WhoWor 93*
Acar, Ahmet 1926- *WhoScE 91-4*
Acar, Jean 1928- *WhoScE 91-2*
Acar, Joseph 1926- *St&PR 93*
Acar, Joseph Nemr 1942- *WhoUN 92*
Acar, Yalcin Bekir 1951- *WhoEmL 93, WhoSSW 93*
Acaster, Linda Diane 1952- *WhoAmW 93*
Acbon, C.P. *WhoScE 91-1*
Accampo, Anthony David 1959- *WhoSSW 93*
Accardi, Michael Vincent 1947- *St&PR 93*
Accardo, Anthony Joseph d1992 *NewYTBS 92 [port]*
Accardo, Anthony Joseph 1906-1992 *BioIn 17*
Accardo, Salvatore 1941- *Baker 92*
Accardo, Salvatore Francis 1937- *WhoWor 93*
Accarino, Joseph Henry 1949- *St&PR 93*
Accas, Gene A. 1926- *St&PR 93*
Accettola, Albert Bernard 1918- *WhoAm 92*
Acciajuoli *OxDcByz*
Acciajuoli, Donato 1428-1478 *BioIn 17*
Acciarri, Giovanni Rossi 1938- *WhoUN 92*
Acconci, Vito 1940- *BioIn 17*
Acconci, Vito Hannibal 1940- *WhoAm 92*
Acconcia, Paula Christine 1951- *WhoEmL 93*
Accordino, Frank Joseph 1946- *WhoAm 92, WhoEmL 93*
Accordino, Margaret Spillane 1948- *WhoAmW 93*
Accorsi, Ernest William, Jr. 1941- *WhoAm 92*
Accrocca, Elio Filippo 1923- *DcLB 128 [port]*
Accuosti, William V. 1934- *St&PR 93*
Accurso, Catherine Josephine 1955- *WhoEmL 93, WhoWor 93*
Ace, Drexel Maurice, Jr. 1950- *WhoE 93, WhoEmL 93*
Ace, Johnny 1929-1954 *SoulM*
Acebo, Luis Gomez- 1934-1991 *BioIn 17*
Acer, David J. *BioIn 17*
Acerra, Angelo T. d1990 *BioIn 17*
Acerra, Michele 1937- *St&PR 93, WhoAm 92*
Acerra, Mike 1937- *WhoAm 92*
Acers, Maurice Wilson *Law&B 92*
Acers, Maurice Wilson 1907- *St&PR 93*
Aceto, Vincent John 1932- *WhoE 93*
Acevedo, Domingo Elio 1936- *WhoE 93*
Acevedo, Hector Eduardo 1964- *WhoSSW 93*
Acevedo, Hector Luis 1947- *WhoAm 92, WhoSSW 93*
Acevedo, Jesus T. 1892-1918 *DcMexL*
Acevedo, Manuel Raul 1945- *WhoE 93*
Acevedo, Rommel Enrique 1952- *WhoWor 93*
Acevedo Escobedo, Antonio 1909-1985 *DcMexL*
Acevedo Peralta, Ricardo de Jesus 1941- *WhoWor 93*
Aceves, Jose 1909- *HispAmA*
Acey, Thomas M. 1946- *St&PR 93*
Ach, Roger Workum, II 1943- *St&PR 93, WhoAm 92*
Achacoso, Theodore Borromeo 1961- *WhoE 93*
Acharia, Basudeb 1942- *WhoAsAP 91*
Acharya, Harsha 1944- *WhoIns 93*
Acharya, Jayaraj 1951- *WhoUN 92*
Acharya, Sagri Vasudeva 1943- *WhoE 93*
Acharya, Tanka Prasad d1992 *NewYTBS 92*
Acharya, Tanka Prasad 1912-1992 *BioIn 17*
Achatz, Hans 1964- *WhoWor 93*
Achatz, John 1948- *WhoE 93*
Achbar, Francine 1946- *WhoAm 92, WhoAmW 93*
Achebe, Chinua 1930- *BioIn 17, BlkAull 92, ConLC 75 [port], CurBio 92 [port], DcTwHis, IntLitE, IntvWPC 92 [port], MagSWL [port], WhoWor 93, WorLitC [port]*
Achebe, (Albert) Chinua(lumogu) 1930- *DcLB 117 [port], MajAI [port]*
Achen, Norman Charles 1942- *St&PR 93*
Achenbach, Hans *WhoScE 91-3*
Achenbach, Jan Drewes 1935- *WhoAm 92*
Achenbach, R. Timothy 1945- *St&PR 93*
Achenbach, Rebecca Sue 1947- *WhoAmW 93*
Achenbaum, Alvin A. 1925- *St&PR 93*
Achenbaum, Alvin Allen 1925- *WhoAm 92, WhoE 93*
Achenbaum, Warren D. 1934- *St&PR 93*
Acheson, Alice 1895- *BioIn 17*
Acheson, Allen Morrow 1926- *St&PR 93, WhoAm 92*
Acheson, David Campion 1921- *WhoAm 92*
Acheson, Dean 1893-1971 *ColdWar 1 [port], PolPar*
Acheson, Dean Gooderham 1893-1971 *DcTwHis*
Acheson, James *WhoAm 92*
Acheson, James C. 1936- *St&PR 93*
Acheson, Louis Kruzan, Jr. 1926- *WhoAm 92*
Acheson, Patricia Castles 1924- *WhoAmW 93*
Acheson, Roy Malcolm 1921- *WhoAm 92*
Achey, Denise Louise 1960- *WhoAmW 93*
Achiek Ibn Oumar, Sayyid 1951- *WhoAfr*
Achikzad, G. Faruq 1936- *WhoUN 92*
Achille, Joyce Herms 1937- *St&PR 93*
Achilleos, Chris 1947- *ScF&FL 92*
Achilles Tatius fl. 2nd cent.- *OxDcByz*
Achin, Milos Kosta 1915- *WhoE 93, WhoWor 93*
Achinstein, Asher 1900- *WhoAm 92*
Achinstein, Peter Jacob 1935- *WhoAm 92*
Achitoff, Louis d1989 *BioIn 17*
Achkar, Maria 1926- *WhoWor 93*
Achmatowicz, Osman 1931- *WhoScE 91-4*
Achmet Ben Sirin *OxDcByz*
Achor, Louis Joseph 1948- *WhoEmL 93, WhoSSW 93*
Achord, James Lee 1931- *WhoAm 92, WhoSSW 93*
Achorn, Robert Comey 1922- *WhoAm 92, WhoWor 93*
Achron, Isidor 1892-1948 *Baker 92*
Achron, Joseph 1886-1943 *Baker 92*
Achte, Kalle 1928- *WhoScE 91-4*
Achtelstetter, Karin Waltraut 1961- *WhoWor 93*
Achtemeier, Gary Lynn 1943- *WhoAm 92*
Achtemeier, Paul John 1927- *WhoSSW 93*
Achtenberg, Joel Franklin 1946- *WhoEmL 93*
Achterberg, Charles Richard 1939- *St&PR 93*
Achterhof, Kathleen L. *Law&B 92*
Achternbusch, Herbert 1938- *DcLB 124 [port]*
Achtert, Walter Scott 1943- *WhoAm 92, WhoWrEP 92*
Achtzehnter, Joachim 1960- *WhoWor 93*
Achtziger, Harold LeRoy 1934- *St&PR 93*
Achucarro, Joaquin 1936- *Baker 92*
Achuthan, Radh M. 1935- *WhoE 93*
Aciman, Andre A. *BioIn 17*
Acin, Jovan 1941- *MiSFD 9*
Acitelli, Linda Katherine 1951- *WhoEmL 93*
Acito, Daniel Joseph 1918- *WhoAm 92*
Ackefors, Hans E.G. 1932- *WhoScE 91-4*
Ackell, Edmund Ferris 1925- *WhoAm 92, WhoSSW 93*
Ackell, Joseph J. *Law&B 92*
Ackelsberg, Martha A. 1946- *ConAu 139*
Acker, Albert Harold 1941- *St&PR 93*
Acker, C. Edward 1929- *EncABHB 8 [port]*
Acker, Charles R. 1912- *St&PR 93*
Acker, Christopher B. *Law&B 92*
Acker, Dieter 1940- *Baker 92*
Acker, Duane Calvin 1931- *WhoAm 92*
Acker, Ernest R. d1992 *NewYTBS 92*
Acker, Frederick George 1934- *WhoAm 92*
Acker, George Harris, Jr. 1956- *WhoSSW 93*
Acker, Herbert William 1942- *WhoAm 92*
Acker, Jon A. 1945- *St&PR 93*
Acker, Joseph Edington 1918- *WhoAm 92*
Acker, Kathy 1948- *ScF&FL 92*
Acker, Lawrence Gene 1950- *WhoAm 92*
Acker, Martin Herbert 1921- *WhoAm 92*
Acker, Nathaniel Hull 1927- *WhoAm 92*
Acker, Paul Arthur 1952- *St&PR 93*
Acker, Robert Flint 1920- *WhoAm 92*
Acker, Robert Wayne 1949- *St&PR 93*
Acker, Virginia Margaret 1946- *WhoAmW 93*
Acker, William Marsh, Jr. 1927- *WhoAm 92*
Acker, Woodrow Louis 1937- *WhoSSW 93*
Ackerberg, Robert Cyril 1934- *WhoE 93*
Ackeri, Ivan *WhoScE 91-4*
Ackerley, Barry *WhoAm 92*
Ackerley, J.R. 1896-1967 *BioIn 17*
Ackerley, Joe Randolph 1896-1967 *BioIn 17*
Ackerly, Howard F. 1928- *St&PR 93*
Ackerly, Robert Saunders, Jr. 1929- *WhoAm 92*
Ackerly, Wendy Saunders 1960- *WhoAmW 93, WhoEmL 93*

Ackerman, Allan Jay 1931- WhoE 93
Ackerman, Bettye Louise 1928- WhoAm 92
Ackerman, Caroline Iverson 1918- WhoAmW 93
Ackerman, Craig St&PR 93
Ackerman, David L. 1943- St&PR 93
Ackerman, David Paul 1949- WhoEmL 93
Ackerman, Diane BioIn 17
Ackerman, Diane 1948- DcLB 120 [port], WhoWrEP 92
Ackerman, Don E. 1933- St&PR 93
Ackerman, Don Eugene 1933- WhoAm 92
Ackerman, Dorothy Lyon AmWomPl
Ackerman, Edgar D. Law&B 92
Ackerman, Emanuel C. BioIn 17
Ackerman, Eugene 1920- WhoAm 92
Ackerman, F. Duane 1942- WhoAm 92
Ackerman, F. Kenneth, Jr. 1939- WhoE 93
Ackerman, Forrest J. 1916- ScF&FL 92
Ackerman, Frank A. Law&B 92
Ackerman, Gary L. 1942- CngDr 91, WhoAm 92, WhoE 93
Ackerman, George S. 1920- St&PR 93
Ackerman, Gerald Martin 1928- WhoAm 92
Ackerman, H. Don 1926- St&PR 93, WhoAm 92
Ackerman, Harold A. 1928- WhoAm 92, WhoE 93
Ackerman, Harry S. 1912-1991 BioIn 17, ConTFT 10
Ackerman, Helen Page 1912- WhoAm 92
Ackerman, Henry Sweets 1942- WhoAm 92
Ackerman, Herbert 1930- St&PR 93
Ackerman, Jack Rossin 1931- WhoAm 92
Ackerman, James F. 1924- St&PR 93
Ackerman, James Nils 1912- WhoAm 92
Ackerman, James Sloss 1919- WhoAm 92
Ackerman, Joel G. Law&B 92
Ackerman, John A. 1937- St&PR 93
Ackerman, John Cyril WhoAm 92
Ackerman, John Cyril 1937- St&PR 93
Ackerman, John Henry 1925- WhoAm 92
Ackerman, John R., Jr. Law&B 92
Ackerman, John Tryon 1941- St&PR 93, WhoAm 92
Ackerman, Jolene Kay 1952- WhoAmW 93
Ackerman, Joseph J. H. 1949- WhoAm 92
Ackerman, Kenneth Benjamin 1932- WhoAm 92
Ackerman, L.C. 1917- St&PR 93
Ackerman, Lennis Campbell 1917- WhoAm 92
Ackerman, Lillian Alice 1928- WhoAmW 93
Ackerman, Lisa Marilyn 1960- WhoE 93, WhoEmL 93
Ackerman, Louise Magaw 1904- WhoAmW 93
Ackerman, Marshall 1925- WhoAm 92
Ackerman, Melvin 1937- WhoAm 92
Ackerman, Mona BioIn 17
Ackerman, Noreen Carol 1944- WhoAmW 93, WhoWrEP 92
Ackerman, Ora Ray 1931- WhoAm 92
Ackerman, Paul Adam 1945- WhoSSW 93
Ackerman, Philip C. Law&B 92
Ackerman, Philip Charles 1944- St&PR 93, WhoAm 92
Ackerman, Ray B. 1922- St&PR 93
Ackerman, Raymond Basil 1922- WhoAm 92
Ackerman, Robert Alan 1951- WhoEmL 93
Ackerman, Robert Jon 1948- WhoE 93
Ackerman, Robert O. 1946- St&PR 93
Ackerman, Robert W. 1938- St&PR 93
Ackerman, Robert Wallace 1938- WhoAm 92, WhoWor 93
Ackerman, Roger G. 1938- St&PR 93
Ackerman, Rosalie J. 1940- WhoAmW 93
Ackerman, Roy Alan 1951- St&PR 93, WhoEmL 93
Ackerman, Samuel 1917- St&PR 93
Ackerman, Sanford Selig 1932- WhoAm 92
Ackerman, Stephanie C. St&PR 93
Ackerman, Therese Maria 1963- WhoSSW 93
Ackerman, Valentine Peter 1926- WhoWor 93
Ackerman, William 1949- Baker 92
Ackermann, Barbara Bogel 1940- WhoE 93
Ackermann, Juergen Ernst 1936- WhoWor 93
Ackermann, Jurgen 1936- WhoScE 91-3
Ackermann, Marsha Ellen 1950- WhoEmL 93
Ackermann, Otto 1909-1960 Baker 92, OxDcOp
Ackers, Gary Keith 1939- WhoAm 92
Ackerson, Duane Wright, Jr. WhoWrEP 92
Ackerson, Garret G. d1992 NewYTBS 92
Ackerson, Jeffrey Townsend 1944- WhoAm 92, WhoE 93
Ackerson, Nels John 1944- WhoAm 92, WhoE 93
Ackery, D.M. WhoScE 91-1
Acklam, Jon Neil 1947- WhoEmL 93
Ackland, Joss 1928- BioIn 17
Ackland, Rodney 1908-1991 AnObit 1991
Acklen, Charles Wayne 1944- St&PR 93
Ackles, Bob BioIn 17
Ackles, Janice Vogel WhoWor 93
Ackles, Robert 1952- St&PR 93
Ackley, Danielle Renee 1970- WhoWrEP 92
Ackley, John Brian 1948- WhoEmL 93, WhoSSW 93
Ackley, Kenneth E. 1938- St&PR 93
Ackley, Marie WhoWrEP 92
Ackley, Mary E. 1842- BioIn 17
Ackley, P.O. 1903-1989 BioIn 17
Ackley, Parker Otto 1903-1989 BioIn 17
Acklie, Duane William WhoAm 92
Acklie, Duane William 1931- St&PR 93
Acklie, Phyllis Ann 1933- St&PR 93, WhoAmW 93
Acklin, Barbara 1943- BioIn 17, SoulM
Acklin, Thomas Patrick 1950- WhoE 93
Ackman, Milton Roy 1932- WhoAm 92
Ackman, Roger S. Law&B 92, St&PR 93
Ackmann, Lowell Eugene 1923- WhoAm 92
Ackoff, Russell Lincoln 1919- WhoAm 92
Ackourey, Paul Philip 1958- WhoEmL 93
Ackroyd, Peter BioIn 17
Ackroyd, Peter 1949- ScF&FL 92
Ackroyd, Ronald Tunstall 1921- WhoWor 93
Ackte, Aino 1876-1944 Baker 92, OxDcOp
Acomb, Dan T. 1956- St&PR 93
Acomba, David MiSFD 9
Acord, Art 1890-1931 BioIn 17
Acord, James L., Jr. BioIn 17
Acord-Skelton, Barbara Burrows 1928- WhoAmW 93
Acorn, Milton 1923-1986 WhoCanL 92
Acosta, Carlos Law&B 92
Acosta, Daniel, Jr. 1945- HispAmA
Acosta, Ivan 1943- HispAmA
Acosta, Julio Bernard 1927- WhoAm 92
Acosta, Nelson John 1947- WhoWor 93
Acosta, Raymond L. 1925- HispAmA [port]
Acosta, Raymond Luis 1925- WhoAm 92, WhoSSW 93
Acosta, Roland Howard Law&B 92
Acosta, Socorro O. 1934- WhoAsAP 91
Acosta, Ursula 1933- WhoAmW 93, WhoSSW 93
Acosta-Belen, Edna 1948- HispAmA
Acosta-Colon, Marie 1949- NotHsAW 93 [port]
Acosta Saignes, Miguel 1908-1989 IntDcAn
Acosta-Sing, Mirian 1948- WhoAmW 93
Acquaah, Jude Attah 1935- WhoWor 93
Acquanetta 1920- BioIn 17
Acquaotta, Henry Francis 1926- St&PR 93
Acquavella, Demian d1990 BioIn 17
Acquavella, William R. BioIn 17
Acquaviva, Charlotte Law&B 92
Acquaviva, Nicholas 1951- St&PR 93
Acree, Margaret Louise 1937- WhoAmW 93
Acres, Mark 1949- ScF&FL 92
Acrivos, Andreas 1928- WhoAm 92
Acton, Charles 1914- WhoWor 93
Acton, Constance Foster 1947- WhoEmL 93
Acton, David 1933- WhoAm 92
Acton, David Lawrence 1949- WhoEmL 93, WhoWor 93
Acton, Harold 1904- BioIn 17, ScF&FL 92
Acton, Norman 1918- WhoAm 92
Acton, Peter M. Law&B 92
Acton, William Anthony 1910- WhoWor 93
Acton, William C. 1953- St&PR 93
Acuff, A. Marshall, Jr. 1939- St&PR 93
Acuff, Eileen Colette 1963- WhoAmW 93
Acuff, John Edgar 1940- WhoSSW 93
Acuff, Robert Vann 1952- WhoEmL 93, WhoSSW 93
Acuff, Roy 1903-1992 NewYTBS 92 [port], News 93-2
Acuff, Roy (Claxton) 1903- Baker 92, WhoAm 92
Acuna, Manuel 1849-1873 DcMexL
Acuna, Richard Miguel Law&B 92
Acuna, Rodolfo 1932- HispAmA
Acworth, Andrew ScF&FL 92
Aczel, Janos Dezso 1924- WhoAm 92
Aczel, Susan Kende 1927- WhoAmW 93
Aczel, Tamas 1921- WhoE 93, WhoWrEP 92
Ada, Joseph Franklin 1943- WhoAm 92
Adachi, Agnes Magdalene 1918- WhoAmW 93
Adachi, Gin-ya 1938- WhoWor 93
Adachi, Hatazo 1884-1947 HarEnMi
Adachi, Janet K. Law&B 92
Adachi, Kozaburo 1933- WhoWor 93
Adachi, Ryohei 1935- WhoAsAP 91
Adachi, Susumu 1925- WhoWor 93
Adaikala Raj, L. 1936- WhoAsAP 91
Adair, Charles E. 1947- WhoAm 92, WhoSSW 93
Adair, Charles Robert, Jr. 1914- WhoAm 92
Adair, Charles Valloyd 1923- WhoAm 92
Adair, Dianna Lynn 1950- WhoEmL 93
Adair, Dwight MiSFD 9
Adair, Gilbert ScF&FL 92
Adair, Glenda R. 1962- WhoAmW 93, WhoEmL 93
Adair, James B. ScF&FL 92
Adair, John Douglas, Jr. 1943- St&PR 93
Adair, John H. Law&B 92
Adair, John Joseph 1941- WhoAm 92
Adair, K. Eric Law&B 92
Adair, Kenneth Jerome Law&B 92
Adair, Red 1915- BioIn 17, WhoAm 92
Adair, Robert Charles 1952- St&PR 93
Adair, Robert Kemp 1924- ConAu 136
Adair, Stephen W. 1947- St&PR 93
Adair, Tony 1953- St&PR 93
Adair, Wendell Hinton, Jr. 1944- WhoAm 92
Adair, Wendy Hilty 1949- WhoEmL 93
Adair, William B. 1949- WhoE 93
Adair, William Benjamin, Jr. 1951- WhoEmL 93
Adair, Yvonne 1946- WhoAmW 93, WhoWor 93
Adalioglu, Ulvi 1937- WhoScE 91-4
Adalsteinsson, Stefan 1928- WhoScE 91-4
Adam BioIn 17
Adam, Adolphe 1803-1856 IntDcOp [port], OxDcOp
Adam, Adolphe (-Charles) 1803-1856 Baker 92
Adam, Alice Law&B 92
Adam, Antal 1929- WhoScE 91-4
Adam, Auguste Villiers de L'Isle ScF&FL 92
Adam, Bruce D. 1956- St&PR 93
Adam, Christopher Michael 1951- WhoWor 93
Adam, Claus 1917-1983 Baker 92
Adam, Cornel 1915- WhoAm 92
Adam, Gary Lee 1946- WhoWor 93
Adam, George F., Jr. 1946- WhoAm 92
Adam, Gerold H. 1933- WhoScE 91-3
Adam, Graeme Mercer 1839-1912 BioIn 17
Adam, Hans O. 1925- WhoScE 91-4
Adam, J. Marc 1938- St&PR 93
Adam, James Vernon 1948- St&PR 93
Adam, Jan 1920- ConAu 38NR
Adam, Jeno 1896-1982 Baker 92
Adam, John 1942- WhoE 93, WhoUN 92
Adam, John, Jr. 1914- St&PR 93, WhoAm 92
Adam, Judy Z. 1955- St&PR 93
Adam, Ken BioIn 17, WhoAm 92
Adam, Laszlo 1950- St&PR 93
Adam, LaVern Lester 1943- WhoSSW 93, WhoWor 93
Adam, (Jean) Louis 1758-1848 Baker 92
Adam, Mary Lou 1933- St&PR 93
Adam, Michael 1919- ConAu 37NR
Adam, Naomi C. Law&B 92
Adam, Orval Michael 1930- WhoAm 92
Adam, Paul James 1934- WhoAm 92
Adam, Peter 1937- WhoScE 91-3
Adam, Robert 1728-1792 BioIn 17
Adam, Robert B. 1918- St&PR 93
Adam, Stephen Ferenc 1929- WhoAm 92
Adam, Theo 1926- Baker 92, OxDcOp
Adam, Thomas Lorenzo 1946- WhoEmL 93
Adam, Thomas R. 1900-1990 BioIn 17
Adam, W. Kay Law&B 92
Adam, Waldemar 1937- WhoScE 91-3
Adam, Z. Alfred 1928- St&PR 93
Adamakos, Arthur Louis 1956- WhoE 93
Adamantopoulos, Konstantinos 1959- WhoWor 93
Adamany, David Walter 1936- WhoAm 92, WhoWor 93
Adamany, Richard C. 1952- St&PR 93
Adamberger, Valentin 1743-1804 OxDcOp
Adamberger, (Josef) Valentin 1743-1804 Baker 92
Adamchek, Janice Lynn 1949- WhoAmW 93, WhoE 93, WhoEmL 93
Adamczak, Eugeniusz 1935- WhoWor 93
Adamczewski, Kazimierz 1936- WhoScE 91-4
Adamczewski, Zdzislaw 1931- WhoScE 91-4
Adamczyk, Bogdan Stanislaw 1930- WhoScE 91-4, WhoWor 93
Adamczyk, Kazimierz 1954- WhoScE 91-4
Adamczyk, Zbigniew 1938- WhoScE 91-4
Adam de la Halle c. 1237-c. 1287 Baker 92
Adam de Marisco d1259 BioIn 17
Adam de St. Victor dc. 1148 Baker 92
Adamec, Constance M. d1992 BioIn 17, NewYTBS 92
Adamec, Joseph Victor 1935- WhoAm 92
Adamec, Ladislav 1926- WhoWor 93
Adamec, Vladimir WhoScE 91-4
Adamenko, Victor Gregory 1936- WhoWor 93
Adami, Giuseppe 1878-1946 OxDcOp
Adamian, Gregory Harry 1926- WhoAm 92
Adami-Charney, Anne Sybell 1949- WhoEmL 93
Adamiecki, Karol 1866-1933 PolBiDi
Adamis, Michael 1929- Baker 92
Adamitis, Donald M. 1944- St&PR 93
Adamkiewicz, Vincent Witold 1924- WhoAm 92
Adamko, Joseph Michael 1932- St&PR 93, WhoAm 92
Adamo, Joseph F. 1946- St&PR 93
Adamo, Mary-Ellen McCann 1942- WhoAmW 93, WhoE 93
Adamo, Ralph 1948- WhoWrEP 92
Adamo, Victor T. 1948- WhoIns 93
Adamonis, Vitold Joseph 1946- St&PR 93
Adamonti, (Josef) Valentin 1743-1804 Baker 92
Adamov, Arthur 1908-1970 BioIn 17
Adamovich, Shirley Gray 1927- WhoAm 92
Adamowicz, Mieczyslaw 1939- WhoScE 91-4
Adamowski, Joseph 1862-1930 Baker 92, PolBiDi
Adamowski, Timothee 1857-1943 Baker 92, PolBiDi
Adams, A. John Bertrand 1931- WhoAm 92, WhoWor 93
Adams, Abigail 1744-1818 BioIn 17
Adams, Aden Cornelius 1939- St&PR 93
Adams, Alan R. Law&B 92
Adams, Albert Willie, Jr. 1948- WhoAm 92
Adams, Alfred Bernard, Jr. 1920- WhoSSW 93
Adams, Alfred Gray 1946- WhoSSW 93
Adams, Alfred Hugh 1928- WhoAm 92
Adams, Alfred Rodney WhoScE 91-1
Adams, Algalee Pool 1919- WhoAm 92
Adams, Alice 1926- BioIn 17, WhoAm 92, WhoAmW 93, WhoWrEP 92
Adams, Alice Patricia 1930- WhoAm 92
Adams, Alton W. 1946- St&PR 93
Adams, Alvin Philip, Jr. 1942- WhoAm 92, WhoWor 93
Adams, Amy Brown 1950- WhoSSW 93
Adams, Andrew Joseph 1909- WhoAm 92
Adams, Andrew Stanford 1922- WhoAm 92
Adams, Andrew W. Law&B 92
Adams, Anna Christie 1952- WhoWrEP 92
Adams, Anne WhoWrEP 92
Adams, Anne Tryon BioIn 17
Adams, Ansel 1902-1984 BioIn 17, ConHero 2 [port]
Adams, Anthony ScF&FL 92
Adams, Anthony Peter WhoScE 91-1
Adams, Arlin Marvin 1921- WhoAm 92, WhoE 93
Adams, Arthur Gray, Jr. 1935- WhoWrEP 92
Adams, Arvil Van 1943- WhoAm 92, WhoE 93
Adams, Aundrea Jasmine Kaye 1954- WhoSSW 93
Adams, Austin A. WhoSSW 93
Adams, Austin Alfred 1943- St&PR 93
Adams, Barbara ConAu 136
Adams, Barbara 1932- WhoAmW 93
Adams, Barbara Johnston 1943-1990 BioIn 17
Adams, Beejay 1920- WhoAmW 93, WhoWor 93
Adams, Bernard Schroder 1928- WhoAm 92
Adams, Bertha Devereux AmWomPl
Adams, Betsy Walker 1962- WhoAmW 93
Adams, Bett Yates 1942- WhoAm 92
Adams, Beverly Josephine 1951- WhoAmW 93, WhoEmL 93
Adams, Bill ScF&FL 92
Adams, Bradway B. 1956- St&PR 93
Adams, Brent Larsen 1949- WhoE 93
Adams, Brent Ray 1967- WhoE 93
Adams, Brock BioIn 17
Adams, Brock 1927- CngDr 91, WhoAm 92
Adams, Brooke 1949- WhoAm 92
Adams, Brooks 1848-1927 GayN
Adams, Bruce 1952- St&PR 93
Adams, Bruce E. 1947- St&PR 93
Adams, Bryan 1959- WhoAm 92
Adams, Buck BioIn 17
Adams, Buel Thomas 1933- WhoAm 92
Adams, C. Clint Law&B 92
Adams, Carl Fillmore, Jr. 1950- WhoWor 93

Adams, Carl Morgan, Jr. 1940- *WhoWor 93*
Adams, Carol Ann Jacobs 1946- *WhoEmL 93*
Adams, Carol Josephine 1951- *WhoSSW 93*
Adams, Carol Twitty 1943- *WhoAmW 93*
Adams, Caroline Jeanette H. 1951- *WhoAmW 93, WhoEmL 93*
Adams, Caroline Sue Gano 1939- *WhoAmW 93*
Adams, Carrie Belle Wilson 1859-1940 *AmWomPl*
Adams, Cary Meredith 1948- *WhoAm 92*
Adams, Catlin 1950- *MiSFD 9*
Adams, Charles 1834-1900 *Baker 92*
Adams, Charles F. 1910- *St&PR 93*
Adams, Charles Francis 1807-1886 *PolPar*
Adams, Charles Francis 1927- *WhoAm 92, WhoWor 93*
Adams, Charles Henry 1918- *WhoAm 92*
Adams, Charles Jairus 1917- *WhoAm 92*
Adams, Charles Jesse 1947- *WhoEmL 93*
Adams, Charles L. *Law&B 92*
Adams, Charles Lynford 1929- *WhoAm 92*
Adams, Charles Marshall 1907-1991 *BioIn 17*
Adams, Charles Preston 1942- *St&PR 93*
Adams, Charles R. 1927- *St&PR 93*
Adams, Charles Siegel 1936- *WhoE 93*
Adams, Charles Wally 1934- *St&PR 93*
Adams, Christine 1952- *St&PR 93*
Adams, Christine Hanson 1950- *WhoEmL 93*
Adams, Christopher *BioIn 17*
Adams, Christopher Steve, Jr. 1930- *WhoAm 92*
Adams, Clara M. 1948- *WhoAmW 93*
Adams, Clinton 1918- *WhoAm 92*
Adams, Conrad Robert, II 1942- *St&PR 93*
Adams, Constance Althea 1953- *WhoWrEP 92*
Adams, Coyote *BioIn 17*
Adams, Daniel *MiSFD 9*
Adams, Daniel Fenton 1922- *WhoAm 92*
Adams, Daniel Lee 1936- *WhoAm 92*
Adams, Darrell R. 1954- *St&PR 93*
Adams, Darryl George 1939- *WhoSSW 93*
Adams, Daryl Brown 1947- *St&PR 93*
Adams, David Bachrach 1939- *WhoAm 92*
Adams, David Brian *Law&B 92*
Adams, David Gray 1961- *WhoSSW 93*
Adams, David Huntington 1942- *WhoSSW 93*
Adams, David John 1949- *WhoEmL 93*
Adams, David L. 1956- *St&PR 93*
Adams, Dean 1957- *WhoE 93, WhoEmL 93*
Adams, Deborah 1956- *WhoWrEP 92*
Adams, Dee Briane 1942- *WhoSSW 93, WhoWor 93*
Adams, Denis Conway *WhoScE 91-1*
Adams, Dennis Paul 1948- *WhoE 93*
Adams, Diane Loretta 1948- *WhoE 93, WhoEmL 93*
Adams, Don M. *Law&B 92*
Adams, Doris Jo 1926- *St&PR 93*
Adams, Doug *MiSFD 9*
Adams, Douglas 1952- *BioIn 17, ScF&FL 92*
Adams, Douglas Fletcher 1937- *St&PR 93*
Adams, Douglas William 1953- *WhoWor 93*
Adams, Douglass Franklin 1935- *WhoAm 92*
Adams, Duncan Dartrey 1925- *WhoWor 93*
Adams, E.C. 1930- *St&PR 93*
Adams, E. Sherman 1910-1991 *BioIn 17*
Adams, Earl William, Jr. 1937- *WhoAm 92*
Adams, Eaton, Jr. 1930- *St&PR 93*
Adams, Edie 1927- *QDrFCA 92 [port]*
Adams, Edie 1929- *BioIn 17*
Adams, Edith *SmATA 71*
Adams, Edmund John 1938- *WhoAm 92*
Adams, Edward Beverle 1939- *WhoAm 92*
Adams, Edward Thomas 1933- *WhoAm 92*
Adams, Edwin Melville 1914- *WhoAm 92*
Adams, Egbert Harrison 1899- *St&PR 93*
Adams, Elaine Parker *WhoSSW 93*
Adams, Elie Maynard 1919- *WhoWrEP 92*
Adams, Elizabeth Shaw Colgan 1950- *WhoAmW 93*
Adams, Ellen *WhoWrEP 92*
Adams, Elliot Quincy 1888-1971 *BioIn 17*
Adams, Emma Hildreth fl. 1883-1886 *BioIn 17*
Adams, Estella *AmWomPl*
Adams, Eva Bertrand d1991 *BioIn 17*
Adams, Evangeline Smith 1868-1932 *BioIn 17*
Adams, Everett Merle 1920- *WhoAm 92*
Adams, F.C. 1938- *WhoScE 91-2*
Adams, F. Edward *Law&B 92*
Adams, F. Gerard 1929- *WhoAm 92*
Adams, Fay 1924- *WhoWrEP 92*
Adams, Faye Litsey 1945- *WhoAmW 93*
Adams, Florence 1932- *BioIn 17*
Adams, Floyd N. 1942- *St&PR 93*
Adams, Frances Grant, II 1955- *WhoAmW 93, WhoE 93, WhoEmL 93*
Adams, Francis A. 1874-1975 *ScF&FL 92*
Adams, Francis W.H. 1904-1990 *BioIn 17*
Adams, Frank H. 1935- *St&PR 93*
Adams, Frank M. d1990 *BioIn 17*
Adams, Franklin Pierce 1881-1960 *JrnUS*
Adams, Franklin V. 1947- *St&PR 93*
Adams, Fred C. *BioIn 17*
Adams, Fred C. 1949- *ScF&FL 92*
Adams, Fred E. 1928- *St&PR 93*
Adams, G.E. *WhoScE 91-1*
Adams, Gail Hayes 1944- *WhoAm 92*
Adams, Gene D. 1933- *St&PR 93*
Adams, Geoffrey Philip 1944- *WhoScE 91-1*
Adams, George Bell 1930- *WhoAm 92, WhoWor 93*
Adams, George F. *Law&B 92*
Adams, George F., Jr. 1948- *St&PR 93*
Adams, George Gabriel 1948- *WhoE 93*
Adams, George Harold 1926- *WhoAm 92, WhoE 93*
Adams, George R. 1936- *St&PR 93*
Adams, George William 1948- *WhoEmL 93*
Adams, Gerard 1948- *WhoWor 93*
Adams, Gerry *BioIn 17*
Adams, Gilbert Ray 1943- *WhoSSW 93*
Adams, Glenda 1939- *ScF&FL 92*
Adams, Glenn A. 1957- *St&PR 93*
Adams, Grantley *DcCPCAm*
Adams, Gregory Burke 1948- *WhoEmL 93, WhoSSW 93*
Adams, Gregory Drake 1949- *St&PR 93*
Adams, H.A.S. 1951- *St&PR 93*
Adams, Hall, Jr. 1933- *WhoAm 92*
Adams, Harold B. 1923- *WhoWrEP 92*
Adams, Harold Dale 1953- *WhoSSW 93*
Adams, Harold Lynn 1939- *WhoAm 92*
Adams, Harriet S(tratemeyer) 1892?-1982 *MajAI [port]*
Adams, Harriet Stratemeyer *BioIn 17*
Adams, Harriet Stratemeyer 1892-1982 *ScF&FL 92*
Adams, Hazard 1926- *ScF&FL 92*
Adams, Hazard Simeon 1926- *WhoAm 92*
Adams, Hazel Greenlee Redfearn 1905- *WhoAmW 93, WhoSSW 93*
Adams, Helen Schmidlen 1935- *WhoAmW 93*
Adams, Henry 1802-1872 *EncAACR*
Adams, Henry 1838-1918 *BioIn 17, GayN, MagSAmL [port]*
Adams, Henry 1949- *WhoAm 92*
Adams, Henry B. 1838-1918 *PolPar*
Adams, Herbert Ryan 1932- *WhoAm 92*
Adams, Howard Glen 1940- *WhoAm 92*
Adams, Hunter *BioIn 17, ScF&FL 92*
Adams, Ian 1937- *ScF&FL 92, WhoCanL 92*
Adams, J. Randy 1956- *St&PR 93*
Adams, J. W. 1929- *WhoAm 92*
Adams, Jack *ScF&FL 92*
Adams, Jack 1952- *WhoEmL 93*
Adams, James A. 1927- *St&PR 93*
Adams, James Allen 1954- *WhoEmL 93*
Adams, James Blackburn 1926- *WhoAm 92*
Adams, James E. 1944- *WhoAm 92*
Adams, James Frederick 1927- *WhoAm 92*
Adams, James G., Jr. 1954- *WhoEmL 93*
Adams, James Hume *WhoScE 91-1*
Adams, James Louis 1928- *WhoAm 92*
Adams, James Luther 1901- *BioIn 17, WhoAm 92*
Adams, James Lyn 1950- *WhoWrEP 92*
Adams, James M. 1952- *St&PR 93*
Adams, James (Macgregor David) 1951- *ConAu 138*
Adams, James Mills 1936- *WhoAm 92, WhoE 93*
Adams, James R. 1939- *WhoAm 92*
Adams, James Richard 1941- *WhoWrEP 92*
Adams, James S. 1959- *St&PR 93*
Adams, James Thomas 1930- *WhoAm 92*
Adams, James W., Jr. *Law&B 92*
Adams, James Wilson 1928- *WhoSSW 93*
Adams, Jane Ellen 1940- *WhoAmW 93*
Adams, Jane F. 1957- *St&PR 93*
Adams, Jane Grant *Law&B 92*
Adams, Jane (Poni) 1921- *SweetSg C*
Adams, Janet Woodbury d1991 *BioIn 17*
Adams, Jay Willette 1953- *WhoSSW 93*
Adams, Jean Ruth 1928- *WhoAm 92, WhoAmW 93*
Adams, Jeffrey Karl 1950- *WhoEmL 93*
Adams, Jennifer A. 1952- *WhoEmL 93*
Adams, Jere Sue *Law&B 92*
Adams, Jerome R(obertson) 1938- *ConAu 139*
Adams, Jerry L. 1946- *WhoEmL 93, WhoSSW 93*
Adams, Jerry Ray 1961- *WhoSSW 93*
Adams, Jill Elaine 1952- *WhoEmL 93*
Adams, Jim Walter 1928- *WhoSSW 93*
Adams, Jimmie Vick 1936- *WhoAm 92*
Adams, Joe D. 1933- *St&PR 93*
Adams, Joey 1911- *WhoAm 92*
Adams, John *BioIn 17, ScF&FL 92*
Adams, John 1735-1826 *BioIn 17, PolPar*
Adams, John 1947- *ConMus 8 [port], IntDcOp, OxDcOp*
Adams, John Allan Stewart 1926- *WhoAm 92*
Adams, John Anthony 1944- *BioIn 17*
Adams, John B. 1947- *St&PR 93*
Adams, John Buchanan, Jr. 1948- *WhoAm 92*
Adams, John C. 1939- *WhoAm 92, WhoSSW 93*
Adams, John Carter, Jr. 1936- *WhoWor 93*
Adams, John (Coolidge) 1947- *Baker 92*
Adams, John David Vessot 1934- *WhoAm 92*
Adams, John Francis, Jr. 1936- *WhoAm 92*
Adams, John H. 1936- *BioIn 17*
Adams, John Hamilton 1936- *WhoAm 92*
Adams, John Hanly 1918- *WhoAm 92*
Adams, John Hubert 1943- *St&PR 93*
Adams, John Hurst 1929- *WhoAm 92*
Adams, John Laurence 1943- *WhoE 93*
Adams, John Lewis *WhoAm 92*
Adams, John M. 1950- *WhoSSW 93*
Adams, John Marshall *Law&B 92*
Adams, John Marshall 1930- *WhoAm 92*
Adams, John Quincy *DcCPCAm*
Adams, John Quincy d1990 *BioIn 17*
Adams, John Quincy 1767-1848 *BioIn 17, OxCSupC, PolPar*
Adams, John Quincy 1938- *WhoAm 92*
Adams, John Quincy, III 1945- *WhoAm 92*
Adams, John R. 1900- *WhoAm 92*
Adams, John Richard 1918- *WhoAm 92*
Adams, John Robert 1938- *WhoAm 92*
Adams, John Stephen 1938- *WhoAm 92*
Adams, John T. 1862-1939 *PolPar*
Adams, John Wayne 1947- *WhoEmL 93*
Adams, John William 1924- *St&PR 93*
Adams, John William 1956- *WhoE 93*
Adams, Johnnie L. 1944- *St&PR 93*
Adams, Johnny 1932- *SoulM*
Adams, Jonathan L. 1947- *WhoAm 92*
Adams, Joseph A. 1960- *St&PR 93*
Adams, Joseph C. *Law&B 92*
Adams, Joseph H. *BioIn 17*
Adams, Joseph Peter 1907- *WhoAm 92, WhoWor 93*
Adams, Joseph T. *Law&B 92*
Adams, Joseph W. 1924- *St&PR 93*
Adams, Joseph William 1966- *WhoSSW 93*
Adams, Joyce Carol 1946- *WhoEmL 93*
Adams, Joyce Marilyn 1934- *WhoAmW 93*
Adams, Judith Ann 1948- *WhoEmL 93*
Adams, Julie 1926?- *SweetSg D [port]*
Adams, Julius Gregg 1957- *WhoE 93*
Adams, June Miller *Law&B 92*
Adams, K. Susie *Law&B 92*
Adams, Karen Cooper 1941- *WhoE 93*
Adams, Kathleen Ann 1953- *WhoAmW 93*
Adams, Kathleen Margaret 1952- *WhoE 93*
Adams, Keith *WhoSSW 93*
Adams, Kenneth Francis 1946- *St&PR 93, WhoAm 92*
Adams, Kenneth R. *Law&B 92*
Adams, Kenneth R. 1941- *St&PR 93*
Adams, Kenneth Stanley, Jr. 1923- *St&PR 93, WhoAm 92, WhoSSW 93*
Adams, Kevin Martin 1964- *WhoSSW 93*
Adams, Kevin Paul 1968- *WhoWor 93*
Adams, Kirby C. 1955- *St&PR 93*
Adams, L. Sherman 1899-1986 *PolPar*
Adams, Laura Ann 1959- *WhoAmW 93*
Adams, Laura Lee 1956- *WhoEmL 93*
Adams, Laura Merrihew *AmWomPl*
Adams, Laura Sitz 1946- *WhoSSW 93*
Adams, Laurie Marie 1941- *WhoE 93*
Adams, Lawrence 1955- *St&PR 93*
Adams, Lawrence Charles 1948- *WhoEmL 93*
Adams, Lee S. *Law&B 92*
Adams, Lee S. 1949- *St&PR 93*
Adams, Lee Stephen 1949- *WhoAm 92, WhoEmL 93*
Adams, Leland J., Jr. *Law&B 92*
Adams, Leon Ashby, III 1951- *WhoWor 93*
Adams, Leon David 1905- *WhoAm 92*
Adams, Leslie Bunn, Jr. 1932- *WhoAm 92*
Adams, Leslie William *Law&B 92*
Adams, Levi 1802?-1832 *BioIn 17*
Adams, Linda Crausby 1961- *WhoAmW 93*
Adams, Linda Susan 1964- *WhoAmW 93*
Adams, Lisa *BioIn 17*
Adams, Louisa Catherine 1775-1852 *BioIn 17*
Adams, Lowell William 1946- *WhoE 93*
Adams, Lucy Shire 1906- *WhoAmW 93*
Adams, Lynda Chuchko 1961- *WhoE 93*
Adams, Malcolm Ritchie 1956- *WhoSSW 93*
Adams, Marcia Howe *Law&B 92*
Adams, Marcia Howe 1948- *WhoEmL 93*
Adams, Marcus Hans Wilhelm 1954- *WhoWor 93*
Adams, Margaret Ann 1935- *WhoAmW 93*
Adams, Margaret Bernice 1936- *WhoAm 92*
Adams, Margaret Diane 1937- *WhoAmW 93*
Adams, Margaret Irene *Law&B 92*
Adams, Margaret Mary 1953- *WhoAmW 93*
Adams, Marian 1843?-1885 *BioIn 17*
Adams, Marilyn Jager *BioIn 17*
Adams, Marilyn Jager 1948- *ConAu 136*
Adams, Marjorie E. 1947- *St&PR 93*
Adams, Marjory Brower 1943- *WhoAmW 93*
Adams, Mark 1925- *WhoAm 92*
Adams, Mark Patrick 1967- *WhoSSW 93*
Adams, Mark R. 1961- *St&PR 93*
Adams, Martha C. *Law&B 92*
Adams, Mary Katherine 1951- *WhoAmW 93*
Adams, Mary Lonergan *Law&B 92*
Adams, Mason 1919- *WhoAm 92*
Adams, Maud *BioIn 17*
Adams, Maude 1872-1953 *BioIn 17*
Adams, Maureen Kay 1948- *WhoAmW 93*
Adams, Michael *BioIn 17*
Adams, Michael B. 1943- *St&PR 93*
Adams, Michael Charles Corringham 1945- *WhoSSW 93*
Adams, Michael F. 1948- *WhoAm 92*
Adams, Michael James *WhoScE 91-1*
Adams, Michael John *WhoScE 91-1*
Adams, Michael L. 1948- *WhoEmL 93*
Adams, Michael R. 1954- *WhoE 93*
Adams, Michael Ross 1957- *WhoEmL 93*
Adams, Michael Thomas 1948- *WhoEmL 93*
Adams, Michelle Florine 1966- *WhoAmW 93*
Adams, Mignon Strickland *WhoE 93*
Adams, Molly Kathryn Smith 1929- *WhoAmW 93*
Adams, Moses 1803-1837 *BioIn 17*
Adams, Myrna D. 1940- *St&PR 93*
Adams, N.Q. 1925- *St&PR 93*
Adams, Nancy Ann 1932- *WhoSSW 93*
Adams, Nancy R. *WhoAmW 93*
Adams, Nathaniel Keene *Law&B 92*
Adams, Neil Douglas 1944- *WhoSSW 93*
Adams, Nicholas *ScF&FL 92*
Adams, Nicholas 1952- *St&PR 93*
Adams, Nick 1931?-1968 *BioIn 17*
Adams, Noah *WhoE 93*
Adams, Norman 1927- *BioIn 17*
Adams, Norman J. 1933- *St&PR 93*
Adams, Norman Joseph 1930- *WhoWor 93*
Adams, O. Edwin 1934- *St&PR 93*
Adams, Oleta *BioIn 17, SoulM*
Adams, Onie H. Powers 1907- *WhoWor 93*
Adams, Oscar William, Jr. 1925- *WhoAm 92, WhoSSW 93*
Adams, Owen Ed, Sr. 1936- *WhoSSW 93*
Adams, Pamela Crippen 1961- *ScF&FL 92*
Adams, Pat 1928- *WhoAm 92, WhoE 93*
Adams, Patricia Anne 1961- *WhoAmW 93*
Adams, Patti Lynn 1952- *WhoSSW 93*
Adams, Paul Ancil 1937- *WhoAm 92*
Adams, Paul G. 1945- *St&PR 93*
Adams, Paul Winfrey 1913- *WhoAm 92*
Adams, Pauline Gordon 1922- *WhoAmW 93*
Adams, Payton F. 1930- *WhoAm 92*
Adams, Perry Ronald 1921- *WhoAm 92*
Adams, Peter *DcCPCAm*
Adams, Peter David 1937- *WhoAm 92*
Adams, Peter Frederick *WhoAm 92*
Adams, Peter Sayles 1953- *WhoEmL 93*
Adams, Peter Webster 1939- *St&PR 93*
Adams, Phelps H. 1902-1991 *BioIn 17*
Adams, Philip 1905- *WhoWor 93*
Adams, Phoebe-Lou *BioIn 17*
Adams, Platt 1885-1961 *BiDAMSp 1989*
Adams, Ralph E. 1935- *St&PR 93*
Adams, Ralph Wyatt, Sr. 1915- *WhoAm 92, WhoWor 93*
Adams, Ranald Trevor, Jr. 1925- *WhoAm 92*
Adams, Randall David 1958- *WhoEmL 93, WhoSSW 93*

Adams, Raymond Edward 1933- *WhoAm 92*
Adams, Raymond Randal 1954- *WhoSSW 93*
Adams, Richard 1920- *BioIn 17, ChlFicS, ScF&FL 92, SmATA 69 [port]*
Adams, Richard B. 1943- *St&PR 93*
Adams, Richard Edward 1921- *WhoAm 92*
Adams, Richard (George) 1920- *MajAI [port], WhoAm 92, WhoWor 93*
Adams, Richard Glenn 1951- *WhoE 93, WhoWrEP 92*
Adams, Richard Gregg 1932- *St&PR 93*
Adams, Richard M. 1947- *WhoAm 92*
Adams, Richard Newbold 1924- *WhoAm 92*
Adams, Richard Towsley 1921- *WhoAm 92*
Adams, Richard Willey 1926- *St&PR 93*
Adams, Robert 1932-1990 *ScF&FL 92*
Adams, Robert Allen 1945- *WhoIns 93*
Adams, Robert Arthur, Jr. 1959- *WhoE 93*
Adams, Robert B. *Law&B 92*
Adams, Robert Bentley *BioIn 17*
Adams, Robert D. *Law&B 92*
Adams, Robert D. 1941- *St&PR 93*
Adams, Robert David *WhoScE 91-1*
Adams, Robert Edward 1941- *WhoAm 92*
Adams, Robert F. 1937- *WhoSSW 93*
Adams, Robert Francis 1947- *St&PR 93*
Adams, Robert H(ickman) 1937- *WhoWrEP 92*
Adams, Robert Hugo 1943- *WhoAm 92*
Adams, Robert J. 1932- *St&PR 93*
Adams, Robert Kitwell, II 1944- *WhoSSW 93*
Adams, Robert M. 1923- *St&PR 93*
Adams, Robert McCormick 1926- *ConAu 39NR, WhoAm 92, WhoE 93*
Adams, Robert Rehmann 1935- *St&PR 93*
Adams, Robert Walker 1950- *WhoWor 93*
Adams, Robert Waugh, Jr. 1936- *WhoAm 92*
Adams, Rodger 1953- *St&PR 93*
Adams, Roger Anthony 1934- *St&PR 93*
Adams, Roger James 1935- *WhoE 93*
Adams, Roger W. 1938- *WhoScE 91-1*
Adams, Ronald Emerson 1943- *WhoAm 92*
Adams, Ronald Roy *St&PR 93*
Adams, Rose Ann 1952- *WhoAmW 93*
Adams, Roy 1933- *St&PR 93, WhoAm 92*
Adams, Roy M. 1940- *WhoAm 92*
Adams, Russell Baird 1910- *WhoAm 92*
Adams, Ruth Salzman 1923- *WhoAm 92*
Adams, Sallyann Kelly 1952- *WhoAmW 93*
Adams, Samuel 1722-1803 *JrnUS, PolPar*
Adams, Samuel Franklin 1958- *WhoEmL 93*
Adams, Samuel Hopkins 1871-1958 *JrnUS*
Adams, Sandra Ann 1948- *WhoEmL 93*
Adams, Sandra Lynn 1946- *WhoAmW 93*
Adams, Sandra Lynn 1958- *WhoSSW 93*
Adams, Sarah Virginia 1955- *WhoAmW 93, WhoEmL 93*
Adams, Scott 1909-1982 *BioIn 17*
Adams, Scott Leslie 1955- *WhoEmL 93*
Adams, Seibert 1934- *St&PR 93*
Adams, Sexton 1936- *ConAu 37NR*
Adams, Shirley Jo 1959- *St&PR 93*
Adams, Stanley 1907- *WhoAm 92*
Adams, Stephen 1939- *WhoAm 92*
Adams, Stephen F. *Law&B 92*
Adams, Steve *WhoAm 92, WhoSSW 93*
Adams, Steven Lee 1957- *WhoSSW 93, WhoWor 93*
Adams, Suzanne 1872-1953 *Baker 92*
Adams, Taggart D. 1941- *WhoAm 92*
Adams, Tammy Downer 1959- *WhoSSW 93*
Adams, Teri Joy 1947- *WhoAmW 93*
Adams, Terry A. *ScF&FL 92*
Adams, Thelma Michelle 1959- *WhoE 93, WhoEmL 93*
Adams, Thomas *BioIn 17*
Adams, Thomas 1785-1858 *Baker 92*
Adams, Thomas Boylston 1910- *WhoAm 92*
Adams, Thomas Brooks 1919- *WhoAm 92*
Adams, Thomas Gerald 1938- *WhoAm 92*
Adams, Thomas Merritt 1935- *WhoAm 92*
Adams, Thomas Randolph 1921- *WhoAm 92*
Adams, Thomas Stanley 1948- *St&PR 93*
Adams, Thomas Tilley 1929- *WhoE 93, WhoWor 93*
Adams, Thomas Walton 1947- *WhoEmL 93, WhoWor 93*
Adams, Timothy D. 1959- *St&PR 93*
Adams, Timothy Dow 1943- *WhoSSW 93*
Adams, Timothy Journay 1948- *WhoEmL 93*
Adams, Timothy Raymond 1951- *WhoEmL 93*
Adams, Todd Porter 1955- *WhoSSW 93*
Adams, Tom 1931-1985 *DcCPCAm*
Adams, Tony 1953- *ConTFT 10*
Adams, Vanessa Marlene 1959- *WhoSSW 93*
Adams, Vergil 1926- *St&PR 93*
Adams, Veronica Wadewitz 1951- *WhoAm 92*
Adams, Victoria Eleanor 1941- *WhoAmW 93, WhoWor 93*
Adams, Vivian 1941- *WhoAmW 93*
Adams, W. Andrew 1945- *WhoAm 92*
Adams, W. Earl *St&PR 93*
Adams, W.G. 1934- *St&PR 93*
Adams, W. Randolph 1944- *St&PR 93*
Adams, Walter 1922- *BioIn 17, ConAu 37NR*
Adams, Warren Sanford, II 1910- *WhoAm 92, WhoWor 93*
Adams, Wayne Verdun 1945- *WhoAm 92*
Adams, Welles V. 1924- *St&PR 93*
Adams, Weston 1938- *WhoAm 92, WhoWor 93*
Adams, Wiley S. *Law&B 92*
Adams, William Alfred 1960- *WhoEmL 93*
Adams, William Carryl 1940- *WhoSSW 93*
Adams, William Duval 1917- *St&PR 93*
Adams, William Gillette 1939- *WhoAm 92*
Adams, William Hensley 1929- *WhoAm 92, WhoWor 93*
Adams, William J. *Law&B 92*
Adams, William J. 1941- *St&PR 93*
Adams, William Jack 1929- *St&PR 93*
Adams, William Jackson, Jr. 1908- *WhoAm 92*
Adams, William Johnston 1934- *WhoAm 92*
Adams, William LeRoy 1929- *St&PR 93, WhoAm 92*
Adams, William Mansfield 1932- *WhoAm 92*
Adams, William Richard 1923- *WhoAm 92*
Adams, William Roger 1935- *WhoAm 92*
Adams, William Taylor 1957- *WhoWrEP 92*
Adams, William V. *St&PR 93*
Adams, William Valere 1948- *WhoEmL 93*
Adams, William W. 1934- *St&PR 93*
Adams, William White 1934- *WhoAm 92, WhoE 93*
Adams, William Yewdale 1927- *WhoAm 92*
Adams-Berry, Kathy 1961- *WhoAmW 93*
Adams-Ender, Clara *BioIn 17*
Adams-Ender, Clara Leach 1939- *AfrAmBi [port], WhoAm 92*
Adams-Jacobson, Nancy 1952- *WhoWrEP 92*
Adams Jones, D. *WhoScE 91-1*
Adamski, Richard J. *WhoAm 92*
Adamski, Robert J. 1935- *St&PR 93*
Adamski, Thomas Joseph 1947- *St&PR 93*
Adamsky, Robert Stephen 1947- *St&PR 93*
Adamson, Al *MiSFD 9*
Adamson, Albert Scott, Jr. 1947- *WhoEmL 93*
Adamson, Arthur Wilson 1919- *WhoAm 92*
Adamson, Carl Theodore, Jr. 1951- *St&PR 93*
Adamson, Dan Klinglesmith 1939- *WhoAm 92, WhoSSW 93*
Adamson, Donald 1939- *ConAu 39NR*
Adamson, Gary Bror 1934- *St&PR 93*
Adamson, Gary M. 1936- *St&PR 93*
Adamson, Gary Milton 1936- *WhoAm 92*
Adamson, Geoffrey David 1946- *WhoAm 92, WhoEmL 93*
Adamson, George *BioIn 17*
Adamson, Grant F. *Law&B 92*
Adamson, Jack 1923- *St&PR 93*
Adamson, James C. *BioIn 17*
Adamson, Jane N. 1931- *WhoAmW 93*
Adamson, Janet Laurel 1882-1962 *BioIn 17*
Adamson, Joe 1945- *WhoWrEP 92*
Adamson, John Ernest 1867-1950 *BioIn 17*
Adamson, John William 1936- *WhoAm 92*
Adamson, Joy 1910-1980 *BioIn 17*
Adamson, Linda Larson *Law&B 92*
Adamson, Mary Anne 1954- *WhoAmW 93*
Adamson, Oscar Charles, II 1924- *WhoAm 92*
Adamson, Peter 1946- *WhoWor 93*
Adamson, Reggie D. 1951- *WhoIns 93*
Adamson, Robin *WhoScE 91-1*
Adamson, Scott 1946- *St&PR 93*
Adamson, Steven B. 1955- *St&PR 93*
Adamson, Terrence Burdett 1946- *WhoAm 92*
Adamson, Thomas Charles, Jr. 1924- *WhoAm 92*
Adamsons, Uldis 1945- *WhoE 93, WhoWor 93*
Adams-Slone, Rita Diane 1949- *WhoEmL 93*
Adams-Staskin, Irene D. 1928- *St&PR 93*
Adam von Fulda c. 1440-1505 *Baker 92*
Adan, Avraham 1926- *BioIn 17, HarEnMi*
Adan, Martin 1908-1985 *SpAmA*
Adanalian, Charles Ronald 1939- *St&PR 93*
Adanio, Louis A. *WhoIns 93*
Adante, David E. 1951- *St&PR 93*
Adante, Richard P. 1946- *St&PR 93*
Adar, Uri 1928- *St&PR 93*
Adare, J. Robert 1927- *St&PR 93*
Adasa, Artemio A. 1952- *WhoAsAP 91*
Adashek, James L. *Law&B 92*
Adaskin, Murray 1906- *Baker 92, WhoAm 92*
Adato, Beverly Zweig 1955- *WhoEmL 93, WhoSSW 93*
Adato, Perry Miller *WhoAm 92*
Adawi, Ibrahim Hasan 1930- *WhoAm 92*
Adawi, Nadia Sharon 1958- *WhoEmL 93*
Adcock, Albert 1929- *St&PR 93*
Adcock, Betty *BioIn 17*
Adcock, David Filmore 1938- *WhoAm 92*
Adcock, David William 1958- *St&PR 93*
Adcock, Elizabeth Sharp 1938- *WhoWrEP 92*
Adcock, J. Michael 1949- *St&PR 93*
Adcock, James Luther 1943- *WhoSSW 93*
Adcock, James Michael 1949- *WhoAm 92*
Adcock, Louie Norman, Jr. 1930- *WhoAm 92*
Adcock, Phil *BioIn 17*
Adcock, Richard Paul *Law&B 92*
Adcock, Thomas 1947- *ConAu 138*
Adcock, William Elton 1931- *St&PR 93*
Adcock, Willis Alfred 1922- *WhoAm 92*
Adcox, Gerald Wayne, Jr. 1955- *St&PR 93*
Adcox, Stephen Irvin 1946- *WhoAm 92, WhoEmL 93*
Addae, Sandra A. *Law&B 92*
Addams, Jane 1860-1935 *BioIn 17, ConHero 2 [port], DcTwHis, GayN, WomChHR [port]*
Addanki, Somasundaram 1932- *WhoE 93*
Addante, Steven M. 1957- *St&PR 93*
Addelson, Kathryn Pyne 1932- *WhoWrEP 92*
Addenbrook, William J. 1938- *St&PR 93*
Addeo, Edmund G. 1907-1980 *ScF&FL 92*
Addeo, John A. 1948- *St&PR 93*
Adder, Dr. *ScF&FL 92*
Adderley, Herb 1939- *BioIn 17*
Adderley, James 1861-1942 *ScF&FL 92*
Adderley, Julian Edwin 1928-1975 *Baker 92*
Adderley, Terence E. 1933- *St&PR 93*
Addes, George 1910-1990 *BioIn 17*
Addessi, Aileen Champion *Law&B 92*
Addesso, Dominic James 1953- *WhoIns 93*
Addicott, Fredrick Taylor 1912- *WhoAm 92*
Addicott, Warren Oliver 1930- *WhoAm 92*
Addiego, James P. 1941- *WhoIns 93*
Addington, Betty Jane 1945- *St&PR 93*
Addington, Bruce 1953- *St&PR 93*
Addington, Graham A. 1949- *St&PR 93*
Addington, James H. 1938- *St&PR 93*
Addington, Kay Frances 1941- *WhoAmW 93*
Addington, Larry *St&PR 93*
Addington, Larry C. 1936- *ConEn*
Addington, Ronda Jo 1958- *WhoAmW 93*
Addington, Sarah 1891-1940 *ScF&FL 92*
Addinsell, Richard (Stewart) 1904-1977 *Baker 92*
Addis, Deborah Jane 1950- *WhoAmW 93*
Addis, Donna Jean 1945- *WhoAmW 93*
Addis, Harold Earl 1930- *St&PR 93*
Addis, Laird Clark, Jr. 1937- *WhoAm 92*
Addis, Lauane Cleo 1956- *St&PR 93*
Addis, Sara Allen 1930- *WhoAmW 93*
Addis, Thomas Richard *WhoScE 91-1*
Addison, Adele 1925- *Baker 92*
Addison, Alexander 1930- *WhoWor 93*
Addison, Brian Michael *Law&B 92*
Addison, Charles H. 1941- *WhoIns 93*
Addison, Charles Henry 1941- *St&PR 93, WhoAm 92*
Addison, David Dunham 1941- *WhoSSW 93*
Addison, Edward L. 1930- *St&PR 93, WhoAm 92, WhoSSW 93*
Addison, Era Scott 1933- *WhoWrEP 92*
Addison, Harry Metcalf 1938- *WhoAm 92*
Addison, Herbert John 1932- *WhoAm 92*
Addison, James Clyde, Jr. 1947- *WhoEmL 93, WhoSSW 93*
Addison, John 1920- *Baker 92*
Addison, John 1946- *WhoScE 91-1*
Addison, Joseph *ScF&FL 92*
Addison, Joseph 1672-1719 *BioIn 17, OxDcOp*
Addison, Linda Leuchter 1951- *WhoAm 92, WhoAmW 93*
Addison, Roger G. *Law&B 92*
Addison, Stephen Oliver, Jr. 1954- *WhoEmL 93*
Addison, Ulysses Zembles, Jr. 1961- *WhoSSW 93*
Addison, William Oscar 1950- *WhoEmL 93*
Addiss, Stephen 1935- *WhoAm 92*
Addiss, Susan Silliman 1931- *WhoAmW 93*
Addlestone, Nathan S. 1913- *St&PR 93*
Addlestone, Nathan Sidney 1913- *WhoAm 92*
Addleton, David Franklin 1954- *WhoEmL 93, WhoSSW 93*
Adducci, Anthony J. 1937- *St&PR 93*
Adducci, Joseph Edward 1934- *WhoAm 92*
Adduci, Vincent James 1920- *WhoAm 92*
Addy, Alva Leroy 1936- *WhoAm 92*
Addy, Frederick S. 1932- *St&PR 93*
Addy, Frederick Seale 1932- *WhoAm 92*
Addy, George Arthur 1915- *WhoAm 92*
Addy, Jo Alison Phears 1951- *WhoAm 92*
Addy, Lowell David 1951- *WhoEmL 93*
Addy, Martin *WhoScE 91-1*
Addy, May *AmWomPl*
Ade, George 1866-1944 *GayN, JrnUS*
Ade, Ginny *WhoWrEP 92*
Ade, James L. 1932- *WhoAm 92, WhoSSW 93*
Ade, Jerome Carroll 1950- *WhoE 93*
Ade, Ronald Charles 1929- *WhoIns 93*
Adebonojo, Festus O. 1931- *WhoAm 92*
Adede, Andronico O. 1937- *WhoUN 92*
Adedeji, Adebayo 1930- *WhoAfr, WhoWor 93*
Adee, Bernard E. 1934- *St&PR 93*
Adegbite, Samson G. 1952- *WhoE 93, WhoEmL 93*
Adegbola, Sikiru Kolawole 1949- *WhoEmL 93, WhoWor 93*
Adekson, Mary Olufunmilayo *WhoAmW 93, WhoWor 93*
Adelberg, Arthur W. *Law&B 92*
Adelberg, Arthur William 1951- *St&PR 93, WhoAm 92*
Adelberg, Edward Allen 1920- *WhoAm 92*
Adelberg, Harry 1906-1990 *BioIn 17*
Adelberg, Philip 1941- *St&PR 93*
Adelburg, August, Ritter von 1830-1873 *Baker 92*
Adelekan, Patricia Ann 1942- *WhoAmW 93*
Adelgren, Kermit Edward 1931- *St&PR 93*
Adelhardt, Andrew J. 1935- *St&PR 93*
Adeli, Hojjat 1950- *WhoAm 92, WhoEmL 93*
Adelis, Nancy C. 1953- *WhoAmW 93*
Adelizzi, Robert F. 1935- *St&PR 93*
Adelizzi, Robert Frederick 1935- *WhoAm 92*
Adell, Hirsch 1931- *WhoAm 92*
Adelman, Adrian d1991 *BioIn 17*
Adelman, Andrew George 1928- *WhoSSW 93*
Adelman, David Isaac 1964- *WhoEmL 93, WhoSSW 93*
Adelman, Deborah Susan 1953- *WhoEmL 93*
Adelman, Gerald S. 1942- *WhoIns 93*
Adelman, Graham L. 1949- *St&PR 93*
Adelman, Graham Lewis *Law&B 92*
Adelman, Graham Lewis 1949- *WhoAm 92*
Adelman, Herbert Bernard 1928- *St&PR 93*
Adelman, Irma *BioIn 17*
Adelman, Irma Glicman 1930- *WhoAm 92*
Adelman, Irving 1926- *WhoE 93*
Adelman, Jonathan Reuben 1948- *WhoEmL 93*
Adelman, Kenneth Allan 1959- *WhoE 93*
Adelman, Kenneth Lee 1946- *WhoAm 92*
Adelman, Michael L. 1952- *St&PR 93*
Adelman, Milton Harris 1910- *WhoE 93*
Adelman, Richard Charles 1940- *WhoAm 92*
Adelman, Rick 1946- *WhoAm 92*
Adelman, Robert Bardwell 1952- *WhoEmL 93*
Adelman, Robert Wharton 1954- *St&PR 93*
Adelman, Saul Joseph 1944- *WhoSSW 93*
Adelman, Stanley Joseph 1942- *WhoAm 92*
Adelman, Stanley R. 1925- *St&PR 93*
Adelman, Steven Allen 1945- *WhoAm 92*
Adelman, Steven Herbert 1945- *WhoAm 92*
Adelman, William John 1932- *WhoAm 92*
Adelmann, Frederick Joseph 1915- *WhoAm 92*

Adelmann, Penelope Owens WhoAm 92, WhoE 93
Adels, Robert Mitchell 1948- WhoAm 92
Adelsheim, Mark Simon 1952- WhoEmL 93
Adelsman, Jean 1944- WhoAmW 93
Adelson, Alan Merrill 1943- WhoE 93
Adelson, Alexander M. 1934- WhoAm 92
Adelson, Gerald H. 1937- St&PR 93
Adelson, Lawrence Seth Law&B 92
Adelson, Lawrence Seth 1950- WhoEmL 93
Adelson, Mark Hirsch 1960- WhoEmL 93
Adelson, Maurice Bernard, IV 1952- WhoEmL 93
Adelson, Mervyn Lee 1929- WhoAm 92
Adelstein, Peter Z. 1924- WhoE 93
Adelstein, Stanford Mark 1931- St&PR 93
Adelstein, Stanley James 1928- WhoAm 92
Adema, E.H. 1927- WhoScE 91-3
Aden, Arthur Laverne 1924- WhoAm 92
Aden, Susan J. Law&B 92
Adenauer, Konrad 1876-1967 BioIn 17, ColdWar 1 [port], DcTwHis
Adenbaum, Robert W. 1928- St&PR 93
Adeney, Howard Martin 1942- WhoWor 93
Adeniran, Dixie Darlene 1943- WhoAmW 93
Adenis, Jacques Andre Marie 1926- WhoWor 93
Ader, Joseph Daniel 1947- WhoEmL 93, WhoSSW 93
Ader, Lisa F. Law&B 92
Ader, Richard Alan 1951- WhoAm 92, WhoEmL 93
Ader, Robert 1932- WhoE 93
Aderhold, John Edward 1925- St&PR 93
Aderholdt, Janet Ann 1966- WhoAmW 93
Aderholt, Ben L. 1942- WhoAm 92
Aderman, Larry James 1952- St&PR 93
Adermann, Albert Evan 1927- WhoAsAP 91
Aders, Robert O. 1927- WhoAm 92
Aderton, Jane Reynolds 1913- WhoAm 92
Adessa, Anthony Thomas 1951- WhoSSW 93
Adessi, G. WhoScE 91-2
Adeva SoulM
Adey, William Ross 1922- WhoAm 92
Adezati, Luciano 1924- WhoWor 93
Adgate, Andrew 1762-1793 Baker 92
Adhemar, Jean 1908-1987 BioIn 17
Adhemar de Monteil, Bishop of Le Puy d1098 HarEnMi
Adherbal d113BC HarEnMi
Adhikari, Ambika P. 1952- WhoEmL 93
Adhikari, Surendra Bir 1954- WhoWor 93
Adhin, Herman Sookdew 1933- WhoWor 93
Adhyatma, M. P. H. 1932- WhoAsAP 91
Adib, Ahmed 1937- WhoUN 92
Adibe, Ernest Chukwuemeka 1950- WhoWor 93
Adickes, Sandra 1933- ConAu 139
Adie, Bryce R. 1938- St&PR 93
Adiel, Ray 1927- St&PR 93
Adiele, Nkwachkwu Moses 1951- WhoEmL 93, WhoWor 93
Adik, Stephen Peter 1943- St&PR 93, WhoAm 92
Adikes, James D. 1962- WhoE 93
Adikes, Park T. 1931- St&PR 93
Adikes, Robert Kirk 1939- St&PR 93
Adikpeto, Kodjo E. 1941- WhoUN 92
Adila, John Law&B 92
Adilardi, G. WhoScE 91-3
Adiletta, Debra Jean Olson 1959- WhoAmW 93, WhoEmL 93
Adiletta, Joseph George 1920- St&PR 93
Adimando, Carmine F. 1944- St&PR 93
Adin, Nancy Edith 1938- WhoAmW 93
Adinolfi, Matteo WhoScE 91-1
Adireksarn, Pramarn 1914- WhoAsAP 91
Adirim, Aaron 1946- WhoEmL 93, WhoWor 93
Adiseshiah, Malcolm Sathianathan 1910- WhoWor 93
Adisman, Irwin Kenneth 1919- WhoAm 92
Aditya, I 870-960 HarEnMi
Adjamah, Kokouvi Michel 1942- WhoWor 93
Adjani, Isabelle BioIn 17
Adjani, Isabelle 1955- IntDcF 2-3 [port]
Adjei, Alex Asiedu 1955- WhoWor 93
Adkerson, Donya Lynn 1959- WhoAmW 93
Adkin, Mark 1936- ConAu 139
Adkins, Arthur William Hope 1929- WhoAm 92
Adkins, Barbara L. 1946- WhoSSW 93, WhoWor 93
Adkins, Ben Frank 1938- WhoWor 93
Adkins, Bertha S. 1906-1983 PolPar
Adkins, Betty A. 1934- WhoAmW 93
Adkins, Bradley W. 1937- St&PR 93
Adkins, C. John WhoScE 91-1
Adkins, Cecil (Dale) 1932- Baker 92
Adkins, Cephas Joe, Jr. 1925- WhoSSW 93
Adkins, Craig Ivan 1963- WhoEmL 93
Adkins, Edward Cleland 1926- WhoAm 92, WhoWor 93
Adkins, Edward James 1947- WhoEmL 93
Adkins, Fredrick Earl, III 1952- WhoSSW 93
Adkins, G. Carlton Law&B 92
Adkins, Gregory D. 1941- WhoAm 92
Adkins, Howard Eugene 1912- WhoAm 92
Adkins, Jan 1944- MajAI [port], SmATA 69 [port]
Adkins, Janet d1990 BioIn 17
Adkins, Jo Ann Yeager 1929- WhoSSW 93
Adkins, John Earl, Jr. 1937- WhoAm 92
Adkins, Leslie John d1991 BioIn 17
Adkins, Luther Pryor 1926- St&PR 93
Adkins, M. Douglas 1936- WhoAm 92
Adkins, Margaret Anne 1957- WhoSSW 93
Adkins, Patrick H. 1948- ScF&FL 92
Adkins, Richard Cyril WhoScE 91-1
Adkins, Robert Thune, Sr. 1926- WhoSSW 93
Adkins, Rosanne Brown 1944- WhoAmW 93
Adkins, Roy Allen 1952- WhoEmL 93
Adkins, Thomas Ronald Law&B 92
Adkins, Walter L. 1937- St&PR 93
Adkinson, Brian Lee 1959- WhoEmL 93
Adkinson, David Keith 1949- St&PR 93
Adkinson, Robert K. ScF&FL 92
Adkinson, Ruth AmWomPl
Adkison, Ronnie Darrell 1958- WhoSSW 93
Adkisson, Davis Whitfield, Jr. Law&B 92
Adkisson, Perry Lee 1929- WhoAm 92, WhoSSW 93
Adlai, Richard S. 1942- St&PR 93
Adland, Marvin Leon 1919- WhoE 93
Adlard, Mark 1932- ScF&FL 92
Adlard, Maxwell Wright WhoScE 91-1
Adlard, Peter M. ScF&FL 92
Adle, Richard S. 1946- WhoE 93
Adleman, Robert H. 1916-1989 ScF&FL 92
Adler, Aaron 1914- WhoAm 92
Adler, Alan 1951- ScF&FL 92
Adler, Allen A. 1916-1964 ScF&FL 92
Adler, Alton A. 1909- St&PR 93
Adler, Arthur M., Jr. 1917- WhoAm 92
Adler, Barbara Walz 1943- WhoAmW 93, WhoSSW 93
Adler, Beatriz Crabb 1929- WhoAmW 93
Adler, Benjamin 1903-1990 BioIn 17
Adler, Bruce Law&B 92
Adler, C. S. 1932- BioIn 17, ScF&FL 92, SmATA 15AS [port]
Adler, C(arole) S(chwerdtfeger) 1932- ConAu 40NR, DcAmChF 1985, MajAI [port], WhoWrEP 92
Adler, Carol Ellen 1938- WhoWrEP 92
Adler, Carole S. 1932- BioIn 17
Adler, Carolyn R. Law&B 92
Adler, Charles Spencer 1941- WhoAm 92, WhoWor 93
Adler, Clarence 1886-1969 Baker 92
Adler, Cyrus 1863-1940 JeAmHC
Adler, Dankmar 1844-1900 BioIn 17
Adler, David A. 1947- MajAI [port], SmATA 70 [port], WhoWrEP 92
Adler, David Avram 1947- WhoAm 92, WhoEmL 93
Adler, David Joseph 1952- WhoEmL 93
Adler, David Leon 1929- St&PR 93
Adler, Diana d1991 BioIn 17
Adler, Didier Jean-Jacques 1955- WhoWor 93
Adler, Donald D. Law&B 92
Adler, Dwain Robert 1955- WhoEmL 93, WhoSSW 93
Adler, Earl 1932- WhoE 93, WhoIns 93
Adler, Edward Andrew Koeppel 1948- WhoEmL 93
Adler, Edward I. 1954- WhoE 93
Adler, Edward Jerome 1932- St&PR 93
Adler, Erwin Ellery 1941- WhoAm 92, WhoWor 93
Adler, Estelle Caroline 1951- WhoAmW 93, WhoE 93
Adler, F. Charles 1889-1959 Baker 92
Adler, Fred Peter 1925- WhoAm 92
Adler, Freda Schaffer 1934- WhoAm 92
Adler, Frederick R. 1925- St&PR 93
Adler, Frederick Richard 1925- WhoAm 92
Adler, Gerald 1924- WhoAm 92
Adler, Guido 1855-1941 Baker 92
Adler, Helen Elise AmWomPl
Adler, Helmut Ernest 1920- WhoE 93
Adler, Herbert d1991 BioIn 17
Adler, Howard, Jr. 1925- WhoAm 92
Adler, Howard Bruce 1951- WhoAm 92
Adler, Ira Jay 1942- WhoAm 92
Adler, Irving 1913- ChlLR 27 [port], MajAI [port], SmATA 15AS [port], WhoE 93, WhoWor 93
Adler, Isidore 1916-1990 BioIn 17
Adler, Jack P. Law&B 92
Adler, Jack Philip 1953- WhoEmL 93
Adler, Jacques Henri 1916- St&PR 93
Adler, James Barron 1932- WhoAm 92
Adler, James R. 1950- WhoEmL 93
Adler, James Richard 1938- St&PR 93
Adler, Jane Eve 1944- WhoE 93
Adler, Jankel 1895-1949 BioIn 17
Adler, Jankiel 1895-1949 PolBiDi
Adler, Jeffrey William 1962- WhoEmL 93
Adler, Jerome M. 1931- St&PR 93
Adler, John Stanley 1948- WhoEmL 93
Adler, Julius 1930- WhoAm 92
Adler, Karl Paul 1939- WhoAm 92
Adler, Kenneth A. 1934- St&PR 93
Adler, Kraig Kerr 1940- WhoAm 92
Adler, Kurt 1907-1977 Baker 92
Adler, Kurt Herbert 1905-1988 Baker 92, OxDcOp
Adler, Kurt S. 1921- St&PR 93
Adler, Larry 1914- Baker 92
Adler, Larry 1938- WhoAm 92
Adler, Laszlo 1932- WhoAm 92
Adler, Lawrence 1923- WhoAm 92
Adler, Lawrence Joel 1939- WhoE 93
Adler, Lee 1926- WhoAm 92
Adler, Lee Paul 1956- WhoEmL 93
Adler, Leonore Loeb 1921- WhoAmW 93
Adler, Lou MiSFD 9
Adler, Marc S. Law&B 92
Adler, Margot Susanna 1946- WhoWrEP 92
Adler, Mark 1955- WhoEmL 93
Adler, Martin 1934- St&PR 93, WhoIns 93
Adler, Marvin 1928- St&PR 93
Adler, Michael F. 1936- St&PR 93
Adler, Michael Richard 1945- St&PR 93
Adler, Michael S. 1943- WhoAm 92
Adler, Mortimer Jerome 1902- BioIn 17, WhoAm 92
Adler, Myron 1924- St&PR 93
Adler, Patricia Ann 1951- WhoEmL 93
Adler, Paul ScF&FL 92
Adler, Peggy 1942- WhoAmW 93, WhoE 93, WhoWor 93
Adler, Peter Herman 1899- OxDcOp
Adler, Peter Herman 1899-1990 Baker 92, BioIn 17
Adler, Philip 1925- WhoAm 92
Adler, Pierre M. 1948- WhoScE 91-2
Adler, Renata BioIn 17
Adler, Renata 1938- WhoAm 92, WhoWrEP 92
Adler, Richard BioIn 17
Adler, Richard 1921- Baker 92, WhoAm 92
Adler, Richard Alan 1942- WhoIns 93
Adler, Richard Brooks 1922-1990 BioIn 17
Adler, Richard J. St&PR 93
Adler, Richard Seth 1958- WhoEmL 93
Adler, Robert 1913- WhoAm 92
Adler, Robert J. 1955- St&PR 93
Adler, Robert M. 1953- St&PR 93
Adler, Rudolf E. 1929- WhoScE 91-3
Adler, Ruth G. St&PR 93
Adler, Samuel (Hans) 1928- Baker 92, WhoAm 92
Adler, Samuel I. 1924- St&PR 93
Adler, Selig St&PR 93
Adler, Sherman 1928- WhoAm 92
Adler, Sidney W. 1952- WhoEmL 93
Adler, Sol 1925- WhoWrEP 92
Adler, Stella 1901-1992 NewYTBS 92 [port]
Adler, Stephen Fred 1930- WhoAm 92
Adler, Stephen Louis 1939- WhoAm 92
Adler, Theodore W. 1906- St&PR 93
Adler, Thomas W. 1929- St&PR 93
Adler, Verda Virginia 1956- WhoE 93
Adler, Warren BioIn 17
Adler, Warren 1927- WhoAm 92
Adler, William F. 1944- St&PR 93
Adlercreutz, C. Herman Th. 1932- WhoScE 91-4
Adlerstein, Jo Anne Chernev 1947- WhoEmL 93
Adlerstein, Lee Alan 1947- WhoEmL 93
Adlgasser, Anton Cajetan 1729-1777 Baker 92
Adlington, John Edward WhoScE 91-1
Adlivankin, Arno Antero 1940- WhoWor 93
Adlman, Monroe 1925- St&PR 93
Adlon, Percy 1935- MiSFD 9
Adlung, Jakob 1699-1762 Baker 92
Admant, Philippe Edmond 1954- WhoWor 93
Adnot, John 1950- WhoEmL 93, WhoSSW 93
Adoff, Arnold 1935- ConAu 37NR, MajAI [port], SmATA 15AS [port]
Adoff, Virginia ScF&FL 92
Adolf, Mary McGinley 1955- WhoAmW 93
Adolfati, Andrea 1721?-1760 OxDcOp
Adolfo 1933- WhoAm 92
Adolph, D.E. Law&B 92
Adolph, Robert J. 1927- WhoAm 92
Adolphe, Rosalie DcCPCAm
Adolphi, Ronald Lee 1946- WhoE 93
Adolphus, Milton 1913-1988 Baker 92
Adom, Edwin Nii Amalai 1941- WhoE 93
Adomeit, Gerhard 1929- WhoScE 91-3
Adomian, George 1932- WhoAm 92, WhoSSW 93
Adomian, Lan 1905-1979 Baker 92
Adomitis, Daniel J. Law&B 92
Adomnan c. 624-704 OxDcByz
Adonizio, Ann Marie Catherine 1945- WhoE 93
Adonizio, Anthony Charles, Jr. Law&B 92
Ador, Thierry Francois 1954- WhoWor 93
Adorjan, Carol (Madden) 1934- SmATA 71 [port], WhoWrEP 92
Adorjan, Julius Joe 1938- WhoAm 92
Adorno, Theodor 1903-1969 Baker 92
Adorno, Theodor Wiesengrund 1903-1969 OxDcOp
Adoum, Jorge Enrique 1926- SpAmA
Adoum, Mahamat Ali 1947- WhoWor 93
Adour, David Lawrence Law&B 92
Adoutte, Andre 1947- WhoScE 91-2
Adovasio, J. M. WhoE 93
Adrain, Robert Stephen 1947- WhoScE 91-1
Adreon, Beatrice Marie Rice 1929- WhoAmW 93
Adreon, Harry Barnes 1929- WhoAm 92
Adri WhoAm 92, WhoAmW 93
Adriaensen, Emanuel c. 1554-1604? Baker 92
Adriaenssen, Emanuel c. 1554-1604? Baker 92
Adrian, Lord WhoScE 91-1
Adrian, Barbara BioIn 17
Adrian, Barbara 1931- WhoAm 92
Adrian, Charles Raymond 1922- WhoAm 92
Adrian, Donna Jean 1940- WhoAm 92
Adrian, Erle Keys, Jr. 1936- WhoSSW 93
Adrian, F.J. WhoScE 91-3
Adrian, Frances ConAu 37NR, MajAI
Adrian, Gary Alan 1951- WhoEmL 93
Adrian, Hal L. 1934- WhoIns 93
Adrian, Iris 1912- QDrFCA 92 [port], SweetSg C [port]
Adrian, Jack 1945- ScF&FL 92
Adrian, Jean 1925- WhoScE 91-2
Adrian, Kristin Law&B 92
Adrian, P. Norbert 1958- St&PR 93
Adrian, Werner ScF&FL 92
Adrian, William Bryan, Jr. 1937- WhoAm 92
Adriance, Anne Altmaier 1957- WhoAmW 93
Adriance, Vanderpoel 1909-1991 BioIn 17
Adrianopoli, Barbara Catherine 1943- WhoAmW 93, WhoWor 93
Adriansen, Emanuel c. 1554-1604? Baker 92
Adriansen, Erik 1935- WhoScE 91-2
Adrianssen, Emanuel c. 1554-1604? Baker 92
Adrianyi, Gabriel Friedrich Michael 1935- WhoWor 93
Adriel, Jeanne 1892-1984 ScF&FL 92
Adrien, Daniel Omer 1942- St&PR 93
Adrien, Jacques Patrick Blondeau 1944- WhoIns 93
Adrine, Ronald B. AfrAmBi [port]
Adrine-Robinson, Kenyette 1951- WhoEmL 93
Adrio, Adam 1901-1973 Baker 92
Adrion, Harold L. Law&B 92
Adrion, William Richards 1943- WhoE 93
Adsersen, Henning Emil 1943- WhoScE 91-2
Adsit, Charles G. 1915-1991 BioIn 17
Adsit, LaVergne Lee 1935- St&PR 93
Adubato, Richard Adam 1937- WhoAm 92, WhoSSW 93
Adubato, Susan Ann 1954- WhoAmW 93, WhoE 93, WhoEmL 93
Aduddle, Larry Steven 1946- WhoEmL 93
Aduja, Peter Aquino 1920- WhoAm 92
Adulyadej, Bhumibol BioIn 17
Adum, Ognjan 1924- WhoScE 91-4
Advani, Dilip 1953- St&PR 93
Advani, Gulu Nanik 1953- WhoEmL 93
Advani, L. K. 1927- BioIn 17
Advani, Lal K. 1927- WhoAsAP 91
Advenier, Charles 1944- WhoScE 91-2
Adwon, Edward R. Law&B 92
Adwon, Phillip Mitchell 1956- WhoSSW 93
Ady, Howard Parmelee, III 1944- WhoSSW 93
Ady, Robert 1935- WhoAm 92
Ady, Robert M. St&PR 93
Adyebo, George WhoWor 93
Adzemovic, Vladimir B. d1990 BioIn 17

Agud, Roger 1926- *WhoE 93*
Aguero, Fernando *DcCPCAm*
Agueros, Victoriano 1854-1911 *DcMexL*
Aguero-Teare, Teresa 1961- *WhoWor 93*
Aguiar, Adam Martin 1929- *WhoAm 92, WhoE 93*
Aguiar, Joao Baptista da Costa 1947- *BioIn 17*
Aguiar, Maria Stella Chorao 1949- *WhoWor 93*
Aguiari, Lucrezia 1743-1783 *OxDcOp*
Aguiar-Velez, Deborah *BioIn 17*
Aguiar-Velez, Deborah 1955- *HispAmA*
Aguilar, Antonio 1926- *WhoScE 91-3*
Aguilar, Carlos A. 1943- *St&PR 93*
Aguilar, Charles, III 1944- *St&PR 93*
Aguilar, Filemon C. 1914- *WhoAsAP 91*
Aguilar, Gale Ramon 1932- *St&PR 93*
Aguilar, George Albert 1930- *St&PR 93*
Aguilar, Isabel 1936- *WhoAmW 93*
Aguilar, Jose Antonio 1943- *DcMexL*
Aguilar, Juan R. 1943- *WhoUN 92*
Aguilar, Manuel 1938- *WhoScE 91-3*
Aguilar, Margaret Hope 1951- *WhoEmL 93*
Aguilar, Mila Deysolong 1949- *WhoWor 93*
Aguilar, Ricardo Alberto 1960- *WhoEmL 93*
Aguilar, Robert P. 1931- *HispAmA, WhoAm 92*
Aguilar, Rodolfo Jesus 1936- *WhoSSW 93*
Aguilar, Silvestre Francisco 1940- *WhoSSW 93*
Aguilar B., L. Enrique 1957- *WhoWor 93*
Aguilar Bulgarelli, Oscar *DcCPCAm*
Aguilar Camin, Hector 1946- *DcMexL*
Aguilar-Hecht, Francis Eric 1954- *WhoIns 93, WhoUN 92*
Aguilar-Mawdsley, Andres 1924- *WhoUN 92*
Aguilar Mora, Jorge 1946- *DcMexL*
Aguilar Perez, Wanda Ivette 1958- *WhoAmW 93*
Aguilar Peris, Jose 1924- *WhoScE 91-3*
Aguilera, Antonio Guzman 1894- *HispAmA*
Aguilera, Bruce A. 1948- *St&PR 93*
Aguilera, Bruce Allen *Law&B 92*
Aguilera, Donna Conant *WhoAm 92*
Aguilera de Heredia, Sebastian 1561-1627 *Baker 92*
Aguilera Diaz, Gaspar 1947- *DcMexL*
Aguilera Malta, Demetrio 1909-1981 *DcMexL, ScF&FL 92, SpAmA*
Aguiluz, Victor Ford *Law&B 92*
Aguinada Carranza, Mario *DcCPCAm*
Aguinaga, Penelope Anne 1958- *WhoE 93*
Aguinaldo, Emilio 1869-1964 *DcTwHis, HarEnMi*
Aguinaldo, Jorge Tansingco 1952- *WhoWor 93*
Aguinsky, Richard Daniel 1958- *WhoWor 93*
Aguirre, Annette *Law&B 92*
Aguirre, Carlos Ernesto 1943- *St&PR 93*
Aguirre, Edgar Heriberto 1940- *WhoWor 93*
Aguirre, Gabriel E. 1935- *St&PR 93*
Aguirre, Gabriel Eloy 1935- *HispAmA*
Aguirre, Igor Ricardo 1965- *WhoWor 93*
Aguirre, Jesse 1944- *St&PR 93, WhoAm 92*
Aguirre, Julian 1868-1924 *Baker 92*
Aguirre, Manuel 1948- *ScF&FL 92*
Aguirre, Manuel J. 1893-1978 *DcMexL*
Aguirre, Mark Anthony 1959- *BiDAMSp 1989, WhoAm 92*
Aguirre, Michael J. 1949- *HispAmA [port]*
Aguirre, Robert 1964- *WhoEmL 93*
Aguirre Bianchi, Renato 1943- *WhoWor 93*
Aguirre-Molina, Marilyn 1948- *NotHsAW 93*
Aguirre-Puente, Jaime 1933- *WhoScE 91-2*
Aguirre Ramirez, Gonzalo *WhoWor 93*
Aguirre-Sacasa, Francisco Xavier 1944- *WhoUN 92*
Agujari, Lucrezia 1743-1783 *Baker 92*
Agullo, Joaquim 1943- *WhoScE 91-3*
Agullo-Lopez, Fernando 1934- *WhoScE 91-3*
Agullo-Rueda, Fernando 1960- *WhoWor 93*
Agursky, Mikhail *BioIn 17*
Agus, Zalman S. 1941- *WhoAm 92*
Agusta, Benjamin J. 1931- *WhoAm 92*
Agusta, Corrado d1989 *BioIn 17*
Agusta, Francesca *BioIn 17*
Agusta, Riccardo *BioIn 17*
Agustin, Jose 1944- *DcMexL, SpAmA*
Agustini, Delmira 1886-1914 *BioIn 17*
Agvan Dorjiev, Khambo Lama 1854-1937? *BioIn 17*
Agypt, Ronald G. 1956- *WhoIns 93*
Ahab *BioIn 17, HarEnMi*
Ahad Ha'am 1856-1927 *BioIn 17*
Ahart, Jan F. 1941- *St&PR 93*
Ahart, Jan Fredrick 1941- *WhoAm 92*
Ahart, Wayne Eugene 1940- *St&PR 93*
Ahasic, Michael 1941- *St&PR 93*
Ahasic, William John 1913- *St&PR 93*
Ahearn, Catherine 1949- *WhoCanL 92*
Ahearn, Charles *Law&B 92*
Ahearn, Charlie *MiSFD 9*
Ahearn, Donald G. 1934- *WhoSSW 93*
Ahearn, Donald Patrick 1929- *WhoWor 93*
Ahearn, James 1931- *WhoAm 92*
A'Hearn, Joan M. 1937- *WhoWrEP 92*
Ahearn, John Edward *Law&B 92*
Ahearn, John Francis, Jr. 1921- *WhoAm 92*
Ahearn, John Stephen 1944- *WhoAm 92*
Ahearn, Joseph August 1936- *WhoAm 92*
Ahearn, Patricia Jean 1936- *WhoAmW 93, WhoWor 93*
Ahearn, Robert John 1961- *WhoE 93*
Ahearn, Terrence James *Law&B 92*
Ahearn, William Barry 1950- *WhoEmL 93, WhoSSW 93*
Ahearne, John Francis 1934- *WhoAm 92*
Ahenobarbus, Lucius Domitius d48BC *HarEnMi*
Ahern, Arch M. *Law&B 92*
Ahern, Barbara Ann 1940- *WhoE 93*
Ahern, Charles W. 1953- *St&PR 93*
Ahern, David (Anthony) 1947- *Baker 92*
Ahern, Donald Hugh 1928- *St&PR 93*
Ahern, F. Gregory 1952- *St&PR 93*
Ahern, Francis Thomas 1953- *WhoEmL 93*
Ahern, Jerome M. *ScF&FL 92*
Ahern, Jerry 1946- *ScF&FL 92*
Ahern, John E. 1935- *St&PR 93*
Ahern, John Joseph 1942- *WhoAm 92*
Ahern, Margaret Ann 1931- *WhoAmW 93*
Ahern, Maureen *WhoE 93*
Ahern, Patrick V. 1919- *WhoAm 92*
Ahern, S.A. *ScF&FL 92*
Ahern, Sharon A. 1948- *ScF&FL 92*
Ahern, Stephen H. *Law&B 92*
Ahern, Thomas Francis 1947- *WhoWrEP 92*
Aherne, Robert E. *Law&B 92*
Ahidjo, Ahmadou 1924-1989 *DcTwHis*
Ahl, Alwynelle Self 1941- *WhoAm 92*
Ahl, David Howard 1939- *WhoAm 92*
Ahl, Marian Antoinette 1952- *WhoEmL 93, WhoSSW 93*
Ahl, Richard A. 1948- *St&PR 93*
Ahl, Roger John 1963- *WhoWor 93*
Ahlberg, Allan *BioIn 17*
Ahlberg, Allan 1938- *ChlFicS, ConAu 38NR, MajAI [port]*
Ahlberg, Harold 1935- *WhoAm 92*
Ahlberg, J.E. *WhoScE 91-1*
Ahlberg, James E. *WhoAm 92*
Ahlberg, James George 1951- *WhoEmL 93*
Ahlberg, Janet *BioIn 17*
Ahlberg, Janet 1944- *MajAI*
Ahlberg, John Harold 1927- *WhoAm 92*
Ahlberg, Jon O. *Law&B 92*
Ahlberg, Per N.I. 1938- *WhoScE 91-4*
Ahlbom, Ruth *WhoScE 91-4*
Ahlbrand, John E. 1927- *St&PR 93*
Ahlbrand, Russell L. 1924- *St&PR 93*
Ahlburg, Kaj 1959- *St&PR 93*
Ahle, Johann Georg 1651-1706 *Baker 92*
Ahle, Johann Rudolf 1625-1673 *Baker 92*
Ahle, Peter 1941- *WhoWor 93*
Ahlem, Lloyd Harold 1929- *WhoAm 92*
Ahlemann, Elizabeth Bottorff *Law&B 92*
Ahlen, John William, III 1947- *WhoAm 92*
Ahlen, Steven Paul 1949- *WhoE 93*
Ahlen, T. Ingemar 1936- *WhoScE 91-4*
Ahlenius, William Matheson 1934- *WhoAm 92*
Ahlers, B. Orwin 1926- *WhoAm 92, WhoE 93*
Ahlers, Eleanor Emily 1911- *WhoAm 92*
Ahlers, Guenter 1934- *WhoAm 92*
Ahlers, Hendrick Christian d1991 *BioIn 17*
Ahlers, Rolf Willi 1936- *WhoAm 92*
Ahlersmeyer, David L. *Law&B 92*
Ahlersmeyer, Mathieu 1896-1979 *Baker 92*
Ahlert, Dieter 1944- *WhoWor 93*
Ahles, Doris L. *St&PR 93*
Ahlf, Thomas J. *Law&B 92*
Ahlfeld, William Joseph 1922- *WhoE 93*
Ahlgren, Johan G.A. 1926- *WhoScE 91-4*
Ahlgren, Roy Bertil 1927- *WhoE 93*
Ahlgren, Sture Gunnar B:son 1930- *WhoWor 93*
Ahlheim, Udo 1960- *WhoWor 93*
Ahlijanian, Martin John *Law&B 92*
Ahlin, Janne 1942- *ConAu 136*
Ahling, Bengt 1944- *WhoScE 91-4*
Ahlrichs, Nancy Surratt 1952- *WhoAmW 93*
Ahlrichs, Reinhart 1940- *WhoScE 91-3*
Ahlschwede, Arthur Martin 1914- *WhoAm 92*
Ahlstone, Arthur 1933- *St&PR 93*
Ahlstroem, G(oesta) W(erner) 1918- *WhoWrEP 92*
Ahlstroem, G(oesta) W(erner) 1918-1992 *ConAu 136*
Ahlstrom, Antti Gustav 1939- *WhoScE 91-4*
Ahlstrom, David 1927- *Baker 92*
Ahlstrom, G(osta) W(erner) *ConAu 136*
Ahlstrom, Gosta W. *BioIn 17*
Ahlstrom, Mary Lou *Law&B 92*
Ahlstrom, Michael Joseph 1953- *WhoEmL 93, WhoSSW 93*
Ahlstrom, Richard Mather 1934- *WhoAm 92*
Ahlstrom, Richard Ward 1924- *St&PR 93*
Ahlstrom, William F. 1944- *WhoAm 92*
Ahluvalia, Jasjit T. 1938- *St&PR 93*
Ahluwalia, Bira 1944- *St&PR 93*
Ahluwalia, S.S. 1951- *WhoAsAP 91*
Ahmad, Shah of Bahmani d1435 *HarEnMi*
Ahmad, Anees 1942- *WhoUN 92*
Ahmad, Eqbal 1931- *WhoAm 92*
Ahmad, Ghulam 1839?-1908 *BioIn 17*
Ahmad, Khalil 1950- *WhoWor 93*
Ahmad, M. Abraham 1953- *WhoE 93*
Ahmad, Naseer 1937- *WhoWor 93*
Ahmad, Rashid 1938- *WhoUN 92*
Ahmad, S. Ehtisham Uddin 1950- *WhoUN 92*
Ahmad, Shair 1935- *WhoAm 92*
Ahmad, Shami *BioIn 17*
Ahmad, Syed Rashid 1949- *WhoWor 93*
Ahmad, Waqar 1953- *WhoWor 93*
Ahmad, Zakaria Haji *ConAu 138*
Ahmadi, Gholam 1955- *St&PR 93*
Ahmad ibn Idris d1837 *BioIn 17*
Ahmad Mattar, Hon. Dr. 1939- *WhoAsAP 91*
Ahmadou Kourouma *BioIn 17*
Ahmad Shah, Ibni Al-Marhum Sultan Abu Bakar 1930- *WhoWor 93*
Ahmad Shah Al-Musta In Billah Ibni Al-M., His Royal Highness Sultan Haji 1930- *WhoAsAP 91*
Ahmad Shah Durani c. 1722-1772 *HarEnMi*
Ahmad Urai Bin Datuk Hakim Abang Haji M., Setia Negara Abang Haji 1933- *WhoAsAP 91*
Ahmad Zaidi Adruce B. Mohamed Noor, Tyt Tun Datuk Patinggi Haji 1921- *WhoAsAP 91*
Ahman, Hans-Erik Verner 1940- *WhoWor 93*
Ahmann, Donald Henry 1930- *WhoSSW 93*
Ahmann, John Stanley 1921- *WhoAm 92*
Ahmann, Mathew Hall 1931- *WhoAm 92*
Ahmann-Leighton, Christine *WhoAmW 93*
Ahmed, I 1590-1617 *HarEnMi*
Ahmed, Abbas Hassan Abbas 1953- *WhoWor 93*
Ahmed, Abdel-Rahim d1991 *BioIn 17*
Ahmed, Abu 1949- *WhoWor 93*
Ahmed, Adel A. *Law&B 92*
Ahmed, Ali 1934- *WhoE 93*
Ahmed, Elsayed Mohamed 1954- *WhoWor 93*
Ahmed, Fakhruddin 1931- *WhoAsAP 91*
Ahmed, Hedayat 1933- *WhoUN 92*
Ahmed, Iftikhar *St&PR 93*
Ahmed, Iqbal 1951- *WhoE 93, WhoEmL 93, WhoWor 93*
Ahmed, Jasim Uddin 1933- *WhoUN 92*
Ahmed, Javed 1960- *WhoE 93, WhoEmL 93*
Ahmed, Kamal Hussein 1934- *WhoUN 92*
Ahmed, Kazi Zafar 1940- *WhoAsAP 91*
Ahmed, Khalil 1934- *WhoAm 92*
Ahmed, Khandakar Moshtaque 1918- *WhoAsAP 91*
Ahmed, Kyle *WhoAm 92*
Ahmed, Manzoor 1940- *WhoUN 92*
Ahmed, Mohamed Ibrahim 1921- *WhoAfr*
Ahmed, Mohammed M.A. 1933- *WhoUN 92*
Ahmed, Mohiuddin 1944- *WhoUN 92*
Ahmed, Moudud *WhoAsAP 91*
Ahmed, Moudud 1940- *WhoWor 93*
Ahmed, Nasim d1990 *BioIn 17*
Ahmed, Saad Attia 1950- *WhoEmL 93*
Ahmed, Salahuddin 1932- *WhoUN 92*
Ahmed, Samir Ahmed 1946- *WhoSSW 93*
Ahmed, Shahabuddin *WhoAsAP 91*
Ahmed, Shaheen 1962- *WhoWor 93*
Ahmed, Shahzada Kabir 1941- *WhoWor 93*
Ahmed, Shaikh Sultan 1937- *WhoE 93*
Ahmed, Shami *BioIn 17*
Ahmed, Sultan 1923- *WhoWor 93*
Ahmed Pasha fl. c. 1799- *HarEnMi*
Ahmose, II d525BC *HarEnMi*
Ahmuty, John R. *Law&B 92*
Ahn, Choong Yong 1941- *WhoWor 93*
Ahn, Ho-Sam 1940- *WhoE 93*
Ahn, Jaehoon 1941- *WhoE 93*
Ahn, Sangwoo 1938- *St&PR 93*
Ahn, Suhn Yung 1934- *WhoWor 93*
Ahna, Heinrich Karl Herman de *Baker 92*
Ahna, Pauline de 1863-1950 *See* Strauss, Richard 1864-1949 *OxDcOp*
Ahn Byung Kyu 1938- *WhoAsAP 91*
Ahn Chan Hee 1932- *WhoAsAP 91*
Ahner, Charles William, Jr. *Law&B 92*
Ahner, David James 1950- *St&PR 93*
Ahnert, Frank 1927- *WhoScE 91-3, WhoWor 93*
Ahnert, W. Peter 1944- *St&PR 93*
Ahn Young-Ki 1937- *WhoAsAP 91*
Aho, Esko Tapani 1954- *WhoWor 93*
Aho, Gary L. 1935- *ScF&FL 92*
Aho, Jean 1942- *WhoE 93*
Aho, Kalevi 1949- *Baker 92*
Aho, Kathleen Gail 1960- *WhoWrEP 92*
Aho, Kauko Johannes 1922- *WhoWor 93*
Ahokas, Jukka Matias 1950- *WhoScE 91-4*
Ahonen, Roy R. 1926- *St&PR 93*
Ahonen, Vaino Axel 1933- *St&PR 93*
Ahonen, William D. *Law&B 92*
Ahrari, M. E. 1945- *WhoAm 92, WhoSSW 93*
Ahrend, Grace Shirley 1942- *WhoAmW 93*
Ahrens, Edward Hamblin, Jr. 1915- *WhoAm 92*
Ahrens, Erick Karl Frederick 1949- *WhoEmL 93*
Ahrens, Franklin Alfred 1936- *WhoAm 92*
Ahrens, Gertine *AmWomPl*
Ahrens, Gilbert Pomeroy 1938- *St&PR 93*
Ahrens, Henry William 1918- *WhoE 93*
Ahrens, John Frederick 1929- *WhoE 93*
Ahrens, Joseph Johannes Clemens 1904- *Baker 92*
Ahrens, Kent *WhoAm 92, WhoE 93*
Ahrens, Leigh P. *WhoAm 92*
Ahrens, Lynn *BioIn 17*
Ahrens, Mary Ann Painovich 1942- *WhoAmW 93*
Ahrens, Paul C. 1952- *St&PR 93*
Ahrens, Paul Joseph, Jr. 1936- *WhoSSW 93*
Ahrens, Rolland William 1933- *WhoSSW 93*
Ahrens, Rudolf Martin 1928- *WhoSSW 93*
Ahrens, Shirley L. 1943- *St&PR 93*
Ahrens, Thomas H. 1919- *WhoAm 92*
Ahrens, William Henry 1925- *WhoAm 92, WhoWor 93*
Ahrensdorf, Robert Edgar 1916- *St&PR 93*
Ahrensfeld, Thomas Frederick 1923- *WhoAm 92*
Ahrland, Sten *WhoScE 91-4*
Ahrnell-Runnquist, Ann Christine 1953- *WhoWor 93*
Ahrold, Kyle Warren 1949- *WhoAm 92*
Ahroni, Jessie Helen 1948- *WhoEmL 93*
Ahronovich, (Georgi) Yuri 1932- *Baker 92*
Ahrons, Constance Ruth 1937- *WhoAmW 93*
Ahrweiler, Helene 1926- *BioIn 17*
Ahsan, Aziz M. *Law&B 92*
Ahsan, Hosne Ara 1952- *WhoWor 93*
Ahsanullah, Mohammad 1936- *WhoE 93*
Ahsberger, Per Thomas Hugo 1935- *WhoWor 93*
Ahti, Teuvo Tapio 1934- *WhoScE 91-4*
Ahto, Thomas N. *Law&B 92*
Ah-Tye, Susan *Law&B 92*
Ahuerga, Carlos de la *St&PR 93*
Ahuja, Jagdish Chand 1927- *WhoAm 92*
Ahuja, Rajendra Kumar 1938- *WhoUN 92*
Ahumada, Anna Lucinda 1949- *WhoEmL 93*
Ahumada, Herminio 1899-1983 *DcMexL*
Ahwoi, Ato Kwamena 1944- *WhoAfr*
Ah-Yoong, Georges 1949- *St&PR 93*
Ai 1947- *DcLB 120 [port]*
Ai, Ch'ing 1910- *BioIn 17*
Ai, David C. *St&PR 93*
Ai, Steven C. 1953- *St&PR 93*
Aia, Michael Alfred 1933- *WhoE 93*
Aibel, Howard James *Law&B 92*
Aibel, Howard James 1929- *St&PR 93, WhoAm 92*
Aibl, Joseph *Baker 92*
Aiblinger, Johann Kaspar 1779-1867 *Baker 92*
Aich, Robert Louis 1953- *WhoEmL 93*
Aicher, Richard Edward 1950- *St&PR 93*
Aicher, Sarah *BioIn 17*
Aichi, Kazuo 1937- *WhoAsAP 91*
Aichinger, Gregor 1564-1628 *Baker 92*
Aickin, Donald Russell 1934- *WhoWor 93*
Aickin, Robert Malcolm 1949- *WhoWor 93*
Aickman, Robert 1914-1981 *BioIn 17, ScF&FL 92*
Aida, Yukie 1953- *WhoSSW 93*
Aidan d606 *HarEnMi*

Aidar, Nelson 1953- WhoWor 93
Aidekman, Alex 1915-1990 BioIn 17
Aidells, Bruce 1944- ConAu 138
Aidelson, Deborah Adele 1968- WhoE 93
Aidik d1257 HarEnMi
Aidinoff, M. Bernard 1929- St&PR 93
Aidinoff, Merton Bernard 1929- WhoAm 92
Aidley, David John 1937- WhoWor 93
Aidlin, Stephen H. 1940- St&PR 93
Aidman, Charles WhoAm 92
Aidoo, (Christina) Ama Ata 1942- DcLB 117 [port]
Aidoo, Kofi Edirisah 1946- WhoWor 93
Aids, Leland Stanford Law&B 92
Aidt, Glenn E. 1940- St&PR 93
Aidun, Debra Law&B 92
Aiello, Danny BioIn 17
Aiello, Danny 1933- CurBio 92 [port]
Aiello, Danny 1936- WhoAm 92
Aiello, David BioIn 17
Aiello, Edward Lawrence 1928- WhoE 93
Aiello, Elizabeth Ann 1922- WhoAmW 93
Aiello, Gennaro C. 1953- WhoE 93, WhoEmL 93
Aiello, John R. 1946- WhoE 93
Aiello, Penelope Anne 1951- WhoAmW 93
Aiello, Pietro 1939- WhoWor 93
Aiello, Ralph J. Law&B 92
Aiello, Ray 1946- St&PR 93
Aiello, Rebecca Garbutt 1936- WhoSSW 93
Aiello, Rick BioIn 17
Aiello, Robert James 1937- St&PR 93
Aiello, Tina Marie 1963- WhoE 93
Aiello-Contessa, Angela M. 1954- WhoAm 92
Aig, Dennis Ira 1950- WhoEmL 93
Aigeldinger, Nancy B. 1931- St&PR 93
Aigen, Betsy Paula 1938- WhoE 93
Aiginger, Johannes 1937- WhoScE 91-4, WhoWor 93
Aigner, Dennis John 1937- WhoAm 92
Aigner, Kurt W. ScF&FL 92
Aigret, C. WhoScE 91-2
Aihara, Cornellia 1926- WhoWrEP 92
Aihara, Herman 1920- WhoWrEP 92
Aihara, Hikaru 1925- WhoWor 93
Aihara, Kazuyuki 1954- WhoWor 93
Aika, Ken-ichi 1942- WhoWor 93
Aikas, Erkki WhoScE 91-4
Aikawa, Jerry Kazuo 1921- WhoAm 92, WhoWor 93
Aiken, Alma W. AmWomPl
Aiken, Bruce A. BioIn 17
Aiken, Charles Moffatt 1934- WhoSSW 93
Aiken, Conrad 1889-1973 BioIn 17
Aiken, Conrad Joseph Law&B 92
Aiken, Dorothy Louise 1924- WhoAmW 93
Aiken, Ednah Robinson 1872- AmWomPl
Aiken, J.S., Mrs. AmWomPl
Aiken, Jefferson Kirksey, Jr. 1941- WhoSSW 93
Aiken, Joan 1924- BioIn 17, ScF&FL 92
Aiken, Joan (Delano) 1924- ChlFicS, MajAI [port], SmATA 73 [port]
Aiken, John 1913-1990 ScF&FL 92
Aiken, Lawrence James 1944- WhoE 93
Aiken, Lewis Roscoe, Jr. 1931- WhoAm 92
Aiken, Linda Harman 1943- WhoAm 92, WhoAmW 93
Aiken, Lisa Anne 1956- WhoAmW 93
Aiken, Michael Thomas 1932- WhoAm 92
Aiken, Peter Haynes 1959- WhoEmL 93, WhoSSW 93
Aiken, Robert Dennis 1950- WhoE 93
Aiken, Robert Morris, Jr. 1942- St&PR 93
Aiken, Scott 1935- St&PR 93
Aiken, Tara L. Law&B 92
Aiken, Tracy BioIn 17
Aiken, William 1806-1887 BioIn 17
Aiken, William 1934- St&PR 93, WhoAm 92
Aiken, William Eric 1935- WhoAm 92, WhoE 93
Aiken, William Minor 1932- WhoWrEP 92
Aikens, Clyde Melvin 1938- WhoAm 92
Aikens, Joan BioIn 17
Aikens, Joan Deacon WhoAm 92, WhoAmW 93
Aikens, Martha Brunette 1949- WhoAmW 93
Aikin, James D. ScF&FL 92
Aikin, Jim 1948- ScF&FL 92
Aikin, Warren St&PR 93
Aikivuori, Anne Marja 1961- WhoWor 93
Aikman, Albert Edward 1922- WhoSSW 93
Aikman, James S. 1951- WhoSSW 93
Aikman, John Rae 1931- St&PR 93
Aikman, Robert E. 1932- St&PR 93
Aikman, Troy BioIn 17
Aikman, Troy 1966- WhoAm 92
Aikman, William Francis 1945- WhoE 93
Aikman, William Henry 1927- St&PR 93
Aikman, Zora Susanne 1945- WhoSSW 93
Ailes, Roger 1940- PolPar
Ailes, Roger Eugene 1940- WhoAm 92
Ailes, Walter A. 1942- St&PR 93
Ailey, Alvin BioIn 17
Ailhaud, Gerard 1936- WhoScE 91-2
Ailios Herodianos OxDcByz
Aillon, Gonzalo Alberto 1940- WhoSSW 93
Ailloni-Charas, Dan 1930- WhoAm 92, WhoWor 93
Ailloni-Charas, Miriam Clara 1935- WhoAmW 93, WhoE 93
Ailly, Pierre d' 1350-1420? BioIn 17
Ailstock, Charles A. Law&B 92
Aime, Albert du ScF&FL 92
Aime, Claude Jean 1946- WhoScE 91-2
Aime, Jean-Claude 1935- WhoUN 92
Aimee, Anouk BioIn 17
Aimee, Anouk 1932- IntDcF 2-3 [port]
Aimilianos OxDcByz
Aimone, Jon C. Law&B 92
Aimone, Richard James 1939- St&PR 93
Ain, Mark S. 1943- St&PR 93
Ain, Mark Stuart 1943- WhoE 93
Ain, Sanford King 1947- WhoEmL 93
Aine, Veli Valo 1919- WhoWor 93
Aineias of Gaza fl. 5th cent.- OxDcByz
Ainge, Daniel Ray 1959- BiDAMSp 1989
Ainley, Janet Mary 1952- WhoWor 93
Aino, Koichiro 1928- WhoAsAP 91
Ainsa, Francis Swinburne 1915- WhoSSW 93
Ainsley, Alix ConAu 39NR
Ainslie, A.R. WhoScE 91-1
Ainslie, Michael L. 1943- St&PR 93
Ainslie, Michael Lewis 1943- WhoAm 92
Ainslie, Ruth W. Law&B 92
Ainslie, Tom WhoWrEP 92
Ainsworth, Catherine Harris 1910- WhoWrEP 92
Ainsworth, David A. 1950- WhoEmL 93
Ainsworth, David V. Law&B 92
Ainsworth, Dick P. 1939- St&PR 93
Ainsworth, Don Ray 1953- WhoEmL 93
Ainsworth, Elaine Marie 1948- WhoAmW 93
Ainsworth, Harriet Crawford 1914- WhoAmW 93
Ainsworth, Henry Alexander WhoScE 91-1
Ainsworth, Jimmy Hiram 1944- St&PR 93
Ainsworth, Kenneth George 1923- WhoE 93
Ainsworth, Mary AmWomPl
Ainsworth, Mary D. Salter 1913- BioIn 17
Ainsworth, Mary Dinsmore Salter 1913- WhoAm 92
Ainsworth, Mavis 1931- WhoWor 93
Ainsworth, Ruth 1908- ScF&FL 92
Ainsworth, Ruth (Gallard) 1908- ConAu 37NR, MajAI [port], SmATA 73 [port]
Ainsworth, Thomas Clayton 1942- St&PR 93
Ainsworth, Walter S. 1928- St&PR 93
Ainsworthy, Roy ScF&FL 92
Ai-Po-Hua 1909-1989 BioIn 17
Ai Qing 1910- BioIn 17
Airaksinen, Mauno M. 1930- WhoScE 91-4
Airapetyan, Ruben Gurghen 1951- WhoWor 93
Airaudo, Charles B. 1941- WhoScE 91-2
Aird, A. Marie 1934- St&PR 93
Aird, Edwin George Anderson WhoScE 91-1
Aird, Eric Ronald 1936- St&PR 93
Aird, Jack A. 1924- St&PR 93
Aird, John Black BioIn 17
Aird, John Black 1923- WhoAm 92, WhoWor 93
Aird, Richard L. 1949- St&PR 93
Aird, Steven Douglas 1952- WhoEmL 93
Aires, Randolf H. Law&B 92
Aires, Randolf Hess 1935- St&PR 93
Airey, Jean ScF&FL 92
Airington, Harold L. 1927- WhoAm 92
Airola, Joe Antonio 1928- WhoSSW 93
Airola, Mark Joseph Law&B 92
Aisawa, Ichiro 1954- WhoAsAP 91
Aisenberg, Irwin Morton 1925- WhoAm 92, WhoE 93
Aisenbrey, Stuart K. 1942- St&PR 93
Aisenbrey, Stuart Keith 1942- WhoAm 92
Aishima, Tetsuo 1946- WhoWor 93
Aisle, Francisco Jose 1934- HispAmA
Aisner, Joseph 1944- WhoAm 92
Aisner, Mark 1910- WhoE 93
Aistars, John 1938- WhoE 93
Aistulf d757 HarEnMi
Aita, Carolyn Rubin 1943- WhoAm 92
Aita, Choei 1928- WhoAsAP 91
Aita, Mary Majella 1958- WhoEmL 93
Aitay, Victor WhoAm 92
Aitchison, Anne Catherine 1939- WhoAmW 93
Aitchison, James 1938- ConAu 137
Aitken, Adelaide MacMurray 1945- WhoAmW 93
Aitken, Bart Aaron 1959- WhoSSW 93
Aitken, D.G. WhoUN 92
Aitken, Denis Gillon 1951- WhoUN 92
Aitken, Diane Legner 1938- WhoAm 92
Aitken, Hugh 1924- Baker 92
Aitken, I.D. WhoScE 91-1
Aitken, Irene M. AmWomPl
Aitken, Margaret Ann Law&B 92
Aitken, Martin J. WhoScE 91-1
Aitken, Maureen Mackenzie WhoScE 91-1
Aitken, Molly Bennett 1944- WhoAmW 93
Aitken, R.J. WhoScE 91-1
Aitken, Robert 1939- Baker 92
Aitken, Robert Andrew Law&B 92
Aitken, Rosemary Theresa 1946- WhoEmL 93
Aitken, Thomas Dean 1939- WhoAm 92
Aitken, Webster 1908-1981 Baker 92
Aitken, William Nelson 1926- St&PR 93
Aitkin, W. Roy 1932- WhoAm 92
Aitmatov, Chingiz BioIn 17
Aitmatov, Chingiz 1928- ConLC 71 [port], ScF&FL 92
Aitmatov, Chingiz (Torekulovich) 1928- ConAu 38NR
Aitomeri, Jaakko Alex 1953- WhoWor 93
Aiton, E.J. 1920-1991 BioIn 17
Aiton, Eric John 1920-1991 BioIn 17
Aittokoski, Margaretha Marina 1934- WhoWor 93
Aittomaki, Antero 1944- WhoScE 91-4
Aitzema, Lieuwe van 1600-1669 BioIn 17
Aiuto, Russell 1934- WhoAm 92
Aiuvalasit, Anthony G., Jr. Law&B 92
Aiuvalasit, Anthony George, Jr. 1949- WhoAm 92, WhoEmL 93
Aiyangar, Srinivasa Ramanujan 1887-1920 BioIn 17
Aizawa, Hideyuki 1919- WhoAsAP 91
Aizawa, Keio 1927- WhoWor 93
Aizawa, Masuo 1942- WhoWor 93
Aizen, Rachel K. WhoAmW 93
Aizenshtat, Anna Yakovlevna 1926- WhoWor 93
Ai Zhisheng 1929- WhoAsAP 91
Aizu, Izumi 1952- WhoWor 93
Ajar, Emile BioIn 17
Ajatasatru fl. c. 500BC- HarEnMi
Ajawara, Augustus Chiedozie 1953- WhoEmL 93
Ajax, Tom R. 1949- St&PR 93
Ajay, Abe 1919- BioIn 17, WhoAm 92
Ajayi, J(acob) F(estus) Ade(niyi) 1929- ConAu 40NR
Ajbani, Prabodh D. 1949- St&PR 93
Ajdukiewicz, Kazimierz 1890-1963 PolBiDi
Ajdukiewicz, Tadeusz 1852-1916 PolBiDi
Ajello, Aldo Romano 1936- WhoUN 92
Ajemian, Diran ScF&FL 92
Ajemian, Robert Myron 1925- WhoAm 92
Ajemian, Warren Haig 1919- St&PR 93
Ajib bin Ahmad, Dato' Abdul 1947- WhoAsAP 91
Ajmanov, Saken 1914-1970 DrEEuF
Ajmone-Marsan, Guido 1947- Baker 92
Ajo, David 1946- WhoScE 91-3
Ajodhia, Jules R. WhoWor 93
Ajzenberg-Selove, Fay 1926- WhoAm 92
Ak, Dogan 1928- WhoE 93
Akagi, Norihiko 1959- WhoAsAP 91
Akagi, Tadaatsu 1938- WhoWor 93
Akagi, Yasuharu 1939- WhoWor 93
Akagiri, Misao 1920- WhoAsAP 91
Akaha, Tsuneo 1949- WhoEmL 93
Akaka, Daniel K. BioIn 17
Akaka, Daniel K. 1924- CngDr 91
Akaka, Daniel Kahikina 1924- WhoAm 92
Akakios OxDcByz
Akakios c. 322-c. 433 OxDcByz
Akalaitis, JoAnne BioIn 17
Akalaitis, JoAnne 1937- ConAu 138, WhoAm 92, WhoAmW 93, WhoE 93
Akam, Michael Edwin WhoScE 91-1
Akamatsu, Hirotaka 1948- WhoAsAP 91
Akar, Ahmet 1947- WhoScE 91-4
Akard, Sarah Ann 1958- WhoAmW 93
Akaruru, Inatio WhoWor 93
Akasaka, Takeshi 1948- WhoWor 93
Akasaki, Toshiro 1925- WhoAm 92
Akashah, Mary Scoboria 1949- WhoWrEP 92
Akashi, Yasushi 1931- WhoUN 92
Akasofu, Syun-Ichi 1930- WhoAm 92
Akavickas, Gary R. Law&B 92
Akayev, Askar WhoWor 93
Akbar 1542-1605 HarEnMi
Akbar, Emperor of Hindustan 1542-1605 BioIn 17
Akbar, Chudary Hameed 1960- WhoWor 93
Akbar Khan d1849 HarEnMi
Akca, Alparslan 1936- WhoScE 91-3
Akcasu, Ahmet Ziyaeddin 1924- WhoAm 92
Ake, H. Worth 1923- WhoIns 93
Ake, John Notley 1941- WhoAm 92
Ake, Simeon 1932- WhoAfr
Ake-Boyer, Catherine Ann 1949- WhoWor 93
Akechi, Mitsumide 1526-1582 HarEnMi
Akeley, Carl Ethan 1864-1926 BioIn 17
Akeley, Delia 1875-1970 Expl 93
Akeley, Mary L. Jobe 1886-1966 BioIn 17
Akell, Robert Berry 1921- WhoE 93
Aken, Harold E., Jr. 1929- St&PR 93
Akenside, Mark 1721-1770 BioIn 17
Akenson, Donald Harman 1941- WhoAm 92, WhoWrEP 92
Akephaloi OxDcByz
Aker, David Law&B 92
Aker, David Orin 1946- WhoSSW 93
Aker, Walter William 1918- St&PR 93
Akera, Tai 1932- WhoAm 92
Akerblom, Malin 1940- WhoScE 91-4
Akerlof, Carl William 1938- WhoAm 92
Akerman, A. WhoScE 91-4
Akerman, Alf Knut Lennart 1923- WhoWor 93
Akerman, Chantal 1950- MiSFD 9
Akerman, Joseph Lax, Jr. 1950- WhoEmL 93
Akerman, Karl Erik Ossian 1950- WhoScE 91-4
Akerman, Nathaniel Howard 1947- WhoEmL 93
Akerman, Susanna (Kristina) 1959- ConAu 139
Akermark, Bjorn Johan 1933- WhoWor 93
Akeroyde, Samuel c. 1650-1706? Baker 92
Akers, Alan Burt ScF&FL 92
Akers, Brock Cordt 1956- WhoEmL 93
Akers, Carolyn Coneida Clary 1951- WhoAmW 93
Akers, CathayAnne Marie 1952- WhoAmW 93
Akers, Charles David 1948- WhoEmL 93
Akers, Diane Spradlin 1964- WhoAmW 93
Akers, Floyd MajAI
Akers, James Arlan 1963- WhoSSW 93
Akers, John F. St&PR 93
Akers, John F. 1934- BioIn 17
Akers, John Fellows 1934- WhoAm 92, WhoE 93, WhoWor 93
Akers, Lawrence C. Law&B 92
Akers, Louis J. 1951- St&PR 93
Akers, Lucille Marie 1936- WhoAmW 93
Akers, M.F. 1939- St&PR 93
Akers, Ottie Clay 1949- WhoE 93, WhoEmL 93
Akers, Sheldon Buckingham, Jr. 1926- WhoAm 92, WhoE 93
Akers, Suzanne Selberg 1947- WhoEmL 93
Akers, Tom, Jr. 1919- WhoAm 92
Akers, William Walter 1922- WhoAm 92
Akerson, Alan W. WhoAm 92
Akerson, Daniel Francis 1948- St&PR 93, WhoAm 92
Akerson, Steve 1954- St&PR 93
Akers-Stahl, Michelle BioIn 17
Akerstrom, Ullie R. AmWomPl
Akesim, Judah 1948- WhoAsAP 91
Akeson, Wayne Henry 1928- WhoAm 92
Akesson, Anders Gustav 1951- WhoWor 93
Akesson, Bjorn O. 1942- WhoScE 91-4
Akesson, Norman Berndt 1914- WhoAm 92
Akhenaton, King of Egypt fl. c. 1388BC-1358BC BioIn 17
Akhmatova, Anna Andreevna 1889-1966 BioIn 17
Akhmedov, Rustam Urmanovic WhoWor 93
Akhmerov, Rustjam Rafaelovich 1951- WhoWor 93
Akhromeyev, Sergei 1923-1991 AnObit 1991, BioIn 17
Akhtar, Abdul Hafeez 1940- WhoWor 93
Akhtar, Afzaal 1955- WhoWor 93
Akhtar, Muhammad WhoScE 91-1
Akhtar, Muhammad 1933- WhoWor 93
Akhtar, Shabbir 1960- ConAu 139
Akhtari, Saeid 1961- WhoWor 93
Akhter, Mohammad Nasir 1944- WhoAm 92
Akhurst, Harold Weldon 1913- St&PR 93
Aki, Keiiti 1930- WhoAm 92
Akiba, Tadatoshi 1942- WhoAsAP 91
Akiba ben Joseph c. 50-c. 132 BioIn 17
Akiga 189-?-1959 IntDcAn
Akihito 1933- DcTwHis
Akihito, Emperor 1933- WhoWor 93
Akihito, Emperor of Japan BioIn 17
Akihito, His Imperial Majesty 1933- WhoAsAP 91
Akil, Akil Eisa 1944- WhoUN 92
Akimenko, Fyodor 1876-1945 Baker 92
Akimoto, Koichi 1958- WhoWor 93
Akin, Bertha AmWomPl
Akin, Billy Larue 1933- WhoIns 93

Akin, Gwendolyn 1950- WhoE 93
Akin, Hikmet 1948- WhoWor 93
Akin, Joan Harris 1944- WhoAmW 93
Akin, John G. 1911- St&PR 93
Akin, Lewis E. 1937- WhoAm 92
Akin, Mary Barbara 1932- WhoAmW 93
Akin, Mary Jane 1948- WhoEmL 93
Akin, Robert M., Jr. 1904- St&PR 93
Akin, William E(rnest) 1936- ConAu 39NR
Akin, William Ernest 1936- WhoE 93
Akinaka, Asa Masayoshi 1938- WhoAm 92
Akindynos & Pegasios OxDcByz
Akindynos, Gregory c. 1300-1348 OxDcByz
Akinjide, Richard Osuolale Abimbola 1931- WhoAfr
Akinkugbe, Oladipo Olujimi 1933- WhoWor 93
Akins, Dwain Allen Law&B 92
Akins, Imogene 1953- WhoAmW 93
Akins, Jerry Wayne 1943- St&PR 93
Akins, Marian AmWomPl
Akins, Melody Anne 1957- WhoAmW 93
Akins, Zane Vernon 1940- WhoAm 92
Akins, Zoe 1886-1958 AmWomPl
Akita, Sadao 1931- WhoWor 93
Akiyama, Atsushi 1927- WhoAsAP 91
Akiyama, Carol Lynn 1946- WhoEmL 93
Akiyama, Hajime 1931- WhoAsAP 91
Akiyama, Hideki 1952- WhoWor 93
Akiyama, Kazuyoshi 1941- Baker 92, WhoAm 92
Akiyama, Saneyuki 1868-1918 HarEnMi
Akiyama, Yoshifuru 1859-1930 HarEnMi
Akiyoshi, Toshiko 1929- WhoAm 92
Akkad, Moustapha MiSFD 9
Akkadevi fl. c. 1047- HarEnMi
Akkapeddi, Kaushik Sharma 1954- WhoE 93
Akkara, Joseph Augustine 1938- WhoWor 93
Akkas, Nuri 1944- WhoScE 91-4
Akkaya, Inci 1936- WhoScE 91-4
Aklonis, John Joseph 1940- WhoAm 92
Akman, Jeffrey Scott 1956- WhoE 93
Akman, Recai 1953- WhoScE 91-4
Akos, Francis 1922- WhoAm 92
Akoto, Yaw 1952- WhoEmL 93
Akoun, Georges 1927- WhoScE 91-2
Akovali, Guneri 1937- WhoScE 91-4
Akpata, Solomon Sunday Osayande 1937- WhoUN 92
Akram, Munir 1945- WhoWor 93
Akrida-Demertzi, Konstantoula 1951- WhoWor 93
Akridge, Frances Goode 1939- WhoSSW 93
Akridge, Paul Bai 1952- WhoWor 93
Akrigg, Alan WhoScE 91-1
Akritidis, Costas 1938- WhoScE 91-3
Akropolites OxDcByz
Akropolites, Constantine dc. 1324 OxDcByz
Akropolites, George 1217-1282 OxDcByz
Aks, Patricia 1926- BioIn 17, ConAu 136
Akselrad, David Martin 1959- WhoEmL 93
Akselsson, Kjell Roland 1940- WhoWor 93
Aksen, Gerald 1930- WhoAm 92
Aksen, Howard Stephen 1936- WhoAm 92
Aksenov, Vasilii ScF&FL 92
Aksenov, Vasilii Pavlovich 1932- BioIn 17
Aksent'Ev, Leonid Aleksandrovich 1932- WhoWor 93
Akses, Necil Kazim 1908- Baker 92
Aksin, Mustafa 1931- WhoUN 92, WhoWor 93
Aksnes, Gunnar 1926- WhoScE 91-4
Aksoy, Vedat 1957- WhoScE 91-4
Aksyonov, Vassily 1932- BioIn 17, ScF&FL 92
Aksyonov, Vassily Pavlovich 1932- WhoAm 92, WhoWrEP 92
Aksyuchits, Victor BioIn 17
Ak Temenggong Jinggot, Datuk Justine WhoAsAP 91
Aktouarios, John OxDcByz
Aktuna, Ibrahim 1944- WhoScE 91-4
Akulichev, Victor Anatolyevich 1939- WhoWor 93
Akutagawa, Donald 1923- WhoAm 92
Akutagawa, Yasushi 1925-1989 Baker 92
Akutsu, Yoshihiro 1932- WhoWor 93
Akyildiz, A. Remzi 1926- WhoScE 91-4
Akyilmaz, Mehmet O. 1944- WhoScE 91-4
Akylas, Triantaphyllos R. 1955- WhoEmL 93
Akyuzalp, Nurgun M. 1937- WhoUN 92
Alabanese Quaas, Isabelle Caroline 1960- WhoAmW 93
Alabouvette, Claude WhoScE 91-2
Alack, James C. 1948- St&PR 93
Al-Adel, Iba Fouad 1948- WhoWor 93
Aladjem, Silvio 1928- WhoAm 92
Alados, Concepcion L. WhoScE 91-3
Alafouzo, Antonia 1952- WhoAmW 93, WhoE 93, WhoEmL 93
Alaghband, Vahid 1952- WhoWor 93
Alagic, Suad 1946- WhoWor 93
Alaia, Azzedine BioIn 17
Alaia, Azzedine 1940?- CurBio 92 [port]
Alaie, Belinda Jean 1954- WhoE 93, WhoEmL 93
Alaimo, Anthony A. 1920- WhoAm 92, WhoSSW 93
Alaimo, Anthony Louis 1954- WhoE 93
Alain 1868-1951 BioIn 17
Alain, Jehan (Ariste) 1911-1940 Baker 92
Alain, Marie-Claire 1926- Baker 92
Alain, Olivier 1918- Baker 92
Alaini, Mohsin Ahmed 1932- WhoAm 92, WhoWor 93
Alajalov, Constantin 1900-1987 BioIn 17
Alakszay, Elizabeth Maria 1963- WhoEmL 93
Alala, Joseph Basil, Jr. 1933- WhoAm 92
Alaleona, Domenico 1881-1928 Baker 92
Alam, Akhter-Ul 1939- WhoWor 93
Alam, Badrul 1945- WhoWor 93
Alam, Maktoob 1942- WhoSSW 93
Alam, Md. Nurul 1953- WhoWor 93
Alam, Mohammad Shahid 1950- WhoEmL 93
Alam, Syed Mahbubul 1956- WhoWor 93
Alaman, Lucas 1792-1853 DcMexL
Alamar, Paul 1924- WhoE 93
Alameda, George Kevin 1955- WhoEmL 93
Al-Ameeri, Raschid Salim BioIn 17
Alamgir, Mohiuddin 1943- WhoUN 92
Alami, Omar Mechiche 1962- WhoWor 93
Al-Amili, Baha' al-Din 1547-1621 BioIn 17
Al-Amoud, Ahmed Ibrahim 1946- WhoWor 93
Alampi, Phillip d1992 NewYTBS 92 [port]
Al-Amri, Hussein Abdullah 1944- WhoWor 93
Alamundarus OxDcByz
Alamundarus d554 OxDcByz
Alan, Jordan MiSFD 9
Alan, Rafique 1929- WhoAsAP 91
Alanbrooke, Alan Francis Brooke, Viscount 1883-1963 BioIn 17, DcTwHis, HarEnMi
Alander, Jyri Maunu 1957- WhoWor 93
Alandt, Franklin D. 1932- St&PR 93
Alanis, Joan Marti WhoWor 93
Alanis, Macedonio 1962- WhoEmL 93
Alanis, Maria Luisa 1948- WhoAmW 93
Alanis, Roy 1939- St&PR 93
Alaniz, Margie Franco 1950- WhoAmW 93
Alanko, Matti L.J. 1935- WhoScE 91-4
Alaoui, Moulay Ahmed 1919- WhoWor 93
Alarcon, Arthur L. 1925- HispAmA
Alarcon, Arthur Lawrence 1925- WhoAm 92
Alarcon, Francisco X. 1954- DcLB 122 [port]
Alarcon, Minella Clutario 1948- WhoWor 93
Alarcon, Norma 20th cent.- HispAmA
Alarcon, Rogelio Alfonso 1926- WhoWor 93
Alarcon, Rogelio Bautista 1937- WhoWor 93
Alarcon, Terry Quentin 1948- WhoEmL 93
Alarcon de Quesada, Ricardo WhoWor 93
Alard, Jean-Delphin 1815-1888 Baker 92
Alardin, Carmen 1933- DcMexL
Alaric c. 370-410 HarEnMi
Alaric 365?-410 OxDcByz
Alaric, II d507 HarEnMi
Alarid, Albert Joseph 1948- WhoEmL 93
Alarie, Pierrette 1921- Baker 92
Alario, John A. 1943- WhoSSW 93
Alario, Robert F. Law&B 92
Alario-Franco, Miguel Angel 1942- WhoScE 91-3
Alary, Jean-Charles 1939- WhoUN 92
Alary, Josette 1934- WhoScE 91-2
Alary, Jules Eugene Abraham 1814-1891 Baker 92
Alasia, Sam L. 1959- WhoAsAP 91
Al Assaad, Al Ayham Abraham 1958- WhoWor 93
al-Assad, Hafez 1930- CurBio 92 [port], News 92 [port]
Al-Assaf, Ibrahim Abdulaziz 1949- WhoE 93
Alatas, Ali 1932- WhoAsAP 91, WhoWor 93
Alatheus d387 HarEnMi
Alatis, James Efstathios 1926- WhoAm 92, WhoE 93
Alatorre, Antonio 1922- DcMexL
Alatorre-Morones, Ernesto 1929- WhoWor 93
Alatriste, Sealtiel 1949- DcMexL
Alattiya, Abdulla Khalid 1953- WhoWor 93
Alatzas, George 1940- WhoWor 93
Ala-Ud-Din Jahanshuz of Ghor fl. c. 1150- HarEnMi
Ala-Ud-Din Kaikobad d1234 HarEnMi
Ala-Ud-Din Khilji d1316 HarEnMi
Alaupovic, Alexandra Vrbanic 1921- WhoAm 92, WhoAmW 93
Alavi, Najmuddin Ahmed 1949- WhoSSW 93
Alaviuhkola, Timo Arvi 1940- WhoScE 91-4
Al-Awadhi, Abdul Hamid Abdullah 1946- WhoUN 92
Alawi, Adnan Abdus-Salam 1940- WhoWor 93
Alayeto, George I. 1926- WhoAm 92
Alayza, Cecilia De Losada 1961- WhoWor 93
Alazraki, Jaime 1934- WhoAm 92, WhoWrEP 92
Alazraki, Naomi 1941- WhoAm 92
Alba, Camilo Benjamin 1956- WhoEmL 93, WhoWor 93
Alba, Guillermo Hernandez de 1906-1988 BioIn 17
Alba, Maria d1992 NewYTBS 92 [port]
Alba, Ray 1918- St&PR 93
Albach, Carl Rudolph 1907- WhoAm 92
Albach, Roger Fred 1932- WhoSSW 93
Albagli, Louise Martha 1954- WhoAmW 93
Al Bahar, Adnan 1955- WhoWor 93
Albaiges, Joan 1942- WhoScE 91-3
Albala, Mark Craig 1955- WhoE 93
Albam, Manny BioIn 17
Alban, Charles E. 1924- St&PR 93
Alban, James Carlton, Jr. 1917- St&PR 93
Alban, Roger C. 1948- St&PR 93
Alban, Roger Charles 1948- WhoEmL 93, WhoWor 93
Albanese, Charles C. 1937- St&PR 93
Albanese, Eda 1901- St&PR 93
Albanese, Ellen Louise 1949- WhoAmW 93
Albanese, Gerard, Jr. 1952- WhoIns 93
Albanese, John Charles 1925- St&PR 93
Albanese, Lee R. 1926- St&PR 93
Albanese, Licia BioIn 17
Albanese, Licia 1909- Baker 92
Albanese, Licia 1913- IntDcOp, OxDcOp, WhoAm 92
Albanese, Naomi G. d1989 BioIn 17
Albanese, Stephen Anthony 1947- WhoE 93
Albanese, Thomas 1957- St&PR 93
Albanesi, Enrico Peter 1938- St&PR 93
Albaneze, David Thomas 1952- WhoSSW 93
Albani, Emma 1847-1930 Baker 92, IntDcOp [port], OxDcOp
Albani, Mattia 1621-1712 Baker 92
Al Banna, Ahmed Abdulrahman 1959- WhoWor 93
Albano, Anne Marie 1957- WhoE 93
Albano, Anthony William 1953- WhoE 93
Albano, Domenico Bruno 1943- St&PR 93
Albano, Peter 1940?- ScF&FL 92
Albano, Rodolfo B. 1934- WhoAsAP 91
Albany, George M. 1945- St&PR 93
Albany, George Martin 1945- WhoIns 93
Albany, James S. 1952- St&PR 93
Albany, John Stuart, Duke of c. 1481-1536 HarEnMi
Albarede, Francis 1947- WhoScE 91-2
Albarella, Joan Katherine 1944- WhoWrEP 92
Albarello, Margherita Law&B 92
Albarran, Alan Brett 1954- WhoSSW 93
Albas, Jose Maria Escriva de Balaguer y 1902-1975 BioIn 17
Albaugh, Fred William 1913- WhoAm 92
Albaugh, Judson K. d1992 NewYTBS 92
Albaugh, Judson K. 1925-1992 BioIn 17
Albaugh, Patricia Johnson 1945- WhoAmW 93, WhoSSW 93
Albaum, Gerald (Sherwin) 1933- ConAu 38NR
Albaum, Jean Stirling 1932- WhoAmW 93
Albeck, Joseph Henry 1946- WhoEmL 93
Albeck, Lorin Henry Law&B 92
Albee, Arden Leroy 1928- WhoAm 92
Albee, Edward 1928- BioIn 17, MagSAmL [port], WorLitC [port]
Albee, Edward Franklin 1928- WhoAm 92, WhoE 93, WhoWor 93, WhoWrEP 92
Albee, George Wilson 1921- WhoAm 92
Albee, Marjory P. Law&B 92
Albella Martin, Jose Maria 1943- WhoScE 91-3
Alben, Alexander David Law&B 92
Albenda, David 1936- WhoAm 92
Albenesius, Richard Joseph 1956- WhoSSW 93
Albeniz, Isaac 1860-1909 Baker 92, OxDcOp
Albeniz, Mateo c. 1755-1831 Baker 92
Albeniz y Basanta, Pedro 1795-1855 Baker 92
Albenque, Michel 1940- WhoScE 91-2
Alber, Fred M. Law&B 92
Alber, Oleg E. Law&B 92
Alber, Phillip George 1948- WhoEmL 93
Alberca, Luis F. 1930- WhoScE 91-3
Alberca Silva, Luis F. WhoScE 91-3
Alberda, Linda Kresge 1956- WhoEmL 93
Alberda Vanekenstein, Peter C.W. 1940- St&PR 93
Alberdi, Maria-Teresa 1942- WhoScE 91-3
Alberding, Gilbert F. Law&B 92
Alberding, Richard C. 1931- WhoAm 92
Alberg, James L. Law&B 92
Alberg, James L. 1952- St&PR 93
Alberg, Mildred Freed 1921- WhoAm 92
Alberg, Tom Austin 1940- WhoAm 92
Alberg, William Gary 1949- St&PR 93
Alberga, Alta Wheat WhoAm 92, WhoAmW 93
Albergati Capacelli, Pirro, Conte d' 1663-1735 Baker 92
Alberger, William Relph 1945- WhoAm 92
Alberghi, Paolo Tommaso 1716?-1785 Baker 92
Albergo, Horace 1932- St&PR 93
Albergo, Horace Maurice 1932- WhoAm 92
Albergo, Paul Francis 1960- WhoEmL 93
Alberici, Gabriel J. 1909- St&PR 93, WhoAm 92
Alberini, Carlos E. St&PR 93
Alberry, Monique Jean 1967- WhoAmW 93
Albers, Anni 1899- WhoAm 92
Albers, Charles BioIn 17
Albers, Charles E. 1940- St&PR 93
Albers, Charles Edgar 1940- WhoAm 92
Albers, Claus 1925- WhoScE 91-3
Albers, Fern B. 1951- St&PR 93
Albers, Fern Beth Law&B 92
Albers, Fern Beth 1951- WhoEmL 93
Albers, Glennon Alvin 1951- St&PR 93
Albers, Greg H. 1949- WhoEmL 93
Albers, Hans 1892-1960 IntDcF 2-3 [port]
Albers, Hans-Georg Law&B 92
Albers, Hermann G. BioIn 17
Albers, Jo-Ann Huff 1938- WhoSSW 93
Albers, John BioIn 17
Albers, John Richard 1931- St&PR 93, WhoAm 92, WhoSSW 93
Albers, Kenneth F.X. 1927- St&PR 93
Albers, Rick M. 1954- WhoEmL 93
Albers, Ruud 1966- WhoWor 93
Albers, William M. 1927- St&PR 93
Albers, William Marion 1932- WhoAm 92
Albersheim, Peter 1934- WhoAm 92
Alberson, Ramsey B. Law&B 92
Alberson, Robert 1951- St&PR 93
Albers-Schonberg, Joyce Marie 1943- St&PR 93
Albert 1819-1861 Baker 92
Albert, Archduke of Austria 1559-1621 HarEnMi
Albert, Archduke of Austria 1817-1895 HarEnMi
Albert, Duke of York 1895-1952 BioIn 17
Albert, Prince Consort of Victoria 1819-1861 BioIn 17
Albert, Prince of Monaco 1958- BioIn 17
Albert, I c. 1100-1170 HarEnMi
Albert, Alan Dale 1956- WhoSSW 93
Albert, Alfred Gerhardt 1920- WhoAm 92
Albert, Bob BioIn 17
Albert, Burton, Jr. 1936- WhoWrEP 92
Albert, Carl 1908- BioIn 17
Albert, Carl B. 1908- PolPar
Albert, Charles Louis Napoleon d' 1809-1886 Baker 92
Albert, Charles Thompson 1930- WhoAm 92
Albert, Conrad Preston 1946- St&PR 93
Albert, Daniel Arthur 1948- WhoWor 93
Albert, Daniel Myron 1936- WhoAm 92
Albert, David H. 1950- WhoWrEP 92
Albert, Deborah Gail Freifeld 1961- WhoWor 93
Albert, Dewey d1992 BioIn 17, NewYTBS 92
Albert, Douglas Mitchell 1956- WhoE 93
Albert, Eddie 1908- BioIn 17, WhoAm 92
Albert, Edward 1951- WhoAm 92
Albert, Edward J. 1933- St&PR 93
Albert, Elizabeth Law&B 92
Albert, Eugen D' IntDcOp
Albert, Eugen d' 1864-1932 OxDcOp
Albert, Eugene d' 1864-1932 Baker 92
Albert, Faye Sharon 1942- WhoAmW 93
Albert, Garett J. 1943- WhoAm 92
Albert, Gerald 1917- WhoE 93, WhoWor 93
Albert, Gerald 1925- St&PR 93, WhoAm 92
Albert, Hans J. 1941- St&PR 93

Albert, Harold William 1949- *WhoEmL 93*
Albert, Harry Francis 1935- *WhoE 93*
Albert, Heinrich 1604-1651 *Baker 92*
Albert, Helen Mary 1953- *WhoAmW 93*
Albert, Herman 1922- *St&PR 93*
Albert, Ira Bernard 1944- *WhoE 93*
Albert, Janet Sue 1947- *WhoAmW 93, WhoE 93*
Albert, John 1942- *WhoE 93*
Albert, Judith Florence 1938- *WhoAmW 93*
Albert, Karel 1901-1987 *Baker 92*
Albert, Kathy Swift 1961- *WhoEmL 93*
Albert, Kevin K. 1952- *St&PR 93*
Albert, Kim Thomas 1953- *St&PR 93*
Albert, Lois Eldora Wilson 1938- *WhoAm 92*
Albert, Marv 1943- *WhoAm 92*
Albert, Mathias 1933- *WhoScE 91-4*
Albert, Michael P. 1940- *St&PR 93*
Albert, Mike 1954- *BioIn 17*
Albert, Neale Malcolm 1937- *WhoAm 92*
Albert, Peter James *Law&B 92*
Albert, Richard H. *Law&B 92*
Albert, Robert Alan 1933- *WhoAm 92*
Albert, Robert V. 1956- *WhoEmL 93*
Albert, Rose 1903- *AmWomPl*
Albert, Ross Alan 1958- *WhoEmL 93*
Albert, Stephen J. 1941-1992 *NewYTBS 92 [port]*
Albert, Stephen (Joel) 1941- *Baker 92, WhoAm 92*
Albert, Stephen W. 1952- *St&PR 93*
Albert, Stuart J. *Law&B 92*
Albert, Susan Wittig 1940- *WhoAm 92*
Albert, Terri Lyn 1962- *WhoAmW 93*
Albert, Vernon E. 1942- *St&PR 93*
Albert, William Eastwood 1951- *St&PR 93*
Albertalli, Roy Charles *Law&B 92*
Albertazzi, Alberto 1940- *WhoWor 93*
Albertazzie, Ralph 1923- *ScF&FL 92*
Albertelli, Guy Leo 1950- *WhoEmL 93*
Albertelli, Lawrence 1946- *St&PR 93*
Albert Garcia, Pablo 1967- *WhoWor 93*
Albert-Goldberg, Nancy 1938- *WhoAm 92*
Alberth, Bela 1925- *WhoScE 91-4*
Alberthal, Lester M. *St&PR 93*
Alberthal, Lester M., Jr. 1944- *WhoAm 92, WhoSSW 93*
Alberti, Domenico 1710-c. 1740 *Baker 92*
Alberti, Donald Wesley 1950- *WhoE 93*
Alberti, Gasparo c. 1480-c. 1560 *Baker 92*
Alberti, Giuseppe Matteo 1685-1751 *Baker 92*
Alberti, Johann Friedrich 1642-1710 *Baker 92*
Alberti, Johanna 1940- *ConAu 136*
Alberti, Kurt G.M.M. *WhoScE 91-1*
Alberti, Leon Battista 1404-1472 *BioIn 17*
Alberti, Peter William 1934- *WhoAm 92*
Alberti, Rafael 1902- *BioIn 17*
Albertine, Kurt H. 1952- *WhoE 93*
Albertini, Gerald Francis 1950- *WhoEmL 93*
Albertini, Joachim (Gioacchino) 1749-1812 *Baker 92*
Albertini, William O. 1943- *St&PR 93*
Albertini, William Oliver 1943- *WhoAm 92*
Albert-Nelson, Ilene 1955- *WhoEmL 93*
Alberto, Pamela Louise 1954- *WhoAmW 93*
Albert of Aachen fl. 12th cent.- *OxDcByz*
Albert of Hohenzollern-Kulmbach, II 1522-1557 *HarEnMi*
Alberts, Andrea Maxine 1951- *WhoE 93*
Alberts, Celia Anne *Law&B 92*
Alberts, Gary R. 1941- *St&PR 93*
Alberts, Irwin N. d1991 *BioIn 17*
Alberts, James Joseph 1943- *WhoAm 92*
Alberts, Jerome 1925- *WhoAm 92*
Alberts, Joop D. 1940- *WhoUN 92*
Alberts, Julien 1916-1986 *BioIn 17*
Alberts, Marion Edward 1923- *WhoAm 92*
Alberts, Robert Carman 1907- *WhoAm 92, WhoWor 93*
Alberts, Robert J. 1952- *St&PR 93*
Alberts, Wolfgang G. 1940- *WhoScE 91-3*
Albertsen, N.C. 1946- *WhoScE 91-2*
Albertsen, Per Hjort 1919- *Baker 92*
Albertson, Charles H. 1946- *St&PR 93*
Albertson, David L. 1942- *St&PR 93*
Albertson, Fred Woodward 1908- *WhoAm 92, WhoWor 93*
Albertson, Paul Allen, Jr. 1932- *St&PR 93*
Albertson, Robert Bernard 1946- *WhoAm 92*
Albertson, Susan L. 1929- *WhoAmW 93*
Albertson, Vernon Duane 1928- *WhoAm 92*
Albertsson, Tomas 1945- *WhoScE 91-4*
Albert von Hohenzollern 1490-1568 *HarEnMi*
Alberty, Robert Arnold 1921- *WhoAm 92*
Alberty, Ron L. 1937- *WhoSSW 93*
Albery, Wyndham John *WhoScE 91-1*
Albetta, Victor F. 1943- *St&PR 93*
Albi, Dominic 1921- *St&PR 93*
Albicastro, Henricus dc. 1738 *Baker 92*
Albin, Arthur M. *Law&B 92*
Albin, George L. 1942- *St&PR 93*
Albin, Joan Elizabeth 1948- *WhoEmL 93*
Albin, Leslie Diane 1954- *WhoEmL 93*
Albin, Randy Clark 1957- *WhoEmL 93*
Albin, Rran Ahskenazy 1952- *WhoE 93*
Albinak, Marvin Joseph 1928- *WhoE 93*
Albinana, Asuncion Izquierdo de 1914- *DcMexL*
Albinger, William J., Jr. *Law&B 92*
Albinger, William J., Jr. 1945- *WhoIns 93*
Albino, E. *WhoScE 91-3*
Albino, George Robert 1929- *WhoAm 92*
Albino, Judith E. N. *WhoAmW 93*
Albinoni, Tomaso 1671-1750 *BioIn 17, OxDcOp*
Albinoni, Tomaso (Giovanni) 1671-1751 *Baker 92*
Albinski, Nan Bowman 1934- *ScF&FL 92*
Albios, Janine 1956- *WhoAmW 93*
Albitz, William E. 1934- *St&PR 93*
Albizu, Olga 1924- *HispAmA*
Albizu Campos, Pedro *DcCPCAm*
Albo, Richard Gerald 1946- *St&PR 93*
Alboin d572 *HarEnMi*
Alboin d572 *OxDcByz*
Albom, Michael Jonathan 1944- *WhoE 93*
Albon, Colin Paul 1936- *WhoScE 91-1*
Albon, Michaela A. *Law&B 92*
Alboni, Marietta 1823-1894 *Baker 92, IntDcOp [port], OxDcOp*
Alborg-Dominguez, Miguel 1946- *WhoWor 93*
Alborzian, Cameron *BioIn 17*
Albosta, Richard Francis 1936- *St&PR 93, WhoAm 92*
Albrant, Daniel Howard 1962- *WhoSSW 93*
Albrecht, Albert Pearson 1920- *WhoAm 92*
Albrecht, Alexander 1885-1958 *Baker 92*
Albrecht, Allan James 1927- *WhoE 93*
Albrecht, Anthony W. 1930- *St&PR 93*
Albrecht, Arthur John 1931- *WhoAm 92*
Albrecht, Charles Frank, Jr. 1939- *St&PR 93*
Albrecht, Duane Taylor 1927- *WhoAm 92*
Albrecht, Edward Daniel 1937- *St&PR 93, WhoAm 92*
Albrecht, Evgeni 1842-1894 *Baker 92*
Albrecht, Felix Robert 1926- *WhoAm 92*
Albrecht, Frederick A. 1955- *St&PR 93*
Albrecht, Frederick Ivan 1917- *WhoAm 92*
Albrecht, Frederick Steven 1949- *WhoAm 92*
Albrecht, Gerd 1935- *Baker 92*
Albrecht, Hans 1902-1961 *Baker 92*
Albrecht, Harold William 1942- *St&PR 93*
Albrecht, Irving Augustine 1954- *WhoEmL 93*
Albrecht, James J. 1932- *St&PR 93*
Albrecht, James L. *Law&B 92*
Albrecht, Johann Lorenz 1732-1768 *Baker 92*
Albrecht, K. *WhoScE 91-3*
Albrecht, Karl 1807-1863 *Baker 92*
Albrecht, Kay Montgomery 1949- *WhoAm 92, WhoSSW 93*
Albrecht, Konstantin 1835-1893 *Baker 92*
Albrecht, Lillie H. Vanderveer *AmWomPl*
Albrecht, Mark Jennings 1950- *WhoAm 92*
Albrecht, Nancy 1945- *WhoAmW 93*
Albrecht, Otto Edwin 1899-1984 *Baker 92*
Albrecht, Paul Abraham 1922- *WhoAm 92*
Albrecht, Peggy Stoddard 1919- *WhoWrEP 92*
Albrecht, Pierre A. 1941- *WhoScE 91-2*
Albrecht, Raymond Paul *Law&B 92*
Albrecht, Richard Raymond 1932- *St&PR 93, WhoAm 92*
Albrecht, Robert Downing 1931- *WhoAm 92*
Albrecht, Ronald Frank 1937- *WhoAm 92*
Albrecht, Ronald Lewis 1935- *WhoE 93*
Albrecht, Sterling Jean 1937- *WhoAm 92*
Albrecht, Susan Lynn 1961- *WhoAmW 93*
Albrecht, Thomas Blair 1943- *WhoSSW 93*
Albrecht, Timothy Edward 1950- *WhoEmL 93, WhoSSW 93*
Albrecht, William Price, Jr. 1935- *WhoAm 92*
Albrechtsberger, Johann Georg 1736-1809 *Baker 92*
Al'brekht, Ernst Heinrich 1937- *WhoWor 93*
Albrektsen, Helge Normann 1950- *WhoWor 93*
Albret, Charles d' c. 1347-1415 *HarEnMi*
Albrethsen, Adrian Edysel 1929- *WhoE 93*
Albrici, Vincenzo 1631-1696 *Baker 92*
Albright, Archie E. 1920- *St&PR 93*
Albright, Archie Earl, Jr. 1920- *WhoAm 92*
Albright, Barbara Joy 1955- *WhoAm 92*
Albright, Beatrice Maria 1929- *WhoSSW 93*
Albright, Carl Wayne 1944- *St&PR 93*
Albright, Chip 1953- *WhoEmL 93*
Albright, Clyde Ballinger *Law&B 92*
Albright, Deborah Elaine 1958- *WhoAmW 93*
Albright, Douglas K. 1925- *St&PR 93*
Albright, Elaine McClay 1946- *WhoAmW 93*
Albright, Glen Patrick 1956- *WhoWrEP 92*
Albright, Grover C. 1938- *St&PR 93*
Albright, Harry Wesley, Jr. 1925- *WhoAm 92*
Albright, Hugh Norton 1928- *WhoAm 92*
Albright, Jack Lawrence 1930- *WhoAm 92*
Albright, James Michael 1940- *WhoE 93*
Albright, Jerry Wallace 1936- *St&PR 93*
Albright, John *BioIn 17*
Albright, Joseph William 1954- *WhoEmL 93*
Albright, Justin W. 1908- *WhoAm 92*
Albright, Kay Dale 1957- *WhoAmW 93*
Albright, Laurie Jo 1952- *WhoEmL 93*
Albright, Lois 1904- *WhoAm 92, WhoWor 93*
Albright, Lola 1925- *SweetSg D*
Albright, Lyle Frederick 1921- *WhoAm 92*
Albright, Marcia Anne 1936- *WhoAmW 93*
Albright, Maureen Terese 1961- *WhoEmL 93*
Albright, Nancy Eggelhof 1940- *WhoWrEP 92*
Albright, Paul Herman 1948- *WhoE 93*
Albright, Raymond Jacob 1929- *WhoAm 92*
Albright, Richard Sheldon, II 1951- *WhoE 93, WhoEmL 93*
Albright, Tenley 1935- *BioIn 17*
Albright, Thomas E. 1951- *St&PR 93*
Albright, Townsend Shaul 1942- *WhoAm 92*
Albright, Warren Edward 1937- *St&PR 93, WhoAm 92*
Albright, William (Hugh) 1944- *Baker 92*
Albrigo, John Louis 1944- *WhoSSW 93*
Albritton, David Donald 1913- *BiDAMSp 1989*
Albritton, Dondi Ortiz 1957- *WhoEmL 93, WhoWor 93*
Albritton, Paul Howard, Jr. 1943- *St&PR 93*
Albritton, Robert Sanford 1914- *WhoAm 92*
Albritton, Sarah Carlyle 1960- *WhoEmL 93*
Albritton, William Harold, III 1936- *WhoAm 92*
Albritton, William Hoyle 1942- *WhoAm 92*
Albritton, William Leonard 1941- *WhoAm 92*
Albrizio, Francesco 1947- *WhoWor 93*
Albro, Harley Marcus 1932- *St&PR 93*
Albro, Phillip William 1939- *WhoSSW 93*
Albro-Schaad, Kathryn Jeanne 1946- *WhoAmW 93*
Albu, Andrei 1928- *WhoScE 91-4*
Albuquerque, Affonso de 1453-1515 *HarEnMi*
Albuquerque, Afonso de 1453?-1515 *Expl 93 [port]*
Albuquerque, Jose C.D. 1935- *WhoScE 91-3*
Albuquerque, Lita 1946- *WhoAm 92*
Alburger, David Elmer 1920- *WhoE 93*
Alburger, James Reid 1950- *WhoEmL 93*
Albyn, Richard Keith 1927- *WhoAm 92*
Alcaide, Tomaz 1901-1967 *Baker 92*
Alcaino, Gonzalo 1936- *WhoWor 93*
Alcala, Fernando Enriquez y Afan de Ribera, duque de 1583-1637 *BioIn 17*
Alcala, Jose Ramon 1940- *HispAmA*
Alcala-Galiano, Dionisio 1760-1805 *BioIn 17*
Alcalay, Adolph Haim 1908- *St&PR 93*
Alcalay, Albert S. 1917- *WhoAm 92*
Alcala Zamora, Niceto 1877-1949 *DcTwHis*
Alcantara, Theo 1941- *Baker 92, WhoAm 92*
Alcaraz Figueroa, Estanislao 1918- *WhoAm 92*
Alcarez, Robert F. 1947- *St&PR 93*
Alcayaga, Lucila Godoy 1889-1957 *BioIn 17*
Al-Chalabi, Margery Lee 1939- *WhoWor 93*
Alchin, Barry Edward 1938- *WhoWor 93*
Alchin, John R. 1948- *St&PR 93*
Alchin, John Reginald 1948- *WhoAm 92*
Al-Chokhachy, Modhaffer Khalaf 1930- *WhoE 93*
Alcibiades c. 450BC-404BC *HarEnMi*
Alcindor, Lew 1947- *BioIn 17*
Alcindor, (Ferdinand) Lew(is) *ConAu 139*
Alcoba-Enciso, Fermin 1940- *WhoUN 92*
Alcocer, Robert J. 1933- *WhoIns 93*
Alcocer Castro, Guillermo Alberto 1961- *WhoWor 93*
Alcock, Charles Benjamin 1923- *WhoAm 92*
Alcock, Gudrun *DcAmChF 1960*
Alcock, John, Sr. 1715-1806 *Baker 92*
Alcock, John, Jr. 1740?-1791 *Baker 92*
Alcock, Sue Ellyn 1959- *WhoEmL 93*
Alcock, Vivian (Dolores) 1924- *ChlFicS*
Alcock, Vivien 1924- *MajAI [port], ScF&FL 92*
Alcon, Sonja Lee de Bey Gebhardt Ryan 1937- *WhoAmW 93*
Alcopley, L. 1910-1992 *BioIn 17*
Alcoriza, Luis 1920- *MiSFD 9*
Alcorn, Charles S. 1954- *St&PR 93*
Alcorn, David S. 1923- *St&PR 93*
Alcorn, David Stewart 1923- *WhoAm 92*
Alcorn, Gordon Dee 1907- *WhoAm 92*
Alcorn, Harold, II 1936- *St&PR 93*
Alcorn, Howard W. d1992 *NewYTBS 92*
Alcorn, Hugh Meade 1907-1992 *BioIn 17*
Alcorn, Hugh Meade, Jr. d1992 *NewYTBS 92*
Alcorn, Hugh Meade, Jr. 1907- *PolPar*
Alcorn, John 1935-1992 *BioIn 17*
Alcorn, John E. d1992 *NewYTBS 92 [port]*
Alcorn, Joseph Nichols, III 1941- *WhoAm 92*
Alcorn, (Hugh) Meade, (Jr.) 1907-1992 *CurBio 92N*
Alcorn, Samuel 1927- *St&PR 93*
Alcosser, Sandra B. 1944- *WhoWrEP 92*
Alcott, Abigail May 1840-1879 *BioIn 17*
Alcott, Amy Strum 1956- *BiDAMSp 1989, WhoAm 92, WhoAmW 93*
Alcott, James Arthur 1930- *St&PR 93, WhoAm 92*
Alcott, Louisa May 1832-1888 *AmWomWr 92, BioIn 17, MagSAmL [port], MajAI [port], WorLitC [port]*
Alcott, Mark Howard 1939- *WhoAm 92*
Alcott, May 1840-1879 *BioIn 17*
Alcott, Rosalind W. d1990 *BioIn 17*
Alcox, Michael T. 1947- *WhoAm 92*
Alcox, Michael Thomas 1947- *St&PR 93*
Alcox, Patrick Joseph 1946- *WhoEmL 93*
Alcudia Gonzalez, Felipe 1943- *WhoScE 91-3*
Alcyone *ConAu 39NR*
Ald, Roy A. *ScF&FL 92*
Alda, Alan *BioIn 17*
Alda, Alan 1936- *ConTFT 10, MiSFD 9, WhoAm 92*
Alda, Frances 1879-1952 *IntDcOp [port]*
Alda, Frances 1883-1952 *Baker 92, OxDcOp*
Alda, Tony *BioIn 17*
Al-Dabass, David *WhoScE 91-1*
Aldag, Edward Karl, Jr. 1963- *WhoSSW 93*
Aldag, Ramon John 1945- *WhoAm 92*
Aldag, Richard Jeffrey 1955- *WhoEmL 93*
Aldag, Rudolf Wilhelm *WhoScE 91-3*
Aldan, Daisy 1923- *WhoWrEP 92*
Aldana, Angelo R. *Law&B 92*
Aldana, Fernando 1944- *WhoScE 91-3*
Aldape, Alina A.C.E. *Law&B 92*
Aldape, Alina Alicia Catalina Elizabeth 1952- *WhoEmL 93*
Aldave, Barbara Bader 1938- *WhoAm 92, WhoAmW 93*
Aldea, Patricia 1947- *WhoAm 92, WhoAmW 93, WhoEmL 93*
Aldeen, Norris A. 1917- *St&PR 93*
Aldemir, Tunc 1947- *WhoWor 93*
Alden, Alice Wight 1865- *AmWomPl*
Alden, David *OxDcOp*
Alden, Douglas William 1912- *WhoAm 92, WhoSSW 93*
Alden, Ebenezer *BioIn 17*
Alden, Elizabeth Joan 1953- *St&PR 93*
Alden, Henry Mills 1836-1917 *GayN*
Alden, Howard *BioIn 17*
Alden, Ingemar Bengt 1943- *WhoWor 93*
Alden, John Edgar 1941- *St&PR 93*
Alden, John Ramon 1945- *St&PR 93*
Alden, John Richard 1908-1991 *BioIn 17*
Alden, John W. *Law&B 92*
Alden, Judith Abato 1946- *WhoEmL 93*
Alden, Mary C. *Law&B 92*
Alden, Michele *ConAu 39NR*
Alden, Phyllis *Law&B 92*
Alden, Priscilla *BioIn 17*
Alden, Raymond William, III 1949- *WhoSSW 93*
Alden, Ruth *AmWomPl*
Alden, Sharyn Louise 1943- *WhoAmW 93*
Alden, Stacia 1945- *WhoAmW 93*

Alden, Vernon Roger 1923- *St&PR 93, WhoAm 92*
Alden, William Livingston 1837-1908 *JrnUS*
Aldenkamp, A.P. 1951- *WhoScE 91-3*
Alder, Althea Alice 1933- *WhoWor 93*
Alder, Berni Julian 1925- *WhoAm 92*
Alder, Richard Welsley 1939- *St&PR 93*
Alder, Zane Griffeth 1926- *WhoWor 93*
Alderdice, John Thomas 1955- *WhoWor 93*
Alderdice, Paul W. 1953- *St&PR 93*
Alderdice, Phyllis Craig 1935- *WhoAmW 93*
Alderete, Joseph Frank 1920- *WhoSSW 93, WhoWor 93*
Alderfer, Clayton Paul 1940- *WhoAm 92*
Alderighi, Sandro 1940- *WhoUN 92*
Alderman, Beatrice *AmWomPl*
Alderman, Bissell 1912- *WhoAm 92*
Alderman, Charles Wayne 1950- *WhoEmL 93, WhoSSW 93*
Alderman, Ellen *BioIn 17*
Alderman, Eric R. *Law&B 92*
Alderman, Eugene Wayne 1936- *WhoSSW 93*
Alderman, Frances Rogers 1939- *WhoAmW 93*
Alderman, Gill 1941- *ScF&FL 92*
Alderman, Janice Mae 1963- *WhoSSW 93*
Alderman, John Richard 1947- *WhoEmL 93*
Alderman, Michael Harris 1936- *WhoAm 92*
Alderman, Michael James 1952- *WhoEmL 93*
Alderman, Minnis Amelia 1928- *WhoAm 92, WhoAmW 93*
Alderman, Myles Harris 1936- *St&PR 93*
Alderman, Richard Mark 1947- *WhoAm 92*
Alderman, Silvia Morell 1952- *WhoEmL 93*
Alderman, Walter A., Jr. 1945- *St&PR 93*
Alderman, Walter Arthur, Jr. 1945- *WhoE 93*
Alders, G. *WhoScE 91-3*
Aldersey-Williams, Hugh 1959- *ConAu 138*
Aldershof, Kent Leroy 1936- *St&PR 93*
Alderson, Arthur Norman 1948- *WhoSSW 93*
Alderson, Carmel Marie *Law&B 92*
Alderson, Creed F., Jr. 1933- *St&PR 93*
Alderson, David P., II 1949- *St&PR 93*
Alderson, G.W. *WhoScE 91-1*
Alderson, Harold B. d1991 *BioIn 17*
Alderson, Jack C. 1930- *St&PR 93*
Alderson, Karen Ann 1947- *WhoEmL 93*
Alderson, Margaret Northrop 1936- *WhoAm 92, WhoAmW 93, WhoSSW 93*
Alderson, Mercedes 1927- *WhoAmW 93*
Alderson, Richard Lynn 1947- *WhoAm 92*
Alderson, Sue Ann 1940- *WhoCanL 92*
Alderson, Thomas 1917- *WhoE 93*
Alderson, William Thomas 1926- *WhoAm 92, WhoSSW 93*
Alderton, Susan Edith 1952- *St&PR 93, WhoAmW 93*
Aldi, Andrew Vincent 1947- *St&PR 93, WhoAm 92*
Aldin, Cecil 1870-1935 *BioIn 17*
Aldin, Peter 1932- *WhoE 93*
Aldinger, William F. 1947- *St&PR 93*
Aldinger, William F., III 1947- *WhoAm 92*
Aldington, Hilda Doolittle *AmWomPl*
Aldington, Richard 1892-1962 *BioIn 17*
Aldis, Henry 1913- *WhoWor 93*
Aldis, Mary Reynolds 1872-1949 *AmWomPl*
Aldis, Will *MiSFD 9*
Aldisert, Ruggero John 1919- *WhoAm 92*
Aldiss, Brian W. 1925- *ScF&FL 92*
Aldiss, Brian Wilson 1925- *BioIn 17, WhoAm 92, WhoWor 93*
Aldiss, Margaret 1933- *ScF&FL 92*
Aldissi, Mahmoud Ali Yousef 1952- *WhoE 93, WhoEmL 93*
Aldon, Adair *MajAI*
Aldous, Allan 1911- *DcChlFi*
Aldous, Joan *WhoAm 92*
Aldred, Jeffrey Kent 1943- *St&PR 93*
Aldred, Kenneth James 1945- *WhoAsAP 91*
Aldred, William M. 1936- *St&PR 93*
Aldredge, Theoni Vachliotis 1932- *WhoAm 92, WhoAmW 93, WhoE 93*
Aldrete, Lori Johnson 1946- *WhoEmL 93*
Aldrich, Adell 1943- *MiSFD 9*
Aldrich, Alexander 1928- *WhoAm 92, WhoE 93*
Aldrich, Ann *ConAu 37NR, MajAI*
Aldrich, Ann 1927- *WhoAm 92*
Aldrich, Azelle M. *AmWomPl*
Aldrich, Bess Streeter 1881-1954 *BioIn 17*
Aldrich, C. Elbert 1923- *WhoSSW 93*
Aldrich, Daniel G. 1918-1990 *BioIn 17*
Aldrich, David Beals 1931- *WhoAm 92, WhoWrEP 92*
Aldrich, David Lawrence 1948- *WhoEmL 93*
Aldrich, Duane Cannon 1943- *WhoAm 92*
Aldrich, Frank Nathan 1923- *WhoAm 92, WhoE 93, WhoWor 93*
Aldrich, Franklin Dalton 1929- *WhoAm 92*
Aldrich, Frederic DeLong 1899- *WhoWor 93*
Aldrich, George E. 1946- *St&PR 93*
Aldrich, Henry 1648-1710 *Baker 92*
Aldrich, James F. *Law&B 92*
Aldrich, James Leonard 1932- *WhoE 93*
Aldrich, Janet Alice 1960- *WhoEmL 93*
Aldrich, Jeffrey William 1942- *St&PR 93*
Aldrich, John Carlson 1937- *WhoWor 93*
Aldrich, John Herbert 1947- *WhoAm 92*
Aldrich, Joseph C(offin) 1940- *ConAu 37NR*
Aldrich, Karen Bailey 1959- *WhoEmL 93*
Aldrich, Larry *NewYTBS 92 [port]*
Aldrich, Lawrence J. *Law&B 92*
Aldrich, Nancy Armstrong 1925- *WhoAm 92, WhoAmW 93, WhoE 93, WhoWor 93*
Aldrich, Nelson W. 1841-1915 *PolPar*
Aldrich, Patricia Anne Richardson 1926- *WhoAm 92, WhoAmW 93*
Aldrich, Putnam (Calder) 1904-1975 *Baker 92*
Aldrich, Ralph Edward 1940- *WhoAm 92*
Aldrich, Richard 1863-1937 *Baker 92*
Aldrich, Richard H. *St&PR 93*
Aldrich, Richard John 1925- *WhoAm 92*
Aldrich, Richard Orth 1921- *WhoAm 92*
Aldrich, Robert 1918-1983 *MiSFD 9N*
Aldrich, Robert Adams 1924- *WhoAm 92, WhoE 93*
Aldrich, Robert Anderson 1917- *WhoAm 92*
Aldrich, Roland W., Jr. 1944- *St&PR 93*
Aldrich, Thomas Albert 1923- *St&PR 93, WhoAm 92*
Aldrich, Thomas Bailey 1836-1907 *GayN*
Aldrich, William C. 1932- *WhoIns 93*
Aldrich, William Rolland 1959- *WhoEmL 93*
Aldridge, Alan 1943- *ScF&FL 92*
Aldridge, Alexandra 1940- *ScF&FL 92*
Aldridge, Alfred Owen 1915- *WhoAm 92*
Aldridge, Andrew C. *Law&B 92*
Aldridge, Charles Ray 1946- *WhoEmL 93*
Aldridge, Delores Patricia *WhoAmW 93*
Aldridge, Donald O'Neal 1932- *WhoAm 92*
Aldridge, Douglas Eugene 1961- *WhoSSW 93*
Aldridge, Edward C., Jr. 1938- *WhoAm 92*
Aldridge, Ira Frederick d1991 *BioIn 17*
Aldridge, (Harold Edward) James 1918- *DcChlFi*
Aldridge, James R. 1930- *St&PR 93*
Aldridge, John Watson 1922- *WhoAm 92, WhoWrEP 92*
Aldridge, John William 1924- *St&PR 93*
Aldridge, Kenneth William 1955- *WhoEmL 93*
Aldridge, Lionel *BioIn 17*
Aldridge, Melvin Dayne 1941- *WhoAm 92*
Aldridge, Myron Anthony 1953- *WhoE 93*
Aldridge, Noel Henry 1924- *WhoWor 93*
Aldridge, Ray 1948- *ScF&FL 92, WhoWrEP 92*
Aldridge, Richard C., Jr. 1925- *St&PR 93*
Aldridge, Roger Merle 1946- *WhoEmL 93*
Aldridge, Rosemary Robinson 1962- *WhoEmL 93*
Aldridge, Sidney A. 1940- *St&PR 93*
Aldridge, Susan Barham 1956- *WhoAm 92, WhoAmW 93*
Aldrin, Buzz *BioIn 17*
Aldrin, Buzz 1930- *WhoAm 92*
Aldrin, Edwin E. *BioIn 17*
Aldringen, Johann 1588-1634 *HarEnMi*
Aldringer, Johann 1588-1634 *HarEnMi*
Aldrovandini, Giuseppe (Antonio Vincenzo) 1671-1707 *Baker 92*
Aldwin, Carolyn Magadelen 1953- *WhoAmW 93*
Aldwinckle, Herb Sanders 1942- *WhoE 93*
Alea, Tomas Gutierrez *MiSFD 9*
Aleandro, Norma 1941- *HispAmA*
Alebua, Ezekiel 1948- *WhoAsAP 91*
Aleck, Kirk 1947- *St&PR 93*
Alecock, David Andrew 1955- *WhoE 93*
Aledort, Paul Jeffrey 1954- *WhoEmL 93*
Alefeld, Georg 1933- *WhoScE 91-3*
Alefeld, Goetz Eberhard 1941- *WhoWor 93*
Alegado, Rolando Baladad 1946- *WhoE 93*
Alegi, August Paul *Law&B 92*
Alegi, August Paul 1943- *St&PR 93*
Alegi, Peter Claude 1935- *WhoAm 92*
Alegre, Francisco Javier 1729-1788 *DcMexL*
Alegre, Julio Cesar 1950- *WhoWor 93*
Alegria, Cesar V., Jr. *Law&B 92*
Alegria, Ciro 1909-1967 *SpAmA*
Alegria, Claribel *BioIn 17*
Alegria, Claribel 1924- *ConLC 75 [port], SpAmA*
Alegria, Fernando 1918- *HispAmA, SpAmA*
Alegria, Lydia Isabel *WhoAmW 93*
Aleichem, Sholem 1859-1916 *BioIn 17*
Aleijadinho 1730-1814 *BioIn 17*
Aleixandre, Vicente 1898-1984 *BioIn 17*
Alejandro, Carlos Frederico Diaz- 1937-1985 *BioIn 17*
Alekhine, Alexander 1892-1946 *BioIn 17*
Alekman, Stanley Lawrence 1938- *WhoAm 92*
Alekna, Zenonas Petras 1938- *WhoWor 93*
Aleksander, Igor *WhoScE 91-1*
Aleksandr Nevski 1220-1263 *HarEnMi*
Aleksandrov, Anatoliy Petrovich 1903- *WhoWor 93*
Aleksandrov, Grigorij 1903-1983 *DrEEuF*
Aleksandrov, Leonid Naumovitsh 1923- *WhoWor 93*
Aleksandrowicz, Jerzy Witold 1936- *WhoScE 91-4*
Aleksandrowicz, Ryszard 1926- *WhoScE 91-4*
Alekseev, Mikhail Vasilievich 1857-1918 *HarEnMi*
Alekseeva, Liudmila 1927- *BioIn 17*
Alekseevskii, N.E. *WhoScE 91-4*
Aleksic, Branko 1951- *WhoWor 93*
Aleksy, Patriarch of Russia *BioIn 17*
Aleksy, Ronald James 1947- *WhoEmL 93, WhoWrEP 92*
Aleman, John Stephen 1935- *St&PR 93*
Aleman, Jose Luis 1928- *WhoWor 93*
Aleman, Miguel 1902-1983 *DcTwHis*
Aleman, Mindy Robin 1950- *WhoAmW 93*
Aleman, Moses Aaron 1931- *WhoUN 92*
Aleman Valdes, Miguel 1900- *DcCPCAm*
Alemar, Jose David 1949- *WhoEmL 93, WhoSSW 93*
Alembert, Jean-le-Rond d' 1717-1783 *Baker 92, BioIn 17*
Alemshah, Kourkene M. 1907-1947 *Baker 92*
Alencon, Charles, IV, Duke of 1489-1525 *HarEnMi*
Alencon, Francis, Duke of 1554-1584 *HarEnMi*
Alenie, Mary 1826-1896 *BioIn 17*
Alenier, Karren LaLonde 1947- *WhoEmL 93, WhoWrEP 92*
Alenitsyn, Alexander Georgievich 1938- *WhoWor 93*
Alenov, Lydia 1948- *BioIn 17*
Aleo, Joseph John 1925- *WhoAm 92*
Aleotti, Raffaella c. 1570-c. 1646 *BioIn 17*
Aleotti, Vittoria c. 1570-c. 1646 *BioIn 17*
Alepian, Taro 1945- *WhoE 93*
Aler, John 1949- *Baker 92, OxDcOp*
Alerte, Frank A. *Law&B 92*
Ale Ruiz, Rafael 1960- *WhoWor 93*
Al-Eryani, Abdul Qawi Abowasi 1954- *WhoUN 92*
Ales, Beverly Gloria 1928- *WhoWrEP 92*
Alesana, Tofilau Eti 1924- *WhoAsAP 91, WhoWor 93*
Aleschus, Justine Lawrence 1925- *WhoAmW 93*
Aleshire, Richard Joe 1947- *WhoEmL 93*
Alesia, James Henry 1934- *WhoAm 92*
Alesia, Patrick L. 1948- *St&PR 93*
Alesia, Patrick Lawrence 1948- *WhoAm 92*
Aleskerov, Fuad Tagi 1951- *WhoWor 93*
Alesky, Pamela Dee 1959- *WhoAmW 93*
Alessandrescu, Alfred 1893-1959 *Baker 92*
Alessandri, Arturo 1868-1950 *DcTwHis*
Alessandri, Felice 1747-1798 *Baker 92, OxDcOp*
Alessandri, Jorge 1896-1987 *DcTwHis*
Alessandri, Ricardo William 1962- *WhoE 93*
Alessandrini, Giovanna 1935- *WhoScE 91-3*
Alessandrini, Walter *St&PR 93*
Alessandro, Raffaele d' 1911-1959 *Baker 92*
Alessandro, Victor (Nicholas) 1915-1976 *Baker 92*
Alessandroni, Venan Joseph 1915- *WhoAm 92*
Alessi, Alberto *BioIn 17*
Alessi, George Anthony 1926- *WhoE 93, WhoWor 93*
Alessi, Keith Ernest 1954- *WhoAm 92*
Alessi, Mario Michele 1931- *WhoUN 92*
Alessio, Debra Ann 1957- *WhoEmL 93*
Alesso, Dominick *Law&B 92*
Alevizos, Susan B. 1936- *WhoAm 92*
Alevizos, Theodore G. 1926- *WhoAm 92*
Alevras, John S. 1929- *St&PR 93*
Alewine, James William 1930- *WhoSSW 93*
Alex, Gary Benninger 1941- *WhoAm 92*
Alex, Robert John 1947- *St&PR 93*
Alexander c. 250-328 *OxDcByz*
Alexander c. 870- *OxDcByz*
Alexander, Meister fl. 13th cent.- *Baker 92*
Alexander, Prince of Yugoslavia 1945- *BioIn 17*
Alexander, I 1777-1825 *HarEnMi*
Alexander, I 1888-1934 *DcTwHis*
Alexander, II 1199-1249 *HarEnMi*
Alexander, II, Emperor of Russia 1818-1881 *BioIn 17*
Alexander, III 1100?-1181 *OxDcByz*
Alexander, III 1241-1286 *HarEnMi*
Alexander, IV d1261 *OxDcByz*
Alexander, Alan 1943- *WhoWor 93*
Alexander, Alec Peter 1923- *WhoAm 92*
Alexander, Allen D. 1940- *St&PR 93, WhoIns 93*
Alexander, Amy Ginty-Ryan *WhoAmW 93*
Alexander, Andrew Lamar 1940- *WhoAm 92, WhoE 93*
Alexander, Anthony J. *Law&B 92*
Alexander, Arthur 1940- *SoulM*
Alexander, Arthur Frank 1948- *WhoSSW 93*
Alexander, Avery C. *AfrAmBi*
Alexander, Barbara Leah Shapiro 1943- *WhoAmW 93*
Alexander, Barbara Toll 1948- *WhoAm 92*
Alexander, Barton 1951- *WhoEmL 93*
Alexander, Benjamin Bates 1920- *St&PR 93*
Alexander, Benjamin Harold 1921- *WhoAm 92*
Alexander, Beverly Moore 1947- *WhoAmW 93*
Alexander, Bill 1934- *CngDr 91*
Alexander, Bob Gene 1933- *St&PR 93*
Alexander, Bruce D. 1943- *St&PR 93*
Alexander, Bruce Donald 1943- *WhoAm 92*
Alexander, Bruce J. 1944- *St&PR 93*
Alexander, Bruce Kirby 1948- *WhoEmL 93*
Alexander, C.M. *ScF&FL 92*
Alexander, Carl Albert 1928- *WhoAm 92, WhoWor 93*
Alexander, Caroline 1956- *BioIn 17*
Alexander, Cecil Abraham 1918- *WhoAm 92*
Alexander, Cecil Frances 1818-1895 *BioIn 17*
Alexander, Cecile *AmWomPl*
Alexander, Charles 1868-1923 *BioIn 17*
Alexander, Charles M. *Law&B 92*
Alexander, Charles Michael 1952- *WhoEmL 93*
Alexander, Charles Thomas 1928- *WhoAm 92*
Alexander, Charlotte Anne *WhoWrEP 92*
Alexander, Cheryl Dyer 1953- *St&PR 93*
Alexander, Christina Lillian 1942- *WhoAmW 93, WhoE 93, WhoWor 93*
Alexander, Clifford L., Jr. 1933- *EncAACR, WhoAm 92*
Alexander, Clifford Leopold, Jr. 1933- *AfrAmBi*
Alexander, D.S. *St&PR 93*
Alexander, Daniel Saunders 1953- *WhoE 93, WhoEmL 93*
Alexander, David *ScF&FL 92*
Alexander, David Alan *WhoScE 91-1*
Alexander, David Cleon, III 1941- *WhoWor 93*
Alexander, David Dale 1903-1979 *BiDAMSp 1989*
Alexander, David M. 1945- *ScF&FL 92*
Alexander, Deborah Radford 1953- *WhoEmL 93, WhoSSW 93*
Alexander, Dennis Beauvais *Law&B 92*
Alexander, Dennis W. *Law&B 92*
Alexander, Diane *WhoWrEP 92*
Alexander, Donald Crichton 1921- *WhoAm 92*
Alexander, Donald Lee 1948- *WhoEmL 93*
Alexander, Donna G. 1954- *St&PR 93*
Alexander, Dorothea Danas *WhoE 93*
Alexander, Doyle Lafayette 1950- *BiDAMSp 1989*
Alexander, Drury Blakeley 1924- *WhoAm 92*
Alexander, Duane Frederick 1940- *WhoAm 92, WhoE 93*
Alexander, E. Curtis 1941- *WhoWrEP 92*
Alexander, Eben, Jr. 1913- *WhoAm 92*
Alexander, Edna M. DeVeaux *WhoAmW 93*
Alexander, Edward B. 1958- *St&PR 93*
Alexander, Edward Porter 1835-1910 *BioIn 17, HarEnMi*
Alexander, Edward Russell 1928- *WhoAm 92*

Alexander, Elaine Harriett 1949- *WhoAmW 93*
Alexander, Elizabeth 1962- *WhoAmW 93*
Alexander, Ellin Dribben 1955- *WhoEmL 93*
Alexander, Eugene Morton 1926- *WhoE 93*
Alexander, Evan Shelby 1767?-1809 *BioIn 17*
Alexander, Fernande Gardner 1910- *WhoE 93*
Alexander, Floyce 1938- *WhoWrEP 92*
Alexander, Frank Lyon 1939- *St&PR 93, WhoAm 92*
Alexander, Frank Scott 1943- *WhoWrEP 92*
Alexander, Fred Calvin, Jr. 1931- *WhoAm 92*
Alexander, Fritz W., II 1926- *WhoAm 92*
Alexander, Gary L. *Law&B 92*
Alexander, Gary Philip 1946- *WhoSSW 93*
Alexander, George Jay 1925- *WhoE 93*
Alexander, George Jonathon 1931- *WhoAm 92*
Alexander, George Martin 1950- *WhoWor 93*
Alexander, Gregory Stewart 1948- *WhoAm 92*
Alexander, Grover Cleveland 1887-1950 *BioIn 17*
Alexander, H. Heath 1954- *WhoEmL 93*
Alexander, Haim 1915- *Baker 92*
Alexander, Harold 1940- *WhoAm 92*
Alexander, Harold Campbell 1920- *WhoSSW 93*
Alexander, Harold Luchsinger 1957- *WhoE 93*
Alexander, Harold Rupert Leofric George 1891-1969 *BioIn 17, DcTwHis*
Alexander, Harry 1953- *WhoEmL 93*
Alexander, Henry 1860-1895 *BioIn 17*
Alexander, Herbert E. 1927- *WhoAm 92*
Alexander, Holmes 1906-1985 *ScF&FL 92*
Alexander, Horace Gundry 1889-1989 *BioIn 17*
Alexander, I.C. 1950- *WhoScE 91-1*
Alexander, Ian Kemp 1947- *WhoWor 93*
Alexander, Ian W. *BioIn 17*
Alexander, J. Crinan M. 1944- *WhoScE 91-1*
Alexander, J.W. *SoulM*
Alexander, James Allen 1940- *WhoAm 92*
Alexander, James Eckert 1913- *WhoAm 92*
Alexander, James Edwin 1930- *WhoWor 93*
Alexander, James Marshall, Jr. 1921- *WhoAm 92*
Alexander, James Morton 1924- *St&PR 93*
Alexander, James Patrick 1944- *WhoSSW 93*
Alexander, James Wesley 1934- *WhoAm 92*
Alexander, Jan 1937- *ScF&FL 92*
Alexander, Jane *BioIn 17*
Alexander, Jane 1939- *WhoAm 92, WhoAmW 93, WhoWor 93*
Alexander, Jason 1959- *WhoAm 92*
Alexander, Jeff *WhoSSW 93*
Alexander, Jeffrey S. *Law&B 92*
Alexander, Jeri Jo 1948- *WhoSSW 93*
Alexander, John d1990 *BioIn 17*
Alexander, John 1923-1990 *Baker 92, OxDcOp*
Alexander, John Charles 1915- *WhoWor 93*
Alexander, John Charles 1943- *WhoAm 92*
Alexander, John D. *Law&B 92*
Alexander, John David, Jr. 1932- *WhoAm 92*
Alexander, John H., Jr. 1928- *St&PR 93*
Alexander, John Hanks 1864-1894 *EncAACR*
Alexander, John J. 1940- *WhoAm 92*
Alexander, John J., Jr. 1935- *WhoAm 92*
Alexander, John Macmillan, Jr. 1931- *WhoAm 92*
Alexander, John Robert 1936- *WhoSSW 93*
Alexander, John Thorndike 1940- *WhoAm 92*
Alexander, John Wesley 1919-1990 *BioIn 17*
Alexander, John William, Jr. 1933- *St&PR 93*
Alexander, Jonathan 1947- *WhoAm 92, WhoE 93, WhoEmL 93*
Alexander, Josef d1992 *NewYTBS 92*
Alexander, Josef 1907-1989 *Baker 92*
Alexander, Josef 1907-1992 *BioIn 17*
Alexander, Joseph Kunkle, Jr. 1940- *WhoAm 92*
Alexander, Joseph Raymond *Law&B 92*
Alexander, Joyce Mary 1927- *WhoAm 92, WhoAmW 93*
Alexander, Judd Harris 1925- *WhoAm 92, WhoSSW 93*
Alexander, Judith Ann 1940- *WhoAm 92, WhoAmW 93*
Alexander, Julie *BioIn 17*
Alexander, Karen *BioIn 17*
Alexander, Karl 1944- *ScF&FL 92*
Alexander, Karl Friedrich 1925- *WhoScE 91-3*
Alexander, Katherine *ScF&FL 92*
Alexander, Kay Marie 1940- *WhoAmW 93*
Alexander, Ken Edward 1956- *WhoSSW 93*
Alexander, Kenneth Lewis 1924- *WhoAm 92*
Alexander, Kobi 1952- *St&PR 93*
Alexander, Lamar *BioIn 17*
Alexander, Lamar 1940- *CngDr 91, WhoAm 92, WhoE 93*
Alexander, Leeland Neill 1945- *WhoSSW 93*
Alexander, Lewis McElwain 1921- *WhoAm 92*
Alexander, Lincoln MacCauley 1922- *WhoAm 92, WhoE 93*
Alexander, Linda Carol 1959- *WhoAmW 93*
Alexander, Linda Marie 1955- *WhoEmL 93*
Alexander, Lloyd *BioIn 17*
Alexander, Lloyd 1924- *ScF&FL 92*
Alexander, Lloyd (Chudley) 1924- *ConAu 38NR, DcAmChF 1960, DcAmChF 1985, MajAI [port], WhoAm 92, WhoWrEP 92*
Alexander, Lois Amy *AmWomPl*
Alexander, Lori Ann 1959- *WhoSSW 93*
Alexander, Lorraine Myles 1950- *WhoAmW 93*
Alexander, Lynn 1938- *WhoAm 92, WhoAmW 93*
Alexander, Lynne 1958- *ScF&FL 92*
Alexander, Marc 1929- *ScF&FL 92*
Alexander, Margaret Walker 1915- *EncAACR [port]*
Alexander, Margo Nickle 1947- *St&PR 93*
Alexander, Marie Bailey 1913- *WhoAmW 93*
Alexander, Marjorie Anne 1928- *WhoAmW 93*
Alexander, Marsha *ScF&FL 92*
Alexander, Martha G. 1920- *MajAI [port], SmATA 70 [port]*
Alexander, Martin 1930- *WhoAm 92*
Alexander, Martin A. 1900-1991 *BioIn 17*
Alexander, Mary Elsie 1947- *WhoAmW 93*
Alexander, Mary Louise 1926- *WhoAmW 93, WhoWor 93*
Alexander, Mary Suffron *Law&B 92*
Alexander, Matthew 1950- *WhoSSW 93*
Alexander, Max W. 1957- *WhoAm 92*
Alexander, Meena 1951- *ConAu 38NR*
Alexander, Melton Lee 1927- *WhoAm 92*
Alexander, Melvin Taylor 1949- *WhoE 93*
Alexander, Meta R.N. 1924- *WhoScE 91-3*
Alexander, Michael David *WhoScE 91-1*
Alexander, Michael Edward *Law&B 92*
Alexander, Michael Lee 1959- *WhoAm 92, WhoEmL 93, WhoSSW 93*
Alexander, Michele Yermack 1947- *WhoAmW 93*
Alexander, Miles Jordan 1931- *WhoAm 92, WhoSSW 93*
Alexander, Molly Mary Bushong 1958- *WhoEmL 93*
Alexander, Myrl Early 1909- *WhoAm 92*
Alexander, Nancy S. *BioIn 17*
Alexander, Nicholas Anthony 1938- *WhoAm 92, WhoWor 93*
Alexander, Nicholas Z. *Law&B 92*
Alexander, Norman D., Jr. 1930- *St&PR 93*
Alexander, Norman E. 1914- *St&PR 93, WhoAm 92*
Alexander, Norman James 1909- *WhoAm 92*
Alexander, Pamela 1948- *WhoWrEP 92*
Alexander, Patrice Elaine 1951- *WhoSSW 93*
Alexander, Patricia Ross 1955- *WhoAmW 93, WhoEmL 93*
Alexander, Patrick 1926- *ScF&FL 92*
Alexander, Patrick Byron 1950- *WhoAm 92*
Alexander, Patrick Lee 1945- *WhoE 93*
Alexander, Patrick Lynch 1955- *WhoSSW 93*
Alexander, Paul *ScF&FL 92*
Alexander, Peter 1917- *ScF&FL 92*
Alexander, Peter Albert 1942- *WhoAm 92, WhoWor 93*
Alexander, Peter F. 1949- *ConAu 138*
Alexander, Phillip Ross 1936- *St&PR 93*
Alexander, R.J. 1955- *St&PR 93*
Alexander, R. McNeill *BioIn 17*
Alexander, Ralph Edward 1946- *St&PR 93*
Alexander, Ralph William, Jr. 1941- *WhoAm 92*
Alexander, Raymond 1929- *St&PR 93*
Alexander, Raymond Jackson, Jr. 1928- *St&PR 93*
Alexander, Richard B. 1920- *St&PR 93*
Alexander, Richard Douglas 1947- *WhoEmL 93*
Alexander, Richard Lon 1954- *WhoSSW 93*
Alexander, Robert 1905-1980 *ScF&FL 92*
Alexander, Robert Clifton 1957- *WhoEmL 93*
Alexander, Robert David 1927- *St&PR 93*
Alexander, Robert Earl 1939- *WhoAm 92*
Alexander, Robert Evans 1907- *WhoAm 92*
Alexander, Robert Harold 1918- *WhoSSW 93*
Alexander, Robert J. 1918- *ConAu 39NR*
Alexander, Robert Jackson 1918- *WhoAm 92, WhoE 93, WhoWor 93*
Alexander, Robert McNeill *WhoScE 91-1*
Alexander, Robert William 1924- *WhoWor 93*
Alexander, Roberta 1949- *Baker 92*
Alexander, Ronald B. *Law&B 92*
Alexander, Ronald B. 1947- *St&PR 93*
Alexander, Ronald Clifford 1949- *WhoEmL 93*
Alexander, Rosemary Elizabeth 1926- *WhoAm 92*
Alexander, Roy 1930- *WhoAm 92*
Alexander, S. Allan 1951- *WhoEmL 93, WhoSSW 93*
Alexander, S. Kanneth 1948- *St&PR 93*
Alexander, Sadie Tanner Mossell 1898-1989 *BioIn 17*
Alexander, Samuel Allen, Jr. 1938- *WhoAm 92, WhoE 93, WhoWor 93*
Alexander, Samuel Craighead 1930- *WhoAm 92*
Alexander, Sander Peter 1929- *WhoAm 92*
Alexander, Saundra Weisband 1944- *WhoE 93*
Alexander, Scott A. *St&PR 93*
Alexander, Scott Emerson 1949- *St&PR 93*
Alexander, Shana *BioIn 17*
Alexander, Shana 1925- *WhoAm 92, WhoWrEP 92*
Alexander, Stacy Ann 1959- *WhoEmL 93*
Alexander, Stanford J. 1928- *St&PR 93*
Alexander, Stanton Malone 1941- *WhoSSW 93*
Alexander, Stephen Winthrop 1941- *St&PR 93*
Alexander, Steve 1947- *WhoWrEP 92*
Alexander, Stewart F. 1914-1991 *BioIn 17*
Alexander, Sue 1933- *SmATA 15AS [port]*
Alexander, Terry James 1946- *St&PR 93*
Alexander, Thea *ScF&FL 92*
Alexander, Theodore Martin 1909- *WhoAm 92*
Alexander, Theodore William, III 1945- *WhoE 93*
Alexander, Theron *WhoAm 92*
Alexander, Thomas B. *Law&B 92*
Alexander, Thomas Benjamin 1918- *WhoAm 92*
Alexander, Thomas F. 1951- *WhoWrEP 92*
Alexander, Thomas M. 1951- *St&PR 93*
Alexander, Thomas Marston 1950- *WhoEmL 93*
Alexander, Tice *BioIn 17*
Alexander, Vera 1932- *WhoAm 92*
Alexander, Vicki *BioIn 17*
Alexander, Victor d1992 *BioIn 17, NewYTBS 92*
Alexander, Victor Theodore 1956- *WhoWor 93*
Alexander, Wayne Taichi 1954- *WhoWor 93*
Alexander, Welborn Excell, Jr. 1941- *WhoAm 92*
Alexander, Will W. 1884-1956 *EncAACR*
Alexander, Willard A. 1931- *WhoAm 92*
Alexander, William 1577?-1640 *DcLB 121 [port]*
Alexander, William 1726-1783 *HarEnMi*
Alexander, William A. *Law&B 92*
Alexander, William B., Jr. 1937- *St&PR 93*
Alexander, William Brooks 1921- *WhoAm 92*
Alexander, William Cameron, II 1938- *WhoIns 93*
Alexander, William Carter 1937- *WhoAm 92*
Alexander, William D. d1991 *BioIn 17*
Alexander, William D., III 1911- *WhoAm 92*
Alexander, William H. 1941- *St&PR 93*
Alexander, William Henry 1902- *WhoAm 92*
Alexander, William Henry 1930- *WhoAm 92*
Alexander, William Herbert 1941- *WhoAm 92*
Alexander, William Louis, Jr. 1961- *WhoEmL 93*
Alexander, William Major, Jr. 1928- *St&PR 93*
Alexander, William Marvin 1912- *BioIn 17*
Alexander, William Olin 1939- *WhoAm 92*
Alexander, William Polk, III 1947- *WhoEmL 93*
Alexander, William Powell 1934- *WhoAm 92*
Alexander, William Vincent 1936- *St&PR 93*
Alexander, William Vollie, Jr. 1934- *WhoAm 92, WhoSSW 93*
Alexander, Wynne *WhoE 93*
Alexander-Guerra, Lycia Lucia 1955- *WhoEmL 93*
Alexander of Battenberg 1857-1893 *HarEnMi*
Alexander of Epirus, I d331BC *HarEnMi*
Alexander of Grernan, Baron 1950- *WhoWor 93*
Alexander of Tralles 525-605 *OxDcByz*
Alexander of Tunis, Harold Rupert Leofric George Alexander, Earl 1891-1969 *HarEnMi*
Alexander of Yugoslavia, Crown Prince 1945- *NewYTBS 92 [port]*
Alexander Schmorell *DcAmChF 1960*
Alexander Severus 208-235 *HarEnMi*
Alexanderson, Alvin 1947- *St&PR 93*
Alexanderson, Gerald Lee 1933- *WhoAm 92*
Alexander the Akoimetos dc. 430 *OxDcByz*
Alexander the Great 356BC-323BC *OxDcOp*
Alexander, the Great 356BC-323BC *BioIn 17, Expl 93, OxDcByz*
Alexander the Great, III 356BC-323BC *HarEnMi*
Alexander The Monk 6th cent.-9th cent. *OxDcByz*
Alexandra, Empress 1872-1918 *BioIn 17*
Alexandra, Liana 1947- *Baker 92*
Alexandratos, Nicholas 1937- *WhoUN 92*
Alexandre, Denis C. 1936- *WhoScE 91-2*
Alexandre, DeWitt Loomis, Jr. 1949- *WhoE 93*
Alexandre, Gilbert Fernand A.E. 1944- *WhoWor 93*
Alexandre, J.M.N. 1925- *WhoScE 91-2*
Alexandre, Jean-Henri 1931- *WhoScE 91-2*
Alexandre, Kristin Kuhns 1948- *WhoAmW 93*
Alexandrenne, Louis *WhoUN 92*
Alexandris, Penelope *Law&B 92*
Alexandropoulos, Nikolaos 1934- *WhoWor 93*
Alexandropoulos, Nikos 1934- *WhoScE 91-3*
Alexandrou, Nicholas E. 1931- *WhoScE 91-3*
Alexandrov, Alexander 1883-1946 *Baker 92*
Alexandrov, Anatoli 1888-1982 *Baker 92*
Alexandrov, Victor Alekseevich 1958- *WhoWor 93*
Alexanian, Diran 1881-1954 *Baker 92*
Alexanian, Raymond 1932- *WhoAm 92*
Alexeev, Dmitri 1947- *Baker 92*
Alexeff, Alexander 1934- *St&PR 93*
Alexeff, Igor 1931- *WhoAm 92, WhoSSW 93*
Alexich, Milton P. 1930- *St&PR 93*
Alexie, Sherman (Joseph, Jr.) 1966- *ConAu 138*
Alexiev, Alexi Dimitrov 1928- *WhoScE 91-4*
Alexim, Jao Carlos 1937- *WhoUN 92*
Alexios Angelos, III c. 1153-1211? *OxDcByz*
Alexios Angelos, IV c. 1182-c. 1204 *OxDcByz*
Alexios Doukas, V dc. 1204 *OxDcByz*
Alexios Homo Dei *OxDcByz*
Alexios Komnenos, I c. 1057-1118 *OxDcByz*
Alexios Komnenos, I c. 1182-1222 *OxDcByz*
Alexios Komnenos, II 1169-c. 1183 *OxDcByz*
Alexios Komnenos, II 1283-1330 *OxDcByz*
Alexios Komnenos, III 1338-1390 *OxDcByz*
Alexios Komnenos, IV 1382-1429 *OxDcByz*
Alexios Stoudites fl. 1025-1043 *OxDcByz*
Alexiou, James 1932- *St&PR 93*
Alexiou, Margaret Beatrice 1939- *WhoAm 92*
Alexis 1629-1676 *HarEnMi*
Alexis, Athena *ScF&FL 92*

Alexis, Francis 1947- *DcCPCAm*
Alexis, Geraldine M. 1948- *WhoAm 92*
Alexis, Katina 1946- *ScF&FL 92*
Alexis, Kim *BioIn 17*
Alexis, Marcus 1932- *St&PR 93*
Alexis, Marcus L., II 1959- *WhoE 93*
Alexius Comnenus, I 1048-1118 *HarEnMi*
Alexopolous, Ayala T. *Law&B 92*
Alexopoulos, Costas George 1939- *WhoWor 93*
Alexopoulos, Helene *WhoAm 92*
Alexopoulos, Nicolaos George 1942- *WhoAm 92*
Alexopoulos, Stathis 1949- *WhoWor 93*
Alexov, Alexander 1951- *BioIn 17*
Alexsy, Steven F. *Law&B 92*
Alexy-Stoll, Patricia Anne 1957- *WhoAmW 93*
Aley, Charles R. 1956- *WhoE 93, WhoEmL 93, WhoWor 93*
Aley, Paul Nathaniel 1944- *St&PR 93*
Al-Faihani, Saeed Mohamed 1960- *WhoUN 92*
Alfakhri, Emad Sadad 1961- *WhoWor 93*
Alfange, Dean, Jr. 1930- *WhoAm 92*
Alfano, A.A. 1949- *St&PR 93*
Alfano, Angel Rosario 1940- *WhoE 93*
Alfano, Blaise Francis 1923- *WhoAm 92*
Alfano, Charles Thomas, Sr. 1920- *WhoAm 92*
Alfano, Franco 1875-1954 *Baker 92, OxDcOp*
Alfano, Jane D. *Law&B 92*
Alfano, Michael Charles 1947- *St&PR 93, WhoAm 92, WhoEmL 93*
Alfarabi, Abu Nasr c. 870-c. 950 *Baker 92*
Alfaro, Agustin 1938- *WhoScE 91-3*
Alfaro, Cordelia Ann 1938- *WhoAmW 93*
Alfaro, Jorge Prince 1927-1990 *BioIn 17*
Alfaro Aguila-Real, Fernando 1954- *WhoWor 93*
Alfaro Pineda, Rafael Angel 1961- *WhoUN 92, WhoWor 93*
Al-Fasi d1837 *BioIn 17*
Alfau, Felipe 1902- *ConAu 137, ScF&FL 92*
Alfaya, Gerardo B. 1967- *WhoWor 93*
Al-Fayed, Mohamed 1933- *BioIn 17*
Alfelor, Ciriaco R. *WhoAsAP 91*
Alferaki, Achilles 1846-1919 *Baker 92*
Alferez, Faust 1930- *St&PR 93*
Alferov, Zhores I. 1930- *WhoWor 93*
Alfers, Gerald Junior 1931- *WhoAm 92*
Alfheim, Roar Lemcke 1935- *WhoWor 93*
Alfidi, Ralph Joseph 1932- *WhoAm 92*
Alfieri, Frank Thomas 1930- *WhoAm 92*
Alfieri, John Joseph 1917- *WhoAm 92*
Alfieri, Katherine Anne 1960- *WhoAmW 93*
Alfieri, Lisa 1969- *WhoAmW 93*
Alfieri, Pietro 1801-1863 *Baker 92*
Alfiero, Sal *BioIn 17*
Alfiero, Sal H. 1937- *St&PR 93*
Alfiero, Salvatore Harry 1937- *WhoAm 92, WhoE 93*
Alfirevic, Ivo 1939- *WhoScE 91-4*
Alfoldi, Lajos 1927- *WhoScE 91-4*
Alfoldi, Laszlo 1928- *WhoScE 91-4*
Alfons, Hans 1933- *WhoScE 91-4*
Alfonseca, Manuel 1946- *WhoWor 93*
Alfonso, VI c. 1042-1109 *HarEnMi*
Alfonso, VII c. 1104-1157 *HarEnMi*
Alfonso, VIII 1155-1214 *HarEnMi*
Alfonso, X, King of Castile and Leon 1221-1284 *BioIn 17*
Alfonso, XI 1311-1350 *HarEnMi*
Alfonso, XIII 1886-1941 *DcTwHis*
Alfonso, XIII, King of Spain 1886-1941 *BioIn 17*
Alfonso, Antonio Escolar 1943- *WhoAm 92*
Alfonso, Carlos 1950- *HispAmA*
Alfonso, Carlos Juan 1955- *WhoSSW 93*
Alfonso, Eduardo 1952- *WhoEmL 93, WhoSSW 93*
Alfonso, Robert John 1928- *WhoAm 92*
Alfonso, Zecconi *WhoScE 91-3*
Alfonso el Grande, III c. 838-910 *HarEnMi*
Alfonso the Magnanimous, V c. 1396-1458 *HarEnMi*
Alfonso the Warrior, I c. 1073-1134 *HarEnMi*
Alfonzo, Carlos 1950-1991 *BioIn 17*
Alford, B.W. 1957- *St&PR 93*
Alford, Beverly Joane 1946- *WhoAmW 93*
Alford, Bobby Ray 1932- *WhoAm 92*
Alford, Brad Alan 1953- *WhoE 93*
Alford, Charles J., Jr. 1922- *St&PR 93*
Alford, Donald E. 1926- *St&PR 93*
Alford, Edna 1947- *WhoCanL 92*
Alford, Fred F., Jr. 1931- *St&PR 93*
Alford, George A. d1990 *BioIn 17*
Alford, George David *WhoScE 91-1*
Alford, J. Keith 1941- *St&PR 93*
Alford, Joan Franz 1940- *WhoAmW 93*
Alford, John W. 1912- *St&PR 93*
Alford, John William 1912- *WhoAm 92*
Alford, Kenneth J. *Baker 92*
Alford, Kenneth W. 1938- *St&PR 93*
Alford, Lamar 1944-1991 *BioIn 17*
Alford, Lionel Devon 1925- *St&PR 93*
Alford, Marcus Richard 1953- *WhoEmL 93*
Alford, Mary Ann *Law&B 92*
Alford, Mary Ann 1954- *WhoEmL 93*
Alford, Michael R. *Law&B 92*
Alford, Nancy Boylan 1941- *WhoAmW 93, WhoSSW 93*
Alford, Neill Herbert, Jr. 1919- *WhoAm 92, WhoWor 93*
Alford, Newell Gilder, Jr. 1920- *WhoAm 92*
Alford, Paul Legare 1930- *WhoAm 92*
Alford, Philip John 1953- *St&PR 93*
Alford, Richard Dana 1951- *WhoEmL 93*
Alford, Robert E. 1926- *St&PR 93*
Alford, Robert Ross 1928- *WhoAm 92, WhoE 93*
Alford, Robert Wilfrid, Jr. 1955- *WhoEmL 93, WhoSSW 93*
Alford, Sandra Elaine 1944- *WhoAmW 93*
Alford, Stephen Todd 1964- *BiDAMSp 1989*
Alford, Thomas Earl 1935- *WhoAm 92*
Alford, Timothy James 1947- *WhoAm 92*
Alford, Walter H. *Law&B 92*
Alford, Walter Helion 1938- *WhoAm 92*
Alford, William Lumpkin 1924- *WhoSSW 93*
Alford, William P. 1948- *WhoAm 92*
Alford, William Parker 1927- *WhoAm 92*
Alfred, Dewitt Clinton, Jr. 1937- *WhoSSW 93*
Alfred, John Samuel 1954- *WhoWor 93*
Alfred, Karl Sverre 1917- *WhoAm 92*
Alfred, Norris W. *BioIn 17*
Alfred, Stephen Jay 1934- *WhoAm 92*
Alfred, Theodore Mark 1925- *St&PR 93*
Alfred, William 1922- *WhoAm 92, WhoWrEP 92*
Alfreds, Joe *WhoWrEP 92*
Alfredson, Jens *WhoWrEP 92*
Alfredsson, Mats Lennart 1946- *WhoWor 93*
Alfred the Great 871-899 *OxDcOp*
Alfrey, Marian Antoinette 1925- *WhoAmW 93*
Alfriend, Kyle Terry 1940- *WhoSSW 93*
Alfs, Matthew Gerd 1956- *WhoWrEP 92*
Alfsen, Annette 1928- *WhoScE 91-2*
Alfsen, Tore K. *WhoScE 91-4*
Alfuth, Terry J. 1945- *WhoIns 93*
Alfuth, Terry James 1945- *St&PR 93*
Alfven, Hannes Olof Gosta 1908- *WhoAm 92, WhoWor 93*
Alfven, Hugo (Emil) 1872-1960 *Baker 92*
Algarin, Miguel 1941- *BioIn 17, HispAmA [port]*
Algarotti, Francesco 1712-1764 *Baker 92, OxDcOp*
Algarra, Maria Luisa 1916-1957 *DcMexL*
Algava-Czik, Esta *Law&B 92*
Algen, Irving 1930- *St&PR 93*
Algen, Jeffrey 1960- *St&PR 93*
Alger, Chadwick Fairfax 1924- *WhoAm 92*
Alger, Derek S. *WhoWrEP 92*
Alger, Esther Marion *AmWomPl*
Alger, Fred M. 1934- *St&PR 93*
Alger, H.C. 1938- *St&PR 93*
Alger, Horatio 1832-1899 *BioIn 17*
Alger, Horatio, Jr. *MajAI*
Alger, Horatio, Jr. 1830-1899 *GayN*
Alger, Leclaire (Gowans) 1898-1969 *MajAI [port]*
Alger, Martin Joseph 1944- *St&PR 93*
Alger, R. Kennedy 1947- *St&PR 93*
Algeri, Sergio 1940- *WhoScE 91-3*
Algermissen, Marie Star 1949- *WhoAmW 93*
Algie, James *WhoScE 91-1*
Algino, Joseph Michael, II 1954- *WhoEmL 93*
Algirdas, Sauclargas 1948- *WhoWor 93*
Algozin, Bruce *ScF&FL 92*
Algra, Ronald James 1949- *WhoEmL 93*
Algren, Nelson 1909-1981 *BioIn 17, MagSAmL [port]*
Alguire, Judith 1946- *ScF&FL 92*
Alhadeff, Benjamin Jay 1948- *St&PR 93*
Alhadeff, Charles D. 1909- *St&PR 93*
Alhadeff, David Albert 1923- *WhoAm 92*
Alhadeff, Gini *BioIn 17*
Alhadeff, Morris Jerome 1914- *WhoAm 92*
Al-Hafeez, Humza 1931- *WhoAm 92*
Al-Hakim, Tawfiq 1898-1987 *BioIn 17*
Alhava, Esko M. 1941- *WhoScE 91-4*
Alho, Antti V. 1935- *WhoScE 91-4*
Al-Hoi, Abu d1991 *BioIn 17*
Al-Hoqail, Abdullah Hamad 1937- *WhoWor 93*
Al-Hudaithi, Abdullah Ibrahim 1939- *WhoWor 93*
Al-Husseini, Faisal *BioIn 17*
Ali 1970-
See Tribe Called Quest, A *ConMus 8*
Ali, Agha Shahid 1949- *WhoWrEP 92*
Ali, Frank *St&PR 93*
Ali, Grace Lucy Moore 1952- *WhoEmL 93*
Ali, Gregory F. 1956- *St&PR 93*
Ali, H. A. Mukti 1923- *WhoWor 93*
Ali, Jaffer *ScF&FL 92*
Ali, Jam Sadiq d1992 *BioIn 17*
Ali, Marie Ida 1948- *WhoEmL 93*
Ali, Mehdi 1944- *WhoAm 92*
Ali, Mehdi Raza 1944- *St&PR 93*
Ali, Mohamed Ibrahim 1944- *WhoUN 92*
Ali, Mohamed Muntaz 1931- *WhoWor 93*
Ali, Mohammad Farhat 1938- *WhoWor 93*
Ali, Muhammad 1942- *AfrAmBi, BioIn 17, WhoAm 92*
Ali, Naseemul 1938- *WhoWor 93*
Ali, Rafath 1944- *St&PR 93, WhoAm 92*
Ali, S. Hadi Raza d1992 *BioIn 17*
Ali, S. Yousuf 1935- *WhoScE 91-1*
Ali, Salem Robaye 1934-1978 *BioIn 17*
Ali, Syed Ibrahim 1941- *WhoWor 93*
Ali, Syed Sadaqat 1953- *WhoWor 93*
Ali, Zine el Abidine ben *BioIn 17*
Alia, Paolo *WhoScE 91-3*
Alia, Ramiz *BioIn 17, NewYTBS 92*
Alia, Ramiz 1925- *ColdWar 2 [port]*
Ali Abdallah Salih 1942- *BioIn 17*
Aliabiev, Alexander (Nikolaievich) 1787-1851 *Baker 92*
Ali Akbar Khan 1922- *Baker 92*
Alianak, Hrant 1950- *WhoCanL 92*
Alias Bin Mohd Ali 1937- *WhoAsAP 91*
Aliber, Robert Z. 1930- *WhoAm 92*
Alibert, G. *WhoScE 91-2*
Alibrandi, Joseph F. 1928- *St&PR 93*
Alibrandi, Joseph Francis 1928- *WhoAm 92*
Alicata, Joseph Everett 1904- *WhoAm 92*
Alice, Mary 1941- *WhoAm 92, WhoAmW 93*
Alice, Ronald *Law&B 92*
Alicea, Nelson Moises 1954- *WhoSSW 93*
Alich, John Arthur, Jr. 1942- *St&PR 93*
Alichniewicz, Andrzej 1918- *WhoScE 91-4*
Alick, Nafe Joe 1936- *St&PR 93, WhoAm 92*
Alicki, Robert 1951- *WhoWor 93*
Alie, Arthur H. 1939- *WhoIns 93*
Alie, Arthur Henry 1939- *St&PR 93, WhoAm 92*
Alie, Pere Ysern y 1875?-1946 *BioIn 17*
Aliengena, Tony *BioIn 17*
Alier, Abel 1933- *WhoAfr*
Aliesan, Jody 1943- *WhoWrEP 92*
Aliev, Fikrat Ahmadali 1949- *WhoWor 93*
Aliferis, James d1992 *BioIn 17, NewYTBS 92*
Alig, Frank Douglas Stalnaker 1921- *WhoWor 93*
Alig, Roger Casanova 1941- *WhoE 93*
Alighieri, Dante 1265-1321 *BioIn 17*
Ali Hassan Mwinyi *BioIn 17*
Ali-Jackson, Kamil *Law&B 92*
Ali Keshtmand, Comrade Sultan 1935- *WhoAsAP 91*
Alikhan, Shahid 1923- *WhoUN 92*
Aliki *MajAI*
Alikpala, Federico Y., Jr. 1932- *WhoWor 93*
Alimanestianu, Calin 1925- *WhoAm 92*
Alimansky, Burt 1943- *WhoAm 92*
Alimaras, Gus 1958- *WhoEmL 93*
Alimchandani, Guloo Mohan 1953- *WhoWor 93*
Alimena, Jim 1952- *St&PR 93*
Alimpij fl. 11th cent.- *OxDcByz*
Alin, Robert David 1952- *St&PR 93*
Alin, Victoria Hastings 1955- *WhoAmW 93*
Alina, Walter Paul 1931- *St&PR 93*
Alinder, James Gilbert 1941- *WhoAm 92*
Aline, Countess of Romanones *BioIn 17*
Alinei, Mario 1926- *WhoWor 93*
Alinsky, Saul *BioIn 17*
Alinsky, Saul D. 1909-1972 *PolPar*
Aliot, Etienne 1946- *WhoWor 93*
Aliprandi, Bernardo c. 1710-c. 1792 *Baker 92*
Aliprandi, Giambattista 1942- *St&PR 93, WhoAm 92*
Al-Iryani, Abdul Karim 1935- *WhoWor 93*
Alisberg, Nancy Beth 1952- *WhoAmW 93*
Alisky, Marvin Howard 1923- *WhoAm 92*
Alison, John Richardson 1956- *WhoEmL 93*
Alison, Paul Nordell 1950- *WhoWor 93*
Alisov, Nikolaj Vasiljevich 1921- *WhoWor 93*
Alitalo, Ilkka Viljo Olavi 1934- *WhoScE 91-4*
Alito, Samuel Anthony, Jr. 1950- *WhoAm 92, WhoE 93*
Alivernini, John M. *Law&B 92*
Alivisatos, Spyridon G. A. 1918- *WhoWor 93*
Alivizatos, A.S. 1948- *WhoScE 91-3*
Alix, Jacquelyn J. 1940- *WhoE 93*
Aliyev, Ramiz Jalal Oglye 1957- *WhoWor 93*
Alizai, Azam 1931- *St&PR 93*
Alizzi, Anthony Joseph 1953- *WhoE 93*
Aljian, James Donovan 1932- *WhoAm 92*
Al-Jubeihi, Hussein Eid *WhoWor 93*
Al-Kabbani, Samir 1954- *WhoSSW 93*
Al-Kadhi, Isam Nouri 1933- *WhoWor 93*
Alkalay-Gut, Karen 1945- *WhoWrEP 92*
Alkamper, Jochen 1927- *WhoScE 91-3*
Alkan, Charles-Valentin 1813-1888 *Baker 92*
Alkemade, Peter Johannes 1939- *WhoWor 93*
Alker, Hayward Rose, Jr. 1937- *WhoAm 92*
Al-Khalidi, Mohammad Towfiq 1945- *WhoUN 92*
Al-Khalifa, Hamad Ibn Isa 1950- *WhoWor 93*
Al-Khalifa, Isa bin Sulman, Amir of Bahrain *BioIn 17*
Al-Khalifa, Isa Ibn Salman 1933- *WhoWor 93*
Al-Khalifa, Khalifa ibn Salman 1935- *WhoWor 93*
Al-Khalifa, Mohamed Bin Khalifa Hamid 1937- *WhoWor 93*
Al-Khalifa, Muhammad Bin Mubarak 1935- *WhoWor 93*
al-Kharrat, Edwar 1926- *ConAu 136*
Al Khateeb, Mohamed Awad 1944- *WhoUN 92*
Al-Khatir, Mubarak Ali *WhoWor 93*
Al-Khawashky, Mohammad Is-Haq 1931- *WhoUN 92*
Al Khayat, Mohamed Haytham 1937- *WhoUN 92*
Al-Khayyal, Faiz Abdullah 1949- *WhoEmL 93*
Al-Khazraji, Abdul Karim Gaidan 1935- *WhoUN 92*
Al Khushashi, Naim Izzat 1939- *WhoWor 93*
Al-Khussaiby, Salim Mohammed 1939- *WhoUN 92*
Alkire, Edward Arthur 1953- *St&PR 93*
Alkire, Richard Charles 1955- *WhoEmL 93*
Alkire, Richard Collin 1941- *WhoAm 92*
Alkire, Sharon Cynthia 1945- *WhoAmW 93*
Alkon, Ellen Skillen 1936- *WhoAm 92*
Alkon, Paul K. 1935- *ScF&FL 92*
Alkon, Paul Kent *WhoAm 92*
Alkov, Len A. *Law&B 92*
Alksnis, Viktor *BioIn 17*
Allaben, William Thomas 1939- *WhoSSW 93*
Allaby, Michael 1933- *ScF&FL 92*
Allaby, Stanley Reynolds 1931- *WhoAm 92*
Alladaye, Michel 1940- *WhoAfr*
Allaid, Voceln *Law&B 92*
Allain, Emery Edgar 1922- *WhoAm 92*
Allain, Leon Gregory 1924- *WhoSSW 93*
Allain, Lynn M. *Law&B 92*
Allain, P. 1934- *WhoScE 91-2*
Allain-Targe, Francois Henri Rene 1832-1902 *BioIn 17*
Allaire, Marion *Law&B 92*
Allaire, Paul A. *BioIn 17*
Allaire, Paul Arthur 1938- *St&PR 93, WhoAm 92, WhoE 93*
Allais, Maurice 1911- *BioIn 17*
Allais, Maurice-Felix 1911- *WhoWor 93*
Allam, Mark Whittier 1908- *WhoAm 92*
Allamong, Betty D. 1935- *WhoAm 92*
Allan, Alex Milroy 1917- *St&PR 93*
Allan, Anthony Havelock- 1904- *BioIn 17*
Allan, Barry David 1935- *WhoAm 92*
Allan, Barry Stewart 1954- *St&PR 93*
Allan, Donald Aspinwall 1922- *WhoAm 92*
Allan, Dorothy C. *AmWomPl*
Allan, Elaine Marie *Law&B 92*
Allan, Frank Kellog 1935- *WhoAm 92*
Allan, Garry Lindsay 1958- *WhoWor 93*
Allan, Harry Thain 1928- *WhoAm 92*
Allan, Hugh James Pearson 1928- *WhoAm 92*
Allan, Jean *BioIn 17*
Allan, Jim *ScF&FL 92*
Allan, John B. *BioIn 17*
Allan, John Dykes 1925- *St&PR 93*
Allan, John Malcolm, Jr. 1955- *WhoEmL 93*
Allan, Jon Whitney 1958- *WhoAm 92*
Allan, Mabel E. 1915- *ScF&FL 92*
Allan, Mabel Esther 1915- *MajAI [port]*
Allan, Margaret Catherine 1947- *WhoAmW 93, WhoSSW 93*
Allan, Mea 1909-1982 *ScF&FL 92*
Allan, Michael L. *Law&B 92*
Allan, Ralph T. MacKinnon 1942- *St&PR 93*
Allan, Ralph Thomas Mackinnon 1942- *WhoAm 92*

Allan, Rebecca S. *Law&B 92*
Allan, Richard J. 1941- *St&PR 93*
Allan, Robert Moffat, Jr. 1920- *WhoWor 93*
Allan, Ronald C. 1937- *St&PR 93*
Allan, Rupert M. d1991 *BioIn 17*
Allan, Stanley Nance 1921- *WhoAm 92*
Allan, Stuart *BioIn 17*
Allan, Ted *ScF&FL 92*
Allan, Ted 1916- *WhoCanL 92*
Allan, Walter Robert 1937- *WhoAm 92*
Allan, William Norman 1925- *St&PR 93*
Allan, Yvonne Leticia 1927- *WhoAmW 93*
Allanbrook, Douglas 1921- *Baker 92*
Alland, Lawrence Martin 1931- *WhoSSW 93*
Allansmith, Mathea Reuter 1930- *WhoAmW 93*
Allanson, Bruce D. 1930- *St&PR 93*
Allard, A. Wayne 1943- *CngDr 91*
Allard, Ann Helmuth 1950- *WhoEmL 93*
Allard, Brenda Jo 1954- *WhoEmL 93*
Allard, David Henry 1929- *WhoAm 92*
Allard, Dean Conrad 1933- *WhoAm 92*
Allard, Harry *ConAu 38NR, MajAI*
Allard, Harry G(rover), Jr. 1928- *ConAu 38NR, MajAI [port]*
Allard, James E. 1942- *St&PR 93*
Allard, James Edward 1942- *WhoAm 92*
Allard, Jean 1924- *St&PR 93, WhoAm 92*
Allard, Judith Louise 1945- *WhoE 93*
Allard, Karen Ann 1955- *WhoAmW 93*
Allard, Leon D. 1938- *WhoAm 92*
Allard, Lucille Roybal *NotHsAW 93*
Allard, Marvel June *WhoE 93*
Allard, Nicholas Leo 1929- *St&PR 93*
Allard, Rene *Law&B 92*
Allard, Richard C. 1945- *St&PR 93*
Allard, Robert Wayne 1919- *WhoAm 92*
Allard, Ronald A. 1946- *St&PR 93*
Allard, Thurman J. 1959- *WhoEmL 93*
Allard, Wayne A. 1943- *WhoAm 92*
Allard, William Kenneth 1941- *WhoAm 92, WhoSSW 93*
Allardice, John McCarrell 1940- *WhoE 93*
Allardice, Robert B., III *WhoAm 92*
Allardt, Erik Anders 1925- *WhoScE 91-4, WhoWor 93*
Allardt, Linda 1926- *WhoWrEP 92*
Allardyce, Dale H. 1949- *St&PR 93*
Allardyce, Fred A. 1941- *St&PR 93*
Allare, John P. *Law&B 92*
Allaster, Kingsley G. 1930- *St&PR 93*
Allavena, Marcel 1930- *WhoScE 91-2*
Allawala, S.M. Idrees 1931- *WhoWor 93*
Allawi, Sabah Hashem 1938- *WhoUN 92*
Allbee, Carlynne Marie 1947- *WhoEmL 93*
Allbee, Sandra Moll 1947- *WhoEmL 93*
Allbery, Debra L. 1957- *WhoWrEP 92*
Allbeury, Ted 1917- *ScF&FL 92*
Allbeury, Theodore *ScF&FL 92*
Allbright, Bruce G. 1928- *St&PR 93*
Allbright, Bruce Galloway 1928- *WhoAm 92*
Allbright, Karan Elizabeth 1948- *WhoAmW 93, WhoEmL 93*
Allbritain, Caddie Bolton *AmWomPl*
Allbritton, Barbara B. 1937- *St&PR 93*
Allbritton, Cliff 1931- *WhoSSW 93, WhoWor 93*
Allbritton, Elwyn James 1937- *St&PR 93*
Allbritton, Joe L. 1924- *St&PR 93*
Allbritton, Joe Lewis 1924- *WhoAm 92*
Allchin, A(rthur) M(acdonald) 1930- *ConAu 38NR*
Allcock, Harry Melvin, Jr. 1932- *St&PR 93*
Allcock, Harry R. 1932- *WhoAm 92*
Allcock, John Bartlett *WhoScE 91-1*
Allcock, Phil *ScF&FL 92*
Allcorn, Seth 1946- *ConAu 138*
Alldahl, Per Gunnar 1943- *Baker 92*
Allday, Martin Lewis 1926- *WhoAm 92*
Alldian, David P. 1955- *St&PR 93*
Alldis, John 1929- *Baker 92*
Alldredge, Alice Louise 1949- *WhoAm 92*
Alldredge, Leroy Romney 1917- *WhoAm 92*
Alldredge, Robert Louis 1922- *WhoWor 93*
Alldredge, William 1940- *St&PR 93*
Alldritt, Keith 1935- *ScF&FL 92*
Alldritt, Virgil Everett 1954- *WhoEmL 93*
Alleborn, James P. 1948- *St&PR 93*
Allee, David Jepson 1931- *WhoAm 92*
Allee, Debra Cole 1939- *WhoE 93*
Allee, Nancy Jane *WhoAmW 93, WhoSSW 93*
Allegaert, Burr 1934- *St&PR 93*
Allegrante, John Philip 1952- *WhoE 93*
Allegranti, Maddalena 1754-c. 1802 *OxDcOp*
Allegre, Claude-Jean 1937- *WhoScE 91-2*
Allegre, M. *WhoScE 91-2*
Allegretti, Albert P. 1954- *St&PR 93*
Allegretti, Joseph Nicholas 1937- *St&PR 93*
Allegretti, Regina M. *Law&B 92*
Allegri, Domenico 1585-1629 *Baker 92*
Allegri, Gregorio c. 1582-1652 *Baker 92*
Allegri, Lorenzo c. 1573-1648 *Baker 92*
Allegro, Gianni 1954- *WhoScE 91-3*
Allegrucci, Donald Lee 1936- *WhoAm 92*
Alleman, Aurelia Rushton 1928- *WhoAmW 93*
Alleman, Raymond Henry 1934- *WhoAm 92*
Alleman, Rodger N. *Law&B 92*
Alleman, Thomas Butler 1952- *WhoSSW 93*
Allemand, Pierre Bernard 1941- *WhoWor 93*
Allemane, Jean 1843-1935 *BioIn 17*
Allemann, Sabina *WhoAm 92*
Allemeier, Daniel R. *Law&B 92*
Allen, A. K. *MiSFD 9*
Allen, Adam *ConAu 39NR*
Allen, Adrian *WhoScE 91-1*
Allen, Albert Lee *Law&B 92*
Allen, Alex B. *MajAI, SmATA 69, WhoWrEP 92*
Allen, Alice 1943- *WhoAmW 93*
Allen, Alice Catherine Towsley 1924- *WhoAm 92*
Allen, Alice E. *AmWomPl*
Allen, Andrew B. *Law&B 92*
Allen, Andrew Marshall 1941- *WhoAm 92*
Allen, Andrew Raymond 1933- *St&PR 93*
Allen, Andrew V. 1941- *St&PR 93*
Allen, Anita Jeanne Litsinger 1937- *WhoAmW 93*
Allen, Anna Foster 1901- *WhoAm 92*
Allen, Anna Jean 1955- *WhoAmW 93, WhoEmL 93*
Allen, Anna Marie 1955- *WhoEmL 93*
Allen, Arly Harrison 1938- *St&PR 93*
Allen, Arthur Bruce 1903-1975 *ScF&FL 92*
Allen, Arthur Clinton, III 1944- *St&PR 93*
Allen, Arthur Hamilton 1928- *St&PR 93*
Allen, Arthur Silsby 1934- *WhoSSW 93*
Allen, B. D. 1935- *WhoAm 92*
Allen, Barbara *SoulM*
Allen, Barbara Ann 1956- *WhoEmL 93*
Allen, Barbara Jane 1948- *WhoAmW 93*
Allen, Barbara Jo 1904?-1974 *ScF&FL 92*
Allen, Barry Morgan 1939- *WhoE 93*
Allen, Beatrice 1917- *WhoAmW 93, WhoE 93*
Allen, Belle *St&PR 93, WhoAm 92, WhoAmW 93*
Allen, Bertha Lee 1908- *WhoWor 93*
Allen, Bessie Malvina 1918- *WhoSSW 93*
Allen, Beth Elaine 1952- *WhoAm 92*
Allen, Betsy *MajAI*
Allen, Bettie Crossfield 1931- *WhoAmW 93*
Allen, Betty *WhoAm 92*
Allen, Betty 1930- *Baker 92, BioIn 17*
Allen, Betty Rea 1937- *WhoSSW 93*
Allen, Blair H. 1933- *WhoWrEP 92*
Allen, Bob 1935- *News 92 [port]*
Allen, Bradley E. *Law&B 92*
Allen, Brian David *Law&B 92*
Allen, Bron M. *St&PR 93*
Allen, Bruce Ethan *Law&B 92*
Allen, Bruce Templeton 1938- *WhoAm 92*
Allen, Bruce Wayne 1953- *WhoSSW 93*
Allen, Buck 1925- *WhoWrEP 92*
Allen, Burnie B. 1952- *St&PR 93*
Allen, Byron *BioIn 17*
Allen, Byron 1961- *ConBlB 3 [port]*
Allen, C. Lee *Law&B 92*
Allen, Carl *BioIn 17*
Allen, Carol 1948- *WhoAmW 93*
Allen, Carolyn Sessions 1939- *WhoWrEP 92*
Allen, Carolyn W. *AfrAmBi*
Allen, Cathy Lou Koenig 1946- *WhoEmL 93*
Allen, Charles 1903- *BioIn 17*
Allen, Charles Crawford, II 1948- *WhoEmL 93*
Allen, Charles Earnest 1940- *St&PR 93*
Allen, Charles Eugene 1939- *WhoAm 92*
Allen, Charles Joseph, II 1917- *WhoAm 92*
Allen, Charles Leffler 1959- *WhoEmL 93, WhoSSW 93*
Allen, Charles Lewis 1946- *WhoIns 93*
Allen, Charles Mengel 1916- *WhoAm 92*
Allen, Charles Richard 1926- *WhoAm 92*
Allen, Charles Upton 1953- *WhoEmL 93*
Allen, Charles W. 1904-1991 *BioIn 17*
Allen, Charles William 1912- *WhoAm 92*
Allen, Charles William 1932- *WhoAm 92*
Allen, Charlotte Vale 1941- *BioIn 17, WhoCanL 92*
Allen, Chesney 1893-1982
See Flanagan, Bud 1896-1968 & Allen, Chesney 1893-1982 *QDrFCA 92*
Allen, Chesney 1894-1982
See Crazy Gang, The *IntDcF 2-3*
Allen, Christina Lynn 1958- *WhoAmW 93*
Allen, Christopher E. *Law&B 92*
Allen, Clarence Richard *WhoEmL 93*
Allen, Clarence Roderic 1925- *WhoAm 92*
Allen, Claxton Edmonds, III 1944- *WhoE 93*
Allen, Clayton Hamilton 1918- *WhoWor 93*
Allen, Clive V. *Law&B 92*
Allen, Clive Victor 1935- *St&PR 93, WhoAm 92*
Allen, Corey 1934- *MiSFD 9*
Allen, Craig Douglas *Law&B 92*
Allen, Crawford Leonard 1952- *WhoEmL 93*
Allen, Cynthia Ann 1959- *WhoAmW 93*
Allen, D.H. 1955- *WhoScE 91-1*
Allen, D.J. 1942- *WhoScE 91-1*
Allen, Dale 1938- *St&PR 93*
Allen, Damian Francis 1962- *WhoWor 93*
Allen, Darina 1948- *WhoWor 93*
Allen, Darryl Frank 1943- *St&PR 93, WhoAm 92*
Allen, Dave
See Gang of Four *ConMus 8*
Allen, Davia M. 1945- *WhoSSW 93*
Allen, David *MiSFD 9*
Allen, David 1942- *WhoE 93, WhoWor 93*
Allen, David 1960- *St&PR 93*
Allen, David Christian 1949- *WhoEmL 93*
Allen, David Christopher 1933- *WhoE 93, WhoWor 93*
Allen, David Donald 1931- *St&PR 93, WhoAm 92, WhoIns 93*
Allen, David Dudley 1925- *WhoWrEP 92*
Allen, David E. 1942- *St&PR 93*
Allen, David Henry 1950- *WhoSSW 93*
Allen, David James 1935- *WhoAm 92, WhoWor 93*
Allen, David M. *WhoAm 92*
Allen, David Robert 1956- *WhoEmL 93*
Allen, David Russell 1942- *WhoAm 92*
Allen, David Woodroffe 1944- *WhoE 93*
Allen, Davis B. *BioIn 17*
Allen, Debbie *BioIn 17, MiSFD 9, WhoAm 92*
Allen, Debbie 1950- *ConMus 8 [port]*
Allen, Debby *BioIn 17*
Allen, Deborah 1950- *AfrAmBi*
Allen, Deborah Ann 1956- *WhoAmW 93*
Allen, Deborah Jean 1959- *WhoSSW 93*
Allen, Deborah Rudisill 1951- *WhoEmL 93*
Allen, Debra Janiece 1953- *WhoAmW 93*
Allen, Delmas James 1937- *WhoAm 92, WhoSSW 93*
Allen, Denny 1939- *WhoSSW 93*
Allen, Derek *ScF&FL 92*
Allen, Diane Renee 1959- *WhoAmW 93*
Allen, Dick 1939- *ScF&FL 92*
Allen, Diogenes 1932- *WhoAm 92*
Allen, Don Lee 1934- *WhoAm 92, WhoSSW 93*
Allen, Donald Merriam 1912- *BioIn 17*
Allen, Donald Vail 1928- *WhoAm 92, WhoWor 93*
Allen, Donald Wayne 1960- *WhoEmL 93, WhoSSW 93*
Allen, Douglas Leslie 1924- *St&PR 93, WhoAm 92*
Allen, Duane David 1943- *WhoAm 92*
Allen, Duncan B. 1953- *St&PR 93*
Allen, Durward Leon 1910- *WhoAm 92*
Allen, Dwight W. 1946- *St&PR 93*
Allen, Dyrck J. *St&PR 93*
Allen, Edith Agnes 1939- *WhoE 93*
Allen, Edna May 1887- *AmWomPl*
Allen, Edward Hathaway 1948- *WhoEmL 93*
Allen, Edward Raymond 1913- *WhoWor 93*
Allen, Elbert Enrico 1921- *WhoAm 92*
Allen, Eliza 1809-1861 *BioIn 17*
Allen, Elizabeth Ann 1954- *WhoEmL 93*
Allen, Elizabeth Maresca 1958- *WhoAmW 93*
Allen, Ethan 1738-1789 *HarEnMi*
Allen, Ethan 1907- *St&PR 93*
Allen, Eugene J., Jr. 1950- *St&PR 93*
Allen, Eugene Murray 1916- *WhoAm 92*
Allen, F.C. *Law&B 92*
Allen, F. C., Jr. 1933- *WhoAm 92*
Allen, F.M. 1856-1937 *ScF&FL 92*
Allen, Frances Elizabeth 1932- *WhoAm 92, WhoAmW 93*
Allen, Frances Jessica 1961- *WhoE 93*
Allen, Frances Michael 1939- *WhoAmW 93*
Allen, Frances Ruth 1929- *WhoSSW 93*
Allen, Francis P., Jr. 1914- *St&PR 93*
Allen, Frank C., Jr. 1934- *St&PR 93*
Allen, Frank Carroll 1913- *WhoAm 92*
Allen, Frank Richard 1922- *St&PR 93*
Allen, Fred 1894-1956 *BioIn 17, QDrFCA 92 [port]*
Allen, Fred Cary 1917- *WhoAm 92*
Allen, Fred E. 1938- *St&PR 93*
Allen, Fred Steven 1949- *WhoSSW 93*
Allen, Frederic W. 1926- *WhoAm 92*
Allen, Frederick Lewis 1890-1954 *JrnUS*
Allen, G. Matthew 1959- *St&PR 93*
Allen, Garland Edward 1936- *WhoAm 92*
Allen, Gary Curtiss 1939- *WhoSSW 93*
Allen, Gary Joe 1946- *WhoEmL 93*
Allen, Gay Wilson 1903- *BioIn 17*
Allen, Gaye Jean Asfahl 1965- *WhoSSW 93*
Allen, Gene Alfred 1953- *WhoE 93*
Allen, Geoffrey 1928- *WhoWor 93*
Allen, Geoffrey, Sir *WhoScE 91-1*
Allen, George *BioIn 17*
Allen, George 1832-1907 *BioIn 17*
Allen, George, Jr. 1952- *WhoSSW 93*
Allen, George F. *BioIn 17*
Allen, George F. 1952- *WhoAm 92*
Allen, George Howard 1914- *WhoAm 92*
Allen, George James 1944- *WhoAm 92*
Allen, George Sewell 1942- *WhoAm 92*
Allen, George Wade *Law&B 92*
Allen, George Whitaker 1928- *WhoWor 93*
Allen, Gerald F. *Law&B 92*
Allen, Gertrude K. *Law&B 92*
Allen, Gilbert Bruce 1951- *WhoSSW 93, WhoWrEP 92*
Allen, Gina *WhoAm 92, WhoAmW 93*
Allen, Glenn A. 1947- *St&PR 93*
Allen, Gloria B. 1926- *St&PR 93*
Allen, Gracie 1902-1964 *QDrFCA 92 [port]*
Allen, Gracie 1906?-1964 *BioIn 17*
Allen, Grant 1848-1899 *BioIn 17*
Allen, H.L., Jr. 1941- *St&PR 93*
Allen, Harold M. *St&PR 93*
Allen, Harold W.G. *ScF&FL 92*
Allen, Harrison 1841-1897 *IntDcAn*
Allen, Harry Franklin 1956- *WhoE 93, WhoEmL 93*
Allen, Harry William 1930- *St&PR 93*
Allen, Heath Ledward 1927- *WhoAm 92*
Allen, Henry 1877-1952 *Baker 92*
Allen, Henry (James, Jr.) 1908-1967 *Baker 92*
Allen, Henry Joseph 1931- *WhoE 93, WhoWor 93*
Allen, Henry Justin 1868-1950 *BioIn 17*
Allen, Henry Muriel 1952- *WhoWrEP 92*
Allen, Henry W. 1912-1991 *BioIn 17*
Allen, Henry Wilson 1912-1991 *ScF&FL 92*
Allen, Herbert 1908- *WhoAm 92, WhoE 93*
Allen, Herbert A., Jr. *BioIn 17*
Allen, Herbert Ellis 1939- *WhoAm 92*
Allen, Hervey 1889-1949 *ScF&FL 92*
Allen, Homer J. 1923- *St&PR 93*
Allen, Howard Godfrey *WhoScE 91-1*
Allen, Howard J. 1941- *WhoE 93*
Allen, Howard P. 1925- *St&PR 93*
Allen, Howard Pfeiffer 1925- *WhoAm 92*
Allen, Hugh Percy 1869-1946 *Baker 92*
Allen, Ira 1751-1814 *BioIn 17*
Allen, Irwin 1916-1991 *AnObit 1991, BioIn 17, MiSFD 9N*
Allen, Ivan d1992 *BioIn 17*
Allen, Ivan, Jr. 1911- *EncAACR, St&PR 93, WhoAm 92*
Allen, Ivan, III d1992 *NewYTBS 92*
Allen, J. Everett 1903- *St&PR 93*
Allen, James, Jr. *Law&B 92*
Allen, James A. *Law&B 92*
Allen, James Albert 1930- *WhoAm 92*
Allen, James B. *Law&B 92*
Allen, James B. 1912- *St&PR 93*
Allen, James de Vere 1936-1990 *BioIn 17*
Allen, James Douglas 1958- *WhoSSW 93*
Allen, James E., Jr. *Law&B 92*
Allen, James Frederick 1950- *WhoAm 92*
Allen, James Harrill 1906- *WhoAm 92*
Allen, James Henry 1935- *WhoSSW 93*
Allen, James L. d1992 *NewYTBS 92*
Allen, James Lane 1904- *St&PR 93*
Allen, James Lee 1957- *WhoEmL 93*
Allen, James Lovic, Jr. 1929- *WhoAm 92, WhoSSW 93, WhoWrEP 92*
Allen, James Madison 1944- *WhoSSW 93*
Allen, James P. 1949- *St&PR 93*
Allen, James R. d1992 *NewYTBS 92 [port]*
Allen, James R. 1925- *WhoAm 92*
Allen, James R. 1949- *St&PR 93*
Allen, James Richard 1956- *WhoEmL 93*
Allen, James Samuel 1941- *WhoAm 92*
Allen, James William, Jr. 1944- *St&PR 93*
Allen, Jane G. *Law&B 92*
Allen, Jane Gould 1925- *WhoE 93*
Allen, Janet Ann 1965- *WhoAmW 93*
Allen, Janet Marjorie 1953- *WhoWor 93*
Allen, Jay Presson 1922- *WhoAm 92*
Allen, Jean *AmWomPl*
Allen, Jean William 1923- *St&PR 93*
Allen, Jefferson F. 1945- *St&PR 93*
Allen, Jeffrey Michael 1948- *WhoAm 92, WhoEmL 93*
Allen, Jeffrey Rodgers 1953- *WhoEmL 93*
Allen, Jennie Elizabeth 1962- *WhoE 93*
Allen, Jeri 1947- *WhoEmL 93*
Allen, Jerry Clark 1939- *St&PR 93, WhoAm 92*
Allen, Jerry Linn 1942- *St&PR 93*
Allen, Jerry Wayne 1948- *WhoSSW 93*

Allen, Jesse Owen, III 1938- WhoSSW 93, WhoWor 93
Allen, Jessie Lee 1923- WhoAmW 93
Allen, Jim Bill 1945- WhoSSW 93
Allen, Joan 1956- WhoAm 92, WhoAmW 93
Allen, Joanna C. Law&B 92
Allen, Joe Bailey, III 1951- WhoEmL 93
Allen, Johannes 1916-1973 ScF&FL 92
Allen, John 1930- News 92 [port]
Allen, John E. d1992 BioIn 17
Allen, John E., Jr. d1992 NewYTBS 92
Allen, John Earling 1949- St&PR 93
Allen, John Edward 1950- WhoEmL 93
Allen, John F. 1944- St&PR 93
Allen, John J. 1936- St&PR 93
Allen, John Logan 1941- WhoAm 92
Allen, John Loyd 1931- WhoAm 92
Allen, John M. Law&B 92
Allen, John Owen 1935- St&PR 93
Allen, John Thomas, Jr. 1935- WhoSSW 93, WhoWor 93
Allen, John W. Law&B 92
Allen, John W. 1923- St&PR 93
Allen, John Walter WhoScE 91-1
Allen, John Whitlock, Sr. 1930- WhoAm 92
Allen, Jonathan 1942- WhoE 93
Allen, Joseph D., III 1945- WhoIns 93
Allen, Joseph Garrott d1992 NewYTBS 92
Allen, Joseph Garrott 1912-1992 BioIn 17
Allen, Joseph Henry 1916- WhoAm 92
Allen, Joyce Smith 1939- WhoAmW 93
Allen, Judith 1938- WhoE 93
Allen, Judith Elaine 1942- WhoAmW 93
Allen, Judith Matkin 1953- WhoAmW 93
Allen, Judith Ruth 1943- WhoAmW 93, WhoWor 93
Allen, Judy ChlFicS, ScF&FL 92
Allen, Julian Myrick, Jr. 1956- WhoEmL 93, WhoSSW 93, WhoWor 93
Allen, Karen Alfstad 1942- WhoAmW 93
Allen, Karen Jane 1951- WhoAm 92, WhoAmW 93
Allen, Keith W. 1953- WhoEmL 93
Allen, Keith William WhoScE 91-1
Allen, Kenneth D. 1939- St&PR 93
Allen, Kenneth Dale Law&B 92
Allen, Kenneth Dale 1939- WhoAm 92
Allen, Kenneth J. WhoAm 92
Allen, Kenneth L. Law&B 92
Allen, Kenneth William WhoScE 91-1
Allen, Kevin John WhoScE 91-1
Allen, L. David 1940- ScF&FL 92
Allen, L. Nash, Jr. 1944- St&PR 93
Allen, Larry Eugene 1948- WhoEmL 93
Allen, Laurie Catherine 1948- WhoAm 92
Allen, Lawrence David, Jr. 1952- WhoEmL 93
Allen, Leatrice Delorice 1948- WhoAmW 93
Allen, Lee SoulM
Allen, Lee H. 1924- St&PR 93
Allen, Lee Harrison 1924- WhoAm 92
Allen, Lee Norcross 1926- WhoAm 92, WhoSSW 93
Allen, Leilani Eleanor 1949- WhoAmW 93
Allen, Leon Arthur, Jr. 1933- WhoAm 92
Allen, Leslie BioIn 17
Allen, Leslie 1935- WhoWor 93
Allen, Lew 1925- BioIn 17
Allen, Lew, Jr. 1925- WhoAm 92
Allen, Lewis 1905-1986 MiSFD 9N
Allen, Linda ChlFicS
Allen, Linda Marie 1952- WhoAmW 93
Allen, Lloyd E. Law&B 92
Allen, Lloyd Edward, Jr. 1943- WhoAm 92
Allen, Lori 1939- ScF&FL 92
Allen, Louis 1922-1991 ConAu 136
Allen, Louis Alexander 1917- St&PR 93, WhoAm 92, WhoWor 93
Allen, Louis La Boiteaux 1925- St&PR 93
Allen, Louise 1910- WhoAmW 93
Allen, Lydia AmWomPl
Allen, Lydia B. Law&B 92
Allen, Lyle Wallace 1924- WhoAm 92
Allen, M.C. 1914- ScF&FL 92
Allen, M(alcolm) D(ennis) 1951- ConAu 138
Allen, Marcus 1960- WhoAm 92
Allen, Margaret F. AmWomPl
Allen, Mariette Pathy 1940- WhoE 93
Allen, Marilyn ScF&FL 92
Allen, Marilyn Lee 1943- WhoAmW 93
Allen, Marilyn Myers Pool 1934- WhoAm 92, WhoAmW 93
Allen, Marjorie J. BioIn 17
Allen, Mark Gerard 1958- WhoEmL 93
Allen, Mark Hill 1956- WhoEmL 93
Allen, Mark Le Gros 1947- WhoUN 92
Allen, Mark Paul 1944- WhoE 93
Allen, Mark R. Law&B 92
Allen, Mark R. 1953- St&PR 93
Allen, Martha Leslie 1948- WhoWrEP 92
Allen, Martha Mitten 1937- WhoSSW 93
Allen, Martin ScF&FL 92
Allen, Martin Joseph, Jr. 1936- St&PR 93
Allen, Martin R. 1955- St&PR 93
Allen, Martin Steven 1947- WhoEmL 93
Allen, Mary Ann ScF&FL 92
Allen, Mary C. 1909- ScF&FL 92
Allen, Mary Catherine Mitchell WhoAmW 93, WhoWor 93
Allen, Mary Kathryn 1953- WhoAmW 93, WhoEmL 93
Allen, Mary Mosher AmWomPl
Allen, Maryon Pittman 1925- BioIn 17, WhoAm 92, WhoAmW 93, WhoSSW 93
Allen, Matthew Arnold 1930- WhoAm 92
Allen, Maurice Bartelle, Jr. 1926- WhoAm 92
Allen, Maxine B. 1942- WhoAmW 93
Allen, Merle Maeser, Jr. 1932- WhoAm 92
Allen, Merrill James 1945- WhoWor 93
Allen, Merton 1929- WhoSSW 93
Allen, Michael BioIn 17
Allen, Michael (Derek) 1939- ConAu 39NR
Allen, Michael G. 1950- St&PR 93
Allen, Michael Glynne 1938- WhoAm 92
Allen, Michael L. ScF&FL 92
Allen, Michael L. 1948- St&PR 93
Allen, Michael Lewis 1937- WhoAm 92
Allen, Michael Patrick 1945- ConAu 137
Allen, Miriam Marx 1927- ConAu 138
Allen, Moira Anderson 1959- WhoEmL 93
Allen, Murray E. 1931- St&PR 93
Allen, N. Sue Law&B 92
Allen, Nancy Kachelriess 1951- WhoEmL 93
Allen, Nancy Schuster 1948- WhoAm 92, WhoAmW 93
Allen, Newton Perkins 1922- WhoAm 92, WhoSSW 93
Allen, Niathan AfrAmBi
Allen, Nicholas Eugene 1907- WhoAm 92
Allen, Nina Irene White 1908- WhoWrEP 92
Allen, Noble Curtis 1954- WhoEmL 93, WhoSSW 93
Allen, Norman W. Law&B 92
Allen, Olive AmWomPl
Allen, Oscar DcCPCAm
Allen, P.W. 1925- WhoScE 91-1
Allen, Patricia 1942- WhoE 93
Allen, Patricia Fisher 1942- WhoAmW 93
Allen, Patricia J. 1940- St&PR 93
Allen, Patrick David 1955- WhoEmL 93
Allen, Patrick J. Law&B 92
Allen, Patrick Joseph 1948- WhoEmL 93
Allen, Paul BioIn 17, WhoAm 92
Allen, Paul Hastings 1883-1952 Baker 92
Allen, Paul Howard 1954- WhoE 93, WhoEmL 93
Allen, Paul James 1955- WhoEmL 93
Allen, Pauline Virginia 1909- WhoAmW 93
Allen, Peter BioIn 17, Law&B 92
Allen, Peter d1992 NewYTBS 92 [port]
Allen, Peter 1944-1992 CurBio 92N, News 93-1
Allen, Peter Ackerman 1940- WhoAm 92
Allen, Peter Henry Gay WhoScE 91-1
Allen, Peter Thomas WhoScE 91-1
Allen, Philip W. 1951- St&PR 93
Allen, Phillip E. 1931- WhoAm 92
Allen, Phillip Richard 1939- WhoAm 92
Allen, Phillip Stephen 1952- WhoE 93
Allen, Phylicia Ayers- BioIn 17
Allen, Phyllis St&PR 93
Allen, R. Lee 1944- St&PR 93
Allen, Ralph 1913-1966 ScF&FL 92
Allen, Ralph D. 1941- St&PR 93
Allen, Ralph Dean 1941- WhoAm 92
Allen, Ralph Gilmore 1934- WhoAm 92
Allen, Ralph Orville, Jr. 1943- WhoSSW 93
Allen, Randy BioIn 17
Allen, Randy Lee 1946- WhoAm 92, WhoAmW 93, WhoE 93
Allen, Ray Wallace 1936- WhoE 93
Allen, Raye Virginia 1929- WhoAmW 93
Allen, Raymond Ralph 1931- St&PR 93
Allen, Rex BioIn 17
Allen, Rex Whitaker 1914- WhoAm 92
Allen, Richard 1760-1831 BioIn 17
Allen, Richard A. Law&B 92
Allen, Richard A. 1932- St&PR 93
Allen, Richard B. Law&B 92
Allen, Richard Blose 1919- WhoAm 92
Allen, Richard C. 1926- WhoAm 92
Allen, Richard Charles 1939- WhoAm 92
Allen, Richard Chester 1926- WhoWrEP 92
Allen, Richard Duane 1942- St&PR 93
Allen, Richard Garrett 1923- WhoAm 92
Allen, Richard M. 1929- St&PR 93
Allen, Richard R. 1940- St&PR 93
Allen, Richard S. ScF&FL 92
Allen, Richard S. 1956- St&PR 93
Allen, Richard Stanley 1939- WhoAm 92, WhoWrEP 92
Allen, Richard Vincent 1936- WhoAm 92, WhoWor 93
Allen, Ricky 1935- BioIn 17
Allen, Robert 1900- JrnUS
Allen, Robert 1946- WhoCanL 92
Allen, Robert Carter 1930- WhoSSW 93
Allen, Robert David 1952- WhoAm 92
Allen, Robert Dee 1928- WhoAm 92
Allen, Robert E. BioIn 17, Law&B 92
Allen, Robert E. 1935- St&PR 93
Allen, Robert E. 1937- WhoIns 93
Allen, Robert Erwin 1941- WhoE 93
Allen, Robert Eugene 1935- WhoAm 92, WhoE 93
Allen, Robert Eugene Barton 1940- WhoWor 93
Allen, Robert Francis 1938- WhoAm 92
Allen, Robert Harold 1928- St&PR 93
Allen, Robert Harold 1948- WhoEmL 93
Allen, Robert Hugh 1924- WhoAm 92
Allen, Robert Lee AfrAmBi
Allen, Robert Smith 1924- WhoAm 92
Allen, Robert Vreeland Law&B 92
Allen, Robert W. 1950- WhoAm 92
Allen, Robert Willard 1943- WhoAm 92
Allen, Roberta WhoWrEP 92
Allen, Roberta L. 1945- WhoAm 92
Allen, Rocelia J. 1924- WhoE 93
Allen, Rodney Desvigne 1957- WhoE 93
Allen, Rodney F. 1938- WhoSSW 93
Allen, Roger Laurance WhoScE 91-1
Allen, Roger MacBride 1957- ScF&FL 92
Allen, Roland Emery 1941- WhoSSW 93
Allen, Ronald John 1940- WhoAm 92
Allen, Ronald Morgan Law&B 92
Allen, Ronald Roger, Jr. 1955- WhoEmL 93
Allen, Ronald Royce 1930- WhoAm 92
Allen, Ronald T. Law&B 92
Allen, Ronald W. 1941- BioIn 17, St&PR 93, WhoAm 92, WhoSSW 93
Allen, Ronald Wesley 1948- WhoSSW 93
Allen, Rose Mary Law&B 92
Allen, Rosemary Alice 1956- WhoAmW 93
Allen, Roy Kevin 1941- St&PR 93
Allen, Roy L., II AfrAmBi [port]
Allen, Roy O. 1921-1992 BioIn 17
Allen, Roy O., Jr. d1992 NewYTBS 92
Allen, Russell Plowman 1951- WhoAm 92
Allen, Sally Lyman 1926- WhoAm 92
Allen, Sally Patricia 1949- WhoWor 93
Allen, Sam WhoWrEP 92
Allen, Samuel J. 1920- St&PR 93
Allen, Sandra Nair 1933- WhoAmW 93
Allen, Sarah Gilbert 1945- WhoAmW 93
Allen, Sharon Amerine 1942- WhoAmW 93
Allen, Sharon Banks 1941- WhoAmW 93
Allen, Sheila WhoScE 91-1
Allen, Sheila Marie 1948- WhoAmW 93
Allen, Sheila Rosalynd 1942- ScF&FL 92
Allen, Stanley Lee 1957- WhoEmL 93
Allen, Stanley M. 1940- St&PR 93
Allen, Stephen Charles 1952- WhoWor 93
Allen, Stephen Dean 1943- WhoWor 93
Allen, Stephen Valentine Patrick William 1921- WhoAm 92
Allen, Steve 1921- BioIn 17
Allen, Stuart 1943- WhoE 93, WhoWor 93
Allen, Sture 1928- WhoWor 93
Allen, Susan J. Law&B 92
Allen, Tami Marie 1967- WhoWrEP 92
Allen, Tandy M. 1935- St&PR 93
Allen, Teddy G. 1936- WhoAm 92
Allen, Terry 1943- Baker 92
Allen, Terry Hall 1946- WhoSSW 93
Allen, Terry Lloyd Law&B 92
Allen, Theodore R. 1926- St&PR 93
Allen, Theresa Ohotnicky 1948- WhoAm 92, WhoAmW 93, WhoEmL 93
Allen, Thomas 1944- Baker 92, IntDcOp, OxDcOp
Allen, Thomas B. ChlBIID [port]
Allen, Thomas Byrd 1933- WhoSSW 93
Allen, Thomas Draper 1926- WhoAm 92
Allen, Thomas E. 1919- WhoAm 92, WhoE 93, WhoWor 93
Allen, Thomas J. Law&B 92
Allen, Thomas John 1931- WhoAm 92
Allen, Thomas Nelson 1938- WhoSSW 93
Allen, Thomas P. St&PR 93
Allen, Thomas S. 1954- St&PR 93
Allen, Tim BioIn 17
Allen, Tim 1953- News 93-1 [port]
Allen, Timothy Andrew 1955- WhoAm 92
Allen, Timothy Charles 1954- WhoEmL 93
Allen, Toby 1941- WhoAm 92
Allen, Tom 1938?-1988 ScF&FL 92
Allen, Tom Chris 1932- WhoSSW 93
Allen, Tom L. St&PR 93
Allen, Toni K. 1940- WhoAm 92
Allen, Trudy B. Law&B 92
Allen, Vicki Ann 1953- WhoEmL 93
Allen, Vicki Thomas 1955- WhoEmL 93, WhoSSW 93
Allen, Vicky 1957- WhoAmW 93, WhoEmL 93
Allen, Virginia Ann 1953- WhoAmW 93, WhoE 93
Allen, Virginia Peterson Law&B 92
Allen, Virginia Rose 1949- WhoAmW 93
Allen, W.P. 1921- St&PR 93
Allen, Wade W. 1912- St&PR 93
Allen, Wells Preston, Jr. 1921- WhoAm 92
Allen, William A. 1944- St&PR 93
Allen, William Bruce 1958- WhoSSW 93
Allen, William Cecil 1919- WhoAm 92
Allen, William D. 1959- St&PR 93
Allen, William Dale 1938- WhoAm 92
Allen, William Dean 1950- WhoWrEP 92
Allen, William E. 1932- St&PR 93
Allen, William F., Jr. 1919- St&PR 93
Allen, William Fletcher 1931- WhoAm 92
Allen, William Frederick, Jr. 1919- WhoAm 92, WhoWor 93
Allen, William George WhoScE 91-1
Allen, William H., Jr. 1935- St&PR 93
Allen, William Hayes 1926- WhoAm 92
Allen, William L., III 1943- St&PR 93
Allen, William Richard WhoScE 91-1
Allen, William Richard 1924- WhoAm 92
Allen, William Richard, Jr. 1940- St&PR 93, WhoAm 92
Allen, William Riley 1953- WhoEmL 93
Allen, William Rodney 1952- ScF&FL 92
Allen, William Sheridan 1932- WhoAm 92
Allen, Winnie 1895-1985 BioIn 17
Allen, Woody BioIn 17
Allen, Woody 1935- Au&Arts 10 [port], ConAu 38NR, JeAmHC, MiSFD 9, QDrFCA 92 [port], WhoAm 92, WhoE 93, WhoWrEP 92
Allen-Bouska, Rebecca Auk 1961- WhoAmW 93
Allenby, Braden R. Law&B 92
Allenby, Edmund Henry Hynman 1861-1936 DcTwHis
Allenby, Edmund Henry Hynman, Viscount 1861-1936 HarEnMi
Allenby, Steven J. 1954- St&PR 93
Allende, Isabel BioIn 17
Allende, Isabel 1942- ScF&FL 92
Allende, Isabel 1946- SpAmA
Allende, Octavio, Jr. 1930- St&PR 93
Allende, Salvador 1908-1973 DcTwHis
Allende (-Saron), Humberto 1885-1959 Baker 92
Allende Gossens, Salvador 1908-1973 BioIn 17, ColdWar 2 [port]
Allender, John Roland 1950- WhoEmL 93
Allender, Julie Ann 1950- WhoE 93, WhoEmL 93
Allender, Patrick W. 1946- St&PR 93, WhoAm 92
Allendorf, Donald A. 1934- St&PR 93
Allen-Langdon, Barbara 1958- WhoWrEP 92
Allen-Leventhal, Judith Anne 1946- WhoAmW 93
Allen-Morano, Susan Elizabeth 1947- WhoAmW 93
Allen-Noble, Rosie Elizabeth 1938- WhoE 93
Allen-Poole, Barbara Helen 1951- WhoAmW 93
Allen-Robinson, Judith 1946- WhoSSW 93
Allenson, Alexandra Chryssomallis 1956- WhoEmL 93
Allenstein, Gloria Gomez 1945- WhoAmW 93
Allensworth, Carl d1991 BioIn 17
Allensworth, Dorothy Alice 1907- WhoAm 92, WhoAmW 93
Allensworth, John Catlett, IV 1918- WhoSSW 93
Aller, Frank d1971 NewYTBS 92 [port]
Aller, Lawrence Hugh 1913- WhoAm 92
Aller, Margo Friedel 1938- WhoAm 92, WhoAmW 93
Aller, Robert Lundeen 1934- St&PR 93, WhoAm 92
Aller, Ronald G. 1937- WhoIns 93
Aller, Wayne Kendall 1933- WhoAm 92
Allerhand, Adam 1937- WhoAm 92
Allers, Franz 1905- Baker 92, WhoAm 92
Allers, Marlene Elaine 1931- WhoAmW 93
Allerton, John Stephen 1926- WhoAm 92
Allerton, Joseph 1919- WhoE 93
Allery, Kenneth Edward 1925- WhoAm 92
Alles, Herman 1922- St&PR 93
Alles, Rodney Neal, Sr. 1950- WhoSSW 93
Alletzhauser, Albert J. 1960- ConAu 136
Alleweldt, Gerhardt Erich 1927- WhoScE 91-3
Alley, A. Kenneth 1943- St&PR 93
Alley, Barrett Le Quatte 1934- WhoSSW 93
Alley, Frederick Don 1940- WhoAm 92
Alley, Gary Thomas 1956- WhoSSW 93

Alley, Henry Melton 1945- WhoWrEP 92
Alley, James Pinckney, Jr. 1942- WhoSSW 93
Alley, Kirstie BioIn 17, WhoAm 92, WhoAmW 93
Alley, Kirstie 1955- ConTFT 10
Alley, Louis E. BioIn 17
Alley, Nancy Patricia 1957- WhoEmL 93
Alley, Ralph L. 1951- St&PR 93
Alley, Richard Kenneth 1931- St&PR 93
Alley, Robert Sutherland 1932- WhoAm 92
Alley, Wayne Edward 1932- WhoAm 92
Alley, William J. 1929- St&PR 93
Alley, William Jack 1929- WhoAm 92, WhoE 93, WhoIns 93, WhoWor 93
Alley-Barros, Elizabeth Dalein 1958- WhoE 93
Alleyn, Ellen MajAI
Alleyne, Albert Burnham 1932- WhoUN 92
Alleyne, Barbara Christina WhoAmW 93, WhoWor 93
Alleyne, Brian 1943- WhoWor 93
Alleyne, John WhoAm 92
Allf, Nancy Lee 1957- WhoEmL 93
Allfrey, Anthony 1930- ConAu 137
Allfrey, John WhoScE 91-1
Allfrey, Phyllis 1908-1986 DcCPCAm
Allgaier, Rand D. Law&B 92
Allgeier, Edward J. 1934- St&PR 93
Allgood, Antoinette Raub 1942- WhoAmW 93
Allgood, Clarence W. 1902-1991 BioIn 17
Allgood, Jimmy Eugene 1955- WhoEmL 93, WhoWor 93
Allgood, John F. Law&B 92
Allgood, John Franklin 1946- WhoSSW 93
Allgood, Molly 1887-1952 BioIn 17
Allgood, Myralyn F(rizzelle) 1939- ConAu 137
Allgood, Sara 1883-1950 BioIn 17
Allgood, Thomas Bowden 1949- WhoSSW 93
Allgyer, Robert Earl 1944- WhoAm 92, WhoWor 93
Allhoff, Fred 1904-1988 ScF&FL 92
Alli 1867-1949 Baker 92
Alli, Al 1933- St&PR 93
Alli, Richard James, Sr. 1932- WhoWor 93
Alliali, Camille 1926- WhoAfr
Allibone, Thomas Edward WhoScE 91-1
Alliger, Howard St&PR 93
Alliger, Jeremy David 1952- WhoAm 92, WhoWor 93
Alligood, David Lamar 1934- St&PR 93
Alligood, Paul St&PR 93
Allik, Michael 1935- WhoAm 92
Alliker, Stanford Arnold 1946- WhoEmL 93
Allileuva, Nadezhda Sergeyevna BioIn 17
Allilueva, Svetlana 1926- WhoWrEP 92
Allin, John Maury 1921- WhoAm 92
Allin, Lawrence Carroll 1932- WhoWor 93
Allin, Norman 1884-1973 Baker 92
Allin, Patrick Joseph 1951- St&PR 93
Allin, Thomas Banbury 1949- St&PR 93, WhoAm 92
Alline, Henry 1748-1784 BioIn 17
Alling, Charles Booth, Jr. 1921- WhoAm 92
Alling, Charles Calvin, III 1923- WhoAm 92
Alling, Janet Dickey 1939- WhoE 93
Alling, Norman Larrabee 1930- WhoAm 92
Allinger, Norman Louis 1928- WhoAm 92
Allingham, Dennis John 1950- St&PR 93, WhoEmL 93
Allingham, Margery 1904-1966 BioIn 17
Allingham, William 1824-1889 BioIn 17
Allington, Gloria Jean Ham 1945- WhoAmW 93, WhoSSW 93
Allington, Robert William 1935- St&PR 93
Allinson, A. Edward 1934- St&PR 93, WhoAm 92
Allinson, Deborah Louise 1950- WhoEmL 93
Allinson, Gary Dean 1942- WhoAm 92
Allio, David Franklin 1955- WhoEmL 93
Allio, Robert John 1931- WhoAm 92
Allison, Adrienne Amelia 1940- WhoE 93
Allison, Albert Ray, III 1960- WhoEmL 93, WhoSSW 93
Allison, Anne Marie 1931- WhoAmW 93, WhoSSW 93
Allison, Arthur Compton WhoScE 91-1
Allison, Audre BioIn 17
Allison, Bobby BioIn 17
Allison, Christine BioIn 17
Allison, Christopher FitzSimons 1927- WhoAm 92
Allison, Clay 1840-1887 BioIn 17
Allison, Clyde d1990 BioIn 17
Allison, Clyde C. 1905-1990 BioIn 17
Allison, Diane Beaudette 1961- WhoAmW 93
Allison, Donald G. 1950- WhoAm 92
Allison, Dwight Leonard, Jr. 1929- WhoAm 92
Allison, Edgar Lee, III 1960- WhoEmL 93
Allison, Elisabeth 1946- St&PR 93
Allison, Elisabeth Kovacs 1946- WhoAm 92, WhoAmW 93
Allison, George Lloyd 1931- St&PR 93
Allison, Grace 1946- WhoEmL 93
Allison, Graham Tillett, Jr. 1940- WhoAm 92
Allison, Harrison Clarke 1917- WhoWrEP 92
Allison, Harry V. 1934- St&PR 93
Allison, Herbert Monroe, Jr. 1943- St&PR 93, WhoAm 92
Allison, Ian Miles WhoScE 91-1
Allison, James Claybrooke, II 1942- WhoAm 92
Allison, James Henry, Jr. 1949- WhoEmL 93
Allison, James Michael 1953- WhoAm 92
Allison, James Richard, Jr. 1924- WhoAm 92
Allison, James Waters, III 1951- WhoEmL 93
Allison, Jane Shawver 1938- WhoAmW 93
Allison, John Andrew, IV 1948- St&PR 93, WhoAm 92, WhoSSW 93
Allison, John C. 1944- St&PR 93, WhoSSW 93
Allison, John Robert 1948- WhoAm 92, WhoSSW 93
Allison, John Rollins, III 1946- WhoEmL 93
Allison, Jonathan 1916- WhoE 93
Allison, Joy Elaine 1953- WhoEmL 93
Allison, Karen Anne 1958- WhoEmL 93
Allison, Karl 1948-1990 BioIn 17
Allison, Laird Burl 1917- WhoWor 93
Allison, Larry Edward 1946- St&PR 93
Allison, Latham Lee 1933- WhoAm 92
Allison, Linda Merz 1951- St&PR 93
Allison, Lynette Elaine Law&B 92
Allison, Mark J. 1955- St&PR 93
Allison, Mark S. St&PR 93
Allison, Mary Ruth 1945- WhoAmW 93
Allison, Mose 1927- Baker 92
Allison, Rachel 1959- St&PR 93
Allison, Richard Clark 1924- WhoAm 92
Allison, Richard D. Law&B 92
Allison, Richard Dale 1957- WhoEmL 93
Allison, Robert Arthur 1937- WhoAm 92
Allison, Robert B. 1943- St&PR 93
Allison, Robert Harry 1952- WhoEmL 93
Allison, Robert J., Jr. 1939- St&PR 93
Allison, Robert James, Jr. 1939- WhoAm 92
Allison, Rufus K. 1918- St&PR 93
Allison, Stacy Marie 1958- WhoAmW 93
Allison, Stephen Galender 1952- WhoEmL 93, WhoSSW 93, WhoWor 93
Allison, Terry Elizabeth 1956- WhoEmL 93, WhoSSW 93
Allison, Wick 1948- WhoAm 92
Allison, William James 1927- St&PR 93
Allison, William Robert 1934- BiDAMSp 1989
Allison, William Whitaker 1933- St&PR 93
Allister, Claud 1891-1970 QDrFCA 92 [port]
Allister, Pamela Jeffcock 1941- WhoE 93
Alliston, April 1959- WhoE 93
Allman, Charles Bradie 1950- St&PR 93
Allman, Duane 1946-1971 SoulM
Allman, Edward Lee 1926- St&PR 93
Allman, Gregg 1947- WhoAm 92
Allman, John 1935- WhoWrEP 92
Allman, Linden Andrea 1958- WhoEmL 93
Allman, William Berthold 1927- WhoE 93, WhoWor 93
Allmand, Linda Faith 1937- WhoAm 92, WhoAmW 93, WhoSSW 93
Allmand, W. Warren 1932- WhoAm 92
Allmann, Rudolf 1931- WhoScE 91-3
Allmann, Rudolf Hans 1931- WhoWor 93
Allman-Ward, A. Peter 1949- St&PR 93
Allman-Ward, Michele Ann 1950- WhoAm 92, WhoEmL 93, WhoWor 93
Allmendinger, Paul Florin 1922- WhoAm 92
Allmighty, Jon 1963- WhoSSW 93
Allmon, Charles 1921- St&PR 93
Allmon, Michael Bryan 1951- WhoEmL 93
Allmon, Rebecca Lea 1956- WhoAmW 93
Allmon, Sue Ann 1960- WhoAmW 93
Allner, Walter Heinz 1909- WhoAm 92
Allnutt, Frank ScF&FL 92
Allnutt, Robert F. 1935- St&PR 93
Allnutt, Robert Frederick 1935- WhoAm 92
Allocca, Giuseppe Law&B 92
Allocca, John Anthony 1948- WhoWor 93
Allocca, Joseph John Law&B 92
Allocca, Michael A. St&PR 93
Alloju, Anand BioIn 17
Allor, Elizabeth Law&B 92
Allott, Kenneth 1912-1973 ScF&FL 92
Allotta, Joseph John 1947- WhoEmL 93
Alloway, Anne Maureen Schubert 1954- WhoAm 92, WhoWor 93
Alloway, Lawrence 1926-1990 BioIn 17
Alloway, Robert Malcombe 1944- WhoE 93, WhoWor 93
Allport, William W. 1944- St&PR 93
Allport, William Wilkens Law&B 92
Allport, William Wilkens 1944- WhoAm 92
Allread, William O. WhoE 93
Allred, B.J. 1932- St&PR 93
Allred, Barry Lee 1947- St&PR 93
Allred, Christine A. 1940- St&PR 93
Allred, Esther Ella 1941- WhoAmW 93
Allred, Forrest Carlson 1955- WhoEmL 93
Allred, George Burton 1914- St&PR 93
Allred, Henry 1929- WhoWor 93
Allred, Ivan D., Jr. 1936- St&PR 93
Allred, John Caldwell 1926- WhoAm 92
Allred, Michael Sylvester 1945- WhoAm 92
Allred, Olen Rudolph 1932- WhoSSW 93
Allred, Rita Reed 1935- WhoAmW 93
Allred, Winston G. 1942- St&PR 93
Alls, Willard Jess 1938- WhoSSW 93
Allsbrook, Ogden Olmstead, Jr. 1940- WhoSSW 93, WhoWor 93
Allsburg, Chris Van ScF&FL 92
Allsep, Larry Michael, Jr. 1958- WhoWor 93
Allshouse, John 1951- WhoWor 93
Allshouse, Merle Frederick 1935- WhoAm 92
Allsop, Kenneth Lee 1939- St&PR 93
Allsop, Theresa H. Law&B 92
Allsopp, Dennis WhoScE 91-1
Allsopp, James Edward, Jr. 1929- St&PR 93
Allston, Aaron 1960- ScF&FL 92
Allswang, John Myers 1937- WhoAm 92
Allswede, Ralph Dahl 1939- St&PR 93
Alltmont, Jack Marks 1947- WhoEmL 93
Allukian, Myron, Jr. 1939- WhoAm 92
Allum, Geoffrey Michael 1957- WhoAm 92
Allums, Brenda Lee French 1950- WhoSSW 93
Allwarden, Christopher J. Law&B 92
Allwarden, Joseph Christopher 1930- St&PR 93
Allwood, Michael Charles WhoScE 91-1
Ally, Carl Joseph BioIn 17
Ally, Carl Joseph 1924- WhoAm 92
Allyn, Angela 1961- WhoEmL 93
Allyn, Barbara WhoWrEP 92
Allyn, Jerome B. 1937- St&PR 93
Allyn, Jerri 1952- WhoE 93
Allyn, Mabel Conklin AmWomPl
Allyn, Susan M. BioIn 17
Allyn, William F. 1935- St&PR 93
Allyn, William Finch 1935- WhoAm 92
Allyson, June 1917- IntDcF 2-3
Alm, Albert 1941- WhoScE 91-4
Alm, Alvin Leroy 1937- WhoAm 92
Alm, James 1937- WhoAm 92
Alm, Philip BioIn 17
Alm, Richard Sanford 1921- WhoAm 92
Almaca, Carlos WhoScE 91-3
Almada, Manuel 1912- WhoWor 93, WhoWrEP 92
Al-Maghaleh, Abdul Aziz Salih 1937- WhoWor 93
Almagro, Diego de 1475?-1538 Expl 93 [port]
al Mahasseni, Mohammad Marwan 1927- WhoWor 93
Al-Mahgoub, Rifaat 1926-1990 BioIn 17
Al-Maktum, Hamdan bin Rashid 1945- WhoWor 93
Al-Maktum, Muhammad ibn Rashid 1946- WhoWor 93
Almaliotis, Dimitrios 1949- WhoScE 91-3
Alman, Emily Arnow 1922- WhoAmW 93, WhoWor 93
Alman, Isadora 1940- WhoAmW 93
Alman, Rex, III 1951- St&PR 93
Alman, Richard D. St&PR 93
Almand, Charles Christopher 1959- WhoSSW 93
Almand, J.D. 1917- WhoWrEP 92
Almand, James Frederick 1948- WhoEmL 93
Almanqour, Nasser Al-Hamad 1927- WhoWor 93
Almansa Pastor, Angel F. 1934- WhoWor 93
Almanza, Hector Raul 1912- DcMexL
Almar, Ivan 1932- WhoScE 91-4
Almaraz, Carlos 1941- HispAmA
Almario, Thelma Z. 1933- WhoAsAP 91
Al-Mashat, Mohammed BioIn 17
Almasi, Elemer 1919- WhoScE 91-4
Almasi, George Stanley WhoAm 92
Alma-Tadema, Lawrence 1836-1912 BioIn 17
Al-Mateen, Cheryl Singleton 1959- WhoEmL 93
Almaula, Prabodh I. Law&B 92
Al-Mawlawi, Abdulwahed Abdullah 1950- WhoWor 93
Almazan, Pascual 1813-1886 DcMexL
Almbladh, Carl-Olof 1943- WhoWor 93
Almdale, James 1952- St&PR 93
Almedina, Fernando Yanez de la fl. 1506-1531 BioIn 17
Almedingen, E.M. 1898-1971 ScF&FL 92
Almeida, Alcino G. St&PR 93
Almeida, Antonio (Jacques) de 1928- Baker 92
Almeida, C. Victoria 1956- WhoEmL 93
Almeida, Damien C. 1927- St&PR 93
Almeida, Fernando d' c. 1600-1660 Baker 92
Almeida, Francisco de c. 1450-1510 HarEnMi
Almeida, John G. 1953- St&PR 93
Almeida, Jose Agustin 1933- WhoSSW 93, WhoWor 93
Almeida, Joseph John 1930- St&PR 93
Almeida, Laurindo 1917- Baker 92, WhoAm 92
Almeida, M. Elisabete M. 1946- WhoScE 91-3
Almeida, Victoria Martin 1951- WhoAmW 93, WhoE 93
Almeida Duran, Rodolfo 1936- WhoUN 92
Almeida Merino, Adalberto 1916- WhoAm 92
Almeida Teixeira, Maria Esmeralda Fernandes de 1950- WhoScE 91-3
Almen, Louis Theodore 1925- WhoAm 92, WhoWor 93
Almen, Lowell Gordon 1941- WhoAm 92
Almen, Lowell Xgordon 1941- WhoWrEP 92
Almendros, Nestor BioIn 17
Almendros, Nestor 20th cent. HispAmA [port]
Almendros, Nestor 1930- MiSFD 9
Almendros, Nestor 1930-1992 ConTFT 10, CurBio 92N
Almenrader, Carl 1786-1843 Baker 92
Almereyda, Michael MiSFD 9
Almering, Mireille Francoise 1960- WhoWor 93
Almgard, Gunnar 1926- WhoScE 91-4
Almgren, Frederick Justin, Jr. 1933- WhoAm 92
Almgren, Gunnar E.E. 1931- WhoScE 91-4
Almgren, Herbert Philip 1916- WhoAm 92
Almgren, Nancy Welch 1948- WhoE 93
Almgren, Vera J. 1910- St&PR 93
Al Mishari, Ahmad Hamad 1949- WhoWor 93
Almlie, Linda Lee 1945- WhoAmW 93
Almoayed, Tawfeeq Abdulrahman 1948- WhoWor 93
Almodovar, Pedro BioIn 17
Almodovar, Pedro 1949- WhoWor 93
Almodovar, Pedro 1951- ConTFT 10, MiSFD 9
Al-Mohawes, Nasser Abdullah 1951- WhoWor 93
Almon, James E. 1932- St&PR 93
Almon, Reneau Pearson 1937- WhoAm 92, WhoSSW 93
Almon, William Joseph 1932- WhoAm 92
Almond, Carl Herman 1926- WhoAm 92
Almond, David R. Law&B 92, WhoAm 92
Almond, David R. 1940- St&PR 93
Almond, Edward Mallory 1892-1979 HarEnMi
Almond, Gabriel Abraham 1911- BioIn 17, WhoAm 92
Almond, Gary Robert 1958- WhoE 93
Almond, Giles Kevin 1956- WhoEmL 93, WhoSSW 93
Almond, Jeffrey William WhoScE 91-1
Almond, Joan 1934- WhoSSW 93
Almond, Jocelyn ScF&FL 92
Almond, Lincoln C. 1936- WhoAm 92
Almond, Matthew John 1960- WhoWor 93
Almond, Paul 1931- MiSFD 9, WhoAm 92
Almonde, Philips van 1644-1711 HarEnMi
Almony, Robert Allen, Jr. 1945- WhoAm 92
Almquist, Bruce Gunnar Law&B 92
Almquist, Carl Jonas Love 1793-1866 Baker 92
Almquist, Don 1929- WhoAm 92
Almquist, Donald John 1933- WhoAm 92
Almquist, Gregg 1948- ScF&FL 92
Almquist, John ScF&FL 92
Almquist, Lars-Olof 1955- WhoScE 91-4

Almquist, Mary Rebecca 1958- *WhoWrEP 92*
Almquist, Sharon Kristina 1962- *WhoWrEP 92*
Almqvist, Fredrik 1945- *WhoScE 91-4*
Alms, Dixie Lee 1952- *WhoEmL 93*
Almstead, Clara J. 1935- *WhoAmW 93*
Al-Muaammar, Faisal Abdurahman 1959- *WhoWor 93*
Al Mualla, Ahmed Ali Hamad Ali 1957- *WhoUN 92*
Al-Mualla, Rashid bin Ahmad 1930- *WhoWor 93*
Al-Mughairy, Lyutha Sultan 1947- *WhoUN 92*
Al Mulhim, Fahed Saleh 1960- *WhoWor 93*
Al-Murr, Michel 1932- *WhoWor 93*
Almy, Marion Marable 1946- *WhoAmW 93, WhoEmL 93*
Almy, Thomas Pattison 1915- *WhoAm 92*
Al-Naeem, Muna Abdulla 1964- *WhoWor 93*
Alnaemi, Nasser Mohd 1960- *WhoWor 93*
Alnaes, Eyvind 1872-1932 *Baker 92*
Al-Nahayan, Zayid ibn Sultan 1918- *WhoWor 93*
Al-Nahhas Pasha, Mustafa 1876?-1965 *BioIn 17*
Al-Nahi, Qussay Maki 1943- *WhoUN 92*
Al Naib, Shafik *WhoScE 91-1*
Alnar, Hasan Ferit 1906-1978 *Baker 92*
Al-Nasser, Nassir Abdel Aziz *WhoUN 92*
Alne, Dennis James 1947- *WhoE 93*
Al-Nekhilan, Ahmed Mohammed 1936- *WhoWor 93*
Alnima, Samir Khairy 1949- *WhoUN 92*
Al-Ni'mah, Hassan Ali Hussain *WhoUN 92*
Al-ni-mah, Hassan Ali Hussain 1940- *WhoWor 93*
Al-Nowaiser, Essa Abdullah 1951- *WhoUN 92*
Al-Nuaimi, Miqdad *WhoScE 91-1*
Al-Nuami, Humaid ibn Rashid 1930- *WhoWor 93*
Aloff, Mindy 1947- *WhoAm 92*
Alogna, John A. 1943- *St&PR 93*
Alogna, John Joseph 1923- *St&PR 93*
Aloia, Richard Paul, Jr. 1967- *WhoE 93*
Alois, Edward J. 1960- *St&PR 93*
Aloisi, Carol Ann 1953- *WhoAmW 93*
Aloisi de Larderel, Jacqueline 1942- *WhoUN 92*
Aloisi de Larderel, Jacqueline Marthe 1942- *WhoWor 93*
Alok, Swatantra Kumar 1940- *WhoUN 92*
Alok Rai *ScF&FL 92*
Aloma, Rene R. 1947-1986 *WhoCanL 92*
Alomar, Roberto *BioIn 17*
Alomar, Roberto Velazquez 1968- *WhoAm 92*
Alomar, Sandy, Jr. *BioIn 17*
Alomar, Santos Velazquez Sandy, Jr. 1966- *WhoAm 92*
Alompra 1714-1760 *HarEnMi*
Aloneftis, Andreas 1945- *WhoWor 93*
Alongi, Charlie 1930- *St&PR 93*
Alonso, Alicia *BioIn 17*
Alonso, Alicia 1921?- *NotHsAW 93 [port]*
Alonso, Armando F. 1958- *WhoEmL 93*
Alonso, Damaso 1898-1990 *BioIn 17*
Alonso, Jesus *Law&B 92*
Alonso, Julio Alfonso 1948- *WhoWor 93*
Alonso, Kenneth B. 1942- *HispAmA*
Alonso, Maria Conchita 1957- *NotHsAW 93 [port]*
Alonso, Odon *WhoSSW 93*
Alonso, William 1933- *WhoAm 92*
Alonso-Alonso, Rafael *WhoAm 92, WhoSSW 93*
Alonso-Amelot, Miguel Enrique 1946- *WhoWor 93*
Alonso Coratella, Manuel 1955- *WhoAm 92*
Alonso-Fernandez, Francisco 1924- *WhoScE 91-3*
Alonso-Fernandez, Jose Ramon 1946- *WhoWor 93*
Alonso Gascon, Pablo Javier 1952- *WhoWor 93*
Alonso Inarra, Javier 1950- *WhoWor 93*
Alonso Perez De Agreda, Eduardo E. 1947- *WhoScE 91-3*
Alonzo, John A. 1934- *ConTFT 10, MiSFD 9*
Alonzo, Martin Vincent 1931- *WhoAm 92*
Alonzo, Richard Lawrence 1939- *St&PR 93*
Alonzo, Ronald 1942- *St&PR 93*
Aloot, Mariano Daniel 1947- *WhoEmL 93*
Alosio, Gregory Ryan *MiSFD 9*
Alost, Robert Allen 1935- *WhoAm 92, WhoSSW 93*
Alotto, Anthony Lee 1950- *WhoEmL 93*
Alou, Felipe Rojas 1935- *WhoAm 92*
Alousianos *OxDcByz*
Alov, Aleksandr 1923-1983 *DrEEuF*
Al Owais, Abdul Aziz Naser 1946- *WhoUN 92*
Aloy, Reynaldo Vilardo 1940- *WhoWor 93*
Alpaerts, Flor 1876-1954 *Baker 92*
Alpaerts, Jef 1904-1973 *Baker 92*
Alp Arslan c. 1030-1073 *OxDcByz*
Alp Arslan, Mohammed ibn Da'ud c. 1030-1072 *HarEnMi*
Alpaugh, Walter G. 1921- *WhoIns 93*
Alpaut, Y. Okyay 1928- *WhoScE 91-4*
Alpen, Edward Lewis 1922- *WhoAm 92*
Alpenheim, Ilse von 1927- *Baker 92*
Alper, Albert 1912- *WhoAm 92*
Alper, Anne Elizabeth 1942- *WhoAm 92*
Alper, Barbara Jeanne 1946- *WhoAmW 93*
Alper, Howard 1941- *WhoAm 92*
Alper, Hyman 1921- *St&PR 93*
Alper, Jerome Milton 1914- *WhoAm 92*
Alper, Jonathan L. d1990 *BioIn 17*
Alper, Keith Michael 1962- *WhoEmL 93*
Alper, Merlin Lionel 1932- *St&PR 93, WhoAm 92*
Alper, Seymour Lewis 1915- *St&PR 93*
Alperin, Barry J. 1940- *St&PR 93*
Alperin, George 1927- *St&PR 93*
Alperin, Goldie Green 1905- *WhoAmW 93, WhoWor 93*
Alperin, Harvey Jacob 1950- *WhoEmL 93*
Alperin, Howard Abraham 1956- *WhoSSW 93*
Alperin, Irwin Ephraim 1925- *WhoAm 92, WhoE 93*
Alperin, Irwin M. 1920-1990 *BioIn 17*
Alperin, Janice A. *Law&B 92*
Alperin, Richard Martin 1946- *WhoE 93, WhoWor 93*
Alperin, Stanley I. 1931- *WhoWor 93*
Alpern, Andrew 1938- *WhoAm 92*
Alpern, Jacob J. d1990 *BioIn 17*
Alpern, Linda Lee Wevodau 1949- *WhoAmW 93, WhoEmL 93*
Alpern, Lynne Shapiro 1944- *WhoWrEP 92*
Alpern, Mathew 1920- *WhoAm 92*
Alpern, Mildred 1931- *WhoAmW 93*
Alpern, Milton 1925- *WhoE 93*
Alpern, Ramona Lenny *WhoE 93*
Alperovitz, Gar 1936- *WhoAm 92, WhoWrEP 92*
Alpers, David Hershel 1935- *WhoAm 92*
Alpers, Edward Alter 1941- *WhoAm 92*
Alpers, Helmut A. 1930- *St&PR 93*
Alpers, John Hardesty, Jr. 1939- *WhoWor 93*
Alpert, A. Sidney 1938- *St&PR 93*
Alpert, Allen Sidney 1938- *WhoE 93*
Alpert, Ann Sharon 1938- *WhoAmW 93, WhoWor 93*
Alpert, Benjamin 1910- *St&PR 93*
Alpert, Caroline Evelyn 1926- *WhoE 93*
Alpert, Daniel 1952- *WhoEmL 93*
Alpert, David E. *Law&B 92*
Alpert, Eugene Jay 1948- *WhoSSW 93*
Alpert, Harry A. 1913- *St&PR 93*
Alpert, Herb 1935- *WhoAm 92*
Alpert, Herbert S. 1918- *St&PR 93*
Alpert, Hollis 1916- *WhoAm 92, WhoWrEP 92*
Alpert, Irene S. *Law&B 92*
Alpert, Jack *Law&B 92*
Alpert, Jane K. *Law&B 92*
Alpert, Janet A. 1946- *St&PR 93*
Alpert, Janet Anne 1946- *WhoEmL 93*
Alpert, Jeffrey Stuart 1944- *WhoE 93*
Alpert, Joel Jacobs 1930- *WhoAm 92*
Alpert, Jon *BioIn 17*
Alpert, Jonathan Louis 1945- *WhoSSW 93*
Alpert, Joseph M. 1938- *St&PR 93*
Alpert, Joseph Stephen 1942- *WhoAm 92*
Alpert, Linda Ruth *Law&B 92*
Alpert, Marc S. 1944- *St&PR 93*
Alpert, Marc Stephen 1944- *WhoAm 92*
Alpert, Marco Moser 1947- *WhoEmL 93*
Alpert, Mark *Law&B 92*
Alpert, Mark Ira 1942- *WhoAm 92*
Alpert, Mark Zachary 1946- *WhoE 93*
Alpert, Michael Edward 1942- *WhoAm 92*
Alpert, Nancy R. *Law&B 92, St&PR 93*
Alpert, Nelson Leigh 1925- *WhoE 93*
Alpert, Norman 1921- *WhoAm 92*
Alpert, Norman Joseph 1931- *WhoAm 92*
Alpert, Peter A. *Law&B 92*
Alpert, Richard H. *Law&B 92*
Alpert, Seymour 1918- *WhoAm 92*
Alpert, Warren 1920- *St&PR 93, WhoAm 92, WhoWor 93*
Alpert, William Harold 1934- *WhoE 93*
Alphabet, Dr. *WhoWrEP 92*
Alpher, Ralph Asher 1921- *WhoAm 92*
Alphin, Elaine Marie 1955- *ScF&FL 92, WhoWrEP 92*
Alphin, Fred, Jr. *Law&B 92*
Alphonsa, Mother 1851-1926 *BioIn 17*
Alphonse, Karen D. *Law&B 92*
Alphonso, Gordon Richard *Law&B 92*
Alphonso, Mervyn Lyttleton 1941- *St&PR 93*
Alpiar, Hal 1941- *WhoE 93, WhoWor 93*
Alpiser, Joanne Duncan 1957- *WhoEmL 93*
Alprin, Brian Dean 1954- *WhoEmL 93*
Alps, Glen Earl 1914- *WhoAm 92*
Al-Qaddafi, Muammar 1942- *BioIn 17, CurBio 92 [port]*
Al-Qasimi, Saqr ibn Muhammad 1920- *WhoWor 93*
Al-Qassimi, Sultan Bin Mohammed 1939- *WhoWor 93*
Al-Quaryoty, Mohammad Qasem 1949- *WhoWor 93*
Alquist, Joan Armstrong *AmWomPl*
Al-Quraishi, Abdul Aziz 1930- *WhoWor 93*
Al-Quwatli, Shukri 1891-1967 *BioIn 17*
Alreck, Pamela Lynn 1950- *WhoEmL 93*
Alrimawi, Ahmad Shukry Lutfi 1946- *WhoWor 93*
Al-Sabah, Abdullah al-Salem 1895-1965 *BioIn 17*
Al-Sabah, Jaber al-Ahmad al-Jaber, Amir of Kuwait 1926- *BioIn 17*
Al-Sabah, Jabir Al-Ahmad Al-Jabir 1926- *WhoWor 93*
Al-Sabah, Nawwaf Al-Ahmad al-Jabir *WhoWor 93*
Al-Sabah, Sa'd al-Abdallah al-Salim 1924- *WhoWor 93*
Al-Sabah, Salem Abdulaziz Al Saud 1951- *WhoWor 93*
Al-Sabah, Salem Jaber Al-Ahmad 1947- *WhoUN 92*
Al-Sabah, Salim al-Sabah al-Salim 1937- *WhoWor 93*
Al-Sabah, Saud Nasir 1944- *WhoAm 92, WhoWor 93*
Alsac, Orhan *WhoScE 91-4*
Al-Said, Fahad Bin Mahmoud 1944- *WhoWor 93*
Al-Sa'id, Nuri 1888-1958 *BioIn 17*
Al-Said, Sayyed Faher Bin Taimur 1926- *WhoWor 93*
Al Salami, Mohamed Abdullah Sultan 1960- *WhoWor 93*
Al Sallal, Mohammad Saad 1949- *WhoUN 92*
Al-Saud, Naif bin Abdualaziz bin Abdulrahman 1934- *WhoWor 93*
Al-Sawsa, Abd al-Raziq *WhoWor 93*
Al-Sawwaf, Monqidh Mohammed 1950- *WhoE 93*
Alsberg, Dietrich Anselm 1917- *WhoAm 92*
Alschbach, Linda Marie 1967- *WhoAmW 93*
Alscher, Ruth Grene 1943- *WhoAmW 93*
Alschuler, Al 1934- *WhoWrEP 92*
Alschuler, Albert W. 1948- *WhoAm 92*
Alschuler, Sam 1913- *WhoAm 92*
Alsdorf, James W. 1913-1990 *BioIn 17*
Al Seif, Khaled Musaed 1953- *WhoWor 93*
Alsentzer, Gerald G. 1947- *St&PR 93*
Alseth, Jane *Law&B 92*
Al-Shaker, Abdullah Jassim d1989 *BioIn 17*
Al-Shara, Farouk 1938- *WhoWor 93*
Al-Sharqi, Hamad ibn Muhammad 1949- *WhoWor 93*
Al-Shewaihy, Mohammed Ali 1933- *WhoWor 93*
Al-Shuaibi, Saleh Mohammad 1948- *WhoWor 93*
Al-Shuwab, Aqil Abdulla 1962- *WhoWor 93*
Alsina, Carlos Roque 1941- *Baker 92*
Als-Nielsen, Jens 1937- *WhoScE 91-2*
Alsobrook, Gail Brown 1942- *WhoSSW 93*
Alsobrook, Henry Bernis, Jr. 1930- *WhoAm 92*
Alsobrook, Rosalyn Rutledge 1952- *WhoWrEP 92*
Al-Solaim, Soliman Abdul-Aziz *WhoWor 93*
Alson, Eli 1929- *WhoE 93*
Alsop, Donald Douglas 1927- *WhoAm 92*
Alsop, Joseph 1910- & Alsop, Stewart 1914-1978 *JrnUS*
Alsop, Joseph 1910-1989 *BioIn 17, ColdWar 1 [port]*
Alsop, Joseph W. *St&PR 93*
Alsop, Mary O'Hara 1885-1980 *MajAI [port]*
Alsop, Robert C. *Law&B 92*
Alsop, Stewart 1914-1978
See Alsop, Joseph 1910- & Alsop, Stewart 1914-1978 *JrnUS*
Alspach, Donn E. 1931- *WhoWor 93*
Alspach, Philip Halliday 1923- *WhoAm 92*
Alspaugh, Robert Eugene 1933- *St&PR 93*
Alspaugh, Robert Odo *WhoAm 92*
Alspaugh, Robert Odo 1912- *St&PR 93*
Alspaw, Dalton E. 1940- *St&PR 93*
Alstadt, Donald M. *BioIn 17*
Alstadt, Donald Martin 1921- *WhoAm 92*
Alston, Archer Sills 1918- *WhoSSW 93*
Alston, Bessie M. *AmWomPl*
Alston, Emmett *MiSFD 9*
Alston, Eugene Benson 1934- *WhoSSW 93*
Alston, Francine Ann Kristian 1962- *WhoAmW 93*
Alston, Gerald *SoulM*
Alston, Jan M. 1955- *St&PR 93*
Alston, John M. 1928- *St&PR 93*
Alston, Jon Paul 1937- *WhoSSW 93*
Alston, Lawrence Leighton 1952- *WhoEmL 93, WhoSSW 93*
Alston, Lela 1942- *WhoAmW 93*
Alston, Mary Elizabeth 1953- *WhoWrEP 92*
Alston, Nigel DeWalt 1951- *WhoSSW 93*
Alston, Paul Perry 1940- *WhoSSW 93*
Alston, Richard John William 1948- *WhoWor 93*
Alston, Richard Kenneth Robert 1941- *WhoAsAP 91*
Alston, Robert A. *Law&B 92*
Alston, Robert Merritt 1949- *WhoEmL 93*
Alston, Samuel 1770-1809 *BioIn 17*
Alston, Timothy John 1950- *WhoWor 93*
Alston, William P(ayne) 1921- *ConAu 37NR*
Alston, William Payne 1921- *WhoAm 92*
Alston, Winston C.H. 1940- *WhoUN 92*
Alstrin, J.C. 1946- *St&PR 93*
Alstrup, Keld 1946- *St&PR 93*
al-Sudeari, Abdelmohsen Mohammed 1936- *WhoWor 93*
Alsultan, Abdullah Sultan 1954- *WhoWor 93*
Al-Suwaidi, Salem Mohammed 1956- *WhoEmL 93, WhoWor 93*
Alsworth, Frances Wilkerson 1927- *WhoSSW 93*
Alsworth, Linda Rae 1955- *WhoAmW 93*
Alt, Arthur Tilo 1931- *WhoSSW 93*
Alt, Betty L. 1931- *WhoAmW 93*
Alt, Daniel Mark 1949- *St&PR 93*
Alt, Dennis M. *Law&B 92*
Alt, Gary *BioIn 17*
Alt, Helmut G. 1944- *WhoScE 91-3*
Alt, James Edward 1946- *WhoAm 92*
Alt, John 1962- *WhoAm 92*
Alt, Julane Brooks *Law&B 92*
Alt, Norman C. *Law&B 92*
Alt, Walter Louis 1926- *St&PR 93*
Alt, William E. 1952- *St&PR 93*
Alt, Willis E. 1944- *St&PR 93*
Alta 1942- *WhoWrEP 92*
Alta, Lina Maria 1961- *WhoEmL 93*
Altabe, Joan Augusta Berg 1935- *WhoAm 92*
Altabef, Richard H. *Law&B 92*
Al-Tahir, Haytham Qasim *WhoWor 93*
Altamirano, Ignacio Manuel 1834-1893 *DcMexL*
Altamura, Carmela Elizabeth 1939- *WhoAmW 93, WhoE 93, WhoWor 93*
Altamura, Michael Victor 1923- *WhoWor 93*
Altamura, Patrick M. *Law&B 92*
Altamura, Robert James 1953- *WhoE 93*
Altan, Taylan 1938- *WhoAm 92*
Altani, Ippolit 1846-1919 *OxDcOp*
Al-Tarifi, Abdul-Rahman Hassan 1946- *WhoWor 93*
Altay, Fahri 1942- *WhoScE 91-4*
Altbach, Philip 1941- *WhoAm 92*
Altchek, Edward Myer 1931- *WhoE 93*
Altekruse, Joan Morrissey 1928- *WhoAm 92*
Altemeyer, Donald Blaine 1946- *WhoEmL 93*
Alten, Felix Charles 1928- *St&PR 93*
Altena, Arnaud d' *ScF&FL 92*
Altenau, Alan Giles 1938- *WhoAm 92, WhoWor 93*
Altenau, Richard Dale 1960- *St&PR 93*
Altenbaumer, Larry F. 1948- *St&PR 93*
Altenburg, Johann Ernst 1734-1801 *Baker 92*
Altenburg, Michael 1584-1640 *Baker 92*
Altenburger, Christian 1957- *Baker 92*
Altenhof, Jeanette Faye 1955- *WhoAmW 93*
Alter, Andrew William *Law&B 92*
Alter, Brian Reid 1956- *St&PR 93*
Alter, David 1923- *WhoAm 92*
Alter, David Emmet, Jr. 1921- *WhoAm 92*
Alter, Dennis Ira 1951- *St&PR 93*
Alter, Edward T. 1941- *WhoAm 92*
Alter, Eleanor Breitel 1938- *WhoAm 92*
Alter, Eleanor Reed 1908- *WhoAmW 93*
Alter, Gerald L. 1910- *WhoWor 93*
Alter, Harvey 1932- *WhoAm 92*
Alter, Jean Victor 1925- *WhoAm 92*
Alter, Jonathan Hammerman 1957- *WhoAm 92*
Alter, Julie *BioIn 17*
Alter, Kathryn *BioIn 17*

Alter, Lynne 1953- WhoAmW 93, WhoEmL 93
Alter, M. Luke Law&B 92
Alter, Milton 1929- WhoAm 92
Alter, Nelson T. 1926- St&PR 93
Alter, Nelson Tobias 1926- WhoSSW 93
Alter, Norman B. 1935- St&PR 93
Alter, Robert BioIn 17
Alter, Robert 1935- JeAmHC
Alter, Shirley Jacobs 1929- St&PR 93, WhoAmW 93
Alter, Simcha B. 1897-1992 NewYTBS 92
Alter, Victor 1890-1941 PolBiDi
Alter, Victor 1890-1942? BioIn 17
Alterman, Dean N. 1960- WhoEmL 93
Alterman, Irwin Michael 1941- WhoAm 92
Alterman, Stanley R. Law&B 92
Altermatt, Paul Barry 1930- WhoAm 92
Alter Muri, Simone Bernette 1954- WhoE 93
Altersitz, Janet Kinahan 1951- WhoAmW 93
Alterton, Margaret 1877-1934 ScF&FL 92
Altes, Ernest-Eugene 1830-1899 Baker 92
Altes, Harvey Cyril 1928- WhoSSW 93
Altes, Joseph-Henri 1826-1895 Baker 92
Altevogt, Rudolf Heinrich 1924- WhoScE 91-3
Altfeld, Sheldon Isaac 1937- WhoAm 92
Altfeld, Theodore Sandford 1943- St&PR 93
Altgeld, John P. 1847-1902 PolPar
Altgeld, John Peter 1847-1902 GayN
Altgelt, Ernest J., III Law&B 92
Altgilbers, Larry Lee 1945- WhoSSW 93
Altglass, Max 1886-1952 Baker 92
Alth, Gerhart WhoScE 91-4
Al-Thani, Abdulla bin Khalifa WhoWor 93
Al-Thani, Hamad Bin Khalifa 1949- WhoWor 93
Al-Thani, Hamad Bin Suham 1940- WhoWor 93
Al-Thani, Khalifa Bin Hamad 1932- WhoWor 93
Althans, John H., Jr. 1935- St&PR 93
Althaus, Barbara Donalson 1937- WhoAmW 93
Althaus, David Steven 1945- St&PR 93, WhoSSW 93
Althaus, Egon 1933- WhoScE 91-3
Althaus, H. WhoScE 91-3
Althauser, Martha G. 1940- St&PR 93
Althaver, Lambert E. 1931- St&PR 93
Althaver, Lambert Ewing 1931- WhoAm 92
Altheimer, Alan J. 1903- St&PR 93, WhoAm 92
Altheimer, Bessie Miriam 1875- AmWomPl
Altheimer, Joseph WhoE 93
Althen, Wayne W. 1937- St&PR 93
Alther, Jack R. 1926- St&PR 93
Alther, Lisa BioIn 17
Altherr, Jack Richard 1926- WhoAm 92
Altherr, Jack Richard, Jr. 1949- WhoAm 92
Althof, Timothy D. 1948- St&PR 93
Althofer, Heinz 1925- BioIn 17
Althoff, Catherine L. 1956- St&PR 93
Althoff, David E. 1941- St&PR 93
Althoff, Gordon 1948- St&PR 93
Althoff, Ronald David 1941- WhoSSW 93
Altholz, Thomas I. 1950- St&PR 93
Althorp, Viscount BioIn 17
Althouse, Janet Marie 1940- WhoE 93
Althouse, Lawrence Wilson 1930- WhoSSW 93
Althouse, Paul (Shearer) 1889-1954 Baker 92
Althuis, Thomas Henry 1941- WhoE 93
Althusser, Louis BioIn 17
Altick, Leslie L. WhoAm 92
Altick, Richard Daniel 1915- ConAu 40NR
Altier, Sabine Patricia Law&B 92
Altier, Theodore J. 1921- St&PR 93
Altier, William John 1935- WhoE 93, WhoWor 93
Altieri, Earl R. 1930- St&PR 93
Altieri, Maria Rita 1957- WhoEmL 93
Altieri, Pablo Ivan 1943- WhoSSW 93
Altieri, Peter Louis 1955- WhoEmL 93
Al-Tikriti, Barzan 1951- WhoUN 92
Altimari, Frank X. 1928- WhoAm 92, WhoE 93
Altimir, Oscar Alberto 1935- WhoUN 92
Altinbilek, H. Dogan 1944- WhoScE 91-4
Alting, Leo L. 1939- WhoScE 91-2
Alting, Leo Larsen 1939- WhoWor 93
Altinok, Tevfik 1943- WhoWor 93
Altizer, Thomas Jonathan Jackson 1927- WhoAm 92
Altman, Adele Rosenhain 1924- WhoAmW 93, WhoWor 93
Altman, Alison 1958- WhoAmW 93
Altman, Allan 1929- WhoE 93
Altman, Arnold David 1917- WhoAm 92
Altman, Barbara Jean Friedman 1947- WhoEmL 93
Altman, Beth Law&B 92
Altman, Cynthia Caroline 1951- WhoAmW 93
Altman, Dan Nixon 1952- WhoE 93
Altman, Dara F. Law&B 92
Altman, Edward Ira 1941- WhoAm 92, WhoWrEP 92
Altman, Ellen 1936- WhoAm 92
Altman, Franc Collier 1926- St&PR 93
Altman, Irwin 1930- WhoAm 92, WhoWrEP 92
Altman, James L. Law&B 92
Altman, Jane Callahan 1949- WhoAmW 93
Altman, Jeff BioIn 17
Altman, Joseph 1925- WhoAm 92
Altman, Kathryn BioIn 17
Altman, Laurence 1933- St&PR 93
Altman, Lawrence Gene 1952- WhoE 93, WhoEmL 93
Altman, Lawrence Kimball 1937- WhoAm 92
Altman, Leo Sidney 1911- WhoAm 92
Altman, Lorin Jay 1946- St&PR 93
Altman, Louis 1933- WhoAm 92
Altman, Ludwig 1910-1990 Baker 92
Altman, Lyle D. 1930- St&PR 93, WhoAm 92
Altman, M.H. 1952- St&PR 93
Altman, Mark A. ScF&FL 92
Altman, Martin S. 1949- St&PR 93
Altman, Mary Ann 1930- WhoAm 92
Altman, Melvin S. Law&B 92
Altman, Milton Hubert 1917- WhoAm 92
Altman, Nathaniel 1948- WhoWrEP 92
Altman, Norman Eugene 1919- St&PR 93
Altman, Norman Jon 1957- St&PR 93
Altman, Randy Allan 1954- WhoEmL 93
Altman, Richard L. 1946- WhoE 93, WhoEmL 93
Altman, Richard Stuart 1933- WhoSSW 93
Altman, Robert BioIn 17
Altman, Robert 1925- BioIn 17, MiSFD 9, News 93-2 [port]
Altman, Robert Alan 1947- WhoEmL 93
Altman, Robert B. 1925- WhoAm 92
Altman, Robert Lee 1935- WhoAm 92
Altman, Robin M. 1958- WhoEmL 93
Altman, Roy Peter 1934- WhoAm 92
Altman, Sheldon 1934- St&PR 93, WhoAm 92
Altman, Sidney 1939- WhoAm 92, WhoE 93, WhoWor 93
Altman, Steven 1945- WhoAm 92
Altman, Steven C. 1947- St&PR 93
Altman, Steven Jay Law&B 92
Altman, Stuart Harold 1937- WhoAm 92
Altman, Thomas ScF&FL 92
Altman, William P. 1938- St&PR 93
Altman-Fischer, Linda Susan 1955- WhoEmL 93
Altman-Kole, LeeAnn 1962- WhoAmW 93
Altmann, Kenneth 1933- St&PR 93
Altmann, Lilo 1951- WhoWor 93
Altmann, Michael Stewart 1952- WhoE 93
Altmann, Stuart Allen 1930- WhoAm 92
Altmann, Wilhelm 1862-1951 Baker 92
Altmeyer, Felicia Law&B 92
Altmeyer, Jeannine (Theresa) 1948- Baker 92
Altmeyer, John W. 1959- St&PR 93
Altmeyer, Theo(dor David) 1931- Baker 92
Altmiller, Jeanne Elizabeth 1960- WhoAmW 93
Altner, Helmut 1934- WhoScE 91-3
Altner, Peter Christian 1932- WhoAm 92
Altnikol, Johann Christoph 1719-1759 Baker 92
Alto, Brian J. 1958- St&PR 93
Alto, Joseph S. Law&B 92
Altobello, Daniel Joseph 1941- St&PR 93, WhoAm 92
Altolaguirre, Manuel 1904-1959 BioIn 17
Altolaguirre, Manuel 1905-1959 DcMexL
Altom, Rhoda Lynn 1957- WhoEmL 93
Altom, William H. 1925- St&PR 93
Altomare, Erica Von Scheven 1950- WhoAmW 93
Alton, Andrea I. 1946- ScF&FL 92
Alton, Ann Leslie 1945- WhoAm 92, WhoAmW 93, WhoWor 93
Alton, Bruce Taylor 1939- WhoAm 92
Alton, David C. 1930- St&PR 93
Alton, Elaine Vivian 1925- WhoAm 92
Alton, Howard Robert, Jr. 1927- St&PR 93
Alton, Howard Robert, III Law&B 92
Alton, Jerald M. Law&B 92
Alton, John G. 1954- WhoWrEP 92
Alton, John W. 1941- St&PR 93
Altonen, Mikko Antero 1929- WhoScE 91-4
Altorfer, H. John 1936- St&PR 93
Al'tov, Genrikh ScF&FL 92
Altrocchi, Julia Cooley 1893- AmWomPl
Altrocchi, Sally Archer 1960- WhoEmL 93
Altrock, Richard Charles 1940- WhoAm 92
Altschaeffl, Adolph George 1930- WhoAm 92
Altscher, Stanley Gary 1952- St&PR 93
Altschuh, Gregory W. Law&B 92
Altschuh, Gregory William 1946- WhoEmL 93
Altschul, Aaron Mayer 1914- WhoAm 92
Altschul, Alfred S. 1939- St&PR 93
Altschul, Alfred Samuel 1939- WhoAm 92
Altschul, Arthur G. 1920- St&PR 93
Altschul, Arthur Goodhart 1920- WhoAm 92
Altschul, B.J. 1948- WhoEmL 93, WhoSSW 93
Altschul, David E. Law&B 92
Altschul, David Edwin 1947- WhoEmL 93
Altschul, James Sloan 1960- WhoEmL 93
Altschul, Selig d1992 NewYTBS 92 [port]
Altschuler, Bruce Robert 1947- WhoE 93
Altschuler, David Edward 1952- WhoEmL 93
Altschuler, Jonathan Bobrow 1936- WhoAm 92
Altschuler, Modest 1873-1963 Baker 92
Altschuler, Stephen 1932- St&PR 93
Altshuler, Alan Anthony 1936- WhoAm 92
Altshuler, J. 1939- St&PR 93
Altshuler, Lanny Stephen 1948- WhoEmL 93, WhoSSW 93
Altshuller, Genrikh ScF&FL 92
Altshuller, Mark Gregory 1929- WhoE 93
Altstadt, Audrey L. WhoE 93
Altstadt, Manfred 1950- St&PR 93
Altstaedt, Hans Volker 1954- WhoWor 93
Altuch, Peter Mark 1952- WhoEmL 93
Altura, Burton Myron 1936- WhoAm 92, WhoWor 93
Al-Turabi, Hassan BioIn 17
Altvater, Arthur William, Jr. 1942- St&PR 93
Altvater, Donald 1921- St&PR 93
Alty, Cathleen Jo 1958- WhoAmW 93
Alty, J.L. WhoScE 91-1
Alty, James Lenton WhoScE 91-1
Aluise, David A. 1953- St&PR 93
Aluise, Timothy John 1956- WhoAm 92
Aluko, Timothy Mofolorunso 1918- DcLB 117 [port]
Alumbaugh, deLyn Ross 1950- WhoEmL 93
Alumbaugh, JoAnn McCalla 1952- WhoAm 92
Alun-Jones, Derek WhoScE 91-1
Alurista 1947- HispAmA [port], WhoAm 92
Alushin, Michael Stephen 1947- WhoEmL 93
Alutto, Joseph Anthony 1924- St&PR 93
Alutto, Joseph Anthony 1941- WhoAm 92, WhoE 93
Alva, Juan 1936- WhoSSW 93
Alva, Luigi 1927- Baker 92, IntDcOp, OxDcOp
Alva, Margaret 1942- WhoAsAP 91
Alva Ixtlixochitl, Fernando de 1577-1648 DcMexL
Alvarado, Francisco 1932- WhoScE 91-2
Alvarado, Jose 1911-1974 DcMexL
Alvarado, Linda 1951- NotHsAW 93
Alvarado, Manuel 1948- ScF&FL 92
Alvarado, Pedro de 1485-1541 Expl 93 [port]
Alvarado, Rafael 1924- WhoScE 91-3
Alvarado, Ricardo Raphael 1927- WhoAm 92
Alvarado, Richard A., Sr. 1943- St&PR 93
Alvarado, Trini BioIn 17
Alvarado, Yolanda H. 1943- NotHsAW 93 [port]
Alvarado, Yolanda Hernandez 1943- WhoAmW 93
Alvarado de Ricord, Elsie 1928- SpAmA
Alvarado Zavala, Jose Antonio 1943- DcMexL
Alvardo, Pablo Mauricio Law&B 92
Alvares, Joe 1935- St&PR 93
Alvarez, Albert 1861-1933 Baker 92
Alvarez, Ambrosio Toval 1959- WhoWor 93
Alvarez, Angel 1947- WhoScE 91-3
Alvarez, Anne Maino 1941- HispAmA
Alvarez, Arthur 1958- St&PR 93
Alvarez, Chico d1992 NewYTBS 92
Alvarez, Danny 1949- WhoEmL 93
Alvarez, Eric Manuel 1950- WhoSSW 93
Alvarez, Everett 1937- BioIn 17
Alvarez, Everett, Jr. 1937- HispAmA
Alvarez, Fernando 1942- WhoScE 91-3
Alvarez, Gregory Eugenio Law&B 92
Alvarez, Griselda 1918- DcMexL
Alvarez, Heherson Turingan 1939- WhoAsAP 91
Alvarez, Joan M. d1990 BioIn 17
Alvarez, Jorge Luis 1944- WhoSSW 93
Alvarez, Jose 1940- WhoSSW 93
Alvarez, Jose Armando 1949- WhoEmL 93, WhoSSW 93
Alvarez, Jose Florencio 1948- WhoEmL 93, WhoSSW 93
Alvarez, Julia BioIn 17, NotHsAW 93 [port]
Alvarez, Laurence Richards 1937- WhoSSW 93
Alvarez, Leonardo 1938- St&PR 93
Alvarez, Linda NotHsAW 93
Alvarez, Louis Basilio 1927- WhoSSW 93
Alvarez, Louis Lefcourt 1955- WhoEmL 93
Alvarez, Luis Miguel 1965- WhoSSW 93
Alvarez, Luis W. BioIn 17
Alvarez, Luis Walter 1911- HispAmA
Alvarez, Manuel J. Law&B 92
Alvarez, Mercedes WhoAmW 93
Alvarez, Paul H. 1942- St&PR 93
Alvarez, Paul Hubert 1942- WhoAm 92
Alvarez, Raymond P. WhoWrEP 92
Alvarez, Robert S. BioIn 17
Alvarez, Robert Smyth 1912- WhoAm 92
Alvarez, Rodolfo 1936- HispAmA, WhoAm 92
Alvarez, Thomas Peter 1967- WhoE 93
Alvarez, Walter 1940- BioIn 17, WhoAm 92
Alvarez Acosta, Miguel 1907- DcMexL
Alvarez Bogaert, Fernando DcCPCAm
Alvarez Bravo, Manuel 1902- BioIn 17
Alvarez-Builla Gomez, Julio 1946- WhoWor 93
Alvarez Constantino, Jesus 1914- DcMexL
Alvarez Cordova, Enrique DcCPCAm
Alvarez-Cullen, Martha 1955- WhoE 93
Alvarez Gardeazabal, Gustavo 1945- SpAmA
Alvarez-Gonzalez, Rafael 1958- WhoSSW 93
Alvarez Gorsira, Francisco Manuel 1942- WhoUN 92
Alvarez-Marques, Desiderio Miguel 1951- WhoWor 93
Alvarez Martinez, Gustavo Adolfo 1937-1989 DcCPCAm
Alvarez Martinez, Luz 1942- NotHsAW 93
Alvarez Miranda, A. WhoScE 91-3
Alvarez-Pellitero, Maria Pilar 1944- WhoScE 91-3
Alvarez Posada, Jose Maria 1911-1965? DcMexL
Alvarez-Recio, Emilio 1938- St&PR 93
Alvarez-Recio, Emilio De La Torre 1938- WhoAm 92
Alvarez Rendueles, Jose Ramon 1940- WhoWor 93
Alvarez-Renta, Luis Rafael 1950- WhoSSW 93, WhoWor 93
Alvarez-Rodrich, Augusto Anibal 1959- WhoWor 93
Alvarez-Santori, Jose 1917- St&PR 93
Alvarino, Angeles 1916- WhoAm 92
Alvarino de Leira, Angeles 1916- HispAmA [port], WhoAm 92
Alvaro, Anthony Joseph 1945- St&PR 93
Alvaro, Ferdinand, Jr. Law&B 92
Alvaro, Filipe Nunes 1945- WhoWor 93
Alvaro, L. Jim Pizarro 1967- WhoWor 93
Alvary, Lorenzo 1909- Baker 92, WhoAm 92
Alvary, Max 1856-1898 Baker 92, OxDcOp
Alva Talledo, Luis Ernesto 1927- Baker 92
Alventosa, Vincent Law&B 92
Alver, Bente Gullveig BioIn 17
Alverson, Ben Earl 1940- WhoWor 93
Alverson, Charles 1935- ScF&FL 92
Alverson, Fred Dwight 1955- WhoEmL 93
Alverson, William H. St&PR 93
Alverson, William H. 1933- WhoAm 92
Alves, Gerald W. 1951- St&PR 93
Alves, Herbert A. 1933- St&PR 93
Alves, Joaquim Paredes 1922- WhoWor 93
Alves, Joe 1938- MiSFD 9
Alves, Joseph Thomas 1921- WhoE 93
Alves, Judith Ann 1949- WhoAmW 93
Alves, Leonard Gustavo 1919- WhoWor 93
Alves Da Silva, Manuel 1925- WhoScE 91-3
Alves Pereira, Jose de Almeida 1945- WhoWor 93
Alvey, Doris May Giordano 1945- WhoAmW 93
Alvey, J. WhoScE 91-1
Alvey, Joseph Earl, Jr. 1937- WhoSSW 93, WhoWor 93
Alvey, Robert J. 1956- WhoSSW 93
Alvi, Zahoor Mohem 1942- WhoAm 92
Alviano, Bartolomeo d' 1455-1515 HarEnMi
Alvin, Dave BioIn 17
Alvin, Robert E. 1946- St&PR 93
Alvinczy, Josef 1735-1810 HarEnMi

Alvine, Robert 1938- *WhoAm 92, WhoE 93, WhoWor 93*
Alvino, Gloria Dora 1931- *WhoE 93*
Alvira Martin, Pilar 1943- *WhoScE 91-3*
Alvirez, Hortensia Maria 1944- *NotHsAW 93*
Alvis, Margaret Olivier 1942- *WhoAmW 93*
Alviset, Lucien 1928- *WhoScE 91-2*
Alvisi, Franco 1927- *WhoScE 91-3*
Alvord, Bethany Jean *Law&B 92*
Alvord, Burt 1866-1910? *BioIn 17*
Alvord, Joel Barnes 1938- *St&PR 93, WhoAm 92*
al-Wahab, Ibrahim Ismael 1928- *WhoWor 93*
Alway, Robert Hamilton 1912-1990 *BioIn 17*
Alwin, Karl 1891-1945 *Baker 92*
Alworth, Lance 1940- *BioIn 17*
Alworth, Sandra Ann 1947- *WhoAm 92*
Al-Wosemer, Turki Salem 1962- *WhoWor 93*
Alwyn, Kenneth 1925- *Baker 92*
Alwyn, William 1905-1985 *Baker 92*
Aly, Herbert 1928- *WhoScE 91-3*
Al-Yaagoub, Ali Husain 1958- *WhoWor 93*
Alyabyev, Alexander 1787-1851 *OxDcOp*
Al Yasiri, Kahtan Abbass 1939- *WhoAm 92*
Alyates *OxDcByz*
Alyea, Hubert Newcombe 1903- *WhoE 93*
Alyer, Philip A. *MajAI*
Alypios fl. 4th cent.- *Baker 92*
Alzado, Lyle *BioIn 17*
Alzado, Lyle 1949-1992 *NewYTBS 92 [port]*
Al-Zarafy, Mohammed Yousuf 1954- *WhoUN 92*
Al-Zarb, Haj Muhammad Hassan Amin d1898 *BioIn 17*
Alzon, Emmanuel Marie Joseph Maurice d' 1810-1880 *BioIn 17*
Al-Zubaidi, Amer Aziz 1945- *WhoSSW 93*
Alzubaidy, Kahtan Hamza 1949- *WhoWor 93*
Am, Magnar 1952- *Baker 92*
Amabile, Anthony A. 1934- *WhoWrEP 92*
Amabile, George 1936- *WhoCanL 92*
Amabile, John Louis 1934- *WhoAm 92, WhoE 93*
Amabile, Ralph J., Jr. 1928- *St&PR 93*
Amacher, Maryanne 1943- *Baker 92*
Amacher, Richard Earl 1917- *WhoAm 92*
Amacher, Ryan C. 1945- *WhoSSW 93*
Amadei, Deborah Lisa 1952- *WhoE 93, WhoEmL 93*
Amadei, Filippo c. 1670-c. 1729 *Baker 92*
Amadei, Filippo fl. 1690-1730 *OxDcOp*
Amadeo, VI 1334-1383 *OxDcByz*
Amadeo, Jose H. 1928- *WhoAm 92*
Amadi, Elechi 1934- *BioIn 17*
Amadi, Elechi (Emmanuel) 1934- *ConAu 38NR, DcLB 117 [port]*
Amadio, Bari Ann 1949- *WhoAmW 93, WhoEmL 93*
Amadio, Ernest Richard 1944- *St&PR 93*
Amado, Jorge 1912- *BioIn 17, ScF&FL 92, WhoWor 93*
Amado, Patricia Ann 1960- *WhoEmL 93*
Amado, Ralph 1932- *HispAmA*
Amado, Renato Giuseppe 1942- *WhoWor 93*
Amadon, Gregory *St&PR 93*
Amador, Elias 1932- *HispAmA*
Amador, Victor John 1928- *St&PR 93*
Amadou, Ali *WhoWor 93*
Amadou, Hama 1950- *WhoAfr*
Amaducci, Bruno 1925- *Baker 92*
Amaiu, Tom 1952- *WhoAsAP 91*
Amalarius of Metz dc. 850 *OxDcByz*
Amalasuntha d535 *OxDcByz*
Amaldi, Edoardo *WhoScE 91-3*
Amaldi, Edoardo 1908-1989 *BioIn 17*
Amalfitano, John Michael 1950- *St&PR 93*
Amali *OxDcByz*
Amalia Catharina 1640-1697 *Baker 92*
Amalia Friederike 1794-1870 *Baker 92*
Amaliksen, Arne S. 1938- *St&PR 93*
Amalric, I 1136-1174 *OxDcByz*
Aman, Alfred Charles, Jr. 1945- *WhoAm 92*
Aman, Craig William 1964- *WhoSSW 93*
Aman, George B. 1943- *St&PR 93*
Aman, George Matthias, III 1930- *WhoAm 92*
Aman, Joseph Patrick 1957- *WhoEmL 93*
Aman, Mohammed Mohammed 1940- *WhoAm 92*
Aman, Reinhold Albert 1936- *WhoAm 92, WhoWrEP 92*
Amani, Mohammad Nabi 1945- *WhoUN 92*
Amani, Nikolai 1872-1904 *Baker 92*
Amaning, Kwadwo Owusu 1956- *WhoSSW 93*
Amann, Charles Albert 1926- *WhoAm 92*
Amann, Cynthia Clair 1948- *WhoAm 92, WhoAmW 93, WhoWor 93*
Amann, Laura Jane 1957- *WhoAmW 93*
Amann, Michael Paul 1949- *St&PR 93*
Amann, Peter Henry 1927- *WhoAm 92*
Amann, R. Scott 1955- *St&PR 93*
Amann, Richard David 1954- *WhoSSW 93*
Amano, Akihiro 1934- *WhoWor 93*
Amano, Yoshitaka *ScF&FL 92*
Amante, Edelmiro A. 1933- *WhoAsAP 91*
Amantea, Rebecca Anne 1955- *WhoAmW 93*
Amantia, Jacquelin Boulanger 1957- *WhoAmW 93*
Amanuddin, Syed 1934- *WhoWrEP 92*
Amanuma, Akira 1927- *WhoWor 93*
Amar, Denis *MiSFD 9*
Amar, Licco 1891-1959 *Baker 92*
Amar, Paula Bram 1934- *WhoAmW 93*
Amara, Lucine 1927- *Baker 92, WhoAm 92*
Amaral, Donald J. 1952- *St&PR 93*
Amaral, Olga Ceballos de *BioIn 17*
Amaral, Suzana *MiSFD 9*
Amaranath, Thota Hewage Ananda 1945- *WhoWor 93*
Amare, Rothayne *ScF&FL 92*
Amarel, Saul 1928- *WhoAm 92*
Amarger, Noelle 1937- *WhoScE 91-2*
Amari, Akira 1949- *WhoAsAP 91*
Amari, Robert Francis 1955- *WhoEmL 93*
Amari, Shun-ichi 1936- *WhoWor 93*
Amari, Takeshi 1942- *WhoWor 93*
Amariglio, Henri 1935- *WhoScE 91-2*
Amarilios, John Alexander 1958- *WhoEmL 93*
Amariutei, Alexandrina 1941- *WhoScE 91-4*
Amar Leonard Linggi Ak Jugah, Datuk *WhoAsAP 91*
Amaro, Ismael de Sousa 1942- *WhoWor 93*
Amartya Kumar Sen *BioIn 17*
Amash, Charles Elias 1932- *St&PR 93*
Amasula, Carlos Baldado, Jr. 1941- *WhoWor 93*
Amat, Elias Rogent y 1821-1897 *BioIn 17*
Amat, Josep 1940- *WhoScE 91-3*
Amat, Juan Carlos c. 1572-1642 *Baker 92*
Amat, Oriol Salas 1957- *WhoWor 93*
Amatayakul, Puripat 1958- *WhoWor 93*
Amateau, Rod 1923- *MiSFD 9*
Amati *Baker 92*
Amati, Andrea 1500?-1580? *Baker 92*
Amati, Antonio c. 1538-c. 1595 *Baker 92*
Amati, Girolamo c. 1561-1630 *Baker 92*
Amati, Girolamo 1649-1740 *Baker 92*
Amati, Nicola 1596-1684 *Baker 92*
Amato, A.J. 1951- *St&PR 93*
Amato, Albert Louis, Jr. 1948- *St&PR 93*
Amato, Camille Jean 1942- *WhoAmW 93*
Amato, Denise *Law&B 92*
Amato, Gary N. 1951- *St&PR 93*
Amato, Guiliano 1938- *WhoWor 93*
Amato, Isabella Antonia 1942- *WhoAm 92*
Amato, Joe *BioIn 17*
Amato, John Gerard *Law&B 92*
Amato, John V. 1930- *St&PR 93*
Amato, Joseph John 1952- *WhoE 93*
Amato, Michele Amateau 1945- *WhoE 93*
Amato, Pasquale 1878-1942 *Baker 92, IntDcOp [port], OxDcOp*
Amato, Paul H. 1939- *St&PR 93*
Amato, Thomas Gabriel 1945- *St&PR 93*
Amato, Victoria Anne 1957- *WhoSSW 93*
Amato, Vincent N. *Law&B 92*
Amato, Vincent Vito 1929- *WhoAm 92*
Amatong, Ernesto S. 1929- *WhoAsAP 91*
Amatori, Michael Louis 1951- *WhoEmL 93*
Amatus c. 1010-c. 1083 *OxDcByz*
Amatya, Dhruba Man Singh 1932- *WhoWor 93*
Amaya, Elias Holguin 1932- *WhoWor 93*
Amazeen, Paul Gerard 1939- *St&PR 93*
Amazing Randi *BioIn 17*
Ambach, Dwight Russell 1931- *WhoAm 92*
Ambach, Gordon Mac Kay 1934- *WhoAm 92*
Ambach, Walter 1927- *WhoWor 93*
Ambach, Walter 1929- *WhoScE 91-4*
Ambasz, Emilio 1943- *WhoAm 92, WhoWor 93*
Ambatchew, Abebe 1934- *WhoUN 92*
Ambeault, David E. 1940- *St&PR 93*
Ambedkar, Bhimrao Ramji 1892-1956 *BioIn 17*
Ambedkar, Bhimrao Ramji 1893-1956 *DcTwHis*
Amber, Douglas George 1956- *WhoEmL 93*
Amber, Rich 1949- *WhoEmL 93*
Amberg, Deborah Ann *Law&B 92*
Amberg, John W. 1931- *St&PR 93*
Amberg, Richard Hiller, Jr. 1942- *St&PR 93, WhoAm 92, WhoSSW 93*
Amberg, Thomas Law 1948- *WhoAm 92*
Ambielli, Adam Frederick 1937- *St&PR 93*
Ambielli, Robert John 1951- *WhoEmL 93*
Ambler, Anthony Peter *WhoScE 91-1*
Ambler, Bruce M. 1939- *St&PR 93*
Ambler, Bruce Melville 1939- *WhoAm 92*
Ambler, David Samuel 1954- *WhoEmL 93*
Ambler, Eric 1909- *BioIn 17, ConAu 38NR, WhoAm 92*
Ambler, Ernest 1923- *WhoAm 92*
Ambler, Richard Penry *WhoScE 91-1*
Ambler, Thomas Wilson *Law&B 92*
Ambler, Thomas Wilson 1953- *WhoEmL 93*
Ambler, Timothy Felix John 1937- *WhoE 93, WhoWor 93*
Amboian, John Peter 1931- *WhoAm 92*
Ambos, Robert 1945- *WhoWor 93*
Ambraseys, Nicholas Nicholas *WhoScE 91-1*
Ambrister, John Charles 1944- *WhoAm 92*
Ambroise-Thomas, Pierre 1937- *WhoScE 91-2*
Ambros, August Wilhelm 1816-1876 *Baker 92*
Ambros, Vladimir 1890-1956 *Baker 92*
Ambrose c. 333-397 *Baker 92*
Ambrose c. 339-397 *OxDcByz*
Ambrose, Saint, Bishop of Milan d397 *BioIn 17*
Ambrose, Amy Christine 1963- *WhoEmL 93*
Ambrose, Brian *WhoScE 91-1*
Ambrose, Charles Clarke 1924- *WhoAm 92*
Ambrose, Charles Stuart 1951- *WhoEmL 93, WhoSSW 93*
Ambrose, Donald Eric 1947- *WhoEmL 93*
Ambrose, Henrietta *AfrAmBi [port]*
Ambrose, James Richard 1922- *WhoAm 92*
Ambrose, Joseph V., Jr. *Law&B 92*
Ambrose, Joseph V., Jr. 1929- *St&PR 93*
Ambrose, Joseph Vincent, Jr. 1929- *WhoAm 92*
Ambrose, Lottie F. *ScF&FL 92*
Ambrose, Marilyn Miller 1946- *WhoAmW 93, WhoE 93*
Ambrose, Myles Joseph 1926- *WhoAm 92*
Ambrose, Samuel Sheridan, Jr. 1923- *WhoAm 92*
Ambrose, Stephen Edward 1936- *WhoAm 92*
Ambrose, Stephen F., Jr. *Law&B 92*
Ambrose, Tommy W. 1926- *WhoAm 92*
Ambrosini, Paul John 1950- *WhoEmL 93*
Ambrosino, Ralph Thomas, Jr. 1940- *WhoAm 92*
Ambrosio, Alfredo d' 1871-1914 *Baker 92*
Ambrosio, Vittorio 1879-1958 *HarEnMi*
Ambrosius c. 333-397 *Baker 92*
Ambrosius, Hermann 1897-1983 *Baker 92*
Ambrosius, James W. *Law&B 92*
Ambroziak, Cezary Andrzej 1935- *WhoScE 91-4*
Ambroziak, Shirley Ann 1953- *WhoEmL 93*
Ambrozic, Aloysius Matthew 1930- *WhoAm 92*
Ambrozy, P. *WhoScE 91-4*
Ambrus, Arpad 1944- *WhoScE 91-4*
Ambrus, Clara Maria 1924- *WhoAm 92*
Ambrus, Gyozo Laszlo 1935- *MajAI [port]*
Ambrus, Julian L. 1924- *WhoAm 92*
Ambrus, Lynda 1963- *WhoE 93*
Ambrus, Victor G. *MajAI*
Ambrusko, John Stephen 1913- *WhoSSW 93*
Ambrusko, Therese *Law&B 92*
Ambruso, Christine Strong 1951- *WhoAmW 93*
Ambruso, Kathleen Lennon 1945- *WhoAmW 93*
Ambruster, John R. 1931- *St&PR 93*
Ambruz, John F. 1955- *St&PR 93*
Ambuhl, Frank Jerrold 1925- *WhoSSW 93*
Ambuhl, Heinz 1928- *WhoScE 91-4*
Ambur, Damodar Reddy 1947- *WhoSSW 93*
Amburn, Ellis 1933- *ConAu 138*
Amcher, Jeannie Webb 1953- *WhoAmW 93*
Amdahl, Byrdelle John 1934- *WhoAm 92*
Amdahl, Douglas Kenneth 1919- *WhoAm 92*
Amdahl, Gene Myron 1922- *St&PR 93, WhoAm 92*
Amdall, William J. 1953- *St&PR 93*
Amdall, William John 1953- *WhoAm 92*
Amdrup, Erik 1923- *WhoScE 91-2*
Amdur, James A. 1936- *St&PR 93*
Amdur, James Austin 1936- *WhoAm 92*
Amdur, Neil 1939- *WhoAm 92*
Amdursky, Robert S. 1937-1990 *BioIn 17*
Amdur Small, Catherine Richardson 1963- *WhoEmL 93*
Ameche, Don 1908- *IntDcF 2-3 [port], WhoAm 92*
Ameen, Elsie Coker 1953- *WhoSSW 93*
Ameen, Lane 1923- *WhoE 93*
Ameen, Mark Joseph 1958- *WhoWrEP 92*
Ameen, Walter Louis 1907- *WhoWor 93*
Ameeri, Raschid Salim al- *BioIn 17*
Amelinckx, Frans Cyriel 1932- *WhoSSW 93*
Ameling, Christine A. 1954- *St&PR 93*
Ameling, Elly 1934- *Baker 92*
Ameling, Elly 1938- *WhoAm 92, WhoWor 93*
Amelio, Carol Lynn *Law&B 92*
Amelio, Gianni 1945- *MiSFD 9*
Amelio, Gilbert F. *BioIn 17*
Amelio, Gilbert Frank 1943- *WhoAm 92*
Amelio, Raymond Carmine 1945- *WhoE 93*
Ameller, Andre (Charles Gabriel) 1912-1990 *Baker 92*
Ameluug, Donald Eugene 1957- *St&PR 93*
Amemiya, Takeshi 1935- *WhoAm 92*
Amen, Irving 1918- *WhoAm 92*
Amen, Paul D. 1934- *St&PR 93*
Amend, A.L. 1916- *St&PR 93*
Amend, Elizabeth Ann *Law&B 92*
Amend, James Michael 1942- *WhoAm 92*
Amend, William John Conrad, Jr. 1941- *WhoAm 92*
Amende, Lynn Meridith 1950- *WhoAm 92, WhoEmL 93*
Amendola, Carl Francis 1963- *WhoE 93*
Amendola, Joseph 1920- *WhoSSW 93*
Amendola, Sal John 1948- *WhoE 93*
Amendt, Marilyn Joan 1928- *WhoAmW 93*
Amengual (-Astaburuaga), Rene 1911-1954 *Baker 92*
Amenhotep, IV, King of Egypt fl. c. 1388BC-1358BC *BioIn 17*
Ament, Mark Steven 1951- *WhoEmL 93, WhoSSW 93*
Ament, Richard 1919- *WhoAm 92*
Ament, Richard Rand 1950- *WhoEmL 93*
Amenta, Joyce Ann 1943- *WhoUN 92*
Amenta, Peter Sebastian 1927- *WhoAm 92*
Amer, Magid Hashim 1941- *WhoWor 93*
Amerasekare, Chandra 1938- *WhoUN 92*
Amerasinghe, Chittharanjan Felix 1933- *WhoWor 93*
Americanos, Petros Georghiou 1935- *WhoScE 91-4*
Americus, Robert Lear 1950- *St&PR 93*
Amerine, Anne Follette 1950- *WhoAm 92*
Amerine, Maynard Andrew 1911- *WhoAm 92*
Amerine, Terry Lee 1964- *WhoEmL 93*
Ameringer, Charles D. 1926- *WhoAm 92*
Amerman, John Ellis 1944- *WhoAm 92*
Amerman, John W. 1932- *St&PR 93, WhoAm 92*
Amerman, Lucy S.L. *Law&B 92*
Amerman, Patricia Anne 1952- *WhoAmW 93*
Amero, Jane Adams 1941- *WhoAmW 93*
Amero, Robert Clayton 1917- *WhoE 93*
Amery, Antoon 1933- *WhoScE 91-2*
Amery, Diane *WhoWrEP 92*
Ames, Adelbert, III 1921- *WhoAm 92*
Ames, Bobbie Hackney 1930- *WhoSSW 93*
Ames, Bruce N. *BioIn 17*
Ames, Bruce Nathan 1928- *WhoAm 92*
Ames, C.J. *WhoScE 91-1*
Ames, Carter S. *Law&B 92*
Ames, Cathi-Lynne 1954- *WhoAmW 93*
Ames, Charles O. 1926- *St&PR 93*
Ames, Christopher 1956- *WhoSSW 93*
Ames, Christopher Norman 1953- *WhoE 93, WhoEmL 93*
Ames, Craig L. *Law&B 92*
Ames, Craig L. 1944- *WhoAm 92*
Ames, Damaris 1944- *St&PR 93, WhoAm 92, WhoAmW 93*
Ames, David Atwater 1938- *WhoE 93*
Ames, David J. 1945- *St&PR 93*
Ames, Donald C. *Law&B 92*
Ames, Donald Paul 1922- *WhoAm 92, WhoWor 93*
Ames, E. Preston *ConTFT 10*
Ames, Evelyn Perkins 1908-1990 *BioIn 17*
Ames, Frank Anthony 1942- *WhoAm 92*
Ames, G. Ronald 1939- *WhoIns 93*
Ames, George J. 1917- *St&PR 93*
Ames, George Joseph 1917- *WhoAm 92*
Ames, George Ronald 1939- *St&PR 93, WhoAm 92*
Ames, Henry T. *Law&B 92*
Ames, J. Edward 1949- *ScF&FL 92*
Ames, James B. 1911- *St&PR 93*
Ames, James Barr 1911- *WhoAm 92*
Ames, Jimmy Ray 1951- *WhoSSW 93*
Ames, John Lewis 1912- *WhoWor 93*
Ames, Lee J. 1921- *ScF&FL 92*
Ames, Leon Kessling 1882-1936 *BiDAMSp 1989*
Ames, Lincoln 1932- *St&PR 93*

Ames, Louise Bates 1908- *ConAu 39NR, WhoAm 92, WhoE 93*
Ames, Marc L. 1943- *WhoE 93*
Ames, Marion P. d1992 *NewYTBS 92 [port]*
Ames, Marshall Howard 1944- *St&PR 93*
Ames, Mary E. Clemmer 1831-1884 *JrnUS*
Ames, Marybeth 1951- *WhoEmL 93*
Ames, Michael Allen 1944- *St&PR 93*
Ames, Michael McClean 1933- *WhoAm 92*
Ames, Mildred 1919- *ScF&FL 92*
Ames, Milton Benjamin, Jr. 1913- *WhoAm 92*
Ames, Oakes 1931- *WhoAm 92*
Ames, Oliver Filley 1920- *St&PR 93*
Ames, Patrick W. 1954- *WhoWrEP 92*
Ames, Peter John 1945- *WhoE 93*
Ames, Preston 1905-1983 *ConTFT 10*
Ames, Richard Scott 1954- *St&PR 93*
Ames, Robert Charles *Law&B 92*
Ames, Robert S. 1919- *St&PR 93*
Ames, Robert San 1919- *WhoAm 92*
Ames, Roger *BioIn 17*
Ames, Sandra Patience 1947- *WhoEmL 93*
Ames, Stanley Arthur *WhoScE 91-1*
Ames, Stanley Richard 1918- *WhoE 93*
Ames, Stephen C. 1938- *St&PR 93*
Ames, Steven Edmund 1940- *WhoWrEP 92*
Ames, Steven Reede 1951- *WhoE 93, WhoEmL 93, WhoWor 93*
Ames, Susan 1945- *WhoWor 93*
Ames, Thomas-Robert Howland 1930- *WhoE 93*
Ames, William 1576-1633 *BioIn 17*
Ames, William Clark 1950- *WhoWor 93*
Ames, William Francis 1926- *WhoAm 92*
Ames, William H. 1944- *St&PR 93*
Ames, William Harold 1944- *WhoAm 92*
Ames, Wilmer *BioIn 17*
Ames, Winslow 1907-1990 *BioIn 17*
Amestoy, Jeffrey Lee 1946- *WhoAm 92, WhoE 93*
Ames-Urie, Patricia Yvonne 1946- *WhoEmL 93*
Amethyst *WhoWrEP 92*
Amey, David Edward 1947- *WhoWrEP 92*
Amey, Lorne James 1940- *WhoAm 92*
Amey, Rae 1947- *WhoAmW 93, WhoEmL 93*
Amey, William Greenville 1918- *WhoAm 92*
Amezcua, Consuelo Gonzalez *NotHsAW 93*
Amfahr, Donald F. 1929- *St&PR 93*
Amfitheatrov, Daniele 1901-1983 *Baker 92*
Amgott, Allen E. *Law&B 92*
Amhaus, Gordon Arthur 1946- *WhoEmL 93*
Amherst, Jeffrey 1717-1797 *HarEnMi*
Amhowitz, Harris J. *Law&B 92*
Amiano, Fred A. 1945- *St&PR 93*
Amicarelli, Debra Lee 1957- *WhoEmL 93*
Amice, Carol Rizzardi 1955- *WhoAmW 93, WhoWrEP 92*
Amichai, Yehuda *BioIn 17*
Amicis, Anna Lucia de 1733-1816 *Baker 92*
Amick, Charles J. d1991 *BioIn 17*
Amick, Martin Sherman 1951- *WhoEmL 93*
Amick, Steven H. *Law&B 92*
Amick, Steven Hammond 1947- *WhoEmL 93*
Amico, Richard Joseph 1953- *WhoEmL 93*
Amiconi, Gino 1940- *WhoScE 91-3*
Amidei, Lester A., Jr. 1944- *St&PR 93*
Amidon, Roger Lyman 1938- *WhoAm 92*
Amiel, Barbara *WhoAm 92*
Amiel, C. *WhoScE 91-2*
Amiel, J.A. 1951- *WhoScE 91-2*
Amiel, Jon *MiSFD 9*
Amiel, Karen Baggett 1950- *WhoEmL 93*
Amiel, Michel *WhoScE 91-2*
Amies, Hardy 1909- *BioIn 17*
Amieva, Celso *DcMexL*
Amihai, Yehuda *BioIn 17*
Amili, Baha' al-Din Muhammad ibn al-Husayn 1547-1621 *BioIn 17*
Amill, Luis A. 1898-1990 *BioIn 17*
Amin, Hassan Mohamed 1933- *WhoUN 92*
Amin, Idi 1925- *BioIn 17*
Amin, Idi 1926- *DcTwHis*
Amin, Idi Dada 1925- *WhoAfr*
Amin, Jamillah Maarij 1947- *WhoAmW 93*
Amin, Mohamed Redha 1948- *WhoUN 92*
Amin, Mohammed 1928- *WhoAsAP 91*
Amin, Samir *BioIn 17*
Amin, Samir 1931- *WhoWor 93*
Amin, Sayed-Hassan 1948- *WhoWor 93*
Amin, Sudhir J. 1944- *St&PR 93*
Amin al-Zarb, Haj Muhammad Hassan d1898 *BioIn 17*
Amini, Bijan Khajehnouri 1943- *WhoAm 92*
Amini, Gordon C. *Law&B 92*
Amini, Majid 1935- *St&PR 93*
Amini, Mohammed Reza 1940- *WhoUN 92*
Amino, Nobuyuki 1940- *WhoWor 93*
Amin Oumee, Idi Dada 1925- *ColdWar 2 [port]*
Aminov, Yuri Achmetovich 1942- *WhoWor 93*
Aminu, Jubril *WhoWor 93*
Aminullah, Sayed Muhammad 1931- *WhoWor 93*
Amioka, Takeshi 1928- *WhoAsAP 91*
Amiot, Jean Joseph Marie 1718-1793 *Baker 92*
Amiot, Michel 1947- *WhoUN 92*
Amiotte, Arthur 1944- *BioIn 17*
Amiotte, Donald Paul 1946- *WhoEmL 93*
Amir, Dov 1924- *St&PR 93*
Amir, Gideon *MiSFD 9*
Amira, Alan J. *Law&B 92*
Amiran, Eyal Yosef 1960- *WhoSSW 93*
Amiran, MindaRae 1932- *WhoE 93*
Amirante, Gianni A. 1938- *WhoScE 91-3*
Amiri, Afsaneh 1962- *WhoEmL 93*
Amiri, Aman F. 1951- *St&PR 93*
Amirian, Carol Christine 1965- *WhoAmW 93*
Amirkhanian, Charles (Benjamin) 1945- *Baker 92*
Amir-Moez, Ali Reza 1919- *WhoSSW 93, WhoWor 93*
Amirouche, Farid M.L. 1954- *WhoEmL 93*
Amiroutzes, George c. 1400-c. 1469 *OxDcByz*
Amirov, Arif Khankishi Oglu 1952- *WhoWor 93*
Amirov, Fikret 1922-1984 *OxDcOp*
Amirov, Fikret Dzhamil 1922-1984 *Baker 92*
Amirtharajah, Appiah 1940- *WhoSSW 93*
Amis, Edward Stephen, Jr. 1941- *WhoAm 92*
Amis, Kingsley 1922- *BioIn 17, BritWr S2, MagSWL [port], ScF&FL 92, WhoAm 92, WhoWor 93*
Amis, Martin *BioIn 17*
Amis, Martin 1949- *MagSWL [port], ScF&FL 92*
Amis, Martin Louis 1949- *WhoWor 93*
Amis, William B. 1937- *St&PR 93*
Amish, Keith Warren 1923- *WhoAm 92*
Amis-Jessup, Jan 1927- *WhoSSW 93*
Amistad, Glenn Repiedad 1955- *WhoEmL 93*
Amitay, Noach 1930- *WhoAm 92*
Amitrano, Sergio 1939- *St&PR 93*
Amla, Tirath Ran 1914- *WhoAsAP 91*
Amlicke, Thos R. 1936- *St&PR 93*
Amling, Frederick 1926- *WhoAm 92*
Amling, Warren 1924- *BiDAMSp 1989*
Ammaccapane, Danielle *WhoAmW 93*
Amman, Elizabeth Jean 1941- *WhoAmW 93*
Amman, John Charles 1935- *WhoAm 92*
Ammann, Benno 1904-1986 *Baker 92*
Ammann, Klaus 1940- *WhoScE 91-4*
Ammann, Lillian Ann Nicholson 1946- *WhoSSW 93*
Ammann, Thomas 1949- *BioIn 17*
Ammann, William R. 1941- *St&PR 93*
Ammannati, Enrico Maria 1946- *WhoWor 93*
Ammar, Alex David 1951- *WhoEmL 93*
Ammar, K.A., Jr. 1933- *St&PR 93*
Ammar, Najeeb A., Jr. 1946- *St&PR 93*
Ammar, Raymond George 1932- *WhoAm 92*
Ammar, Richard Frederick 1938- *St&PR 93*
Ammarell, John S. 1920- *St&PR 93*
Ammarell, John Samuel 1920- *WhoAm 92*
Ammer, Donald Scott 1962- *WhoWrEP 92*
Ammer, Stephen D. *St&PR 93*
Ammeraal, Robert Neal 1936- *WhoWor 93*
Ammerbach, Elias Nicolaus c. 1530-1597 *Baker 92*
Ammerman, Ada Tully *AmWomPl*
Ammerman, Anthony E. 1961- *WhoSSW 93*
Ammerman, Robert Ray 1927- *WhoAm 92*
Ammerman, Robert Thompson 1959- *WhoE 93*
Ammermann, Dieter F. 1937- *WhoScE 91-3*
Ammeter, Debra A.A. *Law&B 92*
Ammeter, John Herbert 1940- *WhoScE 91-4*
Ammianus Marcellinus c. 330-c. 392 *OxDcByz*
Ammon, Harry 1917- *WhoAm 92*
Ammon, Henry J. 1934- *St&PR 93*
Ammon, Hermann Philipp Theodor 1933- *WhoWor 93*
Ammon, Tina K. 1941- *WhoAmW 93*
Ammons, A.R. 1926- *BioIn 17*
Ammons, Archie Randolph 1926- *WhoAm 92, WhoWrEP 92*
Ammons, "Jug" (Eugene) 1925-1974 *Baker 92*
Ammons, Richard Allen 1952- *WhoSSW 93*
Ammons, Robert Bruce 1920- *WhoAm 92*
Ammons, Roger L. 1950- *WhoEmL 93*
Amner, John 1579-1641 *Baker 92*
Amneus, D. A. 1919- *WhoAm 92, WhoAmW 93*
Amoako, Eric *Law&B 92*
Amochaev, Tania 1949- *St&PR 93*
Amodio, Michael P. *Law&B 92*
Amole, Warren Ralph, III 1950- *St&PR 93*
Amolsch, Arthur Lewis 1939- *WhoSSW 93*
Amon, Anton 1943- *WhoAm 92*
Amon, Arthur Howard, Jr. 1927- *WhoAm 92*
Amon, Blasius 1558-1590 *Baker 92*
Amon, Carol Bagley 1946- *WhoAm 92, WhoAmW 93*
Amon, Markus 1959- *BioIn 17*
Amon, Simeon S. *Law&B 92*
Amon, William Frederick, Jr. 1922- *WhoAm 92*
Amond, Chester D. 1926- *St&PR 93*
Amonett, Larry Earl 1952- *WhoEmL 93*
Amonkar, U. *Law&B 92*
Amon Parisi, Cristina Hortensia 1956- *WhoE 93, WhoEmL 93*
Amonson, Johanne Leslie 1949- *WhoAmW 93, WhoEmL 93*
Amo Ortega, Jose M. 1944- *WhoScE 91-3*
Amor, Anthony Roger 1945- *St&PR 93*
Amora, Aderito S. Vieira 1941- *WhoWor 93*
Amore, Ann Marie *WhoAmW 93*
Amore, Joseph Robert 1944- *St&PR 93*
Amore, Michael Joseph 1947- *WhoE 93*
Amoretti Scarcia, BiancaMaria 1938- *WhoWor 93*
Amorevoli, Angelo (Maria) 1716-1798 *Baker 92*
Amorian Dynasty *OxDcByz*
Amorim, Enrique 1900-1960 *SpAmA*
Amorkesos fl. 5th cent.- *OxDcByz*
Amornmarn, Rumpa 1946- *WhoEmL 93, WhoSSW 93*
Amoros, Sandy 1930-1992 *NewYTBS 92 [port]*
Amoroso, Alison Maria 1965- *WhoE 93*
Amoroso, Marie Dorothy 1924- *WhoAmW 93, WhoE 93, WhoWor 93*
Amoroso, Rhonda K. *Law&B 92*
Amoroso, Vincent 1947- *WhoE 93*
Amoruso, Donald Joseph 1937- *WhoE 93*
Amoruso, Marino *MiSFD 9*
Amory, Charles Reginald, Jr. 1940- *St&PR 93*
Amory, Cleveland *BioIn 17*
Amory, Cleveland 1917- *WhoAm 92, WhoWrEP 92*
Amory, Daniel 1946- *WhoEmL 93*
Amory, Joyce Wethered Heathcoat- *BioIn 17*
Amory, Mark 1941- *ScF&FL 92*
Amory, Robert F. 1945- *St&PR 93*
Amory, Thomas Carhart 1933- *WhoAm 92*
Amos *BioIn 17*
Amos, Archie L., Jr. *AfrAmBi [port]*
Amos, Betty Ann 1948- *WhoAmW 93, WhoEmL 93*
Amos, Betty Giles 1941- *WhoSSW 93*
Amos, Charles Weldon 1922- *St&PR 93*
Amos, Christine Wilkens 1961- *WhoSSW 93*
Amos, Daniel Paul 1951- *St&PR 93, WhoSSW 93*
Amos, Dennis B. 1923- *WhoAm 92*
Amos, Harton Douglas 1943- *WhoIns 93*
Amos, James Lysle 1929- *WhoAm 92*
Amos, Janette Garbee 1940- *WhoAmW 93*
Amos, Janice Rae 1953- *WhoEmL 93*
Amos, Jerry W. *Law&B 92*
Amos, John 1941- *WhoAm 92*
Amos, Kent *BioIn 17*
Amos, Larry Charles *Law&B 92*
Amos, Larry Charles 1935- *WhoAm 92*
Amos, Paul Shelby 1926- *WhoAm 92, WhoSSW 93*
Amos, Timothy Franklin 1955- *WhoEmL 93*
Amos, Tori *WhoAmW 93*
Amos, Wally *BioIn 17*
Amos, Wray McMichael, Jr. 1958- *St&PR 93*
Amoss, Benjamin McRae, Jr. 1960- *ConAu 139*
Amoss, Berthe (Marks) 1925- *DcAmChF 1960*
Amoss, Walter James, Jr. 1924- *St&PR 93*
Amoss, Walter James, III 1947- *WhoAm 92, WhoSSW 93*
Amo-Sunkwa, Emmanuel 1962- *WhoWor 93*
Amouroux, Jacques Eugene 1941- *WhoScE 91-2*
Amoyal, Pierre 1949- *Baker 92*
Amparado, Keith D. 1952- *WhoE 93, WhoEmL 93, WhoWor 93*
Ampel, Frederick Jared 1947- *WhoEmL 93*
Ampel, Leon Louis 1936- *WhoAm 92*
Amper, Leslie Ruth 1954- *WhoEmL 93*
Amphilochios of Ikonion c. 340-c. 394 *OxDcByz*
Ampitiya-Nandalal, Hemalie Kalpalatha 1961- *WhoWor 93*
Ampola, Massimo Filippo 1944- *WhoWor 93*
Amprimoz, Alexandre L. 1948- *ScF&FL 92, WhoCanL 92*
Ampthill, Baron 1829-1884 *BioIn 17*
'Amr c. 575-664 *OxDcByz*
Amram, David Werner 1930- *WhoAm 92*
Amram, David (Werner, III) 1930- *Baker 92*
Amram, Philip W. *BioIn 17*
Amram, Raphi *BioIn 17*
Amram, Robert 1930- *MiSFD 9*
Amrhein, Christine B. *Law&B 92*
Amrhein, Mark J. *Law&B 92*
Amrhein, Nikolaus 1942- *WhoScE 91-4*
Amr Ibn Al-As c. 585-664 *HarEnMi*
Amrine, Danny Andrew 1951- *WhoEmL 93*
Amrita Pritam 1919- *BioIn 17*
Amrod, Paul Joseph 1926- *WhoE 93*
Amron, Alan 1948- *St&PR 93*
Amron, Irving 1921- *WhoE 93*
Amsbaugh, Judith 1933- *WhoAmW 93*
Amsden, Ted Thomas 1950- *WhoEmL 93*
Amsel, Abram 1922- *WhoAm 92*
Amsel, Robert Gary 1957- *WhoEmL 93*
Amsel, Steve David 1950- *WhoAm 92*
Amsler, Joseph William, Jr. 1954- *WhoE 93*
Amspaugh, Jerry L. 1931- *St&PR 93*
Amspoker, James Mack 1926- *WhoAm 92*
Amstadter, Laurence 1922- *St&PR 93, WhoAm 92*
Amster, Linda 1938- *WhoWrEP 92*
Amster, Linda Evelyn 1938- *WhoAm 92*
Amster, Robert A. *Law&B 92*
Amsterdam, Adam D. *Law&B 92*
Amsterdam, Anthony Guy 1935- *WhoAm 92*
Amsterdam, Bernard 1904-1991 *BioIn 17*
Amstutz, Arnold Everet 1936- *St&PR 93*
Amstutz, Daniel Gordon 1932- *WhoAm 92*
Amstutz, G. Christian *WhoScE 91-3*
Amstutz, Gary Paul 1955- *WhoEmL 93*
Amstutz, Harold Emerson 1919- *WhoAm 92*
Amstuz, Eric *Law&B 92*
Amter, Robert Frederick 1938- *St&PR 93*
Amthor, Carl Burleigh 1934- *St&PR 93*
Amthor, Terry K. *ScF&FL 92*
Amtmann, James S. 1947- *St&PR 93*
Amtoft-Nielsen, Joan Theresa 1940- *WhoAmW 93, WhoSSW 93, WhoWor 93*
Amuah, Maki Mandela- *BioIn 17*
Amua-Sekyi, E.T. 1957- *St&PR 93*
Amuleru-Marshall, Nancy Richardson 1949- *WhoSSW 93*
Amunategui, Juan 1938- *WhoUN 92*
Amundrud, John K. *Law&B 92*
Amundsen, Arthur L. d1990 *BioIn 17*
Amundsen, Roald 1872-1928 *BioIn 17, ConHero 2 [port], Expl 93 [port]*
Amundsen, Tore 1934- *WhoScE 91-4*
Amundson, Clyde Howard 1927- *WhoAm 92*
Amundson, Gary Robert 1949- *St&PR 93*
Amundson, John Melvin, Jr. 1926- *WhoAm 92*
Amundson, Judith Louise Allison 1921- *WhoSSW 93*
Amundson, Kurt E. *St&PR 93*
Amundson, Neal Russell 1916- *WhoAm 92*
Amundson, Patricia W. 1957- *St&PR 93*
Amundson, Robert A. *WhoAm 92*
Amundson, Roger Keith 1946- *St&PR 93*
Amurri, Franco 1958- *MiSFD 9*
Amy, Gilbert 1936- *Baker 92*
Amy, Jonathan Weekes 1923- *WhoAm 92*
Amylon, Michael David 1950- *WhoAm 92*
Amy-Moreno de Toro, Angel Alberto 1945- *WhoE 93*
Amyot, Genevieve 1945- *WhoCanL 92*
Amyotte, Sherry Jo 1956- *WhoAmW 93*
Amyx, Darrell Arlynn 1911- *WhoAm 92*
Amzar, Gheorghe N. 1938- *WhoScE 91-4*
An, Pham Xuan *BioIn 17*
Anable, Anne Currier Steinert *WhoAmW 93*
Anable, David John 1939- *WhoE 93*

Anacker, August Ferdinand 1790-1854 *Baker 92*
Anacker, George E. 1923- *St&PR 93*
Anacleto, Luis Manuel Pinguinha 1941- *WhoWor 93*
Anadon, A. 1946- *WhoScE 91-3*
Anaebonam, Aloysius Onyeabo 1955- *WhoWor 93*
Anagnost, Maria Athena 1943- *WhoAm 92, WhoAmW 93*
Anagnostakes, Manoles 1925- *BioIn 17*
Anagnostes, John *OxDcByz*
Anagnosti, Dhimiter 1936- *DrEEuF*
Anagnosti, Petar 1934- *WhoScE 91-4*
Anagnostopoulos, Augoustinos 1934- *WhoScE 91-3*
Anagnostopoulos, Constantine E. 1922- *St&PR 93*
Anagnostopoulos, Constantine Emmanuel 1922- *WhoAm 92*
Anagnostopoulos, Constantine Nicholas 1944- *WhoE 93*
Anagnostopoulos, George 1962- *WhoWor 93*
Anagnostopoulos, Stavros Aristidou 1946- *WhoWor 93*
Anagnostopoulos, Takis 1936- *WhoScE 91-2*
Anam, Abul Mohasin Mohammad 1944- *WhoWor 93*
Anami Korechika 1887-1945 *HarEnMi*
Anamosa, Martha *Law&B 92*
Anand, C.J. 1956- *St&PR 93*
Anand, Dev 1923- *IntDcF 2-3 [port]*
Anand, Mulk Raj 1905- *BioIn 17, IntLitE*
Anand, Suresh Chandra 1931- *WhoAm 92, WhoWor 93*
Anandam, Kamala 1929- *WhoAmW 93*
Anand Panyarachun *BioIn 17*
Anand Singh 1939- *WhoAsAP 91*
Anania, Joseph V. *BioIn 17*
Anania, Michael *BioIn 17*
Anania, Michael Angelo 1939- *WhoWrEP 92*
Anania, William Christian 1958- *WhoE 93*
Ananian, Joyce Lucille 1948- *WhoE 93*
Ananias of Sirak fl. 7th cent.- *OxDcByz*
Ananthanarayanan, Venkataraman 1936- *WhoSSW 93*
Anantharam, Venkat 1960- *WhoEmL 93*
Anantharaman, A. 1938- *St&PR 93*
Anaouil, Louise 1953- *WhoCanL 92*
Anaporte-Easton, Jean Boehlke 1942- *WhoWrEP 92*
Anargirou, Pauline 1958- *WhoEmL 93*
Anargyros, Spero 1915- *WhoAm 92*
Anas, Azwar 1931- *WhoAsAP 91*
Anas, Julianne Kay 1941- *WhoAmW 93*
Anast, David George 1955- *WhoEmL 93*
Anastanio, Anthony J. *WhoIns 93*
Anastas, Terrence Joseph 1958- *WhoEmL 93*
Anastasatu, Constantin 1917- *WhoScE 91-4*
Anastasi, Anne 1908- *BioIn 17, WhoAm 92, WhoAmW 93, WhoE 93*
Anastasiia Nikolaevna, Grand Duchess 1901-1918 *BioIn 17*
Anastasijevic, Vojin 1928- *WhoScE 91-4*
Anastasio, James 1930- *St&PR 93, WhoIns 93*
Anastasio, Louis N. 1944- *St&PR 93*
Anastasios fl. 730-754 *OxDcByz*
Anastasios, I d598 *OxDcByz*
Anastasios, I c. 430-518 *OxDcByz*
Anastasios, II d719 *OxDcByz*
Anastasios of Sinai dc. 700 *OxDcByz*
Anastasius Bibliothecarius c. 800-c. 879 *OxDcByz*
Anastasopoulos, John Nicholas 1946- *WhoWor 93*
Anastasopoulou, Maria 1944- *WhoWor 93*
Anastassakis, Evangelos M. 1938- *WhoScE 91-3*
Anastassakis, Evangelos Manthos 1938- *WhoWor 93*
Anastassiou, Effie F. *Law&B 92*
Anastassov, Ivan 1941- *WhoUN 92*
Anastole, Dorothy Jean 1932- *WhoAmW 93*
Anastos, Andrea L. *ScF&FL 92*
Anastos, Peter *BioIn 17*
Anastos, Rosemary Park 1907- *WhoAm 92*
Anatol, Karl W. E. *WhoAm 92*
Anatolios *OxDcByz*
Anaukpetlun d1628 *HarEnMi*
Anawati, Joseph Soliman 1941- *WhoWor 93*
Anawrahta d1077 *HarEnMi*
Anaya, Herbert *DcCPCAm*
Anaya, Jose Vicente 1947- *DcMexL*
Anaya, Richard Alfred, Jr. 1932- *WhoAm 92*
Anaya, Rudolfo 1937- *IntvWPC 92 [port]*
Anaya, Rudolfo A. *BioIn 17*
Anaya, Rudolfo A. 1937- *HispAmA, WhoWrEP 92*
Anaya, Toney 1941- *HispAmA*
Anaya B., Alfonso 1926- *DcMexL*
Anaya Montes, Melida *DcCPCAm*
Anazagasty, Anita Dolores 1944- *WhoWrEP 92*
Anazagasty, Maria Louisa 1950- *WhoEmL 93*
Anbar, Michael 1927- *WhoAm 92*
Anceau, Christine 1962- *WhoScE 91-2*
Ancel, Richard J. *Law&B 92*
Ancell, Nathan S. 1908- *WhoAm 92*
Ancerl, Karel 1908-1973 *Baker 92*
Ances, I. George 1935- *WhoAm 92, WhoE 93*
Anchel, Edward 1939- *St&PR 93*
Ancheta, Bart D. 1927- *St&PR 93*
Anchieta, Juan de 1462-1523 *Baker 92*
Anchin, David C. d1990 *BioIn 17*
Anchlia, Than Mal 1918- *WhoE 93*
Anciaux, Jean 1930- *WhoAsAP 91*
Ancier, Garth *BioIn 17*
Ancina, Giovenale 1545-1604 *Baker 92*
Ancizar-Sordo, Jorge 1908- *WhoWor 93*
Ancker-Johnson, Betsy 1927- *St&PR 93, WhoAm 92, WhoAmW 93*
Ancker-Johnson, Betsy 1929- *BioIn 17*
Anckner, Joseph Edward 1932- *St&PR 93*
Anclien, Jeffrey J. 1961- *St&PR 93*
Ancoli-Israel, Sonia 1951- *WhoEmL 93*
Ancona, Alessandro D' *IntDcAn*
Ancona, Barry 1948- *WhoAm 92*
Ancona, Eligio 1835-1893 *DcMexL*
Ancona, George Ephraim 1929- *WhoAm 92*
Ancona, Joseph I. 1924- *St&PR 93*
Ancona, Leonardo A.D. 1922- *WhoScE 91-3*
Ancona, Mario 1860-1931 *Baker 92*
Ancona, Michael Joseph 1948- *St&PR 93*
Ancona, Sam A. 1922- *St&PR 93*
Ancot *Baker 92*
Ancot, Jean 1779-1848 *Baker 92*
Ancot, Jean 1799-1829 *Baker 92*
Ancot, Louis 1803-1836 *Baker 92*
Ancrum, Cheryl Denise 1958- *WhoAmW 93, WhoEmL 93*
Ancuta, Kathleen Madeline 1953- *WhoAm 92, WhoAmW 93*
Ancy, Richard A. 1936- *St&PR 93*
Anczyc, Wladyslaw 1823-1883 *PolBiDi*
Anda, Geza 1921-1976 *Baker 92*
Anda, Jose Guadalupe de 1880-1950 *DcMexL*
Andac, S. Orhan 1929- *WhoScE 91-4*
Andal, Marian *WhoWrEP 92*
Andaloro, John J. 1956- *St&PR 93*
Andaloro, John Joseph 1956- *WhoEmL 93*
Andary, Raymond 1937- *WhoUN 92*
Andaya, Rolando R. 1937- *WhoAsAP 91*
Andelson, Robert Vernon 1931- *WhoAm 92, WhoSSW 93*
Andelson, Sherman L. 1925- *St&PR 93*
Andemicael, Berhanykun 1935- *WhoUN 92*
Andemicael, Iassu 1933- *WhoUN 92*
Anden, Nils-Erik 1937- *WhoScE 91-4*
Andera, Katherine Anne 1949- *WhoEmL 93*
Anderberg, Carl-Olof 1914-1972 *Baker 92*
Anderberg, Edward C. 1918-1992 *BioIn 17*
Anderberg, Lorraine Jensen 1939- *St&PR 93*
Anderberg, Roy Anthony 1921- *WhoWor 93*
Anderberg, Russell Frank, III 1938- *St&PR 93*
Anderberg, Torgny *MiSFD 9*
Anderca, Constantin 1926- *WhoScE 91-4*
Anderegg, George Francis, Jr. 1937- *WhoAm 92*
Anderegg, John Swift, Jr. 1924- *St&PR 93*
Anderegg, Karen Klok *WhoAm 92*
Anderegg, Karen Klok 1940- *ConAu 137, WhoWrEP 92*
Anderegg, Robert G. *Law&B 92*
Anderer, Friedrich Alfred 1926- *WhoScE 91-3, WhoWor 93*
Anderer, Joseph Henry 1924- *WhoAm 92*
Anderhalter, Oliver Frank 1922- *WhoAm 92*
an der Heiden, Wulf-Uwe 1942- *WhoWor 93*
Anderko, Kurt P. 1926- *WhoScE 91-3*
Anderla, Georges Jiri 1921- *WhoWor 93*
Anderluh, John Russell 1934- *WhoAm 92*
Andermann, Greg *WhoEmL 93*
Anders, Agnetha *ScF&FL 92*
Anders, Allison *MiSFD 9*
Anders, Arthur Fretz, III 1948- *WhoE 93*
Anders, Catherine 1953- *St&PR 93*
Anders, Edward 1926- *WhoAm 92*
Anders, Geoffrey Taylor 1950- *WhoE 93*
Anders, Howard G. 1943- *St&PR 93*
Anders, Jeanne *WhoWrEP 92*
Anders, Mark Leslie 1955- *WhoEmL 93*
Anders, Max Eugene 1947- *WhoSSW 93*
Anders, Merry 1932?- *SweetSg D [port]*
Anders, Nedda Casson d1991 *BioIn 17*
Anders, Peter 1908-1954 *Baker 92, IntDcOp, OxDcOp*
Anders, Sarah Frances 1927- *WhoAmW 93*
Anders, Thomas L. *Law&B 92*
Anders, Wieslaw 1933- *WhoScE 91-4*
Anders, William Alison 1933- *WhoAm 92*
Anders, Wladyslaw 1892-1970 *PolBiDi*
Anders, Wolfhart Hermann 1941- *WhoWor 93*
Andersch, Alfred 1914-1980 *BioIn 17, ConAu 37NR*
Andersdatter, Karla M. 1938- *WhoWrEP 92*
Andersen, Adda Husted- *BioIn 17*
Andersen, Alf R. *Law&B 92*
Andersen, Arna Jacob 1923- *WhoScE 91-2*
Andersen, Arne Skytt 1931- *WhoWor 93*
Andersen, Bill Byron 1936- *WhoAm 92*
Andersen, Burton Robert 1932- *WhoAm 92*
Andersen, Carsten Steen 1943- *St&PR 93, WhoAm 92*
Andersen, Christian Bjorn *WhoScE 91-2*
Andersen, Dale Gordon 1933- *WhoAm 92*
Andersen, Daniel 1929- *WhoScE 91-2*
Andersen, Daniel Johannes 1909- *WhoAm 92*
Andersen, Darian *Law&B 92*
Andersen, David Christian 1948- *WhoSSW 93*
Andersen, David Lee 1951- *WhoEmL 93*
Andersen, David S. *Law&B 92*
Andersen, Donald Edward 1923- *WhoAm 92*
Andersen, Doris 1909- *DcChlFi, WhoCanL 92*
Andersen, Doris Evelyn 1923- *WhoAmW 93, WhoWor 93*
Andersen, Elmer Lee 1909- *WhoAm 92*
Andersen, Flemming Allan 1925- *WhoScE 91-2*
Andersen, Frank Angelius 1953- *WhoWor 93*
Andersen, Frank N. *St&PR 93*
Andersen, Gordon Walter 1934- *St&PR 93*
Andersen, H.A. 1939- *WhoScE 91-2*
Andersen, H. Verlan d1992 *NewYTBS 92*
Andersen, Hans 1805-1875 *OxDcOp*
Andersen, Hans Christian 1805-1875 *BioIn 17, MajAI [port], WorLitC [port]*
Andersen, Hans Christian 1941- *WhoAm 92*
Andersen, Hans Henrik 1937- *WhoScE 91-2, WhoWor 93*
Andersen, Harold R. 1945- *St&PR 93*
Andersen, Harold Wayne 1923- *WhoAm 92*
Andersen, Helge 1929- *WhoScE 91-2*
Andersen, Henning 1934- *WhoAm 92*
Andersen, Henning Haahr 1950- *WhoWor 93*
Andersen, Henrik Joergen 1960- *WhoWor 93*
Andersen, Ib H.P. 1936- *WhoScE 91-2*
Andersen, Ib Steen 1954- *WhoAm 92*
Andersen, James A. 1924- *WhoAm 92*
Andersen, Jan 1945- *WhoWor 93*
Andersen, Janet Linda 1947- *WhoE 93*
Andersen, (Carl) Joachim 1847-1909 *Baker 92*
Andersen, John *BioIn 17*
Andersen, Jorgen *WhoScE 91-2*
Andersen, Juel 1923- *WhoWrEP 92*
Andersen, Karl August 1903-1970 *Baker 92*
Andersen, Karl Terpager 1937- *WhoScE 91-2*
Andersen, Karsten 1920- *Baker 92*
Andersen, Katherine L. *Law&B 92, St&PR 93*
Andersen, Kay *Law&B 92*
Andersen, Kenneth A. 1934- *St&PR 93*
Andersen, Kenneth Benjamin 1905- *WhoAm 92*
Andersen, Kenneth Eldon 1933- *WhoAm 92*
Andersen, Kenneth Joseph 1936- *WhoE 93*
Andersen, Kenneth Kaae 1934- *WhoE 93*
Andersen, Kent Tucker 1942- *WhoAm 92, WhoE 93, WhoWor 93*
Andersen, Kurt 1954- *WhoWrEP 92*
Andersen, Laird Bryce 1928- *WhoAm 92*
Andersen, Lee Dixon 1952- *WhoEmL 93*
Andersen, Leif Percival 1951- *WhoWor 93*
Andersen, Luba 1945- *WhoAmW 93*
Andersen, M. Rita *St&PR 93*
Andersen, Marianne Singer *WhoAmW 93, WhoE 93*
Andersen, Mark Gerald 1959- *WhoEmL 93*
Andersen, Mary Schwartz 1953- *WhoEmL 93*
Andersen, Mathias N. 1958- *WhoScE 91-2*
Andersen, Mogens 1916- *WhoWor 93*
Andersen, Morten 1960- *WhoAm 92*
Andersen, Ole Bedsted *WhoScE 91-2*
Andersen, Olivia Donaldson Cushing 1871- *AmWomPl*
Andersen, Paul Kent 1948- *WhoWor 93*
Andersen, Peder 1952- *WhoWor 93*
Andersen, Per O. 1930- *WhoScE 91-4*
Andersen, Raymond John 1947- *WhoAm 92*
Andersen, Rene 1946- *WhoE 93*
Andersen, Richard 1946- *WhoWrEP 92*
Andersen, Richard Arnold 1946- *WhoAm 92*
Andersen, Richard Esten 1957- *WhoE 93, WhoEmL 93*
Andersen, Richard Lee 1948- *WhoWor 93*
Andersen, Robert Allen 1936- *WhoAm 92*
Andersen, Robert L. *Law&B 92*
Andersen, Ronald Max 1939- *WhoAm 92*
Andersen, Roy Stuart 1921- *WhoE 93*
Andersen, Sheree Hilton 1954- *WhoEmL 93*
Andersen, Shirley Anne 1942- *WhoAmW 93*
Andersen, Steve Richard 1946- *WhoEmL 93, WhoSSW 93*
Andersen, Susan Marie *WhoAmW 93*
Andersen, Tage 1927- *WhoWor 93*
Andersen, Thomas Edward 1952- *St&PR 93*
Andersen, Torgeir Bjorge 1952- *WhoScE 91-4*
Andersen, Torkild 1934- *WhoScE 91-2*
Andersen, Vagn 1929- *WhoAm 92*
Andersen, Warren G. *Law&B 92*
Andersen, Wayne Vesti 1930- *WhoWor 93*
Andersen Karlsson, Eva Elisabeth 1948- *WhoWor 93*
Andersin, Hans E. 1930- *WhoScE 91-4*
Andersland, Orlando Baldwin 1929- *WhoAm 92*
Anderson, A. Elaine 1950- *St&PR 93*
Anderson, A. Helen *AmWomPl*
Anderson, A.J. *Law&B 92*
Anderson, A. Laurie *Law&B 92*
Anderson, Adelaide Mary 1863-1936 *BioIn 17*
Anderson, Adele Konkel 1949- *WhoEmL 93*
Anderson, Alan Brauer 1934- *WhoSSW 93*
Anderson, Alan Julian 1953- *WhoSSW 93*
Anderson, Alan Marshall 1955- *WhoEmL 93*
Anderson, Alan Patrick *WhoScE 91-1*
Anderson, Alan R. 1935- *WhoAm 92*
Anderson, Alan Reinold 1949- *WhoE 93*
Anderson, Alan Stewert 1948- *WhoE 93*
Anderson, Albert Esten 1921- *St&PR 93, WhoAm 92*
Anderson, Albert M., Jr. 1935- *St&PR 93*
Anderson, Alexa Johanna 1961- *WhoE 93*
Anderson, Alexander M. *WhoAm 92*
Anderson, Alexandra C. 1942- *WhoAm 92, WhoWrEP 92*
Anderson, Alfred Oliver 1928- *WhoE 93, WhoWor 93*
Anderson, Alice Jane 1947- *WhoEmL 93*
Anderson, Allamay Eudoris 1933- *WhoAmW 93, WhoE 93*
Anderson, Allan Crosby 1932- *WhoAm 92*
Anderson, Allen Joel 1941- *WhoScE 91-4*
Anderson, Alvin E. 1943- *WhoIns 93*
Anderson, Andre Nelson 1964- *WhoSSW 93*
Anderson, Andrew Edwin 1940- *St&PR 93*
Anderson, Andrew Herbert 1928- *WhoAm 92*
Anderson, Andy *MiSFD 9*
Anderson, Ann 1952- *WhoAmW 93*
Anderson, Anna R. 1948- *St&PR 93*
Anderson, Anne Victoria 1958- *WhoAmW 93*
Anderson, Annethea Elizabeth 1932- *WhoWrEP 92*
Anderson, Ansel Cochran 1933- *WhoAm 92*
Anderson, Arlo C. 1932- *WhoE 93*
Anderson, Armour Axil 1920- *St&PR 93*
Anderson, Arnold S. 1934-1991 *BioIn 17*
Anderson, Arthur Allan 1939- *WhoAm 92*
Anderson, Arthur G., Jr. 1918- *WhoAm 92*
Anderson, Arthur George 1926- *WhoAm 92*
Anderson, Arthur N. 1912- *WhoAm 92*
Anderson, Arthur Roland 1910- *WhoAm 92*
Anderson, Arthur Salzner 1923- *WhoAm 92*
Anderson, Arthur W. 1938- *St&PR 93*
Anderson, Aubrey Lee 1940- *WhoAm 92*
Anderson, Austin Corbin, III 1965- *WhoE 93*
Anderson, Austin Gilman *WhoAm 92*
Anderson, Austin Gilman 1942- *St&PR 93*
Anderson, Austin Gothard 1931- *WhoAm 92*
Anderson, Barbara C. *Law&B 92*
Anderson, Barbara H. *Law&B 92*

Anderson, Barbara Ina 1941- *WhoAmW 93*
Anderson, Barbara Louise 1951- *WhoAmW 93*
Anderson, Belinda Childress 1954- *WhoAmW 93*
Anderson, Benard Harold 1935- *WhoAm 92*
Anderson, Bernard E. *WhoE 93*
Anderson, Beth 1950- *Baker 92, BioIn 17, WhoEmL 93*
Anderson, Betty *ScF&FL 92*
Anderson, Beverly Jo 1953- *WhoAmW 93*
Anderson, Bill *BioIn 17*
Anderson, Blair Richard 1953- *WhoEmL 93*
Anderson, Bob 1932- *WhoWor 93*
Anderson, Bradford Paul *Law&B 92*
Anderson, Bradford William 1956- *WhoEmL 93, WhoWor 93*
Anderson, Bradley Jay 1924- *WhoAm 92*
Anderson, Brian E. 1944- *WhoWrEP 92*
Anderson, Brian L. 1952- *WhoIns 93*
Anderson, Brian R. *WhoScE 91-1*
Anderson, Brian Thomas 1957- *WhoEmL 93*
Anderson, Brierly W. 1932- *St&PR 93*
Anderson, Brocke *WhoWrEP 92*
Anderson, Broncho Billy 1882?-1971 *BioIn 17*
Anderson, Brooke 1939- *St&PR 93*
Anderson, Bruce Kenneth 1943- *WhoE 93*
Anderson, Bruce Morgan 1941- *WhoE 93, WhoWor 93*
Anderson, Bruce Paige 1952- *WhoSSW 93*
Anderson, Bruce Stanley 1952- *WhoEmL 93*
Anderson, Bryce Otis 1936- *WhoE 93*
Anderson, Buist Murfee 1904- *WhoAm 92*
Anderson, Burnside E., III *Law&B 92*
Anderson, Byron Edward 1954- *WhoEmL 93*
Anderson, C. Arnold 1907-1990 *BioIn 17*
Anderson, C. C. *SmATA 72*
Anderson, C.H. *St&PR 93*
Anderson, C. Leonard 1946- *WhoEmL 93*
Anderson, C. Merton 1927- *St&PR 93*
Anderson, C. Robert *Law&B 92*
Anderson, Carl 1905-1991 *AnObit 1991*
Anderson, Carl B. 1922- *St&PR 93*
Anderson, Carl David 1905-1991 *BioIn 17*
Anderson, Carl H. 1938- *St&PR 93*
Anderson, Carl L. 1942- *St&PR 93*
Anderson, Carl Victor 1942- *WhoSSW 93*
Anderson, Carla Lee 1930- *WhoAmW 93*
Anderson, Carol Leslie 1963- *WhoAmW 93*
Anderson, Carol Louise 1943- *WhoAmW 93*
Anderson, Carol Lynn 1952- *WhoEmL 93*
Anderson, Carol McMillan 1938- *WhoAm 92, WhoAmW 93*
Anderson, Carol Patricia 1946- *WhoAmW 93, WhoEmL 93*
Anderson, Carole Ann 1938- *WhoAm 92, WhoAmW 93*
Anderson, Carole Lewis 1944- *WhoAm 92*
Anderson, Carolyn Jennings 1913- *WhoAm 92*
Anderson, Carolyn Joyce 1947- *WhoEmL 93*
Anderson, Carroll Norlin 1924- *WhoSSW 93*
Anderson, Carson Anthony 1951- *WhoEmL 93*
Anderson, "Cat" (William Alonzo) 1916-1981 *Baker 92*
Anderson, Catherine A. 1946- *St&PR 93*
Anderson, Catherine Agnes 1946- *WhoEmL 93*
Anderson, Catherine Baker 1947- *WhoAmW 93*
Anderson, Catherine C. *SmATA 72*
Anderson, Catherine Corley 1909- *SmATA 72 [port]*
Anderson, Catherine M. 1937- *WhoAmW 93*
Anderson, Cathy C. *Law&B 92*
Anderson, Cathy Jean 1953- *WhoAmW 93*
Anderson, Charlene Marie 1952- *WhoEmL 93*
Anderson, Charles Albert 1932- *WhoAm 92*
Anderson, Charles Arnold 1907-1990 *BioIn 17*
Anderson, Charles Arthur 1917- *WhoAm 92*
Anderson, Charles Bernard 1938- *WhoAm 92*
Anderson, Charles D. 1931- *St&PR 93*
Anderson, Charles Edward 1946- *WhoSSW 93*
Anderson, Charles Lester 1960- *WhoEmL 93*
Anderson, Charles Mc Kenna 1933- *St&PR 93*
Anderson, Charles R. S. 1927- *WhoAm 92*
Anderson, Charles Ralph Seibold 1927- *St&PR 93*
Anderson, Charles Roberts 1902- *WhoAm 92*
Anderson, Charles Ross 1937- *WhoWor 93*
Anderson, Charles S. *St&PR 93*
Anderson, Charles S. 1930- *WhoAm 92*
Anderson, Charles W., Jr. 1907-1960 *EncAACR*
Anderson, Charles W., III *Law&B 92*
Anderson, Charles William 1934- *WhoAm 92*
Anderson, Cherine Esperanza 1964- *WhoAmW 93*
Anderson, Cheryl Diane 1954- *WhoAmW 93*
Anderson, Chester 1932-1991 *ScF&FL 92*
Anderson, Chester Grant 1923- *WhoAm 92*
Anderson, Christina Edith *WhoAmW 93*
Anderson, Christine *Law&B 92*
Anderson, Christine Marlene 1947- *WhoAm 92*
Anderson, Christine Pidgeon 1955- *WhoEmL 93*
Anderson, Christine Ruth Minton 1951- *WhoEmL 93*
Anderson, Christopher James 1950- *WhoEmL 93*
Anderson, Cindy *BioIn 17*
Anderson, Claudia Jeanne 1955- *WhoSSW 93*
Anderson, Clifford Hugo 1924- *WhoE 93*
Anderson, Clifford I. 1937- *St&PR 93*
Anderson, Clifton Einar 1923- *WhoWor 93*
Anderson, Clyde Eugene 1923- *St&PR 93*
Anderson, Colin 1904-1980 *ScF&FL 92*
Anderson, Constance Powell *AmWomPl*
Anderson, Court Olof 1942- *St&PR 93*
Anderson, Craig A. *Law&B 92*
Anderson, Craig Alan 1955- *WhoEmL 93*
Anderson, Craig Earl 1941- *WhoAm 92*
Anderson, Craig Edgar 1947- *WhoEmL 93*
Anderson, Craig Lester 1950- *St&PR 93*
Anderson, Craig W. 1945- *ScF&FL 92*
Anderson, Cromwell Adair 1926- *WhoAm 92*
Anderson, Curtiss Martin 1928- *WhoWrEP 92*
Anderson, Cynthia Finkbeiner Sjoberg 1949- *WhoAm 92, WhoAmW 93*
Anderson, Cynthia Harvey 1950- *WhoE 93*
Anderson, D. Kent 1941- *St&PR 93*
Anderson, Dale *WhoWrEP 92*
Anderson, Dale 1933- *WhoAm 92*
Anderson, Dale Arden 1936- *WhoAm 92, WhoSSW 93*
Anderson, Dale Kenneth 1922- *WhoAm 92*
Anderson, Dan Charles 1945- *St&PR 93*
Anderson, Daniel P. 1952- *St&PR 93*
Anderson, Daniel T. *Law&B 92*
Anderson, Daniel William 1960- *WhoAm 92*
Anderson, Danita Ruth 1956- *WhoEmL 93*
Anderson, Darel Burton 1927- *WhoAm 92*
Anderson, Darla R. *Law&B 92*
Anderson, Darlene Yvonne 1953- *WhoEmL 93*
Anderson, Darrell Edward 1932- *WhoAm 92*
Anderson, Darryl Kent 1941- *WhoAm 92*
Anderson, Daryl *WhoAm 92*
Anderson, Dave *BioIn 17*
Anderson, David *BioIn 17*
Anderson, David 1937- *WhoAm 92*
Anderson, David B. *Law&B 92*
Anderson, David B. 1942- *St&PR 93*
Anderson, David Boyd 1942- *WhoAm 92*
Anderson, David Carlson 1948- *WhoSSW 93*
Anderson, David Charles 1931- *WhoWrEP 92*
Anderson, David Coussmaker *WhoScE 91-1*
Anderson, David Coussmaker 1940- *WhoWor 93*
Anderson, David Daniel 1924- *WhoAm 92, WhoWor 93*
Anderson, David E. *WhoAm 92*
Anderson, David Fenimore 1948- *WhoSSW 93*
Anderson, David Franklin 1926- *WhoIns 93*
Anderson, David G. *Law&B 92*
Anderson, David George 1951- *WhoEmL 93*
Anderson, David Gilroy 1930- *WhoAm 92, WhoE 93*
Anderson, David Harold, Jr. 1948- *St&PR 93*
Anderson, David Hugh Tweed 1931- *WhoWor 93*
Anderson, David J. 1949- *St&PR 93*
Anderson, David John 1943- *St&PR 93*
Anderson, David Laron 1955- *St&PR 93*
Anderson, David Lawrence 1948- *WhoAm 92, WhoEmL 93*
Anderson, David Lee 1953- *WhoEmL 93*
Anderson, David Lloyd 1935- *WhoAm 92*
Anderson, David Martin 1930- *WhoE 93*
Anderson, David Osborne 1955- *WhoEmL 93*
Anderson, David Poole 1929- *BiDAMSp 1989, WhoAm 92, WhoWrEP 92*
Anderson, David Prewitt 1934- *WhoAm 92*
Anderson, David R. *Law&B 92*
Anderson, David R. 1952- *WhoSSW 93*
Anderson, David Ralph 1946- *WhoEmL 93*
Anderson, David Trevor 1938- *WhoAm 92*
Anderson, David Turpeau 1942- *WhoAm 92*
Anderson, David W. *Law&B 92*
Anderson, David William *Law&B 92*
Anderson, Davin Charles 1955- *WhoEmL 93, WhoWor 93*
Anderson, Dawn Davis 1956- *WhoSSW 93*
Anderson, Dawn Renee 1962- *WhoEmL 93*
Anderson, Dayle L. *Law&B 92*
Anderson, Dean *St&PR 93*
Anderson, Dean William 1946- *WhoAm 92, WhoE 93*
Anderson, Deborah Ann 1950- *WhoAmW 93*
Anderson, Deborah Eason 1961- *WhoAmW 93*
Anderson, Deborah L. *Law&B 92*
Anderson, Debra Lee 1958- *WhoAmW 93*
Anderson, Delores Faye 1936- *WhoAmW 93*
Anderson, Denice Anna 1947- *WhoAmW 93*
Anderson, Denise d1990 *BioIn 17*
Anderson, Derek H. 1940- *St&PR 93*
Anderson, Diana Dawn 1959- *WhoEmL 93*
Anderson, Diane Lynn 1968- *WhoAmW 93*
Anderson, Don 1939- *ScF&FL 92*
Anderson, Don Lynn 1933- *WhoAm 92*
Anderson, Donald *BioIn 17*
Anderson, Donald 1943- *St&PR 93*
Anderson, Donald Bernard 1919- *WhoAm 92*
Anderson, Donald E. *BioIn 17*
Anderson, Donald Gordon Marcus 1937- *WhoAm 92*
Anderson, Donald Kennedy, Jr. 1922- *WhoAm 92*
Anderson, Donald Lee 1929- *WhoSSW 93*
Anderson, Donald Meredith 1928- *WhoAm 92*
Anderson, Donald Milton *WhoAm 92*
Anderson, Donald Morgan 1930- *WhoAm 92, WhoE 93, WhoWor 93*
Anderson, Donald Paul 1930- *WhoAm 92*
Anderson, Donald R. 1935- *St&PR 93*
Anderson, Donna Kay 1935- *WhoAm 92*
Anderson, Donnald K. 1942- *CngDr 91*
Anderson, Doris Ehlinger 1926- *WhoAmW 93*
Anderson, Doris Elaine *Law&B 92*
Anderson, Dorothea Ann 1944- *WhoUN 92*
Anderson, Dorothy Jean 1926- *WhoAmW 93*
Anderson, Dorrine Ann Petersen 1923- *WhoAmW 93, WhoWor 93*
Anderson, Douglas *BioIn 17*
Anderson, Douglas Arthur 1947- *WhoEmL 93*
Anderson, Douglas Delano 1942- *WhoAm 92*
Anderson, Douglas DeWayne 1957- *WhoE 93*
Anderson, Douglas Poole 1939- *WhoSSW 93*
Anderson, Douglas Richard 1938- *WhoAm 92, WhoSSW 93*
Anderson, Douglas Scranton Helmsley 1929- *WhoE 93, WhoWor 93*
Anderson, Douglas Williams 1932- *WhoE 93, WhoWor 93*
Anderson, Duwayne Marlo 1927- *WhoAm 92*
Anderson, E. Karl 1931- *WhoAm 92*
Anderson, E. Van 1944- *St&PR 93*
Anderson, Earl Milton, Jr. 1925- *St&PR 93*
Anderson, Eddie 1905-1977 *QDrFCA 92 [port]*
Anderson, Edgar William 1931- *WhoSSW 93*
Anderson, Edith Helen 1927- *WhoAm 92*
Anderson, Edmund Perry *Law&B 92*
Anderson, Edna 1922- *WhoAmW 93*
Anderson, Edward Riley 1932- *WhoAm 92, WhoSSW 93*
Anderson, Edwyna 1930- *WhoAm 92*
Anderson, Edwyna G. *Law&B 92*
Anderson, Eileen E. 1931- *St&PR 93*
Anderson, Elaine Janet 1940- *WhoAmW 93*
Anderson, Eleanor June 1914- *St&PR 93*
Anderson, Elisabeth Madge Kehrer *WhoAmW 93*
Anderson, Elizabeth McKee 1957- *WhoEmL 93*
Anderson, Ellis Bernard 1926- *WhoAm 92*
Anderson, Elmer Ebert 1922- *WhoAm 92, WhoSSW 93*
Anderson, Emily 1891-1962 *Baker 92*
Anderson, Emily Ann 1946- *WhoAmW 93*
Anderson, Emily L. *AmWomPl*
Anderson, Emory Dean 1939- *WhoScE 91-2*
Anderson, Eric Edward 1951- *WhoEmL 93*
Anderson, Eric Keith 1957- *WhoEmL 93*
Anderson, Eric Severin 1943- *WhoAm 92, WhoSSW 93, WhoWor 93*
Anderson, Eric William 1923- *WhoAm 92*
Anderson, Ernest Washington 1922- *WhoAm 92*
Anderson, Eskil 1913- *St&PR 93*
Anderson, Ethel Avara *WhoAmW 93*
Anderson, Eugene 1944- *AfrAmBi [port]*
Anderson, Eugene A. 1908- *St&PR 93*
Anderson, Eugene Karl 1935- *St&PR 93*
Anderson, Eugene M., Jr. *Law&B 92*
Anderson, Eva Jean 1939- *WhoE 93*
Anderson, F. Allan 1944- *St&PR 93*
Anderson, Fletcher Neal 1930- *WhoAm 92*
Anderson, Flipper *BioIn 17*
Anderson, Frances Swem 1913- *WhoAmW 93, WhoWor 93*
Anderson, Frank R., Jr. *BioIn 17*
Anderson, Frank Russell 1923- *WhoWrEP 92*
Anderson, Frank T. *St&PR 93*
Anderson, Frank Wayne 1949- *WhoSSW 93*
Anderson, Frederick Randolph, Jr. 1941- *WhoAm 92*
Anderson, G. Ernest, Jr. 1929- *WhoE 93*
Anderson, G. M. 1882?-1971 *IntDcF 2-3 [port]*
Anderson, G. Roderic *Law&B 92*
Anderson, Gary *BioIn 17*
Anderson, Gary 1948- *WhoSSW 93*
Anderson, Gary Dean 1947- *WhoAm 92*
Anderson, Gary F. 1953- *St&PR 93*
Anderson, Gary William 1951- *WhoE 93, WhoEmL 93*
Anderson, Gene Randall 1940- *St&PR 93*
Anderson, Geoffrey Allen *Law&B 92*
Anderson, Geoffrey Allen 1947- *WhoAm 92*
Anderson, George 1944- *WhoScE 91-1*
Anderson, George Alfred 1949- *WhoSSW 93*
Anderson, George Eli 1946- *St&PR 93*
Anderson, George Elliott, Jr. 1935- *WhoSSW 93*
Anderson, George Harding 1931- *WhoAm 92*
Anderson, George Joseph 1960- *WhoEmL 93*
Anderson, George Kenneth 1946- *WhoAm 92*
Anderson, George L. 1941- *WhoUN 92*
Anderson, George Lee 1934- *WhoAm 92*
Anderson, George Ross, Jr. 1929- *WhoAm 92, WhoSSW 93*
Anderson, George W. 1934- *WhoAm 92*
Anderson, George W(helan), Jr. 1906-1992 *CurBio 92N*
Anderson, George Whelan d1992 *NewYTBS 92 [port]*
Anderson, George Whelan 1906-1992 *BioIn 17*
Anderson, Gerald Dwight 1944- *ConAu 37NR*
Anderson, Gerald Edwin 1931- *WhoAm 92*
Anderson, Gerald Leslie 1940- *St&PR 93, WhoAm 92, WhoSSW 93*
Anderson, Gerald M. 1944- *WhoSSW 93*
Anderson, Geraldine Louise 1941- *WhoAmW 93*
Anderson, Gerard Fenton 1951- *WhoEmL 93*
Anderson, Gilbert M. 1882?-1971 *BioIn 17*
Anderson, Girard F. 1932- *St&PR 93, WhoAm 92*
Anderson, Glenn Elwood 1914- *WhoAm 92*
Anderson, Glenn M. 1913- *CngDr 91*
Anderson, Glenn Malcolm *WhoAm 92*
Anderson, Gordon Benjamin 1927- *St&PR 93*
Anderson, Gordon Louis 1947- *WhoEmL 93*
Anderson, Gordon MacKenzie 1932- *WhoAm 92*

Anderson, Gordon Wood 1936- BioIn 17, WhoE 93
Anderson, Gregory Joseph 1944- WhoAm 92
Anderson, Gregory Lyman 1951- WhoSSW 93
Anderson, Grover D. 1942- St&PR 93
Anderson, Guy Irving 1906- WhoAm 92
Anderson, H. Richard 1953- WhoEmL 93
Anderson, Hamish Alexander WhoScE 91-1
Anderson, Hans-Joachim 1931- WhoScE 91-3
Anderson, Harold Albert 1908- WhoAm 92
Anderson, Harold Homer 1897-1990 BioIn 17
Anderson, Harrison Clarke 1932- WhoAm 92
Anderson, Harry BioIn 17
Anderson, Harry Alan 1945- WhoIns 93
Anderson, Harry Frederick, Jr. 1927- WhoAm 92
Anderson, Heather Sue 1965- WhoAmW 93
Anderson, Helen Sharp 1916- WhoSSW 93
Anderson, Henry Fitzgerald 1951- WhoE 93
Anderson, Henry J. WhoIns 93
Anderson, Henry J. 1908- St&PR 93
Anderson, Henry Lee Norman 1934- WhoWor 93
Anderson, Henry Warren 1956- WhoEmL 93, WhoSSW 93
Anderson, Herbert H. 1920- WhoAm 92
Anderson, Herman 1944- WhoSSW 93
Anderson, Herschel Vincent 1932- WhoAm 92
Anderson, Holly L. 1946- WhoAmW 93, WhoWor 93
Anderson, Holly Teas Law&B 92
Anderson, Howard L. 1944- St&PR 93
Anderson, Howard N. 1929- WhoIns 93
Anderson, Howard Palmer 1915- WhoSSW 93
Anderson, Hugh d1873 BioIn 17
Anderson, Hugh Ross WhoScE 91-1
Anderson, Ian 1947- See Jethro Tull ConMus 8
Anderson, Iris Anita 1930- WhoAmW 93
Anderson, Irma Louise 1941- WhoWrEP 92
Anderson, Irvin Charles 1928- WhoAm 92
Anderson, Irving Edward, Jr. 1946- WhoWor 93
Anderson, Isabel Weld Perkins 1876-1948 AmWomPl
Anderson, Ivan Verner, Jr. 1939- WhoSSW 93
Anderson, Ivie 1904-1949 BioIn 17
Anderson, J. Burton 1943- St&PR 93
Anderson, J.C. WhoScE 91-1
Anderson, J(ohn) Kerby 1951- WhoWrEP 92
Anderson, J. Trent 1939- WhoAm 92
Anderson, Jack 1922- BioIn 17, ScF&FL 92
Anderson, Jack A. 1938- St&PR 93
Anderson, Jack G. 1922- St&PR 93
Anderson, Jack L. 1936- St&PR 93
Anderson, Jack Northman 1922- WhoAm 92, WhoWrEP 92
Anderson, Jack Oland 1921- WhoAm 92
Anderson, Jack Roy 1925- WhoAm 92, WhoWor 93
Anderson, Jack Warren 1935- WhoWrEP 92
Anderson, Jackson 1922- JrnUS
Anderson, James 1955- ScF&FL 92
Anderson, James Allen 1959- WhoE 93
Anderson, James Arthur 1935- St&PR 93, WhoAm 92
Anderson, James Arthur 1955- WhoE 93
Anderson, James Brent 1950- WhoE 93, WhoEmL 93, WhoWor 93
Anderson, James Buell 1912- WhoWor 93
Anderson, James C. 1944- St&PR 93
Anderson, James Donald 1952- WhoEmL 93
Anderson, James E. 1935- St&PR 93
Anderson, James E., Jr. Law&B 92
Anderson, James E(lliott) 1933- WhoWrEP 92
Anderson, James F. Law&B 92
Anderson, James Francis, Jr. 1954- WhoEmL 93
Anderson, James Frederick 1927- WhoAm 92
Anderson, James George 1936- WhoAm 92
Anderson, James Gerard 1944- WhoAm 92
Anderson, James Gilbert WhoAm 92
Anderson, James Keith 1924- WhoAm 92
Anderson, James L. 1943- WhoIns 93
Anderson, James Lavalette, Jr. 1954- WhoE 93
Anderson, James Milton 1941- St&PR 93, WhoAm 92
Anderson, James Noel 1951- WhoEmL 93
Anderson, James R. 1953- St&PR 93
Anderson, James S. 1940- St&PR 93
Anderson, James Thomas 1939- St&PR 93
Anderson, James Walter 1931- WhoSSW 93
Anderson, James Warren, III 1958- WhoE 93
Anderson, James William 1918- St&PR 93
Anderson, James William, III 1937- WhoAm 92
Anderson, Jane 1893- BioIn 17
Anderson, Jane Louise Blair 1948- WhoAmW 93
Anderson, Janelle Marie 1954- WhoAmW 93
Anderson, Janet Alm 1952- WhoAmW 93, WhoEmL 93, WhoWor 93
Anderson, Janet B. Law&B 92
Anderson, Janet Isabelle 1950- WhoEmL 93
Anderson, Janet Kathleen 1950- WhoAm 92
Anderson, Janet M. Law&B 92
Anderson, Janet P. Law&B 92
Anderson, Jani 1949- ScF&FL 92
Anderson, Janice Linn 1943- WhoSSW 93
Anderson, Jean Blanche 1940- WhoWrEP 92
Anderson, Jean Lorraine 1945- WhoAmW 93
Anderson, Jeannie St&PR 93
Anderson, Jeffery D. 1947- St&PR 93
Anderson, Jeffery Stuart 1949- WhoEmL 93
Anderson, Jeffrey Alan 1953- WhoE 93
Anderson, Jeffrey Michael 1955- WhoSSW 93
Anderson, Jerry Allen 1947- WhoE 93
Anderson, Jerry Maynard 1933- WhoAm 92
Anderson, Jerry William, Jr. 1926- WhoWor 93
Anderson, Jessica BioIn 17
Anderson, Jessie Ysobel Calhoun AmWomPl
Anderson, Jewel Yergin 1959- WhoAmW 93
Anderson, Joan 1944?- BioIn 17
Anderson, Joan Wellin Freed 1945- WhoAmW 93
Anderson, Joan Wester 1938- WhoWrEP 92
Anderson, Joann Morgan 1933- WhoAmW 93
Anderson, Joanne Leora 1929- WhoAmW 93
Anderson, Jodi BlkAmWO
Anderson, Joel A. St&PR 93
Anderson, John WhoScE 91-1
Anderson, John d1992 NewYTBS 92 [port]
Anderson, John 1917- BioIn 17
Anderson, John A. 1938- St&PR 93
Anderson, John A., Jr. Law&B 92
Anderson, John A., III Law&B 92
Anderson, John Ainslie WhoScE 91-1
Anderson, John Allan Dalrymple WhoScE 91-1
Anderson, John Ansel 1903- WhoAm 92
Anderson, John Arthur 1924- St&PR 93
Anderson, John B. 1922- PolPar
Anderson, John Bailey 1945- WhoAm 92
Anderson, John Bayard 1922- WhoAm 92
Anderson, John C. 1958- St&PR 93
Anderson, John Calvin 1952- WhoEmL 93
Anderson, John Carl 1945- St&PR 93
Anderson, John Charles 1954- WhoWrEP 92
Anderson, John David 1926- WhoAm 92
Anderson, John David, Jr. 1937- WhoAm 92
Anderson, John Edward 1917- WhoAm 92
Anderson, John Edward 1927- WhoAm 92
Anderson, John Erling 1929- WhoAm 92
Anderson, John Filmore 1942- WhoIns 93
Anderson, John Firth 1928- WhoAm 92
Anderson, John G. 1929- St&PR 93
Anderson, John Gaston 1922- WhoAm 92
Anderson, John H. Law&B 92
Anderson, John Harvey, Jr. 1949- WhoEmL 93
Anderson, John Henderson 1929- WhoSSW 93
Anderson, John Kerby 1951- WhoEmL 93, WhoSSW 93
Anderson, John L. 1927- St&PR 93
Anderson, John Leonard 1927- WhoAm 92
Anderson, John Leonard 1945- WhoAm 92
Anderson, John Lothian WhoScE 91-1
Anderson, John M. 1943- St&PR 93
Anderson, John MacKenzie 1938- WhoAm 92
Anderson, John Mueller 1914- WhoAm 92
Anderson, John Murray 1926- WhoAm 92
Anderson, John Pyle Law&B 92
Anderson, John Richard 1931- WhoAm 92
Anderson, John Robert 1928- WhoAm 92
Anderson, John Robert 1936- WhoAm 92
Anderson, John Robert 1947- WhoAm 92
Anderson, John Roy 1919- WhoWor 93
Anderson, John Thomas 1930- WhoAm 92
Anderson, John Weir 1928- WhoAm 92
Anderson, John Whiting 1934- WhoAm 92
Anderson, Jolene Slover WhoAmW 93, WhoWor 93
Anderson, Jon 1940- WhoWrEP 92
Anderson, Jon 1944- See Yes ConMus 8
Anderson, Jon G. 1951- St&PR 93
Anderson, Jon Mac 1937- WhoAm 92
Anderson, Jon Stephen 1936- WhoAm 92
Anderson, Jonpatrick Schuyler 1951- WhoEmL 93, WhoWor 93
Anderson, Joseph 1757-1837 PolPar
Anderson, Joseph Andrew, Jr. 1921- WhoAm 92
Anderson, Joseph Fletcher, Jr. 1949- WhoAm 92, WhoSSW 93
Anderson, Joseph Nelson 1948- WhoEmL 93
Anderson, Joseph Norman 1926- WhoAm 92
Anderson, Judith 1898-1992 BioIn 17, ConTFT 10, CurBio 92N
Anderson, Judith 1899-1992 NewYTBS 92 [port], News 92, -92-3
Anderson, Judith Anne 1943- WhoAmW 93
Anderson, Judith Helena 1940- WhoAm 92
Anderson, Judy BioIn 17
Anderson, Judy M. 1948- St&PR 93
Anderson, Julie Kay 1961- WhoEmL 93
Anderson, June BioIn 17, WhoAm 92
Anderson, June 1952- Baker 92, OxDcOp, WhoAmW 93
Anderson, June 1955- IntDcOp
Anderson, June M. ScF&FL 92
Anderson, Karen 1932- ScF&FL 92
Anderson, Karen (Kruse) 1932- ConAu 136
Anderson, Karen L. 1948- WhoWrEP 92
Anderson, Karl Richard 1917- WhoWor 93
Anderson, Katherine Doster 1932- WhoAmW 93
Anderson, Kathleen Gay 1950- WhoEmL 93
Anderson, Kathleen Janette WhoScE 91-1
Anderson, Kathleen M. Rex 1944- WhoE 93
Anderson, Kathryn Corinn 1959- WhoAmW 93
Anderson, Kay ScF&FL 92
Anderson, Keith 1917- WhoAm 92
Anderson, Keith E. 1936- St&PR 93
Anderson, Keith Graham 1939- WhoWor 93
Anderson, Keith S. 1965- St&PR 93
Anderson, Kelly Elizabeth 1957- WhoEmL 93
Anderson, Kenneth 1957- WhoSSW 93
Anderson, Kenneth Arthur Noel 1891-1959 HarEnMi
Anderson, Kenneth E. 1943- St&PR 93
Anderson, Kenneth Norman 1921- WhoAm 92, WhoE 93, WhoWor 93
Anderson, Kenneth Patrick 1966- WhoE 93
Anderson, Kenneth Ward 1931- WhoSSW 93
Anderson, Kenny 1970- BioIn 17
Anderson, Kent Lee 1949- WhoE 93
Anderson, Kent S. 1962- St&PR 93
Anderson, Kent Taylor Law&B 92
Anderson, Kent Taylor 1953- St&PR 93, WhoAm 92
Anderson, Kent Thomas 1942- St&PR 93
Anderson, Kent Victor 1935- St&PR 93
Anderson, Kerrii B. 1957- St&PR 93
Anderson, Kevin J. 1962- ScF&FL 92
Anderson, Kim R. Law&B 92
Anderson, Kinsey A. 1926- WhoAm 92
Anderson, Kirk S. 1937- St&PR 93
Anderson, Kitty 1966- WhoWor 93
Anderson, Kristian St&PR 93
Anderson, Kurt Michael 1953- WhoEmL 93
Anderson, Kym 1950- WhoUN 92
Anderson, L.G. Law&B 92
Anderson, Larry D. Law&B 92
Anderson, Larry Robert 1960- WhoEmL 93
Anderson, Laura Grant 1943- WhoAmW 93
Anderson, Laurence Alexis 1940- WhoAm 92
Anderson, Laurie MiSFD 9
Anderson, Laurie 1947- Baker 92, BioIn 17, WhoAm 92, WhoE 93
Anderson, LaVerne Eric 1922- WhoAm 92
Anderson, Lawrence Bernhart 1906- WhoAm 92
Anderson, Lawrence Keith 1935- WhoAm 92
Anderson, Lawrence Leslie, Jr. 1930- WhoAm 92
Anderson, Lawrence Richard 1942- WhoAm 92
Anderson, Lea E. 1954- WhoAm 92, WhoE 93
Anderson, Lee Ann 1959- St&PR 93
Anderson, Lee Roger 1945- WhoAm 92
Anderson, Lee Stratton 1925- WhoAm 92, WhoSSW 93
Anderson, Lennart 1928- WhoAm 92
Anderson, Leo E. 1902- WhoAm 92
Anderson, Leonard Gustave 1919- WhoAm 92
Anderson, Leonard Louis 1934- WhoE 93
Anderson, Leroy 1908-1975 Baker 92
Anderson, LeRoy Hagen 1906-1991 BioIn 17
Anderson, Leslie Brian 1948- WhoE 93
Anderson, Lester William 1943- WhoE 93
Anderson, Lewis Daniel 1930- WhoAm 92
Anderson, Lila Daum Law&B 92
Anderson, Linda D. WhoAmW 93
Anderson, Linda Mary 1943- WhoAmW 93
Anderson, Lindsay 1923- MiSFD 9
Anderson, Lindsay Gordon 1923- WhoWor 93
Anderson, Lloyd L. 1933- St&PR 93
Anderson, Lloyd Lee 1933- WhoAm 92, WhoWor 93
Anderson, Logan B. St&PR 93
Anderson, Loni BioIn 17
Anderson, Loni Kaye 1946- WhoAm 92
Anderson, Lorraine M. Law&B 92
Anderson, Louie BioIn 17
Anderson, Louie 1953?- ConAu 139
Anderson, Louis Wilmer, Jr. 1933- WhoAm 92
Anderson, Louise Eleanor 1934- WhoAm 92
Anderson, Louise Goings 1930- WhoAmW 93
Anderson, Lowell Carlton 1937- St&PR 93
Anderson, Lucy 1797-1878 Baker 92
Anderson, Lucy Macdonald 1942- WhoAmW 93
Anderson, Lyle Arthur 1931- WhoAm 92
Anderson, Lynn Law&B 92
Anderson, Lynn 1947- WhoAm 92
Anderson, (Terry) Lynn 1957- WhoWrEP 92
Anderson, Maceo 1910- BioIn 17
Anderson, Madge AmWomPl
Anderson, Maggie 1948- WhoWrEP 92
Anderson, Margaret d1973 BioIn 17
Anderson, Margaret Ellen 1941- WhoAm 92
Anderson, Margaret J. 1931- ScF&FL 92
Anderson, Margaret Lavinia 1941- WhoAm 92
Anderson, Margaret Lynn 1950- WhoEmL 93
Anderson, Margery Lawrence 1949- WhoE 93
Anderson, Margot West 1939- WhoAmW 93
Anderson, Margret Elizabeth 1949- WhoEmL 93
Anderson, Marian 1899- Baker 92
Anderson, Marian 1902- BioIn 17, ConHero 2 [port], ConMus 8 [port], EncAACR, IntDcOp [port], OxDcOp, WhoAm 92, WhoAmW 93
Anderson, Marie Barbara 1934- WhoWrEP 92
Anderson, Marion Cornelius 1926- WhoAm 92
Anderson, Mark Alexander 1953- WhoEmL 93
Anderson, Mark Eugene 1952- WhoWor 93
Anderson, Mark M. 1955- ConAu 139
Anderson, Mark Peter Law&B 92
Anderson, Mark Ransom 1951- WhoE 93
Anderson, Mark Robert 1951- WhoEmL 93
Anderson, Mark S. 1962- St&PR 93
Anderson, Mark T. 1953- WhoEmL 93
Anderson, Marlene Kay 1954- WhoAmW 93
Anderson, Marsha Dale 1952- WhoSSW 93
Anderson, Marshall Lee 1918- St&PR 93
Anderson, Martha Alene 1945- WhoAmW 93
Anderson, Martha Jean 1946- WhoAmW 93, WhoEmL 93
Anderson, Martha O. Law&B 92
Anderson, Martin Carl 1936- WhoAm 92, WhoWor 93

Anderson, Martin H.F. 1949- *St&PR 93*
Anderson, Mary 1859-1940 *AmWomPl*
Anderson, Mary 1872-1964 *BioIn 17, ScF&FL 92*
Anderson, Mary 1929- *ScF&FL 92*
Anderson, Mary Harris 1940- *WhoSSW 93*
Anderson, Mary Jane 1930- *WhoWrEP 92*
Anderson, Mary Jane 1935- *WhoAm 92*
Anderson, Mary Jo *Law&B 92*
Anderson, Mary Leigh 1956- *WhoAm 92*
Anderson, Mary Lou 1949- *WhoAmW 93*
Anderson, Mary M. 1919- *ConAu 136*
Anderson, Mary Rose Scanlan 1950- *WhoWor 93*
Anderson, Mary Virginia 1949- *WhoEmL 93*
Anderson, Mary W. *Law&B 92*
Anderson, Max Elliot 1946- *WhoEmL 93*
Anderson, Maxwell L. *BioIn 17*
Anderson, Megan Bothwell 1944- *WhoAmW 93*
Anderson, Mel 1928- *WhoAm 92*
Anderson, Mel 1952- *St&PR 93*
Anderson, Melissa Sue 1962- *ConTFT 10*
Anderson, Melvern 1929- *WhoIns 93*
Anderson, Melvin, Mrs. *SmATA 72*
Anderson, Michael 1920- *MiSFD 9*
Anderson, Michael Falconer *ScF&FL 92*
Anderson, Michael Falconer 1947- *ConAu 136*
Anderson, Michael George 1951- *WhoEmL 93*
Anderson, Michael James 1943- *WhoWrEP 92*
Anderson, Michael Joseph 1920- *WhoAm 92*
Anderson, Michael L. 1958- *WhoAm 92, WhoEmL 93*
Anderson, Michael Robert 1953- *WhoEmL 93*
Anderson, Michael S. *Law&B 92*
Anderson, Michael Steven 1954- *WhoEmL 93*
Anderson, Michael Thomas 1950- *WhoE 93, WhoEmL 93*
Anderson, Michael William 1954- *St&PR 93*
Anderson, Michael William 1955- *WhoEmL 93*
Anderson, Michelle *Law&B 92*
Anderson, Milada Filko 1922- *St&PR 93*
Anderson, Milton Henry 1919- *WhoAm 92*
Anderson, Minton M. 1898-1990 *BioIn 17*
Anderson, Mitchell 1963- *WhoWor 93*
Anderson, Myles Norman 1931- *WhoAm 92*
Anderson, Myron Kent 1950- *WhoEmL 93*
Anderson, N. Christian, III 1950- *WhoAm 92*
Anderson, Nancy J. *Law&B 92*
Anderson, Nancy Katherine 1948- *WhoEmL 93*
Anderson, Nancy Scott 1939- *ConAu 137*
Anderson, Neal *BioIn 17*
Anderson, Neal 1964- *WhoAm 92*
Anderson, Ned, Sr. 1943- *WhoAm 92, WhoWor 93*
Anderson, Neil 1945- *WhoSSW 93*
Anderson, Nellie Mae 1957- *WhoSSW 93*
Anderson, Nels Eric 1961- *WhoWor 93*
Anderson, Nils, Jr. 1914- *WhoAm 92, WhoWor 93*
Anderson, Noble *St&PR 93*
Anderson, Norman Dean 1928- *WhoSSW 93*
Anderson, Odin Waldemar 1914- *WhoAm 92*
Anderson, Oliver Duncan 1940- *WhoAm 92*
Anderson, Oliver R. 1932- *St&PR 93*
Anderson, Ora Sterling 1931- *WhoAmW 93*
Anderson, Orvil Roger 1937- *WhoAm 92*
Anderson, Owen Raymond 1919- *WhoAm 92*
Anderson, Pamela Jo 1951- *WhoEmL 93*
Anderson, Pamela Jo 1955- *WhoEmL 93*
Anderson, Patricia Etta 1942- *WhoAmW 93*
Anderson, Patricia Francis 1956- *WhoAmW 93*
Anderson, Patricia Joyce 1941- *WhoAmW 93*
Anderson, Patrick Lee 1959- *WhoEmL 93*
Anderson, Patrick Michael 1953- *WhoEmL 93, WhoWor 93*
Anderson, Paul Dale 1944- *ScF&FL 92, WhoWrEP 92*
Anderson, Paul Edward 1921- *WhoAm 92*
Anderson, Paul F. 1938- *St&PR 93*
Anderson, Paul Gustavus 1935- *WhoE 93*
Anderson, Paul Irving 1935- *WhoAm 92*
Anderson, Paul Maurice 1926- *WhoAm 92*
Anderson, Paul Nathaniel 1937- *WhoWor 93*
Anderson, Paul Nathaniel, III 1952- *WhoEmL 93*
Anderson, Paul Stewart 1952- *WhoEmL 93*
Anderson, Paul W. 1946- *St&PR 93*
Anderson, Paul Y. 1893-1938 *JrnUS*
Anderson, Paula *Law&B 92*
Anderson, Paula Lee 1953- *WhoAmW 93*
Anderson, Pauline Harriet 1918- *WhoAmW 93*
Anderson, Peer L. *Law&B 92*
Anderson, Peer L. 1944- *St&PR 93*
Anderson, Peer LaFollette 1944- *WhoAm 92*
Anderson, Peggy Rees 1958- *WhoAmW 93*
Anderson, Peter Dean 1957- *WhoSSW 93*
Anderson, Peter Irving 1950- *WhoE 93, WhoEmL 93*
Anderson, Peter Joseph 1951- *WhoEmL 93*
Anderson, Peter MacArthur 1937- *WhoAm 92*
Anderson, Philip Alden 1948- *WhoEmL 93*
Anderson, Philip Sidney 1935- *WhoAm 92*
Anderson, Philip Warren 1923- *WhoAm 92, WhoE 93, WhoWor 93*
Anderson, Phillip Doak 1923- *St&PR 93*
Anderson, Phyllis Reinhold 1936- *WhoAmW 93*
Anderson, Phyllis Wynn *WhoAmW 93*
Anderson, Porter 1953- *WhoEmL 93*
Anderson, Poul 1926- *BioIn 17, ScF&FL 92*
Anderson, Poul William 1926- *WhoAm 92, WhoWrEP 92*
Anderson, Quentin 1912- *WhoAm 92*
Anderson, R.D. *Law&B 92*
Anderson, R. Duane 1942- *St&PR 93*
Anderson, R.J. *Law&B 92, WhoScE 91-1*
Anderson, R. Quintus 1930- *St&PR 93, WhoAm 92, WhoE 93, WhoWor 93*
Anderson, Rachael Keller 1938- *WhoAm 92*
Anderson, Rachel 1943- *BioIn 17*
Anderson, Randall Keith 1952- *WhoE 93, WhoEmL 93, WhoWor 93*
Anderson, Ray *BioIn 17*
Anderson, Raymond Hilbert, Jr. 1952- *WhoSSW 93*
Anderson, Raymond T. 1932- *St&PR 93*
Anderson, Reid *BioIn 17*
Anderson, Reid Bryce 1949- *WhoAm 92, WhoE 93*
Anderson, Renee Coreen 1957- *WhoAmW 93*
Anderson, Rex *ScF&FL 92*
Anderson, Richard *Law&B 92*
Anderson, Richard A. 1929- *St&PR 93*
Anderson, Richard Alan 1933- *WhoE 93*
Anderson, Richard Allen 1946- *WhoE 93*
Anderson, Richard C. 1929- *WhoAm 92*
Anderson, Richard C. 1938- *WhoSSW 93*
Anderson, Richard Carl 1928- *WhoAm 92*
Anderson, Richard Carl 1932- *St&PR 93*
Anderson, Richard Dean 1950- *HolBB [port]*
Anderson, Richard Edmund *Law&B 92*
Anderson, Richard Edmund 1938- *WhoAm 92*
Anderson, Richard Eugene 1930- *WhoE 93*
Anderson, Richard Gene 1930- *St&PR 93*
Anderson, Richard Graham *WhoScE 91-1*
Anderson, Richard Heron 1821-1879 *HarEnMi*
Anderson, Richard Kim 1956- *WhoEmL 93*
Anderson, Richard Loree 1915- *WhoAm 92*
Anderson, Richard Louis 1927- *WhoAm 92*
Anderson, Richard McLemore 1930- *WhoSSW 93*
Anderson, Richard Norman 1926- *WhoAm 92*
Anderson, Richard Paul 1946- *WhoEmL 93*
Anderson, Richard Powell 1934- *WhoAm 92*
Anderson, Richard R. 1941- *St&PR 93*
Anderson, Richard William 1919- *WhoAm 92*
Anderson, Robbie Jo 1952- *WhoEmL 93*
Anderson, Robbin Gail 1964- *WhoAmW 93*
Anderson, Robert 1750-1830 *BioIn 17*
Anderson, Robert 1805-1871 *HarEnMi*
Anderson, Robert 1920- *St&PR 93, WhoAm 92, WhoSSW 93*
Anderson, Robert 1936- *WhoAsAP 91*
Anderson, Robert 1944- *BioIn 17, WhoAm 92*
Anderson, Robert Alexander 1946- *WhoEmL 93*
Anderson, Robert Bennett 1924- *St&PR 93*
Anderson, Robert Bruce 1956- *WhoEmL 93*
Anderson, Robert Buehn 1926- *WhoAm 92*
Anderson, Robert C. *Law&B 92*
Anderson, Robert C. 1945- *WhoIns 93*
Anderson, Robert Davis 1934- *St&PR 93*
Anderson, Robert Douglas 1939- *WhoSSW 93, WhoWor 93*
Anderson, Robert E. 1919- *St&PR 93*
Anderson, Robert E., III 1934- *St&PR 93*
Anderson, Robert G. *Law&B 92*
Anderson, Robert Gene 1939- *St&PR 93*
Anderson, Robert Geoffrey William 1944- *WhoWor 93*
Anderson, Robert Gregg 1928- *WhoAm 92*
Anderson, Robert H. *Law&B 92*
Anderson, Robert Helms 1939- *WhoAm 92*
Anderson, Robert Henry *WhoScE 91-1*
Anderson, Robert Henry 1918- *WhoAm 92*
Anderson, Robert K. 1935- *WhoAm 92*
Anderson, Robert Kenneth 1935- *St&PR 93*
Anderson, Robert Lanier, III 1936- *WhoAm 92, WhoSSW 93*
Anderson, Robert Morris, Jr. 1939- *WhoAm 92*
Anderson, Robert N. *Law&B 92*
Anderson, Robert Norton 1937- *St&PR 93*
Anderson, Robert O. 1917- *St&PR 93*
Anderson, Robert Orville 1917- *WhoAm 92*
Anderson, Robert Roger 1959- *WhoE 93*
Anderson, Robert Rowand 1834-1921 *BioIn 17*
Anderson, Robert Simpers 1939- *WhoE 93*
Anderson, Robert T. *Law&B 92*
Anderson, Robert Theodore 1934- *WhoAm 92*
Anderson, Robert Wayne 1951- *WhoAm 92*
Anderson, Robert Wesley, Jr. 1949- *WhoSSW 93*
Anderson, Robert Woodruff 1917- *WhoAm 92*
Anderson, Roberta 1942- *ScF&FL 92*
Anderson, Roberta Joan 1943- *WhoAm 92, WhoAmW 93*
Anderson, Robin Latham 1964- *WhoEmL 93*
Anderson, Roderick B. *Law&B 92*
Anderson, Rodney W. *Law&B 92*
Anderson, Roger Burke 1950- *WhoEmL 93*
Anderson, Roger E. 1921- *WhoAm 92*
Anderson, Rolph Ely 1936- *WhoAm 92, WhoE 93*
Anderson, Ron *WhoAm 92*
Anderson, Ron Joe 1946- *WhoAm 92, WhoSSW 93*
Anderson, Ronald A. 1946- *St&PR 93*
Anderson, Ronald C. 1942- *St&PR 93*
Anderson, Ronald D. 1932- *WhoAm 92*
Anderson, Ronald Delaine 1937- *WhoAm 92*
Anderson, Ronald Earl 1948- *WhoSSW 93*
Anderson, Ronald Gordon 1948- *WhoIns 93*
Anderson, Ronald R. 1942- *St&PR 93*
Anderson, Ronald Regis 1942- *WhoAm 92*
Anderson, Ronald Shand *WhoScE 91-1*
Anderson, Ronald Truman 1933- *WhoIns 93*
Anderson, Rosas Enrique 1926- *WhoWor 93*
Anderson, Roscoe Odell Dale 1913- *WhoWor 93*
Anderson, Rosemary Burdette 1953- *WhoEmL 93*
Anderson, Ross Barrett 1951- *WhoE 93, WhoWor 93*
Anderson, Ross Sherwood 1951- *WhoAm 92*
Anderson, Roy, Jr. 1929- *St&PR 93*
Anderson, Roy, III 1957- *St&PR 93*
Anderson, Roy Arnold 1920- *St&PR 93*
Anderson, Roy Everett 1918- *WhoAm 92*
Anderson, Roy H. 1938- *St&PR 93*
Anderson, Roy Kenneth 1952- *WhoEmL 93*
Anderson, Roy Malcolm *WhoScE 91-1*
Anderson, Roy Malcolm 1947- *WhoWor 93*
Anderson, Roy Ryden 1920- *WhoAm 92*
Anderson, Rudolph J., Jr. 1924- *WhoAm 92*
Anderson, Russell Bruce, Sr. 1957- *WhoSSW 93*
Anderson, Russell Karl, Jr. 1943- *WhoE 93*
Anderson, Ruth 1928- *Baker 92*
Anderson, Ruth Carrington 1915- *WhoAmW 93*
Anderson, Sandra Lee 1959- *WhoAmW 93*
Anderson, Sandra Wood 1949- *WhoEmL 93*
Anderson, Sara Lee 1962- *WhoAmW 93*
Anderson, Sarah G. *Law&B 92*
Anderson, Scot W. *Law&B 92*
Anderson, Scott Charles 1951- *WhoEmL 93*
Anderson, Scott D. *BioIn 17*
Anderson, Scott David 1957- *WhoAm 92*
Anderson, Shannon Whitcomb 1955- *WhoSSW 93*
Anderson, Sharon 1950- *St&PR 93*
Anderson, Sharon Anne *WhoAmW 93*
Anderson, Sherwood 1876-1941 *BioIn 17, JrnUS, MagSAmL [port], WorLitC [port]*
Anderson, Shirley Roberts 1951- *WhoAmW 93*
Anderson, Sigurd 1904-1990 *BioIn 17*
Anderson, Simone Marie 1964- *St&PR 93*
Anderson, Sparky 1934- *WhoAm 92*
Anderson, Stacy *BioIn 17*
Anderson, Stanford Owen 1934- *WhoAm 92*
Anderson, Stanton Dean 1940- *WhoAm 92*
Anderson, Stefan S. 1934- *St&PR 93*
Anderson, Stefan Stolen 1934- *WhoAm 92*
Anderson, Stella Miles *Law&B 92*
Anderson, Stephen Carl 1954- *WhoSSW 93*
Anderson, Stephen Francis 1950- *WhoEmL 93*
Anderson, Stephen Hale 1932- *WhoAm 92*
Anderson, Steve *MiSFD 9*
Anderson, Steven Hunter 1962- *WhoSSW 93*
Anderson, Steven Lloyd 1957- *WhoSSW 93*
Anderson, Steven Robert 1955- *WhoEmL 93*
Anderson, Sue Ann 1947- *WhoAmW 93*
Anderson, Suellen 1950- *WhoEmL 93*
Anderson, Susan 1870-1960 *BioIn 17*
Anderson, Susan Holliday 1944- *WhoWor 93*
Anderson, Susan Janice *ScF&FL 92*
Anderson, Susan K. *Law&B 92*
Anderson, Susan Lou 1947- *WhoAm 92*
Anderson, Susan Renita 1958- *WhoEmL 93*
Anderson, Susan Stuebing 1951- *WhoAm 92, WhoAmW 93*
Anderson, Sydney 1927- *WhoAm 92*
Anderson, T(homas) J(efferson, Jr.) 1928- *Baker 92*
Anderson, T. Valfrid *Law&B 92*
Anderson, Tad Stephen 1955- *WhoEmL 93*
Anderson, Ted G. 1930- *St&PR 93*
Anderson, Teresa *BioIn 17*
Anderson, Terri Ann 1949- *WhoEmL 93*
Anderson, Terry *BioIn 17*
Anderson, Terry J. *Law&B 92*
Anderson, Terry L. *Law&B 92*
Anderson, Terry Lee 1947- *WhoEmL 93*
Anderson, Thelma Deane 1920- *WhoWrEP 92*
Anderson, Theodore Robert 1949- *WhoE 93*
Anderson, Theodore Wellington 1941- *WhoE 93, WhoWor 93*
Anderson, Theodore Wilbur 1918- *WhoAm 92*
Anderson, Theresa Lee 1963- *WhoAmW 93*
Anderson, Thomas *WhoScE 91-1*
Anderson, Thomas Caryl 1944- *WhoE 93*
Anderson, Thomas Dunaway 1912- *WhoAm 92*
Anderson, Thomas E. *Law&B 92*
Anderson, Thomas F. 1911-1991 *BioIn 17*
Anderson, Thomas Harold 1924- *WhoAm 92*
Anderson, Thomas J. *St&PR 93*
Anderson, Thomas J. 1910- *WhoAm 92*
Anderson, Thomas J. 1945- *St&PR 93*
Anderson, Thomas Jefferson, Jr. 1924- *WhoSSW 93*
Anderson, Thomas Jefferson, Jr. 1928- *WhoAm 92*
Anderson, Thomas Kemp, Jr. 1926- *WhoAm 92*
Anderson, Thomas Liston *Law&B 92*
Anderson, Thomas P. 1916- *WhoAm 92*
Anderson, Thomas Patrick 1934- *WhoAm 92, WhoE 93*
Anderson, Thomas Peter 1948- *WhoEmL 93*
Anderson, Thomas Robert 1954- *WhoEmL 93*
Anderson, Thomas Willman 1950- *WhoAm 92*
Anderson, Timothy Christopher 1950- *WhoAm 92*
Anderson, Tom Sheridan 1954- *WhoE 93*
Anderson, Tom Troy 1962- *WhoEmL 93*

Anderson, Tommy 1932- *St&PR 93*
Anderson, Totton J. 1909-1992 *ConAu 136*
Anderson, Tracey Allen 1957- *WhoEmL 93*
Anderson, Valerie Lee 1955- *WhoE 93*
Anderson, Vance J. *Law&B 92*
Anderson, Victor O. 1913- *St&PR 93*
Anderson, Vincent *Law&B 92*
Anderson, Violet Henson 1931- *WhoAmW 93*
Anderson, Vivienne d1991 *BioIn 17*
Anderson, W. French 1936- *BioIn 17, WhoAm 92*
Anderson, Walter Dixon 1932- *WhoAm 92, WhoE 93*
Anderson, Walter Herman 1944- *WhoAm 92, WhoE 93*
Anderson, Walter Inglis 1903-1965 *BioIn 17*
Anderson, Walter Lee 1950- *St&PR 93*
Anderson, Wanda Stroud 1939- *WhoSSW 93*
Anderson, Warren Lee, II 1952- *WhoEmL 93*
Anderson, Warren Mattice 1915- *WhoAm 92*
Anderson, Wayne Arthur 1938- *WhoAm 92*
Anderson, Wayne K., Jr. *Law&B 92*
Anderson, Wells Howard *Law&B 92*
Anderson, Wendell Lowrie 1922- *WhoE 93*
Anderson, Wendell William, Jr. 1925- *WhoAm 92*
Anderson, Wes 1952-1991 *BioIn 17*
Anderson, Wesley Lawrence 1942- *St&PR 93*
Anderson, Wessell *BioIn 17*
Anderson, Wilda (Christine) 1951- *ConAu 139, WhoAmW 93*
Anderson, Willam Craig 1946- *WhoEmL 93*
Anderson, William *WhoScE 91-1*
Anderson, William 1771-1811 *BioIn 17*
Anderson, William Alan 1952- *WhoEmL 93*
Anderson, William Albert 1949- *WhoE 93*
Anderson, William Albion, Jr. 1939- *WhoAm 92*
Anderson, William Augustus 1942- *WhoWor 93*
Anderson, William Banks, Jr. 1931- *WhoAm 92*
Anderson, William Bert 1938- *WhoAm 92*
Anderson, William C. *Law&B 92*
Anderson, William Carl 1943- *WhoAm 92*
Anderson, William Carl 1958- *WhoEmL 93*
Anderson, William Clifford *Law&B 92*
Anderson, William Clyde 1934- *WhoSSW 93*
Anderson, William D. 1944- *St&PR 93*
Anderson, William E., II *Law&B 92*
Anderson, William Edward 1922- *WhoAm 92*
Anderson, William Edward 1943- *St&PR 93*
Anderson, William H. *Law&B 92*
Anderson, William H., II 1937- *St&PR 93*
Anderson, William Harold 1919- *WhoWor 93*
Anderson, William Heartly 1930- *WhoAm 92*
Anderson, William Henry 1940- *WhoAm 92*
Anderson, William Hopple 1926- *WhoAm 92*
Anderson, William J. 1946- *St&PR 93*
Anderson, William James *Law&B 92*
Anderson, William Kenneth 1919- *WhoAm 92*
Anderson, William R. 1939- *St&PR 93*
Anderson, William Richard, III 1955- *WhoSSW 93*
Anderson, William Robert 1921- *WhoAm 92*
Anderson, William Scovil 1927- *WhoAm 92*
Anderson, Willie *BioIn 17*
Anderson, Willis M. *Law&B 92*
Anderson, Wyatt Wheaton 1939- *WhoAm 92*
Anderson-Cherry, Sherri Lynn 1965- *WhoE 93*
Anderson-Imbert, Enrique 1910- *WhoAm 92*
Anderson-Mann, Shelley N. 1964- *WhoAmW 93*
Anderson-Papillion, Nathan *Law&B 92*
Anderson-Rodriguez, Joy 1946- *WhoAmW 93*
Andersons, Maris 1937- *St&PR 93*
Anderson Shelton, Margaret Martin 1923- *WhoSSW 93*
Anderson-Tidwell, Mary Ellen 1940- *WhoAmW 93*
Anderssen, Adolf 1818-1879 *BioIn 17*
Andersson, Albin Bertil 1928- *WhoWor 93*
Andersson, B. Lennart 1948- *WhoScE 91-4*
Andersson, Bengt E. 1923- *WhoScE 91-4*
Andersson, Berndt Ake Sigurd 1918- *WhoWor 93*
Andersson, Bibi 1935- *BioIn 17, IntDcF 2-3 [port], WhoWor 93*
Andersson, Billie Venturatos 1947- *WhoEmL 93*
Andersson, Bjorn Leif Andre 1959- *WhoWor 93*
Andersson, C. Dean *ScF&FL 92*
Andersson, Carl Johan 1827-1867 *Expl 93*
Andersson, Craig Remington 1937- *WhoAm 92*
Andersson, Folke O. 1933- *WhoScE 91-4*
Andersson, Gullmar Johan 1936- *WhoUN 92*
Andersson, Hans O.F. 1942- *WhoScE 91-4*
Andersson, Harriet 1932- *BioIn 17, IntDcF 2-3*
Andersson, Henrik 1935- *WhoScE 91-4*
Andersson, Ingvar O. 1933- *WhoScE 91-4*
Andersson, K. Lennart 1925- *WhoScE 91-4*
Andersson, Kurt E. 1938- *WhoScE 91-4*
Andersson, Lars 1956- *BioIn 17*
Andersson, Lars-Olov 1938- *WhoScE 91-4*
Andersson, Leif C. 1944- *WhoScE 91-4*
Andersson, Leif Christer Leander 1944- *WhoWor 93*
Andersson, Leif Per Roland 1923- *WhoWor 93*
Andersson, Matts *WhoScE 91-4*
Andersson, Nina R. *ScF&FL 92*
Andersson, Ola S. 1944- *St&PR 93*
Andersson, Per-Erik 1929- *WhoScE 91-4*
Andersson, Rolf 1949- *WhoScE 91-4*
Andersson, S.A. Hugo 1927- *WhoScE 91-4*
Andersson, Sten 1923- *WhoWor 93*
Andersson, Stig Ingvar 1945- *WhoWor 93*
Andersson, W. Paul 1946- *WhoEmL 93*
Andersson, Yerker Johan Olof 1929- *WhoE 93*
Andert, Jeffrey Norman 1950- *WhoEmL 93, WhoWor 93*
Anderton, Brian Henry *WhoScE 91-1*
Anderton, Charles Harold 1957- *WhoEmL 93*
Anderton, James Franklin, IV 1943- *St&PR 93*
Anderton, Jim 1938- *WhoAsAP 91*
Andert-Schmidt, Darlene Mary 1954- *WhoSSW 93*
Andes, Charles L. 1930- *St&PR 93*
Andes, Charles Lovett 1930- *WhoAm 92, WhoE 93*
Andes, G. Thomas 1942- *St&PR 93, WhoAm 92*
Andes, Joan Keenen 1930- *WhoAmW 93*
Andes, Mary Vivienne 1950- *WhoAmW 93*
Andes, Nancy 1954- *WhoAmW 93*
Andes, Ronald L. *Law&B 92*
Andewelt, Roger B. 1946- *CngDr 91*
Andino, Julio 1919- *St&PR 93*
Andis, Matthew G. 1908- *St&PR 93*
Andlauer, Edgar L. 1923- *St&PR 93*
Andler, Donald Andrew 1938- *WhoAm 92*
Ando, Ainosuke 1947- *WhoWor 93*
Ando, Hirofumi 1937- *WhoUN 92*
Ando, Kiyoshi 1948- *WhoWor 93*
Ando, Motoo 1934- *WhoWor 93*
Ando, Nisuke 1935- *WhoWor 93*
Ando, Sadao 1927- *WhoWor 93*
Ando, Salvador 1945- *WhoWor 93*
Ando, Shigeru 1929- *WhoWor 93*
Ando, Shiro 1928- *WhoWor 93*
Ando, Tadanao 1930- *WhoWor 93*
Ando, Tadao 1941- *BioIn 17, WhoWor 93*
Andoe, Joe Michael 1955- *WhoE 93*
Andoh, Emmanuel Kenneth 1944- *WhoUN 92*
Andolana, Gregorio A. 1947- *WhoAsAP 91*
Andolf, Ellika Margareta 1949- *WhoWor 93*
Andolina, Michael B. *Law&B 92*
Andolsek, Charles Merrick 1947- *WhoAm 92*
Andolsek, Ludwig J. 1910- *WhoAm 92*
Andolshek, Richard Anders 1952- *WhoWor 93*
Andonian, Archie Arsavir Takfor 1950- *WhoEmL 93*
Andonie Fernandez, Miguel *DcCPCAm*
Andonov, Ivan 1934- *DrEEuF*
Andonov, Metodi 1932-1974 *DrEEuF*
Andonov, Vladimir 1934- *WhoScE 91-4*
Andorfer, Donald Joseph 1937- *WhoAm 92*
Andorka, Frank Henry 1946- *WhoAm 92, WhoEmL 93*
Andra, Jurgen H. 1937- *WhoScE 91-3*
Andrade, Antonio de 1580-1634 *Expl 93*
Andrade, C. Roberto 1925- *St&PR 93*
Andrade, Carmen 1947- *WhoScE 91-3*
Andrade, Edna *WhoAm 92*
Andrade, Eloy Campagnone *Law&B 92*
Andrade, Francesco d' 1859-1921 *Baker 92*
Andrade, Jorge 1951- *St&PR 93*
Andrade, Jose Eduardo 1942- *St&PR 93*
Andrade, Kerry McCoy 1945- *St&PR 93*
Andrade, Mario de 1893-1945 *ScF&FL 92*
Andrade, Mario de 1928-1990 *BioIn 17*
Andrade, Stephen Paul 1952- *WhoEmL 93*
Andrae, Theodore E., III 1933- *St&PR 93*
Andras, Ferenc 1942- *DrEEuF*
Andras, Kenneth Bertram 1909- *St&PR 93*
Andrasick, James Stephen 1944- *St&PR 93, WhoAm 92*
Andrasovan, Tibor 1917- *Baker 92*
Andrassy, Istvan 1927- *WhoScE 91-4*
Andrassy, Timothy Francis 1948- *WhoAm 92*
Andrau, Maya Hedda 1936- *WhoAmW 93*
Andrauskas, Donna Marie 1960- *WhoAmW 93*
Andre, Adolf 1855-1910 *Baker 92*
Andre, Anton 1775-1842 *Baker 92*
Andre, Armand A.C. 1924- *WhoScE 91-2*
Andre, Bernard fl. 1500- *BioIn 17*
Andre, Calvin G. 1948- *St&PR 93*
Andre, Carl 1935- *WhoAm 92, WhoWor 93*
Andre, Carl August 1806-1887 *Baker 92*
Andre, Franz 1893-1975 *Baker 92*
Andre, Harvie 1940- *WhoE 93*
Andre, Herman William 1938- *St&PR 93*
Andre, J.M. 1944- *WhoScE 91-2*
Andre, Jean Baptiste 1823-1882 *Baker 92*
Andre, Jean G. 1942- *WhoScE 91-2*
Andre, Johann 1741-1799 *Baker 92, OxDcOp*
Andre, Johann Anton 1775-1842 *OxDcOp*
Andre, Johann August 1817-1887 *Baker 92*
Andre, John 1751-1780 *BioIn 17, HarEnMi*
Andre, Julius 1808-1880 *Baker 92*
Andre, Karl 1853-1914 *Baker 92*
Andre, Kenneth B., Jr. 1933- *St&PR 93, WhoIns 93*
Andre, Lona 1915- *SweetSg C [port]*
Andre, Louis Joseph Nicolas 1838-1913 *BioIn 17*
Andre, Marion *WhoCanL 92*
Andre, Maurice 1933- *Baker 92*
Andre, Michael 1946- *WhoE 93, WhoWrEP 92*
Andre, Oscar Jules 1900- *WhoAm 92*
Andre, Pamela Q. J. 1942- *WhoAm 92*
Andre, Paul Dean 1928- *WhoAm 92, WhoWrEP 92*
Andre, Rae 1946- *WhoEmL 93*
Andre, Richard A. 1950- *St&PR 93*
Andre, Scott E. 1958- *St&PR 93*
Andrea, Douglas John 1951- *WhoSSW 93*
Andrea, Elma Williams *WhoAmW 93*
Andrea, Frank A.D., Jr. 1926- *St&PR 93*
Andrea, Frederick Wilhelm, III 1952- *WhoSSW 93*
Andrea, Mario Iacobucci 1917- *WhoE 93*
Andrea, Paula 1952- *WhoAmW 93*
Andrea, Ronald Kent 1946- *WhoE 93*
Andreacchi, Anthony P. *Law&B 92*
Andreadis, Elaine Catherine 1948- *WhoAmW 93*
Andreadis, Theodore George 1950- *WhoE 93*
Andreae, Marc 1939- *Baker 92*
Andreae, Meinrat O. 1949- *WhoScE 91-3, WhoWor 93*
Andreae, Otto A. 1913- *St&PR 93*
Andreae, Volkmar 1879-1962 *Baker 92*
Andreae, Wayne A. 1912- *St&PR 93*
Andreani, Jacques 1929- *WhoWor 93*
Andreano, Ralph Louis 1929- *WhoAm 92*
Andreanszky, Gabor Lipto Szentandrasi 1942- *WhoWor 93*
Andreas, Bernard fl. 1500- *BioIn 17*
Andreas, David Lowell 1949- *St&PR 93, WhoAm 92*
Andreas, Dwayne 1918- *CurBio 92 [port]*
Andreas, Dwayne O. *BioIn 17*
Andreas, Dwayne O. 1918- *St&PR 93*
Andreas, Dwayne Orville 1918- *WhoAm 92, WhoWor 93*
Andreas, Eulalie *AmWomPl*
Andreas, George C. 1938- *St&PR 93*
Andreas, Glenn Allen 1943- *St&PR 93*
Andreas, Lowell W. 1922- *St&PR 93*
Andreas, Michael Dwayne 1948- *St&PR 93, WhoAm 92*
Andreas, Ray A. 1944- *St&PR 93*
Andreasen, Arman C. 1937- *WhoIns 93*
Andreasen, Charles Peter 1930- *WhoE 93*
Andreasen, Nancy Coover *WhoAm 92, WhoAmW 93*
Andreasen, Niels-Erik Albinns 1941- *WhoAm 92*
Andreasen, Samuel Gene 1927- *WhoSSW 93*
Andreas-Friedrich, Ruth 1901-1977 *BioIn 17*
Andreason, George Edward 1932- *WhoSSW 93, WhoWor 93*
Andreason, John Christian 1924- *WhoAm 92*
Andreas-Salome, Lou 1861-1937 *BioIn 17*
Andreassen, Poul 1928- *St&PR 93, WhoAm 92*
Andreassen, Terje 1961- *WhoWor 93*
Andreassi, Lucio 1934- *WhoScE 91-3*
Andrecic, Marguerite Marie 1958- *WhoEmL 93*
Andre de La Porte, Edward Paul Leonhard 1948- *WhoUN 92*
Andree, Elfrida 1841-1929 *Baker 92*
Andree, Martin Edwin 1938- *WhoSSW 93*
Andreeff, Nickolas P. 1931- *St&PR 93*
Andreen, Aviva Louise 1952- *WhoAmW 93, WhoEmL 93*
Andreen, Carl-Joel Y.G. 1933- *WhoScE 91-4*
Andreev, Victor Alexandrovich 1939- *WhoUN 92*
Andreevich, Demin Andrei 1925- *WhoWor 93*
Andregg, Charles Harold 1917- *WhoSSW 93*
Andreini, Giovanni Battista 1579-1654 *OxDcOp*
Andreini, Virginia 1583-1630 *OxDcOp*
Andreis, Henry Jerome 1931- *St&PR 93*
Andreis, Josip 1909-1982 *Baker 92*
Andreissen, David *ScF&FL 92*
Andrejeski-Cotriss, Joan Louise 1959- *WhoSSW 93*
Andrejevic, M. *WhoScE 91-4*
Andrejkovics, Bernard 1920- *St&PR 93*
Andrej of Bogoljubovo c. 1111-1174 *OxDcByz*
Andrejzchick, Marsha Lorene 1954- *WhoAmW 93, WhoEmL 93*
Andrel, Peter A. 1955- *WhoE 93*
Andren, Karl Goesta 1946- *WhoEmL 93*
Andren-Sandberg, Ake 1947- *WhoScE 91-4*
Andreo, P. 1950- *WhoScE 91-4*
Andreoff, Christopher Andon 1947- *WhoEmL 93*
Andreoli, Carlo 1840-1908 *Baker 92*
Andreoli, Kathleen Gainor 1935- *WhoAm 92, WhoAmW 93*
Andreoli, Mario *WhoScE 91-3*
Andreoni, Aurelio I.P. 1912- *St&PR 93*
Andreopoulos, Spyros 1929- *ScF&FL 92*
Andreopoulos, Spyros George 1929- *WhoWor 93*
Andreose, Mario 1934- *WhoWor 93*
Andreotti, Giulio *BioIn 17*
Andreotti, Giulio 1919- *WhoWor 93*
Andreotti, Rodolfo 1926- *WhoScE 91-3*
Andreou, Klitos 1944- *WhoScE 91-4*
Andreozzi, Gaetano 1755-1826 *OxDcOp*
Andreozzi, Louis Joseph 1959- *WhoEmL 93*
Andreozzi, Sharon Elaine 1944- *WhoE 93*
Andrepont, James A. 1946- *St&PR 93*
Andrepont, Marcus Dwayne 1959- *WhoSSW 93*
Andres, Christian 1950- *WhoWor 93*
Andres, F. William 1906- *St&PR 93*
Andres, John Charles *Law&B 92*
Andres, Joseph E. *Law&B 92*
Andres, Klaus 1934- *WhoScE 91-3, WhoWor 93*
Andres, Marian Gail 1944- *WhoAmW 93*
Andres, Marie Lorraine 1963- *WhoAmW 93*
Andres, Mary Jean *Law&B 92*
Andres, Pedro 1954- *WhoWor 93*
Andres, Prentice Lee 1939- *WhoIns 93*
Andres, Reubin 1923- *WhoAm 92, WhoE 93*
Andres, Robert P. 1930- *St&PR 93*
Andres, Roger Yves 1948- *WhoWor 93*
Andres, Ronald Paul 1938- *WhoAm 92*
Andres, Stephen Michael 1945- *St&PR 93*
Andresakes, George J. 1913- *St&PR 93*
Andresco, Andy B. 1933- *St&PR 93*
Andresen, Edmund Hugh 1949- *WhoAsAP 91*
Andresen, Egon Christian 1928- *WhoScE 91-3*
Andresen, Finn O. 1932- *St&PR 93*
Andresen, Graciela Vazquez 1952- *WhoAmW 93*
Andresen, Ivar 1896-1940 *Baker 92*
Andresen, Linda Skeen 1951- *WhoEmL 93*
Andresen, Malcolm 1917- *WhoE 93*
Andresen, Oystein *WhoScE 91-4*
Andresen, Per Krogh 1943- *St&PR 93*
Andresen, Rolf S. 1935- *St&PR 93*
Andreson, Charles Jeremiah 1947- *WhoE 93*
Andress, Charlotte Frances 1910- *WhoAmW 93*
Andress, James Gillis 1939- *St&PR 93*
Andress, John Barney 1936- *WhoSSW 93*

Andros, Hazel LaVerne 1939- *WhoAmW 93*
Andros, Helen Mary *WhoWor 93*
Andros, Stephen John 1955- *WhoEmL 93*
Androsch, Hannes 1938- *WhoWor 93*
Androsiglio, Charles 1950- *St&PR 93*
Androski, Michael Alan 1949- *WhoEmL 93*
Androutsellis-Theotokis, Paul 1939- *WhoWor 93*
Andrunakievich, Vladimir Alexandrovich 1917- *WhoWor 93*
Andrup, Lars 1961- *WhoWor 93*
Andrus, Cecil Dale 1931- *WhoAm 92*
Andrus, David Clifford 1953- *WhoEmL 93*
Andrus, Donald R. *WhoAm 92*
Andrus, Gerald L. 1904- *St&PR 93*
Andrus, Gerald Louis 1904- *WhoAm 92*
Andrus, James Francis 1953- *WhoEmL 93*
Andrus, John Stebbins 1927- *WhoE 93, WhoWor 93*
Andrus, Leonard C. 1933- *St&PR 93*
Andrus, Leonard Carl 1933- *WhoAm 92*
Andrus, Lisa Katherine 1962- *WhoAmW 93*
Andrus, Lloyd Loyl 1945- *St&PR 93*
Andrushkiw, Roman Ihor 1937- *WhoE 93*
Andrusieczko, Adam Franciszek 1931- *WhoScE 91-4*
Andruskevich, Thomas Anthony 1951- *St&PR 93*
Andruzzi, Ellen Adamson 1917- *WhoAmW 93*
Andrychuk, Dmetro 1918- *WhoSSW 93*
Andrysiak, Janine S. 1953- *WhoAmW 93*
Andryszak, John A. 1951- *St&PR 93*
Andryszak, John Adam *Law&B 92*
Andrzejak-Andre, Marilyn Kathleen 1960- *WhoEmL 93*
Andrzejewski, Jerzy 1909-1983 *PolBiDi*
Andrzejewski, Marceli 1923- *WhoScE 91-4*
Andrzejewski, Margaret Rusek 1953- *WhoWrEP 92*
Andujar, Manuel 1913- *DcMexL*
Andujar, Rafael 1946- *WhoEmL 93*
Aneiro, Richard John 1930- *WhoE 93*
Anell, Lars Evert Roland 1941- *WhoUN 92*
Anelli, Angelo 1761-1820 *OxDcOp*
Anello, Douglas A. d1990 *BioIn 17*
Anello, John Albert, Jr. 1953- *WhoEmL 93*
Anemas *OxDcByz*
Anemone *BioIn 17*
Anerio, Felice c. 1560-1614 *Baker 92*
Anerio, Giovanni Francesco c. 1567-1630 *Baker 92*
Anerousis, John Peter 1949- *WhoE 93, WhoEmL 93*
Anesta, Joseph A. *Law&B 92*
Anestos, Harry Peter 1917- *WhoE 93*
Anet, Baptiste 1676-1755 *Baker 92*
Anet, Jean-Baptiste 1650-1710 *Baker 92*
Anet, N'zi Nanan Koliabo 1942- *WhoUN 92*
Anewalt, Thomas C. 1953- *WhoEmL 93*
Anfield, Frank *BioIn 17*
Anfindsen, Cyrus Peter 1934- *St&PR 93*
Anfinsen, Christian Boehmer 1916- *WhoAm 92, WhoE 93, WhoWor 93*
Anfinson, A.A. 1923- *St&PR 93*
Anfinson, Thomas Elmer 1941- *WhoAm 92*
Anfinson, Verna A. 1929- *St&PR 93*
Anfossi, Pasquale 1727-1797 *Baker 92, OxDcOp*
Anfousse, Ginette 1944- *WhoCanL 92*
Ang, Alfredo Hua-Sing 1930- *WhoAm 92*
Ang, Marcelo Huibonhoa, Jr. 1959- *WhoWor 93*
Ang, Ozdem 1933- *WhoScE 91-4*
Ang, Renato Vicente 1960- *WhoWor 93*
Angalet, Gwendoline Bain 1947- *WhoEmL 93*
Angara, Edgardo J. 1934- *WhoAsAP 91*
Angarola, Robert Joseph 1950- *WhoE 93*
Angarola, Robert Thomas 1945- *WhoAm 92*
Ange, Michael *BioIn 17*
Angel, Albalucia 1939- *BioIn 17, SpAmA*
Angel, Albert David 1937- *St&PR 93*
Angel, Allen Robert 1942- *WhoE 93*
Angel, Arthur Ronald 1948- *WhoAm 92*
Angel, Aubie 1935- *WhoAm 92*
Angel, Benjamin J. 1936- *St&PR 93*
Angel, Daniel Duane 1939- *WhoSSW 93*
Angel, David Edgar, Sr. 1928- *WhoSSW 93*
Angel, Dennis 1947- *WhoEmL 93*
Angel, Elizabeth Jouret 1933- *WhoE 93*
Angel, Frank Philip 1953- *WhoEmL 93*
Angel, Jack E. 1938- *St&PR 93*
Angel, Jack Easton 1938- *WhoWor 93*
Angel, James Roger Prior 1941- *WhoAm 92*
Angel, James Terrance 1945- *WhoAm 92*
Angel, John Lawrence 1915-1986 *IntDcAn*
Angel, Leonard 1945- *WhoCanL 92*
Angel, Martin Vivian 1937- *WhoWor 93*
Angel, Michelle Robin 1963- *WhoAmW 93, WhoEmL 93*
Angel, Milton Israel 1921- *St&PR 93*
Angel, Ralph Michael 1951- *WhoWrEP 92*
Angel, Steven Michael 1950- *WhoEmL 93*
Angelakis, Manos G. 1941- *WhoE 93*
Angelakos, Diogenes James 1919- *WhoAm 92*
Angelakos, Evangelos Theodorou 1929- *WhoAm 92, WhoE 93, WhoWor 93*
Angela Merici, Saint 1474-1540 *BioIn 17*
Angelastro, Jane Ellen 1942- *WhoAmW 93*
Angelastro, Terese Marie 1968- *WhoWrEP 92*
Angele, Alfred Robert 1940- *WhoWor 93*
Angele, Susan M. *Law&B 92*
Angeles, Democrito J. 1922- *WhoAsAP 91*
Angeles, Romeo S. 1930- *WhoAsAP 91*
Angeles, Victoria de los *BioIn 17*
Angeles, Victoria de Los 1923- *Baker 92*
Angeles Torres, Maria de los *NotHsAW 93*
Angeletti, Maria Claire *Law&B 92*
Angeli, Andrea d' 1868-1940 *Baker 92*
Angeli, Gerry 1946- *St&PR 93*
Angeli, Maceo-Giovanni 1951- *WhoScE 91-3*
Angeli, Pier 1932-1971 *BioIn 17*
Angelicchio, David John 1951- *St&PR 93*
Angelicchio, Domenic Louis 1944- *St&PR 93*
Angelich, Anton P. R. 1950- *WhoEmL 93*
Angelich, Mark S. *St&PR 93*
Angelich, Samuel Michael 1924- *St&PR 93*
Angelici, Robert J. 1937- *WhoAm 92*
Angelides, Demosthenes Constantinos 1947- *WhoWor 93*
Angelides, Kikis Michael 1939- *WhoUN 92*
Angelides, Marios Costas 1964- *WhoWor 93*
Angelilli, Frank G. 1948- *St&PR 93*
Angelillo, Lori Ann 1963- *WhoEmL 93*
Angelin, Bo Anders 1949- *WhoWor 93*
Angeline, Karen *BioIn 17*
Angeline, Victor, III *Law&B 92*
Angelini, Arnaldo Maria 1909- *WhoWor 93*
Angelini, Bontempi Giovanni Andrea *Baker 92*
Angelini, Carl A. 1935- *St&PR 93*
Angelini, F.A. 1944- *WhoScE 91-3*
Angelini, Giancarlo *WhoScE 91-3*
Angelini, Jean-Claude 1955- *WhoWor 93*
Angelino, Charles F. 1935- *St&PR 93, WhoIns 93*
Angelino, Henri 1935- *WhoScE 91-2*
Angelino, Steven A.G.F. 1953- *WhoScE 91-3*
Angelis, Flora Mariana de *See* Mariani-Masi, Maddalena 1850-1916 *OxDcOp*
Angelis, Frank *St&PR 93*
Angell, Betty Ruth Johnson 1943- *WhoAmW 93, WhoWor 93*
Angell, Charles Marshall 1946- *WhoIns 93*
Angell, Charles T. 1941- *St&PR 93*
Angell, Granville Williams, III 1947- *WhoSSW 93*
Angell, J. Steven 1949- *St&PR 93*
Angell, James Browne 1924- *WhoAm 92, WhoWor 93*
Angell, Jeanne Simon 1961- *WhoE 93*
Angell, Judie 1937- *ScF&FL 92*
Angell, Karol 1950- *WhoEmL 93, WhoSSW 93*
Angell, Norman Rockefeller 1944- *St&PR 93*
Angell, Richard Bradshaw 1918- *WhoAm 92*
Angell, Richard S. *BioIn 17*
Angell, Roger *BioIn 17*
Angell, Roger 1920- *BiDAMSp 1989, WhoAm 92, WhoWrEP 92*
Angell, Valentine Chauncey 1941- *WhoWrEP 92*
Angell, Wayne *BioIn 17*
Angell, Wayne D. 1939- *WhoAm 92, WhoWor 93*
Angelle, Paul J. 1937- *St&PR 93*
Angelo, Girard Francis 1929- *WhoE 93*
Angelo, Ivan 1936- *ScF&FL 92*
Angelo, J. Victor Da Silva 1949- *WhoUN 92*
Angelo, Louis d' 1888-1958 *Baker 92*
Angelo, Peter Gregory 1947- *WhoE 93, WhoEmL 93*
Angelo, Priscilla J. *WhoE 93*
Angelo, Richard *BioIn 17*
Angelo, Richard John 1940- *St&PR 93*
Angelo, Robert A. *Law&B 92*
Angelo, Ronald John 1952- *WhoEmL 93*
Angelo, Sandra Ann 1952- *WhoEmL 93*
Angelo, Susan Ann 1956- *WhoAmW 93*
Angeloff, Dann V. 1935- *WhoAm 92, WhoWor 93*
Angelone, A.C. 1939- *St&PR 93*
Angelone, Romolo d1991 *BioIn 17*
Angeloni, Carlo 1834-1901 *Baker 92*
Angeloni, Gianni Antonio 1947- *WhoWor 93*
Angelopoulos, Athanasios Anastasios 1939- *WhoWor 93*
Angelopoulos, Theo 1936- *MiSFD 9*
Angelopoulos, Thodoros 1935- *BioIn 17*
Angelos *OxDcByz*
Angelos, Cynthia G. 1955- *WhoSSW 93*
Angelou, Maya *BioIn 17*
Angelou, Maya 1928- *AmWomWr 92, ConTFT 10, WhoAm 92, WhoWrEP 92*
Angelov, Angel Simeonov 1929- *WhoScE 91-4*
Angelov, Vasil Georgiev 1950- *WhoWor 93*
Angelow, Andrey Kirilow 1950- *WhoWor 93*
Angelozzi, Nicholas J. 1942- *St&PR 93*
Angel-Shaffer, Arlene Beth 1951- *WhoEmL 93*
Angelucci, Jeff *MiSFD 9*
Anger, Darol c. 1953- *See* Turtle Island String Quartet *ConMus 9*
Anger, Gottfried Johann 1928- *WhoWor 93*
Anger, Kenneth 1932- *MiSFD 9, WhoWrEP 92*
Anger, Willibald *WhoScE 91-3*
Angerer, Paul 1927- *Baker 92*
Angermuller, Rudolph (Kurt) 1940- *Baker 92*
Angers, Pierre-Jean David d' 1788-1856 *BioIn 17*
Angert, Norbert 1940- *WhoScE 91-3*
Angert, Stuart Henry 1941- *WhoE 93*
Angerville, Edwin Duvanel 1961- *WhoE 93*
Angevine, Eric Neil 1949- *WhoEmL 93, WhoSSW 93*
Anggard, Erik E. 1934- *WhoScE 91-4*
Anggard, K. *WhoScE 91-4*
Anghaie, Samim 1949- *WhoAm 92*
Anghinetti, Joseph Richard 1936- *St&PR 93*
Angier, Natalie Marie 1958- *WhoAm 92, WhoAmW 93, WhoE 93*
Angileri, Antonio 1950- *WhoE 93*
Angino, Ernest Edward 1932- *WhoAm 92*
Angioli, Renata Maria 1962- *WhoEmL 93*
Angiolini, Gaspero 1731-1803 *OxDcOp*
Angione, Howard Francis 1940- *WhoAm 92*
Anglada, Jay Alfred 1939- *WhoAm 92*
Angle, John Charles 1923- *St&PR 93, WhoAm 92, WhoE 93*
Angle, John Edwin 1931- *WhoAm 92*
Angle, Kelly *BioIn 17*
Angle, Lisa Alison 1953- *WhoEmL 93*
Angle, Margaret Susan 1948- *WhoEmL 93, WhoWor 93*
Angle, Richard W. 1941- *St&PR 93*
Angle, Richard Warner, Jr. 1941- *WhoAm 92*
Angle, Roger R. 1938- *WhoWrEP 92*
Anglebert, Jean-Baptiste Henri d' 1661-1735 *Baker 92*
Anglebert, Jean-Henri d' 1628-1691 *Baker 92*
Anglemire, Kenneth Norton *WhoAm 92*
Anglemyer, Grant M. 1946- *St&PR 93*
Angles, Higini 1888-1969 *Baker 92*
Angles, Rafael 1731-1816 *Baker 92*
Anglesey, Zoe R. 1941- *WhoWrEP 92*
Angleton, James *BioIn 17*
Anglewicz, David James 1947- *St&PR 93*
Anglim, John J. d1991 *BioIn 17*
Anglim, Timothy P. 1952- *St&PR 93*
Anglin, Clarence *BioIn 17*
Anglin, J. Michael *Law&B 92*
Anglin, John *BioIn 17*
Anglin, Linda McCluney 1929- *WhoSSW 93, WhoWor 93*
Anglin, Michael Williams 1946- *WhoEmL 93*
Anglin, Richard R. 1938- *St&PR 93*
Angling, Michael 1943- *WhoWor 93*
Anglo, Michael *ScF&FL 92*
Angmar-Mansson, Birgit E. 1939- *WhoScE 91-4*
Angoff, Charles 1902-1979 *JeAmFiW, ScF&FL 92*
Angoff, Marion Brenda 1939- *WhoWrEP 92*
Angotti, Antonio Mario 1958- *WhoEmL 93*
Angotti, Arthur A. 1944- *St&PR 93*
Angotti, Franco 1941- *WhoScE 91-3*
Angove, Tom 1914- *BioIn 17*
Angove-Rogers, Adrian Jean 1965- *WhoSSW 93*
Angremy, Jean-Pierre 1937- *WhoWor 93*
Angrilli, Albert 1917- *WhoE 93*
Angrisani, Frank 1950- *St&PR 93*
Angrisano, Giuseppe *WhoScE 91-3*
Angst, Jules 1926- *WhoScE 91-4*
Angster, John David 1952- *St&PR 93*
Angster, Judit 1951- *WhoWor 93*
Angstman, Clifford W. 1952- *St&PR 93*
Angstrom, Wayne Raymond 1939- *WhoAm 92, WhoWor 93*
Anguiano, Eugenio 1938- *WhoUN 92*
Anguiano, Lupe 1929- *HispAmA, NotHsAW 93 [port], WhoAm 92, WhoAmW 93*
Anguiano, Raul 1915- *WhoWor 93*
Anguier, Michel 1612-1686 *BioIn 17*
Anguisciola, Sofonisba 1527?-1625 *BioIn 17*
Anguizola, Gustavo Antonio 1928- *WhoWor 93*
Angulo, Charles Bonin 1943- *WhoE 93, WhoWor 93*
Angulo, Gerard Antonio 1956- *WhoAm 92, WhoEmL 93*
Angulo, Lawrence George 1948- *WhoEmL 93*
Angulo, Manuel R. 1917- *St&PR 93*
Angulo, Manuel Rafael 1917- *WhoAm 92*
Angulo, Miriam 1955- *NotHsAW 93*
Angus, Bruce 1906- *St&PR 93*
Angus, Chris A.L. *Law&B 92*
Angus, John Cotton 1934- *WhoAm 92*
Angus, Rosalie JoAnn 1939- *WhoAmW 93*
Angus, William Arthur, Jr. 1923- *WhoAm 92*
Angus, William Arthur, III 1946- *St&PR 93*
Angus, William Roger 1949- *St&PR 93*
Angus-Leppan, P.-V. *WhoScE 91-2*
Angus-Leppan, Peter Vincent 1930- *WhoWor 93*
Anhaiser, L.A. 1938- *St&PR 93*
Anhalt, Edward 1914- *ConTFT 10*
Anhalt, Frederic von *BioIn 17*
Anhalt, Istvan 1919- *Baker 92*
Anhang, Abraham *St&PR 93*
Anhut, William Frederick, Jr. 1952- *St&PR 93*
Aniag, Francisco B., Jr. 1948- *WhoAsAP 91*
Anicia Juliana 461?-527? *OxDcByz [port]*
Anicius *OxDcByz*
Aniel, Jan H. *Law&B 92*
Anielewicz, Mordechaj 1919-1943 *PolBiDi*
Anievas, Agustin 1934- *Baker 92*
Anik, Selahattin 1927- *WhoScE 91-4*
Anikeeff, Anthony Hotchkiss 1952- *WhoEmL 93*
Anikonov, Yuri Evgienievich 1933- *WhoWor 93*
Anikulapo-Kuti, Fela 1938- *BioIn 17*
Anil, Sahin 1952- *WhoScE 91-4*
Anile, Angelo Marcello 1948- *WhoScE 91-3*
Animuccia, Giovanni c. 1500-1571 *Baker 92*
Aniot, Andrzej *WhoScE 91-4*
Anishchenko, Vadim Semenovich 1943- *WhoWor 93*
Anisimov, Anatoly Vasylyovich 1948- *WhoWor 93*
Anisimov, Vladimir Vladislavovich 1947- *WhoWor 93*
Anisits, Ferenc 1938- *WhoScE 91-4*
Aniskovich, Paul P. 1936- *WhoIns 93*
Aniskovich, Paul Peter, Jr. 1936- *St&PR 93, WhoAm 92*
Anisman, Martin Jay 1942- *WhoAm 92, WhoSSW 93*
Aniszewski, Tadeusz 1950- *WhoScE 91-4*
Anjard, Ronald Paul, Sr. 1935- *WhoAm 92*
Anjoorian, Rosalie B. 1951- *WhoAmW 93*
Anjum, Ilyas Mohammad 1955- *WhoE 93*
Ank, William 1951- *WhoAsAP 91*
Anka, Paul 1941- *Baker 92, WhoAm 92*
Ankara, Alpay 1938- *WhoScE 91-4*
Ankeny, DeWalt H., Jr. *BioIn 17*
Anker, Peter 1955- *WhoWor 93*
Anker, Peter L. 1935- *St&PR 93*
Anker, Peter Louis 1935- *WhoAm 92*
Anker, Richard Bruce 1943- *WhoUN 92*
Anker, Robert Alvin 1941- *WhoAm 92, WhoIns 93*
Ankerl, Guy Cornelius Thomas 1933- *WhoWor 93*
Ankerman, William Lewis 1947- *WhoEmL 93*
Ankers, Evelyn 1918-1985 *BioIn 17*
Ankerson, Robert William 1933- *WhoE 93*
Ankney, Jeannie Broskey 1954- *WhoAmW 93*
Ankrum, Dorothy Darlene 1933- *WhoAmW 93*
Ankrum, L. Doyle 1928- *St&PR 93*
Ankrum, Morris 1896-1964 *BioIn 17*

Ankrum, William Dean 1930- St&PR 93
Anliker, Rudolf 1926- WhoWor 93
An Lu-Shan d757 HarEnMi
Anlyan, William George 1925- WhoAm 92
Ann, Beatrice 1936- WhoAmW 93
Anna 963-1011 OxDcByz
Anna, Karl Edward 1932- St&PR 93
Anna Amalia 1723-1787 Baker 92
Anna Amalia 1739-1807 Baker 92
Anna Amalia, Duchess of Saxe-Weimar 1739-1807 BioIn 17
Anna Amalie, Princess of Prussia 1723-1787 BioIn 17
Annabi, Hedi 1943- WhoUN 92
Annabi, Kamal 1940- WhoUN 92
Annable, Weldon Grant 1937- WhoAm 92
Annakin, Ken 1914- MiSFD 9
Anna Komnene OxDcByz
Annan, Daniel Francis 1928- WhoAfr
Annan, David ScF&FL 92
Annan, Kofi Atta 1938- WhoUN 92
Annan, Ralph ScF&FL 92
Annand, Iathan T. Law&B 92
Annand, James Earle 1929- WhoAm 92
Anna O. 1859-1936 BioIn 17
Anna of Savoy 1306?-c. 1365 OxDcByz
Annaswamy, Anuradha Mandayam 1956- WhoE 93
Annaud, Jean-Jacques 1943- MiSFD 9, WhoWor 93
Anne, Her Royal Highness 1950- WhoWor 93
Anne, Princess 1950- BioIn 17
Anne, Claire WhoWrEP 92
Anne, David 1930- ScF&FL 92
Annear, Laurence I. 1949- St&PR 93
Anne Boleyn, Queen 1507-1536 BioIn 17
Annechini, William, Jr. 1950- WhoEmL 93
Anneken, William Bernard 1933- St&PR 93
Annenberg, Barnet 1931- St&PR 93
Annenberg, Sophia Morris 1910- St&PR 93
Annenberg, Ted M. Law&B 92
Annenberg, Ted M. 1927- St&PR 93
Annenberg, Walter 1908- JeAmHC, News 92 [port], -92-3 [port]
Annenberg, Walter H. 1908- BioIn 17, WhoAm 92
Anne, of Hanover, Princess of Orange 1709-1759 BioIn 17
Annese, Betsy Jane 1949- WhoSSW 93
Annese, Domenico 1919- WhoAm 92
Annesley, Thomas Michael 1953- WhoEmL 93
Annessi, Jean Ludeman 1958- WhoEmL 93
Annestrand, Stig Alvar 1933- WhoAm 92
Annett, Bruce James, Jr. 1952- WhoWrEP 92
Annett, Cora (Scott) 1931- DcAmChF 1960
Annett, John WhoScE 91-1
Annett, R.D. Law&B 92
Annetta, Catherine 1951- WhoEmL 93
Annetti, Robert J. 1936- St&PR 93
Annetts, Ed 1919- BioIn 17
Anni, Arden S. 1951- WhoAsAP 91
Annibale c. 1527-1575 Baker 92
Annibale (Il Padovano) c. 1527-1575 Baker 92
Annibale, Robert Anthony 1948- St&PR 93
Annibali, Domenico c. 1705-1779 OxDcOp
Annie Johnston DcAmChF 1960
Anniko, Matti 1947- WhoScE 91-4
Annila, Erkki Aulis 1937- WhoScE 91-4
Anning, Raymon Harry 1930- WhoAsAP 91
Annis, Edward R. 1913- WhoSSW 93
Annis, Lawrence Vincent 1946- WhoSSW 93
Annis, Martin 1922- St&PR 93, WhoAm 92
Annis, Robert Lyndon 1949- WhoEmL 93
Ann-Margret 1941- BioIn 17, WhoAm 92
Anno, James Nelson 1934- WhoAm 92
Anno, Mitsumasa ChlBIID [port]
Anno, Mitsumasa 1926- BioIn 17, MajAI [port]
Anns, Arlene Eiserman WhoAmW 93
Anns, Philip Harold 1925- St&PR 93, WhoAm 92
Annunziata, Kimberly Joy 1955- WhoEmL 93
Annunzio, Frank BioIn 17
Annunzio, Frank 1915- CngDr 91, WhoAm 92
Annunzio, Gabriele d' 1863-1938 HarEnMi
Annus, John Augustus 1935- WhoAm 92
Annus, Sandor 1930- WhoScE 91-4
Anobile, Richard J. 1947- ScF&FL 92
Anoff, Jean Schoenstadt 1937- WhoSSW 93
Anokye, Akua Duku 1948- WhoEmL 93
Anon, Julian Louis 1954- WhoEmL 93
Anonsen, Nils Ove Georg 1938- WhoWor 93
Anonsen, P. Denise 1956- WhoAmW 93
Ano Nuevo Kerr, Louise NotHsAW 93
Anosov, Dmitriy Victorovich 1936- WhoWor 93
Anosov, Nikolai 1900-1962 Baker 92
Anouilh, Jean 1910-1987 BioIn 17
Anouilh, Lisa Denise 1962- WhoAmW 93
Anrig, Gregory Richard 1931- WhoAm 92
Anrooij, Peter van 1879-1954 Baker 92
Anrooy, Peter van 1879-1954 Baker 92
Anryon, Julien BioIn 17
Ansa, Tina McElroy BioIn 17
Ansak, Marie-Louise 1928- WhoAm 92
Ansani, Giovanni 1744-1826 OxDcOp
Ansari, Mohammad Aslam 1932- WhoUN 92
Ansari, Mohammed Amin 1934- WhoAsAP 91
Ansari, Nadim Ahmad 1947- WhoWor 93
Ansary, Cyrus A. 1933- WhoAm 92
Ansary, Hassan J. 1949- St&PR 93
Ansary, Hassan Jaber 1949- WhoAm 92, WhoWor 93
Ansbacher, Charles Alexander 1942- WhoAm 92
Ansbacher, Lewis 1928- WhoAm 92
Ansbacher, Max George 1935- WhoE 93
Ansbacher, Rudi 1934- WhoAm 92
Ansbert OxDcByz
Ansbro, James Michael WhoWor 93
Ansbro, John Joseph 1932- WhoE 93
Anscher, Bernard 1922- WhoAm 92, WhoSSW 93, WhoWor 93
Anscher, Marcia Daniel St&PR 93
Anschuetz, Lou John 1952- WhoEmL 93
Anschuetz, Norbert Lee 1915- WhoAm 92
Anschutz, Karl 1815-1870 Baker 92
Anschutz, Mark W. 1952- St&PR 93
Anschutz, Phillip F. 1939- WhoAm 92
Anseaume, Louis d1784 OxDcOp
Ansehl, Robert A. Law&B 92
Ansel, Howard Carl 1933- WhoAm 92
Ansell, Edward Orin 1926- WhoAm 92
Ansell, George Stephen 1934- WhoAm 92
Ansell, Julian S. 1922- WhoAm 92
Ansell, Ruth Elizabeth 1956- WhoEmL 93
Anselm c. 1100-1158 OxDcByz
Anselm, Saint, Archbishop of Canterbury 1033-1109 BioIn 17
Anselme, Jean-Pierre Louis Marie 1936- WhoAm 92
Anselment, Kenneth L., Jr. Law&B 92
Anselmi, Giuseppe 1876-1929 Baker 92, OxDcOp
Anselmi, Robert A. Law&B 92
Anselmini, Jean-Pierre 1940- WhoAm 92
Anselmo, Garry L. 1944- St&PR 93
Anselmo, Giovanni BioIn 17
Anselmo, Philip Shepard 1940- WhoAm 92
Anselmo, Rene BioIn 17
Anseman, Terry Olano 1947- WhoSSW 93
Ansen, David 1945- ConTFT 10
Ansen, David B. 1945- WhoAm 92, WhoE 93
Ansermet, Ernest 1883-1969 Baker 92, OxDcOp
Ansevics, Nancy Leah 1940- WhoAmW 93
Ansfield, Thomas J. 1940- St&PR 93
Ansgar, Rabenalt P. WhoScE 91-4
Anshaw, Carol 1946- WhoAm 92
Anshell, Joseph G. 1946- St&PR 93
Anshen, Melvin 1912- WhoAm 92
Anshen, Ruth Nanda 1914- WhoAmW 93
Ansin, Ronald M. 1934- St&PR 93
Ansle, Dorothy ScF&FL 92
Anslee, Ancella AmWomPl
Ansley, Addie 1933- St&PR 93
Ansley, Campbell Wallace, Jr. 1921- WhoSSW 93
Ansley, Darlene H. 1942- WhoSSW 93
Ansley, Darlyne 1940- St&PR 93
Ansley, David George 1956- WhoEmL 93
Ansley, Georgeanna St&PR 93
Ansley, Kenneth W. St&PR 93
Anslinger, Harry Jacob 1892-1975 BioIn 17
Anslow, D.A. WhoScE 91-1
Ansnes, Terry Law&B 92
Anson, Capt. 1841- ScF&FL 92
Anson, Abraham 1912- WhoWrEP 92
Anson, Barbara ScF&FL 92
Anson, F. Martin 1942- St&PR 93
Anson, Fred Colvig 1933- WhoAm 92
Anson, George 1697-1762 HarEnMi
Anson, George 1797-1857 HarEnMi
Anson, Hugo Philip 1947- WhoUN 92
Anson, Jay 1921-1980 ScF&FL 92
Anson, Michael WhoScE 91-1
Anson, Michael A. 1946- WhoAm 92
Anson, Robert Sam 1945- BioIn 17
Anson, Roger William WhoScE 91-1
Anson-Weber, Joan E. 1927- WhoWrEP 92
Ansorge, Conrad (Eduard Reinhold) 1862-1930 Baker 92
Ansorge, Harry O. Law&B 92
Ansorge, Iona Marie 1927- WhoAmW 93
Ansorge, Richard Eric WhoScE 91-1
Ansorge, Wilhelm 1944- WhoScE 91-3
Anspach, Ernst 1913- WhoAm 92, WhoE 93
Anspach, Herbert Kephart 1926- WhoAm 92
Anspach, Kenneth Gordon 1952- WhoEmL 93
Anspaugh, David MiSFD 9
Anspon, Harry Davis 1917- WhoE 93
Anstadt, George W. 1947- WhoE 93
Anstatt, Peter Jan 1942- WhoAm 92, WhoE 93
Anstee, Margaret Joan 1926- WhoUN 92
Anstett, Alfred 1926- WhoScE 91-2
Anstett, Robert Emory 1933- WhoWrEP 92
Anstine, Mary K. St&PR 93
Anstruther, Eva AmWomPl
Antaky, Donald E. St&PR 93
Antal, Emanuel 1931- WhoScE 91-4
Antal, Jozsef 1919- WhoScE 91-4
Antal, Kimberly Joan 1959- WhoEmL 93
Antal, Martin WhoScE 91-4
Antal, Michael Jerry, Jr. 1947- WhoEmL 93
Antal, Saul Cornel 1927- WhoWor 93
Antal, Stephen J. Law&B 92
Antall, Jozsef BioIn 17, WhoWor 93
Antaloczy, Zoltan 1923- WhoScE 91-4
Antanaitis, Cynthia Emily 1954- WhoAmW 93, WhoEmL 93
Antani, Sunil F. 1947- St&PR 93
Antar, Basil Niman 1942- WhoAm 92
Antar, Eddie 1947- NewYTBS 92 [port]
Antar, Johanna Frances 1953- WhoAmW 93
Antar, Sam Law&B 92
Antaya, Kenneth Francis 1947- St&PR 93
Antczak, Janice 1947- ScF&FL 92
Ante, Jose Lotivio 1947- WhoWor 93
Antegnati, Costanzo 1549-1624 Baker 92
Antekeier, Kristopher BioIn 17
Antell, Darrick Eugene WhoE 93
Antell, Judy BioIn 17
Antell, Maryann F. 1962- St&PR 93
Antelline, Fred F. 1910- St&PR 93
Antenberg, Bruce Franklin 1938- St&PR 93
Anteplioglu, Hayrettin 1924- WhoScE 91-4
Antequera y Castro, Jose 1690-1731 HarEnMi
Antes, Harry W. 1930- St&PR 93
Antes, Horst 1936- BioIn 17, WhoWor 93
Antes, John 1740-1811 Baker 92
Anteunis, Marc Jan Oscar 1932- WhoScE 91-2
Antezana, Fernando S. 1935- WhoUN 92
Antheil, George 1900-1959 Baker 92, BioIn 17, OxDcOp
Anthemios dc. 414 OxDcByz
Anthemios d472 OxDcByz
Anthemios of Tralles dc. 558 OxDcByz
Anthes, Clifford Charles 1907- WhoWor 93
Anthes, John A., Jr. 1949- St&PR 93
Anthes, Richard Allen 1944- WhoAm 92
Anthimos of Nikomedeia d303 OxDcByz
Anthofer, Joseph D. Law&B 92
Anthoine, Robert 1921- WhoAm 92, WhoWor 93
Anthonsen, Karl Martin 1928- WhoScE 91-4
Anthony, Bishop 1935- WhoAm 92
Anthony, A.K. 1940- WhoAsAP 91
Anthony, Adam 1923- WhoE 93
Anthony, Andrew John 1950- WhoEmL 93
Anthony, Beryl F., Jr. 1938- CngDr 91
Anthony, Beryl Franklin, Jr. 1938- WhoAm 92, WhoSSW 93
Anthony, Burton C. 1932- St&PR 93
Anthony, C. L. ConAu 37NR, MajAI
Anthony, Carol A. Law&B 92
Anthony, Carolyn Additon 1949- WhoEmL 93
Anthony, Clarence E. AfrAmBi
Anthony, Clary 1924- St&PR 93
Anthony, David Vincent 1929- WhoAm 92
Anthony, Dean Wade 1948- WhoEmL 93, WhoSSW 93
Anthony, Dee ScF&FL 92
Anthony, Donald Barrett 1948- St&PR 93, WhoAm 92, WhoEmL 93, WhoSSW 93
Anthony, Donald Charles 1926- WhoAm 92
Anthony, Donald Harold 1950- WhoEmL 93
Anthony, Edward Lovell, II 1921- WhoAm 92
Anthony, Edward Mason 1922- WhoAm 92, WhoE 93
Anthony, Elaine Margaret 1932- WhoAmW 93
Anthony, Ethan 1950- WhoE 93, WhoEmL 93
Anthony, Frank 1922- WhoWrEP 92
Anthony, Frank S. Law&B 92
Anthony, Fred Paul 1935- WhoAm 92
Anthony, George Tobey 1824-1896 BioIn 17
Anthony, Graham WhoScE 91-1
Anthony, Greg 1967- BioIn 17
Anthony, Gretchen Wilhelmina Hauser 1936- WhoSSW 93
Anthony, Guy M. 1915- St&PR 93
Anthony, Harris R. Law&B 92
Anthony, Harry Antoniades 1922- WhoAm 92, WhoWor 93
Anthony, Henry B. 1815-1884 PolPar
Anthony, Henry Bowen 1815-1884 JrnUS
Anthony, J. Marshall 1944- St&PR 93
Anthony, Jacqueline 1966- WhoAmW 93, WhoEmL 93
Anthony, James R(aymond) 1922- Baker 92
Anthony, Jan S. 1942- St&PR 93
Anthony, Jane Marie 1950- WhoE 93
Anthony, Jimmy Jess 1952- WhoSSW 93
Anthony, Joe L. 1951- St&PR 93
Anthony, John MajAI
Anthony, John Edward 1932- St&PR 93
Anthony, John Joseph 1940- WhoSSW 93
Anthony, John T. St&PR 93
Anthony, Joseph 1912- MiSFD 9
Anthony, Joseph 1960- WhoWrEP 92
Anthony, Joseph Harry 1949- WhoEmL 93
Anthony, Julian Danford, Jr. 1935- WhoAm 92
Anthony, Kara Lee 1965- WhoEmL 93
Anthony, Kenneth 1942- WhoScE 91-1
Anthony, Len S. Law&B 92
Anthony, Lysette ConTFT 10
Anthony, Mark 1966- ScF&FL 92
Anthony, Michael 1932- BioIn 17, DcLB 125 [port]
Anthony, Michael 1955- See Van Halen ConMus 8
Anthony, Michael Thomas 1959- WhoE 93
Anthony, Page 1935- MiSFD 9
Anthony, Patrick Allan 1954- WhoEmL 93
Anthony, Paul Barrie 1934- WhoE 93
Anthony, Perry 1940- St&PR 93, WhoAm 92
Anthony, Piers BioIn 17
Anthony, Piers 1934- ScF&FL 92
Anthony, Ray 1922- Baker 92
Anthony, Richard E. 1946- St&PR 93
Anthony, Robert Armstrong 1931- WhoAm 92
Anthony, Robert Holland 1948- WhoAm 92, WhoSSW 93
Anthony, Robert J. 1934- St&PR 93
Anthony, Robert Newton 1916- WhoAm 92
Anthony, Ronald T. 1939- St&PR 93
Anthony, Rowland Barney 1918- St&PR 93
Anthony, Roy d1992 BioIn 17, NewYTBS 92
Anthony, Stephen C. Law&B 92
Anthony, Stephen Clay 1951- WhoSSW 93
Anthony, Steven J. Law&B 92
Anthony, Susan B. 1820-1906 GayN, PolPar
Anthony, Susan Brownell 1820-1906 BioIn 17
Anthony, Thomas Dale 1952- WhoEmL 93
Anthony, Thomas Richard 1941- WhoAm 92
Anthony, Vernice Davis 1945- WhoAm 92
Anthony, Virginia Quinn Bausch 1945- WhoAm 92
Anthony, William Graham 1934- WhoAm 92
Anthony, William Ross 1924- St&PR 93
Anthony, Yancey Lamar 1922- WhoWor 93
Anthony Gulden, Kathy Ann 1963- WhoE 93
Anthony-Negron, Dona Lee 1955- WhoAmW 93
Anthony, of Padua, Saint 1195-1231 BioIn 17
Anthony Peter, His Beatitude 1907- WhoAm 92, WhoWor 93
Antic, Michael 1963- WhoEmL 93
Antich, Rose Ann WhoAmW 93
Anticho, Andrea c. 1480-1539? Baker 92
Antico, Andrea c. 1480-1539? Baker 92
Antieau, Kim ScF&FL 92
Antignani, Bonnie Provenzano 1952- WhoWrEP 92
Antigua, Orlando BioIn 17
Antila, Matti Tapio 1926- WhoScE 91-4
Antila, V. Anna WhoWrEP 92
Antila, Veijo A. 1930- WhoScE 91-4

Antill, D.M. WhoScE 91-1
Antill, John 1904-1986 Baker 92
Antill, Keith 1929- ScF&FL 92
Antilla, Susan 1954- WhoAm 92, WhoAmW 93, WhoEmL 93
Antin, Anthony Lenard 1923- WhoE 93
Antin, Arthur J. St&PR 93
Antin, David 1932- WhoAm 92, WhoWrEP 92
Antin, Eleanor 1935- WhoAm 92
Antin, Mary 1881-1949 BioIn 17, JeAmFiW
Antin, Robert L. St&PR 93
Antinori, Dennis J. 1948- St&PR 93
Antinori, Orazio 1811-1882 IntDcAn
Antiochos OxDcByz
Antiochos, Gregory 1125?-c. 1196 OxDcByz
Antiochos Strategos OxDcByz
Antiochus, IV, King of Syria c. 215BC-164BC BioIn 17
Antion, David Stephen 1961- WhoEmL 93
Antipa, Gregory Alexis 1941- WhoAm 92
Antiphon 5th cent.BC- BioIn 17
Antisdale, C. Martin 1932- St&PR 93
Antle, Charles Edward 1930- WhoAm 92
Antle, Ricky Lee 1953- WhoE 93
Antler, Morton 1928- WhoAm 92
Antman, Stuart Sheldon 1939- WhoAm 92
Antoine, Andre 1858-1943 BioIn 17
Antoine, Florence Sheila 1941- WhoAmW 93
Antoine, Georges 1892-1918 Baker 92
Antoine, Nolton 1940- BioIn 17
Antoine, Robert Francis 1927- St&PR 93
Antokol, Joan S. Law&B 92
Antokoletz, Elliott Maxim 1942- WhoAm 92
Antokolski, Mark Matveevich 1843-1902 PolBiDi
Antoku, Norimitsu 1929- WhoWor 93
Antolik, Michael Raymond 1948- WhoE 93
Anton, Bill 1957- BioIn 17
Anton, Bruce Norman 1951- St&PR 93, WhoEmL 93
Anton, Frank A. 1949- WhoAm 92
Anton, Frederick W., III 1934- St&PR 93, WhoIns 93
Anton, George Louis 1923- WhoAm 92
Anton, Harvey 1923- St&PR 93, WhoAm 92, WhoE 93, WhoWor 93
Anton, Ioan 1924- WhoScE 91-4
Anton, John M. 1947- WhoEmL 93
Anton, Lori L. Law&B 92
Anton, Mace Damon 1961- WhoE 93
Anton, Nicholas Guy d1992 NewYTBS 92 [port]
Anton, Nicholas Guy 1906-1992 WhoAm 92, WhoWor 93
Anton, Richard Henry 1946- WhoEmL 93
Anton, Thomas 1931- St&PR 93, WhoAm 92, WhoWor 93
Anton, Thomas Julius 1934- WhoAm 92
Anton, Traci Lynn 1966- WhoAmW 93
Anton, Uwe ScF&FL 92
Anton, William Lloyd 1938- St&PR 93
Anton, William R. WhoAm 92
Antona, Ettore 1931- WhoScE 91-3
Antonacci, Anthony Eugene 1949- WhoWor 93
Antonacci, Greg MiSFD 9
Antonacci, Lori 1947- WhoAmW 93, WhoE 93
Antonaccio, Mario Americo 1930- WhoE 93
Antonacopoulos, N. WhoScE 91-3
Antonakos, Stephen 1926- WhoAm 92
Antonazzi, Frank Joseph, Jr. 1950- WhoWrEP 92
Antonazzo, Nicholas Orlando 1937- St&PR 93, WhoAm 92
Antone, Nahil Peter 1952- WhoEmL 93, WhoWor 93
Antonell, Walter John 1934- St&PR 93, WhoAm 92
Antonelli, Daniel Salvatore 1952- WhoAm 92
Antonelli, Dominic BioIn 17
Antonelli, Ferdinando Giuseppe 1896- WhoAm 92, WhoWor 93
Antonelli, Georgiana Alexa 1948- WhoAmW 93
Antonelli, Giacomo 1806-1876 BioIn 17
Antonelli, John William 1917- St&PR 93
Antonelli, Laura 1942?- BioIn 17
Antonelli, Pattie Ellen 1953- WhoEmL 93
Antonellis, Charlene Adele 1948- WhoAmW 93, WhoEmL 93
Antonellis, Domenic M. 1940- St&PR 93
Antonescu, Ion 1882-1946 DcTwHis
Antonetti, Toni Marie 1952- WhoEmL 93
Antoni, Antonio d' 1801-1859 Baker 92
Antoni, Diane Louise 1940- WhoAmW 93
Antoni, Nils A.T. 1928- WhoScE 91-4
Antoni, Robert (William) 1958- ConAu 139
Antoniades, Harry Nicholas 1923- WhoAm 92
Antoniades, Ioannis Dimitri 1937- WhoUN 92
Antoniadis, Dimitri Alexander 1947- WhoAm 92
Antoniazzi, Franco 1944- WhoScE 91-3, WhoWor 93
Antonich, John Julius 1933- St&PR 93
Antonina c. 484-c. 548 OxDcByz
Antonini, Joseph E. 1941- St&PR 93, WhoAm 92
Antonini, Marion Hugh 1930- St&PR 93, WhoAm 92
Antonini, Michael Joseph 1946- WhoEmL 93
Antonini, Richard Lee 1942- St&PR 93
Antonino, Adelbert W. 1937- WhoAsAP 91
Antoninus, Brother 1912- WhoAm 92
Antoninus, Marcus Aurelius 121-180 BioIn 17
Antonio, Douglas John 1955- WhoEmL 93, WhoWor 93
Antonio, Juan 1945-1990 BioIn 17
Antonio, Lou MiSFD 9
Antonio, Susan Riccio 1963- WhoE 93
Antonioli, Robert St&PR 93
Antonioni, Michelangelo BioIn 17
Antonioni, Michelangelo 1912- MiSFD 9
Antoniorrobles DcMexL
Antoniou, Andreas 1938- WhoAm 92
Antoniou, Lucy D. 1929- WhoAm 92, WhoWor 93
Antoniou, Maria 1952- WhoScE 91-3
Antoniou, N. WhoScE 91-3
Antoniou, Panayotis A. 1962- WhoWor 93
Antoniou, Theodore 1935- Baker 92
Antonis, William Nicholas Law&B 92
Antoniu, Radu 1925- WhoScE 91-4
Antonius, Marcus c. 83BC-30BC BioIn 17
Antoniw, John Frank WhoScE 91-1
Antonoff, Gary L. 1936- WhoAm 92
Antonoff, Steven Ross 1948- WhoAm 92
Antonopoulos, James Peter Law&B 92
Antonopoulos, Nicholas St&PR 93
Antonopoulos-Domis, M. WhoScE 91-3
Antonov, Edouard 1938- WhoUN 92
Antonov, Ljubomir WhoScE 91-4
Antonova, Irina Alexandrovna 1922- WhoWor 93
Antonovitz, Frank A. Law&B 92
Antonow, Joseph P. 1915- St&PR 93
Antonsen, Elmer Harold 1929- WhoAm 92
Antonson, Earl 1930- St&PR 93
Antonson, Joan Margaret 1951- WhoEmL 93
Antonsson, Stefan 1960- WhoE 93
Antonucci, Frank Ralph 1946- WhoE 93
Antonuccio, Joseph Albert 1932- WhoAm 92
Antony d1232 OxDcByz
Antony, IV d1397 OxDcByz
Antony, Franz Joseph 1790-1837 Baker 92
Antony, P.A. 1936- WhoAsAP 91
Antony Kassymatas, I fl. 821-837? OxDcByz
Antony Kauleas, II fl. 893-901 OxDcByz
Antony The Great c. 251-356 OxDcByz
Antony The Younger 785-865 OxDcByz
Antoon, A. J. d1992 NewYTBS 92 [port]
Antoon, A.J. 1944-1992 BioIn 17, ConTFT 10
Antoon, Alfred Joseph 1944-1992 BioIn 17
Antos, Kenneth Martin 1943- St&PR 93
Antosiewicz, Linda A. 1952- St&PR 93
Antosik, Stanley Joseph 1943- WhoE 93
Antoun, Annette Agnes 1927- WhoAm 92
Antoun, M. Lawreace 1927- WhoAmW 93
Antreasian, Garo Zareh 1922- WhoAm 92
Antrim, Richard 1907?-1969 BioIn 17
Antrobus, John 1933- ChlFicS
Anttila, Argo WhoScE 91-4
Anttonen, Hannu Pekka 1948- WhoScE 91-4
Antulay, Abdul Rehman 1942- WhoAsAP 91
Antun, Juan Pablo 1947- WhoWor 93
Antunes, C.F.R. Lemos 1951- WhoScE 91-3
Antunes, Carlos Lemos 1951- WhoWor 93
Antunes, Jose M.V. 1954- WhoScE 91-3
Antupit, Samuel I. 1929- St&PR 93
Antupit, Samuel Nathaniel 1932- WhoAm 92
Antychowicz, Jerzy 1939- WhoScE 91-4
Antymniuk, Paul Law&B 92
Antz, Tracy N. 1960- WhoEmL 93
Antzelevitch, Charles 1951- WhoAm 92
Antzis, Errol Richard 1958- WhoE 93
Anuchin, D.N. 1843-1923 IntDcAn
Anuman Rajadhon 1888-1969 IntDcAn
Anunsen, Cathy Sue BioIn 17
Anuswith, Christopher Edwin 1951- WhoEmL 93, WhoSSW 93
Anuta, Michael Joseph 1901- WhoWor 93
Anutta, Lucile Jamison Law&B 92
Anutta, Lucile Jamison 1943- WhoSSW 93
Anvaripour, M. A. 1935- WhoAm 92
Anvic, Frank ScF&FL 92
Anvie, Frank ScF&FL 92
Anvil, Christopher ScF&FL 92
Anvire, Joachim Djabia 1952- WhoUN 92
Anwar, Imran 1962- St&PR 93
Anwar, Jamshed 1957- WhoWor 93
Anwar, Pervaiz 1947- St&PR 93
Anwar, Usman 1968- St&PR 93
Anwar bin Ibrahim 1947- WhoAsAP 91
Anwyl, Jeremy BioIn 17
Anyaeto, Callistus Chijioke 1962- WhoWrEP 92
Anyanwu, Chukwukre 1943- WhoE 93, WhoWor 93
Anyaoku, Eleazar Chukwuemeka 1933- WhoAfr
Anz, Reg Dean 1942- WhoWor 93
Anzaghi, Davide 1936- Baker 92
Anzai, Yoji 1941- St&PR 93
Anzaldua, Gloria 1942- DcLB 122 [port]
Anzalone, Anthony E. Law&B 92
Anzalone, Carmen James 1927- St&PR 93
Anzas OxDcByz
Anzel, Sanford Harold 1929- WhoAm 92
Anzelone, Paulette Alda WhoAmW 93
Anzini, Ann Elizabeth Urban 1962- WhoE 93
Anzorema, Jorge BioIn 17
Anzuini, Henry G. 1930- St&PR 93
Anzules, Bethany 1952- WhoAmW 93
Aoae, Joseph 1941- WhoAsAP 91
Aoi, Joichi BioIn 17
Aoi, Joichi 1926- WhoWor 93
Aoki, George T. Law&B 92
Aoki, Ichiro 1935- WhoWor 93
Aoki, John H. 1931- WhoAm 92
Aoki, Jun-ichi 1935- WhoWor 93
Aoki, Junjiro 1910- WhoWor 93
Aoki, Keizo 1941- WhoWor 93
Aoki, Masahisa 1923- WhoAsAP 91
Aoki, Masamitsu 1945- WhoWor 93
Aoki, Masanao 1931- WhoAm 92
Aoki, Mikio 1934- WhoAsAP 91
Aoki, Rocky BioIn 17
Aoki, Shinji 1926- WhoAsAP 91
Aoki, Takashi 1930- St&PR 93
Aona, Gretchen Mann 1933- WhoAm 92, WhoAmW 93
Aonuma, Tatsuo 1933- WhoWor 93
Aosaki, Masahiko 1940- WhoWor 93
Aoshima, Shin-ichiro 1958- WhoWor 93
Aosta, Amedeo Umberto, Duke of 1898-1942 HarEnMi
Aosta, Emanuele Filiberto, Duke d' 1869-1931 HarEnMi
Aouita, Said BioIn 17
Aoun, Hacib d1992 BioIn 17, NewYTBS 92
Aoun, Michel BioIn 17
Aoyagi, Dennis S. St&PR 93
Aoyama, Hiroyuki 1932- WhoWor 93
Apa Abraham c. 554-624 OxDcByz
Apacible, Conrado V. 1942- WhoAsAP 91
Apagyi, Geza WhoScE 91-4
Apanasewicz, Stanislaw 1936- WhoScE 91-4
Apanasov, Boris Nikolaevich 1950- WhoSSW 93, WhoWor 93
A-Pao-Chi 872-926 HarEnMi
Aparicio, Angel C. 1949- WhoScE 91-3
Aparicio, Luis 1934- HispAmA
Aparicio, Manuel HispAmA
Apateanu, Vlad 1925- WhoScE 91-4
Apatoff, Michael John 1955- WhoAm 92
Apaydin, Aydin 1957- WhoScE 91-4
Apczynski, John 1942- WhoE 93
Apel, Barbara Jean 1935- WhoE 93
Apel, D. Scott ScF&FL 92
Apel, Donald Matthew 1957- WhoE 93
Apel, Edwin Victor, Jr. Law&B 92
Apel, Harry M. 1931- St&PR 93
Apel, John Paul 1932- St&PR 93
Apel, John Ralph 1930- WhoAm 92
Apel, Myrna L. 1942- WhoAmW 93, WhoWor 93
Apel, Willi 1893-1988 Baker 92
Apelfeld, Aharon BioIn 17
Apelian, Virginia Matosian 1934- WhoAmW 93, WhoE 93, WhoWor 93
Apelt, Jurgen WhoScE 91-3
Apen, Gregory John 1945- St&PR 93
Apen, John Robert 1937- St&PR 93
Aperghis, Georges 1945- Baker 92, OxDcOp
Aperia, Anita Chatarina 1936- WhoScE 91-4, WhoWor 93
Apers, Desire J. 1929- WhoScE 91-2
Apers, J. WhoScE 91-2
Apestegui, Alfredo 1955- WhoWor 93
Apfel, Gary 1952- WhoAm 92
Apfel, Necia 1930- WhoWrEP 92
Apfel, Robert Edmund 1943- WhoAm 92
Apfelbaum, Marian 1931- WhoScE 91-2
Apfelbaum, Percy Max 1900-1991 BioIn 17
Apfelbaum, William BioIn 17
Apfelschnitt, Carl 1948-1990 BioIn 17
Apgar, Arthur Frederick 1939- St&PR 93
Apgar, Barbara Sue 1943- WhoAmW 93
Apgar, Clifford Marshall 1936- St&PR 93
Apgar, Mahlon, IV 1941- WhoAm 92, WhoE 93, WhoWor 93
Apgar, Phillip E. 1953- St&PR 93
Aphelion BioIn 17
Aphrahat dc. 345 OxDcByz
Aphthonios fl. 4th cent.-5th cent. OxDcByz
Apice, Joanne Marie 1959- WhoAmW 93
Apicella, Richard L. Law&B 92
Apion OxDcByz
Apirion, David 1935- WhoAm 92
Apis, Dragutin T. Dimitrijevic- 1876-1917 BioIn 17
ApIvor, Denis 1916- Baker 92, BioIn 17
Apjohn, Nelson George 1956- WhoEmL 93
Apkarian, Harry 1922- St&PR 93
Aplan, Frank Fulton 1923- WhoAm 92, WhoE 93
Aplan, Peter Donaghue 1957- WhoE 93
Aplin, Mary Emily AmWomPl
Apodaca, Jerry 1934- HispAmA
Apodaca, Robert BioIn 17
Apodaca, Rudy Samuel 1939- WhoWrEP 92
Apodaca, Victor Joe BioIn 17
Apokaukos OxDcByz
Apokaukos, Alexios d1345 OxDcByz [port]
Apokaukos, John c. 1155-1233 OxDcByz
Apolinario, Basilio Evangelista, IV 1963- WhoWor 93
Apollinaris c. 310-c. 390 OxDcByz
Apolloni, Giovanni Filippo c. 1635-1688 OxDcOp
Apolloni, Salvatore c. 1704- OxDcOp
Apollonios of Tyana OxDcByz
Apone, Carl Anthony 1923- WhoAm 92
Aponovich, Anastasia BioIn 17
Aponovich, James 1948- BioIn 17
Aponso, Herbert Allan 1925- WhoWor 93
Aponte, Christopher BioIn 17
Aponte, Juan Milton 1952- WhoWor 93
Aponte, Mari Carmen 1946- NotHsAW 93 [port]
Aponte Alsina, Marta 1945- WhoAmW 93
Aponte-Ledee, Rafael 1938- Baker 92
Aponte Martinez, Luis 1922- WhoAm 92, WhoSSW 93, WhoWor 93
Apostel, Hans (Erich) 1901-1972 Baker 92
Apostle, Hippocrates G. 1910-1990 BioIn 17
Apostle, James A. 1956- St&PR 93
Apostolakis, Constantinos 1945- WhoWor 93
Apostolakis, James John 1942- WhoAm 92
Apostolakis, Michael 1931- WhoScE 91-3
Apostolatos, Gerasimos 1948- WhoScE 91-3
Apostoles, Michael c. 1420-c. 1474 OxDcByz
Apostolescu, Nicu 1896- OxDcOp
Apostolides, Anthony Demetrios WhoWor 93
Apostolos, Paul Michael 1936- WhoE 93
Apostolou, John L. 1930- ScF&FL 92
Apostolou, Paul Charles 1942- WhoE 93
Apostolova, Lilia Nikolova 1951- WhoWor 93
App, James Leonard 1936- WhoSSW 93
Appalaraju, Gunasekar V. 1958- WhoEmL 93
Appel, Alfred 1906- St&PR 93, WhoAm 92
Appel, Alfred, Jr. 1934- WhoWrEP 92
Appel, Allen ScF&FL 92
Appel, Allen (R.) 1945- ConAu 138
Appel, Benjamin 1907-1977 ScF&FL 92
Appel, Bernard Sidney 1932- WhoAm 92
Appel, Clare Rostan d1990 BioIn 17
Appel, Denise O. Law&B 92
Appel, Eric Michael 1960- WhoEmL 93
Appel, Florence AmWomPl
Appel, Garry Richard 1952- WhoEmL 93
Appel, Irving Harold 1917- WhoE 93
Appel, John J. 1921- WhoAm 92
Appel, Karel Christian 1921- WhoAm 92, WhoWor 93
Appel, Kenneth I. 1932- WhoAm 92
Appel, Marcia Faye 1950- WhoWrEP 92
Appel, Marsha Ceil 1953- WhoEmL 93
Appel, Marta 1894-1987? BioIn 17
Appel, Michael 1949- WhoAm 92
Appel, Nina S. 1936- WhoAm 92, WhoAmW 93
Appel, Norman 1924- St&PR 93
Appel, Norman 1945- WhoAm 92
Appel, Richard Gilmore 1889-1975 BioIn 17
Appel, Robert Eugene 1958- WhoE 93, WhoEmL 93
Appel, Stuart David 1954- WhoE 93
Appel, Theodore Julius 1936- St&PR 93
Appel, U.J. 1917- St&PR 93

Appel, Wallace Henry 1925- *WhoAm 92*
Appel, William Frank 1924- *WhoAm 92*
Appelbaum, Alan 1936- *WhoAm 92*
Appelbaum, Joel Alan 1941- *WhoAm 92*
Appelbaum, Judith Pilpel 1939- *WhoAmW 93*
Appelbaum, Marc J. *Law&B 92*
Appelbaum, Michael Arthur 1945- *WhoAm 92*
Appelbaum, Murray Clark 1935- *St&PR 93*
Appelbaum, Paul Stuart 1951- *WhoAm 92, WhoEmL 93*
Appelberg, Carl 1930- *WhoWor 93*
Appeldoorn, Dina 1884-1938 *Baker 92*
Appeldorn, Francis R. 1935- *St&PR 93, WhoAm 92*
Appelfeld, Aharon 1932- *MagSWL [port]*
Appelfeld, Aron *BioIn 17*
Appelhof, Ruth Stevens 1945- *WhoAmW 93, WhoSSW 93*
Appell, Daisy R. *AmWomPl*
Appell, Don d1990 *BioIn 17*
Appell, Kathleen Marie 1943- *WhoAmW 93, WhoE 93*
Appell, Lawrence 1949- *St&PR 93*
Appelman, Evan Hugh 1935- *WhoAm 92*
Appelman, L.P. 1929- *St&PR 93*
Appelrath, Hans-Jurgen 1952- *WhoScE 91-3*
Appelroth, Sven-Eric W. 1929- *WhoScE 91-4*
Appelson, Wallace Bertrand 1930- *WhoAm 92*
Appelt, James Mark *Law&B 92*
Appencellers, Benedictus 16th cent.- *Baker 92*
Appenzelder, Benedictus 16th cent.- *Baker 92*
Appenzelders, Benedictus 16th cent.- *Baker 92*
Appenzeller, Benedictus 16th cent.- *Baker 92*
Appenzeller, Immo 1940- *WhoScE 91-3*
Appenzeller, Immo Julius 1940- *WhoWor 93*
Appenzeller, Otto 1927- *WhoAm 92*
Apperley, Mark David 1947- *WhoWor 93*
Apperson, Bernard James 1956- *WhoEmL 93, WhoSSW 93, WhoWor 93*
Apperson, Jack A. 1934- *St&PR 93*
Apperson, Jack Alfonso 1934- *WhoAm 92*
Apperson, Jean 1934- *WhoAm 92, WhoAmW 93*
Apperson, Polly Merrill 1910- *WhoE 93*
Appert, Edward Carl 1944- *St&PR 93*
Appert, Peter P. 1955- *St&PR 93*
Appia, Adolphe 1862-1928 *IntDcOp, OxDcOp*
Appia, Edmond 1894-1961 *Baker 92*
Appiah, Joe 1918-1990 *BioIn 17*
Appiah, Peggy 1921- *ChlFicS*
Appignanesi, Lisa 1946- *ScF&FL 92*
Appignani, Louis Joseph 1933- *St&PR 93*
Appl, Franklin John 1937- *WhoSSW 93*
Appl, Fredric Carl 1932- *WhoAm 92*
Applbaum, Ronald Lee 1943- *WhoAm 92*
Apple, B. Nixon 1924- *St&PR 93, WhoAm 92*
Apple, Billy R. 1938- *St&PR 93*
Apple, Daina Dravnieks 1944- *WhoAmW 93, WhoE 93, WhoSSW 93*
Apple, David Joseph 1941- *WhoAm 92*
Apple, F. Dean 1935- *St&PR 93*
Apple, Jacki 1941- *WhoWrEP 92*
Apple, James Glenn 1937- *WhoE 93*
Apple, John B. 1935- *St&PR 93*
Apple, John Boyd 1935- *WhoAm 92*
Apple, Leslie Mark 1949- *St&PR 93*
Apple, Margot *BioIn 17*
Apple, Mary Florence 1950- *WhoEmL 93*
Apple, Max *BioIn 17*
Apple, Max 1941- *JeAmFiW*
Apple, Max Isaac 1941- *WhoAm 92*
Apple, Raymond Walter, Jr. 1934- *WhoAm 92*
Apple, Robah Warren, Jr. 1955- *WhoEmL 93*
Apple, Roger W. 1956- *WhoEmL 93*
Apple, Steven Anthony 1954- *WhoEmL 93*
Apple, William Marlan 1929- *WhoWrEP 92*
Apple, Willis Wade 1951- *St&PR 93, WhoEmL 93*
Applebaum, Charles *Law&B 92*
Applebaum, Deborah C. *Law&B 92*
Applebaum, Edward 1937- *Baker 92, WhoAm 92*
Applebaum, Edward Leon 1940- *WhoAm 92*
Applebaum, Eugene 1936- *St&PR 93, WhoAm 92*
Applebaum, Harvey Milton 1937- *WhoAm 92*
Applebaum, Louis 1918- *Baker 92, WhoAm 92*
Applebaum, Louis 1936- *St&PR 93*
Applebaum, Michael Murray 1958- *WhoEmL 93*
Applebaum, Ronald Lee 1943- *WhoAm 92*
Applebaum, Stuart S. 1949- *WhoAm 92*
Applebee, Constance 1874?-1981 *BioIn 17*
Appleberry, James Bruce 1938- *WhoAm 92*
Applebroog, Ida *BioIn 17*
Appleby, Alan 1937- *WhoE 93*
Appleby, Audrey Jane 1952- *WhoE 93*
Appleby, Cornwell G. *Law&B 92*
Appleby, Dan *MiSFD 9*
Appleby, Doris Chambers 1930- *WhoAmW 93*
Appleby, H.P. *Law&B 92*
Appleby, James R., Jr. 1945- *St&PR 93*
Appleby, John Winfred 1922- *St&PR 93*
Appleby, Joyce Oldham 1929- *WhoAm 92*
Appleby, Ken 1953- *ScF&FL 92*
Appleby, Marjory Lu 1930- *WhoE 93*
Appleby, Robert Houston 1931- *WhoSSW 93*
Appledorn, Mary Jeanne van *Baker 92*
Applefeld, Laurie Sue 1953- *WhoEmL 93*
Appleford, R. Duncan 1938- *ScF&FL 92*
Applegarth, Margaret Tyson 1886- *AmWomPl*
Applegarth, Paul Vollmer 1946- *WhoAm 92, WhoEmL 93*
Applegarth, Virginia B. 1953- *WhoAmW 93, WhoEmL 93*
Applegate, Allita Emery 1887- *AmWomPl*
Applegate, Arthur Lowrie 1914- *St&PR 93*
Applegate, Christina *BioIn 17*
Applegate, Christina 1972?- *ConTFT 10*
Applegate, Debra Annette 1962- *WhoWrEP 92*
Applegate, Donald Jay 1944- *WhoE 93*
Applegate, Douglas 1928- *CngDr 91, WhoAm 92*
Applegate, E. Timothy *Law&B 92*
Applegate, Edward Timothy 1934- *St&PR 93*
Applegate, Henry M., III 1947- *St&PR 93*
Applegate, James Robert 1943- *WhoSSW 93*
Applegate, John *ScF&FL 92*
Applegate, Malcolm W. 1936- *WhoAm 92*
Applegate, Mary Sollinger 1961- *WhoEmL 93*
Applegate, Robert 1954- *WhoE 93*
Applegate, Steven C. 1948- *St&PR 93*
Applegate, Vicki *Law&B 92*
Applegate, William Joseph 1946- *WhoAm 92*
Appleman, Donald J. 1949- *St&PR 93*
Appleman, Howard C. 1927- *St&PR 93*
Appleman, Marjorie *WhoAm 92*
Appleman, Nathan d1992 *NewYTBS 92*
Appleman, Philip 1926- *ScF&FL 92, WhoAm 92, WhoWrEP 92*
Appleman, Robert D. d1991 *BioIn 17*
Appleman-Vassil, Nanci 1953- *WhoEmL 93*
Applequist, Jon Barr 1932- *WhoAm 92*
Applequist, Virgil H. 1947- *St&PR 93*
Appler, Sandra Gaye 1957- *WhoAmW 93*
Appleton, Arthur Ivar 1915- *WhoAm 92, WhoWor 93*
Appleton, Bill R. 1937- *WhoAm 92*
Appleton, Daniel Randolph, Jr. 1942- *WhoE 93, WhoWor 93*
Appleton, James Robert 1937- *WhoAm 92*
Appleton, Jeffrey Wayne 1959- *WhoSSW 93*
Appleton, John 1935- *St&PR 93*
Appleton, Jon (Howard) 1939- *Baker 92*
Appleton, Joseph Hayne 1927- *WhoAm 92*
Appleton, Kathy Allen 1950- *WhoE 93*
Appleton, Malcolm 1941- *WhoScE 91-1*
Appleton, Myra 1934- *WhoAm 92*
Appleton, R. O., Jr. 1945- *WhoAm 92*
Appleton, Robert Wayne 1953- *WhoEmL 93*
Appleton, Scott d1992 *NewYTBS 92*
Appleton, Scott 1942-1992 *BioIn 17*
Appleton, Thomas Howard, Jr. 1950- *WhoSSW 93*
Appleton, Victor *ScF&FL 92*
Appleton, Victor, II *ScF&FL 92*
Appleton, William James 1928- *WhoE 93*
Applewhite, Clyde C. 1933- *WhoUN 92*
Applewhite, Harriet Branson 1940- *WhoAmW 93, WhoE 93*
Applewhite, James *BioIn 17*
Applewhite, James William 1935- *WhoWrEP 92*
Applewhite, Margaret Patricia 1955- *WhoAmW 93*
Appley, Lawrence A. 1904- *St&PR 93, WhoAm 92, WhoWor 93*
Appley, Mortimer Herbert 1921- *WhoAm 92*
Appleyard, David Frank 1939- *WhoAm 92*
Appleyard, Glenn N. d1992 *NewYTBS 92*
Appleyard, John Harold *WhoScE 91-1*
Applin, Elizabeth A. 1942- *St&PR 93*
Appling, Christine Headrick 1965- *WhoSSW 93*
Appling, Luke 1907-1991 *AnObit 1991, BioIn 17*
Apps, Jerold W(illard) 1934- *ConAu 37NR*
Apps, Jerry *ConAu 37NR*
Apps, Robert Louis *WhoScE 91-1*
Appy, Gerard d1990 *BioIn 17*
Apraksin, Fedor Matveevich 1661-1728 *HarEnMi*
Aprati, Robert *Law&B 92*
Aprea, Sharon Martin 1956- *WhoAmW 93*
Ap Rees, Garth 1934- *WhoUN 92*
ap Rees, Thomas 1930- *WhoWor 93*
Aprenos *OxDcByz*
April, Gary Charles 1940- *WhoSSW 93*
April, Paul Kenneth 1939- *WhoE 93*
April, Rand Scott 1951- *WhoAm 92, WhoEmL 93*
Aprile, Giuseppe 1731-1813 *Baker 92*
Aprile, Giuseppe 1732-1813 *OxDcOp*
Aprill, Jack *BioIn 17*
Aprille, Thomas Joseph, Jr. 1943- *WhoAm 92*
Aprison, Morris Herman 1923- *WhoAm 92*
Aprosio, Norbert Jack 1924- *WhoScE 91-2*
Apruzzese, Vincent John 1928- *WhoAm 92*
Apruzzi, Gene *St&PR 93*
Apruzzi, Gene 1934- *WhoAm 92*
Apseudes, Theodore *OxDcByz*
Apsley, Samuel D. 1931- *WhoScE 91-1*
Apstein, Carl Stephen 1941- *WhoE 93*
Apt, Harold H. 1928- *St&PR 93*
Apt, Leonard 1922- *WhoAm 92*
Apt, Lesley A. *Law&B 92*
Apt, Lesley Ann 1946- *WhoE 93*
Apted, Michael *BioIn 17*
Apted, Michael 1941- *MiSFD 9*
Apted, Michael D. 1941- *WhoAm 92*
Apter, David Ernest 1924- *WhoAm 92*
Apter, Emily (S.) 1954- *ConAu 137*
Apter, J. Scott 1947- *St&PR 93*
Apter, T.E. 1949- *ScF&FL 92*
Apte-Sanders, Sue-Ellen Ilene 1956- *WhoEmL 93, WhoSSW 93*
Aptheker, Herbert 1915- *WhoAm 92*
Apthorp, William Foster 1848-1913 *Baker 92*
Aptidon, Hassan Gouled 1916- *WhoWor 93*
Aptowitzer, Willi Zeev 1918- *WhoWor 93*
Apuron, Anthony Sablan 1945- *WhoAm 92*
Apyan, Roseanne Lucille 1949- *WhoAmW 93, WhoEmL 93*
Aquavella, James Vincent 1932- *WhoE 93*
Aquavia, James *Law&B 92*
Aquila, Francis Joseph 1957- *WhoEmL 93*
Aquilar, Maria *Law&B 92*
Aquilina, Benjamin 1943- *St&PR 93*
Aquiline, Judith 1947- *WhoEmL 93*
Aquilino, Daniel 1924- *WhoAm 92*
Aquilino, Paul Philip 1941- *St&PR 93*
Aquilino, Thomas J., Jr. 1939- *CngDr 91*
Aquilino, Thomas Joseph, Jr. 1939- *WhoAm 92, WhoE 93*
Aquin, Hubert 1929-1977 *BioIn 17*
Aquina, Mary, Sister *ConAu 37NR*
Aquinas, Thomas 1224-1274 *OxDcByz*
Aquinas, Thomas 1225?-1274 *BioIn 17*
Aquino, Agapito A. 1939- *WhoAsAP 91*
Aquino, Antonio L. 1948- *WhoAsAP 91*
Aquino, Carlos Alberto 1959- *WhoWor 93*
Aquino, Corazon *BioIn 17*
Aquino, Corazon C. 1933- *WhoAsAP 91*
Aquino, Corazon Cojuangco 1933- *WhoWor 93*
Aquino, Felix John 1952- *WhoEmL 93*
Aquino, Florante L. 1950- *WhoAsAP 91*
Aquino, Herminio S. 1949- *WhoAsAP 91*
Aquino, Honorato Y. 1941- *WhoAsAP 91*
Aquino, Iva Toguri d' *BioIn 17*
Aquino, John 1949- *ScF&FL 92*
Aquino, John Goddard 1960- *WhoEmL 93*
Aquino, John Thomas 1949- *WhoEmL 93*
Aquino, Joseph Mario 1947- *WhoE 93*
Aquino, Maria Corazon 1933- *DcTwHis*
Aquino-Oreta, Teresa 1944- *WhoAsAP 91*
Aquirre, Juan Lauro, Jr. 1968- *WhoWor 93*
Ara, Ugo 1876-1936 *Baker 92*
Arabia, Joseph V. 1942- *St&PR 93*
Arabia, Paul 1938- *WhoWor 93*
Arabian, Armand 1934- *WhoAm 92*
Arabian, John K. 1943- *St&PR 93*
Arabie, Phipps 1948- *WhoAm 92*
Arabi Pasha 1839-1911 *HarEnMi*
Arabis, Stanley Lawrence *Law&B 92*
Arabshahi, Alireza 1966- *WhoSSW 93*
Arader, Vallijeanne *BioIn 17*
Arader, W. Graham, III *BioIn 17*
Arado, Joseph Edwin 1929- *St&PR 93*
Aradottir, Asa L. 1959- *WhoScE 91-4*
Arafat, Yasir 1929- *BioIn 17, DcTwHis*
Arafat, Yassir 1929- *ColdWar 2 [port]*
Arafe, Robert Howard 1930- *St&PR 93*
Aragall, Giacomo 1939- *OxDcOp*
Aragall (y Garriga), Giacomo (Jaime) 1939- *Baker 92*
Aragno, Anna 1945- *WhoE 93*
Aragon 1897-1982 *BioIn 17*
Aragon, Jean Armand 1942- *WhoUN 92*
Aragon, Jose *HispAmA*
Aragon, Jose Rafael 1796?-1862 *HispAmA*
Aragon, Louis 1897-1982 *BioIn 17*
Aragon, Manuel Gutierrez *MiSFD 9*
Aragon, Ruben Victor 1949- *St&PR 93*
Aragona, John T. *Law&B 92*
Aragon Quinonez, Hector *DcCPCAm*
Aragon Ramirez, Vicente 1950- *WhoWor 93*
Aragosa, Emanuel Joseph 1931- *WhoE 93*
Arai, Ikuo 1935- *WhoWor 93*
Arai, Junichi 1932- *BioIn 17*
Arai, Kiyomitsu 1928- *WhoWor 93*
Arai, Motoko 1960- *ScF&FL 92*
Arai, Shokei 1948- *WhoAsAP 91*
Arai, Thomas Yoshitami 1931- *WhoWor 93*
Araia, Francesco 1709-c. 1770 *OxDcOp*
Araico, Enrique Jesus 1955- *WhoSSW 93*
Araiz, Joseph Michael 1961- *WhoE 93, WhoWor 93*
Araiza, Francesco 1950- *IntDcOp*
Araiza, Francisco 1950- *Baker 92, OxDcOp, WhoAm 92*
Araja, Francesco 1709-1770 *Baker 92*
Arakaki, Wayne S. 1932- *WhoIns 93*
Arakawa, Edward Takashi 1929- *WhoSSW 93*
Arakawa, Kasumi 1926- *WhoAm 92, WhoWor 93*
Arakawa, Morimasa 1925- *WhoWor 93*
Arakelian, Maureen 1934- *WhoE 93*
Araki, Gregg *MiSFD 9*
Araki, Minoru S. 1931- *WhoAm 92*
Araki, Sadao 1877-1966 *HarEnMi*
Araki, Takeo 1934- *WhoWor 93*
Arakishvili, Dmitri 1873-1953 *Baker 92*
Arama, Constantin 1919- *WhoScE 91-4*
Araman, Georges 1941- *WhoUN 92*
Arambasin, Ana Cekic *WhoScE 91-4*
Aramburu, Jennifer Travers 1964- *WhoAmW 93, WhoEmL 93*
Aramburu, Juan Carlos Cardinal 1912- *WhoWor 93*
Aramian, S. Sue 1932- *St&PR 93*
Aramony, William *BioIn 17*
Aramony, William 1927- *WhoAm 92*
Arams, Frank Robert 1925- *WhoAm 92*
Aran, Fernando Santiago 1957- *WhoEmL 93*
Aran, Jean-Marie 1939- *WhoScE 91-2*
Aran, Peter 1928- *WhoUN 92*
Arana, Francisco Javier *DcCPCAm*
Arana, Kimberley Ann Howard 1957- *WhoEmL 93*
Arana, Ric *ScF&FL 92*
Arana, Vicente 1939- *WhoScE 91-3*
Arana-Adams, Therese A. 1945- *St&PR 93, WhoIns 93*
Arana-Adams, Therese Anne 1945- *WhoAmW 93*
Arana Osorio, Carlos 1918- *DcCPCAm*
Aranas, Maria Elena Lizares 1937- *WhoAmW 93*
Aranas, Noel Bautista 1962- *WhoSSW 93*
Aranas, Roberto Lumabi 1968- *WhoWor 93*
Arancia, Louis John 1928- *WhoE 93*
Arancibia, Jaime H. 1946- *WhoWor 93*
Arand, Frederick Francis 1954- *WhoEmL 93*
Arand, Wolfgang Michael Leonhard 1929- *WhoScE 91-3*
Aranda, Charles 1931- *WhoWrEP 92*
Aranda, Miguel Angel 1939- *WhoAm 92, WhoSSW 93*
Aranda, Theodore *DcCPCAm*
Araneta, Manuel 1949- *St&PR 93*
Arangi-Lombardi, Giannina 1891-1951 *Baker 92*
Arango, Jeronimo *BioIn 17*
Arango, Jorge Sanin 1916- *WhoAm 92*
Arango, Judith Wolpert 1928- *WhoSSW 93*
Arango, Maite *BioIn 17*
Arango, Richard Steven 1953- *WhoSSW 93*
Arango y Escandon, Alejandro 1821-1883 *DcMexL*
Arani, Ardy A. 1954- *WhoEmL 93*
Aranibar, Jorge Ernesto 1951- *WhoUN 92*
Aranosian, Lynda Marie 1967- *WhoAmW 93*
Aranow, Peter Jones 1946- *St&PR 93, WhoAm 92*
Aranow, Robert Bittman 1954- *WhoEmL 93*
Aranson, Michael J. 1944- *WhoAm 92*
Aranson, Robert 1953- *WhoEmL 93*

Arant, Eugene Wesley 1920- WhoAm 92, WhoWor 93
Arant, Patricia M. 1930- WhoAm 92
Aranyakananda, Chanond 1938- WhoWor 93
Aranyi, Jelly d' 1893-1966 Baker 92
Aranyi, Peter 1948- WhoScE 91-4
Aranzadi, Telesforo 1860-1945 IntDcAn
Araoz, Alberto B. WhoUN 92
Araoz, Daniel Leon 1930- WhoAm 92
Arapakis, George 1926- WhoWor 93
Arapoglou, Christopher Theodore 1955- St&PR 93
Arapov, Boris (Alexandrovich) 1905- Baker 92
Araquistain, Paul A. 1927- St&PR 93
Aras, Namik K. 1935- WhoScE 91-4
Araskog, Rand V. BioIn 17
Araskog, Rand Vincent 1931- St&PR 93, WhoAm 92, WhoE 93, WhoWor 93
Arasteh, A(bdol) Reza 1927-1992 ConAu 139
Arasteh, Abdal-Reza 1927- WhoAm 92
Arasteh, Kavouss 1941- WhoUN 92
Arastou, Seyed Mojtaba 1955- WhoUN 92
Arata, Foster S. Law&B 92
Arata, Sil Louis, Sr. 1930- WhoWor 93
Aratingi, Michael J. Law&B 92
Aratus of Sicyon 271BC-213BC HarEnMi
Arau, Alfonso MiSFD 9
Araujo, Arturo DcCPCAm
Araujo, Jose Emilio Goncalves 1922- WhoWor 93
Araujo, Manuel Enrique DcCPCAm
Araujo, Marcio Santos Silva 1946- WhoWor 93
Araujo, Severino de Melo 1935- WhoUN 92
Araulo, Maria Teresa Rosario Lopes 1947- WhoUN 92
Arauxo Baker 92
Arauxo, Francisco Baker 92
Arauz, Ines Elmina 1938- WhoAmW 93
Aravot, Rafael St&PR 93
Arax, Christine 1961- WhoWrEP 92
Arazi, Efraim BioIn 17
Arb, Tim K. 1938- St&PR 93
Arbab, Farhad 1952- WhoWor 93
Arbab, Munawar Ali 1940- WhoWor 93
Arban, (Joseph) Jean-Baptiste (Laurent) 1825-1889 Baker 92
Arbanas, Frederick V. 1939- BiDAMSp 1989
Arbantenos OxDcByz
Arbatskii, Konstantin Solimanovich Nagel'- BioIn 17
Arbaugh, Charles H. Law&B 92
Arbaugh, Charles H. 1943- St&PR 93
Arbaugh, Eugene A. 1938- St&PR 93
Arbeau, Thoinot 1520-1595 Baker 92
Arbeene, Michael James 1953- WhoSSW 93
Arbegast, James L. 1932- St&PR 93
Arbeit, Robert David 1947- WhoEmL 93
Arbeiter, Kurt 1929- WhoScE 91-4
Arbeitman, Yoel L. 1941- WhoE 93
Arbeloa, Arancha 1958- WhoScE 91-3
Arbenz Guzman, Jacobo 1913-1970 DcCPCAm
Arbenz Guzman, Jacobo 1913-1971 ColdWar 2 [port], DcTwHis
Arber, Werner 1929- WhoAm 92, WhoWor 93
Arbesu Fraga, Jose Antonio 1940- BioIn 17
Arbhabhirama, Anat 1938- WhoAsAP 91
Arbib, John A. 1924- WhoSSW 93, WhoWor 93
Arbib, Michael Anthony 1940- WhoAm 92
Arbisi, Donna Wiese Law&B 92
Arbit, Beryl Ellen 1949- WhoEmL 93
Arbit, Bruce 1954- WhoAm 92
Arbit, Harvey Marvin 1947- WhoEmL 93
Arbit, Terry Steven 1958- WhoEmL 93
Arbitell, Michelle Renee 1962- WhoAmW 93
Arbiter, Nathaniel 1911- WhoAm 92
Arbitman, William A. Law&B 92
Arblay, Frances Burney d' 1752-1840 BioIn 17
Arbogast d394 OxDcByz
Arbogast, David Harvey 1951- WhoEmL 93
Arbogast, Robert Ernest 1946- St&PR 93
Arboit, Joan 1936-1990 BioIn 17
Arboleda, Amadio Antonio 1934- WhoUN 92
Arboleya, Carlos Jose 1929- HispAmA
Arbos, Enrique Fernandez 1863-1939 Baker 92
Arbour, Alger 1932- WhoAm 92
Arbour, Harold Cyril 1939- WhoAm 92
Arbour, Peter W. Law&B 92
Arbucci, John ScF&FL 92
Arbuckle, Earl Francis, III 1950- WhoEmL 93
Arbuckle, Fatty 1887-1933 BioIn 17
Arbuckle, Georgia Ann 1961- WhoAmW 93
Arbuckle, James Ernest 1939- St&PR 93
Arbuckle, Linda Jane 1950- WhoSSW 93
Arbuckle, Matthew 1828-1883 Baker 92
Arbuckle, Paul Douglas 1959- WhoSSW 93
Arbuckle, Robert Dean 1940- WhoE 93
Arbuckle, Roscoe 1887-1933 IntDcF 2-3 [port], QDrFCA 92 [port]
Arbuckle, Scott G. 1931- WhoAm 92
Arbulu-Neira, Humberto E. 1947- WhoUN 92
Arbur, Rosemarie 1944- ScF&FL 92
Arbury, Andrew Stephen, III 1953- WhoEmL 93
Arbuthnot, John 1667-1735 Baker 92, BioIn 17
Arbuthnot, Marriot 1711-1794 HarEnMi
Arbuthnot, Peter Ivan 1948- WhoEmL 93
Arca, Emil 1960- WhoE 93
Arca, Giuseppe 1949- WhoWor 93
Arca, Gulseren 1953- WhoScE 91-4
Arcadelt, Jacob c. 1505-1568 Baker 92
Arcadet, Jachet c. 1505-1568 Baker 92
Arcamone, Federico M. 1928- WhoScE 91-3
Arcand, Anthony Arthur 1961- WhoE 93
Arcand, Denys BioIn 17
Arcand, Denys 1941- ConTFT 10, MiSFD 9
Arcangel, Alberta Marie 1921- WhoAmW 93
Arcara, Gwen Oliver 1945- WhoAmW 93
Arcara, James Paul 1934- WhoAm 92, WhoE 93
Arcara, Richard Joseph 1940- WhoAm 92
Arcari, John J. 1945- St&PR 93
Arcari, Ralph Donato 1943- WhoAm 92
Arcaro, Harold Conrad, Jr. 1935- WhoAm 92
Arcate, Cynthia A. Law&B 92
Arce, A. Anthony 1923- WhoAm 92
Arce, Bayardo DcCPCAm
Arce, Phillip William 1937- WhoAm 92
Arce, Ramon St&PR 93
Arce, Rebecca E. Law&B 92
Arce-Cacho, Eric Amaury 1940- WhoWor 93
Arcel, Ray 1899- BioIn 17
Arcella, Lisa 1961- WhoWrEP 92
Arcelli, Carlo 1941- WhoScE 91-3
Arceneaux, George, Jr. 1928- WhoAm 92, WhoSSW 93
Arceneaux, Martin Thomas 1951- WhoEmL 93
Arceneaux, Michael d1991 BioIn 17
Arceneaux, William 1941- WhoAm 92
Arceo, Raoul B. 1957- St&PR 93
Arcesi-Dozier, Beverly Ann 1959- WhoSSW 93
Archabal, Nina Marchetti 1940- WhoAm 92, WhoAmW 93
Archadet, Jachet c. 1505-1568 Baker 92
Archambault, Andre 1949- St&PR 93
Archambault, Bennett St&PR 93, WhoAm 92
Archambault, Gilles 1933- WhoCanL 92
Archambault, Guy St&PR 93
Archambault, J.K. 1938- St&PR 93
Archambault, John BioIn 17, MajAI
Archambault, John Kenehan 1938- WhoAm 92
Archambault, Kathleen Ann 1960- WhoAmW 93
Archambault, Louis 1915- WhoAm 92
Archambault, Lynn St&PR 93
Archambeau, Charles Bruce 1933- WhoAm 92
Archambeau, Iwan d' 1879-1955 Baker 92
Archambeau, Jason Rousseau Law&B 92
Archambeau, John Orin 1925- WhoAm 92
Archambeau, Leo Bruce 1932- St&PR 93
Archangelsky, Alexander 1846-1924 Baker 92
Archbold, Douglas P. 1944- St&PR 93
Archbold, Judith Woodard Law&B 92
Archbold, Timothy J. Law&B 92
Archer, Adele W. 1956- St&PR 93
Archer, Anne BioIn 17
Archer, Arthur Elliott 1943- WhoAm 92
Archer, Beverly Jean Crew 1933- WhoAmW 93
Archer, Bill 1928- CngDr 91
Archer, Brian Harrison WhoScE 91-1
Archer, Brian Roper 1929- WhoAsAP 91
Archer, C. WhoScE 91-1
Archer, Carl Marion 1920- WhoSSW 93
Archer, Chalmers, Jr. 1938- ConAu 138
Archer, Dennis Wayne 1942- WhoAm 92
Archer, Desmond Brian WhoScE 91-1
Archer, Douglas Robert 1948- WhoAm 92
Archer, Ellen M. 1946- WhoAmW 93, WhoEmL 93
Archer, Eric D. Law&B 92
Archer, Frederick 1838-1901 Baker 92
Archer, Glenn LeRoy, Jr. 1929- CngDr 91, WhoAm 92
Archer, Hutton Gilbert 1944- WhoUN 92
Archer, Ira Fletcher 1940- WhoSSW 93
Archer, James BioIn 17
Archer, James Elson 1922- WhoAm 92
Archer, Jeffrey 1940- BioIn 17, ScF&FL 92
Archer, Jeffrey Howard 1940- WhoWor 93
Archer, John Stuart WhoScE 91-1
Archer, Judy Ione 1949- WhoAmW 93
Archer, Jules 1915- WhoWrEP 92
Archer, Kathleen Frances 1955- WhoAm 92
Archer, Kathryn Elizabeth 1923- WhoAmW 93
Archer, Kenneth D. Law&B 92
Archer, Laura Phelps Law&B 92
Archer, Lloyd Daniel 1942- WhoSSW 93
Archer, Mary Jane 1949- WhoAmW 93, WhoEmL 93
Archer, Mary Jo 1955- WhoAmW 93
Archer, Myrtle Lilly 1926- WhoWrEP 92
Archer, Nelson BioIn 17
Archer, Nuala Miriam 1955- WhoWrEP 92
Archer, O.R. 1904- St&PR 93
Archer, Peggy Ann 1947- WhoWrEP 92
Archer, Richard A. 1927- WhoIns 93
Archer, Richard D. Law&B 92
Archer, Richard James Goodwin 1939- WhoAm 92
Archer, Richard John 1948- WhoE 93
Archer, Richard Joseph 1922- WhoAm 92
Archer, Ronald Dean 1932- WhoAm 92
Archer, Sarah Elizabeth Brick 1958- WhoAmW 93
Archer, Stephen Hunt 1928- WhoAm 92
Archer, Stephen Murphy 1934- WhoAm 92
Archer, Sydney 1917- WhoAm 92
Archer, Teri Lynn 1965- WhoAmW 93
Archer, Thomas Charles 1940- St&PR 93
Archer, Thomas George Law&B 92
Archer, Victoria Leigh Law&B 92
Archer, Violet 1913- Baker 92, BioIn 17
Archer, Violet Balestreri 1913- WhoAm 92
Archer, Vivian Thomas 1939- WhoAmW 93
Archer, Wallace St&PR 93
Archer, William George 1907-1979 IntDcAn
Archer, William Reynolds, Jr. 1928- WhoAm 92, WhoSSW 93
Archerd, Army WhoAm 92
Archey, Lisa Ann 1957- WhoEmL 93
Archibald, Andrew M. 1945- St&PR 93
Archibald, Andrew Ronald WhoScE 91-1
Archibald, Claudia Jane 1939- WhoAm 92, WhoAmW 93
Archibald, David D. Law&B 92
Archibald, Fred John 1922- WhoE 93
Archibald, George William 1946- WhoAm 92
Archibald, Jean AmWomPl
Archibald, Jeanne S. 1951- WhoAm 92, WhoAmW 93
Archibald, Julius A., Jr. 1931- WhoE 93
Archibald, Nolan D. BioIn 17
Archibald, Nolan D. 1943- St&PR 93, WhoAm 92, WhoE 93
Archibald, Patricia Ann 1931- WhoAmW 93
Archibald, Rae William 1941- St&PR 93
Archibald, Read W. 1940- St&PR 93
Archibald, Reginald Mac Gregor 1910- WhoAm 92
Archibald, Russell D. 1924- St&PR 93
Archibugi, Francesca 1961- MiSFD 9
Archie, David Esden 1925- St&PR 93
Archimedes c. 287BC-212BC BioIn 17, OxDcByz
Archinow, Lisa Jill 1959- St&PR 93
Archinto Marconi, Rosellina 1935- WhoWor 93
Architects Adventure ScF&FL 92
Archuleta, Diego 1814-1884 HispAmA
Archuleta, Edmund G. 1942- St&PR 93
Archuleta, Felipe 1910-1991 BioIn 17
Archuletta, Patti Stolkin 1946- WhoAmW 93
Arcia Hamana, Luis Jose 1940- WhoWor 93
Arcidy, Louis M. 1954- St&PR 93
Arcidy, Mark A. 1958- St&PR 93
Arciello, Michael Joseph 1934- St&PR 93
Arcieri, Sandy Lee 1955- WhoAmW 93, WhoWor 93
Arcilesi, Richard William 1934- St&PR 93
Arcilesi, Vincent Jasper 1932- WhoAm 92
Arcilla, Felisa Bas 1934- WhoWor 93
Arciniega, Tomas A. 1937- HispAmA [port]
Arciniega, Tomas Abel 1937- WhoAm 92
Arciszewski, Krzysztof 1592-1656 PolBiDi
Arciszewski, Tomasz 1877-1955 PolBiDi
Arconti, Richard David 1952- WhoEmL 93
Arcos, Cresencio S. 1943- WhoAm 92, WhoSSW 93, WhoWor 93
Arcruni OxDcByz
Arculf OxDcByz
Arculli, Ronald Joseph 1939- WhoAsAP 91
Arcuri, Leonard Philip 1947- WhoEmL 93
Arcuri, Shirley Copeland 1949- WhoEmL 93
Arcuri, Tammy Louise 1961- WhoEmL 93
Ard, Charles Walter 1932- St&PR 93
Ard, Elizabeth Law&B 92
Ard, Harold Jacob 1940- WhoAm 92
Ard, Marlin D. Law&B 92
Ardabourios d471 OxDcByz
Ardai, Charles 1969- ConAu 136, ScF&FL 92
Ardaillou, Raymond WhoScE 91-2
Ardales, Venancio Berso 1948- WhoWor 93
Ardans, Alexander Andrew 1941- WhoAm 92
Ardant, Fanny BioIn 17
Ardant Du Picq, Charles Jean Jacques Joseph 1831-1870 HarEnMi
Ardash, Garin 1963- WhoWor 93
Arday, Donald K. 1955- WhoEmL 93
Ardeberg, Arne L. 1940- WhoScE 91-4
Arden, Allyn 1941- St&PR 93
Arden, Bruce Wesley 1927- WhoAm 92
Arden, Caroline 1928- WhoAmW 93
Arden, Eugene 1923- WhoAm 92
Arden, Eve 1908?-1990 IntDcF 2-3
Arden, Eve 1912-1990 BioIn 17, QDrFCA 92 [port]
Arden, John 1930- BioIn 17, BritWr S2, WhoWor 93
Arden, Sherry W. 1930- WhoAm 92
Arden, William WhoWrEP 92
Arden, William John Blaine WhoScE 91-1
Ardeni, Pier Giorgio 1959- WhoWor 93
Ardenne, Manfred von 1907- WhoScE 91-3
Ardern, John 1945- WhoWor 93
Ardery, Philip Pendleton 1914- WhoAm 92
Ardevol, Jose 1911-1981 Baker 92
Ardia, Stephen Vincent 1941- St&PR 93, WhoAm 92, WhoE 93
Ardido, Laurie Law&B 92
Ardila, Enrique 1944- WhoWor 93
Ardinger, Richard Kirk 1953- WhoWrEP 92
Ardisano, Rick 1958- BioIn 17
Ardison, Linda Gail 1940- WhoAmW 93
Arditi, Luigi 1822-1903 Baker 92, OxDcOp
Arditi, Ralph Vincent 1927- St&PR 93
Ardito Barletta, Nicolas 1938- DcCPCAm
Arditti, Edward Roger Law&B 92
Arditti, Elliot Robert Law&B 92
Arditti, Fred D. 1939- WhoAm 92, WhoWor 93
Arditti, Sol J. 1928- St&PR 93
Ardizzone, Edward (Jeffrey Irving) 1900-1979 MajAI [port]
Ardley, Neil (Richard) 1937- ConAu 39NR
Ardoin, John Louis 1935- WhoAm 92
Ardolino, Emile ConTFT 10, MiSFD 9, WhoAm 92
Ardolino, George A. 1955- St&PR 93
Ardouin, Daniel A. 1946- WhoScE 91-2
Ardouin, Daniel Andre 1946- WhoWor 93
Ardrey, R. Leigh 1937- St&PR 93
Ardrey, Robert 1908-1980 ScF&FL 92
Ardussi, W. Philip 1934- St&PR 93
Are, Lisa Darryl 1950- WhoEmL 93
Area, Ronald Gilbert 1945- WhoSSW 93
Arecchi, F.T. WhoScE 91-3
Areddy, Joseph Michael 1933- St&PR 93
Areeda, Phillip 1930- WhoAm 92
Areen, Gordon E. 1918- WhoAm 92
Aregio, Pablo de 1447-1520 BioIn 17
Aregood, Richard Lloyd 1942- WhoAm 92
Arehart, Catherine Lee 1954- WhoEmL 93
Areizaga, Juan Carlos fl. c. 1809- HarEnMi
Arekapudi, Kumar Vijaya Vasantha 1957- WhoWor 93
Arekapudi, Vijayalakshmi 1948- WhoEmL 93
Arel, Bulent 1918-1990 Baker 92
Arel, Bulent 1919-1990 BioIn 17
Arel, Karen Marie 1952- WhoAmW 93
Arel, Maurice Louis 1937- St&PR 93
Arellano, Ignacio 1928- WhoAm 92
Arellano, Jesus 1919-1979 DcMexL
Arellano, Juan Estevan 1947- DcLB 122
Arem, Lawrence Jay 1950- WhoEmL 93
Aremberg, Jean de Ligne, Count of 1525-1568 HarEnMi
Arena, Albert A. 1929- WhoAm 92, WhoE 93
Arena, M. Scott 1946- St&PR 93, WhoAm 92
Arena, Nick F. 1939- St&PR 93
Arena, Nick Frank 1939- WhoAm 92

Arenal, Julie *WhoAm 92*
Arenas, Juan Jose 1940- *WhoScE 91-3*
Arenas, Reinaldo 1943-1990 *BioIn 17, ScF&FL 92, SpAmA*
Arenas-Rosado, Juan Francisco 1944- *WhoWor 93*
Arenberg, David 1927- *WhoSSW 93*
Arenberg, Eli 1927- *St&PR 93*
Arenberg, Julius Theodore, Jr. 1923- *WhoAm 92*
Arenberg, Paul M. 1931- *St&PR 93*
Arenberg, Timothy Paul 1957- *St&PR 93*
Arenberg, William Donald 1930- *St&PR 93*
Arencibia, Raul Antonio 1955- *WhoEmL 93*
Arend, John Tim 1940- *St&PR 93*
Arend, Laurence Warren 1945- *WhoSSW 93*
Arend, Mark Bernard 1960- *WhoSSW 93*
Arend, William W. 1934- *St&PR 93*
Arendall, Charles Baker, Jr. 1915- *WhoAm 92, WhoWor 93*
Arendell, Steven L. 1955- *St&PR 93*
Arendes, Michael C., Jr. *Law&B 92*
Arends, Norman Paul 1945- *WhoWor 93*
Arendsen, Glenn Stuart *Law&B 92*
Arendt, Hannah *BioIn 17*
Arendt, Hannah 1906-1975 *JeAmHC*
Arendt, Ronald Henry 1941- *WhoE 93*
Arendts, Franz Joseph 1935- *WhoScE 91-3*
Arenella, Peter Lee 1947- *WhoEmL 93*
Arenella, Roy Edward 1939- *WhoE 93*
Arenhoevel, Hartmuth 1938- *WhoWor 93*
Arenowitz, Albert Harold 1925- *WhoAm 92*
Arens, Franz Xavier 1856-1932 *Baker 92*
Arens, James F. 1934- *WhoAm 92*
Arens, Manfred 1924- *WhoScE 91-3*
Arens, Moshe 1925- *WhoWor 93*
Arens, Nicholas Herman 1937- *WhoE 93, WhoWor 93*
Arens, Stephen Richard 1951- *WhoEmL 93*
Arens, Steven Carlton 1955- *WhoEmL 93*
Arensberg, Conrad M. 1910- *IntDcAn*
Arensky, Anton 1861-1906 *OxDcOp*
Arensky, Anton (Stepanovich) 1861-1906 *Baker 92*
Arenson, Barbara Levine 1947- *WhoEmL 93*
Arenson, Edwin Walker 1950- *WhoEmL 93*
Arenson, Gregory K. 1949- *WhoEmL 93*
Arenson, Karen Wattel 1949- *WhoAm 92*
Arenstein, Marvin 1934- *WhoSSW 93*
Arent, Albert E. 1911- *St&PR 93*
Arent, Albert Ezra 1911- *WhoAm 92*
Arent, Marvin L. 1917- *St&PR 93*
Arent, Richard Joseph 1963- *WhoEmL 93*
Arenth, Linda M. d1992 *NewYTBS 92*
Arenth, Linda M. 1932-1992 *BioIn 17*
Arenth, Linda Magnusson 1932- *WhoAmW 93*
Arentschildt, Alexander Carl Friedrich von 1806-1881 *HarEnMi*
Arentsen, Leonard W. d1991 *BioIn 17*
Arentsschild, Odo von 1921- *WhoScE 91-3*
Areobindus dc. 512 *OxDcByz*
Areskog, Donald Clinton 1926- *WhoE 93, WhoWor 93*
Areskog, Nils-Holger Carl 1929- *WhoScE 91-4*
Areskoug, Kaj 1933- *St&PR 93*
Areson, Peter DeWitt 1950- *WhoE 93*
Arest, Iris Knight 1950- *WhoAmW 93*
Arestie, Edward Alan 1952- *St&PR 93*
Aresty, Esther Bradford *WhoAm 92*
Aresty, Jeffrey 1951- *WhoEmL 93*
Arethas dc. 520 *OxDcByz*
Arethas fl. 529-569 *OxDcByz*
Arethas of Caesarea dc. 932 *OxDcByz*
Arett, Kent A. *BioIn 17*
Aretz (de Ramon y Rivera), Isabel 1909- *Baker 92*
Arevalo, Juan Jose 1904-1990 *BioIn 17*
Arevalo, L. *WhoScE 91-3*
Arevalo Bermejo, Juan Jose 1904- *DcCPCAm*
Arevshatian, Levon 1938- *WhoUN 92*
Arey, Patrick Kane 1947- *WhoEmL 93*
Arey, Robert Jackson, Jr. 1952- *St&PR 93, WhoSSW 93*
Arezzo, Guido d' *Baker 92*
Arfa, Milton 1920- *WhoAm 92*
Arfield, George 1937- *WhoE 93*
Arfin, Ronald R. 1953- *St&PR 93*
Arft, Larry Norman 1946- *WhoEmL 93*
Arfwedson, Anders J. 1940- *WhoUN 92*
Argamasilla, Joaquin 1905?- *BioIn 17*
Argan, Giulio Carlo 1909-1992 *ConAu 139, NewYTBS 92*
Arganbright, A.D. 1930- *St&PR 93*
Arganbright, A. Dean 1930- *WhoAm 92, WhoIns 93*
Arganbright, Nancy *BioIn 17*
Argazzi, Robert A. *Law&B 92*
Argenbright, Debra *Law&B 92*
Argent, Bernard Barry *WhoScE 91-1*
Argent, G.C.G. 1941- *WhoScE 91-1*
Argenta, Craig Jon 1952- *WhoEmL 93*
Argenta (Maza), Ataulfo 1913-1958 *Baker 92*
Argenti, Mario 1954- *St&PR 93*
Argentine, Peter Dominic 1948- *St&PR 93, WhoAm 92*
Argento, Dario 1940- *MiSFD 9*
Argento, Dominick 1927- *Baker 92, IntDcOp, OxDcOp*
Argerich, Martha 1941- *Baker 92*
Argeroplos, William J. *St&PR 93*
Argeroudis, Nick G. 1956- *St&PR 93*
Argersinger, William John, Jr. 1918- *WhoAm 92*
Argetsinger, Gerald Scott 1946- *WhoE 93*
Argibay, Jorge Luis 1953- *WhoWor 93*
Argirion, Michael 1940- *WhoAm 92*
Argiriou, George D. *Law&B 92*
Argiropoulos, Kathleen *Law&B 92*
Argo, Dorothy Peck *WhoSSW 93*
Argo, Linda Kay 1951- *WhoEmL 93*
Argo, William Alexander 1923- *St&PR 93*
Argon, Ali Suphi 1930- *WhoAm 92*
Argow, Keith Angevin 1936- *WhoAm 92*
Argroves, Kenneth W. 1947- *St&PR 93*
Argrow, Brian M. 1960- *WhoSSW 93*
Argudin, Antonio 1953- *DcMexL*
Argue, James B., Jr. 1951- *WhoSSW 93*
Argue, John Clifford 1932- *WhoAm 92, WhoWor 93*
Arguedas, Jose Maria 1911-1969 *SpAmA*
Arguelles, Hugo 1932- *DcMexL*
Arguelles, Ivan 1939- *WhoWrEP 92*
Arguelles, John 1927- *HispAmA [port]*
Arguelles Bringas, Roberto 1875-1915 *DcMexL*
Arguello, Concha Maria de Concepcion 1791-1857 *NotHsAW 93*
Arguello, Leonardo *DcCPCAm*
Arguello, Miriam *DcCPCAm*
Argueta, Manlio 1936- *SpAmA*
Argun, Fatima Hatice 1959- *WhoAm 92*
Argyelan, Michael Charles *St&PR 93*
Argyilan, Kristi Ann 1958- *WhoEmL 93*
Argyll, Archibald Campbell, Earl of 1629-1685 *HarEnMi*
Argyll, Archibald Campbell, Marquis and Earl of 1607-1661 *HarEnMi*
Argyrakis, Panos P. 1950- *WhoWor 93*
Argyriadis, George 1930- *WhoScE 91-3*
Argyris, Chris 1923- *WhoAm 92*
Argyropoulos, John c. 1393-1487 *OxDcByz*
Argyros *OxDcByz*
Argyros c. 1000-c. 1058 *OxDcByz*
Argyros, Isaac 1300?-c. 1375 *OxDcByz*
Argy-Rousseau, Gabriel 1885-1953 *BioIn 17*
Arhan, Pierre 1937- *WhoScE 91-2*
Arhem, Peter 1946- *WhoScE 91-4*
Ari, Bakuji 1922- *WhoWor 93*
Ariadne c. 457-515 *OxDcByz*
Arian, Rahim 1931- *St&PR 93*
Arias, Alberto A. Boyd *BioIn 17*
Arias, Arnulfo 1901- *DcTwHis*
Arias, Arturo 1950- *SpAmA*
Arias, Harmodio *DcCPCAm*
Arias, Irwin Monroe 1926- *WhoAm 92, WhoE 93*
Arias, Pedro Luis 1959- *WhoWor 93*
Arias, Roberto E. 1918-1989 *BioIn 17*
Arias, Ron 1941- *ScF&FL 92*
Arias Calderon, Ricardo 1933- *DcCPCAm*
Arias Madrid, Arnulfo 1901-1988 *DcCPCAm*
Arias-Misson, Alain August 1939- *WhoWrEP 92*
Arias Navarro, Carlos 1908-1989 *BioIn 17*
Arias-Salgado y Montalvo, Fernando 1938- *WhoUN 92*
Arias Sanchez, Oscar *BioIn 17*
Arias Sanchez, Oscar 1941- *DcCPCAm, WhoWor 93*
Aribau, Bonaventura Carles 1798-1862 *BioIn 17*
'Arib ibn Sa'd al-Qurtubi d980? *OxDcByz*
Aribon c. 1000-c. 1078 *Baker 92*
Aribon de Freising c. 1000-c. 1078 *Baker 92*
Aribon de Liege c. 1000-c. 1078 *Baker 92*
Aribon d'Orleans c. 1000-c. 1078 *Baker 92*
Aribo Scholasticus c. 1000-c. 1078 *Baker 92*
Arick, Clarke Douglas 1950- *WhoSSW 93*
Arico, Margaret Mary 1952- *WhoAmW 93*
Aridjis, Homero 1940- *DcMexL, SpAmA*
Aridor, Yoram 1933- *WhoUN 92*
Arie, Thomas Harry David *WhoScE 91-1*
Arienzo, Nicola d' 1842-1915 *Baker 92*
Aries, Lucien Emile 1940- *WhoScE 91-2*
Aries, Philippe 1914-1984 *BioIn 17*
Arieti, James Alexander 1948- *WhoEmL 93, WhoSSW 93*
Arif, Muhammad 1939- *WhoWor 93*
Arifin, Bustanil 1925- *WhoAsAP 91*
Ariga Kosaku 1897-1945 *HarEnMi*
Arigapudi, Premchand 1933- *WhoUN 92*
Arigoni, Duilio 1928- *WhoScE 91-4*
Arik, Baha Engin 1956- *WhoE 93*
Arik, Tali 1956- *WhoEmL 93*
Arikawa, Seiji 1929- *WhoAsAP 91*
Ariki, Soichiro 1929- *WhoWor 93*
Arima, Akito 1930- *WhoWor 93*
Arima, Masafumi 1895-1944 *HarEnMi*
Arima, Michiko 1941- *WhoWor 93*
Arimitsu, Toshihico 1952- *WhoWor 93*
Arimura, Akira 1923- *WhoAm 92*
Arinaga, Susan L. *Law&B 92*
Aring, Charles D. *BioIn 17*
Arinsburg, Larry 1947- *WhoEmL 93*
Arinze, Francis 1932- *ConAu 138*
Arinze, Francis Cardinal 1932- *WhoWor 93*
Ariola, Wayne *St&PR 93*
Arioli, Mario 1953- *WhoWor 93*
Arion, Georges Julien 1920- *WhoWor 93*
Ariosti, Attilio 1666-c. 1729 *Baker 92, OxDcOp*
Ariosto, Lodovico 1474-1535 *OxDcOp*
Aris, J.B.B. *WhoScE 91-1*
Aris, John Bernard Benedict 1934- *WhoWor 93*
Aris, Rutherford 1929- *WhoAm 92*
Aris, Stanley Joseph 1940- *WhoAm 92*
Arison, Micky 1949- *St&PR 93, WhoAm 92, WhoSSW 93*
Arison, Ted 1924- *WhoAm 92*
Ariss, Herbert Joshua 1918- *WhoAm 92*
Aristakesian, Emin 1936- *Baker 92*
Aristakes Lastivertc'i *OxDcByz*
Aristarain, Adolfo 1943- *MiSFD 9*
Aristeides, Ailios 117?-c. 189 *OxDcByz*
Aristenos *OxDcByz*
Aristenos, Alexios 12th cent.- *OxDcByz*
Aristide, Jean-Bertrand *BioIn 17*
Aristide, Jean-Bertrand 1953- *DcCPCAm, WhoWor 93*
Aristides Quintilianus fl. c. 200- *Baker 92*
Aristophanes c. 450BC-c. 385BC *MagSWL [port]*
Aristophanes c. 445BC-c. 388BC *OxDcByz*
Aristotle 384BC-322BC *Baker 92, BioIn 17, MagSWL [port], OxDcByz*
Aristoxenus 354BC- *Baker 92*
Ariturk, Emin 1921- *WhoScE 91-4*
Ariturk, Haluk 1949- *St&PR 93, WhoIns 93*
Arius c. 250-336 *OxDcByz*
Ariwibowo, Tungki 1936- *WhoAsAP 91*
Ariwibowo, Turki 1936- *WhoWor 93*
Ariyoshi, George Ryoichi 1926- *WhoAm 92*
Ariyoshi, Rita Clare 1939- *WhoWrEP 92*
Ariyoshi, Sawako 1931-1984 *BioIn 17*
Ariyoshi, Toshihiko 1930- *WhoWor 93*
Arizaga, Rodolfo 1926-1985 *Baker 92*
Arizumi, Martha Robbins 1952- *WhoWor 93*
Arjani, Anita B. *Law&B 92*
Arjas, Elja 1943- *WhoScE 91-4, WhoWor 93*
Arjona, Sandra Katherine 1947- *WhoAmW 93*
Ark, Connie Eileen 1951- *WhoWrEP 92*
Arkadios 377?-408 *OxDcByz*
Arkai, Peter 1944- *WhoScE 91-4*
Arkas, Nikolai 1853-1909 *Baker 92*
Arkel, Paul Van 1970- *WhoWor 93*
Arkell, John A. 1962- *St&PR 93*
Arkell, Robert B. 1931- *St&PR 93*
Arkell, Robert S. 1933- *St&PR 93*
Arkenberg, Amy Rosalie 1943- *WhoAmW 93*
Arkes, Hadley P. *WhoAm 92*
Arkfeld, Frank John 1945- *St&PR 93*
Arkham, Candice *ScF&FL 92*
Arkhipova, Irina 1925- *OxDcOp*
Arkhipova, Irina (Konstantinovna) 1925- *Baker 92*
Arkhippov, Evgenil IAkovlevich 1882-1950 *BioIn 17*
Arkhurst, Joyce 1921- *BlkAull 92*
Arkilic, Galip Mehmet 1920- *WhoAm 92*
Arkin, Alan 1934- *IntDcF 2-3 [port], MiSFD 9, ScF&FL 92*
Arkin, Alan Wolf 1934- *WhoAm 92*
Arkin, Frances 1904-1991 *BioIn 17*
Arkin, Joseph 1922- *WhoWrEP 92*
Arkin, Joseph 1923- *WhoE 93, WhoWor 93*
Arkin, L. Jules *WhoSSW 93*
Arkin, Michael Barry 1941- *WhoAm 92*
Arkin, Robert David 1954- *WhoEmL 93, WhoSSW 93*
Arkin, Stanley Herbert 1932- *WhoSSW 93, WhoWor 93*
Arkle, Phyllis 1910- *ChlFicS*
Arkles, Barry 1947- *St&PR 93*
Arkles, Barry Charles 1949- *WhoAm 92*
Arkoff, Samuel Z. 1918- *WhoAm 92*
Arkoosh, Fred G. 1914- *St&PR 93*
Arkoosh, Fred G., Jr. 1945- *St&PR 93*
Arkor, Andre d' 1901-1971 *Baker 92*
Arkowitz, Martin Arthur 1935- *WhoAm 92*
Arkus, Allen Sol 1946- *WhoEmL 93, WhoSSW 93*
Arkus, Leon Anthony 1915- *WhoAm 92*
Arkush, Allan 1948- *MiSFD 9*
Arkuss, Neil Philip 1945- *WhoAm 92*
Arkutu, Andrew Ananie 1936- *WhoUN 92*
Arkwright, Richard 1732-1792 *BioIn 17*
Arky, Ronald Alfred 1929- *WhoAm 92*
Arlaud, Gerard *WhoScE 91-2*
Arlea, Michael Nicholas 1944- *St&PR 93*
Arledge, Charles Stone 1935- *St&PR 93, WhoAm 92*
Arledge, Roone *BioIn 17*
Arledge, Roone 1931- *News 92 [port], WhoAm 92*
Arlen, Gary O'Hara 1945- *WhoWrEP 92*
Arlen, Harold 1905-1986 *Baker 92*
Arlen, Jennifer Hall 1959- *WhoEmL 93*
Arlen, Michael J. 1930- *WhoAm 92, WhoWor 93, WhoWrEP 92*
Arles, Henri d' *BioIn 17*
Arlet, Babbette *St&PR 93*
Arlet, Jacques 1920- *WhoScE 91-2*
Arlett, Russell Loris 1899-1964 *BiDAMSp 1989*
Arletty 1898- *IntDcF 2-3 [port]*
Arletty 1898-1992 *NewYTBS 92 [port]*
Arley, Niels Henrik 1911- *WhoWor 93*
Arlidge, John Walter 1933- *St&PR 93, WhoAm 92*
Arlin, Zalmen A. d1992 *NewYTBS 92*
Arling, Bryan Jeremy 1944- *WhoE 93, WhoWor 93*
Arlinghaus, Sandra Judith Lach 1943- *WhoAmW 93, WhoWor 93*
Arlington, William J. 1948- *St&PR 93*
Arlinskii, Yury Moiseevich 1949- *WhoWor 93*
Arlis, Anthony T. 1930- *St&PR 93*
Arlis, Chrissie P. 1932- *St&PR 93*
Arliss, George 1868-1946 *IntDcF 2-3*
Arlott, John 1914-1991 *AnObit 1991*
Arlott, (Leslie Thomas) John 1914-1991 *ConAu 136*
Arlow, Allan Joseph 1944- *WhoAm 92*
Arlow, Arnold Jack 1933- *WhoAm 92*
Arlow, Jacob A. 1912- *WhoAm 92*
Arlow, Seth Martin 1946- *WhoEmL 93*
Arlt, Gottfried 1926- *WhoScE 91-3*
Arlt, Mary Ann *Law&B 92*
Arlt, Roberto 1900-1942 *SpAmA*
Arlt, Wulf (Friedrich) 1938- *Baker 92*
Arluck, Hyman 1905-1986 *Baker 92*
Arm, Jonathan Peter 1953- *WhoWor 93*
Arma, Paul 1904-1987 *Baker 92*
Armacost, John Cooper 1936- *WhoE 93*
Armacost, Michael Hayden 1937- *WhoAm 92, WhoWor 93*
Armacost, Peter Hayden 1935- *WhoAm 92*
Armacost, Samuel Henry 1939- *St&PR 93*
Armagost, Elsa Gafvert *WhoAmW 93, WhoWor 93*
Armah, Ayi Kwei 1938- *BioIn 17*
Armah, Ayi Kwei 1939- *DcLB 117 [port], IntLitE, WhoWrEP 92*
Armah, Joseph 1967- *WhoWor 93*
Armaly, Mansour Farid 1927- *WhoAm 92*
Arman 1928- *BioIn 17, News 93-1 [port]*
Arman, Ara 1930- *WhoAm 92*
Arman, Armand Pierre 1928- *WhoAm 92*
Arman, Theodore W. 1922- *St&PR 93*
Armand, Jean-Pierre 1943- *WhoScE 91-2*
Armand, Patrick *WhoAm 92*
Armando, Armando 1945- *WhoScE 91-3*
Armani, Giacomo 1868-1954 *See* Tess, Giulia 1889-1976 *OxDcOp*
Armani, Giorgio *BioIn 17*
Armani, Giorgio 1934- *WhoAm 92, WhoWor 93*
Armani, Michael F. *Law&B 92*
Armani, Joseph S. *Law&B 92*
Armanini, Louis A. 1930- *St&PR 93*
Armanios, Erian Abdelmessih 1950- *WhoSSW 93*
Armant, Terry Lee 1948- *WhoE 93*
Armantrout, (Mary) Rae 1947- *WhoWrEP 92*
Armario-Garcia, Pedro 1955- *WhoWor 93*
Armaro, Mario *Law&B 92*
Armata, Cheryl Petrucci *Law&B 92*
Armatis, Leo R. 1937- *St&PR 93*
Armato, David N. 1961- *WhoE 93*
Armato, Peter 1953- *WhoE 93, WhoEmL 93*
Armatrading, Joan 1950- *Baker 92, BioIn 17*
Armbrecht, Edward C., Jr. 1932- *St&PR 93*
Armbrecht, Mary Ellyn 1956- *WhoAmW 93*
Armbrecht, William Henry, III 1929- *WhoAm 92*
Armbrister, Monique Martin 1967- *WhoAmW 93*
Armbrust, Bernerd *St&PR 93*
Armbruster, Debra A. *Law&B 92*
Armbruster, James R. *Law&B 92*
Armbruster, Karl 1846-1917 *Baker 92*

Armbruster, R. Lee Law&B 92
Armbuster, Lee D. 1955- St&PR 93
Arme, Christopher WhoScE 91-1
Armellino, Michael Ralph 1940- WhoAm 92
Armen, Robert William 1943- St&PR 93
Armenakas, Anthony Emmanuel 1924- WhoE 93
Armenante, Piero M. 1953- WhoE 93
Armendarez, Peter Xavier 1930- WhoSSW 93
Armendaris, Alex d1992 NewYTBS 92
Armendariz, Pedro 1912-1963 HispAmA, IntDcF 2-3 [port]
Armenise, Giovanni Auletta BioIn 17
Armenise, Mario Nicola 1943- WhoWor 93
Arment, Laura B. Law&B 92
Armenteros, Rafael 1922- WhoScE 91-4
Armenti, Joseph Rocco 1950- WhoE 93, WhoEmL 93, WhoWor 93
Armentia Fructuoso, Javier Esteban 1962- WhoWor 93
Armento, Donald Francis 1956- WhoEmL 93
Armentor, Glenn John 1950- WhoEmL 93
Armentrout, Dede BioIn 17
Armentrout, Donald Smith 1939- WhoSSW 93
Armentrout, Peter Bruce 1953- WhoEmL 93
Armentrout, Steven Alexander 1933- WhoAm 92
Armer, Graham S.T. WhoScE 91-1
Armer, Laura Adams 1874-1963 MajAI [port]
Armer, Sondra Schecter 1944- WhoWrEP 92
Armes, Ethel Marie AmWomPl
Armes, Steven Peter 1962- WhoWor 93
Armesto, Diego 1945- WhoWor 93
Armetta, Joseph James 1943- St&PR 93
Armey, Richard K. BioIn 17
Armey, Richard K. 1940- CngDr 91
Armey, Richard Keith 1940- WhoAm 92, WhoSSW 93
Armga, Carol Joan 1951- WhoAmW 93
Armida SweetSg C [port]
Armida 1913- HispAmA
Armiger, Gene Gibbon 1931- WhoSSW 93
Armiger, George D. 1945- St&PR 93
Armijo, Jacqulyn Doris 1938- WhoAmW 93
Armijo, Lillian Mendoza 1959- WhoAmW 93
Armijo, Nola Margaret 1948- WhoAmW 93
Armillei, Raymond Joseph 1954- WhoE 93
Armin, Georg 1871-1963 Baker 92
Armingaud, Jules 1820-1900 Baker 92
Armington, John Howard 1913- St&PR 93
Armington, Judie Ann 1943- WhoAmW 93
Arminio, Alphonse P. 1942- St&PR 93
Armistead, Ivor Cary, III Law&B 92
Armistead, John Irving 1949- WhoEmL 93
Armistead, Katherine Kelly 1926- WhoAmW 93
Armistead, Mary Kathryn 1952- WhoSSW 93
Armistead, Moss William, III 1915- WhoAm 92
Armistead, Russell Eugene, Jr. 1946- WhoEmL 93
Armistead, William Cole, Jr. 1944- WhoSSW 93
Armistead, Willis William 1916- WhoAm 92
Armitage, Barri June 1937- WhoWrEP 92
Armitage, Brian WhoScE 91-1
Armitage, George MiSFD 9
Armitage, Janet D. 1956- WhoAmW 93
Armitage, John Vernon WhoScE 91-1
Armitage, Karole 1954- WhoAm 92
Armitage, Kenneth Barclay 1925- WhoAm 92
Armitage, P. WhoScE 91-1
Armitage, Robert Allen Law&B 92
Armitage, Robert Allen 1948- WhoEmL 93
Armitt, Lucie 1962- ScF&FL 92
Armknecht, Paul Anthony 1945- WhoE 93
Armocida, Patricia Anne 1956- WhoAmW 93
Armold, Judith Ann 1945- WhoAmW 93
Armon, Gary Leo 1950- WhoEmL 93
Armon, Michael William 1953- St&PR 93
Armon, Norma 1937- WhoWor 93
Armondo, Angelo Anthony 1948- WhoEmL 93
Armor, David J. 1938- WhoAm 92
Armor, James Burton 1926- WhoAm 92
Armour, Carolyn Law&B 92
Armour, David Edward Ponton 1921- WhoAm 92
Armour, David George WhoScE 91-1
Armour, Elizabeth Ann 1952- WhoWor 93
Armour, James WhoScE 91-1
Armour, James A. 1943- St&PR 93
Armour, James Author 1943- WhoAm 92
Armour, James Brown 1841-1928 BioIn 17
Armour, James Lott 1938- WhoAm 92, WhoWor 93
Armour, Justin BioIn 17
Armour, Laurance Hearne, Jr. 1923- WhoAm 92
Armour, Lawrence 1935- St&PR 93
Armour, Lawrence A. 1935- WhoAm 92
Armour, Mary Gooch 1942- WhoAm 92
Armour, Norman E. 1928- St&PR 93
Armour, Peter BioIn 17
Armour, R.J. St&PR 93
Armour, Richard Willard 1906-1989 BioIn 17
Armour, Robert Charles 1936- WhoSSW 93
Armour, Thomas BioIn 17
Armour, Walter B. 1929- St&PR 93
Armpriester, Ginger Gail 1948- WhoEmL 93
Arms, Brewster Lee 1925- WhoAm 92
Arms, Geoffrey Law&B 92
Armstead, Clark A. 1932- St&PR 93
Armstead, George Brooks, Jr. 1927- WhoE 93
Armstead, Joshie Jo 1944- BioIn 17
Armstead, Rhonda R. Law&B 92
Armstrong, A.G. Law&B 92
Armstrong, Abigail M. Law&B 92
Armstrong, Alexandra 1939- WhoAm 92
Armstrong, Alice Catt WhoWrEP 92
Armstrong, Alicia BioIn 17
Armstrong, Anna Dawn 1943- WhoAmW 93
Armstrong, Anna Rebecca AmWomPl
Armstrong, Anne Legendre 1927- WhoAm 92, WhoAmW 93
Armstrong, Anthony 1897-1976 ScF&FL 92
Armstrong, Bess 1953- BioIn 17
Armstrong, Brenda Lee 1945- WhoAmW 93
Armstrong, Bruce Konrad 1944- WhoUN 92
Armstrong, Bunty BioIn 17
Armstrong, Campbell ScF&FL 92
Armstrong, Carl Hines 1926- WhoAm 92
Armstrong, Carolyn Ann 1938- WhoAmW 93
Armstrong, Charles P. 1951- WhoIns 93
Armstrong, Charles W. 1871-1951 ScF&FL 92
Armstrong, Clara Julia Evershed 1911- WhoAmW 93
Armstrong, Clare BioIn 17
Armstrong, Colin WhoScE 91-1
Armstrong, Craig BioIn 17
Armstrong, Craig Stephen 1947- WhoEmL 93
Armstrong, Daniel Wayne 1949- WhoAm 92, WhoEmL 93
Armstrong, Darlene L. 1949- WhoAmW 93, WhoWor 93
Armstrong, David Andrew 1940- WhoAm 92
Armstrong, David Anthony 1930- WhoAm 92
Armstrong, David Ballard 1940- St&PR 93
Armstrong, David Gilford WhoScE 91-1
Armstrong, David Millar WhoScE 91-1
Armstrong, David Millar 1941- WhoWor 93
Armstrong, David William 1954- WhoWor 93
Armstrong, Deanna Frances 1962- WhoAmW 93, WhoEmL 93
Armstrong, Denise Grace WhoE 93
Armstrong, Dickwin Dill 1934- WhoAm 92
Armstrong, Donald Edward, Jr. 1950- WhoEmL 93, WhoSSW 93
Armstrong, Douglas S. 1953- St&PR 93
Armstrong, Edward Bradford, Jr. 1928- WhoWor 93
Armstrong, Edward W. 1921- St&PR 93
Armstrong, Edwin Richard 1921- WhoAm 92
Armstrong, Elizabeth Law&B 92
Armstrong, Elizabeth Neilson 1952- WhoAm 92
Armstrong, Eugene M. 1918- St&PR 93
Armstrong, F. Michael 1942- WhoIns 93
Armstrong, F.W. ScF&FL 92
Armstrong, Fredric Michael 1942- St&PR 93, WhoAm 92
Armstrong, Fytton 1912-1970 ScF&FL 92
Armstrong, Garry Herbert Emile 1942- WhoE 93
Armstrong, Gary Alan 1947- WhoEmL 93, WhoSSW 93
Armstrong, Gary L. 1943- St&PR 93
Armstrong, Gene Lee 1922- WhoAm 92, WhoWor 93
Armstrong, Gillian 1950- MiSFD 9
Armstrong, Graham St&PR 93
Armstrong, Greg L. 1960- St&PR 93
Armstrong, Gregory Timon 1933- WhoAm 92
Armstrong, Hamilton Fish 1893-1973 ColdWar 1 [port]
Armstrong, Henry Conner 1925- WhoAm 92
Armstrong, Herbert Stoker 1915- WhoAm 92
Armstrong, Herbert W. 1902-1986 BioIn 17
Armstrong, Homer D. 1924- St&PR 93
Armstrong, Ingram L., Mrs. AmWomPl
Armstrong, J. Robert Law&B 92
Armstrong, Jack D. Law&B 92
Armstrong, Jack Gilliland 1929- WhoAm 92
Armstrong, James 1924- WhoAm 92
Armstrong, James E. Law&B 92
Armstrong, James Francis, III 1945- WhoE 93
Armstrong, James Franklin WhoAm 92
Armstrong, James R., Sr. 1929- St&PR 93
Armstrong, James Sinclair 1915- WhoAm 92
Armstrong, Jan Maria 1950- WhoE 93
Armstrong, Jan Robert 1953- WhoEmL 93
Armstrong, Jane Botsford WhoAm 92, WhoAmW 93
Armstrong, Jean I. 1941- WhoAmW 93
Armstrong, Jefferson d1992 BioIn 17
Armstrong, Jill Leslie 1952- WhoAmW 93
Armstrong, Joanna 1915- WhoAmW 93
Armstrong, Joanne Marie 1956- WhoAmW 93
Armstrong, John 1717-1795 HarEnMi
Armstrong, John Alexander 1922- WhoAm 92
Armstrong, John Allan 1934- WhoAm 92
Armstrong, John Barclay 1850-1913 BioIn 17
Armstrong, John Dale 1918- WhoAm 92
Armstrong, John Kenaston 1929- WhoAm 92
Armstrong, John Kremer 1934- WhoAm 92, WhoE 93, WhoWor 93
Armstrong, John M. 1943- St&PR 93
Armstrong, Judith E. Law&B 92
Armstrong, Julia A. Law&B 92
Armstrong, Karan 1941- Baker 92
Armstrong, Kathleen E. Law&B 92
Armstrong, Keith Bernard 1931- WhoWor 93
Armstrong, Kenneth Law&B 92
Armstrong, Kenneth E. 1947- St&PR 93
Armstrong, Leonard Otho 1921- St&PR 93
Armstrong, Lloyd, Jr. 1940- WhoAm 92
Armstrong, Louis 1898?-1971 Baker 92
Armstrong, Louis 1900-1971 BioIn 17, ConHero 2 [port]
Armstrong, Louise Van Voorhis 1887-1948 BioIn 17
Armstrong, Louise Van Voorhis 1889- AmWomPl
Armstrong, Margaret Coury 1937- WhoAmW 93
Armstrong, Martha Susan 1954- WhoSSW 93
Armstrong, Martin Keith 1949- WhoWor 93
Armstrong, Mary Vaughn 1934- WhoWrEP 92
Armstrong, Mary W. 1936- St&PR 93
Armstrong, Michael 1944- MiSFD 9
Armstrong, Michael 1956- ScF&FL 92
Armstrong, Michael David 1955- WhoEmL 93, WhoWor 93
Armstrong, Michael Francis 1932- WhoAm 92
Armstrong, Moe 1944- WhoWor 93
Armstrong, Nancy L. 1948- WhoAm 92, WhoEmL 93
Armstrong, Neal Earl 1941- WhoAm 92
Armstrong, Neil 1930- BioIn 17, Expl 93 [port]
Armstrong, Neil A. 1930- WhoAm 92, WhoWor 93
Armstrong, Nelson William, Jr. 1941- St&PR 93, WhoAm 92
Armstrong, Niall A. Law&B 92
Armstrong, Oliver Wendell 1919- WhoAm 92, WhoWor 93
Armstrong, Orville 1929- WhoAm 92
Armstrong, Pamela Gayle 1945- WhoAmW 93
Armstrong, Patricia E. Law&B 92
Armstrong, Patricia Jean Law&B 92
Armstrong, Patricia Kay 1936- WhoWrEP 92
Armstrong, Patrick Hamilton 1941- WhoWor 93
Armstrong, Paul L. Law&B 92
Armstrong, Peg Jean 1943- WhoSSW 93
Armstrong, Peter M. 1954- St&PR 93
Armstrong, Phillip M. Law&B 92
Armstrong, Ralph Henry 1950- WhoSSW 93
Armstrong, Richard 1943- Baker 92, OxDcOp
Armstrong, Richard 1949- WhoAm 92
Armstrong, Richard A. d1992 NewYTBS 92
Armstrong, Richard Alford 1929- WhoAm 92
Armstrong, Richard Burke 1924- WhoAm 92, WhoWor 93
Armstrong, Richard L. 1944- St&PR 93
Armstrong, Richard Q. St&PR 93
Armstrong, Richard Stoll 1924- WhoAm 92
Armstrong, Ricky Lee 1954- WhoSSW 93
Armstrong, Robb BioIn 17
Armstrong, Robert A. Law&B 92
Armstrong, Robert Arnold 1928- WhoAm 92
Armstrong, Robert Baker 1914- WhoAm 92
Armstrong, Robert Dean 1923- WhoWor 93
Armstrong, Robert Douglas Law&B 92
Armstrong, Robert Eddy 1932- WhoE 93
Armstrong, Robert Sitgreaves 1956- WhoEmL 93
Armstrong, Robert Stevenson, Jr. 1954- WhoEmL 93
Armstrong, Robert Wakefield d1992 BioIn 17, NewYTBS 92
Armstrong, Robert Weeks, III 1949- St&PR 93
Armstrong, Robin B. MiSFD 9
Armstrong, Robin Louis 1935- WhoAm 92
Armstrong, Rodney 1923- WhoAm 92
Armstrong, Rosemary 1951- WhoEmL 93
Armstrong, Roxanne Law&B 92
Armstrong, Russell 1916- St&PR 93
Armstrong, Sarah ScF&FL 92
Armstrong, Scott Michael 1964- WhoE 93
Armstrong, Sebert Ray 1935- St&PR 93
Armstrong, Sheila 1942- Baker 92
Armstrong, Stella Morse AmWomPl
Armstrong, Susan S. Law&B 92
Armstrong, Theodore M. 1939- St&PR 93
Armstrong, Theodore Morelock 1939- WhoAm 92
Armstrong, Thomas A. BioIn 17
Armstrong, Thomas Field 1947- WhoEmL 93, WhoSSW 93
Armstrong, Thomas K. 1954- St&PR 93
Armstrong, Thomas Newton 1932- BioIn 17
Armstrong, Thomas Newton, III 1932- WhoAm 92, WhoWor 93
Armstrong, Thomas R. 1944- St&PR 93
Armstrong, Thomas W. Law&B 92
Armstrong, Timothy Joseph 1945- WhoWor 93
Armstrong, Victoria Elizabeth 1950- WhoAmW 93
Armstrong, W. Charles WhoAm 92
Armstrong, W. James 1929- St&PR 93
Armstrong, Wallace Edwin 1896-1980 IntDcAn
Armstrong, Walter Preston, Jr. 1916- WhoAm 92, WhoSSW 93, WhoWor 93
Armstrong, Walter William 1928- St&PR 93, WhoAm 92
Armstrong, Warren Bruce 1933- WhoAm 92
Armstrong, William BioIn 17
Armstrong, William Guy 1924- WhoScE 91-1
Armstrong, William H(oward) 1914- MajAI [port]
Armstrong, William Harold 1954- WhoEmL 93, WhoSSW 93
Armstrong, William Henry 1943- WhoAm 92
Armstrong, William Howard 1914- DcAmChF 1960
Armstrong, William Warren 1935- WhoAm 92
Armstrong, William Weaver 1862-1906 BioIn 17
Armstrong, Willis Coburn 1912- WhoE 93
Armstrong, Zella AmWomPl
Armstrong-Dailey, Ann BioIn 17
Armstrong-Jones, Antony Charles Robert 1930- WhoWor 93
Armstrong-Jones, Tony 1930- BioIn 17
Armytage, David WhoScE 91-1
Armytage, Walter 1915- ScF&FL 92
Arn, Dwight Calvin Law&B 92
Arn, Edward F. 1906- BioIn 17
Arn, Kenneth Dale 1921- WhoAm 92
Arnaboldi, Joseph Paul 1920- WhoE 93
Arnaboldi, Leo Peter, III 1959- WhoEmL 93
Arnalds, Andres 1948- WhoScE 91-4
Arnall, Ellis G. d1992 NewYTBS 92 [port]
Arnall, Patrick James Law&B 92
Arnason, Barry Gilbert Wyatt 1933- WhoAm 92
Arnason, Dale Gordon Law&B 92

Arnason, David 1940- *WhoCanL 92*
Arnason, Eleanor 1942- *ScF&FL 92*
Arnatt, Ronald Kent 1930- *WhoE 93*
Arnaud, Alain 1945- *WhoScE 91-2*
Arnaud, Claude Donald, Jr. 1929- *WhoAm 92*
Arnaud, Dominique 1929- *WhoScE 91-2*
Arnaud, Maurice J. 1942- *WhoScE 91-4*
Arnaud, Maurice Joseph 1942- *WhoWor 93*
Arnauld, Antoine 1612-1694 *BioIn 17*
Arnault, Bernard *BioIn 17*
Arnault, Bernard Jean 1949- *WhoAm 92, WhoWor 93*
Arnaz, Desi 1917- *HispAmA*
Arnaz, Desi 1917-1986 *BioIn 17, ConMus 8 [port]*
Arnaz, Desi, Jr. *BioIn 17*
Arnaz, Lucie *BioIn 17*
Arnaz, Lucie 1951- *NotHsAW 93*
Arnaz, Lucie Desiree 1951- *WhoAm 92*
Arnbak, Jens C. 1943- *WhoScE 91-3*
Arnberg, Robert Lewis 1945- *WhoAm 92*
Arndt, C.C. *WhoWrEP 92*
Arndt, Carmen Gloria 1942- *WhoAmW 93*
Arndt, Darlene Susan 1965- *WhoAmW 93*
Arndt, Dennis R. *Law&B 92*
Arndt, Dianne Joy 1939- *WhoAmW 93, WhoWor 93*
Arndt, Ernst Albert Walter Wilhelm 1927- *WhoWor 93*
Arndt, Ernst Moritz 1769-1860 *BioIn 17*
Arndt, Frances 1919- *WhoAmW 93*
Arndt, Fritz 1938- *WhoScE 91-3*
Arndt, Gunther 1907-1976 *Baker 92*
Arndt, Helmut Hoyer 1911- *WhoWor 93*
Arndt, Joan Marie 1945- *WhoAmW 93*
Arndt, Karl John Richard 1903- *WhoWrEP 92*
Arndt, Kenneth Alfred 1936- *WhoAm 92*
Arndt, Kenneth Eugene 1933- *WhoAm 92*
Arndt, Linda Diane 1949- *WhoAmW 93*
Arndt, Nancy Yvonne 1938- *WhoAm 92, WhoAmW 93*
Arndt, Paul Wilhelm, Jr. 1934- *St&PR 93*
Arndt, Richard T. 1928- *WhoAm 92*
Arndt, Robert H. 1942- *St&PR 93*
Arndt, Roger Edward Anthony 1935- *WhoAm 92*
Arndt, Stephen Allen 1949- *WhoEmL 93*
Arndt, Uwe D. 1935- *WhoScE 91-3*
Arndt, Walter Werner 1916- *WhoAm 92*
Arne, Gary R. 1957- *St&PR 93*
Arne, Jean-Louis 1946- *WhoScE 91-2*
Arne, Marshall C. 1930- *St&PR 93*
Arne, Michael c. 1740-1786 *Baker 92*
Arne, Thomas Augustine 1710-1778 *Baker 92, IntDcOp [port], OxDcOp*
Arneil, Gavin Cranston *WhoScE 91-1*
Arneiro, (Jose Augusto) Ferreira Veiga d' 1838-1903 *Baker 92*
Arnell, Gordon E. 1935- *St&PR 93*
Arnell, Gordon Edwin 1935- *WhoAm 92*
Arnell, Richard Anthony 1938- *WhoAm 92, WhoWor 93*
Arnell, Richard (Anthony Sayer) 1917- *Baker 92*
Arnell, Walter James William 1924- *WhoAm 92*
Arner, Gwen *MiSFD 9*
Arner, Robert David 1943- *WhoWrEP 92*
Arnesen, Eric Andrew 1950- *St&PR 93*
Arnesen, Mark R. *Law&B 92*
Arnesjo, Bo A. 1934- *WhoScE 91-4*
Arneson, D.J. 1935- *ScF&FL 92*
Arneson, Dora Williams 1947- *WhoEmL 93*
Arneson, Gary A. 1948- *WhoIns 93*
Arneson, George Stephen 1925- *WhoAm 92*
Arneson, James Herman 1952- *WhoEmL 93*
Arneson, Jay Clair 1936- *St&PR 93*
Arneson, Kristin *Law&B 92*
Arneson, Marjorie D. *Law&B 92*
Arneson, Mark A. 1915- *St&PR 93*
Arneson, Phillip W. 1936- *St&PR 93*
Arneson, Phillip William 1936- *WhoAm 92*
Arneson, Robert 1930- *BioIn 17*
Arneson, Robert C. 1930-1992 *NewYTBS 92 [port]*
Arneson, Robert Carston 1930- *WhoAm 92*
Arnestad, Finn (Oluf Bjerke) 1915- *Baker 92*
Arnett, Anna Williams *AmWomPl*
Arnett, Carroll D. 1946- *WhoEmL 93*
Arnett, Carroll (Gogisgi) 1927- *WhoWrEP 92*
Arnett, Foster Deaver 1920- *WhoAm 92, WhoWor 93*
Arnett, George W. 1903-1991 *BioIn 17*
Arnett, Gerald Alan 1962- *WhoSSW 93*
Arnett, Harold Edward 1931- *WhoAm 92*
Arnett, Jack *ScF&FL 92*
Arnett, James E. 1951- *St&PR 93*
Arnett, James Edward 1912- *WhoWor 93*
Arnett, Lonnie A. 1946- *St&PR 93*
Arnett, Norman Jeffrey 1953- *WhoEmL 93*
Arnett, Patricia Fryer 1960- *WhoSSW 93*
Arnett, Penelope Pratt 1948- *WhoEmL 93*
Arnett, Peter *BioIn 17*
Arnett, Peter 1934- *WhoAm 92*
Arnett, Thomas L. *Law&B 92*
Arnett, Tom S., Jr. 1951- *St&PR 93*
Arnett, Warren Grant 1923- *WhoAm 92*
Arnette, Christopher Anthony 1956- *WhoSSW 93*
Arnette, Robert *MajAI*
Arney, David Christopher 1949- *WhoEmL 93*
Arney, Jeffrey Alan 1957- *WhoEmL 93*
Arney, William Ray 1950- *WhoEmL 93*
Arnez, Nancy Levi 1928- *WhoAm 92*
Arnheim, Falk Kantor 1917- *WhoE 93*
Arnheim, Rudolf *BioIn 17*
Arnhoff, Franklyn Nathaniel 1926- *WhoAm 92*
Arnhold, Henry H. 1921- *WhoAm 92*
Arnic, Blaz 1901-1970 *Baker 92*
Arnick, John Stephen 1933- *WhoE 93*
Arnim, Bettina von 1785-1859 *BioIn 17, NinCLC 38 [port]*
Arnim, Hans Georg, Count of 1582?-1641 *HarEnMi*
Arnim, Hans-Jurgen von 1889-1962 *BioIn 17*
Arnim, Jurgen von 1889-1971 *HarEnMi*
Arnim, Ludwig Achim, Freiherr von 1781-1831 *BioIn 17*
Arning, John F. 1925- *St&PR 93*
Arning, John Fredrick 1925- *WhoAm 92*
Arnink, Donna Jean 1946- *WhoWrEP 92*
Arno, James Anthony *Law&B 92*
Arno, Raymond 1936- *St&PR 93*
Arnof, Ian 1939- *WhoAm 92, WhoSSW 93*
Arnoff, Judith U. 1946- *St&PR 93*
Arnoff, Judith Unger 1946- *WhoEmL 93*
Arnold, Alan 1922- *ScF&FL 92*
Arnold, Alice Marie 1958- *WhoE 93, WhoEmL 93*
Arnold, Allen J. 1934- *St&PR 93*
Arnold, Arlene 1952- *WhoAmW 93*
Arnold, Armin Herbert 1931- *WhoWrEP 92*
Arnold, Barbara E. *Law&B 92*
Arnold, Barbara Eileen 1927- *WhoAmW 93*
Arnold, Barbara Jean 1950- *WhoEmL 93*
Arnold, Barbara Jeanne 1950- *WhoAmW 93*
Arnold, Benedict 1741-1801 *BioIn 17, HarEnMi*
Arnold, Beverly Sue 1949- *WhoAmW 93*
Arnold, Bob 1952- *WhoWrEP 92*
Arnold, Bruce Robert 1955- *WhoAm 92, WhoE 93*
Arnold, Byron 1901-1971 *Baker 92*
Arnold, Cecil Benjamin 1927- *WhoSSW 93*
Arnold, Charles Burle, Jr. 1934- *WhoAm 92*
Arnold, Charles Parker 1933- *St&PR 93*
Arnold, Christine Annette 1966- *WhoEmL 93*
Arnold, Claire Groemling 1962- *WhoAmW 93*
Arnold, Craig Glen 1949- *WhoWrEP 92*
Arnold, Daniel W. 1954- *WhoIns 93*
Arnold, David *WhoScE 91-1*
Arnold, David Brown 1940- *WhoE 93*
Arnold, David Burton 1939- *St&PR 93, WhoAm 92*
Arnold, David H. *WhoSSW 93*
Arnold, David P. 1942- *St&PR 93*
Arnold, David Walker 1936- *St&PR 93, WhoAm 92*
Arnold, Deborah Grant 1950- *WhoAmW 93*
Arnold, Deborah Kaye 1955- *WhoAm 92*
Arnold, Denis (Midgley) 1926-1986 *Baker 92*
Arnold, Dianne E. 1944- *St&PR 93*
Arnold, Dianne Ekberg 1944- *WhoAm 92*
Arnold, Douglas Norman 1954- *WhoAm 92, WhoEmL 93*
Arnold, Douglas Ray 1948- *St&PR 93, WhoAm 92*
Arnold, Duane Wade-Hampton 1953- *WhoWor 93*
Arnold, Eddy 1918- *Baker 92, WhoAm 92*
Arnold, Eddy 1951- *WhoEmL 93*
Arnold, Edgar Frank, Jr. 1925- *WhoWrEP 92*
Arnold, Edward H. *St&PR 93*
Arnold, Edward Henry 1939- *St&PR 93, WhoAm 92*
Arnold, Edwin Lester 1857-1935 *ScF&FL 92*
Arnold, Edwin Roy 1962- *WhoEmL 93*
Arnold, Edwin Turner, III 1947- *WhoSSW 93*
Arnold, Ellen Holt 1943- *WhoE 93*
Arnold, Emily *WhoWrEP 92*
Arnold, Emily 1939- *MajAI [port]*
Arnold, Esther Watkins *AmWomPl*
Arnold, Eugene, Jr. 1922- *St&PR 93*
Arnold, Eve *BioIn 17*
Arnold, Frances Deupree 1940- *WhoSSW 93*
Arnold, Frances Hamilton 1956- *WhoAmW 93*
Arnold, Frank Edward 1914-1987 *ScF&FL 92*
Arnold, Frederick J. 1931- *St&PR 93*
Arnold, G. Dewey, Jr. 1925- *WhoAm 92*
Arnold, Gary Howard 1942- *WhoAm 92, WhoWrEP 92*
Arnold, George J. *Law&B 92*
Arnold, George John 1942- *St&PR 93*
Arnold, George Lawrence 1942- *WhoAm 92*
Arnold, Gordon R. 1945- *St&PR 93*
Arnold, Harold W. 1930- *St&PR 93*
Arnold, Harry Bartley 1912- *WhoAm 92*
Arnold, Harry J. 1940- *St&PR 93*
Arnold, Harry J., Jr. *Law&B 92*
Arnold, Harry Loren, Jr. 1912- *WhoAm 92*
Arnold, Heinrich 1933- *WhoWor 93*
Arnold, Henri *WhoAm 92*
Arnold, Henry Harley 1886-1950 *HarEnMi*
Arnold, Herbert Anton 1935- *WhoAm 92*
Arnold, Hubert Merrell 1935- *WhoSSW 93*
Arnold, Hugh R. 1943- *St&PR 93*
Arnold, Ilene Debbie 1959- *WhoAmW 93*
Arnold, J. David 1955- *WhoE 93*
Arnold, J.M. *Law&B 92*
Arnold, Jack 1916- *MiSFD 9*
Arnold, Jack 1927- *WhoE 93*
Arnold, Jack Maurice *Law&B 92*
Arnold, Jackie Smith 1932- *WhoWrEP 92*
Arnold, James 1962- *St&PR 93*
Arnold, James Barto, III 1950- *WhoSSW 93*
Arnold, James Ellsworth 1956- *WhoEmL 93*
Arnold, James Leonard 1946- *WhoEmL 93*
Arnold, James Richard 1923- *WhoAm 92*
Arnold, James Walter 1931- *St&PR 93*
Arnold, Janet Nina 1933- *WhoAmW 93*
Arnold, Jasper Henry, III 1944- *WhoAm 92*
Arnold, Jay 1936- *WhoE 93*
Arnold, Jean Ann 1948- *WhoAm 92, WhoAmW 93, WhoEmL 93*
Arnold, Jeanne Gosselin 1917- *WhoAmW 93, WhoE 93*
Arnold, Jeffrey Robert 1946- *St&PR 93*
Arnold, Jerome Gilbert *WhoAm 92*
Arnold, Jill Cleon 1962- *WhoAmW 93*
Arnold, Joanne Easley 1930- *WhoAmW 93*
Arnold, Joe Roger 1942- *St&PR 93*
Arnold, Johann Gottfried 1773-1806 *Baker 92*
Arnold, John David 1933- *WhoE 93*
Arnold, John Dirk 1950- *WhoEmL 93*
Arnold, John Fox 1937- *WhoAm 92*
Arnold, John P. 1946- *WhoAm 92, WhoE 93*
Arnold, John Q. 1944- *St&PR 93*
Arnold, John Robert 1923- *St&PR 93*
Arnold, John Scott *Law&B 92*
Arnold, Joshua David 1951- *WhoEmL 93*
Arnold, Karl 1794-1877 *Baker 92*
Arnold, Karl Werner 1940- *WhoWor 93*
Arnold, Kenneth James 1927- *WhoAm 92*
Arnold, Kenneth Lloyd 1944- *WhoAm 92*
Arnold, Kenneth Mark 1951- *WhoAm 92, WhoEmL 93*
Arnold, Kenneth R. *Law&B 92*
Arnold, Lawrence G. 1941- *St&PR 93*
Arnold, Leonard J. 1947- *WhoWor 93*
Arnold, Leslie Bisger 1956- *WhoAmW 93, WhoEmL 93*
Arnold, Lewis Tracy 1933- *St&PR 93*
Arnold, Linda G. *St&PR 93*
Arnold, Linda Gayle 1947- *WhoEmL 93*
Arnold, Lorna Jean 1945- *WhoSSW 93*
Arnold, Lucy Edith 1862- *AmWomPl*
Arnold, Lynn Ellis 1934- *WhoAm 92*
Arnold, Malcolm 1921- *Baker 92, BioIn 17*
Arnold, Marc Benjamin 1948- *WhoE 93*
Arnold, Margaret Long 1914- *WhoAmW 93*
Arnold, Margot *WhoWrEP 92*
Arnold, Margot 1925- *ScF&FL 92*
Arnold, Mark Alan *ScF&FL 92*
Arnold, Martha G. *St&PR 93*
Arnold, Martin 1929- *WhoAm 92*
Arnold, Martin Leon 1959- *WhoSSW 93*
Arnold, Mary Bertucio 1924- *WhoAm 92*
Arnold, Mary O'Gallagher *WhoAmW 93*
Arnold, Mary Pamela 1949- *WhoAm 92, WhoAmW 93, WhoEmL 93*
Arnold, Matthew 1822-1888 *MagSWL [port], PoeCrit 5 [port], WorLitC [port]*
Arnold, Matthew Charles 1927- *WhoAm 92*
Arnold, Maurice 1865-1937 *Baker 92*
Arnold, Michael Robert 1960- *WhoEmL 93*
Arnold, Monroe d1991 *BioIn 17*
Arnold, Morris F. d1992 *NewYTBS 92*
Arnold, Morris Fairchild 1915- *WhoAm 92*
Arnold, Morris Sheppard 1941- *WhoAm 92, WhoSSW 93*
Arnold, Nancy Nakamura 1949- *WhoSSW 93*
Arnold, Neil David 1948- *St&PR 93*
Arnold, Newt *MiSFD 9*
Arnold, Paul Beaver 1918- *WhoAm 92*
Arnold, Peri Ethan 1942- *WhoAm 92*
Arnold, Peter Gordon 1943- *WhoE 93*
Arnold, Philip Mills 1911- *WhoAm 92, WhoWor 93*
Arnold, Philip Willard 1949- *WhoE 93*
Arnold, Phyllis H. 1948- *St&PR 93*
Arnold, Ralph L. 1951- *St&PR 93*
Arnold, Rana McMurray 1944- *WhoAmW 93*
Arnold, Richard 1845-1918 *Baker 92*
Arnold, Richard L. 1931- *St&PR 93*
Arnold, Richard Sheppard 1936- *WhoAm 92, WhoSSW 93*
Arnold, Richard Warren 1929- *WhoAm 92*
Arnold, Robert Don 1939- *WhoSSW 93*
Arnold, Robert Edwin 1948- *WhoEmL 93*
Arnold, Robert H. 1917- *St&PR 93*
Arnold, Robert H. 1918- *WhoE 93*
Arnold, Robert J. *Law&B 92*
Arnold, Robert L. 1943- *St&PR 93*
Arnold, Robert Lloyd 1952- *WhoEmL 93*
Arnold, Robert Morris 1928- *WhoAm 92*
Arnold, Robert Moses 1948- *WhoAm 92*
Arnold, Rocky Richard 1948- *WhoEmL 93*
Arnold, Roger James 1955- *WhoE 93*
Arnold, Ron R. 1942- *St&PR 93*
Arnold, Ronald Lee 1952- *WhoSSW 93*
Arnold, Rose Mary 1935- *WhoAmW 93*
Arnold, Roseanne *BioIn 17*
Arnold, Roseanne 1952- *ConAu 139*
Arnold, Roseanne 1953- *WhoAm 92, WhoAmW 93*
Arnold, Sally Ann 1948- *WhoAmW 93*
Arnold, Sam *BioIn 17*
Arnold, Samuel 1740-1802 *Baker 92, OxDcOp*
Arnold, Samuel C. 1937- *St&PR 93*
Arnold, Samuel James 1774-1852 *OxDcOp*
Arnold, Sandra Kouns 1941- *WhoAmW 93*
Arnold, Scott Gregory 1961- *WhoEmL 93*
Arnold, Shalynn *BioIn 17*
Arnold, Sharon Ann 1943- *WhoAmW 93*
Arnold, Sheila 1929- *WhoAmW 93*
Arnold, Stanley Norman 1915- *WhoAm 92*
Arnold, Stanley Richard 1932- *WhoAm 92*
Arnold, Susan Ann 1951- *WhoEmL 93*
Arnold, Susan Bird 1951- *WhoAmW 93, WhoEmL 93*
Arnold, Tedd 1949- *ConAu 137, SmATA 69 [port]*
Arnold, Terrence Eugene 1955- *WhoEmL 93*
Arnold, Theresa Janis *Law&B 92*
Arnold, Thomas Brent 1950- *WhoEmL 93*
Arnold, Tom *BioIn 17*
Arnold, Tom 1959- *News 93-2 [port]*
Arnold, Toni Lavalle 1947- *WhoAmW 93*
Arnold, Val *BioIn 17*
Arnold, Valerie Denise 1956- *WhoAmW 93, WhoEmL 93*
Arnold, Vladimir Igorevich 1937- *WhoWor 93*
Arnold, Wallace Cornelius 1938- *AfrAmBi*
Arnold, Walter Martin 1906- *WhoAm 92*
Arnold, Watson Caufield, Jr. 1945- *WhoSSW 93*
Arnold, William Edwin 1938- *WhoAm 92*
Arnold, William Harry *Law&B 92*
Arnold, William Howard 1931- *WhoAm 92*
Arnold, William J. 1945- *St&PR 93*
Arnold, William Lee *Law&B 92*
Arnold, William P. 1946- *St&PR 93*
Arnold, Yuri 1811-1898 *Baker 92*
Arnold Hubert, Nancy Kay 1951- *WhoAmW 93*
Arnoldi, Carl Christian 1921- *WhoScE 91-2*
Arnoldi, Charles Arthur 1946- *WhoAm 92*
Arnold-Nobbman, Mildred Maxine Berry 1936- *WhoAmW 93*
Arnolds, D.M. *Law&B 92*
Arnoldson, Oscar 1830-1881 *Baker 92*
Arnoldson, Sigrid 1861-1943 *Baker 92, IntDcOp, OxDcOp*
Arnon, Daniel Israel 1910- *WhoAm 92*
Arnon, Meir 1951- *WhoWor 93*

Arnon, Michael 1925- St&PR 93
Arnone, Mary Grace 1961- WhoE 93
Arnosky, Jim ChlBIID [port]
Arnosky, Jim 1946- MajAI [port], SmATA 70 [port]
Arnot, David Sheldon 1930- St&PR 93
Arnot, Robert Burns BioIn 17
Arnot, Susan Eileen 1957- WhoAmW 93
Arnott, C.G. 1939- St&PR 93
Arnott, Ellen Marie 1945- WhoAmW 93
Arnott, Eric John 1929- WhoWor 93
Arnott, Howard Joseph 1928- WhoAm 92
Arnott, R. Jackson 1938- St&PR 93
Arnott, Randall Glenn 1953- WhoEmL 93
Arnott, Richard James 1949- WhoE 93
Arnott, Robert Douglas 1954- WhoAm 92
Arnott, Struther WhoScE 91-1
Arnott, Struther 1934- WhoAm 92
Arnould, Marcel 1927- WhoScE 91-2
Arnould, Richard Julius 1941- WhoAm 92
Arnould, Robert E. 1940- WhoScE 91-2
Arnould, Sophie 1740-1802 OxDcOp
Arnould, (Madeleine) Sophie 1740-1802 Baker 92
Arnous, Amjad Zuhdi 1963- WhoSSW 93
Arnove, Robert Frederick WhoAm 92
Arnovitz, Benton Mayer 1942- WhoAm 92, WhoWrEP 92
Arnow, Diana Irene 1958- WhoEmL 93
Arnow, Harriette Louisa Simpson 1908-1986 BioIn 17
Arnow, Leslie Earle 1909- WhoAm 92, WhoE 93
Arnow, Pat Jo 1949- WhoSSW 93
Arnow, Winston Eugene 1911- WhoAm 92
Arns, Paulo Evaristo Cardinal 1921- WhoWor 93
Arnsan, Daniel Carlton 1946- WhoEmL 93
Arnsdorf, Dennis Abraham 1953- WhoEmL 93
Arnsdorf, Morton Frank 1940- WhoAm 92, WhoWor 93
Arnst, Thomas William Law&B 92
Arnstad, Mary Killackey 1948- WhoAmW 93
Arnstam, Leo 1905-1979 DrEEuF
Arnsteen, Katy Keck 1934- BioIn 17, ConAu 136
Arnstein, Daphne Barritt-Vane d1990 BioIn 17
Arnstein, Sherry Phyllis WhoAm 92
Arnstein, Walter Leonard 1930- WhoAm 92
Arnston, Harrison ScF&FL 92
Arnt, Charles 1908-1990 BioIn 17
Arntson, Peter Andrew 1938- WhoAm 92, WhoSSW 93
Arntzen, Charles Joel 1941- WhoAm 92
Arntzen, Helmut 1931- WhoWor 93
Arnulf, of Lisieux d1184 BioIn 17
Arnwine, Don Lee 1932- WhoAm 92
Arnwine, William Carrol 1929- WhoAm 92
Arny, Deane Cedric 1917- WhoAm 92
Arny, Louis Wayne, III 1942- WhoE 93
Aro, Antti V. 1938- WhoScE 91-4
Aro, Seppo L.I. 1948- WhoScE 91-4
Arocena, Eduardo DcCPCAm
Arodz, Henryk Stanislaw 1948- WhoWor 93
Aroesty, Sidney Albert 1946- St&PR 93
Aroesty, Steven Mitchell 1961- WhoEmL 93
Arogyaswamy, Bernard Anthony 1945- WhoE 93
Arola, Burton Charles 1953- St&PR 93
Arom, Simha 1930- ConAu 139
Aromaa, Ulla 1942- WhoScE 91-4
Aromin, Mercedes Fung 1956- WhoAmW 93
Aron, Adam M. 1954- St&PR 93
Aron, Alan Milford 1933- WhoAm 92
Aron, Elaine ScF&FL 92
Aron, Eve Glicka Serenson 1937- WhoAmW 93
Aron, Jaime 1943- WhoWor 93
Aron, Joel Edward 1928- WhoE 93
Aron, Mark G. Law&B 92
Aron, Mark Gidell 1943- St&PR 93
Aron, Paul H. 1912-1991 BioIn 17
Aron, Raymond 1905-1983 BioIn 17
Aron, Susan Marlene 1956- WhoEmL 93
Aronberg, Ronald Jerry 1932- St&PR 93
Arone, Anne 1959- St&PR 93
Aronek, George 1927- St&PR 93
Aronfreed, Jessica Marie 1960- WhoAmW 93
Aroni, Samuel 1927- WhoAm 92
Aroni, Zvee d1990 BioIn 17
Aronica, Lou 1958- ScF&FL 92
Aronin, Ben 1904-1980 ScF&FL 92
Aronin, Irene C. 1951- St&PR 93
Aronin, Lewis Richard 1919- WhoE 93
Aronin, Marc Jacob 1964- WhoE 93
Aronin, Patricia Anne 1948- WhoAm 92
Aronne-Amestoy, Lida Beatriz 1940- WhoAmW 93
Aronoff, Carol R. Law&B 92
Aronoff, Craig Ellis 1951- WhoAm 92, WhoEmL 93, WhoSSW 93
Aronoff, George Rodger 1950- WhoAm 92
Aronoff, Jonathan Ross 1953- WhoE 93
Aronoff, Kenny BioIn 17
Aronoff, Mark H. 1949- WhoAm 92
Aronoff, Michael Stephen 1940- WhoAm 92
Aronoff, Stuart Bertram 1932- St&PR 93
Aronovitch, Roza Law&B 92
Aronovitz, David 1947- ScF&FL 92
Aronovitz, Sidney M. 1920- WhoAm 92
Aronovsky, Ronald George 1955- WhoEmL 93
Aronow, Donald Joel BioIn 17
Aronow, Edward 1945- WhoE 93, WhoWor 93
Aronow, Gil Nicholas Law&B 92
Aronow, Greta L. Law&B 92
Aronow, Jani Allison 1957- WhoEmL 93
Aronow, Judith 1926- WhoSSW 93
Aronow, Leslie 1937-1990 BioIn 17
Aronow, Richard A. Law&B 92
Aronow, Richard Avery 1953- WhoEmL 93
Aronow, Saul 1917- WhoAm 92
Aronow, Stephen A. Law&B 92
Aronowitz, Cecil (Solomon) 1916-1978 Baker 92
Aronowitz, Jack Leon 1940- St&PR 93
Aronowitz, Jerome David 1946- WhoSSW 93
Aronowitz, Marvin 1924- St&PR 93
Aron-Rosa, D.S. 1934- WhoScE 91-2
Arons, Arnold Boris 1916- WhoAm 92
Arons, Jonathan 1943- WhoAm 92
Arons, Mark David 1958- WhoEmL 93
Arons, Michael Eugene 1939- WhoAm 92, WhoE 93
Arons, Michael Jerome 1942- WhoE 93
Aronson, Alan A. 1947- St&PR 93
Aronson, Arnold H. 1935- WhoAm 92
Aronson, Arnold P. 1943- WhoWrEP 92
Aronson, Arthur H. 1935- St&PR 93, WhoAm 92
Aronson, Arthur Lawrence 1933- WhoAm 92
Aronson, Bernard 1946- WhoAm 92
Aronson, Carl Edward 1936- WhoAm 92
Aronson, David 1912- WhoAm 92
Aronson, David 1923- WhoAm 92
Aronson, Deborah Jan 1955- WhoEmL 93
Aronson, Donald Eric 1934- WhoAm 92
Aronson, Edgar David 1934- WhoAm 92, WhoWor 93
Aronson, Elaine Linda 1959- WhoAmW 93
Aronson, Esther Leah 1941- WhoAm 92, WhoAmW 93, WhoWor 93
Aronson, Frederick Rupp 1953- WhoEmL 93
Aronson, Harvey Bear 1945- WhoSSW 93
Aronson, Howard Isaac 1936- WhoAm 92
Aronson, I(rwin) Michael 1942- ConAu 137
Aronson, James Ries 1932- WhoE 93
Aronson, Jonathan David 1949- WhoEmL 93
Aronson, Louis V., II 1923- St&PR 93
Aronson, Louis Vincent, II 1923- WhoAm 92
Aronson, Mark Berne 1941- WhoAm 92, WhoE 93
Aronson, Max 1882?-1971 BioIn 17
Aronson, Michael Andrew 1939- WhoAm 92, WhoWrEP 92
Aronson, Milton Howard 1918- WhoAm 92
Aronson, Miriam Klausner 1940- WhoWor 93
Aronson, Paul Robert 1927- WhoE 93
Aronson, Rebecca 1941- WhoAmW 93
Aronson, Richard Norman 1953- St&PR 93
Aronson, Robert A. 1949- St&PR 93, WhoEmL 93
Aronson, Robert Michael Law&B 92
Aronson, Sidney Herbert 1924- WhoAm 92
Aronson, Stanley Maynard 1922- WhoAm 92
Aronson, Susan Shane 1951- WhoAmW 93
Aronson, Virginia Ruth 1931- WhoAmW 93
Aronsson, Bertil S. 1929- WhoScE 91-4
Aronsson, Herbert A. 1929- St&PR 93
Aronstam, Neil Lee 1945- WhoAm 92
Aronstein, Martin Joseph 1925- WhoAm 92
Aronzon, Kimberle Ann Law&B 92
Arop, Martin Malwal WhoAfr
Arora, Jasbir Singh 1943- WhoAm 92
Arora, Sardari Lal 1929- WhoWor 93
Arora, Shirley L(ease) 1930- DcAmChF 1960
Arora, Shirley Lease 1930- WhoAm 92
Arora, Swarnjit Singh 1940- WhoWor 93
Aros, Jesse Ricardo 1962- WhoSSW 93
Arosio, Alberto 1950- WhoWor 93
Arouch, Salamo BioIn 17
Arouet, Francois-Marie ScF&FL 92
Arouh, Jeffrey Alan 1945- WhoAm 92
Arova, Sonia BioIn 17
Arova, Sonia 1928- WhoAmW 93
Arowesty, Jill 1964- WhoAmW 93
Aroyo, Mois Ilja 1952- WhoWor 93
Arp, Halton Christian 1927- WhoWor 93
Arp, Marilyn LaDean 1940- WhoAmW 93
Arp, Nancy Jo 1963- WhoAmW 93
Arp, Thomas Roscoe 1932- WhoSSW 93
Arpads OxDcByz
Arpagaus, Reto Walter 1940- WhoWor 93
Arpante, Stephen John 1935- St&PR 93
Arpel, John David 1949- WhoWor 93
Arpels, Claude d1990 BioIn 17
Arpigny, Claude 1937- WhoScE 91-2
Arpin, David Allen 1950- St&PR 93
Arpin, Gary Quintin 1944- WhoE 93
Arpin, Noel 1936- WhoScE 91-2
Arpin, Paul 1925- St&PR 93
Arpin, Peter 1957- St&PR 93
Arpino, Gerald Peter 1928- WhoAm 92, WhoE 93
Arp-Lotter, Donna 1950- WhoAmW 93
Arquette, David BioIn 17
Arquette, Lois Duncan ScF&FL 92
Arquette, Rosanna 1959- WhoAm 92
Arquilla, George, Jr. 1921- St&PR 93
Arquilla, Robert 1926- WhoAm 92
Arquit, Kevin James 1954- WhoAm 92, WhoEmL 93
Arra, Raymond Francis 1943- St&PR 93
Arrabal, Fernando 1932- WhoWor 93
Arraiz, Antonio 1903-1962 SpAmA
Arraj, Alfred Albert 1906- WhoAm 92
Arrakoski, Olli 1941- WhoWor 93
Arrathoon, Siran 1915- St&PR 93
Arrathoon, Tigran 1909- St&PR 93
Arrau, Claudio 1903-1991 AnObit 1991, Baker 92, BioIn 17, News 92
Arredondo, David Ernest 1953- WhoE 93
Arredondo, Ines 1928-1989 DcMexL
Arregui Garay, Vicente 1871-1925 Baker 92
Arreguin, Esteban Jose 1958- WhoEmL 93
Arrendale, Thomas A. St&PR 93
Arreola, John Bradley 1935- WhoWor 93
Arreola, Juan Jose 1918- DcMexL, SpAmA
Arreola, Mona Jean 1940- WhoAmW 93
Arreola, Philip 1940- HispAmA [port], WhoAm 92
Arreola Cortes, Raul 1917- DcMexL
Arrett, Jane Head Law&B 92
Arriaga (y Balzola), Juan Crisostomo (Jacobo Antonio de) 1806-1826 Baker 92
Arria Salicetti, Diego Enrique 1938- WhoUN 92
Arrick, Martin D. 1953- St&PR 93
Arrieta, Albert Joseph 1964- WhoSSW 93
Arrieta, Jorge 1954- St&PR 93
Arrieta y Corera, Pascual Juan Emilio 1823-1894 Baker 92
Arrieu, Claude 1903- BioIn 17, OxDcOp
Arrieu, Claude 1903-1990 Baker 92
Arrighi, Mel 1933-1986 ScF&FL 92
Arrighi, Pascal Laurent 1921- BioIn 17
Arrigo, Girolamo 1930- Baker 92
Arrigo, Joseph D. 1923- St&PR 93
Arrigoni, Carlo 1697-1744 Baker 92
Arrigoni, Enrico Lamberto 1937- WhoWor 93
Arrillaga, Josefina 1933- WhoWor 93
Arrindell, Clement Athelston 1931- WhoWor 93
Arrington, Billy Charles 1953- WhoSSW 93
Arrington, Charles Hammond, Jr. 1920- WhoAm 92
Arrington, Christine Denise 1953- WhoAmW 93
Arrington, Doris Banowsky 1933- WhoAmW 93
Arrington, Dorothy Anita Collins 1922- WhoAmW 93, WhoSSW 93, WhoWor 93
Arrington, Edward L., Jr. 1946- St&PR 93
Arrington, Edwin S. 1945- St&PR 93
Arrington, Gerald Lynn 1955- WhoE 93
Arrington, Harriet Ann 1924- WhoAmW 93, WhoWor 93
Arrington, James S. 1930- St&PR 93
Arrington, John Leslie, Jr. 1931- WhoAm 92, WhoSSW 93, WhoWor 93
Arrington, John N. 1939- WhoWor 93
Arrington, Karen Kemp 1953- WhoAmW 93
Arrington, Lawrence Edward 1953- WhoEmL 93
Arrington, Leonard James 1917- WhoAm 92
Arrington, Lloyd Madison, Jr. 1947- WhoEmL 93
Arrington, Marvin S. AfrAmBi
Arrington, Melvin Slay, Jr. 1949- WhoEmL 93, WhoSSW 93
Arrington, Michael Browne 1943- WhoAm 92
Arrington, Pamela Gray 1953- WhoEmL 93
Arrington, Richard, Jr. 1934- AfrAmBi, WhoAm 92, WhoSSW 93
Arrington, Richard W. Law&B 92
Arrington, Tracy Lynn 1966- WhoSSW 93
Arriola, David Bruce 1950- WhoAm 92
Arriola, Juan Jose de 1698-1768 DcMexL
Arriola, Pepito 1896-1954 Baker 92
Arrison, Clement R. 1930- St&PR 93, WhoE 93
Arrizurieta, Jorge L. 1965- WhoEmL 93, WhoSSW 93
Arro, Elmar 1899-1985 Baker 92
Arro, Ilmar 1942- WhoWor 93
Arrol, John 1923- St&PR 93, WhoAm 92
Arron, Judith Hagerty 1942- WhoAm 92
Arroniz, Marcos d1859? DcMexL
Arrott, Anthony Schuyler 1928- WhoAm 92
Arrouet, Dennis 1937- WhoAm 92
Arrow, Jay ScF&FL 92
Arrow, Kenneth Joseph 1921- BioIn 17, WhoAm 92, WhoWor 93
Arrow, William ScF&FL 92
Arrowitz, Linda Wildman 1957- WhoAmW 93
Arrowood, Bennie Noland 1941- WhoSSW 93
Arrowood, Lisa Gayle 1956- WhoEmL 93
Arrowsmith, Marian Campbell 1943- WhoAmW 93
Arrowsmith, Peter Dean 1934- St&PR 93
Arrowsmith, William 1924-1992 BioIn 17
Arrowsmith, William A. d1992 NewYTBS 92 [port]
Arrowsmith, William Ayres 1924- WhoWrEP 92
Arrowsmith, William Ayres 1924-1992 ConAu 136
Arrowsmith-Lowe, Janet Bixby 1949- WhoAmW 93
Arrow Yasko, Amy 1957- WhoAmW 93, WhoEmL 93
Arroyo, Antonio Maria 1928- WhoWor 93
Arroyo, Eduardo 1937- BioIn 17
Arroyo, Francisco Vighi WhoScE 91-3
Arroyo, Joao Marcellino 1861-1930 Baker 92
Arroyo, Martina 1935- OxDcOp
Arroyo, Martina 1936- Baker 92
Arroyo, Martina 1937- IntDcOp
Arroyo, Martina 1940- BioIn 17
Arroyo Ramos, Miguel 1943- WhoScE 91-3
Arruda, John B. 1934- St&PR 93
Arruda-Neto, Joao Dias de Toledo 1943- WhoWor 93
Arrue, Jose L. 1949- WhoScE 91-3
Arrufat, Anton 1935- SpAmA
Arruntius, Lucius c. 60BC-10AD HarEnMi
Arrupe, Pedro 1907-1991 AnObit 1991, BioIn 17
Arsaber 9th cent.- OxDcByz
Arsak OxDcByz
Arscott, David ScF&FL 92
Arsenault, Kate Whitman 1922- WhoE 93
Arseneault, Gerard Armand 1933- St&PR 93
Arseni, Constantin WhoScE 91-4
Arsenijevic, Momcilo 1930- WhoScE 91-4
Arsenios OxDcByz
Arsenios Autoreianos c. 1200-1273 OxDcByz
Arsenios the Great 354-445 OxDcByz
Arsenis, Charalampos 1935- WhoScE 91-3
Arsenovic, Alexander 1928- WhoE 93
Arsenych, S.J. Law&B 92
Arshady, Reza WhoWor 93
Arsht, Leslye Alene 1945- WhoAmW 93
Arsht, S. Samuel 1910- St&PR 93
Arst, Herbert N. WhoScE 91-1
Arst, Lee N. 1946- St&PR 93
Arstark, Lester D. 1924- WhoE 93
Arstingstall, John Edward 1946- WhoSSW 93
Art, Richard C., Jr. Law&B 92
Artabasdos OxDcByz
Artabasdos, Nicholas Rhabdas OxDcByz
Artal, Pablo 1961- WhoWor 93
Artaria Baker 92
Artaria, Carl August d1919 Baker 92
Artaria, Carlo 1747-1808 Baker 92
Artaria, Dominik d1936 Baker 92
Artaria, Francesco 1744-1808 Baker 92
Artaria, Franz d1942 Baker 92
Artaud, Antonin 1896-1948 IntDcF 2-3
Artavasdus d743 HarEnMi
Artaza-Rouxel, Mario 1937- WhoUN 92
Arteaga, Carlos 1951- WhoWor 93
Arteaga, Esteban de 1747-1799 Baker 92
Arteaga, Gertrudis Gomez de Avellaneda y 1814-1873 BioIn 17
Arteaga, Horacio 1948- WhoUN 92

Arteaga Campos, A. Enrique 1939- WhoWor 93
Arteche, Bartolome D. 1935- WhoAsAP 91
Arteche, Romeo Rapsing 1938- WhoWor 93
Artemiadis, Nicolas K. 1917- WhoWor 93
Artemios dc. 362 OxDcByz
Artemiou, Artemis L. 1961- WhoWor 93
Artenstein, Isaac MiSFD 9
Arterberry, Kathryn Ross Law&B 92
Arterbery, Vivian J. 1937- St&PR 93
Arterburn, Katherine Greer 1962- WhoAmW 93
Arterburn, Stephen Forrest 1953- WhoAm 92
Arters, Linda Bromley 1951- WhoAmW 93
Artery, Michael G. Law&B 92
Artevelde, Philip van 1340-1382 HarEnMi
Arth, John Raphael 1936- St&PR 93, WhoAm 92
Arth, Lawrence J. 1943- WhoIns 93
Arth, Lawrence Joseph 1943- St&PR 93, WhoAm 92
Arth, Malcolm J. d1992 BioIn 17, NewYTBS 92 [port]
Arthaud, John C. 1939- St&PR 93
Arther, Cathy Homa Law&B 92
Arthey, Vincent David 1933- WhoScE 91-1
Arthos, John 1908- WhoAm 92
Arthur, King BioIn 17
Arthur, Alan Thorne 1942- WhoE 93
Arthur, Anne 1950- WhoWor 93
Arthur, Anthony Henry 1934- St&PR 93
Arthur, Bea BioIn 17
Arthur, Beatrice 1926- WhoAm 92
Arthur, Chester A. 1829-1886 PolPar
Arthur, Chester Alan 1830-1886 BioIn 17
Arthur, David J. Law&B 92
Arthur, David Stuart ScF&FL 92
Arthur, Donna Carole 1942- WhoWrEP 92
Arthur, Elizabeth 1953- WhoWrEP 92
Arthur, Elizabeth Aldrich 1923- WhoWrEP 92
Arthur, Elizabeth E. Law&B 92
Arthur, Elizabeth Evans 1954- St&PR 93
Arthur, Ellen Law&B 92
Arthur, Ellen Lewis Herndon 1837-1880 BioIn 17
Arthur, Gary David 1950- WhoEmL 93
Arthur, George K. AfrAmBi [port]
Arthur, George K. 1899- See Dane, Karl 1886-1934 & Arthur, George K. 1899- QDrFCA 92
Arthur, George Roland 1925- WhoAm 92
Arthur, Greer Martin 1935- WhoAm 92
Arthur, Hugh Thomas, II Law&B 92
Arthur, Jacquelyn D. 1949- WhoAm 92
Arthur, James Greig 1944- WhoAm 92
Arthur, Jean c. 1901-1991 News 92
Arthur, Jean 1905-1991 AnObit 1991, BioIn 17, ConTFT 10, IntDcF 2-3
Arthur, Jean 1908?- SweetSg C [port]
Arthur, John M. 1922- St&PR 93
Arthur, John Morrison 1922- WhoAm 92
Arthur, John Robert WhoScE 91-1
Arthur, Jonathan Robin Francis WhoScE 91-1
Arthur, Karen 1941- ConTFT 10, MiSFD 9
Arthur, Margaret K. Law&B 92
Arthur, Merrill W. 1955- St&PR 93
Arthur, Michael Elbert 1952- WhoEmL 93
Arthur, Nan Kene 1954- WhoEmL 93
Arthur, Paul Keith 1931- WhoAm 92
Arthur, Ransom J. 1925-1989 BioIn 17
Arthur, Ronald Vance, II 1959- St&PR 93
Arthur, Ruth M. 1905-1979 ScF&FL 92
Arthur, Stanley Roger 1935- BioIn 17
Arthur, Thomas Hahn 1937- WhoSSW 93
Arthur, Wallace WhoScE 91-1
Arthur, Warren Dupree, IV 1948- WhoEmL 93, WhoSSW 93
Arthur, William Bolling 1914- WhoAm 92
Arthur, William Brian 1946- WhoAm 92
Arthur, William Edgar 1929- WhoAm 92
Arthurs, Alberta Bean 1932- WhoAm 92, WhoAmW 93
Arthurs, Arnold Magowan WhoScE 91-1
Arthurs, Arnold Magowan 1934- WhoWor 93
Arthurs, Bruce D. 1952- ScF&FL 92
Arthurs, Eugene Gerard 1947- St&PR 93
Arthurs, Harry William 1935- WhoAm 92
Arthursdotter, Karin Emilia 1926- WhoWor 93
Artigas, Jose Gervasio 1764-1850 HarEnMi
Artigas, Jose Maria 1952- WhoWor 93
Artigliere, Anthony 1961- St&PR 93
Artigue, Ray Joseph 1954- WhoAm 92
Artigues, Carol 1942- WhoSSW 93
Artimez, John Edward, Jr. 1956- WhoEmL 93
Artinger, Istvan 1933- WhoScE 91-4
Artinian, Artine 1907- WhoAm 92
Artioli, Gilberto 1957- WhoWor 93
Artis, Gregory D. Law&B 92
Artis, Katasha BioIn 17
Artison, Richard E. 1933- AfrAmBi [port]
Artist, Everette Ward 1954- WhoEmL 93
Artl, Karen Ann 1950- WhoAmW 93
Artman, Florence Jean 1937- WhoAmW 93
Artmann, William Charlie 1957- WhoEmL 93
Artola, Adan DcCPCAm
Artom, Auro R. 1937- WhoScE 91-3
Arton, Gavin Rendell 1950- St&PR 93
Artone, David B. 1942- St&PR 93
Artot, Alexandre-Joseph Montagney 1815-1845 Baker 92
Artot, Desiree 1835-1907 Baker 92, OxDcOp
Artot, Jean-Desire 1803-1887 Baker 92
Artot, Maurice Montagney Baker 92
Artot, Maurice Montagney 1772-1829 Baker 92
Artot de Padilla, Lola Baker 92
Arts, Herwig Wilhelm 1935- WhoWor 93
Artschwager, Richard 1923- BioIn 17, WhoAm 92
Artsruni OxDcByz
Artucio, Hernan 1929- WhoWor 93
Artukids OxDcByz
Artukovic, Andrija 1899-1988 BioIn 17
Arturi, Anthony Joseph 1937- WhoE 93
Artursson, Per Artur Sven 1956- WhoWor 93
Artus, Jacques R. 1943- WhoUN 92
Artushenia, Marilyn Joanne 1950- WhoWor 93
Artusi, Giovanni Maria c. 1540-1613 Baker 92
Artusi, Steven L. Law&B 92
Artwohl, Paul J. 1953- St&PR 93
Artyomov, Viacheslav 1940- Baker 92
Artz, Arlene Betty 1922- St&PR 93
Artz, Bernice Shirley 1921- St&PR 93
Artz, Frederick J. 1949- St&PR 93
Artz, Frederick James 1949- WhoEmL 93
Artz, Milton 1916- St&PR 93
Artz, Richard Thomas 1953- St&PR 93
Artz, Susan C. 1955- St&PR 93
Artzibushev, Nikolai 1858-1937 Baker 92
Artzt, Alice (Josephine) 1943- Baker 92
Artzt, Edwin Lewis BioIn 17
Artzt, Edwin Lewis 1930- St&PR 93, WhoAm 92
Artzt, Russell M. 1947- WhoAm 92
Aruego, Jose BioIn 17
Aruego, Jose 1932- MajAI [port]
Aruffo, A. James 1932- St&PR 93
Arum, Robert 1931- WhoAm 92
Aruna, Aladi 1933- WhoAsAP 91
Arunachalam, Aladi WhoAsAP 91
Arunachalam, M. 1944- WhoAsAP 91
Arunanondchai, Suphat 1954- WhoWor 93
Arundel, Earl of 1307?-1376 BioIn 17
Arundel, Earl of 1346-1397 BioIn 17
Arundel, Arthur Windsor 1928- St&PR 93
Arundell, Dennis 1898-1988 Baker 92, OxDcOp
Arundell, Dennis Drew 1898-1988 IntDcOp
Arundell, Victor Charles 1931- WhoWor 93
Arunrugstichai, Narong-Rit 1948- WhoWor 93
Arup, Hans WhoScE 91-2
Arutiunian, Alexander 1920- Baker 92
Arutyunyan, Gagik WhoWor 93
Arvanetes, Gregory L. 1935- St&PR 93
Arvanigian, Gregory G. 1961- St&PR 93
Arvanitakis, Constantine S. 1939- WhoWor 93
Arvanitis, Cyril Steven 1926- WhoAm 92, WhoE 93
Arvantinos, S.C. 1938- St&PR 93
Arvay, Attila 1927 WhoScE 91-4
Arvay, Nancy Joan 1952- WhoAmW 93, WhoEmL 93, WhoWor 93
Arven, Andrea ScF&FL 92
Arveson, William Barnes 1934- WhoAm 92
Arvey, Jacob M. 1895-1977 PolPar
Arvidson, Philip R. 1938- St&PR 93
Arvidson, Raymond Ernst 1948- WhoAm 92
Arvieux, Jacques 1940- WhoScE 91-2
Arvilommi, Heikki Sakari 1939- WhoScE 91-4
Arvin, Newton 1900-1963 BioIn 17
Arvis, Gabriel 1934- WhoScE 91-2
Arvonen, Helen ScF&FL 92
Arvystas, Michael Geciauskas 1942- WhoAm 92
Ary, Marjorie Moore 1948- WhoAmW 93
Ary, T.S. 1925- BioIn 17, WhoAm 92, WhoE 93
Arzac, Adriana Maria 1947- WhoE 93
Arzbaecher, Robert Charles 1931- WhoAm 92
Arzner, Dorothy 1900-1979 MiSFD 9N
Arzoumanian, Linda Lee 1942- WhoAmW 93
Arzoumanidis, Gregory G. 1936- WhoAm 92
Arzt, Arthur d1991 BioIn 17
Arzu Irigoyen, Alvaro DcCPCAm
Arz Von Straussenburg, Arthur 1857-1935 HarEnMi
As, Johannes A. 1924- WhoScE 91-3
Asa, Cheryl Suzanne 1945- WhoAm 92
Asabia, Samuel Oyewole 1931- WhoWor 93
Asad, Hafiz al- 1928- DcTwHis
Asada, Akira 1934- WhoWor 93
Asada, Toichiro 1954- WhoWor 93
Asada, Toshi 1919- WhoWor 93
Asadi, Asad 1946- WhoEmL 93, WhoWor 93
Asadi, Eraj Kamber 1963- St&PR 93
Asadullah Khan 1797-1869 BioIn 17
Asaff, Glenn W. 1950- St&PR 93
Asafiey, Boris (Vladimirovich) 1884-1949 Baker 92
Asahara, Stella L. T. WhoAmW 93
Asahi, Chiseki 1932- WhoWor 93
Asahina, Robert James 1950- WhoAm 92, WhoEmL 93
Asai, Hitohisa 1931- WhoSSW 93
Asai, Yoshiyuki 1927- WhoAsAP 91
Asaj, Antun 1929- WhoScE 91-4
Asajima, Shoichi 1931- WhoWor 93
Asaka, Yasuhiko 1887- HarEnMi
Asakawa, Takako 1939- WhoAm 92
Asakura, Hitoshi 1937- WhoWor 93
Asam, James A. Law&B 92
Asami, Yasushi 1960- WhoWor 93
Asamoah, Andrew Kwabena 1940- WhoUN 92
Asamoah, Obed Y. 1936- WhoAfr
Asamoah, Obed Yao 1936- WhoWor 93
Asan OxDcByz
Asano, Katsuhito 1938- WhoAsAP 91
Asanov, Abit 1952- WhoWor 93
Asanova, Dinara 1942-1985 DrEEuF
Asante, Molefi K(ete) 1942- WhoWrEP 92
Asante, Molefi Kete 1942- ConBlB 3 [port]
Asante, Samuel Kwadwo Boaten 1933- WhoUN 92, WhoWor 93
Asanuma, Hiroshi 1926- WhoAm 92, WhoE 93
Asaoka, Ryohei 1927- WhoWor 93
Asaro, John BioIn 17
Asawa, Tatsuro 1932- WhoWor 93
Asay, Jeffrey S. Law&B 92
Asayama, Ken 1930- WhoWor 93
Asbed, Mona H. 1935- WhoAmW 93
Asbell, Bernard 1923- WhoAm 92, WhoWrEP 92
Asbell, Fred Thomas 1948- WhoAm 92
Asberg, Marie 1938- WhoScE 91-4, WhoWor 93
Asberry, Bobbie Jo 1934- WhoAmW 93, WhoWor 93
Asbestas, Gregory OxDcByz
Asbjoernsen, Peter Christen 1812-1885 MajAI [port]
Asbjornson, Ronald Anton 1938- St&PR 93
Asbrand, Karin AmWomPl
Asbury, Arthur Knight 1928- WhoAm 92
Asbury, William E. 1952- St&PR 93
Ascalon, David 1945- WhoE 93
Ascandoni Rivero, Jaime 1932- WhoUN 92
Ascani, Paolo 1957- WhoWor 93
Asch, Arthur L. 1941- St&PR 93
Asch, Arthur Louis 1941- WhoAm 92
Asch, Frank BioIn 17
Asch, Frank 1946- ScF&FL 92
Asch, Leopold 1926- WhoScE 91-2
Asch, Moses 1905-1986 BioIn 17
Asch, Nolan E. 1949- St&PR 93, WhoIns 93
Asch, Peter BioIn 17
Asch, Ricardo Hector 1947- WhoAm 92
Asch, Sholem 1880-1957 JeAmFiW, PolBiDi
Aschaffenburg, Walter (Eugene) 1927- Baker 92, WhoAm 92
Aschan, Ulf 1937- ConAu 138
Aschauer, Charles Joseph, Jr. 1928- WhoAm 92
Aschauer, Mary Ann 1947- WhoEmL 93
Asche, David E. 1937- St&PR 93
Asche, Ronald D. 1949- St&PR 93
Aschenbrenner, Christian Heinrich 1654-1732 Baker 92
Aschenbrenner, Frank Aloysious 1924- WhoWor 93
Aschenbrenner, John E. 1949- WhoIns 93
Aschenbrenner, Lisbeth Law&B 92
Ascher, Amalie Adler WhoAmW 93
Ascher, Barbara Lazear 1946- ConAu 138
Ascher, David Law&B 92
Ascher, Eugene ScF&FL 92
Ascher, James John 1928- WhoWor 93
Ascher, Joseph 1829-1869 Baker 92
Ascher, Leo 1880-1942 Baker 92
Ascher, Marcia 1935- WhoAmW 93
Ascher, Mark Louis 1953- WhoEmL 93
Ascher, Robert 1931- WhoAm 92
Ascher, Sheila 1944- ScF&FL 92
Ascher, Steven Alan Law&B 92
Ascher, Steven Peter 1955- WhoEmL 93
Ascher/Straus ScF&FL 92
Ascher-Svanum, Haya 1948- WhoAmW 93
Aschheim, Deborah S. Law&B 92
Aschheim, Joseph 1930- WhoAm 92
Aschinger, Eric Dean 1947- St&PR 93
Aschinger, Keith Lee, Sr. 1943- St&PR 93
Aschinger, Zdena Anna 1923- St&PR 93
Aschkenasy, Herbert St&PR 93
Aschkinasi, David Law&B 92
Aschner, Michael 1955- WhoE 93
Aschoff, Lorraine Marie 1950- WhoAmW 93, WhoE 93, WhoEmL 93
Aschwanden, Richard Josef 1927- WhoWrEP 92
Ascione, Joseph Anthony 1952- WhoEmL 93
Ascolese, Michael John 1946- WhoEmL 93
Ascoli, Aurelio 1929- WhoScE 91-3
Ascoli, Franca 1931- WhoScE 91-3
Ascoli, Marion Rosenwald d1990 BioIn 17
Ascone, Teresa Palmer 1945- WhoAmW 93
Ascone, Vicente 1897-1979 Baker 92
Ascroft, Peter Gerard WhoScE 91-1
Asculai, Ephraim 1935- WhoUN 92
Asdahl, Kristian 1920- WhoWor 93
Ase, Lars-Erik 1933- WhoScE 91-4
Aseer, Ghulam Nabi 1940- WhoWor 93
Aselage, Susan Seabury 1954- St&PR 93, WhoEmL 93
Asen, I d1196 OxDcByz
Asen, Shel F. 1937- WhoAm 92
Asen, Sheldon F. 1937- St&PR 93
Asencio, Diego C. 1931- WhoAm 92
Asenjo Martinez, Jose Luis 1924- WhoScE 91-3
Asfaw, Lagesse WhoAfr
Asfaw, Tesfaye 1947- WhoWor 93
Asfour, Shawki 1937- WhoWor 93
Asfour, Wilda 1931- WhoE 93
Asfoury, Zakaria Mohammed 1921- WhoWor 93
Asgeirsson, Sigvaldi 1950- WhoScE 91-4
Asgrimsson, Halldor 1947- WhoWor 93
Ash, Alan 1908- ScF&FL 92
Ash, Arlene Sandra 1946- WhoEmL 93
Ash, Barbara Lee 1940- WhoE 93
Ash, Brian 1936- ScF&FL 92
Ash, Carroll L. 1925- St&PR 93
Ash, Cay Van ScF&FL 92
Ash, Constance 1950- ScF&FL 92
Ash, David Charles 1951- St&PR 93
Ash, Dorothy Matthews 1918- WhoAmW 93
Ash, Eric BioIn 17
Ash, Eric Duane 1959- WhoEmL 93
Ash, Erin McNerney 1953- WhoE 93
Ash, Ernest M. 1916- St&PR 93
Ash, Gregory Lee 1952- St&PR 93
Ash, Hiram Newton 1934- WhoE 93
Ash, J. Marshall 1940- WhoAm 92
Ash, James Lee, Jr. 1945- WhoAm 92
Ash, Jerome M. St&PR 93
Ash, Major McKinley, Jr. 1921- WhoAm 92, WhoWor 93
Ash, Mary Kay BioIn 17, St&PR 93
Ash, Mary Kay Wagner WhoAm 92, WhoAmW 93
Ash, Michael S. Law&B 92
Ash, Patricia Tighe Law&B 92
Ash, Paul B. 1950- WhoE 93
Ash, Paul J. 1929- St&PR 93
Ash, Philip 1917- WhoAm 92, WhoSSW 93
Ash, Robert Lee 1954- St&PR 93
Ash, Robert W. WhoWrEP 92
Ash, Robert William 1926- St&PR 93
Ash, Rodney Beryl 1946- St&PR 93
Ash, Rosemary Ann 1946- WhoAmW 93
Ash, Roy Lawrence 1918- WhoAm 92
Ash, Scott Howell 1948- WhoSSW 93
Ash, Sharon Kaye 1943- WhoAmW 93
Ash, Susan Joy 1952- WhoAmW 93
Ash, Susan Violet 1956- WhoSSW 93
Ash, T. Lynn 1951- St&PR 93
Ash, W.R. Law&B 92
Ash, Walter Thompson d1992 BioIn 17, NewYTBS 92
Ashabranner, Brent K. 1921- BioIn 17
Ashabranner, Brent K(enneth) 1921- ChlLR 28 [port]
Ashabranner, Brent (Kenneth) 1921- MajAI [port]
Ashadawi, Ahmed Ali 1939- WhoWor 93
Ashamalla, Medhat Guirguis 1942- WhoAm 92
Ashanti, Baron James 1950- WhoWrEP 92
Ashar, Dev 1942- WhoE 93
Ashauer, Guenter 1934- WhoWor 93

Ashbery, John BioIn 17
Ashbery, John 1927- AmWrS3, MagSAmL [port]
Ashbery, John (Lawrence) 1927- ConAu 37NR, WhoAm 92, WhoWor 93, WhoWrEP 92
Ashbolt, Alfred Anthony 1944- WhoWor 93
Ashbridge, Elizabeth 1713-1755 BioIn 17
Ashbridge, Margaret S. Law&B 92
Ashbrook, Beulah Mae 1934- WhoSSW 93
Ashbrook, Charles William Law&B 92
Ashbrook, Dana BioIn 17
Ashbrook, James Barbour 1925- WhoAm 92
Ashbrook, Jean Spencer 1934- BioIn 17
Ashbrook, William Sinclair, Jr. 1922- WhoWor 93
Ashburn, Anderson 1919- WhoAm 92
Ashburn, Donald George, Jr. 1959- WhoSSW 93
Ashburn, Jo LaZetta 1943- WhoAmW 93
Ashby, Carl Crittenden, III 1946- WhoEmL 93, WhoSSW 93
Ashby, Carol Iris Hill 1953- WhoEmL 93
Ashby, Denise Stewart 1941- WhoAmW 93
Ashby, Donald Wayne, Jr. 1926- WhoAm 92
Ashby, Elizabeth Campbell WhoAmW 93
Ashby, Eric 1904-1992 ConAu 139
Ashby, Gary 1943- St&PR 93
Ashby, Hal 1936-1988 MiSFD 9N
Ashby, Harold R. 1940- St&PR 93
Ashby, Hugh Clinton 1934- WhoAm 92
Ashby, Jerry W. Law&B 92
Ashby, John d1693 HarEnMi
Ashby, John Edmund, Jr. 1936- WhoSSW 93, WhoWor 93
Ashby, John Forsythe 1929- WhoAm 92
Ashby, Linda Sue 1946- WhoEmL 93
Ashby, Lisa Scherry 1963- WhoAmW 93
Ashby, Lynn Cox 1938- WhoAm 92
Ashby, Margery Irene Corbett 1882-1981 BioIn 17
Ashby, Michael F[illegible]s 1935- WhoWor 93
Ashby, Norma Ra[illegible]atty 1935- WhoAmW 93
Ashby, Patricia F. 1927- WhoWor 93
Ashby, Richard J. 1944- St&PR 93
Ashby, Richard James, Jr. 1944- WhoAm 92
Ashby, Roger A. 1940- St&PR 93
Ashby, Roger Arthur 1940- WhoAm 92, WhoE 93
Ashby, Rosemary Gillespy 1940- WhoAmW 93
Ashby, Ruth ScF&FL 92
Ashby, Steven James 1948- WhoSSW 93
Ashby, Teri H. Law&B 92
Ashby, Thomas Todd 1954- WhoEmL 93
Ashby, Turner 1828-1862 HarEnMi
Ashby, William 1889-1991 BioIn 17
Ashcraft, David Lee 1946- St&PR 93
Ashcraft, Elizabeth Eva 1957- WhoAmW 93
Ashcraft, James Harold, Jr. 1957- WhoEmL 93, WhoSSW 93
Ashcraft, Johnny Herbert 1940- St&PR 93
Ashcraft, Patricia Rogers 1944- WhoSSW 93
Ashcraft, Raymond Law&B 92
Ashcraft, Susan Collins 1954- WhoEmL 93
Ashcraft, Thomas J. WhoAm 92
Ashcroft, George Warburton WhoScE 91-1
Ashcroft, John David 1942- WhoAm 92, WhoWor 93
Ashcroft, Kenneth 1935- WhoWor 93
Ashcroft, Neil William 1938- WhoAm 92
Ashcroft, Peggy 1907-1991 AnObit 1991, BioIn 17, ConTFT 10, News 92
Ashcroft, Philip Giles 1926- WhoWor 93
Ashcroft, Richard Carter 1942- WhoWor 93
Ashcroft, Shelley Alane 1953- WhoWrEP 92
Ashdjian, Vilma 1954- WhoEmL 93
Ashdown, Catherine E. Law&B 92
Ashdown, Ellen Abernethy 1945- WhoWrEP 92
Ashdown, Franklin Donald 1942- WhoWor 93
Ashdown, Jeremy John 1941- WhoWor 93
Ashdown, Katherine Conklin Law&B 92
Ashdown, Marie Matranga WhoAmW 93, WhoE 93
Ashdown, Paddy BioIn 17, NewYTBS 92 [port]
Ashdown, Paddy 1941- CurBio 92 [port]
Ashdown, Philomena Saldanha 1958- WhoEmL 93
Ashe, Arthur BioIn 17, NewYTBS 92 [port]
Ashe, Arthur 1943- ConHero 2 [port]
Ashe, Arthur, Jr. 1943- AfrAmBi
Ashe, Arthur James, III 1940- WhoAm 92
Ashe, Arthur Robert, Jr. 1943- WhoAm 92, WhoE 93
Ashe, Bernard Flemming 1936- WhoAm 92, WhoE 93
Ashe, David 1952- St&PR 93
Ashe, Douglas Fulton 1953- WhoE 93
Ashe, Gena L. Law&B 92
Ashe, Gordon ScF&FL 92
Ashe, James Neely, Jr. 1951- WhoEmL 93
Ashe, James S. 1947- WhoAm 92
Ashe, Jeanne Moutoussamy- 1951- BioIn 17
Ashe, Maude Llewellyn 1908- WhoAmW 93
Ashe, Rosalind ScF&FL 92
Ashe, Victor Henderson 1945- WhoAm 92, WhoSSW 93
Ashe, William J. 1920- St&PR 93
Asheim, David C. 1955- St&PR 93
Ashelman, Polly McBryde-Miller 1947- WhoAmW 93
Ashen, Frank Z. 1944- St&PR 93
Ashen, Philip 1915- WhoE 93
Ashenberg, Wayne R. 1947- St&PR 93
Ashenfelder, Barry A. 1949- St&PR 93
Ashenfelter, David Louis 1948- WhoAm 92
Ashenfelter, Jayne Eberly 1955- St&PR 93
Ashenfelter, John William Law&B 92
Ashenfelter, Orley Clark 1942- WhoAm 92
Asher, Aaron WhoAm 92
Asher, Bernard Wolff 1936- WhoE 93
Asher, Betty Turner 1944- WhoAmW 93
Asher, Dale L. 1933- St&PR 93
Asher, David 1946- WhoIns 93
Asher, Duffey Ann 1959- WhoWor 93
Asher, Dustin T. 1942- WhoWrEP 92
Asher, Frederick 1915- St&PR 93, WhoAm 92
Asher, Garland Parker 1944- St&PR 93, WhoAm 92
Asher, James 1944- BioIn 17
Asher, James Leonard 1947- WhoEmL 93, WhoWor 93
Asher, Jeffrey S. 1963- St&PR 93
Asher, Jerome M. 1922- St&PR 93
Asher, Kamlesh 1953- WhoEmL 93
Asher, Lester 1910-1990 BioIn 17
Asher, Lila Oliver 1921- WhoAm 92, WhoE 93
Asher, M. Richard 1932- St&PR 93
Asher, Martin ScF&FL 92
Asher, Martin Richard 1932- BioIn 17
Asher, Marty ScF&FL 92
Asher, Michael 1953- BioIn 17
Asher, Michael John WhoScE 91-1
Asher, Renee 1964- WhoAmW 93, WhoE 93
Asher, Robert B. 1937- St&PR 93
Asher, Robert D. 1927- St&PR 93
Asher, Sandra Darlene 1948- WhoEmL 93
Asher, Sandra Fenichel 1942- MajAI [port], WhoWrEP 92
Asher, Sandy (Fenichel) 1942- SmATA 71 [port]
Asher, Steven Alan 1947- WhoEmL 93
Asher, Steven E. Law&B 92
Asher, Thomas M. 1926- St&PR 93
Asher, William 1919- MiSFD 9
Asherin, Allen Lee St&PR 93
Asherman, Allan 1947- ScF&FL 92
Asheron, Sara ConAu 38NR, MajAI
Asherson, Geoffrey L. 1929- WhoScE 91-1
Ashfield, Keith M. 1946- St&PR 93
Ashford, A.P. Law&B 92
Ashford, Anita Rhea 1950- WhoAmW 93, WhoEmL 93
Ashford, Clinton Rutledge 1925- WhoAm 92
Ashford, Douglas E(lliott) 1928- ConAu 37NR
Ashford, Douglas Elliott 1928- WhoAm 92
Ashford, Evelyn BioIn 17, WhoAm 92, WhoAmW 93
Ashford, Evelyn 1957- BlkAmWO [port]
Ashford, Janet Isaacs 1949- WhoEmL 93
Ashford, Marguerite Kamehaokalani 1953- WhoEmL 93
Ashford, Mary Jane 1948- WhoWrEP 92
Ashford, Nicholas BioIn 17
Ashford, Nicky 1943- See Ashford & Simpson SoulM
Ashford, Nigel (John Gladwell) 1952- ConAu 137
Ashford, Norman Joseph WhoScE 91-1
Ashford, Rosalind Mary 1954- WhoAmW 93, WhoEmL 93
Ashford, Theodore H. 1937- St&PR 93
Ashford, Thomas S. Law&B 92
Ashford & Simpson SoulM
Ashforth, Alden (Banning) 1933- Baker 92
Ashforth, H. Adams 1901-1991 BioIn 17
Ashgriz, Nasser 1957- WhoE 93, WhoEmL 93
Ashhurst, Anna Wayne 1933- WhoWor 93
Ashihara, Yoshinobu 1918- WhoWor 93
Ashikaga, Tadayoshi 1307-1352 HarEnMi
Ashikaga, Takauji 1305-1358 HarEnMi
Ashington-Pickett, Michael Derek 1931- WhoSSW 93
Ashinoff, Susan Jane 1949- WhoAmW 93
Ashizawa, Theodore 1934- WhoE 93
Ashjian, Mesrob 1941- WhoAm 92
Ashkenas, Irving Louis 1916- WhoAm 92
Ashkenazi, Elliott Uriel 1941- WhoE 93
Ashkenazi, Ely Ezra 1922- WhoAm 92
Ashkenazi, Isaac 1953- St&PR 93
Ashkenazi, Vidal WhoScE 91-1
Ashkenazy, Vladimir BioIn 17
Ashkenazy, Vladimir D(avidovich) 1937- ConAu 137
Ashkenazy, Vladimir (Davidovich) 1937- Baker 92, WhoAm 92, WhoWor 93
Ashkin, Marilyn Ann Law&B 92
Ashkin, Roberta Ellen 1953- WhoAmW 93
Ashkin, Ronald Evan 1957- St&PR 93, WhoEmL 93, WhoWor 93
Ashkin, Stephen P. 1955- St&PR 93
Ashkinazy, Larry Robert 1952- WhoE 93, WhoEmL 93, WhoWor 93
Ashlandonian WhoWrEP 92
Ashlee, Ted 1914- ScF&FL 92
Ashler, Philip Frederic 1914- WhoAm 92, WhoSSW 93, WhoWor 93
Ashley, Alvin BioIn 17
Ashley, Amber Kim 1959- WhoEmL 93
Ashley, Austin S. 1916- St&PR 93
Ashley, Bernard 1935- ChlFicS, MajAI [port]
Ashley, C. WhoScE 91-1
Ashley, Charles Gary 1934- WhoSSW 93
Ashley, Darlene Joy 1945- WhoAm 92, WhoAmW 93
Ashley, Diana Gaye 1948- WhoEmL 93
Ashley, Donald D. d1991 BioIn 17
Ashley, Edward Everett 1906- WhoWor 93
Ashley, Eleanor Tidaback 1910- WhoAmW 93
Ashley, Elizabeth 1941- WhoAm 92
Ashley, Ella Jane Rader 1941- WhoAmW 93
Ashley, Fletcher 1926- WhoAm 92
Ashley, Francis Paul WhoScE 91-1
Ashley, George d1991 BioIn 17
Ashley, Holt 1923- WhoAm 92
Ashley, James MacGregor 1941- WhoSSW 93
Ashley, James Robert 1927- WhoAm 92
Ashley, James Wheeler 1923- WhoAm 92
Ashley, Janelle Coleman 1941- WhoAm 92
Ashley, John 1934- BioIn 17
Ashley, John Dewitt, Jr. 1915- WhoSSW 93
Ashley, Lawrence Atwell, Jr. 1929- WhoAm 92
Ashley, Merrill WhoAm 92, WhoAmW 93, WhoE 93
Ashley, Michael ScF&FL 92
Ashley, Mike 1948- ScF&FL 92
Ashley, Nick BioIn 17
Ashley, Ona Christine 1954- WhoEmL 93
Ashley, Pamela J. Law&B 92
Ashley, Paula Claire 1939- WhoAmW 93
Ashley, Robert H. 1948- St&PR 93
Ashley, Robert Paul, Jr. 1915- WhoAm 92
Ashley, Robert (Reynolds) 1930- Baker 92
Ashley, Rosalind Minor 1923- WhoWrEP 92
Ashley, Sharon Anita 1948- WhoAm 92, WhoAmW 93, WhoEmL 93
Ashley, Simon K. WhoWrEP 92
Ashley, Steven 1940- ScF&FL 92
Ashley, Thomas William Ludlow 1923- BioIn 17
Ashley, William Henry 1778-1838 BioIn 17, Expl 93
Ashley, William J. 1955- WhoIns 93
Ashley-Cameron, Sylvia Elaine 1955- WhoEmL 93
Ashley-Farrand, Margalo 1944- WhoWor 93
Ashlock, Robert B. 1930- WhoSSW 93
Ashman, Gary D. Law&B 92
Ashman, Glen Edward 1956- WhoEmL 93
Ashman, Harvey A. Law&B 92
Ashman, Harvey Alan Law&B 92
Ashman, Howard 1950-1991 BioIn 17, ScF&FL 92
Ashman, Hyman 1909-1991 BioIn 17
Ashman, Raymond Donald 1923- St&PR 93
Ashman, Stephen Neil 1948- St&PR 93
Ashmead, John d1992 NewYTBS 92 [port]
Ashmead, John 1917-1992 BioIn 17
Ashmead, John 1950- ScF&FL 92
Ashmead, John, Jr. 1917-1992 ConAu 136
Ashmen, Barry Dennis 1947- WhoE 93
Ashment, Arvil L. 1947- St&PR 93
Ashmore, Charles Wayne 1938- WhoSSW 93
Ashmore, Harry Scott 1916- EncAACR
Ashmore, James Loyd 1951- WhoEmL 93
Ashmore, Ruth AmWomPl
Ashmun, Clifford S., Jr. 1923- St&PR 93
Ashmun, John B. 1923- St&PR 93
Ashmus, Keith Allen 1949- WhoAm 92, WhoEmL 93
Ashner, Marvin 1936- St&PR 93
Ashoo, Waleed K. St&PR 93
Ashorn, Theodore H. 1932- WhoWor 93
Ashot OxDcByz
Ashpes, Philip 1938- St&PR 93
Ashraf, Elizabeth Ann 1947- WhoAmW 93
Ashraf, Saad 1968- WhoWor 93
Ashraf, Syed Javed 1940- WhoWor 93
Ashraff, Muthuwappa Muhammed 1950- WhoWor 93
Ashrafi, Mukhtar 1912-1975 Baker 92
Ashrawi, Hanan BioIn 17
Ashrawi, Hanan 1946- CurBio 92 [port]
ash-Sharif, Muhammad Omar 1930- WhoWor 93
Ashton, Alan C. 1942- & Bastian, Bruce W. 1948- ConEn
Ashton, Algernon (Bennet Langton) 1859-1937 Baker 92
Ashton, Betsy Finley 1944- WhoAmW 93, WhoE 93
Ashton, C. Earl 1944- St&PR 93
Ashton, Charles ScF&FL 92
Ashton, David BioIn 17
Ashton, David John 1921- WhoAm 92
Ashton, Diane Patricia 1948- WhoAmW 93
Ashton, Dore WhoAm 92, WhoWrEP 92
Ashton, Dore 1928- BioIn 17
Ashton, Edward J. Law&B 92
Ashton, Edward Joseph 1941- St&PR 93
Ashton, Geoffrey Cyril 1925- WhoAm 92
Ashton, Harris John 1932- St&PR 93, WhoAm 92
Ashton, Jay ScF&FL 92
Ashton, Jean Willoughby 1938- WhoAmW 93
Ashton, John K., Jr. 1927- WhoE 93
Ashton, Larry James 1941- St&PR 93
Ashton, M. Anthony 1935- St&PR 93
Ashton, M.C. WhoScE 91-1
Ashton, Margaret 1856-1937 BioIn 17
Ashton, Maria Slark 1948- WhoAmW 93
Ashton, Marvin ScF&FL 92
Ashton, Mary Madonna WhoAm 92
Ashton, Nancy Lynn 1950- WhoEmL 93
Ashton, Neil K. 1944- St&PR 93
Ashton, Patricia Teague 1946- WhoAmW 93, WhoSSW 93
Ashton, Peter Jack 1935- St&PR 93
Ashton, Peter Shaw 1934- WhoAm 92
Ashton, Philip T. 1934- St&PR 93
Ashton, Price Richard 1917- WhoWor 93
Ashton, Robert W. 1937- St&PR 93, WhoAm 92
Ashton, Robin G. 1949- WhoWrEP 92
Ashton, Rosemary 1947- ConAu 138
Ashton, S.J. WhoScE 91-1
Ashton, Thomas Walsh 1929- WhoWor 93
Ashton, William J. 1946- WhoEmL 93
Ashton, Winifred ScF&FL 92
Ashton-Warner, Sylvia 1908-1984 BioIn 17
Ashurbanipal d627BC HarEnMi
Ashurnasirpal, II d859BC HarEnMi
Ashwell, David MiSFD 9
Ashwell, Henry 1828-1909 BioIn 17
Ashwell, Margaret 1946- WhoScE 91-1
Ashworth, Barbara J. 1933- WhoAmW 93
Ashworth, Brent Ferrin Law&B 92
Ashworth, Brent Ferrin 1949- St&PR 93, WhoWor 93
Ashworth, Denise Marchant 1917- WhoSSW 93
Ashworth, Emily Yaung 1945- WhoSSW 93
Ashworth, Geoffrey Hugh 1950- WhoIns 93
Ashworth, John Lawrence 1934- WhoAm 92
Ashworth, Kenneth Hayden 1932- WhoAm 92
Ashworth, Mary Wells d1992 NewYTBS 92
Ashworth, Phyllis Corbett 1952- WhoEmL 93
Ashworth, Richard G. 1926- St&PR 93
Ashworth, Richard Goodspeed 1926- WhoAm 92
Ashworth, Willis Louis 1945- WhoE 93
Ashy, Doug Elias, Sr. 1930- St&PR 93
Ashy, Steve M. 1953- St&PR 93
Asidenos, Sabas fl. 1204-1214 OxDcByz
Asiedu, Diane 1954- WhoAmW 93
Asiel, Monique 1919- WhoScE 91-2
Asim, Mohammed 1954- WhoE 93
Asim, Waheed BioIn 17
Asimakopoulos, John L. 1948- St&PR 93
Asimakopulos, A. 1930-1990 BioIn 17
Asimakopulos, Athanasios 1930- WhoAm 92
Asimakopulos, Tom 1930-1990 BioIn 17

Asimov, Isaac 1920- JeAmHC, WhoWrEP 92
Asimov, Isaac 1920-1992 BioIn 17, ConAu 137, CurBio 92N, DcLB Y92N [port], MajAI [port], NewYTBS 92 [port], News 92, -92-3, ScF&FL 92
Asimov, Janet Jeppson 1926- ScF&FL 92
Asimow, Morris 1906-1982 ScF&FL 92
Asin, Carlos Guillermo 1950- WhoWor 93
Asin, Mario 1939- St&PR 93
Asioli, Bonifazio 1769-1832 Baker 92
Asiqpasazade 1400-c. 1484 OxDcByz
Asire, Nancy 1945- ScF&FL 92
Ask, Frede WhoScE 91-2
Ask, Frede A. 1931- WhoScE 91-2
Ask, Sten S. 1943- WhoUN 92
Askaa, Stig 1946- WhoWor 93
Askanas-Engel, Valerie 1937- WhoAm 92
Askeland, Calvin Keith 1954- St&PR 93
Askenase, Stefan 1896-1985 Baker 92
Askenazy, Salomon 1936- WhoScE 91-2
Askenazy, Szymon 1867-1935 PolBiDi
Askew, Arthur John 1942- WhoUN 92
Askew, Bob E. 1942- WhoIns 93
Askew, Emil Boyd 1941- WhoIns 93
Askew, Jonathan Stephen 1950- WhoEmL 93
Askew, Laurin Barker, Jr. 1942- St&PR 93
Askew, Mary Frances 1921- WhoWor 93
Askew, Penny Sue 1967- WhoSSW 93
Askew, Reubin O'Donovan 1928- WhoAm 92
Askew, Thomas Adelbert 1931- WhoE 93
Askew, Walter Herbert 1947- WhoSSW 93
Askew, William E. 1949- St&PR 93
Askey, Arthur 1900-1982 QDrFCA 92 [port]
Askey, Richard Allen 1933- WhoAm 92
Askhabov, Sultan Nazhmudinovich 1954- WhoWor 93
Askham, Janet Mary WhoScE 91-1
Askia Muhammad d1538 HarEnMi
Askidas, Theodore d588 OxDcByz
Askin, Elisa Mullenix 1953- WhoIns 93
Askin, Jacalyn Ann 1954- WhoEmL 93
Askin, Leon 1907- WhoAm 92
Askin, Richard Henry, Jr. 1947- WhoAm 92
Askin, Walter Miller 1929- WhoAm 92
Askinazi, William F. Law&B 92
Askins, Charles 1907- BioIn 17
Askins, Nancy Paulsen 1948- WhoAmW 93, WhoEmL 93
Askins, Wallace Boyd 1930- St&PR 93, WhoE 93
Askonas, Brigitte A. BioIn 17
Askovic, Radomir 1938- WhoScE 91-4
Askren, James D. 1942- St&PR 93
Askwith, Thomas Michael N. 1945- WhoUN 92
Aslam, Javed 1941- WhoUN 92
Aslam, M. WhoScE 91-1
Aslam, Mohammad 1959- WhoWor 93
Aslam, Muhammed Javed 1938- WhoSSW 93
Aslam Watanjar, Mohammad 1946- WhoAsAP 91
Aslaner, Mustafa 1934- WhoScE 91-4
Aslanian, Azed Ozzie 1918- St&PR 93
Aslanian, Samson MiSFD 9
Aslanides, Peter Constantine 1940- WhoAm 92
Aslet, Peter M. 1952- St&PR 93
Asli, Ilsa H. 1944- WhoAmW 93
Aslin, Edna SweetSg C
Aslin, Malcolm M. 1947- St&PR 93
Asling, Clarence Willet 1913- WhoAm 92
Asman, Sanford J. Law&B 92
Asmar, Laila Michelle 1957- WhoEmL 93, WhoSSW 93
Asmus, John BioIn 17
Asmus, John Fredrich 1937- WhoAm 92
Asmus, Klaus-Dieter 1937- WhoScE 91-3
Asmussen, Erik 1942- WhoScE 91-2
Asmuth, Anthony W., III Law&B 92
Asner, Edward 1929- BioIn 17, WhoAm 92
Asnes, Harald 1929- WhoScE 91-4
Asnin, Scott ScF&FL 92
Asnyk, Adam 1838-1897 PolBiDi
Aso, Taro 1940- WhoAsAP 91
Asoka, King of Magadha d232BC BioIn 17
Asola, Giammateo c. 1532-1609 Baker 92
Asolik OxDcByz
Asomoa, Ansa Kwami 1938- WhoWor 93
Asonevich, Walter Jozef 1950- WhoEmL 93, WhoSSW 93
Asot Erkat, II OxDcByz
Asot Olormac', III OxDcByz
Asot the Great, I d890 OxDcByz
Asow, Erich Hermann Muller von Baker 92
Asp, Nils-Georg L. 1944- WhoScE 91-4
Asp, William George 1943- WhoAm 92
Aspa, Mario 1799-1868 Baker 92
Aspar d471 OxDcByz
Asparuch OxDcByz
Aspatore, George A. Law&B 92
Aspatore, George Alfred 1949- WhoEmL 93
Aspaturian, Vernon Varaztat 1922- WhoAm 92
Aspbury, Herbert F. 1944- St&PR 93
Aspbury, Herbert Francis 1944- WhoAm 92
Aspe Armella, Pedro 1950- WhoAm 92, WhoWor 93
Aspect, Alain 1947- WhoWor 93
Aspell, James Fitzgerald 1961- WhoEmL 93
Aspen, Marvin Edward 1934- WhoAm 92
Asper, Israel Harold 1932- WhoAm 92
Asper, Maynard W. Law&B 92
Asper, Vernon Lowell 1956- WhoSSW 93
Asperger, Robert George, Sr. 1937- WhoSSW 93
Aspero, Benedict Vincent 1940- WhoAm 92
Aspestrand, Sigwart 1856-1941 Baker 92
Aspevig, Clyde 1951- BioIn 17
Aspholm, Wilford Thomas 1913- St&PR 93
Aspietes OxDcByz
Aspillaga, Inigo D. Law&B 92
Aspin, Les BioIn 17
Aspin, Les 1938- CngDr 91, WhoAm 92
Aspin, Leslie, Jr. 1938- NewYTBS 92
Aspinall, Arnold WhoScE 91-1
Aspinall, Brian Clifford WhoScE 91-1
Aspinall, Brian E. Law&B 92
Aspinall, D. WhoScE 91-1
Aspinall, Keith Wilton 1953- WhoAm 92
Aspinwall, Marie Law&B 92
Aspinwall, Mark A. Law&B 92
Aspiras, Jose D. 1924- WhoAsAP 91
Aspis, Harold B. Law&B 92
Aspis, Harold B. 1954- St&PR 93
Aspland, Joseph Robert 1928- WhoAm 92
Aspler, Tony 1939- ScF&FL 92, WhoCanL 92
Asplin, Edward W. 1922- St&PR 93
Asplin, Edward William 1922- WhoAm 92
Asplmayr, Franz 1728-1786 Baker 92
Asplund, Bronwyn Lorraine 1947- WhoAmW 93
Asplund, Dan Arvo 1948- WhoScE 91-4
Asplund, Mark J. Law&B 92
Aspnes, David E. 1939- WhoAm 92
Aspray, Joseph M. Law&B 92
Asprin, Robert Lynn 1946- ScF&FL 92
Aspull, George 1813-1832 Baker 92
Asquith, Anthony 1902-1968 MiSFD 9N
Asquith, Don Gaylord 1947- WhoEmL 93
Asquith, H.H. 1852-1928 BioIn 17
Asquith, Herbert Henry 1852-1928 BioIn 17, DcTwHis
Asquith, Margot 1864-1945 BioIn 17
Asquith, Philip Ernest 1940- St&PR 93
Asquith, Ronald H. 1932- WhoAm 92
Asrat, Dereje 1948- WhoUN 92
Asriel, Andre 1922- Baker 92
Assa, Menachem St&PR 93
Assad, Albert Joseph 1915- St&PR 93
Assad, Hafez BioIn 17
Assad, Hafez al- 1930- ColdWar 2 [port]
Assad, Hafiz 1928- WhoWor 93
Assad, Rif'at al- 1937- WhoWor 93
Assael, Dorette Vock d1991 BioIn 17
Assael, Henry 1935- WhoAm 92
Assael, Michael 1949- WhoE 93, WhoEmL 93
Assaf, Emile Joseph 1927- St&PR 93
Assaf, Ronald G. 1935- WhoSSW 93
Assaf, Ronald George 1935- St&PR 93
Assante, Allison ScF&FL 92
Assante, Allison d1992 NewYTBS 92
Assante, Armand BioIn 17
Assante, Armand 1949- WhoAm 92
Assante, Carole Anne 1937- WhoIns 93
Assayas, Olivier MiSFD 9
Asscher, Jean Claude 1928- WhoWor 93
Assef, Sherif Tahsin 1960- WhoE 93
Assefa, Lakew 1937- WhoUN 92
Asselin, John Thomas 1951- WhoEmL 93
Asselin, Martial 1924- WhoE 93
Asselin, Olivar 1874-1937 BioIn 17
Asselin-Dargitz, Anna 1954- WhoAmW 93
Asselineau, Jean 1921- WhoScE 91-2
Asselineau, Roger 1915- ScF&FL 92
Assemat-Tessandier, Joseph Manuel 1947- WhoWor 93
Assen, Nigel St. Dennis 1929- WhoWor 93
Assennato, Vincent Thomas 1950- WhoIns 93
Assensoh, Akwasi B. 1946- WhoWrEP 92
Asseo, Lee A. 1938- St&PR 93
Asseo, Yosef Dov 1956- WhoEmL 93
Asser, Tobias Michael Carel 1935- WhoUN 92
Asseyev, Nikita Zakaravich BioIn 17
Assimakopoulos, Panayotis Adam 1940- WhoScE 91-3, WhoWor 93
siniwi, Bernard 1935- WhoCanL 92
Assink, Anne Hoekstra 1948- WhoEmL 93
Assink, Brent E. 1955- WhoAm 92
Assiri, Abdul-Reda Ali 1946- WhoWor 93
Assmann, Carol Hynes 1963- WhoSSW 93
Assmayer, Ignaz 1790-1862 Baker 92
Assour, Jacques M. 1932- St&PR 93
Assumpcao, Ronald 1949- WhoAm 92
Assunto, Alyne Law&B 92
Ast, Teodor 1940- WhoScE 91-4
Asta, August F. 1931- St&PR 93
Asta, Eduardo Pablo 1957- WhoWor 93
Asta, Richard A. 1956- St&PR 93
Astafjev, Vladimir Ivanovich 1948- WhoWor 93
Astaire, Fred BioIn 17
Astaire, Fred 1899-1987 Baker 92, IntDcF 2-3 [port]
Astakhov, Yevgeni Mikhailovitch 1937- WhoWor 93
Astarita, Gennaro c. 1745-c. 1803 OxDcOp
Astarita, Gianni 1933- WhoWor 93
Astarita, Susan Gallagher 1941- WhoAmW 93
Aste, George James 1939- St&PR 93
Aste, Louis J. Law&B 92
Asteljoki, Jussi Akseli 1945- WhoScE 91-4
Asten, Gail Van ScF&FL 92
Astengo, Giovanni 1915-1990 BioIn 17
Aster, Vera Constance 1945- WhoAmW 93
Asterios of Amaseia 330?-420? OxDcByz
Asterios Sophistes dc. 341 OxDcByz
Astfalk, Leonard Nathaniel 1942- St&PR 93
Astheimer, David Levengood 1951- St&PR 93
Asti, Alison Louise 1954- WhoEmL 93
Asti, Giovanni 1937- WhoScE 91-3
Astie, Henri R.Y. 1939- WhoScE 91-2
Astier de la Vigerie, Emmanuel d' 1900-1969 BioIn 17
Astill, Bernard Douglas 1925- WhoE 93
Astill, Kenneth Norman 1923- WhoAm 92
Astill, Norma Di Lauro WhoWor 93
Astin, Alexander William 1932- WhoAm 92
Astin, John 1930- MiSFD 9
Astin, John Allen 1930- WhoAm 92
Astin, Sean BioIn 17
Astle, Dale L. Law&B 92
Astle, Ian BioIn 17
Astle, Scott S. Law&B 92
Astle, Thora Myrlene 1913- WhoWrEP 92
Astler, Barbara Lynn 1960- WhoSSW 93
Astley, Eugene Roy 1926- St&PR 93
Astley, Jacob 1579-1652 HarEnMi
Astley, Neil Philip 1953- WhoWor 93
Astley, R.E. St&PR 93
Astley, Robert Murray 1944- St&PR 93
Astley, Suzette Lynn 1951- WhoAmW 93
Astley, Thea BioIn 17
Astley, Thea 1925- IntLitE
Astol, Leonardo Garcia 1906- HispAmA
Aston, David Law&B 92
Aston, James ConAu 37NR, MajAI
Aston, James William 1911- St&PR 93, WhoAm 92
Aston, John G. 1902-1990 BioIn 17
Aston, Joseph L. 1937- St&PR 93
Aston, Miriam Elizabeth 1947- WhoEmL 93
Aston, Sheree Jean 1954- WhoEmL 93
Astor, Viscountess 1879-1964 BioIn 17
Astor, Ana Inez d1992 BioIn 17, NewYTBS 92
Astor, Brooke BioIn 17, WhoAm 92, WhoE 93
Astor, Fred G. 1951- St&PR 93
Astor, John Jacob 1763-1848 BioIn 17
Astor, John Jacob, IV 1864-1912 GayN
Astor, John Jacob, V 1912-1992 NewYTBS 92
Astor, Josef 1959- BioIn 17
Astor, Mary 1906-1987 BioIn 17, IntDcF 2-3 [port]
Astor, Peter (George) 1938- Baker 92
Astor, Philip BioIn 17
Astor, Susan Irene 1946- WhoWrEP 92
Astor, Vincent, Mrs. WhoWrEP 92
Astorga, Emanuele d' 1680-1757? Baker 92
Astorino, Louis Don 1946- WhoAm 92
Astrachan, Anthony BioIn 17
Astrachan, Anthony d1992 NewYTBS 92
Astrachan, John M. 1928-1991 BioIn 17
Astrakhan, Dmitry MiSFD 9
Astrakhantsev, Victor Vasilyevich 1948- WhoWor 93
Astraldi, Mario WhoScE 91-3
Astrampsychos OxDcByz
Astrand, (Karl) Hans (Vilhelm) 1925- Baker 92
Astrand, Irma L. 1927- WhoScE 91-4
Astrapas, John OxDcByz
Astrin, Marvin H. 1925- WhoAm 92
Astro, Richard Bruce 1941- WhoAm 92
Astrom, H.U. 1926- WhoScE 91-4
Astrom, Karl Johan 1934- WhoScE 91-4
Astruc, Michel Jean Raymond 1942- WhoScE 91-2
Astrue, Michael James 1956- WhoAm 92
Astudillo, Rafael 1947- WhoScE 91-3
Asturias, Miguel Angel BioIn 17
Asturias, Miguel Angel 1899-1974 SpAmA
Asturias, Rodrigo DcCPCAm
Astuto, Philip Louis 1923- WhoAm 92
Astwood, William Peter 1940- WhoE 93
Asuar, Jose Vicente 1933- Baker 92
Asubeie, Abdulaziz Mohamed 1945- WhoWor 93
Asugar, Henry 1948- WhoAsAP 91
Asuncion, Vargas Pena 1944- WhoWor 93
Asundi, Anand Krishna 1953- WhoWor 93
Asvall, Jo Erik WhoScE 91-2
Aswad, Betsy 1939- WhoAm 92, WhoAmW 93, WhoWor 93
Aswad, Richard Nejm 1936- WhoE 93
Atack, Douglas 1923- WhoAm 92
Atagunduz, Gurbuz 1936- WhoScE 91-4
Ataiifar, Ali Akbar 1952- WhoE 93
Atal, Bishnu Saroop 1933- WhoAm 92
Atal, Yogesh 1937- WhoUN 92
Atam-Alibeckoff, Galib-Bey 1923- St&PR 93
Atamian, Susan 1950- WhoAmW 93, WhoEmL 93
Atanasoff, John V. BioIn 17
Atanasoff, John Vincent 1903- WhoAm 92
Atanasov, Georgi 1881-1931 Baker 92
Atanasov, Georgy 1882-1931 OxDcOp
Atanasov, Nicola 1939- WhoScE 91-4
Atanasov, Nikola 1886-1969 Baker 92
Atanassov, Krassimir Todorov 1954- WhoWor 93
Atapattu, Ranjit Kanista Parakrama 1933- WhoUN 92
Atash, Farhad 1954- WhoEmL 93
Atassi, Ghanem 1936- WhoWor 93
Atassi, Nureddin al- d1992 NewYTBS 92
Ataturk 1881-1938 HarEnMi
Ataturk, Kemal 1881-1938 BioIn 17
Ataturk, Mustafa Kemal 1881-1938 DcTwHis
Atay, Ali Riza 1932- WhoWor 93
Atcher, Randy 1918- WhoWor 93
Atcher, Robert Whitehill 1951- WhoEmL 93
Atcheson, Richard W. 1948- WhoEmL 93
Atchia, Michael 1938- WhoUN 92
Atchinson, Frances Elizabeth 1903- AmWomPl
Atchison, Arthur Mark 1944- WhoWor 93
Atchison, Beth Tillotson 1929- WhoAmW 93
Atchison, David Andrew 1954- WhoWor 93
Atchison, Gregory Mac 1957- WhoEmL 93, WhoSSW 93
Atchison, Joseph E. 1914- St&PR 93
Atchison, Richard Calvin 1932- WhoAm 92
Atchison, Sammy Stone 1943- BioIn 17
Atchison, Thomas Andrew 1937- WhoSSW 93
Atchity, Kenneth J. 1944- WhoWrEP 92
Atchley, Anthony C. 1942- WhoAm 92
Atchley, Daniel Gene 1942- WhoSSW 93
Atchley, William Reid 1942- WhoAm 92
Aten, Ira 1862-1953 BioIn 17
Atencio, Debra Susan 1955- WhoAmW 93
Atencio, Dolores S. 1955- NotHsAW 93
Atencio, Jerry Law&B 92
Atencio, Kathleen Nilon 1959- WhoAmW 93
Atencio, Paulette 1947- NotHsAW 93
Ater, William Clement 1940- St&PR 93, WhoAm 92
Ates, J. Robert 1945- WhoAm 92, WhoSSW 93, WhoWor 93
Ates, Roscoe 1892-1962 QDrFCA 92 [port]
Atger, Pierre Antoine 1930- WhoScE 91-2
Atget, Eugene 1857-1927 ModArCr 3 [port]
Atha, Stuart Kimball, Jr. 1925- WhoAm 92
Athanas, Emanuel Stelios 1907- WhoSSW 93
Athanase, Theodore St&PR 93
Athanasios 295-373 OxDcByz
Athanasios, I c. 1235-c. 1315 OxDcByz
Athanasios, II OxDcByz
Athanasios of Athos 925?-c. 1001 OxDcByz
Athanasios of Meteora 1305-1383 OxDcByz
Athanasius, Saint d373 BioIn 17
Athanason-Dymersky, Nickie Ann 1954- WhoEmL 93
Athanasopulos, Christos 1938- WhoScE 91-3

Athanassiades, Nickolas George 1916- *WhoWor 93*
Athanassiades, Nikos *WhoScE 91-3*
Athanassiades, Ted *WhoAm 92*
Athanassiou, Evangelos Themistoklis 1948- *WhoWor 93*
Athanassoglou, Micholas Panos 1944- *WhoWor 93*
Athanassoulas, Sotirios 1936- *WhoAm 92*
Athans, Michael T. 1937- *WhoAm 92*
Athas, Gus J. *Law&B 92*
Athas, Gus J. 1936- *St&PR 93*
Athas, Gus James 1936- *WhoAm 92*
Athaulf d416 *HarEnMi*
Atheling, William *ConAu 40NR*
Atheling, William, Jr. 1921-1975 *BioIn 17*
Athenais-Eudokia c. 400-460 *OxDcByz*
Athens, J. D. *MiSFD 9*
Atherholt, J. Eric *Law&B 92*
Atherton, Alexander Simpson 1913- *WhoAm 92*
Atherton, Alfred Leroy, Jr. 1921- *WhoAm 92*
Atherton, Charles Henry 1932- *WhoAm 92*
Atherton, David 1944- *Baker 92*
Atherton, David Reed 1952- *WhoEmL 93, WhoSSW 93*
Atherton, Derek Percy *WhoScE 91-1*
Atherton, Gertrude Franklin Horn 1857-1948 *BioIn 17*
Atherton, James Dale 1935- *WhoAm 92*
Atherton, N.M. *WhoScE 91-1*
Atherton, Philip Gwyther 1931- *WhoWor 93*
Atherton, Robert A. *Law&B 92*
Atherton, Roy Thomas 1933- *WhoWor 93*
Atherton, Selwyn I. 1929- *WhoAm 92*
Atherton, Shirley Ann 1943- *WhoAmW 93*
Atherton, William 1947- *WhoAm 92, WhoEmL 93*
Athey, Janet Louise 1957- *WhoSSW 93*
Athey, Louis Lee 1929- *WhoE 93*
Athey, Mary Frances 1944- *WhoAmW 93*
Athey, Michael B. *St&PR 93*
Athey, Paul Rothgeb 1944- *St&PR 93*
Athey, Preston G. 1949- *St&PR 93*
Athey, Rochelle Rene 1964- *WhoAmW 93*
Athithan, R. Dhanuskodi 1953- *WhoAsAP 91*
Athmann, Marilyn *BioIn 17*
Atieh, Michael Gerard 1953- *WhoAm 92*
Atienza, Frank Eng 1951- *WhoWor 93*
Atigbi, Kofitunde Jolomi 1961- *WhoE 93*
Atil, Esin 1938- *WhoAm 92*
Atilgan, Timur Faik 1943- *WhoE 93*
Atisanoe, Salevaa *BioIn 17*
Atisnoe, Salevaa *NewYTBS 92 [port]*
Atiyah, Michael Francis 1929- *BioIn 17, WhoWor 93*
Atiyeh, George Nicholas 1923- *WhoAm 92*
Atkar, Amarjit Singh 1953- *WhoWor 93*
Atkeson, Mary Meek *AmWomPl*
Atkeson, Ray 1907-1990 *BioIn 17*
Atkeson, Timothy Breed 1927- *WhoAm 92*
Atkey, Bertram 1880-1952 *ScF&FL 92*
Atkin, Flora B(lumenthal) 1919- *ConAu 37NR*
Atkin, Gary Eugene 1946- *WhoEmL 93*
Atkin, Gerald Clifford 1936- *St&PR 93, WhoAm 92*
Atkin, J. Myron 1927- *WhoAm 92*
Atkin, James Blakesley 1930- *WhoAm 92*
Atkin, Jerry Clayton 1949- *St&PR 93*
Atkin, Joseph Raymond 1945- *St&PR 93*
Atkin, Louis Phillip 1951- *WhoEmL 93*
Atkin, Sidney Joseph 1934- *St&PR 93*
Atkin, William Walter 1947- *St&PR 93*
Atkins, Anthony George *WhoScE 91-1*
Atkins, Candi 1946- *WhoAmW 93*
Atkins, Chester Burton 1924- *WhoAm 92*
Atkins, Chester G. 1948- *CngDr 91*
Atkins, Chester Greenough 1948- *WhoAm 92, WhoE 93*
Atkins, Chet 1924- *Baker 92*
Atkins, Cholly *BioIn 17*
Atkins, Cholly 1913- *WhoAm 92*
Atkins, Dale Morrell 1922- *WhoAm 92*
Atkins, David *BioIn 17*
Atkins, Deborah Kaye 1958- *WhoAmW 93, WhoEmL 93, WhoWor 93*
Atkins, Doug 1943- *BioIn 17*
Atkins, E. Larry 1946- *St&PR 93*
Atkins, Eileen *BioIn 17*
Atkins, Frank *ScF&FL 92*
Atkins, Fredd Glossie 1952- *AfrAmBi [port]*
Atkins, George L. 1941- *St&PR 93*
Atkins, George W.P., Jr. 1938- *St&PR 93*
Atkins, Jacqueline Marx 1941- *WhoAmW 93*
Atkins, James N. *Law&B 92*
Atkins, Joe T. 1928- *St&PR 93*
Atkins, John 1916- *ScF&FL 92*
Atkins, John 1938- *WhoWor 93*
Atkins, Joseph P. 1940- *WhoAm 92*
Atkins, Kay Roberta 1939- *WhoAm 92, WhoAmW 93*
Atkins, Margaret E. *ScF&FL 92*
Atkins, Marvin Cleveland 1931- *WhoSSW 93*
Atkins, Meg Elizabeth *ScF&FL 92*
Atkins, Michael B. 1914- *WhoWor 93*
Atkins, Michelle Blaine 1953- *WhoEmL 93*
Atkins, Peter 1963- *BioIn 17*
Atkins, Peter Allan 1943- *WhoAm 92*
Atkins, Richard A. d1990 *BioIn 17*
Atkins, Richard Bart 1951- *WhoE 93, WhoEmL 93, WhoWor 93*
Atkins, Richard G. *WhoAm 92*
Atkins, Richard L. 1926- *WhoAm 92*
Atkins, Richard Norman 1948- *WhoEmL 93*
Atkins, Robert *BioIn 17*
Atkins, Robert E., Jr. *Law&B 92*
Atkins, Robert Emmett, Jr. 1936- *St&PR 93, WhoAm 92*
Atkins, Robert Michael 1953- *WhoEmL 93*
Atkins, Ronald Raymond 1933- *WhoAm 92*
Atkins, Russell 1926- *ConAu 16AS [port], WhoWrEP 92*
Atkins, Sally Ann 1959- *WhoEmL 93*
Atkins, Samuel James, III 1944- *St&PR 93, WhoAm 92*
Atkins, Stephen Edward *Law&B 92*
Atkins, Stuart Pratt 1914- *WhoAm 92*
Atkins, Theodore William 1938- *St&PR 93*
Atkins, Thomas Jay 1943- *WhoAm 92, WhoWor 93*
Atkins, Thomas R. 1939- *ScF&FL 92*
Atkins, Victor Kennicott, Jr. 1945- *WhoAm 92*
Atkins, William Allen 1934- *WhoE 93*
Atkins, William Reed, Jr. 1959- *WhoEmL 93*
Atkinson, Allen d1987 *BioIn 17*
Atkinson, Anthony 1945- *WhoScE 91-1*
Atkinson, Anthony Barnes *WhoScE 91-1*
Atkinson, Anthony Curtis *WhoScE 91-1*
Atkinson, Arthur Sheridan 1918- *St&PR 93*
Atkinson, Basil Eric 1926- *St&PR 93*
Atkinson, Bernard 1936- *WhoScE 91-1*
Atkinson, Bill 1916- *WhoAm 92*
Atkinson, Brian 1937- *WhoScE 91-1*
Atkinson, Bruce Wilson *WhoScE 91-1*
Atkinson, Bryan Herbert 1940- *St&PR 93*
Atkinson, Charles 1913- *WhoAm 92*
Atkinson, Charles Ora 1944- *WhoWrEP 92*
Atkinson, Craig *BioIn 17*
Atkinson, David *WhoScE 91-1*
Atkinson, Dewey Franklin 1930- *WhoSSW 93*
Atkinson, Edward Arthur 1948- *St&PR 93*
Atkinson, Frank 1922-1991 *BioIn 17*
Atkinson, Frederick Griswold 1904-1991 *BioIn 17*
Atkinson, Gordon 1930- *WhoAm 92*
Atkinson, Harold Witherspoon 1914- *WhoSSW 93*
Atkinson, Helen Winwick *WhoScE 91-1*
Atkinson, Henry 1782-1842 *HarEnMi*
Atkinson, Holley 1959- *WhoAmW 93*
Atkinson, Holly Gail 1952- *WhoAm 92, WhoE 93, WhoEmL 93*
Atkinson, Howard Phillip 1954- *WhoEmL 93*
Atkinson, J. 1943- *WhoScE 91-4*
Atkinson, James P. *Law&B 92*
Atkinson, James Peter 1947- *WhoEmL 93*
Atkinson, James Vincent 1934- *St&PR 93*
Atkinson, Janet Dora 1955- *WhoAmW 93*
Atkinson, Jeff John Frederick 1948- *WhoEmL 93*
Atkinson, John Bond 1950- *WhoEmL 93*
Atkinson, John Christopher 1948- *WhoWor 93*
Atkinson, John Herbert *WhoScE 91-1*
Atkinson, John Pepper 1942- *WhoSSW 93*
Atkinson, John Scott 1951- *WhoE 93*
Atkinson, John T. 1948- *St&PR 93*
Atkinson, Joseph William 1940- *St&PR 93*
Atkinson, Judith Ruth Elizabeth 1949- *WhoSSW 93*
Atkinson, Kathy Baley *Law&B 92*
Atkinson, Kathy Jo 1951- *WhoEmL 93*
Atkinson, Landis W., III *Law&B 92*
Atkinson, Larry Gordon 1951- *WhoEmL 93*
Atkinson, Laurence V. *WhoScE 91-1*
Atkinson, Lloyd C. 1942- *St&PR 93*
Atkinson, Lloyd Charles 1942- *WhoAm 92*
Atkinson, Lucy Jo 1931- *WhoWrEP 92*
Atkinson, Lynn Ann 1954- *WhoEmL 93*
Atkinson, Mayme Green 1925- *St&PR 93*
Atkinson, Michael Bernard 1949- *WhoSSW 93*
Atkinson, Nancy Lou Sheppeard 1940- *WhoSSW 93*
Atkinson, Paul Anthony *WhoScE 91-1*
Atkinson, Paul Phillip 1924- *WhoSSW 93*
Atkinson, Peter Alan 1952- *WhoE 93*
Atkinson, Regina Elizabeth 1952- *WhoAmW 93*
Atkinson, Richard Chatham 1929- *WhoAm 92, WhoWor 93*
Atkinson, Richard Collier 1942- *St&PR 93*
Atkinson, Richard Lee, Jr. 1942- *WhoSSW 93*
Atkinson, Robert Charles 1953- *WhoE 93*
Atkinson, Robert G. 1945- *WhoE 93*
Atkinson, Ronald *WhoScE 91-1*
Atkinson, Rowan 1955- *ConTFT 10*
Atkinson, Rupert Leigh 1938- *WhoWor 93*
Atkinson, Russell Welsh 1947- *St&PR 93*
Atkinson, Shannon Marlow 1962- *WhoAmW 93*
Atkinson, Stephanie R. *BioIn 17*
Atkinson, Stephen L. *Law&B 92*
Atkinson, Steven Douglas 1947- *WhoEmL 93*
Atkinson, Stuart *ScF&FL 92*
Atkinson, Susan D. 1944- *WhoAmW 93*
Atkinson, Theodore Edward, III 1955- *WhoE 93*
Atkinson, Thomas *WhoScE 91-1*
Atkinson, Valerie Jo 1959- *WhoAmW 93*
Atkinson, Walter Theodore, Jr. 1940- *WhoSSW 93*
Atkinson, William Christopher 1902-1992 *ConAu 139*
Atkinson, William Edward 1939- *WhoAm 92*
Atkinson, William H.W. 1943- *St&PR 93*
Atkinson, William L. *BioIn 17*
Atkinson, William Lee 1953- *WhoEmL 93*
Atkinson-Keen, Susan *ScF&FL 92*
Atkisson, Curtis T., Jr. 1933- *St&PR 93*
Atkisson, Curtis Trumbull, Jr. 1933- *WhoAm 92*
Atkyns, Robert Lee 1948- *WhoE 93*
Atl, Dr. *DcMexL*
Atlan, Guy *WhoScE 91-2*
Atlan, Paul 1942- *WhoWor 93*
Atlantic Starr *SoulM*
Atlantov, Vladimir 1939- *Baker 92, OxDcOp*
Atlas, Alan L. *Law&B 92*
Atlas, Allan Jay 1952- *WhoAm 92*
Atlas, Allan W(arren) 1943- *Baker 92*
Atlas, Allison *BioIn 17*
Atlas, Arthur 1945- *WhoE 93*
Atlas, Charles 1893-1972 *BioIn 17*
Atlas, Craig Mitchell 1959- *WhoEmL 93*
Atlas, David 1924- *WhoAm 92*
Atlas, James (Robert) 1949- *ConAu 138, WhoAm 92, WhoWrEP 92*
Atlas, Liane Wiener *WhoE 93*
Atlas, Randall I. 1953- *WhoEmL 93, WhoSSW 93*
Atlas, Scott Jerome 1950- *WhoAm 92, WhoEmL 93*
Atlas, Seth Jackson 1958- *WhoEmL 93*
Atlas, Vicki S. *Law&B 92*
Atlasov, Vladimir Vasilyevich d1711 *Expl 93*
Atlass, Michael B. *Law&B 92*
Atlee, Debbie Gayle 1955- *WhoAmW 93, WhoEmL 93*
Atlee, Philip 1915-1991 *BioIn 17*
Atler, Marilyn Van Derbur *BioIn 17*
Atlung, Tove 1952- *WhoScE 91-2*
Atluri, Satya Nadham 1945- *WhoAm 92*
Atluru, Sitaramaiah 1936- *St&PR 93*
Atmaca, Necmi 1948- *St&PR 93*
Atneosen, Steven Troy *Law&B 92*
Atnip, Michael Grant 1948- *St&PR 93*
Atobe, Yasuzo 1926- *WhoAm 92*
Aton, Mary Fredericka Lawhon 1930- *WhoAmW 93*
Ator, Donald Wilbur 1930- *WhoSSW 93*
Atran, Scott 1952- *WhoWor 93*
Atreya, Sushil Kumar 1946- *WhoAm 92*
Atsumi, Akio 1927- *WhoWor 93*
Attaignant, Pierre c. 1494-1552 *Baker 92*
Attaingnant, Pierre c. 1494-1552 *Baker 92*
Attal, Gene 1947- *WhoEmL 93, WhoSSW 93*
Attaleiates, Michael c. 1020-c. 1085 *OxDcByz*
Attali, Jacques *BioIn 17*
Attali, Jacques 1943- *WhoWor 93*
Attanasio, A.A. 1951- *ScF&FL 92*
Attanasio, A(lfred) A(ngelo) 1951- *ConAu 137*
Attanasio, John Baptist 1954- *WhoEmL 93*
Attanasio, John R. *Law&B 92*
Attanasio, Virginia 1958- *WhoE 93, WhoWor 93*
Attard, Janet 1944- *WhoWrEP 92*
Attardi, Charles, Jr. 1942- *St&PR 93*
Attardi, Giuseppe M. 1923- *WhoAm 92*
Attardo, Lewis Charles 1950- *WhoEmL 93*
Attardo, Loretta *Law&B 92*
Attardo, Michael J. 1941- *St&PR 93*
Attas, Haydar Abu Bakr al- 1939- *WhoWor 93*
Attaway, John Allen 1930- *WhoSSW 93*
Attaway, Julian J. 1926- *St&PR 93*
Attaway, Le Roy Banks, Jr. 1937- *WhoWrEP 92*
Attaway, William 1911-1986 *EncAACR*
Attea, Frederick G. 1939- *WhoAm 92*
Atteberry, James L. 1923- *WhoSSW 93*
Atteberry, William D. 1920- *St&PR 93*
Atteberry, William Duane 1920- *WhoAm 92*
Atteberry-Luckinbill, Clara DeAnn 1937- *WhoSSW 93*
Attebery, Brian 1951- *ScF&FL 92*
Attebery, Louie Wayne 1927- *WhoAm 92*
Attebury, Janice Marie 1954- *WhoAmW 93, WhoEmL 93*
Attee, Joyce Valerie Jungclas 1926- *WhoAmW 93*
Atteignant, Pierre c. 1494-1552 *Baker 92*
Atten, Pierre *WhoScE 91-2*
Attenborough, Family *BioIn 17*
Attenborough, Keith 1944- *WhoWor 93*
Attenborough, Philip John 1936- *WhoWor 93*
Attenborough, Richard *BioIn 17*
Attenborough, Richard 1923- *IntDcF 2-3 [port], MiSFD 9, WhoAm 92, WhoWor 93*
Attenborough, Richard (Samuel) 1923- *ConAu 139*
Attenhofer, Karl 1837-1914 *Baker 92*
Atterberg, Kurt 1887-1974 *Baker 92, OxDcOp*
Atterbury, Lee Richard 1948- *WhoEmL 93*
Atterbury, Robert Rennie, III *Law&B 92*
Atterbury, Robert Rennie, III 1937- *St&PR 93*
Atterbury, Thomas J. 1931- *St&PR 93*
Attermeier, Fredric Joseph 1946- *WhoSSW 93*
Atterton, P.E. *WhoScE 91-1*
Attewell, Peter Brian *WhoScE 91-1*
Attfield, Robin *ConAu 137*
Atthowe, Jean Fausett 1931- *WhoWrEP 92*
Attias, Daniel *MiSFD 9*
Attias, Diana *ScF&FL 92*
Attias, Sheila Telanoff 1935- *WhoE 93*
Attie, Dotty 1938- *BioIn 17*
Attieh, Bassam Wahab 1936- *WhoWor 93*
Attiga, Ali Ahmed 1931- *WhoUN 92*
Attikos *OxDcByz*
Attila d453 *OxDcByz*
Attila, King of the Huns d453 *BioIn 17*
Attinger, Ernst Otto 1922- *WhoAm 92*
Attix, Frank Herbert 1925- *WhoAm 92*
Attiyeh, Richard Eugene 1937- *WhoAm 92*
Attkisson, Carolyn S. *Law&B 92*
Attlee, Clement 1883-1967 *ColdWar 1 [port]*
Attlee, Clement Richard 1883-1967 *DcTwHis*
Attlee, Martin Richard 1927-1991 *BioIn 17*
Attles, Alvin A., Jr. 1936- *BiDAMSp 1989*
Attles, Joseph E. 1903-1990 *BioIn 17*
Attles, LeRoy 1966- *WhoSSW 93*
Attneave, Carolyn Lewis *BioIn 17*
Attolini, Jose 1916-1957 *DcMexL*
Attramadal, Audun 1931- *WhoScE 91-4*
Attridge, Geoffrey Giles *WhoScE 91-1*
Attridge, George N. 1928- *St&PR 93*
Attridge, Richard Byron 1933- *WhoAm 92*
Attstrom, Rolf Valter 1938- *WhoScE 91-4*
Attwell, Kirby 1935- *St&PR 93, WhoAm 92*
Attwell, Mabel Lucie 1879-1964 *BioIn 17*
Attwood, David Thomas 1941- *WhoAm 92*
Attwood, James Albert 1927- *St&PR 93*
Attwood, James Albert, Jr. 1958- *WhoE 93, WhoEmL 93*
Attwood, Madge Louise 1928- *WhoAmW 93*
Attwood, Thomas 1765-1838 *Baker 92, OxDcOp*
Attwood, Thomas 1783-1856 *BioIn 17*
Attwood, Tony 1947- *ScF&FL 92*
Atumano, Simon d1383? *OxDcByz*
Atwater, Florence Carroll 1896-1979 *BioIn 17*
Atwater, Florence (Hasseltine Carroll) 1896-1979 *MajAI*
Atwater, Franklin S. 1916- *St&PR 93*
Atwater, Harvey Leroy 1951-1991 *BioIn 17*
Atwater, Horace Brewster, Jr. 1931- *St&PR 93, WhoAm 92*
Atwater, James David 1928- *WhoAm 92*
Atwater, John 1954- *BioIn 17*
Atwater, John Richard 1954- *WhoE 93*
Atwater, John Spencer 1913- *WhoAm 92*

Atwater, Lee 1951-1991 *AnObit 1991, BioIn 17*
Atwater, Marshall Anderson 1940- *WhoE 93*
Atwater, N. William 1934- *WhoAm 92*
Atwater, Neil William 1934- *St&PR 93*
Atwater, Phyllis Yvonne 1947- *WhoAmW 93*
Atwater, Richard Merlin 1946- *WhoWrEP 92*
Atwater, Richard Tupper 1892-1948 *BioIn 17, MajAI*
Atwater, Sally *BioIn 17*
Atwater, Verne Stafford 1920- *WhoAm 92*
Atwater, Wilbur Olin 1844-1907 *BioIn 17*
Atwell, Charles McHugh 1939- *St&PR 93*
Atwell, Constance Woodruff 1942- *WhoAm 92, WhoAmW 93*
Atwell, Robert Herron 1931- *WhoAm 92, WhoE 93*
Atwell-Holler, Rita Irene 1941- *WhoAmW 93, WhoWrEP 92*
Atwill, Douglas *BioIn 17*
Atwill, Jane Hickman 1953- *WhoSSW 93*
Atwill, Lionel 1885-1946 *BioIn 17*
Atwill, William Henry 1932- *WhoSSW 93*
Atwood, Ann Margaret 1913- *WhoAm 92*
Atwood, Brian G. *St&PR 93*
Atwood, Bruce Gilbert 1937- *St&PR 93*
Atwood, Carol Ann 1945- *WhoAmW 93*
Atwood, Charles E., III 1946- *St&PR 93*
Atwood, Diana Field 1946- *WhoAmW 93, WhoEmL 93*
Atwood, Donald J. *BioIn 17*
Atwood, Donald J. 1924- *CngDr 91*
Atwood, Donald Jesse, Jr. 1924- *WhoAm 92*
Atwood, Donald Keith 1933- *WhoAm 92*
Atwood, Edward Charles 1922- *WhoAm 92*
Atwood, Genevieve 1946- *WhoAm 92*
Atwood, Harold Leslie 1937- *WhoAm 92*
Atwood, Horace, Jr. 1918- *St&PR 93*
Atwood, James R. 1944- *WhoAm 92*
Atwood, Jane Coles 1952- *WhoEmL 93*
Atwood, Jeffrey B. 1948- *WhoWrEP 92*
Atwood, Jeffrey Nelson 1950- *WhoE 93*
Atwood, Kelly Palmer 1946- *WhoEmL 93*
Atwood, Kimball Chase, III d1992 *NewYTBS 92*
Atwood, Margaret 1939- *BioIn 17, IntLitE, MagSWL [port], ScF&FL 92, WhoCanL 92, WorLitC [port]*
Atwood, Margaret Eleanor 1939- *WhoAm 92, WhoAmW 93, WhoWrEP 92*
Atwood, Margaret Jane 1952- *WhoEmL 93*
Atwood, Mary Sanford 1935- *WhoAmW 93*
Atwood, Peter J. 1965- *WhoWrEP 92*
Atwood, Raymond Percival, Jr. 1952- *WhoEmL 93*
Atwood, Robert Bruce 1907- *WhoAm 92*
Atwood, Susan Jennifer 1956- *WhoAmW 93*
Atwood, Thomas Donald 1940- *St&PR 93*
Atzberger, Frank J. 1937- *St&PR 93*
Atzeff, Efrodita 1912- *WhoAmW 93*
Atzerodt, George d1865 *BioIn 17*
Atzert, Jill L. 1961- *St&PR 93*
Atzmueller, Hugo Johann 1951- *WhoWor 93*
Au, Alice Man-Jing *WhoAmW 93*
Au, Leo Yuin 1949- *St&PR 93*
Au, Patrick Shu-Keung 1950- *WhoWor 93*
Au, Tung 1923- *WhoAm 92*
Au, William August, III 1949- *WhoE 93, WhoEmL 93*
Aub, A. Edgar, Jr. 1928- *St&PR 93*
Aub, Max 1903-1972 *DcMexL*
Aube, Howard James 1961- *WhoEmL 93*
Aube, Randy Alan 1957- *WhoEmL 93*
Aubel, Joseph Lee 1936- *WhoSSW 93*
Auber, Daniel-Francois-Esprit 1782-1871 *Baker 92, IntDcOp [port], OxDcOp*
Auberjonois, Rene Murat 1940- *WhoAm 92*
Auberry, Horace 1931- *St&PR 93*
Aubert, Alvin *BioIn 17*
Aubert, B. 1936- *WhoScE 91-2*
Aubert, Guy 1929- *WhoScE 91-2*
Aubert, Jacques 1689-1753 *Baker 92*
Aubert, Jacques 1947- *St&PR 93*
Aubert, Jean-Jacques 1943- *WhoScE 91-2*
Aubert, Louis-Francois-Marie 1877-1968 *Baker 92*
Aubert, Rosemary 1946- *WhoCanL 92*
Aubert, Y. *WhoScE 91-2*
Aubert de Gaspe, Philippe-Ignace-Francois 1814-1841 *BioIn 17*
Aubert de Gaspe, Philippe-Joseph 1786-1871 *BioIn 17*
Aubery du Boulley, Prudent-Louis 1796-1869 *Baker 92*
Aubin, Bruce R. 1931- *St&PR 93*
Aubin, Denis 1951- *St&PR 93*
Aubin, Gary Paul 1945- *WhoE 93*
Aubin, Horace de Saint- *ScF&FL 92*
Aubin, Napoleon 1812-1890 *BioIn 17*
Aubin, Thomas William 1953- *WhoAm 92*
Aubin, Tony (Louis Alexandre) 1907-1981 *Baker 92*
Aubin, William Mark 1929- *WhoE 93*
Aubke, Friedhelm 1932- *WhoAm 92*
Aubock, Carl *WhoScE 91-4*
Aubouin, Jean Armand 1928- *WhoScE 91-2, WhoWor 93*
Aubrecht, Richard Albert 1944- *St&PR 93*
Aubrey, Crispin 1946- *ScF&FL 92*
Aubrey, Frank 1840-1927 *ScF&FL 92*
Aubrey, John 1626-1697 *BioIn 17*
Aubrey, Oliver Warren 1921- *WhoWor 93*
Aubrey, Robert Joseph 1948- *WhoWor 93*
Aubrey, Roger Frederick 1929- *WhoAm 92*
Aubrook, Edward W. 1915-1990 *BioIn 17*
Aubry, Claude B. 1914-1984 *WhoCanL 92*
Aubry, Eugene Edwards 1935- *WhoAm 92*
Aubry, Lloyd Walter 1924- *St&PR 93*
Aubry, Pierre 1874-1910 *Baker 92*
Aubry, Serge J. 1945- *WhoScE 91-2*
Aubry, Vicki Ann 1953- *WhoEmL 93*
Aubuchon, Bernard W., Sr. 1926- *St&PR 93*
Aubuchon, Jacques d1991 *NewYTBS 92*
Aubuchon, Jacques 1924-1991 *BioIn 17*
Aubuchon, James L. *Law&B 92*
Aubuchon, William Edward, Jr. 1916- *St&PR 93*
Auburn, Norman Paul 1905- *WhoAm 92*
Auburn, Pamela Rae 1954- *WhoSSW 93*
Auburn, Stephen T. *Law&B 92*
Aubut, Marcel 1948- *WhoAm 92, WhoE 93*
Aucella, Peter Joseph 1952- *WhoEmL 93*
Auch, Stephen Edward 1930- *St&PR 93*
Auch, Walter E. 1921- *St&PR 93*
Auch, Walter Edward 1921- *WhoAm 92*
Auchincloss, Adele Lawrence d1991 *BioIn 17*
Auchincloss, Kenneth 1937- *WhoAm 92*
Auchincloss, Louis *BioIn 17*
Auchincloss, Louis 1917- *MagSAmL [port]*
Auchincloss, Louis Stanton 1917- *WhoAm 92, WhoE 93, WhoWor 93, WhoWrEP 92*
Auchincloss, Reginald L., Jr. d1992 *NewYTBS 92*
Auchincloss, Samuel Sloan, Jr. 1942- *WhoAm 92*
Auchincloss, Sarah Sedgwick 1949- *WhoEmL 93*
Auchinleck, Claude John Ayre 1884-1981 *HarEnMi*
Auchinleck, Claude John Eyre 1884-1981 *BioIn 17, DcTwHis*
Auciello, Orlando Hector 1945- *WhoWor 93*
Auckenthaler, Alan *Law&B 92*
Auckerman, Raymond A. 1944- *WhoIns 93*
Auckland, James Craig 1948- *WhoEmL 93, WhoSSW 93*
Auckland, John Neil *WhoScE 91-1*
Auclair, Daniel 1951- *WhoScE 91-2*
Auclair, Jacques Lucien 1923- *WhoAm 92*
Auclair, Joan *BioIn 17*
Auclair, Michel 1950- *St&PR 93*
Auclair, Robert A. 1937- *St&PR 93*
Auclair, Sue 1949- *WhoEmL 93*
Aucoin, John Hubert 1943- *St&PR 93*
AuCoin, Les 1942- *CngDr 91, WhoAm 92*
Aucoin, Lindy Bode *Law&B 92*
Aucone, James Joseph 1941- *WhoAm 92*
Aucott, George W. 1934- *WhoAm 92*
Aucremanne, Daniel Q. 1955- *St&PR 93*
Auda, Antoine 1879-1964 *Baker 92*
Aude, Claudette *WhoCanL 92*
Audema, M. *WhoScE 91-2*
Auden, Renee 1928- *ScF&FL 92*
Auden, W.H. 1907-1973 *BioIn 17, MagSWL [port], OxDcOp, WorLitC [port]*
Auden, W(ystan) H(ugh) 1907-1973 *IntDcOp*
Auden, Wystan Hugh 1907-1973 *BioIn 17*
Audet, Armand Albert 1934- *St&PR 93*
Audet, Barbara Grouls 1930- *WhoAmW 93*
Audet, David Arthur 1957- *WhoE 93*
Audet, Henri 1918- *WhoAm 92*
Audet, Leonard 1932- *WhoAm 92*
Audet, Paul Andre 1923- *WhoAm 92*
Audet, Paul R. *Law&B 92*
Audet, Rene 1920- *WhoAm 92*
Audet, Richard *St&PR 93*
Audett, Theophilus Bernard 1905- *WhoWor 93*
Audhali, Ahmed Abdulla 1945- *WhoWor 93*
Audi, Alfred J. 1938- *St&PR 93*
Audi, Aminy Inati 1937- *St&PR 93*
Audia, Christina 1941- *WhoAm 92*
Audia, Joseph 1958- *WhoSSW 93*
Audiffret-Pasquier, duc d' 1823-1905 *BioIn 17*
Audije, Ana Lee Farcon 1965- *WhoAmW 93*
Audino, Diane Mary 1961- *St&PR 93*
Audino, Joseph Vincent 1949- *WhoEmL 93*
Audley, Barbara Marie 1940- *WhoAmW 93*
Audley-Charles, Michael Geoffrey *WhoScE 91-1*
Audlin, David John, Jr. 1957- *WhoEmL 93*
Audoly, Christian Daniel 1960- *WhoWor 93*
Audone, Bruno *WhoScE 91-3*
Audouze, Francoise *WhoScE 91-2*
Audouze, Jean 1940- *WhoScE 91-2, WhoWor 93*
Audran, Edmond 1840-1901 *Baker 92, OxDcOp*
Audran, Marius-Pierre 1816-1887 *Baker 92*
Audran, Stephane 1932- *IntDcF 2-3 [port]*
Audretsch, Jurgen 1942- *WhoScE 91-3*
Audry, Colette 1906-1990 *BioIn 17*
Audsley, Eric 1949- *WhoScE 91-1*
Audubon, John James 1785-1851 *BioIn 17*
Audunson, Tore 1939- *WhoScE 91-4*
Auel, Jean M. *BioIn 17*
Auel, Jean M. 1936- *ScF&FL 92*
Auel, Jean M(arie) 1936- *WhoWrEP 92*
Auel, Jean Marie 1936- *WhoAm 92, WhoAmW 93*
Auer, Albert K. 1948- *St&PR 93*
Auer, James Matthew 1928- *WhoAm 92*
Auer, John 1937- *St&PR 93*
Auer, Leopold 1845-1930 *Baker 92*
Auer, Ludwig M. *WhoScE 91-4*
Auer, Martin S. d1991 *BioIn 17*
Auer, Max 1880-1962 *Baker 92*
Auer, Mischa 1905-1967 *QDrFCA 92 [port]*
Auerbach, Alan Bruce 1952- *St&PR 93*
Auerbach, Alan Jeffrey 1951- *WhoAm 92, WhoEmL 93*
Auerbach, Anita L. 1946- *WhoSSW 93*
Auerbach, Arnold 1917- *BioIn 17*
Auerbach, Beatrice Fox 1887-1968 *BioIn 17*
Auerbach, Berthold 1812-1882 *BioIn 17*
Auerbach, Boris *Law&B 92*
Auerbach, Boris 1931- *St&PR 93, WhoAm 92*
Auerbach, Bradford Carlton *Law&B 92*
Auerbach, Bradford Carlton 1957- *WhoEmL 93*
Auerbach, Carl Abraham 1915- *WhoAm 92*
Auerbach, Cornelia 1900- *See* Schroder, Hanning 1896-1987 *Baker 92*
Auerbach, David A. 1943- *St&PR 93*
Auerbach, Earl 1922- *St&PR 93*
Auerbach, Ernest Sigmund 1936- *WhoAm 92*
Auerbach, Frank 1931- *WhoWor 93*
Auerbach, Frank H. 1931- *BioIn 17*
Auerbach, Isaac L. d1992 *NewYTBS 92*
Auerbach, Isaac L. 1921- *St&PR 93, WhoAm 92*
Auerbach, Joel Ira 1946- *WhoWor 93*
Auerbach, Jonathan 1954- *ScF&FL 92*
Auerbach, Joseph 1916- *WhoAm 92*
Auerbach, Kay Joan 1936- *WhoAmW 93*
Auerbach, Marci Fay 1955- *WhoAmW 93*
Auerbach, Marshall Jay 1932- *WhoAm 92, WhoWor 93*
Auerbach, Michael Howard 1943- *WhoAm 92*
Auerbach, Norman E. 1920- *St&PR 93*
Auerbach, Paul A. *Law&B 92*
Auerbach, Philip 1926- *St&PR 93*
Auerbach, Philip B. 1923- *WhoE 93*
Auerbach, Red 1917- *BioIn 17, WhoAm 92, WhoE 93*
Auerbach, Seymour 1929- *WhoAm 92*
Auerbach, Sheryl Lynn 1952- *WhoEmL 93*
Auerbach, Stanley Irving 1921- *WhoAm 92*
Auerbach, Stuart Charles 1935- *WhoAm 92*
Auerbach, Sylvia *WhoE 93*
Auerbach, Victor 1917- *WhoE 93*
Auerbach, Victor Hugo 1928- *WhoE 93*
Auerbach, Wendy Evelyne 1942- *WhoSSW 93*
Auerbach, William 1914- *WhoAm 92*
Auerbacher, Peter 1950- *WhoWor 93*
Auerbach-Levy, William 1889-1964 *BioIn 17*
Auerback, Alfred 1915- *WhoAm 92*
Auerback, Sandra Jean 1946- *WhoAmW 93, WhoEmL 93*
Auernhammer, Hermann 1941- *WhoScE 91-3*
Auernheimer, Mark Edward 1964- *WhoSSW 93*
Auerswald, David Christian 1946- *WhoEmL 93*
Aufdenkamp, Jo Ann 1926- *WhoAmW 93*
Aufderheide, Patricia Ann 1948- *WhoAmW 93, WhoE 93*
Auffray, Charles 1951- *WhoScE 91-2*
Aufhauser, Alfred 1910- *St&PR 93*
Aufiero, Vincent James d1990 *BioIn 17*
Aufox, Jerry M. 1942- *St&PR 93*
Aufox, Jerry Michael *Law&B 92*
Aufses, Arthur Harold, Jr. 1926- *WhoAm 92*
Aug, Stephen M. 1936- *WhoAm 92, WhoE 93*
Augarde, Lester William Bryan *WhoScE 91-1*
Augat, Ernest H. 1906- *St&PR 93*
Auge, Bradley Keith 1950- *St&PR 93*
Augelli, John Pat 1921- *WhoAm 92*
Augello, Paul John, Jr. 1966- *WhoE 93*
Augello, William Joseph 1926- *WhoAm 92*
Augenblick, Harry A. 1926- *St&PR 93*
Augener, George 1830-1915 *Baker 92*
Augenstein, Bruno W. 1923- *WhoAm 92*
Auger, Arleen 1939- *OxDcOp, WhoAm 92*
Auger, Arleen (Joyce) 1939- *Baker 92*
Auger, David J. *WhoAm 92*
Auger, Harvey J. 1947- *WhoAm 92*
Auger, Harvey Joseph, Jr. 1947- *St&PR 93*
Auger, Regis *WhoCanL 92*
Auger, Ronald 1942- *St&PR 93*
Auger, Simone *WhoAm 92*
Auger, Yolanda Marshall 1934- *WhoUN 92*
Augereau, Pierre Francois Charles 1757-1816 *HarEnMi*
Augerson, Scott William 1949- *WhoWrEP 92*
Augerson, William S. 1927- *St&PR 93*
Aughinbaugh, Patricia Bartley 1950- *WhoAmW 93*
Augier, Angel 1919- *SpAmA*
Augmon, Stacey *BioIn 17*
Augsburger, Aaron Donald 1925- *WhoAm 92*
Augsburger, Lee D. *Law&B 92*
Augsburger, Myron S. 1929- *WhoE 93*
Augspurger, Karol W. *Law&B 92*
Augspurger, Lynn L. *Law&B 92*
Augstein, Ernst 1934- *WhoScE 91-3*
Augstein, Rudolf 1923- *WhoWor 93*
Augur, Marilyn Hussman 1938- *WhoSSW 93*
Augusciak, Joseph S. *Law&B 92*
August, Bille 1948- *MiSFD 9, WhoAm 92, WhoWor 93*
August, Casey Paul *Law&B 92*
August, Joan Frieda 1948- *WhoAmW 93*
August, Katherine 1948- *WhoEmL 93*
August, Robert Olin 1921- *WhoAm 92*
August, Robert Werner 1952- *St&PR 93*
August, Robin Lynn 1949- *WhoSSW 93*
August, Rudolf 1926- *WhoAm 92, WhoWor 93*
August, Stanley 1931- *St&PR 93*
Auguste, Macdonald 1948- *St&PR 93*
Auguste Le Breton 1913- *WhoWor 93*
Augusti, Giuliano 1935- *WhoScE 91-3, WhoWor 93*
Augustijn, Govert J.P. 1937- *WhoScE 91-3*
Augustin, Antoine 1947- *WhoWor 93*
Augustin, Family *BioIn 17*
Augustin, Raymond William *Law&B 92*
Augustine 354-430 *OxDcByz*
Augustine, Saint, Bishop of Hippo *BioIn 17*
Augustine, Aurelius 354-430 *Baker 92*
Augustine, Bradford Gordon 1959- *WhoEmL 93*
Augustine, Cynthia H. *Law&B 92*
Augustine, Daniel Gerald 1946- *St&PR 93*
Augustine, James Robert 1946- *WhoEmL 93, WhoSSW 93*
Augustine, Jane 1931- *WhoWrEP 92*
Augustine, Jaqueline Rose 1950- *WhoAm 92*
Augustine, Jeffrey B. 1953- *St&PR 93*
Augustine, Jerome Samuel 1928- *WhoAm 92, WhoWor 93*
Augustine, John H. *Law&B 92*
Augustine, Matthew 1944- *St&PR 93*
Augustine, Mildred *MajAI*
Augustine, Norman R. 1935- *BioIn 17, St&PR 93*
Augustine, Norman Ralph 1935- *WhoAm 92, WhoE 93*
Augustine, Richard John 1946- *St&PR 93*
Augustine, Robert Leo 1932- *WhoE 93*
Augustine, Ronald Sylvester 1938- *WhoWor 93*
Augustine, Rose Marie *BioIn 17*
Augustine, Theodore Francis 1946- *St&PR 93*
Augustinus, Aurelius 354-430 *Baker 92*
Augustus, Emperor of Rome 63BC-14AD *BioIn 17*

Augustus, II 1670-1733 *PolBiDi*
Augustus, Gaius Julius Caesar Octavianus 63BC-14AD *HarEnMi*
Augustyn, Frank Joseph 1953- *WhoAm 92*
Augustyn, Frederick John, Jr. 1951- *WhoE 93, WhoEmL 93*
Augustyn, Noel James 1946- *WhoEmL 93*
Auh, Yang John 1934- *WhoWor 93*
Aukerman, Dale H. 1930- *WhoE 93*
Aukland, Duncan Dayton 1954- *WhoEmL 93*
Aukland, Knut 1929- *WhoScE 91-4*
Aukrust, Lars *WhoScE 91-4*
Aukward Hartnett, Monica Elizabeth 1956- *WhoAmW 93*
Aulbach, George Louis 1925- *WhoAm 92, WhoSSW 93, WhoWor 93*
Auld, Bertram Alexander 1922- *WhoAm 92*
Auld, Bruce 1954- *WhoEmL 93*
Auld, Douglas G. 1948- *St&PR 93*
Auld, Frank 1923- *WhoAm 92*
Auld, John Harvey, II 1946- *WhoEmL 93*
Auld, Michael I. 1945- *St&PR 93*
Aulenbach, William Craig 1951- *WhoEmL 93*
Aulenti, Anthony Russell 1950- *St&PR 93*
Aulenti, Gae *BioIn 17*
Auletta, Ken *BioIn 17*
Auletta, Pat V. d1991 *BioIn 17*
Auletta, Patrick Vincent 1950- *St&PR 93*
Auletta, Pietro c. 1698-1771 *Baker 92, OxDcOp*
Auletta, Richard C. 1937- *St&PR 93*
Auletta Armenise, Giovanni *BioIn 17*
Aulette, Judy Root 1948- *WhoEmL 93, WhoSSW 93*
Aulich, Chris *ScF&FL 92*
Aulich, Terence Gordon 1945- *WhoAsAP 91*
Aulin, Laura Valborg 1860-1928 *Baker 92*
Aulin, Tor (Bernhard Vilhelm) 1866-1914 *Baker 92*
Aulitzky, Herbert 1922- *WhoWor 93*
Aull, Elizabeth Berryman 1951- *WhoEmL 93*
Aull, Jeffrey Lee 1949- *St&PR 93*
Aulnoy, Madame d' 1650?-1705 *BioIn 17*
Aulson, Patrick J. 1951- *St&PR 93, WhoIns 93*
Aulson, Patrick Joseph 1951- *WhoSSW 93*
Ault, Charles Rollin 1923- *WhoAm 92*
Ault, Ethyl Lorita 1939- *WhoAmW 93, WhoWor 93*
Ault, Frank H. 1944- *St&PR 93*
Ault, Hugh Joseph 1940- *WhoAm 92*
Ault, James Mase 1918- *WhoAm 92*
Ault, John Brady 1951- *WhoEmL 93*
Ault, John L. 1946- *St&PR 93*
Ault, Lee A., III 1936- *St&PR 93, WhoAm 92*
Ault, Neil Norman 1922- *WhoE 93*
Ault, O. E. 1899- *ScF&FL 92*
Ault, Thomas Jefferson, III 1911- *WhoAm 92*
Ault, Warren Ortman 1887-1989 *BioIn 17*
Aultman, Donnald Boyd 1954- *St&PR 93*
Aultman, Larry Louis 1947- *WhoSSW 93*
Aultman, Mark *ScF&FL 92*
Aultman, William W. 1924- *St&PR 93*
Aumack, Shirley Jean 1949- *WhoAmW 93*
Aumaitre, Louis A. 1935- *WhoScE 91-2*
Aumala, K. Olli 1939- *WhoScE 91-4*
Aumala, Olli 1939- *WhoWor 93*
Aumale, duc d' 1822-1897 *BioIn 17*
Auman, Delbert A. 1926- *St&PR 93*
Auman, Dorothy 1925-1991 *BioIn 17*
Auman, Walter 1926-1991 *BioIn 17*
Aumiller, G.E. 1937- *St&PR 93*
Aumiller, Gary Steven 1956- *WhoE 93*
Aumiller, Sandra Lee 1953- *WhoAmW 93*
Aumont, Jean-Pierre 1911- *WhoAm 92*
Aumuller, Ludwig *WhoScE 91-3*
Aune, Jon Brian 1939- *St&PR 93*
Aune, Thomas Martin 1951- *WhoE 93*
Aung San 1914-1947 *DcTwHis*
Aung San 1916-1947 *HarEnMi*
Aung San Suu Kyi *BioIn 17, WhoAsAP 91*
Aung San Suu Kyi 1945- *CurBio 92 [port]*
Aungst, Bruce Jeffrey 1952- *WhoE 93*
Aunstrup, Knud 1932- *WhoScE 91-2*
Auping, Michael G. 1949- *WhoAm 92*
Aura, Alejandro 1944- *DcMexL*
Aurand, Charles Henry, Jr. 1932- *WhoAm 92*
Auray, Delbert 1962- *St&PR 93*
Aurbach, Gerald D. 1927-1991 *BioIn 17*
Aurbach, Herbert Alexander 1924- *WhoAm 92*
Aured, C. Fred 1934- *St&PR 93*
Aureli, Aurelio d1708 *IntDcOp*
Aureli, Aurelio fl. 1652-1708 *OxDcOp*
Aureli, Giles 1926- *WhoAm 92*
Aureli, Massimo 1946- *WhoUN 92*
Aurelianus Reomensis *Baker 92*
Aurelio, John *BioIn 17*
Aurelio, Richard 1929- *St&PR 93*
Aurelio, Richard Roberto Luigi *BioIn 17*
Aurelius, Brynn F. *Law&B 92*
Aurelius Victor, Sextus c. 320-c. 389 *OxDcByz*
Aurell, John Karl 1935- *WhoAm 92*
Aurell, N. Mattias 1934- *WhoScE 91-4*
Aurer-Kozelj, Jelena 1934- *WhoScE 91-4*
Auriacombe, Louis 1917-1982 *Baker 92*
Auriana, Lawrence *St&PR 93*
Auric, Georges 1899-1983 *Baker 92*
Aurich, Harald 1932- *WhoScE 91-3*
Aurichio, Joseph L. 1931- *St&PR 93*
Aurichio, Joseph Louis 1931- *WhoAm 92*
Auriema, Carlos 1925- *St&PR 93*
Auriemma, Donald Joseph 1942- *St&PR 93*
Auriemma, Geno *BioIn 17*
Auriemma, Louis Francis 1937- *St&PR 93, WhoAm 92*
Auriemmo, Frank J., Jr. 1942- *WhoIns 93*
Auriemmo, Frank Joseph, Jr. 1942- *St&PR 93, WhoAm 92*
Aurientis, Dominique *BioIn 17*
Aurigema, Robert J. *Law&B 92*
Aurin, Robert James 1943- *WhoAm 92*
Auriol, Jean-Marc 1931- *WhoWor 93*
Auriol, Paul J. 1927- *WhoScE 91-3*
Auriol, Vincent 1884-1966 *BioIn 17, DcTwHis*
Auritt, Robert David 1951- *St&PR 93*
Aurner, Robert Ray 1898- *WhoAm 92*
Aurner, Robert Ray, II 1927- *WhoE 93, WhoWor 93*
Aurobindo, Sri 1872-1950 *BioIn 17*
Aurora, Sardar Jagjit Singh 1917- *WhoAsAP 91*
Aurousseau, Michel E. 1926- *WhoScE 91-2*
Aus, Rose Marie Goetz 1934- *WhoAmW 93*
Ausanka, John Joseph, III 1943- *St&PR 93*
Aus der Ohe, Adele 1864-1937 *Baker 92*
Ausefski, James A. 1949- *St&PR 93*
Ausere, Joe Morris 1929- *St&PR 93, WhoAm 92*
Ausfahl, William Friend 1940- *St&PR 93*
Ausland, John C. 1920- *WhoWor 93*
Ausman, LaVerne 1930- *WhoAm 92*
Ausman, Robert K. 1933- *St&PR 93, WhoAm 92*
Ausmus, Jacqueline Rhnea 1958- *WhoAmW 93*
Ausmus, James T. *Law&B 92*
Ausmus, James T. 1937- *St&PR 93*
Ausnehmer, John Edward 1954- *WhoEmL 93*
Ausseil, Jean 1925- *WhoWor 93*
Aussel, Claude 1946- *WhoScE 91-2*
Aussel, Jean-Paul 1956- *WhoWor 93*
Aussenac, Gilbert Christian 1937- *WhoScE 91-2*
Ausserer, Roy Louis 1922- *St&PR 93*
Aussure, Pierre 1952- *WhoWor 93*
Aust, Gerald Aldric 1950- *St&PR 93*
Aust, Joe Bradley 1926- *WhoAm 92*
Aust, Steven Douglas 1938- *WhoAm 92*
Austad, Carol Shaw 1946- *WhoAmW 93*
Austad, David Brian 1960- *St&PR 93*
Austad, Oscar Melvin 1922- *St&PR 93*
Austad, Vigdis 1954- *WhoAm 92, WhoE 93, WhoEmL 93*
Austel, Volkhard 1939- *WhoWor 93*
Austell, Edward Callaway 1937- *St&PR 93, WhoAm 92*
Austell, Elizabeth Garrison 1960- *WhoSSW 93*
Austen, George 1941- *St&PR 93*
Austen, Hallie Iglehart 1947- *WhoEmL 93*
Austen, Jane 1775-1817 *BioIn 17, DcLB 116 [port], MagSWL [port], WorLitC [port]*
Austen, Karl Frank 1928- *WhoAm 92, WhoE 93*
Austen, William Gerald 1930- *WhoAm 92, WhoWor 93*
Auster, Carol Jean 1954- *WhoAmW 93*
Auster, Clark C. 1924- *St&PR 93*
Auster, Douglas *Law&B 92*
Auster, Kenneth 1953- *St&PR 93*
Auster, Lawrence Scott 1947- *WhoIns 93*
Auster, Paul 1947- *BioIn 17, NewYTBS 92 [port], ScF&FL 92, WhoAm 92, WhoWrEP 92*
Austerlade, Evald K. 1932- *St&PR 93*
Austermann, Richard Oates *Law&B 92*
Austill, Allen 1927- *WhoAm 92*
Austin, Alan Douglas 1939- *WhoE 93*
Austin, Alex 1925-1985 *ScF&FL 92*
Austin, Alicia 1942- *ScF&FL 92*
Austin, Allen Earle 1942- *WhoE 93*
Austin, Arthur Donald, II 1932- *WhoAm 92*
Austin, Barbara Elizabeth 1941- *WhoAmW 93, WhoSSW 93*
Austin, Berit Synnove 1938- *WhoAmW 93*
Austin, Brett M. 1944- *St&PR 93*
Austin, Brock J. *Law&B 92*
Austin, Bruce Phillips *Law&B 92*
Austin, Catherine Brannelly 1955- *WhoAmW 93*
Austin, Cathy Kiselyak 1954- *WhoEmL 93*
Austin, Charles A., III 1934- *St&PR 93*
Austin, Charles Edwin 1928- *WhoAm 92*
Austin, Charles John 1934- *WhoAm 92*
Austin, Charles L. d1992 *NewYTBS 92*
Austin, Charles Thomas 1932- *St&PR 93*
Austin, Cheryl Lynne 1955- *WhoAmW 93, WhoEmL 93*
Austin, Dan 1929- *WhoSSW 93*
Austin, Daniel William 1949- *WhoEmL 93*
Austin, Darrel 1907- *WhoAm 92*
Austin, David George 1951- *WhoEmL 93*
Austin, David Mayo 1923- *WhoAm 92*
Austin, Deborah Ruth 1953- *WhoEmL 93*
Austin, Doris Jean *BioIn 17*
Austin, Dorothy Mayover 1931- *WhoAmW 93, WhoWor 93*
Austin, Dwight Warren 1940- *St&PR 93*
Austin, Edward *WhoAm 92*
Austin, Ernest 1874-1947 *Baker 92*
Austin, Florence 1884-1927 *Baker 92*
Austin, Frank Holm 1952- *WhoSSW 93*
Austin, Fred C. *WhoAm 92*
Austin, Fred C. 1926- *St&PR 93*
Austin, Frederic 1872-1952 *Baker 92, OxDcOp*
Austin, Gabriel Christopher 1935- *WhoAm 92*
Austin, Gail A. *Law&B 92*
Austin, Garrett Edward *Law&B 92*
Austin, George Kenneth, Jr. 1931- *St&PR 93*
Austin, Grace Baliunas 1940- *WhoAm 92, WhoAmW 93*
Austin, Grace Jewett 1872-1948 *AmWomPl*
Austin, Gregory Alan 1945- *St&PR 93*
Austin, Harry George, III 1958- *St&PR 93*
Austin, Harry Gregory 1936- *WhoAm 92*
Austin, Harry Guiden 1917- *WhoAm 92*
Austin, Helen Atwood *AmWomPl*
Austin, Helen H. *AmWomPl*
Austin, Henry Richter 1882-1961 *Baker 92*
Austin, Hudson *DcCPCAm*
Austin, Ian George 1951- *St&PR 93*
Austin, Irma Caroline 1941- *WhoAmW 93*
Austin, Jacob 1932- *WhoAm 92*
Austin, James *BioIn 17*
Austin, James E. 1942- *St&PR 93*
Austin, James W., III *Law&B 92*
Austin, James William 1906- *WhoAm 92*
Austin, Jennifer Sue 1963- *WhoAmW 93*
Austin, Jerry L. 1932- *St&PR 93*
Austin, Joan Donna 1931- *St&PR 93*
Austin, John David 1936- *WhoAm 92*
Austin, John Norman 1937- *WhoAm 92*
Austin, John Robert 1951- *WhoEmL 93*
Austin, John Teufel 1925- *St&PR 93*
Austin, John Turnell 1869-1948 *Baker 92*
Austin, Jon Nicholas 1959- *WhoE 93*
Austin, Judith 1940- *WhoAmW 93*
Austin, Judy Essary 1948- *WhoAmW 93*
Austin, Karen Elaine 1949- *WhoAmW 93*
Austin, Karen S. *Law&B 92*
Austin, Larry (Don) 1930- *Baker 92*
Austin, Leland M., Jr. 1943- *St&PR 93*
Austin, Linda LaRue 1945- *WhoAmW 93*
Austin, Lucille Carroll 1950- *WhoEmL 93*
Austin, Margaret Elizabeth 1933- *WhoAsAP 91*
Austin, Margot d1990 *BioIn 17*
Austin, Marion Russell 1927- *WhoE 93*
Austin, Marshall Edward 1957- *WhoE 93, WhoEmL 93*
Austin, Mary 1868-1934 *GayN*
Austin, Mary Hunter 1868-1934 *AmWomPl, AmWomWr 92, BioIn 17*
Austin, Mary Jane 1931- *WhoAmW 93*
Austin, Max Eugene 1933- *WhoAm 92*
Austin, Michael Charles 1955- *WhoE 93, WhoEmL 93, WhoWrEP 92*
Austin, Nancy Elizabeth 1953- *WhoWrEP 92*
Austin, Norman K. 1953- *WhoEmL 93*
Austin, Ormand R. *Law&B 92*
Austin, Page Insley 1942- *WhoAmW 93*
Austin, Patricia *WhoWrEP 92*
Austin, Patricia J. *Law&B 92*
Austin, Patricia Quinn 1958- *WhoE 93*
Austin, Patti 1948- *SoulM*
Austin, Penelope Wilkinson 1951- *WhoAmW 93*
Austin, Philip Edward 1942- *WhoAm 92, WhoSSW 93*
Austin, Phylis Ann 1943- *WhoWrEP 92*
Austin, R.G. 1937- *ScF&FL 92*
Austin, Randolph L. 1940- *St&PR 93*
Austin, Randolph Lee 1940- *WhoAm 92*
Austin, Ray 1932- *MiSFD 9*
Austin, Raymond Darrel 1953- *WhoEmL 93*
Austin, Reginald Henry 1935- *WhoWor 93*
Austin, Richard *ScF&FL 92*
Austin, Richard B. *Law&B 92*
Austin, Richard D. *Law&B 92*
Austin, Richard D. 1936-1990 *BioIn 17*
Austin, Richard Grant 1948- *WhoAm 92*
Austin, Richard H. *AfrAmBi [port]*
Austin, Richard Henry 1913- *WhoAm 92*
Austin, Robert C. 1919- *St&PR 93*
Austin, Robert Clarke 1931- *WhoAm 92*
Austin, Robert Eugene, Jr. 1937- *WhoAm 92, WhoSSW 93, WhoWor 93*
Austin, Robert Fredric 1950- *WhoEmL 93*
Austin, Robert Lee 1918- *St&PR 93*
Austin, Robert M. 1938- *St&PR 93*
Austin, Rodney R.D. *BioIn 17*
Austin, Roger Born 1956- *WhoSSW 93*
Austin, Ross E. *Law&B 92*
Austin, Sam M. 1933- *WhoAm 92*
Austin, Sharon J. *Law&B 92*
Austin, Spencer Peter 1909- *WhoAm 92*
Austin, Stephen Jerome 1939- *St&PR 93*
Austin, Steven G. *Law&B 92*
Austin, Sumner 1888-1981 *OxDcOp*
Austin, Susan Rebecca 1945- *WhoAmW 93*
Austin, T. Edward 1926- *WhoAm 92, WhoSSW 93*
Austin, Terri Dian *Law&B 92*
Austin, Terri Louise 1952- *WhoAmW 93*
Austin, Thomas David 1933- *WhoSSW 93*
Austin, Thomas Howard 1937- *WhoE 93*
Austin, Thomas Nelson 1945- *WhoSSW 93*
Austin, Thomas Noell 1916- *St&PR 93*
Austin, Tom *BioIn 17*
Austin, Tom Noell 1916- *WhoAm 92*
Austin, Tracy Ann 1962- *WhoAm 92*
Austin, Tracy L. *Law&B 92*
Austin, Victor Lee 1956- *WhoE 93*
Austin, Walter Wade 1946- *WhoSSW 93*
Austin, Warren Barker 1910- *WhoSSW 93*
Austin, William Lamont 1915- *WhoAm 92*
Austin, William W(eaver) 1920- *Baker 92*
Austing, Lawrence B. 1925- *St&PR 93*
Austin-Lucas, Barbara Etta 1951- *WhoAmW 93*
Aust-Keefer, Mary Beth 1958- *WhoAmW 93*
Auston, David Henry 1940- *WhoAm 92*
Austral, Florence 1892-1968 *Baker 92*
Austral, Florence 1894-1968 *OxDcOp*
Austrian, Neil R. 1940- *St&PR 93, WhoAm 92*
Austrian, Robert 1916- *WhoAm 92, WhoE 93*
Ausubel, Marvin Victor 1927- *WhoAm 92*
Aut, Warren E. 1932- *St&PR 93*
Auten, David Charles 1938- *WhoAm 92, WhoWor 93*
Auten, John Harold 1922- *WhoAm 92*
Auten, Paul W. 1953- *St&PR 93*
Autera, Michael E. 1938- *St&PR 93*
Autera, Michael Edward 1938- *WhoAm 92*
Auteri, Rose Mary Patti 1928- *WhoE 93, WhoWor 93*
Auteri Manzocchi, Salvatore 1845-1924 *Baker 92*
Auterinen, Iiro Heikki 1957- *WhoWor 93*
Auteuil, Daniel *BioIn 17*
Auth, Tony 1942- *WhoAm 92, WhoE 93*
Authement, Ray P. 1929- *WhoSSW 93*
Author Of "The Realm Of The Ice King" *ScF&FL 92*
Autin, A. Anthony, Jr. 1938- *St&PR 93*
Autin, Ernest Anthony, II 1957- *WhoAm 92, WhoSSW 93*
Autio-Harmainen, Helena Irmeli 1949- *WhoWor 93*
Autolitano, Astrid 1938- *St&PR 93, WhoAm 92, WhoAmW 93*
Auton, J.P. *WhoScE 91-1*
Autoreianos *OxDcByz*
Autori, Franco 1903-1990 *Baker 92, BioIn 17*
Autorino, Anne Turnbull 1914- *WhoAmW 93, WhoE 93*
Autorino, Anthony D. 1938- *St&PR 93*
Autret, Alain 1944- *WhoScE 91-2*
Autrey, Frank Eugene 1924- *St&PR 93, WhoAm 92*
Autrum, Hansjochem Otto 1907- *WhoWor 93*
Autry, Carol 1946- *WhoAmW 93*
Autry, Carolyn 1940- *WhoAm 92*
Autry, Charles T. *Law&B 92*
Autry, Elizabeth Welland 1954- *WhoAmW 93*
Autry, Gene 1907- *BioIn 17, IntDcF 2-3 [port], WhoAm 92*
Autry, Howard Winton 1930- *St&PR 93*
Autry, James Arthur 1933- *WhoAm 92*
Autry, Lana Mathis 1947- *WhoSSW 93*
Autry, Larry Frank 1959- *WhoEmL 93, WhoSSW 93*
Autry, Niles Patterson 1937- *St&PR 93*
Auvinen, Thomas Roger 1939- *WhoIns 93*
Auvray, Bernard *WhoScE 91-2*

Auwarter, Franklin Paul 1934- WhoAm 92
Auwers, Arthur von 1838-1915 BioIn 17
Auwers, Stanley John 1923- WhoAm 92
Auwerx, Johan Henri 1958- WhoWor 93
Auxenfans, Bernard Paul 1944- WhoWor 93
Auxentios c. 420-c. 470 OxDcByz
Auxentios, Bishop 1953- WhoAm 92
Au-Yeung, Hang Stephen 1953- WhoEmL 93
Au-Yeung Fu, Anthony 1935- WhoAsAP 91
Auzepy, Philippe 1931- WhoScE 91-2, WhoWor 93
Auzinger, Winfried 1956- WhoWor 93
Auzins, Igor MiSFD 9
Avagliano, Karen Marie Law&B 92
Avakian, Alexandra 1960- BioIn 17
Avakian, Aram d1987 MiSFD 9N
Avakian, Arlene Voski 1939- ConAu 139
Avakian, Laura Ann 1945- WhoE 93
Avakoff, Joseph Carnegie 1936- WhoWor 93
Avaliani, Pyotr N. 1943- WhoUN 92
Avalle-Arce, Juan Bautista 1927- WhoAm 92
Avallone, John V. 1947- St&PR 93
Avallone, Martin D. Law&B 92
Avallone, Michael 1924- ScF&FL 92
Avallone, Michael Angelo 1924- WhoAm 92
Avallone, Michael (Angelo, Jr.) 1924- ConAu 39NR
Avallone, Michael Nicholas 1951- WhoE 93
Avallone, Riccardo 1915- WhoWor 93
Avalon, Frankie 1940- WhoAm 92
Avalone, Ronnie 1922- WhoSSW 93, WhoWor 93
Avance, Gayland T. 1953- St&PR 93
Avant, David Alonzo, Jr. 1919- WhoAm 92, WhoSSW 93
Avant, Deborah Denise 1958- WhoAmW 93
Avant, Gayle 1940- WhoSSW 93
Avant, Grady, Jr. 1932- WhoAm 92
Avant, Robert Frank 1937- WhoAm 92
Avanzini, Giuliano 1937- WhoScE 91-3
Avari, Family BioIn 17
Avasthi, Ram Bandhu 1941- WhoWor 93
Avati, Pupi 1938- MiSFD 9
Avazian, Richard William 1937- St&PR 93
Avchen, Malvin 1934- St&PR 93
Avdeyeva, Larissa (Ivanovna) 1925- Baker 92
Avdoian, Richard John 1951- WhoEmL 93
Avdonin, Sergey Anatoliy 1948- WhoWor 93
Ave, John Robert 1932- St&PR 93, WhoAm 92
Avebury IntDcAn
Avedis, Howard (Hikmet) MiSFD 9
Avedisian, Archie Harry 1928- WhoE 93
Avedisian, Armen G. 1926- WhoAm 92
Avedisian, Edward 1936- WhoAm 92
Avedon, Richard BioIn 17
Avedon, Richard 1923- WhoAm 92, WhoE 93
Aveleyra Arroyo de Anda, Teresa 1920- DcMexL
Aveling, Edward Bibbins 1851-1898 BioIn 17
Aveling, Eleanor Marx 1855-1898 BioIn 17
Avella, John Vincent 1942- St&PR 93
Avellar, Michael J. Law&B 92
Avellis-Abrams, Rosemary Marisa 1945- St&PR 93
Avenali, Peter 1918- St&PR 93
Avenary, Hanoch 1908- Baker 92
Avenel-Navara, Cheryl Ann 1947- WhoAmW 93
Aveni, Anthony F. BioIn 17
Aveni, Anthony Francis 1938- WhoAm 92
Aveni, Antonino 1939- WhoScE 91-3
Avenick, Karen Reinhardt 1946- WhoEmL 93
Avent, Peggy 1946- WhoSSW 93
Aventinus, Johannes 1477-1534 Baker 92
Avera, Stephen Russell Law&B 92
Average White Band SoulM
Averbach, Benjamin L. 1919- WhoE 93
Averback, Hy 1925- MiSFD 9
Averbah, Il'ja 1934-1986 DrEEuF
Averbeck, Karen Marie 1961- WhoEmL 93
Averbook, Beryl David 1920- WhoWor 93
Averbuch, Gerald 1921- St&PR 93
Averch, Harvey Allan 1935- WhoAm 92
Averdunk, Gottfried 1934- WhoScE 91-3
Averell, Clara Rose AmWomPl
Averell, Lois Hathaway 1917- WhoAm 92
Averett-Short, Geneva Evelyn 1938- WhoAmW 93, WhoE 93
Averill, Bruce Alan 1948- WhoAm 92
Averill, Donald St&PR 93
Averill, Esther Cunningham 1895- AmWomPl
Averill, Esther (Holden) 1902-1992 ConAu 139, SmATA 72
Averill, James Reed 1935- WhoAm 92
Averill, Lloyd James, Jr. 1923- WhoAm 92
Averill, Thomas Fox 1949- WhoWrEP 92
Averiss, Joanne Law&B 92
Averitt, George Ronald 1949- WhoEmL 93
Averitt, Gerald Eastep 1943- St&PR 93
Averitt, Richard Garland, III 1945- WhoWor 93
Averitt, Robert C. 1903- St&PR 93
Averkamp, Anton 1861-1934 Baker 92
Averkieva, Iuliia Pavlovna 1907-1980 IntDcAn
Averoff-Tossizza, Evangelos 1910-1990 BioIn 17
Averroes 1126-1198 BioIn 17
Aversa, Dolores Sejda 1932- WhoAmW 93, WhoE 93
Aversenti, Candida Covino 1952- St&PR 93
Aversenti, Edmund V., Jr. 1944- St&PR 93
Avery, Anne Forster 1938- WhoAmW 93
Avery, Benjamin Parke 1828-1875 JrnUS
Avery, Bruce C. 1940- St&PR 93
Avery, Bruce Edward 1949- WhoEmL 93
Avery, Byllye Y. BioIn 17
Avery, Cameron Scott 1938- WhoAm 92
Avery, Cheryl Brown 1959- WhoWrEP 92
Avery, Christine Ann 1951- WhoAmW 93
Avery, Colin R. 1942- St&PR 93
Avery, David Wayne 1953- WhoSSW 93
Avery, Donald Hills 1937- WhoAm 92, WhoWor 93
Avery, Elaine Elvira 1924- WhoAmW 93
Avery, Family BioIn 17
Avery, Gerald Kenneth 1953- WhoEmL 93
Avery, Gillian (Elise) 1926- MajAI [port]
Avery, Gordon Bennett 1931- WhoAm 92
Avery, Helen Palmer 1910- WhoWrEP 92
Avery, Jack Alexander 1928- St&PR 93
Avery, James Knuckey 1921- WhoAm 92
Avery, James Robert 1940- St&PR 93
Avery, James Stephen 1923- WhoAm 92
Avery, Jeanne 1931- WhoE 93, WhoWor 93
Avery, John E. 1941- St&PR 93
Avery, John T. 1931- St&PR 93
Avery, Julia May 1917- WhoAm 92, WhoAmW 93
Avery, Kenneth Austin 1953- WhoWrEP 92
Avery, Lee Ann 1957- WhoEmL 93
Avery, Luther James 1923- WhoAm 92
Avery, Margaret 1951- WhoAmW 93, WhoEmL 93
Avery, Margaret DuBose Law&B 92
Avery, Martin 1955- WhoCanL 92
Avery, Mary Ellen 1927- WhoAm 92, WhoAmW 93
Avery, Mary Emerson 1953- WhoEmL 93
Avery, Nathan M. 1934- St&PR 93
Avery, Neil Francis 1953- WhoWrEP 92
Avery, Patricia Irene 1951- WhoEmL 93
Avery, Richard ScF&FL 92
Avery, Robert David 1953- WhoWor 93
Avery, Susan Kathryn 1950- WhoAm 92
Avery, William H. 1905- St&PR 93
Avery, William Henry 1911- BioIn 17
Avery, William Hinckley 1912- WhoAm 92
Avery, William J. 1940- St&PR 93
Avery, William Joseph 1940- WhoAm 92
Avery, William P. 1918- WhoWrEP 92
Averyt, Gayle O. 1933- St&PR 93
Averyt, Gayle Owen 1933- WhoAm 92, WhoIns 93
Avey, Harry Thompson, Jr. 1916- WhoSSW 93
Avey, Ruby 1927- ConAu 39NR
Avgerakis, George Harris 1949- WhoEmL 93
Avgerinos, Cecily Terese 1945- WhoWrEP 92
Avi 1937- Au&Arts 10 [port], DcAmChF 1960, DcAmChF 1985, ScF&FL 92, SmATA 71 [port], WhoAm 92
Aviado, Domingo M. 1924- WhoAm 92, WhoE 93
Avian, Bob BioIn 17
Avian, Bob 1937- WhoAm 92
Avice, Claude ScF&FL 92
Avidan, Amos Andrew 1952- WhoE 93
Avidom, Menahem 1908- Baker 92
Avigad, Nachman 1905-1992 ConAu 136
Avigad, Nahman 1905-1992 BioIn 17, NewYTBS 92
Avigliano, Matteo A. 1941- WhoScE 91-3
Avila, Cesar DcCPCAm
Avila, Edgar V. 1949- St&PR 93
Avila, Jac 1952- MiSFD 9
Avila, John 1947- St&PR 93
Avila, William Thaddeus 1954- WhoSSW 93
Avila Camacho, Manuel 1897-1955 DcCPCAm, DcTwHis
Avildsen, Edward B. 1929- St&PR 93
Avildsen, John G. 1935- ConTFT 10
Avildsen, John G. 1936- MiSFD 9
Avildsen, John Guilbert 1935- WhoAm 92
Avildsen, Tom MiSFD 9
Aviles, Alice Alers WhoAmW 93, WhoE 93
Aviles, Pedro Menendez de 1519-1574 BioIn 17
Aviles, Yvette Marie 1966- WhoAmW 93
Aviles Fabila, Rene 1940- SpAmA
Avino-Barracato, Kathleen 1956- WhoAmW 93, WhoEmL 93
Aviola, Louis A., Jr. 1940- St&PR 93
Avioli, James P. 1938- St&PR 93
Avirett, John Williams, II 1902- WhoAm 92
Avirom, Cheryl Ruth 1951- WhoEmL 93
Avis, Deborah Kah 1959- WhoAmW 93
Avis, James C. Law&B 92
Avis, Kenneth Edward 1918- WhoSSW 93
Avis, Meiert MiSFD 9
Avis, Robert Grier 1931- WhoAm 92
Avise, John Charles 1948- WhoAm 92
Avison, Charles 1709-1770 Baker 92
Avison, David 1937- WhoAm 92
Avison, Margaret 1918- BioIn 17, WhoCanL 92
Avizienis, Algirdas BioIn 17
Avnby, Fredd 1944- WhoScE 91-2
Avner, Brett Kim 1949- WhoWor 93
Avner, L.L. 1915- St&PR 93
Avnet, Jon 1947- MiSFD 9
Avni, Tzvi (Jacob) 1927- Baker 92
Avolio, Wendy Freedman 1953- WhoEmL 93
Avon, Earl of 1897-1977 BioIn 17
Avona, Vincent Leonard 1936- WhoAm 92
Avondoglio, Leo 1913- St&PR 93
Avossa, Giuseppe d' 1708-1796 Baker 92
Avraamij of Smolensk fl. 13th cent.- OxDcByz
Avraham, Regina 1935- WhoAmW 93
Avram, Henriette Davidson 1919- WhoAm 92, WhoAmW 93
Avram, Morrell M. 1929- WhoAm 92
Avrameas, Stratis 1930- WhoScE 91-2
Avramovic, Mila 1954- WhoWor 93
Avrashow, Wayne 1950- St&PR 93
Avren, J. David S. Law&B 92
Avrett, John Glenn 1929- WhoAm 92
Avrett, Roz 1933- WhoE 93
Avrick, Stuart J. 1934- St&PR 93
Avriel, Deborah Suzanne 1935- WhoUN 92
Avriett, James R. 1944- St&PR 93
Avril, Carmen WhoCanL 92
Avril, Gary Lawrence Law&B 92
Avril, John G. 1930- St&PR 93
Avril, Prosper 1937- DcCPCAm
Avril, Thomas B. 1925- St&PR 93
Avrit, Richard Calvin 1932- WhoAm 92
Avrit, Tamra Jane 1963- WhoAmW 93
Avruch, Phillip G. Law&B 92
Avrunin, Charlene Pattishall 1946- WhoEmL 93
Avrunin, Dana I. Law&B 92
Avrunin, George Sam'l 1952- WhoEmL 93
Avsar, Efraim 1944- WhoScE 91-4
Avshalomov, Aaron 1894-1965 Baker 92
Avshalomov, Jacob (David) 1919- Baker 92
Avtges, James Peter 1929- St&PR 93
Awad, Adnan BioIn 17
Awad, Issa 1932- WhoUN 92
Awad, Joseph F. 1929- St&PR 93
Awad, Joseph Frederick 1929- WhoSSW 93
Awad, William Michel, Jr. 1927- WhoSSW 93
Awais, George Musa 1929- WhoAm 92, WhoWor 93
Awalt, Elizabeth Grace 1956- WhoE 93
Awalt, Marilene Kay 1942- WhoSSW 93
Awamori, Takashi 1939- WhoAsAP 91
Awan, Ghulam Mustafa 1940- WhoWor 93
Awaya, Toshinobu 1926- WhoAsAP 91
Awbrey, S. Scott 1952- WhoEmL 93
Awdry, Christopher BioIn 17
Awdry, Christopher Vere 1940- ConAu 136
Awdry, W. BioIn 17
Awdry, Wilbert BioIn 17
Awerbuch, Shimon 1946- WhoE 93
Awilda Lopez, Mara NotHsAW 93
Awkwright, Ruth AmWomPl
Awlinson, Richard ScF&FL 92
Awojoodu, Samson Olalekan 1955- WhoE 93, WhoEmL 93
Awolowo, Obafemi 1909-1987 DcTwHis
Awoonor, Kofi 1935- DcLB 117 [port]
Awori, Thelma 1943- WhoUN 92
Awramik, Stanley Michael 1946- WhoEmL 93
Awschalom, Miguel BioIn 17
Awtrey, Jim L. 1943- WhoAm 92
Awwal, Mohammad Abdul 1933- WhoWor 93
Ax, Emanuel 1949- Baker 92, BioIn 17, PolBiDi, WhoAm 92, WhoWor 93
Ax, P. WhoScE 91-3
Ax, Peter 1959- WhoEmL 93
Axam, John Arthur 1930- WhoAm 92
Axe, John Randolph 1938- WhoAm 92
Axel, Bernard 1946- WhoEmL 93, WhoSSW 93, WhoWor 93
Axel, Gabriel 1918- MiSFD 9
Axel, John Werner 1941- St&PR 93
Axel, Marc 1945- WhoSSW 93
Axel, Michael A. Law&B 92
Axel, Robert Jay 1946- WhoEmL 93
Axelrad, Charles Steven 1949- WhoE 93
Axelrad, Irving Irmas 1915- WhoAm 92
Axelrad, James Alan 1950- St&PR 93
Axelrod, A. Bernard 1917- St&PR 93
Axelrod, Alan 1952- ScF&FL 92
Axelrod, Barry Leon 1947- WhoEmL 93
Axelrod, Bart M. 1958- St&PR 93
Axelrod, Bernadette Bonner 1963- WhoAmW 93
Axelrod, Charles Paul 1941- WhoAm 92
Axelrod, Daniel Isaac 1910- WhoAm 92
Axelrod, David Bruce 1943- WhoWrEP 92
Axelrod, G. Carla Law&B 92
Axelrod, George 1922- MiSFD 9
Axelrod, Herbert Richard 1927- WhoWor 93
Axelrod, Jerome 1945- WhoWrEP 92
Axelrod, Jonathan Gans 1946- WhoAm 92
Axelrod, Joseph H. 1916-1991 BioIn 17
Axelrod, Julius 1912- WhoAm 92, WhoWor 93
Axelrod, Leah Joy 1929- WhoAmW 93
Axelrod, Leonard 1950- WhoEmL 93
Axelrod, Lisa 1945- WhoE 93
Axelrod, Mark Richard 1946- WhoWrEP 92
Axelrod, Marvin F. 1927- St&PR 93
Axelrod, Norman Nathan 1934- WhoAm 92, WhoE 93, WhoWor 93
Axelrod, Peter 1948- WhoEmL 93
Axelrod, Ronald J. Law&B 92
Axelrod, Stephen Lee 1951- WhoEmL 93, WhoWor 93
Axelrod, Steven Joseph 1950- WhoE 93
Axelrod, William B. 1910- St&PR 93
Axelrood, Jack Law&B 92
Axelroth, Lynn Robin 1954- WhoEmL 93
Axelsen, Nils Holger 1942- WhoScE 91-2, WhoWor 93
Axelsen, Richard H. 1933- St&PR 93
Axelson, Charles Frederic 1917- WhoAm 92
Axelson, Jeffrey Mark 1951- WhoEmL 93
Axelson, Joseph Allen 1927- WhoAm 92, WhoWor 93
Axelson, Kenneth S. 1922- St&PR 93
Axelson, Olav 1937- WhoScE 91-4
Axelson, Teresa Elaine 1947- St&PR 93
Axer, Otto 1906-1982 PolBiDi
Axford, D.W. 1920- St&PR 93
Axford, David Norman 1934- WhoUN 92
Axford, Roy Arthur 1928- WhoAm 92, WhoWor 93
Axford, W. Ian 1933- WhoScE 91-2, -91-3
Axford, Warren Scott 1956- WhoEmL 93
Axiak, Victor 1950- WhoWor 93
Axilrod, Stephen H. 1926- St&PR 93
Axilrod, Stephen Harvey 1926- WhoAm 92
Axinn, Donald Everett 1929- WhoAm 92, WhoWrEP 92
Axinn, George Harold 1926- WhoAm 92
Axler, James ScF&FL 92
Axley, Frederick William 1941- WhoAm 92
Axline, Robert Paul 1935- WhoAm 92, WhoE 93
Axlund, Richard C. 1941- St&PR 93
Axman, Emil 1887-1949 Baker 92
Axon, Kenneth Stuart 1940- WhoWor 93
Axon, Michael 1957- WhoSSW 93
Axouch OxDcByz
Axt, Harry S. 1935- St&PR 93
Axtell, James Lewis 1941- WhoAm 92
Axtell, John David 1934- WhoAm 92
Axthelm, Pete BioIn 17
Axthelm, Pete 1943- WhoWrEP 92
Axtmann, Robert Clark 1925- WhoAm 92
Axton, David 1945- BioIn 17
Axton, Hoyt Wayne 1938- WhoAm 92
Axton, William Fitch 1926- WhoSSW 93
Axup, Bruce Edward 1954- St&PR 93
Axworthy, Thomas Sydney 1947- WhoAm 92
Aya 1965- BioIn 17
Aya, Roderick Honeyman 1916- WhoE 93, WhoWor 93
Ayad, Boulos Ayad 1928- WhoAm 92

Ayad, Joseph Magdy 1926- *WhoSSW 93, WhoWor 93*
Ayah, Wilson N. *WhoWor 93*
Ayala, Anissa *BioIn 17*
Ayala, Francisco Jose 1934- *WhoAm 92*
Ayala, Marissa 1990- *BioIn 17*
Ayala, Mary *BioIn 17*
Ayala, Rowena Winifred *WhoAmW 93*
Ayala Anguiano, Armando 1928- *DcMexL*
Ayala-Lasso, Jose 1932- *WhoUN 92*
Ayala Oliva, Alejandro Ernesto 1916- *WhoWor 93*
Ayala Perez, Daniel 1906-1975 *Baker 92*
Ayalti, Hanan J. d1992 *NewYTBS 92*
Ayalti, Hanan J. 1910-1992 *BioIn 17*
Ayan, Cosan 1960- *WhoScE 91-4*
Ayandele, Emmanuel Ayankanmi 1936- *WhoUN 92*
Ayano, Katsutoshi 1949- *WhoWor 93*
Ayanru, Grace Hughes 1933- *WhoAmW 93*
Ayars, Albert Lee 1917- *WhoAm 92*
Ayaso, Manuel 1934- *WhoAm 92*
Ayaz, Nevzat 1930- *WhoWor 93*
Aybar, Charles Anton 1956- *WhoSSW 93*
Aybar, Romeo 1930- *WhoAm 92, WhoWor 93*
Ayberk, Savas 1946- *WhoScE 91-4*
Ayca, Ertugrul 1922- *WhoScE 91-4*
Aycardi, Eduardo Rafael 1939- *WhoWor 93*
Ayckbourn, Alan 1939- *BioIn 17, ConLC 74 [port]*
Aycliffe, Jonathan *ScF&FL 92*
Aycock, Alice *BioIn 17*
Aycock, Alice 1946- *WhoAm 92*
Aycock, Dale 1930?- *ScF&FL 92*
Aycock, David Wayne 1955- *WhoSSW 93*
Aycock, Don Milton 1951- *WhoWrEP 92*
Aycock, Edwin Norton 1929- *St&PR 93*
Aycock, Helen P. 1938- *WhoSSW 93*
Aycock, Hugh David 1930- *WhoAm 92*
Aycock, Pamela Gayle 1961- *WhoAmW 93*
Aycock, Robert 1919- *WhoSSW 93*
Aycock, Roger D. *ScF&FL 92*
Aycoth, John Edward 1956- *WhoE 93*
Aydelott, Madison P., III 1954- *WhoEmL 93*
Aydelotte, Myrtle Kitchell 1917- *WhoAm 92, WhoAmW 93*
Aydelotte, William Osgood 1910- *WhoWrEP 92*
Aydy, Catherine *ConAu 38NR*
Aye, Maryon 1903-1951 *SweetSg B [port]*
Ayeni, Olusola Idowu 1944- *WhoUN 92*
Ayer, A.L., Jr. 1925- *St&PR 93*
Ayer, Alton Audie 1947- *WhoAm 92*
Ayer, Anne 1917- *WhoWrEP 92*
Ayer, Donald Belton 1949- *WhoAm 92, WhoEmL 93*
Ayer, Doris Moseley 1909- *St&PR 93*
Ayer, Frederick Latham 1940- *WhoSSW 93*
Ayer, Kristin Vander Meer 1951- *WhoEmL 93*
Ayer, Lloyd M. 1929- *St&PR 93*
Ayer, Ramani *WhoIns 93*
Ayer, Ramani 1947- *St&PR 93*
Ayer, William Alfred 1932- *WhoAm 92*
Ayeroff, Jeff *BioIn 17*
Ayers, A. Merrill 1946- *WhoEmL 93*
Ayers, Anne Louise 1948- *WhoEmL 93*
Ayers, Caroline LeRoy 1941- *WhoAmW 93*
Ayers, Cathie Ientha 1950- *WhoAmW 93*
Ayers, Crimora Witten 1942- *WhoE 93*
Ayers, Donald Walter 1933- *St&PR 93, WhoAm 92*
Ayers, Eben A. 1891-1977 *BioIn 17*
Ayers, Elinor Cocheran d1991 *BioIn 17*
Ayers, Emory Daniel 1928- *WhoAm 92*
Ayers, George Edward Lewis 1938- *WhoAm 92*
Ayers, Gerri Lynn 1955- *WhoSSW 93*
Ayers, Harold Edward 1958- *WhoSSW 93*
Ayers, Harry Brandt 1935- *WhoAm 92, WhoSSW 93*
Ayers, James Edson 1932- *St&PR 93, WhoAm 92*
Ayers, James Lee 1919- *WhoWor 93*
Ayers, James Wilber 1928- *WhoWrEP 92*
Ayers, Jeffrey David 1960- *WhoEmL 93, WhoWor 93*
Ayers, Jennie Lee 1941- *St&PR 93*
Ayers, Joseph Williams 1904- *WhoWor 93*
Ayers, Oscar L. 1927- *WhoIns 93*
Ayers, Oscar Lee 1927- *St&PR 93*
Ayers, Patricia Ann 1958- *WhoEmL 93*
Ayers, Phillip Rex 1948- *WhoSSW 93*
Ayers, Ralston E. 1932- *St&PR 93*
Ayers, Randall Wayne 1954- *WhoEmL 93*
Ayers, Richard H. *BioIn 17*
Ayers, Richard H. 1942- *St&PR 93, WhoAm 92*
Ayers, Richard Winston 1910- *WhoAm 92*
Ayers, Ronald Marvin 1947- *WhoEmL 93, WhoSSW 93*
Ayers, Roy (E., Jr.) 1940- *Baker 92*
Ayers, Scott N. 1944- *St&PR 93*
Ayers, Vicky Willis *Law&B 92*
Ayers, W. Floyd 1938- *St&PR 93*
Ayers, William Borden 1952- *St&PR 93*
Ayers, William McLean 1950- *WhoAm 92*
Ayers-Allen, Phylicia *BioIn 17*
Ayestaran, Lauro 1913-1966 *Baker 92*
Aygen, Nermin *IntDcAn*
Ayik, Celal 1943- *WhoScE 91-4*
Ayim, May 1960- *ConAu 139*
Aykac, M. Kemal 1939- *WhoScE 91-4*
Aykanian, Ara 1928- *St&PR 93*
Aykroyd, Dan *BioIn 17*
Aykroyd, Dan 1951- *QDrFCA 92 [port]*
Aykroyd, Dan 1952- *CurBio 92 [port], HolBB [port], MiSFD 9*
Aykroyd, Daniel Edward 1952- *WhoAm 92*
Ayler, Albert 1936-1970 *Baker 92*
Ayles, Rosemary Anne 1939- *WhoWor 93*
Aylesworth, Jim 1943- *WhoWrEP 92*
Aylesworth, Thomas G. 1927- *ScF&FL 92*
Aylesworth, Thomas Gibbons 1927- *WhoAm 92, WhoWrEP 92*
Aylesworth, William Andrew 1942- *St&PR 93, WhoAm 92*
Aylett, Bernard John *WhoScE 91-1*
Ayling, Campbell L. *Law&B 92*
Ayling, John R. 1944- *St&PR 93*
Aylor, Alan E. 1956- *St&PR 93*
Aylor, R.B. *Law&B 92*
Aylsworth, Joseph Lynn, Jr. 1916- *WhoSSW 93*
Aylward, James Francis 1942- *WhoE 93*
Aylward, Linda Szempruch *Law&B 92*
Aylward, Ronald Lee 1930- *St&PR 93, WhoAm 92*
Aylward, Thomas James, Jr. 1923- *WhoAm 92*
Aylwin, Louise *WhoCanL 92*
Aylwin, Patricio *BioIn 17*
Aylwin, Patricio 1918- *WhoWor 93*
Ayman, Ibrahim *WhoScE 91-4*
Aymar, Brandt 1911- *ConAu 37NR*
Aymard, Michele Andree 1933- *WhoScE 91-2*
Ayme, Segolene 1946- *WhoScE 91-2*
Aymerich, Angela Figuera 1902-1984 *BioIn 17*
Aymerich, Melchoir fl. c. 1822- *HarEnMi*
Aymerich, Ysabel M. *St&PR 93*
Aymond, Gregory Ray 1956- *WhoEmL 93*
Aymond, Pamela Buchmeyer *Law&B 92*
Aynardi, Martha Whitman 1954- *WhoAmW 93*
Aynes, Richard Lee 1949- *WhoEmL 93*
Aynesworth, Paula Butler 1953- *WhoAmW 93*
Aynsley-Green, Albert *WhoScE 91-1*
Ayo, Donald Joseph 1934- *WhoSSW 93*
Ayoob, Richard Joseph 1953- *WhoEmL 93*
Ayoola, Emmanuel Olayinka 1933- *WhoWor 93*
Ayotte, Gaston Arthur, Jr. 1933- *WhoE 93*
Ayoub, Ali Taha 1938- *WhoUN 92*
Ayoub, Catherine C. 1949- *WhoE 93*
Ayoub, Ferida 1943- *WhoUN 92*
Ayoub, Ibrahim T. 1941- *WhoUN 92*
Ayraud, Pierre *ScF&FL 92*
Ayrault, Evelyn West 1922- *WhoAm 92, WhoAmW 93*
Ayrault, Margaret W. 1911-1989 *BioIn 17*
Ayre, John Randolph 1938- *St&PR 93*
Ayres, Barbara Joan 1937- *WhoE 93*
Ayres, Clarence Edwin *BioIn 17*
Ayres, Ed 1941- *WhoWrEP 92*
Ayres, Elizabeth Patricia 1950- *WhoE 93*
Ayres, Frances Lynch 1950- *WhoEmL 93*
Ayres, Frederic 1876-1926 *Baker 92*
Ayres, James Marx 1922- *WhoAm 92*
Ayres, Janice Ruth 1930- *WhoAmW 93, WhoWor 93*
Ayres, Jeffrey Peabody 1952- *WhoEmL 93*
Ayres, Jeremiah Johnston 1932- *St&PR 93*
Ayres, Joe R. 1941- *St&PR 93*
Ayres, Joe Robbins 1941- *WhoAm 92*
Ayres, John Cecil 1919- *WhoAm 92*
Ayres, John James Brevard 1939- *WhoE 93*
Ayres, John Samuel 1914- *St&PR 93, WhoAm 92*
Ayres, Lew 1908- *IntDcF 2-3 [port]*
Ayres, Lyman S. 1908- *St&PR 93*
Ayres, Mary Ellen 1924- *WhoAm 92*
Ayres, Ray Morris 1928- *WhoSSW 93*
Ayres, Robert Moss, Jr. 1926- *WhoAm 92*
Ayres, Robert Underwood 1932- *WhoAm 92, WhoE 93*
Ayres, Russell W., III *Law&B 92*
Ayres, Samuel, III 1919- *WhoAm 92*
Ayres, Stephen McClintock 1929- *WhoAm 92, WhoWor 93*
Ayres, Steven B. 1952- *St&PR 93*
Ayres, Ted Dean 1947- *WhoEmL 93*
Ayres, Virginia Marian 1954- *WhoAmW 93, WhoE 93*
Ayrton, Edmund 1734-1808 *Baker 92*
Ayrton, Elisabeth Walshe 1910?-1991 *ConAu 136*
Ayrton, Elisabeth Walshe 1918-1991 *ScF&FL 92*
Ayrton, William 1777-1858 *Baker 92, OxDcOp*
Ayscough, Peter Brian *WhoScE 91-1*
Ayscue, Brian Thomas 1948- *WhoEmL 93*
Ayscue, Edwin Osborne, Jr. 1933- *WhoAm 92*
Aytekin, Veli 1921- *WhoScE 91-4*
Aytoun, Robert 1570-1638 *DcLB 121 [port]*
Ayub, Zahid Hussain 1954- *WhoEmL 93*
Ayub Khan, Muhammad 1907-1974 *DcTwHis*
Ayyagari, Kamalakar Rao 1944- *WhoE 93*
Ayyala, Sarmas S.V.S. 1940- *St&PR 93*
Ayyildiz, Judy Light 1941- *WhoSSW 93*
Ayza, Jordi 1948- *WhoScE 91-3*
Azaceta, Luis Cruz 1942- *BioIn 17, HispAmA, WhoE 93*
Azad, Abdul Kalam 1888-1958 *BioIn 17*
Azad, Lila Peggy 1933- *WhoAmW 93*
Azadian, Harry Y. 1934- *WhoE 93*
Azadovskii, M.K. 1888-1954 *IntDcAn*
Azaid 1908-1990 *BioIn 17*
Azana, Manuel 1881-1940 *DcTwHis*
Azanchevsky, Mikhail 1839-1881 *Baker 92*
Azano, Warren Bailey *Law&B 92*
Azar, Edward E. 1938-1991 *BioIn 17*
Azar, Hector 1930- *DcMexL*
Azar, Henry Amin 1927- *WhoAm 92, WhoWor 93*
Azar, J. Douglas 1946- *St&PR 93*
Azar, Jimmy 1936- *St&PR 93*
Azar, Mary Ellen 1958- *WhoAmW 93*
Azar, Richard Thomas 1954- *WhoE 93, WhoEmL 93, WhoWor 93*
Azara, Nancy Jean 1939- *WhoE 93*
Azarchs, Tanya Sednew 1951- *St&PR 93*
Azari, Nina Parvin 1959- *WhoAmW 93*
Azarian, Mardiros 1929- *WhoE 93*
Azarian, Martin Vartan 1927- *WhoAm 92*
Azarin, Vladimir Solomonovich 1935- *WhoWor 93*
Azarnoff, Daniel Lester 1926- *St&PR 93, WhoAm 92*
Azaroff, Leonid Vladimirovitch 1926- *WhoAm 92*
Azarow, Charles 1918- *WhoSSW 93*
Azbill, Russell Darrell 1965- *WhoSSW 93*
Azcarraga, Jose A. de 1941- *WhoScE 91-3*
Azcarraga, Jose Adolfo de 1941- *WhoWor 93*
Azcona Hoyo, Jose Simon 1927- *DcCPCAm*
Azcuenaga, Mary Laurie 1945- *WhoAm 92, WhoAmW 93*
Azcuna, Adolfo S. 1939- *WhoAsAP 91*
Azdi, Al- fl. c. 800-810 *OxDcByz*
Azevado, Francisco de 1578-1660 *Expl 93*
Azevedo, Alexis-Jacob 1813-1875 *Baker 92*
Azevedo, Ario Lobo *WhoScE 91-3*
Azevedo, Carlos 1934- *WhoScE 91-3*
Azevedo, Carlos de 1918- *ConAu 136*
Azevedo, Joseph Anthony 1944- *WhoSSW 93*
Azevedo, Thales de 1904- *IntDcAn*
Azfar, Shahida Ikram 1945- *WhoUN 92*
Azhar, Barkat Ali 1927- *WhoWor 93*
Azhari, Ismail al- 1900-1969 *DcTwHis*
Azie, Scott David 1951- *WhoE 93*
Azieres, Claude 1943- *St&PR 93*
Azikiwe, Benjamin Nnamdi 1904- *BioIn 17, DcTwHis*
Azikiwe, Emeka Ayo 1941- *WhoUN 92*
Azikiwe, Nnamdi 1904- *BioIn 17*
Azim, Imran 1954- *WhoWor 93*
Azimov, Isaak I. *ScF&FL 92*
Azine, Sheldon Lee *Law&B 92*
Azinger, Paul *BioIn 17*
Aziz, Omar 1932- *WhoScE 91-3*
Aziz, Tariq 1936- *BioIn 17*
Aziz, Tariq Mikhayl 1936- *WhoWor 93*
Aziz, Ungku Abdul 1922- *WhoWor 93*
Aziz, William E. *St&PR 93*
Aziz, Zahir M. 1937- *WhoUN 92*
Aziza, Mohamed 1940- *WhoUN 92*
Aziz Bin Begawan Pehin Udana Khatib Dato, Yang Berhormat Pehin Orang Kaya Laila *WhoAsAP 91*
Azize, Yamila 1953- *NotHsAW 93*
Azizov, Tomas Yakovievich 1946- *WhoWor 93*
Azkue, Resurreccion Maria de 1864-1951 *Baker 92*
Azlan Muhibbuddin Shah Yussuff Izzuddin, Shah ibni Al-Marhum, Sultan 1928- *WhoWor 93*
Azlan Muhibuddin Shah Ibni Almarhum, Yang DiPertuan Agong Sultan 1928- *WhoAsAP 91*
Azlin, Denise Roxane 1962- *WhoEmL 93*
Azmayparashvili, Shalva 1903-1957 *Baker 92*
Azmeh, Issam 1928- *WhoWor 93*
Azmi, Shabana *IntDcF 2-3*
Azmitia, Maria Margarita 1958- *WhoAmW 93*
Aznavour, Charles 1924- *Baker 92, NewYTBS 92 [port]*
Aznavurian, Charles 1924- *Baker 92*
Azneer, J. Leonard 1921- *WhoAm 92*
Aznoian, Nicholas David 1929- *St&PR 93*
Azodi, Djahangir 1937- *WhoWor 93*
Azofeifa Ch., Carlos E. 1944- *WhoWor 93*
Azoff, Eitan Michael 1956- *WhoWor 93*
Azoff, Irving *BioIn 17*
Azoulay, Guy *BioIn 17*
Azouz, Slaheddine 1938- *WhoUN 92*
Azpeitia, Lynne Marie 1951- *WhoAm 92, WhoEmL 93*
Azpiazu, Aurelio 1945- *WhoSSW 93*
Azrael, Judith Anne 1938- *WhoWrEP 92*
Azrin, Nathan Harold 1930- *WhoAm 92*
Azuela, Arturo 1938- *SpAmA*
Azuela, Mariano 1873-1952 *BioIn 17, DcMexL, SpAmA*
Azuma, Norio 1928- *WhoAm 92*
Azuma, Shozo 1951- *WhoAsAP 91*
Azuma, Takamitsu 1933- *WhoWor 93*
Azure, Leo L., Jr. *St&PR 93*
Azus, Louis 1936- *WhoIns 93*
Azzalina, Charles Samuel 1932- *St&PR 93*
Azzam, Khader Abdel Fattah 1942- *WhoUN 92*
Azzam, Rasheed M.A. 1945- *WhoSSW 93*
Azzara, Andrew J. *Law&B 92*
Azzara, Michael William 1947- *WhoAm 92*
Azzaroli, Augusto 1921- *WhoScE 91-3, WhoWor 93*
Azzarone, Carol Ann 1946- *WhoAmW 93*
Azzato, Louis E. 1930- *St&PR 93*
Azzato, Louis Enrico 1930- *WhoAm 92, WhoWor 93*
Azzi, Angelo Manfredo 1939- *WhoScE 91-4*
Azzone, Giovanni Felice *WhoScE 91-3*
Azzopardi, Francesco 1748-1809 *Baker 92*
Azzopardi, Jennifer Angele 1959- *WhoWor 93*
Azzopardi, Marc Antoine 1940- *WhoWor 93*
Azzopardi, Mario 1950- *MiSFD 9*

B

"B" *ScF&FL 92*
B., Beth *MiSFD 9*
B., Marina *BioIn 17*
B., Scott *MiSFD 9*
Baa, Ion I. 1941- *WhoScE 91-4*
Baack, John Edward 1936- *WhoAm 92*
Baacke, Jurgen 1942- *WhoScE 91-3*
Baader, W. *WhoScE 91-3*
Baal, Jan van 1909- *IntDcAn*
Baal, Shem-Tov 1700-1760 *PolBiDi*
Baalbaki, Mohammed Tahseen 1940- *WhoWor 93*
Ba'al Shem Tov c. 1700-1760 *BioIn 17*
Baang, Young-Min 1948- *WhoWor 93*
Baar, James A. 1929- *WhoAm 92*
Baaren, Kees van 1906-1970 *Baker 92*
Baarli, Johan 1921- *WhoScE 91-4*
Baarova, Lida 1910- *IntDcF 2-3*
Baars, Aalbert Jan 1943- *WhoScE 91-3*
Baartman, John L., III 1930- *St&PR 93*
Baas, Jacquelynn 1948- *WhoAm 92, WhoAmW 93*
Baaset, Tracey Valerie *Law&B 92*
Baasner, Bernd 1950- *WhoWor 93*
Baatrup, Erik *WhoWor 93*
Baatz, Henning *WhoScE 91-3*
Baatz, Stan M. 1952- *St&PR 93*
Baatz, Wilmer H. 1915-1991 *BioIn 17*
Baba, Isamu 1923- *WhoWor 93*
Baba, James Boliba 1945- *WhoUN 92*
Baba, Marietta Lynn 1949- *WhoAm 92, WhoAmW 93, WhoEmL 93*
Baba, Noboru 1925- *WhoAsAP 91*
Baba, Tupeni *WhoAsAP 91*
Baba, Yoshihiko 1933- *WhoWor 93*
Baba, Yoshinobu 1958- *WhoWor 93*
Babadzhanian, Arno 1921-1983 *Baker 92*
Babah, Mohammed S. 1944- *WhoE 93*
Babajko, Susan *Law&B 92*
Babangida, Ibrahim *BioIn 17, WhoWor 93*
Babangida, Ibrahim 1941- *ConBlB 4 [port]*
Babangida, Ibrahim Badamasi 1941- *WhoAfr*
Babangida, Ibrahim Badamosi 1941- *News 92 [port]*
Babaoglu, Rehim 1946- *WhoEmL 93, WhoSSW 93*
Babaoka, Marian L. 1960- *St&PR 93*
Babar, Raza Ali 1947- *WhoEmL 93*
Babashoff, Diane L. 1944- *St&PR 93*
Babatunde, Obba *BioIn 17*
Babayan, Vigen Khachig 1913- *WhoE 93*
Babayev, Andrei 1923-1964 *Baker 92*
Babb, Albert Leslie 1925- *WhoAm 92*
Babb, Alvin Charles 1932- *WhoAm 92*
Babb, Charles Keith 1952- *WhoEmL 93*
Babb, Douglass *Law&B 92*
Babb, Frank Edward 1932- *WhoAm 92*
Babb, Harold 1926- *WhoAm 92*
Babb, James Tinkham 1899-1968 *BioIn 17*
Babb, Judith Ann 1949- *WhoEmL 93*
Babb, Julius Wistar, III 1946- *WhoAm 92*
Babb, Kathleen Marie 1947- *WhoAmW 93*
Babb, Lawrence Alan *WhoAm 92*
Babb, Marion Standahl 1918- *WhoAmW 93*
Babb, Marva Tew 1951- *WhoAmW 93*
Babb, Ralph W. 1949- *St&PR 93*
Babb, Ralph Wheeler, Jr. 1949- *WhoAm 92*
Babb, Sanora 1907- *WhoWrEP 92*
Babb, Steven Craig *Law&B 92*
Babb, William Kay 1957- *WhoSSW 93*
Babb, Wylie Sherrill 1940- *WhoAm 92*
Babbage, Charles 1792-1871 *BioIn 17*
Babbage, Joan Dorothy 1926- *WhoAmW 93, WhoE 93*
Babbage, Robert *WhoAm 92*
Babbel, David Frederick 1949- *WhoAm 92, WhoEmL 93*
Babbi, Cristoforo 1745-1814 *Baker 92*
Babbi, Gregorio (Lorenzo) 1708-1768 *Baker 92*
Babbie, Earl (Robert) 1938- *WhoWrEP 92*
Babbin, Jed Lloyd 1950- *WhoWor 93*
Babbish, Byron C. *Law&B 92*
Babbitt, Arthur d1992 *BioIn 17, NewYTBS 92*
Babbitt, Bruce Edward 1938- *WhoAm 92*
Babbitt, Edward Joseph *Law&B 92*
Babbitt, James E. 1948- *St&PR 93*
Babbitt, Lucy Cullyford *ScF&FL 92*
Babbitt, Milton 1916- *BioIn 17*
Babbitt, Milton (Byron) 1916- *Baker 92, WhoAm 92*
Babbitt, Natalie *BioIn 17*
Babbitt, Natalie 1932- *ScF&FL 92*
Babbitt, Natalie (Moore) 1932- *DcAmChF 1960*
Babbitt, Natalie (Zane Moore) 1932- *ConAu 38NR, MajAI [port]*
Babbitt, Randy *BioIn 17*
Babbitt, Samuel Fisher 1929- *WhoAm 92*
Babbs, Donald Max 1939- *WhoSSW 93*
Babb-Sprague, Kristen *WhoAmW 93*
Babby, Ellen Reisman 1950- *WhoAm 92*
Babchuk, Nicholas 1922- *WhoAm 92*
Babcicky, Karel 1940- *WhoWor 93*
Babcock, Barbara Allen 1938- *WhoAm 92*
Babcock, Barbara Ann 1948- *WhoAmW 93*
Babcock, Bernie Smade, Mrs. 1868- *AmWomPl*
Babcock, Brenda Lynn 1960- *WhoEmL 93*
Babcock, Charles Luther 1924- *WhoAm 92*
Babcock, Charles W., Jr. *Law&B 92*
Babcock, Fred C. 1913- *St&PR 93*
Babcock, George F. 1948- *WhoEmL 93*
Babcock, Horace 1912- *WhoAm 92*
Babcock, Jack Emerson 1915- *WhoAm 92*
Babcock, Jacqueline Eileen 1948- *WhoEmL 93*
Babcock, James F. 1933- *St&PR 93*
Babcock, Janice Beatrice 1942- *WhoAmW 93, WhoWor 93*
Babcock, Judith Ann 1956- *WhoEmL 93*
Babcock, Keith Moss 1951- *WhoEmL 93*
Babcock, Lyndon Ross, Jr. 1934- *WhoAm 92*
Babcock, Madolyn Evelyn 1924- *WhoAmW 93*
Babcock, Michael Joseph 1941- *WhoAm 92*
Babcock, Nellie Jo 1951- *WhoAmW 93*
Babcock, Peter H. 1949- *WhoAm 92, WhoSSW 93*
Babcock, Sherra Walls 1948- *WhoEmL 93*
Babcock, Stephen Lee 1939- *WhoAm 92*
Babcock, Theodore A. 1954- *St&PR 93*
Babcock, Virginia Godwin Moses 1920- *WhoAmW 93*
Babcock, Walter Christian, Jr. 1947- *WhoAm 92*
Babcock, Warner King 1951- *WhoEmL 93*
Babcock, Wendell Keith 1925- *WhoWor 93*
Babcock, William E. 1939- *St&PR 93*
Babcook, Douglas Robert 1927- *St&PR 93*
Babe, David L. 1943- *St&PR 93*
Babecky, Paul 1961- *WhoEmL 93*
Babel, Dietrich 1930- *WhoScE 91-3*
Babel', I. 1894-1941 *BioIn 17*
Babel', Isaac 1894-1941 *BioIn 17*
Babell, William c. 1690-1723 *Baker 92*
Babella, Gyorgy *WhoScE 91-4*
Babelon, Jean-Pierre 1931- *WhoWor 93*
Babenco, Hector 1946- *MiSFD 9*
Baber, Guy Allen 1923- *St&PR 93*
Baber, Harriet Erica 1950- *WhoAmW 93*
Baber, Ralph Peter 1957- *WhoWor 93*
Baber, Robert Henry 1950- *WhoWrEP 92*
Baber, Stanley Roy *WhoScE 91-1*
Baber, Wilbur H., Jr. 1926- *WhoSSW 93, WhoWor 93*
Babero, Andras Fanfiero *Law&B 92*
Babes, Vincent T. 1933- *WhoScE 91-4*
Babey, Jean-Paul 1955- *WhoWor 93*
Babgert, Bruce Antony 1935- *WhoScE 91-1*
Babiarz, Francis Stanley 1948- *WhoEmL 93*
Babiarz, Joseph F. 1927- *St&PR 93*
Babiarz, Joseph Francis, Jr. 1951- *WhoEmL 93*
Babiasz, Judy Lynn 1958- *WhoAmW 93*
Babic, Hrvoje I. 1929- *WhoScE 91-4*
Babic, Joze 1917- *DrEEuF*
Babic, Michael Walter 1951- *WhoEmL 93*
Babich, Adam 1955- *WhoEmL 93*
Babich, Joanne Marie 1951- *WhoAmW 93*
Babich, Leonard Andrew 1935- *St&PR 93*
Babich, Michael Wayne 1945- *WhoSSW 93*
Babich, Nicholas 1930- *St&PR 93*
Babicki, Ryszard 1927- *WhoScE 91-4*
Babij, Mark John 1956- *WhoE 93, WhoEmL 93*
Babik, Paul B. 1947- *St&PR 93*
Babikian, George H. *WhoAm 92*
Babin, Claude 1934- *WhoScE 91-2*
Babin, Claude Hunter 1924- *WhoAm 92*
Babin, Claude Hunter, Jr. 1952- *WhoEmL 93, WhoSSW 93*
Babin, Mara L. 1950- *St&PR 93*
Babin, Maria Teresa 1910- *HispAmA*
Babin, Maria Teresa 1910-1989 *NotHsAW 93 [port]*
Babin, Troy J. *Law&B 92*
Babin, Victor 1908-1972 *Baker 92*
Babin, W. Edward 1935- *St&PR 93*
Babinec, Gehl P. *Law&B 92, WhoAm 92*
Babinec, George Frederick 1957- *WhoEmL 93*
Babinecz, Richard William *Law&B 92*
Babington, Brian Keith 1956- *WhoUN 92*
Babini, G.N. *WhoScE 91-3*
Babini, Matteo 1754-1816 *Baker 92*
Babiniec, Dennis Henry 1956- *WhoEmL 93*
Babitch, Joseph Aaron 1942- *WhoSSW 93*
Babitz, Brenda Lipton 1940- *WhoAmW 93, WhoE 93*
Babitz, Eve *BioIn 17*
Babitz, Sol 1911-1982 *Baker 92*
Babji, Abdul Salam *WhoWor 93*
Babler, Wayne E. 1915- *WhoAm 92*
Babler, Wayne E., Jr. 1942- *WhoAm 92, WhoWor 93*
Bablitch, William A. 1941- *WhoAm 92*
Babock, Ronald Pringle 1936- *St&PR 93*
Babonis, Eleanor Rose 1935- *WhoAmW 93*
Babrowski, Claire Harbeck 1957- *WhoAmW 93*
Babson, Arthur C. 1909- *St&PR 93*
Babson, David Leveau 1911- *WhoAm 92*
Babson, Donald Paul 1924- *St&PR 93*
Babson, Irving K. 1936- *WhoAm 92, WhoWor 93*
Babson, Nicholas C. 1946- *St&PR 93*
Babson, Stanley M., Jr. 1925- *St&PR 93*
Babson, Susan Averill 1924- *St&PR 93*
Babu, Shishir Chandra 1951- *WhoEmL 93*
Babu, Suresh Chandra 1961- *WhoE 93, WhoWor 93*
Babu, Uma Mahesh 1947- *WhoE 93*
Babuder, Maks 1940- *WhoScE 91-4*
Babula, William 1943- *WhoAm 92, WhoWrEP 92*
Babur 1483-1530 *HarEnMi*
Baburek, Ivan *WhoScE 91-4*
Babutia, Ioan 1929- *WhoScE 91-4*
Baby, M.A. 1954- *WhoAsAP 91*
"Baby Doc" *DcCPCAm*
Babyface *BioIn 17, SoulM*
Babylas *ConAu 139*
Babylas dc. 250 *OxDcByz*
Baca, Eduardo 1951- *WhoWor 93*
Baca, Elfego 1865-1949 *BioIn 17*
Baca, Jimmy Santiago 1952- *DcLB 122 [port], MagSAmL [port]*
Baca, Joseph Francis 1936- *HispAmA [port], WhoAm 92*
Baca, Judith F. 1946- *NotHsAW 93 [port]*
Baca, Judy 1946- *HispAmA*
Baca, Linda Todd 1946- *WhoEmL 93*
Baca, Lisa Lu Ann 1967- *WhoAmW 93*
Baca, Polly 1943- *NotHsAW 93 [port]*
Baca, Thomas E. 1952- *WhoAm 92*
Baca-Barragan, Polly 1941- *HispAmA*
Bacal, Glenn Spencer 1953- *WhoEmL 93*
Bacall, Cortland B. 1919- *St&PR 93*
Bacall, Lauren 1924- *BioIn 17, IntDcF 2-3 [port], WhoAm 92*
Bacani, Nicanor-Guglielmo Vila 1947- *WhoWor 93*
Bacanskas, John 1937- *St&PR 93*
Bacares, Alfonso 1943- *St&PR 93*
Bacarisse, Pamela *WhoE 93*
Bacarisse, Salvador 1898-1963 *Baker 92*
Bacay, Danilo Abellanosa 1941- *WhoWor 93*
Baca-Zinn, Maxine 1942- *HispAmA, NotHsAW 93 [port]*
Baccala, James N. 1945- *St&PR 93*
Baccaloni, Salvatore 1900-1969 *Baker 92, IntDcOp, OxDcOp*
Baccanti, Marco 1961- *WhoWor 93*
Baccari, Alberto 1952- *WhoAm 92*
Baccari, Carmella 1945- *WhoE 93*
Bacchetta, Richard Charles Lucien 1951- *WhoScE 91-2*
Bacchus, James L. 1949- *WhoSSW 93*
Bacchus, Jim 1949- *CngDr 91, WhoAm 92*

Bacci, Diana Shawhan Harris 1948- WhoE 93
Bacciarelli, Marcello 1731-1818 PolBiDi
Baccigaluppi, Roger John 1934- WhoAm 92
Baccus Horsley, Diane Christie 1949- WhoEmL 93
Baccusi, Ippolito 1550-1608 Baker 92
Bace, Edward J. 1952- St&PR 93
Bace, Edward J., Jr. 1952- WhoEmL 93
Bacelar, Manuela 1943- BioIn 17
Bacevicius, John Anthony, V 1953- WhoWor 93
Bacewicz, Grazyna BioIn 17
Bacewicz, Grazyna 1909-1969 Baker 92
Bacewicz, Grazyna 1913-1969 PolBiDi
Bach Baker 92
Bach, Albert 1844-1912 Baker 92
Bach, Arthur Law&B 92
Bach, Arthur James 1929- WhoAm 92
Bach, August Wilhelm 1796-1869 Baker 92
Bach, Bernard 1937- WhoScE 91-2
Bach, Carl Philipp Emanuel 1714-1788 Baker 92
Bach, Caspar Baker 92
Bach, Caspar 1570-1640 Baker 92
Bach, Charles L., Jr. 1952- WhoE 93, WhoEmL 93
Bach, Christoph Baker 92
Bach, Christoph 1613-1661 Baker 92
Bach, Claudia Stewart 1956- WhoEmL 93
Bach, Daryl Gene 1936- St&PR 93
Bach, David Charles Law&B 92
Bach, Elizabeth Marie 1952- WhoEmL 93
Bach, Georg Christoph 1642-1697 Baker 92
Bach, George Leland 1915- WhoAm 92
Bach, Gunther 1928- WhoWor 93
Bach, Harold H., Jr. 1932- St&PR 93
Bach, Heinrich Baker 92
Bach, Heinrich 1615-1692 Baker 92
Bach, J.F. WhoScE 91-2
Bach, Jacques 1833-1894 See Kranich & Bach Baker 92
Bach, James A. 1950- St&PR 93, WhoAm 92
Bach, Jan (Morris) 1937- Baker 92, WhoAm 92
Bach, Johann Baker 92
Bach, Johann 1550-1626 Baker 92
Bach, Johann 1604-1673 Baker 92
Bach, Johann Aegidius 1645-1716 Baker 92
Bach, Johann Ambrosius Baker 92
Bach, Johann Ambrosius 1645-1695 Baker 92
Bach, Johann Bernhard 1676-1749 Baker 92
Bach, Johann Christian 1735-1782 Baker 92, BioIn 17, OxDcOp
Bach, Johann Christoph 1642-1703 Baker 92
Bach, Johann Christoph 1645-1693 Baker 92
Bach, Johann Christoph 1671-1721 Baker 92
Bach, Johann Christoph 1732-1795 OxDcOp
Bach, Johann Christoph Friedrich 1732-1795 Baker 92
Bach, Johann Ernst 1722-1777 Baker 92
Bach, Johann Ludwig 1677-1731 Baker 92
Bach, Johann Michael 1648-1694 Baker 92
Bach, Johann Nicolaus 1669-1753 Baker 92
Bach, Johann Sebastian 1685-1750 Baker 92, OxDcOp
Bach, Johannes See Bach Baker 92
Bach, Leonhard Emil 1849-1902 Baker 92
Bach, Marcus 1906- WhoAm 92, WhoWrEP 92
Bach, Matt Howard 1957- WhoE 93
Bach, Melchior See Bach Baker 92
Bach, Nicolaus See Bach Baker 92
Bach, Penelope Caroline 1946- WhoEmL 93
Bach, Peter E. 1935- St&PR 93
Bach, Richard 1936- BioIn 17, ScF&FL 92
Bach, Richard D. 1934- WhoAm 92
Bach, Sebastian 1968- BioIn 17
Bach, Steve Crawford 1921- WhoAm 92
Bach, Veit See Bach Baker 92
Bach, Wilhelm Friedemann 1710-1784 Baker 92, OxDcOp
Bach, Wilhelm Friedrich Ernst 1759-1845 Baker 92
Bacha, James Ronald Law&B 92
Bachand, Jean-Claude Law&B 92
Bachand, Stephen E. 1938- WhoAm 92
Bachand, William Randall 1953- WhoSSW 93
Bachanek, Stanislaw W. 1920- WhoScE 91-4
Bacharach, Burt 1928- Baker 92, BioIn 17
Bacharach, Burt 1929- WhoAm 92
Bacharach, Melvin Lewis 1924- WhoAm 92
Bachauer, Gina 1913-1976 Baker 92
Bachchan, Amitabh 1942- IntDcF 2-3
Bache, Benjamin Franklin 1769-1798 BioIn 17, JrnUS
Bache, Constance 1846-1903 Baker 92
Bache, Ellyn 1942- WhoWrEP 92
Bache, Louise Franklin AmWomPl
Bache, Steven Edward 1955- WhoSSW 93
Bache, Theodore Stephen 1936- St&PR 93, WhoAm 92, WhoE 93
Bachel, Larry F. 1949- WhoIns 93
Bachelard, Herman Stanton WhoScE 91-1
Bachelder, Joseph Elmer, III 1932- WhoAm 92
Bachelder, Thomas 1958- ConAu 139
Bachelet, Alfred 1864-1944 Baker 92
Bachelis, Leonard WhoE 93
Bachelis, Roald Davidovich 1930- WhoWor 93
Bachem-Alent, Rose Marie WhoWrEP 92
Bachenheimer, Cara Conway 1961- WhoEmL 93
Bachenheimer, Ralph James 1928- WhoE 93
Bachenheimer, Steven I. 1942- St&PR 93
Bacher, Francoise 1928- WhoScE 91-2
Bacher, Judith St. George 1946- WhoAm 92, WhoE 93
Bacher, Rosalie Wride 1925- WhoAmW 93, WhoWor 93
Bachhuber, Carl Nelson 1943- St&PR 93
Bachhuber, Theodore Joseph 1913- St&PR 93
Bachicha, Joseph Alfred WhoWor 93
Bachik, Mark 1955- WhoEmL 93
Bachko, Nicholas 1919- WhoWor 93
Bachko, Nicholas 1919-1991 BioIn 17
Bachleder, Louis J. Law&B 92
Bachmacz, Waldemar 1928- WhoScE 91-4
Bachmair, Hans 1943- WhoScE 91-3
Bachman, Bonnie Jean 1950- WhoEmL 93
Bachman, Bruce Michael 1951- WhoSSW 93
Bachman, Carol Christine 1959- WhoAmW 93
Bachman, Charles William St&PR 93
Bachman, David Christian 1934- WhoAm 92
Bachman, Ellen Cathy Law&B 92
Bachman, Gary Eugene 1951- WhoEmL 93
Bachman, George 1933- WhoAm 92
Bachman, Henry L. 1930- St&PR 93
Bachman, Henry Lee 1930- WhoAm 92
Bachman, James Edward 1947- St&PR 93
Bachman, James G. 1948- St&PR 93
Bachman, Jean Collom 1935- WhoAmW 93
Bachman, John Andrew, Jr. 1926- WhoSSW 93
Bachman, John B. 1955- WhoE 93
Bachman, Lee William 1947- St&PR 93
Bachman, Leonard 1925- WhoAm 92
Bachman, Lillian Helen 1938- WhoAmW 93
Bachman, Nathan Dulaney, IV 1935- WhoAm 92
Bachman, Richard ScF&FL 92
Bachman, Richard 1947- BioIn 17
Bachman, Stanley Frederick 1924- St&PR 93
Bachman, Vernon Emil 1937- St&PR 93
Bachman, Walter Crawford 1911-1991 BioIn 17
Bachmann, Albert Edward 1917- WhoSSW 93
Bachmann, Alberto Abraham 1875-1963 Baker 92
Bachmann, Bill 1946- WhoEmL 93, WhoSSW 93, WhoWor 93
Bachmann, Donna Grace 1948- WhoAmW 93
Bachmann, Eric R. d1991 BioIn 17
Bachmann, Fedor Wolfgang 1927- WhoScE 91-4, WhoWor 93
Bachmann, John A. Law&B 92
Bachmann, John W. 1938- St&PR 93
Bachmann, Marc R. 1928- WhoScE 91-4
Bachmann, Mark Edward 1948- St&PR 93
Bachmann, Peter Joseph 1949- WhoE 93
Bachmann, Peter Klaus 1950- WhoWor 93
Bachmann, Richard A. 1944- St&PR 93
Bachmann, Richard Arthur 1944- WhoAm 92, WhoSSW 93
Bachmann, Wolfgang 1932- WhoScE 91-3
Bachmeyer, Robert Wesley 1915- WhoAm 92
Bachmeyer, Thomas John 1942- WhoSSW 93
Bachner, Donald J. 1930- St&PR 93
Bachner, John Philip 1944- WhoE 93
Bachner, Marcia Lynn 1946- WhoAmW 93, WhoE 93
Bachofen, Johann Caspar 1695-1755 Baker 92
Bachofen, Johann Jakob 1815-1887 IntDcAn
Bachofen, Reinhard 1932- WhoScE 91-4
Bachofer, Thomas Law&B 92
Bachop, Martin William 1952- WhoSSW 93
Bachop, William G. 1928- St&PR 93
Bachrach, Alice R. d1991 BioIn 17
Bachrach, Bradford K. d1992 NewYTBS 92 [port]
Bachrach, Bradford K. 1910- WhoAm 92
Bachrach, Charles Lewis 1946- WhoAm 92
Bachrach, David Arthur 1952- WhoEmL 93
Bachrach, David James 1948- WhoSSW 93
Bachrach, Eve Elizabeth 1951- WhoEmL 93
Bachrach, Howard L. 1920- WhoAm 92
Bachrach, Ira Nathaniel 1938- WhoAm 92
Bachrach, L. Fabian, Jr. 1917- St&PR 93
Bachrach, Louis F., III 1950- St&PR 93
Bachrach, Louis Fabian, Jr. 1917- WhoAm 92
Bachrach, Louis Fabian, III 1950- WhoEmL 93
Bachrach, Nancy 1948- WhoAm 92
Bachrach, Robert D. 1954- St&PR 93
Bachrach, Robert Lee 1926- St&PR 93
Bachrich, Sigmund 1841-1913 Baker 92
Bachta, Linda M. 1951- WhoAmW 93
Bachtell, Clifton M. 1937- St&PR 93
Bachtler, John Franz WhoScE 91-1
Bachtold, Thomas Eugene 1935- WhoWor 93
Bachur, Nicholas Robert, Sr. 1933- WhoAm 92
Bachus, Benson Floyd 1917- WhoWor 93
Bachus, Ernest Wayne 1946- WhoEmL 93
Bachus, Larry Glenn 1948- WhoEmL 93
Bachus, Walter Otis 1926- WhoAm 92
Bachynski, Morrel Paul 1930- WhoAm 92
Bach-y-Rita, Paul 1934- WhoAm 92
Bach-Zelewski, Erich von der 1898-1972 HarEnMi
Bacia, Tadeusz 1926- WhoScE 91-4
Bacigalupi, Eusebi Guell y 1847-1918 BioIn 17
Bacigalupo, Charles Anthony 1934- St&PR 93, WhoAm 92
Bacik, Carl Stephen 1925- St&PR 93
Bacilek, Jaromir K. 1946- WhoScE 91-4
Bacilly, Benigne de c. 1625-1690 Baker 92
Bacino, Joseph Nicholas 1930- St&PR 93
Back, George 1796-1878 Expl 93 [port]
Back, Jim 1955- St&PR 93
Back, Ralph J.R. 1949- WhoScE 91-4
Back, Sven-Erik 1919- Baker 92
Back, Wilfried 1939- WhoScE 91-3
Backas, James Jacob 1926- WhoAm 92
Backberg, Bruce A. Law&B 92
Backberg, Bruce Allen 1948- St&PR 93, WhoAm 92
Backe, John David 1932- St&PR 93, WhoAm 92
Backe, John Elliott 1960- WhoE 93, WhoEmL 93
Backe, Pamela Renee 1955- WhoEmL 93
Backeland, Gerald H. 1945- St&PR 93
Backenroth-Ohsako, Gunnel Anne Maj 1951- WhoWor 93
Backenstoss, Henry Brightbill 1912- WhoE 93
Backer, Bruce Everett 1955- WhoEmL 93
Backer, David F. 1940- St&PR 93, WhoAm 92
Backer, Leonard Norman d1991 BioIn 17
Backer, Marjorie K. St&PR 93
Backer, Matthias Henry, Jr. 1926- WhoAm 92
Backer, Morris 1927- St&PR 93
Backer, Rushton O. 1926- WhoAm 92
Backer, Todd Gilbert 1960- WhoEmL 93
Backer, W. Dale 1946- St&PR 93
Backer, William Earnest 1922- St&PR 93
Backer, William Montague 1926- St&PR 93, WhoAm 92, WhoE 93
Backer-Grondahl, Agathe 1847-1907 BioIn 17
Backer-Grondahl, Agathe (Ursula) 1847-1907 Baker 92
Backers, Cor 1910- Baker 92
Backers-Hoyle, Angela Cherie 1958- WhoAmW 93
Backes, Paul Gilbert 1952- WhoAm 92
Backes, Ronald Joseph Law&B 92
Backes, Ruth Emerson 1918- WhoE 93
Backes, Wilfried 1943- St&PR 93
Backes-Gellner, Uschi 1959- WhoWor 93
Backhaus, Betty Jane 1930- WhoSSW 93
Backhaus, Egon R.K. 1927- WhoScE 91-3
Backhaus, Gerald C. Law&B 92
Backhaus, Loren A. 1942- St&PR 93
Backhaus, Wilhelm 1884-1969 Baker 92
Backhus, James Robert 1957- St&PR 93
Backlund, Claudia Mai Law&B 92
Backlund, Jan E. 1944- WhoScE 91-4
Backlund, Jon Oskar 1846-1916 BioIn 17
Backlund, Ralph Theodore 1918- WhoAm 92, WhoWrEP 92
Backman, Alan Gregory 1950- WhoE 93
Backman, Diana ScF&FL 92
Backman, Jean Adele 1931- WhoAmW 93
Backman, Katherine Ruth 1949- WhoAmW 93
Backman, Robert Emil 1917- WhoE 93
Backman, William D., Jr. 1931- St&PR 93
Backman, William Lewis 1947- WhoSSW 93
Backofen, Richard B. Law&B 92
Backscheider, Paula R(ice) 1943- ConAu 138
Backstrand, Drew Steven Law&B 92
Backstrom, Gunnar 1931- WhoScE 91-4
Backus, Ann Swift Newell 1941- WhoAmW 93
Backus, Charles Edward 1937- WhoAm 92
Backus, Debra Marie 1955- WhoE 93
Backus, Emma Henrietta Schermeyer 1876- AmWomPl
Backus, G. Richard 1935- St&PR 93
Backus, George Edward 1930- WhoAm 92
Backus, Helene B. AmWomPl
Backus, Jan 1947- WhoAmW 93
Backus, Jim BioIn 17
Backus, Jim 1913-1989 QDrFCA 92 [port]
Backus, John 1924- WhoAm 92
Backus, John King 1925- WhoAm 92
Backus, Marcia Ellen 1954- WhoAmW 93
Backus, Patricia Mary 1948- WhoAmW 93
Backus, Richard Grant, II 1949- WhoEmL 93, WhoSSW 93
Bacmeister, Rhoda d1991 BioIn 17
Bacon, Abigail R. 1950- St&PR 93
Bacon, Augustus Octavius 1835-1914 PolPar
Bacon, Brett Kermit 1947- WhoAm 92, WhoEmL 93
Bacon, Brian M. Law&B 92
Bacon, Caroline Sharfman 1942- WhoAmW 93
Bacon, Charles L., Jr. Law&B 92
Bacon, Cheryl Mann 1954- WhoAmW 93
Bacon, Darwin Dee 1947- WhoEmL 93
Bacon, David John WhoScE 91-1
Bacon, David Walter 1935- WhoAm 92
Bacon, Deanna Maria 1943- WhoAmW 93
Bacon, Deborah Gale 1942- WhoAmW 93
Bacon, Denis F. 1929- St&PR 93
Bacon, Dennis Ray 1957- WhoEmL 93
Bacon, Dolores Marbourg AmWomPl
Bacon, Donald ScF&FL 92
Bacon, Donald Conrad 1935- WhoAm 92, WhoWrEP 92
Bacon, Donna L. 1951- St&PR 93
Bacon, Edmund Norwood 1910- WhoAm 92
Bacon, Edward Michael, Jr. 1930- St&PR 93
Bacon, Edwin Munroe 1844-1916 JrnUS
Bacon, Ernst 1898-1990 Baker 92, BioIn 17
Bacon, Eva M. AmWomPl
Bacon, Francis d1992 NewYTBS 92 [port]
Bacon, Francis 1909-1992 BioIn 17, CurBio 92N, ModArCr 3 [port]
Bacon, Francis Warner 1920- St&PR 93
Bacon, George A., Jr. 1929- St&PR 93
Bacon, George Edgar 1932- WhoAm 92
Bacon, George Edward WhoScE 91-1
Bacon, George Hughes 1935- WhoE 93, WhoWor 93
Bacon, Hazel AmWomPl
Bacon, James Edmund 1931- St&PR 93, WhoAm 92, WhoE 93
Bacon, James Jeffrey 1956- WhoE 93
Bacon, Janice Lynne 1954- WhoEmL 93
Bacon, Jenny BioIn 17
Bacon, John A. Law&B 92
Bacon, John O. 1950- St&PR 93
Bacon, John Stille 1935- St&PR 93
Bacon, Josephine 1906- AmWomPl
Bacon, Josephine Dodge Daskam 1876-1961 AmWomPl
Bacon, Judd L. Law&B 92
Bacon, Kevin 1958- WhoAm 92
Bacon, Larry Stephen 1946- St&PR 93
Bacon, Lawrence E. 1938- St&PR 93, WhoIns 93
Bacon, Lawrence Edward 1938- WhoAm 92
Bacon, Leonard 1802-1881 BioIn 17
Bacon, Leonard Anthony 1931- WhoWor 93
Bacon, Lloyd 1890-1955 MiSFD 9N
Bacon, Louis Albert 1921- WhoAm 92
Bacon, Martha 1917-1981 ScF&FL 92
Bacon, Martha Brantley 1938- WhoAmW 93
Bacon, Martha (Sherman) 1917-1981 DcAmChF 1960
Bacon, Mary Schell Hoke 1870- AmWomPl
Bacon, Nancy Marie 1946- St&PR 93
Bacon, Nathaniel 1647-1676 HarEnMi

Bacon, Neil F. 1956- *St&PR 93*
Bacon, Paul Caldwell 1945- *WhoWor 93*
Bacon, Peggy 1895-1987 *ScF&FL 92*
Bacon, Phillip 1922- *WhoAm 92, WhoWor 93, WhoWrEP 92*
Bacon, Richard Franklin 1927- *WhoAm 92*
Bacon, Richard Mackenzie 1776-1844 *Baker 92*
Bacon, Robert C. 1940- *St&PR 93*
Bacon, Roger 1926- *WhoSSW 93*
Bacon, Selden D. d1992 *NewYTBS 92*
Bacon, Sylvia 1931- *WhoAm 92*
Bacon, Vicky Lee 1950- *WhoEmL 93*
Bacon, Wallace Alger 1914- *WhoAm 92, WhoWrEP 92*
Bacon, Warren H. 1923-1991 *BioIn 17*
Bacon, Wesley D. 1940- *WhoIns 93*
Bacon, William Francis 1956- *WhoEmL 93*
Bacon, William T., Jr. 1923- *St&PR 93*
Bacorro, Benjamin Tabayoyong 1945- *WhoWor 93*
Bacot, John Carter 1933- *St&PR 93, WhoAm 92*
Bacot, Marie 1942- *WhoSSW 93, WhoWor 93*
Bacque, Angela 1957- *WhoAmW 93*
Bacque, James 1929- *WhoCanL 92*
Bacquier, Gabriel 1924- *IntDcOp, OxDcOp, WhoWor 93*
Bacquier, Gabriel (-Augustin-Raymond-Theodore-Louis) 1924- *Baker 92*
Bacskai Lauro, Istvan 1933- *DrEEuF*
Bacso, George J., III *Law&B 92*
Bacso, Peter 1928- *DrEEuF*
Baczenski, Jacqueline F. 1945- *WhoAmW 93*
Baczynski, Krzysztof Kamil 1921-1944 *PolBiDi*
Baczynski, Zbigniew 1920- *WhoScE 91-4*
Bada, Anthony Dominic 1929- *St&PR 93*
Badain, David I. *Law&B 92*
Badal, Daniel Walter 1912- *WhoAm 92*
Badalamente, Marie Ann 1949- *WhoE 93*
Badalamenti, Angelo *BioIn 17, ConTFT 10*
Badalamenti, Anthony 1940- *WhoWor 93*
Badalamenti, Anthony Francis 1943- *WhoE 93*
Badalamenti, Fred Leopoldo 1935- *WhoE 93*
Badale, Andy *ConTFT 10*
Badali, G.A. *Law&B 92*
Badalian, Mike *St&PR 93*
Badalian, Ray *St&PR 93*
Badalli, Frank J., Sr. 1922- *St&PR 93*
Badamo, Laura M. *Law&B 92*
Badanes, Menke *WhoWrEP 92*
Badanes, Peter Louis *Law&B 92*
Badani, Abdulla 1955- *WhoIns 93*
Badaracco, Cheryl Kay 1962- *WhoEmL 93, WhoSSW 93*
Badar Khan, Agha Mahmood 1928- *WhoWor 93*
Badarzewska, Thekla 1834-1861 *Baker 92*
Badash, Lawrence 1934- *WhoAm 92*
Badat, Randall *MiSFD 9*
Badawi, Samir M. 1933- *WhoUN 92*
Badawi Abdullah bin Haji Ahmad Badawi, Datuk 1939- *WhoAsAP 91*
Badcock, Wogan S., Jr. 1932- *St&PR 93*
Baddeley, Alan David *WhoScE 91-1*
Baddeley, D. Jeffery 1938- *St&PR 93*
Baddeley, D. Jeffrey *Law&B 92*
Baddeley, D. Jeffrey 1938- *WhoAm 92*
Baddeley, Pam *ScF&FL 92*
Baddiley, James *WhoScE 91-1*
Baddiley, James 1918- *WhoWor 93*
Baddock, James 1950- *ConAu 137*
Baddorf, Robert James 1950- *St&PR 93*
Baddour, Anne Bridge *WhoAmW 93, WhoWor 93*
Baddour, Raymond Frederick 1925- *WhoAm 92*
Bade, Robert Alan 1946- *St&PR 93*
Bade, Thomas M. *ScF&FL 92*
Bade, Tom 1946- *ScF&FL 92, WhoEmL 93*
Badea, Christian *WhoAm 92*
Badea, Christian 1947- *Baker 92*
Badeer, Henry Sarkis 1915- *WhoAm 92*
Badel, Julie 1946- *WhoAm 92, WhoAmW 93*
Badell, Colleen Curtis 1951- *WhoAmW 93*
Badellas, Anthimos 1937- *WhoScE 91-3*
Badelles, Mariano 1915- *WhoAsAP 91*
Bademian, Leon 1932- *St&PR 93*
Baden, Conrad 1908-1989 *Baker 92*
Baden, Michael M. 1934- *WhoWor 93*
Baden, Robert 1936- *ConAu 138, SmATA 70 [port]*
Baden, Robert Charles 1942- *WhoAm 92*
Baden-Baden, Louis, Margrave of 1655-1707 *HarEnMi*
Badenoch, Lindsay *ScF&FL 92*
Baden-Powell, Robert Stephenson Smyth 1857-1941 *DcTwHis, HarEnMi*
Baden-Powell of Gilwell, Baron 1857-1941 *BioIn 17*
Bader, Albert Xavier, Jr. 1932- *WhoAm 92*
Bader, Andrea Elizabeth 1955- *WhoEmL 93*
Bader, Cal Joseph, Jr. 1950- *WhoE 93*
Bader, Douglas Robert Steuart 1910-1982 *HarEnMi*
Bader, Fredric George 1947- *St&PR 93*
Bader, Gregory Dennis 1950- *St&PR 93*
Bader, Gregory V. *Law&B 92*
Bader, Harry Frederick 1924- *WhoE 93*
Bader, Hermann Joseph 1927- *WhoWor 93*
Bader, Izaak Walton 1922- *WhoE 93, WhoWor 93*
Bader, John Merwin 1919- *WhoAm 92*
Bader, Jonathan David *Law&B 92*
Bader, Joseph Francis 1939- *St&PR 93*
Bader, Kate 1947- *WhoAmW 93*
Bader, Kenneth Leroy 1934- *WhoAm 92*
Bader, Louis *Law&B 92*
Bader, Martin *St&PR 93*
Bader, Michael Haley 1929- *WhoAm 92*
Bader, Randi J. *Law&B 92*
Bader, Richard F. W. 1931- *WhoAm 92*
Bader, Robert Smith 1925- *WhoAm 92*
Bader, Walter M. 1911- *St&PR 93*
Bader, William Banks 1931- *WhoAm 92*
Badertscher, David Glen 1935- *WhoAm 92, WhoE 93*
Badertscher, Donald 1934- *St&PR 93*
Badescu, A.A. Paul 1943- *WhoScE 91-4*
Badescu, Dinu (Constantin) 1904- *Baker 92*
Badessa, Robert C. 1948- *St&PR 93*
Badet, Josette Francoise 1947- *WhoWor 93*
Badetti, Rolando Emilio 1947- *WhoWor 93*
Badgeley, Clarence Dale 1899-1990 *BioIn 17*
Badger, Beryl Ann 1947- *WhoWor 93*
Badger, Charles H. 1917- *St&PR 93, WhoAm 92*
Badger, David Harry 1931- *WhoWor 93*
Badger, David Russell 1947- *WhoEmL 93*
Badger, Eugene Carroll 1928- *WhoSSW 93*
Badger, George Edmund 1795-1866 *OxCSupC*
Badger, James Winifred 1941- *WhoSSW 93*
Badger, John M. *Law&B 92*
Badger, M.S. *Law&B 92*
Badger, Mildred Rita 1939- *St&PR 93*
Badger, Phil *MiSFD 9*
Badger, Sandra Rae 1946- *WhoAmW 93*
Badger, Sherwin Campbell 1901-1972 *BiDAMSp 1989*
Badger, Thomas Mark 1945- *WhoSSW 93*
Badger, Timothy C. 1949- *St&PR 93*
Badgerow, John Nicholas 1951- *WhoEmL 93*
Badgett, Billy *BioIn 17*
Badgett, Lee Douglas 1939- *WhoAm 92*
Badgett, Tom 1944- *WhoSSW 93*
Badgley, John Roy 1922- *WhoWor 93*
Badgley, Marie Minor Curry 1926- *WhoAmW 93*
Badgley, Mark *BioIn 17*
Badgley, Theodore McBride 1925- *WhoAm 92*
Badgley, William S. 1930- *St&PR 93, WhoAm 92*
Badgro, Red 1903- *BioIn 17*
Badham, John 1939- *MiSFD 9*
Badham, John MacDonald 1939- *WhoAm 92*
Badham, Robert E. 1929- *WhoAm 92*
Badia *BioIn 17*
Badia, Carlo Agostino 1672-1738 *Baker 92*
Badia, Conchita 1897-1975 *Baker 92*
Badia-Batalla, Francesc 1923- *WhoWor 93*
Badian, Ernst 1925- *WhoAm 92, WhoE 93*
Badie, Ronald Peter 1942- *St&PR 93, WhoAm 92*
Badillo, Diana 1946- *WhoEmL 93*
Badillo, Herman 1929- *HispAmA [port]*
Badillo-Sciortino, Olga Esther 1941- *WhoWrEP 92*
Badings, Henk 1907-1987 *Baker 92*
Badini, Aldo Anthony 1958- *WhoEmL 93*
Badini, Carlo Francesco fl. 18th cent.- *OxDcOp*
Badini, Ernesto 1876-1937 *Baker 92*
Badinski, Nicolai 1937- *Baker 92*
Badinter, Elisabeth *BioIn 17*
Badinter, Robert 1928- *BioIn 17*
Badish, Kenneth Michael 1951- *WhoEmL 93*
Badiyi, Reza 1936- *MiSFD 9*
Badler, Norman Ira 1948- *WhoE 93*
Badley, Bernard William David 1933- *WhoAm 92*
Badman, John, III 1944- *WhoE 93, WhoWor 93*
Badmington, Richard R. 1955- *St&PR 93*
Badmington, Richards R. 1955- *WhoE 93*
Badoaro, Giacomo 1602-1654 *OxDcOp*
Badoer, Giacomo *OxDcByz*
Badoglio, Pietro 1871-1956 *DcTwHis, HarEnMi*
Badon, Calvin L. 1935- *St&PR 93*
Badorf, John T. 1920- *St&PR 93*
Badour, Terence Patrick *Law&B 92*
Badoux, Samuel 1930- *WhoScE 91-4*
Badovinus, Wayne L. 1943- *WhoAm 92*
Badr, Gamal Moursi 1924- *WhoE 93, WhoWor 93*
Badran, Adnan 1935- *WhoUN 92*
Badran, Saeed M. 1956- *WhoWor 93*
Badr Muqbil, Saeed Sharae 1943- *WhoUN 92*
Badstue, P.B. 1927- *WhoScE 91-2*
Badstuebner, Hans Alexander 1916- *WhoWor 93*
Badtke, Donald J. 1936- *St&PR 93*
Baduel, R. 1947- *WhoScE 91-2*
Badura, Carl Werner 1937- *WhoE 93*
Badura, Leslaw Arnold 1925- *WhoScE 91-4*
Badura, Paul 1927- *Baker 92*
Badura-Skoda, Paul 1927- *Baker 92, WhoAm 92*
Badwi, Abby F. 1946- *St&PR 93*
Badwound, Elgin *BioIn 17*
Badzik, Carolyn Donna 1967- *WhoE 93*
Badzik, Joan Renee 1960- *WhoAmW 93*
Bae, Myung Ho 1939- *WhoWor 93*
Baebler, Drew Charles 1960- *WhoEmL 93*
Baechel, Kenneth Earl 1941- *WhoE 93*
Baechle, James J. *Law&B 92*
Baechle, James Joseph 1932- *St&PR 93, WhoAm 92*
Baechle, Susan Jean Parks 1946- *WhoEmL 93*
Baechle, Thomas J. *Law&B 92*
Baechli, Otto *DcCPCAm*
Baede, A.P.M. 1940- *WhoScE 91-3*
Baeder, Donald L. 1925- *St&PR 93*
Baeder, Donald Lee 1925- *WhoAm 92*
Baeder, John Alan 1938- *WhoSSW 93*
Baehni, Pierre 1946- *WhoScE 91-4*
Baehr, Barbara Ann 1956- *WhoAmW 93*
Baehr, Hans-Peter 1942- *WhoScE 91-3*
Baehr, Lutz Amand 1939- *WhoUN 92*
Baehr, Patricia Goehner *BioIn 17*
Baehr, Theodore 1946- *WhoSSW 93*
Baehr, Timothy James 1943- *WhoWrEP 92*
Baen, James Patrick 1943- *ScF&FL 92*
Baen, Jim *ScF&FL 92*
Baena, Robert Bob 1930- *WhoE 93*
Baena, Scott Louis 1949- *WhoAm 92*
Baena Soares, Joao Clemente 1931- *WhoWor 93*
Baender, Margaret Woodruff 1921- *WhoAmW 93, WhoWrEP 92*
Baensch, Robert Eduard 1934- *WhoAm 92*
Baenziger, Raymond Emil 1934- *WhoUN 92*
Baer, Albert M. 1905- *St&PR 93*
Baer, Albert Max 1905- *WhoAm 92*
Baer, Alec Jean 1930- *WhoScE 91-4*
Baer, Andrew Rudolf 1946- *WhoAm 92*
Baer, Barbara Sue 1958- *WhoE 93*
Baer, Ben Kayser 1926- *WhoAm 92*
Baer, Benjamin F. 1918-1991 *BioIn 17*
Baer, Bernard Allan 1925- *WhoSSW 93*
Baer, Charles E. 1933- *St&PR 93*
Baer, David, Jr. 1905- *St&PR 93*
Baer, Donald Ray 1947- *WhoEmL 93*
Baer, Edward *Law&B 92*
Baer, Elizabeth Roberts 1946- *WhoAmW 93, WhoE 93*
Baer, Emil 1917- *St&PR 93*
Baer, Eric 1932- *WhoAm 92*
Baer, Eva Maria 1933- *WhoAmW 93*
Baer, Frederick Eugene 1924- *St&PR 93*
Baer, Frederick W. 1948- *St&PR 93*
Baer, George Martin 1936- *WhoAm 92*
Baer, Gregor 1958- *WhoE 93*
Baer, Henry 1930- *WhoAm 92*
Baer, Hilde 1917- *St&PR 93*
Baer, Howard Lee 1918- *WhoWor 93*
Baer, J. Arthur, II 1921- *St&PR 93*
Baer, James Edward 1952- *WhoEmL 93*
Baer, Jerome I. 1936- *WhoIns 93*
Baer, John H. d1990 *BioIn 17*
Baer, John Metz 1908- *WhoWor 93*
Baer, John Richard Frederick 1941- *WhoAm 92*
Baer, Jon Alan 1945- *WhoE 93*
Baer, Joseph d1991 *BioIn 17*
Baer, Joseph Winslow 1917- *WhoAm 92*
Baer, Josh *BioIn 17*
Baer, Judith Abbott 1945- *WhoAmW 93*
Baer, Judy 1951- *SmATA 71 [port]*
Baer, Karl Ernst von 1792-1876 *BioIn 17*
Baer, Karla B. 1935- *St&PR 93*
Baer, Kenneth A. 1946- *St&PR 93*
Baer, Kenneth Peter 1930- *WhoAm 92*
Baer, Leopold S. 1926- *St&PR 93*
Baer, Linda Larson 1949- *WhoAmW 93*
Baer, Luke 1950- *WhoEmL 93*
Baer, Marc (Bradley) 1945- *ConAu 138*
Baer, Marcie M. 1933- *WhoWrEP 92*
Baer, Martha Lynn 1939- *WhoAm 92*
Baer, Max, Jr. 1937- *MiSFD 9*
Baer, Max Frank 1912- *WhoE 93*
Baer, Michael Alan 1943- *WhoAm 92, WhoE 93*
Baer, Norbert Sebastian 1938- *WhoAm 92*
Baer, Ralph August 1933- *St&PR 93, WhoAm 92*
Baer, Robert J. 1937- *WhoAm 92*
Baer, Robert Jacob 1924- *WhoAm 92*
Baer, Robert Joseph 1937- *St&PR 93*
Baer, Roland C., Jr. 1937- *St&PR 93*
Baer, Rudolf Lewis 1910- *WhoAm 92, WhoWor 93*
Baer, Steve H. 1949- *St&PR 93*
Baer, Thomas James 1927- *WhoAm 92*
Baer, Thomas S. 1942- *St&PR 93*
Baer, Timothy M. *Law&B 92*
Baer, Werner 1931- *WhoAm 92*
Baer, William Harold 1947- *WhoEmL 93*
Baer, William P. 1943- *St&PR 93*
Baerg, Richard Henry 1937- *WhoAm 92, WhoWor 93*
Baer-Kaupert, Friedrich-Wilhelm 1930- *WhoWor 93*
Baerlecken, Marta 1909- *WhoWor 93*
Baermann, Donna Lee Roth 1939- *WhoAmW 93*
Baermann, Robert Paul 1929- *St&PR 93*
Baernstein, Albert, II 1941- *WhoAm 92*
Baervoets, Raymond 1930-1989 *Baker 92*
Baerwald, David *BioIn 17*
Baerwald, Eric Harris 1964- *WhoE 93*
Baerwald, John Edward 1925- *WhoAm 92*
Baesch, John Francis 1944- *WhoE 93*
Baesel, Stuart Oliver 1925- *WhoAm 92*
Baessler, Arthur 1857-1907 *IntDcAn*
Baete, Gregory Paul 1953- *WhoEmL 93*
Baetsle, L.H.J.M. 1930- *WhoScE 91-2*
Baettig, Michel 1944- *WhoWor 93*
Baetz, Barbara Shelby *Law&B 92*
Baetzhold, Howard George 1923- *WhoAm 92*
Baeumer, Ludwig 1937- *WhoUN 92*
Baeumer, Max Lorenz *WhoAm 92, WhoWrEP 92*
Baev, Svetlomir V. 1947- *WhoWor 93*
Baev, Svetlomir Velev 1947- *WhoUN 92*
Baevre, Olav Arne 1947- *WhoScE 91-4*
Baey, Lian Peck 1931- *WhoWor 93*
Baeyens, August 1895-1966 *Baker 92*
Baez, Alberto Vinicio 1912- *HispAmA [port]*
Baez, Carmen 1908- *DcMexL*
Baez, Carmen 1957- *WhoAm 92, WhoEmL 93*
Baez, Edmundo 1914- *DcMexL*
Baez, Griselle 1959- *WhoAm 92, WhoSSW 93*
Baez, Joan *BioIn 17*
Baez, Joan 1941- *ConHero 2 [port], NotHsAW 93 [port]*
Baez, Joan (Chandos) 1941- *Baker 92, WhoAm 92, WhoAmW 93*
Baez, Manuel 1941- *WhoAm 92, WhoSSW 93*
Baez, Roberto A. 1962- *WhoE 93*
Baez, Wilfred John 1956- *WhoE 93*
Baeza, Daniel Michael 1952- *WhoEmL 93*
Baeza-Yates, Ricardo A. 1961- *WhoWor 93*
Bafalon, Lee *Law&B 92*
Bafaloukos, Ted 1946- *MiSFD 9*
Baffes, Thomas Gus 1923- *WhoAm 92*
Baffin, William 1584?-1622 *Expl 93*
Bafford, E. Donald 1929- *St&PR 93*
Bafile, Corrado Cardinal 1903- *WhoAm 92, WhoWor 93*
Bafort, Jozef M. 1935- *WhoScE 91-2*
Bagadion, Benjamin Ursua 1923- *WhoWor 93*
Bagai, Eric Paul 1940- *WhoWrEP 92*
Bagan, Merwyn 1936- *St&PR 93*
Bagarazzi, James Michael 1951- *WhoEmL 93*
Bagaria-Rivard, Sabine Marie 1958- *WhoWor 93*
Bagatsing, Amado S. 1947- *WhoAsAP 91*
Bagatsing, Ramon S., Jr. 1950- *WhoAsAP 91*
Bagatta, John J. d1992 *NewYTBS 92*
Bagayev, Gennadyi Nikolayevich 1937- *WhoWor 93*
Bagaza, Jean Baptiste 1946- *WhoAfr*
Bagbeni Adeito Nzengeya 1941- *WhoWor 93*
Bagby, Clarence Watson, Jr. 1937- *St&PR 93*
Bagby, Daniel Gordon 1941- *WhoSSW 93, WhoWor 93*
Bagby, Frederick Lair, Jr. 1920- *WhoAm 92*
Bagby, James Charles Jacob, Sr. 1889-1954 *BiDAMSp 1989*

Bagby, Susan Pound 1943- WhoAmW 93
Bagby, Wesley M(arvin) 1922- ConAu 37NR
Bagby, Wesley St. John 1910- WhoWor 93
Bagby, William Rardin 1910- WhoSSW 93
Bagchi, Kallol Kumar 1951- WhoWor 93
Bagci, Yildirim 1952- WhoScE 91-4
Bagdadi, Amr Ali WhoScE 91-1
Bagdan, Gloria 1929- WhoAmW 93, WhoE 93
Bagdasarian, Michael 1934- WhoScE 91-4
Bagdazian, Richard William 1955- WhoEmL 93
Bagdikian, Ben Haig 1920- WhoAm 92, WhoWrEP 92
Bagdon, Charles Anthony 1946- WhoEmL 93
Bagdon, Paul ScF&FL 92
Bagdonas, John Louis 1950- St&PR 93
Bagdorf, Howard Law&B 92
Bageant, Martha Dyer 1906- WhoAmW 93
Bagehot, Walter 1826-1877 BioIn 17
Bagerdjian, Maig S. Law&B 92
Bageris, John 1924- WhoAm 92
Bages, Jose Torras y 1846-1916 BioIn 17
Bagg, Gladys 1899- AmWomPl
Bagg, Helen F. AmWomPl
Bagg, Kirk Joseph 1959- WhoEmL 93
Bagg, Robert Ely 1935- WhoAm 92
Bagg, Thomas Campbell 1917- WhoE 93
Bagg, Thomas G. Law&B 92
Baggaley, Philip Andrew 1952- St&PR 93
Baggarly, Beverly J. 1950- WhoAmW 93
Bagge, Carl Elmer 1927- WhoAm 92
Bagge, Douglas M. Law&B 92
Bagge, Marla Jean 1952- WhoEmL 93
Bagge, Michael Charles 1950- WhoAm 92, WhoWor 93
Bagge, Pauli Kalervo 1938- WhoScE 91-4
Bagge, Selmar 1823-1896 Baker 92
Bagger, Ole 1933- WhoScE 91-2
Bagger, Richard Hartvig 1960- WhoEmL 93
Baggett, Byrd B. 1949- St&PR 93
Baggett, Judson B. 1944- WhoSSW 93
Baggett, Robert Joseph, Jr. 1920- St&PR 93
Baggett, W. Mike 1946- WhoEmL 93
Baggiani, Guido 1932- Baker 92
Baggio, Sebastiano Cardinal 1913- WhoWor 93
Bagg-Morgan, Kathleen Therese 1959- WhoSSW 93
Baggott, Clifford Deveney 1948- St&PR 93
Baggott, George E. 1942- St&PR 93
Baggott, George Theodore 1909- St&PR 93
Baggott, John Wayne 1918- St&PR 93
Baggott, William K. Law&B 92
Baggs, Fred Taylor 1925- St&PR 93
Baghio'o, Jean-Louis 1910- BioIn 17
Bagian, James Philip 1952- WhoSSW 93
Bagienski, J. WhoScE 91-4
Bagin, Douglas H. 1948- St&PR 93
Baglan, Charles E., Jr. 1951- WhoEmL 93
Bagley, Brian G. 1934- WhoE 93, WhoWor 93
Bagley, Charles Michael 1956- WhoEmL 93
Bagley, Colleen 1954- WhoAmW 93
Bagley, Constance Elizabeth 1952- WhoAmW 93
Bagley, Desmond 1923-1983 ScF&FL 92
Bagley, Edythe Scott 1924- WhoAmW 93, WhoE 93
Bagley, Gailian Dean, Jr. 1945- St&PR 93
Bagley, Harold J. Law&B 92
Bagley, James Maher 1954- WhoEmL 93
Bagley, James Paul 1942- St&PR 93
Bagley, John R. Law&B 92
Bagley, Mary H. 1949- St&PR 93
Bagley, Richard E. 1943- St&PR 93
Bagley, Robert Waller 1921- WhoSSW 93
Bagley, Thomas Steven 1952- WhoEmL 93
Bagley, William Thompson 1928- WhoAm 92
Bagli, Vincent Joseph 1925- WhoAm 92
Baglini, Norman A. 1942- WhoIns 93
Baglio, Ben M. ScF&FL 92
Baglio, Joseph Anthony 1939- WhoE 93
Baglio, Vincent Paul 1960- WhoE 93, WhoEmL 93, WhoWor 93
Baglioni, Camilla See Cavos, Caterino 1775-1840 OxDcOp
Bagnal, Charles Wilson, Jr. 1957- WhoE 93, WhoWor 93
Bagnal, Kimberly Baughman 1949- WhoWrEP 92
Bagnall, Graham Edward 1948- WhoAm 92
Bagnall, Nigel (Thomas) 1927- ConAu 136
Bagnall, R.D. 1945- ScF&FL 92
Bagnall, Roger Shaler 1947- WhoAm 92
Bagnara, Francesco 1784-1866 OxDcOp
Bagnaschi, Charles Louis 1941- St&PR 93
Bagnell, L.H. St&PR 93
Bagneris, Renee Michelle Wing 1949- WhoEmL 93
Bagneschi, Michael T. 1942- St&PR 93
Bagney, Elizabeth 1924- WhoWor 93
Bagnold, Enid 1889-1981 ConAu 40NR, MajAI [port]
Bagnold, Ralph A. 1896-1990 BioIn 17
Bagnoli, Vincent James, Jr. 1952- WhoAm 92
Bagolini, Giorgio 1936- WhoScE 91-3
Bagoon, Robert 1923- St&PR 93
Bagot, William A. 1935- St&PR 93
Bagratids OxDcByz
Bagration, Peter Ivanovich 1765-1812 HarEnMi
Bagration, Teymuraz d1992 NewYTBS 92
Bagration-Mukhransky, Teymuraz, Prince 1912-1992 BioIn 17
Bagrodia, Santosh 1940- WhoAsAP 91
Bagshaw, David A. St&PR 93
Bagshaw, Joseph Charles 1943- WhoAm 92, WhoE 93
Bagshaw, Malcolm A. 1925- WhoAm 92
Bagsik, Boguslaw BioIn 17
Baguelin, Francois 1942- WhoScE 91-2
Bagwell, Clarence L. 1942- St&PR 93
Bagwell, James Franklin 1946- St&PR 93
Bagwell, Kathleen Kay 1951- WhoAmW 93, WhoEmL 93, WhoWor 93
Bagwell, Kenneth L. 1924- WhoAm 92
Bagwell, Marilyn St&PR 93
Bagwell, William C. 1942- St&PR 93
Bagwill, John W., Jr. 1930- St&PR 93
Bagwill, John Williams, Jr. 1930- WhoAm 92
Baha, Daniel Scott 1955- WhoEmL 93
Baha' Al-Din 1145-1235 OxDcByz
Bahador, Sardar Khan 1955- WhoWor 93
Bahadue, George Paul 1954- WhoSSW 93
Bahadur, Birendra 1949- WhoAm 92
Bahadur, Chance 1942- WhoAm 92
Bahadur, Khawaja Ali 1930- WhoWor 93
Bahakel, Cy N. 1921- WhoAm 92
Bahan, Roland Aloysius, Jr. 1930- WhoSSW 93
Bahar, Ezekiel 1933- WhoAm 92
Bahar, Reza 1951- St&PR 93
Baharav, Moshe 1930- WhoWor 93
Baharsjah, Sjarifudin 1933- WhoAsAP 91
Bahary, William Shaul 1936- WhoE 93
Bahash, Robert J. 1945- WhoAm 92
Bahash, Robert Joseph 1945- St&PR 93
Bahcall, John Norris 1934- WhoAm 92
Bahcall, Neta Assaf 1942- WhoAm 92, WhoAmW 93
Baher, Constance Whitman 1942- WhoAmW 93, WhoWor 93
Bahi, Abdelaziz 1938- WhoUN 92
Bahl, John C. 1943- St&PR 93
Bahl, John Charles 1943- WhoSSW 93
Bahl, Om Parkash 1927- WhoAm 92
Bahl, Saroj Mehta 1946- WhoSSW 93
Bahler, Gary M. Law&B 92
Bahler, Nelson E. Law&B 92
Bahlke, Elizabeth Anne 1950- St&PR 93
Bahlke, Valerie ScF&FL 92
Bahlman, David Arthur 1945- WhoE 93
Bahlman, Dudley Ward Rhodes 1923- WhoAm 92
Bahlman, William Thorne, Jr. 1920- WhoAm 92
Bahlmann, David William 1939- WhoAm 92
Bahlmann, Jerome R. Law&B 92
Bahlo, Peter 1959- WhoEmL 93
Bahlouli, Hassan Hamidou 1933- WhoUN 92
Bahls, Gene Charles 1929- WhoAm 92, WhoWor 93
Bahls, Jane Easter 1954- WhoWrEP 92
Bahls, Steven Carl 1954- St&PR 93, WhoEmL 93
Bahm, Archie John 1907- WhoAm 92
Bahme, Myra Anne 1942- WhoAmW 93
Bahmer, Robert H. 1904-1990 BioIn 17
Bahn, Charles Frederick, Jr. 1954- WhoEmL 93
Bahn, David Lowell 1963- WhoE 93
Bahna, Geraldine Frances WhoAmW 93
Bahner, Carl Tabb 1908- WhoSSW 93
Bahner, Gert 1930- Baker 92
Bahner, Thomas Maxfield 1933- WhoAm 92
Bahner, Werner WhoScE 91-3
Bahnik, Roger L. 1944- St&PR 93
Bahniuk, Eugene 1926- WhoAm 92
Bahniuk, Frank Theodore 1937- St&PR 93, WhoAm 92
Bahnson, Henry Theodore 1920- WhoAm 92
Bahouth, Peter A. 1953- WhoAm 92
Bahr, Anne Marie 1950- WhoAmW 93
Bahr, Carman Bloedow 1931- WhoSSW 93
Bahr, Christine Marie 1958- WhoAmW 93
Bahr, Donald Walter 1927- WhoAm 92
Bahr, Eduardo 1940- SpAmA
Bahr, Ehrhard 1932- WhoAm 92
Bahr, Fax MiSFD 9
Bahr, Hermann 1863-1934 DcLB 118 [port]
Bahr, Howard Miner 1938- WhoAm 92
Bahr, James Theodore 1942- WhoE 93
Bahr, (Franz) Josef 1770-1819 Baker 92
Bahr, Klaus 1929- St&PR 93
Bahr, Laren S. 1944- WhoWrEP 92
Bahr, Lauren S. 1944- WhoAm 92
Bahr, Lutz Amand 1939- WhoUN 92
Bahr, Mary 1946- ConAu 136
Bahr, Morton 1926- WhoAm 92
Bahr, Neil E. 1925- St&PR 93
Bahr, Robert Lawrence 1945- WhoE 93
Bahr, Terri Jean 1960- WhoAmW 93
Bahrani, Mustafa David 1927- St&PR 93
Bahrawi, Fouad Bin Abdul Wahab 1943- WhoWor 93
Bahre, Everett T. 1936- St&PR 93
Bahrenburg, Bruce ScF&FL 92
Bahrenburg, D. Claeys BioIn 17
Bahrenburg, D. Claeys 1947- St&PR 93, WhoAm 92
Bahrenburg, Rolf W. 1922- St&PR 93
Bahri, Ahmed 1938- WhoUN 92
Bahrin Bin Pengiran Haji Abbas, Yang Amat Mulia Pengiran Laila Kanun WhoAsAP 91
Bahr-Mildenburg, Anna 1872-1947 IntDcOp [port], OxDcOp
Bahro, Rudolf 1935- BioIn 17
Bahun, Stjepan 1933- WhoScE 91-4
Bai, Tommaso c. 1650-1714 Baker 92
Baian OxDcByz
Baiardi, John Charles 1918- WhoAm 92
Baicu, Tudorel 1931- WhoScE 91-4
Baida, Peter 1950- WhoEmL 93
Baiden, Dawn Lee Law&B 92
Baier, Augusto Carlos 1941- WhoWor 93
Baier, Edward John 1925- WhoAm 92
Baier, Frederick William, Jr. 1945- St&PR 93
Baier, Kurt 1917- WhoE 93
Baierlein, Jean L. 1940- WhoAmW 93
Baiers, Douglas R. Law&B 92
Baif, Jean-Antoine de 1532-1589 Baker 92
Baig, Munawar Waheed 1952- WhoWor 93
Baigent, Julia Marie 1958- WhoEmL 93
Baiget, Tomas 1944- WhoWor 93
Baigi, Marla Jean 1959- WhoAmW 93
Baik, Sung-Hak BioIn 17
Baik Chan Ki WhoAsAP 91
Baikie, William Balfour 1825-1864 Expl 93 [port]
Bail, Christoph 1944- WhoWor 93
Bail, Chuck MiSFD 9
Bail, Joe Paul 1925- WhoAm 92
Bail, Richard A. 1941- St&PR 93
Bail, Richard Nelson, Jr. 1942- WhoUN 92
Bailar, Barbara Ann 1935- WhoAm 92
Bailar, Benjamin Franklin 1934- St&PR 93, WhoAm 92
Bailar, John Christian 1904-1991 BioIn 17
Bailar, John Christian, III 1932- WhoAm 92
Baildon, John David 1943- WhoE 93
Bailer, Albert John 1939- St&PR 93
Bailer, Bonnie Lynn 1946- WhoE 93
Bailer, Lloyd H. 1914-1990 BioIn 17
Bailer, William George 1953- WhoE 93
Bailes, Gordon Lee 1946- WhoEmL 93, WhoSSW 93
Bailes, Margaret BlkAmWO
Bailes, Randall Powell 1950- WhoEmL 93
Bailes, Robert Lee 1932- St&PR 93
Bailey, A.G. WhoScE 91-1
Bailey, Adrian George WhoScE 91-1
Bailey, Alan James 1947- St&PR 93
Bailey, Albert Edward 1871-1951 ScF&FL 92
Bailey, Alfred Goldsworthy 1905- WhoCanL 92
Bailey, Alice Ward 1857- AmWomPl
Bailey, Allen J. WhoScE 91-1
Bailey, Alvin Riley, Jr. 1954- WhoEmL 93
Bailey, Amos Purnell 1918- WhoAm 92, WhoWor 93
Bailey, Angela Jane 1961- WhoAmW 93
Bailey, Anita Irene WhoScE 91-1
Bailey, Ann K. Law&B 92
Bailey, Anna Eliza Clay AmWomPl
Bailey, Anne 1958- SmATA 71 [port]
Bailey, Annette Lee 1958- WhoEmL 93
Bailey, Anthony BioIn 17
Bailey, Barbara Vaughan 1958- WhoAmW 93
Bailey, Barry D. 1954- St&PR 93
Bailey, Bernard Allen 1918- St&PR 93
Bailey, Bernard John WhoScE 91-1
Bailey, Betty Jane 1931- WhoAmW 93
Bailey, Betty Lou 1929- WhoAmW 93, WhoE 93
Bailey, Beverly Ann 1965- WhoAmW 93
Bailey, Brad Duane 1958- WhoEmL 93
Bailey, Bruce Edward 1954- WhoE 93
Bailey, Bruce Stewart 1936- St&PR 93
Bailey, "Buster" (William C.) 1902-1967 Baker 92
Bailey, Calvin Dean 1955- WhoEmL 93
Bailey, Carl d1990 BioIn 17
Bailey, Carl D. Law&B 92
Bailey, Carl Franklin 1930- WhoAm 92, WhoSSW 93
Bailey, Carmine Michael 1958- WhoEmL 93
Bailey, Carolyn Sherwin 1875-1961 AmWomPl, MajAI [port]
Bailey, Catherine Suzanne 1958- WhoAmW 93
Bailey, Cecil Cabaniss 1901- WhoAm 92
Bailey, Cecil Dewitt 1921- WhoAm 92
Bailey, Charles-James Nice 1926- WhoWor 93
Bailey, Charles Lyle 1934- WhoAm 92
Bailey, Charles S. 1924- St&PR 93
Bailey, Charles Stanley 1949- WhoAm 92
Bailey, Charles Waldo 1929- WhoWrEP 92
Bailey, Charles Waldo, II 1929- WhoAm 92
Bailey, Charles William 1932- WhoWor 93
Bailey, Clyde E. Law&B 92
Bailey, Coley L. 1950- St&PR 93, WhoSSW 93
Bailey, Colin 1938- WhoScE 91-1
Bailey, Colin John 1946- WhoAm 92
Bailey, Cynthia Lee 1956- WhoAmW 93
Bailey, Damon BioIn 17
Bailey, Dana Kavanagh 1916- WhoAm 92
Bailey, Daniel A. d1991 BioIn 17
Bailey, Daniel Allen 1953- WhoEmL 93
Bailey, David B. Law&B 92
Bailey, David Clifton 1939- WhoSSW 93
Bailey, David John WhoScE 91-1
Bailey, David John 1944- St&PR 93
Bailey, David Michael 1951- WhoEmL 93, WhoSSW 93
Bailey, David Nelson 1945- WhoAm 92
Bailey, David Roy Shackleton 1917- WhoAm 92
Bailey, Dayle Lee Law&B 92
Bailey, Debra Sue 1953- WhoAm 92, WhoEmL 93
Bailey, Deena Tamara 1947- WhoAmW 93, WhoEmL 93
Bailey, DeFord 1899-1982 BioIn 17
Bailey, Denise Anne Law&B 92
Bailey, Dennis R. ScF&FL 92
Bailey, Dennis Richard 1945- WhoE 93
Bailey, Diana Marion 1951- WhoEmL 93
Bailey, Diane WhoWrEP 92
Bailey, Dick d1991 BioIn 17
Bailey, Don 1942- WhoCanL 92
Bailey, Don M. 1946- St&PR 93
Bailey, Don Matthew 1946- WhoAm 92
Bailey, Donna BioIn 17
Bailey, Donna J. Law&B 92
Bailey, Donna Jean 1951- WhoEmL 93
Bailey, Donna (Veronica Anne) 1938- ConAu 136
Bailey, Douglas & Deardourff, John PolPar
Bailey, Dudley 1918- WhoAm 92
Bailey, Elizabeth Ellery 1938- WhoAm 92
Bailey, Ethel Mc Caslin AmWomPl
Bailey, Ethel V. AmWomPl
Bailey, Exine Margaret Anderson 1922- WhoAm 92
Bailey, Felicia Annette 1955- WhoSSW 93
Bailey, Florence Merriam 1863-1948 BioIn 17
Bailey, Francis 1735-1815 JrnUS
Bailey, Francis Lee 1933- WhoAm 92
Bailey, Frank Henry 1946- WhoEmL 93
Bailey, Fred Coolidge 1925- WhoAm 92
Bailey, Gamaliel 1807-1859 JrnUS, PolPar
Bailey, Gary Bernard 1954- WhoEmL 93
Bailey, Gary C. Law&B 92
Bailey, George 1919- ConAu 38NR
Bailey, George A., Jr. 1925- St&PR 93
Bailey, Gerald Earl 1929- ScF&FL 92
Bailey, Glenn E. 1954- St&PR 93, WhoAm 92
Bailey, Glenn W. 1925- St&PR 93
Bailey, Glenn Waldemar 1925- WhoAm 92, WhoE 93
Bailey, Grace Daniel 1927- WhoAmW 93
Bailey, Greg 1954- WhoWrEP 92
Bailey, Gregory Wayne 1952- WhoEmL 93
Bailey, Guy Vernie 1929- WhoSSW 93
Bailey, Gwen 1930- St&PR 93
Bailey, Harold Stevens, Jr. 1922- WhoAm 92
Bailey, Harry Augustine, Jr. 1932- WhoAm 92
Bailey, Harvey A. 1937- St&PR 93
Bailey, Helen AmWomPl
Bailey, Helen Cheney AmWomPl

Bailey, Helen McShane 1916- WhoAm 92
Bailey, Henry John, III 1916- WhoAm 92
Bailey, Herbert Smith, Jr. 1921- WhoAm 92
Bailey, Hilary 1936- ScF&FL 92
Bailey, Horace C. 1914- St&PR 93
Bailey, Hugh Coleman 1929- WhoAm 92, WhoSSW 93
Bailey, Irving Widmer, II 1941- St&PR 93, WhoAm 92, WhoSSW 93
Bailey, J. Hugh 1936- St&PR 93, WhoIns 93
Bailey, J.O. 1903-1979 ScF&FL 92
Bailey, Jack N. 1950- St&PR 93
Bailey, Jack P., Jr. 1954- St&PR 93
Bailey, Jackson Holbrook 1925- WhoWrEP 92
Bailey, Jacob 1731-1808 BioIn 17
Bailey, James Allen 1955- WhoSSW 93
Bailey, James Curtis 1936- WhoWor 93
Bailey, James Hinton, Jr. 1946- St&PR 93
Bailey, James Lovell 1907- WhoSSW 93, WhoWor 93
Bailey, James Martin 1929- WhoAm 92, WhoWrEP 92
Bailey, James Montgomery 1841-1894 JrnUS
Bailey, James N. Law&B 92
Bailey, James Russell 1935- WhoIns 93
Bailey, Janet Dee 1946- WhoEmL 93
Bailey, Janet Lee 1953- WhoEmL 93
Bailey, Jerry Lynn 1948- WhoEmL 93
Bailey, Jerry Wayne 1948- WhoEmL 93
Bailey, Jill Ann 1955- WhoAmW 93
Bailey, Joan E. 1942- WhoE 93
Bailey, Joel Furness 1913- WhoAm 92
Bailey, John 1942- MiSFD 9, WhoAm 92
Bailey, John 1944- ScF&FL 92
Bailey, John Andrew WhoScE 91-1
Bailey, John C. 1941- St&PR 93
Bailey, John E. Law&B 92
Bailey, John Edward WhoScE 91-1
Bailey, John M. 1905-1975 PolPar
Bailey, John M. 1955- St&PR 93
Bailey, John M., III 1942- WhoIns 93
Bailey, John Martin 1928- WhoAm 92
Bailey, John Maxwell 1927- WhoAm 92
Bailey, John Milton 1925- WhoAm 92
Bailey, John Moran 1904-1975 BioIn 17
Bailey, John Turner 1926- WhoAm 92
Bailey, Joselyn Elizabeth WhoAmW 93
Bailey, Joy Hafner 1928- WhoSSW 93
Bailey, Joyce T. Law&B 92
Bailey, Judy K. Law&B 92
Bailey, K. Ronald 1947- WhoEmL 93, WhoWor 93
Bailey, Kate AmWomPl
Bailey, Kathrine E. 1922- WhoWrEP 92
Bailey, Kathy Clark 1956- WhoEmL 93
Bailey, Keith E. 1942- St&PR 93, WhoAm 92
Bailey, Kendall BioIn 17
Bailey, Kenneth Kyle 1923- WhoAm 92
Bailey, Kenneth Reece 1940- WhoAm 92
Bailey, Kristen 1952- WhoAmW 93, WhoEmL 93
Bailey, L.H. 1858-1954 BioIn 17
Bailey, L. Storm 1931- St&PR 93
Bailey, Larrie 1934- WhoSSW 93
Bailey, Larry Dayton 1937- St&PR 93
Bailey, Larry Douglas 1942- WhoSSW 93
Bailey, Larry Ronald 1944- WhoSSW 93
Bailey, Lawrence E. 1943- St&PR 93
Bailey, Lawrence Randolph, Sr. 1918- WhoAm 92
Bailey, Lawrence Randolph, Jr. 1949- WhoEmL 93
Bailey, Lee E. Law&B 92
Bailey, Lee Edwin 1952- St&PR 93
Bailey, Leonard Lee 1942- WhoAm 92
Bailey, Liberty Hyde 1858-1954 BioIn 17
Bailey, Lillian Baker 92
Bailey, Lonnie Gene 1939- WhoAm 92
Bailey, Loretto Carroll 1908- AmWomPl
Bailey, Louie Lee 1946- WhoEmL 93
Bailey, Louise Slagle 1930- WhoWrEP 92
Bailey, Lynn Gordon 1936- St&PR 93
Bailey, Major Windsor, II 1961- WhoWor 93
Bailey, Malcolm 1942- WhoScE 91-1
Bailey, Margaret Ann 1948- WhoSSW 93
Bailey, Marie St&PR 93
Bailey, Mark Gregory 1954- WhoSSW 93
Bailey, Mark W. Law&B 92
Bailey, Mary Beatrice 1933- WhoAmW 93
Bailey, Michael John 1953- WhoEmL 93
Bailey, Michael Keith 1956- WhoEmL 93, WhoSSW 93
Bailey, Michael Paul 1952- WhoSSW 93
Bailey, Michael R. Law&B 92
Bailey, Michael Robert 1947- WhoE 93
Bailey, Michael Wallace 1968- WhoSSW 93
Bailey, Mildred BioIn 17
Bailey, Mildred 1907-1951 Baker 92
Bailey, Nancy ScF&FL 92
Bailey, Nancy Joyce 1942- WhoE 93
Bailey, Nigel John 1938- WhoWor 93
Bailey, Norma 1949- MiSFD 9
Bailey, Norman 1923- OxDcOp
Bailey, Norman 1933- IntDcOp
Bailey, Norman Alishan 1931- WhoE 93
Bailey, Norman (Stanley) 1933- Baker 92
Bailey, Orville Taylor 1909- WhoAm 92
Bailey, Palmer Kent 1947- WhoEmL 93
Bailey, Patricia Ann 1937- WhoAmW 93
Bailey, Patricia Price 1937- WhoAmW 93
Bailey, Patrick 1947- MiSFD 9
Bailey, Patti BioIn 17
Bailey, Paul 1906-1987 ScF&FL 92
Bailey, Paul 1946- WhoEmL 93
Bailey, Paul E. 1947- St&PR 93
Bailey, Paul Fredrick 1954- WhoEmL 93
Bailey, Paul Townsend 1939- WhoWor 93
Bailey, Pearl 1918-1990 BioIn 17
Bailey, Pearl Mae 1918- AfrAmBi
Bailey, Pearl (Mae) 1918-1990 Baker 92
Bailey, Philip 1951- SoulM
Bailey, Philip Sigmon 1916- WhoAm 92, WhoWor 93
Bailey, Philip Sigmon, Jr. 1943- WhoAm 92, WhoWor 93
Bailey, R.A. WhoScE 91-1
Bailey, Ray H. 1949- St&PR 93
Bailey, Raymond James 1940- St&PR 93
Bailey, Reeve Maclaren 1911- WhoAm 92
Bailey, Reubena Winona 1926- WhoWrEP 92
Bailey, Richard A. Law&B 92
Bailey, Richard Allin 1949- St&PR 93
Bailey, Richard Briggs 1926- WhoAm 92
Bailey, Richard W. 1945- St&PR 93
Bailey, Richard Weld 1939- WhoAm 92
Bailey, Richard Williams 1933- WhoWor 93
Bailey, Rick D. Law&B 92
Bailey, Rick E. Law&B 92
Bailey, Ricky E. 1959- WhoEmL 93
Bailey, Robert, Jr. 1945- WhoAm 92
Bailey, Robert Bartley Law&B 92
Bailey, Robert C. 1936- WhoAm 92
Bailey, Robert C. 1950- St&PR 93
Bailey, Robert David 1939- St&PR 93
Bailey, Robert Donald 1953- WhoEmL 93, WhoWor 93
Bailey, Robert Duke 1944- WhoSSW 93
Bailey, Robert Elliott 1932- WhoAm 92, WhoSSW 93
Bailey, Robert Fred 1932- St&PR 93
Bailey, Robert G. 1943- WhoIns 93
Bailey, Robert George 1943- WhoAm 92
Bailey, Robert Greg 1954- WhoEmL 93
Bailey, Robert Hal 1948- St&PR 93
Bailey, Robert Jay 1952- WhoE 93
Bailey, Robert L. 1937- St&PR 93
Bailey, Robert M. Law&B 92
Bailey, Robert Marland 1930- St&PR 93
Bailey, Robert Marshall 1954- WhoEmL 93
Bailey, Robert Mikell 1955- WhoEmL 93
Bailey, Robert Short 1931- WhoAm 92
Bailey, Robert Sterling 1930- St&PR 93
Bailey, Robert W. ScF&FL 92
Bailey, Robert W. 1944- WhoIns 93
Bailey, Robert W(ilson) 1943- WhoWrEP 92
Bailey, Robert William 1944- WhoAm 92
Bailey, Robert William 1951- WhoEmL 93
Bailey, Roberta 1938- WhoSSW 93
Bailey, Robin W. 1952- ScF&FL 92
Bailey, Rodney N. 1944- St&PR 93
Bailey, Ronald E. 1944- St&PR 93
Bailey, Ronald Wade 1935- WhoAm 92
Bailey, Ruth Hill 1916- WhoWor 93
Bailey, Ryburn H. 1929- WhoIns 93
Bailey, Ryburn Hancock 1929- St&PR 93
Bailey, Scott Arthur 1947- WhoEmL 93
Bailey, Steven Scott 1948- WhoWor 93
Bailey, Sturges W. 1919- BioIn 17
Bailey, Susan Carol 1954- WhoAmW 93, WhoEmL 93
Bailey, Tania 1927- WhoAmW 93
Bailey, Thomas D. 1945- St&PR 93
Bailey, Thomas Edward 1947- WhoSSW 93
Bailey, Timothy Gordon 1950- WhoEmL 93
Bailey, Tommy Ray 1947- WhoSSW 93
Bailey, Vicki L. Law&B 92
Bailey, Wayne Paul Law&B 92
Bailey, Wendell 1940- WhoAm 92
Bailey, Wendy Ann 1956- WhoAmW 93
Bailey, Wesley Lefferts d1990 BioIn 17
Bailey, Wilford Sherrill 1921- WhoAm 92
Bailey, William Harrison 1930- WhoAm 92
Bailey, William Henry 1949- WhoEmL 93, WhoSSW 93
Bailey, William John 1921-1989 BioIn 17
Bailey, William O. 1926- St&PR 93
Bailey, William Scherer 1948- WhoEmL 93
Bailey, William Wesley 1941- WhoAm 92
Bailey, Willis Joshua 1854-1932 BioIn 17
Bailey, Zan Tamar WhoSSW 93
Bailey, Zelda Chapman 1949- WhoEmL 93
Bailey-Carman, Susan Marie 1948- WhoAmW 93
Baileys, Charles Neal 1948- St&PR 93
Baileys, Steven Jeffery 1954- St&PR 93
Bailey Waddick, Sheryl F. Law&B 92
Bailey-Watts, Antony Edward WhoScE 91-1
Bailey-Wilson, Joan Ellen 1953- WhoAmW 93
Bai Lichen 1941- WhoAsAP 91
Bailin, Lionel J. 1928- WhoAm 92
Bailin, Marc L. St&PR 93
Bailin, Toby 1941- St&PR 93
Bailitz, Ronald E. 1941- St&PR 93
Baillargeon, Marie Law&B 92
Baillargeon, Richard 1951- St&PR 93
Baillargeon, Victor Paul 1958- WhoEmL 93, WhoSSW 93
Bailleu, Kenneth Ross 1947- WhoEmL 93
Bailleux, Jean 1935- WhoScE 91-2
Baillie, Alexander Charles, Jr. 1939- WhoAm 92
Baillie, Allan 1943- ChlFicS, DcChlFi
Baillie, Charles Douglas 1918- WhoAm 92
Baillie, Hugh 1890-1966 JrnUS
Baillie, Isobel 1895-1983 Baker 92
Baillie, Joanna 1762-1851 BioIn 17
Baillie, Mary Helen 1926- WhoWor 93
Baillie, Priscilla Woods 1935- WhoAm 92
Baillie, William c. 1595- HarEnMi
Baillie-David, Sonja Kirsteen 1961- WhoAmW 93
Baillie Strong, Stuart 1943- WhoWor 93
Baillieul, John Brouard 1945- WhoAm 92, WhoE 93
Baillio, O. Dallas, Jr. 1940- WhoSSW 93
Baillon, Austin John 1927- WhoWor 93
Baillot, Pierre (-Marie-Francois de Sales) 1771-1842 Baker 92
Baillou, Jean 1924- WhoWor 93
Bailly, Claude 1929- WhoScE 91-2
Bailly, Henri-Claude A. 1946- St&PR 93
Bailly, Henri-Claude Albert 1946- WhoAm 92
Bailly, Louis 1882-1974 Baker 92
Bailly, Richard L. 1934- St&PR 93
Bailor, Mike Eugene 1952- St&PR 93
Baily, Alfred Ewing 1925- WhoAm 92, WhoE 93
Baily, Douglas Boyd 1937- WhoAm 92
Baily, John T. 1944- WhoIns 93
Baily, John Thomas 1944- WhoE 93
Baily, Nathan A. 1920- St&PR 93
Bailyn, Bernard 1922- WhoAm 92, WhoE 93
Bailyn, Charles BioIn 17
Bailyn, Lotte 1930- WhoE 93
Bailys, David M. 1961- St&PR 93
Baiman, Gail 1938- WhoAmW 93
Baiman, Sybil 1939- WhoE 93
Bain, Bruce Kahrs 1931- St&PR 93
Bain, Charles E. Law&B 92
Bain, Clinton Dwight 1960- WhoEmL 93, WhoSSW 93
Bain, Conrad Stafford 1923- WhoAm 92
Bain, Cynthia Ann Law&B 92
Bain, Derek Charles WhoScE 91-1
Bain, Donald Knight 1935- WhoAm 92
Bain, Donald R. 1937- St&PR 93
Bain, Douglas Cogburn, Jr. 1940- WhoSSW 93
Bain, Douglas G. Law&B 92
Bain, Douglas Gilman 1926- St&PR 93
Bain, Douglas John 1924- WhoWor 93
Bain, Douglas John Geddes WhoScE 91-1
Bain, Ethel AmWomPl
Bain, Fairfield Tucker 1957- WhoEmL 93
Bain, George Sayers WhoScE 91-1
Bain, George Sayers 1939- WhoWor 93
Bain, Geri Rhonda 1951- WhoWrEP 92
Bain, Irwin Allen Law&B 92
Bain, James Arthur 1918- WhoAm 92
Bain, John D., III 1940- St&PR 93
Bain, John Harper 1940- St&PR 93
Bain, Judith S. Law&B 92
Bain, Larry Ray 1946- WhoEmL 93
Bain, Lawrence David 1950- WhoAm 92, WhoWor 93
Bain, Linda L. BioIn 17
Bain, Linda Valerie 1947- WhoAmW 93
Bain, Lorne Donald 1941- St&PR 93
Bain, Michael Ronald 1941- WhoWor 93
Bain, Richard Anthony 1942- St&PR 93
Bain, Robert Addison 1932- WhoAm 92, WhoWrEP 92
Bain, Sherwood E. 1922- St&PR 93
Bain, Travis Whitsett, II 1934- WhoAm 92
Bain, W.D., Jr. 1925- St&PR 93
Bain, Wilfred 1908- Baker 92
Bain, Wilfred Conwell 1908- WhoAm 92
Bain, William Donald, Jr. 1925- WhoAm 92
Bain, William Griffing Law&B 92
Bain, William H. WhoScE 91-1
Bain, William J., Jr. 1930- St&PR 93
Bain, William James 1896- WhoAm 92
Bain, William James, Jr. 1930- WhoAm 92
Bainbridge, Beryl 1933- BioIn 17
Bainbridge, Dona Bardelli 1953- WhoAmW 93
Bainbridge, Erika Ohara 1951- WhoAmW 93
Bainbridge, Frederick Freeman, III 1927- WhoAm 92
Bainbridge, George Stanley WhoScE 91-1
Bainbridge, Janet Mary WhoScE 91-1
Bainbridge, John BioIn 17
Bainbridge, John 1913- WhoAm 92, WhoWrEP 92
Bainbridge, John 1913-1992 ConAu 139
Bainbridge, John L. d1992 NewYTBS 92
Bainbridge, Kenneth Tompkins 1904- WhoAm 92
Bainbridge, Simon (Jeremy) 1952- Baker 92
Bainbridge, William 1774-1833 HarEnMi
Bainbridge, William John 1962- St&PR 93
Bainbridge, William Sims 1940- ScF&FL 92, WhoE 93
Baine, James Everett Law&B 92
Baine, James Everitt 1941- St&PR 93, WhoSSW 93
Bainer, Philip La Vern 1931- WhoAm 92
Baines, Anthony 1912- Baker 92
Baines, Cuthbert Edward 1879- ScF&FL 92
Baines, Harold Douglass 1959- BiDAMSp 1989, WhoAm 92
Baines, J.E. WhoScE 91-1
Baines, John (David) 1943- SmATA 71 [port]
Baines, Linda Rando 1957- WhoAmW 93
Baini, Giuseppe 1775-1844 Baker 92
Bainnson, Fredric H. d1990 BioIn 17
Bainov, Drumi Dimitrov 1933- WhoWor 93
Bains, Amalia Mesa NotHsAW 93
Bains, David Paul 1950- WhoEmL 93
Bains, Harrison Mackellar, Jr. 1943- St&PR 93, WhoAm 92
Bains, Lee Edmundson 1912- WhoAm 92, WhoWor 93
Bains, Leslie BioIn 17
Bains, Leslie Elizabeth 1943- WhoAm 92
Bainter, Patricia Ann 1961- WhoAmW 93
Bainton, Denise Marlene 1949- WhoEmL 93
Bainton, Donald J. 1931- St&PR 93, WhoAm 92, WhoWor 93
Bainton, Dorothy Ford 1933- WhoAm 92
Bainton, Edgar Leslie 1880-1956 Baker 92
Bainton, John Joseph 1947- WhoAm 92, WhoE 93, WhoWor 93
Bainum, Peter Montgomery 1938- WhoAm 92, WhoE 93
Bainum, Stewart 1919- St&PR 93, WhoAm 92
Bainum, Stewart, Jr. 1946- St&PR 93
Bainun Binti Mohd Ali, Raja Permaisuri Agong Tunku WhoAsAP 91
Baio-Lagreca, JoAnne Law&B 92
Bair, Bruce Macklem 1943- St&PR 93
Bair, David Alan 1964- WhoSSW 93
Bair, David N. 1940- St&PR 93
Bair, Edward Jay 1922- WhoAm 92
Bair, Frieda Augusta 1904- WhoAm 92, WhoAmW 93, WhoWor 93
Bair, Howard S. 1946- St&PR 93
Bair, James Fridolin 1950- WhoE 93
Bair, Jeffrey Glenn 1950- WhoEmL 93
Bair, Myrna Lynn 1940- WhoAmW 93, WhoE 93
Bair, Patrick ScF&FL 92
Bair, Robert Rippel 1925- WhoAm 92
Bair, Royden Stanley 1924- WhoAm 92
Bair, Sheila Colleen 1954- WhoAm 92
Bair, Stephen L. Law&B 92
Bair, William Alois 1931- WhoE 93
Bair, William J. 1924- WhoAm 92
Bairakov, Gueorgy Nikolov 1939- WhoWor 93
Bairam, Erkin Ibrahim 1958- WhoWor 93
Baird, Alan C. 1951- WhoEmL 93
Baird, Bill BioIn 17
Baird, Brent D. 1939- St&PR 93
Baird, Charles F. 1922- St&PR 93
Baird, Charles Fitz 1922- WhoAm 92
Baird, David 1757-1829 HarEnMi
Baird, David G., Jr. 1924- St&PR 93
Baird, David L., Jr. 1945- St&PR 93
Baird, David Leach, Jr. 1945- WhoAm 92
Baird, David Tennent WhoScE 91-1
Baird, Delpha 1930- WhoAmW 93
Baird, Denise Colleen Law&B 92
Baird, Don Wilson 1940- WhoAm 92
Baird, Donn A. 1941- St&PR 93
Baird, Douglas Gordon 1953- WhoAm 92
Baird, Douglas James 1962- WhoEmL 93
Baird, Dugald Euan 1937- St&PR 93, WhoAm 92, WhoE 93
Baird, Edward Rouzie, Jr. 1936- WhoAm 92
Baird, Emily Nadine Blackwood 1921- WhoAmW 93
Baird, Enid C. d1991 BioIn 17

Baird, Erica B. *Law&B 92*
Baird, Eva R. *AmWomPl*
Baird, George 1938- *WhoWor 93*
Baird, Gerald David 1936- *WhoScE 91-1*
Baird, Gordon Prentiss 1950- *WhoAm 92*
Baird, H. Elizabeth *Law&B 92*
Baird, James Abington 1926- *WhoAm 92*
Baird, James C. 1944- *St&PR 93*
Baird, James Frank 1937- *WhoE 93*
Baird, James Kenneth 1951- *WhoEmL 93*
Baird, James Kern 1941- *WhoSSW 93*
Baird, James L. 1917- *St&PR 93*
Baird, James L. 1947- *WhoE 93*
Baird, John Absalom, Jr. 1918- *WhoAm 92, WhoE 93*
Baird, John Northcote 1940- *St&PR 93*
Baird, John Wyllys 1915- *St&PR 93*
Baird, Jon G. 1941- *St&PR 93*
Baird, Joseph Armstrong, Jr. 1922- *WhoAm 92*
Baird, Keith Alexander 1925- *WhoAm 92*
Baird, Leona Mae 1937- *St&PR 93*
Baird, Lisa Morrison 1954- *WhoEmL 93*
Baird, Lourdes G. *WhoAmW 93*
Baird, Lourdes G. 1935- *NotHsAW 93 [port]*
Baird, Marion Sims, Jr. 1921- *WhoSSW 93*
Baird, Martha 1895-1971 *Baker 92*
Baird, Maurice M. 1916- *St&PR 93*
Baird, Mellon Campbell, Jr. 1931- *WhoAm 92*
Baird, Michael 1945- *WhoSSW 93*
Baird, Neil William 1947- *WhoWor 93*
Baird, Newton D. 1928- *ScF&FL 92*
Baird, Pamela Jo 1948- *WhoEmL 93*
Baird, Patricia Ann *WhoAm 92*
Baird, Perry James 1951- *WhoAm 92*
Baird, Peter D. 1941- *BioIn 17*
Baird, R. Stewart, Jr. *Law&B 92*
Baird, Raymond R. 1943- *WhoSSW 93*
Baird, Richard S. 1951- *St&PR 93*
Baird, Robert A. *St&PR 93*
Baird, Robert B. 1923- *St&PR 93*
Baird, Robert Dahlen 1933- *WhoAm 92*
Baird, Robert M. 1937- *ConAu 139*
Baird, Robert Malcolm 1937- *WhoAm 92*
Baird, Robert R. *Law&B 92*
Baird, Robert R. 1929- *WhoIns 93*
Baird, Roger Allen 1914- *WhoAm 92*
Baird, Rosemarie Annette 1956- *WhoE 93*
Baird, Russell Miller 1916- *WhoAm 92*
Baird, Sandy *BioIn 17*
Baird, Tadeusz 1928-1981 *Baker 92, PolBiDi*
Baird, Terence Alan 1950- *WhoEmL 93*
Baird, Terry 1946- *St&PR 93*
Baird, Thomas P. 1923-1990 *BioIn 17, ScF&FL 92*
Baird, Thomas P. 1954- *St&PR 93*
Baird, William David 1939- *WhoAm 92*
Baird, William McKenzie 1944- *WhoAm 92*
Baird, William Robb 1924- *WhoSSW 93*
Baird, William Stanley 1935- *St&PR 93*
Baird, Zoe *BioIn 17, Law&B 92*
Baird, Zoe 1952- *NewYTBS 92 [port], WhoAmW 93*
Baird, Zoe E. *St&PR 93*
Baireuther, James 1946- *St&PR 93*
Bairlein, Franz 1952- *WhoScE 91-3*
Bairrao, Rogerio P.M.B.S. 1954- *WhoScE 91-3*
Bairstow, Edward (Cuthbert) 1874-1946 *Baker 92*
Bairstow, Frances Kanevsky 1920- *WhoAmW 93, WhoWor 93*
Bairstow, Richard Raymond 1917- *WhoWor 93*
Baisch, Rudolf P. 1957- *St&PR 93*
Baisch, Wister S. 1926- *St&PR 93*
Baisden, Charles Robert 1939- *WhoSSW 93*
Baish, Richard O. 1946- *St&PR 93*
Bai-Shih, Wu 1930- *WhoWor 93*
Baisley, Charles William *Law&B 92*
Baisley, Harriet Esther 1917- *WhoAmW 93*
Baisley, James M. *Law&B 92*
Baisley, James M. 1932- *St&PR 93*
Baisley, James Mahoney 1932- *WhoAm 92*
Baisley, Regina Irene 1947- *WhoAmW 93*
Baisley, Robert William 1923- *WhoAm 92*
Baitinger, David G. 1956- *WhoSSW 93*
Baity, John Cooley 1933- *WhoAm 92*
Baity, Patricia Ann 1946- *WhoEmL 93*
Baitz, Jon Robin *NewYTBS 92 [port]*
Bai Xiuting 1931- *BioIn 17*
Baize, Deborah Ann 1963- *WhoEmL 93*
Baizer, Eric Wyatt 1950- *WhoWrEP 92*
Baizerman, Saul 1889-1957 *BioIn 17*
Baj, Enrico 1924- *BioIn 17*
Baja, Celerino Rosauro, Jr. 1963- *WhoWor 93*
Bajan d609 *HarEnMi*
Bajan, Jerzy 1901-1967 *PolBiDi*
Bajar, Victoria Raquel 1942- *WhoWor 93*
Bajarski, Waclaw 1921-1943 *PolBiDi*
Ba Jin Li Yaotang 1904- *WhoWor 93*
Bajit, Fernando Gamboa 1941- *WhoE 93*
Bajo, Theodore *Law&B 92*
Bajoie, Diana E. 1948- *WhoAmW 93*
Bajon, Filip 1947- *DrEEuF*
Bajoras, Feliksas 1934- *Baker 92*
Bajorek, Christopher Henry 1943- *WhoAm 92*
Bajorinas, Eugene A. 1960- *WhoEmL 93*
Bajorunas, Daiva Regina 1946- *WhoEmL 93*
Bajpai, Rajendra Kumari 1925- *WhoAsAP 91*
Bajpai, Shyam Narayan 1947- *WhoE 93*
Bajraj, Reynaldo Felix 1943- *WhoUN 92*
Bajunid, Junidah *Law&B 92*
Bak, David John 1950- *WhoAm 92*
Bak, Jerzy Brunon 1929- *WhoScE 91-4*
Bak, Mary Magnuson 1953- *WhoEmL 93*
Bakac, Andreja 1946- *WhoEmL 93*
Bakai, Janos 1954- *WhoScE 91-4*
Bakaitis, Vincent William, Jr. 1941- *WhoE 93*
Bakal, Abraham Itshak 1936- *WhoE 93*
Bakal, Carl 1918- *WhoAm 92, WhoWrEP 92*
Bakala, Bretislav 1897-1958 *Baker 92*
Bakalar, John Stephen 1948- *WhoAm 92, WhoEmL 93*
Bakaleinikov, Vladimir 1885-1953 *Baker 92*
Bakalian, Alexander Edward 1957- *WhoE 93*
Bakaly, Charles George, Jr. 1927- *WhoAm 92, WhoE 93*
Bakane, John L. 1951- *St&PR 93*
Bakane, John Louis 1951- *WhoAm 92*
Bakatin, Vadim 1937- *BioIn 17*
Bakay, Louis 1917- *WhoAm 92*
Bakay, Roy Arpad Earle 1949- *WhoAm 92, WhoWor 93*
Bakcheios, Geron fl. 3rd cent.-4th cent. *OxDcByz*
Bake, Arnold Adriaan 1899-1963 *Baker 92*
Bakeer, Dagmar Sigrid 1958- *WhoSSW 93*
Bakele Laore, Albert 1952- *WhoAsAP 91*
Bakeman, Carol Ann 1934- *WhoAmW 93*
Baker, A. Diane *Law&B 92*
Baker, A. Vicki *WhoAmW 93*
Baker, Addison E. 1907-1943 *BioIn 17*
Baker, Adolph 1917- *WhoAm 92*
Baker, Alan 1951- *ConAu 38NR*
Baker, Alan L. 1929- *St&PR 93*
Baker, Alan N. *Law&B 92*
Baker, Alan Parker 1931- *WhoWrEP 92*
Baker, Albert I. 1946- *St&PR 93*
Baker, Alice Coleman 1944- *WhoSSW 93*
Baker, Alton Fletcher, Jr. 1919- *WhoWrEP 92*
Baker, Alton Wesley 1912- *WhoAm 92, WhoWor 93*
Baker, Amanda Sirmon 1934- *WhoAmW 93*
Baker, Andrew Hartill 1948- *WhoAm 92*
Baker, Anita *BioIn 17, SoulM*
Baker, Anita 1958- *ConMus 9 [port], WhoAm 92, WhoAmW 93*
Baker, Anita Diane 1955- *WhoAmW 93, WhoEmL 93, WhoSSW 93*
Baker, Anna G. *AmWomPl*
Baker, Arthur 1955- *SoulM*
Baker, Arthur Barrington 1939- *WhoWor 93*
Baker, Augusta 1911- *BioIn 17, BlkAull 92*
Baker, Ava Jean 1947- *WhoEmL 93*
Baker, Avery D. 1935- *St&PR 93*
Baker, Avery Dean 1935- *WhoIns 93*
Baker, Barbara A. *BioIn 17*
Baker, Barbara Ann 1948- *WhoEmL 93*
Baker, Ben 1955- *WhoSSW 93*
Baker, Benjamin Franklin 1811-1889 *Baker 92*
Baker, Bernard Robert, II 1915- *St&PR 93, WhoAm 92, WhoWor 93*
Baker, Bert O. 1918- *St&PR 93*
Baker, Bessie *AmWomPl*
Baker, Betty 1928-1987 *ScF&FL 92*
Baker, Betty (Lou) 1928- *DcAmChF 1960*
Baker, Betty Lou 1928-1987 *ConAu 38NR, MajAI [port], SmATA 73 [port]*
Baker, Betty Louise 1937- *WhoAmW 93*
Baker, Beverly Joyce *BiDAMSp 1989*
Baker, Brenda Broughel 1944- *WhoAmW 93*
Baker, Brian Arthur 1945- *WhoSSW 93*
Baker, Bruce E. 1934- *St&PR 93*
Baker, Bruce Edward 1937- *WhoE 93, WhoWor 93*
Baker, Bruce J. 1954- *WhoEmL 93*
Baker, Burton Carl 1941- *WhoE 93*
Baker, Byron N. *St&PR 93*
Baker, C. Daniel, Jr. *Law&B 92*
Baker, Ç. Russell 1926- *St&PR 93*
Baker, C.S.L. 1939- *WhoScE 91-1*
Baker, C.W. 1930- *St&PR 93*
Baker, Carl Fleck *Law&B 92*
Baker, Carl Joseph 1950- *WhoE 93*
Baker, Carl L. *Law&B 92*
Baker, Carl Leroy 1943- *WhoAm 92*
Baker, Carleton Harold 1930- *WhoAm 92*
Baker, Carlos 1909-1987 *BioIn 17*
Baker, Carolyn Croom 1946- *WhoWrEP 92*
Baker, Carri Lynn 1962- *WhoAmW 93, WhoEmL 93*
Baker, Carroll 1931- *IntDcF 2-3 [port], WhoAm 92*
Baker, Cecil Lamar 1944- *St&PR 93*
Baker, Charles A. 1932- *St&PR 93*
Baker, Charles Adams 1920-1991 *BioIn 17*
Baker, Charles B. 1933- *St&PR 93*
Baker, Charles D. 1928- *St&PR 93*
Baker, Charles David, Jr. 1951- *WhoE 93*
Baker, Charles DeWitt 1932- *WhoAm 92*
Baker, Charles Douglas, Jr. 1948- *WhoSSW 93*
Baker, Charles Duane 1928- *WhoAm 92*
Baker, Charles Ernest 1946- *WhoAm 92, WhoE 93, WhoEmL 93, WhoWor 93*
Baker, Charles Gary 1946- *WhoEmL 93*
Baker, Charles Ray 1932- *WhoAm 92*
Baker, Charlotte 1910- *DcAmChF 1960*
Baker, Cheryl Louise 1948- *WhoEmL 93*
Baker, Chet (Chesney) 1929-1988 *Baker 92*
Baker, Christopher G.J. 1943- *WhoScE 91-1*
Baker, Claire Zivley *Law&B 92*
Baker, Clive Andrew 1946- *WhoIns 93*
Baker, Colin Arthur *WhoScE 91-1*
Baker, Colin Arthur 1929- *WhoWor 93*
Baker, Cornelia Draves 1929- *WhoAmW 93, WhoE 93, WhoWor 93*
Baker, Crispin S. L. 1939- *WhoWor 93*
Baker, Cullen 1835-1869 *BioIn 17*
Baker, Dale Edwin 1946- *WhoAm 92*
Baker, Daniel Neil 1948- *WhoAm 92, WhoE 93, WhoEmL 93*
Baker, Daniel Richard 1932- *WhoSSW 93, WhoWor 93*
Baker, Darrell Edward, Jr. 1955- *WhoE 93*
Baker, Darrius Gene 1946- *WhoIns 93*
Baker, David A. *Law&B 92*
Baker, David A. 1915- *St&PR 93*
Baker, David Alan 1957- *WhoWrEP 92*
Baker, David (Anthony) 1954- *DcLB 120 [port]*
Baker, David Arthur 1941- *WhoE 93*
Baker, David B., Jr. 1927- *St&PR 93*
Baker, David Harris 1955- *WhoAm 92*
Baker, David Hiram 1939- *WhoAm 92*
Baker, David Johnson 1945- *WhoE 93*
Baker, David Mark *Law&B 92*
Baker, David (Nathaniel) 1931- *Baker 92*
Baker, David R. 1932- *St&PR 93*
Baker, David Remember 1932- *WhoAm 92*
Baker, David S. 1937- *WhoAm 92*
Baker, Deborah Warrington 1949- *WhoAmW 93*
Baker, Debra Fryslie 1955- *WhoAmW 93*
Baker, Delbert Wayne 1953- *WhoAm 92*
Baker, Dennis Anthony *WhoScE 91-1*
Baker, Dennis Jay *Law&B 92*
Baker, Dennis Wayne 1946- *WhoAm 92, WhoEmL 93*
Baker, Denys Val 1917-1984 *ScF&FL 92*
Baker, Dexter F. 1927- *St&PR 93*
Baker, Dexter Farrington 1927- *WhoAm 92, WhoE 93*
Baker, Diane Price 1954- *St&PR 93*
Baker, Don Forrest 1947- *WhoEmL 93*
Baker, Don G. 1934- *WhoAm 92*
Baker, Don James 1946- *WhoEmL 93*
Baker, Don M. 1932- *WhoIns 93, WhoSSW 93*
Baker, Don Marion 1932- *St&PR 93*
Baker, Don R. 1948- *WhoEmL 93*
Baker, Donald 1929- *WhoAm 92*
Baker, Donald A. 1927- *St&PR 93*
Baker, Donald Edward 1944- *WhoAm 92*
Baker, Donald Gardner 1923- *WhoAm 92*
Baker, Donald James 1937- *WhoAm 92, WhoE 93*
Baker, Donald Parks 1932- *WhoAm 92*
Baker, Donald Scott 1939- *St&PR 93, WhoAm 92*
Baker, Donald W. *BioIn 17*
Baker, Donald Whitelaw 1923- *WhoWrEP 92*
Baker, Donna Kashulines 1952- *WhoEmL 93*
Baker, Dorothy Gillam 1906-1990 *BioIn 17*
Baker, Dorothy Scott *BioIn 17*
Baker, Dreama Gail 1948- *WhoAmW 93, WhoWor 93*
Baker, Earl Homer 1946- *WhoEmL 93, WhoSSW 93*
Baker, Earl Russel, II 1950- *WhoEmL 93, WhoWor 93*
Baker, Edith Ellis *AmWomPl*
Baker, Edith Madean 1942- *WhoAmW 93*
Baker, Edward D. *St&PR 93*
Baker, Edward Dickinson 1811-1861 *HarEnMi*
Baker, Edward George 1908- *WhoSSW 93, WhoWor 93*
Baker, Edward Kevin 1948- *WhoAm 92, WhoEmL 93, WhoSSW 93*
Baker, Edward L. 1946- *WhoAm 92*
Baker, Edward Martin 1941- *WhoAm 92*
Baker, Edwin Clarence 1925- *WhoIns 93*
Baker, Edwin Moody 1923- *WhoAm 92*
Baker, Edwin Robert 1930- *St&PR 93*
Baker, Edwin Stuart 1944- *WhoWor 93*
Baker, Elaine Rose 1953- *WhoEmL 93*
Baker, Elbert Hall, II 1910- *WhoWrEP 92*
Baker, Eleanor *AmWomPl*
Baker, Eliott Goodman 1952- *WhoEmL 93*
Baker, Elizabeth *AmWomPl*
Baker, Elizabeth 1928- *WhoAmW 93*
Baker, Elizabeth Calhoun *WhoAm 92, WhoAmW 93, WhoWrEP 92*
Baker, Elizabeth Lentz *WhoAmW 93*
Baker, Ella 1903-1986 *BioIn 17*
Baker, Ella Jo 1903-1986 *EncAACR*
Baker, Ellen Shulman 1953- *WhoAm 92, WhoAmW 93*
Baker, Elliott *BioIn 17*
Baker, Elliott 1922- *ScF&FL 92*
Baker, Elmer Elias, Jr. 1922- *WhoAm 92*
Baker, Emerson 1882-1934 *ScF&FL 92*
Baker, Eric Edward 1933- *WhoAm 92*
Baker, Erin *BioIn 17*
Baker, Erin Y. *Law&B 92*
Baker, Ernest Waldo, Jr. 1926- *WhoAm 92*
Baker, Eugene *St&PR 93*
Baker, Evan 1952- *WhoE 93*
Baker, F. M. 1942- *WhoE 93*
Baker, F.W.G. 1928- *WhoScE 91-2*
Baker, Faith Mero 1941- *WhoAmW 93*
Baker, Florence 1841-1916 *See* Baker, Samuel White 1821-1893 & Baker, Florence 1841-1916 *Expl 93*
Baker, Floyd Wilmer 1927- *WhoAm 92*
Baker, Francis E., Jr. 1929- *St&PR 93*
Baker, Francis Edward, Jr. 1944- *WhoE 93*
Baker, Frank 1908-1982 *ScF&FL 92*
Baker, Frank 1936- *WhoE 93*
Baker, Frank C. 1944- *St&PR 93*
Baker, Frank Hamon 1923- *WhoAm 92*
Baker, Fred *MiSFD 9*
Baker, Fred Greentree 1950- *WhoEmL 93*
Baker, Frederick John 1941- *WhoAm 92*
Baker, Frederick Milton, Jr. 1949- *WhoEmL 93*
Baker, Frederick Waller 1949- *WhoIns 93, WhoWrEP 92*
Baker, Gail Verleen 1952- *WhoWrEP 92*
Baker, Gary Anthony 1945- *WhoSSW 93*
Baker, Gary E. *Law&B 92*
Baker, Gary N. 1946- *St&PR 93*
Baker, Gary Roger 1944- *WhoSSW 93*
Baker, George 1877-1965 *EncAACR*
Baker, George Allen, Jr. 1932- *WhoAm 92*
Baker, George Chisholm 1918- *WhoAm 92*
Baker, George Fisher 1840-1931 *BioIn 17*
Baker, George Pierce 1866-1935 *GayN*
Baker, George Stanley 1950- *WhoEmL 93*
Baker, George T. 1900-1963 *EncABHB 8 [port]*
Baker, Georgetta J. *Law&B 92*
Baker, Gertrude *BioIn 17*
Baker, Gilbert Jens 1946- *WhoEmL 93, WhoWor 93*
Baker, Ginger *BioIn 17*
Baker, Ginger 1939- *See* Cream *ConMus 9*
Baker, Gloria Ann 1939- *WhoAmW 93*
Baker, Gloria Jean 1952- *WhoAmW 93*
Baker, Graham *MiSFD 9*
Baker, Gregory Benjamin 1961- *WhoWor 93*
Baker, Gregory Lynn 1954- *WhoEmL 93*
Baker, Gwendolyn Calvert 1931- *WhoAm 92, WhoAmW 93*
Baker, H. Forrest 1948- *St&PR 93*
Baker, Harold Cecil 1954- *WhoEmL 93*
Baker, Harold Leslie *Law&B 92*
Baker, Harvey Willis 1918- *WhoAm 92*
Baker, Helen Doyle Peil 1943- *WhoAmW 93*
Baker, Helen Hicks 1950- *WhoEmL 93*
Baker, Helen Marie 1946- *WhoAmW 93*
Baker, Henry d1689 *HarEnMi*
Baker, Henry 1890-1990 *BioIn 17*
Baker, Henry 1952- *WhoEmL 93*
Baker, Henry S., Jr. 1926- *St&PR 93, WhoAm 92*
Baker, Herman 1926- *WhoAm 92, WhoE 93*
Baker, Herschel C. 1914-1990 *BioIn 17*
Baker, Hobey *BioIn 17*
Baker, Hollis MacLure 1916- *WhoAm 92*
Baker, Houston A. *BioIn 17*
Baker, Howard 1947- *ScF&FL 92*
Baker, Howard H., Jr. 1925- *PolPar*

Baker, Howard Henry, Jr. 1925- *WhoAm 92*
Baker, Ida Emma Fitch 1858-1948 *AmWomPl*
Baker, Ira Lee 1915- *WhoAm 92*
Baker, Irena Mihelcic 1955- *WhoAmW 93*
Baker, Irene Bailey 1901- *BioIn 17*
Baker, Isaac M., Jr. 1913- *St&PR 93*
Baker, Isadore *ScF&FL 92*
Baker, Ivan Lee Holt 1958- *WhoSSW 93*
Baker, J. A. 1944- *WhoE 93*
Baker, J.M. *WhoScE 91-1*
Baker, J. Richard 1931- *WhoAm 92*
Baker, Jack Sherman 1920- *WhoAm 92*
Baker, James A., III *BioIn 17*
Baker, James A., III 1930- *ColdWar 1 [port]*
Baker, James Addison, III 1930- *CngDr 91, WhoAm 92, WhoE 93, WhoWor 93*
Baker, James Allan 1942- *WhoAm 92*
Baker, James Arthur *Law&B 92*
Baker, James Barnes 1933- *WhoAm 92*
Baker, James Donald 1943- *WhoSSW 93*
Baker, James Edward 1930- *WhoAm 92*
Baker, James Edward Sproul 1912- *WhoAm 92, WhoWor 93*
Baker, James Edyrn 1951- *WhoEmL 93*
Baker, James Estes 1935- *WhoAm 92, WhoUN 92*
Baker, James Eugene 1951- *WhoEmL 93*
Baker, James Gilbert 1914- *WhoAm 92*
Baker, James Heaton 1829-1913 *JrnUS*
Baker, James Jay 1953- *WhoEmL 93*
Baker, James Johnston 1926- *St&PR 93*
Baker, James K. 1931- *St&PR 93*
Baker, James Kendrick 1931- *WhoAm 92*
Baker, James Nettleton 1930- *WhoAm 92*
Baker, James Patrick 1934- *St&PR 93*
Baker, James R. 1945- *St&PR 93*
Baker, James W. 1926- *BioIn 17*
Baker, Jane *ScF&FL 92*
Baker, Janet 1933- *IntDcOp [port], OxDcOp*
Baker, Janet (Abbott) 1933- *Baker 92, WhoWor 93*
Baker, Jean Harvey 1933- *WhoAm 92*
Baker, Jean Mary 1944- *WhoAm 92, WhoAmW 93*
Baker, Jeanette Sledge 1947- *WhoEmL 93*
Baker, Jeannie 1950- *ChlLR 28 [port]*
Baker, Jeannine Ann 1949- *WhoWrEP 92*
Baker, Jeffrey L. *Law&B 92*
Baker, Jeffrey Stephen 1947- *WhoEmL 93*
Baker, Jessie M. *AmWomPl*
Baker, Joan M. *Law&B 92*
Baker, Joanne Evelyn 1933- *WhoE 93, WhoWor 93*
Baker, Joe Don 1936- *WhoAm 92*
Baker, John A. 1939- *WhoAm 92, WhoIns 93*
Baker, John Alexander 1927- *WhoAm 92*
Baker, John C. 1930- *St&PR 93*
Baker, John Cooper 1947- *WhoE 93, WhoEmL 93*
Baker, John D. d1992 *NewYTBS 92*
Baker, John Daniel 1948- *St&PR 93*
Baker, John Daniel, II 1948- *WhoSSW 93*
Baker, John Donald, Jr. 1938- *WhoE 93*
Baker, John E. 1954- *WhoWor 93*
Baker, John Edward 1940- *St&PR 93*
Baker, John Franklin 1886-1963 *BioIn 17*
Baker, John Gatch 1946- *WhoEmL 93*
Baker, John H. 1944- *WhoScE 91-1*
Baker, John L. 1928- *St&PR 93*
Baker, John Milnes 1932- *WhoAm 92*
Baker, John R. 1926- *St&PR 93*
Baker, John Richard 1946- *WhoEmL 93*
Baker, John Russell 1926- *WhoAm 92*
Baker, John Stevenson 1931- *WhoWor 93*
Baker, John Stewart, III 1946- *WhoEmL 93*
Baker, Johnnie B., Jr. 1949- *BiDAMSp 1989*
Baker, Joseph Edmond 1940- *WhoSSW 93*
Baker, Joseph Edward 1917- *WhoWrEP 92*
Baker, Joseph John 1952- *St&PR 93*
Baker, Joseph Lee 1943- *St&PR 93*
Baker, Joseph Preston 1946- *St&PR 93*
Baker, Josephine 1906-1975 *Baker 92, BioIn 17, ConBlB 3 [port]*
Baker, Josephine L. Redenius 1920- *WhoSSW 93*
Baker, Josephine Turck *AmWomPl*
Baker, Joy Lynn 1954- *WhoWor 93*
Baker, Judith Karen 1945- *St&PR 93*
Baker, Julie A. *Law&B 92*
Baker, Julius 1915- *Baker 92*
Baker, Justine Clara 1939- *WhoAmW 93*
Baker, Karen *BioIn 17*
Baker, Katherine June 1932- *WhoAmW 93, WhoSSW 93*
Baker, Kathryn Benes *Law&B 92*
Baker, Keith Michael 1938- *WhoAm 92*
Baker, Kendall L. 1942- *WhoAm 92*
Baker, Kennard C. d1991 *BioIn 17*
Baker, Kenneth Albert 1946- *WhoAm 92*
Baker, Kenneth Percy 1930- *WhoScE 91-3*
Baker, Kenneth Ray *Law&B 92*
Baker, Kenneth Wilfred 1934- *WhoWor 93*
Baker, Kent Alfred 1948- *WhoEmL 93, WhoWor 93*
Baker, Kerry Allen 1949- *WhoEmL 93, WhoSSW 93, WhoWor 93*
Baker, Kimberly Sue 1964- *WhoEmL 93*
Baker, Kristin *BioIn 17*
Baker, Kurt *MiSFD 9*
Baker, L. *ConAu 139*
Baker, Laura Ann 1955- *WhoEmL 93*
Baker, Laurence C. 1946- *St&PR 93*
Baker, Laurence Howard 1943- *WhoAm 92*
Baker, Laurence Spencer 1925- *WhoE 93*
Baker, LaVern *BioIn 17*
Baker, LaVern 1929- *SoulM*
Baker, Lawrence Colby, Jr. 1935- *WhoAm 92, WhoIns 93*
Baker, Lee Cecil Ray 1942- *WhoSSW 93*
Baker, Lee Edward 1924- *WhoAm 92, WhoSSW 93*
Baker, Lenox Dial 1902- *WhoAm 92, WhoWor 93*
Baker, Leonard Morton 1934- *WhoAm 92*
Baker, Leslie Mayo 1942- *St&PR 93*
Baker, Lester 1930- *WhoAm 92*
Baker, Lillian (L.) 1921- *ConAu 139, WhoAm 92, WhoAmW 93, WhoWor 93*
Baker, Linda Leslie 1948- *WhoAmW 93, WhoEmL 93*
Baker, Lori Ann 1957- *WhoAmW 93*
Baker, Lori Kay 1958- *WhoEmL 93*
Baker, Louis, Jr. 1927- *WhoAm 92*
Baker, Louis Coombs Weller 1921- *WhoWor 93*
Baker, Louis W. 1931- *St&PR 93*
Baker, Louisa L. *Law&B 92*
Baker, Lucille Stoeppler 1919- *WhoAmW 93*
Baker, Lynne Rudder 1944- *WhoAm 92*
Baker, M. Gerald 1939- *St&PR 93*
Baker, Margery 1948- *St&PR 93*
Baker, Margery Claire 1948- *WhoAm 92*
Baker, Mari Jean 1965- *WhoAmW 93*
Baker, Mark Allen 1957- *WhoE 93*
Baker, Mark Bruce 1946- *WhoWor 93*
Baker, Mark Early 1953- *WhoEmL 93, WhoSSW 93*
Baker, Mark R. 1957- *St&PR 93*
Baker, Mark William 1948- *St&PR 93*
Baker, Martin Raymond *Law&B 92*
Baker, Martin Roy 1964- *WhoSSW 93*
Baker, Marvin Duane 1937- *St&PR 93*
Baker, Mary Jordan *WhoAmW 93*
Baker, Melvin C. 1920- *WhoAm 92*
Baker, Merl 1924- *WhoAm 92*
Baker, Merrily Dean *WhoAmW 93*
Baker, Mervin Duane 1949- *WhoWor 93*
Baker, Michael 1937- *Baker 92*
Baker, Michael A. 1954?- *BioIn 17*
Baker, Michael Harry 1916- *WhoAm 92*
Baker, Michael John 1935- *WhoWor 93*
Baker, Michael John 1950- *WhoWor 93*
Baker, Mickey *SoulM*
Baker, Mike *ScF&FL 92*
Baker, Milton 1908- *St&PR 93*
Baker, Neil Reeves *WhoScE 91-1*
Baker, Nell Williams 1934- *WhoAmW 93*
Baker, Nevin S. 1922- *St&PR 93*
Baker, Newell A. 1926- *St&PR 93*
Baker, Newell Alden 1926- *WhoAm 92*
Baker, Nicholson *BioIn 17*
Baker, Nick *ScF&FL 92*
Baker, Nikki 1962- *ConAu 137*
Baker, Nina Brown 1888-1957 *ScF&FL 92*
Baker, Norman Henderson 1917- *WhoAm 92*
Baker, Norman Lee 1926- *WhoE 93, WhoWor 93*
Baker, Norman Robert 1937- *WhoAm 92*
Baker, Octavia Ann 1956- *WhoAmW 93*
Baker, Owen Nelson *Law&B 92*
Baker, Pamela Carolyn 1957- *WhoEmL 93, WhoSSW 93*
Baker, Pamela J. 1947- *BioIn 17*
Baker, Patricia Ellis 1938- *WhoE 93*
Baker, Patricia Marie 1959- *WhoAmW 93*
Baker, Patricia O. 1956- *St&PR 93*
Baker, Patrick C. *Law&B 92*
Baker, Patrick H. *Law&B 92*
Baker, Paul Alan 1955- *WhoWrEP 92*
Baker, Paul Raymond 1927- *WhoAm 92*
Baker, Paul Thornell 1927- *WhoAm 92*
Baker, Peter B. 1946- *WhoScE 91-1*
Baker, Peter Edward *WhoScE 91-1*
Baker, Peter Graham *WhoScE 91-1*
Baker, Peter Harrison 1952- *WhoE 93*
Baker, Peter Mitchell 1939- *WhoAm 92*
Baker, Philip Benton 1934- *St&PR 93*
Baker, Philip Douglas 1922- *WhoAm 92*
Baker, Philip F. 1946- *St&PR 93*
Baker, Philip John Noel- 1889-1982 *BioIn 17*
Baker, Pip *ScF&FL 92*
Baker, R. *WhoScE 91-1*
Baker, R.J. *WhoScE 91-1*
Baker, R. Palmer, Jr. 1918- *WhoAm 92*
Baker, R. Robinson 1928- *WhoAm 92*
Baker, Rachel E. *AmWomPl*
Baker, Ray Stannard 1870-1946 *BioIn 17, JrnUS, TwCLC 47 [port]*
Baker, Raymond 1936- *WhoWor 93*
Baker, Raymond R.J. 1938- *St&PR 93*
Baker, Raymond W. *Law&B 92*
Baker, Richard Albert, Jr. 1959- *WhoE 93*
Baker, Richard Brown 1912- *WhoAm 92, WhoE 93*
Baker, Richard C. *Law&B 92*
Baker, Richard E. 1939- *St&PR 93*
Baker, Richard Earl, Jr. 1960- *WhoE 93*
Baker, Richard Eugene 1939- *WhoAm 92*
Baker, Richard Freligh 1910- *WhoAm 92*
Baker, Richard Graves 1938- *WhoAm 92*
Baker, Richard H. 1948- *CngDr 91*
Baker, Richard Hadley 1936- *WhoSSW 93*
Baker, Richard Hugh 1948- *WhoAm 92, WhoSSW 93*
Baker, Richard J. *Law&B 92*
Baker, Richard J. 1931- *WhoIns 93*
Baker, Richard Joint 1931- *St&PR 93, WhoE 93*
Baker, Richard L. 1935- *St&PR 93*
Baker, Richard Lee 1935- *WhoAm 92*
Baker, Richard M. 1945- *St&PR 93*
Baker, Richard Southworth 1929- *WhoAm 92, WhoWor 93*
Baker, Richard W.S. 1933- *WhoIns 93*
Baker, Richard Wheeler, Jr. 1916- *WhoAm 92*
Baker, Robert 1940- *WhoAm 92*
Baker, Robert Andrew 1925- *WhoAm 92*
Baker, Robert C. *Law&B 92*
Baker, Robert Calhoun d1976 *BioIn 17*
Baker, Robert Donald 1927- *WhoSSW 93*
Baker, Robert Edward 1930- *WhoAm 92*
Baker, Robert Ernest, Jr. 1916- *WhoAm 92, WhoSSW 93*
Baker, Robert Francis 1935- *WhoAm 92, WhoE 93*
Baker, Robert Frank 1936- *WhoAm 92*
Baker, Robert Gene 1928- *PolPar*
Baker, Robert Hart 1954- *WhoAm 92, WhoEmL 93*
Baker, Robert Jay 1927- *WhoE 93*
Baker, Robert John 1938- *WhoAm 92*
Baker, Robert Lee, III 1949- *WhoEmL 93, WhoSSW 93*
Baker, Robert Leon 1920- *WhoWrEP 92*
Baker, Robert Leon 1925- *WhoAm 92*
Baker, Robert M. L., Jr. 1930- *WhoAm 92*
Baker, Robert Maurice 1928- *St&PR 93*
Baker, Robert S. 1940- *ScF&FL 92*
Baker, Robert Shelton 1946- *WhoSSW 93*
Baker, Robert Stevens 1916- *WhoAm 92*
Baker, Robert Thomas 1932- *WhoAm 92*
Baker, Robert William *Law&B 92*
Baker, Robert Woodward 1944- *St&PR 93, WhoAm 92, WhoSSW 93*
Baker, Rodney Lee 1950- *WhoEmL 93*
Baker, Roger C. *WhoScE 91-1*
Baker, Roger Thomas *Law&B 92*
Baker, Roger William Weatherburn 1944- *WhoE 93*
Baker, Roland C. 1938- *WhoIns 93*
Baker, Roland Charles 1938- *WhoAm 92*
Baker, Roland Jerald 1938- *WhoAm 92*
Baker, Ronald Dale 1932- *WhoAm 92*
Baker, Ronald James 1924- *WhoAm 92*
Baker, Ronald Lee 1937- *WhoAm 92*
Baker, Ronald Lee 1938- *WhoE 93*
Baker, Ronald R. 1943- *St&PR 93*
Baker, Ronald Ray 1943- *WhoAm 92*
Baker, Roy Ward 1916- *MiSFD 9*
Baker, Russell 1925- *BioIn 17, JrnUS*
Baker, Russell Tremaine, Jr. 1942- *WhoAm 92*
Baker, Russell Wayne 1925- *WhoAm 92, WhoWrEP 92*
Baker, Sally 1932- *WhoWor 93*
Baker, Samm Sinclair 1909- *WhoWrEP 92*
Baker, Samuel Garrard 1950- *WhoSSW 93*
Baker, Samuel White 1821-1893 *BioIn 17*
Baker, Samuel White 1821-1893 & Baker, Florence 1841-1916 *Expl 93 [port]*
Baker, Saul P. 1925- *St&PR 93*
Baker, Saul Phillip 1924- *WhoAm 92, WhoWor 93*
Baker, Scott 1947- *ScF&FL 92*
Baker, Sharlene 1954- *ConAu 136*
Baker, Sharon 1938- *WhoWrEP 92*
Baker, Sharon 1938-1991 *ScF&FL 92*
Baker, Sheldon S. 1936- *WhoAm 92*
Baker, Sheridan 1918- *WhoAm 92, WhoWrEP 92*
Baker, Sherman Nelson 1919- *St&PR 93*
Baker, Shirley Kistler 1943- *WhoAm 92, WhoAmW 93*
Baker, Stanley 1928-1976 *IntDcF 2-3 [port]*
Baker, Stanley Beckwith 1935- *WhoE 93*
Baker, Stephen 1923- *WhoAm 92, WhoWrEP 92*
Baker, Stephen Anthony 1953- *St&PR 93*
Baker, Stephen Richard 1949- *WhoWor 93*
Baker, Steven Robert 1959- *WhoE 93*
Baker, Stuart David 1935- *WhoAm 92*
Baker, Susan Beggs 1939- *WhoSSW 93*
Baker, Susan Betteridge *Law&B 92*
Baker, Susan P. 1930- *WhoAm 92*
Baker, Suzanne Kathleen 1962- *WhoAmW 93*
Baker, Suzanne Schneider 1947- *WhoEmL 93*
Baker, T. Lindsay 1947- *WhoSSW 93*
Baker, T. Neville *WhoScE 91-1*
Baker, Terry G. *WhoScE 91-1*
Baker, Theodore 1851-1934 *Baker 92*
Baker, Theresa Bailey *Law&B 92*
Baker, Thomas A. d1944 *BioIn 17*
Baker, Thomas Edgar 1931- *St&PR 93, WhoAm 92*
Baker, Thomas Edward 1923- *WhoAm 92*
Baker, Thomas Eugene 1953- *WhoEmL 93, WhoSSW 93*
Baker, Thomas F., IV *Law&B 92*
Baker, Thomas Harri 1933- *WhoSSW 93*
Baker, Thomas J. 1945- *St&PR 93*
Baker, Thomas L. 1943- *WhoSSW 93*
Baker, Thomas Lyle 1945- *St&PR 93*
Baker, Thomas Wayne 1946- *WhoEmL 93*
Baker, Thompson Simkins 1905- *St&PR 93, WhoAm 92, WhoSSW 93*
Baker, Timothy *Law&B 92*
Baker, Timothy Alan 1954- *WhoWor 93*
Baker, Timothy Danforth 1925- *WhoAm 92*
Baker, Timothy James 1951- *St&PR 93*
Baker, Timothy John 1948- *WhoEmL 93*
Baker, Tina Patrice Higgins 1959- *WhoEmL 93, WhoSSW 93*
Baker, Valentine 1827-1887 *HarEnMi*
Baker, Vernon Graham, II *Law&B 92*
Baker, Victoria Jean 1955- *WhoAmW 93*
Baker, W. Howard 1925-1991 *ScF&FL 92*
Baker, W.J. *ScF&FL 92*
Baker, Walter Edward 1928- *WhoE 93*
Baker, Walter Louis 1924- *WhoAm 92*
Baker, Warren Joseph 1938- *WhoAm 92*
Baker, Warren W. 1931- *St&PR 93*
Baker, Wayne D. 1932- *WhoAm 92, WhoIns 93*
Baker, Wilder DuPuy 1931- *WhoAm 92*
Baker, Willard L. 1939- *St&PR 93*
Baker, William Buck 1954- *WhoWor 93*
Baker, William C. 1939- *St&PR 93*
Baker, William Costello, Jr. 1959- *WhoEmL 93*
Baker, William D. *St&PR 93*
Baker, William Dunlap 1932- *WhoAm 92*
Baker, William Franklin 1942- *WhoAm 92*
Baker, William Garrett, Jr. 1933- *WhoAm 92*
Baker, William George 1935- *WhoAm 92*
Baker, William J. 1932- *St&PR 93*
Baker, William L. *Law&B 92*
Baker, William L. 1945- *WhoIns 93*
Baker, William Oliver 1915- *WhoAm 92, WhoE 93*
Baker, William Parr 1946- *WhoAm 92, WhoE 93*
Baker, William Radcliffe 1946- *WhoWrEP 92*
Baker, William Thompson, Jr. 1944- *WhoAm 92*
Baker, William Wallace 1921- *WhoAm 92*
Baker, Winda Louise 1952- *WhoSSW 93*
Baker, Winthrop Patterson, Jr. 1931- *WhoAm 92*
Baker-Branton, Camille B. 1950- *WhoAmW 93, WhoEmL 93*
Baker-Erbisch, C. B. *WhoAmW 93*
Baker Knoll, Catherine *WhoAmW 93, WhoE 93*
Baker-Lievanos, Nina Gillson 1950- *WhoAmW 93, WhoEmL 93*
Baker-Mitchell, Althea Ross 1949- *WhoAmW 93, WhoEmL 93*
Baker-Roelofs, Mina Marie 1920- *WhoAmW 93*
Bakes, Robert Eldon 1932- *WhoAm 92*
Bakewell, Peter John 1943- *WhoSSW 93*
Bakewell, William 1908- *BioIn 17*
Bakfark, Valentin 1507-1576 *Baker 92*
Bakhru, Ashok N. 1942- *St&PR 93*
Bakhru, Ashok Naraindas 1942- *WhoAm 92*
Bakhru, Keshoolal 1933- *WhoAm 92*
Bakhsh, Ahmad 1958- *WhoWor 93*
Bakht, Baidar 1940- *WhoAm 92*
Bakhtiar, Shahpur 1916-1991 *BioIn 17*
Bakhtin, M.M. 1895-1975 *BioIn 17*
Bakhtin, Mikhail Mikhailovich 1895-1975 *BioIn 17*
Bakhtin, Nikolai Nikolaevich *BioIn 17*
Bakhvalov, Nikolaj Sergejevich 1934- *WhoWor 93*

Bakis, Charles Emanuel 1959- *WhoE 93*
Bakka, Richard S. 1940- *WhoIns 93*
Bakke, Alf 1927- *WhoScE 91-4*
Bakke, Dennis W. *BioIn 17, St&PR 93*
Bakke, Duwayne Allan 1939- *St&PR 93*
Bakke, Eileen *BioIn 17*
Bakke, Ernst *WhoScE 91-4*
Bakke, Finn Halvor 1927- *WhoWor 93*
Bakke, Jill Hance 1936- *WhoWrEP 92*
Bakke, Tor A. 1943- *WhoScE 91-4*
Bakken, Bruce Michael 1953- *WhoEmL 93*
Bakken, Constance L. 1923- *St&PR 93*
Bakken, Dick 1941- *WhoWrEP 92*
Bakken, Earl Elmer 1924- *WhoAm 92*
Bakken, Petter M. *WhoScE 91-4*
Bakken, Timothy C. 1957- *WhoEmL 93*
Bakkensen, John Reser 1943- *WhoAm 92*
Bakkensen, Ralph *Law&B 92*
Bakker, Cornelis B. 1929- *WhoAm 92*
Bakker, J.J. 1944- *WhoScE 91-3*
Bakker, Jacob Jan 1952- *WhoScE 91-3*
Bakker, Jim *BioIn 17*
Bakker, Tammy *BioIn 17*
Bakker, Thomas Gordon 1947- *WhoAm 92, WhoEmL 93*
Bakketeig, Leiv S. 1938- *WhoScE 91-4*
Bakkis, George 1881-1938 *Baker 92*
Bakko, Orville Edwin 1919- *WhoAm 92*
Baklanoff, Eric Nicholas 1925- *WhoAm 92*
Baklanov, George 1881-1938 *Baker 92*
Baklanov, Oleg Dmitrievich 1932- *BioIn 17*
Bakman, Patrick T. d1990 *BioIn 17*
Bako, Mahmane Sani 1951- *WhoAfr*
Bako, Terezia 1946- *WhoScE 91-4*
Ba Kobhio, Bassek *MiSFD 9*
Bakonyi, Peter 1938- *WhoScE 91-4*
Bakos, John A. 1932- *St&PR 93*
Bakos, Jozsef S. 1932- *WhoScE 91-4*
Bakos, Miklos 1926- *WhoScE 91-4*
Bakr, Abd Al-Wahhab 1933- *ConAu 139*
Bakri, M. Hani Abdul Kader 1960- *WhoWor 93*
Bakrow, William John 1924- *WhoAm 92*
Baksa, J.A. *Law&B 92*
Bakshi, Jayant 1950- *WhoWor 93*
Bakshi, Kamal Nain 1938- *WhoUN 92*
Bakshi, Ralph *WhoAm 92*
Bakshi, Ralph 1938- *ConAu 138, MiSFD 9*
Bakshian, Aram, Jr. 1944- *WhoE 93*
Bakula, Scott *WhoAm 92*
Bakunawa, Luz Cleta R. *WhoAsAP 91*
Bakushinskii, Anatolie Borisovith 1937- *WhoWor 93*
Bakwin, Edward Morris 1928- *WhoAm 92*
Bal, Rajeev Gopal 1952- *St&PR 93*
Bal, Sant Singh 1942- *ScF&FL 92*
Bala, Gary Ganesh 1958- *WhoEmL 93*
Bala, Wladyslaw 1919- *WhoScE 91-4*
Balaam *BioIn 17*
Balaban, Alexander Joseph 1958- *WhoE 93*
Balaban, Alexandru T. 1931- *WhoScE 91-4*
Balaban, Bob 1945- *MiSFD 9, ScF&FL 92*
Balaban, Donald Eugene 1932- *St&PR 93*
Balaban, John B. 1943- *DcLB 120 [port]*
Balaban, Joseph George 1940- *WhoAm 92*
Balaban, Majer 1877-1942 *PolBiDi*
Balaban, Michael Seth 1949- *St&PR 93*
Balabanian, David Mark 1938- *WhoAm 92*
Balabanian, Norman 1922- *WhoAm 92*
Balacek, Thomas Vincent, Jr. 1961- *WhoEmL 93, WhoWor 93*
Balachandiran, Sellathurai 1942- *WhoWor 93*
Balachandran, Bala Venkataraman 1937- *WhoAm 92*
Balachandran, M(adhavarao) 1938- *ConAu 40NR*
Balachandran, Sarojini 1934- *ConAu 40NR*
Balada, Leonardo 1933- *Baker 92, WhoAm 92*
Baladhuri, Al- dc. 892 *OxDcByz*
Baladi, Andre 1934- *WhoWor 93*
Bala Goud, T. 1931- *WhoAsAP 91*
Balagtas, Manuel Marasigan *WhoWor 93*
Balague Domenech, Jose Carlos 1939- *WhoWor 93*
Balaguer, Joaquin 1906- *DcCPCAm*
Balaguer, Joaquin 1907- *DcTwHis, WhoWor 93*
Balahoutis, Linda *BioIn 17*
Balahtsis, Dede Z. 1964- *St&PR 93*
Balahtsis, Jack 1938- *St&PR 93*
Balajan, Roman 1941- *DrEEuF*
Balakauskas, Osvaldas 1937- *Baker 92*
Balakian, Anna 1916- *WhoAm 92*
Balakian, Nona 1919-1991 *BioIn 17*
Balakian, Peter 1951- *WhoWrEP 92*
Balakirev, Mily 1837-1910 *Baker 92*
Balakrishnan, David c. 1954- *See* Turtle Island String Quartet *ConMus 9*
Balan, Jerry 1948- *St&PR 93*
Balanandan, E. 1924- *WhoAsAP 91*
Balanchine, George 1904-1983 *Baker 92, BioIn 17*
Balanchivadze, Andrei (Melitonovich) 1906- *Baker 92*
Balanchivadze, Andrey 1906- *OxDcOp*
Balanchivadze, Meliton 1862-1937 *OxDcOp*
Balanchivadze, Meliton (Antonovich) 1862-1937 *Baker 92*
Balanesi, Christopher Domenic 1950- *WhoE 93*
Balanis, Constantine Apostle 1938- *WhoAm 92*
Balante, Janice Louise 1955- *WhoAmW 93*
Balantzian, Gerard *WhoScE 91-2*
Balaraman, L. 1932- *WhoAsAP 91*
Balaran, N.E. *WhoAsAP 91*
Balaras, Constantinos Agelou 1962- *WhoWor 93*
Balart, Gabriel 1824-1893 *Baker 92*
Balas, Charles 1945- *WhoE 93*
Balas, Deborah Ann 1957- *WhoEmL 93*
Balas, Jan 1923- *WhoScE 91-4*
Balasa, Joseph John 1932- *St&PR 93*
Balasanian, Sergei 1902-1982 *Baker 92*
Balashev, Angel Bogdanov 1925- *WhoScE 91-4*
Balasko, Yves 1945- *WhoWor 93*
Balassa, Bela A. *BioIn 17*
Balassa, Leslie L. d1992 *NewYTBS 92*
Balassa, Leslie L. 1903- *St&PR 93*
Balassa, Sandor 1935- *Baker 92*
Balasubramanyam, V.N. *WhoScE 91-1*
Balatka, Hans 1825-1899 *Baker 92*
Balavender, Richard Joseph 1944- *St&PR 93*
Balay, Robert Elmore 1930- *WhoAm 92*
Balaz, Beverly Ann 1949- *WhoEmL 93*
Balazs, Bela Arpad 1935- *WhoScE 91-4*
Balazs, Endre A. *St&PR 93*
Balazs, Joseph B. *Law&B 92*
Balazs, Mary W. 1939- *WhoWrEP 92*
Balazs, Sandor 1925- *WhoScE 91-4*
Balbach, Anatol B. 1927- *St&PR 93*
Balbach, Stanley Byron 1919- *WhoAm 92*
Balban, Ghiyas-ud-din 1205-1287 *HarEnMi*
Balbastre, Claude (-Benigne) 1727-1799 *Baker 92*
Balbatre, Claude (-Benigne) 1727-1799 *Baker 92*
Balbi, Lodovico 1545-1604 *Baker 92*
Balbi, Melchiore 1796-1879 *Baker 92*
Balbin, Julius 1917- *WhoE 93, WhoWor 93*
Balbino, Luis *WhoScE 91-3*
Balbo, Italo 1896-1940 *HarEnMi*
Balboa, Vasco Nunez de 1475-1519 *BioIn 17, Expl 93 [port]*
Balbuena, Bernardo de 1562?-1627 *DcMexL*
Balbus, Lodovico 1545-1604 *Baker 92*
Balcaltos, Antonio T. 1923- *WhoAsAP 91*
Balcar, Gerald Pierce 1932- *St&PR 93*
Balcazar, Jose Luis 1959- *WhoWor 93*
Balcer, Anne Elaine 1953- *WhoEmL 93*
Balcer, Charles Louis 1921- *WhoAm 92*
Balcer, Rene Chenevert 1954- *WhoEmL 93*
Balcer-Brownstein, Josefine 1948- *WhoAmW 93*
Balcerowicz, Leszek 1947- *BioIn 17*
Balcerski, William J. *Law&B 92*
Balcerzak, Stanley Paul 1930- *WhoAm 92*
Balch, Charles M. 1942- *WhoAm 92*
Balch, Emily Greene 1867-1961 *BioIn 17*
Balch, Frank 1880-1937 *ScF&FL 92*
Balch, Glenn 1902- *WhoWrEP 92*
Balch, Glenn McClain, Jr. 1937- *WhoAm 92*
Balch, Ida M. *AmWomPl*
Balch, Jerold Howard 1943- *WhoE 93*
Balch, John A. 1935- *St&PR 93*
Balch, John Wayne 1947- *WhoE 93, WhoEmL 93*
Balch, Mary Gertrude *AmWomPl*
Balch, Peter D. *Law&B 92*
Balch, Samuel Eason 1919- *WhoAm 92, WhoWor 93*
Balch, William 1946- *WhoE 93*
Balchin, I. David 1940- *St&PR 93*
Balchunas, Gerard Andrew 1955- *WhoE 93*
Balco, George Joseph 1940- *St&PR 93*
Balcom, Gloria Darleen 1939- *WhoAmW 93*
Balcomb, Sara Allen 1938- *WhoAmW 93*
Balcon, Jonathan Michael H. 1931- *WhoWor 93*
Bald, John *BioIn 17*
Bald, William Balfour *WhoScE 91-1*
Balda, Jo 1922- *WhoAmW 93*
Baldacchino, Joseph Francis 1948- *WhoE 93*
Baldacci, Robert Eugene, Jr. 1952- *WhoE 93*
Baldanza, Deb *WhoWrEP 92*
Baldasre, Michael George 1949- *St&PR 93*
Baldassano, Corinne Leslie 1950- *WhoAm 92, WhoAmW 93*
Baldassari, Dennis 1949- *WhoAm 92*
Baldassari, Dennis P. 1949- *St&PR 93*
Baldassari, Fred J. 1932- *St&PR 93*
Baldassarre, Joseph Anthony 1950- *WhoEmL 93*
Baldauf, Richard John 1920- *WhoAm 92*
Balden, John A. 1949- *St&PR 93*
Balden, Rose Ann 1943- *St&PR 93*
Balderson, Lisa 1965- *WhoAmW 93*
Balderson, Margaret 1915- *DcChlFi*
Balderson, S. Clark 1948- *St&PR 93*
Balderston, C. Canby 1897-1979 *BioIn 17*
Balderston, Jean Merrill 1936- *WhoAmW 93, WhoWrEP 92*
Balderston, William, III 1927- *St&PR 93, WhoAm 92*
Baldeschwieler, John Dickson 1933- *WhoAm 92*
Baldessari, John 1931- *BioIn 17*
Baldessari, John Anthony 1931- *WhoAm 92*
Baldi, Angelo C. *Law&B 92*
Baldi, Angelo C. 1942- *WhoAm 92, WhoSSW 93*
Baldi, Ferdinando *MiSFD 9*
Baldi, Gualtiero 1949- *WhoScE 91-3*
Baldi, Joao Jose 1770-1816 *Baker 92*
Baldi, Robert Otjen 1949- *WhoEmL 93*
Baldi, Virgil B. 1928- *St&PR 93*
Baldick, Chris 1954- *ScF&FL 92*
Baldie, William James 1942- *WhoUN 92*
Baldini, Enrico 1925- *WhoScE 91-3*
Baldini, Sanzio 1939- *WhoScE 91-3*
Baldjiev, Dimitar Nickolov 1937- *WhoScE 91-4*
Baldo, Giorgio *WhoScE 91-3*
Baldo, Helen Johnson 1931- *WhoAmW 93*
Baldock, Bobby Ray 1936- *WhoAm 92*
Baldoni, Rudolph C. 1931- *St&PR 93*
Baldovsky, Diane Mary 1954- *WhoAmW 93*
Baldowsky, Frederic George *Law&B 92*
Baldridge, Anita Carol 1956- *WhoAmW 93, WhoEmL 93*
Baldridge, Bobbie D. 1951- *St&PR 93*
Baldridge, Charlene 1934- *WhoWrEP 92*
Baldridge, Harold G. 1936- *WhoE 93*
Baldridge, Mary Humphrey *WhoCanL 92*
Baldridge, Robert Crary 1921- *WhoAm 92*
Baldridge, Terry Jayne 1954- *WhoSSW 93*
Baldrige, Letitia *NewYTBS 92, WhoAm 92, WhoE 93*
Baldry, Cherith *ScF&FL 92*
Baldry, Cherith 1947- *SmATA 72 [port]*
Baldry, David Andrew Thomas 1936- *WhoUN 92*
Balducci, Giuseppe 1796-1845 *OxDcOp*
Balducci, Stephen Watts 1950- *WhoE 93*
Baldunciks, Juris 1950- *WhoWor 93*
Baldus, Herbert 1899-1970 *IntDcAn*
Baldwin, II 1217-1273 *OxDcByz*
Baldwin, III 1129-1163 *OxDcByz*
Baldwin, Alec *BioIn 17, NewYTBS 92 [port]*
Baldwin, Alec 1958- *CurBio 92 [port], HolBB [port]*
Baldwin, Alex *ConAu 40NR*
Baldwin, Alexander Rae, III 1958- *WhoAm 92, WhoEmL 93*
Baldwin, Alfrieda *Law&B 92*
Baldwin, Alice Blackwood c. 1845-1930 *BioIn 17*
Baldwin, Ann T. 1944- *St&PR 93*
Baldwin, Arthur Dwight, Jr. 1938- *WhoAm 92*
Baldwin, Arthur W. *BioIn 17*
Baldwin, Bee *ScF&FL 92*
Baldwin, Betty Jo 1925- *WhoAmW 93*
Baldwin, Bill 1935- *ScF&FL 92*
Baldwin, Brent Winfield 1952- *WhoWor 93*
Baldwin, Bruce Wayne 1953- *WhoWor 93*
Baldwin, C. Stephen 1938- *WhoUN 92*
Baldwin, Calvin Benham, Jr. 1925- *WhoAm 92*
Baldwin, Carol A. *Law&B 92*
Baldwin, Carolyn H. *BioIn 17*
Baldwin, Carrie Marie 1965- *WhoEmL 93*
Baldwin, Charlene Marie 1946- *WhoEmL 93*
Baldwin, Charles A. *Law&B 92*
Baldwin, Charles Carroll, Jr. 1956- *WhoIns 93*
Baldwin, Charles Henry 1942- *WhoAm 92, WhoE 93*
Baldwin, Charles William 1915- *WhoE 93*
Baldwin, Clarence Jones, Jr. 1929- *WhoAm 92*
Baldwin, Cynthia Ann 1951- *WhoEmL 93*
Baldwin, Cyrus S. *Law&B 92*
Baldwin, Daniel *BioIn 17*
Baldwin, David Allen 1936- *WhoE 93*
Baldwin, David Kendrick 1937- *St&PR 93*
Baldwin, David Rawson 1923- *WhoAm 92*
Baldwin, David Shepard 1921- *WhoAm 92*
Baldwin, Deanna Louise 1946- *WhoSSW 93*
Baldwin, Deborah 1949- *WhoAmW 93*
Baldwin, Deidra B. 1945- *WhoWrEP 92*
Baldwin, DeWitt Clair, Jr. 1922- *WhoAm 92, WhoWor 93*
Baldwin, Diane *BioIn 17*
Baldwin, Dick *WhoWrEP 92*
Baldwin, Dorothy Leila 1948- *WhoAmW 93, WhoE 93, WhoEmL 93, WhoWor 93*
Baldwin, Douglas *Law&B 92*
Baldwin, Douglas V. 1939- *St&PR 93*
Baldwin, Edward 1756-1836 *BioIn 17*
Baldwin, Etta *AmWomPl*
Baldwin, Everett N. 1932- *St&PR 93*
Baldwin, Everett Newton 1932- *WhoAm 92*
Baldwin, Francis Gregory 1956- *St&PR 93*
Baldwin, Frank Bruce, III 1939- *WhoAm 92*
Baldwin, Frank Dwight 1842-1923 *BioIn 17*
Baldwin, Gary Eual 1937- *St&PR 93*
Baldwin, Gary Lee 1943- *WhoAm 92*
Baldwin, Garza, Jr. 1921- *WhoAm 92*
Baldwin, George Curriden 1917- *WhoAm 92*
Baldwin, Glen S. *Law&B 92*
Baldwin, Gordon Brewster 1929- *WhoAm 92, WhoWor 93*
Baldwin, H. Furlong 1932- *St&PR 93*
Baldwin, Hanson W(eightman) 1903-1991 *ConAu 136, CurBio 92N*
Baldwin, Hanson Weightman 1903-1991 *BioIn 17*
Baldwin, Henry 1780-1844 *OxCSupC [port]*
Baldwin, Henry Furlong 1932- *WhoAm 92*
Baldwin, Henry Ives d1992 *NewYTBS 92 [port]*
Baldwin, Herbert E. d1990 *BioIn 17*
Baldwin, Huntley *WhoAm 92*
Baldwin, Ian, Jr. 1938- *WhoE 93*
Baldwin, Irene S. 1939- *WhoAmW 93*
Baldwin, Jack Edward *WhoScE 91-1*
Baldwin, James 1924-1987 *BioIn 17, ConGAN, EncAACR, MagSAmL [port], ShSCr 10 [port], WorLitC [port]*
Baldwin, James J. 1937- *St&PR 93*
Baldwin, James Patric 1954- *WhoEmL 93*
Baldwin, Janet DeLage 1933- *St&PR 93*
Baldwin, Janice Murphy 1926- *WhoAmW 93*
Baldwin, Jeanne O'Grady 1956- *WhoAmW 93*
Baldwin, Jeffrey Kenton 1954- *WhoEmL 93*
Baldwin, Jim *BioIn 17*
Baldwin, John *BioIn 17, WhoScE 91-1*
Baldwin, John Ashby, Jr. 1933- *WhoAm 92*
Baldwin, John Charles 1948- *WhoAm 92, WhoWor 93*
Baldwin, John Denison 1809-1883 *JrnUS*
Baldwin, John Evan *WhoScE 91-1*
Baldwin, John Lucian 1926- *St&PR 93*
Baldwin, John Patrick *WhoScE 91-1*
Baldwin, Kathren *St&PR 93*
Baldwin, Kevin J. *Law&B 92*
Baldwin, Kevin P. 1959- *St&PR 93*
Baldwin, Lee G., Jr. 1922- *St&PR 93*
Baldwin, Leona B. 1934- *WhoAmW 93*
Baldwin, Lynne J. 1946- *St&PR 93*
Baldwin, Margaret Morgan 1952- *WhoSSW 93*
Baldwin, Mark Patrick 1950- *St&PR 93*
Baldwin, Max Russell, Jr. 1964- *WhoEmL 93*
Baldwin, Melvin Dana, II 1941- *St&PR 93*
Baldwin, Merl *ScF&FL 92*
Baldwin, Nancy *BioIn 17*
Baldwin, Orval F., III *Law&B 92*
Baldwin, Paul Clay 1914-1990 *BioIn 17*
Baldwin, Peter *MiSFD 9*
Baldwin, Peter Alan Charles 1927- *WhoWor 93*
Baldwin, Peter Arthur 1932- *WhoAm 92*
Baldwin, Peter Jeremy 1951- *WhoAsAP 91*
Baldwin, Phillip B. 1924- *CngDr 91*
Baldwin, Rhoda Louise 1927- *St&PR 93*
Baldwin, Richard W. *Law&B 92*
Baldwin, Robert C. 1934- *St&PR 93*
Baldwin, Robert Davidson 1937- *St&PR 93*
Baldwin, Robert Edward 1924- *WhoAm 92*
Baldwin, Robert Frederick, Jr. 1939- *WhoAm 92*
Baldwin, Robert Lesh 1927- *WhoAm 92*
Baldwin, Robert R. *Law&B 92*
Baldwin, Robert Roy *WhoScE 91-1*

Baldwin, Robert William WhoScE 91-1
Baldwin, Roderick George 1946- St&PR 93
Baldwin, Roger WhoScE 91-1
Baldwin, Roger M. 1953- St&PR 93
Baldwin, Ronald Kent 1947- St&PR 93
Baldwin, Stan(ley C.) 1929- ConAu 38NR
Baldwin, Stanley 1867-1947 DcTwHis
Baldwin, Stanley C. BioIn 17
Baldwin, Stanly Law&B 92
Baldwin, Stephen BioIn 17
Baldwin, Thomas James 1955- WhoE 93
Baldwin, Thomas Richard 1945- WhoAm 92
Baldwin, Velma Neville Wilson 1918- WhoAmW 93, WhoE 93, WhoWor 93
Baldwin, Virgil Clark, Jr. 1940- WhoSSW 93
Baldwin, Wayne Jay 1948- St&PR 93
Baldwin, William BioIn 17, ConTFT 10
Baldwin, William David 1939- WhoIns 93
Baldwin, William Howard 1916- WhoAm 92
Baldwin, William Russell 1926- WhoAm 92
Baldwin, Winnie AmWomPl
Baldwin Of Flanders 1172-1205? OxDcByz
Bale, G.F. ScF&FL 92
Baleela, Moustafa 1941- WhoWor 93
Balek, Thomas J. 1954- St&PR 93
Balemans, Luc J.M. 1961- WhoScE 91-2
Balenciaga BioIn 17
Balent, Joseph M. 1941- St&PR 93
Balentine, Donald C. 1943- St&PR 93
Balentine, Phil H. 1928- St&PR 93
Bales, Flossie Kathleen 1938- WhoAmW 93
Bales, James Douglas 1962- WhoSSW 93
Bales, John Albert Law&B 92
Bales, John Thompson 1941- WhoE 93
Bales, Keith Stuart 1946- WhoWor 93
Bales, Kent Roslyn 1936- WhoAm 92
Bales, Richard (Henry Horner) 1915- Baker 92, WhoAm 92
Bales, Robert Freed 1916- WhoAm 92
Bales, Ronald C. 1938- WhoAm 92
Bales, Royal Eugene 1934- WhoAm 92
Bales, Susan Ford 1957- WhoAmW 93
Bales, Thomas Oren, Jr. 1948- WhoEmL 93
Bales, Velma Jean Reckling 1927- WhoWrEP 92
Bales, William 1910-1990 BioIn 17
Bales, William A. BioIn 17
Bales, William Baxter 1935- St&PR 93
Bales-Courte, Joy Diane 1958- WhoEmL 93
Balestra, Roger A. 1961- St&PR 93
Balestrero, Gregory 1947- WhoAm 92, WhoSSW 93
Balestrini, Aristobulo Enrique 1941- WhoWor 93
Balestrini, Nanni 1935- DcLB 128
Balet, Marc BioIn 17
Balevski, Angel WhoScE 91-4
Balevski, Angel Tonchev 1910- WhoWor 93
Balewa, Abubakar Tafawa 1912-1966 DcTwHis
Baley, Charles P. 1938- St&PR 93
Baley, Thomas Richard 1948- WhoEmL 93
Balfa, Dewey d1992 NewYTBS 92 [port]
Balfanz, Robert Don 1951- WhoWor 93
Balfe, Alan 1956- WhoWor 93
Balfe, Harry, II 1922- WhoE 93
Balfe, Lina Rosa 1808-1888 Baker 92
Balfe, Michael 1808-1870 OxDcOp
Balfe, Michael William 1808-1870 Baker 92, IntDcOp
Balfoort, Dirk Jacobus 1886-1964 Baker 92
Balfour, Ana Maria 1942- WhoAmW 93
Balfour, Arthur James 1848-1930 BioIn 17, DcTwHis
Balfour, B. Gabriel ScF&FL 92
Balfour, Douglas James 1952- WhoEmL 93
Balfour, Henry Hallowell, Jr. 1940- WhoAm 92, WhoWor 93
Balfour, I.M.F. WhoScE 91-1
Balfour, John fl. c. 1679- HarEnMi
Balfour, Katharine d1990 BioIn 17
Balfour, Norman Eugene Law&B 92
Balfour, Peter John Torquil 1959- WhoWor 93
Balfour, Raymond L. Law&B 92
Balfour, Reginald James 1928- WhoAm 92
Balfour, Robert William 1954- St&PR 93
Balfour, St. Clair 1910- St&PR 93
Balfour, William Mayo 1914- WhoAm 92
Balga, John Theodore, Jr. 1958- WhoE 93
Bal Gopal, K.C. 1937- WhoUN 92
Balgord, James R. 1941- St&PR 93
Balhoff, Robert Alan Law&B 92
Bali, Vyjayanthimala 1933- WhoAsAP 91
Balian, Harry 1958- WhoEmL 93
Balian, Lorna 1929- ConAu 40NR
Baliardo, Diego
See Gipsy Kings, The ConMus 8
Baliardo, Paco
See Gipsy Kings, The ConMus 8
Baliardo, Tonino
See Gipsy Kings, The ConMus 8
Balich, Nicholas S. St&PR 93
Balick, Helen Shaffer WhoAmW 93
Balick, Steven Jeffrey 1956- WhoEmL 93
Balicki, Linda Jean Law&B 92
Baliddawa, Zephaniah Mugere 1939- WhoUN 92
Baliga, John Valentine 1962- WhoSSW 93
Balik, Jaroslav 1924- DrEEuF
Balikov, Henry R. Law&B 92
Balikov, Henry R. 1946- WhoWor 93
Baliles, Gerald L. 1940- WhoAm 92
Balin, Ina 1937-1990 BioIn 17
Balin, Marty 1942- Baker 92, WhoAm 92
Balin, Nancy Anne 1954- WhoE 93
Balinky, Jean Lahn 1933- WhoAmW 93
Balino, Tomas Jose Teodoro 1946- WhoUN 92
Balinska, Astrid 1934- BioIn 17
Balinsky, Benjamin 1913- WhoE 93
Balinsky, Edward 1929- St&PR 93
Balint, Andor 1920- WhoScE 91-4
Balint, David Lee 1946- WhoSSW 93
Balint, Emery 1892-1982 ScF&FL 92
Balint, John Alexander 1925- WhoE 93
Balint, Paul Raymond 1948- WhoE 93
Balint, Tibor 1929- WhoScE 91-4
Balinth-Walther, Noemi Beatrix 1956- WhoAmW 93
Balinton, Umpeylia Marsema 1935- BioIn 17
Baliol, Alexander de 1953- ScF&FL 92
Baliol, Edward de c. 1295-1364 HarEnMi
Baliol, John de c. 1250-1314 HarEnMi
Baliotis, George St&PR 93
Baliozian, Mardick 1925- WhoWor 93
Balis, Charles Edward 1935- St&PR 93
Balis, George S. 1947- St&PR 93
Balis, Jennifer Lynn 1946- WhoAmW 93
Balis, Moses Earl 1921- WhoAm 92
Balisacan, Arsenio Molina 1957- WhoWor 93
Bality, Irene Milvius 1925- St&PR 93
Baliunas, Sallie L. 1953- BioIn 17
Balius, Louis Merrill Law&B 92
Balius, Louis Merrill 1936- St&PR 93
Baliva, Sam Patrick 1950- St&PR 93
Balizet, Carol 1933- ScF&FL 92
Balk, Alfred William 1930- WhoAm 92, WhoWrEP 92
Balk, Fairuza BioIn 17
Balk, Melvin W. 1943- St&PR 93
Balka, Sigmund Ronell Law&B 92
Balka, Sigmund Ronell 1935- WhoAm 92, WhoE 93
Balkany, Milton BioIn 17
Balkcom, Carol Ann 1952- WhoAmW 93, WhoEmL 93
Balke, Victor H. 1931- WhoAm 92
Balkin, Jules Arthur Law&B 92
Balkind, Alvin Louis 1921- WhoAm 92
Balkins, A. James 1952- St&PR 93
Balkins, A. James, III Law&B 92
Balkman, James H. 1936- St&PR 93
Balko, Gregg Brian 1951- WhoEmL 93
Balko, Kathleen Marie 1961- WhoAmW 93
Balkovatz, W.M. Law&B 92
Balkwill, Bryan (Havell) 1922- Baker 92
Ball, Allan E. Law&B 92
Ball, Andrew Justin 1949- WhoWor 93
Ball, Angela 1952- WhoWrEP 92
Ball, Angela Sue 1952- WhoAmW 93
Ball, Anna Caroline BioIn 17
Ball, Anne H. 1939- WhoAm 92, WhoAmW 93
Ball, Arlene Fran 1954- WhoAmW 93
Ball, Armand Baer 1930- WhoAm 92
Ball, Bennett Lester 1949- WhoE 93
Ball, Bill 1923- WhoAm 92
Ball, Blair Evan 1954- WhoEmL 93, WhoWor 93
Ball, Brian 1932- ScF&FL 92
Ball, Brian F. 1945- St&PR 93
Ball, Carroll Raybourne 1925- WhoAm 92
Ball, Catherine Ann 1954- WhoEmL 93
Ball, Charles Elihue 1924- WhoAm 92
Ball, Darrell Wayne 1960- WhoEmL 93
Ball, David George 1936- WhoAm 92
Ball, David N. 1955- WhoScE 91-1
Ball, David Simon 1959- WhoSSW 93
Ball, Derrick Frank WhoScE 91-1
Ball, Donald Lewis 1922- WhoAm 92
Ball, Donald Lincoln 1932- St&PR 93
Ball, Donald Maury 1945- WhoSSW 93
Ball, Donald Ray, Jr. 1956- St&PR 93
Ball, Donna 1951- ScF&FL 92
Ball, Douglas Schelling 1920- WhoAm 92
Ball, Duncan 1941- ScF&FL 92, SmATA 73 [port]
Ball, Edna Marion 1944- WhoAmW 93
Ball, Edward L. Law&B 92
Ball, Eric Samuel 1958- WhoEmL 93
Ball, Ernest R. 1878-1927 Baker 92
Ball, Florence E. ScF&FL 92
Ball, Frank Jervey 1919- WhoAm 92
Ball, Fritz Erhard Stefan 1928- WhoScE 91-3
Ball, George Carl 1921- WhoAm 92
Ball, George L. WhoAm 92
Ball, George W. 1909- ColdWar 1 [port]
Ball, George Wildman 1909- WhoAm 92, WhoWrEP 92
Ball, George William 1941- WhoE 93
Ball, Gordon 1948- St&PR 93
Ball, H. Stuart 1943- St&PR 93
Ball, Harley R. Law&B 92
Ball, Henry A. 1915- St&PR 93
Ball, Howard Guy 1930- WhoAm 92
Ball, Howard Lee 1929- WhoE 93
Ball, Ivern Imogene 1926- WhoWrEP 92
Ball, James 1933- WhoWor 93
Ball, James Allan 1943- WhoSSW 93
Ball, James Bryan 1932- WhoSSW 93
Ball, James Herington Law&B 92
Ball, James P. 1950- St&PR 93
Ball, James Peter 1950- WhoEmL 93
Ball, James William 1939- WhoAm 92
Ball, Jennifer (M. V.) 1958- ConAu 136
Ball, Jess Carl 1941- St&PR 93
Ball, Joe Dale 1949- WhoEmL 93, WhoSSW 93, WhoWor 93
Ball, John 1911-1988 ScF&FL 92
Ball, John A. 1928- WhoAm 92
Ball, John Charles 1949- WhoEmL 93
Ball, John Edward Dewar BioIn 17
Ball, John Fleming 1930- WhoAm 92
Ball, John H. 1919- St&PR 93
Ball, John Hanstein 1919- WhoAm 92
Ball, John K. 1958- St&PR 93
Ball, John Macleod WhoScE 91-1
Ball, John Paul 1946- WhoAm 92
Ball, John Robert 1944- WhoAm 92
Ball, John W. 1925- St&PR 93
Ball, K. 1932- St&PR 93
Ball, Katharine 1904-1991 BioIn 17
Ball, Kay Atkinson 1949- WhoAmW 93
Ball, Kay Evans 1952- WhoEmL 93
Ball, Larry Russell 1946- WhoEmL 93, WhoSSW 93
Ball, Leonard F. Law&B 92
Ball, Leonard F. 1939- St&PR 93
Ball, Lewis Edwin, II 1931- St&PR 93, WhoAm 92
Ball, Linda Suzanne 1951- WhoEmL 93
Ball, Louis Oliver, Jr. 1929- WhoSSW 93
Ball, Lucille 1911-1989 BioIn 17, IntDcF 2-3 [port], QDrFCA 92 [port]
Ball, M. Isabel 1929- WhoAm 92
Ball, Marcus Jerome 1944- St&PR 93
Ball, Margaret 1947- ScF&FL 92
Ball, Margaret A. 1938- St&PR 93
Ball, Marguerite Ellen 1963- WhoSSW 93
Ball, Maria-Elena 1940- WhoAmW 93
Ball, Markham 1934- WhoAm 92
Ball, Mary 1708-1789 BioIn 17
Ball, Mary Jane 1926- WhoAmW 93
Ball, Mary Loretta Law&B 92
Ball, Michael 1946- Baker 92
Ball, Michael Lee 1946- St&PR 93
Ball, Murray MiSFD 9
Ball, Ned d1990 BioIn 17
Ball, Nelson 1942- WhoCanL 92
Ball, Nelson T. 1924- St&PR 93
Ball, Owen Keith, Jr. Law&B 92
Ball, Owen Keith, Jr. 1950- WhoEmL 93
Ball, P. WhoScE 91-1
Ball, Patricia Ann 1941- WhoAmW 93
Ball, Philip L. Law&B 92
Ball, Philip L. 1934- St&PR 93
Ball, Randall Eugene 1956- WhoEmL 93, WhoSSW 93
Ball, Rex Martin 1934- St&PR 93, WhoAm 92
Ball, Richard Woodruff 1946- St&PR 93, WhoAm 92
Ball, Robert WhoScE 91-1
Ball, Robert H. 1944- St&PR 93
Ball, Robert L. 1946- St&PR 93
Ball, Robert M. 1914- WhoAm 92, WhoWrEP 92
Ball, Robert Michael 1952- WhoAm 92
Ball, Roger C. St&PR 93
Ball, Ronald Edward 1946- WhoEmL 93
Ball, Royston WhoScE 91-1
Ball, Ruth Warren 1954- WhoSSW 93
Ball, Sheri Beth 1963- WhoAmW 93, WhoEmL 93
Ball, Stanley John WhoScE 91-1
Ball, Stephen Geoffrey WhoScE 91-1
Ball, Susan 1947- WhoAm 92, WhoE 93, WhoEmL 93
Ball, Terence 1944- ConAu 138
Ball, Thomas J. 1936- St&PR 93
Ball, Vincent E., Jr. 1951- St&PR 93
Ball, W. MacMahon 1901- BioIn 17
Ball, Wes T. 1956- WhoEmL 93
Ball, William 1921- WhoE 93
Ball, William 1931-1991 AnObit 1991, BioIn 17, ConTFT 10
Ball, William Amos 1932- St&PR 93
Ball, William Austin 1948- WhoE 93, WhoEmL 93
Ball, William Bentley 1916- WhoAm 92
Ball, William Ernest 1930- WhoAm 92
Ball, William H., Jr. Law&B 92
Ball, William Kenneth 1927- WhoAm 92
Ball, William Lee 1959- WhoEmL 93
Ball, William MacMahon 1901- BioIn 17
Ball, William Paul 1913- WhoWor 93
Ball, Zachary 1897- DcAmChF 1960
Balla, Laslo 1954- WhoScE 91-4
Balla, Laszlo 1933- WhoScE 91-4
Ballada, Antonio 1944- WhoE 93
Balladur, Edouard BioIn 17
Ballagas, Emilio 1908-1954 SpAmA
Ballagh, Russell Joseph 1951- WhoSSW 93
Ballam, Joseph 1917- WhoAm 92
Ballam, Samuel Humes, Jr. 1919- WhoAm 92
Ballance, Frank W., Jr. 1942- WhoSSW 93
Ballance, John 1839-1893 BioIn 17
Ballance, John B. 1941- WhoE 93
Ballance, Robert Howard 1941- WhoUN 92
Ballande, Andre BioIn 17
Ballanfant, Kathleen Gamber 1945- WhoAmW 93
Ballanfant, R. Burt Law&B 92
Ballantine, Edward 1886-1971 Baker 92
Ballantine, Ian BioIn 17
Ballantine, Ian 1916- WhoAm 92, WhoWrEP 92
Ballantine, James Archibald WhoScE 91-1
Ballantine, James C. 1941- St&PR 93
Ballantine, Morley Cowles 1925- WhoAm 92, WhoAmW 93
Ballantine, Thomas Austin, Jr. 1926- WhoAm 92
Ballantyne, David 1913-1990 BioIn 17
Ballantyne, David 1924-1986 ScF&FL 92
Ballantyne, Garth Hadden 1951- WhoE 93
Ballantyne, Joseph Merrill WhoAm 92
Ballantyne, Richard Lee Law&B 92
Ballantyne, Richard Lee 1939- St&PR 93
Ballantyne, Richard Van 1955- St&PR 93
Ballantyne, Robert Jadwin 1925- WhoAm 92
Ballantyne, W.G. 1942- St&PR 93
Ballard Baker 92
Ballard, Ann E. Law&B 92
Ballard, Betty Ruth Wesley 1924- WhoAmW 93
Ballard, Carlos Raymond, Sr. 1907- St&PR 93
Ballard, Carlos Raymond, Jr. 1926- St&PR 93
Ballard, Carroll BioIn 17
Ballard, Carroll 1937- MiSFD 9
Ballard, Charles Alan St&PR 93, WhoAm 92
Ballard, Claude Mark, Jr. 1929- WhoAm 92
Ballard, David Eugene 1949- WhoAm 92
Ballard, Debbi Ann 1949- WhoEmL 93
Ballard, Edward Brooks 1906- WhoAm 92
Ballard, Edward Goodwin 1910- WhoWrEP 92
Ballard, Emmett Jessee, II 1950- WhoEmL 93
Ballard, Eugene H. Law&B 92
Ballard, Eugene Henry 1934- WhoAm 92
Ballard, Florence 1944-1976 BioIn 17
Ballard, Frederick Armstrong 1907- WhoAm 92
Ballard, Geoff WhoScE 91-1
Ballard, Hank 1936- SoulM
Ballard, Harold BioIn 17
Ballard, Holley WhoCanL 92
Ballard, Ian Matheson 1937- WhoE 93
Ballard, J.G. 1930- BioIn 17, ScF&FL 92
Ballard, J(ames) G(raham) 1930- ConAu 39NR
Ballard, John David 1936- WhoIns 93
Ballard, John Houston 1944- St&PR 93
Ballard, John Houston, III 1944- WhoIns 93
Ballard, John Stuart 1922- WhoAm 92
Ballard, John W., Jr. 1922- St&PR 93
Ballard, John William, Jr. 1922- WhoAm 92
Ballard, Judy Thomas 1950- WhoSSW 93
Ballard, Larry Coleman 1935- St&PR 93, WhoAm 92, WhoIns 93
Ballard, Linda Burdick 1958- WhoAmW 93, WhoEmL 93
Ballard, Louis W(ayne) 1931- Baker 92
Ballard, Louis Wayne 1931- WhoAm 92
Ballard, Marshall 1942- St&PR 93
Ballard, Martha W. BioIn 17
Ballard, Mary Melinda 1957- WhoAm 92, WhoAmW 93
Ballard, Melinda 1957- St&PR 93
Ballard, Michael 1942-1991 BioIn 17
Ballard, Michael Eugene 1953- WhoEmL 93
Ballard, Michael P. 1950- St&PR 93
Ballard, Mignon Franklin 1934- BioIn 17

Ballard, Patricia Irene 1950- *WhoAmW 93*
Ballard, Richard Alan 1946- *St&PR 93*
Ballard, Robert D. 1942- *ConHero 2 [port]*
Ballard, Robert Duane 1942- *WhoAm 92*
Ballard, Robert Eugene, Jr. 1943- *WhoE 93*
Ballard, Ronald Michael 1958- *WhoEmL 93, WhoWor 93*
Ballard, S.M. *ScF&FL 92*
Ballard, Sarah *BioIn 17*
Ballard, Stanley Sumner 1908- *WhoAm 92*
Ballard, Thomas Bradford 1946- *WhoSSW 93*
Ballard, Thomas Hickok 1941- *WhoAm 92, WhoSSW 93*
Ballard, Thomas William 1950- *WhoEmL 93, WhoSSW 93*
Ballard, William Hanser *Law&B 92*
Ballauff, Matthias Michael 1952- *WhoWor 93*
Ballay, Denis *WhoScE 91-2*
Balldin, Ulf I. 1939- *WhoScE 91-4*
Balleis, Siegfried Martin 1953- *WhoWor 93*
Ballem, John *WhoCanL 92*
Ballem, John Bishop 1925- *WhoAm 92*
Ballen, John W. 1959- *St&PR 93*
Ballen, Robert Gerald 1956- *WhoEmL 93*
Ballen, Samuel Bernard 1922- *St&PR 93*
Ballengee, Bert 1924- *St&PR 93*
Ballengee, James M. 1923- *St&PR 93*
Ballengee, James McMorrow 1923- *WhoAm 92*
Ballengee, James R. 1935- *St&PR 93*
Ballengee, Jerry Hunter 1937- *St&PR 93*
Ballengee, John M. 1950- *St&PR 93*
Ballenger, Cass 1926- *CngDr 91*
Ballenger, John George 1931- *St&PR 93*
Ballenger, Thomas Cass 1926- *St&PR 93, WhoAm 92, WhoSSW 93*
Ballentine, Carol E. *Law&B 92*
Ballentine, Henry Vern 1955- *WhoEmL 93, WhoSSW 93*
Ballentine, J. Gregory 1948- *WhoAm 92*
Ballentine, James Macallan, Jr. 1933- *St&PR 93*
Ballentine, Lee 1954- *ScF&FL 92*
Ballentine, Lee Kenney 1954- *WhoWor 93, WhoWrEP 92*
Ballentine, Michael C. d1991 *BioIn 17*
Ballentine, Richard O. *Law&B 92*
Ballentine, Richard O. 1936- *St&PR 93*
Ballentine, Rudolph M. 1941- *WhoWrEP 92*
Baller, James 1947- *WhoEmL 93*
Ballerini, Albano *BioIn 17*
Ballerini, Luigi 1940- *DcLB 128 [port]*
Balles, John Joseph 1921- *WhoAm 92*
Ballester, Frank 1908- *St&PR 93*
Ballester, Jose Felix 1944- *St&PR 93*
Ballester, Miguel 1919- *WhoScE 91-3*
Ballester, Pablo J. 1959- *WhoWor 93*
Ballesteros, Juventino Ray, Jr. 1953- *WhoEmL 93, WhoSSW 93, WhoWor 93*
Ballesteros, Seve *BioIn 17*
Ballesteros, Severiano 1957- *WhoAm 92, WhoWor 93*
Ballestra, Gian Nicola Filippi 1954- *WhoWor 93*
Ballestracci, Regis 1937- *WhoScE 91-2*
Ballew, Anthony Robert 1952- *WhoEmL 93*
Ballew, Charles William 1931- *WhoAm 92*
Ballew, David Wayne 1940- *WhoAm 92*
Ballew, Doris Evelyn 1938- *WhoAmW 93*
Ballew, Glenn 1948- *St&PR 93*
Ballew, Glenn L. 1948- *WhoIns 93*
Ballew, Jeffery Allen 1955- *St&PR 93*
Ballew, Nellie Hester 1914- *WhoAmW 93*
Ballew, Patricia Lynn Creamer 1955- *WhoAmW 93*
Balley, Murray 1933- *St&PR 93*
Ballhaus, Michael 1935- *ConTFT 10*
Ballhaus, William Francis 1918- *WhoAm 92*
Ballhaus, William Francis, Jr. 1945- *WhoAm 92*
Ballhausen, C.J. *WhoScE 91-2*
Balli, Heinz H.R. 1929- *WhoScE 91-4*
Balli, Mardick 1925- *WhoWor 93*
Ballico, Edoardo 1955- *WhoWor 93*
Balliet, Marvin Joseph 1957- *WhoEmL 93*
Balliett, Gene 1931- *WhoAm 92*
Balliett, Whitney 1926- *WhoAm 92, WhoWrEP 92*
Ballif, Claude 1924- *Baker 92*
Ballin, Albert 1857-1918 *BioIn 17*
Ballin, Gene 1919- *St&PR 93*
Ballin, William Christopher 1927- *WhoAm 92, WhoWor 93*
Balling, Michael 1866-1925 *Baker 92, OxDcOp*
Balling, Peter 1944- *WhoScE 91-2*
Balling, Robert C., Jr. 1952- *ConAu 138*
Ballinger, Bill S. 1912-1980 *ScF&FL 92*
Ballinger, Charles Kenneth 1950- *WhoEmL 93*
Ballinger, Glenn Thomas 1943- *St&PR 93*
Ballinger, Harry Russell 1892- *WhoAm 92*
Ballinger, James K. 1949- *WhoAm 92*
Ballinger, Janet Lynn 1948- *WhoEmL 93*
Ballinger, Joann Anderson 1946- *WhoAmW 93*
Ballinger, Malcolm George 1947- *St&PR 93*
Ballinger, Walter Francis 1925- *WhoAm 92*
Ballinger, William S. *ScF&FL 92*
Ballington, Leola Pope 1944- *WhoSSW 93*
Ballio, Alessandro 1921- *WhoScE 91-3*
Ballio, Giulio 1940- *WhoScE 91-3*
Ballis, Richard Paul 1940- *St&PR 93*
Ballista, Antonio 1936- *Baker 92*
Ballivet, Marc 1941- *WhoScE 91-4*
Ballivian, Jose 1804-1852 *HarEnMi*
Ballmeyer, William Henry 1946- *St&PR 93*
Ballo, Thomas J. *Law&B 92*
Balloffet, Armando d1992 *BioIn 17, NewYTBS 92*
Ballon, Edward Mahler 1925- *WhoAm 92*
Ballon, Robert J(ean) 1919- *WhoWrEP 92*
Ballon, Thomas A. 1946- *St&PR 93*
Balloni, Antonio Jose 1954- *WhoWor 93*
Ballot, Alissa E. *Law&B 92*
Ballot, Alissa E. 1955- *WhoAmW 93, WhoEmL 93*
Ballou, Arthur W. 1915-1981 *ScF&FL 92*
Ballou, Clinton E. 1923- *WhoAm 92*
Ballou, Earline 1935- *WhoSSW 93*
Ballou, Esther Williamson 1915-1973 *Baker 92*
Ballou, Glen Martin 1935- *WhoE 93*
Ballou, Judith Ann 1959- *WhoAmW 93*
Ballou, Kathy Deanne Taylor 1951- *WhoAmW 93, WhoWor 93*
Ballou, Kenneth Walter 1930- *WhoAm 92*
Ballou, Mark *BioIn 17*
Ballou, Mary 19th cent.- *BioIn 17*
Ballou, Maturin Murray 1820-1895 *JrnUS*
Ballou, Rebecca *Law&B 92*
Ballou, Sullivan d1861 *BioIn 17*
Ballow, Bob *BioIn 17*
Ballowe, James 1933- *WhoAm 92*
Balls, Barbara Bundock *Law&B 92*
Ballway, Joseph H., Jr. *Law&B 92*
Ballweber, Hettie Lou 1944- *WhoAmW 93, WhoE 93, WhoWor 93*
Bally, Laurent Marie Joseph 1943- *WhoWor 93*
Balmages, Fred Ira 1948- *WhoE 93*
Balmages, Michael G. *Law&B 92*
Balmain, Keith George 1933- *WhoAm 92*
Balmas, Carl M. 1940- *St&PR 93*
Balmer, James Walter 1948- *WhoAm 92*
Balmer, Luc 1898- *Baker 92*
Balmer, Norman Louis *Law&B 92*
Balmer, Sandra *Law&B 92*
Balmer, Thomas Ancil 1952- *WhoEmL 93*
Balmes, Edward James 1953- *St&PR 93*
Balmes, Jaime Luciano 1810-1848 *BioIn 17*
Balmforth, Dawn Elizabeth 1964- *WhoAmW 93*
Balmori, Diana 1936- *WhoE 93*
Balmuth, Michael 1950- *St&PR 93*
Balny, C. *WhoScE 91-2*
Balocco, Luciano *WhoScE 91-3*
Baloch, Ghulam Muhammad 1936- *WhoWor 93*
Baloescu, Corneliu 1928- *WhoScE 91-4*
Baloff, Nicholas 1937- *WhoAm 92*
Balog, Betty Enocksen 1932- *WhoWrEP 92*
Balog, Imre *Law&B 92*
Balog, James *BioIn 17*
Balog, James 1928- *St&PR 93, WhoAm 92*
Balog, James Dennis 1952- *WhoAm 92*
Balog, Joseph A. *Law&B 92*
Balog, Linda Marie 1946- *WhoAmW 93, WhoEmL 93*
Balog, Richard Thomas 1951- *WhoEmL 93, WhoWor 93*
Balog, Theresa Gallagher 1937- *WhoAmW 93*
Balogh, Andras 1933- *WhoScE 91-4*
Balogh, Erno 1897-1989 *Baker 92*
Balogh, Gyorgy 1932- *WhoScE 91-4*
Balogh, James 1939- *St&PR 93*
Balogh, Kadosa 1942- *WhoScE 91-4*
Balogh, Karoly 1930- *WhoE 93*
Balogh, Linda Jean 1950- *WhoEmL 93*
Balogh, Sandor 1932- *WhoScE 91-4*
Balogh, Stephen A. *St&PR 93*
Balogh, Thomas 1905-1985 *BioIn 17*
Balogi, Jeno 1945- *WhoScE 91-4*
Balokovic, Zlatko 1895-1965 *Baker 92*
Balose, Charles A. 1946- *St&PR 93*
Balough, Daniel C. *Law&B 92*
Baloun, John Charles 1934- *WhoAm 92*
Baloun, Rosemary Ann 1945- *WhoAmW 93*
Balousek, Jack *BioIn 17*
Balousek, John B. *WhoAm 92*
Balow, Bruce d1989 *BioIn 17*
Balow, Irving Henry 1927- *WhoAm 92*
Balows, Albert 1921- *WhoAm 92*
Baloyra, Enrique Antonio 1942- *WhoAm 92*
Balph, David Filey 1931-1990 *BioIn 17*
Balph, Effie Sammond *AmWomPl*
Balsam, Alan H. d1992 *NewYTBS 92*
Balsam, Artur 1906- *Baker 92*
Balsam, Jerome *Law&B 92*
Balsam, Martin Henry 1919- *WhoAm 92*
Balsamo, Donna Jean 1940- *WhoAmW 93*
Balsamo, Louis J. *Law&B 92*
Balsamon, Theodore c. 1130-c. 1195 *OxDcByz*
Balsaver, Ashok Mukund 1937- *WhoSSW 93*
Balsavich, Donald Keith 1951- *St&PR 93*
Balser, Elnora Marie 1952- *WhoEmL 93*
Balser, John J. *Law&B 92*
Balser, Paul Fisher 1942- *WhoE 93*
Balser, Werner 1946- *WhoWor 93*
Balshi, James D. 1955- *WhoE 93*
Balshi, Philip John *WhoAm 92*
Balsiger, David Wayne 1945- *WhoAm 92, WhoWrEP 92*
Balsiger, John Richard 1932- *St&PR 93*
Balsiger, W. Edwin 1935- *St&PR 93*
Balsis, Eduardas 1919-1984 *Baker 92*
Balslev, Ivar 1937- *WhoScE 91-2*
Balsley, Howard Lloyd 1913- *WhoAm 92, WhoWor 93*
Balsley, James F. 1939- *St&PR 93*
Balsley, Philip 1939- *See* Statler Brothers, The *ConMus 8*
Balsley, Philip Elwood 1939- *WhoAm 92*
Balsman, Wayne 1941- *St&PR 93*
Balswick, Jack Orville *ConAu 136*
Balswick, Judith K. 1939- *ConAu 136*
Baltag, Inokentie 1936- *WhoWor 93*
Baltag, Octavian-Ioan 1945- *WhoScE 91-4*
Baltake, Joe *WhoAm 92*
Baltazar, Romulo Flores 1941- *WhoE 93*
Baltazzi, Evan Serge 1921- *WhoAm 92*
Baltensperger, Peter 1938- *WhoCanL 92*
Baltensperger, Walter 1927- *WhoScE 91-4, WhoWor 93*
Balter, Anita Hart d1991 *BioIn 17*
Balter, Frances Sunstein *WhoAmW 93, WhoE 93*
Balter, James Jonathan 1966- *WhoEmL 93*
Balter, Leslie Marvin 1920- *WhoE 93*
Balter, Marie 1930- *BioIn 17*
Balter, Neil 1960- *ConEn*
Balter, Stuart M. *St&PR 93*
Baltermants, Dmitri 1912-1990 *BioIn 17*
Baltes, Kenneth John 1936- *St&PR 93*
Baltes, Matthias 1940- *WhoWor 93*
Baltes, Werner 1929- *WhoScE 91-3*
Balth, Carel 1939- *WhoWor 93*
Balthasar, Hans Urs von 1905-1988 *BioIn 17*
Balthaser, Gerda Haas 1936- *WhoAmW 93*
Balthazar, Earl Edward 1918- *WhoWor 93*
Balthazard, Mark Joseph 1957- *WhoEmL 93*
Balthazor, Albert, Jr. 1925- *WhoWor 93*
Balthrop, David Albert 1940- *St&PR 93*
Balthrop, Ricky D. *Law&B 92*
Balthus 1908- *BioIn 17*
Baltimore, David 1938- *BioIn 17, WhoAm 92, WhoE 93, WhoWor 93*
Baltimore, J. *ConAu 38NR, MajAI*
Baltin, Charles d1992 *NewYTBS 92*
Baltis, Russell V., Jr. 1928- *St&PR 93*
Balton, Allen R. 1908- *St&PR 93*
Baltsa, Agnes 1944- *Baker 92, OxDcOp*
Baltzar, Thomas c. 1630-1663 *Baker 92*
Baltzell, Edward Digby 1915- *WhoAm 92*
Baltzer, Gerhard F.Th.K. 1933- *WhoScE 91-3*
Baluch, Henryk 1932- *WhoScE 91-4*
Balucki, Michal 1837-1901 *PolBiDi*
Baluk, Robert Raymond *Law&B 92*
Balukas, Jean 1959- *WhoAm 92*
Balun, Chas. *ScF&FL 92*
Balunas, Robert John 1947- *WhoE 93*
Balus, Laurian 1924- *WhoScE 91-3*
Balut, George Samuel 1955- *WhoWor 93*
Balutis, Thomas *St&PR 93*
Baluyot, Cherita Costales 1947- *St&PR 93*
Balvay, Gerard 1941- *WhoScE 91-2*
Balve, Beba Carmen 1931- *WhoWor 93*
Balverde-Sanchez, Laura 1951- *NotHsAW 93*
Bal y Gay, Jesus 1905- *Baker 92*
Balyogeshwar 1957- *BioIn 17*
Balz, Douglas Charles 1943- *WhoAm 92*
Balz, Frank Joseph 1950- *WhoEmL 93*
Balza, Jose 1939- *SpAmA*
Balzac, Audrey FloBelle Adrian 1928- *WhoAmW 93*
Balzac, Honore 1799-1850 *OxDcOp*
Balzac, Honore de 1799-1850 *DcLB 119 [port], MagSWL [port], NinCLC 35 [port], ScF&FL 92, WorLitC [port]*
Balzani, Vincenzo 1936- *WhoScE 91-3*
Balzary, Michael *BioIn 17*
Balzary, Michael c. 1962- *See* Red Hot Chili Peppers, The *News 93-1*
Balzekas, Stanley, Jr. 1924- *WhoAm 92*
Balzer, Bernd Robert 1942- *WhoWor 93*
Balzer, Giorgio 1940- *WhoIns 93*
Balzerano, E. *WhoScE 91-3*
Balzhiser, Richard Earl 1932- *WhoAm 92*
Balzotti, Linda Marie 1961- *WhoAmW 93, WhoEmL 93*
Bam, Foster 1927- *WhoAm 92, WhoE 93*
Bambaataa, Afrika *SoulM*
Bambace, Robert Shelly 1930- *WhoAm 92*
Bambacus, John Nicholas 1945- *WhoE 93*
Bambara, John D. 1932- *St&PR 93*
Bambara, Robert Anthony 1949- *WhoE 93*
Bambara, Toni Cade *BioIn 17*
Bambara, Toni Cade 1939- *AmWomWr 92*
Bamber, Jeffrey V. *Law&B 92*
Bamber, Judie *BioIn 17*
Bamber, Margaret Mary 1953- *WhoAmW 93, WhoEmL 93*
Bamberg, Elmar 1942- *WhoScE 91-4*
Bamberger, Carl 1902-1987 *Baker 92*
Bamberger, Carlos Enrique Leopoldo 1933- *WhoSSW 93*
Bamberger, David 1940- *WhoAm 92*
Bamberger, David Harned 1942- *WhoAm 92*
Bamberger, Fred Hans 1898- *WhoE 93*
Bamberger, Gerald Francis 1920- *WhoAm 92*
Bamberger, J. David *BioIn 17*
Bamberger, J. David 1928- *St&PR 93*
Bamberger, Julia Kathryn 1960- *WhoE 93, WhoEmL 93*
Bamberger, Michael Albert 1936- *WhoAm 92*
Bamberger, Werner d1991 *BioIn 17*
Bambic, Robert M. 1954- *WhoEmL 93*
Bambola, Vincent J. 1942- *St&PR 93*
Bamboschek, Giuseppe 1890-1969 *Baker 92*
Bambrick, James Alan 1946- *St&PR 93, WhoIns 93*
Bambrick, James Joseph 1917- *WhoWor 93*
Bambrick, Joseph Thomas, Jr. *Law&B 92*
Bambrick-Mohorcic, Therese Anne 1958- *WhoAmW 93*
Bambridge, Martin Edward *Law&B 92*
Bambury, Joseph Anthony, Jr. 1932- *St&PR 93*
Bame, Samuel Jarvis, Jr. 1924- *WhoAm 92*
Bamert, Matthias 1942- *Baker 92*
Bamford, Carol Marie 1948- *WhoEmL 93*
Bamford, Colin Grahame *WhoScE 91-1*
Bamford, Edward G. 1932- *St&PR 93*
Bamford, Samuel 1788-1872 *BioIn 17*
Bamford, Thomas Bennett 1928- *WhoE 93*
Bamford, Thomas Horst 1940- *St&PR 93*
Bamisaiye, Emanuel Adewale 1940- *WhoWor 93*
Bamman, Robert H. 1921- *St&PR 93*
Bammel, Brian Paul 1943- *St&PR 93*
Bamonte, Karen *BioIn 17*
Bampton, Betsy Ann 1937- *WhoSSW 93*
Bampton, James William 1909- *WhoAm 92*
Bampton, Rose 1907- *OxDcOp*
Bampton, Rose 1908- *Baker 92*
Bampton, Rose 1909- *IntDcOp*
Ban, Akos 1927- *WhoScE 91-4*
Ban, Edward David 1949- *WhoEmL 93*
Ban, Frigyes 1902-1969 *DrEEuF*
Ban, Joseph D(aniel) 1926- *WhoWrEP 92*
Ban, Miklos I. 1931- *WhoScE 91-4*
Ban, Sadayuki 1949- *WhoWor 93*
Ban, Stephen Dennis 1940- *WhoAm 92*
Ban, Vladimir Sinisa 1941- *WhoE 93*
Ban, Woodrow W. *Law&B 92*
Ban, Zvonimir 1934- *WhoScE 91-4*
Banach, Richard E. 1946- *St&PR 93*
Banach, Stefan 1892-1945 *PolBiDi*
Banafato, Joseph F. 1942- *St&PR 93*
Banal, M. *WhoScE 91-2*
Banas, Conrad Martin 1927- *WhoE 93*
Banas, John *MiSFD 9*
Banas, Marian 1930- *WhoScE 91-4*
Banas, Richard Frederick 1948- *WhoEmL 93*
Banas, Ronald John 1936- *St&PR 93*
Banas, Stanley R. 1927- *St&PR 93*
Banaschewski, Bernhard 1926- *WhoAm 92*

Banasik, Robert Casmer 1942- WhoWor 93
Banasz, Walter Ronald 1943- WhoE 93
Banaszkiewicz, Stanislaw 1932- WhoScE 91-4
Banaszynski, Jacqueline Marie 1952- WhoAmW 93
Banatre, Jean-Pierre 1948- WhoScE 91-2
Banatvala, Jangu 1934- WhoWor 93
Banatvala, Jehangir Edalgi WhoScE 91-1
Banatwalla, Gulam Mehmood 1933- WhoAsAP 91
Banavali, Rajiv Manohar 1958- WhoSSW 93
Bancheri, Christine E. Law&B 92
Banchieri, Adriano (Tomaso) 1568-1634 Baker 92
Banchoff, Thomas Francis 1938- WhoAm 92
Banciu, Louis James Law&B 92
Bancroft, Alexander Clerihew 1938- WhoAm 92
Bancroft, Ann BioIn 17
Bancroft, Anne 1931- IntDcF 2-3, MiSFD 9, WhoAm 92, WhoAmW 93
Bancroft, Arthur M. 1923- St&PR 93
Bancroft, Charles E. 1925- WhoIns 93
Bancroft, Elizabeth Abercrombie 1947- WhoAm 92, WhoAmW 93
Bancroft, George 1882-1956 BioIn 17
Bancroft, George F., Mrs. AmWomPl
Bancroft, George Michael 1942- WhoAm 92
Bancroft, Harding Foster d1992 NewYTBS 92 [port]
Bancroft, Harding Foster 1910-1992 BioIn 17
Bancroft, J.H. WhoScE 91-1
Bancroft, James Ramsey 1919- WhoAm 92
Bancroft, Janet 1936- WhoUN 92
Bancroft, John Basil 1929- WhoAm 92
Bancroft, Joseph C. 1900- St&PR 93
Bancroft, Laura MajAI
Bancroft, Lewis Clinton 1929- WhoE 93
Bancroft, Paul, III 1930- St&PR 93, WhoAm 92, WhoE 93
Bancroft, Paul Marshall 1954- WhoIns 93
Bancroft, Robert Lewis 1947- WhoE 93
Bancroft, Ronald Mann 1943- St&PR 93, WhoAm 92
Banczak, Peggy J. Law&B 92
Band, The ConMus 9 [port]
Band, Albert 1924- MiSFD 9
Band, Charles 1952- MiSFD 9
Band, David 1942- WhoAm 92
Band, Jeffrey D. 1948- WhoEmL 93
Band, Stanley Irving 1930- St&PR 93
Banda, Hastings Kamuzu 1906- WhoAfr
Banda, Hastings Kanuzu 1906- DcTwHis
Banda, Ngwazi Hastings Kamuzu 1906- WhoWor 93
Banda, Scott Law&B 92
Banda Farfan, Raquel 1928- DcMexL
Bandar, Prince of Saudi Arabia BioIn 17
Bandaranaike, Sirimavo R.D. 1916- WhoAsAP 91
Bandaranaike, Sirimavo Ratwatte Dias 1916- DcTwHis
Bandaranaike, Solomon West Ridgeway Dias 1899-1959 DcTwHis
Bandar bin Sultan 1949- NewYTBS 92 [port]
Bandeen, Robert Angus 1930- St&PR 93, WhoAm 92
Bandeen, William Reid 1926- WhoAm 92
Bandel, Manville H. 1930- St&PR 93
Bandelier, Adolph 1840-1914 IntDcAn
Bandemer, Hans Walter 1932- WhoWor 93
Bander, Carol Jean 1945- WhoAmW 93
Bander, Mark B. Law&B 92
Bander, Myron 1937- WhoAm 92
Bander, Norman Robert WhoSSW 93
Bander, Robert Nelson 1944- WhoSSW 93
Bandera, Bob 1956- WhoE 93
Bandera, Cesareo 1934- WhoAm 92
Bandes, Dean 1944- WhoE 93
Bandes, Susan Jane 1951- WhoAm 92
Bandier, Martin WhoAm 92
Bandiere, Richard C. 1943- St&PR 93
Bandiere, Richard Charles 1943- WhoAm 92
Bandieri, Leo P. 1929- St&PR 93
Bandini, Angela BioIn 17
Bandion, Josef WhoScE 91-4
Bandler, Beth M. Law&B 92
Bandler, John William 1941- WhoAm 92
Bandler, Michael Louis 1938- St&PR 93, WhoAm 92
Bandler, Ned Wendell 1929- St&PR 93
Bando, Eiichi 1943- WhoWor 93
Bando, Salvatore Leonard 1944- BiDAMSp 1989
Bando, Yoshichika 1934- WhoWor 93
Bandolik, Steven Dale 1953- WhoEmL 93
Bandon, Alawadin T., Jr. WhoAsAP 91
Bandong, Paul Anthony 1956- WhoWor 93
Bandopadhyaya, Amitava 1957- WhoWor 93
Bandow, Douglas Leighton 1957- WhoAm 92, WhoWrEP 92
Bandrowska-Turska, Eva 1897-1979 Baker 92
Bandrowski, Aleksander 1860-1913 PolBiDi
Bandrowski, James Francis 1948- WhoEmL 93
Bandrowski, Jeffrey A. 1942- St&PR 93
Bandrowski-Sas, Alexander 1860-1913 Baker 92
Bandtke, Jerzy Samuel 1768-1835 PolBiDi
Bandura, Albert 1925- WhoAm 92
Bandurraga, Peter Louis 1944- WhoAm 92
Bandurski, Bruce Lord 1940- WhoE 93, WhoWor 93
Bandus, Randall J. Law&B 92
Bandy, Franklin 1914-1987 ScF&FL 92
Bandy, Gary 1944- WhoE 93
Bandy, Mary Lea 1943- WhoAm 92
Bandy, "Mo" 1944- Baker 92
Bandy, Patricia Ann 1943- WhoAmW 93
Bandy, Thomas William 1954- WhoSSW 93
Bandy-Hedden, Irene Gesa 1940- WhoAmW 93
Bane, Charles Arthur 1913- WhoAm 92
Bane, Keith James 1939- WhoAm 92
Bane, Marilyn A. 1943- St&PR 93
Bane, Richard Corey 1955- WhoE 93
Banegas, Estevan Brown 1941- WhoE 93
Baneham, Sam 1947- ScF&FL 92
Baner, Johan 1596-1641 HarEnMi
Banerjee 1939- WhoWor 93
Banerjee, (Bimal) 1939- WhoAm 92
Banerjee, Biswajit 1950- WhoUN 92
Banerjee, Prashant 1962- WhoWor 93
Banerjee, Samarendranath 1932- WhoAm 92
Banerjee, Somendu Kumar 1944- WhoUN 92
Banerji, Ranan Bihari 1928- WhoAm 92
Banerji, Sara 1932- ScF&FL 92
Banes, Daniel 1918- WhoWrEP 92
Banet, Charles Henry 1922- WhoAm 92
Baneth, Jean 1936- WhoUN 92
Banever, Thomas Clark 1945- WhoE 93
Banevich, Sergei 1941- Baker 92
Baney, Barry BioIn 17
Baney, John Edward 1934- WhoAm 92, WhoE 93
Baney, Richard Neil 1937- WhoSSW 93, WhoWor 93
Banfield, Edward Christie 1916- WhoAm 92
Banfield, Jaime D. Law&B 92
Banfield, Joanne 1954- WhoEmL 93
Banfield, Suzanne Marie 1949- WhoAmW 93
Banford, David 1947- St&PR 93
Bang, Gisle 1927- WhoScE 91-4
Bang, Hans Olaf 1913- WhoWor 93
Bang, Jeanene K. 1937- St&PR 93
Bang, Karl-L. WhoScE 91-4
Bang, Molly 1943- BioIn 17, SmATA 69 [port]
Bang, Molly Garrett 1943- MajAI [port]
Bang, Xu 1931- WhoWor 93
Bangaru, Babu Rajendra Prasad 1947- WhoEmL 93
Bangdiwala, Ishver Surchand 1922- WhoAm 92
Bangel, Edward W. 1942- St&PR 93
Bangen, Bernhard 1928- St&PR 93
Bangert, B.A. WhoScE 91-1
Bangert, Richard Elmer 1920- WhoAm 92
Bangerter, Darrell Howell 1935- St&PR 93
Bangerter, Dee R. 1944- WhoAm 92
Bangerter, Jean M. Law&B 92
Bangerter, Lee R. 1941- St&PR 93
Bangerter, Norman Howard 1933- WhoAm 92
Bangham, Robert Arthur 1942- WhoWor 93
Banghart, Rick D. 1957- WhoEmL 93
Bangou, Henri 1922- DcCPCAm
Bangs, Carol Jane 1949- WhoWrEP 92
Bangs, Cate 1951- WhoWor 93
Bangs, Frank Kendrick 1914- WhoAm 92
Bangs, John Kendrick 1920- WhoAm 92
Bangs, John Wesley, III 1941- WhoWor 93
Bangs, Nelson A. Law&B 92, WhoAm 92
Bangs, Nelson A. 1952- St&PR 93
Bangs, Richard BioIn 17
Bangs, Richard Johnston 1950- WhoEmL 93
Bangs, Will Johnston 1923- WhoAm 92
Bangser, Henry Maimin 1930- St&PR 93
Bangura, Abdul Karim 1953- WhoEmL 93
Banharn Silpa-Archa, Nai 1932- WhoAsAP 91
Banhazi, Gyula 1927- WhoScE 91-4
Banhegyi, Mihaly 1935- WhoScE 91-4
Banhidi, Laszlo 1944- WhoScE 91-4
Banholzer, Frank J. 1929- St&PR 93
Bania, Donald W. Law&B 92
Baniak, Sheila Mary 1953- WhoEmL 93
Banichi, Enrique Law&B 92
Banik, Sambhu Nath 1935- WhoAm 92
Banim, John 1798-1842 DcLB 116 [port]
Banis, Lynn Law&B 92
Banis, Richard P. 1943- WhoAm 92
Banis, Victor J. ScF&FL 92
Banister, Henry Charles 1831-1897 Baker 92
Banister, Jack E. 1929- St&PR 93
Banister, John c. 1625-1679 Baker 92
Banister, John, Jr. c. 1663-c. 1725 Baker 92
Banister, Manly 1914-1986 ScF&FL 92
Banister, Peter Anthony WhoScE 91-1
Banister, Richard Albert 1948- WhoAm 92
Banitt, Peter Frederick 1962- WhoEmL 93
Bank, Edward Paul Law&B 92
Bank, Harvey L. 1943- WhoSSW 93
Bank, Jacques 1943- Baker 92
Bank, Jonathan F. 1943- WhoAm 92
Bank, Joseph 1938- St&PR 93
Bank, Malvin E. 1930- WhoAm 92
Bank, Mirra MiSFD 9
Bank, Steven Barry 1939- WhoAm 92
Bankard, Robert Roy 1937- St&PR 93
Banker, Dave Vinodkumar 1943- WhoSSW 93
Banker, David Wayne 1959- WhoEmL 93
Banker, Gilbert Stephen 1931- WhoAm 92
Banker, Joel I. 1927- St&PR 93
Banker, Martin H. Law&B 92
Banker, Thomas Andrew 1950- WhoE 93
Bankert, Joseph Edward 1949- WhoEmL 93
Bankert, Pamela Beryl 1954- WhoAmW 93, WhoEmL 93
Bankhead, Samuel 1910-1976 BiDAMSp 1989
Bankhead, Tallulah 1902-1968 BioIn 17
Bankhead, William B. 1874-1940 PolPar
Bankhead, William Greer, Jr. 1941- WhoSSW 93
Banko, Bernadette Illona 1951- WhoAmW 93
Bankoff, Seymour George 1921- WhoAm 92, WhoWor 93
Bankole, Isaach de BioIn 17
Bankole-Bright, H.C. d1958 BioIn 17
Bankowski, Dennis R. 1946- St&PR 93
Bankowski, Edward 1942- WhoScE 91-4
Bankowski, Jacek Jan 1940- WhoScE 91-4, WhoWor 93
Banks, Albert Victor, Jr. 1956- WhoAm 92, WhoE 93, WhoEmL 93
Banks, Allen WhoAm 92
Banks, Anna Delceina 1952- WhoAmW 93, WhoE 93, WhoWor 93
Banks, Arthur Sparrow 1926- WhoAm 92
Banks, Bettie Sheppard 1933- WhoAm 92, WhoAmW 93
Banks, Brian R. 1956- ConAu 138
Banks, Bruce J. Law&B 92
Banks, C. Vernon 1937- St&PR 93
Banks, Carolyn WhoWrEP 92
Banks, Carrie Wyatt AmWomPl
Banks, Cecil James 1947- WhoAm 92
Banks, Charles A. WhoAm 92
Banks, Darrell 1938- SoulM
Banks, David ScF&FL 92
Banks, David Owen 1940- WhoE 93
Banks, David R. 1937- St&PR 93
Banks, David Russell 1937- WhoSSW 93
Banks, Dean 1941- St&PR 93
Banks, Delores Johnson 1951- WhoE 93
Banks, Dennis 1932- BioIn 17
Banks, Dennis 1937- CurBio 92 [port]
Banks, Dennns Craig 1948- St&PR 93
Banks, Don(ald Oscar) 1923-1980 Baker 92
Banks, Donald BioIn 17
Banks, Donald B. Law&B 92
Banks, Edward 1903-1988 IntDcAn
Banks, Ephraim 1918- WhoAm 92, WhoE 93
Banks, Eric Kendall 1955- WhoEmL 93
Banks, Ernest 1931- WhoAm 92
Banks, Fred Lee, Jr. 1942- WhoSSW 93
Banks, George, Jr. 1958- WhoEmL 93
Banks, Gretchen Q. Law&B 92
Banks, Harold Ralph 1954- WhoEmL 93, WhoSSW 93
Banks, Helen Ward AmWomPl
Banks, Henry H. 1921- WhoAm 92
Banks, Henry Stephen 1920- WhoE 93
Banks, Homer 1941- SoulM
Banks, Hugh C. d1990 BioIn 17
Banks, Iain M. 1954- ScF&FL 92
Banks, J.E. 1908- St&PR 93
Banks, Jacob William 1918- St&PR 93
Banks, James Albert 1941- WhoAm 92
Banks, James B. 1951- St&PR 93
Banks, James Barber 1951- WhoAm 92
Banks, James Paul 1941- St&PR 93
Banks, James T. Law&B 92
Banks, John ScF&FL 92
Banks, John Archibald 1946- WhoAsAP 91
Banks, John Houston 1911- WhoAm 92
Banks, John L. 1949- St&PR 93
Banks, Joseph 1743-1820 Expl 93 [port]
Banks, Joseph Eugene 1908- WhoAm 92
Banks, Leslie J. 1953- St&PR 93
Banks, Lisa Jean 1956- WhoAmW 93, WhoEmL 93
Banks, Lloyd J. 1923- St&PR 93
Banks, Lynne Reid ScF&FL 92
Banks, Lynne Reid 1929- BioIn 17, ChlFicS
Banks, Margaret Amelia 1928- WhoAmW 93
Banks, Melinda Bruce 1955- WhoAmW 93
Banks, Michael A. 1951- ScF&FL 92
Banks, Michael O. 1959- St&PR 93
Banks, Monty 1897-1950 QDrFCA 92 [port]
Banks, Nathaniel P. 1816-1894 PolPar
Banks, Nathaniel Prentiss 1816-1894 HarEnMi
Banks, Peter WhoScE 91-1
See Also Yes ConMus 8
Banks, Peter Morgan 1937- WhoAm 92
Banks, Philip Francis 1933- St&PR 93
Banks, R.A. 1930- ScF&FL 92
Banks, Ramond E. ScF&FL 92
Banks, Raymond E. 1918- ScF&FL 92
Banks, Rela 1933- WhoAm 92
Banks, Robert C. 1930- St&PR 93
Banks, Robert J. 1928- WhoAm 92
Banks, Robert Sherwood 1934- WhoAm 92
Banks, Robert Thomas 1931- WhoSSW 93
Banks, Roland Fitzgerald, Jr. 1932- WhoAm 92
Banks, Ronald Eric WhoScE 91-1
Banks, Russell 1919- St&PR 93, WhoAm 92, WhoE 93
Banks, Russell 1940- BioIn 17, ConLC 72 [port], CurBio 92
Banks, Susan Mary Law&B 92
Banks, Theodore L. Law&B 92
Banks, Theodore Lee 1951- WhoEmL 93
Banks, Thomas 1735-1805 BioIn 17
Banks, Vanita M. Law&B 92
Banks, Victor DcCPCAm
Banks, Virginia Anne 1949- WhoSSW 93
Banks, William 1934- WhoScE 91-1
Banks, William Louis, Jr. 1936- WhoSSW 93
Banks-Campbell, Linda Diane 1948- WhoAmW 93
Bankson, Douglas 1920- WhoCanL 92
Bankson, Douglas Henneck 1920- WhoWrEP 92
Banks-Tarr, Sharon Elizabeth 1950- WhoEmL 93
Bankston, Archie M. Law&B 92
Bankston, Archie M. 1937- St&PR 93
Bankston, Archie Moore, Jr. 1937- WhoAm 92
Bankston, Gene Clifton 1924- WhoAm 92
Bankvall, Claes WhoScE 91-4
Banky, Vilma 1898- IntDcF 2-3 [port]
Banky, Vilma 1901?-1992 NewYTBS 92 [port]
Bann, Kathleen Winters 1957- WhoEmL 93
Bann, Stephen 1942- ConAu 137
Banna, Mostafa Hasan Omar 1941- WhoWor 93
Bannach, Bryan Eugene 1963- WhoSSW 93
Bannan, Bernard Jerome 1920- St&PR 93
Bannan, Charles F. 1915- St&PR 93
Bannan, Michael P. Law&B 92
Bannard, J.E. 1941- WhoScE 91-3
Bannard, Walter Darby 1934- WhoAm 92
Bannasch, Peter 1934- WhoScE 91-3
Bannat, Edward George 1947- WhoE 93
Banneker, Benjamin 1731-1806 BioIn 17
Bannen, Carol 1951- WhoEmL 93
Bannenberg, Jon BioIn 17
Banner, Bob 1921- WhoAm 92
Banner, Brian Edward Law&B 92
Banner, David L. 1942- WhoUN 92
Banner, David Lee 1942- WhoWor 93
Banner, John 1910-1973 QDrFCA 92 [port]
Banner, John G. Law&B 92
Banner, Stephen E. 1938- St&PR 93
Banner, Stephen Edward 1938- WhoAm 92
Bannerman, Helen (Brodie Cowan Watson) 1862?-1946 ConAu 136, MajAI [port]
Bannerman, Henry Campbell- 1836-1908 BioIn 17
Bannerman, Kay 1919-1991 ConTFT 10
Bannerman, Martha G. 1943- St&PR 93
Bannes, Lawrence J. Law&B 92

Bannes, Stephen William 1958- *WhoEmL 93, WhoWor 93*
Bannett, Lon S. *Law&B 92*
Bannick, Janice C. 1938- *St&PR 93*
Bannigan, Thomas Aloysius 1953- *St&PR 93*
Banning, Margaret Culkin 1891- *AmWomPl*
Bannish, Aaron Philip 1966- *St&PR 93*
Bannish, Harold Michael 1932- *St&PR 93*
Bannish, Marlene Kathryn 1935- *St&PR 93*
Bannish, Matthew 1957- *St&PR 93*
Bannish, Thaddeus John 1961- *St&PR 93*
Bannister, Brian R. *WhoScE 91-1*
Bannister, Brian Roy 1936- *WhoWor 93*
Bannister, Dan R. 1930- *WhoAm 92*
Bannister, Daniel R. 1930- *St&PR 93*
Bannister, Geoffrey 1945- *WhoAm 92*
Bannister, Henry (-Marriott) 1854-1919 *Baker 92*
Bannister, Jo 1951- *ScF&FL 92*
Bannister, Marc A. *Law&B 92*
Bannister, Ralph L. 1921- *St&PR 93*
Bannister, Robert Corwin, Jr. 1935- *WhoAm 92*
Bannister, Roger Gilbert 1929- *WhoWor 93*
Bannister, Ursula Regina 1944- *WhoAmW 93*
Banno, John A. 1940- *St&PR 93*
Bannon, Barbara A. 1928-1991 *BioIn 17*
Bannon, John Charles *WhoAsAP 91*
Bannon, Kathleen Angela 1947- *WhoAmW 93, WhoSSW 93*
Bannon, Mark *ScF&FL 92*
Banny, Jean Konan 1929- *WhoAfr*
Banoczy, Jolan 1929- *WhoScE 91-4*
Banonis, Barbara Ann Cuccioli 1947- *WhoAmW 93, WhoEmL 93*
Banonis, Edward Joseph 1945- *WhoSSW 93*
Banos, J. Luis 1918- *St&PR 93*
Banos, Jose Luis 1918- *WhoSSW 93, WhoWor 93*
Banowetz, David P., Jr. *Law&B 92*
Banowetz, Joseph Murray 1934- *WhoWor 93*
Banquer, Cleve Stephen 1947- *St&PR 93*
Bansak, Stephen A., Jr. 1939- *WhoAm 92, WhoWor 93*
Bansal, Ambrish K. 1947- *WhoE 93*
Bansal, Pawan Kumar 1948- *WhoAsAP 91*
Bansal, Raul 1957- *St&PR 93*
Banse, Amy L. *Law&B 92*
Banse, Karl 1929- *WhoAm 92*
Banse, Robert Lee 1927- *St&PR 93, WhoAm 92*
Bansemer, Jan Marcin 1802-1840 *PolBiDi*
Bansemer, Roger 1948- *ConAu 137*
Banshchikov, Gennadi 1943- *Baker 92*
Bansi Lal 1927- *WhoAsAP 91*
Banski, Douglas A. 1954- *St&PR 93*
Banson, Luis Manuel Tanjangco 1959- *WhoWor 93*
Banstetter, Robert James *Law&B 92*
Banta, Doris B. *Law&B 92*
Banta, Henry David 1938- *WhoAm 92*
Banta, Merle Henry 1932- *WhoAm 92*
Banta, Paul F. *Law&B 92*
Banta, Robert R. 1942- *St&PR 93*
Banta, William Claude 1941- *WhoE 93*
Bantel, Linda Mae 1943- *WhoAm 92, WhoAmW 93*
Bantes, Bonnie *St&PR 93*
Bantey, Bill 1928- *WhoE 93*
Bantham, Russel A. *WhoAm 92*
Bantham, Russel Alvin *Law&B 92*
Banti, Brigida 1759-1806 *Baker 92*
Banti, Brigida Giorgi *OxDcOp*
Bantis, Spiro K. *Law&B 92*
Bantle, Louis Francis 1928- *St&PR 93, WhoAm 92*
Bantock, Granville 1868-1946 *Baker 92, OxDcOp*
Banton, Michael Parker 1926- *WhoWor 93*
Bantry, Bryan 1956- *WhoE 93, WhoEmL 93, WhoWor 93*
Banuelos, Betty Lou 1930- *WhoAmW 93*
Banuelos, Juan 1932- *DcMexL*
Banuelos, Romana Acosta 1925- *HispAmA, NotHsAW 93 [port]*
Banville, John *BioIn 17*
Banville, John 1945- *CurBio 92 [port], WhoWor 93*
Banwart, George Junior 1926- *WhoAm 92*
Banwart, Jakob 1609-c. 1657 *Baker 92*
Banwart, Wayne Lee 1948- *WhoAm 92*
Banyacski, Stephen 1936- *St&PR 93*
Banyai, Geraldine Lepera 1940- *St&PR 93*
Banyai, L. *WhoScE 91-4*
Banyard, Alfred Lothian 1908- *WhoAm 92*
Banyard, Rosemary Elizabeth 1958- *WhoAm 92*
Banyas, Jeffrey Brian 1959- *WhoE 93, WhoEmL 93*
Banyas, Susan Marie 1960- *WhoAmW 93*
Banzer, Jerry Lee 1938- *St&PR 93*
Banzett, Robert Bruce 1947- *WhoE 93*
Banzhaf, Clayton H. 1917-1990 *BioIn 17*
Banzhaf, John F., III 1940- *WhoAm 92*
Banzhaf, Steven Michael 1950- *WhoAm 92*
Bao, Joseph Yue-Se 1937- *WhoWor 93*
Baoda, J. Alberto *Law&B 92*
Bao Dai 1913- *DcTwHis*
Bao Tong *WhoAsAP 91*
Bapatla, Krishna M. *WhoSSW 93*
Baptist, Allwyn J. 1943- *WhoAm 92*
Baptist, Sylvia Evelyn 1944- *WhoAmW 93, WhoWor 93*
Baptista, Artur Lopes 1935- *WhoWor 93*
Baptista, J.L. 1932- *WhoScE 91-3*
Baptista, Pedro Joao fl. 19th cent.- & Jose, Amaro fl. 19th cent.- *Expl 93*
Baptiste, Idella Lou 1952- *WhoEmL 93*
Baptiste, Nancy Ellen 1946- *WhoEmL 93*
Baquerizo, M. 1922- *WhoScE 91-3*
Baquero, Antonio 1949- *WhoScE 91-3*
Baquerot, Maryan 1944- *WhoUN 92*
Baquet, Claudia *BioIn 17*
Baquet, Rene Philippe 1951- *WhoEmL 93*
Baquiaux Gomez, Rolando *DcCPCAm*
Bar, Joshua *Law&B 92*
Bara, Bruno G. 1949- *WhoScE 91-3*
Bara, Ion I. 1941- *WhoScE 91-4*
Bara, Jean Marc 1946- *WhoAm 92*
Bara, Theda 1890?-1955 *IntDcF 2-3 [port]*
Barab, Marvin 1927- *WhoWor 93*
Baraban, Jack 1919- *St&PR 93*
Barabanov, Alexander L. 1955- *WhoUN 92*
Barabanov, Nikita Evgenievich 1954- *WhoWor 93*
Barabas, Frank 1933- *WhoUN 92*
Barabas, Silvio 1920- *WhoAm 92*
Barabas, Zoltan 1926- *WhoScE 91-4*
Barabaschi, Sergio 1930- *WhoWor 93*
Barabba, Vincent Pasquale 1934- *WhoAm 92*
Barabino, William Albert 1932- *WhoE 93, WhoWor 93*
Barac, Bosko A. 1930- *WhoScE 91-4*
Barach, Bruce K. 1956- *WhoE 93*
Barach, Philip G. 1930- *St&PR 93, WhoAm 92*
Barach, Steven *Law&B 92*
Barack, Nathan A. *BioIn 17*
Barack, Robin Sheffman 1946- *WhoE 93*
Baracz, Stanislaw 1864-1936 *PolBiDi*
Barad, Jill E. *BioIn 17*
Barad, Jill Elikann 1951- *St&PR 93, WhoAm 92, WhoAmW 93*
Barad, Judith Adrian 1949- *WhoAmW 93*
Barada, Lajos 1925- *WhoScE 91-4*
Baraga, Frederic 1797-1868 *BioIn 17*
Barager, Wendy Ayrian 1949- *WhoEmL 93*
Baragona, Freddie James, Jr. 1952- *WhoSSW 93*
Baraguay D'Hilliers, Achille 1795-1878 *HarEnMi*
Baragwanath, Albert Kingsmill 1917- *WhoAm 92*
Barak, Deborah *Law&B 92*
Barak, Joanne *Law&B 92*
Barak, Shlomo 1938- *St&PR 93*
Baraka, Amiri 1934- *BioIn 17, ConAu 38NR, MagSAmL [port], WhoAm 92*
Baraka, Imamu Amiri 1934- *BioIn 17*
Barakat, Samir F. 1954- *WhoAm 92*
Baraket, Mark *ScF&FL 92*
Baral, Isvar 1925- *WhoWor 93*
Baram, Peter 1926- *St&PR 93*
Baran, Carolyn Jones 1942- *WhoAm 92*
Baran, E. J. 1936- *WhoAm 92*
Baran, Jan Witold 1948- *WhoAm 92*
Baran, John Morf *Law&B 92*
Baran, Lubomir Wlodzimierz 1937- *WhoScE 91-4*
Baran, Nancy *Law&B 92*
Baran, Paul A. 1910-1964 *BioIn 17*
Baran, Robert J. *Law&B 92*
Baran, S. Askeri 1942- *WhoScE 91-4*
Baran, William Lee 1943- *WhoAm 92, WhoSSW 93*
Baranauckas, Carla May 1955- *WhoAmW 93, WhoEmL 93*
Barancik, Charles 1928- *St&PR 93*
Barancik, Martin B. *Law&B 92*
Baranco, Gregory T. 1948- *AfrAmBi [port]*
Baranczak, Stanislaw 1946- *WhoWrEP 92*
Barandes, Robert 1947- *WhoAm 92*
Barandiaran, Jose Miguel de 1889- *IntDcAn*
Barandiaran, Miguel D. 1933- *WhoScE 91-3*
Baranek, Paul Peter 1914- *WhoWor 93*
Barange, Charles 1897-1985 *BioIn 17*
Baranger, Jacques R. 1940- *WhoScE 91-2*
Baranick, Wilfred John *Law&B 92*
Baranick, Wilfred John 1927- *St&PR 93*
Baranik, Rudolf 1920- *WhoAm 92*
Barannikov, Victor *BioIn 17*
Baranoff, Ed Marc 1957- *St&PR 93*
Baranov, Alexander Andreyevich 1746-1819 *Expl 93 [port]*
Baranov, Alexander Sergeevich 1944- *WhoWor 93*
Baranovic, Kresimir 1894-1975 *Baker 92, OxDcOp*
Baranovskaya, Vera d1935 *IntDcF 2-3*
Baranow, Joan Marie 1958- *WhoWrEP 92*
Baranowski, Edward Alfred 1938- *WhoSSW 93*
Baranowski, Edwin Michael 1947- *WhoEmL 93*
Baranowski, Frank Paul 1921- *WhoAm 92*
Baranowski, Jacek M. 1939- *WhoScE 91-4*
Baranowski, Jan Jozef 1805-1888 *PolBiDi*
Baranowski, Janice Carlson Henske 1952- *WhoEmL 93*
Baranowski, Leslie Boleslaw 1912- *St&PR 93*
Baranowski, Paul Joseph 1950- *WhoE 93*
Baranowski, Tom 1946- *WhoAm 92, WhoEmL 93, WhoSSW 93*
Baranowski, Zenon 1936- *WhoScE 91-4*
Baranski, Andrzej 1934- *WhoScE 91-4*
Baranski, Andrzej 1941- *DrEEuF*
Baranski, Christine 1952- *WhoAm 92, WhoAmW 93*
Baranski, Dennis Anthony 1950- *St&PR 93*
Baranski, Joan Sullivan 1933- *WhoAm 92*
Baranski, Lawrence Anthony 1955- *WhoEmL 93*
Baranski, Zygmunt Guido 1951- *WhoWor 93*
Barany, James Walter 1930- *WhoAm 92, WhoWor 93*
Barany, Kate 1929- *WhoAm 92*
Barany, Nancy 1960- *WhoAmW 93*
Barasch, Clarence Sylvan 1912- *WhoAm 92*
Barasch, Mal Livingston 1929- *WhoAm 92*
Barasch, Marian 1948- *WhoE 93*
Barasch, Shirley Ruth 1933- *WhoE 93*
Barasch, Violette Kasica 1954- *WhoEmL 93*
Barash, Anthony Harlan 1943- *WhoAm 92*
Barash, Paul George 1942- *WhoAm 92*
Barassi, Dario 1940- *WhoWor 93*
Barassin, A. *WhoScE 91-2*
Barat, Jozsef *WhoScE 91-4*
Barata, Gabriel L.S.N. 1944- *WhoScE 91-3*
Barata Pinto, R.H.G. *WhoScE 91-3*
Bara Temes, Javier 1944- *WhoScE 91-3*
Barath, Istvan 1936- *WhoScE 91-4*
Barati, George 1913- *Baker 92*
Baratieri, Oreste 1841-1901 *HarEnMi*
Baratka, Thomas Edward 1946- *St&PR 93*
Baratka, William G. 1934- *St&PR 93*
Baratloo, Mojdeh *BioIn 17*
Baratta, Anthony J., Jr. 1943- *St&PR 93*
Baratta, Joseph Preston 1943- *WhoE 93*
Baratta, Pamela Amelia 1960- *WhoEmL 93*
Baratta, Salvatore Peter 1935- *St&PR 93*
Baratti, Jacques C. 1943- *WhoScE 91-2*
Baratz, Morton Sachs 1923- *WhoAm 92*
Baratz, Robert Sears 1946- *WhoE 93*
Barauski, A. Kathleen 1948- *WhoAmW 93*
Baray, Henry *Law&B 92*
Baraz, Robert H. d1991 *BioIn 17*
Barazabal, Mariano 1772-1807 *DcMexL*
Barazone, Mounque 1948- *WhoEmL 93*
Barazzone, Esther Lynn 1946- *WhoAmW 93*
Barba, Frank Peter 1932- *WhoE 93*
Barba, Harry 1922- *ScF&FL 92, WhoAm 92, WhoWrEP 92*
Barba, J. Brendan 1941- *St&PR 93*
Barba, Joseph A. 1934- *St&PR 93*
Barbaccia, Barbara Lynn 1949- *WhoAmW 93*
Barbachano Ponce, Miguel 1930- *DcMexL*
Barbagelata, Robert Dominic 1925- *WhoAm 92*
Barbaia, Domenico 1778-1841 *OxDcOp*
Barbaja, Domenico c. 1775-1841 *Baker 92*
Barbakoff, Paul 1931- *St&PR 93*
Barbakow, Jeffery C. 1944- *WhoAm 92*
Barbakow, Jeffrey C. 1944- *St&PR 93*
Barbalas, Michael Peter 1955- *WhoWor 93*
Barban, Arnold Melvin 1932- *WhoAm 92*
Barban, Dorys Josefina *WhoE 93*
Barbancon, Diane de d1566 *BioIn 17*
Barbanel, Leon d1990 *BioIn 17*
Barbanell, Robert Louis 1930- *WhoAm 92*
Barbanis, Basil 1926- *WhoScE 91-3*
Barbano, Frances Elizabeth 1944- *WhoWrEP 92*
Barbara *OxDcByz*
Barbaran, Francisco Ramon 1960- *WhoWor 93*
Barbaree, George Ralph 1925- *WhoAm 92*
Barbarelli, Louis Emanuel 1942- *St&PR 93*
Barbarieu, Jacques c. 1420-1491 *Baker 92*
Barbarino, Craig Michael 1962- *WhoE 93*
Barbaro, Nicolo c. 1400-c. 1453 *OxDcByz*
Barbaro, Ronald D. 1931- *WhoE 93*
Barbarosh, Milton Harvey 1955- *WhoEmL 93, WhoSSW 93*
Barbarossa c. 1483-1546 *HarEnMi*
Barbarus Scaligeri *OxDcByz*
Barbasetti Di Prun, Adalberto 1940- *WhoAm 92*
Barbash, Fred 1945- *WhoAm 92*
Barbash, Joseph 1921- *WhoAm 92*
Barbash, Uri *MiSFD 9*
Barbat, Alex Horia 1947- *WhoWor 93*
Barbatelli, Ettore, Sr. 1923- *St&PR 93*
Barbatio, Calypso 1946- *WhoWor 93*
Barbato, Gene A. 1935- *St&PR 93*
Barbato, Joseph Allen 1944- *WhoSSW 93, WhoWrEP 92*
Barbato, Steven A. *BioIn 17*
Barbauld, Anna Letitia Aikin 1743-1825 *BioIn 17*
Barbe, Betty Catherine 1930- *WhoAmW 93, WhoWor 93*
Barbe, David Franklin 1939- *WhoAm 92*
Barbe, Helmut 1927- *Baker 92*
Barbe, Henri 1902-1966 *BioIn 17*
Barbe, Jacques H.A. 1941- *WhoScE 91-2*
Barbe, Pierre 1900- *BioIn 17*
Barbe, Walter Burke 1926- *WhoAm 92*
Barbeau, Clayton C. 1930- *ScF&FL 92*
Barbeau, David C. *St&PR 93*
Barbeau, Dennis William 1947- *WhoSSW 93*
Barbeau, Hubert 1929- *St&PR 93*
Barbeau, Jacques Jean 1938- *WhoWor 93*
Barbeau, Marius 1883-1969 *Baker 92, BioIn 17, IntDcAn*
Barbeau, Susanne 1950- *WhoEmL 93*
Barbee, George E. L. 1943- *WhoAm 92, WhoE 93, WhoWor 93*
Barbee, H. Randoloph, Jr. 1940- *WhoSSW 93*
Barbee, Jeanette H. 1934- *St&PR 93*
Barbee, Joe Ed 1934- *WhoWor 93*
Barbee, Lindsey 1876- *AmWomPl*
Barbee, Lloyd Augustus 1925- *WhoAm 92*
Barbee, Victor 1954- *WhoAm 92*
Barbee, William Clifford, Jr. 1944- *WhoE 93*
Barbenel, Joseph Cyril *WhoScE 91-1*
Barber, Albert F. *BioIn 17*
Barber, Andrew B. 1909- *St&PR 93*
Barber, Andrew Bollons 1909- *WhoAm 92*
Barber, Andrew L. *Law&B 92*
Barber, Ann McDonald 1951- *WhoWor 93*
Barber, Arthur Whiting 1926- *WhoAm 92*
Barber, Ben Bernard Andrew 1944- *WhoAm 92*
Barber, Benjamin R. 1939- *WhoWrEP 92*
Barber, Bonnie A. *Law&B 92*
Barber, Carol Cornsweet 1958- *WhoEmL 93*
Barber, Carol Lee 1949- *WhoAmW 93*
Barber, Charles Andrew d1992 *NewYTBS 92*
Barber, Charles Edward 1840-1917 *GayN*
Barber, Charles Edward 1939- *St&PR 93, WhoSSW 93, WhoWor 93*
Barber, Charles F. 1917- *St&PR 93*
Barber, Charles Finch 1917- *WhoAm 92*
Barber, Charles Turner 1941- *WhoWor 93*
Barber, Clarence Lyle 1917- *WhoAm 92*
Barber, David John *WhoScE 91-1*
Barber, Deborah E. 1939- *St&PR 93*
Barber, Derek *WhoScE 91-1*
Barber, Diane M. *Law&B 92*
Barber, Donald B. 1906- *St&PR 93*
Barber, Donald L. 1953- *St&PR 93*
Barber, Donn Paul 1934- *St&PR 93*
Barber, Douglas Ray 1948- *WhoSSW 93*
Barber, Dulan *ScF&FL 92*
Barber, Earl Eugene 1939- *WhoWor 93*
Barber, Edmund Amaral, Jr. 1916- *WhoE 93*
Barber, Edward Bruce 1937- *WhoWor 93*
Barber, Edwin B. 1927- *WhoIns 93*
Barber, Edwin Barnard 1927- *St&PR 93*
Barber, Edwin Ford 1932- *St&PR 93*
Barber, Frederick R. 1937- *St&PR 93*
Barber, Gail F. *Law&B 92*
Barber, Geoffrey Glenn 1953- *WhoWor 93*
Barber, Gerald E. 1946- *St&PR 93*
Barber, Gordon Keller 1954- *St&PR 93*
Barber, Gregory Paul 1948- *St&PR 93*
Barber, Henry *St&PR 93*
Barber, Ilsa Joan 1945- *WhoE 93*
Barber, Irving K. *St&PR 93*
Barber, James *WhoScE 91-1*

Barber, James Alden 1934- *WhoAm 92, WhoE 93*
Barber, James Arthur 1936- *St&PR 93*
Barber, James C. 1953- *St&PR 93*
Barber, James David 1930- *WhoAm 92*
Barber, James Hill *WhoScE 91-1*
Barber, James Laurance 1951- *St&PR 93*
Barber, James R. 1956- *St&PR 93*
Barber, Janice Ann 1947- *WhoEmL 93*
Barber, Jeffrey Wilson 1953- *St&PR 93*
Barber, Jerry Randel 1940- *WhoAm 92*
Barber, Jim Robert 1952- *WhoEmL 93*
Barber, John *BioIn 17*
Barber, John 1675-1741 *BioIn 17*
Barber, John Anthony 1941- *St&PR 93*
Barber, John Merrell 1935- *WhoAm 92*
Barber, John Steven 1955- *WhoSSW 93*
Barber, Karin *ConAu 138*
Barber, Kenneth W. 1952- *WhoE 93, WhoEmL 93*
Barber, Langdon Laws 1922- *St&PR 93*
Barber, Larry L. 1939- *St&PR 93*
Barber, Larry Marshall *Law&B 92*
Barber, Lloyd Ingram 1932- *WhoAm 92*
Barber, Lynn *BioIn 17*
Barber, Marsha 1946- *WhoAmW 93, WhoEmL 93*
Barber, Mary E. *AmWomPl*
Barber, Mary Foster *AmWomPl*
Barber, Melanie Margaret Cecilia 1958- *WhoEmL 93*
Barber, Monty Clyde 1931- *St&PR 93*
Barber, Nigel William Thomas 1955- *WhoSSW 93*
Barber, Orion Metcalf, II 1935- *WhoAm 92*
Barber, Patricia Ann 1952- *WhoSSW 93*
Barber, Patricia Louise 1953- *WhoEmL 93*
Barber, Perry Oscar, Jr. 1938- *WhoAm 92*
Barber, Peter K. *Law&B 92*
Barber, Phillip R. 1935- *St&PR 93*
Barber, Phyllis (Nelson) 1943- *ConAu 139*
Barber, Red 1908- *WhoAm 92*
Barber, Red 1908-1992 *NewYTBS 92 [port], News 93-2*
Barber, Richard 1941- *ScF&FL 92*
Barber, Richard D. *St&PR 93*
Barber, Robert Allen 1942- *St&PR 93*
Barber, Robert Charles 1936- *WhoAm 92*
Barber, Robert E. 1932- *St&PR 93*
Barber, Robert Latimer 1946- *WhoEmL 93*
Barber, Rosamond *Law&B 92*
Barber, Rupert T. 1903- *St&PR 93*
Barber, Russell Brooks Butler 1934- *WhoAm 92*
Barber, Russell Jeffrey 1950- *WhoEmL 93*
Barber, Salvador 1933- *WhoScE 91-3*
Barber, Samuel 1910-1981 *Baker 92, IntDcOp, OxDcOp*
Barber, Stanley Arthur 1921- *WhoAm 92*
Barber, Stephen Douglas 1955- *WhoWor 93*
Barber, Theodore Francis 1931- *WhoWor 93*
Barber, Thomas King 1923- *WhoAm 92*
Barber, Walter Lanier 1908- *WhoAm 92*
Barber, William Henry *WhoSSW 93*
Barber, William Joseph 1925- *WhoE 93*
Barber, William L. *Law&B 92*
Barbera, Anthony Thomas 1955- *WhoE 93*
Barbera, Augusto Antonio 1938- *WhoWor 93*
Barbera, Jack Joseph 1934- *St&PR 93*
Barbera, Jack Vincent 1945- *WhoSSW 93*
Barbera, Jose Eduardo 1950- *WhoWor 93*
Barbera, Joseph *WhoAm 92*
Barbera, Joseph 1911- *MiSFD 9*
Barbera, Michael Anthony 1952- *WhoEmL 93*
Barbera, Rodney R. 1953- *St&PR 93*
Barbera Moral, Eduardo 1952- *WhoScE 91-3*
Barberi, Francesco 1905-1988 *BioIn 17*
Barberi, Robert O. *Law&B 92*
Barberi, Robert Obed 1945- *St&PR 93, WhoAm 92*
Barberie, Richard C. 1939- *St&PR 93*
Barberini family *OxDcOp*
Barberio, Diane Elizabeth 1945- *WhoWrEP 92*
Barberis, Alessandro 1937- *WhoWor 93*
Barberis, Dana M. *Law&B 92*
Barberis, Dorothy Watkeys 1918- *WhoE 93*
Barberis, Juan Carlos *BioIn 17*
Barberi Squarotti, Giorgio 1929- *DcLB 128*
Barbero, G. *WhoScE 91-3*
Barbero, Jose Alfredo 1950- *WhoWor 93*
Barbero, Robert J. 1929- *St&PR 93*
Barbero, Yves *ScF&FL 92*
Barbero Mari, Paloma 1955- *WhoScE 91-3*
Barbery, Paul S. *Law&B 92*
Barbet, Pierre 1925- *ScF&FL 92*
Barbetta, Maria Ann 1956- *WhoAmW 93*
Barbey, Bertrand *Law&B 92*
Barbey, Daniel Edward 1889-1969 *HarEnMi*
Barbey, Grace Holmes 1907-1990 *BioIn 17*
Barbey d'Aurevilly, Jules-Amedee 1808-1889 *DcLB 119 [port]*
Barbie, Klaus *BioIn 17*
Barbie, Klaus 1913-1991 *AnObit 1991, News 92*
Barbier, Eric *MiSFD 9*
Barbier, Jules 1822-1901 *OxDcOp*
Barbier, Rene (Auguste-Ernest) 1890-1981 *Baker 92*
Barbieri, Carlo Emanuele 1822-1867 *Baker 92*
Barbieri, Cesare *WhoScE 91-3*
Barbieri, Christopher George 1941- *WhoAm 92*
Barbieri, Elaine 1936- *ConAu 138*
Barbieri, Enrique 1959- *WhoSSW 93*
Barbieri, Fedora 1920- *Baker 92, IntDcOp, OxDcOp*
Barbieri, Francesco Giovanni Battista 1942- *WhoWor 93*
Barbieri, Francisco Asenjo 1823-1894 *Baker 92*
Barbieri, Giovanni Francesco 1591-1666 *BioIn 17*
Barbieri, Joseph James 1939- *WhoSSW 93*
Barbieri, Margaret Elizabeth 1947- *WhoWor 93*
Barbieri, Roberta Marie 1966- *WhoAmW 93*
Barbieri, Rocco Anthony 1936- *St&PR 93*
Barbieri, Sante Uberto 1902-1991 *BioIn 17*
Barbieri, YuVonne J. Canter 1940- *WhoAmW 93*
Barbieri-Nini, Marianna 1818-1887 *Baker 92, OxDcOp*
Barbiero, Michael F. 1949- *WhoE 93*
Barbir, Mira *Law&B 92*
Barbirau, Jacques c. 1420-1491 *Baker 92*
Barbireau, Jacques c. 1420-1491 *Baker 92*
Barbirolli, John 1899-1970 *Baker 92, OxDcOp*
Barbis, Elizabeth M. *Law&B 92*
Barblan, Guglielmo 1906-1978 *Baker 92*
Barblan, Otto 1860-1943 *Baker 92*
Barbo, Dorothy Marie 1932- *WhoAm 92, WhoAmW 93*
Barbor, H.R. 1893-1933 *ScF&FL 92*
Barbor, John Howard 1952- *WhoEmL 93*
Barbosa, Geraldo Alexandre 1943- *WhoWor 93*
Barbosa, Raymond *Law&B 92*
Barbosa, Romulo Xavier 1928- *WhoWor 93*
Barbosa-Lima, Carlos 1944- *Baker 92*
Barbot, Joseph-Theodore-Desire 1824-1897 *Baker 92*
Barbour, Alan G. 1933- *ScF&FL 92*
Barbour, Billy Michael 1953- *WhoEmL 93, WhoSSW 93*
Barbour, Charlene 1949- *WhoAmW 93, WhoEmL 93, WhoSSW 93*
Barbour, Douglas 1940- *ScF&FL 92, WhoCanL 92*
Barbour, George H. d1992 *NewYTBS 92 [port]*
Barbour, Hugh Revell 1929- *WhoAm 92*
Barbour, J(ames) Murray 1897-1970 *Baker 92*
Barbour, James 1775-1842 *PolPar*
Barbour, James Keith 1948- *WhoWor 93*
Barbour, James Lewis 1951- *WhoSSW 93*
Barbour, JoAnne 1941- *WhoAmW 93*
Barbour, Karen *BioIn 17*
Barbour, Michael George 1942- *WhoAm 92*
Barbour, Michael Thomas 1947- *WhoAm 92*
Barbour, Philip P. 1783-1841 *PolPar*
Barbour, Philip Pendleton 1783-1841 *OxCSupC [port]*
Barbour, Richard Randolph 1957- *WhoEmL 93*
Barbour, Robert Charles 1935- *St&PR 93*
Barbour, Robert Gordon 1947- *WhoEmL 93*
Barbour, Thomas D. 1928- *St&PR 93*
Barbour, William Ernest, Jr. 1909- *WhoAm 92*
Barbour, William Rinehart, Jr. 1922- *WhoAm 92*
Barbour, Williams H., Jr. 1941- *WhoSSW 93*
Barboza, Anthony 1944- *WhoE 93*
Barboza, Gloria 1951- *WhoEmL 93*
Barboza, Michael J. 1945- *St&PR 93*
Barboza-Flores, Marcelino 1952- *WhoWor 93*
Barbrack, Joanne H. *Law&B 92*
Barbre, John H. 1934- *WhoIns 93*
Barbree, Jay *ScF&FL 92*
Barbry, William Henry, III 1943- *WhoSSW 93*
Barbusse, Henri 1874-1935 *BioIn 17*
Barbuti, Joseph F. 1935- *St&PR 93*
Barbuto, Joseph 1947- *WhoEmL 93*
Barbuy, Beatriz 1950- *WhoWor 93*
Barca, George Gino 1937- *WhoAm 92, WhoWor 93*
Barca, James Joseph 1944- *WhoSSW 93*
Barca, Kathleen 1946- *WhoAmW 93, WhoEmL 93*
Barcan, Reina *Law&B 92*
Barce, Ramon 1928- *Baker 92*
Barcelo, Francois 1941- *WhoCanL 92*
Barcelo, Gabriel Norberto 1946- *WhoWor 93*
Barcelo, John James, III 1940- *WhoAm 92*
Barcelo, Maria Gertrudes 1800-1852 *NotHsAW 93*
Barcelo, Miquel 1957- *BioIn 17*
Barcelo, Miquel Roca 1949- *WhoWor 93*
Barcelo Coll, Juan 1938- *WhoScE 91-3*
Barcelona, Charles B. *WhoAm 92*
Barcelona, Ricardo Go 1955- *WhoWor 93*
Barcena, Alicia 1952- *WhoUN 92*
Barcenas, Roger Candol 1962- *WhoWor 93*
Barcewicz, Stanislaw 1858-1929 *Baker 92, PolBiDi*
Barch, Karen Martin 1954- *St&PR 93, WhoEmL 93*
Barch, Robert Louis 1941- *St&PR 93*
Barchas, Jack David 1935- *WhoAm 92*
Barchers, Charles William 1929- *St&PR 93*
Barchers, Suzanne Inez 1946- *WhoEmL 93*
Barchet, Stephen 1932- *WhoAm 92*
Barchi, Robert Lawrence 1946- *WhoAm 92*
Barchie, Paul F. *Law&B 92*
Barchiesi, Robert 1955- *ConAu 137*
Barci, Robert John 1954- *WhoWrEP 92*
Barcicki, Janusz 1920- *WhoScE 91-4*
Barcikowski, Bernard 1936- *WhoScE 91-4*
Barcinski, Derek Scott 1959- *WhoSSW 93*
Barckert, Lee 1946- *St&PR 93*
Barckley, Robert Eugene 1922- *WhoAm 92*
Barclay, Alan 1910- *ScF&FL 92*
Barclay, Barry 1944- *MiSFD 9*
Barclay, Ben *ScF&FL 92*
Barclay, Bernice 1922- *ScF&FL 92*
Barclay, Bill *ConAu 38NR*
Barclay, Bruce J. *Law&B 92*
Barclay, Carl Archie 1922- *WhoSSW 93*
Barclay, Carrie Marie Voiles 1964- *WhoAmW 93*
Barclay, Glen St. John 1930- *ScF&FL 92*
Barclay, H. Douglas *Law&B 92*
Barclay, Hugh Douglas 1932- *WhoAm 92*
Barclay, Huntington 1939- *St&PR 93*
Barclay, James C.E. *Law&B 92*
Barclay, James Ralph 1926- *WhoAm 92*
Barclay, Joan 1920- *SweetSg C [port]*
Barclay, John Allen 1951- *WhoEmL 93*
Barclay, Joseph Johnson 1933- *St&PR 93*
Barclay, Judith Shaffer 1942- *WhoE 93*
Barclay, Mark Alan 1950- *St&PR 93*
Barclay, Rhoda S. *AmWomPl*
Barclay, Richard Laurence 1951- *St&PR 93*
Barclay, Robert Heriot 1785-1837 *HarEnMi*
Barclay, Ronald David 1934- *WhoAm 92*
Barclay, Steven W. *Law&B 92*
Barclay, Thomas 1824?-1881 *BioIn 17*
Barclay, William Ewert *ConAu 38NR*
Barclay de Tolly, Mikhail Bogdanovich 1761-1818 *HarEnMi*
Barcley, Robert D. *Law&B 92*
Barclift, William C. *Law&B 92*
Barclift, William C. 1949- *St&PR 93*
Barclift, William C., III 1949- *WhoAm 92, WhoEmL 93*
Barcomb, Wayne A. 1933- *St&PR 93*
Barco Vargas, Virgilio *BioIn 17*
Barcus, Anne Sharon 1947- *WhoAmW 93*
Barcus, Benjamin Franklin 1960- *WhoEmL 93, WhoWor 93*
Barcus, Corrinne Locke *AmWomPl*
Barcus, Francis Earle 1927- *WhoE 93*
Barcus, Gilbert Martin 1937- *WhoE 93, WhoWor 93*
Barcus, James Edgar 1938- *WhoAm 92, WhoWrEP 92*
Barcus, Mary Evelyn 1938- *WhoAmW 93*
Barcus, Nancy B(idwell) 1937- *ConAu 40NR*
Barczak, Bernard Gerard 1947- *WhoE 93, WhoEmL 93*
Barczy, Pal 1941- *WhoScE 91-4*
Barczyk, John A. 1947- *St&PR 93*
Bard, Allen Joseph 1933- *WhoAm 92*
Bard, George 1926- *St&PR 93*
Bard, John Franklin 1941- *WhoAm 92*
Bard, Michael *Law&B 92*
Bard, Nelson P. 1908- *St&PR 93*
Bard, Nicholas Van 1955- *St&PR 93*
Bard, Richard H. 1947- *WhoAm 92*
Bard, Stephen H. *Law&B 92*
Bard, Susan M. 1954- *WhoWrEP 92*
Bard, Susan Martha 1954- *WhoEmL 93*
Bard, Theodore 1923- *St&PR 93*
Barda, Jean Francis 1940- *WhoWor 93*
Bardach, Joan Lucile 1919- *WhoAm 92*
Bardach, Sheldon Gilbert 1937- *WhoAm 92*
Bardack, Paul Roitman 1953- *WhoAm 92*
Bardacke, Paul Gregory 1944- *WhoAm 92*
Bardadyn, Ryszard *WhoScE 91-4*
Bardagy, Robert A. 1939- *St&PR 93*
Bardai, Barjoyai Bin 1952- *WhoWor 93*
Bardanes, George dc. 1240 *OxDcByz*
Bardanes Tourkos *OxDcByz*
Bardas d866 *OxDcByz*
Bardasz, Ewa Alice *WhoAm 92*
Bardavelidze, V.V. 1899-1970 *IntDcAn*
Bardeche, Maurice *BioIn 17*
Bardeck, Walter Peter 1910- *WhoWrEP 92*
Bardeen, Bette *Law&B 92*
Bardeen, John 1908-1991 *AnObit 1991, BioIn 17*
Bardeen, William Leonard 1938- *WhoAm 92*
Barden, Don *BioIn 17*
Barden, George Richard 1935- *St&PR 93*
Barden, Janice Kindler *WhoAmW 93, WhoSSW 93*
Barden, John Allan 1936- *WhoAm 92*
Barden, Karl Alvin 1940- *WhoWor 93*
Barden, Kenneth Eugene 1955- *WhoEmL 93*
Barden, Laing *WhoScE 91-1*
Barden, Robert Christopher 1954- *WhoWor 93*
Barden, Thomas E(arl) 1946- *ConAu 136*
Barden, William Charles 1952- *St&PR 93*
Bardenwerper, Walter William 1951- *WhoEmL 93*
Bardfeld, Lawrence R. *Law&B 92*
Bardhan, Pranab 1939- *ConAu 139*
Bardi, Cheryl Morehouse 1950- *WhoAmW 93*
Bardi, Giovanni de 1534-1612 *Baker 92, OxDcOp*
Bardi, Martino 1956- *WhoWor 93*
Bardill, Donald Ray 1934- *WhoAm 92*
Bardin, Christian Andre 1939- *St&PR 93*
Bardin, Claude 1936- *WhoScE 91-2*
Bardin, Clyde Wayne 1934- *WhoAm 92*
Bardin, David J. 1933- *WhoAm 92*
Bardin, Rodney Norman, II 1957- *WhoEmL 93*
Bardin, Rollin Edmond 1932- *WhoSSW 93*
Bardin, W. Earl 1927- *St&PR 93*
Bardins, Kathryn Ballowe 1952- *WhoAmW 93*
Bardis, Panos Demetrios 1924- *WhoAm 92*
Bardo, Charles J. 1938- *St&PR 93*
Bardo, John William 1948- *WhoAm 92*
Bardo, Robert *BioIn 17*
Bardole, Betty Jean 1932- *WhoAmW 93*
Bardolph, Richard 1915- *WhoAm 92*
Bardon, Daniel Russell 1947- *St&PR 93*
Bardon, Jack Irving 1925- *WhoAm 92*
Bardon, Marcel 1927- *WhoAm 92*
Bardon, Stephen M. 1955- *St&PR 93*
Bardos, Denes Istvan 1938- *WhoAm 92*
Bardos, Lajos 1899-1986 *Baker 92*
Bardos, Pierre 1942- *WhoScE 91-2*
Bardos, Thomas Joseph 1915- *WhoAm 92*
Bardosh, N. Larry 1941- *St&PR 93*
Bardot, Brigitte *BioIn 17*
Bardot, Brigitte 1934- *IntDcF 2-3 [port], WhoWor 93*
Bardsley, David M. *Law&B 92*
Bardsley, Richard Geoffrey 1928- *St&PR 93*
Bardwick, Judith Marcia 1933- *WhoAm 92*
Bardwil, Joseph A. 1928- *St&PR 93*
Bardwil, Joseph Anthony 1928- *WhoAm 92*
Bardwil, Steven Craig *Law&B 92*
Bardy, Alexander P. 1930- *St&PR 93*
Bardyguine, Patricia Wilde 1928- *WhoAm 92*
Bare, Bruce 1914- *WhoAm 92*
Bare, Jean-Patrick Claude Lucien 1944- *WhoUN 92*
Bare, Joseph Edward, Jr. 1923- *WhoAm 92*
Bare, Lois Kieffaber 1942- *WhoAmW 93*
Bare, Richard L. *MiSFD 9*
Bare, Robert Joseph 1935- *WhoAm 92*
Bare, Thomas Michael 1942- *WhoE 93*
Barea Navarro, Jose M. *WhoScE 91-3*
Barefield, Eddie 1909-1991 *AnObit 1991, BioIn 17*
Barefield, Thomas A. *WhoIns 93*
Barefoot, Brian Miller 1943- *WhoAm 92*
Barefoot, Donald L. 1954- *St&PR 93*
Bareihs, Dieter Erich 1966- *WhoE 93*
Bareiss, Erwin Hans 1922- *WhoAm 92*
Bareiss, Rolf Eugen 1932- *WhoWor 93*
Barej, Wieslaw 1934- *WhoScE 91-4*

Bareja, Stanislaw 1929-1987 *DrEEuF*
Barel, Alain R.F. 1946- *WhoScE 91-2*
Barel, Phyllis Barbara 1947- *St&PR 93*
Barela, Casimiro 1847-1920 *HispAmA*
Barela, Esmerlindo Jaramillo 1948- *WhoEmL 93*
Barela, Patrocino 1908-1964 *HispAmA*
Barela, Veronica Elizabeth 1945- *WhoAmW 93*
Barenberg, Sumner A. 1945- *St&PR 93*
Barenboim, Daniel *BioIn 17*
Barenboim, Daniel 1942- *Baker 92, OxDcOp, WhoAm 92, WhoWor 93*
Barendrecht, Embrecht 1924- *WhoScE 91-3*
Barendsen, Gerrit Willem 1927- *WhoScE 91-3*
Barendsz, A.W. *WhoScE 91-3*
Barenfeld, Michael 1943- *St&PR 93*
Barenghi, Carlo Ferruccio 1953- *WhoWor 93*
Barenholtz, Ben 1935- *BioIn 17*
Barenholtz, Bernard M. 1914-1989 *BioIn 17*
Barenholtz, Paul Kenneth *Law&B 92*
Barenis, Pat Peaster 1951- *WhoEmL 93*
Barenklau, Keith Edward 1931- *WhoAm 92, WhoSSW 93*
Barentine, W.S. *St&PR 93*
Barents, Brian E. *BioIn 17*
Barents, Brian Edward 1944- *WhoAm 92*
Barents, Willem 1550?-1597 *Expl 93*
Barentyne, Ross 1939- *WhoE 93*
Barentzen, Heinrich Johannes 1940- *WhoWor 93*
Barer, Sol J. 1947- *St&PR 93*
Barere, Simon *BioIn 17*
Barere, Simon 1896-1951 *Baker 92*
Bares, Judith C. *Law&B 92*
Bareth, Camille 1934- *WhoScE 91-2*
Baretich, John Francis 1954- *St&PR 93*
Baretski, Charles Allan 1918- *WhoE 93, WhoWor 93*
Barfield, Clem *BioIn 17*
Barfield, Kenny Dale 1947- *WhoEmL 93, WhoSSW 93*
Barfield, Larry M. 1948- *St&PR 93*
Barfield, Robert F. 1933- *WhoAm 92*
Barfield, Stewart Bayne 1957- *WhoEmL 93*
Barfield, William B. *Law&B 92*
Barfoot, Joan 1946- *WhoCanL 92*
Barford, Norman Charles 1921- *WhoWor 93*
Barford, R.M. 1929- *St&PR 93*
Barford, Ralph MacKenzie 1929- *WhoAm 92*
Barg, David William 1918- *St&PR 93*
Barg, Meredith *Law&B 92*
Bargainer, Paul V. 1954- *WhoEmL 93*
Barganier, Ricky Brent 1963- *WhoSSW 93*
Bargar, Gary 1947-1985 *BioIn 17*
Bargar, Robert S. 1919- *St&PR 93*
Bargar, Robert Sellstrom 1919- *WhoAm 92*
Bargar, William *BioIn 17*
Barge, Daniel Bythewood 1922- *St&PR 93*
Barge, Sylvia Earnestine 1940- *WhoAmW 93*
Bargellini, Pier Luigi 1914- *WhoAm 92*
Bargen, Karl d1990 *BioIn 17*
Bargeon, Herbert Alexander, Jr. 1934- *WhoWor 93*
Barger, Abraham Clifford 1917- *WhoAm 92*
Barger, Benjamin 1920- *WhoSSW 93*
Barger, Carl F. d1992 *NewYTBS 92 [port]*
Barger, Cecil Edwin 1917- *WhoAm 92*
Barger, Donald G. 1943- *St&PR 93*
Barger, Erwin D., Jr. *Law&B 92*
Barger, Eva Catlin 1957- *WhoAmW 93*
Barger, J.P. 1927- *St&PR 93*
Barger, Jack L. 1957- *St&PR 93*
Barger, James Daniel 1917- *WhoAm 92*
Barger, James Edwin 1934- *WhoAm 92*
Barger, John 1953- *BioIn 17*
Barger, Marsha Bunn 1952- *WhoAmW 93*
Barger, Maurice W., Jr. 1931- *WhoIns 93*
Barger, Mitzi Leigh 1961- *WhoAmW 93*
Barger, Myrtle L. *AmWomPl*
Barger, R. Vincent 1942- *St&PR 93*
Barger, Richard Wilson 1934- *WhoAm 92*
Barger, Richards D. 1928- *St&PR 93, WhoIns 93*
Barger, Robert Vincent 1942- *WhoAm 92*
Barger, Stephen Richard 1950- *WhoEmL 93*
Barger, Vernon Duane 1938- *WhoAm 92*
Barger, William James 1944- *WhoAm 92*
Bargetzi, Jean-Pierre 1923- *WhoScE 91-4*
Bargh, John A. *BioIn 17*
Bargholtz, Christoph 1945- *WhoScE 91-4*
Bargholtz, Christoph Hubert 1945- *WhoWor 93*
Barghoorn, Elso Sterrenberg 1915-1984 *BioIn 17*
Barghoorn, Frederick C. *BioIn 17*
Bargiel, Woldemar 1828-1897 *Baker 92*
Bargielski, Zbigniew 1937- *Baker 92*
Bargmann, Valentine 1908-1989 *BioIn 17*
Bargmeyer, Alan K. 1941- *St&PR 93*
Bargon, Ernst *WhoScE 91-3*
Barguirdjian, Henry Ralph 1957- *St&PR 93*
Barham, Charles Dewey, Jr. 1930- *St&PR 93, WhoAm 92, WhoSSW 93*
Barham, Jesse Walter 1924- *WhoWor 93*
Barham, Mack Elwin 1924- *WhoAm 92*
Barham, Mel A. 1937- *St&PR 93*
Barham, Michael R. 1957- *St&PR 93*
Barham, Patte *WhoAm 92, WhoAmW 93*
Barham, Sadie G. *AfrAmBi*
Bar Hebraeus *OxDcByz*
Barhite, Mary Louise *Law&B 92*
Barhorst, Sharon Ann 1952- *St&PR 93*
Bari, Judi *BioIn 17*
Bari, Shamsul 1941- *WhoUN 92*
Baribeau, Michel 1931- *St&PR 93*
Baribeau, Simon 1928- *St&PR 93*
Baric, Ante 1943- *WhoScE 91-4*
Baric, David A. *Law&B 92*
Barich, Dewey Frederick 1911- *WhoAm 92*
Baridon, Philip Clarke 1946- *WhoE 93*
Barie, Philip Steven 1953- *WhoE 93, WhoEmL 93*
Barienbrock, Ronald Charles 1947- *St&PR 93*
Barigelletti, Francesco 1944- *WhoScE 91-3*
Barik, Sudhakar 1949- *WhoAm 92, WhoEmL 93*
Baril, David Chase *Law&B 92*
Baril, Earl Francis 1930- *WhoE 93*
Baril, Karen Kallio *Law&B 92*
Baril, Nancy Ann 1952- *WhoAmW 93*
Barilan, Amiram *St&PR 93*
Barile, Andrew J. 1942- *WhoIns 93*
Barile, Frank D. 1933- *St&PR 93*
Barile, Michael Frederick 1924- *WhoE 93*
Barili, Alfredo 1854-1935 *Baker 92*
Barilich, Thomas Anthony 1955- *WhoEmL 93, WhoWor 93*
Barilier, Etienne *BioIn 17*
Barilka, William Michael 1948- *WhoWor 93*
Bar-Illan, David (Jacob) 1930- *Baker 92, WhoAm 92*
Barillari, Edward R. *Law&B 92*
Barille, Elisabeth 1960- *ConAu 137*
Barilli, Bruno 1880-1952 *Baker 92*
Barilli, Luigi 1767-1824 See Bondini, Pasquale 1737?-1789 *OxDcOp*
Baring, George Rowland Stanley 1918-1991 *BioIn 17*
Bario, Patricia Yaroch 1932- *WhoE 93*
Bariou, Robert 1942- *WhoScE 91-2*
Baris, Cemal *WhoScE 91-4*
Baris, Mubeccel 1942- *WhoScE 91-4*
Barisano, Joseph *WhoWrEP 92*
Barisci, Joseph Norbert 1950- *WhoWor 93*
Barish, Ellen Gail *Law&B 92*
Barish, Jean Ellen 1952- *St&PR 93*
Barish, Jonas Alexander 1922- *WhoAm 92*
Barish, Julian I. 1917- *WhoE 93*
Barish, Keith *ConTFT 10*
Bariso, Angelo 1936- *St&PR 93*
Baritz, Loren 1928- *WhoAm 92*
Barjansky, Alexander 1883-1961 *Baker 92*
Barjavel, Rene 1911-1985 *ScF&FL 92*
Barjokas, Joanne 1957- *WhoAmW 93*
Bark, Conrad Voss *ScF&FL 92*
Bark, Fritz Helge 1942- *WhoWor 93*
Bark, Jan (Helge Guttorm) 1934- *Baker 92*
Barkalow, Carol 1958?- *BioIn 17*
Barkan, Alexander E. 1909-1990 *BioIn 17*
Barkan, Joel David 1941- *WhoAm 92*
Barkan, Leonard *Law&B 92*
Barkan, Leonard 1926- *St&PR 93*
Barkan, Philip 1925- *WhoAm 92*
Barkat, Gourad Hamadou c. 1930- *WhoAfr*
Barkauskas, Vytautas 1931- *Baker 92*
Barkays *SoulM*
Barkel, Charles 1898-1973 *Baker 92*
Barkeley, Norman A. 1930- *St&PR 93*
Barkell, Howard 1914-1990 *BioIn 17*
Barkemeijer de Wit, Jeanne Sandra 1955- *WhoAmW 93*
Barken, Bernard Allen 1924- *WhoWor 93*
Barker, Andrew K. 1949- *St&PR 93*
Barker, Anita Joyce 1947- *St&PR 93*
Barker, Anthony Trevor *WhoScE 91-1*
Barker, Barbara 1938- *WhoAmW 93*
Barker, Barbara Ann 1943- *WhoAm 92, WhoAmW 93*
Barker, Barry W. 1943- *WhoWrEP 92*
Barker, Becky Bean 1963- *WhoAmW 93*
Barker, Bruce Allen 1952- *WhoEmL 93, WhoSSW 93*
Barker, Bruce M. *BioIn 17*
Barker, C. *WhoScE 91-1*
Barker, C. Austin 1911- *St&PR 93*
Barker, Calvin LaRue 1930- *WhoSSW 93*
Barker, Celeste Arlette 1947- *WhoAmW 93, WhoEmL 93, WhoWor 93*
Barker, Charles *WhoAm 92*
Barker, Charles Thomas 1946- *WhoEmL 93*
Barker, Clarence Austin 1911- *WhoAm 92*
Barker, Clayton Robert *Law&B 92*
Barker, Clayton Robert, III 1957- *WhoEmL 93*
Barker, Clive *BioIn 17, MiSFD 9*
Barker, Clive 1952- *Au&Arts 10 [port], ScF&FL 92*
Barker, Clyde Frederick 1932- *WhoAm 92, WhoWor 93*
Barker, Colin George 1939- *WhoSSW 93*
Barker, D.A. 1947- *ScF&FL 92*
Barker, D.C. *WhoScE 91-1*
Barker, D.J.P. *WhoScE 91-1*
Barker, Daniel Stephen 1934- *WhoAm 92*
Barker, David Bertram 1946- *WhoEmL 93*
Barker, Dennis 1929- *ScF&FL 92*
Barker, Douglas Wayne 1952- *St&PR 93*
Barker, Edwin Bogue 1954- *WhoAm 92*
Barker, Elisabeth 1910-1986 *ConAu 136*
Barker, Elspeth 1940- *ConAu 138*
Barker, Emmett Wilson, Jr. 1937- *WhoAm 92*
Barker, Eric 1912-1990 *QDrFCA 92 [port]*
Barker, Ernest G. 1939- *WhoSSW 93*
Barker, Frank H. 1930- *St&PR 93*
Barker, Frank Morehead, III 1963- *WhoSSW 93*
Barker, Frederick Henry, Jr. 1953- *WhoEmL 93*
Barker, Garry G. 1943- *WhoWrEP 92*
Barker, Geoffrey Ronald *WhoScE 91-1*
Barker, George 1913-1991 *AnObit 1991, BioIn 17*
Barker, George Granville 1913- *ConAu 38NR*
Barker, Gregory Kimball 1946- *WhoEmL 93*
Barker, Harley Granville- 1877-1946 *BioIn 17*
Barker, Harold Grant 1917- *WhoAm 92, WhoE 93*
Barker, Harold Kenneth 1922- *WhoAm 92*
Barker, Horace Albert 1907- *WhoAm 92*
Barker, Horace Anthony *WhoScE 91-1*
Barker, Hugh Alton 1925- *St&PR 93*
Barker, James 1946- *WhoWrEP 92*
Barker, James Cathey 1945- *WhoSSW 93*
Barker, James Cecil 1948- *St&PR 93, WhoEmL 93*
Barker, James Rex 1935- *St&PR 93, WhoAm 92*
Barker, Jaryn I. *Law&B 92*
Barker, Jeanne Wilson 1939- *WhoSSW 93*
Barker, Joe F. *Law&B 92*
Barker, John E. 1947- *St&PR 93*
Barker, John Stewart 1947- *WhoSSW 93*
Barker, Jonathan 1949- *ConAu 139*
Barker, Judy 1941- *WhoAm 92, WhoAmW 93*
Barker, Kathleen Marie 1951- *WhoAmW 93*
Barker, Kenneth Joseph 1953- *WhoSSW 93*
Barker, Kenneth Neil 1937- *WhoAm 92*
Barker, Larry Lee 1941- *WhoAm 92, WhoWor 93*
Barker, Laurenn Russell 1945- *WhoAm 92, WhoAmW 93*
Barker, Lee Charles 1952- *WhoEmL 93*
Barker, Len 1955- *BioIn 17*
Barker, Lex 1919-1973 *BioIn 17*
Barker, Linda Gail 1948- *WhoAmW 93*
Barker, Lisa Ann 1965- *WhoSSW 93*
Barker, Llyle James, Jr. 1932- *WhoAm 92*
Barker, M.A.R. 1929- *ScF&FL 92*
Barker, M.H. *Law&B 92*
Barker, M. Theresa *Law&B 92*
Barker, Margaret 1944- *ConAu 138*
Barker, Margaret T. d1992 *BioIn 17, NewYTBS 92*
Barker, Mary Katherine 1921- *WhoAmW 93*
Barker, Michael Charles John *WhoScE 91-1*
Barker, Michael Dean 1960- *WhoWor 93*
Barker, Muhammad Abd Al-Rahman *ScF&FL 92*
Barker, Muhammad Abd-al-Rahman 1929- *WhoAm 92*
Barker, Nancy Lepard 1936- *WhoAm 92*
Barker, Nicholas 1932- *ScF&FL 92*
Barker, Norman, Jr. 1922- *St&PR 93*
Barker, Nugent 1888- *ScF&FL 92*
Barker, Pat 1943- *BioIn 17*
Barker, Patricia Joyce *WhoAm 92*
Barker, Paul 1914- *St&PR 93*
Barker, Peter Frank *WhoScE 91-1*
Barker, Philip Edwin *WhoScE 91-1*
Barker, Philip George 1944- *WhoWor 93*
Barker, R. William *Law&B 92*
Barker, Ralph 1917- *ConAu 38NR*
Barker, Richard Alexander 1947- *WhoWor 93*
Barker, Richard Clark 1926- *WhoAm 92*
Barker, Richard Gordon 1937- *WhoAm 92*
Barker, Richard T. 1932-1991 *BioIn 17*
Barker, Robert 1928- *St&PR 93, WhoAm 92*
Barker, Robert John 1941- *St&PR 93*
Barker, Robert William *WhoAm 92*
Barker, Roger Garlock 1903-1990 *BioIn 17*
Barker, Rolph William Johnson *WhoScE 91-1*
Barker, Ronald C. 1927- *St&PR 93*
Barker, Ronald G. *BioIn 17*
Barker, Ronnie 1929- *QDrFCA 92 [port]*
Barker, Ruth Anne 1945- *WhoE 93*
Barker, Samuel Booth 1912- *WhoAm 92*
Barker, Sandra Stock *Law&B 92*
Barker, Sarah Evans 1943- *WhoAm 92, WhoAmW 93*
Barker, Sidney Alan *WhoScE 91-1*
Barker, Stanley Anthony 1956- *WhoWrEP 92*
Barker, Stephen R. 1955- *St&PR 93*
Barker, Steven Richard 1950- *WhoSSW 93*
Barker, Ted Alan 1947- *St&PR 93*
Barker, Teresa Lynn 1954- *WhoEmL 93*
Barker, Thomas Carl 1931- *WhoAm 92*
Barker, Thomas W. *ScF&FL 92*
Barker, Thomas Watson, Jr. 1944- *St&PR 93, WhoAm 92*
Barker, Tommie Dora 1888-1978 *BioIn 17*
Barker, Wade *ScF&FL 92*
Barker, Walter Lee 1928- *WhoAm 92*
Barker, Walter William, Jr. 1921- *WhoAm 92*
Barker, William Alfred 1919- *WhoAm 92*
Barker, William Benjamin 1947- *St&PR 93, WhoAm 92*
Barker, William Clinton 1950- *St&PR 93*
Barker, William Daniel 1926- *WhoAm 92, WhoWor 93*
Barker, William Gardner 1913-1990 *BioIn 17*
Barker, William Griffith, Jr. 1933- *St&PR 93*
Barker, William Hall, Jr. 1953- *WhoE 93*
Barker, William Henry 1946- *WhoEmL 93*
Barker, Willie G., Jr. 1937- *WhoSSW 93*
Barker, Winona Clinton 1938- *WhoAm 92*
Barker-Griffith, Ann Elizabeth 1942- *WhoAmW 93*
Barkett, Henry Richard Frank 1958- *WhoEmL 93*
Barkett, Rosemary 1939- *WhoAmW 93, WhoSSW 93*
Barkhamer, Josephine Rita 1949- *WhoWrEP 92*
Barkhorn, Henry C., III 1949- *St&PR 93*
Barkhorn, Henry Charles, III 1949- *WhoAm 92*
Barkhorn, Jean Cook 1931- *WhoAm 92, WhoWrEP 92*
Barkhouse, Joyce 1913- *WhoCanL 92*
Barkhuus, Arne 1906- *WhoAm 92*
Barkin, Ben 1915- *WhoAm 92*
Barkin, Elaine R(adoff) 1932- *Baker 92*
Barkin, Ellen *BioIn 17*
Barkin, Ellen 1955- *HolBB [port]*
Barkin, Kay Anita Frohlich 1952- *WhoEmL 93, WhoSSW 93*
Barkin, Martin 1936- *WhoAm 92*
Barkin, Marvin E. 1933- *WhoAm 92*
Barkin, Robert Allan 1939- *WhoAm 92*
Barkin, Solomon 1907- *WhoAm 92*
Barkley, Alben W. 1877-1956 *PolPar*
Barkley, Alben William 1877-1956 *BioIn 17*
Barkley, Barry R. 1943- *St&PR 93*
Barkley, Brian Evan 1945- *WhoAm 92*
Barkley, Charles *BioIn 17*
Barkley, Charles Wade 1963- *BiDAMSp 1989, WhoAm 92*
Barkley, Clint *BioIn 17*
Barkley, Deanne 1931- *ConTFT 10*
Barkley, Drew S. *WhoIns 93*
Barkley, Erich Russell 1948- *WhoE 93*
Barkley, Henry Brock, Jr. 1927- *WhoAm 92, WhoSSW 93, WhoWor 93*
Barkley, Jane *Law&B 92*
Barkley, Kenneth Ray 1940- *St&PR 93*
Barkley, Miriam Corn 1952- *WhoEmL 93*
Barkley, Monika Johanna 1961- *WhoSSW 93*
Barkley, Nella *BioIn 17*
Barkley, Paul Haley, Jr. 1937- *WhoAm 92*
Barkley, Raymond E. 1927- *St&PR 93*
Barkley, Richard Clark 1932- *WhoAm 92, WhoWor 93*
Barkley, Rufus C., Jr. 1930- *St&PR 93*
Barkley, Scott Glenn 1960- *WhoE 93*

Barkley, Theodore Mitchell 1934- WhoAm 92
Barkley, William Donald 1941- WhoAm 92
Barkley, William J. 1941- St&PR 93
Barkman, Jon Albert 1947- WhoE 93, WhoEmL 93
Barko, Randall S. 1951- St&PR 93
Bar-Kochba, Moshe 1930-1992 NewYTBS 92
Barkocy, Andrew Bernard 1932- WhoE 93
Barkoff, Rupert Mitchell 1948- WhoAm 92
Barkofske, Francis Lee 1939- WhoAm 92
Bar Kokhba d135 BioIn 17
Barkow, Robert F. 1942- St&PR 93
Barksdale, Arthur Sydnor, III 1951- St&PR 93
Barksdale, C. Bruce, Jr. 1931- St&PR 93
Barksdale, Charles Beverly 1963- WhoE 93
Barksdale, Clarence Caulfield 1932- WhoAm 92
Barksdale, Darryll Wayne 1954- WhoSSW 93
Barksdale, James H. Law&B 92
Barksdale, James Love 1943- St&PR 93, WhoSSW 93
Barksdale, Milton Kendall, Jr. 1945- WhoSSW 93
Barksdale, Rhesa Hawkins 1944- WhoAm 92, WhoSSW 93
Barksdale, Richard Dillon 1938- WhoAm 92
Barksdale, Shirley BioIn 17
Barksdale, Thomas G. 1937- St&PR 93
Barksdale, William E. 1931- St&PR 93
Barksdale-Hakim, Cynthia Zakiah 1945- WhoAmW 93
Barkuloo, Adria D. AmWomPl
Barkwell, Donald D. 1930- St&PR 93
Barkwill, Linda Klobasa 1947- WhoEmL 93
Barlaam Of Calabria c. 1290-1348 OxDcByz
Barlach, Ernst 1870-1938 BioIn 17, DcLB 118 [port]
Barlage, Harry E. 1941- St&PR 93
Barlament, Robert John 1928- St&PR 93
Barlar, Rebecca Nance 1950- WhoEmL 93
Barlas, Elaine M. Law&B 92
Barlas, Julie Sandall 1944- WhoAm 92
Barla-Szabo, Gabor 1949- WhoScE 91-4
Barlett, Alex 1953- WhoAsAP 91
Barlett, Donald L. BioIn 17
Barlett, Donald L. 1936- WhoAm 92
Barlett, James Edward 1944- WhoAm 92
Barletta, Giuseppe Antonio 1954- WhoWor 93
Barletta, Joseph Francis 1936- WhoAm 92, WhoWrEP 92
Barletta, Robert T. 1946- St&PR 93
Barley, Albert Lawrence 1942- St&PR 93
Barley, Barbara Ann 1954- WhoAmW 93, WhoEmL 93
Barley, Doris Faye 1936- WhoSSW 93
Barley, John Alvin 1940- WhoSSW 93
Barley, Kathryn Myers 1954- WhoEmL 93
Barley, Nena Stewart 1958- WhoEmL 93
Barlich, Gail Lynne 1961- WhoAmW 93
Barlier, Francois 1933- WhoScE 91-2
Barlik, Marcin 1944- WhoScE 91-4
Barlin, Carole Arlene 1935- WhoAmW 93
Barlin, Wayne A. Law&B 92
Barling, Renee Meyers 1935- WhoAmW 93
Barling, Tom ScF&FL 92
Barlis, Thomas K. 1959- WhoE 93
Barloco, Gerard H. 1944- WhoIns 93
Barlow, Alfred Ernest 1861-1914 BioIn 17
Barlow, Alvin Wellington 1961- WhoEmL 93
Barlow, Anne Louise 1925- WhoAm 92
Barlow, August Ralph, Jr. 1934- WhoE 93, WhoWor 93
Barlow, Beth 1950- BioIn 17
Barlow, Carl Morton 1925- WhoE 93
Barlow, Charles Beach 1926- St&PR 93, WhoE 93
Barlow, Charles Franklin 1923- WhoAm 92
Barlow, Clark W. 1938- St&PR 93, WhoAm 92
Barlow, Conrad R. 1920- St&PR 93
Barlow, Curtis Hudson 1948- St&PR 93
Barlow, DeWitt D. 1946- St&PR 93
Barlow, Douglas BioIn 17
Barlow, Frank John 1914- St&PR 93, WhoAm 92
Barlow, Fred 1881-1951 Baker 92
Barlow, Harold 1915- Baker 92
Barlow, Howard 1892-1972 Baker 92
Barlow, James Craig 1946- WhoEmL 93
Barlow, Joel 1754-1812 BioIn 17
Barlow, Joel 1908- WhoAm 92
Barlow, Joel William 1942- WhoAm 92
Barlow, John David, Jr. 1935- St&PR 93
Barlow, John Sutton 1925- WhoE 93
Barlow, Joyce Krutick 1946- WhoEmL 93
Barlow, Kathleen T. Law&B 92
Barlow, Kenneth James 1932- WhoAm 92
Barlow, Kent Michael 1935- St&PR 93
Barlow, Laurie Patricia Hildebrand 1952- WhoEmL 93
Barlow, Leo 1952- St&PR 93
Barlow, Lolete Falck 1932- WhoWrEP 92
Barlow, Matthew R. Joseph 1935- WhoWor 93
Barlow, Michael Joseph 1964- WhoE 93
Barlow, Mildred Devereux d1990 BioIn 17
Barlow, Nadine Gail 1958- WhoAmW 93
Barlow, Nathan B. 1939- St&PR 93
Barlow, Oliver B. 1960- St&PR 93
Barlow, Peter WhoScE 91-1
Barlow, R.H. 1918-1951 ScF&FL 92
Barlow, Robert Dudley 1954- WhoWor 93
Barlow, Robert Hayward 1918-1951 IntDcAn
Barlow, Samuel (Latham Mitchill) 1892-1982 Baker 92
Barlow, Walter Greenwood 1917- WhoAm 92
Barlow, Wayne (Brewster) 1912- Baker 92
Barlow, William 1943- ConAu 139
Barlow, William Edward 1917- WhoAm 92, WhoWrEP 92
Barlow, William H. Law&B 92
Barlow, William J. 1950- St&PR 93
Barlow, William Pusey, Jr. 1934- WhoAm 92
Barlowe, Dorothea 1926- BioIn 17
Barlowe, Dot 1926- BioIn 17
Barlowe, Sy BioIn 17
Barlowe, Wayne Douglas 1958- ScF&FL 92
Barloy, J. WhoScE 91-2
Barma, Haider Hatam Tyebjee 1944- WhoAsAP 91
Barma, Tyebjee Hatam 1933- WhoAsAP 91
Barmak, Mark E. Law&B 92
Barman, Marilyn Joanne 1938- WhoAmW 93
Barman, Mervyn Lee 1933- WhoWor 93
Barmann, Heinrich (Joseph) 1784-1847 Baker 92
Barmann, Karl 1811-1885 Baker 92
Barmann, Karl, Jr. 1839-1913 Baker 92
Barmann, Lawrence Francis 1932- WhoAm 92
Barmeyer, John R. Law&B 92
Barmeyer, John R. 1946- WhoIns 93
Barmore, Gregory Terhune 1941- St&PR 93, WhoAm 92
Barna, B. Peter 1928- WhoScE 91-4
Barna, Douglas Peter 1945- WhoE 93
Barna, Gary Stanley 1940- St&PR 93
Barna, Joel Warren 1951- ConAu 138
Barna, Peter 1943- St&PR 93, WhoAm 92
Barna, Richard A. 1948- St&PR 93
Barna, Richard Allen 1948- WhoE 93
Barnaba, Frank BioIn 17
Barnabas OxDcByz
Barnabas, Beata Maria 1948- WhoScE 91-4
Barnabeo, Susan Law&B 92
Barnaby, Daryl John 1956- WhoWor 93
Barnard, A.M. MajAI
Barnard, Anne 1750-1825 BioIn 17
Barnard, Aubrey D. 1936- St&PR 93
Barnard, Bonnie Marie 1957- WhoAmW 93
Barnard, Charles Francis 1928- St&PR 93
Barnard, Charles Nelson 1924- WhoWrEP 92
Barnard, Charlotte 1830-1869 Baker 92
Barnard, Christiaan 1922- ConHero 2 [port]
Barnard, Christiaan Neethling 1922- WhoWor 93
Barnard, Christopher S. Law&B 92
Barnard, D.R. 1932- St&PR 93
Barnard, David Bruce Law&B 92
Barnard, Donald Edward 1939- St&PR 93
Barnard, Doug, Jr. 1922- CngDr 91
Barnard, Douglas Craig 1958- WhoEmL 93
Barnard, Druie Douglas, Jr. 1922- WhoAm 92, WhoSSW 93
Barnard, E.A. WhoScE 91-1
Barnard, Gustan 1940- WhoUN 92
Barnard, Henry 1811-1900 BioIn 17
Barnard, Henry William 1799-1857 HarEnMi
Barnard, John K. 1940- St&PR 93
Barnard, John Mordaunt 1956- WhoWor 93
Barnard, Judith 1934?- ConAu 139
Barnard, Kate 1875-1930 BioIn 17
Barnard, Kathleen Rainwater 1927- WhoWor 93
Barnard, Kathryn Elaine 1938- WhoAm 92
Barnard, Keith ScF&FL 92
Barnard, Kurt 1927- WhoAm 92
Barnard, Marjorie Faith ScF&FL 92
Barnard, Michael MiSFD 9
Barnard, Michael Dana 1946- WhoAm 92
Barnard, Nicholas 1958- ConAu 139
Barnard, Peter Deane 1932- WhoWor 93
Barnard, Richard Harry WhoScE 91-1
Barnard, Robert BioIn 17
Barnard, Robert C. 1913- WhoWor 93
Barnard, Rollin Dwight 1922- WhoAm 92
Barnard, Sandra Kay 1941- WhoAmW 93
Barnard, Scott Henry 1943- WhoAm 92
Barnard, Seph 1956- WhoEmL 93, WhoWor 93
Barnard, Sheri S. 1937- WhoAmW 93
Barnard, Susan Muller 1935- WhoAm 92
Barnard, Thomas H. 1939- WhoAm 92
Barnard, Tom ConAu 139
Barnard, Tudor Peter Brian 1940- WhoScE 91-4
Barnard, Walther M. 1937- WhoAm 92
Barnard, William Calvert 1914- WhoAm 92
Barnardo, Thomas John 1845-1905 BioIn 17
Barnat, Rhonda Katz 1952- WhoEmL 93
Barnathan, Jack Martin 1959- WhoE 93
Barnathan, Julius 1927- St&PR 93, WhoAm 92
Barnby, Joseph 1838-1896 Baker 92
Barncord, Ronald L. 1947- St&PR 93
Barndorff-Nielsen, Ole Eiler 1935- WhoWor 93
Barnds, John Edward 1932- St&PR 93
Barne, Kitty 1883- AmWomPl
Barnebey, Kenneth Alan 1931- WhoAm 92
Barneby, Mary Rudie St&PR 93
Barnecut, John C. Law&B 92
Barnekow, Christian 1837-1913 Baker 92
Barner, Annabel Monroe 1925- WhoAmW 93
Barner, Brett Lee 1963- WhoEmL 93, WhoSSW 93
Barner, Bruce Monroe 1951- WhoEmL 93, WhoWor 93
Barner, Jennifer Caitlin 1962- WhoAmW 93
Barnes, A. James 1942- WhoAm 92
Barnes, Adrienne Martine- ScF&FL 92
Barnes, Albert Coombs 1872-1951 BioIn 17
Barnes, Allan Randall 1946- WhoEmL 93
Barnes, Alvin F. 1929- St&PR 93
Barnes, Andre LaMont 1957- WhoSSW 93
Barnes, Andrew Earl 1939- WhoAm 92, WhoSSW 93, WhoWrEP 92
Barnes, Barbara Green 1938- WhoSSW 93
Barnes, Ben Blair 1935- WhoSSW 93
Barnes, Benjamin Shields, Jr. 1919- WhoAm 92
Barnes, Benjamin Warren Grant 1948- WhoEmL 93
Barnes, Bernard Ellis 1931- WhoSSW 93
Barnes, Bess AmWomPl
Barnes, Betty Rae 1932- WhoSSW 93
Barnes, Binnie 1905- BioIn 17
Barnes, Brenda St&PR 93
Barnes, Brenda Roney 1947- WhoAmW 93
Barnes, Calvin K. 1929- St&PR 93
Barnes, Candace Eccles 1949- WhoE 93
Barnes, Carla Leddy 1938- WhoAmW 93
Barnes, Carlyle F. 1924- St&PR 93
Barnes, Carlyle Fuller 1924- WhoAm 92
Barnes, Carman Dee 1912- AmWomPl
Barnes, Carol Elizabeth 1938- WhoAmW 93
Barnes, Carol Pardon 1941- WhoAmW 93
Barnes, Carolyn S. Machalec 1957- WhoEmL 93
Barnes, Cathy Lynn 1952- WhoAmW 93
Barnes, Charles Andrew 1921- WhoAm 92
Barnes, Charles D. 1935- WhoAm 92
Barnes, Charles David 1935- St&PR 93
Barnes, Christopher E. 1953- St&PR 93
Barnes, Christopher Richard 1940- WhoAm 92
Barnes, Christopher W. Law&B 92
Barnes, Clare d1992 BioIn 17
Barnes, Clarence A. d1992 BioIn 17
Barnes, Clarence A., Jr. d1992 NewYTBS 92
Barnes, Clarence W. 1938- St&PR 93
Barnes, Clifton Odell 1928- St&PR 93
Barnes, Clive Alexander 1927- WhoAm 92, WhoE 93
Barnes, Constance Ingalls 1903- WhoAmW 93
Barnes, Corinne Ann 1928- WhoAmW 93
Barnes, Craig Martin 1949- WhoEmL 93, WhoSSW 93
Barnes, Cynthia Ann 1949- WhoEmL 93
Barnes, David Robert, Jr. 1952- WhoEmL 93
Barnes, David S. Law&B 92
Barnes, Dawn Cooper 1958- WhoE 93
Barnes, Deborah Dickson 1944- WhoAmW 93
Barnes, Denis Tat WhoAmW 93
Barnes, Dennis Norman 1940- WhoAm 92
Barnes, Diana Marion WhoScE 91-1
Barnes, Dick 1932- WhoWrEP 92
Barnes, Djuna 1892-1982 AmWomPl, AmWr S3, BioIn 17, MagSAmL [port]
Barnes, Donald Frederic 1914- WhoIns 93
Barnes, Donald Gayle 1940- WhoAm 92
Barnes, Donald L. 1943- WhoIns 93
Barnes, Donald Michael 1943- WhoAm 92
Barnes, Donald Winfree 1943- WhoAm 92
Barnes, Douglas J. 1936- St&PR 93
Barnes, Duncan 1935- WhoAm 92, WhoE 93
Barnes, E. Gregory Law&B 92
Barnes, Earl J. Law&B 92
Barnes, Edward F. ConAu 136
Barnes, Edward Larrabee 1915- WhoAm 92
Barnes, Edward Shippen 1887-1958 Baker 92
Barnes, Edwin N. 1946- St&PR 93
Barnes, Eleanor A. AmWomPl
Barnes, Frank Stephenson 1932- WhoAm 92
Barnes, G.W. Law&B 92
Barnes, Gene 1926- WhoWor 93
Barnes, George Elton 1900- WhoAm 92
Barnes, George H., Sr. AfrAmBi
Barnes, George William 1927- WhoAm 92
Barnes, Gloria S. 1922- WhoAmW 93
Barnes, Graham 1935- WhoAsAP 91
Barnes, Grant Alan 1932- WhoAm 92
Barnes, Harris H., III 1946- WhoSSW 93
Barnes, Harry G., Jr. 1926- WhoAm 92
Barnes, Henrietta Lucile 1931- WhoAmW 93
Barnes, Howard G. 1913- WhoAm 92
Barnes, Hubert B. Law&B 92
Barnes, Hubert Lloyd 1928- WhoAm 92
Barnes, Ida M. AmWomPl
Barnes, Iraline G. 1947- St&PR 93
Barnes, Irwin N. Law&B 92
Barnes, Isabel Janet 1936- WhoAm 92
Barnes, James Alford 1944- WhoE 93
Barnes, James Arthur 1954- St&PR 93
Barnes, James E. 1934- St&PR 93, WhoAm 92, WhoSSW 93
Barnes, James Garland, Jr. 1940- WhoAm 92
Barnes, James John 1931- WhoAm 92
Barnes, James McGregor 1953- St&PR 93
Barnes, James Milton 1923- WhoAm 92
Barnes, James R. 1938- St&PR 93
Barnes, Jane Law&B 92
Barnes, Jane Ellen 1943- WhoWrEP 92
Barnes, Jay S. Law&B 92
Barnes, Jay William, Jr. 1924- WhoAm 92
Barnes, Jhane Elizabeth 1954- WhoAm 92, WhoAmW 93
Barnes, Jill 1953- WhoWrEP 92
Barnes, Jim Weaver 1933- WhoWrEP 92
Barnes, Joanna 1934- WhoAm 92
Barnes, John 1957- ScF&FL 92
Barnes, John (Allen) 1957- ConAu 137
Barnes, John Andrew 1960- WhoAm 92
Barnes, John Charles Law&B 92
Barnes, John E. 1935- St&PR 93
Barnes, John Elmer 1948- WhoSSW 93
Barnes, John Fayette 1930- WhoAm 92
Barnes, John H. 1945- St&PR 93
Barnes, John J. 1924- WhoIns 93
Barnes, John Jay 1957- WhoE 93
Barnes, John Joseph 1924- St&PR 93
Barnes, John M. 1924- St&PR 93
Barnes, John R. 1944- St&PR 93
Barnes, John Wadsworth 1920- WhoE 93
Barnes, Jonathan A. 1946- St&PR 93
Barnes, Joy Chappell 1950- WhoEmL 93
Barnes, Judith Anne 1948- WhoEmL 93
Barnes, Judith Elaine 1954- WhoE 93
Barnes, Judy Ann 1950- WhoSSW 93
Barnes, Julian BioIn 17
Barnes, Julian 1946- NewYTBS 92 [port], ScF&FL 92
Barnes, Julian Patrick 1946- WhoWor 93
Barnes, Karen BioIn 17
Barnes, Karen Louise 1942- WhoAmW 93
Barnes, Karen Wink 1958- WhoSSW 93
Barnes, Kate Miller 1953- WhoAmW 93, WhoEmL 93
Barnes, Kay Darlene 1937- WhoAmW 93
Barnes, Keith Allen 1940- St&PR 93
Barnes, Kenneth James WhoScE 91-1
Barnes, Kent Arlyn 1943- WhoSSW 93
Barnes, Kimberly D. Law&B 92
Barnes, L. Burton, III Law&B 92
Barnes, L.V. 1912- St&PR 93
Barnes, Lahna Harris 1947- WhoAmW 93, WhoWor 93
Barnes, Linda 1949- ScF&FL 92
Barnes, Linda Jane 1958- WhoAmW 93
Barnes, Linda Joyce 1949- WhoEmL 93
Barnes, Lisa Graivier Law&B 92

Barnes, Lloyd T. d1992 *NewYTBS 92 [port]*
Barnes, Louie Burton, III 1948- *WhoAm 92, WhoEmL 93, WhoSSW 93*
Barnes, Maggie Lue Shifflett 1931- *WhoAmW 93*
Barnes, Margaret Anderson *WhoAmW 93*
Barnes, Margaret Ayer 1886-1967 *AmWomPl*
Barnes, Mark 1960- *WhoEmL 93*
Barnes, Mark James 1957- *WhoAm 92, WhoEmL 93*
Barnes, Martin E. 1948- *St&PR 93*
Barnes, Martin McRae 1920- *WhoAm 92*
Barnes, Mary 1923- *BioIn 17*
Barnes, Mary Emelia Clark *AmWomPl*
Barnes, Mary Jane 1913- *WhoWrEP 92*
Barnes, Mary Westergaard 1927- *WhoAmW 93*
Barnes, Megan *ScF&FL 92*
Barnes, Melissa Katherine 1952- *WhoAmW 93*
Barnes, Michael (Anthony) 1947- *ConAu 137*
Barnes, Michael C. *Law&B 92*
Barnes, Michael Darr 1943- *WhoAm 92*
Barnes, Michael Edward 1957- *WhoE 93*
Barnes, Michael Francis *Law&B 92*
Barnes, Michael J. *Law&B 92*
Barnes, Michael Robert *WhoScE 91-1*
Barnes, Michelle Annette 1961- *WhoAmW 93*
Barnes, Milton 1931- *Baker 92*
Barnes, Myra Edwards 1933- *ScF&FL 92*
Barnes, Nancy C. *Law&B 92*
Barnes, Nancy Carol 1953- *WhoWrEP 92*
Barnes, Norman Frank 1939- *WhoAm 92*
Barnes, Paul McClung 1914- *WhoAm 92*
Barnes, Paula Carolyn 1952- *WhoEmL 93, WhoSSW 93*
Barnes, Peggy Elizabeth 1958- *WhoAmW 93*
Barnes, Peter 1931- *BioIn 17*
Barnes, Peter A. *Law&B 92*
Barnes, Peter John 1946- *WhoScE 91-1*
Barnes, Philip Andrew *WhoScE 91-1*
Barnes, Randall Curtis 1951- *WhoAm 92*
Barnes, Richard George 1922- *WhoAm 92*
Barnes, Richard Gordon 1932- *WhoAm 92, WhoWrEP 92*
Barnes, Richard J. *St&PR 93*
Barnes, Richard Nearn 1928- *WhoSSW 93*
Barnes, Robert Allan 1927- *St&PR 93*
Barnes, Robert G., Jr. 1929- *St&PR 93*
Barnes, Robert Goodwin 1914- *WhoAm 92, WhoWrEP 92*
Barnes, Robert Lowell 1937- *WhoSSW 93*
Barnes, Robert Merton 1934- *WhoAm 92*
Barnes, Ronald Edwin 1962- *WhoE 93*
Barnes, Rory 1946- *ScF&FL 92*
Barnes, Rosemary Lois 1946- *WhoEmL 93*
Barnes, Roswell Parkhurst 1901-1990 *BioIn 17*
Barnes, Russell Miller 1927- *St&PR 93*
Barnes, Sally Anderson 1955- *WhoSSW 93*
Barnes, Samuel Henry 1931- *WhoAm 92, WhoE 93*
Barnes, Samuel Lee 1941- *St&PR 93*
Barnes, Sandra Henley 1943- *WhoAm 92, WhoAmW 93, WhoWor 93*
Barnes, Sandra Theis 1935- *WhoAmW 93*
Barnes, Scott Andrew 1963- *WhoEmL 93, WhoSSW 93*
Barnes, Scott Martin *Law&B 92*
Barnes, Seaborn d1878 *BioIn 17*
Barnes, Sheryl Lyn 1959- *WhoAmW 93*
Barnes, Sidney W. *BioIn 17*
Barnes, Stephen E. *ScF&FL 92*
Barnes, Stephen E. 1957- *St&PR 93*
Barnes, Stephen Paul 1957- *WhoEmL 93*
Barnes, Steven 1952- *ScF&FL 92*
Barnes, T. Larry *Law&B 92*
Barnes, Teveia R. *Law&B 92*
Barnes, Theodore W. 1931- *WhoAm 92*
Barnes, Thomas E. *Law&B 92*
Barnes, Thomas G. 1930- *WhoAm 92*
Barnes, Thomas Joseph 1930- *WhoAm 92*
Barnes, Thomas V. *AfrAmBi [port]*
Barnes, Thomas Vernon 1936- *WhoAm 92*
Barnes, Timothy Lee 1951- *WhoEmL 93*
Barnes, Tom Mackey 1942- *St&PR 93*
Barnes, V. Lee 1936- *St&PR 93*
Barnes, Veta Richardson 1962- *WhoEmL 93*
Barnes, Veta T. *Law&B 92*
Barnes, Virgil Everett, II 1935- *WhoAm 92*
Barnes, Wade 1917- *WhoWrEP 92*
Barnes, Wallace 1926- *St&PR 93, WhoAm 92, WhoE 93*
Barnes, Wallace R. *Law&B 92*
Barnes, Wallace Ray 1928- *WhoAm 92*
Barnes, Wendell Wright, Jr. 1950- *WhoEmL 93*
Barnes, Wesley Edward 1937- *WhoAm 92*
Barnes, William Arthur, III 1938- *WhoAm 92*
Barnes, William Douglas 1953- *WhoEmL 93*
Barnes, William M. 1925- *St&PR 93*
Barnes, William Oliver, Jr. 1922- *WhoAm 92*
Barnes, William Watson 1936- *WhoSSW 93*
Barnes, Willie R. 1931- *WhoWor 93*
Barnes, Wilson King 1907- *WhoAm 92*
Barnes, Z.E. 1921- *St&PR 93*
Barnes, Zane Edison 1921- *WhoAm 92*
Barnes-Bruce, Mary Hanford *WhoAmW 93*
Barnes-Farrell, Janet Lorraine 1952- *WhoAmW 93, WhoE 93*
Barness, Amnon Shemaya 1924- *WhoAm 92*
Barness, Lewis Abraham 1921- *WhoAm 92*
Bar-Ness, Yeheskel 1932- *WhoAm 92, WhoE 93*
Barnes-Svarney, Patricia *BioIn 17*
Barnet, Boris 1902-1965 *DrEEuF*
Barnet, Charlie 1913- *Baker 92*
Barnet, Charlie 1913-1991 *AnObit 1991, BioIn 17*
Barnet, John H. 1935- *St&PR 93*
Barnet, Miguel 1940- *SpAmA*
Barnet, Peter M. *WhoAm 92*
Barnet, Richard Jackson 1929- *WhoAm 92, WhoWrEP 92*
Barnet, Robert Joseph 1929- *WhoAm 92*
Barnet, Sylvan 1926- *WhoAm 92*
Barnet, Will 1911- *WhoAm 92*
Barnett, Alice 1886-1975 *Baker 92*
Barnett, Allen *BioIn 17*
Barnett, Allen Marshall 1940- *WhoAm 92*
Barnett, Ansley Sartain 1965- *WhoSSW 93*
Barnett, Arthur Doak 1921- *WhoAm 92*
Barnett, Barry Howard 1954- *WhoEmL 93*
Barnett, Benjamin Lewis, Jr. 1926- *WhoAm 92*
Barnett, Bennie Everson 1926- *St&PR 93*
Barnett, Bernard 1920- *WhoAm 92*
Barnett, Bertha L. Strickland 1941- *WhoSSW 93*
Barnett, Betty Gay 1947- *WhoAmW 93*
Barnett, Bill Marvin 1931- *WhoAm 92, WhoWrEP 92*
Barnett, Bonnie 1947- *Baker 92*
Barnett, Bruce H. *Law&B 92*
Barnett, Bruce Philip 1949- *St&PR 93*
Barnett, Burton 1933- *St&PR 93*
Barnett, Camille Cates 1949- *WhoAmW 93*
Barnett, Carol Sue *Law&B 92*
Barnett, Charles E. *Law&B 92*
Barnett, Charles G. *Law&B 92*
Barnett, Charles Robertson 1940- *WhoSSW 93*
Barnett, Christopher Morgan 1955- *WhoEmL 93*
Barnett, Clara *OxDcOp*
Barnett, Clarence F. *BioIn 17*
Barnett, Crawford Fannin, Jr. 1938- *WhoSSW 93, WhoWor 93*
Barnett, Cynthia Ann 1952- *WhoAmW 93*
Barnett, Dana Golden 1941- *St&PR 93*
Barnett, Darlene *Law&B 92*
Barnett, Darrell 1949-1991 *BioIn 17*
Barnett, David Leon 1922- *WhoWrEP 92*
Barnett, Don 1929- *St&PR 93*
Barnett, Edward William 1933- *WhoAm 92*
Barnett, Elizabeth Hale 1940- *WhoAmW 93*
Barnett, Eric Oliver 1929- *WhoWor 93*
Barnett, Gene Austin 1929- *WhoE 93*
Barnett, Gordon James 1921- *WhoE 93*
Barnett, Henry Lewis 1914- *WhoAm 92*
Barnett, Herbert Phillip 1910-1972 *BioIn 17*
Barnett, Hollis 1939- *St&PR 93*
Barnett, Holly Billings 1956- *WhoEmL 93*
Barnett, Homer Garner 1906-1985 *IntDcAn*
Barnett, Howard Albert 1920- *WhoAm 92*
Barnett, Howard Gentry, Jr. 1950- *WhoAm 92*
Barnett, Hoyt Robinson 1943- *St&PR 93*
Barnett, Ida B. Wells- 1862-1931 *BioIn 17*
Barnett, Ida Wells 1862-1931 *EncAACR*
Barnett, Ivan 1947- *SmATA 70 [port]*
Barnett, Jacalyn F. 1952- *WhoAmW 93*
Barnett, Jahnae H. 1946- *WhoAm 92, WhoAmW 93*
Barnett, James *Law&B 92*
Barnett, James Wallace 1930- *WhoAm 92*
Barnett, Jana Ruth 1952- *WhoIns 93*
Barnett, Jane Ayne 1950- *WhoAmW 93*
Barnett, Jerome E. *Law&B 92*
Barnett, Joanne 1954- *WhoEmL 93*
Barnett, John *BioIn 17*
Barnett, John 1802-1890 *Baker 92, OxDcOp*
Barnett, John Francis 1837-1916 *Baker 92*
Barnett, John H. 1942- *WhoAm 92*
Barnett, John (Manley) 1917- *Baker 92*
Barnett, Jonathan 1937- *WhoAm 92*
Barnett, Joseph *OxDcOp*
Barnett, Joyce Perkins 1946- *WhoSSW 93*
Barnett, K.C. *WhoScE 91-1*
Barnett, Karl Fredrick 1927- *St&PR 93*
Barnett, Lauren Ileene 1956- *WhoEmL 93*
Barnett, Lawrence Raymond 1913- *WhoAm 92*
Barnett, Lena Sue 1959- *WhoAmW 93*
Barnett, Lester Alfred 1915- *WhoAm 92*
Barnett, Lisa A. *ScF&FL 92*
Barnett, Lloyd Melville Harcourt 1930- *WhoUN 92*
Barnett, Louis E. *Law&B 92*
Barnett, Marguerite *BioIn 17*
Barnett, Marguerite Ross 1942-1992 *NewYTBS 92 [port]*
Barnett, Mark 1957- *WhoE 93, WhoEmL 93*
Barnett, Mark William 1954- *WhoAm 92*
Barnett, Martha Walters 1947- *WhoAm 92*
Barnett, Mary Louise 1941- *WhoAmW 93*
Barnett, Michael I. 1936- *WhoWor 93*
Barnett, Michael Lancelot 1954- *WhoWor 93*
Barnett, Moneta 1922-1976 *BlkAuII 92*
Barnett, Patricia Ann 1956- *WhoEmL 93*
Barnett, Paul *ScF&FL 92*
Barnett, Peter Ralph 1951- *WhoEmL 93, WhoSSW 93, WhoWor 93*
Barnett, Philip 1937- *St&PR 93*
Barnett, Preston Baker 1946- *St&PR 93*
Barnett, R. David 1926- *WhoAm 92, WhoSSW 93*
Barnett, Ralph Lipsey 1933- *WhoAm 92*
Barnett, Richard Allan *WhoE 93*
Barnett, Richard Blair 1927- *WhoAm 92*
Barnett, Richard Chambers 1932- *WhoAm 92*
Barnett, Richard J. *Law&B 92*
Barnett, Richard Meyer 1934- *St&PR 93*
Barnett, Robert Bruce 1946- *WhoEmL 93*
Barnett, Robert G. *Law&B 92*
Barnett, Robert G. 1933- *St&PR 93*
Barnett, Robert Glenn 1933- *WhoAm 92*
Barnett, Robert Warren 1911- *WhoAm 92*
Barnett, Robert William 1959- *WhoWor 93*
Barnett, Rosalea 1946- *WhoAmW 93*
Barnett, Rosamund *OxDcOp*
Barnett, Stephen *WhoScE 91-1*
Barnett, Stephen G. *Law&B 92*
Barnett, Steve *MiSFD 9*
Barnett, Steven D. *Law&B 92*
Barnett, Steven Dale 1947- *St&PR 93*
Barnett, Stuart Alan 1942- *St&PR 93*
Barnett, Susan Holtzman 1953- *WhoAmW 93*
Barnett, Susanne La Mar 1946- *WhoEmL 93*
Barnett, Theresa A. *Law&B 92*
Barnett, Theresa Ann 1952- *WhoEmL 93*
Barnett, Thomas Buchanan 1919- *WhoAm 92*
Barnett, Thomas Glen 1946- *St&PR 93, WhoEmL 93*
Barnett, Tim *BioIn 17*
Barnett, Trevor N. 1948- *St&PR 93*
Barnett, Tricia Ann *WhoAmW 93*
Barnett, Vic *WhoScE 91-1*
Barnett, Vincent MacDowell, Jr. 1913- *WhoAm 92*
Barnett, Vivian Endicott 1944- *WhoAm 92, WhoAmW 93, WhoE 93*
Barnett, Walter Michael 1903- *WhoAm 92, WhoSSW 93*
Barnett, William A. *Law&B 92*
Barnett, William Arnold 1941- *WhoAm 92*
Barnett, William D., Jr. 1943- *St&PR 93*
Barnett, William Hale 1958- *WhoWor 93*
Barnett, William John 1921- *WhoE 93*
Barnett, Zarah *OxDcOp*
Barnette, C. Joseph 1941- *St&PR 93*
Barnette, Curtis H. 1935- *St&PR 93*
Barnette, Curtis Handley *Law&B 92*
Barnette, Curtis Handley 1935- *WhoAm 92*
Barnette, David Allen 1952- *WhoEmL 93*
Barnette, David J. 1930- *St&PR 93*
Barnette, Dennis Arthur 1941- *WhoAm 92*
Barnette, E.T. *BioIn 17*
Barnette, Elazer J. *BioIn 17*
Barnette, Elbridge Truman *BioIn 17*
Barnette, Henry Wesley 1934- *WhoSSW 93*
Barnette, Joseph D., Jr. 1939- *WhoAm 92*
Barnette, Marge C. 1944- *WhoAmW 93*
Barnette, Martha 1957- *ConAu 136*
Barnett Scharf, Lauren Ileene 1956- *WhoWrEP 92*
Barnev, Petar 1935- *WhoScE 91-4*
Barneva, Margarita 1935- *WhoScE 91-4*
Barnevik, Percy *BioIn 17*
Barnevik, Percy Nils 1941- *WhoAm 92, WhoWor 93*
Barnewall, Gordon Gouverneur 1924- *WhoAm 92*
Barney *ScF&FL 92*
Barney, Amelia A. *Law&B 92*
Barney, Anna Louise 1857?-1931 *AmWomPl*
Barney, C. Lynn 1943- *St&PR 93*
Barney, Carlton Elliott 1946- *St&PR 93*
Barney, Carol Ross 1949- *WhoEmL 93*
Barney, Charles Lester 1925- *WhoAm 92*
Barney, Charles Richard 1935- *WhoAm 92*
Barney, Duane R. 1956- *WhoEmL 93*
Barney, Gerald G. *St&PR 93*
Barney, John A. 1929- *WhoE 93*
Barney, John Charles 1939- *WhoAm 92*
Barney, Joshua 1759-1818 *HarEnMi*
Barney, Lemuel Jackson, Jr. 1945- *BiDAMSp 1989*
Barney, Michael Eugene 1947- *WhoEmL 93, WhoSSW 93*
Barney, Natalie Clifford 1876-1972 *ScF&FL 92*
Barney, Robert John 1952- *WhoEmL 93*
Barney, Thomas McNamee 1938- *WhoAm 92*
Barney, Tina *BioIn 17*
Barney, William Joshua 1911-1991 *BioIn 17*
Barney, William Lesko 1943- *WhoSSW 93*
Barnhard, Ronald Harris 1948- *St&PR 93*
Barnhard, Sherwood A. 1921- *St&PR 93*
Barnhard, Sherwood Arthur 1921- *WhoAm 92, WhoE 93, WhoWor 93*
Barnhardt, D.F. *Law&B 92*
Barnhardt, James Harper 1913- *St&PR 93*
Barnhardt, Robert Alexander 1937- *WhoAm 92*
Barnhardt, T.M. 1932- *St&PR 93*
Barnhardt, Zeb Elonzo, Jr. 1941- *WhoAm 92, WhoSSW 93*
Barnhart, Beverly Jean 1954- *WhoAm 92*
Barnhart, Charles Elmer 1923- *WhoAm 92*
Barnhart, Clarence Lewis 1900- *WhoAm 92, WhoWrEP 92*
Barnhart, David Brown 1956- *WhoEmL 93*
Barnhart, David Knox 1941- *WhoWrEP 92*
Barnhart, Elizabeth Anne 1955- *WhoAmW 93, WhoEmL 93*
Barnhart, Jo Anne B. 1950- *WhoAm 92, WhoAmW 93*
Barnhart, Mary Ann 1930- *WhoSSW 93*
Barnhart, Richard Brown 1933- *WhoE 93*
Barnhart, Steven Robert 1956- *WhoEmL 93*
Barnhill, Barbara Anne 1942- *WhoSSW 93*
Barnhill, Charles Joseph, Jr. 1943- *WhoAm 92*
Barnhill, Charles L. 1934- *St&PR 93*
Barnhill, David Stan 1949- *WhoEmL 93*
Barnhill, Howard Eugene 1923- *WhoAm 92*
Barnhill, John Herschel 1947- *WhoSSW 93*
Barnhill, John W., Jr. 1936- *St&PR 93*
Barnhill, John Warren 1959- *WhoE 93, WhoEmL 93*
Barnhill, Sarah Rives 1949- *WhoSSW 93*
Barnhill, Stephen Fuller 1948- *WhoSSW 93*
Barnholdt, Terry Joseph 1954- *WhoE 93, WhoEmL 93, WhoWor 93*
Barnhouse, Kenneth Jeffrey *Law&B 92*
Barnhouse, Paul E. 1926- *St&PR 93*
Barnhouse, Ruth Tiffany *WhoAmW 93*
Barni, Eduardo Luis 1954- *WhoWor 93*
Barnickol, Karl R. *Law&B 92*
Barnicle, Mike *BioIn 17*
Barnidge, Mary Shen 1948- *WhoWrEP 92*
Barnish, Valerie L. *ScF&FL 92*
Barnoff, Sharon Holloway 1952- *WhoEmL 93*
Barnouw, Dagmar 1936- *ConAu 139*
Barnouw, Erik 1908- *WhoWrEP 92*
Barnouw, Victor 1915-1989 *BioIn 17*
Barns, Doretha Mae Clayton 1917- *WhoAmW 93, WhoWor 93*
Barnstead, William A. 1919- *St&PR 93*
Barnstone, Willis 1927- *WhoAm 92, WhoWrEP 92*
Barnthouse, William Joseph 1948- *WhoEmL 93*
Barnum, Barbara J. 1937- *St&PR 93*
Barnum, Barbara Jun 1937- *WhoWrEP 92*
Barnum, Cheryl *BioIn 17*
Barnum, Daniel Boone 1938- *WhoSSW 93*
Barnum, Donald G. 1931- *St&PR 93*
Barnum, H.B. *SoulM*
Barnum, James Alymer *Law&B 92*
Barnum, John Wallace 1928- *WhoAm 92*
Barnum, Madalene Demarest 1874- *AmWomPl*

Barnum, Mary Ann Mook 1946- WhoAmW 93
Barnum, Nan Martin 1951- WhoEmL 93
Barnum, P.T. 1810-1891 BioIn 17
Barnum, P. T., Jr. MajAI
Barnum, Phineas Taylor 1810-1891 BioIn 17
Barnum, Robert T. 1945- St&PR 93
Barnum, Theodore MajAI
Barnum, Thomas Grossenbach 1932- St&PR 93
Barnum, William Douglas 1946- WhoE 93, WhoEmL 93
Barnum, William H. 1818-1889 PolPar
Barnum, William Henry 1818-1889 BioIn 17
Barnum, William Laird 1916- WhoAm 92
Barnum, William Milo 1927- WhoAm 92, WhoWor 93
Barnwell, Adrienne Knox 1938- WhoAmW 93
Barnwell, D. Robinson 1915- DcAmChF 1960
Barnwell, Franklin Hershel 1937- WhoAm 92
Barnwell, George Morgan, Jr. 1939- WhoSSW 93
Barnwell, Thomas Pinkney, III 1943- WhoAm 92
Barnwell, Virginia Lynn 1961- WhoAmW 93
Barnwell, William 1943- ScF&FL 92
Baro, Ignacio Martin- BioIn 17
Baro, Jose 1927- WhoSSW 93
Barocas, Susan Honey 1952- WhoEmL 93
Barocci, Robert Louis 1942- WhoAm 92
Baroda, Dawna Michele 1967- St&PR 93
Baroda, Marcia Ann 1935- St&PR 93
Baroda, Richard J. 1936- St&PR 93
Baroff, George Stanley 1924- WhoAm 92
Baroff, Lynn Elliott 1949- WhoEmL 93
Baroldi, Giorgio Cesare 1924- WhoWor 93
Barolin, G. WhoScE 91-4
Barolini, Helen 1925- ConAu 39NR, WhoAmW 93, WhoWrEP 92
Barolo, Bruno 1926- WhoScE 91-3
Barolsky, Michael 1947- Baker 92
Barolsky, Paul 1941- WhoAm 92
Baron, Abraham 1922- St&PR 93
Baron, Allen 1935- MiSFD 9
Baron, Allen A. 1941- St&PR 93
Baron, Alma Fay S. 1923- WhoAm 92
Baron, Barbara Ann 1950- WhoAmW 93
Baron, Beth 1958- ConAu 138
Baron, Carolyn 1940- WhoAm 92, WhoE 93, WhoWrEP 92
Baron, Charles Hillel 1936- WhoAm 92
Baron, Christian C.A. 1930- WhoScE 91-2
Baron, Christopher 1943- WhoUN 92
Bar-On, Dan 1938- ConAu 139
Baron, Denis Neville WhoScE 91-1
Baron, Elizabeth Shaw 1951- WhoAmW 93
Baron, Ernst Gottlieb 1696-1760 Baker 92
Baron, Franklin Andrew Merrifield 1923- WhoUN 92, WhoWor 93
Baron, Frederick David 1947- WhoAm 92
Baron, Gino V. 1948- WhoScE 91-2
Baron, Howard N. 1922- St&PR 93
Baron, Ira Saul 1948- WhoSSW 93
Baron, Irwin d1991 BioIn 17
Baron, Ivan BioIn 17
Baron, Jean Claude 1949- WhoScE 91-2
Baron, Jeffrey 1942- WhoAm 92
Baron, Joel R. 1938- St&PR 93
Baron, Judson Richard 1924- WhoAm 92, WhoE 93
Baron, Kim 1949- St&PR 93
Baron, Linda Ann 1943- WhoAmW 93
Baron, Lou BioIn 17
Baron, Martin Raymond 1922- WhoAm 92
Baron, Mary Kelley 1944- WhoWrEP 92
Baron, Maureen Walsh 1930- WhoAmW 93
Baron, Maurice 1889-1964 Baker 92
Baron, Melvin Leon 1927- WhoAm 92
Baron, Naomi Susan 1946- WhoAm 92
Baron, Nick ScF&FL 92
Baron, Paul B. 1921- St&PR 93
Baron, Paul Dulaney 1944- WhoSSW 93
Baron, Robert Adelor 1922- WhoE 93
Baron, Robert Alan 1943- WhoAm 92
Baron, Ron d1991 BioIn 17
Baron, Ronald H. 1950- St&PR 93
Baron, Salo Wittmayer 1895-1989 BioIn 17, JeAmHC
Baron, Samuel 1925- Baker 92, WhoAm 92
Baron, Samuel 1928- WhoAm 92
Baron, Samuel Haskell 1921- WhoAm 92
Baron, Sandra Law&B 92
Baron, Seymour 1923- St&PR 93, WhoAm 92
Baron, Sheldon 1934- WhoAm 92
Baron, Stanley N. BioIn 17
Baron, Steven J. Law&B 92
Baron, Theodore 1928- WhoAm 92
Baron, William J. 1936- St&PR 93
Baron Crespo, Enrique BioIn 17
Barondes, Samuel Herbert 1933- WhoAm 92
Barondess, Jeremiah Abraham 1924- WhoAm 92
Barondess, Linda Hiddemen 1945- WhoAm 92
Baron di Novara 1940- WhoWor 93
Barone, Anthony 1938- WhoE 93
Barone, Anthony A. 1949- St&PR 93
Barone, Anthony L. 1945- St&PR 93
Barone, Antonio 1939- WhoScE 91-3
Barone, Bruce Michael 1949- St&PR 93
Barone, Dennis 1955- WhoWrEP 92
Barone, Donald Anthony 1948- WhoEmL 93
Barone, Edward J. d1992 NewYTBS 92
Barone, Edward J. 1943-1992 BioIn 17
Barone, Francesco Enrico 1923- WhoWor 93
Barone, James George 1947- St&PR 93
Barone, Jeanine Michelle 1953- WhoAmW 93
Barone, John Anthony 1924- WhoAm 92
Barone, Lorenzo 1942- WhoWor 93
Barone, Michael BioIn 17, St&PR 93
Barone, Michael D. 1944- WhoAm 92
Barone, Robert Austin 1942- St&PR 93
Barone, Robert Paul 1937- St&PR 93
Barone, Rose Marie Pace 1920- WhoAm 92, WhoAmW 93, WhoE 93, WhoWrEP 92
Barone, Salvatore V. 1934- St&PR 93
Barone, Sherry Joy 1960- WhoEmL 93
Barone, Stephanie Lynn 1965- WhoAmW 93, WhoE 93
Barone, Stephen Salvatore 1922- WhoAm 92
Barongpa, Sushil 1947- WhoAsAP 91
Baroni, Geno 1930-1984 BioIn 17
Baronner, Robert Francis 1926- St&PR 93, WhoAm 92
Baronnet, Alain Jean 1944- WhoScE 91-2
Baronnet, Jean-Marie 1945- WhoScE 91-2
Baronoff, William Law&B 92
Baronova, Irina 1916- BioIn 17
Barons, Christopher Macon 1953- WhoEmL 93
Baroody, Albert Joseph, Jr. 1952- WhoSSW 93
Baroody, Michael Elias 1946- WhoAm 92
Baroody, Michael Norman, Jr. 1950- WhoE 93
Baroudy, Bahige Mourad 1950- WhoEmL 93, WhoWor 93
Barouh, Victor St&PR 93
Barous, John T. 1933- St&PR 93
Barowsky, Andrew Phillip 1950- St&PR 93
Barowsky, Harris White 1949- WhoEmL 93
Barowsky, Mark St&PR 93
Barozzi, Alva Coplon 1937- WhoE 93
Barpal, I.R. 1940- St&PR 93
Barpal, Isaac Ruben 1940- WhoAm 92
Barquin, Ramon Carlos 1942- WhoAm 92
Barquist, G. Sheldon St&PR 93
Barr, Alfred Lowell 1933- WhoAm 92
Barr, Allan David Stephen WhoScE 91-1
Barr, Amelia E. AmWomPl
Barr, Blaine G. BioIn 17
Barr, Bob BioIn 17
Barr, Carolyn AmWomPl
Barr, Charles F. Law&B 92
Barr, Charles Francis 1950- WhoIns 93
Barr, Charles Joseph Gore 1940- WhoAm 92
Barr, Charlotte A. WhoAmW 93
Barr, Chester Alwyn 1938- WhoSSW 93
Barr, D.I.H. WhoScE 91-1
Barr, Daniel Wayne 1952- WhoEmL 93
Barr, David Charles 1950- WhoAm 92
Barr, David Eric Law&B 92
Barr, David John 1939- WhoAm 92
Barr, David T. 1951- St&PR 93
Barr, Deloris 1950- WhoE 93
Barr, Densil Neve ConAu 40NR
Barr, Donald 1921- ScF&FL 92
Barr, Donald J. WhoAm 92
Barr, Donald Joseph 1935- St&PR 93
Barr, Donald M. 1948- St&PR 93
Barr, Donald Roy 1938- WhoAm 92
Barr, Elisabeth ScF&FL 92
Barr, Frank Forbes Law&B 92
Barr, Fred C. St&PR 93
Barr, Frederick Reichert, Jr. 1956- WhoEmL 93
Barr, Gary Keith 1945- St&PR 93
Barr, George 1937- ScF&FL 92
Barr, George McKinley 1892-1974 BiDAMSp 1989
Barr, Ginger 1947- WhoAmW 93
Barr, Gregory Philip 1949- WhoEmL 93
Barr, Harry Kyle, III Law&B 92
Barr, Henrietta C. AmWomPl
Barr, Howard Raymond 1910- WhoAm 92
Barr, Irwin Robert 1920- WhoAm 92
Barr, J. James 1941- St&PR 93
Barr, Jacob Dexter 1944- WhoAm 92
Barr, James 1924- WhoWor 93
Barr, James David 1943- St&PR 93
Barr, James George 1951- WhoE 93
Barr, James Houston, III 1941- WhoSSW 93
Barr, James Milton 1936- WhoAm 92
Barr, James P. Law&B 92
Barr, Jean G. 1946- WhoAmW 93
Barr, John Baldwin 1932- WhoAm 92
Barr, John D. WhoSSW 93
Barr, John Hanson 1938- St&PR 93
Barr, John Michael 1957- WhoWor 93
Barr, John Robert 1936- WhoAm 92
Barr, John W., III 1921- St&PR 93
Barr, John Watson, III 1921- WhoAm 92
Barr, John Z. 1949- St&PR 93
Barr, Johnnie M. 1952- St&PR 93
Barr, Jon Michael 1938- WhoAm 92
Barr, Joseph W. 1918- St&PR 93
Barr, Joseph Walker 1918- WhoAm 92, WhoWor 93
Barr, Joseph Williston 1949- WhoAm 92
Barr, Katherine Nowell Law&B 92
Barr, Laurence James 1935- St&PR 93
Barr, Marleen S. 1953- ScF&FL 92
Barr, Marlene Joy 1935- WhoAmW 93, WhoWor 93
Barr, Martin 1925- WhoAm 92
Barr, Michael Blanton 1948- WhoAm 92, WhoE 93
Barr, Michael Charles 1947- WhoAm 92, WhoE 93, WhoEmL 93, WhoWor 93
Barr, Michael R. 1949- St&PR 93
Barr, Murray Llewellyn 1908- WhoAm 92
Barr, Nancy Verde 1944- WhoE 93
Barr, Ray D. 1929- St&PR 93
Barr, Rhoda Brooke 1931- WhoAmW 93
Barr, Richard Arthur 1925- WhoE 93
Barr, Richard C. 1934- St&PR 93
Barr, Richard Stuart 1943- WhoSSW 93
Barr, Rita 1929- WhoAmW 93
Barr, Robert 1850-1912 BioIn 17
Barr, Robert Alfred, Jr. 1934- WhoAm 92
Barr, Robert Dale 1939- WhoAm 92
Barr, Robert David 1957- WhoSSW 93
Barr, Robert Edward 1956- WhoSSW 93, WhoWor 93
Barr, Roger Coke 1942- WhoSSW 93
Barr, Roger Moore 1934- WhoE 93
Barr, Roseanne BioIn 17, ConAu 139
Barr, Roseanne 1952- HolBB [port]
Barr, Sanford Lee 1952- WhoEmL 93
Barr, Sheryl Newberry 1950- WhoSSW 93
Barr, Shirley G. 1936- St&PR 93
Barr, Susan Hartline 1942- WhoAmW 93
Barr, Thomas A. 1927- St&PR 93
Barr, Thomas D. 1949- St&PR 93
Barr, Thomas Delbert 1931- WhoAm 92
Barr, Tina 1955- WhoWrEP 92
Barr, Wallace R. 1946- St&PR 93
Barr, William E. Law&B 92
Barr, William G. Law&B 92
Barr, William P. NewYTBS 92 [port]
Barr, William P. 1950- BioIn 17, CurBio 92 [port]
Barr, William Pelham 1950- WhoAm 92, WhoE 93
Barra, Donatella 1941- WhoScE 91-3
Barra, Yves WhoScE 91-2
Barrack, Donald J. Law&B 92
Barrack, Martin Kenneth 1942- WhoE 93
Barrack, Richard M. 1940- St&PR 93
Barrack, William S., Jr. 1929- St&PR 93
Barrack, William Sample, Jr. 1929- WhoAm 92
Barraclough, Charles Arthur 1926- WhoE 93
Barraclough, Elizabeth Dick WhoScE 91-1
Barraclough, Peter Bryan WhoScE 91-1
Barraclough, William George 1935- WhoAm 92
Barraco, Andre 1947- WhoScE 91-2
Barraco, Giuseppe Salvatore Fortunato 1950- WhoWor 93
Barradas, Carlos Helio Barata T. 1927- WhoWor 93
Barragan, Frank, Jr. 1918- St&PR 93
Barragan, Hector M. Law&B 92
Barragan, Linda Diane 1950- WhoEmL 93
Barragan, Luis 1902-1988 BioIn 17
Barragan Munoz, Fernando 1941- WhoWor 93
Barragar, Harvey Claude 1934- WhoAm 92
Barragry, Mary Ann 1948- WhoAmW 93
Barrai, Italo 1931- WhoScE 91-3
Barraine, Elsa 1910- Baker 92
Barraine, Robert J. 1935- WhoScE 91-2
Barrales-Rienda, J.M. 1937- WhoScE 91-3
Barralis, Gilbert 1936- WhoScE 91-2
Barranco, Giuseppe Antonio 1940- WhoWor 93
Barranco, Lisa Antionette 1965- WhoAmW 93
Barranco, Robert George 1940- St&PR 93
Barranger, Milly Slater 1937- WhoAmW 93
Barrante, James Richard 1938- WhoE 93
Barrantes, Barbara Law&B 92
Barrantes, Charles E. 1952- St&PR 93
Barrantes, Francisco Jose 1944- WhoWor 93
Barrantes, Hector d1990 BioIn 17
Barraque, Jean 1928-1973 Baker 92
Barrar, Annette Knight 1939- WhoAmW 93
Barras, Jacques-Melchior Saint Laurent de dc. 1800 HarEnMi
Barrass, Charles Bryan WhoScE 91-1
Barrass, Robert WhoScE 91-1
Barratt, Brian WhoScE 91-1
Barratt, Cynthia Louise 1953- WhoAm 92, WhoAmW 93, WhoEmL 93, WhoSSW 93
Barratt, David ScF&FL 92
Barratt, Donald C. 1937- St&PR 93
Barratt, Eric George 1938- WhoWor 93
Barratt, Ernest Stoelting 1925- WhoAm 92
Barratt, John P. 1944- St&PR 93
Barratt, Louise Bascom AmWomPl
Barratt, Raymond William 1920- WhoAm 92
Barratt-Brown, Michael 1918- ConAu 38NR
Barraud, Henry 1900- Baker 92, OxDcOp
Barraud, J. WhoScE 91-2
Barrault, Jean-Louis 1910- BioIn 17, IntDcF 2-3 [port], OxDcOp
Barrault, Marie-Christine 1944- BioIn 17
Barrax, Gerald William 1933- DcLB 120 [port]
Barraza, Santa 1951- NotHsAW 93
Barrazotto, Mary Elizabeth Law&B 92
Barre, Charles 1950- WhoE 93
Barre, Francoise Sinoussi 1947- WhoWor 93
Barre, Fred D. 1943- St&PR 93
Barre, Georges 1886-1970 HarEnMi
Barre, H. Walter 1948- St&PR 93
Barre, Jean-Paul 1935- WhoWor 93
Barre, Loren D. 1925- St&PR 93
Barre, Raymond BioIn 17
Barre, Raymond 1924- WhoWor 93
Barre, Robert Lawrence 1918- WhoE 93
Barre, Siyad Mohammed 1919- WhoAfr
Barre, Stephen Alan 1938- St&PR 93
Barre, Steven C. Law&B 92
Barre, Steven Craig 1959- WhoE 93
Barre, William Michael 1949- WhoEmL 93
Barrea, Karen Ann 1963- WhoAmW 93
Barreau, Herve Albert 1929- WhoWor 93
Barreau, Jocelyne 1947- WhoScE 91-2
Barreca, Christopher A. Law&B 92
Barreiro, Jose Maria 1793-1819 HarEnMi
Barreiro Del Rio, Laureano 1949- WhoWor 93
Barrelet, Charles Edouard 1934- St&PR 93
Barrell, Bill Douglas 1932- WhoE 93
Barrell, Brigitte BioIn 17
Barrell, Harry Daniel 1941- St&PR 93
Barrellier, Paul 1945- WhoScE 91-2
Barren, Bruce Willard 1942- WhoAm 92, WhoWor 93
Barrenchea, Linda Diane 1958- WhoAmW 93
Barrer, Roger Aaron 1926- WhoAm 92
Barrera, Carl J. Law&B 92
Barrera, Elvira Puig 1943- WhoAmW 93, WhoSSW 93, WhoWor 93
Barrera, Hugo DcCPCAm
Barrera, Laz 1924-1991 AnObit 1991, BioIn 17
Barrera, Oscar BioIn 17
Barrera, Ruben Rivera 1939- WhoWor 93
Barreras del Rio, Petra 1952- NotHsAW 93
Barrere, Clem Adolph 1939- WhoSSW 93
Barrere, Georges 1876-1944 Baker 92
Barrere, Jamie Newton 1946- WhoEmL 93, WhoSSW 93
Barres, Gabriel 1924- WhoScE 91-2
Barres, Maurice 1862-1923 BioIn 17, DcLB 123 [port], TwCLC 47 [port]
Barres, Samuel Lawrence 1924- WhoE 93
Barrese, Robert L. 1947- St&PR 93
Barret, Apollon (Marie-Rose) c. 1803-1879 Baker 92
Barreto, Bruno 1955- MiSFD 9
Barreto, Kathleen Anne Coogan 1954- WhoAmW 93, WhoEmL 93, WhoWor 93
Barreto-Rivera, Rafael 1944- WhoCanL 92
Barrett, A.M., Jr. 1921- St&PR 93
Barrett, Alan H. 1927-1991 BioIn 17
Barrett, Alan John WhoScE 91-1
Barrett, Andrew BioIn 17, WhoAm 92
Barrett, Ann WhoScE 91-1
Barrett, Ann B. 1943- St&PR 93
Barrett, Anthony G. M. 1952- WhoAm 92
Barrett, Arthur Paul 1930- St&PR 93

Barrett, Barbara Bush 1956- *WhoAmW 93*
Barrett, Barbara McConnell 1950- *WhoAm 92, WhoEmL 93*
Barrett, Beatrice Helene 1928- *WhoAm 92, WhoAmW 93, WhoE 93*
Barrett, Benjamin Smith 1920- *WhoSSW 93*
Barrett, Berndan Francis Dominic 1960- *WhoWor 93*
Barrett, Bill 1934- *WhoAm 92*
Barrett, Brian E. 1931- *WhoScE 91-3*
Barrett, Brian James *Law&B 92*
Barrett, Bruce Alan 1950- *WhoEmL 93*
Barrett, Bruce Richard 1939- *WhoAm 92*
Barrett, Carol *St&PR 93*
Barrett, Catherine Glass 1952- *WhoEmL 93*
Barrett, Charles E. 1931- *St&PR 93*
Barrett, Cheryl Lynn 1965- *WhoAmW 93*
Barrett, Clara Hayes *WhoE 93*
Barrett, Colleen C. 1944- *St&PR 93*
Barrett, Colleen Crotty 1944- *WhoAm 92*
Barrett, David D. 1952- *St&PR 93*
Barrett, David Eugene 1955- *WhoEmL 93, WhoSSW 93*
Barrett, David G. 1949- *St&PR 93*
Barrett, David S. 1941- *St&PR 93*
Barrett, David V. 1952- *ScF&FL 92*
Barrett, Deborah Hillman 1962- *WhoEmL 93*
Barrett, Diane Marie 1956- *WhoAmW 93*
Barrett, Dick *ScF&FL 92*
Barrett, Dirk K., Jr. *Law&B 92*
Barrett, Donald V. *St&PR 93*
Barrett, Eaton Stannard 1786-1820 *DcLB 116 [port]*
Barrett, Edward W. 1910-1989 *BioIn 17*
Barrett, Edythe Hart 1915- *WhoAmW 93*
Barrett, Elizabeth Ann Manhart 1934- *WhoAmW 93, WhoE 93*
Barrett, Elizabeth Anne 1961- *WhoEmL 93*
Barrett, Emma 1898-1983 *Baker 92*
Barrett, Eric C. *WhoScE 91-1*
Barrett, Ethel 1892?- *ScF&FL 92*
Barrett, Evelyn Carol 1928- *WhoE 93*
Barrett, Frank Joseph 1932- *WhoAm 92*
Barrett, Frederick Charles 1949- *WhoEmL 93*
Barrett, G.J. 1928- *ScF&FL 92*
Barrett, Gerald R. *ScF&FL 92*
Barrett, Gregory R. 1947- *St&PR 93*
Barrett, Harold C., Jr. 1924- *St&PR 93*
Barrett, Harold Francis, Jr. 1919- *WhoWrEP 92*
Barrett, Herbert 1910- *WhoAm 92*
Barrett, Izadore 1926- *WhoAm 92*
Barrett, Jacquelyn Harrison 1950- *AfrAmBi*
Barrett, James E. 1922- *WhoAm 92*
Barrett, James Lee 1929- *WhoWrEP 92*
Barrett, James P. 1936- *WhoAm 92*
Barrett, James Thomas 1927- *WhoAm 92*
Barrett, Jane Hayes 1947- *WhoAm 92*
Barrett, Jeremiah Joseph 1941- *WhoE 93*
Barrett, Jessica 1952- *WhoAmW 93, WhoEmL 93*
Barrett, Joan 1950- *St&PR 93*
Barrett, John *WhoScE 91-1*
Barrett, John Adams 1937- *WhoAm 92*
Barrett, John Anthony 1942- *WhoAm 92*
Barrett, John F. 1949- *WhoIns 93*
Barrett, John James, Jr. 1948- *WhoEmL 93*
Barrett, John Michael 1963- *WhoSSW 93*
Barrett, John Richard 1928- *WhoSSW 93, WhoWor 93*
Barrett, Joseph Edward 1937- *WhoE 93*
Barrett, Joseph Michael 1934- *WhoAm 92*
Barrett, Joyce Durham 1943- *ConAu 138*
Barrett, Karen Anne 1961- *WhoEmL 93*
Barrett, Karen Moore *Law&B 92*
Barrett, Karen Moore 1950- *WhoEmL 93*
Barrett, Kevin *ScF&FL 92*
Barrett, Laurence 1935- *ScF&FL 92*
Barrett, Laurence Irwin 1935- *WhoAm 92, WhoE 93*
Barrett, Lee Ann 1952- *WhoEmL 93*
Barrett, Lezli-An *MiSFD 9*
Barrett, Lida Kittrell 1927- *WhoAm 92*
Barrett, Lillian *AmWomPl*
Barrett, Linda Ann 1951- *WhoAmW 93*
Barrett, Linda L. 1948- *WhoAmW 93, WhoEmL 93*
Barrett, Loretta Anne 1941- *WhoAm 92*
Barrett, Lucile J. *AmWomPl*
Barrett, Lyle Eugene 1942- *WhoSSW 93, WhoWor 93*
Barrett, Lyn *WhoWrEP 92*
Barrett, M. James *St&PR 93*
Barrett, M. Patricia 1937- *St&PR 93*
Barrett, Mary Sheila 1939- *WhoAmW 93, WhoSSW 93*
Barrett, Matthew W. 1944- *WhoAm 92, WhoE 93, WhoWor 93*
Barrett, Matthew William *BioIn 17*
Barrett, Melanie Taylor 1943- *WhoAmW 93*
Barrett, Michael Dennis 1947- *ScF&FL 92*
Barrett, Michael Henry 1932- *WhoAm 92*
Barrett, Michael J. 1946- *St&PR 93*
Barrett, Michael John 1954- *WhoEmL 93, WhoSSW 93, WhoWor 93*
Barrett, Minna Sara 1948- *WhoEmL 93*
Barrett, Nancy Smith 1942- *WhoAm 92*
Barrett, Neal Jr. 1929- *ScF&FL 92*
Barrett, Nicholas *ScF&FL 92*
Barrett, O'Neill, Jr. 1929- *WhoAm 92*
Barrett, Patricia Louise 1947- *WhoEmL 93*
Barrett, Patricia Ruth 1952- *WhoAmW 93*
Barrett, Patrick J. *Law&B 92*
Barrett, Patrick Joseph *Law&B 92*
Barrett, Paul L. *Law&B 92*
Barrett, Paulette Singer 1937- *WhoAm 92*
Barrett, Peter John *Law&B 92*
Barrett, Philip Roderick Francombe *WhoScE 91-1*
Barrett, Raphael Douglas 1949- *WhoWor 93*
Barrett, Raymond James 1924-1991 *WhoAm 92*
Barrett, Red 1915-1990 *BioIn 17*
Barrett, Richard 1936- *SoulM*
Barrett, Richard David 1931- *WhoAm 92*
Barrett, Richard Hewins 1949- *WhoEmL 93*
Barrett, Richard James 1948- *WhoAm 92*
Barrett, Richard M. *St&PR 93*
Barrett, Robert Daker 1945- *WhoAm 92*
Barrett, Robert James, III 1944- *WhoAm 92*
Barrett, Robert John, Jr. 1917- *WhoAm 92*
Barrett, Robert Mason *Law&B 92*
Barrett, Robert South, IV 1927- *WhoAm 92*
Barrett, Rodney James 1947- *WhoWor 93*
Barrett, Roger Watson 1915- *WhoAm 92*
Barrett, Roland George 1944- *St&PR 93*
Barrett, Ronald Eugene 1923- *St&PR 93*
Barrett, Roy Carmen 1929- *St&PR 93*
Barrett, Samuel Alfred 1879-1965 *IntDcAn*
Barrett, Scott Alexander 1957- *WhoWor 93*
Barrett, Shannon *St&PR 93*
Barrett, Sheila Marie 1967- *WhoAmW 93*
Barrett, "Sid" Roger 1946- *Baker 92*
Barrett, Stephen D. 1941- *St&PR 93*
Barrett, Stephen W. 1956- *WhoIns 93*
Barrett, Steve A. 1952- *AfrAmBi [port]*
Barrett, Susan (Mary) 1938- *ConAu 138*
Barrett, Thomas Rawson 1927- *WhoE 93*
Barrett, Timothy John 1948- *St&PR 93*
Barrett, Tom Hans 1930- *St&PR 93*
Barrett, Tony R. 1939- *St&PR 93*
Barrett, William d1992 *NewYTBS 92 [port]*
Barrett, William (C.) 1913-1992 *CurBio 92N*
Barrett, William (Christopher) 1913-1992 *ConAu 139*
Barrett, William E. 1900-1986 *ScF&FL 92*
Barrett, William E. 1929- *CngDr 91, WhoAm 92*
Barrett, William Hale 1929- *St&PR 93*
Barrett, William Joel 1939- *WhoAm 92, WhoE 93*
Barrett, William Owen 1945- *WhoAm 92*
Barrett, William Thomas 1931- *St&PR 93*
Barretta-Keyser, Jolie 1954- *WhoAmW 93, WhoEmL 93*
Barrett-Connor, Elizabeth Louise 1935- *WhoAm 92, WhoAmW 93*
Barrette, Raymond 1950- *St&PR 93*
Barrett-Kobes, Violet Uline 1955- *WhoE 93*
Barrett Lee, Theresa M. *Law&B 92*
Barrett-Moran, Linda Marie 1947- *WhoE 93*
Barretto, Dennis 1915- *St&PR 93*
Barretto, Gene M. 1929- *St&PR 93*
Barretto, Paulo Marcos de Campos 1939- *WhoUN 92*
Barrett-Watson, Carolyn *BioIn 17*
Barri, Joseph Paul 1946- *St&PR 93*
Barricelli, Jean-Pierre 1924- *WhoWrEP 92*
Barrick, Anita *St&PR 93*
Barrick, William Henry 1916- *WhoAm 92*
Barrick-Pizzo, Victoria Ann *Law&B 92*
Barrie, Barbara Ann 1931- *WhoAm 92*
Barrie, David Scott 1952- *WhoEmL 93*
Barrie, Dennis Ray 1947- *WhoAm 92*
Barrie, Douglas S. 1933- *St&PR 93*
Barrie, George 1943- *St&PR 93*
Barrie, J.M. 1860-1937 *ScF&FL 92*
Barrie, J(ames) M(atthew) 1860-1937 *ConAu 136, MajAI [port]*
Barrie, Jeffrey Edward 1941- *WhoE 93*
Barrie, John Paul 1947- *WhoEmL 93*
Barrie, Monica *ScF&FL 92*
Barrie, Robert 1927- *WhoAm 92*
Barrie, William James 1948- *St&PR 93*
Barrientos, Maria 1884-1946 *Baker 92, IntDcOp*
Barrientos, Robert John 1953- *WhoEmL 93*
Barrier, John Wayne 1949- *WhoEmL 93, WhoSSW 93*
Barrier, Richard George *Law&B 92*
Barriere, Jean c. 1705-1747 *Baker 92*
Barriga Rivas, Rogelio 1912-1961 *DcMexL*
Barrilleaux, Christopher Nissen 1954- *WhoEmL 93, WhoSSW 93*
Barringer, Allen C. *Law&B 92*
Barringer, John Paul 1903- *WhoAm 92, WhoE 93*
Barringer, Margaret Chew 1946- *WhoEmL 93*
Barringer, Paul Brandon 1930- *St&PR 93*
Barringer, Paul Brandon, II 1930- *WhoAm 92, WhoSSW 93*
Barringer, Philip E. 1916- *WhoAm 92*
Barringer, Robert Stewart 1952- *WhoEmL 93*
Barrington, Bruce David 1942- *WhoSSW 93*
Barrington, Daines 1727-1800 *Baker 92*
Barrington, G. Bruce *Law&B 92*
Barrington, James d1992 *BioIn 17*
Barrington, Judith M. 1944- *WhoWrEP 92*
Barrington, Michael *ConAu 38NR*
Barrington, Pauline B. *AmWomPl*
Barrington, Samuel 1729-1800 *HarEnMi*
Barrington-Carlson, Sharyn Marie 1946- *WhoEmL 93*
Barrins, Phyllis Caroline 1921- *WhoAmW 93*
Barrio, Eduardo del *BioIn 17*
Barrio, Jorge Raul 1941- *WhoAm 92*
Barrio, Raymond 1921- *WhoAm 92, WhoWrEP 92*
Barrios, Arturo *BioIn 17*
Barrios, Digby Wayne 1937- *WhoAm 92*
Barrios, Enrique 1945- *ScF&FL 92*
Barrios, George G. 1943- *WhoE 93*
Barrios, Gregg 1945- *DcLB 122 [port]*
Barrios, John Anthony 1969- *WhoEmL 93*
Barrios, Justo Rufino *DcCPCAm*
Barrios, Justo Rufino 1835-1885 *HarEnMi*
Barrios de Chamorro, Violeta *DcCPCAm*
Barrios Fernandez, Angel 1882-1964 *Baker 92*
Barris, Audrey J. *Law&B 92*
Barris, Chuck *MiSFD 9*
Barrish, Beverly Comfort 1935- *WhoAmW 93*
Barriskill, Maudanne Kidd 1932- *WhoAmW 93, WhoWor 93*
Barritt, Evelyn Ruth Berryman 1929- *WhoAm 92*
Barritt, Lester S. 1933- *St&PR 93*
Barro, Mary Helen 1938- *HispAmA*
Barro, Robert Joseph 1944- *WhoAm 92*
Barroin, Guy 1945- *WhoScE 91-2*
Barroll, Katherine Brandt *Law&B 92*
Barron, Almen Leo 1926- *WhoAm 92*
Barron, Anthony Ramirez 1954- *WhoEmL 93*
Barron, Arthur *MiSFD 9*
Barron, Barbara Jane 1959- *WhoEmL 93*
Barron, Barbara Marilyn 1937- *WhoAm 92, WhoAmW 93*
Barron, Bebe 1927- *Baker 92*
Barron, Bruce D. 1952- *St&PR 93*
Barron, Bruce N. 1955- *St&PR 93*
Barron, Caroline 1958- *WhoEmL 93*
Barron, Charles E. 1928- *St&PR 93*
Barron, Charles Elliott 1928- *WhoAm 92*
Barron, Charles Thomas 1950- *WhoE 93, WhoEmL 93*
Barron, Dennis H. 1940- *St&PR 93, WhoAm 92*
Barron, Donald Ray 1947- *St&PR 93*
Barron, Edward L. 1935- *St&PR 93*
Barron, Eugene D. 1958- *WhoEmL 93*
Barron, Frances Marlene 1939- *WhoAmW 93, WhoE 93*
Barron, Francis Patrick 1951- *WhoAm 92, WhoEmL 93*
Barron, Francois 1953- *St&PR 93*
Barron, Gary A. 1944- *St&PR 93*
Barron, Grover Cleveland, III 1948- *WhoEmL 93*
Barron, Harold S. *Law&B 92*
Barron, Harold Sheldon 1936- *WhoAm 92*
Barron, Heidi *Law&B 92*
Barron, Howard Robert 1930- *WhoAm 92*
Barron, Ilona Eleanor 1929- *WhoAmW 93*
Barron, James 1768-1851 *HarEnMi*
Barron, James Turman 1954- *WhoE 93*
Barron, Jerome Aure 1933- *WhoAm 92*
Barron, Joan Marie 1929- *WhoAmW 93*
Barron, John Field 1952- *St&PR 93*
Barron, Judy 1939- *ConAu 137*
Barron, Kenneth George 1942- *WhoE 93*
Barron, Kevin Delgado 1929- *WhoAm 92*
Barron, Laurence David *WhoScE 91-1*
Barron, Laurence David 1944- *WhoWor 93*
Barron, Lisbeth R. 1962- *St&PR 93*
Barron, Lisbeth Rae 1962- *WhoEmL 93*
Barron, Louis 1919-1990 *BioIn 17*
Barron, Louis 1920- *Baker 92*
Barron, Medora Ann 1924- *WhoAmW 93*
Barron, Mel *St&PR 93*
Barron, Michael Peter 1939- *WhoSSW 93*
Barron, Millard E. 1949- *St&PR 93*
Barron, Neil 1934- *ScF&FL 92*
Barron, (Richard) Neil 1934- *ConAu 37NR*
Barron, Patricia C. *St&PR 93*
Barron, Patrick Kenneth 1945- *WhoSSW 93*
Barron, Peggy Pennisi 1958- *WhoAmW 93, WhoEmL 93*
Barron, Peter Mark 1957- *WhoWor 93*
Barron, Randall Franklin 1936- *WhoSSW 93*
Barron, Ray 1925- *WhoWrEP 92*
Barron, Robert A. 1933- *St&PR 93*
Barron, Roberta 1940- *WhoAmW 93*
Barron, Ros 1933- *WhoAm 92*
Barron, Samuel 1809-1888 *HarEnMi*
Barron, Sean *BioIn 17*
Barron, Steve 1956- *MiSFD 9*
Barron, Susan 1940- *WhoAmW 93, WhoE 93*
Barron, Susan 1945- *BioIn 17*
Barron, T.A. *ScF&FL 92*
Barron, Thomas 1949- *WhoEmL 93*
Barron, William Worth, Jr. 1949- *WhoSSW 93*
Barron, Zelda *MiSFD 9*
Barrone, Gerald Doran 1931- *WhoAm 92*
Barrone, Julia A. *Law&B 92*
Barronton, Deward Neal 1937- *St&PR 93*
Barros, Anna Maria 1956- *WhoAmW 93*
Barros, Fernando Correa de 1942- *WhoWor 93*
Barros, Paulo 1958- *WhoScE 91-3*
Barros E. Sousa, Maria Luisa de *WhoScE 91-3*
Barroso, Angel Arevalo *WhoScE 91-3*
Barroso, Augusto Manuel Carvalho 1945- *WhoWor 93*
Barroso Neto, Joaquim Antonio 1881-1941 *Baker 92*
Barrott, John C. 1964- *St&PR 93*
Barrow, Betty Harris 1950- *St&PR 93*
Barrow, C.W.M. *WhoScE 91-1*
Barrow, Charles Herbert 1930- *St&PR 93, WhoAm 92*
Barrow, Charles Wallace 1921- *WhoAm 92*
Barrow, Christopher John 1950- *WhoWor 93*
Barrow, Donald F. d1991 *BioIn 17*
Barrow, Errol 1920-1987 *DcCPCAm*
Barrow, Frank Pearson, Jr. 1928- *WhoAm 92*
Barrow, Hugh Will, Jr. 1949- *WhoSSW 93*
Barrow, Isaac 1630-1677 *BioIn 17*
Barrow, James J. *Law&B 92*
Barrow, John David *WhoScE 91-1*
Barrow, Kal 1933- *WhoE 93*
Barrow, Lionel Ceon, Jr. 1926- *WhoAm 92*
Barrow, Lloyd H. 1942- *SmATA 73 [port]*
Barrow, Louis *ScF&FL 92*
Barrow, Martin G. 1944- *WhoAsAP 91*
Barrow, Mary Claire 1950- *WhoSSW 93*
Barrow, Nita *BioIn 17*
Barrow, Robert Earl 1930- *WhoAm 92*
Barrow, Robert Guy 1936- *St&PR 93*
Barrow, Ruth Nita 1916- *WhoWor 93*
Barrow, Stephen A. 1934- *St&PR 93*
Barrow, Thomas Davies 1924- *WhoAm 92, WhoWor 93*
Barrow, Thomas Francis 1938- *WhoAm 92*
Barrow, Wylie Winfield 1935- *St&PR 93*
Barrowman, Mike *BioIn 17*
Barrows, David Prescott 1873-1954 *IntDcAn*
Barrows, Frank *BioIn 17*
Barrows, Frank Clemence 1946- *WhoSSW 93*
Barrows, John 1913-1974 *Baker 92*
Barrows, Mabel Hay 1873- *AmWomPl*
Barrows, Margaret Ann 1955- *WhoAmW 93*
Barrows, Marjorie *AmWomPl*
Barrows, Richard Lee 1945- *WhoAm 92*
Barrows, Robert Guy 1926- *WhoWor 93*
Barrucand, Dominique 1933- *WhoScE 91-2*
Barrus, Paul Wells *BioIn 17*
Barrus, Tim *ScF&FL 92*
Barry, Alfred E. 1935- *St&PR 93*
Barry, Allan Ronald 1945- *WhoSSW 93, WhoWor 93*
Barry, Arthur J. 1909-1990 *BioIn 17*
Barry, B.T.K. *WhoScE 91-1*
Barry, Ben *WhoWrEP 92*
Barry, Betty Lynn 1946- *WhoEmL 93*
Barry, Bonnie B. 1940- *WhoAmW 93*
Barry, Brent *BioIn 17*
Barry, Brian Michael *WhoScE 91-1*

Barry, Brian William *WhoScE 91-1*
Barry, Christopher John 1947- *WhoEmL 93*
Barry, Colman James 1921- *WhoAm 92*
Barry, Daniel F. 1946- *St&PR 93*
Barry, Daniel Leo 1951- *St&PR 93*
Barry, Daniel Patrick 1947- *St&PR 93*
Barry, Dave *BioIn 17, WhoAm 92, WhoWrEP 92*
Barry, David A. 1946- *St&PR 93*
Barry, David E. 1925- *St&PR 93*
Barry, David N. 1927- *St&PR 93*
Barry, David N., III *Law&B 92, WhoAm 92*
Barry, David Richard 1935- *St&PR 93*
Barry, Desmond Thomas, Jr. 1945- *WhoAm 92*
Barry, Donald H. 1938- *St&PR 93*
Barry, Donald J., Jr. 1946- *St&PR 93*
Barry, Donald Lee 1953- *WhoEmL 93, WhoWor 93*
Barry, Donald Martin 1944- *WhoE 93*
Barry, Douglas Albert 1961- *WhoEmL 93*
Barry, Drew *BioIn 17*
Barry, Edmund D. *Law&B 92*
Barry, Edward William 1937- *St&PR 93, WhoAm 92, WhoWrEP 92*
Barry, Effi *BioIn 17*
Barry, Elizabeth Lottes 1958- *WhoEmL 93*
Barry, Emma Jeannie 1949- *WhoAmW 93*
Barry, Francis Julian, Jr. 1949- *WhoAm 92, WhoEmL 93*
Barry, Franklyn Stanley, Jr. 1939- *St&PR 93*
Barry, Gene 1919- *WhoAm 92*
Barry, George C. *Law&B 92*
Barry, Gerald 1952- *Baker 92*
Barry, Gertrude *AmWomPl*
Barry, Harriet Rita 1933- *WhoE 93*
Barry, Helen Bryant 1918- *WhoAmW 93*
Barry, Herbert, III 1930- *WhoAm 92, WhoWor 93*
Barry, Iris 1895-1969 *ScF&FL 92*
Barry, J. Edward 1912- *St&PR 93*
Barry, James Michael 1956- *WhoEmL 93*
Barry, James Patrick *Law&B 92*
Barry, James Potvin 1918- *WhoWor 93*
Barry, James Russell 1960- *WhoEmL 93*
Barry, James W. d1991 *BioIn 17*
Barry, Jan 1943- *WhoWrEP 92*
Barry, Janet Cecilia 1944- *WhoAmW 93*
Barry, Jeff *SoulM*
Barry, Jerard Michael 1942- *WhoWor 93*
Barry, Jerome 1939- *Baker 92*
Barry, Joan 1953- *WhoEmL 93*
Barry, Joel Mark 1950- *St&PR 93*
Barry, John 1745-1803 *BioIn 17, HarEnMi*
Barry, John A(bbott) 1948- *ConAu 139*
Barry, John Abbott 1948- *WhoWrEP 92*
Barry, John Eduard 1959- *WhoEmL 93*
Barry, John Francis, Jr. *Law&B 92*
Barry, John H. 1931- *St&PR 93*
Barry, John J. *WhoAm 92*
Barry, John Kevin 1925- *WhoAm 92*
Barry, John Reagan 1921- *WhoAm 92, WhoSSW 93*
Barry, John S. *Law&B 92*
Barry, John Stephen 1924- *St&PR 93*
Barry, Jon *BioIn 17*
Barry, Jonathan *ScF&FL 92*
Barry, Joseph Amber 1917- *WhoWor 93*
Barry, Joyce Alice 1932- *WhoAmW 93*
Barry, Kathleen E. *Law&B 92*
Barry, Kenneth Andrew *Law&B 92*
Barry, Lei 1941- *WhoAmW 93*
Barry, Len 1942- *SoulM*
Barry, Lynda *BioIn 17, WhoAm 92*
Barry, Lynda 1956- *Au&Arts 9 [port], News 92 [port]*
Barry, Lynda (Jean) 1956- *ConAu 138*
Barry, Lynne M. *Law&B 92*
Barry, Lynne Marie 1961- *WhoAmW 93*
Barry, Margaret Stuart 1927- *ChlFicS*
Barry, Marilyn White 1936- *WhoE 93*
Barry, Marion 1936- *BioIn 17*
Barry, Marion S. 1936- *EncAACR, PolPar*
Barry, Mark Philip 1952- *WhoE 93*
Barry, Mary Alice 1928- *St&PR 93, WhoAm 92*
Barry, Maryanne Trump 1937- *WhoAm 92, WhoAmW 93*
Barry, Michaela Marie 1960- *WhoEmL 93*
Barry, Mimi Neal *WhoWrEP 92*
Barry, Nancy *BioIn 17*
Barry, Patricia Pound 1941- *WhoAm 92*
Barry, Patrick R. 1949- *WhoSSW 93*
Barry, Peter E. 1927- *St&PR 93*
Barry, Peter Neil 1940- *WhoSSW 93*
Barry, Peter Townsley *WhoScE 91-1*
Barry, Philip Semple 1923- *WhoAm 92*
Barry, Richard *BioIn 17*
Barry, Richard E. *Law&B 92*
Barry, Richard Francis 1917- *WhoAm 92*
Barry, Richard Francis, III 1943- *WhoAm 92, WhoSSW 93, WhoWrEP 92*
Barry, Rick *BioIn 17*
Barry, Rick 1944- *WhoAm 92*
Barry, Robert Louis 1934- *WhoE 93*
Barry, Robertine 1863-1910 *BioIn 17*
Barry, Roger Graham 1935- *WhoAm 92*
Barry, Scooter *BioIn 17*
Barry, Susan Brown 1944- *WhoAmW 93, WhoWor 93*
Barry, Thomas Anthony 1918- *WhoE 93, WhoWor 93*
Barry, Thomas Corcoran 1944- *WhoAm 92*
Barry, Thomas Hubert 1918- *WhoAm 92, WhoWor 93*
Barry, Thomas Joseph 1955- *WhoEmL 93*
Barry, Thomas K. 1945- *St&PR 93*
Barry, Thomas M. 1949- *St&PR 93, WhoE 93, WhoEmL 93*
Barry, Tom 1950- *ConAu 139*
Barry, William A(nthony) 1930- *ConAu 38NR*
Barry, William Anthony 1930- *WhoE 93*
Barry, William Earl 1937- *WhoSSW 93*
Barry, William Edward 1957- *WhoEmL 93*
Barry, William Farquhar 1818-1878 *HarEnMi*
Barry, William Garrett, III 1955- *WhoAm 92*
Barry, William H. 1918- *St&PR 93*
Barry, William James 1927- *St&PR 93*
Barry, William W. 1932- *WhoAm 92*
Barrymore, Blanche Marie Louise Oelrichs *AmWomPl*
Barrymore, Drew *BioIn 17*
Barrymore, Drew 1975- *ConAu 139*
Barrymore, Ethel 1879-1959 *BioIn 17, IntDcF 2-3*
Barrymore, John 1882-1942 *BioIn 17, IntDcF 2-3 [port]*
Barrymore, Lionel 1878-1954 *BioIn 17, IntDcF 2-3, MiSFD 9N*
Bars, Ivars John 1954- *WhoEmL 93*
Barsa, Karyn Odette 1961- *WhoAmW 93*
Barsa, Michael S. 1944- *St&PR 93*
Barsalona, Frank Samuel 1938- *WhoAm 92, WhoE 93, WhoWor 93*
Barsalou, Eric 1935- *WhoScE 91-2*
Barsan, George M. 1937- *WhoScE 91-4*
Barsan, Richard Emil 1945- *WhoWor 93*
Barsan, Robert Blake 1948- *WhoEmL 93, WhoWor 93*
Barsanouphios dc. 545 *OxDcByz*
Barsanti, Francesco c. 1690-1772 *Baker 92*
Barsanti, John Richard, Jr. 1928- *WhoAm 92*
Barsanti, Robert Randolph 1932- *St&PR 93*
Barsauma 415?-496 *OxDcByz*
Bar-Sauma, Rabban 1225?- *Expl 93*
Barschall, Henry Herman 1915- *WhoAm 92*
Barschdorff, Dieter 1935- *WhoScE 91-3, WhoWor 93*
Barselou, Paul Edgar 1922- *WhoAm 92*
Barsh, Gregory Scott 1961- *WhoEmL 93*
Barshad, Yoav 1956- *WhoWor 93*
Barshai, Rudolf (Borisovich) 1924- *Baker 92, WhoAm 92*
Barshay, Robert Howard *ScF&FL 92*
Barshop, Irving d1991 *BioIn 17*
Barshop, Mark N. 1953- *St&PR 93*
Barshop, Ronald Charles 1959- *WhoSSW 93*
Barshop, Samuel Edwin 1929- *St&PR 93*
Barshter, Nancy E. *Law&B 92*
Barsi, Louis Michael 1941- *WhoE 93, WhoWor 93*
Barsimson, Jacob fl. 17th cent.- *BioIn 17*
Barsky, Belle *AmWomPl*
Barsky, Bernard *St&PR 93*
Barsky, David L. 1943- *St&PR 93*
Barsness, John 1952- *ConAu 139*
Barsness, Peggy Ann *BioIn 17*
Barsness, Richard Webster 1935- *WhoAm 92*
Barsocchini, Reno d1986 *BioIn 17*
Barsom, George Martin 1940- *St&PR 93*
Barsony, Istvan 1948- *WhoWor 93*
Barsotti, Sylvia 1956- *WhoAmW 93*
Barsoum, Camelia K. *St&PR 93*
Barsova, Valeria 1892-1967 *Baker 92*
Barsova, Valeriya 1892-1967 *OxDcOp*
Barstis, George A. *St&PR 93*
Barstow, Josephine 1940- *OxDcOp*
Barstow, Josephine (Clare) 1940- *Baker 92*
Barstow, Paul Rogers 1925- *WhoE 93*
Barstow, Roland J. 1919- *St&PR 93, WhoAm 92*
Barsumas 415?-496 *OxDcByz*
Barsy, Imre Joseph, Jr. 1953- *WhoEmL 93*
Barszczewska, Elzbieta 1913-1987 *PolBiDi*
Bart, A. 1937- *WhoScE 91-2*
Bart, Daniel L. *Law&B 92*
Bart, Edward 1917- *WhoIns 93*
Bart, Jan Christiaan Jozef 1941- *WhoWor 93*
Bart, Jean *AmWomPl*
Bart, Jean 1650-1702 *HarEnMi*
Bart, Lionel 1930- *WhoWor 93*
Bart, Margo *Law&B 92*
Bart, Peter *BioIn 17*
Bart, Peter Benton 1932- *WhoAm 92*
Bart, Polly Turner 1944- *WhoAmW 93*
Bart, Randall Kerr 1952- *WhoEmL 93*
Bart, Walter John, Jr. 1943- *St&PR 93*
Barta, Carol Marie 1960- *WhoAmW 93*
Barta, Frank Rudolph, Sr. 1913- *WhoAm 92, WhoWor 93*
Barta, Fredrick Michael 1949- *WhoEmL 93*
Barta, Gyorgy 1915- *WhoScE 91-4*
Barta, James Omer 1931- *WhoAm 92*
Barta, Josef c. 1746-1787 *Baker 92*
Barta, Kent *Law&B 92*
Barta, Lubor 1928-1972 *Baker 92*
Barta, Otto 1916- *WhoScE 91-4*
Barta, Thomas James 1940- *St&PR 93*
Bartak, Gary J. 1953- *WhoEmL 93*
Bartali, Gino *BioIn 17*
Bartalini, C. Richard 1931- *WhoAm 92*
Bartalus, Istvan 1821-1899 *Baker 92*
Bartay, Andreas 1799-1854 *Baker 92*
Bartay, Ede 1825-1901 *Baker 92*
Bartch, Stephen Carl 1965- *WhoE 93*
Bartchy, Rodney Richard 1949- *St&PR 93*
Barte, William B. *Law&B 92*
Barteau, John 1928- *St&PR 93*
Barteau, John Frank 1928- *WhoAm 92*
Barteau, Mary Alice 1963- *WhoEmL 93*
Bartee, Sam 1948- *WhoEmL 93*
Bartee, Stephen William 1950- *WhoE 93*
Bartee, Ted Ray 1938- *WhoSSW 93*
Bartee, Thomas Creson 1926- *WhoAm 92*
Bartek, Gordon Luke 1925- *WhoWor 93*
Bartek, Kevin George 1964- *WhoE 93*
Bartel, Alice J. 1946- *WhoEmL 93*
Bartel, Charles H. *Law&B 92*
Bartel, Fred Frank 1917- *WhoAm 92*
Bartel, Kazimierz 1882-1941 *PolBiDi*
Bartel, Lavon Lee 1951- *WhoEmL 93*
Bartel, Paul 1938- *MiSFD 9*
Bartel, Pauline C. 1952- *WhoWrEP 92*
Bartel, Richard Joseph 1950- *WhoEmL 93, WhoSSW 93*
Bartel, Roger Francis 1951- *WhoEmL 93*
Bartel, Ryszard 1934- *WhoScE 91-4*
Barteld, John T. 1946- *St&PR 93*
Bartelds, Geert 1935- *WhoScE 91-3*
Bartelds, Robert Willem 1947- *WhoWor 93*
Bartell, George D. *St&PR 93*
Bartell, George H., Jr. *St&PR 93*
Bartell, James E. 1942- *St&PR 93*
Bartell, James Elliot 1942- *WhoSSW 93*
Bartell, Jeffrey Bruce 1943- *WhoAm 92*
Bartell, Lawrence Sims 1923- *WhoAm 92*
Bartelmay, Dale Nevin 1926- *St&PR 93*
Bartelme, Joe d1991 *BioIn 17*
Bartelme, Lisa Marie 1967- *WhoAmW 93*
Bartelmus, Peter L.P. 1942- *WhoUN 92*
Bartels, Betty J. 1925- *WhoAmW 93*
Bartels, Bruce Michael 1946- *WhoAm 92*
Bartels, Busso 1940- *WhoUN 92*
Bartels, Donald Hoyt 1948- *WhoEmL 93*
Bartels, G. *WhoScE 91-3*
Bartels, Jean Ellen 1949- *WhoAmW 93*
Bartels, John Ries 1897- *WhoAm 92, WhoE 93*
Bartels, Juergen E. 1940- *St&PR 93, WhoAm 92*
Bartels, Louis J. 1927- *St&PR 93*
Bartels, Millard 1905- *WhoAm 92*
Bartels, Peter T. *WhoAm 92*
Bartels, Polly Elizabeth 1962- *WhoAmW 93*
Bartels, Stanley Leonard 1927- *WhoAm 92*
Bartels, Ursula Brennan *Law&B 92*
Bartels, Wolfgang von 1883-1938 *Baker 92*
Bartelstone, Rona Sue 1951- *WhoAm 92, WhoAmW 93*
Bartelstone, Steven David 1947- *WhoAm 92*
Bartelstone, Ted Henry 1950- *WhoEmL 93*
Bartelt, Wilbert Bruce 1936- *St&PR 93*
Barten, David *BioIn 17*
Bartenstein, Louis 1946- *St&PR 93, WhoIns 93*
Barter, Barbara Ann 1934- *WhoAmW 93, WhoWor 93*
Barter, Catherine J. *Law&B 92*
Barter, John W. 1946- *St&PR 93*
Barter, John William, III 1946- *WhoAm 92*
Barter, Judith Ann 1951- *WhoE 93*
Barter, Robert Henry 1913- *WhoAm 92*
Barter, Ruby Sunshine *WhoAmW 93*
Barter, Scott Torrey 1959- *WhoSSW 93*
Barter, Stephen Leslie 1957- *WhoWor 93*
Barth, Barry Jay *Law&B 92*
Barth, Christian A. 1935- *WhoScE 91-3*
Barth, David E. *Law&B 92*
Barth, David K. 1943- *St&PR 93*
Barth, David Keck 1943- *WhoAm 92*
Barth, Delbert Sylvester 1925- *WhoAm 92*
Barth, Diana *WhoWrEP 92*
Barth, Douglas Kent *Law&B 92*
Barth, Edward X. 1957- *St&PR 93*
Barth, Elmer Ernest 1922- *WhoAm 92*
Barth, Frances D. 1946- *WhoAm 92, WhoEmL 93*
Barth, Hans 1897-1956 *Baker 92*
Barth, Heinrich 1821-1865 *Expl 93, IntDcAn*
Barth, Ilene Joan 1944- *WhoAm 92*
Barth, James Richard 1943- *WhoAm 92*
Barth, Jeffrey Lynn 1951- *WhoEmL 93*
Barth, John *BioIn 17*
Barth, John 1930- *MagSAmL [port], ScF&FL 92, ShSCr 10 [port]*
Barth, John M. 1946- *St&PR 93*
Barth, John Robert 1931- *WhoAm 92*
Barth, John Simmons 1930- *WhoAm 92, WhoE 93, WhoWor 93, WhoWrEP 92*
Barth, Karl Heinrich 1847-1922 *Baker 92*
Barth, Mark Harold 1951- *WhoEmL 93*
Barth, Markus Karl 1915- *WhoWor 93*
Barth, Max 1907- *WhoAm 92*
Barth, Michael Carl 1941- *WhoAm 92*
Barth, Norman Henry 1957- *WhoWor 93*
Barth, Peter 1937- *WhoE 93*
Barth, R(obert) L(awrence) 1947- *WhoWrEP 92*
Barth, Richard 1850-1923 *Baker 92*
Barth, Richard 1931- *St&PR 93, WhoAm 92*
Barth, Roger 1951- *WhoE 93*
Barth, Roger Vincent 1938- *WhoAm 92, WhoWor 93*
Barth, Rolf Frederick 1937- *WhoAm 92*
Barth, Sandra Lynne 1956- *WhoEmL 93*
Barth, Stephen Joseph 1948- *St&PR 93*
Bartha, Adorjan 1923- *WhoScE 91-4*
Bartha, Denes 1908- *Baker 92*
Bartha, Gabor 1947- *WhoScE 91-4*
Bartha, Laszlo 1931- *WhoScE 91-4*
Bartha, Richard 1934- *WhoE 93*
Barthe, Grat-Norbert 1828-1898 *Baker 92*
Barthel, Cheryl Ann 1961- *WhoEmL 93*
Barthel, Edward P. *Law&B 92*
Barthel, F. Ernest 1933- *St&PR 93, WhoAm 92*
Barthel, Henner Lutz 1947- *WhoWor 93*
Barthel, Johannes *WhoScE 91-3*
Barthel, Josef M.G. 1929- *WhoScE 91-3*
Barthelemon, Francois-Hippolyte 1741-1808 *Baker 92*
Barthelemy, Robert R. *BioIn 17*
Barthelemy, Sidney *BioIn 17*
Barthelemy, Sidney John 1942- *WhoAm 92, WhoSSW 93*
Barthelmas, Ned Kelton 1927- *WhoAm 92, WhoWor 93*
Barthelme, Donald *BioIn 17*
Barthelme, Donald 1907- *WhoAm 92*
Barthelme, Donald 1931-1989 *MagSAmL [port], ScF&FL 92*
Barthelme, Frederick *BioIn 17*
Barthelme, Steve(n) 1947- *ConAu 136*
Barthelmes, Richard Brian 1938- *WhoAm 92*
Barthelmes, William Harold 1946- *St&PR 93*
Barthelmess, Richard 1895-1963 *BioIn 17, IntDcF 2-3 [port]*
Barthelmess, Stephan Friedrich 1959- *WhoWor 93*
Barthel-Rosa, Paulo Roberto 1939- *WhoUN 92*
Barthes, Roland *BioIn 17*
Barthold, Clementine B. 1921- *WhoAmW 93*
Barthold, Lionel Olav 1926- *WhoAm 92*
Bartholdson, John Robert 1944- *St&PR 93, WhoAm 92*
Bartholemew, Linda Curry 1948- *St&PR 93*
Bartholet, Elizabeth 1940- *WhoAm 92*
Bartholoma, Manfred *Law&B 92*
Bartholomae, Eric Thompson 1961- *WhoE 93*
Bartholomae, Richard C. 1925- *St&PR 93*
Bartholomaus, Carl G. *Law&B 92*
Bartholomay, William C. 1928- *WhoAm 92, WhoIns 93, WhoSSW 93, WhoWor 93*
Bartholomay, William Conrad 1928- *St&PR 93*
Bartholome, Lloyd W. *BioIn 17*
Bartholomee, Pierre 1937- *Baker 92*
Bartholomew *OxDcByz*
Bartholomew, Alan Alfred 1953- *WhoE 93*
Bartholomew, Anita 1949- *WhoAmW 93, WhoE 93, WhoEmL 93*
Bartholomew, Arthur Peck, Jr. 1918- *WhoAm 92*
Bartholomew, Barbara 1941- *ScF&FL 92*
Bartholomew, Byron Simpson 1927- *St&PR 93*
Bartholomew, Dave *BioIn 17*
Bartholomew, Dave 1920- *SoulM*
Bartholomew, David John *WhoScE 91-1*

Bartholomew, Donald Dekle 1929- WhoWor 93
Bartholomew, Frank H. 1898-1985 DcLB 127 [port]
Bartholomew, Freddie d1992 NewYTBS 92 [port]
Bartholomew, Freddie 1924-1992 BioIn 17
Bartholomew, Gary Alan 1956- WhoEmL 93
Bartholomew, George A. BioIn 17
Bartholomew, George Adelbert 1919- WhoAm 92
Bartholomew, Gilbert Alfred 1922- WhoAm 92
Bartholomew, James J. 1934- St&PR 93
Bartholomew, Jean SmATA 73
Bartholomew, Linda Curry 1948- WhoE 93
Bartholomew, Lloyd Gibson 1921- WhoAm 92
Bartholomew, Reginald 1936- WhoAm 92
Bartholomew, William Lee 1950- WhoEmL 93, WhoWor 93
Barthou, Jean Louis 1862-1934 BioIn 17
Barth-Wehrenalp, Gerhard 1920- WhoAm 92
Bartice, Gregory M. 1951- St&PR 93
Bartilson, William R., Sr. Law&B 92
Bartilucci, Andrew Joseph 1922- WhoAm 92
Bartizal, Robert George 1932- WhoAm 92
Bartko, Pavol 1931- WhoScE 91-4
Bartkowech, Raymond A. 1950- WhoWrEP 92
Bartkowski, Alison Mary 1967- WhoAmW 93
Bartkowski, Eugene H. 1934- WhoIns 93
Bartkowski, Frances 1948- ScF&FL 92
Bartkowski, Stanislaw B. 1933- WhoScE 91-4
Bartkowski, William Patrick 1951- St&PR 93
Bartkus, John Gregory 1960- WhoEmL 93
Bartkus, Richard Anthony 1931- WhoAm 92
Bartl, Hans 1933- WhoScE 91-3
Bartl, James F. Law&B 92
Bartl, James F. 1940- St&PR 93
Bartle, Annette Gruber WhoAm 92, WhoAmW 93, WhoWor 93
Bartle, Emery Warness 1943- WhoAm 92
Bartle, Robert Gardner 1927- WhoAm 92
Bartle, Suzanne Elaine 1962- WhoAmW 93
Bartlemay, Susan Elaine 1946- WhoEmL 93
Bartles, Dean Lynn 1956- WhoSSW 93
Bartlett, Alex 1937- WhoAm 92
Bartlett, Alice Hunt 1870- AmWomPl
Bartlett, Allen Lyman, Jr. 1929- WhoAm 92
Bartlett, Art BioIn 17
Bartlett, Arthur Eugene 1933- WhoAm 92, WhoWor 93
Bartlett, Bob 1875-1946 Expl 93
Bartlett, Brian 1953- WhoCanL 92
Bartlett, Bruce Allen 1948- WhoWrEP 92
Bartlett, Bruce L. 1944- St&PR 93
Bartlett, Bruce Reeves 1951- WhoAm 92, WhoE 93, WhoEmL 93
Bartlett, Byron Allan 1940- WhoWrEP 92
Bartlett, Byron Robert 1952- WhoE 93
Bartlett, C. Scott, Jr. 1933- St&PR 93
Bartlett, Charles Leffingwell 1921- WhoAm 92
Bartlett, Clifford Adams, Jr. 1937- WhoAm 92, WhoWor 93
Bartlett, Cody Blake 1939- WhoAm 92
Bartlett, D. Brook 1937- WhoAm 92
Bartlett, David Farnham 1938- WhoAm 92
Bartlett, David Loomis 1941- St&PR 93
Bartlett, David Vangelder 1959- WhoEmL 93
Bartlett, Debra Marie 1956- WhoE 93
Bartlett, Dede Thompson 1943- St&PR 93, WhoAm 92
Bartlett, Desmond William 1931- WhoAm 92
Bartlett, Diane Sue 1947- WhoAmW 93
Bartlett, Dick MiSFD 9
Bartlett, Edward F. Law&B 92
Bartlett, Elizabeth WhoWrEP 92
Bartlett, Elizabeth Easton 1937- WhoAmW 93
Bartlett, Elizabeth M. AmWomPl
Bartlett, Elizabeth Susan 1927- WhoAm 92
Bartlett, Ethel 1896-1978 Baker 92
Bartlett, Gene E. 1910-1989 BioIn 17
Bartlett, George W. d1991 BioIn 17
Bartlett, George W. 1920- St&PR 93
Bartlett, Glenna M. 1932- St&PR 93
Bartlett, Gregg Edward 1962- WhoSSW 93
Bartlett, Hall 1922- MiSFD 9
Bartlett, Hall 1929- WhoAm 92, WhoWor 93
Bartlett, Harley Harris 1886-1960 IntDcAn
Bartlett, Helen Buck 1959- WhoWrEP 92
Bartlett, Homer Newton 1845-1920 Baker 92
Bartlett, James Holly 1904- WhoSSW 93
Bartlett, James Lowell, III 1945- WhoAm 92
Bartlett, James Theodore 1937- St&PR 93
Bartlett, James Williams 1926- WhoAm 92
Bartlett, James Wilson, III 1946- WhoAm 92, WhoEmL 93
Bartlett, James Yeoman 1951- WhoSSW 93
Bartlett, Janell Alison 1965- WhoEmL 93
Bartlett, Janeth Marie 1946- WhoEmL 93
Bartlett, Jeanne M. Law&B 92
Bartlett, Jeffrey Warner Law&B 92
Bartlett, Jeffrey Warner 1943- St&PR 93
Bartlett, Jennifer 1941- BioIn 17
Bartlett, Jennifer Losch 1941- ConAu 136, WhoAm 92
Bartlett, John B. Law&B 92
Bartlett, John Bruen 1941- St&PR 93, WhoAm 92
Bartlett, John Louis 1929- St&PR 93
Bartlett, John Wesley 1935- WhoAm 92
Bartlett, Joseph T., Jr. 1936- St&PR 93
Bartlett, Joseph W. 1933- BioIn 17
Bartlett, Joseph Warren 1933- WhoAm 92
Bartlett, Landell 1897-1972 ScF&FL 92
Bartlett, Lee Anthony 1950- WhoWrEP 92
Bartlett, Leonard Lee 1930- WhoAm 92
Bartlett, Lynn ScF&FL 92
Bartlett, Lynn Conant 1921- WhoAm 92, WhoWrEP 92
Bartlett, Marie 1949- BioIn 17
Bartlett, Marshall Prentiss Law&B 92
Bartlett, Maurice Stevenson 1910- WhoWor 93
Bartlett, Nancy L. Law&B 92
Bartlett, Neil 1932- WhoAm 92
Bartlett, Paul D., Jr. 1919- St&PR 93
Bartlett, Paul Dana, Jr. 1919- WhoAm 92
Bartlett, Paul Doughty 1907- WhoAm 92
Bartlett, Peter Barry 1934- St&PR 93
Bartlett, Peter Greenough 1930- WhoWor 93
Bartlett, Richard 1935- WhoAm 92, WhoSSW 93
Bartlett, Richard C. 1935- St&PR 93
Bartlett, Richard James 1926- WhoAm 92
Bartlett, Richard W. 1939- St&PR 93
Bartlett, Richmond Jay 1927- WhoAm 92
Bartlett, Ricky Alan 1955- WhoE 93, WhoEmL 93
Bartlett, Robert A. 1917- St&PR 93
Bartlett, Robert Addison, Jr. 1945- St&PR 93
Bartlett, Robert John 1950- WhoAm 92
Bartlett, Robert Perry, Jr. 1938- WhoAm 92
Bartlett, Robert V(irgil) 1953- WhoWrEP 92
Bartlett, Robert W. 1946- St&PR 93
Bartlett, Robert Watkins 1933- WhoAm 92
Bartlett, Rosemary Verhey Law&B 92
Bartlett, Samuel B. 1935- St&PR 93
Bartlett, Scott d1990 BioIn 17
Bartlett, Shirley Anne 1933- WhoAmW 93, WhoWor 93
Bartlett, Stephen Sheppard 1952- WhoEmL 93
Bartlett, Steve BioIn 17
Bartlett, Steve 1947- WhoAm 92, WhoSSW 93
Bartlett, Steven James 1945- WhoWrEP 92
Bartlett, Steven Thade 1962- WhoEmL 93
Bartlett, Thomas Alva 1930- WhoAm 92
Bartlett, Thomas Eastman, Jr. 1948- WhoEmL 93
Bartlett, Vernon 1894-1983 ScF&FL 92
Bartlett, Walter E. 1928- St&PR 93, WhoAm 92
Bartlett, William McGillivray 1932- WhoAm 92
Bartley, Albert Lea, Jr. Law&B 92
Bartley, Burnett Graham, Jr. 1924- St&PR 93, WhoAm 92
Bartley, D. D. 1958- WhoAmW 93
Bartley, David Anthony 1946- St&PR 93, WhoEmL 93
Bartley, Eugene WhoAm 92
Bartley, John T., Jr. 1955- St&PR 93
Bartley, Opelene 1924- WhoWor 93
Bartley, Robert LeRoy 1937- WhoAm 92, WhoE 93, WhoWrEP 92
Bartley, Robert Paul 1926- WhoE 93, WhoWor 93
Bartley, S. Howard 1901-1988 BioIn 17
Bartley, Samuel Howard 1901-1988 BioIn 17
Bartley, Shirley Kay 1955- WhoAmW 93, WhoEmL 93
Bartling, John B., Jr. 1957- St&PR 93
Bartling, Kim K. 1958- St&PR 93
Bartling, Phyllis McGinness 1927- WhoAmW 93
Bartling, Theodore Charles 1922- WhoAm 92
Bartling, William H. Law&B 92
Bartlo, Sam D. 1919- WhoAm 92
Bartlow, Thomas Loren 1942- WhoE 93
Bartman, Jeffrey 1951- WhoWrEP 92
Bartman, Robert E. WhoAm 92
Bartman, William S. MiSFD 9
Bartmann, Flavio Celso 1952- WhoWor 93
Bartmann, Heather BioIn 17
Bartmess, Geary, III 1948- WhoEmL 93
Bartmuss, Richard 1859-1910 Baker 92
Bartner, Bernard I. 1926- St&PR 93
Bartner, Martin 1930- WhoAm 92
Bartness, Becky Ann 1952- WhoAmW 93
Bartnett, Robert Elliott 1929- WhoSSW 93
Bartnicki, Stanley Thomas 1933- WhoWor 93
Bartnicki-Garcia, Salomon 1935- WhoAm 92
Bartnik, Anna Maria 1964- WhoWor 93
Bartnik, Romuald 1938- WhoScE 91-4
Bartnikas, Ray 1936- WhoAm 92
Bartnikowa, Wieslawa Teresa 1938- WhoWor 93
Bartnoff, Judith 1949- WhoAm 92
Barto, J.V. 1935- St&PR 93
Barto, Vincent A. Law&B 92
Bartocci, Barbara BioIn 17
Bartocha, Bodo 1928- WhoAm 92
Bartoe, Otto Edwin, Jr. 1927- WhoAm 92
Bartok, Bela 1881-1945 Baker 92, BioIn 17, IntDcOp [port], OxDcOp
Bartok, Frederick Francis 1943- WhoE 93
Bartok, Leslie Andrews 1951- WhoE 93
Bartok, Linda Louise 1947- WhoAmW 93
Bartok, Michael F. Law&B 92
Bartok, Mihaly 1933- WhoScE 91-4
Bartok, William 1930- WhoAm 92
Bartol, Angela 1923- WhoAmW 93
Bartol, Ernest Thomas 1946- WhoE 93, WhoWor 93
Bartol, Julio R. 1939- St&PR 93
Bartolacci, Guido J. 1929- St&PR 93
Bartolacci, Raymond Anthony 1923- St&PR 93
Bartoletti, Bruno 1926- Baker 92, WhoAm 92, WhoWor 93
Bartolf, Philip S. 1949- St&PR 93
Bartoli, Cecilia 1966- BioIn 17, CurBio 92 [port], OxDcOp
Bartoli, Henry E. 1946- St&PR 93
Bartolini, Anthony Louis 1931- WhoAm 92
Bartolini, Bruce Anthony 1950- WhoE 93
Bartolini, Robert Alfred 1942- WhoAm 92, WhoE 93
Bartolino, John Bruce 1944- WhoAm 92, WhoE 93
Bartolino da Padova fl. 14th cent.- Baker 92
Bartolo, Adolph Marion 1929- St&PR 93, WhoAm 92
Bartolo, Donna M. 1941- WhoAmW 93
Bartolo, Michael 1939- WhoUN 92
Bartolomei, Hector Guido 1941- WhoUN 92
Bartolomeo, Daniel Anthony 1955- WhoE 93
Bartolomeo, Richard Nicholas 1935- St&PR 93
Bartolomeo degli Organi 1474-1539 Baker 92
Bartolone, Joseph Francis, Sr. 1929- WhoAm 92
Bartolozzi, Bruno 1911-1980 Baker 92
Bartolucci, Luis Alberto 1946- WhoEmL 93
Bartolutti, Steven Craig 1955- WhoSSW 93
Barton, Alice L. AmWomPl
Barton, Allan D. Law&B 92
Barton, Allen Hoisington 1924- WhoAm 92
Barton, Ann Elizabeth 1923- WhoAmW 93
Barton, Bernard 1784-1849 BioIn 17
Barton, Blair L. 1953- WhoE 93
Barton, Brett WhoWrEP 92
Barton, Bruce 1886-1967 BioIn 17
Barton, Bruce Glenn 1952- WhoEmL 93
Barton, C. Robert 1926- St&PR 93, WhoAm 92, WhoIns 93
Barton, Carl P. 1916- WhoAm 92
Barton, Charles (Albert) 1920- ConAu 139
Barton, Charles Andrews, Jr. 1916- WhoWor 93
Barton, Charles Rodney 1954- WhoWor 93
Barton, Clara 1821-1912 BioIn 17, ConHero 2 [port], GayN
Barton, Colleen 1923- WhoWrEP 92
Barton, Cynthia A. Law&B 92
Barton, Dan ScF&FL 92
Barton, David Elliott WhoScE 91-1
Barton, David J. Law&B 92
Barton, David Joseph 1956- WhoEmL 93
Barton, David Knox 1927- WhoAm 92
Barton, Derek 1918- BioIn 17
Barton, Derek Harold Richard 1918- WhoAm 92, WhoWor 93
Barton, Dorothea AmWomPl
Barton, Edmund 1849-1920 DcTwHis
Barton, Edward Read 1938- WhoE 93
Barton, Ellen Louise 1946- WhoEmL 93
Barton, Evan Mansfield 1903- WhoAm 92
Barton, Frederick Durrie 1949- WhoEmL 93
Barton, Fredrick Preston 1948- WhoWrEP 92
Barton, Gail Melinda 1937- WhoAm 92
Barton, Gary E. 1941- St&PR 93
Barton, Genie BioIn 17
Barton, Gerald Gaylord 1931- St&PR 93, WhoAm 92
Barton, Gerald Lee 1934- St&PR 93, WhoAm 92
Barton, Greg BioIn 17
Barton, Gregory Edward 1961- WhoEmL 93
Barton, Harold Leonard, III 1960- WhoSSW 93
Barton, Jacqueline K. 1952- WhoAm 92, WhoAmW 93
Barton, James ScF&FL 92
Barton, James Cary 1940- WhoSSW 93, WhoWor 93
Barton, James Miller 1942- WhoAm 92
Barton, Janice Sweeny 1939- WhoAmW 93
Barton, Jay 1922- WhoAm 92
Barton, Jean Marie 1945- WhoAm 92, WhoE 93
Barton, Jerry O'Donnell 1947- WhoAm 92, WhoE 93, WhoEmL 93
Barton, Jo Ann 1949- WhoAmW 93
Barton, Joan Chi-Hung Lo 1944- WhoE 93
Barton, Joe 1949- CngDr 91
Barton, Joe Linus 1949- WhoAm 92, WhoSSW 93
Barton, John BioIn 17
Barton, John 1946- WhoIns 93
Barton, John 1948- ConAu 137
Barton, John 1957- WhoCanL 92
Barton, John A. 1935- WhoScE 91-1
Barton, John Bernard Adie 1928- WhoWor 93
Barton, John Frederick 1932- WhoE 93
Barton, John Hays 1936- WhoAm 92
Barton, John Murray 1921- WhoE 93
Barton, John Richard 1951- WhoScE 91-1
Barton, Justin R. 1942- St&PR 93
Barton, Lewis 1940- WhoAm 92, WhoE 93, WhoWor 93
Barton, Lily Jo 1965- WhoSSW 93
Barton, Lucy 1891- AmWomPl
Barton, Madalene Mayer St&PR 93
Barton, Marie Tidwell 1937- WhoAmW 93
Barton, Mark Quayle 1928- WhoAm 92
Barton, Mary WhoAm 92
Barton, Nancy E. Law&B 92
Barton, Nelda Ann Lambert 1929- WhoAm 92, WhoAmW 93, WhoSSW 93
Barton, Nick 1944- WhoWor 93
Barton, Pat WhoWrEP 92
Barton, Paul 1936- WhoE 93
Barton, Paul Booth, Jr. 1930- WhoAm 92
Barton, Peter Richard, III 1950- WhoAm 92
Barton, R.H. 1935- St&PR 93
Barton, Ralph 1891-1931 BioIn 17
Barton, Ralph G. 1940- St&PR 93
Barton, Raymond Oscar, III 1949- WhoEmL 93, WhoSSW 93
Barton, Robert H. 1933- St&PR 93
Barton, Robert James 1942- St&PR 93
Barton, Robert L., Jr. 1943- WhoE 93
Barton, Robert P. Law&B 92
Barton, Robert Wayne 1948- WhoEmL 93
Barton, Roger 1947- WhoWrEP 92
Barton, Russell William 1923- WhoAm 92, WhoWor 93
Barton, Ruth Ann 1941- WhoWrEP 92
Barton, S.W. 1928- ScF&FL 92
Barton, Samuel 1785-1858 ScF&FL 92
Barton, Sara Law&B 92
Barton, Scott K. 1952- St&PR 93
Barton, Sean MiSFD 9
Barton, Stanley 1927- WhoAm 92
Barton, Suzanne F. Law&B 92
Barton, Thomas Frank, Sr. 1905- WhoWrEP 92
Barton, Thomas H. 1924- St&PR 93
Barton, Thomas Herbert 1926- WhoAm 92
Barton, Thomas Jackson 1940- WhoAm 92
Barton, Thomas L. Law&B 92
Barton, William 1950- ScF&FL 92

Barton, William Arnold 1948- *WhoWor 93*
Barton, William Blackburn 1899- *WhoAm 92*
Barton, William Clyde, Jr. 1931- *St&PR 93*
Barton, William E. 1944- *St&PR 93*
Barton, William Russell 1925- *WhoAm 92*
Bartonicek, Robert 1932- *WhoScE 91-4*
Bartos, Dale J. 1950- *St&PR 93*
Bartos, Frantisek 1837-1906 *Baker 92*
Bartos, Frantisek 1905-1973 *Baker 92*
Bartos, Jan Zdenek 1908-1981 *Baker 92*
Bartos, Jerry Garland 1933- *WhoSSW 93*
Bartos, Josef 1887-1952 *Baker 92*
Bartos, Leonard Francis 1947- *WhoEmL 93*
Bartos, Oldrich 1944- *WhoWor 93*
Bartosek, Ivan 1934- *WhoScE 91-3*
Bartosic, Albert J. *BioIn 17*
Bartosic, Florian 1926- *WhoAm 92*
Bartosik, Marja-Liisa 1946- *WhoScE 91-4*
Bartoszek, Joseph Edward 1952- *WhoE 93*
Bartow, Gene B. 1930- *BiDAMSp 1989*
Bartow, Jerome E. *WhoIns 93*
Bartow, Jerome Edward 1930- *St&PR 93*
Bartow, Randy David 1951- *WhoAm 92*
Bartow, Stuart Allen, Jr. 1951- *WhoWrEP 92*
Bartow, Thomas Mark 1949- *WhoAm 92*
Bartra, Agusti 1908-1982 *DcMexL*
Bartram, George *ScF&FL 92*
Bartram, John 1699-1777 *BioIn 17*
Bartram, M. *Law&B 92*
Bartram, Maynard Cleveland 1926- *St&PR 93*
Bartram, Ralph Herbert 1929- *WhoAm 92*
Bartram, William 1739-1823 *BioIn 17*
Barts, Linda O. 1938- *WhoSSW 93*
Bartsch, David A. 1951- *St&PR 93*
Bartsch, Helmut 1940- *WhoScE 91-2*
Bartsch, James R. d1991 *BioIn 17*
Bartsch, Pierre *WhoScE 91-2*
Bartsch, Richard Alan 1950- *WhoEmL 93*
Bartsch, Richard Allen 1940- *WhoSSW 93*
Bartsch, Susanne *BioIn 17*
Bartsch, William H. 1933- *ConAu 138*
Bartsch, William Henry 1933- *WhoUN 92*
Bartscht, Heri Bert 1919- *WhoAm 92*
Bartter, Brit Jeffrey 1949- *WhoEmL 93*
Bartter, Martha 1932- *ScF&FL 92*
Bartter, Martha Ann 1932- *WhoWrEP 92*
Bartunek, Henrietta Ann 1944- *WhoAmW 93*
Bartunek, Kenneth Steven 1965- *WhoEmL 93*
Bartunek, Robert Richard 1914- *WhoAm 92*
Bartunek, Robert Richard, Jr. 1946- *WhoEmL 93*
Bartunik, Hans-Dieter *WhoScE 91-3*
Bartus, Raymond Thomas 1947- *WhoAm 92*
Bartusiak, Marcia Frances 1950- *WhoE 93*
Bartuska, Doris Gorka 1929- *WhoAmW 93*
Bartyczak, Michael A. *Law&B 92*
Bartynski, Cynthia Lynn 1958- *WhoE 93, WhoEmL 93*
Bartz, Carol *NewYTBS 92 [port], St&PR 93*
Bartz, Carol 1948- *WhoAmW 93*
Bartz, Carol A. *BioIn 17*
Bartz, David John 1955- *WhoEmL 93*
Bartz, Debra Ann 1960- *WhoEmL 93*
Bartz, Freeman Edwin 1930- *St&PR 93*
Bartz, Mary Russo *WhoAm 92, WhoAmW 93*
Bartzatt, Ronald Lee 1953- *WhoEmL 93*
Bartzokis, Chris C. *Law&B 92*
Bartzokis, Spiro C. 1952- *St&PR 93*
Barua, Jahnu 1952- *MiSFD 9*
Baruch *OxDcByz*
Baruch, Andre 1906-1991 *BioIn 17*
Baruch, Bernard 1870-1965 *ColdWar 1 [port]*
Baruch, Bernard M. 1870-1965 *JeAmHC*
Baruch, Bernard M., Jr. d1992 *NewYTBS 92*
Baruch, Bernard Mannes 1870-1965 *BioIn 17, DcTwHis*
Baruch, Eduard 1907- *St&PR 93, WhoAm 92, WhoWor 93*
Baruch, Jacques 1922-1986 *PolBiDi*
Baruch, John Alfred 1926- *St&PR 93, WhoAm 92*
Baruch, Jordan Jay 1923- *WhoAm 92*
Baruch, Michael Amnon 1965- *WhoWor 93*
Baruch, Monica Lobo-Filho 1954- *WhoAmW 93, WhoEmL 93*
Baruch, Pierre 1927- *WhoWor 93*
Baruch, Ralph M. 1923- *WhoAm 92*
Baruch, Renee D. *Law&B 92*
Baruch, Steven *BioIn 17*
Baruh, Haim 1954- *WhoEmL 93*
Baruh, Rosanne J. *Law&B 92*
Barus, Carl 1919-1990 *BioIn 17*
Barus, Vlastimil 1935- *WhoScE 91-4*
Barusch, Lawrence Roos 1949- *WhoEmL 93*
Barut, Asim Orhan 1926- *WhoAm 92*
Baruth, Charlotte d1991 *BioIn 17*
Barvik, Miroslav 1919- *Baker 92*
Barvinok, Alexander I. 1963- *WhoWor 93*
Barvoets, Ernest 1957- *St&PR 93*
Barwahser, Hubert 1906-1985 *Baker 92*
Barwell, Cindy Ann 1957- *WhoEmL 93*
Barwick, B.J., Jr. *St&PR 93*
Barwick, James V. *Law&B 92*
Barwick, JoAnn R. *WhoAm 92*
Barwick, John O., III 1949- *St&PR 93*
Barwick, John Samuel 1962- *WhoEmL 93*
Barwick, Robert Charles 1930- *St&PR 93*
Barwick, Steven James 1947- *St&PR 93*
Barwinski, Richard Conrad 1951- *WhoEmL 93*
Barwood, Hal *MiSFD 9*
Bary, Alfred (Erwin) von 1873-1926 *Baker 92*
Bary, Brian McK. 1919- *WhoScE 91-3*
Baryakhtar, Victor Grigori 1930- *WhoWor 93*
Barylai, Mahmoud 1944- *WhoAsAP 91*
Baryphonus, Henricus 1581-1655 *Baker 92*
Baryshnikov, Mikhail 1948- *BioIn 17, WhoAm 92, WhoWor 93*
Barzach, Michele 1943- *BioIn 17*
Barzaghi, Jacques *NewYTBS 92*
Barzelay, Douglas E. *Law&B 92*
Barzgar, Mohammad Ali 1942- *WhoUN 92*
Barzilay, Isaac Eisenstein 1915- *WhoAm 92*
Barzilay, Zvi 1946- *St&PR 93*
Barzin, Leon (Eugene) 1900- *Baker 92*
Bar-Ziv, Haim Emanuel 1937- *St&PR 93*
Barzman, Ben d1989 *BioIn 17*
Barzman, Ben 1912-1989 *ScF&FL 92*
Barzum, Roger *Law&B 92*
Barzun, Jacques 1907- *Baker 92, WhoAm 92, WhoWor 93, WhoWrEP 92*
Barzune, Dolores 1939- *WhoAmW 93*
Barzyk, Fred *MiSFD 9*
Barzynski, Wincenty M. 1838-1899 *PolBiDi*
Bas, Carlos *WhoScE 91-3*
Bas, Daniel Paul 1932- *WhoUN 92*
Bas, Giulio 1874-1929 *Baker 92*
Basa, Eniko Molnar 1939- *WhoE 93*
Basabarajeswari, S.M.T. 1928- *WhoAsAP 91*
Basalla, John Louis 1954- *WhoEmL 93*
Basanez, Edward Samuel 1930- *WhoSSW 93*
Basanez, Luis 1943- *WhoScE 91-3*
Basar, Haluk 1965- *WhoScE 91-4*
Basar, Tamer 1946- *WhoAm 92*
Basaran, Ali Kadir Temel 1947- *WhoUN 92*
Basaran, Nurettin 1945- *WhoScE 91-4*
Basart, Ann Phillips 1931- *WhoWrEP 92*
Basart, John Philip 1938- *WhoAm 92*
Basavaraj, G.S. 1941- *WhoAsAP 91*
Basawapatna, Ganesh *BioIn 17*
Basaza-Mpyisi, Eldad John 1932- *WhoUN 92*
Basbas, Monte George 1921- *WhoE 93*
Basch, David *WhoAm 92*
Basch, Joseph Martin 1920- *St&PR 93*
Basch, Paul Frederick 1933- *WhoAm 92*
Basch, Reva *BioIn 17*
Basch, Richard Vennard 1945- *WhoE 93, WhoWor 93*
Basch, Sheldon *Law&B 92*
Bascom, Barbara *BioIn 17*
Bascom, Earl Wesley 1906- *WhoWor 93*
Bascom, John G. 1943- *St&PR 93*
Bascom, Louise Rand *AmWomPl*
Bascom, Perry Bagnall 1924- *WhoAm 92*
Bascom, Robert Holden 1940- *WhoE 93*
Bascom, Willard Newell 1916- *WhoAm 92*
Bascom, William R. 1912-1981 *IntDcAn*
Bascones, Antonio 1944- *WhoScE 91-3*
Basconi, E. Wayne *Law&B 92*
Bascunana, Jose Luis 1927- *WhoE 93*
Basden, Cameron *WhoAm 92*
Basdeo, Sahadeo 1945- *WhoWor 93*
Base, Graeme *ChlBIID [port]*
Base, Graeme 1958- *BioIn 17*
Base, Graeme (Rowland) 1958- *MajAI [port]*
Base, Richard G. 1945- *St&PR 93*
Base, Steven W. 1944- *St&PR 93*
Base, Viola Esther 1919- *WhoAmW 93*
Basech, Elinor 1927- *WhoE 93*
Basefsky, Stuart Mark 1949- *WhoEmL 93*
Basehart, Harry W. 1910-1988 *IntDcAn*
Basel, Frances Rita 1933- *WhoAmW 93*
Baselitz, Georg 1938- *WhoWor 93*
Baselt, Fritz 1863-1931 *Baker 92*
Baselt, Randall Clint 1944- *WhoAm 92*
Baseman, Alan Howard 1953- *WhoEmL 93, WhoSSW 93*
Baseman, Robert Lynn 1932- *St&PR 93*
Baser, Steven I. *Law&B 92*
Baserga, Renato Luigi 1925- *WhoAm 92, WhoE 93*
Basevi, Abramo 1818-1885 *Baker 92*
Basford, James O. 1931- *St&PR 93*
Basford, Michael J. *Law&B 92*
Basford, Robert Eugene 1923- *WhoAm 92, WhoE 93*
Basgall, Bernard A., Jr. 1940- *WhoIns 93*
Bash, Charles Dayton 1949- *WhoEmL 93*
Bash, Frank Ness 1937- *WhoAm 92, WhoSSW 93*
Bash, James Francis 1925- *WhoAm 92*
Bash, Philip Edwin 1921- *WhoAm 92*
Bash, Roger Leonard 1947- *WhoE 93*
Bash, Yigal Amir 1938- *WhoAm 92*
Basha, Leigh-Alexandra 1960- *WhoEmL 93*
Basham, Jimmye Kay 1958- *WhoEmL 93*
Basham, Lloyd M. 1947- *St&PR 93*
Basham, Lloyd Moman 1947- *WhoEmL 93*
Basham, Michael Alan 1957- *WhoEmL 93*
Basham, Nancy W. 1944- *St&PR 93*
Basham, Paul E. 1938- *St&PR 93*
Basham, Robert D. *St&PR 93*
Basham-Tooker, Janet Brooks 1919- *WhoAm 92, WhoAmW 93*
Bashant, Floyd Thomas *St&PR 93*
Bashara, George N., Jr. *Law&B 92*
Basharmal, Khodaidad 1945- *WhoUN 92*
Bashe, Gilbert Gregg 1954- *WhoEmL 93*
Bashe, Lawrence Douglas 1944- *St&PR 93*
Basheda, Randall Steven 1958- *St&PR 93*
Basheer, Thalekkunnil 1945- *WhoAsAP 91*
Basher, T.A.M. Fakhrul 1957- *WhoWor 93*
Bashevis, Isaac *ConAu 39NR, MajAI*
Bashevkin, Albert 1907- *St&PR 93*
Bashevkin, Irving 1924- *St&PR 93*
Bashevkin, Robert 1930- *St&PR 93*
Bashford, Eric Rainer 1959- *WhoEmL 93*
Bashinski, Leonard C. 1943- *WhoIns 93*
Bashinsky, Sloan Young 1919- *WhoAm 92*
Bashinsky, Sloan Young, II 1942- *WhoWrEP 92*
Bashir, Omar Hassan Ahmed el 1944- *WhoAfr*
Bashir, Umar Hasan Ahmad al- *WhoWor 93*
Bashizi, Bashige Bafunyembaka 1950- *WhoUN 92*
Bashjawish, Ramzi 1965- *WhoE 93*
Bashkin, Lloyd Scott 1951- *WhoE 93, WhoEmL 93, WhoWor 93*
Bashkirov, Dmitri 1931- *Baker 92*
Bashkirtseff, Marie 1860-1884 *BioIn 17*
Bashkirtseva, Mariia Konstantinovna 1860-1884 *BioIn 17*
Bashkow, Theodore Robert 1921- *WhoAm 92*
Bashmakov, Leonid 1927- *Baker 92*
Bashmakova, Isabella Grigoryevna 1921- *WhoWor 93*
Bashor, Ronald Leslie 1949- *WhoEmL 93, WhoSSW 93*
Bashore, Charles Eicker 1914- *St&PR 93*
Bashore, George Willis 1934- *WhoAm 92*
Bashore, Helen L. 1921- *St&PR 93*
Bashshur, Ramona 1961- *WhoAmW 93*
Bashua, Abiodun Oluremi 1951- *WhoUN 92*
Bashwiner 1944- *WhoWor 93*
Bashwiner, Steven Lacelle 1941- *WhoAm 92*
Basia *BioIn 17*
Basic, Anne Marie *Law&B 92*
Basich, Vladimir Walter 1934- *St&PR 93*
Basichis, Gordon Allen 1947- *WhoEmL 93, WhoWor 93*
Basie, Count 1904-1984 *Baker 92*
Basil dc. 468 *OxDcByz*
Basil, Bishop 1915- *BioIn 17*
Basil, Saint, Bishop of Caesarea c. 329-379 *BioIn 17*
Basil, I 830?-886 *OxDcByz*
Basil, I 1371-1425 *OxDcByz*
Basil, II 958-1025 *OxDcByz [port]*
Basil, Amy Elizabeth 1962- *WhoE 93*
Basil, Douglas Constantine 1923- *WhoAm 92, WhoWrEP 92*
Basil, Marvin B. 1934- *St&PR 93*
Basil, Otto 1901-1983 *ScF&FL 92*
Basil, Stephen Joseph 1950- *WhoWor 93*
Basil, William C. *Law&B 92*
Basilakes *OxDcByz*
Basilakes, Nikephoros c. 1115-c. 1182 *OxDcByz*
Basil Bulgaroctonos, II 958-1025 *HarEnMi*
Basile, Abigail Julia Ellen Herron 1915- *WhoAmW 93*
Basile, Andreana c. 1580-c. 1640 *Baker 92*
Basile, Antoine E. 1938- *WhoE 93*
Basile, Carol Ann 1953- *WhoEmL 93*
Basile, Francis X. *WhoAm 92*
Basile, Giorgio 1942- *WhoWor 93*
Basile, Jean 1932- *WhoCanL 92*
Basile, Joseph John, Jr. 1952- *WhoE 93*
Basile, Michael E. 1923- *St&PR 93*
Basile, Neal F. 1944- *St&PR 93*
Basile, Neal Fahr 1944- *WhoAm 92*
Basile, Paul Louis, Jr. 1945- *WhoAm 92, WhoWor 93*
Basile, Richard Emanuel 1921- *WhoAm 92*
Basile Baroni, Adriana c. 1580-c. 1640 *OxDcOp*
Basil Elachistos *OxDcByz*
Basili, Francesco 1767-1850 *Baker 92*
Basili, Robert Andrew 1934- *St&PR 93*
Basilides, Maria 1886-1946 *Baker 92*
Basilio, Anthony Joseph 1938- *WhoE 93*
Basilio, Eleanor Vasco 1961- *WhoWor 93*
Basiliskos dc. 476 *OxDcByz*
Basilius Pictor *OxDcByz*
Basil Kamateros, II *OxDcByz*
Basil Of Ankyra dc. 364 *OxDcByz*
Basil Of Ialimbana *OxDcByz*
Basil Of Ohrid dc. 1169 *OxDcByz*
Basilone, John *BioIn 17*
Basil The Bogomil dc. 1111 *OxDcByz*
Basil The Copper Hand dc. 932 *OxDcByz*
Basil The Great c. 329-379 *OxDcByz*
Basil the Macedonian, I 812-886 *HarEnMi*
Basil The Nothos c. 925-c. 985 *OxDcByz*
Basil The Younger d944 *OxDcByz*
Basimakopulos, Joanne E. 1945- *WhoUN 92*
Basin, Thomas 1412-1491 *BioIn 17*
Basinger, Cheryl Kathryn Ricketts 1955- *WhoEmL 93*
Basinger, Karen Lynn 1955- *WhoAmW 93*
Basinger, Kim *BioIn 17*
Basinger, Kim 1953- *HolBB [port], WhoAm 92*
Basinger, Malcolm D. 1929- *St&PR 93*
Basinger, Robert 1931- *St&PR 93*
Basinger, Thomas Preston 1947- *St&PR 93*
Basinskas, Justinas 1923- *Baker 92*
Basinski, Anthony Joseph 1947- *WhoAm 92*
Basinski, Ida Rockwood 1927- *WhoAmW 93*
Basinski, John Edward 1949- *WhoE 93*
Basinski, Zbigniew Stanislaw 1928- *WhoAm 92*
Basiola, Mario 1892-1965 *Baker 92*
Basiotis, Panayotis Peter 1947- *WhoE 93*
Basiouny, Fouad M. 1938- *WhoSSW 93*
Basista, Michael Paul 1952- *WhoEmL 93*
Basius, Francis L. 1931- *St&PR 93*
Baska, James Louis 1927- *St&PR 93, WhoAm 92*
Baskakov, Victor Aleksei 1929- *WhoWor 93*
Baskauskas, Asta *BioIn 17*
Baske, C. Alan 1927- *WhoWor 93*
Basker, James Glynn 1952- *WhoE 93*
Basker, Robin Michael *WhoScE 91-1*
Baskervill, Charles Thornton 1953- *WhoSSW 93*
Baskervill, Jane Gibbs 1955- *WhoWrEP 92*
Baskerville, Charles Alexander 1928- *WhoAm 92*
Baskett, James Alvin 1947- *WhoSSW 93*
Baskett, Thomas Sebree 1916- *WhoAm 92*
Baskett, William D., III *Law&B 92*
Baskin, Barbara H(olland) 1929- *WhoWrEP 92*
Baskin, Barbara Holland 1929- *WhoE 93*
Baskin, Cary 1968- *St&PR 93*
Baskin, Charles Richard 1926- *WhoSSW 93*
Baskin, David Stuart 1952- *WhoAm 92*
Baskin, Don C. 1944- *St&PR 93*
Baskin, Ed Swann, Jr. 1950- *WhoSSW 93*
Baskin, Gary A. *Law&B 92*
Baskin, Judith R. 1950- *ConAu 137*
Baskin, Leland Burleson 1952- *WhoAm 92*
Baskin, Leonard 1922- *WhoAm 92*
Baskin, Richard *MiSFD 9*
Baskin, Ronald Joseph 1935- *WhoAm 92*
Baskin, William Gresham 1933- *WhoSSW 93*
Baskin, Yvonne Cecile 1948- *WhoEmL 93*
Baskind, Barry *St&PR 93*
Baskind, Stanley Marvin 1930- *St&PR 93*
Baskinger, Patricia JoAnne 1949- *WhoEmL 93*
Baskins, Ann O. 1955- *St&PR 93*
Baskins, Ann O'Neil *Law&B 92*
Basle, Michel-Felix 1944- *WhoScE 91-2*
Basler, Thomas G. 1940- *WhoAm 92*
Basler, Wayne G. 1930- *St&PR 93*
Basler, Wayne Gordon 1930- *WhoSSW 93*
Basler, William L. 1944- *St&PR 93*

Bateman, Leah Michelle 1968- *WhoWor 93*
Bateman, Maureen Scannell *Law&B 92*
Bateman, Michael John 1969- *WhoE 93*
Bateman, Paul Trevier 1919- *WhoAm 92*
Bateman, Paul William 1957- *WhoAm 92, WhoEmL 93*
Bateman, Robert 1930- *BioIn 17*
Bateman, Robert McLellan 1930- *WhoAm 92*
Bateman, S.F. 1940- *St&PR 93*
Bateman, Samuel M. 1930- *St&PR 93*
Bateman, Sharon Louise 1949- *WhoEmL 93*
Bateman, Sylvia Lilaine *Law&B 92*
Bateman, Veda Mae 1921- *WhoAm 92*
Bateman, William Maxwell 1920- *WhoAm 92*
Batenhorst, Gary R. *Law&B 92*
Batenhorst, Jimmie Ann 1963- *WhoSSW 93*
Bates, Alan 1934- *BioIn 17, IntDcF 2-3, WhoAm 92, WhoWor 93*
Bates, Albert Kealiinui 1947- *WhoEmL 93, WhoSSW 93*
Bates, Anthony Richard *WhoScE 91-1*
Bates, Anthony W. *WhoScE 91-1*
Bates, Barbara J. Neuner 1927- *WhoAmW 93, WhoE 93*
Bates, Baron Kent 1934- *WhoAm 92*
Bates, Beverly Bailey 1938- *WhoSSW 93*
Bates, Blanche 1873-1941 *BioIn 17*
Bates, Bradford L. *Law&B 92*
Bates, Brian *ScF&FL 92*
Bates, Bruce Alan 1958- *WhoEmL 93*
Bates, Bruce B. 1931- *St&PR 93, WhoAm 92*
Bates, Carl Thomas 1950- *St&PR 93*
Bates, Carman Lynn 1948- *WhoEmL 93*
Bates, Carolyn A. *Law&B 92*
Bates, Carolyn May 1955- *WhoSSW 93*
Bates, Catherine 1964- *ConAu 139*
Bates, Catherine Teresa 1964- *WhoWor 93*
Bates, Charles Carpenter 1918- *WhoAm 92*
Bates, Charles Laurance 1924- *St&PR 93*
Bates, Charles Turner 1932- *WhoAm 92*
Bates, Charles Walter 1953- *WhoEmL 93*
Bates, Colin Arthur *WhoScE 91-1*
Bates, Colin Arthur 1935- *WhoWor 93*
Bates, Cynthia *Law&B 92*
Bates, D.B. fl. 1851-1855 *BioIn 17*
Bates, Daniel M. 1951- *St&PR 93*
Bates, David *Law&B 92*
Bates, David 1952- *BioIn 17*
Bates, David M. *Law&B 92*
Bates, David Martin 1934- *WhoAm 92*
Bates, David Mayfield 1946- *WhoEmL 93, WhoSSW 93*
Bates, David Quentin, Jr. 1951- *WhoAm 92*
Bates, David Robert 1916- *WhoWor 93*
Bates, David T. 1947- *St&PR 93*
Bates, David Vincent 1922- *WhoAm 92*
Bates, David Wynn, Sr. 1935- *St&PR 93*
Bates, Don 1939- *WhoAm 92, WhoE 93*
Bates, Donald Vincent 1936- *St&PR 93*
Bates, Donnette Marie 1949- *WhoEmL 93*
Bates, Dwight Lee 1943- *WhoWor 93*
Bates, Edward Brill 1919- *WhoAm 92*
Bates, Ella Skinner *AmWomPl*
Bates, Esther Willard 1884- *AmWomPl*
Bates, Frank 1934- *St&PR 93*
Bates, Frederick Newcomb *Law&B 92*
Bates, Gary A. 1940- *St&PR 93*
Bates, George E. d1992 *NewYTBS 92*
Bates, George William 1940- *WhoAm 92*
Bates, Gerald Earl 1933- *WhoAm 92*
Bates, Gladys Edgerly 1896- *WhoAm 92*
Bates, H.E. 1905-1974 *BioIn 17, ShSCr 10 [port]*
Bates, Harry *ScF&FL 92*
Bates, Henry Walter 1825-1892 *Expl 93 [port]*
Bates, Herbert Ernest 1905-1974 *BioIn 17*
Bates, James Earl 1923- *WhoAm 92, WhoE 93, WhoWor 93*
Bates, James Leonard 1919- *WhoAm 92*
Bates, Janice 1955- *WhoEmL 93*
Bates, Jared Lewis 1941- *WhoAm 92*
Bates, Jeffrey Roberts *Law&B 92*
Bates, Jim 1941- *BioIn 17, WhoAm 92*
Bates, Joah 1741-1799 *Baker 92*
Bates, John Bertram 1914- *WhoAm 92*
Bates, John Burnham 1918- *WhoAm 92*
Bates, John Cecil, Jr. 1936- *WhoAm 92*
Bates, John Coalter 1842-1919 *CmdGen 1991 [port]*
Bates, John Walter 1939- *WhoSSW 93*
Bates, Julius F. 1950- *St&PR 93*
Bates, Katharine Lee 1859-1929 *AmWomPl*
Bates, Kathy *BioIn 17*
Bates, Kathy 1948- *ConTFT 10, WhoAm 92, WhoAmW 93*
Bates, Kenneth R. 1959- *St&PR 93*
Bates, Laura Mae 1933- *WhoWrEP 92*
Bates, Lawrence Fulcher 1954- *WhoEmL 93*
Bates, Lilybell *AmWomPl*
Bates, Lura Wheeler 1932- *WhoAmW 93*
Bates, Malcolm Rowland 1934- *WhoAm 92*
Bates, Mariette J. 1950- *WhoEmL 93*
Bates, Mary L. 1930- *St&PR 93*
Bates, Mary Louise 1930- *WhoAm 92*
Bates, Mary Lynn *Law&B 92*
Bates, Mary Lynn Dovith 1947- *WhoEmL 93*
Bates, Mary Patricia 1951- *WhoAmW 93*
Bates, Michael John 1950- *WhoEmL 93*
Bates, Pamela 1953- *WhoE 93*
Bates, Patricia Stamper 1947- *WhoEmL 93, WhoSSW 93*
Bates, Peg Leg 1907- *BioIn 17*
Bates, Peggy Thorpe- 1914-1989 *BioIn 17*
Bates, Philip S. 1954- *St&PR 93*
Bates, Ralph 1940- *BioIn 17*
Bates, Ralph Samuel 1906- *WhoE 93*
Bates, Rex James 1923- *WhoAm 92*
Bates, Rhonda Barber 1962- *WhoAmW 93*
Bates, Richard A. *Law&B 92*
Bates, Richard Brent *Law&B 92*
Bates, Richard Doane, Jr. 1944- *WhoE 93*
Bates, Richard F. 1923- *St&PR 93*
Bates, Richard Mather 1932- *WhoAm 92*
Bates, Robert Dale, Sr. 1941- *St&PR 93*
Bates, Robert M. 1933- *St&PR 93*
Bates, Robert William 1961- *WhoEmL 93*
Bates, Rodney Lin 1946- *WhoEmL 93*
Bates, Ronald G.N. 1924- *WhoCanL 92*
Bates, Sarah c. 1755-1811 *Baker 92*
Bates, Sarah E. *Law&B 92*
Bates, Scott 1923- *WhoWrEP 92*
Bates, Sheri Lee 1967- *WhoSSW 93*
Bates, Stephanie *BioIn 17*
Bates, Susannah 1941- *ScF&FL 92*
Bates, Terry Bryan 1959- *WhoEmL 93*
Bates, Thomas *BioIn 17*
Bates, Thomas William 1937- *St&PR 93*
Bates, Timothy Mark 1960- *WhoEmL 93*
Bates, Walter Alan 1925- *WhoAm 92*
Bates, Wayne *BioIn 17*
Bates, William fl. 18th cent.- *Baker 92*
Bates, William, III 1949- *WhoEmL 93*
Bates, William H. 1921- *St&PR 93*
Bates, William Hubert 1926- *WhoAm 92*
Bates, William Leroy, Jr. 1921- *WhoSSW 93*
Bateson, Gregory 1904-1980 *IntDcAn*
Bateson, Mary Catherine 1939- *BioIn 17, ConAu 137, WhoAm 92*
Bateson, Richard d1991 *BioIn 17*
Bateson, Thomas d1630 *Baker 92*
Bates-Silva, Mary Louise 1930- *WhoAmW 93*
Batey, Amanda 1950- *WhoEmL 93*
Batey, Douglas Leo 1947- *WhoEmL 93*
Batey, Peter William James *WhoScE 91-1*
Batey, Sharyn Rebecca 1946- *WhoSSW 93*
Bath, Lord d1992 *NewYTBS 92 [port]*
Bath, David A. 1947- *St&PR 93*
Bath, Hubert 1883-1945 *Baker 92*
Bath, James R. *BioIn 17*
Bath, Karen Lee 1947- *WhoAmW 93*
Bathaw d1991 *BioIn 17*
Bathe, William 1564-1614 *Baker 92*
Bathel, Darryl Donald 1949- *WhoEmL 93*
Bather, John Alfred *WhoScE 91-1*
Bather, Paul *AfrAmBi*
Bathias, Claude 1938- *WhoWor 93*
Bathon, Edward G. 1907-1991 *BioIn 17*
Bathon, Thomas Neil 1961- *WhoEmL 93*
Bathori, Jane 1877-1970 *Baker 92*
Bathrick, David 1936- *WhoE 93*
Bathsheba *BioIn 17*
Bathurst, David d1992 *NewYTBS 92 [port]*
Bathy, Anna 1901-1962 *Baker 92*
Batie, Sandra S. *BioIn 17*
Batignani, Laurie A. 1953- *WhoAm 92*
Batin, Christopher Michael 1955- *WhoWrEP 92*
Batina, Lawrence J. 1952- *St&PR 93*
Batis Martinez, Huberto 1934- *DcMexL*
Batista, Eike *BioIn 17*
Batista, Emily Johnson 1954- *WhoEmL 93*
Batista, Fulgencio 1901-1973 *DcTwHis*
Batista, John Veloso 1934- *St&PR 93, WhoAm 92*
Batista, Kenneth 1952- *WhoE 93*
Batista y Zaldivar, Fulgencio 1901-1973 *ColdWar 2 [port], DcCPCAm*
Batiste, Robert Joseph 1950- *WhoEmL 93*
Batistin *Baker 92*
Batiuk, Thomas Martin 1947- *WhoAm 92*
Batiz (Campbell), Enrique 1942- *Baker 92*
Batka, Richard 1868-1922 *Baker 92*
Batkai, Laszlo 1940- *WhoScE 91-4*
Batkiewicz, Raymond J. 1952- *St&PR 93*
Batkin, Bruce D. 1953- *St&PR 93*
Batkin, Sanford Lewis 1923- *St&PR 93*
Batko, Andrzej 1933- *WhoScE 91-4*
Batlin, Alfred Robert 1930- *WhoWrEP 92*
Batlin, Robert Alfred 1930- *WhoAm 92*
Batlivala, Robert Bomi D. 1940- *WhoWor 93*
Batlle Alvarez, C. Nicolas 1942- *WhoWor 93*
Batlle y Ordonez, Jose 1856-1929 *DcTwHis*
Batman, David Reid *Law&B 92*
Batoff, Steven Irving 1951- *WhoEmL 93*
Bator, Francis Michel 1925- *WhoAm 92*
Bator, James M. 1942- *St&PR 93*
Bators, Stiv d1990 *BioIn 17*
Batorski, Judith Ann 1949- *WhoAmW 93, WhoE 93, WhoEmL 93*
Batory, Anne Heineman 1946- *WhoEmL 93*
Batory, Ronald Louis 1950- *WhoAm 92, WhoEmL 93*
Batory, Stefan 1533-1586 *PolBiDi*
Batory, Stephen Stanley 1946- *WhoE 93*
Batow, David P. *Law&B 92*
Batozech, Jeffrey 1960- *WhoIns 93*
Batra, Ashok K.J. 1940- *St&PR 93*
Batres, Eduardo *WhoAm 92*
Batsakis, John George 1929- *WhoAm 92*
Batsanov, Serguei Borisovich 1954- *WhoWor 93*
Batscha, Robert Michael 1945- *WhoAm 92*
Batschelet, Margaret Weathers 1945- *WhoAmW 93*
Batsford, Brian 1910-1991 *AnObit 1991*
Batson, Blair Everett 1920- *WhoAm 92*
Batson, David Warren 1956- *WhoEmL 93*
Batson, Larry Floyd 1930- *WhoAm 92, WhoWrEP 92*
Batson, Raymond Milner 1931- *WhoWor 93*
Batson, Robert D. *Law&B 92*
Batson, Robert Grover 1950- *WhoEmL 93, WhoSSW 93*
Batson, Stephen Wesley 1946- *WhoEmL 93, WhoSSW 93, WhoWor 93*
Batstone Cook, Christopher William 1951- *WhoWor 93*
Batt, Allen Edward 1949- *WhoEmL 93, WhoWrEP 92*
Batt, David M. 1948- *St&PR 93*
Batt, Lourie T. 1927- *St&PR 93*
Batt, Michael *BioIn 17*
Batt, Miles Girard 1933- *WhoSSW 93*
Batt, Nick 1952- *WhoAm 92, WhoEmL 93*
Batt, Richard James 1957- *WhoE 93*
Batt, Ronald Elmer 1933- *WhoE 93*
Batta, Edward J. 1937- *St&PR 93*
Batta, Ronald 1951- *WhoAfr*
Battaglia, Anthony Sylvester 1927- *WhoAm 92*
Battaglia, Biagio 1909-1991 *BioIn 17*
Battaglia, Bruno *WhoScE 91-3*
Battaglia, Bruno 1923- *WhoScE 91-3*
Battaglia, Franco 1953- *WhoWor 93*
Battaglia, Frederick Camillo 1932- *WhoAm 92*
Battaglia, Joseph Paul 1950- *WhoE 93*
Battaglia, Massimo 1948- *WhoWor 93*
Battaglia, Michael Salvatore 1944- *WhoAm 92*
Battaglia, Philip Maher 1935- *WhoAm 92*
Battaglia, Richard J. *Law&B 92*
Battaglini, Frank Paul 1944- *WhoAm 92, WhoE 93*
Battaglini, Linda Jackson 1950- *WhoEmL 93*
Battaille, Charles-Amable 1822-1872 *Baker 92*
Battaner, Enrique 1945- *WhoScE 91-3*
Battarbee, Harold D. 1940- *WhoSSW 93*
Battat, Emile A. 1938- *WhoAm 92, WhoE 93, WhoWor 93*
Batte, Michael C. 1946- *St&PR 93*
Batteast, Robert V. 1931- *St&PR 93*
Battegay, Raymond 1927- *WhoScE 91-4, WhoWor 93*
Batteh, Jad Hanna 1947- *WhoSSW 93*
Battei, Antonio 1949- *WhoWor 93*
Battelle, Beverly Kay 1951- *WhoEmL 93*
Batten, Adrian 1591-1637 *Baker 92*
Batten, Alan Henry 1933- *WhoAm 92*
Batten, Charles Francis 1942- *WhoSSW 93*
Batten, Frank 1927- *St&PR 93, WhoAm 92, WhoWrEP 92*
Batten, George Leemon, Jr. 1952- *WhoSSW 93*
Batten, Jack 1932- *WhoCanL 92*
Batten, James Knox 1936- *St&PR 93, WhoAm 92, WhoSSW 93, WhoWrEP 92*
Batten, James William 1919- *WhoSSW 93, WhoWor 93*
Batten, Jerry Lee 1953- *WhoSSW 93*
Batten, Michael Ellsworth 1940- *St&PR 93, WhoAm 92*
Batten, Ralph *ScF&FL 92*
Batten, W. Howard 1929- *St&PR 93*
Batten, Wayne Carroll 1956- *WhoE 93*
Batten, William Milfred 1909- *WhoAm 92*
Battenberg, Louis Francis, Prince of 1900-1979 *BioIn 17*
Battenberg, Louis of 1854-1921 *HarEnMi*
Battenhouse, Roy Wesley 1912- *WhoAm 92*
Battenson, J. Robert 1937- *St&PR 93*
Batterham, Richard 1936- *BioIn 17*
Batterman, Boris William 1930- *WhoAm 92, WhoE 93*
Batterman, Steven Charles 1937- *WhoAm 92*
Battern, Timothy Hill 1950- *WhoEmL 93*
Battersby, Alan Rushton *WhoScE 91-1*
Battersby, Bradley *MiSFD 9*
Battersby, Charles Tonge 1922- *WhoWor 93*
Battersby, Harold Ronald 1922- *WhoAm 92*
Battersby, James Lyons, Jr. 1936- *WhoAm 92*
Battersby, Roy *MiSFD 9*
Battershall, Philip H. 1930- *St&PR 93*
Batterson, J. Robert 1937- *WhoIns 93*
Batterson, Steven L. 1950- *WhoEmL 93*
Battesti, Christine Denise 1960- *WhoWor 93*
Battestin, Martin Carey 1930- *WhoAm 92*
Battey, Charles *BioIn 17*
Battey, Charles W. 1932- *WhoAm 92*
Battey, Charles Wheaton 1932- *St&PR 93*
Battey, Judith Whitlock 1957- *WhoAmW 93*
Battey, Richard Howard 1929- *WhoAm 92*
Battiato, David Alan 1952- *WhoEmL 93*
Battiato, Giacomo 1943- *MiSFD 9*
Battiato, John Michael *Law&B 92*
Battiau, Michel 1941- *WhoScE 91-2*
Battiau-Queney, Yvonne 1941- *WhoScE 91-2*
Battilana, Raymond E. 1937- *St&PR 93*
Battin, B.W. 1941- *ScF&FL 92*
Battin, Cynthia Ann 1957- *WhoEmL 93*
Battin, James Franklin 1925- *WhoAm 92*
Battin, Richard Horace 1925- *WhoAm 92, WhoE 93*
Battin, Skip 1934- *See* Byrds, The *ConMus 8*
Battin, Wendy J. 1953- *WhoWrEP 92*
Battino, Rubin 1931- *WhoAm 92*
Battishill, Jonathan 1738-1801 *Baker 92*
Battison, John Henry 1915- *WhoAm 92*
Battista, Joseph N. 1955- *St&PR 93*
Battista, Matthew J. 1933- *St&PR 93*
Battista, Nicholas Rudolph 1951- *WhoE 93*
Battista, Orlando Aloysius 1917- *St&PR 93, WhoAm 92*
Battista, Robert James 1939- *WhoAm 92*
Battista, Vito P. 1908-1990 *BioIn 17*
Battistella, Jacques-P. 1948- *WhoScE 91-2*
Battistelli, Joseph John 1930- *WhoWor 93*
Battisti, Eugenio 1924-1989 *BioIn 17*
Battisti, Frank *BioIn 17*
Battisti, Frank Joseph 1922- *WhoAm 92*
Battisti, Oreste Guerino 1951- *WhoWor 93*
Battisti, Paul Oreste 1922- *WhoAm 92*
Battistini, Gaudenzio 1722-1800 *Baker 92*
Battistini, Giacomo 1665-1719 *Baker 92*
Battistini, Mattia 1856-1928 *Baker 92, IntDcOp [port], OxDcOp*
Battistini, Noe 1936- *WhoWor 93*
Battistoni, Alvino 1920- *St&PR 93*
Battistoni, Claudio *WhoScE 91-3*
Battjer, Laura Catherine 1951- *WhoE 93*
Battjes, Jurjen Anno 1939- *WhoScE 91-3*
Battle, Allen Overton, Jr. 1927- *WhoAm 92*
Battle, Carl *Law&B 92*
Battle, Edward G. 1931- *St&PR 93*
Battle, Edward Gene 1931- *WhoAm 92*
Battle, Emery Alford, Jr. 1947- *WhoEmL 93, WhoSSW 93*
Battle, Emily Anne 1934- *WhoSSW 93*
Battle, Gloria Jean 1950- *WhoSSW 93*
Battle, Hinton *BioIn 17*
Battle, Jean Allen 1914- *WhoAm 92, WhoWor 93, WhoWrEP 92*
Battle, Joan Pierce 1935- *WhoAmW 93*
Battle, Joe David 1958- *WhoEmL 93*
Battle, John S., Jr. 1919- *St&PR 93*
Battle, Kathleen 1948- *Baker 92, IntDcOp, OxDcOp*
Battle, Kathleen Deanna *WhoAm 92, WhoAmW 93, WhoWor 93*
Battle, Lucius Durham 1918- *WhoAm 92*
Battle, Lucy Troxell 1916- *WhoAmW 93*
Battle, Mark G. *WhoAm 92*
Battle, Richard Vernon 1951- *WhoSSW 93*
Battle, Thomas P. *Law&B 92*
Battle, Thomas Peyton 1942- *St&PR 93, WhoAm 92*
Battle, Turner Charles, III 1926- *WhoWor 93*
Battle, Valencia Bernita 1965- *WhoAmW 93*

Battle, William R. 1924- *St&PR 93, WhoIns 93*
Battle, William Rainey 1924- *WhoAm 92*
Battle, William Robert 1927- *WhoAm 92, WhoWrEP 92*
Battleman, Murray 1936- *St&PR 93*
Battles, Cliff 1910-1991 *BioIn 17*
Battles, Edith 1921- *ScF&FL 92*
Battles, (Roxy) Edith 1921- *WhoWrEP 92*
Battles, Roxy Edith 1921- *WhoAm 92, WhoAmW 93*
Battles, Roy Edward 1911- *WhoSSW 93*
Battles, Timothy J. 1944- *St&PR 93*
Battocletti, Joseph Henry 1925- *WhoAm 92*
Batton, Desire-Alexandre 1798-1855 *Baker 92*
Batton, Kenneth Duff 1942- *WhoE 93*
Batton, Monica Kim 1956- *WhoE 93, WhoEmL 93, WhoWor 93*
Battram, Richard L. 1934- *WhoAm 92*
Batts, Anne King 1945- *WhoAmW 93*
Batts, Constance Brooks 1954- *WhoE 93*
Batts, James A., Jr. d1992 *NewYTBS 92*
Batts, Michael Stanley 1929- *WhoAm 92, WhoWrEP 92*
Batts, Ronald N. 1949- *St&PR 93*
Batts, Warren L. 1932- *St&PR 93*
Batts, Warren Leighton 1932- *WhoAm 92*
Battson, Bradford Lee 1957- *WhoEmL 93*
Battu, Pantaleon 1799-1870 *Baker 92*
Batty, Gayle Priscilla 1936- *WhoE 93*
Batty, H. Andrew, Jr. 1947- *St&PR 93*
Batty, John Carl 1955- *WhoEmL 93*
Batty, John Michael *WhoScE 91-1*
Batty, Judith Nell *Law&B 92*
Batty, Michael 1945- *WhoWor 93*
Batu Bagan 1924- *WhoAsAP 91*
Batubara, Cosmas 1938- *WhoAsAP 91*
Batu Khan d1255 *HarEnMi*
Baturin, Alexander 1904- *OxDcOp*
Baty, Cecelia Glacy *Law&B 92*
Baty, Peggy June 1956- *WhoAmW 93*
Baty, Vicki Louise 1948- *WhoWrEP 92*
Batyrov, Ravil' 1931- *DrEEuF*
Batz, Hans-Georg 1944- *WhoWor 93*
Batza, Stephen M. 1955- *St&PR 93*
Batzei, William B. *Law&B 92*
Batzel, Roger Elwood 1921- *WhoAm 92*
Batzer, R. Kirk 1915- *WhoAm 92*
Batzli, George Oliver 1936- *WhoAm 92*
Bau, Lawrence *Law&B 92*
Baubles, Richard C. *St&PR 93*
Bauch, Thomas Jay *Law&B 92*
Bauch, Thomas Jay 1943- *St&PR 93, WhoAm 92*
Bauchman, Robert W. 1920- *St&PR 93*
Bauchot, Roland 1929- *WhoScE 91-2*
Bauchspiess, Karl Rudolf 1955- *WhoWor 93*
Bauckham, James Arthur 1936- *St&PR 93*
Baucom, Bill L. 1933- *St&PR 93*
Baucom, Sidney G. 1930- *St&PR 93*
Baucom, Sidney George 1930- *WhoAm 92*
Baucum, William Emmett, Jr. 1945- *WhoSSW 93*
Baucus, Max 1941- *CngDr 91*
Baucus, Max S. 1941- *WhoAm 92*
Baud-Bovy, Samuel 1906-1986 *Baker 92*
Baudean, Aubrey A., Jr. 1959- *WhoSSW 93*
Baudelaire, Charles 1821-1867 *BioIn 17, MagSWL [port], ScF&FL 92, WorLitC [port]*
Baudendistel, Daniel *WhoAm 92*
Bauder, Alfred 1934- *WhoScE 91-4*
Bauder, Marianna 1943- *WhoAmW 93*
Baudet, Jean C. 1944- *WhoScE 91-2*
Baudhuin, Donald Joseph 1949- *St&PR 93*
Baudhuin, Pierre 1934- *WhoScE 91-2*
Baudier, Julian Gerald, Sr. 1919- *St&PR 93*
Baudin, Pierre 1931- *WhoScE 91-2*
Baudino, Gael 1955?- *ScF&FL 92*
Baudiot, (Charles-) Nicolas 1773-1849 *Baker 92*
Baudis, Dominique Pierre Jean Albert 1947- *BioIn 17*
Baudo, Serge 1927- *WhoWor 93*
Baudo, Serge (Paul) 1927- *Baker 92*
Baudoin, Bryan E. 1961- *WhoSSW 93*
Baudoin, Jean-Pierre 1950- *WhoScE 91-2*
Baudoin, Noel c. 1480-1530 *Baker 92*
Baudouin, I 1930- *WhoWor 93*
Baudouin, Richard Evan, Jr. 1953- *WhoSSW 93*
Baudouin de Courtenay Ehrenkreutz-Jedrzejewiczowa, Cezaria 1885-1967 *IntDcAn*
Baudrier, Yves 1906-1988 *Baker 92*
Baudrillard, Jean 1929- *BioIn 17*
Baudry, Alain 1942- *WhoScE 91-2*
Baudy, Romona Theresa 1947- *WhoEmL 93*
Baue, Arthur Edward 1929- *WhoAm 92*
Bauer, Abby Anne 1965- *WhoAmW 93*
Bauer, Allison Shelton 1962- *WhoSSW 93*
Bauer, Arthur James 1947- *WhoEmL 93*
Bauer, August Robert, Jr. 1928- *WhoAm 92, WhoWor 93*
Bauer, Barbara Ann 1955- *WhoAmW 93*
Bauer, Barbara Gae 1958- *WhoAmW 93, WhoE 93, WhoEmL 93, WhoWor 93*
Bauer, Barbara Lois 1957- *WhoAmW 93*
Bauer, Branko 1921- *DrEEuF*
Bauer, Brian H. 1947- *St&PR 93*
Bauer, Bud *BioIn 17*
Bauer, Carl W. 1933- *St&PR 93*
Bauer, Caroline Feller *WhoAm 92*
Bauer, Caroline Feller 1935- *BioIn 17*
Bauer, Catherine E. *Law&B 92*
Bauer, Celeste Joan Coggiola 1949- *WhoAmW 93*
Bauer, Charles T. 1919- *St&PR 93*
Bauer, Chris M. 1948- *St&PR 93*
Bauer, Chris Michael 1948- *WhoAm 92*
Bauer, Christian 1938- *WhoScE 91-4*
Bauer, Cynthia Mary 1955- *WhoEmL 93*
Bauer, Dale R. d1992 *NewYTBS 92*
Bauer, Dale Robert 1928- *WhoAm 92*
Bauer, Daniel George 1960- *WhoE 93, WhoEmL 93*
Bauer, David E. 1929- *St&PR 93*
Bauer, Debra Rosenthal 1952- *WhoEmL 93*
Bauer, Douglas F. *Law&B 92*
Bauer, Douglas F. 1942- *St&PR 93, WhoAm 92*
Bauer, Edward Ewing 1917- *St&PR 93, WhoWor 93*
Bauer, Elaine Louise 1949- *WhoAm 92*
Bauer, Elizabeth Kelley 1920- *WhoAmW 93*
Bauer, Ernst Georg 1928- *WhoWor 93*
Bauer, F. *WhoScE 91-4*
Bauer, Fred 1934- *BioIn 17*
Bauer, Fred A.M. *Law&B 92*
Bauer, Fred C. 1927- *St&PR 93*
Bauer, Frederick Christian 1927- *WhoAm 92*
Bauer, Friedhelm Detlef 1953- *WhoWor 93*
Bauer, Friedrich Ludwig 1924- *WhoWor 93*
Bauer, G.J. *WhoScE 91-1*
Bauer, G. Michael *Law&B 92*
Bauer, Gary Haywood 1950- *WhoEmL 93*
Bauer, Gary Lee 1946- *WhoAm 92*
Bauer, George E. 1920- *St&PR 93*
Bauer, George Victor 1932- *St&PR 93*
Bauer, Gerd Walter 1948- *WhoWor 93*
Bauer, Gerhard H. 1935- *WhoWor 93*
Bauer, Gil L. *BioIn 17*
Bauer, Gordon P. 1938- *St&PR 93*
Bauer, Gunther Ernst 1942- *WhoScE 91-4*
Bauer, Gunther Georg 1928- *WhoWor 93*
Bauer, H. Dan *Law&B 92*
Bauer, Hans Dieter 1929- *WhoScE 91-3*
Bauer, Harold 1873-1951 *Baker 92*
Bauer, Heinz 1933- *WhoScE 91-3*
Bauer, Henry Hermann 1931- *WhoAm 92, WhoSSW 93*
Bauer, James August 1933- *WhoSSW 93*
Bauer, James M. *Law&B 92*
Bauer, James P. 1945- *St&PR 93*
Bauer, Jean-Francois 1955- *St&PR 93*
Bauer, Jeffrey Patrick 1949- *WhoEmL 93*
Bauer, Jerry 1948- *WhoEmL 93*
Bauer, Jobst-Hubertus 1945- *WhoWor 93*
Bauer, Joel J. 1942- *WhoE 93*
Bauer, John J. d1990 *BioIn 17*
Bauer, Joseph W. *Law&B 92*
Bauer, Judy Marie 1947- *WhoAmW 93*
Bauer, Kurt Heinz 1930- *WhoScE 91-3*
Bauer, Larry Alan 1954- *WhoEmL 93*
Bauer, Lawrence Michael 1950- *WhoEmL 93*
Bauer, Lillian Grace 1911- *WhoAmW 93*
Bauer, Malcolm Clair 1914- *WhoWrEP 92*
Bauer, Margaret Spearly 1951- *WhoE 93*
Bauer, Marilyn Wimberley 1936- *WhoSSW 93*
Bauer, Marion 1897-1955 *BioIn 17*
Bauer, Marion Dane 1938- *DcAmChF 1960, DcAmChF 1985, MajAI [port], SmATA 69 [port], WhoAm 92*
Bauer, Marion (Eugenie) 1887-1955 *Baker 92*
Bauer, Mark Eugene 1952- *WhoEmL 93*
Bauer, Max William 1957- *WhoEmL 93*
Bauer, Michael D. 1948- *St&PR 93*
Bauer, Michael John *Law&B 92*
Bauer, Michael John 1951- *St&PR 93*
Bauer, Monica Elizabeth 1953- *WhoE 93*
Bauer, Nancy *BioIn 17*
Bauer, Nancy 1934- *WhoCanL 92*
Bauer, Nancy Elaine 1953- *WhoAm 92, WhoE 93*
Bauer, Nancy Louise 1941- *WhoAmW 93*
Bauer, Neil Stephen 1943- *WhoE 93*
Bauer, Norman James 1929- *WhoE 93*
Bauer, Otto Frank 1931- *WhoAm 92*
Bauer, Paul David 1943- *St&PR 93, WhoAm 92*
Bauer, Pierre 1941- *WhoScE 91-2*
Bauer, Ralph Glenn 1925- *WhoAm 92*
Bauer, Randall Richard 1949- *WhoEmL 93*
Bauer, Raymond Gale 1934- *WhoE 93, WhoWor 93*
Bauer, Raymond W. 1915- *St&PR 93*
Bauer, Reinhard *WhoScE 91-3*
Bauer, Rhonda Leah 1959- *WhoEmL 93*
Bauer, Richard Carlton 1944- *WhoAm 92, WhoE 93*
Bauer, Richard J. 1938- *St&PR 93*
Bauer, Richard K. 1928- *WhoScE 91-3*
Bauer, Robert Albert 1910- *WhoAm 92*
Bauer, Robert Michael 1953- *WhoE 93*
Bauer, Robert Paul 1920- *WhoAm 92*
Bauer, Robin David 1959- *St&PR 93*
Bauer, Roger Duane 1932- *WhoAm 92*
Bauer, Ronald G. *Law&B 92*
Bauer, Ronald Lee 1937- *WhoAm 92*
Bauer, Roy A. 1945- *ConAu 137*
Bauer, Rudolf 1889-1954 *BioIn 17*
Bauer, Ruth Warfield 1936- *WhoAmW 93, WhoE 93, WhoWor 93*
Bauer, Sharon Ann 1947- *WhoEmL 93*
Bauer, Siegfried Josef 1930- *WhoScE 91-4*
Bauer, Stacy L. *Law&B 92*
Bauer, Stephen W. *Law&B 92*
Bauer, Stephen Walter 1960- *WhoEmL 93*
Bauer, Steve *BioIn 17*
Bauer, Steven 1948- *ScF&FL 92*
Bauer, Steven Albert 1948- *WhoWrEP 92*
Bauer, Steven Michael 1949- *WhoEmL 93*
Bauer, Theodore James 1909- *WhoAm 92*
Bauer, Udibert Reinoldo 1956- *WhoWor 93*
Bauer, W. *WhoScE 91-3*
Bauer, W. Neil 1946- *St&PR 93*
Bauer, Walter B. 1916- *St&PR 93*
Bauer, Werner 1943- *WhoScE 91-4*
Bauer, William D. *Law&B 92*
Bauer, William Joseph 1926- *WhoAm 92*
Bauer, Wolfgang 1941- *DcLB 124 [port]*
Bauerle, Barbara Frances 1950- *WhoAm 92*
Bauerle, Dieter 1940- *WhoScE 91-4*
Bauerle, Hermann 1869-1936 *Baker 92*
Bauerle, Todd Alex 1960- *WhoEmL 93*
Bauerlein, Dudley Lawrence, Jr. 1946- *St&PR 93*
Bauerlein, Mark Weightman 1959- *WhoSSW 93*
Bauerly, Ronald John 1953- *WhoEmL 93*
Bauermann, Julius Frank 1932- *St&PR 93*
Bauermeister, Mathilde 1849-1926 *Baker 92*
Bauer-Patitz, D. *WhoWrEP 92*
Bauerschmidt, George Charles 1946- *WhoAm 92*
Bauersfeld, Carl Frederick 1916- *WhoAm 92*
Bauer-Theussl, Franz (Ferdinand) 1928- *Baker 92*
Bauer-Tomich, Faith E. 1957- *WhoAmW 93*
Bauger, Eivind 1919- *WhoScE 91-4*
Baugh, Ann Lawrence 1938- *WhoAmW 93*
Baugh, Charles Milton 1931- *WhoAm 92*
Baugh, Charles R. 1950- *St&PR 93*
Baugh, Constance Marie 1949- *WhoE 93*
Baugh, Coy Franklin 1946- *WhoAm 92*
Baugh, Elaine Dorothy 1953- *WhoEmL 93*
Baugh, Gary J. *St&PR 93*
Baugh, John Frank 1916- *St&PR 93, WhoAm 92*
Baugh, Laura *BioIn 17*
Baugh, Philip Dupont 1948- *WhoSSW 93*
Baugh, Sammy 1914- *BioIn 17*
Baugh, Thomas Willard, III 1962- *WhoSSW 93*
Baugh, William R. 1949- *St&PR 93*
Baughan, Maxie Calloway, Jr. 1947- *BiDAMSp 1989*
Baughcum, Steven Lee 1950- *WhoEmL 93*
Baugher, John Oliver 1937- *St&PR 93*
Baugher, Nancy Anne 1957- *WhoAmW 93*
Baugher, Peter V. 1948- *WhoAm 92, WhoEmL 93*
Baugher, Tara Lou Auxt 1953- *WhoEmL 93*
Baughman, David 1949- *St&PR 93*
Baughman, Dorothy 1940- *BioIn 17*
Baughman, Fred Hubbard 1926- *WhoAm 92*
Baughman, George Fechtig 1915- *WhoAm 92*
Baughman, George Washington 1911- *WhoSSW 93, WhoWor 93*
Baughman, J. Ross 1953- *WhoAm 92, WhoWrEP 92*
Baughman, James Allan 1951- *WhoE 93*
Baughman, James K. *Law&B 92*
Baughman, Jennifer Jane 1967- *WhoAmW 93*
Baughman, Leonora K. *Law&B 92*
Baughman, Leonora Knoblock 1956- *WhoEmL 93*
Baughman, Linda Youtsey 1947- *WhoSSW 93*
Baughman, Michael *Law&B 92*
Baughman, Ray Edward 1925- *WhoWrEP 92*
Baughman, Robert Patrick 1938- *WhoAm 92, WhoWor 93*
Baughman, Ruth L. *AmWomPl*
Baughman, William Allen 1959- *WhoSSW 93*
Baughn, Robert Elroy 1940- *WhoSSW 93*
Baughn, Steven Peyton 1947- *WhoE 93, WhoEmL 93*
Baughn, William Hubert 1918- *WhoAm 92*
Bauguess, Milt *WhoIns 93*
Bauguss, Douglas 1958- *St&PR 93*
Baugut, Gunar E. 1943- *WhoScE 91-3*
Bauhard, William Leland 1945- *WhoWor 93*
Baujan, Robert Raymond 1930- *St&PR 93*
Baukal, Werner 1935- *WhoScE 91-3*
Bauknecht, John Waltner 1930- *St&PR 93*
Bauknight, Clarence Brock 1936- *St&PR 93, WhoAm 92*
Baukol, Ronald Oliver 1937- *WhoAm 92*
Bauld, Alison 1944- *BioIn 17*
Bauld, Alison (Margaret) 1944- *Baker 92*
Bauldeweyn, Noel c. 1480-1530 *Baker 92*
Bauldewijn, Noel c. 1480-1530 *Baker 92*
Bauldoin, Noel c. 1480-1530 *Baker 92*
Bauleke, Howard Paul 1959- *WhoEmL 93*
Baulieu, Etienne-Emile *BioIn 17*
Baulieu, Etienne-Emile 1926- *WhoScE 91-2*
Baum, Alan Stuart 1955- *WhoEmL 93*
Baum, Andrew Ellis *WhoScE 91-1*
Baum, Bernard 1924- *St&PR 93*
Baum, Bernard Helmut 1926- *WhoAm 92*
Baum, Carl Edward 1940- *WhoAm 92, WhoWor 93*
Baum, Casey *Law&B 92*
Baum, Charles C. 1942- *St&PR 93*
Baum, David Roy 1946- *WhoAm 92*
Baum, Dennis A. 1944- *St&PR 93*
Baum, Dwight C. 1912- *St&PR 93*
Baum, Dwight Crouse 1912- *WhoAm 92*
Baum, Edward S. *BioIn 17*
Baum, Elaine Irene 1952- *WhoAmW 93*
Baum, Eleanor *BioIn 17*
Baum, Eleanor 1940- *WhoAm 92, WhoAmW 93*
Baum, Elizabeth Clark 1942- *WhoAmW 93*
Baum, Ernest W. *Law&B 92*
Baum, Friedrich d1777 *HarEnMi*
Baum, Harold *WhoScE 91-1*
Baum, Herbert Mark 1951- *WhoEmL 93*
Baum, Herbert Merrill 1936- *St&PR 93, WhoAm 92*
Baum, Howard Barry 1952- *WhoE 93*
Baum, Jeanne Ann 1937- *WhoAmW 93*
Baum, Jeffrey David 1952- *WhoEmL 93*
Baum, Jerome Barry 1946- *St&PR 93*
Baum, John 1927- *WhoAm 92*
Baum, Jonathan R. 1961- *St&PR 93*
Baum, Joseph Herman 1927- *WhoAm 92*
Baum, Jules Leonard 1931- *WhoAm 92*
Baum, Kenneth R. 1948- *St&PR 93*
Baum, Kurt 1908-1989 *BioIn 17*
Baum, L. Frank 1856-1919 *BioIn 17, ScF&FL 92*
Baum, L(yman) Frank 1856-1919 *MajAI [port]*
Baum, Laura 1948- *WhoE 93*
Baum, Louis 1948- *BioIn 17*
Baum, Louis F. *MajAI*
Baum, Louise A. d1990 *BioIn 17*
Baum, Lyman Frank 1856-1919 *BioIn 17, GayN*
Baum, Manfred 1939- *WhoWor 93*
Baum, Marjorie Carol 1952- *WhoAmW 93*
Baum, Matthew C. 1931- *St&PR 93*
Baum, Michael *WhoScE 91-1*
Baum, Michael Scott 1952- *WhoAm 92*
Baum, Myrna Elaine *WhoAmW 93*
Baum, Neil F. 1942- *St&PR 93*
Baum, Peter Alan 1947- *WhoEmL 93*
Baum, Ralph Augustus 1932- *St&PR 93, WhoE 93*
Baum, Raymond Nathan 1944- *WhoE 93*
Baum, Richard D. 1932- *WhoIns 93*
Baum, Richard Theodore 1919- *WhoAm 92, WhoE 93, WhoWor 93*
Baum, Robert H. *Law&B 92*
Baum, Roger S. *ScF&FL 92*
Baum, Selma 1924- *WhoAmW 93*
Baum, Stanley 1929- *WhoAm 92*
Baum, Stephen *Law&B 92*
Baum, Stephen H. 1941- *St&PR 93*
Baum, Stephen L. *Law&B 92*
Baum, Sue Ann 1948- *WhoAmW 93*
Baum, Sumner G. 1931- *St&PR 93*
Baum, Thomas 1940- *ScF&FL 92*
Baum, Werner A. 1923- *WhoAm 92*
Baum, William Alvin 1924- *WhoAm 92*

Baum, William Wakefield Cardinal 1926- *WhoWor 93*
Bauman, Arnold 1914-1989 *BioIn 17*
Bauman, Bernard Daniel 1946- *WhoE 93*
Bauman, Charles Joseph 1924- *St&PR 93*
Bauman, Dale Elton 1942- *WhoAm 92, WhoE 93*
Bauman, Donald Stephen *Law&B 92*
Bauman, Frederick C. *Law&B 92*
Bauman, Frederick Carl 1952- *WhoEmL 93*
Bauman, George Duncan 1912- *WhoAm 92, WhoWrEP 92*
Bauman, Gus Bloch 1949- *WhoEmL 93*
Bauman, Guy C. 1951-1990 *BioIn 17*
Bauman, James H. *BioIn 17*
Bauman, Jan Josef 1950- *WhoWor 93*
Bauman, Jerome 1943- *St&PR 93*
Bauman, Jerome Alan 1931- *WhoAm 92*
Bauman, John Andrew 1921- *WhoAm 92*
Bauman, John Duane 1930- *WhoAm 92*
Bauman, John E., Jr. 1933- *WhoAm 92*
Bauman, Jonathan Hugh 1948- *WhoEmL 93*
Bauman, Larry A. 1955- *St&PR 93*
Bauman, Le Roy 1925- *St&PR 93*
Bauman, Mark Lee 1952- *WhoE 93*
Bauman, Martin Harold 1929- *WhoAm 92*
Bauman, Mary P. *Law&B 92*
Bauman, Merritt Richard 1923- *St&PR 93*
Bauman, Nancy Anne 1962- *WhoAmW 93*
Bauman, Richard 1940- *WhoAm 92*
Bauman, Richard Arnold 1924- *WhoAm 92*
Bauman, Robert *BioIn 17*
Bauman, Robert D. *Law&B 92*
Bauman, Robert D. 1940- *WhoIns 93*
Bauman, Robert P. 1931- *St&PR 93*
Bauman, Robert Patten 1931- *WhoAm 92*
Bauman, Robert Poe 1928- *WhoAm 92*
Bauman, Robert Warren, Jr. 1953- *WhoEmL 93, WhoSSW 93*
Bauman, Sharon Ann *WhoAmW 93*
Bauman, Walter Ollendorff 1915- *St&PR 93*
Bauman, William Winter 1961- *WhoEmL 93*
Baumanis, Aivars 1937- *WhoUN 92*
Baumann, Angela Lauria 1945- *WhoAm 92*
Baumann, Daniel E. 1937- *St&PR 93*
Baumann, Daniel H., Jr. 1969- *WhoE 93*
Baumann, Edward Robert 1921- *WhoAm 92*
Baumann, Felix Martin Andreas 1937- *WhoWor 93*
Baumann, Frederick William, Jr. 1945- *St&PR 93*
Baumann, Fritz 1931- *WhoScE 91-4*
Baumann, Gary Joseph 1949- *WhoAm 92*
Baumann, Gary N. 1941- *WhoIns 93*
Baumann, Gregory William 1947- *WhoEmL 93*
Baumann, H.D. *St&PR 93*
Baumann, Hanno Lutz 1940- *WhoScE 91-3*
Baumann, Hermann 1902-1972 *IntDcAn*
Baumann, Hermann (Rudolf Konrad) 1934- *Baker 92*
Baumann, Janet Anne 1938- *WhoAm 92*
Baumann, John M., Jr. *Law&B 92*
Baumann, John Scott *Law&B 92*
Baumann, Judith Kravitz 1942- *WhoSSW 93*
Baumann, Kurt 1907-1983 *BioIn 17*
Baumann, Kurt 1927- *WhoScE 91-4*
Baumann, Max Georg 1917- *Baker 92*
Baumann, Minerva Anne 1959- *WhoAmW 93*
Baumann, Nicole Anita 1932- *WhoScE 91-2*
Baumann, Paul David *BioIn 17*
Baumann, Phillip Allen 1949- *WhoEmL 93*
Baumann, Pierre 1944- *WhoScE 91-4*
Baumann, Richard B. *BioIn 17*
Baumann, Richard Gordon 1938- *WhoAm 92*
Baumann, Robert Jay 1940- *WhoAm 92, WhoSSW 93*
Baumann, Roland Theodore, II *Law&B 92*
Baumann, Roxanne Lee 1953- *WhoEmL 93*
Baumann, Theodore Robert 1932- *WhoWor 93*
Baumann, Thomas P. *St&PR 93*
Baumann, Valerie Joan *Law&B 92*
Baumann, Winfried 1929- *WhoWor 93*
Baumbach, Donna Jean Toler 1948- *WhoEmL 93, WhoSSW 93*
Baumbach, Friedrich August 1753-1813 *Baker 92*
Baumbach, Harold 1904- *WhoAm 92*
Baumbach, Jonathan 1933- *BioIn 17, WhoE 93, WhoWrEP 92*
Baumberger, David Lee 1955- *WhoEmL 93*
Baumbich, James J. 1936- *St&PR 93*
Baume, Michael Ehrenfried 1930- *WhoAsAP 91*
Baume, Peter Erne 1935- *WhoAsAP 91*
Baumeister, Alfred J. 1927- *St&PR 93*
Baumeister, Carl F. 1907- *WhoWor 93*
Baumeister, Donald E. 1950- *WhoEmL 93*
Baumeister, Willi 1889-1955 *BioIn 17*
Baumeister, Wolfgang *WhoScE 91-3*
Baumel, Abraham 1926- *WhoE 93*
Baumel, Herbert 1919- *WhoE 93, WhoWor 93*
Baumel, Jacques 1918- *BioIn 17*
Baumel, Joan Patricia French 1930- *WhoAmW 93, WhoE 93*
Baumer, Beverly Belle 1926- *WhoAm 92, WhoAmW 93*
Baumer, Franklin L. 1913-1990 *BioIn 17*
Baumer, Marie 1905- *AmWomPl*
Baumfelder, Friedrich 1836-1916 *Baker 92*
Baumfree, Isabella d1883 *BioIn 17*
Baumgaertel, Hermann Detlef 1932- *WhoWor 93*
Baumgardner, Barbara Ann 1937- *WhoAmW 93*
Baumgardner, Dennis *St&PR 93*
Baumgardner, James Lewis 1938- *WhoAm 92*
Baumgardner, John Dwane 1940- *St&PR 93*
Baumgardner, John Ellwood, Jr. 1951- *WhoAm 92*
Baumgardner, Kandy Diane 1946- *WhoAm 92*
Baumgardner, Karen T. 1953- *WhoAmW 93*
Baumgardner, Roger Leroy 1942- *St&PR 93*
Baumgardner, Russell Howard 1918- *St&PR 93*
Baumgardner, T. Miesse 1904- *St&PR 93*
Baumgardt, Arden C. 1941- *St&PR 93*
Baumgardt, Arden Charles 1941- *WhoIns 93*
Baumgardt, Billy Ray 1933- *WhoAm 92*
Baumgart, Norbert K. 1931- *WhoAm 92*
Baumgartel, Howard J., Jr. 1920- *WhoAm 92*
Baumgarten, Heinrich L. 1941- *WhoWor 93*
Baumgarten, Heinrich Ludwig 1941- *WhoScE 91-3*
Baumgarten, Herbert J. *Law&B 92*
Baumgarten, Herbert J. 1935- *St&PR 93*
Baumgarten, Joseph Russell 1928- *WhoAm 92*
Baumgarten, Lee A. 1918- *St&PR 93*
Baumgarten, Marion Betor 1960- *WhoEmL 93*
Baumgarten, Neil S. *Law&B 92*
Baumgarten, Paul Anthony 1934- *WhoAm 92*
Baumgarten, Reuben Lawrence 1934- *WhoE 93*
Baumgarten, Richard L. 1946- *St&PR 93*
Baumgarten, Ronald Neal 1942- *WhoWor 93*
Baumgarten, Sidney 1933- *WhoAm 92*
Baumgartner, Allan Rodney 1938- *WhoWor 93*
Baumgartner, Daniel Benton 1944- *WhoWrEP 92*
Baumgartner, Donald H. 1941- *St&PR 93*
Baumgartner, Donald W. 1930- *St&PR 93*
Baumgartner, Franz 1929- *WhoScE 91-3*
Baumgartner, Gerhard *WhoScE 91-4*
Baumgartner, Gunter 1924- *WhoScE 91-4*
Baumgartner, J. Peter *Law&B 92*
Baumgartner, James Earl 1943- *WhoAm 92*
Baumgartner, Johann Franz 1929- *WhoWor 93*
Baumgartner, John H. 1936- *WhoAm 92*
Baumgartner, Joy Ann 1946- *WhoAmW 93*
Baumgartner, Leona 1902-1991 *AnObit 1991, BioIn 17*
Baumgartner, Patricia Alfreda 1936- *WhoAmW 93*
Baumgartner, Paul 1903-1976 *Baker 92*
Baumgartner, Robert A. 1947- *St&PR 93*
Baumgartner, Robert P. *Law&B 92*
Baumgartner, Robert V. 1956- *St&PR 93*
Baumgartner, Rudolf 1917- *Baker 92*
Baumgartner, Ulrich 1946- *WhoUN 92*
Baumgartner, Vito H. 1940- *St&PR 93*
Baumgartner, Wilhelm 1820-1867 *Baker 92*
Baumgartner, William Hans, Jr. 1955- *WhoAm 92*
Baumgold, Charles 1912- *St&PR 93*
Baumgratz, Sergio Santos 1957- *WhoWor 93*
Baumhart, Raymond Charles 1923- *WhoAm 92*
Baumheckel, David Allen 1952- *St&PR 93*
Baumhefner, Clarence Herman 1912- *WhoAm 92*
Baumker, Wilhelm 1842-1905 *Baker 92*
Bauml, Franz Heinrich 1926- *WhoAm 92*
Baumler, Johann Andreas 1941- *WhoUN 92*
Baumoel, Joseph 1928- *St&PR 93*
Baumol, William J. *BioIn 17*
Baumol, William Jack 1922- *WhoAm 92*
Baumrin, Bernard Stefan Herbert 1934- *WhoAm 92*
Baumrin, Judith Marti 1935- *WhoE 93*
Baumrind, Diana 1927- *WhoAm 92*
Baumrind, Lydia 1954- *WhoAmW 93*
Baumrind, Seymour d1990 *BioIn 17*
Baumruck, Scott Alan 1952- *WhoEmL 93*
Baumwell, Ivan Adam 1957- *WhoE 93*
Baumwoll, Joel Phillip 1940- *St&PR 93*
Baumy, Beverly Jo 1959- *WhoAmW 93*
Bauner, Ruth Elizabeth *WhoAmW 93*
Baur, Harry 1880-1943 *IntDcF 2-3 [port]*
Baur, Isolde Nacke 1923- *WhoSSW 93*
Baur, James Gerard 1940- *St&PR 93*
Baur, Jurg 1918- *Baker 92*
Baur, Leonard Hubert Bernhard 1957- *WhoWor 93*
Baur, Max P. 1948- *WhoScE 91-3*
Baur, Philip J., Jr. 1930- *St&PR 93*
Baur, Stephen 1922- *St&PR 93*
Baur, Susan 1940- *ConAu 40NR*
Baur, Werner Heinz 1931- *WhoAm 92, WhoWor 93*
Baurer, Frederic Martin 1957- *WhoEmL 93*
Baurs-Krey, Detlev H. U. 1943- *WhoE 93*
Baus, Marc 1942- *WhoWor 93*
Bausch, James John 1936- *WhoAm 92, WhoE 93, WhoWor 93*
Bausch, Janet Jean Taylor *Law&B 92*
Bausch, Ludwig 1829-1871 *Baker 92*
Bausch, Ludwig Christian August 1805-1871 *Baker 92*
Bausch, Otto 1841-1875 *Baker 92*
Bausch, Richard 1945- *BioIn 17, ScF&FL 92*
Bausch, Richard Carl 1945- *WhoWrEP 92*
Bausch, Robert 1945- *ScF&FL 92*
Bause, David Francis 1936- *WhoE 93*
Bause, Richard Marshall 1925- *St&PR 93*
Bausher, Verne Charles *WhoAm 92*
Bausman, S. David 1946- *St&PR 93*
Baustert, James L. *St&PR 93*
Baustian, Robert Frederick 1921- *WhoAm 92*
Bausum, Henry Stover 1924- *WhoSSW 93*
Bausznern, Waldemar von 1866-1931 *Baker 92*
Bautch, Thomas A. 1949- *St&PR 93*
Baute, Joseph A. 1928- *St&PR 93*
Baute, Julia I. *Law&B 92*
Bauter, Robert Theodore 1929- *St&PR 93*
Bautista, Basilio Nery 1935- *WhoWor 93*
Bautista, Benjamin V. 1928- *WhoAsAP 91*
Bautista, Carol Stoney 1949- *WhoAmW 93*
Bautista, Debra Jo 1956- *WhoAmW 93*
Bautista, Florosa Aguinaldo 1928- *WhoWor 93*
Bautista, Julian 1901-1961 *Baker 92*
Bautista, Norman Ronald 1952- *WhoEmL 93*
Bautista, Renato Go 1934- *WhoAm 92*
Bautista-Myers, Lilian *WhoAmW 93*
Bautz, Laura Patricia 1940- *WhoAm 92, WhoAmW 93*
Bauumgartner, Michael Lee 1957- *WhoEmL 93, WhoSSW 93*
Bauverd, Carlos 1953- *WhoUN 92*
Bauwin, Roberta Elizabeth 1960- *WhoE 93*
Bava, Antonio E. 1940- *WhoScE 91-3*
Bava, Lamberto 1944- *MiSFD 9*
Bava, Mario 1914-1980 *MiSFD 9N*
Bavaria, Joan *BioIn 17*
Bavaria, Steven Michael 1947- *St&PR 93*
Bavasi, Peter 1942- *St&PR 93*
Bavasi, Peter Joseph 1942- *WhoAm 92*
Bavcar, Evgen *BioIn 17*
Baverstam, Ulf H. 1940- *WhoScE 91-4*
Bavicchi, John 1922- *Baker 92*
Baviello, Michael Angelo, Jr. 1951- *WhoEmL 93*
Bavinck, Herman 1939- *WhoWor 93*
Bavis, Karen Ann 1962- *WhoAmW 93, WhoSSW 93*
Bavota, Michael Francis 1952- *WhoEmL 93, WhoWrEP 92*
Bawden, Herbert Perry, Jr. 1943- *WhoE 93*
Bawden, James Wyatt 1930- *WhoAm 92*
Bawden, Nina 1925- *ChlFicS, ScF&FL 92, SmATA 16AS [port]*
Bawden, Nina Mary 1925- *WhoAm 92*
Bawden, Nina (Mary Mabey) 1925- *MajAI [port], SmATA 72 [port]*
Bawteau, J.P. *WhoScE 91-2*
Bax, Arnold 1883-1953 *Baker 92*
Bax, Clifford 1886-1962 *BioIn 17*
Bax, Martin 1933- *ScF&FL 92*
Baxandall, Michael David Kighley 1933- *WhoAm 92*
Baxendale, James Edward 1940- *WhoIns 93*
Baxendale, Lily 1924- *WhoScE 91-1*
Baxendale-Baines, George Wilfrid 1940- *WhoWor 93*
Baxendell, Peter Brian 1925- *WhoAm 92, WhoWor 93*
Baxley, Barbara 1927-1990 *BioIn 17*
Baxley, Craig R. *MiSFD 9*
Baxley, Elizabeth Dawn 1963- *WhoSSW 93*
Baxley, Phillip Kent 1957- *WhoEmL 93*
Baxley, William Clegg 1948- *St&PR 93*
Baxt, Victor J. 1917- *St&PR 93*
Baxter, Adrienne M. 1962- *WhoAmW 93*
Baxter, Alfred Xavier 1925- *St&PR 93*
Baxter, Alistair Napier *WhoScE 91-1*
Baxter, Anne *BioIn 17*
Baxter, Anne 1923-1985 *IntDcF 2-3 [port]*
Baxter, Arthur Pearce 1943- *St&PR 93, WhoAm 92, WhoSSW 93*
Baxter, Barbara Miller d1991 *BioIn 17*
Baxter, Barbara Morgan 1939- *WhoAmW 93*
Baxter, Betty Carpenter 1937- *WhoAmW 93*
Baxter, Brian Lee 1948- *St&PR 93*
Baxter, Bruce Osborne 1945- *WhoAm 92, WhoE 93*
Baxter, Carla Louise Chaney 1955- *WhoAmW 93, WhoEmL 93*
Baxter, Catherine Elaine 1964- *WhoE 93*
Baxter, Cecil William, Jr. 1923- *WhoAm 92*
Baxter, Charles 1947- *ConAu 40NR*
Baxter, Donald 1925- *St&PR 93*
Baxter, Donald William 1926- *WhoAm 92*
Baxter, Dorotha Mae 1923- *WhoAmW 93*
Baxter, Duby Yvonne 1953- *WhoAmW 93*
Baxter, E. Denise *WhoScE 91-1*
Baxter, Elaine 1933- *WhoAm 92, WhoAmW 93*
Baxter, Frederica Boatwright 1941- *St&PR 93*
Baxter, Gerald L. *Law&B 92*
Baxter, Gloria Jean 1940- *WhoAmW 93*
Baxter, Gordon 1923- *BioIn 17*
Baxter, Gregory Wayne 1948- *WhoSSW 93*
Baxter, Harry Stevens 1915- *WhoAm 92*
Baxter, Irving Knott 1876-1957 *BiDAMSp 1989*
Baxter, James Edward 1949- *St&PR 93*
Baxter, James George 1948- *St&PR 93*
Baxter, James K. 1926-1972 *BioIn 17*
Baxter, James William, III 1931- *WhoAm 92, WhoWor 93*
Baxter, Janet Schwartz 1947- *WhoEmL 93*
Baxter, Jerrel Clyde 1955- *WhoEmL 93*
Baxter, Joan 1927- *WhoSSW 93*
Baxter, Joe E., Sr. 1924- *St&PR 93*
Baxter, John 1939- *ScF&FL 92*
Baxter, John Darling 1940- *WhoAm 92*
Baxter, John Lincoln, Jr. 1920- *WhoAm 92*
Baxter, Karen Grimsley 1949- *WhoWrEP 92*
Baxter, Leone Smith 1913- See Whitaker and Baker *PolPar*
Baxter, Lorna *ScF&FL 92*
Baxter, Marvin R. 1940- *WhoAm 92*
Baxter, Mary Ann 1956- *WhoAmW 93*
Baxter, Maurice Glen 1920- *WhoAm 92*
Baxter, Meredith *BioIn 17*
Baxter, Meredith 1947- *WhoAmW 93*
Baxter, Michael John 1944- *WhoWrEP 92*
Baxter, Millie McLean 1926- *WhoAmW 93, WhoWor 93*
Baxter, Murdoch Scott *WhoScE 91-1*
Baxter, Nevins D. 1941- *St&PR 93*
Baxter, Ralph Felix 1925- *WhoAm 92*
Baxter, Randolph 1946- *WhoAm 92*
Baxter, Raoul 1950- *WhoAm 92*
Baxter, Reginald Robert 1925- *WhoAm 92*
Baxter, Richard 1615-1691 *BioIn 17*
Baxter, Richard James *Law&B 92*
Baxter, Robert 1930- *BioIn 17*
Baxter, Robert Banning 1946- *WhoE 93*
Baxter, Robert Dale 1953- *WhoEmL 93*
Baxter, Robert Hampton, III 1931- *WhoAm 92*
Baxter, Robert Henry 1940- *WhoAm 92*
Baxter, Rodd M. *Law&B 92*
Baxter, Ruth Sackett 1928- *WhoAmW 93*
Baxter, Seaton Hall *WhoScE 91-1*
Baxter, Stephen 1957- *ScF&FL 92*
Baxter, Stephen Bartow 1929- *WhoAm 92*
Baxter, Stephen Paul 1948- *St&PR 93*
Baxter, Sydney *Law&B 92*
Baxter, Sylvester 1850-1927 *BioIn 17*
Baxter, Terry *ScF&FL 92*
Baxter, Terry Lawrence 1945- *WhoAm 92*
Baxter, Thomas C. 1932- *St&PR 93*
Baxter, Thomas Gregory 1946- *WhoAm 92*
Baxter, Victoria Lynn 1948- *WhoEmL 93*

Baxter, Violet Diane WhoE 93
Baxter, Warner BioIn 17
Baxter, William Alexander 1929- St&PR 93
Baxter, William G. 1952- WhoE 93
Baxter, William MacNeil 1923- WhoAm 92
Baxter-Birney, Meredith 1947- WhoAm 92
Baxter-Hott, Peggy Ann 1952- WhoAmW 93
Baxtresser, Jeanne WhoAm 92
Bay, Christian 1921-1990 BioIn 17
Bay, D. WhoScE 91-2
Bay, Darrell Edward 1942- WhoSSW 93
Bay, Emmanuel 1891-1967 Baker 92
Bay, Niels 1947- WhoWor 93
Bay, Paul Norman 1935- St&PR 93
Bay, Peter 1957- WhoAm 92
Bay, Richard Anthony 1948- WhoEmL 93
Bay, Ronald Hampton 1948- WhoIns 93
Bay, Zoltan L. d1992 NewYTBS 92
Bayada, G. WhoScE 91-2
Bayar, Mahmud Celal 1884-1986 DcTwHis
Bayarbaatar, Sed-Ochiryn 1956- WhoAsAP 91
Bayard, Alton Ernest, III 1952- WhoEmL 93
Bayard, James Ashton 1767-1815 BioIn 17
Bayard, Jean 1923- WhoWrEP 92
Bayard, Nicholas 1644?-1707 BioIn 17
Bayard, Samuel 1767-1840 BioIn 17
Bayard, Susan Shapiro 1942- WhoAmW 93
Bayazit, Mehmetcik 1937- WhoScE 91-4
Baybayan, Ronald Alan 1946- WhoEmL 93
Bayda, Edward Dmytro 1931- WhoAm 92
Baye, Betty Winston BioIn 17
Baye, Kenneth E. Law&B 92
Baye, Nathalie BioIn 17
Baye, Nathalie 1948- IntDcF 2-3
Baye, Sula L. Law&B 92
Bayegan, H. Markus 1944- WhoScE 91-4
Bayer, Berghold 1942- WhoScE 91-4
Bayer, Cary Stuart 1953- WhoWrEP 92
Bayer, D. Lucille St&PR 93
Bayer, Ernst 1927- WhoScE 91-3, WhoWor 93
Bayer, Frederick J. St&PR 93
Bayer, George Herbert 1924- WhoE 93
Bayer, Henry C. d1991 BioIn 17
Bayer, Henry Frederick 1925- St&PR 93
Bayer, Ian Douglas 1939- St&PR 93
Bayer, Istvan 1923- WhoScE 91-4
Bayer, Josef 1852-1913 Baker 92
Bayer, Jules M. St&PR 93
Bayer, Margret Helene Janssen 1931- WhoAm 92
Bayer, Paul 1931- WhoUN 92
Bayer, Raymond George 1935- WhoE 93
Bayer, Richard Stewart 1951- WhoWor 93
Bayer, Robert Clark 1944- WhoE 93
Bayer, Sandra L. ScF&FL 92
Bayer, Sandy 1945- ScF&FL 92
Bayer, Walter A. 1920- St&PR 93
Bayer, Walter J., II Law&B 92
Bayer-Berenbau, Linda 1948- ScF&FL 92
Bayer-Helms, Friedrich 1926- WhoScE 91-3
Bayerlein, Fritz 1899-1970 HarEnMi
Bayers, Hazel Joyce 1947- WhoEmL 93
Bayes, Ginny 1960- WhoAmW 93
Bayes, Ramon 1930- WhoWor 93
Bayes, Ronald Homer 1932- WhoWrEP 92
Bayezid, I 1354-1403 OxDcByz
Bayh, Birch E., Jr. 1928- PolPar
Bayh, Birch Evans, Jr. 1928- WhoAm 92
Bayh, Evan 1955- WhoAm 92, WhoWor 93
Bayh, Susan B. Law&B 92
Bayko, Emil Thomas 1947- WhoAm 92
Baykut, Mehmet Gokhan 1954- WhoWor 93
Baylard-Eidson, Carrie Cunetto 1953- WhoAmW 93
Bayldon, Roger Wood d1992 NewYTBS 92
Bayle, Francois 1932- Baker 92
Bayle, Pierre BioIn 17
Baylen, Joseph Oscar 1920- WhoAm 92
Bayler, Lavon Ann Burrichter 1933- WhoWrEP 92
Bayles, Deborah Leigh 1953- WhoEmL 93
Bayles, Deborah Lynn 1966- WhoAmW 93
Bayles, Librada C. 1936- WhoAm 92, WhoAmW 93
Bayles, Martha B. AmWomPl
Bayles, Samuel Heagan 1910- WhoAm 92
Bayless, Belle AmWomPl
Bayless, Charles Edward 1942- St&PR 93, WhoAm 92
Bayless, Charles F. 1942- St&PR 93
Bayless, Kathryn Reed 1950- WhoEmL 93
Bayless, Theodore Morris 1931- WhoAm 92
Bayless, Thomas A. Law&B 92
Baylet, Rene Jean 1923- WhoScE 91-2
Bayley, Barrington J. 1937- ScF&FL 92
Bayley, Charles Calvert 1907- WhoWrEP 92
Bayley, Christopher T. 1938- St&PR 93, WhoAm 92
Bayley, Fred Wallace 1955- WhoSSW 93
Bayley, Frederick John WhoScE 91-1
Bayley, Iris BioIn 17
Bayley, J.A. WhoScE 91-1
Bayley, Molly Gilbert 1944- WhoAm 92
Bayley, Nancy 1899- BioIn 17
Bayley, Nicola 1949- BioIn 17, ChlBIID [port], MajAI [port], SmATA 69 [port]
Bayley, Ronald E. 1952- St&PR 93
Bayley, Victor ScF&FL 92
Baylin, Sharon Bloodsworth 1946- WhoEmL 93
Baylis, John 1946- ConAu 39NR
Baylis, Lilian 1874-1937 OxDcOp
Baylis, Robert Montague 1938- St&PR 93
Baylis, William Thomas 1952- WhoSSW 93
Bayliss, Clara Kern 1848- AmWomPl
Bayliss, Colin Ernest 1944- St&PR 93
Bayliss, George Vincent 1931- WhoAm 92
Bayliss, John M.H. 1940- St&PR 93
Bayliss, Larry D. 1940- St&PR 93
Bayliss, Larry Dale 1940- WhoAm 92
Bayliss, Wayne 1948- St&PR 93
Baylon, Bayani Villarin 1932- WhoWor 93
Baylor, Byrd 1924- MajAI [port], SmATA 69 [port]
Baylor, David Anton BioIn 17
Baylor, David Anton 1949- St&PR 93
Baylor, Don Edward 1949- BiDAMSp 1989
Baylor, Elgin Gay 1934- WhoAm 92
Baylor, H. Murray 1913- WhoWrEP 92
Baylor, Hugh Murray 1913- WhoAm 92
Baylor, Michael Jay 1961- WhoE 93
Baylor, Sandra Johnson 1960- WhoAmW 93
Baylson, Michael Morris 1939- WhoAm 92
Baylus, Robert F. 1948- ScF&FL 92
Bayly, John Henry, Jr. 1944- WhoAm 92
Bayly, Joseph 1920-1986 ScF&FL 92
Bayly, Martha AmWomPl
Bayly, Rachel Rima 1963- WhoEmL 93
Bayly, Stephen 1942- MiSFD 9
Baym, Gordon Alan 1935- WhoAm 92
Baym, Nina 1936- WhoAm 92
Bayman, Alice Otte 1956- WhoEmL 93
Baymiller, Lynda Doern 1943- WhoAmW 93
Baynard, Ernest Cornish, III 1944- WhoAm 92
Baynard, Mildred Moyer 1902- WhoSSW 93
Bayne, Adele Wehman WhoAmW 93
Bayne, Basil Edward Francis 1941- WhoWor 93
Bayne, David Cowan 1918- WhoAm 92
Bayne, David Lee, Sr. 1931- St&PR 93
Bayne, Donald Storm 1949- WhoEmL 93
Bayne, Harry McBrayer 1955- WhoSSW 93
Bayne, James Elwood 1940- WhoSSW 93, WhoWor 93
Bayne, James Wilmer 1925- WhoAm 92
Bayne, Kathryn Ann Louise 1959- WhoAmW 93
Bayne, Neil ScF&FL 92
Baynes, Curtis Edward 1951- WhoEmL 93, WhoSSW 93
Baynes, Lacy G. 1933- St&PR 93
Baynes, Pauline (Diana) 1922- ConAu 37NR, MajAI [port]
Baynes, Richard C. 1924- St&PR 93
Baynes, Thomas Edward, Jr. 1940- WhoAm 92
Baynham, A.C. WhoScE 91-1
Baynham, Martha Susan 1964- WhoAmW 93
Bayo, Alberto DcCPCAm
Bayog, Margaret Bean- BioIn 17
Bayoglu, Selcuk 1930- WhoScE 91-4
Bayoras, Feliksas 1934- Baker 92
Bayraktar, Hulya 1946- WhoScE 91-4
Bayrle, Hermann 1951- WhoScE 91-3
Bays, Donna Jean 1958- WhoEmL 93
Bays, Edrie Hill 1949- WhoWrEP 92
Bays, Eric 1932- WhoAm 92
Bays, John Theophanis 1947- WhoAm 92
Bays, Karl BioIn 17
Baysal, Fatih Dogan 1955- WhoSSW 93
Baysal, Orhan WhoScE 91-4
Baysek, A.J. 1951- St&PR 93
Bayshore, Charles Alexander 1919- WhoSSW 93
Bayston, Darwin Merle 1940- WhoAm 92
Bayton, James A. 1912-1990 BioIn 17
Bayuk, Jean Lynn 1963- WhoAmW 93
Bayuk, Mary June 1942- WhoAmW 93
Bayulken, Ahmet Rasit 1946- WhoScE 91-4
Bayus, Brian Edward 1945- St&PR 93
Baz, Farouk El- BioIn 17
Baz, Tom 1933- St&PR 93
Bazaine, Achille Francois 1811-1888 HarEnMi
Bazan, Hugo A. 1944- St&PR 93
Bazan, J. D. DcCPCAm
Bazant, Zdenek Pavel 1937- WhoAm 92
Bazany, Le Roy Francis 1932- St&PR 93, WhoAm 92
Bazdorf, Theodore Alan 1939- St&PR 93
Bazdresch, Karen M. Hollmann 1954- WhoAmW 93
Baze, Gloria Kathleen Jones 1942- WhoSSW 93
Bazela, Jean Ann 1947- WhoAm 92, WhoAmW 93, WhoEmL 93
Bazelaire, Paul 1886-1958 Baker 92
Bazelon, David Lionel 1909- WhoAm 92
Bazelon, Irwin (Allen) 1922- Baker 92
Bazemore, Jack G. 1935- St&PR 93
Bazemore, James Robert 1963- WhoEmL 93
Bazerman, Steven Howard 1940- WhoAm 92, WhoE 93, WhoWor 93
Bazer-Schwartz, Jeannine WhoAm 92
Bazigian, Anita Kizirian WhoAmW 93
Bazigos, Michael Nicholas 1957- WhoE 93
Bazil, Anne M. Law&B 92
Bazin, Albert J. 1904-1991 BioIn 17
Bazin, Andre 1918-1958 BioIn 17
Bazin, Francois 1816-1878 OxDcOp
Bazin, Francois-Emmanuel-Joseph 1816-1878 Baker 92
Bazin, Germain 1901-1990 BioIn 17
Bazin, Henri L. 1933- WhoUN 92
Bazin, Herve 1911- BioIn 17
Bazin, Herve 1935- WhoScE 91-2
Bazin, Marc 1932- DcCPCAm
Bazin, Nancy Topping 1934- WhoAmW 93, WhoSSW 93
Bazler, Frank E. Law&B 92
Bazlik, Miroslav 1931- Baker 92
Bazluke, Francine Tilewick 1954- WhoEmL 93
Bazsa, Gyorgy 1940- WhoScE 91-4
Bazzaglia, Rogelio DcCPCAm
Bazzano, Edie 1938- WhoAmW 93, WhoE 93
Bazzarre, John T. 1930- St&PR 93
Bazzarre, John Thomas 1930- WhoSSW 93
Bazzaz, Fakhri A. 1933- WhoAm 92
Bazzini, Antonio 1818-1897 Baker 92
BB ConAu 38NR
BB 1905-1990 BioIn 17
Beabout, Douglas Howard 1950- WhoEmL 93
Beabout, J. Steven Law&B 92
Beach, Amy Marcy Cheney 1867-1944 BioIn 17
Beach, Arthur Thomas 1920- St&PR 93
Beach, Bert Beverly 1928- WhoE 93
Beach, Betty Lynn 1946- WhoAmW 93
Beach, Cecil Prentice 1927- WhoAm 92
Beach, Charles, Jr. BioIn 17
Beach, Charles A. Law&B 92
Beach, Charles Arthur 1953- St&PR 93
Beach, David Louis 1939- St&PR 93
Beach, Dwight Edward, Jr. 1937- St&PR 93
Beach, Edward Latimer 1918- WhoAm 92
Beach, Gary S. 1954- St&PR 93
Beach, H.H.A., Mrs. 1867-1944 Baker 92, BioIn 17
Beach, James David, Jr. 1935- St&PR 93
Beach, John Parsons 1877-1953 Baker 92
Beach, Kevin L. 1948- St&PR 93
Beach, Lani Leroy 1944- WhoAm 92
Beach, Lee Roy 1936- WhoAm 92
Beach, Linda Marie 1949- WhoAmW 93
Beach, Lisa Ann 1964- WhoEmL 93
Beach, Lynn ScF&FL 92
Beach, Margaret Gastaldi 1915- WhoAm 92
Beach, Michele Raymonde 1961- WhoEmL 93
Beach, Milo C. WhoAm 92, WhoE 93
Beach, Moses Yale 1800-1868 JrnUS
Beach, Murray MacDonald 1954- WhoE 93
Beach, Nancy AmWomPl
Beach, Nancy W. 1962- WhoAmW 93
Beach, Pennie 1945- St&PR 93
Beach, Robert C. 1934- ConAu 139
Beach, Robert E. 1952- St&PR 93
Beach, Robert Oliver, II 1932- WhoAm 92
Beach, Robert Preston 1916- WhoE 93
Beach, Roger C. 1936- WhoAm 92
Beach, Stephen Law&B 92
Beach, Walter Alden 1924- St&PR 93
Beach, William Roeder 1938- St&PR 93
Beacha, R. 1926- St&PR 93
Beacham, Jeanne Ellen 1960- WhoAmW 93
Beachcroft, Nina 1931- ScF&FL 92
Beache, Vincent 1931- DcCPCAm
Beachell, Henry Monroe 1906- WhoWor 93
Beachley, Donovan R., Jr. 1925- St&PR 93
Beachley, Michael Charles 1940- WhoAm 92
Beachley, Norman Henry 1933- WhoAm 92
Beachley, Orville Theodore, Jr. 1937- WhoE 93
Beachy, Leo J. BioIn 17
Beacom, Vincent Edward 1929- St&PR 93
Beaconsfield, Earl of 1804-1881 BioIn 17
Beaderstadt, Andrea Anglin 1949- WhoAmW 93
Beadie, Alexander William Law&B 92
Beadle, Alfred Newman 1927- WhoAm 92
Beadle, Charles Wilson 1930- WhoAm 92
Beadle, David John WhoScE 91-1
Beadle, George W. 1903-1989 BioIn 17
Beadle, J. Grant 1932- St&PR 93
Beadle, John Grant 1932- WhoAm 92
Beadle, Robert Sheldon 1949- St&PR 93
Beadle, Sandy J. 1948- WhoEmL 93
Beadles, Larry J. 1941- St&PR 93
Beadsmoore, Michael David 1947- St&PR 93
Beagan, Loretto Bernard d1992 NewYTBS 92 [port]
Beagen, Elizabeth Julia 1963- WhoAmW 93
Beagen, Loretto Bernard d1992 BioIn 17
Beagen, Thomas P. Law&B 92
Beagle, Gary J. 1945- St&PR 93
Beagle, Maude Stewart AmWomPl
Beagle, Peter S. BioIn 17
Beagle, Peter S. 1939- ScF&FL 92
Beagle, Peter Soyer 1939- WhoAm 92, WhoWrEP 92
Beagle, Ronald 1934- BiDAMSp 1989
Beaglehole, Ernest 1906-1965 IntDcAn
Beagley, Karen Grace 1957- WhoEmL 93
Beagrie, George Simpson 1925- WhoAm 92
Beahan, Michael Eamon 1937- WhoAsAP 91
Beahler, John Leroy 1930- WhoAm 92
Beahm, George W. 1953- ScF&FL 92
Beahm, Nancy Elizabeth 1962- WhoAmW 93
Beahrs, Oliver Howard 1914- WhoAm 92
Beaird, Brett 1958- WhoSSW 93
Beaird, Charles T. 1922- St&PR 93, WhoAm 92
Beaird, David MiSFD 9
Beaird, J. Pat, Jr. 1936- St&PR 93
Beaird, James Ralph 1925- WhoAm 92
Beaird, Richard F. ScF&FL 92
Beak, Peter Andrew 1936- WhoAm 92
Beake, John WhoAm 92
Beake, Lesley 1949- DcChlFi
Beakes, John Herbert, Jr. 1943- WhoE 93
Beakley, George Carroll, Jr. 1922- WhoAm 92
Beakley, Robert Paul 1946- WhoEmL 93
Beal, Alice 1950- WhoAmW 93
Beal, Bernard B. BioIn 17
Beal, Bruce Curtis 1950- WhoEmL 93
Beal, Bruce Leonard Law&B 92
Beal, Dallas Knight 1926- WhoAm 92, WhoE 93
Beal, Donald Gordon 1943- WhoSSW 93
Beal, Donna Lee 1952- WhoE 93
Beal, Edward Wescott 1940- WhoE 93
Beal, George W. 1940- St&PR 93
Beal, Graham William John 1947- WhoAm 92
Beal, Ilene WhoAm 92, WhoAmW 93
Beal, Ilene 1946- St&PR 93
Beal, Jack 1931- WhoAm 92
Beal, Jack L. 1923- BioIn 17
Beal, Jeff BioIn 17
Beal, John 1909- WhoAm 92
Beal, John Franklin 1932- St&PR 93
Beal, John M. 1915- WhoAm 92
Beal, John Robinson 1906-1985 ScF&FL 92
Beal, Jules 1953- St&PR 93
Beal, Louis M.S. BioIn 17
Beal, Mary Arthur 1922- WhoE 93
Beal, Mary Evelyn 1947- WhoEmL 93
Beal, Merrill David 1926- WhoAm 92
Beal, Myron Clarence 1920- WhoAm 92
Beal, Pamela K.M. 1956- St&PR 93
Beal, Richard M. Law&B 92
Beal, Robert Joseph 1936- St&PR 93
Beal, Robert Lawrence 1941- WhoAm 92, WhoE 93, WhoWor 93
Beal, Roy Wilson 1918- St&PR 93
Beal, S. Maxwell 1932- St&PR 93
Beal, Virginia ConAu 139
Beal, Winnona Marie 1938- WhoWrEP 92
Beale, Betty WhoAm 92
Beale, Christopher William 1947- St&PR 93, WhoAm 92

Beale, David A. 1949- *WhoE 93*
Beale, Georgia Robison 1905- *WhoAmW 93, WhoE 93*
Beale, Geraline Ann 1953- *WhoWor 93*
Beale, Guy Otis 1944- *WhoSSW 93*
Beale, Guy R., Jr. 1924- *St&PR 93*
Beale, Irene Alleman 1920- *WhoWrEP 92*
Beale, J. Burkhardt 1955- *WhoEmL 93*
Beale, James Haden 1961- *WhoEmL 93*
Beale, Julian *WhoAsAP 91*
Beale, Nathan 1935- *St&PR 93*
Beale, Peter 1943- *St&PR 93*
Beale, Samuel E., III 1950- *WhoSSW 93*
Beale, Susan M. 1948- *St&PR 93*
Beale, Walter Michael 1955- *WhoEmL 93*
Beales, James Alfred Geaves, III 1923- *WhoAm 92*
Beales, Peter Frederick 1935- *WhoUN 92*
Bealey, Laura Ann 1934- *WhoSSW 93*
Bealieu, Elphege Alphonse 1930- *St&PR 93*
Bealke, Linn Hemingway 1944- *WhoAm 92*
Beall, Betty McCullar 1928- *WhoAmW 93*
Beall, Burtch W., Jr. 1925- *WhoAm 92*
Beall, Cynthia M. 1949- *WhoAm 92*
Beall, Dennis Ray 1929- *WhoAm 92*
Beall, Donald R. 1938- *St&PR 93*
Beall, Donald Ray 1938- *WhoAm 92*
Beall, Gary Donald 1946- *WhoSSW 93*
Beall, George 1937- *WhoAm 92*
Beall, Ingrid Lillehei 1926- *WhoAm 92, WhoAmW 93*
Beall, James Howard 1945- *WhoWor 93*
Beall, Joanna May 1935- *WhoAmW 93, WhoE 93*
Beall, John P. *Law&B 92*
Beall, Julianne 1946- *WhoAmW 93*
Beall, Kenneth Sutter, Jr. 1938- *WhoSSW 93*
Beall, Miriam Lloyd 1909- *WhoAmW 93*
Beall, Richard Olin 1931- *St&PR 93*
Beall, Robert Joseph 1943- *WhoAm 92*
Beall, Robert Matthews, II 1943- *WhoAm 92*
Beallor, Fran 1957- *WhoEmL 93*
Bealmear, Michael William 1947- *WhoEmL 93, WhoWor 93*
Beals, Carleton 1893-1979 *ScF&FL 92*
Beals, Clem Kip, III 1949- *WhoEmL 93*
Beals, Cynthia Louise 1957- *WhoEmL 93*
Beals, Deborah Lynn *Law&B 92*
Beals, George Rodney 1935- *WhoSSW 93*
Beals, Jeffrey A. 1947- *St&PR 93*
Beals, Loren Alan 1933- *WhoAm 92, WhoWor 93*
Beals, Ralph 1929- *St&PR 93*
Beals, Ralph Everett 1936- *WhoAm 92*
Beals, Ralph L. 1901-1985 *IntDcAn*
Beals, Ronald Wayne *Law&B 92*
Beals, Vaughn Leroy, Jr. 1928- *St&PR 93, WhoAm 92*
Beam, Alex *ScF&FL 92*
Beam, Beverly Jane 1941- *St&PR 93*
Beam, Bruce A. 1934- *St&PR 93*
Beam, Clarence Arlen 1930- *WhoAm 92*
Beam, Frank Letts 1942- *WhoWor 93*
Beam, J. Wade 1944- *St&PR 93*
Beam, John M., Jr. 1947- *St&PR 93*
Beam, Lee Ann 1958- *St&PR 93*
Beam, Leta Marie 1954- *WhoAmW 93*
Beam, Margaret Anne Ridgeway 1948- *WhoEmL 93*
Beam, Michael Newton 1942- *St&PR 93*
Beam, Robert Thompson 1919- *WhoAm 92*
Beam, Sherilee Francine 1949- *WhoAmW 93*
Beam, William Lawrence 1935- *St&PR 93*
Beaman, Charles Edward 1933- *St&PR 93*
Beaman, Chester Earl 1916- *WhoSSW 93*
Beaman, Frank Lanier, Jr. 1960- *WhoSSW 93*
Beaman, Joyce Proctor 1931- *WhoWrEP 92*
Beaman, Kenneth Dale 1953- *WhoEmL 93*
Beaman, Margarine Gaynell *WhoAmW 93*
Beaman, Mark 1951- *St&PR 93*
Beaman, Robert H. 1947- *St&PR 93*
Beament, Thomas Harold 1941- *WhoAm 92*
Beamer, Charles 1942- *ScF&FL 92*
Beamer, Ralph L. 1952- *St&PR 93*
Beames, Margaret *DcChlFi*
Beames, Peter Anthony 1960- *WhoE 93*
Beamish, James Robert 1936- *St&PR 93*
Beamish, T. Robert 1937- *St&PR 93*
Beamon, Bob *BioIn 17*
Beamon, Eric *BioIn 17*
Beams, Mark *Law&B 92*
Bean, Alan LaVern 1932- *WhoAm 92, WhoWor 93*
Bean, Bennett 1941- *WhoE 93*
Bean, Bob *BioIn 17*
Bean, Bourne 1920- *St&PR 93*
Bean, Bruce W. *Law&B 92*
Bean, Bruce William 1945- *St&PR 93*
Bean, Bruce Winfield 1941- *WhoAm 92*
Bean, Charles Palmer 1923- *WhoAm 92*
Bean, Claire S. 1952- *St&PR 93*
Bean, Clifford A. 1929- *St&PR 93*
Bean, D. Michael *Law&B 92*
Bean, Daryl 1942- *BioIn 17*
Bean, Delcie D. 1942- *St&PR 93*
Bean, Donald W. 1935- *St&PR 93*
Bean, Edwin Temple, Jr. 1926- *WhoAm 92*
Bean, Elvie Spencer *St&PR 93*
Bean, Ethelle Susannah 1950- *WhoEmL 93*
Bean, Frank Dawson 1942- *WhoAm 92*
Bean, Gary 1949- *WhoEmL 93*
Bean, Gregory Richard 1950- *St&PR 93*
Bean, Jacob d1992 *NewYTBS 92*
Bean, Jacob 1923- *WhoAm 92*
Bean, James W. 1941- *St&PR 93*
Bean, James W., Jr. 1947- *St&PR 93*
Bean, Joan P. 1933- *WhoAm 92*
Bean, John David 1947- *WhoIns 93*
Bean, Jonathan Spangler 1963- *WhoEmL 93*
Bean, Linda Lorraine *NewYTBS 92 [port]*
Bean, Mary C. *Law&B 92*
Bean, Maurice Darrow 1928- *WhoAm 92*
Bean, Philip Thomas *WhoScE 91-1*
Bean, Ralph J., Jr. *Law&B 92, St&PR 93*
Bean, Richard A. 1950- *St&PR 93*
Bean, Richard Mark 1948- *WhoWor 93*
Bean, Robert B. *MiSFD 9*
Bean, Roy 1825?-1903 *BioIn 17*
Bean, Roy H. 1943- *St&PR 93*
Bean, Russell Owen 1948- *WhoSSW 93*
Bean, Susan Montgomery 1948- *WhoAmW 93*
Bean, Theo B. 1926- *St&PR 93*
Bean-Bayog, Margaret *BioIn 17*
Beanblossom, David Austin *Law&B 92*
Beane, C. Ernest *Law&B 92*
Beane, Carol Ashworth 1938- *WhoAmW 93*
Beane, Jerry Lynn 1944- *WhoAm 92*
Beane, Kenneth Dewitt 1937- *WhoSSW 93*
Beane, Lois Velleda 1938- *WhoAmW 93*
Beane, Marjorie L. 1946- *WhoAmW 93*
Beane, Robert Lowell 1956- *WhoEmL 93*
Bear, (Clara) Ann 1937- *WhoWrEP 92*
Bear, David 1949- *ScF&FL 92*
Bear, Dinah 1951- *WhoAm 92, WhoAmW 93*
Bear, Frederick Thomas 1937- *WhoSSW 93*
Bear, Greg 1951- *BioIn 17, ScF&FL 92*
Bear, Gregory Dale 1951- *WhoAm 92*
Bear, Hymen *Law&B 92*
Bear, Jon H. 1934- *St&PR 93*
Bear, Joseph Wolfe, III 1955- *WhoSSW 93*
Bear, Larry Alan 1928- *WhoAm 92, WhoE 93, WhoWor 93*
Bear, Lewis, Jr. 1924- *WhoAm 92*
Bear, Mary Qualey 1941- *WhoSSW 93*
Bear, Sun 1929- *WhoWrEP 92*
Bear, The Mama *WhoWrEP 92*
Bear, William Forrest 1927- *WhoAm 92*
Bearb, Michael Edwin 1956- *WhoE 93*
Bearce, Jeana Dale *WhoAm 92*
Beard, A.D. *St&PR 93*
Beard, Ann Southard 1948- *WhoAmW 93*
Beard, Anson McCook, Jr. 1936- *WhoAm 92*
Beard, C. Randolph 1931- *St&PR 93*
Beard, Carla Jeanne 1954- *WhoAmW 93*
Beard, Charles Austin 1874-1948 *BioIn 17, OxCSupC*
Beard, Charles Julian 1943- *WhoAm 92*
Beard, Charles Richard *Law&B 92*
Beard, Charles Walter 1932- *WhoAm 92*
Beard, Cynthia Aldridge 1953- *WhoEmL 93*
Beard, Dan 1850-1941 *GayN*
Beard, Daniel Paul 1948- *WhoEmL 93*
Beard, Edward T. 1828?-1873 *BioIn 17*
Beard, Elizabeth Letitia 1932- *WhoAm 92, WhoSSW 93*
Beard, Ellis Mabry 1925- *St&PR 93*
Beard, Eugene *WhoAm 92*
Beard, Eugene P. *St&PR 93*
Beard, Frederick K. 1941- *St&PR 93*
Beard, Glenda Rainwater *Law&B 92*
Beard, Hazel *WhoAmW 93, WhoSSW 93*
Beard, Howard Leo 1937- *St&PR 93*
Beard, James 1903-1985 *BioIn 17*
Beard, John c. 1717-1791 *Baker 92, OxDcOp*
Beard, John Edwards 1932- *St&PR 93*
Beard, Judi Lynne 1965- *WhoSSW 93*
Beard, Karen E. 1950- *St&PR 93*
Beard, Leo Roy 1917- *WhoAm 92*
Beard, Mary Ritter 1876-1958 *BioIn 17*
Beard, Michael Kenneth 1941- *WhoE 93*
Beard, Michael Roane 1948- *WhoSSW 93*
Beard, Paul Douglas 1962- *WhoSSW 93*
Beard, Peter H. 1938- *BioIn 17*
Beard, Ralph Milton, Jr. 1927- *BiDAMSp 1989*
Beard, Richard Leonard 1909- *WhoAm 92*
Beard, Robert Earl 1938- *WhoE 93*
Beard, Roberta Jane 1929- *St&PR 93*
Beard, Rodney Rau 1911- *WhoAm 92*
Beard, Ronald Stratton 1939- *WhoAm 92*
Beard, Stephen Ross 1950- *WhoEmL 93*
Beard, Thomas D. 1934- *St&PR 93*
Beard, Walker Rankin 1946- *St&PR 93*
Beard, William David 1923- *St&PR 93*
Beard, William James *Law&B 92*
Beard, William Jennings 1926- *St&PR 93*
Beard, William Kelly 1898-1990 *BioIn 17*
Beard, William M. 1928- *St&PR 93*
Beard, William Roger 1958- *WhoSSW 93*
Beardall, Dennis K. 1953- *St&PR 93*
Beardall, James C. 1939- *St&PR 93, WhoAm 92*
Bearde, Chris *MiSFD 9*
Bearden, Dale A. 1958- *St&PR 93*
Bearden, David Christopher 1959- *WhoEmL 93*
Bearden, Donn Robert 1933- *St&PR 93*
Bearden, Fred Burnette, Jr. 1923- *WhoSSW 93*
Bearden, James Hudson 1933- *WhoAm 92*
Bearden, James William 1947- *St&PR 93*
Bearden, Nancy Carpenter 1958- *WhoWrEP 92*
Bearden, Romare 1914-1988 *BioIn 17*
Bearden, Romare H. 1914-1988 *BlkAuII 92*
Beardmore, Harvey Ernest 1921- *WhoAm 92*
Beardmore, John Alec *WhoScE 91-1*
Beardmore, John Alec 1930- *WhoWor 93*
Beardmore, Thomas C. *Law&B 92*
Beards, Peter Henry *WhoScE 91-1*
Beardslee, Bethany 1927- *Baker 92*
Beardslee, Daniel Bain 1960- *WhoEmL 93*
Beardslee, Sheila Margaret 1950- *WhoAmW 93*
Beardslee, William Armitage 1916- *WhoAm 92*
Beardsley, Aubrey 1872-1898 *ScF&FL 92*
Beardsley, Bruce J. 1963- *WhoE 93*
Beardsley, Charles Mitchell 1921- *WhoIns 93*
Beardsley, Dick *BioIn 17*
Beardsley, Douglas 1941- *WhoCanL 92*
Beardsley, George Peter 1940- *WhoAm 92*
Beardsley, John Ray 1937- *WhoAm 92*
Beardsley, Lehman Franklin 1923- *St&PR 93*
Beardsley, Lisa Marie 1958- *WhoAmW 93*
Beardsley, Mary Louise *Law&B 92*
Beardsley, Michael Leigh 1951- *St&PR 93*
Beardsley, Robert Eugene 1923- *WhoAm 92*
Beardsley, Theodore Sterling, Jr. 1930- *WhoAm 92, WhoE 93, WhoWor 93*
Beardsley, William Edward 1950- *WhoE 93*
Beardwood, Bruce A. 1936- *St&PR 93*
Beardwood, Bruce Allan 1936- *WhoAm 92*
Beare, Bruce Riley 1942- *WhoAm 92*
Beare, Gene Kerwin 1915- *St&PR 93, WhoAm 92*
Beare, Jerry Wayne 1946- *WhoSSW 93*
Beare, Larry T. *Law&B 92*
Beare, Patricia Gauntlett 1945- *WhoSSW 93*
Beare-Rogers, Joyce Louise 1927- *WhoAm 92, WhoAmW 93*
Beares, Paul Richard 1946- *St&PR 93*
Bearg, David Warren 1948- *WhoEmL 93*
Bearg, Martin Lee 1952- *WhoEmL 93*
Bearl, Christine M. *Law&B 92*
Bearman, Christina K. 1948- *St&PR 93*
Bearman, Peter William *WhoScE 91-1*
Bearman, Toni Carbo *BioIn 17*
Bearman, Toni Carbo 1942- *WhoAm 92*
Bearmon, Lee *Law&B 92*
Bearn, Alexander Gordon 1923- *WhoAm 92*
Bearr, David William Comer 1945- *WhoE 93*
Bearsch, Jack Max 1927- *St&PR 93*
Bearss, Edwin Cole 1923- *WhoAm 92*
Bearup, Dennis Ray 1953- *St&PR 93*
Bearwald, Jean Haynes 1924- *WhoAmW 93, WhoWor 93*
Beary, John Francis, III 1946- *WhoAm 92*
Beary, Sharon Kolakowski 1962- *WhoAmW 93*
Beasley, Barbara Starin 1955- *WhoAm 92, WhoEmL 93*
Beasley, Bea Cassandra 1942- *WhoAmW 93*
Beasley, Bruce Miller 1939- *WhoAm 92*
Beasley, Cecil Ackmond, Jr. 1911- *WhoAm 92*
Beasley, Charles Merritt, Jr. 1950- *WhoEmL 93*
Beasley, Cloyd Orris, Jr. 1933- *WhoAm 92, WhoWor 93*
Beasley, Conger, Jr. 1940- *ScF&FL 92, WhoWrEP 92*
Beasley, David Lewis 1955- *St&PR 93*
Beasley, Dorothy Toth *WhoAmW 93, WhoSSW 93*
Beasley, Ernest William, Jr. 1924- *WhoSSW 93, WhoWor 93*
Beasley, Faith E. 1958- *ConAu 139*
Beasley, G.E. 1945- *St&PR 93*
Beasley, G. Rex *Law&B 92*
Beasley, Georgia Mae Zeigler 1948- *WhoAmW 93, WhoEmL 93, WhoWor 93*
Beasley, Jim Sanders 1936- *WhoAm 92*
Beasley, John C. 1942- *St&PR 93*
Beasley, John Edward 1953- *WhoWor 93*
Beasley, John F. *Law&B 92*
Beasley, John H. 1943- *St&PR 93*
Beasley, Joyce *Law&B 92*
Beasley, Lawrence H. 1946- *St&PR 93*
Beasley, Lois Rene 1960- *WhoWor 93*
Beasley, Manley d1990 *BioIn 17*
Beasley, Marvin Coleman 1941- *St&PR 93*
Beasley, Mary Catherine 1922- *WhoAmW 93*
Beasley, Maurine Hoffman 1936- *WhoAmW 93, WhoE 93, WhoWor 93*
Beasley, Michael W. *BioIn 17*
Beasley, Oscar H. 1925- *St&PR 93*
Beasley, Oscar Homer *Law&B 92*
Beasley, Rebecca O. *Law&B 92*
Beasley, Rebecca Octavia 1954- *WhoEmL 93*
Beasley, Robert Palmer *WhoAm 92*
Beasley, Robert Scott 1949- *WhoAm 92, WhoE 93, WhoEmL 93*
Beasley, William Howard, III *BioIn 17*
Beasley, William Rex 1934- *WhoAm 92, WhoSSW 93*
Beasom, Catherine Rose 1945- *WhoSSW 93*
Beason, Amos T. 1940- *St&PR 93*
Beason, Amos Theodore 1940- *WhoAm 92*
Beason, Doug 1953- *ScF&FL 92*
Beason, James Douglas 1953- *WhoE 93, WhoEmL 93*
Beason, Robert Curtis 1946- *WhoE 93*
Beason, Robert Gayle 1927- *WhoWrEP 92*
Beason, Rose Ann McDaniel 1939- *WhoAmW 93*
Beastie Boys, The *ConMus 8 [port]*
Beath, Warren Newton 1951- *ConAu 136*
Beathard, Bobby 1937- *WhoAm 92*
Beatie, Russel Harrison, Jr. 1938- *WhoE 93*
Beatles, The *DcTwHis*
Beatley, Janice Carson 1919-1987 *BioIn 17*
Beatman, Leslie Harvey *St&PR 93*
Beato, Antonio fl. c. 1850-c. 1890 *BioIn 17*
Beaton, Cecil 1904-1980 *BioIn 17*
Beaton, Christina *Law&B 92*
Beaton, Edward James 1957- *WhoWor 93*
Beaton, Emily Kimenker *WhoAmW 93*
Beaton, Gregory Thomas 1956- *WhoE 93*
Beaton, Harold Campbell 1930- *WhoAsAP 91*
Beaton, Michael Steve 1950- *WhoEmL 93, WhoSSW 93*
Beaton, Roy Howard 1916- *WhoAm 92, WhoWor 93*
Beatrice, Princess of York 1988- *BioIn 17*
Beatrice, William Daniel, Jr. 1938- *WhoSSW 93*
Beatrice D'este *DcAmChF 1960*
Beatrix, Her Majesty 1938- *WhoWor 93*
Beattie, Alan *MiSFD 9*
Beattie, Allan Leslie 1926- *St&PR 93*
Beattie, Ann *BioIn 17*
Beattie, Ann 1947- *MagSAmL [port], ShSCr 11 [port], WhoAm 92, WhoWrEP 92*
Beattie, David *BioIn 17*
Beattie, David Stuart 1924- *WhoWor 93*
Beattie, Diana Scott 1934- *WhoAm 92*
Beattie, Donald A. 1929- *WhoAm 92*
Beattie, Edward James 1918- *WhoAm 92, WhoE 93, WhoWor 93*
Beattie, Frederick G. *Law&B 92*
Beattie, G. Anthony *WhoScE 91-1*
Beattie, Herbert 1926- *Baker 92*
Beattie, Ian Robert *WhoScE 91-1*
Beattie, James 1735-1803 *BioIn 17*
Beattie, James L. *Law&B 92*
Beattie, Janet Holtzman 1927- *WhoAm 92*
Beattie, Jessie Louise 1896-1985 *WhoCanL 92*
Beattie, Mary B. *Law&B 92*
Beattie, Melody *BioIn 17*
Beattie, Melody Lynn 1948- *WhoWrEP 92*
Beattie, Nora Maureen 1925- *WhoAm 92*
Beattie, Pamela Marie Pash 1944- *WhoAmW 93*
Beattie, Richard Irwin 1939- *WhoAm 92*
Beattie, Scott Stanford 1949- *WhoWor 93*

Beattie, Shane A. *BioIn 17*
Beattie, Ted Arthur 1945- *WhoAm 92*
Beatty, Alan Edwin 1933- *St&PR 93*
Beatty, Bruce Wm. 1948- *St&PR 93*
Beatty, Christine E. *Law&B 92*
Beatty, Curtis Marvin 1954- *St&PR 93*
Beatty, Daniel A. *Law&B 92*
Beatty, David 1871-1936 *DcTwHis, HarEnMi*
Beatty, David Ross 1942- *WhoAm 92*
Beatty, Donald Caldwell *Law&B 92*
Beatty, Frances 1940- *WhoAmW 93*
Beatty, Frances Fielding Lewis 1948- *WhoEmL 93*
Beatty, Garry Hamilton 1935- *WhoAm 92*
Beatty, Henry Perrin 1950- *WhoAm 92, WhoE 93, WhoWor 93*
Beatty, Ida Helm *AmWomPl*
Beatty, Jack J. 1945- *WhoAm 92, WhoWrEP 92*
Beatty, Jeffrey G. 1958- *St&PR 93*
Beatty, Jerome, Jr. 1918- *ScF&FL 92*
Beatty, Jessica *AmWomPl*
Beatty, John Cabeen, Jr. 1919- *WhoAm 92*
Beatty, John Lee 1948- *WhoAm 92*
Beatty, John (Louis) 1922-1975 *DcAmChF 1960*
Beatty, Kenneth Orion, Jr. 1913- *WhoAm 92, WhoSSW 93*
Beatty, Lorne Alan 1955- *St&PR 93*
Beatty, Mark W. 1953- *WhoEmL 93*
Beatty, Michael L. *Law&B 92*
Beatty, Michael L. 1947- *WhoAm 92, WhoSSW 93*
Beatty, Michael Lance 1947- *St&PR 93*
Beatty, Ned 1937- *WhoAm 92*
Beatty, Patricia 1922-1991 *BioIn 17*
Beatty, Patricia Jean *WhoWrEP 92*
Beatty, Patricia (Robbins) 1922- *DcAmChF 1960*
Beatty, Patricia (Robbins) 1922-1991 *DcAmChF 1985, MajAI [port], SmATA 73 [port]*
Beatty, Paul Francis 1934- *WhoAm 92*
Beatty, Perrin *BioIn 17*
Beatty, Richard Paul 1953- *WhoE 93*
Beatty, Richard S. 1934- *St&PR 93*
Beatty, Richard Scott 1959- *St&PR 93*
Beatty, Richard Scrivener 1934- *WhoAm 92*
Beatty, Robert d1992 *NewYTBS 92*
Beatty, Robert 1909-1992 *BioIn 17*
Beatty, Robert D. 1926- *St&PR 93*
Beatty, Robert G. *Law&B 92*
Beatty, Stephen Earl 1951- *St&PR 93*
Beatty, Talley *BioIn 17*
Beatty, Tina Marie 1955- *WhoAmW 93, WhoEmL 93, WhoSSW 93, WhoWor 93*
Beatty, Vander 1941-1990 *BioIn 17*
Beatty, Warren 1937- *BioIn 17, MiSFD 9, WhoAm 92*
Beatty, Warren 1938- *IntDcF 2-3 [port]*
Beatty, Wilbur C. 1942- *WhoE 93*
Beatty, Willard Max 1929- *WhoSSW 93*
Beatty, William Kaye 1926- *WhoAm 92*
Beatty, William Louis 1925- *WhoAm 92*
Beatty-deSana, Jeanne Warren 1920- *WhoSSW 93*
Beaty, Benjamin Brett *Law&B 92*
Beaty, Bill G. 1930- *St&PR 93*
Beaty, David Alvin 1948- *WhoEmL 93*
Beaty, Harry Nelson 1932- *WhoAm 92*
Beaty, Narlin B. 1950- *St&PR 93*
Beaty, Orren, Jr. 1919- *WhoAm 92*
Beaty, Rufus F. *Law&B 92*
Beaubien, Anne Kathleen 1947- *WhoAm 92*
Beaubien, Philippe de Gaspe, II 1928- *WhoAm 92*
Beauce, Thierry de *BioIn 17*
Beauchamp, David F. 1940- *St&PR 93*
Beauchamp, David Fitzgerald 1940- *WhoAm 92*
Beauchamp, Gary Fay 1951- *WhoEmL 93, WhoSSW 93*
Beauchamp, Gorman 1938- *ScF&FL 92*
Beauchamp, Jacques 1948- *St&PR 93, WhoAm 92*
Beauchamp, Jacques Donat *Law&B 92*
Beauchamp, Jeffery Oliver 1943- *WhoWor 93*
Beauchamp, John Herndon 1911- *St&PR 93*
Beauchamp, Patrick Lowell 1933- *St&PR 93*
Beauchamp, Pierre 1943- *WhoAm 92*
Beauchemin, Judith Ann 1939- *WhoE 93*
Beauchemin, Neree 1850-1931 *BioIn 17*
Beauchemin, Susan-Marie 1950- *WhoEmL 93*
Beauchemin, Yves 1941- *BioIn 17, WhoCanL 92*
Beaude, Henri E. 1870-1930 *BioIn 17*
Beaudet, Eugene (Gene) Charles 1924- *WhoWrEP 92*
Beaudette-Lubow, Rhonda Marie 1963- *WhoAmW 93*
Beaudin, Earnest Charles *Law&B 92*
Beaudin, James A. 1944- *St&PR 93*
Beaudin, Monique *St&PR 93*
Beaudine, William 1892-1970 *MiSFD 9N*
Beaudoin, Bernard J. 1940- *St&PR 93*
Beaudoin, Carol Ann 1949- *WhoAmW 93*
Beaudoin, Claude L. *Law&B 92*
Beaudoin, Claude L. 1933- *St&PR 93*
Beaudoin, Cynthia Ann 1940- *WhoE 93*
Beaudoin, Donna Paradis 1955- *WhoAmW 93*
Beaudoin, Gerald-Armand 1929- *WhoAm 92*
Beaudoin, Karen Gracy 1950- *WhoAmW 93*
Beaudoin, Laurent 1938- *St&PR 93, WhoAm 92*
Beaudoin, Patricia E. *St&PR 93*
Beaudoin, Paul E. 1960- *WhoE 93*
Beaudoin, Richard W. 1944- *St&PR 93*
Beaudoin, Robert Lawrence 1933- *WhoWor 93*
Beaudouin, Mark T. *Law&B 92*
Beaudouin, Mark T. 1955- *St&PR 93*
Beaudreau, David Eugene 1929- *WhoAm 92*
Beaudreault, Edgar Joseph, Jr. 1948- *WhoEmL 93*
Beaudry, Agnes Ruth Porter 1932- *WhoAmW 93*
Beaudry, Antoinette *ScF&FL 92*
Beaudry, G. Ward 1941- *WhoSSW 93*
Beaudry, Janis Stonier 1956- *WhoEmL 93*
Beaudway, James E. 1916- *St&PR 93*
Beaufait, Frederick William 1936- *WhoAm 92*
Beaufay, Henri F.C. 1928- *WhoScE 91-2*
Beaufays, Oscar F. 1933- *WhoScE 91-2*
Beauford, Forrest Daniel 1923- *WhoSSW 93*
Beauford, Fred 1939- *WhoE 93*
Beauford, Richard Micheal 1953- *St&PR 93*
Beaufort, John d1992 *NewYTBS 92*
Beaufort, John David 1912- *WhoAm 92, WhoWrEP 92*
Beaufort, Margaret 1443-1509 *BioIn 17*
Beaufranc, Gerard Alexandre 1930- *WhoWor 93*
Beaufre, Andre 1902-1973 *HarEnMi*
Beaugeard, David *BioIn 17*
Beaugrand, Honore 1848-1906 *BioIn 17*
Beaugrand, Michel 1945- *WhoWor 93*
Beauharnais, Eugene de 1781-1824 *HarEnMi*
Beaujon, Paul 1900-1969 *ScF&FL 92*
Beaulac, Willard Leon 1899-1990 *BioIn 17*
Beaulieu, Elphege Alphonse 1930- *St&PR 93*
Beaulieu, Jacques Alexandre 1932- *WhoAm 92*
Beaulieu, Jean Paul 1952- *St&PR 93*
Beaulieu, Jean Pierre de 1725-1819 *HarEnMi*
Beaulieu, Joseph Armand 1934- *WhoE 93*
Beaulieu, Kenneth L. 1948- *St&PR 93*
Beaulieu, Kenneth Leo 1948- *WhoAm 92*
Beaulieu, Leigh P. 1961- *WhoEmL 93*
Beaulieu, Marie-Desire 1791-1863 *Baker 92*
Beaulieu, Michel 1941-1985 *WhoCanL 92*
Beaulieu, Richard 1952- *St&PR 93*
Beaulieu, Roger L. 1924- *St&PR 93*
Beaulieu, Roger Louis 1924- *WhoAm 92*
Beaulieu, Victor Levy 1945- *BioIn 17, WhoCanL 92*
Beaulnes, Aurele 1928- *WhoAm 92*
Beaumarchais, Pierre Augustin Caron de 1732-1799 *OxDcOp*
Beaumont, Charles 1929-1967 *ScF&FL 92*
Beaumont, Donald A. 1935- *WhoAm 92*
Beaumont, Edward Arthur 1951- *WhoEmL 93*
Beaumont, Gabrielle *MiSFD 9*
Beaumont, Grace Beverly 1944- *WhoAmW 93*
Beaumont, Harry 1888-1966 *MiSFD 9N*
Beaumont, John 1583?-1627 *DcLB 121 [port]*
Beaumont, John Garry 1934- *WhoScE 91-1*
Beaumont, John Graham *WhoScE 91-1*
Beaumont, Joseph 1616-1699 *DcLB 126 [port]*
Beaumont, Judith D. *Law&B 92*
Beaumont, Mona *WhoAmW 93*
Beaumont, Neil 1936- *St&PR 93*
Beaumont, Pamela Jo 1944- *WhoAm 92*
Beaumont, Ralph 1926- *ConTFT 10*
Beaumont, Richard Austin 1925- *WhoAm 92, WhoWor 93*
Beaumont, Robert George 1930- *St&PR 93*
Beaumont, Roger 1935- *ScF&FL 92*
Beaumont, Roger Alban 1935- *WhoSSW 93*
Beaumont, Steven Peter *WhoScE 91-1*
Beaumont, Susan Linehan *Law&B 92*
Beaumont, William 1785-1853 *BioIn 17*
Beaumont, William Charles 1943- *WhoScE 91-1*
Beaupain, Elaine Shapiro 1949- *WhoAm 92, WhoAmW 93, WhoE 93*
Beaupre, Paul 1923- *WhoCanL 92*
Beaupre, Vicki Louise 1953- *WhoAmW 93*
Beaupre, Walter Joseph 1925- *WhoE 93*
Beauregard, Charles R. 1919- *St&PR 93*
Beauregard, Luc 1941- *WhoE 93*
Beauregard, Michael R. *Law&B 92*
Beauregard, Pierre Gustave Toutant 1818-1893 *BioIn 17, HarEnMi*
Beausejour, Bruce P. *Law&B 92*
Beausoleil, Claude 1948- *WhoCanL 92*
Beausoleil, Doris Mae 1932- *WhoAmW 93, WhoE 93*
Beauvais, Edward R. 1936- *ConEn*
Beauvais, Kenneth R. 1954- *St&PR 93*
Beauvarlet-Charpentier, Jacques-Marie 1766-1834 *Baker 92*
Beauvarlet-Charpentier, Jean-Jacques 1734-1794 *Baker 92*
Beauvau-Craon, Diane, princesse de *BioIn 17*
Beauvoir, Simone de 1908-1986 *BioIn 17, ConLC 71 [port], WorLitC [port]*
Beaven, John Lewis 1930- *WhoE 93*
Beaven, Mary H. 1936- *WhoE 93*
Beaven, Peter Jamieson 1925- *WhoWor 93*
Beaven, Robert G. *St&PR 93*
Beaven, Robert Pendelton 1917- *St&PR 93*
Beaven, Winton Henry 1915- *WhoAm 92*
Beaver, Bonnie Veryle 1944- *WhoAm 92*
Beaver, Donavon F. 1935- *St&PR 93*
Beaver, Frank Eugene 1938- *WhoAm 92*
Beaver, Howard Oscar, Jr. 1925- *St&PR 93, WhoAm 92*
Beaver, James Addams 1837-1914 *BioIn 17*
Beaver, Jeffrey Thorp 1937- *St&PR 93*
Beaver, Joseph H. 1933- *St&PR 93*
Beaver, Kerry Eugene 1963- *WhoEmL 93*
Beaver, Lester Albert 1923- *St&PR 93*
Beaver, Paul Chester 1905- *WhoAm 92*
Beaver, Paul (Eli) 1953- *ConAu 40NR*
Beaver, R. Pierce 1906-1987 *BioIn 17*
Beaver, Robert Pierce 1906-1987 *BioIn 17*
Beaver, Thomas, Jr. 1923- *St&PR 93*
Beaver, William Henry 1940- *WhoAm 92*
Beaverbrook, Baron 1879-1964 *BioIn 17*
Beavers, Alvin Herman 1913- *WhoAm 92*
Beavers, Chester *St&PR 93*
Beavers, Daniel 1950- *WhoSSW 93*
Beavers, Elizabeth Anne Stewart 1958- *WhoSSW 93*
Beavers, Ellington McHenry 1916- *WhoAm 92*
Beavers, Louise 1902-1962 *IntDcF 2-3 [port]*
Beavers, Robert Franklin 1933- *St&PR 93*
Beavers, Roy L. 1930- *WhoSSW 93*
Beaverson, Roger E. *St&PR 93*
Beazer, Richard *St&PR 93*
Beazley, Hamilton Scott 1943- *WhoAm 92*
Beazley, Kim Christian 1948- *WhoAsAP 91, WhoWor 93*
Beazley, Lillian Stoll 1895- *AmWomPl*
Beazley, William Henry, Jr. 1931- *St&PR 93*
Beban, Gary Joseph 1946- *WhoAm 92*
Bebbington, J.E. *WhoScE 91-1*
Bebchick, Leonard Norman 1932- *WhoWor 93*
Bebear, Claude *BioIn 17*
Bebear, Claude 1935- *WhoWor 93*
Bebee, Gary Richard 1946- *WhoEmL 93*
Bebell, Harlan 1962- *WhoE 93*
Beber, Robert H. *Law&B 92*
Beber, Robert H. 1933- *WhoAm 92*
Becarevic, Aleksandar 1919- *WhoScE 91-4*
Becaud, Gilbert 1927- *Baker 92*
Beccali, Luigi d1990 *BioIn 17*
Beccatelli, Theresa Cecilia 1949- *WhoE 93, WhoEmL 93*
Becci, Michael Nelson *Law&B 92*
Becci, Michele Maria 1961- *WhoAmW 93*
Becci, Noreen B. *Law&B 92*
Beccue, Diana Lynn 1955- *WhoEmL 93*
Becerra (-Schmidt), Gustavo 1925- *Baker 92*
Bechara, Gervasio Henrique 1949- *WhoWor 93*
Bechard, Gorman *ScF&FL 92*
Bechard, Gorman 1959- *MiSFD 9*
Bechaud, Robert L. 1943- *St&PR 93*
Bechdel, Alison 1960- *ConAu 138*
Becher, Alfred Julius 1803-1848 *Baker 92*
Becher, Edmund Theodore 1904- *WhoWor 93*
Becher, N.E.H. 1932- *St&PR 93*
Becher, Paul Ronald 1934- *WhoAm 92, WhoWrEP 92*
Becher, Sheldon Herbert 1929- *St&PR 93*
Becher, William Don 1929- *WhoAm 92*
Becherer, Deborah Zorn 1958- *WhoAmW 93, WhoEmL 93*
Becherer, Hans Walter 1935- *St&PR 93, WhoAm 92, WhoWor 93*
Becherer, Richard John 1951- *WhoE 93*
Becherescu, Dumitru 1929- *WhoScE 91-4*
Bechert, Dietrich Wolfgang 1936- *WhoWor 93*
Bechert, Heinz 1932- *ConAu 136*
Bechet, J.N. 1928- *WhoScE 91-2*
Bechet, Sidney (Joseph) 1897-1959 *Baker 92*
Bechgaard, Julius 1843-1917 *Baker 92*
Bechhofer, Frank *WhoScE 91-1*
Bechi, Gino 1913- *Baker 92, OxDcOp*
Bechler, Adam Krzysztof 1945- *WhoWor 93*
Bechler, Edwin Christopher 1913- *St&PR 93*
Bechler, Johann Christian 1784-1857 *Baker 92*
Bechly, Paul Lorin 1958- *WhoEmL 93*
Bechmann, Roland 1919- *ConAu 136*
Bechstein, (Friedrich Wilhelm) Carl 1826-1900 *Baker 92*
Becht, Adeline Charlotte 1937- *WhoAmW 93*
Becht, Edward F. 1930- *St&PR 93*
Becht, James Humphrey *Law&B 92*
Becht, Marco 1966- *WhoWor 93*
Becht, Richard Paul 1933- *St&PR 93*
Bechtel, Gary H. *WhoAm 92*
Bechtel, H. Robert 1949- *St&PR 93*
Bechtel, Heinrich Philipp Karl 1935- *WhoUN 92*
Bechtel, Laura P. d1992 *NewYTBS 92*
Bechtel, Pierre Robert 1933- *WhoScE 91-2*
Bechtel, Riley *WhoAm 92*
Bechtel, Robert C. 1924- *St&PR 93*
Bechtel, Robert W. 1923-1992 *BioIn 17*
Bechtel, Ronald W. 1903- *St&PR 93*
Bechtel, Sara Elizabeth 1954- *WhoE 93*
Bechtel, Stephen D., Jr. 1925- *St&PR 93*
Bechtel, Stephen Davison, Jr. 1925- *WhoAm 92*
Bechtle, Louis Charles 1927- *WhoAm 92, WhoE 93*
Bechtle, Robert Alan 1932- *WhoAm 92*
Bechtler, Catherine Joy 1960- *WhoAmW 93*
Bechtol, Nancy June 1950- *WhoEmL 93*
Bechtol, William Milton 1931- *WhoAm 92*
Bechtold, Jeroen *BioIn 17*
Bechtold, Linda Helen 1963- *WhoAm 92*
Bechtold, Susan Hatfield 1948- *WhoSSW 93*
Bechtold, Timothy V. 1953- *WhoIns 93*
Becich, Raymond Brice 1945- *WhoAm 92*
Beck, Aaron T. *BioIn 17*
Beck, Aaron Temkin 1921- *WhoAm 92*
Beck, Abe Jack 1914- *WhoAm 92*
Beck, Adrian Robert 1932- *WhoAm 92*
Beck, Alan M(arshall) 1942- *WhoWrEP 92*
Beck, Albert 1928- *St&PR 93, WhoAm 92*
Beck, Anatole 1930- *WhoAm 92*
Beck, Andreas 1948- *WhoScE 91-4*
Beck, Andrew *Law&B 92*
Beck, Andrew James 1948- *WhoE 93, WhoEmL 93, WhoWor 93*
Beck, Anna 1926- *WhoAmW 93*
Beck, Anna Nadine 1922- *WhoAmW 93*
Beck, Anne Landsbury *AmWomPl*
Beck, Art *WhoWrEP 92*
Beck, Audrey 1954- *WhoAmW 93*
Beck, Bertha Reed *AmWomPl*
Beck, Bethany Ann 1948- *St&PR 93*
Beck, Brent Allen 1958- *WhoEmL 93*
Beck, Burt d1990 *BioIn 17*
Beck, C.C. 1910-1989 *BioIn 17*
Beck, Calvin Thomas 1930-1989 *ScF&FL 92*
Beck, Carl A. 1917- *St&PR 93*
Beck, Charles E. *Law&B 92*
Beck, Charles W. d1991 *BioIn 17*
Beck, Charlotte Hudgens 1937- *WhoSSW 93*
Beck, Christoph F. 1941- *WhoScE 91-3*
Beck, Christopher Alan 1953- *WhoEmL 93*
Beck, Connie Kay *Law&B 92*
Beck, Conrad 1901-1989 *Baker 92*
Beck, Curt Buxton 1924- *WhoSSW 93*
Beck, Curt Werner 1927- *WhoAm 92*
Beck, Daniel Edward 1960- *WhoEmL 93, WhoSSW 93*
Beck, Daniel James 1948- *WhoEmL 93*
Beck, David A. 1953- *St&PR 93*
Beck, Dawn Marie *Law&B 92*
Beck, Deborah Berman 1938- *WhoAmW 93*
Beck, Donald R., Jr. 1955- *St&PR 93*
Beck, Dorothy Fahs *WhoAm 92, WhoAmW 93, WhoE 93*
Beck, Earl Ray 1916- *WhoAm 92, WhoSSW 93, WhoWor 93*
Beck, Edward Henry, III *Law&B 92*

Beck, Edward Henry, III 1950- *WhoEmL 93*
Beck, Edward W. *Law&B 92*
Beck, Edward W. 1944- *St&PR 93*
Beck, Edward William 1944- *WhoAm 92*
Beck, Eileen M. 1941- *St&PR 93*
Beck, Erika Piekut 1954- *WhoAmW 93*
Beck, Erwin H. 1937- *WhoScE 91-3*
Beck, Eugen Alexander 1933- *WhoWor 93*
Beck, F.H.A. *WhoScE 91-3*
Beck, Felix M. 1926- *St&PR 93*
Beck, Frances Josephine Mottey 1918- *WhoWor 93*
Beck, Franz 1734-1809 *Baker 92*
Beck, Friedrich H. 1927- *WhoScE 91-3*
Beck, Fritz Paul 1931- *WhoScE 91-3*
Beck, George Eugene 1926- *St&PR 93*
•**Beck**, George L. 1937- *St&PR 93*
Beck, George Preston 1930- *WhoSSW 93, WhoWor 93*
Beck, George R. *Law&B 92*
Beck, George William 1921- *WhoAm 92*
Beck, Guido 1903-1988 *BioIn 17*
Beck, Hans 1939- *WhoScE 91-4*
Beck, Henry Lawrence 1923- *St&PR 93*
Beck, Henry M., Jr. 1951- *WhoEmL 93*
Beck, Howard Fred 1928- *St&PR 93*
Beck, Irwin Y. 1924- *St&PR 93*
Beck, J. Edward, Jr. 1948- *St&PR 93*
Beck, James (Henry) Beck 1930- *WhoWrEP 92*
Beck, James Carl 1939- *St&PR 93*
Beck, James H. 1925- *St&PR 93*
Beck, James P. 1941- *St&PR 93*
Beck, Jan Scott 1955- *WhoAm 92, WhoEmL 93*
Beck, Jean-Baptiste 1881-1943 *Baker 92*
Beck, Jeff *BioIn 17*
Beck, Jeffrey *BioIn 17*
Beck, Jeffrey Dengler 1948- *WhoE 93*
Beck, Jeffrey Haines 1949- *WhoEmL 93*
Beck, Joan Wagner 1923- *WhoAm 92, WhoWrEP 92*
Beck, Joann L. *Law&B 92*
Beck, Joe Eugene 1947- *WhoEmL 93, WhoWor 93*
Beck, Joel *BioIn 17*
Beck, John Christian 1924- *WhoAm 92*
Beck, John E. *Law&B 92*
Beck, John G. 1925- *WhoIns 93*
Beck, John Jacob 1949- *WhoSSW 93*
Beck, John LeRoy 1947- *WhoEmL 93*
Beck, John Ness 1930-1987 *Baker 92*
Beck, Josef 1894-1944 *DcTwHis*
Beck, Joseph James 1946- *WhoEmL 93*
Beck, Jozef 1894-1944 *PolBiDi*
Beck, June Gayle 1956- *WhoSSW 93*
Beck, Karl 1814-1879 *Baker 92*
Beck, Keith Lindell 1946- *WhoEmL 93*
Beck, Klaus Martin 1941- *WhoWor 93*
Beck, Livia Grunwald 1947- *WhoEmL 93*
Beck, Lowell R. 1934- *WhoIns 93*
Beck, Lowell Richard 1934- *WhoAm 92*
Beck, Ludwig 1880-1944 *BioIn 17, HarEnMi*
Beck, Luke Ferrell Wilson 1948- *WhoSSW 93*
Beck, Mae Lucille 1936- *WhoAmW 93*
Beck, Manfred Herman Josef 1943- *WhoE 93*
Beck, Marilyn Mohr 1928- *WhoAm 92*
Beck, Marjorie Ruth 1956- *WhoE 93, WhoEmL 93*
Beck, Marshall G. 1944- *St&PR 93*
Beck, Martha 1900- *Baker 92*
Beck, Mary Constance 1946- *WhoAm 92*
Beck, Mary Lynn Bingham *Law&B 92*
Beck, Mary McLean 1946- *WhoAmW 93*
Beck, Mat *WhoAm 92*
Beck, Maurice Sidney *WhoScE 91-1*
Beck, Mihaly T. 1929- *WhoScE 91-4*
Beck, Miroslav 1928- *WhoScE 91-4*
Beck, Morris 1927- *WhoSSW 93*
Beck, Nancy Flaherty *WhoE 93*
Beck, Nancy Mann McConnico 1933- *WhoAmW 93*
Beck, Neil J. *Law&B 92*
Beck, Neva Ann 1941- *WhoAmW 93*
Beck, Norman Wood 1901- *WhoE 93*
Beck, Paul Adams 1908- *WhoAm 92*
Beck, Paul Allen 1944- *WhoAm 92*
Beck, Paul Augustine 1936- *WhoAm 92*
Beck, Peggy S. *Law&B 92*
Beck, Phyllis Whitman 1927- *WhoAmW 93*
Beck, R. Albert 1919- *St&PR 93*
Beck, Richard R. 1930- *WhoIns 93*
Beck, Robert A. 1925- *WhoIns 93*
Beck, Robert Alfred 1920- *WhoAm 92*
Beck, Robert Arthur 1925- *WhoAm 92*
Beck, Robert Beryl 1935- *WhoSSW 93*
Beck, Robert Charles 1951- *WhoE 93*
Beck, Robert Edward 1941- *WhoE 93*
Beck, Robert James 1938- *WhoSSW 93*
Beck, Robert K. *Law&B 92*
Beck, Robert Louis 1938- *WhoAm 92*
Beck, Robert N. *WhoAm 92*
Beck, Robert Nelson 1924- *WhoWrEP 92*
Beck, Robert Randall 1940- *St&PR 93*
Beck, Roger D. 1936- *St&PR 93*
Beck, Roland Peter 1931- *WhoAm 92*
Beck, Rosemarie 1924- *WhoAm 92*
Beck, Russell *WhoScE 91-1*
Beck, Simone *BioIn 17*
Beck, Stanley Dwight 1919- *WhoAm 92*
Beck, Steven H. *St&PR 93*
Beck, Stuart J. *St&PR 93*
Beck, Susan 1943- *WhoAmW 93*
Beck, Susan Gayle Long 1959- *WhoSSW 93*
Beck, Sydney 1906- *Baker 92*
Beck, Tamara 1947- *WhoEmL 93*
Beck, Terry Lee 1958- *St&PR 93*
Beck, Thomas Edwin 1946- *WhoEmL 93*
Beck, Thomas G. *St&PR 93*
Beck, Thomas Ludvigsen 1899-1963 *Baker 92*
Beck, Timothy Daniel 1953- *WhoEmL 93, WhoWor 93*
Beck, Virginia Lee 1941- *WhoAmW 93*
Beck, Walter 1929- *DrEEuF*
Beck, Walther 1923- *WhoScE 91-4*
Beck, William Austin 1930- *WhoE 93*
Beck, William Harold, Jr. 1928- *WhoSSW 93*
Beck, William Samson 1923- *WhoAm 92*
Beck, Winfried 1943- *WhoWor 93*
Beck, Wolfgang M. 1932- *WhoScE 91-3*
Beck, Wolfgang Maximilian 1932- *WhoWor 93*
Beckedorff, David Lawrence 1940- *WhoAm 92*
Beckel, Charles Leroy 1928- *WhoAm 92*
Beckel, Daniel D. *Law&B 92*
Beckel, Mark Scott *Law&B 92*
Beckel, Robert Gilliland 1948- *WhoE 93*
Beckelheimer, Christine Elizabeth Campbell 1916- *WhoAmW 93, WhoSSW 93*
Beckemeier, Edward A. 1925- *WhoIns 93*
Beckemeyer, Nancy Scott 1953- *WhoEmL 93, WhoSSW 93*
Beckemeyer, W.H. 1946- *St&PR 93*
Becken, Bradford Albert 1924- *WhoAm 92*
Becken, Garold Wallace 1953- *WhoEmL 93*
Beckenbach, William Charles 1937- *St&PR 93*
Beckenstein, Jay Barnet 1951- *WhoE 93*
Beckenstein, Myron 1938- *WhoAm 92, WhoWrEP 92*
Becker, Albert (Ernst Anton) 1834-1899 *Baker 92*
Becker, Alida 1948- *ScF&FL 92*
Becker, Allen Edward 1948- *WhoEmL 93*
Becker, Alta *AmWomPl*
Becker, Amanda Shaw *Law&B 92*
Becker, Arthur B. 1928- *St&PR 93*
Becker, Arthur Frank 1905- *St&PR 93*
Becker, Barbara 1945- *WhoAmW 93*
Becker, Beatrice *AmWomPl*
Becker, Bernard William, Jr. 1926- *St&PR 93*
Becker, Betsy 1939- *WhoAm 92, WhoAmW 93, WhoWor 93*
Becker, Bettie Geraldine 1918- *WhoAm 92, WhoAmW 93*
Becker, Beverly June 1930- *WhoE 93*
Becker, Boris *BioIn 17*
Becker, Boris 1967- *WhoAm 92*
Becker, Brandon 1954- *WhoEmL 93*
Becker, Brian Elden 1949- *WhoE 93*
Becker, Bruce Carl, II 1948- *WhoEmL 93, WhoWor 93*
Becker, Bruce Clare 1929- *WhoE 93*
Becker, Bruce D. *Law&B 92*
Becker, Bud J. *Law&B 92*
Becker, Connie Lynn 1968- *WhoE 93*
Becker, Constantin Julius 1811-1859 *Baker 92*
Becker, David Bruce 1953- *WhoWor 93*
Becker, David Leigh 1960- *WhoEmL 93*
Becker, David Mandel 1935 *WhoAm 92*
Becker, David Manning 1949- *WhoEmL 93*
Becker, David N. 1945- *St&PR 93*
Becker, David Stephen 1954- *WhoEmL 93*
Becker, Deborah *WhoIns 93*
Becker, Deborah Dawn 1950- *WhoAmW 93*
Becker, Deborah R. 1960- *St&PR 93*
Becker, Diane Louise 1950- *WhoEmL 93*
Becker, Dietrich 1623-1679 *Baker 92*
Becker, Don C. 1933- *St&PR 93*
Becker, Don Crandall 1933- *WhoAm 92*
Becker, Donald Eugene 1923- *WhoAm 92*
Becker, Douglas Wesley 1950- *WhoEmL 93, WhoSSW 93*
Becker, Dwight Lowell 1918- *WhoAm 92*
Becker, E. Allen 1938- *St&PR 93*
Becker, Edward A. 1938- *WhoAm 92, WhoSSW 93, WhoWor 93*
Becker, Edward Roy 1933- *WhoAm 92, WhoE 93*
Becker, Edwin Demuth 1930- *WhoAm 92*
Becker, Edwin F. 1946- *St&PR 93*
Becker, Edwin H. 1910- *St&PR 93*
Becker, Erich Peter 1939- *St&PR 93, WhoAm 92*
Becker, Eugene E. *WhoIns 93*
Becker, Eve *ScF&FL 92*
Becker, Frank 1944- *Baker 92*
Becker, Fred Reinhardt, Jr. 1949- *WhoEmL 93*
Becker, Frederick Fenimore 1931- *WhoAm 92, WhoSSW 93*
Becker, G. Ted 1944- *St&PR 93*
Becker, Gail Roselyn 1942- *WhoAmW 93*
Becker, Gary Michael 1958- *WhoEmL 93*
Becker, Gary S. *NewYTBS 92 [port]*
Becker, Gary Stanley 1930- *WhoAm 92*
Becker, George James 1934- *WhoAm 92*
Becker, George Raymond 1931- *St&PR 93*
Becker, Gerhard W. 1927- *WhoScE 91-3*
Becker, Gero *WhoScE 91-3*
Becker, Gert *WhoScE 91-3*
Becker, Gert Otto 1933- *St&PR 93*
Becker, Gordon P. *Law&B 92*
Becker, Gretchen Anne 1959- *WhoAmW 93*
Becker, Gunther (Hugo) 1924- *Baker 92*
Becker, Gustave Louis 1861-1959 *Baker 92*
Becker, H. Merrill, Jr. 1938- *St&PR 93*
Becker, Hans *WhoScE 91-3*
Becker, Harold *MiSFD 9*
Becker, Heinz 1922- *Baker 92*
Becker, Helmut 1927- *WhoScE 91-3*
Becker, Herbert S. 1931- *WhoE 93*
Becker, Herman Eli 1910- *WhoSSW 93*
Becker, Howard Edward 1954- *St&PR 93*
Becker, Howard H. 1940- *WhoE 93*
Becker, Hugo 1863-1941 *Baker 92*
Becker, Irving J. *WhoSSW 93*
Becker, Isidore A. 1926- *WhoAm 92, WhoWor 93*
Becker, Ivan 1948- *WhoEmL 93*
Becker, Ivan E. 1929- *St&PR 93*
Becker, Ivan Endre 1929- *WhoAm 92*
Becker, Jack Douglas 1947- *WhoSSW 93*
Becker, James W. *Law&B 92*
Becker, James W. 1942- *St&PR 93*
Becker, James William 1942- *WhoAm 92*
Becker, Jasper 1956- *ConAu 139*
Becker, Jean 1833-1884 *Baker 92*
Becker, Jerry 1929- *St&PR 93*
Becker, Jill B. 1952- *WhoEmL 93*
Becker, Jim *Law&B 92*
Becker, Joann E. 1948- *St&PR 93*
Becker, JoAnn Elizabeth 1948- *WhoAm 92, WhoAmW 93*
Becker, John 1943- *St&PR 93*
Becker, John A. 1942- *St&PR 93*
Becker, John Alphonsis 1942- *WhoAm 92*
Becker, John J(oseph) 1886-1961 *Baker 92*
Becker, Jon Scott *Law&B 92*
Becker, Jon Scott 1953- *WhoEmL 93*
Becker, Joseph 1923- *WhoAm 92*
Becker, Joseph Scott 1950- *WhoEmL 93*
Becker, Josh *MiSFD 9*
Becker, Julie A. Taylor 1961- *WhoAmW 93*
Becker, Juliette 1938- *WhoAmW 93*
Becker, Julius 1919- *St&PR 93*
Becker, Jurek 1937- *BioIn 17*
Becker, Jurgen 1932- *WhoWor 93*
Becker, K.E. *WhoScE 91-3*
Becker, Karl Martin 1943- *WhoAm 92*
Becker, Kenneth Melvin 1948- *WhoEmL 93*
Becker, Kenneth Richard 1947- *WhoEmL 93*
Becker, Larry Keith 1948- *WhoIns 93*
Becker, Larry Wayne 1946- *WhoEmL 93*
Becker, Lawrence J. *Law&B 92*
Becker, Lawrence M. 1955- *St&PR 93*
Becker, Lawrence Wilfred 1941- *WhoE 93*
Becker, Leander Peter 1938- *WhoScE 91-4*
Becker, Lilliam 1948- *WhoSSW 93*
Becker, Linda Sue 1954- *WhoAmW 93*
Becker, Lisa Tamiris 1967- *BioIn 17*
Becker, M. *WhoScE 91-2*
Becker, Magdalene Neuenschwander 1915- *WhoAmW 93*
Becker, Margot *ScF&FL 92*
Becker, Marie Grace 1926- *St&PR 93*
Becker, Marshall Hilford 1940- *WhoAm 92*
Becker, Marvin Burton 1922- *WhoAm 92*
Becker, Marvin Oren 1930- *St&PR 93*
Becker, Mary Julia 1928- *WhoAmW 93*
Becker, Mary Louise *WhoAm 92, WhoAmW 93, WhoE 93*
Becker, Michael Albert *Law&B 92*
Becker, Michael Charles 1948- *WhoEmL 93*
Becker, Michael Lewis 1940- *WhoAm 92*
Becker, Michael R. 1945- *St&PR 93*
Becker, Muriel R. 1924- *ScF&FL 92*
Becker, Murray Leonard 1933- *WhoE 93*
Becker, Norman H. 1937- *St&PR 93*
Becker, Patricia *Law&B 92*
Becker, Patricia Winifred *WhoAm 92*
Becker, Paul Albert 1939- *WhoWor 93*
Becker, Paul Joseph 1953- *WhoIns 93*
Becker, Paul Leonard *Law&B 92*
Becker, Paula Lee 1941- *WhoAmW 93*
Becker, Paula Modersohn- 1876-1907 *BioIn 17*
Becker, Philip H. *Law&B 92*
Becker, Pierre J.C. 1942- *WhoScE 91-2*
Becker, Quinn Henderson 1930- *WhoAm 92*
Becker, Ralph Edward 1931- *St&PR 93, WhoAm 92*
Becker, Ralph Elihu 1907- *WhoAm 92, WhoE 93*
Becker, Ralph Elihu, Jr. 1952- *WhoEmL 93*
Becker, Randall B. 1942- *St&PR 93*
Becker, Raymond J. 1905- *St&PR 93*
Becker, Raymond John, Jr. 1956- *WhoE 93*
Becker, Rex Louis 1913- *WhoAm 92*
Becker, Rhoda Heffner 1935- *WhoAmW 93*
Becker, Richard Charles 1931- *WhoAm 92*
Becker, Richard J. 1925- *St&PR 93*
Becker, Richard Stanley 1934- *WhoAm 92*
Becker, Robert 1954- *St&PR 93*
Becker, Robert A. 1920- *WhoAm 92*
Becker, Robert Alan 1931- *WhoE 93*
Becker, Robert B. 1949- *St&PR 93*
Becker, Robert C. 1941- *St&PR 93*
Becker, Robert Cappel 1941- *WhoAm 92*
Becker, Robert Clarence 1927- *WhoAm 92*
Becker, Robert Eugene 1929- *St&PR 93*
Becker, Robert J. *Law&B 92*
Becker, Robert Jerome 1922- *WhoAm 92*
Becker, Robert Joseph 1946- *WhoEmL 93, WhoWor 93*
Becker, Robert Otto 1923- *WhoAm 92*
Becker, Robert Richard 1923- *WhoAm 92*
Becker, Roger Vern 1947- *WhoEmL 93*
Becker, Ronald Ivan 1942- *St&PR 93*
Becker, Ronald Leonard 1950- *WhoEmL 93*
Becker, Samuel 1903- *WhoAm 92*
Becker, Samuel L. d1991 *BioIn 17*
Becker, Sandra Neiman Hammer 1947- *WhoEmL 93*
Becker, Seymour 1924- *WhoE 93, WhoWor 93*
Becker, Sherri Craft 1944- *WhoSSW 93*
Becker, Stephen Arnold 1951- *WhoAm 92*
Becker, Stephen David 1927- *WhoSSW 93*
Becker, Stephen Edward 1948- *WhoEmL 93, WhoSSW 93*
Becker, Stephen S. *St&PR 93*
Becker, Steven Allen *WhoE 93*
Becker, Susan Kaplan 1948- *WhoAmW 93, WhoE 93, WhoEmL 93*
Becker, Suzanne Sheehan 1945- *WhoAmW 93*
Becker, Suzy 1962- *WhoAmW 93*
Becker, Thelma *BioIn 17*
Becker, Ulrich J. 1938- *WhoE 93*
Becker, Uwe Eugen 1947- *WhoWor 93*
Becker, Walter Edward 1935- *St&PR 93*
Becker, Wesley Clemence 1928- *WhoAm 92*
Becker, Wilhelm 1937- *WhoScE 91-3*
Becker, William 1909-1992 *BioIn 17*
Becker, William Adolph 1933- *WhoE 93, WhoSSW 93, WhoWor 93*
Becker, William Clifford 1948- *St&PR 93*
Becker, William Watters 1943- *WhoAm 92*
Becker, Wolf-Jurgen 1940- *WhoScE 91-3*
Becker-Castillo, Renee Lyn 1960- *WhoAmW 93*
Beckerdite, A.D. 1926- *St&PR 93*
Becker-Doyle, Eve 1955- *WhoSSW 93*
Beckering, Gerald Elliott 1946- *WhoEmL 93*
Beckerle, Carol A. *Law&B 92*
Becker-Lewke, Laura V. *Law&B 92*
Beckerman, Barry Lee 1941- *WhoE 93*
Beckerman, Edwin Paul 1927- *WhoE 93*
Beckerman, Martin 1942- *WhoSSW 93, WhoWor 93*
Beckerman, Murray 1924- *St&PR 93*
Beckerman, Nancy Greyson 1943- *WhoAmW 93*
Beckerman, Robert Cy 1946- *WhoSSW 93*
Becker-Platen, Jens Dieter 1937- *WhoScE 91-3*
Becker-Roukas, Helane Renee 1957- *WhoAmW 93, WhoE 93, WhoEmL 93*
Beckers, B. *WhoScE 91-2*
Beckers, Carl L.A. 1907- *St&PR 93*
Beckers, H.L. *WhoScE 91-1*
Beckers, Jacques Maurice 1934- *WhoWor 93*
Beckert, Ewald Herbert 1920- *WhoWor 93*
Beckert, John Francis 1940- *St&PR 93*
Beckert, W.J. 1942- *St&PR 93*
Beckervordersandforth, Christian Paul *WhoScE 91-3*

Becket, Jim *ScF&FL 92*
Beckett, Barry 1944- *SoulM*
Beckett, Beverly Baker *BiDAMSp 1989*
Beckett, Eugene Francis 1929- *WhoE 93*
Beckett, Evette *BioIn 17*
Beckett, Gary Roger 1946- *WhoSSW 93*
Beckett, Grace 1912- *WhoAmW 93*
Beckett, J. Overton 1927- *St&PR 93*
Beckett, Jenifer *ScF&FL 92*
Beckett, Joanne M. *Law&B 92*
Beckett, John Angus 1916- *WhoAm 92*
Beckett, John Douglas 1938- *St&PR 93, WhoAm 92*
Beckett, Lee M. *Law&B 92*
Beckett, Mark William 1952- *St&PR 93*
Beckett, Mary Ellen 1933- *WhoAmW 93*
Beckett, Samuel 1906-1989 *BioIn 17, MagSWL [port], WorLitC [port]*
Beckett, Susan Kay 1948- *WhoAmW 93*
Beckett, Theodore Charles 1929- *WhoAm 92, WhoWor 93*
Beckett, Theodore Cornwall 1952- *WhoEmL 93, WhoWor 93*
Beckett, Thomas L. 1953- *WhoWrEP 92*
Beckett, Wheeler 1898-1986 *Baker 92*
Beckett, William Wade 1928- *WhoAm 92*
Beckey, Sylvia Louise 1946- *WhoAm 92, WhoEmL 93*
Beckfeld, William Francis 1933- *St&PR 93*
Beckford, George *DcCPCAm*
Beckham, Edgar Frederick 1933- *WhoAm 92*
Beckham, Howard Richard, Jr. 1955- *WhoEmL 93, WhoSSW 93*
Beckham, Marianne Max *WhoAmW 93*
Beckham, Mary Estes Shelby 1927- *WhoSSW 93*
Beckham, Michael *MiSFD 9*
Beckham, Paul Dearmin 1943- *St&PR 93*
Beckham, Richard F. 1936- *St&PR 93*
Beckham, Stephen Andrew 1959- *WhoEmL 93, WhoSSW 93*
Beckham, Stephen Robert 1952- *WhoEmL 93*
Beckham, William Arthur 1927- *WhoAm 92*
Beckhard, Herbert 1926- *WhoAm 92*
Becking, Gustav (Wilhelm) 1894-1945 *Baker 92*
Beckingham, Kathleen Mary 1946- *WhoSSW 93*
Beckius, Larry V. 1934- *St&PR 93*
Becklake, Margaret Rigsby 1922- *WhoAm 92, WhoAmW 93*
Beckler, David Zander 1918- *WhoAm 92, WhoScE 91-2*
Beckley, H.R. *WhoScE 91-1*
Beckley, Jay Charles 1928- *St&PR 93*
Beckley, John 1757-1807 *PolPar*
Beckley, Michael John 1942- *WhoAm 92*
Beckley, Naomi *BioIn 17*
Beckley, Robert Howard 1920- *WhoSSW 93*
Beckley, William J. *Law&B 92*
Beckman, Aileen Kohn 1933- *WhoE 93*
Beckman, Arnold Orville 1900- *WhoAm 92*
Beckman, Arthur Herman 1930- *St&PR 93*
Beckman, Connie Lewis 1950- *WhoAmW 93*
Beckman, Delores *DcAmChF 1960*
Beckman, Dennis Donald 1952- *WhoEmL 93*
Beckman, Donald 1932- *WhoAm 92*
Beckman, Gail McKnight 1938- *WhoAm 92*
Beckman, Gunhild N.M. 1941- *WhoScE 91-4*
Beckman, Gunnel 1910- *MajAI [port]*
Beckman, James Wallace Bim 1936- *WhoWor 93*
Beckman, Jill Marie *Law&B 92*
Beckman, Joseph Alfred 1937- *WhoAm 92, WhoSSW 93*
Beckman, Judith Kalb 1940- *WhoAm 92, WhoAmW 93, WhoE 93, WhoWor 93*
Beckman, Kenneth Oren 1948- *WhoEmL 93*
Beckman, Kenneth W. 1918- *St&PR 93*
Beckman, Lars E.A. 1928- *WhoScE 91-4*
Beckman, Martin J. 1940- *St&PR 93*
Beckman, Melissa Ann 1964- *WhoAmW 93*
Beckman, Olof 1922- *WhoScE 91-4*
Beckman, Robert 1949- *St&PR 93*
Beckman, Vincent H. 1915- *St&PR 93*
Beckman, Widar Karl Valdemar 1939- *WhoWor 93*
Beckman, William N. *Law&B 92*
Beckman, William Scott 1961- *WhoSSW 93*
Beckmann, Johann Friedrich Gottlieb 1737-1792 *Baker 92*
Beckmann, John William 1960- *WhoE 93*
Beckmann, Jon Michael 1936- *WhoAm 92*
Beckmann, Leo Heinrich Josef Franz 1930- *WhoWor 93*
Beckmann, Max 1884-1950 *BioIn 17, ModArCr 3 [port]*
Beckmann, Michele Lillian 1957- *WhoAmW 93, WhoEmL 93*
Beckmann, Petr 1924- *WhoAm 92*
Beckmann, Poul 1924- *WhoScE 91-1*
Beckmann, Uwe 1942- *WhoWor 93*
Beckmeyer, Henry Ernest 1939- *WhoWor 93*
Becknell, Patricia Ann 1950- *WhoEmL 93*
Beckner, Donald Lee 1939- *WhoAm 92*
Beckner, Everet Hess 1935- *WhoAm 92*
Beckon, Weir Emil 1938- *St&PR 93*
Becks, Cherry Marion 1941- *WhoAmW 93*
Becksford, Dennis 1955- *St&PR 93*
Beckstead, Richard L. 1929- *St&PR 93*
Beckstead, Robert Dale 1959- *WhoWrEP 92*
Beckstrand, Shelley M. *Law&B 92*
Beckstrom, John Michael Smith 1952- *WhoEmL 93*
Beckum, Leonard Charles 1937- *WhoAm 92*
Beckwith, Abijah 1784-1874 *BioIn 17*
Beckwith, Barbara Jean 1948- *WhoAmW 93*
Beckwith, Carol 1945- *BioIn 17*
Beckwith, Catherine S. 1958- *WhoEmL 93*
Beckwith, Charles Emilio 1917- *WhoAm 92*
Beckwith, Christopher I. 1945- *WhoWrEP 92*
Beckwith, Christopher Irving 1945- *WhoAm 92*
Beckwith, David *WhoAm 92*
Beckwith, David M. *Law&B 92*
Beckwith, Don L. 1946- *St&PR 93*
Beckwith, George 1753-1823 *BioIn 17*
Beckwith, Henry Hopkins 1935- *St&PR 93*
Beckwith, Henry L.P., Jr. 1935- *ScF&FL 92*
Beckwith, Herbert L. 1903- *WhoAm 92*
Beckwith, James S., III 1932- *St&PR 93*
Beckwith, John 1750-1809 *Baker 92*
Beckwith, John 1918-1991 *BioIn 17*
Beckwith, John 1927- *Baker 92, WhoAm 92*
Beckwith, John Charles 1941- *St&PR 93*
Beckwith, John H. d1879 *BioIn 17*
Beckwith, Jonathan Roger 1935- *WhoAm 92*
Beckwith, Lewis Daniel 1948- *WhoEmL 93*
Beckwith, Maxine Marie 1939- *WhoAmW 93*
Beckwith, Merle Ray 1942- *WhoWrEP 92*
Beckwith, Robert W. 1858-1978 *BioIn 17*
Beckwith, Rodney Fisk 1935- *St&PR 93, WhoAm 92, WhoE 93, WhoWor 93*
Beckwith, Ronald Lee 1935- *WhoAm 92*
Beckwith, William Hunter 1896- *WhoAm 92*
Beckwith, William L. 1926- *St&PR 93*
Beckwitt, Julie-Ann 1958- *WhoSSW 93*
Beckworth, John Barney 1958- *WhoEmL 93*
Beckwourth, James Pierson 1798-1866 *BioIn 17*
Beckwourth, Jim 1800?-1866 *Expl 93 [port]*
Becnel, Salvatore J. *Law&B 92*
Becofsky, Arthur Luke 1950- *WhoAm 92, WhoE 93*
Becraft, Frank Joseph 1943- *St&PR 93*
Bectel, Maurice Quinn 1935- *WhoAm 92*
Becton, Henry Prentiss, Jr. 1943- *WhoAm 92, WhoE 93*
Becton, John William 1947- *WhoSSW 93*
Becton, Julius W., Jr. 1926- *AfrAmBi [port]*
Becton, Julius Wesley, Jr. 1926- *WhoAm 92*
Becton, Patricia Gupton 1959- *WhoAmW 93*
Becvar, Dorothy Stroh 1941- *WhoAmW 93*
Becvarovsky, Anton Felix 1754-1823 *Baker 92*
Beczak, Thaddeus Thomas 1950- *WhoAm 92*
Beda, Bruce A. 1940- *St&PR 93*
Beda, Gaye Elise 1955- *WhoAmW 93, WhoE 93*
Bedard, Kipp A. 1959- *St&PR 93*
Bedard, Mark D. 1956- *St&PR 93*
Bedard, Michael 1949- *ScF&FL 92*
Bedard, Michele *WhoCanL 92*
Bedard, Myriam *BioIn 17*
Bedard, Patrick Joseph 1941- *WhoAm 92, WhoWrEP 92*
Bedard, R. Richard 1943- *St&PR 93*
Bedard, Raymond R. 1954- *St&PR 93*
Bedarf, George Eugene 1951- *WhoEmL 93*
Bedaske, Angela Margaret 1961- *WhoAmW 93, WhoE 93*
Bedau, Hugo Adam 1926- *WhoAm 92*
Bedaw, Barry Lewis 1959- *WhoE 93*
Beddall, David Peter 1948- *WhoAsAP 91*
Beddall, Gerald Clive 1942- *WhoAm 92*
Beddall, Thomas Henry 1922- *WhoAm 92*
Beddie, Lesley Anne *WhoScE 91-1*
Beddington, John Rex *WhoScE 91-1*
Beddoes, Leslie R., Jr. 1933- *St&PR 93*
Beddoes, Thomas Lovell 1803-1849 *BioIn 17*
Beddoe-Stephens, Clive 1943- *St&PR 93*
Beddome, John Macdonald 1930- *WhoAm 92*
Beddow, David P. 1943- *St&PR 93*
Beddow, David Pierce 1943- *WhoAm 92*
Beddow, Jack W. 1921- *St&PR 93*
Beddow, John Warren 1952- *WhoEmL 93*
Beddow, Margery *BioIn 17*
Beddow, Reid d1992 *BioIn 17*
Beddow, Thomas John 1914- *WhoAm 92*
Beddows, Clifford G. *WhoScE 91-1*
Bede c. 672-735 *OxDcByz*
Bede, Sylvesta *WhoWrEP 92*
Bedeaux, Dick 1941- *WhoWor 93*
Bedeian, Arthur George 1946- *WhoAm 92*
Bedelia, Bonnie *BioIn 17*
Bedelia, Bonnie 1948- *WhoAm 92*
Bedelia, Bonnie 1952- *ConTFT 10*
Bedell, Catherine May *WhoAm 92*
Bedell, Charlotte Ware 1933- *WhoSSW 93*
Bedell, Cheryl Etta 1955- *WhoAmW 93*
Bedell, Conaly Wm. 1936- *St&PR 93*
Bedell, Cynthia Mae 1958- *WhoAmW 93*
Bedell, George Chester 1928- *WhoAm 92, WhoSSW 93*
Bedell, George Noble 1922- *WhoAm 92*
Bedell, Graysanne L. *St&PR 93*
Bedell, James Joseph 1954- *St&PR 93*
Bedell, John J. 1934- *St&PR 93*
Bedell, Madelon (Jane Berns) 1922?-1986 *ConAu 136*
Bedell, Thomas Walter 1950- *St&PR 93*
Bedell, William 1571-1642 *BioIn 17*
Bederka, John Matthew 1928- *St&PR 93*
Bederson, Benjamin 1921- *WhoAm 92*
Bede, the Venerable, Saint 673-735 *BioIn 17*
Bedewi, Elizabeth M. 1937- *St&PR 93*
Bedford, Amy Aldrich 1912- *St&PR 93, WhoAmW 93*
Bedford, Barbara *SweetSg B [port]*
Bedford, Brian 1935- *WhoAm 92*
Bedford, Clay P. 1903-1991 *BioIn 17*
Bedford, Clive *ScF&FL 92*
Bedford, David (Vickerman) 1937- *Baker 92*
Bedford, J.J. 1950- *St&PR 93*
Bedford, John *ScF&FL 92*
Bedford, John N. 1940- *St&PR 93*
Bedford, Madeleine Alann Peckham 1910- *WhoAm 92*
Bedford, Michael *ScF&FL 92*
Bedford, Norman C. 1915- *St&PR 93*
Bedford, Norton Moore 1916- *WhoAm 92*
Bedford, Steuart (John Rudolf) 1939- *Baker 92*
Bedford, Sybille *BioIn 17*
Bedford, Sybille 1911- *ScF&FL 92*
Bedford, Terry 1943- *MiSFD 9*
Bedi, Ashok Ramprakash 1948- *WhoEmL 93*
Bedi, Joyce Elizabeth 1954- *WhoEmL 93*
Bedics, Lynn Fay 1947- *WhoAmW 93*
Bedie, Konan 1934- *WhoAfr*
Bedinger, George Michael 1939- *WhoSSW 93*
Bedini, Silvio A. 1917- *WhoAm 92, WhoWrEP 92*
Bedke, Ernest Alford 1934- *WhoAm 92*
Bedke, Kathryn Lynn 1951- *WhoAmW 93*
Bedlin, Dorothy Roberta 1951- *WhoEmL 93*
Bedman, William L. *Law&B 92*
Bednar, Carolyn Diane 1953- *WhoEmL 93*
Bednar, Charles Sokol 1930- *WhoAm 92*
Bednar, Michael John 1942- *WhoAm 92, WhoSSW 93*
Bednar, Rudy Gerard 1951- *WhoEmL 93, WhoWor 93*
Bednar, Stephen J. *Law&B 92*
Bednarczuk, Ewa Malgorzata 1952- *WhoWor 93*
Bednarek, Alexander Robert 1933- *WhoAm 92*
Bednarek, Jana Maria 1934- *WhoAm 92*
Bednar-Hornyak, Nancy Ellen 1935- *WhoAmW 93*
Bednarik, Chuck 1925- *BioIn 17*
Bednarski, Dennis A. 1947- *St&PR 93*
Bednarski, Stansilaw 1925- *WhoScE 91-4*
Bednarz, Edward Lee *Law&B 92*
Bednarz, Gene Marion 1925- *St&PR 93*
Bednarz, Paul Robert 1950- *WhoIns 93*
Bednarz, Susan Clare 1955- *WhoAmW 93, WhoEmL 93*
Bednash, Geraldine Polly 1943- *WhoE 93*
Bedner, Mark Allen 1948- *WhoWor 93*
Bednorz, J. Georg 1950- *WhoAm 92, WhoWor 93*
Bedogni, Vittorio 1943- *WhoScE 91-3*
Bedol, Marshall Theodore 1925- *St&PR 93*
Bedos de Celles, Francois 1709-1779 *Baker 92*
Bedowitz, Steven D. 1942- *ConEn*
Bedoya, Alfonso 1904-1957 *HispAmA*
Bedoya, Jaime J. 1948- *WhoSSW 93*
Bedregal de Conitzer, Yolanda 1918- *WhoWor 93*
Bedrij, Orest J. 1933- *WhoE 93, WhoWor 93*
Bedrin, Claude 1936- *WhoScE 91-2*
Bedrosian, Edward 1922- *WhoAm 92*
Bedrosian, Edward Robert 1932- *St&PR 93, WhoAm 92*
Bedrosian, John C. 1934- *WhoAm 92*
Bedsole, Ann Smith 1930- *WhoAmW 93*
Bedsworth, Joyce 1950- *BioIn 17*
Bedsworth, O. Diane 1942- *WhoAmW 93*
Bedsworth, Philip 1950- *BioIn 17*
Bedwell, Harvey Guy 1874-1952 *BiDAMSp 1989*
Bee, Barnard Elliot 1824-1861 *HarEnMi*
Bee, Mary Rice 1933- *WhoE 93*
Bee, Noah M. d1992 *NewYTBS 92*
Bee, P. Raymond 1916-1990 *BioIn 17*
Bee, Robert Norman 1925- *WhoAm 92*
Bee, Ronald John 1955- *WhoE 93*
Beebe, Allen John 1950- *WhoSSW 93*
Beebe, Bradford Michael 1960- *WhoSSW 93*
Beebe, Cora Prifold 1937- *WhoAm 92*
Beebe, F. Lisa 1952- *WhoWrEP 92*
Beebe, George H. 1910-1990 *BioIn 17*
Beebe, George Monroe 1836-1927 *BioIn 17*
Beebe, Gilbert Wheeler 1912- *WhoE 93*
Beebe, Jack H. 1942- *St&PR 93*
Beebe, John E. 1923- *St&PR 93*
Beebe, John Eldridge 1923- *WhoAm 92*
Beebe, Joseph E. 1944- *St&PR 93*
Beebe, Larry Eugene 1947- *WhoSSW 93*
Beebe, Leo Clair 1917- *St&PR 93, WhoAm 92*
Beebe, Lydia I. *Law&B 92*
Beebe, Marguerite J. 1939- *WhoAmW 93*
Beebe, Raymond Mark *Law&B 92*
Beebe, Raymond Mark 1942- *St&PR 93, WhoAm 92*
Beebe, Richard Townsend 1902- *WhoAm 92*
Beebe, Robert R. 1928- *WhoAm 92*
Beebe, Steven Arnold 1950- *WhoEmL 93, WhoSSW 93*
Beebe, Susan Kay 1956- *WhoEmL 93*
Beebe, Wilson Hollister, Jr. 1954- *WhoE 93*
Beebee, Chris *ScF&FL 92*
Beeby, Kenneth Jack *Law&B 92*
Beeby, Kenneth Jack 1936- *St&PR 93, WhoAm 92*
Beeby, Thomas H. *WhoAm 92*
Beech, Charles William, Jr. 1961- *WhoEmL 93*
Beech, E. Martin 1950- *WhoEmL 93*
Beech, John Charles *WhoScE 91-1*
Beech, Johnny Gale 1954- *WhoEmL 93, WhoSSW 93*
Beech, Keyes 1913-1990 *BioIn 17*
Beech, Linda *BioIn 17*
Beech, Richard 1957- *St&PR 93*
Beech, Thomas Foster 1939- *WhoSSW 93*
Beech, Webb *ConAu 40NR*
Beecham, Thomas 1879-1961 *Baker 92, BioIn 17, IntDcOp, OxDcOp*
Beechcroft, William *WhoWrEP 92*
Beechcroft, William 1924- *ScF&FL 92*
Beecher, Edward 1803-1895 *BioIn 17*
Beecher, George 1940- *WhoE 93*
Beecher, Graciela 1927- *NotHsAW 93*
Beecher, H. Juanita *Law&B 92*
Beecher, Henry Ward 1813-1887 *BioIn 17, JrnUS, PolPar*
Beecher, Lyman 1775-1863 *BioIn 17*
Beecher, Maureen Ursenbach 1935- *ConAu 137*
Beecher, Robert J. 1935- *St&PR 93*
Beecher, Thomas Wylie 1958- *WhoEmL 93*
Beecher, William John 1914- *WhoAm 92*
Beecher, William Manuel 1933- *WhoE 93*
Beeching, Charles Train, Jr. 1930- *WhoAm 92*
Beeching, Jack 1922- *ScF&FL 92*
Beecke, (Notger) Ignaz (Franz) von 1733-1803 *Baker 92*
Beecken, Ulrich *Law&B 92*
Beeckman, Paul 1941- *WhoScE 91-2*
Beecroft, Jack C. 1927- *St&PR 93*
Beecroft, Norma 1934- *Baker 92*
Beecy, Robert E., Jr. 1950- *WhoSSW 93*
Beed, David James 1945- *St&PR 93, WhoIns 93*
Beeder, David Charles 1930- *WhoAm 92*
Beedie, Albert D., Jr. *St&PR 93*
Beedle, Lynn Simpson 1917- *WhoAm 92*
Beedles, William LeRoy 1948- *WhoAm 92*
Beeferman, Harvey L. 1942- *St&PR 93*

Beegel, Susan Field 1954- WhoAmW 93
Beeghly, P.T. 1922- St&PR 93
Beeghly, R. Thornton 1912- St&PR 93
Beegle, Mary Porter AmWomPl
Beehler, Bruce McPherson 1951- WhoEmL 93
Beehler, Michael Thomas 1950- WhoEmL 93
Beek, Barton 1924- St&PR 93
Beek, Wiero Jan 1932- WhoScE 91-3
Beekley, Cynthia Xanthopoulos 1940- WhoAmW 93
Beekman, Bernadette Theresa Law&B 92
Beekman, Philip E. 1931- WhoAm 92
Beekman, Philip Emmet 1931- St&PR 93
Beekman, William Bedloe 1949- WhoEmL 93
Beekman, Zwanette Margaretha 1927- WhoScE 91-3
Beeks, Clarence 1922-1981 BioIn 17
Beeks, Graydon 1919- ScF&FL 92
Beeks, Graydon Fisher, Jr. 1948- WhoEmL 93
Beeks, Michele Lynn 1953- WhoEmL 93
Beeks, Steven 1956- St&PR 93
Beel, Robert Wayne 1952- St&PR 93
Beel, William Elliott 1910- WhoSSW 93
Beelen, Gerry M. Law&B 92
Beeler, Cecil Freeman 1915- ConAu 139
Beeler, Charles Alan 1939- WhoSSW 93
Beeler, Madison Scott 1910-1989 BioIn 17
Beeler, Myrton Freeman 1922- WhoWrEP 92
Beeler, Thomas J. Law&B 92
Beeler, Thomas J. 1933- St&PR 93
Beeler, Thomas Joseph 1933- WhoAm 92
Beeler, Thomas Taylor, III 1944- WhoWrEP 92
Beeler, Warren Jennings 1932- WhoSSW 93
Beeley, Nigel Robert Arnold 1951- WhoWor 93
Beeley, Robert Alfred 1938- St&PR 93
Beell, Fred d1925 BioIn 17
Beellaerts, Jean Baker 92
Beem, Jack Darrel 1931- WhoAm 92
Beem, Jane A. 1934- WhoWrEP 92
Beem, John Kelly 1942- WhoAm 92, WhoWor 93
Beeman, Greg MiSFD 9
Beeman, John William Law&B 92
Beeman, John William 1940- St&PR 93
Beeman, Keith R. 1915- St&PR 93
Beeman, Richard E. 1945- St&PR 93, WhoAm 92
Beeman, Richard R. 1942- WhoAm 92
Beemon, Karen Louise 1947- WhoEmL 93
Been, Hans Henrik 1949- WhoWor 93
Beenackers, A.A.C.M. 1943- WhoScE 91-3
Beene, Geoffrey BioIn 17
Beene, Geoffrey 1927- WhoAm 92, WhoWor 93
Beeners, Wilbert John 1921- WhoAm 92
Beenken, Samuel Warner 1951- WhoSSW 93
Beenstock, Raymond 1930- St&PR 93
Beentjes, Lucas B. 1930- WhoScE 91-3
Beer, A.E. 1932- St&PR 93
Beer, Alan Earl 1937- WhoAm 92
Beer, Albert John 1950- WhoIns 93
Beer, Alice Stewart 1912- WhoAmW 93
Beer, Andrew Eilers 1932- WhoAm 92
Beer, Barrett Lynn 1936- WhoAm 92
Beer, Clara Louise Johnson 1918- WhoAm 92
Beer, Gyorgy 1927- WhoScE 91-4
Beer, Hans 1932- WhoScE 91-3
Beer, Jacob Liebmann Baker 92
Beer, Jakob Liebmann 1791-1864 BioIn 17
Beer, Janos Miklos 1923- WhoAm 92
Beer, Janusz Zygmunt 1930- WhoE 93
Beer, Jeanette Mary Ayres WhoAm 92
Beer, Johann 1655-1700 Baker 92
Beer, John Vincent 1928- WhoScE 91-1
Beer, Jonathan Hillel 1963- WhoE 93
Beer, Joseph Ernest 1959- WhoEmL 93
Beer, (Johann) Joseph 1744-1812 Baker 92
Beer, Kenneth E. d1989 BioIn 17
Beer, Michael S. Law&B 92
Beer, Murray L. 1928- St&PR 93
Beer, Otto F. 1910- WhoWor 93
Beer, Peter Hill 1928- WhoAm 92, WhoSSW 93
Beer, Reinhard 1935- WhoAm 92
Beer, William R. 1943-1991 BioIn 17
Beerbohm, Max 1872-1956 BioIn 17, BritWr S2
Beerbower, Cynthia Gibson 1949- WhoAmW 93
Beerbower, Douglas O. Law&B 92
Beere, Peter ScF&FL 92
Beerer, Larry D. 1955- WhoEmL 93
Beering, Shokrina Radpour Law&B 92
Beering, Steven Claus 1932- WhoAm 92, WhoWor 93
Beerling, Richard D. Law&B 92
Beerman, Bernard Marvin 1936- WhoAm 92
Beerman, Herman 1901- WhoAm 92, WhoWrEP 92
Beerman, Joel I. Law&B 92
Beermann, Allen J. 1940- WhoAm 92
Beermann, Bjorn A. 1941- WhoScE 91-4
Beermann, Hans J. 1930- WhoScE 91-3
Beernaert, Claude WhoScE 91-2
Beernink, Darrell W. 1937- WhoIns 93
Beers, Charlotte NewYTBS 92 [port]
Beers, Charlotte L. St&PR 93
Beers, Charlotte L. 1935- WhoAm 92, WhoE 93
Beers, David Rogers 1963- WhoE 93
Beers, David Thompson 1953- St&PR 93
Beers, Donald Osborne 1949- WhoEmL 93
Beers, John Henry Law&B 92
Beers, Lewis F., III Law&B 92
Beers, Steven C. 1945- St&PR 93
Beers, Susan Mary 1951- WhoAmW 93
Beers, V. Gilbert 1928- St&PR 93
Beers, Victor Gilbert 1928- WhoAm 92, WhoWrEP 92
Beers, William 1948- ConAu 137
Beers, William O. d1992 NewYTBS 92
Beers, William O. 1914-1992 BioIn 17
Beerup, Robert Dale 1949- WhoEmL 93
Beer-Walbrunn, Anton 1864-1929 Baker 92
Beery, Donald Thomas 1960- WhoEmL 93, WhoSSW 93
Beery, Noah 1884-1946 BioIn 17
Beery, Noah 1916- WhoAm 92
Beery, R. Earl 1947- WhoAm 92
Beery, Roger Lewis, II 1957- WhoSSW 93
Beery, Wallace 1885-1949 BioIn 17, IntDcF 2-3 [port]
Beery, Wallace 1886-1949 QDrFCA 92 [port]
Beery, William Stocktill 1947- WhoE 93
Beese, J. Carter, Jr. 1956- WhoAm 92
Beese, P.J. 1946- ScF&FL 92
Beesemyer, Fritz Timothy 1952- WhoAm 92
Beesley, Charles ScF&FL 92
Beesley, Horace Brent 1946- WhoAm 92
Beesley, Linda Holland 1951- WhoEmL 93
Beesmer, Ronald G. 1958- WhoE 93
Beeson, Frederic L. Law&B 92
Beeson, George H. 1943- St&PR 93
Beeson, Jack 1921- IntDcOp, OxDcOp
Beeson, Jack Hamilton 1921- Baker 92, WhoAm 92
Beeson, Montel Eileen 1939- WhoAmW 93
Beeson, Paul Bruce 1908- WhoAm 92
Beeson, William B. 1927- St&PR 93
Beest, Jacoba van Heemskerck van 1876-1923 BioIn 17
Beestman, Donna M. 1943- WhoE 93
Beestman, George Bernard 1939- WhoE 93
Beeth, Howard 1942- WhoSSW 93
Beeth, Lola 1862-1940 Baker 92
Beetham, Roger Campbell 1937- WhoWor 93
Beetham, Stanley Williams 1933- WhoAm 92, WhoWor 93
Beethoven, Ludwig van 1712-1773 Baker 92
Beethoven, Ludwig van 1770-1827 Baker 92, BioIn 17, IntDcOp, OxDcOp
Beetler, Dianne Lynn 1951- WhoWrEP 92
Beeton, Alfred Merle 1927- WhoAm 92
Beeton, Samuel Orchart 1831-1877 BioIn 17
Beets, Charles N. 1922- WhoScE 91-2
Beets, Freeman Haley 1919- WhoAm 92
Beets, Latin Renee 1959- WhoEmL 93
Beetschen, Jean-Claude 1929- WhoScE 91-2
Beevers, Alec WhoScE 91-1
Beevers, Harry 1924- WhoAm 92
Beevers, Leonard 1934- WhoSSW 93
Beeves, Derril W. St&PR 93
Beezer, Anthony E. WhoScE 91-1
Beezley, Leona Kay 1946- WhoEmL 93
Beezley, Linda D. WhoAmW 93
Beezley, Maxinne AmWomPl
Befera, Mary Rose 1963- WhoAmW 93
Beffara, Louis-Francois 1751-1838 Baker 92
BeFoure, Jeannine Marie 1923- WhoAmW 93
Befus, Albert Dean 1948- WhoAm 92
Beg, M. Rashid 1949- WhoE 93, WhoWor 93
Beg, Mirza Abdul Baqi 1934-1990 BioIn 17
Beg, Mirza Umair 1946- WhoWor 93
Begam, Robert George 1928- WhoAm 92, WhoWor 93
Begamudre, Ven 1956- WhoCanL 92
Begando, Joseph Sheridan 1921- WhoAm 92
Begashaw, Girma 1950- WhoUN 92
Begbie, Robert WhoScE 91-1
Begehr, Heinrich Gottfried Werner WhoWor 93
Begelfer, Constance A. Law&B 92
Begell, Frederick Paul d1992 BioIn 17
Begell, William 1928- WhoWor 93, WhoWrEP 92
Begelman, Mitchell C. WhoAm 92
Begg, Alastair Currie 1954- WhoWor 93
Begg, Hugh MacKemmie WhoScE 91-1
Begg, Peter Robert 1951- WhoEmL 93
Begg, Virginia Lopez 1944- WhoE 93
Beggan, John Francis 1935- WhoAm 92
Beggrow, Dennis BioIn 17
Beggs, Andrea J. Law&B 92
Beggs, Barbara Cass- 1904- BioIn 17
Beggs, David Walker 1929- WhoE 93
Beggs, James Montgomery 1926- WhoAm 92
Beggs, James Randy 1949- WhoSSW 93
Beggs, Mary J. BioIn 17
Beggs, Thomas Montague 1899-1990 BioIn 17
Beggs-Uema, Marck Lewis 1958- WhoWrEP 92
Beghe, Renato 1933- WhoAm 92
Beghin, Barbara Jean Law&B 92
Beghin, C. WhoScE 91-2
Beghini, Victor Gene 1934- St&PR 93
Begian, Harry BioIn 17
Begiebing, Robert J. 1946- ConLC 70 [port]
Begiebing, Robert J(ohn) 1946- ConAu 40NR
Begien, Martin 1928- St&PR 93
Begin, Charles Arthur, Jr. 1952- WhoSSW 93
Begin, Luc A. 1943- WhoCanL 92
Begin, Menachem 1913- DcTwHis, NewYTBS 92 [port], PolBiDi
Begin, Menachem 1913-1992 BioIn 17, News 92, -92-3
Begin, Menahem 1913-1992 CurBio 92N
Begin, Roger Normand 1952- WhoAm 92, WhoE 93, WhoWor 93
Beglarian, Grant 1927- Baker 92, WhoAm 92
Begleiter, Alvin Leon 1933- St&PR 93
Begley, Ed, Jr. BioIn 17
Begley, Ed, Jr. 1949- WhoAm 92
Begley, Evelyn Maria 1953- WhoE 93, WhoEmL 93
Begley, James M. Law&B 92
Begley, Kathleen A. 1948- WhoEmL 93
Begley, Kevin Robert 1958- St&PR 93
Begley, Louis 1933- WhoAm 92, WhoWor 93
Begley, Michael Joseph 1909- WhoAm 92
Begley, Nan Elizabeth 1951- WhoAmW 93
Begley, Patrick Anthony 1932- St&PR 93
Begnis, Giuseppe de OxDcOp
Begnis, Giuseppe Ronzi de OxDcOp
Bego, Jean St&PR 93
Begon, Elisabeth 1696-1755 BioIn 17
Begovic, Miroslav Miodrag 1956- WhoEmL 93, WhoSSW 93
Begovich, Michael 1959- WhoEmL 93
Begovich, Nicholas Anthony 1921- WhoAm 92
Begue, John Samuel 1937- St&PR 93
Beguelin, Mike BioIn 17
Beguier, Jacques Paul 1935- WhoUN 92
Beguin, Bernard Auguste 1923- WhoWor 93
Beguin, Claude G. 1938- WhoScE 91-2
Beguin, Francois 1933- WhoScE 91-4
Beguin, Fred Paul 1909- WhoAm 92
Begum, Forquan 1951- WhoWor 93
Begun, Benson Harris 1932- St&PR 93
Begun, Eric G. Law&B 92
Begun, Semi J. 1905- St&PR 93
Begun, Semi Joseph 1905- WhoAm 92
Beha, James J. 1916- St&PR 93
Beha, James Joseph 1916- WhoAm 92
Beha, Ralph Werner 1950- WhoEmL 93
Behaghel, Joseph WhoScE 91-2
Behague, Gerard (Henri) 1937- Baker 92
Behan, Brendan 1923-1964 BioIn 17, BritWr S2
Behan, David Paul 1939- WhoSSW 93
Behan, Edmund J. 1929- St&PR 93
Behan, John 1919-1991 BioIn 17
Behan, John William Law&B 92
Behan, Michael John 1946- St&PR 93
Behan, Robert Francis 1933- WhoAm 92
Behan, William A. Law&B 92
Behan, William A., Jr. Law&B 92
Behar, Diane Susan 1952- WhoE 93
Behar, Isaac 1946- WhoSSW 93
Behar, Leon Isidore 1956- WhoEmL 93
Beharriell, Frederick John 1918- WhoAm 92
Behbehani, Abbas M. 1925- WhoAm 92
Behbehanian, Mahin Fazeli WhoAmW 93
Beheim, Michel 1416-1474 Baker 92
Beheler, Carlan Mueller 1943- WhoSSW 93
Behen, Edward Nicholas 1948- WhoEmL 93
Behham, John F. 1921- St&PR 93
Behi, Ruhi Habib 1948- WhoWor 93
Behl, Wolfgang 1918- WhoAm 92
Behle, Alfred Paul 1935- WhoScE 91-3
Behlen, Charles William 1949- WhoWrEP 92
Behler, Diana Ipsen 1938- WhoAm 92
Behler, Ernst Heitmar 1928- WhoAm 92
Behling, Charles Frederick 1940- WhoAm 92, WhoE 93
Behling, George Rogers 1938- St&PR 93
Behling, Howard L. 1945- St&PR 93
Behling, J. Haigler 1931- St&PR 93
Behling, Roland Herbert 1925- WhoAm 92
Behlke, Charles Edward 1926- WhoAm 92
Behlmann, Richard Alan 1954- WhoWor 93
Behm, Eduard 1862-1946 Baker 92
Behm, Edward J. 1933- St&PR 93
Behm, Forrest Edwin 1919- WhoAm 92
Behm, Mark Andrew 1954- WhoE 93
Behm, Mark Edward 1945- WhoE 93
Behm, Richard H. 1948- WhoWrEP 92
Behm, Ronald Thomas 1938- St&PR 93
Behn, Aphra 1640-1689 BioIn 17, WorLitC [port]
Behn, Harry 1898-1973 DcAmChF 1960
Behn, Robert Dietrich 1941- ConAu 137, WhoWrEP 92
Behn, Sally A. 1928- St&PR 93
Behnam, Awni 1940- WhoUN 92
Behncke, David L. d1953 BioIn 17
Behncke, David L. 1897-1953 EncABHB 8 [port]
Behne, Noel David 1936- St&PR 93
Behne, Thomas David 1931- St&PR 93
Behner, Elton Dale 1952- WhoEmL 93
Behnke, Bruce I. 1944- St&PR 93
Behnke, Carl Gilbert 1945- WhoAm 92
Behnke, Elizabeth Doelker 1926- WhoAmW 93
Behnke, Harlan James 1929- St&PR 93
Behnke, James Ralph 1943- St&PR 93, WhoAm 92
Behnke, Leigh 1946- WhoEmL 93
Behnke, Marylou 1950- WhoAm 92
Behnke, Michael Clare 1943- WhoE 93
Behnke, Roy Herbert 1921- WhoAm 92, WhoWor 93
Behnke, Wallace Blanchard, Jr. 1926- WhoAm 92, WhoSSW 93
Behnke, William Alfred 1924- WhoAm 92
Behr, Alan Law&B 92
Behr, Claus 1926- St&PR 93
Behr, Edward BioIn 17
Behr, Franz 1837-1898 Baker 92
Behr, Heather Ashley 1967- WhoE 93
Behr, Ralph Steven 1951- WhoEmL 93
Behr, Raymond Anthony 1948- WhoE 93, WhoEmL 93
Behr, Richard Alan 1933- St&PR 93
Behr, Richard Henry 1942- WhoAm 92, WhoE 93
Behrakis, George D. 1934- St&PR 93
Behrenberg, John P. 1930- St&PR 93
Behrenbruch, William David 1946- WhoEmL 93
Behrend, Donald Fraser 1931- WhoAm 92
Behrend, (Gustav) Fritz 1889-1972 Baker 92
Behrend, Itzig 1766-1845 BioIn 17
Behrend, Jeanne 1911-1988 Baker 92
Behrend, Leslie G. 1931- St&PR 93
Behrend, Siegfried 1933-1990 Baker 92
Behrend, William 1861-1940 Baker 92
Behrend, William Louis 1923- WhoAm 92, WhoWor 93
Behrends, Ralph E. 1926-1988 BioIn 17
Behrends, Steve 1959- ScF&FL 92
Behrends, Wolfgang 1926- WhoWor 93
Behrendt, Bill Lee 1958- WhoEmL 93
Behrendt, David Frogner 1935- WhoAm 92, WhoWrEP 92
Behrendt, Ernst d1990 BioIn 17
Behrendt, John Charles 1932- WhoAm 92
Behrendt, John Thomas 1945- WhoAm 92
Behrendt, Thomas Rudolf 1951- WhoWor 93
Behrenf, James B. Law&B 92
Behrens, Albert Paul 1934- St&PR 93
Behrens, Arno W. 1936- WhoScE 91-3
Behrens, Barbara Lee Law&B 92
Behrens, Berel Lyn 1940- WhoAmW 93
Behrens, David A. 1943- St&PR 93
Behrens, Frank Herman 1959- WhoWor 93
Behrens, Heinrich 1937- WhoScE 91-3
Behrens, Hildegard 1937- Baker 92, IntDcOp [port], WhoAm 92, WhoWor 93
Behrens, Hildegard 1941- OxDcOp
Behrens, Howard BioIn 17
Behrens, Jack 1935- Baker 92
Behrens, Laura Suzanne 1956- WhoEmL 93
Behrens, Peter 1868-1940 BioIn 17

Behrens, Peter 1954- WhoCanL 92
Behrens, Peter G. 1927- St&PR 93
Behrens, Phyllis Irene 1955- WhoSSW 93
Behrens, Raymond A. 1947- St&PR 93
Behrens, Richard John 1946- WhoEmL 93, WhoWor 93
Behrens, Sam BioIn 17
Behrens, Warner 1935- WhoUN 92
Behrens, Wayne C. 1956- St&PR 93
Behrens, William Blade 1956- WhoEmL 93, WhoSSW 93
Behrensmeyer, J.H. 1957- St&PR 93
Behret, Heinz M. 1940- WhoScE 91-3
Behret, Heinz Michael 1940- WhoWor 93
Behring, Kenneth E. 1928- WhoAm 92
Behringer, Scott Martin 1952- WhoEmL 93
Behringer, Thomas Edward, Jr. 1930- St&PR 93
Behrins, Harriet Frances 19th cent.- BioIn 17
Behrle, Franklin Charles 1922- WhoAm 92
Behrman, Beatrice d1990 BioIn 17
Behrman, Carol H(elen) 1925- WhoWrEP 92
Behrman, Daniel 1923- WhoWrEP 92
Behrman, Daniel 1923-1990 BioIn 17
Behrman, Edward Joseph 1930- WhoAm 92
Behrman, Harold Richard 1939- WhoAm 92, WhoE 93
Behrman, Jack Newton 1922- WhoAm 92, WhoWor 93
Behrman, Jere Richard 1940- WhoAm 92
Behrman, Martin 1864-1926 PolPar
Behrman, Myron M. 1906- WhoAm 92, WhoSSW 93
Behrman, Richard Elliot 1931- WhoAm 92
Behrmann, Christine A. d1991 BioIn 17
Behrmann, Joan Metzner WhoAmW 93
Behrstock, Bruce 1947- St&PR 93
Behrstock, Herbert A. 1942- WhoUN 92
Behrstock, Julian Robert 1916- WhoAm 92
Behuniak, Peter, Jr. 1950- WhoE 93, WhoEmL 93
Beiabure, Meita 1953- WhoWor 93
Beichelt, Frank Erich 1942- WhoWor 93
Beichman, Arnold 1913- WhoAm 92
Beicke, Robert William Law&B 92
Bei Dao 1949- ConAu 139
Beidel, Hyun Sook 1935- WhoWrEP 92
Beider, Andrew Michael 1951- WhoEmL 93
Beiderbecke, Bix 1903-1931 Baker 92, BioIn 17
Beiderwell, Bruce 1952- ConAu 137
Beidler, George A. 1944- St&PR 93
Beidler, John Nathan Law&B 92
Beidler, Peter Grant 1940- WhoAm 92
Beidler, Sheppard 1918- St&PR 93
Beier, David Jay 1934- WhoSSW 93
Beier, Eric Henry 1945- St&PR 93
Beier, Karl A. 1947- St&PR 93
Beier, Thomas E. 1945- St&PR 93
Beierle, Thomas R. Law&B 92
Beierwaltes, William Henry 1916- WhoAm 92, WhoWor 93
Beig, Robert Erich 1948- WhoWor 93
Beigbeder, Jean-Michel 1938- St&PR 93
Beigel, Allan 1940- WhoAm 92
Beighey, Lawrence Jerome 1938- St&PR 93, WhoAm 92
Beighle, Douglas P. Law&B 92
Beighle, Douglas Paul 1932- St&PR 93, WhoAm 92
Beighley, Ruthanne Law&B 92
Beighley, Ruthanne 1946- St&PR 93
Beight, Janice Marie 1947- WhoAmW 93
Beights, Nancy Craik 1951- WhoEmL 93
Beigie, Carl Emerson 1940- WhoAm 92
Beigl, William 1950- WhoWor 93
Beijersbergen, J.C.M. WhoScE 91-3
Beikirch, Gary BioIn 17
Beikman, Dennis Wayne 1940- St&PR 93
Beil, Barry Jay 1947- St&PR 93
Beil, Karen Magnuson 1950- WhoAmW 93
Beil, Marshall Howard 1946- WhoE 93, WhoEmL 93
Beil, Ralph Edwin 1927- St&PR 93
Beil, Sheldon L. 1928- St&PR 93
Beilby, Margaret Glenn 1949- WhoEmL 93
Beilenson, Anthony C. 1932- CngDr 91
Beilenson, Anthony Charles 1932- WhoAm 92
Beiler, Edna 1923- BioIn 17
Beiles, David Michael St&PR 93
Beiles, Herbert Noel 1939- St&PR 93
Beilig, Richard Henry 1930- St&PR 93
Beilke, James Ernest 1929- WhoAm 92
Beilke, Marlan 1940- WhoWrEP 92
Beilke, Steven J. Law&B 92
Beilman, Mary Louise St&PR 93
Beilschmidt, Curt 1886-1962 Baker 92
Beim, David Odell 1940- WhoAm 92
Beim, Elizabeth Artz 1940- WhoAmW 93
Beim, Norman WhoAm 92, WhoWrEP 92
Beima, Janice Carol 1937- WhoAmW 93
Bein, Otmar WhoScE 91-4
Beinecke, Candace Krugman 1946- WhoEmL 93
Beinecke, Frederick William 1943- WhoAm 92
Beinecke, Joy Dewey d1989 BioIn 17
Beinecke, William S. 1914- WhoAm 92
Beineix, Jean-Jacques BioIn 17
Beineix, Jean-Jacques 1946- MiSFD 9
Beineke, Lowell Wayne 1939- WhoAm 92
Beinfield, Robert Harvey 1960- WhoEmL 93
Beinhard, Pierre WhoScE 91-2
Beinhart, Larry 1947- ConAu 138
Beinhauer, Rudolf 1932- WhoScE 91-3
Beinhocker, Gilbert David 1932- WhoAm 92, WhoE 93, WhoWor 93
Beinicke, Steve 1956- SmATA 69
Beinker, Dale J. 1931- St&PR 93
Beinstein, Arnold Robert 1920- St&PR 93
Beinum, Eduard van 1900-1959 Baker 92
Beirn, Terence U. d1991 BioIn 17
Beirne, Barbara 1933- SmATA 71 [port]
Beirne, Charles J. BioIn 17
Beirne, Kenneth Joseph 1946- WhoAm 92
Beirne, Martin Douglas 1944- WhoSSW 93
Beirne, Paul Roe 1961- WhoEmL 93
Beirnes, David W. 1952- St&PR 93
Beis, Isidoros 1946- WhoScE 91-3
Beisang, Arthur A. 1932- St&PR 93
Beiseigel, Shirley-Ann 1927- WhoAm 92
Beiseker, Thomas C. 1920- St&PR 93
Beisel, Daniel Cunningham 1916- WhoAm 92
Beisel, James Richard, Jr. 1955- WhoEmL 93
Beiser, Gerald Jay 1930- St&PR 93
Beiser, Helen Ruth 1914- WhoAm 92
Beiser, Leo 1924- WhoE 93
Beisler, Henry, Jr. 1920- St&PR 93
Beisler, Peter C. 1942- St&PR 93
Beisler, Ted 1949- WhoSSW 93
Beisman, James Joseph 1933- St&PR 93
Beiss, Ulrich 1927- WhoScE 91-3
Beissel, Henry 1929- WhoCanL 92
Beissel, Johann Conrad 1690-1768 Baker 92
Beisser, Frederick G. 1942- St&PR 93
Beisser, Judith Kay 1946- WhoAmW 93, WhoEmL 93
Beisswenger, Harry Louis, Jr. 1935- WhoE 93
Beistegui, Carlos de BioIn 17
Beistline, Earl Hoover 1916- WhoAm 92
Beitel, Joseph M. 1952-1991 BioIn 17
Beiter, Sean T. Law&B 92
Beithon, Patricia A. Law&B 92
Beiting, John Morgan 1938- St&PR 93
Beiting, Michael R. Law&B 92
Beitinger, Thomas Lee 1945- WhoSSW 93
Beitins, Inese Zinta 1937- WhoAm 92
Beito, G.A. 1933- St&PR 93
Beittenmiller, J.G. 1959- St&PR 93
Beitz, Alexandra Grigg 1960- WhoAmW 93
Beitzel, George B. 1928- St&PR 93, WhoAm 92
Beitzel, J.E. 1939- St&PR 93
Beizer, Boris ScF&FL 92
Beizer, Richard L. 1942- WhoAm 92
Beja, Morris 1935- WhoAm 92
Bejarano, Fausto 1960- WhoWor 93
Bejarano, Luis Enrique 1917- WhoE 93
Bejart, Maurice Jean 1927- WhoWor 93
Bejblik, Alois 1926-1990 BioIn 17
Bejczy, Antal Karoly 1930- WhoAm 92
Bejian, Donna Virginia 1951- WhoE 93
Bejnar, Thaddeus Putnam 1948- WhoEmL 93
Bejot, Francis Edwin 1934- St&PR 93
Bek, Werner K. 1934- WhoScE 91-3
Bekal Utsahi 1928- WhoAsAP 91
Bekaroglu, Ozer 1933- WhoScE 91-4
Bekavac, Nancy Yavor 1947- WhoAm 92, WhoAmW 93
Bekefi, George 1925- WhoAm 92
Bekelnitzky, Seymour Gerald Law&B 92
Bekendam, J. 1926- WhoScE 91-3
Bekenstein, Susan 1952- WhoEmL 93
Bekes, Carolyn Ethel 1947- WhoAm 92, WhoEmL 93
Bekes, Pal 1956- BioIn 17
Bekesi, Pal 1939- WhoScE 91-4
Bekey, George Albert 1928- WhoAm 92
Bekey, Ivan 1931- WhoE 93
Bekhor, David Law&B 92
Bekic, Zoran 1959- WhoWor 93
Bekir, Nagwa Esmat 1944- WhoWor 93
Bekkedahl, Brad Douglas 1957- WhoEmL 93
Bekken, Amy BioIn 17
Bekken, Arne WhoScE 91-4
Bekker, Mieczyslaw G. 1905- PolBiDi
Bekker, P.C.F. WhoScE 91-3
Bekker, (Max) Paul (Eugen) 1882-1937 Baker 92
Bekku, Sadao 1922- Baker 92
Bekkum, Owen D. 1924- WhoAm 92, WhoWor 93
Bekoff, Anne C. 1947- WhoAmW 93
Bekritsky, Bruce Robert 1946- WhoEmL 93
Beks, J.W.F. 1928- WhoScE 91-3
Bel, Patricia Damian 1957- WhoSSW 93
Bela, III c. 1148-1196 OxDcByz
Belack, James Paul 1933- St&PR 93
Beladi, Ilona 1925- WhoScE 91-4
Belafonte, Harry BioIn 17
Belafonte, Harry 1927- AfrAmBi, Baker 92, ConBlB 4 [port], ConMus 8 [port], WhoAm 92, WhoWor 93
Belafonte, Shari BioIn 17
Belafsky, Mark Lewis 1939- WhoE 93
Belaich, Jean-Pierre 1937- WhoScE 91-2
Belaieff, Mitrofan (Petrovich) 1836-1904 Baker 92
Belaiev, Victor 1888-1968 Baker 92
Belaiey, Mitrofan (Petrovich) 1836-1904 Baker 92
Bel Air, Roger 1946- WhoWrEP 92
Belak, Michael James 1961- WhoE 93
Belan, William Wells 1950- WhoEmL 93
Beland, Pierre BioIn 17
Belaney, William Louis 1926- St&PR 93
Belanger, A. Douglas 1953- St&PR 93
Belanger, Arthur Cyril 1925- St&PR 93
Belanger, Francine 1959- St&PR 93
Belanger, Gerard 1940- WhoAm 92
Belanger, Louise-Marie Law&B 92
Belanger, Marcel 1943- WhoCanL 92
Belanger, O. Frank St&PR 93
Belanger, Paul 1939- WhoUN 92
Belanger, Pierre Rolland 1937- WhoAm 92
Belanger, Richard J. Law&B 92
Belanger, Sharlene ScF&FL 92
Belanger, Wayne Jean 1957- WhoEmL 93
Belanger, William Joseph 1925- WhoAm 92
Belanoff, Stuart B. Law&B 92
Belardi, Gene Piero Law&B 92
Belardi, James Richard 1957- St&PR 93
Belasco, David 1853-1931 BioIn 17, GayN
Belasco, Simon 1918- WhoAm 92
Belasco, Steven R. Law&B 92
Belash, Judith Glaser Law&B 92
Belasky, Michael Bruce 1945- St&PR 93
Belau, Jane Carol Gullickson 1934- WhoAmW 93, WhoWor 93
Belau, Jane Gullickson 1934- St&PR 93
Belaunde, Terry Fernando 1912- DcTwHis
Belaval, Emilio S. 1903-1972 SpAmA
Belbas, Dean 1932- St&PR 93
Belbeck, Kenneth George 1928- St&PR 93
Belbel, Elic 1950- WhoScE 91-2
Belberov, Zdravko WhoScE 91-4
Belbruno, Diana Rousseau Law&B 92
Bel Bruno, Joseph James 1952- WhoE 93
Belcamino, Beverley A. Law&B 92
Belcastro, Frank A. 1936- St&PR 93
Belcastro, Patrick Frank 1920- WhoAm 92
Belcher, Afsaneh G. 1958- WhoAmW 93
Belcher, Brent 1949- St&PR 93
Belcher, Carl W. Law&B 92
Belcher, Dennis Irl 1951- WhoEmL 93
Belcher, Diana Steinbach 1952- WhoEmL 93
Belcher, Donald David 1938- St&PR 93, WhoAm 92
Belcher, Donald W. 1922- St&PR 93
Belcher, Edward L. 1926- St&PR 93
Belcher, Gerald L. 1941-1991 BioIn 17
Belcher, Grace (Ruth) Daley 1902- WhoWrEP 92
Belcher, James Michael 1947- WhoSSW 93
Belcher, Jennifer Marion 1944- WhoAmW 93
Belcher, John Arthur 1956- WhoEmL 93
Belcher, Kenneth A. 1931- St&PR 93
Belcher, La Jeune 1960- WhoAmW 93, WhoEmL 93
Belcher, Louis David 1939- WhoAm 92
Belcher, Marilyn Kay 1938- WhoAmW 93
Belcher, Murray C. 1914- St&PR 93
Belcher, Nancy Foote 1921- WhoWor 93
Belcher, Supply 1751-1836 Baker 92
Belcher, Taylor Garrison 1920-1990 BioIn 17
Belcher, William Walter, Jr. 1943- WhoWor 93
Belcher-Redebaugh-Levi, Caroline Louise 1910- WhoWor 93
Belcher-Williams, Patricia Ann 1951- WhoAmW 93
Belchic, Katherine Mitchell 1953- WhoAmW 93
Belcke, Friedrich August 1795-1874 Baker 92
Belcourt, Alain B.C. 1943- WhoScE 91-2
Beldecos, Ariadne Law&B 92
Beldegreen, Karen J. 1950- St&PR 93
Belden, Arthur B. 1945- St&PR 93
Belden, Bob BioIn 17
Belden, Catherine Ellen 1941- WhoSSW 93
Belden, Daniel M. 1944- St&PR 93
Belden, David 1949- ScF&FL 92
Belden, David Leigh 1935- WhoAm 92
Belden, H. Reginald 1907- WhoAm 92
Belden, Jeffrey Lynn 1952- St&PR 93
Belden, Louis de Keyser 1926- WhoWor 93
Belden, Stephen Frederic 1954- WhoEmL 93
Belden, Wilanne Schneider 1925- ScF&FL 92, WhoWrEP 92
Belden, William H., Jr. 1942- St&PR 93
Belden, William Hinchliffe 1914- St&PR 93
Belderbos, C.M.N. WhoScE 91-3
Belding, Daniel Russell 1956- WhoSSW 93
Belding, Meric W. 1922- St&PR 93
Belding, Stephen T. 1952- St&PR 93
Beldner, Richard S. Law&B 92
Beldner, Richard Steven 1942- St&PR 93
Beldock, D.T. 1934- St&PR 93
Beldock, Donald Travis 1934- WhoAm 92
Beldock, Myron 1929- WhoAm 92
Beldon, Sanford T. 1932- WhoAm 92, WhoWrEP 92
Beldowski, Tadeusz 1929- WhoScE 91-4
Bele, Raphael 1942- WhoAsAP 91
Belen, Frederick Christopher 1913- WhoAm 92
Belenke, Burton 1926- St&PR 93
Beleno, Joaquin 1922-1988 SpAmA
Belenson, Allen G. Law&B 92
Belenson, Allen George 1935- St&PR 93
Beleslin, Dusan 1931- WhoScE 91-4
Beleson, Robert Brian 1950- WhoEmL 93
Beless, Rosemary June 1947- WhoEmL 93
Belet, Jacques H. 1948- St&PR 93
Belet, Jacques Henry, III 1948- WhoAm 92
Beletz, Elaine Ethel 1944- WhoAmW 93
Belew, Adrian WhoAm 92
Belew, David Lee 1931- WhoAm 92
Belew, David Owen, Jr. 1920- WhoAm 92
Belew, John Seymour 1920- WhoAm 92
Belew-Irwin, Valerie Suzanne 1960- WhoAmW 93
Belfield, Judith Ann 1946- WhoWrEP 92
Belfiglio, Edward E. 1938- St&PR 93
Belfiglio, Valentine John 1934- WhoSSW 93
Belfitt, William John WhoScE 91-1
Belford, Barbara 1935- ConAu 136
Belford, Gary Cinney 1948- St&PR 93
Belford, Jeffrey Bryon 1947- St&PR 93
Belford, Ken WhoCanL 92
Belford, Richard David 1945- WhoAm 92
Belford, Roz 1929- WhoSSW 93
Belfort-Chalat, Jacqueline 1930- WhoAmW 93
Belforte, David Arthur 1932- WhoE 93
Belfour, Ed BioIn 17
Belfrage, Cedric 1904-1990 BioIn 17
Belfrage, Goran WhoScE 91-4
Belfrage, Jan Kurt Henrik 1944- WhoWor 93
Belfrage, Per A. 1940- WhoScE 91-4
Belfrage, Sally 1936- BioIn 17
Belfus, Isaac Lou 1925- St&PR 93
Bel Geddes, Barbara 1922- WhoAm 92, WhoAmW 93
Bel Geddes, Joan WhoAm 92
Bel Geddes, Joan 1916- WhoWrEP 92
Belgin, Harvey Harry 1912- WhoSSW 93, WhoWor 93
Belgion, Montgomery 1892-1973 ScF&FL 92
Belgrave, Joyce Mary Cynthia 1935- WhoAmW 93
Bel Hadj Amor, Mohsen 1935- WhoUN 92
Beliaev, Aleksandr 1884-1942 ScF&FL 92
Beliaev, Yuri Nicholaevitch 1944- WhoUN 92
Belica, Marina Elena 1959- WhoE 93
Belica, Paul 1921- WhoAm 92
Belica, Paul M. 1946- St&PR 93
Belich, John Patrick 1938- WhoAm 92
Belichick, Bill WhoAm 92
Beliczay, Julius (Gyula) von 1835-1893 Baker 92
Beligratis, Steven D. 1931- St&PR 93
Belik, G. 1947- St&PR 93
Belille, Ronald 1947- WhoEmL 93
Belin, David William 1928- WhoAm 92, WhoWor 93
Belin, Gaspard d'Andelot 1918- WhoAm 92
Belin, J.C. 1914- St&PR 93
Belin, Jacob Chapman 1914- WhoAm 92, WhoSSW 93

Belin, Marc *WhoScE 91-2*
Belin, Rene 1898-1977 *BioIn 17*
Belinfante, Geoffrey Warren 1947- *WhoEmL 93*
Beling, Gregory N. 1945- *St&PR 93*
Beling, Helen 1914- *WhoAm 92*
Belinger, Harry Robert 1927- *St&PR 93, WhoAm 92*
Belinski, William J. 1950- *WhoIns 93*
Belinskiy, Boris Pavlovitch 1946- *WhoWor 93*
Belisarios c. 505-565 *OxDcByz*
Belisarius c. 505-565 *HarEnMi*
Belisle, Gilles 1923- *WhoAm 92*
Belissary, Karen 1959- *WhoAmW 93*
Belitsky, Melvin J. 1946- *St&PR 93*
Belitt, Ben 1911- *WhoAm 92, WhoWrEP 92*
Belitz, Hans-Dieter 1931- *WhoScE 91-3*
Belitz, Martin Jerome 1937- *St&PR 93*
Beliveau, Daniele 1951- *St&PR 93*
Beliveau, L.C. 1917- *St&PR 93*
Beliveau-Jones, Marguerite Anita *WhoAmW 93*
Beliveau Muchnicki, Margaret Anne 1954- *WhoAmW 93*
Beljan, John Richard 1930- *WhoAm 92, WhoWor 93*
Belk, Audrey Marie Walters 1938- *WhoAmW 93*
Belk, Colleen G. Webb 1929- *WhoWrEP 92*
Belk, Gene Denton 1938- *WhoSSW 93*
Belk, John Anthony *WhoScE 91-1*
Belk, John Blanton 1925- *WhoAm 92*
Belk, John M. 1920- *St&PR 93, WhoAm 92*
Belk, Lowell Warner 1937- *St&PR 93*
Belk, Nancy Ann 1957- *WhoAmW 93*
Belk, Thomas M. 1925- *St&PR 93*
Belk, Thomas Milburn 1925- *WhoAm 92, WhoSSW 93*
Belkin, Bernard *Law&B 92*
Belkin, Boris 1948- *Baker 92*
Belkin, Boris David 1948- *WhoAm 92*
Belkin, Harvey *Law&B 92*
Belkin, Janet Ehrenreich 1938- *WhoAmW 93, WhoWor 93*
Belkin, Michael 1941- *WhoWor 93*
Belkin, Samuel 1911-1976 *JeAmHC*
Belkin, Stanley 1936- *St&PR 93*
Belknap, Jeremy 1744-1798 *BioIn 17*
Belknap, John Corbould 1946- *WhoAm 92*
Belknap, Norton 1925- *WhoAm 92*
Belknap, Robert Lamont 1929- *WhoAm 92*
Belkora, Abdelhak 1933- *WhoUN 92*
Bell, Acton 1820-1849 *BioIn 17*
Bell, Al *SoulM*
Bell, Alan Robert 1952- *WhoEmL 93*
Bell, Alan Russell 1939- *St&PR 93*
Bell, Albert E. 1949- *St&PR 93*
Bell, Albert Jerome *Law&B 92*
Bell, Albert Jerome 1960- *St&PR 93, WhoAm 92*
Bell, Alexander Graham 1847-1922 *BioIn 17, GayN*
Bell, Alison *BioIn 17*
Bell, Andrew Michael 1946- *WhoEmL 93*
Bell, Ann 1951- *WhoAmW 93, WhoEmL 93, WhoWor 93*
Bell, Archie, & the Drells *SoulM*
Bell, Arthur 1926- *WhoWor 93*
Bell, Barbara Dillard 1936- *WhoAmW 93*
Bell, Battle, III 1945- *WhoSSW 93*
Bell, Becky *BioIn 17*
Bell, Bert 1894-1959 *BioIn 17*
Bell, Blake Allen 1958- *WhoEmL 93*
Bell, Bobby 1940- *BioIn 17*
Bell, Bradley J. 1952- *WhoAm 92*
Bell, Bradley John 1952- *St&PR 93*
Bell, Brian Dutcher 1937- *St&PR 93*
Bell, Brian J. *Law&B 92*
Bell, Brian M. *Law&B 92*
Bell, Brittian Dudley, III 1942- *WhoE 93*
Bell, Bruce Raymond King 1954- *WhoSSW 93*
Bell, Bryan 1918- *WhoSSW 93*
Bell, Buddy F.E. 1938- *St&PR 93*
Bell, Byron 1935- *WhoE 93*
Bell, Carl Compton 1947- *WhoEmL 93*
Bell, Carleton L. 1928- *St&PR 93*
Bell, Carol Jean *Law&B 92*
Bell, Carol Willsey 1939- *WhoAm 92*
Bell, Carola *AmWomPl*
Bell, Carole Allen 1949- *WhoAmW 93*
Bell, Carolyn Shaw 1920- *WhoAm 92, WhoE 93*
Bell, Catherine L. *Law&B 92*
Bell, Charles Anderson 1925- *St&PR 93*
Bell, Charles Eugene, Jr. 1932- *WhoWor 93*
Bell, Charles F. *Law&B 92*
Bell, Charles Greenleaf 1916- *WhoWrEP 92*
Bell, Charles Ray 1941- *WhoAm 92*
Bell, Charles Robert, Jr. 1930- *WhoAm 92*
Bell, Charlotte Dorothy 1931- *WhoWrEP 92*
Bell, Charlotte Jean 1950- *WhoAmW 93*
Bell, Charolette Renee 1949- *WhoAmW 93*
Bell, Cheryl Jane 1946- *WhoAm 92*
Bell, Chester Gordon 1934- *WhoAm 92, WhoWor 93*
Bell, Clare 1952- *DcAmChF 1960, ScF&FL 92*
Bell, Clare Louise 1952- *WhoAm 92*
Bell, Clarence Deshong 1914- *WhoE 93*
Bell, Clarence Elmo 1912- *WhoSSW 93*
Bell, Clarence R. *Law&B 92*
Bell, Clive 1881-1964 *BioIn 17, DcLB DS10*
Bell, Colleen Larkin *Law&B 92*
Bell, Cool Papa 1903-1991 *BioIn 17*
Bell, Corinne Reed 1943- *WhoAmW 93*
Bell, Craig Wilson 1950- *WhoEmL 93*
Bell, Currer 1816-1855 *BioIn 17*
Bell, Cynthia Sue 1959- *WhoEmL 93*
Bell, D.A. *WhoScE 91-1*
Bell, Daniel *BioIn 17*
Bell, Daniel 1919- *WhoAm 92*
Bell, Daniel L., Jr. *Law&B 92*
Bell, Daniel L., Jr. 1929- *St&PR 93*
Bell, Daniel Long, Jr. 1929- *WhoAm 92*
Bell, Daphne Ann *WhoAmW 93*
Bell, Darla Dee 1946- *WhoEmL 93*
Bell, David A. 1942- *St&PR 93*
Bell, David Andrew *WhoScE 91-1*
Bell, David Arthur 1943- *WhoAm 92*
Bell, David Fowler 1947- *WhoSSW 93*
Bell, David John 1933- *WhoWor 93*
Bell, David Julian 1951- *WhoEmL 93*
Bell, David L. *Law&B 92*
Bell, David Victor John 1944- *ConAu 38NR*
Bell, Dawn Louise 1961- *WhoAmW 93*
Bell, Deborah Jean 1954- *WhoAmW 93*
Bell, Deborah Marie 1955- *WhoAmW 93*
Bell, Dennis Arthur 1934- *St&PR 93*
Bell, Derrick *NewYTBS 92 [port]*
Bell, Derrick A. *BioIn 17*
Bell, Derrick Albert 1930- *WhoAm 92*
Bell, Devasirvatham Jesudas 1951- *WhoUN 92*
Bell, Diane Robin 1943- *WhoE 93*
Bell, Dick 1938- *WhoSSW 93*
Bell, Donald (Munro) 1934- *Baker 92*
Bell, Donna Louise 1953- *WhoSSW 93*
Bell, Dorothy *WhoScE 91-1*
Bell, Dorothy Hagler 1935- *WhoAmW 93*
Bell, Douglas *ScF&FL 92*
Bell, Douglas Clarkson *Law&B 92*
Bell, Douglas Haldane *WhoScE 91-1*
Bell, Douglas McCall 1955- *WhoEmL 93*
Bell, E. John 1937- *St&PR 93*
Bell, Edward, Jr. 1939- *St&PR 93, WhoAm 92*
Bell, Edward Francis 1930- *St&PR 93*
Bell, Eldrin A. *BioIn 17*
Bell, Elise Stone *WhoWrEP 92*
Bell, Ellis 1818-1848 *BioIn 17*
Bell, Emerson *MajAI*
Bell, Emma A. *AmWomPl*
Bell, Ernest Lorne, III 1926- *WhoAm 92*
Bell, Frances Louise 1926- *WhoAm 92, WhoAmW 93, WhoE 93, WhoWor 93*
Bell, Frank *MajAI*
Bell, Frank A. 1935- *St&PR 93*
Bell, Frank Joseph, III 1955- *WhoE 93, WhoEmL 93*
Bell, Frank Ouray, Jr. 1940- *WhoAm 92*
Bell, Frank S., Jr. 1937- *St&PR 93*
Bell, Fredric J. 1941- *St&PR 93*
Bell, Geo. Robert 1912- *St&PR 93*
Bell, George *BioIn 17*
Bell, George 1814-1890 *BioIn 17*
Bell, George Antonio 1959- *WhoAm 92*
Bell, George deBenneville d1992 *NewYTBS 92*
Bell, George Edwin 1923- *WhoAm 92*
Bell, George Irving 1926- *WhoAm 92*
Bell, George Macdonald *WhoScE 91-1*
Bell, Gertrude 1868-1926 *Expl 93 [port]*
Bell, Gertrude Margaret Lowthian 1868-1926 *BioIn 17*
Bell, Gordon B. 1934- *ScF&FL 92*
Bell, Greg *BioIn 17*
Bell, Gregory Curtis 1930- *BiDAMSp 1989*
Bell, Gus Kaiser 1927- *WhoSSW 93*
Bell, Haney H., III *Law&B 92*
Bell, Haney Hardy, III 1944- *WhoAm 92*
Bell, Harrison B. 1925- *WhoWrEP 92*
Bell, Harry Edward 1947- *WhoEmL 93*
Bell, Harry Fullerton, Jr. 1954- *WhoEmL 93, WhoSSW 93*
Bell, Harry Satcher 1927- *WhoAm 92*
Bell, Henry Marsh, Jr. 1928- *St&PR 93, WhoAm 92, WhoSSW 93*
Bell, Herbert Aubrey Frederick 1921- *WhoAm 92*
Bell, Howard Earl 1934- *St&PR 93*
Bell, Howard Hughes *BioIn 17*
Bell, Howard Hughes 1926- *WhoAm 92*
Bell, Howard Wesley, Jr. 1948- *WhoEmL 93*
Bell, Hugh H. 1941- *St&PR 93*
Bell, I. C., Jr. 1939- *WhoSSW 93*
Bell, Ian *ScF&FL 92*
Bell, Irving 1912- *WhoE 93*
Bell, J.C. *WhoScE 91-1*
Bell, J. Frank 1938- *St&PR 93*
Bell, Jack 1952- *WhoSSW 93*
Bell, Jack P. 1940- *WhoE 93*
Bell, Jack William 1946- *St&PR 93*
Bell, Jacqueline S. 1941- *St&PR 93*
Bell, James A. 1917-1992 *BioIn 17*
Bell, James Adrian 1917- *WhoAm 92, WhoWrEP 92*
Bell, James Alton 1947- *WhoEmL 93, WhoSSW 93*
Bell, James Bacon 1952- *WhoWor 93*
Bell, James E. 1940- *St&PR 93*
Bell, James Franklin 1856-1919 *CmdGen 1991 [port]*
Bell, James Frederick 1914- *WhoAm 92*
Bell, James Frederick 1922- *WhoAm 92*
Bell, James H. d1992 *BioIn 17, NewYTBS 92 [port]*
Bell, James Keith 1955- *WhoE 93*
Bell, James Milton 1921- *WhoAm 92, WhoE 93, WhoWor 93*
Bell, James Milton 1925- *WhoE 93*
Bell, James Milton 1943- *WhoSSW 93*
Bell, James R. *Law&B 92*
Bell, James R. 1933- *St&PR 93*
Bell, James Russell *Law&B 92*
Bell, James T. 1921- *St&PR 93*
Bell, James Tyler 1960- *WhoE 93*
Bell, Jane Matlack 1949- *WhoWrEP 92*
Bell, Jeanne Lower 1934- *WhoAmW 93, WhoE 93*
Bell, Jeanne Viner 1923- *WhoAmW 93*
Bell, Jeffrey Donald 1956- *WhoAm 92*
Bell, Jewel Hairston d1990 *BioIn 17*
Bell, John 1797-1869 *PolPar*
Bell, John 1928-1990 *BioIn 17*
Bell, John 1952- *ScF&FL 92*
Bell, John Boyle, Jr. 1933- *St&PR 93*
Bell, John Cromwell 1892-1974 *BioIn 17*
Bell, John David 1954- *WhoEmL 93*
Bell, John Frantz 1914- *WhoAm 92*
Bell, John Lewis McCulloch 1942- *WhoAm 92, WhoWor 93*
Bell, John Milton 1922- *WhoAm 92*
Bell, John N. 1931- *St&PR 93*
Bell, John Nigel Berridge *WhoScE 91-1*
Bell, John Richard 1959- *WhoEmL 93*
Bell, Jonathan Robert 1947- *WhoAm 92*
Bell, Joseph 1949- *ScF&FL 92*
Bell, Joseph A. 1936- *St&PR 93*
Bell, Joseph Charles 1940- *WhoE 93*
Bell, Joseph Edmund, Jr. *Law&B 92*
Bell, Joshua *BioIn 17*
Bell, Joshua 1967- *Baker 92*
Bell, Judith A. *Law&B 92*
Bell, Judith Virginia 1949- *WhoAmW 93*
Bell, Judy Kay 1947- *WhoAmW 93*
Bell, Julius W. d1992 *NewYTBS 92*
Bell, Karen *BioIn 17*
Bell, Keith Allen *Law&B 92*
Bell, Kelly Denny 1958- *WhoWrEP 92*
Bell, Kenneth John 1930- *WhoAm 92*
Bell, Kenneth R. *Law&B 92*
Bell, Larry John 1940- *WhoE 93*
Bell, Larry Stuart 1939- *WhoAm 92*
Bell, Laura Jeane 1922- *WhoWor 93*
Bell, Lawrence Miller 1927- *St&PR 93*
Bell, Lawrence R. 1941- *WhoIns 93*
Bell, Lee Phillip *WhoAm 92, WhoWor 93*
Bell, Leland 1922-1991 *BioIn 17*
Bell, Leslie Frank *Law&B 92*
Bell, Lilian Lida 1867-1929 *AmWomPl*
Bell, Linda Flounders 1952- *WhoWrEP 92*
Bell, Linda R. 1949- *WhoEmL 93*
Bell, M.A. *Law&B 92*
Bell, M. Shayne 1957- *ScF&FL 92*
Bell, Madeleine *SoulM*
Bell, Madison Smartt 1957- *WhoWrEP 92*
Bell, Margaret Couvillon 1943- *St&PR 93*
Bell, Marja-Liisa Sanelma 1930- *WhoWor 93*
Bell, Mark Gerald 1950- *WhoEmL 93*
Bell, Martin *MiSFD 9*
Bell, Martin Allen 1951- *WhoAm 92*
Bell, Martin David *Law&B 92*
Bell, Marvin 1937- *BioIn 17*
Bell, Mary Allison 1936- *WhoAmW 93, WhoSSW 93*
Bell, Mary Ann Elizabeth 1943- *WhoSSW 93*
Bell, Mary E. Beniteau 1937- *WhoSSW 93*
Bell, Mary Kathleen 1922- *WhoAmW 93*
Bell, May *AmWomPl*
Bell, Merton I. 1935- *St&PR 93*
Bell, Michael A. *BioIn 17*
Bell, Michael L. *Law&B 92*
Bell, Michael Steven 1946- *WhoWrEP 92*
Bell, Mildred Bailey 1928- *WhoAmW 93, WhoSSW 93*
Bell, Millicent *BioIn 17*
Bell, Morris L. 1924- *St&PR 93*
Bell, Muriel *Law&B 92*
Bell, Mylle *BioIn 17*
Bell, Nancy Elizabeth 1949- *WhoAmW 93*
Bell, Neil 1887-1964 *ScF&FL 92*
Bell, Norman Howard 1931- *WhoAm 92*
Bell, Normand W. 1930- *WhoIns 93*
Bell, Ovid H. 1917- *St&PR 93*
Bell, P. Jackson 1941- *St&PR 93, WhoAm 92*
Bell, Palmer H. 1948- *St&PR 93*
Bell, Patricia Mondello 1956- *WhoE 93*
Bell, Paul Burton, Jr. 1946- *WhoSSW 93*
Bell, Paul David 1953- *WhoSSW 93*
Bell, Paul David 1955- *WhoEmL 93*
Bell, Paul W. d1990 *BioIn 17*
Bell, Paul W. 1933- *ScF&FL 92*
Bell, Peter M. 1934- *St&PR 93*
Bell, Peter Mayo 1934- *WhoAm 92*
Bell, Peter Robert Frank *WhoScE 91-1*
Bell, Philip Dale *WhoScE 91-1*
Bell, Philip Wilkes 1924- *WhoAm 92*
Bell, Phillip Michael 1942- *WhoAm 92*
Bell, R.L. *WhoScE 91-1*
Bell, R.M. *WhoScE 91-1*
Bell, R.W. *Law&B 92*
Bell, Randall 1943- *WhoSSW 93*
Bell, Randall William 1938- *WhoAm 92*
Bell, Raymond Joseph 1949- *WhoE 93*
Bell, Regina Jean *WhoAmW 93*
Bell, Richard 1920- *WhoSSW 93*
Bell, Richard Chevalier 1928- *WhoAm 92*
Bell, Richard E. 1934- *St&PR 93*
Bell, Richard Eugene 1934- *WhoAm 92, WhoSSW 93*
Bell, Richard G. *Law&B 92*
Bell, Richard G. 1947- *St&PR 93, WhoEmL 93*
Bell, Richard Trent 1946- *WhoE 93*
Bell, Richard V. 1922- *St&PR 93*
Bell, Richard W. *Law&B 92*
Bell, Rickey Charles 1949- *WhoEmL 93*
Bell, Rob *ScF&FL 92*
Bell, Robbie Hancock 1955- *WhoEmL 93*
Bell, Robert *BioIn 17*
Bell, Robert, Jr. *Law&B 92*
Bell, Robert Arnold 1950- *WhoE 93, WhoEmL 93*
Bell, Robert Austin 1933- *St&PR 93, WhoAm 92*
Bell, Robert Brooks 1953- *WhoEmL 93*
Bell, Robert Cecil 1951- *WhoWor 93*
Bell, Robert Collins 1912- *WhoE 93*
Bell, Robert E. 1947- *St&PR 93*
Bell, Robert E(ugene) 1926- *ConAu 138*
Bell, Robert Eugene 1914- *WhoAm 92*
Bell, Robert Holmes 1944- *WhoAm 92*
Bell, Robert L. 1919- *St&PR 93*
Bell, Robert Lawrence 1919- *WhoE 93*
Bell, Robert Lewis 1951- *WhoEmL 93*
Bell, Robert Maurice 1944- *WhoAm 92*
Bell, Robert S., Jr. *Law&B 92*
Bell, Robert Taylor *WhoScE 91-1*
Bell, Ronald 1937- *St&PR 93*
Bell, Roseanne 1946- *WhoAmW 93*
Bell, Sam Hanna 1909-1990 *BioIn 17*
Bell, Samuel H. 1925- *WhoAm 92*
Bell, Sarah Ann 1961- *WhoSSW 93*
Bell, Sarah Virginia 1955- *WhoAmW 93*
Bell, Sharon Kaye 1943- *WhoAmW 93, WhoWor 93*
Bell, Sharon Teresa Echerd 1950- *WhoAmW 93*
Bell, Stanley R. 1946- *St&PR 93*
Bell, Stephen 1946- *St&PR 93*
Bell, Stephen M. 1948- *St&PR 93*
Bell, Stephen Robert 1942- *WhoAm 92*
Bell, Stephen Scott 1935- *WhoAm 92*
Bell, Steve *BioIn 17*
Bell, Stoughton 1923- *WhoAm 92*
Bell, Stuart John 1944- *St&PR 93*
Bell, Susan Jane 1946- *WhoAmW 93, WhoEmL 93*
Bell, Teresa M. *Law&B 92*
Bell, Terrel Howard 1921- *WhoAm 92*
Bell, Thaddeus John *BioIn 17*
Bell, Theodore Augustus 1946- *WhoAm 92*
Bell, Thom 1941- *SoulM*
Bell, Thomas *St&PR 93, WhoScE 91-1*
Bell, Thomas D., Jr. 1949- *St&PR 93*
Bell, Thomas Devereaux, Jr. 1949- *WhoAm 92*
Bell, Thomas E. 1943- *St&PR 93*
Bell, Thomas Eugene 1945- *WhoSSW 93*
Bell, Thomas Rowe 1928- *St&PR 93, WhoAm 92*
Bell, Timothy Harwell 1949- *WhoEmL 93*
Bell, Tom 1856- *BioIn 17*
Bell, Trudy E. *ScF&FL 92*
Bell, Van W. 1946- *St&PR 93*
Bell, Vanessa 1879-1961 *BioIn 17, DcLB DS10*
Bell, Veda V. 1929- *WhoAmW 93*
Bell, Victor Altmark, Jr. 1942- *St&PR 93*
Bell, Victor Leroy 1935- *WhoWrEP 92*
Bell, Vincent G., Jr. 1925- *St&PR 93*
Bell, Vito L. 1945- *St&PR 93*
Bell, W.D.M. 1880-1954 *BioIn 17*
Bell, W. Douglas 1921- *St&PR 93*

Belt, Bradley Deck 1958- *WhoEmL 93*
Belt, Donald Clifford 1947- *St&PR 93*
Belt, Donald E. 1924- *St&PR 93*
Belt, Edward Scudder 1933- *WhoAm 92*
Belt, J.E. 1933- *St&PR 93*
Belt, Megan Patricia 1964- *WhoAmW 93*
Belt, Percy Keith 1948- *St&PR 93*
Belt, Ralph C. 1930- *WhoIns 93*
Belt, Robert Howard, Jr. 1951- *WhoE 93*
Beltagy, Mohammad Abdel-Maksoud 1950- *WhoWor 93*
Beltaire, Beverly Ann 1926- *WhoAm 92, WhoAmW 93*
Belter, Edgar William 1929- *WhoWor 93*
Belth, Joseph M. 1929- *WhoIns 93*
Belth, Joseph Morton 1929- *WhoAm 92*
Belthoff, Richard Charles, Jr. 1958- *WhoEmL 93*
Belton, Beth Marie 1955- *WhoAmW 93*
Belton, Betty Rose 1934- *WhoWrEP 92*
Belton, Deborah Carolyn Knox 1962- *WhoAmW 93, WhoEmL 93*
Belton, Edward Lee 1915- *WhoSSW 93*
Belton, John G. 1947- *WhoSSW 93*
Belton, John Thomas 1947- *WhoEmL 93*
Belton, Kepka Hochman *WhoWrEP 92*
Belton, Linda Weber 1950- *WhoAmW 93*
Belton, Sharon Sayles *AfrAmBi*
Beltrame, James Michael 1943- *St&PR 93*
Beltrame, Joseph Robert 1943- *St&PR 93*
Beltrame, Paolo 1930- *WhoScE 91-3*
Beltrami, Pier Angelo 1950- *WhoWor 93*
Beltran, Eusebius Joseph 1934- *WhoAm 92, WhoSSW 93*
Beltran, Luis Fernando 1952- *WhoWor 93*
Beltran, Michael R. 1940- *St&PR 93*
Beltran, Natalio M., Jr. 1937- *WhoAsAP 91*
Beltran, Neftali 1916- *DcMexL*
Beltran, Porter Daniel 1947- *WhoWor 93*
Beltran De Heredia Onis, Jose M. 1921- *WhoScE 91-3*
Beltrao, Alexandre Fontana 1924- *WhoWor 93*
Beltritti, Giacomo Giuseppe 1910-1992 *NewYTBS 92*
Beltz, Charles Robert 1913- *WhoAm 92*
Beltz, Herbert Allison 1926- *WhoAm 92*
Beltz, Hernan Peralta 1939- *WhoWor 93*
Beltz, John David 1961- *WhoE 93*
Beltz, William Albert 1929- *St&PR 93, WhoAm 92, WhoWrEP 92*
Beltzer, Herman M. 1927- *St&PR 93*
Beltzer, Herman Martin 1927- *WhoAm 92*
Beltzner, Gail Ann 1950- *WhoAmW 93, WhoE 93, WhoEmL 93, WhoWor 93*
Belushi, James 1954- *WhoAm 92*
Belushi, John 1949-1982 *BioIn 17, IntDcF 2-3, QDrFCA 92 [port]*
Belushi, Judith Jacklin 1951- *WhoEmL 93*
Belushi, Judy *BioIn 17*
Belville, Barbara Ann *Law&B 92*
Belville, Barbara Ann 1957- *WhoEmL 93*
Belvin, Donald Lynnwood 1953- *WhoSSW 93*
Belvin, Jesse 1933-1960 *SoulM*
Bely, Victor 1904-1983 *Baker 92*
Belyakov, Velju Nachev 1931- *WhoWor 93*
Belyea, Robert C. 1925- *St&PR 93*
Belyi, Gennadij Vladimirovitch 1951- *WhoWor 93*
Belyi, Vladimir Ivanovitch 1938- *WhoWor 93*
Belytschko, Ted Bohdan 1943- *WhoAm 92*
Belz, Carl Irvin 1937- *WhoE 93*
Belz, Stephen Robert 1953- *St&PR 93*
Belza, Igor *Baker 92*
Belza, Wladyslaw 1847-1913 *PolBiDi*
Belzberg, Brent Stanley 1951- *WhoAm 92*
Belzberg, Samuel 1928- *St&PR 93, WhoAm 92, WhoWor 93*
Belzer, Alan 1932- *St&PR 93, WhoAm 92*
Belzer, Burton E. 1926- *St&PR 93*
Belzer, Ellen J. 1951- *WhoAmW 93, WhoEmL 93*
Belzer, Folkert Oene 1930- *WhoAm 92*
Belzer, John D. 1951- *St&PR 93*
Belzer, Judith *BioIn 17*
Belzile, M.L. *Law&B 92*
Bem, Daniel Jozef 1933- *WhoScE 91-4*
Bem, Eugene S. 1966- *WhoE 93*
Bem, Jozef 1795-1850 *PolBiDi*
Bem, Pavel 1935- *WhoScE 91-4*
Bem, Sandra Lipsitz 1944- *BioIn 17*
Bemak, Fred Paul 1948- *WhoE 93*
Beman, Deane Randolph 1938- *WhoAm 92*
Beman, Leland H. 1951- *St&PR 93*
Beman, Lynn Susan 1942- *WhoE 93*
Bemben, Brenda J. *Law&B 92*
Bembenek, Alan Roger 1960- *WhoEmL 93*
Bembenek, Lawrencia *BioIn 17*
Bemberg, Gerald Francis 1945- *St&PR 93*
Bemberg, Herman 1859-1931 *Baker 92*
Bemberg, Maria Luisa 1940- *MiSFD 9*
Bembo, Antonia c. 1670- *Baker 92, BioIn 17*
Bemelmans, Ludwig 1898-1962 *BioIn 17, MajAI [port]*
Bemelmans, Th.M.A. 1943- *WhoScE 91-3*
Bemelmans, Theo M. A. 1943- *WhoWor 93*
Bement, Arden Lee, Jr. 1932- *WhoAm 92*
Bemis, Alan C. 1907-1991 *BioIn 17*
Bemis, Bradford Scott *Law&B 92*
Bemis, F. Gregg, Jr. 1928- *St&PR 93*
Bemis, Hal L. 1912- *St&PR 93*
Bemis, Hal Lawall 1912- *WhoAm 92, WhoE 93, WhoWor 93*
Bemis, John Howard *Law&B 92*
Bemis, Katharine Isabel *AmWomPl*
Bemis, Linda Ruth 1943- *WhoAmW 93*
Bemis, Mary 1961- *WhoAmW 93*
Bemis, Mary Ferguson 1961- *WhoAm 92*
Bemis, Michael B. 1947- *St&PR 93*
Bemis, Royce Edwin 1941- *WhoSSW 93*
Bemis, Stephen Theodore *Law&B 92*
Bemis, Thomas Bruce 1953- *WhoEmL 93*
Bemmann, Hans *ScF&FL 92*
Bemvenutti, Joao Carlos 1947- *WhoWor 93*
Ben Abdallah, Moncef 1946- *WhoWor 93*
Benabid, Alim Louis 1942- *WhoScE 91-2*
Benacerraf, Baruj 1920- *WhoAm 92, WhoE 93, WhoWor 93*
Benacerraf, Paul 1931- *WhoAm 92*
Benach, Henry 1917- *St&PR 93*
Benach, Sharon Ann 1944- *WhoAmW 93*
Benacin, Philippe 1958- *St&PR 93*
Benackova, Gabriela 1944- *OxDcOp*
Benackova, Gabriela 1947- *Baker 92*
Benade, Leo Edward 1916- *WhoAm 92*
Benagiano, Giuseppe P. 1937- *WhoScE 91-3*
Benaich, Evelyne *Law&B 92*
Benaim, Jose Carlos De Amarante 1947- *WhoWor 93*
Benaim-Deman, Mireya *WhoAmW 93*
Benais, Christian *BioIn 17*
Benaissa, Hamdan 1935- *WhoUN 92*
Benak, James Donald 1954- *WhoEmL 93*
Benak, Mari L. *WhoAmW 93*
Ben Ak Panggi, Michael 1935- *WhoAsAP 91*
Benaksas-Schwartz, Elaine Julie 1959- *WhoAmW 93*
Ben Ali, Zine Al-Abidine 1936- *WhoWor 93*
Ben Ali, Zine el Abidine *BioIn 17*
Benally, Raymond A. 1953- *WhoEmL 93*
Ben Amara, Taoufik Mohamed 1946- *WhoUN 92*
Benamati, Dennis Charles 1948- *WhoEmL 93*
Benammar, Raouf Mohammed 1945- *WhoUN 92*
Ben Amor, Ismail 1937- *WhoWor 93*
Benamrane, Djilali 1942- *WhoUN 92*
Benanav, Gary G. 1945- *St&PR 93*
Benanto, Ronald R. *St&PR 93*
Benapfl, William Joseph 1956- *WhoEmL 93*
Benard, Bruce Raymond 1949- *WhoEmL 93*
Benaresh, Ehsanollah 1934- *WhoE 93*
Ben-Ari, Yehezkel *WhoScE 91-2*
Benario, Herbert William 1929- *WhoAm 92, WhoSSW 93*
Benaroya, Haym 1954- *WhoEmL 93*
Benaroya, Raphael *BioIn 17*
Benary, Margot *MajAI*
Benary-Isbert, Margot 1889-1979 *MajAI [port], ScF&FL 92*
Ben-Asher, Daniel Lawrence 1946- *WhoE 93, WhoEmL 93*
Benassy, Jean-Pascal 1948- *WhoWor 93*
Benasutti, Marion *BioIn 17*
Benatar, Leo 1930- *St&PR 93, WhoAm 92, WhoSSW 93*
Benatar, Pat 1953- *ConMus 8 [port], WhoAm 92, WhoAmW 93*
Benatre, Andre 1930- *WhoScE 91-2*
Benatzky, Ralph 1884-1957 *Baker 92*
Benavente, Toribio de d1569 *DcMexL*
Benavente y Martinez, Jacinto 1866-1954 *BioIn 17*
Benavides, Jaime Miguel 1923- *WhoSSW 93, WhoWor 93*
Benavides, Luis Jordan 1949- *WhoEmL 93*
Benavides, Mariana *Law&B 92*
Benavides, Oscar R. 1876-1945 *BioIn 17*
Benavides, Patrick R. 1953- *St&PR 93*
Benavides, Rodolfo 1907- *DcMexL*
Benavides, Roy 1935- *HispAmA*
Benavidez, Celina Garcia 1954- *WhoAmW 93*
Benavidez, Roy *BioIn 17*
Benbassat, Mario 1933- *WhoWor 93*
Ben Bella, Ahmed 1918?- *BioIn 17, ColdWar 2 [port]*
Ben Bella, Mohammed Ahmed 1916- *DcTwHis*
Benbenek, Janeen Louise 1969- *WhoAmW 93*
Benberry, Cuesta Ray 1923- *WhoAm 92, WhoAmW 93, WhoWor 93*
Benbouali, Abdenour 1939- *WhoUN 92*
Benbow, Camilla Persson 1956- *WhoAm 92, WhoEmL 93*
Benbow, Charles Clarence 1929- *WhoAm 92, WhoWrEP 92*
Benbow, John Robert 1931- *WhoAm 92*
Benbridge, Henry 1743-1812 *BioIn 17*
Benbrook, Charles Mallard 1949- *WhoE 93*
Bencastro, Mario *BioIn 17*
Bencat, Jan 1943- *WhoScE 91-4*
Bence, Kenneth C. 1928- *St&PR 93*
Bence, Kevin James 1961- *St&PR 93*
Bence, William Jackson 1948- *WhoSSW 93*
Bench, Dan A. 1934- *St&PR 93, WhoIns 93*
Bench, Johnny *BioIn 17*
Bench, Johnny Lee 1947- *WhoAm 92*
Benchimol, Alberto 1932- *WhoWor 93*
Benchley, Nathaniel 1915-1981 *ScF&FL 92*
Benchley, Nathaniel (Goddard) 1915-1981 *DcAmChF 1960*
Benchley, Peter *BioIn 17*
Benchley, Peter 1940- *ScF&FL 92*
Benchley, Peter Bradford 1940- *WhoAm 92, WhoWrEP 92*
Benchley, Robert 1889-1945 *QDrFCA 92 [port]*
Benchoff, James Martin 1927- *WhoAm 92*
Bencini, Sara Haltiwanger 1926- *WhoAmW 93*
Bencivenga, Ernest V. 1918- *St&PR 93*
Bencivengo, Elaine Palusci 1942- *WhoE 93*
Bencke, Ronald L. 1940- *St&PR 93*
Benckendorf, Glenn E. 1929- *St&PR 93*
Bencks, Rodney N. 1934- *St&PR 93*
Bencomo, Jose Antonio, Jr. 1946- *WhoSSW 93*
Bencrowsky, Anna M. 1951- *St&PR 93*
Bencsath, Katalin Agnes *WhoE 93*
Bencze, Eva Ivanyos 1932- *WhoAmW 93*
Bencze, Gyula 1936- *WhoScE 91-4*
Bencze, Pal 1929- *WhoScE 91-4*
Benda, Carl Thomas 1937- *St&PR 93*
Benda, Franz 1709-1786 *Baker 92*
Benda, Friedrich 1745-1814 *Baker 92*
Benda, Friedrich 1754-1814 *OxDcOp*
Benda, Friedrich Ludwig 1752-1792 *Baker 92, OxDcOp*
Benda, Georg Anton 1722-1795 *Baker 92*
Benda, Hans von 1888-1972 *Baker 92*
Benda, Irmgard 1927- *WhoScE 91-3*
Benda, Jiri 1722?-1795 *OxDcOp*
Benda, Julien 1867-1956 *BioIn 17*
Benda, Karl Hermann Heinrich 1748-1836 *Baker 92*
Benda, Leopold A. 1933- *WhoScE 91-3*
Benda, Marilyn Virginia 1935- *WhoAmW 93*
Benda, Sten 1935- *WhoWor 93*
Benda, Vladimir 1944- *WhoScE 91-4*
Benda, Wladyslaw Theodor 1873-1948 *PolBiDi*
Bendahou, Taoufik Noreddine 1935- *WhoUN 92*
Ben Daniel, David Jacob 1931- *WhoAm 92, WhoE 93*
Bendat, Cindy *Law&B 92*
Bendau, Clifford P. 1950- *ScF&FL 92*
Ben-David, Joseph *BioIn 17*
Bende, Andras V. 1938- *St&PR 93*
Bendel, Franz 1833-1874 *Baker 92*
Bendelac, Roger Emile 1956- *WhoE 93, WhoWor 93*
Bendeler, Johann Philipp 1654-1709 *Baker 92*
Bendelius, Albert 1913- *St&PR 93*
Bendelius, Arthur George 1936- *WhoAm 92*
Bendell, A. *WhoScE 91-1*
Benden, Norman E. 1958- *St&PR 93*
Bender, Adam Norman 1942- *WhoE 93*
Bender, Angela Marie 1967- *WhoAmW 93*
Bender, Arthur Stillman 1938- *WhoSSW 93*
Bender, Bert *BioIn 17*
Bender, Betty Barbee 1932- *WhoAmW 93*
Bender, Betty Wion 1925- *WhoAm 92*
Bender, Bruce Dean 1951- *WhoEmL 93*
Bender, Bruce F. 1949- *St&PR 93, WhoAm 92*
Bender, Byron Wilbur 1929- *WhoAm 92*
Bender, Carl Martin 1943- *WhoAm 92*
Bender, Charles C. 1936- *St&PR 93*
Bender, Charles Christian 1936- *WhoAm 92*
Bender, David Ray 1942- *WhoAm 92*
Bender, Douglas Ray 1953- *WhoWor 93*
Bender, Edward C. 1937- *St&PR 93*
Bender, Eleanor M. 1941- *WhoWrEP 92*
Bender, Elizabeth Melchert 1960- *WhoEmL 93*
Bender, Ernest 1919- *BioIn 17*
Bender, Esther Louise 1942- *WhoWrEP 92*
Bender, Gary Nedrow 1940- *WhoAm 92*
Bender, Gary William 1948- *WhoE 93, WhoEmL 93, WhoWor 93*
Bender, Graham I. 1939- *St&PR 93, WhoAm 92*
Bender, H. David 1938- *St&PR 93*
Bender, Harold 1910- *WhoWor 93*
Bender, Harvey W., Jr. 1933- *WhoAm 92*
Bender, Henry Elias 1938- *WhoWor 93*
Bender, Jack *MiSFD 9*
Bender, James Frederick 1905- *WhoAm 92*
Bender, James Joseph *Law&B 92*
Bender, Jay Mitchell 1935- *St&PR 93*
Bender, Joel *MiSFD 9*
Bender, Joel R. 1947- *St&PR 93*
Bender, John C. *Law&B 92*
Bender, John Henry, Jr. 1931- *WhoSSW 93, WhoWor 93*
Bender, Joseph J. *BioIn 17*
Bender, Martin 1947- *WhoUN 92*
Bender, Michael A. 1929- *WhoE 93*
Bender, Michael Allen *Law&B 92*
Bender, Michael Keith 1947- *WhoEmL 93, WhoSSW 93*
Bender, Miles D. 1937- *St&PR 93*
Bender, Pamela Ann 1961- *WhoAmW 93*
Bender, Paul 1875-1947 *Baker 92*
Bender, Paul Edward 1951- *WhoAm 92*
Bender, Phoebe Powell 1933- *WhoAm 92, WhoAmW 93*
Bender, Ray *BioIn 17*
Bender, Raymond P. *Law&B 92*
Bender, Richard 1930- *WhoAm 92*
Bender, Roberta E. *Law&B 92*
Bender, Ross Thomas 1929- *WhoAm 92*
Bender, Susan Letitia 1961- *WhoAmW 93*
Bender, Susan Marie 1953- *WhoAmW 93*
Bender, Theodore J., III 1947- *St&PR 93*
Bender, Thomas 1944- *WhoAm 92, WhoWrEP 92*
Bender, Thomas Richard 1939- *WhoAm 92*
Bender, Thomas V. *Law&B 92*
Bender, Timothy A. 1943- *St&PR 93*
Bender, Virginia Best 1945- *WhoAmW 93, WhoWor 93*
Bender, Wayne F. *Law&B 92*
Benderly, Ziva *BioIn 17*
Bendernagel, Donald A. *Law&B 92*
Benders, Kris *ScF&FL 92*
Benderson, Bruce 1952- *WhoWrEP 92*
Bendetson, Robert Rome 1951- *St&PR 93*
Bendheim, C.H. 1917- *St&PR 93*
Ben Dhia, Abdelaziz *WhoWor 93*
Bendich, Adrianne 1944- *WhoE 93*
Bendick, Jeanne 1919- *BioIn 17, MajAI [port]*
Bendick, Marc, Jr. 1946- *WhoEmL 93*
Bendig, William Charles 1927- *WhoAm 92*
Bendikas, Omar Jurgis 1927- *St&PR 93*
Bendikov, Alexander Davidovitch 1950- *WhoWor 93*
Bendiksen, Kjell Hugo 1947- *WhoScE 91-4*
Bendinelli, Agostino 1550-1598 *Baker 92*
Bendinelli, Agostino 1635-1703 *Baker 92*
Bendinelli, Cesare d1617 *Baker 92*
Bendinelli, Mauro G. 1934- *WhoScE 91-3*
Bendinelli, Mauro Giuseppe 1934- *WhoWor 93*
Bendiner, Robert 1909- *WhoAm 92, WhoWrEP 92*
Bendis, Jay S. 1946- *St&PR 93*
Bendit, Daniel Cohn- *BioIn 17*
Benditt, Theodore Matthew 1940- *WhoAm 92*
Bendix, Linda Ann 1951- *WhoAmW 93*
Bendix, Max 1866-1945 *Baker 92*
Bendix, Otto 1845-1904 *Baker 92*
Bendix, Reinhard *BioIn 17*
Bendix, Richard C. 1948- *St&PR 93*
Bendix, Victor Emanuel 1851-1926 *Baker 92*
Bendix, William 1906-1964 *IntDcF 2-3 [port], QDrFCA 92 [port]*
Bendix, William E. 1935- *St&PR 93*
Bendix, William Emanuel 1935- *WhoAm 92*
Bendixen, Alfred 1952- *ScF&FL 92*
Bendixen, Henrik Holt 1923- *WhoAm 92*
Bendixen, Warren E. 1930- *WhoE 93*
Bendjedid Chadli *BioIn 17*
Bendl, Karel 1839-1897 *OxDcOp*
Bendl, Karl 1838-1897 *Baker 92*
Bendler, Salomon 1683-1724 *Baker 92*
Bendo, Gerald Michael *Law&B 92*
Bendorf, Angela S. 1962- *WhoAmW 93*
Bendowski, Joseph Adam 1943- *St&PR 93*
Bendrihem, Elliott 1948- *WhoAm 92*
Bendumb, Mathew 1947- *WhoAsAP 91*
Bendzin, Leonard John 1925- *St&PR 93*
Bene, Adriana Gabrieli del c. 1755-c. 1799 *IntDcOp*
Bene, Georges 1919- *WhoScE 91-4*

Benecke, Gary Edward 1953- WhoSSW 93
Benecke, Marc BioIn 17
Benecki, Anita 1934- WhoE 93
Benecki, Walter T. 1939- St&PR 93
Benedeczky, Istvan 1931- WhoScE 91-4
Benedek, Elissa P. BioIn 17
Benedek, Laslo d1992 NewYTBS 92
Benedek, Laslo 1907- MiSFD 9
Benedek, Laslo 1907-1992 BioIn 17
Benedek, Ludwig August von 1804-1881 HarEnMi
Benedek, Melinda 1951- St&PR 93
Benedek, S.J. 1952- St&PR 93
Benedetti, David J. 1956- St&PR 93
Benedetti, Ettore 1940- WhoScE 91-3
Benedetti, Gaetano 1920- WhoScE 91-4
Benedetti, Joseph C. 1942- St&PR 93
Benedetti, Mario 1920- SpAmA
Benedetti, Michele 1778- OxDcOp
Benedetti, Richard 1949- St&PR 93
Benedetti, Thomas Joseph 1947- WhoAm 92
Benedetti Michelangeli, Arturo Baker 92
Benedetto, Donna A. 1962- WhoWrEP 92
Benedetto, Lorraine Ann 1949- WhoAmW 93, WhoE 93, WhoEmL 93
Benedetto, M. William 1941- St&PR 93, WhoAm 92
Benedetto, Peter P. 1930- St&PR 93
Benedetto, Salvatore A. 1937- St&PR 93
Benedick, Dale Raymond 1941- WhoSSW 93
Benedick, Richard Elliot 1935- WhoAm 92
Benedict, Andrew Bell, Jr. 1914- St&PR 93
Benedict, Anthony Wayne Law&B 92
Benedict, Bruce Whitlock 1937- St&PR 93
Benedict, Burton 1923- WhoAm 92
Benedict, C.M. 1934- St&PR 93
Benedict, Clyde 1927- St&PR 93
Benedict, Donwayne 1933- St&PR 93
Benedict, Elinor Divine 1931- WhoWrEP 92
Benedict, Francis E. 1939- St&PR 93
Benedict, Fred K. 1923- St&PR 93
Benedict, Helen Elizabeth 1946- WhoAm 92
Benedict, Jack R. 1931- St&PR 93
Benedict, James Nelson 1949- WhoAm 92
Benedict, Jeffrey Law&B 92
Benedict, Jeril Robert Law&B 92
Benedict, John G. d1990 BioIn 17
Benedict, Julius 1804-1885 Baker 92, IntDcOp, OxDcOp
Benedict, Laura Watson 1861-1932 IntDcAn
Benedict, Linda J. 1942- WhoIns 93
Benedict, Linda Sherk 1945- WhoAm 92
Benedict, Manson 1907- WhoAm 92
Benedict, Mark J. 1951- WhoEmL 93
Benedict, Paul C. 1943- St&PR 93
Benedict, Peter Folger 1943- St&PR 93
Benedict, Robert C. 1938- St&PR 93
Benedict, Robert C. 1951- WhoIns 93
Benedict, Rodman Wesley Law&B 92
Benedict, Ronald L. Law&B 92
Benedict, Ruth 1887-1948 IntDcAn
Benedict, Samuel S. 1930- WhoAm 92
Benedict, Ulrich G. 1930- WhoScE 91-3
Benedict, Walter J. 1902-1991 BioIn 17
Benedictus Appenzeller Baker 92
Benedik, Kenneth Joseph 1946- WhoEmL 93, WhoSSW 93
Benedikt, Bozidar D. 1938- WhoWor 93
Benedikt, Michael 1935- BioIn 17, WhoAm 92, WhoWrEP 92
Benedikz, Thorarinn 1939- WhoScE 91-4
Benedini, Marcello 1932- WhoScE 91-3
Benedito y Vives, Rafael 1885-1963 Baker 92
Benedosso, Anthony Nechols 1949- WhoEmL 93
Benefield, James Dewey, Jr. 1931- St&PR 93
Beneigh, John J., Jr. 1950- St&PR 93
Benejam, Gustavo Ricardo 1955- WhoE 93
Beneke, Tex 1914- Baker 92
Beneken, Gerhard 1953- BioIn 17
Beneken, Jan E.W. 1934- WhoScE 91-3
Benelbas, Leon Amram 1952- WhoWor 93
Benelli, Antonio Peregrino 1771-1830 Baker 92
Benenson, Claire Berger WhoE 93
Benenson, David Maurice 1927- WhoAm 92
Benenson, Edward Hartley 1914- WhoAm 92, WhoWor 93
Benenson, Esther Siev 1925- WhoWor 93
Benenson, James, Jr. 1936- St&PR 93, WhoAm 92
Benenson, Jennifer Law&B 92
Benenson, Mark Keith 1929- WhoAm 92
Benenson, Peter 1921- BioIn 17
Benenson, Walter 1936- WhoAm 92
Benerito, Ruth Rogan 1916- WhoAm 92
Benerofe, Stanley 1933- St&PR 93
Benes, Edvard 1884-1948 DcTwHis
Benes, Marcia Elizabeth 1949- WhoAm 92, WhoEmL 93
Benes, Patricia Ellen 1950- WhoEmL 93
Benes, Susan Carleton 1948- WhoWor 93
Benesch, Katherine 1946- WhoEmL 93
Benesch, Ruth Erica 1925- WhoAm 92
Benesch, Ryszard 1930- WhoScE 91-4
Benesch, William Milton 1922- WhoAm 92
Benesi, Betty-Ann Branca 1952- WhoEmL 93
Benestad, Finn 1929- Baker 92
Benestad, Haakon B. 1940- WhoScE 91-4
Benet, Edmond 1936- WhoScE 91-3
Benet, John fl. 15th cent.- Baker 92
Benet, Laura 1884-1979 BioIn 17, ScF&FL 92
Benet, Leslie Zachary 1937- WhoAm 92, WhoWor 93
Benet, Stephen Vincent 1898-1943 BioIn 17, ShSCr 10 [port]
Benet, Sula 1906-1982 IntDcAn
Benet, Thomas Carr 1926- WhoAm 92, WhoWrEP 92
Benetti, Federico Jose 1947- WhoWor 93
Benevenia, Michael A. 1956- WhoIns 93
Benevento, Francis O. 1942- St&PR 93
Benevento, Lois Victoria 1930- WhoAmW 93
Benevoli, Orazio 1605-1672 Baker 92
Beney, Gilbert R. 1934- WhoUN 92
Benezet, Louis Tomlinson 1915- WhoAm 92, WhoWor 93
Benezra, Claude 1939- WhoScE 91-2
Benezra, Neal 1953- WhoAm 92
Benezra, Raymond Leon 1930- St&PR 93
Benfatti, Irene 1948- WhoAmW 93, WhoEmL 93
Benfell, V. Stanley 1934- St&PR 93
Benfenati, Emilio 1954- WhoWor 93
Benfer, David William 1946- WhoAm 92
Benfey, Otto Theodor 1925- WhoAm 92, WhoWrEP 92
Benfield, Ann Kolb 1946- WhoEmL 93
Benfield, David William 1941- WhoE 93
Benfield, James H. 1953- St&PR 93
Benfield, Jeanette Louise 1955- WhoAmW 93
Benfield, John Richard 1931- WhoAm 92
Benfield, Marion Wilson, Jr. 1932- WhoAm 92
Benforado, David M. 1925- WhoAm 92
Benford, Gregory 1941- BioIn 17, ScF&FL 92
Benford, Gregory Albert 1941- WhoAm 92, WhoWrEP 92
Benford, Harry Bell 1917- WhoAm 92
Benford, Norman J. 1938- WhoAm 92
Benford, Timothy B. 1941- ScF&FL 92
Benford, William Lee 1942- WhoAm 92
Ben-Gal, Joseph 1951- St&PR 93
Bengali, Yunus Hashim 1949- WhoWor 93
Benge, James Edward 1952- WhoE 93
Benge, Mary Cecelia Riley 1952- WhoEmL 93
Benge, Phillip James 1949- WhoWor 93
Bengels, Barbara Natalie 1943- WhoE 93
Bengelsdorf, Peter A. 1946- St&PR 93
Benger, Scott C. 1949- St&PR 93
Benghiat, Russell 1948- WhoEmL 93
Benglis, Lynda 1941- BioIn 17, WhoAm 92, WhoE 93
Bengmark, Stig Bertil Samuel 1929- WhoScE 91-4
Bengoechea, Mariano 1944- WhoWor 93
Bengoechea, Shane Orin 1956- WhoEmL 93
Bengston, Billy Al BioIn 17
Bengston, Billy Al 1934- WhoAm 92
Bengtson, Betty Grimes 1940- WhoAmW 93
Bengtson, Bruce D. 1938- WhoAm 92
Bengtson, J.N. 1945- St&PR 93
Bengtson, Karl Wayne 1955- WhoEmL 93
Bengtson, Kathleen Ann 1949- WhoAmW 93
Bengtson, Roger Dean 1941- WhoAm 92, WhoSSW 93
Bengtson, Roger H. 1930- St&PR 93
Bengtson, Staffan WhoScE 91-4
Bengtson, Vern L. 1941- WhoAm 92
Bengtsson, Beng-Erik U. 1945- WhoScE 91-4
Bengtsson, Bengt-Goran 1950- WhoWor 93
Bengtsson, Bengt O. 1946- WhoScE 91-4
Bengtsson, Bo WhoScE 91-4
Bengtsson, Bo M.L. 1939- WhoScE 91-4
Bengtsson, Elias 1918- WhoScE 91-4
Bengtsson, Ewert W. 1948- WhoScE 91-4
Bengtsson, Ewert Waldemar 1948- WhoWor 93
Bengtsson, Frans 1894-1954 TwCLC 48
Bengtsson, Goran 1947- WhoWor 93
Bengtsson, Gunnar 1941- WhoScE 91-4
Bengtsson, Gustaf Adolf Tiburtius 1886-1965 Baker 92
Bengtsson, (Lars) Ingmar (Olof) 1920-c. 1989 Baker 92
Bengtsson, J. Stellan Y. 1935- WhoScE 91-4
Bengtsson, Lennart WhoScE 91-1
Bengtsson, Nils E. 1925- WhoScE 91-4
Bengtsson, Sven Gosta 1929- WhoScE 91-4
Benguerel, Xavier 1931- Baker 92
Benguigui, Yehuda 1951- WhoUN 92
Benguria, Rafael D. 1951- WhoWor 93
Ben-Gurion, David 1886-196-? HarEnMi
Ben-Gurion, David 1886-1973 BioIn 17, ColdWar 2 [port], DcTwHis, PolBiDi
Bengzon, Antonio E., III 1941- WhoAsAP 91
Benhabyles, Abdelmalek 1921- WhoWor 93
Ben-Haim, Paul 1897-1984 Baker 92
Benham, Alice Welles AmWomPl
Benham, Christopher Bruce 1948- WhoSSW 93
Benham, Douglas Neal 1956- WhoEmL 93
Benham, Isabel Hamilton 1909- WhoAm 92
Benham, James Mason 1935- WhoAm 92
Benham, Lee Kenneth 1940- WhoAm 92
Benham, Neil Roger 1936- St&PR 93
Benham, Priscilla Carla 1950- WhoAmW 93
Benham, Robert AfrAmBi [port], WhoAm 92, WhoSSW 93
Benham, Robert S. 1938- St&PR 93
Benham, Webster Lance 1949- St&PR 93
Benhamou, Jean-Pierre 1927- WhoScE 91-2
Benhard, F. Gordon 1934- St&PR 93
Benhart, Coralyn M. Law&B 92
Benhima, El Ghali 1934- WhoUN 92
Beni, Gerardo 1946- WhoAm 92, WhoEmL 93, WhoWor 93
Beni, John Joseph 1932- WhoE 93
Benicewicz, Brian Chester 1954- WhoEmL 93
Benichou, Claudie WhoScE 91-2
Benichou, Pascal WhoAm 92
Benidickson, Agnes WhoAm 92
Benigni, Roberto BioIn 17
Benigni, Roberto 1952- MiSFD 9
Benigno, Thomas Daniel 1954- WhoEmL 93
Benik, Tina C. Law&B 92
Benik, Tina C. 1959- St&PR 93
Beninati, Francis Anthony 1947- WhoEmL 93
Benincasa, Louis 1927- St&PR 93
Benincori, Angelo Maria 1779-1821 Baker 92
Bening, Annette BioIn 17
Bening, Annette c. 1958- News 92 [port]
Benington, George Beaubien 1959- WhoWrEP 92
Benini 1941- WhoWor 93
Benini, Lorraine Francis 1947- WhoAmW 93
Beninson, D. WhoScE 91-1
Benirschke, Kurt 1924- WhoAm 92
Benisek, John Paul 1935- St&PR 93
Benison, John E. 1926- St&PR 93
Benison, Peter 1950- WhoEmL 93
Ben-Israel, Shabtal WhoWrEP 92
Benite, Kathleen Berke AmWomPl
Benitez, Dawn Patrice 1955- WhoSSW 93
Benitez, Fernando 1912- DcMexL
Benitez, Gonzalo A. 1955- St&PR 93
Benitez, Isidro Basa 1927- WhoWor 93
Benitez, Jesus Luis 1949-1980 DcMexL
Benitez, John Griswold 1957- WhoEmL 93, WhoWor 93
Benitez, Jose Maria 1888-1967 DcMexL
Benitez, Maria BioIn 17
Benitez, Shirley Ann 1943- WhoAmW 93
Benitez-Rojo, Antonio 1931- ConAu 137, SpAmA
Benito De Las Heras, Manuel R. 1950- WhoScE 91-3
Benjamin, I c. 590-665 OxDcByz
Benjamin, Adelaide Wisdom 1932- WhoSSW 93, WhoWor 93
Benjamin, Albert, III 1904- WhoAm 92
Benjamin, Andy BioIn 17
Benjamin, Anne Elizabeth WhoScE 91-1
Benjamin, Arthur 1893-1960 Baker 92
Benjamin, Ben d1991 BioIn 17
Benjamin, Benny SoulM
Benjamin, Bernard WhoScE 91-1
Benjamin, Beth E. Law&B 92
Benjamin, Beverly Paschke 1928- WhoAmW 93
Benjamin, Bezaleel Solomon 1938- WhoAm 92
Benjamin, Bruce Michael 1952- St&PR 93
Benjamin, Christopher Edwin 1950- WhoEmL 93
Benjamin, Clarence B. 1907- St&PR 93
Benjamin, Colin Henry 1936- St&PR 93
Benjamin, David WhoWrEP 92
Benjamin, David Joel, III 1947- WhoAm 92
Benjamin, Edward A. 1938- WhoAm 92
Benjamin, Edward Alan 1938- St&PR 93
Benjamin, Edward Bernard, Jr. 1923- WhoAm 92, WhoSSW 93, WhoWor 93
Benjamin, Ernst 1937- WhoAm 92
Benjamin, G.P. 1930- St&PR 93
Benjamin, George 1960- Baker 92
Benjamin, George David 1933- St&PR 93, WhoAm 92
Benjamin, George S. 1935- St&PR 93
Benjamin, Gerald Roger 1939- WhoSSW 93
Benjamin, Gilbert Leon 1936- WhoE 93
Benjamin, Gina G. 1959- WhoAmW 93
Benjamin, Harvey E. 1941- WhoAm 92
Benjamin, Irma A. AmWomPl
Benjamin, Jacob ScF&FL 92
Benjamin, James Cover 1952- St&PR 93, WhoAm 92, WhoEmL 93
Benjamin, James Gilbert 1949- WhoEmL 93
Benjamin, James Leo 1941- St&PR 93
Benjamin, Janice Yukon 1951- WhoEmL 93
Benjamin, Jeffrey Law&B 92
Benjamin, Jeffrey 1945- WhoAm 92
Benjamin, John 1945- WhoWor 93
Benjamin, Joseph Wilmer, Jr. 1929- WhoWrEP 92
Benjamin, Judah P. 1811-1884 JeAmHC, PolPar
Benjamin, Judah Philip 1811-1884 BioIn 17
Benjamin, Karl Stanley 1925- WhoAm 92
Benjamin, Lorna Smith 1934- WhoAm 92
Benjamin, Louis 1926- St&PR 93
Benjamin, Louis Kuhn 1954- WhoEmL 93
Benjamin, Mary Lynn 1942- WhoWrEP 92
Benjamin, Michele ScF&FL 92
Benjamin, Raymond 1945- WhoUN 92
Benjamin, Richard 1938- MiSFD 9, WhoAm 92
Benjamin, Richard Walter 1935- WhoSSW 93
Benjamin, Robba Lee 1947- WhoAmW 93
Benjamin, Robert Irving 1949- WhoWor 93
Benjamin, Robert John 1938- St&PR 93
Benjamin, Robert L. 1923- WhoWrEP 92
Benjamin, Robert S. 1909-1979 BioIn 17
Benjamin, Robert Spiers 1917- WhoAm 92, WhoWrEP 92
Benjamin, Roger Stuart Law&B 92
Benjamin, Ruth WhoWrEP 92
Benjamin, S. Rodgers 1926- St&PR 93
Benjamin, Sheila Pauletta 1948- WhoAmW 93
Benjamin, Theodore Simon 1926- WhoAm 92
Benjamin, Thomas Brooke WhoScE 91-1
Benjamin, Walter 1892-1940 BioIn 17
Benjamin, Wesley Steven 1951- WhoSSW 93
Benjamin, William E(mmanuel) 1944- Baker 92
Benjamin, William Joseph, Jr. 1955- WhoSSW 93
Benjamin of Tudela fl. 12th cent.- Expl 93, OxDcByz
Ben Jelloun, Tahar 1944- BioIn 17, ScF&FL 92
Benke, Norman R. 1931- WhoAm 92
Benke, Paul Arthur 1921- WhoAm 92
Benke, Robin Paul 1953- WhoEmL 93
Benker, Hans Otto 1942- WhoWor 93
Benke-Smith, Clayton 1959- BioIn 17
Benkirane, Adbelhak Mohamed 1933- WhoUN 92
Benko, Donald James 1954- WhoE 93
Benko, Ralph J. 1952- WhoEmL 93
Benkov, Deborah Law&B 92
Benkow, Josef 1924- WhoWor 93
Benlifer, Ginger Engel 1949- WhoEmL 93
Benlowes, Edward 1602-1676 DcLB 126
Ben-Meir, Marc 1946- WhoSSW 93
Ben-Menachem, Yoram 1934- WhoAm 92
Ben-Menashe, Ari BioIn 17
Benmosche, Robert H. 1944- St&PR 93
Ben-Moshe, Baoz 1946- St&PR 93
Benn, Anthony Wedgwood 1925- DcTwHis
Benn, Ben 1884-1983 BioIn 17
Benn, Cynthia D. Law&B 92
Benn, Denis Martin 1937- WhoUN 92
Benn, Sally Ann 1956- WhoAmW 93
Benn, Terrence B. Law&B 92
Benn, Theodore Alexander 1918- WhoAm 92
Benn, Tony 1925- BioIn 17
Bennack, Frank Anthony, Jr. 1933- WhoAm 92, WhoE 93
Ben-Naftali, Abraham 1935- WhoWor 93
Bennard, George 1873-1958 Baker 92
Bennardo, Michael L. Law&B 92
Bennardo, S.A. 1951- St&PR 93

Benne, Kenneth D(ean) 1908-1992 *ConAu 139*
Benne, Kenneth Dean 1908- *WhoAm 92, WhoWor 93*
Bennell, John Sutherland 1893-1992 *CurBio 92N*
Benneman, Marion Anna *Law&B 92*
Benner, Bruce 1927- *St&PR 93*
Benner, Carol Ann 1948- *WhoE 93*
Benner, David J. *Law&B 92*
Benner, Dorothy Spurlock 1938- *WhoAmW 93*
Benner, James E. 1939- *St&PR 93*
Benner, M. William *St&PR 93*
Benner, Mary Wright 1956- *WhoAmW 93*
Benner, Randall Ray 1952- *WhoSSW 93*
Benner, Richard 1946-1990 *MiSFD 9N*
Benner, Richard Edward, Jr. 1932- *WhoAm 92*
Benner, Robbert 1948- *WhoScE 91-3*
Bennert, Arthur James 1926- *St&PR 93, WhoAm 92*
Bennet, Carl Christian 1954- *WhoWor 93*
Bennet, Douglas Joseph, Jr. 1938- *WhoAm 92*
Bennet, John c. 1570- *Baker 92*
Bennet, Pamela Dyer- *ScF&FL 92*
Bennet, Richard Dyer- 1913-1991 *BioIn 17*
Bennet, Robert Ames 1870-1954 *ScF&FL 92*
Bennett, Alan *WhoScE 91-1*
Bennett, Alan 1934- *BioIn 17*
Bennett, Alan C. 1924- *St&PR 93*
Bennett, Alan Jerome 1941- *St&PR 93, WhoAm 92*
Bennett, Albert Edward 1931- *WhoScE 91-2*
Bennett, Albert Farrell 1944- *WhoAm 92*
Bennett, Alden S. 1919- *St&PR 93*
Bennett, Alexander Elliot 1940- *WhoAm 92*
Bennett, Alvoid Rickey 1956- *WhoSSW 93*
Bennett, Anna Elizabeth 1914- *WhoWrEP 92*
Bennett, Antoinette *Law&B 92*
Bennett, Arnold 1867-1931 *BioIn 17, MagSWL [port]*
Bennett, Barbara Curry *ScF&FL 92*
Bennett, Barry Steven 1953- *St&PR 93*
Bennett, Bernice Spitz *WhoWrEP 92*
Bennett, Betsy *BioIn 17*
Bennett, Bettie McKinney 1951- *WhoEmL 93*
Bennett, Betty T. *WhoAm 92, WhoAmW 93, WhoE 93*
Bennett, Bill *MiSFD 9*
Bennett, Billye Jean 1946- *WhoEmL 93*
Bennett, Bo *BioIn 17*
Bennett, Bobbie Jean 1940- *WhoSSW 93*
Bennett, Bradford Carl 1953- *WhoEmL 93*
Bennett, Brian O'Leary 1955- *WhoAm 92*
Bennett, Brian Timothy 1951- *WhoEmL 93*
Bennett, Brian Timothy 1962- *WhoE 93*
Bennett, Bruce David 1948- *WhoEmL 93*
Bennett, Bruce S. 1944- *St&PR 93*
Bennett, Bruce Scott 1958- *WhoEmL 93*
Bennett, Bruce W. 1930- *St&PR 93*
Bennett, Bruce W., Jr. 1930- *WhoAm 92*
Bennett, Bryce H., Jr. 1953- *WhoEmL 93*
Bennett, Burton George 1939- *WhoUN 92, WhoWor 93*
Bennett, C. Leonard 1939- *WhoAm 92*
Bennett, Carl 1920- *WhoAm 92*
Bennett, Carl Edward 1918- *WhoWrEP 92*
Bennett, Carol Elise 1938- *WhoAmW 93, WhoE 93*
Bennett, Carol Elizabeth 1951- *WhoAm 92*
Bennett, Carolyn Linda 1950- *WhoWrEP 92*
Bennett, Catherine Cecilia 1958- *WhoAmW 93*
Bennett, Catherine Dorris 1963- *WhoEmL 93*
Bennett, Catherine June 1950- *WhoAmW 93*
Bennett, Cathy E. d1992 *NewYTBS 92*
Bennett, Cedric Eugene 1926- *WhoWor 93*
Bennett, Charles Alan 1947- *WhoEmL 93*
Bennett, Charles E. 1910- *CngDr 91*
Bennett, Charles Edward 1910- *WhoAm 92, WhoSSW 93*
Bennett, Charles Franklin, Jr. 1926- *WhoAm 92*
Bennett, Charles Leo 1920- *WhoAm 92*
Bennett, Charles Turner 1932- *WhoAm 92*
Bennett, Charles Wilfred, Jr. 1947- *WhoEmL 93*
Bennett, Charlotte McCalla *BioIn 17*
Bennett, Christopher Martin *Law&B 92*
Bennett, Claire Richardson 1928- *WhoAm 92*
Bennett, Clara Marion *AmWomPl*
Bennett, Clarence Henry 1946- *WhoWor 93*
Bennett, Claude F. 1936- *WhoAm 92*
Bennett, Colin J. 1955- *ConAu 138*
Bennett, Compton 1900-1974 *MiSFD 9N*
Bennett, Connie Sue 1955- *WhoAmW 93, WhoEmL 93*
Bennett, Cornelius 1965- *WhoAm 92*
Bennett, Craig W. 1959- *WhoEmL 93*
Bennett, Cynthia 1957- *WhoWor 93*
Bennett, Dale L. 1936- *St&PR 93*
Bennett, Darlene B. 1930- *St&PR 93*
Bennett, Dave 1930- *WhoSSW 93*
Bennett, David *Law&B 92*
Bennett, David Joel 1935- *WhoAm 92*
Bennett, David McAlpine 1954- *WhoEmL 93*
Bennett, David Spencer 1935- *WhoWor 93*
Bennett, DeAnn Auman 1959- *WhoEmL 93*
Bennett, Dennis Alan *Law&B 92*
Bennett, Dick *BioIn 17*
Bennett, Donald Dalton 1936- *WhoAm 92, WhoSSW 93*
Bennett, Doris Margaret *Law&B 92*
Bennett, Dorothea 1929-1990 *BioIn 17*
Bennett, Douglas Carleton 1946- *WhoAm 92*
Bennett, Douglas Marshall 1947- *WhoWor 93*
Bennett, Duane Arthur 1950- *WhoEmL 93*
Bennett, Edmund Taylor 1932- *St&PR 93*
Bennett, Edna d1991 *BioIn 17*
Bennett, Edward *BioIn 17*
Bennett, Edward A. *Law&B 92*
Bennett, Edward A. 1920-1983 *BioIn 17*
Bennett, Edward Henry 1917- *WhoE 93*
Bennett, Edward Herbert, Jr. 1915- *WhoAm 92*
Bennett, Edward J., Jr. 1932- *St&PR 93*
Bennett, Edward James *Law&B 92*
Bennett, Edward James 1941- *WhoAm 92, WhoWor 93*
Bennett, Edward Moore 1927- *WhoAm 92*
Bennett, Edward Virdell, Jr. 1947- *WhoE 93, WhoEmL 93*
Bennett, ElDean 1928- *WhoAm 92*
Bennett, Elizabeth McSpadden 1943- *WhoAm 92*
Bennett, Elizabeth Saakvitne 1949- *WhoAmW 93*
Bennett, Elizabeth Susan 1950- *WhoSSW 93*
Bennett, Ellen Corrinne *AmWomPl*
Bennett, Elsie Margaret 1919- *WhoAmW 93*
Bennett, Enoch Arnold 1867-1931 *BioIn 17*
Bennett, Ernest D., III 1952- *St&PR 93*
Bennett, Eugene F. 1923- *WhoIns 93*
Bennett, Frank Cantelo, Jr. 1930- *WhoAm 92, WhoWor 93*
Bennett, Fred Alus 1939- *St&PR 93*
Bennett, Fred Lawrence 1939- *WhoAm 92*
Bennett, Frederick Elwood 1934- *St&PR 93*
Bennett, G. Delmar 1915- *St&PR 93*
Bennett, G. Kirk, Jr. 1955- *St&PR 93*
Bennett, Gary *MiSFD 9*
Bennett, Gary L. 1940- *ConAu 138, ScF&FL 92*
Bennett, Gary Lee 1940- *WhoAm 92, WhoWrEP 92*
Bennett, Gary Paul 1941- *St&PR 93, WhoAm 92*
Bennett, Gary R. 1951- *St&PR 93*
Bennett, Gemma Morrison *Law&B 92*
Bennett, Geoffrey M. *ScF&FL 92*
Bennett, Geoffrey W. *St&PR 93*
Bennett, George D. *Law&B 92*
Bennett, George F. 1911- *St&PR 93*
Bennett, George F., Jr. 1941- *St&PR 93*
Bennett, George Frederick 1911- *WhoAm 92*
Bennett, George H., Jr. *Law&B 92*
Bennett, George O. 1958- *St&PR 93*
Bennett, Georgette 1946- *St&PR 93, WhoAm 92, WhoE 93, WhoEmL 93*
Bennett, Geraldine Eudora 1921- *WhoAmW 93*
Bennett, Gladys Jenkins 1929- *WhoWrEP 92*
Bennett, Gordon Clowe 1922- *WhoWrEP 92*
Bennett, Grant *St&PR 93*
Bennett, Grover Bryce 1921- *WhoAm 92*
Bennett, Gwendolyn 1902-1981 *BioIn 17*
Bennett, H. Stanley d1992 *NewYTBS 92*
Bennett, H(enry) Stanley 1910-1992 *CurBio 92N*
Bennett, Hal Zina 1936- *ConAu 40NR*
Bennett, Harold Clark 1924- *WhoAm 92*
Bennett, Harold Zina *ConAu 40NR*
Bennett, Harriet Cook 1945- *WhoSSW 93*
Bennett, Harry 1895-1990 *BioIn 17*
Bennett, Harry Louis 1923- *WhoAm 92*
Bennett, Harve 1930- *WhoAm 92*
Bennett, Helen Donele 1948- *WhoEmL 93*
Bennett, Henry James 1942- *St&PR 93*
Bennett, Howard *BioIn 17*
Bennett, Howard Allen 1919- *WhoSSW 93*
Bennett, Hugh Hammond 1881-1960 *BioIn 17*
Bennett, Hywel 1944- *WhoWor 93*
Bennett, Irving 1923- *WhoWrEP 92*
Bennett, Ivan Frank 1919- *WhoAm 92, WhoWor 93*
Bennett, Ivan L. 1922-1990 *BioIn 17*
Bennett, J.A. *WhoScE 91-1*
Bennett, Jack 1934- *DcChlFi*
Bennett, Jack Franklin 1924- *St&PR 93, WhoAm 92*
Bennett, Jacqueline Beekman 1946- *WhoEmL 93*
Bennett, James *BioIn 17*
Bennett, James Austin 1915- *WhoAm 92*
Bennett, James Brown, III 1940- *St&PR 93*
Bennett, James D., Jr. 1936- *St&PR 93*
Bennett, James E. 1920- *St&PR 93*
Bennett, James Edward 1925- *WhoAm 92*
Bennett, James Franklin 1955- *WhoE 93*
Bennett, James Gordon 1795-1872 *JrnUS*
Bennett, James Gordon 1841-1918 *GayN*
Bennett, James Gordon, Jr. 1841-1918 *JrnUS*
Bennett, James Jefferson 1920- *WhoAm 92*
Bennett, James L. 1934- *St&PR 93*
Bennett, James Marvin 1939- *WhoE 93*
Bennett, James Patrick 1957- *WhoEmL 93, WhoSSW 93*
Bennett, James Paul *Law&B 92*
Bennett, James Richard 1932- *WhoSSW 93*
Bennett, James Stark 1947- *WhoAm 92*
Bennett, James T. 1942- *WhoAm 92*
Bennett, Janice *ScF&FL 92*
Bennett, Jarratt Graham 1935- *WhoSSW 93*
Bennett, Jay 1912- *Au&Arts 10 [port], DcAmChF 1960, DcAmChF 1985*
Bennett, Jay 1922- *ScF&FL 92*
Bennett, Jay Brett 1961- *WhoSSW 93*
Bennett, Jean Louise McPherson 1930- *WhoAm 92*
Bennett, Jeff *ScF&FL 92*
Bennett, Jeffrey Alan 1949- *WhoEmL 93*
Bennett, Jeffrey Richard 1948- *WhoEmL 93*
Bennett, Jeremy Bennett 1960- *WhoWor 93*
Bennett, Jerome D. *Law&B 92*
Bennett, Jill 1947- *ScF&FL 92*
Bennett, Jim 1921- *WhoAm 92*
Bennett, Joan 1910-1990 *BioIn 17, IntDcF 2-3 [port]*
Bennett, Joanne Carol 1931- *WhoAmW 93*
Bennett, JoAnne Williams 1945- *WhoCanL 92*
Bennett, Joe Claude 1933- *WhoAm 92*
Bennett, Joel H. 1936- *St&PR 93*
Bennett, Joel Herbert 1936- *WhoAm 92*
Bennett, John *WhoScE 91-1*
Bennett, John 1937- *WhoUN 92*
Bennett, John A. 1943- *St&PR 93*
Bennett, John Caister *BioIn 17*
Bennett, John Campbell White 1948- *WhoEmL 93*
Bennett, John Edward 1954- *WhoE 93*
Bennett, John Frederic 1920- *WhoWrEP 92*
Bennett, John Henry 1947- *WhoSSW 93*
Bennett, John J. 1938- *WhoWrEP 92*
Bennett, John Joseph 1923- *WhoAm 92*
Bennett, John L. 1920- *WhoE 93*
Bennett, John M. 1942- *WhoWrEP 92*
Bennett, John Morrison 1933- *WhoAm 92*
Bennett, John R. 1922- *St&PR 93*
Bennett, John Richard 1952- *WhoEmL 93*
Bennett, John Roscoe 1922- *WhoAm 92*
Bennett, John Townsend, Jr. 1939- *WhoWor 93*
Bennett, Joseph 1831-1911 *Baker 92*
Bennett, Joseph P. 1929- *St&PR 93*
Bennett, Josephine *BioIn 17*
Bennett, Joshua Henry 1952- *WhoE 93*
Bennett, Josiah Quincy 1913-1991 *BioIn 17*
Bennett, Josiah W. d1992 *NewYTBS 92*
Bennett, Josiah W. 1916-1992 *BioIn 17*
Bennett, Kathleen 1946- *ConAu 138*
Bennett, Keith Ervin 1948- *WhoEmL 93*
Bennett, Keith Harry *WhoScE 91-1*
Bennett, Kenneth Alan 1935- *WhoAm 92*
Bennett, Kevin D. *Law&B 92*
Bennett, LaFell Dickinson 1954- *WhoEmL 93*
Bennett, Lance Jay *Law&B 92*
Bennett, Laura *ScF&FL 92*
Bennett, Laura Gilmour *ScF&FL 92*
Bennett, Laurie Jane *Law&B 92*
Bennett, Lawrence Allen 1923- *WhoAm 92*
Bennett, Lawrence Herman 1930- *WhoAm 92*
Bennett, Lawrence T. *Law&B 92*
Bennett, Leeman *BioIn 17*
Bennett, Lerone, Jr. 1928- *BlkAuII 92, WhoAm 92, WhoWrEP 92*
Bennett, Lewis Tilton, Jr. 1940- *WhoWor 93*
Bennett, Lloyd 1935- *WhoSSW 93*
Bennett, Lois 1933- *WhoAmW 93*
Bennett, Lois Carol 1942- *WhoAmW 93*
Bennett, Lonnie Joe 1931- *WhoSSW 93*
Bennett, Louis Lowell 1909-1991 *BioIn 17*
Bennett, Louise (Simone) 1919- *DcLB 117 [port]*
Bennett, Lowell Howard 1913- *WhoWor 93*
Bennett, Lynne Dee 1953- *WhoAmW 93*
Bennett, M.J. *ScF&FL 92*
Bennett, M. Julie 1962- *St&PR 93*
Bennett, Mable Keightley *AmWomPl*
Bennett, Maisha Bobbie Hamilton 1948- *WhoEmL 93*
Bennett, Marcia J. 1945- *ScF&FL 92*
Bennett, Marcia Joanne 1945- *WhoWrEP 92*
Bennett, Marcus C. 1936- *St&PR 93*
Bennett, Margaret Airola 1950- *WhoAmW 93*
Bennett, Margaret Ethel Booker 1923- *WhoAm 92*
Bennett, Margaret Theresa 1950- *WhoEmL 93*
Bennett, Margot 1903-1980 *ScF&FL 92*
Bennett, Marianne *Law&B 92*
Bennett, Marion T. 1914- *CngDr 91*
Bennett, Marion Tinsley 1914- *WhoAm 92*
Bennett, Mark Alan 1959- *WhoSSW 93*
Bennett, Mark Jay 1954- *WhoEmL 93*
Bennett, Marshall Alton, Jr. 1955- *WhoEmL 93*
Bennett, Marshall Goodloe, Jr. 1943- *WhoAm 92, WhoSSW 93*
Bennett, Marsi Ann 1960- *WhoEmL 93*
Bennett, Mary 1918- *WhoAmW 93, WhoWor 93*
Bennett, Mary Connell 1944- *WhoAmW 93*
Bennett, Mary Patrick *Law&B 92*
Bennett, Melanie R. *Law&B 92*
Bennett, Michael *BioIn 17*
Bennett, Michael David 1943- *WhoScE 91-1*
Bennett, Michael Edward 1958- *WhoSSW 93*
Bennett, Michael P. *Law&B 92*
Bennett, Michael Steven 1961- *WhoE 93*
Bennett, Michele *DcCPCAm*
Bennett, Mike *ScF&FL 92*
Bennett, Mildred Jane Martin 1930- *WhoAmW 93, WhoSSW 93*
Bennett, Mildred R. 1909-1989 *BioIn 17*
Bennett, Miriam Frances 1928- *WhoAm 92*
Bennett, Monty Clare 1938- *St&PR 93*
Bennett, Nancy Elaine 1941- *WhoAmW 93*
Bennett, Nancy McCullough 1942- *WhoAmW 93*
Bennett, Nicholas C. 1942- *St&PR 93*
Bennett, Noel McKenzie 1931- *WhoWor 93*
Bennett, Norman E. 1917- *WhoAm 92, WhoWrEP 92*
Bennett, Norman Robert 1932- *ConAu 39NR*
Bennett, Olga Salowich 1925- *WhoAmW 93*
Bennett, Otes 1921- *St&PR 93*
Bennett, Pamela Gale 1938- *WhoAmW 93*
Bennett, Pamela Kay 1957- *WhoAmW 93*
Bennett, Pamela Yvonne 1959- *WhoAmW 93*
Bennett, Patricia Ann Work 1947- *WhoWrEP 92*
Bennett, Paul Lester 1946- *WhoEmL 93*
Bennett, Paul (Lewis) 1921- *WhoWrEP 92*
Bennett, Peggy Elizabeth 1935- *WhoAmW 93*
Bennett, Peter Brian 1931- *WhoAm 92*
Bennett, Peter Dunne 1933- *WhoAm 92*
Bennett, Phil E. 1953- *St&PR 93*
Bennett, Philaeta Virginia 1937- *WhoAmW 93*
Bennett, Philip Anthony 1947- *WhoScE 91-1*
Bennett, Phyllis Dixon 1950- *WhoSSW 93*
Bennett, Ralph Kinney *BioIn 17*
Bennett, Ralph Stephen 1940- *St&PR 93*
Bennett, Ransom, Jr. 1923- *St&PR 93*
Bennett, Rebecca *AmWomPl*
Bennett, Reginald *WhoScE 91-1*
Bennett, Reynold 1918- *WhoAm 92*
Bennett, Richard Bedford 1870-1947 *DcTwHis*
Bennett, Richard C. *MiSFD 9*
Bennett, Richard Clark 1941- *WhoWor 93*
Bennett, Richard Douglas 1948- *WhoEmL 93*
Bennett, Richard E. 1933- *St&PR 93*
Bennett, Richard Earle 1919- *WhoAm 92*

Bennett, Richard Edward 1954- WhoEmL 93
Bennett, Richard Gerald 1942- WhoSSW 93
Bennett, Richard Henry 1939- St&PR 93
Bennett, Richard J. Law&B 92
Bennett, Richard Joseph 1917- WhoAm 92
Bennett, Richard L. 1952- WhoEmL 93
Bennett, Richard Rodney 1936- Baker 92, BioIn 17, CurBio 92 [port], OxDcOp
Bennett, Richard T. 1945- St&PR 93
Bennett, Richard Thomas 1930- WhoAm 92
Bennett, Rita 1951- St&PR 93
Bennett, Robert 1952- WhoEmL 93
Bennett, Robert Alvin 1947- WhoEmL 93
Bennett, Robert Cobb 1941- WhoSSW 93
Bennett, Robert Earl, Jr. 1952- WhoSSW 93
Bennett, Robert Frederick 1927- BioIn 17, WhoAm 92
Bennett, Robert J. 1941- St&PR 93
Bennett, Robert John WhoScE 91-1
Bennett, Robert John 1941- WhoAm 92
Bennett, Robert LeRoy 1937- WhoE 93
Bennett, Robert Louis 1925- WhoWor 93
Bennett, Robert Menzies 1926- WhoAm 92
Bennett, Robert Putnam 1932- WhoSSW 93
Bennett, Robert Royce 1926- WhoAm 92
Bennett, Robert Russell 1894-1981 Baker 92, BioIn 17
Bennett, Robert S. BioIn 17, Law&B 92
Bennett, Robert Stephen 1939- NewYTBS 92 [port]
Bennett, Robin L. Law&B 92
Bennett, Roderick WhoScE 91-1
Bennett, Rodney MiSFD 9
Bennett, Roger Edman 1955- WhoEmL 93, WhoSSW 93
Bennett, Ron Stephan 1953- WhoEmL 93
Bennett, Ronald Lee 1942- St&PR 93
Bennett, Ronald Thomas 1944- WhoAm 92
Bennett, Roy 1912-1989 BioIn 17
Bennett, Roy F. 1928- St&PR 93
Bennett, Russell Odbert 1915- WhoAm 92
Bennett, Sabrina Ross 1966- WhoAmW 93
Bennett, Saul 1936- WhoAm 92
Bennett, Scott Boyce 1939- WhoAm 92
Bennett, Scott L. Law&B 92
Bennett, Scott Lawrence 1949- St&PR 93
Bennett, Shannon Rae 1952- WhoAmW 93
Bennett, Sharon Kay 1947- WhoEmL 93, WhoSSW 93
Bennett, Shirley Ann 1952- WhoAmW 93
Bennett, Stanley T. 1949- St&PR 93
Bennett, Stephen A. 1938- WhoE 93
Bennett, Steven Alan 1953- St&PR 93
Bennett, Steven Fredrick 1959- WhoWor 93
Bennett, Stuart C. 1949- WhoScE 91-1
Bennett, Susan Carroll 1953- WhoEmL 93
Bennett, Susan Elizabeth 1961- WhoAmW 93
Bennett, Susan Fentress 1947- WhoAmW 93
Bennett, T. Wesley 1913- BiDAMSp 1989
Bennett, Terence WhoScE 91-1
Bennett, Terry Joe 1953- WhoSSW 93
Bennett, Thea ScF&FL 92
Bennett, Thomas A. St&PR 93
Bennett, Thomas Albert 1949- WhoEmL 93
Bennett, Thomas B., III 1947- St&PR 93
Bennett, Thomas E. 1929- WhoAm 92
Bennett, Thomas Edward 1929- St&PR 93
Bennett, Thomas H. Law&B 92
Bennett, Thomas LeRoy, Jr. 1942- WhoAm 92
Bennett, Thomas Peter 1937- WhoAm 92, WhoSSW 93
Bennett, Thomas R. Law&B 92
Bennett, Thomas William 1954- WhoWor 93
Bennett, Tony BioIn 17
Bennett, Tony 1926- Baker 92, WhoAm 92
Bennett, Tracy d1991 BioIn 17
Bennett, W. Craig d1990 BioIn 17
Bennett, Ward BioIn 17
Bennett, Wendell Clark 1905-1953 IntDcAn
Bennett, William WhoAm 92
Bennett, William E. WhoAm 92
Bennett, William E. 1946- St&PR 93
Bennett, William G. 1924- St&PR 93, WhoAm 92
Bennett, William Henry BioIn 17
Bennett, William Henry, III Law&B 92
Bennett, William John 1943- BioIn 17
Bennett, William Leo, Jr. 1921- WhoSSW 93
Bennett, William Michael 1938- WhoAm 92
Bennett, William Ralph, Jr. 1930- WhoAm 92
Bennett, William S. Law&B 92
Bennett, William Sterndale 1816-1875 Baker 92
Bennett, Winfield Scott, III 1946- WhoEmL 93, WhoSSW 93
Bennett, Winslow Wood 1925- WhoAm 92
Bennett-Brown, Mary 1958- St&PR 93
Bennett-Smith, Stephanie M. 1941- WhoAmW 93
Bennewitz, Antonin 1833-1926 Baker 92
Benney, Douglas Mabley 1922- WhoAm 92, WhoE 93, WhoWor 93
Benney, Robert 1904- WhoAm 92
Benni, Stefano 1947- ScF&FL 92
Bennia, Denise Carty- 1947-1990 BioIn 17
Bennice, Angelo Philip 1931- WhoE 93
Bennici, Andrea 1942- WhoWor 93
Bennie, R.T. 1933- St&PR 93
Bennigsen, Levin August 1745-1826 HarEnMi
Bennigsen-Foerder, Rudolf von 1926-1989 BioIn 17
Benning, Arthur E. 1929- St&PR 93
Benning, James David 1957- WhoSSW 93
Benning, John A. Law&B 92
Benning, John Alan 1934- St&PR 93
Benning, Joseph Francis, Jr. 1922- WhoAm 92
Benninger, Edward C., Jr. 1942- WhoAm 92
Benninger, Edward Charles, Jr. 1942- St&PR 93
Benninger, Fred 1917- St&PR 93, WhoAm 92
Benningfield, Anna Beth 1940- WhoAmW 93
Benninghoff, William Shiffer 1918- WhoAm 92
Benninghoven, Alfred 1932- WhoScE 91-3
Bennington, Leslie Orville, Jr. 1946- WhoEmL 93
Bennington, Ronald Kent 1936- WhoAm 92
Bennington, Timothy R. 1944- St&PR 93
Bennington, William Jay 1939- WhoAm 92
Bennink, Jan 1956- WhoWor 93
Bennion, Douglas Noel 1935- WhoAm 92
Bennion, Milton 1870-1953 BioIn 17
Bennion, Sherilyn Cox 1935- ConAu 137
Bennis, Susan BioIn 17
Bennis, Warren Gameliel 1925- WhoAm 92, WhoWor 93
Bennis, William Joseph 1946- St&PR 93
Bennison, Allan Parnell 1918- WhoSSW 93
Bennison, W.D. 1944- St&PR 93
Bennitt, Michael Paul 1955- WhoEmL 93
Benno, II, Bishop of Osnabruck c. 1020-1088 BioIn 17
Bennon, Saul 1914- WhoAm 92
Benns, Robin Anise 1958- WhoE 93
Benny, Jack 1894-1974 BioIn 17, QDrFCA 92 [port]
Benny, Jeffrey Allan 1956- St&PR 93
Benny, Mike BioIn 17
Beno-Clark, Candice Lynn 1951- WhoAmW 93, WhoEmL 93
Benois, Alexandre 1870-1960 IntDcOp, OxDcOp
Benois, Nadia 1894-1975 OxDcOp
Benois, Nicola 1901-1988 IntDcOp, OxDcOp
Benoist, Alain de 1943- BioIn 17
Benoist, Andre 1879-1953 Baker 92
Benoist, Charles Augustin 1861-1936 BioIn 17
Benoist, Elizabeth S. 1901- ScF&FL 92
Benoist, Francois 1794-1878 Baker 92
Benoist, Jean-Marie BioIn 17
Benoit, Andre 1938- St&PR 93
Benoit, Carolyn Fay 1945- WhoAmW 93
Benoit, Donald Anthony 1936- WhoWor 93
Benoit, Francois DcCPCAm
Benoit, Hendra ScF&FL 92
Benoit, Henri 1928- WhoWor 93
Benoit, Henri Charles 1921- WhoScE 91-2
Benoit, Jacques 1941- WhoCanL 92
Benoit, Jacques W. 1941- MiSFD 9
Benoit, James Leo 1951- WhoSSW 93
Benoit, Jean-Pierre Robert 1930- WhoWor 93
Benoit, Joan BioIn 17
Benoit, Leroy James 1913- WhoAm 92
Benoit, Nancy Louise 1944- WhoAmW 93
Benoit, Normand George 1949- WhoEmL 93
Benoit, Paul Law&B 92
Benoit, Peter 1834-1901 Baker 92
Benoit, R.E. 1947- St&PR 93
Benoit, Richard Armand 1942- WhoE 93
Benoit, Victor DcCPCAm
Benoit-Guyod, Jean-Louis Alain 1938- WhoWor 93
Benoliel, Peter Andre 1932- WhoAm 92
Benovic, Adam 1943- WhoScE 91-4
Benowitz, Robert Barry 1934- WhoE 93
Benoy, Gaston J.P. 1931- WhoScE 91-2
Ben-Porath, Yoram d1992 NewYTBS 92
Benque, J.P. 1947- WhoScE 91-2
Ben Raphael, David d1992 BioIn 17, NewYTBS 92
Benrubi, Bonni 1953- WhoE 93
Bensaid, M. WhoScE 91-2
Bensaid-Mrejen, Dody 1936- WhoWor 93
Bensch, Klaus George 1928- WhoAm 92
Bensch, Leonard Ernest 1946- St&PR 93
Benscheidt, Steven Eugene 1954- WhoEmL 93
Benscher, Walter 1923- St&PR 93
Benschip, Gary John 1947- WhoEmL 93
Benschneider, Don Carl 1946- WhoSSW 93
Benscuter, Thomas Donald 1950- St&PR 93
Bensel, Carolyn Kirkbride 1941- WhoAm 92, WhoAmW 93
Bensen, D.R. 1927- ScF&FL 92
Bensen, Robert George 1929- St&PR 93
Bensen, Roger D. 1935- St&PR 93
Benserade, Isaac de 1613?-1691 OxDcOp
Ben-Shir, Rya Helen 1955- WhoEmL 93
Benshoof, Janet BioIn 17
Benshoof, Janet L. 1947- WhoAmW 93
Benshoof, Terrence James 1946- WhoEmL 93
Bensiker, Tina Renee Johns Law&B 92
Bensimon, Gilles BioIn 17
Bensimon, Rachel 1933- St&PR 93
Bensinger, David August 1926- WhoAm 92
Bensinger, Lenore Cooper 1943- WhoWrEP 92
Bensinger, Peter Benjamin 1936- WhoAm 92
Bensinger, Steven J. 1955- WhoIns 93
Bensink, John ScF&FL 92
Bensink, John Robert 1948- WhoWrEP 92
Bensko, John 1949- WhoWrEP 92
Bensko, Robert Ray, Jr. 1959- WhoSSW 93
Bensky, Jonathan Michael 1946- WhoWor 93
Bensman, Charles J. 1933- WhoSSW 93
Benso, William Eldon 1937- St&PR 93
Bensol, Oscar ConAu 37NR
Benson, Alvin K. 1944- WhoWor 93
Benson, Andrew Alm 1917- WhoAm 92
Benson, Andrew B. 1940- St&PR 93
Benson, AnnDrea McFarlane Law&B 92
Benson, Arthur Christopher 1862-1925 BioIn 17
Benson, Barbara Ellen 1943- WhoAm 92, WhoAmW 93, WhoE 93
Benson, Barbara S. Law&B 92
Benson, Bernice LaVina WhoAmW 93
Benson, Betty G. 1943- WhoAmW 93
Benson, Betty Jones 1928- WhoSSW 93
Benson, Bradley Duane 1959- WhoEmL 93
Benson, Brian Joseph 1941- WhoSSW 93
Benson, Carla Louise WhoAmW 93
Benson, Charles Edward 1912- WhoWor 93
Benson, Charles Everett 1937- WhoE 93
Benson, Charles Scott 1922- WhoAm 92
Benson, Clara Mays 1932- WhoWrEP 92
Benson, Colleen Kragelund 1941- WhoAmW 93
Benson, David F. 1949- St&PR 93
Benson, David William 1931- WhoAm 92
Benson, Debra Ann 1953- WhoAmW 93, WhoEmL 93, WhoWor 93
Benson, Dee Vance 1948- WhoAm 92
Benson, Dennis N. 1943- St&PR 93
Benson, Donald E. 1930- St&PR 93
Benson, Donald Erick 1930- WhoAm 92, WhoWor 93
Benson, E.F. 1867-1940 BioIn 17, ScF&FL 92
Benson, Edward Frederic 1867-1940 BioIn 17
Benson, Edwin Welburn, Jr. 1945- WhoSSW 93
Benson, Eliot H. d1991 BioIn 17
Benson, Elizabeth P. BioIn 17
Benson, Eugene 1928- WhoCanL 92
Benson, Ezra Taft BioIn 17
Benson, Family BioIn 17
Benson, George BioIn 17
Benson, George 1943- ConMus 9 [port], WhoAm 92
Benson, George Charles Sumner 1908- WhoAm 92
Benson, George Leonard 1934- WhoAm 92
Benson, Gordon, Jr. 1936- ScF&FL 92
Benson, Gregg Carl Law&B 92
Benson, Gregory Vincent 1954- St&PR 93
Benson, Harry J. Law&B 92
Benson, I. John 1946- St&PR 93
Benson, J. Jeffrey 1957- WhoEmL 93
Benson, Jack M. 1933- St&PR 93
Benson, Jackson J. BioIn 17
Benson, James Albert 1930- St&PR 93
Benson, James B. Law&B 92
Benson, James Carl 1935- WhoAm 92
Benson, James DeWayne 1925- WhoAm 92
Benson, James O. 1933- St&PR 93
Benson, Janet Elizabeth 1954- WhoEmL 93
Benson, Jeffrey L. Law&B 92
Benson, Jerry S. 1932- St&PR 93
Benson, Joan 1929- Baker 92
Benson, Joanne 1943- WhoAmW 93
Benson, John Alexander, Jr. 1921- WhoAm 92
Benson, John Schuler 1927- St&PR 93
Benson, Jon G. St&PR 93
Benson, Joseph 1919-1991 BioIn 17
Benson, Judith Anne 1951- WhoWor 93
Benson, Judith K. 1950- St&PR 93
Benson, Julie Morton 1937- St&PR 93
Benson, K. Blair d1990 BioIn 17
Benson, Karen Elizabeth 1957- WhoSSW 93
Benson, Kathleen BioIn 17
Benson, Kenneth Peter 1927- St&PR 93, WhoAm 92
Benson, Kenneth S. 1937- St&PR 93
Benson, Kenneth Samuel 1937- WhoAm 92
Benson, Kenneth Victor 1929- WhoAm 92
Benson, Kim Derrick 1954- WhoWrEP 92
Benson, Larry Dean 1929- WhoWrEP 92
Benson, Laura F. 1950- WhoEmL 93
Benson, Lenni Beth 1958- WhoEmL 93
Benson, Lenore J. WhoAm 92, WhoAmW 93
Benson, Leo, III 1938- St&PR 93
Benson, Linda Kay 1947- WhoAmW 93
Benson, Louis BioIn 17
Benson, Lucy Peters Wilson 1927- WhoAm 92, WhoAmW 93
Benson, Lucy Wilson 1927- St&PR 93
Benson, Lyle Charles 1949- WhoEmL 93, WhoSSW 93
Benson, Marie Chapman 1909- WhoAmW 93
Benson, Mark James 1955- St&PR 93
Benson, Mary A. AmWomPl
Benson, Mary Ellen 1945- WhoAmW 93
Benson, Matthew T. 1957- WhoWrEP 92
Benson, Michael ScF&FL 92
Benson, Michael Kent 1954- BiDAMSp 1989
Benson, Michaela Chasser 1948- WhoAmW 93
Benson, Mildred 1905- BioIn 17
Benson, Mildred (Augustine Wirt) 1905- MajAI
Benson, Mildred Wirt MajAI
Benson, Morton 1924- WhoAm 92
Benson, Nancy Jane 1953- WhoEmL 93
Benson, Nannette I. 1954- St&PR 93
Benson, Nella ScF&FL 92
Benson, Nettie Lee 1905- WhoAm 92
Benson, Patricia A. 1958- St&PR 93
Benson, Paul 1918- WhoAm 92
Benson, Peter 1956- ConAu 137
Benson, Peter Allen 1950- St&PR 93
Benson, Priscilla Jenkins 1940- WhoE 93
Benson, Purnell Handy 1913-1992 BioIn 17
Benson, Raymond Ellis 1924- WhoE 93
Benson, Richard BioIn 17
Benson, Richard A. 1943- St&PR 93
Benson, Richard Edward 1936- St&PR 93
Benson, Robby BioIn 17
Benson, Robby 1956- MiSFD 9
Benson, Robert Clinton, Jr. 1946- WhoE 93, WhoWor 93
Benson, Robert Elliott 1916- WhoAm 92
Benson, Robert Eugene 1940- WhoAm 92
Benson, Robert Frederick 1935- WhoE 93
Benson, Robert L. 1942- WhoAm 92
Benson, Robert Leslie 1947- WhoAm 92
Benson, Robert Slater 1942- St&PR 93
Benson, Robert W. Law&B 92, St&PR 93
Benson, Ronald Edward 1936- WhoAm 92, WhoSSW 93
Benson, Sandra Jean 1949- WhoAmW 93
Benson, Sidney William 1918- WhoAm 92
Benson, Steve 1949- WhoWrEP 92
Benson, Steven Clark 1954- WhoWor 93
Benson, T.R. Law&B 92
Benson, Thomas Avery 1953- St&PR 93
Benson, Thomas Hayden 1945- WhoAm 92
Benson, Thomas Quentin 1943- WhoAm 92
Benson, Tom 1927- WhoAm 92, WhoSSW 93
Benson, Tom Erlin 1937- St&PR 93
Benson, Valerie Estes 1958- WhoAmW 93
Benson, Warren Frank 1924- WhoAm 92
Benson, Wendy BioIn 17
Benson, William E. 1876-1915 EncAACR
Benson, William Edward 1923- WhoSSW 93
Benson, William Edward Barnes 1919- WhoAm 92, WhoE 93

Benson, William Jeffrey 1922- *St&PR 93*
Benson, Willie McWhorter 1949- *WhoE 93*
Benson, Woodruff Whitman 1942- *WhoWor 93*
Benson O'Connor, Sara Elizabeth 1960- *WhoAmW 93*
Bensoussan *WhoScE 91-2*
Bensoussan, Yves Daniel 1947- *WhoUN 92*
Benster, Brian M. *WhoScE 91-1*
Benstock, Bernard 1930- *WhoSSW 93*
Benstock, Gerald M. 1930- *St&PR 93*
Benstock, Gerald Martin 1930- *WhoAm 92*
Benstock, Marcy *BioIn 17*
Benston, Alice Naomi 1931- *WhoAmW 93*
Benston, George James 1932- *WhoAm 92*
Bensussen, Estelle Esther 1926- *WhoAm 92*
Bent, Alan Edward 1939- *WhoAm 92*
Bent, Daniel A. 1947- *WhoAm 92*
Bent, Devin 1940- *WhoSSW 93*
Bent, Gardner L. 1923- *St&PR 93*
Bent, Henry Albert 1926- *WhoAm 92*
Bent, Ian D(avid) 1938- *Baker 92*
Bent, Jan Brigham 1939- *WhoAmW 93*
Bent, Jennifer *BlkAuII 92*
Bent, Jorj *ScF&FL 92*
Bent, Margaret (Hilda) 1940- *Baker 92*
Bent, Michael William 1951- *WhoEmL 93*
Bent, Noreen C. *Law&B 92*
Bent, Robert Demo 1928- *WhoAm 92*
Bentall, H. Clark 1915- *St&PR 93*
Bentall, Robert Gilmour 1922- *St&PR 93*
Bentall, Shirley Franklyn 1926- *WhoAm 92*
Bentcliffe, Eric 1927?-1992 *ScF&FL 92*
Bentcover, Bruce Jay 1954- *WhoAm 92, WhoEmL 93*
Bente, Wolfgang 1927- *WhoWor 93*
Bentel, Dwight 1909- *WhoAm 92*
Bentel, Frederick Richard 1928- *WhoAm 92*
Bentel, Maria-Luise Ramona Azzarone 1928- *WhoAm 92, WhoAmW 93*
Bentel, Robert B. 1938- *St&PR 93*
Bentele, Raymond F. 1936- *WhoAm 92*
Bentele, Raymond Frank 1936- *St&PR 93*
Benten, Leona *NewYTBS 92 [port]*
Benter, George H. 1942- *St&PR 93*
Benthall, Deedra 1946- *WhoEmL 93, WhoSSW 93*
Bentham, Ethel 1861-1931 *BioIn 17*
Bentham, George Wesley 1944- *St&PR 93*
Bentham, Jeremy 1748-1832 *BioIn 17, NinCLC 38 [port]*
Bentham, Jeremy 1956- *ScF&FL 92*
Bentinck, George 1802-1848 *BioIn 17*
Bentinck-Smith, William 1914- *WhoAm 92, WhoE 93*
Bentine, Michael 1922- *ScF&FL 92*
Bentini, G.G. 1939- *WhoScE 91-3*
Bentini, Gian Giuseppe *WhoScE 91-3*
Bentivegna, Gerald J. 1949- *St&PR 93*
Bentivegna, Peter Ignatius 1941- *WhoE 93*
Bentivegna, Santo William 1955- *WhoE 93*
Bentlage, Debra S. 1957- *WhoE 93*
Bentley, Annette Camnetar 1939- *WhoE 93*
Bentley, Antoinette C. 1937- *WhoIns 93*
Bentley, Antoinette Cozell *Law&B 92*
Bentley, Antoinette Cozell 1937- *St&PR 93, WhoAm 92, WhoAmW 93*
Bentley, Barbara *WhoScE 91-1*
Bentley, Carolyn E. 1923- *St&PR 93*
Bentley, Charles Fred 1914- *WhoAm 92*
Bentley, Charles Raymond 1929- *WhoAm 92*
Bentley, Charles W., Sr. 1915- *St&PR 93*
Bentley, Clarence Edward 1921- *WhoAm 92*
Bentley, Danny L. 1958- *St&PR 93, WhoIns 93*
Bentley, David Michael 1959- *WhoEmL 93*
Bentley, Dewey Jordan 1933- *WhoSSW 93*
Bentley, Earl Wilson, Jr. 1920- *St&PR 93*
Bentley, Edward Nelson 1948- *WhoEmL 93*
Bentley, Eric 1916- *BioIn 17, WhoAm 92, WhoWrEP 92*
Bentley, Eric Jon *Law&B 92*
Bentley, Fred Douglas, Sr. 1926- *WhoSSW 93, WhoWor 93*
Bentley, G. Firman 1934- *St&PR 93*
Bentley, George 1936- *WhoScE 91-1*
Bentley, Gerald Eades 1901- *WhoAm 92*
Bentley, Gladys *BioIn 17*
Bentley, Gordon W. 1946- *St&PR 93*
Bentley, Gregory S. *Law&B 92*
Bentley, Harry Thomas, III 1942- *WhoSSW 93*
Bentley, Helen Delich *CngDr 91, WhoAm 92, WhoAmW 93, WhoE 93*
Bentley, Helen Delich 1923?- *BioIn 17, JrnUS*
Bentley, J.D. *Law&B 92*
Bentley, James Daniel 1945- *WhoAm 92*
Bentley, James Luther 1937- *WhoAm 92*
Bentley, James Robert 1942- *WhoSSW 93*
Bentley, Jayne *ConAu 139*
Bentley, Jeanette B. *Law&B 92*
Bentley, John Gregory 1961- *WhoEmL 93, WhoSSW 93*
Bentley, John Joseph 1934- *St&PR 93*
Bentley, Judith (McBride) 1945- *WhoWrEP 92*
Bentley, Julia 1958- *St&PR 93*
Bentley, Kenneth Chessar 1935- *WhoAm 92*
Bentley, Kenton Earl 1927- *WhoAm 92*
Bentley, Lee M. *WhoAm 92*
Bentley, Margaret Esplin 1947- *WhoE 93*
Bentley, Ormond L. 1935- *WhoIns 93*
Bentley, Orville George 1918- *WhoAm 92*
Bentley, Peter *ScF&FL 92*
Bentley, Peter 1915- *St&PR 93, WhoAm 92*
Bentley, Peter John Gerald 1930- *WhoAm 92*
Bentley, Richard 1794-1871 *BioIn 17*
Bentley, Richard Norcross 1937- *WhoE 93*
Bentley, Sean Singer 1954- *WhoWrEP 92*
Bentley, Sharon Ruth 1947- *WhoAmW 93*
Bentley, Stephen *BioIn 17*
Bentley, Susan E. 1950- *WhoSSW 93*
Bentley, Thomas H., Jr. 1923- *St&PR 93*
Bentley, Thomas Roy 1931- *WhoAm 92*
Bentley, Tim 1953- *WhoEmL 93, WhoSSW 93*
Bentley, William Elbert 1941- *St&PR 93*
Bentley, William H. 1931- *St&PR 93*
Bentley, William Ross 1938- *WhoE 93*
Bently, Donald E. 1924- *St&PR 93*
Bently, Donald Emery 1924- *WhoWor 93*
Bento, Luis Filipe Lopes 1960- *WhoWor 93*
Bentoera, Raymond *DcCPCAm*
Bentoiu, Pascal 1927- *Baker 92*
Benton, Allen Haydon 1921- *WhoAm 92*
Benton, Andrew Keith 1952- *WhoEmL 93*
Benton, Anthony Stuart 1949- *WhoEmL 93*
Benton, Auburn Edgar 1926- *WhoAm 92*
Benton, Bozena Maria 1955- *WhoWor 93*
Benton, Brook 1931-1988 *SoulM*
Benton, David Charles 1954- *WhoEmL 93*
Benton, Deborah Sally 1958- *WhoEmL 93*
Benton, Edward Henry 1950- *WhoE 93, WhoEmL 93*
Benton, Edward M. 1906- *St&PR 93*
Benton, Eric R. *Law&B 92*
Benton, Faye Louise 1939- *WhoAmW 93*
Benton, Fletcher 1931- *WhoAm 92*
Benton, Gene Ray 1933- *St&PR 93*
Benton, George Stock 1917- *WhoAm 92*
Benton, Geraldine Ann 1960- *WhoEmL 93*
Benton, Gladys Gay 1906- *WhoWor 93*
Benton, Hugh Arthur 1929- *WhoAm 92*
Benton, Jack Mitchell 1941- *St&PR 93, WhoWor 93*
Benton, Jean Elizabeth 1943- *WhoAmW 93*
Benton, Jeffrey T. 1953- *St&PR 93*
Benton, Jesse L. 1942- *WhoSSW 93*
Benton, Joel 1832-1911 *JrnUS*
Benton, Joseph *Baker 92*
Benton, Joseph C. *Law&B 92*
Benton, Joseph (Horace) 1898-1975 *Baker 92*
Benton, Juliette T. d1991 *BioIn 17*
Benton, Lyn L. 1950- *WhoEmL 93*
Benton, Mary Josephine 1925- *WhoE 93*
Benton, Nicholas 1926- *WhoE 93*
Benton, Nicholas Frederick 1944- *WhoSSW 93*
Benton, Philip Eglin, Jr. 1928- *St&PR 93, WhoAm 92, WhoWor 93*
Benton, Rita 1881- *AmWomPl*
Benton, Rita 1918-1980 *Baker 92*
Benton, Robert 1932- *MiSFD 9*
Benton, Robert Austin, Jr. 1921- *WhoAm 92*
Benton, Robert Dean 1929- *WhoAm 92*
Benton, Ronald J. 1957- *St&PR 93*
Benton, Thomas Hart 1782-1858 *PolPar*
Benton, Thomas Hart 1889-1975 *BioIn 17*
Benton, Timothy Thomas 1948- *WhoEmL 93*
Benton, William Pettigrew 1923- *WhoAm 92*
Benton-Borghi, Beatrice Hope 1946- *WhoAmW 93, WhoEmL 93*
Bentonelli, Joseph (Horace) 1898-1975 *Baker 92*
Bento Silva, Jorge Manuel 1961- *WhoWor 93*
Bentrup, Friedrich W. 1935- *WhoScE 91-3*
Bentsen, Bent Guttorm 1926- *WhoScE 91-4*
Bentsen, Cheryl 1950- *ConAu 138*
Bentsen, Harry Richard 1932- *St&PR 93*
Bentsen, Kenneth Edward 1926- *WhoAm 92*
Bentsen, Lloyd 1921- *CngDr 91, WhoAm 92, WhoSSW 93*
Bentsen, Lloyd M. 1921- *PolPar*
Bentsen, Lloyd Millard, Jr. 1921- *NewYTBS 92*
Bentsen, Martin James 1954- *St&PR 93*
Bentyne, Cheryl c. 1954- See Manhattan Transfer, The *ConMus 8*
Bentz, Catherine M. *Law&B 92*
Bentz, Dale Monroe 1919- *WhoAm 92*
Bentz, Frederick Jacob 1922- *WhoAm 92*
Bentz, Hans-Joachim 1946- *WhoWor 93*
Bentz, Henry William 1930- *St&PR 93*
Bentz, Susan Marie 1952- *WhoAmW 93*
Bentz, William Frederick 1940- *WhoAm 92*
Bentzen, Niels 1920- *WhoWor 93*
Bentzin, Charles Gilbert 1932- *WhoAm 92, WhoIns 93*
Bentzlin, Stephen E. *BioIn 17*
Bentzon, Jorgen 1897-1951 *Baker 92*
Bentzon, Michael Weis *WhoScE 91-2*
Bentzon, Niels Viggo 1919- *Baker 92*
Benua, Richard Squier 1921- *WhoAm 92*
Benucci, Francesco c. 1745-1824 *Baker 92, IntDcOp, OxDcOp*
Benuzzi, Felice *BioIn 17*
Ben Vannah, Joan 1967- *WhoEmL 93*
Benveniste, Asa 1925-1990 *BioIn 17*
Benveniste, Jacob 1921- *WhoAm 92*
Benveniste, Jacques 1935- *WhoScE 91-2*
Benveniste, Teri Ann 1958- *WhoAmW 93*
Benvenuti, Paolo *WhoScE 91-3*
Benvenuti, Tommaso 1838-1906 *Baker 92*
Benvenuto, Adriano 1933- *WhoWor 93*
Benvenuto, Charles J. *Law&B 92*
Benvenuto, Edoardo G.B. 1940- *WhoScE 91-3*
Benvenuto, Elaine Elizabeth 1943- *WhoAmW 93*
Benvenuto, Watler Raymond 1955- *WhoWor 93*
Benway, Alfred J. 1939- *St&PR 93*
Ben Yahia, Habib 1938- *WhoWor 93*
Benyas, Pamela Fran 1953- *WhoAmW 93*
Ben-Yehuda, Eliezer 1858-1922 *BioIn 17*
Ben-Yehuda, Nachman *ScF&FL 92*
Benyei, Candace Reed 1946- *WhoAm 92, WhoEmL 93*
Benyo, Joseph *St&PR 93*
Benyo, Richard Stephen 1946- *WhoAm 92, WhoWor 93, WhoWrEP 92*
Ben-Yohanan, Asher 1929- *Baker 92*
Benz, Arnold Otto 1945- *WhoWor 93*
Benz, Barry A. 1955- *WhoEmL 93*
Benz, Carl Friedrich 1844-1929 *BioIn 17*
Benz, Charles *St&PR 93*
Benz, Edmund Woodward, Sr. 1911- *WhoSSW 93*
Benz, Edward John 1923- *WhoAm 92*
Benz, Gary David *Law&B 92*
Benz, Georg A. 1926- *WhoScE 91-4*
Benz, George Albert 1926- *WhoAm 92*
Benz, Gregory Paul 1953- *WhoEmL 93*
Benz, Harry R. 1937- *St&PR 93*
Benz, Joan Ryder 1948- *WhoAmW 93*
Benz, Linda Lou 1957- *WhoEmL 93*
Benz, Obie *MiSFD 9*
Benz, Paul A. 1938- *St&PR 93*
Benz, Walter 1931- *WhoWor 93*
Benza, Louis Lawrence *Law&B 92*
Benze, James Gauss, Jr. 1952- *WhoE 93*
Benzell, Mimi 1922-1970 *Baker 92*
Benzenhafer, Del A. 1959- *St&PR 93*
Benzer, Seymour 1921- *WhoAm 92*
Benzi, Gianmartino 1931- *WhoScE 91-3*
Benzi, Roberto 1937- *Baker 92*
Benzian, John *Law&B 92*
Benziger, Robert A. *Law&B 92*
Benzin, Michael Eric 1964- *WhoE 93*
Benzine, Mostapha 1943- *WhoUN 92*
Benzing, Cynthia Dell 1951 *WhoE 93*
Benzing, Louis Henry 1926- *St&PR 93*
Benzinger, Michael 1951- *ConEn*
Benzinger, Ray Anthony 1955- *St&PR 93*
Benzinger, Raymond Burdette 1938- *WhoAm 92, WhoWor 93*
Benzinger, Rolf Hans 1935- *WhoSSW 93*
Ben-Zion 1897-1987 *BioIn 17*
Benzle, Curtis Munhall 1949- *WhoEmL 93, WhoWor 93*
Benzle, Suzan 1950- *WhoEmL 93*
Benzon, Honorio Tabal 1946- *WhoEmL 93*
Ben-Zvi, Phillip N. 1942- *St&PR 93*
Ben-Zvi, Phillip Norman 1942- *WhoAm 92, WhoIns 93*
Ben-Zvi, Yitzhak 1884-1963 *DcTwHis*
Beohm, Richard Thomas 1943- *WhoSSW 93*
Beoletto, James A. *Law&B 92*
Beona, Gerard Motawiya 1950- *WhoAsAP 91*
Beozzo, Sylvester Anthony 1952- *WhoEmL 93*
Bepko, Gerald Lewis 1940- *WhoAm 92*
Bepler, Stephen Edward 1942- *St&PR 93*
Beque, Robert Roger 1927- *WhoWor 93*
Bequette, B. Wayne 1957- *WhoE 93*
Bequette, Doris Elaine 1934- *WhoAmW 93*
Bera, Regina Helen 1938- *WhoE 93*
Beracha, Barry Harris 1942- *WhoAm 92*
Berain, Jean 1637-1711 *OxDcOp*
Beral, Harold 1939- *St&PR 93*
Berall, Frank Stewart 1929- *WhoAm 92, WhoWor 93*
Beran, Denis Carl 1935- *WhoAm 92, WhoE 93*
Beran, James T. *Law&B 92*
Beran, Norbert 1930- *WhoScE 91-3*
Beran, Rudolf Jaroslav Vaclav 1943- *WhoAm 92*
Beranek, Bruce Frank 1938- *St&PR 93*
Beranek, Leo Leroy 1914- *WhoAm 92, WhoWor 93*
Beranger, Clara *AmWomPl*
Berard, Andre *BioIn 17*
Berard, Andre 1940- *St&PR 93, WhoAm 92*
Berard, Armand 1904-1989 *BioIn 17*
Berard, Clement A. *Law&B 92*
Berard, Guy 1955- *WhoWor 93*
Berard, Paul Michael 1946- *WhoEmL 93*
Berard, William Burnet 1921- *St&PR 93*
Berardelli, Francis Mario 1930- *St&PR 93*
Berardi, Angelo c. 1630-1694 *Baker 92*
Berardi, Michael Anthony, Jr. 1959- *WhoEmL 93*
Berardi, Ronald Stephen 1943- *WhoE 93, WhoWor 93*
Berardino, Thomas Joseph 1941- *St&PR 93*
Berardo, Felix Mario 1934- *WhoSSW 93*
Berasategui, Vicente Ernesto 1934- *WhoUN 92*
Berat, Frederic 1800-1855 *Baker 92*
Beraud, Nancy Kathleen 1936- *WhoAmW 93*
Berbary, Maurice Shehadeh 1923- *WhoAm 92, WhoSSW 93, WhoWor 93*
Berbenich, William Alfred 1961- *WhoSSW 93*
Berbente, Corneliu 1938- *WhoScE 91-4*
Berber, Arturo Cecilio 1960- *WhoWor 93*
Berberian, Cathy 1925-1983 *Baker 92*
Berberich, Douglas A. *Law&B 92*
Berberich, Raymond W 1947- *St&PR 93*
Berberick, Nancy Varian 1951- *ScF&FL 92*
Berbie, Jane 1931- *OxDcOp*
Berbie, Jane 1934- *Baker 92*
Berbiguier, Antoine (Benoit-) Tranquille 1782-1838 *Baker 92*
Berbrich, Joan D. 1925- *ScF&FL 92, WhoWrEP 92*
Bercan, Gheorghe-Iosif 1949- *WhoWor 93*
Bercaw, John Edward 1944- *WhoAm 92*
Bercel, Danielle Suzanne 1951- *WhoEmL 93*
Bercel, Nicholas Anthony 1911- *WhoWor 93*
Berch, Rebecca White 1955- *WhoEmL 93*
Berche, Stephane Jacques 1944- *WhoWor 93*
Berchem, Douglas M. 1951- *St&PR 93*
Berchem, Jachet c. 1505-c. 1565 *Baker 92*
Berchem, Theodor 1935- *WhoWor 93*
Bercher, Thomas Eugene Owen 1944- *WhoE 93*
Berchin, Holly Ann 1953- *WhoEmL 93*
Berchtold, Gladys B. 1922- *St&PR 93*
Berchtold, Max 1931- *WhoScE 91-4*
Berchtold, Peter 1934- *WhoScE 91-4*
Berchuck, Ivy Schiff 1933- *WhoE 93*
Berck, Martin Gans 1928- *WhoWrEP 92*
Berckhemer, Hans F. 1926- *WhoScE 91-3*
Berckman, Evelyn 1900-1978 *ScF&FL 92*
Bercovici, Luca *MiSFD 9*
Bercovitch, Hanna Margareta 1934- *WhoAm 92, WhoAmW 93, WhoWrEP 92*
Bercovitch, Sacvan 1933- *WhoAm 92*
Bercow, Paul d1990 *BioIn 17*
Bercow, Paul M. *Law&B 92*
Bercowetz, Bonnie S. 1947- *St&PR 93*
Bercowetz, Bonnie Shane 1947- *WhoAmW 93, WhoEmL 93*
Bercq, Alexis Claude 1960- *WhoEmL 93*
Bercsenyi, L. Gyorgy 1924- *WhoScE 91-4*
Berczi, Andrew Stephen 1934- *WhoAm 92*
Berd, Morris 1914- *WhoE 93*
Berdahl, Robert Max 1937- *WhoAm 92*
Berdan, Robert J. *Law&B 92*
Berdanier, Carolyn Dawson 1936- *WhoAm 92*
Berdela, Edmund Zenon 1925- *St&PR 93*
Berdnik, Carl Oliver 1940- *WhoE 93*
Berdnyk, Oleksandr *ScF&FL 92*
Berdnyk, Oles 1927- *ScF&FL 92*
Berdolt, Herman G. d1991 *BioIn 17*
Berdon, Robert Irwin 1929- *WhoAm 92*
Berdy, Jack M. 1946- *WhoAm 92*
Bere, James F. *BioIn 17*

Berger, Hans G. 1947- St&PR 93
Berger, Harold 1925- WhoAm 92, WhoE 93, WhoWor 93
Berger, Harold 1926- WhoAm 92
Berger, Harold 1928- St&PR 93
Berger, Harold L. 1923- ScF&FL 92
Berger, Harold Phillip 1947- WhoEmL 93
Berger, Harvey James 1950- WhoAm 92
Berger, Harvey L. 1938- St&PR 93
Berger, Harvey Robert 1927- WhoE 93
Berger, Henry 1947- WhoEmL 93
Berger, Herbert 1909- WhoAm 92
Berger, Homer Ferrell 1946- WhoSSW 93
Berger, Howard Stephen 1941- WhoE 93
Berger, Ian Bruce 1942- WhoSSW 93
Berger, Ivan Bennett 1939- WhoWrEP 92
Berger, J. Walter 1947- St&PR 93
Berger, Jean 1909- Baker 92
Berger, Jennifer Law&B 92
Berger, Jerry Allen 1943- WhoAm 92
Berger, John 1926- BioIn 17
Berger, John Peter 1926- WhoWor 93
Berger, John Torrey, Jr. 1938- WhoAm 92
Berger, Joseph WhoAm 92
Berger, Joseph Herman 1904- St&PR 93
Berger, Karen S. Law&B 92
Berger, Kenneth Walter 1924- WhoAm 92
Berger, Lawrence Douglas 1947- WhoEmL 93
Berger, Lawrence Howard 1947- WhoEmL 93
Berger, Leo 1907- St&PR 93
Berger, Lionel Law&B 92
Berger, Louis 1914- St&PR 93
Berger, Ludwig 1777-1839 Baker 92
Berger, Mary J. Law&B 92
Berger, Maureen 1941- WhoAmW 93
Berger, Maurice 1927- WhoWor 93
Berger, Mel ScF&FL 92
Berger, Melvyn Stuart 1939- WhoE 93
Berger, Meyer 1898-1959 JrnUS
Berger, Michael P. Law&B 92
Berger, Michel Jean Henri 1920- WhoScE 91-2
Berger, Miles 1930- St&PR 93
Berger, Miriam Roskin 1934- WhoAmW 93, WhoE 93, WhoWor 93
Berger, Murray H. 1924- St&PR 93
Berger, Murry P. 1926- WhoAm 92
Berger, Nancy Osburn 1951- WhoAmW 93
Berger, Natalie Stelle 1950- WhoEmL 93
Berger, Nina Jacqueline 1959- WhoAmW 93
Berger, Norman L. 1917- St&PR 93
Berger, Oscar 1901- WhoAm 92, WhoE 93, WhoWor 93
Berger, Pamela MiSFD 9
Berger, Pamela C. St&PR 93
Berger, Patricia Wilson 1926- WhoAm 92
Berger, Paul Charles Joseph Marie 1956- WhoWor 93
Berger, Paul Eric 1948- WhoAm 92
Berger, Paula Kaplan Law&B 92
Berger, Peter Ludwig 1929- WhoAm 92
Berger, Phil BioIn 17
Berger, Philip Jeffrey 1943- WhoAm 92
Berger, Raoul 1901- WhoAm 92
Berger, Raymond H. 1931- St&PR 93
Berger, Richard L. 1947- St&PR 93
Berger, Richard Laurence 1939- WhoAm 92
Berger, Rick MiSFD 9
Berger, Rick 1958- WhoEmL 93
Berger, Robert Bertram 1924- WhoAm 92
Berger, Robert Canavan 1951- WhoE 93
Berger, Robert J. 1946- St&PR 93
Berger, Robert Lewis 1925- WhoAm 92
Berger, Robert Michael 1942- WhoAm 92
Berger, Robert S. 1917- St&PR 93
Berger, Roland WhoScE 91-2
Berger, Roman 1930- Baker 92
Berger, Ron Ariel 1948- St&PR 93
Berger, Rudolf 1874-1915 Baker 92
Berger, Sanford Jason 1926- WhoAm 92
Berger, Sarah J. Law&B 92
Berger, Senta 1941- BioIn 17
Berger, Sergey Michael 1960- WhoWor 93
Berger, Seymour Maurice 1928- WhoAm 92
Berger, Seymour P. 1923- St&PR 93
Berger, Spencer S. 1913- St&PR 93
Berger, Stanislaw 1923- WhoScE 91-4
Berger, Stanley Allan 1934- WhoAm 92
Berger, Stephen 1939- St&PR 93, WhoAm 92
Berger, Stephen C. 1934- St&PR 93
Berger, Steven John 1957- WhoAm 92, WhoEmL 93
Berger, Susan L. Law&B 92
Berger, Suzanne 1939- WhoAm 92
Berger, Theodor 1905- Baker 92
Berger, Thomas 1924- BioIn 17, ScF&FL 92
Berger, Thomas Jan 1952- WhoAm 92, WhoWor 93
Berger, Thomas Louis 1924- WhoAm 92, WhoWrEP 92
Berger, Toby 1940- WhoAm 92
Berger, Ulrich 1919- WhoWor 93
Berger, Victor L. 1860-1929 PolPar
Berger, Wayne L. 1947- St&PR 93
Berger, Wilhelm 1861-1911 Baker 92
Berger, Wilhelm Georg 1929- Baker 92, WhoWor 93
Berger, William Ernest 1918- WhoAm 92
Berger, William Merriam Bart 1925- St&PR 93
Berger, Yves 1934- ScF&FL 92
Bergerbest, Nathan Steven Law&B 92
Bergerbest, Nathan Steven 1957- WhoEmL 93
Bergere, C. Wendell 1945- St&PR 93
Bergere, C. Wendell, Jr. Law&B 92
Bergere, Clifford Wendell, Jr. 1945- WhoAm 92
Bergeret, Albert Hamilton 1948- WhoEmL 93
Bergeron, Andre 1922- BioIn 17
Bergeron, Bruce Joseph 1953- WhoE 93
Bergeron, Charles E. 1945- St&PR 93
Bergeron, Clifton George 1925- WhoAm 92
Bergeron, David F. 1957- St&PR 93
Bergeron, Francis A. 1935- St&PR 93
Bergeron, J. Donald 1944- St&PR 93
Bergeron, Jan Paul 1937- St&PR 93
Bergeron, Jeanne Paulette 1955- WhoAmW 93
Bergeron, Kathleen Yvonne 1953- WhoWrEP 92
Bergeron, Lin Paul 1948- WhoE 93
Bergeron, Louis E. 1934- WhoIns 93
Bergeron, Maurice Andre Law&B 92
Bergeron, Peter L. St&PR 93
Bergeron, Philippe 1959- WhoEmL 93
Bergeron, R. Thomas 1931- WhoAm 92
Bergeron, Yvette Tucker 1944- WhoE 93
Bergerson, David R. Law&B 92
Bergerson, David Raymond 1939- WhoAm 92
Bergerson, J. Steven Law&B 92
Bergerson, J. Steven 1942- WhoAm 92
Bergery, Gaston 1892-1974 BioIn 17
Bergesen, Christopher Echols 1952- WhoE 93
Bergesen, Robert Nelson 1937- St&PR 93
Bergeson, Karla K. Law&B 92
Bergeson, Marian WhoAmW 93
Bergeson, Scott 1938- St&PR 93, WhoAm 92
Bergethon, Kaare Roald 1918- WhoAm 92
Bergethon, Peter Roald 1955- WhoE 93
Bergevin, Gyl WhoCanL 92
Bergevin, Yvon J. 1942- St&PR 93
Bergevin, Yvon Joseph 1942- WhoAm 92
Bergevine, George John 1948- WhoE 93
Bergey, Gregory Kent 1949- WhoE 93
Bergeyck, Jac IntDcAn
Bergfeld, V. Alan Law&B 92
Bergfelt, Allan 1915- WhoWor 93
Bergfield, Gene Raymond 1951- WhoSSW 93
Berggreen, Andreas Peter 1801-1880 Baker 92
Berggren, Bo Erik Gunnar 1936- WhoWor 93
Berggren, Bonnie Lee 1940- WhoAmW 93
Berggren, Paulette Therese 1939- WhoAmW 93
Berggren, Ronald Bernard 1931- WhoAm 92
Berggren, Thage 1932- WhoSSW 93
Berggren, Thommy 1937- WhoWor 93
Berggren, William Alfred 1931- WhoAm 92
Berggren Lowe, Margareteva Ruth 1919- WhoWrEP 92
Berggruen, Gretchen BioIn 17
Berggruen, John BioIn 17
Berggruen, John Henry 1943- WhoAm 92
Bergh, Andrew G. 1950- St&PR 93
Bergh, Arpad Albert 1930- WhoAm 92
Bergh, Arthur 1882-1962 Baker 92
Bergh, Henry 1811-1888 BioIn 17
Bergh, Kjell 1945- St&PR 93
Bergh, Marcus B., Jr. Law&B 92
Bergh, Rudolph 1859-1924 Baker 92
Berghammer, John Michael 1958- WhoSSW 93
Berghaus, Ruth d1927 OxDcOp
Berghaus, Ruth 1927- IntDcOp
Bergheim, Donna Rose Feldman 1925- WhoAmW 93, WhoSSW 93
Bergheim, Laura Ann 1962- WhoEmL 93
Berghel, Victoria Smouse 1952- WhoEmL 93
Berghem, Jachet de Baker 92
Bergher, Karen Sheryl 1953- WhoAmW 93
Bergh Johansen, Sverre J. 1939- WhoUN 92
Berghof, Herbert 1909-1990 BioIn 17
Berghoff, Karin S. Law&B 92
Berghoff, Paul Johannes 1943- WhoSSW 93
Berghold, Joseph Philip 1938- St&PR 93, WhoAm 92, WhoSSW 93
Bergholm, Ernst Tauno Herman 1935- WhoWor 93
Bergholtz, Peter 1940- St&PR 93
Bergholz, David 1938- WhoAm 92
Bergholz, Richard Cady 1917- WhoAm 92
Bergholz, Warren Ernest, Jr. 1945- WhoSSW 93
Berghuis, Peter Lange 1951- WhoEmL 93
Berghuis, Thomas G. 1945- St&PR 93
Berghuser, Hugo Erich 1935- WhoAsAP 91
Bergia, Fred L. 1940- St&PR 93
Bergier, Jacques 1912-1978 ConAu 37NR
Bergin, Allen E. 1934- BioIn 17
Bergin, Allen Eric 1934- WhoAm 92
Bergin, Carolyn 1954- WhoSSW 93
Bergin, Daniel Timothy Law&B 92
Bergin, Daniel Timothy 1930- WhoAm 92
Bergin, John Francis 1924- St&PR 93, WhoAm 92
Bergin, John M. Law&B 92
Bergin, Kay V. 1921- WhoAmW 93
Bergin, Kyra K. Law&B 92
Bergin, Patrick 1954- BioIn 17
Bergin, Thomas F. 1924- WhoAm 92
Bergins, Lewis A. 1939- St&PR 93
Bergiron de Briou, Nicolas-Antoine 1690-c. 1768 Baker 92
Berg-Johnson, Karen Ann 1959- WhoAmW 93
Bergklint, Karl Gustaf 1955- WhoEmL 93, WhoSSW 93
Bergknut, Krister 1942- WhoScE 91-4
Bergkvist, Jan Peter 1957- WhoWor 93
Bergl, Nancy 1959- WhoWrEP 92
Berglas, Frank E. 1940- WhoIns 93
Berglas, Stephen S. St&PR 93
Berglas, Steven 1950- WhoEmL 93
Bergleitner, George Charles, Jr. 1935- WhoAm 92, WhoE 93, WhoWor 93
Bergles, Arthur Edward 1935- WhoAm 92
Berglin, Brian P. 1950- St&PR 93
Berglin, Linda 1944- WhoAmW 93
Berglund, Alice Mae 1943- WhoE 93
Berglund, Bjorn 1935- WhoScE 91-4
Berglund, Carl Neil 1938- WhoAm 92
Berglund, Edward P. 1942- ScF&FL 92
Berglund, Erik 1924- WhoScE 91-4
Berglund, Fredrik 1924- WhoScE 91-4
Berglund, Joel 1903- IntDcOp
Berglund, Joel (Ingemar) 1903- Baker 92
Berglund, Paavo (Allan Engelbert) 1929- Baker 92, WhoWor 93
Berglund, Robin G. 1945- WhoAm 92
Berglund, Sharon 1956- St&PR 93
Bergman, A. Barrie 1942- St&PR 93
Bergman, Alan ConTFT 10, WhoAm 92
Bergman, Allan H. 1934- St&PR 93
Bergman, Andrew 1945- MiSFD 9, WhoAm 92
Bergman, Anne Newberry 1925- WhoAmW 93
Bergman, Barrie 1942- WhoAm 92
Bergman, Benjamin S. 1921- St&PR 93
Bergman, Bruce John 1941- St&PR 93
Bergman, Carl A. 1921- St&PR 93
Bergman, Charles Cabe 1933- WhoAm 92
Bergman, Clifford Irvin 1937- St&PR 93
Bergman, Dani L. 1949- WhoEmL 93
Bergman, Daniel MiSFD 9
Bergman, David 1950- WhoWrEP 92
Bergman, David Lewis 1950- WhoE 93
Bergman, David Marc 1948- St&PR 93
Bergman, Donna 1934- SmATA 73 [port]
Bergman, Elliot J. 1926- St&PR 93
Bergman, Erik 1911- Baker 92
Bergman, Ernest L. 1922- WhoAm 92
Bergman, Garrett Edward 1946- WhoE 93, WhoEmL 93
Bergman, George Mark 1943- WhoAm 92
Bergman, Harlan W. 1932- WhoIns 93
Bergman, Harlan Wayne 1932- St&PR 93
Bergman, Harold John 1935- St&PR 93
Bergman, Harry St&PR 93
Bergman, Harry 1912 WhoAm 92, WhoWor 93
Bergman, Harry Richard 1914- St&PR 93
Bergman, Hermas John 1926- WhoAm 92
Bergman, Howard J. Law&B 92
Bergman, Ingmar 1918- BioIn 17, ConLC 72 [port], IntDcOp, MiSFD 9, OxDcOp, WhoAm 92, WhoWor 93
Bergman, Ingrid 1915-1982 BioIn 17, IntDcF 2-3 [port]
Bergman, Jacque Lynn Law&B 92
Bergman, Janet E. 1959- WhoAm 92
Bergman, Janet Eisenstein 1959- WhoAmW 93
Bergman, Jeroen 1966- WhoWor 93
Bergman, Jules 1929-1987 BioIn 17
Bergman, Kathryn Carey Foster 1955- WhoAmW 93
Bergman, Klaus 1931- St&PR 93, WhoAm 92, WhoE 93
Bergman, Laurence Richard 1956- St&PR 93
Bergman, Marilyn ConTFT 10
Bergman, Marilyn Keith WhoAm 92
Bergman, Mark Steven 1956- WhoE 93, WhoEmL 93
Bergman, Marvin Elliot 1941- St&PR 93
Bergman, Nancy Palm 1938- WhoAm 92
Bergman, Naomi Miron 1963- WhoE 93
Bergman, Norma Wolk Law&B 92
Bergman, Philip S. 1921-1990 BioIn 17
Bergman, Richard Isaac 1934- WhoAm 92, WhoE 93
Bergman, Robert Edward 1944- St&PR 93
Bergman, Robert George 1942- WhoAm 92
Bergman, Robert Ira 1954- WhoEmL 93
Bergman, Robert L. 1935- St&PR 93
Bergman, Robert Paul 1945- WhoAm 92, WhoE 93
Bergman, Robert Scribner 1934- WhoWor 93
Bergman, Stefan 1898-1977 BioIn 17
Bergman, Tamar 1939- ConAu 138
Bergman, Walter Chester 1949- WhoEmL 93
Bergman, William I. 1931- WhoAm 92
Bergmann, Arthur M. 1927- WhoE 93, WhoWor 93
Bergmann, Barbara Rose 1927- WhoAm 92
Bergmann, Burckhard 1943- WhoWor 93
Bergmann, Carl 1821-1876 Baker 92
Bergmann, Carl K. 1929- St&PR 93
Bergmann, Charles Randolph 1944- WhoSSW 93
Bergmann, Donald Gerald 1949- WhoE 93, WhoEmL 93
Bergmann, Fred Heinz 1928- WhoAm 92
Bergmann, Fredrick Louis 1916- WhoAm 92
Bergmann, Fritz WhoScE 91-3
Bergmann, Gerhard 1923- WhoScE 91-3
Bergmann, Hans WhoScE 91-4
Bergmann, Heinz 1933- WhoScE 91-4
Bergmann, Paul T. Law&B 92
Bergmann, Richard Ronald 1935- WhoAm 92
Bergmann, Richard Willis 1937- St&PR 93
Bergmann, Trish 1953- WhoAmW 93, WhoEmL 93
Bergmann, Valentina 1846-1924 See Serov, Alexander 1820-1871 OxDcOp
Bergmans, Paul (Jean Etienne Charles Marie) 1868-1935 Baker 92
Bergner, Amos 1935- St&PR 93
Bergner, Cathy L. 1951- WhoAmW 93, WhoEmL 93
Bergner, David 1902-1991 BioIn 17
Bergner, Elisabeth 1897-1986 IntDcF 2-3 [port]
Bergner, Marilyn Neufeld d1992 NewYTBS 92
Bergner, Wilhelm 1837-1907 Baker 92
Bergner, William H. 1944- St&PR 93
Bergner, William Joseph 1948- WhoEmL 93
Bergoffen, Charles R. Law&B 92
Bergold, Harry Earl, Jr. 1931- WhoAm 92
Bergold, Orm 1925- WhoWor 93
Bergomi, Joseph G. 1933- St&PR 93
Bergonia, Raymond David 1951- WhoAm 92, WhoEmL 93
Bergonzi, Bernard 1929- ScF&FL 92
Bergonzi, Carlo Baker 92
Bergonzi, Carlo c. 1683-1747 Baker 92
Bergonzi, Carlo 1924- Baker 92, CurBio 92 [port], IntDcOp, OxDcOp, WhoAm 92
Bergonzi, Frank Michael 1945- WhoAm 92
Bergonzi, Franklyn Michael 1945- St&PR 93
Bergonzi, Michael Angelo Baker 92
Bergonzi, Nicola Baker 92
Bergonzi, Zosimo Baker 92
Bergonzini, Emore 1927- WhoScE 91-3
Bergonzoli, Anibale 1884-1973 HarEnMi
Bergovoy, Richard R. Law&B 92
Bergquist, Arnold Everett 1935- WhoE 93
Bergquist, Bruce Orville 1948- St&PR 93
Bergquist, David W. 1941- St&PR 93
Bergquist, Gordon Neil 1932- WhoAm 92
Bergquist, Harold B. 1937- St&PR 93
Bergquist, James Manning 1934- WhoE 93
Bergquist, Lloyd Frederick 1929- WhoAm 92
Bergquist, Nils Robert 1939- WhoUN 92, WhoWor 93
Bergquist, Stephen A. Law&B 92
Bergreen, Bernard D. Law&B 92
Bergreen, Laurence Roger 1950- WhoE 93
Bergren, Sheila Jo 1957- St&PR 93
Bergs, William F. 1947- WhoIns 93
Bergseth, Harald 1923- WhoScE 91-4
Bergsjo, Per B. 1932- WhoScE 91-4
Bergsland, Katherine Smith 1934- St&PR 93
Bergsland, Thomas Grant 1933- St&PR 93

Bergsma, Daniel 1909- WhoAm 92
Bergsma, Jitze 1932- WhoScE 91-3
Bergsma, William (Laurence) 1921- Baker 92, WhoAm 92
Bergsmark, Edwin Martin 1941- St&PR 93, WhoAm 92, WhoWor 93
Bergson, Abram 1914- BioIn 17, WhoAm 92
Bergson, Goran 1934- WhoScE 91-4
Bergson, Henri 1859-1941 BioIn 17
Bergson, Henry Paul 1942- WhoE 93
Bergson, Lisa Marie 1950- St&PR 93
Bergson, Maria WhoAm 92
Bergson, Maria 1914- BioIn 17
Bergstedt, Jan-Erik 1935- St&PR 93
Bergstein, Harry Benjamin 1916- WhoAm 92
Bergstein, Melvyn E. St&PR 93
Bergstein, Sol d1990 BioIn 17
Bergstein, Stanley Francis 1924- WhoE 93
Bergsteiner, Harald 1944- WhoWor 93
Bergsteinsson, Paul 1942- St&PR 93
Bergsten, C. Fred 1941- WhoAm 92
Bergsten, Staffan 1932 ScF&FL 92
Bergstrand, Henri 1952- WhoWor 93
Bergstrand, Wilton Everet 1909- WhoAm 92
Bergstresser, John L. 1903-1991 BioIn 17
Bergstresser, Paul Richard 1941- WhoSSW 93
Bergstrom, Albion Andrew 1947- WhoE 93
Bergstrom, Betty Howard 1931- WhoAmW 93
Bergstrom, Dedric Waldemar 1919- WhoAm 92
Bergstrom, Elaine 1946- ScF&FL 92
Bergstrom, Erik BioIn 17
Bergstrom, George Frederick 1950- WhoEmL 93
Bergstrom, Hans Olof Oskar 1930- WhoWor 93
Bergstrom, Helen Marie 1930- WhoAm 92
Bergstrom, Ingvar Erik 1913- WhoWor 93
Bergstrom, James David 1933- St&PR 93
Bergstrom, Jan BioIn 17
Bergstrom, Janet ScF&FL 92
Bergstrom, Joan Margosian 1940- WhoE 93
Bergstrom, Jonas 1929- WhoScE 91-4
Bergstrom, K. Gunnar ScF&FL 92
Bergstrom, K. Sune D. 1916- WhoAm 92, WhoWor 93
Bergstrom, Richard Norman 1921- WhoAm 92
Bergstrom, Robert Benton Law&B 92
Bergstrom, Robert William 1918- WhoAm 92
Bergstrom, Roy E. 1935- St&PR 93
Bergstrom, Sten Rudolf 1934- WhoWor 93
Bergstrom, Stig Magnus 1935- WhoAm 92
Bergstrom, William Hugo 1921- WhoE 93
Bergsund, Richard T. 1927- WhoIns 93
Bergt, Neil Gradon 1936- WhoAm 92
Bergter, F. WhoScE 91-3
Bergthorsson, Pall 1923- WhoScE 91-4
Bergtold, James L. 1930- St&PR 93
Bergtraum, Howard Michael 1946- WhoEmL 93
Bergum, Patricia E. Law&B 92
Bergum, Steven John 1945- St&PR 93
Berg-Wilion, Elayne Law&B 92
Berhalter, Kathleen Anne 1938- WhoAmW 93
Berhanu, Bayih WhoAfr
Beria, Lavrenti BioIn 17
Beria, Lavrenti Pavlovich 1899-1953 DcTwHis
Beric, Berislav 1927- WhoScE 91-4
Berick, James H. Law&B 92
Berick, James H. 1933- St&PR 93
Berick, James Herschel 1933- WhoAm 92
Berigan, Bunny 1908-1942 BioIn 17
Berigan, Patrick Tierney 1956- WhoEmL 93
Berigan, Rory Ann 1954- WhoE 93, WhoEmL 93
Berigan, Rowland Bernart 1908-1942 Baker 92
Berinbaum, Martin 1942- Baker 92
Bering, Carol Gretchen 1938- WhoAmW 93
Bering, Edgar Andrew, III 1946- WhoEmL 93
Bering, Vitus 1681-1741 Expl 93 [port]
Beringer, H. WhoScE 91-3
Beringer, John Evelyn WhoScE 91-1
Beringer, Oscar 1844-1922 Baker 92
Beringer, Robert McGinnis 1957- WhoEmL 93
Beringer, Stuart M. 1923- St&PR 93
Beringer, Stuart Marshall 1923- WhoAm 92
Beringer, William E. Law&B 92
Beringer, William Ernst 1928- St&PR 93, WhoAm 92, WhoSSW 93
Beringhaus, Kerry L. Law&B 92
Berins, Maurice H. d1990 BioIn 17
Berinsky, Burton d1991 BioIn 17
Berinstein, William Paul 1935- WhoE 93
Berio, Luciano BioIn 17
Berio, Luciano 1925- Baker 92, IntDcOp, OxDcOp, WhoAm 92, WhoWor 93
Beriot, Charles (-Auguste) de 1802-1870 Baker 92
Beriot, Charles-Wilfride de 1833-1914 Baker 92
Berish, Barry M. 1932- St&PR 93
Berish, Sharon Lynne McMeans 1951- WhoSSW 93
Beristain de Souza, Jose Mariano 1756-1817 DcMexL
Beritic, Tihomil 1919- WhoScE 91-4
Berk, Alan 1940- St&PR 93
Berk, Alan S. 1934- WhoAm 92
Berk, Allen Joel 1940- WhoAm 92
Berk, Ann E. WhoAm 92
Berk, Burton Benjamin 1930- WhoWor 93
Berk, Carole Doull 1950- WhoEmL 93
Berk, Howard 1926- ScF&FL 92
Berk, Jack Edward WhoAm 92
Berk, James Edward 1945- St&PR 93, WhoAm 92
Berk, Mindy Lynn 1965- WhoE 93
Berk, Nicole Susan 1950- WhoAmW 93
Berk, Paul David 1938- WhoAm 92
Berk, Peggy Faith 1951- WhoAmW 93, WhoE 93, WhoEmL 93
Berk, Richard Charles 1948- WhoEmL 93, WhoSSW 93
Berk, Steven Lee 1949- WhoAm 92, WhoWor 93
Berk, William Stewart 1957- WhoEmL 93
Berka, Antonin 1931- WhoScE 91-4
Berka, Dusan 1945- St&PR 93
Berka, Marianne Guthrie 1944- WhoAmW 93
Berka, Richard J. Law&B 92
Berkbigler, Marsha Lee 1950- WhoAm 92
Berke, Alison Debra 1955- WhoAm 92
Berke, Anita Diamant WhoAmW 93
Berke, Beth Law&B 92
Berke, Erwin M. 1917- St&PR 93
Berke, Ivan H. 1943- St&PR 93
Berke, Jerrold I. 1934- WhoUN 92
Berke, Jerry St&PR 93
Berke, Jules 1926- WhoAm 92
Berke, Kent Russell Law&B 92
Berke, Michael 1939- St&PR 93
Berke, Steven Leigh 1954- WhoE 93, WhoEmL 93
Berke, Yvette Nancy 1961- WhoEmL 93
Berkebile, Guy 1961- St&PR 93
Berkel, Charles John 1925- St&PR 93
Berkel, Joseph Anthony 1956- WhoSSW 93
Berkeley, Bernard 1923- St&PR 93
Berkeley, Betty Life 1924- WhoAmW 93
Berkeley, Busby 1895-1976 MiSFD 9N
Berkeley, Edmund C. 1912- ScF&FL 92
Berkeley, Francis Lewis, Jr. 1911- WhoSSW 93
Berkeley, Frederick D. 1928- St&PR 93
Berkeley, George 1685-1753 BioIn 17
Berkeley, Lennox 1903-1989 OxDcOp
Berkeley, Lennox (Randall Francis) 1903-1989 Baker 92
Berkeley, Marvin H. 1922- WhoAm 92
Berkeley, Michael 1948- Baker 92
Berkeley, Norborne, Jr. 1922- St&PR 93
Berkeley, Robert David 1945- WhoSSW 93
Berkeley, William 1606-1677 BioIn 17, HarEnMi
Berkelhammer, Gerald 1931- St&PR 93, WhoE 93
Berkelhammer, Robert Bruce 1949- WhoEmL 93
Berkell, Dianne E. 1948- WhoE 93
Berkelman, Karl 1933- WhoAm 92
Berkemeier, F.X. Law&B 92
Berkemeyer, Thomas G. Law&B 92
Berken, Mitchell Lloyd 1937- St&PR 93
Berkenes, Joyce Marie Poore 1953- WhoEmL 93
Berkenfield, Steven L. Law&B 92
Berkenhead, John L. fl. 18th cent.- Baker 92
Berkenkamp, Fred Julius 1925- WhoAm 92
Berkenkamp, John 1936- St&PR 93
Berkenstock, Howard Roy, Jr. Law&B 92
Berkery, Michael John 1945- WhoAm 92
Berkery, Rosemary T. Law&B 92
Berkes, Howard 1954- WhoAm 92
Berkes, Istvan 1930- WhoScE 91-2
Berkes, Leslie John 1946- WhoEmL 93
Berkey, Catherine Susan 1951- WhoE 93
Berkey, Dennis A. Law&B 92
Berkey, Dennis D. 1947- WhoE 93
Berkey, John 1932- ScF&FL 92
Berkey, Judith Osterhoudt 1943- WhoAmW 93, WhoSSW 93
Berkey, Richard H. 1952- St&PR 93
Berkey, Sharon ScF&FL 92
Berkhan, Sharon Lee 1954- WhoEmL 93
Berki, R.N. BioIn 17
Berkich, Donald Rodney 1946- WhoE 93
Berkin, Laurie Rose Law&B 92
Berkin, Rona St&PR 93
Berkland, James Omer 1930- WhoWor 93
Berkley, Alison Joan 1970- WhoAmW 93
Berkley, Burton 1934- WhoE 93
Berkley, E.B. 1923- St&PR 93
Berkley, Elizabeth BioIn 17
Berkley, Eugene Bertram 1923- WhoAm 92
Berkley, Florence Pfullmann 1953- WhoAmW 93
Berkley, Herbert Ronald 1933- St&PR 93
Berkley, John Lee 1948- WhoEmL 93
Berkley, Nancy M. Law&B 92
Berkley, Peter Lee 1939- WhoAm 92
Berkley, Richard L. BioIn 17, WhoAm 92
Berkley, Robert Lee 1946- St&PR 93
Berkley, Ronald S. 1931- St&PR 93
Berkley, Stephen M. 1944- St&PR 93
Berkley, Stephen Mark 1944- WhoAm 92
Berkley, William R. 1945- St&PR 93, WhoIns 93
Berkley, William Robert 1945- WhoAm 92
Berkley, William S. 1956- St&PR 93
Berkman, Aaron 1900-1991 BioIn 17
Berkman, Claire Fleet 1942- WhoAmW 93
Berkman, Edwina ScF&FL 92
Berkman, Eileen J. Law&B 92
Berkman, Gerald R. 1949- St&PR 93
Berkman, Harold W(illiam) 1926- WhoWrEP 92
Berkman, Harold William 1926- WhoAm 92, WhoSSW 93
Berkman, Jack Neville 1905- St&PR 93
Berkman, James Israel 1913- WhoE 93
Berkman, Jerome 1931- WhoWor 93
Berkman, Lillian WhoAm 92
Berkman, Louis 1909- St&PR 93
Berkman, Marshall L. 1936- WhoAm 92
Berkman, Marshall Lee 1936- St&PR 93
Berkman, Michael G. 1917- WhoAm 92
Berkman, Morland Edward 1931- St&PR 93
Berkman, Seymour J. 1925- St&PR 93
Berkman, Susan C. Josephs 1953- WhoAmW 93, WhoEmL 93
Berkman, William Roger 1928- WhoAm 92
Berkner, Klaus Hans 1938- WhoAm 92
Berko, Ferenc 1916- WhoAm 92
Berko, Stephan 1924-1991 BioIn 17
Berkoff, Charles Edward 1932- WhoAm 92
Berkoff, Steven 1937- ConTFT 10
Berkolaiko, Mark Zinov'evich 1945- WhoWor 93
Berkon, Martin 1932- WhoE 93
Berkovic, Zvonimir 1928- DrEEuF
Berkovitch, Boris S. 1921- WhoAm 92
Berkovits, Eliezer 1908- ConAu 37NR
Berkow, Albert J. 1923- St&PR 93
Berkow, Ira Harvey 1940- WhoAm 92, WhoE 93, WhoWrEP 92
Berkow, Michael 1955- WhoEmL 93
Berkowe, Kathleen Hawkins Law&B 92
Berkowicz, Joseph 1789-1846 PolBiDi
Berkowitz, A. Menachem 1962- WhoE 93
Berkowitz, Alan Ira BioIn 17
Berkowitz, Alan R. 1956- WhoEmL 93
Berkowitz, Barry Alan 1942- WhoE 93
Berkowitz, Bernard Joseph 1945- WhoE 93
Berkowitz, Bernard Solomon 1930- WhoAm 92
Berkowitz, David Andrew 1952- WhoE 93
Berkowitz, Donald Allen 1948- St&PR 93, WhoAm 92
Berkowitz, Edward H. Law&B 92
Berkowitz, Eric Neal 1949- WhoEmL 93
Berkowitz, Evelyn S. Law&B 92
Berkowitz, George BioIn 17
Berkowitz, Herbert Mattis 1947- WhoEmL 93
Berkowitz, J. 1928- St&PR 93
Berkowitz, Joan B. 1931- St&PR 93
Berkowitz, Kenneth Paul 1942- WhoAm 92, WhoE 93
Berkowitz, Leonard 1926- WhoAm 92
Berkowitz, Leonard M. 1921- St&PR 93
Berkowitz, Michael H. WhoIns 93
Berkowitz, Michael H. 1942- St&PR 93
Berkowitz, Michael Harold 1942- WhoAm 92
Berkowitz, Mortimer, Jr. 1915- St&PR 93
Berkowitz, Murray Richard 1952- WhoSSW 93
Berkowitz, Pamela 1963- St&PR 93
Berkowitz, Phil 1930- St&PR 93
Berkowitz, Philip Joseph 1965- WhoE 93
Berkowitz, Ralph Steven 1949- WhoEmL 93, WhoSSW 93, WhoWor 93
Berkowitz, Richard Alan 1951- WhoSSW 93
Berkowitz, Robert Howard 1922- St&PR 93
Berkowitz, Steven Paul 1940- St&PR 93
Berkowitz, Terry WhoE 93
Berkowitz, Victor 1942- St&PR 93
Berkshire, Francis Howard WhoScE 91-1
Berkshire, Gerald Lynn 1951- WhoEmL 93
Berkson, Jacob Benjamin 1925- WhoE 93
Berkson, Marshall H. 1925- St&PR 93
Berkwitt, George Joseph 1921- WhoAm 92, WhoWrEP 92
Berkwitz, Robert S. Law&B 92
Berl, Howard Stephen 1947- St&PR 93
Berl, John David 1927- St&PR 93
Berlacher, Phyllis O'Brien 1958- WhoEmL 93
Berlage, Gai Ingham 1943- WhoAm 92, WhoAmW 93, WhoE 93, WhoWor 93
Berlamont, Jean 1946- WhoScE 91-2
Berland, Abel E. 1915- St&PR 93
Berland, Abel Edward 1915- WhoAm 92
Berland, James Fred 1943- WhoAm 92
Berland, Karen Ina 1947- WhoAm 92, WhoAmW 93
Berland, Sanford Neil Law&B 92
Berlanga, Luis Garcia 1921- MiSFD 9
Berlangieri, Nicholas Joseph 1946- WhoSSW 93
Berlant, Anthony 1941- WhoAm 92
Berlant, Tony 1941- BioIn 17
Berlatsky, David MiSFD 9
Berle, Milton 1908- QDrFCA 92 [port], WhoAm 92
Berle, Peter Adolf Augustus 1937- WhoAm 92
Berleant, Arnold 1932- WhoAm 92
Berleant-Schiller, Riva 1935- WhoE 93
Berlekamp, Elwyn Ralph 1940- WhoAm 92
Berler, Beatrice (Adele) 1915- ConAu 139
Berles, James John 1957- WhoWrEP 92
Berlet, Nancy Weir 1949- WhoAmW 93, WhoE 93, WhoEmL 93, WhoWor 93
Berley, David Richard 1942- WhoWor 93
Berliant, Ronald 1932- St&PR 93
Berlie, Elizabeth Marie 1966- WhoEmL 93
Berlier, John C. 1936- St&PR 93
Berlijn, Anton 1817-1870 Baker 92
Berlik, Leonard J. 1947- St&PR 93
Berlin, Alan Daniel 1939- WhoAm 92, WhoE 93
Berlin, Andrew WhoAm 92
Berlin, Barry Neil 1954- WhoEmL 93
Berlin, Bruce Atkisson 1920- St&PR 93
Berlin, Caren Ann 1959- WhoEmL 93
Berlin, Charles 1936- WhoE 93
Berlin, Charles Seder 1947- WhoEmL 93
Berlin, Cheston Milton, Jr. 1936- WhoE 93
Berlin, Daniel 1920- St&PR 93
Berlin, David Nelson 1949- St&PR 93
Berlin, Doris Ada 1919- WhoAmW 93
Berlin, Edward Law&B 92
Berlin, Fred Saul 1941- WhoAm 92
Berlin, Howard Richard 1935- WhoAm 92
Berlin, Ira 1941- WhoWrEP 92
Berlin, Irving 1888-1989 Baker 92, BioIn 17, ConMus 8 [port], OxDcOp
Berlin, Isaiah 1909- WhoWor 93
Berlin, Jerome Clifford 1942- WhoSSW 93
Berlin, Johan Daniel 1714-1787 Baker 92
Berlin, Kenneth Darrell 1933- WhoAm 92
Berlin, Lorna Chumley 1938- WhoAm 92, WhoAmW 93
Berlin, Martin Henry 1934- St&PR 93
Berlin, Max 1956- St&PR 93
Berlin, Meredith Rise 1955- WhoE 93, WhoWor 93
Berlin, Richard L. 1915- St&PR 93
Berlin, Stanton Henry 1934- WhoAm 92
Berlin, Steven R. 1944- St&PR 93
Berlin, Steven Ritt 1944- WhoAm 92
Berlind, Bruce Peter 1926- WhoAm 92
Berlind, Jeffrey P. 1939- St&PR 93
Berlind, Robert Elliot 1938- WhoAm 92
Berlind, Roger S. 1930- St&PR 93
Berlind, Roger Stuart 1930- WhoAm 92
Berline, James H. 1946- WhoAm 92
Berline, Jeffrie B. 1948- St&PR 93
Berliner, Allen Irwin 1947- WhoAm 92
Berliner, Don 1930- WhoWrEP 92
Berliner, Emile 1851-1929 BioIn 17
Berliner, Ernst 1915- WhoAm 92
Berliner, Hans Jack 1929- WhoAm 92
Berliner, Henry Adler, Jr. 1934- St&PR 93, WhoAm 92
Berliner, Herman Albert 1944- WhoAm 92
Berliner, Joseph Scholom 1921- WhoAm 92
Berliner, Michael Alan 1954- St&PR 93
Berliner, Patricia Mary 1946- WhoAm 92, WhoE 93, WhoEmL 93
Berliner, Robert W. Law&B 92

Berliner, Robert William 1915- WhoAm 92
Berliner, Ruth Shirley 1928- WhoAmW 93, WhoE 93, WhoWor 93
Berliner, William Michael 1923- WhoAm 92, WhoE 93, WhoWor 93
Berling, Zygmunt 1898-1980 PolBiDi
Berlinger, Warren 1937- WhoAm 92
Berlinger, William G., Jr. 1916- St&PR 93
Berlinghof, Charles Overton 1930- St&PR 93
Berlinguer, Giovanni 1924- WhoScE 91-3
Berlinski, Edward C. 1942- St&PR 93
Berlinski, Herman 1910- Baker 92
Berlinski, Jacques 1913-1988 Baker 92
Berlioz, Gabriel Pierre 1916- Baker 92
Berlioz, Georges Louis 1943- WhoWor 93
Berlioz, Hector 1803-1869 BioIn 17, IntDcOp [port], OxDcOp
Berlioz, (Louis-) Hector 1803-1869 Baker 92
Berlioz, Louis Hector 1803-1869 BioIn 17
Berlis, Douglas A. 1920- St&PR 93
Berlitz, Charles Frambach 1914- WhoWrEP 92
Berlon, Henry G. Law&B 92
Berlow, Robert Alan Law&B 92
Berlow, Robert Alan 1947- St&PR 93, WhoAm 92
Berlowitz Tarrant, Laurence 1934- WhoAm 92
Berls, Robert Edwin, Jr. 1939- WhoE 93
Berlucchi, Giovanni 1935- WhoScE 91-3, WhoWor 93
Berly, Joel Anderson, III 1956- WhoEmL 93
Berlyn, Michael 1949- ScF&FL 92
Berlyne, Geoffrey Merton 1931- WhoE 93
Berman, Abraham 1926- St&PR 93
Berman, Alan 1925- WhoAm 92
Berman, Alec S. Law&B 92
Berman, Allan 1940- WhoAm 92
Berman, Andrew 1959- St&PR 93
Berman, Ann Muriel 1951- WhoWrEP 92
Berman, Ariane R. 1937- WhoAm 92
Berman, Arthur Irwin 1925- WhoWor 93
Berman, Arthur Jerome 1928- WhoE 93
Berman, Arthur Malcolm 1935- WhoAm 92
Berman, Avis BioIn 17
Berman, Barbara Sandra 1938- WhoAmW 93
Berman, Barnett 1922- WhoAm 92
Berman, Barry David 1937- WhoAm 92
Berman, Barry I. 1942- St&PR 93
Berman, Barry Louis 1936- WhoE 93
Berman, Baruch 1925- WhoAm 92
Berman, Bennett I. 1918- WhoAm 92
Berman, Bennett Irwin 1918- St&PR 93
Berman, Brad Laurence 1957- WhoEmL 93
Berman, Bruce WhoAm 92
Berman, Bruce Judson 1946- WhoSSW 93
Berman, Bud d1991 BioIn 17
Berman, Carol May 1949- WhoE 93
Berman, Chris BioIn 17
Berman, Claire 1936- WhoWrEP 92
Berman, Colleen Ann 1950- WhoEmL 93
Berman, Cynthia Ann Law&B 92
Berman, Daniel Lewis 1934- WhoAm 92, WhoWor 93
Berman, Daniel Micah 1957- WhoEmL 93
Berman, David 1934- WhoAm 92
Berman, Edgar BioIn 17
Berman, Edward Henry 1940- WhoSSW 93
Berman, Elliot H. Law&B 92
Berman, Eric M. 1948- WhoEmL 93
Berman, Fred Jean 1926- WhoAm 92
Berman, Gary Scott 1956- WhoE 93
Berman, H. Lawrence 1937- St&PR 93
Berman, Harvey Paul Law&B 92
Berman, Howard Allen 1949- WhoEmL 93
Berman, Howard L. 1941- CngDr 91
Berman, Howard Lawrence 1941- WhoAm 92
Berman, Janis Gail 1946- WhoAm 92
Berman, Jay Arnold 1950- St&PR 93
Berman, Jay Harris 1958- WhoEmL 93
Berman, Jay Michael 1952- WhoEmL 93
Berman, Jeffrey L. 1943- WhoE 93
Berman, Joanna WhoAm 92
Berman, Joshua Mordecai 1938- WhoAm 92
Berman, Kenneth Everett 1932- St&PR 93
Berman, Lawrence J. 1927- St&PR 93
Berman, Lazar 1930- WhoAm 92, WhoWor 93
Berman, Lazar (Naumovich) 1930- Baker 92
Berman, Leo 1917- WhoWor 93
Berman, Lewis Paul 1937- WhoAm 92
Berman, Linda Fran 1952- WhoAmW 93
Berman, Lori Beth Law&B 92
Berman, Lori Beth 1958- WhoEmL 93
Berman, Louise Marguerite 1928- WhoAm 92
Berman, Marcelo Samuel 1945- WhoWor 93
Berman, Mark Edward 1945- St&PR 93
Berman, Mark Niles 1952- WhoEmL 93
Berman, Marla A. Law&B 92
Berman, Marla Ilyse Law&B 92
Berman, Marlene Oscar 1939- WhoAm 92, WhoE 93
Berman, Marshall Fox 1939- WhoAm 92
Berman, Marshall Howard 1940- WhoAm 92
Berman, Michael David 1948- WhoEmL 93
Berman, Milton 1924- WhoAm 92
Berman, Mira 1928- WhoAm 92
Berman, Mitch 1956- ConAu 136, ScF&FL 92
Berman, Mona S. 1925- WhoAm 92, WhoAmW 93
Berman, Morris 1944- BioIn 17, ConAu 139
Berman, Muriel Mallin WhoAm 92
Berman, Myra E. St&PR 93
Berman, Myron J. St&PR 93
Berman, Neil Sheldon 1933- WhoAm 92
Berman, Noel B. 1932- St&PR 93
Berman, Pamela Joy 1962- WhoEmL 93
Berman, Patricia Karatsis 1953- WhoAmW 93
Berman, Paul 1937- WhoE 93
Berman, Paul 1949- BioIn 17
Berman, Paula Kay 1967- WhoSSW 93
Berman, Peter Alan 1951- WhoE 93
Berman, Peter Henry 1931- WhoE 93
Berman, Philip I. 1915- WhoAm 92
Berman, Richard Angel 1945- WhoAm 92
Berman, Richard Bruce 1951- WhoEmL 93
Berman, Richard Michael Law&B 92
Berman, Richard Miles 1943- WhoAm 92
Berman, Robert Howard 1944- St&PR 93
Berman, Robert I. 1938- St&PR 93
Berman, Robert M. Law&B 92
Berman, Robert S. 1932- WhoAm 92
Berman, Robert Samuel 1953- St&PR 93
Berman, Ronald Charles 1949- WhoEmL 93
Berman, Ronald Stanley 1930- WhoWrEP 92
Berman, Ruth ScF&FL 92
Berman, Sabina 1953- DcMexL
Berman, Samuel d1991 BioIn 17
Berman, Samuel 1923- St&PR 93
Berman, Sanford 1933- BioIn 17, WhoWrEP 92
Berman, Saul J. 1946- WhoWor 93
Berman, Sheryl Hope 1957- WhoAmW 93
Berman, Shirley d1992 BioIn 17, NewYTBS 92
Berman, Sidney 1908- WhoAm 92
Berman, Siegrid Visconti 1944- WhoAmW 93
Berman, Simeon Moses 1935- WhoAm 92
Berman, Stanley 1934- WhoAm 92
Berman, Stanley G. 1934- St&PR 93
Berman, Steve William 1954- WhoEmL 93
Berman, Steven P. Law&B 92
Berman, Steven Todd Law&B 92
Berman, Stuart M. 1923- St&PR 93
Berman, Ted MiSFD 9
Berman, Todd Robert 1957- WhoWor 93
Berman, Vivian 1928- WhoE 93
Berman, William H. 1936- WhoAm 92
Berman, William Howard 1936- St&PR 93
Berman-Hammer, Susan 1950- WhoAmW 93
Bermann, George Alan 1945- WhoAm 92
Bermann, Leslie Kay 1966- WhoEmL 93
Bermann, Nancy Stewart 1957- WhoEmL 93
Bermann, Patty Pemberton AmWomPl
Bermant, Chaim 1929- ScF&FL 92
Bermant, Charles Mark 1954- WhoWrEP 92
Bermant, George Wilson 1926- WhoAm 92
Bermant, Oser Irvin 1927- WhoE 93
Bermanzohn, Francis R. Law&B 92
Bermas, Neal F. 1950- WhoE 93
Bermas, Stephen Law&B 92
Bermas, Stephen 1925- St&PR 93, WhoAm 92
Bermejo Zeropa, Luis 1927- WhoScE 91-3
Bermeo, Rodrigo Alejandro 1957- WhoWor 93
Bermeo-Estrella, Miguel Angel 1950- WhoUN 92
Bermeo-Lanas, Vicente 1921- WhoWor 93
Bermingham, Debra Pandell 1953- WhoE 93
Bermingham, John Anthony 1944- WhoE 93
Bermingham, John Scott 1951- WhoWor 93
Bermingham, Peter WhoAm 92
Bermingham, Richard P. 1939- St&PR 93
Bermon, Michael F. 1944- St&PR 93
Bermond, Jean-Claude 1945- WhoScE 91-2
Bermudez, Enrique DcCPCAm
Bermudez, Enrique d1991 BioIn 17
Bermudez, Eugenia M. 1932- WhoAm 92
Bermudez, Jorge Alberto 1951- WhoE 93
Bermudez, Maria Elvira 1916-1988 DcMexL
Bermudez, Ricardo J. 1914- SpAmA
Bermudez Rodriguez, Jorge Emilio 1943- WhoWor 93
Bermudo, Juan c. 1510-c. 1555 Baker 92
Bern, Howard Alan 1920- WhoAm 92
Bern, Murray Morris 1944- WhoE 93
Bern, Paul 1889-1932 BioIn 17
Bern, Ronald L. 1936- St&PR 93
Bern, Ronald Lawrence 1936- WhoAm 92
Bern, Victoria ConAu 138
Berna, Paul 1910- ScF&FL 92
Bernabe, Juliana Thesalonica 1962- WhoAmW 93
Bernabei, Ercole 1622-1687 Baker 92
Bernabei, Giuseppe Antonio 1649-1732 Baker 92
Bernabeu, Eusebio 1944- WhoScE 91-3
Bernabini, Marcello WhoScE 91-3
Bernac, Pierre 1899-1979 Baker 92
Bernacchi, Antonio Maria 1685-1756 Baker 92, IntDcOp, OxDcOp
Bernacchi, Richard Lloyd 1938- WhoAm 92
Bernacka, Krystyna 1927- WhoScE 91-4
Bernacki, Henryk 1923- WhoScE 91-4
Bernadet, Paul 1930- St&PR 93
Bernadotte, Folke 1895-1948 BioIn 17, DcTwHis
Bernadotte, Jean Baptiste Jules 1763-1844 HarEnMi
Bernadou, Michel Jean-Marie 1943- WhoWor 93
Bernal, Arthur W. 1913-1991 BioIn 17
Bernal, Ernesto M. BioIn 17
Bernal, Gabriel 1945- WhoUN 92
Bernal, Ignacio 1910- IntDcAn
Bernal, Rafael 1915-1972 DcMexL
Bernal (y Garcia y Pimentel), Ignacio 1910-1992 ConAu 136
Bernalte-Miralles, Antoni 1927- WhoWor 93
Bernanos, Georges 1888-1948 BioIn 17, ScF&FL 92
Bernar, Juan 1956- WhoWor 93
Bernard, Alexander 1952- WhoEmL 93, WhoWor 93
Bernard, Andrea Present Law&B 92
Bernard, Annette M. 1959- WhoAmW 93
Bernard, Bess Mary WhoE 93
Bernard, Cathy S. 1949- WhoAmW 93, WhoEmL 93
Bernard, Charles Julien 1966- WhoAm 92
Bernard, Charles Keith 1938- WhoAm 92
Bernard, Chris MiSFD 9
Bernard, Crystal BioIn 17
Bernard, David George 1921- WhoAm 92
Bernard, David Kane 1956- WhoWrEP 92
Bernard, Dominique P. 1942- WhoScE 91-2
Bernard, Donald Arthur 1933- St&PR 93
Bernard, Donald Ray 1932- WhoSSW 93, WhoWor 93
Bernard, Eddie Nolan 1946- WhoAm 92
Bernard, Eric BioIn 17
Bernard, Eric 1943-1991 AnObit 1991
Bernard, Ernest Stephen 1944- WhoSSW 93
Bernard, Georges 1904- WhoWor 93
Bernard, Glen Richard 1955- WhoEmL 93
Bernard, H. Russell 1940- WhoAm 92
Bernard, Harry 1898-1979 BioIn 17
Bernard, Jack A. 1947- WhoEmL 93
Bernard, Jacques 1959- WhoWor 93
Bernard, James Harvey, Jr. 1951- WhoEmL 93
Bernard, James M. 1951- St&PR 93
Bernard, James Robert 1952- WhoE 93
Bernard, James William 1937- St&PR 93
Bernard, Jami 1956- WhoAm 92
Bernard, Jean-Leon 1922- WhoScE 91-2
Bernard, Jessie Shirley 1903- BioIn 17
Bernard, Joseph Antoine 1866-1931 BioIn 17
Bernard, Judd Benjamin 1962- WhoE 93
Bernard, Judith Ann 1942- WhoAmW 93
Bernard, Jules Frank 1920- St&PR 93
Bernard, Julie Johnstone Law&B 92
Bernard, Kenneth 1930- WhoAm 92, WhoWrEP 92
Bernard, Kenneth John 1958- WhoEmL 93
Bernard, Kent S. Law&B 92
Bernard, Lewis W. WhoAm 92
Bernard, Lola Diane 1928- WhoAm 92
Bernard, Louis 1937- St&PR 93
Bernard, Louis Joseph 1925- WhoAm 92
Bernard, Lowell Francis 1931- WhoAm 92
Bernard, Marie BioIn 17
Bernard, Moritz (Matvey) 1794-1871 Baker 92
Bernard, Myron Jules 1930- St&PR 93
Bernard, Nancy S. 1934- WhoAm 92, WhoAmW 93
Bernard, Norman P. 1945- St&PR 93
Bernard, Oliver WhoScE 91-2
Bernard, Philippe 1931- WhoAm 92
Bernard, Richard K. Law&B 92
Bernard, Richard Lawson 1926- WhoAm 92
Bernard, Robert WhoWrEP 92
Bernard, Robert 1900-1971 Baker 92
Bernard, Robert A. 1952- St&PR 93
Bernard, Ronald Allan 1953- WhoE 93, WhoEmL 93, WhoWor 93
Bernard, Ronald C. 1943- St&PR 93
Bernard, Sharon Elaine 1943- St&PR 93, WhoAmW 93
Bernard, Steven F. 1947- St&PR 93
Bernard, Thomas J(oseph) 1945- ConAu 138
Bernard, Viola Wertheim 1907- WhoAm 92
Bernard, William Bekker 1914- WhoSSW 93
Bernard-Dagan, Colette 1929- WhoScE 91-2
Bernardeau, Christine 1943- WhoSSW 93
Bernardez, Alexander Ruiz 1957- WhoWor 93
Bernardez, Romulo Catris 1935- St&PR 93
Bernardez, Rudolfo A. 1933- WhoAsAP 91
Bernardez, Teresa 1931- HispAmA [port]
Bernardi, Bartolomeo c. 1660-1732 Baker 92
Bernardi, Bernardo 1916- IntDcAn
Bernardi, Francesco Baker 92
Bernardi, G. WhoScE 91-2
Bernardi, Giorgio 1929- WhoWor 93
Bernardi, Mario 1930- WhoAm 92
Bernardi, Mario (Egidio) 1930- Baker 92
Bernardi, Stefano c. 1585-1636 Baker 92
Bernardin, George Flynn 1933- St&PR 93
Bernardin, James Irwin 1929- WhoAm 92
Bernardin, Joseph L. BioIn 17
Bernardin, Joseph Louis Cardinal 1928- WhoAm 92, WhoWor 93
Bernardini, Allen J. 1938- St&PR 93
Bernardini, Isa 1943- WhoAm 92
Bernardini, Joe 1937- ConAu 136
Bernardini, Marcello c. 1740-c. 1799 OxDcOp
Bernardini, Richard Albert 1951- WhoEmL 93
Bernardo, Jeannette Lim 1963- WhoAmW 93
Bernardo, Jose Miguel 1950- WhoWor 93
Bernardo, Raymond Francis 1917- WhoE 93
Bernardone, Jeffrey John 1958- WhoE 93
Bernards, Neal 1963- SmATA 71 [port]
Bernards, Solomon Schnair 1914- WhoAm 92
Bernardus Guidonis, Bishop of Lodeve 1261?-1331 BioIn 17
Bernart de Ventadorn fl. 12th cent.- Baker 92
Bernas, Harry WhoScE 91-2
Bernas, Lilian Helen 1948- WhoAm 92, WhoAmW 93, WhoEmL 93
Bernasconi, Andrea c. 1706-1784 Baker 92
Bernasconi, F.A. WhoScE 91-3
Bernasek, Steven Lynn 1949- WhoE 93
Bernat, Mary K. 1958- St&PR 93
Bernath, Gabor 1933- WhoScE 91-4
Bernath, Jeno 1944- WhoScE 91-4
Bernatowicz, Felix Jan Brzozowski 1920- WhoE 93, WhoWor 93
Bernatowicz, Frank Allen 1954- WhoEmL 93, WhoWor 93
Bernatowicz, Rita Elizabeth 1946- WhoAmW 93
Bernau, George 1945- ScF&FL 92
Bernau, Simon John 1937- WhoAm 92, WhoSSW 93
Bernauer, Carol Candice 1956- WhoEmL 93
Bernauer, Louise Boethling 1945- WhoAmW 93
Bernay, Betti 1926- WhoAm 92, WhoAmW 93
Bernays, Anne 1930- WhoWrEP 92
Bernays, Anne Fleischman 1930- WhoAm 92
Bernays, Edward L. 1891- BioIn 17, WhoAm 92
Bernays, Elizabeth Anna 1940- WhoAm 92
Bernbach, John Lincoln 1944- St&PR 93, WhoAm 92, WhoE 93
Bernbach, William 1911-1982 BioIn 17
Bernberg, Bruce Arthur 1943- St&PR 93, WhoAm 92
Bernbom, John Law&B 92
Bernd, August 1950- WhoScE 91-3
Bernd, David LeMoine 1949- WhoAm 92
Bernd, James D. 1933- St&PR 93
Bernds, Edward MiSFD 9
Berndt, Catherine Helen 1918- IntDcAn

Berndt, Ellen German *Law&B 92*
Berndt, Ernst Rudolf 1946- *WhoE 93*
Berndt, Jane Ann 1954- *WhoEmL 93*
Berndt, John Edward 1940- *WhoAm 92*
Berndt, Joyce L. 1929- *St&PR 93*
Berndt, Kim Lawrence 1956- *WhoEmL 93*
Berndt, Richard E. 1930- *St&PR 93*
Berndt, Ronald M. 1916-1990 *IntDcAn*
Berndt, Ronald Murray 1916-1990 *BioIn 17*
Berndt, Scott D. 1951- *St&PR 93*
Berndt, Thomas Theodore, Jr. 1947- *WhoEmL 93*
Berne, Bruce J. 1940- *WhoAm 92*
Berne, Clement H. *Law&B 92*
Berne, Eric 1910-1970 *BioIn 17*
Berne, Karin *WhoWrEP 92*
Berne, Max L. 1921- *St&PR 93*
Berne, Patricia Higgins 1934- *WhoE 93*
Berne, Robert Matthew 1918- *WhoAm 92, WhoSSW 93*
Berne, Stanley 1923- *WhoWrEP 92*
Berne, Tim *BioIn 17*
Bernecker, Larry O. 1948- *St&PR 93*
Bernee, Andrea Lorel 1960- *WhoEmL 93*
Berneike, Richard H. *Law&B 92*
Berneker, Constanz 1844-1906 *Baker 92*
Bernell, Sue 1942- *WhoWrEP 92*
Bernens, Donald L. 1929- *St&PR 93*
Berner, Arthur Samuel *Law&B 92*
Berner, Arthur Samuel 1943- *St&PR 93*
Berner, Carl Walter 1902- *ConAu 37NR*
Berner, David Paul 1949- *WhoE 93*
Berner, Elizabeth A. *Law&B 92*
Berner, Frederic George, Jr. 1943- *WhoAm 92*
Berner, G. Gary 1948- *St&PR 93*
Berner, George Luis Soren 1948- *WhoWor 93*
Berner, Jan 1932- *WhoScE 91-4*
Berner, Lawrence M. *St&PR 93*
Berner, Leo De Witte, Jr. 1922- *WhoAm 92*
Berner, Richard Brian 1946- *WhoE 93*
Berner, Robert Arbuckle 1935- *WhoAm 92*
Berner, Robert Frank 1917- *WhoAm 92*
Berner, Robert Lee, Jr. 1931- *WhoAm 92*
Berner, Sargent H. 1941- *St&PR 93*
Berner, Stephen P. 1934-1990 *BioIn 17*
Berner, T. Roland 1910-1990 *BioIn 17*
Berner, Thomas Franklyn 1954- *WhoEmL 93*
Berners, Lord 1883-1950 *Baker 92*
Berners, Edgar Hubert 1898- *WhoAm 92*
Bernert, Jan Paul 1951- *WhoWor 93*
Bernet Kempers, Karel Philippus 1897-1974 *Baker 92*
Berney, Arnold E. 1943- *St&PR 93*
Berney, Betty Lou 1932- *WhoWrEP 92*
Berney, Elizabeth Gottlieb 1957- *WhoE 93*
Berney, Gail S. *Law&B 92*
Berney, Jean 1928- *WhoScE 91-4*
Berney, Joseph H. 1932- *St&PR 93*
Berney, Joseph Henry 1932- *WhoAm 92*
Berney, S.R. 1938- *St&PR 93*
Bernfeld, Jeffrey A. *St&PR 93*
Bernfeld, Jules E. 1917- *St&PR 93*
Bernfeld, Peter Harry William 1912- *WhoAm 92*
Bernfeld, William Steven 1950- *WhoE 93*
Bernfield, Merton Ronald 1938- *WhoE 93*
Bernhagen, Lillian Flickinger 1916- *WhoAm 92, WhoWor 93*
Bernhang, Arthur M. 1934- *WhoE 93*
Bernhard, Duke of Saxe-Weimar 1604-1639 *HarEnMi*
Bernhard, Prince 1911- *WhoWor 93*
Bernhard, Alexander Alfred 1936- *WhoAm 92*
Bernhard, Arnold 1901- *WhoWrEP 92*
Bernhard, Berl 1929- *WhoAm 92*
Bernhard, Christine A. *Law&B 92*
Bernhard, Christoph 1628-1692 *Baker 92*
Bernhard, Harry Barnett 1933- *WhoSSW 93, WhoWor 93*
Bernhard, Herbert Ashley 1927- *WhoAm 92*
Bernhard, Janet K. 1904- *St&PR 93*
Bernhard, Jeffrey David 1951- *WhoE 93*
Bernhard, Jon Casper 1961- *WhoEmL 93*
Bernhard, Linda Anne 1947- *WhoAmW 93*
Bernhard, Richard Harold 1933- *WhoSSW 93*
Bernhard, Robert Arthur 1928- *St&PR 93, WhoAm 92*
Bernhard, Sandra *BioIn 17*
Bernhard, Sandra 1955?- *ConAu 137, ConTFT 10*
Bernhard, Thomas *BioIn 17*
Bernhard, Thomas 1931-1989 *DcLB 124 [port]*
Bernhard, William Francis 1924- *WhoAm 92*
Bernhard der Deutsche d1459 *Baker 92*
Bernhard Jackson, Gabriele Johanna 1934- *WhoE 93*
Bernhardson, Ivy Schutz *Law&B 92*
Bernhardson, Ivy Schutz 1951- *St&PR 93, WhoAmW 93, WhoEmL 93*
Bernhardt, Arthur Dieter 1937- *WhoAm 92, WhoE 93, WhoWor 93*
Bernhardt, Curtis 1899-1981 *MiSFD 9N*
Bernhardt, Donald John 1937- *WhoAm 92*
Bernhardt, Gregory Ralph 1948- *WhoEmL 93*
Bernhardt, Herbert Nelson *WhoAm 92*
Bernhardt, Jay 1943- *St&PR 93*
Bernhardt, John Bowman 1929- *St&PR 93, WhoAm 92*
Bernhardt, Kirsten Ingrid *Law&B 92*
Bernhardt, Lewis Jules 1937- *WhoWor 93*
Bernhardt, Maciej *WhoScE 91-4*
Bernhardt, Marcia Brenda 1938- *WhoSSW 93*
Bernhardt, Melvin *WhoAm 92*
Bernhardt, Richard Bruce 1961- *WhoEmL 93*
Bernhardt, Robert *WhoAm 92*
Bernhardt, Sarah 1844-1923 *BioIn 17*
Bernhardt, Warren *BioIn 17*
Bernhart, Dennis G. 1945- *St&PR 93*
Bernheim, Alain 1947- *WhoScE 91-2*
Bernheim, Elinor K. 1907-1992 *NewYTBS 92 [port]*
Bernheim, Heather Stanchfield Peterson *WhoAmW 93*
Bernheim, Jacques 1924- *WhoScE 91-4*
Bernheim, Jean L. 1941- *WhoScE 91-2*
Bernheim, Joyce Mary 1952- *WhoEmL 93*
Bernheimer, Alan Weyl 1913- *WhoE 93*
Bernheimer, Martin 1936- *Baker 92, WhoAm 92*
Bernheimer, Walter S., II 1940- *St&PR 93*
Bernheisel, Donald Paul 1945- *St&PR 93*
Bernholtz, Bryan Alan *Law&B 92*
Bernich, Mary Gabrielle 1963- *WhoAmW 93*
Bernick, Carol Lavin 1952- *St&PR 93*
Bernick, Howard B. 1952- *St&PR 93*
Bernick, Randal N. 1958- *St&PR 93*
Bernie, Bruce Jeremy 1948- *WhoEmL 93*
Bernie, John A. 1940- *WhoScE 91-1*
Bernier, George Matthew, Jr. 1934- *WhoAm 92*
Bernier, Georges 1934- *WhoScE 91-2*
Bernier, Jean 1936- *WhoAm 92*
Bernier, Jean-Pierre *Law&B 92*
Bernier, John Gerard 1958- *WhoEmL 93*
Bernier, John Rodrigue 1945- *St&PR 93*
Bernier, Nicolas 1665-1734 *Baker 92*
Bernier, Patrick Pierre 1943- *WhoWor 93*
Bernier, Rene 1905-1984 *Baker 92*
Bernier, Rosamond *BioIn 17*
Bernier, Wilfred Alcide 1943- *WhoE 93*
Berniere, Jacques Jean 1937- *WhoWor 93*
Bernieres, Louis de *ScF&FL 92*
Berning, Charles F. 1945- *St&PR 93*
Berning, Randall Karl 1950- *WhoEmL 93*
Berning, Susan Maxwell 1941- *BiDAMSp 1989*
Berninger, Lori Dobbs 1961- *WhoEmL 93*
Berninger, Virginia Wise 1946- *WhoEmL 93*
Bernini, Dante 1926- *WhoWor 93*
Bernini, Gian Lorenzo 1598-1680 *BioIn 17*
Bernitt, Sven Robert Hans 1963- *WhoWor 93*
Bernknopf, Al d1991 *BioIn 17*
Bernkopf, Jeanne d1992 *BioIn 17*
Bernkopf, Jeanne F. d1992 *NewYTBS 92*
Bernkrant, M.C. 1927- *St&PR 93*
Bernlohr, Kurt W. *Law&B 92*
Bernlohr, Robert William 1933- *WhoAm 92*
Bernobich, H. Elizabeth 1959- *WhoAmW 93*
Bernoco, Domenico 1935- *WhoWor 93*
Bernofsky, Carl 1933- *WhoSSW 93*
Bernosky, Herman George 1921- *WhoE 93*
Bernot, Jacques 1929- *WhoScE 91-2*
Bernoulli, Eduard 1867-1927 *Baker 92*
Berno von Reichenau c. 970-1048 *Baker 92*
Berns, Bert 1929-1967 *SoulM*
Berns, Ellen Marsha Schimmel 1948- *WhoEmL 93*
Berns, Eugene H. 1936- *St&PR 93*
Berns, Joseph J. 1946- *St&PR 93*
Berns, Kenneth Ira 1938- *WhoAm 92*
Berns, Margie 1949- *WhoAmW 93*
Berns, Peter Vernon 1956- *WhoE 93*
Berns, Walter Fred 1919- *WhoAm 92*
Bernsen, Collin *BioIn 17*
Bernsen, Corbin *BioIn 17*
Bernsen, Corbin 1954- *WhoAm 92*
Bernsen, Harold John 1936- *WhoAm 92*
Bernshtam, A.N. 1910-1956 *IntDcAn*
Bernstein, Abraham 1918-1990 *BioIn 17*
Bernstein, Abraham 1932- *St&PR 93*
Bernstein, Alan Arthur 1944- *WhoAm 92*
Bernstein, Alan Barry 1947- *WhoAm 92, WhoSSW 93*
Bernstein, Alfred S. 1914- *St&PR 93*
Bernstein, Alison *BioIn 17*
Bernstein, Alvin Stanley 1929- *WhoE 93*
Bernstein, Andrea *Law&B 92*
Bernstein, Andrew J. *Law&B 92*
Bernstein, Anne Carolyn 1944- *WhoAmW 93*
Bernstein, Anne Elayne 1937- *WhoAm 92*
Bernstein, Armyan *MiSFD 9*
Bernstein, Arnold Robert 1920- *St&PR 93*
Bernstein, Arthur Dan 1926- *St&PR 93*
Bernstein, Arthur J. 1947- *WhoEmL 93, WhoSSW 93*
Bernstein, Arthur Jay 1937- *WhoAm 92*
Bernstein, Barbara Jane 1961- *WhoEmL 93*
Bernstein, Benedict Jacob 1910-1991 *BioIn 17*
Bernstein, Bernard 1908-1990 *BioIn 17*
Bernstein, Bernard 1929- *St&PR 93, WhoAm 92*
Bernstein, Bernard Alexander 1938- *WhoE 93*
Bernstein, Beth Anspach d1992 *BioIn 17*
Bernstein, Betsy Bennett 1950- *WhoEmL 93*
Bernstein, Brad *Law&B 92*
Bernstein, Burt 1937- *St&PR 93*
Bernstein, Burton 1932- *WhoWrEP 92*
Bernstein, Carl *BioIn 17*
Bernstein, Carl 1944- *JrnUS, WhoAm 92, WhoWrEP 92*
Bernstein, Carol Ann 1947- *WhoEmL 93*
Bernstein, Caryl S. *Law&B 92*
Bernstein, Caryl Salomon 1933- *St&PR 93, WhoAm 92, WhoAmW 93*
Bernstein, Charles 1950- *WhoE 93, WhoWrEP 92*
Bernstein, Charles Marc 1952- *WhoEmL 93*
Bernstein, Claire Marie 1943- *WhoAmW 93*
Bernstein, Daniel J. *Law&B 92*
Bernstein, Daniel Lewis 1937- *WhoAm 92*
Bernstein, David d1992 *BioIn 17*
Bernstein, David H. 1935- *St&PR 93*
Bernstein, David Howard 1956- *WhoAm 92*
Bernstein, Debra L. *Law&B 92*
Bernstein, Donald Chester *Law&B 92*
Bernstein, Donald Chester 1942- *WhoAm 92*
Bernstein, Donald H. 1938- *St&PR 93*
Bernstein, Douglas Lon 1958- *WhoEmL 93*
Bernstein, Eduard 1850-1932 *BioIn 17, DcTwHis*
Bernstein, Edwin S. 1930- *WhoAm 92*
Bernstein, Elaine Handlin 1926- *WhoSSW 93*
Bernstein, Ellen 1946- *WhoAmW 93*
Bernstein, Elliot 1923- *St&PR 93*
Bernstein, Elliot Louis 1934- *WhoAm 92*
Bernstein, Elliot Roy 1941- *WhoAm 92*
Bernstein, Elmer 1922- *Baker 92, WhoAm 92*
Bernstein, Emil Steven 1946- *St&PR 93, WhoAm 92*
Bernstein, Eric Martin 1957- *WhoEmL 93*
Bernstein, Esther 1921- *St&PR 93*
Bernstein, Eugene Felix 1930- *WhoAm 92*
Bernstein, Eugene Merle 1931- *WhoAm 92*
Bernstein, Eva Gould 1918- *WhoAmW 93*
Bernstein, George L. 1932- *WhoAm 92*
Bernstein, H. Bruce 1943- *WhoAm 92*
Bernstein, H. Carol *Law&B 92*
Bernstein, Harold L. *Law&B 92*
Bernstein, Harold Lintz 1921- *St&PR 93*
Bernstein, Harvey Michael 1945- *WhoAm 92, WhoE 93*
Bernstein, Harvey N. *Law&B 92*
Bernstein, Herbert J. 1944- *WhoWrEP 92*
Bernstein, Herbert Joseph 1943- *WhoE 93*
Bernstein, Herman Joel 1941- *St&PR 93*
Bernstein, I. Leonard 1924- *WhoAm 92*
Bernstein, I. Melvin 1938- *WhoAm 92*
Bernstein, Ileane Janis 1956- *WhoE 93*
Bernstein, Ira Borah 1924- *WhoAm 92*
Bernstein, Ira Harvey 1938- *WhoSSW 93*
Bernstein, Irving 1921- *WhoAm 92, WhoE 93*
Bernstein, Irwin Frederick 1933- *St&PR 93*
Bernstein, Isadore Abraham 1919- *WhoAm 92*
Bernstein, Jane 1949- *WhoEmL 93, WhoWrEP 92*
Bernstein, Jay 1927- *WhoAm 92*
Bernstein, Jean *Law&B 92*
Bernstein, Jerald Jack 1934- *WhoE 93*
Bernstein, Jeremy 1929- *BioIn 17*
Bernstein, Jeremy Marshall 1952- *WhoEmL 93*
Bernstein, Jerry Daniel 1949- *WhoEmL 93*
Bernstein, Joan Z. *Law&B 92*
Bernstein, Joe 1932- *WhoAm 92*
Bernstein, John T. *Law&B 92*
Bernstein, Jonathan E. 1944- *St&PR 93*
Bernstein, Joseph 1930- *WhoSSW 93, WhoWor 93*
Bernstein, Kenneth Alan 1956- *WhoEmL 93*
Bernstein, Larry R. *Law&B 92*
Bernstein, Laurel 1945- *WhoAm 92*
Bernstein, Lawrence 1940- *WhoAm 92, WhoE 93*
Bernstein, Lawrence F. 1939- *Baker 92*
Bernstein, Leonard *WhoScE 91-1*
Bernstein, Leonard d1990 *NewYTBS 92*
Bernstein, Leonard 1918-1990 *Baker 92, BioIn 17, ConHero 2 [port], IntDcOp, JeAmHC, OxDcOp*
Bernstein, Lester 1920- *WhoAm 92*
Bernstein, Louis 1927- *WhoAm 92*
Bernstein, Louis B. *Law&B 92*
Bernstein, Marc Alan 1955- *WhoEmL 93*
Bernstein, Martin 1904- *Baker 92*
Bernstein, Martin L. 1941- *St&PR 93*
Bernstein, Marver H. 1919-1990 *BioIn 17*
Bernstein, Mashey Maurice 1946- *WhoWrEP 92*
Bernstein, Merton Clay 1923- *WhoAm 92*
Bernstein, Michael Howard 1943- *St&PR 93*
Bernstein, Michael Joel 1938- *WhoSSW 93*
Bernstein, Myron Elliott 1938- *St&PR 93*
Bernstein, Neil David 1945- *St&PR 93*
Bernstein, Neil S. 1938- *St&PR 93*
Bernstein, Norman d1992 *NewYTBS 92*
Bernstein, Norman Ralph 1927- *WhoAm 92*
Bernstein, Patricia Robin 1956- *WhoAmW 93, WhoEmL 93*
Bernstein, Paul 1927- *WhoAm 92*
Bernstein, Paul M. 1929-1990 *BioIn 17*
Bernstein, Phyliss Louise 1940- *WhoAmW 93*
Bernstein, R. Victor *Law&B 92*
Bernstein, Ralph 1933- *WhoAm 92*
Bernstein, Richard 1928- *St&PR 93*
Bernstein, Richard A. 1946- *St&PR 93, WhoAm 92*
Bernstein, Richard Barry 1923-1990 *BioIn 17*
Bernstein, Richard Mark 1957- *WhoE 93, WhoEmL 93*
Bernstein, Robert 1920- *WhoAm 92*
Bernstein, Robert Alan *BioIn 17*
Bernstein, Robert Alan 1958- *WhoEmL 93*
Bernstein, Robert I. 1927- *St&PR 93*
Bernstein, Robert Jay 1948- *WhoEmL 93*
Bernstein, Robert Louis 1923- *WhoAm 92, WhoWrEP 92*
Bernstein, Seymour 1911- *St&PR 93*
Bernstein, Sidney 1938- *WhoAm 92*
Bernstein, Sidney Ralph 1907- *WhoAm 92, WhoWrEP 92*
Bernstein, Sol 1927- *WhoAm 92, WhoWor 93*
Bernstein, Stanley Joseph *WhoAm 92*
Bernstein, Stephen L. *Law&B 92*
Bernstein, Stephen L. 1933- *St&PR 93*
Bernstein, Stephen Michael 1941- *WhoE 93*
Bernstein, Steven 1957- *St&PR 93*
Bernstein, Steven Michael 1953- *WhoE 93*
Bernstein, Susan Powell 1938- *WhoAm 92*
Bernstein, Theodore 1926- *WhoAm 92*
Bernstein, Theresa 1896- *BioIn 17*
Bernstein, Victor H. d1992 *NewYTBS 92*
Bernstein, Vigdor D. *Law&B 92*
Bernstein, Walter 1929- *MiSFD 9*
Bernstein, William 1933- *St&PR 93*
Bernstein, William J. *Law&B 92*
Bernstein, Zalman C. 1926- *St&PR 93*
Bernstine, Daniel O'Neal 1947- *WhoAm 92*
Bernt, Benno Anthony 1931- *WhoAm 92*
Bernthal, David Gary 1950- *WhoEmL 93*
Bernthal, Frederick W. 1928- *St&PR 93*
Bernthal, Harold George 1928- *WhoAm 92*
Bernthal, Russell Lee 1957- *WhoEmL 93*
Bernt Hazzard, Charlotte Irene 1953- *WhoAmW 93, WhoEmL 93*
Berntsen, Bjarne T. 1935- *St&PR 93*
Berntsen, Drude *WhoScE 91-4*
Bernucca, Louis F. 1938- *St&PR 93*
Bernuth, Ernest Patrick, Jr. 1939- *WhoWrEP 92*
Bernuth, Julius von 1830-1902 *Baker 92*
Bero, Marilyn Procino 1937- *WhoAmW 93*
Bero, Ronald Arthur 1935- *St&PR 93, WhoAm 92*
Bero, William Burke 1932- *St&PR 93*
Beroff, Michel 1950- *Baker 92*
Berolzheimer, Karl *Law&B 92*
Berolzheimer, Karl 1932- *WhoAm 92*
Beron, Gail Laskey 1943- *WhoAmW 93*
Beron, Petar Kirilov 1940- *WhoScE 91-4*
Beron, Philip, Jr. *St&PR 93*
Beronio, Janet Marie *Law&B 92*
Beroza, Anne *Law&B 92*
Beroza, Morton 1917- *WhoE 93*

Berquist, James Richard 1928- *WhoIns 93*
Berr, Friedrich 1794-1838 *Baker 92*
Berr, Stephen Frederick 1936- *WhoE 93*
Berr, Ulrich Rudolf 1927- *WhoScE 91-3, WhoWor 93*
Berra, Lawrence Peter 1925- *WhoAm 92*
Berra, P. Bruce 1935- *WhoAm 92*
Berra, Robert Louis 1924- *WhoAm 92*
Berra, William 1952- *BioIn 17*
Berra, Yogi 1925- *BioIn 17, WhoAm 92*
Berrada, Mohammed 1944- *WhoWor 93*
Berreby, David 1958- *WhoE 93*
Berres, Frances Brandes *WhoAmW 93, WhoWor 93*
Berres, Gerald J. *Law&B 92*
Berres, Roger Edward *Law&B 92*
Berresford, Susan Vail 1943- *WhoAm 92, WhoAmW 93, WhoE 93*
Berretta, Horacio 1926- *WhoWor 93*
Berrettone, Robert J. 1948- *WhoE 93*
Berrey, Bedford Hudson, Jr. 1950- *WhoE 93*
Berrey, Robert Forrest 1939- *St&PR 93, WhoAm 92*
Berrezoug, Mohamed 1941- *WhoUN 92*
Berri, Claude 1934- *MiSFD 9*
Berriault, Gina 1926-1991 *ScF&FL 92*
Berridge, George B. 1928- *St&PR 93*
Berridge, George Bradford *Law&B 92*
Berridge, George Bradford 1928- *WhoAm 92*
Berridge, Jesse 1874-1966 *ScF&FL 92*
Berridge, Michael John *WhoScE 91-1*
Berridge, Thomas E. *Law&B 92*
Berridge, Thomas E. 1946- *WhoIns 93*
Berrie, A.D. *WhoScE 91-1*
Berrie, Russell 1933- *WhoAm 92*
Berrien, Edith Heal *AmWomPl*
Berrien, James S. *BioIn 17*
Berrien, James S. 1952- *St&PR 93*
Berrien, James Stuart 1952- *WhoAm 92*
Berrier, Erwin F., Jr. *Law&B 92*
Berrier, Ronald G. 1943- *St&PR 93*
Berrigan, A. John 1943- *St&PR 93*
Berrigan, Daniel *BioIn 17*
Berrigan, Daniel 1921- *WhoWrEP 92*
Berrigan, Philip 1923- *BioIn 17*
Berrigan, Ted 1934-1983 *BioIn 17*
Berrill, Norman John 1903- *WhoAm 92*
Berriman, W. Thomas 1930- *St&PR 93*
Berring, Robert Charles, Jr. 1949- *WhoEmL 93*
Berringer, Gary Revere 1952- *WhoE 93*
Berringer, Oscar, Mrs *AmWomPl*
Berrington, Hugh Bayard *WhoScE 91-1*
Berrio, William John 1937- *St&PR 93*
Berrios Martinez, Ruben 1939- *DcCPCAm*
Berriozabal, Maria Antonietta 1941- *NotHsAW 93*
Berritt, Harold Edward 1936- *St&PR 93*
Berro, Karen Lynn 1959- *WhoAmW 93*
Berro, Michael Bruce 1955- *WhoEmL 93*
Berroa, Ignacio *BioIn 17*
Berroir, Andre *WhoScE 91-2*
Berrow, Michael Lloyd 1932- *WhoScE 91-1*
Berruguete, Alonso c. 1486-1561 *BioIn 17*
Berruguete, Pedro 1450-1504 *BioIn 17*
Berrut, Jean-Paul 1952- *WhoWor 93*
Berry, Adaline Hohf *AmWomPl*
Berry, Adrian 1937- *ScF&FL 92*
Berry, Alan Lindsay 1954- *WhoE 93*
Berry, Ambrose 1954- *St&PR 93*
Berry, Ann Roper 1934- *WhoAm 92*
Berry, Bill *MiSFD 9*
Berry, Brenda Gail 1949- *WhoAmW 93*
Berry, Brewton 1901- *WhoAm 92*
Berry, Brian Joe Lobley 1934- *WhoAm 92*
Berry, Brian Shepherd 1929- *WhoE 93*
Berry, Bryan 1930-1955 *ScF&FL 92*
Berry, Buford Preston 1935- *WhoAm 92, WhoSSW 93*
Berry, C.S. 1910- *St&PR 93*
Berry, Carol A. 1950- *WhoAmW 93*
Berry, Carrie Adams *AmWomPl*
Berry, Catherine R. *Law&B 92*
Berry, Charlene Helen 1941- *WhoAmW 93*
Berry, Charles Gordon 1950- *WhoAm 92, WhoEmL 93*
Berry, Charles Oscar 1907- *WhoAm 92*
Berry, "Chu" 1908-1941 *Baker 92*
Berry, Chuck 1926- *Baker 92, SoulM, WhoAm 92*
Berry, Clarence G. 1927- *St&PR 93*
Berry, Constance I. *Law&B 92*
Berry, D. Bruce *ScF&FL 92*
Berry, David E. 1932- *St&PR 93*
Berry, David Holmes 1951- *WhoEmL 93*
Berry, David J. 1944- *WhoAm 92*
Berry, David Lawton 1926- *St&PR 93*
Berry, David Richard *WhoScE 91-1*
Berry, Dean C. 1952- *St&PR 93*
Berry, Dean Lester 1935- *WhoAm 92*
Berry, Debra L. 1949- *WhoAmW 93*
Berry, Don H. 1931- *St&PR 93*
Berry, Donald Kent 1953- *WhoEmL 93, WhoSSW 93*
Berry, Donald Lee 1940- *WhoSSW 93*
Berry, Donald Reese 1953- *WhoEmL 93*
Berry, Doyle G. 1930- *St&PR 93*
Berry, Edna Janet 1917- *WhoAm 92*
Berry, Eliot 1949- *ConAu 139*
Berry, Erlinda Gonzales *NotHsAW 93*
Berry, Eugene Dwight 1952- *AfrAmBi*
Berry, Francine J. *Law&B 92*
Berry, George A., III 1918- *St&PR 93*
Berry, George Abbott 1951- *WhoSSW 93*
Berry, George B. 1936- *St&PR 93*
Berry, Gerard 1948- *WhoScE 91-2*
Berry, Guy Curtis 1935- *WhoAm 92*
Berry, H. *WhoScE 91-1*
Berry, Halle 1967?- *ConBlB 4 [port]*
Berry, Harold James 1913- *St&PR 93*
Berry, Henry Arnold, Jr. 1945- *WhoWrEP 92*
Berry, Henry G. 1936- *St&PR 93*
Berry, Henry T., Jr. *Law&B 92*
Berry, Ian J.G. *WhoScE 91-1*
Berry, Ilona M. *Law&B 92*
Berry, Isabel Ethel 1941- *WhoAmW 93*
Berry, J. Bill 1945- *ConAu 137*
Berry, Jack 1918-1980 *IntDcAn*
Berry, James *BioIn 17, BlkAuII 92*
Berry, James 1914- *BioIn 17*
Berry, James 1925- *ChlFicS*
Berry, James C.P. *Law&B 92*
Berry, James Frederick 1927- *WhoAm 92*
Berry, James R. 1933- *ScF&FL 92*
Berry, Jan 1941- *Baker 92*
Berry, Janet Claire 1948- *WhoSSW 93*
Berry, Janis Marie 1949- *WhoEmL 93*
Berry, Jay 1928- *St&PR 93*
Berry, Jeffery R. *Law&B 92*
Berry, Joan Elizabeth 1956- *WhoEmL 93*
Berry, Joe Gene 1944- *WhoSSW 93*
Berry, Joe Wilkes 1938- *WhoAm 92*
Berry, John *WhoWrEP 92*
Berry, John 1917- *MiSFD 9*
Berry, John Aloysius *Law&B 92*
Berry, John Charles 1938- *WhoWor 93*
Berry, John Coltrin 1937- *WhoAm 92*
Berry, John F. 1943- *St&PR 93*
Berry, John J., III *Law&B 92*
Berry, John Nichols, III 1933- *JrnUS, WhoAm 92, WhoWrEP 92*
Berry, John Widdup 1939- *WhoAm 92*
Berry, John Willard 1947- *WhoAm 92*
Berry, John William 1922- *St&PR 93, WhoAm 92*
Berry, Jonas *ConAu 37NR*
Berry, Joni Ingram 1953- *WhoSSW 93*
Berry, Joseph J. 1946- *St&PR 93*
Berry, Joyce Charlotte 1937- *WhoAm 92, WhoWrEP 92*
Berry, Joyce T. *WhoAm 92*
Berry, Jules 1883-1951 *IntDcF 2-3 [port]*
Berry, Julianne Elward 1946- *WhoAm 92*
Berry, Julie Merritt 1963- *WhoEmL 93*
Berry, Karen Smith 1958- *WhoAmW 93*
Berry, Kristin *BioIn 17*
Berry, Lemuel, Jr. 1946- *WhoAm 92, WhoEmL 93, WhoSSW 93*
Berry, Leonard 1930- *WhoSSW 93*
Berry, Leonidas Harris 1902- *WhoAm 92*
Berry, Leslie Ellis 1952- *WhoEmL 93*
Berry, Leslie Thomas McCloud 1937- *WhoWor 93*
Berry, Lettie Amanda 1966- *WhoSSW 93*
Berry, Linden Farrar 1944- *WhoWrEP 92*
Berry, Lisa C. *Law&B 92*
Berry, Lucile Blackburn *AmWomPl*
Berry, Martin *WhoScE 91-1*
Berry, Mary Douglas Poindexter 1943- *WhoAmW 93*
Berry, Mary Frances 1938- *EncAACR*
Berry, Michael James 1947- *WhoAm 92, WhoWor 93*
Berry, Michael John 1951- *WhoWor 93*
Berry, Michael Victor *WhoScE 91-1*
Berry, N.L. *ScF&FL 92*
Berry, Nancy Michaels 1928- *WhoAm 92*
Berry, Nelson Scott 1942 *St&PR 93*
Berry, Norma Jean 1946- *WhoAmW 93*
Berry, Nyas 1912- *BioIn 17*
Berry, Paul Sherman 1934- *WhoUN 92*
Berry, Peter DuPre 1943- *WhoSSW 93*
Berry, Phillip Reid 1950- *WhoEmL 93, WhoWor 93*
Berry, Phillip Samuel 1937- *WhoWor 93*
Berry, Raymond 1933- *BioIn 17*
Berry, Richard *BioIn 17*
Berry, Richard 1946- *BioIn 17*
Berry, Richard C. 1928- *St&PR 93*
Berry, Richard Cameron 1927- *WhoSSW 93*
Berry, Richard Chisholm 1928- *WhoAm 92*
Berry, Richard Douglas 1926- *WhoAm 92*
Berry, Richard Lewis 1946- *WhoAm 92, WhoWrEP 92*
Berry, Richard Louis *Law&B 92*
Berry, Richard Stephen 1931- *WhoAm 92*
Berry, Robert Bass 1948- *WhoEmL 93, WhoSSW 93*
Berry, Robert H. 1944- *St&PR 93*
Berry, Robert John 1947- *WhoE 93, WhoEmL 93*
Berry, Robert T. 1949- *St&PR 93*
Berry, Robert Vaughan 1933- *St&PR 93, WhoAm 92*
Berry, Robert Worth 1926- *WhoAm 92, WhoWor 93*
Berry, Scyld 1954- *ConAu 136*
Berry, Shelley Dutton *ScF&FL 92*
Berry, Shirley Nichols 1930- *WhoAmW 93*
Berry, Sidney Bryan 1926- *WhoAm 92*
Berry, Stephen Ames 1947- *ScF&FL 92*
Berry, Stephen Gardner 1951- *WhoEmL 93*
Berry, Thomas Ernest 1947- *WhoEmL 93*
Berry, Thomas Harrison 1944- *WhoE 93*
Berry, Thomas Joseph 1925- *WhoAm 92*
Berry, Thomas Robert 1931- *WhoAm 92*
Berry, Timothy Brooks 1948- *St&PR 93*
Berry, Timothy J. *Law&B 92*
Berry, Todd Andrew 1951- *WhoEmL 93*
Berry, Tom *MiSFD 9*
Berry, Vickie Lee 1954- *WhoEmL 93*
Berry, Virgil J. 1928- *St&PR 93*
Berry, Virgil Jennings, Jr. 1928- *WhoAm 92*
Berry, Wallace (Taft) 1928- *Baker 92*
Berry, Walter 1929- *Baker 92, IntDcOp, OxDcOp, WhoAm 92*
Berry, Warren 1922- *BioIn 17*
Berry, Wendell 1934- *BioIn 17, MagSAmL [port], WhoAm 92, WhoWrEP 92*
Berry, William Benjamin Newell 1931- *WhoAm 92*
Berry, William Deck 1940- *WhoSSW 93*
Berry, William James, III 1950- *WhoEmL 93, WhoSSW 93*
Berry, William L., Jr. *Law&B 92*
Berry, William Lee 1935- *WhoAm 92*
Berry, William Martin 1920- *St&PR 93, WhoAm 92, WhoWor 93*
Berry, William S. 1941- *St&PR 93*
Berry, William W. 1932- *St&PR 93*
Berry, William Wells 1917- *WhoAm 92, WhoSSW 93*
Berry, William Willis 1932- *WhoAm 92, WhoSSW 93*
Berry Caban, Cristobal Santiago 1953- *WhoEmL 93, WhoSSW 93*
Berryessa, Richard Greaves 1947- *WhoEmL 93*
Berryhill, Dennis G. 1947- *St&PR 93*
Berryhill, Henry Lee, Jr. 1921- *WhoAm 92*
Berry Hill, James *BioIn 17*
Berryman, David Homer 1952- *St&PR 93*
Berryman, Jane Ann 1962- *WhoWor 93*
Berryman, John 1914-1972 *BioIn 17, MagSAmL [port]*
Berryman, Karen Louise 1953- *WhoAmW 93*
Berryman, Patricia Lord 1953- *WhoAmW 93*
Berryman, Richard Byron 1932- *WhoAm 92*
Berryman, Treva Griffith 1952- *WhoEmL 93, WhoSSW 93*
Berry-Smith, Bridgette A. *Law&B 92*
Bers, Abraham 1930- *WhoE 93*
Bers, Donald Martin 1953- *WhoEmL 93*
Bers, John A. 1946- *WhoSSW 93*
Bersa, Blagoje 1873-1934 *Baker 92, OxDcOp*
Bersa, Josip *OxDcOp*
Bersa, Vladimir 1864-1927 *OxDcOp*
Bersak, Robert A. *Law&B 92*
Bersch, Charles Frank 1927- *WhoSSW 93*
Berscheid, Ellen S. 1936- *WhoAm 92, WhoAmW 93*
Berset, Claudette 1941- *WhoScE 91-2*
Bersh, Philip Joseph 1921- *WhoAm 92*
Bershad, Jack R. 1930- *St&PR 93, WhoAm 92*
Bershad, Neil Jeremy 1937- *WhoAm 92*
Bershon, Barbara Luck 1946- *WhoAmW 93*
Bershtel, Sara 1947- *ConAu 139*
Bersianik, Louky 1930- *BioIn 17, WhoCanL 92*
Bersoff, Donald Neil 1939- *WhoAm 92, WhoE 93*
Bersohn, Matthias 1823-1908 *PolBiDi*
Berson, David William 1954- *WhoAm 92*
Berson, Eliot Lawrence 1937- *WhoAm 92*
Berson, F.A. *BioIn 17*
Berson, Felician Andrzej *BioIn 17*
Berson, Garry Zalmanovich 1935- *WhoWor 93*
Berson, Jerome Abraham 1924- *WhoAm 92*
Berson, Nancy S. *Law&B 92*
Berson, Robert M. *Law&B 92*
Berson, Robert M. 1939- *St&PR 93*
Berssenbrugge, Mei-Mei 1947- *WhoWrEP 92*
Berst, Barb Jo 1957- *WhoWrEP 92*
Berstein, Florence *AmWomPl*
Berstein, Irving Aaron 1926- *WhoAm 92, WhoE 93*
Berstein, Richard William *Law&B 92*
Berstein, Robert Louis 1923- *St&PR 93*
Berstell, Gerald N. 1949- *WhoEmL 93*
Berster, Carol Ann 1949- *WhoAmW 93*
Bersticker, Albert Charles 1934- *St&PR 93, WhoAm 92*
Bert, Carol Lois 1938- *WhoAmW 93*
Bert, Charles Wesley 1929- *WhoAm 92, WhoSSW 93*
Bert, Clara Virginia 1929- *WhoAmW 93, WhoSSW 93, WhoWor 93*
Bert, Debbie DeAnne 1954- *WhoAmW 93*
Bert, Eddie *BioIn 17*
Berta, Carolyn P. 1954- *St&PR 93*
Berta, Robert Michael 1955- *WhoEmL 93*
Berta, Vince 1958- *St&PR 93*
Berta, William Michael d1991 *BioIn 17*
Bertacchi, Paolo 1926- *WhoScE 91-3*
Bertagnolli, Emil J. 1925- *St&PR 93*
Bertain, George Joseph, Jr. 1929- *WhoAm 92*
Bertalan, Attila *MiSFD 9*
Bertali, Antonio 1605-1669 *Baker 92, OxDcOp*
Bertalotti, Angelo Michele 1666-1747 *Baker 92*
Bertan, Howard S. 1935- *St&PR 93*
Bertani, Alcide *WhoScE 91-3*
Bertani, Lelio c. 1550-c. 1620 *Baker 92*
Bertati, Giovanni 1735-1815 *OxDcOp*
Bertau, Ronald 1945- *WhoScE 91-2*
Bertch, David Paul 1945- *WhoSSW 93*
Bertch, Robert B. 1952- *St&PR 93*
Berte, Dennis James 1950- *St&PR 93*
Berte, Heinrich 1857-1924 *Baker 92*
Berte, Loredana *BioIn 17*
Berte, Neal Richard 1940- *WhoAm 92*
Berteau, David John 1949- *WhoAm 92*
Berteau, Martin c. 1700-1771 *Baker 92*
Bertel, Charles G. 1926- *St&PR 93*
Bertel, John W. 1965- *St&PR 93*
Bertele, William 1935- *WhoE 93*
Bertell, Mary Katherine 1925- *WhoE 93*
Bertell, Patricia Mari 1948- *WhoAmW 93*
Bertelle, Jeanne T. 1947- *WhoAm 92, WhoAmW 93, WhoEmL 93*
Bertelli, David Laurence 1944- *St&PR 93*
Bertellotti, Christopher Paul 1950- *WhoEmL 93*
Bertellotti, Edward A. 1952- *St&PR 93*
Bertels, William Charles 1951- *WhoEmL 93*
Bertelsen, Christian Cameron 1943- *St&PR 93*
Bertelsen, Rodeen Penny *Law&B 92*
Bertelsen, Thomas Elwood, Jr. 1940- *WhoAm 92*
Bertelsman, William Odis 1936- *WhoSSW 93*
Bertenshaw, Bobbi Cherrelle 1961- *WhoAmW 93, WhoEmL 93*
Bertenshaw, William Howard, III 1930- *WhoE 93*
Bertero, Vitelmo V. *BioIn 17, WhoAm 92*
Berth, Donald Frank 1935- *WhoE 93*
Bertha, Csilla *ScF&FL 92*
Bertha Of Sulzbach dc. 1160 *OxDcByz*
Bertheaume, Isidore c. 1752-1802 *Baker 92*
Berthelemy, Claude 1934- *WhoScE 91-2*
Berthelot, Henry J. *Law&B 92*
Berthelot, John 1930- *St&PR 93*
Berthelot, Yves Henri 1957- *BioIn 17*
Berthelot, Yves M. 1937- *WhoScE 91-4, WhoUN 92*
Berthelsdorf, Siegfried 1911- *WhoAm 92, WhoWor 93*
Berthelsen, Asger 1928- *WhoScE 91-2*
Berthelsen, John Robert 1954- *WhoAm 92, WhoEmL 93*
Berthelsen, Thomas *WhoScE 91-2*
Berthet, Paul 1933- *WhoScE 91-2*
Berthet, Philippe R. 1926- *St&PR 93*
Berthezene, Francois 1939- *WhoWor 93*
Berthiaume, Terry J. 1953- *St&PR 93*
Berthiaume, Wayne Henry 1955- *WhoE 93*
Berthier, Louis Alexandre 1753-1815 *HarEnMi*
Berthier, Michel *Law&B 92*
Berthoff, Rowland Tappan 1921- *WhoAm 92*
Berthold, Claes-Henric 1937- *WhoScE 91-4*
Berthold, Dennis Alfred 1942- *WhoSSW 93*
Berthold, James K. 1938- *St&PR 93*
Berthold, Thomas R. *Law&B 92*
Berthold-Rosen, Bonnie Madeline 1950- *WhoAmW 93*
Berthomieu, Claude 1939- *WhoWor 93*
Berthot, Jake 1939- *WhoAm 92*
Berthou, Jean-Marie 1940- *WhoScE 91-2*
Berthoz, Alain 1939- *WhoScE 91-2*
Berthrong, Frederick Morgan 1943- *St&PR 93*
Berti, Arturo Luis 1912- *WhoWor 93*

Berti, Carlo c. 1555-1602 Baker 92
Berti, Giancarlo 1924- WhoScE 91-3
Berti, Giovanni Pietro d1638 Baker 92
Berti, Luciano 1922- WhoWor 93
Berticat, Philippe 1939- WhoScE 91-2
Bertiger, Karen Lee 1954- WhoAmW 93, WhoEmL 93
Bertin, Antonio 1939- WhoScE 91-3
Bertin, Giuseppe 1952- WhoWor 93
Bertin, John Joseph 1938- WhoAm 92
Bertin, Louise 1805-1877 BioIn 17
Bertin, Louise (-Angelique) 1805-1877 Baker 92
Bertin de la Doue, Thomas c. 1680-1745 Baker 92
Bertinelli, Valerie 1960?- BioIn 17
Bertini, (Benoit-) Auguste 1780-1830 Baker 92
Bertini, Domenico 1829-1890 Baker 92
Bertini, Francesca 1888?-1985 IntDcF 2-3 [port]
Bertini, Gary 1927- Baker 92, WhoWor 93
Bertini, Giuseppe 1759-1852 Baker 92
Bertini, Henri (-Jerome) 1798-1876 Baker 92
Bertini, Salvatore 1721-1794 Baker 92
Bertino, Joseph Rocco 1930- WhoAm 92
Bertino, Shieila Elaine 1949- WhoSSW 93
Bertino, Thomas Law&B 92
Bertinotti (-Radicati), Teresa 1776-1854 Baker 92
Bertler, Ake 1931- WhoScE 91-4
Bertles, John Francis 1925- WhoAm 92
Bertness, Janette Ann 1957- WhoEmL 93
Berto, Gene WhoWrEP 92
Berto, Juliet d1990 BioIn 17
Bertocchi, Luciano 1933- WhoScE 91-3
Bertocci, D.A. St&PR 93
Bertocci, Peter Anthony 1910-1989 BioIn 17
Bertoch, David J. Law&B 92
Bertoch, Ronald Henry 1929- St&PR 93
Bertok, Janos 1934- WhoScE 91-4
Bertola, Francesco 1937- WhoScE 91-3
Bertoldo, Joseph Ramon 1950- WhoEmL 93
Bertoldo, Sperindio c. 1530-1570 Baker 92
Bertolet, Paul SmATA 73
Bertolett, Craig Randolph 1936- WhoSSW 93
Bertoli, Paolo Cardinal 1908- WhoAm 92, WhoWor 93
Bertolin, Mario 1957- WhoWor 93
Bertolini, Fernando 1925- WhoWor 93
Bertolini, Henry 1921- St&PR 93
Bertolino, James D. 1942- WhoWrEP 92
Bertolino, Rosaleen 1956- WhoWrEP 92
Bertolli, Eugene Emil 1923- WhoAm 92
Bertolli, Francesca d1767 Baker 92
Bertolli, Lisa Marie 1958- WhoEmL 93
Bertolote, Jose Manoel 1948- WhoUN 92
Bertolotti, Mario 1933- WhoScE 91-3, WhoWor 93
Bertolucci, Attilio 1911- DcLB 128 [port]
Bertolucci, Bernardo BioIn 17
Bertolucci, Bernardo 1940- MiSFD 9
Bertolucci, Bernardo 1941- WhoAm 92, WhoWor 93
Bertolucci, Kenneth John 1956- WhoEmL 93
Berton, Adolphe 1817-1857 OxDcOp
Berton, Henri 1784-1832 OxDcOp
Berton, Henri-Montan 1767-1844 Baker 92, OxDcOp
Berton, Lee 1931- WhoAm 92
Berton, Pierre 1920- BioIn 17, WhoAm 92, WhoCanL 92, WhoWrEP 92
Berton, Pierre-Montan 1727-1780 Baker 92, OxDcOp
Bertonazzi, Louis Peter 1933- WhoE 93
Bertoni, Ferdinand 1752-1813 OxDcOp
Bertoni, Ferdinando Gioseffo 1725-1813 Baker 92
Bertoni, Henry Louis 1938- WhoAm 92
Bertorello, Hector Eduardo 1932- WhoWor 93
Bertos, Rigas Nicholas 1929- WhoAm 92
Bertot, Ted F. 1945- WhoE 93
Bertouille, Gerard 1898-1981 Baker 92
Bertouille, Robert William 1930- St&PR 93
Bertram, Bonnie Jeanne 1964- WhoSSW 93
Bertram, C. Brent Law&B 92
Bertram, Deborah Kay 1949- WhoAmW 93
Bertram, Frederic Amos 1937- WhoAm 92
Bertram, H. Neal 1941- WhoAm 92
Bertram, Irving S. Law&B 92
Bertram, Joan Marie 1947- WhoAmW 93
Bertram, Manya M. WhoWor 93
Bertram, Philip William 1954- WhoAm 92
Bertram, Richard Garth WhoScE 91-1
Bertram, Robert Whitcomb 1948- WhoEmL 93
Bertram, Theodor 1869-1907 Baker 92
Bertram, Vedah 1891-1912 SweetSg A
Bertramson, B. Rodney 1914- WhoAm 92
Bertran, Ross Frederick 1952- WhoEmL 93
Bertran Armand, Beatriz A. 1958- WhoEmL 93
Bertrand, Aline 1798-1835 Baker 92
Bertrand, Annabel Hodges 1915- WhoAmW 93, WhoSSW 93, WhoWor 93
Bertrand, Antoine de c. 1540-c. 1581 Baker 92
Bertrand, Charles A. 1925- WhoE 93
Bertrand, Donald Ernest Law&B 92
Bertrand, Frederic H. 1936- St&PR 93
Bertrand, Frederic Howard 1936- WhoAm 92
Bertrand, Gabrielle 1923- WhoAmW 93
Bertrand, Jean 1925- WhoScE 91-2
Bertrand, Joseph BioIn 17
Bertrand, Marcel P.E. 1944- WhoScE 91-2
Bertrand, Michel 1924- WhoScE 91-2
Bertrand, Pierre 1938- WhoScE 91-2
Bertrand, Robert D. Law&B 92
Bertrand, Roger Robert 1954- WhoWor 93
Bertrand, Scott Richard 1954- WhoSSW 93
Bertrandon De La Broquiere d1459 OxDcByz
Bertranou, Enrique German 1937- WhoWor 93
Bertran Rusca, Juan 1931- WhoScE 91-3
Bertran-Salvans, Miquel 1945- WhoScE 91-3
Bertsch, Frank Henry 1925- St&PR 93, WhoAm 92
Bertsch, Frederick Charles, III 1942- WhoAm 92
Bertsch, Gene C. Law&B 92
Bertsch, James Allen 1947- WhoE 93
Bertsch, James L. 1943- St&PR 93
Bertsch, James L. 1944- WhoAm 92
Bertsch, Robert B. 1952- St&PR 93
Bertsch, Robert Joseph 1948- WhoEmL 93
Bertsche, Bernard B. 1942- St&PR 93
Bertsche, Copeland Gray Law&B 92
Bertschinger, Hans Ulrich 1932- WhoScE 91-4
Bertschinger, Jeffrey 1956- St&PR 93
Bertucci, Guido 1948- WhoUN 92
Bertucelli, Robert Edward 1948- WhoWor 93
Berty, John Jeffry 1953- WhoEmL 93
Berube, Margery Stanwood 1943- WhoAmW 93
Berube, Maurice R. 1933- ConAu 139
Berube, Maurice Ralph 1933- WhoSSW 93
Berube, Yves 1940- WhoWor 93
Beruriah 2nd cent.- BioIn 17
Berutti, Arturo 1862-1938 Baker 92
Bervaes, Jan C.A.M. 1947- WhoScE 91-3
Berven, Norman Lee 1945- WhoWor 93
Berwald, Franz 1796-1868 OxDcOp
Berwald, Franz (Adolf) 1796-1868 Baker 92
Berwald, Helen Dorothy 1925- WhoAm 92
Berwald, Johan Fredrik 1787-1861 Baker 92
Berwald, William 1864-1948 Baker 92
Berwaldt, Carl P. 1956- St&PR 93
Berwanger, John Jay Law&B 92
Berwick, Virginia G. 1939- St&PR 93
Berwind, C. Graham, Jr. 1928- St&PR 93
Berwyn, Cynthia Kathleen Hughes 1957- WhoAmW 93
Berz, Michael MiSFD 9
Berzak, Arlyne Levinson 1936- WhoAmW 93
Berzborn, Richard J. 1937- WhoScE 91-3
Berzeviczy-Pallavicini, Federico von 1909-1989 BioIn 17
Berzins, Erna Marija 1914- WhoAmW 93, WhoWor 93
Berzok, Robert Martin 1944- WhoE 93
Berzon, Betty 1928- WhoAm 92
Berzon, Faye Clark 1926- WhoAmW 93
Berzsenyi, Zoltan 1943- WhoScE 91-4
Besag, Julian E. WhoScE 91-1
Besan, Janos 1942- WhoScE 91-4
Besancon, Francois J. 1927- WhoScE 91-2
Besant, Annie 1847-1933 DcTwHis
Besant, Colin Bowden WhoScE 91-1
Besant, Larry Xon 1935- WhoAm 92, WhoSSW 93
Besanzoni, Gabriella 1888-1962 Baker 92
Besard, Jean-Baptiste 1567-1625 Baker 92
Besas c. 480-c. 560 HarEnMi
Besaw, Vic ScF&FL 92
Besaw, Victor 1916- ScF&FL 92
Besbeck, S.M. 1948- St&PR 93
Besbris, Ava M. Law&B 92
Besch, Emerson Louis 1928- WhoAm 92
Besch, Everett Dickman 1924- WhoAm 92
Beschel, Robert Paine, Jr. 1957- WhoEmL 93
Bescherer, Ed BioIn 17
Bescherer, Edwin A., Jr. 1933- WhoAm 92
Bescherer, Jane BioIn 17
Beschi, M.C. Law&B 92
Beschle, Donald L. 1951- WhoEmL 93
Beschloss, Michael R. 1955- BioIn 17
Bescos, Julian 1947- WhoScE 91-3
Beseiso, Fouad Hamdi 1943- WhoUN 92
Besekirsky, Vasili Baker 92
Beseler, Hans Hartwig von 1850-1921 HarEnMi
Beseman, Arlene Elizabeth 1931- WhoAmW 93
Besen, Aaron Jay 1958- WhoEmL 93
Besen, Stanley Martin 1937- WhoAm 92
Besenhard, Jurgen Otto 1944- WhoScE 91-3, WhoWor 93
Beser, Jacob d1992 NewYTBS 92
Beser, Jacques 1950- WhoEmL 93
Beserra, Wendy Colby 1947- WhoAmW 93
Beshar, Christine 1929- WhoAm 92
Beshar, Robert Peter 1928- WhoAm 92
Besharo, Peter Attie 1899?-1960? BioIn 17
Beshear, Steven L. 1944- WhoAm 92
Beshears, Charles Daniel 1917- WhoAm 92, WhoWor 93
Beshears, James MiSFD 9
Beshears, Robert Gene 1931- WhoAm 92
Besicovitch, Abram Samoilovitch 1891-1970 BioIn 17
Besing, Ray Gilbert 1934- WhoAm 92, WhoWor 93
Besio, Josephine M. AmWomPl
Beskos, Dimitri Efthimios 1946- WhoWor 93
Beskos, Dimitrios 1946- WhoScE 91-3
Beskow, Elsa (Maartman) 1874-1953 MajAI [port]
Besl, Alfred B. 1924- St&PR 93
Besler, Samuel 1574-1625 Baker 92
Besley, Kathleen M. H. AmWomPl
Beslity, James M. Law&B 92
Besman, Douglas Brian Law&B 92
Besner, Bram 1932- St&PR 93
Besner, Neil K. 1949- ConAu 137
Besnoff, Larry 1951- WhoEmL 93
Besonen, Joanne Frances 1946- WhoAmW 93
Besore, George Raleigh, Jr. 1924- WhoSSW 93
Besore, Richard L. Law&B 92
Besozzi, Alessandro 1702-1793 Baker 92
Besozzi, Paul Charles 1947- WhoEmL 93
Besrat, Abraham 1938- WhoUN 92
Bess, Charles Wayne 1958- WhoEmL 93
Bess, Clayton 1944- BioIn 17
Bess, E. Tamu d1991 BioIn 17
Bess, Harold Leon 1924-1992 WhoE 93
Bess, Henry David 1939- WhoWor 93
Bess, James Lawrence 1934- WhoE 93
Bess, Paul William 1949- WhoEmL 93
Bess, Robert Wade 1958- WhoWrEP 92
Bessant, John Robert WhoScE 91-1
Bessaraboff, Nicholas 1894-1973 Baker 92
Bessarion 1399?-1472 OxDcByz
Bessborough, Mary 1915- WhoWor 93
Besse, Ralph Moore 1905- WhoAm 92
Besse, Ronald Duncan 1938- WhoAm 92
Besse, William Michael 1949- WhoSSW 93
Bessel, Vasili 1842-1907 Baker 92
Besseler, Heinrich 1900-1969 Baker 92
Bessems, Antoine 1809-1868 Baker 92
Bessent, Don 1931-1990 BioIn 17
Bessenyey, Francis B. 1925- St&PR 93, WhoAm 92, WhoE 93
Besser, Albert Gordon 1924- WhoAm 92
Besser, Amy Helene 1956- WhoEmL 93
Besser, Bruno Philipp 1962- WhoWor 93
Besser, Fannie Bear d1992 NewYTBS 92
Besser, Howard R. Law&B 92
Besser, Howard Russell 1941- WhoAm 92
Besser, John Edward Law&B 92
Besser, John Edward 1942- St&PR 93, WhoAm 92
Besser, Lawrence Wayne 1948- WhoSSW 93
Besserman, Ellen Rae 1958- WhoE 93
Bessette, Frederick W. Law&B 92
Bessette, Gerard 1920- BioIn 17, WhoCanL 92
Bessette, Joseph Thomas 1925- WhoAm 92
Bessette, Thomas E. Law&B 92
Bessey, B. Thomas 1936- St&PR 93
Bessey, Edward Cushing 1934- St&PR 93, WhoAm 92
Bessey, Jeffrey L. 1957- WhoE 93
Bessey, William Higgins 1913- WhoAm 92
bes Shahar, Eluki 1956- ScF&FL 92
Bessie, Dan MiSFD 9
Bessieres, Jean-Baptiste 1768-1813 HarEnMi
Bessinger, Jess Balsor, Jr. 1921- WhoAm 92
Bessire, Henry Edmond 1935- St&PR 93
Bessis, Georges 1931- WhoScE 91-2
Bessis, Roger 1933- WhoScE 91-2
Bessler, Stephen Craig 1951- WhoEmL 93
Besslich, Philipp W. 1929- WhoScE 91-3
Bessman, Alice N. 1922- WhoAmW 93
Bessman, Samuel Paul 1921- WhoAm 92
Bessmertnova, Natalya Igorevna 1941- WhoWor 93
Bessmertnykh, Aleksandr A. 1933- BioIn 17
Besso, Marc Joseph 1931- St&PR 93
Besso, Michelangelo 1873-1955 BioIn 17
Besso, W. James 1935- St&PR 93
Bessolo, James Peter Law&B 92
Besson, Jean-Marie WhoScE 91-2
Besson, Luc 1959- MiSFD 9
Besson, Michel Louis 1934- St&PR 93, WhoAm 92
Bessor, Bryan W. 1955- St&PR 93
Bessor, Joyce M. 1931- St&PR 93
Bessor, William D. 1927- St&PR 93
Best, Carl BioIn 17
Best, Charles L. Law&B 92
Best, Connie Lee 1951- WhoSSW 93
Best, David Peter 1952- WhoWor 93
Best, Edgar Everett 1904- WhoE 93
Best, Elizabeth Allaire 1956- WhoEmL 93
Best, Elsdon 1856-1931 IntDcAn
Best, Eugene Crawford, Jr. 1939- WhoAm 92
Best, Franklin L., Jr. Law&B 92
Best, Franklin Luther, Jr. 1945- WhoE 93
Best, Frederick Napier 1943- WhoSSW 93
Best, G. WhoScE 91-1
Best, Gary Dean 1936- ConAu 40NR
Best, Gordon Trevor WhoScE 91-1
Best, Gordon Trevor 1934- WhoWor 93
Best, Herbert 1894-1980 ScF&FL 92
Best, James L. 1959- St&PR 93
Best, James W. 1945- St&PR 93
Best, Janna Luebkemann 1960- WhoEmL 93
Best, Joan Elizabeth 1940- WhoAmW 93
Best, Joel 1946- ConAu 139
Best, Joel Gordon 1946- WhoAm 92
Best, John, Jr. 1932- St&PR 93
Best, Judah 1932- WhoAm 92
Best, Kathleen Francis 1946- WhoEmL 93, WhoSSW 93
Best, Laurence John 1950- WhoEmL 93
Best, Linda Reed 1945- WhoAmW 93
Best, Lloyd 1934- DcCPCAm
Best, Mary Sue 1930- WhoWrEP 92
Best, Michael K. 1936- St&PR 93
Best, Nicholas 1948- ConAu 138
Best, Pete 1941- BioIn 17
Best, Raymond Merle 1938- St&PR 93
Best, Rhys John 1946- WhoSSW 93
Best, Robert A. 1937- WhoE 93
Best, Robert Glen 1958- WhoSSW 93
Best, Robert Henry 1896-1952 BioIn 17
Best, Robert John WhoScE 91-1
Best, Robert Mulvane 1922- St&PR 93, WhoAm 92
Best, Robert W. Law&B 92
Best, Robert Wayne 1946- St&PR 93, WhoAm 92, WhoSSW 93
Best, Roberta Louise 1941- WhoWor 93
Best, Roger Norman 1949- WhoEmL 93, WhoWor 93
Best, Ronald 1936- St&PR 93
Best, Sharon Louise Peckham 1940- WhoE 93
Best, Thirza Louise 1934- WhoE 93
Best, Thomas c. 1570-c. 1638 HarEnMi
Best, Travis BioIn 17
Best, W(illiam) T(homas) 1826-1897 Baker 92
Best, Wayne Allison, Jr. 1927- WhoSSW 93
Best, William 1829?-1863 BioIn 17
Best, William Andrew, III 1961- WhoE 93
Best, Willis D. 1923- WhoAm 92
Best, Wim 1956- WhoWor 93
Best, Winfield Judson 1919- WhoAm 92, WhoWrEP 92
Beste, Harold E. d1990 BioIn 17
Beste, James G. Law&B 92
Bestehorn, Ute Wiltrud 1930- WhoAmW 93
Besten, Robert Bruce 1929- St&PR 93
Besteni, Barbara Amnerys 1958- WhoEmL 93, WhoWor 93
Bester, Alfred 1913-1987 BioIn 17, ScF&FL 92
Bester, Helmut 1953- WhoWor 93
Bestercy, Robert John 1931- St&PR 93
Bestgen, William Henry, Jr. 1947- WhoEmL 93
Besthoff, Anthony Warren 1935- St&PR 93
Bestler, Gerald M. 1929- St&PR 93
Bestler, Gerald Milton 1929- WhoAm 92, WhoWor 93
Best-Louther, Mary Jane 1954- WhoAmW 93
Bestmann, Jay W. Law&B 92

Beyer, Frank Michael 1928- Baker 92
Beyer, Gerry Wayne 1956- WhoEmL 93
Beyer, Gordon Robert 1930- WhoAm 92
Beyer, H. Otley 1883-1966 IntDcAn
Beyer, Henryka 1782-1855 PolBiDi
Beyer, Herbert Albert 1923- St&PR 93
Beyer, Jane Magdalyn 1959- WhoAmW 93
Beyer, Janice Mary 1934- WhoAmW 93
Beyer, Jeffrey C. 1954- St&PR 93
Beyer, Johanna Magdalena 1888-1944 Baker 92
Beyer, John Treacy 1943- St&PR 93
Beyer, Jurgen Hans Karl 1936- WhoScE 91-3
Beyer, Karen Ann 1942- WhoAmW 93
Beyer, Karl Henry, Jr. 1914- WhoAm 92
Beyer, Karol 1818-1877 PolBiDi
Beyer, Klaus Dietrich 1937- WhoE 93
Beyer, Lawrence Gerald 1933- St&PR 93
Beyer, Linda M. Law&B 92
Beyer, Manfred 1924- WhoScE 91-3
Beyer, Michael 1957- WhoWor 93
Beyer, Michael J. 1946- St&PR 93
Beyer, Morten S. 1921- St&PR 93
Beyer, Norma Warren 1926- WhoWor 93
Beyer, Robert Thomas 1920- WhoAm 92, WhoE 93
Beyer, Sandra Lynn 1960- WhoAmW 93
Beyer, Sonya von Zitzewitz 1931- WhoAmW 93
Beyer, Suzanne 1928- WhoAmW 93, WhoE 93
Beyer, Wayne Cartwright 1946- WhoE 93, WhoWor 93
Beyer, Wayne Herman 1956- WhoEmL 93
Beyer, William H. Law&B 92
Beyerhaus, Peter (Paul Johannes) 1929- ConAu 38NR, WhoWor 93
Beyerlein, Douglas Craig 1950- WhoEmL 93
Beyerlein, Fred Gordon 1947- St&PR 93
Beyer-Mears, Annette 1941- WhoAm 92, WhoAmW 93, WhoWor 93
Beyers, Daryl A. BioIn 17
Beyers, Patricia Joan WhoAmW 93
Beyers, William Bjorn 1940- WhoAm 92
Beyersdorf, Marguerite Mulloy 1922- WhoAmW 93, WhoWor 93
Beyersmann, Detmar 1939- WhoScE 91-3
Beyette, Donald Leslie 1945- St&PR 93
Beyman, Jonathan Eric 1955- WhoAm 92, WhoE 93, WhoEmL 93
Beymer, William 1881-1969 ScF&FL 92
Beynon, David J. 1932- St&PR 93
Beynon, John ScF&FL 92
Beynon, John 1903-1969 BioIn 17
Beyreis, James Robert 1944- St&PR 93
Beysens, Daniel Andre-Marie 1945- WhoWor 93
Beystehner, John J. Law&B 92
Beyster, John Robert 1924- St&PR 93
Beytagh, Francis Xavier, Jr. 1935- WhoAm 92
Beyzym, Jan 1850-1912 PolBiDi
Bezahler, Donald J. 1932- St&PR 93
Bezahler, Donald Jay 1932- WhoAm 92
Bezanski, Ilia Metodiev 1941- WhoWor 93
Bezanson, Elaine Ruth Croyle 1946- WhoAmW 93
Bezanson, Peter Floyd 1915- WhoAm 92
Bezar, Gilbert Edward 1930- WhoAm 92
Bezard, Jean 1930- WhoScE 91-2
Bezard, Max Jack 1965- WhoWor 93
Bezark, Richard Samuel 1922- St&PR 93
Bezdek, Jan 1896- Baker 92
Bezdicek, Albert J. 1929- St&PR 93
Bezekirsky, Vasili 1835-1919 Baker 92
Bezik, Cynthia Burns 1953- WhoEmL 93
Bezikos, Lynne A. Law&B 92
Bezille, Guy WhoScE 91-2
Bezjak, Richard G. 1945- St&PR 93
Bezmen, Pamir 1936- WhoWor 93
Bezroudnoff, Jean-Basile WhoCanL 92
Bezrukov, Sergej Leonidovich 1958- WhoWor 93
Bezubik, Bernard 1919- WhoScE 91-4
Bezucha, Robert Joseph 1940- WhoAm 92
Bezuglyi, Sergey Ivanovich 1954- WhoWor 93
Bezuidenhout, Pieter Jacobus 1947- WhoUN 92
Bezursik, Edward Anthony, Jr. 1951- WhoE 93
Bezzina, Alexander 1958- WhoWor 93
Bezzone, Albert Paul 1931- WhoAm 92
Bhabra, H.S. 1955- WhoCanL 92
Bhaduri, Amit BioIn 17
Bhagat, H.K.L. 1921- WhoAsAP 91
Bhagat, Surinder Kumar 1935- WhoAm 92
Bhagwan, Sudhir 1942- WhoWor 93
Bhajan Lal 1930- WhoAsAP 91
Bhakta, Manoranjan 1939- WhoAsAP 91
Bhalla, Ajit Singh 1939- WhoUN 92
Bhalla, Deepak Kumar 1946- WhoWor 93
Bhalodkar, Narendra Chandrakant 1948- WhoAm 92
Bhamani, Noor Mohammad 1925- WhoWor 93
Bhamji WhoAsAP 91
Bhandare, Murlidhar Chandrakant 1928- WhoAsAP 91
Bhandari, Arvind 1950- WhoAm 92
Bhandari, Sunder Singh 1921- WhoAsAP 91
Bhanot, Manohar Lal 1934- WhoUN 92
Bhansali, Siddarth BioIn 17
Bhansali, Yashodhara BioIn 17
Bharadwaj, Krishna 1935- BioIn 17
Bharadwaj, Radha MiSFD 9
Bharati, Agehananda 1923- WhoWrEP 92
Bharati, Agehananda 1923-1991 BioIn 17
Bharati, Saroja WhoAm 92, WhoAmW 93
Bharatiya, Pat 1942- St&PR 93
Bhardwaj, Hans Raj 1937- WhoAsAP 91
Bhardwaj, Paras Ram 1948- WhoAsAP 91
Bhargava, Anju Page 1956- WhoE 93, WhoEmL 93
Bhargava, Ashok 1943- WhoAm 92
Bhargava, Ashok K. 1939- St&PR 93
Bhargava, Pradeep 1943- St&PR 93
Bhargava, Pushpa Mittra 1928- WhoWor 93
Bhargava, Rameshwar Nath 1939- WhoAm 92
Bhartia, Prakash 1944- WhoAm 92
Bharvaney, Tahilram Rochiram Govind 1930- WhoWor 93
Bhat, Ramachandra K. 1941- WhoE 93
Bhathal, R.S. ScF&FL 92
Bhatia, Anil Kumar 1945- WhoWor 93
Bhatia, Dil Mohan Singh 1939- WhoSSW 93
Bhatia, Jeet 1945- St&PR 93
Bhatia, June WhoCanL 92
Bhatia, Madan 1929- WhoAsAP 91
Bhatia, Peter K. 1953- WhoAm 92
Bhatia, Ram Nath 1942- WhoSSW 93
Bhatia, Rattan Jethanand 1930- WhoUN 92
Bhatia, Sonia Singh WhoAmW 93
Bhatkhande, Vishnu Narayan 1860-1936 Baker 92
Bhatla, Manmohan N. 1939- St&PR 93
Bhatnagar, Gopal Mohan 1937- WhoE 93
Bhatt, Jitendrabhai Labhshanker 1927- WhoAsAP 91
Bhatt, Kavery Ragunandan DcChlFi
Bhatt, Prakash C. 1947- St&PR 93
Bhattacharjee, Kanalendu 1946- WhoAsAP 91
Bhattacharjee, Sourendra 1926- WhoAsAP 91
Bhattacharya, Bhabani 1906- BioIn 17
Bhattacharya, Pallab Kumar 1949- WhoAm 92
Bhattacharya, Pradeep Kumar 1945- WhoSSW 93
Bhattacharya, Purna 1946- St&PR 93
Bhattacharya, Syamal Kanti 1949- WhoEmL 93
Bhattacharya-Chatterjee, Malaya 1946- WhoAm 92, WhoE 93, WhoEmL 93
Bhattacharyya, S.K. WhoScE 91-1
Bhattacharyya, Santosh Kumar 1927- WhoWor 93
Bhattacharyya, Shankar Prashad 1946- WhoAm 92
Bhattacherjee, Parimal 1937- WhoAm 92, WhoSSW 93
Bhattarai, Khem Raj 1962- WhoWor 93
Bhattarai, Krishna Prasad WhoAsAP 91, WhoWor 93
Bhatti, Muhammad Saleh 1948- WhoWor 93
Bhatti, Neeloo 1955- WhoWor 93
Bhatty, Margaret R. DcChlFi
Bhaumik, Mani Lal 1932- WhoAm 92
Bhavaraju, Murty Parabrahma 1940- WhoAm 92
Bhave, Vinoba 1896-1982 DcTwHis
Bhavsar, Natvar Prahladji 1934- WhoAm 92
Bhayani, Harin 1936- St&PR 93
Bhayani, Kiran Lilachand 1944- WhoWor 93
Bhowmik, Prasanta Chitta 1943- WhoE 93
Bhuiyan, Muhammad N. 1931- WhoUN 92
Bhukanchana, Sombati 1948- WhoWor 93
Bhumibol, Adulyadej 1927- DcTwHis
Bhumibol Adulyadej, His Majesty 1927- WhoWor 93
Bhumibol Adulyadej, King of Thailand BioIn 17
Bhumibol Adulyadej, King Rama IX of Thailand 1927- WhoAsAP 91
Bhuria, Dileep Singh 1944- WhoAsAP 91
Bhutta, Tariq Iqbal 1940- WhoWor 93
Bhutto, Begum Nusrat 1934- WhoAsAP 91
Bhutto, Benazir BioIn 17
Bhutto, Benazir 1953- DcTwHis, WhoAsAP 91, WhoWor 93
Bhutto, Zulfikar Ali 1928-1979 BioIn 17, ColdWar 2 [port], DcTwHis
Bhuva, Bharat Laxmidas 1960- WhoEmL 93
Bhuyan, Muhammad Ayubur Rahman 1938- WhoWor 93
Biacs, Peter A. 1940- WhoScE 91-4
Biacs, Peter Akos 1940- WhoScE 91-4
Biaett, Doddridge Hewitt Law&B 92
Biaett, Doddridge Hewitt, III 1942- WhoE 93
Biafora, Joseph R. 1920- St&PR 93
Biagetti, Richard Victor 1940- WhoE 93
Biaggi, Cristina Shelley 1937- WhoAm 92
Biagi, L.D. ScF&FL 92
Biagi, Richard Charles 1925- WhoAm 92
Biagini, Andrea 1947- WhoWor 93
Biagioni, Gloria M. 1928- St&PR 93
Biagiotti, Laura BioIn 17
Bial, Morrison David 1917- BioIn 17
Bial, Raymond Steven 1948- WhoWrEP 92
Bial, Rudolf 1834-1881 Baker 92
Bialas, Gunter 1907- Baker 92
Bialas, Paul Anthony 1949- WhoEmL 93
Bialeck, Alan R. Law&B 92
Bialek, Ryszard 1932- WhoScE 91-4
Bialer, Seweryn 1926- WhoAm 92
Bialick, David W. 1942- St&PR 93
Bialik, Ezra I. Law&B 92
Bialik, Mayim BioIn 17
Bialk, Elisa 1912-1990 BioIn 17
Bialkin, Kenneth J. 1929- St&PR 93
Bialkin, Kenneth Jules 1929- WhoAm 92
Bialkowski, Grzegorz 1932- WhoScE 91-4
Bialkowski, Marek Edward 1951- WhoWor 93
Biallo, Thomas M. d1991 BioIn 17
Biallozor, Swetlana 1932- WhoScE 91-4
Bialo, Walter 1917- St&PR 93
Bialosky, David L. Law&B 92
Bialy, Linda Lee 1947- WhoE 93
Bialynicki-Birula, Iwo 1933- WhoScE 91-4
Bian, Beverly E. Law&B 92
Bianca, Andrew Michael 1956- WhoEmL 93
Biancardi, Enrico 1942- WhoScE 91-3
Biancardi, Paul A. Law&B 92
Biancardi, Peter A. 1933- St&PR 93
Biancheri, John Joseph 1930- St&PR 93
Bianchi, Al BioIn 17
Bianchi, Alberto Maria 1955- WhoWor 93
Bianchi, Angelo 1926- WhoScE 91-3
Bianchi, Bettie S. 1931- St&PR 93
Bianchi, Bianca 1855-1947 Baker 92
Bianchi, Carmine Paul 1927- WhoAm 92
Bianchi, Christophe Jacques 1965- WhoWor 93
Bianchi, Donald Ernest 1933- WhoAm 92
Bianchi, Edward 1942- MiSFD 9
Bianchi, Ettore 1920- WhoWor 93
Bianchi, Francesco c. 1752-1810 Baker 92, OxDcOp
Bianchi, Giorgio 1936- WhoWor 93
Bianchi, Giuseppe 1933- WhoScE 91-3
Bianchi, Laurie Ann 1964- WhoAmW 93, WhoEmL 93
Bianchi, Marco Berkeley 1939- WhoAm 92
Bianchi, Massimo 1951- WhoScE 91-3
Bianchi, Nestor Oscar 1931- WhoWor 93
Bianchi, Patrizio Unincenzo 1952- WhoWor 93
Bianchi, Richard A. 1940- WhoIns 93
Bianchi, Robert Michael 1956- WhoSSW 93
Bianchi, Robert N. 1944- St&PR 93
Bianchi, Ronald F. Law&B 92
Bianchi, Ted J., Jr. 1940- WhoIns 93
Bianchi, Valentina 1839-1884 Baker 92
Bianchi, Vincenz Ferrerius Friedrich, Baron von 1768-1855 HarEnMi
Bianchi-Bigelow, Cheryl Ann 1957- WhoAmW 93
Bianchine, Joseph R. 1929- St&PR 93
Bianchine, Joseph Raymond 1929- WhoAm 92
Bianchini, Domenico c. 1510-c. 1576 Baker 92
Bianchini, Peter Albert 1963- St&PR 93
Bianchino, Bernard A. Law&B 92
Bianchino, Bernard Anthony 1948- WhoAm 92
Bianchi Porro, Gabriele 1938- WhoWor 93
Bianco, Anthony Joseph, III 1953- WhoAm 92
Bianco, Antonio 1948- WhoSSW 93
Bianco, Jose 1908-1986 SpAmA
Bianco, Joseph Paul, Jr. 1936- WhoAm 92
Bianco, Lucio 1941- WhoScE 91-3
Bianco, Margery MajAI
Bianco, Margery Williams 1881-1944 MajAI [port]
Bianco, Nicole Ann 1949- WhoEmL 93
Bianco, Peter 1963- WhoEmL 93
Bianco, Pietro Antonio c. 1540-1611 Baker 92
Bianco, Roberto Corrado 1953- WhoWor 93
Bianco, S. Anthony Law&B 92
Biancolli, Louis d1992 NewYTBS 92
Biancolli, Louis 1907- WhoWrEP 92
Biancolli, Louis Leopold 1907-1992 ConAu 139
Bianconi, Charles 1786-1875 BioIn 17
Bianconi, Gregory Frederick 1952- WhoE 93
Bianconi, Lynne Schmidt Law&B 92
Biancosino, Anthony F. 1945- St&PR 93
Biancotti, Peter Joel 1943- St&PR 93
Biard, James Robert 1931- WhoAm 92
Biardo, John Charles 1950- WhoWrEP 92
Biars, Mark M. Law&B 92
Bias, Dana G. 1959- WhoEmL 93
Bias, Jay BioIn 17
Bias, Lonise BioIn 17
Biasca, Rodolfo Eduardo 1944- WhoWor 93
Biasco, Salvatore 1939- WhoWor 93
Biasi, Gino P. 1931- St&PR 93
Biasone, Danny 1909-1992 BioIn 17, NewYTBS 92 [port]
Biava, Luis WhoAm 92
Biays, Pierre 1921- WhoScE 91-2
Biba, Yuriy Igorevich 1961- WhoWor 93
Bibalitsch, Antonio (Gino) 1922- Baker 92
Bibalo, Antonio (Gino) 1922- Baker 92
Bibart, Richard Lee 1942- WhoAm 92
Bibaud, Adele 1854-1941 BioIn 17
Bibaud, Michel 1782-1857 BioIn 17
Bibaud, Richard Edgar 1937- St&PR 93
Bibb, Daniel Roland 1951- WhoSSW 93, WhoWor 93
Bibb, Mervyn James WhoScE 91-1
Bibb, Peyton D., Jr. Law&B 92
Bibb, Richard T. 1925- St&PR 93
Bibbo, Marluce 1939- WhoAm 92
Bibbs, Karol Lee 1935- WhoE 93
Bibby, Douglas Martin 1946- St&PR 93, WhoAm 92
Bibby, Michele Alexander 1961- WhoAmW 93
Bibby, Regina Nanette 1960- WhoAmW 93
Bibeault, Donald B. St&PR 93
Bibel, Debra Jan 1945- WhoAm 92
Bibel, Wolfgang Leonhard 1938- WhoWor 93
Biber, Heinrich 1644-1704 OxDcOp
Biber, Heinrich (Ignaz Franz von) 1644-1704 Baker 92
Biber, Stanley H. BioIn 17
Biberfeld, Alfred G. 1924- St&PR 93
Biberman, Herbert J. 1900-1971 MiSFD 9N
Biberman, Lucien Morton 1919- WhoAm 92
Biberstein, Ernst Ludwig 1922- WhoAm 92
Bibicoff, Harvey 1939- St&PR 93
Bibikov, Sergei Jonasovitch 1960- WhoWor 93
Bibl, Andreas 1807-1878 Baker 92
Bibl, Rudolf 1832-1902 Baker 92
Bible, Charles 1937- BlkAuII 92
Bible, Frances 1927- Baker 92
Bible, Francis Lillian WhoAm 92
Bible, Geoffrey Cyril 1937- WhoAm 92
Bible, John Bruner 1940- WhoSSW 93
Bibling, John Henry 1958- St&PR 93
Biblowitz, Joshua 1920- St&PR 93
Bibulus, Marcus Calpurnius d48BC BioIn 17
Bibus, Thomas William 1949- WhoEmL 93
Bice, Debra Louise 1953- WhoEmL 93
Bice, Michael David 1956- WhoEmL 93, WhoSSW 93
Bice, Ruth Ann 1958- WhoAmW 93
Bice, Scott Haas 1943- WhoAm 92
Bicego, Valerio 1953- WhoWor 93
Bicehouse, Henry James 1943- WhoSSW 93
Bicelli, Luisa Peraldo WhoScE 91-3
Bicerano, Jozef 1952- WhoEmL 93
Bich, Bruno 1946- WhoAm 92
Bich, Genevieve Law&B 92
Bich, Marcel L. 1914- WhoAm 92
Bicha, Karel Denis 1937- WhoAm 92
Bichakjian, Bernard H. 1937- ConAu 136
Bichan, H.R. WhoScE 91-1
Bichat, Henry Herve 1938- WhoScE 91-2
Bichelonne, Jean 1904-1945 BioIn 17
Bicheno, Tracey L. Law&B 92
Bicher, George A. 1929- St&PR 93
Bicheron, Gilberte 1933- WhoScE 91-2
Bichsel, Dean E. 1938- St&PR 93
Bichsel, Terrence Earl 1949- St&PR 93
Bichurin, N.IA. 1777-1853 IntDcAn
Bick, Cort L. 1941- St&PR 93
Bick, David Greer 1953- WhoAm 92, WhoEmL 93
Bick, Frank C. 1927- St&PR 93
Bick, Katherine Livingstone 1932- WhoAm 92
Bick, Robert Steven 1961- WhoWor 93
Bick, Vincent F., Jr. Law&B 92

Bickart, Theodore Albert 1935- *WhoAm 92*
Bickel, Alexander 1924-1974 *OxCSupC*
Bickel, Bruce Douglas 1952- *WhoEmL 93*
Bickel, Catherine Mary 1959- *WhoAmW 93*
Bickel, Gordon 1944- *St&PR 93*
Bickel, Hans 1925- *WhoScE 91-4*
Bickel, Henry Joseph 1929- *WhoAm 92*
Bickel, Herbert Jacob, Jr. 1930- *WhoAm 92*
Bickel, John Frederick 1928- *WhoE 93*
Bickel, Lauren Elizabeth 1956- *WhoAmW 93*
Bickel, Lillian *BioIn 17*
Bickel, Peter John 1940- *WhoAm 92*
Bickel, Stephen Douglas 1939- *St&PR 93, WhoIns 93*
Bickel, Sue 1944- *WhoAmW 93*
Bickel, William Jon 1955- *WhoWrEP 92*
Bickelhaupt, Herbert Ernst 1924- *St&PR 93*
Bickers, David Rinsey 1941- *WhoAm 92*
Bickerstaff, David L. 1956- *St&PR 93*
Bickerstaff, George W. 1955- *St&PR 93*
Bickerstaff, Isaac 1735-1812 *BioIn 17*
Bickerstaff, Mina March Clark 1936- *WhoAmW 93, WhoSSW 93*
Bickerstaffe, Isaac 1735-c. 1812 *OxDcOp*
Bickerstaffe, Roger 1947- *WhoScE 91-3*
Bickert, Jock *BioIn 17*
Bickert, Robert H. 1939- *St&PR 93*
Bickerton, Ashley 1959- *BioIn 17*
Bickerton, Derek 1926- *ScF&FL 92*
Bickerton, Evan J. *Law&B 92*
Bickerton, John Thorburn 1930- *WhoAm 92*
Bickford, Andrew Thomas 1952- *St&PR 93, WhoAm 92*
Bickford, Christopher Penny 1943- *WhoAm 92, WhoE 93*
Bickford, Clarence E., Jr. 1935- *St&PR 93*
Bickford, Gail Holmgren 1930- *WhoAmW 93, WhoE 93*
Bickford, James Gordon 1928- *St&PR 93, WhoAm 92, WhoE 93*
Bickford, Jewelle Wooten 1941- *WhoAm 92*
Bickford, John V. 1934-1991 *BioIn 17*
Bickford, John Van Buren 1934- *St&PR 93*
Bickford, Karin *St&PR 93*
Bickford, Maria A. 1824-1845 *BioIn 17*
Bickford, Nathaniel Judson 1940- *St&PR 93*
Bickford-Swarthout, Doris Louise *WhoWrEP 92*
Bickham, Ben William 1929- *WhoSSW 93*
Bickham, Jack M. 1930- *ScF&FL 92*
Bickham, Jack M(iles) 1930- *WhoWrEP 92*
Bickham, W.K. *Law&B 92*
Bickimer, Patricia L. *Law&B 92*
Bickis, Nellie 1929- *St&PR 93*
Bickle, Thomas Anthony 1940- *WhoWor 93*
Bickley, David Thomas *WhoScE 91-1*
Bickley, Robert Bruce 1942- *WhoSSW 93*
Bickman, Leonard B. 1941- *WhoSSW 93*
Bickmore, Danford Earl Lloyd *Law&B 92*
Bickmore, Deborah Talmadge- *ScF&FL 92*
Bickmore, J. Grant 1916- *WhoAm 92*
Bicknell, Arthur *ScF&FL 92*
Bicknell, Dorothy Joan *WhoScE 91-1*
Bicknell, Joseph McCall 1933- *WhoAm 92*
Bicknell, Kirby Neal 1959- *WhoSSW 93*
Bicknell, Neil Clement 1942- *WhoE 93*
Bickner, Bruce Pierce 1943- *St&PR 93, WhoAm 92*
Bicks, David Peter 1933- *WhoAm 92*
Bicks, Henrietta Isaacson d1990 *BioIn 17*
Bicofsky, David Marc 1947- *WhoE 93*
Bicserdy, Gyula 1938- *WhoScE 91-4*
Bidault, Georges 1899-1982 *DcTwHis*
Bidault, Georges 1899-1983 *BioIn 17*
Biddick, Bradley D. 1947- *St&PR 93*
Biddick, Roger Dean 1923- *St&PR 93*
Biddick-Liepins, Diane Kay 1954- *WhoAmW 93*
Biddinger, Paul Williams 1953- *WhoAm 92*
Biddington, William Robert 1925- *WhoAm 92*
Biddison, Alan McCauley *Law&B 92*
Biddix, Sharon Yvonne 1947- *WhoAmW 93*
Biddle, Adrian *WhoAm 92*
Biddle, Anthony Joseph Drexel 1896-1961 *BioIn 17*
Biddle, Anthony Joseph Drexel, III 1948- *WhoEmL 93, WhoWor 93*
Biddle, Arthur William 1936- *WhoE 93*
Biddle, Bruce Jesse 1928- *WhoAm 92*
Biddle, Daniel R. *WhoAm 92, WhoE 93*
Biddle, David 1944- *WhoWor 93*
Biddle, Ellen McGowan 1841- *BioIn 17*
Biddle, Flora Miller *WhoAm 92, WhoE 93*
Biddle, Gary James 1938- *St&PR 93*
Biddle, H.W. *WhoScE 91-1*
Biddle, Livingston Ludlow, Jr. 1918- *WhoAm 92, WhoWrEP 92*
Biddle, Melvin E. *BioIn 17*
Biddle, Stanton Fields 1943- *WhoAm 92*
Biddle, Wayne Thomas 1924- *St&PR 93*
Biddlecome, Jack Eugene 1927- *St&PR 93*
Biddy, Ernest C., Jr. 1945- *WhoIns 93*
Bidelman, Wayne D. 1947- *St&PR 93*
Bidelman, William Pendry 1918- *WhoAm 92*
Biden, Joseph R. *BioIn 17*
Biden, Joseph R., Jr. 1942- *CngDr 91*
Biden, Joseph Robinette, Jr. 1942- *WhoAm 92, WhoE 93*
Bideno, Juan d1871 *BioIn 17*
Biderman, Charles Israel 1946- *WhoEmL 93*
Bidinger, Jerome Raymond *Law&B 92*
Bidinger, Lawrence Paul 1946- *WhoEmL 93*
Bidlack, Jerald Dean 1935- *St&PR 93, WhoAm 92*
Bidlack, Russell Eugene 1920- *WhoAm 92*
Bidlake, Mark Forrest 1954- *WhoWor 93*
Bidle, Dean E. 1953- *St&PR 93*
Bidlen, Beryl C. 1925- *St&PR 93*
Bidmead, Christopher H. *ScF&FL 92*
Bidney, David 1908-1987 *IntDcAn*
Bidwell, Annie Ellicott 1841?-1918 *BioIn 17*
Bidwell, Bennett E. *BioIn 17*
Bidwell, Charles Edward 1932- *WhoAm 92*
Bidwell, Charles W. 1895-1947 *BioIn 17*
Bidwell, Donald 1930- *St&PR 93*
Bidwell, Jacalyn 1946- *WhoAmW 93*
Bidwell, James Truman, Jr. 1934- *WhoAm 92*
Bidwell, Karen Rubino 1957- *WhoE 93*
Bidwell, Lita *ConAu 40NR*
Bidwell, Robert Ernest 1926- *WhoE 93, WhoWor 93*
Bidwell, Roger Grafton Shelford 1927- *WhoAm 92*
Bidwell, Thomas L. 1932- *St&PR 93*
Bidwill, William V. *WhoAm 92*
Bie, Oskar 1864-1938 *Baker 92*
Biebel, Curt Fred, Jr. 1947- *WhoEmL 93*
Biebel, John 1943- *WhoAm 92, WhoSSW 93*
Bieber, Brigid O. *Law&B 92*
Bieber, C.N. *St&PR 93*
Bieber, Connie 1954- *BioIn 17*
Bieber, Irying 1908-1991 *BioIn 17*
Bieber, Mark Allan 1946- *WhoE 93*
Bieber, Owen *BioIn 17*
Bieber, Owen F. 1929- *WhoAm 92*
Bieber, Paul D. 1949- *St&PR 93*
Bieber, Tim *BioIn 17*
Bieber, William F. 1942- *St&PR 93*
Bieber-Meek, Susan Kay 1951- *WhoEmL 93*
Biebuyck, Daniel Prosper 1925- *WhoAm 92*
Biebuyck, Julien Francois 1935- *WhoAm 92*
Bieck, Gary L. 1947- *St&PR 93*
Bieck, Louis F., Jr. 1944- *St&PR 93*
Bieck, P.R. *WhoScE 91-3*
Bieck, Robert Barton, Jr. 1952- *WhoEmL 93*
Bied, Dan 1925- *WhoWrEP 92*
Biede, Herman Charles 1928- *WhoSSW 93*
Biedenharn, Eric C., Jr. 1950- *St&PR 93*
Biedenharn, Lawrence C., Jr. 1922- *WhoAm 92, WhoSSW 93*
Biederman, Barron Zachary 1930- *WhoAm 92*
Biederman, Charles Joseph 1906- *WhoAm 92*
Biederman, Donald E. *Law&B 92*
Biederman, Donald Ellis 1934- *WhoAm 92*
Biederman, Edwin Williams, Jr. 1930- *WhoWor 93*
Biederman, James *BioIn 17*
Biederman, Ronald R. 1938- *WhoAm 92*
Biedermann, Bernd 1956- *WhoWor 93*
Biedermann, Gunter 1940- *WhoScE 91-3*
Biederstadt, Lynn *ScF&FL 92*
Biediger, George Edward 1949- *WhoSSW 93*
Biedinger, Henry Jacob 1929- *St&PR 93*
Biedinger, Karl Benton 1957- *WhoSSW 93*
Biedma, Jaime Gil de 1929- *BioIn 17*
Biedron, Theodore John 1946- *WhoAm 92*
Bieganski, Tadeusz 1944- *WhoScE 91-4*
Biegel, Eileen Mae 1937- *WhoAmW 93*
Biegel, Joseph David *Law&B 92*
Biegel, Paul 1925- *ChlLR 27 [port], ScF&FL 92*
Biegel, Paul 1930- *St&PR 93*
Biegel, Paul (Johannes) 1925- *ChlFicS*
Biegeleisen, H.I. 1904-1991 *BioIn 17*
Biegen, Arnold Irwin 1933- *WhoAm 92*
Biegen, Elaine Ruth 1939- *WhoAmW 93*
Bieger, Elaine Mindich 1932- *WhoE 93*
Biegler, Antonius Michael 1945- *St&PR 93*
Biegler, David W. 1946- *WhoAm 92*
Biegler, David Wayne 1946- *St&PR 93*
Biegler, Louis W. 1914- *WhoIns 93*
Biehl, John C. *Law&B 92*
Biehl, Kathy Anne 1956- *WhoEmL 93*
Biehl, Michael M. 1951- *WhoEmL 93*
Biehl, Robert John 1950- *St&PR 93*
Biehl, Ruth Berneice *WhoAmW 93*
Biehl, Vicki 1956- *WhoWrEP 92*
Biehle, Karen Jean 1959- *WhoAmW 93, WhoEmL 93*
Biehler, Steven G. *St&PR 93*
Biehn, Michael *BioIn 17*
Biehn, Michel *BioIn 17*
Bieker, Richard Francis 1944- *WhoE 93*
Bieker-Brady, Kristina Lee 1964- *WhoAmW 93*
Biekkola, Lee Raymond 1947- *St&PR 93*
Biel, Howard Steven 1947- *WhoE 93*
Biel, Jack Harold 1943- *WhoSSW 93*
Biel, Michael Jay 1946- *WhoEmL 93*
Biela, Edward John, Jr. 1953- *WhoSSW 93*
Biela, Joseph A. *Law&B 92*
Bielanski, Adam 1912- *WhoWor 93*
Bielawa, Herbert 1930- *Baker 92*
Bielawiec, Michal 1927- *WhoWor 93*
Bielawski, Elizabeth Anne 1950- *WhoAmW 93*
Bielawski, Kazimierz 1815-1905 *PolBiDi*
Bielawski, Shraga Feivel 1916- *BioIn 17*
Bielawski, Stephen M. 1949- *St&PR 93*
Bielby, Lorence Jon 1956- *WhoEmL 93*
Biele, Hugh Irving 1942- *WhoWor 93*
Bielecka-Fordos, Ewa 1944- *WhoScE 91-4*
Bielecki, Paul Michael 1947- *WhoEmL 93*
Bielecky, Andrew Roman, III 1937- *St&PR 93*
Bielefeldt, Catherine C. *WhoAmW 93*
Bielek, Milan 1938- *WhoScE 91-4*
Bielema, Dale L. *St&PR 93*
Bielenberg, Douglas O. 1929- *St&PR 93*
Bielenstein, Hans Henrik August 1920- *WhoAm 92*
Bieler, Charles Linford 1935- *WhoAm 92*
Bieler, Thomas A. 1942- *WhoUN 92*
Bielewicz, Eugeniusz 1923- *WhoScE 91-4*
Bieliauskas, Vytautas Joseph 1920- *WhoAm 92*
Bielich, Nadine 1947- *WhoAmW 93*
Bielicki, Tadeusz *WhoScE 91-4*
Bielicky, Michael 1954- *BioIn 17*
Bielik, Pal'o 1910-1983 *DrEEuF*
Bielinski, Donald E. 1949- *St&PR 93*
Bielinski, Donald Edward 1949- *WhoAm 92*
Bielinski, Peter Anthony *Law&B 92*
Bielke, Patricia Anne 1949- *WhoEmL 93*
Biellik, Robin Julian 1949- *WhoUN 92*
Biellmann, Jean-Francois 1934- *WhoScE 91-2*
Biello, Stephen Joseph, III 1940- *WhoE 93*
Biel-Nielsen, Kim Erik 1949- *WhoWor 93*
Bielory, Abraham Melvin 1946- *WhoE 93, WhoEmL 93, WhoWor 93*
Bielory, Leonard 1954- *WhoEmL 93*
Bielous, J.W. *WhoScE 91-1*
Bielowsky, Sol 1925- *St&PR 93*
Bielski, Ben W., Jr. 1953- *St&PR 93*
Bielski, Donald Joseph 1959- *WhoEmL 93*
Bielski, Janusz 1924- *WhoScE 91-4*
Bielski, Marcin 1495-1575 *PolBiDi*
Bielski, Mozelle M. *Law&B 92*
Bielss, Otto William, Jr. 1933- *WhoSSW 93*
Bieluch, Philip James 1955- *WhoE 93, WhoEmL 93*
Bieluch, William Charles 1918- *WhoAm 92, WhoWor 93*
Bielun, John A. 1951- *St&PR 93*
Biely, Ali Ismail 1938- *WhoUN 92*
Biely, Debra Marie 1957- *WhoE 93*
Bieman, Elizabeth 1923- *ConAu 137*
Biemann, Klaus 1926- *WhoAm 92*
Biemeck, Bruce J. 1949- *St&PR 93*
Biemer, Linda Hill 1942- *WhoAmW 93, WhoE 93*
Biemiller, Carl L. 1912-1979 *ScF&FL 92*
Bien, Amos 1951- *WhoWor 93*
Bien, Cheryl Frances 1959- *WhoAmW 93*
Bien, Guenther 1936- *WhoWor 93*
Bien, Joseph Julius 1936- *WhoAm 92*
Bien, Michael W. 1955- *WhoEmL 93*
Bien, Peter Adolph 1930- *WhoAm 92, WhoWrEP 92*
Bien, Robert Lowell 1923- *St&PR 93*
Bien, Zeungnam 1943- *WhoWor 93*
Bien-Austerman, Sue Ellen 1950- *WhoAmW 93*
Biencourt, Christopher John *Law&B 92*
Bieneck, Bjorn 1943- *St&PR 93*
Bienen, Leigh Buchanan 1938- *WhoWrEP 92*
Bienenfeld, Marvin S. 1932- *St&PR 93*
Bienenstock, Arthur Irwin 1935- *WhoAm 92*
Bienenstock, George 1945- *WhoE 93*
Bienenstock, John 1936- *WhoAm 92*
Bienert, Walter B. 1931- *St&PR 93*
Bienes, Nicholas Peter 1952- *ConAu 136*
Bienfait, Jean M. Gilbert 1927- *WhoScE 91-2*
Bienfait, Michel 1939- *WhoScE 91-2*
Bieniarz, Krzysztof 1933- *WhoWor 93*
Bieniasz, Bogumil 1940- *WhoScE 91-4*
Bieniawski, Zdzislaw Tadeusz 1936- *WhoAm 92*
Bieniewski, Janusz 1931- *WhoScE 91-4*
Bienkiewicz, Krzystof *WhoScE 91-4*
Bienkowski, Sigmund John 1941- *WhoE 93*
Bienvenu, Yves C. 1947- *WhoScE 91-2*
Bienz, Darrel Rudolph 1926- *WhoAm 92*
Bier, Barry 1945- *St&PR 93*
Bier, Carol Manson 1947- *WhoEmL 93*
Bier, Charles James 1945- *WhoSSW 93*
Bier, Horace 1918- *St&PR 93*
Bier, John Leo 1936- *WhoIns 93*
Bier, Rob 1949- *WhoEmL 93*
Bier, Thomas Phillip *BioIn 17*
Bierals, Gregory Paul 1946- *WhoSSW 93*
Bierbauer, Charles *BioIn 17*
Bierbaum, Dennis Robert 1937- *St&PR 93*
Bierbaum, J. Armin 1924- *WhoAm 92*
Bierbaum, Janith Marie 1927- *WhoAm 92*
Bierbaum, Paul Martin, Jr. 1946- *WhoEmL 93*
Bierbaum, Philip James 1942- *WhoAm 92*
Bierbaum, Robert 1912- *St&PR 93*
Bierbrier, Doreen 1946- *WhoWrEP 92*
Bierce, Ambrose 1842-1914? *BioIn 17, GayN, JrnUS, MagSAmL [port], ScF&FL 92, WorLitC [port]*
Bierce, Ambrose (Gwinett) 1842-1914? *ConAu 139*
Bierce, Charles Richard 1944- *WhoSSW 93*
Bierce, William B. 1949- *WhoEmL 93*
Biercuk, Jeffrey A. 1945- *St&PR 93*
Bierdeman, Brenda Lee 1954- *WhoAmW 93*
Bierdeman, Louise J. 1949- *St&PR 93*
Bierdiajew, Walerian 1885-1956 *Baker 92, PolBiDi*
Bierds, Linda Louise 1945- *WhoWrEP 92*
Bierdziewski, Daniel A. 1959- *St&PR 93*
Bierens De Haan, Jack 1938- *WhoScE 91-4*
Bierey, Gottlob Benedikt 1772-1840 *Baker 92*
Bierich, Jurgen R. 1921- *WhoScE 91-3*
Bierig, Jack R. 1947- *WhoEmL 93*
Biering, Niels Gustav 1943- *WhoUN 92*
Bieringer, Leonard Mark *Law&B 92*
Bieringer, Walter H. 1899-1990 *BioIn 17*
Bierkan, Dean A. *Law&B 92*
Bierkan, Dean Andrew 1945- *WhoE 93*
Bierlein, Dieter 1928- *WhoWor 93*
Bierley, John Charles 1936- *WhoAm 92*
Bierley, Paul Edmund 1926- *WhoAm 92*
Bierlin, Thelma Pauline 1927- *St&PR 93*
Bierly, Eugene Wendell 1931- *WhoAm 92*
Biermacher, Kenneth Wayne 1953- *WhoEmL 93*
Bierman, Carl A. 1914- *St&PR 93*
Bierman, Charles John 1938- *WhoSSW 93*
Bierman, Charles Warren 1924- *WhoAm 92*
Bierman, Edwin Lawrence 1930- *WhoAm 92*
Bierman, George William 1925- *WhoAm 92*
Bierman, James Norman 1945- *WhoAm 92*
Bierman, Jane Carl 1919- *St&PR 93*
Bierman, Judith Ann 1950- *WhoEmL 93*
Bierman, Norman 1907- *WhoAm 92*
Bierman, Robert *MiSFD 9*
Bierman, Robert d1990 *BioIn 17*
Bierman, Tamara Jo 1966- *WhoSSW 93*
Biermann, Charles H. 1930- *St&PR 93*
Biermann, Wolf 1936- *BioIn 17*
Biermann, Wolfgang *WhoScE 91-3*
Biernacki, Halina T. *WhoE 93, WhoWor 93*
Biernacki, Michal Marian 1855-1936 *PolBiDi*
Biernacki, Tomasz 1924- *WhoScE 91-4*
Biernacki-Poray, Wlad Otton 1924- *St&PR 93*
Biernat, James David *Law&B 92*
Biernat, Jan F. 1937- *WhoScE 91-4, WhoWor 93*
Biernat, Lillian M. Nahumenuk 1931- *WhoE 93*
Bierne, Jacques *WhoScE 91-2*
Biers, William Richard 1938- *WhoWrEP 92*
Biersack, Hans J. 1946- *WhoScE 91-3*
Bierstadt, Albert 1830-1902 *BioIn 17*
Bierstedt, Klaus Dieter 1945- *WhoWor 93*
Bierstedt, Peter Richard 1943- *WhoAm 92*

Bierstedt, Robert 1913- *WhoAm 92, WhoWrEP 92*
Bierstedt, Robin *Law&B 92*
Biersteker, Klaas 1925- *WhoScE 91-3*
Biersteker, Melvin C. 1950- *St&PR 93*
Bierut, Boleslaw 1892-1956 *ColdWar 2 [port], DcTwHis, PolBiDi*
Bierwirth, John C. 1924- *St&PR 93*
Bierwirth, John Cocks 1924- *WhoAm 92*
Biery, Evelyn Hudson 1946- *WhoAmW 93*
Biery, Galen Eugene *Law&B 92*
Bies, David Alan 1925- *WhoWor 93*
Bies, Susan Schmidt 1947- *St&PR 93, WhoAmW 93*
Biesecker, James Robert 1950- *WhoEmL 93*
Biesel, David Barrie 1931- *WhoE 93*
Biesel, Diane Jane 1934- *WhoAmW 93*
Biesele, John Julius 1918- *WhoAm 92, WhoWor 93*
Biesenbach, Ginn M. 1924- *St&PR 93*
Bieser, Harold Leslie 1928- *St&PR 93*
Biesinger, John William, III 1949- *WhoEmL 93*
Biess, Barbara Dziedzic 1963- *WhoAmW 93, WhoEmL 93*
Biestek, Tadeusz 1926- *WhoScE 91-4*
Biesterfeld, Craig Stewart 1953- *WhoEmL 93*
Bieth, Joseph G. 1940- *WhoScE 91-2*
Biette, Jean-Claude *MiSFD 9*
Biety, Sarah Anne *Law&B 92*
Bietz, Ralph L. R. 1953- *WhoEmL 93*
Biever, Angela Mary 1953- *WhoEmL 93*
Biever, Robert Henry 1931- *St&PR 93*
Biewen, Robert *St&PR 93*
Biewen, Robert L. 1936- *WhoWrEP 92*
Biezup, John Thomas 1929- *WhoAm 92*
Biffi, Giacomo Cardinal 1928- *WhoWor 93*
Biffle, Richard Lee, III 1949- *WhoEmL 93*
Bifulco, Michael *ScF&FL 92*
Big, Susan Nagy 1946- *WhoAmW 93, WhoEmL 93*
Big Apple Band *SoulM*
Bigard, "Barney" (Alban Leon) 1906-1980 *Baker 92*
Bigart, Homer 1907-1991 *AnObit 1991, BioIn 17*
Bigback, Bonnie Dee Woodward 1950- *WhoAmW 93, WhoEmL 93*
Bigbie, John Taylor 1923- *WhoAm 92*
Bigby, Michael Elliott 1949- *WhoE 93*
Bigda, John Paul 1938- *St&PR 93*
Bigda, Rudolph A. 1916- *WhoSSW 93*
Bigeard, Marcel Maurice 1916- *HarEnMi*
Bigeleisen, Jacob 1919- *WhoAm 92, WhoE 93*
Bigelow, Beverly 1947- *WhoAmW 93*
Bigelow, Charles Cross 1928- *WhoAm 92*
Bigelow, Christopher Bruce 1953- *WhoEmL 93*
Bigelow, Dana Francis *Law&B 92*
Bigelow, Daniel James 1935- *WhoWor 93*
Bigelow, David Skinner, III 1931- *WhoWor 93*
Bigelow, Donald Nevius 1918- *WhoAm 92*
Bigelow, E. Thayer *BioIn 17*
Bigelow, E. Thayer, Jr. 1941- *St&PR 93*
Bigelow, Eugene Thayer, Jr. 1941- *WhoAm 92, WhoE 93*
Bigelow, George H. 1942- *St&PR 93*
Bigelow, J.A. 1945- *St&PR 93*
Bigelow, Jonathan Lehr 1950- *WhoEmL 93*
Bigelow, Julie Helene *AmWomPl*
Bigelow, Kathryn *BioIn 17, ConTFT 10*
Bigelow, Kathryn 1951- *MiSFD 9*
Bigelow, Kathryn 1952?- *ConAu 139*
Bigelow, Lynne Thayer 1942- *WhoAmW 93*
Bigelow, Martha Mitchell 1921- *WhoAm 92*
Bigelow, Michael *WhoAm 92*
Bigelow, Newton J.T. 1904-1991 *BioIn 17*
Bigelow, Page Elizabeth 1948- *WhoAmW 93, WhoEmL 93*
Bigelow, Peter Thomas 1949- *WhoSSW 93*
Bigelow, Richard A. 1931- *St&PR 93*
Bigelow, Robert O. 1926- *St&PR 93*
Bigelow, Robert P. 1927- *WhoAm 92*
Bigelow, Stephen D. *Law&B 92*
Bigelow, William Frederick 1879-1966 *BioIn 17*
Bigelow-Lourie, Anne Edwige 1946- *WhoAm 92, WhoEmL 93*
Biggar, Barry P. 1952- *WhoAm 92*
Biggar, James McCrea 1928- *St&PR 93, WhoAm 92, WhoE 93*
Biggar, John R. 1944- *St&PR 93*
Biggar, Robert McCrea 1932- *St&PR 93, WhoAm 92*
Biggart, Eleanor Marie 1926- *WhoWrEP 92*
Biggart, Robert K. *Law&B 92*
Bigger, B. Frank 1942- *St&PR 93*
Bigger, John P. 1934- *St&PR 93, WhoAm 92*
Bigger, John Thomas, Jr. 1935- *WhoAm 92*
Bigger, Margaret Goldsborough 1939- *WhoWrEP 92*
Bigger, Richard Andrew, Jr. 1937- *WhoSSW 93*
Biggers, Ann Peeples 1943- *WhoWrEP 92*
Biggers, Carole L. *Law&B 92*
Biggers, Edwin L. 1935- *WhoAm 92*
Biggers, Emory Melvin 1951- *WhoE 93, WhoEmL 93*
Biggers, John A., Sr. 1940- *St&PR 93*
Biggers, Neal Brooks, Jr. 1935- *WhoAm 92, WhoSSW 93*
Biggers, W.J. 1928- *St&PR 93*
Biggers, William Joseph 1928- *WhoAm 92, WhoSSW 93*
Biggerstaff, Charlotte Jean 1945- *WhoAmW 93*
Biggerstaff, Kathy *BioIn 17*
Biggerstaff, Marilyn Anne 1946- *WhoEmL 93*
Biggerstaff, Randy Lee 1951- *WhoWor 93*
Biggert, Susan Lynnette 1959- *WhoAmW 93*
Biggins, Charles Clyde 1935- *St&PR 93*
Biggins, Edward Joseph, Jr. 1947- *St&PR 93*
Biggins, James J. 1928- *St&PR 93*
Biggio, Sara Leigh 1955- *WhoSSW 93*
Biggle, Lloyd 1923- *BioIn 17*
Biggle, Lloyd Jr. 1923- *ScF&FL 92*
Biggles, Richard Robert 1946- *WhoAm 92*
Biggott, Robert B. 1952- *St&PR 93*
Biggs, Alton L. 1951- *WhoSSW 93*
Biggs, Antoinette Bailey 1936- *WhoAmW 93*
Biggs, Arthur Edward 1930- *WhoAm 92*
Biggs, Barry Hugh 1935- *WhoAm 92*
Biggs, Barton Michael 1932- *WhoAm 92*
Biggs, Cheryl *ScF&FL 92*
Biggs, Clinton A. 1911- *St&PR 93*
Biggs, David H. 1945- *St&PR 93*
Biggs, Donald Anthony 1936- *WhoAm 92*
Biggs, E. Glenn 1933- *St&PR 93*
Biggs, E(dward George) Power 1906-1977 *Baker 92*
Biggs, Edmund Logan 1938- *WhoE 93, WhoWor 93*
Biggs, Electra Waggoner 1916- *BioIn 17*
Biggs, Hugh Lawry 1904- *WhoAm 92*
Biggs, J. O. 1925- *WhoAm 92*
Biggs, James L. 1960- *St&PR 93*
Biggs, James Pearson 1940- *St&PR 93, WhoAm 92*
Biggs, Jeremy Hunt 1935- *St&PR 93, WhoAm 92*
Biggs, Joel Gilson, Jr. 1947- *WhoEmL 93*
Biggs, John, Jr. 1895-1979 *ScF&FL 92*
Biggs, John H. 1936- *St&PR 93, WhoIns 93*
Biggs, John Herron 1936- *WhoAm 92*
Biggs, Lawrence Raymond, Jr. 1959- *WhoEmL 93*
Biggs, Margaret Key 1933- *WhoWrEP 92*
Biggs, Mark McCampbell 1954- *WhoEmL 93*
Biggs, Mary 1944- *ConAu 137, WhoWrEP 92*
Biggs, Michael Wilson *Law&B 92*
Biggs, Murchison Bolton 1954- *St&PR 93*
Biggs, Paul Joseph 1952- *WhoEmL 93*
Biggs, Robert Dale 1934- *WhoAm 92*
Biggs, Thomas Jones 1912- *WhoAm 92*
Biggs, Thomas Wayne *Law&B 92*
Biggs, Thomas Wylie 1950- *WhoEmL 93*
Biggs, Wellington Allen 1923- *WhoWrEP 92*
Biggs-Williams, Evelyn Ann 1950- *WhoAmW 93*
Biggy, Mary Virginia 1924- *WhoAm 92*
Bigham, James E. 1951- *WhoEmL 93*
Bigham, James John 1937- *St&PR 93*
Bigham, Michael F. *St&PR 93*
Bigham, Wanda Durrett *WhoAmW 93*
Bighley, Mark Steven 1954- *WhoEmL 93, WhoSSW 93*
Bighorse, Gus 1846?-1939 *BioIn 17*
Biging, Elizabeth Ann *Law&B 92*
Bigland, Eileen *ScF&FL 92*
Biglari, Haik 1951- *WhoSSW 93*
Bigler, David Alan 1936- *St&PR 93*
Bigler, Harold Edwin, Jr. 1931- *WhoAm 92*
Bigler, Harold S. 1926- *St&PR 93*
Bigler, John C. *Law&B 92*
Bigler, M. Jayn 1958- *WhoWrEP 92*
Bigler, Suzanne Coyle *Law&B 92*
Bigler, William 1814-1880 *BioIn 17*
Bigley, Frank *Law&B 92*
Bigley, Nancy Jane 1932- *WhoAm 92, WhoAmW 93*
Bigley, William Joseph, Jr. 1924- *WhoAm 92, WhoE 93*
Biglieri, Edward George 1925- *WhoAm 92*
Biglieri, Ezio 1944- *WhoWor 93*
Bigman, Anton W. 1929- *WhoE 93*
Big Maybelle 1924-1972 *SoulM*
Big Money Odis *See* Digital Underground *ConMus 9*
Bignami, Carlo 1808-1848 *Baker 92*
Bignens, Max 1912- *OxDcOp*
Bignier, Michel C.M. 1926- *WhoScE 91-2*
Bignier, Michel Charles Maurice 1926- *WhoScE 91-2*
Bignon, Jean 1929- *WhoScE 91-2*
Bigo, Pierre (Auguste) 1906- *ConAu 136*
Bigombe, Samusoni *WhoUN 92*
Bigongiari, Piero 1914- *DcLB 128 [port]*
Bigot, Bernard M.J. 1950- *WhoScE 91-2*
Bigot, Charles *WhoScE 91-2*
Bigot, Charles 1932- *BioIn 17*
Bigot, Claude 1933- *WhoScE 91-2*
Bigot (de Morogues), Marie 1786-1820 *Baker 92*
Bigot, Eugene 1888-1965 *Baker 92*
Bigot, Jean-Yves 1956- *WhoWor 93*
Bigot, Marie Healy 1843- *AmWomPl*
Bigourd, Jean U. 1936- *WhoScE 91-2*
Bigras, Julien 1932-1989 *WhoCanL 92*
Biguenet, John Joseph 1949- *WhoWrEP 92*
Biguet, Robert 1945- *WhoScE 91-2*
Bigus, Lawrence Weaver 1955- *WhoEmL 93*
Bigwood, Robert William 1956- *WhoEmL 93*
Bihary, Joyce 1950- *WhoAmW 93*
Bihldorff, John Pearson 1945- *WhoAm 92*
Bihlmeyer, Larry Lee 1946- *WhoEmL 93, WhoSSW 93*
Bihn, Willi Rudolf 1929- *WhoWor 93*
Bihova, Diana 1947- *WhoAmW 93*
Bihovsky, Ron Hans 1948- *WhoE 93*
Bihr, James Elwood 1927- *WhoAm 92*
Bijaoui, Albert 1943- *WhoScE 91-2*
Bijkerk, Cornelis 1927- *WhoScE 91-3*
Bijl, Marco *Law&B 92*
Bijleveld, Anne Willem 1946- *WhoUN 92*
Bijou, Sidney William 1908- *WhoAm 92*
Bijsterbosch, Bert H. 1934- *WhoScE 91-3*
Bijur, Peter I. *WhoAm 92*
Bijur, Peter I. 1942- *St&PR 93*
Bijvanck, Henk 1909-1969 *Baker 92*
Bikales, Norbert M. 1929- *WhoE 93*
Bikales, Norman Allen 1935- *WhoAm 92*
Bikbaev, Ramil Faritovich 1961- *WhoWor 93*
Bike, William Stanley 1957- *WhoWrEP 92*
Bikel, Theodore 1924- *Baker 92, WhoAm 92, WhoE 93*
Bikerman, Michael *WhoE 93*
Bikle, Paul F. 1916-1991 *BioIn 17*
Biklen, Douglas 1945- *WhoE 93*
Biklen, Paul 1915- *WhoAm 92*
Biko, Stephen 1946-1977 *ConHero 2 [port]*
Biko, Steve 1956-1977 *DcTwHis*
Biko, Steven 1946-1977 *ConBlB 4 [port]*
Bilajbegovic, Asim 1950- *WhoScE 91-4*
Bilak, Myron 1951- *WhoSSW 93*
Biland, Alan Thomas 1958- *WhoEmL 93*
Bilandic, Michael A. 1923- *WhoAm 92*
Bilaniuk, Larissa Tetiana 1941- *WhoAm 92*
Bilaniuk, Oleksa Myron 1926- *WhoAm 92*
Bilardello, John Joseph 1959- *St&PR 93*
Bilas, Jeffrey P. *Law&B 92*
Bilawsky, Mark A. 1947- *St&PR 93*
Bilawsky, Mark Allen *Law&B 92*
Bilbao, Guillermo G. *Law&B 92*
Bilbeisi, Munther Ismael *BioIn 17*
Bilbie, Vlad *WhoScE 91-4*
Bilbo, Theodore G. 1877-1947 *PolPar*
Bilbow, James Robert 1923- *WhoE 93*
Bilbray, Fred Richard 1939- *St&PR 93*
Bilbray, James H. 1938- *CngDr 91*
Bilbray, James Hubert 1938- *WhoAm 92*
Bilbro, Mathilde *AmWomPl*
Bilby, Bruce Alexander *WhoScE 91-1*
Bilby, Cindy Melton 1958- *WhoAmW 93*
Bilchev, Svetoslav Jordanov 1946- *WhoWor 93*
Bilde, Anders 1600-1657 *HarEnMi*
Bilderbach, Joe 1938- *St&PR 93*
Bilderbeek, Jan 1943- *WhoWor 93*
Bilderdijk, Willem 1756-1831 *ScF&FL 92*
Bildersee, Robert Alan 1942- *WhoAm 92*
Bildman, Lars Erik 1945- *WhoAm 92*
Bildner, James Lebson 1954- *WhoE 93*
Bildstein, Hieronymus c. 1580-c. 1626 *Baker 92*
Bildt, Carl 1949- *WhoWor 93*
Bile, Abdi *BioIn 17*
Bilello, John Charles 1938- *WhoAm 92*
Bilenkin, Dmitri 1933-1987 *ScF&FL 92*
Biler, Piotr Cezary 1958- *WhoWor 93*
Biles, Jack I. 1920- *ScF&FL 92*
Biles, John Alexander 1923- *WhoAm 92*
Biles, Marilyn Marta 1935- *WhoAmW 93*
Biles, Murray Robert 1931- *St&PR 93*
Biles, Robert Erle 1942- *WhoSSW 93*
Biles, Susan Rebecca 1951- *WhoSSW 93*
Biletnikoff, Fred *BioIn 17*
Bilezikjian, Edward Andrew 1950- *WhoEmL 93*
Bilfinger, Thomas Victor 1952- *WhoE 93*
Bilge, Aytekin 1929- *WhoScE 91-4*
Bilgen, Ahmet Munir *WhoScE 91-4*
Bilger, Jeffrey M. 1960- *St&PR 93*
Bilger, Robert C. 1952- *St&PR 93*
Bilgore, P.S. *Law&B 92*
Bilhardt, Diane Marie 1952- *WhoEmL 93*
Bilhartz, Skip L. 1947- *St&PR 93*
Bilhon, Jhan de fl. 1534-1556 *Baker 92*
Bilhorn, William W. 1930- *WhoAm 92*
Bilianis, Alexandra 1964- *St&PR 93*
Bilibin, Ivan IAkovlevich 1876-1942 *BioIn 17*
Bilich, Marion Yellin 1949- *WhoE 93*
Bilinski, Alfred 1926- *WhoScE 91-4*
Bilinski, John Nestor 1947- *WhoEmL 93*
Bilinski, Mieczyslaw 1942- *WhoScE 91-4*
Bilinski, Raynold Joseph 1946- *WhoEmL 93*
Bilinsky, Yaroslav 1932- *WhoAm 92, WhoWor 93*
Bilirakis, Michael 1930- *CngDr 91, WhoAm 92, WhoSSW 93*
Biljetina, Richard 1947- *St&PR 93*
Bilka, Paul Joseph 1919- *WhoAm 92*
Bilker, Audrey *ScF&FL 92*
Bilker, Harvey L. *ScF&FL 92*
Bilkey, Beverly Yvonne 1926- *WhoAm 92*
Bill, Anders 1931- *WhoScE 91-4*
Bill, Andrew *ScF&FL 92*
Bill, G. Dana 1926- *St&PR 93*
Bill, Hans 1935- *WhoScE 91-4*
Bill, J(ohn) Brent 1951- *WhoWrEP 92*
Bill, Joseph G. 1934- *St&PR 93*
Bill, Max 1908- *WhoWor 93*
Bill, Tony 1940- *MiSFD 9, WhoAm 92*
Billam, Dale J. *Law&B 92*
Billam, Rosemary 1952- *BioIn 17*
Billante, Samuel J. 1942- *St&PR 93*
Billard, Jean 1933- *WhoScE 91-2*
Billard, Roland 1934- *WhoScE 91-2*
Billau, Robin Louise 1951- *WhoAmW 93, WhoEmL 93*
Billauer, Barbara Pfeffer 1951- *WhoAm 92*
Billaz, Rene Maurice 1933- *WhoScE 91-2*
Bill, Buffalo 1846-1917 *BioIn 17*
Bille, Jean-Georges 1931- *WhoWor 93*
Bille, Nils 1937- *WhoScE 91-2*
Bille, Sten Fredrik 1913- *WhoWor 93*
Billeaud, Richard D. *Law&B 92*
Billecci, Tom *BioIn 17*
Billen, Thomas Raymond 1945- *St&PR 93, WhoAm 92*
Biller, Carmen George 1953- *WhoEmL 93*
Biller, Frank Joseph 1953- *St&PR 93*
Biller, Gregory L. *St&PR 93*
Biller, Henry Burt 1940- *WhoAm 92*
Biller, Hugh Frederick 1934- *WhoAm 92*
Biller, Joel Wilson 1929- *WhoAm 92*
Biller, Leslie Stuart 1948- *WhoAm 92*
Biller, Morris 1915- *WhoAm 92*
Biller, Rainer H. 1944- *WhoScE 91-3*
Biller, Scott *St&PR 93*
Billeres, Rene 1910- *BioIn 17*
Billes, D.G. 1938- *St&PR 93*
Billet, Kevin R. *Law&B 92*
Billfalk, Lennart 1946- *WhoScE 91-4*
Billgert, Stig Nils 1928- *WhoWor 93*
Billharz, Constance Ellen Clark 1921- *WhoAm 92, WhoAmW 93, WhoE 93*
Billhon, Jhan de *Baker 92*
Billias, George Athan 1919- *WhoAm 92*
Billias, Stephen *ScF&FL 92*
Billiau, Alfons J.D.A. 1937- *WhoScE 91-2*
Billick, L. Larkin 1948- *WhoSSW 93*
Billick, Timothy Richard *Law&B 92*
Billie, L. Clark 1938- *St&PR 93*
Billig, Michael *WhoScE 91-1*
Billig, Robert Emmanuel 1946- *WhoWor 93*
Billig, Thomas Clifford 1930- *WhoAm 92*
Billik, Eugene 1927- *St&PR 93*
Billing, Barbara Heap *WhoScE 91-1*
Billing, Grant D. 1951- *St&PR 93*
Billinge, Roy 1937- *WhoScE 91-4, WhoWor 93*
Billinger, Richard 1890-1965 *DcLB 124 [port]*
Billingham, John *BioIn 17, WhoScE 91-1*
Billingham, Rupert Everett 1921- *WhoAm 92*
Billings, Alan Reginald 1925- *WhoWor 93*
Billings, Barbara Lee 1946- *WhoAmW 93*
Billings, Brian Francis 1939- *WhoAm 92*
Billings, Bruce Hadley 1915- *WhoAm 92*
Billings, Charles Edgar 1929- *WhoAm 92*
Billings, Clarence David 1943- *WhoSSW 93*
Billings, Clyde A., Jr. *Law&B 92*
Billings, David S. 1942- *St&PR 93*
Billings, Donald Franklin 1957- *WhoAm 92*
Billings, Edward Robert 1913- *WhoAm 92*
Billings, Edwin C. 1933- *St&PR 93*
Billings, Eric R. *Law&B 92*

Billings, Franklin Swift, Jr. 1922- *WhoAm 92, WhoE 93*
Billings, Harold Wayne 1931- *WhoAm 92, WhoSSW 93, WhoWrEP 92*
Billings, John F. *Law&B 92*
Billings, Judith *WhoAm 92*
Billings, Karen S. 1943- *St&PR 93*
Billings, Marland Pratt 1902- *WhoAm 92*
Billings, Patricia Ann Collins 1946- *WhoAmW 93*
Billings, Peggy Marie 1928- *WhoAm 92, WhoAmW 93*
Billings, Peter Watson 1917- *St&PR 93*
Billings, Richard Whitten 1924- *WhoE 93*
Billings, Robert *BioIn 17*
Billings, Robert 1949- *WhoEmL 93*
Billings, Robert 1949-1987 *WhoCanL 92*
Billings, Robert Northrop 1947- *WhoIns 93*
Billings, Stephen Alec *WhoScE 91-1*
Billings, Thomas Neal 1931- *WhoWor 93*
Billings, Thomas Trevor 1951- *WhoEmL 93*
Billings, Warren M. 1940- *WhoSSW 93*
Billings, William 1746-1800 *Baker 92, BioIn 17*
Billings, William Dwight 1910- *WhoAm 92*
Billingslea, William, Jr. *Law&B 92*
Billingslea, William, Jr. 1940- *St&PR 93*
Billingsley, C.E. 1933- *St&PR 93*
Billingsley, Charles Edward 1933- *WhoAm 92*
Billingsley, Daniel Ray 1951- *WhoSSW 93*
Billingsley, Gary L. 1950- *St&PR 93*
Billingsley, James E. 1953- *St&PR 93*
Billingsley, James Ray 1927- *St&PR 93*
Billingsley, John *WhoScE 91-1*
Billingsley, John C. 1941- *St&PR 93*
Billingsley, John R. *Law&B 92*
Billingsley, Robert Thaine 1954- *WhoEmL 93, WhoSSW 93*
Billingsley, Thaine 1925- *BioIn 17*
Billingsley, Weyland Dee, Jr. 1946- *WhoEmL 93, WhoSSW 93*
Billings-Nolan, LuAnn 1960- *WhoAmW 93*
Billington, Barry E. 1940- *WhoSSW 93*
Billington, C.J. *WhoScE 91-1*
Billington, David Perkins 1927- *WhoAm 92*
Billington, David Rex 1939- *WhoUN 92*
Billington, Deborah Gail 1949- *WhoAmW 93*
Billington, Elizabeth 1765-1818 *Baker 92, OxDcOp*
Billington, James H. 1929- *BioIn 17*
Billington, James Hadley 1929- *WhoAm 92, WhoE 93, WhoWor 93*
Billington, Kevin 1933- *MiSFD 9*
Billington, Rachel *BioIn 17*
Billington, Steven Miles 1952- *WhoEmL 93*
Billington, William Howard, Jr. 1924- *St&PR 93, WhoAm 92*
Billinsky, Ignatius M. d1992 *NewYTBS 92*
Billinsley, Charles Edward 1933- *St&PR 93*
Billinson, Brian K. *Law&B 92*
Billinton, Roy 1935- *WhoAm 92*
Billion, Richard Edmund *Law&B 92*
Billis, Euripides Christos 1936- *WhoWor 93*
Billiter, Freda Delorous 1937- *WhoAmW 93*
Billiter, William Overton, Jr. 1934- *WhoAm 92, WhoWrEP 92*
Billman, Irwin Edward 1940- *WhoAm 92, WhoWrEP 92*
Billman, John A. 1948- *St&PR 93*
Billmeier, Sarah *BioIn 17*
Billmeyer, Kurt Conrad 1955- *St&PR 93*
Billod, Jacques P.X. 1948- *WhoScE 91-2*
Billot, Christian *WhoScE 91-2*
Billot, Eric Guy 1952- *WhoWor 93*
Billotte, Gaston Herve Gustave 1875-1940 *HarEnMi*
Billoux, Francois 1903-1976 *BioIn 17*
Billow, Marvin L. 1929- *St&PR 93*
Billroth, Theodor 1829-1894 *Baker 92*
Bills, Daniel G. 1924- *St&PR 93*
Bills, Elizabeth R. *AmWomPl*
Bills, Gerald Fremont 1955- *WhoE 93*
Bills, Mitchell Edward 1950- *WhoE 93*
Bills, Robert Edgar 1916- *WhoSSW 93*
Bills, Robert Howard 1944- *WhoAm 92*
Bills, Scott L(aurence) 1948- *ConAu 38NR*
Bills, Scott Laurence 1948- *WhoSSW 93*
Bills, Sheryl Jean 1945- *WhoWrEP 92*
Billson, Anne *ScF&FL 92*
Billups, Charles Edward 1929- *St&PR 93*
Billups, Clinton Ford, Jr. 1947- *WhoEmL 93*
Billups, Norman Fredrick 1934- *WhoAm 92*
Bill W. 1895-1971 *BioIn 17*
Billy, Michel Francois 1928- *WhoScE 91-2*
Billy, the Kid *BioIn 17*
Bilney, Gordon Neil 1939- *WhoAsAP 91*
Biloa Tang, Pascal 1937- *WhoUN 92*
Bilodeau, Alain 1950- *St&PR 93*
Bilodeau, Caroline *Law&B 92*
Bilodeau, Louis E. 1952- *St&PR 93*
Bilodeau, Steven Jules 1958- *St&PR 93*
Bilofsky, Howard Steven 1943- *WhoWor 93*
Bilotta, Diane Briley 1953- *WhoAmW 93*
Bilotta, Peter Francis 1960- *WhoE 93*
Bilotti, Eugene 1949- *St&PR 93*
Bilotti, Michael Joseph 1941- *St&PR 93*
Bilotti, Richard 1942- *WhoAm 92, WhoE 93*
Bilow, Steven Craig 1960- *WhoEmL 93*
Bilozerchev, Dmitri *BioIn 17*
Bilpuch, Edward George 1927- *WhoAm 92, WhoWor 93*
Bils, Charles F. *Law&B 92*
Bilsborough, Alan *WhoScE 91-1*
Bilsborough, David Haley 1955- *WhoScE 91-1*
Bilse, Benjamin 1816-1902 *Baker 92*
Bilsing, David Charles 1933- *St&PR 93, WhoAm 92*
Bilsky, Earl 1928- *St&PR 93*
Bilson, Bruce 1928- *MiSFD 9*
Bilson, Danny *MiSFD 9*
Bilson, F. Barry 1953- *St&PR 93*
Bilson, Malcolm 1935- *Baker 92*
Bilstrom, Jon W. *Law&B 92*
Bilt, Peter van der 1936-1983 *Baker 92*
Biltcliffe, George Henry 1935- *St&PR 93*
Biltis, Marvin 1941- *WhoAm 92*
Biltis, Marvin Leon 1941- *WhoSSW 93*
Bilton, Stuart Douglas 1946- *St&PR 93*
Bilton, William George 1944- *WhoSSW 93*
Biltonen, Rodney Lincoln 1937- *WhoAm 92*
Biltz, Ralph Edward 1944- *WhoE 93*
Biltz, Stuart James 1946- *WhoEmL 93*
Bilus, Benjamin S. *Law&B 92*
Bilyea, M.E. 1947- *St&PR 93*
Bilyeu, Charles Pierce 1954- *WhoEmL 93*
Bilyeu, Dick 1921- *BioIn 17*
Bilyeu, Don G., 1927- *St&PR 93*
Bilyeu, Richard *ScF&FL 92*
Bilyi, Mikhail Ulianovich *WhoWor 93*
Bimblick, Warren N. 1954- *St&PR 93*
Bimboni, Alberto 1882-1960 *Baker 92*
Bimson, Carl Alfred 1900- *WhoAm 92, WhoWor 93*
Bimstein, Benjamin William 1917- *WhoSSW 93*
Bimstein, Irving I. 1926- *St&PR 93*
Bimstein, Ronnie Irving 1956- *St&PR 93*
Bimstein, Whitey 1897?-1969 *BioIn 17*
Bina, Cyrus 1946- *WhoEmL 93*
Binau, Donald C. 1927- *St&PR 93*
Bincer, Adam Marian 1930- *WhoAm 92*
Binch, Gilles (de) c. 1400-1460 *Baker 92*
Binche, Gilles (de) c. 1400-1460 *Baker 92*
Binchois, Gilles (de) c. 1400-1460 *Baker 92*
Binchy, Maeve *BioIn 17*
Binde, Beth Esther 1953- *WhoAmW 93*
Binde, Jerome 1951- *WhoUN 92*
Binder, Abraham Wolfe 1895-1966 *Baker 92*
Binder, Amy Finn 1955- *WhoAm 92, WhoAmW 93, WhoE 93*
Binder, B. *WhoScE 91-4*
Binder, Christlieb Siegmund 1723-1789 *Baker 92*
Binder, David Franklin 1935- *WhoAm 92, WhoE 93*
Binder, David George 1936- *St&PR 93*
Binder, Earl Andrew 1904-1965 *ScF&FL 92*
Binder, Elaine Kotell 1938- *WhoE 93*
Binder, Frederick William 1926- *St&PR 93*
Binder, Gordon M. 1935- *St&PR 93*
Binder, Herbert R. 1937- *WhoAm 92*
Binder, J. Morris 1939- *St&PR 93*
Binder, Jeffrey J. *Law&B 92*
Binder, John *MiSFD 9*
Binder, Karl 1816-1860 *Baker 92*
Binder, Kurt 1944- *WhoScE 91-3*
Binder, Leonard James 1926- *WhoAm 92, WhoWor 93*
Binder, Lucy S. 1937- *St&PR 93*
Binder, Lucy Simpson 1937- *WhoAm 92*
Binder, Madeline Dotti 1942- *WhoAmW 93*
Binder, Mark W. *Law&B 92*
Binder, Martin R. 1918- *St&PR 93*
Binder, Mary S. *Law&B 92*
Binder, Maurice 1925?-1991 *BioIn 17*
Binder, Michael Alan 1955- *WhoE 93*
Binder, Mike *MiSFD 9*
Binder, Mildred Katherine 1918- *WhoAmW 93*
Binder, Mitchell Barry 1955- *St&PR 93*
Binder, Nancy Deborah 1951- *WhoAmW 93*
Binder, Richard Allen 1937- *WhoAm 92*
Binder, Robert Henri 1932- *WhoE 93*
Binder, Timothy Robert *Law&B 92*
Bindereif, Albrecht *WhoScE 91-3*
Binderman, Melvin David 1940- *WhoE 93*
Binding, Horst 1939- *WhoScE 91-3*
Bindley, William *MiSFD 9*
Bindley, William Edward 1940- *St&PR 93, WhoAm 92, WhoWor 93*
Bindra, Tejinder Singh *Law&B 92*
Bindseil, Edwin R. 1930- *St&PR 93*
Bindseil, Lee Anton, III 1938- *WhoE 93*
Binegar, Diane *St&PR 93*
Binenbaum, Janco 1880-1956 *Baker 92*
Biner, Margaret Lavin 1952- *WhoE 93*
Bines, Harvey Ernest 1941- *WhoAm 92*
Bines, Richard D. *WhoScE 91-1*
Binet, Jean 1893-1960 *Baker 92*
Binet, Jean-Paul 1924- *WhoScE 91-2*
Binet, Luc Desire 1951- *WhoWor 93*
Binford, Chapman H. 1900-1990 *BioIn 17*
Binford, Jesse Stone, Jr. 1928- *WhoSSW 93*
Binford, Joseph Robert *Law&B 92*
Bing, Dave *BioIn 17*
Bing, Dave 1943- *ConBlB 3 [port]*
Bing, David 1943- *ConEn*
Bing, Janet Mueller 1937- *WhoSSW 93*
Bing, Leon 1950- *BioIn 17*
Bing, Mack *MiSFD 9*
Bing, Oscar Harold Lee 1935- *WhoE 93*
Bing, Richard J. 1909- *BioIn 17*
Bing, Richard McPhail 1950- *WhoWor 93*
Bing, Roland Edward, Jr. 1921- *WhoAm 92*
Bing, Rudolf 1902- *BioIn 17, OxDcOp*
Bing, Rudolf (Franz Joseph) 1902- *Baker 92*
Bing, Stanley *BioIn 17*
Binga, Jesse 1865-1950 *BioIn 17*
Bingaman, Jeff 1943- *CngDr 91, WhoAm 92*
Bingaman, Steven W. 1956- *St&PR 93*
Bingde, Tan 1928- *WhoWor 93*
Bingeman, Alison *ScF&FL 92*
Bingen, Franz Marie Jacques *WhoWor 93*
Bingen, Hildegard von 1098-1179 *BioIn 17*
Bingenheimer, Charles G. 1953- *St&PR 93*
Binger, Eugene Thomas 1923- *St&PR 93*
Binger, Louis-Gustave 1856-1936 *Expl 93*
Binger, Wilson Valentine 1917- *WhoAm 92*
Bingham, Barry 1906-1988 *BioIn 17*
Bingham, Barry 1933- *BioIn 17*
Bingham, (George) Barry 1906-1988 *DcLB 127 [port]*
Bingham, Billy Elias 1931- *WhoSSW 93*
Bingham, Carson *ScF&FL 92*
Bingham, Charles W. 1933- *WhoAm 92*
Bingham, Christopher 1937- *WhoAm 92*
Bingham, Edwin Theodore 1936- *WhoAm 92*
Bingham, Eleanor Miller 1946- *BioIn 17*
Bingham, Eula 1929- *WhoAm 92*
Bingham, George Barry 1906-1988 *BioIn 17*
Bingham, George Barry 1933- *BioIn 17*
Bingham, George Barry, Jr. 1933- *WhoAm 92, WhoSSW 93*
Bingham, George Walter Chandler 1925- *WhoWor 93*
Bingham, Henry J. *St&PR 93*
Bingham, Hiram 1789-1869 *BioIn 17*
Bingham, Hiram 1831-1908 *BioIn 17*
Bingham, Hiram 1875-1956 *Expl 93*
Bingham, Hiram A. 1935- *WhoWrEP 92*
Bingham, James Hugh 1946- *St&PR 93*
Bingham, Jinsie Scott 1935- *WhoAm 92, WhoAmW 93*
Bingham, John A. 1815-1900 *BioIn 17*
Bingham, John Ferguson 1952- *WhoScE 91-1*
Bingham, Jonathan Worth 1942-1964 *BioIn 17*
Bingham, June 1919- *WhoAmW 93, WhoE 93*
Bingham, Kathleen S. 1939- *St&PR 93*
Bingham, Mary Lily Kenan Flagler 1867-1917 *BioIn 17*
Bingham, Nicholas Hugh *WhoScE 91-1*
Bingham, Nicholas Hugh 1945- *WhoWor 93*
Bingham, Paris Edward, Jr. 1957- *WhoWor 93*
Bingham, Paul M. 1942- *St&PR 93*
Bingham, Robert A. *Law&B 92*
Bingham, Robert S. 1948- *St&PR 93*
Bingham, Robert Worth 1871-1937 *BioIn 17, JrnUS*
Bingham, Robert Worth 1932-1966 *BioIn 17*
Bingham, Roger *BioIn 17, ScF&FL 92*
Bingham, Russell Nevins 1944- *WhoE 93*
Bingham, Sallie *BioIn 17*
Bingham, Sallie 1937- *WhoWrEP 92*
Bingham, Seth (Daniels) 1882-1972 *Baker 92*
Bingham, Walter D. 1921- *WhoAm 92*
Bingham, Wayne M. 1954- *St&PR 93*
Bingle, Donald J. 1954- *WhoEmL 93*
Bingler, Aimee *BioIn 17*
Bingley, Edward J. 1934- *WhoIns 93*
Bingley, Margaret 1947- *ScF&FL 92*
Bingley, Margaret (Jane) 1947- *SmATA 72 [port]*
Bingman, Bradlee Ann 1959- *WhoAmW 93*
Bingman, Mark Allen 1958- *WhoSSW 93*
Bingo-Duggins, Michael Oneil 1946- *WhoSSW 93*
Binh, Nguyen Thi, Madame 1927- *DcTwHis*
Bini, Dante Natale 1932- *WhoWor 93*
Binicki, Stanislav 1872-1942 *Baker 92, OxDcOp*
Biniek, Joseph Paul 1922- *WhoWrEP 92*
Binion, Beatrice Marie 1958- *WhoWor 93*
Binion, Linda Diane 1948- *WhoAmW 93*
Binion, Lula 1938- *WhoAmW 93*
Bink, Frederik Albert 1937- *WhoScE 91-3*
Binkerd, Gordon (Ware) 1916- *Baker 92, WhoAm 92*
Binkert, Alvin John 1910- *WhoAm 92*
Binkert, Christopher C. 1949- *St&PR 93*
Binkhorst, Robert A. 1931- *WhoScE 91-3*
Binkin, Irving 1906?-1989? *ScF&FL 92*
Binkley, G.P. *Law&B 92*
Binkley, James Arthur 1930- *St&PR 93*
Binkley, Janet Ramage 1930- *WhoWrEP 92*
Binkley, Nicholas Burns 1945- *WhoAm 92*
Binkley, Olin Trivette 1908- *WhoAm 92*
Binkley, Thomas (Eden) 1931- *Baker 92*
Binkowski, Edward Stephan 1948- *WhoAm 92, WhoEmL 93*
Binkowski, Lisa Mary 1953- *WhoAmW 93*
Binkowski, Richard O. *St&PR 93*
Binks, Rebecca Anne 1955- *WhoAmW 93, WhoEmL 93*
Bin Mohamad, Mahathir 1925- *WhoAsAP 91*
Binmore, Kenneth George *WhoScE 91-1*
Binn, Moreton I. 1936- *St&PR 93*
Binnendijk, Hans *WhoScE 91-1*
Binnette, Owens Joseph 1930- *St&PR 93*
Binney, Robert Harry 1945- *WhoAm 92, WhoWor 93*
Binnie, Alan G. 1906- *St&PR 93*
Binnie, David Morison *WhoScE 91-1*
Binnig, Gerd 1947- *WhoScE 91-4*
Binnig, Gerd Karl 1947- *WhoAm 92, WhoWor 93*
Binning, Bette Finese 1927- *WhoWor 93*
Binning, John Harlan 1923- *WhoIns 93*
Binninger, George A. 1948- *St&PR 93*
Binnion, John Edward 1918- *WhoAm 92*
Binns, Carol Ann 1955- *WhoE 93*
Binns, Edward 1916-1990 *BioIn 17*
Binns, James Edward 1931- *WhoAm 92*
Binns, James W. 1946- *WhoAm 92, WhoE 93*
Binns, James Wallace 1940- *WhoWor 93*
Binns, John 1772-1860 *JrnUS*
Binns, Kenneth John *WhoScE 91-1*
Binns, Kenneth John 1934- *WhoWor 93*
Binns, Malcolm 1936- *Baker 92*
Binns, Matthew McKinley *WhoScE 91-1*
Binns, Ottwell 1872- *ScF&FL 92*
Binns, R. *WhoScE 91-1*
Binns, Ronald W. 1956- *St&PR 93*
Binns, Walter Gordon, Jr. 1929- *WhoAm 92, WhoWor 93*
Binoux, Michel *WhoScE 91-2*
Binowitz, Charles 1905- *St&PR 93*
Binsfeld, Connie Berube 1924- *WhoAm 92, WhoAmW 93*
Bin Shakir, Sharif Zayd 1934- *WhoWor 93*
Bin Siddiq, Mohammed Mustafa 1948- *WhoWor 93*
Binstein, Mark P. *BioIn 17*
Binstock, R. C. 1958- *ConAu 138*
Binstock, Robert Henry 1935- *WhoAm 92, WhoWrEP 92*
Binstock, Ruth Atlas *AmWomPl*
Binswanger, David R. 1956- *St&PR 93*
Binswanger, Frank d1991 *BioIn 17*
Binswanger, Frank G., Jr. 1928- *St&PR 93*
Binswanger, John K. 1932- *St&PR 93, WhoAm 92*
Bintliff, Barbara Ann 1953- *WhoEmL 93*
Bintz, Jacques 1927- *WhoScE 91-3*
Bintz, Joan Heiderer 1931- *St&PR 93*
Bintz, John Carl 1931- *St&PR 93*
Binyon, Hal O., III 1940- *St&PR 93*
Binzen, Peter (Husted) 1922- *ConAu 136, WhoAm 92, WhoWrEP 92*
Binzet, Ahmet 1953- *WhoScE 91-4*
Biobaku, Saburi Oladeni 1918- *WhoWor 93*
Biolchini, Robert Fredrick 1939- *WhoSSW 93, WhoWor 93*

Biondi, Frank J., Jr. 1945- *St&PR 93, WhoAm 92*
Biondi, Lawrence 1938- *WhoAm 92*
Biondi, Manfred Anthony 1924- *WhoAm 92*
Biondi, Matthew Nicolas 1965- *BiDAMSp 1989*
Biondillo, Philip 1947- *WhoEmL 93*
Biondo, Bradley Edward 1953- *WhoE 93*
Biondo, Dino Dominick 1958- *WhoEmL 93, WhoWor 93*
Biondo, Joseph Del 1926- *St&PR 93*
Biondo, Michael Thomas 1928- *WhoAm 92*
Biondo, Raymond Vitus 1936- *WhoSSW 93*
Bioni, Antonio 1698-c. 1738 *OxDcOp*
Biordi, Giovanni 1691-1748 *Baker 92*
Bioy Casares, Adolfo 1914- *BioIn 17, ScF&FL 92, SpAmA*
Bippus, David Paul 1949- *WhoAm 92*
Bir, Michelle Marie 1965- *WhoAmW 93, WhoWor 93*
Biraben, Pierre 1945- *WhoAm 92*
Birardi, Giuseppe R. 1918- *WhoScE 91-3*
Birbari, Adil Elias 1933- *WhoWor 93*
Birbaum, Joseph Louis 1939- *St&PR 93*
Birbeck, Mike *BioIn 17*
Birch, Bill 1934- *WhoAsAP 91*
Birch, Bryan 1937- *St&PR 93*
Birch, Bryan John *WhoScE 91-1*
Birch, David William 1913- *WhoE 93*
Birch, Douglas Malcolm *WhoE 93*
Birch, Elizabeth Miller *Law&B 92*
Birch, Eric Norman 1942- *St&PR 93*
Birch, Francis d1992 *NewYTBS 92*
Birch, Francis 1903-1992 *BioIn 17*
Birch, Grace Morgan 1925- *WhoAmW 93, WhoE 93*
Birch, Gregory Mark 1952- *WhoE 93*
Birch, H. *WhoScE 91-1*
Birch, Jack Willard 1915- *WhoAm 92*
Birch, John Paul 1939- *St&PR 93*
Birch, Keith G. 1934- *WhoScE 91-1*
Birch, Murray Patrick 1953- *WhoAm 92*
Birch, Nicholas John *WhoScE 91-1*
Birch, Norman John 1930- *St&PR 93*
Birch, P. *WhoScE 91-1*
Birch, Patricia *MiSFD 9*
Birch, Patricia 1934?- *ConTFT 10*
Birch, Stanley F., Jr. 1945- *WhoAm 92*
Birch, Stanley Francis, Jr. 1945- *WhoSSW 93*
Birch, William Charles 1932- *St&PR 93*
Birch, William Dunham, Jr. 1940- *WhoAm 92, WhoE 93, WhoWor 93*
Birchak, James Robert 1939- *WhoSSW 93*
Birchak, Michael Joseph 1954- *WhoEmL 93*
Birchall, David W. *WhoScE 91-1*
Birchall, Robert 1760-1819 *Baker 92*
Bircham, Deric Neale 1934- *WhoWor 93*
Birch-Andersen, Aksel *WhoScE 91-2*
Birchard, Clarence C. 1866-1946 *Baker 92*
Birchard, Guy 1949- *WhoCanL 92*
Birchard, Kendon Thomas 1938- *St&PR 93*
Birchby, Kenneth L. 1915- *St&PR 93*
Birchby, Kenneth Lee 1915- *WhoAm 92*
Birchem, Regina 1938- *WhoAm 92*
Bircher, Edgar Allen 1934- *WhoAm 92*
Bircher, James A. 1944- *St&PR 93*
Bircher, Wayne C. 1955- *St&PR 93*
Birchette, Gerald Craig *Law&B 92*
Birchfield, Dorothy Melton 1928- *WhoAmW 93*
Birchfield, J. Kermit, Jr. *Law&B 92*
Birchfield, John Kermit, Jr. 1940- *St&PR 93, WhoAm 92, WhoE 93*
Birchfield, Mary Eva 1909- *WhoAmW 93, WhoSSW 93*
Birchler, Thomas Alan 1961- *WhoSSW 93*
Birchman, David 1949- *SmATA 72 [port]*
Birck, Michael John 1938- *WhoAm 92*
Birckbichler, Richard Dean 1948- *St&PR 93, WhoAm 92*
Birckhead, Fannie W. *AfrAmBi*
Bird, Agnes Thornton 1921- *WhoAm 92, WhoWor 93*
Bird, Alan Charles 1938- *WhoScE 91-1*
Bird, Ana M. *Law&B 92*
Bird, Angus Graham 1950- *WhoWor 93*
Bird, Antoinette Kelsall *ScF&FL 92*
Bird, Arthur 1856-1923 *Baker 92*
Bird, Barbara Elizabeth Irma *WhoScE 91-1*
Bird, Caroline 1915- *WhoAm 92, WhoWrEP 92*
Bird, Charles Albert 1947- *WhoEmL 93*
Bird, Christopher G. 1957- *St&PR 93*
Bird, Claudia Storm 1954- *St&PR 93*
Bird, Colin Carmichael *WhoScE 91-1*
Bird, David Jacobs 1954- *WhoEmL 93*
Bird, Donna Clarice 1950- *WhoEmL 93*
Bird, Edward Dennis 1926- *WhoAm 92*
Bird, Eugene Hall 1925- *WhoE 93*
Bird, Grace Electra *AmWomPl*
Bird, Harrie Waldo, Jr. 1917- *WhoAm 92*
Bird, Harry H. 1933- *WhoAm 92, WhoE 93*
Bird, Herbert R. 1912-1989 *BioIn 17*
Bird, Howard 1916- *BioIn 17*
Bird, Ian Bruce *Law&B 92*
Bird, Isabella 1831-1904 *Expl 93*
Bird, Ivor *DcCPCAm*
Bird, Jacqueline Faye 1954- *WhoEmL 93*
Bird, James T. 1949- *St&PR 93*
Bird, Jerry Joe d1991 *BioIn 17*
Bird, John Adams 1937- *WhoAm 92*
Bird, John Malcolm 1931- *WhoAm 92*
Bird, John William Clyde 1932- *WhoAm 92*
Bird, John Williston *BioIn 17*
Bird, Jon Arthur 1939- *St&PR 93*
Bird, Juanita Delores 1942- *WhoE 93*
Bird, Junius Bouton 1907-1982 *IntDcAn*
Bird, Kenneth D. 1917-1991 *BioIn 17*
Bird, L. Raymond 1914- *WhoE 93, WhoWor 93*
Bird, Larry *BioIn 17, NewYTBS 92 [port]*
Bird, Larry (Joe) 1956- *ConAu 139, WhoAm 92, WhoE 93*
Bird, Leonard Arthur 1910- *WhoWor 93*
Bird, Lester 1938- *DcCPCAm, WhoWor 93*
Bird, Luther Smith 1921- *WhoSSW 93*
Bird, Margaret Helena 1954- *WhoE 93*
Bird, Mary Lynne Miller 1934- *WhoAm 92*
Bird, Matthew Alexius 1957- *WhoEmL 93*
Bird, Nancy 1915- *BioIn 17*
Bird, Patricia Amy 1941- *WhoWrEP 92*
Bird, Peter 1951- *WhoAm 92*
Bird, Peter G. 1944- *St&PR 93*
Bird, Phylis Shuttleworth 1941- *WhoE 93*
Bird, R. Curtman 1957- *St&PR 93*
Bird, Ralph G. 1933- *St&PR 93*
Bird, Ralph Gordon 1933- *WhoAm 92*
Bird, Robert Byron 1924- *WhoAm 92, WhoWrEP 92*
Bird, Robert E. 1929- *St&PR 93*
Bird, Robert Hutchins 1932- *St&PR 93*
Bird, Robert Wilson 1918- *WhoAm 92*
Bird, Rose Elizabeth 1936- *WhoAm 92, WhoAmW 93*
Bird, Sandra Lopez *Law&B 92*
Bird, Sarah Ann *WhoWrEP 92*
Bird, Stephen J. *Law&B 92*
Bird, Stewart *MiSFD 9*
Bird, Terence C. 1945- *St&PR 93*
Bird, Thomas Edward 1935- *WhoE 93*
Bird, Vere, Jr. 1936- *DcCPCAm*
Bird, Vere C. 1909- *DcCPCAm*
Bird, Vere Cornwall, Sr. 1909- *WhoWor 93*
Bird, Wendell R(aleigh) *ConAu 40NR*
Bird, Wendell Raleigh 1954- *WhoEmL 93, WhoSSW 93, WhoWor 93*
Bird, Whitworth F. 1932- *WhoIns 93*
Bird, Whitworth F., Jr. 1932- *St&PR 93*
Bird, Will Richard 1891-1984 *WhoCanL 92*
Birdman, Jerome Moseley 1930- *WhoAm 92*
Bird-Porto, Patricia Anne 1952- *WhoAmW 93*
Birds, John Richard 1948- *WhoWor 93*
Birdsall, Arthur Anthony 1947- *WhoEmL 93*
Birdsall, Blair 1907- *WhoAm 92*
Birdsall, Charles Kennedy 1925- *WhoAm 92*
Birdsall, David Lee 1954- *WhoWor 93*
Birdsall, Peter 1948- *ScF&FL 92*
Birdsall, William Forest 1937- *WhoAm 92*
Birdsell, Regina Sullivan 1946- *WhoEmL 93*
Birdsell, Sandra 1942- *WhoCanL 92*
Birdsey, Anna Campas 1949- *WhoAmW 93*
Birdsey, George J. 1947- *St&PR 93*
Birdseye, Tom *BioIn 17*
Birdsong, David Persons 1952- *WhoSSW 93*
Birdsong, George Yancy 1939- *St&PR 93, WhoAm 92*
Birdsong, McLemore, Jr. 1943- *St&PR 93*
Birdsong, Randall George 1951- *WhoEmL 93*
Birdsong, William Herbert, Jr. 1918- *WhoAm 92*
Birdsong, William M., Jr. 1934- *St&PR 93*
Birdwell, Carolyn Campbell 1947- *WhoEmL 93*
Birdwell, Daniel Martin *Law&B 92*
Birdwell, Donald Wayne 1952- *St&PR 93*
Birdwell, James Edwin, Jr. 1924- *WhoAm 92*
Birdwell, Randall Patrick 1956- *WhoAm 92*
Birdwell, Roy Dean 1937- *St&PR 93*
Birdwell, Russell 1903-1977 *ScF&FL 92*
Birdwhistell, Anne Davison 1944- *WhoE 93*
Birdwhistell, Ray L. 1918- *WhoAm 92*
Bird Woman 1786-1884 *BioIn 17*
Birdwood, William Riddell 1865-1951 *HarEnMi*
Birdzell, Donald T. d1991 *BioIn 17*
Birdzell, Samuel Henry 1916- *WhoAm 92*
Bireley, Robert 1933- *ConAu 137*
Birely, William Cramer 1919- *WhoAm 92*
Biren, David Robert 1937- *WhoE 93*
Biren, Matthew Bennett 1948- *WhoEmL 93*
Biren, Melissa H. *Law&B 92*
Birenbaum, Barbara 1941- *BioIn 17, ConAu 136*
Birenbaum, Barbara Joan 1941- *WhoAmW 93*
Birenbaum, David Elias 1937- *WhoAm 92, WhoE 93*
Birenbaum, H.A. *Law&B 92*
Birenbaum, William M. 1923- *WhoAm 92*
Birendra Bir Bikram Shah Dev, His Majesty 1945- *WhoWor 93*
Birendra Bir Bikram Shah Dev, King of Nepal 1945- *WhoAsAP 91*
Birendra Bir Bikram Shah Deva, King of Nepal 1945- *BioIn 17*
Bires, Dennis Eugene 1954- *WhoEmL 93*
Birge, Anne Constantin 1952- *WhoEmL 93*
Birge, Pamela Adair 1954- *WhoAmW 93*
Birge, Robert R. 1946- *BioIn 17*
Birge, Robert Richards 1946- *WhoAm 92, WhoWor 93*
Birgeneau, Robert Joseph 1942- *WhoAm 92*
Biribauer, Richard Frank *Law&B 92*
Birindelli, Luca Maria 1956- *WhoWor 93*
Biringer, Paul Peter 1924- *WhoAm 92*
Biriotti, Leon 1929- *Baker 92*
Birish, George James 1928- *St&PR 93*
Biriukov, Yuri 1908-1976 *Baker 92*
Birk, Bernhard William 1926- *St&PR 93*
Birk, David R. *Law&B 92*
Birk, David R. 1947- *St&PR 93*
Birk, John R. 1951- *WhoAm 92, WhoEmL 93*
Birk, Joseph E. *Law&B 92*
Birk, Kathy *BioIn 17*
Birk, Robert Eugene 1926- *WhoAm 92*
Birk, Roger E. *BioIn 17*
Birk, Sharon Anastasia 1937- *WhoAm 92*
Birk, Timothy Edward 1951- *WhoEmL 93*
Birkan, Marcel 1942- *WhoScE 91-2*
Birkby, Evelyn *BioIn 17*
Birkdale, Lisa M. *Law&B 92*
Birkel, Bernard L. *Law&B 92*
Birkeland, K. *WhoScE 91-4*
Birkeland, Rolf 1938- *WhoScE 91-4*
Birkelbach, Albert Ottmar 1927- *WhoAm 92*
Birkelo, Ralph J. 1929- *St&PR 93*
Birkelund, John P. 1930- *St&PR 93*
Birkelund, John Peter 1930- *WhoAm 92*
Birkenhead, Earl of 1872-1930 *BioIn 17*
Birkenhead, Frederick Edwin Smith, Earl of 1872-1930 *DcTwHis*
Birkenhead, Thomas Bruce 1931- *WhoAm 92, WhoE 93, WhoWor 93*
Birkenkamp, Dean F. 1956- *St&PR 93*
Birkenkamp, Dean Frederick 1956- *WhoAm 92*
Birkenmeier, Gary Francis 1946- *WhoEmL 93, WhoSSW 93*
Birkenruth, Harry H. 1931- *St&PR 93*
Birkenshaw, David J. 1955- *St&PR 93*
Birkenshaw, J.W. 1947- *WhoScE 91-1*
Birkenstock, Arthur O. 1928- *WhoIns 93*
Birkenstock, James Warren 1912- *WhoAm 92*
Birkenstock, Johann Adam 1687-1733 *Baker 92*
Birkerts, Gunnar 1925- *WhoAm 92*
Birket-Smith, Kaj 1893-1977 *IntDcAn*
Birkett, James Davis 1936- *WhoE 93*
Birkett, John Hooper 1925- *WhoAm 92*
Birkett, Maria Grace Liggiera 1956- *WhoAmW 93, WhoEmL 93*
Birkey, Lou Ann 1958- *St&PR 93*
Birkhahn, Jonathan *Law&B 92*
Birkhead, Guthrie Sweeney, Jr. 1920- *WhoAm 92*
Birkhed, Dowen 1946- *WhoScE 91-4*
Birkhofer, A. *WhoScE 91-3*
Birkhofer, Carrie Lynne 1961- *WhoAmW 93*
Birkhoff, Garrett 1911- *WhoAm 92*
Birkholm, Michael Peter 1952- *St&PR 93*
Birkholz, E. Terry 1937- *St&PR 93*
Birkholz, Fred Ray *Law&B 92*
Birkholz, Gabriella Sonja 1938- *WhoAm 92, WhoAmW 93, WhoWor 93*
Birkholz, Raymond J. 1936- *St&PR 93*
Birkholz, Raymond James 1936- *WhoAm 92*
Birkin, Andrew *MiSFD 9*
Birkin, Charles 1907-1985 *ScF&FL 92*
Birkinbine, John, II 1930- *WhoAm 92, WhoWor 93*
Birkins, R. Parker 1926- *St&PR 93*
Birkins, Rodney Mann 1930- *WhoAm 92*
Birkinshaw, Alan *MiSFD 9*
Birkinshaw, Colin 1947- *WhoScE 91-3*
Birkland, Robert M. 1951- *St&PR 93*
Birkle, M. *WhoScE 91-3*
Birkmaier, Robert David 1955- *WhoEmL 93*
Birkner, Edward Charles 1920- *WhoAm 92*
Birks, Donna S. 1955- *St&PR 93*
Birks, Drummond 1919- *St&PR 93*
Birks, H. Jonathan 1945- *St&PR 93*
Birks, Neil 1935- *WhoAm 92*
Birky, John Edward 1934- *WhoAm 92*
Birla family *DcTwHis*
Birle, James R. 1936- *WhoAm 92*
Birle, James Robb 1936- *WhoAm 92*
Birler, Ali Sencer 1935- *WhoScE 91-4*
Birley, Arthur William *WhoScE 91-1*
Birman, Joan S. 1927- *WhoAmW 93*
Birman, Joseph Leon 1927- *WhoAm 92*
Birman, Ronnie Rathkopf 1947- *WhoE 93*
Birmelin, August Robert 1933- *WhoAm 92*
Birmelin, Robert 1933- *BioIn 17*
Birmingham, Anthony Terence *WhoScE 91-1*
Birmingham, Bascom Wayne 1925- *WhoAm 92*
Birmingham, Carolyn 1953- *WhoSSW 93*
Birmingham, Fletcher Ansil 1956- *WhoEmL 93*
Birmingham, Gina Maria 1965- *WhoAmW 93*
Birmingham, John J. 1939- *WhoIns 93*
Birmingham, John James 1939- *St&PR 93*
Birmingham, Keith 1934- *St&PR 93*
Birmingham, Richard Francis 1949- *WhoEmL 93*
Birmingham, Richard Gregory 1929- *WhoAm 92*
Birmingham, Richard Joseph 1953- *WhoEmL 93*
Birmingham, Stephen *BioIn 17*
Birmingham, Stephen 1931- *WhoAm 92, WhoWrEP 92*
Birn, Raymond Francis 1935- *WhoAm 92*
Birnbach, Gerald Marshall 1931- *St&PR 93*
Birnbach, Heinrich 1793-1879 *Baker 92*
Birnbach, Karl Joseph 1751-1805 *Baker 92*
Birnbaum, Alfred 1957- *ScF&FL 92*
Birnbaum, Allan S. 1937- *St&PR 93*
Birnbaum, Burton H. 1942- *St&PR 93*
Birnbaum, David Mark *Law&B 92*
Birnbaum, Denise Barbara 1951- *WhoEmL 93*
Birnbaum, Edward Lester 1939- *WhoAm 92*
Birnbaum, Eleazar 1929- *WhoAm 92, WhoWrEP 92*
Birnbaum, Gisele Blankstein d1989 *BioIn 17*
Birnbaum, Henrik 1925- *WhoAm 92*
Birnbaum, Henry 1917- *WhoAm 92*
Birnbaum, Hermann 1905- *WhoE 93*
Birnbaum, Howard Kent 1932- *WhoAm 92*
Birnbaum, Irwin Morton 1935- *WhoAm 92, WhoE 93*
Birnbaum, Jane H. 1948- *WhoAmW 93*
Birnbaum, Joan Welker 1923- *WhoAmW 93*
Birnbaum, Leon *Law&B 92*
Birnbaum, Lester H. *Law&B 92*
Birnbaum, Max 1919- *St&PR 93*
Birnbaum, Milton 1919- *ScF&FL 92*
Birnbaum, Robert *Law&B 92*
Birnbaum, Robert 1936- *WhoAm 92*
Birnbaum, Robert Jack 1927- *WhoAm 92*
Birnbaum, Roy Bennett *Law&B 92*
Birnbaum, Roy Bennett 1953- *WhoEmL 93*
Birnbaum, Stephen *BioIn 17*
Birnbaum, Stephen Norman 1937- *WhoWrEP 92*
Birnbaum, Stephen (Norman) 1937-1991 *ConAu 136*
Birnbaum, Theodore d1990 *BioIn 17*
Birnbaum, Zdzislaw 1880-1921 *PolBiDi*
Birnbaum, Zygmunt William 1903- *WhoAm 92*
Birnberg, Howard Gene 1950- *WhoEmL 93*
Birnberg, Jack 1937- *WhoE 93*
Birne, Cindy Frank 1956- *WhoSSW 93*
Birney, Arthur A. 1927- *St&PR 93*
Birney, David Bell 1825-1864 *HarEnMi*
Birney, David Edwin *WhoAm 92*
Birney, David G. 1943- *St&PR 93*
Birney, Earle 1904- *BioIn 17, WhoCanL 92*
Birney, (Alfred) Earle 1904- *WhoWrEP 92*
Birney, James G. 1792-1857 *PolPar*
Birney, Margaret Linda Hamilton 1954- *WhoEmL 93*
Birney, Meredith Baxter *BioIn 17*
Birney, Robert Charles 1925- *WhoAm 92*
Birnhak, Jack *St&PR 93*

Birnhak, Sam 1950- St&PR 93
Birnhak, Sandra Jean 1945- WhoAmW 93, WhoE 93, WhoWor 93
Birnholz, Francoise M. Law&B 92
Birnholz, Jack 1931- St&PR 93
Birnholz, Jason Cordell 1942- WhoAm 92
Birnholz, Richard Joseph 1945- WhoSSW 93
Birnie, Carel Frederik Theodoor 1925- WhoWor 93
Birnie, Daryl Elmer 1933- WhoAm 92
Birnie, Richard V. 1952- WhoScE 91-1
Birnie, Richard Williams 1944- WhoE 93
Birnie, Tessa (Daphne) 1934- Baker 92
Birnkammer, Hermann 1938- WhoScE 91-3
Birnkrant, Henry Joseph 1955- WhoEmL 93
Birns, Mark Theodore 1949- WhoAm 92, WhoEmL 93
Birnstiel, Charles WhoAm 92
Birnstiel, Max L. 1933- WhoScE 91-4
Birnstiel, Max Luciano 1933- WhoWor 93
Biro, Attila Gyorgy 1931- WhoScE 91-4
Biro, B. MajAI
Biro, B(alint) S(tephen) 1921- ConAu 39NR, MajAI [port]
Biro, Bruce-Michael 1950- WhoEmL 93, WhoSSW 93
Biro, David BioIn 17
Biro, Emery J., III Law&B 92
Biro, Endre N.A. 1919- WhoScE 91-4
Biro, Ferenc 1928- WhoScE 91-4
Biro, Geza 1933- WhoScE 91-4
Biro, Gy WhoScE 91-4
Biro, Gyorgy 1928- WhoScE 91-4
Biro, Joan S. 1955- St&PR 93
Biro, Lajos 1856-1931 IntDcAn
Biro, Laszlo 1929- WhoAm 92
Biro, Peter 1930- WhoScE 91-4
Biro, Peter 1943- WhoScE 91-4
Biro, Sari 1912-1990 BioIn 17
Biro, Tamas 1936- WhoScE 91-4
Biro, Val ConAu 39NR, MajAI
Biro, Val 1921- BioIn 17, ChlLR 28 [port]
Biroc, Joe ConTFT 10
Biroc, Joseph 1903?- ConTFT 10
Biroc, Joseph F. ConTFT 10
Birol, Andrew John 1959- WhoE 93
Biron, Cemal 1919- WhoScE 91-4
Biron, Christine Anne 1951- WhoAmW 93, WhoE 93, WhoEmL 93
Biros, Lorraine 1946- WhoAmW 93
Birosik, Patti 1956- WhoEmL 93
Birrell, Augustine 1850-1933 BioIn 17
Birrell, Robert Warren 1930- St&PR 93
Birren, Faber ScF&FL 92
Birren, James Emmett 1918- WhoAm 92
Birrenkott, Pete S. 1948- St&PR 93
Birrer, Richard Bruce 1953- WhoEmL 93
Birschel, Dee Baltzer 1947- WhoAmW 93
Birschtein, Barbara Ann WhoAmW 93
Birsh, Arthur Thomas 1932- WhoAm 92, WhoE 93, WhoWrEP 92
Birsic, Linda Marie 1964- WhoAmW 93
Birss, David Nevin 1942- St&PR 93
Birss, Edward W. 1952- St&PR 93
Birstein, Ann WhoWrEP 92
Birstein, Seymour Joseph 1927- WhoE 93, WhoWor 93
Birt, Cecil Jerome Law&B 92
Birt, Diane Feickert 1949- WhoEmL 93
Birtel, Frank Thomas 1932- WhoAm 92
Birtles, Anthony Bruce WhoScE 91-1
Birtles, Dora (Toll) 1903?- DcChlFi
Birtner, Herbert 1900-1942 Baker 92
Birtwell, Kathleen Ayres Law&B 92
Birtwistle, Donald B. 1920- St&PR 93
Birtwistle, Harrison 1934- IntDcOp, OxDcOp
Birtwistle, Harrison (Paul) 1934- Baker 92
Birtwistle, Margaret Anne 1948- WhoE 93
Biruni, Al 973-1048? OxDcByz
Birx, H. James 1941- WhoAm 92, WhoE 93, WhoWor 93
Birza, Rob BioIn 17
Birzon, Gerald 1929- St&PR 93
Bis, Kazimierz 1930- WhoScE 91-4
Bisaccio, Martha Louise 1939- WhoAmW 93
Bisanar, Robert M. Law&B 92
Bisarnsin, Tanongsak 1948- WhoEmL 93, WhoSSW 93
Bisbee, David George 1947- WhoEmL 93
Bisbee, David Wise 1950- WhoEmL 93
Bisbee, Gerald E. 1942- St&PR 93
Bisbee, Gerald Elftman, Jr. 1942- WhoAm 92, WhoE 93
Bisbee, J.E. 1935- St&PR 93
Bisbee, Madge Cranston 1939- WhoAmW 93
Bisbing, Steven B. 1956- WhoE 93
Bisby, Mark Ainley 1946- WhoAm 92
Biscamp, Walter B., Jr. 1961- St&PR 93
Biscardi, Chester 1948- WhoAm 92
Biscaye, Pierre Eginton 1935- WhoE 93
Bisceglio, Anthony F. 1947- St&PR 93
Bisch, John J. 1928- St&PR 93
Bisch, Richard Michel Marie 1943- WhoWor 93
Bischak, Kathleen Huff 1951- WhoAmW 93
Bischi, Gian-Italo 1960- WhoWor 93
Bischko, Johannes J. 1922- WhoScE 91-4
Bischof, Hansjoachim WhoScE 91-3
Bischof, Harrington 1935- St&PR 93
Bischof, Henrik 1934- WhoWor 93
Bischof, Merriem Lanova WhoAm 92
Bischof, Rainer 1947- Baker 92
Bischofberger, Guido 1924- WhoWor 93
Bischoff, David 1951- ScF&FL 92
Bischoff, David Canby 1930- WhoAm 92
Bischoff, Elmer 1916-1991 BioIn 17
Bischoff, Franz Arthur 1864-1929 BioIn 17
Bischoff, Frederic John 1939- St&PR 93
Bischoff, Gerhard O. 1925- WhoScE 91-3
Bischoff, Heather Woodard ScF&FL 92
Bischoff, Hermann 1868-1936 Baker 92
Bischoff, Ilse 1903?-1990 BioIn 17
Bischoff, James R. 1936- St&PR 93
Bischoff, Janet E. WhoAmW 93
Bischoff, Joyce Arlene 1938- WhoAmW 93, WhoWor 93
Bischoff, Kenneth Bruce 1936- WhoAm 92
Bischoff, Lutz 1938- WhoScE 91-3
Bischoff, Marie Baker 92
Bischoff, Marilyn Brett 1930- WhoE 93
Bischoff, Robert Henry 1922- WhoAm 92
Bischoff, Susan Ann 1951- WhoAm 92
Bischoff, Wendy Winona 1960- WhoEmL 93
Bischoff, Winfried Franz Wilhelm 1941- WhoAm 92
Bischofsberger, Wolfgang O.L. 1925- WhoScE 91-3
Biscoe, John 1794-1849 Expl 93
Biscoe, Timothy John WhoScE 91-1
Bisdale, Ralph d1991 BioIn 17
Bisdale, Thomas Arthur Law&B 92
Bisel, Harry Ferree 1918- WhoAm 92
Bisenius, Charles J. 1931- St&PR 93
Bisesi, Jan BioIn 17
Bisgaard, Edward Lawrence, Jr. 1946- WhoWor 93
Bisgaard, Sverre WhoScE 91-4
Bisgard, Gerald Edwin 1937- WhoAm 92
Bish, Donna Louise 1949- WhoE 93
Bish, John Arthur 1939- WhoUN 92
Bish, Milan David 1929- WhoAm 92
Bish, Robert Leonard 1941- WhoWor 93
Bish, Tedi Lori 1956- WhoAm 92
Bishaf, Morris 1926- St&PR 93
Bishara, Amin Tawadros 1944- WhoWor 93
Bishara, Angele 1948- WhoEmL 93
Bishara, Louis Yousif 1939- WhoWor 93
Bishara, Samir Edward 1935- WhoAm 92
Bisharat, Leila Thayer 1943- WhoUN 92
Bishea, Ann Elizabeth 1961- WhoAmW 93
Bisher, James Furman 1918- WhoAm 92, WhoSSW 93, WhoWrEP 92
Bishof, John S., Jr. Law&B 92
Bishoff, Candace Law&B 92
Bishop, Albert Bentley 1929- WhoAm 92
Bishop, Albert Jeffry 1931- St&PR 93
Bishop, Amelia Morton 1920- WhoSSW 93
Bishop, Andre NewYTBS 92 [port]
Bishop, Andre 1948- WhoAm 92, WhoE 93
Bishop, Ann 1899-1990 BioIn 17
Bishop, Anna 1810-1884 Baker 92, OxDcOp
Bishop, Anne 1912- WhoWrEP 92
Bishop, Anne Hughes 1935- WhoSSW 93
Bishop, Barbara N. WhoAmW 93
Bishop, Barney Tipton, III 1951- WhoEmL 93, WhoSSW 93
Bishop, Bert BioIn 17
Bishop, Betty Josephine 1947- WhoAmW 93, WhoEmL 93, WhoWor 93
Bishop, Bronwyn Kathleen 1942- WhoAsAP 91
Bishop, Bruce Howard 1928- St&PR 93
Bishop, Bruce Taylor 1951- WhoSSW 93
Bishop, Budd Harris 1936- WhoAm 92, WhoSSW 93
Bishop, C. Diane 1943- WhoAm 92, WhoAmW 93
Bishop, Calvin Thomas 1929- WhoAm 92
Bishop, Carla J. Law&B 92
Bishop, Carly ScF&FL 92
Bishop, Catherine B. 1949- WhoAmW 93
Bishop, Charles E. 1930- WhoIns 93
Bishop, Charles Edwin 1921- WhoAm 92
Bishop, Charles Johnson 1920- WhoAm 92
Bishop, Charles Joseph 1941- St&PR 93, WhoAm 92
Bishop, Charles Landon 1938- WhoAm 92
Bishop, Charles W. 1951- St&PR 93
Bishop, Claude Titus 1925- WhoAm 92
Bishop, Connie Bossons 1953- WhoEmL 93
Bishop, Curtis 1912-1967 DcAmChF 1960
Bishop, Daniel S. Law&B 92
Bishop, David 1928-1989 BioIn 17
Bishop, David Fulton 1937- WhoAm 92
Bishop, David Nolan 1940- WhoSSW 93
Bishop, Deborah Lee 1950- WhoEmL 93
Bishop, Don C. Law&B 92
Bishop, Donald WhoScE 91-1
Bishop, Donald S. 1932- St&PR 93
Bishop, Donna Johnson 1952- WhoAmW 93
Bishop, E. Eugene BioIn 17
Bishop, E. William 1939- St&PR 93
Bishop, Elizabeth 1911-1979 BioIn 17, MagSAmL [port]
Bishop, Elizabeth Shreve 1951- WhoEmL 93
Bishop, Ernest Eugene 1930- St&PR 93
Bishop, Ernest L. Law&B 92
Bishop, Ethel Mae 1908- WhoAmW 93, WhoE 93
Bishop, Eugene E. 1930- WhoSSW 93
Bishop, Gavin 1946- BioIn 17
Bishop, Gene H. 1930- St&PR 93
Bishop, Gene Herbert 1930- WhoAm 92, WhoSSW 93
Bishop, George 1924- ScF&FL 92
Bishop, George Franklin 1942- WhoAm 92
Bishop, George Reginald, Jr. 1922- WhoE 93
Bishop, George Robert 1927- WhoScE 91-3
Bishop, Gerald 1949- ScF&FL 92
Bishop, Gloria Stenson 1937- WhoAm 92
Bishop, Gordon Bruce 1938- WhoAm 92
Bishop, Grant William 1961- WhoWor 93
Bishop, Harry Craden 1921- WhoAm 92
Bishop, Henry 1786-1855 OxDcOp
Bishop, Henry Rowley 1786-1855 Baker 92
Bishop, Henry S. 1942- St&PR 93
Bishop, Herbert William WhoScE 91-1
Bishop, Howard Stuart 1938- WhoAm 92, WhoE 93
Bishop, Iola Getchell AmWomPl
Bishop, Ivan D. 1940- WhoIns 93
Bishop, J. Richard 1952- St&PR 93
Bishop, James St&PR 93
Bishop, James A. 1922- WhoAm 92
Bishop, James C., Jr. Law&B 92
Bishop, James C., Jr. 1936- St&PR 93
Bishop, James Francis 1937- WhoE 93
Bishop, James Joseph 1936- WhoAm 92
Bishop, Jemma Won-Ja 1944- WhoE 93
Bishop, Jill W. 1946- St&PR 93
Bishop, Jim B. 1944- St&PR 93
Bishop, Joey 1918- WhoAm 92
Bishop, John F. 1924- St&PR 93
Bishop, John J. 1950- St&PR 93
Bishop, John M. 1945- St&PR 93
Bishop, John Michael 1936- WhoAm 92, WhoWor 93
Bishop, Joy Voncile Mahana 1934- WhoSSW 93
Bishop, Joyce Ann 1935- WhoAmW 93
Bishop, Katherine Elizabeth 1952- WhoAmW 93, WhoEmL 93
Bishop, Kathryn Elizabeth 1945- WhoAm 92, WhoAmW 93
Bishop, Larry Alan 1936- St&PR 93
Bishop, Leah Margaret 1954- WhoAmW 93
Bishop, Lee Law&B 92
Bishop, Leo Kenneth 1911- WhoAm 92
Bishop, Leonard 1922- ScF&FL 92
Bishop, Lester Law&B 92
Bishop, Lon A. 1942- St&PR 93
Bishop, Louise Williams AfrAmBi [port]
Bishop, Louise Williams 1933- WhoAmW 93
Bishop, Luther Doyle 1921- WhoAm 92
Bishop, Margaret 1920 WhoAmW 93
Bishop, Marvin 1945- WhoWor 93
Bishop, Mary Chambers 1955- WhoEmL 93
Bishop, Mary Lou 1929- WhoAmW 93
Bishop, Mary Robinson 1922- WhoAmW 93
Bishop, Maurice 1944-1983 ColdWar 2 [port], DcCPCAm
Bishop, Maurice c. 1945-1983 DcTwHis
Bishop, Michael BioIn 17
Bishop, Michael 1945- ScF&FL 92
Bishop, Michael Joseph 1951- WhoEmL 93
Bishop, Morchard 1903- ScF&FL 92
Bishop, Nancy Ventress Rider 1920- WhoAmW 93
Bishop, Oliver Richard 1928- WhoWor 93
Bishop, Patricia Hoover 1935- WhoAmW 93
Bishop, Paul Edward 1940- WhoAm 92
Bishop, Peter 1932- St&PR 93
Bishop, Peter G. 1944- WhoScE 91-1
Bishop, Pike WhoWrEP 92
Bishop, R.E.D. 1925-1989 BioIn 17
Bishop, Rand 1933- WhoE 93
Bishop, Raymond Francis WhoScE 91-1
Bishop, Raymond Francis 1945- WhoWor 93
Bishop, Raymond Holmes, Jr. 1925- WhoAm 92
Bishop, Richard Evelyn Donohue 1925-1989 BioIn 17
Bishop, Richard James WhoScE 91-1
Bishop, Robert C. 1943- St&PR 93
Bishop, Robert Calvin 1943- WhoAm 92
Bishop, Robert Charles BioIn 17
Bishop, Robert Charles 1929- WhoWor 93
Bishop, Robert D. St&PR 93
Bishop, Robert Lyle 1916- WhoAm 92
Bishop, Robert Milton 1921- WhoAm 92
Bishop, Robert Vance 1949- WhoSSW 93
Bishop, Robert Welch 1955- WhoEmL 93
Bishop, Robert Whitsitt 1949- WhoEmL 93, WhoWor 93
Bishop, Robert Willis 1943- St&PR 93
Bishop, Roy Lovitt 1939- WhoAm 92
Bishop, Ruth d1990 BioIn 17
Bishop, Ruth Ann 1942- WhoAmW 93
Bishop, Sally WhoAmW 93
Bishop, Sid Glenwood 1923- WhoSSW 93
Bishop, Sidney W. 1926- St&PR 93
Bishop, Sidney Willard 1926- WhoAm 92, WhoIns 93
Bishop, Stephen 1952- WhoAm 92
Bishop, Stephen Richard 1953- WhoWrEP 92
Bishop, Sue 1953- WhoAmW 93, WhoEmL 93
Bishop, Sue Marquis 1939- WhoAm 92, WhoSSW 93
Bishop, Susan Katharine 1946- WhoAmW 93
Bishop, Thomas Harrell 1936- WhoAm 92
Bishop, Thomas Ray 1925- WhoSSW 93
Bishop, Thomas Walter 1929- WhoAm 92, WhoE 93
Bishop, Timothy Neal 1947- WhoEmL 93, WhoSSW 93
Bishop, Vernon Richard 1937- St&PR 93
Bishop, Virginia Wakeman 1927- WhoAmW 93
Bishop, Warner Bader 1918- WhoAm 92
Bishop, Wayne C. Law&B 92
Bishop, Wayne Staton 1937- WhoAm 92
Bishop, Wendy 1953- ConAu 137
Bishop, Wendy S. 1953- WhoWrEP 92
Bishop, William Hardy 1935- St&PR 93
Bishop, William P. 1956- St&PR 93
Bishop, William Paul 1956- WhoE 93, WhoEmL 93
Bishop, William Peter 1940- WhoAm 92
Bishop, William Squire 1947- WhoAm 92
Bishop, William T. 1940- WhoAm 92
Bishop, William Wade 1939- WhoAm 92
Bishop, Zealia B. 1897-1968 ScF&FL 92
Bishop-Kovacevich, Stephen 1940- Baker 92
Bishopric, Karl 1925- WhoAm 92
Bishopric, Marjorie Lee Collins d1991 BioIn 17
Bisht, Desh Bandhu 1927- WhoUN 92
Bisiewicz, Alan Walter 1951- WhoEmL 93
Bisineeru, Jayadev Revanna 1952- WhoE 93
Bisk, Anatole 1919- WhoWor 93
Biskin, Bruce Howard 1950- WhoE 93
Biskin, Miriam Marcia Newell 1920- WhoWrEP 92
Biskup, Steven F. Law&B 92
Bisling, Peter Godehard Franz 1953- WhoWor 93
Bismarck, Astrid M. Law&B 92
Bismarck, Herbert, Furst von 1849-1904 BioIn 17
Bismarck, Otto, Furst von 1815-1898 BioIn 17
Bismillah Khan 1916- Baker 92
Bismuth, Henri 1934- WhoScE 91-2
Bisnar, Miguel Chiong 1953- WhoWor 93
Bisno, Alan Lester 1936- WhoSSW 93
Bisno, Alice Cohen Law&B 92
Bisno, Alison Peck 1955- St&PR 93, WhoAm 92, WhoEmL 93
Bisoffi, Stefano 1954- WhoScE 91-3
Bispham, David (Scull) 1857-1921 Baker 92
Bisping, Bernward 1954- WhoWor 93
Bisping, Bruce Henry 1953- WhoAm 92
Biss, Gerald 1876- ScF&FL 92
Bissada, Nabil Kaddis 1938- WhoWor 93
Bissell, Betty Dickson 1932- WhoAm 92, WhoAmW 93
Bissell, Brent John 1950- WhoWor 93
Bissell, George Arthur 1927- WhoAm 92
Bissell, George S. 1929- WhoAm 92
Bissell, James Dougal, III 1951- WhoEmL 93
Bissell, Jean Galloway 1936-1990 BioIn 17
Bissell, John Howard 1935- WhoAm 92
Bissell, John W. 1940- WhoE 93
Bissell, John Wm. 1929- St&PR 93
Bissell, Keith 1912- Baker 92

Bissell, Leclair 1928- *WhoWrEP 92*
Bissell, Phil 1926- *WhoAm 92*
Bissell, Philip Raymond *WhoScE 91-1*
Bissell, Richard Etter 1946- *WhoAm 92*
Bissell, Richard Mervin, Jr. 1909- *WhoAm 92*
Bissell, Sumner F. 1928- *St&PR 93*
Bissell, Thomas J. *Law&B 92*
Bissen, Charmaine Ramona 1956- *WhoAmW 93*
Bissen, Gregory John 1953- *WhoEmL 93*
Bisset, Charles W. *Law&B 92*
Bisset, Davies W., Jr. 1930- *St&PR 93, WhoIns 93*
Bisset, Jacqueline *BioIn 17*
Bisset, Jacqueline 1946- *WhoAm 92*
Bisset, Karen I. *Law&B 92*
Bissett, Alexander Forbes 1933- *St&PR 93*
Bissett, Barbara Anne 1950- *WhoAmW 93, WhoEmL 93, WhoWor 93*
Bissett, Bill 1939- *BioIn 17, WhoCanL 92*
Bissette, Samuel Delk 1921- *WhoSSW 93*
Bissette, Winston Louis, Jr. 1943- *WhoAm 92*
Bissinger, Frederick Lewis 1911- *WhoAm 92*
Bissinger, H.G. *BioIn 17*
Bissinger, Harry Gerard 1954- *WhoAm 92*
Bissmeyer, Albert J. 1945- *St&PR 93*
Bisson, Andre 1929- *BioIn 17*
Bisson, Claude 1931- *WhoAm 92*
Bisson, Edmond Emile 1916- *WhoAm 92, WhoWor 93*
Bisson, Linda Gale Stevens 1946- *WhoAmW 93, WhoE 93, WhoWor 93*
Bisson, Lise 1942- *St&PR 93*
Bisson, Terry 1942- *ScF&FL 92*
Bissonette, D.P. 1939- *St&PR 93*
Bissonette, William Theadore 1942- *WhoSSW 93*
Bissonnette, Marsha O. *Law&B 92*
Bissoondath, Neil 1955- *WhoCanL 92*
Bissoondath, Neil (Devindra) 1955- *ConAu 136*
Bistany, Diane V. 1939- *WhoIns 93*
Bisti, Silvia 1946- *WhoScE 91-3*
Bisticci, Vespasiano da 1421-1498 *BioIn 17*
Bistline, F. Walter, Jr. 1950- *WhoEmL 93*
Bistline, Stephen 1921- *WhoAm 92*
Bistline, Thomas M. *Law&B 92*
Biston, R. *WhoScE 91-2*
Bistram, Gregory M. *Law&B 92*
Biswas, Abdur Rahman 1926- *WhoWor 93*
Biszick, Doris A. M. 1963- *WhoAm 92, WhoAmW 93, WhoEmL 93*
Bisztricsany, Ede 1925- *WhoScE 91-4*
Bita, Lili 1935- *WhoWrEP 92*
Bitan, Giora Y. 1954- *WhoAm 92*
Bitar, Abdul-Rahman 1938- *WhoUN 92*
Bitar, Mohammad Adnan M. 1938- *WhoWor 93*
Bitar, Salah al-Din 1912-1980 *BioIn 17*
Bitar, Sergio *BioIn 17*
Bitar, Thomas J. 1932- *St&PR 93*
Bitar Liebers, Karen Yasmine *Law&B 92*
Bitas, Basil C. *Law&B 92*
Bitek, Okot p' 1931-1982 *BioIn 17*
Biter, Linda Ann 1939- *WhoAmW 93*
Bitetti (Ravina), Ernesto (Guillermo) 1943- *Baker 92*
Bithell, Thomas C. 1946- *St&PR 93*
Bither, Eve M. *WhoAm 92*
Bither, Richard A. 1946- *St&PR 93*
Bitker, Marjorie M. d1990 *BioIn 17*
Bitko, Sheldon 1927- *St&PR 93*
Bitler, Harold Paul 1942- *St&PR 93*
Bitner, John Howard 1940- *WhoAm 92*
Bitner, John William 1948- *St&PR 93, WhoE 93, WhoEmL 93, WhoWor 93*
Bitner, William Lawrence, III 1931- *St&PR 93, WhoAm 92*
Bitney, Mayme Riddle *AmWomPl*
Bitoff, John William 1936- *WhoAm 92*
Biton, Michel *WhoScE 91-2*
Bitondo, Domenic 1925- *WhoAm 92*
Bitov, Andrei *BioIn 17*
Bitowft, Robert John 1932- *WhoSSW 93*
Bitsadze, Andrej 1916- *WhoWor 93*
Bitsch, Marcel 1921- *Baker 92*
Bitsch, Roland 1937- *WhoWor 93*
Bitsch-Larsen, Lars Kristian 1945- *WhoWor 93*
Bittante, Giovanni 1953- *WhoScE 91-3*
Bittel, Lester Robert 1918- *WhoSSW 93, WhoWrEP 92*
Bittel, Muriel Helene *WhoAmW 93*
Bittel, Patricia Thomas 1951- *WhoEmL 93*
Bittel, Raymond Herman 1942- *WhoSSW 93*
Bittell, James Edward *Law&B 92*
Bitten, Mary Josephine 1942- *WhoAmW 93*
Bittenbender, Brad James 1948- *WhoEmL 93, WhoWor 93*
Bittenbender, Charles A. *Law&B 92*
Bittenbender, Charles A. 1949- *St&PR 93*
Bittence, Mary M. 1952- *WhoAmW 93*
Bittencourt, Clovis Ramos 1947- *WhoWor 93*
Bitter, Benita R. 1925- *St&PR 93*
Bitter, Carl Hermann 1813-1885 *Baker 92*
Bitter, Edwin Ward 1930- *St&PR 93*
Bitter, Frank Gordon 1943- *WhoAm 92*
Bitter, Gehart Leonard 1921- *WhoAm 92*
Bitter, Harold Hugo 1922- *St&PR 93*
Bitter, Istvan 1941- *WhoScE 91-4*
Bitter, John 1909- *WhoAm 92*
Bitter, Mark Joseph 1958- *St&PR 93*
Bitterman, Morton Edward 1921- *WhoAm 92*
Bitting, Larry L. 1948- *WhoSSW 93*
Bittinger, Allen Walter 1953- *St&PR 93*
Bittinger, Donald S. d1987 *BioIn 17*
Bittinger, Douglas Edward 1966- *WhoE 93*
Bittker, Donald L. *Law&B 92*
Bittle, Bonnie Jean 1950- *WhoSSW 93*
Bittleman, Dolores Dembus *WhoE 93*
Bittman, James Michael 1936- *WhoWor 93*
Bittmann, Susan Wilkins 1946- *WhoAmW 93*
Bittner, Amy Margaret *Law&B 92*
Bittner, Barbara Jane 1947- *WhoAmW 93*
Bittner, Carl S. *WhoAm 92*
Bittner, George Russell 1928- *St&PR 93*
Bittner, Harlan Fletcher 1951- *WhoEmL 93*
Bittner, James W. 1921-1977 *ScF&FL 92*
Bittner, Julius 1874-1939 *Baker 92*
Bittner, Katherine Louise 1960- *WhoEmL 93*
Bittner, Richard Russell 1950- *WhoE 93*
Bittner, Ronald Joseph 1954- *WhoE 93*
Bittner, Ronald L. 1941- *St&PR 93*
Bittner, William 1921-1977 *ScF&FL 92*
Bittone, Richard Edward 1929- *St&PR 93*
Bittourna, Bert K. *Law&B 92*
Bittremieux, Leo 1880-1946 *IntDcAn*
Bittrich, Hans-Joachim 1923- *WhoWor 93*
Bittrich, Louis Edward 1937- *WhoSSW 93*
Bitts, Todd Michael 1946- *WhoAm 92*
Bitz, Gerald M. 1935- *St&PR 93*
Bitzer, Donald Lester 1934- *WhoAm 92*
Bitzer, Jeffrey T. 1952- *WhoE 93*
Bitzer, Joan Louise 1952- *WhoAmW 93*
Bitzer, John Frederick, Jr. 1936- *WhoAm 92*
Biurrun Salanueva, Francisco Javier 1946- *WhoWor 93*
Bivens, Constance Ann 1938- *WhoAmW 93, WhoWor 93*
Bivens, Donald Wayne 1952- *WhoEmL 93*
Bivens, Loren *MiSFD 9*
Bivens, Lydia Ruth 1939- *WhoSSW 93*
Bivins, C. Benny 1956- *WhoEmL 93*
Bivins, Daniel Eugene 1932- *WhoSSW 93*
Bivins, John 1940- *BioIn 17*
Bivins, William Pannill, Jr. *Law&B 92*
Bivona, Virginia Siena 1931- *WhoAmW 93*
Bixby, Allan Barton 1936- *St&PR 93, WhoAm 92*
Bixby, Bill 1934- *MiSFD 9, WhoAm 92*
Bixby, E. Rew 1920?- *ScF&FL 92*
Bixby, Edward K. 1935- *St&PR 93*
Bixby, Ethel Amy 1916- *WhoAmW 93*
Bixby, Harold Glenn 1903- *WhoAm 92*
Bixby, J.E. 1922- *St&PR 93*
Bixby, Joseph Nathan 1950- *WhoEmL 93*
Bixby, Joseph R. 1925- *WhoAm 92*
Bixby, Joseph Reynolds 1925- *WhoIns 93*
Bixby, R. Burdell 1914-1991 *BioIn 17*
Bixby, R. Phillip 1953- *St&PR 93*
Bixby, Ray Z. *ConAu 40NR*
Bixby, Richard W. 1936- *St&PR 93*
Bixby, Robert Jay 1952- *WhoWrEP 92*
Bixby, Robert William *WhoScE 91-1*
Bixby, Tom 1947- *WhoEmL 93*
Bixby, Walter E. 1932- *WhoAm 92, WhoIns 93*
Bixby, Walter Edwin 1932- *St&PR 93*
Bixby-Smith, Sarah 1871-1935 *BioIn 17*
Bixenstine, Kim Fenton 1958- *WhoAmW 93, WhoEmL 93*
Bixler, Andrew Loy Moore 1909- *WhoSSW 93*
Bixler, David 1929- *WhoAm 92*
Bixler, Diana Lee *Law&B 92*
Bixler, Herbert Edwards 1911- *WhoE 93*
Bixler, Howard *WhoWrEP 92*
Bixler, John Mourer 1927- *WhoE 93*
Bixler, Joseph H. 1945- *WhoIns 93*
Bixler, Lois Jane 1958- *WhoEmL 93*
Bixler, Margaret Triplett 1917- *WhoAmW 93*
Bixler, Michael T. 1947- *St&PR 93*
Bixler, Paul 1899- *WhoWrEP 92*
Bixler, Paul Howard *BioIn 17*
Bixler, Roland M. 1913- *St&PR 93*
Bixler, William Elwell 1947- *St&PR 93*
Biya, Paul 1933- *WhoAfr, WhoWor 93*
Biyarov, Bazarcan Nuroldinovich 1957- *WhoWor 93*
Biyidi, Alexandre 1932- *BioIn 17*
Bizar, Irving 1932- *WhoAm 92, WhoE 93, WhoWor 93*
Bizar, Scott *ScF&FL 92*
Bizart, Guy *WhoScE 91-2*
Bizet, Georges 1838-1875 *Baker 92, IntDcOp [port], OxDcOp*
Bizic, Peter, Jr. 1937- *WhoSSW 93*
Bizily, Dale Francis 1945- *St&PR 93*
Bizimungu, Casimir 1951- *WhoAfr, WhoWor 93*
Bizios, John Dimitrios 1938- *WhoWor 93*
Bizub, Johanna Catherine 1957- *WhoAmW 93, WhoEmL 93*
Bizzano, Joseph D., Jr. *Law&B 92*
Bizzarro, Angleo D. *St&PR 93*
Bizzell, Bobby Gene 1940- *WhoAm 92, WhoSSW 93*
Bizzell, Patricia (Lynn) 1948- *ConAu 139*
Bizzi, Emilio 1933- *WhoAm 92*
Bizzoco, Daniel Joseph 1953- *WhoE 93, WhoEmL 93*
Bjarnason, D.C. *Law&B 92*
Bjarnason, Gudmundur 1944- *WhoWor 93*
Bjelinski, Bruno 1909- *Baker 92*
Bjelke, Donald K. *Law&B 92*
Bjelke, Erik 1934- *WhoScE 91-4*
Bjelke-Petersen, Florence Isabel 1920- *WhoAsAP 91*
Bjelke-Petersen, Johannes 1911- *BioIn 17*
Bjelland, Cato 1957- *WhoWor 93*
Bjelland, Ronald Wiggo *Law&B 92*
Bjelle, Anders Otto *WhoScE 91-4*
Bjercke, Alf Richard 1921- *WhoWor 93*
Bjerg, Nils 1933- *St&PR 93*
Bjerke, Harold William 1940- *WhoE 93*
Bjerke, Odd *ScF&FL 92*
Bjerkedal, Tor 1926- *WhoScE 91-4*
Bjerknes, Michael Leif 1956- *WhoAm 92*
Bjerre, Jens 1903-1986 *Baker 92*
Bjerregaard, Ritt *BioIn 17*
Bjersing, Lars 1929- *WhoScE 91-4*
Bjoner, Ingrid 1927- *Baker 92, OxDcOp*
Bjontegard, Arthur Martin, Jr. 1938- *St&PR 93, WhoAm 92, WhoSSW 93*
Bjoraker, Walter Thomas 1920- *WhoAm 92*
Bjorck, AndersPer-Arne 1944- *WhoWor 93*
Bjorck, Eva Birgitta 1937- *WhoWor 93*
Bjorhovde, Reidar 1941- *WhoAm 92*
Bjork, Carl Kenneth, Jr. 1956- *WhoEmL 93*
Bjork, Christina *BioIn 17*
Bjork, Glenn 1939- *WhoScE 91-4*
Bjork, Gordon Carl 1935- *WhoAm 92*
Bjork, Lars 1924- *WhoScE 91-4*
Bjork, Philip Reese 1940- *WhoAm 92*
Bjork, Robert Allen 1939- *WhoAm 92*
Bjork, Robert David, Jr. 1946- *WhoEmL 93, WhoWor 93*
Bjork, Robert William 1926- *St&PR 93*
Bjorke, Oyvind 1933- *WhoScE 91-4*
Bjorkegren, Lars-Erik 1943- *WhoScE 91-4*
Bjorkelo, Anders 1947- *ConAu 138*
Bjorkerud, Soren 1930- *WhoScE 91-4*
Bjorkholm, John Ernst 1939- *WhoAm 92*
Bjorklund, Alf Johan 1939- *WhoScE 91-4*
Bjorklund, Brenda A. *Law&B 92*
Bjorklund, Frederick 1913- *WhoAm 92*
Bjorklund, Gunnar 1935- *WhoScE 91-4*
Bjorklund, Hank *Law&B 92*
Bjorklund, Harold P. 1940- *St&PR 93*
Bjorklund, Janet Vinsen 1947- *WhoEmL 93*
Bjorklund, Katharine Browne 1952- *WhoEmL 93*
Bjorklund, Kjell R. 1943- *WhoScE 91-4*
Bjorklund, Lars Goran 1962- *St&PR 93*
Bjorklund, Lennart Bo 1945- *St&PR 93*
Bjorkman, Arlene Doris 1947- *WhoEmL 93*
Bjorkman, Dale A. *Law&B 92*
Bjorkman, Henry C. *Law&B 92*
Bjorkman, Julie Marie 1968- *WhoAmW 93*
Bjorkman, Olle Erik 1933- *WhoAm 92*
Bjorksten, Bengt 1940- *WhoScE 91-4*
Bjorlin, Ulf 1933- *BioIn 17*
Bjorlin, (Mats) Ulf (Stefan) 1933- *Baker 92*
Bjorling, Jussi 1911-1960 *Baker 92, BioIn 17, IntDcOp, OxDcOp*
Bjorling, Sigurd 1907-1983 *Baker 92*
Bjorlo, Thorbiorn Johan 1940- *WhoScE 91-4*
Bjorlykke, Knut O. 1938- *WhoScE 91-4*
Bjorn, Anna-Lisa 1932- *WhoScE 91-4*
Bjorn, Dinna *WhoWor 93*
Bjorn-Andersen, Niels 1944- *WhoWor 93*
Bjornbak, Mark Philip 1958- *WhoEmL 93*
Bjorndahl, David Lee 1927- *St&PR 93*
Bjorndal, Earl Martin 1951- *St&PR 93*
Bjorneberg, Paul Grant 1953- *WhoAm 92*
Bjornholm, Sven 1927- *WhoScE 91-2*
Bjornland, Dag *WhoScE 91-4*
Bjorno, Leif *WhoWor 93*
Bjorno, Leif 1937- *WhoScE 91-2*
Bjornsen, George S. *Law&B 92*
Bjornson, Carroll Norman 1929- *WhoSSW 93, WhoWor 93*
Bjornson, Edward Lee 1931- *St&PR 93*
Bjornson, Maria *WhoAmW 93*
Bjornson, Maria 1949- *OxDcOp*
Bjornsson, Arni 1905- *Baker 92*
Bjornsson, Holmgeir 1937- *WhoScE 91-4*
Bjornsson, Sigurdur 1942- *WhoWor 93*
Bjornstad, Brad 1952- *WhoSSW 93*
Bjornstad, James 1940- *ScF&FL 92*
Bjornstad, Karen Jean 1950- *WhoAmW 93*
Bjornstrand, Gunnar 1909-1986 *IntDcF 2-3*
Bjorntorp, Per A. 1931- *WhoScE 91-4*
Bjornvig, Thorkild Strange 1918- *WhoWor 93*
Bjoro, Edwin Francis, Jr. 1928- *WhoE 93*
Bjoro, Knut Jahr 1925- *WhoScE 91-4*
Bjorseth, Alf *WhoScE 91-4*
Bjurman, George 1906-1990 *BioIn 17*
Bjurman, George Andrew 1948- *St&PR 93*
Bjurulf, Per 1932- *WhoScE 91-4*
Blaauboer, James William 1938- *St&PR 93*
Blaauw, Gerrit A. 1924- *WhoScE 91-3*
Blaauw, Russell Wayne 1944- *WhoWor 93*
Blab, Josef S. 1949- *WhoScE 91-3*
Blach, Harold B., Jr. 1931- *St&PR 93*
Blach, R. *WhoScE 91-1*
Blache, Klaus Michael 1951- *WhoEmL 93*
Blacher, Boris 1903-1975 *Baker 92, OxDcOp*
Blacher, Richard Stanley 1924- *WhoAm 92*
Blachere, Henri T. 1926- *WhoScE 91-2*
Blachford, Peter Carl Howard 1949- *WhoAm 92*
Blachly, Jack Lee 1942- *WhoAm 92, WhoSSW 93, WhoWor 93*
Blachman, Nelson Merle 1923- *WhoAm 92*
Blachman, Rochel Sara *Law&B 92*
Blachnik, Roger O.G. 1936- *WhoScE 91-3*
Blachnik, Roger Otto Gotz 1936- *WhoWor 93*
Blachut, Beno 1913-1985 *Baker 92, IntDcOp, OxDcOp*
Blachut, Teodor Josef 1915- *WhoAm 92*
Blacik, Stephen Mark 1951- *WhoWrEP 92*
Black, Alexander 1914- *WhoAm 92*
Black, Alexander Chisholm 1954- *WhoEmL 93*
Black, Alice Verner 1942- *WhoAmW 93*
Black, Allen Decatur 1942- *WhoAm 92*
Black, Andrew 1859-1920 *Baker 92*
Black, Andrew Patrick 1951- *WhoWor 93*
Black, Angus 1943- *ScF&FL 92*
Black, Ann Nix 1945- *WhoSSW 93*
Black, Arthur Geiger 1948- *WhoEmL 93*
Black, Arthur Leo 1922- *WhoAm 92*
Black, Arthur (Raymond) 1943- *ConAu 138*
Black, Asa Calvin, Jr. 1943- *WhoSSW 93*
Black, Barbara Aronstein 1933- *WhoAm 92*
Black, Barbara Crowder 1922- *WhoAmW 93*
Black, Barbara E. *Law&B 92*
Black, Barry Martin 1946- *St&PR 93, WhoAm 92*
Black, Barton Tyler 1953- *WhoEmL 93*
Black, Benjamin F. 1908- *St&PR 93*
Black, Betty Lynne 1946- *WhoAmW 93*
Black, Beverly Holstun 1942- *WhoAmW 93*
Black, Boyd C. 1926- *St&PR 93*
Black, Boyd Carson 1926- *WhoWor 93*
Black, Bradford 1936- *St&PR 93*
Black, Brady Forrest 1908- *WhoWrEP 92*
Black, Campbell 1944- *ScF&FL 92*
Black, Carl Clifton, II 1955- *WhoSSW 93*
Black, Cathleen P. 1944- *St&PR 93*
Black, Cathleen Prunty 1944- *WhoAm 92, WhoAmW 93, WhoE 93, WhoSSW 93, WhoWrEP 92*
Black, Charles *BioIn 17*
Black, Charles Alvin 1920- *WhoAm 92*
Black, Charles Robert 1935- *WhoAm 92*
Black, Charlie J. 1934- *AfrAmBi*
Black, Christopher *ScF&FL 92*
Black, Claire Alexander 1953- *WhoEmL 93*
Black, Clanton Candler, Jr. 1931- *WhoAm 92*
Black, Clementina 1853-1922 *BioIn 17*
Black, Clint *BioIn 17, WhoAm 92*
Black, Clyde Edward 1938- *WhoSSW 93*
Black, Clyde Joseph, III 1945- *St&PR 93*
Black, Cobey 1922- *WhoAmW 93, WhoWor 93*
Black, Conrad 1944- *CurBio 92 [port]*
Black, Conrad M. *BioIn 17, NewYTBS 92 [port]*

Black, Conrad Moffat 1944- St&PR 93, WhoAm 92
Black, Craig Call 1932- WhoAm 92
Black, Creed Carter 1925- WhoAm 92, WhoWrEP 92
Black, Curtis Doersam 1951- WhoEmL 93
Black, Cyril 1902-1991 AnObit 1991
Black, Cyril Edwin 1915-1989 BioIn 17
Black, Daniel Hugh 1947- WhoEmL 93, WhoSSW 93, WhoWor 93
Black, Daniel James 1931- St&PR 93
Black, David 1945- ConAu 136, WhoAm 92
Black, David A. 1949- St&PR 93
Black, David P. 1949- WhoAm 92
Black, David R. 1952- St&PR 93
Black, David Randall 1947- WhoEmL 93
Black, David Scott 1961- WhoEmL 93
Black, Dawn 1943- WhoAmW 93
Black, Deven Keith 1953- WhoE 93
Black, Don G. AfrAmBi
Black, Donald Bruce 1932- WhoAm 92
Black, Donald Chain 1935- WhoWrEP 92
Black, Donald E. 1942- St&PR 93
Black, Donna Hall 1961- WhoSSW 93
Black, Donna R. 1947- WhoAmW 93
Black, Dorothy 1899-1985 ScF&FL 92
Black, Douglas D. 1961- WhoEmL 93
Black, Earl 1942- WhoSSW 93
Black, Eileen Mary 1944- WhoAmW 93, WhoWor 93
Black, Eli DcCPCAm
Black, Eugene Charlton 1927- WhoAm 92
Black, Eugene F. 1903-1990 BioIn 17
Black, Eugene R. 1898-1992 NewYTBS 92 [port]
Black, Eugene R(obert) 1898-1992 CurBio 92N
Black, Eugene Robert 1873-1934 BioIn 17
Black, Eugene Robert 1898-1992 BioIn 17
Black, Fischer BioIn 17
Black, Frances Patterson 1949- WhoAmW 93
Black, Frank 1894-1968 Baker 92
Black, Gary Michael Law&B 92
Black, Gavin ConAu 39NR
Black, Gerald Joseph 1946- WhoEmL 93
Black, Gerald Robin Law&B 92
Black, Gerry WhoAm 92
Black, Gladys AmWomPl
Black, Glenn A. 1900-1964 IntDcAn
Black, Harry George 1933- WhoWrEP 92
Black, Hillel Moses 1929- WhoAm 92, WhoWrEP 92
Black, Howard 1947- WhoEmL 93
Black, Hugo LaFayette 1886-1971 BioIn 17, OxCSupC [port]
Black, Hugo Lafayette, Jr. 1922- WhoAm 92
Black, Ian Stuart 1915- ScF&FL 92
Black, James A., Jr. 1942- St&PR 93
Black, James Allen, Jr. 1951- WhoEmL 93, WhoSSW 93
Black, James Harold, Jr. 1944- WhoSSW 93
Black, James Isaac, III 1951- WhoAm 92, WhoEmL 93
Black, James M., II Law&B 92
Black, James R. 1943- St&PR 93
Black, James Sinclair 1940- WhoAm 92
Black, James Whyte 1924- BioIn 17, WhoWor 93
Black, Janet Knecht 1942- WhoAmW 93
Black, Janice T. 1946- St&PR 93
Black, Jean Blashfield 1939- WhoAmW 93
Black, Jeannie ScF&FL 92
Black, Jeremiah Sullivan 1810-1883 OxCSupC
Black, Jeremy Joseph 1952- WhoEmL 93
Black, Jeremy (Martin) 1955- ConAu 136
Black, Jerry Ray 1948- WhoSSW 93
Black, Jesse M., Jr. 1942- St&PR 93
Black, Joanne BioIn 17
Black, Joe 1945- St&PR 93
Black, Joe Bernard 1933- WhoSSW 93
Black, John Arthur, Jr. 1949- WhoEmL 93
Black, John C. St&PR 93
Black, John D. 1919- St&PR 93
Black, John Franklin, Jr. 1953- WhoSSW 93
Black, John M. Law&B 92
Black, John Rees 1952- WhoAsAP 91
Black, John Sheldon 1948- WhoAm 92
Black, John W. 1937- St&PR 93
Black, Jonathan 1943- WhoAm 92
Black, Joseph 1924- WhoAm 92
Black, Joseph Richard, Jr. Law&B 92
Black, Joseph Thomas, Jr. 1967- WhoE 93
Black, Joyce Macwatty d1992 NewYTBS 92 [port]
Black, Karen 1942- IntDcF 2-3, WhoAm 92
Black, Kathleen Anderson 1951- WhoAmW 93
Black, Kathryn Ann 1951- WhoAmW 93
Black, Kathryn N. 1933- WhoAmW 93
Black, Kathryn Stechert BioIn 17
Black, Kay Freeman 1936- WhoAmW 93
Black, Kenneth, Jr. 1925- WhoAm 92, WhoIns 93
Black, Kent M. 1939- St&PR 93
Black, Kent March 1939- WhoAm 92
Black, Kirby Samuel 1954- WhoEmL 93
Black, Kristine Mary 1953- WhoEmL 93
Black, L.K. 1930- St&PR 93
Black, Larry David 1949- WhoAm 92
Black, Leon BioIn 17
Black, Leon David, Jr. 1926- WhoAm 92
Black, Leonard J. 1919- WhoAm 92
Black, Leota Hulse AmWomPl
Black, Lindsay MacLeod 1907- WhoE 93
Black, Lois Mae 1931- WhoAm 92
Black, Lydia T. 1925- WhoAm 92
Black, M.H. WhoScE 91-1
Black, Malacai ScF&FL 92
Black, Margaret Mary 1966- WhoAmW 93
Black, Martin 1956- BioIn 17
Black, Martin Morris WhoScE 91-1
Black, Mary Ann 1953- WhoSSW 93
Black, Mary C. 1922-1992 BioIn 17
Black, Mary Canny 1960- WhoAmW 93
Black, Mary Childs d1992 NewYTBS 92 [port]
Black, Mary (Childs) 1922-1992 ConAu 137
Black, Maureen 1937- WhoAmW 93
Black, Merry Beth AmWomPl
Black, Michael WhoScE 91-1
Black, Michael R. 1960- WhoEmL 93
Black, Naomi Ruth 1957- WhoEmL 93
Black, Natalie A. Law&B 92
Black, Natalie A. 1949- St&PR 93
Black, Neil Spencer 1960- St&PR 93
Black, Noel 1937- MiSFD 9
Black, Noel Anthony 1937- WhoAm 92
Black, Norman M., III 1947- St&PR 93
Black, Norman William 1931- WhoAm 92, WhoSSW 93
Black, Page Morton WhoAmW 93, WhoE 93, WhoWor 93
Black, Patricia Jean 1954- WhoAmW 93
Black, Patricia Reed 1957- WhoEmL 93
Black, Patti Carr 1934- WhoAm 92
Black, Paul Martin 1953- WhoSSW 93
Black, Paul Stephen 1953- WhoEmL 93, WhoSSW 93
Black, Paul William 1934- WhoSSW 93
Black, Percy 1922- WhoAm 92, WhoE 93
Black, Peter 1938- St&PR 93
Black, Randy 1961- BioIn 17
Black, Randy D. 1952- St&PR 93
Black, Rebecca Jane 1946- WhoEmL 93
Black, Richard B. d1992 NewYTBS 92
Black, Richard Bruce 1933- WhoAm 92
Black, Richard E. Law&B 92
Black, Robert ScF&FL 92
Black, Robert d1992 BioIn 17
Black, Robert Alan 1944- WhoSSW 93
Black, Robert Bliss 1944- St&PR 93
Black, Robert Coleman 1934- WhoAm 92
Black, Robert David Law&B 92
Black, Robert Frederick 1920- WhoAm 92
Black, Robert Irvin 1923- St&PR 93
Black, Robert James 1955- WhoEmL 93
Black, Robert L., Jr. 1917- WhoWor 93
Black, Robert Lincoln 1930- WhoAm 92
Black, Robert P. 1927- St&PR 93
Black, Robert Perry 1927- WhoAm 92
Black, Robert W. Law&B 92
Black, Ronnie Delane 1947- WhoAm 92
Black, Rosalie Jean 1938- WhoAmW 93
Black, Rosemary Law&B 92
Black, Roy E. 1945- BioIn 17
Black, Samuel Harold 1930- WhoAm 92
Black, Sandra Kay 1942- WhoWrEP 92
Black, Sherry Joe 1950- WhoWor 93
Black, Shirley Norman 1916- WhoWor 93
Black, Shirley Renee 1960- WhoEmL 93
Black, Shirley Sharp 1940- St&PR 93
Black, Shirley Temple 1928- BioIn 17, WhoAm 92, WhoAmW 93, WhoWor 93
Black, Stan A. 1937- St&PR 93
Black, Stanley 1913- Baker 92
Black, Stanley Warren, III 1939- WhoAm 92
Black, Stephen F. 1944- WhoAm 92
Black, Steven D. 1952- St&PR 93
Black, Stuart M. 1926- St&PR 93
Black, Susan Faye 1937- WhoSSW 93
Black, Susan Harrell 1943- WhoAmW 93
Black, Suzanne Alexandra 1958- WhoAmW 93, WhoEmL 93, WhoWor 93
Black, Sydney Doree 1915- WhoE 93
Black, Terrance 1944- St&PR 93
Black, Theodore Halsey 1928- St&PR 93, WhoAm 92, WhoE 93
Black, Theodore Michael 1919- WhoWrEP 92
Black, Theodore Michael, Sr. 1919- WhoAm 92
Black, Thomas Donald 1920- WhoAm 92
Black, Topper 1951- St&PR 93
Black, W.G. 1927- St&PR 93
Black, Walter Evan, Jr. 1926- WhoAm 92, WhoE 93
Black, Walter Kerrigan 1915- WhoAm 92
Black, Wendell Walter 1957- WhoSSW 93
Black, William Alan 1953- St&PR 93
Black, William D. ScF&FL 92
Black, William Earl 1951- WhoEmL 93
Black, William Edward 1947- WhoEmL 93
Black, William Gordon 1927- WhoAm 92
Black, William Harman, II 1925- St&PR 93
Black, William James Murray WhoScE 91-1
Black, William R. 1926- St&PR 93
Black, William S. 1919- St&PR 93
Black, Winifred Sweet 1863-1936 JrnUS
Blackadar, Alfred Kimball 1920- WhoAm 92
Blackall, Eric A. 1914-1989 BioIn 17
Blackall, Kathleen Ann 1957- WhoAmW 93
Blackburn, Barbara Ann 1942- WhoWrEP 92
Blackburn, Bonnie 1939- Baker 92
Blackburn, Bonnie S. WhoIns 93
Blackburn, Bonnie S. 1949- St&PR 93
Blackburn, Catherine Elaine 1953- WhoEmL 93, WhoSSW 93
Blackburn, Chancey 1947- WhoSSW 93
Blackburn, Charles Frank Law&B 92
Blackburn, Charles Franklin 1951- St&PR 93
Blackburn, Charles Lee 1928- St&PR 93, WhoAm 92
Blackburn, Christine Louise 1948- WhoAmW 93
Blackburn, D.H. WhoScE 91-1
Blackburn, D. Joann 1941- St&PR 93
Blackburn, David Alan 1944- St&PR 93
Blackburn, David Ralph 1955- WhoSSW 93
Blackburn, Deloris Gail 1954- WhoSSW 93
Blackburn, Donald F. 1927- St&PR 93
Blackburn, Edward J. 1923- St&PR 93
Blackburn, Elizabeth Helen 1948- WhoAm 92, WhoAmW 93
Blackburn, Gary Wayne 1958- St&PR 93
Blackburn, George Lincoln 1936- WhoE 93
Blackburn, Greg V. Law&B 92
Blackburn, Henry Webster, Jr. 1925- WhoAm 92
Blackburn, Jack 1883-1941 BioIn 17
Blackburn, Jack Bailey 1922- WhoAm 92
Blackburn, James Ross, Jr. 1930- WhoAm 92, WhoWor 93
Blackburn, Jeffrey R. 1952- St&PR 93
Blackburn, John 1923- ScF&FL 92
Blackburn, John H. 1942- St&PR 93
Blackburn, John Leslie 1924- WhoSSW 93
Blackburn, John Lewis 1913- WhoAm 92
Blackburn, John Oliver 1929- WhoAm 92
Blackburn, Marsh Hanly 1929- St&PR 93
Blackburn, Martha Grace 1944- WhoAm 92
Blackburn, Mary Johnson AmWomPl
Blackburn, Michael James 1957- WhoEmL 93
Blackburn, Myrle St&PR 93
Blackburn, Neal 1926- St&PR 93
Blackburn, Norman d1990 BioIn 17
Blackburn, Paul P., Jr. d1992 NewYTBS 92 [port]
Blackburn, Paul Pritchard 1937- WhoAm 92
Blackburn, Richard S. 1927- St&PR 93
Blackburn, Richard W. Law&B 92
Blackburn, Richard Wallace 1942- St&PR 93
Blackburn, Robert Barnett 1930- St&PR 93
Blackburn, Robert McGrady 1919- WhoAm 92
Blackburn, Robert P. Law&B 92
Blackburn, Roger Lloyd 1946- WhoEmL 93
Blackburn, Simon 1944- ConAu 40NR
Blackburn, Steven Peter 1952- WhoEmL 93
Blackburn, Susan Stone- ScF&FL 92
Blackburn, Thomas C(arl) 1936- WhoWrEP 92
Blackburn, Thomas Harold 1932- WhoAm 92
Blackburn, Thomas Irven 1949- WhoEmL 93
Blackburn, Tom 1912- BioIn 17
Blackburn, Ulric 1926- WhoE 93
Blackburn, W.R. Law&B 92
Blackburn, William Martin 1939- WhoAm 92
Black Elk 1863-1950 BioIn 17
Blacker, Harriet 1940- WhoAm 92, WhoWrEP 92
Blacker, Ian T. 1954- WhoEmL 93
Blackert, Virginia Rose 1948- WhoAmW 93
Blackett, Stanley E. 1938- St&PR 93
Blackett, Tina Marie 1961- WhoAmW 93
Blackfield, Cecilia Malik 1915- WhoAmW 93
Blackford, David Elliott 1948- WhoAm 92
Blackford, Gary D. Law&B 92
Blackford, James Mathew 1952- St&PR 93
Blackford, Jenny 1957- ScF&FL 92
Blackford, Leo Price 1951- St&PR 93, WhoAm 92
Blackford, Robert Newton 1937- St&PR 93, WhoAm 92, WhoSSW 93
Blackford, Russell 1954- ScF&FL 92
Blackford, Staige D. 1931- WhoWrEP 92
Blackham, Ann Rosemary 1927- WhoAmW 93, WhoE 93
Black Hawk 1767-1838 HarEnMi
Blackhurst, Eric Paul 1961- WhoEmL 93
Blackie, William 1906- BioIn 17
Blackin, Jack M. 1942- St&PR 93
Blackin, Jack Milton 1942- WhoAm 92
Blacking, John BioIn 17
Black-Keefer, Sharon Kay 1949- WhoAmW 93, WhoEmL 93, WhoWor 93
Blackledge, Kenneth Allen 1950- St&PR 93
Blackledge, Sheri Dione 1968- WhoAmW 93
Blackledge, William d1828 BioIn 17
Blackler, Antonie William Charles 1931- WhoAm 92
Blackler, Sharon Renda 1947- WhoAm 92
Blackley, Neil Ramsay 1955- WhoWor 93
Blacklidge, James B. 1943- St&PR 93
Blacklidge, Raymond Mark 1960- WhoEmL 93, WhoWor 93
Blacklidge, Richard Henry 1914- WhoWrEP 92
Blacklin, Malcolm MajAI, ScF&FL 92, SmATA 69
Blacklock, Charles B. 1924- St&PR 93
Blacklock, Gordon BioIn 17
Blacklock, Steven M. 1958- St&PR 93
Blacklow, Neil Richard 1938- WhoE 93
Blacklow, Robert Stanley 1934- WhoAm 92
Blackman, Audrey 1907-1990 BioIn 17
Blackman, Charles 1928- BioIn 17
Blackman, David Ira 1951- WhoEmL 93
Blackman, Derek Ernest WhoScE 91-1
Blackman, Don 1935- DcCPCAm
Blackman, Dorman R. 1935- St&PR 93
Blackman, Dorothy Loyte 1935- WhoWrEP 92
Blackman, George Raymond 1960- WhoEmL 93
Blackman, Ghita Waucheta 1932- WhoAmW 93
Blackman, James Ray 1942- St&PR 93
Blackman, James Timothy 1951- WhoEmL 93
Blackman, Jeanne A. 1943- WhoAm 92, WhoAmW 93
Blackman, Joan 1948- WhoE 93
Blackman, John Calhoun, IV 1944- WhoSSW 93
Blackman, John M. 1942- St&PR 93
Blackman, Kenneth E. 1938- St&PR 93
Blackman, Kenneth Robert 1941- WhoAm 92
Blackman, Michael Lee 1943- St&PR 93
Blackman, Murray Ivan 1945- WhoE 93
Blackman, Patricia Ann 1946- WhoEmL 93
Blackman, Richard Gus, Jr. 1948- WhoSSW 93
Blackman, Robert Irwin 1928- WhoAm 92
Blackman, Samuel William 1913- WhoE 93
Blackman, Sonya d1990 BioIn 17
Blackman, Steven Theodore 1945- St&PR 93
Blackman, Sue Anne Batey 1948- WhoAmW 93
Blackman, Vernon Harold 1929- WhoAm 92
Blackmann, Linda J. 1950- St&PR 93
Blackmar, Beatrice AmWomPl
Blackmar, Charles Blakey 1922- WhoAm 92
Blackmer, Donald Laurence Morton 1929- WhoAm 92
Blackmere, Peter G. 1946- St&PR 93
Blackmon, Antonia A. WhoWrEP 92
Blackmon, James Donald 1941- WhoSSW 93
Blackmon, John Jerry 1928- WhoSSW 93
Blackmon, Joyce McAnulty 1937- St&PR 93
Blackmon, Larry SoulM
Blackmon, Michael James 1946- WhoEmL 93
Blackmon, W. E. B. 1951- WhoEmL 93, WhoWor 93
Blackmoor, Edmund ScF&FL 92
Blackmore, Josiah H. 1934- WhoAm 92

Blackmore, Leigh *ScF&FL 92*
Blackmore, Madeline *AmWomPl*
Blackmore, Paul J. *Law&B 92*
Blackmore, R.D. 1939- *St&PR 93*
Blackmore, Vivienne J. 1948- *WhoAmW 93*
Blackmun, Harry A. *BioIn 17*
Blackmun, Harry A. 1908- *CngDr 91*
Blackmun, Harry Andrew 1908- *OxCSupC [port], WhoAm 92, WhoE 93, WhoWor 93*
Blackmun, Sally A. *Law&B 92*
Blackner, Boyd Atkins 1933- *WhoAm 92*
Black-Rhodes, Diana Karen 1953- *WhoEmL 93*
Black Sabbath *ConMus 9 [port]*
Blackshear, A. T., Jr. 1942- *WhoAm 92*
Blackshear, Helen Friedman 1911- *WhoWrEP 92*
Blackshire, E. Ann *Law&B 92*
Blacksmith, Sara *WhoWrEP 92*
Blacksmith, William August, IV 1963- *WhoE 93*
Blackson, Benjamin Franklin 1933- *WhoE 93*
Blackstock, Charity 1888- *ScF&FL 92*
Blackstock, James Fielding 1947- *WhoEmL 93*
Blackstock, Jerry Byron 1945- *WhoAm 92, WhoSSW 93*
Blackstock, LeRoy 1914- *WhoAm 92, WhoWor 93*
Blackstock, Rebecca 1943- *WhoSSW 93*
Blackstock, Virginia Lee Lowman 1917- *WhoAmW 93*
Blackstone, Franklin *Law&B 92*
Blackstone, Franklin, Jr. *Law&B 92*
Blackstone, George Arthur 1922- *WhoAm 92*
Blackstone, Harry Bouton, Jr. 1934- *WhoAm 92*
Blackstone, James *ScF&FL 92*
Blackstone, Jay *Law&B 92*
Blackstone, Patricia Clark 1952- *WhoE 93, WhoEmL 93*
Blackstone, Paul Carroll 1930- *WhoE 93*
Blackstone, R. Loring 1926- *St&PR 93*
Blackstone, Richmond Loring 1926- *WhoAm 92*
Blackstone, Sandra Lee *WhoAm 92, WhoAmW 93*
Blackstone, Vicky Lee 1958- *WhoAmW 93*
Blackton, Charles Stuart 1913- *WhoAm 92*
Blackton, James Stuart 1875-1941 *BioIn 17*
Blacktree, Barbara *WhoWrEP 92*
Blackwelder, John Norris 1936- *St&PR 93*
Blackwelder, Richard E. 1909- *ScF&FL 92*
Blackwelder, Richard Eliot 1909- *WhoAm 92*
Blackwelder, Ron Forest 1941- *WhoAm 92*
Blackwell, Alice Stone 1857-1950 *BioIn 17, PolPar*
Blackwell, Annie Louise 1929- *WhoAmW 93*
Blackwell, Antoinette Louisa Brown 1825-1921 *BioIn 17*
Blackwell, Barbara Jane 1956- *WhoAmW 93*
Blackwell, Bernard Constantine 1940- *WhoWor 93*
Blackwell, Bumps 1922-1985 *SoulM*
Blackwell, Cecil 1924- *WhoAm 92, WhoSSW 93*
Blackwell, Christopher Mark 1962- *WhoWor 93*
Blackwell, Dan Page 1952- *WhoEmL 93*
Blackwell, David Alan 1957- *WhoSSW 93*
Blackwell, David Jefferson 1927- *WhoAm 92*
Blackwell, Debbie L. *Law&B 92*
Blackwell, Don W. 1958- *St&PR 93*
Blackwell, Donald Eustace *WhoScE 91-1*
Blackwell, Douglas L. 1933- *St&PR 93*
Blackwell, Earl 1913- *WhoAm 92, WhoWor 93, WhoWrEP 92*
Blackwell, Ed 1929-1992 *NewYTBS 92 [port]*
Blackwell, Elizabeth 1821-1910 *BioIn 17*
Blackwell, F.B. 1930- *WhoScE 91-1*
Blackwell, G.W. *WhoScE 91-1*
Blackwell, Harolyn *BioIn 17*
Blackwell, Henry Barlow, II 1928- *WhoAm 92*
Blackwell, Jacqueline Pflughoeft 1936- *WhoAmW 93*
Blackwell, James Augusta, Jr. 1940- *WhoAm 92*
Blackwell, James Britt 1956- *WhoSSW 93*
Blackwell, James Madison, IV 1931- *WhoE 93*
Blackwell, Jeffrey David 1943- *St&PR 93*
Blackwell, John 1942- *WhoAm 92*
Blackwell, John Adrian, Jr. 1940- *WhoSSW 93*
Blackwell, John C. 1935- *WhoScE 91-1*
Blackwell, John Wesley 1941- *WhoAm 92*
Blackwell, Karen J. *Law&B 92*
Blackwell, Kathryn D. 1950- *St&PR 93*
Blackwell, Kent *St&PR 93*
Blackwell, Lelia Elisabeth 1955- *WhoEmL 93*
Blackwell, Linda Christine 1953- *WhoWrEP 92*
Blackwell, Lucien *BioIn 17*
Blackwell, Lucien E. *WhoAm 92, WhoE 93*
Blackwell, Marlin Earl, Jr. 1941- *WhoIns 93*
Blackwell, Menefee Davis 1916- *WhoAm 92*
Blackwell, Morton Clyde 1939- *WhoSSW 93*
Blackwell, Neil Harold 1950- *WhoWor 93*
Blackwell, Nigel Stirling 1947- *St&PR 93*
Blackwell, Paul Eugene 1941- *WhoAm 92*
Blackwell, Richard Manning 1940- *St&PR 93, WhoAm 92*
Blackwell, Roland John *WhoScE 91-1*
Blackwell, Ronald Eugene 1933- *WhoAm 92, WhoSSW 93*
Blackwell, Saundra Cochran 1946- *WhoEmL 93*
Blackwell, Searcy Van *Law&B 92*
Blackwell, Stanley Michael 1951- *WhoEmL 93*
Blackwell, Thomas F. 1961- *WhoEmL 93*
Blackwell, Unita *NewYTBS 92 [port]*
Blackwell, Virginia Anne 1942- *WhoAmW 93*
Blackwell, William Allen 1920- *WhoAm 92*
Blackwell, William Ernest 1932- *St&PR 93, WhoAm 92, WhoSSW 93*
Blackwell-Williams, Linda *Law&B 92*
Blackwood, Alan 1932- *SmATA 70*
Blackwood, Albemarle 1881-1921 *BioIn 17*
Blackwood, Algernon 1869-1951 *ScF&FL 92*
Blackwood, Arthur Leonard 1932- *WhoSSW 93*
Blackwood, Brett N. 1959- *St&PR 93*
Blackwood, Caroline *BioIn 17*
Blackwood, Christian *MiSFD 9*
Blackwood, Christian 1942-1992 *NewYTBS 92*
Blackwood, Easley 1903-1992 *BioIn 17, NewYTBS 92 [port]*
Blackwood, Easley 1933- *Baker 92*
Blackwood, Gary L. *ScF&FL 92*
Blackwood, Gary L. 1945- *SmATA 72 [port]*
Blackwood, Lois Anne 1949- *WhoAmW 93, WhoEmL 93*
Blackwood, Michael *BioIn 17*
Blackwood, Ronald A. *AfrAmBi*
Blackwood, Russell Thorn, III 1928- *WhoAm 92*
Blackwood, William Jonathan 1953- *WhoE 93, WhoWor 93*
Blacque, Taurean *BioIn 17, WhoAm 92*
Blad, Blaine L. 1939- *WhoAm 92*
Blade, Alexander *MajAI*
Blade, Martin Alan 1947- *St&PR 93*
Blade, Melinda Kim 1952- *WhoAmW 93, WhoEmL 93*
Blade-Font, Artur 1932- *WhoWor 93*
Blades, A.T. 1908- *St&PR 93*
Blades, Ann 1947- *SmATA 69 [port], WhoAm 92, WhoCanL 92, WhoWrEP 92*
Blades, Ann (Sager) 1947- *MajAI [port]*
Blades, Brian 1955- *St&PR 93*
Blades, Herbert William 1908- *WhoAm 92*
Blades, Jane M. 1953- *WhoAmW 93*
Blades, Jim *BioIn 17*
Blades, John Donaldson 1936- *WhoWrEP 92*
Blades, Ruben 1948- *Baker 92, HispAmA, WhoAm 92*
Bladis, Richard P. 1930- *St&PR 93*
Bladis, Robert F. 1924- *St&PR 93*
Bladon, Peter 1926- *WhoWor 93*
Blady Szwajger, Adina 1917- *BioIn 17*
Blaedel, Walter John 1916- *WhoAm 92*
Blaeker, Felix 1935- *WhoWor 93*
Blaes, Arnold Joseph 1814-1892 *Baker 92*
Blaes, Elisa 1817-1878 *Baker 92*
Blaes-Bernard, Nelly 1953- *WhoScE 91-2*
Blaese, Robert Michael 1939- *WhoE 93*
Blaesi, Mary Virginia 1953- *WhoEmL 93*
Blaess, Darrell L. *St&PR 93*
Blaess, Darrell L. 1937- *WhoIns 93*
Blaess, Donna Adele 1948- *WhoEmL 93, WhoSSW 93*
Blaga, Aurel Ioan Stefan 1930- *WhoScE 91-4*
Blaga, Lucian 1895-1961 *ConLC 75 [port]*
Blagden, Olga Gates *AmWomPl*
Blager, Florence Berman *WhoAm 92, WhoAmW 93*
Blagg, Christopher Robin 1931- *WhoAm 92*
Blagg, Gary Delance 1950- *WhoSSW 93*
Blagg, Jim *BioIn 17*
Blagojevic, Milan 1920- *WhoScE 91-4*
Blagojevich, Robert R. 1955- *St&PR 93*
Blagrove, Henry Gamble 1811-1872 *Baker 92*
Blaha, Ivo 1936- *Baker 92*
Blaha, Jan 1934- *WhoScE 91-4*
Blaha, John E. *BioIn 17*
Blaha, Verle Dennis 1929- *St&PR 93*
Blahd, William Henry 1921- *WhoAm 92*
Blahetka, Marie Leopoldine 1811-1887 *Baker 92, BioIn 17*
Blahetka, Russell Ernest 1952- *WhoEmL 93*
Blahnik, Bernard E. 1928- *WhoIns 93*
Blahous, Charles Paul 1935- *St&PR 93*
Blahovec, Jiri 1942- *WhoScE 91-4*
Blahut, Richard Edward 1937- *WhoAm 92*
Blai, Bertha 1915- *WhoE 93*
Blaich, Robert Ian 1930- *WhoAm 92*
Blaich, Rolf E. 1943- *WhoScE 91-3*
Blaich, Ruediger 1955- *WhoWor 93*
Blaier, Andrei 1933- *DrEEuF*
Blaikie, Robert B. 1906-1992 *BioIn 17, NewYTBS 92 [port]*
Blain, Alexander, III 1918- *WhoAm 92*
Blain, Bradley Gordon 1953- *WhoAm 92*
Blain, Francis Rene 1943- *WhoUN 92*
Blain, Peter George *WhoScE 91-1*
Blain, Sonia M. *Law&B 92*
Blain, W. Edward 1951- *ConAu 139*
Blaine, Charles G. 1925- *St&PR 93*
Blaine, Charles Gillespie 1925- *WhoAm 92*
Blaine, David Bradley 1946- *St&PR 93*
Blaine, Davis Robert 1943- *WhoAm 92*
Blaine, Devon 1947- *WhoEmL 93*
Blaine, Dorman 1939- *St&PR 93*
Blaine, Dorothea Constance Ragette 1930- *WhoAm 92, WhoAmW 93*
Blaine, Frederick Matthew 1947- *WhoE 93*
Blaine, Gloria Beckwith 1924- *WhoAmW 93*
Blaine, Hal *BioIn 17*
Blaine, James *ConAu 39NR*
Blaine, James G. 1830-1893 *GayN, PolPar*
Blaine, Joan C. 1931- *St&PR 93*
Blaine, John 1914-1990 *BioIn 17, ScF&FL 92*
Blaine, Marjorie *AmWomPl*
Blaine, Nell 1922- *BioIn 17*
Blaine, Nell Walden 1922- *WhoAm 92*
Blaine, William D. 1929- *St&PR 93*
Blaine, William McKinley, Jr. 1931- *St&PR 93*
Blainville, Charles-Henri de 1710-c. 1770 *Baker 92*
Blair, Alan J. 1924- *St&PR 93*
Blair, Alvin Francis 1931- *St&PR 93*
Blair, Andrew d1885 *ScF&FL 92*
Blair, Andrew Lane, Jr. 1946- *WhoAm 92*
Blair, Ballard Glenn 1957- *WhoE 93*
Blair, Barbara Anne 1926- *WhoSSW 93*
Blair, Barbara D. 1938- *St&PR 93*
Blair, Bonnie *BioIn 17*
Blair, Bonnie 1964- *BiDAMSp 1989, CurBio 92 [port], News 92 [port], -92-3 [port], WhoAmW 93*
Blair, Bowen 1918- *St&PR 93, WhoAm 92*
Blair, Calvin Patton 1924- *WhoAm 92*
Blair, Charles Lee 1954- *WhoE 93, WhoEmL 93*
Blair, Charles Melvin 1910- *WhoAm 92*
Blair, Charles Michael 1942- *WhoAm 92*
Blair, Christopher David 1944- *St&PR 93*
Blair, Clay Drewry 1925- *WhoWrEP 92*
Blair, Clyde Edmon 1950- *WhoEmL 93*
Blair, Craig John 1943- *St&PR 93, WhoAm 92*
Blair, Culverson 1947- *BlkAuII 92*
Blair, Cynthia 1953- *ScF&FL 92*
Blair, David William 1929- *WhoE 93*
Blair, Dennis Earl 1947- *WhoEmL 93*
Blair, Diana 1947- *WhoWrEP 92*
Blair, Diane Divers 1938- *WhoSSW 93*
Blair, Donald Robert 1928- *St&PR 93*
Blair, Earl F. 1943- *St&PR 93*
Blair, Earl Henry 1951- *WhoEmL 93, WhoSSW 93*
Blair, Edward Joseph 1944- *St&PR 93*
Blair, Edward McCormick 1915- *St&PR 93, WhoAm 92*
Blair, Elaine Judith 1957- *WhoEmL 93*
Blair, Eric *ScF&FL 92*
Blair, Eric 1903-1950 *BioIn 17*
Blair, Ernest *Law&B 92*
Blair, Francis Preston 1791-1876 *JrnUS*
Blair, Fred 1940- *AfrAmBi [port]*
Blair, Fred Edward 1933- *WhoAm 92*
Blair, Frederick David 1946- *WhoEmL 93, WhoWor 93*
Blair, Fredrika *BioIn 17*
Blair, Gary Charles 1938- *WhoAm 92*
Blair, Glenn Myers 1908- *WhoAm 92*
Blair, Gloria Christine 1946- *WhoEmL 93*
Blair, Gordon Purves *WhoScE 91-1*
Blair, Graham Kerin 1951- *WhoWor 93*
Blair, Jack R. 1942- *St&PR 93*
Blair, James Burton 1935- *WhoSSW 93, WhoWor 93*
Blair, James F. 1941- *St&PR 93*
Blair, James Pease 1931- *WhoAm 92*
Blair, James Walter, Jr. 1936- *WhoAm 92*
Blair, Jim *Law&B 92*
Blair, Joane Ellen 1929- *WhoAmW 93*
Blair, John 1929- *WhoAm 92*
Blair, John 1961- *ScF&FL 92*
Blair, John, Jr. 1732-1800 *OxCSupC [port]*
Blair, John D. 1944- *WhoAm 92*
Blair, John Norman 1926- *St&PR 93*
Blair, John R. 1946- *St&PR 93*
Blair, John Thomas 1951- *WhoEmL 93*
Blair, Jon Harlan 1933- *St&PR 93*
Blair, Joseph E., Jr. 1931- *WhoIns 93*
Blair, Joseph Edward, Jr. 1931- *St&PR 93*
Blair, Karin *ScF&FL 92*
Blair, Kathie Lynn 1951- *WhoAmW 93*
Blair, Kerrie Jane 1956- *WhoEmL 93*
Blair, Lachlan Ferguson 1919- *WhoAm 92*
Blair, Les 1941- *MiSFD 9*
Blair, Lester Winston 1949- *WhoE 93*
Blair, Lorne *MiSFD 9*
Blair, Marie Lenore 1931- *WhoAmW 93*
Blair, Mary Josephine d1991 *BioIn 17, NewYTBS 92*
Blair, Patricia Wohlgemuth 1929- *WhoE 93*
Blair, Paula Wyatt 1944- *WhoAmW 93*
Blair, Pauline Hunter *MajAI, ScF&FL 92*
Blair, Peter Hunter 1912-1982 *ScF&FL 92*
Blair, Philip Joseph 1955- *WhoEmL 93*
Blair, Prentice Randol 1928- *St&PR 93*
Blair, R. *WhoScE 91-3*
Blair, R. Cary 1939- *St&PR 93, WhoIns 93*
Blair, R. Gregory 1947- *St&PR 93*
Blair, Richard *St&PR 93*
Blair, Richard Eugene 1923- *WhoSSW 93*
Blair, Robert 1933- *WhoAm 92*
Blair, Robert Noel 1912- *WhoAm 92*
Blair, Robin Elise Farbman 1951- *WhoAmW 93*
Blair, Robin Leitch *WhoScE 91-1*
Blair, Roy Thomas 1946- *St&PR 93*
Blair, Russell Madison 1929- *St&PR 93*
Blair, Ruth Reba 1934- *WhoSSW 93*
Blair, Ruth Virginia Van Ness 1912- *WhoAmW 93*
Blair, Samuel Davidson 1927- *WhoAm 92*
Blair, Samuel Rufus 1932- *WhoWrEP 92*
Blair, Sandra Simko 1940- *WhoAmW 93*
Blair, Sidney Robert 1929- *WhoAm 92, WhoE 93*
Blair, Sloan Blackmon 1929- *WhoSSW 93*
Blair, Steven N. *BioIn 17*
Blair, Steven Noel 1939- *WhoAm 92, WhoSSW 93*
Blair, Stewart D. 1949- *St&PR 93*
Blair, Tammy Jeanette 1963- *WhoSSW 93*
Blair, Thomas S. 1922- *St&PR 93*
Blair, Virginia Ann 1925- *WhoAmW 93*
Blair, Walter d1992 *NewYTBS 92*
Blair, Walter 1900-1992 *ConAu 139, SmATA 72*
Blair, Watson Bayard 1954- *WhoEmL 93*
Blair, William Draper, Jr. 1927- *WhoAm 92*
Blair, William Granger 1925- *WhoAm 92*
Blair, William H. *Law&B 92*
Blair, William McCormick, Jr. 1916- *WhoAm 92*
Blair, William Richardson 1908- *WhoAm 92*
Blair, William Sutherland 1917- *WhoAm 92*
Blair, William Travis 1925- *WhoAm 92*
Blair-Hastings, Fredrika 1918-1990 *WhoWor 93*
Blair-Larsen, Susan Margaret 1950- *WhoAmW 93, WhoE 93, WhoEmL 93*
Blais, Jacques 1937- *WhoCanL 92*
Blais, Madeleine Helena 1949- *WhoWrEP 92*
Blais, Marie-Claire 1939- *BioIn 17, ConAu 38NR, MagSWL [port], WhoAmW 93, WhoCanL 92*
Blais, Norman J. 1929- *St&PR 93*
Blais, Pierre 1948- *WhoE 93*
Blais, Roger Nathaniel 1944- *WhoSSW 93, WhoWor 93*
Blaisdell, Bruce 1945- *St&PR 93*
Blaisdell, Deborah 1955- *St&PR 93*
Blaisdell, Durwood Alton d1991 *BioIn 17*
Blaisdell, Ernest Atwell 1940- *WhoE 93*
Blaisdell, Jack D. 1933- *St&PR 93*
Blaisdell, Nancy S. *Law&B 92*
Blaise, Adolfe Benoit d1772 *OxDcOp*
Blaise, Clark 1940- *WhoCanL 92*
Blaise, Clark Lee 1940- *WhoWrEP 92*
Blaise, Jean Edmond 1921- *WhoWor 93*
Blaize, Herbert *BioIn 17*
Blaize, Herbert 1918-1989 *DcCPCAm*
Blaize, Samuel Allen 1946- *St&PR 93*

Blake, Alan C. 1952- *St&PR 93*
Blake, Ann Beth 1944- *WhoAm 92*
Blake, Bertram Thorp d1990 *BioIn 17*
Blake, Buckeye 1946- *BioIn 17*
Blake, Bud 1918- *WhoAm 92*
Blake, Carl 1935- *WhoE 93*
Blake, Christopher Robert 1951- *WhoEmL 93*
Blake, Cicero 1938- *BioIn 17*
Blake, Connie Marie 1955- *WhoAmW 93*
Blake, Darlene Evelyn 1947- *WhoAmW 93, WhoEmL 93*
Blake, David B. *Law&B 92*
Blake, David Bevan *Law&B 92*
Blake, David (Leonard) 1936- *Baker 92*
Blake, Diane Adams 1950- *WhoAmW 93, WhoSSW 93*
Blake, Donald George 1929- *St&PR 93*
Blake, Dorothy 1936- *WhoUN 92*
Blake, Dorothy Mae 1931- *WhoAmW 93*
Blake, Elias, Jr. 1929- *WhoAm 92*
Blake, Eubie 1883-1983 *Baker 92*
Blake, Eugene Carson 1906-1985 *EncAACR*
Blake, Francis S. *Law&B 92*
Blake, Fred D. *Law&B 92*
Blake, George *BioIn 17*
Blake, George Rowell 1945- *St&PR 93*
Blake, George Rowland 1918- *WhoAm 92*
Blake, Gerald K. 1934- *St&PR 93*
Blake, Gerald Rutherford 1939- *WhoAm 92*
Blake, Gilbert Easton 1953- *WhoEmL 93*
Blake, Gwyn Adams 1927- *St&PR 93*
Blake, Howard 1938- *BioIn 17*
Blake, Irene Elvin 1947- *WhoEmL 93*
Blake, James Joseph 1939- *WhoE 93*
Blake, James P. *Law&B 92*
Blake, Jane Salley 1937- *WhoWrEP 92*
Blake, Jeannette Belisle 1920- *WhoE 93*
Blake, Jeffrey Michael 1954- *WhoE 93*
Blake, Jerry A. 1938- *St&PR 93*
Blake, Joan Johnston Wallman 1930- *WhoAm 92, WhoAmW 93, WhoWor 93*
Blake, John Ballard 1922- *WhoAm 92, WhoWrEP 92*
Blake, John Edward 1933- *St&PR 93, WhoAm 92*
Blake, John Francis 1922- *WhoAm 92*
Blake, John Freeman 1950- *WhoEmL 93*
Blake, John Herman 1934- *WhoAm 92*
Blake, Jonathan Daniels 1946- *St&PR 93*
Blake, Judith 1926- *WhoAm 92*
Blake, Jules 1924- *St&PR 93, WhoAm 92*
Blake, Katherine *ScF&FL 92*
Blake, Kevin E. 1958- *WhoEmL 93*
Blake, Lamont Vincent 1913- *WhoAm 92*
Blake, Larry Jay 1930- *WhoAm 92*
Blake, Laura 1959- *WhoAmW 93*
Blake, Lee Scott *Law&B 92*
Blake, Margaret Tate 1927- *WhoAmW 93*
Blake, Maxine *Law&B 92*
Blake, Michael *WhoAm 92*
Blake, Michael 1943- *BioIn 17*
Blake, Michael James 1956- *WhoEmL 93*
Blake, Mildred Riorden d1990 *BioIn 17*
Blake, Nicholas 1904-1972 *BioIn 17*
Blake, Nick *BioIn 17*
Blake, Norman P., Jr. *BioIn 17*
Blake, Norman Perkins 1941- *St&PR 93*
Blake, Norman Perkins, Jr. 1941- *WhoAm 92*
Blake, O.A. *Law&B 92*
Blake, Owen, Jr. *Law&B 92*
Blake, Pamela 1916- *SweetSg C*
Blake, Pamela Diane 1958- *WhoEmL 93*
Blake, Peter Jost 1920- *WhoAm 92*
Blake, Quentin 1932- *BioIn 17, ChlBIID [port]*
Blake, Quentin (Saxby) 1932- *ConAu 37NR, MajAI [port]*
Blake, Ran 1935- *Baker 92, WhoAm 92*
Blake, Ray Edward, III 1947- *St&PR 93*
Blake, Renee *WhoWrEP 92*
Blake, Richard *AfrAmBi [port]*
Blake, Richard Allan 1945- *WhoWrEP 92*
Blake, Robert 1599-1657 *HarEnMi*
Blake, Robert Frederick 1915- *WhoE 93*
Blake, Robert M. 1931- *St&PR 93*
Blake, Robert Rogers 1918- *WhoAm 92*
Blake, Robert Wallace 1921- *WhoAm 92*
Blake, Rockwell 1951- *OxDcOp*
Blake, Rockwell (Robert) 1951- *Baker 92*
Blake, Ronald A. 1946- *WhoWor 93*
Blake, Russell C. 1943- *WhoAm 92*
Blake, Stacey 1878-1964 *ScF&FL 92*
Blake, Stephanie *ScF&FL 92*
Blake, Stephen P. 1942- *ConAu 139*
Blake, Stewart Prestley 1914- *WhoAm 92*
Blake, Stuart *Law&B 92*
Blake, Stuart B. *Law&B 92*
Blake, Susan *ScF&FL 92*
Blake, Thomas Clinton 1927- *St&PR 93*
Blake, Thomas E. 1938- *St&PR 93*
Blake, Thomas Hughes 1950- *WhoEmL 93, WhoSSW 93*
Blake, Tona *BioIn 17*
Blake, Trudi Odella 1921- *WhoAm 92*
Blake, Veronica Elizabeth 1953- *WhoWrEP 92*
Blake, Victor Harold 1935- *St&PR 93, WhoIns 93, WhoWor 93*
Blake, Vincent Patrick 1932- *St&PR 93, WhoAm 92*
Blake, Walker E. *ConAu 40NR*
Blake, Walter Samuel 1951- *WhoSSW 93*
Blake, Webb Thomas, Jr. 1963- *WhoSSW 93*
Blake, William 1757-1827 *BioIn 17, MagSWL [port], MajAI [port], NinCLC 37 [port], WorLitC [port]*
Blake, William 1862?-1895 *BioIn 17*
Blake, William Dorsey *ScF&FL 92*
Blake, William Ernest, Jr. 1930- *WhoSSW 93*
Blake, William George 1949- *WhoEmL 93*
Blake, William Henry 1913- *WhoAm 92*
Blake, William J. *Law&B 92*
Blakeburn, Dave Lowry, II 1960- *WhoSSW 93*
Blake-Greenaway, Veronica *Law&B 92*
Blakeley, Helen Beatty 1954- *WhoE 93*
Blakeley, Katherine M. *Law&B 92*
Blakeley, Linda 1941- *WhoAmW 93*
Blakeley, William Thomas Frederick *WhoScE 91-1*
Blakelock, Ralph Albert 1847-1919 *GayN*
Blakely, Bryan William *Law&B 92*
Blakely, Carolyn Frazier 1936- *WhoAmW 93*
Blakely, Christine Marie 1951- *WhoAmW 93*
Blakely, Edward James 1938- *WhoAm 92*
Blakely, Hugh W. 1951- *St&PR 93*
Blakely, James Russell 1935- *WhoE 93*
Blakely, Jane McCarthy 1948- *WhoAmW 93*
Blakely, Kip 1961- *WhoSSW 93*
Blakely, Marilyn *BioIn 17*
Blakely, Marvin *Law&B 92*
Blakely, Mary Kay *BioIn 17*
Blakely, Pamela Higgitt 1952- *WhoAmW 93*
Blakely, Robert John 1915- *WhoAm 92, WhoWrEP 92*
Blakely, Ronald Lyle 1931- *WhoAm 92*
Blakely, T.T., Jr. 1937- *St&PR 93*
Blake-MacIntosh, Monica Bernadette 1957- *WhoE 93*
Blakeman, Beth Renee 1951- *WhoWrEP 92*
Blakeman, D.G. 1932- *St&PR 93*
Blakeman, Jeffrey Allen 1963- *St&PR 93*
Blakeman, John Peter *WhoScE 91-1*
Blakeman, Marie Barbara 1917- *St&PR 93*
Blakeman, Royal Edwin 1923- *WhoAm 92*
Blakemore, Claude Coulehan 1909- *WhoAm 92*
Blakemore, Colin *WhoScE 91-1*
Blakemore, Colin Brian 1944- *WhoWor 93*
Blakemore, Felix J. 1872- *ScF&FL 92*
Blakemore, Harold *BioIn 17*
Blakemore, James Roberts, II 1952- *WhoEmL 93*
Blakemore, Mark *Law&B 92*
Blakemore, Michael 1928- *MiSFD 9*
Blakemore, Michael John *WhoScE 91-1*
Blakemore, Ralph W. 1946- *St&PR 93*
Blakemore, Sally Gay 1947- *WhoEmL 93*
Blakemore, Steven Michael 1954- *St&PR 93*
Blakemore, Terry G. 1944- *St&PR 93*
Blakeney, Allan Emrys 1925- *WhoAm 92*
Blakeney, Jay D. 1957- *ScF&FL 92*
Blakeney, Tom A., Jr. 1929- *St&PR 93*
Blakeney, Whiteford Carlyle, Jr. 1944- *WhoSSW 93*
Blakenham, Viscount 1938- *WhoWor 93*
Blakenship, Wesley F., Jr. 1957- *St&PR 93*
Blaker, Charles William 1918- *WhoWrEP 92*
Blaker, Jill *Law&B 92*
Blakeslee, Albert Francis 1874-1954 *BioIn 17*
Blakeslee, Alton Lauren 1913- *WhoAm 92, WhoWrEP 92*
Blakeslee, Carolyn Denise 1957- *WhoSSW 93*
Blakeslee, Edward Eaton 1921- *WhoAm 92*
Blakeslee, George Edward 1948- *WhoE 93*
Blakeslee, Leroy Lawrence 1935- *WhoAm 92*
Blakeslee, Mermer *ScF&FL 92*
Blakesley, David M. 1944- *St&PR 93*
Blakey, Art *BioIn 17*
Blakey, Art 1919-1990 *Baker 92*
Blakey, Tom *St&PR 93*
Blakley, Benjamin Spencer, III 1952- *WhoE 93, WhoEmL 93*
Blakley, George Robert, Jr. 1932- *WhoAm 92, WhoSSW 93*
Blakley, John Clyde 1955- *WhoEmL 93*
Blakley, Ronee 1946- *MiSFD 9*
Blakney, Hurley *St&PR 93*
Blakney-Richards, Bettye Ruth 1939- *WhoAmW 93*
Blalock, Donna K. *Law&B 92*
Blalock, Hubert M. 1926-1991 *BioIn 17*
Blalock, James Edward 1943- *WhoUN 92*
Blalock, Jane 1945- *BiDAMSp 1989*
Blalock, Lois Lorayne *Law&B 92*
Blalock, Marion Gale 1948- *WhoEmL 93*
Blalock, Michael David 1951- *WhoEmL 93*
Blalock, Sherrill 1945- *WhoAm 92*
Blalock, Wallace Davis 1931- *St&PR 93*
Blamey, Richard Lyle 1941- *St&PR 93*
Blamey, Roger Wallas *WhoScE 91-1*
Blamey, Thomas Albert 1884-1951 *HarEnMi*
Blamont, Francois Colin de 1690-1760 *Baker 92*
Blamont, Francois Collin de 1690-1760 *OxDcOp*
Blampied, P. J. 1942- *WhoAm 92*
Blampied, Peter J. 1942- *St&PR 93*
Blan, Ollie Lionel, Jr. 1931- *WhoAm 92*
Blanc, Daniel 1927- *WhoScE 91-2*
Blanc, Daniel Louis 1927- *WhoWor 93*
Blanc, Denise *WhoScE 91-2*
Blanc, Dominique *BioIn 17*
Blanc, Esther Silverstein 1913- *BioIn 17*
Blanc, Louis 1811-1882 *BioIn 17*
Blanc, Martin D. 1925- *St&PR 93*
Blanc, Mel 1908-1989 *BioIn 17*
Blanc, Noel *BioIn 17*
Blanc, Peter 1912- *WhoAm 92, WhoE 93*
Blanc, Robert *Law&B 92*
Blanc, Robert H. 1930- *WhoScE 91-2*
Blanc, Roger David 1945- *WhoAm 92*
Blanca, Antoine 1936- *WhoUN 92*
Blancafort (de Rossello), Manuel 1897-1987 *Baker 92*
Blancarte, James E. 1953- *HispAmA*
Blancato, Ken *MiSFD 9*
Blancato, Robert Benedict 1951- *WhoE 93*
Blance, R. Bruce *Law&B 92*
Blancett-Maddock, V. Diane 1956- *WhoEmL 93*
Blanch, Andrea *BioIn 17*
Blanch, E.W., Jr. 1936- *WhoIns 93*
Blanch, Lesley *BioIn 17*
Blanch, Stuart Yarworth 1918- *WhoWor 93*
Blanchard, Alan Franklin 1939- *WhoAm 92*
Blanchard, Allen 1929- *WhoAsAP 91*
Blanchard, Amy Ella 1856-1926 *AmWomPl*
Blanchard, Andy *BioIn 17*
Blanchard, Bruce Charles *WhoScE 91-1*
Blanchard, Carl Richard 1912- *WhoAm 92*
Blanchard, Charles Elton 1868-1945 *ScF&FL 92*
Blanchard, Charles H. 1937- *St&PR 93*
Blanchard, Colleen Diana 1945- *WhoAmW 93*
Blanchard, Craig A. 1942- *St&PR 93*
Blanchard, Daniel S. 1943- *WhoUN 92*
Blanchard, David Andrew 1958- *WhoEmL 93, WhoSSW 93*
Blanchard, David Beresford 1943- *WhoAm 92*
Blanchard, David Lawrence 1931- *WhoAm 92*
Blanchard, Dorothy *AmWomPl*
Blanchard, Duane Everett 1938- *St&PR 93*
Blanchard, Elizabeth Louise 1961- *WhoAmW 93*
Blanchard, Elwood P. 1931- *St&PR 93*
Blanchard, Elwood P., Jr. *WhoAm 92, WhoE 93*
Blanchard, Eric Alan *Law&B 92*
Blanchard, Esprit Joseph Antoine 1696-1770 *Baker 92*
Blanchard, Frances Jones 1926- *WhoAmW 93*
Blanchard, George Samuel 1920- *WhoAm 92*
Blanchard, Georges Marie Jean 1877-1954 *HarEnMi*
Blanchard, Gerald L. *Law&B 92*
Blanchard, Harry Russell, Jr. 1950- *WhoE 93*
Blanchard, Helen Margaret 1932- *WhoAmW 93*
Blanchard, Isaac 1772-1794 *BioIn 17*
Blanchard, James Hubert 1941- *St&PR 93*
Blanchard, James J. 1942- *WhoAm 92*
Blanchard, Jayne M. 1957- *WhoE 93*
Blanchard, Jerry Clifton 1950- *WhoEmL 93, WhoSSW 93*
Blanchard, Joseph Bateman 1946- *St&PR 93*
Blanchard, Joseph Procter 1945- *WhoE 93*
Blanchard, Joyce Ruth 1949- *WhoWrEP 92*
Blanchard, Kenneth E. 1940- *St&PR 93*
Blanchard, Kirk F. 1949- *St&PR 93*
Blanchard, Lawrence E., Jr. 1921- *St&PR 93*
Blanchard, Lawrence Eley, Jr. 1921- *WhoAm 92*
Blanchard, Mari 1927-1970 *SweetSg D [port]*
Blanchard, Martin Glenn 1946- *St&PR 93*
Blanchard, Michael D. *Law&B 92*
Blanchard, Michel 1934- *WhoScE 91-2*
Blanchard, Norman H. 1930- *St&PR 93*
Blanchard, Norman Harris 1930- *WhoAm 92, WhoE 93, WhoWor 93*
Blanchard, Richard Emile, Sr. 1928- *WhoWor 93*
Blanchard, Richard F. 1920- *St&PR 93*
Blanchard, Richard F. 1933- *St&PR 93*
Blanchard, Robert Johnstone Weir 1934- *WhoAm 92*
Blanchard, Robert T. 1944- *St&PR 93*
Blanchard, Ronald Joseph 1946- *WhoE 93*
Blanchard, Thomas 1788-1864 *BioIn 17*
Blanchard, Townsend Eugene 1931- *St&PR 93, WhoAm 92*
Blanchard, William Clifford 1933- *St&PR 93*
Blanchard, William Henry 1922- *WhoWor 93*
Blanche, John *ScF&FL 92*
Blanchemain, Antoine 1925- *WhoScE 91-2*
Blanchet, Bertrand 1932- *WhoAm 92*
Blanchet, Jean Paul 1938- *WhoScE 91-2*
Blanchet, Madeleine 1934- *WhoAmW 93*
Blanchet, Peter 1957- *WhoAm 92*
Blanchet, Rene 1941- *WhoScE 91-2*
Blanchet, Robert Paul 1927- *WhoScE 91-2*
Blanchet-Sadri, Francine 1953- *WhoSSW 93*
Blanchette, James Edward 1924- *WhoWor 93*
Blanchette, Jeanne E. Maxant 1944- *WhoAm 92*
Blanchette, Jeanne Ellene Maxant 1944- *WhoAmW 93*
Blanchette, Oliva 1929- *WhoAm 92*
Blanchette, Rita T. Billings 1913- *WhoWrEP 92*
Blanchette, Robert Wilfred 1932- *WhoAm 92*
Blanchfield, James Edward 1945- *St&PR 93*
Blanchford, Jeff Auld 1939- *WhoE 93*
Blanck, Gertrude Sacks *WhoAmW 93*
Blanck, Lorraine Theresa 1957- *WhoAmW 93*
Blanckenburg, Christian Friedrich von 1744-1796 *BioIn 17*
Blanckenhagen, Peter Heinrich von 1909-1990 *BioIn 17*
Blanc-Louvel, Christiane 1932- *WhoScE 91-2*
Blanco, Alberto 1951- *DcMexL*
Blanco, Alvaro 1946- *WhoScE 91-3*
Blanco, Anna 1955- *WhoEmL 93*
Blanco, Betty Mintz 1927- *WhoWor 93*
Blanco, Bruce M. 1949- *St&PR 93*
Blanco, Dianne Hayes 1947- *St&PR 93*
Blanco, Griselda *BioIn 17*
Blanco, Jeanette H. *Law&B 92*
Blanco, Jorge Luis 1928- *St&PR 93*
Blanco, Josefa Joan-Juana 1954- *WhoEmL 93, WhoWor 93*
Blanco, Juan 1920- *Baker 92*
Blanco, Laura 1956- *WhoAmW 93*
Blanco, Raymond D., Jr. 1932- *WhoIns 93*
Blanco, Richard L. *BioIn 17*
Blanco, Victor 1936- *WhoAm 92*
Blanco, William *Law&B 92*
Blanco-Bazan, Agustin 1949- *WhoUN 92*
Blanco Lopez, Desiderio 1929- *WhoWor 93*
Blanco Moheno, Roberto 1920- *DcMexL*
Blancos, Roberto *WhoWrEP 92*
Bland, Bob *St&PR 93*
Bland, Bobby 1930- *SoulM, WhoAm 92*
Bland, Charles *OxDcOp*
Bland, Edith Nesbit *ConAu 137, MajAI*
Bland, Edith Nesbit 1858-1924 *BioIn 17*
Bland, Edward Albert 1930- *WhoAm 92*
Bland, Edward Franklin 1901- *WhoAm 92*
Bland, Eveline Mae 1939- *WhoAmW 93*
Bland, Fabian *ConAu 137, MajAI*
Bland, Gilbert Tyrone 1955- *WhoSSW 93*
Bland, James 1798-1861 *OxDcOp*
Bland, James A. 1854-1911 *Baker 92*
Bland, Jane d1991 *BioIn 17*
Bland, Jay 1945- *ScF&FL 92*
Bland, Jeffrey Reid 1941- *WhoSSW 93*
Bland, John Hannam 1930- *WhoWor 93*
Bland, Margaret *AmWomPl*
Bland, Maria Theresa 1769-1838 *OxDcOp*
Bland, Mark M. 1958- *WhoSSW 93*
Bland, Peter George 1937- *St&PR 93, WhoAm 92*
Bland, Richard *Law&B 92*
Bland, Richard C. 1922- *St&PR 93*
Bland, Robert E. 1943- *St&PR 93*
Bland, Stephen S. 1960- *St&PR 93*

Bland, Terry D. Law&B 92
Bland, Thomas Richard, Jr. 1955- WhoEmL 93
Bland, William Marshall, Jr. 1922- WhoSSW 93
Bland, William W. 1907- St&PR 93
Bland, Yvonne Sacripant 1961- WhoAmW 93
Blanda, George 1927- BioIn 17
Blanda, George F. 1927- WhoAm 92
Blandau, Richard Julius 1911- WhoAm 92
Blandford, Marquess of 1955- BioIn 17
Blandford, Donald Joseph 1938- WhoAm 92, WhoSSW 93
Blandford, Donald W. 1946- St&PR 93
Blandford, Gregory McAdoo 1962- WhoEmL 93
Blandford, Roger David 1949- WhoAm 92
Blandford, Teresa J. St&PR 93
Blandin, Nanette Marie 1948- WhoEmL 93
Blandin, Patrick WhoScE 91-2
Blanding, Sandra Ann 1951 WhoEmL 93
Blandino, Ramon Arturo 1956- WhoE 93
Blandy, Doug(las E.) 1951- ConAu 138
Blandy, John Peter WhoScE 91-1
Blandy, William Henry George 1890-1954 HarEnMi
Blane, Amy Ann Cowan 1949- WhoAmW 93
Blane, Sally 1910- SweetSg B [port]
Blane, William Roy Law&B 92
Blaney, Connie Gayle 1955- WhoAmW 93
Blaney, Elizabeth Charlotte 1954- WhoAmW 93
Blaney, Geoffrey 1948- WhoEmL 93
Blaney, Harry Clay d1990 BioIn 17
Blaney, Harry Clay, III 1938- WhoE 93
Blaney, James Bernard 1961- WhoEmL 93
Blaney, Maureen T. Law&B 92
Blaney, Michael Law&B 92
Blaney, Thomas George 1941- WhoScE 91-1, WhoWor 93
Blaney-Tisbury, Alan Martin 1948- WhoWor 93
Blanford, John William 1940- St&PR 93, WhoAm 92
Blangiforti, Fino 1943- St&PR 93
Blangini, Felice 1781-1841 OxDcOp
Blangini, (Giuseppe Marco Maria) Felice 1781-1841 Baker 92
Blank, Allan 1925- Baker 92
Blank, Andrew Russell 1945- WhoSSW 93, WhoWor 93
Blank, Arthur M. 1942- WhoAm 92, WhoSSW 93
Blank, Benjamin 1929- St&PR 93, WhoAm 92
Blank, Blanche Davis WhoAm 92
Blank, Charles E. Law&B 92
Blank, Clair 1915-1965 BioIn 17
Blank, Cynthia Fisher 1925- WhoAm 92
Blank, David 1943- St&PR 93
Blank, Dennis Ray 1942- St&PR 93
Blank, Franklin 1921- WhoWrEP 92
Blank, H. Robert 1914- WhoAm 92
Blank, Harvey 1918- WhoAm 92
Blank, Howard E. 1909- St&PR 93
Blank, Howard Steven 1948- WhoE 93
Blank, Jack Maurice 1930- St&PR 93
Blank, Jan Antoni 1785-1884 PolBiDi
Blank, Jeremy Brendon St&PR 93
Blank, Joan Gill 1928- WhoAmW 93
Blank, John P. 1950- St&PR 93
Blank, Jonathan William 1960- WhoE 93, WhoEmL 93
Blank, Karen ScF&FL 92
Blank, Leo d1992 BioIn 17, NewYTBS 92
Blank, Leo Joseph 1917- St&PR 93
Blank, Leon W. 1932- St&PR 93
Blank, Les 1935- MiSFD 9
Blank, Marion Sue 1933- WhoAm 92
Blank, Mark B. 1954- WhoSSW 93
Blank, Martin 1933- WhoE 93
Blank, Martin J. 1947- St&PR 93
Blank, Matthew Charles BioIn 17
Blank, Melody Hollen 1956- WhoEmL 93
Blank, Melvin E. 1944- St&PR 93
Blank, Michael Lvovich 1954- WhoWor 93
Blank, Raymond Michael 1933- WhoE 93
Blank, Rebecca Margaret 1955- WhoEmL 93
Blank, Richard Glenn 1935- WhoSSW 93
Blank, Robert Gerhard 1942- St&PR 93
Blank, Robert Henry 1943- WhoAm 92
Blank, Robert P. Law&B 92
Blank, Rolf Georg 1948- WhoScE 91-4
Blank, Ronald M. 1947- St&PR 93
Blank, Steven Paul 1952- WhoE 93
Blank, Thomas Craig 1956- WhoEmL 93
Blank, Thomas Rannels 1952- WhoE 93
Blank, Walter 1930- WhoScE 91-3
Blank, Wanda WhoWrEP 92
Blanke, Jordan Matthew 1954- WhoEmL 93, WhoSSW 93
Blanke, Richard Donald 1940- WhoE 93
Blanke, Walter 1931- WhoScE 91-3
Blankemeyer, Robert H. 1946- St&PR 93
Blankenbaker, Robert E. Law&B 92
Blankenbaker, Ronald Gail 1941- WhoAm 92, WhoWor 93
Blankenbaker, Virginia Murphy 1933- WhoAmW 93
Blankenburg, Gunter 1931- WhoScE 91-3
Blankenburg, Judith B. 1933- WhoSSW 93
Blankenburg, Quirin van 1654-1739 Baker 92
Blankenburg, William Burl 1932- WhoAm 92
Blankenburg, Wolfgang 1928- WhoScE 91-3
Blankenhorn, David George, III 1955- WhoE 93
Blankenhorn, David Henry 1924- WhoAm 92
Blankenhorn, M. Barbara AmWomPl
Blankenhorn, Timothy Lee 1963- WhoSSW 93
Blankenship, Asa L. 1926- St&PR 93
Blankenship, Barbara Stewart 1949- WhoEmL 93, WhoSSW 93
Blankenship, Darla Kay 1963- WhoAmW 93
Blankenship, David Bruce 1949- St&PR 93
Blankenship, David L. 1951- St&PR 93
Blankenship, Edward G. 1943- WhoAm 92
Blankenship, Gilmer Leroy 1945- WhoAm 92
Blankenship, J. Randall 1953- WhoWrEP 92
Blankenship, John L. 1948- WhoWrEP 92
Blankenship, Joseph E. 1942- St&PR 93
Blankenship, Marie 1925- St&PR 93
Blankenship, Raymond Earl 1956- WhoEmL 93
Blankenship, Richard Eugene 1948- WhoEmL 93
Blankenship, Terry Lee 1945- WhoSSW 93
Blankenship, Wanda B. 1939- St&PR 93
Blankenship, William D. 1934- ScF&FL 92
Blankensopp, Diane Holt 1942- WhoSSW 93
Blanker, Charles H. 1951- St&PR 93
Blankers-Koen, Fanny 1918- BioIn 17
Blankert, John Joel 1935- WhoWor 93
Blankfield, Bryan J. Law&B 92
Blankfort, Lowell Arnold 1926- WhoWor 93
Blankfort, Michael 1907-1982 BioIn 17
Blankinship, Henry Massie 1942- WhoSSW 93, WhoWor 93
Blankinship, Kathleen Flo 1947- WhoAmW 93
Blankinship, Rachel Ann 1947- WhoAmW 93
Blankley, Walter Elwood 1935- St&PR 93, WhoAm 92, WhoE 93
Blankmeyer, Kurt Van Cleave Law&B 92
Blanks, Mary Ann Law&B 92
Blanks, Naomi Mai 1917- WhoAmW 93, WhoSSW 93
Blankson, Naadu I. BioIn 17
Blanksteen, Merrill B. 1953- St&PR 93
Blanning, Lyn AmWomPl
Blanpied, Pamela Wharton 1937- ScF&FL 92
Blanpied, William Antoine 1933- WhoE 93
Blanqui, Auguste 1805-1881 BioIn 17
Blanqui, Louis Auguste 1805-1881 BioIn 17
Blanscet, Glen Alan Law&B 92
Blanshei, Sarah Rubin 1938- WhoAm 92
Blanson, Vincent Price 1959- WhoEmL 93
Blanter, Matvei (Isaakovich) 1903- Baker 92
Blanton, Amelia Norman Law&B 92
Blanton, Bobbie Jean 1966- WhoSSW 93
Blanton, Edward Lee, Jr. 1931- WhoAm 92
Blanton, Fred, Jr. 1919- WhoSSW 93
Blanton, Graham Brinson 1935- St&PR 93
Blanton, Henry BioIn 17
Blanton, Hoover Clarence 1925- WhoAm 92, WhoSSW 93, WhoWor 93
Blanton, Jack Christopher 1935- WhoAm 92
Blanton, Jack S. 1927- St&PR 93
Blanton, Jack Sawtelle 1927- WhoAm 92
Blanton, Jack Sawtelle, Jr. 1953- St&PR 93
Blanton, James C. 1930- St&PR 93
Blanton, Jeremy 1939- WhoAm 92
Blanton, Jesse William 1923- St&PR 93
Blanton, Jimmy 1918-1942 Baker 92
Blanton, John Arthur 1928- WhoWor 93
Blanton, John Richard, Jr. 1946- WhoEmL 93
Blanton, Lawton Walter 1914- WhoE 93, WhoWor 93
Blanton, Nancy Eileen 1956- WhoSSW 93
Blanton, Patricia Louise 1941- WhoAmW 93, WhoWor 93
Blanton, Raymond 1950- St&PR 93
Blanton, Robert D'Alden 1943- WhoAm 92
Blanton, W. C. 1946- WhoEmL 93
Blanton, William N., III Law&B 92
Blanz, Robert Carl 1932- WhoAm 92
Blaramberg, Pavel (Ivanovich) 1841-1907 Baker 92
Blas, Alfred F. Law&B 92
Blasbalg, Larry B. St&PR 93
Blasbalg, Morton L. 1946- St&PR 93
Blasch, Howard F. 1928- WhoIns 93
Blasch, Robert Edward 1931- WhoSSW 93
Blaschke, Gottfried 1937- WhoScE 91-3
Blaschke, Lyn Rochelle 1961- WhoSSW 93
Blaschke, Renee Dhossche 1938- WhoSSW 93
Blasco, Alfred Joseph 1904- WhoAm 92
Blasco Ibanez, Vicente 1867-1928 BioIn 17
Blascovich, James Joseph 1946- WhoE 93
Blase, William Thomas 1949- WhoE 93, WhoEmL 93
Blasek, William Edward, III 1952- WhoE 93
Blaser, Cathy B. 1950- WhoWrEP 92
Blaser, J.P. WhoScE 91-4
Blaser, Kurt 1940- WhoWor 93
Blaser, Richard John 1946- St&PR 93
Blaser, Robin 1925- WhoCanL 92
Blaser, Werner 1924- ConAu 136
Blasgen, Sharon Walther Law&B 92
Blashfield, Evangeline Wilbour d1918 AmWomPl
Blashfield, Jean ScF&FL 92
Blashford-Snell, John Nicholas 1936- WhoWor 93
Blasi, Alberto 1931- WhoAm 92
Blasi, Christoph J. 1950- WhoWor 93
Blasi, Francesco 1937- WhoScE 91-3
Blasi, Rafe d1992 NewYTBS 92
Blasiak, James L. Law&B 92
Blasier, Cole 1925- WhoAm 92, WhoE 93
Blasier, John W. 1932- St&PR 93
Blasier, P.C. 1953- St&PR 93
Blasier, Peter Cole Law&B 92
Blasingame, Barbara Pyle 1941- St&PR 93
Blasingame, Benjamin Paul 1918- WhoAm 92
Blasingame, David Thomas 1947- WhoEmL 93
Blasingim, Mary B. Law&B 92
Blasios Of Amorion dc. 912 OxDcByz
Blasiotti, Robert Vincent 1949- WhoE 93
Blasius, Donald C. 1929- St&PR 93
Blasius, Donald Charles 1929- WhoAm 92
Blask, Christopher Ernst 1965- WhoEmL 93
Blaske, Steven A. Law&B 92
Blaskie, Henry Peter, Jr. 1934- St&PR 93
Blaskiewicz, John A. 1948- St&PR 93
Blaskiewicz, Kathleen St&PR 93
Blasko, Leonard 1939- St&PR 93
Blaskovic, Dionyz 1913- WhoWor 93
Blaskowitz, Johannes von 1883-1948 HarEnMi
Blasland, Warren Vincent, Jr. 1945- WhoE 93
Blasor, Scott Ellis 1949- St&PR 93
Blasor-Bernhardt, Donna Jo 1944- WhoWor 93
Blass, Bill BioIn 17
Blass, Bill 1922- WhoAm 92, WhoE 93
Blass, Gerhard Alois 1916- WhoAm 92, WhoWor 93, WhoWrEP 92
Blass, John Paul 1937- WhoAm 92
Blass, Marcus Gabriel 1950- WhoEmL 93
Blass, Noland, Jr. 1920- WhoAm 92
Blass, Paul Joseph 1943- St&PR 93
Blass, Walter Paul 1930- WhoE 93
Blass, William Errol 1937- WhoAm 92, WhoSSW 93
Blastares, Matthew dc. 1346 OxDcByz
Blaszczyk, Pawel WhoScE 91-4
Blatch, Mari Ann Rhodes 1941- St&PR 93
Blatch, Mary Ann Law&B 92
Blatchford, Samuel 1820-1893 OxCSupC [port]
Blatchley, Robert Leo Law&B 92
Blate, Michael 1938- WhoSSW 93
Blate, Samuel Robert 1944- WhoWrEP 92
Blatecky, Alan Rudolph 1946- WhoEmL 93, WhoSSW 93
Blatherwick, David Elliott Spiby 1941- WhoWor 93
Blatherwick, Gerald D. 1936- St&PR 93, WhoAm 92
Blathwayt, William 1649?-1717 BioIn 17
Blatner, Barbara Ann 1949- WhoWrEP 92
Blatner, Sherry Diane 1947- WhoEmL 93
Blatnik, John A. 1911-1991 BioIn 17
Blatnik, John A(nton) 1911-1991 CurBio 92N
Blatnik, Thais Frances 1919- WhoAmW 93
Blatny, Josef 1891-1980 Baker 92
Blatny, Pavel 1931- Baker 92
Blatt, Allison Quensen 1962- WhoEmL 93
Blatt, Beverly Faye 1944- WhoAm 92
Blatt, David William Eli 1949- WhoWor 93
Blatt, Edward A. 1905-1991 BioIn 17
Blatt, Ethel Shames 1931- WhoE 93
Blatt, Frantisek Tadeas 1793-1856 Baker 92
Blatt, Jeremiah Lion 1920- WhoSSW 93
Blatt, Lee N. 1928- St&PR 93
Blatt, Lola St&PR 93
Blatt, Melanie Judith 1946- WhoAmW 93
Blatt, Neil A. 1954- St&PR 93, WhoAm 92
Blatt, Richard Lee 1940- WhoAm 92
Blatt, S. Leslie 1935- WhoE 93
Blatt, Sidney I. 1921- St&PR 93
Blatt, Sidney Jules 1928- WhoAm 92
Blatt, Solomon, Jr. 1921- WhoAm 92
Blattberg, Robert Charles 1942- WhoAm 92
Blatteis, Clark Martin 1932- WhoSSW 93
Blattenberg, Robert C. 1919- WhoIns 93
Blatter, Frank Edward 1939- WhoAm 92
Blatter, William B. 1934- St&PR 93
Blatterman, Alan Lee 1948- WhoSSW 93
Blattman, H. Eugene 1936- St&PR 93
Blattmann, Margot Conrad WhoE 93
Blattner, Christopher J. 1943- St&PR 93
Blattner, Jeffrey Hirsh 1954- WhoEmL 93
Blattner, Joseph Lorne, Jr. 1945- St&PR 93, WhoAm 92
Blattner, Julie Meyer d1991 BioIn 17
Blattner, Meera McCuaig 1930- WhoAmW 93, WhoWor 93
Blattner, Robert, II d1992 NewYTBS 92
Blattner, Stephen Christian 1941- St&PR 93
Blatty, William Peter 1928- MiSFD 9, ScF&FL 92, WhoAm 92, WhoWrEP 92
Blatz, Laurie Lynn 1962- WhoEmL 93
Blatz, Linda Jeanne 1950- WhoAmW 93, WhoE 93, WhoEmL 93
Blau, Barry 1927- St&PR 93, WhoAm 92
Blau, Bruno 1881-1954 BioIn 17
Blau, Charles William 1943- WhoAm 92
Blau, E.L. St&PR 93
Blau, Edward B. d1991 BioIn 17
Blau, Francine Dee 1946- WhoAm 92, WhoEmL 93
Blau, Harvey Ronald 1935- WhoAm 92, WhoSSW 93
Blau, Helen Margaret 1948- WhoEmL 93
Blau, Jeffrey Alan 1951- WhoEmL 93
Blau, Joel 1945- ConAu 137
Blau, Joel Michael 1959- WhoEmL 93
Blau, Jonathon Law&B 92
Blau, Monte 1926- WhoAm 92
Blau, Murray 1921- St&PR 93
Blau, Peter Michael 1918- WhoAm 92, WhoSSW 93
Blau, Stanley M. 1937- St&PR 93
Blauensteiner, Albert 1949- WhoWor 93
Blauer, Charles L. 1929- St&PR 93
Blauert, Jens P. 1938- WhoScE 91-3, WhoWor 93
Blaufarb, Gerard Alan Law&B 92
Blaufox, Morton Donald 1934- WhoAm 92, WhoE 93
Blaufuss, David Ronald 1941- WhoE 93
Blaugrund, Clifford Earl 1945- St&PR 93
Blaugrund, Lee S. 1947- St&PR 93
Blaukopf, Kurt 1914- Baker 92
Blauner, Bob 1929- WhoAm 92
Blauner, Laurie Ann 1953- WhoWrEP 92
Blauner, Peter BioIn 17
Blauner, Peter 1959- ConAu 136
Blauschild, Doreen J. Law&B 92
Blaustein, Albert P. 1921- BioIn 17
Blaustein, Albert Paul 1921- WhoAm 92
Blaustein, Bruce Robert 1948- St&PR 93
Blaustein, Julian 1913- BioIn 17
Blaustein, Matthew I. 1955- St&PR 93
Blaustein, Mordecai P. 1935- WhoE 93
Blaustein, Morton K. d1990 BioIn 17
Blauvelt, Brian Mourrie 1956- WhoEmL 93
Blauvelt, John Clifford 1920- WhoAm 92
Blauvelt, Lillian Evans 1874-1947 Baker 92
Blauvelt, Melinda 1949- WhoAmW 93
Blauvelt, Ralph 1942- WhoWrEP 92
Blauvelt, Reginald T. d1991 BioIn 17
Blauw, Pieter Wilhelmus 1942- ConAu 137
Blauw, Wim ConAu 137
Blauwhoff, Matthieu Paul 1954- WhoWor 93
Blavat, Jerry 1940- WhoE 93
Blavet, Michel 1700-1768 Baker 92
Blaxland, Gregory 1778-1853 Expl 93
Blaxter, H. Vaughan, III Law&B 92
Blaxter, John H.S. 1929- WhoScE 91-1

Blaxter, Kenneth Lyon 1919- *WhoWor 93*
Blay, John E. *Law&B 92*
Blaydes, David Fairchild 1934- *WhoSSW 93*
Blaydes, James Elliott 1927- *WhoSSW 93*
Blaydes, Sophia Boyatzies 1933- *WhoAm 92, WhoSSW 93*
Blaydon, Colin Campbell 1940- *WhoAm 92*
Blaylock, Denny Alan 1946- *St&PR 93*
Blaylock, James P. 1950- *ScF&FL 92*
Blayn, Hugo *ScF&FL 92*
Blayton-Taylor, Betty 1937- *WhoE 93*
Blaz, Ben 1928- *CngDr 91, HispAmA [port], WhoAm 92*
Blazak, Paige Gayle 1947- *WhoE 93*
Blazakis, M. Chris *BioIn 17*
Blaze, Francois-Henri-Joseph 1784-1857 *Baker 92*
Blaze, Henri 1813-1888 *Baker 92*
Blazek, Doris Defibaugh 1943- *WhoAm 92*
Blazek, Douglas David 1941- *WhoWrEP 92*
Blazek, Frank E. *St&PR 93*
Blazek, Jizi 1923- *WhoWor 93*
Blazek, Joseph Lawrence 1957- *WhoWrEP 92*
Blazek, Wayne Joseph 1950- *WhoE 93, WhoEmL 93*
Blazek, Zdenek 1905-1988 *Baker 92*
Blazer, Dennis Wayne 1947- *St&PR 93*
Blazer, Sallie Marie 1957- *WhoAmW 93*
Blazewicz, Jacek 1951- *WhoScE 91-4*
Blazey, Mark Lee 1948- *WhoEmL 93*
Blazier, John Edward 1950- *WhoIns 93*
Blazin, Michael Joseph 1955- *WhoE 93*
Blazina, Janice Fay 1953- *WhoEmL 93*
Blazina, Vay John 1941- *WhoE 93*
Blazon, Denise G. 1952- *WhoAmW 93, WhoEmL 93*
Blazquez, Rafael *WhoScE 91-3*
Blazy, Diane Edith 1952- *WhoEmL 93*
Blazzard, Norse Novar 1937- *WhoAm 92*
Bleach, Gail Ann 1949- *WhoAmW 93*
Bleakley, Jim *BioIn 17*
Bleakley, Marjorie Sue 1921- *WhoAmW 93*
Bleakley, Peter Kimberley 1936- *WhoAm 92*
Bleam, Laura Jane *WhoE 93*
Bleasdale, Alan 1946- *ConTFT 10*
Bleau, Barbara Lee *WhoSSW 93*
Blech, Harry 1910- *Baker 92*
Blech, Leo 1871-1958 *Baker 92, IntDcOp, OxDcOp*
Blecha, Diane Louise 1949- *WhoAmW 93*
Blecha, Karl 1933- *WhoWor 93*
Blechar, Stephen T. 1941- *St&PR 93*
Blecharczyk, Stephanie Russell Adams 1935- *WhoE 93*
Blecher, Anthony Foster 1945- *St&PR 93*
Blecher, Melvin 1922- *WhoAm 92*
Blecher, Reuven Nota 1952- *WhoWor 93*
Blecher, Steven Donald 1942- *St&PR 93*
Blecher, Wilfried 1930- *BioIn 17*
Blechinger, Peter Hans 1939- *St&PR 93*
Blechman, Corey *MiSFD 9*
Blechman, R. O. 1930- *WhoAm 92*
Blechschmidt, Edward A. 1952- *St&PR 93*
Blechschmidt, Edward Allan 1952- *WhoAm 92*
Blechschmidt, Horst 1939- *WhoScE 91-3*
Bleck, Max Emil 1927- *WhoAm 92, WhoE 93*
Bleck, Phyllis Claire 1936- *WhoAmW 93*
Bleck, Virginia Eleanore 1929- *WhoAm 92, WhoAmW 93*
Blecker, Ira David *Law&B 92*
Blecker, Naomi Perle 1956- *WhoAmW 93*
Bleckert, Heinz Gerhard 1926- *WhoWor 93*
Bleckner, Edward, Jr. 1933- *St&PR 93, WhoAm 92*
Bleckner, Jeff 1943- *MiSFD 9*
Bleckner, Ross 1949- *BioIn 17*
Bledsoe, Ann Bishop 1950- *WhoAmW 93*
Bledsoe, Bryan Edward 1955- *WhoSSW 93*
Bledsoe, Garry Paul 1947- *St&PR 93*
Bledsoe, Gilbert H. 1940- *St&PR 93*
Bledsoe, Jane Kathryn 1937- *WhoAm 92, WhoAmW 93, WhoSSW 93*
Bledsoe, Janeva Leigh 1949- *WhoEmL 93*
Bledsoe, Jessie 1865-1951 *BioIn 17*
Bledsoe, Jules 1898-1943 *Baker 92, BioIn 17*
Bledsoe, June Elizabeth Jaycox 1958- *WhoEmL 93*
Bledsoe, Marilyn M. 1943- *WhoAmW 93*
Bledsoe, Matt d1876 *BioIn 17*
Bledsoe, Ralph Champion 1933- *WhoAm 92*
Bledsoe, Steven Roy *Law&B 92*
Bledsoe, Walter Arthur, Jr. 1916- *St&PR 93*
Bledsoe, Woodrow Wilson 1921- *WhoAm 92*
Bleecker, John Andrew, III 1951- *WhoEmL 93*
Bleecker, Theodore 1923- *WhoAm 92*
Bleehen, Norman Montague *WhoScE 91-1*
Bleeke, Joel Allen 1953- *WhoEmL 93*
Bleeker, J.A.M. *WhoScE 91-3*
Bleeker-Wagemakers, E.M. 1940- *WhoScE 91-3*
Bleetstein, Gary 1953- *St&PR 93*
Blegen, Bryce C. *Law&B 92*
Blegen, Judith 1940- *Baker 92*
Blegvad, Erik *BioIn 17*
Blegvad, Erik 1923- *MajAI [port]*
Blegvad, Lenore *BioIn 17*
Blehert, (Maurice) Dean 1942- *WhoWrEP 92*
Blei, Gary 1940- *St&PR 93*
Blei, Peter 1949- *St&PR 93*
Bleiberg, Robert Marvin 1924- *WhoAm 92, WhoWrEP 92*
Bleibtrey, Ethelda *BiDAMSp 1989*
Bleich, David 1936- *ScF&FL 92*
Bleich, David Lloyd 1943- *WhoAm 92*
Bleicher, Ann G. *Law&B 92*
Bleicher, Richard D. *Law&B 92*
Bleicher, Sheldon Joseph 1931- *WhoAm 92, WhoWor 93*
Bleichert, Adolf 1926- *WhoScE 91-3*
Bleichmann, Yuli 1868-1910 *Baker 92*
Bleidt, Barry Anthony 1951- *WhoEmL 93, WhoSSW 93*
Bleier, Michael E. *Law&B 92*
Bleier, Richard M. 1913-1990 *BioIn 17*
Bleier, Robert Patrick 1946- *BiDAMSp 1989*
Bleier, Rocky *BioIn 17*
Bleifeld, Stanley 1924- *WhoAm 92*
Bleiler, E.F. 1920- *ScF&FL 92*
Bleiler, Everett Franklin 1920- *WhoAm 92*
Bleiler, Richard 1959- *ScF&FL 92*
Bleiman, Junius Jay d1991 *BioIn 17*
Bleiman, Wendy Anne *Law&B 92*
Bleimann, Alexander A. 1918- *WhoE 93*
Bleimann, Karl Richard 1934- *St&PR 93*
Bleitner, Gary D. 1954- *St&PR 93*
Bleiweiss, Herbert Irving 1931- *WhoAm 92, WhoWrEP 92*
Bleiweiss, Irene 1960- *WhoEmL 93*
Bleiweiss, Robert Morton 1934- *WhoAm 92*
Blem, Charles Robert 1943- *WhoSSW 93*
Blem, Joe L. 1936- *St&PR 93*
Blemaster, Norman Lee 1940- *St&PR 93*
Blemmydes, Nikephoros 1197-c. 1269 *OxDcByz*
Blencowe, Paul Sherwood 1953- *WhoAm 92, WhoWor 93*
Blenderman, Ronald J. 1927- *St&PR 93*
Blendl, Heribert Michael 1927- *WhoScE 91-3*
Blendon, Robert Jay 1942- *WhoAm 92*
Blendy, Michael M. 1946- *St&PR 93*
Blenis, Barry G. 1943- *St&PR 93*
Blenke, Heinz 1920- *WhoScE 91-3*
Blenke, John Walter, Jr. *Law&B 92*
Blenkinsop, Gordon Penrhyn 1931- *WhoAsAP 91*
Blenko, Richard Deakin 1953- *St&PR 93*
Blenko, Walter John, Jr. 1926- *WhoE 93*
Blenko, William H., Jr. 1921- *St&PR 93*
Blenman, Laura Ruth 1947- *WhoAmW 93*
Blennemann, Friedhelm 1943- *WhoScE 91-3*
Blenner, Leslie Kay 1959- *WhoAmW 93*
Blenner, Susan Mary 1953- *WhoAmW 93*
Blennerhassett, Margaret Agnew 1773?-1842 *BioIn 17*
Blesch, Christopher John 1958- *WhoEmL 93*
Blesch, Robert William 1959- *WhoEmL 93*
Bleser, Joseph G. 1945- *WhoAm 92*
Bleser, Rita Elizabeth *Law&B 92*
Blesius, Rita Fae 1948- *WhoAmW 93*
Bless, Robert Charles 1927- *WhoAm 92*
Bless, Robert Richard 1965- *WhoSSW 93*
Blessed Virgin Mary, Saint *BioIn 17*
Blessen, Karen *WhoAm 92, WhoAmW 93*
Blessey, Walter Emanuel, Jr. 1944- *WhoSSW 93*
Blessing, Carole Anne 1945- *WhoAmW 93*
Blessing, Charles A. d1992 *NewYTBS 92*
Blessing, Donald Carl 1955- *WhoEmL 93*
Blessing, Edward Warfield 1936- *WhoAm 92, WhoSSW 93, WhoWor 93*
Blessing, Gene S. 1939- *St&PR 93*
Blessing, Gene Swart 1939- *WhoSSW 93*
Blessing, Gerald Vincent 1942- *WhoE 93*
Blessing, Scott Francis 1957- *WhoE 93, WhoEmL 93*
Blessinger, Karl 1888-1962 *Baker 92*
Blessing-Moore, Joann Catherine 1946- *WhoEmL 93*
Blethen, David Lawrence 1959- *WhoEmL 93*
Blethen, Frank A. 1945- *WhoAm 92*
Blethen, Harold Tyler, III 1945- *WhoSSW 93*
Blethen, John *Law&B 92*
Blethen, William Kingsley, Jr. 1945- *St&PR 93*
Bleumink, Eric 1935- *WhoScE 91-3*
Bleveans, John 1938- *WhoAm 92, WhoWor 93*
Blevins, Andy d1887 *BioIn 17*
Blevins, Anne Helen 1908- *WhoE 93*
Blevins, Bradley Edward 1960- *WhoEmL 93*
Blevins, Bryan O'Donnell 1939- *WhoSSW 93*
Blevins, Carolyn DeArmond 1936- *WhoSSW 93*
Blevins, Charles Russell 1942- *WhoSSW 93*
Blevins, Charlie R. 1921- *St&PR 93*
Blevins, Gary Lynn 1941- *WhoAm 92*
Blevins, James Ray 1949- *WhoEmL 93*
Blevins, James V. 1912- *St&PR 93*
Blevins, Jeffrey Alexander 1955- *WhoEmL 93*
Blevins, Jerry R. 1946- *St&PR 93*
Blevins, Karla *BioIn 17*
Blevins, Larry Joe 1952- *WhoSSW 93*
Blevins, William Edward 1927- *St&PR 93, WhoAm 92*
Bleviss, Alan David 1941- *WhoE 93*
Bleviss, Morris 1942- *St&PR 93*
Blewer, John MacGregor d1991 *BioIn 17*
Blewett, Carolyn Sue 1941- *WhoAmW 93*
Blewett, John Paul 1910- *WhoAm 92*
Blewett, Neal 1933- *WhoAsAP 91*
Blewett, Patrick Bernard 1928- *WhoAm 92*
Blewett, Robert Noall 1915- *WhoAm 92*
Blewett, Stephen Douglas 1942- *WhoWrEP 92*
Blewitt, George Augustine 1937- *WhoAm 92*
Blewitt, J. Justin, Jr. *Law&B 92*
Blewitt, Jonathan 1782-1853 *Baker 92, OxDcOp*
Blewitt, Richard Francis 1947- *WhoEmL 93*
Bley, Carla *BioIn 17*
Bley, Carla 1938- *ConMus 8 [port]*
Bley, Carla Borg 1938- *WhoAm 92*
Bley, Elmer O. 1936- *St&PR 93*
Bley, Joseph Russell, Jr. *Law&B 92*
Bleyberg, Maria Zamfir 1938- *WhoAmW 93*
Bleyen, Luc-Jean 1956- *WhoWor 93*
Bleyer, Georg 1647?-c. 1694 *Baker 92*
Bleyer, Nicolaus 1591-1658 *Baker 92*
Bleyle, John A. 1944- *WhoIns 93*
Bleyle, John Allen 1944- *St&PR 93*
Bleyle, Karl 1880-1969 *Baker 92*
Bleyman, Lea Kanner 1936- *WhoE 93*
Bleznick, Donald William 1924- *WhoAm 92*
Blicher, Adolph 1907- *WhoE 93*
Blicher, Bert 1943- *St&PR 93, WhoAm 92*
Blichert-Toft, Mogens 1936- *WhoScE 91-2*
Blick, Ambler Montquire 1947- *WhoE 93*
Blick, Freda Lulf 1946- *WhoUN 92*
Blick, Kenneth Edward 1944- *WhoSSW 93*
Blickens, Robert P. 1948- *St&PR 93*
Blickenstaff, Bradley Smith 1929- *St&PR 93*
Blickenstaff, Nancy Lou Diviney 1935- *WhoAmW 93*
Blickle, Tibor 1931- *WhoScE 91-4*
Blickman, Bernard d1991 *BioIn 17*
Blicksilver, Edith 1926- *WhoSSW 93*
Blickwede, Donald Johnson 1920- *WhoAm 92*
Blide, Todd David Foster 1959- *WhoEmL 93*
Blieberg, Helene Andrea 1955- *WhoEmL 93*
Bliedung, Dorothea *AmWomPl*
Bliek, Leendert M. 1940- *WhoScE 91-3*
Blier, Bernard 1916-1989 *IntDcF 2-3 [port]*
Blier, Bertrand *BioIn 17*
Blier, Bertrand 1939- *MiSFD 9*
Bligh, Jasmine 1913-1991 *AnObit 1991*
Bligh, William 1754-1817 *BioIn 17, HarEnMi*
Blight, Margaret Mary *WhoScE 91-1*
Blight, Philip Arthur *WhoScE 91-1*
Blight, Samuel S. *Law&B 92*
Bliley, John Earle 1919- *St&PR 93*
Bliley, Mark A. 1958- *St&PR 93*
Bliley, Thomas J., Jr. 1932- *CngDr 91*
Bliley, Thomas Jerome, Jr. 1932- *WhoAm 92, WhoSSW 93*
Blim, Richard Don 1927- *WhoAm 92*
Blind, MaryAnn 1947- *WhoAmW 93*
Blind, William Charles 1911- *St&PR 93, WhoAm 92*
Blinde, Gene A. 1944- *St&PR 93*
Blinder, Abe Lionel 1909- *WhoAm 92*
Blinder, Eduardo R. 1951- *WhoUN 92*
Blinder, James F. 1934- *St&PR 93*
Blinder, Mark Fisher 1948- *St&PR 93*
Blinder, Martin S. 1946- *St&PR 93, WhoAm 92, WhoEmL 93*
Blinder, Meyer *BioIn 17*
Blinder, Richard Lewis 1935- *WhoAm 92*
Blinder, Robert *Law&B 92*
Blinder, Rosalind Kaplan 1945- *WhoAmW 93*
Blinder, Seymour Michael 1932- *WhoAm 92*
Blinder, Stuart M. 1950- *St&PR 93*
Blindheim, Sandra Lee 1942- *WhoAmW 93*
Blind Tom *Baker 92*
Blinka, Gary Lane 1941- *St&PR 93*
Blinken, Donald 1925- *WhoAm 92*
Blinken, Robert J. 1929- *St&PR 93*
Blinken, Robert James 1929- *WhoAm 92*
Blinkoff, Sharon *Law&B 92*
Blinks, John Rogers 1931- *WhoAm 92*
Blinn, Linda Segal *Law&B 92*
Blinn, Stephen M. 1947- *St&PR 93*
Blinn, William 1937- *ConTFT 10*
Blish, James 1921-1975 *BioIn 17, ScF&FL 92*
Blish, Nelson Adrian *Law&B 92*
Blishen, Edward 1920- *BioIn 17, ChlFicS, ScF&FL 92*
Bliss, Anthony 1913-1991 *AnObit 1991*
Bliss, Anthony Addison 1913-1991 *BioIn 17*
Bliss, Arthur 1891-1975 *OxDcOp*
Bliss, Arthur (Edward Drummond) 1891-1975 *Baker 92*
Bliss, Carol Louise 1949- *WhoE 93*
Bliss, Charles M. 1904-1991 *BioIn 17*
Bliss, Corinne Demas 1947- *WhoWrEP 92*
Bliss, David James 1942- *WhoAm 92*
Bliss, Eric Marshall 1960- *WhoSSW 93*
Bliss, G.R. 1931- *St&PR 93*
Bliss, Harry F. d1990 *BioIn 17*
Bliss, James C. 1933- *St&PR 93*
Bliss, Jerry Evan 1949- *WhoEmL 93*
Bliss, Kathleen *BioIn 17*
Bliss, Lawrence Carroll 1929- *WhoAm 92*
Bliss, Nancy E. 1945- *WhoAmW 93*
Bliss, P. Paul 1872-1933 *Baker 92*
Bliss, Philip Paul 1838-1876 *Baker 92*
Bliss, Ray C. 1907-1981 *PolPar*
Bliss, Richard Donald 1947- *WhoEmL 93*
Bliss, Robert Harms 1940- *WhoAm 92*
Bliss, Robert Lewis 1921- *WhoAm 92*
Bliss, Rodney David, III 1942- *WhoIns 93*
Bliss, Roland Boyd 1934- *St&PR 93*
Bliss, Ronald Gene 1942- *WhoWrEP 92*
Bliss, Sidney H. 1947- *St&PR 93*
Bliss, Stanley Michael 1939- *St&PR 93*
Bliss, Tasker Howard 1853-1930 *CmdGen 1991 [port], HarEnMi*
Bliss, William E. 1936- *St&PR 93*
Bliss, William Stanley, Jr. 1932- *WhoAm 92*
Blissert, Julie Harrison 1954- *WhoE 93, WhoEmL 93*
Blissett, William Frank 1921- *WhoAm 92*
Blissitt, Patricia Ann 1953- *WhoAmW 93, WhoEmL 93, WhoSSW 93, WhoWor 93*
Blitch, Iris Faircloth 1912- *BioIn 17*
Blitch, James Buchanan 1923- *WhoAm 92*
Blitch, Ronald Buchanan 1953- *WhoSSW 93*
Blitheman, John c. 1525-1591 *Baker 92*
Blitman, Bruce Alan 1956- *WhoEmL 93*
Blitman, Howard Norton 1926- *WhoAm 92*
Blitshteyn, Mark 1950- *St&PR 93*
Blitstein, Barry 1938- *St&PR 93*
Blitz, Daniel 1920- *WhoE 93*
Blitz, Gerard 1912-1990 *BioIn 17*
Blitz, Peggy Sanderfur 1940- *WhoAmW 93*
Blitz, Stephen M. 1941- *WhoAm 92*
Blitzer, Andrew 1946- *WhoAm 92, WhoE 93, WhoEmL 93*
Blitzer, Charles 1927- *WhoAm 92*
Blitzer, David Mayers 1948- *St&PR 93, WhoE 93*
Blitzer, Wolf *BioIn 17*
Blitzer, Wolf 1948- *ConAu 136*
Blitzstein, Marc 1905-1964 *Baker 92, IntDcOp, OxDcOp*
Bliven, Bruce, Jr. 1916- *WhoAm 92, WhoE 93, WhoWrEP 92*
Bliven, Naomi 1925- *WhoAm 92*
Blivess, Michael P. 1947- *WhoIns 93*
Bliwas, Ronald Lee 1942- *WhoAm 92*
Bliwise, Lester Martin 1945- *WhoAm 92*
Blix, Hans Martin 1928- *WhoUN 92, WhoWor 93*
Blixen, Karen 1885-1962 *BioIn 17*
Blixen-Finecke, Bror, baron von 1886-1946 *BioIn 17*
Blixt, Charles A. *Law&B 92*
Blizard, Marjorie Claire 1950- *WhoAmW 93*
Blizkovsky, Milan 1934- *WhoScE 91-4*

Bliznakov, Emile George 1926- WhoAm 92, WhoSSW 93
Bliznakov, Georgi Manuilov 1920- WhoScE 91-4
Bliznakov, Milka Tcherneva 1927- WhoAm 92, WhoAmW 93
Blizorukov, Michail Gennadievich 1958- WhoWor 93
Blizzard, Alan 1939- WhoAm 92
Blizzard, Henry Wallace 1940- WhoSSW 93
Blizzard, Richard Tyrone 1947- WhoE 93
Blizzard, Robert M. 1924- WhoAm 92
Blobel, Gunter 1936- WhoAm 92
Blobel, Hans Georg 1929- WhoScE 91-3
Bloch, Alan 1915- WhoE 93
Bloch, Alan L. 1930- St&PR 93
Bloch, Alan Neil 1932- WhoAm 92, WhoE 93
Bloch, Andre 1873-1960 Baker 92
Bloch, Andrea Lynn 1952- WhoAm 92, WhoAmW 93, WhoEmL 93
Bloch, Antoine 1938- WhoWor 93
Bloch, Augustyn 1929- PolBiDi
Bloch, Augustyn (Hippolit) 1929- Baker 92
Bloch, Barbara Joyce 1925- WhoAmW 93, WhoWrEP 92
Bloch, Bertram 1892-1987 ScF&FL 92
Bloch, Daniel 1938- WhoScE 91-2
Bloch, Douglas 1949- ConAu 138
Bloch, Douglas George 1949- WhoWrEP 92
Bloch, Elmer M. d1990 BioIn 17
Bloch, Eric 1928- WhoE 93
Bloch, Erich BioIn 17
Bloch, Erich 1925- WhoAm 92
Bloch, Ernest 1880-1959 Baker 92, IntDcOp, OxDcOp
Bloch, Ernest 1921- WhoAm 92
Bloch, Felix S. BioIn 17
Bloch, Henry Wollman 1922- BioIn 17, St&PR 93, WhoAm 92, WhoWor 93
Bloch, Herman S. 1912-1990 BioIn 17
Bloch, Howard M. 1927- St&PR 93
Bloch, J. Thomas 1938- St&PR 93
Bloch, Jeffrey Marlon Law&B 92
Bloch, Julia Chang 1942- WhoAm 92, WhoAmW 93, WhoE 93, WhoWor 93
Bloch, Konrad Emil 1912- WhoAm 92, WhoWor 93
Bloch, Kurt Julius 1929- WhoAm 92
Bloch, Lester Bernard 1930- St&PR 93
Bloch, Marc 1886-1944 BioIn 17
Bloch, Marie Halun 1910- DcAmChF 1960, WhoAmW 93
Bloch, Martin B. 1935- St&PR 93, WhoAm 92
Bloch, Milton Joseph 1937- WhoAm 92
Bloch, Moise B. 1907- St&PR 93
Bloch, Patrick 1942- WhoScE 91-2
Bloch, Paul 1939- WhoAm 92
Bloch, Peter 1921- WhoE 93
Bloch, Rene M. 1923- WhoWor 93
Bloch, Richard A. 1926- BioIn 17
Bloch, Richard Isaac 1943- WhoAm 92
Bloch, Robert 1917- BioIn 17, ScF&FL 92
Bloch, Robert Albert 1917- WhoAm 92, WhoWrEP 92
Bloch, Suzanne 1907- Baker 92
Bloch, Thomas Anthony 1939- WhoWor 93
Bloch, Thomas M. 1954- St&PR 93
Blocher, Kenyon Raymond 1937- St&PR 93
Blocher, Robert Moulton 1933- St&PR 93
Bloch-Laine, Francois 1912- BioIn 17
Block, Alan Jay 1938- WhoAm 92
Block, Allan James 1954- WhoAm 92
Block, Alvin V. 1926- St&PR 93
Block, Amanda Roth 1912- WhoAm 92
Block, Arnold 1927- St&PR 93
Block, Arthur R. Law&B 92
Block, Barry Herbert 1949- WhoE 93
Block, Bob ScF&FL 92
Block, Bruce MiSFD 9
Block, Curtis 1938- St&PR 93
Block, Dennis B. 1940- St&PR 93
Block, Dennis Jeffery 1942- WhoAm 92
Block, Diane Zuern 1946- WhoAmW 93
Block, Donald 1936- St&PR 93
Block, Doug MiSFD 9
Block, Edward Martel 1927- WhoAm 92
Block, Emil Nathaniel, Jr. 1930- WhoAm 92
Block, Eric 1942- WhoAm 92
Block, Eva Sully d1990 BioIn 17
Block, Francesca Lia 1962- ScF&FL 92
Block, Francine Ellen 1947- WhoE 93
Block, Franklin Lee 1936- WhoSSW 93
Block, Gary Brooks 1964- WhoE 93
Block, Gene David 1948- WhoAm 92
Block, Gene R. 1937- St&PR 93
Block, George Edward 1926- WhoAm 92
Block, Harvey 1924- St&PR 93
Block, Haskell Mayer 1923- WhoAm 92
Block, Herbert 1909- JrnUS
Block, Herbert Lawrence 1909- BioIn 17, WhoAm 92, WhoE 93
Block, Hermann WhoScE 91-1
Block, Ilene Goldstein Law&B 92
Block, Isaac Edward 1924- WhoAm 92, WhoWor 93
Block, James BioIn 17
Block, James P. 1930- St&PR 93
Block, Janet Leven WhoAmW 93
Block, Jay Lloyd d1990 BioIn 17
Block, Jeanne H. 1923-1981 BioIn 17
Block, Jochen H. 1929- WhoScE 91-3
Block, John Douglas 1948- St&PR 93, WhoAm 92
Block, John Robinson 1954- St&PR 93, WhoAm 92, WhoE 93
Block, John Rusling 1935- WhoAm 92
Block, Joseph K. 1955- St&PR 93
Block, Joseph L. 1902-1992 NewYTBS 92 [port]
Block, Jules Richard 1930- WhoAm 92
Block, Julian 1934- WhoWrEP 92
Block, Karen Joyce 1960- WhoEmL 93
Block, Kenneth L. 1920- St&PR 93
Block, Lawrence 1938- WhoAm 92, WhoWrEP 92
Block, Leonard N. 1911- St&PR 93
Block, Leonard Nathan 1911- WhoAm 92
Block, Leslie C. 1945- St&PR 93
Block, Linda Elizabeth 1934- WhoAmW 93
Block, Louis Stuart 1947- WhoEmL 93, WhoSSW 93
Block, Lynne Wood 1943- WhoAmW 93
Block, Macy T. St&PR 93
Block, Manfred Stemmer Law&B 92
Block, Marc Sandy Law&B 92
Block, Marguerite Beck 1889- AmWomPl
Block, Mary Ann 1945- WhoSSW 93
Block, Maxinne AmWomPl
Block, Melvin August 1921- WhoAm 92
Block, Michael I. 1956- WhoIns 93
Block, Michael Kent 1942- WhoAm 92, WhoWor 93
Block, Michael S. 1945- St&PR 93
Block, Michel 1937- Baker 92
Block, Murray Harold 1924- WhoAm 92
Block, Myrna 1946- St&PR 93
Block, Myron W. 1947- St&PR 93
Block, Ned 1942- WhoAm 92
Block, Nelson Richard 1951- WhoEmL 93
Block, Pamela Jo 1947- WhoAmW 93, WhoEmL 93
Block, Paul St&PR 93
Block, Philip Dee, III 1937- WhoAm 92
Block, Pierre 1940- WhoScE 91-2
Block, Radean G. 1938- St&PR 93
Block, Ralph A. 1936- St&PR 93
Block, Richard Earl 1931- WhoAm 92, WhoWor 93
Block, Richard Raphael 1938- WhoE 93, WhoWor 93
Block, Robert B. Law&B 92
Block, Robert Charles 1929- WhoAm 92
Block, Robert I. 1951- WhoWor 93
Block, Robert Jackson 1922- WhoAm 92, WhoWor 93
Block, Robert Michael 1947- WhoEmL 93, WhoSSW 93
Block, Ruth 1930- WhoAm 92
Block, Ruth S. 1930- St&PR 93
Block, S. Lester 1917- WhoAm 92
Block, Simon Anthony Allen 1935- WhoWor 93
Block, Stanley Marlin 1922- WhoAm 92
Block, Stephen A. St&PR 93
Block, Stephen Andrew Law&B 92
Block, Steven Robert 1955- WhoAm 92
Block, Thomas H. 1945- ScF&FL 92
Block, Thomas M. 1954- WhoAm 92
Block, Thomas Ray 1953- WhoEmL 93
Block, Walter (Edward) 1941- WhoWrEP 92
Block, William 1915- St&PR 93, WhoAm 92, WhoE 93
Block, William Karl, Jr. 1944- WhoAm 92
Block, William Kenneth 1950- WhoE 93, WhoWor 93
Block, Zenas 1916- WhoAm 92
Blocker, DeeDee BioIn 17
Blocker, Helmut 1945- WhoScE 91-3
Blocker, Riddick Richard, III 1961- WhoSSW 93
Blocker, Robert Lewis 1946- WhoAm 92
Blocker-Hunter, Margaret 1927- WhoAmW 93
Blockhus, Wanda A. BioIn 17
Blockley, David Ian WhoScE 91-1
Blocksma, Mary 1942- WhoWrEP 92
Blockx, Jan 1851-1912 Baker 92, OxDcOp
Blodek, Vilem 1834-1874 OxDcOp
Blodek, Wilhelm 1834-1874 Baker 92
Blodgett, Anne Washington 1940- WhoAm 92
Blodgett, E.D. 1935- WhoCanL 92
Blodgett, Eleanor D. 1896-1990 BioIn 17
Blodgett, Forrest Clinton 1927- WhoWor 93
Blodgett, Frank Caleb 1927- WhoAm 92
Blodgett, Karen Pisc: tta 1958- WhoAmW 93
Blodgett, Mark Stephen 1954- WhoSSW 93
Blodgett, Mark Wentworth 1957- WhoEmL 93
Blodgett, Omer William 1917- WhoAm 92
Blodgett, Todd Alan 1960- WhoE 93
Blodgett, Vernon L., Jr. 1946- St&PR 93
Blodgett, Warren Terrell 1923- WhoAm 92
Blodgett, William Arthur 1937- WhoAm 92
Bloebaum, William Douglas, Jr. 1939- St&PR 93
Bloede, Merle Huie 1921- WhoE 93
Bloede, Victor Carl 1917- WhoAm 92
Bloede, Victor Gustav 1920- WhoAm 92, WhoWor 93
Bloedel, Kurt Robert Law&B 92
Bloem, James H. 1950- St&PR 93
Bloembergen, Nicolaas 1920- WhoAm 92, WhoE 93, WhoWor 93
Bloemendaal, Dirk C. Law&B 92
Bloemendaal, Marilyn Kay 1945- WhoAmW 93
Bloemendal, Lee Charles 1943- WhoSSW 93
Bloemer, Rosemary Celeste 1930- WhoWor 93
Bloemsma, Marco Paul 1924- WhoWor 93
Bloes, Richard Kenneth 1951- WhoE 93
Bloesch, Maureen Lee 1942- WhoAmW 93
Blogna, Charles 1928- St&PR 93
Blohm, Douglas L. 1953- St&PR 93
Blok, Regina Dyanne Kulzer 1951- WhoEmL 93
Blokhin, Nikolai Nikolaevitch 1912- WhoWor 93
Blokhuis, Harry J. 1955- WhoScE 91-3
Bloksberg, Fran Ellen 1957- WhoE 93
Bloland, Paul Anson 1923- WhoAm 92
Blom, Anders Fredrik 1955- WhoWor 93
Blom, Daniel C. 1919- St&PR 93
Blom, Daniel Charles 1919- WhoAm 92, WhoIns 93
Blom, Donald, Jr. 1944- St&PR 93
Blom, Eric (Walter) 1888-1959 Baker 92
Blom, Frans 1893-1963 IntDcAn
Blom, Gaston Eugene 1920- WhoAm 92
Blom, Gertrude Duby 1901- IntDcAn
Blom, J.L. 1938- WhoScE 91-3
Blom, Jack 1927- St&PR 93
Blom, Johannes 1928- WhoE 93
Blom, Nicole Jan 1958- WhoAm 92
Blom, Richard Frederick 1932- WhoE 93
Blomback, Erik Gustaf Birger 1926- WhoScE 91-4
Blomback, Margareta 1925- WhoScE 91-4
Blomberg, Erik 1922- Baker 92
Blomberg, Robert N. 1956- WhoEmL 93
Blomberg, Werner von 1878-1943 HarEnMi
Blomberg, Werner von 1878-1946 BioIn 17
Blombery, Peter Alexander 1947- WhoWor 93
Blomdahl, Karl-Birger 1916-1968 Baker 92, IntDcOp, OxDcOp
Blome, Anthony E. 1935- St&PR 93
Blomen, Leo Josef Maria Joannes 1955- WhoWor 93
Blomfield, Muriel May 1948- WhoAmW 93
Blomgren, Bruce Holmes 1945- WhoAm 92, WhoSSW 93
Blomgren, Ronald Walter 1934- WhoE 93
Blomhoff, Rune 1955- WhoWor 93
Blomker-Manucci, Doris Kathryn 1955- WhoAmW 93
Blommer, Henry 1906- St&PR 93
Blomquist, Bernard L. 1926- St&PR 93
Blomquist, Carl Arthur 1947- WhoWor 93
Blomquist, Carl Gunnar 1931- WhoAm 92
Blomquist, David Wels 1956- WhoEmL 93
Blomquist, Ernest R., III 1946- WhoAm 92
Blomquist, Harold A. 1952- St&PR 93
Blomquist, Jan 1941- WhoScE 91-4
Blomquist, Jane Ann 1958- WhoAmW 93
Blomquist, Richard Frederick 1912- WhoAm 92
Blomquist, Richard T. 1952- St&PR 93
Blomquist, Robert Oscar 1930- St&PR 93, WhoAm 92
Blomstedt, Herbert 1927- BioIn 17
Blomstedt, Herbert (Thorson) 1927- Baker 92, WhoAm 92, WhoWor 93
Blomstedt, Robert Kent 1931- WhoAm 92
Blomstrom, Bruce A. 1937- St&PR 93
Blomstrom, John Joseph Law&B 92
Blomstrom, Magnus Conrad 1952- WhoWor 93
Blon, Franz von 1861-1945 Baker 92
Blondeau, Dominique 1942- WhoCanL 92
Blondeau, Jacques Patrick Adrien 1944- WhoWor 93
Blondeau, Pierre-Auguste-Louis 1784-1865 Baker 92
Blondek, John 1943- St&PR 93
Blondel, Marc 1938- BioIn 17
Blondel, Michel 1940- WhoScE 91-2
Blondel, Nathalie 1960- ConAu 138
Blondell, Joan 1909-1979 IntDcF 2-3 [port]
Blonder, Lloyd 1939- St&PR 93
Blondin, Ethel D. 1951- WhoAmW 93
Blondin, Nancy Sue 1957- WhoAmW 93
Blonski, Kerry Christopher 1962- WhoSSW 93
Blonsky, Stephen Lawrence 1955- WhoE 93
Blonstein, Marshall St&PR 93
Blonston, Gary Lee 1942- WhoAm 92
Blood, Antoinette Marie 1941- WhoAmW 93, WhoE 93
Blood, Archer Kent 1923- WhoAm 92
Blood, Edward Linford 1945- St&PR 93, WhoAm 92
Blood, Johnny 1904-1985 BioIn 17
Blood, Karen Angela 1959- WhoEmL 93
Blood, Marilyn Kay 1942- WhoAmW 93
Blood, Opal Sue 1939- WhoWrEP 92
Blood, Peter WhoScE 91-1
Blood, Thomas Hanson 1957- WhoEmL 93
BloodBaker, Kimberly Sue 1964- WhoEmL 93
Bloodstone SoulM
Bloodworth, Albert William Franklin 1935- WhoAm 92, WhoSSW 93, WhoWor 93
Bloodworth, Donald A. 1956- St&PR 93
Bloodworth, Gerald B. 1936- St&PR 93
Bloodworth, J. M. Bartow, Jr. 1925- WhoAm 92
Bloodworth, Linda ConTFT 10
Bloodworth, William Andrew, Jr. 1942- WhoAm 92
Bloodworth-Thomason, Linda BioIn 17
Bloodworth-Thomason, Linda 1947?- ConTFT 10
Bloodworth-Thomason, Linda 1948- WhoAm 92, WhoAmW 93
Bloom, A. William 1923- St&PR 93
Bloom, Alan Law&B 92
Bloom, Alan 1945- St&PR 93, WhoAm 92
Bloom, Alfred Howard 1946- WhoAm 92, WhoE 93
Bloom, Allan 1930- WhoAm 92
Bloom, Allan 1930-1992 NewYTBS 92
Bloom, Allan (David) 1930- WhoWrEP 92
Bloom, Allan (David) 1930-1992 ConAu 139, CurBio 92N
Bloom, Allen Law&B 92
Bloom, Allen J. 1935- St&PR 93
Bloom, Arnold S. Law&B 92
Bloom, Arnold Sanford 1942- WhoAm 92
Bloom, Arthur Leslie WhoScE 91-1
Bloom, Barry Malcolm 1928- St&PR 93, WhoAm 92
Bloom, Benjamin Harris 1946- WhoEmL 93
Bloom, Bernard 1912- St&PR 93
Bloom, Britton ScF&FL 92
Bloom, Bryan Scott 1955- WhoEmL 93
Bloom, C. Hugh 1933- St&PR 93
Bloom, Charles Andrew 1952- WhoSSW 93
Bloom, Claire 1931- IntDcF 2-3, WhoAm 92
Bloom, Clive 1953- ScF&FL 92
Bloom, D. A. 1958- WhoE 93
Bloom, Dan A. St&PR 93
Bloom, David Edward 1938- WhoE 93
Bloom, David Myron 1928- WhoSSW 93
Bloom, David Ronald 1943- WhoAm 92
Bloom, Debby Lee Whitehill 1955- WhoAmW 93
Bloom, Deborah M. Law&B 92
Bloom, Donald Eugene 1928- WhoIns 93
Bloom, Edward Alan 1914- WhoAm 92, WhoWrEP 92
Bloom, Edwin John, Jr. 1931- WhoAm 92
Bloom, Eugene Charles 1933- WhoWor 93
Bloom, Floyd Elliott 1936- WhoAm 92
Bloom, Frank 1937- WhoAm 92
Bloom, George I. d1991 BioIn 17
Bloom, Harold 1930- BioIn 17, ConAu 39NR, JeAmHC, ScF&FL 92, WhoAm 92, WhoWrEP 92
Bloom, Herbert 1930- WhoWrEP 92
Bloom, Hyman 1913- WhoAm 92
Bloom, James Edward 1941- WhoWor 93
Bloom, Jane Ira BioIn 17
Bloom, Janet K. WhoWrEP 92
Bloom, Jeffrey MiSFD 9
Bloom, Joanne G. Law&B 92
Bloom, Joel N. 1925- St&PR 93
Bloom, John ScF&FL 92
Bloom, John Porter 1924- WhoAm 92
Bloom, Ken(neth) 1949- ConAu 38NR
Bloom, Kenneth A. St&PR 93
Bloom, Kenneth M. 1951- St&PR 93
Bloom, Kerry Steven 1953- WhoSSW 93
Bloom, Lary Roger 1943- WhoAm 92, WhoWrEP 92

Bloom, Lawrence Stephen 1930- *St&PR 93, WhoAm 92*
Bloom, Lee Hurley 1919- *WhoAm 92*
Bloom, Lillian S. *AmWomPl*
Bloom, Luka *BioIn 17*
Bloom, Lynn Marie Zimmerman 1934- *WhoWrEP 92*
Bloom, Margo Judith 1953- *WhoE 93*
Bloom, Mark *ScF&FL 92*
Bloom, Martha Louise 1951- *WhoE 93*
Bloom, Martin J. 1930- *St&PR 93*
Bloom, Maude Mc Fie *AmWomPl*
Bloom, Max 1909-1990 *BioIn 17*
Bloom, Max Robert 1916- *WhoE 93*
Bloom, Michael Eugene 1947- *WhoEmL 93, WhoWor 93*
Bloom, Miriam Krasnick 1920- *WhoAmW 93*
Bloom, Murray Teigh 1916- *WhoAm 92*
Bloom, Myer 1928- *WhoAm 92*
Bloom, Paul 1944- *WhoE 93*
Bloom, Pauline *WhoWrEP 92*
Bloom, Peter Herbert 1949- *WhoEmL 93*
Bloom, Robert 1930- *ScF&FL 92*
Bloom, Robert M. 1923- *St&PR 93*
Bloom, Rodney M. 1933- *St&PR 93*
Bloom, Rodney Merlin 1933- *WhoAm 92*
Bloom, Ruth Elsa 1954- *WhoE 93, WhoEmL 93*
Bloom, Sam *BioIn 17*
Bloom, Samuel Michael 1908- *WhoE 93*
Bloom, Samuel W. 1924- *BioIn 17*
Bloom, Sara Lambert 1944- *WhoAmW 93*
Bloom, Sherman 1934- *WhoAm 92*
Bloom, Shirley Gordon 1944- *St&PR 93*
Bloom, Stephanie Ann 1966- *WhoAmW 93*
Bloom, Stephanie M. *Law&B 92*
Bloom, Stephen Edward 1955- *WhoEmL 93, WhoSSW 93*
Bloom, Stephen Joel 1936- *WhoAm 92*
Bloom, Stephen Robert *WhoScE 91-1*
Bloom, Steve *Law&B 92*
Bloom, Steven *Law&B 92*
Bloom, Ursula 1893-1984 *ScF&FL 92*
Bloom, Walter Russell 1948- *WhoWor 93*
Bloom, William *ScF&FL 92*
Bloom, William J. 1947- *St&PR 93*
Bloom, William John 1949- *St&PR 93*
Bloomberg, Anthony 1948- *WhoUN 92*
Bloomberg, Jeffrey Marc *Law&B 92*
Bloomberg, Mary Beth 1947- *WhoEmL 93*
Bloomberg, Michael *BioIn 17*
Bloomberg, Robert Joseph 1947- *WhoEmL 93*
Bloomberg, Stuart *BioIn 17*
Bloomberg, Warner, Jr. 1926- *WhoAm 92*
Bloomburg, Shelley H. *Law&B 92*
Bloome, J.A. 1949- *St&PR 93*
Bloomer, Harold Franklin, Jr. 1933- *WhoAm 92, WhoE 93*
Bloomer, Hiram Reynolds 1845-1911 *BioIn 17*
Bloomer, J.M. 1842-1923 *ScF&FL 92*
Bloomer, Jack 1935- *St&PR 93*
Bloomer, James Lawrence 1939- *WhoE 93*
Bloomer, Nona *BioIn 17*
Bloom-Feshbach, Jonathan Stephen 1950- *WhoE 93*
Bloom-Feshbach, Sally 1953- *WhoAmW 93, WhoE 93*
Bloomfield, Arthur Irving 1914- *WhoAm 92, WhoE 93*
Bloomfield, Clara Derber 1942- *WhoAm 92*
Bloomfield, Coleman *WhoIns 93*
Bloomfield, Coleman 1926- *WhoAm 92*
Bloomfield, Daniel Kermit 1926- *WhoAm 92*
Bloomfield, David Peter *WhoScE 91-1*
Bloomfield, Fannie *Baker 92*
Bloomfield, George 1930- *MiSFD 9*
Bloomfield, Keith Martin 1951- *WhoEmL 93*
Bloomfield, Kevin Lawrence *Law&B 92*
Bloomfield, Leonard 1887-1949 *IntDcAn*
Bloomfield, Lincoln Palmer 1920- *WhoAm 92*
Bloomfield, Louis J. 1936- *WhoIns 93*
Bloomfield, Maxwell Herron, III 1931- *WhoAm 92*
Bloomfield, Mel C. *Law&B 92*
Bloomfield, Michael *BioIn 17*
Bloomfield, Michael Ivan 1950- *WhoE 93*
Bloomfield, Michaela 1966- *SmATA 70 [port]*
Bloomfield, Paul 1898- *ScF&FL 92*
Bloomfield, Peter 1946- *WhoEmL 93*
Bloomfield, Robert 1766-1823 *BioIn 17*
Bloomfield, Ronald James 1948- *WhoEmL 93*
Bloomfield, Serena Lurie 1953- *WhoAm 92, WhoEmL 93*
Bloomfield, Theodore (Robert) 1923- *Baker 92*
Bloomfield, Victor Alfred 1938- *WhoAm 92*
Bloomfield, William Mendel 1948- *WhoEmL 93*
Bloomgarden, Gary Michael 1954- *WhoE 93*
Bloomgarden, Kathy Finn 1949- *WhoAm 92, WhoAmW 93, WhoE 93*
Bloomgarden, Nancy L. *Law&B 92*
Bloomingdale, Arthur Lee, Jr. 1930- *WhoIns 93*
Bloomingdale, Teresa 1930- *WhoWrEP 92*
Bloomquist, Aldrich Carl 1921- *St&PR 93*
Bloomquist, Dennis H. *Law&B 92*
Bloomquist, John Hayes 1946- *WhoEmL 93*
Bloomquist, Kenneth Gene 1931- *WhoAm 92*
Bloor, David *WhoScE 91-1*
Bloor, Ella Reeve 1862-1951 *BioIn 17*
Bloor, Malcolm I.G. *WhoScE 91-1*
Bloor, William Spencer 1918- *WhoAm 92*
Bloquel, Jose 1934- *WhoScE 91-2*
Blore, Eric 1887-1959 *QDrFCA 92 [port]*
Blos, Joan W. 1928- *SmATA 69 [port], WhoAm 92, WhoWrEP 92*
Blos, Joan W(insor) 1928- *DcAmChF 1960, MajAI [port]*
Blose, Frances W. *AmWomPl*
Bloskas, John D. 1928- *WhoSSW 93*
Blosl, Thomas Louis 1934- *St&PR 93*
Bloss, Donald R. *Law&B 92*
Bloss, Julie L. 1959- *WhoEmL 93*
Bloss, Wallace O. 1947- *WhoEmL 93*
Blosser, Henry Gabriel 1928- *WhoAm 92*
Blosser, Henry L. 1952- *WhoEmL 93*
Blosser, Patricia Ellen 1931- *WhoAm 92*
Blossman, Alfred Rhody, Jr. 1931- *WhoAm 92*
Blossom, Beth 1926- *WhoWrEP 92*
Blossom, Charles N. 1935- *WhoIns 93*
Blotekjaer, Kjell 1933- *WhoScE 91-4, WhoWor 93*
Blotner, Joseph Leo 1923- *BioIn 17, WhoAm 92*
Blotner, Norman David 1918- *WhoAm 92*
Blotnick, Srully (D.) 1941- *ConAu 136*
Blottner, Myra Ann 1935- *WhoAmW 93*
Blouch, G.B. 1946- *St&PR 93*
Blouch, Timothy Craig 1954- *WhoEmL 93*
Blouch, William Edward 1951- *WhoE 93*
Blough, Donald S. 1929- *WhoAm 92*
Blough, Douglas Duane 1949- *WhoEmL 93*
Blough, Freeman, Jr. 1946- *WhoE 93*
Blough, Glenn Orlando 1907- *WhoWrEP 92*
Blough, Richard John 1947- *WhoE 93*
Blough, Roy 1901- *WhoAm 92*
Blouin, Francis Xavier, Jr. 1946- *WhoEmL 93*
Blouin, Maurice F. 1905- *St&PR 93*
Blount, Ben B., Jr. *WhoAm 92*
Blount, Ben B., Jr. 1939- *St&PR 93*
Blount, Dan S. 1928- *St&PR 93*
Blount, Don H. 1929- *WhoAm 92*
Blount, Evelyn 1942- *WhoAm 92*
Blount, Gordon Neil *WhoScE 91-1*
Blount, Herman *Baker 92*
Blount, J.T. *Law&B 92*
Blount, Joseph L. *Law&B 92*
Blount, Luther Hammond 1916- *St&PR 93*
Blount, Mel *BioIn 17*
Blount, Melesina Mary *AmWomPl*
Blount, Michael Eugene 1949- *WhoAm 92*
Blount, Robert Arthur 1949- *WhoEmL 93*
Blount, Robert Grier 1938- *St&PR 93, WhoAm 92*
Blount, Robert Haddock 1922- *WhoAm 92*
Blount, Roy *BioIn 17*
Blount, Stanley Freeman 1929- *WhoAm 92*
Blount, Susan L. *Law&B 92*
Blount, Terry Jacob 1943- *St&PR 93*
Blount, William d1534 *BioIn 17*
Blount, William Allan 1954- *WhoAm 92*
Blount, William H. 1922- *St&PR 93*
Blount, William Houston 1922- *WhoAm 92, WhoSSW 93*
Blount, Willie 1768-1835 *BioIn 17*
Blount, Winton M. 1921- *PolPar*
Blount, Winton Malcolm 1921- *St&PR 93*
Blount, Winton Malcolm, Jr. 1921- *WhoAm 92, WhoSSW 93*
Blount, Winton Malcolm, III 1943- *WhoAm 92*
Blount-Clark, Juanita Elizabeth 1952- *WhoAmW 93*
Blouse, Ben U. 1950- *WhoE 93*
Bloustein, Francis J. 1907?-1984 *BioIn 17*
Bloustein, Peter Edward 1937- *WhoWor 93*
Blout, Bart Boyd 1943- *St&PR 93*
Blout, Elkan Rogers 1919- *WhoAm 92*
Blovits, Larry *BioIn 17*
Blow, David Mervyn *WhoScE 91-1*
Blow, John 1648?-1708 *IntDcOp [port]*
Blow, John 1649?-1708 *Baker 92, OxDcOp*
Blow, Kurtis 1959- *SoulM*
Blow, Robert G. *St&PR 93*
Blower, Bruce Gregory 1937- *WhoWor 93*
Blowers, A.E. 1948- *St&PR 93*
Blowers, Andrew Thomas *WhoScE 91-1*
Blowers, Carl H. 1939- *St&PR 93*
Blowfield, Ian Stuart 1947- *WhoWor 93*
Bloxberg, Michael H. *Law&B 92*
Bloxham, Eleanor Joan Earle 1957- *WhoEmL 93*
Bloxham, Paul Anthony *WhoScE 91-1*
Bloxom, David Leon 1950- *St&PR 93*
Bloy, Leon 1846-1917 *DcLB 123 [port]*
Blozis, Albert C. 1919-1945 *BiDAMSp 1989*
Blozis, Jolene McCoy 1941- *WhoWrEP 92*
Bloznalis, Peter James 1963- *WhoE 93*
Blucher, Gebhard Leberecht von 1742-1819 *HarEnMi*
Blucher, Lillian H. 1933- *WhoE 93*
Blucher, Rodney J. 1935- *St&PR 93*
Bludman, Sidney Arnold 1927- *WhoAm 92*
Bludson-Francis, Vernett 1951- *AfrAmBi [port]*
Bludworth, David H. *BioIn 17*
Blue, Ben 1901-1975 *QDrFCA 92 [port]*
Blue, Charles Toomey 1952- *WhoEmL 93, WhoSSW 93*
Blue, Dan, Jr. *WhoSSW 93*
Blue, Edwin Gene 1934- *WhoSSW 93*
Blue, Elmer 1925- *St&PR 93*
Blue, Frank W. *Law&B 92*
Blue, James N. 1935- *St&PR 93*
Blue, Luzerne Atwell 1897-1958 *BiDAMSp 1989*
Blue, Monte 1890-1963 *BioIn 17*
Blue, Phillip Edwin 1940- *St&PR 93*
Blue, Robert Donald 1898-1989 *BioIn 17*
Blue, Robert Lee 1920- *WhoWor 93*
Blue, Rose 1931- *DcAmChF 1960, WhoAmW 93*
Blue, Sherwood 1905- *WhoWor 93*
Blue, Tyson 1952- *ScF&FL 92*
Blue, Vida *BioIn 17*
Blue, Warren Grant 1926- *St&PR 93*
Bluebello, James Joseph 1926- *St&PR 93*
Blue Cloud, Peter (Aroniawenrate) 1933- *ConAu 40NR*
Bluefarb, Samuel Mitchell 1912- *WhoAm 92*
Bluege, Oswald Louis 1900-1985 *BiDAMSp 1989*
Bluejay *ScF&FL 92*
Bluemink, J.G. *WhoScE 91-3*
Bluemke, David W. 1953- *St&PR 93*
Bluemke, John Albert, Jr. 1949- *St&PR 93*
Bluemle, Lewis William, Jr. 1921- *WhoAm 92*
Bluemle, Robert Louis 1933- *WhoAm 92, WhoWor 93*
Bluemner, Oscar Florianus 1867-1938 *BioIn 17*
Blue Notes *SoulM*
Bluestein, Abram Isaac 1948- *St&PR 93*
Bluestein, Claire 1926- *WhoAmW 93, WhoE 93*
Bluestein, Daniel Thomas 1943- *WhoWrEP 92*
Bluestein, Edwin A., Jr. 1930- *WhoAm 92*
Bluestein, Herman W. 1947- *St&PR 93*
Bluestein, Joan S. 1920- *St&PR 93*
Bluestein, Judith A. 1948- *St&PR 93*
Bluestein, Judith Ann 1948- *WhoAmW 93*
Bluestein, Paul H. 1923- *St&PR 93*
Bluestein, Paul Harold 1923- *WhoAm 92*
Bluestein, Steve Franklin 1947- *WhoEmL 93*
Bluestein, Venus Weller 1933- *WhoAm 92, WhoAmW 93*
Bluestone, Andrew Lavoott 1951- *WhoEmL 93*
Bluestone, Hugh Lawrence 1948- *WhoAm 92, WhoEmL 93*
Bluestone, Irving 1917- *ConAu 136*
Bluestone, Stanton J. 1944- *WhoAm 92*
Bluford, Guion S. 1942- *BioIn 17*
Bluford, Guion Stewart, Jr. 1942- *AfrAmBi [port], WhoAm 92*
Bluford, Lucile *BioIn 17*
Bluhm, Barbara Jean 1925- *WhoAm 92*
Bluhm, David Rodney *Law&B 92*
Bluhm, Heinz 1907- *WhoAm 92, WhoE 93*
Bluhm, Nathan Mark 1954- *WhoE 93*
Bluhm, Neil Gary 1938- *WhoAm 92*
Bluhm, Norman 1920- *WhoAm 92*
Bluhm, Ursula Schultze- 1921- *BioIn 17*
Bluhm, William Theodore 1923- *WhoAm 92*
Bluing, Karen Louise 1962- *WhoAmW 93*
Bluitt, Karen 1957- *WhoAmW 93, WhoEmL 93*
Blum, Arthur 1926- *WhoAm 92*
Blum, Barbara Davis *WhoAm 92, WhoAmW 93*
Blum, Barbara Meddock 1938- *WhoAmW 93*
Blum, Bruce Ivan 1931- *WhoE 93*
Blum, Carol Francis 1958- *WhoAmW 93*
Blum, Carol Kathlyn *WhoE 93*
Blum, Cheryl Ann 1966- *WhoAmW 93*
Blum, Chris *MiSFD 9*
Blum, David 1920- *St&PR 93*
Blum, David Lawrence 1962- *WhoEmL 93*
Blum, Deborah *WhoAmW 93*
Blum, Donald R. 1931- *St&PR 93*
Blum, Dorothy Kathleen *WhoSSW 93*
Blum, Ethel Halsey d1991 *BioIn 17*
Blum, Eva Tansky 1949- *WhoEmL 93*
Blum, Fred Andrew 1939- *WhoAm 92*
Blum, Geoffrey Carl 1951- *WhoWrEP 92*
Blum, Gerald H. 1926- *St&PR 93*
Blum, Gerald Henry 1926- *WhoAm 92*
Blum, Gerald S. 1932- *St&PR 93*
Blum, Gerald Saul 1922- *WhoAm 92*
Blum, Herbert M. *Law&B 92*
Blum, Howard 1948- *BioIn 17*
Blum, Howard L. 1945- *St&PR 93*
Blum, Howard Robert 1951- *WhoE 93, WhoEmL 93*
Blum, Irving 1930- *WhoAm 92*
Blum, Jacob Joseph 1926- *WhoAm 92, WhoSSW 93*
Blum, James Arnold 1942- *WhoIns 93*
Blum, Jay Herman 1965- *WhoE 93*
Blum, Jean-Claude 1928- *WhoScE 91-2*
Blum, Jeffrey Stuart 1947- *WhoEmL 93*
Blum, John A. 1915- *St&PR 93*
Blum, John Alan 1933- *WhoAm 92*
Blum, John Curtis 1915- *WhoAm 92*
Blum, John Morton 1921- *WhoAm 92*
Blum, John Robert Halsey 1929- *WhoE 93*
Blum, Jordyn *BioIn 17*
Blum, Lawrence Philip 1917- *WhoAm 92*
Blum, Leon 1872-1950 *BioIn 17, DcTwHis*
Blum, Linda Marie 1949- *WhoAmW 93*
Blum, Manuel 1938- *WhoAm 92*
Blum, Marc Paul 1942- *St&PR 93*
Blum, Mark J. 1953- *St&PR 93*
Blum, Melvin 1936- *WhoE 93*
Blum, Michael Stephen 1939- *WhoAm 92*
Blum, Nancy Allison 1959- *WhoAmW 93*
Blum, Patricia Rae 1948- *WhoAmW 93*
Blum, Peter *BioIn 17*
Blum, Peter 1950- *WhoEmL 93*
Blum, Richard C. *BioIn 17*
Blum, Richard Hosmer Adams 1927- *WhoAm 92*
Blum, Richard I. 1953- *WhoEmL 93*
Blum, Richard L. d1991 *BioIn 17*
Blum, Robert 1900- *Baker 92*
Blum, Robert Allan 1938- *WhoAm 92*
Blum, Robert Edward 1899- *WhoAm 92, WhoWor 93*
Blum, Robert S. 1958- *ScF&FL 92*
Blum, Ronald Joseph 1948- *WhoE 93*
Blum, Rosalind F. 1910- *WhoE 93*
Blum, Saralee 1939- *WhoAmW 93*
Blum, Seymour 1916- *St&PR 93*
Blum, Seymour L. 1925- *WhoAm 92*
Blum, Sharon Dukette 1946- *WhoAmW 93*
Blum, Steven B. 1951- *WhoEmL 93*
Blum, Virgil C. 1913-1990 *BioIn 17*
Blum, Volker 1937- *WhoScE 91-3*
Blum, Walter J. 1918- *WhoAm 92*
Blum, William Lee 1920- *WhoAm 92*
Blumberg, Adele Rosenberg 1916- *WhoAmW 93*
Blumberg, Alyse Neiburg 1946- *WhoEmL 93*
Blumberg, Avrom Aaron 1928- *WhoAm 92*
Blumberg, Barbara Salmanson 1927- *WhoAmW 93, WhoE 93, WhoWor 93*
Blumberg, Baruch Samuel 1925- *WhoAm 92, WhoE 93, WhoWor 93*
Blumberg, David 1925- *St&PR 93, WhoAm 92*
Blumberg, Diane Susan 1952- *WhoAmW 93*
Blumberg, Donald D. 1929- *St&PR 93*
Blumberg, Edward J. *Law&B 92*
Blumberg, Edward J. 1908- *St&PR 93*
Blumberg, Edward Robert 1951- *WhoSSW 93, WhoWor 93*
Blumberg, Gerald 1911- *WhoAm 92*
Blumberg, Gunar John *Law&B 92*
Blumberg, Herbert K. 1925- *St&PR 93*
Blumberg, Herbert Kurt 1925- *WhoAm 92*
Blumberg, Joan M. *Law&B 92*
Blumberg, Joel Myron 1940- *WhoE 93*
Blumberg, John Philip 1949- *WhoEmL 93*
Blumberg, Julia Baum *WhoAmW 93*
Blumberg, June Beth 1959- *WhoE 93*
Blumberg, Lawrence 1947- *WhoE 93*
Blumberg, Leda 1956- *WhoWrEP 92*
Blumberg, Leroy Norman 1929- *WhoE 93*
Blumberg, Lisa B. *Law&B 92*
Blumberg, Mark Stuart 1924- *WhoAm 92*
Blumberg, Marvin E. 1926- *St&PR 93*
Blumberg, Michael S. 1926- *St&PR 93*
Blumberg, Michael Zangwill 1945- *WhoSSW 93*
Blumberg, Nathan(iel) Bernard 1922- *WhoWrEP 92*

Blumberg, Nathaniel Bernard 1922- *WhoAm 92*
Blumberg, Peter S. 1944- *St&PR 93*
Blumberg, Peter Steven 1944- *WhoE 93*
Blumberg, Philip Flayderman 1957- *WhoEmL 93, WhoSSW 93*
Blumberg, Phillip Irvin 1919- *WhoAm 92*
Blumberg, Rhoda 1917- *MajAI [port], ScF&FL 92, SmATA 70 [port]*
Blumberg, Richard M. *Law&B 92*
Blumberg, Robert H. *Law&B 92*
Blumberg, Robert H. 1939- *St&PR 93*
Blumberg, Stanley A. 1912- *ConAu 136*
Blumberg, Stephen 1944- *St&PR 93*
Blumberg, Stuart Lester 1947- *WhoEmL 93*
Blumberg, Walter B. 1911- *St&PR 93*
Blume, (Ferdinand Anton) Clemens 1862-1932 *Baker 92*
Blume, Clinton W., Jr. 1934- *St&PR 93*
Blume, Clinton W., III 1957- *WhoEmL 93*
Blume, Clinton Willis, Jr. 1932- *WhoE 93*
Blume, Cynthia Ann 1949- *WhoAmW 93*
Blume, Friedrich 1893-1975 *Baker 92*
Blume, Gerald W. *Law&B 92*
Blume, Hans-Peter 1933- *WhoScE 91-3*
Blume, Helmut 1920- *ConAu 138*
Blume, Jack Paul 1915- *WhoAm 92*
Blume, Jay Donald, Jr. 1940- *WhoAm 92*
Blume, John August 1909- *WhoAm 92*
Blume, Judy *BioIn 17*
Blume, Judy 1938- *ChlFicS*
Blume, Judy (Sussman) 1938- *ConAu 37NR, MajAI [port], WhoAm 92, WhoAmW 93, WhoWrEP 92*
Blume, Judy (Sussman Kitchens) 1938- *DcAmChF 1960*
Blume, Kathryn Alice 1947- *WhoEmL 93*
Blume, Lawrence Dayton 1948- *WhoE 93*
Blume, Mark Gregory 1962- *WhoEmL 93*
Blume, Marshall Edward 1941- *WhoAm 92*
Blume, Martin 1932- *WhoAm 92*
Blume, Myron R. 1931- *St&PR 93*
Blume, Peter 1906- *BioIn 17, WhoAm 92*
Blume, Peter 1906-1992 *NewYTBS 92 [port]*
Blume, Peter Frederick 1946- *WhoAm 92, WhoE 93*
Blume, Richard L. *Law&B 92*
Blume, Stephen Craig 1948- *WhoEmL 93*
Blume, Teddy d1992 *BioIn 17*
Blume, Theodore d1992 *NewYTBS 92*
Blume, Walter Manley 1958- *WhoEmL 93*
Blumel, Joseph Carlton 1928- *WhoAm 92*
Blumell, R.C. *Law&B 92*
Blumen, Norman H. *Law&B 92*
Blumenfeld, Alfred Morton 1919- *WhoAm 92*
Blumenfeld, Esther Richter 1936- *WhoSSW 93*
Blumenfeld, Felix (Mikhailovich) 1863-1931 *Baker 92*
Blumenfeld, Harold 1905?-1991 *BioIn 17*
Blumenfeld, Harold 1923- *Baker 92*
Blumenfeld, Henry Alexander 1925- *WhoWor 93*
Blumenfeld, Jack Barry 1952- *WhoEmL 93*
Blumenfeld, Jeffry Alan 1952- *WhoEmL 93*
Blumenfeld, John A., Jr. *Law&B 92*
Blumenfeld, Laura R. *BioIn 17*
Blumenfeld, Philip Martin 1931- *WhoAm 92*
Blumenfeld, Seth David 1940- *St&PR 93, WhoAm 92*
Blumenfeld, Yorick 1932- *ScF&FL 92*
Blumenkopf, Todd Andrew 1956- *WhoSSW 93*
Blumenkrantz, Nelly 1930- *WhoScE 91-2*
Blumenreich, Martin Sigvart 1949- *WhoSSW 93*
Blumenreich, Patricia Estela 1954- *WhoEmL 93, WhoSSW 93*
Blumenschein, Ulrich E. 1929- *WhoWor 93*
Blumenshine, J. Wesley *Law&B 92*
Blumenson, Martin 1918- *WhoWrEP 92*
Blumenstiel, Gilbert 1955- *WhoWor 93*
Blumenstock, David Albert 1927- *WhoAm 92*
Blumenstock, Marvin Walter 1932- *WhoE 93*
Blumental, Felicja 1911-1991 *BioIn 17, NewYTBS 92*
Blumental, Felicja 1918- *Baker 92*
Blumenthal, Andy *MiSFD 9*
Blumenthal, Bruce 1952- *WhoE 93*
Blumenthal, Carol 1951- *WhoEmL 93*
Blumenthal, Fritz 1913- *WhoAm 92*
Blumenthal, Gerald Paul 1945- *WhoE 93*
Blumenthal, Harold Jay 1926- *WhoAm 92*
Blumenthal, Herman 1915- *St&PR 93*
Blumenthal, Herman Bertram 1916- *WhoAm 92*
Blumenthal, Howard J. 1952- *ConAu 136*
Blumenthal, Isidor 1909- *St&PR 93*
Blumenthal, Jack 1919- *St&PR 93*
Blumenthal, Jeffrey Michael *Law&B 92*
Blumenthal, John Frederick 1949- *WhoEmL 93*
Blumenthal, Joseph 1897-1990 *BioIn 17*
Blumenthal, Karl Konstantin Albrecht Leonhard von 1810-1900 *HarEnMi*
Blumenthal, Kurt Douglas 1944- *St&PR 93*
Blumenthal, Max 1911-1990 *BioIn 17*
Blumenthal, Mortimer Jacob 1921-1990 *BioIn 17*
Blumenthal, Norman B. *Law&B 92*
Blumenthal, Richard *WhoAm 92, WhoE 93*
Blumenthal, Richard Cary 1951- *WhoEmL 93*
Blumenthal, Robert S. 1928- *St&PR 93*
Blumenthal, Sidney 1909-1990 *BioIn 17*
Blumenthal, Stanley Len 1946- *WhoWrEP 92*
Blumenthal, Steven 1948- *WhoEmL 93, WhoWor 93*
Blumenthal, Susan Jane 1952- *WhoAmW 93*
Blumenthal, Sydney C., Jr. 1916- *St&PR 93*
Blumenthal, Terry Dale 1954- *WhoEmL 93*
Blumenthal, W. Michael *BioIn 17*
Blumenthal, W. Michael 1926- *St&PR 93*
Blumenthal, Werner Michael 1926- *WhoAm 92*
Blumenthal, William 1955- *WhoEmL 93*
Blumentritt, Ferdinand 1853-1913 *IntDcAn*
Blumentritt, Gunther von 1892- *HarEnMi*
Blumer, Anne Marie 1956- *WhoAmW 93, WhoEmL 93*
Blumer, Frederick Elwin 1933- *WhoAm 92*
Blumer, James William 1924- *St&PR 93*
Blumer, Theodor 1881-1964 *Baker 92*
Blum-Goldstein, Susan Ruth 1963- *WhoEmL 93*
Blumhardt, Rodney S. 1935- *St&PR 93*
Blumkin, Linda Ruth 1944- *WhoAm 92*
Blumlein, Michael 1948- *ScF&FL 92*
Blumner, Martin 1827-1901 *Baker 92*
Blumofe, Robert Fulton *WhoAm 92*
Blumrich, Josef Franz 1913- *WhoWor 93*
Blumstein, Alfred 1930- *WhoAm 92*
Blumstein, David d1990 *BioIn 17*
Blumstein, James Franklin 1945- *WhoAm 92*
Blumstein, Jerome 1930- *St&PR 93*
Blumstein, Renee 1957- *WhoAm 92, WhoE 93, WhoEmL 93*
Blumstein, Renee J. 1957- *WhoAmW 93*
Blumstein, Rita Blattberg 1937- *WhoE 93*
Blumstein, Sheila Ellen 1944- *WhoAm 92*
Blumstein, Susan Bender 1943- *WhoE 93*
Blumstein, William A. 1948- *WhoAm 92*
Blunck, Lawrence Paul 1956- *WhoEmL 93*
Blundell, Derek John *WhoScE 91-1*
Blundell, George 1935- *WhoWor 93*
Blundell, Phyllis Q. d1992 *BioIn 17*
Blundell, Thomas Leon *WhoScE 91-1*
Blundell, Thomas Leon 1942- *WhoWor 93*
Blundell, William Edward 1934- *WhoAm 92*
Blundell, William Richard Charles 1927- *WhoAm 92*
Blunden, Brian William 1938- *WhoScE 91-1*
Blunden, Edmund 1896-1974 *BioIn 17*
Blunden, Gerald *WhoScE 91-1*
Blunden-Willms, Margot H. 1937- *WhoScE 91-1*
Blunderland Cartoonist *ScF&FL 92*
Blundon, Jill M. *Law&B 92*
Blundon, Jill M. 1953- *St&PR 93*
Blunier, Doris E. 1952- *St&PR 93*
Blunk, Forrest Stewart 1913- *WhoAm 92*
Blunk, Nancy M. *St&PR 93*
Blunt, Anne 1837-1917 & Blunt, Wilfrid Scawen 1840-1922 *Expl 93 [port]*
Blunt, Anthony 1907-1983 *BioIn 17, ColdWar 1 [port]*
Blunt, Charles William *WhoAsAP 91*
Blunt, Charles William 1951- *WhoWor 93*
Blunt, Giles *ScF&FL 92*
Blunt, James Gilpatrick 1826-1881 *HarEnMi*
Blunt, Kathleen S. *Law&B 92*
Blunt, Peter 1941- *St&PR 93*
Blunt, Roger Reckling 1930- *St&PR 93*
Blunt, Roy D. 1950- *WhoAm 92*
Blunt, Tom *BioIn 17*
Blunt, Wilfrid 1901-1987 *ScF&FL 92*
Blunt, Wilfrid Scawen 1840-1922 *See* Blunt, Anne 1837-1917 & Blunt, Wilfrid Scawen 1840-1922 *Expl 93*
Blurton, Keith Frederick 1940- *WhoSSW 93*
Blust, John Louis 1944- *St&PR 93*
Blust, Raymond E. d1991 *BioIn 17*
Blute, Joseph Galvin 1957- *WhoEmL 93*
Bluteau, L.M. 1927- *St&PR 93*
Bluth, B. J. 1934- *WhoAm 92*
Bluth, Dewey C. 1922- *St&PR 93*
Bluth, Don 1938- *MiSFD 9*
Bluth, Edmund W. *Law&B 92*
Bluth, Irene Picasso 1927- *WhoAmW 93*
Bluthner, Julius (Ferdinand) 1824-1910 *Baker 92*
Blutig, Eduard *MajAI, SmATA 70*
Blutnick, Milton d1992 *BioIn 17, NewYTBS 92*
Bluto, Chuck *BioIn 17*
Blutstein, Harvey M. 1927- *WhoE 93, WhoIns 93*
Blutter, Joan Wernick 1929- *WhoAm 92*
Bluvas, William J. 1943- *St&PR 93*
Bly, Allison *BioIn 17*
Bly, Carol McLean 1930- *WhoWrEP 92*
Bly, Charles Albert 1952- *WhoE 93*
Bly, David Alan 1953- *WhoEmL 93*
Bly, Herbert Arthur 1929- *St&PR 93, WhoAm 92*
Bly, James Charles, Jr. 1952- *WhoE 93*
Bly, Janet (Chester) 1945- *ConAu 40NR*
Bly, Margaret Anne 1942- *WhoAmW 93, WhoSSW 93*
Bly, Mark John 1949- *WhoWrEP 92*
Bly, Nellie 1867-1922 *BioIn 17, GayN*
Bly, P.H. *WhoScE 91-1*
Bly, Peter A(nthony) 1944- *ConAu 38NR*
Bly, Robert *BioIn 17*
Bly, Robert 1926- *MagSAmL [port], News 92 [port]*
Bly, Robert Elwood 1926- *WhoAm 92, WhoWrEP 92*
Bly, Robert W(ayne) 1957- *ConAu 40NR*
Bly, Sharon Vernice 1963- *WhoE 93*
Bly, Stephen A(rthur) 1944- *ConAu 40NR*
Bly, Stephen Arthur 1944- *WhoWrEP 92*
Blyholder, George Donald 1931- *WhoSSW 93*
Blyleven, Bert *BioIn 17*
Blyleven, Rik Aalbert 1951- *BiDAMSp 1989*
Blyn, George 1919- *WhoE 93*
Blyn, Stefany 1953- *WhoE 93, WhoEmL 93*
Blynn, Guy M. *Law&B 92*
Blynn, Guy M. 1945- *St&PR 93*
Blynn, Guy Marc 1945- *WhoAm 92*
Blystone, F. Lynn 1935- *St&PR 93*
Blystone, Jane Marie 1951- *WhoWrEP 92*
Blystone, Richard *BioIn 17*
Blystone, Robert Vernon 1943- *WhoAm 92, WhoSSW 93*
Blyth, Ann Marie 1949- *WhoAmW 93, WhoEmL 93, WhoWor 93*
Blyth, David 1956- *MiSFD 9*
Blyth, Jeff *MiSFD 9*
Blyth, Michael Leslie 1950- *WhoAm 92, WhoEmL 93*
Blyth, Myrna Greenstein 1939- *St&PR 93, WhoAm 92, WhoAmW 93, WhoE 93, WhoWrEP 92*
Blyth, Thomas Scott *WhoScE 91-1*
Blythe, Angela D. 1960- *WhoAmW 93, WhoEmL 93*
Blythe, Anne Montague 1948- *WhoAmW 93*
Blythe, Dean H. *Law&B 92*
Blythe, Edward E. *Law&B 92*
Blythe, Ernest 1889-1975 *BioIn 17*
Blythe, Gary 1959- *BioIn 17*
Blythe, Harold Urquhart 1942- *WhoSSW 93*
Blythe, James W. 1946- *St&PR 93*
Blythe, Joseph John 1947- *WhoEmL 93*
Blythe, Kay Lankford 1945- *WhoAmW 93*
Blythe, Richard N., Jr. 1948- *St&PR 93*
Blythe, Ronald 1922- *ScF&FL 92*
Blythe, Ronald R. 1948- *St&PR 93*
Blythe, Sue Duncan 1947- *WhoAmW 93*
Blyton, Enid (Mary) 1897-1968 *MajAI [port]*
Blyveis, Barry 1939- *WhoAm 92*
Boaden, James 1762-1839 *BioIn 17*
Boadicea, Queen d62 *BioIn 17*
Boado, Heriberto Jose 1944- *WhoWor 93*
Boadway, W.A., Mrs. *AmWomPl*
Boag, Thomas Johnson 1922- *WhoAm 92*
Boagni, Lois Glasscock 1937- *WhoAmW 93*
Boak, Jeffrey L. *Law&B 92*
Boak, Ruth Alice 1906- *WhoAm 92*
Boake, Corwin, III 1953- *WhoSSW 93*
Boal, Augusto *BioIn 17*
Boal, Bernard Harvey 1937- *WhoWor 93*
Boal, Dean 1931- *WhoAm 92*
Boal, Jan List 1930- *WhoSSW 93*
Boal, Peter Cadbury 1965- *WhoAm 92*
Boam, Jeffrey 1949- *ConTFT 10*
Boan, Bobby Jack 1945- *WhoAm 92*
Board, Dwight V. *Law&B 92*
Board, Dwight Vernon 1944- *WhoAm 92*
Board, Elizabeth I. 1952- *WhoAmW 93*
Board, Frederick Allen 1941- *St&PR 93*
Board, Howard E. 1943- *St&PR 93*
Board, Joseph Breckinridge, Jr. 1931- *WhoAm 92*
Board, Kenneth *WhoScE 91-1*
Board, Prudence F. *ScF&FL 92*
Board, Warren Lee 1942- *WhoAm 92*
Boardman, Arthur G. 1910-1991 *BioIn 17*
Boardman, Eleanor 1898-1991 *BioIn 17*
Boardman, Elijah 1760-1823 *BioIn 17*
Boardman, Eunice 1926- *WhoAm 92*
Boardman, Harold F. *Law&B 92*
Boardman, Harold F. 1939- *St&PR 93*
Boardman, Harold Frederick, Jr. 1939- *WhoAm 92, WhoE 93, WhoWor 93*
Boardman, James Paul 1947- *WhoE 93*
Boardman, John Michael 1938- *WhoAm 92*
Boardman, John Turner *WhoScE 91-1*
Boardman, Linda Irene 1948- *WhoEmL 93, WhoSSW 93*
Boardman, Mark Seymour 1958- *WhoEmL 93*
Boardman, Michael Neil 1942- *WhoE 93*
Boardman, Norman D. 1932- *WhoIns 93*
Boardman, Richard Stanton 1923- *WhoAm 92*
Boardman, Robert A. *Law&B 92*
Boardman, Robert (B.) 1943- *ConAu 138*
Boardman, Robert Emmett 1932- *St&PR 93*
Boardman, Rosanne Virginia 1946- *WhoAmW 93, WhoEmL 93, WhoWor 93*
Boardman, Seymour 1921- *WhoAm 92*
Boardman, Thomas *ScF&FL 92*
Boardman, Thomas Alan *Law&B 92*
Boardman, Tom 1930- *ScF&FL 92*
Boardman, William Penniman 1941- *St&PR 93, WhoAm 92*
Boarman, Gerald Jude 1940- *WhoE 93*
Boarman, Marjorie Ruth 1953- *WhoAmW 93*
Boarman, Patrick Madigan 1922- *WhoAm 92*
Boarman, William Dale 1949- *St&PR 93*
Boas, Andrew M. 1955- *St&PR 93*
Boas, Frank 1930- *WhoWor 93*
Boas, Franz 1858-1942 *BioIn 17, IntDcAn*
Boas, Kathleen Lawrence 1925- *WhoE 93*
Boas, Norman Francis 1922- *WhoE 93*
Boas, Robert A. *Law&B 92*
Boas, Robert Sanford 1923- *WhoAm 92*
Boas, Robert Sanford 1923-1992 *NewYTBS 92 [port]*
Boas, Roger 1921- *WhoAm 92*
Boasberg, Leonard W. 1923- *WhoAm 92*
Boase, Ian Alexander *Law&B 92*
Boast, Keith Edwin 1940- *St&PR 93*
Boast, Molly S. 1948- *WhoAmW 93*
Boat, Thomas Frederick 1939- *WhoAm 92*
Boateng, Adwoa Achia 1955- *WhoEmL 93*
Boateng, Joshua Yaw 1947- *WhoE 93*
Boates, Christopher Reid 1950- *WhoEmL 93*
Boatman, Bonny E. 1950- *St&PR 93*
Boatman, Garrett *ScF&FL 92*
Boatman, Michael *BioIn 17*
Boatner, Haydon L. 1900- *HarEnMi*
Boatner, Theresa M. *Law&B 92*
Boatright, Ann Long 1947- *WhoAm 92, WhoAmW 93*
Boatright, James Francis 1933- *WhoAm 92*
Boatright, Joanna Morson 1958- *WhoEmL 93*
Boatti, Stephen J. *Law&B 92*
Boatwright, Charlotte Jeanne 1937- *WhoAmW 93*
Boatwright, Christopher Monroe 1954- *WhoAm 92*
Boatwright, H. Lee, III 1933- *St&PR 93*
Boatwright, Helen *Baker 92*
Boatwright, Howard (Leake, Jr.) 1918- *Baker 92*
Boatwright, John G. P. 1936- *WhoAm 92*
Boatwright, McHenry 1928- *Baker 92*
Boatwright, P.J. 1927-1991 *BioIn 17*
Boatwright, Purvis J. 1927-1991 *BioIn 17*
Boatwright, William Heard 1933- *St&PR 93*
Boatwright-McEvoy, Margaret Roberta 1950- *WhoE 93*
Boaventura, Rui Alfredo Rocha 1944- *WhoWor 93*
Boayue, Wilfred Sei 1938- *WhoUN 92*
Boaz, Daniel York 1959- *WhoEmL 93*
Boaz, David Douglas 1953- *WhoAm 92*
Boaz, Doniella 1934- *WhoAm 92, WhoAmW 93*
Boaz, Stephen Scott 1948- *WhoEmL 93*
Boazman, Franklin Meador 1939- *WhoSSW 93, WhoWor 93*
Bob, Indiana *WhoWrEP 92*
Bob, Sharon Helene 1949- *WhoEmL 93*
Boba, Denise Anne 1961- *WhoEmL 93*
Boba, Imre 1919- *WhoAm 92*
Boban, Kathleen 1962- *WhoEmL 93*
Bob & Earl *SoulM*
Bobay, Donald L. 1946- *St&PR 93*

Bobb, Harold Daniel 1952- WhoEmL 93
Bobb, L. Edward 1951- WhoIns 93
Bobb, Richard Allen 1937- WhoAm 92
Bobb, Richard M. 1938- St&PR 93
Bobbitt, Finley Marvin, Jr. 1931- St&PR 93
Bobbitt, Gary Lee 1951- WhoEmL 93
Bobbitt, James McCue 1930- WhoAm 92
Bobbitt, Max E. 1945- WhoAm 92
Bobbitt, Nancy Marie 1951- WhoAmW 93, WhoEmL 93, WhoSSW 93
Bobbitt, Philip Chase 1948- WhoAm 92
Bobbs, John C. 1943- St&PR 93
Bobby, Theodore N. Law&B 92
Bobby Z BioIn 17
Bobco, William David, Jr. 1946- WhoEmL 93
Bobe, Henry Dale 1952- St&PR 93
Bob-Egbe, Rita Omono 1960- WhoWor 93
Bobenhouse, Nellie Ruth 1936- WhoAmW 93
Bober, Bernard R. 1934- St&PR 93
Bober, Jack d1991 BioIn 17
Bober, Kenneth Frank 1948- St&PR 93
Bober, Lawrence H. 1924- St&PR 93
Bober, Lawrence Harold 1924- WhoAm 92
Bober, Raymond Hans 1923- WhoWrEP 92
Boberg, James Odell 1959- WhoEmL 93
Bobersky, Pamela Lynn 1966- WhoAmW 93
Bobier, Harold d1985 BioIn 17
Bobier, Joan Kuech 1951- WhoAmW 93
Bobillier, Pierre WhoScE 91-2
Bobinchuck, William R. 1927- St&PR 93
Bobins, Norman R. WhoAm 92
Bobinski, George Sylvan 1929- WhoAm 92, WhoE 93
Bobinski, Henryk 1861-1914 PolBiDi
Bobis, Arthur H. 1936- St&PR 93
Bobisud, Larry Eugene 1940- WhoAm 92
Bobleter, Ortwin 1924- WhoScE 91-4
Bobo, Donald Arthur 1918- WhoAm 92
Bobo, Jack C. 1940- St&PR 93
Bobo, Jack E. 1924- WhoIns 93
Bobo, Jack Edward 1924- WhoAm 92
Bobo, James Robert 1923- WhoAm 92
Bobo, Leslie Joyner 1958- WhoEmL 93
Bobo, Leslie Renee 1963- WhoEmL 93, WhoSSW 93
Bobo, Melvin 1924- WhoAm 92
Bo-Boliko, Lokonga 1934- WhoAfr
Bobosky, W. Brand 1939- St&PR 93
Bobrinskoy, George V. 1933-1991 BioIn 17
Bobroff, Harold 1920- WhoAm 92
Bobrow, Alvan Lee 1949- St&PR 93, WhoEmL 93
Bobrow, Davis Bernard 1936- WhoAm 92
Bobrow, Henry Bernard 1924- WhoE 93
Bobrow, Laura Judith 1928- WhoE 93
Bobrow, Martin WhoScE 91-1
Bobrow, Martin 1938- WhoWor 93
Bobrowski, Dobieslaw Alexander 1927- WhoWor 93
Bobruff, Carole Marks 1935- WhoAmW 93
Bobruk, Toni Sue 1948- WhoAmW 93
Bobryk, Michal L. Law&B 92
Bobst, Isaac 1847- BioIn 17
Bobula, Edward Michael 1915- St&PR 93
Bobulinski, Gregory Alexander 1950- WhoE 93
Bobye, Wayne I. 1947- St&PR 93
Bobyk, John Michael 1934- St&PR 93
Bocage, Ronald Joseph Law&B 92
Bocage, Ronald Joseph 1946- St&PR 93
Bocan, Hynek 1938- DrEEuF
Bocanegra, Matias de 1612-1668 DcMexL
Bocarsly, Andrew Bruce 1954- WhoE 93
Bocca, Julio BioIn 17, WhoAm 92
Boccabadati, Cecilia 1825-1906 See Varesi, Felice 1813-1889 OxDcOp
Boccabadati, Luigia c. 1800-1850 See Varesi, Felice 1813-1889 OxDcOp
Boccabadati, Virginia 1828-1922 See Varesi, Felice 1813-1889 OxDcOp
Boccaccio, Giovanni 1313-1375 BioIn 17, MagSWL [port], ShSCr 10
Boccaletti, Mario WhoScE 91-3
Boccard, Frederick A. 1951- St&PR 93
Boccard, Roger L. 1929- WhoScE 91-2
Boccardi, Louis D. 1937- St&PR 93
Boccardi, Louis Donald 1937- WhoAm 92
Boccella, Claire M. Law&B 92
Boccella, Claire Marie Law&B 92
Boccherini, (Ridolfo) Luigi 1743-1805 Baker 92
Bocchetti, Mark G. Law&B 92
Bocchi, Luigi 1934- WhoScE 91-3
Bocchimuzzo, Vincent Louis 1952- WhoE 93
Bocchino, Frances Lucia 1944- WhoAmW 93
Bocchino, Linda Elizabeth 1948- WhoEmL 93
Bocci, Marc S. Law&B 92
Boccia, Judy Elaine 1955- WhoAmW 93
Boccia Rosado, Ann Marie 1958- WhoEmL 93
Boccieri, Monica Litwin 1942- WhoSSW 93
Boccio, Barbara Ann 1958- WhoEmL 93
Boccio, Karen Corinne 1954- WhoWrEP 92
Boccitto, Bonnie L. 1949- WhoIns 93
Boccitto, Elio WhoAm 92
Boccone, Adriano 1931- WhoScE 91-3
Boccone, Andrew A. St&PR 93
Boccone, Andrew Albert 1945- WhoE 93
Bocell, James Russell 1921- St&PR 93
Boch, Philippe 1938- WhoScE 91-2
Bocharov, Gennadii Nikolaevich BioIn 17
Bochat, Kenneth Law&B 92
Bochco, Steve 1943- WhoAm 92
Bochco, Steven BioIn 17
Bochco, Steven 1943- ConAu 138
Bochco, Steven (Ronald) 1943- WhoWrEP 92
Boche, Gernot 1938- WhoScE 91-3, WhoWor 93
Bochero, Peter 1899?-1960? BioIn 17
Bochicchio, Paul Law&B 92
Bochicchio-Ausura, Jill Arden 1951- WhoAm 92, WhoAmW 93, WhoEmL 93
Bochin, Hal W(illiam) 1942- ConAu 137
Bochnacki, Zbigniew WhoScE 91-4
Bochnak, Mary Louise 1951- WhoEmL 93
Bochner, Hart 1956- WhoAm 92
Bochner, Lloyd 1924- WhoAm 92
Bochner, Martin Barry 1934- WhoE 93
Bochner, Mel 1940- WhoAm 92
Bochnowski, Jean Elise 1962- WhoE 93
Bochow, Carl Evans 1928- St&PR 93
Bochroch, Albert R(obert) 1909- ConAu 39NR
Bochsa, (Robert-) Nicolas-Charles 1789-1856 Baker 92
Bochsa, Robert Nicolas Charles 1789-1856 BioIn 17
Bock, Annie Sara AmWomPl
Bock, Carolyn Ann 1942- WhoAmW 93
Bock, Charles Walter 1945- WhoE 93
Bock, Dale E. Law&B 92
Bock, David Ruick 1943- WhoUN 92
Bock, Eduard d1871 See Bote & Bock Baker 92
Bock, Edward John 1916- WhoAm 92
Bock, Fedor von 1880-1945 HarEnMi
Bock, Frances Ann 1939- WhoAmW 93
Bock, Gisela 1942- ConAu 138
Bock, Gordon Honold 1952- WhoWrEP 92
Bock, Gustav 1813-1863 See Bote & Bock Baker 92
Bock, Gustav 1882-1953 See Bote & Bock Baker 92
Bock, Hans 1928- WhoScE 91-3, WhoWor 93
Bock, Hans Hermann 1940- WhoScE 91-3, WhoWor 93
Bock, Harvey N. Law&B 92
Bock, Hugo 1848-1932 See Bote & Bock Baker 92
Bock, J. Kathryn 1948- WhoEmL 93
Bock, Jacques 1932- St&PR 93
Bock, Jay Lawrence 1950- WhoEmL 93
Bock, Jeffrey William 1950- WhoEmL 93
Bock, Jerry 1928- Baker 92, WhoAm 92
Bock, John Louis 1945- WhoSSW 93
Bock, Joseph Reto 1929- St&PR 93, WhoAm 92
Bock, Klaus 1944- WhoScE 91-2, WhoWor 93
Bock, Michael 1950- WhoWor 93
Bock, Peter 1937- WhoScE 91-3
Bock, Richard W. 1865-1949 BioIn 17
Bock, Robert Howard 1932- WhoAm 92
Bock, Robert J. St&PR 93
Bock, Robert M. 1923-1991 BioIn 17
Bock, Rudolf M. 1927- WhoScE 91-3
Bock, Russell Samuel 1905- WhoAm 92, WhoWrEP 92
Bock, Steen 1962- WhoWor 93
Bock, Walter Joseph 1933- WhoAm 92
Bock, William Richard, Jr. 1939- WhoAm 92
Bockart, Richard L. 1934- St&PR 93
Bockbrader, Robert Harold 1938- St&PR 93
Bocke, John J. 1947- St&PR 93
Bockelman, Charles Kincaid 1922- WhoE 93
Bockelman, John Richard 1925- WhoAm 92, WhoWor 93
Bockelmann, Rudolf 1892-1958 IntDcOp, OxDcOp
Bockelmann, Rudolf (August Louis Wilhelm) 1892-1958 Baker 92
Bockemuhl, Jochen 1939- WhoScE 91-3
Bocken, Hubert Felix 1944- WhoWor 93
Bocker, Hans Jurgen 1939- WhoWor 93
Bockerstette, Joseph A. 1957- WhoAm 92
Bockewitz, Wilma Gertrude WhoAmW 93
Bockey, Pamela Sue 1952- WhoEmL 93
Bockhoff, Frank James 1928- WhoAm 92
Bockhop, Clarence William 1921- WhoAm 92
Bockhorn, Robert K. 1935- St&PR 93
Bockian, Donna Marie 1946- WhoAmW 93
Bockian, James Bernard 1936- WhoE 93
Bockius, Louis V., III 1935- St&PR 93
Bockli, Urs 1952- WhoEmL 93
Bockmuhl, Klaus BioIn 17
Bockstein, Herbert 1943- WhoAm 92
Bockstoce, John R. BioIn 17
Bockstruck, Arnold Herbert 1927- St&PR 93
Bockstruck, Robert H. 1958- St&PR 93
Bockus, C. Barry 1934- St&PR 93, WhoAm 92
Bockus, Harry N., Jr. 1926- St&PR 93
Bockwoldt, Todd Shane 1967- WhoWor 93
Bocobo, Christian Reyes 1954- WhoWor 93
Boczar, Jerzy 1924- WhoScE 91-4
Boczek, Jan H. 1927- WhoScE 91-4
Boczek, Paul 1937- St&PR 93
Boczkaj, Bohdan Karol 1930- WhoWor 93
Bod, Peter A. BioIn 17
Boda, Domokos Istvan 1921- WhoScE 91-4
Boda, John 1922- Baker 92
Boda, Koloman 1927- WhoScE 91-4
Boda, Veronica Constance 1952- WhoAmW 93, WhoEmL 93
Bodaan, Harry Jacobus 1951- WhoAm 92
Bodager, Barbara Aileen Law&B 92
Bodalo, Antonio 1940- WhoScE 91-3
Bodalski, Richard A. 1939- St&PR 93
Bodansky, David 1924- WhoAm 92
Bodanszky, Miklos 1915- WhoAm 92
Bodanza, Joseph Frank 1947- St&PR 93
Bodanzky, Artur 1877-1939 Baker 92, IntDcOp, OxDcOp
Bodarski, Zdzislaw 1931- WhoScE 91-4
Bodart, Jean-Marc Claude 1964- WhoWor 93
Bodart, Philippe Joseph Ghislain 1960- WhoWor 93
Bodart, William Roger 1931- St&PR 93
Bodart-Talbot, Joni (Jomi Bodart) 1947- WhoWrEP 92
Bodde, David L. 1943- St&PR 93
Bodde, William, Jr. 1931- WhoAm 92, WhoWor 93
Boddecker, Philipp Friedrich 1607-1683 Baker 92
Boddecker, Philipp Jakob 1642-1707 Baker 92
Boddeke, Rudolf 1934- WhoScE 91-3
Boddeker, Edward William, III 1929- WhoSSW 93
Boddeker, Karl W. 1934- WhoScE 91-3
Bodden, Jane Ellen 1948- WhoEmL 93, WhoSSW 93
Bodden, Jim 1930-1988 DcCPCAm
Bodden, John M. 1930- St&PR 93
Bodden, Norman 1935- DcCPCAm
Bodden, William Michael 1929- WhoAm 92
Boddenberg, Bruno 1938- WhoScE 91-3
Boddens-Hosang, J.F. 1929- WhoUN 92
Boddewyn, J(ean) J. 1929- ConAu 39NR
Boddez, Gerard R.V. 1928- WhoScE 91-2
Boddie, Benjamin F. 1925- WhoSSW 93
Boddie, Don O'Mar 1944- WhoWor 93
Boddie, Grace Collins 1917- St&PR 93
Boddie, Reginald Alonzo 1959- WhoEmL 93
Boddiger, George Cyrus 1917- WhoAm 92
Boddington, Craig Thornton 1952- WhoWrEP 92
Boddy, Clive Roland 1959- WhoWor 93
Boddy, Fred 1952- St&PR 93
Bode, Barbara WhoAm 92
Bode, Carl 1911- WhoAm 92, WhoWrEP 92
Bode, Christoph Albert-Maria 1955- WhoWor 93
Bode, Dietrich Karl Ernst 1934- WhoWor 93
Bode, Hans Ragnar 1938- WhoAm 92
Bode, Henry Joseph 1934- St&PR 93
Bode, Janet BioIn 17
Bode, Johann Joachim Christoph 1730-1793 Baker 92
Bode, Ken BioIn 17
Bode, Richard Albert 1931- WhoAm 92
Bode, Roy Evan 1948- WhoAm 92
Bode, Rudolf 1881-1970 Baker 92
Bode, Sara Giddings 1935- WhoAmW 93
Bode, Vaughn 1941-1975 ScF&FL 92
Bode, Walter Albert 1950- WhoAm 92
Bodecker, N(iels) M(ogens) 1922-1988 ConAu 40NR, MajAI, SmATA 73 [port]
Bodeen, George H. 1924- St&PR 93
Bodek, Arie 1947- WhoE 93
Bodek, Gordon S. 1920- St&PR 93
Bodek, Norman 1932- WhoWrEP 92
Bodeker, Robert Allen 1936- St&PR 93
Bodell, Gerald H. 1939- St&PR 93
Bodell, Mark B. 1952- St&PR 93
Bodell, Michael James 1949- St&PR 93
Bodem, Dennis Richard 1937- WhoAm 92
Boden, Constantin Robert 1936- St&PR 93
Boden, William David 1941- St&PR 93, WhoE 93
Bodenbender, Douglas 1945- St&PR 93
Bodenburg, Angela Sommer- BioIn 17, ScF&FL 92
Bodenheimer, Henry C., Jr. 1950- WhoEmL 93
Bodenmann, John 1936- St&PR 93
Bodenschatz, Erhard 1576-1636 Baker 92
Bodenschatz, John BioIn 17
Bodensieck, Raymond Alan 1959- WhoE 93
Bodensiek, Herbert K. 1927- St&PR 93
Bodenstedt, A. Andreas 1934- WhoScE 91-3
Bodenstedt, Erwin Friedrich 1926- WhoScE 91-3
Bodenstein, Ira 1954- WhoEmL 93
Bodenstein, Nancy Miller St&PR 93
Bodenstein, Robert Q. 1936- St&PR 93
Bodenstein, Robert Quentin 1936- WhoIns 93
Bodet, Jaime Torres 1902-1974 BioIn 17
Bodett, Tom 1955- SmATA 70 [port]
Bodey, Gerald Paul 1934- WhoAm 92
Bodey, Richard Allen 1930- WhoWrEP 92
Bodey, Vicki Darlene 1956- WhoAmW 93
Bodge, Clifford A. 1935- St&PR 93
Bodi, Sonia Ellen 1940- WhoAmW 93
Bodian, David d1992 NewYTBS 92
Bodian, David 1910- WhoAm 92
Bodian, Nat G. 1921- WhoAm 92
Bodie, Carroll Alexander Law&B 92
Bodie, Idella Fallaw 1925- WhoWrEP 92
Bodiford, Charlene 1953- WhoEmL 93
Bodiford, David Wayne 1955- St&PR 93
Bodily, David Martin 1933- WhoAm 92
Bodin, Lars-Gunnar 1935- Baker 92
Bodin, Richelle Lynn 1967- WhoSSW 93
Bodine, Bernadette 1935- WhoAmW 93
Bodine, David Butterfield 1952- St&PR 93
Bodine, Della L. 1951- WhoAmW 93
Bodine, Edward F. 1921- St&PR 93
Bodine, James Forney 1921- WhoAm 92
Bodine, Laurence 1950- WhoAm 92, WhoEmL 93
Bodine, Paul J., Jr. 1924- St&PR 93
Bodine, Richard P. 1926- St&PR 93
Bodine, Robert J. 1924- St&PR 93
Bodini, Daniele Damaso 1945- WhoAm 92
Bodini, Vittorio 1914-1970 DcLB 128 [port]
Bodker, Cecil 1927- MajAI [port]
Bodker, Stuart Eliot 1953- WhoEmL 93
Bodkin, Henry Grattan, Jr. 1921- WhoAm 92
Bodkin, Lawrence Edward 1927- WhoWor 93
Bodkin, Lynn M. Law&B 92
Bodkin, M.E. 1942- St&PR 93
Bodkin, Ruby Pate 1926- WhoAmW 93
Bodky, Erwin 1896-1958 Baker 92
Bodlaj, Viktor 1928- WhoWor 93
Bodlender, Jonathan Andrew 1938- WhoWor 93
Bodley, Harley Ryan, Jr. 1936- WhoAm 92
Bodley, Seoirse 1933- Baker 92
Bodlund, R.R. 1940- St&PR 93
Bodman, Edward Dunham d1991 BioIn 17
Bodman, Richard Stockwell 1938- WhoAm 92
Bodman, Roger A. 1952- St&PR 93
Bodman, Samuel W. BioIn 17
Bodman, Samuel W. 1938- St&PR 93
Bodman, Samuel Wright, III 1938- WhoAm 92, WhoE 93
Bodmer, Johann Jakob 1698-1783 BioIn 17
Bodmer, Karl 1809-1893 BioIn 17
Bodmer, Michael Anthony 1944- WhoSSW 93
Bodmer, Walter WhoScE 91-4
Bodmer, Walter 1936- WhoScE 91-1
Bodmer, Walter Fred 1936- WhoWor 93
Bodnar, John, III 1958- WhoEmL 93
Bodnar, Lora Lynn 1971- WhoAmW 93
Bodnar, Paul Zoltan 1950- WhoEmL 93
Bodnar, Priscilla Marlene Law&B 92
Bodnar, Richard 1946- WhoE 93
Bodnar, Tadeusz 1922- WhoScE 91-4
Bodne, Ben B. d1992 BioIn 17, NewYTBS 92
Bodner, Emanuel 1947- WhoSSW 93
Bodner, Herbert 1948- St&PR 93, WhoAm 92
Bodner, John, Jr. 1927- WhoAm 92
Bodner, M. Gayle Law&B 92
Bodner, Seymour S. 1927- WhoE 93

Bodo, Imre 1932- *WhoScE 91-4*
Bodo, Joseph Paul, Jr. 1931- *WhoSSW 93*
Bodo, Murray 1937- *WhoWrEP 92*
Bodofsky, Gary Allen 1958- *WhoSSW 93*
Bodoni, Philip P. 1952- *St&PR 93*
Bodony, Stephen Gerald 1947- *WhoEmL 93*
Bodor, Bruce Timothy 1959- *WhoEmL 93*
Bodor, Nicholas S. 1939- *St&PR 93*
Bodow, Wayne R. *Law&B 92*
Bodrov, Sergej 1948- *DrEEuF*
Bodson, Bernard 1955- *WhoScE 91-2*
Bodson, F.J. 1947- *WhoWor 93*
Bodson, Marc 1957- *WhoEmL 93*
Bodsworth, Charles Frederick 1918- *WhoAm 92*
Bodsworth, Colin *WhoScE 91-1*
Bodsworth, Fred *WhoCanL 92*
Bodtcher, Ronald Keith 1959- *WhoSSW 93*
Bodwell, Russell S. 1921- *St&PR 93*
Body, Jack 1944- *Baker 92*
Bodzy, Allen N. 1953- *St&PR 93*
Bodzy, Glen A. *Law&B 92*
Bodzy, Glen Alan 1952- *St&PR 93*
Boe, Barbara Louise 1935- *WhoAmW 93*
Boe, David Stephen 1936- *WhoAm 92*
Boe, Eugene *BioIn 17*
Boe, Eugene d1992 *NewYTBS 92*
Boe, Eugene H. 1937- *St&PR 93*
Boe, Gerard Patrick 1936- *WhoAm 92*
Boe, Myron Timothy 1948- *WhoEmL 93, WhoSSW 93, WhoWor 93*
Boe, Nils A. d1992 *NewYTBS 92 [port]*
Boe, Nils A. 1913- *CngDr 91*
Boe, Nils Andreas 1913- *WhoAm 92*
Boe, Ralph Jacob 1944- *WhoAm 92, WhoSSW 93*
Boe, Thomas Daniel 1960- *WhoEmL 93*
Boebel, Carl Paul 1931- *St&PR 93*
Boechler, Paul M. 1958- *St&PR 93*
Boeck, August de 1865-1937 *Baker 92*
Boeck, Phil H. 1948- *St&PR 93*
Boecke, Donald W. *Law&B 92*
Boeckel, Florence Brewer 1855- *AmWomPl*
Boecker, Jeffrey Allen *Law&B 92*
Boeckh, Jurgen 1934- *WhoScE 91-3*
Boeckman, Frances Blissard 1921- *WhoAmW 93, WhoSSW 93*
Boeckman, James Wallace *Law&B 92*
Boeckman, L. Michelle *Law&B 92*
Boeckman, Robert Kenneth, Jr. 1944- *WhoAm 92*
Boeckmann, Delores 1904-1989 *BiDAMSp 1989*
Boeckner, Robert G. 1941- *St&PR 93*
Boeddeker, Timothy Mark 1948- *WhoEmL 93*
Boedecker, Anne Louise 1951- *WhoE 93, WhoEmL 93*
Boedeker, Harold W. 1913- *St&PR 93*
Boeder, Jennie G. *Law&B 92*
Boeding, Jo Diane *Law&B 92*
Boegen, Anne S. d1989 *BioIn 17*
Boegner, Dieter K.H. 1932- *St&PR 93*
Boegner, Mary Elizabeth Blanche 1925- *WhoAmW 93*
Boehe, Ernst 1880-1938 *Baker 92*
Boeheim, James Arthur, Jr. 1944- *BiDAMSp 1989*
Boehk, Paul E. 1931- *St&PR 93*
Boehle, William Randall 1919- *WhoAm 92*
Boehlefeld, Heidi *Law&B 92*
Boehler, Peter 1712-1775 *BioIn 17*
Boehler, William L. 1930- *St&PR 93*
Boehlert, Sherwood L. 1936- *CngDr 91*
Boehlert, Sherwood Louis 1936- *WhoAm 92, WhoE 93*
Boehm, C. Norman, Jr. 1928- *WhoE 93*
Boehm, David A. 1914- *St&PR 93*
Boehm, David Alfred 1914- *WhoAm 92*
Boehm, Eric H. 1918- *St&PR 93*
Boehm, Eric Hartzell 1918- *WhoAm 92, WhoWor 93*
Boehm, Felix Hans 1924- *WhoAm 92*
Boehm, Frederick T. *Law&B 92*
Boehm, George August Westall 1922- *WhoE 93*
Boehm, Hanns-Peter 1928- *WhoScE 91-3*
Boehm, Harald 1938- *WhoScE 91-3*
Boehm, Josef Franz 1944- *St&PR 93*
Boehm, K.H. 1935- *WhoScE 91-3*
Boehm, Klaus Juergen 1949- *St&PR 93*
Boehm, Marlys Gladen 1951- *St&PR 93*
Boehm, Richard d1992 *NewYTBS 92*
Boehm, Richard Wood 1926- *WhoWor 93*
Boehm, Robert Foty 1940- *WhoAm 92*
Boehm, Ronald James 1953- *St&PR 93*
Boehm, Steven Bruce 1954- *WhoEmL 93*
Boehm, Theodore R. *Law&B 92*
Boehm, Werner William 1913- *WhoAm 92, WhoWor 93*
Boehm, William J. 1936- *St&PR 93*
Boehme, Donna C. *Law&B 92*
Boehme, Hilary C. 1935- *St&PR 93*
Boehme, Ronald Edward 1937- *WhoWor 93*
Boehme, Sarah Elizabeth 1948- *WhoEmL 93*
Boehme, Vernon P. 1953- *St&PR 93*
Boehmer, Daniel R. 1949- *St&PR 93*
Boehmer, Raquel Davenport 1938- *WhoAmW 93*
Boehmer, Ronald Glenn 1947- *WhoEmL 93*
Boehmler, E. William 1940- *St&PR 93*
Boehn, Dieter L. 1938- *WhoWor 93*
Boehncke, Engelhard 1935- *WhoScE 91-3*
Boehne, Edward G. 1940- *St&PR 93*
Boehne, Edward George 1940- *WhoAm 92*
Boehne, Patricia Jeanne 1940- *WhoWrEP 92*
Boehnen, David Leo 1946- *St&PR 93, WhoAm 92*
Boehner, David L. *Law&B 92*
Boehner, John A. 1949- *CngDr 91, WhoAm 92*
Boehning, Joseph Frederick 1931- *WhoAm 92*
Boehr, Dorothy J. 1942- *St&PR 93*
Boehs, Kenneth Robert 1947- *St&PR 93*
Boeing, John K. d1990 *BioIn 17*
Boeka, Adriana M. *St&PR 93*
Boeke, Eugene H., Jr. 1925- *St&PR 93, WhoAm 92, WhoWor 93*
Boeke, Lee G. *BioIn 17*
Boeke, Norbert Henry 1940- *WhoWor 93*
Boeke, Robert William 1925- *St&PR 93*
Boekelheide, Virgil Carl 1919- *WhoAm 92*
Boekenheide, Russell W. 1930- *St&PR 93*
Boekenheide, Russell William 1930- *WhoAm 92*
Boeker, Paul Harold 1938- *WhoAm 92*
Boelaert, Edmond 1899-1966 *IntDcAn*
Boele, C.M.A. *WhoScE 91-3*
Boelen, Charles 1941- *WhoUN 92*
Boelens, Otto Cornelis 1945- *WhoWor 93*
Boelens, Simon Wigger 1957- *WhoWor 93*
Boeler, Jan B. 1938- *WhoScE 91-4*
Boell, Edgar John 1906- *WhoAm 92*
Boella, Giuliano *WhoScE 91-3*
Boellmann, Leon 1862-1897 *Baker 92*
Boelman, Mahnaz *Law&B 92*
Boelter, John Dolliff *Law&B 92*
Boelts, Kenneth J. 1935- *St&PR 93*
Boely, Alexandre Pierre Francois 1785-1858 *Baker 92*
Boely, Bernard 1948- *WhoWor 93*
Boelza, Igor 1904- *Baker 92*
Boemi, A. Andrew 1915- *St&PR 93*
Boemi, Andrew Anthony 1944- *St&PR 93*
Boenker, Alvin Charles 1920- *WhoSSW 93*
Boenning, Henry Dorr, Jr. 1914- *WhoAm 92*
Boentje, John D., Jr. 1916- *St&PR 93*
Boepple, Paul 1896-1970 *Baker 92*
Boer, F. Peter 1941- *WhoAm 92*
Boer, G.J. 1942- *WhoScE 91-3*
Boergers, Mary H. 1946- *WhoAmW 93*
Boeri, Fernand 1936- *WhoScE 91-2*
Boeri, Renato Raimondo 1922- *WhoWor 93*
Boering, Geert 1929- *WhoScE 91-3*
Boermeester, Donald Alan 1967- *WhoE 93*
Boerner, Jo M. 1944- *WhoAmW 93, WhoSSW 93*
Boerner, John M. 1934- *St&PR 93*
Boerner, Peter 1926- *WhoAm 92*
Boero, Felipe 1884-1958 *Baker 92*
Boerrigter, Glenn Charles 1932- *WhoAm 92*
Boers, Arthur Paul 1957- *ConAu 138*
Boers, Terry John 1950- *WhoAm 92*
Boersma, Burton Harry 1929- *WhoAm 92*
Boersma, Diana Lurie *Law&B 92*
Boersma, Diana Lurie 1956- *WhoEmL 93*
Boersma, Lawrence Allan 1932- *WhoWor 93*
Boersma, Mark A. 1950- *St&PR 93*
Boersma, Sipko Luu 1921- *WhoWor 93*
Boerste, Michael Stephan 1963- *WhoSSW 93*
Boerstler, Barry L. 1947- *St&PR 93*
Boerstler, Barry Lee 1947- *WhoEmL 93*
Boerstler, Richard William 1923- *WhoWrEP 92*
Boertje, Stanley Benjamin 1930- *WhoSSW 93*
Boes, Francis Xavier 1939- *St&PR 93*
Boes, Lawrence William 1935- *WhoAm 92*
Boesak, Allan 1945- *WhoAfr*
Boesak, Allan Aubrey 1946- *BioIn 17, WhoWor 93*
Boesch, Christian 1941- *Baker 92*
Boesch, Francis Theodore 1936- *WhoAm 92, WhoE 93*
Boesch, Lawrence Michael 1951- *WhoEmL 93*
Boesch, Rainer 1938- *Baker 92*
Boesch, Richard John 1963- *WhoWor 93*
Boesche, Fenelon 1910- *St&PR 93*
Boeschenstein, William Wade 1925- *WhoAm 92*
Boeschenstein, Wm. W. 1925- *St&PR 93*
Boese, Frederick C. *Law&B 92*
Boese, Gilbert Karyle 1937- *WhoAm 92*
Boese, James Stephen 1940- *St&PR 93, WhoAm 92*
Boese, Kathleen Carol 1942- *WhoAmW 93*
Boese, Martha *AmWomPl*
Boese, Robert Alan 1934- *WhoAm 92*
Boese, Sandra Jean 1940- *WhoAmW 93*
Boesel, Kenneth S. 1912- *St&PR 93*
Boesel, Milton Charles, Jr. 1928- *WhoAm 92, WhoWor 93*
Boesel, Stephen W. 1944- *St&PR 93*
Boesen, John Michael 1946- *WhoEmL 93*
Boesen, Melvin Peter 1931- *St&PR 93*
Boeser, William F. *St&PR 93*
Boesgaard, Ann 1939- *BioIn 17*
Boeshaar, Patricia Chikotas 1947- *WhoEmL 93*
Boeshe, Barbara Louise *WhoE 93*
Boesiger, Peter 1946- *WhoWor 93*
Boesken, Dietrich H. 1927- *WhoWor 93*
Boesky, Ivan F. *BioIn 17*
Boesky, S.J. 1956- *St&PR 93*
Boesman, Gabriel 1926- *WhoScE 91-2*
Boesmans, Philippe 1936- *Baker 92*
Boessenecker, John 1953- *ConAu 138*
Boesset, Antoine 1586-1643 *Baker 92*
Boessneck, Kathleen Susan 1958- *WhoAmW 93*
Boethius c. 480-c. 524 *OxDcByz*
Boethius, Anicius Manlius Torquatus Severinus c. 480-524 *Baker 92*
Boetig, Donna Byrnes 1950- *WhoWrEP 92*
Boetius, Anicius Manlius Torquatus Severinus c. 480-524 *Baker 92*
Boettcher, Barbara E. *Law&B 92*
Boettcher, Bryan Clair 1956- *WhoEmL 93*
Boettcher, Diane Ruth 1957- *WhoEmL 93*
Boettcher, Harold Paul 1923- *WhoAm 92*
Boettcher, Norbe Birosel 1932- *WhoAm 92, WhoAmW 93*
Boettcher, Robert Richard, II 1944- *WhoSSW 93*
Boettcher, Wilfried 1929- *Baker 92*
Boettger, Hermann 1923- *WhoScE 91-3*
Boettger, Susan Doris 1952- *WhoEmL 93*
Boetticher, Budd 1916- *MiSFD 9*
Boetticher, Wolfgang 1914- *Baker 92*
Boev, Metodi 1935- *WhoScE 91-4*
Boeve, Helena Michalek 1943- *WhoSSW 93*
Boex-Borel, Joseph *ScF&FL 92*
Boff, Kenneth Richard 1947- *WhoEmL 93*
Boff, Leonardo *DcCPCAm*
Boffa, Louis A. 1948- *St&PR 93*
Boffa, Maurice 1939- *WhoWor 93*
Boffey, Stephen Arthur *WhoScE 91-1*
Boffi, Giandomenico 1953- *WhoWor 93*
Boffi, S. *WhoScE 91-3*
Boffi, Vinicio *WhoScE 91-3*
Bofill, Rano Solidum 1942- *WhoSSW 93, WhoWor 93*
Bofill, Ricardo *DcCPCAm*
Bofill, Ricardo 1939- *BioIn 17, WhoWor 93*
Bogaard, William J. *Law&B 92*
Bogaard, William Joseph 1938- *St&PR 93, WhoAm 92*
Bogacki, Michael Francis 1954- *St&PR 93*
Bogacki, Miroslaw 1932- *WhoScE 91-4*
Bogaczyk, Stanley J. 1942- *St&PR 93*
Bogaert, Harmen Meyndertsz van den *BioIn 17*
Bogaerts, M.J.M. 1934- *WhoScE 91-3*
Bogajewski, Jerzy 1938- *WhoScE 91-4*
Bogan, Charles E. *Law&B 92*
Bogan, Dagmar Anne 1956- *WhoAmW 93*
Bogan, Elizabeth Chapin 1944- *WhoAm 92*
Bogan, John J. *Law&B 92*
Bogan, Louise 1897-1970 *AmWrS3, BioIn 17*
Bogan, Mary Flair 1948- *WhoAmW 93*
Bogan, Neil Earnest 1945- *WhoAm 92*
Bogan, Ralph A.L., Jr. 1922- *St&PR 93, WhoAm 92*
Bogan, Willie Clyde *Law&B 92*
Boganda, Barthelemy Yangongo 1944- *WhoUN 92*
Bogar, John A. 1918- *WhoIns 93*
Bogard, Carole Christine *WhoAm 92*
Bogard, Donald P. *Law&B 92*
Bogard, Harry Gene 1932- *St&PR 93*
Bogard, Terry Lee 1936- *WhoE 93*
Bogarde, Dirk 1921- *BioIn 17, IntDcF 2-3 [port]*
Bogarde, John Bengt Torgny 1950- *WhoWor 93*
Bogardus, Carl Robert, Jr. 1933- *WhoAm 92*
Bogardus, E. Hal 1931- *WhoE 93*
Bogardus, John A., Jr. 1927- *St&PR 93, WhoIns 93*
Bogardus, Raymond B. 1946- *St&PR 93*
Bogart, Brendan James 1967- *WhoE 93*
Bogart, Carol Lynn 1949- *WhoAmW 93*
Bogart, Charles Henry 1940- *WhoSSW 93*
Bogart, E. A. *ConAu 137*
Bogart, Eleanor A(nne) 1928- *ConAu 137*
Bogart, Homer Gordon 1922- *WhoAm 92*
Bogart, Humphrey 1899-1957 *BioIn 17, IntDcF 2-3 [port]*
Bogart, James Willoughby 1946- *St&PR 93*
Bogart, John d1992 *NewYTBS 92*
Bogart, John 1900-1986 *BioIn 17*
Bogart, Kenneth Paul 1943- *WhoE 93*
Bogart, Larry 1914-1991 *BioIn 17*
Bogart, Neil 1943-1982 *BioIn 17*
Bogart, Paul 1919- *MiSFD 9, WhoAm 92*
Bogart, Peter T. 1937- *St&PR 93*
Bogart, Robert B. 1944- *WhoAm 92*
Bogart, Robert W. 1946- *St&PR 93*
Bogart, W. Humphrey 1944- *St&PR 93*
Bogart, Wanda Lee 1939- *WhoAmW 93, WhoWor 93*
Bogart, William G. 1903-1977 *ScF&FL 92*
Bogart, William Harry 1931- *WhoWor 93*
Bogas, Ed *ScF&FL 92*
Bogash, Richard 1922- *WhoAm 92*
Bogash, Richard R. 1948- *WhoEmL 93*
Bogatay, Paul 1905-1972 *BioIn 17*
Bogaty, Lisa Bradford 1952- *WhoEmL 93*
Bogatyrev, Anatoly (Vasilievich) 1913- *Baker 92*
Bogatyrev, P.G. 1893-1971 *IntDcAn*
Bogatyrev, Semyon(ovich) 1890-1960 *Baker 92*
Bogayevicz, Yurek *MiSFD 9*
Bogdahn, Joseph R. 1962- *WhoEmL 93*
Bogdan, Carolyn Louetta 1941- *WhoAmW 93*
Bogdan, James Thomas 1938- *WhoWor 93*
Bogdan, Mircea 1943- *WhoScE 91-4*
Bogdan, Norbert A. 1902-1991 *BioIn 17*
Bogdan, Victor Michael 1933- *WhoAm 92*
Bogdanich, Walt 1950- *WhoAm 92*
Bogdanoff, John Lee 1916- *WhoAm 92*
Bogdanov, Alexander 1873-1928 *ScF&FL 92*
Bogdanov, Michael 1938- *ConTFT 10*
Bogdanov, Peter Atanassov 1933- *WhoScE 91-4*
Bogdanov, Rifkat Ibragimovich 1950- *WhoWor 93*
Bogdanov-Berezovsky, Valerian (Mikhailovich) 1903-1971 *Baker 92*
Bogdanovich, Joseph James 1912- *WhoAm 92*
Bogdanovich, Peter 1939- *BioIn 17, MiSFD 9, WhoAm 92*
Bogdasarian, John Robert 1944- *WhoAm 92*
Bogden, James Michael *Law&B 92*
Bogdon, Bernard D. *Law&B 92*
Bogdon, Eugene C. 1925- *St&PR 93*
Bogdonoff, Morton David 1925- *WhoAm 92*
Bogdonoff, Seymour Moses 1921- *WhoAm 92*
Boge, Herbert E. 1921- *St&PR 93*
Bogen, Claudia H. *Law&B 92*
Bogen, Don 1949- *WhoWrEP 92*
Bogen, Laurel Ann 1950- *WhoWrEP 92*
Bogen, Leslie A. 1954- *St&PR 93*
Bogen, Mark David 1959- *WhoEmL 93*
Bogen, Samuel Adams 1913- *WhoAm 92*
Bogenrief, Paul *Law&B 92*
Bogenstadt, Ludwig Von. *WhoWrEP 92*
Boger, Dale L. 1953- *WhoAm 92*
Boger, Dan Calvin 1946- *WhoEmL 93*
Boger, David Vernon 1939- *WhoWor 93*
Boger, Gail Green Parsons 1914- *WhoAm 92*
Boger, Joshua *St&PR 93*
Boger, Kenneth Snead 1946- *WhoE 93*
Boger, Lawrence Leroy 1923- *WhoAm 92*
Boger, Peter *WhoScE 91-3*
Boger, Peter Heinrich *WhoWor 93*
Boger, William Pierce, III 1945- *WhoWor 93*
Bogers, Robert J. 1946- *WhoScE 91-3*
Bogert, Charles M. d1992 *NewYTBS 92*
Bogert, Charles M. 1908-1992 *BioIn 17*
Bogert, George Taylor 1920- *WhoAm 92*
Bogert, Ivan Lathrop 1918- *WhoAm 92*
Bogert, Jeremiah Milbank 1941- *St&PR 93*
Bogert, Joan N. 1934- *St&PR 93*
Bogert, John Allen 1945- *St&PR 93*
Bogert, John Rogers 1924- *St&PR 93*
Bogert, Richard D. 1933- *St&PR 93*
Boggan, Bridgitt Fredia 1960- *WhoE 93*
Boggan, E. Carrington d1992 *NewYTBS 92*
Boggan, E. Carrington 1943-1992 *BioIn 17*
Boggan, Jeffrey Scott 1960- *WhoSSW 93*
Boggess, Albert *BioIn 17*
Boggess, Jerry R. 1944- *St&PR 93*
Boggess, Jerry Reid 1944- *WhoAm 92*
Boggess, John J. 1928- *WhoE 93*
Boggess, Thomas Phillip, III 1921- *WhoAm 92, WhoWor 93*
Boggess, William Talbot 1940- *St&PR 93*

Boggiani, Guido 1861-1901 *IntDcAn*
Boggio, Dennis Ray 1953- *WhoEmL 93*
Boggio, Miriam A. 1952- *WhoIns 93*
Boggs, Clifford G. 1939- *St&PR 93*
Boggs, Corinne Claiborne 1916- *WhoAmW 93*
Boggs, D.W. *ScF&FL 92*
Boggs, Danny Julian 1944- *WhoAm 92, WhoSSW 93*
Boggs, Duane Gary 1945- *WhoE 93*
Boggs, Edward Louis, III 1951- *WhoEmL 93*
Boggs, Elizabeth Monroe 1913- *WhoAmW 93*
Boggs, Jack Aaron 1935- *WhoAm 92*
Boggs, Jacqueline A. *Law&B 92*
Boggs, James Ernest 1921- *WhoAm 92*
Boggs, James T. *Law&B 92*
Boggs, Joseph Dodridge 1921- *WhoAm 92, WhoWor 93*
Boggs, Josiah Clendennen 1927- *St&PR 93*
Boggs, L. Kennedy *Law&B 92*
Boggs, Larry A. *Law&B 92*
Boggs, Lindy *BioIn 17*
Boggs, Marcus Livingstone, Jr. 1947- *WhoAm 92, WhoWrEP 92*
Boggs, Martha Ann 1928- *WhoSSW 93*
Boggs, Mary Louise 1956- *WhoAmW 93*
Boggs, N. Cornell, III *Law&B 92*
Boggs, Phil d1990 *BioIn 17*
Boggs, Ralph Stuart 1917- *WhoAm 92*
Boggs, Robert Newell 1930- *WhoAm 92, WhoWrEP 92*
Boggs, Sam, Jr. 1928- *WhoAm 92*
Boggs, Thomas Hale, Jr. 1940- *WhoAm 92, WhoWor 93*
Boggs, Wade *BioIn 17*
Boggs, Wade Anthony 1958- *WhoAm 92, WhoE 93*
Boggs, William Dixon 1933- *WhoAm 92*
Boggs, William Morris 1952- *WhoE 93*
Bog-Hansen, Thorkild Christian 1939- *WhoScE 91-2*
Boghosian, Paula der 1933- *WhoAmW 93, WhoWor 93*
Boghosian, Varujan Yegan 1926- *WhoAm 92*
Boghossian, P.O., III 1955- *St&PR 93*
Bogi, Imre 1939- *WhoScE 91-4*
Bogia, Benjamin Preston 1934- *WhoSSW 93*
Bogianckino, Massimo 1922- *Baker 92, OxDcOp*
Bogild Hansen, John 1950- *WhoScE 91-2*
Bogin, Linda A. *Law&B 92*
Bogino. Charles Hoover 1959- *WhoSSW 93*
Bogle, Chester Vernon 1924- *St&PR 93*
Bogle, Dick *AfrAmBi [port]*
Bogle, Edra Charlotte 1934- *WhoSSW 93*
Bogle, Hugh Andrew 1909- *WhoAm 92*
Bogle, John C. 1929- *St&PR 93*
Bogle, John Clifton 1929- *WhoAm 92*
Bogle, Mary Elizabeth Anderson 1927- *WhoSSW 93*
Bogle, Robert Angell, Jr. 1937- *St&PR 93*
Bogle, T.G. *St&PR 93*
Bogle, William Yates, IV 1957- *WhoE 93*
Bognar, Gyozo 1930- *WhoScE 91-4*
Bogner, M. Eugene 1946- *St&PR 93*
Bogner, Norman 1935- *ScF&FL 92*
Bogner, Willy *MiSFD 9*
Bognon, Pierre Desire 1940- *St&PR 93*
Bogoevici, Nicolae 1928- *WhoScE 91-4*
Bogomil, Pop fl. 10th cent.- *OxDcByz*
Bogomolny, Richard Joseph 1935- *WhoAm 92*
Bogomolny, Robert L. *Law&B 92*
Bogomolny, Robert Lee 1938- *St&PR 93, WhoAm 92*
Bogorad, Barbara Ellen *WhoAmW 93*
Bogorad, Lawrence 1921- *WhoAm 92, WhoE 93*
Bogorad, Samuel Nathaniel 1917- *WhoAm 92*
Bogoras, Waldemar 1865-1936 *IntDcAn*
Bogosian, Eric *BioIn 17*
Bogosian, Eric 1953- *ConAu 138, WhoAm 92, WhoE 93*
Bogosian, Richard Wayne 1937- *WhoAm 92, WhoWor 93*
Bogossian, Gail *Law&B 92*
Bograd, Michele Louise 1952- *WhoEmL 93*
Bograd, Samuel d1991 *BioIn 17*
Bogrand, Randall K. 1954- *St&PR 93*
Bogre, Janos 1927- *WhoScE 91-4*
Bogren, Hugo Gunnar 1933- *WhoAm 92*
Bogrov, Dmitrii 1887-1911 *BioIn 17*
Bogsch, Arpad 1919- *WhoUN 92*
Bogstahl, Deborah Marcelle 1950- *WhoAmW 93*
Bogtstra, Frits Robert 1937- *WhoScE 91-3*
Boguchwal, Stephen F. *Law&B 92*
Bogue, Allan G. 1921- *WhoAm 92*
Bogue, Andrew Wendell 1919- *WhoAm 92*
Bogue, Barbara Ann Tyus 1945- *WhoAmW 93*
Bogue, Carrie Anne 1952- *WhoAmW 93, WhoEmL 93*
Bogue, Lucille Maxfield 1911- *WhoWrEP 92*
Bogue, Philip R. 1924- *St&PR 93*
Bogue, Philip Roberts 1924- *WhoAm 92*
Bogue, Ronald Lynn 1948- *WhoSSW 93*
Bogues, Muggsy *BioIn 17*
Bogumill, Michael Thomas 1938- *WhoE 93*
Bogusky, Alf 1947- *WhoAm 92*
Boguslaski, Mary G. *Law&B 92*
Boguslavsky, Leonid 1951- *WhoWor 93*
Boguslaw, Robert 1919- *WhoAm 92*
Boguslawski, Alexander Prus 1951- *WhoEmL 93*
Boguslawski, Edward 1940- *Baker 92*
Boguslawski, Wladyslaw 1757-1829 *PolBiDi*
Boguslawski, Wladyslaw 1838-1909 *PolBiDi*
Bogusz, Maciej Jozef 1940- *WhoWor 93*
Bogut, John Carl, Jr. 1961- *WhoEmL 93*
Bogutsky, Paul Harold 1952- *St&PR 93*
Bogutz, Jerome Edwin 1935- *WhoAm 92*
Bogy, David Beauregard 1936- *WhoAm 92*
Bogy, John W. *Law&B 92*
Boh, Ivan 1930- *WhoAm 92*
Boh, Robert Henry 1930- *St&PR 93*
Bohac, Josef 1929- *Baker 92*
Bohac, Martin McCormick *Law&B 92*
Bohacek, Nenad 1920- *WhoScE 91-4*
Bohamed, Gary M. 1960- *St&PR 93*
Bohan, Jack L. *Law&B 92*
Bohan, Janis Sue 1945- *WhoAmW 93*
Bohan, John E. 1931- *St&PR 93*
Bohan, Marc 1926- *WhoWor 93*
Bohan, Richard W. *Law&B 92*
Bohan, Stephen John 1957- *WhoEmL 93*
Bohanan, David John 1946- *WhoE 93, WhoEmL 93*
Bohane, Michael John 1936- *WhoAm 92*
Bohannan, Paul James 1920- *WhoAm 92*
Bohannon, David D. 1898- *WhoAm 92*
Bohannon, John 1936- *WhoWrEP 92*
Bohannon, Joseph Elton, III 1960- *WhoSSW 93*
Bohannon, Marcia Marie 1960- *WhoAmW 93*
Bohannon, Raymond Lawrence 1954- *WhoWor 93*
Bohannon, Richard Leland 1907- *WhoAm 92*
Bohannon, Sarah Virginia 1947- *WhoAmW 93*
Bohanon, Luther L. 1902- *WhoAm 92*
Bohanon, Richard Lee 1935- *WhoAm 92*
Bohanske, Robert Thomas 1953- *WhoWor 93*
Bohata, Emil Anton 1918- *WhoWor 93*
Bohaterewicz, Bronislaw 1880-1941 *PolBiDi*
Bohdan, Stalinski 1924- *WhoScE 91-4*
Bohemund c. 1050-1109 *OxDcByz*
Bohince, Judith Ann 1940- *WhoSSW 93*
Bohjalian, Chris 1960- *ConAu 139*
Bohl, H. *WhoScE 91-3*
Bohl, Michael E. 1956- *St&PR 93*
Bohlander, Robert F. 1934- *St&PR 93*
Bohle, Bruce William 1918- *WhoAm 92, WhoWrEP 92*
Bohle, Daniel James 1946- *WhoEmL 93*
Bohlemann, Rolando Guillermo 1952- *WhoWor 93*
Bohlen, Charles E. 1904-1974 *BioIn 17, ColdWar 1 [port]*
Bohlen, Christopher Wayne 1949- *WhoEmL 93*
Bohlen, Jeanne Louise 1938- *WhoE 93*
Bohlen, Nina 1931- *WhoAm 92*
Bohlen, Richard William 1935- *WhoAm 92*
Bohlen, Walter Franklin 1938- *WhoE 93*
Bohlender, Hugh D. *Law&B 92*
Bohlender, Hugh Darrow 1951- *WhoEmL 93*
Bohler, Torstein *WhoScE 91-4*
Bohler, Tyrus Augustus 1947- *WhoEmL 93*
Bohler, Wallace H. 1927- *St&PR 93*
Bohlin, Carol Fry 1958- *WhoAmW 93*
Bohlin, Daniel James 1949- *WhoEmL 93*
Bohlin, Gunnar 1929- *WhoScE 91-4*
Bohlin, Peter Quarfordt 1937- *WhoAm 92*
Bohlin, R. Paul 1936- *WhoAm 92, WhoE 93*
Bohlin, Torgny 1925- *WhoWor 93*
Bohling, Raymond Frank 1915- *WhoSSW 93*
Bohlinger, Alfred J. d1992 *NewYTBS 92 [port]*
Bohlinger, Alfred J. 1902-1992 *BioIn 17*
Bohling-Philippi, Vicki Dee 1964- *WhoAmW 93*
Bohlke, Gary Lee 1941- *WhoE 93*
Bohlken, Deborah Kay 1952- *WhoAmW 93, WhoSSW 93*
Bohlmann, Daniel Robert 1948- *WhoEmL 93, WhoWor 93*
Bohlmann, Paul F. 1925- *St&PR 93*
Bohlmann, Ralph Arthur 1932- *WhoAm 92*
Bohlmann, Rodney John 1948- *WhoEmL 93*
Bohm, David J. d1992 *NewYTBS 92 [port]*
Bohm, Eberhard 1941- *WhoScE 91-3*
Bohm, Georg 1661-1733 *Baker 92*
Bohm, H. *WhoScE 91-3*
Bohm, Henry Victor 1929- *WhoAm 92*
Bohm, James Glenn 1962- *WhoWor 93*
Bohm, Joel Lawrence *Law&B 92*
Bohm, Joel Lawrence 1942- *St&PR 93*
Bohm, Joseph 1795-1876 *Baker 92*
Bohm, Karl 1894-1981 *Baker 92, IntDcOp [port], OxDcOp*
Bohm, Karl-Heinz Hermann 1923- *WhoAm 92*
Bohm, Theobald 1794-1881 *Baker 92*
Bohm, Werner 1939- *St&PR 93*
Bohman, Michael 1917- *WhoScE 91-4*
Bohman, Per Rickard 1943- *WhoWor 93*
Bohme, Diethard Kurt 1941- *WhoAm 92*
Bohme, Franz Magnus 1827-1898 *Baker 92*
Bohme, G. 1942- *WhoScE 91-3*
Bohme, Jakob 1575-1624 *BioIn 17*
Bohme, Johann F. 1940- *WhoScE 91-3*
Bohme, Kurt (Gerhard) 1908-1989 *Baker 92*
Bohmer, Einar 1930- *WhoScE 91-4*
Bohmer, William T. 1947- *St&PR 93*
Bohmont, Dale Wendell 1922- *WhoAm 92*
Bohmrich, Marion Letcher d1991 *BioIn 17*
Bohn, Barbara Ann 1943- *WhoSSW 93*
Bohn, Charlotte Galitz 1930- *WhoAmW 93*
Bohn, Corinn J. *Law&B 92*
Bohn, Donna F. *Law&B 92*
Bohn, Henry George 1796-1884 *BioIn 17*
Bohn, John *St&PR 93*
Bohn, John A., Jr. 1937- *St&PR 93*
Bohn, John Augustus, Jr. 1937- *WhoAm 92*
Bohn, Karen M. 1953- *St&PR 93*
Bohn, Peter N. 1919- *St&PR 93*
Bohn, Ralph Carl 1930- *WhoAm 92*
Bohn, Sarah A. 1956- *WhoEmL 93*
Bohn, Udo 1939- *WhoScE 91-3*
Bohne, Carl John, Jr. 1916- *WhoAm 92*
Bohne, Dieter 1935- *WhoScE 91-3*
Bohnen, Blythe 1940- *WhoE 93*
Bohnen, Michael 1887-1965 *IntDcOp*
Bohnen, (Franz) Michael 1887-1965 *Baker 92*
Bohnenkamp, Jeffry Joseph 1955- *WhoEmL 93*
Bohner, Charles H. 1927- *BioIn 17*
Bohner, Charles Henry 1927- *WhoAm 92*
Bohner, Hal Jay *Law&B 92*
Bohner, (Johann) Ludwig 1787-1860 *Baker 92*
Bohnert, Betty Louise 1941- *WhoAmW 93*
Bohnert, Lea 1919-1990 *BioIn 17*
Bohnert, Lester L. *Law&B 92*
Bohnet, Armin 1936- *WhoScE 91-3*
Bohnet, Matthias W. 1933- *WhoScE 91-3*
Bohnett, William H. *St&PR 93*
Bohnhoff, William John 1938- *St&PR 93*
Bohning, Elizabeth Edrop 1915- *WhoAm 92*
Bohning, Gerry 1934- *WhoSSW 93*
Bohning, Wolf-Rudiger 1942- *WhoUN 92*
Bohnke, Emil 1888-1928 *Baker 92*
Bohnsack, M. Gregory 1950- *St&PR 93*
Bohny, Robert William 1939- *St&PR 93*
Bohon, Roy L. 1953- *St&PR 93*
Bohon, Scott E. *Law&B 92*
Bohorfoush, Joseph George 1907- *WhoWor 93*
Bohorquez, Fernando Augusto 1945- *WhoE 93*
Bohoskey, Bernice Fleming 1918- *WhoAm 92*
Bohr, Aage Niels 1922- *WhoAm 92, WhoWor 93*
Bohr, Jakob 1957- *WhoWor 93*
Bohr, Niels Henrik David 1885-1962 *BioIn 17*
Bohr, Ryszard 1926- *WhoScE 91-4*
Bohren, Janet Linderoth *WhoAmW 93*
Bohren, Kevin L. 1957- *St&PR 93*
Bohren, Michael Oscar 1947- *WhoEmL 93*
Bohrer, Betty 1962- *WhoEmL 93*
Bohrer, Michael Steven 1945- *St&PR 93*
Bohrer, Richard William 1926- *WhoSSW 93, WhoWrEP 92*
Bohrer, Tom *BioIn 17*
Bohrnstedt, George William 1938- *WhoAm 92*
Bohrod, Aaron d1992 *NewYTBS 92*
Bohrod, Aaron 1907-1992 *BioIn 17, CurBio 92N*
Bohs, G. Lee 1959- *St&PR 93*
Bohunicky, Debra Ann 1954- *WhoEmL 93*
Bohuon, Claude *WhoScE 91-2*
Boiarski, Philip S. 1945- *WhoWrEP 92*
Boica, Adelino Artur Manuel Duarte 1924- *WhoWor 93*
Boice, Craig Kendall 1952- *WhoE 93, WhoEmL 93, WhoWor 93*
Boice, John Kyle 1961- *WhoE 93, WhoEmL 93*
Boice, Margaret Rockwell 1947- *WhoSSW 93*
Boice, Stephen Crosby 1951- *St&PR 93*
Boichut, Edmund Just Victor 1864-1941 *HarEnMi*
Boie, Heinrich Christian 1744-1806 *BioIn 17*
Boieldieu, Adrien 1775-1834 *IntDcOp [port], OxDcOp*
Boieldieu, Adrien-Louis-Victor 1815-1883 *Baker 92*
Boieldieu, Adrien-Louis-Victor 1816-1883 *OxDcOp*
Boieldieu, Francois-Adrien 1775-1834 *Baker 92*
Boies, Wilber H. 1944- *WhoAm 92*
Boies, William Wesley 1957- *WhoSSW 93*
Boiffin, Jean *WhoScE 91-2*
Boigne, Benoit le Borgne, Count de 1751-1830 *HarEnMi*
Boigny, Felix Houphouet- *BioIn 17*
Boigny, Marie-Therese Houphouet- *BioIn 17*
Boijsen, Erik 1922- *WhoScE 91-4*
Boike, Edward Joseph 1923- *St&PR 93*
Boiko, Anatoly V. 1939- *WhoScE 91-4*
Boiko, Anatoly Vladimirovich 1939- *WhoUN 92*
Boilanger, Mitzi Lu 1953- *WhoAmW 93, WhoEmL 93*
Boilard, David W. *BioIn 17*
Boileau, Leo Victor 1944- *St&PR 93*
Boileau, Marie *AmWomPl*
Boileau, Nathaniel Britton 1763-1850 *BioIn 17*
Boileau, Oliver C. 1927- *BioIn 17*
Boileau, Oliver Clark, Jr. 1927- *WhoAm 92*
Boileau, Pierre 1906- *ScF&FL 92*
Boiles, John W. 1945- *St&PR 93*
Boillat, Guy Maurice Georges 1937- *WhoWor 93*
Boillot, Gilbert 1934- *WhoScE 91-2*
Boillot, Pierre 1941- *WhoWor 93*
Boilly, Louis-Leopold 1761-1845 *BioIn 17*
Boily, Jeffrey O. 1955- *St&PR 93*
Boiman, Donna Rae 1946- *WhoAmW 93*
Boime, Albert Isaac 1933- *WhoAm 92*
Boineau, Elizabeth Lloyd 1956- *WhoEmL 93*
Boineau, Franklin Girard 1943- *WhoAm 92*
Boinest, William Calhoun 1933- *St&PR 93*
Boioannes *OxDcByz*
Boioannes, Basil *OxDcByz*
Bois, Claude *WhoScE 91-2*
Bois, Curt 1901-1991 *BioIn 17*
Bois, Pierre 1924- *WhoAm 92*
Bois, Rob du 1934- *Baker 92*
Boisclair, Joan 1956- *WhoWrEP 92*
Boise, Audrey Lorraine 1933- *WhoE 93*
Boise, Otis Bardwell 1844-1912 *Baker 92*
Boisfontaine, Curtis Rich 1929- *WhoAm 92*
Boismare, Francis 1934- *WhoScE 91-2*
Boismortier, Joseph Bodin de 1689-1755 *Baker 92*
Boisonnault, Jean 1939- *St&PR 93*
Boisot, Louis de d1576 *HarEnMi*
Boisse, Joseph Adonias 1937- *WhoAm 92*
Boisseau, Jerry Philip 1939- *WhoE 93, WhoWor 93*
Boisseau, Leon Hardy 1945- *WhoSSW 93*
Boisselle, Allan Albert 1947- *WhoE 93*
Boissevain, Inez Milholland *AmWomPl*
Boissevain, Jean Tennyson 1905-1991 *BioIn 17*
Boisson, Pierre 1894-1948 *HarEnMi*
Boisson, Robert Richard 1946- *St&PR 93*
Boisture, W.W., Jr. 1944- *St&PR 93*
Boisvert, Craig Stephen 1956- *WhoSSW 93*
Boisvert, William E. 1942- *WhoAm 92*
Boisvert, Yves 1950- *WhoCanL 92*
Boisvieux, J.-F. *WhoScE 91-2*
Boit, Christian Ulrich 1952- *WhoE 93*
Boitani, Piero 1947- *ConAu 137*
Boitano, Brian *BioIn 17, NewYTBS 92 [port]*
Boitel, Ana Maria 1952- *WhoEmL 93*
Boiter, Donald Harry 1935- *St&PR 93*
Boiteux, Marcel 1922- *WhoScE 91-2*
Boito, Arrigo 1842-1918 *Baker 92, IntDcOp [port], OxDcOp*

Boivin, Claude 1934- St&PR 93, WhoAm 92
Boivin, Georges Law&B 92
Boivin, Jerome MiSFD 9
Boivin, M. WhoScE 91-2
Boivin Filion, Pierrette Law&B 92
Bojack, Audrey D. Law&B 92
Bojack, Stephen D. 1937- St&PR 93
Bojanin, Stevan 1921- WhoScE 91-4
Bojanov, Borislav Dechev 1944- WhoWor 93
Bojanowski, Jan S. 1921- WhoScE 91-4
Bojarczuk, David Charles 1956- WhoE 93
Bojarski, Czeslaw 1923- WhoScE 91-4
Bojarski, Edmund Anthony 1924- WhoSSW 93
Bojarski, Jeanne Frances 1951- WhoAmW 93
Bojarski, Wladyslaw 1931- WhoWor 93
Bojarski, Wlodzimierz 1930- WhoScE 91-4
Bojarski, Zbigniew Jacek 1921- WhoScE 91-4
Bojaxhiu, Agnes Gonxha 1910- WhoWor 93
Boje, David Leonard 1965- WhoE 93
Bojkov, Rumen Dimiter 1931- WhoUN 92
Bojorquez, Juan de Dios 1892-1967 DcMexL
Bojsen-Moller, Finn 1933- WhoScE 91-2
Bojtos, Peter 1949- St&PR 93
Bok, Alexander Toland 1959- WhoEmL 93
Bok, Dean 1939- WhoAm 92
Bok, Derek 1930- WhoAm 92, WhoWor 93
Bok, Derek Curtis BioIn 17
Bok, Edward 1863-1930 GayN, JrnUS
Bok, Edward William 1863-1930 BioIn 17
Bok, Hannes 1914-1964 ScF&FL 92
Bok, Joan T. 1929- St&PR 93
Bok, Joan Toland 1929- WhoAm 92, WhoE 93
Bok, John Fairfield 1930- WhoAm 92
Bok, Mary Louise Curtis 1876-1970 Baker 92
Bok, Sissela BioIn 17
Bok, Sissela 1934- WhoAm 92, WhoAmW 93
Bokaemper, Stefan 1936- WhoAm 92
Bokassa, I 1921- BioIn 17
Bokassa, Jean Bedel 1921- DcTwHis, WhoAfr
Bokat, Stephen Arthur 1946- WhoE 93, WhoEmL 93
Boke, Norman Hill 1913- WhoAm 92
Bokelmann, Gary Wayne 1949- WhoEmL 93
Bokemeyer, Heinrich 1679-1751 Baker 92
Bokerman, M. Jeanne 1921- WhoAmW 93
Bokhari, Ashfaque Hussain 1956- WhoWor 93
Bokhari, Ejaz Ali Shah 1924- WhoWor 93
Bokhari, Habib 1948- St&PR 93
Bokhari, Muhammad Ashfaq 1950- WhoWor 93
Bokhoven, Willem 1924- WhoScE 91-3
Bokn, Tor L. 1943- WhoScE 91-4
Boknecht, Louis H. 1941- St&PR 93
Bokoch, Gary Michael 1954- WhoEmL 93
Bokori, Jozsef 1927- WhoScE 91-4
Bokovoy, R.D. 1943- St&PR 93
Bokros, Paul 1928- WhoAm 92
Boksay, Zoltan 1927- WhoScE 91-4
Boksenberg, A. WhoScE 91-1
Boksenberg, Alexander 1936- WhoWor 93
Bokser, Baruch M. BioIn 17
Bokser, Lewis 1904- WhoE 93, WhoWor 93
Bokx, Cornelis 1939- WhoWor 93
Bol, Jan Willem 1951- WhoEmL 93
Bol, Manute BioIn 17
Bola, Marybeth Marx 1959- WhoEmL 93
Bolaffi, Janice Lerner 1933- WhoAm 92
Bolan, Robert S. 1941- WhoAm 92
Bolan, Thomas A. 1924- St&PR 93
Bolan, Thomas Anthony 1924- WhoAm 92, WhoWor 93
Boland, Brian P. Law&B 92
Boland, Christopher Thomas, II 1915- WhoAm 92
Boland, Edward P. 1911- ColdWar 1 [port]
Boland, Ellen Clark 1955- WhoEmL 93
Boland, Gerald Lee 1946- WhoE 93, WhoEmL 93
Boland, Jack Edward, IV 1942- St&PR 93
Boland, Janet Lang 1924- WhoAm 92
Boland, John 1913-1976 ScF&FL 92
Boland, John A. 1946- St&PR 93
Boland, John Francis, Jr. 1915- WhoAm 92
Boland, John Joseph, Jr. 1920- St&PR 93
Boland, John Thomas 1944- WhoE 93
Boland, Joseph Patrick Law&B 92
Boland, Joseph Patrick 1959- WhoSSW 93
Boland, Lois Walker 1919- WhoSSW 93
Boland, Mark Sheridan 1955- WhoWor 93
Boland, Mary 1880-1965 QDrFCA 92 [port]
Boland, Matthew Frederick 1962- WhoE 93
Boland, Michael J. Law&B 92
Boland, P. 1936- WhoScE 91-3
Boland, Patricia Ann 1935- WhoE 93
Boland, Raymond James 1932- WhoAm 92
Boland, Robert James 1937- St&PR 93
Boland, Thomas Edwin 1934- St&PR 93, WhoAm 92
Boland, Tom 1929- St&PR 93
Boland, Veronica Grace 1899-1982 BioIn 17
Bolande, Robert Paul 1926- WhoAm 92
Bolander, Glen S. 1946- St&PR 93
Bolander, Glen S., Jr. 1946- WhoEmL 93
Boland-Robillard, Virginia Anne 1958- WhoEmL 93
Bolanos, Alvaro Felix 1955- WhoSSW 93
Bolanos, Magtangol Hilario 1930- WhoWor 93
Bolanowski, Boleslaw 1932- WhoScE 91-4
Bolanowski, Stanley John, Jr. 1950- WhoE 93
Bolar, Larry D. 1936- St&PR 93
Bolarin, M.C. 1952- WhoScE 91-3
Bolas, Edward S. 1952- WhoEmL 93
Bolas, Gerald Douglas 1949- WhoAm 92
Bolce, Donn W. 1928- St&PR 93
Bolch, Carl Edward, Jr. 1943- St&PR 93, WhoAm 92
Bolcik, Charles Gabriel 1932- WhoAm 92
Bolcom, William BioIn 17
Bolcom, William (Elden) 1938- Baker 92, WhoAm 92
Bolcsvolgyi, Ferenc WhoScE 91-4
Bold, Frances Ann 1930- WhoAm 92
Bold, Mary Ellender 1952- WhoEmL 93, WhoWrEP 92
Bolda, Peter G. 1930- St&PR 93
Boldemann, Laci 1921-1969 Baker 92
Bolden, "Buddy" (Charles Joseph) 1877-1931 Baker 92
Bolden, Charles F., Jr. 1946- AfrAmBi [port]
Bolden, Jeanette BlkAmWO
Bolden, Leo F. 1938- St&PR 93
Bolden, Michael Geronia 1953- WhoEmL 93
Bolden, R.D. 1941- St&PR 93
Bolden, Rosamond 1938- WhoAmW 93
Bolden, Theodore Edward 1920- WhoAm 92
Bolden, Timothy H. Law&B 92
Boldensele, Wilhelm Von dc. 1337 OxDcByz
Bolding, Alene Marsha 1949- WhoAmW 93
Bolding, Cecil L. 1921- WhoSSW 93
Bolding, David Christian 1953- WhoEmL 93
Bolding, James C. Law&B 92
Bolding, James McCollum Law&B 92
Boldingh, Mary Jo Law&B 92
Boldini, Giovanni 1842?-1931 BioIn 17
Boldirev, Victor 1936- WhoUN 92
Boldischar, Paul J., Jr. 1941- St&PR 93
Boldizsar, Laszlo Law&B 92
Boldosser, Nancy Shilay 1957- WhoEmL 93
Boldridge, David William 1954- WhoEmL 93
Boldrin, Laurie-Anne 1964- WhoEmL 93
Boldry, Joseph Stuart, Jr. 1956- WhoEmL 93
Boldt, David Rhys 1941- WhoAm 92
Boldt, Dennise Marie 1951- WhoWor 93
Boldt, Donald Bernard 1934- St&PR 93
Boldt, Gary L. 1944- St&PR 93
Boldt, Heinz 1923- WhoWor 93
Boldt, James Robert 1951- St&PR 93
Boldt, Michael Herbert 1950- WhoAm 92
Boldt, Oscar Charles 1924- St&PR 93, WhoAm 92
Boldt, Peter 1927- WhoScE 91-3, WhoWor 93
Bolduc, Bruce Joseph 1958- WhoE 93
Bolduc, Donald Raymond 1946- St&PR 93
Bolduc, Ernest Joseph 1924- WhoAm 92
Bolduc, Gerald J. St&PR 93
Bolduc, J.P. 1939- St&PR 93, WhoAm 92, WhoE 93, WhoWor 93
Bolduc, James Philip 1949- WhoAm 92
Bolduc, Jerome M. 1929- St&PR 93
Bolduc, Joseph Patrick 1943- St&PR 93
Bolduc, L.M. 1939- St&PR 93
Bolduc, Michele Law&B 92
Bolduc, Rene BioIn 17
Bole, Alan G. WhoScE 91-1
Bole, Clifford MiSFD 9
Bole, Filipe 1936- WhoAsAP 91
Bole, Filipe Nagera 1936- WhoWor 93
Bole, Giles G. 1928- WhoAm 92
Bolebruch, Jeffrey John 1963- WhoE 93
Bolebruch, Lori Ann 1957- WhoEmL 93
Bolen, Amos Alonzo 1909- WhoAm 92
Bolen, Bob 1926- WhoAm 92
Bolen, Charles Warren 1923- WhoAm 92
Bolen, David B. 1923- WhoAm 92, WhoWor 93
Bolen, David J. Law&B 92
Bolen, Eric George 1937- WhoSSW 93
Bolen, Kenneth James 1947- WhoIns 93
Bolen, Max Carlton 1919- WhoSSW 93
Bolen, Waldo Emerson, Jr. 1931- St&PR 93
Bolender, Carroll Herdus 1919- WhoAm 92
Bolender, James Henry 1937- WhoAm 92
Bolender, Mark J. Law&B 92
Bolender, Todd BioIn 17
Bolender, Todd 1919- WhoAm 92
Bolene, Margaret Rosalie Steele 1923- WhoAm 92, WhoAmW 93
Bolerjack, Stephen D. Law&B 92
Boles, Christina Lynn 1950- St&PR 93
Boles, Dennis Ray 1956- WhoEmL 93
Boles, Donald Michael 1951- WhoEmL 93
Boles, Gary Thomas 1945- WhoSSW 93
Boles, John Culson 1953- WhoEmL 93, WhoSSW 93
Boles, Roger 1928- WhoAm 92
Boles-Carenini, Bruno 1925- WhoScE 91-3
Boleslaw, I 966-1025 PolBiDi
Boleslaw, II 1039-1081 PolBiDi
Boleslaw, III 1085-1139 PolBiDi
Boleslaw, IV 1120-1173 PolBiDi
Boleslaw, V 1221-1279 PolBiDi
Boleslawski, Richard 1889-1937 MiSFD 9N, PolBiDi
Bolet, Jorge 1914-1990 Baker 92, BioIn 17
Boley, Bruno Adrian 1924- WhoAm 92
Boley, Dennis Lynn 1951- WhoEmL 93, WhoSSW 93
Boley, Donna Jean 1935- WhoAmW 93
Boley, Eugene Conlee 1928- St&PR 93
Boley, Jacqueline 1954- WhoEmL 93
Boley, Robert Lee, Jr. 1958- WhoSSW 93
Boley, Theresa Maria 1951- WhoEmL 93
Boley Bolaffio, Rita WhoAm 92, WhoAmW 93, WhoWor 93
Boleyn, Anne 1507-1536 BioIn 17
Bolf, Ron Bruce 1954- WhoEmL 93
Bolgan, Anne C(atherine) 1923-1992? ConAu 136
Bolger, Bernadette L. Law&B 92
Bolger, Brenna Mercier 1942- WhoAm 92
Bolger, David P. 1957- St&PR 93
Bolger, James Brendan 1935- WhoWor 93
Bolger, Jim 1935- WhoAsAP 91
Bolger, Mary Kenealy 1949- WhoEmL 93
Bolger, Rita M. Law&B 92
Bolger, Robert Joseph 1922- WhoSSW 93
Bolgiano, Ralph, Jr. 1922- WhoAm 92
Bolian, George Clement 1930- WhoAm 92
Bolich, Gregory Gordon 1953- WhoEmL 93
Bolick, Steven Gregory 1958- WhoSSW 93
Bolie, Victor Wayne 1924- WhoAm 92, WhoWor 93
Bolin, Alpha E., Jr. 1927- St&PR 93
Bolin, Bert R.J. 1925- WhoScE 91-4
Bolin, Bertil Axel 1923- WhoWor 93
Bolin, Charles William 1926- St&PR 93
Bolin, Edmund Mike 1944- WhoSSW 93
Bolin, Jewel N. 1926- St&PR 93
Bolin, John Seelye 1943- WhoSSW 93
Bolin, Olof 1941- WhoScE 91-4
Bolin, Shirley Judith 1928- St&PR 93, WhoAmW 93
Bolin, William Harvey 1922- WhoAm 92
Bolind, Lawrence, Jr. 1954- WhoEmL 93
Bolinder, E. Folke 1922- WhoScE 91-4
Bolinder, Robert Donald 1931- St&PR 93, WhoAm 92
Bolinder, William H. WhoIns 93
Boling, Beth A. 1960- WhoEmL 93
Boling, Carole Joan 1943- WhoAmW 93
Boling, Edward Joseph 1922- WhoAm 92, WhoSSW 93
Boling, James Earl 1928- WhoSSW 93
Boling, Jewell 1907- WhoAmW 93, WhoSSW 93, WhoWor 93
Boling, Joseph Edward 1942- WhoAm 92, WhoWor 93
Boling, Judy Atwood 1921- WhoAmW 93
Boling, Mark Edward 1954- WhoEmL 93, WhoSSW 93
Bolingbroke, Viscount 1678-1751 BioIn 17
Bolingbroke, Robert A. 1938- St&PR 93, WhoAm 92
Bolinger, Corbin Eugene 1929- St&PR 93, WhoAm 92
Bolinger, Dwight 1907-1992 BioIn 17
Bolinger, Dwight L. d1992 NewYTBS 92
Bolinger, Dwight (L.) 1907-1992 ConAu 137
Bolinger, George James 1950- St&PR 93
Bolinger, John C., Jr. 1922- St&PR 93, WhoAm 92
Bolinger, Robert Stevens 1936- St&PR 93, WhoAm 92
Bolino, John Vincent 1941- WhoAm 92
Bolitho, Louise Greer 1927- WhoAmW 93
Bolivar, Simon 1783-1830 BioIn 17, HarEnMi
Bolk, Deborah Marie 1960- WhoAmW 93
Bolk, Louis 1866-1930 IntDcAn
Bolka, Bernard J. 1955- St&PR 93
Bolker, Henry Irving 1926- WhoAm 92
Bolkiah, Mohamed 1947- WhoWor 93
Bolkiah, Muda Hassanal 1946- BioIn 17
Bolkiah, Paduka Seri Pengiran Digadong Sahibul Mal Pengir WhoAsAP 91
Bolkiah, Paduka Seri Pengiran Perdana Wazir Sahibul Himma WhoAsAP 91
Bolks, Ervin J. 1941- St&PR 93
Bolks, Ervin Jay 1941- WhoAm 92
Bolkus, Nick WhoAsAP 91
Boll, Charles Raymond 1920- WhoAm 92
Boll, Heinrich 1917-1985 BioIn 17, ConLC 72 [port], MagSWL [port], WorLitC [port]
Boll, James C. Law&B 92
Boll, Per M. 1929- WhoScE 91-2
Boll, Roger W. 1942- St&PR 93
Bolla, Jim BioIn 17
Bolla, William Joseph 1947- WhoEmL 93
Bollack, Claude G. 1925- WhoScE 91-2
Bollag, Jean-Marc 1935- WhoAm 92
Bollag, Thierry Gaston 1960- WhoWor 93
Bolle, Donald Martin 1933- WhoAm 92
Bolle, Hans-Jurgen 1929- WhoScE 91-3
Bolle, James Dougan 1931- WhoE 93
Bolle, Leon M.R. 1944- WhoScE 91-2
Bolle, Michael D. 1941- WhoWor 93
Bollen, Alex 1940- WhoScE 91-2
Bollen, Peter Douglas 1948- WhoWrEP 92
Bollen, Roger 1941- WhoAm 92
Bollenbach, Stephen Frasier BioIn 17
Bollenbach, Stephen Frasier 1942- St&PR 93, WhoAm 92
Bollenbacher, Michael Kenneth 1954- WhoSSW 93
Boller, Francois 1938- WhoScE 91-2
Boller, George L. Law&B 92
Boller, Margaret Mary 1956- WhoEmL 93
Boller, Ronald Cecil 1939- WhoAm 92
Boller, Thomas Peter 1949- WhoWor 93
Bollerer, Fred L. St&PR 93
Bollerman, James Michael 1954- St&PR 93
Bolles, Charles Avery 1940- WhoAm 92
Bolles, John W. 1945- St&PR 93
Bolles, Peter Piper 1937- St&PR 93
Bolles, Richard Nelson 1927- WhoAm 92
Bolles, Ronald Kent 1948- WhoEmL 93
Bollet, Alfred Jay 1926- WhoAm 92
Bollheimer, Denise 1950- WhoEmL 93, WhoSSW 93
Bollhoefer, Carolyn J. 1936- St&PR 93
Bollich, Elridge Nicholas 1941- WhoSSW 93
Bolliger, Arthur Philipp 1948- WhoWor 93
Bolliger, Erwin 1929- WhoWor 93
Bollimpalli, Rao G. 1938- St&PR 93
Bollin, William Robert 1949- St&PR 93
Bolline, Peter E. 1948- St&PR 93
Bolling, Alexander Russell, Jr. 1922- WhoAm 92
Bolling, Claude 1930- Baker 92
Bolling, Eddie Newman 1945- St&PR 93
Bolling, H. WhoScE 91-3
Bolling, John Randolph 1935- St&PR 93
Bolling, Landrum Rymer 1913- WhoAm 92
Bolling, Richard 1916- PolPar
Bolling, Richard 1916-1991 AnObit 1991
Bolling, Richard Norman 1926- St&PR 93
Bolling, Richard Walker 1916-1991 BioIn 17
Bolling, Robert 1738-1775 BioIn 17
Bolling, Robert D'Arcy 1923- WhoAm 92
Bolling, Roger 1926- St&PR 93
Bollinger, Alfred 1932- WhoScE 91-4
Bollinger, Bob James 1953- WhoEmL 93
Bollinger, Don M. 1914- St&PR 93
Bollinger, Don Mills 1914- WhoAm 92
Bollinger, Jane C. 1949- WhoAmW 93
Bollinger, John Gustave 1935- WhoAm 92
Bollinger, Lee C. 1946- ConAu 138
Bollinger, Lee Carroll 1946- WhoAm 92
Bollinger, Lowell Moyer 1923- WhoAm 92
Bollinger, Margaret L. Law&B 92
Bollinger, Pamela Beemer 1947- WhoAmW 93, WhoEmL 93
Bollinger, Patti Theresa 1967- WhoAmW 93
Bollinger, Sheryl Lea 1957- St&PR 93
Bollinger, Taree 1949- WhoWrEP 92
Bollinger, Thomas Richard 1943- St&PR 93
Bollius, Daniel c. 1590-c. 1642 Baker 92
Bollman, Mark Brooks, Jr. 1925- St&PR 93, WhoAm 92
Bollmann, Henry P. 1935- St&PR 93

Bollmann, Juergen 1943- *St&PR 93*
Bollom, Daniel Arthur 1936- *St&PR 93*
Bollon, Arthur Peter 1942- *WhoAm 92*
Bollon Mourier, Monique 1955- *WhoWor 93*
Bollum, Frederick James 1927- *WhoAm 92*
Bolm, Deborah Dell 1951- *WhoAmW 93*
Bolman, Pieter Simon Heinrich 1941- *WhoAm 92*
Bolmarcich, Gene G. *Law&B 92*
Bolmer, John Edwin, II 1958- *WhoEmL 93*
Bolnick, Howard J. 1945- *WhoIns 93*
Bolnick, Howard Jeffrey 1945- *WhoAm 92*
Bologa, Alexandru S. 1947- *WhoScE 91-4*
Bologna, Calogero Antonio 1957- *WhoEmL 93*
Bologna, Jacopo da *Baker 92*
Bologna, Joseph 1936- *MiSFD 9*
Bologna, Joseph 1938- *WhoAm 92*
Bologna, Peter Andrew *Law&B 92*
Bologna, T.A. 1948- *St&PR 93*
Bolognani, Lorenzo Alfonso Maria 1928- *WhoWor 93*
Bolognani Fantin, Anna Maria 1936- *WhoScE 91-3*
Bolognese, Don(ald Alan) 1934- *MajAI, SmATA 71*
Bolognesi, Dani Paul 1941- *WhoAm 92*
Bolognini, Louis Thomas *Law&B 92*
Bolognini, Mauro 1922- *MiSFD 9*
Bolomey, Jean Charles 1942- *WhoScE 91-2*
Bolomey, Roger Henry 1918- *WhoAm 92*
Boloni, Istvan 1928- *WhoScE 91-4*
Bolooki, Hooshang 1937- *WhoAm 92*
Bolos I. Capdevila, Jose Oriol de 1924- *WhoScE 91-3*
Bolotin, Craig *MiSFD 9*
Bolotin, Irving 1932- *St&PR 93*
Bolotin, Lora M. *WhoAmW 93*
Bolotowsky, Andrew Ilyitch 1949- *WhoEmL 93, WhoWor 93*
Bolotowsky, Ilya 1907-1981 *BioIn 17*
Boloyan, Myron B. 1957- *WhoEmL 93*
Bolsche, Franz 1869-1935 *Baker 92*
Bolsen, Barbara Ann 1950- *WhoAmW 93*
Bolshakov, Nikolai 1874-1958 *Baker 92*
Bolsky, Abraham S. 1922- *St&PR 93*
Bolsky, Abraham S. 1922-1991 *BioIn 17*
Bolsover, George Henry 1910-1990 *BioIn 17*
Bolstad, Greta 1938- *WhoScE 91-4*
Bolster, Archie Milburn 1933- *WhoAm 92*
Bolster, Arthur Stanley, Jr. 1922- *WhoAm 92*
Bolster, Jacqueline Neben *WhoAmW 93*
Bolster, Stephen Clark 1951- *WhoEmL 93, WhoSSW 93*
Bolster, William Lawrence 1943- *BioIn 17, WhoAm 92*
Bolsterli, Margaret Jones *BioIn 17*
Bolsterli, Margaret Jones 1931- *WhoAm 92*
Bolstridge, June C. *WhoE 93*
Bolt, Alan *BioIn 17*
Bolt, Ben 1952- *MiSFD 9*
Bolt, Bruce Alan 1930- *WhoAm 92*
Bolt, Carmen Maria 1947- *WhoSSW 93*
Bolt, Carol 1941- *WhoCanL 92*
Bolt, Charles Murphy 1930- *St&PR 93*
Bolt, David Bruce 1954- *WhoEmL 93*
Bolt, Eunice Mildred DeVries 1926- *WhoAmW 93*
Bolt, Gerard H. 1925- *WhoScE 91-3*
Bolt, Gordon John *WhoScE 91-1*
Bolt, Hermann M. 1943- *WhoScE 91-3*
Bolt, Joe De *ScF&FL 92*
Bolt, Katherine Heym 1944- *WhoAmW 93*
Bolt, M. Ronald 1948- *St&PR 93*
Bolt, Michael Gerald 1953- *WhoE 93*
Bolt, Richard Henry 1911- *WhoAm 92*
Bolt, Robert *BioIn 17*
Bolt, Robert 1924- *MiSFD 9*
Bolt, Robert Oxton 1924- *WhoWor 93*
Bolt, Thomas Alvin Waldrep 1956- *WhoEmL 93, WhoSSW 93*
Bolt, Tommy 1916- *BiDAMSp 1989*
Bolt, William J. 1930- *WhoAm 92*
Boltacz, Susan R. *Law&B 92*
Boltanski, Christian 1944- *WhoWor 93*
Bolte, Achim 1928- *WhoScE 91-3*
Bolte, Brown 1908- *St&PR 93, WhoAm 92*
Bolte, Charles Guy 1920- *WhoWrEP 92*
Bolten, Hermann J. *Law&B 92*
Bolten, John, Jr. 1920- *St&PR 93*
Bolter, Eugene Paul 1932- *WhoAm 92, WhoE 93*
Bolthouse, William J. 1940- *St&PR 93*
Boltin, Lee 1917-1991 *BioIn 17*
Boltman, Robin *BioIn 17*
Bolton, Anne Heaney *Law&B 92*
Bolton, Anthony E. *WhoScE 91-1*
Bolton, Brian *WhoScE 91-1*
Bolton, Brian J. 1938- *St&PR 93*
Bolton, Charles Thomas 1943- *WhoAm 92*
Bolton, David J. 1929- *St&PR 93*
Bolton, Dorothy Grover 1929- *WhoAmW 93*
Bolton, Earl Clinton 1919- *WhoAm 92*
Bolton, Eldon L., Jr. *Law&B 92*
Bolton, Elizabeth 1919- *WhoAmW 93*
Bolton, Evelyn *MajAI*
Bolton, F.M. *ScF&FL 92*
Bolton, Frances Payne Bingham 1885-1977 *BioIn 17*
Bolton, Harvey Verndale 1938- *St&PR 93*
Bolton, Hugh Robert *WhoScE 91-1*
Bolton, Ivy May 1879- *AmWomPl*
Bolton, James R. 1945- *St&PR 93*
Bolton, Jan E. 1945- *St&PR 93*
Bolton, Johanna M. *ScF&FL 92*
Bolton, John R. *BioIn 17*
Bolton, John Robert 1948- *WhoAm 92*
Bolton, John Roger 1950- *WhoAm 92*
Bolton, Julia Gooden 1940- *WhoE 93*
Bolton, Julian T. *AfrAmBi*
Bolton, Kenneth Albert 1941- *WhoE 93, WhoWor 93*
Bolton, Kevin Michael 1951- *WhoSSW 93*
Bolton, Martha O. 1951- *WhoAmW 93, WhoEmL 93, WhoWor 93*
Bolton, Mary Jane 1934- *WhoAmW 93*
Bolton, Michael *BioIn 17, NewYTBS 92 [port], WhoAm 92*
Bolton, Michael 1953- *News 93-2 [port]*
Bolton, Michael G. 1949- *St&PR 93*
Bolton, Paul L. *Law&B 92*
Bolton, Robert Edward 1951- *WhoScE 91-1*
Bolton, Robert H. 1908- *St&PR 93*
Bolton, Robert Harvey 1908- *WhoAm 92, WhoSSW 93*
Bolton, Robert Horatious 1964- *WhoSSW 93*
Bolton, Roger Edwin 1938- *WhoAm 92*
Bolton, Ronald McLean 1933- *WhoE 93*
Bolton, Ruth Ann 1952- *WhoAmW 93*
Bolton, Thaddeus L. 1865-1948 *BioIn 17*
Bolton, Thomas B. *WhoScE 91-1*
Bolton, Thyrza LaVerne Wilcox 1927- *WhoSSW 93*
Bolton, W.F. 1930- *ScF&FL 92*
Bolton, William Elvin, III 1946- *St&PR 93*
Bolton, William J. 1937- *St&PR 93*
Bolton, William W. 1900-1966 *ScF&FL 92*
Bolton-Smith, Carlile, Jr. *Law&B 92*
Bolton-Smith, Carlile, Jr. 1937- *St&PR 93, WhoAm 92*
Boltuck, Richard Dale 1955- *WhoEmL 93*
Boltz, Gerald Edmund 1931- *WhoAm 92*
Boltz, Mary Ann 1923- *WhoAm 92, WhoAmW 93, WhoWor 93*
Boltz, Ronald R. 1945- *St&PR 93*
Boltzmann, Ludwig 1844-1906 *BioIn 17*
Bolus, Debra Ann 1963- *WhoAmW 93*
Bolusky, Eric Bruce 1949- *WhoSSW 93*
Bolvig, C.P. 1929- *St&PR 93*
Bolvin, John Orvard 1929- *WhoE 93*
Bolwell, H.J. 1925- *St&PR 93*
Bolyai, Stephen 1951- *WhoE 93*
Bolyard, Gary M. 1935- *St&PR 93*
Bolyn, Jacques Henri Louis 1926- *WhoScE 91-2*
Bolz, Michael Richard *Law&B 92*
Bolz, Sanford Hegleman 1915-1991 *BioIn 17*
Bolzoni, Giovanni 1841-1919 *Baker 92*
Boman, Eric 1867-1924 *IntDcAn*
Boman, Fred Hjalmar 1943- *WhoWor 93*
Boman, Gunnar 1941- *WhoScE 91-4*
Boman, Hans G. 1924- *WhoScE 91-4*
Boman, John Harris, Jr. 1910- *WhoAm 92*
Boman, Mogens 1933- *WhoScE 91-2*
Boman, P.O. 1926- *WhoScE 91-4*
Boman, Primavera Roxan 1946- *WhoEmL 93*
Bomani, Paul Nimage 1925- *WhoAfr*
Bomar, Anne E. *Law&B 92*
Bomar, Clifton Patrick, Jr. 1942- *St&PR 93*
Bomar, Patricia M. 1938- *St&PR 93*
Bomar, Samuel G. 1945- *St&PR 93*
Bomba, Lisa *St&PR 93*
Bomba, Margaret Ann 1947- *WhoAmW 93*
Bombace, Giovanni 1929- *WhoScE 91-3*
Bombal, Jacques *St&PR 93*
Bombal, Maria Luisa 1910-1980 *BioIn 17, ScF&FL 92, SpAmA*
Bombardelli, Silvije 1916- *Baker 92*
Bombaugh, Karl Jacob 1922- *WhoWor 93*
Bombay, Sidi Mubarak 1820?-1885 *Expl 93*
Bombeck, Erma *BioIn 17*
Bombeck, Erma (Louise) 1927- *ConAu 39NR, WhoAm 92, WhoAmW 93, WhoWrEP 92*
Bombei, Gary V. 1941- *St&PR 93*
Bombelli, Luca 1957- *WhoWor 93*
Bomberg, David 1890-1957 *BioIn 17*
Bomberg, Thomas James 1928- *WhoAm 92*
Bomberger, David R., Jr. 1948- *WhoAm 92*
Bomberger, Glen R. 1937- *WhoAm 92*
Bomberger, Gregory *Law&B 92*
Bomberger, Russell Branson 1934- *WhoAm 92*
Bomberger, Samuel William 1927- *WhoAm 92*
Bombino, Isabel Pinera 1954- *WhoEmL 93*
Bomboko, Lokumba is Elenge (Justin-Marie) 1928- *WhoAfr*
Bomgardner, John H., III *Law&B 92*
Bomgardner, William Earl 1925- *WhoAm 92*
Bomhof, Martin A. M. 1948- *WhoWor 93*
Bommel, Hans Eberhard 1912- *WhoWor 93*
Bommelaer, Alain 1947- *WhoAm 92, WhoWor 93*
Bommer, Gerhard 1946- *WhoWor 93*
Bommer, Jurgen Dieter Guido 1942- *WhoWor 93*
Bompart, Bill Earl 1933- *WhoSSW 93*
Bompiani, Valentino d1992 *NewYTBS 92*
Bompiani, Valentino 1898-1992 *BioIn 17*
Bomstead, Beulah Eugenia 1896- *AmWomPl*
Bomstein, Alan Charles 1945- *WhoSSW 93*
Bomstein, Brian Eric 1964- *WhoSSW 93*
Bomtempo, Joao Domingos 1775-1842 *Baker 92*
Bomzer, David J. 1961- *WhoEmL 93*
Bon, Maarten 1933- *Baker 92*
Bon, Willem Frederik 1940-1983 *Baker 92*
Bona, Christian Maximilian 1937- *WhoWor 93*
Bona, Frederick E. 1939- *St&PR 93*
Bona, Frederick Emil 1939- *WhoAm 92*
Bona, Giovanni 1609-1674 *Baker 92*
Bona, Thomas Mark 1955- *WhoEmL 93*
Bona, Valerio c. 1560- *Baker 92*
Bonaca, Paul Luciano 1941- *St&PR 93*
Bonacci, Carla 1959- *WhoE 93*
Bonacci, Eugene Charles 1939- *St&PR 93*
Bonaccorsi, R. *WhoScE 91-3*
Bonach, Edward J. *St&PR 93*
Bonacorsi, Gregory James 1955- *WhoE 93, WhoEmL 93*
Bonacorsi, Larry Joseph 1948- *WhoEmL 93*
Bonadonna, Gianni 1934- *WhoScE 91-3*
Bonaduce, Danny *BioIn 17*
Bonafont, R.L. *WhoScE 91-1*
Bonaguide, John M. 1935- *St&PR 93*
Bonaguidi, Orland 1914- *St&PR 93*
Bonaiuto, John A. *WhoAm 92*
Bonald, Jose Manuel Caballero 1926- *BioIn 17*
Bonaldi, Jane Gayle 1942- *WhoAmW 93*
Bonaly, Roger 1937- *WhoScE 91-2*
Bonami, E. Andre *Law&B 92*
Bonan, Seon Pierre 1917- *WhoAm 92, WhoWor 93*
Bonander, John V. 1935- *St&PR 93*
Bonann, Gregory J. *MiSFD 9*
Bonanni, Ann L. 1953- *WhoAmW 93*
Bonanno, Jacqueline 1944- *WhoE 93*
Bonanno, Margaret Wander 1950- *ConAu 40NR, ScF&FL 92*
Bonanno, Robert Donald 1927- *WhoE 93*
Bonanno, Robert S. *Law&B 92*
Bonanto, Paul J. *Law&B 92*
Bonapart, Alan David 1930- *WhoAm 92*
Bonaparte, Eugene Louis Jean Joseph Napoleon 1856-1879 *HarEnMi*
Bonaparte, Jerome 1784-1860 *HarEnMi*
Bonaparte, Joseph 1768-1844 *HarEnMi*
Bonaparte, Josephine 1763-1814 *BioIn 17*
Bonaparte, Louis 1778-1846 *HarEnMi*
Bonaparte, Louis-Napoleon 1808-1873 *BioIn 17*
Bonaparte, Napoleon 1769-1821 *BioIn 17*
Bonaparte, Norton N., Jr. 1953- *AfrAmBi*
Bonaparte, Robert d1990 *BioIn 17*
Bonaparte, Tony Hillary 1939- *WhoAm 92*
Bonar, L. George 1934- *St&PR 93*
Bonar, Linda Louise 1949- *WhoAmW 93*
Bonar, Lucian George 1934- *WhoAm 92*
Bonar, Robert Addison 1925- *WhoSSW 93*
Bonar, Veronica *ConAu 136*
Bonaros, Thomas P. 1941- *St&PR 93*
Bonaros, Thomas Patrick *Law&B 92*
Bonarrigo, Domenick M. *Law&B 92*
Bonarrigo, Rocco *Law&B 92*
Bonart, Richard F. 1925- *WhoScE 91-3*
Bonasia, John J. 1933- *St&PR 93*
Bonastia, Peter Joseph 1938- *St&PR 93*
Bonath, Klaus H. 1936- *WhoScE 91-3*
Bonaventura *BioIn 17, NinCLC 35*
Bonaventura, Anthony di 1930- *Baker 92*
Bonaventura, Arnaldo 1862-1952 *Baker 92*
Bonaventura, Celia J..an 1941- *WhoAmW 93*
Bonaventura, Joseph 1942- *WhoAm 92*
Bonaventura, Mario di 1924- *Baker 92*
Bonaventure, Jacques 1955- *St&PR 93*
Bonavia, Ferruccio 1877-1950 *Baker 92*
Bonavita, Elena 1944- *WhoAmW 93*
Bonazinga, Marie T. 1948- *St&PR 93*
Bonazinga, Marie Therese 1948- *WhoAmW 93, WhoE 93, WhoEmL 93*
Bonazzi, Elaine Claire *WhoAm 92*
Bonazzo, Anthony Henry, II 1957- *WhoE 93, WhoEmL 93*
Boncan, Raul A. 1928- *WhoAsAP 91*
Boncher, Mary 1946- *WhoAmW 93*
Bonci, Alessandro 1870-1940 *Baker 92, IntDcOp [port], OxDcOp*
Boncol, Gheorghe 1935- *WhoScE 91-4*
Boncour, Joseph Paul- 1873-1972 *BioIn 17*
Boncy, R. Richard *Law&B 92, St&PR 93*
Bonczar, Elizabeth Semon 1949- *St&PR 93*
Bonczek, Robert R. *Law&B 92*
Bond, Alan *BioIn 17, WhoAm 92, WhoWor 93*
Bond, Alan Brian 1961- *WhoAm 92*
Bond, Alma Halbert 1923- *WhoSSW 93*
Bond, Amanda Odessa 1942- *WhoE 93, WhoWor 93*
Bond, Arthur D., Jr. 1933- *St&PR 93*
Bond, Audrey Mae 1932- *WhoAmW 93*
Bond, Bruce *BioIn 17*
Bond, Bruce R. 1946- *St&PR 93*
Bond, C. James *Law&B 92*
Bond, Calhoun 1921- *WhoAm 92*
Bond, Carrie Jacobs- 1862-1946 *BioIn 17*
Bond, Carrie (Minetta) Jacobs 1862-1946 *Baker 92*
Bond, Cathy Louise Elizabe 1952- *WhoEmL 93*
Bond, Chapel 1730-1790 *Baker 92*
Bond, Charles C., Jr. 1923- *St&PR 93*
Bond, Charles Eugene 1930- *WhoAm 92*
Bond, Charles H., Sr. 1944- *St&PR 93*
Bond, Christopher S. 1939- *CngDr 91*
Bond, Christopher Samuel 1939- *WhoAm 92*
Bond, Cornelius Combs, Jr. 1933- *WhoAm 92*
Bond, Dan Murray 1937- *St&PR 93*
Bond, Edlyne *ScF&FL 92*
Bond, Edward *BioIn 17*
Bond, Edward 1934- *ConAu 38NR*
Bond, Edward Anthony 1957- *St&PR 93*
Bond, Elaine R. 1935- *St&PR 93*
Bond, Elizabeth Hunt 1953- *WhoAmW 93*
Bond, Floyd Alden 1913- *WhoAm 92*
Bond, Gary M. *Law&B 92*
Bond, Geoffrey Colin *WhoScE 91-1*
Bond, George Clement 1936- *WhoE 93*
Bond, George Thomas *Law&B 92*
Bond, Hannah Elizabeth 1964- *WhoAmW 93*
Bond, Harley William 1935- *St&PR 93*
Bond, Harold Herant 1939- *WhoWrEP 92*
Bond, I.J. 1947- *St&PR 93*
Bond, J. Max 1902-1991 *BioIn 17*
Bond, J. Max, Jr. 1935- *WhoAm 92*
Bond, James 1900-1989 *BioIn 17*
Bond, James, III *BioIn 17, MiSFD 9*
Bond, James Joseph 1937- *St&PR 93*
Bond, Jean Carey *BlkAuII 92*
Bond, John *WhoScE 91-1*
Bond, John Adikes 1955- *WhoEmL 93*
Bond, John P., III 1937- *AfrAmBi [port]*
Bond, John R. 1912-1990 *BioIn 17*
Bond, John Walter 1933- *WhoE 93*
Bond, Judith S. 1940- *WhoAmW 93*
Bond, Julian *BioIn 17*
Bond, Julian 1940- *PolPar, WhoAm 92, WhoSSW 93*
Bond, (Horace) Julian 1940- *EncAACR [port]*
Bond, Kelli Lorraine 1959- *WhoAmW 93*
Bond, Kendell Herran 1945- *WhoSSW 93*
Bond, Larry *ScF&FL 92*
Bond, Lewis H. 1921- *St&PR 93*
Bond, Lilian 1910-1991 *BioIn 17*
Bond, Lora 1917- *WhoAmW 93*
Bond, Louis J. 1959- *St&PR 93*
Bond, Marc Douglas 1954- *WhoEmL 93*
Bond, Marjorie Hyde d1991 *BioIn 17*
Bond, Martin Lafayette 1944- *WhoSSW 93*
Bond, Marvin Andrew 1949- *WhoEmL 93*
Bond, Mary Bligh 1895- *ScF&FL 92*
Bond, Mary G. 1923- *St&PR 93*
Bond, Michael Richard *WhoScE 91-1*
Bond, (Thomas) Michael 1926- *ChlFicS, MajAI [port]*
Bond, Morris Lindsay 1936- *St&PR 93*
Bond, Myron Humphrey 1938- *WhoSSW 93*
Bond, Nancy 1945- *ScF&FL 92*
Bond, Nancy (Barbara) 1945- *DcAmChF 1960, DcAmChF 1985, MajAI [port]*
Bond, Nelson 1908- *ScF&FL 92*
Bond, Nelson Leighton, Jr. 1935- *WhoE 93*
Bond, Niles Woodbridge 1916- *WhoAm 92*
Bond, Olive P. *AmWomPl*

Bond, Peter Danford 1940- *WhoAm 92*
Bond, Philip 1909-1991 *BioIn 17*
Bond, Randall Clay 1953- *WhoE 93, WhoWor 93*
Bond, Rebecca Rose 1957- *WhoE 93*
Bond, Richard C. 1909-1989 *BioIn 17*
Bond, Richard C., Jr. *Law&B 92*
Bond, Richard Ewing *Law&B 92*
Bond, Richard Norman 1950- *WhoAm 92*
Bond, Richard O. 1946- *St&PR 93*
Bond, Richard Randolph 1927- *WhoAm 92*
Bond, Sarah Ann 1955- *WhoAmW 93*
Bond, Stanley John 1943- *St&PR 93*
Bond, Thomas 1913- *WhoAm 92, WhoWor 93*
Bond, Thomas Alden 1938- *WhoAm 92*
Bond, Thomas Jefferson, Jr. 1936- *WhoE 93, WhoSSW 93*
Bond, Timothy 1942- *MiSFD 9*
Bond, Tommy David *Law&B 92*
Bond, Victoria 1945- *Baker 92*
Bond, Victoria Ellen 1945- *WhoAm 92, WhoAmW 93, WhoSSW 93*
Bond, Virginia F. 1919- *WhoWrEP 92*
Bond, Walter Dayton 1932- *WhoSSW 93*
Bond, Ward 1905-1960 *IntDcF 2-3 [port]*
Bond, William Edward 1943- *St&PR 93*
Bond, William Henry 1915- *WhoAm 92*
Bond, William J. *Law&B 92*
Bondar, Roberta Lynn 1945- *WhoAm 92, WhoAmW 93*
Bondarchuk, Sergei 1920- *IntDcF 2-3 [port], MiSFD 9*
Bondarchuk, Sergey Fedorovich 1920- *WhoWor 93*
Bondarcuk, Sergej 1920- *DrEEuF*
Bondareff, William 1930- *WhoAm 92*
Bondarev, Boris Vladimirovich 1945- *WhoWor 93*
Bondareva, Olga Nikolaevna 1937- *WhoWor 93*
Bondarowicz, John Frank 1961- *WhoEmL 93*
Bonde, Allen *BioIn 17*
Bonde, James R. 1932- *St&PR 93*
Bonde, Olaf Carl 1927- *WhoAm 92*
Bonde, Peder Carlsson 1923- *WhoWor 93*
Bonde-Petersen, Flemming 1930- *WhoScE 91-2*
Bonder, Annette Gertrude 1929- *WhoAmW 93*
Bonder, Daniel L. 1953- *St&PR 93*
Bonder, Joel F. *Law&B 92*
Bonderman, David *St&PR 93*
Bonderman, David 1942- *NewYTBS 92 [port]*
Bondeville, Emmanuel 1898- *OxDcOp*
Bondeville, Emmanuel (Pierre Georges) de 1898-1987 *Baker 92*
Bondi, A.M. 1913- *St&PR 93*
Bondi, Beulah 1892-1981 *IntDcF 2-3*
Bondi, Enrico 1933- *WhoWor 93*
Bondi, Hermann 1919- *BioIn 17, WhoWor 93*
Bondi, James Oliver 1949- *WhoSSW 93*
Bondi, Joseph Charles, Jr. 1936- *WhoAm 92, WhoSSW 93*
Bondi, Kathleen 1952- *WhoAmW 93, WhoEmL 93*
Bondi, Ken *BioIn 17*
Bondi, Nikki C. 1950- *WhoEmL 93*
Bondi, Thomas A. *Law&B 92*
Bondi-Greeley, Cindi L. 1961- *WhoAmW 93*
Bondin, Ray Anthony 1956- *WhoAm 92, WhoWor 93*
Bondinell, Stephanie 1948- *WhoAmW 93, WhoEmL 93, WhoSSW 93, WhoWor 93*
Bondini, Marianna 1780-1813 *OxDcOp*
Bondini, Pasquale 1737?-1789 *OxDcOp*
Bondon, Jacques (Lauret Jules Desire) 1927- *Baker 92*
Bondor, Antal 1932- *WhoScE 91-4*
Bondroff, Ben F. 1942- *St&PR 93*
Bondrop, Torben von Muderspach 1958- *WhoWor 93*
Bond-Roxborough, Mildred 1927- *St&PR 93*
Bonds, Barry *BioIn 17*
Bonds, Barry Lamar 1964- *WhoAm 92*
Bonds, Bill *BioIn 17*
Bonds, John D. 1941- *St&PR 93*
Bonds, Michael Scott 1954- *WhoSSW 93*
Bonds, Paula *Law&B 92*
Bonds, Rosie *BioIn 17, BlkAmWO*
Bonds, Suzanne M. 1950- *St&PR 93*
Bonds, Thyra Verle 1927- *WhoAmW 93*
Bonds, William Kenneth 1929- *WhoAm 92*
Bond-Upson, Deborah Gwendolyn 1949- *WhoEmL 93*
Bondur, John Maurice 1943- *WhoE 93*
Bondurant, David William 1948- *WhoEmL 93*
Bondurant, Emmet Jopling, II 1937- *WhoAm 92*
Bondurant, Freida W. *Law&B 92*
Bondurant, Kathleen Alice 1958- *WhoEmL 93*
Bondurant, Stuart 1929- *WhoAm 92*
Bondurant, Teresa N. 1957- *WhoSSW 93*
Bondy, Egon *BioIn 17*
Bondy, Eugene L., Jr. 1920- *St&PR 93*
Bondy, Martin 1929- *St&PR 93*
Bondy, Michael Frank 1923- *WhoE 93*
Bondy, Peter J. 1944- *St&PR 93*
Bondy, Philip Kramer 1917- *WhoAm 92*
Bondy, Philip L. d1990 *BioIn 17*
Bone, Amy Clarke *AmWomPl*
Bone, B.C. 1928- *St&PR 93*
Bone, Brenda Kay 1960- *WhoWrEP 92*
Bone, Bruce Charles 1928- *WhoAm 92*
Bone, Diane Elizabeth Baker 1955- *WhoEmL 93*
Bone, Glenn Daniel, III 1963- *WhoWor 93*
Bone, J.F. 1916- *ScF&FL 92*
Bone, J.J. *BioIn 17*
Bone, James R., Jr. 1942- *St&PR 93*
Bone, Janet Witmeyer 1930- *WhoAmW 93*
Bone, Jay Jasper *BioIn 17*
Bone, M. *WhoScE 91-1*
Bone, Roger Conley 1941- *WhoAm 92*
Boneau, C. Alan 1926- *WhoAm 92*
Bonebrake, Merrill L. 1937- *St&PR 93*
Bonee, John Leon, III 1947- *WhoE 93*
Bonehill, Captain Ralph *MajAI*
Bonehill, Ralph 1862-1930 *BioIn 17*
Bonel, Gilbert 1929- *WhoScE 91-2*
Bonella, John J. 1934- *St&PR 93*
Bonelli, Richard 1887-1980 *Baker 92*
Bonelli, Robert Allen 1950- *St&PR 93*
Bonelli, Ronald J. 1952- *St&PR 93*
Bonem, Rena Mae 1948- *WhoAmW 93*
Bonen, Norma Jean 1951- *WhoAmW 93*
Boner, Bill *BioIn 17*
Boner, Donald Leslie 1944- *WhoWor 93*
Boner, J. Russell 1930- *WhoUN 92*
Boner, Linda Hearne 1959- *WhoAmW 93*
Boner, William H. 1945- *WhoAm 92*
Bonerz, Peter 1938- *MiSFD 9, WhoAm 92*
Boneschanscher, Eppo Johannes 1957- *WhoWor 93*
Bonesio, Woodrow Michael 1943- *WhoAm 92*
Bonesso, Carmel Burke 1960- *WhoAmW 93*
Bonesteel, Michael John 1939- *WhoAm 92*
Bonestell, Chesley *BioIn 17*
Bonestell, Chesley 1888-1986 *ScF&FL 92*
Bonet, Frank Joseph 1937- *WhoAm 92*
Bonet, Lisa *BioIn 17, WhoAm 92*
Bonet, Lisa 1967- *ConTFT 10*
Bonet-Sugranes, Juan-Julio 1940- *WhoScE 91-3*
Bonetti, Giovanni *WhoScE 91-3*
Bonetti, Kay Jacqueline 1940- *WhoWrEP 92*
Bonetti, Mattia *BioIn 17*
Bonetto, Frank J. 1950- *St&PR 93*
Boneu, Bernard 1942- *WhoScE 91-2*
Bonev, B. *WhoScE 91-4*
Bonev, Evlogui 1931- *WhoUN 92*
Boney, W.A. 1933- *St&PR 93*
Bonfante, Larissa *WhoAm 92*
Bonfatti, Flavio *WhoScE 91-3*
Bonfichi, Paolo 1769-1840 *Baker 92*
Bonfield, Arthur Earl 1936- *WhoAm 92*
Bonfield, Barbara Goldstein 1937- *WhoSSW 93*
Bonfield, Edward Harvey 1938- *WhoE 93*
Bonfield, Gordon Bradley, Jr. 1926- *WhoAm 92*
Bonfield, Phyllis Kline 1942- *WhoE 93*
Bonfield, W. *WhoScE 91-1*
Bonfiglio, Joel David 1958- *WhoEmL 93*
Bonfiglio, Michael 1917- *WhoAm 92*
Bonfiglio, Robert Anthony 1954- *WhoE 93*
Bonfiglio, Salvatore J. 1959- *WhoEmL 93*
Bonfils, Frederick Gilman 1860-1933 *JrnUS*
Bonforte, Richard James 1940- *WhoAm 92*
Bong, Richard I. 1920-1945 *BioIn 17*
Bonga, Timothy 1956- *WhoAsAP 91*
Bongard, C. Mark *Law&B 92*
Bongianino, Piero 1925- *WhoWor 93*
Bongie, Christopher Laurence 1960- *WhoSSW 93*
Bongiorno, Andrew W. *Law&B 92*
Bongiorno, Angelo 1923- *St&PR 93*
Bongiorno, Anthony M. *Law&B 92*
Bongiorno, James William 1943- *WhoAm 92*
Bongiorno, John Anthony 1951- *WhoWor 93*
Bongiorno, John J. 1938- *St&PR 93*
Bongiorno, John Jacques 1938- *WhoAm 92*
Bongiorno, Joseph John, Jr. 1936- *WhoAm 92*
Bongiovanni, David A. *Law&B 92*
Bongiovanni, Elaine *Law&B 92*
Bongiovanni, George Edward 1949- *WhoWor 93*
Bongiovanni, Michael 1920- *St&PR 93*
Bongo, Albert-Bernard Omar 1935- *WhoWor 93*
Bongo, Ali (Martin) 1940- *WhoAfr*
Bongo, Omar *BioIn 17*
Bongo, Omar (Albert Bernard) 1935- *WhoAfr*
Bongo, Pascaline *WhoWor 93*
Bongoy, Mpekesa 1938- *WhoUN 92*
Bongrand, Pierre 1950- *WhoScE 91-2*
Bong Way Wong *BioIn 17*
Bonhag, Thomas Edward 1952- *WhoE 93, WhoEmL 93*
Bonhagen, Jerry C. *Law&B 92*
Bonham, Ben B. 1944- *St&PR 93*
Bonham, Clifford Vernon 1921- *WhoAm 92*
Bonham, Dwight Mendon 1925- *WhoAm 92*
Bonham, Ellen Rice 1941- *WhoAmW 93*
Bonham, Frank *BioIn 17*
Bonham, Frank 1914- *DcAmChF 1960*
Bonham, Frank 1914-1988 *ScF&FL 92*
Bonham, Frank 1914-1989 *MajAI [port]*
Bonham, George Wolfgang 1924- *WhoAm 92, WhoWrEP 92*
Bonham, Gordon Clinton 1957- *WhoAm 92, WhoEmL 93*
Bonham, James Butler 1807-1836 *BioIn 17*
Bonham, James Paul 1940- *St&PR 93*
Bonham, John 1948-1980 *BioIn 17*
Bonham, Kristine Carlson 1959- *WhoSSW 93*
Bonham, Margaret Rion 1958- *WhoAmW 93*
Bonham, Mary *AmWomPl*
Bonham, Robert G. 1918- *St&PR 93*
Bonham-Yeaman, Doria 1932- *WhoAmW 93, WhoSSW 93*
Bonheim, Frank Werner 1926- *St&PR 93*
Bonheur, Rosa 1822-1899 *BioIn 17*
Bonhoeffer, Dietrich 1906-1945 *BioIn 17, DcTwHis*
Bonhomme, Pierre c. 1555-1617 *Baker 92*
Bonhomme, Pierre 1941- *WhoScE 91-2*
Boni, Guillaume fl. 16th cent.- *Baker 92*
Boni, Miki 1938- *WhoAmW 93*
Boni, Robert Eugene 1928- *St&PR 93*
Bonica, John Joseph 1917- *WhoAm 92*
Bonie, Kathleen Avegno 1949- *WhoAmW 93*
Boniello, Michael P. 1955- *St&PR 93*
Boniface, Christian Pierre 1962- *WhoWor 93*
Boniface, Rudolph Harold 1926- *WhoWor 93*
Boniface, Thomas John 1944- *St&PR 93*
Boniface Of Montferrat 115-?-1207 *OxDcByz*
Bonifacius c. 380-432 *HarEnMi*
Bonifas, Barbara J. 1947- *WhoAmW 93, WhoEmL 93*
Bonifas, Jane Marie 1935- *WhoAmW 93*
Bonifay, E. *WhoScE 91-2*
Bonifazi, Stephen 1924- *WhoSSW 93*
Bonifaz Nuno, Alberto 1911- *DcMexL*
Bonifaz Nuno, Ruben 1923- *DcMexL*
Bonifer, Michael *ScF&FL 92*
Bonifield, Eugene 1933- *WhoIns 93*
Bonifield, John D. 1942- *St&PR 93*
Bonifield, William C. 1934- *WhoAm 92*
Bonilla, Bobby *NewYTBS 92 [port]*
Bonilla, Bobby 1963- *BioIn 17, News 92 [port]*
Bonilla, Frank 192-?- *HispAmA*
Bonilla, Jose Luis 1946- *WhoWor 93*
Bonilla, Luis Lopez 1956- *WhoWor 93*
Bonilla, Mary Ann 1956- *WhoEmL 93*
Bonilla, Policarpo *DcCPCAm*
Bonilla, Roberto Martin Antonio 1963- *WhoAm 92*
Bonilla, Ruben, Jr. 20th cent.- *HispAmA*
Bonilla, Tony 1936- *HispAmA [port], WhoAm 92*
Bonilla-Santiago, Gloria *HispAmA*
Bonilla-Santiago, Gloria 1954- *NotHsAW 93*
Bonilla Vargas, Jose Alberto 1955- *WhoWor 93*
Bonime, Florence 1907-1990 *BioIn 17*
Bonime, Jonathan D. *Law&B 92*
Bonime, Walter Raymond 1909- *WhoE 93*
Bonime-Blanc, Andrea 1957- *WhoE 93*
Bonin, Bernard 1936- *WhoAm 92*
Bonin, Bernard 1948- *WhoScE 91-2*
Bonin, Daniel J. 1938- *WhoScE 91-2*
Bonin, Georges Robert 1930- *WhoWor 93*
Bonin, Paul Joseph 1929- *WhoAm 92*
Bonina, Mary 1950- *WhoWrEP 92*
Bonine, Dan R. 1940- *St&PR 93*
Boning, Dieter Georg 1939- *WhoScE 91-3*
Bonini, Frank J. 1937- *St&PR 93*
Bonini, Jean F. *Law&B 92*
Bonini, Severo 1582-1663 *Baker 92*
Bonini, Victor L. 1934- *St&PR 93*
Bonini, Victor Louis 1958- *WhoWrEP 92*
Bonino, Fernanda 1927- *WhoAm 92*
Boninsegna, Celestina 1877-1947 *Baker 92, IntDcOp [port]*
Boniol, Eddie Eugene 1931- *WhoSSW 93*
Bonior, David E. *BioIn 17*
Bonior, David E. 1945- *CngDr 91*
Bonior, David Edward 1945- *WhoAm 92*
Bonis, Ferenc 1932- *Baker 92*
Bonis, Melanie 1858-1937 *Baker 92*
Bonis Fast, Francine Dale 1951- *WhoEmL 93*
Bonistalli, Donald Raymond 1948- *St&PR 93*
Bonita, Joseph C. *Law&B 92*
Bonitsis, Theologos Homer 1953- *WhoE 93*
Bonitz, Richard Eric *Law&B 92*
Boniuk, Vivien *BioIn 17*
Boniventi, Giuseppe c. 1670-c. 1727 *OxDcOp*
Boniver, Jacques 1945- *WhoScE 91-2*
Bonjean, Charles Michael 1936- *WhoAm 92*
Bonjiovanni, Kim Rice *Law&B 92*
Bonjour, Edgar 1898-1991 *BioIn 17*
Bonjour, Jean-Philippe 1936- *WhoScE 91-4*
Bon Jovi, Jon *BioIn 17*
Bon Jovi, Jon 1962- *WhoAm 92*
Bonk, David Thomas 1956- *WhoEmL 93*
Bonk, Joseph J. *Law&B 92*
Bonk, Joseph John, II 1957- *WhoEmL 93*
Bonk, Kathleen Lynn 1953- *WhoAmW 93*
Bonk, Kathy *BioIn 17*
Bonke, Felix I.M. 1940- *WhoScE 91-3*
Bonkoski, Kenneth John 1941- *St&PR 93*
Bonkoski, R.J. 1946- *St&PR 93*
Bonkovsky, Herbert Lloyd 1941- *WhoAm 92, WhoE 93*
Bonkowski, Ronald Lawrence 1938- *WhoAm 92*
Bonn, Edward Joseph 1953- *WhoAm 92, WhoSSW 93*
Bonn, Ethel May 1925- *WhoAm 92*
Bonn, Joseph A. 1943- *St&PR 93*
Bonn, Mark Andrew 1950- *WhoSSW 93*
Bonn, Paul Douglas 1934- *St&PR 93*
Bonn, Paul Verne 1939- *WhoAm 92*
Bonn, Theodore Hertz 1923- *WhoAm 92*
Bonn, Walter 1927- *St&PR 93*
Bonnaffe, Jacques *BioIn 17*
Bonnamour, Luc Jacques 1946- *WhoWor 93*
Bonnamy, Ernest 1896-1991 *BioIn 17*
Bonnar, John 1934- *WhoScE 91-3, WhoWor 93*
Bonnard, Pierre 1867-1947 *BioIn 17*
Bonnaure, Pierre E. 1929- *WhoScE 91-3*
Bonne, Francoise Daniele 1951- *WhoWor 93*
Bonneau, Frederic Daniel 1962- *WhoSSW 93*
Bonneau, Louis 1851-1938 *HarEnMi*
Bonnechere, Francois J. 1937- *WhoScE 91-2*
Bonnefoy, Yves *BioIn 17*
Bonnefoy, Yves Jean 1923- *WhoWor 93*
Bonnell, John S. 1893-1992 *NewYTBS 92 [port]*
Bonnell, John Sutherland 1893-1992 *BioIn 17, ConAu 136*
Bonnell, R.E. 1930- *St&PR 93*
Bonnell, Thomas H. *St&PR 93*
Bonnell, Victoria Eileen 1942- *WhoAm 92*
Bonnell, William M. *Law&B 92*
Bonner, Barbara 1948- *WhoE 93*
Bonner, Barbara Groce *WhoSSW 93*
Bonner, Bester Davis 1938- *WhoAmW 93*
Bonner, Beverly Ann 1953- *WhoEmL 93*
Bonner, Boyd Lee 1925- *St&PR 93*
Bonner, C.D. 1934- *St&PR 93*
Bonner, Charles William, III 1928- *WhoAm 92*
Bonner, Cindy 1953- *ConAu 139*
Bonner, Craig Alan 1956- *WhoE 93*
Bonner, Daniel Patrick 1945- *WhoE 93*
Bonner, David C. 1946- *St&PR 93*
Bonner, David Calhoun 1946- *WhoAm 92*
Bonner, Elena *BioIn 17*
Bonner, Francis Truesdale 1921- *WhoAm 92*
Bonner, Geraldine 1870-1930 *AmWomPl*
Bonner, Grace Linnell *Law&B 92*
Bonner, Jack 1948- *WhoAm 92*
Bonner, Jack Wilbur, III 1940- *WhoAm 92, WhoSSW 93, WhoWor 93*
Bonner, Joel E. *Law&B 92*
Bonner, John Arthur 1929- *WhoWor 93*
Bonner, John Tyler 1920- *WhoAm 92*
Bonner, Lewis E. 1944- *St&PR 93*
Bonner, Marita 1899-1971 *AmWomWr 92, BioIn 17*
Bonner, Marita Occomy *AmWomPl*
Bonner, Monica Rossi 1946- *WhoE 93*
Bonner, Patricia Jane 1935- *WhoSSW 93*
Bonner, Peter *WhoScE 91-1*
Bonner, Robert Cleve 1942- *WhoAm 92*
Bonner, Robert F. d1991 *BioIn 17*
Bonner, Robert William 1920- *WhoAm 92*

Bonner, Shirley Harrold 1929- *WhoAmW 93*
Bonner, Stephen B. 1946- *WhoIns 93*
Bonner, Terry Nelsen *WhoWrEP 92*
Bonner, Thomas, Jr. 1942- *WhoSSW 93, WhoWrEP 92*
Bonner, Thomas Neville 1923- *WhoAm 92*
Bonner, Thomas Perry 1958- *WhoEmL 93*
Bonner, Walter Daniel, Jr. 1919- *WhoAm 92*
Bonner, Walter Joseph 1925- *WhoAm 92*
Bonner, William Andrew 1919- *WhoAm 92*
Bonner, William Neely, Jr. 1923- *WhoAm 92*
Bonner, William Russell 1942- *St&PR 93*
Bonnes, Charles A. *Law&B 92*
Bonnes, Charles Andrew 1941- *St&PR 93, WhoAm 92*
Bonnes, David Ralph 1930- *St&PR 93*
Bonneson, Mary Elisabeth 1961- *WhoAmW 93*
Bonnet, Alain *WhoScE 91-2*
Bonnet, Andre 1953- *WhoWor 93*
Bonnet, Beatriz Alicia 1959- *WhoAm 92, WhoEmL 93*
Bonnet, Claude 1938- *WhoScE 91-2*
Bonnet, Georges 1889-1973 *BioIn 17*
Bonnet, Georges 1925- *WhoScE 91-2*
Bonnet, Jean-Jacques 1939- *WhoScE 91-2*
Bonnet, Joseph (Elie Georges Marie) 1884-1944 *Baker 92*
Bonnet, Juan Amedee 1939- *WhoAm 92, WhoWor 93*
Bonnet, Paul *BioIn 17*
Bonnet, Roger-Maurice 1937- *WhoScE 91-2, WhoWor 93*
Bonnetain, Lucien 1926- *WhoScE 91-2*
Bonnett, Kendra R. 1955- *WhoWrEP 92*
Bonnett, Raymond *WhoScE 91-1*
Bonnett, Raymond 1931- *WhoWor 93*
Bonnette, Augustus Kennerley 1944- *WhoAm 92*
Bonneville, Benjamin Louis Eulalie de 1796-1878 *Expl 93 [port]*
Bonneville, Julie A. *Law&B 92*
Bonneville, Kenneth J., Jr. *Law&B 92*
Bonneville, Richard Briggs 1942- *WhoAm 92*
Bonney, Brian Edward *Law&B 92*
Bonney, Donald Ernest 1952- *WhoEmL 93*
Bonney, Hal James, Jr. 1929- *WhoAm 92*
Bonney, John Dennis 1930- *St&PR 93, WhoAm 92*
Bonney, Maurice Charles *WhoScE 91-1*
Bonney, Samuel Robert 1943- *WhoAm 92*
Bonney, Weston L. 1925- *St&PR 93*
Bonney, Weston Leonard 1925- *WhoAm 92*
Bonney, William H. *BioIn 17*
Bonnie, Richard Jeffrey 1945- *WhoAm 92*
Bonnier, Charlotte *BioIn 17*
Bonnier, Karl-Adam 1934- *WhoSSW 93*
Bonnin, Jean 1939- *WhoScE 91-2*
Bonnivet, Guillaume Gouffier, Lord of c. 1488-1525 *HarEnMi*
Bonniwell, George Barton 1939- *St&PR 93*
Bonniwell, Katherine *WhoAm 92, WhoE 93*
Bonno, Giuseppe 1711-1788 *Baker 92, OxDcOp*
Bonnot, Bernard Robert 1941- *WhoE 93*
Bonnot, G.G. 1939- *WhoScE 91-2*
Bonnot, Jacques *WhoScE 91-2*
Bonny 1957- *BioIn 17*
Bonnycastle, Lawrence Christopher 1907- *WhoAm 92*
Bonnyman, George Gordon 1919- *WhoAm 92*
Bono, Anthony Salvatore Emanuel, II 1946- *WhoEmL 93*
Bono, B. Charles, III 1948- *St&PR 93*
Bono, Charlene Cecilia 1949- *WhoAmW 93*
Bono, Emilio de 1866-1944 *HarEnMi*
Bono, Philip 1921- *WhoAm 92*
Bono, Sonny *BioIn 17*
Bono, Sonny 1935- *News 92 [port]*
Bono, Sonny Salvatore 1935- *WhoAm 92*
Bonofiglio, Marie Carolyn 1961- *WhoAmW 93*
Bonomelli, Charles James 1948- *WhoWrEP 92*
Bonomi, John Gurnee 1923- *WhoAm 92*
Bonomo, Joe 1901-1978 *BioIn 17*
Bonomo, Joseph Ralph 1951- *WhoE 93, WhoEmL 93*
Bonomo, Lorenzo 1924- *WhoScE 91-3*
Bonomo, Marne Louise 1947- *WhoEmL 93*
Bononcini, Antonio Maria 1677-1726 *Baker 92, OxDcOp*
Bononcini, Giovanni 1670-1747 *Baker 92, OxDcOp*
Bononcini, Giovanni Maria 1642-1678 *Baker 92, OxDcOp*
Bononcini, Marco Antonio *Baker 92*
Bonosaro, Carol Alessandra 1940- *WhoAm 92*
Bonporti, Francesco Antonio 1672-1748 *Baker 92*
Bonsa, Viola 1897-1991 *BioIn 17*
Bonsack, Rose Mary Hatem 1933- *WhoAmW 93*
Bonsaing, Edward Jerry *BioIn 17*
Bonsal, David F. 1939- *St&PR 93*
Bonsal, Dudley Baldwin 1906- *WhoE 93*
Bonsal, Richard I. 1920- *St&PR 93*
Bonsal, Richard Irving 1920- *WhoAm 92*
Bonsall, Edward H., III 1930- *St&PR 93*
Bonsall, Joseph Sloan, Jr. 1948- *WhoAm 92*
Bonsanti, Giorgio 1944- *WhoWor 93*
Bonse, Ulrich K. 1928- *WhoScE 91-3*
Bonse, Ulrich Karl 1928- *WhoWor 93*
Bonsel, Adriaan 1918- *Baker 92*
Bonsembiante, Mario 1928- *WhoScE 91-3*
Bonser, Sidney H. 1924- *St&PR 93*
Bonser, Sidney Henry 1924- *WhoAm 92*
Bonsib, Richard E. 1931- *St&PR 93*
Bonsignore, Joseph John 1920- *WhoAm 92*
Bonsignore, Michael Robert 1941- *WhoAm 92*
Bonsky, Jack Alan *Law&B 92*
Bonsky, Jack Alan 1938- *WhoAm 92*
Bonstead, Douglas Lyal 1947- *WhoEmL 93*
Bonta, Ivan L. 1922- *WhoScE 91-3*
Bonta, Ray Withers 1913- *WhoSSW 93*
Bontchev, Panayot Rankov 1933- *WhoScE 91-4*
Bonte, Frederick James 1922- *WhoAm 92*
Bonte, Jean-Paul 1947- *WhoScE 91-2*
Bonte-Friedheim, C. *WhoScE 91-3*
Bonte-Friedheim, C.H. *WhoScE 91-3*
Bontempi, Giovanni c. 1624-1705 *OxDcOp*
Bontempi, Giovanni Andrea c. 1624-1705 *Baker 92*
Bontemps, Arna(ud Wendell) 1902-1973 *MajAI [port]*
Bontemps, Arna Wendell 1902-1973 *BioIn 17, BlkAull 92, EncAACR*
Bonting, Sjoerd Lieuwe 1924- *WhoAm 92*
Bontly, Thomas 1939- *ScF&FL 92*
Bontos, George Emmanuel 1924- *WhoSSW 93*
Bontoyan, Warren Roberts 1932- *WhoAm 92*
Bontrager, Robert Marion 1956- *WhoSSW 93*
Bontz, Maruita Carolyn 1930- *WhoE 93*
Bonuccelli, Charles Louis 1955- *WhoE 93*
Bonucci, Ermanno 1930- *WhoScE 91-3*
Bonura, Larry Samuel 1950- *WhoSSW 93*
Bonus, Holger 1935- *WhoWor 93*
Bonus, Robert Harold 1927- *St&PR 93*
Bonutti, Alexander Carl 1951- *WhoEmL 93*
Bonvalet, Jean-Pierre 1937- *WhoScE 91-2*
Bonventre, Joseph Vincent 1949- *WhoAm 92*
Bonventre, Vincent Martin 1948- *WhoEmL 93*
Bonvillian, William Boone 1947- *WhoAm 92, WhoEmL 93*
Bonvino, Frank W. *Law&B 92*
Bonwell, Miner Welsh 1925- *St&PR 93*
Bonyhadi, Ernest 1924- *WhoAm 92*
Bonynge, Richard 1930- *OxDcOp, WhoAm 92, WhoWor 93*
Bonynge, Richard (Alan) 1930- *Baker 92*
Bonz, Margaret Huling 1941- *WhoAmW 93*
Bonzagni, Vincent Francis 1952- *WhoEmL 93, WhoSSW 93*
Bonzani, Peter Lawrence 1945- *St&PR 93*
Boo, Ben 1925- *WhoAm 92*
Boo, Betty *BioIn 17*
Boobyer, Don J. 1953- *WhoEmL 93*
Boochever, Robert 1917- *WhoAm 92*
Boock, H. Frank 1942- *St&PR 93*
Boocker, Lee K. *Law&B 92*
Boocks Neff, Nancy Louise 1952- *WhoEmL 93*
Boocock, Sarane Spence 1935- *WhoAm 92*
Boocock, Stephen William 1948- *WhoEmL 93*
Boodey, Cecil Webster, Jr. 1931- *WhoAm 92, WhoWor 93*
Boodhoo, Martin Jagdeo 1931- *WhoUN 92*
BoodhooSingh, Yasmin Shanta 1950- *WhoE 93*
Boodman, David M. 1923- *St&PR 93*
Boodman, David Morris 1923- *WhoAm 92*
Boody, Irving R., Jr. 1917- *St&PR 93*
Booe, Karen Phyllis 1952- *WhoAmW 93*
Booh Booh, Jacques Roger *WhoWor 93*
Booh Booh, Jacques Roger 1938- *WhoAfr*
Booher, Alice Ann 1941- *WhoAmW 93, WhoE 93*
Booher, Barbara *BioIn 17*
Booher, Charles Forest 1944- *WhoWor 93*
Booher, Deborah L. *BioIn 17*
Booher, E.S. *St&PR 93*
Booher, Edward E. 1911-1990 *BioIn 17*
Booher, John P. 1946- *St&PR 93*
Booher, Lawrence J., Jr. *Law&B 92*
Book, Edward R. 1931- *WhoAm 92*
Book, John Kenneth 1950- *WhoEmL 93, WhoSSW 93, WhoWor 93*
Book, Kenneth Merten 1938- *St&PR 93*
Book, Samuel Howard 1940- *WhoAm 92, WhoE 93*
Book, Stephen Mark 1954- *WhoEmL 93*
Bookataub, S. Joseph 1948- *St&PR 93*
Bookatz, Samuel 1910- *WhoAm 92*
Bookbinder, Hyman Harry 1916- *WhoAm 92*
Booke, Henry Edward 1932- *WhoE 93*
Booker, Alvin Eugene 1928- *WhoE 93, WhoWor 93*
Booker, Betty Mae 1948- *WhoAmW 93*
Booker, Bodley, Jr. 1918- *St&PR 93*
Booker, Bruce E. *WhoIns 93*
Booker, Christopher (John Penrice) 1937- *ConAu 136*
Booker, Deirdre Elizabeth 1965- *WhoEmL 93*
Booker, Donald Brandon 1942- *WhoWor 93*
Booker, Henry Marshall 1935- *WhoSSW 93*
Booker, John Franklin 1934- *WhoAm 92*
Booker, John William 1942- *St&PR 93*
Booker, Larry Frank 1950- *WhoEmL 93*
Booker, Lewis Thomas 1929- *WhoAm 92*
Booker, Mary 1897-1974 *BioIn 17*
Booker, Nana Laurel 1946- *WhoAmW 93, WhoEmL 93*
Booker, Stephen B. 1957- *St&PR 93*
Booker, W. Wayne 1934- *St&PR 93*
Booker, William Jeffrey 1963- *WhoSSW 93*
Booker-Davis, Janet Marie 1954- *WhoAmW 93*
Booker T & the MGs *SoulM*
Bookhammer, Eugene Donald 1918- *WhoAm 92*
Bookhardt, Fred Barringer, Jr. 1934- *WhoAm 92, WhoE 93, WhoWor 93*
Bookhart, Samuel Wingard, Jr. 1931- *WhoE 93*
Bookman, Charlotte *ConAu 38NR, MajAI*
Bookman, Dale George 1921- *St&PR 93*
Bookman, George B. 1914- *WhoAm 92*
Bookout, John Frank, Jr. 1922- *WhoAm 92*
Bookout, John Garber 1935- *St&PR 93*
Books, Earl James 1942- *WhoSSW 93*
Books, Glen *Law&B 92*
Books, Joy Ann 1937- *WhoAmW 93*
Bookspan, Martin 1926- *Baker 92*
Bookspan, Michael Lloyd 1929- *WhoAm 92*
Bookwalter, J.R. *MiSFD 9*
Bookwalter, Richard Leroy 1942- *St&PR 93*
Boolel, Satcam 1920- *WhoAfr*
Boolell, Satcam 1920- *WhoWor 93*
Boolos, George Stephen 1940- *WhoAm 92*
Boom, Glenn Leonard 1926- *St&PR 93*
Boomer, Walter 1938- *BioIn 17*
Boomer, Walter Eugene 1938- *WhoAm 92*
Boomershine, Donald Eugene 1931- *WhoAm 92*
Boon, Christopher Routley *WhoScE 91-1*
Boon, Jaap J. 1947- *WhoScE 91-3*
Boon, Jean Pierre 1935- *WhoWor 93*
Boon, Nancy Ridenhour 1928- *WhoSSW 93*
Boon, Thierry Robert 1941- *WhoScE 91-2*
Boon, Yves M. *Law&B 92*
Boon, Yves Marie 1947- *WhoWor 93*
Boone, Alan Lee 1945- *St&PR 93*
Boone, Anthony *Law&B 92*
Boone, "Blind" (John William) 1864-1927 *Baker 92*
Boone, Bruce 1940- *ConGAN*
Boone, Celia Trimble 1953- *WhoAmW 93, WhoEmL 93*
Boone, Charles 1939- *Baker 92*
Boone, Charles S. 1953- *St&PR 93*
Boone, Clifford Scott 1948- *WhoEmL 93*
Boone, Daniel *BioIn 17*
Boone, Daniel 1734-1820 *BioIn 17, Expl 93 [port], HarEnMi*
Boone, Daniel, Jr. *Law&B 92*
Boone, David E. *Law&B 92*
Boone, David Edwin 1946- *St&PR 93*
Boone, David Ridgway 1952- *WhoEmL 93*
Boone, Debby 1956- *Baker 92*
Boone, Debra George 1958- *WhoEmL 93*
Boone, Dorothy Mae 1919- *WhoAmW 93*
Boone, Douglas Larry 1945- *WhoSSW 93*
Boone, Eddie H. 1944- *St&PR 93*
Boone, Edgar John 1930- *WhoWor 93*
Boone, Eugene Lawrence 1937- *WhoSSW 93*
Boone, Franklin Delano Roosevelt, Sr. 1942- *WhoSSW 93*
Boone, Franklin Delanor Roosevelt, Sr. 1942- *WhoAm 92*
Boone, Frans Robert 1940- *WhoScE 91-3*
Boone, Gary W. 1947- *St&PR 93*
Boone, Gregory Kay *Law&B 92*
Boone, Harold Thomas 1921- *WhoAm 92*
Boone, J. William 1952- *WhoEmL 93*
Boone, James Leroy, Jr. 1923- *WhoSSW 93*
Boone, James Virgil 1933- *WhoWor 93*
Boone, Janice Fowler 1945- *WhoAmW 93*
Boone, Jefferson Wentworth 1950- *WhoEmL 93*
Boone, Jeffrey S. *Law&B 92*
Boone, Joel A. *Law&B 92*
Boone, John A. 1923- *St&PR 93*
Boone, John Carter 1952- *WhoEmL 93*
Boone, John Clay 1947- *WhoEmL 93*
Boone, Kenneth Ray 1949- *WhoSSW 93*
Boone, Kimberlie Ann 1960- *WhoAmW 93*
Boone, Kurt Bradley 1959- *WhoE 93*
Boone, Lalia Phipps 1907- *WhoWrEP 92*
Boone, Laura Virginia 1956- *WhoEmL 93*
Boone, Levi D., III *Law&B 92*
Boone, Lois Ann 1941- *St&PR 93*
Boone, Louis Eugene 1941- *WhoAm 92*
Boone, Marshall Nolan, Jr. 1942- *WhoSSW 93*
Boone, Marvin Lester, Sr. 1931- *WhoWor 93*
Boone, Mary *BioIn 17*
Boone, Mary Ann 1961- *WhoEmL 93*
Boone, Michael Mauldin 1941- *WhoAm 92*
Boone, Morell Douglas 1942- *WhoAm 92*
Boone, Oliver Kiel 1922- *WhoAm 92*
Boone, Pat 1934- *BioIn 17, WhoAm 92*
Boone, Pat (Charles Eugene) 1934- *Baker 92*
Boone, Patricia Cash 1955- *WhoAmW 93*
Boone, Pierre M. 1944- *WhoScE 91-2*
Boone, Pierre Michel 1941- *WhoWor 93*
Boone, Ray 1923- *BioIn 17*
Boone, Richard Winston, Sr. 1941- *WhoSSW 93*
Boone, Robert Edward 1933- *St&PR 93*
Boone, Robert Raymond 1947- *BiDAMSp 1989*
Boone, Susan Hobbs 1952- *St&PR 93*
Boone, Taylor Scott 1948- *WhoEmL 93*
Boone, Thomas Caleb 1957- *WhoEmL 93*
Boone, Thomas John 1957- *WhoWor 93*
Boone, William Roy 1938- *St&PR 93*
Boone Family *BioIn 17*
Boonekamp, Piet M. 1950- *WhoScE 91-3*
Boon-Falleur, Thierry 1944- *WhoScE 91-2*
Boonin, Nicholas Philip 1950- *WhoEmL 93*
Boon Poh, Cheah 1930- *WhoWor 93*
Boonshaft-Lewis, Hope Judith 1949- *WhoAm 92*
Boonstra, Mark Thomas 1957- *WhoEmL 93*
Boontje, Albertus Hendrikus 1933- *WhoScE 91-3*
Boop, Robert Lee, Sr. 1945- *WhoSSW 93*
Boor, Myron Vernon 1942- *WhoWor 93*
Booraem, Jonathan W. 1938- *St&PR 93*
Boord, Les 1947- *St&PR 93*
Boorda, Jeremy Michael 1938- *WhoAm 92*
Boorem, Mary Teresa 1955- *WhoEmL 93*
Booren, Jo van den 1935- *Baker 92*
Boorkman, Jo Anne 1947- *WhoEmL 93*
Boorman, Howard Lyon 1920- *WhoAm 92*
Boorman, Jack T. 1941- *WhoUN 92*
Boorman, John 1933- *MiSFD 9, WhoAm 92*
Boorman, Philip Michael 1939- *WhoAm 92*
Boorman, Reg 1935- *WhoAsAP 91*
Booros, James L. 1929- *WhoIns 93*
Boorstein, James *BioIn 17*
Boorstein, Laurence 1951- *WhoEmL 93*
Boorstin, Daniel J. 1914- *BioIn 17, WhoAm 92, WhoWor 93, WhoWrEP 92*
Boorstin, Jon *ConTFT 10*
Boorstin, Paul 1944- *ScF&FL 92*
Boorstin, Samuel A. *BioIn 17*
Boorstin, Sharon 1945- *ScF&FL 92*
Boos, Arthur Charles 1954- *WhoEmL 93*
Boos, Florence S. 1943- *ScF&FL 92*
Boos, Florence Saunders 1943- *WhoAmW 93*
Boos, Francis Henry, Jr. *Law&B 92*
Boos, H. Gordon *MiSFD 9*
Boos, Julian H. 1925- *WhoSSW 93*
Boos, Wilbur F. 1928- *St&PR 93*
Booser, Earl Richard 1922- *WhoE 93*
Boosey, John A. 1929- *St&PR 93*
Boosey, John Arthur 1929- *WhoAm 92*
Boosey, Thomas *Baker 92*
Boosey & Hawkes *Baker 92*
Boost, Renee Mary 1965- *WhoAmW 93*

Boostrom, William C. 1949- *WhoEmL 93*
Boot, John C. G. 1936- *WhoE 93*
Boot, Rene Gerardus Antonius 1956- *WhoWor 93*
Boot, William *ConAu 39NR*
Booth, Albert Edward, II 1942- *WhoAm 92*
Booth, Andrew Donald 1918- *WhoAm 92*
Booth, Anna Belle 1912- *WhoE 93*
Booth, Anne *AmWomPl*
Booth, Barbara Ribman 1928- *WhoAmW 93*
Booth, Beatrice Giorlando 1955- *WhoAmW 93*
Booth, Bonnie Nelson 1942- *WhoE 93, WhoWor 93*
Booth, Bradford A. 1909-1968 *ScF&FL 92*
Booth, Brian G. 1936- *St&PR 93*
Booth, Brian Geddes 1936- *WhoAm 92*
Booth, Charles Loomis, Jr. 1933- *St&PR 93, WhoAm 92*
Booth, Chesley P.W. 1939- *St&PR 93*
Booth, Chesley Peter Washburn 1939- *WhoAm 92*
Booth, David A. *WhoScE 91-1*
Booth, Diane Elizabeth 1948- *WhoWrEP 92*
Booth, E.W. 1944- *St&PR 93*
Booth, Edgar Hirsch 1926- *WhoAm 92*
Booth, Edwina d1991 *BioIn 17*
Booth, Eric D. 1944- *WhoAm 92*
Booth, Gary E. 1940- *St&PR 93*
Booth, George 1926- *WhoAm 92*
Booth, George Geoffrey 1942- *WhoAm 92*
Booth, George Henry 1954- *St&PR 93*
Booth, Gifford Marsden, Jr. 1913- *St&PR 93*
Booth, Glenna Greene 1928- *WhoAm 92, WhoWor 93*
Booth, Gordon Dean, Jr. 1939- *WhoAm 92, WhoSSW 93, WhoWor 93*
Booth, Harold W. 1934- *WhoIns 93*
Booth, Harold Waverly 1934- *WhoAm 92*
Booth, Henry G. 1941- *St&PR 93*
Booth, Henry Michael 1925- *WhoWor 93*
Booth, Herb 1942- *WhoSSW 93*
Booth, Hilda Earl Ferguson 1943- *WhoSSW 93*
Booth, Hilliard *AmWomPl*
Booth, Israel MacAllister 1931- *St&PR 93, WhoAm 92*
Booth, James Albert 1946- *WhoEmL 93*
Booth, James Ford *Law&B 92*
Booth, Jane Schuele *WhoSSW 93*
Booth, Janet Jayne 1924- *WhoAmW 93*
Booth, Jean Anne 1962- *WhoAmW 93*
Booth, John Edwin 1927- *St&PR 93*
Booth, John Lord 1907- *WhoAm 92*
Booth, John Nicholls 1912- *WhoAm 92*
Booth, John Samuel, III 1944- *WhoSSW 93*
Booth, John T. 1929- *St&PR 93*
Booth, John Thomas 1929- *WhoAm 92, WhoWor 93*
Booth, John Wayne 1948- *WhoSSW 93*
Booth, John Wilkes 1838-1865 *BioIn 17*
Booth, Laurence Ogden 1936- *WhoAm 92*
Booth, Lila 1930- *WhoE 93*
Booth, M.R. 1942- *WhoScE 91-1*
Booth, Malcolm Aaron 1936- *WhoE 93*
Booth, Marcell Alphonse 1927- *St&PR 93*
Booth, Margaret Ann 1946- *WhoE 93, WhoEmL 93*
Booth, Martin 1936- *St&PR 93*
Booth, Mitchell B. 1927- *WhoAm 92*
Booth, Monique Nicole *Law&B 92*
Booth, Neil 1946- *St&PR 93*
Booth, Nicholas Henry 1923- *WhoSSW 93*
Booth, Patricia Vogt 1947- *WhoEmL 93*
Booth, Philip 1925- *WhoAm 92, WhoWrEP 92*
Booth, R.F. 1935- *St&PR 93*
Booth, Rachel Zonelle 1936- *WhoAm 92*
Booth, Randolph Lee 1952- *WhoAm 92*
Booth, Richard Earl 1919- *WhoAm 92*
Booth, Richard H. *WhoIns 93*
Booth, Robert Alan 1952- *WhoEmL 93*
Booth, Robert H. *Law&B 92*
Booth, Robert Harrison 1932- *WhoSSW 93*
Booth, Robert Lee, Jr. 1936- *WhoAm 92*
Booth, Robert V.D. 1908- *St&PR 93*
Booth, Roger George 1942- *WhoWor 93*
Booth, Rosemary 1941- *WhoAmW 93*
Booth, Roy Sims 1938- *WhoScE 91-4*
Booth, Sara Daniel 1964- *WhoAmW 93*
Booth, Shirley d1992 *NewYTBS 92 [port]*
Booth, Shirley 1898-1992 *News 93-2*
Booth, Stanley 1942- *ConAu 136*
Booth, Stephen M. *Law&B 92*
Booth, T.C. *WhoScE 91-1*
Booth, Thomas Geofffrey *WhoScE 91-1*
Booth, Thomas M. 1931- *St&PR 93*
Booth, Tony Hood, Jr. 1948- *WhoEmL 93, WhoSSW 93*
Booth, Wallace William, III 1952- *WhoWor 93*
Booth, Wallace Wray 1922- *St&PR 93*
Booth, Wayne Clayson 1921- *WhoAm 92*
Booth, William Ray 1941- *WhoSSW 93*
Booth, William Roland 1942- *WhoAm 92*
Booth, William Thomas 1920- *St&PR 93*
Boothby, Guy 1867-1905 *ScF&FL 92*
Boothby, Robert John Graham 1900-1986 *BioIn 17*
Boothby, Willard Sands, III 1946- *WhoEmL 93*
Boothby, William Munger 1918- *WhoAm 92*
Boothe, Barbara Ann 1949- *WhoSSW 93*
Boothe, Brownell K. *Law&B 92*
Boothe, Clare 1903-1987 *BioIn 17*
Boothe, Dawn Merton 1953- *WhoAmW 93*
Boothe, Edward Milton 1935- *WhoSSW 93*
Boothe, Fred D. 1948- *St&PR 93*
Boothe, Garland C., Jr. *Law&B 92*
Boothe, Leon Estel 1938- *WhoAm 92, WhoSSW 93*
Boothe, Power 1945- *WhoAm 92*
Boothe, Roger K. *Law&B 92*
Boothe, Sabrina Anne 1958- *WhoAmW 93*
Boothroyd, Alan D. 1933- *WhoUN 92*
Boothroyd, Betty 1929- *WhoWor 93*
Boothroyd, G. 1932- *BioIn 17*
Boothroyd, Geoffrey 1932- *BioIn 17*
Boothroyd, Herbert J. 1928- *WhoAm 92*
Bootle, William Augustus 1902- *WhoAm 92*
Boots, Sharon G. 1939- *WhoWrEP 92*
Bootsy *SoulM*
Booty, John Everitt 1925- *WhoAm 92*
Booty, Mervyn Douglas *WhoAm 92*
Boova, Augustus A. 1924- *St&PR 93*
Boova, Thomas F. 1949- *St&PR 93*
Booz, Gretchen Arlene 1933- *St&PR 93, WhoAmW 93*
Booze, Rosemarie Marilyn 1957- *WhoAmW 93*
Booze, Thomas Franklin 1955- *WhoEmL 93*
Boozer, Brenda Lynn 1948- *WhoAm 92*
Boozer, Carol Sue Neely 1944- *WhoAmW 93*
Boozer, Grant William 1951- *St&PR 93*
Boozer, Howard Rai 1923- *WhoAm 92*
Boozer, Linda B. *Law&B 92*
Boozer, Robert Charles 1930- *WhoAm 92*
Boozer, Young J. 1948- *St&PR 93*
Boozer, Young Jacob, III 1948- *WhoAm 92*
Bopp, Edward Sidney 1930- *WhoSSW 93*
Bopp, Franz 1791-1867 *IntDcAn*
Bopp, Fritz Welhelm 1945- *WhoScE 91-3*
Bopp, Martin 1923- *WhoScE 91-3*
Bopp, Mary *Law&B 92*
Bopp, Mary Ann 1955- *WhoAmW 93, WhoE 93*
Bopp, William C. 1943- *St&PR 93*
Boppart, Shari Beth *Law&B 92*
Boppe, Charles William 1948- *WhoEmL 93*
Boppe, Larry Eugene 1942- *St&PR 93*
Bopst, David Bruce 1937- *St&PR 93*
Boquet, Robert Wayne 1943- *St&PR 93*
Boquet, Yves Andre 1956- *WhoE 93*
Boquist, L. Lennart V. 1937- *WhoScE 91-4*
Bor, Jonathan Steven 1953- *WhoAm 92*
Bor, Mehmet 1958- *WhoWor 93*
Bor, Zsolt 1949- *WhoScE 91-4*
Bora, Alexander 1916- *WhoAm 92*
Boraczek, Walter M. 1941- *St&PR 93*
Borah, Frederic 1941- *St&PR 93*
Borah, William E. 1865-1940 *PolPar*
Borak, Robert Lawrence 1947- *St&PR 93*
Boran, Rayanne Marie 1968- *WhoE 93*
Boranic, Milivoj 1936- *WhoScE 91-4*
Boraston, Ian George *WhoScE 91-1*
Boratyn, Martin T. *Law&B 92*
Borau, Jose Luis 1929- *MiSFD 9*
Borawski, John Henry 1957- *WhoWor 93*
Borax, Sigmund 1930- *St&PR 93*
Boraz, Robert Alan 1951- *WhoEmL 93, WhoWor 93*
Borbely, Gyorgy 1943- *WhoScE 91-4*
Borch, Gaston Louis Christopher 1871-1926 *Baker 92*
Borch, Richard Frederic 1941- *WhoAm 92*
Borchard, Adolphe 1882-1967 *Baker 92*
Borchard, Craig Lee 1962- *WhoE 93*
Borchard, Klaus 1938- *WhoScE 91-3*
Borchard, Tom *BioIn 17*
Borchard, Werner 1935- *WhoScE 91-3*
Borchardt, Anne *WhoE 93*
Borchardt, Frank A. 1935- *St&PR 93*
Borchardt, Herbert H. 1906- *St&PR 93*
Borchardt, John Keith 1946- *WhoSSW 93*
Borchardt, Paul Douglas 1942- *WhoSSW 93*
Borchardt, Robert L. *BioIn 17*
Borchardt, Robert L. 1938- *St&PR 93*
Borchardt, Ronald Terrance 1944- *WhoAm 92*
Borchelt, M.L. 1926- *St&PR 93*
Borchers, Edward L. 1939- *St&PR 93*
Borchers, Hans Werner 1949- *WhoWor 93*
Borchers, Leon J. 1940- *St&PR 93*
Borchers, Orville William, Jr. 1946- *St&PR 93*
Borchers, Robert Reece 1936- *WhoAm 92*
Borchert, Donald Marvin 1934- *WhoAm 92*
Borchert, Doug *Law&B 92*
Borchert, Gunter 1926- *WhoScE 91-3*
Borchert, John Robert 1918- *WhoAm 92*
Borchert, Wolfgang 1921-1947 *DcLB 124 [port]*
Borchetta, Michael Joseph 1965- *WhoEmL 93*
Borchgrave, Arnaud de *ScF&FL 92*
Borchman, Norman John 1923- *St&PR 93*
Borck, Chester E. 1913- *St&PR 93*
Borck, Edmund von 1906-1944 *Baker 92*
Borcoman, James Willmott 1926- *WhoAm 92*
Borcover, Alfred Seymour 1931- *WhoAm 92*
Borda, Daniel Jean 1932- *St&PR 93*
Borda, Deborah 1949- *WhoAm 92, WhoAmW 93*
Borda, Richard Joseph 1931- *WhoAm 92*
Bordacs Irwin, Krisztina 1956- *WhoAmW 93, WhoEmL 93*
Bordallo, Madeleine Mary 1933- *WhoAm 92*
Borde, Jean Benjamin de la *Baker 92*
Bordeaux, Pierre William Harriston 1948- *WhoEmL 93, WhoSSW 93*
Bordelon, Cheryl Ann 1947- *WhoEmL 93*
Bordelon, Geraldine Lopez 1968- *WhoEmL 93*
Bordelon, Guy *BioIn 17*
Borden, Brenda Jane 1958- *WhoEmL 93*
Borden, Bruce F. 1951- *St&PR 93*
Borden, Donald Wayne 1959- *WhoWor 93*
Borden, Enid A. 1950- *WhoEmL 93*
Borden, Ernest Carleton 1939- *WhoAm 92*
Borden, Gavin Gail d1991 *BioIn 17*
Borden, George Asa 1932- *WhoAm 92*
Borden, Joseph 1931- *St&PR 93*
Borden, Kathleen Elizabeth Pedder 1955- *WhoAmW 93, WhoEmL 93*
Borden, Lizzie 1860-1927 *NewYTBS 92 [port]*
Borden, Lizzie 1954- *MiSFD 9*
Borden, Louise 1949- *BioIn 17*
Borden, Louise (Walker) 1949- *ConAu 136*
Borden, Mary *AmWomPl*
Borden, Robert Laird 1854-1937 *DcTwHis*
Borden, Sandra McClister 1946- *WhoAmW 93, WhoE 93, WhoWor 93*
Borden, Sherman T. 1929- *St&PR 93*
Borden, Spencer, IV 1941- *WhoE 93*
Borden, Weston Thatcher 1943- *WhoAm 92*
Borden, William S. d1990 *BioIn 17*
Borden, William Vickers 1938- *WhoWrEP 92*
Bordenick, Stephanie Elaine 1962- *WhoEmL 93*
Border, James Robert 1956- *WhoEmL 93*
Border, Norma Lynne 1946- *WhoAmW 93*
Border, Rosemary 1943- *ScF&FL 92*
Borderies, Nicole 1950- *WhoScE 91-2*
Borderon, J.C. 1934- *WhoScE 91-2*
Borders, Bruce 1959- *BioIn 17*
Borders, Carol Lee *WhoAmW 93*
Borders, Charles Edward 1925- *WhoAm 92*
Borders, Gary B. 1955- *ScF&FL 92*
Borders, John Gillespie 1946- *WhoEmL 93*
Borders, John Kenneth 1921- *St&PR 93*
Borders, Robert L. 1928- *St&PR 93*
Borders, William Alexander 1939- *WhoAm 92*
Borders, William Donald 1913- *WhoAm 92*
Bordes, Adrienne *WhoE 93*
Bordes, Charles (Marie Anne) 1863-1909 *Baker 92*
Bordes, John L., Jr. *Law&B 92*
Bordes, Peter Anthony 1927- *WhoAm 92*
Bordetsky, Diana M. 1948- *WhoEmL 93*
Bordett, Daniel Leonard 1923- *St&PR 93*
Bordett, Robert Daniel 1948- *WhoEmL 93*
Bordewick, James R., Jr. *Law&B 92*
Bordie, John George 1931- *WhoAm 92, WhoSSW 93*
Bordier, Jacques 1950- *WhoWor 93*
Bordiga, Benno 1920- *St&PR 93, WhoAm 92, WhoWor 93*
Bordiga, Jeffrey Scott 1952- *St&PR 93*
Bordin, Gelindo *BioIn 17*
Bordini, Ernest John 1957- *WhoEmL 93, WhoSSW 93*
Bordner, Gregory Wilson 1959- *WhoEmL 93, WhoWor 93*
Bordogna, Joseph 1933- *WhoAm 92, WhoWor 93*
Bordogni, Giulio Marco 1789-1856 *Baker 92, OxDcOp*
Bordon, Robert L. *Law&B 92*
Bordoni, Faustina *Baker 92*
Bordoni, Faustina 1693-1783 *BioIn 17*
Bordoni, Faustina c. 1700-1781 *IntDcOp [port], OxDcOp*
Bordua, Adrien *Law&B 92*
Bordy, Bill 1930- *WhoWor 93*
Bordyn, James M. 1948- *St&PR 93*
Borecek, Dennis Ladislov 1946- *St&PR 93*
Borecki, Kenneth Michael 1955- *WhoE 93, WhoEmL 93*
Borecky, Ladislav 1924- *WhoScE 91-4*
Boreham, Roland S. 1924- *St&PR 93*
Boreham, Roland S., Jr. *BioIn 17*
Boreham, Roland Stanford, Jr. 1924- *WhoAm 92, WhoSSW 93*
Borel, Anne Christine *Law&B 92*
Borel, Armand 1923- *WhoAm 92*
Borel, Emile 1871-1956 *BioIn 17*
Borel, G. *WhoScE 91-3*
Borel, Georges Antoine 1936- *WhoWor 93*
Borel, J. *WhoScE 91-2*
Borel, Jacques 1925- *WhoWor 93*
Borel, Jacques Paul 1931- *WhoScE 91-2*
Borel, James David 1951- *WhoEmL 93*
Borel, Joseph Boex- *ScF&FL 92*
Borel, Marguerite 1883- *BioIn 17*
Borel, Petrus 1809-1859 *DcLB 119 [port]*
Borel, Philippe 1942- *WhoUN 92*
Borel, Rene C. 1948- *St&PR 93*
Borel, Richard Wilson 1943- *WhoAm 92, WhoE 93*
Borel-Clerc, Charles 1879-1959 *Baker 92*
Borella, Luis Enrique 1930- *WhoE 93*
Borella, Mary Dorothy 1919- *WhoAmW 93*
Borelli, Francis Joseph 1935- *WhoAm 92*
Borelli, Frank J. 1935- *St&PR 93*
Borelli, Marco 1961- *WhoScE 91-3*
Borello, Patrick J. 1946- *St&PR 93*
Boren, Arthur Rodney 1916- *WhoAm 92*
Boren, Arthur Rodney, Jr. 1946- *WhoAm 92*
Boren, Benjamin N. 1909- *WhoAm 92*
Boren, Charles Sidney 1943- *St&PR 93*
Boren, David L. *BioIn 17*
Boren, David L. 1941- *CngDr 91, PolPar*
Boren, David Lyle 1941- *WhoAm 92, WhoSSW 93*
Boren, Hollis Grady 1923- *WhoAm 92*
Boren, Hugo 1943- *St&PR 93*
Boren, James Edgar 1949- *WhoEmL 93*
Boren, James Lewis, Jr. 1928- *St&PR 93, WhoSSW 93*
Boren, Judith Rita Knox 1949- *WhoAmW 93*
Boren, Kenneth E. *St&PR 93*
Boren, Leland Emerson 1923- *St&PR 93*
Boren, Lyle H. d1992 *NewYTBS 92*
Boren, Lynda Sue 1941- *WhoAmW 93, WhoSSW 93, WhoWor 93*
Boren, Sunny Truss *Law&B 92*
Boren, Thomas Garner 1949- *WhoAm 92*
Boren, William Meredith 1924- *St&PR 93, WhoAm 92, WhoSSW 93*
Borenfreund, Ellen 1922- *WhoE 93*
Borenstein, Abe Isaac 1957- *WhoAm 92*
Borenstein, Emily Ruth 1923- *WhoWrEP 92*
Borenstein, Eve Rose 1955- *WhoEmL 93*
Borenstein, Milton Conrad 1914- *WhoAm 92, WhoE 93, WhoWor 93*
Borensztein, Eduardo Roberto 1954- *WhoE 93, WhoEmL 93*
Borer, Edward Turner 1938- *St&PR 93, WhoAm 92, WhoE 93, WhoWor 93*
Borer, Jeffrey Stephen 1945- *WhoAm 92, WhoE 93, WhoWor 93*
Borer, W.J. *WhoScE 91-4*
Boresi, Arthur Peter *WhoAm 92, WhoWrEP 92*
Boresi, Janet Carlson 1954- *St&PR 93*
Boresi, Richard Leo 1951- *WhoEmL 93*
Boretsky, Bonnie *Law&B 92*
Boretz, Benjamin (Aaron) 1934- *Baker 92*
Boretz, Naomi Messinger 1935- *WhoE 93*
Boreus, Lars O. 1930- *WhoScE 91-4*
Borey, Nadine Marie 1966- *WhoE 93*
Borg, Alan Charles Nelson 1942- *WhoWor 93*
Borg, Bjorn 1956- *BioIn 17, WhoAm 92, WhoWor 93*
Borg, Carl Oscar 1879-1947 *BioIn 17*
Borg, Donn *Law&B 92*
Borg, Gavin *WhoWrEP 92*
Borg, John W. *Law&B 92*
Borg, Joseph Philip 1952- *WhoEmL 93*
Borg, Kim 1919- *Baker 92, WhoWor 93*
Borg, Malcolm Austin 1938- *St&PR 93, WhoAm 92*
Borg, Martin Joseph 1950- *WhoWor 93*
Borg, Robert Martin 1956- *WhoWor 93*
Borg, Sandra A. 1939- *St&PR 93*
Borg, Sidney Fred 1916- *WhoAm 92*

Borg, Stefan 1954- *WhoEmL 93*
Borg, Stefan Lennart 1945- *WhoWor 93*
Borg, Tonia *Law&B 92*
Borg, Veda Ann d1973 *SweetSg C [port]*
Borg, Walter R. *BioIn 17*
Borg, Wayne M. 1923- *St&PR 93*
Borga, Tricia *Law&B 92*
Borgaonkar, Digamber Shankarrao 1932- *WhoAm 92*
Borgardt, Steven Edward 1952- *St&PR 93*
Borgatta, Edgar F. 1924- *WhoAm 92*
Borgatti, Anthony A., Jr. 1916- *St&PR 93*
Borgatti, Giuseppe 1871-1950 *Baker 92, IntDcOp, OxDcOp*
Borgatti, Renata 1894-1964 *Baker 92*
Borge, Victor 1909- *Baker 92, WhoAm 92*
Borgefors, Gunilla M. 1952- *WhoWor 93*
Borgel, James *Law&B 92*
Borgelt, Burton C. 1933- *WhoAm 92*
Borgelt, Burton Cook 1933- *St&PR 93*
Borge Martinez, Tomas 1930- *ColdWar 2 [port], DcCPCAm*
Borgen, Bjorn K. 1937- *St&PR 93*
Borgen, Ole Edvard 1925- *WhoWor 93*
Borgenicht, Miriam *BioIn 17*
Borger, Egon 1946- *WhoScE 91-3*
Borger, Henry Adolph 1933- *WhoE 93*
Borger, John E. *Law&B 92*
Borger, John Emory 1952- *WhoEmL 93*
Borger, Michael Hinton Ivers 1951- *WhoWor 93*
Borger, Mitchell F. *Law&B 92*
Borgerding, Bruce *Law&B 92*
Borgerding, George N. 1928- *St&PR 93*
Borgers, Leo Peter 1956- *WhoWor 93*
Borges, Cindy Schultze *BioIn 17*
Borges, David Joseph 1955- *WhoEmL 93*
Borges, Francisco L. *AfrAmBi [port]*
Borges, Francisco Lopes 1951- *WhoAm 92*
Borges, Jacobo 1931- *WhoWor 93*
Borges, Jorge Luis 1899-1986 *BioIn 17, DcTwHis, MagSWL [port], ScF&FL 92, SpAmA, WorLitC [port]*
Borges, Wanda 1950- *WhoAmW 93*
Borges, William, III 1948- *WhoEmL 93*
Borgese, Elisabeth Mann 1918- *WhoAm 92*
Borgese, John A. *Law&B 92*
Borgeson, Amy Louise 1953- *WhoEmL 93*
Borgeson, Bruce William *Law&B 92*
Borgeson, Donald Robert 1923- *St&PR 93*
Borgeson, Earl Charles 1922- *WhoAm 92*
Borgeson, Richard D. *Law&B 92*
Borgeson, Steven E. *Law&B 92*
Borgeson, Wallace R. 1945- *St&PR 93*
Borges Perez, Andres *WhoScE 91-3*
Borget, Lloyd George 1913- *WhoAm 92*
Borg-Evans, Michele Lee 1958- *WhoAmW 93, WhoEmL 93*
Borggreven, Jozef M.P.M. 1943- *WhoScE 91-3*
Borghese, Antonio 1944- *WhoScE 91-3*
Borghese, Elisabeth Mann 1918- *ScF&FL 92*
Borghese, Livio M. 1938- *St&PR 93*
Borghese, Valerio 1912-1974 *HarEnMi*
Borghi, Adelaide 1829-1901 *Baker 92*
Borghi, Giovanni Battista 1738-1796 *Baker 92*
Borghi, Peter T. 1950- *St&PR 93*
Borgia, B. *WhoScE 91-3*
Borgia, Cesare 1475-1507 *HarEnMi*
Borgia, Mary Regina Seber 1955- *WhoEmL 93*
Borgia, Nancy Adriana 1943- *WhoAmW 93*
Borginis, Walter William, III 1955- *WhoEmL 93*
Borgioli, Armando 1898-1945 *Baker 92*
Borgioli, Dino 1891-1960 *Baker 92, IntDcOp [port], OxDcOp*
Borgiotti, Giorgio Vittorio 1932- *WhoAm 92*
Borglum, Gutzon 1867-1941 *BioIn 17*
Borgman, Dean C. 1941- *St&PR 93*
Borgman, Eric Bruno 1970- *WhoE 93*
Borgman, George Allan 1928- *WhoE 93*
Borgman, James Mark 1954- *WhoAm 92*
Borgman, Janet Jean 1962- *WhoEmL 93*
Borgman, Jim 1954- *BioIn 17*
Borgman, Patricia E. 1948- *WhoAmW 93*
Borgmeyer, Robert J. 1947- *St&PR 93*
Borgnine, Ernest 1917?- *IntDcF 2-3 [port], WhoAm 92*
Borgofia, Juan de fl. 1495-1533 *BioIn 17*
Borg Olivier de Puget, Albert 1932- *WhoWor 93*
Borgonovo, Mauricio *DcCPCAm*
Borgstahl, Kaylene Denise 1951- *WhoAm 92, WhoAmW 93*
Borgstedt, Douglas 1911- *WhoAm 92*
Borgstedt, Harold Heinrich 1929- *WhoAm 92, WhoE 93*
Borgstrom, Georg Arne 1912-1990 *BioIn 17*
Borgstrom, Hjalmar 1864-1925 *Baker 92*
Borgwing, Lars Weiron 1953- *WhoEmL 93*
Borhidi, Attila L. 1932- *WhoScE 91-4*
Bori, Lucrezia 1887-1960 *Baker 92, IntDcOp [port], NotHsAW 93, OxDcOp*
Boria, Jorge Luis 1948- *WhoWor 93*
Boriani, Attilio Carlo 1936- *WhoScE 91-3*
Borich, Michael 1949- *WhoWrEP 92*
Borie, Bernard Simon, Jr. 1924- *WhoWor 93*
Borie, John Stewart 1956- *WhoE 93*
Bories, George F. 1939- *WhoScE 91-2*
Bories, Serge-Alain 1938- *WhoScE 91-2*
Boril dc. 1218 *OxDcByz*
Borillo, M. 1934- *WhoScE 91-2*
Boring, John Wayne 1929- *WhoAm 92*
Boring, Marvin R. 1930- *St&PR 93*
Boris d1015
See Boris and Gleb *OxDcByz*
Boris, I d907 *OxDcByz*
Boris, II c. 930-c. 976 *OxDcByz*
Boris, III 1894-1943 *DcTwHis*
Boris, III, Czar of Bulgaria 1894-1943 *BioIn 17*
Boris, Bessie 1917- *WhoE 93*
Boris, Etienne Alain 1956- *WhoWor 93*
Boris, Howard *Law&B 92*
Boris, Robert *MiSFD 9*
Boris, Robert Elliot 1947- *WhoWrEP 92*
Boris, Ruthanna 1918- *WhoAm 92*
Boris, Walter R. 1921- *St&PR 93*
Boris, William O. 1939- *WhoAm 92*
Boris and Gleb *OxDcByz*
Borisenko, Eugene Nikitich 1941- *WhoUN 92*
Borish, Arnold Peter 1948- *WhoEmL 93*
Boris Kalamanovic c. 1113-c. 1155 *OxDcByz*
Boriskie, Helen Ann 1949- *WhoAmW 93, WhoEmL 93*
Borisoff, Norman *ScF&FL 92*
Borison, Adam Bruce 1953- *WhoEmL 93*
Borison, Herbert Leon 1922-1990 *BioIn 17*
Borisov, Georgi *WhoScE 91-4*
Borisov, Igor 1951- *WhoWor 93*
Borisov, Lilcho 1925- *Baker 92*
Borisov, Milko 1921- *WhoScE 91-4*
Borissoff, Erast 1946- *WhoE 93*
Borisy, Gary G. 1942- *WhoAm 92*
Boritt, Gabor Szappanos 1940- *WhoAm 92, WhoE 93*
Borja Cevallos, Radrigo 1935- *BioIn 17*
Borja Cevallos, Rodrigo 1935- *WhoWor 93*
Borjas, George Jesus 1950- *WhoAm 92, WhoEmL 93*
Borja y Gonzalez de Riancho, Lucrecia 1887-1960 *Baker 92*
Borjeson, Lena 1940- *WhoWor 93*
Bork, Jeff S. *Law&B 92*
Bork, Ned Lawrence, III 1955- *WhoEmL 93*
Bork, Robert Heron 1927- *OxCSupC, WhoAm 92, WhoE 93*
Borkan, Lionel 1925- *St&PR 93*
Borke, Louise Ilene 1955- *WhoAmW 93*
Borkenstein, Donald M. 1936- *St&PR 93*
Borker, Wallace J. 1919- *St&PR 93*
Borkh, Inge 1917- *Baker 92, IntDcOp [port]*
Borkh, Inge 1921- *OxDcOp*
Borko, Harold 1922- *WhoAm 92*
Bor-Komorowski, Tadeusz 1895-1966 *PolBiDi*
Borkosky, Bruce Glenn 1954- *WhoEmL 93, WhoSSW 93*
Borkovec, Pavel 1894-1972 *Baker 92*
Borkowska, Maria *WhoScE 91-4*
Borkowski, Adam 1942- *WhoScE 91-4*
Borkowski, Bohdan 1852-1901 *Baker 92*
Borkowski, Francis Thomas 1936- *WhoAm 92, WhoSSW 93*
Borkowski, Janusz Leonard 1938- *WhoScE 91-4*
Borkowski, John J. 1926- *St&PR 93*
Borkowski, Joseph 1938- *St&PR 93*
Borkowski, Jozef A. 1943- *WhoScE 91-4*
Borkowski, Michael William *Law&B 92*
Borkowski, Szczepan Franciszek 1929- *WhoWor 93*
Borkowski, Tomasz 1925- *WhoScE 91-4*
Borkowsky, William 1947- *WhoE 93*
Borland, Barbara Dodge d1991 *BioIn 17*
Borland, Clifford R. 1937- *St&PR 93*
Borland, Hal 1900-1978 *BioIn 17*
Borland, Kathryn Kilby 1916- *WhoAm 92*
Borland, Michael D. *Law&B 92*
Borland, Ona Winants *AmWomPl*
Borland, William K. *Law&B 92*
Borland, William K. 1942- *WhoIns 93*
Borlaug, Norman Ernest 1914- *WhoAm 92, WhoSSW 93, WhoWor 93*
Borle, Andre Bernard 1930- *WhoAm 92, WhoE 93*
Borling, Peter Alexander, III 1949- *St&PR 93*
Borman, Arthur Charles, Jr. 1927- *St&PR 93*
Borman, Bonnie M. *Law&B 92*
Borman, C.A. 1952- *St&PR 93*
Borman, Deborah Lynn 1961- *WhoAmW 93*
Borman, Earle Kirkpatrick, Jr. 1930- *St&PR 93, WhoAm 92*
Borman, Frank 1928- *EncABHB 8 [port], St&PR 93, WhoAm 92, WhoWor 93*
Borman, Iris 1943- *WhoAmW 93*
Borman, Karen Therese 1960- *WhoAmW 93*
Borman, Lisa S. 1950- *WhoEmL 93*
Borman, Merle Douglas 1936- *St&PR 93*
Borman, Paul 1932- *WhoAm 92*
Borman, Terry Reed 1949- *WhoE 93*
Bormann, Martin 1900-c. 1945 *DcTwHis*
Bormaster, Lisa Curtis 1960- *WhoEmL 93*
Born, Allen 1933- *WhoAm 92*
Born, Brooksley Elizabeth 1940- *WhoAm 92*
Born, C. Allen 1933- *St&PR 93*
Born, David Pearson 1954- *WhoEmL 93*
Born, Emily Marie 1959- *WhoAm 92, WhoAmW 93, WhoWrEP 92*
Born, Ethel Wolfe 1924- *WhoAmW 93*
Born, Franz 1912- *ScF&FL 92*
Born, Gary Brian 1955- *WhoEmL 93*
Born, Gernot K.C. 1944- *WhoScE 91-3*
Born, Gunthard Karl 1935- *WhoWor 93*
Born, Helena 1860-1901 *BioIn 17*
Born, Jorge, Jr. 1962- *WhoWor 93*
Born, Kathryn W. *St&PR 93*
Born, Richard L. *St&PR 93*
Born, Richard W. *St&PR 93*
Born, Samuel Roydon, II 1945- *WhoAm 92*
Born, Willy E.C. 1923- *WhoScE 91-3*
Bornancin, Mary Janet 1953- *WhoEmL 93*
Bornand, Ruth Chaloux 1901- *WhoAm 92, WhoE 93*
Borne, Alan B. 1943- *St&PR 93*
Borne, Allen Helwick, Jr. 1959- *WhoEmL 93*
Borne, Bonita H. 1953- *WhoAm 92*
Borne, Ludwig 1786-1837 *BioIn 17*
Borne, Maureen *St&PR 93*
Borneas, Marius 1921- *WhoScE 91-4*
Bornefeld, Helmut 1906-1990 *Baker 92*
Borneff, Joachim O. 1920- *WhoScE 91-3*
Borneff, Marianne 1951- *WhoScE 91-3*
Borneman, Alice Gregory 1940- *WhoAmW 93*
Bornemann, Alfred H. 1908-1991 *BioIn 17*
Bornemisza, Francesca Thyssen- *BioIn 17*
Bornemisza, Paul 1960- *WhoWor 93*
Borneo, Rudolph John 1941- *WhoAm 92*
Borner, Achim-Rudiger 1955- *WhoWor 93*
Borner, Klaus 1929- *WhoWor 93*
Borner, William J. 1959- *WhoEmL 93*
Bornet, Stephen Folwell 1947- *WhoAm 92, WhoE 93*
Bornet, Vaughn Davis 1917- *WhoAm 92*
Borngesser, C. Vance *Law&B 92*
Bornheimer, Allen Millard 1942- *WhoAm 92*
Bornholdt, Kenneth C. *Law&B 92*
Bornholdt, Laura Anna 1919- *WhoAm 92*
Bornholdt, Robert Mark 1961- *WhoWor 93*
Bornhorst, Joseph F. 1937- *St&PR 93*
Bornhorst, Michael Edward 1949- *WhoEmL 93*
Bornhorst, Walter John 1941- *St&PR 93*
Bornhuetter, Ronald L. 1932- *WhoIns 93*
Bornino, Anna Maria 1946- *WhoAmW 93*
Bornkamm, Reinhard 1931- *WhoScE 91-3, WhoWor 93*
Bornmann, Carl Malcolm 1936- *WhoAm 92, WhoE 93, WhoWor 93*
Bornmann, Robert Clare 1931- *WhoSSW 93*
Borns, Harold William, Jr. 1927- *WhoAm 92*
Borns, Robert Aaron 1935- *WhoWor 93*
Bornschein, Franz Carl 1879-1948 *Baker 92*
Bornscheuer, George Charles 1922- *WhoE 93*
Bornstead, Beulah *AmWomPl*
Bornstein, Arnold Fredrick 1953- *WhoE 93*
Bornstein, Eli 1922- *WhoAm 92*
Bornstein, George Jay 1941- *WhoAm 92*
Bornstein, Jeffrey Victor 1950- *WhoEmL 93*
Bornstein, Leslie F. *St&PR 93*
Bornstein, Lester Milton 1925- *WhoAm 92*
Bornstein, Linda Upham 1952- *WhoE 93*
Bornstein, Morris 1927- *WhoAm 92*
Bornstein, Paul 1934- *WhoAm 92*
Bornstein, Rita 1936- *WhoAm 92, WhoAmW 93*
Bornstein, Robert Joseph 1937- *WhoE 93, WhoWor 93*
Bornstein, Steve *BioIn 17*
Bornstein, Steven M. 1952- *WhoE 93*
Bornstein, William G. *Law&B 92*
Borny, Walter Michael 1948- *WhoEmL 93, WhoWor 93*
Boro, Stephen Andrew 1966- *WhoE 93*
Boro, William Jeffrey 1948- *WhoE 93*
Boroch, Anthony Walter 1937- *St&PR 93*
Borochoff, Daniel *BioIn 17*
Borochoff, Ida Sloan 1922- *WhoWor 93*
Borod, Donald L. 1947- *St&PR 93*
Borod, Ronald Sam 1941- *WhoAm 92*
Borodin, Alexander 1833-1887 *IntDcOp, OxDcOp*
Borodin, Alexander (Porfirievich) 1833-1887 *Baker 92*
Borodin, Mikhail Markovich 1884-1951 *BioIn 17*
Borodin, Oleg Veniaminovich 1951- *WhoWor 93*
Borofsky, Jonathan *BioIn 17*
Borofsky, Jonathan 1942- *WhoAm 92*
Borofsky, Mark Howard *Law&B 92*
Borojevic, Katarina 1928- *WhoScE 91-4*
Borojevic Edler Von Bojna, Svetozar 1856-1920 *HarEnMi*
Boron, Piotr 1920- *WhoScE 91-4*
Boron, Sandra *Law&B 92*
Boronat, Olimpia 1867-1934 *OxDcOp*
Boroni, Antonio 1738-1792 *Baker 92*
Boros, Andrea Clare 1958- *WhoAmW 93*
Borosini, Francesco c. 1690- *OxDcOp*
Boroson, Florence 1927- *WhoE 93*
Borovik, Artem 1960- *BioIn 17*
Borovikov, Viktor Maximovitsh 1946- *WhoUN 92*
Borovoy, Roger Stuart 1935- *WhoAm 92*
Borovsky, Alexander 1889-1968 *Baker 92*
Borovsky, Havel 1821-1856 *BioIn 17*
Borow, Leonard J. 1947- *St&PR 93*
Borow, Richard Henry 1935- *WhoAm 92*
Borow, Wendy Meri 1951- *WhoAmW 93*
Borowczyk, Walerian 1923- *MiSFD 9*
Borowick, Tami Caryl 1968- *WhoAmW 93*
Borowiec, Saturnin 1926- *WhoScE 91-4*
Borowiec, Stanley Paul 1955- *WhoE 93, WhoEmL 93*
Borowiecki, Lawrence R. *Law&B 92*
Borowiecki, Lucjan 1925- *WhoScE 91-4*
Borowitz, Albert Ira 1930- *WhoAm 92, WhoWrEP 92*
Borowitz, Grace Burchman 1934- *WhoAm 92*
Borowitz, Irving Julius 1930- *WhoE 93*
Borowitz, Joseph Leo 1932- *WhoAm 92*
Borowitz, Sidney 1918- *WhoE 93*
Borowska, Zofia Kurylo 1928- *WhoE 93*
Borowski, David V. 1947- *St&PR 93*
Borowski, Eileen Frances 1959- *WhoAmW 93*
Borowski, Felix 1872-1956 *Baker 92*
Borowski, Jennifer Lucile 1934- *WhoAmW 93*
Borowski, Jerzy 1929- *WhoScE 91-4*
Borowski, John Michael 1948- *WhoEmL 93*
Borowski, Norman Michael 1937- *St&PR 93*
Borowski, Tadeusz 1922-1951 *PolBiDi*
Borowsky, Allen C. 1937- *St&PR 93*
Borowsky, Ben A. 1930- *WhoWrEP 92*
Borowsky, Philip 1946- *WhoAm 92, WhoWor 93*
Borowsky, Richard Lewis 1943- *WhoE 93*
Borowy, Frank Rhine 1948- *WhoEmL 93*
Borowy, Richard 1960- *WhoEmL 93*
Borowy, Sandra Ann 1955- *WhoEmL 93*
Borpujari, Jitendra Gopal 1942- *WhoUN 92*
Borra, Pier C. 1940- *St&PR 93*
Borraccini, Janet Marie 1961- *WhoEmL 93*
Borras, Caridad 1942- *HispAmA*
Borrebaek, Borgar 1932- *WhoScE 91-4*
Borreca, John Peter 1953- *WhoEmL 93*
Borrego, Carlos S. 1948- *WhoScE 91-3*
Borrego, Fernando A. *Law&B 92*
Borrel, Andre 1936- *WhoAm 92*
Borrell, Anthony J., Jr. 1940- *St&PR 93*
Borrell, Jerry 1952- *WhoEmL 93*
Borrell, Jose I. 1957- *WhoScE 91-3*
Borrell, Paul Nicholas 1949- *WhoE 93, WhoEmL 93*
Borrelli, John Francis 1955- *WhoEmL 93, WhoWor 93*
Borrelli, Joseph L. 1947- *St&PR 93*
Borrelli, Mario Alfredo 1922- *WhoWor 93*
Borrelli, Nicholas Francis 1936- *WhoE 93*
Borrelli, Vincent Alphonse 1931- *St&PR 93*
Borrello, Alfred 1931- *ScF&FL 92*
Borresen, (Aksel Ejnar) Hakon 1876-1954 *Baker 92*
Borresen, Leif J. 1947- *St&PR 93*
Borresen, Thor Erik 1952- *WhoSSW 93*
Borresen, Torger *WhoScE 91-2*
Borriello, Edoardo 1940- *WhoWor 93*
Borris, Clay 1950- *MiSFD 9*
Borris, Jacques *BioIn 17*
Borris, Siegfried 1906-1987 *Baker 92*
Borris, Thomas Jude 1961- *WhoSSW 93*

Borrmann, Werner A. 1939- *St&PR 93*
Borroff, Edith 1925- *Baker 92*
Borromeo, Theodore C. *Law&B 92*
Borromini, Francesco 1599-1667 *BioIn 17*
Borrow, George 1803-1881 *BioIn 17*
Borrowman, Merle L. 1920- *WhoAm 92*
Borrus, Amy S. 1956- *WhoE 93*
Borrus, Bruce Joseph 1950- *WhoEmL 93*
Borrus, Jack 1928- *WhoE 93*
Borruso, Thomas C. 1944- *St&PR 93*
Borry, Carol Ann 1925- *WhoAmW 93*
Bors, Linda Jean 1955- *WhoAmW 93*
Borsa, Ferdinando 1939- *WhoWor 93*
Borsari, George Robert, Jr. 1940- *WhoAm 92*
Borsch, Falk K. 1946- *WhoScE 91-3*
Borsch, Frederick Houk 1935- *WhoAm 92*
Borschke, August J. *Law&B 92*
Borschke, Bernard Gregory 1944- *St&PR 93*
Borschke, Daniel Christopher 1952- *WhoWor 93*
Borsellino, Charles Clifford 1952- *WhoEmL 93*
Borsheim, Roger M. *ScF&FL 92*
Borsick, Marlin Lester 1953- *WhoEmL 93*
Borsinger, Deborah D. *Law&B 92*
Borski, Robert A., Jr. 1948- *CngDr 91*
Borski, Robert Anthony 1948- *WhoAm 92, WhoE 93*
Borsody, Robert Peter 1937- *WhoAm 92*
Borson, Daniel Benjamin 1946- *WhoWor 93*
Borson, Roo 1952- *WhoCanL 92*
Borsos, Janos *WhoScE 91-4*
Borsos, John Donald 1914- *WhoWrEP 92*
Borsos, Phillip 1953- *MiSFD 9*
Borst, David Wellington 1918- *WhoAm 92*
Borst, Donald Vincent 1936- *St&PR 93*
Borst, Hans Georg 1927- *WhoScE 91-3*
Borst, John, Jr. *Law&B 92*
Borst, John, Jr. 1927- *St&PR 93, WhoAm 92*
Borst, K. Max *BioIn 17*
Borst, Lyle Benjamin 1912- *WhoAm 92*
Borst, Philip West 1928- *WhoAm 92*
Borst, Richard Allen 1941- *St&PR 93*
Borst, Stephen Lyle *Law&B 92*
Borstein, Carole A. *Law&B 92*
Borstein, Michael Lawrence 1939- *St&PR 93*
Borsting, Jack Raymond 1929- *WhoAm 92*
Borst Jzn, P.J. *WhoScE 91-3*
Borst-Manning, Diane Gail 1937- *WhoAmW 93*
Borsum, James Carl 1958- *WhoEmL 93*
Bortak, John J. 1947- *St&PR 93*
Borteck, Robert D. 1947- *WhoAm 92, WhoEmL 93*
Bortel, Edgar 1927- *WhoWor 93*
Bortel, Robert William 1954- *WhoEmL 93*
Bortemark, Ingvar 1941- *WhoScE 91-4*
Borten, William H. 1935- *WhoAm 92*
Bortfeld, Reinhard K. 1927- *WhoScE 91-3*
Borth, John Cleve 1935- *St&PR 93*
Borthwick, David Lumsden 1935- *St&PR 93*
Borthwick, J.M. 1936- *St&PR 93*
Bortin, Mortimer M. 1922- *WhoAm 92*
Bortis, William Francis, II 1946- *WhoEmL 93*
Bortka, Lynn Alan *Law&B 92*
Bortkiewicz, Sergei (Eduardovich) 1877-1952 *Baker 92*
Bortman, Eli C. 1943- *St&PR 93*
Bortman, Michael *MiSFD 9*
Bortner-Wandling, Deborah Ann 1949- *WhoAm 92*
Bortnes, Gunhild 1948- *WhoScE 91-4*
Bortniansky, Dimitri (Stepanovich) 1751-1825 *Baker 92*
Bortnichak, Edward Arnold 1951- *WhoEmL 93*
Bortnyansky, Dmitry 1751-1825 *OxDcOp*
Bortolami, Ruggero 1926- *WhoScE 91-3*
Bortolan, Peter Roger 1937- *WhoE 93*
Bortolani, Virginio 1934- *WhoScE 91-3*
Bortolazzo, Julio Lawrence 1915- *WhoAm 92*
Bortoli, Mario 1927- *St&PR 93*
Bortolotto, David *BioIn 17*
Bortoluzzi, Paolo 1938- *WhoWor 93*
Borton, D.B. *ConAu 138*
Borton, Douglas 1960- *ScF&FL 92*
Borton, Elizabeth *MajAI*
Borton, George Robert 1922- *WhoWor 93*
Borton, John Carter, Jr. 1938- *WhoAm 92*
Borts, George Herbert 1927- *WhoE 93*
Borts, Robert Edward 1962- *WhoEmL 93*
Bortz, Daniel 1943- *Baker 92*
Bortz, Donald Richard 1935- *WhoE 93*
Bortz, Laurie R. *Law&B 92*
Bortz, Paul Isaac 1937- *WhoAm 92*
Bortz, Phyllis E. 1926- *WhoAmW 93*
Bortz, Robert Henry 1949- *St&PR 93*
Boruch, Marianne 1950- *WhoWrEP 92*
Boruch, Mieczyslaw Stefan 1930- *WhoScE 91-4*
Borum, Olin Henry 1917- *WhoSSW 93*
Borum, Rodney Lee 1929- *WhoAm 92*
Borun, Victor Marek 1943- *WhoE 93*
Borup, Eric Einar 1948- *St&PR 93*
Borup-Jorgensen, (Jens) Axel 1924- *Baker 92*
Borut, Donald Jay 1941- *WhoAm 92*
Borut, Josephine 1942- *WhoAmW 93*
Borutta, William Earl 1938- *St&PR 93*
Borvendeg, Janos 1935- *WhoScE 91-4*
Borwein, David 1924- *WhoAm 92*
Borwick, Leonard 1868-1925 *Baker 92*
Borwick, Richard 1908- *WhoE 93*
Bory, Robert 1891-1960 *Baker 92*
Borys, Henry James 1952- *WhoWrEP 92*
Borys, Theodor James 1954- *WhoE 93, WhoEmL 93*
Borysewicz, Mary Louise *WhoAmW 93*
Borysiewicz, Leszek Krzysztof *WhoScE 91-1*
Borzage, Frank 1893-1962 *MiSFD 9N*
Borzillo, Michelle Marie 1956- *WhoEmL 93*
Borzovs, Juris 1950- *WhoWor 93*
Borzsonyi, Sandor 1944- *WhoScE 91-4*
Borzymowski, Andrzej 1932- *WhoWor 93*
Bos, Coenraad Valentyn 1875-1955 *Baker 92*
Bos, Jan Dositheus 1951- *WhoWor 93*
Bos, Lambert Jan Van Den 1964- *WhoWor 93*
Bos, Marinus G. 1943- *WhoScE 91-3*
Bos, Polly *Law&B 92*
Bos, Willem 1921- *WhoWor 93*
Bosack, Theodore Nicholas 1940- *WhoE 93*
Bosacki, Emil C. 1932- *WhoAm 92*
Bosak, Donald *St&PR 93*
Bosakov, Joseph Blagoev 1942- *WhoAm 92*
Bosanquet, Nick *WhoScE 91-1*
Bosanquet, Nick Francis Gustavus 1942- *WhoWor 93*
Bosatra, Andrea 1925- *WhoScE 91-3*
Bosboom, Anthony J. 1923- *St&PR 93*
Bosc, Jacques Felix 1931- *WhoScE 91-2*
Bosca, Christopher 1959- *St&PR 93*
Boscaino, Giuliano 1961- *WhoWor 93*
Boscamp, Stephen Carl 1955- *St&PR 93*
Boscawen, Edward 1711-1761 *HarEnMi*
Bosch, Berthold G. 1930- *WhoScE 91-3*
Bosch, Clement A. *Law&B 92*
Bosch, Clement A. 1938- *St&PR 93*
Bosch, Gerald J. *St&PR 93*
Bosch, Hieronymus d1516 *BioIn 17*
Bosch, Jorge Jose 1925- *WhoAm 92*
Bosch, Juan 1909- *DcCPCAm, DcTwHis, SpAmA*
Bosch, Leendert 1924- *WhoScE 91-3*
Bosch, Orlando *DcCPCAm*
Bosch, Pieter Joseph van den c. 1736-1803 *Baker 92*
Bosch, Samuel Henry 1934- *WhoAm 92*
Boschan, Charlotte d1990 *BioIn 17*
Boschee, Catharine *Law&B 92*
Boschen, William O. 1921- *St&PR 93*
Boscher, Donald Harry 1932- *St&PR 93*
Bosch Gavino, Juan 1909- *ColdWar 2 [port]*
Boschi, Enzo *WhoScE 91-3*
Boschi, Giuseppe fl. 1698-1744 *OxDcOp*
Boschi, Valentino 1922- *WhoScE 91-3*
Boschma, Gerald A. 1938- *St&PR 93*
Boschot, Adolphe 1871-1955 *Baker 92*
Bosch Roura, Lluis 1940- *WhoScE 91-3*
Boschwitz, Kenneth S. *Law&B 92*
Boschwitz, Rudy 1930- *WhoAm 92*
Boscia, Jon Andrew 1952- *St&PR 93, WhoAm 92*
Bosco, Anthony Gerard 1927- *WhoAm 92, WhoE 93*
Bosco, Anthony Joseph, Jr. 1957- *St&PR 93*
Bosco, Cassandra John 1957- *WhoEmL 93*
Bosco, Clyde *ScF&FL 92*
Bosco, Henry A. 1922- *St&PR 93*
Bosco, Jay William 1951- *WhoEmL 93*
Bosco, Luigi Paolo 1929- *WhoWor 93*
Bosco, Monique 1927- *WhoCanL 92*
Bosco, Philip 1930- *BioIn 17*
Bosco, Philip Michael 1930- *WhoAm 92, WhoE 93*
Boscoe, Claudia Frances 1948- *WhoE 93, WhoWor 93*
Boscoe, Richard William 1950- *WhoE 93*
Boscovich, Alexander Uriah 1907-1964 *Baker 92*
Bose, Ajay Kumar 1925- *WhoAm 92*
Bose, Amar Gopal 1929- *St&PR 93, WhoAm 92*
Bose, Animesh 1953- *WhoWor 93*
Bose, Anjan 1946- *WhoAm 92, WhoEmL 93*
Bose, Arup Kumar *Law&B 92*
Bose, Bimal Kumar 1932- *WhoAm 92*
Bose, Fritz 1906-1975 *Baker 92*
Bose, Hans-Jurgen von 1953- *Baker 92*
Bose, Henry E. *St&PR 93*
Bose, Nirmal Kumar 1940- *WhoAm 92*
Bose, Pradip 1955- *WhoE 93*
Bose, Ryan L. *Law&B 92*
Bose, Sarat Chandra 1889-1950 *BioIn 17*
Bose, Somesh K. *Law&B 92*
Bose, Subhas Chandra 1897-1945 *BioIn 17, DcTwHis*
Bose, Subir Kumar 1931- *WhoAm 92*
Boseman, Glenn 1941- *WhoAm 92*
Bosendorfer *Baker 92*
Bosendorfer, Ignaz 1794-1859 *Baker 92*
Bosendorfer, Ludwig 1835-1919 *Baker 92*
Bosh, Teddy George 1945- *St&PR 93*
Boshell, Buris Raye 1926- *WhoAm 92*
Boshell, Edward Owen, Jr. 1935- *St&PR 93*
Boshell, Gordon 1908- *ScF&FL 92*
Bosher, David E. 1953- *St&PR 93*
Bosher, Paul Leonard 1945- *WhoWor 93*
Boshes, Louis D. 1908- *WhoAm 92*
Boshier, Maureen Louise 1946- *WhoAmW 93, WhoEmL 93*
Boshinski, Thomas A. *Law&B 92*
Boshka, Wayne Phillip 1931- *St&PR 93*
Boshkov, Stefan Hristov 1918- *WhoAm 92*
Boshkov, Stefan Robert 1949- *WhoE 93*
Boshoven, Stephen John 1955- *St&PR 93*
Bosi, Carlo *WhoScE 91-3*
Bosi, Robert A. 1955- *St&PR 93*
Bosiljevac, Joseph Edward 1951- *WhoEmL 93*
Bosilovic, Robert J. *Law&B 92*
Bosin, Adeline Vallosio 1945- *WhoAmW 93*
Bosin, Stephen Roger *Law&B 92*
Bosio, Angelo 1955- *WhoWor 93*
Boskello, Dennis Jon 1953- *WhoE 93, WhoEmL 93*
Bosken, James Edward 1958- *St&PR 93*
Boskey, Bennett 1916- *WhoAm 92*
Boskin, Michael J. *BioIn 17*
Boskin, Michael Jay 1945- *WhoAm 92*
Boskind, Paul Arthur 1929- *WhoAm 92*
Boskovich, John *MiSFD 9*
Boskovsky, Willi 1909-1991 *Baker 92, BioIn 17*
Boslaugh, Leslie 1917- *WhoAm 92*
Bosler, Charles Walter, Jr. 1949- *WhoEmL 93*
Bosler, Robert Lawrence 1951- *St&PR 93*
Bosley, Harold A. 1907-1975 *BioIn 17*
Bosley, Karen Lee 1942- *WhoAmW 93*
Bosley, Lawrence Nevel 1947- *St&PR 93*
Bosley, Tom 1927- *WhoAm 92*
Bosling, Bent *WhoWor 93*
Bosma, Lee A. 1950- *St&PR 93*
Bosma, Marinus Bernard 1951- *St&PR 93*
Bosmajian, Haig Aram 1928- *WhoAm 92*
Bosman, C.J.L.M. 1947- *WhoScE 91-3*
Bosman, Giel Johannes Cornelius Gerardus Maria 1954- *WhoWor 93*
Bosmans, Henriette (Hilda) 1895-1952 *Baker 92*
Bosner, Kevin Charles 1951- *WhoEmL 93*
Bosniak, Morton Arthur 1929- *WhoAm 92*
Bosnic, Ante 1928- *WhoScE 91-4*
Bosomworth, Peter Palliser 1930- *WhoAm 92*
Bosone, Reva Zilpha Beck 1895-1983 *BioIn 17*
Bosque, George d1991 *BioIn 17*
Bosquet, Alain 1919- *WhoWor 93*
Bosquet, Emile 1878-1958 *Baker 92*
Bosquet, Pierre Francois Joseph 1810-1861 *HarEnMi*
Bosquez, John 1943- *St&PR 93*
Boss, Bradford R. 1933- *St&PR 93*
Boss, Janusz 1938- *WhoScE 91-4*
Boss, Kenneth Jay 1935- *WhoAm 92*
Boss, Pauline Grossenbacher 1934- *WhoAmW 93*
Boss, Russel Wayne 1943- *WhoAm 92, WhoWor 93*
Boss, Shelly Jeanne 1950- *WhoWrEP 92*
Bossa, Francesco 1941- *WhoScE 91-3*
Bossano, Joseph John 1939- *WhoWor 93*
Bossard, Andres 1944-1992 *BioIn 17, NewYTBS 92*
Bosschere, Jean de 1878-1953 *ScF&FL 92*
Bosse, Fred C. *Law&B 92*
Bosse, Fred Charles 1949- *WhoIns 93*
Bosse, Gustave 1884-1943 *Baker 92*
Bosse, Harriet *BioIn 17*
Bosse, Malcolm J. 1932- *ScF&FL 92*
Bosse, Malcolm Joseph, Jr. 1926- *WhoAm 92*
Bosse, Peter Alan 1960- *WhoEmL 93*
Bosseau, Donald Lee 1936- *WhoAm 92*
Bosselman, Fred Paul 1934- *WhoAm 92*
Bossemeyer, William John, III 1950- *WhoEmL 93*
Bossen, David August 1927- *St&PR 93, WhoAm 92*
Bossen, Wendell J. 1933- *St&PR 93*
Bossen, Wendell John 1933- *WhoAm 92*
Bosserman, Joseph Norwood 1925- *WhoAm 92*
Bossert, Carol Jo 1956- *WhoEmL 93*
Bossert, Edythe Hoy 1908- *WhoE 93*
Bossert, James P. 1953- *St&PR 93*
Bosses, Mark David 1962- *St&PR 93*
Bosseur, Jean-Yves 1947- *Baker 92*
Bosshardt, Robert *ScF&FL 92*
Bossi, Enrico 1861-1925 *Baker 92*
Bossi, Pietro 1834-1896 *Baker 92*
Bossi, (Rinaldo) Renzo 1883-1965 *Baker 92*
Bossi, William J., Jr. 1956- *WhoIns 93*
Bossidy, Lawrence A. *BioIn 17*
Bossidy, Lawrence Arthur 1935- *St&PR 93, WhoAm 92, WhoE 93*
Bossier, Albert Louis, Jr. 1932- *St&PR 93, WhoAm 92, WhoSSW 93*
Bossinger-Garwin, June Ann 1950- *WhoEmL 93*
Bossio, Salvatore 1928- *St&PR 93*
Bossley, Burton B., Jr. *Law&B 92*
Bossmeyer, Glenn D. 1949- *St&PR 93*
Bossmeyer, Glenn David *Law&B 92*
Bossom, Joel *Law&B 92*
Bosson, Barbara *WhoAm 92*
Bossow-Lueders, Donna Christine 1950- *WhoAmW 93*
Boss Tweed 1823-1878 *BioIn 17*
Bossu, Maximilien de Hennin-Lietard, Count of d1578 *HarEnMi*
Bossy, J.G.M. 1929- *WhoScE 91-2*
Bossy, Michael 1957- *WhoAm 92*
Bossy, Nick 1936- *WhoAsAP 91*
Bost, David Lee 1944- *St&PR 93*
Bost, Francis William 1950- *WhoSSW 93*
Bost, Glenn E., II *Law&B 92*
Bost, Harold Clifford, Jr. 1961- *WhoSSW 93*
Bost, Jack 1925- *WhoScE 91-2*
Bost, Jane Morgan 1953- *WhoSSW 93*
Bost, Lloyd Cleveland 1920- *St&PR 93*
Bost, Ralph Herman, Jr. 1954- *WhoEmL 93*
Bost, Raymond Morris 1925- *WhoAm 92*
Bost, Ted Roby 1924- *WhoSSW 93*
Bost, Timothy R. 1947- *St&PR 93*
Bost, Tom F., Jr. 1916- *St&PR 93*
Bost, Walter L. 1927- *St&PR 93*
Bost, Wiley Eugene 1929- *St&PR 93*
Bostan, Elisabeta 1931- *DrEEuF*
Bosted, Dorothy Stack 1953- *WhoAmW 93, WhoEmL 93*
Bostek-Brady, Eva Maria 1961- *WhoAmW 93, WhoEmL 93*
Bostel, Luca von 1649-1716 *OxDcOp*
Bostelman, Janice Lynn 1958- *WhoAmW 93*
Bostelmann, Gert 1944- *WhoScE 91-3*
Bostelmann, Otto 1907-1981 *Baker 92*
Boster, Constanza Helena G. 1944- *WhoE 93*
Bostian, Frieda Farmer 1942- *WhoSSW 93*
Bostian, Keith Allan 1951- *WhoAm 92*
Bostian, Nancy Lenora 1940- *St&PR 93*
Bostic, Mary Louise Price 1939- *WhoAm 92*
Bostic, Steven R. 1943- *ConEn*
Bostic, W. Wayne 1950- *WhoEmL 93*
Bostich, June M. *Law&B 92*
Bostick, Barbara *BioIn 17*
Bostick, Charles Dent 1931- *WhoAm 92, WhoSSW 93*
Bostick, W.H. 1916-1991 *BioIn 17*
Bostick, Winston Harper 1916-1991 *BioIn 17*
Bostin, Marvin Jay 1933- *WhoE 93*
Bostleman, Richard Lee 1944- *WhoAm 92*
Bostock, C.J. *WhoScE 91-1*
Bostock, Richard Matthew 1952- *WhoEmL 93*
Bostock, Roy Jackson 1940- *WhoAm 92, WhoE 93*
Bostock, Stephen John *WhoScE 91-1*
Boston, Ben 1961- *WhoEmL 93*
Boston, Betty Lee 1935- *WhoSSW 93*
Boston, Billie 1939- *WhoAmW 93, WhoSSW 93, WhoWor 93*
Boston, Bruce 1943- *ScF&FL 92, WhoWrEP 92*
Boston, Bruce Ormand 1940- *WhoSSW 93*
Boston, Charles Ray 1928- *WhoAm 92*
Boston, Edward William 1949- *WhoE 93*
Boston, James Robert, Jr. 1958- *WhoEmL 93*
Boston, John William 1933- *St&PR 93*
Boston, Kirby L. *Law&B 92*
Boston, L.M. 1892-1990 *BioIn 17, ScF&FL 92*
Boston, L(ucy) M(aria Wood) 1892-1990 *MajAI [port]*
Boston, Leona 1914- *WhoAm 92, WhoAmW 93*
Boston, Lucy Maria 1892-1990 *BioIn 17*
Boston, Lucy (Marie) 1892- *ChlFicS*
Boston, Thomas R. *Law&B 92*
Boston, W. Geoffrey 1949- *St&PR 93*

Boston, Wallace Ellsworth, Jr. 1954- *WhoEmL 93*
Boston, William Clayton 1934- *WhoSSW 93, WhoWor 93*
Bostrom, Carl Otto 1932- *WhoAm 92*
Bostrom, Kurt G.V. 1932- *WhoScE 91-4*
Bostrom, Rolf G. 1936- *WhoScE 91-4*
Bosttwick, Gerald 1924- *St&PR 93*
Bostwick, Barry 1945- *WhoAm 92*
Bostwick, Burdette Edwards 1908- *WhoWrEP 92*
Bostwick, Eddie Dwayne 1965- *St&PR 93*
Bostwick, Henry *DcCPCAm*
Bostwick, Randell A. 1922- *WhoAm 92*
Boswell, Bernell Nephi 1925- *WhoWor 93*
Boswell, Celia Cole 1933- *WhoSSW 93*
Boswell, Connee 1907-1976 *Baker 92*
Boswell, Connee 1912-1976 *BioIn 17*
Boswell, Dan Alan 1947- *WhoWor 93*
Boswell, Edwin Clair 1909- *St&PR 93*
Boswell, Gary Taggart 1937- *St&PR 93, WhoAm 92, WhoE 93*
Boswell, George Worley 1919- *WhoSSW 93*
Boswell, James 1740-1795 *BioIn 17, WorLitC [port]*
Boswell, James Douglas 1942- *WhoAm 92*
Boswell, Jeanetta 1922- *WhoWrEP 92*
Boswell, John J. 1947- *St&PR 93*
Boswell, Kenneth Boyd 1938- *WhoSSW 93*
Boswell, Marion Lillard 1923- *WhoAm 92*
Boswell, Mark Ward *Law&B 92*
Boswell, Martha *AmWomPl*
Boswell, Martha 1908-1958 *BioIn 17*
Boswell, Mary Rose *WhoE 93*
Boswell, Philip John 1949- *WhoAm 92*
Boswell, Robert 1953- *ConAu 136*
Boswell, Robert S. 1949- *St&PR 93*
Boswell, Roderick William *WhoWor 93*
Boswell, Ronald Leslie Doyle 1940- *WhoAsAP 91*
Boswell, Rupert Dean, Jr. 1929- *WhoAm 92*
Boswell, Thomas Murray 1947- *BiDAMSp 1989, WhoAm 92*
Boswell, Thomas W. 1944- *St&PR 93*
Boswell, Thomas Wayne 1944- *WhoAm 92*
Boswell, Vet *BioIn 17*
Boswell, Wade M. *Law&B 92*
Boswell, William P. 1946- *St&PR 93*
Boswell, William Paret *Law&B 92*
Boswell, William Paret 1946- *WhoEmL 93*
Boswell, Winthrop Palmer 1922- *WhoAmW 93, WhoWor 93*
Boswinkel, J.A. 1952- *WhoScE 91-3*
Bosworth, Brian *BioIn 17*
Bosworth, Bruce Leighton 1942- *WhoWor 93*
Bosworth, C.J.A. *WhoScE 91-1*
Bosworth, David 1947- *WhoWrEP 92*
Bosworth, Derek Leonard *WhoScE 91-1*
Bosworth, Douglas LeRoy 1939- *WhoAm 92*
Bosworth, George Joseph, Jr. 1938- *St&PR 93*
Bosworth, Hobart 1867-1943 *BioIn 17, IntDcF 2-3 [port]*
Bosworth, Jeffrey Willson 1948- *WhoEmL 93*
Bosworth, Mary Annsenetta 1950- *WhoAmW 93*
Bosworth, Michael Francis 1950- *WhoEmL 93*
Bosworth, Michael K. *Law&B 92*
Bosworth, Stephen R. *Law&B 92*
Bosze, Jean-Pierre *BioIn 17*
Bosznay, Adam 1926- *WhoScE 91-4*
Bot, G.P.A. *WhoScE 91-3*
Bota, Liviu Aurelian 1936- *WhoUN 92*
Bota, Valentin I. 1928- *WhoScE 91-4*
Botafogo, Ana *BioIn 17*
Botaish, Janet *BioIn 17*
Botana, Philip C. 1945- *St&PR 93*
Botaneiates *OxDcByz*
Botas, Juan Suarez d1992 *NewYTBS 92*
Botchwey, Kwesi 1942- *WhoAfr*
Bote, Eduard *Baker 92*
Bote & Bock *Baker 92*
Botel, Max *St&PR 93*
Botelho Gosalvez, Raul 1917- *SpAmA*
Botero, Fernando 1932- *WhoAm 92, WhoWor 93*
Botev, Kostadin Borissov 1948- *WhoWor 93*
Botez, Dan 1948- *WhoAm 92*
Both, Robert Allen 1952- *WhoEmL 93*
Both, Zoia 1956- *WhoWor 93*
Botha, C. John 1937- *St&PR 93*
Botha, Elna *BioIn 17*
Botha, Louis 1862-1919 *DcTwHis, HarEnMi*
Botha, Pieter W. *BioIn 17*
Botha, Pieter Willem 1916- *DcTwHis, WhoAfr, WhoWor 93*
Botha, R.F. 1932- *BioIn 17*
Botha, Roelof Frederik 1932- *BioIn 17, WhoAfr, WhoWor 93*
Bothe, Brooke 1945- *St&PR 93*
Bothe, Davis Ross 1950- *WhoEmL 93*
Bothell, Diane J. *ScF&FL 92*
Bothfeld, Edward Elms 1924- *St&PR 93*
Bothfeld, Henry *BioIn 17*
Bothfeld, Liz *BioIn 17*
Bothig, Barbara 1934- *WhoScE 91-3*
Bothmer, Dietrich Felix von 1918- *WhoAm 92*
Bothmer, Felix von 1852-1937 *HarEnMi*
Bothner-By, Aksel Arnold 1921- *WhoAm 92*
Bothorel, Pierre 1930- *WhoScE 91-2*
Bothwell, Alfred Lester Meador 1949- *WhoE 93*
Bothwell, Dorr 1902- *WhoAm 92*
Bothwell, John Charles 1926- *WhoAm 92*
Bothwell, Joseph C., Jr. 1923- *St&PR 93*
Bothwell, Robert Otto 1937- *WhoE 93*
Bothwell-Murphy, Linda Ann 1954- *WhoEmL 93*
Botica, Luke F. 1950- *St&PR 93*
Botifoll, Luis J. 1908- *WhoSSW 93*
Botkin, Daniel B. 1937- *ConAu 136*
Botkin, Gregg A. 1960- *St&PR 93*
Botkin, Monty Lane 1951- *WhoEmL 93, WhoSSW 93*
Botoe, Carlotta *WhoAmW 93*
Botombele, Bokonga Ekanga 1932- *WhoUN 92*
Botos, Erno Peter 1954- *WhoScE 91-4*
Botquin, Gaston *WhoScE 91-2*
Botsai, Elmer Eugene 1928- *WhoAm 92, WhoWor 93*
Botsch, Sharyn 1950- *WhoEmL 93*
Botsco, Margaret Anna 1950- *WhoAmW 93*
Botsford, Keith 1928- *WhoE 93*
Botsford, Susi 1947- *WhoEmL 93*
Botsford, Ward *BioIn 17*
Botshon, Ann 1942- *WhoWrEP 92*
Botsko, Patricia M. *Law&B 92*
Botsko, Terri T. *Law&B 92*
Botstein, David 1942- *WhoAm 92*
Botstein, Leon *NewYTBS 92 [port]*
Botstein, Leon 1946- *BioIn 17*
Botstiber, Hugo 1875-1941 *Baker 92*
Bott, E. Joyce 1957- *WhoAmW 93*
Bott, Harold Sheldon 1933- *WhoAm 92, WhoWor 93*
Bott, Harvey John 1933- *WhoSSW 93*
Bott, Jean Joseph 1826-1895 *Baker 92*
Bott, Martin Harold Phillips *WhoScE 91-1*
Bott, Patricia Allen 1911- *WhoE 93*
Bott, Raoul 1923- *WhoAm 92*
Bott, Rebecca Marie 1967- *WhoSSW 93*
Botta, Louis Henry 1953- *WhoE 93*
Bottalico, Antonio 1939- *WhoScE 91-3*
Bottarelli, Giovanni fl. 1740-1780 *OxDcOp*
Bottari, George L. 1919- *WhoWrEP 92*
Bottari, George Leo 1919- *WhoSSW 93*
Bottcher, Albrecht 1954- *WhoWor 93*
Bottcher, Ron d1991 *BioIn 17*
Botte, Kurt Franz *Law&B 92*
Botte, Samuel F. 1950- *St&PR 93*
Bottee de Toulmon, Auguste 1797-1850 *Baker 92*
Bottel, Helen Alfea *WhoAm 92, WhoWrEP 92*
Bottelier, Pieter Paul 1937- *WhoUN 92*
Bottelli, Richard 1937- *WhoAm 92*
Bottelli, Richard Joseph, Jr. 1959- *WhoEmL 93*
Bottemiller, Donald Louis 1939- *St&PR 93*
Botten, David S. 1944- *St&PR 93*
Bottenberg, Wolfgang 1930- *Baker 92*
Botter, Constant H. 1928- *WhoScE 91-3*
Botterbusch, Hope Roland 1950- *WhoEmL 93*
Botterill, Joyce 1939- *ConAu 138*
Bottero, Laura Ann 1961- *WhoEmL 93*
Botterud, Karen F. *Law&B 92*
Bottesini, Giovanni 1821-1889 *Baker 92*
Bottge, Peggy Ann 1956- *WhoAmW 93, WhoEmL 93*
Bottger, Otto Werner 1923- *WhoScE 91-3*
Botticelli, Denise E. *Law&B 92*
Botticelli, Denise Ellen 1951- *St&PR 93*
Botticelli, Sandro 1444?-1510 *BioIn 17*
Botticher, Bernhard 1956- *WhoScE 91-3*
Bottiger, H. Margareta 1927- *WhoScE 91-4*
Bottiger, Lars Erik 1924- *WhoScE 91-4*
Bottigheimer, Ruth B. 1939- *ScF&FL 92*
Bottiglia, Frank Robert 1946- *WhoE 93*
Bottiglia, William Filbert 1912- *WhoAm 92*
Bottiglier, Janet Ellen 1952- *WhoWrEP 92*
Botting, Douglas (Scott) 1934- *ConAu 37NR*
Botting, R.A. *WhoScE 91-1*
Bottini, Ernesto Enrique 1947- *WhoWor 93*
Bottino, A. *WhoScE 91-3*
Bottisti, Deborah Ann 1967- *WhoWrEP 92*
Bottje, Will Gay 1925- *Baker 92*
Bottke, Heinz 1924- *WhoScE 91-3*
Bottner, Irving Joseph 1916- *WhoAm 92*
Botto, Antony Alan 1938- *WhoE 93*
Botto, Robert Irving 1949- *WhoSSW 93*
Botto de Barros, Adwaldo Cardoso 1925- *WhoUN 92*
Bottom, Dale Coyle 1932- *WhoAm 92*
Bottomley, Lois S. 1943- *St&PR 93*
Bottomley, Paul A. *BioIn 17*
Bottomley, Virginia Hilda Brunette Maxwell 1948- *WhoWor 93*
Bottoms, David 1949- *DcLB 120 [port], WhoWrEP 92*
Bottoms, Robert Garvin 1944- *WhoAm 92*
Bottoms, Timothy 1951- *WhoAm 92*
Bottoms, William Clay, Jr. 1946- *WhoEmL 93*
Bottoni, Robert J. 1923- *St&PR 93*
Bottorff, Dennis C. 1944- *St&PR 93, WhoAm 92*
Bottorff, Michele Lynette Stanford 1952- *WhoEmL 93*
Bottrigari, Ercole 1531-1612 *Baker 92*
Botts, David M. *St&PR 93*
Botts, Ellen Alberta 1947- *WhoEmL 93*
Botts, Guy Warren 1914- *WhoAm 92*
Botts, John H. 1929- *St&PR 93*
Botts, John Minor 1802-1869 *PolPar*
Botts, Kenneth Charles 1926- *St&PR 93*
Botts, Pamela Jean 1943- *WhoAmW 93*
Bottum, C.E., Jr. 1927- *St&PR 93*
Bottum, Thomas George 1950- *WhoIns 93*
Botty, Kenneth John 1927- *WhoAm 92, WhoE 93*
Botvinnik, M.M. 1911- *BioIn 17*
Botvinnik, Mikhail Moiseevich 1911- *BioIn 17*
Botway, Jaclyn Cooper 1935- *WhoAmW 93*
Botway, Lloyd Frederick 1947- *WhoSSW 93*
Botwinick, Allen George 1943- *St&PR 93*
Botwinick, Michael 1943- *WhoAm 92*
Botwinick, Moshe Lev 1953- *WhoE 93*
Botwinik, Diane Joy Blitt 1945- *WhoAmW 93*
Bouab, Abdelhamid 1943- *WhoUN 92*
Boualga, Mohamed 1939- *WhoWor 93*
Bouayad, Abderrahmane 1933- *WhoUN 92*
Bouaziz, Roger 1929- *WhoScE 91-2*
Boubai, Wilfred Brass 1947- *WhoEmL 93, WhoWor 93*
Boubals, Denis 1926- *WhoScE 91-2*
Boubelik, Henry F., Jr. 1936- *St&PR 93*
Boubelik, Henry Fredrick, Jr. 1936- *WhoAm 92*
Boublik, Miloslav 1927- *WhoE 93*
Bouc, David C. *Law&B 92*
Bouc, Robert *WhoScE 91-2*
Boucek, Robert J. 1936- *St&PR 93*
Bouchard, Benoit 1940- *WhoAm 92*
Bouchard, Chislain 1941- *St&PR 93*
Bouchard, Jacques 1930- *WhoAm 92*
Bouchard, Lucien *BioIn 17*
Bouchard, Lynda M. 1956- *WhoWrEP 92*
Bouchard, Marie P. *Law&B 92*
Bouchard, Norman Roger 1948- *St&PR 93*
Bouchard, Richard Joseph 1936- *St&PR 93*
Bouchard, Stephen Alfred 1958- *WhoE 93*
Bouchard, Thomas *BioIn 17*
Bouchard, Thomas Joseph, Jr. 1937- *WhoAm 92*
Bouchardeau, Huguette 1935- *BioIn 17*
Boucharlat, Pierre-Yves 1939- *WhoWor 93*
Bouche, Marcel B. 1937- *WhoScE 91-2*
Bouchenaki, Mounir 1943- *WhoUN 92*
Boucher, Alexandre-Jean 1778-1861 *Baker 92*
Boucher, Allen C. 1922- *St&PR 93*
Boucher, Anthony 1911-1968 *BioIn 17*
Boucher, Celeste Suzette 1956- *WhoAmW 93*
Boucher, Claude G. 1949- *WhoScE 91-2*
Boucher, D. Louise *Law&B 92*
Boucher, David H. 1954- *WhoE 93*
Boucher, Denise 1935- *BioIn 17*
Boucher, Dorothy L. 1936- *St&PR 93*
Boucher, Eric *Law&B 92*
Boucher, Francine B. *Law&B 92*
Boucher, Guy Louis *Law&B 92*
Boucher, Henry Joseph 1947- *WhoAm 92, WhoE 93, WhoEmL 93*
Boucher, Jean-Marie 1943- *WhoUN 92*
Boucher, John Henri 1956- *WhoE 93*
Boucher, Joseph Lee 1934- *St&PR 93*
Boucher, Joseph William 1951- *WhoEmL 93*
Boucher, Laurence James 1938- *WhoAm 92*
Boucher, Louis Jack 1922- *WhoAm 92*
Boucher, Michel 1941- *WhoScE 91-2*
Boucher, Miriam Cherny 1954- *WhoEmL 93*
Boucher, Raymond Gabriel 1947- *WhoAm 92*
Boucher, Rick 1946- *CngDr 91, WhoAm 92, WhoSSW 93*
Boucher, Robb *BioIn 17*
Boucher, Robert F. *WhoScE 91-1*
Boucher, Roberta Mary 1951- *WhoAmW 93, WhoEmL 93*
Boucher, Roger Andre *Law&B 92*
Boucher, Roland A. 1945- *St&PR 93*
Boucher, Serge 1944- *WhoScE 91-2*
Boucher, Stephen G. 1946- *St&PR 93*
Boucher, Tania Kunsky *WhoE 93*
Boucher, Thomas Owen 1942- *WhoE 93*
Boucher, Thomas W. 1955- *St&PR 93*
Boucher, Wayne Irving 1934- *WhoAm 92*
Boucher, Yvon 1946- *WhoCanL 92*
Boucher de Boucherville, Georges 1814-1894 *BioIn 17*
Boucherle, Robert H. *St&PR 93*
Boucherville, Georges Boucher de 1814-1894 *BioIn 17*
Bouchie, L. Kirk 1958- *St&PR 93*
Bouchier, Ian Arthur Dennis 1932- *WhoScE 91-1*
Bouchikhi, Chico
See Gipsy Kings, The *ConMus 8*
Bouchillon, Bill Gene 1928- *WhoSSW 93*
Bouchitey, Patrick *MiSFD 9*
Boucicaut 1366-1421 *OxDcByz*
Bouciquault, Jean le Meingre, II c. 1366-1421 *HarEnMi*
Bouckaert, J.P.C.O. 1930- *WhoScE 91-2*
Bouckley, Sandra Lynn 1959- *WhoEmL 93*
Boucolon, Maryse 1937- *BioIn 17*
Boucourechliev, Andre 1925- *Baker 92*
Boucouvalas, Marcie 1947- *WhoAm 92, WhoAmW 93, WhoEmL 93*
Boucque, Ch.V. 1935- *WhoScE 91-2*
Boudarel, Georges *BioIn 17*
Boudart, Michel 1924- *WhoAm 92*
Boudicca d62 *BioIn 17*
Boudin, Guy d1991 *BioIn 17*
Boudin, Leonard B. 1912-1989 *BioIn 17*
Boudin, Michael *NewYTBS 92 [port]*
Boudinot, Elias 1740-1821 *OxCSupC*
Boudoulas, Harisios 1935- *WhoAm 92*
Boudreau, A. Allan 1936- *WhoE 93*
Boudreau, Aileen T. *St&PR 93*
Boudreau, Edna Mae 1935- *WhoWrEP 92*
Boudreau, Edward Joseph, Jr. 1944- *St&PR 93, WhoAm 92*
Boudreau, Gregory G. 1948- *St&PR 93*
Boudreau, James Karle *Law&B 92*
Boudreau, James Lawton 1935- *St&PR 93, WhoAm 92*
Boudreau, JoAnne 1936- *WhoAmW 93*
Boudreau, Kevin Paul 1964- *WhoEmL 93*
Boudreau, Marcel Leopold 1936- *St&PR 93*
Boudreau, N. Cason *Law&B 92*
Boudreau, Paul J. 1938- *WhoIns 93*
Boudreau, Robert (Austin) 1927- *Baker 92*
Boudreau, Robert James 1950- *WhoWor 93*
Boudreau, Robert W. 1937- *St&PR 93*
Boudreau, Rolland *Law&B 92*
Boudreault, Eugene 1932- *St&PR 93*
Boudreaux, C. Kathleen 1934- *St&PR 93*
Boudreaux, Gloria Marie 1935- *WhoAmW 93*
Boudreaux, Jeffrey L. 1951- *St&PR 93*
Boudreaux, John 1946- *WhoAm 92*
Boudreaux, Kenneth Justin 1943- *WhoAm 92*
Boudreaux, Laura Goerlitz 1955- *WhoWrEP 92*
Boudreaux, Robert Palmer 1922- *St&PR 93*
Boudreaux, Ronald Paul 1951- *WhoSSW 93*
Boudreaux, Thomas Lee 1947- *St&PR 93*
Boudreaux, Warren Louis 1918- *WhoAm 92, WhoSSW 93*
Boudria, Cherylanne 1959- *WhoAmW 93, WhoEmL 93*
Boue, Andre *WhoScE 91-2*
Boueil, Sylvain R. 1952- *WhoIns 93*
Boueiz, Fares 1955- *WhoWor 93*
Bouer, Judith 1942- *WhoAmW 93, WhoWor 93*
Bouet, J.P. Thibault d1990 *BioIn 17*
Bouey, Ora James 1931- *WhoAmW 93*
Bouez, Faris 1955- *WhoWor 93*
Boufflers, Louis Francois, Marquis and Duke de 1644-1711 *HarEnMi*
Bougainville, Louis Antoine de 1729-1811 *BioIn 17, Expl 93 [port]*
Bougard, Jacques 1937- *WhoScE 91-2*
Bougere, C. Anthony 1945- *WhoE 93*
Bough, Dale Eugene 1930- *St&PR 93*
Boughan, Constance McManus 1951- *WhoAmW 93*
Bougher, Aubrey Nelson 1943- *WhoE 93*
Boughner, Howard R. 1908- *WhoWrEP 92*

Boughner, Leslie C. *WhoIns 93*
Boughs, Susan S. *Law&B 92*
Boughton, James Kenneth 1922- *WhoSSW 93*
Boughton, Joe A. 1934- *St&PR 93*
Boughton, Ross Byron 1960- *WhoE 93*
Boughton, Rutland 1878-1960 *Baker 92, IntDcOp, OxDcOp*
Boughton, William (Paul) 1948- *Baker 92*
Bougie, Jacques 1947- *WhoAm 92, WhoE 93, WhoWor 93*
Bougie, Roger *Law&B 92*
Bougie, Roger M. 1933- *St&PR 93*
Bouhafa, Moncef M. 1947- *WhoUN 92*
Bouhageb, A. 1945- *WhoScE 91-2*
Bouher, Margaret Ann 1955- *WhoEmL 93*
Bouhet, Jacques Emile 1942- *WhoE 93*
Bouhoutsos, Jacqueline Cotcher *WhoAmW 93, WhoWor 93*
Bouhy, Jacques 1848-1929 *OxDcOp*
Bouhy, Jacques (-Joseph Andre) 1848-1929 *Baker 92*
Bouic, Robert 1937- *WhoWor 93*
Bouigue, R.C.-M. 1920- *WhoScE 91-2*
Bouilhet Family *BioIn 17*
Bouilliant-Linet, Francis Jacques 1932- *WhoSSW 93, WhoWor 93*
Bouillon, Robert de la Marck, II, Duke de d1536 *HarEnMi*
Bouilly, Jean-Nicolas 1763-1842 *OxDcOp*
Bouissac, Paul Antoine 1934- *WhoAm 92*
Bouisson, Fernard 1874-1959 *BioIn 17*
Bouix, Jean E.H. 1940- *WhoScE 91-2*
Boukas, Andreas 1961- *WhoWor 93*
Bouknight, Barbara Elvira 1946- *WhoEmL 93*
Boulaine, Jean 1922- *WhoScE 91-2*
Bouland, Harold 1943- *St&PR 93*
Boulanger, Debra Ann 1956- *WhoAm 92*
Boulanger, Donald Richard 1944- *St&PR 93, WhoAm 92*
Boulanger, Georges 1837-1891 *HarEnMi*
Boulanger, Georges-Ernest-Jean-Marie 1837-1891 *BioIn 17*
Boulanger, Lili 1893-1918 *BioIn 17*
Boulanger, Lili (Juliette Marie Olga) 1893-1918 *Baker 92*
Boulanger, Nadia 1887-1979 *BioIn 17*
Boulanger, Nadia (Juliette) 1887-1979 *Baker 92*
Boulanger, Philippe 1940- *WhoWor 93*
Boulanger, Pierre Alain 1940- *WhoScE 91-2*
Boulanger, Robert Norman 1933- *St&PR 93*
Boulanger, Rodney Edmund 1940- *WhoAm 92*
Boulares, Mohsen 1939- *WhoUN 92*
Boulay, Robert A. 1953- *St&PR 93*
Boulaye, Guy G. 1937- *WhoScE 91-2*
Bould, Sally 1941- *WhoAmW 93*
Boulden, Anne Marion 1961- *WhoE 93*
Boulden, Judith Ann 1948- *WhoAmW 93*
Bouldin, Joel Ray, Jr. 1956- *St&PR 93*
Bouldin, Marshall, III *BioIn 17*
Bouldin, Regina Diane 1964- *WhoAmW 93*
Bouldin, Richard Hindman 1942- *WhoSSW 93*
Boulding, Elise Marie 1920- *WhoAm 92, WhoAmW 93*
Boulding, Kenneth Ewart 1910- *BioIn 17, WhoAm 92*
Boulerice, Jacques 1945- *WhoCanL 92*
Boulesteix, Claude 1937- *WhoScE 91-2*
Boulet, Lionel 1919- *WhoAm 92*
Boulet, Roger Henri 1944- *WhoAm 92*
Bouletreau, Michel 1943- *WhoScE 91-2*
Bouley, C. Alan 1928- *St&PR 93*
Bouley, David *BioIn 17, NewYTBS 92 [port]*
Bouley, William L. 1945- *St&PR 93*
Boulez, Pierre 1925- *Baker 92, BioIn 17, IntDcOp [port], OxDcOp, WhoAm 92, WhoWor 93*
Boulger, Francis William 1913- *WhoAm 92*
Boulger, James Daniel, Jr. 1924- *St&PR 93*
Boulin, Robert 1920-1979 *BioIn 17*
Bouline, Stephen Eric 1957- *WhoEmL 93*
Boulle, Philippe L. 1943- *WhoUN 92*
Boulle, Pierre 1912- *ScF&FL 92*
Boullet, Eric-Marie 1948- *WhoWor 93*
Boullianne, George Emile 1931- *St&PR 93*
Boullion, Lois A. *Law&B 92*
Boullosa, Carmen 1954- *DcMexL*
Boulloud, Andre 1927- *WhoScE 91-2*
Boulnois, Graham John *WhoScE 91-1*
Boulnois, Joseph 1884-1918 *Baker 92*
Boulouard, Raymond 1928- *WhoScE 91-2*
Bouloukos, Don P. *WhoE 93*
Bouloukos, Don Peter *St&PR 93*
Boulpaep, Emile Louis J. B. 1938- *WhoAm 92*
Boult, Adrian (Cedric) 1889-1983 *Baker 92*
Boult, Reber Fielding 1907- *St&PR 93*
Boult, S. Kye *ScF&FL 92*
Boultbee, J.A. 1943- *St&PR 93*
Boultbee, John Arthur 1943- *WhoAm 92, WhoE 93, WhoWor 93*
Boulter, Cedric Gordon 1912-1989 *BioIn 17*
Boulter, Donald *WhoScE 91-1*
Boulter, Michael Charles *WhoScE 91-1*
Boulter, Patrick Stewart 1927- *WhoWor 93*
Boulting, John 1913-1985 *MiSFD 9N*
Boulting, Roy 1913- *MiSFD 9*
Boultinghouse, Beate Carola 1949- *WhoEmL 93*
Boultinghouse, Marion Craig Bettinger 1930- *WhoAm 92*
Boulton, Donald Arthur 1930- *WhoSSW 93*
Boulton, Edwin Charles 1928- *WhoAm 92*
Boulton, Frank Ernest *WhoScE 91-1*
Boulton, Robert George 1928- *St&PR 93*
Boulton, Shauna Dee 1949- *WhoAmW 93*
Boulton-Lewis, Gillian Marie 1940- *WhoWor 93*
Boulud, Daniel *BioIn 17*
Boulware, Clayton William *Law&B 92*
Boulware, Lemuel R. *BioIn 17*
Boulware, Richard Stark 1935- *WhoWor 93*
Boulware-Miller, Kay *Law&B 92*
Bouma, J. 1940- *WhoScE 91-3*
Bouma, Jack Q. 1928- *St&PR 93*
Bouma, Robert Edwin 1938- *WhoAm 92*
Bouman, Aries 1937- *WhoScE 91-3*
Bouman, Lennart N. 1937- *WhoScE 91-3*
Boumann, Robert L. *Law&B 92*
Boumann, Robert Lyle 1946- *WhoEmL 93*
Boumedienne, Houari 1927-1978 *BioIn 17, ColdWar 2 [port], DcTwHis*
Boumis, Evangelos 1937- *WhoWor 93*
Bounds, Doris Swayze 1904- *St&PR 93, WhoAmW 93*
Bounds, E.M. 1835-1913 *BioIn 17*
Bounds, Edward McKendree 1835-1913 *BioIn 17*
Bounds, Julia-Anna Green 1946- *WhoSSW 93*
Bounds, Nancy 1928- *WhoAmW 93*
Bounds, Sarah Etheline 1942- *WhoAmW 93, WhoSSW 93, WhoWor 93*
Boundy, David Eric 1957- *WhoE 93, WhoEmL 93*
Boundy, Donna J. 1949- *WhoWrEP 92*
Bounhoure, Jean-Paul 1933- *WhoScE 91-2*
Bounty, Thomas M. *Law&B 92*
Bouquegneau, Christian R.G. 1945- *WhoScE 91-2*
Bouquet, Francis Lester 1926- *WhoAm 92*
Bour, Daniele 1939- *BioIn 17*
Bour, Ernest 1913- *Baker 92*
Bouraoui, Hedi 1932- *WhoCanL 92*
Bouras, James Charles 1941- *St&PR 93*
Bourasaw, Noel V. 1944- *WhoWrEP 92*
Bourassa, Andre 1936- *WhoCanL 92*
Bourassa, Napoleon 1827-1916 *BioIn 17*
Bourassa, Richard *BioIn 17*
Bourassa, Robert 1933- *BioIn 17, WhoAm 92, WhoE 93*
Bourbaki, Charles Denis Sauter 1816-1897 *HarEnMi*
Bourbeau, Nina Marie 1957- *WhoEmL 93*
Bourbin, Yannic Pierre 1954- *WhoWor 93*
Bourbon, Antoine de 1518-1562 *HarEnMi*
Bourbon, Bruce Robert 1941- *St&PR 93*
Bourbon, Charles, Cardinal de 1523-1590 *HarEnMi*
Bourbon, Charles, Count of Montpensier and Duke of 1490-1527 *HarEnMi*
Bourbonnais, Michel *Law&B 92*
Bourcier, Jacques Adair 1927- *WhoWor 93*
Bourdaire, Jean-Marie 1946- *WhoWor 93*
Bourdais de Charbonniere, Eric 1939- *WhoAm 92*
Bourdeau, Bernard N. 1948- *WhoIns 93*
Bourdeau, Paul T. *WhoIns 93*
Bourdeau, Paul Turgeon 1932- *WhoAm 92*
Bourdeau, Philippe F.J. 1926- *WhoScE 91-2*
Bourdeau, Yvan J.P. 1948- *St&PR 93*
Bourdeaux, Norma Earle 1930- *WhoAmW 93*
Bourdelle, Emile Antoine 1861-1929 *BioIn 17*
Bourdieu, Pierre Felix 1930- *WhoWor 93*
Bourdin, Roger 1900-1973 *Baker 92*
Bourdin, Thomas Francis 1931- *WhoWrEP 92*
Bourdon, David 1934- *WhoAm 92, WhoWrEP 92*
Bourdon, Denise Teresa 1967- *WhoAmW 93*
Bourdon, Joseph Henry, III 1930- *St&PR 93*
Bourdon, Paul Stephen 1959- *WhoSSW 93*
Bourdow, Daniel G. 1933- *St&PR 93*
Bourdow, Patricia A. 1935- *St&PR 93*
Bourdu, Robert 1924- *WhoScE 91-2*
Bourel, Michel 1920- *WhoScE 91-2*
Bourg, James Bradford 1946- *WhoSSW 93*
Bourg, Robert T. 1939- *St&PR 93*
Bourgain, Rene-Henri 1926- *WhoScE 91-2*
Bourgaize, Linda Harper 1947- *WhoAmW 93, WhoEmL 93*
Bourgaize, Robert G. *WhoAm 92*
Bourgault, Lise 1950- *WhoAmW 93*
Bourgault-Ducoudray, Louis-Albert 1840-1910 *Baker 92*
Bourgeacq, Christian A. *Law&B 92*
Bourgeau, Jean-Paul Leonce 1939- *WhoWor 93*
Bourgelais, Donna Chamberlain 1948- *WhoEmL 93*
Bourgeois, Andre Marie Georges 1902- *WhoAm 92*
Bourgeois, Anne Mary 1940- *WhoAmW 93*
Bourgeois, Claude Marcel 1936- *WhoScE 91-2*
Bourgeois, David P. 1945- *St&PR 93*
Bourgeois, Douglas *BioIn 17*
Bourgeois, Leon Victor Auguste 1851-1925 *BioIn 17*
Bourgeois, Louise *BioIn 17, WhoAm 92*
Bourgeois, Louise 1911- *WhoAmW 93, WhoWor 93*
Bourgeois, Loys c. 1510-c. 1561 *Baker 92*
Bourgeois, Marc L. *WhoScE 91-2*
Bourgeois, Paulette *BioIn 17*
Bourgeois, Paulette 1951- *ConAu 137, WhoCanL 92*
Bourgeois, R. Flint *Law&B 92*
Bourgeois, Richard Denis *Law&B 92*
Bourgeois, Roger Robert 1943- *WhoSSW 93*
Bourgeois, Thomas-Louis (-Joseph) 1676-1750 *Baker 92*
Bourgery, Marc Edmond Clement 1941- *WhoWor 93*
Bourges, Herve 1933- *WhoWor 93*
Bourges-Maunoury, Maurice 1914- *BioIn 17*
Bourget, Paul 1852-1935 *DcLB 123 [port]*
Bourget, Robert Bernard 1946- *WhoEmL 93*
Bourgin, Frank P. *BioIn 17*
Bourgin, Jean-Pierre 1944- *WhoWor 93*
Bourgraf, Elroy Edwin 1931- *St&PR 93*
Bourguet, Alan F. 1955- *St&PR 93*
Bourguiba, Habib 1903- *BioIn 17*
Bourguiba, Habib Ben Ali 1903- *ColdWar 2 [port]*
Bourguiba, Habib ibn Ali 1903- *DcTwHis*
Bourguignon, Erika Eichhorn 1924- *WhoAm 92*
Bourguignon, Francis de 1890-1961 *Baker 92*
Bourguignon, Francois Jean 1945- *WhoWor 93*
Bourguignon, Jean-Pierre 1947- *WhoWor 93*
Bourguignon, Philippe Etienne 1948- *WhoEmL 93, WhoWor 93*
Bourguignon, Serge 1928- *MiSFD 9*
Bourin, Michel Sylvain 1944- *WhoScE 91-2*
Bourinot, John George 1837-1902 *BioIn 17*
Bouriquet, Robert 1925- *WhoScE 91-2*
Bouris, Michael Lee 1942- *WhoIns 93*
Bourjaily, Vance 1922- *WhoAm 92, WhoWrEP 92*
Bourke, Clyde Edwin, Jr. 1928- *WhoSSW 93*
Bourke, Dale Hanson *BioIn 17*
Bourke, Geoffrey J. 1929- *WhoScE 91-3*
Bourke, George Mitchell 1923- *St&PR 93*
Bourke, Sara M. *AmWomPl*
Bourke, Vernon Joseph 1907- *WhoAm 92*
Bourke, William Oliver 1927- *St&PR 93, WhoAm 92, WhoSSW 93*
Bourke-White, Margaret 1904-1971 *BioIn 17, WomChHR [port]*
Bourke-White, Margaret 1906-1971 *JrnUS*
Bourland, Charles Thomas 1937- *WhoSSW 93*
Bourland, Pamela Gale 1958- *WhoSSW 93*
Bourlas, M. *WhoScE 91-4*
Bourlioux, Pierre 1940- *WhoScE 91-2*
Bourmont, Louis Auguste Victor de 1773-1846 *HarEnMi*
Bourn, Alan Michael *WhoScE 91-1*
Bourn, John *WhoUN 92*
Bournaud, Michel 1936- *WhoScE 91-2*
Bourne, Alan Miles 1945- *St&PR 93*
Bourne, Carol Elizabeth Mulligan 1948- *WhoAmW 93*
Bourne, Cecil John 1920-1990 *BioIn 17*
Bourne, Charles Percy 1931- *WhoAm 92*
Bourne, Daniel Carter 1955- *WhoWrEP 92*
Bourne, Duncan Stewart 1959- *WhoEmL 93*
Bourne, Francis Stanley 1919- *WhoAm 92*
Bourne, Frederick John *WhoScE 91-1*
Bourne, Henry Clark, Jr. 1921- *WhoAm 92*
Bourne, James Edwin 1929- *St&PR 93*
Bourne, John 1918- *ScF&FL 92*
Bourne, John Russell 1932- *WhoScE 91-4*
Bourne, Kenneth Allen 1942- *St&PR 93*
Bourne, Lyle Eugene, Jr. 1932- *WhoAm 92*
Bourne, Malcolm Cornelius 1926- *WhoE 93*
Bourne, Martha Flowers 1943- *WhoAmW 93*
Bourne, Mary Bonnie Murray 1903- *WhoAm 92, WhoAmW 93, WhoE 93*
Bourne, Mel *BioIn 17*
Bourne, Mel 1923- *ConTFT 10*
Bourne, Miriam Anne *BioIn 17*
Bourne, Peter Geoffrey 1939- *WhoAm 92*
Bourne, R. Wiley, Jr. *St&PR 93*
Bourne, Ralph W., Jr. 1936- *WhoIns 93*
Bourne, Randolph Silliman 1886-1918 *BioIn 17*
Bourne, Russell 1928- *WhoAm 92*
Bourne, Samuel G. 1916- *WhoAm 92*
Bourne, Victoria Tyson 1952- *WhoEmL 93*
Bourne, Willie R. 1931- *St&PR 93*
Bournjini, Salah 1938- *WhoUN 92*
Bournonville, Alexandre Hippolyte, Prince de fl. c. 1674- *HarEnMi*
Bournonville, Jacques de c. 1675-c. 1754 *Baker 92*
Bournonville, Jean de c. 1585-1632 *Baker 92*
Bournonville, Valentin de c. 1610-1663 *Baker 92*
Bourns, Marsha *ScF&FL 92*
Bourns, Richard T. 1934- *St&PR 93*
Bourquardez, Earl Constant 1948- *WhoEmL 93, WhoSSW 93*
Bourque, Andre J. 1947- *St&PR 93*
Bourque, Charles Henry 1945- *St&PR 93*
Bourque, Irby 1942- *St&PR 93*
Bourque, Linda Anne Brookover 1941- *WhoAmW 93*
Bourque, Michael H. 1948- *WhoE 93, WhoEmL 93*
Bourque, Michael T. *Law&B 92*
Bourque, Philip John 1922- *WhoAm 92*
Bourque, Ray 1960- *WhoAm 92*
Bourquien, Louis fl. c. 1800- *HarEnMi*
Bourquin, David Ray 1941- *ScF&FL 92*
Bourquin, Maurice 1941- *WhoScE 91-4*
Bourquin, Paul A. 1921- *St&PR 93*
Bourre, Jean-Marie 1945- *WhoScE 91-2*
Bourrelly, Henri d1991 *BioIn 17*
Bourseiller, Marie Sara *BioIn 17*
Bourton, Michel 1935- *WhoScE 91-2*
Bourtzes *OxDcByz*
Bourtzes, Michael dc. 996 *OxDcByz*
Bouscaren, Anthony Trawick 1920- *WhoE 93*
Bouscaren, Remy *WhoScE 91-2*
Bouseman, John Keith 1936- *WhoWor 93*
Bouser, Juanita Watts 1945- *WhoAmW 93*
Bousfield, Barry *BioIn 17*
Bousfield, Edward Lloyd 1926- *WhoAm 92*
Bousfield, H.T.W. 1891- *ScF&FL 92*
Boushie, Raymond W. 1940- *St&PR 93*
Boushy, John 1954- *St&PR 93*
Bousono, Carlos 1923- *BioIn 17*
Bousoulengas, Alexandros *WhoScE 91-3*
Bousquet, Bernard 1939- *WhoScE 91-2*
Bousquet, Georges 1818-1854 *Baker 92*
Bousquet, Henri *St&PR 93*
Bousquet, Jean 1924- *WhoScE 91-2*
Bousquet, Thomas Gourrier 1934- *WhoAm 92*
Bousquette, William C. 1936- *WhoAm 92*
Bousquette, William Charles 1936- *St&PR 93*
Boussard, Jean-Claude L. 1938- *WhoScE 91-2*
Boussauw, Luc H.A. 1944- *St&PR 93*
Boussel, Pierre 1920- *BioIn 17*
Bousset, Jean-Baptiste 1662-1725 *Baker 92*
Bousset, Rene Drouard de 1703-1760 *Baker 92*
Boussuge, Michel 1956- *WhoScE 91-2*
Boustead, William Henry *Law&B 92*
Boutelee, Charles Addison 1839-1901 *JrnUS*
Boutell, C.B. 1908-1981 *ScF&FL 92*
Boutell, Michael D. *Law&B 92*
Boutelle, Clarence M. 1851-1903 *ScF&FL 92*
Boutelle, Grace *AmWomPl*
Boutelle, Jane Cronin 1926- *WhoAmW 93*
Bouthillier, Yves Marie 1901-1977 *BioIn 17*
Boutilier, Scott Eugene 1956- *St&PR 93*
Boutillette, Leroy Bruce, Jr. 1950- *St&PR 93*
Boutillier, Robert John 1924- *WhoAm 92*
Boutin, Pierre A.R. 1933- *WhoScE 91-2*
Boutissou, Serge 1939- *WhoWor 93*

Boutmy, Emile Gaston 1835-1906 *BioIn 17*
Boutmy, Josse 1697-1779 *Baker 92*
Bouton, James Alan 1939- *WhoAm 92*
Bouton, Janet Laura 1943- *WhoAmW 93*
Bouton, Jim *BioIn 17*
Boutoumites *OxDcByz*
Boutoussov, Mikhail Mikhailovitch 1937- *WhoUN 92*
Boutris, Demetrios A. 1961- *WhoEmL 93*
Boutros-Ghali, Boutros 1922- *BioIn 17, CurBio 92 [port], WhoUN 92*
Boutross, Denise M. 1952- *WhoAm 92*
Boutry, Roger 1932- *Baker 92*
Boutte, David Gray 1944- *WhoWor 93*
Bouttens, Frank 1952- *WhoWor 93*
Boutton, Thomas William 1951- *WhoSSW 93*
Boutwell, Florence Rose 1934- *WhoAmW 93*
Boutwell, George S. 1818-1905 *BioIn 17*
Boutwell, Herbert Chauncey, III 1948- *WhoEmL 93*
Boutwell, Roswell Knight 1917- *WhoAm 92*
Boutwell, Wayne Allison 1944- *WhoE 93*
Bouvard, Marguerite Gusman 1937- *WhoWrEP 92*
Bouve, Howard A., Jr. 1930- *St&PR 93*
Bouvet, Charles (Rene Clement) 1858-1935 *Baker 92*
Bouvier, Jane Alpert 1945- *WhoE 93*
Bouvier, Janet Laubach 1930- *WhoAmW 93, WhoE 93*
Bouvier, Marcelle 1942- *St&PR 93*
Bouw, Jacob 1926- *WhoScE 91-3*
Bouw, Pieter 1941- *WhoWor 93*
Bouwer, Herman 1927- *WhoAm 92*
Bouwer, John D. 1938- *St&PR 93*
Bouwhuis, D.G. 1942- *WhoScE 91-3*
Bouwma, J. 1946- *WhoScE 91-3*
Bouws, Everard 1941- *WhoScE 91-3*
Bouwsma, William James 1923- *WhoAm 92*
Bouyea, Peter A. 1948- *St&PR 93*
Bouyoucos, John Vinton 1926- *WhoAm 92*
Bouysse, Philippe 1938- *WhoScE 91-2*
Bouzakis, Konstantin-Dionysios 1948- *WhoScE 91-3*
Bouzianis, Melissa Farrah 1957- *WhoEmL 93*
Bouzignac, Guillaume fl. 17th cent.- *Baker 92*
Bova, Ben 1932- *BioIn 17, ScF&FL 92*
Bova, Ben(jamin William) 1932- *MajAI [port]*
Bova, Benjamin William 1932- *WhoAm 92*
Bova, Jeffrey Stephen 1953- *WhoE 93, WhoWor 93*
Bova, Linda Carol 1947- *WhoAmW 93*
Bova, Paul Peter 1941- *St&PR 93*
Bova, Thomas William 1942- *St&PR 93*
Bova, Vincent Arthur, Jr. 1946- *WhoEmL 93*
Bovaird, Brendan Peter 1948- *WhoAm 92, WhoE 93*
Bovallius, Ake 1937- *WhoScE 91-4*
Bovard, Carl M. 1930- *St&PR 93*
Bovard, Oliver K. 1872-1945 *JrnUS*
Bovarnick, Ellen 1954- *WhoEmL 93*
Bovasso, Julie 1930-1991 *BioIn 17, ConTFT 10*
Bovay, Harry Elmo, Jr. 1914- *WhoAm 92, WhoWor 93*
Bovbjerg, Dana H. 1951- *WhoE 93*
Bove, Alfred Anthony 1938- *WhoE 93*
Bove, Carol Mastrangelo 1949- *WhoE 93*
Bove, Jan A.J. 1948- *WhoUN 92*
Bove, Januar D., Jr. 1920- *WhoAm 92*
Bove, John Louis 1928- *WhoAm 92*
Bove, Luiz Eduardo *Law&B 92*
Bove, Marylou Goodman 1958- *WhoEmL 93*
Bove, Peter W. d1990 *BioIn 17*
Bove, Robert Charles 1951- *WhoEmL 93*
Bove, Roseann 1942- *WhoE 93*
Bovee, Eugene Cleveland 1915- *WhoAm 92*
Bovee, Gerald N. 1939- *St&PR 93*
Bovee, Jan Merrill 1938- *St&PR 93*
Bovee, Spence 1962- *WhoEmL 93*
Bovee, Warren R. *Law&B 92*
Bovell, Carlton Rowland 1924- *WhoAm 92*
Bovender, Jack O. 1945- *St&PR 93*
Bovender, Jack Oliver, Jr. 1945- *WhoSSW 93*
Bovenizer, Bruce 1945- *St&PR 93, WhoIns 93*
Bovenkerk, Henry G. d1990 *BioIn 17*
Boveroux, Brooks 1943- *St&PR 93*
Boves, Joaquin Lorenzo 1949- *WhoE 93, WhoEmL 93, WhoWor 93*
Boves, Jose Tomas d1821? *HarEnMi*
Bovet, Daniel 1907-1992 *BioIn 17*
Bovet, Daniele 1907-1992 *CurBio 92N, NewYTBS 92 [port]*
Bovet, Joseph 1879-1951 *Baker 92*
Bovetti, Raimondo 1945- *WhoWor 93*
Bovey, Rodney William 1934- *WhoSSW 93*
Bovey, Terry Robinson 1948- *WhoEmL 93*
Bovik, Harry Q. 1943- *WhoE 93*
Boville, Byron *BioIn 17*
Bovin, Denis Alan 1947- *WhoAm 92, WhoEmL 93*
Bovingdon, George Geil 1934- *WhoWor 93*
Bovino, Charles A. 1940- *St&PR 93*
Bovit, Jeffrey 1953- *St&PR 93*
Bovit, R. Lionel 1927- *St&PR 93*
Bovo, Mary Jane 1946- *WhoE 93*
Bovoso, Carole Ione Lewis 1937- *WhoWrEP 92*
Bovre, Odd 1933- *WhoScE 91-2*
Bovy, Vina 1900-1983 *Baker 92*
Bovy-Lysberg, Charles-Samuel 1821-1873 *Baker 92*
Bow, Clara 1905-1965 *IntDcF 2-3 [port]*
Bow, Sing Tze 1924- *WhoWor 93*
Bow, Stephen Tyler, Jr. 1931- *WhoAm 92, WhoWor 93*
Bowcock, John E. *WhoScE 91-1*
Bowcut, Michael Jerry 1953- *St&PR 93*
Bowden, Alan Leslie *WhoScE 91-1*
Bowden, Ann 1924- *WhoAmW 93, WhoSSW 93, WhoWor 93*
Bowden, Benjamin John 1932- *St&PR 93*
Bowden, Bobby *BioIn 17*
Bowden, Bobby 1930- *WhoAm 92*
Bowden, Charles Edgar 1929- *St&PR 93*
Bowden, Charles Malcolm 1933- *WhoSSW 93*
Bowden, Edward F. *St&PR 93*
Bowden, Elbert Victor 1924- *WhoAm 92, WhoSSW 93*
Bowden, Elizabeth Ann 1948- *WhoAmW 93*
Bowden, Etta 1893-1973 *ScF&FL 92*
Bowden, Garrett R. 1950- *St&PR 93*
Bowden, Gordon Townley 1915- *WhoE 93*
Bowden, Henry James Charles 1901- *BioIn 17*
Bowden, Henry Lumpkin 1910- *WhoAm 92*
Bowden, Henry Lumpkin, Jr. 1949- *WhoAm 92*
Bowden, Hugh Kent 1933- *WhoAm 92*
Bowden, James Alvin 1948- *St&PR 93, WhoAm 92*
Bowden, Jesse Earle 1928- *WhoAm 92, WhoWrEP 92*
Bowden, Jon M. *Law&B 92*
Bowden, Margaret D. *Law&B 92*
Bowden, Maxine 1943- *WhoAmW 93*
Bowden, Michael Albert 1944- *WhoWor 93*
Bowden, Phil 1906-1980 *ScF&FL 92*
Bowden, Richard Keane 1952- *St&PR 93*
Bowden, Robert 1929- *BiDAMSp 1989*
Bowden, Sally Ann 1943- *WhoAm 92*
Bowden, Susan 1936- *WhoWrEP 92*
Bowden, Travis J. 1938- *St&PR 93, WhoAm 92*
Bowden, William Darsie 1920- *WhoAm 92*
Bowdin, Harby Glenn 1951- *WhoEmL 93*
Bowditch, Nathaniel 1773-1838 *BioIn 17*
Bowditch, Nathaniel Rantoul 1932- *WhoAm 92*
Bowditch, Robert Shaw 1909- *St&PR 93*
Bowdler, Anthony John 1928- *WhoAm 92*
Bowdler, George Albert 1920- *WhoSSW 93*
Bowdre, Charlie 1859?-1880 *BioIn 17*
Bowdre, John Birch, Jr. 1954- *WhoEmL 93*
Bowdre, Paul Reid 1958- *WhoEmL 93, WhoSSW 93*
Bowe, Carol Ann 1953- *WhoE 93*
Bowe, Edward Louis 1946- *WhoEmL 93*
Bowe, James Joseph 1927- *St&PR 93*
Bowe, Jeffrey John 1963- *St&PR 93*
Bowe, Peter Armistead 1956- *St&PR 93, WhoE 93*
Bowe, Richard E. 1921- *St&PR 93*
Bowe, Richard Eugene 1921- *WhoAm 92, WhoE 93*
Bowe, Riddick *BioIn 17*
Bowe, Riddick c. 1967- *News 93-2 [port]*
Bowe, Thomas Edward, III 1954- *WhoEmL 93*
Bowe, William John 1942- *St&PR 93, WhoAm 92*
Bowen, A. Grant 1930- *St&PR 93*
Bowen, Alanson G. *Law&B 92*
Bowen, Albert Reeder 1905- *WhoAm 92*
Bowen, Asta 1955- *WhoWrEP 92*
Bowen, Barbara Cherry 1937- *WhoAm 92, WhoAmW 93, WhoSSW 93*
Bowen, Barbara Lynn 1945- *WhoAmW 93*
Bowen, Barry *St&PR 93*
Bowen, Berry D. *Law&B 92*
Bowen, Billy M. 1935- *WhoIns 93*
Bowen, Brett H. 1941- *St&PR 93*
Bowen, Carol Ewald *Law&B 92*
Bowen, Carol Snow 1956- *WhoSSW 93*
Bowen, Charles Revelle 1926- *WhoE 93*
Bowen, Clotilde Dent 1923- *WhoAm 92*
Bowen, David Hywel Michael 1939- *WhoE 93*
Bowen, David Keith *WhoScE 91-1*
Bowen, David Reece 1932- *WhoAm 92*
Bowen, David Vaughan 1945- *WhoWor 93*
Bowen, Debra Jean 1955- *WhoAmW 93*
Bowen, Derrick 1930- *St&PR 93*
Bowen, Donald Edgar 1939- *WhoAm 92*
Bowen, Dudley Hollingsworth, Jr. 1941- *WhoAm 92, WhoSSW 93*
Bowen, Elizabeth 1899-1973 *BioIn 17, BritWr S2, MagSWL [port]*
Bowen, Eva Joyce 1934- *WhoSSW 93*
Bowen, Frank Weston, Jr. 1952- *WhoEmL 93*
Bowen, Fred Pasco, II 1958- *St&PR 93*
Bowen, Gail 1942- *ConAu 138*
Bowen, Gary L. *Law&B 92*
Bowen, Gary Lee 1953- *WhoSSW 93*
Bowen, George Hamilton, Jr. 1925- *WhoAm 92*
Bowen, George L. 1896-1991 *BioIn 17*
Bowen, Glenn Ainsworth 1956- *WhoUN 92*
Bowen, Glenn H. *Law&B 92*
Bowen, Gordon Stewart 1950- *WhoAm 92, WhoEmL 93*
Bowen, H. Kent 1941- *WhoAm 92*
Bowen, Harrold Pasco 1934- *St&PR 93*
Bowen, Harry T. 1930- *St&PR 93*
Bowen, Howard Rothmann 1908-1989 *BioIn 17*
Bowen, Ian Hamilton *WhoScE 91-1*
Bowen, Ivor Delme *WhoScE 91-1*
Bowen, J. David 1930- *WhoSSW 93*
Bowen, Jack 1948- *St&PR 93*
Bowen, James E. 1948- *St&PR 93*
Bowen, James Harold, Jr. 1948- *WhoE 93*
Bowen, James Ronald 1941- *WhoAm 92*
Bowen, James Thomas 1948- *WhoEmL 93*
Bowen, James Thomas, Jr. 1948- *WhoSSW 93*
Bowen, Jean 1927- *WhoAmW 93*
Bowen, Jeanne Gay 1946- *WhoAmW 93*
Bowen, Jeffrey A. 1948- *St&PR 93*
Bowen, Jeffrey Byron 1950- *WhoSSW 93*
Bowen, Jenny *MiSFD 9*
Bowen, Jewell Ray 1934- *WhoAm 92*
Bowen, Jill Veronica 1947- *WhoWrEP 92*
Bowen, Joan Martin 1939- *WhoAm 92*
Bowen, Joe d1991 *BioIn 17*
Bowen, John E., III 1931- *St&PR 93*
Bowen, John J. 1948- *St&PR 93*
Bowen, John Joseph 1952- *WhoE 93*
Bowen, John Metcalf 1933- *WhoAm 92*
Bowen, John Richard 1934- *St&PR 93, WhoAm 92*
Bowen, Kelley Bailey 1962- *WhoAmW 93, WhoEmL 93, WhoWor 93*
Bowen, Kim *Law&B 92*
Bowen, Lionel Frost 1922- *WhoAsAP 91*
Bowen, Lowell Reed 1931- *WhoAm 92*
Bowen, Marcia Kay 1957- *WhoAmW 93*
Bowen, Margaret Elizabeth *AmWomPl*
Bowen, Margretta Jeffers *Law&B 92*
Bowen, Marjorie *ScF&FL 92*
Bowen, Marjorie Estelle 1960- *WhoAmW 93*
Bowen, Martin C. 1943- *St&PR 93*
Bowen, Murray *BioIn 17*
Bowen, Norman Wayne 1942- *St&PR 93*
Bowen, Patrick G. *Law&B 92*
Bowen, Patrick Harvey 1939- *WhoAm 92*
Bowen, Paul Rhys 1951- *WhoE 93*
Bowen, Philip M. *Law&B 92*
Bowen, Richard Lee 1933- *WhoAm 92*
Bowen, Richard Mayo, III 1947- *WhoAm 92*
Bowen, Robert Allen 1946- *WhoIns 93*
Bowen, Robert John *Law&B 92*
Bowen, Robert Morchart 1913- *WhoAm 92*
Bowen, Robert William 1960- *WhoE 93, WhoEmL 93, WhoWor 93*
Bowen, Ronald Scott 1943- *WhoE 93*
Bowen, Sandra Cobb 1952- *WhoSSW 93*
Bowen, Stephen Francis, Jr. 1932- *WhoAm 92*
Bowen, Stephen Stewart 1946- *WhoAm 92*
Bowen, Sybil Spande *AmWomPl*
Bowen, Thomas Allan 1951- *WhoEmL 93*
Bowen, Thomas E. 1932- *St&PR 93*
Bowen, Thomas Edwin 1934- *WhoAm 92*
Bowen, W.J. 1922- *St&PR 93, WhoSSW 93*
Bowen, Walter E. 1942- *St&PR 93*
Bowen, William Augustus 1930- *WhoAm 92*
Bowen, William Gordon 1933- *WhoAm 92, WhoWor 93*
Bowen, William H. 1933- *WhoAm 92*
Bowen, William Harvey 1923- *WhoAm 92*
Bowen, William Joseph 1934- *WhoAm 92*
Bowen, William Richard *WhoScE 91-1*
Bowen, (Edwin) York 1884-1961 *Baker 92*
Bowen, Zack R. 1934- *WhoSSW 93*
Bowen, Zeddie Paul 1937- *WhoAm 92*
Bower, Allan Maxwell 1936- *WhoAm 92*
Bower, Brock 1931- *ScF&FL 92*
Bower, Bruce Edward 1950- *WhoEmL 93*
Bower, Catherine Downes 1947- *WhoEmL 93*
Bower, Christopher James 1957- *WhoAm 92, WhoEmL 93*
Bower, David Harrison 1947- *WhoE 93*
Bower, Dorothy E.A. *Law&B 92*
Bower, Douglas *BioIn 17*
Bower, Douglas William 1948- *WhoEmL 93, WhoSSW 93*
Bower, Fay Louise 1929- *WhoAmW 93*
Bower, Geoffrey Donald 1946- *WhoWor 93*
Bower, Glen Landis 1949- *WhoEmL 93*
Bower, Harold Eugene, Jr. 1955- *WhoE 93*
Bower, Haywood W. 1948- *St&PR 93*
Bower, Henry E. *Law&B 92*
Bower, Janie Pittman 1955- *WhoEmL 93*
Bower, Jean Ramsay 1935- *WhoAm 92, WhoAmW 93*
Bower, John Arthur 1943- *WhoWor 93*
Bower, John Joseph 1925- *WhoAm 92*
Bower, John W. 1930- *St&PR 93*
Bower, Joseph Lyon 1938- *WhoAm 92, WhoE 93*
Bower, Kathleen Ann 1962- *WhoAmW 93, WhoEmL 93*
Bower, Kenneth Francis 1942- *WhoWor 93*
Bower, Leonard Ernest 1947- *WhoEmL 93*
Bower, Mark Victor 1953- *WhoEmL 93*
Bower, Marvin 1903- *St&PR 93, WhoAm 92*
Bower, Marvin D. 1924- *St&PR 93, WhoIns 93*
Bower, Paul George 1933- *WhoAm 92*
Bower, Peggy Joyce 1957- *WhoAmW 93*
Bower, Peter Thomas A. 1946- *St&PR 93*
Bower, Regina Patricia 1950- *St&PR 93*
Bower, Richard James 1939- *WhoAm 92*
Bower, Richard Stuart 1928- *WhoAm 92*
Bower, Robert Hewitt 1949- *WhoEmL 93*
Bower, Robert T. 1919-1990 *BioIn 17*
Bower, Rose Janet 1919- *WhoAmW 93*
Bower, Ruth Lawther 1917- *WhoSSW 93*
Bower, Sandra Irwin 1946- *WhoAm 92, WhoEmL 93*
Bower, Ward *Law&B 92*
Bower, William A. *Law&B 92*
Bower, William Richard 1955- *WhoE 93*
Bower, Willis Herman 1916- *WhoAm 92*
Bowerfind, Edgar Sihler, Jr. 1924- *WhoAm 92*
Bowering, George 1935- *ConAu 16AS [port]*
Bowering, George 1936- *WhoCanL 92*
Bowering, George Harry 1936- *WhoAm 92, WhoWrEP 92*
Bowering, Marilyn 1949- *WhoCanL 92*
Bowering, Peter 1926- *ScF&FL 92*
Bowerman, Bill 1911- *BioIn 17*
Bowerman, Bryan Peter 1942- *WhoAm 92*
Bowerman, C.L. 1939- *St&PR 93*
Bowerman, Charles Leo 1939- *WhoAm 92*
Bowerman, Donald Bradley 1934- *WhoAm 92*
Bowerman, P. *WhoScE 91-1*
Bowerman, Richard H. 1917- *St&PR 93*
Bowerman, Richard Henry 1917- *WhoAm 92*
Bowerman, William J. 1909- *WhoAm 92*
Bowerman, William Jay 1911- *BioIn 17*
Bowermaster, Michael 1949- *WhoSSW 93*
Bowers, Albert 1930-1990 *BioIn 17*
Bowers, Arthur Stutz, Jr. 1932- *St&PR 93*
Bowers, B.L. *ScF&FL 92*
Bowers, Bradley Roy 1956- *WhoSSW 93*
Bowers, Carl Richard 1931- *St&PR 93*
Bowers, Charles R. 1940- *WhoAm 92, WhoWor 93*
Bowers, Charlotte A. 1936- *WhoAmW 93*
Bowers, Claud G. 1878-1958 *JrnUS*
Bowers, Clyde T. 1914- *St&PR 93*
Bowers, Daniel Kent 1947- *St&PR 93*
Bowers, David A. 1946- *St&PR 93*
Bowers, David Alan *Law&B 92*
Bowers, David Alexander *WhoAm 92*
Bowers, David C. 1937- *St&PR 93*
Bowers, Debbi Kaye 1964- *WhoAmW 93*
Bowers, Dorothea Ellen 1925- *WhoAmW 93*
Bowers, Edward Albert 1941- *WhoSSW 93*
Bowers, Elliott Toulmin 1919- *WhoSSW 93*
Bowers, Eloise B. 1912- *WhoAmW 93*
Bowers, Emmett Wadsworth 1926- *WhoAm 92*
Bowers, Francis Robert 1920- *WhoAm 92*
Bowers, Frank N. d1991 *BioIn 17*
Bowers, Fredson Thayer 1905-1991 *BioIn 17*
Bowers, G. Roger *Law&B 92*
Bowers, George *MiSFD 9*

Bowers, George Robert 1935- WhoWor 93
Bowers, Glenn Lee 1921- WhoAm 92
Bowers, Grayson Hunter 1897- WhoE 93, WhoWor 93
Bowers, Gregory L. 1951- St&PR 93
Bowers, J. Milton, Mrs. ConAu 139
Bowers, James Edward Law&B 92
Bowers, James Kenneth 1941- St&PR 93
Bowers, James O. 1948- St&PR 93
Bowers, James Robert, III 1945- WhoWor 93
Bowers, James Thomas 1958- WhoE 93
Bowers, James W. Law&B 92
Bowers, Jane McCormick 1941- WhoAmW 93
Bowers, John H. 1945- St&PR 93
Bowers, John Waite 1935- WhoAm 92
Bowers, John Zimmerman 1913- WhoAm 92
Bowers, June Eleanore 1922- WhoSSW 93
Bowers, Klaus Dieter 1929- WhoAm 92
Bowers, Lanny Ross 1951- WhoSSW 93
Bowers, Lee Ailes 1950- WhoEmL 93
Bowers, M. Blair 1930- WhoAmW 93
Bowers, Melissa Kay 1968- WhoSSW 93
Bowers, Michael Joseph 1941- WhoAm 92, WhoSSW 93
Bowers, Michelle Anne 1961- WhoSSW 93
Bowers, Mildred Maxine 1931- WhoAmW 93
Bowers, Patricia Eleanor Fritz 1928- WhoAm 92, WhoAmW 93, WhoE 93
Bowers, Patricia Newsome 1944- WhoAmW 93, WhoE 93, WhoWor 93
Bowers, Paul Alan 1947- WhoEmL 93
Bowers, Paul Duane, Jr. 1931- WhoAm 92
Bowers, Peter George 1937- WhoE 93
Bowers, Phillip Frederick 1947- WhoE 93
Bowers, Q(uentin) David 1938- ConAu 37NR
Bowers, R. Todd 1956- St&PR 93
Bowers, Richard L. 1942- St&PR 93
Bowers, Richard Lee 1939- WhoSSW 93
Bowers, Richard Philip 1931- WhoAm 92
Bowers, Richard S. 1946- St&PR 93
Bowers, Richard Stewart, Jr. Law&B 92
Bowers, Richard Stewart, Jr. 1946- WhoAm 92, WhoEmL 93
Bowers, Robert Bruce 1948- WhoAm 92
Bowers, Robert E. 1956- St&PR 93
Bowers, Sabra Elaine 1948- WhoSSW 93
Bowers, Stanley Jacob 1912- WhoAm 92
Bowers, Thomas Arnold 1942- WhoAm 92, WhoSSW 93
Bowers, Thomas Glenn 1950- WhoE 93
Bowers, Thomas J. c. 1823-1885 Baker 92
Bowers, Thomas R. 1940- St&PR 93
Bowers, Trudy Marilyn 1948- WhoAmW 93
Bowers, William A. WhoIns 93
Bowers, William Clare 1951- WhoEmL 93
Bowers, William Frederick 1944- St&PR 93
Bowers, William James 1928- St&PR 93
Bowers, William R. 1944- St&PR 93
Bowers, Zella Zane 1929- WhoAmW 93
Bowersock, Glen Warren 1936- WhoAm 92, WhoWor 93, WhoWrEP 92
Bowersock, Von K. 1943- St&PR 93, WhoIns 93
Bowersox, Judith Jeane 1949- WhoEmL 93
Bowersox, Thomas H. 1941- St&PR 93
Bowery, N.G. WhoScE 91-1
Bowery Boys, The QDrFCA 92 [port]
Bowes, Arlene Dannenberg 1950- WhoEmL 93
Bowes, Charles A. Law&B 92
Bowes, David Dwight 1951- WhoAm 92
Bowes, Donald Ralph WhoScE 91-1
Bowes, Florence 1925- WhoAmW 93
Bowes, Frederick, III 1941- WhoAm 92
Bowes, George Ernest 1942- WhoSSW 93
Bowes, Gregory B. 1954- St&PR 93
Bowes, Henry Edward 1915- WhoAm 92
Bowes, Joseph 1923-1990 BioIn 17
Bowes, Richard 1944- ScF&FL 92
Bowes, Robert C. Law&B 92
Bowes, Russell C., Jr. 1937- St&PR 93
Bowes, William K., Jr. St&PR 93
Bowey, Donald F., Jr. 1933- St&PR 93
Bowey, John R. 1958- MiSFD 9
Bowey, Olwyn BioIn 17
Bowie, Cameron 1945- WhoWor 93
Bowie, David BioIn 17
Bowie, David 1947- Baker 92, WhoAm 92
Bowie, David Bernard 1954- WhoEmL 93
Bowie, Douglas B. 1943- St&PR 93
Bowie, Edward John Walter 1925- WhoAm 92
Bowie, James 1796-1836 HarEnMi
Bowie, Jim DcAmChF 1960, MajAI
Bowie, Joseph Wayne 1958- WhoSSW 93
Bowie, Lenard Connell 1937- WhoSSW 93, WhoWor 93
Bowie, Lester BioIn 17
Bowie, Lester 1941- Baker 92
Bowie, Norman Ernest 1942- WhoAm 92
Bowie, Thomas P. 1944- WhoIns 93
Bowie, Timothy Jon 1963- WhoEmL 93
Bowinski, Peter N. 1948- St&PR 93
Bowker, Albert Hosmer 1919- WhoAm 92
Bowker, Ann Marta 1935- WhoAmW 93
Bowker, Cynthia Ann 1948- WhoAmW 93
Bowker, Laura Lee 1957- WhoEmL 93
Bowker, Lee Harrington 1940- WhoAm 92
Bowker, Michael WhoScE 91-1
Bowker, Richard 1950- ScF&FL 92
Bowker, Susan Thayer AmWomPl
Bowkett, Gerald Edson 1926- WhoWrEP 92
Bowkett, Stephen BioIn 17
Bowkett, Stephen 1953- ScF&FL 92
Bowlan, Marian AmWomPl
Bowlby, John BioIn 17
Bowlby, Orin L. 1942- St&PR 93
Bowlby, R. Floyd 1959- St&PR 93
Bowlby, Richard Eric 1939- WhoWor 93
Bowlby, Richard Evans 1928- St&PR 93
Bowlen, Patrick Dennis 1944- WhoAm 92
Bowler, E. Joseph 1936- St&PR 93
Bowler, Jan Brett MajAI, SmATA 71
Bowler, Kenneth WhoScE 91-1
Bowler, Marianne Bianca 1947- WhoE 93
Bowler, Mary E. Law&B 92
Bowler, Shirley 1949- WhoAmW 93
Bowler, W. Scane 1925- St&PR 93
Bowles, A. Eugene 1934- St&PR 93
Bowles, Alan Derek 1960- WhoE 93, WhoWor 93
Bowles, Aubrey Russell, III 1933- WhoAm 92, WhoWor 93
Bowles, Barbara L. 1947- St&PR 93
Bowles, Barbara Landers 1947- WhoAm 92
Bowles, Camilla Parker BioIn 17
Bowles, Chester 1901-1985 PolPar
Bowles, Daniel Allan 1949- St&PR 93
Bowles, Deborah Ann 1949- WhoEmL 93
Bowles, Deborah Ann 1958- WhoAmW 93
Bowles, Edward L. 1897-1990 BioIn 17
Bowles, Ella Shannon 1886- AmWomPl
Bowles, George McMillan 1944- WhoE 93
Bowles, Gordon T. 1904- IntDcAn
Bowles, Howard Dean 1943- St&PR 93
Bowles, Jane Auer 1917-1973 BioIn 17
Bowles, John 1916- WhoAm 92
Bowles, John L. Law&B 92
Bowles, Larry David 1944- St&PR 93
Bowles, Lawrence Thompson 1931- WhoAm 92
Bowles, Margie H. St&PR 93
Bowles, Margo La Joy 1949- WhoEmL 93
Bowles, Patricia Mary 1950- WhoE 93, WhoEmL 93
Bowles, Paul 1910- BioIn 17, MagSAmL [port], WhoWrEP 92
Bowles, Paul Frederic 1910- Baker 92
Bowles, Paul Frederick 1910- WhoAm 92, WhoWor 93
Bowles, Paul Richard 1953- WhoEmL 93
Bowles, Romald E. 1924- St&PR 93
Bowles, Samuel BioIn 17
Bowles, Samuel, III 1826-1878 JrnUS
Bowles, Steve ScF&FL 92
Bowles, Susan Law&B 92
Bowles, Ted 1947- St&PR 93
Bowles, Walter Donald 1923- WhoAm 92
Bowles, William Lisle 1762-1850 BioIn 17
Bowles, William R. Law&B 92
Bowley, Donovan Aidan Robin 1945- WhoE 93
Bowley, Norman W. 1951- St&PR 93
Bowlin, Jerry C. Law&B 92
Bowlin, Kendall Duane 1933- St&PR 93
Bowlin, Melissa Anne 1959- WhoSSW 93
Bowlin, Michael Ray 1943- WhoAm 92
Bowlin, Mike R. 1943- St&PR 93
Bowline, Dwain Virgil 1957- WhoSSW 93
Bowling, B.J. 1941- St&PR 93
Bowling, Bruce Thomas 1937- WhoAm 92
Bowling, David J. Law&B 92
Bowling, Douglas William 1953- WhoSSW 93
Bowling, Evelyn Burge 1931- WhoAm 92
Bowling, Harold T. 1935- St&PR 93
Bowling, James Chandler 1928- WhoAm 92, WhoE 93
Bowling, James Merle 1940- WhoSSW 93
Bowling, James W. St&PR 93
Bowling, John Robert 1943- WhoSSW 93
Bowling, John Selby 1944- WhoSSW 93
Bowling, Kathleen E. 1946- WhoEmL 93
Bowling, Lance Christopher 1948- WhoEmL 93, WhoWor 93
Bowling, Nina Richardson 1956- WhoEmL 93
Bowling, Randy Oather 1955- WhoSSW 93
Bowling, Rita Joan 1949- WhoEmL 93
Bowling, Rod A. 1949- St&PR 93
Bowling, Thomas B. 1932- WhoIns 93
Bowling, Thomas Barksdale 1932- St&PR 93
Bowling, Walter Scott 1945- WhoIns 93
Bowling, William Dennis 1949- WhoSSW 93
Bowling, William Glasgow 1902- WhoAm 92
Bowlly, Art BioIn 17
Bowls, Karen Frances 1940- WhoAmW 93
Bowlus, Dale Richard 1948- WhoE 93
Bowlus, Douglas B. 1944- St&PR 93
Bowman, Anthony J. MiSFD 9
Bowman, Barbara Ann 1944- WhoAmW 93
Bowman, Barbara Ann 1954- WhoAmW 93
Bowman, Barbara Hyde 1930- WhoAm 92
Bowman, Barbara Taylor 1928- WhoAm 92
Bowman, Betsey Jean 1923- WhoSSW 93
Bowman, Bob 1936- WhoWrEP 92
Bowman, Brad 1949- St&PR 93
Bowman, Bruce H. St&PR 93
Bowman, Carol Ann 1952- WhoEmL 93
Bowman, Carroll Clyde 1946- WhoSSW 93
Bowman, Charles Harwood, Jr. 1936- WhoSSW 93
Bowman, Christine 1948- WhoAmW 93
Bowman, Christopher BioIn 17, NewYTBS 92 [port]
Bowman, Connie L. 1954- St&PR 93
Bowman, Daniel Oliver 1931- WhoSSW 93
Bowman, David W. Law&B 92
Bowman, David Wesley 1940- St&PR 93, WhoAm 92
Bowman, Dean Orlando 1909- WhoAm 92
Bowman, Don Jerry 1935- St&PR 93
Bowman, Donald E. 1948- St&PR 93
Bowman, Dorothy Louise 1927- WhoAm 92
Bowman, Dorothy Marie 1937- WhoAmW 93
Bowman, Edward Harry 1925- WhoAm 92
Bowman, Edward L. Law&B 92
Bowman, Elena Irene 1960- WhoAmW 93
Bowman, Elizabeth Sue 1954- WhoEmL 93
Bowman, Erin Gardner 1948- WhoAmW 93
Bowman, Euday (Louis) 1887-1949 Baker 92
Bowman, George Arthur, Jr. 1917- WhoWor 93
Bowman, George Leo 1935- WhoE 93
Bowman, Georgiana Hood 1937- WhoAmW 93
Bowman, Gerald L. St&PR 93
Bowman, Glenn D. Law&B 92
Bowman, H.L. 1928- St&PR 93
Bowman, Hazel Lois 1917- WhoAmW 93
Bowman, Helga BioIn 17
Bowman, J.C. WhoScE 91-1
Bowman, Jacqueline Bonnie WhoAmW 93
Bowman, James 1941- OxDcOp
Bowman, James Donald 1933- WhoAm 92
Bowman, James Edward 1923- WhoAm 92
Bowman, James Henry 1931- WhoAm 92, WhoWrEP 92
Bowman, James Kinsey 1933- WhoAm 92
Bowman, James S. 1934- St&PR 93
Bowman, James Scarboro, III 1952- WhoEmL 93, WhoSSW 93
Bowman, James (Thomas) 1941- Baker 92
Bowman, Jeanne Mangum 1925- WhoSSW 93
Bowman, Jim 1946- WhoSSW 93
Bowman, John St&PR 93
Bowman, John B. 1902- St&PR 93
Bowman, John Felipe 1931- St&PR 93
Bowman, John Maxwell 1925- WhoAm 92
Bowman, John R. Law&B 92
Bowman, Jon Robert 1954- WhoAm 92
Bowman, Joseph Searles 1920- WhoAm 92
Bowman, L. Allen 1932- St&PR 93
Bowman, Laird Price 1927- WhoAm 92
Bowman, Larry Alan 1948- WhoEmL 93
Bowman, Leah 1935- WhoAm 92
Bowman, Lorene AmWomPl
Bowman, Louise Morey AmWomPl
Bowman, Martha Alexander 1945- WhoAmW 93
Bowman, Martha Dietrich 1947- WhoAmW 93, WhoEmL 93
Bowman, Marvis 1936- WhoAm 92
Bowman, Mary Ann 1940- WhoAmW 93, WhoWrEP 92
Bowman, Mary Beth 1948- WhoEmL 93
Bowman, Mary Delia 1924- WhoAmW 93
Bowman, Michael Allen 1952- WhoEmL 93
Bowman, Michael Floyd 1953- WhoEmL 93
Bowman, Monroe Bengt 1901- WhoWor 93
Bowman, Neil O'Kane Law&B 92
Bowman, Neil O'Kane 1948- WhoSSW 93
Bowman, Pasco Middleton, II 1933- WhoAm 92
Bowman, Patricia 1961- BioIn 17
Bowman, Patricia Ann 1949- WhoWor 93
Bowman, Patricia Ann 1960- WhoAmW 93
Bowman, Patricia L. Law&B 92
Bowman, Peyton Graham, III 1929- WhoAm 92, WhoE 93
Bowman, R. Peter BioIn 17
Bowman, Rebecca Nipper 1955- WhoAmW 93
Bowman, Richard Andrew 1936- WhoSSW 93
Bowman, Richard Carl 1926- WhoAm 92
Bowman, Richard Frederick 1952- St&PR 93
Bowman, Robert Allott 1955- WhoAm 92
Bowman, Robert F. 1933- St&PR 93
Bowman, Robert G. 1921- St&PR 93
Bowman, Robert Gibson 1921- WhoAm 92
Bowman, Robert Henry 1915- St&PR 93
Bowman, Robert K. 1937- St&PR 93
Bowman, Robert William 1947- WhoSSW 93
Bowman, Roger M. 1950- St&PR 93, WhoIns 93
Bowman, Roger Manwaring 1916- WhoAm 92
Bowman, Ronald Paul 1956- WhoEmL 93
Bowman, Sarah A. 1812-1866 BioIn 17
Bowman, Scott WhoAm 92
Bowman, Susan D. Law&B 92
Bowman, Thea d1990 BioIn 17
Bowman, Ward Simon, Jr. 1911- WhoAm 92
Bowman, William Cameron WhoScE 91-1
Bowman, William Jackson, Jr. Law&B 92
Bowman, William Pepper 1956- WhoEmL 93
Bowman, William Scott 1933- WhoAm 92
Bowman-Dalton, Burdene Kathryn 1937- WhoAmW 93
Bowman-Randall, Gayle Darlene 1964- WhoAmW 93
Bowmer, Christopher Kenneth John 1946- St&PR 93
Bowmer, John Vance 1931- St&PR 93
Bown, Cyril John WhoScE 91-1
Bown, Jane 1925- BioIn 17
Bown, Oliver Hutchins 1921- WhoSSW 93
Bown, Robert T. Law&B 92
Bown, Thomas H., II 1944- St&PR 93
Bownan, David Tilden Law&B 92
Bowne, Dale Russell 1934- WhoE 93
Bowne, Martha Hoke 1931- WhoAm 92
Bownes, Hugh Henry 1920- WhoAm 92
Bowness, Rick 1955- WhoAm 92
Bowring, Eva 1892-1985 BioIn 17
Bowron, Edgar Peters 1943- WhoAm 92
Bowron, James BioIn 17
Bowron, Lottie Mabel 1879-1964 BioIn 17
Bowron, Richard Anderson 1924- WhoAm 92
Bowron, William A., Jr. 1953- St&PR 93
Bowron-White, Susan Law&B 92
Bows, Robert Alan 1949- WhoEmL 93
Bowser, Anita Olga 1920- WhoAmW 93
Bowser, James William 1929- WhoWrEP 92
Bowser, Kenneth MiSFD 9
Bowsher, Charles Arthur 1931- WhoAm 92, WhoE 93
Bowtell, Rita Evans 1931- WhoAmW 93
Bowyer, Adrian 1952- WhoWor 93
Bowyer, Allen Frank 1932- WhoWor 93
Bowyer, Bob d1992 NewYTBS 92
Bowyer, Charles Stuart 1934- WhoAm 92
Bowyer, D.E. WhoScE 91-1
Bowyer, Joan Elizabeth 1944- WhoAmW 93
Bowyer, John Robert WhoScE 91-1
Bowyer, Mark Alan 1963- WhoSSW 93
Bowyer, Shirley Caroline Smith 1949- WhoSSW 93
Bowyer, W.H. 1940- WhoScE 91-1
Bowyer, Worthy Lee, Jr. 1938- St&PR 93
Box, Barry Glenn 1958- WhoAm 92, WhoEmL 93, WhoSSW 93
Box, Brian Wayne 1965- WhoEmL 93
Box, Cloyce K. 1923- St&PR 93
Box, Duane Herbert 1927- St&PR 93
Box, Dwain D. 1916- WhoAm 92
Box, George Edward Pelham 1919- WhoAm 92
Box, George Lee 1934- St&PR 93
Box, James C. 1931- St&PR 93
Box, James Ellis, Jr. 1931- WhoAm 92
Box, Jerry Don 1942- St&PR 93
Box, Jerry W. 1938- St&PR 93
Box, John 1920- ConTFT 10
Box, John Harold 1929- WhoAm 92
Box, Michael Allister 1947- WhoWor 93
Box, Muriel 1905-1991 AnObit 1991
Box, Roger H. 1942- St&PR 93
Box, Roger Hayward 1942- WhoSSW 93
Box, Thadis Wayne 1929- WhoAm 92
Box, Tom D. Law&B 92
Box, Vernon George S. 1946- WhoE 93
Boxall, R.R. WhoScE 91-1

Boxall, Richard George 1936- WhoAm 92
Boxberg, Christian Ludwig 1670-1729 Baker 92
Boxberger, Matthew Dean 1959- WhoEmL 93
Boxberger, Michael D. WhoAm 92
Boxberger, Michael Dwight 1946- St&PR 93
Boxdorfer, James Jay 1957- St&PR 93
Boxenhorn, Burton 1928- WhoE 93
Boxer, Barbara 1940- BioIn 17, CngDr 91, NewYTBS 92, WhoAm 92, WhoAmW 93
Boxer, Jerome Harvey 1930- WhoAm 92, WhoWor 93
Boxer, Jonathan A. Law&B 92
Boxer, Matthew Law&B 92
Boxer, Robert Jacob 1935- WhoSSW 93
Boxer, Robert William 1933- WhoAm 92
Boxer, Rubin 1927- St&PR 93, WhoAm 92
Boxer, Stanley Robert 1926- WhoAm 92, WhoE 93
Boxill, Herbert John 1931- St&PR 93
Boxill, Nancy A. AfrAmBi [port]
Boxleitner, Bruce 1950- HolBB [port]
Boxler, Dorothy Bacino 1956- WhoAmW 93
Boxler, Patricia Ann 1947- WhoAmW 93
Boxus, Ph. WhoScE 91-2
Boy, Stephen Francis 1952- WhoE 93
Boya, Luis Joaquin 1936- WhoWor 93
Boya Balet, Luis J. 1936- WhoScE 91-3
Boyaci, Suleyman 1943- WhoScE 91-4
Boyadjieff, George Ivan 1938- St&PR 93
Boyadzhiev, Ljubomir WhoScE 91-4
Boyajian, Carole L. 1948- WhoEmL 93
Boyajian, Jerel ScF&FL 92
Boyajian, Jerry 1953- ScF&FL 92
Boyan, Norman John 1922- WhoAm 92
Boyan, William L., Jr. 1937- St&PR 93
Boyanovsky, Harold D. 1944- St&PR 93
Boyanton, Janet Shafer 1954- WhoWrEP 92
Boyars, Albert St&PR 93
Boyarsky, Alvin 1928-1990 BioIn 17
Boyarsky, Benjamin William 1934- WhoAm 92, WhoWrEP 92
Boyarsky, Rose Eisman 1924- WhoAmW 93
Boyarsky, Val David 1960- WhoEmL 93
Boyatt, Thomas David 1933- WhoAm 92
Boyatzis, Richard Eleftherios 1946- WhoEmL 93
Boyazis, James Law&B 92, WhoAm 92
Boyazis, James 1936- St&PR 93
Boyce, Allan R. 1943- WhoAm 92
Boyce, Bert Roy 1938- WhoAm 92
Boyce, C.B.C. WhoScE 91-1
Boyce, Chris 1943- ScF&FL 92
Boyce, Daniel Hobbs 1953- WhoEmL 93
Boyce, David Edward 1938- WhoAm 92
Boyce, Donald Nelson 1938- St&PR 93, WhoAm 92
Boyce, Edward Wayne, Jr. 1926- WhoAm 92
Boyce, Emily Stewart 1933- WhoAm 92, WhoAmW 93
Boyce, Gerald G. 1925- WhoAm 92
Boyce, Gerard Robert 1954- WhoEmL 93
Boyce, Ira F. 1910- St&PR 93
Boyce, James A., Jr. Law&B 92
Boyce, Joseph Nelson 1937- WhoAm 92
Boyce, Laura Ellen 1962- WhoAmW 93
Boyce, Loretta U. d1991 BioIn 17
Boyce, Mary AmWomPl
Boyce, Mary Elizabeth 1956- WhoAmW 93
Boyce, Meherwan Phiroz 1942- WhoSSW 93
Boyce, Meredith Ann 1946- WhoE 93
Boyce, Neith 1872-1951 AmWomPl
Boyce, Peter Bradford 1936- WhoAm 92, WhoE 93
Boyce, R.S.M. BioIn 17
Boyce, Randall C. Law&B 92
Boyce, Thomas C. St&PR 93
Boyce, Tracy Davenport 1966- WhoEmL 93
Boyce, Wayne 1926- WhoWrEP 92
Boyce, William 1711-1779 Baker 92
Boychenko, Anthony Steven 1948- St&PR 93
Boychuk, Michael Ted 1955- St&PR 93
Boycks, Barbara Elizabeth 1944- St&PR 93
Boycott, B.B. WhoScE 91-1
Boyd, Alan Conduitt 1926- WhoAm 92
Boyd, Alberta Jeannine 1950- WhoAmW 93
Boyd, Ann Fisher 1933- WhoAmW 93
Boyd, Ann Fisher 1937- St&PR 93
Boyd, Anne (Elizabeth) 1946- Baker 92
Boyd, Arnold David 1946- St&PR 93
Boyd, Asadullah BioIn 17
Boyd, Belle 1844-1900 BioIn 17
Boyd, Betty 1924- WhoAmW 93
Boyd, Billy Carl 1950- WhoSSW 93
Boyd, Billy Willard 1948- WhoEmL 93
Boyd, Bob 1926- BioIn 17
Boyd, Bobbie Marguerite 1957- WhoAmW 93, WhoEmL 93
Boyd, Brian (David) 1952- ConAu 139, WhoWor 93
Boyd, Bruce L. 1938- St&PR 93, WhoIns 93
Boyd, C. Edward 1936- St&PR 93
Boyd, Candy Dawson DcAmChF 1985
Boyd, Candy Dawson 1946- BlkAull 92, ConAu 138, SmATA 72 [port]
Boyd, Catherine Emma 1918- WhoWrEP 92
Boyd, Charles BioIn 17
Boyd, Charles Graham 1938- WhoAm 92
Boyd, Charles H. 1934- St&PR 93
Boyd, Clarence 1942- St&PR 93
Boyd, Clarence Elmo 1911- WhoAm 92, WhoSSW 93
Boyd, Crowther M. 1908- St&PR 93
Boyd, Daniel BioIn 17
Boyd, Daniel 1956- MiSFD 9
Boyd, Danny Douglass 1933- WhoSSW 93
Boyd, David Malcolm 1951- WhoWor 93
Boyd, David Parker 1957- WhoEmL 93
Boyd, David Walter Law&B 92
Boyd, David William 1941- WhoAm 92
Boyd, Dawn Michele 1952- WhoAm 92, WhoEmL 93
Boyd, Deborah Ann 1955- WhoAmW 93
Boyd, Dennis BioIn 17
Boyd, Derek Raymond WhoScE 91-1
Boyd, Don MiSFD 9
Boyd, Edson 1912- St&PR 93
Boyd, Edward George Charles Arthur WhoScE 91-1
Boyd, Edward Lee 1930- St&PR 93, WhoAm 92, WhoSSW 93
Boyd, Edward Lee 1932- WhoWor 93
Boyd, Edwin Louis 1932- St&PR 93
Boyd, Eleanor Elizabeth H. 1935- WhoAmW 93
Boyd, Emilie Lou 1935- WhoSSW 93
Boyd, Eva Philips AmWomPl
Boyd, Francis Virgil 1922- WhoAm 92
Boyd, Frank E., Jr. 1923- St&PR 93
Boyd, Frank E., III 1951- St&PR 93
Boyd, Fred 1938- St&PR 93
Boyd, Frolly 1950- WhoIns 93
Boyd, Gary Delane 1932- WhoAm 92
Boyd, Gary Don 1947- WhoSSW 93
Boyd, George Edward 1911- WhoAm 92
Boyd, George Golden 1944- St&PR 93
Boyd, Gordon McArthur 1946- WhoE 93
Boyd, Graham Gregory Law&B 92
Boyd, Hallam 1928- St&PR 93
Boyd, Harry Dalton 1923- WhoAm 92
Boyd, Herbert Reed, Jr. 1925- WhoSSW 93
Boyd, Howard Taney 1909- WhoAm 92
Boyd, Ian Alexander WhoScE 91-1
Boyd, Ian William 1958- WhoWor 93
Boyd, J. Cookman, Jr. 1906- St&PR 93
Boyd, James Brown 1937- WhoAm 92
Boyd, James E. 1948- St&PR 93
Boyd, James Emory 1906- WhoSSW 93
Boyd, James R. 1921- St&PR 93
Boyd, James R. 1946- St&PR 93
Boyd, James Rice 1952- WhoSSW 93
Boyd, James Robert 1946- WhoAm 92
Boyd, Jane Elizabeth 1946- WhoEmL 93
Boyd, Jerry Lee 1955- St&PR 93
Boyd, Jimmie d1991 BioIn 17
Boyd, Joanne E. Law&B 92
Boyd, Joe Dan 1934- WhoSSW 93
Boyd, John 1912- BioIn 17
Boyd, John 1919- ScF&FL 92
Boyd, John A. 1928- WhoIns 93
Boyd, John Hamilton 1924- WhoAm 92, WhoSSW 93
Boyd, John Howard 1950- WhoE 93
Boyd, John Kent 1910- WhoWor 93
Boyd, John Parker 1764-1830 HarEnMi
Boyd, John Patrick 1949- WhoEmL 93
Boyd, John S. WhoScE 91-1
Boyd, John S. 1946- St&PR 93
Boyd, John Thomas 1927- WhoSSW 93
Boyd, John Wells 1950- WhoEmL 93
Boyd, John Willard 1925- WhoSSW 93
Boyd, Joseph A. 1921- St&PR 93
Boyd, Joseph Arthur, Jr. 1916- WhoAm 92
Boyd, Joseph Don 1926- WhoAm 92
Boyd, Josephine Watson 1927- WhoAmW 93
Boyd, Julia Greer 1925- WhoAmW 93
Boyd, Julianne Mamana 1944- WhoAmW 93
Boyd, Julius 1923- St&PR 93
Boyd, Kelly Alvis Law&B 92
Boyd, Kenneth Wade 1938- WhoSSW 93
Boyd, Landis Lee 1923- WhoAm 92
Boyd, Larry Chester 1958- WhoE 93, WhoEmL 93
Boyd, Lauren Denise Law&B 92
Boyd, Leona Potter 1907- WhoAmW 93
Boyd, Linda Joyce 1946- WhoEmL 93
Boyd, Linda Smith 1961- WhoE 93
Boyd, Linn 1800-1859 PolPar
Boyd, Liona Maria WhoAm 92
Boyd, Louis Jefferson 1928- WhoAm 92
Boyd, Louise Arner 1887-1972 Expl 93 [port]
Boyd, Louise Mason 1947- WhoSSW 93
Boyd, Louise Yvonne 1959- WhoEmL 93
Boyd, Malcolm 1923- WhoAm 92, WhoWrEP 92
Boyd, Marcia Lynn 1959- WhoAmW 93
Boyd, Martha Law&B 92
Boyd, Mary BioIn 17
Boyd, Mary Dexter 1913- WhoAmW 93
Boyd, Mary Jo 1940- WhoSSW 93
Boyd, Michael Alan Law&B 92
Boyd, Michael Alan 1937- St&PR 93, WhoAm 92
Boyd, Michael C. Law&B 92
Boyd, Michael Delen 1956- St&PR 93
Boyd, Michael Joel 1938- WhoIns 93
Boyd, Mildred Wernet 1947- WhoE 93
Boyd, Milton John 1941- WhoAm 92
Boyd, Morton 1936- St&PR 93, WhoAm 92, WhoSSW 93
Boyd, Nancy AmWomPl
Boyd, Oil Can BioIn 17
Boyd, Orsemus Bronson, Mrs. BioIn 17
Boyd, Peter MacKerer 1955- St&PR 93
Boyd, Ralph E. 1936- St&PR 93
Boyd, Randall M. 1946- St&PR 93, WhoIns 93
Boyd, Rhonda Weiderspon 1958- WhoEmL 93
Boyd, Richard Alfred 1927- WhoAm 92
Boyd, Robert Arthur 1918- St&PR 93
Boyd, Robert David Hugh WhoScE 91-1
Boyd, Robert E., Jr. 1926- St&PR 93
Boyd, Robert Ernest 1958- WhoSSW 93
Boyd, Robert Friend 1927- St&PR 93
Boyd, Robert Giddings, Jr. 1940- WhoAm 92
Boyd, Robert Jamison 1930- St&PR 93
Boyd, Robert Methven, Jr. 1933- St&PR 93
Boyd, Robert Sprott 1941- WhoWor 93
Boyd, Robert T. Law&B 92
Boyd, Robert T. 1933- St&PR 93
Boyd, Robert Thompson 1914- WhoE 93
Boyd, Robert William 1948- WhoE 93
Boyd, Robert Wright, III 1945- WhoAm 92
Boyd, Saifullah BioIn 17
Boyd, Sally 1947- WhoAmW 93
Boyd, Shirley R. Law&B 92
Boyd, Stephen Blake 1954- WhoSSW 93
Boyd, Stephen Curtis 1949- WhoEmL 93
Boyd, Stephen Fayen 1952- St&PR 93
Boyd, Stephen Mather 1934- WhoAm 92
Boyd, Stuart Robert 1939- WhoAm 92
Boyd, Susan Isabel 1946- WhoAmW 93
Boyd, Theophilus Bartholomew, III 1947- WhoWor 93
Boyd, Thomas, III 1936- St&PR 93
Boyd, Thomas James Morrow 1932- WhoWor 93
Boyd, Thomas Marshall 1946- WhoAm 92
Boyd, Timothy John 1967- WhoSSW 93
Boyd, Virginia Ann 1954- WhoAm 92
Boyd, Virginia Ann Lewis 1944- WhoE 93
Boyd, Wallace M., Jr. BioIn 17
Boyd, Waymon Lewis 1933- St&PR 93
Boyd, Willard L. 1927- St&PR 93
Boyd, Willard Lee 1927- WhoAm 92
Boyd, William 1895-1972 BioIn 17
Boyd, William 1952- BioIn 17, ConLC 70 [port]
Boyd, William, Jr. 1915- St&PR 93, WhoAm 92
Boyd, William Beaty 1923- WhoAm 92
Boyd, William Douglas, Jr. 1929- WhoWor 93
Boyd, William Richard 1916- WhoAm 92
Boyda, Kenneth L. 1944- St&PR 93
Boyda, Robert G. Law&B 92
Boyde, Alan WhoScE 91-1
Boydell, Brian (Patrick) 1917- Baker 92
Boyden, Allen Marston 1908- WhoAm 92
Boyden, Bruce Robert 1949- WhoEmL 93
Boyden, David Dodge 1910-1986 Baker 92
Boyden, Frederick B. Law&B 92
Boyden, Joel Michael 1937- WhoAm 92, WhoWor 93
Boyden, Robert W. 1932- St&PR 93
Boyden, Walter Lincoln 1932- WhoAm 92
Boyd-Kray, Peggy 1934- St&PR 93
Boyd-Meis, Betty Sue 1952- WhoEmL 93
Boyd-Webb, Sandra Elaine 1964- WhoAmW 93
Boyea, Bruce Walter 1951- St&PR 93
Boyen, Hermann von 1771-1848 HarEnMi
Boyer, Alan R. 1946- St&PR 93
Boyer, Calvin James 1939- WhoAm 92
Boyer, Carl, III 1937- WhoWor 93
Boyer, Charles 1897-1978 IntDcF 2-3 [port]
Boyer, Cheryl Talley 1959- WhoAmW 93
Boyer, Clell Crittenden, Jr. Law&B 92
Boyer, Daniel Christopher St&PR 93
Boyer, David Creighton 1930- WhoAm 92
Boyer, David S. 1942- St&PR 93
Boyer, David Scott 1942- WhoAm 92
Boyer, Dawn Doty 1964- WhoAmW 93
Boyer, Edith E.L. AmWomPl
Boyer, Edwin Lyman 1939- WhoE 93
Boyer, Elizabeth ScF&FL 92
Boyer, Eric 1939- WhoAsAP 91
Boyer, Ernest L. BioIn 17
Boyer, Ernest LeRoy 1928- WhoAm 92
Boyer, Ford Sylvester 1934- WhoWor 93
Boyer, George Edward, Jr. 1955- WhoEmL 93
Boyer, George T. 1928- St&PR 93
Boyer, Gregory Martin 1954- WhoE 93
Boyer, Gregory Myron 1956- WhoSSW 93
Boyer, Guy H. 1954- St&PR 93
Boyer, H. Stacey Law&B 92
Boyer, Herbert Wayne 1936- WhoAm 92
Boyer, James Lorenzen 1936- WhoAm 92
Boyer, James Rahn 1933- St&PR 93
Boyer, Jean 1935- WhoScE 91-2
Boyer, John H. 1950- St&PR 93
Boyer, John W., Jr. 1928- St&PR 93
Boyer, Katherine Elizabeth 1942- WhoSSW 93
Boyer, Kaye Kittle 1942- WhoAmW 93
Boyer, Laura Mercedes 1934- WhoAmW 93
Boyer, Lenora Leone 1945- WhoAmW 93
Boyer, Lester Leroy, Jr. 1937- WhoAm 92
Boyer, Lillian Buckley 1916- WhoAm 92, WhoAmW 93
Boyer, Marcel 1943- WhoAm 92
Boyer, Nicodemus Elijah 1925- WhoWor 93
Boyer, Peter Jay 1950- WhoEmL 93
Boyer, Philip B. 1940- St&PR 93
Boyer, Raymond Foster 1910- WhoAm 92
Boyer, Robert Allan 1934- WhoE 93, WhoWor 93
Boyer, Robert Allen 1916- WhoAm 92
Boyer, Robert Ernst 1929- WhoAm 92
Boyer, Robert H. 1937- ScF&FL 92
Boyer, Robert Jay 1951- WhoEmL 93
Boyer, Robert Malcolm Law&B 92
Boyer, Ronald E. 1937- St&PR 93
Boyer, Stephan P. 1956- St&PR 93
Boyer, Susan Ruth 1961- WhoAmW 93
Boyer, Susan Spark 1943- WhoWrEP 92
Boyer, Thomas G. Law&B 92
Boyer, Timothy Howard 1941- WhoE 93
Boyer, Vincent Saull 1918- WhoAm 92
Boyer, Wilbur B., Jr. 1945- St&PR 93
Boyer, William Davis 1924- WhoSSW 93
Boyer, William H(arrison) 1924- WhoWrEP 92
Boyers, Charles Frank 1942- St&PR 93
Boyers, Robert 1942- WhoAm 92
Boyes, Fred Howard 1933- WhoE 93
Boyes, Stephen Richard 1950- WhoSSW 93, WhoWor 93
Boyesen, H.H. 1848-1895 GayN
Boyett, Bob BioIn 17
Boyett, Gary Quin 1950- WhoSSW 93
Boyett, Shirley Ann 1938- WhoAmW 93
Boyett, Steven R. 1960- ScF&FL 92
Boyette, Charles Otis 1935- WhoSSW 93
Boyette, Flip Huntus 1920- St&PR 93
Boyette, Ivern WhoWrEP 92
Boyette, Judith W. Law&B 92
Boyette, Marsha Ann 1952- WhoEmL 93
Boy George 1961- Baker 92
Boyher, Jeffery L. Law&B 92
Bo Yibo 1908- WhoWor 93
Boyington, Gregory 1912-1988 BioIn 17
Boyington, Pappy 1912-1988 BioIn 17
Boyk, Fredric Michael 1953- St&PR 93
Boykan, Martin 1931- Baker 92, WhoAm 92
Boyke, Paul 1940- St&PR 93
Boyken, Donald Richard 1952- WhoSSW 93
Boykin, A. Hugh 1925- St&PR 93
Boykin, Frances Lewis WhoE 93, WhoWor 93
Boykin, Hamilton Haight 1939- St&PR 93
Boykin, Joseph Floyd, Jr. 1940- WhoAm 92
Boykin, Lykes M. 1919- WhoAm 92
Boykin, Melanie Poe 1960- WhoAmW 93
Boykin, Raymond Francis 1953- WhoEmL 93
Boykin, Robert Heath 1926- WhoAm 92
Boykin, Robert N., Jr. 1947- St&PR 93
Boykin, Susan Bell 1957- WhoAmW 93
Boykin, Wilburn Tinsley, Jr. 1955- WhoEmL 93
Boykin, William Johnson 1919- St&PR 93
Boykins, Genora Kendrick Law&B 92
Boyko, Christopher Allan 1954- WhoEmL 93, WhoWor 93
Boyko, Gregory Andrew 1951- St&PR 93, WhoAm 92, WhoIns 93
Boyko, Yelena Aleksandrovna 1933- WhoWor 93
Boylan, Anne Mary 1947- WhoAmW 93
Boylan, Brian Richard 1936- WhoWor 93
Boylan, Clare 1948- ConAu 136
Boylan, D.J., Jr. 1924- St&PR 93

Boylan, David Ray 1922- WhoAm 92
Boylan, Dean M. 1926- St&PR 93
Boylan, Elizabeth Shippee 1946- WhoAm 92, WhoAmW 93, WhoEmL 93
Boylan, Gary Lynn 1952- WhoEmL 93
Boylan, Glenn Gerard 1959- WhoEmL 93, WhoSSW 93
Boylan, Gwendolyn Anne 1946- WhoAmW 93
Boylan, James Finney 1958- ScF&FL 92
Boylan, James George 1937- WhoSSW 93
Boylan, James J. Law&B 92
Boylan, Jeanne-Marie 1949- St&PR 93
Boylan, John L. 1955- St&PR 93
Boylan, John Lester 1955- WhoEmL 93
Boylan, John Patrick 1941- WhoAm 92
Boylan, John Wilson 1914-1991 BioIn 17
Boylan, MaryAnn Hair 1949- WhoAmW 93
Boylan, Merle Nelson 1925- WhoAm 92
Boylan, Michael J. Law&B 92, St&PR 93
Boylan, Paul Charles 1939- WhoAm 92
Boylan, Peter James 1936- WhoAm 92
Boylan, Roger Brendan 1951- WhoWrEP 92
Boylan, Stanley Louis 1941- WhoE 93
Boylan, William Alvin 1924- WhoAm 92, WhoE 93, WhoWor 93
Boyland, Joseph Francis 1931- St&PR 93, WhoAm 92
Boyle, Alexander Robert Mills 1937- St&PR 93
Boyle, Amy Christine 1963- WhoAmW 93
Boyle, Andrew 1919-1991 AnObit 1991, BioIn 17
Boyle, Anna Marie 1926- WhoAmW 93
Boyle, Barbara Dorman 1935- WhoAm 92, WhoAmW 93
Boyle, Barbara Jane 1936- WhoAmW 93
Boyle, Barbara Merle Princelau 1923- WhoAmW 93, WhoE 93
Boyle, Beth C. 1965- WhoAmW 93
Boyle, Bradley C. 1956- St&PR 93
Boyle, Bruce James 1931- WhoAm 92
Boyle, C.R., III 1948- St&PR 93
Boyle, Carolyn A. 1940- St&PR 93
Boyle, Carolyn Anne 1940- WhoIns 93
Boyle, Charles Keith 1930- WhoAm 92
Boyle, Clyde Frank 1923- St&PR 93
Boyle, Daniel E. 1931- St&PR 93
Boyle, Daniel Edward, Jr. 1931- WhoAm 92
Boyle, David P. 1964- St&PR 93
Boyle, Dennis O'Neil 1952- St&PR 93
Boyle, Donna Davis 1962- WhoEmL 93
Boyle, Edward James, Jr. 1940- St&PR 93
Boyle, Edward Patrick 1912- St&PR 93
Boyle, Elizabeth Mary Hunt 1956- WhoEmL 93
Boyle, Francis Anthony 1950- WhoEmL 93
Boyle, Francis Joseph 1927- WhoAm 92, WhoE 93
Boyle, Francis Joseph 1945- WhoAm 92
Boyle, Francis William, Jr. 1951- WhoWor 93
Boyle, George Frederick 1886-1948 Baker 92
Boyle, Glenn Edward 1952- WhoEmL 93
Boyle, Harry J. 1915- WhoCanL 92
Boyle, Howard H. 1921- St&PR 93
Boyle, Ira Lee 1950- St&PR 93
Boyle, James Joseph 1951- WhoE 93
Boyle, James Torrance WhoScE 91-1
Boyle, Jane A. Law&B 92
Boyle, JoAnne Woodyard 1935- WhoAmW 93
Boyle, Joanne Xenia 1945- WhoAmW 93
Boyle, John David 1946- WhoWrEP 92
Boyle, John E. Whiteford 1915- WhoWrEP 92
Boyle, John Edward 1948- WhoEmL 93
Boyle, John Edward Whiteford 1915- WhoAm 92
Boyle, John F. Law&B 92
Boyle, John J. 1930- St&PR 93
Boyle, John L. 1934- St&PR 93
Boyle, John Raymond 1941- WhoAm 92
Boyle, John T. 1921- WhoIns 93
Boyle, John William 1929- WhoAm 92
Boyle, John William 1937- St&PR 93
Boyle, Joseph E. 1921- St&PR 93
Boyle, Joseph F. d1992 NewYTBS 92
Boyle, Joseph Francis 1924- WhoAm 92
Boyle, Joseph T. Law&B 92
Boyle, Josephine ScF&FL 92
Boyle, Kathleen M. Law&B 92
Boyle, Kay 1902- BioIn 17, WhoAm 92, WhoAmW 93, WhoWrEP 92
Boyle, Kay 1902-1992 NewYTBS 92 [port]
Boyle, Kay 1903- AmWomWr 92
Boyle, Kevin John 1955- WhoE 93, WhoEmL 93, WhoWor 93
Boyle, Lara Flynn BioIn 17
Boyle, Lara Flynn 1971?- ConTFT 10
Boyle, Larry Monroe 1943- WhoAm 92
Boyle, Lawrence D. 1942- St&PR 93
Boyle, Lynnette Zellner 1952- WhoEmL 93
Boyle, M. Katheryn Law&B 92
Boyle, M. Ross 1935- WhoAm 92
Boyle, Mark St&PR 93
Boyle, Mark Cameron Law&B 92
Boyle, Mark S. Law&B 92
Boyle, Mary Ann Josette 1949- WhoAmW 93
Boyle, Matthew A. Law&B 92
Boyle, Matthew Anthony 1944- St&PR 93
Boyle, Michael F. 1955- St&PR 93
Boyle, Michael John 1944- WhoAm 92
Boyle, Patricia Jean WhoAm 92, WhoAmW 93
Boyle, Peter 1933- WhoAm 92
Boyle, Pyotr J. 1951- WhoE 93
Boyle, Renee Kent 1926- WhoAm 92, WhoAmW 93, WhoE 93
Boyle, Richard Guy 1938- St&PR 93, WhoAm 92
Boyle, Richard James 1943- St&PR 93, WhoAm 92
Boyle, Richard John 1932- WhoAm 92
Boyle, Robert 1627-1691 BioIn 17
Boyle, Robert Daniel 1965- WhoE 93, WhoWor 93
Boyle, Robert H. BioIn 17
Boyle, Robert Patrick 1913- WhoAm 92
Boyle, Scott Alan 1955- St&PR 93
Boyle, Stephen P. 1940- St&PR 93
Boyle, Susan M. 1948- St&PR 93
Boyle, T. Coraghessan BioIn 17
Boyle, T. Coraghessan 1948- MagSAmL [port], ScF&FL 92
Boyle, Terence Law&B 92
Boyle, Terence 1952- WhoEmL 93
Boyle, Terrence W. 1945- WhoSSW 93
Boyle, Thomas C. Law&B 92
Boyle, Willard Sterling 1924- WhoAm 92
Boyle, William A. d1990 BioIn 17
Boyle, William C.H., Jr. 1953- WhoEmL 93, WhoSSW 93
Boyle, William Charles 1936- WhoAm 92
Boyle, William George 1930- WhoSSW 93
Boyle, William Leo, Jr. 1933- WhoAm 92, WhoE 93
Boyle, William M., Jr. 1902-1961 PolPar
Boyle, William Marshall 1902-1961 BioIn 17
Boyle, William Pickard, Jr. 1933- St&PR 93, WhoAm 92
Boyle, William R. 1932- WhoAm 92
Boyle, William W. 1934- St&PR 93
Boyles, Beatrice C. 1915- WhoAmW 93
Boyles, Carol Ann Patterson 1932- WhoSSW 93
Boyles, David Charles, Jr. 1953- WhoSSW 93
Boyles, Diane Horton 1948- WhoAmW 93
Boyles, Donna Lou Cochran 1935- WhoAmW 93
Boyles, Harlan Edward 1929- WhoAm 92, WhoSSW 93
Boyles, James Kenneth 1916- WhoAm 92
Boyles, William Archer 1951- WhoEmL 93
Boyles, William Ray 1948- St&PR 93
Boyles-Sprenkel, Carolee Anita 1953- WhoWrEP 92
Boyll, David Lloyd 1940- WhoAm 92
Boyll, Randall 1962- ScF&FL 92
Boylston, Adrian F. 1927- St&PR 93
Boylston, Arthur William WhoScE 91-1
Boylston, Benjamin Calvin 1932- St&PR 93, WhoAm 92, WhoE 93, WhoWor 93
Boylston, Helen Dore 1895-1984 MajAI [port]
Boylston, John 1920- St&PR 93
Boylston, Robert Judson 1931- WhoSSW 93
Boym, Svetlana 1959- ConAu 139
Boyman, John Edward George 1937- WhoAm 92
Boyne, Allan L. 1936- St&PR 93
Boyne, Robert D. 1930- St&PR 93
Boyne, Walter James 1929- WhoAm 92
Boynton, Bruce Ryland 1948- WhoEmL 93
Boynton, Harry Gene 1928- WhoSSW 93
Boynton, Lisa Passey BioIn 17
Boynton, Lois Ann 1959- WhoSSW 93
Boynton, Nancy H. 1933- St&PR 93
Boynton, Rex Powell 1951- WhoSSW 93
Boynton, Richard S. 1934- St&PR 93
Boynton, Robert Granville 1951- WhoEmL 93
Boynton, Wyman Pender 1908- WhoWor 93
Boyom, Bodie Michel Nguiffo 1940- WhoWor 93
Boyriven, Mariette Hartley 1940- WhoAm 92, WhoAmW 93
Boyse, Edward Arthur 1923- WhoAm 92
Boysen, Connie Jean 1958- WhoEmL 93
Boysen, Harry 1904- WhoAm 92
Boysen, Lars 1948- WhoEmL 93
Boysen, Melicent Pearl 1943- WhoAmW 93
Boyt, Patrick Elmer 1940- WhoSSW 93
Boyt, Rose 1958- BioIn 17
Boyter, Scott M. 1947- WhoEmL 93
Boytim, James Alvin 1937- WhoE 93
Boytim, Thomas Edward 1948- WhoE 93
Boyum, Joy Gould 1934- WhoE 93
Boyvin, Jacques c. 1649-1706 Baker 92
Boz MajAI
Boza, Clara Brizeida 1952- WhoAmW 93, WhoEmL 93
Boza, Enrrique Agustin 1963- WhoSSW 93
Bozac, A.N. Law&B 92
Bozack, Michael James 1952- WhoEmL 93, WhoSSW 93
Bozarov, Mihail WhoScE 91-4
Bozarth, Robert S. Law&B 92
Bozay, Attila 1939- Baker 92
Bozcuk, Ali Nihat 1941- WhoScE 91-4
Bozdech, Marek Jiri 1946- WhoAm 92
Bozec, Patrick P.M. 1940 WhoScE 91-2
Bozeman, Adda Bruemmer 1908- WhoAm 92, WhoWor 93
Bozeman, Carlton Michael 1957- WhoEmL 93, WhoSSW 93
Bozeman, Frank Carmack 1933- WhoAm 92, WhoSSW 93
Bozeman, Lynne Norman 1961- WhoEmL 93
Bozeman, Sylvia Trimble 1947- WhoEmL 93
Bozeman, Thomas Hunt 1958- WhoEmL 93
Bozer, Ahmet Yuksel 1928- WhoScE 91-4
Bozhinov, Nikolai Sashov 1950- WhoWor 93
Bozic, Darijan 1933- Baker 92
Bozic, Michael C. WhoAm 92
Bozic, Streten ScF&FL 92
Bozich, Anthony Thomas 1924- WhoAm 92
Bozich, Robert 1942- WhoE 93
Bozigian, Howard Kirk 1951- WhoEmL 93
Bozin, James Andrew 1953- WhoSSW 93
Boznanska, Olga 1865-1940 PolBiDi
Bozniak, Murray M. 1945- WhoAm 92
Boznos, William P. Law&B 92
Bozo, Sandor 1933- WhoScE 91-4
Bozone, Billie Rae 1935- WhoAm 92, WhoAmW 93
Bozorgmanesh, H. 1943- St&PR 93
Bozorth, Squire Newland 1935- WhoAm 92
Bozovich, Vesna Law&B 92
Bozoyan, Sylvia 1953- WhoAmW 93
Bozsa, Deborah Ann 1953- WhoEmL 93
Bozza, Eugene 1905- Baker 92
Bozza, Linda Susan 1949- WhoWrEP 92
Bozzacchi, Gianni MiSFD 9
Bozzay, William 1923- St&PR 93
Bozzelli, Andrew Joseph, Jr. 1931- WhoAm 92
Bozzelli, John Wolf 1947- WhoEmL 93
Bozzelli, Joseph W. 1942- WhoE 93
Bozzi, Nicholas C. 1938- St&PR 93
Bozzo, Ana Cristina d1991 BioIn 17
Bozzo, Stephen E. Law&B 92
Bozzola, Furio WhoScE 91-3
Bozzone, Robert Peter 1933- St&PR 93
Bozzuto, Adam 1916- St&PR 93
Bozzuto, Carl Richard 1947- WhoEmL 93
Bozzuto, Michael Adam 1956- St&PR 93, WhoAm 92
Braakman, Reinder 1926- WhoScE 91-3
Braam, Geert Pieter Adriaan 1930- WhoWor 93
Braasch, George H. Law&B 92
Braasch, John William 1922- WhoAm 92
Braasch, Steven Mark 1954- WhoSSW 93
Braasch, William Michael 1947- WhoEmL 93
Braathe, Peder B. 1919- WhoScE 91-4
Braathen, Ole Sigmund 1933- WhoScE 91-4
Braatz, Clayton Ross 1940- St&PR 93
Braatz, Gary Orlon 1959- St&PR 93
Braatz, Thomas Drew 1962- WhoEmL 93
Brabander, R. G. R. Law&B 92
Brabec, Barbara 1937- WhoWrEP 92
Brabec, Rosemary Jean 1951- WhoAmW 93
Brabec, Vlastislav 1932- WhoScE 91-4
Brabham, Peggy Jean WhoAmW 93
Brabham, William Lewis 1945- St&PR 93
Brabin, Charles J. 1883-1957 MiSFD 9N
Brabourne, John Ulick Knatchbull 1924- WhoWor 93
Braboy, Barbara Ann 1952- WhoAmW 93
Brabson, Max LaFayette 1926- WhoAm 92
Brabston, Mary Elizabeth 1948- WhoEmL 93
Braby, Thomas Richard 1931- WhoSSW 93
Braccesi, Alessandro 1937- WhoWor 93
Braccini, Lisa Ann 1963- WhoE 93
Bracciolini, Poggio 1380-1459 BioIn 17
Bracco, Frediano Vittorio 1937- WhoAm 92
Bracco, Lorraine BioIn 17
Bracco, Lorraine 1955?- ConTFT 10
Bracco, Umberto 1930- WhoScE 91-4
Brace, Allen St&PR 93
Brace, Elizabeth Hanchett AmWomPl
Brace, Gladys AmWomPl
Brace, James Frederick 1945- St&PR 93
Brace, Robert Dewitt 1930- St&PR 93
Bracebridge, Clarence E. d1991 BioIn 17
Bracefield, Hilary Maxwell 1938- WhoWor 93
Braceful, Brenda Bogerty 1951- WhoAmW 93
Braceland, John G. St&PR 93
Bracete, Juan Manuel 1951- WhoEmL 93, WhoSSW 93
Bracewell, Ronald Newbold 1921- BioIn 17, WhoAm 92
Bracewell, William Riley 1938- WhoSSW 93
Bracewell-Milnes, (John) Barry 1931- ConAu 37NR
Bracey, Cookie Frances Lee 1945- WhoAmW 93, WhoE 93, WhoWor 93
Bracey, Michael Alan 1954- WhoEmL 93
Bracey, Nettie Louise 1939- WhoAmW 93
Bracey, Willie Earl 1950- WhoEmL 93
Brach, Brian D. 1970- St&PR 93
Brach, Gerard 1927- ConAu 138
Brachamios OxDcByz
Bracher, Karl Dietrich 1922- ConAu 40NR
Bracher, Paul H. 1956- St&PR 93
Brachet, Christian 1943- WhoUN 92
Brachet, Marc Etienne 1953- WhoWor 93
Brachet, Marcelle WhoScE 91-2
Brachet, Philippe WhoScE 91-2
Brachman, Malcolm K. 1926- St&PR 93, WhoSSW 93
Brachman, Philip Sigmund 1927- WhoAm 92
Brachman, Richard John, II 1951- WhoWor 93
Bracho, Salvador 1944- WhoScE 91-3
Bracho del Pino, Salvador 1944- WhoWor 93
Brachtenbach, Robert F. 1931- WhoAm 92
Brachtl, Susan P. 1941- St&PR 93, WhoAmW 93
Brack, Andre 1938- WhoScE 91-2
Brack, Ben BioIn 17
Brack, Manfred 1943- WhoWor 93
Brack, O. M., Jr. 1938- WhoAm 92
Brack, Pat BioIn 17
Brack, Reginald Kufeld, Jr. 1937- WhoAm 92
Brack, William Dennis 1939- ConAu 136, WhoAm 92
Bracke, Alexandre Marie 1861-1955 BioIn 17
Bracke, James W. St&PR 93
Bracke, W. WhoScE 91-2
Brackeen, Richard E. BioIn 17
Brackeen, Richard E. d1992 NewYTBS 92 [port]
Bracken, Barton William 1955- WhoIns 93
Bracken, Brendan 1901-1958 BioIn 17
Bracken, Charles Herbert 1921- WhoAm 92
Bracken, Eddie 1920- QDrFCA 92 [port], WhoAm 92
Bracken, Frank A. 1934- WhoAm 92
Bracken, Gary K. 1939- St&PR 93
Bracken, George R. 1945- St&PR 93
Bracken, Harold Ronnie 1946- WhoSSW 93
Bracken, Harry McFarland 1926- WhoAm 92
Bracken, Jeanne Munn 1946- WhoWrEP 92
Bracken, John H. Law&B 92
Bracken, Kathleen Ann 1947- WhoAmW 93
Bracken, L. Anthony 1933- St&PR 93
Bracken, Lawrence Joseph 1944- WhoSSW 93
Bracken, Linda Law&B 92
Bracken, Louis Everett 1947- WhoE 93, WhoEmL 93, WhoSSW 93, WhoWor 93
Bracken, Nancy Jean 1944- WhoE 93
Bracken, Nanette Beattie 1950- WhoEmL 93
Bracken, Peg 1918- WhoAm 92, WhoAmW 93
Brackenbury, Alison 1953- ConAu 136
Brackenbury, Ian F. 1946- WhoScE 91-1
Brackenbury, Ian Furnival 1946- WhoWor 93
Brackett, Edward Boone, III 1936- WhoWor 93
Brackett, F. David 1957- St&PR 93
Brackett, Gail Burger 1950- WhoAmW 93, WhoEmL 93

Brackett, Leigh 1915-1978 *BioIn 17, ScF&FL 92*
Brackett, Sally Lee Martin 1932- *WhoAmW 93*
Brackett, Tracey Smith 1961- *WhoEmL 93*
Brackett, William Savage 1931- *WhoSSW 93*
Brackin, Phyllis Jean 1946- *WhoSSW 93*
Brackin, Robert Elton 1953- *WhoSSW 93*
Brackley, William Lowell 1919- *WhoAm 92*
Brackman, Al d1992 *NewYTBS 92*
Brackman, Raphael M. 1925- *St&PR 93*
Brackman, Roberta R. *Law&B 92*
Brackman, Selma 1922- *WhoE 93*
Brackmann, Holly Jean 1947- *WhoEmL 93*
Brackney, Margaret Louise 1963- *WhoAmW 93*
Brackney, William Austin 1928- *St&PR 93*
Brackney, William Henry 1948- *WhoAm 92*
Braconier, Fredrik 1947- *WhoWor 93*
Bracy, John C. *Law&B 92*
Bracy, Michael Blakeslee 1941- *WhoAm 92*
Bradbeer, Clive 1933- *WhoAm 92, WhoSSW 93*
Bradbeer, Joseph William *WhoScE 91-1*
Bradberry, Richard Paul 1951- *WhoE 93*
Bradbrook, Muriel Clara 1909- *WhoWor 93*
Bradburd, Arnold William 1924- *St&PR 93*
Bradburn, David Denison 1925- *WhoAm 92*
Bradburn, Norman M. 1933- *WhoAm 92*
Bradbury, Alan Keith 1949- *WhoWrEP 92*
Bradbury, Bianca (Ryley) 1908-1982 *ConAu 37NR, MajAI [port]*
Bradbury, Bill J. 1932- *St&PR 93*
Bradbury, C.K. *WhoScE 91-1*
Bradbury, Daniel Joseph 1945- *WhoAm 92*
Bradbury, David E. 1946- *St&PR 93*
Bradbury, Edward P. *ConAu 38NR*
Bradbury, Edwin Morton 1933- *WhoAm 92*
Bradbury, James Loren 1924- *St&PR 93*
Bradbury, Kathleen Charlotte 1949- *WhoEmL 93*
Bradbury, Keith P. 1933- *St&PR 93*
Bradbury, Louise A. *AmWomPl*
Bradbury, Malcolm 1932- *BioIn 17, ConTFT 10*
Bradbury, Malcolm Stanley 1932- *WhoWor 93*
Bradbury, Michael William Blackburn *WhoScE 91-1*
Bradbury, Norris Edwin 1909- *WhoAm 92*
Bradbury, Ray 1920- *BioIn 17, ConTFT 10, MagSAmL [port], ScF&FL 92, WorLitC [port]*
Bradbury, Ray Douglas 1920- *WhoAm 92, WhoWrEP 92*
Bradbury, Richard R. 1939- *St&PR 93*
Bradbury, William Batchelder 1816-1868 *Baker 92*
Bradby, Tanya M. 1960- *WhoAmW 93*
Braddell, Maurice *BioIn 17*
Braddock, Edward 1695-1755 *HarEnMi*
Braddock, Richard *BioIn 17*
Braddock, Richard S. 1941- *WhoAm 92, WhoE 93*
Braddock, William Haskell 1935- *St&PR 93*
Braddy, Ann Wishart *AmWomPl*
Brade, Colleen Anne Swierczneski 1964- *WhoE 93*
Brade, William 1560-1630 *Baker 92*
Brademan, Victoria J. *Law&B 92*
Brademas, John *BioIn 17*
Brademas, John 1927- *PolPar, WhoAm 92*
Braden, Alice E. *AmWomPl*
Braden, Anne McCarty 1924- *WhoSSW 93*
Braden, Berwyn Bartow 1928- *WhoAm 92*
Braden, Betty Jane 1943- *WhoAmW 93*
Braden, Charles Hosea 1926- *WhoAm 92*
Braden, David Rice 1924- *WhoAm 92*
Braden, Dennis Ray 1949- *WhoWrEP 92*
Braden, James Dale 1934- *WhoAm 92*
Braden, Joan Kay 1934- *WhoAm 92*
Braden, John A. 1945- *WhoSSW 93*
Braden, K.G. 1938- *St&PR 93*
Braden, Michael *WhoScE 91-1*
Braden, Nancy Adele 1940- *WhoSSW 93*
Braden, Samuel Edward 1914- *WhoAm 92*
Braden, Stanton Connell 1960- *WhoEmL 93*
Braden, Thomas Wardell 1918- *WhoAm 92*
Braden, Verlon Patrick 1934- *WhoWor 93*
Braden, Victoria Jane 1955- *WhoEmL 93, WhoSSW 93*
Brader, Lukas 1935- *WhoScE 91-3*
Brader, Ruth Jennings *Law&B 92*
Brader, Thomas Edward 1953- *WhoSSW 93*
Bradfield, C.J. 1934- *St&PR 93*
Bradfield, Geoffrey *BioIn 17*
Bradfield, J.C. *ScF&FL 92*
Bradfield, J.R. 1943- *St&PR 93*
Bradfield, Joe Lewis 1934- *St&PR 93*
Bradfield, John Walter *WhoScE 91-1*
Bradfield, Michael 1934- *WhoAm 92*
Bradfield, Scott 1955- *ScF&FL 92*
Bradfield, William S. 1937- *St&PR 93*
Bradford, Alex 1927-1978 *Baker 92*
Bradford, Andrew 1686-1742 *BioIn 17, JrnUS*
Bradford, Anita *AmWomPl*
Bradford, Barbara Reed 1948- *WhoEmL 93*
Bradford, Barbara Taylor *WhoAm 92, WhoAmW 93, WhoE 93*
Bradford, Barbara Taylor 1933- *BioIn 17*
Bradford, Brad R. 1950- *St&PR 93*
Bradford, Carl O. 1932- *WhoAm 92*
Bradford, Charles Steven 1956- *WhoEmL 93*
Bradford, Christina 1942- *WhoAmW 93*
Bradford, Claude A. 1944- *St&PR 93*
Bradford, Columbus 1887-1975 *ScF&FL 92*
Bradford, Curtis Delano 1940- *WhoSSW 93*
Bradford, David Frantz 1939- *WhoAm 92*
Bradford, David Jeffrey *Law&B 92*
Bradford, David Jeffrey 1952- *WhoEmL 93*
Bradford, David Paul 1955- *WhoWor 93*
Bradford, David R. *Law&B 92*
Bradford, David R. 1950- *St&PR 93*
Bradford, Dennis Doyle 1945- *St&PR 93, WhoSSW 93, WhoWor 93*
Bradford, Derek Thomas *WhoScE 91-1*
Bradford, Donald Wray 1944- *WhoIns 93*
Bradford, Edmund James 1952- *WhoEmL 93*
Bradford, Edward Anthony 1814-1872 *OxCSupC*
Bradford, Elsa H. 1932- *St&PR 93*
Bradford, Gail Idona 1947- *WhoAmW 93*
Bradford, George E. *Law&B 92*
Bradford, George Francis 1942- *St&PR 93*
Bradford, Gordon *ScF&FL 92*
Bradford, H. Eugene 1942- *St&PR 93*
Bradford, Hal R. *Law&B 92*
Bradford, Henry Francis *WhoScE 91-1*
Bradford, Hilary P. 1929- *St&PR 93*
Bradford, Howard 1919- *WhoAm 92*
Bradford, James, Jr. *Law&B 92*
Bradford, James C., Jr. 1933- *St&PR 93, WhoAm 92*
Bradford, James Herbert 1950- *WhoWor 93*
Bradford, James W. *St&PR 93*
Bradford, Jane Turner 1946- *WhoAmW 93*
Bradford, John 1749-1830 *JrnUS*
Bradford, John Carroll 1924- *WhoAm 92*
Bradford, John T., Sr. *Law&B 92*
Bradford, Judson T. 1928- *St&PR 93*
Bradford, Karleen 1936- *WhoCanL 92*
Bradford, Kent M. *Law&B 92*
Bradford, Larry Glenn 1952- *WhoSSW 93*
Bradford, Larry Newell 1938- *St&PR 93*
Bradford, Leland Powers *BioIn 17*
Bradford, Louise Mathilde 1925- *WhoAmW 93, WhoWor 93*
Bradford, Marjorie Odell 1952- *WhoWrEP 92*
Bradford, Martina L. *BioIn 17*
Bradford, Matthew C. *ScF&FL 92*
Bradford, Michael *ConAu 39NR*
Bradford, Michael Lee 1942- *WhoSSW 93*
Bradford, Milton Douglas 1930- *St&PR 93*
Bradford, Orcelia Sylvia 1953- *WhoAmW 93, WhoEmL 93*
Bradford, Peter Amory 1942- *WhoAm 92*
Bradford, Peter Corey 1935- *WhoWor 93*
Bradford, Reagan Howard, Jr. 1954- *WhoSSW 93*
Bradford, Richard Headlee 1938- *WhoSSW 93*
Bradford, Richard Roark 1932- *WhoAm 92, WhoWrEP 92*
Bradford, Robert *ScF&FL 92*
Bradford, Robert Edward 1931- *St&PR 93, WhoAm 92*
Bradford, Robert Ernest *WhoAm 92*
Bradford, Robert P. 1934- *St&PR 93*
Bradford, Roger R. 1928- *St&PR 93*
Bradford, Samuel *MiSFD 9*
Bradford, Sheri Jones 1964- *WhoAmW 93*
Bradford, Steven M. *Law&B 92*
Bradford, Teresa Ann 1964- *WhoAmW 93*
Bradford, Tutt Sloan 1917- *WhoSSW 93*
Bradford, William 1588-1657 *BioIn 17*
Bradford, William 1663-1752 *JrnUS*
Bradford, William 1722-1791 *JrnUS*
Bradford, William 1729-1808 *PolPar*
Bradford, William 1823-1892 *BioIn 17*
Bradford, William Dalton 1931- *WhoAm 92*
Bradford, William E. 1917- *St&PR 93*
Bradford, William Edward 1935- *WhoAm 92*
Bradford Family *BioIn 17*
Bradford Mathews, Felita Renee 1959- *WhoEmL 93*
Bradham, James V. 1940- *St&PR 93*
Bradic, Ivan 1932- *WhoScE 91-4*
Bradigan, Brian Jay 1951- *WhoEmL 93*
Brading, D. A. 1936- *ConAu 136*
Bradish, Frank *BioIn 17*
Bradish, Warren Allen 1937- *WhoSSW 93*
Bradlee, Benjamin C. 1921- *BioIn 17*
Bradlee, Benjamin Crowninshield 1921- *WhoAm 92, WhoE 93, WhoWrEP 92*
Bradlee, Benjamin P. 1921- *JrnUS*
Bradlee, Dudley H., II 1915- *St&PR 93*
Bradler, Bob *BioIn 17*
Bradler, James Edward 1935- *WhoAm 92*
Bradley, Alice 1875-1946 *AmWomPl*
Bradley, Amelia Jane 1947- *WhoE 93, WhoEmL 93*
Bradley, Amy Lorraine 1949- *WhoAmW 93*
Bradley, Andrew G. *Law&B 92*
Bradley, Andrew Mortimer 1951- *WhoEmL 93*
Bradley, Arthur Harold 1936- *St&PR 93*
Bradley, Beulah M. *AmWomPl*
Bradley, Bill *BioIn 17, NewYTBS 92 [port]*
Bradley, Bill 1943- *CngDr 91, WhoAm 92, WhoE 93, WhoWor 93*
Bradley, Bob *BioIn 17*
Bradley, Bonnie 1951- *WhoAmW 93*
Bradley, Buddy d1972 *BioIn 17*
Bradley, Carol Ann 1953- *WhoEmL 93*
Bradley, Charles Ernest 1962- *WhoSSW 93, WhoWor 93*
Bradley, Charles J. 1935- *St&PR 93*
Bradley, Charles James, Jr. 1935- *WhoAm 92*
Bradley, Charles MacArthur 1918- *WhoWor 93*
Bradley, Charles S. 1931- *St&PR 93*
Bradley, Charles William 1923- *WhoAm 92, WhoWor 93*
Bradley, Christine *ScF&FL 92*
Bradley, Clarence d1972 *BioIn 17*
Bradley, D. Scott 1949- *St&PR 93*
Bradley, Daniel J. 1928- *WhoScE 91-3*
Bradley, Daniel O. *Law&B 92*
Bradley, David *ScF&FL 92*
Bradley, David Gilbert 1916- *WhoAm 92*
Bradley, David Henry, Jr. 1950- *WhoAm 92, WhoWrEP 92*
Bradley, David John *WhoScE 91-1*
Bradley, David Quentin 1936- *St&PR 93*
Bradley, David R. 1950- *WhoIns 93*
Bradley, David Rall, Jr. 1949- *St&PR 93*
Bradley, Derek *WhoScE 91-1*
Bradley, Diane Rose 1956- *WhoEmL 93*
Bradley, Don Bell, III 1945- *WhoSSW 93*
Bradley, Donald *AfrAmBi*
Bradley, Donald Charles 1932- *St&PR 93*
Bradley, Donald Charlton *WhoScE 91-1*
Bradley, Duane 1914- *DcAmChF 1960*
Bradley, E. Michael 1939- *WhoE 93, WhoWor 93*
Bradley, Ed *BioIn 17*
Bradley, Edward 1941- *AfrAmBi, JrnUS*
Bradley, Edward James, I 1946- *WhoEmL 93*
Bradley, Edward R. 1941- *WhoAm 92*
Bradley, Edward William 1927- *WhoAm 92, WhoE 93*
Bradley, Eugene Bradford 1932- *WhoSSW 93*
Bradley, F. Joseph 1943- *St&PR 93*
Bradley, Florence Frances 1934- *WhoWrEP 92*
Bradley, Florene Jordan 1917- *WhoSSW 93*
Bradley, Floyd Henry, III 1951- *St&PR 93*
Bradley, Francis Xavier 1915- *WhoAm 92*
Bradley, Frank L., Jr. 1924- *St&PR 93*
Bradley, Gail Louise 1951- *WhoAmW 93*
Bradley, George E., Jr. 1957- *WhoE 93*
Bradley, George H. 1932- *WhoAm 92*
Bradley, George J. 1916- *St&PR 93*
Bradley, Gerard W. 1927- *St&PR 93*
Bradley, Gilbert Francis 1920- *WhoAm 92*
Bradley, Gwendolyn *WhoAmW 93*
Bradley, Gwendolyn 1952- *Baker 92*
Bradley, Hugh Edward 1928- *St&PR 93*
Bradley, Ian 1950- *ScF&FL 92*
Bradley, Inez Mayo 1935- *WhoAm 92*
Bradley, J.F., Jr. 1930- *St&PR 93, WhoAm 92*
Bradley, James E. 1944- *ConAu 136*
Bradley, Jan 1943- *BioIn 17*
Bradley, Janie R. *BioIn 17*
Bradley, Jerry (Wayne) 1948- *ConAu 137*
Bradley, John 1933- *WhoWor 93*
Bradley, John A. 1937- *St&PR 93*
Bradley, John Andrew 1930- *WhoAm 92*
Bradley, John D., Jr. 1945- *St&PR 93*
Bradley, John Ed(mund, Jr.) 1958- *ConAu 139*
Bradley, John Edmund 1906- *WhoAm 92*
Bradley, John Miller, Jr. 1925- *WhoAm 92, WhoSSW 93*
Bradley, Joseph Anderson, III 1964- *WhoSSW 93*
Bradley, Joseph P. 1813-1892 *OxCSupC [port]*
Bradley, Kathy Annette 1956- *WhoEmL 93*
Bradley, Kenneth Daniel 1949- *WhoEmL 93*
Bradley, Kirk Jackson 1962- *WhoEmL 93*
Bradley, Larry Edwin 1944- *WhoSSW 93*
Bradley, Laurence Alan 1949- *WhoEmL 93, WhoSSW 93*
Bradley, Lawrence D., Jr. 1920- *WhoAm 92*
Bradley, Lee Carrington, Jr. 1897- *WhoAm 92*
Bradley, Lester Eugene 1921- *WhoAm 92*
Bradley, Lillian Trimble 1875- *AmWomPl*
Bradley, Lisa G. *Law&B 92*
Bradley, Lisa M. 1951- *WhoAm 92*
Bradley, Lorraine 1946- *St&PR 93*
Bradley, M. *Law&B 92*
Bradley, M.R. *WhoScE 91-1*
Bradley, Marilynne Gail 1938- *WhoAmW 93, WhoWor 93*
Bradley, Marion Zimmer *BioIn 17*
Bradley, Marion Zimmer 1930- *Au&Arts 9 [port], ScF&FL 92, WhoAm 92, WhoWrEP 92*
Bradley, Mark Andrew 1955- *WhoSSW 93*
Bradley, Mark Edmund 1936- *WhoAm 92*
Bradley, Martha Washington Nutter *WhoWor 93*
Bradley, Marvin R. 1914- *WhoAm 92*
Bradley, Mary E. *AmWomPl*
Bradley, Maud Menefree *AmWomPl*
Bradley, Melvin LeRoy 1938- *WhoAm 92*
Bradley, Michael 1944- *ScF&FL 92*
Bradley, Michael John 1933- *WhoWor 93*
Bradley, Mitchell Hugh 1935- *WhoAm 92*
Bradley, Myra James 1924- *WhoAmW 93*
Bradley, Nolen Eugene, Jr. 1925- *WhoSSW 93, WhoWor 93*
Bradley, Omar Nelson 1893-1981 *CmdGen 1991 [port], DcTwHis, HarEnMi*
Bradley, Patricia 1951- *BiDAMSp 1989*
Bradley, Patricia Ellen 1951- *WhoAmW 93*
Bradley, Paul William 1961- *WhoWor 93*
Bradley, Philip Charles 1936- *St&PR 93*
Bradley, Randall T. 1953- *St&PR 93*
Bradley, Raymond *WhoScE 91-1*
Bradley, Raymond Joseph 1920- *WhoAm 92*
Bradley, Richard Edwin 1926- *WhoAm 92*
Bradley, Robert Franklin 1920- *WhoAm 92*
Bradley, Robert Lee 1920- *WhoAm 92*
Bradley, Roger William 1944- *WhoE 93*
Bradley, Ronald A. 1932- *St&PR 93*
Bradley, Ronald Calvin 1915- *WhoAm 92*
Bradley, Ronald James 1943- *WhoAm 92, WhoSSW 93*
Bradley, Samuel McKnight 1956- *WhoE 93*
Bradley, Sandra S. 1951- *St&PR 93*
Bradley, Scott *BioIn 17*
Bradley, Shawn *BioIn 17*
Bradley, Stephen *BioIn 17*
Bradley, Stephen R. 1754-1830 *PolPar*
Bradley, Sterling Gaylen 1932- *WhoAm 92, WhoWor 93*
Bradley, Terrye Ann 1950- *WhoSSW 93*
Bradley, Thomas 1917- *EncAACR, PolPar, WhoAm 92*
Bradley, Thomas Andrew 1957- *WhoAm 92, WhoIns 93*
Bradley, Thomas Gerald 1931- *St&PR 93*
Bradley, Thomas Reid 1923- *St&PR 93*
Bradley, Tom *BioIn 17*
Bradley, Tom 1917- *AfrAmBi [port], BioIn 17, CurBio 92 [port]*
Bradley, Velma Jean 1951- *WhoEmL 93*
Bradley, Virginia Biart 1925- *WhoAmW 93*
Bradley, Walter D. *Law&B 92*
Bradley, Wanda Louise 1953- *WhoAmW 93, WhoE 93*
Bradley, Ward R., Jr. 1929- *St&PR 93*
Bradley, Wesley Holmes 1922- *WhoAm 92*
Bradley, William John 1929- *St&PR 93*
Bradman, Tony 1954- *ScF&FL 92*
Bradna, Joanne Justice 1952- *WhoEmL 93*
Bradner, James H., Jr. *Law&B 92*
Brado, Michael Wayne 1958- *WhoEmL 93*
Brado, W. *WhoScE 91-3*
Bradrick, Roy Burton, Jr. 1953- *WhoEmL 93*
Bradshaw, Alan *WhoScE 91-1*

Bradshaw, Alexander M. 1944- *WhoScE 91-3*
Bradshaw, Anthony David 1926- *WhoWor 93*
Bradshaw, Beverly Jean 1946- *WhoEmL 93*
Bradshaw, Billy Dean 1940- *WhoWor 93*
Bradshaw, Carl John 1930- *WhoAm 92, WhoWor 93*
Bradshaw, Carolyn Sue 1935- *WhoAmW 93*
Bradshaw, Charles Robert *WhoScE 91-1*
Bradshaw, Clark C. 1944- *St&PR 93*
Bradshaw, Conrad Allan 1922- *WhoAm 92*
Bradshaw, Cynthia Helene 1954- *WhoEmL 93*
Bradshaw, D. Lynn *Law&B 92*
Bradshaw, D. Lynn 1941- *St&PR 93*
Bradshaw, Dennis Eric 1960- *WhoSSW 93*
Bradshaw, Dove 1949- *WhoEmL 93*
Bradshaw, Elizabeth Shepperd Morin 1947- *WhoEmL 93*
Bradshaw, Elvis Bobby 1954- *BioIn 17*
Bradshaw, Eugene B. *Law&B 92*
Bradshaw, Eugene Barry 1938- *St&PR 93, WhoAm 92*
Bradshaw, Gillian 1956- *ScF&FL 92*
Bradshaw, Howard Holt 1937- *WhoSSW 93*
Bradshaw, Ira Webb 1929- *WhoWor 93*
Bradshaw, James Edward 1940- *WhoSSW 93*
Bradshaw, James Vearl 1956- *WhoEmL 93*
Bradshaw, James W. 1935- *St&PR 93*
Bradshaw, Janelle F. *St&PR 93*
Bradshaw, Jean Paul, II 1956- *WhoAm 92*
Bradshaw, Jeffrey C. 1947- *WhoSSW 93*
Bradshaw, Jerry C. 1931- *St&PR 93*
Bradshaw, Jerry Marcus 1946- *WhoEmL 93*
Bradshaw, John 1933- *BioIn 17, ConAu 138, News 92 [port]*
Bradshaw, John 1952- *MiSFD 9*
Bradshaw, John Pilcher, Jr. 1933- *St&PR 93*
Bradshaw, John Robert 1954- *WhoE 93*
Bradshaw, Jonathan Richard *WhoScE 91-1*
Bradshaw, Kevin *BioIn 17*
Bradshaw, Lillian Moore 1915- *WhoAm 92, WhoAmW 93*
Bradshaw, Mark Davis 1954- *WhoEmL 93*
Bradshaw, Merrill (Kay) 1929- *Baker 92*
Bradshaw, Murray Charles 1930- *WhoAm 92*
Bradshaw, Nanci Marie 1940- *WhoAmW 93*
Bradshaw, Paul C. 1926- *St&PR 93*
Bradshaw, Paul Stephen 1937- *St&PR 93*
Bradshaw, Penni Pearson 1954- *WhoEmL 93*
Bradshaw, Perry D. *Law&B 92*
Bradshaw, Peter 1935- *WhoAm 92*
Bradshaw, Ralph Alden 1941- *WhoAm 92*
Bradshaw, Randy *MiSFD 9*
Bradshaw, Raymond Stanley, Jr. 1933- *St&PR 93*
Bradshaw, Richard Eugene 1950- *WhoE 93*
Bradshaw, Richard James 1944- *WhoAm 92*
Bradshaw, Richard John 1948- *St&PR 93, WhoAm 92*
Bradshaw, Richard Rotherwood 1916- *WhoAm 92*
Bradshaw, Robert 1916-1978 *DcCPCAm*
Bradshaw, Robert Walker 1929- *St&PR 93*
Bradshaw, Rod Eric 1951- *WhoEmL 93, WhoSSW 93, WhoWor 93*
Bradshaw, Stanley J. 1957- *WhoAm 92*
Bradshaw, Terry *BioIn 17*
Bradshaw, Terry 1948- *WhoAm 92*
Bradshaw, Thomas William 1954- *WhoScE 91-1*
Bradshaw, Wayne Robert 1949- *St&PR 93*
Bradshaw, William David 1928- *WhoAm 92*
Bradshaw, William Peter *WhoScE 91-1*
Bradshaw-Isherwood, Christopher William 1904-1986 *BioIn 17*
Bradsky, Wenzel Theodor 1833-1881 *Baker 92*
Bradstreet, Anne 1612?-1672 *BioIn 17, MagSAmL*
Bradstreet, Bernard Francis 1945- *WhoAm 92*
Bradstreet, Dennis 1948- *St&PR 93*
Bradt, Hale Van Dorn 1930- *WhoAm 92*
Bradt, L. Jack 1928- *St&PR 93*
Bradway, William S. 1946- *St&PR 93*
Bradwell, Baron 1905-1976 *BioIn 17*
Bradwell, James 1925- *ScF&FL 92*
Bradwell, John Joseph 1934- *WhoSSW 93*
Brady, Adelaide Burks 1926- *WhoAm 92, WhoAmW 93*
Brady, Aidan 1928- *WhoScE 91-3*
Brady, Alexander *WhoAm 92*
Brady, Alfred R. 1937- *St&PR 93*
Brady, Andrew John 1955- *St&PR 93*
Brady, Ann 1947- *ConAu 138*
Brady, Ann Marie *Law&B 92*
Brady, B. 1947- *St&PR 93*
Brady, Barbara Jeanne 1967- *WhoAmW 93*
Brady, Betsy J. *Law&B 92*
Brady, Bruce L. 1939- *St&PR 93*
Brady, Carl Franklin 1919- *St&PR 93, WhoAm 92*
Brady, Christopher James 1950- *St&PR 93*
Brady, Colleen Anne 1951- *WhoEmL 93*
Brady, Dan Phillip 1952- *WhoWrEP 92*
Brady, David Sharp *Law&B 92*
Brady, Deborah A. 1954- *St&PR 93*
Brady, Donna Elizabeth 1955- *WhoEmL 93, WhoWor 93*
Brady, Eamonn Feeney 1964- *WhoE 93*
Brady, Edmund Matthew, Jr. 1941- *WhoAm 92*
Brady, Edward G. 1930- *St&PR 93*
Brady, Edward J. *Law&B 92*
Brady, Elbert Leroy 1941- *WhoAm 92*
Brady, Eugene F. *Law&B 92*
Brady, Francis *WhoAm 92*
Brady, Francis C. 1944- *St&PR 93*
Brady, Frank 1924-1986 *BioIn 17*
Brady, Frank Benton 1914- *WhoAm 92*
Brady, Frank R. 1934- *WhoWrEP 92*
Brady, Gail P. 1945- *St&PR 93*
Brady, Gene Franklyn 1932- *WhoE 93*
Brady, George Moore 1922- *WhoAm 92*
Brady, Harry Albert 1925- *WhoAm 92*
Brady, Helen Jennifer 1952- *WhoSSW 93*
Brady, Henry Grady *WhoWrEP 92*
Brady, Holly Wheeler 1947- *WhoEmL 93, WhoWrEP 92*
Brady, Jack D. 1943- *St&PR 93*
Brady, James 1928- *BioIn 17*
Brady, James 1941- *JrnUS*
Brady, James F. *Law&B 92*
Brady, James Joseph 1936- *WhoAm 92*
Brady, James M. 1955- *St&PR 93*
Brady, James S. *BioIn 17*
Brady, James S. 1944- *WhoAm 92*
Brady, James Winston 1928- *WhoAm 92*
Brady, Jane *ScF&FL 92*
Brady, Jane Frances 1935- *WhoAm 92, WhoAmW 93*
Brady, Jane Mariette 1955- *WhoEmL 93*
Brady, Jennie M. 1948- *WhoAmW 93, WhoEmL 93, WhoWor 93*
Brady, Jim 1940- & Brady, Sarah 1942- *ConHero 2 [port]*
Brady, John B. 1929- *St&PR 93*
Brady, John David, Jr. 1958- *WhoEmL 93*
Brady, John Joseph, Jr. 1923- *WhoAm 92*
Brady, John Michael *WhoScE 91-1*
Brady, John Paul 1928- *ScF&FL 92, WhoAm 92*
Brady, Joseph F. 1946- *St&PR 93*
Brady, Joseph John 1926- *WhoAm 92*
Brady, Joseph Vincent 1922- *WhoAm 92*
Brady, Kent Mason 1941- *WhoE 93*
Brady, Kim 1951- *WhoEmL 93*
Brady, Lawrence J. 1943- *St&PR 93*
Brady, Lawrence Peter 1940- *WhoE 93, WhoWor 93*
Brady, Luther W., Jr. 1925- *WhoAm 92*
Brady, Lynn Robert 1933- *WhoAm 92*
Brady, Lynne Ellen 1946- *WhoEmL 93*
Brady, Mariel *AmWomPl*
Brady, Martin R., Jr. 1938- *WhoIns 93*
Brady, Mary Gerard 1959- *WhoWrEP 92*
Brady, Mary Rolfes 1933- *WhoAmW 93*
Brady, Mathew B. 1823-1896 *JrnUS*
Brady, Maureen 1943- *WhoWrEP 92*
Brady, Melvin Michael 1933- *WhoWor 93*
Brady, Michael 1928- *ScF&FL 92*
Brady, Michael Wade 1948- *WhoEmL 93*
Brady, Nancy Sammartino 1955- *WhoEmL 93*
Brady, Nelvia *BioIn 17*
Brady, Nicholas F. 1930- *BioIn 17, CngDr 91*
Brady, Nicholas Frederick 1930- *WhoAm 92, WhoE 93, WhoWor 93*
Brady, Nyle C. 1920- *WhoAm 92*
Brady, Patricia 1943- *ConAu 136*
Brady, Patricia Maureen 1943- *WhoSSW 93*
Brady, Patrick 1933- *WhoAm 92, WhoSSW 93*
Brady, Patrick E. 1941- *St&PR 93*
Brady, Patrick Henry *BioIn 17*
Brady, Paul *BioIn 17*
Brady, Paul 1947- *ConMus 8 [port]*
Brady, Philip 1916- *WhoWrEP 92*
Brady, Phillip Donley 1951- *WhoAm 92*
Brady, Richard *ScF&FL 92*
Brady, Richard Alan 1934- *WhoAm 92*
Brady, Richard P. *St&PR 93*
Brady, Robert Edward 1938- *WhoAm 92*
Brady, Robert Frederick, Jr. 1942- *WhoE 93*
Brady, Robert H. 1936- *St&PR 93*
Brady, Robert L. 1944- *St&PR 93*
Brady, Robert Leo 1961- *WhoWor 93*
Brady, Robert Lindsay 1946- *WhoEmL 93*
Brady, Rodney Howard 1933- *St&PR 93, WhoAm 92*
Brady, Roscoe O. 1923- *WhoAm 92*
Brady, Sarah *BioIn 17*
Brady, Sarah 1942- *WhoAmW 93*
Brady, Sarah 1942- See Brady, Jim 1940- & Brady, Sarah 1942- *ConHero 2*
Brady, Scott 1924-1985 *BioIn 17*
Brady, Sharon Elizabeth 1963- *WhoAmW 93*
Brady, Sheila Ann 1935- *St&PR 93*
Brady, Sue Carol Pipes 1947- *WhoAmW 93, WhoEmL 93, WhoWor 93*
Brady, Terence Christian 1931- *St&PR 93*
Brady, Teresa Patricia 1956- *WhoE 93*
Brady, Thomas *Law&B 92*
Brady, Thomas Arthur, Jr. 1946- *WhoEmL 93*
Brady, Thomas Carl 1947- *WhoE 93*
Brady, Thomas Denis 1955- *WhoEmL 93*
Brady, Upton Birnie 1938- *WhoAm 92*
Brady, Viola Catt *Law&B 92*
Brady, Walter Michael 1935- *St&PR 93, WhoAm 92*
Brady, William A. *Law&B 92*
Brady, William John, Jr. 1946- *WhoEmL 93*
Brady, Wray Grayson 1918- *WhoAm 92*
Brady-Amoon, Peggy 1956- *WhoE 93*
Braein, Edvard 1887-1957 *Baker 92*
Braein, Edvard Fliflet 1924-1976 *Baker 92*
Braekhus, Jon 1947- *WhoWor 93*
Braekke, Finn Harald 1938- *WhoScE 91-4*
Braekman-Danheux, Colette 1939- *WhoScE 91-2*
Braem, Lee A. *Law&B 92*
Braen, Bernard Benjamin 1928- *WhoAm 92*
Braestrup, Claus 1945- *WhoScE 91-2*
Braestrup, Peter 1929- *WhoAm 92, WhoE 93*
Braeuninger, William Frederick *Law&B 92*
Braeuninger, William Frederick 1938- *St&PR 93*
Braeutigam, Ronald Ray 1947- *WhoWor 93*
Braff, Howard 1952- *WhoE 93, WhoEmL 93*
Braff, Mark Russell 1955- *WhoEmL 93*
Braff, Sharman *Law&B 92*
Braffet, Bentley T. 1934- *St&PR 93*
Brafford, William Charles 1932- *St&PR 93, WhoAm 92*
Brafman, Bruce J. *Law&B 92*
Braga, Daniel 1946- *WhoEmL 93, WhoWor 93*
Braga, (Antonio) Francisco 1868-1945 *Baker 92*
Braga, Gaetano 1829-1907 *Baker 92*
Braga, Marigildo de Camargo 1924- *WhoWor 93*
Braga, Sonia *BioIn 17*
Bragadino, Marcantonio 1523?-1571 *HarEnMi*
Bragalone, Ellen Marie 1961- *WhoAmW 93*
Braganini, David R. 1951- *St&PR 93*
Braganti, Nancy (Sue) 1941- *ConAu 40NR*
Braganza, Constantine de 1528-1575 *HarEnMi*
Bragard, Roger 1903-1985 *Baker 92*
Braga-Santos, (Jose Manuel) Joly *Baker 92*
Bragason, Arni 1953- *WhoScE 91-4*
Bragaw, George Driver 1957- *WhoE 93*
Bragdon, Allen Davenport 1930- *WhoE 93*
Bragdon, Bruce Richard 1948- *WhoE 93*
Bragdon, Edwin W. 1922- *St&PR 93*
Bragdon, Paul Errol 1927- *WhoAm 92*
Brager, Walter S. 1925- *WhoAm 92*
Bragg, Billy *BioIn 17*
Bragg, Braxton 1817-1876 *BioIn 17, HarEnMi*
Bragg, Charles Fred, II 1910- *St&PR 93*
Bragg, David Gordon 1933- *WhoAm 92*
Bragg, David Kenneth 1948- *St&PR 93*
Bragg, Donald George 1935- *BiDAMSp 1989*
Bragg, Ellis Meredith, Jr. 1947- *WhoEmL 93, WhoSSW 93*
Bragg, George Albert 1942- *WhoAm 92*
Bragg, George Lee 1932- *St&PR 93*
Bragg, Holly Jean *Law&B 92*
Bragg, Jeffrey S. 1949- *WhoIns 93*
Bragg, John Mackie 1921- *WhoAm 92*
Bragg, John Woodbury 1943- *St&PR 93*
Bragg, Melvyn 1939- *BioIn 17*
Bragg, Michael E. *Law&B 92*
Bragg, Michael Ellis 1947- *WhoAm 92, WhoEmL 93, WhoWor 93*
Bragg, Ninette Sturgis *Law&B 92*
Bragg, Patricia D. *St&PR 93*
Bragg, Robert Henry 1919- *WhoAm 92*
Bragg, Sanford B. 1953- *St&PR 93*
Bragg, Steven Russell 1953- *WhoAm 92*
Bragg, T. Steve 1945- *St&PR 93*
Bragin, D.H. 1944- *St&PR 93*
Bragin, David Held 1944- *WhoAm 92*
Braginton-Smith, Brian S. 1953- *WhoEmL 93*
Bragole, Robert A. 1936- *St&PR 93*
Bragole, Robert Anthony 1936- *WhoE 93*
Braha, Thomas I. 1947- *WhoAm 92, WhoE 93, WhoEmL 93, WhoWor 93*
Braham, Delphine Doris 1946- *WhoAmW 93, WhoEmL 93*
Braham, John 1774-1856 *Baker 92, OxDcOp*
Braham, Randolph Lewis 1922- *WhoAm 92*
Brahaney, Thomas Frank 1951- *BiDAMSp 1989*
Brahe, Tycho 1546-1601 *BioIn 17*
Brahier, Milton J. *St&PR 93*
Brahimi, Lakhdar 1934- *WhoWor 93*
Brahm, John 1893-1982 *MiSFD 9N*
Brahma, Chandra Sekhar 1941- *WhoAm 92*
B. Rahmat, Dato' Mohamed 1938- *WhoAsAP 91*
Brahm Dutt 1926- *WhoAsAP 91*
Brahme, Anders 1944- *WhoScE 91-4*
Brahms, Caryl 1901-1982 *ScF&FL 92*
Brahms, Johannes 1833-1897 *Baker 92, BioIn 17*
Brahms, Thomas Walter 1945- *WhoAm 92*
Brahmstedt, Howard Kenneth 1936- *WhoSSW 93*
Brahney, Carolyn Ann 1939- *WhoAmW 93*
Brahs, Stuart J. 1940- *WhoIns 93*
Braibanti, Ralph John 1920- *WhoAm 92*
Braid, Frederick Donald 1946- *WhoEmL 93*
Braid, Katharine F. *Law&B 92*
Braide, Robert David 1953- *WhoAm 92*
Braiden, Paul Mayo *WhoScE 91-1*
Braidish, Joseph Anthony 1951- *WhoSSW 93*
Braids, Olin Capron 1938- *WhoSSW 93*
Braidwood, Linda Schreiber 1909- *WhoAm 92*
Braidwood, Robert J. 1907- *IntDcAn*
Braig, Betty Lou 1931- *WhoAmW 93*
Braille, Louis 1809-1852 *BioIn 17*
Brailoiu, Constantin 1893-1958 *Baker 92*
Brailowsky, Alexander 1896-1976 *Baker 92*
Brailsford, David Frank *WhoScE 91-1*
Brailsford, June Evelyn 1939- *WhoAmW 93*
Brailsford, Marvin Delano 1939- *AfrAmBi*
Brailsford, Timothy John 1964- *WhoWor 93*
Brailski, Christo 1924- *WhoScE 91-4*
Braim, Paul Francis 1926- *WhoSSW 93*
Brain, Aubrey (Harold) 1893-1955 *Baker 92*
Brain, Dennis 1921-1957 *Baker 92*
Brain, Donald Chester 1917- *WhoIns 93*
Brain, George Bernard 1920- *WhoAm 92*
Brain, Joseph David 1940- *WhoAm 92*
Brain, Paul Fredric *WhoScE 91-1*
Brain, Philip *WhoScE 91-1*
Brain, T.J.S. 1941- *WhoScE 91-1*
Brainard, Bradford Peabody 1957- *St&PR 93*
Brainard, Edward Axdal 1931- *WhoAm 92*
Brainard, Elizabeth A. *Law&B 92*
Brainard, Frank Samuel 1917- *St&PR 93*
Brainard, James C. 1954- *WhoEmL 93*
Brainard, Jayne Dawson *WhoAm 92, WhoSSW 93*
Brainard, Katharine *BioIn 17*
Brainard, Lawrence J. 1944- *St&PR 93*
Brainard, Marian E. *Law&B 92*
Brainard, Paul Henry 1928- *WhoAm 92*
Brainard, Thomas D. *Law&B 92*
Brainard, William Crittenden 1935- *WhoAm 92*
Brainbeau, J.C. *WhoWrEP 92*
Braine, Clinton Ellis 1920- *St&PR 93*
Braine, John 1922-1986 *BioIn 17*
Braine, Robert D. 1861-1943 *ScF&FL 92*
Brainer, Susan Langenberg 1957- *WhoEmL 93*
Brainerd, David 1718-1747 *BioIn 17*
Brainerd, Howard R. 1942- *St&PR 93*
Brainerd, John W. 1918- *BioIn 17*
Brainerd, Paul 1947- *St&PR 93*
Brainerd, Stanford Howard 1931- *St&PR 93*
Brainerd, Winthrop John 1939- *WhoWor 93*
Brainin, Frederick 1913- *WhoE 93, WhoWor 93*
Brainin, Reuven 1862-1939 *BioIn 17*

Brainov, Milcho Neshev 1922- *WhoScE 91-4*
Braislin, Gordon S. 1901-1990 *BioIn 17*
Braisted, Madeline Charlotte 1936- *WhoAmW 93*
Brait, A.A. 1924- *St&PR 93*
Brait, Richard A. *Law&B 92*
Braiterman, Thea Gilda 1927- *WhoAmW 93*
Braithwaite, A. Bevan M. 1939- *WhoScE 91-1*
Braithwaite, Derek *WhoScE 91-1*
Braithwaite, Eustace Adolphe 1922- *WhoWor 93*
Braithwaite, George Roger *WhoScE 91-1*
Braithwaite, J. Lorne 1941- *WhoAm 92*
Braithwaite, Jeanine Dolan 1960- *WhoEmL 93*
Braithwaite, John James 1932- *St&PR 93*
Braithwaite, John Michael 1958- *WhoE 93*
Braithwaite, Keith G. 1931- *St&PR 93*
Braithwaite, Max 1911- *WhoCanL 92*
Braithwaite, Nicholas 1939- *OxDcOp*
Braithwaite, Nicholas (Paul Dallon) 1939- *Baker 92*
Braithwaite, R.B. 1900-1990 *BioIn 17*
Braithwaite, Raymond Allen 1933- *WhoAsAP 91*
Braithwaite, Richard B. 1900-1990 *BioIn 17*
Braithwaite, Warwick 1898-1971 *OxDcOp*
Braithwaite, (Henry) Warwick 1896-1971 *Baker 92*
Braithwaite, William Stanley Beaumont 1878-1962 *EncAACR*
Braithwaite-Mott, Derek *BioIn 17*
Braitmayer, John Watson 1930- *St&PR 93*
Brajder, Antonio 1942- *WhoWor 93*
Brajdic, Margie Katherine Badrov 1966- *WhoAmW 93*
Brak, Syd *BioIn 17*
Bra Kanon, Denis 1936- *WhoAfr*
Brake, Barbara Whitaker 1946- *WhoEmL 93*
Brake, Cecil Clifford 1932- *WhoAm 92, WhoWor 93*
Brake, John Ronald 1932- *WhoE 93*
Brake, Laurel 1941- *ConAu 138*
Brake, Pamela Downing *Law&B 92*
Brake, Timothy L. 1948- *WhoEmL 93*
Brakeall, Mary Jane 1939- *WhoAmW 93*
Brakel, Jacques C. 1931- *WhoScE 91-2*
Brakeley, George Archibald, Jr. 1916- *WhoAm 92, WhoE 93*
Brakeley, George Archibald, III 1939- *St&PR 93*
Brakell, John Russell 1935- *WhoWor 93*
Brakeman, Fred Ellis 1950- *WhoEmL 93*
Brakeman, Louis Freeman 1932- *WhoAm 92*
Brakeman, Mark Allan 1957- *WhoWrEP 92*
Brakensiek, Warren Niles *Law&B 92*
Brakensiek, Warren Niles 1946- *St&PR 93*
Braker, Otto Ulrich 1944- *WhoScE 91-4*
Braker, Ulrich 1735-1798 *BioIn 17*
Braker, William Paul 1926- *WhoAm 92*
Brakey, Robert G. 1938- *WhoIns 93*
Brakhage, James Stanley 1933- *WhoAm 92*
Brakke, Myron Kendall 1921- *WhoAm 92*
Brakman, P. *WhoScE 91-3*
Brakoniecki, David A. *Law&B 92*
Braley, Berton 1882-1966 *ScF&FL 92*
Braley, Peter W. 1956- *St&PR 93*
Braley, Richard Donald 1949- *WhoWor 93*
Braley, Robert Bruce 1957- *WhoWrEP 92*
Braley, Russell Norton 1921- *WhoE 93*
Bralich, Richard Allen 1957- *WhoEmL 93*
Bralla, James G. 1926- *St&PR 93*
Bralow, Dawn 1962- *WhoSSW 93*
Bralver, Robert *MiSFD 9*
Braly, Byron Duke 1930- *WhoSSW 93*
Braly, David Duane 1949- *WhoEmL 93*
Braly, Jack E. 1941- *St&PR 93*
Braly, Terrell Alfred 1953- *WhoEmL 93, WhoWor 93*
Bram, Christopher 1952- *ConGAN*
Bram, Dana D. 1947- *St&PR 93*
Bram, Elizabeth 1948- *WhoWrEP 92*
Bram, Isabelle Mary Rickey McDonough *WhoAmW 93, WhoWor 93*
Bram, Leon Leonard 1931- *WhoAm 92, WhoWor 93*
Bram, Stephen Bennett 1942- *St&PR 93*
Braman, Grenville C., Jr. 1946- *WhoE 93*
Braman, Heather Ruth 1934- *WhoAmW 93, WhoWor 93*
Braman, Norman 1932- *WhoAm 92*
Braman, Sandra 1951- *WhoWrEP 92*
Bramann, Jorn K. 1938- *WhoWrEP 92*
Bramante, Pietro Ottavio 1920- *WhoAm 92*
Brambach, Caspar Joseph 1833-1902 *Baker 92*
Brambach, Wilhelm 1841-1932 *Baker 92*
Brambell, Wilfrid 1912-1985 *QDrFCA 92 [port]*
Brambilla, Amalia 1811-1880 *OxDcOp*
Brambilla, Marietta 1807-1875 *Baker 92, OxDcOp*
Brambilla, Paolo 1787-1838 *Baker 92, OxDcOp*
Brambilla, Teresa 1813-1895 *Baker 92*
Brambilla, Teresa 1818-1895 *OxDcOp*
Brambilla, Teresina 1845-1921 *OxDcOp*
Bramble, Austin 1931- *DcCPCAm*
Bramble, Barry B. 1953- *St&PR 93*
Bramble, James Henry 1930- *WhoAm 92*
Bramblett, William Thomas 1932- *St&PR 93*
Brame, Bill 1928- *MiSFD 9*
Brame, Marillyn A. 1928- *WhoAmW 93, WhoWor 93*
Brame, Scott O. 1928- *St&PR 93, WhoAm 92*
Bramel, Jene E., II 1948- *St&PR 93*
Bramel, Tamara Ann 1961- *WhoEmL 93*
Bramer, Kurt Richard 1935- *St&PR 93*
Bramesco, Julienne W. *Law&B 92*
Bramesco, Norton J. 1924-1991 *BioIn 17*
Bramfitt, Bruce Livingston 1938- *WhoE 93*
Bramhall, Eugene Hulbert *WhoAm 92*
Bramlett, Christin Jarvis *Law&B 92*
Bramlett, Christopher Lewis 1938- *WhoAm 92*
Bramlett, Ernest 1921- *St&PR 93*
Bramlett, James Dolphus 1930- *WhoWrEP 92*
Bramlett, John W. 1949- *St&PR 93*
Bramlett, Shirley Marie Wilhelm 1945- *WhoAmW 93, WhoSSW 93, WhoWor 93*
Bramley, Alan Neville *WhoScE 91-1*
Bramley, Andrew John *WhoScE 91-1*
Bramley, Christopher W. 1941- *St&PR 93*
Brammar, William J. 1939- *WhoScE 91-1*
Brammell, Stephen H. *Law&B 92*
Brammell, William Hartman 1955- *WhoEmL 93*
Brammer, Forest Evert 1913- *WhoAm 92*
Brammer, James E. *Law&B 92*
Brammer, Lawrence Martin 1922- *WhoAm 92*
Brams, Marvin Robert 1937- *WhoAm 92*
Brams, Steven John 1940- *WhoAm 92*
Bramsen, James E. 1936- *St&PR 93*
Bramson, Berenice Louise 1929- *WhoAmW 93*
Bramson, Edward J. 1952- *WhoAm 92*
Bramson, Leon 1930- *WhoAm 92*
Bramson, Robert S. 1958- *St&PR 93*
Bramson, Robert Sherman 1938- *WhoAm 92, WhoWor 93*
Bramson, William M. 1926- *St&PR 93*
Bram-Soroko, George 1903- *WhoWor 93*
Bramwell, George Y. *Law&B 92*
Bramwell, Henry 1919- *WhoAm 92, WhoE 93*
Bramwell, Marvel Lynnette 1947- *WhoAmW 93, WhoEmL 93, WhoWor 93*
Bramwell, Neil D. *Law&B 92*
Bramwell, Philip N. *Law&B 92*
Bramwell, Ruby Phillips *AmWomPl*
Branagan, James Joseph 1943- *WhoAm 92*
Branagh, Kenneth *BioIn 17*
Branagh, Kenneth 1960- *MiSFD 9, News 92 [port], WhoAm 92*
Branaman, Amy *Law&B 92*
Branaman, David Edward 1932- *St&PR 93*
Branan, Carolyn Benner 1953- *WhoAmW 93, WhoSSW 93, WhoWor 93*
Branas *OxDcByz*
Branas, Alexios d1187 *OxDcByz*
Branca, Frank Joseph 1948- *WhoE 93*
Branca, John Gregory 1950- *WhoAm 92*
Branca, Ralph M. 1935- *St&PR 93*
Brancaccio, Raymond F. 1927- *St&PR 93*
Brancaforte, Benito 1934- *WhoAm 92*
Brancato, Carolyn Kay 1945- *WhoAm 92*
Brancato, Emanuel Leonard 1914- *WhoAm 92*
Brancato, Leo John 1922- *WhoAm 92*
Brancato, Paul 1923-1992 *BioIn 17*
Brancato, Robin F. *BioIn 17*
Brancato, Robin F. 1936- *Au&Arts 9 [port]*
Branch, Anna Hempstead 1875-1937 *AmWomPl*
Branch, Barrington Heath 1940- *WhoWor 93*
Branch, Ben Shirley 1943- *WhoAm 92*
Branch, Billy H. 1928- *St&PR 93*
Branch, Colin David 1936- *WhoWor 93*
Branch, Daniel Hugh 1958- *WhoEmL 93*
Branch, David Reed 1942- *WhoSSW 93*
Branch, David W. 1965- *WhoE 93*
Branch, Donald Lee 1951- *WhoSSW 93*
Branch, John 1782-1863 *PolPar*
Branch, John Curtis 1934- *WhoSSW 93*
Branch, Judson B. 1906-1989 *BioIn 17*
Branch, Kay E. 1945- *St&PR 93*
Branch, M. Kenya 1957- *WhoE 93*
Branch, Norman L. *St&PR 93*
Branch, Norman Lee 1919- *WhoSSW 93*
Branch, Robert Lee 1924- *WhoAm 92*
Branch, Taylor 1947- *WhoAm 92*
Branch, Thomas Broughton, III 1936- *WhoAm 92, WhoWor 93*
Branch, William (Blackwell) 1927- *ConAu 40NR, WhoAm 92*
Branch, William Dean 1950- *WhoSSW 93*
Branch, William H. 1926- *St&PR 93*
Branche, Stanley d1992 *NewYTBS 92*
Brancheau, Joan M. 1951- *St&PR 93*
Branchini, Frank Caesar 1951- *WhoEmL 93*
Branchu, Alexandrine 1780-1850 *OxDcOp*
Branciforte, Joseph L. 1946- *St&PR 93*
Branco, James 1951- *WhoIns 93*
Branco, James J. 1951- *St&PR 93*
Branco, James Joseph 1951- *WhoE 93, WhoEmL 93*
Branco, Paulo Antonio Neves 1954- *WhoWor 93*
Brancone, Louis Maria 1915- *WhoE 93*
Branconnier, Rene J. 1953- *St&PR 93*
Brancour, Rene 1862-1948 *Baker 92*
Brancusi, Constantin 1876-1957 *BioIn 17*
Brand, Albert Gerard 1960- *WhoSSW 93*
Brand, Betsy 1954- *WhoAm 92*
Brand, Betty L. 1919- *St&PR 93*
Brand, C. Dan 1944- *WhoSSW 93*
Brand, Charles Macy 1932- *WhoAm 92*
Brand, Christian Carl 1949- *WhoWor 93*
Brand, Christianna 1907-1988 *BioIn 17, ScF&FL 92*
Brand, Corinne L. *Law&B 92*
Brand, Daniel 1937- *WhoE 93*
Brand, Dennis Leon 1948- *WhoAm 92*
Brand, Dionne *WhoCanL 92*
Brand, Donald A. 1940- *WhoAm 92*
Brand, Donald Ayres 1940- *St&PR 93*
Brand, Edward Cabell 1923- *WhoAm 92*
Brand, Eugene J. 1934- *St&PR 93*
Brand, Frank A. 1924- *St&PR 93*
Brand, Frank Amery 1924- *WhoAm 92*
Brand, Garrison *ConAu 38NR*
Brand, George Edward, Jr. 1918- *WhoAm 92*
Brand, Helen E. 1954- *WhoAmW 93*
Brand, Helmut Rainer 1952- *WhoWor 93*
Brand, Irene Beard 1929- *WhoWrEP 92*
Brand, James W. 1924- *St&PR 93*
Brand, Jesse R. 1948- *St&PR 93*
Brand, John Charles 1921- *WhoAm 92*
Brand, Jonathan E. 1958- *WhoEmL 93*
Brand, Joseph Lyon 1936- *WhoAm 92*
Brand, Joshua *MiSFD 9*
Brand, Julia Marie 1925- *WhoSSW 93*
Brand, Karen Harrison *Law&B 92*
Brand, Karl Albert 1931- *WhoScE 91-3*
Brand, Kurt 1917- *ScF&FL 92*
Brand, Larry *MiSFD 9, ScF&FL 92*
Brand, Leonard 1923- *WhoAm 92*
Brand, Leonard Roy 1941- *WhoAm 92*
Brand, Louise Fenton *AmWomPl*
Brand, Marcia Ceperly 1962- *WhoAmW 93, WhoEmL 93*
Brand, Mary Lou 1934- *WhoAmW 93, WhoWor 93*
Brand, Max 1892-1944 *ScF&FL 92*
Brand, Max 1896-1980 *Baker 92*
Brand, Michael Dean 1961- *WhoE 93*
Brand, Michael Edward 1950- *WhoEmL 93*
Brand, Myles 1942- *WhoAm 92*
Brand, Natan *BioIn 17*
Brand, Neville d1992 *NewYTBS 92 [port]*
Brand, Neville 1920-1992 *BioIn 17*
Brand, Oscar 1920- *Baker 92, WhoAm 92*
Brand, Othal E. 1919- *St&PR 93*
Brand, Paul W. 1914- *BioIn 17*
Brand, Raymond Manning 1922-1991 *BioIn 17*
Brand, Robert Allyn 1920- *WhoAm 92*
Brand, Robert J. *Law&B 92*
Brand, Robert Joseph 1947- *WhoEmL 93*
Brand, Robert Lawrence 1938- *St&PR 93*
Brand, Robert N. 1936- *St&PR 93*
Brand, Ronald Alvah 1952- *WhoEmL 93*
Brand, S. Richard 1939- *St&PR 93*
Brand, Steve Aaron 1948- *WhoAm 92, WhoEmL 93*
Brand, Stewart 1938- *WhoAm 92, WhoWrEP 92*
Brand, Vance Devoe 1931- *WhoAm 92*
Brand, W. Calvert 1918- *St&PR 93*
Brand, Wilhelm *WhoScE 91-3*
Brandalise, Silvia Regina 1943- *WhoWor 93*
Brandanger, Nancy Ann 1955- *WhoEmL 93*
Brandano, Phyllis Teresa 1952- *WhoAmW 93*
Brandao, Ignacio de Loyola 1936- *ScF&FL 92*
Brandao, M. *WhoScE 91-3*
Brandau, Herman *Law&B 92*
Brandau, Seawell 1903- *St&PR 93*
Brandauer, Frederick Paul 1933- *WhoAm 92*
Brandauer, Klaus Maria *BioIn 17*
Brandauer, Klaus-Maria 1944- *IntDcF 2-3, MiSFD 9, WhoAm 92*
Brandborg, Stewart Monroe 1925- *WhoAm 92*
Brandeberry, Mike E. *Law&B 92*
Brandegee, Frank B. 1864-1924 *PolPar*
Brandeis, Louis D. 1856-1941 *PolPar*
Brandeis, Louis Dembitz 1856-1941 *BioIn 17, JeAmHC, OxCSupC [port]*
Brandel, Barbara *BioIn 17*
Brandel, Donald Joseph 1940- *St&PR 93*
Brandel, Konstanty 1880-1970 *PolBiDi*
Brandel, Marc 1919- *ScF&FL 92, SmATA 71*
Brandel, Nancy *Law&B 92*
Brandell, Sol Richard *WhoWor 93*
Brandely, Louis F. 1906- *St&PR 93*
Branden, Barbara *ScF&FL 92*
Branden, Nathaniel 1930- *ScF&FL 92*
Branden, Victoria *WhoCanL 92*
Brandenberg, Aliki (Liacouras) 1929- *MajAI [port]*
Brandenberg, Franz 1932- *MajAI [port]*
Brandenberger, Robert Hans 1954- *WhoE 93*
Brandenburg, Brent L. *Law&B 92*
Brandenburg, Carl Albert, Sr. 1946- *St&PR 93*
Brandenburg, David W. 1944- *St&PR 93*
Brandenburg, Glen Ray 1950- *WhoEmL 93*
Brandenburg, Jeffrey A. 1959- *WhoEmL 93*
Brandenburg, John Nelson 1929- *WhoAm 92*
Brandenburg, Richard George 1935- *WhoAm 92*
Brandenburg, Robert Fairchild, Jr. 1938- *WhoSSW 93, WhoWor 93*
Brandenburg, Roger Gene 1932- *St&PR 93*
Brandenburg, Ronald William 1954- *WhoEmL 93*
Brandenburg, Sally J. *St&PR 93*
Brandenburger, Erich 1894-1970 *HarEnMi*
Brandenstein, Daniel Charles 1943- *WhoAm 92*
Brander, D.E. *St&PR 93*
Brander, John Morran 1932- *WhoWrEP 92*
Brander, Laurence 1903- *ScF&FL 92*
Brander, Thomas W. 1949- *St&PR 93*
Brandes, JoAnne *Law&B 92*
Brandes, Lisa 1957- *WhoEmL 93*
Brandes, Norman Scott 1923- *WhoAm 92*
Brandes, Raymond Stewart 1924- *WhoAm 92*
Brandes, Richard David 1935- *St&PR 93*
Brandes, Stanley Howard 1942- *WhoAm 92*
Brandes, Zita Judith Miller *WhoAm 92*
Brandewyne, Rebecca 1955- *ScF&FL 92*
Brandham, Peter Edward 1937- *WhoScE 91-1*
Brandhorst, Wesley Theodore 1933- *WhoAm 92*
Brandhuber, W.F. *Law&B 92*
Brandi, John 1943- *WhoWrEP 92*
Brandi, Maria Luisa 1953- *WhoWor 93*
Brandin, Ake H. 1924- *WhoIns 93*
Brandin, Alf Elvin 1912- *WhoAm 92, WhoWor 93*
Brandin, Donald N. 1921- *St&PR 93*
Brandin, Donald Nelson 1921- *WhoAm 92*
Brandin, Patricia Anne *Law&B 92*
Brandin, Seymour *St&PR 93*
Brandinger, Jay Jerome 1927- *WhoAm 92*
Brandis, Albrecht Max 1932- *WhoWor 93*
Brandis, Bernardine *Law&B 92*
Brandis, Marianne *WhoCanL 92*
Brandis, Marianne 1938- *DcChlFi*
Brandis, Pamela 1946- *WhoAm 92*
Brandl, James H. 1948- *St&PR 93*
Brandl, James Martin 1943- *St&PR 93*
Brandl, Johann Evangelist 1760-1837 *Baker 92*
Brandl, John Edward 1937- *WhoAm 92*
Brandl, Robert W. 1933- *St&PR 93*
Brandl, Rolf 1952- *WhoWor 93*
Brandland, Caryn Marie 1961- *WhoE 93*
Brandle, Anne Marie 1951- *WhoAmW 93*
Brandley, Clarence 1952- *BioIn 17*
Brandli, Heinrich 1938- *WhoScE 91-4*
Brandmeier, Jonathon *BioIn 17*
Brandmeyer, Donald Wayne 1919- *WhoWor 93*
Brandner, Gary 1933- *ConAu 38NR, ScF&FL 92*
Brandner, J. William 1937- *St&PR 93*
Brando, Cheyenne *BioIn 17*
Brando, Christian *BioIn 17*

Brando, Marlon 1924- BioIn 17, ConTFT 10, IntDcF 2-3 [port], MiSFD 9
Brando, Marlon, Jr. 1924- WhoAm 92
Brandolese, Armando 1941- WhoScE 91-3
Brandolini, Anita Jean 1956- WhoEmL 93
Brandolini, Aureliano WhoScE 91-3
Brandom, Lisa Sims 1944- WhoAmW 93
Brandon c. 483-577 BioIn 17
Brandon, Barbara BioIn 17
Brandon, Barbara 1958- WhoAmW 93
Brandon, Barbara 1960?- ConBlB 3 [port]
Brandon, Clark MiSFD 9
Brandon, Claudia A. 1956- St&PR 93
Brandon, Dorothy AmWomPl
Brandon, Edward B. 1931- St&PR 93
Brandon, Elvis Denby, III 1954- WhoSSW 93
Brandon, George Maxwell 1931- St&PR 93
Brandon, Guilbert Lepage, Jr. 1946- St&PR 93
Brandon, Henry 1912-1990 BioIn 17
Brandon, Ida Gillard WhoAmW 93
Brandon, Jack Lee Law&B 92
Brandon, Jay Robert 1953- WhoEmL 93
Brandon, Jeffery Alan 1944- St&PR 93
Brandon, Joseph P. 1959- WhoIns 93
Brandon, Katherine Swint 1952- WhoEmL 93
Brandon, Lawrence G. 1936- WhoIns 93
Brandon, Liane WhoAm 92, WhoE 93
Brandon, Lisa O'Neill 1962- WhoAmW 93
Brandon, Mark Edward 1954- WhoEmL 93
Brandon, Paul Stanley 1946- WhoEmL 93
Brandon, Peter A. d1990 BioIn 17
Brandon, Peter S. WhoScE 91-1
Brandon, Raymond Wilson 1959- WhoSSW 93
Brandon, Robert Allan Law&B 92
Brandon, Robert Eugene 1920- St&PR 93
Brandon, Ruth 1943- ScF&FL 92
Brandon, Stephen Douglas Law&B 92
Brandon, Thomas L. 1945- St&PR 93
Brandow, George Everett 1913- WhoAm 92
Brandow, Theo 1925- WhoAm 92
Brandreth, Paulina AmWomPl
Brandrup, Douglas Warren 1940- WhoE 93
Brands, Allen Jean 1914- WhoAm 92
Brands, George Bernard 1925- St&PR 93
Brands, James Edwin 1937- WhoAm 92, WhoSSW 93
Brandsma, Jeffrey Melvin 1943- WhoSSW 93
Brandsma, Titus 1881-1942 BioIn 17
Brandstadter-Palmer, Georgia White 1940- WhoSSW 93
Brandstaetter, Roman 1906-1987 PolBiDi
Brandstedter, Rodney 1944- St&PR 93
Brandstetter, Bruce George 1956- WhoEmL 93
Brandstetter, Holly N. Law&B 92
Brandstetter, Pavel 1955- WhoScE 91-4
Brandstrom, Charlotte 1959- MiSFD 9
Brandt, Alvin George 1922- WhoWrEP 92
Brandt, Andrew Curtis 1951- WhoWrEP 92
Brandt, Andrzej M. 1930- WhoScE 91-4
Brandt, Barbara Kinman 1954- WhoEmL 93
Brandt, Bernd-August 1929- WhoWor 93
Brandt, Blanch Marie 1937- WhoAmW 93
Brandt, Brenda Joyce 1961- WhoEmL 93
Brandt, Carl D. 1935- St&PR 93
Brandt, Catherine Ann 1962- WhoEmL 93
Brandt, David DcCPCAm
Brandt, David Dean 1947- WhoEmL 93
Brandt, Deborah 1951- ConAu 138
Brandt, Di 1952- WhoCanL 92
Brandt, Donald Edward 1954- WhoAm 92
Brandt, Edward Newman, Jr. 1933- WhoAm 92, WhoSSW 93, WhoWrEP 92
Brandt, Frederick T. 1942- St&PR 93
Brandt, Frederick William 1933- WhoAm 92
Brandt, Grace Borgenicht 1915- WhoAm 92, WhoE 93
Brandt, Harry 1925- WhoAm 92
Brandt, I. Marvin 1942- WhoSSW 93, WhoWor 93
Brandt, Ira Kive 1923- WhoAm 92
Brandt, James Andrew 1927- St&PR 93
Brandt, Jeffrey Lawrence Law&B 92
Brandt, Jobst vom 1517-1570 Baker 92
Brandt, Joel A. Law&B 92
Brandt, John Ashworth 1950- WhoEmL 93
Brandt, John Edward 1946- WhoWor 93
Brandt, John Henry 1940- WhoE 93
Brandt, Joseph A. 1899-1984 BioIn 17
Brandt, Jozef 1841-1915 PolBiDi
Brandt, Karen J. Law&B 92
Brandt, Kirsten 1960- WhoScE 91-2
Brandt, Leslie F. 1919- WhoWrEP 92
Brandt, Louis J. 1904- St&PR 93
Brandt, Marianne 1842-1921 Baker 92, OxDcOp
Brandt, Mary Kathleen 1946- WhoE 93
Brandt, Paul A. 1938- St&PR 93
Brandt, Peter H. 1896-1990 BioIn 17
Brandt, Philip Ronald 1942- St&PR 93
Brandt, Ramona Margaret 1963- WhoAmW 93
Brandt, Reinhard 1932- WhoWor 93
Brandt, Rexford Elson 1914- WhoAm 92
Brandt, Richard 1927- St&PR 93
Brandt, Richard Booker 1910- WhoAm 92
Brandt, Richard Martin 1922- WhoAm 92
Brandt, Richard Paul 1927- WhoAm 92
Brandt, Robert Frederic, III 1946- WhoAm 92
Brandt, Ronald Lee 1947- WhoEmL 93
Brandt, Ronald Marvin 1946- WhoE 93, WhoEmL 93
Brandt, Ronald Stirling 1932- WhoSSW 93
Brandt, Siegmund 1936- WhoScE 91-3
Brandt, Susan 1941- St&PR 93
Brandt, Thomas K. Law&B 92
Brandt, Truman L. 1931- St&PR 93
Brandt, Warren 1918- WhoAm 92
Brandt, Werner W. 1938- WhoE 93
Brandt, William Arthur, Jr. 1949- WhoEmL 93, WhoWor 93
Brandt, William Charles 1957- WhoEmL 93
Brandt, Willy 1913- BioIn 17, DcTwHis, WhoWor 93
Brandt, Willy 1913-1992 ColdWar 1 [port], CurBio 92N, NewYTBS 92 [port], News 93-2
Brandt, Yale M. 1930- WhoAm 92, WhoSSW 93
Brandtjen, Henry A. 1928- St&PR 93
Brandtjen, Henry Albert, III 1959- St&PR 93
Brandt-Sarif, Theodore Sonian 1959- WhoE 93
Brandts-Buys, Jan 1868-1933 Baker 92
Brandukov, Anatol (Andreievich) 1856-1930 Baker 92
Brandveen, Antonio I. 1946- AfrAmBi
Brandveen, Antonio Isadore 1946- WhoEmL 93
Brandvold, Richard J. 1922- St&PR 93
Brandwein, Daniel Scott 1964- WhoE 93
Brandwein, David I. Law&B 92
Brandwein, Debra J. Law&B 92
Brandwein, Larry 1931- WhoAm 92
Brandwein, Steve Craig 1948- St&PR 93
Brandwynne, Marcia BioIn 17
Brandzel, Jacob Reuben 1939- WhoAm 92
Branea, Ioan Dorel 1938- WhoWor 93
Branegan, James Augustus, III 1950- WhoAm 92
Branemark, Per-Ingvar 1929- WhoScE 91-4
Branflick, Robert Andrew 1948- St&PR 93
Branfman, Eric Jay 1947- WhoEmL 93
Branford, Kester Adrian 1950- WhoUN 92
Brangenberg, Albert 1944- St&PR 93
Branges, Louis de 1932- WhoAm 92
Branham, Andrew Law&B 92
Branham, Andrew Criddle 1953- WhoEmL 93
Branham, Mack Carison, Jr. 1931- WhoWor 93
Branham, Richard Lacy, Jr. 1943- WhoWor 93
Branham, William 1909-1965 BioIn 17
Branica, Marko 1931- WhoScE 91-4
Braniff, Thomas E. 1883-1954 EncABHB 8 [port]
Braniff, William WhoAm 92
Branigan, Craig Wolfe 1951- WhoAm 92
Branigan, Helen Marie 1944- WhoAmW 93
Branigan, Keith 1940- WhoWor 93
Branigin, William Joseph 1952- WhoAm 92
Branin, Francis Sunfield, Jr. 1947- WhoE 93
Branin, Joan Julia 1944- WhoAmW 93
Branin, Lora B. 1941- WhoE 93
Branion, John Marshall BioIn 17
Brankov, Georgi 1913- WhoScE 91-4
Brankov, James Preston WhoSSW 93
Brankovich, Mark J. 1922- WhoWor 93
Branley, Franklyn M. 1915- SmATA 16AS [port]
Branley, Franklyn M(ansfield) 1915- ConAu 39NR, MajAI [port]
Branley, Franklyn Mansfield 1915- BioIn 17
Branman, Martin Jeffrey 1955- WhoE 93
Brann, Alton J. 1941- St&PR 93
Brann, Eva Toni Helene 1929- WhoE 93
Brann, Lester William, Jr. 1925- WhoAm 92
Brann, William Cowper 1855-1898 GayN
Brann, William Paul 1916- WhoAm 92
Brannan, David Alexander WhoScE 91-1
Brannan, David Alexander 1942- WhoWor 93
Brannan, Donald J. Law&B 92
Brannan, Eulie Ross 1928- WhoAm 92
Brannan, James Bernard, Jr. 1951- WhoEmL 93
Brannan, Peggy L. 1937- WhoAmW 93
Brannan, Robert D. 1942- St&PR 93
Brannan, William 1925- WhoAm 92
Brannan, William Breece 1958- WhoEmL 93
Brannen, Charles A. 1944- St&PR 93
Brannen, Malcolm Erskine 1946- WhoEmL 93
Brannen, Melissa Lee BioIn 17
Brannen, Tammy BioIn 17
Brannen, William Thomas 1936- St&PR 93
Branner, John Casper 1850-1992 BioIn 17
Branner, Peter T.S. 1934- WhoUN 92
Brannian, Ross Edwin 1925- WhoSSW 93
Brannick, Ellen Marie 1934- WhoAmW 93
Brannick, J.E. 1955- St&PR 93
Brannigan, Gary G(eorge) 1947- ConAu 139
Brannigan, James Hugh 1932- St&PR 93
Brannigan, Michael Christopher 1948- WhoE 93
Brannigan, Owen 1908-1973 Baker 92, OxDcOp
Brannland, Rolf C.A. 1926- WhoScE 91-4
Brannock, Geary Steven Law&B 92
Brannon, Claudia AmWomPl
Brannon, Clifton Woodrow 1912- WhoAm 92
Brannon, Hezzie Raymond, Jr. 1926- WhoAm 92
Brannon, James L. 1945- St&PR 93
Brannon, Jean Marilyn WhoWrEP 92
Brannon, Jean Thomas 1950- WhoSSW 93
Brannon, Judith A. 1948- WhoIns 93
Brannon, Lester Travis, Jr. 1926- WhoAm 92
Brannon, Michael George WhoSSW 93
Brannon, Rachel Ann 1954- WhoSSW 93
Brannon-Peppas, Lisa 1962- WhoAm 92
Branny, Jerzy 1937- WhoScE 91-4
Branom, Debra E. Law&B 92
Bransby, Eric James 1916- WhoAm 92
Bransby, P.L. WhoScE 91-1
Branscheid, Wolfgang 1947- WhoScE 91-3
Branscomb, Anne Wells 1928- WhoAm 92, WhoAmW 93, WhoWor 93
Branscomb, Harvie, Jr. 1922- WhoAm 92
Branscomb, Lewis Capers, Jr. 1911- WhoAm 92
Branscomb, Lewis McAdory 1926- St&PR 93, WhoAm 92
Branscombe, Gena 1881- AmWomPl
Branscombe, Gena 1881-1977 Baker 92
Branscombe, Nyla Ruth 1956- WhoAmW 93, WhoEmL 93
Branscome, James Glenn 1946- St&PR 93
Branscum, Christine Maria 1951- WhoAmW 93
Branscum, Robbie 1937- DcAmChF 1960, MajAI [port], SmATA 72 [port]
Bransden, Brian Harold WhoScE 91-1
Bransdorfer, Stephen Christie 1929- WhoAm 92
Bransfield, John J. 1922- St&PR 93
Bransfield, Robert Carroll 1946- WhoEmL 93
Bransford, Stephen 1949- ScF&FL 92
Bransgrove, Linda Lee 1962- WhoSSW 93
Bransome, Edwin Dagobert, Jr. 1933- WhoSSW 93
Branson, Branley Allan 1929- WhoAm 92
Branson, Branley Allen 1929- WhoWrEP 92
Branson, Brenda Sullens 1961- WhoEmL 93
Branson, Dan Earle 1928- WhoAm 92
Branson, Herman Russell 1914- WhoAm 92
Branson, James Richard 1940- WhoWor 93
Branson, Karen Marie 1956- WhoAmW 93
Branson, Margaret Stimmann 1922- WhoAmW 93
Branson, Mary Lou 1932- WhoAm 92, WhoAmW 93
Branson, Richard 1950- WhoAm 92
Branson, Rusty Scott 1960- St&PR 93
Branstad, Paul A. 1944- St&PR 93
Branstad, Terry Edward 1946- WhoAm 92, WhoWor 93
Branstetter, C. Burton Law&B 92
Brant, Austin E., Jr. 1929- St&PR 93
Brant, David W. 1950- St&PR 93
Brant, Dawn Mary 1965- WhoEmL 93
Brant, George H. Law&B 92
Brant, Henry 1913- Baker 92, WhoAm 92
Brant, Jan 1554-1602 Baker 92
Brant, John Getty 1946- WhoEmL 93
Brant, Joseph 1742-1807 HarEnMi
Brant, L. Ray 1909- St&PR 93
Brant, Marjorie Hasselback Law&B 92
Brant, Murray 1910- St&PR 93
Brant, Peter Reginald 1915- St&PR 93
Brant, Philip Edwin, Jr. 1945- WhoSSW 93
Brant, Richard Ross 1934- St&PR 93
Brant, Sandra WhoAm 92
Brant, William Morton 1937- WhoE 93, WhoWrEP 92
Brant, William W. 1933- St&PR 93
Brantenberg, Gerd 1941- ScF&FL 92
Brantingham, Barney 1932- WhoAm 92
Brantingham, Charles Ross 1917- WhoWor 93
Brantl, James S. Law&B 92
Brantley, Bruce Barton 1933- WhoE 93
Brantley, Charles F. 1933- St&PR 93
Brantley, David Lehmon 1949- St&PR 93
Brantley, Geraldine 1958- WhoSSW 93
Brantley, Helen Thomas 1942- WhoSSW 93
Brantley, Jeffrey Garland 1949- WhoEmL 93, WhoSSW 93
Brantley, Jerry Lee, Jr. 1962- WhoSSW 93
Brantley, Lee Reed 1906- WhoAm 92
Brantley, Nancy Simpson 1938- WhoSSW 93
Brantley, Oliver Wiley 1915- WhoAm 92
Brantley, Sandra J. Law&B 92
Brantley, William Stanley 1956- WhoEmL 93
Brantlinger, F. Herbert 1939- St&PR 93
Branton, Calvin Franklin Law&B 92
Branton, Daniel 1932- WhoAm 92
Branton, Sandra Louise 1956- WhoAmW 93
Brantz, George M. 1930- St&PR 93
Brantzell, Aura Woodin AmWomPl
Branum, William Howell 1941- WhoAm 92
Branyan, Helen Baird 1927- WhoAmW 93
Branyan, Robert Lester 1930- WhoAm 92
Branz, Louis Raymond Law&B 92
Branzell, Karin 1891-1974 OxDcOp
Branzell, Karin Maria 1891-1974 Baker 92
Branzer, John Paul 1942- WhoSSW 93, WhoWor 93
Braque, Georges 1882-1963 BioIn 17
Bras, Antonio B. Law&B 92
Bras, Rafael Luis 1950- WhoAm 92
Brasca, Eugenio 1933- WhoScE 91-3
Brasch, Frederick E. 1875-1967 BioIn 17
Brasch, Jerome F. 1925- St&PR 93
Brasch, John Michael 1955- WhoEmL 93
Brasch, Walter Milton 1945- WhoWrEP 92
Braschi, Nicoletta BioIn 17
Brasel, Jo Anne 1934- WhoAm 92
Brasel, Michael Louis 1958- WhoSSW 93
Brasell, Harold Keary 1922- WhoWor 93
Brasfield, David Williamson 1956- WhoEmL 93, WhoSSW 93
Brasfield, Evans Booker 1932- St&PR 93, WhoAm 92
Brasfield, James 1952- WhoWrEP 92
Brasfield, John Michael 1948- WhoEmL 93
Brasfield, Sam T. 1941- St&PR 93
Brash, Sally Miller 1911- WhoAmW 93
Brashaw, Gerald L. 1941- St&PR 93
Brashear, David Mark 1961- WhoEmL 93
Brashear, Diane Lee 1933- WhoAm 92, WhoAmW 93
Brashear, James F. Law&B 92
Brashear, John A. 1840-1920 BioIn 17
Brashears, Bobby Fuller 1934- WhoAm 92
Brashears, David Fredrick 1946- St&PR 93
Brashears, Kent Baker 1953- WhoEmL 93, WhoSSW 93
Brashears, Wilford Session, Jr. 1925- WhoSSW 93
Brasher, Diane 1949- St&PR 93
Brasher, George Walter 1936- WhoSSW 93
Brasher, James E. Law&B 92
Brasher, James E. 1948- St&PR 93
Brasher, Phyllis Law&B 92
Brasher, Richard Curtis 1931- St&PR 93
Brasher, Thomas Evans 1938- WhoSSW 93
Brashers, (Howard) Charles 1930- WhoWrEP 92
Brashers, Gary Boyd 1947- St&PR 93
Brashier, Edward Martin 1954- WhoSSW 93
Brashier, Robert Steven 1954- WhoEmL 93
Brashler, Anne 1924- WhoWrEP 92
Brashler, William 1947- WhoAm 92
Brasic, Gregory Lee 1961- WhoEmL 93
Brasic, James Robert 1948- WhoEmL 93
Brasidas d422BC HarEnMi
Brasillach, Robert 1909-1945 BioIn 17
Brasket, Curt Justin 1932- WhoAm 92

Braslau, Sophie 1892-1935 *Baker 92*
Brasler, Robert M. 1936- *St&PR 93*
Brasley, Amy Jordan 1956- *WhoAmW 93*
Brass, Hugh Simon *Law&B 92*
Brass, Perry Manuel 1947- *WhoWrEP 92*
Brass, Tinto 1933- *MiSFD 9*
Brass, Wilhelm 1926- *WhoScE 91-3*
Brassard, Christopher J. 1956- *WhoEmL 93*
Brassard, Roger Paul 1913- *WhoE 93*
Brass Construction *SoulM*
Brasseale, Kent A. 1941- *St&PR 93*
Brasseaux, Belinda Sue 1948- *WhoAmW 93*
Brasseaux, Mary Therese 1951- *WhoEmL 93*
Brassel, Kurt E. 1943- *WhoScE 91-4*
Brassel, P. *WhoScE 91-4*
Brassell, Roselyn Strauss 1930- *WhoAm 92*
Brassens, Georges 1921-1981 *Baker 92*
Brassett, Leo Lieux 1923- *St&PR 93*
Brasseur, Pierre 1903?-1972 *IntDcF 2-3 [port]*
Brassey, Laurel Kaye 1954- *WhoAmW 93*
Brassfield, Karen F. 1947- *St&PR 93*
Brassfield, Patricia Ann *WhoAmW 93*
Brassfield, William Charles 1940- *WhoSSW 93*
Brassil, Jean Ella 1933- *WhoAm 92*
Brassin, Louis 1840-1884 *Baker 92*
Brast, Calvin 1933- *St&PR 93*
Brasunas, Anton de Sales 1919- *WhoAm 92*
Brasure, Ralph James, III 1953- *WhoSSW 93*
Braswell, Albert M., Jr. 1920- *St&PR 93*
Braswell, Arnold Webb 1925- *WhoAm 92*
Braswell, George Wilbur 1936- *WhoSSW 93*
Braswell, James C. 1946- *St&PR 93*
Braswell, Kern F. 1956- *WhoSSW 93*
Braswell, Louis Erskine 1937- *WhoAm 92*
Braswell, Pearl Eva 1914- *WhoAmW 93, WhoWor 93*
Braswell, Robert Neil 1932- *WhoAm 92*
Braswell, Walter M. *Law&B 92*
Braszcynski, Janusz 1931- *WhoScE 91-4*
Braszczynski, Janusz 1931- *WhoWor 93*
Bratanata, Slamet d1992 *BioIn 17, NewYTBS 92*
Bratby, John 1928-1992 *NewYTBS 92*
Bratcher, Carla Elizabeth 1942- *WhoAmW 93*
Bratcher, Keith Glenn 1958- *WhoEmL 93*
Bratcher, Twila Langdon *WhoAm 92, WhoAmW 93*
Braten, Stein Leif 1934- *WhoWor 93*
Brathwaite, Edward (Kamau) 1930- *DcLB 125 [port]*
Brathwaite, Faye Anne 1953- *WhoSSW 93*
Brathwaite, Fred 1958?- *BioIn 17*
Brathwaite, Harriet Louisa 1931- *WhoAmW 93*
Brathwaite, Jorge Alonso 1944- *St&PR 93*
Brathwaite, Mellissa Annette 1961- *WhoAmW 93, WhoE 93*
Brathwaite, Nicholas 1925- *DcCPCAm, WhoWor 93*
Bratianu, Ionel 1864-1927 *DcTwHis*
Bratishchev, Alexandr Vasiljevich 1949- *WhoWor 93*
Braton, David Allen 1951- *St&PR 93*
Bratsford, R. *WhoScE 91-1*
Bratsos-Shaw, Diane 1958- *WhoEmL 93*
Bratt, Bengt Erik 1922- *WhoAm 92*
Bratt, C. Griffith 1914- *WhoWor 93*
Bratt, John Albert 1938- *St&PR 93*
Bratt, Nicholas 1948- *St&PR 93, WhoAm 92, WhoEmL 93*
Brattain, Arlene Jane Clark 1938- *WhoAmW 93, WhoWor 93*
Brattain, Donald R. *St&PR 93*
Brattain, Freda Smith 1965- *WhoAmW 93*
Bratten, Craig K. 1953- *St&PR 93*
Bratter, Peter 1935- *WhoWor 93*
Bratter, Thomas Edward *BioIn 17*
Bratter, Thomas Edward 1939- *WhoE 93*
Bratthauar, Ted John 1946- *St&PR 93*
Brattin, Elvin Price 1948- *WhoEmL 93*
Brattin, Joel James 1956- *WhoE 93*
Brattin, Kathleen Ann 1957- *WhoAmW 93, WhoEmL 93*
Brattle, Thomas 1658-1713 *BioIn 17*
Bratton, Ann R. *Law&B 92*
Bratton, Conrad Christopher 1941- *WhoSSW 93*
Bratton, Ida Frank 1933- *WhoAmW 93, WhoSSW 93, WhoWor 93*
Bratton, James Henry, Jr. 1931- *WhoAm 92*
Bratton, Johnny *BioIn 17*
Bratton, Joseph Key 1926- *WhoAm 92*
Bratton, Kevin J. 1949- *St&PR 93*
Bratton, Robert O. 1948- *St&PR 93*
Bratton, William Edward 1919- *St&PR 93, WhoWor 93*
Brattstrom, Bayard Holmes 1929- *WhoAm 92*
Brattstrom, Stig 1931- *WhoWor 93*
Bratzel, Andrew D. *Law&B 92*
Braubach, Mary Ann *MiSFD 9*
Brauch, Charles Peter 1937- *St&PR 93*
Brauch, Merry Ruth Moore 1920- *WhoAm 92*
Braucher, Jane Alberta Elliott *WhoWor 93*
Braucher, Jean 1950- *WhoAmW 93*
Braucher, Richard *Law&B 92*
Braucher, Richard Harold 1936- *St&PR 93*
Brauchitsch, Walter von 1881-1948 *BioIn 17, DcTwHis*
Brauchitsch, Walther von 1881-1948 *HarEnMi*
Brauchle, Walter R. 1943- *St&PR 93*
Brauchli, Marcus Walker 1961- *WhoWor 93*
Braucht, David William 1954- *WhoEmL 93*
Braucht, La Vere T., Jr. 1929- *WhoIns 93*
Braucht, Stephanie Ann Sirotnak 1948- *WhoEmL 93*
Brauckmann, F. Paul 1947- *WhoEmL 93*
Braud, Bert Stephen 1959- *WhoEmL 93*
Braud, Kenneth Warren 1952- *WhoEmL 93, WhoSSW 93*
Braud, Michel *WhoScE 91-2*
Braud, Samuel Philip, III 1930- *St&PR 93*
Braude, Abraham S. 1910- *St&PR 93*
Braude, Anne Janet *ScF&FL 92*
Braude, Edwin S. 1927- *WhoAm 92*
Braude, Keith Z. 1962- *St&PR 93*
Braude, Kenneth Z. 1936- *St&PR 93*
Braude, Kevin Z. 1964- *St&PR 93*
Braude, Michael 1936- *WhoAm 92*
Braude, Robert Michael 1939- *WhoAm 92*
Braude, Stuart 1936- *St&PR 93*
Braude, Theodore R. 1952- *WhoEmL 93*
Braudel, Fernand *BioIn 17*
Braudo, Evgeniy Evgenyevich 1934- *WhoWor 93*
Braudy, Leo Beal 1941- *WhoAm 92, WhoWrEP 92*
Brauer, Amie Ruth 1962- *WhoAmW 93*
Brauer, Arik 1929- *WhoWor 93*
Brauer, Barbara Ann 1937- *WhoE 93*
Brauer, Earle W. 1918-1991 *BioIn 17*
Brauer, Erich 1895-1942 *IntDcAn*
Brauer, Eugene Richard 1936- *St&PR 93*
Brauer, Evald 1904-1961 *Baker 92*
Brauer, Evan Zack 1957- *St&PR 93*
Brauer, Frank 1929- *St&PR 93*
Brauer, Harrol Andrew, Jr. 1920- *WhoWor 93*
Brauer, Heinz Peter 1923- *WhoWor 93*
Brauer, Herbert Julien 1920- *St&PR 93*
Brauer, Jane Zion 1952- *WhoEmL 93*
Brauer, Michael 1949- *WhoEmL 93, WhoWor 93*
Brauer, Ralph Werner 1921- *WhoAm 92*
Brauer, Robert H. *Law&B 92*
Brauer, William H. 1926- *St&PR 93*
Brauff, Lavinia E. *AmWomPl*
Braugh, Scott S. *Law&B 92*
Braugher, Andre *BioIn 17*
Brault, Gayle Lorain 1944- *WhoAmW 93, WhoWor 93*
Brault, Gerard Joseph 1929- *WhoAm 92*
Brault, Jacques 1933- *WhoCanL 92*
Brault, Mary E. 1942- *WhoAmW 93*
Brault, Michel 1928- *MiSFD 9*
Braum, Erich 1931- *WhoScE 91-3*
Brauman, Henry C. 1920- *WhoScE 91-2*
Brauman, John I. 1937- *WhoAm 92*
Braumiller, Allen Spooner 1934- *St&PR 93, WhoAm 92*
Braun, Adolphe 1811-1877 *BioIn 17*
Braun, Alan Joseph 1953- *WhoE 93*
Braun, Andrew James 1962- *WhoEmL 93, WhoSSW 93*
Braun, Armand Aron 1937- *WhoWor 93*
Braun, Arthur David 1952- *WhoSSW 93*
Braun, Bonnie Sue 1947- *WhoEmL 93*
Braun, Carl 1885-1960 *Baker 92*
Braun, Carl August 1927- *BiDAMSp 1989*
Braun, Carol Elizabeth Moseley 1947- *NewYTBS 92 [port]*
Braun, Carol Moseley 1947- *BioIn 17, ConBlB 4 [port], News 93-1 [port], WhoAmW 93*
Braun, Charles Louis 1937- *WhoAm 92*
Braun, Charles R. 1933- *St&PR 93*
Braun, Charles Stuart 1941- *WhoAm 92, WhoSSW 93*
Braun, Christine Ann 1961- *WhoSSW 93*
Braun, Claire S. 1931- *WhoWrEP 92*
Braun, Craig Allen 1939- *WhoE 93*
Braun, Daniel Carl 1905- *WhoAm 92*
Braun, David Adlai 1931- *WhoAm 92*
Braun, Dianne Blocker *Law&B 92*
Braun, Dietrich 1930- *WhoScE 91-3, WhoWor 93*
Braun, Earl Edward, Jr. 1941- *WhoSSW 93*
Braun, Erich F. 1938- *WhoScE 91-3*
Braun, Eunice Hockspeier *WhoAmW 93*
Braun, F.H. *Law&B 92*
Braun, Hans-Gert 1942- *WhoWor 93*
Braun, Harald W. 1952- *WhoWor 93*
Braun, Helmut J. 1924- *WhoScE 91-3*
Braun, Henry 1930- *WhoWrEP 92*
Braun, Hermann Erich 1942- *St&PR 93*
Braun, Janet L. *Law&B 92*
Braun, Jean-Claude 1943- *WhoScE 91-2*
Braun, Jeffrey N. *Law&B 92*
Braun, Jerome 1918- *St&PR 93*
Braun, Jerome Irwin 1929- *WhoAm 92, WhoWor 93*
Braun, Joseph C. *WhoAm 92*
Braun, Kazimierz 1924- *WhoScE 91-4*
Braun, Kazimierz Pawel 1936- *WhoWor 93*
Braun, L. Erich 1944- *St&PR 93*
Braun, Lisa 1951- *WhoAmW 93*
Braun, Lois 1949- *WhoCanL 92*
Braun, Loretta Carol 1933- *St&PR 93*
Braun, Ludwig 1926- *WhoAm 92*
Braun, Manfred 1941- *WhoScE 91-3*
Braun, Martin 1941- *WhoE 93*
Braun, Matthew 1932- *ScF&FL 92*
Braun, Maura Tracey 1966- *WhoEmL 93*
Braun, Maurice 1877-1941 *BioIn 17*
Braun, Michael A. d1992 *NewYTBS 92*
Braun, Michael Alan 1949- *WhoAm 92, WhoEmL 93*
Braun, Michael Russell 1957- *St&PR 93*
Braun, Nancy Lynn 1952- *WhoEmL 93*
Braun, Neil S. 1952- *St&PR 93*
Braun, Norma Mai Tsen Wang 1937- *WhoAmW 93*
Braun, Norman L. 1931- *St&PR 93*
Braun, Peter Michael 1936- *Baker 92*
Braun, Phyllis Cellini 1953- *WhoAmW 93, WhoEmL 93*
Braun, Pinkas 1923- *WhoWor 93*
Braun, Raymond E. 1946- *St&PR 93*
Braun, Reto 1944- *WhoAm 92*
Braun, Richard 1933- *WhoScE 91-4*
Braun, Richard Edward 1937- *St&PR 93*
Braun, Richard L. 1947- *St&PR 93*
Braun, Richard Lane 1917- *WhoAm 92*
Braun, Robert Alexander 1910- *WhoWor 93*
Braun, Robert Denton 1943- *WhoSSW 93*
Braun, Robert Duncan 1939- *WhoWor 93*
Braun, Robert E. *Law&B 92*
Braun, Sheldon Richard 1943- *WhoAm 92*
Braun, Terrance *ScF&FL 92*
Braun, Theodore E. D. 1933- *WhoAm 92*
Braun, Thomas Henry 1943- *St&PR 93*
Braun, Timothy Charles 1957- *St&PR 93*
Braun, Virginia Vickers 1947- *WhoAmW 93*
Braun, Volker 1939- *DcLB 124 [port]*
Braun, Walter Johann Kaspar *WhoWor 93*
Braun, Warren Lloyd 1922- *WhoAm 92*
Braun, Wendy *BioIn 17*
Braun, Wilhelm *Baker 92*
Braun, William J. 1925- *WhoIns 93*
Braun, William Joseph 1925- *WhoAm 92*
Braun, Yvan *Law&B 92*
Braun, Zev *WhoAm 92*
Braunberger, Pierre 1905-1990 *BioIn 17*
Braun-Brashares, Barbara Sue 1948- *WhoEmL 93*
Braunecker, James L. 1953- *St&PR 93*
Braun-Elwert, Wilhelm 1915- *WhoWor 93*
Braunfels, Walter 1882-1954 *Baker 92, OxDcOp*
Braungart, Richard Gottfried 1935- *WhoAm 92*
Braunig, Martha J. *St&PR 93*
Braunitzer, Gerhard 1921- *WhoScE 91-3*
Braunlich, Helmut Karl 1929- *WhoE 93*
Braunschweiger, Robert Welty 1937- *St&PR 93*
Braunsdorf, Mary *Law&B 92*
Braunstein, Barry David 1953- *WhoEmL 93*
Braunstein, Donnie *Law&B 92*
Braunstein, Lee J. 1936- *St&PR 93*
Braunstein, Mark Mathew 1951- *WhoE 93*
Braunstein, Martin Lewis 1944- *St&PR 93*
Braunstein, Nora *St&PR 93*
Braunstein, Phillip 1930- *WhoAm 92*
Braunstein, Richard *Law&B 92*
Braunsweg, Julian 1897-1978 *PolBiDi*
Braunwald, Eugene 1929- *WhoAm 92*
Brausa, G. Steven 1951- *WhoAm 92*
Brause, Donna Carlene 1958- *WhoEmL 93*
Brautigam, Kurt Richard 1957- *WhoSSW 93*
Brautigan, Richard *BioIn 17*
Brautigan, Richard 1933-1984 *ScF&FL 92*
Brautigan, Richard 1935-1984 *MagSAmL [port]*
Brautman, Morton d1991 *BioIn 17*
Brauweiler, Daniel Charles 1961- *WhoEmL 93*
Bravaldo, Donald Henry, Jr. 1934- *St&PR 93*
Bravar, Mladen 1926- *WhoScE 91-4*
Bravard, Robert S. 1935- *ScF&FL 92*
Bravard, Robert Staton 1935- *WhoE 93*
Braver, Moshe 1954- *St&PR 93*
Braverman, Amiel 1926- *St&PR 93*
Braverman, Burt Alan 1946- *WhoEmL 93*
Braverman, Charles 1944- *MiSFD 9*
Braverman, David George 1959- *WhoSSW 93*
Braverman, Donna Caryn 1947- *WhoEmL 93*
Braverman, Doreen *Law&B 92*
Braverman, Ed *BioIn 17*
Braverman, Harold 1921- *St&PR 93*
Braverman, Harry 1920-1976 *BioIn 17*
Braverman, Irwin Merton 1929- *WhoAm 92*
Braverman, Kate *BioIn 17*
Braverman, Larry Jay *Law&B 92*
Braverman, Lois 1950- *WhoEmL 93*
Braverman, Louise Marcia 1948- *WhoE 93*
Braverman, Melvin 1927- *St&PR 93*
Braverman, Michael R. 1951- *St&PR 93*
Braverman, Philip *Law&B 92*
Braverman, Philip 1933- *WhoAm 92*
Braverman, Richard *Law&B 92*
Braverman, Robert Carl 1935- *WhoSSW 93*
Braverman, Robert Jay 1933- *WhoAm 92*
Braverman, Sidney 1928- *St&PR 93*
Braverman, Susan Plavin 1937- *WhoAmW 93*
Bravery, Anthony Frederick *WhoScE 91-1*
Bravman, Richard Edward 1955- *St&PR 93*
Bravmann, Ludwig 1925- *WhoAm 92*
Bravnicar, Matija 1897-1977 *Baker 92*
Bravo, Anthony John 1938- *WhoAm 92, WhoE 93*
Bravo, Carlos Eduardo 1959- *WhoEmL 93*
Bravo, Claudio 1936- *BioIn 17*
Bravo, Manuel Alvarez 1902- *BioIn 17*
Bravo, Rose Marie 1951- *WhoAm 92, WhoAmW 93*
Bravo, Rui *WhoScE 91-3*
Bravo-Casas, German Antonio 1939- *WhoUN 92*
Bravo De Laguna, Jeronimo 1948- *WhoScE 91-3*
Brawer, Catherine Coleman 1943- *St&PR 93, WhoAmW 93*
Brawer, Robert A. *BioIn 17*
Brawerman, George 1927- *WhoE 93*
Brawley, Benjamin 1882-1939 *BlkAuII 92*
Brawley, Edith Mitchell 1936- *WhoAmW 93*
Brawley, Ernest Charles 1937- *WhoWrEP 92*
Brawley, Phyllis L. 1936- *St&PR 93*
Brawley, Robert Julius 1937- *WhoAm 92*
Brawley, Tawana *BioIn 17*
Brawley, Thomas *St&PR 93*
Brawn, Anna *ScF&FL 92*
Brawn, Linda Curtis 1947- *WhoAmW 93, WhoE 93*
Brawne, Michael *WhoScE 91-1*
Brawner, Lee Basil 1935- *WhoAm 92, WhoSSW 93*
Braxen, Gustov *WhoScE 91-4*
Braxton, Anthony 1945- *Baker 92*
Braxton, Karrye Yvonne 1960- *WhoE 93*
Braxton-Kallenbach, Mary Ellen 1946- *WhoEmL 93*
Bray, Absalom Francis, Jr. 1918- *WhoAm 92*
Bray, Anna Eliza 1790-1883 *DcLB 116 [port]*
Bray, Anthos 1924- *WhoScE 91-3*
Bray, Arthur Philip 1933- *WhoAm 92*
Bray, Barry Daniel 1946- *St&PR 93*
Bray, Bonnie Anderson 1929- *WhoAm 92, WhoAmW 93*
Bray, Carolyn Scott 1938- *WhoAmW 93*
Bray, Charles William, III 1933- *WhoAm 92*
Bray, David E. 1938- *St&PR 93*
Bray, David Maurice 1941- *WhoAm 92*
Bray, Douglas Weston *BioIn 17*
Bray, George August 1931- *WhoAm 92, WhoSSW 93*
Bray, Gordon Louis 1953- *WhoE 93*
Bray, Grady P. 1944- *WhoE 93*
Bray, Janet Baltuch 1950- *WhoEmL 93*
Bray, John Joseph 1937- *St&PR 93*
Bray, John Roger 1929- *WhoWor 93*
Bray, Kenneth N.C. *WhoScE 91-1*
Bray, Laurack Doyle 1949- *WhoE 93, WhoEmL 93*
Bray, Louise Whitefield *AmWomPl*
Bray, Melvyn Kenneth 1946- *WhoE 93*
Bray, Oscar S. 1905- *WhoAm 92*
Bray, Philip J. *Law&B 92*
Bray, Philip James 1925- *WhoAm 92*
Bray, Pierce 1924- *WhoAm 92*
Bray, R.N. 1942- *WhoScE 91-1*
Bray, Robert *BioIn 17*
Bray, Robert Bruce 1924- *WhoAm 92*
Bray, Ronald L. 1932- *St&PR 93*
Bray, Rosemary L. *NewYTBS 92 [port]*
Bray, Thomas Lee 1914- *St&PR 93*

Bray, William Harold 1958- WhoWor 93
Braybrooke, David 1924- WhoAm 92, WhoSSW 93, WhoWrEP 92
Braybrooke, Geoffrey Bernard 1935- WhoAsAP 91
Braybrooks, Colin Law&B 92
Brayczewski, Bohdan 1932- WhoWor 93
Brayer, Donald J. 1942- WhoIns 93
Brayer, Kenneth 1941- WhoAm 92
Brayer, Menachem Mendel 1922- WhoAm 92
Brayer, Patrick A. St&PR 93
Brayfield, April Ann 1959- WhoAmW 93
Brayman, Alan Linwood 1951- St&PR 93
Braymer, Marguerite 1911- St&PR 93
Braymer, Marguerite Annetta 1911- WhoAm 92
Brayshaw, Thomas Carlton 1946- WhoAm 92
Brayson, Albert Aloysius, II 1953- WhoE 93, WhoEmL 93
Brayton, Charles R. 1840-1910 PolPar
Brayton, John Summerfield, Jr. 1924- St&PR 93
Brayton, Robert Clayton 1942- St&PR 93
Brayton, Roswell, Sr. 1917- St&PR 93
Brayton, Tammy Ann 1962- WhoE 93
Braza, Francisco 1949- WhoScE 91-3
Braza, Mary Kathryn 1956- WhoAmW 93
Brazaitis, Edna Carey Law&B 92
Brazaitis, Peter John 1936- WhoE 93
Brazaitis, Thomas Joseph 1940- WhoAm 92
Brazauskas, Algirdas BioIn 17
Brazda, Frederick Wicks 1945- WhoSSW 93
Brazeal, Aurelia E. 1943- WhoAmW 93
Brazeal, Carrie Trotter 1956- WhoAmW 93
Brazeal, Donna Smith 1947- WhoAm 92, WhoAmW 93, WhoEmL 93, WhoSSW 93
Brazeal, Earl Henry, Jr. 1939- WhoE 93
Brazeal, Michael Ray 1947- WhoAm 92
Brazeau, Philip R. Law&B 92
Brazeau, Richard 1940- St&PR 93
Brazeau, Willoughby F. d1991 BioIn 17
Brazell, James Ervin 1926- St&PR 93, WhoAm 92
Brazell, John L. 1939- St&PR 93, WhoIns 93
Brazell, Karen Woodard 1938- WhoAm 92
Brazelton, Eugenia Louise 1919- WhoWrEP 92
Brazelton, Roy Dale 1941- St&PR 93, WhoAm 92
Brazelton, Thomas Berry 1918- WhoAm 92
Brazelton, William Thomas 1921- WhoAm 92
Brazener, Ronald D. 1945- St&PR 93
Brazer, Bruce Alan 1952- St&PR 93
Brazer, Harvey Elliot 1922-1991 BioIn 17
Brazer, Mara Hope 1955- WhoAmW 93
Brazer, Marjorie Cahn 1927- WhoWrEP 92
Brazier, C.W. 1910- St&PR 93
Brazier, Don Roland 1921- WhoAm 92
Brazier, Mary Margaret 1956- WhoAmW 93, WhoEmL 93, WhoSSW 93
Brazier, Robert G. WhoAm 92
Brazier, Robert George 1937- St&PR 93
Brazil, Harold Edmund 1920- WhoAm 92
Brazil, John Russell 1946- WhoAm 92
Brazil, Sharon Kay 1956- WhoAmW 93
Brazza, Pierre Savorgnan de 1852-1905 Expl 93 [port]
Brazzale, John Peter 1961- WhoEmL 93
Brazzel, Ronald D. 1940- St&PR 93
Brazzel, William Sherwood 1956- WhoSSW 93
Brazzi, Rossano 1916- ConTFT 10, IntDcF 2-3
Brcic, Josip 1923- WhoScE 91-4
Brdlik, Carola Emilie 1930- WhoAmW 93
Breach, Mark Christopher WhoScE 91-1
Breach, William David 1948- WhoSSW 93
Breading, Robert Picket 1933- WhoE 93
Bready, Richard L. 1944- St&PR 93
Bready, Richard Lawrence 1944- WhoAm 92
Breakenridge, William M. 1846-1931 BioIn 17
Breaker, Richard C. 1926- St&PR 93
Breakey, Jeffrey M. 1959- WhoWrEP 92
Breakstone, Arnold 1933- WhoE 93
Breakstone, Jay L. T. 1951- WhoEmL 93
Breakstone, Kay Louise 1936- WhoAmW 93
Breakstone, Robert Albert 1938- WhoAm 92, WhoWor 93
Breakstone, Ronald Irving 1953- St&PR 93
Breakwell, Glynis Marie WhoScE 91-1
Bream, Julian 1933- ConMus 9 [port], WhoAm 92, WhoWor 93
Bream, Julian (Alexander) 1933- Baker 92
Brean, George Albert 1942- St&PR 93
Brean, J.L. Law&B 92
Breanski, Felix Klemens 1794-1884 PolBiDi
Breard, Jack Hendricks 1939- St&PR 93
Brearley, Candice 1944- WhoE 93
Breart, Gerard L. 1946- WhoScE 91-2
Brearton, James Joseph 1950- WhoEmL 93
Brearton, Robert David 1949- St&PR 93
Breasted, James Henry 1865-1935 IntDcAn
Breathed, Berkeley 1957- WhoAm 92
Breathett, George 1926-1988 BioIn 17
Breathitt, Edward Thompson, Jr. 1924- WhoAm 92
Breathnach, Aodan Seosamh WhoScE 91-1
Breathnach, Caoimghin S. WhoScE 91-3
Breault, David J. 1928- St&PR 93
Breault, Paul Armand 1947- St&PR 93, WhoAm 92
Breault, Theodore Edward 1938- WhoE 93, WhoWor 93
Breaux, Anna Marie 1958- WhoAmW 93, WhoE 93
Breaux, David Lee 1954- WhoSSW 93
Breaux, James Albert 1934- St&PR 93
Breaux, John 1944- CngDr 91
Breaux, John B. 1944- WhoAm 92, WhoSSW 93
Breaux, Paul Joseph 1942- WhoSSW 93
Breazeale, Mack Alfred 1930- WhoAm 92, WhoSSW 93
Breazeale, Robert David 1935- WhoE 93
Brebbia, John Henry 1932- WhoAm 92
Brebels, Adriaan 1952- WhoWor 93
Brebner, John P. 1924- St&PR 93
Brebner, Philip 1955- ConAu 139
Breburda, Josef 1931- WhoScE 91-3
Brech, Donald Lewis 1935- St&PR 93
Brechbill, Bonnie Hellum 1954- WhoWrEP 92
Brechbill, Susan Reynolds 1943- WhoAmW 93
Brechbuhler, Hans 1907-1989 BioIn 17
Brecheen, Harry David 1914- BiDAMSp 1989
Brecher, Arthur Seymour 1928- WhoAm 92
Brecher, Bernd 1932- WhoE 93
Brecher, Edward M. 1911-1989 BioIn 17
Brecher, Ephraim Fred 1931- WhoE 93
Brecher, Ephraim M. Law&B 92
Brecher, Gustav 1879-1940 Baker 92
Brecher, Howard Arthur Law&B 92
Brecher, Irving 1923- WhoAm 92
Brecher, Kenneth 1943- WhoAm 92, WhoE 93
Brecher, Martha L. Law&B 92
Brecher, Michael 1925- WhoAm 92
Brecher, Ronald 1941- St&PR 93
Brechlin, Thomas W. 1934- St&PR 93
Brechon, Edwin Joseph 1940- St&PR 93
Brecht, Bertolt 1898-1956 BioIn 17, DcLB 124 [port], DcTwHis, DramC 3 [port], IntDcOp [port], MagSWL [port], OxDcOp, WorLitC [port]
Brecht, Blaine Richard 1958- WhoEmL 93, WhoSSW 93
Brecht, Donald L. 1935- St&PR 93
Brecht, Martin Bryan 1953- WhoEmL 93
Brecht, Sally Ann 1951- WhoAmW 93, WhoEmL 93
Brecht, Warren Frederick 1932- WhoAm 92
Brechtel, Horst Michael 1935- WhoScE 91-3
Breck, Allen du Pont 1914- WhoAm 92
Breck, Howard Rolland 1912- WhoAm 92
Breck, Katherine Anne 1964- WhoAmW 93
Breck, Robert 1713-1784 BioIn 17
Breck, Sylvia Thorington 1922- WhoE 93
Breckel, Alvina Hefeli 1948- WhoAmW 93, WhoEmL 93
Breckendridge, Franklin Eugene Law&B 92
Breckenridge, Bryan Craig 1951- WhoEmL 93
Breckenridge, Donald E. 1931- St&PR 93
Breckenridge, James R. 1928- St&PR 93
Breckenridge, John Cabell 1821-1875 HarEnMi
Breckenridge, Klindt Duncan 1957- WhoEmL 93
Breckenridge, Neil 1944- WhoSSW 93
Breckenridge, Robert Jerald 1933- St&PR 93
Breckenridge, Robert Markley 1931- St&PR 93
Breckenridge, Sally A. 1958- WhoEmL 93
Brecker, Manfred 1927- St&PR 93, WhoAm 92
Brecker, Michael BioIn 17
Brecker, Randy BioIn 17
Breckheimer, Mark Lewis 1955- St&PR 93
Breckinridge, James Bernard 1939- WhoAm 92
Breckinridge, John 1760-1806 BioIn 17
Breckinridge, John C. 1821-1875 PolPar
Breckinridge, John Cabell 1821-1875 BioIn 17
Breckinridge, Sophonisba Preston 1866-1948 BioIn 17
Breckle, Siegmar-Walter 1938- WhoScE 91-3
Breckner, Deborah Jeanne 1962- WhoEmL 93
Breckner, Jane McMillin 1915- WhoAmW 93, WhoWor 93
Breckner, William John, Jr. 1933- WhoAm 92
Brecknock, John 1937- Baker 92
Breckon, Donald John 1939- WhoAm 92
Breckwoldt, Meinert 1934- WhoScE 91-3
Breczinski, Michael Joseph 1953- WhoEmL 93
Bredahl, Janice Ann 1957- WhoAmW 93, WhoEmL 93
Bredar, Marcia A. Law&B 92
Breddan, Joe 1950- WhoEmL 93
Bredehoft, Elaine Charlson 1958- WhoEmL 93, WhoSSW 93, WhoWor 93
Bredehoft, John Michael 1958- WhoWor 93
Bredemeier, Chet L. 1955- St&PR 93
Bredemeier, Mark David 1964- WhoEmL 93
Bredemeyer, Loretta Jeane 1942- WhoWor 93
Bredemeyer, Reiner 1929- Baker 92
Bredemeyer, Ronald Gordon 1942- St&PR 93, WhoSSW 93
Bredenbeck, Rudolf 1931- St&PR 93
Bredenberg, Carl E. 1940- WhoE 93
Bredenberg, Jeff 1953- ScF&FL 92
Bredenberg, Johan B-son 1930- WhoScE 91-4
Bredenkamp, Richard L. 1945- St&PR 93
Bredesen, Philip Norman 1943- WhoAm 92, WhoSSW 93
Bredesen, Roger T. St&PR 93
Bredeson, Jane R. 1929- WhoAmW 93
Bredeson, John Patrick 1942- St&PR 93
Bredeweg, Judith Senkel 1941- WhoAmW 93
Bredfeldt, John Creighton 1947- WhoEmL 93
Bredhoff, Nancy 1958- St&PR 93
Brediceanu, Tiberiu 1877-1968 Baker 92
Bredin, John Bruce 1914- WhoAm 92, WhoE 93
Bredmose, Niels 1942- WhoScE 91-2
Bredow, Adalbert von 1814-1890 HarEnMi
Bredow, Ilse, Grafin von 1922- BioIn 17
Bredow, Marjorie Y. 1940- St&PR 93
Bredt, Jack Bourquoin 1926- St&PR 93
Bredt, Wolfgang 1937- WhoScE 91-3
Bree, Germaine 1907- WhoSSW 93
Bree, Jean Bernard van 1801-1857 Baker 92
Breece, Robert William, Jr. 1942- WhoAm 92
Breecher, Sheila Rae 1953- WhoEmL 93
Breed, Allen Forbes 1920- WhoAm 92
Breed, David Scranton 1938- WhoE 93
Breed, Eileen Judith 1945- WhoAmW 93
Breed, Ernest Mark, III 1955- WhoEmL 93
Breed, Helen Illick 1925- WhoAm 92, WhoAmW 93
Breed, Joseph R. Law&B 92
Breed, Joseph Rosser 1943- St&PR 93
Breed, Michael Dallam 1951- WhoEmL 93
Breed, Nathaniel Preston 1908- WhoAm 92
Breed, Ria 1944- WhoAm 92
Breeden, Chris David 1955- WhoEmL 93
Breeden, Daniel Franklin 1936- St&PR 93
Breeden, David WhoAm 92
Breeden, Kenneth Ray 1938- WhoWor 93
Breeden, Rex Earl 1920- WhoAm 92
Breeden, Richard BioIn 17
Breeden, Richard C. 1949- WhoAm 92, WhoE 93
Breeden, Robert Lewis 1925- WhoAm 92
Breedijk, Frans Nico 1941- WhoWor 93
Breeding, Carl Wayne 1954- WhoEmL 93
Breeding, David C. 1952- WhoE 93, WhoEmL 93
Breeding, Robert Leroy 1926- St&PR 93
Breedlove, Cindy Graham 1944- WhoAmW 93
Breedlove, Jill M. Law&B 92
Breedlove, Nancy Jean Free 1960- WhoAmW 93
Breedlove, Paul Michael 1943- St&PR 93
Breedlove, Sarah 1867-1919 BioIn 17
Breedlove, William Byron 1953- WhoSSW 93
Breedlove, William Davis 1940- St&PR 93
Breedon, Richard 1955- WhoWor 93
Breedveld, Dick 1939- St&PR 93
Breem, Wallace 1926-1990 BioIn 17
Breen, Ann E. 1940- WhoWrEP 92
Breen, Bernice AmWomPl
Breen, David Neil 1943- St&PR 93
Breen, David V. Law&B 92
Breen, Donald T. Law&B 92
Breen, Edward Grimes 1908-1991 BioIn 17
Breen, F. Glenn 1912- St&PR 93, WhoAm 92
Breen, Faith Fei-Mei Lee 1951- WhoAmW 93, WhoE 93, WhoEmL 93
Breen, Gerald Joseph 1945- St&PR 93
Breen, James J. Law&B 92
Breen, James Joseph 1929- St&PR 93
Breen, James Joseph 1932- WhoAm 92
Breen, John Edward 1932- WhoAm 92
Breen, John Francis 1929- WhoAm 92
Breen, John Gerald 1934- St&PR 93, WhoAm 92
Breen, Jon L. 1943- ScF&FL 92
Breen, Kevin W. Law&B 92
Breen, Laura Law&B 92
Breen, Marilyn 1944- WhoSSW 93
Breen, Mary P. Law&B 92
Breen, Michael 1961- WhoE 93
Breen, Myles Patrick 1939- WhoWor 93
Breen, Robert d1990 BioIn 17
Breen, Thomas A. 1956- St&PR 93
Breen, Thomas J. 1948- St&PR 93
Breen, Thomas John 1948- WhoAm 92
Breen, Timothy Alan 1951- WhoEmL 93
Breen, Timothy Hall 1942- WhoAm 92, WhoWrEP 92
Breen, Walter 1930- ScF&FL 92
Breen, Walter Henry 1928- WhoAm 92
Breene, Bessie Springer AmWomPl
Breene, Samuel A. 1915- St&PR 93
Breer, Carmen Eileen 1936- WhoAmW 93
Brees, Arthur Lee 1949- WhoSSW 93
Breese, Donald Edward 1930- St&PR 93
Breese, Frank Chandler 1944- St&PR 93
Breese, Frank Chandler, III 1944- WhoAm 92
Breese, John Allen 1951- WhoWor 93
Breeze, Frank V. 1924- WhoAm 92
Breeze, Grace Wilkie 1934- WhoWrEP 92
Breeze, William Hancock 1923- WhoAm 92, WhoIns 93, WhoSSW 93
Breezley, Roger L. 1938- St&PR 93
Breezley, Roger Lee 1938- WhoAm 92
Breffeilh, Louis Andrew 1913- WhoAm 92
Brega, Charles Franklin 1933- WhoAm 92
Bregant, Davide 1930- WhoScE 91-3
Bregar, Billy Lee 1951- St&PR 93
Bregar, Raymond E. 1947- St&PR 93
Bregel, Lawrence Edward 1960- WhoSSW 93
Bregenzer, Don 1888-1931 ScF&FL 92
Breger, Herbert 1946- WhoWor 93
Breger, Herbert Joseph 1920- WhoWor 93
Breger, Joseph L. 1916- St&PR 93
Breger, Marshall J. 1946- WhoAm 92
Breger Lee, Donna Eva 1942- WhoAmW 93
Breggin, Peter Roger 1936- WhoAm 92, WhoWrEP 92
Breglio, John F. 1946- WhoAm 92
Bregman, Jacob Israel 1923- WhoAm 92
Bregman, Larry 1922- WhoSSW 93
Bregman, Lucy 1944- WhoAmW 93
Bregman, Martin WhoAm 92
Bregman, Martin J. Law&B 92
Breguet, Abraham-Louis 1747-1823 BioIn 17
Bre'gy, Katherine Marie Cornelia 1888- AmWomPl
Breh, Donald J. Law&B 92
Brehaut, C. Henry 1938- St&PR 93
Brehaut, Charles Henry 1938- WhoAm 92
Breheman, Debra Lynn 1955- WhoAmW 93
Brehm, Alvin 1925- Baker 92
Brehm, Denise Leigh 1959- WhoAmW 93
Brehm, Henry 1953- WhoE 93
Brehm, James G. Law&B 92
Brehm, James Gordon 1956- St&PR 93
Brehm, John Edmund 1931- St&PR 93
Brehm, John Joseph 1934- WhoE 93
Brehm, John R. 1953- St&PR 93
Brehm, Sharon Stephens 1945- WhoAm 92
Brehman, Penny Ann 1947- WhoAmW 93, WhoEmL 93
Brehme, Hans 1904-1957 Baker 92
Brehmer, Steven Lester 1952- WhoEmL 93
Brehy, Hercule 1673?-1737 Baker 92
Breidbart, Stuart R. Law&B 92
Breidegam, Delight Edgar 1926- St&PR 93
Breidegam, DeLight Edgar, Jr. 1926- WhoAm 92
Breidenbach, Cherie Elizabeth 1952- WhoEmL 93
Breidenbach, David Carl Law&B 92

Breidenbach, David John 1957- *WhoEmL 93*
Breidenbach, Don Howard 1947- *WhoEmL 93*
Breidenbach, Francis Anthony 1930- *WhoAm 92*
Breidenbach, Rowland William 1935- *WhoAm 92*
Breidert, Wolfgang 1937- *WhoWor 93*
Breien, Anja 1940- *MiSFD 9*
Breien, Thor 1947- *WhoWor 93*
Breier, Barbara Elizabeth 1948- *WhoAmW 93*
Breier, Harvey 1936- *St&PR 93*
Breihan, Erwin Robert 1918- *WhoAm 92*
Breil, Joseph Carl 1870-1926 *Baker 92*
Breiland, Leslie Kent 1944- *St&PR 93*
Breillat, Catherine 1948- *MiSFD 9*
Breiman, Valerie *MiSFD 9*
Breimer, Douwe D. 1973- *WhoScE 91-3*
Breimyer, Harold Frederick 1914- *WhoAm 92*
Breinburg, Petronella 1927- *BlkAuII 92*
Breindel, Eric Marc 1955- *WhoAm 92*
Breindel, Robert A. *Law&B 92*
Breindler, Gerald 1946- *St&PR 93*
Breiner, James M. 1918- *St&PR 93*
Breiner, Sheldon 1936- *St&PR 93*
Breines, Estelle Borgman 1936- *WhoAmW 93*
Breines, Simon 1906- *WhoAm 92*
Breinin, Goodwin M. 1918- *WhoAm 92*
Breinin, Raymond 1910- *WhoAm 92*
Breininger, Thomas M. *Law&B 92*
Breipohl, Walter Eugene 1953- *WhoEmL 93*
Breisach, Ernst *WhoAm 92*
Breiseth, Christopher Neri 1936- *WhoAm 92*
Breit, Jeffrey Arnold 1955- *WhoEmL 93*
Breitbarth, Gary Glen 1950- *WhoE 93*
Breitbarth, Larry Allen 1963- *WhoEmL 93*
Breitbarth, S. Robert 1925- *WhoAm 92*
Breitbarth, Steven Eldor 1949- *WhoEmL 93*
Breitberg, Freddie 1947- *St&PR 93*
Breitel, Charles D. 1908-1991 *BioIn 17*
Breiten, John W. 1943- *St&PR 93*
Breitenbach, Arthur 1942- *St&PR 93*
Breitenbach, Mary Louise McGraw 1936- *WhoAm 92, WhoAmW 93*
Breitenbach, Thomas George 1947- *WhoAm 92*
Breitenecker, Rudiger 1929- *WhoAm 92, WhoE 93*
Breitenfeld, Frederick, Jr. 1931- *WhoAm 92*
Breitengraser, Wilhelm c. 1495-1542 *Baker 92*
Breitenhuber, Ludwig F.G. 1926- *WhoScE 91-4*
Breitenstein, Fredrick Wilhelm 1933- *WhoUN 92*
Breitenwischer, Ann Louise 1942- *WhoAmW 93*
Breiter, Thomas Herman 1960- *WhoSSW 93*
Breithaupt, David Evans 1940- *WhoAm 92*
Breithaupt, Rudolf 1873-1945 *Baker 92*
Breithaupt, Stephen Allan 1954- *WhoEmL 93*
Breitinger, Johann Jakob 1701-1776 *BioIn 17*
Breitkopf, Bernhard Christoph 1695-1777 *Baker 92*
Breitkopf, Christoph Gottlob 1750-1800 *Baker 92*
Breitkopf, Johann Gottlob Immanuel 1719-1794 *Baker 92*
Breitkopf, Laurel D. *Law&B 92*
Breitkopf & Hartel *Baker 92*
Breitman, Alan M. *Law&B 92*
Breitman, Alan M. 1930- *St&PR 93*
Breitman, Leo R. *WhoAm 92*
Breitman, Leo R. 1941- *St&PR 93*
Breitman, Richard D(avid) 1947- *WhoWrEP 92*
Breitmeyer, Jo Anne 1947- *WhoAm 92, WhoAmW 93*
Breitnauer, Paul J. 1939- *St&PR 93, WhoIns 93*
Breitner, Gerard T. 1947- *WhoE 93*
Breitrose, Henry S. 1936- *WhoAm 92*
Breitschwerdt, Edward Bealmear 1948- *WhoSSW 93*
Breitschwerdt, Kurt G. 1930- *WhoScE 91-3*
Breitschwerdt, Kurt Guenther 1930- *WhoWor 93*
Breitstein, Paul T. *Law&B 92*
Breitwieser, Charles John 1910- *WhoAm 92*
Breitzman, Joel David 1954- *St&PR 93*
Breivik, Harald P. 1940- *WhoScE 91-4*
Breiwa, John Norbert 1950- *WhoSSW 93*
Brejcha, Robert Allen *Law&B 92*
Brejchova, Jana 1940- *IntDcF 2-3 [port]*
Breker, Arno 1900-1991 *AnObit 1991, BioIn 17*
Breker-Cooper, Steven Mark 1947- *WhoEmL 93*
Brel, Jacques 1929-1978 *Baker 92*
Breland, Anita Lesser 1947- *WhoAmW 93*
Breland, Jabe Armistead, II 1949- *WhoEmL 93*
Breland, Jake D. 1946- *St&PR 93*
Brelet, Gisele 1915-1973 *Baker 92*
Brelich, Angelo 1913-1977 *IntDcAn*
Brelis, Dean Constantine 1924- *WhoE 93*
Brelis, Matthew Dean Burns 1957- *WhoAm 92, WhoE 93*
Brellen, Marc *ScF&FL 92*
Breloer, Bernd Jobst *WhoScE 91-3*
Brelsford, Gates Grissom 1950- *St&PR 93*
Brelsford, William Joseph, Jr. 1941- *St&PR 93*
Brema, Marie 1856-1925 *Baker 92, OxDcOp*
Breman, Henle 1943- *WhoScE 91-3*
Breman, Joseph Eliot 1945- *WhoAm 92*
Brembeck, Winston Lamont 1912- *WhoAm 92*
Bremberg, Virginia *WhoAm 92, WhoAmW 93*
Bremehr, Norbert A. 1927- *St&PR 93*
Bremen, Ronald David 1950- *WhoEmL 93, WhoWor 93*
Bremenkamp, Victor Dale 1935- *WhoE 93*
Bremer, Charles A. 1944- *St&PR 93*
Bremer, Frances Winfield 1942- *WhoE 93*
Bremer, Francis John 1947- *WhoEmL 93*
Bremer, John M. *Law&B 92*
Bremer, John M. 1947- *St&PR 93*
Bremer, Jon *WhoScE 91-4*
Bremer, Karen Ingrid 1959- *WhoEmL 93, WhoSSW 93*
Bremer, L. Paul, III 1941- *WhoE 93*
Bremer, Louis Henry, Jr. 1951- *WhoSSW 93*
Bremer, Marlene Schubert *WhoE 93*
Bremer, Per Oscar 1944- *WhoScE 91-4*
Bremer, Ralph M. *Law&B 92*
Bremer, Richard C. *Law&B 92*
Bremer, Richard H. 1948- *WhoAm 92*
Bremer, Thomas R. *Law&B 92*
Bremi, Ulrich 1929- *WhoWor 93*
Bremkamp, Gloria Howe 1924- *WhoWrEP 92*
Bremner, Blanche Irbe 1871- *AmWomPl*
Bremner, Bruce Barton 1939- *WhoAm 92*
Bremner, Frederick 1863-1941 *BioIn 17*
Bremner, Gail K. 1949- *St&PR 93*
Bremner, Geoffrey 1930- *ConAu 38NR*
Bremner, Ian *WhoScE 91-1*
Bremner, John Barnard 1943- *WhoWor 93*
Bremner, John McColl 1922- *WhoAm 92*
Bremner, Mary Elizabeth Thompson 1936- *WhoAmW 93*
Bremond, Francois 1844-1925 *Baker 92*
Brems, Hans Julius 1915- *WhoAm 92*
Bremser, Albert Heinrich 1937- *WhoSSW 93*
Bremser, George, Jr. 1928- *WhoAm 92*
Bremser, Rudolph E. 1931- *St&PR 93*
Bren, Donald L. *BioIn 17*
Bren, Joel 1949- *St&PR 93*
Bren, Shirley 1918- *St&PR 93*
Brenan, Kevin D. *Law&B 92*
Brenchley, Jean Elnora 1944- *WhoAm 92*
Brendan, the Voyager, Saint c. 483-577 *BioIn 17*
Brendel, Albert Edward 1936- *St&PR 93*
Brendel, Alfred 1931- *Baker 92, WhoAm 92, WhoWor 93*
Brendel, El 1890-1964 *QDrFCA 92 [port]*
Brendel, (Karl) Franz 1811-1868 *Baker 92*
Brendel, Klaus 1928- *WhoScE 91-3*
Brendel, Wolfgang 1947- *Baker 92*
Brendel Family *BioIn 17*
Brenden, Mary Jo *Law&B 92*
Brenden, Rita Ann 1953- *WhoEmL 93*
Brenders, Carl *BioIn 17*
Brending, Jacqueline Sue 1960- *WhoSSW 93*
Brendle, Douglas David 1928- *St&PR 93*
Brendle, Kenneth Lee *WhoIns 93*
Brendle, Patricia Ruth 1955- *WhoEmL 93*
Brendler, (Frans Fredric) Eduard 1800-1831 *Baker 92*
Brendler, Walter Clark 1949- *WhoE 93*
Brendlinger, LeRoy R. 1918- *WhoAm 92*
Brendon, Rupert Timothy Rundle 1943- *WhoAm 92*
Brendow, Klaus Johann 1933- *WhoUN 92*
Brendsel, Leland *BioIn 17*
Brendsel, Leland C. *WhoSSW 93*
Brendsel, Leland C. 1942- *St&PR 93*
Brendtro, Larry Kay 1940- *WhoAm 92*
Brendzel, Henry T. *Law&B 92*
Brendzel, Michael L. *Law&B 92*
Brendzel, Ronald I. 1949- *St&PR 93*
Breneman, David Clinton, II 1959- *WhoEmL 93*
Breneman, David Worthy 1940- *WhoAm 92, WhoE 93*
Breneman, Suzanne 1960- *WhoAmW 93*
Brener, Max Donald 1941- *WhoSSW 93*
Brener, Rochelle 1945- *WhoWrEP 92*
Brener, William 1948- *WhoSSW 93*
Brenet, Michel 1858-1918 *Baker 92*
Brengel, Fred L. 1923- *St&PR 93*
Brengel, Fred Lenhardt 1923- *WhoAm 92*
Brengelmann, Johannes C. 1920- *WhoScE 91-3*
Brengle, Thomas Alan 1952- *WhoEmL 93*
Brenin, Jules 1936- *St&PR 93*
Brenke, Herbert *WhoWor 93*
Brenkman, Guy L. 1947- *St&PR 93*
Brenman, Albert 1926- *St&PR 93*
Brenna, Carol Diane 1959- *WhoEmL 93*
Brennan, Alice Comins *Law&B 92*
Brennan, Bernard Francis 1938- *St&PR 93, WhoAm 92*
Brennan, Charles Kevin 1949- *WhoE 93*
Brennan, Charles Martin, III 1942- *St&PR 93, WhoAm 92*
Brennan, Ciaran Brendan 1944- *WhoWor 93*
Brennan, Daniel Christopher 1954- *WhoEmL 93*
Brennan, Daniel L. 1943- *WhoAm 92*
Brennan, David Daniel 1938- *WhoWrEP 92*
Brennan, David S. *Law&B 92*
Brennan, Denise Peters *Law&B 92*
Brennan, Donald P. 1940- *St&PR 93, WhoAm 92*
Brennan, Donna Lesley 1945- *WhoAm 92*
Brennan, Dorothea Elizabeth 1950- *WhoEmL 93*
Brennan, Edward A. *BioIn 17*
Brennan, Edward A. 1934- *St&PR 93, WhoAm 92, WhoWor 93*
Brennan, Eileen Hughes 1951- *WhoAmW 93, WhoEmL 93, WhoSSW 93*
Brennan, Eileen Muench 1943- *WhoAmW 93*
Brennan, Eileen Regina 1935- *WhoAm 92*
Brennan, Elizabeth 1922- *ScF&FL 92*
Brennan, Elizabeth Lane 1951- *WhoEmL 93*
Brennan, Ella *NewYTBS 92 [port]*
Brennan, Eugene G. *Law&B 92*
Brennan, Fanny *BioIn 17*
Brennan, Francis E. d1992 *NewYTBS 92*
Brennan, Francis P. 1917- *St&PR 93*
Brennan, Francis W. 1919- *WhoAm 92*
Brennan, Frank J. d1992 *BioIn 17*
Brennan, Gail Mary 1964- *St&PR 93*
Brennan, Gale 1927- *BioIn 17*
Brennan, George Gerard 1931- *WhoE 93*
Brennan, George J. *Law&B 92*
Brennan, Glen 1929- *WhoE 93*
Brennan, Henry Higginson 1932- *WhoAm 92*
Brennan, Herbert Joseph *Law&B 92*
Brennan, Herbert Joseph 1935- *St&PR 93*
Brennan, J.H. 1940- *ScF&FL 92*
Brennan, James Beach 1947- *WhoEmL 93*
Brennan, James G. 1927- *WhoAm 92*
Brennan, James Joseph 1936- *WhoAm 92*
Brennan, James Joseph 1950- *WhoAm 92*
Brennan, James Patrick *Law&B 92*
Brennan, James Patrick, Sr. 1947- *WhoEmL 93*
Brennan, Jan *ScF&FL 92*
Brennan, John D. 1947- *St&PR 93*
Brennan, John E. 1928- *St&PR 93*
Brennan, John Edward 1928- *WhoAm 92*
Brennan, John Lindsay 1949- *WhoWor 93*
Brennan, John M. 1935- *St&PR 93*
Brennan, John Merritt 1935- *WhoAm 92*
Brennan, John V. 1934- *WhoIns 93*
Brennan, Joseph Francis Xavier 1939- *WhoIns 93*
Brennan, Joseph Gerard 1910- *WhoAm 92*
Brennan, Joseph Payne 1918- *WhoWrEP 92*
Brennan, Joseph Payne 1918-1990 *ScF&FL 92*
Brennan, Joseph Thomas 1931- *WhoE 93*
Brennan, Josephine Annette 1932- *WhoAmW 93*
Brennan, Karen 1941- *WhoWrEP 92*
Brennan, Karen Anne 1948- *St&PR 93*
Brennan, Kathleen M. *Law&B 92*
Brennan, Kathleen Noelle 1966- *WhoWrEP 92*
Brennan, Lane P. *Law&B 92*
Brennan, Lawrence Brian 1953- *WhoEmL 93*
Brennan, Lawrence Edward 1927- *WhoAm 92*
Brennan, Leo Joseph, Jr. 1930- *WhoAm 92*
Brennan, Leo Thomas 1935- *St&PR 93*
Brennan, Martin A. 1946- *WhoIns 93*
Brennan, Martin Joseph 1929- *St&PR 93*
Brennan, Mary Alice 1937- *WhoAmW 93*
Brennan, Mary M. 1954- *WhoAmW 93*
Brennan, Maryellen 1959- *St&PR 93*
Brennan, Maureen A. 1949- *WhoAmW 93*
Brennan, Michael Edward 1962- *WhoE 93*
Brennan, Michael G. *St&PR 93*
Brennan, Michael R. *Law&B 92*
Brennan, Molly *Law&B 92*
Brennan, Murray F. *BioIn 17*
Brennan, Murray Frederick 1940- *WhoAm 92*
Brennan, Nancy Hough *WhoAm 92*
Brennan, Neil James 1947- *WhoWor 93*
Brennan, Noel-Anne 1948- *ScF&FL 92*
Brennan, Noel-Anne Gerson 1948- *WhoE 93*
Brennan, Norma Jean 1939- *WhoAmW 93, WhoE 93*
Brennan, Norman P. 1930- *St&PR 93*
Brennan, Patrick Francis 1931- *St&PR 93, WhoAm 92*
Brennan, Patrick J. *BioIn 17*
Brennan, Patrick Thomas 1952- *WhoAm 92, WhoE 93, WhoEmL 93*
Brennan, Paul Joseph 1920- *WhoAm 92, WhoWor 93*
Brennan, Peter James 1911- *St&PR 93*
Brennan, Richard Grey 1956- *WhoWor 93*
Brennan, Richard S. 1938- *St&PR 93*
Brennan, Richard Snyder 1938- *WhoAm 92*
Brennan, Robert F. 1947- *St&PR 93*
Brennan, Robert J. 1936- *WhoAm 92*
Brennan, Robert Lawrence 1944- *WhoAm 92*
Brennan, Robert T. 1929- *St&PR 93*
Brennan, Roger *Law&B 92*
Brennan, Ruth Almeda 1934- *WhoAmW 93*
Brennan, Ruth Gonchar 1944- *WhoAmW 93*
Brennan, Sheila Ann *Law&B 92*
Brennan, Terence Kelley 1952- *St&PR 93*
Brennan, Terrence Michael 1947- *WhoAm 92, WhoE 93*
Brennan, Terrence Paul 1955- *WhoEmL 93*
Brennan, Theresa Milore *Law&B 92*
Brennan, Thomas A., Jr. *Law&B 92*
Brennan, Thomas Emmett 1929- *WhoAm 92*
Brennan, Thomas John 1923- *WhoE 93, WhoWor 93*
Brennan, Timothy John 1952- *WhoE 93*
Brennan, Timothy William 1951- *WhoAm 92*
Brennan, W. Neil 1962- *WhoE 93*
Brennan, Walter 1894-1974 *IntDcF 2-3 [port]*
Brennan, Walter 1938- *St&PR 93*
Brennan, William F. 1936- *St&PR 93*
Brennan, William J. 1928- *St&PR 93*
Brennan, William J., Jr. *BioIn 17*
Brennan, William J., Jr. 1906- *CngDr 91*
Brennan, William John 1940- *WhoAm 92, WhoE 93*
Brennan, William John, Jr. 1961- *WhoE 93*
Brennan, William Joseph 1928- *WhoAm 92*
Brennan, William Joseph, Jr. 1906- *OxCSupC [port], WhoAm 92, WhoE 93*
Brennan, William Philip 1936- *WhoE 93*
Brennand, James d1992 *BioIn 17*
Brennan-Sparks, Jennifer Anne 1935- *WhoWor 93*
Brennecke, Allen Eugene 1937- *WhoAm 92*
Brenneman, Austin Russell 1932- *WhoSSW 93*
Brenneman, Christine Dee 1960- *WhoE 93*
Brenneman, Cloyd E. 1934- *St&PR 93*
Brenneman, David L. 1943- *St&PR 93*
Brenneman, Delbert Jay 1950- *WhoEmL 93*
Brenneman, Howard L. 1940- *St&PR 93*
Brenneman, Hugh Warren, Jr. 1945- *WhoAm 92*
Brenneman, Mary Beth 1950- *WhoEmL 93*
Brenneman, Ronald A. *St&PR 93*
Brenneman, Terry Richard 1950- *WhoEmL 93*
Brennen, Charles M. 1942- *St&PR 93*
Brennen, Patrick Wayne 1940- *WhoAm 92*
Brennen, Stephen Alfred *WhoAm 92*
Brenner, Alan Ira 1942- *WhoE 93*
Brenner, Albert 1926- *WhoAm 92*
Brenner, Alfred Ephraim 1931- *WhoAm 92*
Brenner, Amy Rebecca 1958- *WhoE 93*
Brenner, Arnold S. 1937- *WhoAm 92*
Brenner, Barbara (Johnes) 1925- *DcAmChF 1985, MajAI [port], WhoWrEP 92*
Brenner, Barry Morton 1937- *WhoAm 92*
Brenner, Barry Scott 1948- *WhoWor 93*
Brenner, Betty *WhoAmW 93*
Brenner, Betty Ann 1950- *WhoAmW 93*
Brenner, Daeg Scott 1939- *WhoAm 92*
Brenner, Daniel Leon 1904- *WhoAm 92*
Brenner, David 1944- *St&PR 93*

Brenner, David 1945- *BioIn 17, WhoAm 92*
Brenner, David Hugh 1950- *WhoAm 92*
Brenner, David Israel 1944- *WhoAm 92*
Brenner, Donald Robert 1936- *St&PR 93, WhoAm 92*
Brenner, Edgar H. 1930- *WhoAm 92*
Brenner, Edward John 1923- *WhoAm 92*
Brenner, Egon 1925- *WhoAm 92*
Brenner, Erma 1911- *WhoAm 92*
Brenner, Esther Hannah 1940- *WhoAmW 93*
Brenner, Esther Lerner 1931- *WhoAmW 93*
Brenner, Frank 1927- *WhoAm 92*
Brenner, Frank 1930- *St&PR 93*
Brenner, Fred 1920- *MajAI [port]*
Brenner, Gail V. *Law&B 92*
Brenner, Glenn d1992 *BioIn 17*
Brenner, Gunter 1928- *WhoWor 93*
Brenner, Henry 1914- *WhoAm 92*
Brenner, Howard 1929- *WhoAm 92*
Brenner, Howard Martin 1933- *WhoAm 92*
Brenner, Janet Maybin Walker *WhoAmW 93, WhoWor 93*
Brenner, Jean S. *Law&B 92*
Brenner, Jerry H. *Law&B 92*
Brenner, Keith E. 1944- *St&PR 93*
Brenner, Kenneth James 1923- *St&PR 93*
Brenner, Marshall Leib 1933- *WhoE 93*
Brenner, Marten Withmar 1926- *WhoScE 91-4*
Brenner, Mary Ellen 1960- *WhoEmL 93*
Brenner, Mayer Alan 1956- *ScF&FL 92*
Brenner, Michael L. *Law&B 92*
Brenner, Raymond *Law&B 92*
Brenner, Rena Claudy *WhoAmW 93*
Brenner, Richard L. 1935- *St&PR 93*
Brenner, Robert *BioIn 17*
Brenner, Robert Charles 1941- *WhoWrEP 92*
Brenner, Robert David 1953- *WhoAm 92*
Brenner, Rodolfo Roberto 1922- *WhoWor 93*
Brenner, Ronald John 1933- *St&PR 93, WhoAm 92*
Brenner, Sten-Olof 1946- *WhoScE 91-4*
Brenner, Stephen Mark 1948- *WhoEmL 93*
Brenner, Sydney *WhoScE 91-1*
Brenner, Theodor Eduard 1942- *WhoE 93*
Brenner, Theodore Engelbert 1930- *WhoAm 92*
Brenner, Thomas Edward 1955- *WhoEmL 93*
Brenner, William Bower 1944- *WhoE 93*
Brenner, William Edward 1936- *WhoAm 92*
Brennerstd, Turid *WhoScE 91-4*
Brennert, Alan 1954- *ScF&FL 92*
Brennessel, Barbara Anne 1948- *WhoAmW 93, WhoEmL 93*
Brennfoerder, Roxann R. 1951- *St&PR 93*
Brenny, Mary Clare 1950- *WhoAmW 93*
Brenoe, Per Tutein 1941- *WhoScE 91-2*
Brenon, Herbert 1880-1958 *MiSFD 9N*
Brent, Andrew J. *Law&B 92*
Brent, Andrew J. 1918- *St&PR 93*
Brent, Andrew Jackson 1918- *WhoAm 92*
Brent, Andrew Mason 1950- *St&PR 93*
Brent, Arthur C. 1942- *St&PR 93*
Brent, Carolyn Maas 1925- *WhoE 93*
Brent, Charlotte c. 1735-1802 *Baker 92, OxDcOp*
Brent, Christopher Joseph 1952- *WhoE 93*
Brent, Donita May 1939- *WhoAmW 93*
Brent, Douglas Beckett 1958- *WhoAm 92*
Brent, Evelyn 1899-1975 *SweetSg B [port]*
Brent, Frank Nevil 1934- *WhoSSW 93*
Brent, Graham John 1954- *WhoSSW 93*
Brent, Hal Preston 1955- *WhoE 93*
Brent, Jeffrey 1947- *St&PR 93*
Brent, Joleene Adalie 1920- *WhoAm 92, WhoSSW 93*
Brent, Keith Joseph *WhoScE 91-1*
Brent, Leslie 1925- *WhoWor 93*
Brent, Linda 1813-1896? *BioIn 17*
Brent, Nancy Jean 1947- *WhoEmL 93*
Brent, Paul Leslie 1916- *WhoAm 92*
Brent, Peter L. *ScF&FL 92*
Brent, Robert Leonard 1927- *WhoAm 92*
Brent, Ruth Stumpe 1951- *WhoEmL 93*
Brent, Timothy 1950- *WhoWor 93*
Brent, William Thomas 1926- *St&PR 93*
Brenta, Gaston 1902-1969 *Baker 92*
Brentano, Clemens 1778-1842 *BioIn 17*
Brentlinger, Paul S. 1927- *St&PR 93*
Brentlinger, Paul Smith 1927- *WhoAm 92*
Brentlinger, William Brock 1926- *WhoAm 92*
Brentnall, Terence David 1946- *St&PR 93*
Brenton, Donald Leverett 1935- *St&PR 93*
Brenton, Frank Howard 1925- *St&PR 93*
Brenton, Howard 1942- *BioIn 17*
Brenton, Marianne Webber 1933- *WhoAmW 93*
Brenton, Michael Scott 1952- *WhoEmL 93*
Brenton, Virginia Mary 1961- *WhoE 93*
Breon, Paul Douty 1915- *WhoE 93*
Brereton, Lewis Hyde 1890-1967 *HarEnMi*
Bres, Philip Wayne 1950- *WhoEmL 93*
Bresadola, Silvano 1931- *WhoScE 91-3*
Bresani, Federico Fernando 1945- *WhoAm 92, WhoE 93, WhoWor 93*
Bresch, Carsten 1921- *WhoScE 91-3*
Bresch, Carsten J. 1921- *WhoWor 93*
Bresch, Saul Robert *Law&B 92*
Brescher, Joseph L., Jr. *Law&B 92*
Breschi, Fabian Rene 1960- *WhoWor 93*
Brescia, Anthony Joseph 1950- *WhoEmL 93, WhoSSW 93, WhoWor 93*
Brescia, Bernardo Fort- *BioIn 17*
Brescia, Frank Joseph 1942- *WhoE 93*
Brescia, James A. 1945- *St&PR 93*
Brescia, James Andrew 1945- *WhoAm 92*
Brescia, Mary Elizabeth 1955- *WhoE 93*
Brescia, Michael Joseph 1933- *WhoAm 92, WhoE 93, WhoWor 93*
Brescianello, Giuseppe Antonio c. 1690-1758 *Baker 92*
Bresee, James Collins 1925- *WhoAm 92*
Bresee, Marc W. *St&PR 93*
Bresee, Philip W. 1924- *St&PR 93*
Bresee, Wilmer E. 1910- *St&PR 93*
Breselor, Franklin K. *Law&B 92*
Bresenham, Jack Elton 1937- *WhoSSW 93*
Bresgen, Cesar 1913- *OxDcOp*
Bresgen, Cesar 1913-1988 *Baker 92*
Breshears, Ronald G. *St&PR 93*
Breshears, Sarah Grigsby 1943- *WhoSSW 93*
Breskman, Joseph S. 1917- *St&PR 93*
Breskovska, Vesselina 1928- *WhoScE 91-4*
Bresky, H. Harry 1925- *WhoAm 92*
Breslauer, Grace Koehler d1990 *BioIn 17*
Breslauer, Marianne 1909- *BioIn 17*
Breslauer, Suzanne Eisen 1938- *WhoAmW 93*
Breslawsky, Marc C. 1942- *WhoAm 92*
Breslawsky, Marc Carl 1942- *St&PR 93*
Bresler, Boris 1918- *WhoAm 92*
Bresler, Charles S. 1927- *St&PR 93*
Bresler, Charles Sheldon 1927- *WhoAm 92*
Bresler, Mark Irwin 1953- *WhoAm 92, WhoEmL 93, WhoSSW 93*
Bresler, Martin I. 1931- *WhoAm 92*
Bresler, Sidney Alan 1923- *WhoE 93*
Breslin, A.C. 1945- *WhoScE 91-3*
Breslin, Barbara Lee 1958- *WhoAmW 93, WhoEmL 93*
Breslin, Donald Joseph 1929- *WhoE 93, WhoWor 93*
Breslin, Edward Francis 1947- *WhoAm 92*
Breslin, James Bernard Leo 1938- *WhoUN 92*
Breslin, Jimmy *BioIn 17*
Breslin, Jimmy 1929- *WhoAm 92, WhoE 93, WhoWrEP 92*
Breslin, Leo Harold 1932- *St&PR 93*
Breslin, Marianne Sonnenbrodt 1918- *WhoAmW 93*
Breslin, Michael E. *Law&B 92*
Breslin, Michael Edward 1937- *WhoAm 92*
Breslin, Michael Joseph, III 1949- *WhoE 93*
Breslin, Nancy Ann 1957- *WhoEmL 93*
Breslin, Patricia 1959- *WhoEmL 93*
Breslin, Theresa *ConAu 138, SmATA 70*
Bresloff, Paul 1942- *WhoScE 91-1*
Breslouf, Morris 1924- *St&PR 93*
Breslow, Andrew B. *Law&B 92*
Breslow, Jan Leslie 1943- *WhoAm 92*
Breslow, Jerome W. 1934- *St&PR 93*
Breslow, Jerome Wilfred 1934- *WhoAm 92*
Breslow, Lester 1915- *WhoAm 92*
Breslow, Marilyn Ganon 1944- *WhoAmW 93*
Breslow, Maurice 1935- *WhoCanL 92*
Breslow, Maurice (A.) 1935- *SmATA 72 [port]*
Breslow, Maurice Alen 1935- *SmATA 72*
Breslow, Norman Edward 1941- *WhoAm 92*
Breslow, Ronald Charles 1931- *WhoAm 92*
Breslow, Stuart J.M. *Law&B 92*
Breslow, Susan 1951- *ConAu 137, SmATA 69 [port]*
Breslow, Tina 1946- *WhoEmL 93*
Bresnahan, David Parsons 1930- *St&PR 93, WhoIns 93*
Bresnahan, James Francis 1926- *WhoAm 92*
Bresnahan, Jill A. *Law&B 92*
Bresnahan, Mark Patrick *Law&B 92*
Bresnahan, William J. 1950- *St&PR 93*
Bresnahan, William W. 1918- *St&PR 93*
Bresnick, Martin 1946- *Baker 92*
Bress, Michael E. 1933- *WhoAm 92*
Bressack, Mitchell Leslie 1953- *WhoEmL 93*
Bressan, Paul Louis 1947- *WhoAm 92, WhoEmL 93*
Bressand, Friedrich Christian c. 1670-1699 *OxDcOp*
Bressanelli, Jerome P. 1936- *St&PR 93*
Bressant, Michele Renee 1956- *WhoAm 92*
Bressi-Stoppe, Elizabeth Rita 1946- *WhoE 93*
Bresslaw, Bernard 1933- *QDrFCA 92 [port]*
Bressler, Barry Evan 1947- *WhoEmL 93*
Bressler, Bernard 1928- *St&PR 93, WhoAm 92, WhoE 93*
Bressler, Charles 1926- *Baker 92*
Bressler, Gary David 1956- *WhoEmL 93*
Bressler, Howard Jay 1941- *St&PR 93*
Bressler, Lee M. 1959- *St&PR 93*
Bressler, Linda Ann *WhoAmW 93*
Bressler, Martin Schmeisser 1951- *WhoE 93*
Bressler, Richard David 1957- *WhoAm 92*
Bressler, Richard M. 1930- *St&PR 93*
Bressler, Richard Main 1930- *WhoAm 92, WhoSSW 93*
Bressler, Steven L. 1951- *WhoAm 92*
Bressler-Gianoli, Clotilde 1875-1912 *Baker 92*
Bresslour, Gerald *Law&B 92*
Bressman, Arthur Y. 1928- *St&PR 93*
Bresson, Henri Cartier- 1908- *BioIn 17*
Bresson, Robert 1901- *WhoWor 93*
Bresson, Robert 1907- *MiSFD 9*
Brest, Albert N. 1928- *WhoAm 92*
Brest, Joel Ira 1938- *WhoE 93*
Brest, Martin 1951- *MiSFD 9, WhoAm 92*
Brest, Paul 1940- *WhoAm 92*
Bresticker, Stanley 1926- *WhoE 93*
Bretan, Hal *Law&B 92*
Bretan, Nicolae 1887-1968 *Baker 92, OxDcOp*
Bret-Day, Robin Carew *WhoScE 91-1*
Breteler, Hans 1943- *WhoScE 91-3*
Breth, James Raymond 1929- *St&PR 93, WhoAm 92*
Brethen, Charles A., III 1946- *St&PR 93*
Brethen, Robert Herschell 1926- *St&PR 93*
Bretherton, Evangeline Lent *AmWomPl*
Bretherton, Eve *AmWomPl*
Bretherton, Patricia Ann 1932- *St&PR 93*
Bretl, Mark A. *St&PR 93*
Bretl, Paul G. 1934- *St&PR 93*
Bretnall, Arthur John 1911- *St&PR 93*
Bretnall, Arthur John, Jr. 1943- *St&PR 93*
Bretnor, Reginald 1911-1992 *ScF&FL 92*
Breton, Albert A. 1929- *WhoAm 92*
Breton, Andre 1896-1966 *BioIn 17, ConAu 40NR*
Breton, Frances Irene 1936- *WhoAmW 93*
Breton, Joseph Raymond 1931- *WhoE 93*
Breton, Tracy Ann 1951- *WhoEmL 93*
Breton y Hernandez, Tomas 1850-1923 *Baker 92*
Bretscher, Mark Steven *WhoScE 91-1*
Bretschneider, Ann Margery 1934- *WhoAm 92*
Bretschneider, Barry Eastburn 1947- *WhoE 93*
Bretsen, Stephen Norris *Law&B 92*
Brett, Annabelle 1947- *WhoEmL 93*
Brett, Arthur Cushman, Jr. 1928- *WhoAm 92*
Brett, Barbara Jeanne *WhoAm 92*
Brett, Brian 1950- *ConAu 139, ScF&FL 92, WhoCanL 92*
Brett, Cliff *WhoAm 92*
Brett, David 1937- *ScF&FL 92*
Brett, Dorothy 1883-1977 *BioIn 17*
Brett, Edwin J. 1828-1895 *BioIn 17*
Brett, George *BioIn 17*
Brett, George Howard 1953- *WhoAm 92*
Brett, George Wendell 1912- *WhoAm 92*
Brett, Guilford Harold 1931- *St&PR 93*
Brett, Jacquelyn Ann 1947- *WhoEmL 93*
Brett, Jan *ChlBIID [port]*
Brett, Jan 1949- *ChlLR 27 [port]*
Brett, Jan (Churchill) 1949- *MajAI [port], SmATA 71 [port]*
Brett, Jeremy 1935- *WhoAm 92*
Brett, John Harold, Jr. 1942- *WhoSSW 93*
Brett, John P. *Law&B 92*
Brett, Lisa Farrell 1956- *WhoEmL 93*
Brett, Patricia Ellen 1954- *WhoAmW 93*
Brett, Peter D. 1943- *WhoWrEP 92*
Brett, Philip 1937- *Baker 92*
Brett, Richard John 1921- *WhoWor 93*
Brett, Robin 1935- *WhoAm 92*
Brett, Stephen *ScF&FL 92*
Brett, Stephen M. *Law&B 92, WhoAm 92*
Brett, Stephen N. 1946- *St&PR 93*
Brett, Stephen Noel 1946- *WhoIns 93*
Brett, Thomas Rutherford 1931- *WhoAm 92, WhoSSW 93*
Brette, Rene 1920- *WhoScE 91-2*
Brettell, Caroline B. 1950- *WhoEmL 93, WhoSSW 93*
Brettell, Richard Robson 1949- *WhoAm 92, WhoSSW 93*
Brett-Elspas, Janis E. 1956- *WhoEmL 93*
Bretthauer, Erich Walter 1937- *WhoAm 92*
Bretthauer, Judith 1949- *WhoAmW 93*
Brettle, Roger *WhoScE 91-1*
Brett-Major, Lin 1943- *WhoSSW 93*
Brettner, Donald M. 1936- *St&PR 93*
Bretton, Barbara 1950- *WhoWrEP 92*
Bretton, Henry L. 1916- *WhoAm 92*
Bretuo, Akwasi *WhoWrEP 92*
Bretz, John W. 1936- *St&PR 93*
Bretz, Linda M. 1934- *WhoAm 92*
Bretz, Ronald James 1951- *WhoEmL 93*
Bretz, Thurman *Law&B 92*
Bretz, Thurman Wilbur 1934- *St&PR 93, WhoAm 92*
Bretzfelder, Deborah May 1932- *WhoAm 92*
Bretzfelder, Robert Benjamin 1929- *WhoE 93*
Bretzlaff, Katherine Nelle 1956- *WhoEmL 93*
Bretzloff, P.D. *Law&B 92*
Bretzner, Christoph Friedrich 1748-1807 *OxDcOp*
Breu, George 1954- *WhoEmL 93*
Breuel, Birgit 1937- *WhoWor 93*
Breuer, Adam A. 1925- *St&PR 93*
Breuer, Bert J. 1936- *WhoScE 91-3*
Breuer, Hans 1868-1929 *Baker 92*
Breuer, Hans Dieter 1939- *WhoScE 91-3*
Breuer, Hans-Peter 1939- *WhoE 93*
Breuer, Helmut B. 1936- *St&PR 93*
Breuer, Helmut W. 1940- *WhoScE 91-3*
Breuer, Josef 1842-1925 *BioIn 17*
Breuer, Lee *WhoAm 92*
Breuer, M.J. 1888-1947 *ScF&FL 92*
Breuer, Melvin Allen 1938- *WhoAm 92*
Breuer, Reinhard 1946- *ConAu 38NR*
Breuer, Richard Ervin 1936- *St&PR 93*
Breuer, Theodore J. *St&PR 93*
Breuer Baculis, Diana Ruth 1949- *WhoEmL 93*
Breughel, Pieter 1522?-1569 *BioIn 17*
Breuil, Henri 1877-1961 *IntDcAn*
Breukink, H.J. 1937- *WhoScE 91-3*
Breuls, P. N. 1951- *WhoWor 93*
Breunig, Carla C. 1956- *St&PR 93*
Breunig, Richard H. 1943- *St&PR 93*
Breunig, Sharon Day 1957- *WhoEmL 93, WhoSSW 93*
Breuning, Oswald von Nell- 1890-1991 *BioIn 17*
Breuninger, Tyrone 1939- *WhoAm 92*
Breur, Lester Mons 1939- *WhoWrEP 92*
Breur, Wim 1940- *WhoUN 92*
Breval, Jean-Baptiste Sebastien 1753-1823 *Baker 92*
Breval, Lucienne 1869-1935 *Baker 92, OxDcOp*
Brevard, Elizabeth B. 1923- *St&PR 93*
Brevard, Henry Clyde, Jr. 1921- *St&PR 93*
Brevard, Jacqueline E. *Law&B 92*
Breve, Franklin Stephen 1955- *WhoE 93, WhoEmL 93*
Breverman, Harvey 1934- *WhoAm 92*
Brevick, Bernard William 1945- *St&PR 93*
Brevick, Lonnie L. 1946- *St&PR 93*
Brevig, Eric *WhoAm 92*
Brevignon, Jean-Pierre 1948- *WhoWor 93*
Brevik, E. Lawrence 1920- *St&PR 93*
Brevik, J. Albert 1920- *WhoAm 92, WhoWor 93*
Brevik, Tor 1932- *Baker 92*
Breville, Pierre (-Onfroy de) 1861-1949 *Baker 92*
Brew, George William 1947- *WhoE 93*
Brew, John Otis 1906-1988 *BioIn 17*
Brew, Richard Douglas *Law&B 92*
Brewbaker, Dick L. 1961- *St&PR 93*
Brewbaker, William Styne, Jr. 1934- *St&PR 93*
Brewda, Joanne Keiran 1946- *St&PR 93*
Brewer, Albert Preston 1928- *WhoAm 92*
Brewer, Amy Austin 1958- *WhoSSW 93*
Brewer, Andrea B. *Law&B 92*
Brewer, Andrea Bordiga 1953- *WhoEmL 93*
Brewer, Arthur Bruce 1951- *WhoSSW 93*
Brewer, Boyd Clarence, Jr. 1936- *WhoE 93*
Brewer, Brooke E. 1941- *St&PR 93*
Brewer, Byron Eugene 1948- *WhoEmL 93, WhoSSW 93*
Brewer, Carey 1927- *WhoAm 92*
Brewer, Charles L. *BioIn 17*
Brewer, Charles Moulton 1931- *WhoAm 92*
Brewer, Cheryl Ann 1959- *WhoAmW 93, WhoEmL 93*
Brewer, Cornelia B. *Law&B 92*
Brewer, Curtis 1925-1991 *BioIn 17*
Brewer, David Josiah 1837-1910 *OxCSupC [port]*

Brewer, David Madison 1953- WhoE 93, WhoEmL 93
Brewer, David Meredith 1934- WhoAm 92
Brewer, David R. Law&B 92
Brewer, David R. 1945- St&PR 93
Brewer, Debra Catherine 1957- WhoEmL 93
Brewer, Diane BioIn 17
Brewer, Don 1930- St&PR 93
Brewer, Doris Raye 1934- WhoAmW 93
Brewer, Douglas Forbes WhoScE 91-1
Brewer, Douglas Forbes 1925- WhoWor 93
Brewer, Edward Cage, III 1953- WhoAm 92
Brewer, Edward E. 1925- St&PR 93
Brewer, Frances Joan 1913-1965 ScF&FL 92
Brewer, George Eugene Francis 1909- WhoAm 92
Brewer, Glynn Douglas, Jr. 1961- WhoEmL 93
Brewer, Harold Martin 1948- WhoEmL 93
Brewer, Helen D. AmWomPl
Brewer, (Alfred) Herbert 1865-1928 Baker 92
Brewer, Herbert L. 1926- St&PR 93
Brewer, Hugh Hudson, Jr. 1936- WhoSSW 93
Brewer, Jackie W. 1954- St&PR 93
Brewer, James T. 1934- St&PR 93
Brewer, James W. St&PR 93
Brewer, Janice 1963- WhoEmL 93
Brewer, Janice Kay 1944- WhoAmW 93
Brewer, Jeanne Pickering 1962- WhoEmL 93
Brewer, Jeutonne P. 1939- ScF&FL 92
Brewer, John Charles 1947- WhoAm 92
Brewer, John H. St&PR 93
Brewer, John Isaac 1903- WhoWrEP 92
Brewer, John Michael 1938- WhoSSW 93
Brewer, John Nolan, III 1954- WhoE 93
Brewer, Kathleen Finney 1958- WhoAmW 93
Brewer, Kathleen Joy 1954- WhoEmL 93
Brewer, Kenneth Wayne 1941- WhoWrEP 92
Brewer, Leo 1919- WhoAm 92
Brewer, LeRoy Earl 1936- WhoE 93
Brewer, Leslie G. 1945- WhoAm 92
Brewer, Linda Law&B 92
Brewer, Lisa Law&B 92
Brewer, Lorraine Carol 1949- WhoAmW 93
Brewer, Madeleine Price 1942- WhoWrEP 92
Brewer, Marilyn J. Law&B 92
Brewer, Marion Alyce 1949- WhoEmL 93
Brewer, Mark Arnold 1953- WhoSSW 93
Brewer, Mary Morland 1947- WhoAmW 93
Brewer, Michael A. 1956- St&PR 93
Brewer, Michael Andrew 1956- WhoSSW 93
Brewer, Michael C. Law&B 92
Brewer, Nancy Tomlinson 1950- WhoEmL 93
Brewer, O. Gordon, Jr. 1936- St&PR 93
Brewer, Oliver David 1919- St&PR 93
Brewer, Oliver Gordon, Jr. 1936- WhoAm 92
Brewer, Oscar S. 1915- St&PR 93
Brewer, Paul Huie 1934- St&PR 93
Brewer, Richard George 1928- WhoAm 92
Brewer, Richard M. 1852-1878 BioIn 17
Brewer, Richard W. 1947- St&PR 93
Brewer, Ricky Lee 1948- WhoSSW 93
Brewer, Robert Malcolm WhoScE 91-1
Brewer, Roy Edward 1949- WhoEmL 93
Brewer, Rubell Essien 1935- WhoUN 92
Brewer, Russell L. Law&B 92
Brewer, Sally E. 1934- St&PR 93
Brewer, Sheryl Anne 1946- WhoEmL 93, WhoSSW 93
Brewer, Stanley R. 1937- St&PR 93, WhoAm 92
Brewer, T. Eugene 1938- St&PR 93
Brewer, Thomas A. 1920- St&PR 93
Brewer, Thomas Bowman 1932- WhoAm 92
Brewer, Thomas Phillips 1947- WhoWrEP 92
Brewer, Timothy Francis, III 1931- WhoE 93
Brewer, Timothy Scot 1952- WhoEmL 93
Brewer, William D. 1936- St&PR 93
Brewer, William Dean WhoSSW 93
Brewer, William Dixon 1936- WhoAm 92
Brewer, William Dodd 1922- WhoAm 92
Brewer, William M., III Law&B 92
Brewer, William Robert, Jr. 1940- WhoSSW 93
Brewer, William W. 1924- St&PR 93
Brewer, William Wallace 1937- WhoWor 93
Brewer, William Ward 1954- WhoSSW 93
Brewerton, Timothy David 1953- WhoEmL 93, WhoSSW 93
Brew-Graves, Samuel Henry 1934- WhoUN 92
Brewin, Austin D. 1937- St&PR 93
Brewin, Nicholas J. WhoScE 91-1
Brewington, Robert Lee 1948- St&PR 93
Brewis, Jesse A. Law&B 92
Brews, Jenny Lynne 1960- WhoAmW 93
Brewster, Bernadette Heidt 1942- WhoWrEP 92
Brewster, Bill 1941- WhoAm 92
Brewster, Bill K. 1941- CngDr 91
Brewster, Carroll Worcester 1936- WhoAm 92
Brewster, Clark Otto 1956- WhoEmL 93
Brewster, David (C.) 1939- ConAu 139
Brewster, Donald P. Law&B 92
Brewster, Dorothy 1883-1979 ScF&FL 92
Brewster, Elizabeth 1922- WhoCanL 92
Brewster, Elizabeth Winifred 1922- WhoAm 92, WhoAmW 93
Brewster, Emma E. AmWomPl
Brewster, Geri Ann Law&B 92
Brewster, Gerry Leiper 1957- WhoEmL 93
Brewster, Graham 1945- St&PR 93
Brewster, Havelock R. 1937- WhoUN 92
Brewster, James Henry 1922- WhoAm 92
Brewster, John 1766-1854 BioIn 17
Brewster, Marcus Eli 1957- WhoAm 92, WhoSSW 93
Brewster, May M. AmWomPl
Brewster, Olive Nesbitt 1924- WhoAmW 93, WhoSSW 93, WhoWor 93
Brewster, Patience ChlBIID [port]
Brewster, Robert Charles 1921- WhoAm 92
Brewster, Robert Gene 1938- WhoAm 92
Brewster, Rudi Milton 1932- WhoAm 92
Brewster, Sadie B. AmWomPl
Brewster, Susan d1992 BioIn 17
Brewster, Townsend Tyler 1924- WhoWrEP 92
Brewster, W(illiam) Herbert, Sr. 1899-1987 Baker 92
Brewster, Wayne E. St&PR 93
Brewster, William 1566?-1644 BioIn 17
Brewster, William K. 1941- WhoSSW 93
Brewster-Walker, Sandra JoAnn 1942- WhoAm 92, WhoE 93
Brewton, Patricia Morris WhoAmW 93
Brewton, Powell 1934- WhoSSW 93
Brewton, Robin Denise 1964- WhoEmL 93
Brewton, Samuel Alton, Jr. 1931- WhoSSW 93
Brewton, Wilbur Emmanuel 1941- WhoSSW 93
Brey, Kathleen Lillian 1948- WhoAmW 93
Breyer, Allan David 1939- St&PR 93
Breyer, James William 1961- WhoEmL 93
Breyer, Joanna 1942- WhoAmW 93
Breyer, Karl J. Law&B 92
Breyer, Karl J. 1947- St&PR 93
Breyer, Norman Nathan 1921- WhoAm 92
Breyer, Stephen Gerald 1938- WhoAm 92
Breyfogle, Peter Nicholas 1935- WhoAm 92
Breymaier, Ann Meredith 1925- WhoAm 92
Breymann, Heinrich von d1777 HarEnMi
Breytspraak, John, Jr. 1929- WhoSSW 93
Breza, Tadeusz 1905-1970 PolBiDi
Brezack, Irving 1923- St&PR 93
Brezack, John Charles 1954- St&PR 93
Brezenoff, Stanley 1937- WhoAm 92
Brezhnev, Leonid 1906-1982 ColdWar 2 [port]
Brezhnev, Leonid Ilyich 1906-1982 DcTwHis
Brezianu, Andrei Petre 1934- WhoE 93
Brezic, Richard F. Law&B 92
Brezina, Valorie Jane 1953- WhoEmL 93
Brezinski, Darlene Rita 1941- WhoAmW 93
Brialmont, Henri Alexis 1821-1903 HarEnMi
Briamonte, Barbara E. Law&B 92
Brian, Alexis Morgan, Jr. 1928- WhoAm 92, WhoWor 93
Brian, Boroimhe, King of Ireland 926-1014 BioIn 17
Brian, Douglas Richard 1945- WhoE 93
Brian, Havergal 1876-1972 Baker 92, OxDcOp
Brian, James Sanford 1947- St&PR 93, WhoEmL 93
Brian, Mark Wendell 1956- WhoEmL 93
Brian, Mary 1908- SweetSg B [port]
Brian, Pierre Leonce Thibaut 1930- St&PR 93, WhoAm 92
Brian, Richard Bruce 1947- St&PR 93
Brian Boru 926-1014 BioIn 17
Briand, Aristide 1862-1932 BioIn 17, DcTwHis
Briand, Claudette 1942- WhoScE 91-2
Briand, Donna Marie 1957- WhoSSW 93
Briand, Per 1932- WhoScE 91-2
Briand, Robert Louis, Jr. 1943- St&PR 93
Brians, Michael Alan 1960- WhoWor 93
Brians, Paul 1942- ScF&FL 92
Briant, Clyde Leonard 1948- WhoAm 92
Briante, Nicholas Michael 1937- WhoIns 93
Briar, George 1950- St&PR 93
Briard, Etienne fl. 16th cent.- Baker 92
Briarton, Grendel ScF&FL 92
Briat, Gudrun Law&B 92
Bricaud, Henri J. 1925- WhoWor 93
Bricaud, Henri Jean 1925- WhoScE 91-2
Briccetti, Joan Therese 1948- WhoAm 92, WhoAmW 93
Briccetti, Thomas 1936- Baker 92
Brice, Bill Eugene 1930- WhoAm 92
Brice, Calvin S. 1845-1898 PolPar
Brice, Calvin Stewart 1845-1898 BioIn 17
Brice, Carol 1918-1985 Baker 92
Brice, Claude Robert 1940- WhoWor 93
Brice, Cliff Verne, Jr. 1939- St&PR 93
Brice, Fanny 1891-1951 Baker 92, BioIn 17, QDrFCA 92 [port]
Brice, Harvey R. 1938- St&PR 93
Brice, Houston A., Jr. 1917- St&PR 93
Brice, James John 1925- WhoAm 92
Brice, Janet Kay 1954- WhoWrEP 92
Brice, Martin H. 1935- ScF&FL 92
Brice, Walter Miller, III 1933- St&PR 93
Bricel, Mark Leon 1929- WhoWor 93
Briceland, Alan Vance 1939- WhoSSW 93
Briceland, Patrick James 1948- WhoSSW 93
Brice-Means, Peggy Jane 1953- WhoWrEP 92
Briceno, Raul 1946- WhoWor 93
Briceno, Salvano Jose 1949- WhoUN 92
Brichford, Maynard Jay 1926- WhoAm 92
Brick, Barrett Lee 1954- WhoEmL 93
Brick, David Joseph 1947- WhoIns 93
Brick, Donald Bernard 1927- WhoAm 92
Brick, Leroy William 1927- St&PR 93
Brick, Robert Thomas 1950- WhoEmL 93
Brick, Thomas G. 1935- St&PR 93
Brickach, Alice Alexandra 1924- WhoE 93
Brickell, Charles Hennessey, Jr. 1935- WhoAm 92, WhoWor 93
Brickell, Edward Ernest, Jr. 1926- WhoAm 92
Bricken, Carl Ernest 1898-1971 Baker 92
Bricker, Donald Lee 1935- WhoAm 92
Bricker, Dusty P. 1954- WhoEmL 93
Bricker, Gerald Wayne 1947- WhoEmL 93
Bricker, Harvey Miller 1940- WhoAm 92
Bricker, James 1935- St&PR 93
Bricker, John W. 1893-1986 PolPar
Bricker, Larry R. 1937- St&PR 93
Bricker, Neal S. 1927- WhoAm 92
Bricker, Richard E. 1934- St&PR 93
Bricker, Seymour Murray 1924- WhoAm 92
Bricker, Victoria Reifler 1940- WhoAm 92, WhoAmW 93
Bricker, William Rudolph 1923- WhoAm 92
Brickey, Kathleen Fitzgerald 1944- WhoAm 92
Brickfield, Cyril Francis 1919- WhoAm 92
Brickford, Andrew T. 1952- St&PR 93
Brickhill, Christopher John 1946- WhoEmL 93
Brickhill, Paul 1916-1991 AnObit 1991, BioIn 17
Brickhouse, John B. 1916- WhoAm 92
Brickhouse, Todd Craig 1952- WhoE 93
Brickle, Barrie Vaughan WhoScE 91-1
Brickle, Lizabeth Scott 1964- St&PR 93
Brickle, Max 1966- St&PR 93
Brickley, Helen L. 1911- St&PR 93
Brickley, Richard Agar 1925- WhoAm 92
Brickley, Robert Larkin 1934- St&PR 93
Brickley, Ronald Jay 1941- St&PR 93
Bricklin, Mark Harris 1939- WhoWrEP 92
Bricklin, Patricia Ellen 1932- WhoAm 92
Brickman, Arlyne BioIn 17
Brickman, Charles Alfred 1932- St&PR 93
Brickman, David 1910- St&PR 93
Brickman, Jane Pacht 1946- WhoEmL 93
Brickman, Joel J. Law&B 92
Brickman, Kristopher Ray 1956- WhoEmL 93
Brickman, Marshall WhoAm 92
Brickman, Marshall 1941- MiSFD 9
Brickman, Paul MiSFD 9
Brickman, Ravelle 1936- WhoAm 92
Brickman, Walter A. 1945- St&PR 93
Brickmann, Juergen A.W. 1939- WhoScE 91-3
Brickner, Martin G. 1939- St&PR 93
Brickner, Ralph Gregg 1951- WhoEmL 93
Brickner, Ronald J. 1934- St&PR 93
Brickson, Richard Alan Law&B 92
Brickson, Richard Alan 1948- St&PR 93, WhoAm 92, WhoEmL 93
Bricktop, Ada Beatrice Baker 92
Brickwedde, Ferdinand Graft 1903-1989 BioIn 17
Brico, Antonia 1902-1989 Baker 92
Briddell, E. Talbot 1942- St&PR 93
Bride, John William 1937- WhoE 93
Bride, Robert Fairbanks 1953- WhoWor 93
Bride, Thomas Patrick 1948- WhoE 93
Brideau, Leo Paul 1947- WhoE 93, WhoEmL 93
Bridegam, Willis Edward, Jr. 1935- WhoAm 92
Bridel, Robert W., Jr. 1947- St&PR 93
Bridell, R.J. 1935- St&PR 93
Briden, James Christopher 1938- WhoScE 91-1
Bridenbaugh, Carl d1992 NewYTBS 92
Bridenbaugh, Carl 1903-1992 BioIn 17, ConAu 136
Bridenbaugh, Peter R. 1940- St&PR 93
Bridenbaugh, Peter Reese 1940- WhoAm 92
Bridenbaugh, Phillip Owen 1932- WhoAm 92
Bridenbaugh, Sharon Graham 1957- WhoAmW 93
Bridenbaugh, William 1932- St&PR 93, WhoAm 92
Bridendall, John P. 1950- St&PR 93
Bridendall, John Philip 1950- WhoAm 92, WhoEmL 93
Bridenstine, Louis Henry, Jr. Law&B 92
Bridenstine, Louis Henry, Jr. 1940- St&PR 93
Bridenstine, Wayne Russell 1948- WhoSSW 93
Bridenstine, William M. Law&B 92
Bridge, Carl James 1922- WhoE 93
Bridge, Edward W., Jr. St&PR 93
Bridge, Frank 1879-1941 Baker 92, BioIn 17
Bridge, (John) Frederick 1844-1924 Baker 92
Bridge, Herbert Marvin 1925- WhoWor 93
Bridge, Jack L. Law&B 92
Bridge, John B. 1950- St&PR 93
Bridge, Jonathan J. Law&B 92
Bridge, Jonathan Joseph 1950- WhoEmL 93
Bridge, Joseph (Cox) 1853-1929 Baker 92
Bridge, Margaret S. 1887- AmWomPl
Bridge, Peter J. 1935- WhoWrEP 92
Bridge, Robert Frederick 1942- St&PR 93
Bridge, Susan BioIn 17
Bridgecross, Peter ConAu 40NR
Bridgeford, Gary James 1947- WhoEmL 93
Bridgeford, John A. St&PR 93
Bridgeland, James Ralph, Jr. 1929- WhoAm 92
Bridgeman, Garry Wayne 1953- WhoSSW 93
Bridgeman, Robert Craig 1951- WhoEmL 93
Bridger, Baldwin, Jr. 1928- WhoAm 92
Bridger, Janice Christine WhoScE 91-1
Bridger, Robert N. 1936- St&PR 93
Bridger, Wagner H. 1928- WhoAm 92
Bridger, William Aitken 1941- WhoAm 92
Bridgers, Ann Preston AmWomPl
Bridgers, Elizabeth Abbott 1963- WhoAmW 93
Bridgers, Sue Ellen 1942- DcAmChF 1960, DcAmChF 1985, MajAI [port], WhoWrEP 92
Bridgers, William Frank 1932- WhoAm 92
Bridges, Alan 1928- MiSFD 9
Bridges, Alan Lynn WhoAm 92
Bridges, Albert Peyton 1925- WhoAm 92
Bridges, Audrey Elaine 1956- WhoSSW 93
Bridges, B. Ried 1927- WhoAm 92
Bridges, Beau BioIn 17
Bridges, Beau 1941- ConTFT 10, MiSFD 9, WhoAm 92
Bridges, Beryl Clarke 1941- WhoAm 92, WhoAmW 93
Bridges, Betty BioIn 17
Bridges, Bryn A. WhoScE 91-1
Bridges, Charles Walter 1943- St&PR 93
Bridges, David M. 1954- WhoE 93
Bridges, David Manning 1936- WhoAm 92, WhoWor 93
Bridges, Edwin Clifford 1945- WhoAm 92, WhoSSW 93
Bridges, Eleutheria 1905- WhoWor 93
Bridges, Gary Wayne BioIn 17
Bridges, H. Styles 1898-1961 PolPar
Bridges, Harold Andrew 1946- WhoEmL 93, WhoSSW 93
Bridges, Harry 1901-1990 BioIn 17
Bridges, Jack Edgar 1925- WhoAm 92
Bridges, Jack L. 1838?- BioIn 17
Bridges, James 1936- MiSFD 9
Bridges, James R. 1943- WhoSSW 93
Bridges, James Wilfrid WhoScE 91-1

Bridges, Jean Bolen 1934- *WhoSSW 93*
Bridges, Jeff *BioIn 17*
Bridges, Jeff 1949?- *ConTFT 10, HolBB [port], IntDcF 2-3*
Bridges, Jeff 1951- *WhoAm 92*
Bridges, Jeffrey Otis 1958- *WhoE 93*
Bridges, Joe M. 1941- *St&PR 93*
Bridges, Julian Curtis 1931- *WhoE 93*
Bridges, L. Michael 1950- *St&PR 93*
Bridges, Laura S. 1945- *St&PR 93*
Bridges, Laurie 1921- *ScF&FL 92*
Bridges, Leon 1932- *WhoAm 92, WhoE 93*
Bridges, Lisa Jane 1958- *WhoAm 92*
Bridges, Lloyd *WhoAm 92*
Bridges, Lloyd 1913- *BioIn 17*
Bridges, Madeline *AmWomPl*
Bridges, Marilyn *BioIn 17*
Bridges, Marshall 1931-1990 *BioIn 17*
Bridges, Neal Julian 1946- *WhoEmL 93*
Bridges, Patricia Ann 1952- *WhoWrEP 92*
Bridges, Peter John 1937- *WhoScE 91-1*
Bridges, Rebecca Davis 1944- *WhoAmW 93*
Bridges, Robert 1844-1930 *BioIn 17*
Bridges, Robert Lysle 1909- *St&PR 93, WhoAm 92*
Bridges, Ronald C. 1944- *St&PR 93*
Bridges, Roy Dubard, Jr. 1943- *WhoAm 92*
Bridges, Russell Brian 1955- *WhoEmL 93*
Bridges, Shelle Ronnelle 1964- *WhoSSW 93*
Bridges, Susan A. 1956- *St&PR 93*
Bridges, T.C. 1868-1944 *ScF&FL 92*
Bridges, Thomas Westcott 1938- *WhoSSW 93*
Bridges, Timothy Arthur 1957- *WhoWor 93*
Bridges, Todd *BioIn 17*
Bridges, William Bruce 1934- *WhoAm 92*
Bridges, William Russell, III 1958- *St&PR 93*
Bridgesmith, Larry Wayne 1948- *WhoEmL 93*
Bridgetower, George (Auguste Polgreen) 1778-1860 *Baker 92*
Bridgewater, Albert Louis 1941- *WhoAm 92*
Bridgewater, Bernard A., Jr. 1934- *St&PR 93*
Bridgewater, Bernard Adolphus, Jr. 1934- *WhoAm 92*
Bridgewater, Cecil *BioIn 17*
Bridgewater, Cynthia Fish 1954- *WhoAmW 93*
Bridgewater, Herbert Jeremiah, Jr. 1942- *WhoAm 92*
Bridgford, Hugh W. 1931- *St&PR 93*
Bridgforth, Allen Cabaniss *Law&B 92*
Bridgforth, Joe K. *Law&B 92*
Bridgforth, Robert Moore, Jr. 1918- *WhoWor 93*
Bridgforth, William A., Jr. 1948- *WhoEmL 93, WhoSSW 93*
Bridgham, Gladys Ruth *AmWomPl*
Bridgham, Lilian Clisby *AmWomPl*
Bridgman, Elizabeth Klein *WhoAmW 93*
Bridgman, George Ross 1947- *WhoEmL 93*
Bridgman, James Campbell 1950- *WhoEmL 93*
Bridgman, P.W. 1882-1961 *BioIn 17*
Bridgman, Percy Williams 1882-1961 *BioIn 17*
Bridgman, Victor *Law&B 92*
Bridgman, William L. *St&PR 93*
Bridgwater, David 1934- *WhoScE 91-2*
Bridgwater, John *WhoScE 91-1*
Bridgwater, Sue *ScF&FL 92*
Bridson, John G. 1935- *St&PR 93*
Bridson, Martin Robert 1964- *WhoEmL 93*
Bridston, Paul Joseph 1928- *WhoAm 92*
Bridwell, Margaret *WhoWrEP 92*
Bridwell, Norman 1928- *BioIn 17*
Bridwell, Norman (Ray) 1928- *MajAI [port]*
Bridwell, R. Kennedy 1943- *St&PR 93*
Bridwell, Robert Kennedy *Law&B 92*
Bridwell, Robert Kennedy 1943- *WhoAm 92*
Brieant, Charles La Monte, Jr. 1923- *WhoAm 92*
Briedis, Laura Marija 1964- *WhoWrEP 92*
Brief, Henry 1924- *WhoAm 92, WhoE 93*
Briefel, Robert E. 1944- *St&PR 93*
Briefer, Dennis K. 1942- *St&PR 93*
Briegel, Richard Carl 1944- *St&PR 93*
Briegel, William Eugene 1949- *WhoWrEP 92*
Briegel, Wolfgang Carl 1626-1712 *Baker 92*
Brieger, Gert Henry 1932- *WhoAm 92*
Briegleb, Wolfgang 1928- *WhoScE 91-3*
Briegs, David Michael 1965- *WhoE 93*
Brien, James Howard 1946- *WhoSSW 93*
Brieno, Linda *ScF&FL 92*
Brienza, Anthony John 1945- *WhoE 93*
Brier, Beth J. *Law&B 92*
Brier, Charles James 1937- *WhoWor 93*
Brier, Daniel Lewis 1932- *WhoSSW 93, WhoWor 93*
Brier, Pamela Sara 1945- *WhoAm 92*
Briere, Ronald Armand 1952- *WhoE 93*
Brierley, J.D.M. *Law&B 92*
Brierley, James Alan 1938- *WhoAm 92*
Brierley, John E. C. 1936- *WhoAm 92*
Brierley, Richard Greer 1915- *St&PR 93*
Brierton, Cheryl L. Wootton Black 1947- *WhoAmW 93, WhoEmL 93*
Briery, Traci *ScF&FL 92*
Briese, Leonard Arden 1933- *WhoWor 93*
Briess, Roger Charles 1937- *WhoAm 92, WhoE 93*
Briet, Marguerite de c. 1510-c. 1560 *BioIn 17*
Brietstein, Howard Abraham 1946- *WhoSSW 93*
Briffaux, Jean-Paul 1952- *WhoScE 91-2*
Brigadier, Maurice C. 1902-1991 *BioIn 17*
Brigance 1913-1990 *BioIn 17*
Briganti, Stephen Anthony 1941- *WhoE 93*
Brigantic, Patricia E. *Law&B 92*
Brigden, Richard N. 1939- *St&PR 93*
Brigden, Richard Nevius Combs 1939- *WhoAm 92*
Brigeois, Evelyne B. 1946- *WhoAmW 93*
Brigg, Peter 1942- *ScF&FL 92*
Briggie, Clifford Randall 1952- *WhoE 93*
Briggs, Arthur d1991 *BioIn 17*
Briggs, Arthur 1899-1991 *AnObit 1991*
Briggs, Asa 1921- *BioIn 17, WhoWor 93*
Briggs, Barry John *Law&B 92*
Briggs, Bunny 1922- *BioIn 17*
Briggs, Caroline *AmWomPl*
Briggs, Charles Frederick 1804-1877 *BioIn 17, JrnUS*
Briggs, Charlie Irwin 1927- *WhoWrEP 92*
Briggs, Clarence E., III 1960- *ConAu 136*
Briggs, Curtis G. *Law&B 92*
Briggs, Cynthia Anne 1950- *WhoAmW 93*
Briggs, David *SoulM*
Briggs, David John *WhoScE 91-1*
Briggs, Dean Winfield 1953- *WhoEmL 93*
Briggs, Donald Knowles 1924- *WhoE 93*
Briggs, E. Janette 1931- *WhoAmW 93*
Briggs, Eddie 1949- *WhoAm 92, WhoSSW 93*
Briggs, Edward Samuel 1926- *WhoAm 92*
Briggs, Everett Ellis 1934- *WhoAm 92, WhoWor 93*
Briggs, Frank P. d1992 *NewYTBS 92 [port]*
Briggs, Gary Lewis 1951- *St&PR 93*
Briggs, Geoffrey Hugh 1926- *WhoAm 92*
Briggs, George Madison 1927- *WhoAm 92*
Briggs, George Oliver 1926- *St&PR 93*
Briggs, Harold Melvin 1904- *WhoAm 92*
Briggs, Herbert W. 1900-1990 *BioIn 17*
Briggs, Ian *ScF&FL 92*
Briggs, Jack L. *Law&B 92*
Briggs, Janet Marie Louise 1951- *WhoEmL 93*
Briggs, Jean Audrey 1943- *WhoAm 92*
Briggs, Joe Bob 1953- *ScF&FL 92*
Briggs, John, Jr. *BioIn 17*
Briggs, John Gurney, Jr. 1916- *WhoWrEP 92*
Briggs, John Philip 1945- *WhoE 93*
Briggs, John V. 1951- *St&PR 93*
Briggs, Julia 1943- *ScF&FL 92*
Briggs, K.M. 1898-1980 *ScF&FL 92*
Briggs, Lloyd C. 1942- *St&PR 93*
Briggs, Lloyd Clark 1942- *WhoIns 93*
Briggs, Marjorie Crowder 1946- *WhoEmL 93*
Briggs, Michael D. *Law&B 92*
Briggs, Michael G. *Law&B 92*
Briggs, Morton Winfield 1915- *WhoAm 92*
Briggs, Patty Ann *WhoWrEP 92*
Briggs, Paul W. 1922- *St&PR 93*
Briggs, Peter 1944- *WhoScE 91-1*
Briggs, Peter Stromme 1946- *WhoAm 92*
Briggs, Philip 1904- *ScF&FL 92*
Briggs, Philip 1928- *St&PR 93, WhoAm 92, WhoIns 93*
Briggs, Philip James 1938- *WhoWor 93*
Briggs, Philip Terry 1934- *WhoAm 92*
Briggs, Phyllis *ScF&FL 92*
Briggs, Raymond *BioIn 17*
Briggs, Raymond (Redvers) 1934- *ChlFicS, MajAI [port]*
Briggs, Reginald Peter 1929- *WhoE 93*
Briggs, Richard Peter 1945- *WhoScE 91-1*
Briggs, Robert Mervyn 1939- *WhoE 93*
Briggs, Robert Oel d1990 *BioIn 17*
Briggs, Robert Peter 1903- *WhoAm 92*
Briggs, Robert Stearns 1944- *St&PR 93*
Briggs, Robert Stephen 1949- *WhoIns 93*
Briggs, Rodney Arthur 1923- *WhoAm 92*
Briggs, Roger Selwyn James *WhoScE 91-1*
Briggs, Sandra S. *Law&B 92*
Briggs, Sherry Welch 1945- *WhoAmW 93, WhoE 93*
Briggs, Shirley Ann 1918- *WhoAm 92*
Briggs, Stanley Austin 1941- *St&PR 93*
Briggs, Steven Russell 1941- *WhoAm 92*
Briggs, Susan Shadinger 1941- *WhoAm 92*
Briggs, Taylor Rastrick 1933- *WhoAm 92*
Briggs, Terry William 1955- *WhoEmL 93*
Briggs, Thomas 1933- *WhoSSW 93*
Briggs, Thomas C. *Law&B 92*
Briggs, Thomas Edward 1945- *St&PR 93*
Briggs, Tom 1952- *WhoE 93*
Briggs, Vernon Mason, Jr. 1937- *WhoAm 92, WhoE 93*
Briggs, William Benajah 1922- *WhoAm 92*
Briggs, William Egbert 1925- *WhoAm 92*
Briggs, Winslow Russell 1928- *WhoAm 92*
Briggs-Bivens, Deborah Susan 1950- *WhoAmW 93*
Briggum, Sue Marie *Law&B 92*
Briggum, Sue Marie 1950- *WhoAmW 93*
Brigham, Bill *BioIn 17*
Brigham, Daniel T. d1990 *BioIn 17*
Brigham, Deirdre Davis 1934- *WhoAmW 93*
Brigham, E. Oran 1940- *St&PR 93, WhoAm 92*
Brigham, Francis Gorham, Jr. 1915- *St&PR 93*
Brigham, H. Day, Jr. 1926- *St&PR 93*
Brigham, James R. 1922- *St&PR 93*
Brigham, James R. 1945- *St&PR 93*
Brigham, John Allen, Jr. 1942- *WhoWor 93*
Brigham, Linda Jane 1963- *WhoAmW 93*
Brigham, Michael F. 1960- *St&PR 93*
Brigham, Robert Cyril 1934- *WhoSSW 93*
Brigham, S.T. Jack, III *Law&B 92*
Brigham, S.T. Jack, III 1939- *St&PR 93*
Brigham, Samuel Townsend Jack, III 1939- *WhoAm 92*
Brigham, Thomas B., Jr. *Law&B 92*
Brigham, William Tufts 1841-1926 *IntDcAn*
Brigham-Grette, Julie 1955- *WhoE 93*
Brigham-Manley, Debra Ann 1965- *WhoAmW 93*
Brighenti, Luigi 1924- *WhoScE 91-3*
Bright, Betty Suida *WhoAmW 93*
Bright, Bill 1921- *BioIn 17*
Bright, Craig Bartley 1931- *WhoAm 92*
Bright, D.A. *Law&B 92*
Bright, David Forbes 1942- *WhoAm 92*
Bright, David R. 1939- *St&PR 93*
Bright, Donald Bolton 1930- *WhoWor 93*
Bright, Donald Lee 1928- *St&PR 93*
Bright, Edgar Allen Gordon 1929- *St&PR 93*
Bright, Edward David 1936- *St&PR 93*
Bright, Elise Marie *WhoSSW 93*
Bright, Freda 1929- *ConAu 136*
Bright, Gerald *Law&B 92*
Bright, Gerald 1923- *St&PR 93, WhoAm 92*
Bright, H.C. Bankole- d1958 *BioIn 17*
Bright, Harold Frederick 1913- *WhoAm 92*
Bright, Harvey R. 1920- *BioIn 17*
Bright, Harvey Roberts 1920- *St&PR 93*
Bright, Heather Elizabeth 1965- *WhoSSW 93*
Bright, Jane M. *Law&B 92*
Bright, Jerlene Ann 1942- *WhoAmW 93*
Bright, Jesse D. 1812-1875 *PolPar*
Bright, John *BioIn 17*
Bright, John Willis 1932- *WhoAm 92*
Bright, Jonathan K. *Law&B 92*
Bright, Margaret 1918- *WhoAm 92*
Bright, Mary 1859-1945 *BioIn 17*
Bright, Mary S. *Law&B 92*
Bright, Myron H. 1919- *WhoAm 92*
Bright, N.J. *WhoScE 91-1*
Bright, Nancy Elizabeth 1944- *WhoWrEP 92*
Bright, Robert 1902-1988 *BioIn 17*
Bright, Royal E. *Law&B 92*
Bright, Sam Raymond 1936- *St&PR 93*
Bright, Sarah *SmATA 71*
Bright, Simeon Miller 1925- *WhoAm 92*
Bright, Stanley J. 1940- *St&PR 93, WhoAm 92*
Bright, Thomas Lynn 1948- *WhoEmL 93*
Bright, Thomas Rhodes 1952- *WhoE 93*
Bright, Willard Mead 1914- *WhoAm 92*
Bright, William Oliver 1928- *WhoAm 92*
Bright, William Townsend 1938- *St&PR 93*
Brightbill, L.O., III 1936- *St&PR 93*
Brightbill, William Robert 1947- *St&PR 93*
Brightfield, Glory *ScF&FL 92*
Brightfield, Richard 1927- *BioIn 17, ScF&FL 92*
Brightfield, Rick *ScF&FL 92*
Brightfield, Rick 1927- *BioIn 17*
Brightman, Mary 1950- *St&PR 93*
Brightman, Richard Warren 1948- *WhoE 93*
Brightman, Robert Lloyd 1920- *WhoAm 92*
Brightman, Samuel C. d1992 *NewYTBS 92*
Brightman, Samuel C. 1911-1992 *BioIn 17*
Brightman, Sarah *BioIn 17, WhoAm 92*
Brightmire, Paul William 1924- *WhoAm 92*
Brighton, Carl Theodore 1931- *WhoAm 92*
Brighton, Catherine *BioIn 17*
Brighton, Gerald David 1920- *WhoAm 92*
Brightwell, John William *WhoScE 91-1*
Brightwell, Judith Ann 1958- *WhoAmW 93*
Brigid, Saint dc. 525 *BioIn 17*
Brigida, Carlo Joseph 1938- *St&PR 93*
Brigit of Kildare, Saint dc. 525 *BioIn 17*
Brignac, Karen Ruth 1960- *WhoAmW 93*
Brignac, Michele Marie 1961- *WhoAmW 93*
Brignac, Wanda Anne 1942- *WhoAmW 93*
Brignell, John Ernest *WhoScE 91-1*
Brignoli, Paolo Marcello 1942- *WhoScE 91-3*
Brignon, Walter L. *Law&B 92*
Brihat, Denis 1928- *WhoWor 93*
Brija-Towery, David Malcolm 1958- *St&PR 93*
Brijs, Bonnie 1953- *WhoAmW 93*
Bril, Elim Evseevich 1939- *WhoWor 93*
Briles, Judith 1946- *WhoAmW 93*
Briley, George Clifton 1925- *St&PR 93*
Briley, J.W. 1954- *St&PR 93*
Briley, John 1925- *ConTFT 10*
Briley, John Marshall 1905-1990 *BioIn 17*
Briley, John Marshall, Jr. 1940- *WhoWrEP 92*
Briley, Martha Clark 1949- *St&PR 93, WhoAmW 93, WhoEmL 93*
Briley, Rebecca Luttrell 1956- *WhoSSW 93*
Brilioth, Helge 1931- *Baker 92*
Brill, A. Bertrand 1928- *WhoAm 92*
Brill, Alan Edward 1947- *WhoE 93*
Brill, Alan Richard 1942- *WhoAm 92*
Brill, Alice Sara 1944- *WhoAmW 93*
Brill, Arthur Sylvan 1927- *WhoAm 92*
Brill, Bonnie 1948- *WhoEmL 93*
Brill, Cynthia M. *Law&B 92*
Brill, David 1941- *St&PR 93*
Brill, Edgar Lewis 1951- *WhoE 93*
Brill, Ernest 1945- *WhoWrEP 92*
Brill, Frank P. 1957- *WhoSSW 93*
Brill, Henry 1906-1990 *BioIn 17*
Brill, James L. 1951- *St&PR 93*
Brill, James Lathrop 1951- *WhoAm 92*
Brill, Jana Alena 1944- *WhoSSW 93*
Brill, Jeffrey A. *Law&B 92*
Brill, Jeffrey A. 1943- *St&PR 93*
Brill, Jesse Miles *Law&B 92*
Brill, Joel Victor 1956- *WhoEmL 93*
Brill, John J. 1931- *St&PR 93*
Brill, Lawrence Lee 1954- *WhoEmL 93*
Brill, Lesley 1943- *WhoAm 92*
Brill, Martin Robert 1951- *WhoE 93*
Brill, Mary A. *St&PR 93*
Brill, Ralph David 1944- *WhoAm 92*
Brill, Richard J. 1939- *St&PR 93*
Brill, Robert H. *BioIn 17*
Brill, Robert Jonathan *Law&B 92*
Brill, Robert Michael *Law&B 92*
Brill, Ronald M. 1943- *St&PR 93*
Brill, Sidney d1990 *BioIn 17*
Brill, Steven *BioIn 17*
Brill, Steven Charles 1953- *WhoAm 92*
Brill, Thomas R. *Law&B 92*
Brill, Walter A. *Law&B 92*
Brill, William Franklin 1923- *WhoE 93*
Brill, Winston Jonas 1939- *WhoAm 92*
Brill, Yvonne Claeys 1924- *WhoAm 92, WhoAmW 93, WhoE 93*
Brilla, Maureen *BioIn 17*
Brilliant, Barbara 1935- *WhoE 93*
Brilliant, Eleanor Luria 1930- *WhoAmW 93*
Brilliant, Neil Lane *Law&B 92*
Brilliant, Richard 1929- *WhoAm 92*
Brilliant, Robert Lee 1948- *WhoAm 92*
Brillinger, David Ross 1937- *WhoAm 92*
Brillion, Steven Matthew 1959- *WhoEmL 93*
Briloff, Abraham Jacob 1917- *WhoAm 92*
Brilon, Robert J. 1960- *St&PR 93*
Brilz, Stephen E. *Law&B 92*
Brim, Armand Eugene 1930- *WhoAm 92*
Brim, Orville Gilbert, Jr. 1923- *WhoAm 92*
Brimacombe, James Keith 1943- *WhoAm 92, WhoWor 93*
Brimacombe, Joseph 1959- *ScF&FL 92*
Brimberry, Woodrow Michael 1945- *WhoSSW 93*
Brimble, Alan 1930- *WhoAm 92*
Brimble, Michael John 1928- *WhoUN 92*
Brimblecombe, Wilfred Ross 1962- *WhoWor 93*
Brimelow, Peter 1947- *WhoAm 92*

Brimer, Jeffrey A. *Law&B 92*
Brimer, Jeffrey A. 1953- *St&PR 93*
Brimer, Philip G. 1950- *WhoIns 93*
Brimhall, Dennis C. 1948- *WhoAm 92*
Brimhall, George H., Jr. 1947- *WhoAm 92*
Brimkov, Valentin Enev 1959- *WhoWor 93*
Brimley, Wilford 1934- *WhoAm 92*
Brimmer, Andrew F. *BioIn 17*
Brimmer, Andrew Felton 1926- *St&PR 93*
Brimmer, Andrew Fenton 1926- *EncAACR*
Brimmer, Clarence Addison 1922- *WhoAm 92*
Brimmer, Martin 1829-1896 *BioIn 17*
Brimmer, Steven Richard 1949- *WhoEmL 93, WhoWor 93*
Brims, John Sinclair 1933- *WhoAm 92*
Brin, David 1950- *BioIn 17, ScF&FL 92, WhoAm 92*
Brin, Royal Henry, Jr. 1919- *WhoAm 92, WhoSSW 93*
Brinberg, Herbert Raphael 1926- *WhoAm 92*
Brinberg, Sybil Wuletich- *ScF&FL 92*
Brincat, John N. 1936- *St&PR 93*
Brincat, John Nicholas 1961- *WhoAm 92*
Brinck, Keith 1955- *WhoWor 93*
Brincker, Hans 1937- *WhoScE 91-2*
Brinckerhoff, Burt 1936- *MiSFD 9*
Brinckerhoff, Richard Charles 1931- *WhoAm 92*
Brinckman, Donald W. 1931- *St&PR 93*
Brinckman, Donald Wesley 1931- *WhoAm 92*
Brincks, Cynthia Ann 1958- *WhoEmL 93*
Brind, Ira 1941- *St&PR 93*
Brinda, Wayne 1950- *WhoEmL 93*
Brindel, June Rachuy 1919- *ScF&FL 92, WhoWrEP 92*
Brindell, Charles R., Jr. 1949- *St&PR 93*
Brindeu, Liviu 1934- *WhoScE 91-4*
Brindisi, Donna Elizabeth 1964- *WhoAmW 93*
Brindisi, Joseph J. *Law&B 92*
Brindisi, Louis J., Jr. d1992 *NewYTBS 92*
Brindle, James 1907-1991 *BioIn 17*
Brindley, David Norman *WhoScE 91-1*
Brindley, G.S. *WhoScE 91-1*
Brindley, Jennifer *St&PR 93*
Brindley, Thomas M. 1952- *St&PR 93*
Brindus, Nicolae 1935- *Baker 92*
Brine, Dolores Randolph 1945- *WhoAmW 93*
Brine, John Alfred Seymour 1926- *WhoWor 93*
Brine, Kevin R. 1950- *St&PR 93*
Brine, Mark Vincent 1948- *WhoE 93*
Brinegar, Claude Stout 1926- *St&PR 93, WhoAm 92, WhoWor 93*
Brinegar, Willard Clouse 1913- *WhoAm 92*
Briner, Daniel G. 1946- *St&PR 93*
Briner, Pamela Joan 1950- *WhoAmW 93*
Brines, Seymour 1927- *WhoE 93*
Briney, Frank E. 1928- *St&PR 93*
Briney, Lester Stafford 1944- *WhoE 93*
Briney, R.E. 1933- *ScF&FL 92*
Briney, Roger A. *Law&B 92*
Briney, Roger Albert 1949- *WhoEmL 93*
Bring, Dale Vincent 1949- *WhoEmL 93*
Bring, Karl E. *Law&B 92*
Bring, Murray H. *Law&B 92*
Bringard, Jerry D. 1936- *St&PR 93*
Bringard, Jerry Dwight *Law&B 92*
Bringas, Joseph d965 *OxDcByz*
Bringham, William Talbert, Jr. 1953- *WhoAm 92*
Bringhurst, Robert *BioIn 17*
Bringhurst, Robert 1946- *WhoCanL 92, WhoWrEP 92*
Bringle, Emmett Watson 1924- *St&PR 93*
Bringmann, Gerhard 1951- *WhoScE 91-3*
Brings, Lawrence Martin 1897- *WhoAm 92*
Bringsjord, Selmer 1958- *ScF&FL 92*
Brinig, Myron 1896-1991 *BioIn 17, ScF&FL 92*
Brink, Allan 1940- *WhoAm 92*
Brink, Andre 1935- *IntLitE*
Brink, Andre Philippus 1935- *BioIn 17, ConAu 39NR*
Brink, Arthur M. 1943- *WhoE 93*
Brink, Carl William 1947- *WhoEmL 93*
Brink, Carol 1895-1981 *ScF&FL 92*
Brink, Carol Ryrie 1895-1981 *AmWomPl, MajAI [port]*
Brink, Charles Patrick 1955- *WhoEmL 93*
Brink, David Ryrie 1919- *WhoAm 92*
Brink, Dennis R. 1941- *St&PR 93*
Brink, Frank, Jr. 1910- *WhoAm 92*
Brink, Ingemar 1952- *WhoWor 93*
Brink, Jean R. 1942- *ConAu 137*
Brink, John W. 1945- *St&PR 93*
Brink, Judith Kay 1947- *WhoEmL 93, WhoWor 93*
Brink, Marion Alice 1928- *WhoAmW 93*
Brink, Marion Francis 1932- *WhoAm 92*
Brink, Richard Edward 1923- *WhoAm 92*
Brink, Richard H. *Law&B 92*
Brink, Thomas C. 1927- *St&PR 93*
Brink, William Joseph, Jr. 1916- *WhoWrEP 92*
Brink, William P. 1916- *WhoAm 92*
Brinker, Edward Jesse 1950- *WhoE 93*
Brinker, John Thomas *Law&B 92*
Brinker, Juergen 1940- *St&PR 93*
Brinker, Kenneth Chris 1953- *WhoEmL 93*
Brinker, Linda *Law&B 92*
Brinker, Lynn John 1931- *St&PR 93*
Brinker, Maureen Connolly *BioIn 17*
Brinker, Nancy *BioIn 17*
Brinker, Norman *NewYTBS 92 [port]*
Brinker, Norman E. 1931- *St&PR 93*
Brinker, Robert Sawyer 1932- *St&PR 93*
Brinker, Thomas Michael 1933- *WhoAm 92, WhoE 93, WhoWor 93*
Brinker, William John 1935- *WhoSSW 93*
Brinkerhoff, Peter John 1945- *WhoAm 92, WhoE 93*
Brinkerhoff, Philip Richard 1943- *St&PR 93, WhoAm 92*
Brinkerhoff, Robert Beveir 1925- *St&PR 93*
Brinkerhoff, Tom J. 1939- *WhoAm 92*
Brinkhaus, Armand J. 1935- *WhoSSW 93*
Brinkhous, Kenneth Merle 1908- *WhoAm 92, WhoWor 93*
Brinkler, John Henry 1914- *WhoAm 92*
Brinkley, Charles Alexander 1929- *WhoAm 92*
Brinkley, Christie *BioIn 17*
Brinkley, David 1920- *JrnUS, WhoAm 92, WhoE 93, WhoWor 93*
Brinkley, Fred Sinclair, Jr. 1938- *WhoAm 92, WhoSSW 93*
Brinkley, Jack Thomas 1930- *WhoAm 92*
Brinkley, James W. 1937- *St&PR 93*
Brinkley, James Wellons 1937- *WhoAm 92*
Brinkley, Janet Daughtrey 1952- *WhoSSW 93*
Brinkley, Joseph Willard 1926- *WhoAm 92*
Brinkley, Phyllis 1926- *WhoAmW 93*
Brinkley, Sterling B. *St&PR 93*
Brinkley, William 1917- *ScF&FL 92*
Brinkley, William Clark 1917- *WhoAm 92, WhoWrEP 92*
Brinkman, Allan 1948- *WhoIns 93*
Brinkman, Carl Alexander 1932- *WhoE 93*
Brinkman, Cornelius Maria 1951- *WhoEmL 93*
Brinkman, Dale Thomas *Law&B 92*
Brinkman, Dirk *Law&B 92*
Brinkman, Henk-Jan 1961- *WhoE 93*
Brinkman, Herbert Charles 1926- *WhoAm 92*
Brinkman, John Anthony 1934- *WhoAm 92*
Brinkman, Judy Kay 1947- *WhoAmW 93*
Brinkman, Karen Elaine 1950- *St&PR 93, WhoAm 92*
Brinkman, Lloyd D. 1929- *St&PR 93*
Brinkman, Ned Eugene 1934- *St&PR 93*
Brinkman, Paul Delbert 1937- *WhoAm 92*
Brinkman, Richard J. 1930- *WhoAm 92*
Brinkman, Richard James 1930- *St&PR 93*
Brinkman, Robert A. 1947- *St&PR 93*
Brinkman, William Frank 1938- *WhoAm 92, WhoE 93*
Brinkmann, A.F. Gunther 1931- *WhoScE 91-3*
Brinkmann, Don *BioIn 17*
Brinkmann, Heinz-Volker *Law&B 92*
Brinkmann, Karl Dwane 1957- *WhoEmL 93*
Brinkmann, Klaus 1937- *WhoScE 91-3*
Brinkmann, Klaus Gerhard 1946- *WhoWor 93*
Brinkmann, Klaus P. 1931- *St&PR 93*
Brinkmann, Richard A. 1921- *WhoWor 93*
Brinkmann, Robert Joseph 1950- *WhoEmL 93*
Brinkmann, Sabra Rose 1962- *St&PR 93*
Brinkmeier, Roger Gene 1942- *St&PR 93*
Brinkmeyer, Robert Herman, Jr. 1951- *WhoSSW 93*
Brinko, Kathleen Therese 1951- *WhoSSW 93*
Brinks, Kenneth J.H. 1935- *St&PR 93*
Brinkworth, Brian Joseph *WhoScE 91-1*
Brinley, Charles Edward 1940- *St&PR 93*
Brinley, David R. *Law&B 92*
Brinley, G. Robert 1949- *St&PR 93*
Brinley, Timothy DeLane 1954- *WhoE 93*
Brinner, Roger E. 1947- *St&PR 93*
Brinnin, John Malcolm 1916- *WhoWrEP 92*
Brinning, Nancy Gillespie 1927- *St&PR 93, WhoAm 92*
Brinsfield, S.D. 1922- *St&PR 93*
Brinsfield, Shirley D. 1922- *WhoAm 92*
Brinsmade, Herman Hine 1876-1968 *ScF&FL 92*
Brinsmade, Lyon Louis 1924- *WhoAm 92*
Brinsmead, Edgar d1907 *Baker 92*
Brinsmead, H(esba) F(ay) 1922- *DcChlFi, MajAI [port]*
Brinsmead, Hesba (Fay) 1922- *ChlFicS*
Brinsmead, John 1814-1908 *Baker 92*
Brinsmead, Thomas *Baker 92*
Brinson, Benjamin Thomas 1948- *WhoEmL 93*
Brinson, Gary P. 1943- *St&PR 93*
Brinson, Gary Paul 1943- *WhoAm 92*
Brinson, Gay Creswell, Jr. 1925- *WhoAm 92, WhoWor 93*
Brinson, Harold Thomas 1930- *WhoAm 92*
Brinson, Mark McClellan 1943- *WhoSSW 93*
Brinson, Michael Ernest *WhoScE 91-1*
Brinster, Barry *WhoE 93*
Brinster, Ralph Lawrence 1932- *WhoAm 92*
Brint, R. Paul 1949- *WhoScE 91-3*
Brintnall, John Robert 1953- *St&PR 93*
Brinton, Bradford 1880-1936 *BioIn 17*
Brinton, Daniel Garrison 1837-1899 *IntDcAn*
Brinton, Edgar Harry 1916-1990 *BioIn 17*
Brinton, Henry 1901-1977 *ScF&FL 92*
Brinton, Margo Ann 1945- *WhoAm 92, WhoSSW 93*
Brinton, Richard K. 1946- *St&PR 93*
Brinton, Richard Kirk 1946- *WhoEmL 93*
Brinton, Tina Ree 1956- *WhoEmL 93*
Brintz, Robert S. *Law&B 92*
Brintzinger, Hans-Herbert 1935- *WhoScE 91-3*
Brinzo, John S. 1942- *St&PR 93, WhoAm 92*
Briody, Laurence Patrick 1936- *WhoE 93*
Brion, Alain *St&PR 93*
Brion, John Martin 1922- *WhoE 93*
Briones, Ellen Margaret 1962- *WhoAmW 93*
Brioschi, Edoardo Teodoro 1941- *WhoWor 93*
Briotte, Kristin E. *Law&B 92*
Brisbane, Arthur 1864-1936 *GayN, JrnUS*
Brisbin, Georgia Faye 1933- *WhoAmW 93*
Brisbin, Robert Edward 1946- *WhoEmL 93*
Brisbois, Richard Anthony 1952- *WhoSSW 93*
Brisbon, Eric Stephen 1954- *St&PR 93*
Brisby, Stewart Paul 1945- *WhoWrEP 92*
Brisch, James John 1953- *St&PR 93*
Brisco, Pat A. *ScF&FL 92*
Brisco, Rodney E. *Law&B 92*
Brisco, Valerie *BioIn 17*
Briscoe, Anne M. 1918- *WhoWor 93*
Briscoe, Bimbo 1955- *WhoEmL 93*
Briscoe, Brian James 1945- *WhoWor 93*
Briscoe, Jack Clayton 1920- *WhoAm 92*
Briscoe, James S. 1932- *St&PR 93*
Briscoe, John 1948- *WhoEmL 93*
Briscoe, John Frederick, Jr. 1952- *WhoEmL 93*
Briscoe, John Hanson 1934- *WhoAm 92*
Briscoe, Joseph R. *Law&B 92*
Briscoe, Keith G. 1933- *WhoAm 92, WhoWor 93*
Briscoe, Margaret Sutton 1864- *AmWomPl*
Briscoe, Mary Rebecca 1957- *WhoEmL 93*
Briscoe, Patricia Ann 1941- *WhoAmW 93*
Briscoe, Ralph O. 1927- *St&PR 93*
Briscoe, Ralph Owen 1927- *WhoAm 92*
Briscoe, Robert John 1941- *St&PR 93*
Brisco-Hooks, Valerie 1960- *AfrAmBi, BlkAmWO [port]*
Brisebois, Marcel 1933- *WhoAm 92*
Briseid, Kjell 1921- *WhoScE 91-4*
Briseno, Rosa M. 1950- *St&PR 93*
Brisentine, Cecilia Kay 1952- *WhoAmW 93*
Brisk, David C. 1930- *St&PR 93*
Briskin, Bernard 1924- *St&PR 93, WhoAm 92*
Briskin, Madeleine 1932- *WhoWor 93*
Briskman, Louis J. *Law&B 92*
Briskman, Robert David 1932- *WhoAm 92*
Brisolara, Ashton 1924- *WhoAm 92*
Brisolla, Thyrso A. 1940- *BioIn 17*
Brissenden, Priscilla Arthur 1925- *WhoE 93, WhoWor 93*
Brissette, Francois *Law&B 92*
Brissette, Gregory Paul 1955- *WhoEmL 93, WhoSSW 93*
Brissette, Martha Blevins 1959- *WhoEmL 93*
Brissey, Ruben Marion 1923- *WhoAm 92*
Brissie, Eugene Field, Jr. 1949- *WhoAm 92*
Brissman, Bernard Gustave 1919- *WhoAm 92*
Brissman, Charles Philip *Law&B 92*
Brisson, Eugene Henri 1835-1912 *BioIn 17*
Brisson, Pat *BioIn 17*
Brisson, Violette *WhoScE 91-2*
Brister, Bill H. 1930- *WhoAm 92*
Brister, Bubby *BioIn 17*
Bristol, Earl of 1730-1803 *BioIn 17*
Bristol, Arlen A. 1952- *WhoEmL 93*
Bristol, Betty Jane 1946- *WhoE 93*
Bristol, Edith *AmWomPl*
Bristol, Horace *BioIn 17*
Bristol, James E. d1992 *NewYTBS 92*
Bristol, Johnny *SoulM*
Bristol, Kelly Gene 1950- *St&PR 93*
Bristol, Louise Fitzgerald 1935- *WhoAmW 93*
Bristol, Marie Mahoney 1942- *WhoAmW 93*
Bristol, Norman 1924- *WhoAm 92*
Bristol, Raymond Curtis 1932- *WhoE 93*
Bristol, Robert Francis 1940- *WhoE 93*
Bristor, Valerie Jayne 1954- *WhoEmL 93*
Bristow, Allan *WhoAm 92*
Bristow, Allan Mercer 1951- *WhoSSW 93*
Bristow, Ann 1940- *WhoAmW 93*
Bristow, Benjamin H. 1832-1896 *PolPar*
Bristow, David Ian 1931- *WhoAm 92*
Bristow, George Frederick 1825-1898 *Baker 92*
Bristow, James Edward 1934- *St&PR 93*
Bristow, James Randle 1950- *WhoEmL 93*
Bristow, Matthew 1945- *St&PR 93*
Bristow, Matthew M. 1945- *WhoE 93*
Bristow, Robert O'Neil 1926- *WhoAm 92, WhoWor 93, WhoWrEP 92*
Bristow, William Harvey, Jr. *WhoE 93*
Bristow, William Richard *Baker 92*
Britain, Radie 1903- *Baker 92*
Britain, Radie 1908- *WhoAm 92*
Britcher, Trina Rose 1960- *WhoAmW 93*
Brite, David Alan 1948- *St&PR 93*
Brite, Donald L. 1933- *St&PR 93*
Brite, Mary Alice 1930- *WhoWrEP 92*
Brito, Aristeo 1942- *DcLB 122 [port]*
Brito, Dagobert Llanos 1941- *WhoAm 92, WhoSSW 93*
Brito, Maria 1947- *NotHsAW 93*
Brito, Mariano *WhoWor 93*
Brito, Odoardo Jose 1948- *WhoWor 93*
Brito, Silvia 1933- *NotHsAW 93*
Brito Cruz, Carlos Henrique 1956- *WhoWor 93*
Brito Selvera, Norma *NotHsAW 93*
Brito y Nicote, Philip d1613 *HarEnMi*
Britt, David Tillman 1955- *WhoSSW 93*
Britt, David V.B. 1937- *St&PR 93*
Britt, David Van Buren 1937- *WhoAm 92*
Britt, Donald R. 1924- *St&PR 93*
Britt, Earl Thomas 1940- *WhoAm 92*
Britt, George Gittion, Jr. 1949- *WhoEmL 93, WhoWor 93*
Britt, Gerald F. 1932- *St&PR 93*
Britt, Glenn A. 1949- *St&PR 93*
Britt, Glenn Alan 1949- *WhoAm 92, WhoEmL 93*
Britt, Henry Middleton 1919- *WhoAm 92*
Britt, J. Stephen 1951- *WhoAm 92*
Britt, Jacquelyn G. *WhoE 93*
Britt, James Thomas 1904- *WhoAm 92*
Britt, Janeann *Law&B 92*
Britt, John Robert *Law&B 92*
Britt, John Roy 1937- *WhoAm 92*
Britt, Julia C. 1952- *WhoEmL 93*
Britt, Julie *BioIn 17, WhoAmW 93*
Britt, Kathleen Ann 1963- *WhoAmW 93*
Britt, Leigh *WhoWrEP 92*
Britt, Maisha Dorrah *WhoAmW 93, WhoE 93, WhoWor 93*
Britt, Maurice *BioIn 17*
Britt, Paul A., Jr. *Law&B 92*
Britt, Robert Louis 1943- *WhoSSW 93*
Britt, Russell William 1926- *WhoAm 92*
Britt, Susan Deanne 1961- *WhoSSW 93*
Britt, Thomas *BioIn 17*
Britt, Timothy Mayo 1948- *WhoSSW 93*
Britt, W. Earl 1932- *WhoAm 92, WhoSSW 93*
Britt, William R. 1948- *St&PR 93*
Brittain, Alfred 1922- *St&PR 93*
Brittain, Alfred, III 1922- *WhoAm 92*
Brittain, Bill *MajAI*
Brittain, Bill 1930- *DcAmChF 1960, ScF&FL 92*
Brittain, Bruce Bennett 1957- *WhoEmL 93, WhoSSW 93*
Brittain, C. Dale 1948- *ScF&FL 92*
Brittain, Carol A. *Law&B 92*
Brittain, Clifford Mark 1958- *WhoSSW 93*
Brittain, James Edward 1931- *WhoAm 92*
Brittain, John 1935- *St&PR 93*
Brittain, John A. 1937- *St&PR 93*
Brittain, John Edward 1946- *WhoScE 91-4, WhoWor 93*
Brittain, John Oliver 1920- *WhoSSW 93*
Brittain, Kerry R. *Law&B 92*
Brittain, Nancy Hammond 1954- *WhoAmW 93*
Brittain, Rasa 1960- *WhoWrEP 92*
Brittain, Ross 1951- *WhoE 93*
Brittain, Vera 1893-1970 *BioIn 17*
Brittain, William E. *ScF&FL 92*

Brittain, William (E.) 1930- *MajAI [port], WhoWrEP 92*
Brittan, Leon 1939- *WhoWor 93*
Brittan, Patrick John 1958- *WhoEmL 93*
Britten, Benjamin 1913-1976 *BioIn 17, IntDcOp [port], OxDcOp*
Britten, (Edward) Benjamin 1913-1976 *Baker 92*
Britten, Gerald Hallbeck 1930- *WhoAm 92*
Britten, John Randall *WhoScE 91-1*
Britten, Roy John 1919- *WhoAm 92*
Brittenham, Raymond Lee 1916- *WhoAm 92*
Brittin, Helen Clark 1938- *WhoAmW 93*
Brittin, L. H. 1877-1952 *EncABHB 8 [port]*
Brittin, Norman Aylsworth 1906- *WhoSSW 93*
Brittingham, David Louis 1959- *WhoEmL 93*
Britto, Ronald 1937- *WhoE 93*
Britto Garcia, Luis 1940- *SpAmA*
Britton, Anthony R. 1960- *St&PR 93*
Britton, Barbara 1920-1980 *SweetSg D [port]*
Britton, Barbara Ann 1959- *WhoEmL 93*
Britton, Carla Boden 1941- *WhoAmW 93*
Britton, Charles Price, III 1939- *St&PR 93*
Britton, Clarold Lawrence 1932- *WhoAm 92*
Britton, David 1945- *ScF&FL 92*
Britton, David Carl 1946- *WhoEmL 93*
Britton, Dennis A. 1940- *WhoAm 92*
Britton, Donald W. 1948- *WhoAm 92*
Britton, Donald Wayne 1948- *St&PR 93*
Britton, Eddie Wayne 1953- *WhoSSW 93*
Britton, Edward Charles 1955- *WhoEmL 93*
Britton, Erwin Adelbert 1915- *WhoAm 92*
Britton, Harold F. *Law&B 92*
Britton, Janet Lorene 1947- *WhoWrEP 92*
Britton, Jennifer June 1960- *WhoAmW 93*
Britton, Joanne Hess *WhoE 93*
Britton, Joanne Marie 1950- *WhoEmL 93*
Britton, John 1940- *WhoScE 91-3*
Britton, John E. 1921- *St&PR 93*
Britton, John Edgar 1921- *WhoE 93*
Britton, John Leslie *WhoScE 91-1*
Britton, Laurence George 1951- *WhoEmL 93, WhoSSW 93*
Britton, Leonard *WhoAm 92*
Britton, Lewis W. *BioIn 17*
Britton, Marla Lynn 1960- *WhoEmL 93*
Britton, Melvin Creed, Jr. 1935- *WhoAm 92*
Britton, Nicholas Ferris 1953- *WhoWor 93*
Britton, Patricia A. *Law&B 92*
Britton, Patricia R. *Law&B 92*
Britton, Peter Ewart 1936- *ConAu 40NR*
Britton, Richard L. 1949- *St&PR 93*
Britton, Robert A. 1946- *St&PR 93*
Britton, Robert Austin 1946- *WhoAm 92*
Britton, Robert Eugene 1924- *St&PR 93*
Britton, Scott Richard 1960- *WhoEmL 93*
Britton, Wesley Alan 1953- *WhoSSW 93*
Britton-Riley, Deborah Alexis 1953- *WhoE 93*
Britts, George M. *Law&B 92*
Britts, William Carlyle 1932- *St&PR 93*
Britz, Diane Edward 1952- *WhoAmW 93, WhoE 93, WhoEmL 93, WhoWor 93*
Brix, Cheri Lee *Law&B 92*
Brixen, Martin Gerald 1927- *WhoAm 92*
Brixey, Stephen S., Jr. 1936- *St&PR 93*
Brixi, Franz Xaver 1732-1771 *Baker 92*
Brizan, George 1943- *DcCPCAm*
Brizek, Robert *St&PR 93*
Brizel, Michael A. *Law&B 92*
Brizendine, Lyle W. 1952- *St&PR 93*
Brizius, Janice Jane 1935- *WhoAmW 93*
Brizuela, Graciela Petra 1959- *WhoWor 93*
Brizzi, Mary T. 1940- *ScF&FL 92*
Brizzolara, Bruce J. 1942- *St&PR 93*
Brizzolara, Charles Anthony 1929- *WhoAm 92*
Brizzolara, John *ScF&FL 92*
Brizzolara, Marco Aurelio 1922- *St&PR 93*
Brizzolara, Mary Suydam 1935- *WhoAmW 93*
Brizzolara, Michael *St&PR 93*
Brizzolara, Paul *Law&B 92*
Brkanovic, Ivan 1906-1987 *Baker 92*
Brna, Susan Eileen 1956- *WhoE 93*
Bro, Bernard (Gerard Marie) 1925- *ConAu 39NR*
Bro, Margueritte Harmon 1894- *AmWomPl*
Broad, David Martin 1947- *St&PR 93*
Broad, Edward M. 1921- *St&PR 93*
Broad, Eli *BioIn 17*
Broad, Eli 1933- *St&PR 93, WhoAm 92, WhoWor 93*
Broad, Joseph A. *St&PR 93*
Broad, Matthew R. *Law&B 92*
Broad, Michael 1951- *WhoEmL 93*
Broadbent, Amalia Sayo Castillo 1956- *WhoAmW 93*
Broadbent, Edward *BioIn 17*
Broadbent, J. Streett 1942- *WhoE 93, WhoWor 93*
Broadbent, Peter Allan 1939- *WhoAm 92*
Broadbent, Peter Edwin, Jr. 1951- *WhoEmL 93*
Broadbent, Sara 1954- *WhoAmW 93*
Broadbent, Thomas V. 1935- *St&PR 93*
Broadbent, Thomas Valentine 1935- *WhoAm 92*
Broadbridge, K. *WhoUN 92*
Broadcorens, Yvonne Ramaut 1905- *WhoWrEP 92*
Broaddhead, Robert L. 1949- *St&PR 93*
Broaddus, Charles David 1930- *WhoAm 92*
Broaddus, Colleen Marie *Law&B 92*
Broaddus, John Alfred 1939- *St&PR 93*
Broaddus, Robert Lewis 1935- *WhoAm 92*
Broadfoot, Albert Lyle 1930- *WhoAm 92*
Broadfoot, Eleanora *Baker 92*
Broadfoot, Robert Earl 1953- *WhoSSW 93*
Broadhead, Caroline 1950?- *BioIn 17*
Broadhead, James Lowell 1935- *WhoAm 92, WhoSSW 93*
Broadhurst, Austin 1917- *St&PR 93, WhoAm 92*
Broadhurst, Austin, Jr. 1947- *WhoEmL 93, WhoWor 93*
Broadhurst, David John 1947- *WhoWor 93*
Broadhurst, Jerome Anthony 1945- *WhoAm 92*
Broadhurst, Kent 1940- *ConAu 137*
Broadhurst, Martin Gilbert 1932- *WhoE 93*
Broadhurst, Norman Neil 1946- *WhoAm 92, WhoEmL 93*
Broadie, Stephen W. *Law&B 92*
Broadley, David C. 1943- *St&PR 93*
Broadman, Howard R. *BioIn 17*
Broadman, Lynn M. 1940- *WhoSSW 93*
Broadman, Richard *MiSFD 9*
Broadright, Sheryl Schuck 1962- *WhoAmW 93*
Broadstreet, Jeff 1954- *MiSFD 9*
Broadus, Betty Russell 1933- *St&PR 93*
Broadus, James Matthew 1947- *WhoE 93, WhoEmL 93*
Broadus, Joseph Edward 1946- *WhoEmL 93, WhoSSW 93, WhoWor 93*
Broadus, Robert Newton 1922- *WhoSSW 93*
Broadwater, James E. 1945- *WhoAm 92*
Broadwater, John Ralph, Jr. 1955- *WhoEmL 93*
Broadwater, Shirley Marie 1937- *WhoAmW 93*
Broadway, Nancy Ruth 1946- *WhoAmW 93*
Broadway, Roxanne Meyer 1951- *WhoEmL 93*
Broadway, William Davis 1930- *WhoSSW 93*
Broadwell, Milton Edward 1938- *WhoWor 93*
Broadwell, Richard Dow 1945- *WhoE 93*
Broadwin, Joseph Louis 1930- *St&PR 93, WhoAm 92*
Broadwood, Henry John Tschudi d1911 *Baker 92*
Broadwood, James Shudi 1772-1851 *Baker 92*
Broadwood, John 1732-1812 *Baker 92*
Broadwood, Thomas *Baker 92*
Broadwood & Sons *Baker 92*
Broas, Donald Sanford 1940- *WhoAm 92*
Brobeck, John Raymond 1914- *WhoAm 92*
Brobeck, Stephen James 1944- *WhoAm 92*
Broberg, Gustave, Jr. 1920- *BiDAMSp 1989*
Brobst, Vernon D. 1943- *St&PR 93*
Brobst, William Keplinger 1928- *WhoWrEP 92*
Broca, Laurent Antoine 1928- *WhoWor 93*
Broca, Paul 1824-1880 *IntDcAn*
Brocato, Andrew, Jr. 1965- *WhoE 93*
Brocato, Joseph Myron 1917- *WhoAm 92*
Brocchini, Ronald Gene 1929- *WhoAm 92*
Broccoli, Albert Romolo 1909- *WhoAm 92, WhoWor 93*
Broccoli, Louis Viscardo 1931- *St&PR 93*
Broch, Henri 1950- *WhoScE 91-2*
Broch, Hermann 1886-1951 *DcLB 124 [port]*
Broche, Charles 1752-1803 *Baker 92*
Broches, Aron 1914- *WhoAm 92*
Brochier, J. 1940- *WhoScE 91-2*
Brochier, Jean G. 1940- *WhoWor 93*
Brochin, Frank M. 1965- *WhoWor 93*
Brochin, Leona Nelkin 1932- *WhoAmW 93*
Brochmann, Elizabeth 1938- *DcChlFi, WhoCanL 92*
Brochstein, Samuel J. 1906- *St&PR 93*
Brochu, Andre 1942- *WhoCanL 92, WhoWrEP 92*
Brochu, Claude Renaud *WhoAm 92, WhoE 93*
Brochu, Pierre 1952- *St&PR 93*
Brochu, Robert A. 1939- *St&PR 93*
Brociner, R.E. *WhoScE 91-1*
Brock, A. Clutton- *ScF&FL 92*
Brock, Alice May 1941- *WhoAm 92*
Brock, Andrew 1934- *WhoScE 91-3*
Brock, Anthony Newton 1939- *WhoSSW 93*
Brock, Arthur Clutton- 1868-1924 *BioIn 17*
Brock, Carolyn Pratt 1946- *WhoAmW 93, WhoSSW 93*
Brock, Charles Lawrence 1943- *WhoAm 92, WhoE 93*
Brock, Charles M. *Law&B 92*
Brock, Christopher John 1954- *WhoScE 91-1*
Brock, Dan Willets 1937- *WhoAm 92*
Brock, Darrell Lee 1957- *WhoEmL 93*
Brock, Darryl *ScF&FL 92*
Brock, David Allen 1936- *WhoAm 92*
Brock, David J.H. *WhoScE 91-1*
Brock, Deborah *MiSFD 9*
Brock, Dee Sala 1930- *WhoAm 92*
Brock, Diane Johnson 1953- *WhoAmW 93*
Brock, Ealy Harris 1941- *St&PR 93*
Brock, Edward Eldon 1954- *WhoSSW 93*
Brock, Eunice Lee Miller 1930- *WhoSSW 93*
Brock, Frank Edgar 1932- *St&PR 93*
Brock, Gerald Wayne 1948- *WhoAm 92*
Brock, Gregory Winters 1946- *WhoSSW 93*
Brock, Harry B., Jr. 1926- *St&PR 93*
Brock, Harry Blackwell, Jr. 1926- *WhoAm 92, WhoSSW 93*
Brock, Horace Rhea 1927- *WhoAm 92*
Brock, Isaac 1769-1812 *HarEnMi*
Brock, James Daniel 1916- *WhoAm 92*
Brock, James H., Jr. *St&PR 93*
Brock, James Hassel 1941- *St&PR 93*
Brock, James Lee 1936- *BiDAMSp 1989*
Brock, James Robert 1944- *WhoAm 92*
Brock, James Rush 1931- *WhoAm 92*
Brock, James Sidney 1913- *St&PR 93, WhoAm 92*
Brock, Jayne 1959- *WhoWrEP 92*
Brock, Jeffrey Stewart 1950- *WhoEmL 93, WhoSSW 93*
Brock, John David 1944- *St&PR 93*
Brock, John Grove 1959- *WhoEmL 93*
Brock, John M. 1913- *St&PR 93*
Brock, John Malcolm, Jr. 1948- *St&PR 93*
Brock, Karena Diane 1942- *WhoAm 92*
Brock, Kathi 1939- *St&PR 93*
Brock, Larry Raymond 1946- *WhoEmL 93*
Brock, Lawrence Ephraim 1913- *St&PR 93*
Brock, Lina Lee d1991 *BioIn 17*
Brock, Lonnie R. 1950- *St&PR 93*
Brock, Lonnie Rex 1950- *WhoEmL 93, WhoWor 93*
Brock, Lorena Rowan 1921- *St&PR 93*
Brock, Louis 1939- *AfrAmBi*
Brock, Louis Clark 1939- *WhoAm 92*
Brock, Lucy Ray Brannen 1950- *WhoAmW 93*
Brock, Lynmar, Jr. 1934- *St&PR 93*
Brock, Mario 1938- *WhoScE 91-3*
Brock, Mary Anne 1932- *WhoAm 92*
Brock, Michael *BioIn 17*
Brock, Mitchell 1927- *WhoAm 92*
Brock, Pat *St&PR 93*
Brock, Paul Warrington 1928- *WhoAm 92*
Brock, Ralph D. 1945- *St&PR 93*
Brock, Randall J. 1943- *WhoWrEP 92*
Brock, Randolph David, III 1943- *St&PR 93*
Brock, Raymond Theodore 1927- *WhoSSW 93*
Brock, Robert Lee 1924- *WhoAm 92*
Brock, Stanton G. 1908- *St&PR 93*
Brock, Thomas Dale 1926- *WhoAm 92*
Brock, Thomas Walter 1931- *WhoAm 92*
Brock, William Allen, III 1941- *WhoAm 92*
Brock, William Alton 1946- *WhoE 93*
Brock, William E., III 1930- *PolPar*
Brock, William Emerson 1930- *WhoAm 92*
Brock, William George 1928- *WhoAm 92*
Brocka, Bruce 1959- *WhoEmL 93*
Brocka, Lino *BioIn 17*
Brocka, Lino 1940-1991 *AnObit 1991, MiSFD 9N*
Brockardt, John I. 1949- *St&PR 93*
Brockbank, T. William 1893-1990 *BioIn 17*
Brockberg, Karen Lee 1945- *WhoAmW 93*
Brockenbrough, Barry W. 1934- *St&PR 93*
Brockenbrough, Henry Watkins 1923- *WhoAm 92*
Brockenbrough, Roger Lewis 1934- *WhoE 93*
Brocker, Sandra Lee Potish 1947- *WhoAmW 93, WhoEmL 93*
Brockes, Jeremy Patrick *WhoScE 91-1*
Brockett, Alice Whitney *AmWomPl*
Brockett, Jessie Faye 1948- *WhoAmW 93*
Brockett, Louise Brewster 1961- *WhoEmL 93*
Brockett, Oscar Gross 1923- *WhoAm 92, WhoWrEP 92*
Brockett, Patrick Lee 1948- *WhoSSW 93*
Brockett, Peter Charles 1946- *WhoAm 92*
Brockett, Roger Ware 1938- *WhoAm 92*
Brockette, Ann Harrington 1940- *WhoAmW 93*
Brockey d1862? *BioIn 17*
Brockey, Harold d1991 *BioIn 17*
Brockhard, Douglas Lee 1947- *St&PR 93*
Brockhaus, William Dillon 1945- *WhoWor 93*
Brockhouse, Bertram Neville 1918- *WhoAm 92*
Brockie, Donald Peter 1931- *WhoAm 92*
Brockie, Keith *BioIn 17*
Brockington, Donald Leslie 1929- *WhoAm 92*
Brockington, Horace 1954- *WhoE 93*
Brockington, Ian F. *WhoScE 91-1*
Brockland-Nease, Margaret Ann 1963- *WhoSSW 93*
Brocklehurst, Keith *WhoScE 91-1*
Brocklesby, Paula Ruth 1948- *WhoAmW 93*
Brockley, Fenton *ScF&FL 92*
Brockman, Donald Charles 1942- *St&PR 93*
Brockman, Keith W. 1944- *St&PR 93*
Brockman, L. Carol *Law&B 92*
Brockman, Leslie Richard 1940- *WhoSSW 93*
Brockman, Murray Wilson 1945- *WhoAm 92*
Brockman, Ronald E. 1941- *St&PR 93*
Brockman, Shirley Blow 1950- *WhoSSW 93*
Brockman, Ted S. *WhoIns 93*
Brockman, Terry James 1955- *WhoEmL 93*
Brockman, Vincent C. *Law&B 92*
Brockman, W.L. *Law&B 92*
Brockmann, Heinz-Wilhelm 1947- *WhoWor 93*
Brockmann, Helen Jane 1947- *WhoEmL 93*
Brockmann, S.E. 1928- *St&PR 93*
Brockmans, J.F. *WhoScE 91-3*
Brockmeyer, John d1990 *BioIn 17*
Brocks, Eric Randy 1946- *WhoE 93*
Brockschmidt, Henry F. 1920- *St&PR 93*
Brocksmith, James G., Jr. 1942- *WhoAm 92*
Brockway, Donald Lee 1939- *WhoSSW 93*
Brockway, Duncan 1932- *WhoAm 92*
Brockway, F.M. *WhoScE 91-1*
Brockway, Fenner 1888-1988 *ScF&FL 92*
Brockway, George Pond 1915- *WhoAm 92*
Brockway, Howard A. 1870-1951 *Baker 92*
Brockway, John Martin *WhoScE 91-1*
Brockway, Laurie Sue 1956- *WhoAmW 93, WhoEmL 93*
Brockway, Merrill LaMonte 1923- *WhoAm 92*
Brockway, Peter Craig 1956- *St&PR 93, WhoEmL 93, WhoSSW 93*
Brockway, William Robert 1924- *WhoAm 92*
Brockwell, Charles Wilbur, Jr. 1937- *WhoAm 92*
Brockwell, John William, Jr. 1953- *WhoEmL 93*
Brod, Albert Thomas 1913- *St&PR 93*
Brod, Daniel 1959- *WhoEmL 93*
Brod, Ernest *Law&B 92*
Brod, Hans-Georg 1949- *WhoScE 91-3*
Brod, Harold J. 1912- *St&PR 93*
Brod, Irven J. 1909- *St&PR 93*
Brod, Max 1884-1968 *Baker 92*
Brod, Michael L. 1945- *St&PR 93*
Brod, Morton Shlevin 1926- *WhoAm 92*
Brod, Spencer Grant 1962- *St&PR 93*
Brod, Stanford 1932- *WhoAm 92*
Broda, Frederick Charles 1937- *St&PR 93*
Broda, Paul *WhoScE 91-1*
Broda, Rafal Jan 1944- *WhoWor 93*
Brodax, Al *MiSFD 9*
Brodbeck, Charles Richard 1949- *WhoEmL 93*
Brodbeck, John Friedrich 1960- *WhoEmL 93*
Brodbeck, Nancy Elizabeth 1962- *WhoEmL 93*
Brodbeck, Urs 1938- *WhoScE 91-4*
Brodbeck, William J. 1944- *St&PR 93*

Brodbent, Bill 1942- *St&PR 93*
Brode, Kevin *Law&B 92*
Brode, Marvin Jay 1931- *WhoAm 92*
Brode, William Edward 1929- *WhoSSW 93*
Brodecki, Joseph Michael 1946- *WhoEmL 93*
Brodecki, Richard J. *Law&B 92*
Brodehl, Johannes 1931- *WhoScE 91-3, WhoWor 93*
Brodell, Albert P. 1923- *St&PR 93*
Brodell, Anne Rayne 1956- *WhoAmW 93*
Brodenova, Lida d1990 *BioIn 17*
Broder, Aaron J. 1924- *WhoAm 92*
Broder, Cliff 1948- *St&PR 93*
Broder, David S. 1929- *JrnUS, PolPar*
Broder, David Salzer 1929- *WhoAm 92, WhoE 93, WhoWrEP 92*
Broder, Douglas Fisher 1948- *WhoE 93*
Broder, Jerry 1927- *St&PR 93*
Broder, Nathan 1905-1967 *Baker 92*
Broder, Patricia Janis 1935- *WhoAm 92, WhoAmW 93, WhoWor 93*
Broder, Samuel 1945- *CurBio 92 [port]*
Broderick, Betty *BioIn 17*
Broderick, Carlfred Bartholomew 1932- *WhoAm 92, WhoWor 93*
Broderick, Cathy *BioIn 17*
Broderick, Damien 1944- *ScF&FL 92*
Broderick, Dan *BioIn 17*
Broderick, David Francis 1958- *WhoEmL 93*
Broderick, Dennis J. *WhoAm 92*
Broderick, Dennis John *Law&B 92*
Broderick, Donald Leland 1928- *WhoWor 93*
Broderick, Edward M., III 1947- *WhoIns 93*
Broderick, Edward Michael, III 1947- *WhoEmL 93*
Broderick, Francis L. d1992 *NewYTBS 92 [port]*
Broderick, Francis L(yons) 1922-1992 *ConAu 139*
Broderick, Gregory Philip 1952- *WhoE 93*
Broderick, Harold Christian 1925- *WhoWor 93*
Broderick, James A. *Law&B 92*
Broderick, James Anthony 1943- *St&PR 93*
Broderick, John *MiSFD 9*
Broderick, John 1935- *St&PR 93*
Broderick, John Caruthers 1926- *WhoAm 92, WhoWrEP 92*
Broderick, Joseph A. 1881-1959 *BioIn 17*
Broderick, Judith Ann 1943- *WhoAmW 93*
Broderick, Matthew *BioIn 17*
Broderick, Matthew 1962- *WhoAm 92*
Broderick, Mick 1959- *ScF&FL 92*
Broderick, Raymond Joseph 1914- *WhoAm 92*
Broderick, Richard James 1921- *St&PR 93*
Broderick, Robert L. 1911- *St&PR 93*
Broderick, Terry 1945- *WhoIns 93*
Broderick, Thomas F. *Law&B 92*
Broderick, Thomas Robert 1952- *WhoSSW 93*
Broderick, Vincent Lyons 1920- *WhoAm 92, WhoE 93*
Broders, Laura Comiskey *Law&B 92*
Brodersen, Arthur James 1939- *WhoAm 92*
Brodersen, Klaus 1926- *WhoScE 91-3*
Brodersen, Rolf 1921- *WhoScE 91-2*
Broderson, Moshe 1890-1956 *PolBiDi*
Brodeur, Alphonse Toner 1902- *St&PR 93, WhoAm 92*
Brodeur, Armand Edward 1922- *WhoAm 92*
Brodeur, Arthur Gilchrist 1888-1968? *ScF&FL 92*
Brodeur, J.H. 1932- *St&PR 93*
Brodeur, John Homer 1935- *WhoE 93*
Brodeur, Margaret R. *Law&B 92*
Brodeur, Patricia Elizabeth Hart 1955- *WhoAmW 93*
Brodeur, Paul Adrian 1931- *WhoE 93*
Brodey, Jim 1942- *WhoWrEP 92*
Brodhay, O. Chester 1874-1954 *ScF&FL 92*
Brodhead, Cynthia *Law&B 92*
Brodhead, David Crawmer 1934- *WhoAm 92, WhoE 93, WhoWor 93*
Brodhead, William McNulty 1941- *WhoAm 92*
Brodhun, Andrew R. 1940- *WhoAm 92*
Brodhurst, Albert Edward 1934- *WhoE 93*
Brodian, Laura 1947- *WhoAm 92*
Brodie, Christina Oakley 1951- *WhoEmL 93*
Brodie, David *BioIn 17*
Brodie, David Alan *WhoScE 91-1*
Brodie, Donald G. 1938- *St&PR 93*
Brodie, Donald Gibbs 1938- *WhoAm 92*
Brodie, Fawn McKay 1915-1981 *BioIn 17*
Brodie, Harlow Keith Hammond 1939- *WhoAm 92, WhoSSW 93, WhoWor 93*
Brodie, Howard 1915- *WhoAm 92, WhoWor 93*
Brodie, Jonathan Michael 1955- *WhoE 93*
Brodie, Kevin *MiSFD 9*
Brodie, M. J. 1936- *WhoAm 92*
Brodie, Martha Jane *Law&B 92*
Brodie, Norman 1920- *WhoAm 92*
Brodie, Paul (Zion) 1934- *Baker 92*
Brodie, R. Bruce *Law&B 92*
Brodie, Robert G. 1931- *St&PR 93*
Brodie, Walter Scott 1868-1935 *BiDAMSp 1989*
Brodie, Wanda Colleen 1935- *WhoAmW 93*
Brodie-Innes, J.W. 1848-1923 *ScF&FL 92*
Brodin, Gunnar 1931- *WhoScE 91-4*
Brodine, Charles Edward 1925- *WhoAm 92, WhoWor 93*
Brodkey, Amy Catherine 1949- *WhoEmL 93*
Brodkey, Andrew Alan 1956- *St&PR 93*
Brodkey, Harold *BioIn 17*
Brodkey, Harold 1930- *MagSAmL [port]*
Brodkey, Harold Roy 1930- *WhoAm 92*
Brodkey, M. Ronald 1936- *St&PR 93*
Brodkey, Robert Stanley 1928- *WhoAm 92*
Brodkin, A. Keith 1935- *St&PR 93*
Brodkin, Adele Ruth Meyer 1934- *WhoAmW 93*
Brodkin, Alan Keith 1935- *WhoAm 92, WhoWor 93*
Brodkin, Herbert 1912-1990? *ConTFT 10*
Brodkin, Herbert Harrison *BioIn 17*
Brodkin, Roger Harrison 1932- *WhoWor 93*
Brodl, Raymond Frank 1924- *WhoAm 92*
Brodman, Estelle 1914- *WhoAm 92, WhoAmW 93*
Brodnan, David S. *Law&B 92*
Brodnax, Margaret O'Bryan 1932- *WhoSSW 93*
Brodovitch, Alexey 1898-1971 *BioIn 17*
Brodowicz, Kazimierz Andrzej 1928- *WhoScE 91-4*
Brodowski, Antoni 1784-1832 *PolBiDi*
Brodowski, Jozef 1775-1842 *PolBiDi*
Brodrick, Nancy Ann 1944- *WhoAmW 93*
Brodsky, Abraham H. d1992 *NewYTBS 92*
Brodsky, Adolf 1851-1929 *Baker 92*
Brodsky, Alexander 1955- *BioIn 17*
Brodsky, Allen 1928- *WhoE 93*
Brodsky, Arthur James 1946- *WhoE 93, WhoEmL 93*
Brodsky, Bernard Steven 1939- *St&PR 93*
Brodsky, David M. 1943- *WhoAm 92*
Brodsky, Frank 1933- *WhoE 93*
Brodsky, Iosif Alexandrovich 1940- *ConAu 37NR, WhoWrEP 92*
Brodsky, Irving 1915- *WhoE 93*
Brodsky, Irwin Abel 1910- *WhoAm 92*
Brodsky, Isadore 1930- *WhoAm 92*
Brodsky, Joseph *ConAu 37NR*
Brodsky, Joseph 1940- *BioIn 17*
Brodsky, Joseph Alexandrovich 1940- *WhoAm 92, WhoE 93, WhoWor 93*
Brodsky, Julian A. 1933- *St&PR 93, WhoAm 92*
Brodsky, Marc Herbert 1938- *WhoAm 92*
Brodsky, Philip Hyman 1942- *WhoAm 92*
Brodsky, Robert Fox 1925- *WhoAm 92*
Brodsky, Samuel 1912- *WhoAm 92*
Brodsky, Stanley L. 1939- *ScF&FL 92*
Brodsky, Sylvia Arlene 1924- *WhoAmW 93*
Brodsky, Vera *Baker 92*
Brodsky, Vlastimil 1920- *IntDcF 2-3 [port]*
Brodsky, William J. 1944- *St&PR 93, WhoAm 92*
Brodsley, Laurel Harriet Chilk 1939- *WhoAmW 93*
Brodt, John D. 1954- *St&PR 93*
Brodt, Phillip David 1963- *WhoSSW 93*
Brody, Aaron Leo 1930- *WhoAm 92, WhoE 93*
Brody, Alan Jeffrey 1952- *WhoAm 92*
Brody, Alexander 1933- *St&PR 93, WhoAm 92*
Brody, Alfred Walter 1920- *WhoAm 92*
Brody, Anita Blumstein 1935- *WhoAmW 93*
Brody, Arthur 1920- *WhoAm 92*
Brody, Bernard B. 1922- *WhoAm 92*
Brody, Charisse *BioIn 17*
Brody, Christopher W. 1944- *St&PR 93*
Brody, David E. *Law&B 92*
Brody, Eugene B. 1921- *WhoAm 92, WhoE 93*
Brody, Eugene David 1931- *WhoAm 92*
Brody, Harold 1923- *WhoAm 92*
Brody, Harold David 1939- *WhoE 93*
Brody, Harry Philip 1952- *WhoWrEP 92*
Brody, Hugh *MiSFD 9*
Brody, Jacob Allan 1931- *WhoAm 92*
Brody, Jacqueline 1932- *WhoAm 92, WhoWrEP 92*
Brody, James Patrick 1920- *WhoAm 92*
Brody, Jane Ellen 1941- *WhoAm 92, WhoAmW 93, WhoWrEP 92*
Brody, Kenneth D. 1943- *St&PR 93*
Brody, Marcia Bernice Auerbach 1937- *WhoE 93*
Brody, Mark A. *Law&B 92*
Brody, Mark S. *Law&B 92*
Brody, Martin 1921- *St&PR 93, WhoAm 92*
Brody, Michael J. *BioIn 17*
Brody, Michael J. 1934-1990 *BioIn 17*
Brody, Michael W. *Law&B 92*
Brody, Morton Aaron 1933- *WhoAm 92*
Brody, Nancy Louise 1954- *WhoAm 92, WhoEmL 93*
Brody, Randy 1951- *WhoEmL 93*
Brody, Richard David 1952- *WhoEmL 93*
Brody, Robert *BioIn 17*
Brody, Robert 1925- *St&PR 93*
Brody, Samuel M. 1926-1992 *NewYTBS 92 [port]*
Brody, Samuel Mandell 1926- *WhoAm 92*
Brody, Saul Nathaniel 1938- *WhoAm 92*
Brody, Sigmund A. 1941- *WhoIns 93*
Brody, Stephen J. 1946- *St&PR 93*
Brody, Steven Martin 1948- *WhoSSW 93*
Brody, Stuart Martin 1936- *WhoE 93*
Brody, Theodore Meyer 1920- *WhoAm 92*
Brody, Wayne *Law&B 92*
Brodzinski, Frederick Ronald 1948- *WhoE 93*
Broe, Steven 1955- *St&PR 93*
Broecker, Eugene W. 1931- *WhoIns 93*
Broecker, Hans Christoph 1936- *WhoScE 91-3*
Broecker, Howard William 1940- *WhoAm 92*
Broedling, Laurie Adele 1945- *WhoAm 92*
Broeg, Bob 1918- *WhoAm 92*
Broeg, Robert William 1918- *BiDAMSp 1989*
Broegger, Fredrik Chr(istian) 1945- *ConAu 138*
Broek, Henri Van Den 1936- *WhoWor 93*
Broekman, David 1899-1958 *Baker 92*
Broelsch, Christoph Erich 1944- *WhoAm 92*
Broene, Gilbert Richard 1948- *WhoEmL 93*
Broeniman, Clifford Scott 1960- *WhoE 93*
Broening, Angela M. d1972 *BioIn 17*
Broening, Gerald F. 1934- *St&PR 93*
Broer, Carleton G., Jr. 1933- *St&PR 93*
Broer, Eileen Dennery 1946- *St&PR 93*
Broer, Lawrence R. 1938- *ScF&FL 92*
Broering, Naomi Cordero 1929- *WhoAm 92*
Broers, Alec Nigel *WhoScE 91-1*
Broers, J. Terry 1939- *WhoAm 92*
Broers, Kimberly Ann 1956- *WhoAmW 93*
Brofferio, Angelo 1802-1866 *BioIn 17*
Brofman, Lance Mark 1949- *WhoAm 92, WhoE 93, WhoEmL 93*
Brofman, Woody 1935- *WhoAm 92*
Brog, David 1933- *WhoAm 92*
Brogan, Eileen M. *Law&B 92*
Brogan, Howard Oakley *WhoAm 92*
Brogan, James 1941- *WhoE 93*
Brogan, James F. 1941- *St&PR 93*
Brogan, Kevin Herbert 1953- *WhoEmL 93*
Brogan, Paul V. *St&PR 93*
Brogan, Rita 1951- *WhoAmW 93, WhoEmL 93*
Brogan, Roy Alan 1940- *St&PR 93*
Brogan, Thomas Edward 1919- *St&PR 93*
Brogan-Werntz, Bonnie Bailey 1941- *WhoAmW 93*
Brogard, Jean-Marie 1935- *WhoScE 91-2*
Brogden, Jill Susan 1957- *WhoSSW 93*
Brogdon, Byron Gilliam 1929- *WhoAm 92*
Brogdon, Jimi *BioIn 17*
Brogdon, Joan Lee 1951- *WhoAmW 93*
Brogdon, Lynda Ann 1947- *WhoAmW 93*
Brogdon, William Alvin *Law&B 92*
Brogelman, Wayne H. *Law&B 92*
Brogger, Fredrik Chr. *ConAu 138*
Broggi, Giorgio 1957- *WhoWor 93*
Broggi, Giovanni 1941- *WhoScE 91-3*
Broggi, Mario F. 1945- *WhoScE 91-4*
Brogi, Antonio 1947- *WhoWor 93*
Brogi, Renato 1873-1924 *Baker 92*
Brogla, Martha Leone 1955- *WhoEmL 93*
Brogli, Rudolf 1936- *WhoScE 91-4*
Brogliatti, Barbara Spencer 1946- *WhoAm 92*
Broglie, Jacques Victor Albert, duc de 1821-1901 *BioIn 17*
Brogna, Luanne Elizabeth 1957- *WhoEmL 93*
Brogno, August 1935- *St&PR 93*
Brogue, Roslyn 1919-1981 *Baker 92*
Brohammer, Richard Frederic 1934- *WhoSSW 93*
Brohan-Lombardi, Julia Ann 1941- *WhoAmW 93*
Brohaugh, William Edward 1953- *WhoWrEP 92*
Broich, Larry D. 1943- *St&PR 93*
Broich, Ulrich 1932- *WhoWor 93*
Broida, Helen *WhoWrEP 92*
Broida, Theodore R. 1928- *St&PR 93*
Broide, Mace Irwin 1924- *WhoAm 92*
Broido, Alvin d1990 *BioIn 17*
Broido, Arnold Peace 1920- *St&PR 93, WhoAm 92*
Broido, Michael W. *Law&B 92*
Broin, Kenneth Edwin 1924- *St&PR 93*
Broin, Mark Stuart 1945- *St&PR 93*
Broitman, Jessica *WhoAmW 93*
Broitman, Selwyn Arthur 1931- *WhoAm 92*
Bro-Jorgensen, Klaus *WhoScE 91-2*
Brok, Sergio Fabian *Law&B 92*
Brokate, Brian William 1954- *WhoEmL 93*
Brokaw, Charles Jacob 1934- *WhoAm 92*
Brokaw, Clifford V., III 1928- *St&PR 93*
Brokaw, Clifford Vail, III 1928- *WhoAm 92, WhoWor 93*
Brokaw, Donald C. 1929- *St&PR 93*
Brokaw, Kathryn Louise Zimmer 1946- *WhoAmW 93*
Brokaw, Norman Robert 1927- *WhoAm 92*
Brokaw, R. Miriam 1917- *WhoWrEP 92*
Brokaw, Thomas John 1940- *WhoAm 92, WhoE 93*
Brokaw, Tom *BioIn 17*
Brokaw, Tom 1940- *JrnUS*
Broke, Philip Bowes Vere 1776-1841 *HarEnMi*
Brokenshire, Terence 1950- *WhoScE 91-1*
Broker, Michael J. *Law&B 92*
Brokken, James Redalen 1941- *WhoAm 92*
Brokl, Thomas Raymond 1948- *WhoEmL 93*
Brokman, Lech 1931- *WhoScE 91-4*
Brokop, Donald Samuel 1939- *St&PR 93*
Brolin, Donn E. *BioIn 17*
Brolin, James *WhoAm 92*
Brolin, Josh *BioIn 17*
Broll, Norbert 1947- *WhoWor 93*
Brollier, David S. *Law&B 92*
Brom, Libor 1923- *WhoAm 92, WhoWor 93*
Brom, Robert H. 1938- *WhoAm 92*
Bromage, William Thomas 1946- *St&PR 93*
Broman, Gunnar E. 1924- *WhoScE 91-4*
Broman, Keith Leroy 1922- *WhoAm 92*
Broman, Natanael 1887-1966 *Baker 92*
Broman, P.G. *WhoScE 91-4*
Broman, Sten 1902-1983 *Baker 92*
Brombacher, Paul J. 1930- *WhoScE 91-3*
Bromberg, Alan Robert 1928- *WhoAm 92, WhoSSW 93, WhoWor 93*
Bromberg, Debra E. *St&PR 93*
Bromberg, Frank M. *St&PR 93*
Bromberg, Frank Wallace, Jr. 1955- *St&PR 93*
Bromberg, Henri Louie, Jr. 1911- *WhoAm 92*
Bromberg, John E. 1946- *WhoAm 92*
Bromberg, Marcia Weinstock 1946- *WhoAmW 93*
Bromberg, Michael A. *Law&B 92*
Bromberg, Murray H. 1924- *WhoE 93*
Bromberg, Myron James 1934- *WhoAm 92*
Bromberg, Robert 1921- *WhoAm 92*
Bromberg, Robert Sheldon 1935- *WhoAm 92*
Bromberg, Walter 1900- *WhoAm 92*
Brombert, Victor H. *BioIn 17*
Brombert, Victor Henri 1923- *WhoAm 92, WhoWrEP 92*
Brome, Robert Harrison 1911- *WhoAm 92*
Brome, Vincent 1910- *ScF&FL 92*
Bromeley, Robert B. 1910- *St&PR 93*
Bromelkamp, Michael Louis 1953- *WhoEmL 93*
Bromery, Randolph Wilson 1926- *WhoAm 92*
Bromfield, Rex *MiSFD 9*
Bromhal, Robert L. 1940- *St&PR 93*
Bromige, David 1935- *WhoCanL 92*
Bromige, David M. 1933- *WhoWrEP 92*
Bromilow, Richard Hampson *WhoScE 91-1*
Bromley, C. Corwin *Law&B 92*
Bromley, D. Allan 1926- *BioIn 17*
Bromley, Daniel Wood 1940- *WhoAm 92*
Bromley, David Allan 1926- *BioIn 17, WhoAm 92*
Bromley, Dudley 1948- *ScF&FL 92*
Bromley, Isaac Hill 1833-1898 *JrnUS*
Bromley, James Hancock 1938- *St&PR 93*
Bromley, Marilyn Modlin 1951- *WhoE 93*
Bromley, Michael Ladd 1963- *WhoSSW 93*
Bromley, Nancy Johnson *Law&B 92*
Bromley, R. Scott *BioIn 17*
Bromley, Richard *Law&B 92*
Bromley, Richard G. 1939- *WhoScE 91-2*

Bromley, Richard H. 1940- *St&PR 93*
Bromley, Wayne Leon, Jr. 1951- *St&PR 93, WhoAm 92, WhoEmL 93*
Bromm, Burkhart 1935- *WhoScE 91-3*
Bromm, Burkhart F. 1935- *WhoWor 93*
Bromm, Frederick Whittemore 1953- *WhoEmL 93*
Bromm, Robert Dale, Sr. 1950- *WhoEmL 93*
Brommelle, Norman Spencer 1915-1989 *BioIn 17*
Brommer, Gerald F(rederick) 1927- *WhoWrEP 92*
Brommer, Jere Joseph 1929- *St&PR 93*
Brommundt, Eberhard Wolfgang 1932- *WhoScE 91-3*
Broms, Bo 1919- *WhoWor 93*
Broms, Nils G. 1924- *St&PR 93*
Bromsen, Maury Austin 1919- *WhoAm 92*
Bromwich, Michael *WhoScE 91-1*
Bronarski, Ludwik 1890-1975 *PolBiDi*
Bronarski, Ludwik (Ryszard Marian) 1890-1975 *Baker 92*
Bronaugh, Edwin Lee 1932- *WhoAm 92*
Brondo, Robert Stanley 1951- *WhoAm 92*
Brondum, Frank 1945- *WhoWor 93*
Brondum, William Charles, Jr. 1919- *St&PR 93*
Broneer, Oscar 1894-1992 *BioIn 17*
Broneer, Oscar T. d1992 *NewYTBS 92 [port]*
Broner, E. M. 1930- *JeAmFiW*
Broner, Mathew 1924- *WhoE 93*
Brones, Lynn A. 1954- *WhoEmL 93*
Bronfen, Elisabeth Eve 1958- *WhoWor 93*
Bronfenbrenner, Martin 1914- *WhoWor 93*
Bronfenbrenner, Urie 1917- *WhoAm 92*
Bronfman, Charles Rosner 1931- *St&PR 93, WhoAm 92*
Bronfman, Edgar M. *WhoE 93*
Bronfman, Edgar Miles 1929- *St&PR 93, WhoAm 92*
Bronfman, Peter Frederick 1929- *WhoAm 92, WhoE 93*
Bronfman, Yefim 1958- *Baker 92, BioIn 17*
Bronheim, Harold E. 1952- *WhoEmL 93*
Broniewski, Wladyslaw 1897-1962 *PolBiDi*
Bronitsky, Martha G. *Law&B 92*
Bronk, John Ramsey *WhoScE 91-1*
Bronk, William *BioIn 17*
Bronk, William 1918- *WhoAm 92*
Bronkan, Janine Ann 1953- *WhoSSW 93*
Bronkesh, Annette Cylia 1956- *WhoE 93*
Bronley, Glenn I. 1953- *WhoE 93*
Bronn, Leslie Joan Boyle 1948- *WhoAm 92*
Bronnen, Arnolt 1895-1959 *DcLB 124 [port]*
Bronner, Edwin B(laine) 1920- *WhoWrEP 92*
Bronner, Edwin Blaine 1920- *WhoAm 92*
Bronner, Ethan Samuel 1954- *WhoE 93*
Bronner, Felix 1921- *WhoAm 92, WhoE 93*
Bronner, Georg 1667?-1720 *Baker 92*
Bronner, Michael B. 1936- *WhoE 93*
Bronner, William R. *Law&B 92*
Bronnimann, Alfred 1936- *WhoScE 91-4*
Bronocco, Terri Lynn 1953- *WhoAmW 93*
Brons, Carel 1931-1983 *Baker 92*
Bronsard, Joseph A. 1933- *St&PR 93*
Bronsart (von Schellendorf), Hans 1830-1913 *Baker 92*
Bronsart (von Schellendorf), Ingeborg 1840-1913 *Baker 92*
Bronsart von Schellendorf, Ingeborg 1840-1913 *BioIn 17*
Bronsberg-Adas, Thomas Joseph 1951- *WhoEmL 93*
Bronsch, Kurt 1924- *WhoScE 91-3*
Bronsdon, Melinda Ann 1940- *WhoAm 92*
Bronskaya, Evgenya 1882-1953 *Baker 92*
Bronski, Eugene William 1936- *WhoAm 92*
Bronson, Barbara June 1949- *WhoEmL 93*
Bronson, Charles *WhoAm 92*
Bronson, Charles 1920- *BioIn 17, IntDcF 2-3 [port]*
Bronson, Cynthia *Law&B 92*
Bronson, Daniel Braid 1943- *St&PR 93*
Bronson, Franklin H. 1932- *WhoAm 92, WhoSSW 93*
Bronson, Frazier L. 1943- *St&PR 93*
Bronson, Henry D. 1935- *St&PR 93*
Bronson, Kenneth C. 1933- *St&PR 93*
Bronson, Kenneth Caldean 1933- *WhoAm 92*
Bronson, Kenneth P. 1951- *St&PR 93*
Bronson, Millard E. 1928- *St&PR 93*
Bronson, Neal Barry 1948- *WhoEmL 93*
Bronson, Oswald P., Sr. *AfrAmBi [port]*
Bronson, Oswald Perry 1927- *WhoAm 92*
Bronson, Randolph Clifton 1944- *WhoAm 92, WhoE 93*
Bronson, Rebecca B. 1947- *WhoAmW 93*
Bronson, Wolfe *WhoWrEP 92*
Bronsteen, Peter 1954- *WhoEmL 93*
Bronstein, Aaron Jacob 1905- *WhoAm 92*
Bronstein, Alvin J. 1928- *WhoE 93*
Bronstein, Arthur J. 1914- *WhoAm 92*
Bronstein, Arturo Sergio 1945- *WhoUN 92*
Bronstein, Gerald Morton 1927- *St&PR 93*
Bronstein, Glen Max 1960- *WhoEmL 93, WhoWor 93*
Bronstein, Herman 1928- *St&PR 93*
Bronstein, Melvin 1924- *WhoE 93, WhoWor 93*
Bronstein, Michail Davidovich 1949- *WhoWor 93*
Bronstein, Peter C. *Law&B 92*
Bronstein, Toby J. 1951- *WhoEmL 93*
Bronstrup, C.R. 1933- *St&PR 93*
Bronte, Anne 1820-1849 *BioIn 17*
Bronte, Branwell 1817-1848 *BioIn 17*
Bronte, Charlotte 1816-1855 *BioIn 17, MagSWL [port], WorLitC [port]*
Bronte, Emily 1818-1848 *BioIn 17, MagSWL [port], NinCLC 35 [port], WorLitC [port]*
Bronte, Louisa *ScF&FL 92, WhoWrEP 92*
Bronte, Patrick 1777-1861 *BioIn 17*
Bronte, Patrick Branwell 1817-1848 *BioIn 17*
Bronto, Hannah *ScF&FL 92*
Bronzaft, Arline L. 1936- *WhoAmW 93, WhoE 93*
Bronzina, Isabel Azucena 1948- *WhoEmL 93*
Bronzino, Joseph D. 1937- *ConAu 136*
Bronzino, Joseph Daniel 1937- *WhoAm 92*
Bronzo, John F. *Law&B 92*
Bronzo, Mark Peter 1960- *WhoIns 93*
Broo, Kenneth Richard 1924- *St&PR 93*
Broodthaers, Marcel 1924-1976 *BioIn 17*
Brook, Adrian Gibbs 1924- *WhoAm 92*
Brook, Alan Henry *WhoScE 91-1*
Brook, Barry S(helley) 1918- *Baker 92*
Brook, Charles Groves Darville *WhoScE 91-1*
Brook, Charles Groves Darville 1940- *WhoWor 93*
Brook, Claire 1925- *St&PR 93*
Brook, David William 1936- *WhoAm 92*
Brook, Henry W. *Law&B 92*
Brook, Henry Wagner 1934- *WhoAm 92, WhoWor 93*
Brook, Leonard *BioIn 17*
Brook, Margaret *ScF&FL 92*
Brook, Marx 1920- *WhoAm 92*
Brook, Peter 1925- *BioIn 17, ConTFT 10, IntDcOp, MiSFD 9, OxDcOp*
Brook, Peter (Stephen Paul) 1925- *Baker 92, ConAu 38NR*
Brook, R.A. *WhoScE 91-1*
Brook, Richard J. *WhoScE 91-3*
Brook, Robert Henry 1943- *WhoAm 92*
Brook, Susan G. 1949- *WhoEmL 93*
Brooke, Avery Rogers 1923- *WhoAm 92, WhoWrEP 92*
Brooke, Baron Ainslie 1918- *WhoWor 93*
Brooke, Basil Stanlake 1888-1973 *BioIn 17*
Brooke, Charlotte 1740-1793 *BioIn 17*
Brooke, Christopher N(ugent) L(awrence) 1927- *ConAu 40NR*
Brooke, David Stopford 1931- *WhoAm 92*
Brooke, Edna Mae 1923- *WhoWor 93*
Brooke, Edward 1919- *BioIn 17*
Brooke, Edward W. 1919- *PolPar*
Brooke, Edward William 1919- *EncAACR, WhoAm 92*
Brooke, Elizabeth *AmWomPl*
Brooke, F. Dixon, Jr. 1948- *St&PR 93*
Brooke, Frances 1724?-1789 *BioIn 17*
Brooke, Francis John, III 1929- *WhoAm 92*
Brooke, Frank A. 1943- *St&PR 93*
Brooke, George Mercer, Jr. 1914- *WhoSSW 93*
Brooke, James 1803-1868 *HarEnMi*
Brooke, Jocelyn 1908-1966 *ScF&FL 92*
Brooke, Keith 1966- *ScF&FL 92*
Brooke, L(eonard) Leslie 1862-1940 *MajAI [port]*
Brooke, Patrick Teal 1953- *WhoEmL 93*
Brooke, Peter Leonard 1934- *WhoWor 93*
Brooke, Ralph Ian 1934- *WhoAm 92*
Brooke, Richard, Jr. 1926- *St&PR 93, WhoIns 93*
Brooke, Robert Zachary 1956- *WhoWor 93*
Brooke, Rupert 1887-1915 *BioIn 17, MagSWL [port], WorLitC [port]*
Brooke, Stephen M. *Law&B 92*
Brooke, Susan Rogers 1951- *WhoAmW 93, WhoEmL 93*
Brooke, William W. *Law&B 92*
Brookeborough, Viscount 1888-1973 *BioIn 17*
Brooke-Davidson, Jennifer 1960- *WhoEmL 93*
Brooke-Popham, Henry Robert Moore 1878-1953 *HarEnMi*
Brooker, Brian Edward *WhoScE 91-1*
Brooker, Eric Lionel 1927- *St&PR 93*
Brooker, Gerard T. 1936- *WhoE 93*
Brooker, Grant R. *Law&B 92*
Brooker, Jewel Spears 1940- *WhoSSW 93*
Brooker, Lena Epps 1941- *WhoSSW 93*
Brooker, M.P. *WhoScE 91-1*
Brooker, Robert Elton 1905- *WhoAm 92*
Brooker, Robert Elton, Jr. 1937- *WhoAm 92*
Brooker, Susan Gay 1949- *WhoAmW 93*
Brooker, Thomas Kimball 1939- *WhoAm 92*
Brooker, Wallace *ScF&FL 92*
Brooker, Walter Eric 1916- *WhoE 93, WhoWor 93*
Brooke-Rose, Christine 1923- *ScF&FL 92*
Brookes, Charles Erwin 1925- *WhoAm 92*
Brookes, Chris 1943- *WhoCanL 92*
Brookes, Christopher Anthony *WhoScE 91-1*
Brookes, Graham Robert *WhoScE 91-1*
Brookes, John A. 1933- *ConAu 137*
Brookes, Murray *WhoScE 91-1*
Brookes, Owen 1940- *ScF&FL 92*
Brookes, Peter *WhoScE 91-1*
Brookes, Robert J. *Law&B 92*
Brookes, Roger *BioIn 17*
Brookes, Valentine 1913- *WhoAm 92, WhoWor 93*
Brookes, Warren T. *BioIn 17*
Brookfield, David Alan 1946- *St&PR 93*
Brookfield, Donald W. 1911- *St&PR 93*
Brookhart, John E. 1936- *St&PR 93*
Brookhiser, Richard 1955- *ConAu 139*
Brookhuis, John G. 1921-1991 *BioIn 17*
Brooking, E. Lynwood 1944- *St&PR 93*
Brooking, Frederick Russell *Law&B 92*
Brookins, Carolyn Seman 1943- *St&PR 93*
Brookins, Dana 1931- *ScF&FL 92*
Brookins, Dana (Martin) 1931- *DcAmChF 1960*
Brookins, Dewey C. 1904-1982 *ScF&FL 92*
Brookins, James Robert 1942- *WhoSSW 93*
Brookman, Amber *St&PR 93*
Brookman, Anthony Raymond 1922- *WhoWor 93*
Brookman, Katharine Barron *AmWomPl*
Brookmeyer, Philip R. *Law&B 92*
Brookner, Anita *BioIn 17, WhoAm 92, WhoWor 93*
Brookner, Anita 1928- *ConAu 37NR*
Brookner, Eli 1931- *WhoAm 92*
Brookover, Barbara Ruth 1956- *WhoAmW 93*
Brookover, J. Gordon 1922- *St&PR 93*
Brooks, A. Raymond 1895-1991 *BioIn 17*
Brooks, A. Raymond 1896-1991 *AnObit 1991*
Brooks, Adam 1956- *MiSFD 9*
Brooks, Alan 1950- *WhoSSW 93*
Brooks, Albert *BioIn 17, ConAu 37NR*
Brooks, Albert 1947- *MiSFD 9, WhoAm 92*
Brooks, Alfred C. 1940- *St&PR 93*
Brooks, Andree Aelion 1937- *WhoAm 92, WhoAmW 93*
Brooks, Andrew Arnold 1953- *St&PR 93*
Brooks, Anne Lee 1948- *WhoSSW 93*
Brooks, Annie Sills *AmWomPl*
Brooks, Arthur Raymond 1895?- *BioIn 17*
Brooks, Arthur T. 1917- *St&PR 93*
Brooks, Audrey Vera 1933- *WhoWor 93*
Brooks, Babert Vincent 1926- *WhoAm 92*
Brooks, Barbara T. 1906- *St&PR 93*
Brooks, Barnett Q. *Law&B 92*
Brooks, Barry Charles 1932- *St&PR 93*
Brooks, Ben 1948- *WhoWrEP 92*
Brooks, Ben L. 1923- *St&PR 93*
Brooks, Bob 1927- *MiSFD 9*
Brooks, Brian Walter *WhoScE 91-1*
Brooks, Bruce *ScF&FL 92*
Brooks, Bruce 1950- *BioIn 17, ConAu 137, DcAmChF 1985, MajAI [port], SmATA 72 [port]*
Brooks, Bruce Delos 1950- *WhoAm 92*
Brooks, Burton 1929- *St&PR 93*
Brooks, C.W., Jr. *ScF&FL 92*
Brooks, Carl E. 1937- *St&PR 93*
Brooks, Carla Jo 1956- *WhoEmL 93, WhoSSW 93*
Brooks, Catherine Ellis 1953- *WhoSSW 93*
Brooks, Cecil *ScF&FL 92*
Brooks, Charles A. *Law&B 92*
Brooks, Charles Joseph William *WhoScE 91-1*
Brooks, Christine Ann 1953- *WhoAmW 93, WhoEmL 93*
Brooks, Claudia Marie 1952- *WhoAmW 93*
Brooks, Cleanth 1906- *BioIn 17, WhoAm 92*
Brooks, Clifton Rowland 1923- *WhoSSW 93*
Brooks, Clyde Speer *WhoE 93*
Brooks, Craig Charles 1946- *St&PR 93*
Brooks, D.W. 1901- *St&PR 93*
Brooks, Daisy *WhoAm 92, WhoAmW 93*
Brooks, Daniel Townley 1941- *WhoAm 92*
Brooks, David Barry 1934- *WhoAm 92*
Brooks, David Michael 1954- *WhoEmL 93*
Brooks, David Neil *WhoScE 91-1*
Brooks, David William 1901- *WhoAm 92*
Brooks, Dawne Lea *WhoAmW 93, WhoWor 93*
Brooks, Deborah Ann 1949- *WhoAmW 93*
Brooks, Deborah Dee 1951- *WhoWor 93*
Brooks, Delores Stallcup Ann 1954- *WhoSSW 93*
Brooks, Dennis Matthew 1934- *WhoAm 92*
Brooks, Diana D. 1950- *St&PR 93, WhoAmW 93*
Brooks, Donald 1955- *WhoAm 92*
Brooks, Donald A. 1941- *St&PR 93*
Brooks, Donald S. *Law&B 92*
Brooks, E. R. 1937- *WhoAm 92, WhoSSW 93*
Brooks, Edward 1942- *WhoAm 92*
Brooks, Edward Howard 1921- *WhoAm 92*
Brooks, Edward Pennell 1895-1991 *BioIn 17*
Brooks, Eleanor Idelle 1951- *WhoEmL 93*
Brooks, Elizabeth Spencer 1954- *WhoEmL 93*
Brooks, Erastus 1815-1886 *JrnUS*
Brooks, Frank C. 1919- *St&PR 93*
Brooks, Frank P. 1920-1991 *BioIn 17*
Brooks, Frank Pickering 1920- *WhoWrEP 92*
Brooks, Frederic H. *St&PR 93*
Brooks, Frederic Henry 1934- *WhoAm 92*
Brooks, Frederick Phillips, Jr. 1931- *WhoAm 92*
Brooks, Garth *BioIn 17, WhoAm 92*
Brooks, Garth 1962- *ConMus 8 [port], CurBio 92 [port], News 92 [port]*
Brooks, Gary Leon 1950- *WhoEmL 93*
Brooks, Gene C. *Law&B 92*
Brooks, Gene Edward 1931- *WhoAm 92*
Brooks, Geoffrey d1990 *BioIn 17*
Brooks, George *MajAI*
Brooks, George H. *BioIn 17*
Brooks, George S., II *Law&B 92*
Brooks, Gerald R. 1936- *St&PR 93*
Brooks, Gerald Thomas 1931- *WhoWor 93*
Brooks, Geraldine 1955- *WhoAm 92*
Brooks, Gladys Sinclair 1914- *WhoAmW 93*
Brooks, Glenn Allen 1960- *WhoEmL 93*
Brooks, Glenn Ellis 1931- *WhoAm 92*
Brooks, Gwendolyn *BioIn 17*
Brooks, Gwendolyn 1917- *AmWrS3, BlkAull 92, ChlLR 27 [port], EncAACR, WhoAm 92, WhoAmW 93, WhoWrEP 92, WorLitC [port]*
Brooks, H. Allen 1925- *WhoAm 92*
Brooks, Harry A. 1913- *St&PR 93*
Brooks, Harry Angelo 1913- *WhoAm 92*
Brooks, Harvey 1931- *WhoE 93*
Brooks, Helen Lee *AmWomPl*
Brooks, Helene Margaret 1942- *WhoAmW 93*
Brooks, Henry Wilson 1949- *WhoE 93*
Brooks, Herbert 1924- *St&PR 93*
Brooks, Herbert Paul 1937- *WhoAm 92, WhoE 93*
Brooks, Howard Zachary 1956- *WhoE 93, WhoEmL 93*
Brooks, J. Andree 1946- *WhoSSW 93*
Brooks, Jack 1922- *BioIn 17, CngDr 91, CurBio 92 [port]*
Brooks, Jack Bascom 1922- *WhoAm 92, WhoSSW 93*
Brooks, James 1906-1992 *BioIn 17, NewYTBS 92 [port]*
Brooks, James A. *Law&B 92*
Brooks, James A., III 1943- *St&PR 93*
Brooks, James Byron 1967- *WhoSSW 93*
Brooks, James (D.) 1906-1992 *CurBio 92N*
Brooks, James E., Jr. 1948- *WhoSSW 93*
Brooks, James Elwood 1925- *WhoAm 92*
Brooks, James Joe, III 1948- *WhoEmL 93, WhoSSW 93*
Brooks, James L. 1940- *ConTFT 10, MiSFD 9, WhoAm 92*
Brooks, James Sprague 1925- *WhoAm 92*
Brooks, James W.F. 1948- *St&PR 93*
Brooks, Jane Peyser 1936- *WhoAmW 93*
Brooks, Janice Young 1943- *ConAu 39NR*
Brooks, Jeffrey Martin 1958- *WhoSSW 93*
Brooks, Jerome Bernard 1932- *WhoAm 92, WhoWor 93*
Brooks, Jerry Claude 1936- *WhoSSW 93*
Brooks, Jo 1949- *WhoEmL 93*
Brooks, Joae Graham 1926- *WhoAm 92*

Brooks, John 1920- *WhoAm 92, WhoWrEP 92*
Brooks, John Allan 1961- *WhoEmL 93*
Brooks, John Bill 1929- *WhoSSW 93*
Brooks, John C. 1951- *St&PR 93*
Brooks, John Edward 1923- *WhoAm 92, WhoE 93*
Brooks, John F. 1919- *St&PR 93*
Brooks, John Lawrence, III 1951- *WhoEmL 93*
Brooks, John Robinson 1918- *WhoAm 92*
Brooks, John Stuart *WhoScE 91-1*
Brooks, John White 1936- *WhoAm 92*
Brooks, Joseph *MiSFD 9*
Brooks, Joseph Barlow 1874-1952 *BioIn 17*
Brooks, Joseph N. 1957- *St&PR 93*
Brooks, Julie Agnes 1941- *WhoAm 92, WhoAmW 93*
Brooks, Julie Anne 1945- *WhoAm 92, WhoWor 93*
Brooks, Karyn *BioIn 17*
Brooks, Kate *ScF&FL 92*
Brooks, Katherine R. *AmWomPl*
Brooks, Keith 1923- *WhoAm 92*
Brooks, Kendra Lee 1948- *WhoAmW 93*
Brooks, Kevin B. 1946- *St&PR 93*
Brooks, Kevin P. 1944- *WhoIns 93*
Brooks, Leslie V. 1941- *St&PR 93*
Brooks, Lewis Alexander 1931- *WhoE 93*
Brooks, Linda Grace 1945- *WhoWrEP 92*
Brooks, Linda Marie 1942- *WhoSSW 93*
Brooks, Linda Thomas 1963- *WhoEmL 93*
Brooks, Lloyd William, Jr. 1949- *WhoSSW 93*
Brooks, Lorenzo 1942- *WhoAm 92*
Brooks, Lorimer Page 1917- *WhoAm 92*
Brooks, Lorraine Elizabeth 1936- *WhoAmW 93*
Brooks, Louise 1906-1985 *BioIn 17, IntDcF 2-3 [port]*
Brooks, Louise Cromwell *BioIn 17*
Brooks, Maggie 1955- *WhoE 93*
Brooks, Mark Hunter 1960- *WhoE 93*
Brooks, Marleen L. *Law&B 92*
Brooks, Martha *ConAu 136, WhoCanL 92*
Brooks, Martha 1944- *BioIn 17*
Brooks, Martin 1950- *WhoAm 92, WhoE 93, WhoEmL 93*
Brooks, Marvin Alan 1945- *WhoE 93*
Brooks, Mary Anna 1939- *WhoAmW 93*
Brooks, Mary Campbell 1964- *WhoEmL 93*
Brooks, Mary Catherine 1962- *WhoAmW 93*
Brooks, Maurice Edward 1922- *WhoAm 92*
Brooks, Mel 1926- *MiSFD 9, QDrFCA 92 [port], WhoAm 92*
Brooks, Michael Lee 1955- *WhoE 93, WhoEmL 93*
Brooks, Michael Paul 1937- *WhoAm 92, WhoSSW 93*
Brooks, Noah 1830-1903 *JrnUS*
Brooks, Nora V. *Law&B 92*
Brooks, Norman Herrick 1928- *WhoAm 92*
Brooks, Otis McDonald 1953- *WhoSSW 93*
Brooks, Patricia 1937- *Baker 92*
Brooks, Paul C. 1942- *St&PR 93*
Brooks, Peter Heath 1945- *WhoWor 93*
Brooks, Peter Preston 1938- *WhoAm 92*
Brooks, Peter Stuyvesant 1942- *WhoE 93*
Brooks, R. Daniel 1946- *WhoIns 93*
Brooks, R.G. *WhoScE 91-1*
Brooks, Ralph J. *St&PR 93*
Brooks, Randy L. 1950- *St&PR 93*
Brooks, Richard d1992 *NewYTBS 92 [port]*
Brooks, Richard 1912-1992 *BioIn 17, ConAu 137, ConTFT 10, MiSFD 9*
Brooks, Richard Alan 1960- *WhoSSW 93*
Brooks, Richard J. *Law&B 92*
Brooks, Richard L. 1939- *St&PR 93*
Brooks, Richard M. 1928- *St&PR 93*
Brooks, Richard Thomas *Law&B 92*
Brooks, Robert D. *Law&B 92*
Brooks, Robert D. 1942- *St&PR 93*
Brooks, Robert Eugene 1946- *WhoEmL 93*
Brooks, Robert Franklin 1928- *WhoSSW 93*
Brooks, Robert Franklin 1939- *WhoAm 92*
Brooks, Robert H. d1990 *BioIn 17*
Brooks, Robert L. 1944- *St&PR 93*
Brooks, Robert Leslie 1944- *WhoAm 92*
Brooks, Robert Liss 1936- *WhoAm 92*
Brooks, Robert Owen 1936- *St&PR 93*
Brooks, Robert Patrick 1929- *WhoSSW 93*
Brooks, Robert R.R. d1992 *NewYTBS 92*
Brooks, Robert Romano Ravi 1905-1992 *BioIn 17*
Brooks, Robert S. *Law&B 92*
Brooks, Robert William 1935-1991 *BioIn 17*
Brooks, Rodney Allen *BioIn 17*
Brooks, Roger Charles 1947- *WhoE 93, WhoEmL 93*
Brooks, Roger K. 1937- *WhoIns 93*
Brooks, Roger Kay 1937- *St&PR 93, WhoAm 92*
Brooks, Roger Leon 1927- *WhoAm 92, WhoSSW 93*
Brooks, Ronald E. 1937- *WhoAm 92*
Brooks, Sam Allen 1939- *St&PR 93*
Brooks, Sarah 1920- *WhoAmW 93*
Brooks, Sharon Lynn 1944- *WhoAmW 93*
Brooks, Stephanie G. *Law&B 92*
Brooks, Stephanie Schaltenbrand 1959- *WhoAmW 93*
Brooks, Susan Ann 1963- *WhoAmW 93*
Brooks, Terrence D. *ScF&FL 92*
Brooks, Terry 1944- *BioIn 17, ScF&FL 92*
Brooks, Thomas Aloysius, III 1937- *WhoAm 92*
Brooks, Thomas D. *Law&B 92*
Brooks, Thomas Joseph, Jr. 1916- *WhoAm 92*
Brooks, Timothy H. 1942- *WhoAm 92*
Brooks, Tonda Hoke 1947- *WhoEmL 93*
Brooks, Tyrone *WhoAm 92*
Brooks, Tyrone, Sr. 1945- *AfrAmBi [port]*
Brooks, Van Wyck 1886-1963 *BioIn 17, ScF&FL 92*
Brooks, Vera Ramey 1952- *WhoAmW 93, WhoEmL 93, WhoWor 93*
Brooks, Vernon Bernard 1923- *WhoAm 92*
Brooks, Vicki L. *Law&B 92*
Brooks, Virginia K. 1953- *WhoWrEP 92*
Brooks, Virginia Solomon 1940- *WhoAmW 93*
Brooks, Walter P. 1951- *St&PR 93*
Brooks, Walter R. 1886-1958 *ScF&FL 92*
Brooks, Wendell Wilkie *Law&B 92*
Brooks, William A. *Law&B 92*
Brooks, William Bryan 1936- *WhoSSW 93*
Brooks, William Charles 1936- *St&PR 93*
Brooks, William D. 1932- *St&PR 93*
Brooks, William Dexter *Law&B 92*
Brooks, William H. *WhoIns 93*
Brooks, William James, III 1953- *WhoEmL 93*
Brooks, William L. d1874 *BioIn 17*
Brooks, William Oliver 1951- *WhoEmL 93, WhoSSW 93*
Brooks, William Robert 1844-1921 *BioIn 17*
Brooks, William W. 1952- *St&PR 93*
Brooksbank, Randolph Wood 1947- *WhoAm 92*
Brooksby, Wade Ford 1941- *St&PR 93*
Brooks-Gunn, Jeanne 1946- *WhoAm 92, WhoAmW 93, WhoE 93*
Brookshaw, George 1751-1823 *BioIn 17*
Brookshaw, Valjean B., Jr. 1931- *St&PR 93*
Brookshaw, Valjean Bispham, Jr. 1931- *WhoSSW 93*
Brooksher, K. Dane *WhoAm 92*
Brookshier, Monty G. *Law&B 92*
Brooks-Hill, Frederick James 1944- *St&PR 93*
Brookshire, Britton Parker 1955- *WhoAm 92*
Brookshire, Jerry Hardman 1943- *WhoSSW 93*
Brookshire, Wiley Eugene 1929- *St&PR 93*
Brooks-Janowiak, Jean 1955- *ScF&FL 92*
Brookstone, Arnold F. 1930- *St&PR 93*
Broom, Donald Maurice *WhoScE 91-1*
Broom, Gerald M. 1940- *St&PR 93*
Broom, Margaret *WhoAmW 93*
Broom, Odell Ammon, III 1953- *WhoEmL 93*
Broom, Todd *BioIn 17*
Broom, William Wescott 1924- *WhoAm 92*
Broomall, Lowell d1991 *BioIn 17*
Broome, Arthur M. 1944- *St&PR 93*
Broome, Burton Edward 1935- *St&PR 93, WhoAm 92*
Broome, C. Charles *Law&B 92*
Broome, Charlotte Stackhouse 1954- *WhoAmW 93*
Broome, Claire Veronica 1949- *WhoAm 92, WhoEmL 93*
Broome, George Calvin, III 1938- *WhoAm 92*
Broome, James P. *Law&B 92*
Broome, John William 1923- *WhoAm 92*
Broome, Linton Dale 1933- *St&PR 93*
Broome, Oscar Whitfield, Jr. 1940- *WhoAm 92*
Broome, Paul W. 1932- *St&PR 93*
Broome, Paul Wallace 1932- *WhoAm 92*
Broome, Richard D. *Law&B 92*
Broome, Samuel Platt d1811 *BioIn 17*
Broome, Theodore B. *Law&B 92*
Broome, William Edward 1868-1932 *Baker 92*
Broomfield, Anthony M. *WhoScE 91-1*
Broomfield, John Philip 1953- *WhoWor 93*
Broomfield, Nicholas *MiSFD 9*
Broomfield, William S. 1922- *CngDr 91, WhoAm 92*
Broomhall, Edith J. *AmWomPl*
Broomhead, Ann 1947- *ScF&FL 92*
Broonzy, "Big Bill" 1893-1958 *Baker 92*
Brooten, Gary 1938- *WhoE 93*
Brooten, Kenneth Edward, Jr. 1942- *WhoWor 93*
Brophy, B.E. *Law&B 92*
Brophy, Brigid 1929- *BioIn 17, ScF&FL 92*
Brophy, Francis L. 1925- *St&PR 93, WhoAm 92*
Brophy, George Thomas 1935- *St&PR 93*
Brophy, James David, Jr. 1926- *WhoAm 92*
Brophy, James John 1926-1991 *BioIn 17*
Brophy, Jere Hall 1934- *WhoAm 92*
Brophy, Jeremiah Joseph 1930- *WhoAm 92*
Brophy, Joseph F. 1939- *St&PR 93*
Brophy, Joseph T. *WhoIns 93*
Brophy, Joseph Thomas 1933- *St&PR 93, WhoAm 92*
Brophy, Mary Nona 1959- *WhoEmL 93*
Brophy, Melonie C. 1954- *St&PR 93*
Brophy, Michael 1963- *WhoSSW 93*
Brophy, Moira Letitia *Law&B 92*
Brophy, Nannette 1963- *SmATA 73 [port]*
Brophy, P.J. *Law&B 92*
Brophy, Pollyann L. *Law&B 92*
Brophy, Theodore F. 1923- *WhoAm 92*
Brophy, Thomas Joseph 1935- *St&PR 93*
Brophy, Todd Randall 1954- *WhoEmL 93*
Broqua, Alfonso 1876-1946 *Baker 92*
Broquetas-Ibars, Antoni 1959- *WhoWor 93*
Bro-Rasmussen, Finn 1928- *WhoScE 91-2*
Brorby, Wade 1934- *WhoAm 92*
Brorsen, Barton Wade 1957- *WhoEmL 93*
Bros, Carol L. *Law&B 92*
Bros, Jan 1918- *WhoScE 91-4*
Brosa, Antonio 1894-1979 *Baker 92*
Brosa, Carol Joanne 1933- *WhoAmW 93, WhoWor 93*
Brosa Bellesteros, Carme 1947- *WhoScE 91-3*
Brosche, Peter Rudolf 1936- *WhoWor 93*
Broschi, Carlo *Baker 92*
Broschi, Riccardo c. 1698-1756 *Baker 92, OxDcOp*
Brosco Christian, Michelle 1966- *WhoAmW 93*
Brose, E. Jerome 1926- *St&PR 93*
Brose, John Adolph 1950- *WhoEmL 93*
Brosen, Frederick *BioIn 17*
Brosens, Frank P. 1959- *St&PR 93*
Brosens, Frank Peter 1957- *WhoAm 92*
Brosens, Ivo 1931- *WhoScE 91-2*
Broser, Hansjoerg 1941- *St&PR 93*
Brosh, Kenneth C. 1914- *St&PR 93*
Brosh, Kent 1941- *St&PR 93*
Brosh, Stephanie Deborah 1964- *WhoEmL 93*
Broshar, Robert Clare 1931- *WhoAm 92*
Brosig, Michael Francis, Sr. 1950- *St&PR 93*
Brosig, Moritz 1815-1887 *Baker 92*
Brosilow, Coleman Bernard 1934- *WhoAm 92*
Brosin, Henry Walter 1904- *WhoAm 92*
Brosius, Edward J. *Law&B 92*
Brosius, Nancy Bancroft *AmWomPl*
Brosky, John G. 1920- *WhoE 93*
Brosky, Robert E. 1940- *St&PR 93*
Brosman, Catharine Savage 1934- *WhoSSW 93, WhoWrEP 92*
Brosmann (a Sancto Hieronymo), Damasus 1731-1798 *Baker 92*
Brosnahan, James Jerome 1934- *WhoAm 92*
Brosnahan, Roger Paul 1935- *WhoAm 92*
Brosnahan, William P. 1940- *St&PR 93*
Brosnan, Carol Raphael Sarah 1931- *WhoAmW 93, WhoE 93*
Brosnan, John 1947- *ScF&FL 92*
Brosnan, Pierce 1953- *WhoAm 92*
Bross, Albert Louis, Jr. 1921- *WhoE 93*
Bross, Helmut A. 1931- *WhoScE 91-3*
Bross, Irwin Dudley Jackson 1921- *WhoAm 92*
Bross, James B., Sr. 1938- *WhoSSW 93*
Bross, John Adams 1911-1990 *BioIn 17*
Bross, John Joseph 1939- *WhoE 93, WhoWor 93*
Bross, Steward Richard, Jr. 1922- *WhoAm 92, WhoWor 93*
Bross, William 1813-1890 *JrnUS*
Brossard, Jacques 1933- *WhoCanL 92*
Brossard, Liane D. *Law&B 92*
Brossard, Nicole 1943- *BioIn 17, ConAu 16AS [port], WhoCanL 92*
Brossard, Sebastien de 1655-1730 *Baker 92*
Brosseau, Alden Wilfrid 1927- *St&PR 93*
Brosseau, Irma Finn 1930- *WhoAm 92*
Brosses, Charles de 1709-1777 *Baker 92*
Brossier, Marthe c. 1577- *BioIn 17*
Brossman, Mark Edward 1953- *WhoEmL 93*
Brossolette, Pierre 1903-1944 *BioIn 17*
Brosstad, Frank 1940- *WhoScE 91-4*
Brost, Gerard Robert 1949- *WhoEmL 93, WhoSSW 93*
Brostoff, Alan Jay 1933- *St&PR 93*
Brostowitz, James M. 1952- *St&PR 93*
Brostrom, Paul G. 1931- *St&PR 93*
Bros y Bertomeu, Juan (Joaquin Pedro Domingo) 1776-1852 *Baker 92*
Brosz, Don Gayle, Jr. 1954- *WhoEmL 93*
Broszat, Martin 1926-1989 *BioIn 17*
Brot, Claude 1929- *WhoScE 91-2*
Brotbeck, George Nathan 1946- *WhoEmL 93*
Broten, Delores 1948- *ScF&FL 92*
Broth, Ray 1930- *WhoSSW 93*
Brothers, Barbara Ann 1968- *WhoAmW 93*
Brothers, Barry 1955- *WhoE 93, WhoEmL 93*
Brothers, Jack Anthony 1943- *WhoWor 93*
Brothers, Jill A. 1963- *St&PR 93*
Brothers, John Alfred 1940- *WhoAm 92*
Brothers, John Wayne 1950- *WhoEmL 93*
Brothers, Joyce *BioIn 17*
Brothers, Joyce Diane *WhoAm 92, WhoAmW 93*
Brothers, Karen Elizabeth 1946- *WhoEmL 93*
Brothers, Kathy Elaine 1959- *WhoAmW 93*
Brothers, Milton J. 1926-1989 *BioIn 17*
Brothers, Ronald J. *Law&B 92*
Brothers Grimm *BioIn 17*
Brothers Johnson *SoulM*
Brotherson, Larry B. *Law&B 92*
Brotherton, Alice Williams *AmWomPl*
Brotherton, Maureen Saltzer 1959- *WhoAmW 93, WhoEmL 93*
Brotherton, Naomi *BioIn 17*
Brotherton, William T., Jr. 1926- *WhoAm 92, WhoSSW 93*
Brotkin, Linda M. *Law&B 92*
Brotman, Alison Beth *Law&B 92*
Brotman, Barbara Louise 1956- *WhoAm 92*
Brotman, Lynne Ann Shapiro 1960- *WhoAmW 93*
Brotman, Phyllis B. 1934- *St&PR 93*
Brotman, Phyllis Block 1934- *WhoAm 92*
Brotman, Stanley Seymour 1924- *WhoAm 92, WhoE 93*
Brotodiningrat, Soemadi D.M. 1941- *WhoUN 92*
Brott, Alexander 1915- *Baker 92*
Brott, Boris 1944- *Baker 92*
Brott, Denis 1950- *Baker 92*
Brott, Irving Deerin, Jr. 1930- *WhoAm 92*
Brott, Walter Howard 1933- *WhoAm 92, WhoWor 93*
Brotzen, Franz Richard 1915- *WhoAm 92, WhoSSW 93*
Brotzman, Donald Glenn 1922- *WhoAm 92*
Brou, Elizabeth Emerson Howell 1956- *WhoAmW 93, WhoEmL 93*
Broucek, William M. 1934- *St&PR 93*
Broucek, William Samuel 1950- *WhoEmL 93*
Brouck, Janet *Law&B 92*
Broud, Ronald L. 1936- *St&PR 93*
Broude, Richard Frederick 1936- *WhoAm 92*
Broudy, Harry Samuel 1905- *WhoAm 92*
Broudy, Nat d1991 *BioIn 17*
Brouet, Jean-Claude *WhoScE 91-2*
Brough, Anthony Thomas 1932- *WhoUN 92*
Brough, Gregory K. 1947- *St&PR 93*
Brough, John Albert 1946- *St&PR 93*
Brough, Michael Bannon 1947- *WhoEmL 93*
Brougham, Kathryn C. 1954- *WhoEmL 93*
Brougham, Robert Powers 1943- *WhoE 93*
Brougham and Vaux, Baron 1778-1868 *BioIn 17*
Brougher, Jerry Ward 1928- *WhoSSW 93*
Broughton, Alan 1942- *St&PR 93*
Broughton, Ann A. *Law&B 92*
Broughton, Bradford Browne 1926- *WhoE 93*
Broughton, Carl L. 1910- *St&PR 93*
Broughton, Carl Louis 1910- *WhoAm 92*
Broughton, Cynthia Elaine 1961- *WhoAmW 93*
Broughton, James 1913- *WhoWrEP 92*
Broughton, Jane *ScF&FL 92*
Broughton, John Marcus 1947- *WhoE 93*
Broughton, N.W. *WhoScE 91-1*
Broughton, Pamela Kay 1946- *WhoWrEP 92*
Broughton, Phillip Charles 1930- *WhoAm 92*
Broughton, Robert B. *Law&B 92*

Broughton, Robert Stephen 1934- *WhoAm 92*
Broughton, Spencer Arthur 1926- *WhoIns 93*
Broughton, T. Alan 1936- *WhoE 93, WhoWrEP 92*
Brouilette, Yves 1951- *WhoE 93*
Brouillard, Freddy 1937- *WhoScE 91-2*
Brouillard, John Charles 1948- *WhoAm 92*
Brouillet, Chrystine 1958- *WhoCanL 92*
Brouillette, Donald G. 1930- *WhoAm 92*
Brouillette, Donald George 1930- *St&PR 93*
Brouillette, Gary Joseph 1940- *WhoAm 92*
Brouillon-Lacombe, Louis *Baker 92*
Broujos, Frank Nicholas, Jr. *Law&B 92*
Brouman, Alvin *Law&B 92*
Broumas, John George 1917- *WhoE 93*
Broumas, Olga 1949- *ConLC 73 [port], WhoWrEP 92*
Broumas, Theodore 1942- *WhoScE 91-3*
Broumas, Theodoros Efthimios 1942- *WhoWor 93*
Broun, Elizabeth 1946- *WhoAm 92, WhoAmW 93, WhoE 93*
Broun, Georges 1928- *WhoScE 91-2*
Broun, Helen *AmWomPl*
Broun, Heywood 1888-1939 *JrnUS*
Broun, Heywood Hale 1918- *WhoAm 92*
Broun, Kenneth Stanley 1939- *WhoAm 92*
Brounoff, Platon 1863-1924 *Baker 92*
Brountas, Paul Peter 1932- *WhoAm 92*
Brous, Bernard 1924- *St&PR 93*
Brous, Charles 1954- *St&PR 93*
Brous, Philip 1930- *WhoAm 92*
Brouse, Brian E. 1950- *St&PR 93*
Brouse, Deborah Elizabeth 1950- *WhoE 93*
Brouse, Jenny R. 1924- *St&PR 93*
Brouse, Robert Clayton 1942- *St&PR 93*
Brouse, Sidney M. 1922- *St&PR 93*
Broussard, Allen E. 1929- *WhoAm 92*
Broussard, Bernard 1929- *WhoSSW 93*
Broussard, Carol Madeline *WhoAmW 93, WhoWor 93*
Broussard, Cassandra Maria 1963- *WhoAmW 93*
Broussard, David N. 1948- *St&PR 93*
Broussard, Debra K. *Law&B 92*
Broussard, Eldridge John, Jr. *BioIn 17*
Broussard, Elsie Rita 1924- *WhoAm 92*
Broussard, Huby J. 1927- *St&PR 93*
Broussard, Jana K. 1961- *St&PR 93*
Broussard, Joseph Otto, III 1938- *WhoAm 92*
Broussard, Louis 1922- *ScF&FL 92*
Broussard, Malcolm Joseph 1953- *WhoSSW 93*
Broussard, Margaret *Law&B 92*
Broussard, Robert R. *Law&B 92*
Broussard, Sharon Foran 1947- *WhoAmW 93*
Broussard, Suzanne Marie 1954- *WhoAmW 93*
Broussard, Thomas Rollins 1943- *WhoAm 92*
Broussard, Vernon James 1932- *St&PR 93*
Broussard, Wendy Faye 1962- *WhoAmW 93*
Broussard, William Arren 1956- *WhoEmL 93*
Broussard, William Joseph 1934- *WhoSSW 93, WhoWor 93*
Brousse, Paul 1844-1912 *BioIn 17*
Brousseau, James Edward 1931- *St&PR 93*
Broutman, Lawrence Jay 1938- *WhoAm 92*
Brouw, W.N. 1940- *WhoScE 91-3*
Brouwenstijn, Gre 1915- *IntDcOp*
Brouwenstijn, Gre (van Swol) 1915- *Baker 92*
Brouwer, Leo 1939- *Baker 92*
Brovarski, Edward Joseph 1943- *WhoAm 92*
Brovas, D. 1928- *WhoScE 91-3*
Brovetto, Gary 1946- *WhoEmL 93*
Brovkin, Vladimir N. 1951- *ConAu 137*
Brow, Thea 1934- *BioIn 17*
Browar, Lisa M. 1951- *WhoAmW 93*
Browde, Anatole 1925- *St&PR 93, WhoAm 92*
Browder, Earl R. 1891-1973 *PolPar*
Browder, Eva Tislowitz 1929- *WhoE 93*
Browder, Felix Earl 1927- *WhoAm 92, WhoE 93, WhoWor 93*
Browder, Glen 1943- *CngDr 91*
Browder, James Steve 1939- *WhoSSW 93*
Browder, John Glen 1943- *WhoAm 92, WhoSSW 93*
Browder, Lesley Hughes, III 1962- *WhoE 93*
Browder, Monte R. *Law&B 92*
Browder, William Barr, Jr. 1910- *WhoSSW 93*
Browdy, Alvin 1917- *WhoAm 92*
Brower, Alan G. *Law&B 92*
Brower, Alice K. *AmWomPl*
Brower, Charles Harry 1948- *WhoEmL 93*
Brower, Charles Nelson 1935- *WhoAm 92*
Brower, Cheryl Diane 1958- *WhoWrEP 92*
Brower, Corwin Lee 1956- *WhoSSW 93*
Brower, David A. 1952- *St&PR 93*
Brower, David Charles 1945- *WhoE 93*
Brower, David John 1930- *WhoWor 93*
Brower, David Ross 1912- *BioIn 17, WhoAm 92, WhoWor 93*
Brower, Edgar Seymour 1930- *St&PR 93*
Brower, Edward E., Jr. 1928- *St&PR 93*
Brower, George David 1948- *WhoEmL 93*
Brower, George R. 1940- *St&PR 93*
Brower, James Calvin 1914- *WhoWor 93*
Brower, John Harold 1940- *WhoSSW 93*
Brower, Joy Daniels 1941- *WhoAmW 93*
Brower, Lincoln Pierson 1931- *WhoSSW 93*
Brower, Paul Gordon 1938- *St&PR 93*
Brower, Ronald Edward 1944- *WhoSSW 93*
Brower, Sharen *BioIn 17*
Brower, Stuart L. 1945- *St&PR 93*
Brower, Wesley Allen 1949- *St&PR 93*
Brower, William L., Jr. 1944- *St&PR 93*
Browes, Pauline 1938- *WhoAm 92, WhoAmW 93*
Browicz, Kazimierz 1925- *WhoScE 91-4*
Browing, Colin Arrott 1935- *St&PR 93*
Browkin, Jerzy 1934- *WhoWor 93*
Browman, David Ludvig 1941- *WhoAm 92*
Brown, A.J. *WhoScE 91-1*
Brown, A(lfred) Peter 1943- *Baker 92*
Brown, A. Whitney *BioIn 17*
Brown, A. Worley 1928- *St&PR 93*
Brown, Aaron Carl 1956- *WhoE 93*
Brown, Abbie Farwell 1871-1927 *AmWomPl*
Brown, Abbott Louis 1943- *WhoAm 92*
Brown, Abbott S. 1955- *WhoEmL 93*
Brown, Adrian Worley 1928- *WhoAm 92*
Brown, Adrienne Baptiste 1940- *WhoAmW 93*
Brown, Adrienne Jean 1950- *WhoAm 92*
Brown, Alan Anthony 1936- *WhoE 93*
Brown, Alan Charles 1948- *St&PR 93*
Brown, Alan Charlton 1929- *WhoAm 92*
Brown, Alan Crawford 1956- *WhoWor 93*
Brown, Alan Geoffrey *WhoScE 91-1*
Brown, Alan Johnson 1951- *WhoSSW 93*
Brown, Alan Marshall, Jr. 1947- *WhoEmL 93*
Brown, Alan N. 1950- *WhoEmL 93*
Brown, Albert Joseph, Jr. 1934- *St&PR 93, WhoAm 92*
Brown, Albert Thaddeus 1941- *WhoE 93*
Brown, Alex 1900-1962 *ScF&FL 92*
Brown, Alexander *WhoScE 91-1*
Brown, Alice *BlkAmWO*
Brown, Alice 1857-1948 *AmWomPl, AmWomWr 92*
Brown, Alice Dalton 1939- *WhoE 93*
Brown, Alice H. *AmWomPl*
Brown, Alice Roberta 1952- *WhoAmW 93*
Brown, Alicia M. *Law&B 92*
Brown, Alistair John 1939- *WhoWor 93*
Brown, Alistair Ross 1941- *WhoSSW 93*
Brown, Allan A. *Law&B 92*
Brown, Allen D. 1951- *St&PR 93*
Brown, Allen Leon, Jr. 1946- *WhoE 93*
Brown, Allyn Stephens 1916- *WhoSSW 93*
Brown, Alpha Estes 1952- *WhoEmL 93*
Brown, Alta Britton Palmer 1935- *WhoSSW 93*
Brown, Amelia Gail 1947- *WhoAmW 93*
Brown, Ames d1991 *BioIn 17*
Brown, Amy J. 1967- *WhoEmL 93*
Brown, Andreas Le 1933- *WhoWor 93*
Brown, Ann Catherine 1935- *WhoAm 92*
Brown, Ann Lenora 1955- *WhoSSW 93*
Brown, Anne Ensign 1937- *BioIn 17*
Brown, Annie K. *AmWomPl*
Brown, Anthony Cave 1930?- *ConAu 139*
Brown, Anthony Lemar 1957- *WhoEmL 93*
Brown, Anthony S. 1934- *St&PR 93*
Brown, Archie 1911-1990 *BioIn 17*
Brown, Arlene Patricia Theresa 1953- *WhoAmW 93*
Brown, Arnold 1939- *WhoAm 92, WhoSSW 93*
Brown, Arnold A. 1929- *St&PR 93*
Brown, Arnold Lanehart, Jr. 1926- *WhoAm 92*
Brown, Arthur 1940- *St&PR 93, WhoAm 92*
Brown, Arthur Edmon, Jr. 1929- *WhoAm 92*
Brown, Arthur Edward, Jr. 1951- *WhoE 93*
Brown, Arthur Frederick *WhoScE 91-1*
Brown, Arthur Hugh Fillingham *WhoScE 91-1*
Brown, Arthur Thomas 1900- *WhoAm 92*
Brown, Arvin Bragin 1940- *WhoAm 92*
Brown, Aubrey Neblett, Jr. 1908- *WhoAm 92*
Brown, Ava Colleen 1952- *WhoEmL 93*
Brown, B. Alex 1948- *WhoEmL 93*
Brown, B. Peter 1922- *WhoIns 93*
Brown, B.R. 1932- *St&PR 93, WhoAm 92*
Brown, B. Warren 1933- *St&PR 93*
Brown, Bailey 1917- *WhoSSW 93*
Brown, Barbara Berger 1930- *WhoAmW 93*
Brown, Barbara Berish 1946- *WhoAmW 93*
Brown, Barbara Black 1928- *WhoWrEP 92*
Brown, Barbara Jean 1936- *WhoAmW 93, WhoE 93*
Brown, Barbara Jeanne 1941- *WhoAm 92*
Brown, Barbara June 1933- *WhoAmW 93*
Brown, Barry *BioIn 17, MiSFD 9*
Brown, Barry 1939- *WhoAm 92*
Brown, Barry Alexander *MiSFD 9*
Brown, Barry Lee 1944- *St&PR 93*
Brown, Barry S. 1949- *St&PR 93*
Brown, Bart A., Jr. 1933- *WhoAm 92*
Brown, Barton 1924- *WhoAm 92*
Brown, Beatrice 1917- *WhoAm 92*
Brown, Benjamin 1794-1853 *BioIn 17*
Brown, Benjamin A. 1943- *St&PR 93, WhoAm 92*
Brown, Benjamin Andrew 1933- *WhoAm 92*
Brown, Benjamin Francis 1946- *WhoUN 92*
Brown, Benjamin Thomas 1948- *WhoSSW 93*
Brown, Benjamin Young 1948- *St&PR 93*
Brown, Bennett Alexander 1929- *St&PR 93*
Brown, Bernard Beau 1925- *St&PR 93*
Brown, Bernard E(dward) 1925- *WhoWrEP 92*
Brown, Bernard G. 1924- *St&PR 93*
Brown, Bert Mahlon 1914- *WhoWor 93*
Brown, Beth *WhoWrEP 92*
Brown, Beth Anne *Law&B 92*
Brown, Beth Marie 1952- *WhoSSW 93*
Brown, Betty Jo 1949- *WhoEmL 93*
Brown, Betty L. 1943- *St&PR 93*
Brown, Betty Louise 1942- *WhoAmW 93*
Brown, Betty Marie 1952- *WhoE 93*
Brown, Bettye Faye 1942- *WhoAmW 93*
Brown, Beulah *AmWomPl*
Brown, Beulah Louise 1917- *WhoAmW 93*
Brown, Beverly C. 1949- *St&PR 93*
Brown, Beverly Eugene 1927- *WhoSSW 93*
Brown, Blair *BioIn 17*
Brown, Bobbi *BioIn 17*
Brown, Bobbie E. 1907-1971 *BioIn 17*
Brown, Bobby *BioIn 17, SoulM*
Brown, Bobby Wayne 1955- *WhoEmL 93*
Brown, Bonnie Joan *WhoAmW 93*
Brown, Bonnie Maryetta 1953- *WhoEmL 93*
Brown, Bradford Stearns 1931- *WhoSSW 93*
Brown, Bradley Bower 1965- *WhoWor 93*
Brown, Bradley David 1961- *WhoEmL 93*
Brown, Brenda Gabioud 1963- *WhoSSW 93*
Brown, Brent W. 1942- *St&PR 93*
Brown, Brian Hilton *WhoScE 91-1*
Brown, Brice Norman 1945- *WhoAm 92*
Brown, Britt 1927- *WhoAm 92*
Brown, Britt Murdock 1952- *St&PR 93*
Brown, Bruce 1931- *WhoAm 92*
Brown, Bruce Allen 1948- *WhoEmL 93*
Brown, Bruce Maitland 1947- *WhoAm 92, WhoE 93, WhoEmL 93*
Brown, Bryan *BioIn 17*
Brown, Bryan T(urner) 1952- *ConAu 139*
Brown, Byron Leslie 1946- *WhoEmL 93*
Brown, Byron William, Jr. 1930- *WhoAm 92*
Brown, C.E. 1938- *WhoIns 93*
Brown, C. Harold 1931- *WhoAm 92*
Brown, Calissa W. *Law&B 92*
Brown, Cameron 1914- *St&PR 93, WhoAm 92, WhoWor 93*
Brown, Candace 1950- *WhoAmW 93*
Brown, Carl Curtis 1947- *WhoEmL 93*
Brown, Carl S. d1991 *BioIn 17*
Brown, Carol A. 1950- *WhoEmL 93*
Brown, Carol Ann 1944- *WhoAmW 93*
Brown, Carol Kapelow 1945- *WhoSSW 93*
Brown, Carole D. *Law&B 92*
Brown, Carolyn P. 1923- *WhoAm 92*
Brown, Carolyn Rink 1946- *WhoAmW 93*
Brown, Carolyn Smith 1946- *WhoAmW 93*
Brown, Carolyn Spencer 1962- *WhoAmW 93*
Brown, Carroll 1928- *WhoAm 92*
Brown, Carroll Edker 1938- *St&PR 93*
Brown, Carter *ScF&FL 92*
Brown, Cary Douglas 1946- *WhoE 93*
Brown, Catherine *BioIn 17*
Brown, Cee *BioIn 17*
Brown, Celeste Gwendolyn 1952- *WhoAmW 93*
Brown, Channing Bolton, III 1958- *WhoEmL 93*
Brown, Charles A. 1942- *St&PR 93*
Brown, Charles B. *Law&B 92*
Brown, Charles D. *Law&B 92*
Brown, Charles Daniel 1927- *WhoAm 92*
Brown, Charles Dodgson 1928- *WhoAm 92*
Brown, Charles E. *Law&B 92*
Brown, Charles Earl 1919- *WhoAm 92*
Brown, Charles Eric 1946- *WhoWor 93*
Brown, Charles Foster, III 1947- *St&PR 93, WhoAm 92*
Brown, Charles Freeman 1914- *WhoAm 92*
Brown, Charles Hawkins 1947- *WhoSSW 93*
Brown, Charles Malcolm *WhoScE 91-1*
Brown, Charles N. 1937- *ScF&FL 92*
Brown, Charles Samuel 1940- *WhoE 93*
Brown, Charles Stuart 1918- *WhoAm 92*
Brown, Charles Theodore 1912- *WhoE 93*
Brown, Charles Timothy *Law&B 92*
Brown, Charles Victor *WhoScE 91-1*
Brown, Charlesey Whitehead 1926- *WhoSSW 93*
Brown, Charlie 1938- *AfrAmBi*
Brown, Charlina Pierce 1935- *WhoAmW 93*
Brown, Charline Hayes 1919- *WhoWrEP 92*
Brown, Charlotte Frances 1956- *WhoAmW 93, WhoEmL 93*
Brown, Charnele *BioIn 17*
Brown, Cheli Ann 1966- *WhoSSW 93*
Brown, Cherri Louise 1949- *WhoWrEP 92*
Brown, Chet 1938- *St&PR 93*
Brown, Chris A. 1962- *WhoIns 93*
Brown, Christine *WhoWrEP 92*
Brown, Christopher 1951- *BioIn 17*
Brown, Christy 1932-1981 *BioIn 17, ConHero 2 [port]*
Brown, Cindy Lu 1958- *WhoAmW 93*
Brown, Claire Louise 1947- *WhoAmW 93*
Brown, Clarence 1890-1987 *BioIn 17, MiSFD 9N*
Brown, Clarence 1924- *BioIn 17*
Brown, Claude 1937- *BioIn 17*
Brown, Claude Lamar, Jr. 1923- *WhoSSW 93*
Brown, Clifford 1930-1956 *Baker 92, BioIn 17*
Brown, Clinton Egbert 1953- *WhoE 93*
Brown, Colin Campbell *WhoScE 91-1*
Brown, Colin Wegand 1949- *St&PR 93, WhoAm 92*
Brown, Colleen A. *Law&B 92*
Brown, Connell Jean 1924- *WhoAm 92*
Brown, Connie Carol 1959- *WhoAmW 93*
Brown, Connie Yates 1947- *WhoAmW 93*
Brown, Conny Ray 1947- *WhoEmL 93, WhoSSW 93*
Brown, Constance C. *AfrAmBi*
Brown, Constance M. *Law&B 92*
Brown, Constance M. 1953- *WhoAmW 93, WhoWor 93*
Brown, Corrine 1946- *WhoAmW 93*
Brown, Courtney C. 1904-1990 *BioIn 17*
Brown, Craig D. 1951- *St&PR 93*
Brown, Craig Jay 1951- *WhoSSW 93*
Brown, Craig Jeffrey 1949- *St&PR 93*
Brown, Craig McFarland 1947- *SmATA 73 [port]*
Brown, Crispin R.W. 1951- *St&PR 93*
Brown, Crosland *ScF&FL 92*
Brown, Cynthia June 1959- *WhoAmW 93*
Brown, Dale 1956- *BioIn 17, ConAu 138, ScF&FL 92*
Brown, Dale Marius 1931- *WhoAm 92*
Brown, Dale Patrick 1947- *WhoAm 92*
Brown, Dale Susan 1954- *WhoAmW 93, WhoE 93, WhoEmL 93, WhoWor 93*
Brown, Dale Weaver 1926- *WhoAm 92*
Brown, Dallas Coverdale, Jr. 1932- *WhoAm 92*
Brown, Dan *BioIn 17*
Brown, Daniel 1946- *WhoEmL 93, WhoWor 93*
Brown, Daniel Clayton 1961- *WhoSSW 93*
Brown, Daniel D. 1929- *St&PR 93*
Brown, Daniel H. 1933- *St&PR 93*
Brown, Daniel Herbert 1933- *WhoAm 92*
Brown, Darmae Judd 1952- *WhoAmW 93*
Brown, Darrell E. 1944- *St&PR 93*
Brown, David *WhoScE 91-1*
Brown, David c. 1896- *BiDAMSp 1989*
Brown, David 1916- *BioIn 17, WhoAm 92, WhoWrEP 92*
Brown, David 1917- *WhoAm 92*
Brown, David A. 1929- *WhoScE 91-3*
Brown, David A. 1945- *WhoAm 92*
Brown, David A. 1957- *St&PR 93*
Brown, David Anthony *WhoScE 91-1*
Brown, David Arthur 1929- *WhoWor 93*
Brown, David Arthur 1934- *St&PR 93*
Brown, David Brent 1960- *WhoSSW 93*
Brown, David Charles 1940- *St&PR 93*
Brown, David (Clifford) 1929- *Baker 92*
Brown, David F. 1941- *St&PR 93*
Brown, David Grant 1936- *WhoAm 92*
Brown, David K. *Law&B 92*

Brown, David Lee 1932- *WhoSSW 93*
Brown, David M. 1935- *WhoAm 92*
Brown, David M. 1938- *St&PR 93*
Brown, David MaGill *Law&B 92*
Brown, David Randolph 1923- *WhoAm 92*
Brown, David Rupert 1934- *WhoAm 92*
Brown, David S. 1952- *St&PR 93*
Brown, David Springer 1915- *WhoAm 92*
Brown, David Taylor 1947- *St&PR 93*
Brown, David W. 1944- *St&PR 93*
Brown, David Warfield 1937- *WhoAm 92*
Brown, David Wesley 1951- *WhoSSW 93*
Brown, Dayton Talmagg 1934- *St&PR 93*
Brown, Deborah Dunn *Law&B 92*
Brown, Deborah Elizabeth 1952- *WhoAmW 93, WhoEmL 93*
Brown, Deborah Susan 1956- *WhoAmW 93*
Brown, Dee Alexander *BioIn 17*
Brown, Dee Alexander 1908- *WhoAm 92, WhoWrEP 92*
Brown, Deming Bronson 1919- *WhoAm 92*
Brown, Denise Scott 1931- *WhoAm 92, WhoAmW 93, WhoWor 93*
Brown, Dennis Phillip *ScF&FL 92*
Brown, Dennis Taylor 1941- *WhoAm 92*
Brown, Dennis Woodfin 1953- *WhoEmL 93*
Brown, Dennison Robert 1934- *WhoAm 92*
Brown, Denny L. 1944- *St&PR 93*
Brown, Dewey Dwight 1946- *WhoEmL 93*
Brown, Diana 1928- *ConAu 40NR, WhoWrEP 92*
Brown, Diane Gillfillan *Law&B 92*
Brown, Don E. 1933- *St&PR 93*
Brown, Don H. d1992 *BioIn 17, NewYTBS 92*
Brown, Don Irvin 1935- *St&PR 93*
Brown, Donald *BioIn 17*
Brown, Donald Arthur 1929- *WhoAm 92*
Brown, Donald David 1931- *WhoAm 92*
Brown, Donald Douglas 1931- *WhoAm 92*
Brown, Donald Edward *WhoScE 91-1*
Brown, Donald James, Jr. 1955- *WhoSSW 93, WhoWor 93*
Brown, Donald Nelson 1937- *WhoSSW 93*
Brown, Donald Ray 1935- *WhoAm 92*
Brown, Donald Robert *Law&B 92*
Brown, Donald Robert 1945- *WhoAm 92*
Brown, Donald Spencer 1928- *WhoUN 92*
Brown, Donald Warren 1939- *St&PR 93*
Brown, Doris *BlkAmWO*
Brown, Doris Jean 1953- *WhoAmW 93*
Brown, Dorothea Williams 1918- *WhoAmW 93*
Brown, Dorothy A. 1953- *WhoEmL 93*
Brown, Dorothy Nell Doss 1946- *WhoAmW 93*
Brown, Douglas A. *Law&B 92*
Brown, Douglas Benedict 1954- *WhoEmL 93*
Brown, Douglas E. *Law&B 92*
Brown, Douglas E. 1956- *St&PR 93*
Brown, Drew T. *BioIn 17*
Brown, Duart Vinson 1912- *WhoWrEP 92*
Brown, Dudley Earl, Jr. 1928- *WhoAm 92*
Brown, Dwight Edward 1945- *St&PR 93*
Brown, E.J. 1909-1991 *ScF&FL 92*
Brown, E(ugene) Richard 1942- *ConAu 40NR*
Brown, Earl Kent 1925- *WhoAm 92*
Brown, Earl Stanley 1953- *WhoSSW 93*
Brown, Earle 1926- *WhoAm 92*
Brown, Earle (Appleton, Jr.) 1926- *Baker 92*
Brown, Earle O., III *Law&B 92*
Brown, Earle Palmer 1922- *WhoAm 92*
Brown, Earlene *BlkAmWO [port]*
Brown, Earlene 1935- *BioIn 17*
Brown, Earlene Dennis 1935- *BiDAMSp 1989*
Brown, Eddie *BioIn 17*
Brown, Eddie d1992 *NewYTBS 92*
Brown, Eddie F. 1945- *WhoAm 92*
Brown, Eddy 1895-1974 *Baker 92*
Brown, Edgar Cary 1916- *WhoAm 92*
Brown, Edgar G. 1898-1954 *EncAACR*
Brown, Edgar Henry, Jr. 1926- *WhoAm 92*
Brown, Edith 1935- *WhoAm 92, WhoAmW 93*
Brown, Edith Toliver *WhoAmW 93*
Brown, Edmund G. 1905- *PolPar*
Brown, Edmund G., Jr. 1938- *PolPar*
Brown, Edmund G., III *Law&B 92*
Brown, Edmund Gerald 1905- *WhoAm 92*
Brown, Edmund Gerald 1938- *BioIn 17*
Brown, Edmund Gerald, Jr. 1938- *WhoAm 92*
Brown, Edward D., Jr. *Law&B 92*
Brown, Edward Duncan *WhoScE 91-1*
Brown, Edward Evan Nelson 1960- *WhoEmL 93*
Brown, Edward G. 1947- *St&PR 93*
Brown, Edward J. *Law&B 92*
Brown, Edward James 1937- *WhoE 93, WhoWor 93*
Brown, Edward Maurice 1909- *WhoAm 92, WhoWor 93*
Brown, Edward Randolph 1933- *WhoAm 92*
Brown, Edward Stanton, III 1949- *WhoEmL 93*
Brown, Edward William *Law&B 92*
Brown, Edwin *Law&B 92*
Brown, Edwin Wilson, Jr. 1926- *WhoAm 92*
Brown, Eileen Thaler 1939- *WhoAmW 93*
Brown, Eleanor McMillen 1890-1991 *BioIn 17*
Brown, Eli Matthew 1923- *WhoAm 92*
Brown, Elizabeth Ann 1918- *WhoAm 92*
Brown, Elizabeth Swift 1919- *St&PR 93*
Brown, Elizabeth Taylor 1930- *WhoAmW 93*
Brown, Ellsworth Howard 1943- *WhoAm 92*
Brown, Elmo Pope d1991 *BioIn 17*
Brown, Elvin J. 1922- *WhoAm 92*
Brown, Elzie Lee 1914- *WhoSSW 93*
Brown, Ephraim Taylor, Jr. 1920- *WhoAm 92*
Brown, Eric 1960- *ScF&FL 92*
Brown, Eric A. 1946- *St&PR 93*
Brown, Eric Berton *Law&B 92*
Brown, Eric David 1953- *WhoEmL 93*
Brown, Eric Gradwell *WhoScE 91-1*
Brown, Eric Joseph 1939- *WhoScE 91-2*
Brown, Eric Steven 1953- *WhoEmL 93*
Brown, Eric Vandyke, Jr. 1940- *WhoAm 92*
Brown, Eric W. *St&PR 93*
Brown, Eric Warren 1959- *WhoEmL 93*
Brown, Ernest Hugh 1943- *St&PR 93*
Brown, Estelle Aubrey *AmWomPl*
Brown, Esther *AmWomPl*
Brown, Esther Lucile 1898-1990 *BioIn 17*
Brown, Ethel Eldridge 1928- *WhoE 93*
Brown, Eugene *St&PR 93*
Brown, Eve *AmWomPl*
Brown, Faith Gideon 1942- *WhoAmW 93*
Brown, Fannie Eleanor Garrett 1924- *WhoAmW 93*
Brown, Fayette 1943- *St&PR 93*
Brown, Fern G. 1918- *ConAu 40NR*
Brown, Firman Hewitt, Jr. 1926- *WhoAm 92*
Brown, Florence Stewart 1929- *WhoE 93*
Brown, Forbes Taylor 1934- *WhoE 93*
Brown, Fornan 1901- *SmATA 71*
Brown, Foster Edward 1952- *St&PR 93*
Brown, Frances Anne 1946- *WhoAmW 93*
Brown, Francis Cabell, Jr. 1936- *WhoAm 92*
Brown, Francis Gordon, Jr. 1879-1911 *BiDAMSp 1989*
Brown, Francis H., III 1959- *WhoEmL 93*
Brown, Francis Robert 1914- *WhoAm 92*
Brown, Frank 1935- *WhoAm 92*
Brown, Frank C. d1992 *BioIn 17*
Brown, Frank R. *WhoScE 91-1*
Brown, Franklin C. *Law&B 92*
Brown, Fred A. 1941- *WhoAm 92*
Brown, Fred E. 1913- *St&PR 93*
Brown, Fred E. 1941- *St&PR 93*
Brown, Fred Elmore 1913- *WhoAm 92*
Brown, Fred Grant 1953- *WhoEmL 93*
Brown, Fred I., Jr. 1923- *St&PR 93*
Brown, Freddie 1907-1986 *BioIn 17*
Brown, Freddie 1910-1991 *AnObit 1991*
Brown, Frederic Joseph 1934- *WhoAm 92*
Brown, Frederick Calvin 1924- *WhoAm 92*
Brown, Frederick Gramm 1932- *WhoAm 92*
Brown, Frederick H. 1927- *WhoIns 93*
Brown, Frederick Harold 1927- *St&PR 93, WhoAm 92, WhoE 93, WhoWor 93*
Brown, Frederick L. *BioIn 17*
Brown, Frederick Lee 1940- *WhoAm 92*
Brown, Frederick W. *Law&B 92*
Brown, Fredric 1906-1972 *ScF&FL 92*
Brown, Freezell, Jr. 1957- *WhoEmL 93*
Brown, Frieda Farfour 1948- *WhoSSW 93*
Brown, Fritz 1949- *WhoSSW 93*
Brown, G. Robert 1933- *St&PR 93*
Brown, Garrett Edward, Jr. 1943- *WhoAm 92*
Brown, Garry Leslie 1942- *WhoWor 93*
Brown, Gary Estle 1941- *WhoAm 92*
Brown, Gary N. *Law&B 92*
Brown, Gary Sandy 1940- *WhoAm 92*
Brown, Gene L. 1950- *St&PR 93*
Brown, Gene W. 1936- *WhoAm 92*
Brown, Georg Stanford *MiSFD 9*
Brown, George *ConAu 39NR*
Brown, George 1914-1985 *ColdWar 1 [port]*
Brown, George E., Jr. 1920- *CngDr 91*
Brown, George Edward, Jr. 1920- *WhoAm 92*
Brown, George Franklin, Jr. 1946- *St&PR 93*
Brown, George Hay 1910- *WhoAm 92*
Brown, George James 1930- *WhoSSW 93*
Brown, George King 1925- *St&PR 93*
Brown, George Leslie 1926- *St&PR 93, WhoAm 92*
Brown, George M. 1908- *St&PR 93*
Brown, George Mackay *BioIn 17*
Brown, George Mackay 1921- *ConAu 37NR, ScF&FL 92*
Brown, George Rhamy 1937- *WhoSSW 93*
Brown, George S. 1930- *St&PR 93*
Brown, George Scratchley 1918-1978 *HarEnMi*
Brown, George Sheldon *ScF&FL 92*
Brown, George Stephen 1945- *WhoAm 92*
Brown, George W. 1830-1889 *BioIn 17*
Brown, George William *WhoScE 91-1*
Brown, Georgia d1992 *NewYTBS 92 [port]*
Brown, Georgia Elizabeth 1963- *WhoWor 93*
Brown, Georgia L. 1948- *NotHsAW 93*
Brown, Gerald Curtis 1942- *WhoAm 92*
Brown, Gerald Eugene 1949- *WhoEmL 93*
Brown, Geraldine 1945- *WhoAmW 93, WhoE 93, WhoWor 93*
Brown, Geraldine Marie 1952- *WhoScE 91-1*
Brown, Geraldine Reed 1947- *WhoAm 92*
Brown, Gerard S. *Law&B 92, St&PR 93*
Brown, Giles Tyler 1916- *WhoAm 92, WhoWor 93*
Brown, Glenda Ann Walters 1937- *WhoAmW 93, WhoSSW 93*
Brown, Glenda Hodgson 1945- *WhoAmW 93*
Brown, Glenn Arthur 1953- *WhoE 93*
Brown, Glenn Robbins, Jr. 1930- *WhoAm 92*
Brown, Glenn William, Jr. 1937- *St&PR 93*
Brown, Glenn William, Jr. 1955- *WhoAm 92, WhoE 93, WhoEmL 93, WhoWor 93*
Brown, Gordon *BioIn 17*
Brown, Gordon E. 1931- *WhoE 93*
Brown, Gordon E., Jr. 1943- *WhoAm 92*
Brown, Gordon Edgar, Jr. 1952- *WhoSSW 93*
Brown, Gordon S. 1931- *St&PR 93*
Brown, Grace Overton *AmWomPl*
Brown, Grady Michael *Law&B 92*
Brown, Gregg C. *Law&B 92*
Brown, Gregg G. 1963- *WhoEmL 93*
Brown, Gregory *MiSFD 9*
Brown, Gregory Neil 1938- *WhoAm 92*
Brown, Guy Eastman, II 1940- *WhoSSW 93*
Brown, H. 1943- *PolPar*
Brown, H. Lowell *Law&B 92*
Brown, H. William 1933- *WhoWor 93*
Brown, Hank 1940- *BioIn 17, CngDr 91, WhoAm 92*
Brown, Harley Procter, Jr. 1921- *WhoSSW 93*
Brown, Harold *BioIn 17*
Brown, Harold 1927- *ColdWar 1 [port], WhoAm 92*
Brown, Harold J., Jr. 1940- *St&PR 93*
Brown, Harriet *BioIn 17*
Brown, Harris Robert 1950- *WhoEmL 93, WhoWor 93*
Brown, Harrison 1917-1986 *ScF&FL 92*
Brown, Harry DeArman 1925- *WhoSSW 93*
Brown, Harry Matthew 1921- *WhoSSW 93*
Brown, Heather *WhoScE 91-1*
Brown, Heidi *Law&B 92*
Brown, Helen Bennett 1902- *WhoAm 92*
Brown, Helen Gurley *BioIn 17*
Brown, Helen Gurley 1922- *WhoAm 92, WhoAmW 93, WhoE 93, WhoWor 93, WhoWrEP 92*
Brown, Helene Gurian 1929- *WhoAmW 93*
Brown, Henry 1907- *WhoWor 93*
Brown, Henry Arthur, Jr. 1921- *St&PR 93*
Brown, Henry Bedinger Rust 1926- *WhoAm 92*
Brown, Henry Billings 1836-1913 *OxCSupC [port]*
Brown, Henry Chapman, III 1959- *WhoSSW 93*
Brown, Henry E. *Law&B 92*
Brown, Henry J. 1941- *St&PR 93*
Brown, Henry Newton 1857-1884 *BioIn 17*
Brown, Henry William *WhoScE 91-1*
Brown, Herbert Charles 1912- *WhoAm 92, WhoWor 93*
Brown, Herbert H. *Law&B 92*
Brown, Herbert Russell 1931- *WhoAm 92*
Brown, Hermione Kopp 1915- *WhoAm 92*
Brown, Himan 1910- *ScF&FL 92*
Brown, Hobson, Jr. 1942- *WhoAm 92*
Brown, Homer Buford 1921- *St&PR 93*
Brown, Howard Bernard 1924- *WhoSSW 93, WhoWor 93*
Brown, Howard C. 1921- *WhoAm 92*
Brown, Howard Carter, III 1951- *WhoEmL 93*
Brown, Howard Earl 1920- *St&PR 93*
Brown, Howard L. 1906- *St&PR 93*
Brown, Howard Mayer 1930- *Baker 92*
Brown, Hubert Gerold 1943- *EncAACR*
Brown, I.A.C. *WhoScE 91-1*
Brown, I. Stephen 1940- *WhoE 93*
Brown, Ian *WhoScE 91-1*
Brown, Ian Alexander 1951- *WhoEmL 93*
Brown, Iona 1941- *Baker 92, WhoAm 92, WhoAmW 93*
Brown, Irene Bennett 1932- *DcAmChF 1960*
Brown, Isabel Zakrzewski 1953- *WhoSSW 93*
Brown, Ivan Douglas *WhoScE 91-1*
Brown, Ivory Lee *BioIn 17*
Brown, J. Callaway 1928- *St&PR 93*
Brown, J. Carter *NewYTBS 92 [port]*
Brown, J. Carter 1934- *BioIn 17*
Brown, J.D. *Law&B 92*
Brown, J. Duncan d1991 *BioIn 17*
Brown, J. Duncan 1923- *St&PR 93*
Brown, J. E. 1940- *WhoSSW 93*
Brown, J. Kathleen *WhoWrEP 92*
Brown, J. Melissa *Law&B 92*
Brown, J.W. 1911- *St&PR 93*
Brown, Jack 1927- *WhoAm 92, WhoWrEP 92*
Brown, Jack Ainsworth 1930- *St&PR 93*
Brown, Jack B. 1924- *St&PR 93*
Brown, Jack C. 1919- *St&PR 93*
Brown, Jack Cole 1930- *WhoAm 92*
Brown, Jack Ernest 1914- *WhoAm 92*
Brown, Jack H. 1939- *WhoAm 92*
Brown, Jack Harold Upton 1918- *WhoAm 92*
Brown, Jack W. 1939- *St&PR 93*
Brown, Jack Wyman 1922- *WhoAm 92*
Brown, Jacob A. 1926- *WhoAm 92*
Brown, Jacob Jennings 1775-1828 *CmdGen 1991 [port], HarEnMi*
Brown, James *BioIn 17, WhoScE 91-1*
Brown, James d1992 *NewYTBS 92*
Brown, James 1920-1992 *BioIn 17*
Brown, James 1928- *Baker 92, WhoAm 92*
Brown, James 1933- *CurBio 92 [port], SoulM*
Brown, James 1957- *ConAu 139*
Brown, James Ace 1942- *WhoSSW 93*
Brown, James Andrew 1914- *WhoAm 92*
Brown, James Anthony 1932- *WhoSSW 93*
Brown, James Arthur *Law&B 92*
Brown, James Arthur 1943- *St&PR 93*
Brown, James Barrow 1932- *WhoAm 92*
Brown, James Briggs 1922- *WhoAm 92*
Brown, James Brooking *WhoScE 91-1*
Brown, James Carrington, III 1939- *WhoWor 93*
Brown, James Cooke 1921-1987 *ScF&FL 92*
Brown, James Curtiss 1921- *WhoSSW 93*
Brown, James D. *ScF&FL 92*
Brown, James Douglas 1958- *St&PR 93*
Brown, James Duff 1862-1914 *Baker 92*
Brown, James Edward *Law&B 92*
Brown, James Edward 1952- *St&PR 93*
Brown, James Elliott 1947- *WhoEmL 93*
Brown, James Eugene, III 1942- *WhoSSW 93*
Brown, James Francis *Law&B 92*
Brown, James Frederick 1943- *St&PR 93*
Brown, James Garland 1933- *WhoSSW 93*
Brown, James Glenn *Law&B 92*
Brown, James H., Jr. 1940- *WhoAm 92*
Brown, James Harlow 1937- *St&PR 93*
Brown, James Harvey 1936- *WhoAm 92*
Brown, James Hugh 1947- *St&PR 93*
Brown, James Joseph 1928- *St&PR 93, WhoAm 92*
Brown, James-Keith 1962- *WhoE 93*
Brown, James LaVelle 1943- *WhoSSW 93*
Brown, James Melton 1925- *WhoAm 92*
Brown, James Michael 1957- *WhoWrEP 92*
Brown, James Monroe, III 1917- *WhoAm 92*
Brown, James Nelson, Jr. 1929- *WhoE 93*
Brown, James O. d1992 *NewYTBS 92*
Brown, James Robert 1930- *WhoAm 92*
Brown, James Robert 1944- *WhoSSW 93*
Brown, James Roy 1950- *WhoSSW 93*
Brown, James Toner 1949- *WhoE 93*
Brown, James W. 1947- *St&PR 93*
Brown, James Ward 1934- *WhoAm 92*
Brown, James Wilcox 1948- *WhoEmL 93*
Brown, James William 1944- *WhoSSW 93, WhoWor 93*
Brown, Jamie 1945- *DcChlFi*
Brown, Jan W. 1942- *WhoAmW 93*
Brown, Jane Delano 1950- *WhoSSW 93*
Brown, Jane Elizabeth *WhoScE 91-1*
Brown, Jane G. 1941- *WhoAm 92*
Brown, Jane Martin Thornton 1951- *WhoEmL 93*
Brown, Janet 1936- *WhoAmW 93*
Brown, Janet Ann 1959- *WhoAmW 93*
Brown, Janet McNalley 1960- *WhoAmW 93, WhoEmL 93*

Brown, Janet R. 1933- WhoAmW 93, WhoE 93
Brown, Jason Walter 1938- WhoAm 92
Brown, Jay M. Law&B 92
Brown, Jay Marshall 1933- WhoE 93
Brown, Jay W. 1945- St&PR 93
Brown, Jean Bush 1947- WhoEmL 93
Brown, Jean Mc Brayer 1908- WhoWrEP 92
Brown, Jean R. Law&B 92
Brown, Jean Rae 1956- WhoEmL 93
Brown, Jean William 1928- WhoAm 92
Brown, Jeanette Snyder 1925- WhoAmW 93
Brown, Jeff ChlFicS
Brown, Jeffrey 1946- WhoE 93, WhoEmL 93
Brown, Jeffrey L. 1955- WhoEmL 93
Brown, Jeffrey S. Law&B 92
Brown, Jeremy Earle 1946- WhoAm 92
Brown, Jeremy James 1954- WhoIns 93
Brown, Jeremy Ronald Coventry 1948- WhoWor 93
Brown, Jerome BioIn 17
Brown, Jerome Miles 1941- WhoE 93
Brown, Jerome R. St&PR 93
Brown, Jerrold Stanley 1953- WhoEmL 93
Brown, Jerry 1938- BioIn 17, News 92 [port], WhoAm 92
Brown, Jerry Earl 1940- ScF&FL 92
Brown, Jerry Glenn 1933- St&PR 93
Brown, Jerry Milford 1938- WhoWor 93
Brown, Jerry William 1925- WhoAm 92, WhoSSW 93
Brown, Jim BioIn 17, MiSFD 9
Brown, Jim 1936- BioIn 17, News 93-2 [port], WhoAm 92
Brown, Jo Ann Law&B 92
Brown, Joan 1938-1990 BioIn 17
Brown, Joan Hudson 1935- WhoSSW 93
Brown, Joan Mazzaferro 1956- WhoAmW 93
Brown, Joan Myers BioIn 17
Brown, Joanne Carlson 1953- WhoEmL 93
Brown, Joanne L. 1953- WhoAmW 93
Brown, Jobeth G. 1950- St&PR 93
Brown, JoBeth Goode 1950- WhoAm 92, WhoAmW 93
Brown, Joe Blackburn 1940- WhoAm 92
Brown, Joe D. St&PR 93
Brown, Joe E. 1892-1973 IntDcF 2-3, QDrFCA 92 [port]
Brown, Joel Edward 1937- WhoAm 92
Brown, John Law&B 92
Brown, John 1715-1766 Baker 92
Brown, John 1757-1837 PolPar
Brown, John 1800-1859 BioIn 17, PolPar
Brown, John C. 1921- WhoIns 93
Brown, John Callaway 1928- WhoAm 92
Brown, John Campbell WhoScE 91-1
Brown, John Carey 1948- WhoEmL 93
Brown, John Carter 1934- BioIn 17, WhoAm 92, WhoE 93
Brown, John E. 1922- St&PR 93
Brown, John Edward 1936- WhoAm 92, WhoE 93
Brown, John Edward 1939- WhoAm 92
Brown, John Fred 1941- WhoSSW 93, WhoWor 93
Brown, John Gilbert Newton 1916- WhoWor 93
Brown, John H. Law&B 92
Brown, John Hampton 1945- WhoAm 92
Brown, John J. 1946- WhoEmL 93
Brown, John Joseph 1931- WhoAsAP 91
Brown, John L. Law&B 92
Brown, John Lackey 1914- WhoE 93
Brown, John Lawrence, Jr. 1925- WhoAm 92
Brown, John Lott 1924- WhoAm 92
Brown, John M. 1924- WhoAm 92
Brown, John Martin 1924- St&PR 93
Brown, John Maxwell 1934- WhoWor 93
Brown, John O. 1934- St&PR 93, WhoAm 92
Brown, John Patrick 1925- WhoAm 92
Brown, John R. BioIn 17
Brown, John Robert 1909- EncAACR, WhoAm 92, WhoSSW 93
Brown, John Robert 1935- St&PR 93
Brown, John Robert 1947- WhoAm 92, WhoEmL 93, WhoWor 93
Brown, John Terrell 1940- St&PR 93
Brown, John Thomas 1948- WhoWor 93
Brown, John W. 1922- St&PR 93
Brown, John Wayne 1949- WhoEmL 93
Brown, John Wilford 1934- St&PR 93, WhoAm 92
Brown, Johnnie Edward 1962- WhoEmL 93
Brown, Jonathan 1939- WhoAm 92
Brown, Joseph A. 1926- WhoAm 92
Brown, Joseph Gordon 1927- WhoAm 92
Brown, Joseph Samuel 1943- WhoE 93
Brown, Joseph Warner, Jr. 1949- St&PR 93
Brown, Joshua BioIn 17
Brown, Joyce Ann BioIn 17
Brown, Joyce Christine 1956- WhoEmL 93
Brown, Juanita Ora Luckett 1948- WhoEmL 93
Brown, Judi BlkAmWO
Brown, Judith d1992 NewYTBS 92
Brown, Judith 1931-1992 BioIn 17
Brown, Judith A. d1991 BioIn 17
Brown, Judith Arner 1947- WhoE 93, WhoEmL 93
Brown, Judith C(ora) ConAu 136
Brown, Judith Ellen 1950- WhoEmL 93
Brown, Judith Olans 1941- WhoAm 92
Brown, Judy Marie 1957- WhoAmW 93
Brown, Julia BioIn 17
Brown, Julie BioIn 17
Brown, June 1923- WhoAm 92
Brown, June Gibbs 1933- WhoAm 92
Brown, June Wilcoxon 1914- WhoAmW 93
Brown, Karen 1955- WhoAmW 93
Brown, Karen Howard 1945- WhoAmW 93
Brown, Karen Kay 1944- WhoAm 92
Brown, Karl 1897-1990 BioIn 17
Brown, Kathaleen Ruth 1937- St&PR 93
Brown, Katharine B. Law&B 92
Brown, Katharine Eisenhart 1921- WhoE 93
Brown, Katharine S. AmWomPl
Brown, Katherine Elizabeth 1948- St&PR 93
Brown, Kathie Hays 1953- WhoSSW 93
Brown, Kathleen BioIn 17, WhoAm 92, WhoAmW 93
Brown, Kathleen Sitley 1955- WhoAmW 93
Brown, Kathryn Ann Smith 1926- WhoAmW 93, WhoSSW 93
Brown, Katy ScF&FL 92
Brown, Kay 1932- BlkAuII 92
Brown, Kay 1950- WhoAmW 93
Brown, Keirn Clarke, Jr. 1947- WhoE 93, WhoEmL 93
Brown, Keith d1991 BioIn 17
Brown, Keith 1933- WhoAm 92
Brown, Keith Allen 1937- St&PR 93
Brown, Keith Lapham 1925- WhoAm 92, WhoWor 93
Brown, Kelly 1955- St&PR 93
Brown, Ken ScF&FL 92
Brown, Kenneth Alan 1951- WhoEmL 93
Brown, Kenneth Allen 1950- WhoSSW 93
Brown, Kenneth Allen 1954- WhoEmL 93, WhoSSW 93
Brown, Kenneth Ashley, Jr. 1946- WhoSSW 93
Brown, Kenneth Charles 1952- WhoAm 92, WhoEmL 93
Brown, Kenneth H. WhoWrEP 92
Brown, Kenneth Henry 1939- WhoSSW 93
Brown, Kenneth Jay Law&B 92
Brown, Kenneth Joseph 1945- WhoWor 93
Brown, Kenneth L. 1936- WhoAm 92, WhoWor 93
Brown, Kenneth Lloyd 1927- WhoAm 92
Brown, Kenneth R. 1936- St&PR 93
Brown, Kenneth Ray 1936- WhoAm 92
Brown, Kent Louis, Sr. 1916- WhoAm 92
Brown, Kent Louis, Jr. 1943- WhoAm 92, WhoWrEP 92
Brown, Kent Robert 1945- St&PR 93
Brown, Kevin Michael 1948- WhoE 93, WhoEmL 93
Brown, Kyle Nelson 1958- WhoEmL 93
Brown, L. Alex 1952- WhoE 93
Brown, L. Baxter Law&B 92
Brown, L. Edwin 1933- WhoSSW 93
Brown, LaRita Early Dawn Ma-Ka-Lani 1937- WhoAmW 93
Brown, Larry BioIn 17, WhoAm 92
Brown, Larry 1951- BioIn 17, ConLC 73 [port]
Brown, Larry Don 1953- WhoSSW 93
Brown, Larry Eddie 1941- WhoSSW 93, WhoWor 93
Brown, Larry G. Law&B 92
Brown, Larry G. 1942- St&PR 93
Brown, Laura Norton AmWomPl
Brown, Laurence A. Law&B 92
Brown, Laurie Mark 1923- WhoAm 92
Brown, Lavelle Shelly 1961- WhoEmL 93
Brown, Lawrence, Jr. 1947- BiDAMSp 1989
Brown, Lawrence B. Law&B 92
Brown, Lawrence Charles 1951- WhoEmL 93
Brown, Lawrence Clifton, Jr. 1950- WhoE 93
Brown, Lawrence David 1926- WhoWor 93
Brown, Lawrence Haas 1934- St&PR 93, WhoAm 92
Brown, Lawrence Harvey 1940- WhoSSW 93
Brown, Lawrence Michael WhoScE 91-1
Brown, Lawrence Murl, Jr. 1958- WhoSSW 93
Brown, Lawrence Raymond, Jr. 1928- WhoAm 92
Brown, Lawrence S., Jr. 1949- WhoE 93
Brown, Leanna 1935- WhoAmW 93, WhoE 93
Brown, Lee Patrick BioIn 17
Brown, Lee Patrick 1937- WhoAm 92, WhoE 93
Brown, Leo d1991 BioIn 17
Brown, Leo C., Jr. 1942- AfrAmBi [port]
Brown, Leon 1907- WhoAm 92
Brown, Leon Carl 1928- WhoAm 92
Brown, Leon T. 1920- St&PR 93
Brown, Leonard Bernard 1932- St&PR 93
Brown, Leonard Franklin 1928- WhoSSW 93
Brown, Les BioIn 17
Brown, Les 1912- BioIn 17
Brown, Les 1928- WhoAm 92
Brown, Les(ter Raymond) 1912- Baker 92
Brown, Leslie Law&B 92
Brown, Leslie Ann 1961- WhoE 93, WhoEmL 93
Brown, Lesly BioIn 17
Brown, Lester L. 1928- WhoWrEP 92
Brown, Lester Russell 1934- WhoAm 92
Brown, Lewis Arnold 1931- WhoAm 92
Brown, Lewis J. 1932- St&PR 93
Brown, Lewis Nathan 1953- WhoAm 92
Brown, Lida M. AmWomPl
Brown, Linda Cockerham 1946- WhoEmL 93
Brown, Linda Joan 1941- WhoAmW 93
Brown, Linda Kay 1948- WhoAmW 93
Brown, Linda Lione 1949- WhoAmW 93
Brown, Linda Lockett 1954- WhoAmW 93
Brown, Linda Susan 1956- WhoAmW 93
Brown, Lisa B. Law&B 92
Brown, Lisa Claire 1954- WhoEmL 93
Brown, Lisa Patton 1958- WhoEmL 93
Brown, Logan R. 1927- St&PR 93, WhoAm 92
Brown, Lois Heffington 1940- WhoAmW 93
Brown, Lorene Byron 1933- WhoAm 92
Brown, Loretta Ann Port 1945- WhoAm 92
Brown, Lorraine Ann 1947- WhoAmW 93, WhoEmL 93
Brown, Louis James WhoScE 91-1
Brown, Louis M. 1909- WhoAm 92
Brown, Louis M. 1943- St&PR 93
Brown, Lowell Severt 1934- WhoAm 92
Brown, Lucy Kennedy AmWomPl
Brown, Lutcher Slade d1991 BioIn 17
Brown, Luther 1939- St&PR 93
Brown, Lydie Szabo Law&B 92
Brown, Lyman R. Law&B 92
Brown, Lynda Marie 1950- WhoAmW 93
Brown, Lynette Ralya 1926- WhoAm 92, WhoAmW 93, WhoWor 93
Brown, Lynn Curtis 1954- WhoEmL 93
Brown, Lynne McKenzie 1952- WhoAmW 93
Brown, Lynne P. 1952- ConAu 138
Brown, Madeleine BioIn 17
Brown, Malcolm Ferrie, Jr. 1926- St&PR 93
Brown, Marc 1946- ChlLR 29 [port]
Brown, Marc Laurence 1951- WhoEmL 93
Brown, Marc Tolon BioIn 17
Brown, Marc (Tolon) 1946- MajAI [port]
Brown, Marcia (Joan) 1918- MajAI [port], WhoAm 92
Brown, Margaret 1891-1990 BioIn 17
Brown, Margaret deBeers Law&B 92
Brown, Margaret Ree 1949- WhoAmW 93, WhoEmL 93
Brown, Margaret Ruth Anderson 1944- WhoAmW 93
Brown, Margaret Wise 1910-1952 BioIn 17, ConAu 136, MajAI [port]
Brown, Marian Elsa 1962- WhoE 93
Brown, Marian Katherine AmWomPl
Brown, Marilyn Branch 1944- WhoAmW 93
Brown, Marilyn Jeanne 1951- WhoAmW 93
Brown, Marilyn Ruth 1951- WhoAmW 93
Brown, Marion Lipscomb, Jr. 1925- WhoAm 92
Brown, Mark L. 1954- St&PR 93
Brown, Mark Terrill 1953- WhoEmL 93
Brown, Marlene Lorraine 1953- WhoAmW 93
Brown, Marsha Ann Stokes 1952- WhoE 93
Brown, Martha Constable 1954- WhoEmL 93
Brown, Martin David 1956- WhoE 93
Brown, Martin Howard 1953- WhoE 93, WhoEmL 93
Brown, Martin R. Law&B 92
Brown, Martin Raymond 1954- WhoAm 92
Brown, Marty BioIn 17
Brown, Marvin S. 1935- St&PR 93, WhoAm 92
Brown, Mary 1847-1935 BioIn 17
Brown, Mary 1929- ScF&FL 92
Brown, Mary C. AmWomPl
Brown, Mary Eleanor 1906- WhoAm 92, WhoAmW 93
Brown, Mary Jo 1958- WhoEmL 93
Brown, Mary Mitchell AmWomPl
Brown, Mary Oliver 1953- WhoWrEP 92
Brown, Matthew 1905- WhoAm 92
Brown, Matthews 1952- WhoEmL 93
Brown, Maude Bass AmWomPl
Brown, Maurice J(ohn) E(dwin) 1906-1975 Baker 92
Brown, Maxine SoulM
Brown, May AmWomPl
Brown, May Belleville AmWomPl
Brown, May Wale 1918- WhoAmW 93
Brown, McTeer 1927- St&PR 93
Brown, Melanie L. Law&B 92
Brown, Melinda J. Law&B 92
Brown, Melissa Kern 1959- WhoEmL 93
Brown, Melissa Mather ScF&FL 92
Brown, Melissa McNeil 1964- WhoAmW 93
Brown, Melissa Rose 1957- WhoAmW 93
Brown, Melvin F. 1935- St&PR 93, WhoAm 92
Brown, Merton (Luther) 1913- Baker 92
Brown, Michael ScF&FL 92, WhoScE 91-1
Brown, Michael 1943- WhoAm 92
Brown, Michael Alan WhoScE 91-1
Brown, Michael Arthur 1938- WhoAm 92
Brown, Michael David 1950- WhoSSW 93
Brown, Michael DeWayne 1954- WhoEmL 93
Brown, Michael Eugene 1954- WhoEmL 93
Brown, Michael George 1951- WhoEmL 93, WhoSSW 93
Brown, Michael Irwin 1943- St&PR 93
Brown, Michael Jay 1956- St&PR 93
Brown, Michael L. 1958- WhoEmL 93
Brown, Michael Lynn 1950- WhoEmL 93
Brown, Michael Lynn 1958- WhoEmL 93
Brown, Michael Marshall 1955- WhoE 93
Brown, Michael Richard 1959- WhoEmL 93
Brown, Michael Robert Withington WhoScE 91-1
Brown, Michael Ross 1941- WhoWor 93
Brown, Michael Stephen 1942- St&PR 93
Brown, Michael Stephen 1948- WhoEmL 93
Brown, Michael Stuart 1941- WhoAm 92, WhoSSW 93, WhoWor 93
Brown, Michael Wayne 1955- WhoEmL 93, WhoSSW 93
Brown, Michelle P(atricia) 1959- ConAu 139
Brown, Mickey Jackson 1946- St&PR 93
Brown, Milton O. 1929- St&PR 93
Brown, Milton Wolf 1911- WhoAm 92
Brown, Mitchell Swift 1950- St&PR 93
Brown, Mollie Margaret 1931- WhoAmW 93
Brown, Molly d1934 BioIn 17
Brown, Mona Wright 1958- WhoAmW 93
Brown, Mordecai 1876-1948 BioIn 17
Brown, Morris Jonathan WhoScE 91-1
Brown, Morton B. 1941- WhoAm 92
Brown, Moses ConAu 139
Brown, Muriel AmWomPl, BioIn 17
Brown, Murray BioIn 17
Brown, Myra 1933- St&PR 93
Brown, Myra Leann 1952- WhoAmW 93
Brown, Nacio (Ignatio) Herb 1896-1964 Baker 92
Brown, Nadine Maynard 1944- WhoSSW 93
Brown, Nancy Alice 1934- WhoAmW 93
Brown, Nancy Ann WhoAm 92
Brown, Nancy G. Law&B 92
Brown, Nancy J. Law&B 92
Brown, Nancy J. 1942- WhoAmW 93
Brown, Nancy Jeanne 1942- WhoAmW 93
Brown, Nancy McIntire 1965- WhoAmW 93
Brown, Nancy V. Law&B 92
Brown, Naola A. Law&B 92
Brown, Naomi Yanagi 1920- WhoAmW 93, WhoSSW 93
Brown, Natalie Joy 1962- WhoWrEP 92
Brown, Neil Anthony 1940- WhoAsAP 91
Brown, Newel Kay 1932- Baker 92
Brown, Nigel Leslie WhoScE 91-1
Brown, Norma ScF&FL 92
Brown, Norman 1921- WhoE 93
Brown, Norman A. 1938- WhoAm 92
Brown, Norman Donald 1935- WhoAm 92
Brown, Norman H. WhoWrEP 92
Brown, Norman Howard 1929- WhoE 93
Brown, Norman James 1942- WhoSSW 93
Brown, Norman L. WhoIns 93
Brown, Norman L. 1930- St&PR 93
Brown, Norman Wesley 1931- St&PR 93

Brown, Olen Ray 1935- *WhoAm 92, WhoWor 93*
Brown, Olivia *ScF&FL 92*
Brown, Ollie Dawkins 1941- *WhoAm 92, WhoSSW 93, WhoWor 93*
Brown, Omer Forrest, II 1947- *WhoEmL 93*
Brown, Oscar *BioIn 17*
Brown, Oscar, Jr. 1926- *WhoAm 92*
Brown, Owsley, II 1942- *WhoSSW 93*
Brown, Palmer *BioIn 17*
Brown, Pamela Anne 1953- *WhoAmW 93*
Brown, Pamela Beatrice 1924-1989 *BioIn 17*
Brown, Pamela Joy Clark 1954- *WhoE 93*
Brown, Pamela S. *Law&B 92*
Brown, Pamela Wedd 1928- *WhoE 93*
Brown, Para Jean 1946- *WhoAmW 93*
Brown, Patricia *AmWomPl*
Brown, Patricia Anne 1962- *WhoE 93*
Brown, Patricia Cochran 1955- *WhoE 93, WhoEmL 93*
Brown, Patricia Griffith 1953- *WhoAmW 93*
Brown, Patricia Irene *WhoAmW 93, WhoE 93, WhoWor 93*
Brown, Patricia L. *Law&B 92*
Brown, Patricia Leonard 1950- *WhoEmL 93*
Brown, Patricia MacDonald 1947- *WhoAmW 93*
Brown, Patricia Mary 1945- *WhoAmW 93*
Brown, Paul 1908-1991 *AnObit 1991, BioIn 17, News 92*
Brown, Paul A. 1938- *WhoAm 92, WhoSSW 93*
Brown, Paul Appleton 1938- *St&PR 93*
Brown, Paul B. 1954- *ConAu 138*
Brown, Paul Bradley 1912- *WhoAm 92*
Brown, Paul Edmondson 1915- *WhoWor 93*
Brown, Paul G. 1955- *St&PR 93*
Brown, Paul Lee 1938- *WhoE 93*
Brown, Paul M. 1938- *WhoAm 92*
Brown, Paul Neeley 1926- *WhoAm 92, WhoSSW 93*
Brown, Paul Sherman 1921- *WhoWor 93*
Brown, Paul Truett 1954- *WhoEmL 93*
Brown, Paul W. 1915- *WhoAm 92*
Brown, Paul Woodrow 1919- *WhoE 93*
Brown, Paula Kinney 1953- *WhoAmW 93*
Brown, Peggy 1936- *WhoE 93*
Brown, Peggy Sims 1950- *WhoAmW 93*
Brown, Peter A. 1949- *ConAu 138*
Brown, Peter Campbell 1913- *WhoWor 93*
Brown, Peter David Gilson 1943- *WhoE 93*
Brown, Peter Duke 1948- *WhoAm 92*
Brown, Peter E. *WhoScE 91-1*
Brown, Peter Gilbert 1940- *WhoAm 92*
Brown, Peter John *WhoScE 91-1*
Brown, Peter John 1951- *WhoSSW 93*
Brown, Peter Megargee 1922- *WhoAm 92*
Brown, Peter Ogden 1940- *WhoE 93*
Brown, Peter Stone 1951- *WhoE 93*
Brown, Peter T. *Law&B 92*
Brown, Philip Henry 1952- *WhoE 93, WhoEmL 93, WhoWor 93*
Brown, Phillip S. *Law&B 92*
Brown, Phillip S. 1936- *St&PR 93*
Brown, Phyllis George *BioIn 17*
Brown, Polly Sarah 1952- *WhoAmW 93, WhoWor 93*
Brown, Preston 1936- *WhoAm 92*
Brown, Quincalee 1939- *WhoAm 92, WhoAmW 93*
Brown, R. *WhoScE 91-1*
Brown, R. Harper 1923- *WhoAm 92*
Brown, R.J., Mrs. *AmWomPl*
Brown, R. Jess *BioIn 17*
Brown, Ralph 1914-1990 *BioIn 17*
Brown, Ralph Edward 1943- *St&PR 93*
Brown, Ralph Evan 1920- *WhoAm 92*
Brown, Ralph S., Jr. *Law&B 92*
Brown, Ralph Sawyer, Jr. 1931- *WhoAm 92*
Brown, Randolph Graham 1942 *St&PR 93*
Brown, Randy Lee 1963- *WhoWor 93*
Brown, Ray *BioIn 17*
Brown, Ray Kent 1924- *WhoAm 92*
Brown, Ray(mond Matthews) 1926- *Baker 92*
Brown, Ray Nowlin 1951- *WhoEmL 93*
Brown, Ray William 1929- *St&PR 93*
Brown, Raymond Jessie 1944- *WhoSSW 93, WhoWor 93*
Brown, Raymond Lloyd 1936- *WhoAm 92*
Brown, Raymond Martin 1946- *WhoEmL 93*
Brown, Raymond Paul 1927- *St&PR 93*
Brown, Raymond R. *Law&B 92*
Brown, Rayner 1912- *Baker 92*
Brown, Rebecca 1956- *ScF&FL 92*
Brown, Rebecca Bard *ScF&FL 92*
Brown, Reginald Harvey 1933- *WhoWor 93*
Brown, Reginald Jude 1940- *WhoAm 92*
Brown, Rhonda *BioIn 17*
Brown, Rhonda Rochelle 1956- *WhoAmW 93*
Brown, Rich 1942- *ScF&FL 92*
Brown, Richard *St&PR 93*
Brown, Richard A. 1940- *St&PR 93*
Brown, Richard Burton, Jr. 1946- *WhoSSW 93*
Brown, Richard C. 1937- *WhoAm 92, WhoWor 93*
Brown, Richard Clark 1939- *WhoSSW 93*
Brown, Richard Dean 1941- *WhoSSW 93*
Brown, Richard Dee 1938- *WhoSSW 93*
Brown, Richard Eric 1946- *BioIn 17*
Brown, Richard Frederick *BioIn 17*
Brown, Richard George 1923- *St&PR 93*
Brown, Richard H. 1947- *St&PR 93*
Brown, Richard H(arvey) 1940- *ConAu 38NR*
Brown, Richard Harris 1947- *WhoAm 92*
Brown, Richard Holbrook 1927- *WhoAm 92*
Brown, Richard James 1944- *St&PR 93, WhoAm 92*
Brown, Richard Jess, Sr. 1912-1989 *EncAACR*
Brown, Richard Kevin 1956- *WhoEmL 93*
Brown, Richard L. 1938- *WhoIns 93*
Brown, Richard Laurence 1962- *WhoE 93*
Brown, Richard LaVerne 1943- *WhoE 93*
Brown, Richard Lawrence 1932- *WhoWor 93*
Brown, Richard Lee 1925- *WhoAm 92*
Brown, Richard M. *Law&B 92*
Brown, Richard M. 1942- *WhoAm 92*
Brown, Richard Maurice 1924- *WhoAm 92*
Brown, Richard N. 1933- *St&PR 93*
Brown, Richard Oliver 1952- *WhoSSW 93*
Brown, Richard P., Jr. 1920- *WhoAm 92*
Brown, Richard Paul 1935- *St&PR 93*
Brown, Richard S. *Law&B 92*
Brown, Richard Searl 1946- *WhoEmL 93*
Brown, Richard Stanley 1951- *St&PR 93*
Brown, Richard T., III *Law&B 92*
Brown, Richard W. 1943- *St&PR 93*
Brown, Rick 1946- *BioIn 17*
Brown, Rita Mae *BioIn 17*
Brown, Rita Mae 1944- *ScF&FL 92, WhoAm 92, WhoWrEP 92*
Brown, Robert 1931- *WhoAm 92*
Brown, Robert 1949- *WhoEmL 93*
Brown, Robert A. *WhoScE 91-1*
Brown, Robert A. 1930- *St&PR 93*
Brown, Robert Alan 1930- *WhoAm 92*
Brown, Robert Alan 1943- *WhoAm 92*
Brown, Robert Allen 1954- *WhoEmL 93*
Brown, Robert Arthur 1951- *WhoAm 92*
Brown, Robert Cecil *Law&B 92*
Brown, Robert Cecil 1928- *WhoE 93*
Brown, Robert Charles 1926- *St&PR 93*
Brown, Robert Charles 1954- *WhoEmL 93*
Brown, Robert Curtis 1920- *WhoAm 92*
Brown, Robert Delford 1930- *WhoAm 92*
Brown, Robert Edward 1930- *WhoSSW 93*
Brown, Robert Edward 1949- *WhoE 93*
Brown, Robert Ellis 1945- *WhoAm 92*
Brown, Robert Francis 1934- *WhoScE 91-1*
Brown, Robert Frederick 1944- *WhoSSW 93*
Brown, Robert Glenn 1940- *WhoAm 92*
Brown, Robert Goodell 1923- *St&PR 93, WhoAm 92*
Brown, Robert Graham *WhoScE 91-1*
Brown, Robert Grover 1926- *WhoAm 92*
Brown, Robert Haines 1938- *WhoE 93*
Brown, Robert Harold 1921- *WhoAm 92*
Brown, Robert Horatio 1917- *WhoAm 92*
Brown, Robert Howard 1947- *WhoEmL 93*
Brown, Robert Howard 1967- *WhoSSW 93*
Brown, Robert Hugh 1959- *WhoWrEP 92*
Brown, Robert James 1933- *WhoAsAP 91*
Brown, Robert James 1935- *WhoIns 93*
Brown, Robert K. 1922- *St&PR 93*
Brown, Robert L. 1945- *St&PR 93*
Brown, Robert L. 1947- *AfrAmBi [port]*
Brown, Robert L., Jr. *AfrAmBi [port]*
Brown, Robert Laidlaw 1941- *WhoAm 92, WhoSSW 93*
Brown, Robert Larry *Law&B 92*
Brown, Robert Lee 1908- *WhoAm 92*
Brown, Robert Lyle 1920- *WhoAm 92*
Brown, Robert M. 1947- *St&PR 93*
Brown, Robert McAfee 1920- *WhoAm 92*
Brown, Robert Mott, III 1947- *WhoE 93*
Brown, Robert Parkin, Jr. 1943- *St&PR 93*
Brown, Robert Richard 1937- *St&PR 93*
Brown, Robert Scott 1959- *WhoSSW 93*
Brown, Robert T. 1936- *St&PR 93*
Brown, Robert Tennant 1932- *WhoUN 92*
Brown, Robert Tindall 1940- *WhoSSW 93*
Brown, Robert W. *Law&B 92*
Brown, Robert Wallace 1925- *WhoAm 92*
Brown, Robert Wayne 1942- *WhoAm 92*
Brown, Robert Weaver, Jr. 1946- *St&PR 93*
Brown, Robert William 1924- *WhoAm 92*
Brown, Rodney Howard 1956- *WhoSSW 93*
Brown, Rodney Morgan 1949- *WhoEmL 93*
Brown, Roger 1915- *WhoSSW 93*
Brown, Roger Alan *Law&B 92*
Brown, Roger Alan 1948- *WhoEmL 93*
Brown, Roger L. 1957- *St&PR 93*
Brown, Roger Oscar 1925- *WhoAm 92*
Brown, Roger Philip 1940- *WhoScE 91-1, WhoWor 93*
Brown, Roger S. 1927- *St&PR 93*
Brown, Roger W. 1929- *St&PR 93*
Brown, Roger William 1925- *WhoAm 92*
Brown, Ron *BioIn 17*
Brown, Ronald *WhoScE 91-1*
Brown, Ronald 1930- *WhoAm 92*
Brown, Ronald 1933- *WhoAm 92*
Brown, Ronald 1941- *AfrAmBi*
Brown, Ronald A. 1935- *St&PR 93*
Brown, Ronald Arthur 1954- *WhoWrEP 92*
Brown, Ronald C. *Law&B 92*
Brown, Ronald C. 1929- *St&PR 93*
Brown, Ronald Craig 1954- *St&PR 93*
Brown, Ronald Dean 1950- *WhoEmL 93*
Brown, Ronald Dee 1933- *St&PR 93*
Brown, Ronald Earl 1950- *St&PR 93*
Brown, Ronald G. 1938- *St&PR 93*
Brown, Ronald Harmon 1941- *WhoAm 92*
Brown, Ronald James 1953- *WhoE 93*
Brown, Ronald Lee 1946- *WhoEmL 93*
Brown, Ronald Osborne 1941- *WhoE 93*
Brown, Ronnie Louis 1951- *St&PR 93*
Brown, Roosevelt 1932- *BioIn 17*
Brown, Rosalie *WhoWrEP 92*
Brown, Rosellen *BioIn 17*
Brown, Rosemary 1917- *Baker 92*
Brown, Roswyn Ann *WhoScE 91-1*
Brown, Rowine Hayes 1913- *WhoAm 92*
Brown, Rowland Chauncey Widrig 1923- *WhoAm 92*
Brown, Roxanne 1947- *WhoAmW 93*
Brown, Roy *WhoSSW 93*
Brown, Roy 1925-1981 *SoulM*
Brown, Rupert *ScF&FL 92*
Brown, Russell Wayne 1949- *St&PR 93*
Brown, Ruth *BioIn 17, WhoAm 92, WhoAmW 93*
Brown, Ruth 1928- *SoulM*
Brown, S.M. Henry, Jr. 1938- *WhoE 93*
Brown, S. Spencer N. 1920- *St&PR 93*
Brown, Sally *Law&B 92*
Brown, Samuel 1908- *WhoSSW 93*
Brown, Samuel, Jr. 1939- *WhoSSW 93*
Brown, Samuel Joseph, Jr. 1941- *WhoAm 92, WhoSSW 93, WhoWor 93*
Brown, Samuel Preston 1913- *St&PR 93, WhoAm 92*
Brown, Sandra 1948- *ConAu 139*
Brown, Sandra Ann 1953- *WhoAmW 93*
Brown, Sandra Jean 1936- *St&PR 93, WhoAm 92, WhoAmW 93*
Brown, Sandra L. 1942- *St&PR 93*
Brown, Sandra Louise Palmer *WhoAmW 93*
Brown, Sandy *BioIn 17*
Brown, Sara Lou 1942- *WhoAmW 93*
Brown, Sarah Carnes 1926- *WhoSSW 93*
Brown, Sarah Ruth 1956- *WhoEmL 93*
Brown, Scott Hamilton *Law&B 92*
Brown, Scott Keith 1960- *WhoWrEP 92*
Brown, Scott M. *Law&B 92*
Brown, Scott M. 1945- *St&PR 93*
Brown, Seymour R. 1924- *WhoAm 92*
Brown, Seymour William 1914- *WhoAm 92*
Brown, Seyom 1933- *WhoAm 92*
Brown, Sharie Anita *Law&B 92*
Brown, Sharon *WhoWrEP 92*
Brown, Sharon Elizabeth 1960- *WhoAmW 93, WhoEmL 93*
Brown, Sharon Gail 1941- *WhoAmW 93, WhoWor 93*
Brown, Sharon Hendrickson 1944- *WhoAmW 93*
Brown, Shelley B. *Law&B 92*
Brown, Shirley *AmWomPl*
Brown, Shirley 1947- *SoulM*
Brown, Shirley Ann 1935- *WhoAmW 93*
Brown, Shirley Mark 1924- *WhoAmW 93*
Brown, Sidney DeVere 1925- *WhoSSW 93*
Brown, Sneaky Pie *ScF&FL 92*
Brown, Spencer 1909- *WhoWrEP 92*
Brown, Spencer, Jr. 1954- *St&PR 93*
Brown, Spencer Hunter 1928- *WhoAm 92*
Brown, Stanley *DcCPCAm*
Brown, Stanley B. *WhoScE 91-1*
Brown, Stanley G. 1945- *St&PR 93*
Brown, Stephanie B. 1943- *WhoAmW 93*
Brown, Stephanie Barry 1943- *St&PR 93*
Brown, Stephanie Diane 1944- *WhoAmW 93*
Brown, Stephen 1952- *WhoAm 92*
Brown, Stephen Andrew 1955- *WhoE 93*
Brown, Stephen B. *Law&B 92*
Brown, Stephen Bernard 1939- *St&PR 93*
Brown, Stephen C. *Law&B 92*
Brown, Stephen C. 1947- *St&PR 93*
Brown, Stephen Frederick *WhoScE 91-1*
Brown, Stephen Frederick 1939- *WhoWor 93*
Brown, Stephen Ira 1938- *WhoAm 92*
Brown, Stephen Joseph 1957- *WhoEmL 93*
Brown, Stephen Kevin 1951- *WhoWor 93*
Brown, Stephen Lamar 1949- *WhoEmL 93*
Brown, Stephen Landesman 1938- *WhoAm 92, WhoE 93*
Brown, Stephen Lee 1937- *St&PR 93, WhoAm 92*
Brown, Stephen Michael 1950- *WhoE 93*
Brown, Stephen Neal 1952- *WhoEmL 93*
Brown, Stephen Smiley 1952- *WhoEmL 93*
Brown, Stephen Thomas 1947- *WhoEmL 93, WhoSSW 93*
Brown, Stephen William 1952- *WhoWor 93*
Brown, Sterling Allen 1901-1989 *BioIn 17*
Brown, Steven Ford 1952- *WhoE 93, WhoWrEP 92*
Brown, Steven Odell 1951- *WhoEmL 93*
Brown, Steven Spencer 1948- *WhoEmL 93*
Brown, Steven Thomas 1961- *WhoSSW 93*
Brown, Steven Wayne *Law&B 92*
Brown, Steven Wesley 1955- *WhoEmL 93*
Brown, Stillman B. 1933- *St&PR 93*
Brown, Stratton Shartel 1923- *WhoAm 92*
Brown, Stuart I. 1933- *WhoAm 92*
Brown, Susan Ann 1948- *St&PR 93*
Brown, Susan Franklin *St&PR 93*
Brown, Susan Gary 1956- *WhoSSW 93*
Brown, Susan L. *BioIn 17*
Brown, Susan O'Connor 1952- *WhoAm 92*
Brown, Susan Silver *BioIn 17*
Brown, Suzanne *BioIn 17*
Brown, Suzanne C. 1956- *St&PR 93*
Brown, Suzanne Wiley 1938- *WhoAmW 93*
Brown, Sybil Arlene 1959- *WhoAmW 93*
Brown, Sylvia 1946- *WhoEmL 93*
Brown, Tamil Lewis *Law&B 92*
Brown, Ted Leon, Jr. 1956- *WhoEmL 93, WhoSSW 93*
Brown, Temple Nix 1930- *St&PR 93*
Brown, Terence Michael 1941- *WhoAm 92*
Brown, Teresa A. *AmWomPl*
Brown, Terrence C. *Law&B 92*
Brown, Terrence Charles 1949- *WhoAm 92*
Brown, Terrezene *BlkAmWO*
Brown, Terry Ellis *Law&B 92*
Brown, Tex *BioIn 17*
Brown, Theodore Lawrence 1928- *WhoAm 92*
Brown, Theodore Morey 1925- *WhoAm 92*
Brown, Theodore Ralph 1951- *WhoEmL 93*
Brown, Thoedore D. 1944- *WhoE 93*
Brown, Thomas Allan 1942- *WhoIns 93*
Brown, Thomas Andrew 1932- *WhoAm 92*
Brown, Thomas B. 1927- *St&PR 93, WhoAm 92*
Brown, Thomas D., Jr. *Law&B 92*
Brown, Thomas E., Jr. *AfrAmBi [port]*
Brown, Thomas Ellis 1946- *WhoEmL 93*
Brown, Thomas Glenn 1948- *WhoE 93*
Brown, Thomas H. 1941- *WhoE 93*
Brown, Thomas Huntington 1945- *WhoE 93*
Brown, Thomas J. 1949- *WhoAm 92*
Brown, Thomas James 1949- *St&PR 93*
Brown, Thomas Neil 1951- *WhoEmL 93*
Brown, Thomas O. 1929- *St&PR 93*
Brown, Thomas Philip, III 1931- *WhoAm 92*
Brown, Timothy Bruce 1960- *WhoEmL 93*
Brown, Timothy Charles 1950- *St&PR 93, WhoSSW 93*
Brown, Timothy Donnell 1966- *BiDAMSp 1989*
Brown, Timothy Glynn *Law&B 92*
Brown, Timothy J. 1949- *St&PR 93*
Brown, Timothy L. 1940- *WhoIns 93*
Brown, Timothy Louis 1950- *WhoEmL 93*
Brown, Timothy Shawn 1961- *WhoE 93*
Brown, Timothy Stuart 1949- *WhoE 93*
Brown, Tina *BioIn 17, NewYTBS 92 [port]*
Brown, Tina 1953- *News 92 [port], WhoAm 92, WhoAmW 93, WhoE 93*
Brown, Tod David 1936- *WhoAm 92*
Brown, Tom 1913-1990 *BioIn 17*
Brown, Tony *MiSFD 9*
Brown, Tony 1933- *ConBlB 3 [port]*
Brown, Tony R. 1939- *St&PR 93*
Brown, Trevor Ernest 1939- *WhoWor 93*
Brown, Trisha *BioIn 17, WhoAm 92, WhoAmW 93*
Brown, Troy Anderson, Jr. 1934- *St&PR 93, WhoAm 92*

Brown, Valerie Anne 1951- *WhoAmW 93*
Brown, Vanessa J. *Law&B 92*
Brown, Victoria Regenia 1952- *WhoAmW 93*
Brown, Vincent *BioIn 17*
Brown, Vincent G. 1940- *St&PR 93*
Brown, Viola Gardner *AmWomPl*
Brown, Virginia *WhoAmW 93*
Brown, Virginia Mae 1923-1991 *BioIn 17*
Brown, Virginia Royall Inness- d1990 *BioIn 17*
Brown, Virginia Suggs 1924- *BlkAuII 92*
Brown, Vivian D. *BlkAmWO [port]*
Brown, W.G. *Law&B 92*
Brown, Wallace Lamar 1926- *WhoSSW 93*
Brown, Wally 1898-1961 & Carney, Alan 1911-1973 *QDrFCA 92 [port]*
Brown, Walston S. 1908- *St&PR 93*
Brown, Walston Shepard 1908- *WhoAm 92*
Brown, Walter E. 1915- *St&PR 93*
Brown, Walter Folger 1869-1961 *BioIn 17, EncABHB 8 [port]*
Brown, Walter Franklin 1952- *WhoEmL 93*
Brown, Walter Lyons 1924- *WhoAm 92*
Brown, Walter Ward 1939- *St&PR 93*
Brown, Warren Joseph 1924- *WhoAm 92*
Brown, Warren Ted 1951- *St&PR 93*
Brown, Wayne W. 1940- *St&PR 93*
Brown, Weir Messick 1914- *WhoE 93*
Brown, Wendy Elaine 1956- *WhoAmW 93*
Brown, Wendy R. *BioIn 17*
Brown, Wentworth 1905-1991 *BioIn 17*
Brown, Wenzell 1911-1981 *ScF&FL 92*
Brown, Wesley Ernest 1907- *WhoAm 92*
Brown, Willet Henry 1905- *WhoAm 92*
Brown, William fl. 18th cent.- *Baker 92*
Brown, William A. *Law&B 92*
Brown, William A. 1957- *WhoEmL 93*
Brown, William A., Jr. *St&PR 93*
Brown, William Anthony 1933- *AfrAmBi*
Brown, William Avon 1924- *St&PR 93*
Brown, William Clifford 1911- *St&PR 93, WhoAm 92*
Brown, William Edward 1904-1989 *BioIn 17*
Brown, William Ernest 1922- *WhoAm 92*
Brown, William Ewart 1928- *St&PR 93*
Brown, William F. *Law&B 92*
Brown, William Ferdinand 1928- *WhoAm 92*
Brown, William G. *St&PR 93*
Brown, William Gardner 1942- *WhoAm 92*
Brown, William Glenn *ScF&FL 92*
Brown, William H. 1941- *St&PR 93*
Brown, William Hill, III 1928- *WhoAm 92*
Brown, William Holmes 1929- *WhoAm 92*
Brown, William J. *Law&B 92*
Brown, William Jones, II 1947- *St&PR 93*
Brown, William L. 1922- *St&PR 93, WhoAm 92*
Brown, William Lacy 1913-1991 *BioIn 17*
Brown, William Lee Lyons, Jr. 1936- *St&PR 93, WhoAm 92, WhoSSW 93*
Brown, William Lewis 1926- *WhoE 93*
Brown, William M. 1942- *St&PR 93, WhoIns 93*
Brown, William Milton 1932- *WhoAm 92*
Brown, William Morris, Jr. 1926- *WhoSSW 93*
Brown, William P. 1919- *St&PR 93*
Brown, William Paul 1919- *WhoAm 92*
Brown, William R. *Law&B 92*
Brown, William R. 1939- *WhoAm 92, WhoIns 93*
Brown, William Randall 1913- *WhoAm 92*
Brown, William Robert 1926- *WhoAm 92*
Brown, William Thacher 1947- *WhoAm 92*
Brown, Willie *BioIn 17*
Brown, Willie L., Jr. 1934- *AfrAmBi [port]*
Brown, Willie Lewis, Jr. *BioIn 17*
Brown, Willie Lewis, Jr. 1934- *WhoAm 92*
Brown, Wilson 1882-1957 *HarEnMi*
Brown, Wilson Gordon 1914- *WhoAm 92*
Brown, Winfield J., Jr. *Law&B 92*
Brown, Wood, III 1936- *WhoAm 92*
Brown, Wynford 1934- *WhoScE 91-4*
Brown, Yvonne Lynn *Law&B 92*
Brown, Zack *BioIn 17*
Brown, Zane Eric 1957- *WhoEmL 93*
Brownawell, Carolyn Elizabeth 1959- *WhoAmW 93*
Brownback, Thomas Samuel 1946- *WhoWor 93*
Brown-Cochrane, Andrea Kane 1962- *WhoAmW 93, WhoEmL 93*
Browne, Aldis J., Jr. 1912- *St&PR 93*
Browne, Aldis Jerome, Jr. 1912- *WhoWor 93*
Browne, Alice Pauline 1918- *WhoWrEP 92*
Browne, Alice Wilson *AmWomPl*
Browne, Anna Therese 1958- *WhoEmL 93*
Browne, Anthony *BioIn 17*
Browne, Anthony 1946- *WhoAm 92*
Browne, Anthony (Edward Tudor) 1946- *MajAI [port]*
Browne, Barum 1898-1951 *ScF&FL 92*
Browne, Brooks Halsey 1949- *St&PR 93, WhoAm 92, WhoEmL 93*
Browne, C.J. *ScF&FL 92*
Browne, Charles Farrar 1834-1867 *NinCLC 37 [port]*
Browne, Charles Idol 1922- *WhoAm 92*
Browne, Charlie 1948- *WhoE 93, WhoEmL 93*
Browne, Coral 1913-1991 *AnObit 1991, BioIn 17, ConTFT 10*
Browne, Cornelius Payne 1923- *WhoAm 92*
Browne, Diana Gayle 1924- *WhoAm 92, WhoAmW 93*
Browne, Dik 1917-1989 *BioIn 17*
Browne, Donald Roger 1934- *WhoAm 92*
Browne, Donald Victor *BioIn 17*
Browne, Donald Victor 1943- *WhoE 93*
Browne, Edmond Patrick 1939- *St&PR 93*
Browne, Edmund John Phillip 1948- *WhoWor 93*
Browne, Edward 1946- *St&PR 93*
Browne, F. Sedgwick 1942- *WhoAm 92*
Browne, Frances 1816-1879 *BioIn 17*
Browne, G. Morgan 1935- *St&PR 93*
Browne, George Sheldon *ScF&FL 92*
Browne, Gerald A. 1928- *ScF&FL 92*
Browne, Gerald Michael 1943- *WhoAm 92*
Browne, Gregory Stephen 1949- *WhoWor 93*
Browne, Henriette *AmWomPl*
Browne, Howard Storm 1925- *WhoE 93*
Browne, Jackson *WhoAm 92*
Browne, Jackson 1948- *Baker 92*
Browne, James J. 1953- *WhoScE 91-3*
Browne, Jeffrey Francis 1944- *WhoAm 92, WhoE 93*
Browne, John Charles 1942- *WhoAm 92*
Browne, John Lewis 1864-1933 *Baker 92*
Browne, John Paul *Law&B 92*
Browne, John R., Sr. 1914- *St&PR 93*
Browne, John Robinson 1914- *WhoAm 92*
Browne, Jonathan Herbert 1954- *St&PR 93*
Browne, Joseph *ScF&FL 92*
Browne, Joseph Peter 1929- *WhoWor 93*
Browne, Juanita Kathryn 1929- *WhoAmW 93*
Browne, Kingsbury 1922- *WhoAm 92*
Browne, Larry Robert 1948- *WhoEmL 93*
Browne, Larry W. *Law&B 92*
Browne, Larry W. 1945- *St&PR 93*
Browne, Leslie 1957- *WhoAm 92*
Browne, Lucile 1907-1976 *SweetSg C [port]*
Browne, Mabel Montgomery *AmWomPl*
Browne, Malcolm Wilde 1931- *WhoAm 92*
Browne, Marshall Gilmore 1926- *St&PR 93*
Browne, Martin Robert 1950- *St&PR 93*
Browne, Matthew *Law&B 92*
Browne, Michael Dennis 1940- *WhoAm 92, WhoWrEP 92*
Browne, Michael Leon 1946- *WhoAm 92, WhoWor 93*
Browne, Millard Child 1915- *WhoAm 92*
Browne, Morgan Trew 1919- *WhoAm 92, WhoWrEP 92*
Browne, Nelson 1908- *ScF&FL 92*
Browne, Orla M. 1933- *WhoScE 91-3*
Browne, Peter Francis *ScF&FL 92*
Browne, Ray B. 1922- *ScF&FL 92*
Browne, Ray Broadus 1922- *WhoAm 92*
Browne, Renni 1939- *WhoWrEP 92*
Browne, Reno Blair *SweetSg C [port]*
Browne, Richard F. *Law&B 92*
Browne, Robert *ScF&FL 92*
Browne, Robert 1550?-1633? *BioIn 17*
Browne, Robert G. 1941- *St&PR 93*
Browne, Robert Span 1924- *WhoAm 92*
Browne, Robert Thomas 1950- *St&PR 93*
Browne, Roger Michael *WhoScE 91-1*
Browne, Roscoe Lee *WhoAm 92*
Browne, Shirley Annette 1952- *WhoAm 92*
Browne, Spencer I. 1949- *St&PR 93*
Browne, Stanhope Stryker 1931- *WhoAm 92*
Browne, Stephen Francis 1949- *WhoUN 92*
Browne, Steven Emery 1950- *WhoEmL 93*
Browne, Thomas L. 1930- *St&PR 93*
Browne, Walter Shawn 1949- *WhoAm 92*
Browne, William Bitner 1914- *WhoAm 92*
Browne, William Thomas 1934- *St&PR 93*
Browne-Evans, Lois 1927- *DcCPCAm*
Brownell, Blaine Allison 1942- *WhoAm 92, WhoSSW 93*
Brownell, Charles E(dward), III 1943- *ConAu 139*
Brownell, David Paul 1944- *St&PR 93, WhoAm 92*
Brownell, David Wheaton 1941- *WhoAm 92, WhoWrEP 92*
Brownell, Edwin Rowland 1924- *WhoAm 92, WhoSSW 93*
Brownell, Eugene Bronson 1908- *St&PR 93*
Brownell, Evelyn B. *AmWomPl*
Brownell, Gordon Lee 1922- *WhoAm 92*
Brownell, Herbert 1904- *BioIn 17*
Brownell, Herbert, Jr. 1904- *PolPar*
Brownell, Hiram Henry 1952- *WhoE 93*
Brownell, James Garland 1933- *WhoWrEP 92*
Brownell, John Arnold 1924- *WhoAm 92*
Brownell, Joyce E. Tarrier 1942- *WhoWrEP 92*
Brownell, Kelly David 1951- *WhoE 93*
Brownell, Lloyd 1912- *St&PR 93*
Brownell, Mary Alice *AmWomPl*
Brownell, Michael Patrick *Law&B 92*
Brownell, Richard *Law&B 92*
Brownell, Samuel Miller 1900-1990 *BioIn 17*
Brownell, W.C. 1851-1928 *GayN*
Browne-Miller, Angela Christine 1952- *WhoAmW 93*
Browne of Tavistock, William c. 1590-1645 *DcLB 121 [port]*
Browner, Carole Helen 1947- *WhoEmL 93*
Browner, Francine 1945- *WhoAmW 93*
Browner, George Robert, Jr. 1932- *St&PR 93*
Browner, Julius Harvey 1930- *WhoSSW 93*
Browner, Richard Frederick 1944- *WhoSSW 93*
Browner, Ross 1954- *BiDAMSp 1989*
Browner, William Allen *Law&B 92*
Brown-Evarts, Edith *AmWomPl*
Browne-Wilkinson, Hilary Isabel Jane 1941- *WhoWor 93*
Brownfield, Charles William 1941- *WhoWor 93*
Brownfield, Debbie 1954- *St&PR 93*
Brownfield, Irma 1931- *WhoAmW 93*
Brownfield, Jeri M. 1960- *WhoSSW 93*
Brownfield, Thomas Allen 1943- *St&PR 93*
Brown-Foster, Arnita Christine 1950- *WhoEmL 93*
Brown-Griffin, Shelley Elizabeth 1949- *WhoE 93*
Brown-Guillory, Elizabeth *BioIn 17*
Brown-Guillory, Elizabeth 1954- *WhoSSW 93*
Brownhill, Bud H. 1941- *WhoWor 93*
Brownhill, David Gordon Cadell 1935- *WhoAsAP 91*
Brownhill, Toni Robeck 1946- *WhoAmW 93*
Browning, Alan Dwight 1940- *St&PR 93*
Browning, Bernard S. 1923- *St&PR 93*
Browning, Calvin 1937- *St&PR 93*
Browning, Carroll Welles 1916- *WhoAm 92*
Browning, Charles Benton 1931- *WhoAm 92*
Browning, Christine *BioIn 17*
Browning, Christopher Corwin 1956- *WhoEmL 93*
Browning, Colin A. 1935- *St&PR 93*
Browning, Colin Arrott 1935- *WhoAm 92, WhoE 93, WhoWor 93*
Browning, Colleen Applegate 1938- *WhoAmW 93*
Browning, Daniel Dwight 1921- *WhoAm 92*
Browning, Daphne *ScF&FL 92*
Browning, David S. *Law&B 92*
Browning, David Stuart 1939- *St&PR 93, WhoAm 92*
Browning, Deborah Lea 1955- *WhoEmL 93*
Browning, Dick Emerson 1950- *WhoEmL 93*
Browning, Dixie 1930- *ScF&FL 92*
Browning, Don Spencer 1934- *WhoAm 92*
Browning, Edmond Lee *WhoAm 92*
Browning, Elizabeth 1933- *WhoWrEP 92*
Browning, Elizabeth Barrett 1806-1861 *BioIn 17, MagSWL [port], PoeCrit 6 [port], WorLitC [port]*
Browning, Frank W. 1937- *WhoIns 93*
Browning, Frederick M. *St&PR 93*
Browning, Grayson Douglas 1929- *WhoAm 92*
Browning, Henry Prentice 1911- *WhoAm 92*
Browning, Iben *BioIn 17*
Browning, James Alexander 1922- *WhoAm 92*
Browning, James Franklin 1923- *WhoAm 92*
Browning, James Robert 1918- *WhoAm 92*
Browning, Jean H. *St&PR 93*
Browning, John 1933- *Baker 92, WhoAm 92*
Browning, John Huntington 1933- *St&PR 93*
Browning, John Moses 1855-1926 *BioIn 17*
Browning, K.A. *WhoScE 91-1*
Browning, Kirk 1921- *MiSFD 9*
Browning, Kurt *BioIn 17*
Browning, Leslie Chadwick *AmWomPl*
Browning, Linda Kathryn *Law&B 92*
Browning, Michael Gorry *WhoAm 92*
Browning, Norma Lee 1914- *WhoAm 92*
Browning, Pamela 1942- *ScF&FL 92, WhoWrEP 92*
Browning, Peter Crane 1941- *WhoAm 92, WhoSSW 93, WhoWor 93*
Browning, Reed S. 1938- *WhoAm 92*
Browning, Reyburn Engle 1933- *St&PR 93*
Browning, Richard Arlen 1941- *WhoAm 92*
Browning, Richard Edward 1955- *WhoEmL 93*
Browning, Robert 1812-1889 *BioIn 17, MagSWL [port], OxDcOp*
Browning, Robert 1928- *ScF&FL 92*
Browning, Robert Masters 1912- *WhoAm 92*
Browning, Roberta Fullerton 1937- *WhoAmW 93*
Browning, Roderick Hanson 1925- *WhoAm 92*
Browning, Ronald C. *St&PR 93*
Browning, Scot R. 1962- *St&PR 93*
Browning, Susan 1939- *St&PR 93*
Browning, Tod 1882-1962 *MiSFD 9N*
Browning, Tom *BioIn 17*
Browning, Tom 1949- *BioIn 17*
Browning, Walter Graham *Law&B 92*
Browning, Warren W. 1927- *St&PR 93*
Browning, William Docker 1931- *WhoAm 92*
Browning, William E.S. 1932- *St&PR 93*
Browning, William Elkins *Law&B 92*
Browning, Wilt *BioIn 17*
Browning-Sletten, Melissa Ann 1947- *WhoAmW 93*
Brown-Jagnow, Betty J.H. 1929- *St&PR 93*
Brownjohn, Alan 1931- *ScF&FL 92*
Brownlee, David W. *Law&B 92*
Brownlee, Don Robert 1951- *WhoEmL 93*
Brownlee, Donald Eugene, II 1943- *WhoAm 92*
Brownlee, George Gow *WhoScE 91-1*
Brownlee, John 1900-1969 *Baker 92*
Brownlee, John 1901-1969 *OxDcOp*
Brownlee, Judith Marilyn 1940- *WhoAm 92, WhoAmW 93*
Brownlee, Karen Jeanne 1949- *WhoSSW 93*
Brownlee, Michael Carl 1949- *WhoSSW 93*
Brownlee, Paula P. *BioIn 17*
Brownlee, Paula Pimlott 1934- *WhoAm 92, WhoE 93*
Brownlee, Robert Calvin 1922- *WhoAm 92*
Brownlee, Robert James 1946- *WhoEmL 93, WhoSSW 93*
Brownlee, Thomas Marshall 1926- *WhoAm 92*
Brownlee, W.D. 1930- *BioIn 17*
Brownlee, Walter D. 1930- *BioIn 17*
Brownley, Edwin Allen, Jr. 1948- *St&PR 93*
Brownley, Floyd Irving, Jr. 1918- *WhoAm 92*
Brownley, John Forrest 1942- *St&PR 93*
Brownlie, Edward Carter 1937- *St&PR 93*
Brownlie, Ian 1932- *WhoWor 93*
Brownlie, Ian T. 1939- *St&PR 93*
Brownlie, John *WhoScE 91-1*
Brownlow, Donald Grey 1923- *WhoE 93, WhoWor 93*
Brownlow, Frank Walsh 1934- *WhoAm 92*
Brownlow, James Merritt 1920-1991 *BioIn 17*
Brownlow, Kevin *BioIn 17*
Brownlow, Kevin 1938- *CurBio 92 [port]*
Brownman, Charles H. *Law&B 92*
Brown Manrique, Gerardo 1949- *WhoEmL 93*
Brown Michelson, Linda *WhoWrEP 92*
Brownmiller, Susan *BioIn 17*
Brownmiller, Susan 1935- *WhoAmW 93, WhoWrEP 92*
Brown-Olmstead, Amanda 1943- *WhoAmW 93*
Brown-Paul, Brenda Elaine 1959- *WhoAmW 93*
Brown Premo, Lisa Ann 1956- *WhoEmL 93*
Brownrigg, Judith Hamilton 1950- *WhoAmW 93, WhoEmL 93*
Brownrigg, Walter Grant 1940- *WhoAm 92*
Brownrout, Harvey M. *Law&B 92*
Brown-Sanders, Dorothy Mae 1951- *WhoAmW 93*

Brownson, Anna Louise Harshman 1926- *WhoSSW 93*
Brownson, Bruce B. 1955- *WhoSSW 93*
Brownson, Charles 1945- *WhoWrEP 92*
Brownson, E. Ramona Lidstone Brady 1930- *WhoAmW 93*
Brownson, Jacques Calmon 1923- *WhoAm 92*
Brownson, Mary Wilson *AmWomPl*
Brownson, William Clarence 1928- *WhoAm 92*
Brownstein, Barbara Lavin 1931- *WhoAm 92*
Brownstein, David Kenneth *Law&B 92*
Brownstein, David M. 1958- *St&PR 93*
Brownstein, Howard 1933- *WhoE 93*
Brownstein, Howard Brod 1950- *WhoEmL 93*
Brownstein, Kenneth R. *Law&B 92*
Brownstein, Martin Herbert 1935- *WhoAm 92*
Brownstein, Philip N. 1917- *St&PR 93*
Brownstein, Philip Nathan 1917- *WhoAm 92*
Brownstein, Vivian Carmel 1930- *WhoE 93*
Brownstein-Santiago, Cheryl 1951- *NotHsAW 93 [port]*
Brownstone, Clyde R. 1935- *St&PR 93*
Brownstone, David M. 1928- *WhoWrEP 92*
Brownstone, Hugh Michael 1957- *WhoE 93, WhoEmL 93, WhoWor 93*
Brownstone, Paul Lotan 1923- *WhoAm 92*
Brown Thrush d1992 *BioIn 17*
Brown Thrush, Princess d1992 *NewYTBS 92*
Brown-West, Orikaye Gogo 1945- *WhoE 93*
Brownwood, David Owen 1935- *WhoAm 92, WhoE 93, WhoWor 93*
Browse, Nicholas 1954- *WhoEmL 93*
Browser, Edward M. *St&PR 93*
Brox, Eleanor Andrea 1959- *WhoWrEP 92*
Broxon, Mildred Downey 1944- *ScF&FL 92*
Broxson, Evelyn Lipscomb 1948- *WhoEmL 93*
Broyard, Anatole *BioIn 17*
Broyde, Bernice Andrea 1940- *WhoAmW 93*
Broyden, C.G. 1933- *WhoScE 91-3*
Broyhill, Craig Gary 1948- *St&PR 93*
Broyhill, James Edgar 1954- *ConEn*
Broyhill, Linda Sharon 1951- *WhoEmL 93*
Broyhill, Paul Hunt 1924- *St&PR 93*
Broyhill, Roy F. 1919- *St&PR 93*
Broyhill, Roy Franklin 1919- *WhoWor 93*
Broyles, Arthur Augustus 1923- *WhoSSW 93*
Broyles, John Allen 1934- *WhoSSW 93*
Broyles, Laura Jane 1958- *WhoEmL 93*
Broyles, R.L. *ScF&FL 92*
Broyles, Ruth Rutledge 1912- *WhoSSW 93*
Broyles, Susan Irene 1949- *WhoEmL 93*
Broyles, T.M. 1937- *St&PR 93*
Broyles, Waymon Carroll 1943- *WhoSSW 93*
Broyles, William Dodson, Jr. 1944- *WhoAm 92, WhoWrEP 92*
Broz, Joseph Stephen 1956- *WhoWor 93*
Brozek, Josef 1913- *WhoAm 92, WhoE 93*
Brozek, Richard Carl 1953- *WhoEmL 93*
Brozman, Robert F. d1991 *BioIn 17*
Brozman, Tina L. 1952- *WhoAmW 93*
Brozon, Charles A. 1946- *St&PR 93*
Brozost, Jay A. *Law&B 92*
Brozovic, Dalibor 1927- *WhoWor 93*
Brozovich, Matthew William 1930- *St&PR 93*
Brozozka, Zbigniew 1953- *WhoWor 93*
Brozyna, Jeffry H. *Law&B 92*
Brozzetti, Jacques 1940- *WhoScE 91-2*
Brubach, David J. 1916- *St&PR 93*
Brubach, Holly Beth 1953- *WhoEmL 93*
Brubaker, Anita Faye 1954- *WhoSSW 93*
Brubaker, Beryl Mae Hartzler 1942- *WhoSSW 93*
Brubaker, Carl H., Jr. 1925- *WhoAm 92*
Brubaker, Charles William 1926- *WhoAm 92*
Brubaker, Crawford Francis, Jr. 1924- *WhoAm 92*
Brubaker, David H. 1939- *St&PR 93*
Brubaker, Donald 1935- *St&PR 93*
Brubaker, Earl J. 1922- *St&PR 93*
Brubaker, Edward Stehman 1924- *WhoWrEP 92*
Brubaker, Edwin H. *St&PR 93*
Brubaker, Herman Wallace, Jr. 1954- *WhoEmL 93*
Brubaker, James Clark 1947- *WhoEmL 93*
Brubaker, James Edward 1935- *WhoE 93*
Brubaker, James Robert 1955- *St&PR 93*
Brubaker, John D. 1930- *St&PR 93*
Brubaker, Karen Sue 1953- *WhoAmW 93*
Brubaker, Lauren Edgar 1914- *WhoAm 92*
Brubaker, Lee *BioIn 17*
Brubaker, Michael William 1957- *WhoE 93*
Brubaker, Peter P. 1946- *St&PR 93, WhoEmL 93*
Brubaker, R.C. 1921- *St&PR 93*
Brubaker, Robert Paul 1934- *St&PR 93, WhoAm 92*
Brubaker, Ruth 1959- *WhoEmL 93*
Brubaker, Stephen Charles 1954- *WhoEmL 93*
Brubeck, Anne Elizabeth Denton 1918- *WhoWor 93*
Brubeck, Dave 1920- *Baker 92, BioIn 17, ConMus 8 [port]*
Brubeck, David Haughey 1942- *St&PR 93*
Brubeck, David Warren 1920- *WhoAm 92, WhoWor 93*
Brubeck, Howard R(engstorff) 1916- *Baker 92*
Bruccoli, Matthew J. 1931- *ScF&FL 92*
Bruccoli, Matthew Joseph 1931- *BioIn 17, WhoAm 92, WhoWrEP 92*
Bruce, Alexander *WhoScE 91-1*
Bruce, Amos Jerry, Jr. 1942- *WhoSSW 93*
Bruce, Aundray *BioIn 17*
Bruce, Blanche K. 1841-1898 *EncAACR [port]*
Bruce, Blanche Kelso 1841-1898 *BioIn 17*
Bruce, Charles J. 1953- *WhoIns 93*
Bruce, Charlotte 1921- *WhoE 93*
Bruce, Dania Gayle 1937- *WhoAmW 93*
Bruce, David K.E. 1898-1977 *BioIn 17*
Bruce, David Lionel 1933- *WhoAm 92*
Bruce, David R. 1925- *St&PR 93*
Bruce, David Ray *Law&B 92*
Bruce, Debra 1951- *WhoWrEP 92*
Bruce, Dennis *BioIn 17*
Bruce, Duane N. 1963- *WhoEmL 93*
Bruce, Elizabeth Garnett *Law&B 92*
Bruce, Estel Edward 1938- *WhoAm 92*
Bruce, Evangeline *BioIn 17*
Bruce, F.F 1910-1990 *BioIn 17*
Bruce, Frank B. 1918- *St&PR 93*
Bruce, Frederick Fyvie 1910-1990 *BioIn 17*
Bruce, Gail Clyde 1953- *WhoEmL 93*
Bruce, George Walter, Jr. 1958- *WhoWor 93*
Bruce, Herbert L. d1990 *BioIn 17*
Bruce, I.G. *WhoScE 91-1*
Bruce, Ian James 1956- *WhoWor 93*
Bruce, Jack *BioIn 17*
Bruce, Jack 1943- *See Cream ConMus 9*
Bruce, Jackson Martin, Jr. 1931- *WhoAm 92*
Bruce, James *MiSFD 9*
Bruce, James 1730-1794 *Expl 93 [port]*
Bruce, James Donald 1936- *WhoAm 92*
Bruce, James Edmund 1920- *WhoAm 92*
Bruce, James M. 1942- *WhoScE 91-1*
Bruce, James Masson *WhoScE 91-1*
Bruce, James W. *Law&B 92*
Bruce, James William *WhoScE 91-1*
Bruce, Jill Renee 1956- *WhoAmW 93*
Bruce, Joanna *ScF&FL 92*
Bruce, John Anthony 1931- *WhoWor 93*
Bruce, John Berry 1955- *WhoSSW 93*
Bruce, John Foster 1940- *WhoE 93*
Bruce, John Martin 1930- *WhoAm 92*
Bruce, John Phillip 1932- *WhoSSW 93*
Bruce, Kerry William 1948- *WhoE 93*
Bruce, Kimberly Sue 1959- *St&PR 93*
Bruce, Laurie B. *Law&B 92*
Bruce, Lawrence E., Jr. d1992 *NewYTBS 92 [port]*
Bruce, Lawrence Everett, Jr. 1945- *WhoAm 92*
Bruce, Lenny 1925-1966 *BioIn 17*
Bruce, Lenny 1926-1966 *JeAmHC*
Bruce, Leonard John 1920- *St&PR 93*
Bruce, Linda Faye 1946- *WhoAmW 93, WhoEmL 93*
Bruce, Liza *BioIn 17*
Bruce, Martin Marc 1923- *WhoE 93*
Bruce, Marvin Ernest 1928- *WhoAm 92*
Bruce, Mary Beth 1956- *WhoAmW 93, WhoEmL 93*
Bruce, Nadine Cecile 1942- *WhoAm 92*
Bruce, Neal Douglas 1969- *WhoE 93*
Bruce, (Frank) Neely 1944- *Baker 92*
Bruce, Neil Curtis 1953- *WhoEmL 93*
Bruce, Norman MacDonald 1941- *St&PR 93*
Bruce, Patricia Gray 1953- *WhoEmL 93*
Bruce, Peter W. 1945- *St&PR 93*
Bruce, Peter Wayne 1945- *WhoAm 92*
Bruce, R. Jeffrey 1959- *St&PR 93*
Bruce, Ralph 1916- *St&PR 93*
Bruce, Randall Alton 1954- *St&PR 93*
Bruce, Robert A. *St&PR 93*
Bruce, Robert B. 1931- *St&PR 93*
Bruce, Robert Cecil 1950- *WhoEmL 93*
Bruce, Robert James 1937- *WhoAm 92*
Bruce, Robert R. *Law&B 92*
Bruce, Robert Rockwell 1944- *WhoAm 92*
Bruce, Robert Thomas 1950- *WhoAm 92*
Bruce, Robert Vance 1923- *WhoAm 92, WhoE 93, WhoWrEP 92*
Bruce, Sandra *BioIn 17*
Bruce, Stanley 1883-1967 *DcTwHis*
Bruce, Terry L. 1944- *CngDr 91, WhoAm 92*
Bruce, Thomas Allen 1930- *WhoAm 92, WhoWor 93*
Bruce, Tom Smith 1948- *WhoEmL 93*
Bruce, Victoria Geraldine *WhoScE 91-1*
Bruce, Willa Marie 1938- *WhoAmW 93*
Bruce, William David 1928- *WhoIns 93*
Bruce, William Rankin 1915- *St&PR 93*
Bruce, William Robert 1929- *WhoAm 92*
Brucefoot, Robert *IntDcAn*
Bruce-Novoa, Juan 1944- *HispAmA*
Bruce-Radcliffe, Godfrey Martin 1945- *WhoWor 93*
Bruce-Sanford, Gail Clotilda 1955- *WhoSSW 93*
Bruch, Carol Sophie 1941- *WhoAm 92*
Bruch, Hans-Peter 1947- *WhoScE 91-3*
Bruch, Max 1838-1920 *OxDcOp*
Bruch, Max (Karl August) 1838-1920 *Baker 92*
Brucher, Ernst 1926- *BioIn 17*
Bruchet, Gilbert 1935- *WhoScE 91-2*
Bruchollerie, Monique de la 1915-1972 *Baker 92*
Bruci, Rudolf 1917- *Baker 92*
Bruck, Arnold von c. 1500-1554 *Baker 92*
Bruck, Charles 1911- *Baker 92*
Bruck, Connie Jane 1946- *WhoE 93*
Bruck, Eva Doman 1950- *WhoEmL 93*
Bruck, Ferdinand Frederick 1921- *WhoAm 92*
Bruck, Kurt 1925- *WhoScE 91-3*
Bruck, Lorraine *ScF&FL 92*
Bruck, Peter Michael 1940- *WhoScE 91-3*
Bruck, Phoebe Ann Mason 1928- *WhoAm 92, WhoAmW 93*
Bruck, Rodney L. 1945- *WhoIns 93*
Bruck, Stephen Desiderius 1927- *WhoAm 92*
Bruck, Terry E. 1945- *St&PR 93*
Bruckart, Walter E. 1937- *WhoAm 92*
Brucken, Eleanor Elizabeth 1929- *WhoAm 92*
Brucken, Nancy Elizabeth 1961- *WhoAmW 93*
Brucken, Robert Matthew 1934- *WhoAm 92*
Bruckenstein, Stanley 1927- *WhoAm 92, WhoE 93*
Brucker, Andrew G. *Law&B 92*
Brucker, David Lee 1938- *St&PR 93*
Brucker, Eric 1941- *WhoAm 92*
Brucker, Henry J. 1916- *St&PR 93*
Brucker, Janet Mary 1946- *WhoAmW 93*
Brucker, Robert Louis 1935- *St&PR 93*
Brucker, Victoria *BioIn 17*
Brucker, Wilber Marion 1926- *WhoAm 92*
Bruckheim, Stan 1960- *WhoEmL 93*
Bruckheimer, Jerry *BioIn 17, WhoAm 92*
Bruck-Lieb, Lilly 1918- *WhoAmW 93*
Bruckmann, Donald J. 1929- *St&PR 93*
Bruckmann, Donald John 1929- *WhoAm 92*
Bruckmann, Klaus Peter 1943- *WhoWor 93*
Bruckmeier, Kurt Fredrick 1956- *WhoSSW 93*
Bruckner, Aleksander 1856-1939 *PolBiDi*
Bruckner, (Josef) Anton 1824-1896 *Baker 92*
Bruckner, Ferdinand 1891-1958 *DcLB 118 [port]*
Bruckner, Heinz Wilhelm 1949- *WhoWor 93*
Bruckner, Howard Leon 1941- *WhoSSW 93*
Bruckner, John Joseph 1960- *WhoSSW 93*
Bruckner, K. Jeffrey 1955- *WhoE 93*
Bruckner, Willa Cohen *Law&B 92*
Bruckner, Willa Cohen 1954- *WhoEmL 93*
Bruckner, William Joseph *Law&B 92*
Bruckner-Ruggeberg, Wilhelm 1906-1985 *Baker 92*
Brud, Wladyslaw S. 1939- *WhoWor 93*
Bruder, George Frederick 1938- *WhoAm 92*
Bruder, Harold Jacob 1930- *WhoAm 92*
Bruder, William Paul 1946- *WhoAm 92*
Brudereck, William C. 1916- *St&PR 93*
Brudieu, Joan c. 1520-1591 *Baker 92*
Brudnak, Peggy Helene 1923- *WhoAmW 93*
Brudner, Harvey Jerome 1931- *WhoAm 92*
Brudner, Helen Gross *WhoAm 92, WhoE 93*
Brudvig, Glenn Lowell 1931- *WhoAm 92*
Brudzinski, Jozef 1874-1917 *PolBiDi*
Brueckheimer, William Rogers 1921- *WhoAm 92*
Brueckner, Bonnie Lichtenstein 1936- *WhoAmW 93*
Brueckner, Keith Allan 1924- *WhoAm 92*
Brueggeman, Edward P. *Law&B 92*
Brueggemann, Wolfgang 1963- *WhoWor 93*
Brueghel, Pieter 1522?-1569 *BioIn 17*
Bruehl, George W. 1919- *BioIn 17*
Bruehl, Heidi 1941-1991 *BioIn 17*
Bruehl, Margaret Ellen 1935- *WhoAmW 93*
Bruel, Iris Barbara 1933- *WhoAm 92*
Bruell, Eric d1991 *BioIn 17*
Bruels, Mark Charles 1941- *WhoSSW 93*
Bruemmer, Arlon W. 1944- *St&PR 93*
Bruemmer, Fred 1929- *WhoAm 92, WhoWrEP 92*
Bruemmer, Lorraine Venskunas *WhoAmW 93*
Bruen, John Dermot 1930- *WhoAm 92*
Bruen, Lawrence S. 1949- *St&PR 93*
Bruene, Warren Benz 1916- *WhoAm 92*
Bruenell, Deborah Derow *Law&B 92*
Bruenger, Leona *St&PR 93*
Bruenger, M.W. 1944- *St&PR 93*
Bruenig, E.F. 1926- *WhoScE 91-3*
Bruening, Deborah Sue 1954- *WhoEmL 93*
Bruening, Richard P. *Law&B 92*
Bruening, Richard P. 1939- *St&PR 93*
Bruening, Richard Patrick *Law&B 92*
Bruening, Richard Patrick 1939- *WhoAm 92*
Bruenn, Howard Gerald 1905- *WhoAm 92, WhoE 93*
Bruenner, Eric William 1949- *WhoEmL 93*
Bruenner, Frederick Herman 1920- *WhoAm 92*
Bruenunger-Buskop, Wendy K. *Law&B 92*
Bruer-Susina, Jacquelyn Jean 1957- *WhoEmL 93*
Brues, Austin Moore 1906-1991 *BioIn 17*
Brueschke, Erich Edward 1933- *WhoAm 92*
Bruesewitz, Lynn Joy 1952- *WhoAmW 93*
Bruesewitz-Lopinto, Gail Cecelia 1956- *WhoAmW 93, WhoEmL 93*
Bruess, Charles Edward 1938- *WhoAm 92*
Bruett, Karen Diesl 1945- *WhoAmW 93*
Bruett, Till Arthur 1938- *WhoAm 92*
Bruett, William H., Jr. 1944- *St&PR 93*
Bruff, Beverly Olive 1926- *WhoAmW 93*
Bruford, Bill 1948- *See Yes ConMus 8*
Brugess, George T. *Law&B 92*
Bruggeman, Douglas 1960- *St&PR 93*
Bruggeman, J.-P. *WhoScE 91-2*
Bruggeman, Jacob Hendrik Gerrit 1950- *WhoWor 93*
Bruggeman, Terrance John 1946- *St&PR 93, WhoAm 92, WhoEmL 93*
Bruggemann, Ingar G.F. 1933- *WhoUN 92*
Bruggemann, Werner H. F. 1936- *WhoWor 93*
Bruggen, Coosje van *BioIn 17*
Bruggen, Frans 1934- *Baker 92*
Brugger, David John 1943- *WhoE 93*
Brugger, Eugene Christian *Law&B 92*
Brugger, George Albert 1941- *WhoAm 92*
Brugger, Heidi Nack 1950- *WhoWrEP 92*
Brugger, Robert J(ohn) 1943- *ConAu 38NR*
Bruggere, Thomas H. 1946- *ConEn*
Bruggink, Eric G. 1949- *CngDr 91, WhoE 93*
Brugh, Thomas B. 1939- *St&PR 93*
Brugioni, Dino A. 1921- *ConAu 137*
Brugirard, Jacques 1923- *WhoScE 91-2*
Brugiroux, Andre *BioIn 17*
Brugler, John C. 1942- *St&PR 93*
Brugler, Richard K. 1928- *St&PR 93*
Brugmann, Wendy Lee 1956- *St&PR 93*
Brugnatelli, Bruno E. 1935- *WhoAm 92*
Brugnoli, Attilio 1880-1937 *Baker 92*
Bruha, William Anton 1930- *St&PR 93*
Bruhn, Gary Lee 1952- *WhoSSW 93*
Bruhn, John Glyndon 1934- *WhoAm 92, WhoSSW 93*
Bruhn, Milt d1991 *BioIn 17*
Bruhnke, Howard W. 1928- *St&PR 93*
Bruhns, Nicolaus 1665-1697 *Baker 92*
Bruhns, Otto-T. 1942- *WhoScE 91-3*
Bruijnes, Eduard 1950- *WhoWor 93*
Bruin, G. 1944- *WhoScE 91-3*
Bruin, Jack *BioIn 17*
Bruin, Linda Lou 1938- *WhoAmW 93*
Bruin, Sally *BioIn 17*
Bruiniers, Terence L. 1946- *St&PR 93*
Bruins, Paul Fastenau 1905- *WhoSSW 93*
Bruinsma, Theodore August 1921- *WhoAm 92*
Bruinvels, Jacques 1932- *WhoScE 91-3*
Bruk, John 1930- *WhoAm 92*
Bruker, Davenport Sanford 1950- *WhoEmL 93*
Bruker, Deborah Willis 1951- *WhoAmW 93*
Bruland, Debra Keosa Maack 1955- *WhoEmL 93*

Brule, A. Lorraine 1925- WhoAmW 93
Brule, Etienne 1592?-1633 Expl 93 [port]
Brule, Gerard WhoScE 91-2
Brule, John D. 1927- WhoAm 92
Brule, Michael Raoul 1953- WhoEmL 93
Brule, Thomas Raymond 1954- WhoEmL 93, WhoSSW 93
Bruley, Duane Frederick 1933- WhoAm 92, WhoWor 93
Brull, Ignaz 1846-1907 Baker 92
Bruller, Jean ScF&FL 92
Bruller, Jean 1902-1991 BioIn 17
Brullo, Robert Angelo 1948- WhoEmL 93
Brulo, Sandra Marie 1952- WhoAmW 93
Brulotte, Gaetan 1945- WhoCanL 92
Brulotte, Gaetan A. 1945- WhoSSW 93
Brum, James F. 1943- St&PR 93
Brumbach, Mary Alice 1947- WhoEmL 93, WhoSSW 93
Brumback, Charles Tiedtke 1928- St&PR 93, WhoAm 92
Brumback, Clarence Landen 1914- WhoAm 92
Brumback, Roger Alan 1948- WhoEmL 93, WhoSSW 93
Brumback-Henry, Sarah Elizabeth 1948- WhoAm 92, WhoEmL 93
Brumbaugh, David Lynn 1952- WhoEmL 93
Brumbaugh, Granville M. 1901-1992 BioIn 17
Brumbaugh, James 1946- ScF&FL 92
Brumbaugh, Jana Jo 1959- WhoEmL 93
Brumbaugh, John Maynard 1927- WhoAm 92
Brumbaugh, Martin Grove 1862-1930 BioIn 17
Brumbaugh, R. Bruce 1952- St&PR 93
Brumbaugh, Robert Dan, Jr. WhoAm 92
Brumbaugh, Robert Sherrick 1918- WhoAm 92, WhoWrEP 92
Brumbelow, Donald Morris 1948- WhoSSW 93
Brumbelow, Norman Ray 1948- St&PR 93
Brumber, K. Richard 1940- St&PR 93
Brumberg, G. David 1939- WhoAm 92
Brumby, Colin (James) 1933- Baker 92
Brumby, John Mansfield 1953- WhoAsAP 91
Brumby, Sewell 1952- WhoEmL 93
Brumel, Antoine 1460-c. 1520 Baker 92
Brumelle, Kenneth Coy 1945- WhoSSW 93
Brumfield, Craig Andrew 1952- St&PR 93
Brumfield, Richard B. 1952- St&PR 93
Brumgardt, John Raymond 1946- WhoAm 92, WhoSSW 93
Brumley, David L. 1949- St&PR 93
Brumley, David Lee 1949- WhoAm 92
Brumley, Larry Don 1958- WhoSSW 93
Brumley, Steven Donald 1941- WhoSSW 93
Brumm, Brian A. 1954- St&PR 93
Brumm, James Earl Law&B 92
Brumm, James Earl 1942- St&PR 93, WhoAm 92
Brumm, Joseph Daniel 1916- WhoAm 92
Brumm, Marcia Cowles 1921- WhoAmW 93
Brumm, Paul Michael 1947- St&PR 93, WhoAm 92, WhoEmL 93
Brumme, Marjorie Vivian 1917- WhoWrEP 92
Brummel, Audrey B. 1935- St&PR 93
Brummel, Mark Joseph 1933- WhoAm 92, WhoWrEP 92
Brummels, J.V. ScF&FL 92
Brummer, Arlene Law&B 92
Brummer, Bernhard Hermann 1935- WhoWor 93
Brummer, Robert Craig 1945- WhoAm 92
Brummet, Richard Lee 1921- WhoAm 92
Brummet, Shauna Renea 1955- WhoAmW 93
Brummett, Ray L. Law&B 92
Brummett, Robert Eddie 1934- WhoAm 92
Brummond, David Joseph 1950- WhoEmL 93
Brumwell, Robin Arnold 1944- St&PR 93
Brun, Andre 1934- WhoScE 91-2
Brun, Fritz 1878-1959 Baker 92
Brun, Herbert 1918- Baker 92, WhoAm 92
Brun, Jean-Pierre 1949- WhoScE 91-2
Brun, Leslie Adolphe 1952- WhoE 93
Brun, Margaret Ann Charlene 1945- WhoWor 93
Brun, Philippe WhoScE 91-2
Brun, Reto 1947- WhoScE 91-4
Bruna, Dick 1927- MajAI [port]
Brunacini, Alan Vincent 1937- WhoAm 92
Brunale, Vito John 1925- WhoAm 92, WhoE 93, WhoWor 93
Brunas, John 1949- ScF&FL 92
Brunas, Michael 1952- ScF&FL 92
Brunda, Michael John 1950- WhoE 93
Brundage, Gertrude Barnes 1941- WhoE 93
Brundage, Howard Denton 1923- WhoAm 92
Brundage, Michael Robert 1942- WhoAm 92
Brundage, Russell Archibald 1929- WhoAm 92
Brundage, Susan 1949- WhoAm 92
Brundage, Warner F., Jr. Law&B 92
Brundell, Per-Olof 1929- WhoScE 91-4
Brundin, Jan Royal 1938- WhoE 93
Brundrett, George Lee, Jr. 1921- WhoAm 92
Brundtland, Gro Harlem BioIn 17
Brundtland, Gro Harlem 1939- DcTwHis, WhoWor 93
Brundy, James M. Law&B 92
Brune, David A. Law&B 92
Brune, David Hamilton 1930- St&PR 93, WhoAm 92
Brune, Eva 1952- WhoAmW 93
Brune, Guillaume Marie Anne 1763-1815 HarEnMi
Brune, H. WhoScE 91-3
Brune, Kay 1941- WhoScE 91-3
Bruneau, Alfred 1857-1934 IntDcOp, OxDcOp
Bruneau, (Louis-Charles-Bonaventure-) Alfred 1857-1934 Baker 92
Bruneau, Arthur Andrew 1923- WhoAm 92
Bruneau, Bill 1948- WhoEmL 93, WhoWor 93
Bruneau, Claude 1931- WhoAm 92
Bruneaux, Debra Louise 1953- WhoAmW 93
Brunei, Sultan of DcCPCAm
Brunel, Wilson 1920- St&PR 93
Brunell, Donald A., Jr. 1944- St&PR 93
Brunell, Jerry Albert 1926- WhoWor 93
Brunell, Jonathan 1955- WhoAm 92
Brunell, Paul F. 1957- St&PR 93
Brunell, Philip A. 1931- WhoAm 92
Brunell, Richard F. 1944- St&PR 93
Brunelle, A. Law&B 92
Brunelle, Jan ScF&FL 92
Brunelle, John B. 1924- St&PR 93
Brunelle, Michael Joseph 1965- WhoE 93
Brunelle, Robert L. 1924- WhoAm 92
Brunelle, Thomas Eugene 1935- St&PR 93
Brunelli, Antonio c. 1575-c. 1630 Baker 92
Brunelli, Jean 1934- ConAu 138
Brunello, Rosanne 1960- WhoAmW 93, WhoWor 93
Bruner, Charlotte Hughes 1917- WhoAm 92
Bruner, Edward M. 1924- WhoAm 92
Bruner, Harry Clair, Jr. Law&B 92
Bruner, Jeffrey A. Law&B 92
Bruner, Jerome Seymour BioIn 17
Bruner, Philip Lane 1939- WhoAm 92
Bruner, Richard Wallace 1926- WhoWrEP 92
Bruner, Robert B. 1933- WhoAm 92
Bruner, Sewell A. 1943- St&PR 93
Bruner, Van Buren, Jr. WhoAm 92
Bruner, William Evans, II 1949- WhoEmL 93
Bruner, William Gwathmey, III 1951- WhoE 93
Brunes, L.L. 1940- WhoScE 91-4
Brunet, Barrie K. 1925- St&PR 93
Brunet, Jean-Jacques 1945- WhoScE 91-2
Brunet, Jett BioIn 17
Brunet, Marta 1897-1967 BioIn 17, SpAmA
Brunet, Pierre 1902-1991 AnObit 1991, BioIn 17
Brunet, Pierre 1939- St&PR 93
Brunet, Randy Michael 1955- WhoEmL 93, WhoSSW 93
Brunet, Tan BioIn 17
Brunett, Karen Elizabeth 1961- WhoAmW 93
Brunette, Bruce Jonathan 1946- WhoEmL 93
Brunette, John S. Law&B 92
Brunette, Marqua Lee 1950- WhoAmW 93, WhoEmL 93, WhoWor 93
Brunette, Ray Leo 1929- St&PR 93
Brunette, Steven Edward 1949- WhoEmL 93
Brunetti, Alfred J. Law&B 92
Brunetti, Bennett E. 1922- St&PR 93
Brunetti, Carlo Enrico 1952- WhoWor 93
Brunetti, Claire F. 1943- WhoSSW 93
Brunetti, Domenico c. 1580-1646 Baker 92
Brunetti, Frank A. 1941- St&PR 93
Brunetti, Gaetano 1744-1798 Baker 92
Brunetti, Giorgio 1937- WhoWor 93
Brunetti, John A. 1924- St&PR 93
Brunetti, Melvin T. 1933- WhoAm 92
Brunetti, Rosalie Z. 1929- St&PR 93
Brunetti, W.H. 1942- St&PR 93
Brunetti, Wayne Henry 1942- WhoAm 92
Bruney, Laura Ann 1957- WhoAmW 93
Brungard, Donald G. 1939- St&PR 93
Brungraber, Robert J. 1929- WhoE 93
Brunhammer, Yvonne Suzanne 1927- WhoWor 93
Brunhard, Glenn R. 1948- St&PR 93
Brunhart, Hans 1945- WhoWor 93
Brunhoff, Jean de 1899-1937 ConAu 137, MajAI [port]
Brunhoff, Laurent de 1925- MajAI [port], SmATA 71 [port]
Bruni, Alessandro 1931- WhoScE 91-3
Bruni, Antonio 1757-1821 OxDcOp
Bruni, Antonio Bartolomeo 1757-1821 Baker 92
Bruni, Carla BioIn 17
Bruni, Carlo 1939- WhoScE 91-3
Bruni, Gennaro Law&B 92
Bruni, Rudolph Hanney, Jr. 1925- WhoSSW 93
Bruni, Stephen Thomas 1949- WhoAm 92, WhoE 93
Bruni, Victoria Hall Law&B 92
Brunie, Charles Henry 1930- WhoAm 92, WhoWor 93
Brunig, Robert Arthur 1946- WhoEmL 93
Bruning, Alfred Aaron, Jr. 1963- WhoEmL 93
Bruning, Anthony Steven 1955- WhoEmL 93
Bruning, Donald Francis 1942- WhoE 93
Bruning, Heinrich 1885-1970 DcTwHis
Bruning, James Leon 1938- WhoAm 92
Bruning, Jochen Wulf 1947- WhoWor 93
Bruning, John H. 1942- St&PR 93
Bruning, Nancy P(auline) 1948- WhoWrEP 92
Bruning, Richard C. Law&B 92
Brunjes, Peter Crawford 1953- WhoSSW 93
Brunk, Kenneth A. 1946- St&PR 93
Brunk, Max Edwin 1914- WhoAm 92
Brunk, Samuel Frederick 1932- WhoAm 92, WhoWor 93
Brunk, Ulf T. 1937- WhoScE 91-4
Brunk, William Edward 1928- WhoAm 92
Brunken, Gerald Walter, Sr. 1938- WhoWor 93
Brunn, Frederick A. 1945- St&PR 93
Brunn, Lottie BioIn 17
Brunn, Robert ScF&FL 92
Brunn, Wolfgang WhoScE 91-3
Brunnell, Jonathan 1955- St&PR 93
Brunner, Alois BioIn 17
Brunner, C.U. WhoScE 91-4
Brunner, Charlotte Marie 1956- WhoAmW 93
Brunner, Curtis J. 1943- St&PR 93
Brunner, David Lee 1953- WhoEmL 93, WhoSSW 93
Brunner, Donald L. 1934- St&PR 93
Brunner, Edward P. 1933- St&PR 93
Brunner, Elizabeth Anne 1959- WhoAmW 93
Brunner, Emma Beatrice Kaufman AmWomPl
Brunner, George Matthew 1925- WhoAm 92
Brunner, Gordon F. 1938- St&PR 93
Brunner, Gordon Francis 1938- WhoAm 92
Brunner, H. Joseph 1942- St&PR 93
Brunner, Hans R. 1937- WhoScE 91-4
Brunner, Hedvig 1933- WhoScE 91-4
Brunner, Henri 1935- WhoScE 91-3
Brunner, J.E. Law&B 92
Brunner, James G. 1949- St&PR 93
Brunner, Jeri Lynn Marion 1947- WhoEmL 93
Brunner, John 1934- BioIn 17, ScF&FL 92
Brunner, John J. 1938- St&PR 93
Brunner, John (Kilian Houston) 1934- ConAu 37NR
Brunner, John M. Law&B 92
Brunner, Karl 1916-1989 BioIn 17
Brunner, Kim Law&B 92
Brunner, Lillian Sholtis WhoAm 92, WhoAmW 93
Brunner, Mary Martinez 1945- WhoAmW 93
Brunner, Merlin A. 1924- St&PR 93
Brunner, Mikael 1933- WhoScE 91-4
Brunner, Neal Herbert 1939- St&PR 93
Brunner, Ralph William 1964- WhoE 93
Brunner, Richard Francis 1926- St&PR 93
Brunner, Robert Francis 1938- WhoAm 92, WhoWor 93
Brunner, Sam Aage 1920- WhoScE 91-2
Brunner, Thomas Rudolph, Jr. 1946- WhoAm 92
Brunner, Vernon Anthony 1940- St&PR 93
Brunngraber, Eric H. 1957- St&PR 93
Brunnstein, Klaus 1937- WhoWor 93
Bruno, Adrian Anthony 1939- St&PR 93
Bruno, Aileen Law&B 92
Bruno, Anthony D. Law&B 92
Bruno, Anthony J. 1929- WhoSSW 93
Bruno, Audrei Ann 1946- WhoAmW 93
Bruno, Cathy Eileen 1947- WhoAmW 93
Bruno, David Alfonse 1950- WhoE 93, WhoEmL 93, WhoWor 93
Bruno, Eli T. Law&B 92
Bruno, Francesco 1939- St&PR 93
Bruno, Frank N. 1943- St&PR 93
Bruno, Gary Robert 1951- WhoEmL 93
Bruno, Gino J. Law&B 92
Bruno, Giordano 1548-1600 BioIn 17
Bruno, Grace Angelia 1935- WhoAmW 93, WhoE 93
Bruno, Harold Robinson, Jr. 1928- WhoAm 92
Bruno, Jim 1935- St&PR 93
Bruno, Jim Neil 1946- WhoEmL 93
Bruno, Joseph S. 1914- WhoSSW 93
Bruno, Judyth Ann 1944- WhoAmW 93
Bruno, Michael 1932- WhoWor 93
Bruno, Richard D. 1943- St&PR 93
Bruno, Richard Louis 1954- WhoE 93
Bruno, Richard McDaniel 1952- St&PR 93
Bruno, Ronald G. WhoAm 92
Bruno, Ronald G. 1952- WhoSSW 93
Bruno, Ronald Gregory 1951- St&PR 93
Bruno, Susan Friedman Law&B 92
Bruno, Vincent John 1926- WhoAm 92
Bruno, Vincenzo 1946 WhoWor 93
Bruno, Virginia V. 1947- St&PR 93
Brunold, Paul 1875-1948 Baker 92
Brunori, Maurizio 1937- WhoScE 91-3
Brunow, Goesta 1936- WhoScE 91-4
Brunow, Gordon Peter 1926- WhoE 93, WhoWor 93
Bruns, Aida Maria 1925- WhoAmW 93
Bruns, Brenton Dane, Sr. 1945- WhoSSW 93
Bruns, David Eugene 1941- WhoSSW 93
Bruns, Debra Foust Law&B 92
Bruns, Edward Albert 1941- WhoWor 93
Bruns, George 1959- St&PR 93
Bruns, George Henry, Jr. 1918- St&PR 93
Bruns, Gerald L. 1938- WhoAm 92
Bruns, Gregory A. Law&B 92
Bruns, Klaus Heinrich 1930- WhoWor 93
Bruns, Linda Marie 1946- WhoEmL 93
Bruns, Maria Reyes 1947- WhoAmW 93, WhoEmL 93
Bruns, Michael F. 1949- St&PR 93
Bruns, Michael L. 1956- St&PR 93
Bruns, Michael Willi Erich 1945- WhoWor 93
Bruns, Nicolaus, Jr. 1926- WhoAm 92
Bruns, Paul 1946- WhoE 93
Bruns, Robert W. Law&B 92
Bruns, William John, Jr. 1935- WhoAm 92
Brunschvicg, Cecile 1877-1946 BioIn 17
Brunschwig, Henri 1904-1989 BioIn 17
Brunsdale, Anne E. 1923- WhoAm 92, WhoAmW 93
Brunsden, Denys WhoScE 91-1
Brunson, Burlie Allen 1945- WhoAm 92
Brunson, Dorothy 1938- BioIn 17
Brunson, Dorothy E. AfrAmBi [port]
Brunson, Dorothy Edwards 1938- WhoAm 92
Brunson, Jack E. 1956- WhoIns 93
Brunson, Jack Edward 1956- St&PR 93
Brunson, Jack Rushing 1928- St&PR 93, WhoIns 93
Brunson, Joel Garrett 1923- WhoWor 93
Brunson, John S. 1934- St&PR 93
Brunson, Martha Luan 1931- WhoAmW 93, WhoSSW 93
Brunsting, Keith Allen 1955- WhoEmL 93
Brunsting, Melody Ann 1955- WhoWrEP 92
Brunswick, Ann Finkenberg 1926- WhoAmW 93
Brunswick, Charles William Ferdinand 1735-1806 HarEnMi
Brunswick, Eve C. Law&B 92
Brunswick, Ferdinand, Duke of 1721-1792 HarEnMi
Brunswick, Frederick William, Duke of 1771-1815 HarEnMi
Brunswick, Mark 1902-1971 Baker 92
Brunswick, Paul L. 1939- St&PR 93
Brunswik, Else Frenkel- 1908-1958 BioIn 17
Brunt, George Law&B 92
Brunt, Harry Herman, Jr. 1921- WhoAm 92
Brunt, Manly Yates, Jr. 1926- WhoAm 92, WhoWor 93
Brunt, Steven Lewis 1947- WhoWor 93
Brunt, Yvonne Brady 1964- WhoSSW 93
Bruntjen, Worth 1936- St&PR 93
Brunton, Gerald W. 1927- St&PR 93
Brunton, John Thomas 1941- St&PR 93
Brunton, Jolee Jeanice 1953- WhoAmW 93
Brunton, Mason Lee 1935- St&PR 93
Brunton, Maude AmWomPl
Brunton, Paul Edward 1922- WhoAm 92
Bruntrager, Edward Charles Law&B 92
Bruorton, Josephine Van Tassel AmWomPl
Brupbacher, Frederick Arnold, II 1954- WhoEmL 93
Brusati, Franco 1922- MiSFD 9

Brusati, Roberto 1850-1935 HarEnMi
Brusca, Donald Richard 1939- St&PR 93
Brusca, Janet Rita 1950- WhoEmL 93
Brusca, Richard C. 1945- WhoAm 92
Brusca, Robert Andrew 1950- WhoAm 92
Bruscantini, Sesto 1919- Baker 92, IntDcOp, OxDcOp
Bruschi, Mireille 1941- WhoScE 91-2
Bruscino, Anita Marie 1963- St&PR 93
Bruse, John Charles Law&B 92
Brusegard, R.H. Law&B 92
Brusenhan, Robert Lee, Jr. 1931- WhoSSW 93
Brusewitz, Gerald Henry 1942- WhoAm 92
Brush, A. Louise d1990 BioIn 17
Brush, Andrew Francis 1950- WhoE 93
Brush, Carey Wentworth 1920- WhoAm 92
Brush, Charles Francis 1923- WhoAm 92
Brush, Clinton E., III 1911- WhoAm 92
Brush, Craig Balcombe 1930- WhoAm 92
Brush, David Elden 1950- WhoEmL 93
Brush, Dorothy Hamilton 1894-1968 AmWomPl
Brush, Frank John, Jr. 1948- St&PR 93
Brush, George W. 1921- WhoAm 92
Brush, John Dwight 1926- St&PR 93
Brush, Karen A. 1960- ScF&FL 92
Brush, Louis Frederick 1946- WhoEmL 93
Brush, Lucien Munson, Jr. 1929- WhoAm 92
Brush, Martyn Thomas 1963- St&PR 93
Brush, Peter Norman 1944- WhoAm 92
Brush, Richard Frank 1930- St&PR 93
Brush, Robert A. 1937- St&PR 93
Brush, Robert Paul 1962- WhoSSW 93
Brush, Sally Anderson 1934- WhoAmW 93
Brush, Stephanie 1954- ConAu 138
Brush, Susan Evelyn 1954- WhoAmW 93
Brush, Thomas S. d1992 NewYTBS 92
Brushwood, David Benson 1948- WhoEmL 93
Brusilov, Aleksei Alekseevich 1853-1926 HarEnMi
Brusilov, Aleksey 1853-1926 DcTwHis
Brusilovsky, Anshel 1928- Baker 92
Brusilovsky, Evgeni 1905-1981 Baker 92
Brusilow, Anshel 1928- Baker 92
Brusilow, Saul 1927- WhoAm 92, WhoE 93
Brusin, Joyce Helena 1958- WhoWrEP 92
Bruski, Fred John 1929- WhoE 93
Bruski, Paul Steven 1949- WhoEmL 93
Bruski-Maus, Betty Jean 1927- WhoAmW 93
Brusko, Marlene Guimond 1940- WhoAmW 93
Brusky, George J. Law&B 92
Bruso, William F. St&PR 93
Bruson, Renato 1936- Baker 92, OxDcOp
Bruss, Franz Thomas 1949- WhoWor 93
Bruss, Howard G., Jr. Law&B 92
Bruss, Katherine Vivian 1961- WhoAmW 93
Brussaard, Gerrit 1942- WhoWor 93
Brussaard, Lijbert 1951- WhoScE 91-3
Brussel, I.R. 1895- ScF&FL 92
Brusselmans, Christiane BioIn 17
Brusselmans, Michel 1886-1960 Baker 92
Brussel-Smith, Bernard 1914- BioIn 17
Brust, David 1935- WhoWor 93
Brust, Steven 1955- ScF&FL 92
Brust, Steven K. (Zoltan) 1955- ConAu 37NR
Brust, Susan Elizabeth 1958- St&PR 93
Brust, Susan Melinda 1951- WhoAmW 93, WhoE 93
Brustad, Bjarne 1895-1978 Baker 92
Brustad, Orin Daniel 1941- WhoAm 92
Brustein, Abram Isaac 1946- WhoE 93, WhoEmL 93
Brustein, Lawrence 1936- WhoAm 92
Brustein, Martin 1924- St&PR 93, WhoE 93
Brustein, Michael Labe 1949- WhoEmL 93
Brustein, Robert Sanford 1927- WhoAm 92, WhoWrEP 92
Brustein, Susan Jane 1948- WhoAmW 93
Bruster, Herbert 1928- WhoScE 91-3
Brustowicz, Paul M. 1944- WhoIns 93
Brustowicz, Robert Marjan 1951- WhoE 93
Brustrom, Jean Mary 1920- WhoAmW 93
Brusven, Arland Duane 1932- St&PR 93
Bruter, Claude Paul 1937- WhoWor 93
Brutian, Georg Abel 1926- WhoWor 93
Brutlag, Michael Lowell 1955- WhoEmL 93
Brutlag, Rodney Sheldon 1938- WhoAm 92
Bruton, Bill 1925- BioIn 17
Bruton, Eric Moore 1915- WhoWor 93
Bruton, F.X., Jr. Law&B 92
Bruton, James DeWitt, Jr. 1908- WhoAm 92, WhoWor 93
Bruton, John Macaulay 1937- WhoWor 93
Bruton, Michael Gerard 1960- WhoEmL 93
Bruton, Virginia Treppendahl 1951- WhoAmW 93
Brutsaert, Dirk 1937- WhoScE 91-2
Brutsche, Ernst W. 1937- St&PR 93
Brutus, Decimus Junius c. 84BC-43BC HarEnMi
Brutus, Dennis 1924- BioIn 17, DcLB 117 [port]
Brutus, Dennis Vincent 1924- WhoAm 92
Brutus, Marcus Junius 85BC-42BC HarEnMi
Brutvan, Cheryl Ann 1955- WhoAm 92
Bruun, Peter 1946- WhoScE 91-2
Bruusgaard, Dag 1940- WhoScE 91-4
Bruyelle, Pierre 1930- WhoScE 91-2
Bruyland, Ignace 1936- WhoScE 91-2
Bruyn, Henry Bicker 1918- WhoAm 92
Bruynel, Ton 1934- Baker 92
Bruynseraede, Yvan Julien 1938- WhoWor 93
Bruzas, Theodore E. 1935- St&PR 93
Bruzda, Francis Joseph 1935- WhoAm 92
Bruzdowicz, Joanna 1943- Baker 92
Bruzelius, Caroline Astrid 1949- WhoEmL 93
Bruzelius, Nils Johan Axel 1947- WhoAm 92
Bruzga, Jill M. Law&B 92
Bruzs, Boris Olgerd 1933- St&PR 93, WhoAm 92, WhoE 93
Bruzzone, Edward Joseph 1946- WhoEmL 93
Bry, Edith 1898-1991 BioIn 17
Bry, Gerhard 1911- BioIn 17
Bry, Michel 1947- WhoScE 91-2
Bryan, A. Bradford, Jr. WhoAm 92
Bryan, Adelbert M. 1943- DcCPCAm
Bryan, Alice I. d1992 NewYTBS 92
Bryan, Alison R. 1891-1992 NewYTBS 92
Bryan, Anthony John Adrian 1923- St&PR 93
Bryan, Ashley 1923- BioIn 17, BlkAuII 92
Bryan, Ashley F. 1923- MajAI [port], SmATA 72 [port]
Bryan, Billie Marie 1932- WhoAm 92, WhoAmW 93, WhoE 93
Bryan, C. Clark 1910- WhoIns 93
Bryan, Caroline Elizabeth 1951- WhoAmW 93
Bryan, Carter Byrd 1945- WhoIns 93
Bryan, Charles Faulkner, Jr. 1946- WhoAm 92, WhoSSW 93
Bryan, Colgan Hobson 1909- WhoAm 92
Bryan, Courtlandt Dixon Barnes 1936- WhoAm 92, WhoWrEP 92
Bryan, Curtis Eugene AfrAmBi
Bryan, D. Tennant 1906- St&PR 93
Bryan, Darrell Ernest 1948- WhoEmL 93
Bryan, David Barclay 1933- WhoWor 93
Bryan, David Tennant 1906- WhoAm 92
Bryan, Earl Watkins 1941- St&PR 93
Bryan, Elizabeth P. 1960- St&PR 93
Bryan, Eric Reginald WhoScE 91-1
Bryan, Eugene Edward 1957- WhoEmL 93
Bryan, F.S., Jr. 1938- St&PR 93
Bryan, G. Howard 1913- St&PR 93
Bryan, Gloria Elaine 1946- WhoEmL 93
Bryan, Gloria Jane 1959- WhoAmW 93
Bryan, Henry Clark, Jr. 1930- WhoAm 92
Bryan, Hob 1952- WhoSSW 93
Bryan, J. Shepard, Jr. 1922- St&PR 93
Bryan, J. Stewart 1938- St&PR 93
Bryan, J. Timothy 1961- St&PR 93
Bryan, Jacob F., IV WhoAm 92
Bryan, Jacob F., IV 1943- WhoIns 93
Bryan, James MiSFD 9
Bryan, James Edward 1906- WhoAm 92
Bryan, James Lee 1936- WhoAm 92
Bryan, Janice 1943- WhoSSW 93
Bryan, Jesse Dwain 1936- WhoSSW 93
Bryan, Jessica ScF&FL 92
Bryan, John Gilbert 1932- St&PR 93
Bryan, John Gilley Law&B 92
Bryan, John Henry 1936- St&PR 93, WhoAm 92
Bryan, John Leland 1926- WhoAm 92
Bryan, John Stewart, III 1938- WhoAm 92, WhoSSW 93
Bryan, Joseph 1845-1908 BioIn 17
Bryan, Joseph, III 1904- WhoAm 92
Bryan, Joseph McKinley 1896- WhoAm 92
Bryan, Joseph Shepard, Jr. 1922- WhoAm 92
Bryan, Katherine Byram WhoE 93
Bryan, Katherine C. AmWomPl
Bryan, Kathryn Timmins 1941- WhoSSW 93
Bryan, Laquey Phillip 1930- St&PR 93
Bryan, Lawrence Donald, III 1943- St&PR 93
Bryan, Lawrence Dow 1945- WhoAm 92
Bryan, Leona Biering 1943- WhoAmW 93
Bryan, Mary Ann 1929- WhoAmW 93
Bryan, Mary Edwards 1842-1913 JrnUS
Bryan, Michael WhoCanL 92
Bryan, Michelle V. 1956- St&PR 93
Bryan, Mildred Gott WhoWor 93
Bryan, Monk 1914- WhoAm 92
Bryan, Norman E. 1947- WhoEmL 93
Bryan, Paul Robey, Jr. WhoAm 92
Bryan, Percival BioIn 17
Bryan, Richard H. 1937- CngDr 91, WhoAm 92
Bryan, Richard Ray 1932- WhoAm 92
Bryan, Robert Armistead 1926- WhoAm 92
Bryan, Robert Fessler 1913- WhoAm 92
Bryan, Robert J. 1934- WhoAm 92
Bryan, Robert Russell 1943- WhoWor 93
Bryan, Sam Neal 1951- WhoEmL 93
Bryan, Sharon 1943- ConAu 37NR, WhoWrEP 92
Bryan, Sharon M. 1959- St&PR 93
Bryan, Shawn William 1948- St&PR 93
Bryan, Susan Almon 1938- WhoAmW 93
Bryan, Thomas L. 1935- St&PR 93
Bryan, Thomas Lynn 1935- WhoAm 92
Bryan, William Alonzo 1938- WhoSSW 93
Bryan, William F., III 1943- WhoIns 93
Bryan, William Jennings 1860-1925 BioIn 17, DcTwHis, GayN, PolPar
Bryan, William Royal 1932- WhoAm 92
Bryan, William Wright 1905-1991 BioIn 17
Bryans, John Thomas 1924- WhoAm 92
Bryant, Alan Willard 1940- WhoWor 93
Bryant, Andrea Pair Law&B 92
Bryant, Anita Law&B 92
Bryant, Ann Aleace 1961- WhoAmW 93
Bryant, Anne Lincoln 1949- WhoAm 92
Bryant, Anthony W. 1930- St&PR 93
Bryant, Arthur H. 1954- WhoAm 92
Bryant, Arthur Herbert, II 1942- WhoAm 92
Bryant, Arthur L. 1934- WhoIns 93
Bryant, Arthur Lee 1934- St&PR 93
Bryant, Barbara Everitt 1926- WhoAm 92, WhoAmW 93
Bryant, Barbara Phyfe 1943- St&PR 93
Bryant, Bear BioIn 17
Bryant, Bertha Estelle 1927- WhoAm 92
Bryant, Beth Ann 1962- WhoAmW 93
Bryant, Beverly A. Law&B 92
Bryant, Blaise BioIn 17
Bryant, Bonnie Lee 1953- WhoE 93
Bryant, Brenda C. 1948- St&PR 93
Bryant, Brenda Joyce 1950- WhoEmL 93
Bryant, C.E., Jr. St&PR 93
Bryant, Calvin Don 1948- WhoEmL 93
Bryant, Cameron Edward, Jr. 1934- WhoAm 92
Bryant, Cecil Farris 1914- WhoAm 92
Bryant, Celia Mae Small 1913- WhoAm 92
Bryant, Charles d1891 BioIn 17
Bryant, Charles Austin, IV 1946- WhoAm 92
Bryant, Cheryl Jean 1949- WhoSSW 93
Bryant, Christopher WhoScE 91-1
Bryant, Christopher Gordon Alastair 1944- WhoWor 93
Bryant, Clifton Dow 1932- WhoAm 92, WhoWor 93
Bryant, Daniel C., Jr. Law&B 92
Bryant, David 1951- WhoEmL 93
Bryant, David Ernest 1922- WhoWrEP 92
Bryant, David Stuart 1948- WhoE 93, WhoEmL 93
Bryant, Debra Suzanne 1953- WhoAmW 93
Bryant, Deloris Sue 1937- WhoAmW 93
Bryant, Demetrius Edward 1956- WhoEmL 93, WhoWor 93
Bryant, Denise Delisle 1946- WhoEmL 93
Bryant, Dennis Michael 1947- WhoEmL 93, WhoSSW 93
Bryant, Don Estes 1917- WhoWor 93
Bryant, Donald Loudon 1908- WhoAm 92, WhoWor 93
Bryant, Donald Loyd 1919- WhoAm 92
Bryant, Doris Law&B 92
Bryant, Dorothy 1930- ScF&FL 92
Bryant, Douglas Wallace 1913- WhoAm 92
Bryant, E.T. d1990 BioIn 17
Bryant, Edward 1945- ScF&FL 92
Bryant, Edward Clark 1915- WhoAm 92
Bryant, Edward Curtis 1925- WhoE 93
Bryant, Edward K. 1902-1991 BioIn 17
Bryant, Edward Winslow, Jr. 1945- WhoWrEP 92
Bryant, Emma Spaulding BioIn 17
Bryant, Eric Thomas d1990 BioIn 17
Bryant, Felice WhoAm 92
Bryant, G.F. WhoScE 91-1
Bryant, G. Preston 1933- WhoWrEP 92
Bryant, Gary David 1949- WhoEmL 93
Bryant, Gary Wayne 1949- St&PR 93
Bryant, Gay 1945- WhoAm 92, WhoWrEP 92
Bryant, George M. Law&B 92
Bryant, George Macon 1926- WhoSSW 93
Bryant, Harry L. 1909- BioIn 17
Bryant, Harry M., Jr. 1940- St&PR 93
Bryant, Harry Miller, Sr. 1921- St&PR 93
Bryant, Harvey Lee 1929- St&PR 93
Bryant, Howard Louis 1921- WhoSSW 93
Bryant, Howard Sewall 1928- St&PR 93, WhoE 93
Bryant, Hubert Hale 1931- WhoAm 92
Bryant, Ira Houston, III 1942- WhoSSW 93
Bryant, Jack G. 1936- St&PR 93
Bryant, James Mitchell 1942- WhoWor 93
Bryant, James Montgomery 1954- WhoE 93, WhoEmL 93
Bryant, James Wesley 1921- WhoAm 92
Bryant, James William WhoScE 91-1
Bryant, Janice E. 1950- St&PR 93
Bryant, Jeannette Marie 1939- WhoAmW 93
Bryant, Jerry W. 1941- St&PR 93
Bryant, John 1943- WhoSSW 93, WhoWor 93
Bryant, John 1947- CngDr 91
Bryant, John Allen WhoScE 91-1
Bryant, John Bradbury 1947- WhoAm 92
Bryant, John Hulon 1941- WhoSSW 93
Bryant, John Wiley 1947- WhoAm 92, WhoSSW 93
Bryant, Joseph Allen, Jr. 1919- WhoAm 92
Bryant, Josephine Harriet 1947- WhoAm 92, WhoAmW 93
Bryant, Juanita Roberson 1924- WhoAmW 93
Bryant, Karen Law&B 92
Bryant, Karen Worstell 1942- WhoAmW 93
Bryant, Kathy Ann 1942- WhoWrEP 92
Bryant, Keith Lynn, Jr. 1937- WhoAm 92
Bryant, Larre 1942- WhoWrEP 92
Bryant, Leon O. 1923- St&PR 93
Bryant, Lester R. 1930- WhoAm 92
Bryant, Lina Antonetta 1960- WhoEmL 93
Bryant, Louise Frances Stevens 1885-1956? AmWomPl
Bryant, Lynn Andrea 1952- WhoEmL 93
Bryant, Lynwood 1908- ConAu 139
Bryant, Mark BioIn 17
Bryant, Martha J. 1949- WhoAm 92, WhoEmL 93
Bryant, Marvin Pierce 1925- WhoAm 92
Bryant, Melissa Dunbar 1957- WhoAmW 93
Bryant, Michael Nolan 1968- WhoSSW 93
Bryant, Nancy White 1957- WhoAmW 93
Bryant, Oscar Sims, Jr. 1920- WhoAm 92
Bryant, Pamela Kaye 1953- WhoAmW 93, WhoEmL 93
Bryant, Paul Thompson 1928- WhoSSW 93
Bryant, Paul W. BioIn 17
Bryant, Perrin Cranford 1941- WhoSSW 93
Bryant, Peter Elwood WhoScE 91-1
Bryant, Peter Jude 1960- WhoEmL 93
Bryant, Phyllis Crudup 1942- WhoSSW 93
Bryant, Randal Everitt 1952- WhoAm 92
Bryant, Randolph William Law&B 92
Bryant, Rebecca Smith 1955- WhoSSW 93
Bryant, Richard James 1928- St&PR 93
Bryant, Richard L. 1952- St&PR 93
Bryant, Richard Todd 1952- WhoEmL 93
Bryant, Rikki Julia 1959- WhoAmW 93
Bryant, Rob 1955- BioIn 17
Bryant, Robert 1958- WhoEmL 93
Bryant, Robert John 1948- WhoWor 93
Bryant, Robert Lee 1926- St&PR 93
Bryant, Robert Parker 1922- WhoAm 92
Bryant, Robert Vernon 1948- WhoAm 92
Bryant, Rosalyn BlkAmWO
Bryant, Ruth Alyne 1924- WhoAm 92
Bryant, Sandra Renee 1959- WhoEmL 93
Bryant, Sharon SoulM
Bryant, Shirley Rhea 1935- WhoSSW 93
Bryant, Stephen R. 1950- St&PR 93
Bryant, Stewart James 1939- WhoWor 93
Bryant, Susan Dolores Niemeyer 1952- WhoAmW 93
Bryant, Susan E. Law&B 92
Bryant, Susan Lynn Zuhl 1960- WhoAmW 93
Bryant, Sylvia Leigh 1947- WhoWrEP 92
Bryant, Sylvie Alpert 1940- WhoUN 92
Bryant, Tamera Sue 1955- WhoWrEP 92
Bryant, Terry G. St&PR 93
Bryant, Thos Lee 1943- WhoAm 92
Bryant, Timothy Weldon 1948- WhoSSW 93
Bryant, Wayne R. AfrAmBi
Bryant, Willard F., Jr. 1960- WhoE 93
Bryant, William B. 1911- WhoAm 92, WhoE 93
Bryant, William Benson 1911- CngDr 91
Bryant, William Cullen 1794-1878 JrnUS
Bryant, William L. Law&B 92
Bryant, Winston 1938- WhoAm 92, WhoSSW 93
Bryars, Gavin 1943- Baker 92

Bryars, Gladyn Cameron 1933- WhoSSW 93
Bryars, W.C. 1922- St&PR 93
Bryce, Catherine Turner 1871- AmWomPl
Bryce, Charles Forsyth Anderson WhoScE 91-1
Bryce, David T. 1947- St&PR 93
Bryce, Graham C. 1940- St&PR 93
Bryce, Graham Watt WhoScE 91-1
Bryce, James 1838-1922 BioIn 17
Bryce, Josephine Hartford d1992 BioIn 17, NewYTBS 92 [port]
Bryce, Sharon Law&B 92
Bryce Echenique, Alfredo 1939- SpAmA
Bryceland, Yvonne BioIn 17
Bryceland, Yvonne 1925-1992 ConTFT 10, NewYTBS 92 [port]
Bryce-Smith, Derek WhoScE 91-1
Bryce-Smith, Derek 1926- WhoWor 93
Brych, Josef 1933- WhoScE 91-2
Brydak, Dobieslaw Jerzy 1935- WhoWor 93
Bryden, Bill 1942- MiSFD 9
Brydges, Samuel Egerton 1762-1837 BioIn 17
Brydon, Donald James 1922- WhoAm 92
Brydon, Donald Lithgow WhoScE 91-1
Brydon, Harold Wesley 1923- WhoWor 93
Bryennios OxDcByz
Bryennios, Joseph c. 1350-c. 1430 OxDcByz
Bryennios, Manuel fl. c. 1300- OxDcByz
Bryennios, Nikephoros 11th cent.- OxDcByz
Bryennios, Nikephoros, The Younger c. 1064-c. 1136 OxDcByz
Bryenton, Elisabeth Ann 1961- WhoAmW 93
Bryer, Anthony Applemore Mornington 1937- WhoWor 93
Bryer, Bruce 1966-1983 BioIn 17
Bryer, Diana 1942- BioIn 17
Bryer, Jackson R(obert) 1937- ConAu 40NR
Bryer, Jackson Robert 1937- WhoE 93
Bryer, Richard H. Law&B 92
Bryfonski, Dedria Anne 1947- St&PR 93, WhoAm 92, WhoAmW 93
Bryggman, Ulf O.G. 1953- WhoScE 91-4
Brygoo, Edouard Raoul 1920- WhoScE 91-2
Bryher 1894-1983 ScF&FL 92
Bryja, Frank J. 1942- St&PR 93
Bryk, William 1955- WhoWrEP 92
Brykalov, Sergei Arkadievich 1954- WhoWor 93
Brymer, Jack 1915- Baker 92
Brymer, Robert L. 1932- St&PR 93
Bryndum, Helge 1925- WhoScE 91-2
Brynelson, Floyd Arvold 1914- St&PR 93
Bryner, Peggy Culbertson 1943- WhoE 93
Bryngil, Judith Anne 1958- WhoEmL 93
Bryn-Julson, Phyllis (Mae) 1945- Baker 92
Brynn, Edward Paul 1942- WhoWor 93
Brynner, Kathy Lee BioIn 17
Brynner, Yul 1915-1985 IntDcF 2-3 [port]
Brynsolfsson, Ari WhoScE 91-3
Brynych, Zbynek 1927- DrEEuF
Bryon, Leslie Enrique 1942- WhoSSW 93
Bryson, Allen Lee 1947- WhoEmL 93
Bryson, Bill BioIn 17
Bryson, Brady Oliver 1915- WhoAm 92
Bryson, David C. Law&B 92
Bryson, Dewey Talmadge, Jr. 1954- WhoSSW 93
Bryson, Dorothy Printup 1894- WhoAmW 93
Bryson, Gary Alton Law&B 92
Bryson, Gary Spath 1943- WhoAm 92
Bryson, George Mitchell 1940- St&PR 93
Bryson, James Edward 1961- WhoEmL 93
Bryson, John 1923- WhoAm 92
Bryson, John D. 1941- St&PR 93
Bryson, John E. 1943- St&PR 93, WhoAm 92
Bryson, Neil Francis Law&B 92
Bryson, Peabo 1951- SoulM
Bryson, Reid Allen 1920- WhoAm 92
Bryson, Sara BioIn 17
Bryson, Stephen 1942- St&PR 93
Bryson, Vaughn D. WhoAm 92
Bryson, Vern Elrick 1920- WhoWor 93
Bryson-Israel, Doris Lorraine 1938- WhoE 93
Bryt, Albert 1913- WhoE 93
Brytczuk, Gary Albert 1947- WhoEmL 93
Bryzinski, Mark Francis 1953- WhoEmL 93
Brzana, Stanislaus Joseph 1917- WhoAm 92
Brzecki, Andrzej 1921- WhoScE 91-4
Brzekowski, Jan 1903-1983 PolBiDi
Brzenk, Richard S. 1942- St&PR 93
Brzeska, Henri Gaudier- 1891-1915 BioIn 17
Brzezinski, Andrzej M. 1932- WhoScE 91-4
Brzezinski, Jerzy 1922- WhoScE 91-4
Brzezinski, Ronald Thomas 1938- St&PR 93
Brzezinski, Zbigniew 1928- ColdWar 1 [port], PolBiDi, WhoAm 92, WhoE 93, WhoWor 93
Brzezinski-Stein, Katharine Anne 1947- WhoAmW 93
Brzoska, Zbigniew Stanislaw 1916- WhoScE 91-4
Brzowska, Zofia 1800-1879 See Kurpinski, Karol 1785-1857 OxDcOp
Brzozowski, Lester 1952- St&PR 93
Brzozowski, Linda Sue 1950- WhoAmW 93
Brzozowski, Ronald C. 1952- St&PR 93
Brzuskiewicz, John Edward 1955- WhoEmL 93
Brzustowicz, Richard John 1917- WhoAm 92
Brzustowicz, Stanislaw Henry 1919- WhoAm 92
Brzyska, Wanda 1931- WhoScE 91-4
Bseiso, Atef d1992 BioIn 17
Bstan-'dzin-rgya-mtsho 1935- BioIn 17
Bua, Nicholas John 1925- WhoAm 92
Buatta, Mario 1935- BioIn 17
Bub, Alexander David 1949- WhoWor 93
Buba, Eugenia Z. 1951- St&PR 93
Buba, Tony MiSFD 9
Bubar, Benjamin C. 1918- PolPar
Bubaris, Gus John 1952- WhoE 93, WhoEmL 93
Bubb, Frank William, III Law&B 92
Bubb, Harry G. 1924- St&PR 93
Bubb, Harry Geiple 1924- WhoAm 92
Bubb, William D. Law&B 92
Bubba, Joseph L. 1938- WhoE 93
Bubbs, Roy H. 1949- St&PR 93
Bube, Richard Howard 1927- WhoAm 92
Bubec, Bob Auwi 1952- WhoAsAP 91
Bubeck, Roy R. 1946- St&PR 93, WhoIns 93
Buben, Arlene Carol 1948- WhoEmL 93
Bubenik, Mark L. Law&B 92
Bubenzer, Gary Dean 1940- WhoAm 92
Bubenzer, Peter St&PR 93
Buber, Martin 1878-1965 BioIn 17
Buber, Mordekhai Martin 1878-1965 BioIn 17
Bubernak, Jon Paul 1935- St&PR 93
Bubert, James Fredrick 1931- St&PR 93
Bubien, Stanley C. 1946- St&PR 93
Bubis, Bess Rosenblum 1922- St&PR 93
Bubis, Marvin R. 1921- St&PR 93
Bubka, Sergei BioIn 17
Bubka, Sergei 1964- WhoWor 93
Bublys, Algimantas Vladas 1941- WhoAm 92
Bubnic, Anne Marie 1949- WhoAm 92
Bubnick, J.J. 1939- St&PR 93
Bubnicki, Zdzislaw 1938- WhoScE 91-4
Bubolz, John Sever 1941- St&PR 93
Bubp, Gregory 1955- St&PR 93
Bubrick, George J. 1947- St&PR 93
Bubrick, George Joseph 1947- WhoAm 92
Buc, Henri 1934- WhoScE 91-2
Buc, Jerzy WhoScE 91-4
Buc, Jerzy Bronislaw 1934- WhoScE 91-4
Buc, Michele Rene 1966- WhoAmW 93
Buc, Nancy Lillian 1944- WhoAmW 93
Bucaille, Marc Louis 1942- WhoWor 93
Bucaille, Maurice 1920- ConAu 137
Bucar, Cary A. ScF&FL 92
Bucard, Marcel 1895-1946 BioIn 17
Bucaro, Robert N. 1951- St&PR 93
Buccella, William Victor 1943- WhoAm 92
Buccello, Henry Louis 1920- WhoAm 92
Bucchere, Victor Sal 1956- WhoE 93
Buccheri, Anthony Thomas 1953- WhoE 93
Bucchi, Mark 1955- WhoEmL 93
Bucchi, Renato 1929- WhoScE 91-3
Bucchi, Valentino 1916-1976 Baker 92
Bucchieri, Peter Charles 1955- WhoEmL 93, WhoWor 93
Bucchignano, John J. 1947- St&PR 93
Bucchioni, J. Dennis 1951- St&PR 93
Bucci, Dick 1944- St&PR 93
Bucci, Elaine Theresa 1957- WhoAmW 93
Bucci, Mark 1924- Baker 92
Buccigrossi, David Eric 1956- WhoEmL 93
Buccinna, Isabel M. 1936- St&PR 93
Buccino, Alphonse 1931- WhoAm 92, WhoSSW 93
Buccino, G.J. 1961- St&PR 93
Buccino, Gerald P. 1938- WhoAm 92
Buccino, Salvatore George 1933- WhoAm 92
Buceck, D.T. 1932- St&PR 93
Bucek, Dennis C. 1945- St&PR 93
Buceta, Joseph Benito 1950- WhoEmL 93
Bucey, David K. 1950- St&PR 93
Buch, David Leslie 1952- WhoE 93
Buch, Donald Noel 1946- WhoSSW 93
Buch, Robert Hansen 1929- St&PR 93
Bucha, Edward Richard 1954- WhoE 93, WhoEmL 93
Bucha, Vaclav 1928- WhoScE 91-4
Buchai, Gregory 1945- St&PR 93
Buchakjian, Serge D. 1954- St&PR 93
Buchakjian, Serge Dikran 1954- WhoE 93
Buchalter, Martin 1932- St&PR 93
Buchalter, Stuart D. 1937- St&PR 93
Buchalter, Stuart David 1937- WhoAm 92
Buchan, Alan Bradley 1936- WhoAm 92
Buchan, Anna 1878-1948 BioIn 17
Buchan, Bryan 1945- ScF&FL 92
Buchan, Graeme David 1948- WhoWor 93
Buchan, Hamish Noble 1944- WhoAm 92
Buchan, John 1875-1940 BioIn 17, ScF&FL 92
Buchan, John Stuart ScF&FL 92
Buchan, Ronald Forbes 1915- WhoAm 92, WhoE 93
Buchan, Russell Paul 1947- WhoEmL 93, WhoWor 93
Buchan, Vivian Eileen 1911- WhoWrEP 92
Buchanan, Alida Law&B 92
Buchanan, Angela M. BioIn 17
Buchanan, Bay BioIn 17
Buchanan(-Berrigan), Dawna Lisa 1954- ConAu 137
Buchanan, Brenda J. WhoAmW 93, WhoWor 93
Buchanan, Bruce, II 1945- WhoAm 92
Buchanan, Buck 1940-1992 BioIn 17, NewYTBS 92 [port]
Buchanan, Candice Lynn 1952- WhoAmW 93
Buchanan, Charles Breneman 1931- St&PR 93, WhoAm 92
Buchanan, D.J. 1945- WhoScE 91-1
Buchanan, Daniel Harvey 1923- WhoAm 92
Buchanan, David 1944- St&PR 93
Buchanan, David R. 1932- St&PR 93
Buchanan, David Royal 1934- WhoSSW 93
Buchanan, Dennis Langston WhoScE 91-1
Buchanan, Dennis Michael 1945- WhoAm 92
Buchanan, Diane Kay 1960- WhoAmW 93
Buchanan, Dianne Jean Johnson 1948- WhoAmW 93
Buchanan, Dodds Ireton 1931- WhoAm 92
Buchanan, Ed Buck 1948- WhoEmL 93
Buchanan, Edna WhoAm 92, WhoAmW 93
Buchanan, Ellery R. 1950- St&PR 93
Buchanan, Ellery Rives 1950- WhoAm 92, WhoE 93
Buchanan, Fannie Rebecca 1875- AmWomPl
Buchanan, Floyd BioIn 17
Buchanan, Franklin 1800-1874 HarEnMi
Buchanan, George WhoScE 91-1
Buchanan, George D. 1937- St&PR 93
Buchanan, George Francis 1924- WhoAm 92
Buchanan, Gloria Jean 1950- WhoAmW 93
Buchanan, Hubert A. 1905- WhoWrEP 92
Buchanan, Isobel 1954- Baker 92
Buchanan, Jack 1890-1957 IntDcF 2-3 [port]
Buchanan, Jack Willard 1923- St&PR 93
Buchanan, James 1791-1868 BioIn 17, PolPar
Buchanan, James Blythe 1933- St&PR 93
Buchanan, James Delbert 1941- WhoSSW 93
Buchanan, James Junkin 1925- WhoAm 92
Buchanan, James M. 1919- BioIn 17
Buchanan, James McGill 1919- WhoAm 92, WhoSSW 93, WhoWor 93, WhoWrEP 92
Buchanan, James William, III 1948- WhoEmL 93
Buchanan, Jerry Major 1923- WhoWrEP 92
Buchanan, Jessica ScF&FL 92
Buchanan, John A. 1925- St&PR 93
Buchanan, John Donald 1927- WhoAm 92
Buchanan, John Edward 1939- St&PR 93
Buchanan, John Edward, Jr. 1953- WhoSSW 93
Buchanan, John Grant WhoScE 91-1
Buchanan, John Grant 1926- WhoWor 93
Buchanan, John Machlin 1917- WhoAm 92
Buchanan, John MacLennan 1931- WhoAm 92
Buchanan, John R. 1929- St&PR 93
Buchanan, John Robert 1928- WhoAm 92
Buchanan, John Thomson WhoScE 91-1
Buchanan, Keith Deans WhoScE 91-1
Buchanan, Larry MiSFD 9
Buchanan, Lee Ann 1955- WhoEmL 93
Buchanan, Lillian 1896-1991 BioIn 17
Buchanan, Lisa Cyr WhoE 93
Buchanan, Lisa M. 1968- WhoEmL 93
Buchanan, Lovell 1949- WhoE 93
Buchanan, Maggie WhoWrEP 92
Buchanan, Margaret AmWomPl
Buchanan, Marie 1922- ScF&FL 92
Buchanan, Marney E. Law&B 92
Buchanan, Maurice J. 1937- St&PR 93
Buchanan, Minor Ferris 1951- WhoEmL 93
Buchanan, Nancy L. Law&B 92
Buchanan, Neil Harold 1959- WhoE 93
Buchanan, Patrick BioIn 17
Buchanan, Patrick 1938- JrnUS
Buchanan, Patrick Joseph 1938- NewYTBS 92 [port], WhoAm 92, WhoE 93
Buchanan, Paul BioIn 17
Buchanan, Paul 1920- BioIn 17
Buchanan, Peggy Carr 1925- WhoAmW 93
Buchanan, Percy d1990 BioIn 17
Buchanan, Peter McEachin 1935- WhoAm 92, WhoE 93
Buchanan, Phillip Hoge 1960- WhoEmL 93, WhoSSW 93
Buchanan, Ranald Dennis 1932- WhoWor 93
Buchanan, Ray Allen 1947- WhoWrEP 92
Buchanan, Rhonda Lee Dahl 1954- WhoSSW 93
Buchanan, Richard Robertson Trail 1944- WhoWor 93
Buchanan, Robert Alexander 1932- WhoAm 92
Buchanan, Robert Angus WhoScE 91-1
Buchanan, Robert Angus 1930- WhoAm 92
Buchanan, Robert Campbell 1940- St&PR 93, WhoAm 92
Buchanan, Robert Edgar 1919- WhoAm 92
Buchanan, Robert McLeod 1932- WhoAm 92
Buchanan, Robert Taylor 1944- WhoAm 92
Buchanan, Ron Joe 1944- WhoSSW 93
Buchanan, Susan Shaver 1954- WhoAm 92
Buchanan, Teri Bailey 1946- WhoAmW 93
Buchanan, Thomas G. 1919-1988 ScF&FL 92
Buchanan, Vera Daerr 1902-1955 BioIn 17
Buchanan, William Burdett 1949- WhoEmL 93
Buchanan, William E. 1903- St&PR 93
Buchanan, William Eugene 1903- WhoAm 92
Buchanan, William H., Jr. Law&B 92
Buchanan, William Hobart, Jr. 1937- St&PR 93, WhoAm 92
Buchanan, William J(esse) 1926- ConAu 39NR
Buchanan, William Walter 1927- WhoAm 92
Buchanan Tomlinson, Dawn Ann 1960- WhoEmL 93, WhoSSW 93
Bucharoff, Simon 1881-1955 Baker 92
Buchberger, Bruno 1942- WhoScE 91-4
Buchberger, Josef F. 1930- WhoScE 91-4
Buchbinder, Darrell B. Law&B 92
Buchbinder, Rudolf 1946- Baker 92, WhoWor 93
Buchbinder, Sharon Bell 1951- WhoEmL 93
Buchbinder-Green, Barbara Joyce 1944- WhoAmW 93
Buchborn, Eberhard 1921- WhoScE 91-3
Buche, Robert H. d1992 BioIn 17
Bucheister, Patricia Louise 1942- WhoWrEP 92
Buchek, Kathleen A. 1958- WhoWrEP 92
Buchel, Karl Heinz 1931- WhoScE 91-3
Buchele, Bonnie Jean 1942- WhoAmW 93
Buchele, Brentley Allen 1955- WhoEmL 93
Buchele, Wesley Fisher 1920- WhoAm 92
Buchelos, Constantin 1941- WhoScE 91-3
Buchen, Edwin Morrisey 1912- St&PR 93
Buchen, John Gustave 1920- WhoAm 92
Buchenroth, Stephen Richard 1948- WhoEmL 93
Bucher, Carol Anne 1948- WhoEmL 93
Bucher, G. Harold 1922- St&PR 93
Bucher, George Scott 1942- WhoIns 93
Bucher, Hans R. 1936- St&PR 93
Bucher, Ingrid Yvonne 1931- WhoAmW 93
Bucher, J. WhoScE 91-4
Bucher, Jan BioIn 17
Bucher, Jeffrey M. 1933- BioIn 17
Bucher, Jeffrey Martin 1933- WhoAm 92
Bucher, John Henry 1939- WhoAm 92
Bucher, Jurg B. 1943- WhoScE 91-4
Bucher, Karl 1847-1930 Baker 92

Bucher, Nancy Leslie Rutherfurd 1913- *WhoAmW 93, WhoE 93*
Bucher, Richard David 1949- *WhoE 93*
Bucher, Suzanne *BioIn 17*
Bucherl, Emil Sebastian 1919- *WhoScE 91-3*
Bucherre-Frazier, Veronique 1951- *WhoAm 92, WhoAmW 93, WhoEmL 93, WhoWor 93*
Buchert, Jean Ruth 1922- *WhoSSW 93*
Buchhalter, Simon 1881-1955 *Baker 92*
Buchholz, Barbara Ballinger 1949- *WhoAmW 93*
Buchholz, Carolyn Leigh 1955- *WhoAmW 93, WhoEmL 93*
Buchholz, David Louis 1936- *WhoAm 92*
Buchholz, Don A. *St&PR 93*
Buchholz, Donald Alden 1929- *WhoAm 92*
Buchholz, Douglas N. 1949- *St&PR 93*
Buchholz, H.E. *WhoScE 91-3*
Buchholz, Jeffrey Carl 1947- *WhoEmL 93*
Buchholz, Kristi Michelle Atchley 1962- *WhoEmL 93*
Buchholz, Richard F. 1930- *St&PR 93*
Buchholz, Robert B. *St&PR 93*
Buchholz, Roger John 1943- *St&PR 93*
Buchholz, Suzanne *ScF&FL 92*
Buchholz, William Edward 1942- *St&PR 93, WhoAm 92*
Buchholz, William James 1945- *WhoE 93, WhoWor 93*
Buchholz-Shaw, Donna Marie 1950- *WhoEmL 93*
Buchi, George Hermann 1921- *WhoAm 92*
Buchi, Gualtiero Amedeo 1930- *WhoWor 93*
Buchi, James 1922- *WhoWor 93*
Buchignani, Leo Joseph 1922- *WhoAm 92*
Buchin, Jean 1920- *WhoE 93*
Buchin, Stanley Ira 1931- *WhoAm 92, WhoE 93, WhoWor 93*
Buchko, Michael Scott 1946- *WhoEmL 93, WhoWor 93*
Buchla, Donald (Frederick) 1937- *Baker 92*
Buchler, Jean-Robert 1942- *WhoSSW 93*
Buchler, Johann Walter 1935- *WhoScE 91-3*
Buchler, Justus 1914-1991 *BioIn 17*
Buchler, Kathleen Ann *Law&B 92*
Buchler, Peter R. *Law&B 92*
Buchler, Ronald Michael 1944- *St&PR 93*
Buchman, Adele S. *Law&B 92*
Buchman, Donald L. 1939- *St&PR 93*
Buchman, Elwood 1923- *WhoAm 92*
Buchman, Heather Rebecca 1965- *WhoAm 92*
Buchman, Kenneth William 1956- *WhoEmL 93*
Buchman, Mark Edward 1937- *St&PR 93*
Buchman, Roberta L. *Law&B 92*
Buchman, Rosalind Solon d1990 *BioIn 17*
Buchman, Seth Barry 1955- *WhoEmL 93, WhoWor 93*
Buchmann, Alan Paul 1934- *WhoAm 92*
Buchmann, Gary John 1957- *WhoEmL 93*
Buchmeier, Michael Joseph 1948- *WhoEmL 93*
Buchmeier, Ronald Wayne *Law&B 92*
Buchmeyer, Jerry 1933- *WhoAm 92, WhoSSW 93*
Buchner, Areta 1951- *WhoE 93*
Buchner, Georg 1813-1837 *OxDcOp*
Buchner, Hans 1483-1538 *Baker 92*
Buchner, Marvin 1929- *St&PR 93*
Buchner, Orville W. 1936- *St&PR 93*
Buchner, Philipp Friedrich 1614-1669 *Baker 92*
Buchner, Piotr *BioIn 17*
Bucholtz, Harold Ronald 1952- *WhoEmL 93*
Bucholtz, Jefferey d1990 *BioIn 17*
Buchroithner, Manfred Ferdinand 1950- *WhoScE 91-4*
Buchs, Armand 1930- *WhoScE 91-4*
Buchsbaum, Betty Cynthia 1927- *WhoAmW 93*
Buchsbaum, Craig M. *Law&B 92*
Buchsbaum, Frank 1923- *St&PR 93*
Buchsbaum, Gershon 1949- *WhoE 93*
Buchsbaum, Jay 1953- *St&PR 93*
Buchsbaum, Michael C. *Law&B 92*
Buchsbaum, Peter A. 1945- *WhoAm 92*
Buchsbaum, Solomon Jan 1929- *WhoAm 92*
Bucht, Birgitta Elisabet 1943- *WhoUN 92*
Bucht, Gunnar 1927- *Baker 92*
Buchta, Stanislav 1931- *WhoScE 91-4*
Buchtela, Karl 1932- *WhoScE 91-4*
Buchter, Thomas 1949- *WhoAm 92*
Buchtger, Fritz 1903-1978 *Baker 92*
Buchwald, Art *BioIn 17*
Buchwald, Art 1925- *JrnUS, WhoAm 92, WhoE 93, WhoWor 93, WhoWrEP 92*
Buchwald, Caryl Edward 1937- *WhoAm 92*
Buchwald, Elias 1924- *WhoAm 92*
Buchwald, Henry 1932- *WhoAm 92*
Buchwald, James Paul 1928- *St&PR 93*
Buchwald, Jennifer Sullivan 1930- *WhoAm 92*
Buchwald, Lee E. 1958- *St&PR 93*
Buchwald, Max Stanton 1956- *WhoSSW 93*
Buchwald, Nathaniel Avrom 1925- *WhoAm 92*
Buchwald, Sara P. 1941- *WhoWrEP 92*
Buchwald, Vagn Fabritius 1929- *WhoScE 91-2*
Buchwalter, Lawrence M. *Law&B 92*
Bucich, Alexandra *St&PR 93*
Bucino, Tony Gerard *St&PR 93*
Buck, Albert R. 1946- *St&PR 93*
Buck, Alfred Andreas 1921- *WhoAm 92*
Buck, Alfred Charles d1991 *BioIn 17*
Buck, Alison Jennifer 1952- *WhoAmW 93, WhoEmL 93*
Buck, Anne Marie 1939- *WhoAmW 93*
Buck, Arthur Charles 1927- *WhoSSW 93*
Buck, Bradford Harold *Law&B 92*
Buck, Carol Kathleen 1925- *WhoAm 92, WhoAmW 93*
Buck, Carolyn Felter 1941- *St&PR 93*
Buck, Charles H. 1915- *ScF&FL 92*
Buck, Charles Theodore 1936- *St&PR 93*
Buck, Christian Brevoort Zabriskie 1914- *WhoWor 93*
Buck, David C. *St&PR 93*
Buck, David D., Jr. 1941- *St&PR 93*
Buck, David W. 1937- *St&PR 93*
Buck, Donald Tirrell 1931- *WhoE 93*
Buck, Dudley 1839-1909 *Baker 92*
Buck, Elizabeth Jane 1957- *WhoAmW 93*
Buck, Fred A. 1945- *WhoIns 93*
Buck, Genevieve Carol 1932- *WhoAm 92*
Buck, Gertrude 1871-1922 *AmWomPl*
Buck, Gurdon Hall 1936- *WhoAm 92*
Buck, Jack *WhoAm 92*
Buck, James E. *St&PR 93, WhoE 93*
Buck, James M., Jr. 1934- *St&PR 93*
Buck, Jan Andrew *Law&B 92*
Buck, Jane Louise 1933- *WhoAmW 93, WhoE 93*
Buck, Jane R. *Law&B 92*
Buck, Jari Holland 1950- *WhoEmL 93*
Buck, Jay Keatley 1928- *WhoAm 92*
Buck, Jeffrey Clark 1959- *WhoEmL 93*
Buck, Joan Juliet *BioIn 17*
Buck, John Bonner 1912- *WhoAm 92*
Buck, K.W. *WhoScE 91-1*
Buck, Lawrence Paul 1944- *WhoAm 92*
Buck, Lee Albert 1923- *WhoAm 92, WhoWor 93*
Buck, Lilli 1950- *WhoWrEP 92*
Buck, Linda Dee 1946- *WhoAmW 93*
Buck, Linda Susan 1949- *WhoEmL 93*
Buck, Louise Zierdt 1919- *WhoAm 92*
Buck, M. Alison 1951- *WhoEmL 93*
Buck, Manfred 1928- *WhoScE 91-3*
Buck, Merle K. 1932- *St&PR 93*
Buck, Monica 1962- *BioIn 17*
Buck, Nancy Margaret Timma 1945- *WhoAmW 93*
Buck, Ole 1945- *Baker 92*
Buck, Paul 1927- *WhoSSW 93*
Buck, Paul Burns 1953- *WhoSSW 93*
Buck, Pearl 1892-1973 *ConHero 2*
Buck, Pearl S. 1892-1973 *BioIn 17*
Buck, Percy Carter 1871-1947 *Baker 92*
Buck, Peter *BioIn 17*
Buck, Peter 1880-1951 *DcTwHis*
Buck, Peter Henry *IntDcAn*
Buck, Richard Clay 1962- *WhoSSW 93*
Buck, Robert Follette 1917- *WhoAm 92*
Buck, Robert R. 1947- *St&PR 93*
Buck, Robert Treat, Jr. 1939- *WhoAm 92, WhoE 93*
Buck, Robert W. 1940- *St&PR 93*
Buck, Rodney Allen 1948- *St&PR 93*
Buck, Rosemary Alice 1953- *WhoAmW 93*
Buck, Roswell Seymour 1904- *WhoE 93*
Buck, Rufus d1896 *BioIn 17*
Buck, Sharon Klein *Law&B 92*
Buck, Stephen Clark 1948- *St&PR 93*
Buck, Steven Edward 1942- *St&PR 93*
Buck, Steven Louis 1949- *WhoEmL 93*
Buck, Susan Jane 1947- *WhoEmL 93*
Buck, Thomas Randolph 1930- *WhoAm 92*
Buck, William Boyd 1933- *WhoAm 92*
Buck, William Franklin, Jr. 1936- *St&PR 93*
Buck, William R. *Law&B 92*
Bucka, Hans Gunter 1925- *WhoScE 91-3*
Buckalew, James M. 1940- *St&PR 93*
Buckalew, Judith Adele 1947- *WhoAm 92*
Buckalew, Robert Joseph 1924- *WhoE 93*
Buckardt, Everett L. *WhoAm 92*
Buckaway, Catherine Margaret 1919- *WhoCanL 92*
Buckaway, William Allen, Jr. 1934- *WhoSSW 93*
Buckbee, Albert W. 1939- *St&PR 93*
Buckbee, Albert W., II 1939- *WhoIns 93*
Buckbee, Edward O'Dell 1936- *WhoAm 92, WhoSSW 93*
Bucke, Charles 1781-1846 *BioIn 17*
Bucke, Christopher *WhoScE 91-1*
Bucke, Richard Maurice 1837-1902 *BioIn 17*
Buckee, Geoffrey K. 1938- *WhoScE 91-1*
Buckee, James William 1946- *St&PR 93*
Buckel, Werner Rudolf Gottfried 1920- *WhoScE 91-3*
Buckels, Marvin Wayne 1929- *WhoAm 92*
Buckely, Robert 1928- *St&PR 93*
Bucken, Ernst 1884-1949 *Baker 92*
Bucker, Rodney G. *Law&B 92*
Buckett, Bonnie-jean 1948- *WhoEmL 93, WhoSSW 93*
Buckey, Peggy McMartin *BioIn 17*
Buckey, Raymond 1958- *BioIn 17*
Buckey, Robert V. 1925- *St&PR 93*
Buckham, Kirk Darryl 1949- *St&PR 93*
Buckhold, William Charles 1953- *WhoEmL 93*
Buckholts, Claudia 1944- *WhoWrEP 92*
Buckholtz, Eileen 1949- *ScF&FL 92*
Buckholtz, Eileen Brenda Garber 1949- *WhoAmW 93*
Buckholz, Durene Marie *WhoAmW 93*
Buckholz, Gary *BioIn 17*
Buckholz, Jeffrey William 1956- *WhoSSW 93*
Buckholz, Linda *BioIn 17*
Buckhout, Robert 1935-1990 *BioIn 17*
Bucki, Carl Leo 1953- *WhoEmL 93*
Buckinger, Sandra Waters 1959- *WhoAmW 93*
Buckingham, Amyand David *WhoScE 91-1*
Buckingham, Amyand David 1930- *WhoWor 93*
Buckingham, Charles H. 1950- *St&PR 93*
Buckingham, Douglas A. 1943- *St&PR 93*
Buckingham, E.J., III *Law&B 92*
Buckingham, Edwin John, III 1947- *St&PR 93, WhoAm 92, WhoEmL 93*
Buckingham, Fannie Louise *AmWomPl*
Buckingham, Fred P. 1953- *St&PR 93*
Buckingham, George Villiers, Duke of 1592-1628 *HarEnMi*
Buckingham, Harold Canute, Jr. 1930- *WhoAm 92*
Buckingham, Isabel *AmWomPl*
Buckingham, James (William) 1932-1992 *ConAu 136*
Buckingham, Jamie *BioIn 17, ConAu 136*
Buckingham, Jamie W. d1992 *NewYTBS 92 [port]*
Buckingham, Julia Clare *WhoScE 91-1*
Buckingham, Julia Clare 1950- *WhoWor 93*
Buckingham, Lindsey 1949?- *ConMus 8 [port], WhoAm 92*
See Also Fleetwood, Mick 1942- *Baker 92*
Buckingham, M.E. *ScF&FL 92*
Buckingham, Richard Leroy 1945- *WhoAm 92*
Buckingham, Richard Sherwood 1932- *St&PR 93*
Buckingham, Stephen Wayne *Law&B 92*
Buckingham, Wayne *BioIn 17*
Buckingham, William Forrest 1951- *WhoAm 92*
Buckla, John D. 1953- *St&PR 93*
Buckla, John David 1953- *WhoE 93*
Buckland, Bonnie Kay 1949- *WhoSSW 93*
Buckland, Charles Smillie 1934- *WhoAm 92*
Buckland, Michael Keeble 1941- *WhoAm 92*
Buckland, Roger Basil 1942- *WhoAm 92*
Buckland, Tamara Smith 1964- *WhoAmW 93*
Buckland, William Henry 1945- *St&PR 93, WhoAm 92*
Buckle, Anthony E. 1949- *WhoScE 91-1*
Buckle, Daphne *WhoCanL 92*
Buckle, David *BioIn 17*
Buckle, Frederick Tarifero 1949- *WhoAm 92*
Buckle, June M. 1951- *WhoEmL 93*
Buckle, Kwame, III 1940- *St&PR 93*
Buckle, Peter William *WhoScE 91-1*
Bucklen, George B. 1941- *St&PR 93*
Buckler, Beatrice 1933- *WhoAm 92, WhoWrEP 92*
Buckler, Bruce 1917- *St&PR 93*
Buckler, Ernest 1908-1984 *WhoCanL 92*
Buckler, Leroy M. 1930- *St&PR 93*
Buckler, Phyllis L. 1922- *St&PR 93*
Buckler, Robert B. 1950- *WhoEmL 93*
Buckler, Sheldon A. 1931- *St&PR 93, WhoAm 92*
Buckler, William Earl 1924-1990 *BioIn 17*
Buckles, Howard E. *Law&B 92*
Buckles, Robert Edwin 1917- *WhoAm 92*
Buckles, Robert Howard 1932- *WhoAm 92*
Buckles, Rodney G. *Law&B 92*
Buckles, Stephen Gary 1943- *WhoAm 92*
Buckles, William R. 1941- *St&PR 93*
Buckles-Deans, Delora Elizabeth 1940- *WhoAmW 93*
Bucklew, Larry L. 1942- *St&PR 93*
Bucklew, Neil S. 1940- *WhoAm 92, WhoSSW 93*
Buckley, Alice I. *Law&B 92*
Buckley, Anthony John 1937- *WhoSSW 93*
Buckley, Betty Bob 1925- *WhoAm 92, WhoAmW 93*
Buckley, C. Brian 1933- *WhoScE 91-1*
Buckley, Carol Joy 1931- *WhoAmW 93*
Buckley, Charles A. 1890-1967 *PolPar*
Buckley, Charles Eugene 1945- *WhoAm 92*
Buckley, Cheryl Rae 1947- *WhoAmW 93*
Buckley, Christopher 1952- *ScF&FL 92*
Buckley, Christopher Taylor 1952- *BioIn 17, ConAu 139*
Buckley, Cornelius M(ichael) 1925- *ConAu 138*
Buckley, D.J. 1917- *St&PR 93*
Buckley, Daniel G. 1936- *St&PR 93*
Buckley, Devin G. *Law&B 92*
Buckley, Donald J. *Law&B 92*
Buckley, Doug 1934- *ScF&FL 92*
Buckley, Edward Joseph 1920- *WhoE 93*
Buckley, Edwin J. *Law&B 92*
Buckley, Edwin T. *WhoAm 92*
Buckley, Elliot Ross 1921- *WhoAm 92*
Buckley, Emerson 1916-1989 *Baker 92, BioIn 17*
Buckley, Esther Gonzalez-Arroyo 1948- *WhoAmW 93*
Buckley, F.C. 1921- *St&PR 93*
Buckley, Frank Wilson 1914- *WhoAm 92*
Buckley, G.J. 1925- *St&PR 93*
Buckley, Gail Geary 1951- *WhoE 93*
Buckley, Gerard Duke 1940- *St&PR 93*
Buckley, Harry W. 1913- *St&PR 93*
Buckley, Helen Ann 1926- *WhoAmW 93*
Buckley, Hilda Mayer 1948- *WhoEmL 93*
Buckley, J. Stephen 1942- *St&PR 93*
Buckley, Jacqueline L. *St&PR 93*
Buckley, James Gary 1953- *WhoEmL 93*
Buckley, James L. 1923- *PolPar*
Buckley, James Lane 1923- *CngDr 91, WhoAm 92, WhoE 93*
Buckley, Jeremiah Stephen 1944- *WhoAm 92*
Buckley, Jerome Hamilton 1917- *WhoAm 92*
Buckley, Joanne (Lorna) 1953- *WhoWrEP 92*
Buckley, Jody Russelle 1965- *WhoAmW 93*
Buckley, Joe 1945- *WhoScE 91-3*
Buckley, John Edward 1940- *St&PR 93*
Buckley, John Edward 1953- *WhoEmL 93*
Buckley, John Joseph, Jr. 1944- *WhoAm 92*
Buckley, John Joseph, Jr. 1947- *WhoEmL 93*
Buckley, Joseph Paul 1924- *WhoAm 92*
Buckley, Joseph Paul, III 1949- *WhoAm 92*
Buckley, Joseph W. 1943- *St&PR 93, WhoAm 92*
Buckley, Joseph Walter 1955- *WhoE 93*
Buckley, Kathleen *ScF&FL 92*
Buckley, Kathleen Marie 1964- *WhoAmW 93*
Buckley, Kevin Joseph 1957- *WhoEmL 93*
Buckley, Lee 1947- *WhoEmL 93*
Buckley, Lisa Louise 1958- *WhoAmW 93, WhoEmL 93*
Buckley, Marta 1946- *St&PR 93*
Buckley, Mary Elizabeth 1950- *WhoAmW 93*
Buckley, Michael Edward 1950- *WhoEmL 93, WhoWor 93*
Buckley, Michael Francis 1943- *WhoE 93, WhoWor 93*
Buckley, Michael P. 1941- *WhoAm 92*
Buckley, Mike Clifford 1944- *WhoAm 92*
Buckley, Page Scott 1918- *WhoAm 92*
Buckley, Peter 1938-1991 *BioIn 17*
Buckley, Peter Jennings *WhoScE 91-1*
Buckley, Peter John 1937- *WhoWor 93*
Buckley, Priscilla Langford 1921- *WhoAm 92, WhoWrEP 92*
Buckley, R. Lawrence *Law&B 92*
Buckley, Rebecca Hatcher 1933- *WhoAm 92*
Buckley, Richard Edward 1953- *WhoAm 92*
Buckley, Richard Francis, Jr. *Law&B 92*
Buckley, Robert *Law&B 92*
Buckley, Robert 1931- *St&PR 93*
Buckley, Robert David 1938- *St&PR 93*
Buckley, Robert E. 1944- *St&PR 93*
Buckley, Robert John 1949- *WhoE 93*
Buckley, Robert Paul 1947- *WhoAm 92, WhoE 93*
Buckley, Ronald 1963- *WhoSSW 93*
Buckley, Samuel Olliphant, III 1947- *WhoEmL 93*

Buckley, Stanley Joseph, Jr. 1957- *WhoEmL 93*
Buckley, T. *WhoScE 91-1*
Buckley, Theresa Louise Riley 1932- *WhoSSW 93*
Buckley, Thomas 1933- *St&PR 93*
Buckley, Thomas Hugh 1932- *WhoAm 92*
Buckley, Timothy Andrew 1950- *WhoEmL 93, WhoSSW 93*
Buckley, Timothy White 1948- *St&PR 93*
Buckley, Virginia Laura 1929- *St&PR 93, WhoAm 92, WhoWrEP 92*
Buckley, William *BioIn 17*
Buckley, William Edwin 1937- *WhoIns 93*
Buckley, William Elmhirst 1913- *WhoAm 92*
Buckley, William F. 1925- *BioIn 17*
Buckley, William F., Jr. 1925- *JrnUS, PolPar*
Buckley, William Frank, Jr. 1925- *WhoAm 92, WhoWrEP 92*
Buckley, William H. *Law&B 92*
Buckley, William Hunt *Law&B 92*
Buckley-Brawner, Kathryn Yolande 1953- *WhoAmW 93*
Buckley-Golder, I.M. *WhoScE 91-1*
Bucklin, Dennis Arthur 1949- *WhoEmL 93*
Bucklin, Patricia Kerr 1954- *WhoEmL 93*
Bucklo, Elaine Edwards 1944- *WhoAmW 93*
Bucklo, Michael Paul *Law&B 92*
Buck-Luce, Carolyn *BioIn 17*
Buckman, James Edward 1944- *WhoAm 92*
Buckman, R.E. *WhoScE 91-4*
Buckman, Repha Joan 1942- *WhoWrEP 92*
Buckman, Robert H. 1937- *St&PR 93*
Buckman, Robert Henry 1937- *WhoAm 92*
Buckman, Thomas Richard 1923- *WhoAm 92*
Buckman, Thomas Warren *Law&B 92*
Buckmaster, Carl E. 1950- *St&PR 93*
Buckmaster, Henrietta 1909-1983 *ScF&FL 92*
Buckmaster, Thomas L. 1956- *WhoEmL 93*
Buckmiller, Gary Lee 1941- *St&PR 93*
Buckmore, Alvah Clarence, Jr. 1944- *WhoAm 92, WhoE 93, WhoWor 93*
Bucknall, Barbara J. 1933- *ScF&FL 92*
Bucknall, Clifford Adrian 1956- *WhoWor 93*
Bucknall, Clive Brian *WhoScE 91-1*
Bucknam, James Romeo 1911- *WhoAm 92*
Bucknam, Mary Olivia Caswell 1914- *WhoAm 92, WhoAmW 93*
Bucknell, Anita 1934- *WhoE 93, WhoWor 93*
Bucknell, Katherine 1957- *WhoWor 93*
Bucknell, Larry Alan 1950- *WhoEmL 93*
Buckner, Bill 1949- *BioIn 17*
Buckner, Charles A., Jr. *Law&B 92*
Buckner, Elmer La Mar 1922- *WhoAm 92*
Buckner, Fred Lynn 1932- *St&PR 93*
Buckner, Helen Watson d1991 *BioIn 17*
Buckner, James Lee 1940- *WhoSSW 93*
Buckner, James Lowell 1934- *WhoAm 92*
Buckner, Jan Allyson *Law&B 92*
Buckner, Jan J. 1942- *St&PR 93*
Buckner, Jennie *BioIn 17*
Buckner, John Hugh 1919- *WhoAm 92*
Buckner, John Kendrick 1936- *WhoSSW 93*
Buckner, John Knowles 1936- *St&PR 93, WhoAm 92*
Buckner, Layton Ray 1932- *St&PR 93*
Buckner, Leonard Wayne 1943- *St&PR 93*
Buckner, Linda Iverson 1950- *WhoEmL 93*
Buckner, Milt(on) 1915-1977 *Baker 92*
Buckner, Philip Franklin 1930- *WhoAm 92*
Buckner, Phillip Alfred 1942- *WhoWrEP 92*
Buckner, Robert 1906-1989 *ScF&FL 92*
Buckner, Robert P. *Law&B 92*
Buckner, Sally Beaver 1931- *WhoWrEP 92*
Buckner, Simon 1823-1914 *BioIn 17*
Buckner, Wesley M. *St&PR 93*
Bucko, John J. 1937- *St&PR 93*
Bucko, John Joseph 1937- *WhoAm 92*
Buckridee, Patricia Ilona 1960- *WhoAmW 93, WhoEmL 93*
Bucks, Charles A. 1927- *St&PR 93*
Bucks, Charles Alan 1927- *WhoAm 92*
Bucksbaum, Martin 1920- *St&PR 93*
Bucksey, Colin *MiSFD 9*
Buckshon, Joseph, Jr. 1959- *St&PR 93*
Buckshon, Joseph J. 1934- *St&PR 93*
Buckstein, Mark A. *Law&B 92*
Buckstein, Mark Aaron 1939- *WhoAm 92*
Buckton, Alice Mary *AmWomPl*
Buckvar, Felice 1938- *WhoWrEP 92*
Buckwalter, Charles Q. *Law&B 92*
Buckwalter, John M. 1931- *St&PR 93*
Buckwalter, Ronald Lawrence 1936- *WhoAm 92, WhoE 93*
Buckwalter, Wayne Clark 1955- *WhoEmL 93*
Buckwell, Allan Edgar *WhoScE 91-1*
Buckwheat Zydeco *BioIn 17*
Bucove, Arnold David 1934- *WhoE 93*
Bucur, John Charles 1925- *WhoAm 92, WhoSSW 93*
Bucur, Nicholas Alan 1939- *St&PR 93*
Bucur, Nicholas Anthony, III 1950- *WhoEmL 93*
Bucur, Voichita 1940- *WhoWor 93*
Bucus, Uldis *Law&B 92*
Bucus, Uldis 1942- *St&PR 93, WhoAm 92*
Bucy, J. Fred 1928- *WhoAm 92*
Bucy, Pamela Lundy 1928- *WhoAmW 93*
Bucy, Paul C. 1904- *WhoAm 92*
Bucy, Richard Snowden 1935- *WhoAm 92*
Buczak, Douglas Chester 1949- *WhoEmL 93*
Buczek, Barbara (Kazimiera Zofia) 1940- *Baker 92*
Buczko, Wlodzimierz 1942- *WhoScE 91-4*
Buczkowna, Barbara (Kazimiera Zofia) 1940- *Baker 92*
Buczkowski, David John 1954- *WhoEmL 93*
Buczkowski, Joseph 1927- *St&PR 93*
Buczkowski, Leonard 1900-1967 *DrEEuF*
Buczynski, Walter 1933- *Baker 92*
Buda, Aleks 1910- *WhoWor 93*
Buda, James Bernard *Law&B 92*
Buda, T.J., Jr. *Law&B 92*
Budacz, Ronald Richard 1946- *St&PR 93*
Budai, Csaba 1941- *WhoScE 91-4*
Budai, Ivan 1953- *WhoUN 92*
Budai, Livia 1950- *WhoWor 93*
Budalur, Thyagarajan Subbanarayan 1929- *WhoAm 92, WhoSSW 93*
Budan, C.D. 1931- *WhoScE 91-4*
Budash, Ronald F. 1940- *St&PR 93*
Budashkin, Nikolai 1910-1988 *Baker 92*
Buday, Ferdinand 1928- *WhoScE 91-4*
Budd, Bernadette Smith 1943- *WhoAmW 93, WhoE 93*
Budd, Caroline H. *AmWomPl*
Budd, Charles A. 1951- *St&PR 93*
Budd, Chester Francis 1933- *St&PR 93*
Budd, David 1927-1991 *BioIn 17*
Budd, David Glenn 1934- *WhoSSW 93, WhoWor 93*
Budd, Edward H. 1933- *St&PR 93, WhoIns 93*
Budd, Edward Hey 1933- *WhoAm 92, WhoE 93*
Budd, Harold 1936- *Baker 92*
Budd, John H. 1938- *WhoIns 93*
Budd, John Henry 1908- *WhoAm 92*
Budd, John Herbert *Law&B 92*
Budd, John Herbert 1938- *St&PR 93*
Budd, Louis John 1921- *WhoAm 92*
Budd, Michael K. 1933- *WhoScE 91-1*
Budd, Mike 1944- *ScF&FL 92*
Budd, Patricia Ann *Law&B 92*
Budd, Patricia Jean 1947- *WhoE 93*
Budd, Richard L. 1937- *St&PR 93*
Budd, Richard Wade 1934- *WhoAm 92, WhoE 93*
Budd, Steven William *Law&B 92*
Budd, Thomas 1934- *St&PR 93*
Budd, W.B. 1935- *St&PR 93*
Budd, Wayne A. *WhoAm 92*
Budd, William Karl 1955- *WhoEmL 93*
Budd, Zola *BioIn 17*
Budde, Frederick Leo *Law&B 92*
Budde, Rollo L. 1917- *St&PR 93*
Budde, Thomas E. 1938- *St&PR 93*
Budde, William R., Jr. 1950- *St&PR 93*
Buddecke, Wolfram Werner 1926- *WhoWor 93*
Buddemeier, Maurice R. 1930- *St&PR 93*
Buddemeyer, David Allan 1957- *St&PR 93*
Budden, Julian (Midforth) 1924- *Baker 92*
Buddenbohm, Harold William 1959- *WhoEmL 93*
Buddensieg, Daphne *BioIn 17*
Buddensieg, Tilmann 1928- *ConAu 138*
Buddha, Gautama *BioIn 17*
Buddhdev, Sharad N. 1951- *St&PR 93*
Buddicom, Jacintha 1901- *ScF&FL 92*
Buddie, James Anthony *Law&B 92*
Buddy, Lee Clinton 1948- *WhoSSW 93*
Budeiri, Ahmed A. 1960- *WhoWor 93*
Budelis, Joseph John 1943- *WhoE 93*
Budelman, Robert Burns, Jr. 1937- *WhoAm 92*
Budelov, Peter Roy 1947- *WhoEmL 93*
Buden, Rosemary Vidale 1931- *WhoAm 92*
Budenholzer, Frank Edward 1945- *WhoWor 93*
Budenholzer, Roland Anthony 1912- *WhoAm 92, WhoWor 93*
Budenny, Semen Mikhailovich 1883-1973 *HarEnMi*
Budevski, Evgeni Bogdanov 1922- *WhoScE 91-4*
Budge, Bruce Penwell 1930- *St&PR 93*
Budge, Hamer Harold 1910- *WhoAm 92*
Budge, Hamilton W. 1928- *St&PR 93*
Budge, Hamilton Whithed 1928- *WhoAm 92*
Budge, Ian *WhoScE 91-1*
Budge, Larry Donald 1939- *WhoAm 92*
Budgell, Rodger C. 1935- *St&PR 93*
Budgie
See Siouxsie and the Banshees *ConMus 8*
Budgor, Aaron Bernard 1948- *WhoEmL 93*
Budiansky, Bernard 1925- *WhoAm 92*
Budick, Cynthia Cherner 1942- *WhoE 93*
Budig, Gene Arthur 1939- *WhoAm 92, WhoWor 93*
Budik, Edith Mary 1948- *WhoAmW 93*
Budin, Josko 1928- *WhoScE 91-4*
Budin, Philip S. 1940- *St&PR 93*
Budinger, Charles Jude 1940- *WhoWor 93*
Budington, William Stone 1919- *WhoAm 92*
Budinich-Diez, Maria Valeria 1958- *WhoAmW 93*
Budisan, Nicolae 1927- *WhoScE 91-4*
Budish, Andrew *Law&B 92*
Budke, Camilla Eunice 1928- *WhoAmW 93*
Budkevics, Girts Janis 1952- *WhoEmL 93*
Budkin, Alexander Ivanovich 1951- *WhoWor 93*
Budman, Cathy Linda 1957- *WhoAmW 93, WhoEmL 93*
Budney, William J. 1940- *St&PR 93*
Budnick, Ernest Joseph 1948- *WhoE 93, WhoEmL 93, WhoWor 93*
Budnitz, Arron Edward 1949- *WhoEmL 93*
Budny, Clement Leonard, Jr. *Law&B 92*
Budny, Eugeniusz 1935- *WhoScE 91-4*
Budny, James Charles 1948- *WhoEmL 93*
Budny, Marco Michael 1954- *St&PR 93*
Budny, Patricia L. *St&PR 93*
Budoff, Penny Wise 1939- *WhoAmW 93*
Budovitch, Brenda Louise 1950- *St&PR 93*
Budow, Terri Hunter *Law&B 92*
Budrevics, Alexander 1925- *WhoAm 92*
Budrow, Nancy Elizabeth 1936- *WhoWrEP 92*
Budrys, Algirdas *ScF&FL 92*
Budrys, Algis 1931- *BioIn 17, ScF&FL 92*
Budrys, Grace 1943- *WhoAmW 93*
Budsworth, J.P. *WhoScE 91-1*
Budtz-Jorgensen, Ejvind 1938- *WhoWor 93*
Budwick, Jeanine Elster 1948- *WhoAmW 93*
Budy, Andrea Hollander 1947- *WhoWrEP 92*
Budy, Edward *Law&B 92*
Budy, Sonia Lim 1937- *WhoE 93*
Budyak, John Joseph 1952- *St&PR 93*
Budzanowski, Andrzej 1933- *WhoScE 91-4*
Budzeika, George 1921- *WhoE 93*
Budzikiewicz, Herbert 1933- *WhoScE 91-3, WhoWor 93*
Budzinski, James Edward 1953- *WhoEmL 93*
Budzinski, Roman Joseph 1949- *WhoEmL 93*
Budzinsky, A. Alexander 1942- *St&PR 93*
Budzinsky, Armin Alexander 1942- *WhoWor 93*
Budzynski, Antoni Feliks 1935- *WhoScE 91-4*
Budzynski, Marian Jerzy 1935- *WhoScE 91-4*
Bue, Carl Olaf, Jr. 1922- *WhoAm 92*
Bue, Christian Jean 1938- *WhoWor 93*
Bueche, Ronald J. *St&PR 93*
Bueche, Wendell Francis 1930- *St&PR 93*
Buechel, Donald Robert 1924- *WhoAm 92*
Buechele, Robert Harold *Law&B 92*
Buechlein, Daniel Mark 1938- *WhoAm 92, WhoSSW 93*
Buechler, Bradley Bruce 1948- *St&PR 93, WhoAm 92*
Buechler, C. Matthew 1933- *St&PR 93*
Buechler, Jean Ann 1945- *WhoAmW 93*
Buechler, John Carl *MiSFD 9*
Buechler, Mark Alan 1952- *WhoSSW 93*
Buechler, Neal Merlyn 1935- *St&PR 93*
Buechner, Barry Lee 1944- *St&PR 93*
Buechner, Carl Frederick 1926- *WhoAm 92*
Buechner, Frederick 1926- *BioIn 17*
Buechner, (Carl) Frederick 1926- *ConAu 39NR*
Buechner, Howard Albert 1919- *WhoAm 92*
Buechner, Margaret 1922- *WhoWor 93*
Buechner, Thomas Scharman 1926- *WhoAm 92, WhoE 93*
Buegeler, Barbara Stephanie 1945- *WhoAmW 93*
Buehl, Elizabeth Anne 1950- *WhoAmW 93*
Buehler, Bernice Alice 1904- *WhoAmW 93*
Buehler, Donald R. *Law&B 92*
Buehler, Sara L. *Law&B 92*
Buehler, Thomas L. *Law&B 92*
Buehler, Thomas Lee 1948- *WhoEmL 93*
Buehlmann, Walbert 1916- *ConAu 38NR*
Buehlmeier, Harry Scott 1949- *WhoE 93*
Buehner, Manfred P.G. 1940- *WhoScE 91-3*
Buehner, Robert William, Jr. 1952- *WhoEmL 93*
Buehner, Suzanne G. 1945- *St&PR 93*
Buehrer, Beverley Bare 1947- *WhoWrEP 92*
Buehrer, Elaine Emilie 1929- *WhoAmW 93*
Buehrig, Gordon M. 1904-1990 *BioIn 17*
Buekens, Alfons G. 1942- *WhoScE 91-2*
Buel, James Wes 1937- *WhoWor 93*
Buel, Richard Van Wyck, Jr. 1933- *WhoAm 92*
Buell, Ardin P. *Law&B 92*
Buell, Bruce Temple 1932- *WhoAm 92*
Buell, Cynthia Louise 1944- *WhoSSW 93*
Buell, Duncan Alan 1950- *WhoEmL 93*
Buell, Ellen Lewis 1905-1989 *BioIn 17*
Buell, Emmett H., Jr. 1941- *ConAu 138*
Buell, Frederick Henderson 1942- *WhoWrEP 92*
Buell, Harold L. *BioIn 17*
Buell, John 1927- *WhoCanL 92*
Buell, Lawrence Ingalls 1939- *WhoAm 92*
Buell, Margaret A. *AmWomPl*
Buell, Rodd Russell 1946- *WhoEmL 93*
Buell, Thomas Allan 1931- *WhoAm 92*
Buell, Victor Paul 1914- *WhoAm 92*
Buell, William Ackerman 1925- *WhoAm 92*
Buelow, David L. 1945- *St&PR 93*
Buelow, George J(ohn) 1929- *Baker 92*
Buelow, George John 1929- *WhoAm 92*
Buelow, Robert J. 1945- *St&PR 93*
Buelow, Roger M. *Law&B 92*
Buenaflor, Matthew Timothy 1957- *WhoEmL 93, WhoSSW 93*
Buenaventura, Milagros Paez 1943- *WhoE 93*
Buenaventura, Rafael B. 1938- *St&PR 93*
Buendia, Gloria Maria 1957- *WhoWor 93*
Buenerd, Michel J. 1942- *WhoScE 91-2*
Buenger, Caroline B. *Law&B 92*
Buenger, Clement Lawrence 1926- *St&PR 93, WhoAm 92*
Bueno, Mary Ann 1951- *WhoAmW 93*
Buente, Victor Otto, Jr. *Law&B 92*
Buenz, John Buechler 1933- *WhoAm 92*
Buenzly, Robert Charles 1943- *WhoE 93*
Buerge, Robin Kenyon 1953- *WhoAm 92*
Buergenthal, Thomas 1934- *WhoAm 92*
Buerger, Charles Alter 1938- *WhoE 93*
Buerger, David B. 1909- *St&PR 93*
Buerger, David Bernard 1909- *WhoAm 92, WhoE 93, WhoWor 93*
Buerger, E. *St&PR 93*
Buerger, Mark Thomas 1948- *St&PR 93*
Buerger, Wolfgang Arnold 1931- *WhoWor 93*
Buergermeister, Hebert 1933- *St&PR 93*
Buerk, Donald Gene 1946- *WhoE 93*
Buerk, Richard K. 1934- *St&PR 93*
Buerkel-Rothfuss, Nancy Louise 1951- *WhoEmL 93*
Buerkle, Jack Vincent 1923- *WhoAm 92*
Buermann, Peter Bruce 1938- *WhoE 93*
Buero Vallejo, Antonio 1916- *BioIn 17, WhoWor 93*
Bueschel, David Alan 1942- *WhoAm 92*
Bueschel, Richard T. 1933- *St&PR 93*
Bueschen, Anton Joslyn 1940- *WhoAm 92, WhoWor 93*
Buescher, Charles Albert, Jr. 1932- *St&PR 93*
Buescher, Thomas Paul 1949- *WhoEmL 93*
Buesing, Mary Donai 1931- *WhoAmW 93*
Buesinger, Ronald Ernest 1933- *St&PR 93, WhoAm 92*
Bueso Rosa, Jose *DcCPCAm*
Buesseler, John Aure 1919- *WhoAm 92*
Buesser, Anthony Carpenter 1929- *WhoAm 92*
Buetens, Eric D. 1953- *WhoEmL 93*
Buetow, Dennis Edward 1932- *WhoAm 92*
Buettner, Carol Ann 1948- *WhoAmW 93*
Buettner, Deborah Anne 1957- *WhoWrEP 92*
Buettner, Gerald Hugo, Jr. 1955- *WhoEmL 93*
Buettner, Kurt H.J. 1926- *WhoScE 91-3*
Buettner, Mary Elizabeth *Law&B 92*
Buettner, Michael Lewis 1957- *WhoE 93, WhoEmL 93*
Buettner, Robert Douglas *Law&B 92*
Buettner, Vicki Jean 1951- *WhoAmW 93*

Buettner-Janusch, John d1992 *NewYTBS 92 [port]*
Buettner-Janusch, John 1924-1992 *ConAu 138*
Bufalini, David Anthony 1952- *WhoEmL 93*
Bufalino, Brenda 1937- *BioIn 17*
Bufalino, Gesualdo 1920?- *ConLC 74*
Bufalino, William E. 1918-1990 *BioIn 17*
Bufe, Mary Elizabeth 1961- *WhoEmL 93*
Bufe, Uwe-Ernst 1944- *St&PR 93*
Bufe, William John 1953- *WhoSSW 93*
Buff, Conrad 1886-1975 *MajAI [port]*
Buff, Ernest Dorchester *Law&B 92*
Buff, Frank Paul 1924- *WhoAm 92*
Buff, Mary (E. Marsh) 1890-1970 *MajAI [port]*
Buffalo, William L. *Law&B 92*
Buffalo Bill 1846-1917 *BioIn 17*
Buffaloe, Neal Dollison 1924- *WhoSSW 93*
Buffalow, Oscar Thomas 1924- *St&PR 93*
Buffardin, Pierre-Gabriel c. 1690-1768 *Baker 92*
Buffat, Philippe-Andre 1942- *WhoScE 91-4*
Buffery, Judith 1943- *ScF&FL 92*
Buffet, Bernard 1928- *WhoWor 93*
Buffet, Louis-Joseph 1818-1898 *BioIn 17*
Buffet, Pierre 1946- *WhoWor 93*
Buffett, Jimmy 1946- *WhoAm 92*
Buffett, Warren E. *BioIn 17*
Buffett, Warren E. 1930- *St&PR 93*
Buffett, Warren Edward 1930- *WhoAm 92*
Buffie, Margaret *DcChlFi, ScF&FL 92*
Buffie, Margaret 1945- *SmATA 71 [port]*
Buffin, Carol 1957- *WhoWrEP 92*
Buffin, David Gareth 1961- *WhoWor 93*
Buffington, Audrey Virginia 1931- *WhoAmW 93*
Buffington, Dean 1940- *St&PR 93*
Buffington, Dennis Elvin 1944- *WhoAm 92*
Buffington, Eliza d1938 *AmWomPl*
Buffington, Gary Lee Roy 1946- *WhoEmL 93*
Buffington, Jack Eugene 1938- *WhoAm 92*
Buffington, Jody Lynn 1959- *WhoE 93*
Buffington, Ralph Meldrim 1907- *WhoAm 92, WhoWor 93*
Buffington, Susan H. *Law&B 92*
Buffinton, Keith William 1957- *WhoE 93*
Buffkin, Beverly Edith 1961- *WhoAmW 93, WhoEmL 93*
Buffkins, Archie Lee 1934- *WhoAm 92*
Buffo, Dennis Daniel 1948- *St&PR 93*
Buffon, Charles Edward 1939- *WhoAm 92*
Buffoni, Franca 1925- *WhoScE 91-3*
Buffum, Charles Walbridge, Jr. 1939- *WhoE 93*
Buffum, Elizabeth V. 1941- *WhoAmW 93*
Buffum, Nancy Kay 1941- *WhoAm 92, WhoAmW 93*
Buffum, Paul *Law&B 92*
Buffum, Paul 1945- *St&PR 93*
Bufler, Hans 1928- *WhoWor 93*
Bufman, Zev 1930- *WhoAm 92*
Buford, Abraham 1749-1833 *HarEnMi*
Buford, Brenda Louise 1951- *WhoEmL 93*
Buford, Edwin Rucker 1935- *St&PR 93*
Buford, Evelyn Claudene Shilling 1940- *WhoAmW 93*
Buford, Floyd Moye, Jr. 1957- *WhoEmL 93, WhoSSW 93*
Buford, Lucy E. Hanson *AmWomPl*
Buford, Robert John 1948- *WhoEmL 93*
Buford, Robert Pegram 1925- *WhoSSW 93*
Buford, Ronetta Marie 1946- *WhoEmL 93, WhoWor 93*
Buford, T. Mark 1953- *St&PR 93*
Buford, Thomas Oliver 1932- *WhoSSW 93*
Bugajski, Jan 1928- *WhoScE 91-4*
Bugajski, Richard 1943- *MiSFD 9*
Bugala, Wladyslaw 1924- *WhoScE 91-4*
Bugalho Semedo, Claudie Manuel 1922- *WhoScE 91-3*
Bugarcic, Helmut 1931- *WhoScE 91-3*
Bugatti, Siobhan *WhoWrEP 92*
Bugbee, Alan Campbell, Jr. 1950- *WhoE 93*
Bugbee, Helen Louise 1909- *WhoWrEP 92*
Bugbee, Joan Barthelme 1932- *WhoAmW 93, WhoSSW 93*
Bugbee, Myra Jane 1952- *WhoEmL 93*
Bugbee, Victoria Jean 1951- *WhoAmW 93, WhoEmL 93*
Bugbee-Jackson, Joan 1941- *WhoAm 92*
Bugeaud de la Piconnerie, Thomas Robert 1784-1849 *HarEnMi*
Bugeja, Michael J. *ConAu 138*
Bugeja, Michael Joseph *WhoWrEP 92*
Bugel, Joe 1940- *WhoAm 92*
Bugenhagen, Thomas Gordon 1932- *WhoE 93*
Buget, Ugur *WhoScE 91-4*
Bugg, Alan Kyle 1956- *WhoSSW 93*
Bugg, Charles Edward 1941- *WhoAm 92*
Bugg, Cheryl H. *Law&B 92*
Bugg, David V. *WhoScE 91-1*
Bugg, June Moore 1919- *WhoAmW 93*
Bugg, Randy 1951- *WhoEmL 93*
Bugg, William A. 1937- *St&PR 93*
Bugg, William J. 1939- *WhoIns 93*
Bugg, William Joseph, Jr. 1939- *St&PR 93, WhoAm 92*
Bugge, Anne M. 1953- *St&PR 93*
Bugge, Hans Chr. *WhoScE 91-4*
Bugge, Lawrence John 1936- *WhoAm 92*
Buggeln, Leigh E. *Law&B 92*
Buggenhout, Christian 1948- *St&PR 93*
Buggey, Lesley JoAnne 1938- *WhoWor 93*
Buggie, Frederick Denman 1929- *WhoWor 93*
Bugglin, Carol Stephanie 1958- *WhoE 93*
Buggy, Martin 1949- *WhoScE 91-3*
Bugh, Mary Lou 1942- *WhoWrEP 92*
Bugher, Mark *WhoAm 92*
Bugher, Robert Dean 1925- *WhoAm 92*
Bughici, Dumitru 1921- *Baker 92*
Bugie, Robert Scott 1954- *St&PR 93*
Bu Giron, Efrain *DcCPCAm*
Bugley, Richard L. *Law&B 92*
Bugliarello, George 1927- *WhoAm 92*
Bugliosi, Ramon L. 1930- *St&PR 93*
Bugliosi, Vincent T. 1934- *WhoAm 92, WhoWrEP 92*
Bugnet, Georges 1879-1981 *BioIn 17*
Bugos, Joseph V. *WhoAm 92*
Bugosh, John 1924- *WhoE 93*
Bugul, Ken *ConAu 139*
Buhagiar, Marion 1932- *WhoAm 92, WhoWrEP 92*
Buhari, Muhammadu 1942- *WhoAfr*
Buhe 1926- *WhoAsAP 91*
Buhite, Thomas Jesse, Sr. 1946- *WhoE 93, WhoEmL 93, WhoWor 93*
Buhl, Bessie M. *AmWomPl*
Buhl, David 1936- *WhoE 93*
Buhl, Edward R. 1951- *St&PR 93*
Buhl, Jean-Louis 1945- *WhoWor 93*
Buhl, Karl Franz 1953- *WhoEmL 93*
Buhl, Lynn Y. *Law&B 92*
Buhl, Robert Carl 1931- *St&PR 93*
Buhle, Mari Jo 1943- *WhoAmW 93*
Buhler, Brice G. *Law&B 92*
Buhler, Charlotte Bertha 1893-1974 *BioIn 17*
Buhler, Frank H. 1926- *St&PR 93*
Buhler, Fred Carl 1933- *St&PR 93*
Buhler, Gregory Wallace 1949- *WhoEmL 93*
Buhler, James Warren 1959- *WhoE 93*
Buhler, Jill Lorie 1945- *WhoAmW 93, WhoWor 93*
Buhler, Joan Elizabeth 1961- *WhoEmL 93*
Buhler, Lucy Jane Ford d1991 *BioIn 17*
Buhler, Lynn Bledsoe 1949- *WhoEmL 93*
Buhler, Nelson d1992 *NewYTBS 92*
Buhler, Patricia Marlene 1953- *WhoE 93*
Buhler, Violetta Kapsalis *Law&B 92*
Buhlig, James Russell 1947- *St&PR 93*
Buhlig, Richard 1880-1952 *Baker 92*
Buhlinger, Linda Louann 1960- *WhoEmL 93*
Buhmann, Robert R. 1922- *St&PR 93*
Buhner, Byron Bevis 1950- *WhoEmL 93*
Buhner, David Allan 1948- *WhoEmL 93*
Buhr, Florence D. 1933- *WhoAmW 93*
Buhr, Sheila Ann 1947- *WhoAmW 93*
Buhrfeind, Susan Marie 1968- *WhoAmW 93*
Buhring, Wolfgang 1932- *WhoScE 91-3*
Buhrman, Larry Stelle 1946- *WhoSSW 93*
Buhrmaster, Robert C. 1947- *St&PR 93*
Buhrow, Stanley E. 1952- *WhoEmL 93*
Buhrow, William Carl 1934- *WhoAm 92*
Buhse, Howard E. 1906- *St&PR 93*
Buhse, Howard Edward 1906- *WhoAm 92*
Buhsmer, John H. 1932- *St&PR 93*
Buhsmer, John Henry 1932- *WhoAm 92*
Bu-Hulaiga, Mohammed-Ihsan Ali 1956- *WhoWor 93*
Bui, H.D. 1937- *WhoScE 91-2*
Bui, Khoi Tien 1937- *WhoWor 93*
Bui, Phong Huy 1960- *WhoEmL 93*
Buice, Bonnie Carl 1932- *WhoSSW 93*
Buice, R. Edward *Law&B 92*
Buice, R. Edward 1946- *St&PR 93*
Buice, William Ramsey 1926- *WhoSSW 93*
Buick, James Gordon 1932- *St&PR 93, WhoAm 92*
Buidang, George *WhoWor 93*
Buie, Stuard Finley, III 1941- *WhoSSW 93*
Buies, Arthur 1840-1901 *BioIn 17*
Bui-Quang, Hung 1948- *St&PR 93*
Buis, Joyce 1930- *WhoSSW 93*
Buis, Michael W. 1949- *St&PR 93*
Buis, Otto J. 1931- *St&PR 93*
Buissink, John Donald 1921- *WhoScE 91-3*
Buisson, Ferdinand 1841-1932 *BioIn 17*
Buisson, Jean 1952- *WhoScE 91-2*
Buist, Jean Mackerley 1919- *WhoAm 92, WhoAmW 93*
Buist, Richardson 1921- *WhoE 93, WhoWor 93*
Buitekant, Allan *BioIn 17*
Buitenhuis, Peter Martinus 1925- *WhoAm 92*
Buiter, Jeanne 1946- *WhoAmW 93*
Buiter, Mike Raymond 1955- *St&PR 93*
Buiteweg, Johannes A. 1926- *St&PR 93*
Bui-Thi-Mai 1944- *WhoScE 91-2*
Buitrago, Fanny 1940- *BioIn 17*
Buitrago, Fanny 1946- *SpAmA*
Buja, Giuseppe Silvio 1946- *WhoWor 93*
Bujak, Franciszek 1875-1953 *PolBiDi*
Bujake, John Edward, Jr. 1933- *WhoAm 92*
Bujakiewicz, Aleksandra 1938- *WhoScE 91-4*
Bujang Bin Haji Ulis Bujang Hadziri 1948- *WhoAsAP 91*
Bujarski, Richard J. *Law&B 92*
Bujarski, Zbigniew 1933- *Baker 92*
Bujniewicz, Zbigniew Antoni 1917- *WhoScE 91-4*
Bujold, Genevieve *WhoAm 92*
Bujold, Genevieve 1942- *IntDcF 2-3*
Bujold, Lois McMaster 1949- *ConAu 139, ScF&FL 92*
Bujones, Fernando *BioIn 17*
Bujones, Fernando Calleiro 1955- *WhoAm 92*
Bukantz, Samuel Charles 1911- *WhoAm 92*
Bukar, Margaret Witty 1950- *WhoAmW 93, WhoEmL 93*
Buker, Margaret R. *Law&B 92*
Buker, Robert *Law&B 92*
Buker, Robert Hutchinson, Sr. 1928- *WhoAm 92*
Buker, Robert L. 1947- *St&PR 93*
Buketoff, Igor 1915- *Baker 92*
Bukey, Erol Dervis 1926- *WhoWor 93*
Bukey, Evan Burr 1940- *WhoSSW 93*
Bukh, Per Nikolaj Drachmann 1965- *WhoWor 93*
Bukhari, Atif Yehya *WhoUN 92*
Bukhari, S. Haider Shah 1939- *WhoWor 93*
Bukharin, Nikolai Ivanovich 1888-1938 *BioIn 17, DcTwHis*
Bukhtiyarov, Yuri Eugene 1964- *WhoWor 93*
Bukhvalov, Alexander Vasilievich 1948- *WhoWor 93*
Buki, Dennis Gabor *Law&B 92*
Buki, Gary A. *Law&B 92*
Bukiet, Melvin Jules *ScF&FL 92*
Bukley, Angelia P. 1957- *WhoEmL 93*
Bukman, Piet 1934- *WhoWor 93*
Bukofzer, Manfred F(ritz) 1910-1955 *Baker 92*
Bukovac, Martin John 1929- *WhoAm 92*
Bukovi, Dennis Frank 1939- *St&PR 93*
Bukovski, John C. 1942- *St&PR 93*
Bukovsky, Vladimir 1942- *WhoWor 93*
Bukow, Ronald 1944- *St&PR 93*
Bukowczyk, Adam P. 1923- *WhoScE 91-4*
Bukowska-Strzyzewska, Maria 1929- *WhoScE 91-4*
Bukowski, Andrzej *WhoScE 91-4*
Bukowski, Charles *BioIn 17*
Bukowski, Charles 1920- *ConAu 40NR, MagSAmL [port], WhoAm 92, WhoWrEP 92*
Bukowski, Daniel J. 1963- *St&PR 93*
Bukowski, Elaine Louise 1949- *WhoAm 92, WhoAmW 93, WhoEmL 93*
Bukowski, Gary Donald 1950- *St&PR 93*
Bukowski, Julia Victoria 1953- *WhoE 93*
Bukowski, Romuald d1992 *NewYTBS 92*
Bukowy, Stanislaw 1922- *WhoScE 91-4*
Bukry, John David 1941- *WhoAm 92*
Buksbaum, David Eugene 1935- *WhoE 93*
Bula, Michael S. *Law&B 92*
Bula, Raymond J. 1927- *WhoAm 92*
Bulabois, Jean M. 1937- *WhoScE 91-2*
Bulajic, Veljko 1928- *DrEEuF*
Bulat, Marijan 1945- *WhoWor 93*
Bulatovic, Miodrag 1930-1991 *BioIn 17*
Bulazel, Kira *BioIn 17*
Bulbul *WhoWrEP 92*
Bulbulian, Arthur H. 1900- *WhoAm 92*
Bulcke, Robert 1945- *WhoScE 91-2*
Bulette, Julia 1832-1867 *BioIn 17*
Buley, Mary Therse 1956- *WhoEmL 93*
Bulfield, Graeme *WhoScE 91-1*
Bulfin, Michael 1939- *WhoScE 91-3*
Bulfin, Preston Edward 1941- *WhoWor 93*
Bulgakov, Mikhail Afanas'evich 1891-1940 *BioIn 17*
Bulganin, Nikolai 1895-1975 *ColdWar 2 [port]*
Bulganin, Nikolai Alekandrovich 1895-1975 *DcTwHis*
Bulgarelli, Rolando 1917- *WhoScE 91-3*
Bulgari, Marina *BioIn 17*
Bulger, Dennis Bernard 1938- *WhoAm 92*
Bulger, John T. 1949- *St&PR 93*
Bulger, Michael Edward 1948- *WhoEmL 93*
Bulger, Whitey *BioIn 17*
Bulger, William Michael *BioIn 17*
Bulger, William Michael 1934- *WhoAm 92*
Bulgo, Joe *BioIn 17*
Bulgren, William Gerald 1937- *WhoAm 92*
Bulhoes, Otavio Gouveia de 1906-1990 *BioIn 17*
Bulich, Antone S., Jr. *Law&B 92*
Bulington, Dennis L. 1955- *St&PR 93*
Bulinski, Daniel J. 1943- *St&PR 93*
Bulinski, Gregory Paul 1953- *WhoEmL 93*
Bulinski, Romuald 1929- *WhoScE 91-4*
Bulinsky, Mirko Ewald 1961- *WhoWor 93*
Bulitko, Valerij Konstantin 1943- *WhoWor 93*
Bulkeley, Bill W. 1949- *St&PR 93*
Bulkeley, Christy Claire 1942- *WhoAm 92*
Bulkeley, John Duncan 1911- *WhoAm 92*
Bulkeley, John Z. 1938- *St&PR 93*
Bulkin, Bernard Joseph 1942- *WhoWor 93*
Bulkin, Michael Herbert 1938- *WhoE 93*
Bulkley, Charles S. *Law&B 92*
Bulkley, David Robert *Law&B 92*
Bulkley, Gregory Bartlett 1943- *WhoE 93*
Bulkley, Robert Ellsworth 1921- *St&PR 93*
Bulkow, Lisa Ruth 1959- *WhoAmW 93*
Bulkowski, Robert 1948- *St&PR 93*
Bulkowski, Virginia 1948- *St&PR 93*
Bull, Alan Thomas *WhoScE 91-1*
Bull, Angela 1936- *ScF&FL 92*
Bull, Bergen Ira *Law&B 92*
Bull, Bergen Ira 1940- *St&PR 93, WhoAm 92*
Bull, Brian Stanley 1937- *WhoAm 92*
Bull, Clara Durland *AmWomPl*
Bull, Clinton LeRoy 1929- *WhoAm 92*
Bull, David 1934- *WhoAm 92*
Bull, Dennis Lee 1946- *WhoEmL 93, WhoSSW 93*
Bull, Donald Arthur 1944- *St&PR 93*
Bull, Edvard Hagerup *Baker 92*
Bull, Emma 1954- *ScF&FL 92*
Bull, Fran 1938- *WhoE 93*
Bull, Frank James 1922- *WhoSSW 93*
Bull, George Albert 1927- *St&PR 93, WhoAm 92*
Bull, George (Anthony) 1929- *ConAu 39NR*
Bull, Gerald *BioIn 17*
Bull, Henrik Helkand 1929- *WhoAm 92*
Bull, Howard I. 1940- *St&PR 93*
Bull, Howard L. *Law&B 92*
Bull, James Robert 1941- *St&PR 93*
Bull, John c. 1562-1628 *Baker 92*
Bull, Katharine Thomas Jarboe *AmWomPl*
Bull, Katherine 1903?-1918 *AmWomPl*
Bull, Marshall R. 1941- *St&PR 93*
Bull, Ole (Bornemann) 1810-1880 *Baker 92*
Bull, Raymond Henry Charles *WhoScE 91-1*
Bull, Sandy 1941- *WhoWor 93*
Bull, Stephen *Law&B 92*
Bull, Walter Stephen 1933- *WhoSSW 93*
Bulla, Ben F. 1920- *St&PR 93*
Bulla, Clyde Robert 1914- *ConAu 40NR, DcAmChF 1960, MajAI [port], WhoAm 92*
Bulla, Robert Baxter 1939- *St&PR 93*
Bullant, Antoine c. 1750-1821 *OxDcOp*
Bullard, Ben B. 1935- *WhoSSW 93*
Bullard, Clark W. *BioIn 17*
Bullard, Claude Earl 1920- *WhoAm 92*
Bullard, David K. 1942- *WhoIns 93*
Bullard, Edgar John, III 1942- *WhoAm 92, WhoSSW 93*
Bullard, Edward Dickinson 1948- *St&PR 93, WhoEmL 93, WhoSSW 93*
Bullard, Fred Bascom, Jr. 1934- *St&PR 93*
Bullard, George 1945- *WhoAm 92*
Bullard, George Woodrow, Jr. 1950- *WhoEmL 93, WhoSSW 93*
Bullard, Helen 1902- *WhoAm 92*
Bullard, James 1951- *WhoEmL 93*
Bullard, Janet 1935- *St&PR 93*
Bullard, Jennie Knepp 1936- *WhoE 93*
Bullard, John Kilburn 1947- *WhoAm 92, WhoE 93, WhoEmL 93*
Bullard, John Moore 1932- *WhoSSW 93*
Bullard, John Wilbur 1938- *St&PR 93*
Bullard, Judith Eve 1945- *WhoAmW 93*
Bullard, Mary Boykin 1933- *WhoAmW 93, WhoSSW 93*
Bullard, Ray Elva, Jr. 1927- *WhoAm 92*
Bullard, Ricky J. 1947- *St&PR 93*
Bullard, Robert Lee 1861-1947 *HarEnMi*
Bullard, Robert Oliver, Jr. 1943- *WhoAm 92*
Bullard, Roland Keith, II 1944- *St&PR 93*
Bullard, Sharon Welch 1943- *WhoAmW 93*
Bullard, Susanna M. 1938- *WhoAmW 93*

Bullard, Todd Hupp 1931- *WhoAm 92*
Bullard, Wanda Messer 1952- *WhoAmW 93*
Bullard, Willis Clare, Jr. 1943- *WhoAm 92*
Bullata, Jamil Yousif 1934- *WhoWor 93*
Bulle, Ralph J. *St&PR 93*
Bullen, Leigh M. 1944- *St&PR 93*
Bullen, Leigh M., Jr. 1944- *WhoAm 92*
Bullen, Richard Hatch 1919- *WhoAm 92*
Buller, Antony T. 1944- *WhoScE 91-4*
Buller, Herman 1923- *WhoCanL 92*
Buller, Jack C. 1933- *St&PR 93*
Buller, John 1927- *Baker 92*
Buller, Redvers Henry 1839-1908 *HarEnMi*
Bullerjahn, Eduard Henri 1920- *WhoAm 92*
Bullett, David B. 1938- *WhoIns 93*
Bullett, David W. *WhoScE 91-1*
Bulletti, Anton Leone c. 1824-c. 1885 *BioIn 17*
Bullick, Margaret M. 1949- *St&PR 93*
Bulliet, Richard Williams 1940- *WhoAm 92*
Bullin, Christine Neva 1948- *WhoAm 92*
Bulliner, P. Alan *Law&B 92*
Bullinger, Hans-Jorg 1944- *WhoScE 91-3*
Bullington, James R. 1940- *WhoAm 92*
Bullins, Ed 1935- *BioIn 17, ConAu 16AS [port], WhoAm 92*
Bullis, John Douglas 1948- *WhoE 93*
Bullister, Edward Theodore 1957- *WhoEmL 93*
Bullitt, Harriett Stimson *BioIn 17*
Bullitt, Pascale Georgia *Law&B 92*
Bullivant, Cecil H. 1882- *ScF&FL 92*
Bullmore, R. Steven 1950- *St&PR 93*
Bulloch, John Frederick Devon 1933- *WhoAm 92*
Bulloch, Steven Nolen *Law&B 92*
Bullock, Abby *AmWomPl*
Bullock, Alistair M. 1941- *WhoScE 91-1*
Bullock, Anna Keller 1929- *WhoAmW 93*
Bullock, Charles Spencer, III 1942- *WhoAm 92*
Bullock, David Fraser 1955- *WhoAm 92*
Bullock, Deborah L. *AfrAmBi [port]*
Bullock, Donald Wayne 1947- *WhoEmL 93*
Bullock, Ellis F. 1945- *St&PR 93*
Bullock, Ellis Way, Jr. 1928- *WhoAm 92*
Bullock, Eric Lynn 1957- *WhoWor 93*
Bullock, Ernest 1890-1979 *Baker 92*
Bullock, Francis Jeremiah 1937- *WhoAm 92*
Bullock, Frank William, Jr. 1938- *WhoAm 92, WhoSSW 93*
Bullock, Frederick William *WhoScE 91-1*
Bullock, Gale Jeaneane 1954- *WhoEmL 93*
Bullock, Geoffrey Norman *WhoScE 91-1*
Bullock, George 1782?-1818 *BioIn 17*
Bullock, Gwendolyn Catrina 1956- *WhoEmL 93*
Bullock, H. Ridgely 1934- *St&PR 93, WhoAm 92*
Bullock, Hugh 1898- *WhoAm 92*
Bullock, Jack 1942- *St&PR 93*
Bullock, James Howard 1953- *WhoSSW 93*
Bullock, James R., Jr. 1948- *St&PR 93*
Bullock, James Roeder 1915- *St&PR 93*
Bullock, Jay *Law&B 92*
Bullock, Jerry McKee 1932- *WhoSSW 93*
Bullock, Jerry Ross 1950- *St&PR 93*
Bullock, Jill *BioIn 17*
Bullock, Jimmie Bruce 1940- *WhoAm 92*
Bullock, John C. *Law&B 92*
Bullock, John McDonell 1932- *WhoAm 92*
Bullock, Linda Sue 1951- *WhoAmW 93*
Bullock, Lottie Molly *WhoAmW 93*
Bullock, Lyndal Marvin *WhoSSW 93*
Bullock, Marianne Patrice 1956- *WhoAmW 93, WhoSSW 93*
Bullock, Marie 1941- *WhoAmW 93*
Bullock, Maurice Randolph 1913- *WhoAm 92*
Bullock, Michael 1918- *ConAu 38NR, WhoCanL 92*
Bullock, Norma Kathryn Rice 1945- *WhoAm 92*
Bullock, Orin Miles, Jr. 1905- *WhoAm 92*
Bullock, Paul S. 1942- *St&PR 93*
Bullock, Peter Bradley 1934- *WhoWor 93*
Bullock, Randall Curtis 1948- *St&PR 93*
Bullock, Robert Crossley 1924- *WhoSSW 93*
Bullock, Robert D. 1929- *WhoAm 92, WhoSSW 93*
Bullock, Robert Daniel 1947- *WhoEmL 93*
Bullock, Ronald Morris 1957- *WhoE 93*
Bullock, Theodore Holmes 1915- *WhoAm 92*
Bullock, Thomas Abbott 1922- *St&PR 93*
Bullock, W.E., Sr. 1923- *St&PR 93*
Bullock, Warren M. 1931- *St&PR 93*
Bullock, William Clapp, Jr. 1936- *St&PR 93*
Bullock, William H. 1927- *WhoAm 92*
Bullock, William Joseph 1943- *WhoSSW 93*
Bullock, William Norris 1953- *St&PR 93*
Bulloff, Aaron Harley 1948- *WhoEmL 93*
Bulloff, Jack John 1914- *WhoAm 92*
Bulloff, Steven Marc *Law&B 92*
Bullough, Bonnie 1927- *WhoAm 92*
Bullough, John Frank 1928- *WhoAm 92*
Bullough, Vern L. 1928- *WhoE 93*
Bullrich, Silvina 1915- *BioIn 17, SpAmA*
Bulluck, Vic *ScF&FL 92*
Bulmahn, Lynn 1955- *WhoAmW 93*
Bulmahn, T. Paul 1943- *St&PR 93*
Bulman, Richard B. 1942- *St&PR 93*
Bulman, William Patrick 1925- *WhoE 93*
Bulmash, Jack Martin 1946- *WhoEmL 93*
Bulmer, Glenn Stuart 1931- *WhoWor 93*
Bulmer, Judith Nicola 1956- *WhoWor 93*
Bulmer, Kenneth 1921- *ScF&FL 92*
Bulnes, Sara Maria 1954- *WhoWrEP 92*
Bulnheim, Hans-Peter *WhoScE 91-3*
Buloff, Joseph 1899-1985 *BioIn 17*
Bulos, Marjorie A. *WhoScE 91-1*
Bulow, Bernhard Heinrich Martin Karl, Furst von 1849-1929 *BioIn 17*
Bulow, Dietrich Adam Heinrich von 1757-1807 *HarEnMi*
Bulow, Friedrich Wilhelm von 1755-1816 *HarEnMi*
Bulow, George M. 1949- *WhoEmL 93*
Bulow, Hans von 1830-1894 *BioIn 17, IntDcOp [port], OxDcOp*
Bulow, Hans (Guido) von 1830-1894 *Baker 92*
Bulow, Karl von 1846-1921 *HarEnMi*
Bulow, Katherine 1943- *WhoAm 92*
Bulsara, C(avas) N(owshirwan) 1927- *DcChlFi*
Bulsara, Frederick *BioIn 17*
Bulsiewicz, William J. *Law&B 92*
Bult, Albert J. 1936- *St&PR 93*
Bulters, Pieter Johannes Maria 1944- *WhoWor 93*
Bulthuis, K. 1937- *WhoScE 91-3*
Bultje, Ronald Alan 1953- *WhoEmL 93*
Bultmann, Rudolf Karl 1884-1976 *BioIn 17*
Bultynck, Pierre L. 1938- *WhoScE 91-2*
Bulwer Lytton, Edward Robert 1831-1891 *BioIn 17*
Bulwer-Lytton, Rosina 1802-1882 *BioIn 17*
Bulychev, Kirill 1934- *ScF&FL 92*
Bulyk, John-Conrad 1949- *WhoE 93*
Bulyzhenkov, Victor Edmundovich 1948- *WhoUN 92*
Bulzacchelli, John G. 1939- *WhoAm 92*
Buma, T.J. 1929- *WhoScE 91-3*
Bumanglag, Alejandro Guira 1950- *WhoEmL 93, WhoWor 93*
Bumann, Paul Fredrick 1930- *WhoSSW 93*
Bumann, Steve L. 1953- *St&PR 93*
Bumba, Lincoln *BioIn 17*
Bumbacher, Beat Karl 1958- *WhoWor 93*
Bumbasirevic, Zivojin V. 1920- *WhoScE 91-4*
Bumbery, Joseph Lawrence 1929- *WhoAm 92*
Bumbry, Grace 1937- *IntDcOp, OxDcOp, WhoAm 92*
Bumbry, Grace (Melzia Ann) 1937- *Baker 92*
Bumby, Adain James 1926- *St&PR 93*
Bumby, Edward Wells 1946- *St&PR 93*
Bumby, John Edgar 1920- *St&PR 93*
Bumcrot, Robert Judson 1936- *WhoE 93*
Bumgardner, David Q. 1950- *St&PR 93*
Bumgardner, Gene David *Law&B 92*
Bumgardner, John Owens *WhoSSW 93*
Bumgardner, Larry G. 1957- *WhoEmL 93*
Bumgarner, John Carson, Sr. 1908- *WhoAm 92*
Bumgarner, John E. 1945- *St&PR 93*
Bumgarner, Marlene Anne 1947- *WhoEmL 93*
Bumiller, Donald Robert 1955- *WhoEmL 93*
Bumler, Georg Heinrich 1669-1745 *Baker 92*
Bump, Mark William *Law&B 92*
Bump, Stanley Earl 1936- *WhoAm 92*
Bump, Wilbur Neil 1929- *WhoAm 92*
Bumpas, M. Stevens 1937- *St&PR 93*
Bumpas, Stuart Maryman 1944- *WhoAm 92*
Bumpass, Larry Lee 1942- *WhoAm 92*
Bumpers, Dale 1925- *CngDr 91*
Bumpers, Dale L. 1925- *WhoAm 92, WhoSSW 93*
Bumpers, W. Carroll *WhoAm 92*
Bumpous, Earle Thomas, III 1943- *WhoSSW 93*
Bumpus, Charles H. 1938- *St&PR 93*
Bumpus, Frank *BioIn 17*
Bumpus, Frederick J. 1929- *St&PR 93, WhoIns 93*
Bumpus, Frederick Joseph 1929- *WhoAm 92*
Bumpus, Jerry Don 1937- *WhoWrEP 92*
Bumpus, Linda Doster 1946- *WhoAmW 93*
Bumpus, Raymond Conrad 1937- *St&PR 93*
Bumstead, Dawn D. 1965- *WhoAmW 93*
Bumstead, Henry 1915- *ConTFT 10*
Bumstead, R. Glenn *Law&B 92*
Bumsted, Robert Milton 1944- *WhoAm 92*
Bunaes, Bard E. 1935- *WhoIns 93*
Bunak, V.V. 1891-1979 *IntDcAn*
Bunbury, John Dennis 1929- *St&PR 93*
Bunce, Alan *MiSFD 9*
Bunce, Donald Fairbairn MacDougal, II 1920- *WhoAm 92*
Bunce, Donald George, Sr. 1938- *WhoE 93*
Bunce, Martha Curtiss 1943- *WhoAmW 93*
Bunce, Richard Alan 1953- *WhoEmL 93, WhoSSW 93*
Bunce, Robert Gerald Henry *WhoScE 91-1*
Bunce, Stanley Chalmers 1917- *WhoAm 92*
Bunch, Austin Warren 1945- *WhoSSW 93*
Bunch, Carol Denise 1960- *WhoSSW 93*
Bunch, Chris 1943- *ScF&FL 92*
Bunch, David R. 1925?- *ScF&FL 92*
Bunch, Doyle R., II 1946- *St&PR 93*
Bunch, Drexel R. 1944- *St&PR 93*
Bunch, Franklin Swope 1913- *WhoAm 92*
Bunch, James Terrance 1942- *WhoAm 92*
Bunch, Jennings Bryan, Jr. 1929- *WhoAm 92*
Bunch, John Blake 1940- *WhoAm 92*
Bunch, Karen Shore 1957- *WhoEmL 93*
Bunch, Kenneth Alan 1961- *WhoEmL 93*
Bunch, Louie Michael 1970- *BioIn 17*
Bunch, Michael Anthony 1949- *WhoSSW 93*
Bunch, Phillip Gene 1938- *St&PR 93*
Bunch, Walter Edward 1955- *WhoEmL 93*
Bunch, William 1902-1941 *BioIn 17*
Bunch, William Jesse *Law&B 92*
Bunche, Ralph 1904-1971 *DcTwHis*
Bunche, Ralph J. 1904-1971 *BioIn 17*
Bunche, Ralph Johnson 1904-1971 *EncAACR [port]*
Buncher, Alan 1946- *WhoEmL 93*
Buncher, James Edward 1936- *WhoAm 92*
Bunda, Donald William 1952- *WhoEmL 93*
Bundgaard, Jorgen 1943- *WhoScE 91-2*
Bundgaard, Nils 1952- *WhoWor 93*
Bundgard, Paul M. *Law&B 92*
Bundi, Renee 1962- *WhoE 93, WhoEmL 93*
Bundick, Glenda Haddox 1946- *WhoSSW 93*
Bundick, William Ross 1917- *WhoAm 92*
Bundles, A'Lelia P. *BioIn 17*
Bundschuh, George A.W. 1933- *WhoIns 93*
Bundschuh, George August William 1933- *St&PR 93, WhoAm 92*
Bundschuh, John J., Jr. 1932- *St&PR 93*
Bundschuh, Marjorie Gurevitz 1952- *WhoEmL 93, WhoWor 93*
Bundu, Abbas 1944- *WhoAfr*
Bundy, Charles Alan 1930- *WhoAm 92*
Bundy, David Hollister 1947- *WhoEmL 93*
Bundy, Elizabeth Campbell 1960- *WhoAmW 93, WhoEmL 93*
Bundy, Freda Graham *AmWomPl*
Bundy, Hallie Flowers 1925- *WhoAmW 93*
Bundy, Harvey H., III 1944- *St&PR 93*
Bundy, Harvey Hollister 1916- *WhoAm 92*
Bundy, Jonas Mills 1835-1891 *JrnUS*
Bundy, Judith Cox 1941- *WhoE 93*
Bundy, Kenneth Alvin 1910- *WhoWor 93*
Bundy, Kirk Jon 1947- *WhoSSW 93*
Bundy, Mary L. 1925- *St&PR 93*
Bundy, Mary Lothrop 1925- *WhoE 93*
Bundy, McGeorge 1919- *ColdWar 1 [port], WhoAm 92*
Bundy, Michael Lyman 1947- *WhoEmL 93, WhoSSW 93*
Bundy, Phil 1945- *St&PR 93*
Bundy, Ralph *ScF&FL 92*
Bundy, Robert Mayne 1932- *St&PR 93*
Bundy, Robert Wendel 1924- *WhoSSW 93*
Bundy, Ronald Floyd 1941- *St&PR 93*
Bundy, William Hatler, Jr. 1940- *St&PR 93*
Bune, Karen Louise 1954- *WhoAmW 93, WhoEmL 93, WhoSSW 93*
Bungard, S.J. *WhoScE 91-1*
Bungay, K.G. *Law&B 92*
Bunge, Charles Albert 1936- *BioIn 17, WhoAm 92*
Bunge, Charles Herman 1944- *St&PR 93*
Bunge, Hans-Joachim 1929- *WhoScE 91-3*
Bunge, Kenneth E. *Law&B 92*
Bunge, Mario Augusto 1919- *WhoWrEP 92*
Bunge, Shelly K. *Law&B 92*
Bungener, Johannes Hendrik 1934- *St&PR 93*
Bunger, Richard Joseph 1942- *Baker 92*
Bungert, August 1845-1915 *OxDcOp*
Bungert, (Friedrich) August 1845-1915 *Baker 92*
Bungert, John Jacob, III 1934- *St&PR 93*
Bungo, Michael William 1950- *WhoAm 92*
Bunim, Mary-Ellis 1946- *WhoAm 92*
Bunin, Erica *Law&B 92*
Bunin, Jeffrey Howard 1948- *WhoE 93, WhoEmL 93*
Bunin, Revol 1924-1976 *Baker 92*
Bunin, Sherry 1925- *BioIn 17*
Bunin, Vladimir 1908-1970 *Baker 92*
Bunio, Russell J. 1947- *St&PR 93*
Bunk, George Mark 1952- *WhoE 93, WhoEmL 93*
Bunke, Robert Werner 1927- *St&PR 93*
Bunker, Andrew F. 1916-1979 *BioIn 17*
Bunker, Anthony Louis 1933- *WhoSSW 93*
Bunker, Caroline Clendening Laise 1917-1991 *BioIn 17*
Bunker, Chang 1811-1874 *BioIn 17*
Bunker, Clive 1946- See Jethro Tull *ConMus 8*
Bunker, Eng 1811-1874 *BioIn 17*
Bunker, Frederick William 1946- *WhoEmL 93*
Bunker, John Birkbeck 1926- *WhoAm 92*
Bunker, Robert B. 1943- *St&PR 93*
Bunker, Samuel Emmet 1927- *WhoE 93*
Bunker, Theodore James 1947- *St&PR 93*
Bunkowski, Kenneth D. 1947- *St&PR 93*
Bunn, Alfred 1798?-1860 *OxDcOp*
Bunn, Derek William *WhoScE 91-1*
Bunn, Derek William 1949- *WhoWor 93*
Bunn, Dorothy Irons 1948- *WhoAmW 93*
Bunn, George 1925- *WhoAm 92*
Bunn, George H. 1945- *WhoE 93*
Bunn, Joe E. 1943- *St&PR 93*
Bunn, Joe Millard 1932- *WhoSSW 93*
Bunn, John R. 1959- *St&PR 93*
Bunn, Patricia Marie *Law&B 92*
Bunn, Paul Grayson 1933- *WhoSSW 93*
Bunn, Philip Robertson *WhoScE 91-1*
Bunn, Philip Robertson 1943- *WhoWor 93*
Bunn, Richard L. 1936- *St&PR 93, WhoAm 92*
Bunn, Ronald Freeze 1929- *WhoAm 92*
Bunn, T. Davis 1952- *ScF&FL 92*
Bunn, Timothy David 1946- *WhoAm 92*
Bunn, Tom Cade 1936- *WhoE 93*
Bunn, W.B. 1952- *St&PR 93*
Bunn, Wallace R. 1922- *St&PR 93*
Bunn, Willard, III 1943- *St&PR 93*
Bunn, William Bernice, III 1952- *WhoAm 92*
Bunnag, Tej 1943- *WhoUN 92*
Bunnel, David S. *Law&B 92*
Bunnell, Dale L. 1936- *St&PR 93*
Bunnell, David M. *Law&B 92*
Bunnell, Donald R. 1947- *St&PR 93*
Bunnell, Paul Joseph 1946- *WhoWrEP 92*
Bunnell, Peter Curtis 1937- *WhoAm 92*
Bunnell, Roderick *Law&B 92*
Bunnell, Roderick 1930- *St&PR 93*
Bunnell, Sandra Jean 1945- *WhoAmW 93*
Bunner, Anne *AmWomPl*
Bunner, H.C. 1855-1896 *GayN*
Bunner, Patricia Andrea 1953- *WhoEmL 93*
Bunnett, Jane *BioIn 17*
Bunnett, Joseph Frederick 1921- *WhoAm 92*
Bunney, Benjamin Stephenson 1938- *WhoAm 92*
Bunney, William Edward 1902-1992 *BioIn 17*
Bunney, William Edward, Sr. d1992 *NewYTBS 92*
Bunni, Nael Georges 1939- *WhoWor 93*
Bunning, David John 1949- *St&PR 93*
Bunning, Jim *BioIn 17*
Bunning, Jim 1931- *CngDr 91, WhoAm 92, WhoSSW 93*
Bunning-Stevens, Barbara A. *Law&B 92*
Bunny, John 1863-1915 *IntDcF 2-3 [port], QDrFCA 92 [port]*
Bunsell, Anthony Roland 1945- *WhoScE 91-2*
Bunshaft, Gordon 1909-1990 *BioIn 17*
Bunshaft, Robert 1947- *WhoE 93*
Bunshaft, Robert S. 1918- *St&PR 93*
Bunshah, Keki Framroze *Law&B 92*
Bunt, A.C. 1924-1991? *BioIn 17*
Bunt, Arthur Christopher 1924-1991? *BioIn 17*
Bunt, James Richard 1941- *St&PR 93, WhoAm 92*
Bunt, Lynne Joy 1948- *WhoAmW 93*

Bunta, James A. Law&B 92
Buntain, David Robert 1948- WhoEmL 93
Bunte, Rhonda Gayle 1954- WhoAmW 93
Bunten, William Daniel 1931- St&PR 93, WhoAm 92
Buntin, Stephen G. 1954- St&PR 93
Buntin, William Lee 1943- St&PR 93
Bunting, A.E. MajAI
Bunting, Anne Eve 1928- BioIn 17
Bunting, Anne Evelyn 1928- WhoWrEP 92
Bunting, Arthur Hugh 1917- WhoWor 93
Bunting, Basil BioIn 17
Bunting, Bruce Gordon 1948- WhoEmL 93
Bunting, Charles I. 1942- WhoAm 92
Bunting, Christopher Henry 1951- WhoAm 92
Bunting, Dana Leigh 1961- St&PR 93
Bunting, Edward 1773-1843 BioIn 17
Bunting, Eve WhoWrEP 92
Bunting, Eve 1928- BioIn 17, ChILR 28 [port], ScF&FL 92
Bunting, (Anne) Eve(lyn) 1928- MajAI [port]
Bunting, (Anne) Eve(Lyn Bolton) 1928- DcAmChF 1985
Bunting, Gary Glenn 1947- WhoWor 93
Bunting, J. Pearce 1929- St&PR 93
Bunting, John Pearce 1929- WhoAm 92, WhoE 93
Bunting, John R., Jr. 1925- St&PR 93
Bunting, Kimberly S. Law&B 92
Bunting, Lee 1915- St&PR 93
Bunting, Melody 1946- WhoAmW 93
Bunting, Robert L. 1928- St&PR 93
Bunting, Robert L. 1946- WhoAm 92
Bunting, William BioIn 17
Bunton, Claire Jennifer Law&B 92
Bunton, Lucius Desha, III 1924- WhoAm 92, WhoSSW 93
Bunton, Mildred Settle 1906- WhoWor 93
Bunton, Terry R. 1940- St&PR 93
Buntrock, Dean L. 1931- St&PR 93
Buntrock, Dean Lewis WhoAm 92, WhoWor 93
Buntrock, Gerhard Friedrich Richard 1954- WhoWor 93
Bunts, Frank Emory 1932- WhoAm 92
Buntyn, Ralph E. 1941- St&PR 93
Buntzman, Mark MiSFD 9
Bunuan, Josefina Santiago 1935- WhoE 93
Bunuel, Juan 1934- MiSFD 9
Bunuel, Luis 1900-1983 MiSFD 9N
Bunyan, John 1628-1688 MagSWL [port], WorLitC [port]
Bunyard, Alan Donald 1931- WhoWor 93
Bunyi, Milagros Calderon 1942- WhoWor 93
Bunzel, John Harvey 1924- WhoAm 92
Bunzel, Ruth Leah 1898-1990 IntDcAn
Bunzi, Rudolph H. 1922- St&PR 93
Bunzl, Rudolph Hans 1922- WhoAm 92, WhoSSW 93
Buo, Jose Oraliza 1942- WhoWor 93
Buo, Sammy Kum 1952- WhoUN 92
Buoch, William Thomas 1923- WhoSSW 93, WhoWor 93
Buonajuti, Amedeo 1947- WhoUN 92
Buonamente, Giovanni Battista c. 1600-1642 Baker 92
Buonamici, Giuseppe 1846-1914 Baker 92
Buonanni, Brian Francis 1945- WhoE 93, WhoWor 93
Buonanno, Vincent J. 1943- St&PR 93
Buonarroti, Michel Angelo 1475-1564 BioIn 17
Buoncore, Richard James 1956- WhoE 93
Buondelmonti, Cristoforo de' fl. 1420- BioIn 17
Buongiorno, Joseph A. 1939- St&PR 93
Buoniconti, Marc BioIn 17
Buoniconti, Nicholas BioIn 17
Buoniconti, Nicholas 1940- BiDAMSp 1989
Buonicore, Anthony Joseph 1950- WhoEmL 93
Buono, A. George 1930- St&PR 93
Buonocore, Richard Antonio 1946- WhoE 93
Buononcini Baker 92
Buonpastore, Joseph L. 1962- St&PR 93
Buontalenti, Bernardo 1531-1608 OxDcOp
Bur, M.P. 1945- St&PR 93
Burachik, Moises 1932- WhoWor 93
Burack, Elmer H(oward) 1927- ConAu 37NR
Burack, Elmer Howard 1927- WhoAm 92
Burack, Michael Leonard 1942- WhoAm 92
Burack, Steven I. 1931- St&PR 93
Burack, Sylvia E. Kamerman 1916- WhoAm 92, WhoWrEP 92
Buraczewski, Adam Tadeusz 1926- WhoWor 93
Buraczewski, Stanislaw 1925- WhoScE 91-4
Burada, Theodor 1839-1923 Baker 92
Burak, Janet Law&B 92
Burakoff, Steven James 1942- WhoAm 92
Burakoff, William L. Law&B 92
Burakowski, Tadeusz 1934- WhoScE 91-4
Buran, Dennis Francis 1941- St&PR 93
Buran, Sandra Lee 1957- WhoAmW 93
Burandt, Gary E. 1943- St&PR 93
Burandt, Gary Edward 1943- WhoE 93, WhoWor 93
Buranelli, Nan 1917- WhoWrEP 92
Buranelli, Vincent 1919- ScF&FL 92
Buranello, Raymond Terrence 1950- WhoEmL 93
Burani, Sergio 1946- WhoEmL 93
Buras-Elsen, Brenda Allynn 1954- WhoAmW 93, WhoEmL 93, WhoSSW 93
Buratti, Bonnie J. 1953- WhoEmL 93
Buravkin, Guennadi N. 1936- WhoUN 92
Burba, Edwin Hess, Jr. 1936- WhoAm 92
Burbach, Stuart P. 1952- St&PR 93
Burbank, Barbara AmWomPl
Burbank, Gladys Verena 1947- WhoEmL 93
Burbank, James Clarke 1946- WhoWrEP 92
Burbank, John Thorn 1939- WhoWor 93
Burbank, Kershaw 1914- WhoSSW 93
Burbank, Luther 1849-1926 BioIn 17, GayN
Burbank, Maude AmWomPl
Burbank, Nelson Stone 1920- WhoAm 92
Burbank, Paul 1928- WhoSSW 93
Burbank, Peter 1917- St&PR 93
Burbank, Robinson Derry 1921- WhoWor 93
Burbank, Rosalind A. Law&B 92
Burbank, Russell King 1943- St&PR 93
Burbea, Jacob N. 1942- WhoE 93, WhoWor 93
Burberry, P.J. WhoScE 91-1
Burbey, Gene P. 1937- St&PR 93
Burbidge, Derek MiSFD 9
Burbidge, Eleanor Margaret Peachey WhoAm 92, WhoAmW 93
Burbidge, John L. 1932- St&PR 93
Burbidge, Kenneth Parry, Jr. 1930- St&PR 93
Burbidge, Nicolas W.R. 1946- St&PR 93
Burbridge, Benjamin Nicholas 1951- WhoScE 91-1
Burbridge, Janet Carol Peters 1950- WhoAmW 93
Burbridge, John L. Law&B 92
Burbridge, John Leonard WhoScE 91-1
Burbulis, Gennady 1945- WhoWor 93
Burbure de Wesembeek, Leon-Philippe-Marie 1812-1889 Baker 92
Burch, Arthur Leroy 1936- St&PR 93
Burch, Arthur Merritt 1935- St&PR 93
Burch, C.R. 1901-1983 BioIn 17
Burch, Craig Alan 1954- WhoWor 93
Burch, D. Russell 1941- St&PR 93
Burch, Dana Adrienne Law&B 92
Burch, Dean 1927- PolPar
Burch, Dean 1927-1991 AnObit 1991, BioIn 17
Burch, Dwayne Lee 1946- WhoEmL 93
Burch, Florine 1941- St&PR 93
Burch, Helen AmWomPl
Burch, James L. Law&B 92
Burch, James Leo 1942- WhoAm 92, WhoSSW 93
Burch, John Thomas, Jr. 1942- WhoAm 92
Burch, John Walter 1925- WhoE 93, WhoWor 93
Burch, Karl D. 1929- St&PR 93
Burch, Lucius Edward, Jr. 1912- WhoAm 92
Burch, Mariel Rae 1934- WhoWrEP 92
Burch, Mark Hetzel 1953- WhoEmL 93
Burch, Melvin Earl 1949- St&PR 93, WhoAm 92, WhoEmL 93
Burch, Michael I. 1941- St&PR 93
Burch, Michael Ira 1941- WhoAm 92
Burch, Ralph Law&B 92, ScF&FL 92
Burch, Robert WhoScE 91-1
Burch, Robert 1925- DcAmChF 1960
Burch, Robert Dale 1928- WhoAm 92
Burch, Robert J. 1943- St&PR 93
Burch, Robert J(oseph) 1925- MajAI [port]
Burch, Robert Joseph 1925- WhoAm 92
Burch, Robert L. 1934- St&PR 93
Burch, Robert Stuart 1959- WhoE 93
Burch, Ruth Marie 1940- WhoAmW 93
Burch, Sarena D. Law&B 92
Burch, Thaddeus Joseph, Jr. 1930- WhoAm 92
Burcham, Barbara June 1952- WhoAmW 93, WhoEmL 93
Burcham, Carroll Franklin 1935- WhoSSW 93
Burcham, Eva Helen 1941- WhoWor 93
Burcham, James Edward 1941- WhoSSW 93
Burcham, Jay Martin 1953- WhoEmL 93, WhoSSW 93
Burcham, Jeffrey Glen 1959- WhoEmL 93
Burcham, Stephen Dale 1956- WhoEmL 93
Burcham, Thomas H. 1936- WhoIns 93
Burcham, Timothy Ray 1953- WhoSSW 93
Burchard, John Kenneth 1936- WhoAm 92
Burchard, Peter Duncan 1921- ConAu 39NR, DcAmChF 1960, MajAI [port]
Burchard, Rachael C. 1921- WhoWrEP 92
Burchardt, Clara Chavez 1932- WhoSSW 93
Burcharth, Hans Falk 1938- WhoScE 91-2
Burchell, Albert Robert 1932- WhoE 93
Burchell, Brendan Joseph 1958- WhoWor 93
Burchell, Brian WhoScE 91-1
Burchell, Herbert Joseph 1930- WhoAm 92
Burchell, Howard Bertram 1907- WhoAm 92
Burchell, Mary Cecilia WhoAm 92
Burchell, Vicki Jo 1961- WhoAmW 93
Burchell, William Irvin 1934- St&PR 93
Burchenal, Joan Riley 1925- WhoE 93
Burcher, Hilda Beasley 1938- WhoAmW 93
Burcher, Robert Douglas, Jr. 1946- WhoEmL 93
Burchett, Donald Keith 1943- WhoSSW 93
Burchett, H.L. 1956- St&PR 93
Burchett, Jay ScF&FL 92
Burchett, John C. Law&B 92
Burchett, Kenneth Eugene 1942- WhoSSW 93
Burchfiel, Burrell Clark 1934- WhoAm 92, WhoE 93
Burchfield, Bruce Allen 1947- WhoEmL 93
Burchfield, Donald Francis 1932- WhoSSW 93
Burchfield, Harry Phineas, Jr. 1915- WhoAm 92
Burchfield, James R. 1924- WhoIns 93
Burchfield, Judy Kay 1945- WhoAmW 93
Burchfield, Patricia Crosby 1930- WhoAmW 93
Burchfield, R.W. WhoScE 91-1
Burchfield, William H. 1935- St&PR 93
Burchill, Donn St&PR 93
Burchill, Jeffrey A. 1952- St&PR 93
Burchill, John Brabazon 1938- WhoE 93
Burchill, Julie 1960- BioIn 17, ScF&FL 92
Burchill, Monte L. 1940- St&PR 93
Burchill, Thomas Francis 1942- WhoAm 92
Burchill, William Roberts, Jr. 1947- WhoEmL 93
Burchinal, Robert Nixon 1925- St&PR 93
Burchinow, Naran U. Law&B 92
Burchman, Leonard 1925- WhoAm 92
Burciaga, Cecilia Preciado de 1945- NotHsAW 93 [port]
Burciaga, Juan C. 1929- HispAmA
Burciaga, Juan Guerrero 1929- WhoAm 92
Burck, Arthur Albert 1913- WhoAm 92
Burck, Cyril B., Jr. 1950- WhoEmL 93
Burck, Joachim a 1546-1610 Baker 92
Burck, William Alexander, III Law&B 92
Burckhardt, Dieter L. 1932- WhoScE 91-4
Burckhardt, Jean Louis 1784-1817 Expl 93 [port]
Burckhardt, Johann Jakob 1903- WhoWor 93
Burckhardt, Lucius 1925- WhoWor 93
Burckhardt, Peter 1939- WhoScE 91-4
Burckhardt, Rudy 1914- WhoAm 92
Burcky, Klaus 1950- WhoScE 91-3
Burczyk, Mary Elizabeth 1953- St&PR 93
Burd, John Stephen 1939- WhoAm 92, WhoSSW 93
Burd, Patricia Ayers 1940- WhoSSW 93
Burd, Robert Meyer 1937- WhoE 93, WhoWor 93
Burda, John Alan Law&B 92
Burda, Marianne Louise 1959- WhoEmL 93
Burdack, Karen A. Law&B 92
Burde, Mart Lou 1951- St&PR 93
Burde, Ronald Marshall 1938- WhoAm 92
Burdekin, David A. 1934- WhoScE 91-1
Burdekin, F.M. WhoScE 91-1
Burdekin, Katharine 1896-1963 ScF&FL 92
Burdekin, Kay ScF&FL 92
Burden, Alfred Lionel, Jr. 1934- WhoSSW 93
Burden, Carolyn Prentice 1953- WhoAmW 93
Burden, Chris 1946- BioIn 17
Burden, Douglas BioIn 17
Burden, Erica Elisabeth 1941- WhoAmW 93
Burden, Geneva Louvenia 1950- WhoEmL 93, WhoSSW 93
Burden, I. Townsend, III 1943- St&PR 93
Burden, Jean Prussing WhoAm 92, WhoAmW 93
Burden, Jean (Prussing) 1914- WhoWrEP 92
Burden, Jeffrey Keith 1956- WhoEmL 93
Burden, Laurance T. 1940- WhoAm 92
Burden, Laurance Treat 1940- St&PR 93
Burden, Nancy Caswell 1946- WhoWrEP 92
Burden, Ronald Garland Law&B 92
Burden, S. Carter 1941- WhoAm 92
Burdeshaw, William Brooksbank 1930- WhoE 93, WhoWor 93
Burdetsky, Ben 1928- WhoAm 92
Burdett, Barbra Elaine 1947- WhoAmW 93
Burdett, Howard William 1939- WhoAm 92
Burdett, Marie Y. Law&B 92
Burdett, Philip Hawley 1914- WhoAm 92
Burdette, Bruce M. 1955- St&PR 93
Burdette, Charles M. 1932- St&PR 93
Burdette, Everette Clifton 1950- St&PR 93
Burdette, Forbes Willard 1932- St&PR 93
Burdette, Ila Leola 1959- WhoSSW 93
Burdette, J.R., Jr. 1948- St&PR 93
Burdette, Jane Elizabeth 1955- WhoAmW 93, WhoEmL 93
Burdette, Keith 1955- WhoSSW 93
Burdette, Lew 1926- BioIn 17
Burdette, Sandra Ivester 1942- WhoAmW 93
Burdette, Walter James 1915- WhoAm 92
Burdge, Jeffrey J. WhoAm 92
Burdge, Larry F. 1934- St&PR 93
Burdge, Rabel James 1937- WhoAm 92
Burdge, Ronald Everett 1938- St&PR 93
Burdi, Alphonse Rocco 1935- WhoAm 92
Burdick, Alison Mae 1958- WhoAmW 93
Burdick, Allan Bernard 1920- WhoAm 92
Burdick, Ariane Neiman 1945- WhoWrEP 92
Burdick, Bruce E. Law&B 92
Burdick, Bruce Emerald 1947- WhoEmL 93
Burdick, David Charles 1954- WhoE 93
Burdick, Eugene Allan 1912- WhoAm 92
Burdick, G.S. ScF&FL 92
Burdick, Glenn Arthur 1932- WhoAm 92
Burdick, Jonathan R. 1958- St&PR 93
Burdick, Lou Brum 1943- WhoAm 92
Burdick, Nancy Lee 1956- WhoAmW 93
Burdick, Quentin N. 1908- CngDr 91
Burdick, Quentin N. 1908-1992 NewYTBS 92 [port]
Burdick, Quentin N(orthrop) 1908-1992 CurBio 92N
Burdick, Quentin Northrop 1908- WhoAm 92
Burdick, Robert William 1943- WhoAm 92
Burdick, Stephen Arthur 1952- WhoEmL 93
Burdick, William MacDonald 1952- WhoE 93
Burditt, George Miller, Jr. 1922- WhoAm 92
Burdon, Jonathan Gareth William 1946- WhoWor 93
Burdon, Philip Ralph 1939- WhoAsAP 91
Burdon, Roy Hunter WhoScE 91-1
Burdon, Roy Hunter 1938- WhoWor 93
Burdsall, Clarice W. 1909- WhoWrEP 92
Bureau, Francoise Law&B 92
Bureau, G. WhoScE 91-2
Bureau, Michel Andre 1943- WhoAm 92
Bureau, William H. BioIn 17
Burege, Esorom 1952- WhoAsAP 91
Burek, Vitomir 1945- WhoScE 91-4
Burek, Walter Gerald 1942- WhoAm 92
Buren, Daniel BioIn 17
Burenga, Kenneth L. 1944- WhoAm 92, WhoE 93
Bures, Joseph Edward 1936- St&PR 93
Buresch, Charles Edward 1947- WhoWor 93
Buresh, Thomas Gordon 1951- WhoEmL 93
Buretta, Thomas J. WhoAm 92
Burette, Pierre-Jean 1665-1747 Baker 92
Burfeindt, Judith Grace 1943- WhoAmW 93
Burford, Alexander Mitchell, Jr. 1929- WhoSSW 93
Burford, Anne McGill 1942- WhoAm 92
Burford, Byron Leslie 1920- WhoAm 92
Burford, Frederick W. 1950- St&PR 93
Burford, Marsha Ann 1951- WhoAmW 93
Burford, Robert Fitzpatrick 1923- WhoAm 92
Burford, Roger Lewis 1930- WhoSSW 93
Burford, Russel E., Jr. Law&B 92
Burg, C. WhoScE 91-2
Burg, Dale R(onda) 1942- WhoWrEP 92
Burg, Fred Murray 1951- WhoE 93, WhoEmL 93

Burg, Fredric David 1940- *WhoAm 92*
Burg, George P. 1948- *St&PR 93*
Burg, George Roscoe 1916- *WhoAm 92*
Burg, James Allen 1966- *WhoSSW 93*
Burg, John Parker 1931- *WhoAm 92*
Burg, Maurice Benjamin 1931- *WhoAm 92*
Burg, Mitchell Marc 1954- *WhoAm 92*
Burg, R.A. 1932- *St&PR 93*
Burg, Ruth Cooper 1926- *WhoAm 92, WhoAmW 93*
Burg, Steven L. 1950- *WhoE 93*
Burgan, Jack A. *Law&B 92*
Burgan, John S. d1991 *BioIn 17*
Burgan, Mary Alice 1935- *WhoAm 92*
Burganger, Judith 1939- *Baker 92*
Burgard, Debora Lynn 1957- *WhoAmW 93*
Burgard, Harold Morgan 1929- *St&PR 93*
Burgart, Herbert Joseph 1932- *WhoE 93*
Burgasser, Irma 1918- *WhoAmW 93*
Burgdoerfer, Jerry 1958- *WhoWor 93*
Burgdoerfer, Jerry J. 1935- *St&PR 93, WhoAm 92*
Burge, Aletha Anne 1949- *WhoAmW 93*
Burge, David James 1960- *WhoEmL 93*
Burge, David (Russell) 1930- *Baker 92, WhoAm 92*
Burge, Edward L. *Law&B 92*
Burge, F. Weldon 1956- *WhoE 93*
Burge, Hazel Andersen 1919- *WhoAmW 93*
Burge, Henry Charles 1911- *WhoAm 92*
Burge, Henry H. 1934- *St&PR 93*
Burge, James D. 1934- *St&PR 93*
Burge, James Darrell 1934- *WhoAm 92*
Burge, Joan Marie 1952- *WhoSSW 93*
Burge, John H. 1949- *WhoEmL 93*
Burge, John Kenneth 1926- *WhoSSW 93*
Burge, John Wesley, Jr. 1932- *St&PR 93, WhoAm 92*
Burge, Robert A. *MiSFD 9*
Burge, Ronald Edgar *WhoScE 91-1*
Burge, Ronald Edgar 1932- *WhoWor 93*
Burge, Stuart 1918- *MiSFD 9*
Burge, William Lee 1918- *WhoAm 92*
Burgee, John Henry 1933- *WhoAm 92*
Burgen, Michele *BioIn 17*
Burgener, Francis Andre 1942- *WhoAm 92*
Burgener, Louis W. 1943- *St&PR 93*
Burgenmeier, Beat 1943- *WhoWor 93*
Burger, Alewyn Petrus 1951- *WhoWor 93*
Burger, Ambrose William 1923- *WhoAm 92*
Burger, Amy Louise 1956- *WhoEmL 93*
Burger, Andre 1920- *WhoScE 91-4*
Burger, Anna 1931- *WhoScE 91-4*
Burger, Artur 1943- *WhoScE 91-4*
Burger, C.J. 1940- *St&PR 93*
Burger, Carol Joan 1944- *WhoAmW 93*
Burger, Carolyn S. 1940- *St&PR 93, WhoAm 92, WhoAmW 93*
Burger, Chester 1921- *WhoAm 92*
Burger, Christa 1935- *WhoWor 93*
Burger, Dionys 1892- *ScF&FL 92*
Burger, Edmund Ganes 1930- *WhoAm 92*
Burger, Emily S. *Law&B 92*
Burger, Gary C. 1943- *WhoE 93*
Burger, Gerald K. 1952- *St&PR 93*
Burger, Gerald Keith 1952- *WhoEmL 93*
Burger, Gottfried August 1747-1794 *BioIn 17*
Burger, Hans-Jurgen 1937- *WhoScE 91-3*
Burger, Henry G. 1923- *WhoAm 92, WhoWor 93, WhoWrEP 92*
Burger, Herbert Francis 1930- *St&PR 93, WhoAm 92*
Burger, Isabel Cuellar 1960- *WhoAmW 93*
Burger, James M. *Law&B 92*
Burger, Janette Marie 1958- *WhoAmW 93*
Burger, Joanna 1941- *ConAu 136*
Burger, Joanne 1938- *ScF&FL 92*
Burger, Kalman 1929- *WhoScE 91-4*
Burger, Lane W. 1941- *St&PR 93*
Burger, Leslie Morton 1940- *WhoAm 92*
Burger, Lowell G. *Law&B 92*
Burger, Lowell G. 1928- *St&PR 93*
Burger, Mark A. *Law&B 92*
Burger, Mark Elliott 1952- *WhoEmL 93*
Burger, Mary Louise *WhoAm 92*
Burger, Neal R. *ScF&FL 92*
Burger, Norbert d1992 *NewYTBS 92*
Burger, Richard Melton 1941- *WhoE 93*
Burger, Robert Eugene 1931- *WhoAm 92, WhoWrEP 92*
Burger, Robert Mercer 1927- *WhoAm 92*
Burger, Suzanne Leslie 1960- *WhoE 93*
Burger, Tibor 1925- *WhoScE 91-4*
Burger, Ulrich 1938- *WhoScE 91-4*
Burger, Van Vechten 1905- *St&PR 93*
Burger, Warren E. 1907- *BioIn 17, CngDr 91, DcTwHis*
Burger, Warren Earl 1907- *OxCSupC [port], WhoAm 92, WhoE 93*
Burger, Werner Carl 1925- *WhoE 93*
Burger, Wolfgang 1931- *WhoScE 91-3*
Burger-Muhlfeld, Fritz 1882-1969 *BioIn 17*

Burgert, David Lee 1959- *WhoEmL 93*
Burgert, Joanne Cree 1945- *WhoAmW 93*
Burges, Richard Joseph 1954- *WhoSSW 93*
Burgeson, Joyce Ann 1936- *WhoAmW 93, WhoWor 93*
Burgeson, Noreen Theresa 1953- *St&PR 93*
Burgess, Alan 1930- *St&PR 93*
Burgess, Allen H. 1934- *St&PR 93*
Burgess, Andrew Scott 1951- *St&PR 93*
Burgess, Anthony 1917- *Baker 92, BioIn 17, MagSWL [port], ScF&FL 92, WhoWor 93*
Burgess, Anthony Rex 1935- *WhoWor 93*
Burgess, Arthur *St&PR 93*
Burgess, Barbara Hood 1926- *BioIn 17, ConAu 138, SmATA 69 [port]*
Burgess, Benjamin L., Jr. *Law&B 92*
Burgess, Benjamin L., Jr. 1943- *WhoAm 92*
Burgess, Beth Brown 1959- *WhoEmL 93, WhoSSW 93*
Burgess, Bethany Jane 1959- *WhoAmW 93*
Burgess, Betty J. 1940- *St&PR 93*
Burgess, Brian 1950- *St&PR 93*
Burgess, Brian Robert 1951- *WhoEmL 93*
Burgess, Bruce Howland 1950- *WhoEmL 93*
Burgess, Carl David 1946- *WhoWor 93*
Burgess, Charles Monroe, Jr. 1951- *WhoSSW 93*
Burgess, Charles Orville 1932- *WhoAm 92, WhoWor 93*
Burgess, Christopher M. 1958- *WhoScE 91-1*
Burgess, David 1948- *WhoAm 92, WhoE 93, WhoEmL 93, WhoWor 93*
Burgess, David Albert *WhoScE 91-1*
Burgess, David Lowry 1940- *WhoAm 92*
Burgess, Dean 1937- *WhoSSW 93*
Burgess, Diane Glenn 1935- *WhoSSW 93*
Burgess, Dixie 1961- *WhoEmL 93*
Burgess, Donald David *WhoScE 91-1*
Burgess, Douglas Holmes 1942- *St&PR 93*
Burgess, Edward Francis, VIII *WhoWrEP 92*
Burgess, Eric 1912- *ScF&FL 92*
Burgess, Forrest Harrill 1927-1991 *BiDAMSp 1989*
Burgess, Frederick Manley 1908- *WhoE 93*
Burgess, Gelett Frank 1866-1951 *GayN*
Burgess, Gloria Jean 1953- *WhoEmL 93*
Burgess, Granville Wyche 1947- *ConAu 137*
Burgess, Guy 1911-1963 *ColdWar 1 [port]*
Burgess, Guy Francis de Moncy 1911-1963 *BioIn 17*
Burgess, Harry C. *Law&B 92*
Burgess, Harvey Waites 1948- *WhoSSW 93*
Burgess, Hayden Fern 1946- *WhoEmL 93*
Burgess, James E. 1936- *St&PR 93*
Burgess, James Edward 1936- *WhoAm 92*
Burgess, James Harland 1929- *WhoAm 92*
Burgess, James Scott 1959- *St&PR 93*
Burgess, Janet Helen 1933- *WhoAm 92, WhoAmW 93*
Burgess, Jay G. 1929- *St&PR 93*
Burgess, Jeanne Llewellyn 1923- *WhoAmW 93*
Burgess, John Frank 1917- *WhoAm 92*
Burgess, John Herbert 1933- *WhoAm 92*
Burgess, John M. 1936- *St&PR 93*
Burgess, Julia E. *Law&B 92*
Burgess, Julia Marshall 1929- *WhoAmW 93*
Burgess, Katherine Stanberry *AmWomPl*
Burgess, Larry Charles 1956- *St&PR 93*
Burgess, Leonard Randolph 1919- *WhoAm 92*
Burgess, Lloyd Albert 1917- *WhoAm 92*
Burgess, Lucinda Anne 1960- *WhoAmW 93*
Burgess, Lynne A. *Law&B 92*
Burgess, Madgelene Jones 1948- *WhoEmL 93, WhoSSW 93*
Burgess, Malcolm Stewart, Jr. 1945- *St&PR 93*
Burgess, Margaret *WhoWrEP 92*
Burgess, Mary A. 1938- *ScF&FL 92*
Burgess, Mary Alice 1938- *WhoAm 92*
Burgess, Mary Elizabeth Schiding Warner 1932- *WhoWrEP 92*
Burgess, Mason *ScF&FL 92*
Burgess, Michael *ScF&FL 92*
Burgess, Michael 1942- *WhoWor 93*
Burgess, Michael 1948- *WhoAm 92, WhoEmL 93, WhoWor 93*
Burgess, Minnie C. *AmWomPl*
Burgess, Myrtle Marie 1921- *WhoAmW 93*
Burgess, Peggy Anne *Law&B 92*
Burgess, Peter Malcolm 1950- *WhoSSW 93*

Burgess, Philip Robert 1960- *WhoAm 92*
Burgess, Phillip M. 1963- *St&PR 93*
Burgess, Ralph K. 1926- *St&PR 93*
Burgess, Richard B. 1943- *St&PR 93*
Burgess, Richard Ball 1943- *WhoAm 92*
Burgess, Richard H. *Law&B 92*
Burgess, Richard Joseph 1931- *St&PR 93*
Burgess, Richard Ray 1942- *WhoAm 92*
Burgess, Richard Robert 1937- *WhoSSW 93*
Burgess, Robert Frederick, Jr. 1958- *WhoEmL 93*
Burgess, Robert George *WhoScE 91-1*
Burgess, Robert K. 1944- *St&PR 93*
Burgess, Robert Kyle 1948- *WhoEmL 93*
Burgess, Robert Lester, Jr. 1949- *WhoSSW 93*
Burgess, Robert Lewis 1931- *WhoAm 92*
Burgess, Robert Ragsdale 1931- *St&PR 93*
Burgess, Robert Ronald 1943- *WhoSSW 93*
Burgess, Rodney Stephen *WhoScE 91-1*
Burgess, Roger 1927- *WhoAm 92*
Burgess, Sally 1953- *OxDcOp*
Burgess, Scott Alan 1964- *ScF&FL 92*
Burgess, Smoky 1927-1991 *BioIn 17*
Burgess, Susie May 1950- *WhoAmW 93*
Burgess, Thornton Waldo 1874-1965 *MajAI [port]*
Burgess, Wayne T. 1942- *St&PR 93*
Burgess, Wayne Thomas 1942- *WhoAm 92*
Burgess, William Patrick 1955- *WhoEmL 93*
Burgess Fongsam, Carole Sharon 1956- *WhoEmL 93*
Burget, Mark Edward 1954- *WhoEmL 93*
Burget, Rosemarie 1957- *St&PR 93*
Burget, Vincent D. 1941- *St&PR 93*
Burgett, Charles Allen 1947- *St&PR 93*
Burgett, Dolores Mary 1935- *WhoAmW 93*
Burgett, Janet Ellyn 1959- *WhoAmW 93*
Burggraf, Frank Bernard, Jr. 1932- *WhoAm 92*
Burggraf, Odus Roy 1929- *WhoAm 92*
Burgh, Hubert de d1243 *BioIn 17*
Burgh, Richard W. 1945- *WhoE 93*
Burghard, Sharon Laws 1946- *WhoWrEP 92*
Burghardt, Andrzej 1928- *WhoScE 91-4*
Burghardt, Ann M. 1932- *St&PR 93*
Burghardt, Erich 1921- *WhoScE 91-4*
Burghardt, Jacob J. 1924- *St&PR 93*
Burghardt, Kurt Josef 1935- *St&PR 93, WhoAm 92*
Burghardt, Walter Francis, Jr. 1952- *WhoEmL 93, WhoSSW 93, WhoWor 93*
Burghart, James Henry 1938- *WhoAm 92*
Burghart, Philip 1926- *St&PR 93*
Burghauser, Jarmil 1921- *Baker 92*
Burgheim, Richard Allan 1933- *WhoAm 92*
Burghersh, Lord 1784-1859 *OxDcOp*
Burghersh, John Fane 1784-1859 *Baker 92*
Burghley, William Cecil, Baron 1520-1598 *BioIn 17*
Burghoff, Christine Grace *Law&B 92*
Burgin, E.J. 1927- *St&PR 93*
Burgin, George Hans 1930- *WhoAm 92*
Burgin, Mark Semjonovich 1946- *WhoWor 93*
Burgin, Richard 1892-1981 *Baker 92*
Burgin, Robert A., Jr. 1924- *St&PR 93*
Burgin, Victor 1941- *BioIn 17, ScF&FL 92*
Burgio, Brian James 1962- *WhoSSW 93*
Burgio, Giuseppe Roberto 1919- *WhoWor 93*
Burgkart, Maxmilian 1930- *WhoScE 91-3*
Burgman, Dierdre Ann 1948- *WhoAmW 93, WhoE 93, WhoWor 93*
Burgmeier, James Alphonse 1923- *St&PR 93*
Burgmuller, Johann August Franz 1766-1824 *Baker 92*
Burgmuller, Johann Friedrich Franz 1806-1874 *Baker 92*
Burgmuller, Norbert 1810-1836 *Baker 92, BioIn 17*
Burgo, Joseph *ScF&FL 92*
Burgon, Barre G. *Law&B 92*
Burgon, Barre Glade 1950- *WhoEmL 93*
Burgon, Geoffrey (Alan) 1941- *Baker 92*
Burgoon, Richard Piper, Jr. *Law&B 92*
Burgos, Hector Hugo 1954- *WhoEmL 93, WhoSSW 93*
Burgos, Julia de 1916-1953 *BioIn 17*
Burgos, Julia de 1917-1953 *SpAmA*
Burgos-Sasscer, Ruth 1931- *WhoAmW 93*
Burgoyne, Edward Eynon 1918- *WhoAm 92*
Burgoyne, J. Albert 1914- *WhoIns 93*
Burgoyne, J. Albert, Jr. *Law&B 92*
Burgoyne, James Frederick 1936- *St&PR 93*
Burgoyne, John 1722-1792 *BioIn 17, HarEnMi*

Burgoyne, John Graves *WhoScE 91-1*
Burgoyne, John Neil 1958- *WhoSSW 93*
Burgoyne, Robert Dennis *WhoScE 91-1*
Burgraff, Donna Lynn 1961- *WhoEmL 93*
Burgstaller, Alois 1871-1945 *Baker 92, OxDcOp*
Burgstresser, Richard Albert, Jr. 1954- *WhoEmL 93*
Burguieres, John Bercham, Jr. *Law&B 92*
Burguieres, Philip Joseph 1943- *St&PR 93, WhoAm 92, WhoSSW 93*
Burgum, Bradley Joseph 1952- *WhoEmL 93*
Burgun, J. Armand 1925- *WhoAm 92*
Burgunder, Thomas *Law&B 92*
Burgundio Of Pisa c. 1110-1193 *OxDcByz*
Burgweger, Francis Joseph Dewes, Jr. 1942- *WhoAm 92*
Burhan, A. Michael 1956- *St&PR 93*
Burhans, Ira N. 1929- *St&PR 93*
Burhenne, Hans Joachim 1925- *WhoAm 92, WhoWor 93*
Burhoe, Brian W. 1941- *WhoAm 92*
Burhoe, Brian Walter 1941- *St&PR 93*
Burhoe, Ralph Wendell 1911- *BioIn 17, WhoAm 92, WhoWor 93*
Buri, Pierre 1935- *WhoScE 91-4*
Buri, William Peter 1948- *St&PR 93*
Burian, Emil 1876-1926 *Baker 92, OxDcOp*
Burian, Emil Frantisek 1904-1959 *Baker 92, OxDcOp*
Burian, Karel 1870-1924 *IntDcOp [port], OxDcOp*
Burian, Zdenek *ScF&FL 92*
Buriau, Karl 1939- *WhoScE 91-4*
Burigana, Enus Anthony 1928- *St&PR 93, WhoAm 92*
Burik, Michael A. *Law&B 92*
Burish, Ben Charles 1925- *St&PR 93*
Burish, Thomas Gerard 1950- *WhoSSW 93*
Burk, A.R. *WhoWrEP 92*
Burk, Bernard Alan 1957- *WhoEmL 93*
Burk, Carl John 1935- *WhoAm 92*
Burk, Carole Adrianne 1945- *WhoSSW 93*
Burk, Dana Prag 1960- *WhoEmL 93*
Burk, David Lynn 1944- *St&PR 93*
Burk, James William *Law&B 92*
Burk, John N(aglee) 1891-1967 *Baker 92*
Burk, Kenneth J. 1933- *St&PR 93*
Burk, Kenneth M. 1952- *WhoEmL 93*
Burk, Linda Janet 1948- *WhoAmW 93*
Burk, Melvyn I. 1941- *St&PR 93*
Burk, Norman 1937- *WhoAm 92*
Burk, Sylvia Joan 1928- *WhoAm 92, WhoAmW 93*
Burka, Maria Karpati 1948- *WhoAmW 93*
Burka, Mark B. 1950- *WhoIns 93*
Burkart, Alan Ray 1930- *WhoAm 92*
Burkart, Burke 1933- *WhoAm 92*
Burkart, Michael F. 1946- *St&PR 93*
Burkart, Robert Edward 1943- *WhoE 93*
Burkart, Walter Mark 1921- *WhoAm 92*
Burkart, Werner 1946- *WhoScE 91-3*
Burkat, Leonard 1919-1992 *NewYTBS 92*
Burkdoll, Frank B. 1923- *St&PR 93*
Burke, Aimee L. *Law&B 92*
Burke, Alan d1992 *NewYTBS 92*
Burke, Andrew John 1955- *WhoE 93*
Burke, Ann M. *Law&B 92*
Burke, Ann McFarland 1952- *WhoE 93*
Burke, Anthony Reid 1954- *WhoSSW 93*
Burke, Arleigh A. 1901- *BioIn 17*
Burke, Arleigh Albert 1901- *HarEnMi*
Burke, Arnold D. 1938- *St&PR 93*
Burke, Barbara Florence 1935- *WhoAmW 93*
Burke, Bernard Flood 1928- *WhoAm 92*
Burke, Betty Joan Schumpert 1932- *WhoAmW 93*
Burke, Beverly Ann *WhoSSW 93*
Burke, Beverly Gail 1952- *WhoEmL 93*
Burke, Billie 1885-1970 *QDrFCA 92 [port]*
Burke, C. Kevin 1937- *St&PR 93*
Burke, Celestine George d1990 *BioIn 17*
Burke, Charles Henry 1922- *St&PR 93*
Burke, Charles Richard 1949- *WhoEmL 93*
Burke, Charles W. 1934- *St&PR 93*
Burke, Cheryl Lea 1963- *WhoAmW 93*
Burke, Chris *BioIn 17*
Burke, Chris 1965- *ConHero 2 [port]*
Burke, Christine Eleanor 1948- *WhoEmL 93*
Burke, Colleen A. 1961- *WhoAmW 93*
Burke, Daniel B. *BioIn 17*
Burke, Daniel B. 1929- *St&PR 93*
Burke, Daniel Barnett 1929- *WhoAm 92, WhoE 93*
Burke, Daniel Harold 1942- *St&PR 93*
Burke, Daniel Valentine 1942- *WhoE 93*
Burke, Daniel William 1926- *WhoAm 92*
Burke, David E. *Law&B 92*
Burke, David W. *BioIn 17*
Burke, Delta *BioIn 17*
Burke, Denise Williamson 1947- *WhoAmW 93*

Burke, Dennis *Law&B 92*
Burke, Diana *WhoWrEP 92*
Burke, Donald Francis *Law&B 92*
Burke, Donald Robert 1921- *WhoAm 92*
Burke, Donna Jensen 1935- *WhoAmW 93*
Burke, Dorothy Bonner *Law&B 92*
Burke, E. Ainslie 1922- *WhoAm 92*
Burke, Edgar Patrick 1944- *WhoWrEP 92*
Burke, Edmond Wayne 1935- *WhoAm 92*
Burke, Edmund 1729?-1797 *BioIn 17, WorLitC [port]*
Burke, Edmund Charles 1921- *WhoAm 92*
Burke, Edmund James, III 1949- *WhoEmL 93*
Burke, Edmund William 1948- *St&PR 93*
Burke, Edward M. *Law&B 92*
Burke, Edward Newell 1916- *WhoAm 92*
Burke, (Carol) Elizabeth 1946- *WhoWrEP 92*
Burke, Elizabeth H. Ferguson 1950- *WhoEmL 93*
Burke, Ellen Smith 1952- *WhoEmL 93*
Burke, Felton Gene 1941- *WhoSSW 93*
Burke, Frank *BioIn 17*
Burke, Frank Gerard 1927- *WhoAm 92*
Burke, Frank Harper *Law&B 92*
Burke, Franklin L. 1941- *St&PR 93*
Burke, Franklin Leigh 1941- *WhoAm 92, WhoSSW 93*
Burke, Fred 1965- *ScF&FL 92*
Burke, Gay Ann Wolesensky 1954- *WhoEmL 93*
Burke, George *St&PR 93*
Burke, George, Abbot 1940- *ScF&FL 92*
Burke, Gerald Thomas 1941- *St&PR 93*
Burke, Grace R. 1925- *WhoE 93*
Burke, Harold E. *Law&B 92*
Burke, Harry Brian 1940- *WhoE 93*
Burke, Inez M. *AmWomPl*
Burke, Irene *Law&B 92*
Burke, J. Grant 1943- *WhoE 93*
Burke, Jack L. 1949- *St&PR 93, WhoIns 93*
Burke, Jacqueline Yvonne 1949- *WhoAm 92, WhoAmW 93, WhoE 93, WhoEmL 93*
Burke, James 1941- *WhoAm 92*
Burke, James D. *BioIn 17*
Burke, James Donald 1939- *WhoAm 92*
Burke, James E. *BioIn 17*
Burke, James Edward 1925- *WhoAm 92, WhoWor 93*
Burke, James Gordon 1943- *St&PR 93*
Burke, James Joseph 1928- *WhoAm 92*
Burke, James Joseph, Jr. 1951- *WhoAm 92*
Burke, James Lee 1936- *BioIn 17, WhoWrEP 92*
Burke, James R. 1938- *St&PR 93*
Burke, Jerome Clarence 1944- *St&PR 93*
Burke, Joanne *BioIn 17*
Burke, Jodi Larcombe 1929- *WhoAmW 93*
Burke, Joe d1992 *BioIn 17, NewYTBS 92*
Burke, Joel Howard 1961- *St&PR 93*
Burke, John *Law&B 92*
Burke, John 1922- *ScF&FL 92*
Burke, John 1947- *WhoAm 92*
Burke, John Francis 1922- *WhoE 93*
Burke, John G. *BioIn 17*
Burke, John J. *Law&B 92*
Burke, John James 1857-1945 *BioIn 17*
Burke, John James 1928- *St&PR 93, WhoAm 92*
Burke, John Joseph, Jr. 1942- *WhoSSW 93*
Burke, John Michael 1946- *WhoE 93*
Burke, John Patrick 1953- *WhoE 93*
Burke, John Thomas 1921- *St&PR 93*
Burke, John W. *Law&B 92*
Burke, Joseph A., Jr. *Law&B 92*
Burke, Joseph C. 1932- *WhoAm 92*
Burke, Joseph Eldrid 1914- *WhoE 93*
Burke, Kathleen Mary 1950- *WhoE 93*
Burke, Kelly Howard 1929- *WhoAm 92, WhoSSW 93*
Burke, Kenneth 1897- *BioIn 17*
Burke, Kenneth A. *Law&B 92*
Burke, Kenneth (Duva) 1897- *ConAu 39NR*
Burke, Kerry 1942- *WhoWor 93*
Burke, Kerry 1943- *WhoAsAP 91*
Burke, Kevin Charles Antony 1929- *WhoAm 92*
Burke, Kevin Michael 1946- *WhoEmL 93*
Burke, Kim Kenneth 1955- *WhoEmL 93*
Burke, Laurence Gerard 1934- *St&PR 93*
Burke, Lee Scott 1951- *St&PR 93*
Burke, Lillian Walker 1917- *WhoAm 92, WhoWor 93*
Burke, Linda Beerbower *Law&B 92*
Burke, Lois Adele *Law&B 92*
Burke, Lucille Pennucci 1938- *WhoAmW 93*
Burke, Margaret Ann 1961- *WhoAmW 93*
Burke, Marguerite Jodi Larcombe *WhoSSW 93*
Burke, Marian *BioIn 17*
Burke, Marianne King 1938- *WhoAmW 93*
Burke, Mark 1944- *St&PR 93*
Burke, Martyn *MiSFD 9*
Burke, Mary *WhoAm 92*
Burke, Mary 1959- *St&PR 93*
Burke, Mary Joan Thompson 1933- *WhoAmW 93*
Burke, Mary Thomas 1930- *WhoAm 92*
Burke, Michael Donald 1944- *St&PR 93, WhoAm 92*
Burke, Michael Richard 1949- *WhoEmL 93*
Burke, Michael Thomas 1946- *WhoEmL 93*
Burke, Michael Walter *Law&B 92*
Burke, Mildred *BiDAMSp 1989*
Burke, Ned *WhoWrEP 92*
Burke, Noel R. *Law&B 92*
Burke, Patricia 1943- *WhoE 93*
Burke, Patrick D. 1949- *St&PR 93*
Burke, Paul Bradford 1956- *St&PR 93*
Burke, Paul Edmund 1948- *WhoEmL 93*
Burke, Paul Robert *Law&B 92*
Burke, Peter Arthur 1948- *WhoAm 92*
Burke, Peter Frederick 1951- *St&PR 93*
Burke, Peter Michael 1948- *WhoEmL 93*
Burke, Peter Sibley 1946- *WhoEmL 93*
Burke, Philip George *WhoScE 91-1*
Burke, Quentin *BioIn 17*
Burke, Ralph *MajAI*
Burke, Raymond F. *Law&B 92*
Burke, Raymond W. *WhoWrEP 92*
Burke, Redmond A. 1914- *WhoAm 92*
Burke, Richard Kitchens 1922- *WhoAm 92*
Burke, Richard Lawrence 1950- *St&PR 93*
Burke, Richard Thomas 1947- *WhoE 93*
Burke, Richard William 1933- *WhoAm 92*
Burke, Rita Denise 1950- *WhoE 93*
Burke, Rita Hoffmann 1925- *WhoE 93*
Burke, Robert *Law&B 92*
Burke, Robert E. *Law&B 92*
Burke, Robert Eugene 1921- *WhoAm 92*
Burke, Robert Harry 1945- *WhoWor 93*
Burke, Robert James 1934- *St&PR 93*
Burke, Robert Lawrence 1916- *St&PR 93*
Burke, Robert O'Hara 1820-1861 & Wills, William John 1834-1861 *Expl 93 [port]*
Burke, Robert S. *Law&B 92*
Burke, Roger M. 1930- *St&PR 93*
Burke, Ronald G. 1932- *WhoAm 92*
Burke, Rosann Margaret 1927- *WhoAmW 93*
Burke, Ruth 1933- *WhoWrEP 92*
Burke, Sharon Jeanette 1955- *WhoAmW 93*
Burke, Shawn Patrick 1958- *WhoE 93*
Burke, Solomon 1936- *SoulM*
Burke, Stephen S. 1945- *WhoIns 93*
Burke, Steve *BioIn 17*
Burke, Steven Charles 1951- *WhoEmL 93*
Burke, Steven P. *Law&B 92*
Burke, Teresa Louise 1966- *WhoAmW 93*
Burke, Teresa Mary 1956- *WhoAmW 93*
Burke, Thomas C. 1941- *WhoIns 93*
Burke, Thomas Edmund 1875-1929 *BiDAMSp 1989*
Burke, Thomas Edmund 1932- *WhoAm 92*
Burke, Thomas John 1947- *WhoEmL 93, WhoWor 93*
Burke, Thomas Joseph, Jr. 1941- *WhoAm 92*
Burke, Thomas Michael 1956- *WhoEmL 93*
Burke, Tom Clifton 1954- *WhoEmL 93, WhoSSW 93*
Burke, Virginia Eileen 1948- *WhoE 93*
Burke, Virginia May 1933- *WhoAmW 93*
Burke, Warren *ScF&FL 92*
Burke, William *BioIn 17*
Burke, William A. 1939- *AfrAmBi*
Burke, William J. *Law&B 92*
Burke, William James 1912- *WhoAm 92*
Burke, William John 1941- *St&PR 93*
Burke, William Marion, 3rd *Law&B 92*
Burke, William T.J. *Law&B 92*
Burke, William Temple, Jr. 1935- *WhoAm 92*
Burke, Yvette Marie 1965- *WhoAmW 93, WhoEmL 93*
Burke, Yvonne Brathwaite 1932- *AfrAmBi, BioIn 17, EncAACR*
Burke, Yvonne Watson Brathwaite 1932- *WhoAm 92, WhoAmW 93*
Burkee, Irvin 1918- *WhoWor 93*
Burkehart, Byron Cleveland 1947- *St&PR 93*
Burkel, Eberhard 1952- *WhoWor 93*
Burkemper, Ronald William 1950- *WhoEmL 93*
Burken, Ruth Marie 1956- *WhoAmW 93, WhoEmL 93*
Burkert, Nancy Ekholm 1933- *MajAI [port]*
Burkert, Robert Randall 1930- *WhoAm 92*
Burkert, Walter 1931- *WhoWor 93*
Burkes, Leisa Jeanotta 1961- *WhoAmW 93, WhoEmL 93*
Burkes, Sarah Beatrice 1948- *WhoEmL 93*
Burket, Gail Brook 1905- *WhoAmW 93, WhoWor 93*
Burket, George Edward, Jr. 1912- *WhoAm 92*
Burket, Harriet *WhoAm 92, WhoWrEP 92*
Burket, Patricia Krise 1952- *WhoE 93*
Burket, Richard Andrew 1925- *St&PR 93*
Burket, Roger Clair 1948- *WhoSSW 93*
Burkett, Cathy Crapps 1959- *WhoAmW 93*
Burkett, Charles William, IV 1961- *WhoEmL 93*
Burkett, Christine Louise 1952- *WhoAmW 93*
Burkett, David Ingram 1948- *WhoEmL 93*
Burkett, Deborah Ann 1951- *St&PR 93*
Burkett, Edward Eugene 1955- *WhoEmL 93*
Burkett, Elizabeth Gayle 1964- *WhoSSW 93*
Burkett, James Wendell 1930- *St&PR 93*
Burkett, Joe Wylie 1945- *WhoWor 93*
Burkett, John *BioIn 17*
Burkett, Lawrence V., Jr. *Law&B 92*
Burkett, Marvin Dan 1942- *St&PR 93*
Burkett, Mary Frances 1939- *WhoE 93*
Burkett, Rachelle Ann 1958- *WhoEmL 93*
Burkett, Randy James 1955- *WhoEmL 93*
Burkett, Robert E. 1954- *St&PR 93*
Burkett, Robert E., Jr. *Law&B 92*
Burkett, Robert L. 1945- *BioIn 17*
Burkett, Steve *BioIn 17*
Burkett, Steven Louis 1958- *WhoEmL 93*
Burkett, Thomas L. 1950- *St&PR 93*
Burkett, William A. 1913- *St&PR 93*
Burkett, William Andrew 1913- *WhoAm 92, WhoWor 93*
Burkey, J. Brent *Law&B 92*
Burkey, J. Brent 1946- *St&PR 93*
Burkey, Jacob Brent 1946- *WhoAm 92, WhoEmL 93*
Burkey, Lee Melville 1914- *WhoAm 92*
Burkhalter, Gary Allen 1955- *WhoSSW 93*
Burkhalter, James Clark 1939- *St&PR 93*
Burkham, Lucie Tousey *AmWomPl*
Burkhammer, Stewart Curtis 1943- *WhoE 93*
Burkhard, Paul 1911-1977 *Baker 92, OxDcOp*
Burkhard, Ronald L. *Law&B 92*
Burkhard, Willy 1900-1955 *Baker 92, OxDcOp*
Burkhardt, Andreas G. 1958- *St&PR 93*
Burkhardt, Bernhard G. 1959- *St&PR 93*
Burkhardt, Bruce *BioIn 17*
Burkhardt, Charles Henry 1915- *WhoE 93*
Burkhardt, Dolores Ann 1932- *WhoAmW 93*
Burkhardt, Eva G. 1930- *St&PR 93*
Burkhardt, Guenter H. 1931- *St&PR 93*
Burkhardt, Guenter M. 1963- *St&PR 93*
Burkhardt, Gwenda M. *Law&B 92*
Burkhardt, Hans Gustav 1904- *WhoAm 92*
Burkhardt, Hugh *WhoScE 91-1*
Burkhardt, James Kevin 1954- *WhoEmL 93*
Burkhardt, John Leonard, Jr. 1937- *WhoE 93*
Burkhardt, Lawrence, III 1932- *WhoAm 92*
Burkhardt, Max 1871-1934 *Baker 92*
Burkhardt, Peter Jon 1957- *WhoEmL 93*
Burkhardt, Robert F. 1936- *St&PR 93*
Burkhardt, Ronald Robert 1948- *WhoEmL 93*
Burkhardt, Walter Heinrich 1928- *WhoWor 93*
Burkhart, Beverly Joanne 1947- *WhoEmL 93*
Burkhart, Bobbie Newman 1948- *WhoAm 92*
Burkhart, Charles Barclay 1914- *WhoAm 92*
Burkhart, D. Arthur 1956- *St&PR 93*
Burkhart, Edward Allen 1959- *St&PR 93*
Burkhart, Harold Eugene 1944- *WhoSSW 93*
Burkhart, Jeffrey A. 1956- *St&PR 93*
Burkhart, Jennifer Ellen 1955- *WhoE 93*
Burkhart, Jo Ann Virginia 1926- *WhoWrEP 92*
Burkhart, John Henry 1920- *WhoAm 92*
Burkhart, John W. 1937- *St&PR 93*
Burkhart, Linda Sue 1953- *WhoAmW 93, WhoEmL 93*
Burkhart, Paul James 1956- *WhoEmL 93*
Burkhart, Rinold W. 1946- *St&PR 93*
Burkhart, Robert Edward 1937- *WhoSSW 93, WhoWrEP 92*
Burkhead, J. Gary 1941- *St&PR 93*
Burkhead, Marie Brown 1934- *WhoAmW 93*
Burkhead, Rebecca Rose 1959- *WhoEmL 93*
Burkholder, Alfred Lee 1934- *WhoSSW 93*
Burkholder, Barry C. 1940- *St&PR 93*
Burkholder, Donald Lyman 1927- *WhoAm 92*
Burkholder, John *BioIn 17*
Burkholder, John Richard 1928- *ConAu 37NR*
Burkholder, Joseph Mark 1956- *WhoEmL 93*
Burkholder, Paul C. *Law&B 92*
Burkholder, Peter Miller 1933- *WhoAm 92*
Burkholder, Walter Edward 1945- *St&PR 93*
Burkholder, Wendell Eugene 1928- *WhoAm 92*
Burkholz, Herbert 1932- *ScF&FL 92*
Burki, Fred Albert 1926- *WhoAm 92*
Burkin, Alfred Richard *WhoScE 91-1*
Burkin, Alfred Richard 1923- *WhoWor 93*
Burkin, Mary *WhoWrEP 92*
Burkland, Elizabeth Ann *Law&B 92*
Burkland, Pamela Rodgers 1943- *WhoAmW 93*
Burkle, Andrew C., Jr. 1943- *St&PR 93*
Burkle, Ronald *BioIn 17*
Burkley, Diane E. 1952- *WhoAmW 93*
Burkley, George G. 1902-1991 *BioIn 17*
Burklow, Ernest Gerald 1942- *WhoSSW 93*
Burklund, Dale E. 1926- *St&PR 93*
Burkman, Ernest, Jr. 1929- *WhoSSW 93*
Burkoth, Terry Lee 1941- *St&PR 93*
Burkov, Vladimir Nicolaevich 1939- *WhoWor 93*
Burkowsky, Mitchell Roy 1931- *WhoE 93*
Burks, Ardath Walter 1915- *WhoE 93*
Burks, Ashby Quinton *Law&B 92*
Burks, Daniel Seamus 1942- *St&PR 93*
Burks, Diane Ruth 1943- *WhoSSW 93*
Burks, Frank E. 1946- *St&PR 93*
Burks, Harry G. 1899-1992 *BioIn 17*
Burks, Jack D. 1951- *WhoE 93, WhoEmL 93, WhoWor 93*
Burks, Ramsey M. 1933- *St&PR 93*
Burks, Richard Thomas 1961- *WhoEmL 93*
Burks, Verner Irwin 1923- *WhoAm 92*
Burks, Winston Watts, III *Law&B 92*
Burkut, Yilmaz 1935- *WhoScE 91-4*
Burlaga, Leonard Francis 1938- *WhoE 93*
Burlage, James Edward 1934- *St&PR 93*
Burlage, Matthew James 1963- *WhoE 93*
Burland, Brian Berkeley 1931- *WhoAm 92, WhoWor 93*
Burland, John Alexis 1931- *WhoE 93*
Burland, John Boscawen *WhoScE 91-1*
Burlant, Brian L. *Law&B 92*
Burlant, William Jack 1928- *WhoAm 92*
Burlas, Ladislav 1927- *Baker 92*
Burlatskii, Fedor Mikhailovich *BioIn 17*
Burlaud, Alain Jean 1946- *WhoWor 93*
Burlbaw, Lynn Matthew 1948- *WhoSSW 93*
Burleigh, Cecil 1885-1980 *Baker 92*
Burleigh, Harry T. 1866-1949 *BioIn 17*
Burleigh, Henry Thacker 1866-1949 *Baker 92*
Burleigh, Joan Billger 1949- *WhoEmL 93*
Burleigh, Joseph Gaynor 1942- *WhoSSW 93*
Burleigh, Louise 1890- *AmWomPl*
Burleigh, William Henry 1812-1871 *JrnUS*
Burleigh, William Robert 1935- *WhoAm 92*
Burle-Marx, Roberto *BioIn 17*
Burle Marx, Roberto 1909- *WhoWor 93*
Burles, Kenneth Thomas 1946- *WhoEmL 93*
Burleski, Joseph Anthony, Jr. 1960- *WhoWor 93*
Burleson, Carolyn Odom 1942- *WhoAmW 93*
Burleson, Claude Alfred 1924- *St&PR 93*
Burleson, Clay O. 1944- *St&PR 93*
Burleson, Donald R. 1941- *ScF&FL 92*
Burleson, Edward 1798-1851 *BioIn 17*
Burleson, Elizabeth *DcAmChF 1960*
Burleson, Gene E. *St&PR 93*
Burleson, Karen Tripp 1955- *WhoAmW 93*
Burleson, Michael Delane 1953- *WhoSSW 93*
Burleson, Omar 1906-1991 *BioIn 17*
Burleson, Terri Lynne 1956- *WhoAmW 93*
Burleson, Willard McKenzie, Jr. 1937- *WhoAm 92*
Burlew, John Swalm 1910- *WhoAm 92*
Burley, Alan John 1956- *WhoEmL 93*
Burley, Charles Frederick 1919- *St&PR 93*
Burley, Dexter Lishon 1944- *WhoE 93*
Burley, Eldon *WhoScE 91-1*
Burley, J. *WhoScE 91-1*
Burley, Jack Lynn 1942- *WhoAm 92*

Burley, John Michael 1944- *WhoUN 92*
Burley, Kathleen Mary 1942- *WhoWrEP 92*
Burley, Mark Alan 1951- *WhoEmL 93*
Burley, Nancy Tyler 1949- *WhoAm 92*
Burley, Timothy Alan 1958- *WhoE 93*
Burley, W.J. 1914- *ScF&FL 92*
Burlin, Natalie Curtis *IntDcAn*
Burlin, Zerita G. 1921- *WhoAmW 93*
Burling, Daniel James 1947- *WhoE 93*
Burling, Irving Ray 1928- *St&PR 93*
Burling, James Sherman 1954- *WhoEmL 93*
Burling, Judith Wilmot 1946- *WhoAmW 93*
Burling, Robbins 1926- *WhoAm 92*
Burlingame, Anson d1991 *BioIn 17*
Burlingame, Edward Livermore 1935- *WhoAm 92*
Burlingame, Eugene Edward 1924- *St&PR 93*
Burlingame, James Montgomery, III 1926- *WhoAm 92*
Burlingame, John Francis 1922- *WhoAm 92, WhoWor 93*
Burlingame, John Hunter 1933- *WhoAm 92*
Burlingame, Leroy James 1929- *WhoAm 92*
Burlingame, Lloyd Lamson 1934- *WhoAm 92*
Burlingham, Eleanor F. d1991 *BioIn 17*
Burlinson, Robert Francis 1939- *St&PR 93*
Burlison, James David 1958- *WhoEmL 93*
Burlison, Joe *BioIn 17*
Burm, Forrest H. 1930- *St&PR 93*
Burman, Ben Lucien 1895-1984 *ScF&FL 92*
Burman, David John 1952- *WhoEmL 93*
Burman, DeeAnn Schaumberg 1949- *WhoEmL 93*
Burman, Diane Berger 1936- *WhoAmW 93*
Burman, John Peter *WhoScE 91-1*
Burman, Kenneth Dale 1944- *WhoE 93*
Burman, Marsha Linkwald 1949- *WhoEmL 93*
Burman, Marshall Lyle 1929- *St&PR 93*
Burman, Robert 1916- *St&PR 93*
Burman, Tom *MiSFD 9*
Burman Todd, Cynthia *Law&B 92*
Burmaster, M.R. *Law&B 92*
Burmaster, M.R. 1934- *St&PR 93, WhoAm 92*
Burmeister, David Lee 1949- *St&PR 93*
Burmeister, Edwin 1939- *WhoAm 92*
Burmeister, James T. 1948- *St&PR 93*
Burmeister, Joachim 1564-1629 *Baker 92*
Burmeister, John Luther 1938- *WhoAm 92*
Burmeister, Jon 1933- *ScF&FL 92*
Burmeister, Kristen Schnelle 1960- *WhoEmL 93*
Burmeister, Norman William 1939- *St&PR 93*
Burmeister, Richard 1860-1944 *Baker 92*
Burmeister, Tracy Lee 1942- *St&PR 93*
Burmester, William Frederick 1923- *WhoWrEP 92*
Burmistrov, Yevgeni Semenovich 1941- *WhoUN 92*
Burn, D.J. *WhoScE 91-1*
Burn, Diane *BioIn 17*
Burn, Helen Jean 1926- *WhoE 93*
Burn, Ian John 1927- *WhoWor 93*
Burn, Malcolm 1949- *WhoEmL 93*
Burnaby, Davy 1881-1949 *QDrFCA 92 [port]*
Burnacini, Giovanni c. 1605-1655 *OxDcOp*
Burnacini, Ludovico 1636-1707 *OxDcOp*
Burnacz, Kornel Anthony 1957- *WhoE 93*
Burnage, Henri 1935- *WhoScE 91-2*
Burnam, Paul Wayne 1913- *WhoAm 92*
Burnam, Tom 1913- *WhoAm 92, WhoWor 93*
Burnap, John B. 1918- *St&PR 93*
Burnard, Bonnie *WhoCanL 92*
Burnbaum, Michael William 1949- *WhoEmL 93*
Burnel, Daniel 1940- *WhoScE 91-2*
Burnell, Bates Cavanaugh 1923- *WhoAm 92*
Burnell, Brian L. 1935- *St&PR 93*
Burnell, Elvin Wallace 1938- *WhoWrEP 92*
Burnell, George A. 1929- *St&PR 93*
Burnell, James McIndoe 1921- *WhoAm 92*
Burnell, Louis Alexander 1928- *WhoWor 93*
Burnes, Carol Ganson 1942- *WhoWrEP 92*
Burnes, Kennett F. 1943- *St&PR 93*
Burnes, Kennett Farrar 1943- *WhoAm 92, WhoE 93*
Burnes, Linda Jane 1949- *WhoAmW 93*
Burnes, Suzie 1946- *WhoAmW 93*
Burness, Don 1941- *WhoWrEP 92*
Burness, James Hubert 1949- *WhoE 93*
Burness, Wallace B(inny) 1933- *WhoWrEP 92*
Burnet, Arthur Hazen 1944- *St&PR 93*
Burnet, George, Jr. 1924- *WhoAm 92*
Burnet, Gilbert 1643-1715 *BioIn 17*
Burnet, Mabelle P. *AmWomPl*
Burnett, Alister Douglas 1943- *WhoSSW 93*
Burnett, Angela 1955- *WhoEmL 93*
Burnett, Anne Berkeley Axton 1960- *WhoAmW 93, WhoEmL 93*
Burnett, Arthur Louis, Sr. 1935- *WhoAm 92*
Burnett, Audrey Lahoma Arnold 1935- *WhoSSW 93*
Burnett, Billie J. 1931- *St&PR 93*
Burnett, Boyd P. *Law&B 92*
Burnett, Carol *BioIn 17*
Burnett, Carol 1936- *WhoAm 92, WhoAmW 93*
Burnett, Charles *BioIn 17*
Burnett, Charles 1944- *MiSFD 9*
Burnett, Chester Arthur 1910-1976 *BioIn 17*
Burnett, Clarence Aubrey 1941- *WhoWor 93*
Burnett, David 1941- *WhoWor 93*
Burnett, Deborah Becher 1949- *WhoEmL 93*
Burnett, Emma *WhoSSW 93*
Burnett, Frances Eliza Hodgson 1849-1924 *AmWomPl*
Burnett, Frances Hodgson 1849-1924 *BioIn 17*
Burnett, Frances (Eliza) Hodgson 1849-1924 *ConAu 136, MajAI [port]*
Burnett, Francis Allan 1932- *WhoE 93*
Burnett, Frank W. 1917-1991 *BioIn 17*
Burnett, Frederick William 1911- *St&PR 93*
Burnett, Gordon Arthur 1934- *St&PR 93*
Burnett, Greg *St&PR 93*
Burnett, Hallie Southgate 1908-1991 *BioIn 17*
Burnett, Hallie Southgate (Zeisel) *ConAu 37NR*
Burnett, Henry 1927- *WhoAm 92*
Burnett, I. Compton- 1884-1969 *BioIn 17*
Burnett, James *Law&B 92*
Burnett, James Robert 1925- *St&PR 93*
Burnett, James Rufus 1949- *WhoAm 92, WhoEmL 93*
Burnett, John G. d1991 *BioIn 17*
Burnett, John Thomas 1931- *St&PR 93*
Burnett, Kathleen A. *Law&B 92*
Burnett, Leo *BioIn 17*
Burnett, Lonnie Sheldon 1927- *WhoAm 92*
Burnett, Lowell Jay 1941- *WhoAm 92*
Burnett, Lynn Barkley 1948- *WhoWor 93*
Burnett, Mary Parham 1956- *WhoEmL 93*
Burnett, Michele Marie 1956- *WhoEmL 93*
Burnett, Nancy C. *Law&B 92*
Burnett, Paul David 1963- *WhoSSW 93*
Burnett, Ralph W. *Law&B 92*
Burnett, Rita Marline 1954- *WhoAmW 93*
Burnett, Robert A. 1927- *WhoAm 92*
Burnett, Robert Adair 1934- *WhoAm 92*
Burnett, Robert Sherwin 1940- *St&PR 93*
Burnett, Roger Macdonald 1941- *WhoE 93*
Burnett, Rosa Scott 1945- *WhoWor 93*
Burnett, Susan Cleary *Law&B 92*
Burnett, Susan Walk 1946- *WhoAmW 93*
Burnett, Virgil 1928- *WhoCanL 92*
Burnett, W.E., Jr. 1927- *St&PR 93*
Burnett, William E., Jr. 1927- *WhoIns 93*
Burnett, William Earl, Jr. 1927- *WhoAm 92, WhoSSW 93*
Burnett, William J. *Law&B 92*
Burnett-Appe, Dana Marie 1948- *WhoSSW 93*
Burnette, Edward L. 1930- *St&PR 93*
Burnette, Guy Ellington, Jr. 1952- *WhoEmL 93*
Burnette, Ikey Scott 1960- *WhoEmL 93, WhoWor 93*
Burnette, Joe Edward 1918- *WhoSSW 93*
Burnette, Linda Lee 1961- *WhoAmW 93*
Burnette, M. Lawrence *Law&B 92*
Burnette, Mary Malissa 1950- *WhoEmL 93*
Burnette, Monica Frances 1960- *WhoAmW 93*
Burnette, Ollen Lawrence, Jr. 1927- *WhoAm 92, WhoSSW 93*
Burnette, Ralph Edwin, Jr. 1953- *WhoEmL 93*
Burnette, Smiley 1911-1967 *QDrFCA 92 [port]*
Burney, Charles 1726-1814 *Baker 92, OxDcOp*
Burney, Derek H. 1939- *WhoWor 93*
Burney, Fanny 1752-1840 *BioIn 17*
Burney, Frank Burleson 1954- *WhoEmL 93*
Burney, Victoria Kalgaard 1943- *WhoAmW 93*
Burnford, Sheila 1918-1984 *DcChlFi, ScF&FL 92, WhoCanL 92*
Burnford, Sheila (Philip Cochrane Every) 1918-1984 *MajAI [port]*
Burnham, Beatrice *SweetSg B [port]*
Burnham, Bonnie *BioIn 17*
Burnham, Bruce Nelson 1938- *WhoSSW 93*
Burnham, Bryson Paine 1917- *WhoAm 92*
Burnham, Charles Wilson 1933- *WhoAm 92*
Burnham, Christine Elizabeth 1958- *St&PR 93*
Burnham, Clara Louise Root 1854-1927 *AmWomPl*
Burnham, Crispin Reed 1949- *WhoWrEP 92*
Burnham, Daniel Hudson 1846-1912 *GayN*
Burnham, Daniel Patrick 1946- *St&PR 93, WhoAm 92*
Burnham, David Bright 1933- *WhoAm 92*
Burnham, Donald Clemens 1915- *WhoAm 92*
Burnham, Douglass Lawrence 1932- *St&PR 93*
Burnham, Duane L. 1942- *St&PR 93*
Burnham, Duane Lee 1942- *WhoAm 92*
Burnham, Gregory Alan 1954- *WhoWrEP 92*
Burnham, Harold Arthur 1929- *WhoAm 92, WhoWor 93*
Burnham, Helen *AmWomPl*
Burnham, Hugo
See Gang of Four *ConMus 8*
Burnham, I.W., II *BioIn 17*
Burnham, I.W., II 1909- *St&PR 93*
Burnham, James 1905-1987 *BioIn 17*
Burnham, Jed James 1944- *St&PR 93*
Burnham, Jeremy *ScF&FL 92*
Burnham, John Chynoweth 1929- *WhoAm 92*
Burnham, Linden Forbes Sampson 1923-1985 *DcTwHis*
Burnham, Noel C. *Law&B 92*
Burnham, Norman James 1951- *WhoEmL 93*
Burnham, Patricia White 1933- *WhoAmW 93*
Burnham, Philip d1991 *BioIn 17*
Burnham, Philip E. d1992 *BioIn 17, NewYTBS 92*
Burnham, Richard E. *Law&B 92*
Burnham, Robert Alan 1928- *WhoE 93*
Burnham, Robert Danner 1944- *WhoAm 92*
Burnham, Robert J. 1930- *St&PR 93*
Burnham, Sheila Kay 1955- *WhoEmL 93*
Burnham, Sophy *WhoWrEP 92*
Burnham, Sophy 1936- *BioIn 17, ConAu 38NR, WhoAmW 93*
Burnham, Stephen John 1948- *WhoEmL 93*
Burnham, Steven James 1947- *WhoEmL 93*
Burnham, Virginia Schroeder 1908- *WhoWor 93*
Burnham, Walter Dean 1930- *WhoAm 92*
Burnham, William W. 1942- *St&PR 93*
Burniaux, Robert *ScF&FL 92*
Burnick, Barrie Sue *Law&B 92*
Burnie, James Peter *WhoScE 91-1*
Burniece, Thomas F., III 1941- *St&PR 93*
Burnight, Susan Robin *Law&B 92*
Burnim, Kalman Aaron 1928- *WhoAm 92*
Burningham, John 1936- *BioIn 17*
Burningham, John (Mackintosh) 1936- *MajAI [port]*
Burnip, Malcolm Stuart *WhoScE 91-1*
Burnison, Boyd Edward 1934- *WhoAm 92, WhoWor 93*
Burniston, Karen Sue 1939- *WhoAmW 93*
Burnley, (John) David 1941- *ConAu 40NR*
Burns, Aaron 1922-1991 *BioIn 17*
Burns, Alan 1929- *ScF&FL 92, WhoWrEP 92*
Burns, Alexandra Darrow 1946- *WhoEmL 93*
Burns, Allan *MiSFD 9*
Burns, Allan Fielding 1936- *WhoE 93*
Burns, Alpha Ward *Law&B 92*
Burns, Alta Marie 1936- *WhoSSW 93*
Burns, Anne Marie 1964- *WhoAmW 93*
Burns, Anneliese 1965- *WhoEmL 93*
Burns, Annelu *AmWomPl*
Burns, Archibaldo 1914- *DcMexL*
Burns, Arnold Irwin 1930- *St&PR 93, WhoE 93*
Burns, Arthur F. 1904-1987 *BioIn 17*
Burns, Arthur Lee 1924- *WhoAm 92, WhoSSW 93*
Burns, Barbara *Law&B 92*
Burns, Barbara Belton 1944- *WhoAmW 93*
Burns, Bertha *BioIn 17*
Burns, Betty-Ann 1941- *WhoAmW 93*
Burns, Beverly K. 1948- *St&PR 93*
Burns, Bill 1963- *St&PR 93*
Burns, Billye Jane 1940- *WhoAmW 93*
Burns, Bob 1890-1956 *QDrFCA 92 [port]*
Burns, Brian Patrick 1936- *WhoAm 92*
Burns, Brian Patrick 1962- *WhoE 93, WhoEmL 93, WhoWor 93*
Burns, Britt *BioIn 17*
Burns, Bryant Robert 1929- *WhoAsAP 91*
Burns, Byron Bernard, Jr. *Law&B 92*
Burns, Campbell Blain *WhoScE 91-1*
Burns, Carol J. 1954- *WhoEmL 93*
Burns, Carroll D. 1932- *WhoIns 93*
Burns, Carroll Dean 1932- *St&PR 93, WhoAm 92*
Burns, Catherine Elizabeth 1953- *WhoAm 92, WhoAmW 93, WhoEmL 93*
Burns, Charles Patrick 1937- *WhoAm 92*
Burns, Charles Sloan 1926- *St&PR 93*
Burns, Chester Ray 1937- *WhoAm 92, WhoSSW 93*
Burns, Christopher 1944- *ScF&FL 92*
Burns, Cliff 1963- *ScF&FL 92*
Burns, Conrad 1935- *CngDr 91*
Burns, Conrad Ray 1935- *BioIn 17, WhoAm 92*
Burns, Cornelius 1951- *WhoWor 93*
Burns, Dan 1925- *St&PR 93*
Burns, Dan W. 1925- *WhoAm 92, WhoWor 93*
Burns, Daniel B. 1932- *St&PR 93*
Burns, Daniel Hobart 1928- *WhoWor 93*
Burns, Daniel K. 1956- *St&PR 93*
Burns, Daniel T. *Law&B 92*
Burns, David Craig 1949- *WhoEmL 93*
Burns, David Mitchell 1928- *WhoAm 92*
Burns, Denise Moretti 1957- *St&PR 93, WhoAmW 93*
Burns, Dennis Raymond 1943- *WhoE 93*
Burns, Donald Carlton 1929- *WhoIns 93*
Burns, Donald E. 1939- *St&PR 93*
Burns, Duncan Thorburn *WhoScE 91-1*
Burns, Edward Bradford 1932- *WhoAm 92*
Burns, Edward C. 1942- *St&PR 93*
Burns, Edward Charles 1942- *WhoE 93*
Burns, Elizabeth A. *Law&B 92*
Burns, Elizabeth Mary 1927- *WhoAm 92*
Burns, Ellen Bree 1923- *WhoAm 92, WhoAmW 93, WhoE 93*
Burns, Eric Grimsley *Law&B 92*
Burns, Florence M. 1905-1988 *BioIn 17*
Burns, Francis *ConTFT 10*
Burns, Fredric Jay 1937- *WhoE 93*
Burns, G. Webster *Law&B 92*
Burns, Geoffrey P. *Law&B 92*
Burns, Geoffrey P. 1950- *St&PR 93*
Burns, George 1896- *BioIn 17, QDrFCA 92 [port], WhoAm 92*
Burns, George Washington 1913- *WhoAm 92*
Burns, Gerald Allen *Law&B 92*
Burns, Gerald Patrick 1940- *WhoWrEP 92*
Burns, Gerald Phillip 1918- *WhoAm 92*
Burns, Glenn Richard 1951- *WhoEmL 93*
Burns, Grant Francis 1947- *WhoEmL 93*
Burns, Harlan Allen 1934- *St&PR 93*
Burns, Harmon E. 1945- *St&PR 93*
Burns, Harold W. 1926- *WhoE 93*
Burns, Harrison 1946-1991 *BioIn 17*
Burns, Harry A. 1943- *St&PR 93*
Burns, Harry R. d1990 *BioIn 17*
Burns, Heather Lee 1951- *WhoEmL 93*
Burns, Helene Barbara 1953- *WhoAmW 93*
Burns, Howard Joseph 1963- *WhoSSW 93*
Burns, Ivan Alfred 1935- *St&PR 93, WhoAm 92*
Burns, J.K. 1926- *WhoScE 91-3*
Burns, Jack Hancock 1920- *WhoAm 92*
Burns, Jacqueline 1927- *WhoAmW 93, WhoE 93*
Burns, James *WhoScE 91-1*
Burns, James 1808-1871 *BioIn 17*
Burns, James Alan, Jr. 1955- *WhoEmL 93*
Burns, James M. 1924- *WhoAm 92*
Burns, James MacGregor 1918- *WhoAm 92*
Burns, James Thomas *Law&B 92*
Burns, James W. 1929- *St&PR 93*
Burns, James William 1929- *WhoAm 92, WhoWor 93*
Burns, Jeffrey Robert 1956- *WhoEmL 93*
Burns, Jim 1948- *ScF&FL 92*
Burns, John 1904- *St&PR 93*
Burns, John A. 1909-1975 *PolPar*
Burns, John Dudley 1933- *St&PR 93, WhoAm 92, WhoSSW 93*
Burns, John Edward, III 1951- *St&PR 93*
Burns, John Elliott 1858-1943 *DcTwHis*
Burns, John F. *BioIn 17*
Burns, John Joseph 1920- *WhoAm 92*
Burns, John Joseph 1924- *WhoAm 92, WhoWor 93*
Burns, John Joseph, Jr. 1925- *WhoE 93*
Burns, John Joseph, Jr. 1931- *WhoAm 92*
Burns, John Luther 1932- *WhoSSW 93*
Burns, John M. d1992 *NewYTBS 92*

Burns, John M. 1924-1992 *BioIn 17*
Burns, John Scott 1947- *WhoAm 92*
Burns, John Thomas 1943- *WhoSSW 93*
Burns, John Tolman 1922- *WhoAm 92*
Burns, John V. d1991 *BioIn 17*
Burns, John William 1945- *WhoAm 92*
Burns, Joseph Arthur 1941- *WhoAm 92*
Burns, Joseph Dennis 1940- *St&PR 93*
Burns, Joseph M. 1938- *WhoE 93*
Burns, Joseph William 1908- *WhoAm 92*
Burns, Keith 1956- *WhoEmL 93*
Burns, Ken *BioIn 17, MiSFD 9*
Burns, Ken 1953- *CurBio 92 [port]*
Burns, Ken Lauren 1953- *WhoAm 92*
Burns, Kenneth Dean 1930- *WhoAm 92*
Burns, Kenneth J., Jr. *Law&B 92*
Burns, Kenneth Jones, Jr. 1926- *St&PR 93, WhoAm 92*
Burns, Kerry Lee 1959- *WhoE 93*
Burns, Latham C. 1930- *St&PR 93*
Burns, Laura Elizabeth 1942- *WhoSSW 93*
Burns, Lawrence Aloysius, Jr. 1949- *WhoEmL 93*
Burns, Lawrence R. 1927- *St&PR 93*
Burns, Linda Ann 1950- *WhoAmW 93*
Burns, Lisamarie 1966- *WhoAmW 93*
Burns, M. Anthony 1942- *St&PR 93*
Burns, Marian Law 1954- *WhoAmW 93*
Burns, Marion G. 1924- *WhoSSW 93*
Burns, Marla Jo 1964- *WhoAmW 93, WhoEmL 93*
Burns, Martin L. 1933- *St&PR 93*
Burns, Marvin Gerald 1930- *WhoAm 92, WhoWor 93*
Burns, Mary Ann *BioIn 17*
Burns, Mary Elizabeth 1946- *WhoEmL 93*
Burns, Mary Ellen *Law&B 92*
Burns, Mary Frances 1949- *WhoEmL 93, WhoSSW 93*
Burns, Mary Modena *AmWomPl*
Burns, Mary Thelma *WhoAmW 93*
Burns, MaryAnn 1961- *WhoAmW 93*
Burns, Maryann Margaret 1944- *WhoAmW 93*
Burns, Marylee *WhoE 93*
Burns, Michael Joseph 1943- *WhoAm 92*
Burns, Michael Keith 1940- *WhoE 93*
Burns, Michael William 1947- *WhoEmL 93*
Burns, Mitchel Anthony 1942- *WhoAm 92, WhoSSW 93*
Burns, Muriel 1933- *St&PR 93*
Burns, Nancy Ann 1936- *WhoSSW 93*
Burns, Nancy M. *AmWomPl*
Burns, Ned Hamilton 1932- *WhoAm 92*
Burns, Olive Ann *BioIn 17*
Burns, Oliver B., Jr. 1930- *St&PR 93*
Burns, Padraic 1929- *WhoAm 92, WhoWor 93*
Burns, Pat 1952- *WhoAm 92*
Burns, Pat Ackerman Gonia 1938- *WhoAmW 93, WhoWor 93*
Burns, Patricia Henrietta 1934- *WhoWrEP 92*
Burns, Patricia Williamee 1941- *WhoAmW 93*
Burns, Patrick A. *Law&B 92*
Burns, Paul M. 1949- *St&PR 93*
Burns, Peter Francis 1949- *WhoEmL 93*
Burns, Phillip O. *Law&B 92*
Burns, Phyllis Ann 1935- *WhoWrEP 92*
Burns, Ralph M. 1916- *St&PR 93*
Burns, Raymond E. 1952- *St&PR 93*
Burns, Rebecca Ann 1946- *WhoE 93, WhoEmL 93*
Burns, Richard *Law&B 92*
Burns, Richard 1958-1992 *ScF&FL 92*
Burns, Richard Dale 1955- *WhoEmL 93*
Burns, Richard Dean 1929- *WhoAm 92*
Burns, Richard Keith 1935- *WhoWrEP 92*
Burns, Richard Michael 1937- *St&PR 93, WhoAm 92*
Burns, Richard Ramsey 1946- *WhoEmL 93*
Burns, Richard (William) 1958-1992 *ConAu 139*
Burns, Rita A. *Law&B 92*
Burns, Robert *Law&B 92, WhoScE 91-1*
Burns, Robert 1759-1796 *BioIn 17, MagSWL [port], PoeCrit 6 [port], WorLitC [port]*
Burns, Robert, Jr. 1936- *WhoSSW 93*
Burns, Robert Ambrose, Jr. 1955- *WhoE 93*
Burns, Robert E(lliott) 1891?-1955 *ConAu 138*
Burns, Robert Edward 1919- *WhoAm 92, WhoWor 93, WhoWrEP 92*
Burns, Robert Edward 1953- *WhoEmL 93*
Burns, Robert Francis 1928- *WhoAm 92*
Burns, Robert Harrison 1941- *WhoIns 93*
Burns, Robert Henry 1929- *WhoAm 92*
Burns, Robert Ignatius 1921- *WhoAm 92*
Burns, Robert Matthew 1948- *WhoAm 92*
Burns, Robert Michael 1938- *WhoSSW 93*
Burns, Robert P. *Law&B 92*
Burns, Robert Paschal 1933- *WhoAm 92*
Burns, Robert Patrick 1947- *WhoEmL 93*
Burns, Robert T. *Law&B 92*
Burns, Robin *BioIn 17, WhoAm 92, WhoAmW 93*
Burns, Roger George 1937- *WhoAm 92, WhoE 93*
Burns, Roland O. 1960- *St&PR 93*
Burns, Roland Stephen *WhoScE 91-1*
Burns, Ronald A. Duffy 1959- *WhoE 93*
Burns, Russell MacBain 1926- *WhoE 93*
Burns, Sally Ann 1959- *WhoAmW 93, WhoEmL 93, WhoSSW 93, WhoWor 93*
Burns, Sandra Flynn 1939- *WhoAmW 93, WhoE 93*
Burns, Sarah Rose 1949- *WhoE 93*
Burns, Scott 1940- *WhoSSW 93*
Burns, Stan Z. d1990 *BioIn 17*
Burns, Stephen Gilbert 1953- *WhoAm 92, WhoEmL 93*
Burns, Stephen James 1939- *WhoAm 92*
Burns, Steven Dwight 1948- *WhoEmL 93*
Burns, Stuart L. 1932- *WhoWrEP 92*
Burns, Teresa Lynn 1958- *WhoSSW 93*
Burns, Terrence Michael 1954- *WhoEmL 93*
Burns, Terry Dee 1956- *WhoEmL 93*
Burns, Tex *ConAu 40NR*
Burns, Tex 1908-1988 *BioIn 17*
Burns, Thagrus Asher 1917- *WhoAm 92*
Burns, Thomas C. *St&PR 93*
Burns, Thomas C. 1928- *WhoAm 92*
Burns, Thomas David 1921- *WhoAm 92, WhoWor 93*
Burns, Thomas G. 1940- *St&PR 93*
Burns, Thomas J. 1945- *St&PR 93*
Burns, Thomas Joseph *Law&B 92*
Burns, Thomas M. *Law&B 92*
Burns, Thomas Roy 1925- *WhoWor 93*
Burns, Thomas Samuel 1945- *WhoAm 92*
Burns, Virginia Law 1925- *WhoAmW 93, WhoWrEP 92*
Burns, W. Haywood 1940- *WhoE 93*
Burns, Ward 1928- *WhoAm 92*
Burns, William A. 1909- *WhoAm 92*
Burns, William Carl, Jr. 1953- *WhoSSW 93*
Burns, William Glenn 1949- *WhoEmL 93*
Burns, William Kenneth 1925- *WhoE 93*
Burns, William Loomis, Jr. 1928- *St&PR 93*
Burns, William O. 1930- *St&PR 93, WhoAm 92*
Burns, William Patrick 1947- *WhoEmL 93*
Burns, William Robert 1922- *WhoIns 93*
Burns, Williams J. *Law&B 92*
Burnsed-Geffen, Adelle 1948- *WhoAmW 93*
Burnshaw, Stanley 1906- *WhoAm 92*
Burnside, Ambrose Everett 1824-1881 *BioIn 17, HarEnMi*
Burnside, Frank Boyle 1950- *WhoEmL 93*
Burnside, John Wayne 1941- *WhoAm 92*
Burnside, Mary *St&PR 93*
Burnside, Mary Beth 1943- *WhoAm 92*
Burnside, Orvin Charles 1932- *WhoAm 92*
Burnside, Pershing Elliott 1946- *WhoAm 92*
Burnside, R.L. *BioIn 17*
Burnside, Waldo Howard 1928- *WhoAm 92*
Burns-Larson, Mary Ward 1952- *WhoAmW 93*
Burns-Love, Darlene Louise 1959- *WhoAmW 93*
Burnstein, Daniel 1946- *WhoWor 93*
Burnstein, Jack D. 1945- *St&PR 93*
Burnstock, Geoffrey *WhoScE 91-1*
Burnworth, Ann 1962- *WhoAmW 93*
Burny, Franz 1938- *WhoScE 91-2*
Buroughs, Edward Elliott 1951- *WhoEmL 93*
Burpeau, George O. *Law&B 92*
Burpee, Robert E. *St&PR 93*
Burr, Aaron 1756-1836 *OxCSupC, PolPar*
Burr, Alan Carleton 1926- *St&PR 93*
Burr, Amelia Josephine 1878- *AmWomPl*
Burr, Borden H., II 1937- *St&PR 93*
Burr, Carleton 1921- *St&PR 93*
Burr, Charles Roger 1948- *WhoE 93*
Burr, Craig Lee 1945- *St&PR 93*
Burr, Dan 1951- *BioIn 17*
Burr, Diane Lynnette 1961- *WhoAmW 93*
Burr, Donald C. *BioIn 17*
Burr, Donald C. 1941- *ConEn, EncABHB 8 [port]*
Burr, Donald Calvin 1941- *WhoE 93*
Burr, Donald D. 1923-1990 *BioIn 17*
Burr, Edward B. 1923- *WhoIns 93*
Burr, Edward Benjamin 1923- *WhoAm 92*
Burr, Francis H. 1914- *St&PR 93*
Burr, Francis Hardon 1914- *WhoAm 92, WhoWor 93*
Burr, Frank W. 1932- *St&PR 93*
Burr, George S. 1917- *WhoAm 92*
Burr, Gray 1919- *WhoWrEP 92*
Burr, Harry Lawson, III 1952- *WhoEmL 93*
Burr, Henry I. 1928- *St&PR 93*
Burr, Hiram Hale, Jr. 1943- *WhoAm 92*
Burr, James Hugh 1948- *St&PR 93*
Burr, Jeff *MiSFD 9*
Burr, John Roy 1933- *WhoAm 92*
Burr, Laurie Diane 1953- *WhoAmW 93, WhoEmL 93*
Burr, Maxwell Arthur 1939- *WhoAsAP 91*
Burr, Michael *WhoAm 92*
Burr, Nanci Singer 1938- *WhoAmW 93*
Burr, Patricia Allyn 1950- *St&PR 93*
Burr, Raymond 1917- *WhoAm 92*
Burr, Robert Elliott *Law&B 92*
Burr, Robert Lyndon 1944- *WhoAm 92*
Burr, Stanley A. 1943- *St&PR 93*
Burr, Stewart S. d1969 *BioIn 17*
Burr, Susanna *WhoScE 91-1*
Burr, Tamara Jill 1967- *WhoAmW 93*
Burr, Thomas M. 1942- *St&PR 93*
Burr, Timothy Fuller 1952- *WhoSSW 93*
Burrage, A. Harcourt 1899- *ScF&FL 92*
Burrage, A.M. 1889-1956 *ScF&FL 92*
Burrage, Harold 1931-1966 *BioIn 17*
Burrard, Harry 1755-1813 *HarEnMi*
Burrasca, Raymond P. *Law&B 92*
Burrchett, Sandy Sue Curtis 1942- *WhoSSW 93*
Burrell, Barbara *BioIn 17*
Burrell, Betty Jean 1960- *WhoAmW 93*
Burrell, Craig Donald 1926- *WhoAm 92*
Burrell, David Bakewell 1933- *WhoAm 92*
Burrell, E. William 1927- *WhoE 93*
Burrell, J.A. 1946- *WhoScE 91-1*
Burrell, Kenneth Earl 1931- *WhoAm 92*
Burrell, Leroy *BioIn 17*
Burrell, Lewis *BioIn 17*
Burrell, Lizabeth Lorie 1952- *WhoEmL 93*
Burrell, Nancy Bradbury 1948- *WhoWrEP 92*
Burrell, Regina Holbrook 1936- *WhoSSW 93*
Burrell, Roy E(ric) C(harles) 1923- *SmATA 72 [port]*
Burrell, Sidney Alexander 1917- *WhoAm 92*
Burrell, Stan Kirk *BioIn 17*
Burrell, Stephen Clark 1942- *St&PR 93*
Burrell, Thomas *BioIn 17*
Burrell, Thomas J. *WhoAm 92*
Burrell, Victor Gregory, Jr. 1925- *WhoAm 92*
Burrell, William 1861-1958 *BioIn 17*
Burrell, William Gibson *WhoScE 91-1*
Burrello, Daniel M. 1961- *WhoSSW 93*
Burress, Angela Malee 1967- *WhoAmW 93*
Burress, Kenneth R. 1934- *St&PR 93*
Burress, Robert C. 1938- *St&PR 93*
Burress, Sharon Baker 1942- *WhoAmW 93*
Burri, Alberto 1915- *BioIn 17*
Burri, Betty Jane 1955- *WhoEmL 93*
Burri, Peter Hermann 1938- *WhoWor 93*
Burridge, David 1944- *WhoScE 91-1*
Burridge, H.J. 1930- *St&PR 93*
Burridge, Robert 1937- *WhoE 93*
Burridge, Trevor David 1932- *ConAu 137*
Burrier, Gail Warren 1927- *WhoWor 93*
Burrill, Bertha Y. *AmWomPl*
Burrill, Christine *MiSFD 9*
Burrill, G. Steven *BioIn 17*
Burrill, Janice Hilary 1957- *WhoEmL 93*
Burrill, Kathleen R. F. 1924- *WhoAm 92*
Burrill, Mary 1879-1946 *AmWomPl*
Burrill, Melinda Jane 1947- *WhoEmL 93*
Burrington, David Edson 1931- *WhoAm 92*
Burrington, Robert P. 1929- *St&PR 93*
Burris, Beth Conley 1959- *WhoSSW 93*
Burris, Bill Buchanan, Jr. 1957- *WhoEmL 93*
Burris, Frances White 1933- *WhoAmW 93*
Burris, James Frederick 1947- *WhoAm 92, WhoE 93, WhoWor 93*
Burris, Johnny Clark 1953- *WhoEmL 93*
Burris, Joseph Stephen 1942- *WhoAm 92*
Burris, Kathryn Ann 1957- *WhoAmW 93, WhoEmL 93*
Burris, Paul D. *St&PR 93*
Burris, Robert E. 1937- *St&PR 93*
Burris, Robert H. 1914- *BioIn 17*
Burris, Robert Harza 1914- *WhoAm 92*
Burris, Roland W. *AfrAmBi [port]*
Burris, Roland Wallace 1937- *WhoAm 92*
Burris, Steven Michael 1952- *WhoWor 93*
Burris, Thelma Ruth 1921- *WhoWrEP 92*
Burritt, Lloyd (Edmund) 1940- *Baker 92*
Burritt, Victor S. 1943- *St&PR 93*
Burros, Donald d1991 *BioIn 17*
Burrough, Harold Martin 1888-1977 *HarEnMi*
Burroughs, Bobbie J. *St&PR 93*
Burroughs, Bruce Douglas 1944- *WhoWor 93*
Burroughs, Edgar Rice 1875-1950 *BioIn 17, ScF&FL 92*
Burroughs, Eric d1992 *NewYTBS 92*
Burroughs, Eugene B. *BioIn 17*
Burroughs, Ida Benjamin *AmWomPl*
Burroughs, Jack Eugene 1926- *WhoAm 92*
Burroughs, Jack Eugene 1946- *WhoSSW 93*
Burroughs, John 1837-1921 *BioIn 17, GayN*
Burroughs, John Coleman 1913-1979 *ScF&FL 92*
Burroughs, John David 1947- *WhoSSW 93*
Burroughs, Jonnie Carmen 1927- *WhoSSW 93*
Burroughs, Margaret Taylor G. 1917- *BlkAuII 92*
Burroughs, Miggs 1946- *WhoE 93, WhoEmL 93*
Burroughs, Richard Hansford, III 1946- *WhoE 93, WhoEmL 93*
Burroughs, Richard Ray 1946- *WhoEmL 93*
Burroughs, Thomas *WhoAm 92*
Burroughs, William Ellis 1951- *WhoEmL 93*
Burroughs, William S. 1914- *AmWrS3, BioIn 17, ConLC 75 [port], ConTFT 10, ScF&FL 92, WorLitC [port]*
Burroughs, William Seward 1857-1898 *GayN*
Burroughs, William Seward 1914- *WhoAm 92, WhoWrEP 92*
Burroughs, William Seward, II 1914- *ConGAN*
Burrow, Claude Hoke 1947- *WhoEmL 93*
Burrow, Harold 1914- *St&PR 93*
Burrow, Terry Bruce 1943- *St&PR 93*
Burroway, Janet G. 1936- *WhoAm 92, WhoSSW 93*
Burroway, Janet Gay 1936- *WhoWrEP 92*
Burrowbridge, Susan Tate 1947- *WhoAmW 93*
Burrowes, Geoff *MiSFD 9*
Burrowes, Norma 1944- *Baker 92, OxDcOp*
Burrows, Arthur Andrews, 3rd 1942- *WhoE 93*
Burrows, Barbara Ann 1947- *WhoAmW 93*
Burrows, Benjamin 1927- *WhoAm 92*
Burrows, Brenda Lee 1960- *WhoE 93*
Burrows, Brian William 1939- *St&PR 93, WhoAm 92*
Burrows, Clifford Robert *WhoScE 91-1*
Burrows, Daniel J. 1954- *St&PR 93*
Burrows, Daniel L. d1990 *BioIn 17*
Burrows, Dennis J. 1945- *WhoSSW 93*
Burrows, Donald Albert 1937- *WhoAm 92*
Burrows, Donald Francis, Jr. 1945- *St&PR 93*
Burrows, Edith Maie 1887- *AmWomPl*
Burrows, Elizabeth MacDonald 1930- *WhoAm 92, WhoAmW 93, WhoWor 93*
Burrows, F. Robert 1933- *St&PR 93*
Burrows, Gates Wilson 1899- *WhoAm 92*
Burrows, George Reynolds Scott 1827-1917 *HarEnMi*
Burrows, James 1940- *ConTFT 10, MiSFD 9, WhoAm 92*
Burrows, Jay Edward 1949- *WhoEmL 93*
Burrows, John Edward 1950- *WhoE 93, WhoEmL 93*
Burrows, John W. *St&PR 93*
Burrows, Jon Hanes 1946- *WhoSSW 93*
Burrows, Kenneth David 1941- *St&PR 93*
Burrows, Lawton A., Jr. *Law&B 92*
Burrows, Lewis 1931- *WhoAm 92*
Burrows, Malcolm *WhoScE 91-1*
Burrows, Michael Donald 1944- *WhoAm 92, WhoWor 93*
Burrows, Reuben Houston 1853-1889 *BioIn 17*
Burrows, Ronald George 1912- *St&PR 93*
Burrows, Selig S. 1913- *St&PR 93*
Burrows, Selig Saul 1913- *WhoAm 92*
Burrows, Stephen J. 1952- *St&PR 93*
Burrows, Stuart 1933- *Baker 92, IntDcOp, OxDcOp*
Burrows, Terry L. 1948- *St&PR 93*
Burrows, W.R., III 1931- *St&PR 93*
Burrows, William Claude 1925- *WhoAm 92*
Burrs, Mick 1940- *WhoCanL 92*
Burrud, Bill 1925-1990 *BioIn 17*
Burrud, William James 1925-1990 *BioIn 17*
Burrus, Charles Andrew, Jr. 1927- *WhoAm 92*
Burrus, Charles Sidney 1934- *WhoAm 92*
Burrus, Clark *AfrAmBi*
Burrus, John Newell 1920- *WhoAm 92*
Burrus, Robert L., Jr. 1934- *St&PR 93*
Burrus, Robert Lewis, Jr. 1934- *WhoAm 92, WhoSSW 93*
Burruss, Darrell E. *Law&B 92*
Burruss, Terry Gene 1950- *WhoSSW 93*
Burry, Allen J. d1990 *BioIn 17*
Burry, Judith Mesnick 1942- *WhoSSW 93*
Burry, William Charles 1911- *WhoE 93*
Bursa, Stanislaw 1865-1947 *PolBiDi*

Bursa, Stanislaw Teodor 1921- WhoScE 91-4
Bursch, Ruby Boothe AmWomPl
Burschel, Peter 1927- WhoScE 91-3, WhoWor 93
Burse, Raymond Malcolm 1951- WhoAm 92
Bursey, Joan Tesarek 1943- WhoAm 92, WhoSSW 93
Bursey, Maurice M. 1939- WhoAm 92
Bursiek, Ralph David 1937- WhoAm 92, WhoE 93
Bursik, Carol Jean 1948- WhoEmL 93
Bursinger, JoEllen 1958- WhoAmW 93
Bursk, Edward C. 1907-1990 BioIn 17
Bursky, Herman Aaron 1938- WhoAm 92
Bursley, Kathleen A. Law&B 92
Bursley, Kathleen A. 1954- WhoAmW 93
Bursma, Albert, Jr. 1937- WhoAm 92
Burson, Charles W. WhoAm 92, WhoSSW 93
Burson, Harold 1921- St&PR 93, WhoAm 92, WhoE 93
Burson, Linda 1942- WhoE 93
Burson, Scott Foster 1952- WhoEmL 93
Burson, William Ralph, Jr. 1938- St&PR 93
Burssens, Amaat F.S. 1897-1983 IntDcAn
Burstall, Clare BioIn 17
Burstall, Rodney Martineau WhoScE 91-1
Burstall, Tim 1929- MiSFD 9
Burstein, Alan Stuart 1940- WhoE 93
Burstein, Chaya M. 1923- BioIn 17
Burstein, David 1947- WhoEmL 93
Burstein, David M. Law&B 92
Burstein, Elias 1917- WhoAm 92
Burstein, Jack David 1945- WhoAm 92, WhoSSW 93
Burstein, Laurie Joan 1951- WhoAmW 93
Burstein, Lawrence St&PR 93
Burstein, Lucien 1922- St&PR 93
Burstein, Melvin L. Law&B 92
Burstein, Melvin L. 1933- St&PR 93
Burstein, Richard Joel 1945- WhoAm 92
Burstein, Sharon Ann Palma 1952- WhoAmW 93, WhoE 93, WhoEmL 93
Burstein, Sol 1922- WhoAm 92
Burston, Richard Mervin 1924- WhoE 93
Burstyn, Ellen 1932- IntDcF 2-3, WhoAm 92, WhoAmW 93
Burstyn, Harold Lewis 1930- WhoWor 93
Burszta, Jozef 1914-1987 IntDcAn
Bursztajn, Harold Jonah 1950- WhoEmL 93
Burt, Alice G. Law&B 92
Burt, Alice Louise 1925- WhoIns 93
Burt, Alvin Miller, III 1935- WhoAm 92
Burt, Alvin Victor, Jr. 1927- WhoAm 92
Burt, Barbara Swett 1955- WhoAmW 93
Burt, Christopher Murray 1933- WhoAm 92
Burt, Cynthia Marie Maultsby 1951- WhoEmL 93
Burt, David Arlin 1949- WhoIns 93
Burt, David Sill 1917- WhoE 93
Burt, Donald X(avier) 1929- ConAu 39NR
Burt, Earl Daniel, Jr. 1948- WhoEmL 93
Burt, Francis 1926- Baker 92
Burt, James Edward, III 1937- St&PR 93
Burt, James Melvin 1933- St&PR 93, WhoAm 92, WhoWor 93
Burt, James Robertson 1933- WhoScE 91-1
Burt, Janice Carol Cockrell 1960- WhoSSW 93
Burt, Jeffrey Amsterdam 1944- WhoAm 92
Burt, John Harris 1918- WhoAm 92
Burt, Karen Rose 1948- WhoAmW 93
Burt, Linda K. 1951- WhoEmL 93
Burt, Marjorie Lombard 1956- WhoAmW 93
Burt, Nathaniel 1913- WhoWrEP 92
Burt, Olive F. Wooley 1894- AmWomPl
Burt, Richard M. Law&B 92
Burt, Richard Max 1944- St&PR 93
Burt, Robert Amsterdam 1939- WhoAm 92
Burt, Robert N. 1937- St&PR 93
Burt, Robert Norcross 1937- WhoAm 92
Burt, Steven Earl 1949- WhoWrEP 92
Burt, Sue Marie Law&B 92
Burt, Wallace Joseph, Jr. 1924- St&PR 93, WhoIns 93
Burt, Wallace Lockwood 1948- WhoIns 93
Burt, Wayne V. 1917-1991 BioIn 17
Burt, William Henry 1903-1987 BioIn 17
Burtch, Robert Lee 1925- St&PR 93
Burtch, Thomas Darrold 1949- WhoEmL 93
Burti, Christopher Louis 1950- WhoEmL 93
Burtin, Margaret Irene 1939- WhoAm 92
Burtin, Pierre WhoScE 91-2
Burtis, John Michael Law&B 92
Burtis, Theodore Alfred 1922- St&PR 93, WhoAm 92
Burtius, Nicolaus c. 1445-1518? Baker 92
Burtle, Gary Jerome 1953- WhoEmL 93, WhoSSW 93
Burtle, James Lindley 1919- WhoE 93, WhoWor 93
Burtle, Paul Walter 1950- WhoEmL 93, WhoWor 93
Burtnick, Ronald 1946- WhoE 93
Burtoft, John Nelson, Jr. 1944- WhoSSW 93
Burton, Al WhoAm 92, WhoWor 93
Burton, Alan G. Law&B 92
Burton, Alexander Martin Grant 1932- WhoWrEP 92
Burton, Anna Marjorie 1931- WhoAmW 93
Burton, Anna Meister WhoE 93
Burton, Arthur H., Jr. 1934- St&PR 93
Burton, Arthur Henry, Jr. 1934- WhoAm 92
Burton, Asa 1752-1836 BioIn 17
Burton, Barbara Anne 1948- WhoAmW 93
Burton, Barbara Susan 1951- WhoSSW 93
Burton, Benjamin Theodore 1919- WhoAm 92
Burton, Boyd Breil 1959- WhoSSW 93
Burton, Brandie WhoAmW 93
Burton, Bruce Clement 1952- St&PR 93
Burton, Byron Scott Law&B 92
Burton, Charles Arthur 1945- WhoE 93
Burton, Charles Edward 1946- WhoEmL 93
Burton, Charles Henning 1915- WhoAm 92
Burton, Charles T. St&PR 93
Burton, Charles Victor 1935- WhoAm 92
Burton, Courtney 1912- St&PR 93
Burton, Dan 1938- CngDr 91
Burton, Daniel F., Jr. BioIn 17
Burton, Daniel G. 1935- WhoIns 93
Burton, Daniel S. 1953- St&PR 93
Burton, Danny Lee 1938- WhoAm 92
Burton, Darrell Irvin 1926- WhoAm 92
Burton, David Philip 1943- WhoScE 91-3
Burton, David R. 1959- St&PR 93
Burton, Diana E. St&PR 93
Burton, Donald H. 1937- WhoE 93
Burton, Donald Joseph 1934- WhoAm 92
Burton, Donna M. WhoWrEP 92
Burton, Earl Gillespie, III 1952- WhoEmL 93
Burton, Edward C., Jr. 1928- St&PR 93
Burton, Edward L., III 1933- St&PR 93
Burton, Edward Lewis 1935- WhoWor 93
Burton, Edwin T. 1942- St&PR 93
Burton, Elizabeth C. Law&B 92
Burton, Eric 1932- DcCPCAm
Burton, Frederick Russell 1861-1909 Baker 92
Burton, Gwendolyn R. Wilson WhoAmW 93
Burton, Harold Hitz 1888-1964 OxCSupC [port]
Burton, Hester (Wood-Hill) 1913- MajAI [port]
Burton, Hugh Malcolm 1932- WhoWor 93
Burton, Ian 1935- WhoAm 92
Burton, J.L. 1927- St&PR 93
Burton, Jack WhoScE 91-1
Burton, James H. 1956- St&PR 93
Burton, James Harold 1956- WhoAm 92
Burton, James Harper 1940- WhoSSW 93
Burton, Janet Ferree 1955- WhoEmL 93
Burton, Janet Landau 1948- WhoAmW 93
Burton, John Campbell 1932- WhoAm 92
Burton, John F. 1951- St&PR 93
Burton, John Lane 1952- WhoEmL 93
Burton, John Lee 1927- WhoSSW 93
Burton, John Reginald 1912- St&PR 93
Burton, John Routh 1917- WhoAm 92
Burton, John Scott Law&B 92
Burton, John Scott 1955- WhoEmL 93
Burton, Joseph Randolph 1951- WhoEmL 93
Burton, Julienne M. Law&B 92
Burton, Kay Fox 1938- WhoAmW 93
Burton, Kenneth Lee 1948- St&PR 93
Burton, Larry 1944- St&PR 93
Burton, Lela Mae 1959- WhoAmW 93
Burton, Lena Dalkeith AmWomPl
Burton, Leone 1936- WhoWor 93
Burton, Levardis Robert Martyn, Jr. WhoAm 92
Burton, Mark 1960- St&PR 93
Burton, Mary Alice 1954- WhoWrEP 92
Burton, Mary Louise Himes 1948- WhoE 93
Burton, Maurice 1898-1992 ConAu 139
Burton, Michael F. 1948- St&PR 93
Burton, Michael Graham 1961- WhoWor 93
Burton, Michael Ladd 1942- WhoAm 92
Burton, Nanci L. 1942- WhoAm 92
Burton, Paul Denison 1929- St&PR 93
Burton, Philip Henry 1904- WhoSSW 93
Burton, Philip Ward 1910- WhoAm 92
Burton, Ralph Gaines 1955- WhoSSW 93
Burton, Ralph Joseph 1911- WhoAm 92
Burton, Ray Berry d1991 BioIn 17
Burton, Raymond C., Jr. 1938- St&PR 93
Burton, Raymond Charles, Jr. 1938- WhoAm 92
Burton, Richard 1821-1890 Expl 93 [port]
Burton, Richard 1925-1984 BioIn 17, IntDcF 2-3 [port]
Burton, Richard A. Law&B 92
Burton, Richard Francis 1821-1890 BioIn 17, IntDcAn
Burton, Richard Irving 1936- WhoAm 92, WhoWor 93
Burton, Robbyn E. Law&B 92
Burton, Robert BioIn 17
Burton, Robert Eugene 1948- WhoEmL 93, WhoSSW 93
Burton, Robert F. 1944- WhoSSW 93
Burton, Robert Gene 1938- WhoAm 92
Burton, Robert George 1929- St&PR 93
Burton, Robert Jones 1946- WhoEmL 93
Burton, Robert Lee 1943- WhoSSW 93
Burton, Robert W. 1927- St&PR 93
Burton, Robert William 1927- WhoAm 92
Burton, Roger Vernon 1928- WhoAm 92
Burton, Ron D. 1946- WhoAm 92, WhoSSW 93
Burton, Roy H. 1933- St&PR 93
Burton, Russell Rohan 1932- WhoAm 92
Burton, S.H. 1919- ScF&FL 92
Burton, Sala 1925-1987 BioIn 17
Burton, Samuel Richard Manfred 1960- WhoEmL 93, WhoSSW 93
Burton, Scot 1953- WhoEmL 93
Burton, Scott 1939-1989 BioIn 17
Burton, Shearor Fay 1938- WhoAmW 93
Burton, Shirley Ann Thrasher 1935- WhoAmW 93
Burton, Sigrid 1951- WhoEmL 93
Burton, Stephen Douglas 1943- Baker 92, WhoSSW 93
Burton, Steven Bruce 1950- WhoE 93
Burton, Steven Bryant 1952- St&PR 93, WhoAm 92
Burton, Thomas Arthur 1934- WhoAm 92
Burton, Thomas H. Law&B 92
Burton, Tim BioIn 17, MiSFD 9
Burton, Tim 1959- News 93-1 [port]
Burton, Tim 1960- WhoAm 92
Burton, Vernon James 1962- WhoEmL 93
Burton, Virginia Lee 1909-1968 MajAI [port]
Burton, William C. Law&B 92
Burton, William de K. 1926- St&PR 93
Burton, William Joseph 1931- WhoE 93
Burton-Bradley, Burton Gyrth 1914- WhoWor 93
Burts, Stephen L. St&PR 93
Burtt, Ben 1948- ConTFT 10, WhoAm 92
Burtt, Benjamin Pickering 1921- WhoAm 92
Burtt, Shelley 1959- ConAu 139
Burud, Sandra Lee 1948- WhoEmL 93
Burwell, Adam Hood 1790-1849 BioIn 17
Burwell, Charles L. 1950- St&PR 93
Burwell, Dudley Sale 1931- WhoAm 92
Burwell, R. Geoffrey WhoScE 91-1
Burwell, Robert Anda 1938- St&PR 93
Burwell, Robert Lemmon, Jr. 1912- WhoAm 92
Burwell, Robin Anderson 1956- WhoEmL 93
Burwell, Stanley B. 1955- St&PR 93
Burwell, Wayne Gregory 1933- WhoAm 92
Burwick, Leo 1911- St&PR 93
Burwinkel, Jack 1931- St&PR 93
Burwood, Linnea Grace 1954- WhoAmW 93
Bury, Charlotte 1775-1861 DcLB 116 [port]
Bury, Edward 1919- Baker 92
Bury, Henri Blaze de 1813-1886 See Castil-Blaze, Francois 1784-1857 OxDcOp
Bury, Jacques A. 1940- WhoUN 92
Bury, Jeffrey Dale 1956- St&PR 93
Bury, John 1925- OxDcOp, WhoAm 92, WhoWor 93
Bury, Pol 1922- BioIn 17
Buryk, Michael John 1950- St&PR 93
Burzen, Don N. 1948- St&PR 93
Burzio, Nicolaus c. 1445-1518? Baker 92
Burzynski, Jerzy Adam 1922- WhoScE 91-4
Burzynski, Norman Stephen 1928- WhoAm 92
Burzynski, Peter Raymond 1948- WhoEmL 93, WhoSSW 93
Burzynski, Stanislaw Rajmund 1943- WhoWor 93
Burzynski, Zbigniew Jozef 1902-1971 PolBiDi
Bus, Roger Jay 1953- WhoEmL 93
Bus, Theodorus A. 1954- St&PR 93
Busa, Darwin Dante 1943- St&PR 93
Busacca, David W. Law&B 92
Busalacchi, Daniel L. 1942- St&PR 93
Busath, David Don 1952- WhoE 93
Busbee, George Dekle 1927- WhoAm 92
Busbee, Kline Daniel, Jr. 1933- WhoWor 93
Busbey, Douglas Earle 1948- WhoEmL 93
Busbin, O. Mell 1937-1991 BioIn 17
Busboom, Larry D. 1942- WhoAm 92
Busby, Bruce Lee 1943- St&PR 93
Busby, David 1926- WhoAm 92
Busby, Edward Oliver 1926- WhoAm 92
Busby, F.M. 1921- ScF&FL 92
Busby, Gerald Lee 1935- St&PR 93
Busby, James L. 1946- St&PR 93
Busby, Jheryl 1949?- ConBlB 3 [port], ConMus 9 [port]
Busby, John 1928- ConAu 39NR
Busby, John Arthur, Jr. 1933- WhoAm 92
Busby, Kathleen BioIn 17
Busby, Marjorie Jean 1931- WhoAm 92
Busby, Mary Alice Law&B 92
Busby, Morris D. WhoAm 92, WhoWor 93
Busby, Nita June 1932- WhoAmW 93
Busby, Richard W. 1945- St&PR 93
Busby, Robert Andrew 1929- St&PR 93
Busby, Robert L., III 1937- St&PR 93
Busby, Shannon Nixon 1955- WhoEmL 93, WhoSSW 93
Busby, Thomas 1755-1838 Baker 92
Busca, Barbara Lou 1945- WhoUN 92
Buscaglia, Adolfo Edgardo 1930- WhoWor 93
Buscaglia, Frank M. Law&B 92
Buscaglia, Leo F. BioIn 17
Buscaglia, (Felice) Leo(nardo) 1924- WhoWrEP 92
Buscaglia, Leonardo 1924- WhoAm 92
Buscaino, Giuseppe Andrea 1922- WhoScE 91-3
Buscemi, Mary Catherine 1959- WhoE 93
Buscemi, Paul 1952- St&PR 93
Busch, Adolf (Georg Wilhelm) 1891-1952 Baker 92
Busch, Allen Cyril 1931- WhoE 93
Busch, Anthony W. 1943- St&PR 93
Busch, Arthur Allen 1954- WhoEmL 93
Busch, Arthur Winston 1926- WhoAm 92
Busch, August A., III 1937- St&PR 93
Busch, August Adolphus, III 1937- WhoAm 92
Busch, Briton Cooper 1936- WhoAm 92
Busch, Carl J. Law&B 92
Busch, Carl (Reinholdt) 1862-1943 Baker 92
Busch, Charles BioIn 17
Busch, Charles 1954- ConTFT 10
Busch, Chester C. St&PR 93
Busch, Christine 1947- WhoEmL 93
Busch, David Truett 1954- WhoSSW 93
Busch, Edwin 1929- St&PR 93
Busch, Frederick 1941- WhoWrEP 92
Busch, Frederick Matthew 1941- WhoAm 92
Busch, Fritz 1890-1951 Baker 92, IntDcOp, OxDcOp
Busch, Harris 1923- WhoAm 92
Busch, Harry 1919- St&PR 93
Busch, Hermann 1897-1975 Baker 92
Busch, James Randall 1960- WhoEmL 93
Busch, John Arthur 1951- WhoEmL 93
Busch, John F. 1919- St&PR 93
Busch, John H. 1927- St&PR 93
Busch, Joyce Ida 1934- WhoAmW 93, WhoWor 93
Busch, Julia 1940- ConAu 39NR
Busch, Nancy Rae Law&B 92
Busch, Niven 1903-1991 AnObit 1991, BioIn 17, ConLC 70
Busch, Peter Jonathan 1952- WhoEmL 93
Busch, Richard 1941- WhoAm 92
Busch, Robert A. 1947- St&PR 93
Busch, Robert Charles 1932- St&PR 93
Busch, Robert Douglas 1949- WhoEmL 93
Busch, Sayde Brenner d1990 BioIn 17
Busch, Thomas Anthony 1947- WhoEmL 93
Busch, Ulrich Bernd 1951- WhoWor 93
Busch, William 1901-1945 Baker 92
Buschbach, Thomas Charles 1923- WhoAm 92
Busche, Eugene Marvin 1926- St&PR 93, WhoAm 92
Busche, Jeffry Francis 1953- WhoEmL 93
Buschenfeld, Herbert 1925- WhoScE 91-3
Buscher, Nancy 1941- WhoAmW 93
Busching, Allen E. 1932- St&PR 93
Buschinger, Alfred 1940- WhoScE 91-3
Buschke, Herman 1932- WhoAm 92
Buschmann, Ben S. 1929- St&PR 93
Buschmann, Johann Carl Eduard von 1805-1880 IntDcAn
Buschmann, Raymond Peter Law&B 92
Buschmann, Siegfried 1937- St&PR 93, WhoAm 92
Busch-Rossnagel, Nancy Ann 1951- WhoE 93
Busch Vannatta, Rita Marie 1956- WhoAmW 93, WhoEmL 93
Busciglio, Richard 1935- WhoAm 92
Busck, Ole Arnold 1937- WhoWor 93
Busdicker, Gordon G. 1933- WhoAm 92

Buse, D(ieter) K(urt) 1941- *ConAu 137*
Buse, Gerhard 1935- *WhoScE 91-3*
Buse, Raymond Leo, Jr. 1925- *St&PR 93*
Buseck, Peter Robert *WhoAm 92*
Busek, Robert Henry 1947- *WhoE 93*
Buselmeier, Bernard J. 1956- *St&PR 93*
Buselmeier, Bernard Joseph 1956- *WhoAm 92*
Buselt, John Paul 1954- *WhoEmL 93*
Busemann, Herbert 1905- *WhoAm 92*
Busenello, Gian Francesco 1598-1659 *OxDcOp*
Busenello, Giovanni Francesco 1598-1659 *IntDcOp*
Buser, Andres A. 1940- *St&PR 93*
Buser, Sue 1949- *WhoEmL 93*
Busey, Gary 1944- *WhoAm 92*
Busey, Irene De Reath Byrd *AmWomPl*
Busey, J. Craig *Law&B 92*
Busey, James B. *BioIn 17*
Busfield, Timothy *BioIn 17*
Busfield, Timothy 1957- *WhoAm 92*
Bush, Alan 1900- *OxDcOp*
Bush, Alan (Dudley) 1900- *Baker 92*
Bush, Allen Julian 1932- *St&PR 93*
Bush, Alvin Bruce 1930- *WhoAm 92*
Bush, Anita Marie 1951- *WhoWrEP 92*
Bush, Ann Kathleen 1960- *WhoAmW 93, WhoEmL 93*
Bush, Arthur W. 1956- *St&PR 93*
Bush, Barbara 1925- *BioIn 17*
Bush, Barbara Pierce 1925- *WhoAm 92, WhoAmW 93, WhoE 93, WhoWor 93*
Bush, Bertha Evangeline 1866- *AmWomPl*
Bush, Brendalee 1949- *WhoEmL 93*
Bush, Carl Gage, Jr. 1944- *WhoE 93*
Bush, Charles Meigs 1928- *WhoAm 92*
Bush, Charles Vernon 1939- *WhoAm 92*
Bush, Craig R. *Law&B 92*
Bush, David Frederic 1942- *WhoE 93*
Bush, David James 1948- *St&PR 93*
Bush, David Victor 1948- *WhoEmL 93*
Bush, Dennis M. 1951- *St&PR 93*
Bush, Donald D. *Law&B 92*
Bush, Donald P. 1931- *St&PR 93*
Bush, Dorothy Vredenburgh *BioIn 17*
Bush, Dorothy W. 1901-1992 *NewYTBS 92 [port]*
Bush, Edward Philip, III 1953- *WhoEmL 93*
Bush, Edwin F., II *Law&B 92*
Bush, Eileen Marie 1936- *WhoAmW 93*
Bush, Eugene Nyle 1952- *WhoWor 93*
Bush, Frank Bradner *Law&B 92*
Bush, Fred Marshall, Jr. 1917- *WhoAm 92*
Bush, Frederick Morris 1949- *WhoAm 92*
Bush, G. Kenner 1934- *St&PR 93*
Bush, Geoffrey 1920- *Baker 92, WhoWor 93*
Bush, George *DcCPCAm, NewYTBS 92 [port]*
Bush, George 1924- *BioIn 17, ColdWar 1 [port], DcTwHis*
Bush, George H. W. 1924- *PolPar*
Bush, George Herbert Walker 1924- *CngDr 91, WhoAm 92, WhoE 93, WhoWor 93*
Bush, George R. *Law&B 92*
Bush, George Ray 1938- *WhoIns 93*
Bush, George W. *BioIn 17, WhoAm 92, WhoSSW 93*
Bush, Gregory John 1956- *St&PR 93*
Bush, Guy Louis 1929- *WhoAm 92*
Bush, Harrison *Law&B 92*
Bush, Howard James 1953- *WhoEmL 93*
Bush, Hugh Sutton 1957- *St&PR 93*
Bush, James R. *Law&B 92*
Bush, James Sloan 1936- *St&PR 93*
Bush, Jeb *BioIn 17*
Bush, Jeffrey *BioIn 17*
Bush, Joanne Tadeo 1947- *WhoAmW 93*
Bush, John Arthur *Law&B 92*
Bush, John Arthur H. *St&PR 93*
Bush, John Arthur Henry *WhoAm 92*
Bush, John B., Jr. 1933- *St&PR 93*
Bush, John Charles 1938- *WhoWrEP 92*
Bush, John David 1955- *WhoSSW 93*
Bush, John Lawrence 1930- *St&PR 93*
Bush, John S., Jr. 1930- *St&PR 93*
Bush, John William 1909- *WhoAm 92, WhoWor 93*
Bush, Jonathan *BioIn 17*
Bush, Joseph Ernest, III 1952- *WhoSSW 93*
Bush, Judy Lynn 1938- *WhoAmW 93*
Bush, June Lee 1942- *WhoAmW 93*
Bush, Karen Michaela 1947- *WhoE 93*
Bush, Kate *BioIn 17*
Bush, Kate 1958- *Baker 92*
Bush, Kenneth Alan 1948- *WhoEmL 93*
Bush, Lance Bryan 1963- *WhoSSW 93*
Bush, Leslie Ambrose 1892-1974 *BiDAMSp 1989*
Bush, Lori Hermelin 1956- *WhoAmW 93*
Bush, Lowell Palmer 1939- *WhoSSW 93*
Bush, Martha H. 1956- *WhoAmW 93*
Bush, Martin Ernest 1958- *WhoWor 93*
Bush, Marvin *BioIn 17*
Bush, Mary Hannah 1946- *WhoAmW 93*
Bush, Mary Kathleen 1935- *WhoSSW 93*
Bush, Mary R. 1955- *St&PR 93*
Bush, Melinda Johnson 1942- *WhoE 93, WhoWor 93*
Bush, Michael J. 1943- *St&PR 93*
Bush, Millie 1987?- *News 92 [port]*
Bush, Neil *BioIn 17*
Bush, Norman 1929- *St&PR 93, WhoAm 92*
Bush, Olivia Ward 1869- *AmWomPl*
Bush, Patricia A. 1941- *St&PR 93*
Bush, Paul Stanley 1936- *St&PR 93, WhoAm 92*
Bush, Paul V. *St&PR 93*
Bush, Pauline 1886-1969 *SweetSg A [port]*
Bush, Prescott *BioIn 17*
Bush, Ralph W. 1938- *St&PR 93*
Bush, Richard Charles 1955- *WhoSSW 93*
Bush, Richard Clarence, III 1947- *WhoEmL 93*
Bush, Richard James 1921- *WhoAm 92*
Bush, Richard N. 1951- *St&PR 93*
Bush, Richard Wayne 1934- *WhoE 93*
Bush, Robert Benjamin 1928- *St&PR 93*
Bush, Robert Bradford 1953- *WhoEmL 93*
Bush, Robert Donald 1939- *WhoAm 92*
Bush, Robert E. 1926- *BioIn 17*
Bush, Robert Thomas 1928- *WhoE 93*
Bush, Robert W. 1947- *St&PR 93*
Bush, Ronald 1946- *ConAu 136*
Bush, Ronald L. 1946- *WhoAm 92*
Bush, S.F. *WhoScE 91-1*
Bush, Sam 1926-1992 *BioIn 17*
Bush, Sarah Lillian 1920- *WhoAmW 93, WhoWor 93*
Bush, Schuyler D. 1938- *St&PR 93*
Bush, Solomon 1753-1796 *BioIn 17*
Bush, Spencer Harrison 1920- *WhoAm 92*
Bush, Stephanie R. *AfrAmBi*
Bush, Steven 1944- *WhoCanL 92*
Bush, Thomas Norman 1947- *WhoAm 92*
Bush, Warren V. d1991 *BioIn 17*
Bush, Warren Van Ness 1931- *WhoSSW 93*
Bush, Werner Frederick 1939- *St&PR 93*
Bush, William 1954- *WhoEmL 93*
Bush, William Arden 1948- *WhoWor 93*
Bush, William M., Jr. 1951- *St&PR 93*
Bush, William Paul, II 1950- *WhoAm 92*
Bush, William Wallace 1914- *St&PR 93*
Bush, Wm. Paul, II 1950- *St&PR 93*
Bush-Brown, Albert 1926- *St&PR 93, WhoAm 92, WhoE 93*
Bushee, Ward *BioIn 17*
Bushek, George J. 1945- *St&PR 93*
Bushell, Alan 1941- *St&PR 93*
Bushelman, John A. *MiSFD 9*
Bushey, A. Scott 1930- *WhoIns 93*
Bushey, Alan Scott 1930- *St&PR 93, WhoAm 92*
Bushey, Francis B. d1991 *BioIn 17*
Bushey, Gerald Blair 1950- *WhoIns 93*
Bushey, Michael Edmond 1949- *WhoEmL 93*
Bushey, Peter F., Jr. 1947- *St&PR 93*
Bushey, Richard D. 1934- *St&PR 93*
Bushey, Richard Kenneth 1940- *St&PR 93, WhoAm 92*
Bushey, Robert Francis 1939- *WhoWrEP 92*
Bushfield, Vera Cahalan 1889-1976 *BioIn 17*
Bushinsky, David Allen 1949- *WhoE 93*
Bushinsky, Jay 1932- *WhoAm 92*
Bush-Joseph, Victoria L. *Law&B 92*
Bushkin, Merle J. 1935- *St&PR 93*
Bushkin, Yuri 1949- *WhoE 93*
Bushman, Brad J. 1960- *WhoEmL 93*
Bushman, Claudia L(auper) 1934- *WhoWrEP 92*
Bushman, David Mark 1962- *WhoSSW 93*
Bushman, Francis X. 1885?-1966 *IntDcF 2-3 [port]*
Bushman, Joseph Charles 1954- *WhoEmL 93*
Bushman, Mary Laura Jones 1946- *WhoEmL 93*
Bushman, Melvin Creed *Law&B 92*
Bushman, Richard L(yman) 1931- *WhoWrEP 92*
Bushman, Robert C. 1935- *St&PR 93*
Bushman, Robert R. 1927- *St&PR 93*
Bushman, Stephen S. 1962- *St&PR 93*
Bushnell, Adelyn 1894- *ScF&FL 92*
Bushnell, Carolyn Suzanne 1940- *WhoAmW 93*
Bushnell, Catharine 1950- *WhoAmW 93*
Bushnell, Clarence William 1916- *WhoAm 92*
Bushnell, David 1742-1824 *BioIn 17*
Bushnell, David Ives, Jr. 1875-1941 *IntDcAn*
Bushnell, Dennis Meyer 1941- *WhoSSW 93*
Bushnell, George E., III *Law&B 92*
Bushnell, George Edward, III 1952- *WhoE 93*
Bushnell, Horace 1802-1876 *BioIn 17*
Bushnell, John Alden 1933- *WhoAm 92*
Bushnell, William, Jr. *MiSFD 9*
Bushner, Norma Lee 1943- *WhoAmW 93*
Bushno, Lila Joan 1931- *WhoWrEP 92*
Bushore, Martha *BioIn 17*
Bushotter, George 1864-1892 *IntDcAn*
Bushway, Rodney John 1949- *WhoWor 93*
Bushyager, Linda E. 1947- *ScF&FL 92*
Busi, Nat Peter 1929- *St&PR 93*
Busia, Kofi Abrefa 1913-1978 *IntDcAn*
Busick, Denzel Rex 1945- *WhoWor 93*
Busick, Rita Johnson 1945- *WhoAmW 93*
Busico, Louis Frank 1935- *St&PR 93*
Businelli, Mario 1934- *WhoScE 91-3*
Businger, Joost Alois 1924- *WhoAm 92*
Busk, Chadwick Christian *Law&B 92*
Busk, Robert Scholley 1915- *WhoSSW 93*
Buskas, Robert James 1932- *St&PR 93*
Busker, Gary Leon 1946- *WhoEmL 93*
Busker, Leroy Henry 1929- *WhoAm 92*
Buskey, James E. *AfrAmBi*
Buskirk, Elsworth Robert 1925- *WhoAm 92, WhoE 93*
Buskirk, Richard Hobart 1927- *WhoAm 92, WhoWor 93*
Busko, William Devin 1929- *St&PR 93*
Buskuhl, Carl Thomas 1952- *WhoEmL 93*
Buslaev, Alexander Pavlovich 1953- *WhoWor 93*
Buslowicz, Mikolaj 1950- *WhoWor 93*
Busnaina, Ahmed Ali 1953- *WhoE 93, WhoEmL 93, WhoWor 93*
Busner, Philip H. 1927- *WhoAm 92*
Busnois, Antoine c. 1430-c. 1492 *Baker 92*
Buso, Eduardo L. *Law&B 92*
Busoni, Ferruccio 1866-1924 *Baker 92, BioIn 17, IntDcOp [port], OxDcOp*
Busowski, John Dennis 1955- *WhoSSW 93*
Busquet, Anne M. *BioIn 17*
Buss, Claude Albert 1903- *WhoAm 92*
Buss, Daniel Frank 1943- *WhoAm 92*
Buss, Dennis A. *Law&B 92*
Buss, Dennis A. 1946- *St&PR 93*
Buss, Edward George 1921- *WhoE 93*
Buss, Eugene L. *Law&B 92*
Buss, J. Ronald 1940- *St&PR 93*
Buss, Jerry Hatten *BioIn 17, WhoAm 92*
Buss, Kate *AmWomPl*
Buss, Leo William 1953- *WhoAm 92*
Buss, Martin John 1930- *WhoSSW 93*
Buss, Volker 1942- *WhoScE 91-3*
Buss, Walter Richard 1905- *WhoAm 92*
Buss, William Charles 1938- *WhoAm 92*
Bussani, Dorothea 1763-c. 1810 *Baker 92*
Bussani, Francesco 1743-1807? *Baker 92, OxDcOp*
Bussani, Giacomo c. 1640-c. 1680 *OxDcOp*
Bussard, Clarence Lease 1911- *WhoAm 92*
Bussard, David Andrew 1955- *WhoE 93*
Bussard, Richard Earl 1934- *WhoAm 92*
Bussard, Robert William 1928- *WhoAm 92, WhoSSW 93*
Bussard, Wayne M. 1958- *St&PR 93*
Busscher, A. Brad *Law&B 92*
Busse, Ewald William 1917- *WhoAm 92*
Busse, George R. 1928- *St&PR 93*
Busse, James P. 1943- *St&PR 93*
Busse, Janis D. 1951- *St&PR 93*
Busse, Leonard Wayne 1938- *WhoAm 92*
Busse, Lu Ann 1956- *WhoAm 92, WhoEmL 93*
Busse, Michael P. 1948- *St&PR 93*
Busse, Michael Philip 1948- *WhoE 93*
Bussel, Bernard 1938- *WhoScE 91-2*
Busselen, Paul V.C. 1942- *WhoScE 91-2*
Bussell, Annette Troup 1945- *WhoAmW 93*
Bussell, Darcey *BioIn 17*
Bussell, Donald E. 1940- *St&PR 93*
Bussell, E. Wayne *Law&B 92*
Bussell, Sally Carney 1958- *WhoEmL 93*
Bussell, T. Alan 1944- *St&PR 93*
Bussem, Albrecht 1930- *WhoWor 93*
Busser, Henri 1872-1973 *OxDcOp*
Busser, Henri-Paul 1872-1973 *Baker 92*
Bussey, Charles David 1933- *WhoAm 92, WhoWrEP 92*
Bussey, George Davis 1949- *WhoEmL 93*
Bussey, Holly Jean 1954- *WhoAmW 93*
Busshoff, Heinrich 1936- *WhoWor 93*
Bussiere, Tadema Whaley 1891- *AmWomPl*
Bussieres, Arthur de 1887-1913 *BioIn 17*
Bussing, Sabine 1960- *ScF&FL 92*
Busskohl, Charles Deforest 1932- *St&PR 93*
Busskohl, Doyle 1928- *St&PR 93*
Busskohl, Steve 1951- *St&PR 93*
Bussler, Ludwig 1838-1900 *Baker 92*
Bussler, Wolfgang 1925- *WhoScE 91-3*
Bussman, John Wood 1924- *WhoAm 92*
Bussone, David Eben 1947- *WhoAm 92, WhoSSW 93*
Bussotti, Sylvano 1931- *Baker 92, OxDcOp*
Busta, Paul Timothy 1952- *WhoEmL 93*
Bustabo, Guila 1917- *Baker 92*
Bustad, Leo Kenneth 1920- *WhoAm 92*
Bustamante, Albert G. 1935- *CngDr 91, HispAmA*
Bustamante, Albert Garza 1935- *WhoAm 92, WhoSSW 93*
Bustamante, Alexander *DcCPCAm*
Bustamante, Bruce W. 1957- *St&PR 93*
Bustamante, Carlos Maria de 1774-1884 *DcMexL*
Bustamante, J.W. Andre *St&PR 93*
Bustamante, Jose Luis *DcCPCAm*
Bustamante, Octaviano N. 1903-1966 *DcMexL*
Bustamante, Ricardo *BioIn 17*
Bustamante, Richard *WhoAm 92*
Bustamante, William Alexander 1884-1977 *BioIn 17, DcTwHis*
Bustani, Myrna 1937- *WhoWor 93*
Bustani, Nancy Kurth 1945- *WhoAmW 93*
Bustard, R. David *Law&B 92*
Bustard, Thomas Stratton 1934- *WhoE 93*
Busteed, Robert Thomas 1939- *St&PR 93*
Buster, Carolyn 1942- *WhoAmW 93*
Buster, Edmond Bate 1918- *WhoAm 92, WhoWor 93*
Busterud, John W. *Law&B 92*
Bustillo, Juan Rafael *BioIn 17*
Bustin, Beverly Miner 1936- *WhoAmW 93*
Bustin, Edouard Jean 1933- *WhoAm 92*
Bustini, Alessandro 1876-1970 *Baker 92*
Bustos Cerecedo, Miguel 1912- *DcMexL*
Busuoli, Gilberto 1937- *WhoScE 91-3*
Busuttil, Anthony 1945- *WhoWor 93*
Busuttil, James Joseph 1958- *WhoE 93, WhoEmL 93, WhoWor 93*
Busuttil, Victor Philip 1945- *WhoUN 92*
Buswell, Debra Sue 1957- *WhoAmW 93, WhoEmL 93*
Buswell, James Oliver, IV 1946- *Baker 92*
Buswink, Anthony Allen 1940- *WhoWrEP 92*
Buszko, Henryk Bronislaw 1924- *WhoWor 93*
Buszko, Irene Joan 1947- *WhoEmL 93*
Buszuwski, Mary L. 1954- *St&PR 93*
Butala, Sharon 1940- *WhoCanL 92*
Butare, Joseph J., Jr. 1942- *St&PR 93*
Butazzoni, Fernando 1952- *SpAmA*
Butch, James Nicholas 1951- *WhoSSW 93*
Butch, William Louis 1932- *St&PR 93, WhoIns 93, WhoSSW 93*
Butchart, F.D., Mrs. *AmWomPl*
Butchart, Mary Beckwith *AmWomPl*
Butchart, Robert L. 1928- *St&PR 93*
Butcher, Amanda Kay 1936- *WhoAmW 93*
Butcher, Bernard B. 1928- *St&PR 93*
Butcher, Bobby Gene 1936- *WhoAm 92*
Butcher, Brian Ronald 1947- *WhoWor 93*
Butcher, Bruce Cameron 1947- *WhoEmL 93*
Butcher, David John 1948- *WhoAsAP 91*
Butcher, Devereux 1906-1991 *BioIn 17*
Butcher, Dick 1946- *St&PR 93*
Butcher, Donald Franklin 1937- *WhoAm 92*
Butcher, Edward Carl 1938- *St&PR 93*
Butcher, Fred R. 1943- *WhoAm 92*
Butcher, Grace 1934- *WhoWrEP 92*
Butcher, Harry William 1948- *WhoSSW 93*
Butcher, Herbert P. *Law&B 92*
Butcher, Howard, III *BioIn 17*
Butcher, Jack Robert 1941- *WhoWor 93*
Butcher, James Walter 1917- *WhoAm 92*
Butcher, John B. *WhoScE 91-1*
Butcher, John Kimberlin 1937- *St&PR 93*
Butcher, Judith M. *WhoScE 91-1*
Butcher, Mary Ellen 1935- *WhoE 93*
Butcher, Michael Andrew Jonathan 1943- *WhoAm 92*
Butcher, P.N. *WhoScE 91-1*
Butcher, Paul D. d1992 *NewYTBS 92*
Butcher, Paul Newman *WhoScE 91-1*
Butcher, Philip 1918- *WhoAm 92*
Butcher, Robert Gilliam, Jr. 1934- *St&PR 93*
Butcher, Sharon A. *Law&B 92*
Butcher, Solomon D. *BioIn 17*
Butcher, Susan *BioIn 17*
Butcher, Susan Howlet 1954- *WhoAmW 93*
Butcher, Thomas W. 1938- *St&PR 93*
Butcher, W.W. Keen 1916- *St&PR 93*
Butcher, Willard C. *BioIn 17*
Butcher, Willard C. 1926- *St&PR 93*
Butcher, Willard Carlisle 1926- *WhoAm 92, WhoWor 93*
Butcher, William 1951- *ScF&FL 92*
Butcher, William Robert, Jr. 1942- *WhoSSW 93*
Butcher-Towzey, David Joseph 1948- *WhoSSW 93*
Butchkes, Sydney 1922- *WhoAm 92*
Butchko, Emil Joseph 1935- *St&PR 93*

Butchko, Robert Edward 1946- *WhoEmL 93*
Butchvarov, Panayot Krustev 1933- *WhoAm 92*
Bute, John Stuart, Earl of 1713-1792 *BioIn 17*
Buteau, Michelle Diane 1952- *WhoAmW 93*
Buten, Max 1932- *St&PR 93*
Butenandt, Adolf 1903- *St&PR 93*
Butenandt, Adolf Friedrich Johann 1903- *WhoWor 93*
Butenas, John Philip *Law&B 92*
Buter, Havery 1923- *St&PR 93*
Butera, Ann Michele 1958- *WhoAmW 93, WhoEmL 93*
Butera, Joseph G. 1945- *St&PR 93*
Butera, Lawrence Thomas *Law&B 92*
Butera, Thomas L. *Law&B 92*
Buterakos, Kathleen Ann 1951- *WhoE 93, WhoEmL 93, WhoWor 93*
Buterbaugh, Noel L. *St&PR 93*
Buteux, Patricia Ann 1944- *St&PR 93, WhoAmW 93*
Buth, David Martin 1952- *WhoEmL 93*
Buth, Donald George 1949- *WhoEmL 93*
Buthelezi, Gatsha 1928- *BioIn 17*
Buthelezi, Gatsha Mangosuthu 1928- *DcTwHis, WhoAfr*
Butherus, Marjorie Elaine 1927- *WhoAmW 93*
Buths, Julius (Emil Martin) 1851-1920 *Baker 92*
Buthusiem, Edward J. *Law&B 92*
Butigan, William Clay 1957- *WhoEmL 93*
Butin, H. *WhoScE 91-3*
Butina, Mary Ann 1949- *WhoE 93*
Buting, Walter E. *Law&B 92*
Butinov, N.A. 1914- *IntDcAn*
Butkevicius, Audrius 1960- *WhoWor 93*
Butkiewicz, James Leon 1949- *WhoEmL 93*
Butkus, Dick *BioIn 17*
Butkus, Dick 1942- *WhoAm 92*
Butkus, Donald Eugene 1934- *WhoSSW 93*
Butland, S.D. *WhoScE 91-1*
Butler, Albert L., Jr. 1918- *St&PR 93*
Butler, Albert R. *Law&B 92*
Butler, Alistair d1992 *NewYTBS 92*
Butler, Andrew J. 1934- *WhoAm 92*
Butler, Anina Liberty *St&PR 93*
Butler, Barbara Kay 1961- *WhoAmW 93*
Butler, Becky Brandt 1948- *WhoSSW 93*
Butler, Benjamin F. 1818-1893 *PolPar*
Butler, Benjamin Franklin 1818-1893 *BioIn 17, EncAACR [port], HarEnMi*
Butler, Betty Rae 1948- *WhoEmL 93*
Butler, Beverly 1932- *ScF&FL 92*
Butler, Billy d1991 *BioIn 17*
Butler, Billy 1945- *BioIn 17*
Butler, Brett *BioIn 17*
Butler, Brian 1949- *WhoE 93, WhoEmL 93*
Butler, Brinton Lee 1953- *WhoEmL 93*
Butler, Broadus Nathaniel 1920- *WhoAm 92*
Butler, Bruce W. 1939- *WhoIns 93*
Butler, Bryan V. 1938- *St&PR 93*
Butler, Byron Clinton 1918- *WhoWor 93*
Butler, Candace Gayle 1951- *WhoEmL 93*
Butler, Carl Ernest 1938- *WhoE 93*
Butler, Carol King 1952- *WhoAmW 93*
Butler, Catherine Jo 1954- *WhoAmW 93*
Butler, Cecile Anne *Law&B 92*
Butler, Charles David 1936- *WhoAm 92*
Butler, Charles Henry 1859-1940 *OxCSupC*
Butler, Charles Thomas 1951- *WhoAm 92*
Butler, Christopher Williams 1950- *WhoEmL 93, WhoSSW 93*
Butler, Claire Draper 1928- *St&PR 93, WhoIns 93*
Butler, Cliff *Law&B 92*
Butler, Cynthia Calibani 1959- *WhoAmW 93*
Butler, Daniel Patrick 1939- *WhoE 93, WhoWor 93*
Butler, David 1894-1979 *MiSFD 9N*
Butler, David 1930- *WhoAm 92*
Butler, David 1941- *ScF&FL 92*
Butler, David Edward 1937- *St&PR 93*
Butler, David Louis 1940- *WhoSSW 93*
Butler, David Robert *WhoScE 91-1*
Butler, Deborah Ann 1949- *WhoAmW 93*
Butler, Dennis E. *Law&B 92*
Butler, Derinda Faye 1969- *WhoWrEP 92*
Butler, Donald E. 1927- *St&PR 93*
Butler, Dorothy 1925- *SmATA 73*
Butler, Dwayne *BioIn 17*
Butler, E. Bruce *Law&B 92*
Butler, Edgar Buell, Jr. 1945- *St&PR 93*
Butler, Edward Lee 1945- *WhoE 93*
Butler, Edward Scannell 1934- *WhoAm 92*
Butler, Elizabeth Brewer 1941- *WhoAmW 93*
Butler, Elizabeth Maire 1948- *WhoEmL 93*
Butler, Ernest, Jr. 1928- *St&PR 93*
Butler, Ernest Alton 1926- *St&PR 93*
Butler, Eugene 1894- *WhoAm 92*
Butler, Eugene L. 1941- *WhoAm 92*
Butler, Eulous Sonny 1939- *WhoSSW 93*
Butler, Evelyn Anne 1940- *WhoWor 93*
Butler, Francelia McWilliams 1913- *WhoAm 92, WhoWor 93*
Butler, Francine 1940- *WhoAmW 93*
Butler, Francis Joseph 1945- *WhoE 93*
Butler, Frank Joseph 1932- *St&PR 93*
Butler, Fred Jay, Jr. 1929- *WhoAm 92*
Butler, Frederick George 1919- *WhoAm 92, WhoWor 93*
Butler, Frederick Karlton *Law&B 92*
Butler, Fredrick Myron 1935- *St&PR 93*
Butler, George *MiSFD 9*
Butler, George A. 1928- *St&PR 93*
Butler, George E. *St&PR 93*
Butler, George Harrison 1917- *WhoAm 92*
Butler, George W., III *Law&B 92*
Butler, George Washington, Jr. 1944- *WhoWor 93*
Butler, Grace Caroline 1937- *WhoAmW 93*
Butler, Gwendoline *ScF&FL 92*
Butler, Harold C. 1940- *St&PR 93*
Butler, Henry *BioIn 17*
Butler, Herbert Edwin 1949- *WhoEmL 93*
Butler, Herbert Fuller 1959- *WhoWor 93*
Butler, I. Ernest, Jr. 1928- *St&PR 93*
Butler, Ivan 1909- *ScF&FL 92*
Butler, Ivan Scott 1962- *WhoWor 93*
Butler, J. Alden 1930- *St&PR 93*
Butler, J.K. 1939- *WhoScE 91-1*
Butler, J. Karen *Law&B 92*
Butler, J. Murfree 1942- *St&PR 93*
Butler, Jack 1944- *ScF&FL 92*
Butler, Jack Armand 1944- *WhoSSW 93*
Butler, Jack Fairchild 1933- *WhoAm 92*
Butler, James 1610-1688 *BioIn 17*
Butler, James Albert 1945- *WhoE 93*
Butler, James C. 1937- *St&PR 93*
Butler, James E. *Law&B 92*
Butler, James Joseph, Jr. 1927- *St&PR 93*
Butler, James Keith 1961- *WhoSSW 93*
Butler, James Newton 1934- *WhoAm 92, WhoE 93*
Butler, James Robert 1930- *WhoAm 92*
Butler, James Robertson, Jr. 1946- *WhoEmL 93*
Butler, Jeremy Edward 1930- *WhoAm 92*
Butler, Jerry *BioIn 17*
Butler, Jerry 1939- *AfrAmBi, SoulM*
Butler, Jesse Lee 1953- *WhoE 93*
Butler, Jimmie H. *ScF&FL 92*
Butler, Jimmie Leon 1935- *St&PR 93*
Butler, Jo Ann *Law&B 92*
Butler, Joan *ScF&FL 92*
Butler, John *BioIn 17*
Butler, John 1728-1796 *HarEnMi*
Butler, John A. 1932- *St&PR 93*
Butler, John Alden 1930- *WhoAm 92*
Butler, John Benson 1938- *WhoWor 93*
Butler, John Carleton 1954- *WhoEmL 93*
Butler, John Joseph 1957- *WhoEmL 93*
Butler, John L., Jr. 1931- *WhoWor 93*
Butler, John Marion 1934- *St&PR 93*
Butler, John Michael 1959- *WhoEmL 93*
Butler, John Michael, II 1969- *WhoWor 93*
Butler, John Musgrave 1928- *WhoAm 92*
Butler, John Paul 1935- *WhoSSW 93*
Butler, John Russ 1936- *St&PR 93*
Butler, Jon Terry 1943- *WhoAm 92*
Butler, Jonathan Putnam 1940- *WhoAm 92*
Butler, Joseph 1929- *St&PR 93*
Butler, Joseph Patrick 1957- *WhoWrEP 92*
Butler, Josephine Elizabeth 1828-1906 *BioIn 17*
Butler, Josiah P. 1936- *St&PR 93*
Butler, Judith Eileen 1957- *WhoEmL 93*
Butler, Karla 1933- *WhoAm 92*
Butler, Katharine Gorrell 1925- *WhoAm 92*
Butler, Katharine S. *Law&B 92*
Butler, Katherine E. *Law&B 92*
Butler, Kenneth Van 1934- *WhoAm 92*
Butler, Kent Alan 1958- *WhoEmL 93*
Butler, L. Chris *Law&B 92*
Butler, Larnell Custis 1941- *WhoWrEP 92*
Butler, Larry Gene 1933- *WhoAm 92*
Butler, Laurie Josey 1957- *St&PR 93*
Butler, Leon N. 1917- *St&PR 93*
Butler, Leslie Richard 1940- *St&PR 93*
Butler, Linda Rae Axelson 1959- *WhoAmW 93*
Butler, Lindley Smith 1939- *WhoSSW 93*
Butler, Luther Dale 1929- *WhoWrEP 92*
Butler, M. Christina 1934- *SmATA 72 [port]*
Butler, Malcolm Lee 1958- *WhoEmL 93*
Butler, Manley Caldwell 1925- *WhoAm 92*
Butler, Margaret Dent 1943- *WhoAmW 93*
Butler, Margaret Kampschaefer 1924- *WhoAm 92*
Butler, Marion 1863-1938 *PolPar*
Butler, Mark S. *Law&B 92*
Butler, Marshall D. 1927- *St&PR 93*
Butler, Mary *BioIn 17*
Butler, Mary Anne 1946- *WhoAmW 93*
Butler, Mary Jane 1946- *WhoE 93*
Butler, Melinda Ann *Law&B 92*
Butler, Michael *ScF&FL 92, WhoScE 91-1*
Butler, Michael Francis 1935- *WhoAm 92*
Butler, Mike W. 1911- *St&PR 93*
Butler, Mildred Allen *AmWomPl*
Butler, Milton C. *Law&B 92*
Butler, Mitchell Danny 1950- *St&PR 93*
Butler, Nancy Taylor 1942- *WhoAmW 93*
Butler, Nathan *ScF&FL 92, WhoWrEP 92*
Butler, Nicholas Murray 1862-1947 *PolPar*
Butler, Norman d1990 *BioIn 17*
Butler, O'Brien c. 1870-1915 *Baker 92*
Butler, Octavia E. *BioIn 17*
Butler, Octavia E. 1947- *ScF&FL 92*
Butler, Octavia E(stelle) 1947- *ConAu 38NR*
Butler, Octavia Estelle 1947- *WhoEmL 93*
Butler, Owen B. 1923- *St&PR 93*
Butler, Owen Bradford 1923- *WhoAm 92*
Butler, Patricia Ann 1952- *WhoUN 92*
Butler, Patricia O. 1953- *WhoAmW 93*
Butler, Patrick d1990 *BioIn 17*
Butler, Patrick Daniel 1959- *WhoEmL 93*
Butler, Patrick Hampton *Law&B 92*
Butler, Patrick Harold 1949- *St&PR 93*
Butler, Patrick John *WhoScE 91-1*
Butler, Paul Bascomb, Jr. 1947- *WhoEmL 93*
Butler, Paul M. 1905-1961 *BioIn 17*
Butler, Paul M. 1906-1961 *PolPar*
Butler, Paul William 1961- *WhoE 93, WhoEmL 93, WhoWor 93*
Butler, Peter A. 1935- *St&PR 93*
Butler, Philip *BioIn 17*
Butler, Philip Howard 1947- *WhoWor 93*
Butler, Pierce 1866-1939 *OxCSupC [port]*
Butler, R.H., Jr. *BioIn 17*
Butler, Rab 1902-1982 *ColdWar 1 [port]*
Butler, Rachel Barton *AmWomPl*
Butler, Richard d1638 *BioIn 17*
Butler, Richard A., Jr. 1927- *St&PR 93*
Butler, Richard Austen 1902-1982 *DcTwHis*
Butler, Richard Colburn 1910- *WhoAm 92*
Butler, Richard Dean 1930- *WhoAm 92*
Butler, Richard John 1951- *WhoWor 93*
Butler, Richard N. 1942- *WhoScE 91-3*
Butler, Robert 1927- *MiSFD 9*
Butler, Robert Allan 1923- *WhoAm 92*
Butler, Robert Andrews 1955- *WhoEmL 93*
Butler, Robert Arthur *Law&B 92*
Butler, Robert Clifton 1930- *WhoAm 92*
Butler, Robert Francis 1935- *WhoWrEP 92*
Butler, Robert Leonard 1931- *WhoAm 92*
Butler, Robert Neil 1927- *WhoAm 92*
Butler, Robert Olen 1945- *WhoWrEP 92*
Butler, Robert Thomas 1925- *St&PR 93, WhoAm 92*
Butler, Roberta Cecilia 1947- *WhoAmW 93*
Butler, Russell 1949- *WhoEmL 93*
Butler, Russell Paul 1959- *WhoEmL 93*
Butler, S.R. *WhoScE 91-1*
Butler, Samuel 1612-1680 *BioIn 17, DcLB 126 [port]*
Butler, Samuel 1835-1902 *BioIn 17, BritWr S2, WorLitC [port]*
Butler, Samuel C. 1930- *St&PR 93*
Butler, Samuel Coles 1930- *WhoAm 92*
Butler, Scot *BioIn 17*
Butler, Smedley Darlington 1881-1940 *HarEnMi*
Butler, Stanley *WhoScE 91-1*
Butler, Stanley W. 1947- *St&PR 93*
Butler, Stephanie Ann *Law&B 92*
Butler, Stuart *WhoScE 91-1*
Butler, Stuart Raymond 1941- *WhoWor 93*
Butler, Susan Lowell 1944- *WhoAm 92, WhoAmW 93*
Butler, Suzanne 1919- *DcChlFi*
Butler, Ted *ConAu 39NR*
Butler, Teresa Lynn 1955- *WhoAmW 93*
Butler, Terry 1949- *See* Black Sabbath *ConMus 9*
Butler, Thomas E. *Law&B 92*
Butler, Thomas P., Jr. *Law&B 92*
Butler, Tim *Law&B 92*
Butler, Tom, Jr. 1914- *St&PR 93*
Butler, Toni Jean 1963- *WhoAmW 93*
Butler, Tubal Uriah 1897-1977 *DcCPCAm*
Butler, Vickie Burkhart 1955- *WhoAmW 93, WhoSSW 93*
Butler, Viggo 1942- *St&PR 93*
Butler, Vincent Paul, Jr. 1929- *WhoAm 92*
Butler, Walter 1752?-1781 *HarEnMi*
Butler, Wilford Arthur 1937- *WhoAm 92*
Butler, Wilfrid Barry 1935- *WhoWor 93*
Butler, William A. *Law&B 92*
Butler, William A. 1951- *St&PR 93, WhoAm 92*
Butler, William E. 1929- *WhoAm 92*
Butler, William E(lliot, II) 1939- *ConAu 38NR*
Butler, William Hill 1943- *WhoSSW 93*
Butler, William Joseph 1924- *WhoAm 92*
Butler, William K. 1952- *St&PR 93*
Butler, William Langdon 1939- *WhoE 93*
Butler, William M. 1861-1937 *PolPar*
Butler, William Morgan 1861-1937 *BioIn 17*
Butler, William Orlando 1791-1880 *HarEnMi*
Butler, William T. 1936- *St&PR 93*
Butler, William Thomas 1932- *WhoAm 92*
Butlin, J.G. *WhoScE 91-1*
Butlin, Phil Pearson 1929- *WhoIns 93*
Butlin, Philip Pearson 1938- *St&PR 93*
Butlin, Ron 1949- *ConAu 136*
Butlin, Roy Norman *WhoScE 91-1*
Butman, Hillel 1932- *BioIn 17*
Butner, Fred Washington, Jr. 1927- *WhoAm 92*
Butner, Linda Roberta 1959- *WhoWrEP 92*
Butner, Robert Westbrook 1942- *WhoSSW 93*
Butor, Michel *BioIn 17*
Butor, Michel 1926- *WhoWor 93*
Butorac, Andelko 1932- *WhoScE 91-4*
Butorac, Frank George 1927- *WhoWor 93*
Butorac, Terry M. *St&PR 93*
Butour, Jean-Luc 1946- *WhoWor 93*
Butow, Robert Joseph Charles 1924- *WhoAm 92*
Butowsky, David Martin 1936- *WhoAm 92*
Butoy, Hendel *MiSFD 9*
Butrum, Herbert L. 1949- *St&PR 93*
Butry, Paul John 1946- *WhoE 93*
Butrymowicz, Zofia 1904- *PolBiDi*
Butsan, George Petrovich 1945- *WhoWor 93*
Butschek, Felix 1932- *WhoScE 91-4*
Butscher, Edward John 1945- *WhoE 93*
Butscher, Laura Clay 1951- *WhoAmW 93*
Butsikares, Socrates K. 1923-1991 *BioIn 17*
Butson, Alton Thomas 1926- *WhoAm 92, WhoSSW 93*
Butson, Elizabeth 1938- *WhoAm 92*
Butt, Bradley D. 1943- *St&PR 93*
Butt, Clara 1872-1936 *OxDcOp*
Butt, Clara (Ellen) 1872-1936 *Baker 92*
Butt, Edward Thomas, Jr. 1947- *WhoEmL 93*
Butt, George Franklin 1928- *St&PR 93*
Butt, Howard Edward 1895-1991 *BioIn 17*
Butt, Howard Edward, Jr. 1927- *WhoAm 92*
Butt, Hugh Roland 1910- *WhoAm 92*
Butt, Isaac 1813-1879 *BioIn 17*
Butt, Jimmy Lee 1921- *WhoAm 92*
Butt, John Baecher 1935- *WhoAm 92*
Butt, Mian Khadim Hussain 1911- *WhoWor 93*
Butt, Norman David 1952- *WhoEmL 93*
Butt, P. Lawrence *Law&B 92*
Butt, P. Lawrence 1941- *St&PR 93*
Butt, Peter D. 1929- *St&PR 93*
Butt, T.R. *WhoScE 91-1*
Butta, Enzo 1925- *WhoScE 91-3*
Buttaci, Sal St. John 1941- *WhoWrEP 92*
Buttaci, Salvatore Michael 1941- *WhoE 93*
Buttafuoco, Joey *BioIn 17*
Buttafuoco, Mary Jo *BioIn 17*
Buttazzo, Giuseppe 1954- *WhoWor 93*
Buttchen, Terry Gerard 1958- *WhoWor 93*
Buttel, Patricia Ann 1960- *WhoEmL 93*
Buttemeyer, Wilhelm 1940- *WhoWor 93*
Buttenheim, Edgar Marion 1922- *WhoAm 92*
Buttenwieser, Benjamin J. d1991 *NewYTBS 92*
Buttenwieser, Benjamin J(oseph) 1900-1991 *CurBio 92N*
Buttenwieser, Benjamin Joseph 1900-1991 *BioIn 17*
Buttenwieser, Helen Lehman 1905-1989 *BioIn 17*
Buttenwieser, Lawrence Benjamin 1932- *WhoAm 92*
Butter, H.D. 1935- *St&PR 93*
Butterbrodt, John 1929- *St&PR 93*
Butterbrodt, John Ervin 1929- *WhoAm 92*
Butterbrodt, Thomas C. 1934- *St&PR 93*
Butterfield, Lord *WhoScE 91-1*
Butterfield, Bruce 1940- *WhoSSW 93*
Butterfield, Bruce Scott 1949- *WhoAm 92*
Butterfield, Carol C. d1991 *BioIn 17*
Butterfield, Charles Edward, Jr. 1928- *WhoE 93*

Butterfield, Craig Irwin 1947- WhoEmL 93
Butterfield, David H. 1938- St&PR 93
Butterfield, Diane Marie 1950- WhoAmW 93
Butterfield, Edith Hadley AmWomPl
Butterfield, Elizabeth Stanford 1954- WhoE 93
Butterfield, John H. ScF&FL 92
Butterfield, Laura Louise 1952- WhoAm 92
Butterfield, Marie AmWomPl
Butterfield, Melissa Ann 1963- WhoAmW 93
Butterfield, R. WhoScE 91-1
Butterfield, R. Keith 1941- St&PR 93, WhoAm 92
Butterfield, Rachel Sue 1965- WhoAmW 93
Butterfield, Roger Place 1907-1981 BioIn 17
Butterfield, Samuel Hale 1924- WhoAm 92
Butterfield, Stephen Alan 1948- WhoE 93
Butterfield, Tommy Wayne 1952- WhoEmL 93
Butterick, Merle Waldron 1946- WhoEmL 93
Butterick, Thomas R. 1954- St&PR 93
Butterley, Nigel (Henry) 1935- Baker 92
Butterlin, Jacques A. 1916- WhoScE 91-2
Butterly, Edward R. 1946- St&PR 93
Butterman, Mark B. Law&B 92
Buttermore, Bradley S. 1956- St&PR 93
Buttermore, Bradley Scott 1956- WhoAm 92, WhoEmL 93
Buttermore, Rodney Everett 1950- WhoEmL 93
Buttermore, Steve Mark 1950- St&PR 93
Buttermore, William Joseph 1941- St&PR 93
Butters, Dorothy Gilman ScF&FL 92
Butters, Dorothy Gilman 1923- WhoAm 92
Butters, Nancy Lee 1950- WhoEmL 93
Butters, Ronald Richard 1940- WhoSSW 93
Butterweck, Hans J. 1932- WhoScE 91-3
Butterweck, Hans Juergen 1932- WhoWor 93
Butterworth, Alan Randolph 1952- WhoEmL 93
Butterworth, Charles 1896-1946 QDrFCA 92 [port]
Butterworth, Edward Livingston 1914- St&PR 93, WhoAm 92
Butterworth, George Esmond WhoScE 91-1
Butterworth, George (Sainton Kaye) 1885-1916 Baker 92
Butterworth, George Warren 1942- WhoAm 92
Butterworth, Jane Rogers Fitch 1937- WhoAm 92, WhoAmW 93, WhoWor 93
Butterworth, Katharine M. BioIn 17
Butterworth, Kenneth W. 1925- St&PR 93, WhoAm 92, WhoE 93
Butterworth, Michael 1947- ScF&FL 92
Butterworth, Oliver 1915- DcAmChF 1960
Butterworth, Oliver 1915-1990 BioIn 17, ConAu 37NR, MajAI [port], ScF&FL 92
Butterworth, Peter 1919-1979 QDrFCA 92 [port]
Butterworth, Robert A. 1942- WhoAm 92
Butterworth, Robert Roman 1946- WhoEmL 93
Butterworth, W(illiam) E(dmund), III 1929- ConAu 40NR
Butterworth, William E. 1929- ScF&FL 92
Buttery, Henry C. 1924- St&PR 93
Buttery, Peter John WhoScE 91-1
Buttet, Jean 1937- WhoScE 91-4
Buttigieg, Joseph J., III 1945- St&PR 93
Buttimer, Edna AmWomPl
Buttin, Gerard 1931- WhoScE 91-2
Butting, Max 1888-1976 Baker 92
Buttinger, Catharine Sarina Caroline 1951- WhoAm 92, WhoEmL 93
Buttinger, Joseph 1906-1992 BioIn 17, ConAu 138
Buttinger, Joseph A. d1992 NewYTBS 92
Buttinger, Muriel Gardiner 1901-1985 ConAu 39NR
Buttion, Thomas Robert 1925- WhoAm 92
Buttlar, Rudolph Otto 1934- WhoAm 92
Buttle, Eugene H. 1927- St&PR 93
Buttler, Peter Haviland 1942- St&PR 93
Buttner, Edgar Mott 1929- St&PR 93
Buttner, Jean Bernhard 1934- St&PR 93, WhoAm 92
Buttner, Johannes 1931- WhoWor 93
Buttner, Steven G. 1948- St&PR 93
Buttner, W. Murray 1932- St&PR 93
Buttner-Ennever, Jean A. 1944- WhoScE 91-3
Buttolph, David Daniels 1957- WhoE 93, WhoEmL 93
Button, A. Dwight 1917- St&PR 93
Button, Bruce Alan 1958- St&PR 93
Button, Daniel Evan 1917- WhoAm 92
Button, Dick BioIn 17
Button, James A. Law&B 92
Button, John 1933- WhoAsAP 91
Button, Kenneth John WhoScE 91-1
Button, Kenneth John 1922- WhoAm 92
Button, Kenneth Rodman 1946- WhoAm 92, WhoE 93, WhoEmL 93
Button, Rena Pritsker 1925- WhoAm 92
Button, Richard Totten 1929- WhoAm 92, WhoE 93
Button, Robert Easton 1915- WhoE 93
Button, Robert Ralph 1938- St&PR 93
Buttons, Red 1918- QDrFCA 92 [port]
Buttorf, Harry William 1952- WhoEmL 93
Buttorff, Curtis Deen 1948- WhoEmL 93
Buttoud, Gerard 1949- WhoScE 91-2
Buttram, J. Alan 1953- St&PR 93
Buttram, Jack Emerson 1932- WhoSSW 93
Buttram, James Alan 1953- WhoEmL 93, WhoSSW 93
Buttram, James Walter 1926- St&PR 93
Buttrey, Claude Thaddeus 1959- WhoEmL 93
Buttrey, Donald Wayne 1935- WhoAm 92
Buttrey, Douglas N(orton) ConAu 40NR
Buttrick, David Gardner 1927- WhoAm 92, WhoSSW 93
Buttrick, George A. BioIn 17
Buttrick, Harold 1931- WhoE 93
Buttrick, John Arthur 1919- WhoAm 92
Buttrum, David A. 1952- St&PR 93
Buttrum, Jack 1929- St&PR 93
Butts, Arthur Edward 1947- WhoEmL 93
Butts, Barbara Loretta 1941- WhoE 93
Butts, Barbara Rosalyn 1955- WhoAm 92
Butts, Brian B. St&PR 93
Butts, Calvin O., III BioIn 17
Butts, David Phillip 1932- WhoSSW 93
Butts, Dorothy AmWomPl
Butts, Edward A. Law&B 92
Butts, Edward Eugene 1938- WhoIns 93
Butts, Evan K. Law&B 92
Butts, George Francis 1923- WhoAm 92
Butts, Herbert Clell 1924- WhoAm 92
Butts, Jane ScF&FL 92
Butts, Leonard Culver 1950- WhoSSW 93
Butts, Lester Wayne WhoSSW 93
Butts, Lorraine Denise Law&B 92
Butts, Mary Johanna 1950- WhoSSW 93
Butts, Sherman R. 1938- St&PR 93
Butts, Virginia WhoAm 92, WhoAmW 93
Butts, William L. 1930- St&PR 93
Buttstett, Johann Heinrich 1666-1727 Baker 92
Buttykay, Akos 1871-1935 Baker 92
Buttz, Charles William 1932- WhoE 93
Butusov, Mikhail Mikhailovitch 1937- WhoWor 93
Butynski, William 1944- WhoAm 92
Butz, Geneva Mae 1944- WhoAmW 93
Butz, Ilse 1942- WhoScE 91-4
Butz, Jeffrey Ralph 1947- WhoE 93
Butz, Otto William 1923- WhoAm 92
Butzberger, Paul T. 1954- St&PR 93
Butzer, Harold Godfrey 1921- St&PR 93
Butzer, Paul Leo 1928- WhoWor 93
Butzlaff Voss, Bambi Lyn 1962- WhoEmL 93
Butzler, Jean-Paul 1941- WhoScE 91-2
Butzner, John Decker, Jr. 1917- WhoAm 92
Butzow, G.N. 1929- St&PR 93
Butzow, Norman Gayle 1946- St&PR 93
Buuck, Roland John 1935- WhoAm 92
Buunen, T.J.F. 1949- WhoScE 91-3
Buurman, Eloise Bernhoft 1915- WhoAmW 93
Buus, Jacques c. 1500-1565 Baker 92
Buus, Jens 1952- WhoWor 93
Buus, Merete 1957- WhoScE 91-2
Buvens, J.L., Jr. Law&B 92
Bux, William John 1946- WhoEmL 93
Buxbaum, Alexandra 1962- WhoEmL 93
Buxbaum, Frederick David 1946- WhoEmL 93
Buxbaum, Henry 1900-1979 BioIn 17
Buxbaum, Katherine AmWomPl
Buxbaum, Otto 1935- WhoScE 91-3
Buxbaum, Richard M. 1930- WhoAm 92
Buxbaum, Robert S. 1929- St&PR 93
Buxer, Constance Gertrude 1923- WhoAmW 93
Buxmann, Joachim 1933- WhoScE 91-3
Buxtehude, Dietrich c. 1637-1707 Baker 92
Buxton, Anne Marie 1968- WhoAmW 93
Buxton, Barry Miller 1949- WhoWrEP 92
Buxton, C.I., II 1924- St&PR 93
Buxton, Charles Ingraham, II 1924- WhoAm 92, WhoIns 93
Buxton, Douglas Francisco 1952- WhoE 93
Buxton, Edward d1990 BioIn 17
Buxton, Elliott L. 1924- St&PR 93
Buxton, James ScF&FL 92
Buxton, John 1912-1989 BioIn 17
Buxton, John Noel WhoScE 91-1
Buxton, Jorge Norman 1921- WhoAm 92
Buxton, Marilyn Philbrick 1947- WhoEmL 93
Buxton, Meg ScF&FL 92
Buxton, Ralph MajAI, SmATA 69
Buxton, Robert Stevens 1925- WhoE 93
Buxton, Thomas Fowell 1786-1845 BioIn 17
Buxton, Winslow H. WhoAm 92
Buxton, Zane Kelly 1946- WhoEmL 93
Buya, Wallace Joseph 1925- St&PR 93, WhoAm 92
Buyers, John William Amerman 1928- St&PR 93, WhoAm 92
Buyers, William James Leslie 1937- WhoAm 92
Buyniski, Victoria B. 1951- ConEn
Buyok, John Paul 1957- WhoEmL 93
Buyoya, Pierre 1949- WhoAfr, WhoWor 93
Buys, Donna Onstad 1944- WhoAmW 93
Buyse, Emile Jules 1927- WhoAm 92
Buyse, Leone Karena 1947- WhoAm 92
Buyske, Donald A. 1927-1990 BioIn 17
Buyske, Steven George 1961- WhoE 93
Buysse, F.X. 1926- WhoScE 91-2
Buysse, James T. 1955- WhoIns 93
Buyst, Ludo 1931- WhoScE 91-2
Buyukataman, Kayaalp 1941- WhoE 93
Buyukyilmaz, Mustafa 1942- WhoScE 91-4
Buzacott, John Alan 1937- WhoAm 92
Buzaid, Larry Law&B 92
Buzaljko, Grace Wilson 1922- WhoAmW 93
Buzan, Norma Jeanne Stephens 1924- WhoWrEP 92
Buzard, James Albert 1927- WhoAm 92
Buzas, Istvan 1942- WhoScE 91-4
Buzas, Joe BioIn 17
Buzawa, Carl G. Law&B 92
Buzbee, Minnie A. AmWomPl
Buzbee, R. Robert 1942- St&PR 93
Buzbee, Richard Edgar 1931- WhoAm 92, WhoWrEP 92
Buzby, Gordon P. 1948- WhoE 93
Buzby, Russell Conwell 1934- St&PR 93
Buzby, Zane MiSFD 9
Buzek, Otokar 1934- WhoScE 91-4
Buzen, Jeffrey P. 1943- St&PR 93
Buziak, Frank T. 1947- St&PR 93, WhoIns 93
Buzick, William A., Jr. 1920- St&PR 93
Buzick, William Alonson, Jr. 1920- WhoAm 92
Buzina, Ratko 1920- WhoScE 91-4, WhoWor 93
Buzinkay, Gezai 1941- WhoWor 93
Buzinky, Edward P. Law&B 92
Buzney, Sheldon Marc 1945- WhoE 93
Buzo, Alexander (John) 1944- ConAu 39NR
Buzo, William R. Law&B 92
Buzunis, Constantine Dino 1958- WhoEmL 93, WhoWor 93
Buzzard, Steven Ray 1946- WhoEmL 93
Buzzcocks, The ConMus 9
Buzzell, Edward 1897-1985 MiSFD 9N
Buzzell, Robert Dow 1933- WhoAm 92
Buzzelli, Charlotte Grace 1947- WhoEmL 93
Buzzelli, David T. 1941- WhoAm 92
Buzzelli, Elizabeth Kane 1936- ScF&FL 92, WhoWrEP 92
Buzzi, Peter L. 1960- St&PR 93
Buzzitta, Louis V. 1931- St&PR 93
Buzzolla, Antonio 1815-1871 Baker 92
Bwint, Derek Shway 1941- St&PR 93
By, Andre Bernard 1955- WhoE 93
Byabafumu, Deo Gratias 1953 WhoUN 92
Byakutaga, Sam Musinguzi 1956- WhoUN 92
Byall, Lynne Ann 1953- WhoE 93
Byam, Marie Elizabeth 1949- WhoAmW 93, WhoEmL 93
Byam, Milton S. 1922-1991 BioIn 17
Byam, Seward Groves, Jr. 1928- WhoAm 92, WhoE 93
Byambasuren, Dashiyn 1933- WhoAsAP 91
Byambasuren, Dashiyn 1942- WhoWor 93
Byard, Carole BlkAuII 92
Byard, Carole 1941- BioIn 17
Byard, Spencer d1992 NewYTBS 92
Byarlay, Matthew Starr 1965- WhoSSW 93
Byars, Betsy 1928- ChlFicS, ScF&FL 92
Byars, Betsy Cromer 1928- BioIn 17, DcAmChF 1960, DcAmChF 1985, MajAI [port], WhoAm 92
Byars, Harold 1941- St&PR 93
Byars, John Buford, Jr. 1928- St&PR 93
Byars, Keith 1963- WhoAm 92
Byars, Linda Joyce 1963- WhoAmW 93
Byars, Walter Ryland, Jr. 1928- WhoAm 92
Byas, Teresa Ann 1955- WhoAmW 93
Byatt, A.S. 1936- BioIn 17
Byatt, Antonia Susan 1936- BioIn 17, WhoWor 93
Byatt, Ronald Archer Campbell Robin 1930- WhoWor 93
Bybee, Jay Scott 1953- WhoAm 92
Bybee, Jimmy L. 1937- St&PR 93
Bybee, O. Lynn 1937- St&PR 93
Bybee, Rodger Wayne 1942- WhoAm 92
Bybee, Shannon Larmer, Jr. 1938- WhoAm 92
Byberg, Patricia J. 1937- St&PR 93
Bycer, Max 1925- St&PR 93
Bych, Barbara Ann 1962- St&PR 93
Bychkov, Semyon 1952- Baker 92, WhoWor 93
Bychkoz, Valerij 1946- WhoUN 92
Byck, Robert Samuel 1933- WhoAm 92
Byckling, Eero Arvi 1936- WhoScE 91-4
Bycott, James Franklin Law&B 92
Bycraft, John Thomas, III 1936- St&PR 93
Bycroft, Barrie Walsham WhoScE 91-1
Bydder, Graeme Mervyn WhoScE 91-1
Bydzovsky, Viktor 1944- WhoWor 93
Bye, Arthur Edwin, Jr. 1919- WhoAm 92
Bye, James Edward 1930- WhoAm 92
Bye, Kari 1937- WhoWor 93
Bye, Ranulph DeBayeux 1916- WhoAm 92
Bye, Raymond Erwin, Jr. 1944- WhoAm 92
Bye, William H. 1921- St&PR 93
Byelick, Stephen C. 1948- St&PR 93
Byer, Allan J. 1933- St&PR 93
Byer, Diana BioIn 17
Byer, Diana 1946- WhoAmW 93
Byer, James L. 1932- St&PR 93
Byer, Kathryn Stripling 1944- WhoWrEP 92
Byer, P. Roger St&PR 93
Byer, Peter Law&B 92
Byer, Robert Louis 1942- WhoAm 92
Byerley, Curt Joseph 1956- WhoE 93
Byerlotzer, Jim J. 1946- St&PR 93
Byerly, F. Hanes 1935- St&PR 93
Byerly, Jean-Marie Law&B 92
Byerly, John A. Law&B 92
Byerly, Kenneth C. 1932- St&PR 93
Byerly, LeRoy James 1931- WhoAm 92
Byerly, Phyllis 1961- St&PR 93
Byerly, Radford, Jr. 1936- WhoAm 92
Byerly, Thomas J. 1947- St&PR 93
Byerly, V. Lois 1932- WhoAmW 93
Byerly, Wesley Grimes, Jr. 1926- WhoSSW 93
Byerly, William Jackson, III 1951- WhoEmL 93
Byerrum, Richard Uglow 1920- WhoAm 92
Byers, Brent Eugene 1950- WhoAm 92, WhoSSW 93
Byers, Brook H. St&PR 93
Byers, Donna Jean 1956- WhoAmW 93
Byers, Edward A. 1939-1989 ScF&FL 92
Byers, George William 1923- WhoAm 92
Byers, Horace Robert 1906- WhoAm 92
Byers, Jane Law&B 92
Byers, Jerome Leon 1926- WhoSSW 93
Byers, Jo Ann 1947- WhoAmW 93
Byers, Mary Helen 1946- WhoSSW 93
Byers, Nina 1930- WhoAm 92
Byers, Richard George 1937- St&PR 93
Byers, Richard Lee 1950- ScF&FL 92
Byers, Robert Allan 1936- WhoE 93
Byers, Thomas Lee Law&B 92
Byers, Timothy Patrick 1954- WhoWrEP 92
Byers, Vic L., III Law&B 92
Byers, Walter 1922- WhoAm 92
Byers, Wayne C. Law&B 92
Byers, William Sewell 1925- WhoSSW 93
Byers Brown, William WhoScE 91-1
Byers-Pevitts, Beverley 1939- WhoAmW 93
Byfield, Bruce 1958- ScF&FL 92
Bygdeman, Marc A. 1934- WhoScE 91-4
Bygren, L.O. 1936- WhoScE 91-4
Byham, Edgar Kimberly Law&B 92
Byington, Alice AmWomPl
Byington, Homer Morrison, III 1934- WhoAm 92
Byington, Robert Lee 1951- WhoEmL 93
Byington, S. John WhoAm 92
Byington, Sally Ruth 1935- WhoAmW 93
Bykat, Alexander 1940- WhoSSW 93
Bykerk, Cecil Dale 1944- St&PR 93
Bykhovsky, Arkadi G. 1943- St&PR 93
Bykhovsky, Arkadi Gregory 1943- WhoAm 92
Bykov, Rolan 1929- DrEEuF
Bykovskii, Valerii Fedorovich 1934- BioIn 17
Bykowski, Anthony Law&B 92
Bykowski, J.A. 1948- St&PR 93

Bykowski, Piotr J. 1939- *WhoScE 91-4*
Byland, Peter *WhoAm 92*
Byler, Jennifer Curtis 1958- *WhoEmL 93*
Byles, Robert Valmore 1937- *WhoSSW 93*
Bylewski, Anthony Walter 1948- *WhoE 93*
Bylica, Andrzej Stefan 1936- *WhoScE 91-4*
Bylinsky, Gene Michael 1930- *WhoAm 92, WhoWrEP 92*
Bylot, Robert fl. 1610-1616 *Expl 93*
Bylsma, Anner 1934- *Baker 92*
Bylsma, Carol Ann 1941- *WhoAmW 93*
Bylund, B. Goran 1937- *WhoScE 91-4*
Bymel, Suzan Yvette *WhoAmW 93*
Bymun, Dennis T. 1945- *St&PR 93*
Bynagle, Hans Edward 1946- *WhoEmL 93*
Byng, G.G. *WhoScE 91-1*
Byng, John 1704-1757 *HarEnMi*
Byng, Julian Hedworth George 1862-1935 *HarEnMi*
Bynoe, Carol Ann *Law&B 92*
Bynoe, Justine *BioIn 17*
Bynoe, Peter Charles Bernard 1951- *WhoAm 92*
Bynoe, Philip Earl 1961- *WhoE 93*
Bynon, Cynthia Jean 1958- *WhoAmW 93*
Bynum, Barbara Stewart 1936- *WhoAm 92*
Bynum, Cheryl Dianne 1960- *WhoWrEP 92*
Bynum, Douglas, Jr. 1934- *WhoSSW 93*
Bynum, George T., III 1951- *WhoSSW 93*
Bynum, Hal B. 1947- *St&PR 93*
Bynum, Harry Lynell 1953- *St&PR 93*
Bynum, Horace Charles 1916- *WhoSSW 93*
Bynum, Jack Edward, Jr. 1929- *WhoAm 92*
Bynum, Randy Jon 1950- *WhoEmL 93*
Byorick, Judith Lynn *Law&B 92*
Byoung Sun 1926- *WhoAsAP 91*
Byram, James Asberry, Jr. 1954- *WhoEmL 93*
Byram, Jim L. 1948- *WhoSSW 93*
Byram, Kim 1959- *St&PR 93*
Byram, Robert G. 1945- *St&PR 93*
Byramji, Homi M. *St&PR 93*
Byrd, Adam Hann- *BioIn 17*
Byrd, Andrew Wayne 1954- *WhoEmL 93, WhoSSW 93*
Byrd, Barbara Ann 1953- *WhoAmW 93*
Byrd, Benjamin Franklin, Jr. 1918- *WhoAm 92*
Byrd, Bette Jean 1928- *WhoAm 92*
Byrd, Bill d1991 *BioIn 17*
Byrd, C. Don 1940- *WhoIns 93*
Byrd, Carolyn Covington 1967- *WhoSSW 93*
Byrd, Catherine Doscher *Law&B 92*
Byrd, Chester Lamar 1936- *St&PR 93*
Byrd, Christine Waterman Swent 1951- *WhoAmW 93*
Byrd, Dan Richard *Law&B 92*
Byrd, David Lamar 1922- *WhoAm 92*
Byrd, Donald(son Toussaint L'Overture) 1932- *Baker 92*
Byrd, Flossie M. *BioIn 17*
Byrd, Gisele Marie 1956- *WhoAmW 93*
Byrd, Guy W. 1941- *WhoAm 92*
Byrd, Harry F., Sr. 1887-1966 *PolPar*
Byrd, Harry F., Jr. 1914- *PolPar*
Byrd, Harry Flood 1887-1966 *BioIn 17*
Byrd, Harry Flood, Jr. 1914- *WhoAm 92*
Byrd, Henry Roeland 1918-1980 *Baker 92*
Byrd, Irene De Reath *AmWomPl*
Byrd, Isaac Burlin 1925- *WhoAm 92*
Byrd, James William 1936- *WhoSSW 93*
Byrd, Jay *WhoWrEP 92*
Byrd, Joann Kathleen 1943- *WhoAmW 93*
Byrd, Jonathan Eugene 1952- *WhoEmL 93*
Byrd, Joseph D. 1943- *St&PR 93*
Byrd, Kathleen Mary 1949- *WhoAm 92*
Byrd, Larry Donald 1936- *WhoAm 92, WhoSSW 93*
Byrd, Laura Jeanne 1963- *WhoEmL 93*
Byrd, LaVerne 1957- *WhoSSW 93*
Byrd, Linda Joyce 1954- *WhoSSW 93*
Byrd, Linward Tonnett 1921- *WhoAm 92*
Byrd, Lloyd Garland 1923- *WhoAm 92*
Byrd, Marc Robert 1954- *WhoEmL 93*
Byrd, Marion Everton 1936- *St&PR 93*
Byrd, Mark Alan 1957- *WhoE 93*
Byrd, Martha Hunter 1930- *WhoWrEP 92*
Byrd, Mary Jane 1946- *WhoAmW 93*
Byrd, Mary Laager 1935- *WhoAm 92, WhoAmW 93*
Byrd, Melvin Leon 1935- *AfrAmBi*
Byrd, Michaele Abner 1949- *WhoAmW 93*
Byrd, Milton Bruce 1922- *WhoAm 92*
Byrd, Odell Richard, Jr. *WhoWrEP 92*
Byrd, Phillip Eugene 1942- *AfrAmBi*
Byrd, Richard Edward 1931- *WhoAm 92*
Byrd, Richard Evelyn 1888-1957 *BioIn 17, Expl 93 [port]*
Byrd, Richard Hays 1939- *WhoAm 92*
Byrd, Richard T. 1935- *St&PR 93*
Byrd, Robert C. *BioIn 17*
Byrd, Robert C. 1917- *CngDr 91, PolPar*
Byrd, Robert Carlyle 1917- *WhoAm 92, WhoSSW 93*
Byrd, Robert Ernest 1919- *St&PR 93*
Byrd, Robert J. 1942- *WhoWrEP 92*
Byrd, Robert W. 1935- *St&PR 93*
Byrd, Ronald Dicky *Law&B 92*
Byrd, Sandra Judith 1960- *WhoAmW 93, WhoEmL 93*
Byrd, Stephen Fred 1928- *WhoAm 92*
Byrd, Stephen Timothy 1957- *WhoEmL 93, WhoSSW 93*
Byrd, Sue Gibson 1953- *WhoEmL 93*
Byrd, Viola J. 1921- *WhoAmW 93*
Byrd, William 1543-1623 *Baker 92*
Byrd, William Levan 1953- *WhoSSW 93*
Byrd, William Thomas, Jr. 1942- *WhoE 93*
Byrde, William 1543-1623 *Baker 92*
Byrd-Lawler, Barbara *BioIn 17*
Byrd-Lawler, Barbara Ann 1952- *WhoAm 92, WhoAmW 93, WhoEmL 93*
Byrds, The *ConMus 8 [port]*
Byres, Marshall Henry 1951- *WhoWor 93*
Byres, Nicole M. *Law&B 92*
Byrkit, Donald Raymond 1933- *WhoSSW 93*
Byrn, Mary Ellen McAdam d1990 *BioIn 17*
Byrn, Stephen R. 1944- *WhoAm 92*
Byrne, Barbara Moakler 1954- *WhoAmW 93*
Byrne, Beverly *ScF&FL 92*
Byrne, Bill Weyman 1929- *St&PR 93*
Byrne, Bradley Roberts 1955- *WhoEmL 93*
Byrne, Charles S. 1944- *St&PR 93*
Byrne, Chris J. *Law&B 92*
Byrne, Daniel William 1958- *WhoE 93, WhoWor 93*
Byrne, David *BioIn 17*
Byrne, David 1952- *Baker 92, ConMus 8 [port], MiSFD 9, WhoAm 92*
Byrne, David Francis 1932- *St&PR 93*
Byrne, Dennis Joseph 1940- *St&PR 93*
Byrne, Dennis William 1946- *WhoEmL 93*
Byrne, Dolly *AmWomPl*
Byrne, Donn Erwin 1931- *WhoAm 92*
Byrne, Dorothy E. *Law&B 92*
Byrne, Edward d1988 *BioIn 17*
Byrne, Edward Blake 1935- *WhoAm 92*
Byrne, Frank Loyola 1928- *WhoAm 92*
Byrne, Gabriel *BioIn 17*
Byrne, Gary C. 1942- *St&PR 93*
Byrne, Gary Cecil 1942- *WhoAm 92*
Byrne, George Dennis 1933- *WhoE 93*
Byrne, George Melvin 1933- *WhoWor 93*
Byrne, Gerard Anthony 1944- *WhoAm 92*
Byrne, H. Richard 1947- *St&PR 93, WhoAm 92*
Byrne, J. Desmond *Law&B 92*
Byrne, James Curran 1947- *WhoE 93*
Byrne, James Frederick 1931- *WhoAm 92*
Byrne, James Joseph 1908- *WhoAm 92*
Byrne, James T. 1939- *St&PR 93*
Byrne, James T., Jr. *Law&B 92*
Byrne, James Thomas, Jr. 1939- *WhoAm 92*
Byrne, Jamie Maria 1961- *WhoE 93*
Byrne, Jane 1933?- *BioIn 17, PolPar*
Byrne, Janet Gail 1952- *WhoAmW 93*
Byrne, Jeffrey Edward 1939- *WhoE 93*
Byrne, Jerome Camillus 1925- *WhoAm 92*
Byrne, John Edward 1925- *WhoAm 92*
Byrne, John J. 1932- *St&PR 93*
Byrne, John James 1920- *WhoAm 92*
Byrne, John Keyes *BioIn 17*
Byrne, John L. *ScF&FL 92*
Byrne, John N. 1925- *WhoAm 92*
Byrne, John P. 1936- *WhoIns 93*
Byrne, John Patrick 1951- *WhoEmL 93*
Byrne, John Vincent 1928- *WhoAm 92*
Byrne, Joseph 1923- *WhoAm 92*
Byrne, Joseph Ahern, Jr. 1953- *WhoEmL 93*
Byrne, Joseph J. 1946- *St&PR 93*
Byrne, Joseph Patrick 1956- *WhoSSW 93*
Byrne, Kevin Francis 1952- *WhoE 93*
Byrne, Leslie Larkin 1946- *WhoAmW 93*
Byrne, Michael C. 1954- *St&PR 93*
Byrne, Michael Joseph 1928- *WhoWor 93*
Byrne, Noel Thomas 1943- *WhoWor 93*
Byrne, Olivia Sherrill 1957- *WhoE 93*
Byrne, Patricia A. *Law&B 92*
Byrne, Patrick F. 1919- *ScF&FL 92*
Byrne, Patrick Francis 1952- *WhoEmL 93*
Byrne, Patrick James 1949- *WhoEmL 93*
Byrne, Patrick Michael 1952- *WhoAm 92, WhoEmL 93*
Byrne, Patrick Michael 1962- *WhoE 93*
Byrne, Richard Hill 1915- *WhoAm 92*
Byrne, Robert 1930- *ScF&FL 92*
Byrne, Robert D., Jr. *Law&B 92*
Byrne, Robert William 1958- *WhoEmL 93*
Byrne, Stewart C. *Law&B 92*
Byrne, Stuart J. 1913- *ScF&FL 92*
Byrne, Thomas M. *Law&B 92*
Byrne, Thomas Ray 1958- *WhoE 93*
Byrne, William Matthew, Jr. 1930- *WhoAm 92*
Byrnes, Arthur E. 1945- *St&PR 93*
Byrnes, Arthur Francis 1917- *WhoAm 92*
Byrnes, Christine Ann 1951- *WhoAmW 93*
Byrnes, Christopher Ian 1949- *WhoAm 92*
Byrnes, David Thomas 1940- *WhoSSW 93*
Byrnes, Donald J. 1926- *St&PR 93, WhoAm 92, WhoSSW 93*
Byrnes, Edward G., Jr. 1941- *St&PR 93*
Byrnes, Frederick Joseph *WhoWrEP 92*
Byrnes, Gary Michael 1948- *St&PR 93*
Byrnes, George D. *Law&B 92*
Byrnes, James Bernard 1917- *WhoAm 92*
Byrnes, James F. 1879-1972 *ColdWar 1 [port], PolPar*
Byrnes, James Francis 1879-1972 *DcTwHis, OxCSupC [port]*
Byrnes, James J. 1941- *St&PR 93*
Byrnes, Jim *BioIn 17*
Byrnes, Joseph F., Jr. *Law&B 92*
Byrnes, Kathleen Ann 1950- *WhoEmL 93*
Byrnes, Kerry Joseph 1945- *WhoE 93*
Byrnes, Lawrence P. *Law&B 92*
Byrnes, Mary Patricia *Law&B 92*
Byrnes, Michael Francis 1957- *WhoEmL 93*
Byrnes, R. John 1948- *St&PR 93*
Byrnes, Ralph Robert 1942- *St&PR 93*
Byrnes, Robert Charles, Jr. 1958- *WhoE 93*
Byrnes, Robert Francis 1917- *WhoAm 92, WhoWrEP 92*
Byrnes, Robert John, III 1948- *WhoEmL 93*
Byrnes, Robert Michael 1937- *WhoAm 92*
Byrnes, Shirley May 1947- *WhoEmL 93*
Byrnes, Thomas C. 1948- *St&PR 93*
Byrnes, Victor Allen 1906- *WhoAm 92*
Byrnes, William Joseph 1940- *WhoWor 93*
Byrnes, William L. 1921- *St&PR 93*
Byrns, Amy Ejercito *Law&B 92*
Byrns, Joseph W. 1869-1936 *PolPar*
Byrnside, Oscar Jehu, Jr. 1935- *WhoAm 92*
Byrom, David Paul 1956- *WhoSSW 93*
Byrom, Fletcher L. 1918- *St&PR 93*
Byrom, Fletcher Lauman 1918- *WhoAm 92*
Byrom, Jack Edwards 1929- *WhoSSW 93, WhoWor 93*
Byrom, Jack L. 1946- *St&PR 93*
Byron, Lord 1788-1824 *MagSWL [port], WorLitC [port]*
Byron, Amanda *ScF&FL 92*
Byron, Beverly B. 1932- *BioIn 17, CngDr 91*
Byron, Beverly Butcher 1932- *WhoAm 92, WhoAmW 93, WhoE 93*
Byron, David John *WhoScE 91-1*
Byron, Don 1958- *WhoAm 92*
Byron, Frederick William, Jr. 1938- *WhoAm 92*
Byron, George Gordon 1788-1824 *BioIn 17, OxDcOp*
Byron, Gloria Blum 1937- *WhoWrEP 92*
Byron, James Stephen 1957- *WhoE 93*
Byron, John c. 1600-1652 *HarEnMi*
Byron, John 1723-1786 *Expl 93, HarEnMi*
Byron, Katharine Edgar 1903-1976 *BioIn 17*
Byron, Richard J. *Law&B 92*
Byron, Richard J. 1938- *WhoIns 93*
Byron, Robert Welton 1925- *St&PR 93, WhoAm 92*
Byron, Stuart 1941- *WhoWrEP 92*
Byron, Thomas William 1947- *WhoEmL 93*
Byron, William James 1927- *WhoAm 92, WhoE 93*
Byrum, James Edward 1945- *St&PR 93*
Byrum, Joe B. 1946- *St&PR 93*
Byrum, John 1947- *MiSFD 9*
Bys, Donna Marie 1955- *WhoAmW 93*
Bysouth, Anthony John *WhoScE 91-1*
Bystrom, John d1991 *BioIn 17*
Bystrom, Oscar Fredrik Bernadotte 1821-1909 *Baker 92*
Bystron, Jan Stanislaw 1892-1964 *IntDcAn*
Bystryn, Jean-Claude 1938- *WhoAm 92*
Byun, Hang S. 1940- *WhoE 93*
Bywater, D.L. *WhoScE 91-1*
Bywater, George Pilsbury 1929- *St&PR 93*
Bywater, William Glen, Jr. 1940- *WhoE 93*
Bywater, Willis McNeill 1939- *St&PR 93*
Bywaters, David R. 1932- *St&PR 93*
Byyny, Richard Lee 1939- *WhoAm 92*
Bzdula, Wayne Barry 1951- *St&PR 93*
Bzura, Greg George 1937- *St&PR 93*

C

Caamano, Roberto 1923- *Baker 92*
Caamano Deno, Francisco 1932-1973 *DcCPCAm*
Caan, James *BioIn 17*
Caan, James 1939- *IntDcF 2-3 [port], MiSFD 9*
Caan, James 1940- *WhoAm 92*
Cabacungan, Florencio Cabatu 1960- *WhoWor 93*
Cabada, Juan de la 1903-1986 *SpAmA*
Cabada, Juan de la 1903-1987 *DcMexL*
Cabadaj, Rudolf 1940- *WhoScE 91-4*
Cabaj, Robert Paul 1948- *WhoAm 92*
Cabak, Michael R. 1933- *St&PR 93*
Caballe, Montserrat *BioIn 17*
Caballe, Montserrat 1933- *Baker 92, IntDcOp, OxDcOp, WhoWor 93*
Caballero, Benjamin Humberto 1948- *WhoWor 93*
Caballero, Carlo 1964- *WhoE 93*
Caballero, Gaston 1927- *WhoUN 92*
Caballero, Manuel Fernandez 1835-1906 *OxDcOp*
Caballero Bonald, Jose Manuel 1926- *BioIn 17*
Caballero Calderon, Eduardo 1910- *SpAmA*
Caballero Stafford, Rosamaria *Law&B 92*
Cabalquinto, Luis Carrazcal 1935- *WhoWrEP 92*
Caban, John d1992 *NewYTBS 92*
Cabana, Veneracion Garganta 1942- *WhoAmW 93*
Cabanas, Elizabeth Ann 1948- *WhoAmW 93, WhoEmL 93*
Cabanas, Humberto 1947- *HispAmA*
Cabanas Barrientos, Lucio *DcCPCAm*
Cabane, Jean Paul 1949- *WhoWor 93*
Cabani, Sergio 1927- *WhoScE 91-3, WhoWor 93*
Cabanillas Gallas, Pio 1923-1991 *BioIn 17*
Cabanilles, Juan Bautista Jose 1644-1712 *Baker 92*
Cabanis, Jose 1922- *WhoWor 93*
Cabaniss, William Jelks, Jr. 1938- *WhoSSW 93*
Cabanya, Mary Louise 1947- *WhoEmL 93*
Cabarcas, Elina 1932- *WhoWrEP 92*
Cabaret, Joseph Ronald 1934- *St&PR 93, WhoAm 92*
Cabarrot, E. 1937- *WhoScE 91-2*
Cabasso, Artie 1957- *St&PR 93*
Cabasso, Ike *St&PR 93*
Cabbabe, Edmond Bechir 1947- *WhoEmL 93*
Cabbibo, Ronald *Law&B 92*
Cabbiness, Carl Owen 1940- *St&PR 93*
Cabe, Linda Sue 1944- *WhoAmW 93*
Cabecon, Antonio de 1510-1566 *Baker 92*
Cabecon, Hernando 1541-1602 *Baker 92*
Cabeen, Samuel Kirkland 1931- *WhoAm 92*
Cabell, Elizabeth Arlisse 1947- *WhoAm 92*
Cabell, James Branch 1879-1958 *ScF&FL 92*
Cabello, Mercedes de Carbonera 1845-1909 *BioIn 17*
Cabello de Carbonera, Mercedes 1845-1909 *BioIn 17*
Cabeney, Jerald W. *Law&B 92*
Cabet, Etienne 1788-1856 *BioIn 17*
Cabey, Alfred Arthur, Jr. 1935- *WhoSSW 93, WhoWor 93*
Cabeza de Baca, Fernando E. 1937- *HispAmA*
Cabeza de Baca, Manuel 1853-1915 *DcLB 122 [port]*
Cabeza de Baca Gilbert, Fabiola *NotHsAW 93*
Cabeza de Baca Gilbert, Fabiola 1898- *DcLB 122 [port]*
Cabeza de Vaca, Alvar Nunez 1490-1556? *Expl 93 [port]*
Cabezas, Jose Antonio 1929- *WhoWor 93*
Cabezas, Robert Thomas 1940- *St&PR 93*
Cabezon, Antonio de c. 1510-1566 *Baker 92*
Cabezon, Hernando 1541-1602 *Baker 92*
Cabibbo, Nicola 1935- *WhoScE 91-3*
Cabic, Edward J. *Law&B 92*
Cabiro, Richard J. 1943- *St&PR 93*
Cable, Carole Law-Gagnon 1944- *WhoAmW 93*
Cable, Charles Allen 1932- *WhoAm 92*
Cable, Dale A. 1947- *St&PR 93*
Cable, Donald Aubrey 1927- *WhoAm 92*
Cable, George Washington 1844-1925 *EncAACR, GayN*
Cable, Howard Reid 1920- *WhoAm 92*
Cable, Howard W., Jr. *Law&B 92*
Cable, Howard Wilson, Jr. 1937- *St&PR 93*
Cable, Jane Nicholson 1935- *WhoAmW 93*
Cable, John A. 1922- *St&PR 93*
Cable, John Franklin 1941- *WhoAm 92*
Cable, Mabel Elizabeth 1935- *WhoE 93*
Cable, Michael *WhoScE 91-1*
Cable, Nevyle R. 1952- *St&PR 93*
Cable, Thomas Hamilton, Jr. 1935- *WhoWor 93*
Cabler, James A., Jr. *Law&B 92*
Cabochan, Gerardo P. 1926- *WhoAsAP 91*
Cabochan, Jose L. 1949- *WhoAsAP 91*
Cabon, Pierre 1928- *WhoWor 93*
Cabot, Charles C., Jr. 1930- *St&PR 93*
Cabot, Charles Codman, Jr. 1930- *WhoAm 92*
Cabot, Ellen *MiSFD 9*
Cabot, George 1751-1823 *PolPar*
Cabot, Harold 1929- *WhoAm 92*
Cabot, Joaquim 1861-1951 *BioIn 17*
Cabot, John 1451?-1498 *Expl 93*
Cabot, John fl. 1497- *DcChlFi*
Cabot, John G.L. 1934- *St&PR 93, WhoAm 92, WhoE 93*
Cabot, Joseph 1921- *WhoWor 93*
Cabot, Lewis Pickering 1937- *WhoE 93*
Cabot, Louis Wellington 1921- *WhoAm 92, WhoE 93, WhoWor 93*
Cabot, Powell M. 1931- *St&PR 93*
Cabot, Powell Mason 1931- *WhoAm 92*
Cabot, Samuel, III 1940- *St&PR 93*
Cabot, Sebastian 1484-1557 *Expl 93 [port]*
Cabot, Thomas Dudley 1897- *WhoAm 92*
Cabot, Walter M. 1933- *St&PR 93*
Cabo Torres, Jesus 1922- *WhoScE 91-3*
Caboz, Regis F.A. 1933- *WhoScE 91-2*
Cabral, Amilcar 1924-1973 *DcTwHis*
Cabral, Amilcar Lopes 1924-1973 *ColdWar 2 [port]*
Cabral, Brian 1956- *BioIn 17*
Cabral, Ciruelo *ScF&FL 92*
Cabral, Cleverson 1941- *WhoWor 93*
Cabral, J.M. Peixoto *WhoScE 91-3*
Cabral, Joao 1599-1669 *Expl 93*
Cabral, Joao de Pina *ConAu 136*
Cabral, Judith Ann 1951- *WhoAm 92, WhoAmW 93*
Cabral, Luis de Almedia 1931- *WhoAfr*
Cabral, Luis Martins 1961- *WhoWor 93*
Cabral, Manuel del 1907- *SpAmA*
Cabral, Pedro Alvares 1467-1519? *Expl 93 [port]*
Cabral, Siegfried J. 1934- *St&PR 93*
Cabral, Theresa L. *Law&B 92*
Cabral, Vasco 1924- *WhoAfr*
Cabranes, Jose A. 1940- *HispAmA [port]*
Cabranes, Jose Alberto 1940- *WhoAm 92, WhoE 93*
Cabrera, Alejandro Leopoldo 1950- *WhoWor 93*
Cabrera, Angelina *NotHsAW 93*
Cabrera, Carmen 1948- *WhoAmW 93*
Cabrera, James C. 1935- *St&PR 93*
Cabrera, Jose Ismael 1947- *WhoSSW 93*
Cabrera, Juan J. 1959- *St&PR 93*
Cabrera, Lydia 1900-1991 *BioIn 17, NotHsAW 93, SpAmA*
Cabrera, Rafael 1884-1943 *DcMexL*
Cabrera, Ramon 1806-1877 *HarEnMi*
Cabrera, Tomas d1991 *BioIn 17*
Cabrera, Victor F. *Law&B 92*
Cabrera Hidalgo, Alfonso *DcCPCAm*
Cabrera Infante, G. 1929- *BioIn 17*
Cabrera Infante, Guillermo 1922- *SpAmA*
Cabrera Infante, Guillermo 1929- *BioIn 17*
Cabreros-Sud, Veena *BioIn 17*
Cabridenc, Roger Alexis Jules 1934- *WhoScE 91-2*
Cabrillo, Juan Rodriguez d1543 *BioIn 17, Expl 93*
Cabrinety, Patricia Butler 1932- *WhoE 93, WhoWrEP 92*
Cabrini, Frances Xavier 1850-1917 *BioIn 17*
Cabrita, Ezequiel *WhoScE 91-3*
Cabrita, Isabel *WhoScE 91-3*
Cacace, John 1939- *St&PR 93*
Cacanindin, Milo Santiago 1956- *WhoWor 93*
Cacavio, Anne R. 1919- *St&PR 93*
Caccamise, Alfred Edward 1919- *WhoSSW 93*
Caccamise, Genevra Louise Ball 1934- *WhoAmW 93, WhoSSW 93*
Caccamo, Nicholas James 1944- *St&PR 93, WhoAm 92*
Caccavale, Judith Lansdowne 1941- *WhoWrEP 92*
Caccia, Harold Anthony 1905-1990 *BioIn 17*
Caccia, Silvio 1950- *WhoScE 91-3*
Cacciamani, Eugene Richard, Jr. 1936- *WhoAm 92*
Cacciapuoti, Beniamino 1929- *WhoScE 91-3*
Cacciatore, Ronald Keith 1937- *WhoSSW 93*
Cacciatore, S. Sammy, Jr. 1942- *WhoAm 92*
Cacciavillan, Agostino 1926- *WhoAm 92, WhoWor 93*
Caccini, Francesca 1587-c. 1626 *OxDcOp*
Caccini, Francesca 1587-c. 1640 *Baker 92, BioIn 17*
Caccini, Giulio c. 1550-1618 *IntDcOp*
Caccini, Giulio 1551-1610 *OxDcOp*
Caccini, Giulio 1551-1618 *Baker 92*
Caccini, Settimia 1591-1638 *OxDcOp*
Cacciolfi, William Peter, Jr. 1960- *WhoEmL 93*
Cacciotti, Joseph John 1930- *St&PR 93*
Caccuro, John A. *Law&B 92*
Caceres, Cesar A. 1927- *HispAmA*
Caceres, Eduardo Jorge 1943- *WhoWor 93*
Cachan, Manuel 1942- *WhoSSW 93*
Cachao 1918?- *BioIn 17*
Cachera, Jean-Paul 1930- *WhoScE 91-2*
Cacheris, James C. 1933- *WhoAm 92*
Cacheris, Plato 1929- *WhoWor 93*
Cachia, Pierre Jacques 1921- *WhoAm 92, WhoWrEP 92*
Cachin, Marcel 1869-1958 *BioIn 17*
Cacho, Wilka V. *Law&B 92*
Cacioppo, George (Emanuel) 1927-1984 *Baker 92*
Cacioppo, John Terrance 1951- *WhoAm 92*
Cacioppo, Joseph Michael 1951- *St&PR 93*
Cacioppo, Lisa Jane 1960- *WhoEmL 93*
Cackener, Helen Elizabeth Lewis 1926- *WhoWrEP 92*
Cacopardo, Marco 1969- *BioIn 17*
Cacouris, Elias Michael 1929- *WhoWor 93*
Cacoyannis, Michael 1922- *MiSFD 9, WhoWor 93*
Cada, Dorothy Ann 1942- *WhoAmW 93*
Cada, Gregory A. *Law&B 92*
Cadafalch, Joseph Puig i 1869?-1957? *BioIn 17*
Cadag, Christina Tejero 1956- *WhoWor 93*
Cadagan, Dan John, III 1949- *WhoEmL 93*
Cadahia, Jose Ramon 1925- *WhoScE 91-3*
Cadamosto, Alvise da 1432-1488 *Expl 93*
Cadaval, Olivia 1943- *NotHsAW 93*
Cadbury, William Edward 1909-1992 *BioIn 17*
Cadbury, William Edward, Jr. d1992 *NewYTBS 92*
Caddel, Linda Blake 1953- *WhoAmW 93*
Caddel, Richard (Ivo) 1949- *ConAu 137*
Caddell, Debbie Eileen 1957 *WhoEmL 93*
Caddell, Foster 1921- *WhoE 93, WhoWor 93*
Caddell, John A. 1910- *WhoAm 92*
Caddell, John A. 1930- *St&PR 93*
Caddell, Michael Jon *Law&B 92*
Caddell, Patrick *BioIn 17*
Caddell, Patrick H. *NewYTBS 92 [port]*
Cadden, Thomas W. 1933- *St&PR 93*
Cadden, Vivian Liebman 1917- *WhoAm 92*
Caddy, (Michael) Douglas 1938- *ConAu 136*
Caddy, Edmund Harrington Homer, Jr. 1928- *WhoAm 92*
Caddy, Michael Douglas 1938- *WhoWor 93*
Cade, Edwin Paul 1965- *WhoSSW 93*
Cade, Frances Renee 1946- *WhoE 93, WhoEmL 93*
Cade, Henry *BioIn 17*
Cade, Jack Carlton 1948- *WhoWor 93*

Cade, John A. 1929- *WhoE 93*
Cadek, Josef 1925- *WhoScE 91-4*
Cadell, Thomas 1742-1802 *BioIn 17*
Cadena, Alvaro 1943- *St&PR 93*
Cadena, Jose S. *Law&B 92*
Cadenasso, Giuseppe 1858?-1918 *BioIn 17*
Cadenhead, Alfred Paul 1926- *WhoAm 92*
Cadenhead, Ben C. *Law&B 92*
Cadenhead, Randall J. *Law&B 92*
Cades, Julius Russell 1904- *WhoAm 92*
Cades, Stewart Russell 1942- *WhoAm 92*
Cadge, William Fleming 1924- *WhoAm 92*
Cadgene, George H. 1919- *St&PR 93*
Cadick, John 1945- *WhoSSW 93*
Cadieux, Marcel J.L.R. 1939- *WhoUN 92*
Cadieux, Pauline *WhoCanL 92*
Cadieux, Pierre H. 1948- *WhoAm 92, WhoE 93*
Cadieux, Robert D. 1937- *St&PR 93*
Cadieux, Roger Joseph 1945- *WhoAm 92*
Cadigan, Pat 1953- *ScF&FL 92*
Cadigan, Patrick Finbar 1935- *St&PR 93*
Cadigan, Patrick Joseph 1936- *WhoAm 92*
Cadigan, Richard Foster 1930- *WhoE 93*
Cadiot, Paul 1923- *WhoScE 91-2*
Cadish, Robert D. *Law&B 92*
Cadle, Nancy Massey 1953- *WhoEmL 93*
Cadle, Steven Howard 1946- *WhoEmL 93*
Cadman, Alan Glyndwr 1937- *WhoAsAP 91*
Cadman, Charles Wakefield 1881-1946 *Baker 92, OxDcOp*
Cadman, Theodore Wesley 1940- *WhoAm 92, WhoE 93*
Cadman, Thomas Lee 1947- *St&PR 93*
Cadman, William L. 1950- *St&PR 93*
Cadman, Wilson K. 1927- *St&PR 93*
Cadman, Wilson Kennedy 1927- *WhoAm 92*
Cadmus, Paul 1904- *WhoAm 92*
Cadmus, Robert B. 1933- *St&PR 93*
Cadnum, Michael 1949- *ScF&FL 92*
Cadogan, John 1930- *WhoScE 91-1*
Cadogan, William J. 1948- *St&PR 93*
Cadoria, Sherian G. *BioIn 17*
Cadoria, Sherian Grace 1940- *AfrAmBi*
Cadorna, Luigi 1850-1928 *HarEnMi*
Cadorna, Raffaele 1815-1897 *HarEnMi*
Cadorniga Carro, Rafael 1927- *WhoScE 91-3*
Cadou, Peter Brosius 1931- *St&PR 93*
Cadow, William Schuyler, Jr. 1936- *WhoE 93*
Cadra, Michael Edward 1953- *WhoEmL 93*
Cadranel, Samy 1939- *WhoWor 93*
Cadrecha, Charles William 1928- *St&PR 93*
Caduff, Sylvia 1937- *Baker 92*
Cadwallader, A.H., III 1928- *St&PR 93*
Cadwallader, Brian James *Law&B 92*
Cadwallader, Chester Samuel, Jr. 1920- *WhoSSW 93*
Cadwell, Carlton Morgan 1944- *St&PR 93*
Cadwell, Floralyn *AmWomPl*
Cadwell, Franchellie Margaret 1937- *WhoAm 92, WhoAmW 93*
Cadwell, Jeffery James 1956- *WhoEmL 93*
Cady, Diane 1955- *St&PR 93*
Cady, Edwin Harrison 1917- *BioIn 17, WhoAm 92, WhoWor 93*
Cady, Elwyn Loomis, Jr. 1926- *WhoWor 93*
Cady, George Hamilton 1906- *WhoAm 92*
Cady, George Leonard, Jr. 1950- *WhoEmL 93*
Cady, Howard 1914-1990 *BioIn 17*
Cady, Jack 1932- *ScF&FL 92, WhoWrEP 92*
Cady, John Lodge 1922- *WhoAm 92*
Cady, John Ramsden 1930- *WhoAm 92*
Cady, Lyle Edward, Jr. 1950- *WhoEmL 93*
Cady, Ruthie 1984-1991 *BioIn 17*
Cady, Verena 1984-1991 *BioIn 17*
Cady, Walter Guyton 1874-1974 *BioIn 17*
Cadzow, James Archie 1936- *WhoAm 92*
Caecina, Aulus c. 90BC-40BC *HarEnMi*
Caeiro, Alberto 1888-1935 *BioIn 17*
Caen, Herb 1916- *JrnUS, WhoAm 92*
Caen, Jacques Philippe 1927- *WhoScE 91-2*
Caenepeel, Stefaan 1956- *WhoWor 93*
Caepio, Quintus Servilius c. 149BC-100BC *HarEnMi*
Caesar, Gaius Julius 100BC-44BC *HarEnMi*
Caesar, Henry A., II 1914- *WhoAm 92*
Caesar, Julius 100BC-44BC *BioIn 17*
Caesar, Knud 1925- *WhoScE 91-3*
Caesar, Neil Benjamin 1957- *WhoEmL 93*
Caesar, Patricia Louise 1946- *WhoE 93*
Caesar, Rolf Julius Erich 1944- *WhoWor 93*
Caesar, Shirley *BioIn 17*
Caesar, Shirley 1938- *WhoAmW 93*
Caesar, Sid 1922- *QDrFCA 92 [port], WhoAm 92*
Caesar, Vance Roy 1944- *WhoAm 92*
Caetano, Marcello Jose das Neves Alves 1904-1981 *DcTwHis*
Cafarchio, Louis Michael 1931- *St&PR 93*
Cafarella, Robert A. 1925- *St&PR 93*
Cafaro, Kim Michele *Law&B 92*
Cafaro, Pasquale 1716-1787 *Baker 92, OxDcOp*
Caffall, Joseph Edward *WhoScE 91-1*
Caffarel, Randal Cyril 1948- *WhoEmL 93, WhoSSW 93*
Caffarelli 1710-1783 *Baker 92, IntDcOp, OxDcOp*
Caffarelli, Joseph J. 1945- *St&PR 93*
Caffarelli, Luis Angel 1948- *WhoAm 92*
Caffaro *OxDcByz*
Caffaro, Pasquale 1716-1787 *Baker 92*
Caffarone, Douglas Peter 1946- *St&PR 93, WhoEmL 93*
Caffee, Lorren Dale 1947- *WhoEmL 93*
Caffee, Marcus Pat 1948- *WhoEmL 93, WhoSSW 93*
Cafferata, Patricia Ann 1944- *WhoAm 92, WhoAmW 93*
Cafferata, Roxane 1955- *WhoWrEP 92*
Cafferty, Pastora San Juan 1940- *HispAmA*
Caffey, Horace Rouse 1929- *WhoAm 92*
Caffey, M. Douglas 1939- *St&PR 93*
Caffey, Michael *MiSFD 9*
Caffey, Rick 1956- *WhoSSW 93*
Caffi, Francesco 1778-1874 *Baker 92*
Caffin, Caroline *AmWomPl*
Caffin, Louise Anne 1943- *WhoE 93*
Caffin, Roger Neil 1945- *WhoWor 93*
Caffrey, Andrew Augustine 1920- *WhoAm 92, WhoE 93*
Caffrey, Francis David 1927- *St&PR 93, WhoAm 92*
Caffrey, James Edward *Law&B 92*
Caffrey, Ronald J. *BioIn 17*
Caffrey, Stephen *BioIn 17*
Caffry, John William 1928- *St&PR 93*
Cafiero, Albert F. 1922- *WhoE 93*
Cafiero, Eugene A. *St&PR 93*
Cafiero, Eugene Anthony 1926- *WhoAm 92*
Cafiero, Tom A. 1946- *St&PR 93*
Cafini, Regenia Dayree 1962- *WhoAmW 93*
Caflisch, Jacob Crawford, Sr. 1938- *WhoSSW 93*
Caflisch, Lucius Conrad 1936- *WhoWor 93*
Cafritz, Conrad *BioIn 17*
Cafritz, Peggie Cooper *BioIn 17*
Cafritz, Peggy Cooper 1947- *WhoAm 92, WhoEmL 93, WhoWor 93*
Cagan, Carol Platt *Law&B 92*
Cagan, Penny 1958- *WhoAmW 93*
Cagan, Richard Dennis 1951- *WhoSSW 93*
Cagan, Robert H. 1938- *WhoAm 92*
Cagan, Stephen M(ichael) 1943- *ConAu 139*
Cage, Chris B. *Law&B 92*
Cage, Gary Wayne 1944- *St&PR 93*
Cage, John *BioIn 17*
Cage, John 1912- *WhoAm 92*
Cage, John 1912-1992 *ConMus 8 [port], NewYTBS 92 [port], News 93-1*
Cage, John (Milton, Jr.) 1912- *Baker 92*
Cage, John (Milton, Jr.) 1912-1992 *CurBio 92N*
Cage, Leo Spaulding 1934- *St&PR 93*
Cage, Nicholas 1965- *WhoAm 92*
Cage, Nicolas *BioIn 17*
Cagelli, Luisa 1960- *WhoScE 91-3*
Cagenello, Donald 1930- *St&PR 93*
Caggia, Alfred R. 1931- *St&PR 93*
Caggiano, Carl 1918- *St&PR 93*
Caggiano, Joseph 1925- *WhoAm 92*
Caggiano, Michael V. 1936- *St&PR 93*
Caggins, Ruth Porter 1945- *WhoAmW 93*
Caginalp, Gunduz 1952- *WhoEmL 93*
Caginalp, Oguz A. *Law&B 92*
Cagle, Gerald D. 1944- *St&PR 93*
Cagle, Joni *WhoWrEP 92*
Cagle, Pamela Hall 1957- *WhoAmW 93*
Cagle, Wesley Jackson 1930- *St&PR 93*
Cagle, William David 1954- *WhoEmL 93*
Cagle, William Howard, Jr. 1943- *St&PR 93*
Cagle, William Rea 1933- *WhoAm 92*
Caglione, Alexander d1992 *NewYTBS 92*
Cagney, James 1899-1986 *BioIn 17, IntDcF 2-3 [port]*
Cagney, Nanette Heath 1957- *WhoEmL 93*
Cagney, Richard Blane, Jr. *Law&B 92*
Cagney, William Robert 1937- *WhoE 93*
Cagnoli, Sherry A. 1949- *St&PR 93*
Cagnoni, Antonio 1828-1896 *Baker 92, OxDcOp*
Cahal, Mac Fullerton 1907- *WhoAm 92*
Cahalane, Thomas P. *BioIn 17*
Cahan, Abraham 1860-1951 *GayN, JeAmFiW, JeAmHC, JrnUS*
Cahan, Bruce Brian 1954- *WhoEmL 93*
Cahan, Bruce I. 1949- *WhoEmL 93*
Cahan, Cora *BioIn 17*
Cahan, Emily Davis 1956- *WhoAmW 93*
Cahan, Jerry R. *Law&B 92*
Cahan, Judith E. 1951- *WhoEmL 93*
Cahan, Leslie Daryll 1946- *WhoEmL 93*
Cahan, William G. 1914- *ConAu 139*
Cahan, William George 1914- *BioIn 17, WhoAm 92*
Cahen, D. *WhoScE 91-2*
Cahen, Pierre-Michel 1936- *WhoScE 91-2*
Cahier, Charles, Mme. 1870-1951 *Baker 92*
Cahill, Barton Joseph 1961- *WhoEmL 93*
Cahill, Calvin David 1956- *St&PR 93*
Cahill, Charles L. 1933- *WhoAm 92*
Cahill, Clyde S. 1923- *WhoAm 92*
Cahill, David M. 1951- *WhoSSW 93*
Cahill, Donald R. *WhoIns 93*
Cahill, Donald R. 1930- *St&PR 93*
Cahill, Edward Eugene 1931- *WhoAm 92*
Cahill, Edward R., Jr. 1937- *St&PR 93*
Cahill, Elizabeth M. d1991 *BioIn 17*
Cahill, George Francis, Jr. 1927- *WhoAm 92*
Cahill, Harry Amory 1930- *WhoAm 92*
Cahill, J. Michael 1945- *St&PR 93*
Cahill, Jack Lauren 1949- *WhoAm 92*
Cahill, James Francis 1926- *WhoAm 92*
Cahill, John C. *WhoAm 92*
Cahill, John Edward 1939- *St&PR 93*
Cahill, John G. 1957- *St&PR 93*
Cahill, John J. 1932- *St&PR 93*
Cahill, John Michael 1947- *WhoEmL 93*
Cahill, Kevin E. 1955- *St&PR 93*
Cahill, Kevin Michael 1936- *ConAu 40NR*
Cahill, Laurence James, Jr. 1924- *WhoAm 92*
Cahill, Lisa Shaffer 1959- *WhoAmW 93*
Cahill, Mary Patricia *Law&B 92*
Cahill, Michael B. 1953- *St&PR 93*
Cahill, Michael Edward 1951- *WhoEmL 93*
Cahill, Michael John 1961- *St&PR 93*
Cahill, Pamela Lee 1953- *WhoAmW 93*
Cahill, Patricia Deal 1947- *WhoAmW 93*
Cahill, Philip L. 1938- *St&PR 93*
Cahill, Richard E. 1943- *St&PR 93*
Cahill, Richard Frederick 1953- *WhoWor 93*
Cahill, Richard M. *Law&B 92*
Cahill, Richard M. 1939- *St&PR 93*
Cahill, Richard Morton 1957- *WhoEmL 93*
Cahill, Robert A. *Law&B 92*
Cahill, Robert H. 1943- *St&PR 93*
Cahill, Thomas Andrew 1937- *WhoAm 92*
Cahill, Thomas Brendan *Law&B 92*
Cahill, Thomas E. 1935- *St&PR 93*
Cahill, Thomas Edward 1935- *WhoAm 92*
Cahill, Thomas J. 1935- *WhoIns 93*
Cahill, Tim *BioIn 17*
Cahill, Tom d1992 *NewYTBS 92*
Cahill, William J., Jr. *Law&B 92*
Cahill, William J., Jr. 1923- *St&PR 93*
Cahill, William Joseph, Jr. 1923- *WhoAm 92*
Cahill, William Walsh, Jr. 1927- *WhoAm 92*
Cahir, John Joseph 1933- *WhoAm 92*
Cahir, Joseph M. 1956- *St&PR 93*
Cahlan, John F. *Law&B 92*
Cahlan, John Forest 1957- *WhoEmL 93*
Cahn, Abry S. 1930- *St&PR 93*
Cahn, David Stephen 1940- *St&PR 93, WhoAm 92*
Cahn, Edward N. 1933- *WhoAm 92, WhoE 93*
Cahn, Glenn Evan 1953- *WhoE 93*
Cahn, Harold A. 1916- *St&PR 93*
Cahn, Jean Camper 1935-1991 *BioIn 17*
Cahn, Jeffrey Barton 1943- *WhoAm 92*
Cahn, John Werner 1928- *WhoAm 92*
Cahn, Joshua Binion 1915- *WhoAm 92*
Cahn, Julius Norman 1922- *WhoAm 92*
Cahn, Michael Donald *Law&B 92*
Cahn, Miles *BioIn 17*
Cahn, Sammy *BioIn 17*
Cahn, Sammy 1913- *Baker 92, WhoAm 92*
Cahn, Stanley Eric Ollendorff 1939- *WhoE 93*
Cahn, Steven M. 1942- *WhoAm 92*
Cahners, Dawn 1962- *WhoE 93*
Cahners, Norman L. 1914-1986 *BioIn 17*
Cahones, Carolyn *WhoWrEP 92*
Cahoon, D.B. 1933- *St&PR 93*
Cahoon, Herbert Thomas Fuller 1918- *WhoE 93*
Cahoon, James Preston 1926- *St&PR 93*
Cahoon, Jean Mitchell 1959- *WhoEmL 93*
Cahoon, Richard Stuart 1954- *WhoE 93, WhoEmL 93*
Cahouet, Frank Vondell 1932- *St&PR 93, WhoAm 92*
Cai, Haitao 1934- *WhoWor 93*
Caiazza, Philip J. 1936- *St&PR 93*
Caiazza, Ronald A. *Law&B 92*
Caiazza, Stephen S. d1990 *BioIn 17*
Caiazzo, Frank Louis 1929- *St&PR 93*
Caicedo, Andres 1951-1976 *SpAmA*
Caicedo, Harry 1928- *HispAmA [port]*
Caicedo, Juana Esther 1949- *WhoAm 92, WhoE 93*
Cai Cheng 1927- *WhoAsAP 91*
Caidin, Martin 1927- *ScF&FL 92*
Cai Jinqing *BioIn 17*
Caillaux, Denis Joseph-Marie 1950- *WhoUN 92*
Caillaux, Henriette *BioIn 17*
Caillaux, Joseph 1863-1944 *BioIn 17, DcTwHis*
Caillavet, Gaston Arman de 1869-1915 *BioIn 17*
Caille, Alain 1945- *WhoAm 92*
Caille, Andre 1943- *St&PR 93, WhoAm 92*
Caillere, Louis 1940- *WhoScE 91-2*
Caillet, David Anthony 1952- *WhoEmL 93*
Caillet, Marcel 1937- *WhoScE 91-2*
Cailletaud, Georges 1953- *WhoScE 91-2*
Caillie, Rene 1799-1838 *Expl 93 [port]*
Cailliet, Lucien 1891-1985 *Baker 92*
Cailliez, Francis *WhoScE 91-2*
Caillois, Roger 1913-1978 *ScF&FL 92*
Caillouette, James Clyde 1927- *WhoAm 92*
Caimi, August W. *Law&B 92*
Cain *BioIn 17*
Cain, Albert Clifford 1933- *WhoAm 92*
Cain, April A. 1956- *St&PR 93*
Cain, Arthur James *WhoScE 91-1*
Cain, Beatrice Naff 1957- *WhoSSW 93*
Cain, Bob 1924- *BioIn 17*
Cain, Burton Edward 1942- *WhoE 93, WhoWor 93*
Cain, Byron W. 1918- *St&PR 93*
Cain, Charles Alan 1943- *WhoAm 92*
Cain, Christine Lee 1948- *St&PR 93*
Cain, Christopher 1943- *MiSFD 9*
Cain, Clifford Chalmers 1950- *WhoEmL 93*
Cain, Craig J. 1923- *St&PR 93*
Cain, Curtis Alan 1958- *WhoSSW 93*
Cain, Darrell Ward 1956- *WhoSSW 93*
Cain, David Lee 1941- *WhoE 93*
Cain, David M. *Law&B 92*
Cain, David P. 1945- *St&PR 93*
Cain, Donald Ames 1928- *WhoSSW 93*
Cain, Donald Ezell 1921- *WhoAm 92*
Cain, Douglas Mylchreest 1938- *WhoAm 92*
Cain, Edmund J. 1945- *WhoUN 92*
Cain, Edmund Joseph 1918- *WhoAm 92*
Cain, Elise Gasque 1920- *WhoSSW 93*
Cain, Esta L. *Law&B 92*
Cain, Felicia Tope 1957- *WhoEmL 93*
Cain, Gary M. 1943- *WhoIns 93*
Cain, George 1930- *St&PR 93*
Cain, George Harvey 1920- *WhoAm 92*
Cain, Gerry Dyke 1952- *WhoE 93*
Cain, Gloria C. 1950- *WhoEmL 93*
Cain, Gordon A. 1912- *St&PR 93*
Cain, Gordon R. *Law&B 92*
Cain, Herman *BioIn 17*
Cain, Herman Wilton 1922- *WhoSSW 93*
Cain, Howard M. 1926- *St&PR 93*
Cain, James Allan 1935- *WhoAm 92*
Cain, James C. d1992 *NewYTBS 92*
Cain, James C. 1913-1992 *BioIn 17*
Cain, James M. 1892-1977 *BioIn 17, MagSAmL [port]*
Cain, James Marshall 1933- *St&PR 93, WhoSSW 93*
Cain, James Nelson 1930- *WhoAm 92*
Cain, Joan Terese 1929- *WhoAmW 93*
Cain, John 1931- *WhoAsAP 91*
Cain, Joseph T. *Law&B 92*
Cain, Kenny *SoulM*
Cain, Laurel Stephanie 1960- *WhoAmW 93*
Cain, Laverne Wallace 1937- *St&PR 93*
Cain, Leo Francis 1909- *WhoAm 92*
Cain, Madeline Ann 1949- *WhoAmW 93*
Cain, Margaret 1946- *WhoIns 93*
Cain, Margaret O'Leary 1946- *St&PR 93*
Cain, Maurice Edward 1934- *WhoScE 91-1*
Cain, Michael Morrison 1949- *WhoEmL 93*
Cain, Michelle Marie 1958- *WhoAmW 93*
Cain, Nancy Lynne 1951- *WhoAmW 93*
Cain, Patricia Jean 1931- *WhoAmW 93, WhoWor 93*
Cain, Patrick J. *Law&B 92*
Cain, Paul W. 1939- *St&PR 93*
Cain, R. Wayne 1937- *St&PR 93*
Cain, Randy 1945- *See* Delfonics *SoulM*
Cain, Raymond Frederick 1937- *WhoAm 92*
Cain, Richard Edward 1939- *WhoWrEP 92*
Cain, Richard Harvey 1825-1887 *BioIn 17, EncAACR*
Cain, Rita M. *Law&B 92*
Cain, Robert *ScF&FL 92*

Cain, Robert Gaynor 1951- WhoEmL 93
Cain, Stanley Robert 1954- WhoEmL 93
Cain, Thomas A. 1930- St&PR 93
Cain, Tim J. 1958- WhoEmL 93
Cain, Victor Ralph 1934- WhoAm 92
Cain, Walker O. 1915- WhoAm 92
Cain, Walter L. 1929- St&PR 93
Cain, William Stanley 1941- WhoE 93
Caine, Carol Whitacre 1925- WhoWor 93
Caine, Conway N. 1937- St&PR 93
Caine, Franklyn A. 1950- St&PR 93
Caine, Geoffrey ScF&FL 92
Caine, Jeffrey 1944- ScF&FL 92
Caine, Michael 1933?- BioIn 17, IntDcF 2-3 [port], WhoAm 92, WhoWor 93
Caine, Nelson 1939- WhoAm 92
Caine, Peter ScF&FL 92
Caine, R.S. 1929- St&PR 93
Caine, Raymond William 1932- St&PR 93
Caine, Shulamith W. 1930- WhoWrEP 92
Caine, Stanley Paul 1940- WhoAm 92
Caine, Stephen Howard 1941- WhoWor 93
Caine, Tedson Michael WhoSSW 93
Caine, W.P. 1935- St&PR 93
Caines, Eric BioIn 17
Caines, Jeannette Franklin 1938- BlkAuII 92
Cainglet, Wilfredo G. 1928- WhoAsAP 91
Cains, Josephine ScF&FL 92
Caiola, James C. 1933- St&PR 93
Caird, Edward 1835-1908 BioIn 17
Caird, Francis Irvine WhoScE 91-1
Caird, J.B. 1927- St&PR 93
Caird, Janet 1913- ScF&FL 92
Caire, William 1946- WhoEmL 93
Cairncross, Alexander Kirkland 1911- WhoAm 92, WhoWor 93
Cairncross, John BioIn 17
Cairnes, Joseph Francis 1907- WhoAm 92
Cairns, Brian Lee 1939- St&PR 93
Cairns, David (Adam) 1926- Baker 92
Cairns, David Allen 1946- WhoAm 92
Cairns, Donald Fredrick 1924- WhoAm 92
Cairns, Elton James 1932- WhoAm 92
Cairns, H. Alan C. 1930- WhoAm 92
Cairns, Helen Smith 1938- WhoAm 92
Cairns, I.R. Law&B 92
Cairns, Ivan Robert 1946- St&PR 93
Cairns, Jack H. WhoScE 91-1
Cairns, James Allan Law&B 92
Cairns, James Robert 1930- WhoAm 92
Cairns, Jeffrey Peter 1954- WhoEmL 93
Cairns, John, Jr. 1923- WhoAm 92
Cairns, John J. 1927- St&PR 93
Cairns, Kelly Andrew Law&B 92
Cairns, Laura Jane 1961- WhoWrEP 92
Cairns, Laurence Howard 1949- St&PR 93
Cairns, Raymond Eldon, Jr. 1932- WhoAm 92
Cairns, Robert Alan WhoScE 91-1
Cairns, Sara Albertson 1939- WhoAmW 93
Cairns, Scott Clifford 1954- WhoSSW 93
Cairns, Suzan Siekmann 1941- WhoE 93
Cairns, Theodore LeSueur 1914- WhoAm 92
Cairone, David C. 1953- St&PR 93
Cairone, Mathew C. Law&B 92
Cairone, Regina H. 1944- St&PR 93
Caister, Richard L. 1938- St&PR 93
Caithamer, Claire S. 1955- WhoIns 93
Caitone, Arlene Elizabeth 1967- WhoAmW 93
Caix d'Hervelois, Louis de c. 1680-1760 Baker 92
Cai Yuanpei 1868-1940 BioIn 17
Cajal, Nicolae 1919- WhoScE 91-4
Cajal, Santiago Ramon 1852-1934 BioIn 17
Cajati, Roberto 1953- WhoWor 93
Cajes, Eugenio 1577-1642 BioIn 17
Cajigal, Joseph A. 1953- St&PR 93, WhoAm 92, WhoEmL 93, WhoWor 93
Cajko, Jerry 1941- BioIn 17
Cajori, Charles Florian 1921- WhoAm 92
Cakala, Stanislaw 1920- WhoScE 91-4
Cakars, Maris BioIn 17
Cakars, Maris d1992 NewYTBS 92
Cakert, Thomas Francis Xavier, Jr. 1947- WhoEmL 93
Cakir, Ali Fuat 1938- WhoScE 91-4
Cakir, Osman 1955- WhoScE 91-4
Cakmak, Ahmet Sefik 1934- WhoAm 92
Cakmak, Ibrahim Turan 1942- WhoScE 91-4
Cal, Guillermo Luis 1945- WhoWor 93
Calabrese, Arnold Joseph 1960- WhoEmL 93
Calabrese, Brian Paul 1959- WhoE 93
Calabrese, Clement A. 1943- St&PR 93
Calabrese, Diane Marie 1949- WhoAm 92, WhoEmL 93
Calabrese, Michael Raphael 1956- WhoEmL 93
Calabrese, P.J. 1927- St&PR 93
Calabrese, Rosalie Sue 1938- WhoAm 92, WhoE 93
Calabrese, Thomas A. 1950- St&PR 93
Calabresi, Guido 1932- WhoAm 92
Calabria, Alfred David 1947- WhoEmL 93
Calabria, Daniel 1936- St&PR 93
Calabro, Frank C. 1943- St&PR 93
Calabro, Jack Louis 1941- St&PR 93
Calabro, Joseph John, III 1955- WhoE 93
Calabro, Louis 1926- Baker 92
Calabro, Natalie WhoAmW 93
Calabro, Nicholas Anthony 1949- St&PR 93
Calado, Jorge C.G. 1938- WhoScE 91-3
Calafati, Gabriel R. 1932- St&PR 93
Calafati, Gabriel Raffele 1932- WhoAm 92
Calafell, Ramon Clark, Jr. 1949- WhoSSW 93
Calahan, Donald Albert 1935- WhoAm 92
Calam, D.H. 1936- WhoScE 91-1
Calamar, Gloria 1921- WhoAm 92
Calamaras, Louis Basil 1908- WhoWor 93
Calamari, John Daniel 1921- WhoAm 92
Calamari-Righi, Maryellen Law&B 92
Calamaro, Raymond Stuart 1944- WhoAm 92
Calame, Alexandre Emile 1913- WhoAm 92
Calame, Byron Edward 1939- WhoAm 92
Calame, Gene D. Law&B 92
Calame, Tracy Calvin 1923- St&PR 93
Calamitsis, Evangelos Anthony 1933- WhoUN 92
Caland, Elisabeth 1862-1929 Baker 92
Calandra, Claire L. Law&B 92
Calandro, Joseph John, Jr. 1930- St&PR 93
Calano, Barbara Bemis 1947- WhoAmW 93
Calapai, Letterio WhoAm 92
Calarco, Margaret Marie 1956- WhoEmL 93
Calarco, N. Joseph 1938- WhoWor 93
Calarco, Patricia Gillam WhoAm 92
Calarco, Vincent A. 1942- St&PR 93
Calarco, Vincent Anthony 1942- WhoAm 92
Calardo, Nick Anthony 1929- St&PR 93
Calas, Carl-Eric 1924- WhoWor 93
Calas, Georges 1948- WhoScE 91-2
Calatchi, Ralph Franklin 1944- WhoAm 92
Calautti, Thomas F. 1949- St&PR 93
Calavera, Jose 1931- WhoScE 91-3
Calaway, Bill 1929- St&PR 93
Calaway, Dennis Louis 1960- WhoEmL 93, WhoSSW 93, WhoWor 93
Calaway, John BioIn 17
Calaway, John Eric 1957- WhoEmL 93
Calbick, Ian MacKinnon 1938- WhoAm 92
Calbo, Leonard J. 1941- St&PR 93
Calboli, Gualtiero Federico 1932- WhoWor 93
Calbom, Cherie 1947- ConAu 138
Calcagni, Edwin G. 1925- St&PR 93
Calcagni, John 1949- WhoAm 92
Calcagni, Thomas Frank 1953- WhoE 93
Calcagnie, Kevin Frank 1955- WhoEmL 93
Calcagno, Lawrence 1913- WhoAm 92
Calcano, Jose Antonio 1900-1980 Baker 92
Calcaterra, Edward L. 1930- St&PR 93
Calcaterra, Mark P. Law&B 92
Calcott, Karen Dawn 1963- WhoSSW 93
Calda, Pavel 1932- WhoE 93
Caldabaugh, Karl 1946- St&PR 93
Caldamone, Anthony Angelo 1950- WhoE 93
Caldara, Anna Maria 1954- WhoWrEP 92
Caldara, Antonio 1670-1736 Baker 92, OxDcOp
Caldarazzo, Richard Joseph 1948- WhoAm 92
Caldarelli, David Donald 1941- WhoAm 92
Caldas, Jose Zanine 1919- BioIn 17
Caldas, Maria 1956- St&PR 93
Caldas, Waltercio 1946- BioIn 17
Caldas Lima, Jose Manuel 1942- WhoUN 92
Caldecott, Ernest John 1922- St&PR 93
Caldecott, Moyra 1927- ScF&FL 92
Caldecott, Randolph (J.) 1846-1886 MajAI [port]
Caldecott, Richard Stanley 1924- WhoAm 92
Caldeira, Gustavo C.N. 1934- WhoScE 91-3
Caldeira, Paulo da Terra 1944- WhoWor 93
Caldeira-Sarava, Fernando WhoScE 91-1
Caldemeyer, Marjorie Janet 1952- WhoEmL 93
Calder, A. WhoScE 91-1
Calder, Alexander 1916-1991 BioIn 17
Calder, Andrew Alexander 1945- WhoWor 93
Calder, Angus 1942- ConAu 38NR
Calder, Daniel Gillmore 1939- WhoAm 92
Calder, Elizabeth AmWomPl
Calder, Gordon S., Jr. Law&B 92
Calder, Iain Wilson 1939- WhoAm 92
Calder, Jenni 1941- ConAu 38NR, ScF&FL 92
Calder, Jennifer Ann Marie 1960- WhoAmW 93
Calder, John Mackenzie 1927- WhoE 93
Calder, Kenneth Thomas 1918- WhoAm 92
Calder, Kent Eyring 1948- WhoE 93, WhoEmL 93, WhoWor 93
Calder, Nigel 1931- BioIn 17
Calder, Nigel (David Ritchie) 1931- ConAu 38NR
Calder, Robert ScF&FL 92
Calder, Robert 1745-1818 HarEnMi
Calder, Robert Mac 1932- WhoWor 93
Caldera, Donald L. 1935- St&PR 93
Calderaro, Leonard Joseph 1935- St&PR 93, WhoAm 92
Calderazzo, Joey BioIn 17
Calderbank, Ian George 1938- WhoScE 91-1
Calderhead, William Dickson 1919- WhoAm 92
Calderini, John Joseph 1935- St&PR 93
Calder-Marshall, Arthur 1908-1992 ConAu 137
Calderon, Alberto P. 1920- WhoAm 92
Calderon, Cesar, Jr. 1944- St&PR 93
Calderon, Fernando 1809-1845 DcMexL
Calderon, Howard St&PR 93
Calderon, John Paul 1961- WhoEmL 93
Calderon, Nissim 1933- St&PR 93, WhoAm 92
Calderon, Ricardo R. Law&B 92
Calderon, Stephen I. 1951- St&PR 93
Calderon de la Barca, Pedro 1600-1681 DramC 3 [port], MagSWL [port]
Calderone, Marlene Elizabeth 1940- WhoAmW 93
Calderone, Mary Steichen 1904- WhoAm 92, WhoAmW 93, WhoWor 93
Calderonello, Alice ScF&FL 92
Calderon Fournier, Rafael Angel 1949- DcCPCAm, WhoWor 93
Calderon Guardia, Rafael Angel 1900-1970 DcCPCAm
Calderwood, James Albert 1941- WhoWor 93
Calderwood, James Henry WhoScE 91-1
Calderwood, James Lee 1930- WhoAm 92
Calderwood, Stanford Matson 1920- WhoAm 92
Calderwood, William Arthur 1941- WhoWor 93
Caldicott, Alfred James 1842-1897 Baker 92
Caldicott, Helen BioIn 17
Caldiero, Raymond Paul 1935- St&PR 93
Caldin, Edward Francis WhoScE 91-1
Caldini, Maria Pia 1931- WhoAm 92
Caldow, June A. 1928- WhoAmW 93
Caldron, Royce Gene 1947- WhoEmL 93, WhoSSW 93
Caldwell, Alethea Otti 1941- WhoAmW 93
Caldwell, Alfred 1903- BioIn 17
Caldwell, Andrew Adam 1966- WhoWrEP 92
Caldwell, Anne 1867-1936 AmWomPl
Caldwell, Bettye McDonald 1924- WhoAm 92, WhoSSW 93
Caldwell, Billy Ray 1932- WhoSSW 93, WhoWor 93
Caldwell, Carlyle G. 1914- WhoAm 92
Caldwell, Cathryn Lynn 1952- WhoAmW 93
Caldwell, Chase L. 1950- St&PR 93
Caldwell, Clara Jane 1929- WhoAmW 93
Caldwell, Courtney Lynn 1948- WhoAmW 93, WhoEmL 93, WhoWor 93
Caldwell, Craig 1922- St&PR 93
Caldwell, Craig Hoskins 1951- WhoEmL 93
Caldwell, Curtis Irvin 1947- WhoWor 93
Caldwell, Daniel Ralston 1936- WhoAm 92
Caldwell, Dean Stephen 1946- St&PR 93
Caldwell, Delmar Ray 1935- WhoSSW 93
Caldwell, Donald R. 1946- WhoAm 92
Caldwell, Doreen (Mary) 1942- SmATA 71 [port]
Caldwell, E. Gerald 1928- St&PR 93
Caldwell, Eleanor Baird AmWomPl
Caldwell, Elwood Fleming 1923- WhoAm 92
Caldwell, Erskine 1903-1987 BioIn 17, MagSAmL [port]
Caldwell, Excetral K. Law&B 92
Caldwell, Frank B., Jr. 1918- St&PR 93
Caldwell, Garnett Ernest 1934- WhoAm 92
Caldwell, George Bruce 1930- WhoAm 92
Caldwell, Gerald Dee 1942- WhoSSW 93
Caldwell, Gladys 1884-1979 BioIn 17
Caldwell, Glyn Gordon 1934- WhoSSW 93
Caldwell, Grant G. 1942- St&PR 93
Caldwell, H. Allan Law&B 92
Caldwell, H. Allan 1944- St&PR 93
Caldwell, Helen Lee 1908-1991 BioIn 17
Caldwell, Howard Bryant 1944- WhoWor 93
Caldwell, James D. 1928- St&PR 93
Caldwell, James Richard 1929- St&PR 93
Caldwell, James W. 1935- St&PR 93
Caldwell, James Wiley 1923- WhoAm 92
Caldwell, Jean Leonora 1928- WhoAmW 93
Caldwell, Jesse Burgoyne, Jr. 1917- WhoWor 93
Caldwell, Jim M. 1903- St&PR 93
Caldwell, John 1947- WhoWor 93
Caldwell, John Bernard WhoScE 91-1
Caldwell, John David 1937- St&PR 93
Caldwell, John Gilmore 1931- WhoAm 92
Caldwell, John L. Law&B 92
Caldwell, John L. 1940- WhoAm 92
Caldwell, John Thomas, Jr. 1932- WhoAm 92
Caldwell, John Tyler 1911- WhoAm 92
Caldwell, John Warwick 1949- WhoEmL 93
Caldwell, Joni 1948- WhoWor 93
Caldwell, Joyce M. 1944- WhoE 93
Caldwell, Judy Carol 1946- WhoAmW 93, WhoEmL 93, WhoSSW 93
Caldwell, Kathleen J. 1947- WhoSSW 93
Caldwell, Kenneth S. 1957- St&PR 93
Caldwell, L. Scott WhoAmW 93
Caldwell, Lynton Keith 1913- WhoAm 92
Caldwell, Marjorie L. Law&B 92
Caldwell, Mary Alice 1949- WhoEmL 93
Caldwell, Mary Linton Pittard 1948- WhoEmL 93, WhoSSW 93
Caldwell, Mary Peri 1935- WhoAm 92, WhoSSW 93
Caldwell, Michael DeFoix 1943- WhoAm 92
Caldwell, Patricia Frances 1942- WhoAmW 93
Caldwell, Patty Jean Grosskopf 1937- WhoAmW 93
Caldwell, Paula Day 1954- WhoAmW 93
Caldwell, Peter BioIn 17
Caldwell, Philip 1920- St&PR 93, WhoAm 92
Caldwell, Richard Clark 1944- St&PR 93
Caldwell, Robert Joseph 1939- St&PR 93
Caldwell, Robert L. 1933- WhoIns 93
Caldwell, Robert S. 1941- St&PR 93
Caldwell, Roger BioIn 17
Caldwell, Sandra Marie 1959- WhoAmW 93
Caldwell, Sarah 1924- Baker 92, IntDcOp, OxDcOp, WhoAm 92, WhoAmW 93
Caldwell, Steven 1947- ScF&FL 92
Caldwell, Stratton F(ranklin) 1926- ConAu 136
Caldwell, Stratton Franklin 1926- WhoAm 92, WhoWrEP 92
Caldwell, Susan Hanes 1938- WhoAm 92, WhoE 93
Caldwell, Taylor 1900-1985 ScF&FL 92
Caldwell, Thomas Andrew 1949- WhoSSW 93
Caldwell, Thomas Howell, Jr. 1934- WhoSSW 93, WhoWor 93
Caldwell, Walter Edward 1941- WhoWor 93
Caldwell, Warren Frederick 1928- WhoAm 92
Caldwell, Wiley N. 1927- St&PR 93
Caldwell, Wiley North 1927- WhoAm 92
Caldwell, Wilfred G. Law&B 92
Caldwell, Will M. 1925- WhoAm 92
Caldwell, William Mackay, III 1922- WhoAm 92, WhoWor 93
Caldwell, William Wilson 1925- WhoAm 92, WhoE 93
Caldwell, Zoe 1933- ConTFT 10, WhoAmW 93
Caldwell-Colbert, A. Toy 1951- WhoAmW 93
Caldwell-Lee, Laurie Neilson 1947- WhoAmW 93, WhoWor 93
Cale, Charles Griffin 1940- WhoAm 92
Cale, John 1940- Baker 92
Cale, John 1942?- ConMus 9 [port]
Cale, William Graham, Jr. 1947- WhoE 93
Calegari, Antonio 1757-1828 Baker 92, OxDcOp
Calegari, Giuseppe c. 1750-1812 OxDcOp
Calegari, Luigi Antonio c. 1780-1849 OxDcOp
Calegari, Maria BioIn 17
Calegari, Maria 1957- WhoAm 92

Calenberg, Jeff BioIn 17
Calenberg, Laura Krauss BioIn 17
Calenoff, Leonid 1923- WhoAm 92
Calentine, Mary Edith 1952- WhoAmW 93
Caler, Alan Bruce 1956- WhoEmL 93
Calero Portocarrero, Adolfo 1931- DcCPCAm
Calfa, Marian 1946- WhoWor 93
Calfas, William Law&B 92
Calfee, John B., Jr. 1945- St&PR 93
Calfee, John Beverly, Sr. 1913- WhoAm 92
Calfee, Robert Chilton 1933- WhoAm 92
Calfee, William Howard 1909- WhoAm 92
Calfee, William Lewis 1917- WhoAm 92, WhoWor 93
Calfee, William Rushton 1947- WhoAm 92
Calfo, Jason Philemon 1954- WhoE 93
Calgaard, Ronald Keith 1937- WhoAm 92, WhoSSW 93
Calhern, Louis 1895-1956 IntDcF 2-3 [port]
Calhoon, Barry A. 1936- St&PR 93
Calhoon, Donald F. 1951- St&PR 93
Calhoun, Alexander D. 1925- St&PR 93
Calhoun, Blue 1936- ScF&FL 92
Calhoun, Calvin Lee, Sr. 1927- WhoAm 92
Calhoun, Carol Victoria 1953- WhoEmL 93
Calhoun, Charles SoulM
Calhoun, Clayne Marsh 1950- WhoEmL 93
Calhoun, Donald Eugene, Jr. 1926- WhoAm 92
Calhoun, Dorothy Donnell AmWomPl
Calhoun, Ellsworth L. 1928- WhoIns 93
Calhoun, Frank Wayne 1933- WhoAm 92
Calhoun, Fred Lee 1931- St&PR 93
Calhoun, Harold 1906- WhoAm 92
Calhoun, Harry L. 1953- WhoWrEP 92
Calhoun, Henry Clay, III 1932- St&PR 93
Calhoun, Jackie 1936- ConAu 138
Calhoun, James Lawrence 1931- St&PR 93
Calhoun, John Alfred 1939- WhoAm 92, WhoE 93, WhoWor 93
Calhoun, John C. 1782-1850 BioIn 17, PolPar
Calhoun, John C., Jr. 1917- WhoAm 92
Calhoun, John Cozart 1937- WhoAm 92, WhoE 93
Calhoun, John H. Law&B 92
Calhoun, John H. 1941- St&PR 93
Calhoun, John R. Law&B 92
Calhoun, Karen Hall 1952- WhoAmW 93
Calhoun, Kitty BioIn 17
Calhoun, Lawrence Eugene 1939- St&PR 93
Calhoun, Madeleine S. Abler 1961- WhoAmW 93
Calhoun, Martin Lewis 1961- WhoAm 92
Calhoun, Mary Diane Mason 1954- WhoAmW 93, WhoSSW 93
Calhoun, Milburn 1930- WhoSSW 93
Calhoun, Monica Dodd 1953- WhoEmL 93
Calhoun, Nancy P. 1944- WhoAmW 93
Calhoun, Noah Robert 1921- WhoAm 92
Calhoun, Peggy J. 1957- WhoSSW 93
Calhoun, Richard James 1926- WhoAm 92, WhoSSW 93
Calhoun, Robert B. 1928- St&PR 93
Calhoun, Robert Lathan 1937- WhoAm 92
Calhoun, Susan Gayle 1960- WhoAmW 93
Calhoun-Senghor, Keith 1955- WhoE 93, WhoWor 93
Cali, Joseph John 1928- WhoAm 92
Cali, Leonard J. Law&B 92
Cali, Salih 1952- WhoScE 91-4
Cali, Salvatore Joseph 1943- St&PR 93
Calia, Mary Elizabeth 1954- WhoEmL 93
Calia, Vincent Frank 1926- WhoE 93
Caliandro, Gloria Brown 1936- WhoAmW 93
Calicchia, Vincent Francis, Jr. 1968- WhoSSW 93
Calice, Mark Allen 1947- St&PR 93
Caliendo, G.D. 1941- St&PR 93
Caliendo, G.D. (Jerry) Law&B 92
Caliendo, James Gerard 1953- St&PR 93
Calienes, Armando Luis 1940- WhoSSW 93, WhoWor 93
Calif, R.C. 1922- ScF&FL 92
Calif, Ruth BioIn 17
Califano, Joseph A. 1931- BioIn 17
Califano, Joseph Anthony, Jr. 1931- WhoAm 92
Califia, Pat 1954- ScF&FL 92
Caligan, Judith Rebecca 1944- WhoAmW 93
Caligari, Peter Douglas Savaria WhoScE 91-1
Caligiuri, Joseph Frank 1928- St&PR 93, WhoAm 92
Caligula, Emperor of Rome 12-41 BioIn 17
Calille, Albert Law&B 92
Calimani, Riccardo 1946- ConAu 137
Calinescu, Adriana Gabriela 1941- WhoAm 92
Calingaert, Michael 1933- WhoAm 92
Calingasan, Jose E. 1934- WhoAsAP 91
Calinger, Ronald Steve 1942- WhoAm 92
Calio, Anthony John 1929- WhoAm 92
Calio, Nicholas Edmund NewYTBS 92 [port]
Calip, Roger E. 1941- WhoWrEP 92
Caliri, David Joseph 1929- WhoSSW 93
Calis, G.N.M. WhoScE 91-3
Calise, Charles Joseph 1959- WhoSSW 93
Calise, Nicholas J. Law&B 92
Calise, Nicholas James 1941- St&PR 93, WhoAm 92
Calise, Ronald Jan 1948- WhoAm 92
Calisher, Hortense BioIn 17
Calisher, Hortense 1911- AmWomWr 92, JeAmFiW, WhoAm 92, WhoAmW 93, WhoWrEP 92
Calisher, Kathleen Anne 1953- St&PR 93
Caliskan, Ahmet 1940- WhoScE 91-4
Caliskan, Sevda 1955- WhoWor 93
Calitri, Joseph Constant 1924- St&PR 93
Calixto, Sergio Arturo 1950- WhoWor 93
Calkin, Brant BioIn 17
Calkin, John Baptiste 1827-1905 Baker 92
Calkin, Joy Durfee 1938- WhoAm 92
Calkin, Parker Emerson 1933- WhoE 93
Calkins, Benjamin 1956- WhoEmL 93
Calkins, Brenda Lynne 1964- WhoAmW 93
Calkins, Charles C. 1950- St&PR 93
Calkins, David Ross 1948- WhoE 93
Calkins, Evan 1920- WhoAm 92, WhoWor 93
Calkins, Gary Nathan 1911- WhoAm 92
Calkins, Harlan D. 1932- St&PR 93
Calkins, Hugh 1924- WhoAm 92
Calkins, James E. 1951- St&PR 93
Calkins, Jerry Milan 1942- WhoAm 92
Calkins, JoAnn Ruby 1934- WhoAmW 93
Calkins, Judith Moritz 1942- WhoAmW 93
Calkins, Judson Wells Law&B 92
Calkins, Kevin L. 1958- St&PR 93
Calkins, Mark Law&B 92
Calkins, Mary Whiton 1863-1930 BioIn 17
Calkins, Paul R. 1926- St&PR 93
Calkins, Richard Laurin 1944- WhoE 93
Calkins, Rita M. 1931- St&PR 93
Calkins, Robert D. d1992 NewYTBS 92
Calkins, Robert D(e Blois) 1903-1992 CurBio 92N
Calkins, Spencer BioIn 17
Calkins, Stephen 1950- WhoEmL 93
Calkins, Susannah Eby 1924- WhoAm 92
Calkins, Therese Maureen 1955- WhoEmL 93
Call, Barbara Jo 1960- WhoEmL 93
Call, Bernice Anderson AmWomPl
Call, David Lincoln 1932- WhoAm 92
Call, Douglas William 1942- WhoSSW 93
Call, Dwight Vincent 1934- WhoWor 93
Call, Harry M. St&PR 93
Call, Jack Stanley 1949- WhoWrEP 92
Call, Judith K. 1943- WhoAmW 93
Call, Larry A. 1934- St&PR 93
Call, Laval J. 1937- St&PR 93
Call, Lawrence Michael 1942- WhoAm 92
Call, Miles R. 1948- St&PR 93
Call, Neil Judson 1933- WhoAm 92
Call, Osborne Jay 1940- St&PR 93
Call, Osborne Jay 1941- WhoAm 92
Call, Reuel WhoAm 92
Call, Reuel T. 1908- St&PR 93
Call, Richard W. 1924- St&PR 93
Call, Robert W. 1945- St&PR 93
Call, William A. 1938- St&PR 93
Calladine, Christopher Reuben WhoScE 91-1
Callaerts, Joseph 1838-1901 Baker 92
Callagan, Dwight A. 1917- WhoAm 92
Callaghan, Barry 1937- WhoCanL 92
Callaghan, Daniel Judson 1890-1942 HarEnMi
Callaghan, Georgann Mary 1944- WhoAmW 93
Callaghan, J. Clair 1933- WhoAm 92
Callaghan, James 1912- ColdWar 1 [port]
Callaghan, John Edward 1942- WhoWor 93
Callaghan, Leonard James 1912- DcTwHis, WhoWor 93
Callaghan, Lori 1953- St&PR 93
Callaghan, Mary Ellen 1950- WhoEmL 93
Callaghan, Michael Sean 1942- St&PR 93
Callaghan, Morley BioIn 17
Callaghan, Morley 1903-1990 WhoCanL 92
Callaghan, Patrick J. 1951- St&PR 93
Callaghan, Susan J. Law&B 92
Callaghan, Terence Vincent WhoScE 91-1
Callaghan, William Joseph 1959- St&PR 93
Callaghan, William McCombe 1897-1991 BioIn 17
Callaham, Betty Elgin 1929- WhoAm 92, WhoSSW 93
Callaham, Gene 1923?-1990 ConTFT 10
Callaham, Thomas Hunter 1915- WhoAm 92
Callahan, Aileen Loughlin WhoE 93
Callahan, Alfred J. d1992 BioIn 17, NewYTBS 92 [port]
Callahan, Alston 1911- WhoWor 93
Callahan, Bob 1942- ConAu 138
Callahan, Bobbie Yolanda 1949- WhoEmL 93
Callahan, Bradley R. 1953- St&PR 93
Callahan, Bud Edward 1932- St&PR 93
Callahan, Carl G. 1924- St&PR 93
Callahan, Carroll Bernard 1908- WhoAm 92
Callahan, Charles Edmund, Jr. 1951- WhoEmL 93
Callahan, Charles V. 1946- St&PR 93
Callahan, Daniel J., III 1932- St&PR 93
Callahan, Daniel John 1930- WhoAm 92
Callahan, David Michael 1958- WhoE 93
Callahan, Edward William 1930- St&PR 93, WhoAm 92
Callahan, Elias Richard, Jr. 1938- WhoAm 92
Callahan, Frank Thomas, Jr. 1928- St&PR 93
Callahan, Gene d1990 BioIn 17
Callahan, Gerald W. Law&B 92
Callahan, Gerald W. 1936- St&PR 93
Callahan, Gerald William 1936- WhoAm 92
Callahan, H. L. 1932- WhoAm 92, WhoSSW 93
Callahan, Harold Robert 1925- St&PR 93
Callahan, Harry Leslie 1923- WhoAm 92
Callahan, Harry Morey 1912- WhoAm 92, WhoWor 93
Callahan, James E. 1942- St&PR 93
Callahan, James Francis 1954- WhoE 93
Callahan, James Lawrence 1935- St&PR 93
Callahan, Jay ScF&FL 92
Callahan, Joan 1939- WhoE 93
Callahan, John BioIn 17
Callahan, John 1951- NewYTBS 92 [port]
Callahan, John William 1947- WhoEmL 93
Callahan, Joseph Murray WhoAm 92
Callahan, Joseph Patrick 1945- WhoAm 92
Callahan, Kathleen Elisabeth 1957- WhoE 93
Callahan, Linda Jeanne 1951- WhoE 93
Callahan, Mary Reynolds WhoAmW 93
Callahan, Michael J. 1939- WhoAm 92
Callahan, Michael Ray 1961- WhoSSW 93
Callahan, Michael Sean Law&B 92
Callahan, Michael Thomas 1948- WhoEmL 93
Callahan, Nancy K. Law&B 92
Callahan, Norman M., Jr. 1920- St&PR 93
Callahan, Norman Mattock, Jr. 1920- WhoE 93
Callahan, North 1908- WhoAm 92
Callahan, Patrick Michael 1947- WhoEmL 93
Callahan, Paul V. d1990 BioIn 17
Callahan, Peter J. St&PR 93
Callahan, Pia Laaster 1955- WhoAm 92, WhoAmW 93, WhoE 93
Callahan, Ralph W. 1906- St&PR 93
Callahan, Ralph Wilson, Jr. 1942- WhoAm 92
Callahan, Rebecca Lynne 1965- WhoEmL 93
Callahan, Richard Law&B 92
Callahan, Richard Frederick 1952- St&PR 93
Callahan, Richard J. 1941- WhoAm 92
Callahan, Rickey Don 1956- WhoEmL 93, WhoSSW 93
Callahan, Robert F. Law&B 92
Callahan, Robert F., Jr. WhoAm 92, WhoE 93
Callahan, Robert J. 1930- WhoAm 92
Callahan, Robert L. Law&B 92
Callahan, Robert L. 1928- St&PR 93
Callahan, Robert L., Jr. 1932- WhoAm 92
Callahan, Robert Lee 1932- St&PR 93
Callahan, Ronald E. 1926- WhoAm 92
Callahan, Shannon M. 1956- WhoAmW 93
Callahan, Shirley Elizabeth 1930- WhoSSW 93
Callahan, Sonny 1932- CngDr 91
Callahan, Stephen Vincent 1950- WhoEmL 93
Callahan, Thomas Dennis 1952- WhoIns 93
Callahan, William Edward 1918- St&PR 93
Callahan, William F., III 1941- St&PR 93
Callan, Byron King d1992 NewYTBS 92
Callan, Byron King 1914-1992 BioIn 17
Callan, Clair Marie 1940- WhoAmW 93
Callan, Dianne Law&B 92
Callan, Edwin Joseph 1922- WhoSSW 93
Callan, Elizabeth Koda- BioIn 17
Callan, Harold Garnet WhoScE 91-1
Callan, J. Michael Law&B 92
Callan, James Michael 1944- St&PR 93
Callan, James Ruskin 1932- WhoE 93
Callan, Jill M. Law&B 92
Callan, John Garling 1946- WhoWor 93
Callan, Joseph Patrick 1944- WhoSSW 93
Callan, Melinda Ann 1954- WhoAmW 93
Callan, Robert E. 1955- St&PR 93
Callan, Robert Edward Law&B 92
Callan, Stephen S. St&PR 93
Callan, Terrence A. 1939- WhoAm 92
Callan, Thomas M. Law&B 92
Callanan, Anne McGuire 1958- WhoEmL 93
Callanan, Carol Lynn 1961- WhoEmL 93
Callanan, Catherine Frances 1952- WhoAmW 93
Callanan, Gerard Joseph Law&B 92
Callanan, Joseph Alfred 1920- WhoWrEP 92
Callanan, Kathleen Joan 1940- WhoAmW 93, WhoWor 93
Callanan, Thomas B. 1953- St&PR 93
Calland, Diana Baker 1935- WhoAm 92
Callander, Bruce Douglas 1923- WhoAm 92
Callander, Kay Eileen Paisley 1938- WhoAmW 93, WhoWor 93
Callander, Robert John 1931- WhoAm 92
Callant, Marcel Alphonse 1919- WhoAm 92
Callard, Carole Crawford 1941- WhoAmW 93
Callard, David Jacobus 1938- St&PR 93, WhoAm 92
Callas, Darcy G. Law&B 92
Callas, John Alexander 1953- WhoE 93
Callas, John Peter 1950- WhoEmL 93
Callas, Maria 1923-1977 Baker 92, BioIn 17, IntDcOp [port], OxDcOp
Callaway, Ben Anderson 1927- WhoAm 92
Callaway, C. Wayne 1941- ConAu 138
Callaway, Clifford Wayne 1941- WhoAm 92
Callaway, David Henry 1912- St&PR 93
Callaway, David Henry, Jr. 1912- WhoAm 92
Callaway, Douglas Darrell Law&B 92
Callaway, Ely BioIn 17
Callaway, Emilie H. AmWomPl
Callaway, Howard Hollis 1927- WhoAm 92
Callaway, Jack BioIn 17
Callaway, James T. 1937-1990 BioIn 17
Callaway, Jasper Lamar 1911- WhoAm 92
Callaway, Karen Alice 1946- WhoAm 92
Callaway, Kathy Jean 1943- WhoWrEP 92
Callaway, Kenneth Hodges 1955- WhoEmL 93
Callaway, Llewellyn L., Jr. d1992 NewYTBS 92
Callaway, Lois Jean Cunningham 1930- WhoAmW 93
Callaway, Paul (Smith) 1909- Baker 92
Callaway, Reeves BioIn 17
Callaway, Richard Charles, III 1956- WhoSSW 93
Callaway, Thomas BioIn 17
Callaway, William H. 1925- St&PR 93
Callbeck, Catherine 1939- WhoAmW 93
Callcott, John Wall 1766-1821 Baker 92
Calle, Carlos I. 1945- WhoSSW 93
Calle, Craig R.L. 1959- St&PR 93, WhoAm 92
Calle, I.K. Law&B 92
Calle, Robert M. 1920- WhoScE 91-2
Callea, Donna L. 1930- St&PR 93
Callebaut, F.A.I. 1949- WhoScE 91-2
Callebaut, Piwnica Carole 1958- WhoWor 93
Calleja, Edwin 1939- WhoWor 93
Calleja, Gomez Rafael 1874-1938 Baker 92
Calleja, John M. 1931- WhoWor 93
Calleja, Jose Manuel 1948- WhoWor 93
Calleja Del Rey, Felix Maria 1759-1828 HarEnMi
Callejas, Rafael Leonardo WhoWor 93
Callejas, Rafael Leonardo 1943- DcCPCAm
Callen, Casper R. d1991 BioIn 17
Callen, Claire 1956- St&PR 93
Callen, Craig Randall 1950- WhoEmL 93
Callen, David H. 1952- St&PR 93
Callen, Elizabeth A. Law&B 92
Callen, Gillian 1951- WhoEmL 93
Callen, Herbert Bernard 1919- WhoAm 92
Callen, James Donald 1941- WhoAm 92

Callen, Jeffrey Phillip 1947- *WhoAm 92*
Callen, John Holmes, Jr. 1932- *St&PR 93, WhoAm 92*
Callen, Michael (Lane) 1955- *ConAu 139*
Callen, Robinson 1925- *St&PR 93*
Callen, Tarquin 1958- *St&PR 93*
Callenbach, Ernest 1929- *ScF&FL 92, WhoAm 92, WhoWrEP 92*
Callenbach, Georg Frans 1933- *WhoWor 93*
Callender, Calvin Duane *Law&B 92*
Callender, Charles Victor 1931- *WhoUN 92*
Callender, Clive O. 1936- *ConBlB 3 [port]*
Callender, Clive Orville 1936- *WhoAm 92, WhoWor 93*
Callender, George 1916- *ConAu 136*
Callender, George Sylvester d1992 *NewYTBS 92*
Callender, James Thomson 1758-1803 *BioIn 17*
Callender, John Francis 1944- *WhoSSW 93*
Callender, John Hancock 1908- *WhoAm 92*
Callender, Norma Anne 1933- *WhoAmW 93, WhoSSW 93, WhoWor 93*
Callender, Red *ConAu 136*
Callender, Red 1916-1992 *BioIn 17*
Callender, Romaine *AmWomPl*
Callender, Rosheen 1948- *WhoWor 93*
Callender, William L. 1933- *St&PR 93*
Callender, William Lacey 1933- *WhoAm 92*
Calles, Plutarcho Elias 1877-1945 *DcTwHis*
Calles, Plutarco Elias 1877-1945 *BioIn 17, DcCPCAm*
Callesen, Ole 1948- *WhoScE 91-2*
Calleton, Theodore Edward 1934- *WhoAm 92*
Calleux, Philippe *BioIn 17*
Callewaert, Denis Marc 1947- *WhoAm 92*
Calliauw, L.J.E. 1928- *WhoScE 91-2*
Callicratidas d406BC *HarEnMi*
Callier, Frank Maria 1942- *WhoScE 91-2*
Callieri, Juan Carlos 1943- *WhoE 93*
Callies, David Lee 1943- *WhoAm 92*
Calligan, William Dennis 1925- *WhoAm 92*
Calligaris, Sergio 1941- *Baker 92*
Callihan, C. Michael 1947- *WhoAm 92, WhoWor 93*
Callihan, Clayton Arthur 1954- *WhoEmL 93*
Callihan, James Marion 1925- *St&PR 93*
Callil, Carmen *BioIn 17*
Callim, Acacio Pontes 1960- *WhoWor 93*
Callimachus d490BC *HarEnMi*
Callin, Grant 1941- *ScF&FL 92*
Callin, Lura Warner *AmWomPl*
Callinet, Claude-Ignace *Baker 92*
Callinet, Francois 1754-1820 *Baker 92*
Callinet, Joseph *Baker 92*
Callinet, Louis 1786-1845 *Baker 92*
Callinet, Louis-Francois *Baker 92*
Calliott, William F. 1944- *St&PR 93*
Callis, Bruce *WhoIns 93*
Callis, Bruce 1939- *St&PR 93, WhoAm 92*
Callis, Clayton Fowler 1923- *WhoAm 92*
Callis, Jerry Jackson 1926- *WhoAm 92*
Callis, Robert *BioIn 17*
Callis, T. Keith 1953- *WhoSSW 93*
Callis, Victoria D. 1953- *WhoWrEP 92*
Callison, Charles Hugh 1913- *WhoAm 92*
Callison, Charles Stuart 1939- *WhoE 93*
Callison, James W. 1928- *St&PR 93, WhoAm 92*
Callison, James William 1955- *WhoEmL 93*
Callison, John Wesley 1939- *BiDAMSp 1989*
Callison, Miriam Anderson 1943- *WhoAmW 93*
Callison, Russell James 1954- *WhoEmL 93*
Callison, Scott Dale 1961- *WhoEmL 93*
Callister, Marion Jones 1921- *WhoAm 92*
Callister, Susan P. *Law&B 92*
Callmer, James Peter 1919- *WhoAm 92*
Callmeyer, Ferenc 1928- *WhoWor 93*
Callner, Bruce Warren 1948- *WhoEmL 93*
Callner, Robert Mark 1951- *WhoEmL 93*
Callo, Joseph Francis 1929- *WhoAm 92*
Callomon, John H. *WhoScE 91-1*
Callon, Frederick Lindsey 1950- *St&PR 93*
Callon, John S. 1920- *St&PR 93*
Callon, Lawrence Michael *St&PR 93*
Callow, A.J. *ScF&FL 92*
Callow, Allan Dana 1916- *WhoAm 92*
Callow, James Arthur *WhoScE 91-1*
Callow, Keith McLean 1925- *WhoAm 92, WhoWor 93*
Callow, Simon *MiSFD 9*
Callow, Simon 1949- *ConAu 138*
Callow, Thomas Edward 1954- *WhoEmL 93*
Callow, William Grant 1921- *WhoAm 92*
Calloway, Cab 1907- *BioIn 17*
Calloway, Cab(ell) 1907- *Baker 92*
Calloway, D. Wayne *BioIn 17*
Calloway, D. Wayne 1935- *St&PR 93, WhoAm 92, WhoE 93*
Calloway, Dawn Kelly 1958- *WhoWrEP 92*
Calloway, Dionne Cliche 1956- *WhoAmW 93*
Calloway, Doris Howes 1923- *WhoAm 92, WhoAmW 93*
Calloway, Jean Mitchener 1923- *WhoAm 92*
Calloway, Maureen 1964- *WhoEmL 93*
Calloway, Northern J. d1990 *BioIn 17*
Calloway, Vanessa Bell *BioIn 17*
Calloway, Warren Lester, Jr. 1942- *WhoSSW 93*
Callsen, Christian E. 1938- *WhoAm 92*
Callsen, Christian Edward 1938- *St&PR 93*
Callum, Myles 1934- *WhoAm 92*
Calman, Donald R. 1928- *St&PR 93*
Calman, Herbert I. 1914-1991 *BioIn 17*
Calman, Robert Frederick 1932- *St&PR 93, WhoAm 92*
Calmell del Solar, Fernando Javier 1949- *WhoWor 93*
Calmenson, Stephanie 1952- *ScF&FL 92*
Calmes, Jean 1926- *WhoScE 91-2*
Calmes, John Wintle 1942- *WhoSSW 93*
Calmes, Richard Allen 1932- *St&PR 93*
Calmese, Linda 1947- *WhoAmW 93, WhoEmL 93*
Calmet, Dominique Pierre 1953- *WhoScE 91-4*
Calmette, Gaston 1858-1914 *BioIn 17*
Calnan, Arthur Francis 1926- *WhoE 93, WhoWor 93*
Calnan, Dennis John 1948- *St&PR 93*
Calnan, Peter Thomas 1929-1989 *BioIn 17*
Calnan, William H., IV *Law&B 92*
Calne, Roy Yorke 1930- *BioIn 17*
Calnon, Guin Corinne 1943- *WhoWrEP 92*
Calo, Antonio 1935- *WhoScE 91-3*
Calo, Joseph Manuel 1944- *WhoAm 92, WhoE 93*
Calof, David Lorne 1949- *WhoEmL 93*
Calogero, Francesco 1935- *WhoScE 91-3*
Calogero, Pascal Frank, Jr. 1931- *WhoAm 92, WhoSSW 93*
Calore, James John 1948- *WhoWrEP 92*
Calori, Fausto 1937- *WhoUN 92*
Calovski, Naste 1933- *WhoUN 92*
Calow, Peter 1947- *WhoWor 93*
Calpin, Martin J. 1934- *WhoIns 93*
Calpin, William Joseph, Jr. 1949- *St&PR 93*
Calpini, John Robert 1943- *WhoSSW 93*
Calson, Clayton Elwood, II 1939- *St&PR 93*
Calta, Louis d1990 *BioIn 17*
Caltagirone, Paul 1952- *WhoEmL 93*
Caltagirone, Salvatore James 1942- *St&PR 93*
Calton, Gary Jim 1943- *WhoAm 92*
Calton, Sandra Jeane 1945- *WhoE 93*
Caltrider, Arthur P. 1935- *St&PR 93*
Caltrider, William Chichester, Sr. 1941- *WhoSSW 93*
Calueanu, Dumitru 1934- *WhoScE 91-4*
Calusdian, Richard Frank 1935- *WhoE 93*
Calvaer, Andre Jules 1921- *WhoWor 93*
Calvani, Alessandro 1952- *WhoUN 92*
Calvani, Terry 1947- *WhoAm 92*
Calvanico, Thomas Paul 1955- *WhoEmL 93*
Calvano, Conrad Anthony 1939- *St&PR 93*
Calvano, Michael Alan 1946- *WhoUN 92*
Calvaruso, Joseph Anthony 1949- *WhoEmL 93*
Calve, Emma 1858-1942 *Baker 92, IntDcOp [port], OxDcOp*
Calvelli, Rick T. *Law&B 92*
Calver, George W. *Law&B 92*
Calver, John *BioIn 17*
Calver, Richard Allen 1939- *WhoSSW 93*
Calverley, John Robert 1932- *WhoAm 92*
Calvert, Barbara Jean 1954- *WhoEmL 93*
Calvert, C. Emmett 1937- *WhoSSW 93*
Calvert, Collin Michael 1952- *WhoEmL 93*
Calvert, Crispina *BioIn 17*
Calvert, Dale 1937- *WhoIns 93*
Calvert, David Victor 1934- *WhoSSW 93*
Calvert, Delbert William 1927- *WhoAm 92*
Calvert, Gordon Lee 1921- *WhoAm 92*
Calvert, Horace Alton 1953- *St&PR 93*
Calvert, Jack George 1923- *WhoAm 92*
Calvert, James Francis 1920- *WhoAm 92*
Calvert, Jane Eleanor 1955- *WhoWor 93*
Calvert, John *MajAI*
Calvert, John David 1952- *WhoEmL 93*
Calvert, John Michael 1950- *WhoEmL 93*
Calvert, Jon Channing 1941- *WhoAm 92*
Calvert, Larrie S. 1935- *St&PR 93*
Calvert, Lloyd P. 1936- *St&PR 93*
Calvert, Lois Wilson 1924- *WhoAmW 93*
Calvert, Mark *BioIn 17*
Calvert, Mark S. *Law&B 92*
Calvert, Mary *ConAu 39NR, ScF&FL 92*
Calvert, Melanie A. 1954- *WhoEmL 93*
Calvert, Patricia 1931- *MajAI [port], SmATA 69 [port], WhoWrEP 92*
Calvert, Paul Henry 1940- *WhoAsAP 91*
Calvert, Philip A. *Law&B 92*
Calvert, Richard Worcester 1931- *St&PR 93*
Calvert, Rosalie Stier 1778-1821 *BioIn 17*
Calvert, Sam J., Jr. 1928- *WhoAm 92*
Calvert, Shirley C. 1928- *St&PR 93*
Calvert, Terry Lynn 1950- *WhoEmL 93*
Calvert, Tok *Law&B 92*
Calvert, William Preston 1934- *WhoAm 92, WhoSSW 93, WhoWor 93*
Calves, Jean-Yves 1948- *WhoScE 91-2*
Calvet, Jacques Yves Jean 1931- *WhoWor 93*
Calvet de Roquer, Emma 1858-1942 *Baker 92*
Calvi, Leesa G. Wood 1957- *WhoEmL 93*
Calviello, Joseph Anthony 1933- *WhoAm 92*
Calvillo, Manuel 1918- *DcMexL*
Calvillo Madrigal, Salvador 1901- *DcMexL*
Calvin, Allen David 1928- *WhoAm 92, WhoWor 93*
Calvin, Boyd Allen, II 1950- *St&PR 93*
Calvin, Dorothy Ver Strate 1929- *WhoAmW 93, WhoWor 93*
Calvin, Jean 1509-1564 *BioIn 17*
Calvin, John 1509-1564 *BioIn 17*
Calvin, Leon *BioIn 17*
Calvin, Melvin 1911- *BioIn 17, WhoAm 92, WhoWor 93*
Calvin, Monte D. 1944- *St&PR 93*
Calvin, Roderick 1963- *WhoSSW 93*
Calvin, Ronald L. 1941- *St&PR 93*
Calvin, Stafford Richard 1931- *WhoWor 93*
Calvin, Virginia Sparks 1928- *WhoSSW 93*
Calvino, Italo *BioIn 17*
Calvino, Italo 1923-1985 *ConLC 73 [port], MagSWL [port], ScF&FL 92*
Calvino, Philippe Andre Marie 1939- *WhoWor 93*
Calvinus, Gnaeus Domitius 96?BC-15?BC *HarEnMi*
Calvisius, Sethus 1556-1615 *Baker 92*
Calvo, Raymond B. 1953- *St&PR 93*
Calvocoressi, Michel Dimitri 1877-1944 *Baker 92*
Calvocoressi, Thomas J. *Law&B 92*
Calvo-Roth, Fortuna Claire 1934- *WhoAmW 93*
Calvo Sotelo, Leopoldo 1926- *WhoWor 93*
Calwell, Arthur 1896-1973 *DcTwHis*
Calzabigi, Ranieri de 1714-1795 *IntDcOp, OxDcOp*
Calzabigi, Ranieri (Simone Francesco Maria) di 1714-1795 *Baker 92*
Calzaretta, Frank G. 1936- *St&PR 93*
Calzetta, Frances Annette 1935- *WhoAmW 93, WhoWor 93*
Camac, Margaret Victoria 1946- *WhoAmW 93*
Camacci, Michael A. 1951- *WhoEmL 93*
Camacho, Alfredo 1951- *WhoEmL 93, WhoSSW 93*
Camacho, Frank E. 1947- *St&PR 93*
Camacho, Hector *BioIn 17*
Camacho, Henry Stephen, III 1947- *WhoE 93*
Camacho, James, Jr. 1956- *WhoEmL 93*
Camacho, Juan *BioIn 17*
Camacho, P. Bruce *WhoIns 93*
Camacho, Richard G. 1933- *St&PR 93*
Camaglia, Ron 1950- *St&PR 93*
Camann, Carl George 1946- *WhoSSW 93*
Camara, Assan Musa 1923- *WhoAfr*
Camara, Helder 1909- *BioIn 17*
Camara, Luiz Cesar Bittencourt 1949- *WhoWor 93*
Camara, Ousmane 1933- *WhoAfr*
Camarata, Anna 1967- *WhoAmW 93*
Camarata, Salvador 1913- *Baker 92*
Camardella, John 1944- *St&PR 93*
Camaree, James P. 1959- *St&PR 93*
Camarena, Enrique *DcCPCAm*
Camargo, Affonso 1929- *WhoWor 93*
Camargo, Alberto Lleras 1906-1990 *BioIn 17*
Camargo, Erney Plessmann 1935- *WhoWor 93*
Camargo, J.C. *Law&B 92*
Camargo, Martin J. 1950- *WhoWrEP 92*
Camargo, Orlando L. 1960- *WhoWor 93*
Camarillo, Albert Michael 1948- *HispAmA [port], WhoEmL 93*
Camarillo y Roa de Pereyra, Maria Enriqueta 1872-1968 *DcMexL*
Camarinha, Alberto *WhoScE 91-3*
Camastro, Frank P. d1990 *BioIn 17*
Camasura, Juanito G., Jr. 1939- *WhoAsAP 91*
Camayd-Freixas, Yohel 1948- *WhoEmL 93*
Cambel, Ali Bulent 1923- *WhoAm 92*
Cambel, Halet 1916- *IntDcAn*
Cambell, John F. 1917- *St&PR 93*
Cambert, Robert c. 1627-1677 *OxDcOp*
Cambert, Robert c. 1628-1677 *Baker 92*
Cambest, Lynn M. 1944- *St&PR 93*
Cambiaire, C.P. 1880- *ScF&FL 92*
Cambias, James Leslie 1966- *WhoSSW 93*
Cambiaso, Luca 1527-1585 *BioIn 17*
Cambier, Penelope Howland 1935- *WhoAmW 93*
Cambini, Giuseppe Maria 1746-1825 *Baker 92*
Camblak, Grigorij c. 1365-1419 *OxDcByz*
Cambon, Jacques 1934- *WhoUN 92*
Cambon, Jules Martin 1845-1935 *BioIn 17*
Cambouris, Arthur Theodore *Law&B 92*
Cambre, Ronald C. 1938- *St&PR 93*
Cambreling, Sylvain 1948- *Baker 92, WhoWor 93*
Cambrice, Robert Louis 1947- *WhoEmL 93*
Cambridge, George William Frederick Charles, Duke of 1819-1904 *HarEnMi*
Cambridge, Robert M. *Law&B 92*
Cambridge, William G. 1931- *WhoAm 92*
Cambron, James Roy 1947- *St&PR 93*
Camden, Archie 1888-1979 *Baker 92*
Camden, David George 1951- *WhoE 93*
Camden, William 1551-1623 *IntDcAn*
Camdessus, Michel *NewYTBS 92*
Camdessus, Michel Jean 1933- *WhoAm 92, WhoUN 92*
Cameira, Germano Silva 1950- *WhoScE 91-3*
Camel, Lisa Martha *Law&B 92*
Camelio, Cosmo Renato 1941- *St&PR 93*
Camell, Paul G. 1947- *St&PR 93*
Cameo *SoulM*
Camer, Mary Martha 1932- *WhoE 93*
Camera, Gerardo Agustin 1946- *WhoWor 93*
Camera, Joan Ann 1955- *WhoEmL 93*
Camera, Sharon Ketcham *Law&B 92*
Cameron, Alastair Duncan 1920- *St&PR 93, WhoAm 92*
Cameron, Alastair Graham Walter 1925- *WhoAm 92*
Cameron, Alison Stilwell d1991 *BioIn 17*
Cameron, Allan Williams 1938- *WhoE 93*
Cameron, Ann *ChlFicS*
Cameron, Ann 1943- *DcAmChF 1985*
Cameron, Anne 1938- *WhoCanL 92*
Cameron, (Barbara) Anne 1938- *ConAu 136*
Cameron, Averil Millicent 1940- *WhoWor 93*
Cameron, Barbara Anne *ScF&FL 92*
Cameron, (George) Basil 1884-1975 *Baker 92*
Cameron, Bruce 1937- *St&PR 93*
Cameron, Bruce Francis 1934- *WhoAm 92*
Cameron, Bruce William 1963- *WhoSSW 93*
Cameron, Charles Clifford 1920- *St&PR 93*
Cameron, Charles Metz, Jr. 1923- *WhoAm 92*
Cameron, Cherylan S. *Law&B 92*
Cameron, Claud Geoghegan 1954- *WhoSSW 93*
Cameron, Colin Campbell d1992 *NewYTBS 92*
Cameron, Colleen Irene 1952- *WhoAm 92, WhoAmW 93, WhoEmL 93*
Cameron, Cordon Donald 1950- *WhoEmL 93*
Cameron, Daniel Forrest 1944- *WhoSSW 93*
Cameron, David *BioIn 17*
Cameron, Dennis Scott *Law&B 92*
Cameron, Don N. *Law&B 92*
Cameron, Don R. 1937- *WhoAm 92*
Cameron, Donald 1946- *WhoAm 92, WhoE 93*
Cameron, Donald Allan *WhoCanL 92*
Cameron, Donald James 1947- *WhoEmL 93, WhoSSW 93*
Cameron, Donald Milner 1940- *WhoAsAP 91*
Cameron, Donald Ross 1947- *WhoWor 93*
Cameron, Douglas G. *Law&B 92*
Cameron, Douglas William *Law&B 92*
Cameron, Douglas Winston 1947- *WhoEmL 93*
Cameron, Duane Harold 1927- *St&PR 93*
Cameron, Duke Edward 1952- *WhoE 93*
Cameron, Duncan Hume 1934- *WhoAm 92*
Cameron, Edward Madison, III 1933- *WhoIns 93*
Cameron, Eleanor *AmWomPl*

Cameron, Eleanor 1912- *BioIn 17, ScF&FL 92*
Cameron, Eleanor (Butler) 1912- *DcAmChF 1960*
Cameron, Eleanor (Frances) 1912- *MajAI [port], WhoAm 92, WhoWrEP 92*
Cameron, Elspeth 1943- *WhoCanL 92*
Cameron, Emmet G. 1911- *St&PR 93*
Cameron, Evelyn *BioIn 17*
Cameron, Ewen Colin 1930- *WhoAsAP 91*
Cameron, George Frederick 1854-1885 *BioIn 17*
Cameron, George Gordon *WhoScE 91-1*
Cameron, Gerald Thomas, Sr. 1924- *St&PR 93*
Cameron, Gerry B. 1938- *St&PR 93, WhoAm 92*
Cameron, Glenn Nilsson 1956- *WhoEmL 93, WhoSSW 93*
Cameron, Gordon C. 1937-1990 *BioIn 17*
Cameron, Heather Anne 1951- *St&PR 93*
Cameron, Helen *AmWomPl*
Cameron, Herbert Daniel, Jr. 1950- *WhoEmL 93*
Cameron, Ian 1924- *ScF&FL 92*
Cameron, Ian Milne Dixon 1938- *WhoAsAP 91*
Cameron, Irma Kyllikki 1948- *WhoAmW 93*
Cameron, J.D. *ScF&FL 92*
Cameron, J. Elliot 1923- *WhoAm 92*
Cameron, James *BioIn 17*
Cameron, James 1954- *Au&Arts 9 [port], ConAu 137, ConTFT 10, MiSFD 9, ScF&FL 92*
Cameron, James Donald 1833-1918 *BioIn 17, PolPar*
Cameron, James Duke 1925- *WhoAm 92*
Cameron, James Sorel *ConAu 136*
Cameron, James William, Jr. 1947- *St&PR 93*
Cameron, Joan *ScF&FL 92*
Cameron, JoAnna *WhoAm 92, WhoWor 93*
Cameron, John *BioIn 17*
Cameron, John Clifford 1946- *WhoEmL 93*
Cameron, John Lansing 1916- *WhoAm 92*
Cameron, John M. 1943- *St&PR 93*
Cameron, John Stewart *WhoScE 91-1*
Cameron, John Thurston *WhoAm 92*
Cameron, John W. 1948- *St&PR 93*
Cameron, Joseph J. 1936- *St&PR 93*
Cameron, Judith Lynne 1945- *WhoAm 92, WhoAmW 93, WhoWor 93*
Cameron, Judy Lea 1948- *WhoEmL 93*
Cameron, Julia *MiSFD 9*
Cameron, Julia Margaret Pattle 1815-1879 *BioIn 17*
Cameron, Julie *ScF&FL 92*
Cameron, Karen Ann 1958- *WhoEmL 93*
Cameron, Kate *ScF&FL 92*
Cameron, Kate 1932- *ScF&FL 92*
Cameron, Keith Gordon 1947- *WhoWor 93*
Cameron, Ken *MiSFD 9*
Cameron, Kenneth A. *St&PR 93*
Cameron, Kenneth M. 1931- *ScF&FL 92*
Cameron, Kirk *BioIn 17*
Cameron, Kirk 1970?- *ConTFT 10*
Cameron, Larry Melvin 1951- *St&PR 93*
Cameron, Linda E. Slotnick 1937- *WhoAmW 93*
Cameron, Lou 1924- *ScF&FL 92, WhoWrEP 92*
Cameron, Lucille Wilson 1932- *WhoAmW 93, WhoE 93*
Cameron, Margaret 1867-1947 *AmWomPl*
Cameron, Marie 1948- *ScF&FL 92*
Cameron, Marion A. 1950- *St&PR 93*
Cameron, Marjorie Kohler *WhoSSW 93*
Cameron, Mark Alan 1954- *WhoEmL 93*
Cameron, Mary King 1940- *St&PR 93*
Cameron, Nicholas Allen 1939- *St&PR 93, WhoAm 92, WhoE 93, WhoWor 93*
Cameron, Nora Nancy 1946- *WhoAmW 93*
Cameron, Peter Alfred Gordon 1930- *WhoAm 92*
Cameron, Peter Jephson *WhoScE 91-1*
Cameron, Richard Douglas 1937- *WhoAm 92*
Cameron, Richfield J. 1921- *WhoIns 93*
Cameron, Rita Giovannetti *WhoAm 92*
Cameron, Robert George 1931- *WhoE 93*
Cameron, Robert J. *Law&B 92*
Cameron, Robert William 1937- *WhoSSW 93*
Cameron, Ronald W. 1934- *St&PR 93*
Cameron, Rondo 1925- *WhoAm 92, WhoSSW 93*
Cameron, Roy Eugene 1929- *WhoAm 92*
Cameron, Ruth Allen 1929- *WhoE 93*
Cameron, Samuel 1956- *WhoWor 93*
Cameron, Sandy R. *Law&B 92*
Cameron, Silver Donald 1937- *WhoCanL 92*
Cameron, Simon 1799-1889 *PolPar*
Cameron, Susan Kay 1960- *WhoAmW 93*
Cameron, Thomas F., III 1944- *WhoSSW 93*
Cameron, Thomas S. 1935- *St&PR 93*
Cameron, Thomas William Lane 1927- *WhoAm 92*
Cameron, Verney Lovett 1844-1894 *Expl 93 [port]*
Cameron, William Bleasdell 1862-1951 *BioIn 17*
Cameron, William Duncan 1925- *WhoSSW 93, WhoWor 93*
Camesas, Adrienne Muller 1956- *WhoE 93*
Camese, Wanda Green 1954- *WhoAmW 93, WhoEmL 93*
Cametti, Alberto 1871-1935 *Baker 92*
Camfield, William Arnett 1934- *WhoAm 92*
Camhi, Rita *Law&B 92*
Camic, David Edward 1954- *WhoEmL 93*
Camicia, Nicholas T. 1916- *St&PR 93*
Camidge, Matthew 1764-1844 *Baker 92*
Camiel, Edwin Peter, Jr. 1950- *WhoEmL 93*
Camiel, Peter J. 1910-1991 *BioIn 17*
Camilion, Oscar H. 1930- *WhoUN 92*
Camille, Michael 1958- *ConAu 137*
Camilleri, Carmel Joseph 1922- *WhoScE 91-2*
Camilleri, John Peter 1957- *WhoEmL 93*
Camilleri, Paul Joachim *Law&B 92*
Camilleri, Paul Joachim 1947- *WhoEmL 93*
Camilleri, Victor 1942- *WhoUN 92*
Camilli, Adolph Louis 1907- *BiDAMSp 1989*
Camilli, Carlo 1946- *WhoWor 93*
Camillo, John R. *Law&B 92*
Camillus, Marcus Furius 440?BC-365BC *HarEnMi*
Camilo, Michel *BioIn 17*
Caminals-Heath, Roser 1956- *ConAu 137*
Caminas, J.A. *WhoScE 91-3*
Camino, Alejandro 1949- *WhoWor 93*
Camino, Rafael *BioIn 17*
Camino Galicia, Leon Felipe 1884-1968 *DcMexL*
Caminos, Ricardo A. d1992 *NewYTBS 92*
Caminos, Ricardo A. 1915-1992 *BioIn 17*
Camisa, George Lincoln 1929- *WhoAm 92*
Camisa, Kenneth Peter 1938- *St&PR 93, WhoE 93*
Camisa, Raymond L. *BioIn 17*
Camisa, Vance G. *Law&B 92*
Camishion, Rudolph C. 1927- *WhoE 93*
Camiz, Sergio 1946- *WhoWor 93*
Camlin, Michael S. 1947- *WhoScE 91-1*
Camm, Alan John *WhoScE 91-1*
Camm, Mary Ellen 1944- *WhoAmW 93*
Camm, Robert James 1923- *WhoE 93*
Camm, Sydney 1893-1966 *BioIn 17*
Cammack, Dennis Robert 1948- *WhoEmL 93*
Cammack, James W. 1943- *St&PR 93*
Cammack, Richard *WhoScE 91-1*
Cammack, Trank Emerson 1919- *WhoAm 92*
Cammaerts, Emile 1878-1953 *ScF&FL 92*
Cammaker, Sheldon I. *Law&B 92*
Cammaker, Sheldon I. 1939- *St&PR 93*
Cammaker, Sheldon Ira 1939- *WhoAm 92*
Cammarano, Luigi c. 1800-1854 *OxDcOp*
Cammarano, Salvadore 1801-1852 *IntDcOp, OxDcOp*
Cammarata, Angelo 1936- *WhoE 93*
Cammarata, Bernard 1940- *St&PR 93*
Cammarata, Joseph 1958- *WhoEmL 93*
Cammarata, Richard John 1950- *WhoE 93*
Cammarota, Michael J. *Law&B 92*
Cammell, Donald *MiSFD 9*
Cammermeyer, Margarethe 1942- *WhoAmW 93*
Cammett, Stuart Hyland 1931- *St&PR 93*
Cammisa, Laurie *BioIn 17*
Cammock, Earl E. 1926- *WhoAm 92*
Camner, Per J.H. 1938- *WhoScE 91-4*
Camo, Bonnie Lou 1942- *WhoAmW 93*
Camoin, Charles 1879-1965 *BioIn 17*
Camona, Gianangelo 1936- *WhoScE 91-3*
Camosse, Henry J. 1930- *St&PR 93*
Camosy, Raymond J. 1950- *St&PR 93*
Camozzi, Victor E. 1916- *St&PR 93*
Camp, Alethea Taylor 1938- *WhoAmW 93*
Camp, Antwone Denise 1960- *WhoAmW 93*
Camp, Barbara Ann 1943- *WhoAmW 93*
Camp, Billy Joe 1938- *WhoAm 92*
Camp, Carolyn Hopkins 1939- *WhoAmW 93, WhoSSW 93*
Camp, Catherine 1965- *WhoWor 93*
Camp, Catherine Crook de *ScF&FL 92*
Camp, Clifton Durrett, Jr. 1927- *WhoAm 92*
Camp, Colleen 1953- *ConTFT 10*
Camp, Constance Willis *AmWomPl*
Camp, Craig Charles 1958- *WhoEmL 93*
Camp, Dave 1953- *CngDr 91, WhoAm 92*
Camp, Deborah *ScF&FL 92*
Camp, Donald Eugene 1940- *WhoE 93*
Camp, Ehney Addison, III 1942- *WhoSSW 93*
Camp, Elizabeth W. *Law&B 92*
Camp, Frances Spencer 1924- *WhoAmW 93, WhoE 93, WhoWor 93*
Camp, Hazel Lee Burt 1922- *WhoAm 92, WhoAmW 93, WhoE 93, WhoSSW 93*
Camp, Jack Tarpley, Jr. 1943- *WhoAm 92, WhoSSW 93*
Camp, Joe 1939- *MiSFD 9, ScF&FL 92*
Camp, John 1944- *BioIn 17, ConAu 138*
Camp, Joseph E. *Law&B 92*
Camp, Joseph S. *ScF&FL 92*
Camp, Joseph Shelton, Jr. 1939- *WhoAm 92, WhoSSW 93*
Camp, L. Sprague de *ScF&FL 92*
Camp, Larry Michael 1948- *WhoEmL 93*
Camp, Leonard Norman, III 1942- *WhoSSW 93*
Camp, Lewis F., Jr. *Law&B 92*
Camp, Lewis Forman, Jr. 1928- *St&PR 93*
Camp, Linda Joyce *WhoAmW 93*
Camp, Max Wayne 1935- *WhoSSW 93*
Camp, Mitch Owen 1964- *WhoSSW 93*
Camp, Orton P. 1922- *St&PR 93*
Camp, Randy Coleman 1952- *WhoEmL 93*
Camp, Richard Doyle Reginal *WhoScE 91-1*
Camp, Robert H. *Law&B 92*
Camp, Roderic A. *BioIn 17*
Camp, Roger *BioIn 17*
Camp, Ruth Suzanne Adams 1937- *WhoE 93*
Camp, Susan K. 1959- *WhoAmW 93*
Camp, Thomas Harley 1929- *WhoSSW 93*
Camp, Walter 1859-1925 *BioIn 17*
Camp, Warren Victor 1946- *WhoEmL 93*
Camp, William Ragsdale 1945- *St&PR 93*
Campa, Arthur L(eon) 1905- *ConAu 40NR*
Campa, Arthur Leon 1905-1978 *HispAmA [port]*
Campa, Valentin *DcCPCAm*
Campagna, Claudio 1955- *WhoWor 93*
Campagna, Joanne Marie 1964- *WhoAmW 93*
Campagna, Lisa A. *Law&B 92*
Campagna, Richard P. 1955- *St&PR 93*
Campagna, Richard Vincent 1952- *WhoEmL 93*
Campagne, Thomas Elmer 1950- *WhoEmL 93*
Campagnoli, Bartolommeo 1751-1827 *Baker 92*
Campagnuolo, Benjamin 1941- *St&PR 93*
Campaigne, Ernest Edwin 1914- *WhoAm 92*
Campaignolle, Jean *WhoScE 91-2*
Campana, Ana Isabel 1934- *WhoAmW 93, WhoE 93, WhoWor 93*
Campana, Fabio 1819-1882 *Baker 92*
Campana, Joseph E. 1952- *WhoEmL 93*
Campana, Patricia *Law&B 92*
Campana, Pedro de 1503-c. 1580 *BioIn 17*
Campana, Richard John 1918- *WhoAm 92*
Campanacci, Luciano 1930- *WhoScE 91-3*
Campanalie, Richard Anthony 1946- *St&PR 93*
Campanari, Giuseppe 1855-1927 *Baker 92*
Campanari, Leandro 1857-1939 *Baker 92*
Campanella, Anton Joseph 1932- *St&PR 93*
Campanella, Carl 1947- *St&PR 93*
Campanella, Donna Madeline 1952- *WhoAm 92, WhoAmW 93*
Campanella, Francis Barry 1936- *WhoE 93*
Campanella, Joseph 1927- *WhoAm 92*
Campanella, Joseph Alex 1942- *St&PR 93*
Campanella, Juan Jose *MiSFD 9*
Campanella, Luigi 1938- *WhoScE 91-3*
Campanella, Michele 1947- *Baker 92*
Campanella, Peter F. 1945- *St&PR 93*
Campanella, Roy 1921- *BioIn 17*
Campanella, Roy, II *MiSFD 9*
Campanelli, Anthony Joseph 1935- *St&PR 93*
Campanelli, Dan 1949- *WhoE 93*
Campanelli, Pauline Eble 1943- *WhoE 93*
Campanie, Samuel John 1952- *WhoEmL 93*
Campanile, Pasquale Festa 1927-1986 *MiSFD 9N*
Campanile, Rita P. *Law&B 92*
Campanini, Cleofonte 1860-1919 *Baker 92, IntDcOp, OxDcOp*
Campanini, Italo 1845-1896 *Baker 92, IntDcOp, OxDcOp*
Campanino, Massimo 1952- *WhoScE 91-3*
Campanioni, Raul A. 1956-1990 *BioIn 17*
Campano, Fred 1937- *WhoUN 92*
Campbel, Ernest 1904- *St&PR 93*
Campbell, A.N. 1913- *St&PR 93*
Campbell, Alan Keith 1923- *St&PR 93, WhoAm 92*
Campbell, Alastair F.S. *Law&B 92*
Campbell, Alexander George MacPherson *WhoScE 91-1*
Campbell, Alexander John 1904- *St&PR 93*
Campbell, Aline *Baker 92*
Campbell, Alistair Matheson 1905- *WhoAm 92*
Campbell, Allan Adams, Jr. *Law&B 92*
Campbell, Allan McCulloch 1929- *WhoAm 92*
Campbell, Allan R. 1942- *St&PR 93*
Campbell, Alma Jacqueline Porter 1948- *WhoE 93*
Campbell, Alta M. 1948- *St&PR 93*
Campbell, Alvin Dean 1947- *St&PR 93*
Campbell, Amy Alise 1963- *WhoAmW 93*
Campbell, Andrew Hamilton 1932- *St&PR 93*
Campbell, Andrew Morton *Law&B 92*
Campbell, Anita *Law&B 92*
Campbell, Anita C. *Law&B 92*
Campbell, Anita Joyce 1953- *WhoAmW 93*
Campbell, Anne *WhoCanL 92*
Campbell, Anne 1940- *WhoScE 91-1*
Campbell, Anne Catherine 1956- *WhoAmW 93*
Campbell, Archibald 1739-1791 *HarEnMi*
Campbell, Archibald 1769-1843 *HarEnMi*
Campbell, Arlington Fichtner 1939- *WhoAm 92*
Campbell, Arthur 1742-1811 *BioIn 17*
Campbell, Arthur Andrews 1924- *WhoAm 92*
Campbell, Arthur V. 1954- *St&PR 93*
Campbell, Avril Kim 1947- *WhoAm 92, WhoAmW 93*
Campbell, B. *WhoScE 91-1*
Campbell, Barbara *SoulM*
Campbell, Barbara 1929- *BlkAuII 92*
Campbell, Barbara Helen 1945- *WhoAmW 93*
Campbell, Barbara Vaughan 1947- *WhoEmL 93*
Campbell, Barry L. 1946- *St&PR 93*
Campbell, Bartley 1843-1888 *JrnUS*
Campbell, Beatrice Murphy *ConAu 137*
Campbell, Beatrix 1947- *ConAu 138*
Campbell, Bebe Moore 1950- *ConAu 139*
Campbell, Ben D. *Law&B 92*
Campbell, Ben Nighthorse *BioIn 17*
Campbell, Ben Nighthorse 1933- *CngDr 91, WhoAm 92*
Campbell, Betty Jean 1951- *WhoEmL 93*
Campbell, Betty Jo 1933- *WhoAmW 93*
Campbell, Beverly Ann 1938- *WhoSSW 93*
Campbell, Beverly-Claire 1954- *WhoAm 92*
Campbell, Bill *BioIn 17*
Campbell, Bonnie Jean 1948- *WhoAm 92, WhoAmW 93*
Campbell, Brian Scott 1959- *WhoSSW 93*
Campbell, Bruce *ConAu 39NR*
Campbell, Bruce Crichton 1947- *WhoAm 92*
Campbell, Bruce Henry 1930- *St&PR 93*
Campbell, Bruce Henry 1940- *WhoE 93*
Campbell, Bruce Irving 1947- *WhoEmL 93*
Campbell, Bryan Clifford *Law&B 92*
Campbell, Byron Chesser 1934- *WhoAm 92*
Campbell, C. John 1935- *St&PR 93*
Campbell, Calvin Arthur, Jr. 1934- *St&PR 93, WhoAm 92, WhoWor 93*
Campbell, Carl L. 1943- *St&PR 93*
Campbell, Carl Lester 1943- *WhoAm 92*
Campbell, Carol Norton 1944- *WhoAmW 93*
Campbell, Carol Sue 1956- *WhoAmW 93*
Campbell, Carolyn Milburn 1961- *WhoEmL 93*
Campbell, Carroll Ashmore, Jr. *BioIn 17*
Campbell, Carroll Ashmore, Jr. 1940- *WhoAm 92, WhoSSW 93, WhoWor 93*
Campbell, Catherine Jeanne 1958- *WhoE 93*
Campbell, Catherine Marie *Law&B 92*
Campbell, Charles A. 1944- *St&PR 93*
Campbell, Charles Alton 1944- *WhoSSW 93*
Campbell, Charles Bryan 1922- *WhoAm 92*
Campbell, Charles Edgar 1921- *WhoSSW 93*
Campbell, Charles Edwin 1942- *WhoAm 92*
Campbell, Charles H. 1931- *WhoAm 92*
Campbell, Charles J. 1915- *WhoAm 92*
Campbell, Charles Mel 1959- *WhoSSW 93*
Campbell, Charles Philip, Jr. 1948- *WhoEmL 93*
Campbell, Charles R. 1939- *St&PR 93*
Campbell, Charles William, Jr. *Law&B 92*

Campbell, Chris Lane 1957- St&PR 93
Campbell, Christian L. Law&B 92
Campbell, Christian L. 1950- St&PR 93
Campbell, Christopher Jay 1950- WhoEmL 93
Campbell, Christopher Joseph 1955- WhoEmL 93
Campbell, Cindy Lou 1960- WhoEmL 93
Campbell, Clair Gilliland 1961- WhoEmL 93
Campbell, Claire Patricia 1933- WhoAmW 93
Campbell, Clara Shiver 1931- St&PR 93
Campbell, Clive S. ScF&FL 92
Campbell, Clyde Del 1930- WhoAm 92
Campbell, Colin 1792-1863 HarEnMi
Campbell, Colin 1927- WhoAm 92
Campbell, Colin Dearborn 1917- WhoAm 92
Campbell, Colin Goetze 1935- WhoAm 92
Campbell, Colin Herald 1911- WhoWor 93
Campbell, Colin Kydd 1927- WhoAm 92
Campbell, Colin Matthew 1942- WhoWor 93
Campbell, Colin McLeod 1945- WhoAm 92
Campbell, Coline WhoAmW 93
Campbell, Constance AmWomPl
Campbell, Courtney Lee 1957- WhoEmL 93
Campbell, Craig Sherman 1935- St&PR 93, WhoSSW 93
Campbell, Crom B. 1928- St&PR 93
Campbell, D.J. 1938- WhoScE 91-1
Campbell, D. Ross St&PR 93
Campbell, David A. Law&B 92
Campbell, David Colin 1873-1949 BiDAMSp 1989
Campbell, David George 1949- WhoE 93, WhoEmL 93, WhoWor 93
Campbell, David Gwynne 1930- WhoAm 92, WhoSSW 93
Campbell, David N. 1941- St&PR 93
Campbell, David Ned 1929- WhoAm 92
Campbell, David Norbert 1932- WhoE 93
Campbell, David P. 1939- WhoSSW 93
Campbell, David Spence WhoScE 91-1
Campbell, David Stetson 1943- WhoAm 92
Campbell, Debe L. 1957- WhoWrEP 92
Campbell, Debra Ellen 1956- WhoAmW 93
Campbell, Debra Lynn 1954- WhoAmW 93, WhoEmL 93
Campbell, Dennis George 1949- WhoAm 92
Campbell, Dennis Marion 1945- WhoAm 92
Campbell, Dennis Miles 1952- WhoSSW 93
Campbell, Dexter McPherson, Jr. 1949- St&PR 93
Campbell, Donald WhoScE 91-1
Campbell, Donald Broughton 1929- St&PR 93
Campbell, Donald E. 1943- ConAu 138
Campbell, Donald Graham 1925- St&PR 93, WhoAm 92
Campbell, Donald John WhoScE 91-1
Campbell, Donald K. 1926- WhoAm 92
Campbell, Donald Thomas 1916- WhoAm 92
Campbell, Donald W. 1934- St&PR 93
Campbell, Donald Wesley 1936- WhoAm 92
Campbell, Donn Melvin 1931- St&PR 93
Campbell, Donna Marie 1949- WhoSSW 93
Campbell, Doris Klein WhoAmW 93
Campbell, Doug MiSFD 9
Campbell, Douglas 1896-1990 BioIn 17
Campbell, Douglas 1920- St&PR 93
Campbell, Douglas Argyle 1929- WhoAm 92
Campbell, Douglass 1919- WhoAm 92, WhoWor 93
Campbell, Dow L. Law&B 92
Campbell, E. E. 1949- WhoE 93
Campbell, E. Wayne Law&B 92
Campbell, Earl BioIn 17
Campbell, Edmund Douglas 1899- WhoAm 92
Campbell, Edward Clinton 1929- WhoE 93, WhoWor 93
Campbell, Edward Fay, Jr. 1932- WhoAm 92
Campbell, Edward Francis 1908- WhoWor 93
Campbell, Edward George 1916- St&PR 93
Campbell, Edward Irving 1942- WhoE 93
Campbell, Edward J. 1928- St&PR 93
Campbell, Edward Joseph 1928- WhoAm 92
Campbell, Edward Patrick 1949- St&PR 93
Campbell, Edwin Denton 1927- WhoAm 92
Campbell, Elden BioIn 17
Campbell, Elizabeth Ann Law&B 92
Campbell, Elizabeth Pfohl 1902- WhoE 93
Campbell, Elizabeth Thurber 1942- WhoAmW 93
Campbell, Eric QDrFCA 92
Campbell, Eric Eldon 1929- WhoAm 92
Campbell, Erma d1991 BioIn 17
Campbell, Evangeline AmWomPl
Campbell, Ewing 1940- WhoSSW 93, WhoWrEP 92
Campbell, Fenton Gregory 1939- WhoAm 92
Campbell, Fergus William WhoScE 91-1
Campbell, Ffyona 1967- BioIn 17
Campbell, Finley Alexander 1927- WhoAm 92
Campbell, Fran 1947- St&PR 93
Campbell, Frances Alexander 1933- WhoAmW 93
Campbell, Frances Harvell WhoAmW 93
Campbell, Francis James 1924- WhoAm 92
Campbell, Frank, Jr. Law&B 92
Campbell, Frank Andrew Scott 1955- WhoEmL 93
Campbell, Frank B., Jr. 1917- St&PR 93
Campbell, Frank Carter 1916- WhoAm 92
Campbell, Frank Paul 1931- St&PR 93
Campbell, G. Anthony Law&B 92
Campbell, G.G. d1991 BioIn 17
Campbell, Gary J. 1944- St&PR 93
Campbell, George Emerson 1932- WhoAm 92
Campbell, George Leroy 1940- St&PR 93
Campbell, Gerard Michael 1951- St&PR 93
Campbell, Gilbert Sadler 1924- WhoAm 92
Campbell, Glen 1936- WhoAm 92
Campbell, Glen (Travis) 1938- Baker 92
Campbell, Gordon Wallace 1932- St&PR 93
Campbell, Graeme 1939- WhoAsAP 91
Campbell, Graeme 1954- MiSFD 9
Campbell, Gregory Scott 1948- St&PR 93
Campbell, Grover Stollenwerck 1954- WhoSSW 93
Campbell, H.J. 1925- ScF&FL 92
Campbell, H. Stuart St&PR 93
Campbell, H. Stuart 1929- WhoAm 92
Campbell, Harold Andrew, III 1947- WhoSSW 93
Campbell, Harry C. 1912- St&PR 93
Campbell, Harry Woodson 1946- WhoEmL 93
Campbell, Harvey A. 1930- St&PR 93
Campbell, Harvey E. 1928- St&PR 93
Campbell, Helen Louise 1939- WhoAmW 93
Campbell, Henry Cummings 1919- WhoAm 92
Campbell, Herbert R. 1927- St&PR 93
Campbell, Hope 1925- ScF&FL 92
Campbell, Hugh D. Law&B 92
Campbell, Hugh L. 1937- St&PR 93
Campbell, Hugh Lyle 1937- WhoAm 92
Campbell, Hugh P. 1934- St&PR 93
Campbell, Ian A. 1939- WhoScE 91-2
Campbell, Ian B. 1928- St&PR 93
Campbell, Ian David 1945- WhoAm 92
Campbell, Ian David 1953- WhoEmL 93
Campbell, J.B. St&PR 93
Campbell, J.D., Jr. 1941- St&PR 93
Campbell, Jack James Ramsay 1918- WhoAm 92
Campbell, Jack Thomas 1937- St&PR 93
Campbell, Jackson Justice 1920- WhoAm 92
Campbell, James Albert Barton 1940- WhoSSW 93
Campbell, James Arthur 1924- WhoAm 92
Campbell, James Batchelder 1944- WhoSSW 93
Campbell, James Boyd 1931- WhoAm 92
Campbell, James D. 1946- St&PR 93
Campbell, James E. 1935- St&PR 93
Campbell, James Edward 1943- WhoWor 93
Campbell, James Howard, Jr. 1958- WhoEmL 93
Campbell, James M. 1943- St&PR 93
Campbell, James P. 1939- St&PR 93
Campbell, James Phillip 1961- WhoE 93
Campbell, James Robert 1942- WhoAm 92
Campbell, James Sargent 1938- WhoAm 92
Campbell, Jane WhoWrEP 92
Campbell, Jane Turner 1931- WhoAmW 93
Campbell, Janet Elaine 1942- WhoAmW 93
Campbell, Janet Louise 1926- WhoAmW 93
Campbell, Jean 1925- WhoAmW 93
Campbell, Jean 1943- WhoAmW 93
Campbell, Jeanna WhoWrEP 92
Campbell, Jefferey James 1952- St&PR 93
Campbell, Jeffrey ScF&FL 92
Campbell, Jeffrey Alan 1956- St&PR 93
Campbell, Jerry Dean 1945- WhoAm 92
Campbell, Jerry Franklin 1936- WhoIns 93
Campbell, Jerry Lee 1934- WhoSSW 93
Campbell, Jill Frost 1948- WhoAmW 93, WhoEmL 93
Campbell, Jo 1950- WhoEmL 93
Campbell, Joan 1937- WhoAmW 93
Campbell, Joan Brown WhoAmW 93
Campbell, Joan Brown 1931- BioIn 17
Campbell, Joanne Lois 1938- WhoAmW 93
Campbell, John BioIn 17
Campbell, John 1653-1728 JrnUS
Campbell, John 1949- BioIn 17
Campbell, John A. WhoScE 91-1
Campbell, John Archibald 1811-1889 OxCSupC [port]
Campbell, John B. 1922- St&PR 93
Campbell, John Coert 1911- WhoAm 92
Campbell, John David 1954- St&PR 93
Campbell, John De Vries 1949- WhoEmL 93
Campbell, John Duncan 1946- WhoEmL 93
Campbell, John Elliot 1959- WhoE 93
Campbell, John Francis 1822-1885 BioIn 17
Campbell, John Gavin 1935- WhoWor 93
Campbell, John H. 1942- St&PR 93
Campbell, John Hone Fitzgerald 1936- WhoWor 93
Campbell, John Kelly 1929- WhoAm 92
Campbell, John L. 1950- St&PR 93
Campbell, John Michael Law&B 92
Campbell, John Morgan 1922- WhoAm 92
Campbell, John N. Law&B 92
Campbell, John Nathan 1930- St&PR 93
Campbell, John Richard 1932- WhoAm 92
Campbell, John Roy 1933- WhoAm 92, WhoSSW 93
Campbell, John S. 1950- St&PR 93
Campbell, John Tucker 1912-1991 BioIn 17
Campbell, John W. Law&B 92
Campbell, John W. 1910-1971 ScF&FL 92
Campbell, John William 1954- WhoEmL 93, WhoSSW 93
Campbell, John Wood 1910-1971 BioIn 17
Campbell, Joseph 1904-1987 BioIn 17
Campbell, Joseph H. 1908- St&PR 93
Campbell, Joseph Howard, Jr. 1952- WhoEmL 93
Campbell, Joseph Leonard 1938- WhoAm 92
Campbell, Joseph Leonard, II 1938- St&PR 93
Campbell, Joseph R. 1934- St&PR 93
Campbell, Josephine Elizabeth AmWomPl
Campbell, Judith Lowe 1946- WhoAm 92, WhoAmW 93, WhoEmL 93
Campbell, Judith May 1938- WhoAm 92
Campbell, K. WhoScE 91-1
Campbell, Karen Mathena 1964- WhoAmW 93
Campbell, Karen Meyer 1958- WhoAmW 93
Campbell, Karlyn Kohrs 1937- ConAu 39NR, WhoAm 92
Campbell, Kathleen 1943- WhoAmW 93
Campbell, Kathleen Mary 1948- WhoEmL 93
Campbell, Katie 1957- ConAu 136
Campbell, Keith Allen 1948- WhoEmL 93
Campbell, Keith S. 1954- St&PR 93
Campbell, Kenneth 1919- St&PR 93
Campbell, Kenneth Eugene, Jr. 1943- WhoAm 92
Campbell, Kenneth L. 1947- St&PR 93
Campbell, Kevin 1943- WhoSSW 93
Campbell, Kim BioIn 17
Campbell, Larry E. 1941- WhoAm 92
Campbell, Laura Casteel 1960- WhoAmW 93
Campbell, Lawrence 1914- WhoE 93
Campbell, Lawrence Claire 1929- St&PR 93
Campbell, Lawrence W. Law&B 92
Campbell, Leonard Martin 1918- WhoAm 92
Campbell, Lesley Ann 1959- WhoEmL 93
Campbell, Levin Hicks 1927- WhoAm 92, WhoE 93
Campbell, Lillian Hawkins (Hankins) AmWomPl
Campbell, Linzy Leon 1927- WhoAm 92
Campbell, Lois Foster 1933- WhoSSW 93
Campbell, Lon Overton Law&B 92
Campbell, Lorraine Marie Peterson 1954- WhoAmW 93
Campbell, Lou Ellen 1943- WhoAmW 93
Campbell, Louis Lorne 1928- WhoAm 92
Campbell, Louise 1937- WhoWrEP 92
Campbell, Luther BioIn 17
Campbell, Lyle Richard 1942- WhoAm 92
Campbell, M.P. Law&B 92
Campbell, M. Steve 1949- St&PR 93
Campbell, Mack W. 1929- St&PR 93
Campbell, Malcolm Murray WhoScE 91-1
Campbell, Malcolm Osborn, Jr. Law&B 92
Campbell, Margaret 1886-1952 ScF&FL 92
Campbell, Margaret M. 1928- WhoAm 92
Campbell, Maria 1940- WhoCanL 92
Campbell, Maria B. Law&B 92
Campbell, Maria Bouchelle 1944- St&PR 93, WhoAm 92, WhoAmW 93
Campbell, Marian A. Law&B 92
Campbell, Marian D. AmWomPl
Campbell, Mark Alan 1953- WhoEmL 93
Campbell, Marsha Mulford 1946- WhoAmW 93
Campbell, Martin MiSFD 9
Campbell, Martin Hoyt BioIn 17
Campbell, Marvin Lynn 1962- WhoSSW 93
Campbell, Mary Anita 1950- WhoEmL 93
Campbell, Mary Ann 1920- WhoWor 93
Campbell, Mary B(aine) 1954- ConAu 136
Campbell, Mary Baine 1954- WhoAmW 93
Campbell, Mary Beth 1952- WhoEmL 93
Campbell, Mary Grace 1928- St&PR 93
Campbell, Mary Kathryn 1939- WhoAm 92
Campbell, Mary Rose 1934- St&PR 93
Campbell, Mary Schmidt BioIn 17
Campbell, Mary Virginia 1946- WhoWrEP 92
Campbell, Maryanne Milstead 1959- WhoAmW 93
Campbell, Melvin Ray, Jr. 1958- WhoSSW 93
Campbell, Michael E. 1947- St&PR 93
Campbell, Michael Edward 1947- WhoAm 92, WhoEmL 93
Campbell, Michael Joseph 1964- WhoE 93, WhoEmL 93
Campbell, Michael Wayne 1964- WhoSSW 93
Campbell, Mildred Corum 1934- WhoAmW 93
Campbell, Milo D. 1851-1923 BioIn 17
Campbell, Milton, Jr. 1934- BioIn 17
Campbell, Milton Grey 1933- BiDAMSp 1989
Campbell, Milton Hugh 1928- WhoAm 92
Campbell, Mona Louise 1919- WhoAm 92
Campbell, Munson d1992 BioIn 17, NewYTBS 92
Campbell, Nancy Ann 1950- WhoAmW 93
Campbell, Nancy Edinger 1957- WhoAm 92, WhoAmW 93, WhoE 93, WhoEmL 93
Campbell, Nancy Irene Barr 1955- WhoEmL 93
Campbell, Nancy L. 1939- St&PR 93, WhoAm 92
Campbell, Naomi BioIn 17
Campbell, Newton Allen 1928- St&PR 93, WhoAm 92
Campbell, Norman 1924- MiSFD 9
Campbell, Olga Margaret 1943- WhoAmW 93, WhoSSW 93
Campbell, Paddy WhoCanL 92
Campbell, Patricia Ann 1941- WhoWrEP 92
Campbell, Patricia Barbara 1947- WhoEmL 93
Campbell, Patricia Forsythe 1948- WhoE 93
Campbell, Patricia J. 1930- BioIn 17
Campbell, Patrick, Mrs. 1865-1940 BioIn 17
Campbell, Patton 1926- WhoAm 92
Campbell, Paul Barton 1930- St&PR 93, WhoAm 92
Campbell, Peter Nelson WhoScE 91-1
Campbell, Phillip J., Jr. 1932- St&PR 93
Campbell, Pollyann S. 1949- WhoEmL 93
Campbell, R. Nelson 1964- WhoEmL 93
Campbell, R(obert) Wright 1927- WhoWrEP 92
Campbell, Rachel Harris AmWomPl
Campbell, Ramsey 1946- ScF&FL 92
Campbell, Randall Marvin 1927- St&PR 93
Campbell, Raymond, III 1948- WhoEmL 93
Campbell, Raymond McKinly 1942- WhoE 93
Campbell, Raymond W. Law&B 92
Campbell, Rea Burne 1954- WhoEmL 93
Campbell, Rebecca Lynn 1957- WhoEmL 93
Campbell, Rebecca Renno 1947- WhoE 93
Campbell, Renoda Gisele 1963- WhoAmW 93
Campbell, Richard Alden 1926- WhoAm 92
Campbell, Richard H. 1936- WhoAm 92

Campbell, Richard P. 1947- WhoAm 92
Campbell, Richard Rice 1923- WhoAm 92
Campbell, Rita Ricardo NotHsAW 93
Campbell, Robert 1937- WhoAm 92
Campbell, Robert, Jr. 1924- St&PR 93
Campbell, Robert Andrew 1947- WhoWor 93
Campbell, Robert Ayerst 1940- WhoAm 92
Campbell, Robert Charles 1924- WhoAm 92
Campbell, Robert Dale 1914- WhoAm 92
Campbell, Robert E. 1933- WhoAm 92
Campbell, Robert Emmett 1933- St&PR 93
Campbell, Robert H. 1937- WhoAm 92, WhoE 93
Campbell, Robert H., Jr. 1934- St&PR 93
Campbell, Robert Hedgcock 1948- WhoEmL 93
Campbell, Robert K. 1930-1990 BioIn 17
Campbell, Robert L. 1922- St&PR 93
Campbell, Robert L. 1951- St&PR 93
Campbell, Robert Patrick 1956- WhoEmL 93
Campbell, Robert W. 1922- St&PR 93
Campbell, Robert Walter 1934- WhoAm 92
Campbell, Robert William Duncan 1951- WhoEmL 93
Campbell, Robin BlkAmWO
Campbell, Roger Keith 1951- WhoEmL 93, WhoSSW 93
Campbell, Ronald Bruce 1946- WhoEmL 93, WhoWor 93
Campbell, Ronald F. 1949- St&PR 93
Campbell, Ronald Neil 1926- WhoAm 92
Campbell, Rosemary Garst 1917- WhoE 93
Campbell, Roy E. 1926- St&PR 93
Campbell, Russell G. 1940- St&PR 93
Campbell, Samuel Gordon 1933- WhoAm 92
Campbell, Sandra S. 1943- WhoAmW 93
Campbell, Sandy 1956- WhoEmL 93
Campbell, Scot R. Law&B 92
Campbell, Scott Eugene 1957- WhoEmL 93, WhoSSW 93
Campbell, Scott Robert 1946- WhoAm 92
Campbell, Scott Steven 1947- WhoSSW 93
Campbell, Sean 1955- St&PR 93
Campbell, Sean E. Law&B 92
Campbell, Selaura Joy 1944- WhoAmW 93, WhoWor 93
Campbell, Sharon Lynn 1955- WhoWrEP 92
Campbell, Sheree Vay 1961- WhoAmW 93
Campbell, Stephen D. Law&B 92
Campbell, Stephen Lee 1965- WhoSSW 93
Campbell, Stephen Mercer 1941- St&PR 93
Campbell, Steven B. 1948- St&PR 93
Campbell, Steven J. 1953- St&PR 93
Campbell, Stewart Fred 1931- WhoAm 92
Campbell, Stuart V.M. 1953- St&PR 93
Campbell, Susan Carrigg 1946- WhoAmW 93
Campbell, Susan L. 1956- WhoIns 93
Campbell, Susan Pannill 1947- WhoAmW 93
Campbell, Suzann Kay 1943- WhoAmW 93
Campbell, Sybil Eileene 1933- WhoUN 92
Campbell, T. Scott 1940- St&PR 93
Campbell, Terry Allen 1957- WhoEmL 93
Campbell, Terry Leland 1941- St&PR 93
Campbell, Terry M. 1950- St&PR 93
Campbell, Thomas 1777-1844 BioIn 17
Campbell, Thomas Colin 1934- WhoAm 92
Campbell, Thomas Corwith, Jr. 1920- WhoAm 92
Campbell, Thomas Douglas 1951- WhoSSW 93
Campbell, Thomas J. BioIn 17
Campbell, Thomas J. 1952- WhoAm 92
Campbell, Thomas Jefferson, Jr. 1956- WhoSSW 93
Campbell, Thomas Justin 1959- WhoE 93
Campbell, Thomas Louis 1959- WhoE 93
Campbell, Thomas M. 1952- St&PR 93
Campbell, Thomas R.B. 1938- St&PR 93
Campbell, Thomas Raymond 1939- St&PR 93
Campbell, Thomas Richardson Brown 1938- WhoE 93
Campbell, Thomas W. 1943- St&PR 93
Campbell, Thomas Wood 1930- St&PR 93
Campbell, Timothy J. 1942- St&PR 93
Campbell, Tom 1952- CngDr 91
Campbell, Tom J. 1943- St&PR 93
Campbell, Van C. 1938- St&PR 93, WhoAm 92
Campbell, Vincent Walter Law&B 92
Campbell, Wallace Arnold 1918- St&PR 93
Campbell, Wallace Justin 1910- WhoAm 92
Campbell, Walter Benjamin 1921- WhoAsAP 91
Campbell, Walter J. d1991 BioIn 17
Campbell, Wendell Jerome 1927- WhoAm 92
Campbell, Wendy L. 1953- WhoWrEP 92
Campbell, Wesley Glenn 1924- WhoAm 92
Campbell, Wilfred 1861-1918 BioIn 17
Campbell, Will D. BioIn 17
Campbell, Will D(avis) 1924- WhoWrEP 92
Campbell, William 1745-1781 HarEnMi
Campbell, William Buford, Jr. 1935- WhoSSW 93
Campbell, William Cecil 1930- WhoAm 92
Campbell, William Clarke 1918- St&PR 93, WhoAm 92
Campbell, William David 1929- St&PR 93
Campbell, William Edward 1927- WhoAm 92
Campbell, William Henry, Jr. 1947- WhoEmL 93
Campbell, William I. 1944- WhoE 93
Campbell, William Ian 1944- St&PR 93
Campbell, William J. d1992 NewYTBS 92
Campbell, William Leander, Jr. 1946- WhoEmL 93, WhoSSW 93
Campbell, William Lester 1931- St&PR 93
Campbell, William McClure 1949- St&PR 93
Campbell, William Michael 1948- WhoSSW 93
Campbell, William Steen 1919- WhoAm 92, WhoWor 93
Campbell, William Wilfred 1861-1918 BioIn 17
Campbell, Winnie B. 1925- St&PR 93
Campbell-Bannerman, Henry 1836-1908 BioIn 17
Campbell Davis, Trevor Fraser 1950- WhoWor 93
Campbell-Platt, Geoffrey WhoScE 91-1
Campbell-Root, Colleen Law&B 92
Campbell-Tipton, Louis 1877-1921 Baker 92
Campbell-Traxler, Donna Lea 1945- WhoAmW 93
Campbell-Watson, Frank 1898-1980 Baker 92
Campbell-White, Annette Jane 1947- WhoAm 92, WhoEmL 93
Camp-Brewer, Laura Marie 1962- WhoAmW 93
Campeau, Jean 1931- WhoAm 92, WhoE 93
Campeau, L. Gerald 1935- St&PR 93
Campeau, Robert 1923- BioIn 17
Campendonk, Heinrich 1889-1957 BioIn 17
Campenhout, Francois van 1779-1848 Baker 92
Campenni, Thomas Felix 1953- WhoE 93, WhoWor 93
Camper, John Jacob 1943- WhoAm 92
Camper, Petrus 1722-1789 IntDcAn
Campero, Narciso 1815-1896 HarEnMi
Campfield, William 1766-1812 BioIn 17
Campian, Thomas 1567-1620 Baker 92
Campiere, Margaret S. Law&B 92
Campigli, Massimo 1895-1971 BioIn 17
Campigotto, Corrado Marco 1962- WhoWor 93
Campin, Elisabeth A. Law&B 92
Campion, Carol-Mae Sack 1950- WhoE 93
Campion, Daniel Ray 1949- WhoWrEP 92
Campion, Edmund John 1949- WhoEmL 93, WhoSSW 93
Campion, Francois c. 1686-1748 Baker 92
Campion, Jane BioIn 17, ConAu 138
Campion, Jane 1955?- ConTFT 10, MiSFD 9
Campion, Joan Berengaria WhoWrEP 92
Campion, John E. Law&B 92
Campion, John F. 1952- WhoEmL 93
Campion, Robert Thomas 1921- WhoAm 92
Campion, Rose AmWomPl
Campion, Sidney 1891- ScF&FL 92
Campion, Thomas 1567-1620 Baker 92
Campioni, Carlo Antonio 1720-1788 Baker 92
Campioni, Inigo 1878-1944 HarEnMi
Campise, Tony BioIn 17
Camplan, Jean 1931- WhoScE 91-2
Campman, Christopher Kuller 1949- WhoE 93, WhoEmL 93
Campney, C.L. Law&B 92
Campney, Lisa Janine Law&B 92
Campo, Angel del 1868-1908 DcMexL
Campo, Angelo 1979- BioIn 17
Campo, Fred S. 1949- St&PR 93
Campo, J. M. 1943- WhoWor 93
Campo, John W., Jr. Law&B 92
Campo, John William 1920- St&PR 93
Campo, Julian 1943- BioIn 17
Campo, Maria Veronica 1957- WhoWor 93
Campo (y Zabaleta), Conrado del 1879-1953 Baker 92
Campobello, Nellie 1900- BioIn 17
Campobello, Nellie Francisca Ernestina 1909- DcMexL
Campolettano, Thomas Alfred 1946- WhoEmL 93
Campoli, Alfredo 1906-1991 AnObit 1991, BioIn 17
Campoli, Ella Frances 1906- WhoAmW 93
Campoli, Lisa Maria 1957- WhoEmL 93
Campolo, Anthony BioIn 17
Campolongo, James Michael 1962- WhoE 93
Campolongo, Vincent Netal 1938- St&PR 93
Campolucci, Roger L. Law&B 92
Campora, Giuseppe 1923- Baker 92
Camporese, Giovanni 1943- St&PR 93
Camporese, Violante 1785-1839 OxDcOp
Campos, Alvaro de 1888-1935 BioIn 17
Campos, Antonio C. 1930- St&PR 93
Campos, Chris BioIn 17
Campos, Francesco Law&B 92
Campos, Javier Francisco 1963- WhoWor 93
Campos, Julieta 1932- BioIn 17, DcMexL, SpAmA
Campos, Luis Manuel Braga da Costa 1950- WhoWor 93
Campos, Marco Antonio 1949- DcMexL
Campos, Michael John 1944- WhoE 93
Campos, Palmira Sandoval 1961- WhoSSW 93
Campos, Paulo Campana 1921- WhoWor 93
Campos, Rosario Yvonne 1948- WhoAmW 93
Campos, Ruben M. 1876-1945 DcMexL
Campos, Santiago E. 1926- HispAmA
Campos-Parsi, Hector 1922- Baker 92
Campos Ramirez, Alejandro 1919- DcMexL
Campra, Andre 1660-1744 Baker 92, OxDcOp
Camps, Francisco 1935- WhoScE 91-3
Camps, Luis 1928- BioIn 17
Camps, Pompeyo 1924- Baker 92
Campton, David 1924- ScF&FL 92
Campus, A. WhoScE 91-1
Campus, Michael MiSFD 9
Campuzano, Juan R. 1912- DcMexL
Camras, Marvin 1916- WhoAm 92
Camron, Roxanne WhoAm 92, WhoWrEP 92
Camu, Frederic 1942- WhoScE 91-2
Camus, Albert 1913-1960 BioIn 17, MagSWL [port], WorLitC [port]
Camus, Daniel 1946- WhoScE 91-2
Camus, Daniel E.J. 1946- WhoScE 91-2
Camus, Mario MiSFD 9
Camussi, Ezio 1877-1956 Baker 92
Can, Cu Huy 1919- WhoWor 93
Canabal, Maria Enilda 1944- WhoAmW 93
Canada, Anne McGee 1965- WhoSSW 93
Canada, Karyn E. 1948- WhoSSW 93
Canada, Linda A. Law&B 92
Canada, Mary Whitfield 1919- WhoAm 92
Canadeo, Ernest Gerard 1955- WhoEmL 93
Canadeo, Tony 1919- BioIn 17
Canady, John Edward, Jr. Law&B 92
Canady, Paul Allen 1938- WhoSSW 93
Canaga, Gayle Suzanne 1961- WhoAmW 93
Canal, Marguerite 1890-1978 Baker 92
Canal, Nicholas 1931- WhoScE 91-3
Canale, Dee James 1932- WhoAm 92
Canale-Parola, Ercole 1929- WhoAm 92
Canales, Herbert Glenn 1954- WhoAm 92, WhoSSW 93
Canales, Judy 1962- NotHsAW 93
Canan, Janine Burford 1942- WhoWrEP 92
Canan, Michael J. 1941- WhoAm 92, WhoWor 93
Canant, Louis Milton 1935- St&PR 93
Canapary, Herbert C. 1932- WhoIns 93
Canapary, Herbert Carton 1932- WhoAm 92
Canardo, Hernando Vicente 1957- WhoEmL 93, WhoWor 93
Canarie, J. David, Jr. Law&B 92
Canarios, Michael Chris 1953- St&PR 93
Canaris, Wilhelm 1887-1945 DcTwHis, HarEnMi
Canary, Brenda Brown ScF&FL 92
Canary, John Joseph 1925- WhoAm 92
Canary, Nancy Halliday 1941- WhoAm 92
Canary, Thomas Lynch, Jr. 1959- WhoEmL 93
Canas, Maria Martinez NotHsAW 93
Canatella, Carl E. 1941- St&PR 93
Canavan, Bernard 1936- St&PR 93, WhoAm 92, WhoE 93
Canavan, Ellen McGee 1941- WhoAmW 93
Canavan, James McGregor, Jr. 1937- St&PR 93
Canavan, John James, Jr. 1933- WhoE 93
Canavan, Kevin Edward 1951- WhoE 93
Canavan, Patricia Ann 1948- WhoAmW 93
Canavan, Thomas Gerard 1953- WhoEmL 93
Canavesio, David C. St&PR 93
Canby, Henry Seidel 1878-1961 BioIn 17, JrnUS
Canby, Joan Alexander 1948- WhoSSW 93
Canby, Vincent 1924- WhoAm 92
Canby, William Cameron, Jr. 1931- WhoAm 92
Canby, William P. 1949- St&PR 93
Cancalosi, Mark Francis 1954- WhoSSW 93
Cancelarich, John 1930- St&PR 93
Cancell, Leonard Nathan 1933- St&PR 93
Cancelli, Christine BioIn 17
Cancelli, John Joseph 1952- WhoE 93
Cancelliere, F.P. 1925- St&PR 93
Cancelliere, Joseph Albert 1923- St&PR 93
Cancellieri, Alfred J. 1939- St&PR 93
Cancienne, Donald Paul 1933- WhoE 93
Cancilla, Edward 1921- St&PR 93
Cancio, Marta 1928- HispAmA
Cancro, Robert 1932- WhoAm 92
Candace, Gratien 1873-1953 BioIn 17
Candage, Howard Everett 1952- WhoE 93, WhoEmL 93, WhoWor 93
Candaux, Pauline A. Law&B 92
Candee, Richard Alexander, Jr. 1947- WhoWor 93
Candeille, Julie 1767-1834 OxDcOp
Candeille, Pierre Joseph 1744-1827 OxDcOp
Candel, Miguel 1945- WhoWor 93
Candela, Frank Michael 1951- WhoE 93, WhoEmL 93, WhoWor 93
Candela, Gregory Paul Law&B 92
Candela, John A. 1934- St&PR 93
Candela, Lucila 1953- WhoScE 91-3
Candelaria, Alberto 1941- St&PR 93
Candelaria, Cordelia 1943- NotHsAW 93 [port]
Candelaria, Fred 1929- WhoCanL 92
Candelaria, John Robert 1953- BiDAMSp 1989
Candelas, Graciela 1922- HispAmA [port]
Candenquist, Arthur 1946- WhoE 93
Cander, Leon 1926- WhoAm 92
Candia, Oscar A. 1935- HispAmA, WhoAm 92
Candib, Murray A. 1915- WhoAm 92, WhoWor 93
Candib, Susan B. Law&B 92
Candido, Larry Steven 1957- WhoEmL 93
Candido, Michael A., Jr. Law&B 92
Candiello, Martha E. Law&B 92
Candilis, Georges 1913- WhoWor 93
Candiotti, Alan 1947- WhoEmL 93
Candland, Douglas Keith 1934- WhoAm 92
Candle, M. Eugene 1947- St&PR 93
Candler, Asa Griggs 1851-1929 GayN
Candler, John Slaughter, II 1908- WhoAm 92, WhoSSW 93
Candlish, Malcolm 1935- St&PR 93, WhoAm 92
Candris, Laura A. 1955- WhoAm 92, WhoEmL 93
Candura, Francesco Nicola 1929- WhoScE 91-3
Candy, David Charles Alexander WhoScE 91-1
Candy, John BioIn 17
Candy, John 1950- QDrFCA 92 [port]
Candy, John Franklin 1950- WhoAm 92
Cane, Carles 1960- WhoWor 93
Cane, Paula P. 1945- WhoAm 92, WhoAmW 93
Canedo, David Lawrence 1945- St&PR 93
Canedo, Lino Gomez 1908-1990 BioIn 17
Canelas, Dale Brunelle 1938- WhoAm 92
Canell, Beverly June 1949- WhoE 93
Canellakis, A. John 1958- WhoEmL 93
Canellakis, Zoe Nakos 1927- WhoE 93
Canellos, George P. 1934- WhoAm 92
Canelos, Nicholas S. Law&B 92
Canemaker, John 1943- BioIn 17
Canepa, Fernando 1947- St&PR 93
Canepa, John Charles 1930- St&PR 93, WhoAm 92
Canepa, Robert F. 1947- St&PR 93
Caner, George Colket, Jr. 1925- WhoAm 92
Canes, Michael Edwin 1941- WhoAm 92
Canessa, Sonia Edith 1964- WhoAmW 93
Canestrari, Renzo 1924- WhoScE 91-3
Canestri, Giovanni Cardinal 1918- WhoWor 93

Canet, Gerardo *St&PR 93*
Canete, Rogelio Calleno 1957- *WhoWor 93*
Canetti, Elias 1905- *BioIn 17, ConLC 75 [port], DcLB 124 [port], WhoWor 93*
Canetto, Silvia Sara 1955- *WhoAmW 93*
Caneva, Carlo 1845-1922 *HarEnMi*
Caneva-Biggane, Terri Denise 1955- *WhoAmW 93, WhoEmL 93*
Canevari, Charles Daniel 1920- *WhoAm 92*
Canever, William F. *Law&B 92*
Caney, Peter Richard 1946- *WhoWor 93*
Canfield, Andrew Trotter 1953- *WhoE 93, WhoWor 93*
Canfield, Brian A. 1938- *WhoWor 93*
Canfield, Constance Dale 1940- *WhoAmW 93*
Canfield, Deborah Ann 1953- *WhoWrEP 92*
Canfield, Debra Beth McKay 1955- *WhoEmL 93*
Canfield, Dorothea F. *ConAu 136, MajAI*
Canfield, Dorothea Frances *ConAu 136, MajAI*
Canfield, Dorothy *ConAu 136, MajAI*
Canfield, Dorothy May 1963- *WhoE 93*
Canfield, Earle Lloyd 1918- *WhoAm 92*
Canfield, Edward Francis 1922- *WhoAm 92*
Canfield, Ethel *BioIn 17*
Canfield, Francis Xavier 1920- *WhoAm 92*
Canfield, Frederick Weber 1930- *St&PR 93, WhoAm 92*
Canfield, Glenn, Jr. 1935- *WhoSSW 93*
Canfield, Gordon R. 1939- *St&PR 93*
Canfield, Grant Wellington, Jr. 1923- *WhoAm 92*
Canfield Joan Giltner 1921- *WhoWrEP 92*
Canfield, Judy Ohlbaum 1947- *WhoAmW 93*
Canfield, Louise Monette *WhoAmW 93*
Canfield, Lynda Rae 1947- *WhoAmW 93*
Canfield, Mary Cass *AmWomPl*
Canfield, Maurice C. 1920- *St&PR 93*
Canfield, Muriel Jean Nixon 1928- *WhoAmW 93, WhoWor 93*
Canfield, Peter Crane 1954- *WhoEmL 93, WhoSSW 93*
Canfield, Richard Grant 1928- *St&PR 93*
Canfield, Thomas F. 1942- *St&PR 93*
Canfield, William 1766-1812 *BioIn 17*
Canganelli, Michael Antonio 1951- *WhoEmL 93*
Cangelosi, Carl J. 1942- *St&PR 93*
Cangemi, Joseph Peter 1936- *WhoAm 92, WhoSSW 93*
Cangemi, Michael Paul 1948- *WhoAm 92, WhoE 93, WhoEmL 93*
Cangiamilla, Bette Frances 1957- *WhoAmW 93*
Cangurel, Susan Stone 1946- *WhoAmW 93*
Canham, Donald N. 1947- *St&PR 93*
Canham, Erwin D(ain) 1904-1982 *DcLB 127 [port]*
Canham Rogers, Julie A. *Law&B 92*
Canidius, Publius Crassus d30BC *HarEnMi*
Caniff, Milton Arthur 1907-1988 *BioIn 17*
Caniglia, Alan Scott 1956- *WhoEmL 93*
Caniglia, Maria 1905-1979 *Baker 92, IntDcOp, OxDcOp*
Caniglia, Richard Gary 1948- *WhoAm 92, WhoE 93, WhoEmL 93*
Canike, Anthony Christopher 1946- *WhoE 93*
Canin, Stuart Victor 1926- *WhoAm 92*
Canino, Bruno 1935- *Baker 92*
Canino, Joel M. 1939- *St&PR 93*
Canion, Joseph R. *BioIn 17*
Canion, Joseph R. 1945- *ConEn*
Canion, Joseph Rod 1945- *WhoSSW 93*
Canion, Rod *BioIn 17*
Caniparoli, Val William 1951- *WhoAm 92*
Canipe, Stephen Lee 1946- *WhoSSW 93*
Canisius, Peter 1929- *WhoScE 91-3*
Canizares, Claude Roger 1945- *WhoE 93*
Canizares, Robert M. 1949- *WhoEmL 93*
Canizio, Candida L. *Law&B 92*
Canlas, Benjamin D., Jr. 1925- *WhoWor 93*
Canlas, Luzano Pancho, Sr. 1940- *WhoE 93*
Cann, Brian 1951- *St&PR 93*
Cann, Howard 1895-1992 *NewYTBS 92 [port]*
Cann, Louise Gebhard *AmWomPl*
Cann, Nancy Timanus *WhoAmW 93*
Cann, Rachel P. 1942- *WhoWrEP 92*
Cann, Sharon Lee 1935- *WhoAmW 93*
Cann, William Francis 1922- *WhoAm 92*
Cann, William Hopson 1916- *WhoAm 92*
Canna, Joseph John 1950- *St&PR 93*
Cannabich, (Johann) Christian (Innocenz Bonaventura) 1731-1798 *Baker 92*
Cannada, Charles T. 1958- *St&PR 93*
Cannaday, Marilyn *ScF&FL 92*
Cannady, Brett Phillips 1956- *St&PR 93*
Cannady, Bruce Riordan 1941- *St&PR 93*
Cannady, Edward Wyatt, Jr. 1906- *WhoWor 93*
Cannady, Frances P. 1920- *St&PR 93*
Cannady, Nathaniel Ellis, Jr. 1920- *St&PR 93*
Cannady, William Tillman 1937- *WhoAm 92*
Cannaliato, Vincent 1941- *St&PR 93*
Cannaliato, Vincent, Jr. 1941- *WhoAm 92, WhoE 93*
Cannamela, David *St&PR 93*
Cannat, Arlette *WhoScE 91-2*
Cannavino, James *NewYTBS 92*
Cannavino, James A. *BioIn 17*
Cannavo, Sal Michael 1928- *St&PR 93*
Cannedy, Curtis Dwight 1953- *St&PR 93*
Cannegieter, Cornelis Antonius 1913- *WhoWor 93*
Cannell, Charles Frederick 1913- *WhoAm 92*
Cannell, Charles H. *ScF&FL 92*
Cannell, John Redferne 1937- *WhoAm 92*
Cannell, Lee Ora 1947- *St&PR 93*
Cannell, Melvin Gilbert Richard *WhoScE 91-1*
Cannell, Peter B. 1926- *St&PR 93*
Cannell, Stephen J. 1941- *Au&Arts 9 [port]*
Cannell, Stephen J(oseph) 1941- *ConAu 138*
Cannell, Stephen Joseph 1941- *WhoAm 92*
Cannell, Tim A. 1949- *St&PR 93*
Cannella, John M. 1908- *HispAmA*
Cannella, John Matthew 1908- *WhoAm 92, WhoE 93*
Cannella, Philip 1933- *WhoAm 92*
Cannella, Vincent David 1938- *St&PR 93*
Cannerelli, Kenneth A. 1948- *St&PR 93*
Canney, Donald James 1930- *WhoAm 92*
Canney, Walter A. 1934- *St&PR 93*
Canniff, Edward Timothy, Jr. 1942- *St&PR 93*
Canniff, Kiki 1948- *WhoWrEP 92*
Canning, Elizabeth Ursula *WhoScE 91-1*
Canning, Fred W. 1931- *St&PR 93*
Canning, George 1770-1827 *BioIn 17*
Canning, Gerald W. 1948- *St&PR 93*
Canning, Jessie Marie *WhoAm 92*
Canning, John A., Jr. *St&PR 93*
Canning, John B. *Law&B 92*
Canning, John Beckman 1943- *WhoE 93*
Canning, John J. 1941- *St&PR 93, WhoAm 92*
Canning, John Rafton 1927- *WhoAm 92*
Canning, Lisa *BioIn 17*
Canning, Simon *St&PR 93*
Canning, Victor 1911-1986 *ScF&FL 92*
Cannings, Christopher *WhoScE 91-1*
Cannistra, Linda M. 1955- *WhoAmW 93*
Cannistra, Philip 1954- *WhoEmL 93*
Cannistraci, Anthony 1951- *WhoE 93*
Cannistraro, Nicholas, Jr. 1939- *WhoAm 92*
Cannizzaro, Paul Peter 1925- *WhoAm 92, WhoE 93*
Cannizzaro, Peter Louis 1944- *St&PR 93*
Canno, Leonard E. 1912- *St&PR 93*
Cannon, Allen Lee 1961- *WhoEmL 93*
Cannon, Annie Jump 1863-1941 *BioIn 17*
Cannon, Benjamin Winton 1944- *WhoWor 93*
Cannon, Bradford 1907- *WhoAm 92*
Cannon, Carl N. 1943- *St&PR 93*
Cannon, Charles C. 1928- *WhoAm 92*
Cannon, Charles Dale 1928- *WhoAm 92*
Cannon, Christine Anne 1952- *WhoAmW 93, WhoEmL 93*
Cannon, Christopher L. *Law&B 92*
Cannon, Christopher L. 1946- *St&PR 93*
Cannon, Christopher Perry 1953- *WhoEmL 93*
Cannon, Curt *ConAu 38NR*
Cannon, Daniel Willard 1920- *WhoAm 92, WhoE 93, WhoWor 93*
Cannon, Darrell Jay 1955- *WhoEmL 93, WhoSSW 93*
Cannon, David C., Jr. *Law&B 92*
Cannon, David Frank 1944- *WhoWor 93*
Cannon, David Price 1946- *WhoEmL 93*
Cannon, Deborah Lynn 1961- *WhoAmW 93*
Cannon, Denise Thornsberry 1949- *WhoEmL 93*
Cannon, Dyan *BioIn 17*
Cannon, Dyan 1937- *MiSFD 9, WhoAm 92*
Cannon, Fanny Venable 1876- *AmWomPl*
Cannon, Faye Ellen 1949- *St&PR 93*
Cannon, Francis V., Jr. 1935- *WhoAm 92*
Cannon, Garland 1924- *WhoAm 92, WhoSSW 93*
Cannon, Gerald N. 1929- *St&PR 93*
Cannon, Glenn Scott 1949- *WhoEmL 93*
Cannon, Grace Bert 1937- *WhoE 93*
Cannon, Harold Dunbar, II 1951- *St&PR 93*
Cannon, Helen Leighton 1911- *WhoAm 92*
Cannon, Herbert Seth 1931- *WhoAm 92, WhoSSW 93*
Cannon, Howard Walter 1912- *WhoAm 92*
Cannon, Hugh 1931- *WhoSSW 93, WhoWor 93*
Cannon, Hugh Michau 1947- *WhoEmL 93*
Cannon, Isabella Walton 1904- *WhoAm 92*
Cannon, J.W. 1943- *St&PR 93*
Cannon, James 1864-1944 *BioIn 17*
Cannon, James A. 1938- *St&PR 93*
Cannon, James F. *AfrAmBi*
Cannon, James J., Jr. *Law&B 92*
Cannon, James W. 1927- *WhoAm 92*
Cannon, Janet 1945- *WhoWrEP 92*
Cannon, Joan M. *Law&B 92*
Cannon, John 1927- *WhoAm 92*
Cannon, John, III 1954- *WhoEmL 93*
Cannon, John Cornelius 1925- *WhoSSW 93*
Cannon, John Haile 1942- *St&PR 93*
Cannon, John Joseph 1954- *WhoE 93, WhoEmL 93*
Cannon, John Kemper 1932- *WhoAm 92*
Cannon, Joseph A. *BioIn 17*
Cannon, Joseph G. 1836-1926 *PolPar*
Cannon, Judy Martha 1946- *WhoSSW 93*
Cannon, Kenneth Dean 1943- *St&PR 93*
Cannon, Lynne M. 1955- *St&PR 93*
Cannon, Lynne Marple 1955- *WhoE 93, WhoWor 93*
Cannon, Margaret Herold 1943- *WhoAmW 93*
Cannon, Mark Wilcox 1928- *WhoAm 92*
Cannon, Martin *ScF&FL 92*
Cannon, Marvin Samuel 1940- *WhoSSW 93*
Cannon, Mary E. *Law&B 92*
Cannon, Mary Ellen 1956- *WhoEmL 93*
Cannon, Maurice L. 1949- *St&PR 93*
Cannon, Michael *Law&B 92*
Cannon, Michael John 1940- *St&PR 93*
Cannon, Nancy Gladstein *WhoAmW 93*
Cannon, Norman Lawrence 1936- *WhoAm 92*
Cannon, Patrick Francis 1938- *WhoAm 92*
Cannon, Paul John 1922- *WhoScE 91-3*
Cannon, Peter 1932- *WhoAm 92*
Cannon, Peter 1951- *ScF&FL 92*
Cannon, (Jack) Philip 1929- *Baker 92*
Cannon, Richard D. 1928- *St&PR 93*
Cannon, Richard Dyson 1928- *WhoE 93*
Cannon, Robert Edwin 1947- *St&PR 93*
Cannon, Robert Eugene 1945- *WhoAm 92, WhoSSW 93*
Cannon, Robert L. 1936- *St&PR 93*
Cannon, Robert Leo 1947- *WhoEmL 93*
Cannon, Robert P. *Law&B 92*
Cannon, Robert William 1931- *WhoAm 92*
Cannon, Samantha Karrie 1948- *WhoAmW 93*
Cannon, Sebren Hatley 1922- *St&PR 93*
Cannon, Sharon McMillen 1959- *WhoAmW 93*
Cannon, Sheila *BioIn 17*
Cannon, Stacey Margaret *Law&B 92*
Cannon, Thomas Burt 1944- *St&PR 93*
Cannon, William Bernard 1920- *WhoAm 92*
Cannon, William Harold 1930- *St&PR 93*
Cannon, William Ragsdale 1916- *WhoAm 92*
Cannon, Woodrow Wilson 1911- *WhoSSW 93*
Cannon, Yolanda J. 1957- *WhoEmL 93*
Cannone-McGill, Rosalie Antoinette 1943- *WhoAmW 93*
Cannon-Geary, Irene Sheila *Law&B 92*
Cannon-Ryan, Susan Kaye 1950- *WhoEmL 93*
Canny, James R. *ScF&FL 92*
Canny, Marie Claire 1938- *WhoAmW 93*
Cano, Alonso 1601-1667 *BioIn 17*
Cano, Kristin Maria 1951- *WhoEmL 93*
Cano, Linda Dulce 1949- *WhoEmL 93, WhoSSW 93*
Cano, Maria Victoria 1960- *WhoEmL 93*
Cano, Mario Stephen 1953- *WhoEmL 93*
Cano, Sylvia *Law&B 92*
Cano-Ballesta, Juan 1932- *WhoAm 92, WhoSSW 93*
Canoff, Karen Huston 1954- *WhoEmL 93*
Canolty, Nancy Lemmon *WhoAmW 93*
Canon, Jack *ScF&FL 92*
Canon, L. Barton, Jr. 1953- *WhoEmL 93*
Canon, Robert Morris 1941- *WhoAm 92, WhoE 93*
Canoni, John David 1939- *WhoAm 92*
Canopari, Gerald Eugene 1944- *St&PR 93*
Canosa, Albert Anthony 1946- *St&PR 93, WhoAm 92*
Canosa, David J. 1952- *St&PR 93*
Canosa, Jorge Mas *BioIn 17*
Canova, Antonio 1757-1822 *BioIn 17*
Canova, Judy 1916-1983 *QDrFCA 92 [port]*
Canovas, Isabel *BioIn 17*
Canovas, Isabel 1945- *WhoWor 93*
Canovas Robles, Jose d1992 *BioIn 17, NewYTBS 92*
Canozer, Ozgul 1944- *WhoScE 91-4*
Canseco, Jose *BioIn 17*
Canseco, Jose 1964- *WhoAm 92*
Canseco-Malloy, Javier 1960- *WhoWor 93*
Cansler, Leslie Ervin 1920- *WhoAm 92*
Cantacuzene, Jean Michel 1933- *WhoWor 93*
Cantagrel, Roger 1946- *WhoScE 91-2*
Cantalupo, James Richard 1943- *WhoAm 92*
Cantaluppi, Stefano Carlo 1954- *WhoWor 93*
Cantarella, Francesco Paquin 1932- *WhoAm 92, WhoWor 93*
Cantarella, Michael John 1940- *St&PR 93*
Cantarelli, Corrado 1926- *WhoScE 91-3*
Cantees, Abe J. 1911- *St&PR 93*
Cantek, Leszek 1927- *WhoScE 91-4*
Cantell, Kari Juhani 1932- *WhoScE 91-4*
Cantell, Lilia Mackay *AmWomPl*
Cantella, Vincent Michele 1917- *WhoAm 92*
Cantelli, Guido 1920-1956 *Baker 92, OxDcOp*
Cantelmo, John R. 1947- *St&PR 93*
Cantelmo, Marilee Ann 1948- *WhoEmL 93*
Cantelmo, Patricia Ann 1944- *WhoE 93*
Cantelo, April (Rosemary) 1928- *Baker 92*
Cantelon, John Edward 1924- *WhoAm 92*
Cantelou, M. Dexter 1958- *WhoSSW 93*
Canteloube (de Malaret), (Marie-) Joseph 1879-1957 *Baker 92*
Canter, Carol Grobman *Law&B 92*
Canter, Deborah Dean 1950- *WhoEmL 93*
Canter, Esther A. *AmWomPl*
Canter, Jerome Wolf 1930- *WhoAm 92*
Canter, Mark A. 1948- *St&PR 93*
Canter, Mark Alan *Law&B 92*
Canter, Ralph Raymond 1921- *WhoAm 92*
Canter, Stanley D. 1923- *WhoAm 92*
Canter, Stanley Stanton 1933- *WhoAm 92*
Canter, Stephen Edward 1945- *WhoAm 92*
Canterac, Jose c. 1785-1835 *HarEnMi*
Cantilli, Edmund Joseph 1927- *WhoAm 92, WhoWor 93*
Cantillon, Richard 1680-1734 *BioIn 17*
Cantilo, Patrick Herrera 1954- *WhoAm 92, WhoEmL 93*
Cantin, Lucille Julienne 1939- *WhoAmW 93*
Cantin, Serge A. *Law&B 92*
Cantine, Susan Lauree Willms 1949- *WhoAmW 93*
Cantinflas 1913- *IntDcF 2-3*
Cantlay, George Gordon 1920- *WhoAm 92*
Cantliffe, Daniel James 1943- *WhoAm 92, WhoSSW 93*
Cantliffe, Jeri Miller 1927- *WhoAm 92, WhoAmW 93, WhoE 93*
Cantlon, Floyd 1932- *St&PR 93*
Canto, Benjamin Joseph 1932- *St&PR 93*
Canto, Diana Catherine 1939- *WhoAmW 93*
Canton, David R. *Law&B 92*
Canton, Frank 1849-1927 *BioIn 17*
Canton, Mark *BioIn 17*
Canton, Mark 1949- *WhoAm 92*
Canton, Michael Henry 1941- *WhoWor 93*
Canton, Wilberto 1923-1979 *DcMexL*
Cantone, Vic 1933- *ConAu 138, WhoAm 92*
Cantoni, Carlo 1936- *WhoScE 91-3*
Cantoni, Giampiero *BioIn 17*
Cantoni, Giampiero 1939- *WhoWor 93*
Cantoni, Louis Joseph 1919- *WhoAm 92*
Cantoni, Virginio 1948- *WhoScE 91-3, WhoWor 93*
Cantor, Alan Everett 1950- *WhoEmL 93*
Cantor, Alexandra S. E. 1961- *WhoAm 92*
Cantor, Bernard Gerald 1916- *WhoAm 92, WhoWor 93*
Cantor, Bernard Jack 1927- *WhoAm 92*
Cantor, Charles Robert 1942- *WhoAm 92*
Cantor, Eddie 1892-1964 *Baker 92, JeAmHC, QDrFCA 92 [port]*
Cantor, Eddie 1893-1964 *IntDcF 2-3 [port]*
Cantor, Edward A. 1928- *St&PR 93*
Cantor, Eleanor Weschler 1913- *WhoAmW 93, WhoE 93*
Cantor, Eli *ScF&FL 92*
Cantor, Eli 1913- *WhoWrEP 92*
Cantor, George (Nathan) 1941- *ConAu 138*
Cantor, Harold 1926- *ConAu 136*
Cantor, Harvey Ira 1942- *WhoE 93*
Cantor, Irvin Victor 1953- *WhoEmL 93*

Cantor, Jay ScF&FL 92
Cantor, Jerome Owen 1949- WhoE 93
Cantor, Johanna T. ScF&FL 92
Cantor, Kathy Jo 1959- WhoAmW 93
Cantor, Leonard St&PR 93
Cantor, Lester Irving 1932- WhoE 93
Cantor, Mara Judith 1940- WhoAmW 93
Cantor, Melanie Gale 1954- WhoAmW 93
Cantor, Mira 1944- WhoE 93
Cantor, Morton B. 1924- WhoE 93
Cantor, Muriel Goldsman 1923- WhoAm 92, WhoAmW 93
Cantor, Norman Frank 1929- WhoAm 92
Cantor, Norman Marshall 1950- St&PR 93
Cantor, Pamela Corliss 1944- WhoAm 92, WhoAmW 93
Cantor, Richard Ira 1944- WhoAm 92, WhoE 93
Cantor, Robert Law&B 92
Cantor, Samuel C. 1919- WhoAm 92
Cantor, Sheldon Gary 1946- St&PR 93
Cantoral-Uriza, Gilberto Eduardo 1949- WhoWor 93
Cantrall, Edward Warren 1931- WhoAm 92
Cantrall, Irving James 1909- WhoWor 93
Cantrell, Charles Leonard 1948- WhoEmL 93
Cantrell, Charles Riley 1945- WhoWrEP 92
Cantrell, Charles Thomas 1944- WhoAm 92
Cantrell, Coleen Sharon 1952- WhoAmW 93
Cantrell, Constance H. Law&B 92
Cantrell, Deborah O. Law&B 92
Cantrell, Dorothy 1940- St&PR 93
Cantrell, Dorothy Treadwell 1942- WhoAmW 93
Cantrell, James F. 1938- St&PR 93
Cantrell, John D. 1933- St&PR 93
Cantrell, John L. St&PR 93
Cantrell, Joseph D. 1944- St&PR 93
Cantrell, Joseph Doyle 1944- WhoAm 92
Cantrell, Lana 1943- WhoAm 92
Cantrell, Lisa W. 1945- ScF&FL 92
Cantrell, Mary 1915- WhoAm 92, WhoAmW 93
Cantrell, Michelle Renee 1956- WhoAmW 93
Cantrell, Robert Wendell 1933- WhoAm 92
Cantrell, Sharron Caulk 1947- WhoAmW 93, WhoSSW 93
Cantrell, Wesley Eugene, Sr. 1935- WhoAm 92, WhoSSW 93
Cantrell, William Allen 1920- WhoAm 92
Cantrell, William Arch, II 1953- WhoEmL 93, WhoSSW 93
Cantril, Albert Hadley 1940- WhoAm 92, WhoE 93
Cantu, E.L. Law&B 92
Cantu, John Maurice 1928- St&PR 93
Cantu, Joseph A. 1950- St&PR 93
Cantu, Patricia Ann Law&B 92
Cantus, H. Hollister 1937- WhoAm 92
Cantwell, Alice Catherine 1927- WhoAmW 93
Cantwell, Dan BioIn 17
Cantwell, Dennis Michael 1943- St&PR 93, WhoAm 92
Cantwell, Don 1935- WhoSSW 93
Cantwell, John Dalzell, Jr. 1909- WhoAm 92
Cantwell, John Walsh 1922- WhoAm 92
Cantwell, Lawrence Michael 1953- WhoIns 93
Cantwell, Linda Walsh 1938- WhoAmW 93
Cantwell, Lois WhoAmW 93, WhoE 93, WhoWor 93
Cantwell, Lois 1951- ScF&FL 92
Cantwell, Maria WhoAmW 93
Cantwell, Mary WhoAm 92
Cantwell, P. Drew 1953- St&PR 93
Cantwell, R.W. 1943- St&PR 93
Cantwell, Robert 1931- WhoAm 92
Cantwell, Robert Crawford 1957- St&PR 93
Cantwell, William Patterson 1921- WhoAm 92
Canty, Brian 1931- WhoWor 93
Canty, Eileen Maxwell 1933- WhoAmW 93
Canty, James Joseph, Jr. 1931- WhoE 93
Canty, Thomas ScF&FL 92
Cantzler, Klaus Martin 1930- WhoWor 93
Canut, A. Louis 1927- St&PR 93
Canvin, David Thomas 1931- WhoAm 92
Can Xue ConAu 139
Canzano, Edward D., Jr. 1907- St&PR 93
Canziani, Arnaldo Maria 1951- WhoWor 93
Canzoneri, Matthew B. WhoAm 92
Canzoneri, Robert 1925- WhoWrEP 92
Canzoniero, Joseph A. 1923- St&PR 93
Cao, Chong Guang 1940- WhoWor 93
Cao, Diogo 1450?-1486 Expl 93
Cao, Feiyu 1924- WhoWor 93
Cao, Jia Ding 1940- WhoWor 93
Cao, Thai-Hai 1954- WhoEmL 93, WhoWor 93
Cao, Yu 1910- BioIn 17
Cao, Zhi-Hao 1937- WhoWor 93
Caos, Antonio 1952- WhoSSW 93
Caouette, David Paul 1960- WhoE 93
Caouette, John Bernard 1944- WhoAm 92, WhoE 93
Cap, Frantisek 1913-1972 DrEEuF
Capablanca, Jose Raul 1888-1942 BioIn 17
Capalbo, Carmen Charles 1925- WhoAm 92
Capalbo, Francis A. St&PR 93
Capaldi, Elizabeth Ann Deutsch 1945- WhoAm 92, WhoSSW 93
Capaldini, Mark Laurence 1954- WhoSSW 93
Capaldo, Guy 1950- WhoEmL 93
Capani, Peter Michael 1951- WhoEmL 93
Capanna, Mark Anthony 1963- WhoE 93
Capanzano, Charles Thomas 1949- WhoEmL 93
Caparas, Mateo WhoAsAP 91
Caparn, Rhys 1909- WhoAm 92
Caparros, Ann Mary 1952- St&PR 93
Capasso, Federico 1949- WhoAm 92
Capasso, Philip Joseph 1943- St&PR 93
Capasso, Stephen E. 1953- St&PR 93
Capasso, Vincent 1934- St&PR 93
Capaul, Raymond W. 1912- St&PR 93
Capdevielle, Pierre 1906-1969 Baker 92
Capdevila, Ramon 1948- WhoScE 91-3
Cape, Arthur St&PR 93
Cape, Judith ScF&FL 92, WhoCanL 92
Cape, Randall E. Law&B 92
Cape, Ronald Elliot 1932- St&PR 93, WhoAm 92
Cape, Safford 1906-1973 Baker 92
Cape, William Robert 1950- St&PR 93
Capecchi, Renato 1923- Baker 92, OxDcOp
Capecelatro, Mark John 1948- WhoE 93, WhoEmL 93
Capece Minutolo, Francesco 1937- WhoWor 93
Capeci, Claire BioIn 17
Capecki, Zenon 1925- WhoScE 91-4
Capehart, Barney Lee 1940- WhoAm 92
Capehart, Craig Earl Law&B 92
Capehart, Homer Earl, Jr. 1922- WhoAm 92
Capehart, Martin Ellis, Jr. 1957- WhoWor 93
Capek, Antoinette A. 1926- WhoWrEP 92
Capek, Karel 1890-1938 BioIn 17, OxDcOp, ScF&FL 92, WorLitC [port]
Capek, Milic 1909- WhoAm 92
Capek, Miroslav 1927- WhoScE 91-4
Capel, Arthur 1631-1683 BioIn 17
Capel, Guy B. Law&B 92
Capelan, Carl R. 1950- St&PR 93
Capeling-Alakija, Sharon 1944- WhoUN 92
Capell, Cydney Lynn 1956- WhoAmW 93, WhoSSW 93
Capell, Richard 1885-1954 Baker 92
Capella, Raul Garcia ScF&FL 92
Capellan, Angel 1942- WhoE 93
Capellaro, John Joseph 1951- St&PR 93
Capelle, A. WhoScE 91-3
Capelle, Edouard von 1855-1931 HarEnMi
Capelli, Catherine Ann 1961- WhoAmW 93
Capelli, Elizabeth A. 1963- WhoAmW 93
Capelli, John Placido 1936- WhoAm 92
Capellmann, Herbert 1942- WhoScE 91-3
Capello, Gene A. Law&B 92
Capello, Luigi Attilio 1859-1941 HarEnMi
Capellos, Chris Spiridon 1934- WhoWor 93
Capelo, Antonio WhoScE 91-3
Capelo, Hermenegildo de Brito 1841-1917 & Ivens, Roberto 1850-1898 Expl 93
Capen, Charles Chabert 1936- WhoAm 92
Capen, Richard Goodwin, Jr. 1934- St&PR 93, WhoAm 92
Caper, Samuel Philip 1938- WhoAm 92
Capers, Charlotte 1913- WhoAm 92
Capers, Mark Verdier 1955- WhoEmL 93
Caperton, Albert Franklin 1936- WhoAm 92
Caperton, Gaston 1940- WhoAm 92, WhoWor 93
Caperton, George Coble 1950- WhoEmL 93
Caperton, Richard Walton 1948- WhoWor 93
Caperton, S. Austin, III Law&B 92
Caperton, W. Gaston 1940- WhoSSW 93
Capes, Bernard 1854-1918 ScF&FL 92
Capes, Rebecca Ellen 1956- WhoAmW 93
Capet, Lucien 1873-1928 Baker 92
Capetillo, Luisa 1879-1922 NotHsAW 93
Capezza, Joseph C. 1955- WhoIns 93
Capice, Philip Charles 1931- WhoAm 92, WhoWor 93
Capie, Forrest Hunter WhoScE 91-1
Capie, Susan Alvera 1953- WhoE 93
Capin, Harlan 1930- St&PR 93
Capistrano, Ricardo Felix 1959- WhoWor 93
Capitan, William Harry 1933- WhoAm 92
Capitant, Rene 1901-1970 BioIn 17
Capitman, Barbara Baer 1919-1990 BioIn 17
Capizzi, Anthony 1954- WhoEmL 93
Capizzi, John A. 1954- WhoIns 93
Capizzi, Robert Lawrence 1938- WhoAm 92
Capizzi, Tracey Leigh Quante 1959- WhoE 93
Caplan, Albert Joseph 1908- WhoAm 92
Caplan, Arnold I. 1942- WhoAm 92
Caplan, Arthur L(eonard) 1950- WhoWrEP 92
Caplan, Benjamin 1916- St&PR 93
Caplan, Constance Rose 1935- WhoE 93
Caplan, David I. Law&B 92
Caplan, Edwin Harvey 1926- WhoAm 92
Caplan, Elinor 1944- WhoAmW 93
Caplan, Frank 1919- St&PR 93
Caplan, Gerald 1917- ConAu 40NR
Caplan, John David 1926- WhoAm 92
Caplan, Judith Shulamith Langer 1945- WhoWrEP 92
Caplan, Lazarus David 1940- WhoAm 92
Caplan, Lester 1924- WhoAm 92, WhoSSW 93
Caplan, Lincoln 1950- ConAu 138
Caplan, Louis Robert 1936- WhoAm 92
Caplan, Mark J. Law&B 92
Caplan, Ralph 1925- WhoAm 92, WhoE 93
Caplan, Richard V. 1937- WhoAm 92
Caplan, Ronald BioIn 17
Caplan, Sherri G. Law&B 92
Caplan, Stanley H. 1944- St&PR 93
Caplen, Harry A. 1911- St&PR 93
Caplen, Larry 1963- St&PR 93
Caplen, Mary Ann 1961- WhoAmW 93
Caplen, Stanley B. 1935- St&PR 93
Caples, John 1900-1990 BioIn 17
Caples, Michael Edward 1951- WhoEmL 93
Caples, Richard James 1949- WhoAm 92, WhoWor 93
Caples, William Goff, IV 1946- WhoEmL 93
Caplet, Andre 1878-1925 Baker 92
Caplin, Barbara Ellen 1954- WhoEmL 93
Caplin, Jerrold Leon 1930- WhoE 93
Caplin, Lee 1946- WhoEmL 93
Caplin, Loren-Paul 1948- WhoEmL 93
Caplin, Michael Andrew 1951- WhoEmL 93
Caplin, Mortimer Maxwell 1916- WhoAm 92
Caplinger, Debra Ann 1954- WhoEmL 93, WhoSSW 93
Caplinger, Kenneth Travers 1912- WhoWor 93
Caplinger, Paula Ruth 1948- WhoAmW 93, WhoEmL 93
Caplovitz, Coleman David 1925- WhoSSW 93
Caplovitz, David d1992 NewYTBS 92 [port]
Caplovitz, David 1928-1992 ConAu 139
Caplow, Peter Joseph 1943- St&PR 93
Caplow, Theodore 1920- WhoAm 92
Capobianco, Cesare 1960- WhoWor 93
Capobianco, Daniel Lauro 1962- WhoEmL 93
Capobianco, Eva Mary 1954- WhoAm 92
Capobianco, Lucia 1938- St&PR 93
Capobianco, Michael 1950- ScF&FL 92
Capobianco, Sheila Marie 1961- WhoAmW 93
Capobianco, Tito 1931- OxDcOp, WhoAm 92
Capocaccia, Lilia 1931- WhoScE 91-3, WhoWor 93
Capocci, Gaetano 1811-1898 Baker 92
Capodanno, Paul J. 1935- St&PR 93
Capodilupo, Elizabeth Jeanne Hatton 1940- WhoAmW 93, WhoE 93, WhoWor 93
Capoferri, Marco Alessandro 1943- WhoWor 93
Capoianu, Dumitru 1929- Baker 92
Capolarello, Joe R. 1961- WhoE 93, WhoEmL 93, WhoWor 93
Capon, Dale E. 1929- St&PR 93
Capon, Robert Farrar 1925- ConAu 136
Capone, Al(fonso) 1899-1947 DcTwHis
Capone, Alphonse William 1919- WhoAm 92
Capone, Antonio 1926- WhoE 93, WhoWor 93
Capone, Donald William 1943- St&PR 93
Capone, Jimmy BioIn 17
Capone, Lori Annette Law&B 92
Capone, Lucien, Jr. WhoAm 92, WhoWor 93
Capone, Margaret Lynch 1907- WhoAmW 93
Caponegro, Candace ScF&FL 92
Caponegro, Ernest Mark 1957- WhoEmL 93
Caponegro, Mary 1956- WhoAmW 93
Caponetti, James Dante 1932- WhoSSW 93
Caponi, Donna Young 1945- BiDAMSp 1989
Caponi, Thomas A. 1930- St&PR 93
Caponigro, Ralph Angelo 1932- St&PR 93, WhoAm 92
Caporale, Charles Michael 1950- WhoIns 93
Caporale, D. Nick 1928- WhoAm 92
Caporale, Patricia Jeane 1947- WhoWrEP 92
Caporale, Robert Stephen 1945- WhoE 93
Caporali, Renso L. 1933- St&PR 93
Caporella, Joseph G. St&PR 93
Caporella, Nick A. St&PR 93
Caporella, Nick A. 1937- WhoAm 92
Capos, Claudia Ruth 1951- WhoAmW 93
Caposela, Ernest Michael 1953- WhoE 93
Capossela, Fred d1991 BioIn 17
Capossela, James P. 1949- WhoWrEP 92
Capote, Truman 1924-1984 AmWrS3, BioIn 17, ConGAN, MagSAmL [port], WorLitC [port]
Capote-Mir, Roberto E. 1935- WhoUN 92
Capoul, (Joseph-Amedee-) Victor 1839-1924 Baker 92
Capozza, Richard Carl 1942- St&PR 93
Capozzi, John St&PR 93
Capp, Al 1909-1979 BioIn 17
Capp, Michael Paul 1930- WhoAm 92
Capp, Morris R. 1951- St&PR 93
Capp, Patrick O. 1951- St&PR 93
Capp, Robert R. 1946- St&PR 93
Cappa, Carl M. 1923- St&PR 93
Cappabianca, Rosemarie Law&B 92
Cappallo, Roger James 1949- WhoE 93
Capparis, Michael C. Law&B 92
Capparucci, Edmund Michael 1957- WhoEmL 93
Cappel, C. Robert 1942- WhoE 93
Cappel, Constance 1936- WhoAmW 93, WhoWor 93
Cappeline, Gary Anthoney 1949- St&PR 93, WhoAm 92
Cappell, Dennis G. 1953- St&PR 93
Cappelletti, Grace 1939- St&PR 93
Cappelletti, John Peter 1936- St&PR 93
Cappelletti, Joseph R. 1951- St&PR 93
Cappelletti, Mauro 1927- WhoAm 92
Cappelletti, Vincenzo 1930- WhoWor 93
Cappelli, Henry Charles 1934- St&PR 93
Cappelli, Louis Joseph 1931- St&PR 93, WhoAm 92
Cappelli, Mario ScF&FL 92
Cappelli, Paul 1955- WhoAm 92
Cappellini, Louis A. St&PR 93
Cappellini, Vito 1938- WhoScE 91-3
Cappello, A. Barry 1942- WhoWor 93
Cappello, Eve 1922- WhoAmW 93
Cappello, Gerard Karam 1961- WhoEmL 93
Cappello, Rosemary C. 1935- WhoWrEP 92
Cappello-Lorca, Juan Carlos 1938- St&PR 93
Cappenberg, Thomas E. 1938- WhoScE 91-3
Capper, Aloysius Joseph, III 1955- WhoE 93, WhoEmL 93
Capper, Arthur 1865-1951 BioIn 17
Capper, Leonard WhoScE 91-1
Capperauld, Ian WhoScE 91-1
Cappetta, Anna Maria 1949- WhoAmW 93
Cappiello, Angela 1954- WhoAmW 93, WhoEmL 93
Cappiello, Frank A., Jr. 1926- St&PR 93
Cappiello, Frank Anthony, Jr. 1926- WhoAm 92
Cappitella, Mauro John 1934- WhoE 93
Cappo, Joseph C. 1936- WhoAm 92, WhoE 93
Cappon, Alexander Patterson 1900- WhoAm 92
Cappon, Andre Alfred 1948- WhoAm 92, WhoE 93, WhoEmL 93
Cappon, Rene Jacques 1924- WhoAm 92
Capps, Benjamin 1922- BioIn 17
Capps, Brenda Gale Harden 1964- WhoEmL 93, WhoSSW 93
Capps, Carroll M. ScF&FL 92
Capps, Ethan LeRoy 1924- WhoAm 92
Capps, James Austin, Jr. 1940- WhoSSW 93
Capps, Patricia 1951- WhoSSW 93
Capps, Richard Huntley 1928- WhoAm 92
Capps, Sherrill Maynard 1941- St&PR 93
Capps, Stephen David 1965- WhoSSW 93

Capps, Thomas Edward 1935- St&PR 93, WhoAm 92, WhoSSW 93
Cappucci, Joseph D. 1931- St&PR 93
Cappuccilli, Piero 1929- Baker 92, IntDcOp, OxDcOp
Cappuccini, Franco 1923- WhoScE 91-3
Cappuccio, Ronald Joseph 1954- WhoEmL 93
Cappuccitti, Rocco 1957- St&PR 93
Cappy, Ralph Joseph 1943- WhoAm 92
Capra, Bernt MiSFD 9
Capra, Frank 1897-1991 AnObit 1991, BioIn 17, MiSFD 9N, News 92
Capranico, Giovanni 1959- WhoWor 93
Caprara, Aeneas Sylvius, de 1631-1701 HarEnMi
Caprari, Juan Jose 1940- WhoWor 93
Capraro, Franz 1941- WhoSSW 93
Capre, Alfred 1946- St&PR 93
Capriata, Jorge A. 1939- WhoUN 92
Capriati, Jennifer BioIn 17, NewYTBS 92 [port]
Capriati, Jennifer Maria 1976- WhoAm 92, WhoAmW 93
Capricci, Samuel Clement 1955- WhoE 93
Caprio, Anthony S. 1945- WhoAm 92, WhoSSW 93
Caprio, Betsy 1933- ScF&FL 92
Caprio, Elaine A. Law&B 92
Caprio, Elizabeth B. ScF&FL 92
Caprio, Gabriel P. 1938- St&PR 93
Caprio, Joseph Giuseppe Cardinal 1914- WhoAm 92, WhoWor 93
Caprio, Lois Ott 1948- WhoAmW 93
Caprio, Nicholas Frank 1939- WhoE 93
Caprioli, Alberto 1956- Baker 92
Capriolo, John Anthony 1957- WhoE 93, WhoEmL 93
Caprio-Stilwell, Julie Ann 1963- WhoEmL 93
Capriotti, Marcia Swanson 1951- WhoSSW 93
Caprivi, Leo 1831-1899 BioIn 17
Caprivi de Caprara de Montecuculi, Georg Leo, Graf von 1831-1899 BioIn 17
Capriz, Gianfranco 1925- WhoWor 93
Caproiu, Stefan 1929- WhoScE 91-4
Capron, Alexander Morgan 1944- WhoAm 92
Capron, Andre WhoScE 91-2
Capron, Henri Baker 92
Capron, Rosewell G. 1953- St&PR 93
Caproni, Giorgio 1912-1990 DcLB 128 [port]
Capsalis, Barbara D. 1943- St&PR 93
Capsalis, Barbara Damon 1943- WhoAm 92
Capshaw, John Chandler 1932- St&PR 93
Capshaw, Tommie Dean 1936- WhoAm 92
Capsouras, Barbara Ellen 1951- WhoAmW 93
Capstick, John Anthony 1939- WhoAm 92
Captain Young of Yale MajAI
Captal De Buch 1321-1376 HarEnMi
Capua, James Vincent 1949- WhoE 93, WhoEmL 93
Capuana, Franco 1894-1969 Baker 92, OxDcOp
Capuana, Maria 1891-1955 OxDcOp
Capuano, Christine Marie 1953- WhoAm 92, WhoAmW 93
Capucine 1933-1990 BioIn 17
Capurro, Laurel Beth BioIn 17
Caputa, Lewis Anthony 1924- WhoSSW 93
Capute, Joseph 1942- St&PR 93
Caputi, Anthony 1924- WhoAm 92
Caputi, Marie Antoinette 1935- WhoAmW 93
Caputi, William James, Jr. 1936- WhoAm 92
Caputo, Anne Spencer 1947- WhoAmW 93
Caputo, Carmen Michael 1940- St&PR 93
Caputo, Cynthia Jane 1950- WhoAmW 93
Caputo, Daniel Vincent 1933- WhoE 93
Caputo, David Armand 1943- WhoAm 92
Caputo, Frank 1937- St&PR 93
Caputo, Gildo 1904-1987 BioIn 17
Caputo, Giuseppe 1926- WhoScE 91-3
Caputo, Joseph Anthony 1940- WhoAm 92, WhoE 93
Caputo, Kathryn Mary 1948- WhoAmW 93
Caputo, Lucio 1935- WhoWor 93
Caputo, Michael A. Law&B 92
Caputo, Philip BioIn 17
Caputo, Philip 1941- ConAu 40NR
Caputo, Philip Joseph 1941- WhoAm 92, WhoWrEP 92
Caputo, Richard K. 1948- ConAu 139
Caputo, Ruggero 1938- WhoScE 91-3
Caputo, Wayne James 1956- WhoE 93
Capzzoli, Matthew J. Law&B 92
Car, Michael Anthony 1946- WhoEmL 93
Car, Milivoj 1918- WhoScE 91-4
Car, Roberto 1947- WhoWor 93
Car, Stanislaw c. 1885-1938 PolBiDi
Cara, Michel 1949- WhoScE 91-2
Caraballo, Wilfredo 1947- HispAmA [port]
Carabatos-Nedelec, Constantin 1940- WhoScE 91-2
Carabell, Robert S. Law&B 92
Carabello, Vincent J. 1942- St&PR 93
Caraberis, George Peter 1955- St&PR 93
Carabillo, Joseph A. Law&B 92
Carabillo, Joseph Anthony 1946- WhoEmL 93, WhoIns 93
Carabillo, Laura E. Law&B 92
Carabillo, Virginia A. 1926- WhoAm 92
Caracalla 186-217 HarEnMi
Caracci, Christine Marie 1960- WhoEmL 93
Caraccio, Babette B. 1957- WhoEmL 93
Caracciolo, Andrew Bernard 1950- WhoEmL 93, WhoSSW 93
Caracciolo, Francis Samuel 1929- WhoSSW 93, WhoWor 93
Caracciolo, Franco 1920- Baker 92
Caracena, Fernando 1936- HispAmA
Caracena, Luis de Benavides Carillo y Toledo, Marquis of d1668 HarEnMi
Caraci, Philip D. Law&B 92
Caraci, Philip D. 1938- St&PR 93
Caradine, Sally Elizabeth 1940- WhoAmW 93
Caradon, Hugh Foot, Baron 1907-1990 BioIn 17
Caradori-Allan, Maria 1800-1865 OxDcOp
Carafa (de Colobrano), Michele (Enrico-Francesco-Vincenzo-Aloisio-Paolo 1787-1872 Baker 92
Carafa, Michele 1787-1872 OxDcOp
Carafello, William V. 1956- St&PR 93
Carafoli, Ernesto 1932- WhoScE 91-4, WhoWor 93
Caragiulo, Nicholas 1930- St&PR 93
Carague, Guillermo N. 1939- WhoAsAP 91
Caraion, Ion 1923-1986 BioIn 17
Caraker, Mary ScF&FL 92
Caraley, Demetrios 1932- WhoAm 92
Caram, Eve 1934- WhoWrEP 92
Caramandi, Nicholas BioIn 17
Caramello, Anne Olszewski 1951- WhoEmL 93
Carameros, George Demitrius, Jr. 1924- St&PR 93, WhoAm 92
Caranfa, Angelo 1942- WhoE 93
Carani, Dorothy Miriam 1927- WhoWrEP 92
Carano, John J. 1954- St&PR 93
Caranti, Andreas 1952- WhoWor 93
Caranza, Ernest de fl. c. 1850-1863 BioIn 17
Carapella, Victor P. 1949- St&PR 93
Carapellucci, Daniel A. 1946- St&PR 93
Carapetyan, Armen 1908- Baker 92, WhoAm 92
Carapezzi, William R., Jr. Law&B 92
Caras, Constantine George 1938- St&PR 93
Caras, Joseph Sheldon 1924- WhoAm 92
Caras, Rhea Law&B 92
Caras, Roger Andrew 1928- WhoAm 92, WhoWrEP 92
Carassiti, Vittorio WhoScE 91-3
Carausius, Marcus Aurelius Mausaeus d293 HarEnMi
Caraux, Jean Gerard Marie 1951- WhoWor 93
Caravaggio, Michelangelo Merisi da 1573-1610 BioIn 17
Caravale, Giovanni Alfredo 1935- WhoWor 93
Caravasos, Nikolaos 1938- WhoE 93
Caravatt, Paul Joseph, Jr. 1922- WhoAm 92
Caravela, Jack ScF&FL 92
Caraveo, Joseph Richard 1931- St&PR 93
Caraway, Betty Jones 1928- WhoAmW 93
Caraway, Hattie W. 1878-1950 PolPar
Caraway, Hattie Wyatt 1878-1950 BioIn 17
Caraway, Yolanda H. 1950- WhoAmW 93
Carax, Leos 1961- MiSFD 9
Caray, Harry Christopher 1919- WhoAm 92
Carayon, Jacques 1916- WhoScE 91-2
Carayon, Pierre 1945- WhoScE 91-2
Carazo Odio, Rodrigo 1926- DcCPCAm
Carb, Evan Daniel 1960- WhoEmL 93
Carb, Stephen Ames 1930- WhoAm 92
Carbajal, Michael BioIn 17
Carbajales, Jose Antonio 1956- WhoWor 93
Carballes, Jean Claude 1942- WhoScE 91-2
Carballido, Emilio 1925- DcMexL
Carballido, Reynaldo 1949- DcMexL
Carballo, Emmanuel 1929- DcMexL
Carballo, Jose 1919- WhoScE 91-3
Carbary, James Franklin 1951- WhoE 93
Carbaugh, John Edward, Jr. 1945- WhoE 93, WhoWor 93
Carbee, Patricia Lee 1952- WhoAmW 93
Carberry, Deirdre WhoAm 92
Carberry, John A. WhoWrEP 92
Carberry, Judith Bower 1936- WhoAmW 93
Carberry, Michael Glen 1941- WhoAm 92, WhoE 93
Carberry, Patricia Ann 1928- WhoAmW 93
Carbery, Thomas Francis WhoScE 91-1
Carbine, Eugene J. 1936- St&PR 93
Carbine, James Edmond 1945- WhoWor 93
Carbine, Judith BioIn 17
Carbo, Gaius Papirius d82BC HarEnMi
Carbo, Kimberly Monique 1960- WhoEmL 93
Carbo, Ramon 1940- WhoWor 93
Carbo, Ramon Casas 1866-1932 BioIn 17
Carbo, Robert Michael 1946- St&PR 93
Carbo-Fite, Rafael 1942- WhoWor 93
Carbognin, Laura 1945- WhoScE 91-3
Carbon, Max William 1922- WhoAm 92
Carbonar, V. Anthony 1934- St&PR 93
Carbonara, Angelo WhoScE 91-3
Carbonari, Bruce A. 1955- St&PR 93
Carbonari, F.J. 1948- St&PR 93
Carbonari, James J. 1941- St&PR 93
Carbonaro, Paul Anthony 1951- WhoEmL 93
Carbone, Alexander A. 1944- St&PR 93
Carbone, Edward A. 1940- St&PR 93
Carbone, Egidio 1940- St&PR 93
Carbone, James A. 1952- WhoAm 92
Carbone, Larry Law&B 92
Carbone, Lewis Peter 1949- WhoAm 92, WhoEmL 93
Carbone, Paul Peter 1931- WhoAm 92
Carbone, Peter Francis, Jr. 1930- WhoSSW 93
Carbone, Richard A. Law&B 92
Carbone, Vincent Peter 1951- St&PR 93
Carbonell, Frieda Wollmann WhoSSW 93
Carbonell, Joaquin R. Law&B 92
Carbonell, Ramiro M. 1962- WhoE 93
Carbonello, Karen DelSpina 1956- WhoE 93
Carboni, Edwin Peters 1939- WhoAm 92
Carboni, Robert O. 1929- St&PR 93
Carboni, Teresa Maria 1961- WhoEmL 93
Carbonneau, Alain Jean-Luc 1948- WhoWor 93
Carcano, Donato WhoScE 91-3
Carcassi, Ugo Efisio Francesco 1921- WhoWor 93
Carcassonne, Yves 1924- WhoScE 91-2, WhoWor 93
Carcaterra, Lorenzo 1954- BioIn 17, WhoWrEP 92
Carcaterra, Mario BioIn 17
Carceles-Breis, Gabriel 1935- WhoUN 92
Carchano, Herve Henri 1940- WhoScE 91-2
Carchano, Herve Henri Vincent Jean 1940- WhoWor 93
Carchidi, Victoria 1958- WhoSSW 93
Carcich, James J. 1941- St&PR 93
Carcieri, Jeanne F. 1946- St&PR 93
Card, Andrew H., Jr. 1947- WhoAm 92, WhoE 93
Card, David M. Law&B 92
Card, David Noel 1952- WhoE 93
Card, Evelyn Gray Whiting AmWomPl
Card, Joseph Bartow 1941- St&PR 93
Card, Lamar 1942- MiSFD 9
Card, Larry J. 1950- WhoIns 93
Card, Lewis WhoWrEP 92
Card, Orson Scott BioIn 17
Card, Orson Scott 1951- ScF&FL 92, WhoAm 92
Card, Richard Otis 1932- WhoE 93
Card, Robert L. 1937- St&PR 93
Card, Wesley Roy 1947- WhoEmL 93
Cardamone, Louis J. 1926- St&PR 93
Cardamone, Richard J. 1925- WhoAm 92, WhoE 93
Cardan, Paul ConAu 138
Cardani, Cesare WhoScE 91-3
Cardarelli, Michael 1958- WhoEmL 93
Carde, Patrice 1948- WhoScE 91-2
Cardellina, John Henry, II 1947- WhoE 93
Cardemil, Leonardo A. 1945- WhoUN 92
Carden, Arnold Eugene 1930- WhoSSW 93
Carden, Charles B. 1944- St&PR 93
Carden, Charles Buford 1944- WhoAm 92
Carden, George Patrick 1929- St&PR 93
Carden, James Matthew, Jr. 1956- WhoEmL 93
Carden, John Lewis, Jr. 1943- St&PR 93
Carden, John M. 1938- St&PR 93
Carden, Sackville Hamilton 1857-1930 HarEnMi
Cardenal, Ernesto 1925- BioIn 17, SpAmA
Cardenal, Jose Francisco DcCPCAm
Cardenas, Anna Laura 1965- WhoAmW 93
Cardenas, Carlos Federico 1946- WhoWor 93
Cardenas, Cuauhtemoc BioIn 17
Cardenas, Cuauhtemoc 1934- DcCPCAm
Cardenas, Diana Delia 1947- WhoAmW 93
Cardenas, Eliecer 1950- SpAmA
Cardenas, Gilberto M. Law&B 92
Cardenas, Judith Frances 1961- WhoAmW 93
Cardenas, Lazaro 1895-1970 DcCPCAm, DcTwHis
Cardenas, Mary Janet M. 1942- HispAmA
Cardenas, Nancy 1934- DcMexL
Cardenas, Norma Alicia 1952- WhoAmW 93, WhoEmL 93
Cardenas, Rene F. 1933- St&PR 93
Cardenas, Rene Fernando 1933- WhoSSW 93
Cardenas, Reyes 1948- DcLB 122 [port]
Cardenas-Falcon, Luis 1934- WhoUN 92
Cardenas Pena, Jose 1918-1963 DcMexL
Cardenas Ramirez, Blandina NotHsAW 93
Cardenes, Andres Jorge 1957- WhoAm 92
Carder, David Allen 1961- WhoEmL 93
Carder, Paul Charles 1941- WhoAm 92
Carder, Thomas Allen 1949- WhoEmL 93, WhoSSW 93
Cardew, Christopher ScF&FL 92
Cardew, Cornelius 1936-1981 Baker 92
Cardew, William J. 1926- St&PR 93
Cardew, William Joseph WhoAm 92
Cardi, Vincenzo 1948- WhoE 93
Cardiff, Jack 1914- ConTFT 10, MiSFD 9
Cardiff, Larry Oliver 1941- St&PR 93
Cardigan, James Thomas Brudenell, Earl of 1797-1868 HarEnMi
Cardile, Joseph S. 1953- St&PR 93
Cardile, Paul Julius 1948- WhoE 93
Cardile, Thomas C. 1937- St&PR 93
Cardillo, Anthony Thomas 1953- WhoEmL 93
Cardillo, Giuliana WhoScE 91-3
Cardillo, Joe 1951- WhoWrEP 92
Cardillo, Joe Alfred 1951- WhoE 93
Cardillo, Robert Francis, Jr. 1952- WhoE 93
Cardillo, Susan Maria 1958- WhoE 93
Cardin, Benjamin L. 1943- CngDr 91
Cardin, Benjamin Louis 1943- WhoAm 92, WhoE 93
Cardin, Herschel 1926- St&PR 93
Cardin, Pierre BioIn 17
Cardin, Pierre 1922- WhoWor 93
Cardin, Shoshana Shoubin 1926- WhoAm 92
Cardin, Tommie Sullivan 1961- WhoEmL 93
Cardina, Claire Armstrong 1931- WhoSSW 93
Cardinael, Georges C.J.M. 1935- WhoScE 91-2
Cardinal, Anthony J. 1934- St&PR 93
Cardinal, Claus 1943- WhoIns 93
Cardinal, Dick St&PR 93
Cardinal, John Robert 1943- WhoE 93
Cardinal, Lawrence Michael, Jr. 1951- St&PR 93
Cardinal, Marcelin 1920- WhoAm 92
Cardinal, Marie BioIn 17
Cardinal, Norman St&PR 93
Cardinal, Robert 1952- St&PR 93
Cardinal, Roger Joseph 1950- WhoE 93
Cardinal, Roger (Thomas) 1940- ConAu 40NR
Cardinal, Shirley Mae 1944- WhoAmW 93
Cardinal, Tantoo BioIn 17
Cardinale, Claudia 1939- BioIn 17, IntDcF 2-3 [port], WhoWor 93
Cardinale, Kathleen Carmel 1933- WhoE 93, WhoWor 93
Cardinale, Robert Law&B 92
Cardinale, Robert Lee 1939- WhoAm 92
Cardinali, Albert John 1934- WhoAm 92
Cardinalli, Carl T. Law&B 92
Cardine, Godfrey Joseph 1924- WhoAm 92
Cardis, Thomas Michael 1945- WhoSSW 93
Cardman, Frank A. d1991 BioIn 17
Cardman, Lawrence S. 1944- WhoAm 92
Cardman, Phillip N. 1948- St&PR 93
Cardoen, Carlos BioIn 17
Cardon, Phillip W. 1935- St&PR 93
Cardona, Alice NotHsAW 93
Cardona, Blanca Alicia 1950- WhoAmW 93
Cardona, Florencia Bisenta de Casillas Martinez WhoAm 92
Cardona, George S. 1951- WhoWor 93
Cardona, Manuel 1934- HispAmA [port], WhoScE 91-3
Cardona, Mildred Law&B 92
Cardona, Ramon Folch de 1467-1522 HarEnMi
Cardona, Rodolfo 1924- WhoAm 92

Cardona-Caines, Ramonita 1943- WhoSSW 93
Cardone, Bonnie Jean 1942- WhoAm 92
Cardone, J. S. MiSFD 9
Cardone, Janine C. 1959- St&PR 93
Cardoni, Horace R. 1916- St&PR 93
Cardoni, Horace Robert 1916- WhoAm 92
Cardos, John (Bud) MiSFD 9
Cardosa, John 1940- St&PR 93
Cardoso, Anthony Antonio 1930- WhoSSW 93, WhoWor 93
Cardoso, Camilo Dias 1929- WhoScE 91-3
Cardoso, Jose Luis Goncalves 1944- WhoScE 91-3
Cardoso, Manuel 1566-1650 Baker 92
Cardoso, Salvador Massano 1951- WhoWor 93
Cardoso Franco, E.P. 1925- WhoScE 91-3
Cardot, Joseph James 1954- WhoSSW 93
Cardoza, Anne de Sola 1941- WhoAm 92
Cardoza, Desdemona 1953- WhoEmL 93
Cardoza, Robert J. 1943- St&PR 93
Cardoza y Aragon, Luis 1904- DcMexL, SpAmA
Cardozier, Virgus R. 1923- WhoAm 92
Cardozo, Benjamin Mordecai 1915- WhoAm 92
Cardozo, Benjamin Nathan BioIn 17
Cardozo, Benjamin Nathan 1870-1938 OxCSupC [port]
Cardozo, Benjamin Nathan 1870-1939 JeAmHC
Cardozo, Francis L. 1836-1903 EncAACR
Cardozo, Michael Hart 1910- WhoAm 92
Cardozo, Miguel Angel 1932- WhoWor 93
Cardozo, Richard Nunez 1936- WhoAm 92
Carducci, Bartolomeo 1560-1608 BioIn 17
Carducci, Eleanor Whalen 1942- WhoE 93
Carducci, Olivia Marie 1961- WhoEmL 93
Carducho, Bartolome 1560-1608 BioIn 17
Carducho, Vicente 1578-1638 BioIn 17
Carduff, Thomas Jerome 1940- St&PR 93
Cardullo, Alice Cecilia 1955- WhoEmL 93
Cardullo, Joseph St&PR 93
Carduner, Jean 1926-1990 BioIn 17
Cardus, David 1922- HispAmA [port], WhoAm 92
Cardus, Neville (John Frederick) 1888-1975 Baker 92
Cardwell, Charles Evan 1944- WhoSSW 93
Cardwell, David Earl 1951- WhoEmL 93
Cardwell, John J. 1931-1990 BioIn 17
Cardwell, Kenneth Donald 1936- St&PR 93
Cardwell, Kenneth Harvey 1920- WhoAm 92
Cardwell, Maude Eileen 1927- WhoSSW 93
Cardwell, Michael Steven 1954- WhoEmL 93
Cardwell, Nancy Lee 1947- WhoAm 92, WhoE 93
Cardwell, Sandra Gayle Bavido 1943- WhoAmW 93, WhoWor 93
Cardwell, Sue Poole 1952- WhoEmL 93, WhoSSW 93
Cardwell, Thomas Augusta, III 1943- WhoE 93, WhoWor 93
Cardwell, Vernon Bruce 1936- WhoAm 92
Cardy, Andrew Gordon WhoAm 92
Cardy, Robert W. 1936- St&PR 93
Cardy, Robert Willard 1936- WhoAm 92
Care, Anthony Deuchar WhoScE 91-1
Carek, Donald John 1931- WhoAm 92
Careless, Hugh Powell 1941- St&PR 93
Carella, Joseph Dino 1955- WhoEmL 93
Carelli, Cara AmWomPl
Carelli, Gabor Paul 1915- WhoAm 92
Carello, William J. Law&B 92
Caren, Robert P. 1932- St&PR 93
Caren, Robert Poston 1932- WhoAm 92
Caressa, J.P. 1942- WhoScE 91-2
Carestini, Giovanni c. 1705-c. 1760 Baker 92, OxDcOp
Caret, Robert Laurent 1947- WhoAm 92
Carette, Bruno 1956-1989 BioIn 17
Caretti, Richard Louis 1953- WhoEmL 93
Caretto, Albert Alexander 1928- WhoAm 92, WhoE 93
Caretto, Vanessa Margaret 1966- WhoAmW 93
Carew, Jan R. 1925- ScF&FL 92
Carew, Jan Rynveld 1920- WhoAm 92
Carew, Jan Rynveld 1925- BlkAull 92
Carew, John C. 1947- St&PR 93
Carew, Lucretia 1778- BioIn 17
Carew, Peter 1514-1575 HarEnMi
Carew, Rod BioIn 17
Carew, Rod 1945- HispAmA [port]
Carew, Rodney Cline 1945- WhoAm 92
Carew, Thomas 1595?-1639? BioIn 17
Carew, Thomas 1595?-1640 DcLB 126
Carew, Topper 1943- MiSFD 9
Carewe, John (Maurice Foxall) 1933- Baker 92
Carey, Ann BioIn 17
Carey, Anthony Morris 1935- WhoAm 92
Carey, Arthur Bernard, Jr. 1950- WhoAm 92
Carey, Barbara 1955- WhoCanL 92
Carey, Barbara I. 1946- WhoIns 93
Carey, Barbara Jane Law&B 92
Carey, Bruce Douglas 1923- WhoAm 92
Carey, Charles W. 1941- St&PR 93
Carey, Chase BioIn 17
Carey, Christopher Chad 1957- WhoEmL 93
Carey, Christopher Edwin 1958- WhoEmL 93
Carey, Cynthia 1947- WhoEmL 93
Carey, David Edward 1913- WhoSSW 93
Carey, Dean L. 1925- St&PR 93
Carey, Dean Lavere 1925- WhoAm 92
Carey, Dennis Clarke 1949- WhoAm 92, WhoWor 93
Carey, Dennis Paul 1945- WhoSSW 93
Carey, Diane ScF&FL 92
Carey, Donal WhoScE 91-3
Carey, Edward John 1944- St&PR 93, WhoAm 92
Carey, Edward Marshel, Jr. 1942- WhoAm 92
Carey, Emily Anne 1948- WhoAmW 93
Carey, Emily Norris 1958- WhoAmW 93
Carey, Emily St. Germain 1934- WhoAmW 93
Carey, Ernestine Gilbreth 1908- WhoAm 92, WhoAmW 93
Carey, Evangeline Ruth 1949- WhoEmL 93
Carey, Ezekiel 1933- See Flamingos SoulM
Carey, Frances Elizabeth 1945- WhoAm 92
Carey, Francis J., Jr. 1926- St&PR 93
Carey, Francis James 1926- WhoAm 92, WhoWor 93
Carey, G. Cheston, Jr. 1930- St&PR 93
Carey, George BioIn 17
Carey, George 1935- News 92 [port], -92-3 [port]
Carey, George Leonard 1935- WhoWor 93
Carey, Gerald E. 1937- WhoIns 93
Carey, Gerald John, Jr. 1930- WhoAm 92
Carey, Gerard V. 1926- WhoAm 92
Carey, Glenn Owaroff 1919- WhoSSW 93
Carey, Gregory Brian 1942- WhoAm 92
Carey, Gregory Dale 1950- WhoWrEP 92
Carey, Harry 1878-1947 BioIn 17, IntDcF 2-3 [port]
Carey, Harry M., Jr. Law&B 92
Carey, Henry c. 1687-1743 Baker 92, BioIn 17
Carey, Howard H. AfrAmBi
Carey, Hugh J. 1941- St&PR 93
Carey, Hugh L. WhoAm 92
Carey, J. Edwin 1923- WhoAm 92
Carey, J. Paul 1958- St&PR 93
Carey, Jack R. 1952- St&PR 93
Carey, Jacob 1926- See Flamingos SoulM
Carey, James d1990 BioIn 17
Carey, James Henry 1932- WhoAm 92
Carey, James William 1934- WhoAm 92
Carey, Jane Quellmalz 1952- St&PR 93, WhoEmL 93
Carey, Jean Lebeis 1943- WhoAmW 93, WhoE 93
Carey, John 1924- WhoAm 92
Carey, John 1934- WhoAm 92
Carey, John A. 1949- St&PR 93
Carey, John Andrew 1949- WhoEmL 93
Carey, John Edward 1949- WhoEmL 93
Carey, John H. 1937- St&PR 93
Carey, John J. 1928- WhoIns 93
Carey, John J. 1931- WhoAm 92
Carey, John Jesse 1931- WhoAm 92
Carey, John Joseph 1928- St&PR 93
Carey, John Leo 1920- WhoAm 92
Carey, John M. 1933- St&PR 93
Carey, Kathryn Ann 1949- WhoAm 92, WhoAmW 93, WhoEmL 93
Carey, Kevin F. Law&B 92
Carey, Kevin Michael 1956- WhoE 93
Carey, Larry Campbell 1933- WhoAm 92
Carey, Lionel DcCPCAm
Carey, M. V. ConAu 38NR
Carey, Macdonald 1913- BioIn 17, WhoAm 92
Carey, Marcia J. 1941- WhoAmW 93
Carey, Margaret Standish 1926- WhoWrEP 92
Carey, Margaret Theresa Logan 1931- WhoAmW 93
Carey, Mariah BioIn 17, WhoAmW 93
Carey, Mariah 1970?- CurBio 92 [port], SoulM
Carey, Marsha Clifton 1951- WhoEmL 93
Carey, Martin Conrad 1939- WhoE 93, WhoWor 93
Carey, Mary 1925- ScF&FL 92
Carey, Mary V(irginia) 1925- ConAu 38NR
Carey, Mathew 1760-1839 BioIn 17
Carey, Max BioIn 17
Carey, Michael J. St&PR 93
Carey, Michael L. 1942- WhoScE 91-3
Carey, Milburn Ernest 1912- WhoAm 92
Carey, Nancy Bunting 1949- WhoAmW 93, WhoEmL 93
Carey, Norman B. 1936- St&PR 93
Carey, Olive Fuller Golden d1988 SweetSg A [port]
Carey, Omer L. 1929- WhoWrEP 92
Carey, Paul Richard 1945- WhoAm 92
Carey, Pauline WhoCanL 92
Carey, Peter BioIn 17, NewYTBS 92 [port]
Carey, Peter 1943- IntLitE, ScF&FL 92
Carey, Peter Kevin 1940- WhoAm 92
Carey, Peter Philip 1943- WhoWor 93
Carey, Richard 1950- St&PR 93
Carey, Richard Adams 1951- WhoWrEP 92
Carey, Richard Neal 1953- St&PR 93
Carey, Robert 1941- St&PR 93
Carey, Robert M. 1945- St&PR 93
Carey, Robert Munson 1940- WhoAm 92
Carey, Robert R. 1937- St&PR 93
Carey, Robert Williams 1918- WhoAm 92
Carey, Ron BioIn 17
Carey, Ron 1936- CurBio 92 [port]
Carey, Ronald WhoAm 92
Carey, Roy WhoScE 91-1
Carey, Sarah Collins 1938- WhoAm 92
Carey, T. Murray Law&B 92
Carey, Thomas Devore 1931- WhoAm 92
Carey, Thomas H. BioIn 17
Carey, Thomas Hilton 1944- WhoAm 92
Carey, Valerie Scho 1949- BioIn 17
Carey, Willard Keith 1929- WhoAm 92
Carey, William 1761-1834 BioIn 17
Carey, William Bacon 1926- WhoAm 92
Carey, William Joseph 1922- WhoAm 92
Carey, William P. 1941- St&PR 93
Carey, William Peter 1941- WhoE 93
Carey, William Polk 1930- St&PR 93, WhoAm 92, WhoWor 93
Carey, William R., Jr. BioIn 17
Carey-McElligott, Renee Suzanne 1961- WhoAmW 93
Carfagno, Anthony Michael St&PR 93
Carfagno, Marian Harvard 1944- WhoAmW 93
Carfagno, Robert F. 1951- St&PR 93
Carfagno, Salvatore Pasquale 1925- WhoE 93
Carfolite, David Warren 1954- WhoEmL 93
Carfora, John Michael 1950- WhoE 93
Cargas, Harry J(ames) 1932- WhoWrEP 92
Cargas, Martin de Porres Law&B 92
Cargian, Donald 1935- St&PR 93
Cargile, James Thomas 1938- WhoAm 92
Cargill, Fidelia Burnell AmWomPl
Cargill, Leslie Irene 1955- WhoE 93
Cargill, Linda Kay 1955- WhoWrEP 92
Cargill, Virginia Knapp 1952- St&PR 93
Cargiulo, Ralph J. St&PR 93
Cargiulo, Ralph J. 1935- WhoIns 93
Cargo, David Francis 1929- WhoAm 92
Cargo, William Ira 1917- WhoAm 92
Carhart, Arthur H. ScF&FL 92
Caria, Jose M. 1947- St&PR 93
Cariani, Paul Raymond 1940- St&PR 93
Cariappa, Padma Tatta Law&B 92
Carias, Marcos 1905-1949 SpAmA
Carias, Mario 1941- WhoWor 93
Carias Andino, Tiburcio 1876-1960 DcCPCAm
Caric, Louis Stephen 1945- St&PR 93
Caricari, Carl 1938- WhoAm 92, WhoSSW 93
Caricato, Gaetano 1922- WhoScE 91-3
Caridad, Jose Maria 1949- WhoWor 93
Carideo, James Joseph 1964- WhoE 93
Carideo, James V. Law&B 92
Carideo, James V. 1935- St&PR 93
Carideo, James Vincent 1935- WhoAm 92
Caridis, Andrew Anthony 1921- St&PR 93
Caridis, Miltiades 1923- Baker 92
Carifio, Michael Sweet 1957- WhoEmL 93, WhoSSW 93
Cariglia, Michael Anthony 1930- St&PR 93
Carignan, Jeffery K. 1959- St&PR 93
Carignan, Luc 1945- St&PR 93
Carigo, Venetia Thomas 1961- WhoSSW 93
Carim, Enver 1938- ConAu 136
Carin, Arthur A. 1928- WhoE 93
Carinci, Gabriele Giustino 1951- WhoSSW 93, WhoWor 93
Carinci, Paolo 1937- WhoScE 91-3
Carini, Robert M. 1943- St&PR 93
Carini, Sandra 1962- WhoScE 91-3
Carino, Aurora Lao 1940- WhoAmW 93
Carino, Donald Lawrence 1948- WhoEmL 93
Carino, Felipe 1956- WhoEmL 93
Carino, Isidro Dimaranan 1926- WhoAsAP 91
Carino, Linda Susan 1954- WhoAmW 93
Carinus, Marcus Aurelius c. 257-285 HarEnMi
Cariola, Robert Joseph 1927- WhoAm 92
Carioti, Bruno Mario 1929- WhoWor 93
Cariou, Len Joseph 1939- WhoAm 92
Carisi, Johnny d1992 NewYTBS 92
Cariss, Richard J. 1943- St&PR 93
Carisse, Johanne Marguerite 1953- WhoWrEP 92
Carissimi, Giacomo 1605-1674 Baker 92
Carissimo, Giovanni 1936- WhoUN 92
Carithers, Hugh Alfred 1913- WhoAm 92
Carithers, Jeanine Rutherford 1933- WhoAm 92
Carity, Susan L. Law&B 92
Carius, Jeffrey R. Law&B 92
Carius, Robert Wilhelm 1929- WhoAm 92, WhoSSW 93
Carkeet, David 1946- ConAu 38NR, ScF&FL 92
Carkner, Ronald Earle Law&B 92
Carl, Glenda Warren 1954- WhoSSW 93
Carl, Hans 1940- WhoUN 92
Carl, Jean Geralyn 1959- WhoEmL 93
Carl, John 1932- St&PR 93
Carl, Judith Lee 1944- WhoAm 92
Carl, Lillian Stewart 1949- ScF&FL 92
Carl, Mary Jo ScF&FL 92
Carl, Robert D., III 1954- St&PR 93
Carl, Seth William 1961- WhoE 93
Carl, Thomas B. 1917- St&PR 93
Carl, Tommie Ewert 1921- WhoAm 92
Carl, William Crane 1865-1936 Baker 92
Carlberg, Ingrid Ann 1960- WhoSSW 93
Carlberg, James Edwin 1950- WhoEmL 93
Carlberg, Nancy Ellen 1947- WhoEmL 93
Carlberg, Ralph 1943- St&PR 93
Carlberg, Robert Judson 1940- WhoE 93
Carlborg, Cynthia Ann Law&B 92
Carlcano, Carlotta Miguelina WhoAmW 93
Carle, Eric BioIn 17, ChlBIID [port]
Carle, Eric 1929- MajAI [port]
Carle, Gilles 1929- MiSFD 9
Carle, Jean-Pierre Law&B 92
Carle, John Rexford 1939- St&PR 93
Carle, Remy WhoScE 91-2
Carlebach, Eli Chaim d1990 BioIn 17
Carlen, Claudia 1906- WhoAm 92
Carlen, Jan C. 1934- St&PR 93
Carleno, Ray B. Law&B 92
Carles, Arthur B. BioIn 17
Carles, Emilie 1900-1979 BioIn 17
Carleson, Robert Bazil 1931- WhoAm 92, WhoWor 93
Carleton, Barbee Oliver 1917- DcAmChF 1960, ScF&FL 92
Carleton, Bukk Griffith 1909- WhoE 93, WhoWor 93
Carleton, Charles Webster d1991 BioIn 17
Carleton, Don Edward 1947- WhoAm 92
Carleton, Gordon Robert 1955- WhoEmL 93
Carleton, Guy 1724-1808 HarEnMi
Carleton, John T. 1944- St&PR 93
Carleton, Leonard B. 1946- St&PR 93
Carleton, Mary Ruth 1948- WhoAmW 93
Carleton, Paul Hunter 1948- WhoEmL 93
Carleton, Richard Allyn 1931- WhoAm 92
Carleton, Richard W. Law&B 92
Carleton, Robert L. 1940- St&PR 93
Carleton, Willard Tracy 1934- WhoAm 92
Carleton, William 1794-1869 BioIn 17
Carletti, Eleonora 1955- WhoScE 91-3
Carley, Charles Team, Jr. 1932- WhoAm 92
Carley, Eileen A. Law&B 92
Carley, Harold Edwin WhoE 93
Carley, James French 1923- WhoAm 92
Carley, James Patrick, Jr. 1949- St&PR 93
Carley, John Blythe 1934- WhoAm 92
Carley, John Halliday 1941- WhoAm 92
Carley, John L. Law&B 92
Carley, John Terrell 1923- WhoSSW 93
Carley, Kurt 1962- WhoEmL 93
Carley, L. David 1928- WhoAm 92
Carley, Larry W. 1950- ConAu 139
Carley, Laura Ann 1950- WhoEmL 93
Carley, Stephen E. 1952- St&PR 93
Carl Gustaf, XVI 1946- WhoWor 93
Carlhian, Jean Paul 1919- WhoAm 92
Carli, Audrey Marilyn 1932- WhoWrEP 92
Carli, Giancarlo 1938- WhoScE 91-3
Carlid, Gote 1920-1953 Baker 92
Carlier, Eugene Norman 1932- St&PR 93
Carlier, Jean Joachim 1926- WhoWor 93
Carlier, John Carmelo 1957- WhoEmL 93
Carlier, Michel Alexandre 1919- WhoScE 91-2
Carlier, Yves 1947- WhoScE 91-2
Carlier De Lavalle, Manuel 1955- WhoScE 91-3
Carlile, Brian R. 1938- WhoIns 93
Carlile, Clancy 1930- ScF&FL 92
Carlile, Clarence ScF&FL 92
Carlile, Henry David 1934- WhoWrEP 92
Carlile, Lloyd A. 1927- St&PR 93

Carlile, Marybeth Toole 1931- WhoAmW 93
Carlile, Richard 1790-1843 BioIn 17
Carlin, Bruce Michael 1952- WhoEmL 93
Carlin, Clair Myron 1947- WhoEmL 93
Carlin, David R., Jr. 1938- WhoE 93
Carlin, Donald W. Law&B 92
Carlin, Donald Walter 1934- St&PR 93, WhoAm 92
Carlin, Edward R. 1940- St&PR 93
Carlin, Edward Robert 1940- WhoAm 92
Carlin, Gabriel S. 1921- WhoAm 92
Carlin, George Denis 1937- WhoAm 92
Carlin, Herbert J. 1917- WhoAm 92
Carlin, Ira Saul 1948- WhoAm 92
Carlin, Jane D. Law&B 92
Carlin, Jerry Fay 1946- WhoEmL 93
Carlin, John Bernard, Jr. 1939- WhoAm 92
Carlin, John William 1940- BioIn 17, WhoAm 92
Carlin, Kellie Colleen Philbrick 1956- WhoAmW 93
Carlin, Michele Diane Duncan 1965- WhoE 93
Carlin, Paul Victor 1945- WhoAm 92
Carlin, Robin H. Law&B 92
Carlin, Sidney Alan 1925- WhoWor 93
Carlin, Stewart Henry 1952- WhoSSW 93
Carlin, Thomas A. d1991 BioIn 17
Carlin, Timothy James Law&B 92
Carline, Joseph J. Law&B 92
Carliner, David 1918- WhoAm 92
Carliner, Geoffrey Owen 1944- WhoE 93
Carliner, Michael Simon 1945- WhoAm 92
Carling, Paul Joseph 1945- WhoE 93
Carlini, James 1954- WhoEmL 93
Carlini, John Louis 1945- WhoE 93
Carlini, Lawrence J. 1949- St&PR 93
Carlini, Lawrence John Law&B 92
Carlino, Lewis John 1932- MiSFD 9
Carlinsky, Dan 1944- ScF&FL 92, WhoWrEP 92
Carlioz, Henri 1932- WhoScE 91-2
Carlis, George W. Law&B 92
Carlise, Carris ConAu 38NR
Carlisle, Countess of 1845-1921 BioIn 17
Carlisle, Albert E. St&PR 93
Carlisle, Anne 1956- ScF&FL 92
Carlisle, Belinda BioIn 17
Carlisle, Belinda 1958- ConMus 8 [port]
Carlisle, Calvin Ernest Law&B 92
Carlisle, Charles Roger 1929- WhoUN 92
Carlisle, Christopher E. 1948- St&PR 93
Carlisle, Dean W. 1929- St&PR 93
Carlisle, Dwight L., Jr. 1935- WhoAm 92
Carlisle, Ervin Frederick 1935- WhoAm 92
Carlisle, George D. 1913- St&PR 93
Carlisle, George Richard, Jr. 1949- WhoEmL 93
Carlisle, George W. 1919- St&PR 93
Carlisle, James Patton 1946- WhoEmL 93
Carlisle, Jerry Dean 1946- St&PR 93
Carlisle, Jock Alan 1924- WhoWrEP 92
Carlisle, John G. 1835-1910 PolPar
Carlisle, Joyce Ellen 1954- WhoWrEP 92
Carlisle, Kitty BioIn 17
Carlisle, Lilian Matarose Baker 1912- WhoAm 92, WhoAmW 93
Carlisle, M. Eugene, Jr. 1933- St&PR 93
Carlisle, Margo Duer Black WhoAm 92
Carlisle, Patricia Kinley 1949- WhoAmW 93, WhoEmL 93
Carlisle, Robert Paul 1960- WhoEmL 93
Carlisle, Shirley Carolyn 1932- St&PR 93
Carlisle, Thomas John 1913-1992 ConAu 40NR
Carlisle, W. Scott, III Law&B 92
Carlisle, William Aiken 1918- WhoAm 92
Carlisle, William G. 1930- St&PR 93
Carlisle, Woodson Studebaker, Jr. 1934- St&PR 93
Carll, Elizabeth Kassay 1950- WhoE 93
Carlnas, Bengt Eric WhoWor 93
Carlo, George Louis 1953- WhoWor 93
Carlock, Lynn 1927- ScF&FL 92
Carlock, Richard B. 1951- St&PR 93
Carlock, Roger E. 1935- St&PR 93
Carlock, Thomas E. Law&B 92
Carlo Emmanuel 1562-1630 BioIn 17
Carlomagno, Giovanni Maria 1940- WhoWor 93
Carlon, Patrick John 1947- WhoEmL 93
Carlos 1945- WhoWor 93
Carlos, I, King of Spain 1500-1558 BioIn 17
Carlos, John BioIn 17
Carlos, Michael C. 1927- St&PR 93
Carlos, Wendy 1939- Baker 92
Carlos Estrella, Victor 1954- WhoWor 93
Carlot, Maxim WhoWor 93
Carloto, Angel M. 1935- WhoAsAP 91
Carlotti, Carl M. Law&B 92
Carlotti, Stephen Jon 1942- WhoAm 92
Carlough, Edward Joseph 1932- WhoE 93
Carlow, John Sydney 1943- WhoWor 93
Carlozzi, Carlo, Jr. 1958- WhoE 93
Carlozzi, Nicholas 1952- St&PR 93
Carlquist, Sherwin 1930- WhoAm 92
Carls, Alice Catherine 1950- WhoSSW 93
Carls, David Henry 1938- St&PR 93
Carlsen, Bent Erik 1945- WhoWor 93
Carlsen, Chris ScF&FL 92
Carlsen, Clifford N., Jr. 1927- St&PR 93
Carlsen, Clifford Norman, Jr. 1927- WhoAm 92
Carlsen, Douglas Michael 1950- WhoEmL 93
Carlsen, Henning 1927- MiSFD 9
Carlsen, James Law&B 92
Carlsen, James Caldwell 1927- WhoAm 92
Carlsen, Janet Haws 1927- WhoAmW 93
Carlsen, June Marie 1959- WhoEmL 93
Carlsen, Kenneth Leroy 1939- WhoAm 92
Carlsen, Robert Charles Law&B 92
Carlsmith, James Merrill 1936- WhoAm 92
Carlsmith, Lawrence Allan 1928- WhoE 93
Carlson, Alan Douglas 1951- WhoEmL 93
Carlson, Alan R. 1921- St&PR 93
Carlson, Anita Lynne 1952- WhoAmW 93
Carlson, Ann Marie 1954- WhoAmW 93
Carlson, Arne Helge 1934- WhoAm 92
Carlson, Arnold R., Jr. 1928- St&PR 93
Carlson, Arnold W. 1928- St&PR 93
Carlson, Barbara Jean 1926- WhoAmW 93
Carlson, Ben 1936- St&PR 93
Carlson, Bradley Reed 1956- WhoEmL 93
Carlson, Brian Jay 1956- WhoEmL 93
Carlson, Bruce St&PR 93
Carlson, Bruce Arne 1946- WhoE 93
Carlson, C.H. Law&B 92
Carlson, C. Herbert 1940- St&PR 93
Carlson, Carl J. d1991 BioIn 17
Carlson, Carmen Elizabeth 1963- WhoEmL 93
Carlson, Carolin McCormick Furst 1934- WhoE 93
Carlson, Charles A. 1933- St&PR 93, WhoAm 92
Carlson, Charles K. 1937- St&PR 93
Carlson, Charlotte Booth 1920- WhoAm 92
Carlson, Christine Mills 1937- WhoAmW 93
Carlson, Claudine 1937- Baker 92
Carlson, Clayton E. 1939- St&PR 93
Carlson, Curt Douglas 1953- St&PR 93
Carlson, Curtis Eugene 1942- WhoWor 93
Carlson, Curtis Keith 1946- WhoEmL 93
Carlson, Curtis L. 1914- St&PR 93
Carlson, Curtis LeRoy BioIn 17
Carlson, Curtis LeRoy 1914- WhoAm 92
Carlson, Curtis M. 1927- St&PR 93
Carlson, Cynthia Joanne 1942- WhoAm 92
Carlson, D.O. 1928- St&PR 93
Carlson, Dale 1935- ScF&FL 92
Carlson, Dale A. 1956- St&PR 93
Carlson, Dale Alan 1959- WhoEmL 93
Carlson, Dale Arvid 1925- WhoAm 92
Carlson, Dale Bick 1935- WhoAm 92, WhoAmW 93
Carlson, Dale Lynn Law&B 92
Carlson, Dale Lynn 1946- WhoE 93, WhoEmL 93, WhoWor 93
Carlson, Daniel A. 1945- St&PR 93
Carlson, Daniel B. ScF&FL 92
Carlson, Danny 1960- ScF&FL 92
Carlson, Darryl Dean 1938- WhoWor 93
Carlson, Dave 1952- BioIn 17
Carlson, David Bret 1918- WhoAm 92
Carlson, David Emil 1942- WhoAm 92
Carlson, David George 1959- WhoEmL 93
Carlson, David Gilbert 1961- WhoEmL 93
Carlson, David M. 1940- St&PR 93
Carlson, David Martin 1940- WhoAm 92
Carlson, Dawn Marie 1956- WhoEmL 93
Carlson, Deborah Ann 1948- WhoEmL 93
Carlson, Deborah Ann 1957- WhoAmW 93
Carlson, DeVon McElvin 1917- WhoAm 92
Carlson, Dianne Elizabeth Law&B 92
Carlson, Don Marvin 1931- WhoAm 92
Carlson, Douglas John 1955- St&PR 93
Carlson, Drew Emil 1948- WhoE 93
Carlson, Dudley Louis 1932- WhoAm 92
Carlson, Dwain C. 1942- St&PR 93
Carlson, E. Jerome BioIn 17
Carlson, Edgar M. d1992 NewYTBS 92
Carlson, Edgar Magnus 1908-1992 BioIn 17
Carlson, Edward C. 1942- WhoAm 92
Carlson, Edward Elmer 1911-1990 BioIn 17
Carlson, Edwin Theodore 1946- WhoEmL 93
Carlson, Eileen Harte 1952- WhoAmW 93
Carlson, Elof Axel 1931- WhoAm 92, WhoWrEP 92
Carlson, Elvin Palmer 1950- WhoE 93
Carlson, Eric W. 1910- ScF&FL 92
Carlson, Eric Walter 1910- WhoE 93
Carlson, Erik B. Law&B 92
Carlson, Evans Fordyce 1896-1947 HarEnMi
Carlson, Frank 1893-1987 BioIn 17
Carlson, Frederick Paul 1938- WhoAm 92
Carlson, Gary 1950- St&PR 93
Carlson, Gary Albert 1946- WhoEmL 93
Carlson, Gary Lee 1954- WhoEmL 93
Carlson, George Arthur 1940- WhoAm 92
Carlson, George L. Law&B 92
Carlson, George Lewis 1946- WhoEmL 93
Carlson, Gerald K. 1943- St&PR 93
Carlson, Gerald Michael 1946- WhoSSW 93
Carlson, Gerald Wesley 1947- WhoEmL 93
Carlson, Glen A., Jr. 1935- St&PR 93
Carlson, Graham B. 1927- St&PR 93
Carlson, Guy Raymond 1918- WhoAm 92
Carlson, Hannah Bick 1963- WhoE 93
Carlson, Harald D. 1952- St&PR 93
Carlson, Harold S. 1903-1990 BioIn 17
Carlson, Harry Law&B 92
Carlson, Harry 1919- WhoAm 92
Carlson, Irene A. Law&B 92
Carlson, Jack 1933-1992 NewYTBS 92
Carlson, Jack Wilson 1933- WhoAm 92
Carlson, James Albert 1933- WhoSSW 93
Carlson, James Ellsworth 1934- WhoAm 92
Carlson, James Leslie 1932- WhoSSW 93
Carlson, James R. 1942- St&PR 93
Carlson, James William 1951- St&PR 93
Carlson, Jane A. 1928- St&PR 93
Carlson, Jane Rise 1949- St&PR 93
Carlson, Jeannie Ann 1955- WhoAm 92, WhoAmW 93, WhoEmL 93, WhoSSW 93
Carlson, Jeffrey B. Law&B 92
Carlson, Jerilyn BioIn 17
Carlson, Jerome Walter 1936- St&PR 93
Carlson, Jerry Alan 1936- WhoAm 92, WhoWrEP 92
Carlson, John A. 1945- St&PR 93
Carlson, John E., Sr. 1930- St&PR 93
Carlson, John F. 1938- St&PR 93
Carlson, John Gregory 1951- WhoE 93
Carlson, John H. Law&B 92
Carlson, John Henry 1945- WhoAm 92
Carlson, John P. St&PR 93
Carlson, John Roy 1909-1991 BioIn 17
Carlson, John Stephen Law&B 92
Carlson, John Tyler 1963- WhoEmL 93
Carlson, Joseph Maxwell 1942- WhoE 93
Carlson, Jud L. 1942- St&PR 93
Carlson, Karen St&PR 93
Carlson, Karin J. St&PR 93
Carlson, Kathleen Law&B 92
Carlson, Keith B. 1948- St&PR 93
Carlson, Kenneth George 1949- WhoEmL 93
Carlson, Kenneth W. 1933- St&PR 93
Carlson, Kristi Mork 1955- WhoAmW 93
Carlson, Lanette Anne 1952- WhoWrEP 92
Carlson, Larry E. 1943- St&PR 93
Carlson, Larry G. ScF&FL 92
Carlson, Larry Paul 1942- St&PR 93
Carlson, Lars A. 1928- WhoScE 91-4
Carlson, Laura Benedict 1965- WhoAmW 93
Carlson, Leland Victor Law&B 92
Carlson, Leroy T. 1916- St&PR 93
Carlson, Leroy T. 1946- St&PR 93
Carlson, LeRoy Theodore Sheridan, Sr. 1916- WhoAm 92
Carlson, Loren Dale 1943- WhoAm 92
Carlson, Loren Merle 1923- WhoAm 92
Carlson, Marian Bille 1952- WhoAm 92, WhoEmL 93
Carlson, Martin Thomas 1950- St&PR 93
Carlson, Marvin Albert 1935- WhoAm 92
Carlson, Mary Ann 1944- WhoAmW 93, WhoE 93
Carlson, Mary Anne Jerow 1957- WhoEmL 93
Carlson, Mary Eileen 1946- WhoAmW 93
Carlson, Mary Susan 1949- WhoEmL 93
Carlson, Michael E. Law&B 92
Carlson, Mickie Asma 1947- WhoAmW 93
Carlson, Nancy Busk 1948- WhoE 93
Carlson, Nancy Lee 1950- WhoEmL 93, WhoWor 93
Carlson, Nancy Lynn 1936- WhoAmW 93
Carlson, Natalie Savage 1906- BioIn 17, DcAmChF 1960, MajAI [port], WhoAm 92, WhoWrEP 92
Carlson, Norman A. 1933- WhoAm 92
Carlson, Oscar Norman 1920- WhoAm 92
Carlson, Paul Richard Law&B 92
Carlson, Per J. 1938- WhoScE 91-4, WhoWor 93
Carlson, Ralph Lawrence 1944- WhoAm 92
Carlson, Ralph W. St&PR 93
Carlson, Randy Eugene 1948- WhoEmL 93
Carlson, Ria Marie 1961- WhoEmL 93
Carlson, Richard A. Law&B 92
Carlson, Richard Ernest 1953- WhoEmL 93
Carlson, Richard George 1930- WhoAm 92
Carlson, Richard Gregory 1949- WhoEmL 93
Carlson, Richard Warner 1941- WhoAm 92, WhoE 93, WhoWor 93
Carlson, Robert A. Law&B 92
Carlson, Robert A. 1932- St&PR 93
Carlson, Robert Brian 1943- St&PR 93
Carlson, Robert Charles 1957- WhoE 93, WhoEmL 93
Carlson, Robert Codner 1939- WhoAm 92
Carlson, Robert E. 1936- WhoIns 93
Carlson, Robert Frederick, Jr. 1952- WhoEmL 93
Carlson, Robert Gideon 1938- WhoAm 92
Carlson, Robert James 1944- WhoAm 92
Carlson, Robert John 1929- WhoAm 92
Carlson, Robert Lee 1924- WhoAm 92
Carlson, Robert Marshall 1950- WhoEmL 93
Carlson, Robert Oskar 1921- WhoAm 92, WhoWor 93
Carlson, Robert P. Law&B 92
Carlson, Robert W., Jr. 1947- St&PR 93
Carlson, Roderick 1928- St&PR 93
Carlson, Roger Allan 1932- St&PR 93, WhoWor 93
Carlson, Roger Charles 1937- WhoIns 93
Carlson, Rolland Sigfrid 1932- St&PR 93, WhoAm 92
Carlson, Ronald J. Law&B 92
Carlson, Roy Perry Merritt 1923- WhoAm 92
Carlson, Ruggles B. 1933- St&PR 93
Carlson, Russell Charles 1926- WhoAm 92
Carlson, Samuel La Verne 1936- St&PR 93
Carlson, Scott Alexander 1955- St&PR 93, WhoAm 92
Carlson, Sharon Lee 1949- WhoEmL 93
Carlson, Stanley A. Law&B 92
Carlson, Stanley A. 1939- WhoAm 92
Carlson, Stanley David 1934- WhoAm 92
Carlson, Stephen Curtis 1951- WhoEmL 93
Carlson, Susan Gay 1944- WhoSSW 93
Carlson, Susan Spevack 1945- WhoAmW 93
Carlson, Suzanne Olive 1939- WhoAm 92
Carlson, Terrance L. 1953- WhoEmL 93
Carlson, Terry A. 1942- St&PR 93
Carlson, Theodore Joshua 1919- WhoAm 92, WhoE 93
Carlson, Thomas B. 1943- St&PR 93
Carlson, Thomas Joseph 1953- WhoAm 92
Carlson, Timothy P. 1938- St&PR 93
Carlson, Virginia E. Law&B 92
Carlson, Wayne Edward 1946- WhoEmL 93
Carlson, Wendell R. 1936- WhoWrEP 92
Carlson, William Clifford 1937- WhoAm 92
Carlson, William Dwight 1928- WhoAm 92, WhoE 93
Carlson, William Hugh 1898-1990 BioIn 17
Carlson, William K. ScF&FL 92
Carlson, Zeke 1953- WhoEmL 93
Carlson-Pickering, Jane 1954- WhoE 93, WhoEmL 93
Carlsson, A. Janne 1932- WhoScE 91-4
Carlsson, Bertil 1928- WhoScE 91-4
Carlsson, Birgitta Kerstin Maria 1948- WhoWor 93
Carlsson, Bo A. V. 1942- WhoAm 92
Carlsson, C. Goran 1954- WhoScE 91-4
Carlsson, Ebbe d1992 NewYTBS 92 [port]
Carlsson, Gunnar E. 1930- WhoScE 91-4
Carlsson, Gunnar Erik 1952- WhoAm 92
Carlsson, Ingvar Gosta 1934- WhoWor 93
Carlsson, Jan Olof 1935- WhoScE 91-4
Carlsson, Marten C. 1936- WhoScE 91-4
Carlsson, Percy Allan 1927- WhoSSW 93
Carlstedt, Jan 1926- Baker 92
Carlstedt, Linda Marie 1941- WhoAmW 93
Carlstrom, David E. St&PR 93
Carlstrom, Elis 1952- WhoScE 91-4
Carlstrom, Lawrence W. 1949- St&PR 93
Carlstrom, Richard A. 1943- St&PR 93
Carlton, Alan R. Law&B 92
Carlton, Alfred Pershing, Jr. 1947- WhoAm 92, WhoEmL 93
Carlton, Ardith ScF&FL 92
Carlton, Bruce C. 1935- St&PR 93
Carlton, Carl 1953- SoulM
Carlton, Carol Lee 1941- WhoAmW 93
Carlton, Charles Merritt 1928- WhoAm 92, WhoE 93
Carlton, Dean 1928- WhoAm 92

Carlton, Dennis William 1951- *WhoAm 92*
Carlton, Diane Michele 1950- *WhoEmL 93*
Carlton, Donald Morrill 1937- *WhoAm 92*
Carlton, Georgann Perock 1955- *WhoSSW 93*
Carlton, Harley Earl 1947- *WhoSSW 93*
Carlton, Helen Louise 1926- *WhoAmW 93*
Carlton, James D. 1948- *WhoAm 92*
Carlton, James Joseph *WhoAsAP 91*
Carlton, Joe R. 1923- *St&PR 93*
Carlton, Larry 1948- *SoulM*
Carlton, Lonnie Calvin 1949- *WhoEmL 93*
Carlton, Louise Hoskins *WhoAmW 93*
Carlton, Mabel Mason *AmWomPl*
Carlton, Mark L. *Law&B 92*
Carlton, Mary Powell 1925- *St&PR 93, WhoAm 92*
Carlton, Melinda *BioIn 17*
Carlton, Michael Will 1936- *St&PR 93*
Carlton, Patrick William 1937- *WhoSSW 93*
Carlton, Paul Kendall 1921- *WhoAm 92*
Carlton, Richard Anthony 1951- *WhoWor 93*
Carlton, Robert Bruce 1948- *WhoAm 92*
Carlton, Roger *ScF&FL 92*
Carlton, Roy David *Law&B 92*
Carlton, Sara Boehlke 1937- *WhoAmW 93*
Carlton, Steven Norman 1944- *WhoAm 92*
Carlton, Terry Scott 1939- *WhoAm 92*
Carlton, William L. 1945- *St&PR 93*
Carlucci, Angela *Law&B 92*
Carlucci, Frank 1930- *ColdWar 1 [port]*
Carlucci, Frank Charles, III 1930- *WhoAm 92, WhoE 93*
Carlucci, Marie Ann 1953- *WhoAmW 93*
Carluccio, Charles Goldhammer 1926- *WhoAm 92*
Carluccio, Frank 1919- *WhoE 93*
Carlyle, Blanche D. *AmWomPl*
Carlyle, Jane Welsh 1801-1866 *BioIn 17*
Carlyle, Joan (Hildred) 1931- *Baker 92*
Carlyle, Thomas 1795-1881 *BioIn 17*
Carlyle, William J. 1927- *WhoScE 91-1*
Carlyon, Kathrine F. *AmWomPl*
Carlyon, Richard *ScF&FL 92*
Carlyss, Earl Winston 1939- *WhoAm 92*
Carmack, Comer A., Jr. 1932- *St&PR 93*
Carmack, George 1907- *WhoAm 92*
Carmack, Mildred Jean 1938- *WhoAm 92*
Carmagnola, Francesco Bussone, Count of c. 1385-1432 *HarEnMi*
Carman, Anne 1942- *WhoE 93*
Carman, Bliss 1861-1929 *BioIn 17, GayN*
Carman, Charles Jerry 1938- *WhoWor 93*
Carman, Elaine Marion 1950- *WhoEmL 93*
Carman, Gary Michael 1949- *WhoAm 92*
Carman, George Henry 1928- *WhoAm 92*
Carman, Gregory W. 1937- *CngDr 91*
Carman, Gregory Wright 1937- *WhoAm 92, WhoE 93*
Carman, Holly Lynn 1953- *WhoEmL 93*
Carman, Hoy Fred 1938- *WhoAm 92*
Carman, John Elwin 1946- *WhoAm 92*
Carman, Juanita Chenault 1923- *WhoWrEP 92*
Carman, LauraLee 1964- *WhoAmW 93*
Carman, Michael Dennis 1938- *WhoAm 92*
Carman, Robert Griffin 1947- *WhoSSW 93*
Carman, Ronald Townsend *Law&B 92*
Carman, Susan Lea 1952- *WhoWrEP 92*
Carman, Thomas W. 1951- *St&PR 93*
Carman, Warren Earl, Jr. 1948- *WhoE 93*
Carmany, James P. *St&PR 93*
Carmazzi, Robert Frank 1950- *St&PR 93, WhoEmL 93, WhoSSW 93*
Carmean, D.W. 1944- *St&PR 93*
Carmean, Jerry Richard 1938- *WhoWor 93*
Carmean, Michael L. 1945- *St&PR 93*
Carmel, Alan Stuart 1944- *WhoAm 92*
Carmel, Simon Jacob 1938- *WhoAm 92*
Carmel, Thomas D. *Law&B 92*
Carmell, Pamela Lee 1950- *WhoWrEP 92*
Carmella, Bradley Ray 1954- *WhoEmL 93*
Carmen, Dave 1948- *WhoE 93*
Carmen, Ira Harris 1934- *WhoAm 92, WhoWor 93*
Carmen, Jean 1914- *SweetSg C [port]*
Carmen, Jeanne *BioIn 17*
Carmer, James Edward 1956- *St&PR 93*
Carmi, Shlomo 1937- *WhoAm 92*
Carmichael, Alexander Douglas 1929- *WhoAm 92*
Carmichael, Ann Crocker 1955- *WhoEmL 93*
Carmichael, Anne Gaye 1961- *WhoEmL 93*
Carmichael, Bruce Fenton 1946- *WhoEmL 93*
Carmichael, Carson, Jr. 1928- *St&PR 93*
Carmichael, Carson, III 1954- *WhoEmL 93*
Carmichael, Charles Wesley 1919- *WhoWor 93*
Carmichael, Daniel Peter *Law&B 92*
Carmichael, David Burton 1923- *WhoAm 92*
Carmichael, David Edward 1947- *St&PR 93*
Carmichael, David M. 1938- *St&PR 93*
Carmichael, David R. *St&PR 93*
Carmichael, David Richard *Law&B 92*
Carmichael, David Richard 1942- *WhoIns 93*
Carmichael, Deborah Murray 1956- *WhoEmL 93*
Carmichael, Donald Scott 1912- *WhoAm 92*
Carmichael, Elizabeth *BioIn 17*
Carmichael, Franklin H. 1890-1945 *BioIn 17*
Carmichael, Harry W. 1922- *St&PR 93*
Carmichael, Hoagy 1899-1981 *Baker 92*
Carmichael, Hugh 1906- *WhoAm 92*
Carmichael, Ian 1920- *QDrFCA 92 [port]*
Carmichael, Ian Stuart Edward 1930- *WhoAm 92*
Carmichael, J.W. *BioIn 17*
Carmichael, James Dolph 1947- *WhoEmL 93*
Carmichael, James H. 1907-1983 *EncABHB 8 [port]*
Carmichael, Joseph Patrick 1954- *St&PR 93*
Carmichael, Judy Lea 1952- *WhoE 93*
Carmichael, Mary Mulloy 1916- *WhoAm 92*
Carmichael, Nancy S. 1958- *WhoE 93*
Carmichael, Paul D. *Law&B 92*
Carmichael, Richard Dudley 1942- *WhoSSW 93*
Carmichael, Robert William 1958- *WhoE 93, WhoEmL 93*
Carmichael, Stokely 1941- *BioIn 17, EncAACR, PolPar*
Carmichael, Vicki 1950- *St&PR 93*
Carmichael, Virgil Wesly 1919- *WhoAm 92, WhoWor 93*
Carmichael, William Charles, II 1950- *WhoSSW 93*
Carmichael, William Clyde 1942- *St&PR 93*
Carmichael, William Daniel 1929- *WhoAm 92*
Carmichael, William Jerome 1920- *WhoAm 92*
Carmien, J. Allen 1919- *St&PR 93*
Carmin, Robert Leighton 1918- *WhoAm 92*
Carmines, Pamela Kay 1955- *WhoAmW 93*
Carmirelli, Pina 1914- *Baker 92*
Carmody, Arthur Roderick, Jr. 1928- *WhoAm 92, WhoWor 93*
Carmody, Charles Stuart 1960- *WhoSSW 93*
Carmody, Cora Lackey 1957- *WhoAmW 93*
Carmody, Dennis Patrick 1948- *WhoEmL 93*
Carmody, George Edward 1931- *WhoE 93*
Carmody, Isobelle 1958- *ScF&FL 92*
Carmody, James Albert 1945- *WhoWor 93*
Carmody, Margaret Jean 1924- *WhoE 93*
Carmody, Robert Edward 1942- *WhoE 93*
Carmody, Thomas Gaughan 1932- *St&PR 93*
Carmody, Thomas R. 1933- *St&PR 93*
Carmody, Thomas Roswell 1933- *WhoSSW 93*
Carmody-Arey, Christine 1938- *WhoAmW 93*
Carmon, Christopher Joseph 1969- *St&PR 93*
Carmon, James Foster 1941- *St&PR 93*
Carmona, Antonio Oscar de Fragoso 1869-1951 *DcTwHis*
Carmona, Maria Manuela *WhoScE 91-3*
Carmony, Donald Duane 1935- *WhoAm 92*
Carmony, Kevin Brackett 1959- *WhoEmL 93, WhoWor 93*
Carmony, Larry Glen 1960- *St&PR 93*
Carmony, Marvin Dale 1923- *WhoAm 92*
Carnaggio, Chatles Samuel 1948- *St&PR 93*
Carnahan, C. Earl 1935- *St&PR 93*
Carnahan, Clarence Earl 1935- *WhoIns 93*
Carnahan, David E. 1943- *St&PR 93*
Carnahan, Flint Jason 1966- *WhoSSW 93*
Carnahan, Frances Morris 1937- *WhoAm 92*
Carnahan, Frances Morris 1947- *WhoWrEP 92*
Carnahan, Jay F. 1949- *St&PR 93*
Carnahan, John Anderson 1930- *WhoAm 92*
Carnahan, John Mitchell 1934- *St&PR 93*
Carnahan, Lew Wallace 1946- *WhoEmL 93*
Carnahan, Marvin R. 1941- *WhoWor 93*
Carnahan, Mel 1934- *WhoAm 92*
Carnahan, Mel Eugene 1934- *WhoAm 92*
Carnahan, Orville Darrell 1929- *WhoAm 92*
Carnahan, Susan Bush *Law&B 92*
Carnall, John Victor 1948- *WhoEmL 93*
Carnam, Allyn Myles *Law&B 92*
Carnap, Rudolf 1891-1970 *BioIn 17*
Carnase, Thomas Paul 1939- *WhoAm 92*
Carnaval, Charles William 1952- *St&PR 93*
Carne, Carolyn Lee 1943- *WhoE 93*
Carne, Judy *ConAu 138*
Carne, Marcel *BioIn 17*
Carne, Marcel 1909- *MiSFD 9*
Carne, Marcel Albert 1906- *WhoWor 93*
Carneal, Ann Holland Stambaugh 1947- *WhoEmL 93, WhoSSW 93*
Carneal, George Upshur 1935- *WhoAm 92*
Carneal, James William 1918- *WhoAm 92*
Carneghi, Letitia Anne 1961- *WhoAmW 93*
Carnegie, Andrew 1835-1919 *BioIn 17, GayN*
Carnegie, Christa L. *Law&B 92*
Carneiro, Kim da Costa 1946- *WhoScE 91-2, WhoWor 93*
Carnell, Corbin Scott 1929- *ScF&FL 92*
Carnell, John 1912-1972 *ScF&FL 92*
Carnell, Judith M. 1943- *WhoWrEP 92*
Carnell, Patricia Sue 1935- *WhoSSW 93*
Carnell, Paul Herbert 1917- *WhoAm 92*
Carnella, Frank Thomas 1934- *St&PR 93*
Carner, Mosco 1904-1985 *Baker 92, ConAu 38NR*
Carner, William John 1948- *WhoEmL 93*
Carnero, Guillermo 1947- *BioIn 17*
Carnes, Edward E. *BioIn 17*
Carnes, Edward Earl 1950- *NewYTBS 92*
Carnes, James E. 1939- *St&PR 93*
Carnes, James Edward 1939- *WhoAm 92*
Carnes, Linda Anne 1948- *WhoSSW 93*
Carnes, Luisa 1905-1964 *DcMexL*
Carnes, Mabel Hamric 1912- *WhoAmW 93*
Carnes, Patty *BioIn 17*
Carnes, Ralph L. 1931- *ScF&FL 92*
Carnes, Thomas Alton 1953- *WhoEmL 93*
Carnes, Valerie 1944- *ScF&FL 92*
Carnes, Wilson Woodrow 1924- *WhoAm 92*
Carnesecca, Luigi 1925- *BiDAMSp 1989*
Carnesoltas, Ana-Maria 1948- *WhoEmL 93*
Carnevali, Doris L(orrain) *WhoWrEP 92*
Carney, Alan 1911-1973 *See* Brown, Wally 1898-1961 & Carney, Alan 1911-1973 *QDrFCA 92*
Carney, Alfonso L., Jr. *Law&B 92*
Carney, Arthur William Matthew 1918- *WhoAm 92*
Carney, Bruce William 1946- *WhoSSW 93*
Carney, Charles Seymour 1920- *WhoWrEP 92*
Carney, Claire T. *St&PR 93*
Carney, David Mitchel *WhoAm 92*
Carney, Deborah Leah Turner 1952- *WhoEmL 93*
Carney, Dennis Joseph 1921- *WhoAm 92*
Carney, Dennis Ray 1947- *St&PR 93*
Carney, Donald Francis, Jr. 1948- *WhoEmL 93*
Carney, Edward James 1930- *St&PR 93*
Carney, Faith E. *Law&B 92*
Carney, Frank Thomas 1956- *WhoEmL 93*
Carney, Gregory John 1946- *St&PR 93*
Carney, Heath Joseph 1955- *WhoEmL 93*
Carney, Henry Allen 1939- *St&PR 93*
Carney, James A. *Law&B 92*
Carney, James Francis *DcCPCAm*
Carney, Jane Carol 1947- *WhoSSW 93*
Carney, Jean Kathryn 1948- *WhoAm 92, WhoAmW 93, WhoEmL 93, WhoWor 93*
Carney, Jeffrey Dean 1967- *WhoEmL 93*
Carney, John D. 1944- *St&PR 93*
Carney, John Henry, Jr. 1964- *WhoEmL 93*
Carney, Joseph D. 1938- *St&PR 93*
Carney, Joseph E. 1945- *WhoIns 93*
Carney, Joseph Patrick 1939- *WhoE 93*
Carney, Karen Lynne 1959- *WhoEmL 93*
Carney, Kathleen 1953- *WhoAmW 93*
Carney, Kathleen L. 1947- *WhoAm 92*
Carney, Kay 1933- *WhoAmW 93*
Carney, Kim 1925- *WhoAm 92*
Carney, Lynn Rose 1955- *WhoE 93*
Carney, Nell Cardwell 1945- *WhoAm 92, WhoAmW 93*
Carney, Patrick 1948- *St&PR 93*
Carney, Peter Roy 1931- *St&PR 93*
Carney, Raymond 1950- *ConAu 137*
Carney, Richard D. *BioIn 17*
Carney, Robert Alfred 1916- *WhoAm 92*
Carney, Robert Arthur 1937- *St&PR 93, WhoWor 93*
Carney, Robert Bostwick 1895-1990 *BioIn 17*
Carney, Roger Francis Xavier 1933- *WhoE 93*
Carney, T(homas) F(rancis) 1931- *ConAu 39NR*
Carney, Thomas 1824-1888 *BioIn 17*
Carney, Thomas J T. 1952- *WhoEmL 93*
Carney, Thomas Quentin 1949- *WhoEmL 93*
Carney, Vaughn A. *Law&B 92*
Carney, Victor M. *Law&B 92*
Carney, W. Peter 1932- *St&PR 93*
Carney, William M. 1950- *ScF&FL 92*
Carney, William V. 1937- *St&PR 93*
Carney-Brown, Phillita Toyia 1952- *WhoAmW 93*
Carneyro, Claudio 1895-1963 *Baker 92*
Carnicer, Ramon 1789-1855 *OxDcOp*
Carnicer (y Batlle), Ramon 1789-1855 *Baker 92*
Carnicero, Jorge E. 1921- *St&PR 93*
Carnicero, Jorge Emilio 1921- *WhoAm 92, WhoSSW 93*
Carnicke, Sharon Marie 1949- *WhoEmL 93*
Carnicom, Gene E. 1944- *WhoWor 93*
Carniglia, Stephen Davis 1950- *WhoAm 92*
Carnine, Roy Leland 1949- *WhoEmL 93*
Carnino-Le Moigne, Annick 1940- *WhoUN 92*
Carniol, Paul J. 1951- *WhoEmL 93*
Carnival, John A. 1944- *St&PR 93*
Carnley, Samuel Fleetwood 1918- *WhoWor 93*
Carnochan, Walter Bliss 1930- *WhoAm 92*
Carnot, Lazare Nicolas Marguerite 1753-1823 *HarEnMi*
Carnot, Sadi 1837-1894 *BioIn 17*
Carnovale, Marco 1959- *WhoWor 93*
Carnovsky, Morris 1897-1992 *BioIn 17, CurBio 92N, NewYTBS 92 [port]*
Carnow, Bertram W. 1922- *St&PR 93*
Carnow, Bertram Warren 1922- *WhoAm 92*
Carnoy, Martin 1938- *WhoAm 92*
Carns, Michael Patrick Chamberlain 1937- *WhoAm 92*
Carns, W.H. 1912- *WhoIns 93*
Caro, Albert Joseph 1938- *St&PR 93*
Caro, Alfred 1931- *St&PR 93*
Caro, Anthony 1924- *WhoWor 93*
Caro, Charles Crawford 1946- *WhoEmL 93, WhoSSW 93*
Caro, Colin Gerald *WhoScE 91-1*
Caro, Dennis R. 1944- *ScF&FL 92*
Caro, Ivor 1946- *WhoAm 92, WhoEmL 93*
Caro, Jodi J. *Law&B 92*
Caro, Lucien Guy 1928- *WhoScE 91-4*
Caro, Marc *MiSFD 9*
Caro, Maria C. 1962- *St&PR 93*
Caro, Robert A. *BioIn 17*
Caro, Robert A. 1935- *ConAu 40NR*
Caro, Robert Allan *WhoAm 92*
Caro, Warren 1907- *WhoAm 92*
Caro, William Allan 1934- *WhoAm 92*
Caro Baroja, Julio 1914- *IntDcAn*
Carobene, Joseph G. 1938- *WhoAm 92*
Caro Fernandez, Manuel 1937- *WhoScE 91-3*
Caroff, Phyllis M. 1924- *WhoAm 92*
Carol, II 1893-1953 *DcTwHis*
Carolan, Douglas M. 1942- *St&PR 93*
Carolan, Geraldine Patricia *Law&B 92*
Carolan, Turlough 1670-1738 *Baker 92, BioIn 17*
Carolan, Vincent L. 1930- *St&PR 93*
Carol-Berard 1881-1942 *Baker 92*
Caroldo, Gian Giacomo c. 1480-1538 *OxDcByz*
Caroli, Claude J. *Law&B 92*
Carolin, Charles R. 1915- *St&PR 93*
Caroline, Princess of Monaco *BioIn 17*
Carollo, James Paul 1946- *St&PR 93, WhoIns 93*
Carolus, James P. 1951- *St&PR 93*
Caron, Alan R. 1951- *St&PR 93*
Caron, Arthur Eugene 1937- *St&PR 93*
Caron, David Dennis 1952- *WhoEmL 93*
Caron, Donald Alvin, Jr. 1966- *WhoE 93*
Caron, Glenn Gordon *MiSFD 9*
Caron, Jean 1944- *WhoScE 91-2*
Caron, Leslie *BioIn 17*
Caron, Leslie 1931- *IntDcF 2-3 [port]*
Caron, Leslie Clare Margaret 1931- *WhoAm 92*
Caron, Louis 1942- *WhoCanL 92*
Caron, Michelle Denise 1968- *WhoAmW 93*
Caron, Paul Lawrence 1957- *WhoEmL 93*
Caron, Philippe fl. 15th cent.- *Baker 92*
Caron, Pierre O. *Law&B 92*
Caron, Raymond 1905- *St&PR 93*
Caron, Rose 1857-1930 *OxDcOp*
Caron, Rose (Lucille) 1857-1930 *Baker 92*

Carone, Frank 1927- *WhoAm 92*
Carone, Richard C. *St&PR 93*
Caronna, Anthony J. *Law&B 92*
Carosella, Maria Pia 1925- *WhoScE 91-3*
Caroselli, Remus F(rancis) 1916- *DcAmChF 1960*
Carosmun, Jean R. *Law&B 92*
Carossa, Hans 1878-1956 *TwCLC 48 [port]*
Carosso, Vincent Phillip 1922- *WhoAm 92*
Carota, Richard J. 1937- *St&PR 93*
Carotenuto, Cav. Romolo 1942- *WhoScE 91-3*
Carothers, Charles Omsted 1923- *WhoAm 92*
Carothers, Christiev *BioIn 17*
Carothers, Durell 1909- *St&PR 93*
Carothers, J. Scott *Law&B 92*
Carothers, Richard Alton 1935- *WhoAm 92*
Carothers, Robert Lee 1942- *WhoAm 92*
Carothers, Sean Brown *St&PR 93*
Carothers, Steven Michael 1954- *WhoAm 92, WhoEmL 93, WhoSSW 93*
Carovano, John Martin 1935- *WhoAm 92*
Carow, Heiner 1929- *DrEEuF*
Carozza, Davy Angelo 1926- *WhoAm 92*
Carozza, Gerald Nicholas, Jr. 1960- *WhoEmL 93*
Carozza, William Victor 1961- *WhoE 93*
Carp, Daniel A. *St&PR 93*
Carp, Richard Lawrence 1926- *WhoAm 92*
Carpani, Giuseppe (Antonio) 1752-1825 *Baker 92*
Carpathios, Neil Emmanuel 1961- *WhoWrEP 92*
Carpel, Kenneth Richard 1941- *St&PR 93*
Carpelan, Bo 1926- *ScF&FL 92*
Carpena Artes, Octavio 1920- *WhoScE 91-3*
Carpency, Gerard Joseph *Law&B 92*
Carpender, Arthur S. 1884-1960 *HarEnMi*
Carpenter, Alfred Nicholas Francis Blakeney 1881-1955 *HarEnMi*
Carpenter, Allan 1917- *BioIn 17, WhoAm 92, WhoWrEP 92*
Carpenter, Alvin Rauso 1942- *WhoAm 92*
Carpenter, Amy B. *Law&B 92*
Carpenter, Amy B. 1956- *St&PR 93*
Carpenter, Angelica Shirley 1945- *SmATA 71 [port]*
Carpenter, Archie H. 1926- *St&PR 93*
Carpenter, Barbara Ann 1958- *WhoSSW 93*
Carpenter, Barry Keith 1949- *WhoE 93*
Carpenter, Ben 1936- *WhoWrEP 92*
Carpenter, Ben H. 1924- *St&PR 93*
Carpenter, Benjamin Harrison, Jr. 1921- *WhoSSW 93*
Carpenter, Bobby R. 1947- *St&PR 93*
Carpenter, Brian George *WhoScE 91-1*
Carpenter, Bruce Gregory *Law&B 92*
Carpenter, Bruce H. 1932- *WhoAm 92*
Carpenter, C. Neal 1932- *St&PR 93*
Carpenter, Carol Settle 1953- *WhoAmW 93*
Carpenter, Catherine E. *Law&B 92*
Carpenter, Chadwick H., Jr. *St&PR 93*
Carpenter, Charles Bernard 1933- *WhoAm 92*
Carpenter, Charles Colcock Jones 1931- *WhoAm 92*
Carpenter, Charles Congden 1921- *WhoAm 92, WhoSSW 93*
Carpenter, Charles D. 1946- *St&PR 93*
Carpenter, Charles Elford, Jr. 1944- *WhoSSW 93, WhoWor 93*
Carpenter, Charles Francis 1957- *WhoEmL 93*
Carpenter, Charles L. *Law&B 92*
Carpenter, Christine A. *Law&B 92*
Carpenter, Christopher *ScF&FL 92*
Carpenter, Christopher Jenns 1940- *WhoUN 92*
Carpenter, Clark Gilbert 1936- *St&PR 93*
Carpenter, Clayton *BioIn 17*
Carpenter, Clayton D. 1940- *St&PR 93*
Carpenter, Daniel Edwin 1946- *WhoEmL 93*
Carpenter, Darrell Franklin 1955- *WhoEmL 93*
Carpenter, David 1941- *WhoCanL 92*
Carpenter, David J. d1991 *BioIn 17*
Carpenter, David Lloyd 1947- *WhoEmL 93*
Carpenter, David R. 1939- *WhoIns 93*
Carpenter, David Roland 1939- *St&PR 93, WhoAm 92*
Carpenter, David William 1950- *WhoEmL 93*
Carpenter, Deborah *Law&B 92*
Carpenter, Delbert Stanley 1950- *WhoAm 92*
Carpenter, Delores Bird 1942- *WhoE 93*
Carpenter, Derr Alvin 1931- *WhoAm 92*
Carpenter, Dorothy Fulton 1933- *WhoAmW 93*
Carpenter, Douglas Bruce 1936- *St&PR 93*
Carpenter, Edmund M. 1941- *St&PR 93*
Carpenter, Edmund Mogford 1941- *WhoAm 92, WhoE 93*
Carpenter, Edmund Nelson, II 1921- *WhoE 93*
Carpenter, Edward 1844-1929 *BioIn 17*
Carpenter, Edward F. d1992 *BioIn 17, NewYTBS 92*
Carpenter, Edward Monroe 1930- *St&PR 93*
Carpenter, Edwin H. 1915- *BioIn 17*
Carpenter, Elizabeth Jane 1949- *WhoAmW 93*
Carpenter, Elizabeth Sutherland 1920- *WhoAm 92, WhoWrEP 92*
Carpenter, Ernest A. *Law&B 92*
Carpenter, Esther 1903- *WhoAmW 93*
Carpenter, Flo 1947- *WhoAmW 93*
Carpenter, Frank Mason 1939- *WhoE 93*
Carpenter, Frank Morton 1902- *WhoAm 92*
Carpenter, Frank Wilkinson 1931- *WhoAm 92*
Carpenter, Frederic Ives 1903-1991 *BioIn 17*
Carpenter, Frederic Ives, (Jr.) 1903-1991 *ConAu 38NR*
Carpenter, Gene Blakely 1922- *WhoAm 92, WhoE 93*
Carpenter, Gene F. 1931- *St&PR 93*
Carpenter, Gerald Edwin 1949- *WhoSSW 93*
Carpenter, Ginger 1955- *WhoAmW 93*
Carpenter, Gordon Russell 1920- *WhoSSW 93*
Carpenter, H. Paul *Law&B 92*
Carpenter, Harry A., Mrs. *AmWomPl*
Carpenter, Henry A. *Law&B 92*
Carpenter, Henry Alan 1950- *St&PR 93*
Carpenter, Howard Grant, Jr. *Law&B 92*
Carpenter, Howard Grant, Jr. 1939- *St&PR 93, WhoAm 92*
Carpenter, Hoyle Dameron 1909- *WhoE 93*
Carpenter, Humphrey *BioIn 17*
Carpenter, Humphrey 1946- *ChlFicS, ScF&FL 92*
Carpenter, J.D. 1948- *WhoCanL 92*
Carpenter, J.G.D. *WhoScE 91-1*
Carpenter, J. Robert 1936- *WhoSSW 93, WhoWor 93*
Carpenter, James 1949- *BioIn 17*
Carpenter, James Arthur 1939- *St&PR 93*
Carpenter, James Craig 1949- *WhoEmL 93*
Carpenter, James Edward 1946- *WhoE 93*
Carpenter, James H. *Law&B 92*
Carpenter, James M. d1992 *NewYTBS 92*
Carpenter, James M. 1914-1992 *BioIn 17*
Carpenter, James Willard *Law&B 92*
Carpenter, Jane Rossman 1952- *WhoAmW 93*
Carpenter, Jeannine Nuttall 1934- *WhoAmW 93*
Carpenter, Jewel Cave 1946- *WhoEmL 93*
Carpenter, Joann *Law&B 92*
Carpenter, John 1948- *MiSFD 9*
Carpenter, John Alden 1876-1951 *Baker 92*
Carpenter, John Howard 1948- *WhoAm 92*
Carpenter, John Marland 1935- *WhoAm 92*
Carpenter, John (Randell) 1936- *ConAu 38NR, WhoWrEP 92*
Carpenter, John W., III 1952- *WhoAm 92*
Carpenter, John Wilson, III 1916- *WhoAm 92*
Carpenter, Joseph E., Jr. *Law&B 92*
Carpenter, Joseph E., Jr. 1953- *St&PR 93*
Carpenter, Joseph Robert 1934- *St&PR 93*
Carpenter, Jot David 1938- *WhoAm 92*
Carpenter, Karen 1950-1983 *Baker 92*
Carpenter, Karen H. 1943- *St&PR 93*
Carpenter, Kenneth E. 1936- *WhoAm 92*
Carpenter, Kenneth E(dward) 1936- *ConAu 137*
Carpenter, Kenneth John 1923- *WhoAm 92*
Carpenter, Kevin Starr 1954- *WhoEmL 93*
Carpenter, Larry H. 1947- *St&PR 93*
Carpenter, Leonard 1948- *ScF&FL 92*
Carpenter, Linda Leigh 1960- *WhoAmW 93*
Carpenter, Lisa Diane 1960- *WhoE 93*
Carpenter, Lon P. 1936- *St&PR 93*
Carpenter, Lynette 1951- *ConAu 138, ScF&FL 92*
Carpenter, M. Michael *Law&B 92*
Carpenter, M. Michael 1936- *St&PR 93*
Carpenter, Malcolm Breckenridge 1921- *WhoAm 92*
Carpenter, Malcolm Scott 1925- *WhoAm 92*
Carpenter, Marj Collier 1926- *WhoAmW 93*
Carpenter, Mark Joseph 1953- *WhoEmL 93*
Carpenter, Marshall L. 1937- *St&PR 93*
Carpenter, Mary-Chapin *BioIn 17*
Carpenter, Mary E. *AmWomPl*
Carpenter, Mary Laure 1953- *WhoAmW 93*
Carpenter, Mary Paige Abeel 1950- *WhoEmL 93*
Carpenter, Mary Pitynski 1926- *WhoAmW 93, WhoSSW 93*
Carpenter, Melissa *BioIn 17*
Carpenter, Michael Alan 1947- *St&PR 93, WhoAm 92, WhoE 93*
Carpenter, Michael E. 1947- *WhoAm 92, WhoE 93*
Carpenter, Michele Annette 1964- *WhoWrEP 92*
Carpenter, Miriam Charlotte 1932- *WhoAmW 93*
Carpenter, Molly *Law&B 92*
Carpenter, Myron Arthur 1938- *St&PR 93, WhoAm 92*
Carpenter, Myrtle Barber *AmWomPl*
Carpenter, Nancy A. 1944- *St&PR 93*
Carpenter, Nancy Carol 1956- *WhoAmW 93*
Carpenter, Nancy Sumrall 1955- *WhoEmL 93*
Carpenter, Nate *St&PR 93*
Carpenter, Noble O. 1929- *St&PR 93*
Carpenter, Noble Olds 1929- *WhoAm 92*
Carpenter, Norman Roblee 1932- *WhoAm 92, WhoWor 93*
Carpenter, Patricia 1920- *WhoWrEP 92*
Carpenter, Patricia 1923- *WhoAm 92*
Carpenter, Paul Leonard 1920- *St&PR 93, WhoAm 92*
Carpenter, Paul Samuel 1956- *WhoE 93*
Carpenter, Peter 1940- *St&PR 93*
Carpenter, Peter William 1942- *WhoWor 93*
Carpenter, Philip David 1943- *WhoAm 92*
Carpenter, Ray Warren 1934- *WhoAm 92*
Carpenter, Richard 1929- *ScF&FL 92*
Carpenter, Richard Amon 1926- *WhoAm 92*
Carpenter, Richard Lynn 1946- *WhoEmL 93*
Carpenter, Richard M. 1927- *WhoAm 92*
Carpenter, Richard Michael 1943- *St&PR 93*
Carpenter, Robert *Law&B 92*
Carpenter, Robert Douglas 1925- *St&PR 93*
Carpenter, Robert Eddy 1924- *St&PR 93*
Carpenter, Robert Hunt 1948- *WhoSSW 93*
Carpenter, Robert R. 1955- *St&PR 93*
Carpenter, Robert Ruliph Morgan 1917-1990 *BioIn 17*
Carpenter, Robert Wayne 1949- *WhoEmL 93*
Carpenter, Roxanne Sue 1952- *WhoAmW 93*
Carpenter, Russell LeGrand 1901-1991 *BioIn 17*
Carpenter, Sandra Mitchell 1934- *St&PR 93*
Carpenter, Scott 1925- *ScF&FL 92*
Carpenter, Sheri Lynn 1956- *WhoAmW 93*
Carpenter, Stanley Hammack 1926- *WhoSSW 93*
Carpenter, Stanley Waterman 1921- *WhoE 93*
Carpenter, Stephen *MiSFD 9*
Carpenter, Susan Karen 1951- *WhoAm 92, WhoAmW 93*
Carpenter, Ted Galen 1947- *WhoAm 92*
Carpenter, Thomas A. 1947- *St&PR 93*
Carpenter, Thomas Oliver 1952- *WhoEmL 93*
Carpenter, Tom L. *St&PR 93*
Carpenter, Vernon John *Law&B 92*
Carpenter, Wallace Wright 1923- *St&PR 93*
Carpenter, Will Dockery 1930- *St&PR 93, WhoAm 92*
Carpenter, William 1940- *WhoWrEP 92*
Carpenter, William C., Jr. 1951- *WhoAm 92*
Carpenter, William Geoffrey *Law&B 92*
Carpenter, William Levy 1926- *WhoAm 92*
Carpenter, William Morton 1940- *WhoE 93*
Carpenter, William Stanley, Jr. 1937- *BiDAMSp 1989*
Carpenter, William Ward 1949- *WhoEmL 93*
Carpenter, Woodrow Wilson 1915- *St&PR 93*
Carpenter-Mason, Beverly Nadine 1933- *WhoAmW 93, WhoE 93*
Carpenter-Meister, Carolyn Evelyn 1946- *WhoE 93*
Carpenter-Phinney, Connie *BioIn 17*
Carpentier, Alejo 1904-1980 *ScF&FL 92, SpAmA*
Carpentier, Andre 1947- *WhoCanL 92*
Carpentier, Jean *WhoScE 91-2*
Carpentras c. 1470-1548 *Baker 92*
Carper, Freda Smith 1953- *WhoAmW 93*
Carper, Gertrude Esther 1921- *WhoAmW 93, WhoE 93, WhoWor 93*
Carper, Robert Allen 1947- *St&PR 93*
Carper, Thomas R. 1947- *CngDr 91*
Carper, Thomas Richard 1947- *WhoAm 92, WhoE 93*
Carper, William Barclay 1946- *WhoEmL 93, WhoSSW 93*
Carpi, Janice E. *Law&B 92*
Carpignano, Josephine Leonora 1928- *WhoAmW 93*
Carpinelli, R. Anthony 1963- *WhoE 93*
Carpini, Giovanni di Piano 1182?-1252 *Expl 93*
Carpino, Barbara Ann 1938- *WhoE 93*
Carpino, Francesco Cardinal 1905- *WhoWor 93*
Carpino, Louis A. 1927- *WhoAm 92*
Carpio, Graham *Law&B 92*
Carpio, Manuel 1791-1860 *DcMexL*
Carpio Nicolle, Jorge *DcCPCAm*
Carpitella, Diego 1924- *Baker 92*
Carples, Charles E. d1990 *BioIn 17*
Carples, Steven Arthur 1954- *WhoEmL 93*
Carpman, Stephen M. *Law&B 92*
Carpozi, George, Jr. 1920- *ScF&FL 92*
Carpp, Edward Daniel 1952- *WhoEmL 93*
Carpus, Robert Joseph 1949- *WhoSSW 93*
Carr, Aaron J. *Law&B 92*
Carr, Albert Bernard 1930- *WhoWrEP 92*
Carr, Albert V., Jr. *Law&B 92*
Carr, Allan *WhoAm 92*
Carr, Andy 1935- *WhoSSW 93*
Carr, Ann Smith *Law&B 92*
Carr, Anne Elizabeth 1939- *WhoSSW 93*
Carr, Arthur Charles 1918- *WhoAm 92*
Carr, Arthur Henry 1947- *St&PR 93*
Carr, Audri Joan 1936- *WhoAmW 93*
Carr, Barbara Comyns- *ScF&FL 92*
Carr, Barbara Kunkel 1945- *WhoAm 92, WhoAmW 93*
Carr, Barry Lynn 1953- *WhoEmL 93*
Carr, Benjamin 1768-1831 *Baker 92*
Carr, Bentley 1946- *ScF&FL 92*
Carr, Bernadette Patricia *WhoAm 92*
Carr, Bernard Francis 1919- *WhoAm 92*
Carr, Bessie 1920- *WhoSSW 93*
Carr, Bob 1943- *CngDr 91*
Carr, Bonnie Jean 1947- *WhoAmW 93, WhoEmL 93, WhoWor 93*
Carr, C.A., Jr. 1944- *St&PR 93*
Carr, C. Wesley *St&PR 93*
Carr, Candy Jeane 1965- *WhoAmW 93*
Carr, Carol Dickinson 1945- *WhoAmW 93*
Carr, Carolyn Kehlor 1948- *WhoEmL 93*
Carr, Carolyn Sue Dean 1943- *WhoSSW 93*
Carr, Cassandra C. 1944- *St&PR 93*
Carr, Cassandra Colvin 1944- *WhoAm 92, WhoAmW 93*
Carr, Catherine A. *Law&B 92*
Carr, Charles F. 1925- *St&PR 93*
Carr, Charles Jelleff 1910- *WhoAm 92*
Carr, Charles William 1917- *WhoAm 92*
Carr, Chris *BioIn 17*
Carr, Christopher C. 1950- *WhoEmL 93*
Carr, Dabney Smith 1802-1854 *JrnUS*
Carr, Daniel Barry 1948- *WhoWor 93*
Carr, Daniel Paul 1951- *WhoWrEP 92*
Carr, David F. *St&PR 93*
Carr, David Turner 1914- *WhoAm 92*
Carr, David Wildon 1945- *WhoE 93*
Carr, Doleen Pellett 1950- *WhoAmW 93, WhoWor 93*
Carr, Edward Albert, Jr. 1922- *WhoAm 92*
Carr, Edward Gary 1947- *WhoE 93*
Carr, Emily 1871-1945 *BioIn 17*
Carr, Eric d1991 *BioIn 17*
Carr, Ernest *BioIn 17*
Carr, F.J. *WhoScE 91-1*
Carr, Frank 1903-1991 *AnObit 1991*
Carr, Fred 1931- *WhoAm 92*
Carr, George 1939- *St&PR 93*
Carr, George Francis, Jr. *Law&B 92*
Carr, George Francis, Jr. 1939- *WhoAm 92*
Carr, George Leroy 1927- *WhoAm 92*
Carr, George Watts, Jr. 1918- *St&PR 93*
Carr, Gerald Paul 1932- *WhoAm 92*
Carr, Geraldine Marie 1955- *WhoEmL 93*
Carr, Gilbert Randle 1928- *WhoAm 92*
Carr, Gladys Justin *WhoAm 92*
Carr, Glenna Dodson 1927- *WhoSSW 93*
Carr, Gwenn L. *Law&B 92*
Carr, Hal N. 1921- *St&PR 93*
Carr, Harold Noflet 1921- *WhoAm 92, WhoSSW 93*
Carr, Harriett (Helen) 1899- *DcAmChF 1960*
Carr, Helen *ScF&FL 92*
Carr, Henry L. 1913- *WhoSSW 93*

Carr, Herbert 1920-1991 BioIn 17
Carr, Howard BioIn 17
Carr, Howard Earl 1915- WhoAm 92
Carr, Howard Ernest 1908- WhoSSW 93
Carr, J(ames Joseph) L(loyd) 1912- ConAu 37NR
Carr, Jack WhoScE 91-1
Carr, Jack David 1938- St&PR 93
Carr, Jack Richard 1937- St&PR 93, WhoAm 92
Carr, Jacquelyn B. 1923- WhoAmW 93
Carr, James 1942- SoulM
Carr, James C. 1933- WhoScE 91-3
Carr, James Francis 1946- WhoEmL 93
Carr, James Herbert 1941- WhoSSW 93
Carr, James McRae 1951- WhoSSW 93
Carr, James Michael 1950- WhoEmL 93
Carr, James Norris, Jr. 1952- WhoE 93
Carr, James Patrick 1950- WhoEmL 93
Carr, James T. 1937- WhoIns 93
Carr, Jay Phillip 1936- WhoAm 92
Carr, Jayge 1940- ScF&FL 92
Carr, Jean D. 1925- St&PR 93
Carr, Jesse Metteau, III 1952- WhoEmL 93, WhoWor 93
Carr, Joanne Klopfer 1954- WhoAmW 93
Carr, John Dickson 1906-1977 BioIn 17
Carr, John F. 1944- ScF&FL 92
Carr, John L. 1932- WhoAm 92
Carr, John L. 1945- ScF&FL 92
Carr, John Mark 1953- WhoEmL 93
Carr, John P. 1945- St&PR 93, WhoIns 93
Carr, John S. Law&B 92
Carr, John Wesley 1945- WhoAm 92
Carr, Joseph E. 1880-1939 BioIn 17
Carr, Judith Weichsel 1942- WhoAmW 93
Carr, Karen Frances 1961- WhoSSW 93
Carr, Kathryne Elizabeth 1955- WhoEmL 93
Carr, Kenneth C. 1937- St&PR 93
Carr, Kenneth L. 1932- St&PR 93
Carr, Kenneth Lloyd 1932- WhoAm 92
Carr, Kenneth Monroe 1925- WhoAm 92, WhoWor 93
Carr, Kirby ScF&FL 92
Carr, Larry Dean 1947- WhoEmL 93
Carr, Lawrence Edward, Jr. 1923- WhoAm 92
Carr, Les 1935- WhoAm 92
Carr, Lewis Bruce 1914-1991 BioIn 17
Carr, Lewis Charles 1946- WhoE 93
Carr, Lois Green 1922- WhoAmW 93
Carr, Louis J., Jr. Law&B 92
Carr, M. Emily 1871-1945 BioIn 17
Carr, M. Robert 1943- WhoAm 92
Carr, Margaret Nell 1933- WhoSSW 93
Carr, Marie Pinak 1954- WhoAmW 93, WhoEmL 93
Carr, Marjorie Barnwell 1949- WhoSSW 93
Carr, Mark Edmund 1962- WhoE 93
Carr, Mary Lucretia AmWomPl
Carr, Michael ScF&FL 92
Carr, Michael A. 1954- St&PR 93
Carr, Michael Fabian 1935- WhoE 93
Carr, Mike ScF&FL 92
Carr, Nick ScF&FL 92
Carr, Noel Gordon WhoScE 91-1
Carr, Pat 1932- WhoWrEP 92
Carr, Patricia Warren 1947- WhoAmW 93, WhoEmL 93
Carr, Patrick E. 1922- WhoAm 92, WhoSSW 93
Carr, Patrick F. 1951- St&PR 93
Carr, Paul Henry 1935- WhoAm 92
Carr, Peggy d1989 BioIn 17
Carr, Peter Emile 1950- WhoWrEP 92
Carr, Peter John 1941- WhoWor 93
Carr, Rich WhoWrEP 92
Carr, Richard Joseph 1935- WhoWrEP 92
Carr, Richard L. 1929- St&PR 93
Carr, Robert Allen 1917- WhoAm 92
Carr, Robert C. 1926- St&PR 93
Carr, Robert Clifford 1940- WhoAm 92
Carr, Robert David 1948- WhoAm 92
Carr, Robert Edward 1949- WhoSSW 93
Carr, Robert Locke 1930- WhoWor 93
Carr, Robert Stuart 1946- WhoAm 92
Carr, Robert Wilson, Jr. 1934- WhoAm 92
Carr, Robin 1953- WhoEmL 93
Carr, Robyn 1951- ConAu 38NR
Carr, Ronald Edward 1932- WhoAm 92
Carr, Roy Arthur 1929- WhoAm 92
Carr, Ruby Louise 1948- WhoEmL 93, WhoSSW 93
Carr, Ruth Anne 1947- WhoAmW 93
Carr, Sandra T. Law&B 92
Carr, Sara Adnee 1963- WhoAmW 93
Carr, Sarah Pratt 1850- AmWomPl
Carr, Sharon Jacqueline 1946- WhoAmW 93
Carr, Sherry Manning Law&B 92
Carr, Shirley G. E. WhoAm 92
Carr, Stephen Hamilton 1947- St&PR 93
Carr, Stephen Howard 1942- WhoAm 92
Carr, Steven Law&B 92
Carr, Susan Jean St&PR 93
Carr, Susan Price 1946-1991 BioIn 17
Carr, Terry MiSFD 9
Carr, Terry 1937-1987 ScF&FL 92
Carr, Thomas E. 1949- St&PR 93
Carr, Thomas Eldridge 1953- WhoEmL 93
Carr, Thomas J. BioIn 17
Carr, Thomas Jefferson, Jr. 1942- St&PR 93, WhoAm 92
Carr, Thomas Michael 1953- WhoWor 93
Carr, Thos. C. 1932- St&PR 93
Carr, Vickie Ann 1956- WhoAmW 93
Carr, Vikki WhoAm 92
Carr, Vikki 1940- HispAmA [port], NotHsAW 93 [port]
Carr, Virginia Colleen 1955- WhoAmW 93
Carr, Virginia Spencer BioIn 17
Carr, Walter James, Jr. 1918- WhoAm 92
Carr, Wayne 1948- St&PR 93
Carr, Wendell Hampton 1953- WhoEmL 93
Carr, Willard Zeller, Jr. 1927- WhoAm 92
Carr, William 1930- St&PR 93, WhoAm 92
Carr, William Anthony 1938- St&PR 93, WhoAm 92
Carr, William G. 1930- St&PR 93
Carr, William Henry A. 1924- WhoWor 93
Carr, William L. Law&B 92
Carr, Wooda N. ScF&FL 92
Carr, Yvonne Denise 1970- WhoE 93
Carra, Andrew Joseph 1943- WhoAm 92
Carra, Carlo 1881-1966 BioIn 17
Carracino, Eugene 1951- St&PR 93
Carracino, Eugene Joseph 1951- WhoSSW 93
Carrada, Gian Carlo 1937- WhoScE 91-3
Carradine, David 1936- MiSFD 9, WhoAm 92
Carradine, John 1906-1988 BioIn 17, IntDcF 2-3
Carradine, Keith 1949- ConTFT 10
Carradine, Keith 1950- BioIn 17
Carradine, Keith Ian 1949- WhoAm 92
Carradini, Lawrence 1953- WhoWor 93
Carragher, Frank A. 1932- St&PR 93
Carragher, Frank Anthony 1932- WhoAm 92
Carraher, Charles Eugene, Jr. 1941- WhoAm 92, WhoSSW 93
Carraher, Mark Stephen 1953- WhoWor 93
Carran, William M., Jr. 1931- St&PR 93
Carranco, Lynwood 1921- WhoWrEP 92
Carranza, Eduardo 1913-1985 SpAmA
Carranza, Juan 1959- WhoWor 93
Carranza, Mary Martha 1963- WhoAmW 93
Carranza, Octavio Alberto 1924- WhoWor 93
Carranza, Ruth 1949- NotHsAW 93
Carranza, Sergio Amilcar 1937- WhoWor 93
Carranza, Venustiano DcCPCAm
Carranza, Venustiano 1859-1920 DcTwHis, HarEnMi
Carrara, Arthur Alfonso 1914- WhoAm 92
Carrara, John Joseph Law&B 92
Carrara, Sidney L. A. 1960- WhoWor 93
Carrasco, Carlos Antonio 1935- WhoUN 92
Carrasco, Gilbert Paul 1953- WhoAm 92
Carrasco, Ricardo Cruz 1943- WhoSSW 93
Carrasco Belmonte, D. Jaime WhoScE 91-3
Carrasquillo, Carlos R. Law&B 92
Carrasquillo, Peggy Musser 1961- WhoSSW 93
Carratala, Jordi 1956- WhoWor 93
Carrato, J. Thomas 1934- Law&B 92
Carraud, Michel-Gaston 1864-1920 Baker 92
Carraway, Andrew 1947- St&PR 93
Carr-DeRamus, Denise 1951- WhoE 93
Carre, Albert 1852-1938 Baker 92, OxDcOp
Carre, Jean-Claude 1931- WhoWor 93
Carre, Jose E.A.E.G. 1936- WhoScE 91-2
Carre, Marguerite 1880-1947 OxDcOp
Carre, Michel 1819-1872 OxDcOp
Carrel, Clarence Wayne 1937- St&PR 93
Carrel, Frederic 1869- ScF&FL 92
Carrel, Jeffrey Mack 1942- WhoE 93
Carrel, Mark ScF&FL 92
Carrell, Betty Lou 1941- WhoAmW 93, WhoWor 93
Carrell, Daniel Allan 1941- WhoAm 92
Carrell, David William 1950- WhoEmL 93
Carrell, Nancy Law&B 92
Carrell, Robin W. WhoScE 91-1
Carrell, Stewart 1934- St&PR 93
Carrell, Terry Eugene 1938- WhoWor 93
Carren, David Bennett 1952- WhoEmL 93
Carrender, Michael Wendell 1953- St&PR 93
Carreno, Alberto Maria 1875-1962 DcMexL
Carreno, Inocente 1919- Baker 92
Carreno, Ricardo Mark 1954- WhoSSW 93
Carreno, Richard Dennis 1946- WhoEmL 93
Carreno, Teresa 1853-1917 BioIn 17
Carreno, (Maria) Teresa 1853-1917 Baker 92
Carreno de Miranda, Juan 1614-1685 BioIn 17
Carrera, Alessandro 1954- WhoSSW 93
Carrera, Joan Judith 1928- WhoE 93
Carrera, Jose Miguel de 1785-1821 HarEnMi
Carrera, Victor Manuel 1954- WhoEmL 93
Carrera Andrade, Jorge 1903-1978 SpAmA
Carreras, Eduardo M. Law&B 92
Carreras, Francisco Jose 1932- WhoAm 92
Carreras, James 1910-1990 BioIn 17
Carreras, Jose 1943- WhoScE 91-3
Carreras, Jose 1946- BioIn 17, ConMus 8 [port], IntDcOp, OxDcOp
Carreras, Jose 1947- WhoAm 92, WhoWor 93
Carreras, Jose (Maria) 1946- Baker 92
Carreras, Michael 1927- MiSFD 9
Carreras-Matas, Luis M. 1921- WhoScE 91-3
Carreras Puigdengolas, Josep M. 1942- WhoWor 93
Carrere, Emmanuel 1957- ScF&FL 92
Carretta, Albert Aloysius 1907- WhoAm 92
Carretta, Richard L. 1939- St&PR 93
Carretta, Richard Louis 1939- WhoAm 92
Carrey, Bernard S. Law&B 92
Carrey, Jim BioIn 17
Carrick, B. Cramton 1913- WhoIns 93
Carrick, Benjamin Lane 1958- WhoSSW 93, WhoWor 93
Carrick, Bruce Robert 1937- St&PR 93, WhoAm 92
Carrick, Carol BioIn 17
Carrick, Carol (Hatfield) 1935- ConAu 37NR, DcAmChF 1985, MajAI [port]
Carrick, Donald BioIn 17
Carrick, Donald (F.) 1929-1989 ConAu 37NR, MajAI
Carrick, John 1819-1890 BioIn 17
Carrick, Paula S. Law&B 92
Carrick, Paula Strecker 1944- WhoAm 92, WhoAmW 93, WhoWor 93
Carrick, Roger John 1937- WhoWor 93
Carrick, Ronald W. St&PR 93
Carrick, Warren F.R. St&PR 93
Carrico, Christine Kathryn 1950- WhoEmL 93
Carrico, Deborah Jean 1948- WhoAmW 93
Carrico, Fred A. 1943- St&PR 93
Carrico, Fred Allen 1943- WhoAm 92
Carrico, Harry Lee 1916- WhoAm 92, WhoSSW 93
Carrie, Allan Stewart WhoScE 91-1
Carrie, Jacques Felix 1939- WhoWrEP 92
Carrier, Bruce A. Law&B 92
Carrier, Constance Virginia 1908- WhoWrEP 92
Carrier, Estelle Stacy 1913- WhoAm 92
Carrier, George Bigelow Law&B 92
Carrier, George Francis 1918- WhoAm 92
Carrier, Glass Bowling, Jr. 1931- WhoAm 92
Carrier, J. T. 1952- WhoSSW 93
Carrier, Lark 1947- SmATA 71 [port]
Carrier, Roch 1937- BioIn 17, WhoCanL 92
Carrier, Ronald Edwin 1932- WhoAm 92, WhoSSW 93
Carrier, Samuel Crowe, III 1945- WhoAm 92
Carrier, W.P. 1923- St&PR 93
Carrier, Warren Pendleton 1918- WhoAm 92
Carrier, William David, III 1943- WhoAm 92
Carriere, Jacques 1924- St&PR 93
Carriere, Patrick Roger 1946- WhoUN 92
Carriere, Rolf Charles 1944- WhoUN 92
Carriero, Peter C. 1949- St&PR 93
Carrig, James Joseph 1930- WhoE 93
Carrig, John A. Law&B 92
Carrig, Wayne Kenneth 1946- St&PR 93
Carrigan, Daniel James 1960- WhoE 93
Carrigan, David Owen 1933- WhoAm 92, WhoWrEP 92
Carrigan, Jerry SoulM
Carrigan, Jim Richard 1929- WhoAm 92
Carrigan, Martha Loretto 1961- WhoAmW 93, WhoEmL 93
Carriger, Albert Clayton, II 1945- WhoSSW 93
Carriger, Phillip R. St&PR 93
Carrigg, C. Eddie 1965- St&PR 93
Carrigg, James A. 1933- WhoAm 92
Carrigg, James Andrew 1933- St&PR 93
Carriker, Edward Henry 1925- St&PR 93
Carriker, Mary Ann Sloop 1957- WhoEmL 93
Carriker, Roy C. 1937- WhoAm 92
Carril, Peter James 1958- WhoAm 92
Carrillo, Adolfo 1855-1926 DcLB 122 [port]
Carrillo, Carmen 1943- WhoAmW 93
Carrillo, Donna Gribben 1954- WhoAmW 93, WhoEmL 93
Carrillo, Francisco J. 1944- WhoUN 92
Carrillo, Leo 1880-1961 HispAmA
Carrillo, M.A. WhoScE 91-3
Carrillo (-Trujillo), Julian (Antonio) 1875-1965 Baker 92
Carrillo Estevez, Manuel 1944- WhoScE 91-3
Carrillo Vargas, Guillermo 1928- WhoScE 91-3
Carrillo y Ancona, Crescencio 1837-1897 DcMexL
Carringer, Paul Timothy 1958- WhoEmL 93
Carrington, Dora de Houghton 1893-1932 BioIn 17
Carrington, Elaine Sterne 1892-1958 AmWomPl
Carrington, Elizabeth Ellen 1943- WhoWrEP 92
Carrington, Frances Grummond 1845-1911 BioIn 17
Carrington, Frank BioIn 17
Carrington, Frank d1992 NewYTBS 92
Carrington, Grant 1938- ScF&FL 92
Carrington, Grant Clark 1938- WhoWrEP 92
Carrington, Henry A. 1929- St&PR 93
Carrington, Hereward 1880-1958 ScF&FL 92
Carrington, John K. 1943- St&PR 93
Carrington, Leonora 1917- BioIn 17, ScF&FL 92
Carrington, McKen Vincent 1949- WhoEmL 93
Carrington, Patricia Ann 1945- WhoSSW 93
Carrington, Peter Alexander Rupert 1919- WhoWor 93
Carrington, Samuel Macon, Jr. 1939- WhoAm 92
Carrington, Susan Schell 1951- WhoEmL 93
Carrington, Sylvia 1960- WhoEmL 93, WhoWor 93
Carrington Da Costa, Rui Braga 1932- WhoWor 93
Carrino, A. Greg 1948- St&PR 93
Carrion, Alejandro 1915- SpAmA
Carrion, Arturo Morales BioIn 17
Carrion, Arturo Morales 1913-1989 HispAmA
Carrion, Audrey J. Sylvia 1958- WhoEmL 93
Carrion, Luis DcCPCAm
Carrion, Richard L. BioIn 17
Carrion, Richard L. 1952- St&PR 93
Carrion, Ulises 1941- DcMexL
Carrion, Ulises 1941-1989 BioIn 17
Carriquiry, Alicia Laura 1957- WhoAmW 93
Carris, James F. Law&B 92
Carris, William H. 1944- St&PR 93
Carrithers, Gale Hemphill 1932- WhoSSW 93
Carriveau, Michael Jon 1956- WhoEmL 93
Carro, Carl Rafael 1961- WhoE 93
Carro, Jorge Luis 1924- WhoAm 92
Carro, Paul Russell d1991 BioIn 17
Carro, Teresita 1959- WhoAmW 93
Carro de Prada, Fernando 1964- WhoWor 93
Carrodus, John (Tiplady) 1836-1895 Baker 92
Carrol, Louis Leon 1923- St&PR 93
Carrol, Regina d1992 NewYTBS 92
Carroll, Adorna Occhialini 1952- WhoAmW 93, WhoEmL 93
Carroll, Albert 1914- WhoAm 92
Carroll, Alison Hope 1965- WhoAmW 93
Carroll, Anna Ella 1815-1894 BioIn 17, PolPar
Carroll, Annie AmWomPl
Carroll, Anthony Quentin 1944- WhoE 93
Carroll, Barbara Anne 1945- WhoAmW 93
Carroll, Barry Joseph 1944- St&PR 93, WhoAm 92
Carroll, Bernard James 1940- WhoAm 92
Carroll, Betty Wilder 1921- WhoE 93
Carroll, Billy Price 1920- WhoAm 92
Carroll, Bonnie 1941- WhoAmW 93
Carroll, Bonnie Cooper 1947- WhoEmL 93
Carroll, Brian Dale 1944- St&PR 93, WhoE 93

Carroll, Brion Michael 1957- WhoEmL 93
Carroll, Bruce E. 1951- WhoE 93
Carroll, Carmal Edward 1923- WhoAm 92
Carroll, Carole Makeig 1941- WhoSSW 93
Carroll, Carroll 1902-1991 BioIn 17
Carroll, Catherine North 1948- WhoEmL 93
Carroll, Charles Lemuel, Jr. 1916- WhoSSW 93
Carroll, Charles Michael 1921- WhoSSW 93
Carroll, Clifford Andrew 1906- WhoAm 92
Carroll, Cynthia Louise 1960- WhoE 93, WhoEmL 93
Carroll, Daniel Law&B 92
Carroll, Daniel T. 1926- St&PR 93
Carroll, David d1992 BioIn 17, NewYTBS 92
Carroll, David McKenzie 1954- WhoEmL 93
Carroll, David S. Law&B 92
Carroll, David Shields 1917- WhoAm 92
Carroll, David Todd 1959- WhoEmL 93, WhoWor 93
Carroll, Dennis D. 1947- WhoEmL 93
Carroll, Dennis Patrick 1941- WhoSSW 93
Carroll, Dennis W. 1947- St&PR 93
Carroll, Diahann BioIn 17
Carroll, Diahann 1935- WhoAm 92
Carroll, Don E. 1942- St&PR 93
Carroll, Douglas WhoScE 91-1
Carroll, Dyer Edmund 1921- WhoE 93
Carroll, Earl Hamblin 1925- WhoAm 92
Carroll, Edward P. Law&B 92
Carroll, Edwin Winford 1912- WhoAm 92
Carroll, Elizabeth J. 1955- WhoEmL 93
Carroll, Elizabeth Joan 1944- St&PR 93
Carroll, Elsie C. AmWomPl
Carroll, George A. Law&B 92
Carroll, George Joseph 1917- WhoAm 92, WhoSSW 93
Carroll, Gerald A. Law&B 92
Carroll, Gerald J. 1934- St&PR 93
Carroll, Gladys Hasty 1904- WhoAm 92
Carroll, Harriet Hunt 1954- WhoAmW 93
Carroll, Holbert Nicholson 1921- WhoAm 92
Carroll, Irwin Dixon 1934- WhoSSW 93
Carroll, J. Douglas BioIn 17
Carroll, J. Larry 1946- MiSFD 9
Carroll, J. Roy 1904-1990 BioIn 17
Carroll, J. Speed 1936- WhoAm 92
Carroll, J. Terry 1945- St&PR 93
Carroll, James BioIn 17
Carroll, James 1943- WhoAm 92
Carroll, James F.L. 1934- WhoE 93
Carroll, James G. Law&B 92
Carroll, James Joseph 1935- WhoE 93
Carroll, James Joseph 1946- WhoEmL 93
Carroll, James Langton 1931- St&PR 93
Carroll, James Larry 1946- WhoEmL 93
Carroll, James Michael 1950- WhoEmL 93
Carroll, James S. 1925- St&PR 93
Carroll, James Vincent, III 1940- WhoAm 92
Carroll, Jane Hammond 1946- WhoWrEP 92
Carroll, Janice Ann Hicks 1957- WhoEmL 93
Carroll, Jeanne 1929- WhoAm 92, WhoAmW 93
Carroll, Jim BioIn 17
Carroll, John 1735-1815 BioIn 17
Carroll, John 1809-1884 BioIn 17
Carroll, John Bissell 1916- WhoAm 92, WhoSSW 93
Carroll, John C. d1990 BioIn 17
Carroll, John D. 1930- St&PR 93
Carroll, John Douglas 1939- WhoAm 92
Carroll, John Henry, Jr. Law&B 92
Carroll, John M. 1939- St&PR 93
Carroll, John Moore 1911- WhoWor 93
Carroll, John Patrick 1928- St&PR 93
Carroll, John Sawyer 1942- WhoAm 92
Carroll, Jon BioIn 17
Carroll, Jonathan 1949- BioIn 17, ScF&FL 92, WhoWrEP 92
Carroll, Joseph Francis 1910-1991 BioIn 17
Carroll, Joseph J. 1931- St&PR 93
Carroll, Joseph John 1936- WhoAm 92
Carroll, Joy 1924- ScF&FL 92
Carroll, Joy 1929- WhoCanL 92
Carroll, Judith Ann 1947- WhoWrEP 92
Carroll, Judy Lynn 1953- WhoAmW 93
Carroll, Julian Morton 1931- WhoAm 92
Carroll, Karen Norman 1962- WhoSSW 93
Carroll, Kathleen F. Law&B 92
Carroll, Kenneth Augustine 1959- WhoWor 93
Carroll, Kenneth Kitchener 1923- WhoAm 92
Carroll, Kent Jean 1926- WhoAm 92
Carroll, Kevin BioIn 17
Carroll, Kim Marie 1958- WhoAmW 93
Carroll, L. James 1940- St&PR 93
Carroll, Latrobe 1894- ScF&FL 92
Carroll, Laura Elizabeth 1956- WhoAmW 93
Carroll, Laurence B., III Law&B 92
Carroll, Lee Francis 1937- WhoE 93
Carroll, Lee S. 1942- St&PR 93
Carroll, Leo Rodgers Law&B 92
Carroll, Leonard M. 1942- St&PR 93
Carroll, Leslie Law&B 92
Carroll, Lewis MajAI
Carroll, Lewis 1832-1898 BioIn 17, MagSWL [port], WorLitC [port]
Carroll, Lillian Esther 1942- WhoAmW 93
Carroll, Linda Louise 1949- WhoSSW 93
Carroll, Lucy Ellen 1946- WhoAmW 93, WhoE 93, WhoWrEP 92
Carroll, Madeleine 1906-1987 IntDcF 2-3 [port]
Carroll, Malcolm W. 1922- St&PR 93
Carroll, Margaret Ann 1929- WhoAm 92
Carroll, Marilyn Jeanne 1950- WhoEmL 93
Carroll, Mark Thomas 1956- WhoEmL 93
Carroll, Marshall Elliott 1923- WhoAm 92
Carroll, Mary Ann 1934- WhoAmW 93
Carroll, Mary Colvert 1940- WhoAm 92
Carroll, MaryBeth Ann 1953- WhoEmL 93
Carroll, Maureen Collins 1960- WhoAmW 93
Carroll, Maureen P. Law&B 92
Carroll, Megan Elizabeth 1967- WhoE 93
Carroll, Michael Adrian 1946- WhoAm 92
Carroll, Michael Dennis 1955- WhoEmL 93
Carroll, Michael M. 1936- WhoAm 92
Carroll, Michael Peter 1946- WhoAm 92
Carroll, Noel 1947- ScF&FL 92
Carroll, Oscar Franklin 1950- WhoE 93
Carroll, P.K. 1926- WhoScE 91-3
Carroll, Patricia L. 1958- WhoWrEP 92
Carroll, Patricia Mary 1939- WhoAmW 93
Carroll, Patricia Whitehead 1954- WhoEmL 93, WhoWor 93
Carroll, Patrick J. 1939- St&PR 93
Carroll, Paul Ferguson 1928- St&PR 93
Carroll, Paula Marie 1933- WhoAmW 93, WhoWor 93
Carroll, Philip Joseph 1937- St&PR 93, WhoAm 92
Carroll, Phillip M. Law&B 92
Carroll, Raoul Lord 1950- WhoAm 92
Carroll, Ray 1937- St&PR 93
Carroll, Raymond James 1949- WhoEmL 93
Carroll, Rebecca Ann 1946- WhoAm 92
Carroll, Rebecca Lois 1952- WhoEmL 93
Carroll, Richard A. 1933- St&PR 93
Carroll, Richard Ellis 1955- WhoEmL 93
Carroll, Richard John 1940- St&PR 93
Carroll, Richard Joseph, Jr. Law&B 92
Carroll, Richard P. 1925- St&PR 93
Carroll, Robert Bruce 1949- WhoEmL 93
Carroll, Robert C. Law&B 92
Carroll, Robert C. 1930- St&PR 93
Carroll, Robert Courtney 1946- WhoE 93
Carroll, Robert Eugene 1957- WhoAm 92
Carroll, Robert Graham 1954- WhoSSW 93
Carroll, Robert Henry 1932- WhoAm 92
Carroll, Robert Lynn 1938- WhoAm 92
Carroll, Robert Martin MiSFD 9
Carroll, Robert R. 1927- St&PR 93
Carroll, Robert W. 1923- WhoAm 92
Carroll, Robert Wayne 1930- WhoAm 92
Carroll, Roger Clinton 1947- WhoSSW 93
Carroll, Ronald Frank WhoScE 91-1
Carroll, Rosemary Lalevee 1945- WhoAm 92
Carroll, Ruth 1899- ScF&FL 92
Carroll, S. F., Mrs. AmWomPl
Carroll, Scott Marshall 1956- WhoEmL 93
Carroll, Shirley deVaux Strong 1930- WhoAmW 93
Carroll, Stephen Douglas 1943- WhoSSW 93
Carroll, Stephen John, Jr. 1930- WhoAm 92
Carroll, Terese Adele Law&B 92
Carroll, Theodus 1928- ScF&FL 92
Carroll, Theodus Catherine 1928- WhoWrEP 92
Carroll, Thomas F. Law&B 92
Carroll, Thomas J. 1941- St&PR 93
Carroll, Thomas John 1929- WhoAm 92
Carroll, Thomas Joseph 1912- WhoAm 92
Carroll, Thomas Joseph 1941- WhoAm 92
Carroll, Thomas Phillip 1955- WhoEmL 93
Carroll, Thomas S. 1919- St&PR 93
Carroll, Thomas Sylvester 1919- WhoAm 92
Carroll, Timothy Wayne 1951- WhoEmL 93
Carroll, Tracy Lynne McLain 1963- WhoAmW 93
Carroll, Virginia SweetSg C [port]
Carroll, Virginia Beckham 1930- WhoAmW 93
Carroll, Wallace E. BioIn 17
Carroll, Wallace E. 1907- St&PR 93
Carroll, Wayne Douglas 1938- WhoE 93
Carroll, Willard MiSFD 9
Carroll, William A. St&PR 93
Carroll, William Alexander 1923- WhoSSW 93
Carroll, William F.G. 1936- St&PR 93
Carroll, William H. 1930- St&PR 93
Carroll, William Jerome 1923- WhoAm 92
Carroll, William Joseph 1947- WhoEmL 93
Carroll, William Kenneth 1927- WhoAm 92
Carroll, William T. d1992 NewYTBS 92
Carroll-Dovenmuehle, Bettye Turpin 1943- WhoSSW 93
Carron, Andrew S. 1951- St&PR 93
Carron, Andrew Sharpe 1951- WhoAm 92
Carron, Arthur 1900-1967 Baker 92
Carron, Charles M. Law&B 92
Carron, Theodore Joseph 1918- WhoSSW 93
Carrondo, M. Armenia 1948- WhoWor 93
Carrothers, Alfred William Rooke 1924- WhoAm 92
Carrothers, Gerald Arthur Patrick 1925- WhoAm 92
Carrott, John Arden 1947- WhoEmL 93, WhoSSW 93
Carrow, Leon Albert 1924- WhoAm 92
Carrow, Milton Michael 1912- WhoAm 92
Carrow, Robert Duane 1934- WhoWor 93
Carrowan, Erwin Raeford 1937- St&PR 93
Carrozzella, Louise Bailey 1934- WhoAmW 93, WhoE 93
Carr Ribeiro, Stella ScF&FL 92
Carrubba, Eugene Roy 1934- WhoE 93
Carrubba, Paul Anthony 1949- St&PR 93
Carrubba, Sandra J. McPherson 1943- WhoWrEP 92
Carruth, Allen Higgins 1919- WhoSSW 93
Carruth, Charles Weldon 1921- WhoAm 92
Carruth, David Barrow 1926- WhoAm 92
Carruth, Ella Kaiser AmWomPl
Carruth, Gorton Veeder 1925- WhoWrEP 92
Carruth, Grant F. 1939- St&PR 93
Carruth, Hayden 1921- BioIn 17, ConAu 38NR, CurBio 92 [port], WhoAm 92, WhoWrEP 92
Carruth, John Campbell St&PR 93
Carruth, Lenox, Jr. 1940- WhoSSW 93
Carruth, Lloyd Brent 1933- St&PR 93
Carruth, W. M., Mrs. AmWomPl
Carruthers, Garrey Edward 1939- WhoWor 93
Carruthers, Ian Douglas WhoScE 91-1
Carruthers, John Baker 92
Carruthers, John Robert 1935- WhoAm 92
Carruthers, Mary C. 1962- WhoAmW 93
Carruthers, Norman Harry 1935- WhoAm 92
Carruthers, Peter Ambler 1935- WhoAm 92
Carruthers, S. George 1945- WhoAm 92
Carruthers, Sara Procter 1962- WhoAmW 93
Carruthers, Walter Edward Royden 1938- WhoAm 92
Carry, L. Ray 1932- WhoSSW 93
Carse, Adam (von Ahn) 1878-1958 Baker 92
Carse, Alice Fetzer d1991 BioIn 17
Carsey, Marcia Lee Peterson 1944- WhoAm 92, WhoAmW 93
Carsey, Marcy BioIn 17
Carsia, Gene Vincent 1961- WhoSSW 93
Carski, Theodore Robert 1930- WhoE 93
Carsley, John F. 1931- St&PR 93
Carson, Ada Lou 1932- WhoAmW 93
Carson, Albert Gus, IV 1960- WhoSSW 93, WhoWor 93
Carson, Ann Katherine 1948- WhoAmW 93
Carson, Ben 1951- ConHero 2 [port]
Carson, Benjamin BioIn 17
Carson, Beth Wilkow 1963- WhoAmW 93
Carson, Charles Henry 1930- WhoE 93
Carson, Cheryl Dawn 1961- WhoEmL 93
Carson, Cynthia Lynn 1961- WhoAmW 93
Carson, Daniel M. Law&B 92
Carson, Dave WhoAm 92
Carson, David ScF&FL 92
Carson, David Allen 1956- WhoE 93
Carson, David Costley 1921- WhoSSW 93
Carson, David E. Law&B 92
Carson, David E.A. 1934- St&PR 93
Carson, David H. Law&B 92
Carson, David M. ScF&FL 92
Carson, Dennis R. 1948- St&PR 93
Carson, Donald Prescott 1949- St&PR 93
Carson, Edward Henry 1854-1935 BioIn 17, DcTwHis
Carson, Edward Mansfield 1929- St&PR 93
Carson, Ewart Robert WhoScE 91-1
Carson, Ginger Roberts 1957- WhoEmL 93
Carson, Gordon Bloom 1911- WhoAm 92, WhoWor 93
Carson, Hamilton C. 1928- St&PR 93
Carson, Harry Albert 1913- WhoAm 92
Carson, Howard C. 1932- St&PR 93
Carson, Jack 1910-1963 QDrFCA 92 [port]
Carson, James 1968- BiDAMSp 1989
Carson, James Donald 1929- WhoAm 92
Carson, James Elijah 1923- WhoAm 92
Carson, James Tyson 1925- St&PR 93
Carson, Jerry L. 1940- WhoAm 92
Carson, Jim BioIn 17
Carson, Jody BioIn 17
Carson, John Congleton 1927- WhoAm 92
Carson, John F. 1920- ScF&FL 92
Carson, John R. 1940- WhoSSW 93
Carson, John Robert 1935- St&PR 93
Carson, John Thompson, Jr. 1916- WhoE 93
Carson, Johnnie 1943- WhoAm 92, WhoWor 93
Carson, Johnny NewYTBS 92 [port]
Carson, Johnny 1925- BioIn 17, WhoAm 92
Carson, Joseph M., Jr. 1931- St&PR 93
Carson, Julia M. Porter 1938- AfrAmBi
Carson, Kathryn L. Law&B 92
Carson, Kenneth A. Law&B 92
Carson, Kent 1930- WhoAm 92
Carson, Kent L. 1930- St&PR 93
Carson, Kit 1809-1868 BioIn 17
Carson, Kit 1858-1957 BioIn 17
Carson, Larry E. 1954- St&PR 93
Carson, Leonard Allen 1940- WhoAm 92, WhoSSW 93, WhoWor 93
Carson, Lettie Gay d1992 NewYTBS 92
Carson, Lettie Gay 1901-1992 BioIn 17
Carson, Linda Frances 1952- WhoAmW 93
Carson, Margaret Marie 1944- WhoAmW 93
Carson, Marvin Wayne 1955- WhoEmL 93
Carson, Mary Silvano 1925- WhoAmW 93
Carson, Matt W. Law&B 92
Carson, Maureen Michelle 1963- WhoAmW 93
Carson, Michael ScF&FL 92
Carson, Nina ScF&FL 92
Carson, Nolan Wendell 1924- WhoAm 92
Carson, Philip L., Sr. 1941- St&PR 93
Carson, Rachel 1907-1964 BioIn 17, ConLC 71 [port], WomChHR [port]
Carson, Richard Dean 1956- WhoE 93
Carson, Richard Nathaniel 1933- St&PR 93
Carson, Rick BioIn 17
Carson, Robert William 1948- WhoEmL 93
Carson, Ronald 1943- St&PR 93
Carson, Ronald Frank 1947- WhoWrEP 92
Carson, Royal Willis, III 1949- WhoSSW 93
Carson, Russell L. 1943- St&PR 93
Carson, Samuel Goodman 1913- WhoAm 92
Carson, Sara 1927- St&PR 93
Carson, Sharon Lynn 1959- WhoSSW 93
Carson, T.C. BioIn 17
Carson, Terrence BioIn 17
Carson, Terry David 1943- WhoSSW 93
Carson, Thomas BioIn 17
Carson, Tom C. 1941- St&PR 93
Carson, Victor John Law&B 92
Carson, Vincent A. d1990 BioIn 17
Carson, Virginia Gottschall WhoAmW 93
Carson, Wallace Preston, Jr. 1934- WhoAm 92
Carson, Wayne Gary 1946- WhoSSW 93
Carson, William 1825-1912 BioIn 17
Carson, William 1858-1957 BioIn 17
Carson, William L. 1918- St&PR 93
Carson, William M. 1947- St&PR 93
Carson, William Morris WhoE 93
Carstairs, John Esdale 1933- WhoAm 92
Carstairs, Sharon 1942- WhoAmW 93
Carstedt, Nancy Sylvia 1940- WhoAmW 93
Carsten, Arlene Desmet 1937- WhoAm 92, WhoAmW 93
Carsten, Mary Nash 1958- WhoEmL 93
Carstens, Donald D. 1935- St&PR 93
Carstens, Harold Henry 1925- WhoAm 92, WhoWor 93
Carstens, Jane Ellen 1922- WhoSSW 93
Carstens, Karl 1914-1992 BioIn 17, NewYTBS 92 [port]

Carstens, Karl (Walter) 1914-1992 CurBio 92N
Carstensen, Bernice ScF&FL 92
Carstensen, Edwin Lorenz 1919- WhoAm 92
Carstensen, Harold B. 1943- St&PR 93
Carstensen, Jens 1943- WhoWor 93
Carstensen, Laurence William, Jr. 1954- WhoEmL 93
Carswell, Allan Ian 1933- WhoAm 92
Carswell, Bruce 1930- St&PR 93
Carswell, Donald 1929- St&PR 93
Carswell, G. Harrold d1992 NewYTBS 92 [port]
Carswell, George Harrold 1919- OxCSupC
Carswell, Harmon 1926- St&PR 93
Carswell, Jane Triplett 1932- WhoAm 92
Carswell, Lois Malakoff 1932- WhoE 93
Carswell, Philip John, Jr. 1939- St&PR 93
Carswell, Robert 1928- WhoAm 92
Carswell, Robert Francis WhoScE 91-1
Carswell, Robert Wayne 1933- WhoSSW 93
Carswell, William Steven WhoScE 91-1
Cart, Dorothy Cariker 1923- WhoWrEP 92
Carta, Franklin Oliver 1930- WhoE 93
Cartagena, Angel M., Jr. Law&B 92
Cartaino, Carol Ann 1944- WhoAmW 93
Cartales, John A. 1928- St&PR 93
Cartan, Jean 1906-1932 Baker 92
Cartaya, Mario 1951- WhoSSW 93
Cartaya, Pedro Pablo 1936- WhoSSW 93
Carte, Richard D'Oyly 1844-1901 Baker 92, BioIn 17, OxDcOp
Carte, Suzanne Lewis 1943- WhoAmW 93
Cartee, Leanne 1962- WhoEmL 93
Cartee, Thomas Edward, Jr. 1960- WhoEmL 93
Cartelli, Antonio 1954- WhoWor 93
Cartelli, Michael A. Law&B 92
Carten, Thomas Francis 1942- WhoE 93
Cartenuto, David J. Law&B 92
Carter, A.B. 1939- St&PR 93
Carter, A. Boyd 1950- St&PR 93
Carter, A.P. 1891-1960 BioIn 17
Carter, Alan John 1929- WhoAsAP 91
Carter, Albert Howard, III 1943- ScF&FL 92, WhoSSW 93
Carter, Albert Marvin 1951- WhoEmL 93
Carter, Alden R. BioIn 17
Carter, Aldia Spiers 1936- WhoAmW 93
Carter, Alice P. AmWomPl
Carter, Angela 1940-1992 BioIn 17, NewYTBS 92 [port], ScF&FL 92
Carter, Angela (Olive) 1940-1992 ConAu 136, SmATA 70
Carter, Anne Cohen 1919- WhoAm 92
Carter, Annette AfrAmBi [port]
Carter, Anthony 1960- WhoAm 92
Carter, Antony Arthur WhoScE 91-1
Carter, Arnold N., Jr. 1929- St&PR 93
Carter, Arthur Franklin 1935- St&PR 93
Carter, Asa d1979 BioIn 17
Carter, Ashton B. 1954- ConAu 137
Carter, Ashton Baldwin 1954- WhoAm 92
Carter, Barbara Vatrt 1943- WhoAmW 93
Carter, Barry Edward 1942- WhoAm 92, WhoWor 93
Carter, Benjamin Carroll 1916- WhoSSW 93
Carter, Bennett Lester 1907- WhoAm 92
Carter, Benny BioIn 17
Carter, Benny 1907- Baker 92
Carter, Bernard A. 1926- St&PR 93
Carter, Bernard T. 1926-1990 BioIn 17
Carter, Betsy L. 1945- WhoAm 92
Carter, Betty BioIn 17
Carter, Betty 1929- WhoAm 92, WhoAmW 93
Carter, Betty 1930- Baker 92
Carter, Billy BioIn 17
Carter, Blanchard Lee 1964- WhoEmL 93
Carter, Brandon WhoScE 91-2
Carter, Brian 1937- ScF&FL 92
Carter, Bruce 1922- ScF&FL 92
Carter, C. Michael Law&B 92
Carter, Calvin 1925- BioIn 17
Carter, Calvin W. 1934- WhoIns 93
Carter, Carla Cifelli 1949- WhoAmW 93, WhoSSW 93
Carter, Carlene 1955- BioIn 17, ConMus 8 [port]
Carter, Carmen 1954- ScF&FL 92
Carter, Carolyn Houchin 1952- WhoAmW 93
Carter, Carolyn Howard 1950- WhoEmL 93
Carter, Carolyn Marie 1954- WhoE 93
Carter, Cary Warren 1947- WhoAm 92
Carter, Catherine Mary 1963- WhoAmW 93
Carter, Cecil Clark 1941- WhoSSW 93
Carter, Charles McLean 1936- WhoAm 92
Carter, Charlotte 1943- WhoAmW 93
Carter, Cheryl C. 1950- St&PR 93
Carter, Churchhill 1930- St&PR 93
Carter, Clarence BioIn 17
Carter, Clarence 1936- SoulM
Carter, Clarence Holbrook 1904- WhoAm 92
Carter, Clifford Clay Law&B 92
Carter, Connie Beverly 1926- WhoAmW 93
Carter, Craig Nash 1949- WhoEmL 93, WhoSSW 93, WhoWor 93
Carter, Curtis Harold, Jr. 1939- WhoWrEP 92
Carter, D.L. 1933-1990 BioIn 17
Carter, Dale William 1949- WhoSSW 93
Carter, Dan T. 1940- WhoAm 92
Carter, Daniel F. 1935- St&PR 93
Carter, Darrell Lewis 1946- WhoEmL 93
Carter, Dauton Odell, Jr. 1943- WhoSSW 93
Carter, David C. d1990 BioIn 17
Carter, David Craig WhoScE 91-1
Carter, David Craig 1940- WhoWor 93
Carter, David Edward 1942- WhoWor 93
Carter, David George, Sr. 1942- WhoE 93
Carter, David J. 1953- WhoSSW 93
Carter, David Kent 1938- WhoSSW 93
Carter, David L. 1933-1990 BioIn 17
Carter, David Martin 1936- WhoAm 92
Carter, David R. St&PR 93
Carter, David Ray 1951- WhoAm 92
Carter, Dean 1922- WhoAm 92
Carter, Debra Hope 1956- WhoSSW 93
Carter, Denis George 1947- WhoEmL 93
Carter, Dennis E. 1956- St&PR 93
Carter, Dennis L. 1930- St&PR 93
Carter, Dick MiSFD 9
Carter, Dixie BioIn 17, WhoAm 92
Carter, Don Earl 1917- WhoAm 92
Carter, Donald WhoAm 92, WhoSSW 93
Carter, Donald Lee 1937- WhoSSW 93
Carter, Donald Patton 1927- WhoAm 92
Carter, Doug C. 1952- St&PR 93
Carter, Douglas Andrew Law&B 92
Carter, E. Leo St&PR 93
Carter, Edith AmWomPl
Carter, Edith Houston 1936- WhoAmW 93
Carter, Edward Carlos, II 1928- WhoAm 92
Carter, Edward Fenton, III 1948- WhoSSW 93
Carter, Edward W. 1911- St&PR 93
Carter, Edward William 1911- BioIn 17
Carter, Eleanor Elizabeth 1954- WhoAmW 93, WhoEmL 93
Carter, Elizabeth 1717-1806 BioIn 17
Carter, Elizabeth Marie 1963- WhoEmL 93
Carter, Elliott 1908- BioIn 17
Carter, Elliott Cook, Jr. 1908- WhoAm 92
Carter, Elliott (Cook, Jr.) 1908- Baker 92
Carter, Elsie Hobart AmWomPl
Carter, Emily Ann 1960- WhoEmL 93
Carter, Emily Suzanne 1942- WhoSSW 93
Carter, Erskine 1948- WhoWrEP 92
Carter, Eugene Currin 1929- WhoSSW 93
Carter, Eugene Hudson 1912- St&PR 93
Carter, Forrest d1979 BioIn 17
Carter, Frances Tunnell WhoAm 92
Carter, Frank H. Law&B 92
Carter, Gary BioIn 17
Carter, Gary Kibler 1936- St&PR 93
Carter, Gary Lynn 1947- St&PR 93
Carter, Gene 1935- WhoAm 92, WhoE 93
Carter, George WhoScE 91-1
Carter, George C. 1940- St&PR 93
Carter, George Carson 1957- WhoE 93, WhoEmL 93
Carter, George Goldsmith- 1911- ScF&FL 92
Carter, George Henry, IV 1955- WhoEmL 93
Carter, George Kent 1935- WhoAm 92
Carter, Georgia B. Law&B 92
Carter, Gerald Emmett 1912- WhoAm 92, WhoE 93, WhoWor 93
Carter, Gina Lee 1962- WhoAmW 93, WhoEmL 93
Carter, Gordon Thomas Law&B 92
Carter, Gordon Thomas 1956- WhoEmL 93
Carter, Granville W. d1992 NewYTBS 92
Carter, Granville W. 1920- BioIn 17
Carter, Granville Wellington 1920- WhoAm 92
Carter, Graydon 1950- WhoE 93
Carter, Gregg Lee 1951- WhoE 93
Carter, Gwendolen Margaret 1906-1991 BioIn 17
Carter, Harlon BioIn 17
Carter, Harold Dee 1939- St&PR 93
Carter, Harold Lloyd WhoWor 93
Carter, Harold O. 1932- WhoAm 92
Carter, Harriet Vanessa WhoSSW 93
Carter, Harry Robert 1947- WhoE 93
Carter, Harvey 1945- St&PR 93
Carter, Helen Maxine 1926- WhoAmW 93
Carter, Henry Moore, Jr. 1932- WhoAm 92
Carter, Herbert Edmund 1910- WhoAm 92
Carter, Hodding, Jr. 1907-1972 DcLB 127 [port], EncAACR
Carter, Hodding, III 1935- JrnUS, WhoAm 92
Carter, Horace BioIn 17
Carter, Howard 1874-1939 BioIn 17
Carter, Hugh Clendenin 1925- WhoAm 92
Carter, Ian Ronald 1943- WhoWor 93
Carter, Imogene Armstrong 1929- WhoAmW 93
Carter, J. Howard 1904-1991 BioIn 17
Carter, J. Wesley 1940- St&PR 93
Carter, Jack L. 1947- St&PR 93
Carter, Jaine Marie 1946- WhoAm 92, WhoWor 93
Carter, James Able 1926- WhoSSW 93
Carter, James Alfred 1941- WhoSSW 93
Carter, James Clarence 1927- WhoAm 92, WhoSSW 93
Carter, James E(dward) 1935- WhoWrEP 92
Carter, James Earl 1924- BioIn 17, DcTwHis
Carter, James Earl, Jr. 1924- WhoAm 92, WhoSSW 93, WhoWor 93
Carter, James Edward, Jr. 1906- WhoSSW 93, WhoWor 93
Carter, James Hal, Jr. 1943- WhoAm 92
Carter, James J. 1949- St&PR 93
Carter, James McCord 1952- WhoAm 92, WhoEmL 93, WhoSSW 93
Carter, James Rose, Jr. 1933- WhoAm 92
Carter, James Sumter 1948- WhoSSW 93
Carter, James W., Jr. Law&B 92
Carter, Jane Foster 1927- WhoAmW 93
Carter, Janice 1946- WhoAmW 93
Carter, Janice Joene 1948- WhoAmW 93, WhoEmL 93, WhoWor 93
Carter, Janis BioIn 17
Carter, Jared 1939- WhoWrEP 92
Carter, Jean Gordon 1955- WhoAmW 93
Carter, Jeffrey Thomas 1959- WhoWor 93
Carter, Jimmy 1924- BioIn 17, ColdWar 1 [port], PolPar, WhoAm 92, WhoSSW 93, WhoWor 93
Carter, Jimmy 1924- & Carter, Rosalynn 1927- ConHero 2 [port]
Carter, Joan P. 1943- St&PR 93
Carter, JoAnn Martin 1932- WhoSSW 93
Carter, Joe BioIn 17
Carter, Joel Steven Law&B 92
Carter, John ScF&FL 92
Carter, John 1929-1991 Baker 92, BioIn 17
Carter, John 1950- WhoAsAP 91
Carter, John Allen, Jr. 1934- St&PR 93
Carter, John Avery 1924- WhoAm 92
Carter, John Bernard 1934- St&PR 93
Carter, John Bernard 1934-1991 BioIn 17
Carter, John Boyd, Jr. 1924- WhoAm 92
Carter, John Coles 1920- WhoAm 92, WhoSSW 93
Carter, John Dale 1944- WhoAm 92, WhoWor 93
Carter, John DeLaney 1956- WhoSSW 93
Carter, John Douglas 1946- WhoAm 92, WhoEmL 93
Carter, John Francis, II 1939- WhoSSW 93
Carter, John Hugh Law&B 92
Carter, John J. 1920- St&PR 93
Carter, John M. 1918- St&PR 93
Carter, John Mack 1928- WhoAm 92, WhoE 93
Carter, John Michael Law&B 92
Carter, John Phillip 1950- WhoWor 93
Carter, John Swain 1950- WhoAm 92
Carter, John Tilton, Jr. 1950- WhoEmL 93
Carter, Jonna Carol 1965- WhoSSW 93
Carter, Joseph A., III 1936- St&PR 93
Carter, Joseph C., Jr. 1927- St&PR 93
Carter, Joseph Carlyle, Jr. 1927- WhoAm 92
Carter, Joseph Chris 1960- WhoAm 92
Carter, Joseph Edwin 1915- WhoAm 92
Carter, Joseph Emerson 1920- St&PR 93
Carter, Joseph H(enry, Sr.) 1932- ConAu 139
Carter, Joseph Robert 1951- WhoAm 92
Carter, Josephine Howell AmWomPl
Carter, Joy Eaton 1923- WhoAmW 93
Carter, Joyce Lee 1929- WhoWrEP 92
Carter, Judy L. 1942- WhoSSW 93
Carter, Julie 1956- WhoEmL 93
Carter, K.B. WhoScE 91-1
Carter, K.C. Law&B 92
Carter, Kathy Diane 1957- WhoEmL 93
Carter, Kathy Ellen 1955- WhoAmW 93
Carter, Kevin Andre Law&B 92
Carter, Lark P. 1930- WhoAm 92
Carter, Larry J. St&PR 93
Carter, Larry Vince 1962- WhoEmL 93
Carter, Lawrence Wayne 1942- WhoSSW 93
Carter, Leigh 1925- St&PR 93
Carter, Leslie H. AmWomPl
Carter, Lewis Aaron, Jr. 1941- WhoE 93
Carter, Liane Kupferberg 1954- WhoWrEP 92
Carter, Lila Mae WhoAmW 93
Carter, Lin 1930-1988 ScF&FL 92
Carter, Linda Michelle 1949- WhoE 93
Carter, Loren James, Jr. 1938- WhoSSW 93
Carter, Louise AmWomPl
Carter, Lynda BioIn 17
Carter, Lynda 1951?- NotHsAW 93
Carter, Lynda Cordoba 20th cent.- HispAmA [port]
Carter, Lynn J. Law&B 92
Carter, Mae Riedy 1921- WhoAmW 93
Carter, Manley Lanier d1991 BioIn 17
Carter, Margaret AmWomPl
Carter, Margaret L. AfrAmBi
Carter, Margaret L. 1935- WhoAmW 93
Carter, Margaret L. 1948- ScF&FL 92
Carter, Marilyn Jean 1935- WhoE 93
Carter, Marshall Nichols 1940- WhoAm 92
Carter, Marshall Sylvester 1909- WhoAm 92
Carter, Martin (Wylde) 1927- DcLB 117 [port]
Carter, Mary 1931- WhoE 93
Carter, Mary Arkley WhoWrEP 92
Carter, Mary Eddie 1925- WhoAm 92, WhoAmW 93
Carter, Mary Kennedy 1934- BlkAull 92
Carter, Mason Carlton 1933- WhoAm 92
Carter, Mason N. St&PR 93
Carter, Maybelle 1909-1978 Baker 92
Carter, Melanie S. Law&B 92
Carter, Melvin Whitsett 1941- WhoWor 93
Carter, Michael Allen 1947- WhoAm 92
Carter, Michael Powell WhoScE 91-1
Carter, Mildred Brown 1927- WhoAmW 93
Carter, Nancy Lee Law&B 92
Carter, Nanette 1954- BioIn 17
Carter, Nanette Carolyn 1954- WhoE 93
Carter, Nell 1948- WhoAm 92
Carter, Neville Louis 1934- WhoAm 92
Carter, Nicholas S.F. 1935- St&PR 93
Carter, Nick ConAu 37NR, -39NR, MajAI, ScF&FL 92
Carter, Noel 1942- St&PR 93
Carter, Noel Vreeland ScF&FL 92
Carter, Nolan 1941- WhoSSW 93
Carter, Norma Annie WhoScE 91-1
Carter, Norma Binder Law&B 92
Carter, Norman Wynne WhoScE 91-1
Carter, O.K. 1943- St&PR 93
Carter, Olive Marie 1910- WhoSSW 93
Carter, Orwin L. 1942- WhoAm 92
Carter, Orwin Lee 1942- St&PR 93
Carter, P.C. WhoScE 91-1
Carter, Pamela Lynn 1949- WhoAmW 93, WhoEmL 93
Carter, Patricia Ann 1945- WhoAmW 93
Carter, Patricia G. 1960- WhoAmW 93
Carter, Patti L. 1952- WhoAmW 93
Carter, Paul A. 1926- ScF&FL 92
Carter, Paul R. 1940- St&PR 93, WhoAm 92
Carter, Paul Richard 1922- WhoAm 92
Carter, Phil Norman 1934- St&PR 93
Carter, Powell Frederick 1931- WhoAm 92
Carter, R. Faye 1942- WhoAmW 93
Carter, R.M.H. 1955- ScF&FL 92
Carter, Rand 1937- WhoE 93
Carter, Rebecca Davilene 1932- WhoAm 92
Carter, Renee BioIn 17
Carter, Richard 1918- WhoAm 92, WhoWrEP 92
Carter, Richard Duane WhoAm 92
Carter, Richard Herrick 1920- St&PR 93
Carter, Richard Lawrance 1934- WhoScE 91-1
Carter, Richard William Gale WhoScE 91-1
Carter, Robert Daniel 1927- WhoSSW 93
Carter, Robert Edward 1946- St&PR 93
Carter, Robert Lee 1917- WhoAm 92
Carter, Robert Powell 1957- St&PR 93
Carter, Robert Ray 1932- WhoWrEP 92
Carter, Roberta Eccleston WhoAmW 93
Carter, Rodney 1957- WhoEmL 93, WhoSSW 93
Carter, Roger William WhoScE 91-1
Carter, Ron 1937- BioIn 17
Carter, Ron(ald Levin) 1937- Baker 92
Carter, Ronald 1937- WhoAm 92
Carter, Ronald D. 1938- St&PR 93
Carter, Ronald Dale 1948- WhoEmL 93
Carter, Ronald Martin, Sr. 1925- St&PR 93, WhoAm 92
Carter, Rosalynn BioIn 17
Carter, Rosalynn 1927- See Carter, Jimmy 1924- & Carter, Rosalynn 1927- ConHero 2

Carter, Rosalynn Smith 1927- WhoAm 92, WhoAmW 93, WhoSSW 93
Carter, Roy Ernest, Jr. 1922- WhoAm 92
Carter, Russell Paul, Jr. 1927- WhoSSW 93
Carter, Russell Webster 1918- WhoE 93
Carter, Ruth B. WhoAmW 93, WhoE 93
Carter, Samuel 1904-1988 BioIn 17
Carter, Samuel Booker, Jr. Law&B 92
Carter, Samuel Leewitt, II 1937- WhoSSW 93
Carter, Sandra Ann 1963- WhoAmW 93
Carter, Sara Kebe 1932- WhoAmW 93
Carter, Saralee Lessman 1951- WhoAm 92, WhoAmW 93
Carter, Scott Hays 1960- WhoEmL 93
Carter, Sharon Cross 1944- WhoAmW 93
Carter, Stephen L. BioIn 17
Carter, Stephen L. 1954- ConBlB 4 [port]
Carter, Stephen Michael 1946- St&PR 93
Carter, Stephen P. Law&B 92
Carter, Steven 1956- ConAu 137
Carter, Steven Fitzgerald 1957- WhoWor 93
Carter, Steven Horace Law&B 92
Carter, Stuart David 1952- WhoWor 93
Carter, Susan Mason 1949- WhoSSW 93
Carter, Susan R. 1956- WhoAmW 93
Carter, Susie BioIn 17
Carter, Sylvia WhoE 93
Carter, Terry L. 1948- St&PR 93
Carter, Thomas BioIn 17, MiSFD 9
Carter, Thomas Allen 1935- WhoSSW 93, WhoWor 93
Carter, Thomas Barton 1949- WhoEmL 93, WhoWor 93
Carter, Thomas Bence 1960- WhoSSW 93
Carter, Thomas F. d1991 BioIn 17
Carter, Thomas H. 1854-1911 PolPar
Carter, Thomas Henry 1854-1911 BioIn 17
Carter, Thomas Heyward, Jr. 1946- WhoEmL 93
Carter, Thomas Lee 1952- WhoAm 92
Carter, Thomas Smith, Jr. 1921- WhoAm 92, WhoWor 93
Carter, Thomas W. 1948- St&PR 93
Carter, Timothy Howard 1944- WhoE 93
Carter, Tonya R. ScF&FL 92
Carter, Velma Eileen 1952- WhoAmW 93
Carter, Vic AfrAmBi
Carter, Victor M. 1909- St&PR 93
Carter, W. Minor 1940- WhoIns 93
Carter, Warrick Livingston 1942- WhoE 93
Carter, Wilbur Lee, Jr. 1922- WhoAm 92
Carter, Wilfred Wilson 1923- St&PR 93, WhoAm 92
Carter, William Allen 1932- WhoAm 92
Carter, William C. BioIn 17
Carter, William Caswell 1917- WhoAm 92
Carter, William Geoffrey WhoScE 91-1
Carter, William George, III 1944- WhoAm 92
Carter, William Harold, Sr. 1938- WhoE 93
Carter, William Joseph 1949- WhoEmL 93
Carter, William Minor 1940- St&PR 93
Carter, William R. 1928- St&PR 93
Carter, William Walton 1921- WhoAm 92
Carter-Clayton, Connie Lynn 1956- WhoEmL 93
Carteret, Philip 1734-1796 Expl 93
Carterette, Edward (Calvin) 1921- Baker 92
Carterette, Edward Calvin Hayes 1921- WhoAm 92
Carter Family BioIn 17
Carter-Miller, Jocelyn BioIn 17
Carter-Ruck, Peter F. 1914- BioIn 17
Carter-White, Kathy Jean 1957- WhoAmW 93
Cartey, Wilfred d1992 NewYTBS 92
Cartey, Wilfred 1931- BlkAuII 92
Cartey, Wilfred 1931-1992 BioIn 17
Cartey, Wilfred (George Onslow) 1931-1992 ConAu 137
Carthaus, James A. 1940- St&PR 93
Carthaus, James Arthur 1940- WhoAm 92
Carthel, Anne Fawver 1952- WhoAmW 93, WhoEmL 93
Carthen, Billy Burton 1950- WhoEmL 93, WhoSSW 93, WhoWor 93
Carthew, Lily AmWomPl
Carthew, Philip 1948- WhoWor 93
Carthy, Margaret d1992 NewYTBS 92 [port]
Carthy, Mark Patrick 1960- WhoEmL 93
Cartianu, Ana ScF&FL 92
Cartier, Benoit 1946- St&PR 93
Cartier, Celine Paule 1930- WhoAm 92
Cartier, David Robert 1954- WhoE 93
Cartier, Edd 1914- ScF&FL 92
Cartier, George Thomas, Jr. 1924- WhoE 93
Cartier, Jacques 1491-1557 Expl 93 [port]
Cartier, Jean-Baptiste 1765-1841 Baker 92
Cartier, Kerry Lee 1947- WhoSSW 93
Cartier, Matthew Roland 1957- WhoSSW 93
Cartier, Richard Wrye 1920- St&PR 93
Cartier, Rudolph 1908- BioIn 17
Cartier-Bresson, Henri 1908- BioIn 17, WhoWor 93
Cartisano, Linda Ann 1953- WhoEmL 93
Cartland, Barbara 1901- ScF&FL 92, WhoAm 92, WhoWor 93
Cartland, Barbara 1902- BioIn 17
Cartland, John Everett, III 1944- St&PR 93
Cartledge, J. Cole Law&B 92
Cartledge, Raymond Eugene 1929- St&PR 93, WhoAm 92
Cartlidge, Richard L. 1954- St&PR 93
Cartmell, James Robert 1931- St&PR 93
Cartmell, Jennifer B. 1953- St&PR 93
Cartmell, Vinton Aikins 1925- WhoAm 92
Cartmill, Cleve 1908-1964 ScF&FL 92
Cartmill, George Edwin, Jr. 1918- WhoAm 92
Cartmill, Matt 1943- WhoAm 92
Cartmill, Rick T. 1948- St&PR 93
Cartner, John A., III 1947- WhoAm 92
Carto, Willis Allison 1926- WhoE 93, WhoWor 93
Carton, Barbara Wells 1950- WhoAmW 93
Carton, Barry F. 1942- St&PR 93
Carton, Laurence Alfred 1918- WhoAm 92
Carton, Margaret F. St&PR 93
Carton, Marvyn 1917- St&PR 93
Carton, Michel 1933- WhoScE 91-2
Carton De Wiart, Adrian 1880-1963 HarEnMi
Cartoni, G. Paolo 1929- WhoScE 91-3
Cartoni, Giampaolo 1929- WhoWor 93
Cartron, Jean-Pierre WhoScE 91-2
Cartun, Joel 1939- St&PR 93
Cartwright, Albert Thomas 1917- WhoE 93
Cartwright, Alton Stuart 1922- WhoAm 92
Cartwright, B. WhoScE 91-1
Cartwright, Bettye Atkins 1925- WhoSSW 93
Cartwright, Carol Ann 1941- WhoAmW 93
Cartwright, Charles Nelson 1933- WhoAm 92, WhoSSW 93
Cartwright, David 1943- WhoWor 93
Cartwright, Derek WhoScE 91-1
Cartwright, Frances Lynn 1948- WhoEmL 93
Cartwright, Gregory Clark Law&B 92
Cartwright, Howard Eugene 1924- WhoAm 92
Cartwright, James Franklin 1948- WhoEmL 93
Cartwright, Jarold Phillip 1952- WhoEmL 93
Cartwright, Jeffrey Robert Law&B 92
Cartwright, Jerry Lee 1958- WhoSSW 93
Cartwright, Joseph Michael 1954- WhoEmL 93
Cartwright, Mabel Irene 1945- WhoAmW 93
Cartwright, Madeline BioIn 17
Cartwright, Mary L. BioIn 17
Cartwright, Mary Lou 1923- WhoAm 92, WhoAmW 93
Cartwright, Michael Wayne 1962- WhoEmL 93
Cartwright, Paul WhoScE 91-1
Cartwright, Peter Swain 1937- St&PR 93
Cartwright, Reg BioIn 17
Cartwright, Rhonda Delrie 1952- St&PR 93
Cartwright, Roberta A. 1938- St&PR 93
Cartwright, Ronald Harris 1946- WhoSSW 93
Cartwright, Scyrus 1953- WhoE 93
Cartwright, Thomas C. Law&B 92
Cartwright, Thomas Harold 1953- St&PR 93
Cartwright, Walter Joseph 1922- WhoAm 92
Cartwright, William c. 1611-1643 DcLB 126 [port]
Cartwright, William Holman 1915- WhoAm 92
Carty, Arthur John 1940- WhoAm 92
Carty, David 1955- ConAu 139
Carty, Gerard James 1932- St&PR 93, WhoAm 92
Carty, Helen Mary Louise WhoScE 91-1
Carty, John L. 1945- St&PR 93
Carty, John Lydon 1945- WhoAm 92, WhoE 93
Carty, John Wesley 1923- WhoWor 93
Carty, Leo 1931- BlkAuII 92
Carty, Paul Vernon 1954- WhoEmL 93
Carty, Raymond Wesley 1956- WhoEmL 93
Carty, Ruth Agnes 1925- WhoSSW 93
Carty-Bennia, Denise 1947-1990 BioIn 17
Caruana, Joan 1941- WhoAmW 93
Caruana, Louis Bartholomew 1937- WhoSSW 93
Caruana, Patrick Peter 1939- WhoAm 92
Caruba, Sandra L. Law&B 92
Carubelli, Raoul 1929- WhoSSW 93
Carucci, Samuel Anthony 1935- WhoAm 92
Carulli, Ferdinando 1770-1841 Baker 92
Carus, Andre W. 1953- St&PR 93
Carus, Frederick Leonard 1941- St&PR 93
Carus, M. Blouke 1927- St&PR 93
Carus, Marcus Aurelius d283 HarEnMi
Carus, Marianne 1928- WhoAm 92, WhoAmW 93
Carus, Marianne S. 1928- St&PR 93
Carus, Milton Blouke 1927- WhoAm 92
Carus, Paul 1923- St&PR 93
Carusillo, Joan Gloria 1931- WhoAmW 93
Caruso, Anthony Robert 1960- WhoEmL 93
Caruso, Barbara 1937- WhoCanL 92
Caruso, Charles M. Law&B 92
Caruso, Charles Michael 1950- WhoEmL 93
Caruso, Christine Ann 1954- WhoSSW 93
Caruso, David A. Law&B 92
Caruso, David R. 1956- WhoE 93
Caruso, Debra Jean 1959- WhoAmW 93
Caruso, Enrico 1873-1921 Baker 92, BioIn 17, IntDcOp [port], OxDcOp
Caruso, Enrico 1904-1987 BioIn 17
Caruso, Jane Allen 1947- WhoSSW 93
Caruso, Jean Carol D. 1952- WhoAmW 93
Caruso, Marie Therese 1931- WhoAm 92
Caruso, Martin I. Law&B 92
Caruso, Nicholas Dominic 1957- WhoE 93, WhoEmL 93
Caruso, Richard Ernest 1943- WhoAm 92
Caruso, Rosario 1936- WhoWor 93
Caruso, Victor Guy 1948- WhoAm 92, WhoE 93, WhoEmL 93
Caruso, Vincent John 1947- St&PR 93
Carusone, Joseph R. 1945- St&PR 93
Carusone, L. Michael 1936- St&PR 93
Caruthers, Donald McIlvaine 1953- WhoE 93
Caruthers, Frank Eugene 1963- WhoEmL 93
Caruthers, Judith Ann 1943- WhoSSW 93
Caruthers, Marilynn Laird 1922- WhoAmW 93
Caruthers, William F. 1920- St&PR 93
Carvaille, Leon 1825-1897 Baker 92
Carvainis, Maria 1946- WhoWrEP 92
Carvajal, Hugo Francisco, Jr. 1941- WhoSSW 93
Carvalhinhos, H.J.G. 1936- WhoScE 91-3
Carvalho, Alcides 1913- WhoWor 93
Carvalho, Antonio Pedro 1960- WhoWor 93
Carvalho, Apolonio de 1913- BioIn 17
Carvalho, Caroline 1827-1895 Baker 92
Carvalho, Claire AmWomPl
Carvalho, Delfim de 1942- WhoScE 91-3
Carvalho, Eleazar de 1912- Baker 92
Carvalho, Frederico Gama WhoScE 91-3
Carvalho, Gaspar Soares de 1920- WhoScE 91-3
Carvalho, Joao de Sousa 1745-1798 Baker 92
Carvalho, Leon 1825-1897 Baker 92, OxDcOp
Carvalho, Solomon Nunes 1815-1897 BioIn 17
Carvalho Minez, Carlos Manuel 1945- WhoScE 91-3
Carvalho Rodrigues, F. 1947- WhoScE 91-3
Carvalko, Joseph R., Jr. Law&B 92
Carvallo, Jorge Nicolas 1945- St&PR 93
Carvallo, Marc Evangelista 1934- WhoWor 93
Carvallo, Mauricio 1944- WhoWor 93
Carvel, Elbert N. 1910- St&PR 93
Carvel, Elbert Nostrand 1910- WhoAm 92
Carvel, Tom 1906-1990 BioIn 17
Carver, Ada Jack 1890-1972 AmWomPl
Carver, Calvin R. 1925- St&PR 93
Carver, Calvin Reeve 1925- WhoAm 92
Carver, Carol Ann 1949- WhoAmW 93
Carver, Charles Clifford, Jr. 1954- WhoEmL 93
Carver, Charles Mark 1960- WhoEmL 93
Carver, Darlene Terry 1954- WhoEmL 93
Carver, David Harold 1930- WhoAm 92
Carver, Earl 1954- WhoSSW 93
Carver, Eugene Pendleton, II 1928- St&PR 93
Carver, George Malone, Jr. 1923- WhoSSW 93
Carver, George Washington 1861?-1943 ConBlB 4 [port], GayN
Carver, George Washington 1864?-1943 BioIn 17, ConHero 2 [port]
Carver, Gordon Howard 1953- WhoE 93
Carver, J. Phillip Law&B 92
Carver, Jeffrey A. 1949- ScF&FL 92
Carver, Jeffrey Penn 1961- St&PR 93
Carver, Joan Sacknitz 1931- WhoSSW 93
Carver, John William, Jr. 1952- WhoSSW 93
Carver, Kate Lee AmWomPl
Carver, Kendall Lynn 1936- WhoWor 93
Carver, Kevin Scott 1953- WhoEmL 93
Carver, Larry A. Law&B 92
Carver, Loyce Cleo 1918- WhoAm 92
Carver, Lyell Henry Law&B 92
Carver, Margaret Miller 1953- WhoAmW 93
Carver, Martin Gregory 1948- St&PR 93, WhoAm 92, WhoEmL 93
Carver, Martin Oswald Hugh WhoScE 91-1
Carver, Michael 1915- BioIn 17
Carver, Norman Francis, Jr. WhoAm 92
Carver, Raymond BioIn 17
Carver, Raymond 1938-1988 AmWrS3, MagSAmL [port]
Carver, Richard D. 1950- St&PR 93
Carver, Robert 1487-c. 1546 Baker 92
Carver, Robert Dale 1936- St&PR 93
Carver, Roy James, Jr. 1943- St&PR 93
Carver, Samuel Webster Law&B 92
Carver, Steve 1945- MiSFD 9
Carver, Thomas William 1938- WhoSSW 93
Carver, Todd Law&B 92
Carver, Todd B. 1958- WhoEmL 93
Carvey, Dana BioIn 17, NewYTBS 92 [port]
Carvey, Dana 1955- ConTFT 10, CurBio 92 [port]
Carville, Chester James, Jr. 1944- NewYTBS 92 [port]
Carville, James BioIn 17
Carville, James G. 1932- St&PR 93
Carwell, Hattie Virginia 1948- WhoEmL 93
Carwell, L'Ann ConAu 38NR, MajAI, SmATA 73
Carwell, Robert Michael Law&B 92
Cary, Alice 1820-1871 AmWomWr 92
Cary, Alice V. AmWomPl
Cary, Angelita DeSilva Law&B 92
Cary, Annie Louise 1841-1921 Baker 92
Cary, Arthur Joyce Lunel 1888-1957 BioIn 17
Cary, Boyd Balford, Jr. 1923- WhoAm 92
Cary, C. Wilbur, Mrs. AmWomPl
Cary, Charles Muse 1948- WhoEmL 93
Cary, Charles Oswald 1917- WhoAm 92
Cary, Elton Mikell 1929- St&PR 93
Cary, Emily Pritchard 1931- WhoWrEP 92
Cary, Frank Taylor 1920- WhoAm 92
Cary, Freeman Hamilton 1926- WhoAm 92
Cary, Gene Leonard 1928- WhoAm 92
Cary, George Rives, Jr. 1930- WhoSSW 93
Cary, Hunsdon, III 1945- WhoSSW 93
Cary, James Donald 1919- WhoAm 92, WhoWrEP 92
Cary, James William 1941- WhoE 93
Cary, John Howard Law&B 92
Cary, John William 1945- WhoWor 93
Cary, Joyce 1888-1957 BioIn 17
Cary, Kevin E. 1955- WhoEmL 93
Cary, Linda Kaye 1963- WhoAmW 93
Cary, Lorene BioIn 17
Cary, Lorene 1956- ConBlB 3 [port]
Cary, Mary Katherine 1953- WhoEmL 93
Cary, Nicolas Robert Hugh 1955- WhoWor 93
Cary, Richard, Jr. 1918- WhoE 93
Cary, Roy 1955- WhoSSW 93
Cary, Sharon L. 1950- WhoEmL 93
Cary, Victor Lee 1917- St&PR 93
Cary, Walter L. 1935- St&PR 93
Cary, William Sterling AfrAmBi
Cary, William Sterling 1927- WhoAm 92
Carydis, Panayotis 1940- WhoScE 91-3, WhoWor 93
Casabal, Melecia Luna 1928- WhoWrEP 92
Casabona, Francisco 1894- Baker 92
Casabonne, Peter G. 1932- St&PR 93
Casaburro, John E. 1951- WhoE 93
Casaccia, Gabriel 1907-1980 SpAmA
Casad, Robert Clair 1929- WhoAm 92
Casada, James Allen 1942- WhoSSW 93, WhoWrEP 92
Casadesus, Francois Louis 1870-1954 Baker 92
Casadesus, Gaby 1901- Baker 92
Casadesus, Henri 1879-1947 Baker 92
Casadesus, Jean 1927-1972 Baker 92
Casadesus, Jean-Claude 1935- Baker 92
Casadesus, Marius 1892-1981 Baker 92
Casadesus, Robert 1899-1972 Baker 92
Casadevall, Eliette Louise 1921- WhoScE 91-2, WhoWor 93
Casado, Antonio Francisco 1913- WhoAm 92

Casado, John *BioIn 17*
Casady, Cort (Boon) 1947- *WhoWrEP 92*
Casady, Timothy T. *Law&B 92*
Casaer, Paul J.M. 1940- *WhoScE 91-2*
Casaer, Piet 1948- *WhoWor 93*
Casaglia, Gianfranco Augusto 1942- *WhoWor 93*
Casagrande, Joseph Bartholomew 1915-1982 *IntDcAn*
Casagrande, Leo 1903-1990 *BioIn 17*
Casal, Lourdes 1938-1981 *NotHsAW 93*
Casal, Manuel 1946- *WhoScE 91-3*
Casalaspro-Couls, Debra Ann 1956- *WhoEmL 93*
Casalbuoni, Roberto 1942- *WhoScE 91-3*
Casale, George N. 1947- *WhoIns 93*
Casale, Karen Ann 1959- *WhoAmW 93*
Casale, Michael J. *WhoIns 93*
Casale, Paul Peter 1950- *WhoE 93*
Casale, Ralph P. 1928- *St&PR 93*
Casale, Ralph Patrick 1928- *WhoAm 92*
Casale, Robert D. *Law&B 92*
Casale, Robert J. 1938- *WhoAm 92*
Casali, Richard A. 1947- *St&PR 93*
Casals, Alicia 1955- *WhoScE 91-3*
Casals, Juan Federico 1930- *WhoWor 93*
Casals, Pablo 1876-1973 *BioIn 17, ConMus 9 [port]*
Casals, Pablo (Pau Carlos Salvador Defillo) 1876-1973 *Baker 92*
Casals, Rosemary 1948- *HispAmA, NotHsAW 93 [port], WhoAm 92*
Casals-Ariet, Jordi 1911- *WhoAm 92*
Casalveri, Frank J. 1929- *St&PR 93*
Casamassima, Salvatore J. *Law&B 92*
Casamassimo, Paul P. 1912-1990 *BioIn 17*
Casamayou, Jean-Marie 1947- *WhoWor 93*
Casamento, Maria M. 1955- *WhoAmW 93*
Casamorata, Luigi Fernando 1807-1881 *Baker 92*
Casanas, Francesco 1952- *WhoScE 91-3*
Casani, John Richard 1932- *WhoAm 92*
Casanova, Aldo John 1929- *WhoAm 92*
Casanova, Andre 1919- *Baker 92*
Casanova, Danielle 1909-1943 *BioIn 17*
Casanova, Jeffrey Steven 1971- *WhoE 93, WhoEmL 93*
Casanova, Laurent 1906-1972 *BioIn 17*
Casanova de Seingalt, Giovanni Jacopo 1725-1798 *OxDcOp*
Casanova de Seingalt, Jacques 1725-1798 *ScF&FL 92*
Casanovas, Enrique 1882-1948 *BioIn 17*
Casanovas, Narciso 1747-1799 *Baker 92*
Casanovas-Rodriguez, Juan S. 1948- *WhoScE 91-3*
Casarella, William Joseph 1937- *WhoAm 92*
Casares, Adolfo Bioy *ScF&FL 92*
Casares, Adolfo Bioy 1914- *BioIn 17*
Casares, Marcelo Ricardo 1936- *WhoWor 93*
Casares, Ricardo Jose 1931- *BiDAMSp 1989*
Casarez-Levison, Rosa 1951- *WhoAmW 93*
Casari, Irene Marie 1950- *WhoAmW 93*
Casariego, Jorge Isaac 1945- *WhoAm 92*
Casarino, John Philip 1940- *WhoE 93*
Casaroli, Agostino *BioIn 17*
Casaroli, Agostino Cardinal 1914- *WhoAm 92, WhoWor 93*
Casas, Bartolome de las 1474-1566 *BioIn 17*
Casas, Melesio 1929- *HispAmA*
Casas, Salvador G. 1950- *WhoEmL 93*
Casasa, Barbara A. 1958- *WhoAmW 93, WhoSSW 93*
Casas Carbo, Ramon 1866-1932 *BioIn 17*
Casasent, David Paul 1942- *WhoAm 92*
Casasin, Trini 1949- *WhoAmW 93*
Casassas, Enric 1920- *WhoScE 91-3*
Casasus, Joaquin D. 1858-1916 *DcMexL*
Casati, Gaetano 1838-1902 *Expl 93*
Casati, Giulio 1942- *WhoWor 93*
Casaus, Victor 1944- *SpAmA*
Casavis, David Bingham 1952- *WhoE 93, WhoEmL 93*
Casavola, Franco 1891-1955 *Baker 92, OxDcOp*
Casazza, Carol A. *Law&B 92*
Casazza, Carol A. 1957- *WhoAmW 93, WhoEmL 93*
Casazza, Elvira 1887-1965 *Baker 92*
Casazza, John Andrew 1924- *WhoAm 92*
Casburn, Mark E. *Law&B 92*
Cascanet, Timothy David 1954- *St&PR 93*
Cascella, Roberto A. *St&PR 93*
Casciani, Patricia Nada *ScF&FL 92*
Casciano, Daniel Anthony 1941- *WhoAm 92*
Casciano, Frank D. *Law&B 92*
Casciari, Raoul Joseph 1934- *St&PR 93*
Cascieri, Arcangelo 1902- *WhoAm 92*
Cascino, Anthony Elmo, Jr. 1948- *WhoEmL 93*
Cascino, James Madison 1951- *WhoEmL 93*
Cascio, Anna Theresa 1955- *WhoAm 92, WhoAmW 93*
Cascio, Mary A. *Law&B 92*
Cascio, Michael Joseph 1950- *WhoEmL 93*
Cascio, Michael P. 1961- *WhoE 93*
Cascio, Sam *BioIn 17*
Cascio-Houston, Grace Catherine 1944- *WhoSSW 93*
Casco, Hector Americo 1951- *WhoWor 93*
Casco, Janis Diane 1955- *WhoAmW 93*
Cascorbi, Helmut Freimund 1933- *WhoAm 92*
Casden, Ron *MiSFD 9*
Case, Anne Catherine 1958- *WhoE 93, WhoEmL 93*
Case, Bonnie Nally 1949- *WhoSSW 93*
Case, Charles Carroll 1914- *WhoAm 92*
Case, Charles Dixon 1952- *WhoEmL 93*
Case, Clyde Willard, Jr. *WhoWor 93*
Case, Colleen Mae 1952- *WhoEmL 93*
Case, Daniel H., III 1957- *St&PR 93*
Case, David 1937- *ScF&FL 92*
Case, David Knowlton 1938- *WhoAm 92*
Case, David Leon 1948- *WhoEmL 93*
Case, Dianne 1955- *DcChlFi*
Case, Douglas Manning 1947- *WhoEmL 93*
Case, Dwight Leland 1929- *WhoAm 92*
Case, Elizabeth 1930- *WhoAm 92*
Case, Eugene Lawrence 1937- *WhoAm 92*
Case, Everett Needham 1901- *WhoAm 92*
Case, Gayrie P. 1931- *St&PR 93*
Case, George David 1947- *WhoSSW 93*
Case, George W. 1940- *St&PR 93*
Case, Gordon Thomas Martin 1941- *St&PR 93*
Case, Hadley 1909- *St&PR 93, WhoAm 92, WhoWor 93*
Case, James Hebard 1920- *WhoAm 92*
Case, James Stewart 1955- *WhoSSW 93*
Case, James Vincent, Jr. 1938- *WhoE 93*
Case, Jean 1930- *St&PR 93*
Case, Jeffrey D. *BioIn 17*
Case, John 1926- *St&PR 93*
Case, John D. *BioIn 17, Law&B 92*
Case, John Danford 1945- *St&PR 93*
Case, John Howard 1955- *WhoEmL 93*
Case, John J. 1930- *St&PR 93*
Case, John Philip 1952- *WhoEmL 93*
Case, Joni Allison 1944- *WhoAmW 93*
Case, Karen Ann 1944- *WhoAm 92*
Case, Kenneth Eugene 1944- *WhoAm 92*
Case, Larry D. *Law&B 92*
Case, Larry D. 1943- *WhoAm 92*
Case, Laura Ferguson 1951- *WhoEmL 93, WhoSSW 93*
Case, Manning Eugene, Jr. 1916- *WhoAm 92*
Case, Mary Elizabeth 1925- *WhoAmW 93*
Case, Matthew A. *Law&B 92*
Case, Michael Leslie *Law&B 92*
Case, Nan Barkin 1936- *WhoE 93*
Case, Pamela Jane 1944- *WhoE 93*
Case, Paul Watson, Jr. 1949- *WhoEmL 93*
Case, Richard Ian 1945- *WhoScE 91-1*
Case, Richard Maynard *WhoScE 91-1*
Case, Richard Paul 1935- *WhoAm 92*
Case, Richard Thomas 1949- *WhoEmL 93*
Case, Robert Brown 1920- *WhoE 93*
Case, Rosalind 1933- *WhoE 93*
Case, Stephen W. *St&PR 93*
Case, Steve K. 1949- *St&PR 93*
Case, Thomas Louis 1947- *WhoEmL 93, WhoSSW 93, WhoWor 93*
Case, Thomas S. 1941- *WhoIns 93*
Case, Tom *ScF&FL 92*
Casebeer, Doug *BioIn 17*
Casebeer, Edwin Frank, Jr. 1933- *WhoAm 92*
Casebeer, R. Scott 1955- *St&PR 93*
Casebere, James Edward 1953- *WhoE 93*
Casebere, Sharon Sue 1944- *WhoAmW 93*
Casebolt, Victor Alan 1935- *St&PR 93, WhoAm 92*
Casebolt, Wayne C. 1929- *St&PR 93*
Casei, Nedda *WhoAm 92*
Caseley, John Charles *WhoScE 91-1*
Casel-Hastings, Mary Lynn 1943- *WhoAmW 93*
Casella, Alfredo 1883-1947 *Baker 92, OxDcOp*
Casella, Max *BioIn 17*
Casella, Ross R. 1931- *St&PR 93*
Casellas, Joaquin 1925- *WhoScE 91-3*
Caselles, Antonio 1945- *WhoScE 91-3*
Caselli, Virgil P. 1940- *WhoAm 92*
Casement, Roger *BioIn 17*
Casement, Roger David 1864-1916 *DcTwHis*
Casement, William Rowley 1947- *WhoE 93*
Case-Pall, Deena 1945- *WhoAmW 93*
Caserta, Maria Theresa 1949- *WhoAmW 93*
Casewit, Curtis W. 1927- *WhoWrEP 92*
Casey, Albert 1915- *BioIn 17*
Casey, Albert Vincent 1920- *WhoAm 92*
Casey, Barbara A. Perea 1951- *WhoAmW 93*
Casey, Beatrice Marie *AmWomPl*
Casey, Bernard J. 1942- *WhoAm 92*
Casey, Beverly Ann 1949- *WhoAmW 93*
Casey, Catherine Elizabeth 1941- *WhoAm 92*
Casey, Charles A. *Law&B 92*
Casey, Charles F. 1927- *St&PR 93*
Casey, Charles Philip 1942- *WhoAm 92*
Casey, Coleman Hampton 1947- *WhoE 93*
Casey, Colleen Sue 1956- *WhoEmL 93*
Casey, Daniel J(oseph) 1937- *WhoWrEP 92*
Casey, Daniel P. *Law&B 92*
Casey, Deborah *Law&B 92*
Casey, Donald Michael 1935- *WhoAm 92*
Casey, Dorcas C. 1935- *St&PR 93*
Casey, Douglas R. *St&PR 93*
Casey, Douglas Robert 1946- *WhoWrEP 92*
Casey, E. Paul 1930- *St&PR 93*
Casey, Edward Dennis 1931- *WhoAm 92*
Casey, Edward G. 1948- *St&PR 93*
Casey, Edward Paul 1930- *WhoAm 92*
Casey, Elizabeth Jane 1941- *WhoE 93*
Casey, Ethel Laughlin 1926- *WhoAm 92, WhoWor 93*
Casey, Everett F. *Law&B 92*
Casey, Genevieve M(ary) 1916- *ConAu 39NR*
Casey, George Edward, Jr. 1946- *WhoEmL 93*
Casey, Gerald Wayne 1940- *WhoWrEP 92*
Casey, Gerard W. *Law&B 92*
Casey, Gerard William 1942- *WhoAm 92*
Casey, Harold Wayne 1951- *See* KC & the Sunshine Band *SoulM*
Casey, Horace Craig, Jr. 1934- *WhoAm 92*
Casey, James E. 1888-1983 *BioIn 17*
Casey, James J. 1915- *St&PR 93*
Casey, James Joseph 1943- *St&PR 93*
Casey, James McLean 1930- *St&PR 93*
Casey, James Neal *Law&B 92*
Casey, Jennifer M. *Law&B 92*
Casey, Jerald Francis 1926- *St&PR 93*
Casey, John 1939- *BioIn 17*
Casey, John A. 1927- *St&PR 93*
Casey, John Dudley 1939- *WhoAm 92, WhoWrEP 92*
Casey, John Joseph 1918- *WhoAm 92, WhoWor 93*
Casey, John L. 1938- *St&PR 93*
Casey, John P. 1920- *WhoAm 92*
Casey, John P. 1945- *St&PR 93*
Casey, John Patrick 1928- *WhoAm 92*
Casey, John Richard 1944- *St&PR 93*
Casey, John W. *Law&B 92*
Casey, Joseph Michael 1948- *WhoE 93*
Casey, Joseph T. 1931- *St&PR 93, WhoAm 92*
Casey, Joseph Thomas, Jr. *Law&B 92*
Casey, Judy Carolyn 1944- *WhoAmW 93*
Casey, June B. 1924- *WhoAmW 93*
Casey, Karen Anne 1955- *WhoAmW 93, WhoE 93, WhoEmL 93*
Casey, Keith Allen 1961- *WhoEmL 93*
Casey, Kenneth Lyman 1935- *WhoAm 92*
Casey, Kevin *BioIn 17*
Casey, Kevin 1956- *St&PR 93*
Casey, Kevin V.E. *St&PR 93*
Casey, Lawrence David 1946- *WhoE 93*
Casey, Linda M. *ConAu 136*
Casey, Madelyn Bennett 1951- *WhoAmW 93*
Casey, Mary Ann 1949- *WhoAmW 93*
Casey, Mary Louise *Law&B 92*
Casey, Maureen Therese 1953- *WhoEmL 93*
Casey, Michael Joseph 1949- *WhoE 93, WhoEmL 93*
Casey, Michael Kirkland 1940- *WhoAm 92, WhoSSW 93*
Casey, Monica Mary 1947- *WhoAmW 93*
Casey, Murray Joseph 1936- *WhoWor 93*
Casey, Phillip E. 1942- *St&PR 93*
Casey, Phillip Earl 1942- *WhoAm 92*
Casey, Randall Charles 1954- *WhoEmL 93, WhoSSW 93*
Casey, Raymond R. 1935- *St&PR 93*
Casey, Raymond Richard 1935- *WhoAm 92*
Casey, Richard Gardiner 1890-1976 *DcTwHis*
Casey, Robert J. *Law&B 92*
Casey, Robert J. 1923- *WhoE 93*
Casey, Robert P. *BioIn 17*
Casey, Robert P. 1932- *WhoAm 92, WhoWor 93*
Casey, Robin Emmett 1953- *St&PR 93*
Casey, Roger Neal 1961- *WhoSSW 93*
Casey, Ronald Bruce 1951- *WhoAm 92, WhoSSW 93*
Casey, Samuel Alexander 1914- *St&PR 93, WhoAm 92*
Casey, Shawn V. 1954- *St&PR 93*
Casey, T.J. 1933- *WhoScE 91-3*
Casey, Theresa Marie 1956- *WhoAmW 93*
Casey, Thomas F. 1952- *St&PR 93*
Casey, Thomas Joseph, III 1951- *WhoEmL 93*
Casey, Thomas Warren 1942- *WhoE 93*
Casey, Timothy Daniel *Law&B 92*
Casey, Walter Hamilton 1940- *St&PR 93*
Casey, William *DcCPCAm*
Casey, William J. *BioIn 17*
Casey, William J. 1913-1987 *ColdWar 1 [port]*
Casey, William Robert, Jr. 1944- *WhoAm 92*
Casey, William Van Etten 1914-1990 *BioIn 17*
Casey, Wilson 1954- *St&PR 93*
Cash, Alana 1950- *WhoAmW 93*
Cash, Alvin 1939- *BioIn 17, SoulM*
Cash, Audrey Sutton 1926- *WhoAmW 93*
Cash, Carl G. 1929- *St&PR 93*
Cash, Carol Vivian 1929- *WhoAm 92, WhoAmW 93, WhoSSW 93, WhoWor 93*
Cash, Christopher Keatley *Law&B 92*
Cash, Ellen Lewis Buell 1905-1989 *BioIn 17*
Cash, Francis W. 1942- *St&PR 93*
Cash, Francis Winford 1942- *WhoAm 92*
Cash, Frank Errette, Jr. 1921- *WhoAm 92*
Cash, Joe Lynn 1939- *WhoSSW 93*
Cash, John D. *WhoScE 91-1*
Cash, Johnny *BioIn 17*
Cash, Johnny 1932- *Baker 92, WhoAm 92*
Cash, Joseph L. 1941- *WhoIns 93*
Cash, June Carter 1929- *Baker 92, WhoAm 92*
Cash, LaVerne 1956- *WhoAmW 93, WhoEmL 93, WhoWor 93*
Cash, Leonore Sullivan 1951- *WhoAmW 93*
Cash, Linda Carol 1951- *WhoAmW 93*
Cash, Loraine Leach *Law&B 92*
Cash, Paul E. 1932- *St&PR 93*
Cash, Paul Thalbert 1911- *WhoAm 92, WhoWor 93*
Cash, Phyllis 1935- *WhoAmW 93*
Cash, R.D. 1942- *St&PR 93*
Cash, Renee M. 1941- *St&PR 93*
Cash, Robert Edward 1933- *St&PR 93*
Cash, Robert Joseph 1955- *WhoEmL 93*
Cash, Rosanne 1955- *Baker 92, BioIn 17, WhoAmW 93*
Cash, Roy Don 1942- *WhoAm 92*
Cash, Wilbur Joseph 1900-1941 *BioIn 17, EncAACR, JrnUS*
Cashel, Martha Frances 1955- *WhoWor 93*
Cashel, Thomas William 1930- *WhoAm 92*
Cashel, William S., Jr. 1920- *St&PR 93*
Cashell, Jane Gering 1948- *WhoEmL 93*
Cashen, Eric *WhoWrEP 92*
Cashen, Henry Christopher, II 1939- *WhoAm 92*
Cashen, J. Frank *WhoAm 92, WhoE 93*
Cashier-Corso, Maria Anne 1946- *WhoE 93*
Cashin, Bonnie 1915- *WhoAm 92, WhoAmW 93*
Cashin, Edward A. 1905- *St&PR 93*
Cashin, Edward Joseph 1927- *WhoAm 92*
Cashin, Francis Joseph 1924- *WhoE 93*
Cashin, J. Patrick *Law&B 92*
Cashin, John Gregory 1925- *WhoSSW 93*
Cashin, John Richard 1946- *WhoAm 92, WhoEmL 93*
Cashin, Richard Marshall 1924- *WhoAm 92*
Cashin, William A., Jr. 1933- *St&PR 93*
Cashion, Herschell A. *St&PR 93*
Cashion, James H. 1941- *WhoSSW 93*
Cashion, James Taylor 1940- *St&PR 93*
Cashion, Joe Mason 1938- *WhoSSW 93*
Cashion, Marvin J. *Law&B 92*
Cashion, Marvin J. 1945- *St&PR 93, WhoIns 93*
Cashion, Robert Nesbit 1947- *WhoAm 92*
Cashion, Shelley Jean 1955- *WhoEmL 93*
Cashion, William Neil 1946- *St&PR 93*
Cashku, Kujtim 1950- *DrEEuF*
Cashman, Edmund Joseph, Jr. 1936- *St&PR 93, WhoAm 92*
Cashman, G.D. 1953- *St&PR 93*
Cashman, John G. 1931- *St&PR 93*
Cashman, John Richard 1935- *WhoWrEP 92*
Cashman, John W. 1923- *WhoAm 92*
Cashman, Michael Edward 1935- *WhoE 93*
Cashman, Michael Richard 1926- *WhoWor 93*
Cashman, Michael W., Sr. 1949- *WhoIns 93*
Cashman, Ray Dudley 1945- *St&PR 93*
Cashman, Robert J. *BioIn 17*
Cashman, Thomas J., Jr. 1952- *St&PR 93*
Cashmore, Patsy Joy 1943- *WhoAm 92, WhoAmW 93*

Casida, John Edward 1929- WhoAm 92
Casida, Lester Earl, Jr. 1928- WhoE 93
Casier, Francis David 1918- St&PR 93
Casillas, Mark 1953- WhoEmL 93, WhoWor 93
Casimir, I 1016-1058 PolBiDi
Casimir, II 1138-1194 PolBiDi
Casimir, III 1310-1370 PolBiDi
Casimir, IV 1427-1492 PolBiDi
Casimiri, Raffaele Casimiro 1880-1943 Baker 92
Casimir-Perier, Jean Paul Pierre 1847-1907 BioIn 17
Casines, Gisela 1951- WhoSSW 93
Casini, Giovanni Maria 1652-1719 Baker 92
Casiraghi, Stefano BioIn 17
Casken, John 1949- OxDcOp
Casken, John (Arthur) 1949- Baker 92
Caskey, Bethany Anne 1950- WhoAmW 93
Caskey, Gary Milton 1952- WhoE 93
Caskey, Micki Morgan 1954- WhoAmW 93
Caskey, W.J. 1949- St&PR 93
Caskey, William Joslin 1949- WhoAm 92, WhoEmL 93
Caskie, Cabot Robison 1944- St&PR 93
Caslav dc. 960 OxDcByz
Caslavska, Vera Barbara 1934- WhoAm 92
Casmere, Vicki L. Law&B 92
Casner, A. James 1907-1990 BioIn 17
Casner, Andrew James 1907-1990 BioIn 17
Caso, Adolph 1934- WhoE 93, WhoWrEP 92
Caso, Alfonso 1896-1970 IntDcAn
Caso, Antonio 1883-1946 DcMexL
Caso, Gasper 1933- WhoAm 92
Caso, George William 1942- WhoSSW 93
Caso, Philip Michael 1958- WhoSSW 93
Caso, William James Law&B 92
Casolari, Antonio 1936- WhoScE 91-3
Casolaro, Daniel 1947-1991 BioIn 17
Casolo, Jennifer Jean BioIn 17
Cason, Barbara d1990 BioIn 17
Cason, Dick Kendall 1922- WhoSSW 93, WhoWor 93
Cason, Ellen Pearre 1948- WhoAmW 93
Cason, Frederick Leon 1928- St&PR 93
Cason, James E. BioIn 17
Cason, June Macnabb 1930- WhoE 93
Cason, Marilynn Jean 1943- St&PR 93
Cason, Marsden Starbuck 1942- WhoAm 92
Cason, Neal Martin 1938- WhoAm 92
Cason, Roger Lee 1930- WhoE 93
Casorati, Felice 1886-1963 BioIn 17
Casoria, Giuseppe Cardinal 1908- WhoAm 92, WhoWor 93
Casowitz, Marilyn F. Law&B 92
Caspar, Donald Louis Dvorak 1927- WhoAm 92
Caspar, George J. 1933- St&PR 93
Caspar, George J., III 1933- WhoAm 92
Caspar, George John Law&B 92
Caspar, Karl 1879-1956 BioIn 17
Caspari, Ernst Wolfgang 1909- BioIn 17
Caspary, Vera 1904- AmWomPl
Caspe, Lynda Wendy 1939- WhoE 93
Casper, Barry Michael 1939- WhoAm 92
Casper, Billy 1931- WhoSSW 93
Casper, Cheri Luann 1949- WhoEmL 93
Casper, Daniel David 1959- St&PR 93
Casper, David 1949- WhoWor 93
Casper, David Bernard 1936- St&PR 93
Casper, David John 1951- BiDAMSp 1989
Casper, Donald Law&B 92
Casper, Eric Michael 1959- WhoEmL 93
Casper, George L. 1908- St&PR 93
Casper, Gerhard BioIn 17
Casper, Gerhard 1937- NewYTBS 92 [port], News 93-1 [port], WhoAm 92
Casper, Jeffrey Elliot 1956- WhoEmL 93
Casper, Joseph W. Law&B 92
Casper, Leonard Ralph 1923- WhoAm 92, WhoWrEP 92
Casper, Marie Lenore 1954- WhoAmW 93
Casper, Marjorie Helen 1938- St&PR 93
Casper, Michael David 1959- St&PR 93
Casper, Paul Alexander 1947- WhoAm 92
Casper, Philip Wilson 1914- St&PR 93
Casper, Richard d1990 BioIn 17
Casper, Richard 1927- St&PR 93
Casper, Robert J. 1943- St&PR 93, WhoAm 92, WhoIns 93
Casper, Rudolf 1930- WhoScE 91-3
Casper, Steven Lee 1958- St&PR 93
Casper, Stewart Michael 1953- WhoEmL 93
Casper, Susan 1947- ScF&FL 92
Caspersen, Barbara Morris 1945- St&PR 93
Caspersen, Finn M.W. 1941- St&PR 93
Caspersen, Finn Michael Westby 1941- WhoAm 92, WhoWor 93
Caspersen, Freda Resika d1991 BioIn 17
Casperson, John R. Law&B 92
Caspi, David Joshua WhoWrEP 92
Caspian, Jonatha Ariadne ScF&FL 92
Cass, April Lorraine 1957- WhoE 93, WhoEmL 93
Cass, David 1937- WhoAm 92
Cass, DeLysle Ferree 1887-1973 ScF&FL 92
Cass, E. R. Peter 1941- WhoE 93
Cass, Edmund Francis, Jr. 1934- St&PR 93
Cass, Edward F. 1947- St&PR 93
Cass, George F. 1939- St&PR 93
Cass, George Frank 1939- WhoAm 92, WhoIns 93
Cass, James d1992 NewYTBS 92
Cass, Jeffrey Dean 1958- WhoSSW 93
Cass, Lewis 1782-1866 PolPar
Cass, Millard 1916- WhoAm 92
Cass, Oliver Wilfred 1949- WhoEmL 93
Cass, Penny Sue 1945- WhoAmW 93
Cass, Richard S. 1928- St&PR 93
Cass, Robert Michael 1945- WhoWor 93
Cass, Ronald Andrew 1949- WhoAm 92
Cass, Thomas Richardson 1930- WhoE 93
Cassaba, Carlos ScF&FL 92
Cassaday, Michael Milliet 1944- WhoE 93
Cassademont Perich, Gloria 1957- WhoScE 91-3
Cassado (Moreau), Gaspar 1897-1966 Baker 92
Cassado (Valls), Joaquin 1867-1926 Baker 92
Cassady, B.W. 1921- St&PR 93
Cassady, Carolyn BioIn 17
Cassady, Cheryl Gale 1949- WhoEmL 93
Cassady, Donald Raymond Law&B 92
Cassady, John Mac 1938- WhoAm 92
Cassady, Laura Taulbee 1958- WhoEmL 93
Cassady, Marsh 1936- ConGAN
Cassady, Marsh Gary 1936- WhoWrEP 92
Cassady, Neal BioIn 17
Cassady, Shawn Lawrence 1958- WhoEmL 93
Cassagnes, Paul Henri 1933- WhoScE 91-2
Cassagnol, Francois 1947- WhoWor 93
Cassan, Jacques 1939- WhoScE 91-2
Cassan, Michel 1943- WhoWor 93
Cassander c. 358BC-297BC HarEnMi
Cassandro, Robert John Law&B 92
Cassanego, Michael John Law&B 92
Cassanego, Michael John 1950- WhoIns 93
Cassani, Giovanni Rodolfo 1933- WhoScE 91-3
Cassano, Linda N. Law&B 92
Cassano, Peter V. 1932- St&PR 93
Cassano, Phyllis A. M. 1949- WhoAmW 93, WhoEmL 93
Cassano, Vincent Frank 1943- St&PR 93
Cassar, Joseph 1947- WhoUN 92
Cassar, Nigel Selwyn 1947- WhoUN 92
Cassar, Richard Douglas 1930- WhoE 93
Cassara, Frank 1913- WhoAm 92
Cassara, James Joseph 1956- WhoSSW 93
Cassaro, Irene Dolores 1951- WhoE 93
Cassatt, Alexander Johnston 1839-1906 BioIn 17
Cassatt, Mary 1844-1926 BioIn 17, ConHero 2 [port]
Cassatt, Mary 1845-1926 GayN
Cassavetes, John 1929-1989 MiSFD 9N
Cass-Beggs, Barbara 1904- BioIn 17
Cassedy, John H. 1930- St&PR 93
Cassedy, Patrick J. 1949- St&PR 93
Cassedy, Sylvia 1930- WhoWrEP 92
Cassedy, Sylvia 1930-1989 BioIn 17, DcAmChF 1985, ScF&FL 92
Cassel, Chester 1918- WhoSSW 93
Cassel, Christine Karen 1945- WhoAm 92
Cassel, Cynthia Lou 1962- WhoEmL 93
Cassel, Daniel 1920- St&PR 93
Cassel, Dona Julian 1946- WhoAmW 93, WhoEmL 93, WhoSSW 93, WhoWor 93
Cassel, Donald Keith 1940- WhoAm 92
Cassel, Edith Hertha Sophie 1940- WhoE 93
Cassel, Harrison H. 1917- St&PR 93
Cassel, James Anders Law&B 92
Cassel, Jean-Pierre 1932- IntDcF 2-3 [port]
Cassel, John Elden 1934- WhoSSW 93
Cassel, Neil Jonathon 1961- WhoEmL 93
Cassel, Randee L. Law&B 92
Cassel, Raymond L. 1957- St&PR 93
Cassel, Robert Thomas 1931- St&PR 93
Cassel, Thomas A.V. 1946- St&PR 93
Cassel, Walter 1910- Baker 92
Cassel, Walter 1920- WhoAm 92
Cassel, William Alwein 1924- WhoSSW 93
Cassell, Benjamin F. St&PR 93
Cassell, Dana Kay WhoWrEP 92
Cassell, Dean George 1928- WhoE 93
Cassell, Eric J. 1928- ConAu 137
Cassell, Eric Jonathan 1928- WhoAm 92
Cassell, Frank Hyde 1916- WhoAm 92
Cassell, Hilda Jane 1942- WhoSSW 93
Cassell, John 1817-1865 BioIn 17
Cassell, Kay Ann 1941- WhoAm 92
Cassell, Merrill Elmo 1942- WhoUN 92
Cassell, Richard Emmett 1949- WhoEmL 93
Cassell, Robert Bernard 1918- WhoSSW 93
Cassell, William Comyn 1934- WhoAm 92
Cassell, William Walter 1917- WhoAm 92
Cassella, Anthony St&PR 93
Cassella, William Nathan, Jr. 1920- WhoAm 92
Cassells, Alan C. 1942- WhoScE 91-3
Cassells, Cyrus Curtis 1957- WhoWrEP 92
Cassells, Donald WhoScE 91-1
Casselman, Cindy Lynn Law&B 92
Casselman, Gary Richard 1948- WhoSSW 93
Casselman, William Allen 1941- WhoAm 92
Casselman, William E., II 1941- WhoAm 92, WhoE 93
Cassels, Edith R. Law&B 92
Cassels, John 1928- BioIn 17
Cassels, Peter Andrew 1943- WhoE 93
Cassen, Philip Jonathan 1960- WhoWor 93
Cassens, Robert Gene 1937- WhoAm 92
Casser, Claudia Law&B 92
Casserleigh, Douglas Washburn Law&B 92
Casserly, Alvaro Alonso 1932- St&PR 93
Casserly, Charley 1949- WhoAm 92, WhoE 93
Casserly, Joseph William 1929- WhoAm 92
Casserly, Sandra Racine 1932- WhoAmW 93
Cassese, John 1934- WhoE 93
Cassese, John J. 1945- St&PR 93
Cassett, Larry R. Law&B 92
Cassetta, Sebastian Ernest 1948- WhoEmL 93, WhoWor 93
Cassetty, Fred Joseph 1938- St&PR 93
Cassey, John Calvin, Jr. 1951- WhoE 93
Cassian, John c. 360-c. 432 OxDcByz
Cassibry, Fred James 1918- WhoAm 92
Cassiday, Benjamin Buckles, Jr. 1922- WhoAm 92
Cassiday, Bruce 1920- ScF&FL 92
Cassiday, Karen Lynn 1960- WhoAmW 93
Cassidy, Butch 1866?- BioIn 17
Cassidy, Carl Eugene 1924- WhoAm 92
Cassidy, David BioIn 17
Cassidy, Edward Idris 1924- WhoWor 93
Cassidy, Francis E. 1928- WhoSSW 93, WhoWor 93
Cassidy, George Thomas 1939- WhoE 93
Cassidy, Gladys BioIn 17
Cassidy, James Edward 1928- WhoWor 93
Cassidy, James Joseph 1916- WhoAm 92, WhoSSW 93
Cassidy, James Joseph 1959- WhoSSW 93
Cassidy, John Harold 1925- WhoAm 92
Cassidy, Kevin H. Law&B 92
Cassidy, Lee M. 1933- WhoE 93
Cassidy, Leigh S. Law&B 92
Cassidy, Nancy Kathleen Law&B 92
Cassidy, Patrick Edward 1937- WhoSSW 93
Cassidy, Richard J. d1990 BioIn 17
Cassidy, Richard Thomas 1916- WhoAm 92
Cassidy, Robert Charles, Jr. 1946- WhoAm 92
Cassidy, Robert Edward 1931- WhoAm 92
Cassidy, Robert Joseph 1930- WhoAm 92
Cassidy, Samuel M. 1932- St&PR 93
Cassidy, Suzanne Bletterman 1944- WhoAmW 93
Cassidy, Thomas Law&B 92
Cassidy, Thomas Joseph 1925- St&PR 93
Cassidy, Thomas Louis 1928- St&PR 93
Cassidy, Thomas Owen 1946- St&PR 93
Cassidy, Tom 1949-1991 BioIn 17
Cassidy, W.D., III 1941- St&PR 93
Cassidy, William 1815-1873 JrnUS
Cassidy, William Arthur 1928- WhoE 93
Cassidy, William Dunnigan, III 1941- WhoE 93
Cassidy, William Louis 1945- St&PR 93
Cassie WhoWrEP 92
Cassiers, Juan 1931- WhoAm 92
Cassiers, Leon 1930- WhoScE 91-2
Cassilis, Ina Leon AmWomPl
Cassill, Herbert Carroll 1928- WhoAm 92
Cassill, Karilyn Kay WhoWrEP 92
Cassill, R.V. 1919- WhoWrEP 92
Cassill, Ronald Verlin 1919- WhoAm 92
Cassilly, Richard 1927- Baker 92, WhoAm 92
Cassiman, Jean-Jacques S.N. 1943- WhoScE 91-2
Cassimatis, Peter John 1928- WhoAm 92
Cassin, Kimberley Jean 1954- WhoSSW 93
Cassin, Rene 1887-1976 BioIn 17
Cassin, Thomas Conway 1938- St&PR 93
Cassin, William Bourke 1931- WhoAm 92, WhoSSW 93, WhoWor 93
Cassinelli, Giuseppe Mario 1932- WhoWor 93
Cassinelli, Joseph Patrick 1940- WhoAm 92
Cassingham, Randy C. 1959- WhoWrEP 92
Cassini, Oleg BioIn 17
Cassini, Oleg Lolewski 1913- WhoAm 92
Cassiodorus c. 487-c. 580 OxDcByz
Cassiodorus, Magnus Aurelius c. 485-c. 580 Baker 92
Cassioppi, Gerald A. Law&B 92
Cassirer, Ernst 1874-1945 BioIn 17
Cassirer, Fritz 1871-1926 Baker 92
Cassirer, Nadine Gordimer 1923- BioIn 17
Cassity, Turner BioIn 17
Cassius, Gaius Avidius d175 HarEnMi
Cassius Longinus, Gaius d42BC HarEnMi
Cassivellaunus fl. c. 54BC- HarEnMi
Cassman, Marvin 1936- WhoAm 92
Cassner, Alvin B. 1913- St&PR 93
Cassner, John Daniel 1940- St&PR 93
Casso, Raul, IV 1958- WhoSSW 93
Casson, Gary Law&B 92
Casson, Hugh Maxwell 1910- BioIn 17
Casson, Richard Frederick 1939- St&PR 93
Cassone, Dominick Joseph 1954- WhoEmL 93
Cassoni, Vittorio WhoScE 91-3
Cassoni, Vittorio d1992 NewYTBS 92 [port]
Cassoux, Patrick J.-C. 1941- WhoScE 91-2
Cassuto, Albert E.L. 1934- WhoScE 91-2
Cassuto, Alvaro (Leon) 1938- Baker 92
Cassutt, Michael 1954- ScF&FL 92
Cassutt, Thomas Gerard 1960- St&PR 93
Cast, Anita Hursh 1939- WhoAmW 93
Castagna, Bruna 1905-1983 Baker 92
Castagna, Edwin 1909-1983 BioIn 17
Castagna, William John 1924- WhoAm 92
Castagnaro, Marie Renee 1944- WhoAmW 93
Castagne, Allan 1943- St&PR 93
Castagnede, Bernard Roger 1956- WhoWor 93
Castagnetta, Grace Sharp 1912- WhoAm 92
Castagnini, Gene Joseph 1949- WhoEmL 93
Castagno, Anthony Joseph 1949- WhoE 93
Castagnoli, Carlo WhoScE 91-3
Castagnoli, Ferdinando 1917-1988 BioIn 17
Castaing, Francois J. BioIn 17
Castaing, Jacques 1943- WhoScE 91-2
Castaldi, Alexander Richard 1950- St&PR 93
Castaldi, Alfonso 1874-1942 Baker 92
Castaldi, David Lawrence 1940- WhoAm 92
Castaldo, John N. 1956- WhoEmL 93
Castaldo, Joseph 1927- Baker 92
Castaldo, Peter James 1948- WhoE 93
Castan, Armand de Baker 92
Castaneda, Antonia I. 1942- HispAmA
Castaneda, Carlos BioIn 17
Castaneda, Carlos Eduardo 1896-1958 HispAmA
Castaneda, Hector-Neri 1924-1991 WhoAm 92
Castaneda, Omar S. 1954- SmATA 71 [port]
Castaneda, Roberto Rudolph 1956- WhoEmL 93
Castaner, Luis M. 1948- WhoScE 91-3
Castanie, Francis S. 1947- WhoScE 91-2
Castano, David Gary Law&B 92
Castano, Elvira Palmerio 1929- WhoAmW 93, WhoE 93, WhoWor 93
Castano, Gregory Joseph 1929- WhoE 93
Castano, John Roman 1926- WhoSSW 93
Castano, Juanita 1949- WhoUN 92
Castano, Sylvia Elizabeth 1953- WhoEmL 93
Castano, Thomas C. Law&B 92
Castanon Tessey, Hector Albino 1912- WhoWor 93
Castanos y Aragon, Francisco Javier 1758-1852 HarEnMi
Caste, Jean F. 1929- WhoAm 92
Casteborn, Lars Goran 1942- St&PR 93
Castedo, Elena BioIn 17
Castedo, Elena 1937- NotHsAW 93, WhoSSW 93

Casteel, Angela Michele 1960- *WhoSSW 93*
Casteel, Bette 1920- *WhoWrEP 92*
Casteel, Catherine McKnight 1949- *WhoAmW 93, WhoSSW 93*
Casteel, Clyde Terrel 1953- *WhoEmL 93*
Casteel, DiAnn Brown 1953- *WhoEmL 93, WhoSSW 93*
Casteel, J. Kenneth 1939- *St&PR 93*
Casteel, Phillip Thomas 1951- *St&PR 93*
Casteel, Thomas Joseph 1948- *WhoE 93*
Casteen, John T., III 1943- *WhoAm 92, WhoSSW 93, WhoWor 93*
Castel, Gerard Joseph 1934- *WhoWor 93*
Castel, Jean Gabriel 1928- *WhoAm 92*
Castel, John C. 1954- *St&PR 93*
Castel, Kenneth R. 1953- *St&PR 93*
Castel, Louis-Bertrand 1688-1757 *Baker 92*
Castel, Moshe 1909-1991 *BioIn 17*
Castel, Nico 1935- *WhoAm 92*
Castel, P. Kevin 1950- *WhoEmL 93*
Castelan, Benjamin *BioIn 17*
Castele, Theodore John 1928- *WhoAm 92*
Castell, Anton-Wolfgang von Faber- *BioIn 17*
Castell, David Gerard 1945- *St&PR 93*
Castell, Mary Elizabeth von Faber- *BioIn 17*
Castella, Xavier 1958- *WhoWor 93*
Castellan, Carl Patrick *Law&B 92*
Castellan, Gilbert William 1924- *WhoAm 92*
Castellan, Jeanne 1819-c. 1858 *OxDcOp*
Castellan, Norman John, Jr. 1939- *WhoAm 92*
Castellani, Armand J. 1917- *WhoAm 92*
Castellani, Robert Joseph 1941- *WhoSSW 93*
Castellani, Vittorio 1937- *WhoScE 91-3*
Castellano, Andrea *BioIn 17*
Castellano, Joseph *Law&B 92*
Castellano, Michel *BioIn 17*
Castellano, Norma Linda 1946- *WhoAmW 93*
Castellano, Olivia 1944- *DcLB 122 [port]*
Castellano, Paul *BioIn 17*
Castellanos, Dario 1937- *WhoWor 93*
Castellanos, Julio Jesus 1910- *WhoE 93*
Castellanos, Rosario *BioIn 17*
Castellanos, Rosario 1925-1974 *DcMexL, SpAmA*
Castellanos Gonzalez, Julian 1939- *WhoWor 93*
Castellanos Quinto, Erasmo 1879-1955 *DcMexL*
Castellarin, Sheila A. 1935- *St&PR 93*
Castelli, Alexander Gerard 1929- *WhoAm 92*
Castelli, Carlo 1938- *WhoWor 93*
Castelli, Edoardo 1938- *WhoScE 91-3*
Castelli, Francis Anthony 1951- *WhoEmL 93*
Castelli, Frank Rafael 1948- *St&PR 93*
Castelli, Leo 1907- *BioIn 17, WhoAm 92, WhoE 93*
Castellino, Francis Joseph 1943- *WhoAm 92*
Castellino, James J. 1956- *St&PR 93*
Castellino, Ronald Augustus Dietrich 1938- *WhoAm 92, WhoE 93*
Castello, Hugo M. 1914- *HispAmA*
Castello, Joli Marion 1963- *WhoEmL 93*
Castello Branco, Mario Monjardim 1931- *WhoWor 93*
Castellon, Augustin d1990 *BioIn 17*
Castellon, Christine New 1957- *WhoAmW 93*
Castells, Manuel 1942- *ConAu 37NR*
Castells, Manuel F. 1942- *St&PR 93*
Castelluzzi, Donato Dan Michael 1949- *St&PR 93*
Castelmary 1834-1897 *Baker 92*
Castelmary, Armand 1834-1897 *OxDcOp*
Castelnau, Francis de la Porte, Comte de 1812-1880 *Expl 93*
Castelnau, Jacques de 1620-1658 *HarEnMi*
Castelnau, Noel Marie Joseph Edouard de Curieres de 1851-1944 *BioIn 17, HarEnMi*
Castelnuovo-Tedesco, Mario 1895-1968 *Baker 92, BioIn 17*
Castelo, Carlos Alberto Monteiro 1943- *WhoWor 93*
Castelo, Henry L. *WhoIns 93*
Castelo-Branco, Camil 1960- *WhoWor 93*
Castelo Branco, Paulo Mauricio 1948- *WhoWor 93*
Casteloes, Susan Chambers 1939- *WhoAmW 93, WhoWor 93*
Castel-Rodrigo, marques de d1651 *BioIn 17*
Casten, Richard Francis 1941- *WhoE 93*
Castenholz, Anton 1930- *WhoScE 91-3*
Castens, Christopher Cole *Law&B 92*
Castens, Christopher Cole 1951- *St&PR 93*
Castenschiold, Rene 1923- *WhoAm 92*
Castenskiold, Holger 1931- *WhoWor 93*
Caster, Bernard Harry 1921- *WhoE 93*
Castera, Pedro 1838-1906 *DcMexL*
Castera, Rene d'Avezac 1873-1955 *Baker 92*
Casterella, Anthony J. 1945- *St&PR 93*
Casterline, Bob E. 1946- *St&PR 93*
Casterline, William Hale, Jr. 1951- *WhoEmL 93*
Castevano, Roman *ScF&FL 92*
Casti, Giovanni Battista 1724-1803 *OxDcOp*
Castiello D'Antonio, Andrea 1954- *WhoWor 93*
Castiglia, Athan F. *St&PR 93*
Castiglia, Joseph J. 1934- *St&PR 93*
Castiglione, Lawrence Virgil, Jr. 1938- *WhoE 93*
Castiglione, Tanya Shriver 1944- *WhoAmW 93*
Castiglioni, Niccolo 1932- *Baker 92*
Castil-Blaze *Baker 92*
Castil-Blaze, Francois 1784-1857 *OxDcOp*
Castile, Rand 1938- *ConAu 138, WhoAm 92, WhoWor 93*
Castilla, Alberto 1883-1937 *Baker 92*
Castilla, Clyde Andre 1907-1983 *ScF&FL 92*
Castilla, Craig K. 1961- *St&PR 93*
Castille, Philip Dubuisson 1948- *WhoSSW 93*
Castillo, Adelaida Del *NotHsAW 93*
Castillo, Ana 1953- *DcLB 122 [port], NotHsAW 93*
Castillo, Carlos 1940- *WhoUN 92*
Castillo, Carlos Manuel *DcCPCAm*
Castillo, Debra A(nn Garsow) 1953- *ConAu 136*
Castillo, Florencio M. del 1828-1863 *DcMexL*
Castillo, Gloria Jean 1954- *WhoEmL 93*
Castillo, Hal Stephen 1947- *WhoEmL 93*
Castillo, Heberto *DcCPCAm*
Castillo, Jenny Maria Teresa 1959- *WhoE 93*
Castillo, Jose Luis 1955- *WhoWor 93*
Castillo, Karen Sue 1948- *WhoEmL 93*
Castillo, Leonard *Law&B 92*
Castillo, Leonel J. 1939- *HispAmA*
Castillo, Leonel Jabier 1939- *WhoAm 92*
Castillo, Lucy Narvaez 1943- *WhoAmW 93, WhoWor 93*
Castillo, Luis Enrique 1950- *WhoEmL 93*
Castillo, Madre 1671-1742 *BioIn 17*
Castillo, Mario Enrique 1945- *WhoWor 93*
Castillo, Martha *Law&B 92*
Castillo, Max *WhoSSW 93*
Castillo, Rafael C. 1950- *WhoWrEP 92*
Castillo, Rafael Ernest 1952- *WhoEmL 93*
Castillo, Raymond Adolph 1935- *WhoE 93*
Castillo, Rolando *DcCPCAm*
Castillo, Sylvia L. 1951- *NotHsAW 93 [port]*
Castillo, Tersa Regalado 1958- *WhoWor 93*
Castillo Armas, Carlos 1914-1957 *DcCPCAm*
Castillo Garcia, Luis Fernando 1936- *WhoWor 93*
Castillo-Guzman, Gonzalo Mario 1966- *WhoWor 93*
Castillo Lara, Rosalio Jose Cardinal 1922- *WhoWor 93*
Castillo Ledon, Amalia *DcMexL*
Castillo Ledon, Luis 1879-1944 *DcMexL*
Castillon (de Saint-Victor), (Marie) Alexis 1838-1873 *Baker 92*
Castillo Najera, Francisco 1886-1954 *DcMexL*
Castillo-Speed, Lillian 1949- *NotHsAW 93*
Castillo y Lanzas, Joaquin M. del 1801-1878 *DcMexL*
Castillo y Saavedra, Antonio del 1603-1667 *BioIn 17*
Castilow, H. Carter 1943- *St&PR 93*
Castine, Michael Patrick 1954- *WhoEmL 93*
Castino, Mario 1934- *WhoScE 91-3*
Castinus fl. c. 421- *HarEnMi*
Castle, Alfred L. 1948- *ConAu 139*
Castle, Bruce Edward 1958- *WhoEmL 93*
Castle, Damon *ScF&FL 92*
Castle, David R. 1949- *St&PR 93*
Castle, Donald Robert 1936- *WhoSSW 93*
Castle, Douglas A. 1942- *WhoScE 91-1*
Castle, Emery Neal 1923- *WhoAm 92*
Castle, Frank Allen 1934- *St&PR 93*
Castle, Frank E. 1932- *St&PR 93*
Castle, Frederick Ted 1938- *ConAu 137*
Castle, Grant Berkeley 1952- *WhoAm 92*
Castle, Gray 1931- *St&PR 93*
Castle, Gregory L. *Law&B 92*
Castle, Harriet Davenport 1843- *AmWomPl*
Castle, Ian Maxwell 1944- *St&PR 93*
Castle, James Cameron 1936- *St&PR 93, WhoAm 92*
Castle, Jayne *ConAu 139*
Castle, John K. 1940- *St&PR 93*
Castle, John Krob 1940- *WhoAm 92, WhoWor 93*
Castle, John Raymond, Jr. 1943- *WhoAm 92*
Castle, Lee d1990 *BioIn 17*
Castle, Marian Johnson *WhoWrEP 92*
Castle, Michael N. 1939- *WhoAm 92, WhoE 93, WhoWor 93*
Castle, Mort 1946- *ScF&FL 92*
Castle, Nick 1947- *MiSFD 9*
Castle, Paul *ConAu 139, SmATA 73*
Castle, Peggie 1927?-1973 *SweetSg D [port]*
Castle, Raymond Nielson 1916- *WhoAm 92*
Castle, Robert Woods 1925- *WhoAm 92*
Castle, Shara Ann 1964- *WhoAmW 93*
Castle, Sharon Denise 1952- *WhoEmL 93*
Castle, Stephen Neil 1952- *WhoEmL 93, WhoWor 93*
Castle, William 1914-1977 *MiSFD 9N*
Castle, William Bosworth 1897-1990 *BioIn 17*
Castle, William Eugene 1929- *WhoAm 92*
Castleberry, May Lewis 1954- *WhoAm 92*
Castleberry, Robert Holmes 1955- *WhoEmL 93*
Castleden, Rodney 1945- *ConAu 138*
Castle-Kidd, Catherine 1942- *WhoAmW 93*
Castleman, Albert Welford, Jr. 1936- *WhoAm 92, WhoE 93*
Castleman, Charles (Martin) 1941- *Baker 92*
Castleman, Curtis H., Jr. *Law&B 92*
Castleman, Harry Weissinger 1911- *WhoSSW 93*
Castleman, Louis Samuel 1918- *WhoAm 92*
Castleman, Melvin 1910- *St&PR 93*
Castleman, Riva 1930- *WhoAm 92*
Castleman, (Esther) Riva 1930- *ConAu 40NR*
Castlen, Peggy Lou 1939- *WhoAmW 93*
Castlereagh, Viscount 1769-1822 *BioIn 17*
Castles, John William 1947- *WhoEmL 93*
Castles, Leone Dexter Strickland 1923- *WhoAmW 93*
Castleton, David J. 1954- *WhoEmL 93*
Castleton, Lane J. 1956- *St&PR 93*
Castner, Lawrence V. *Law&B 92*
Castner, Stephan C. 1939- *WhoSSW 93*
Casto, Dale G. 1936- *St&PR 93*
Casto, Dennis Lee 1954- *WhoEmL 93*
Casto, Jackie *ScF&FL 92*
Casto, James Edward 1941- *WhoSSW 93*
Casto, James John 1960- *WhoSSW 93*
Casto, Leo V. 1933- *St&PR 93*
Caston, Hoite *MiSFD 9*
Caston, Jesse Douglas 1932- *WhoAm 92*
Caston, Ray Allen 1947- *St&PR 93*
Caston, Saul 1901-1970 *Baker 92*
Castonguay, Claude 1929- *St&PR 93, WhoAm 92, WhoWor 93*
Castor, C. William, Jr. 1925- *WhoAm 92*
Castor, Carol Jean 1944- *WhoSSW 93*
Castor, Charles O. 1935- *St&PR 93*
Castor, Jimmy 1943- *SoulM*
Castor, Richard Gilbert 1927- *WhoIns 93*
Castor, Susan Dee 1946- *WhoEmL 93*
Castor, William Stuart, Jr. 1926- *WhoAm 92*
Castoriadis, Cornelius 1922- *ConAu 138*
Castoro, Laura *ScF&FL 92*
Castren, Matthias Alexander 1813-1852 *IntDcAn*
Castries, Christian de 1902-1991 *AnObit 1991, BioIn 17*
Castrignano, Robert Anthony 1920- *WhoE 93*
Castrilla, Gregory John 1949- *St&PR 93*
Castriota, George 1403-1468 *HarEnMi*
Castro, Adolphe de *ScF&FL 92*
Castro, Alberto 1933- *HispAmA*
Castro, Amado Alejandro 1924- *WhoWor 93*
Castro, Armando Fernandes de Morais E 1918- *WhoWor 93*
Castro, Bernard 1904-1991 *BioIn 17*
Castro, Bertrand R. 1938- *WhoScE 91-2*
Castro, Claudio de Moura 1938- *WhoUN 92*
Castro, David M. *Law&B 92*
Castro, Dolores 1923- *DcMexL*
Castro, Fidel 1927- *BioIn 17, DcTwHis, WhoWor 93*
Castro, George 1939- *HispAmA [port]*
Castro, Guillen de 1569-1631 *LitC 19*
Castro, Hugo A. 1943- *St&PR 93*
Castro, Jan Garden 1945- *WhoAm 92, WhoWrEP 92*
Castro, Jean de c. 1540-c. 1611 *Baker 92*
Castro, Joaquim Paulo Lalanda 1957- *WhoWor 93*
Castro, Jose Agustin 1730-1814 *DcMexL*
Castro, Jose Maria 1892-1964 *Baker 92*
Castro, Joseph Armand 1927- *WhoWor 93*
Castro, Joseph Ronald 1934- *WhoAm 92*
Castro, Juan Jose 1895-1968 *Baker 92, OxDcOp*
Castro, Manuel *BioIn 17*
Castro, Marjorie Ellen *WhoAmW 93*
Castro, Nadine Berthe 1944- *WhoAmW 93*
Castro, Peter 1943- *HispAmA*
Castro, Raul *WhoWor 93*
Castro, Ricardo 1864-1907 *Baker 92*
Castro, Sophie Elizabeth 1965- *WhoAmW 93*
Castro, Vincent Robert 1948- *WhoE 93*
Castro, Washington 1909- *Baker 92*
Castro-Brauer, Sylvia Elizabeth 1953- *WhoAmW 93*
Castro-Caldas, Alexandre 1948- *WhoScE 91-3*
Castrodad, Felix A. *WhoAm 92*
Castro Diaz, Luis Enrique 1943- *WhoWor 93*
Castro-Fernandez, F.R. 1950- *WhoScE 91-3*
Castro-Gutierrez, Alvaro 1943- *WhoUN 92*
Castro-Klaren, Sara 1942- *WhoE 93*
Castro Leal, Antonio 1896-1981 *DcMexL*
Castronova, Jeri Benita *WhoAmW 93*
Castronovo, David 1945- *WhoE 93*
Castronovo, Thomas Nicholas 1959- *WhoEmL 93*
Castro Ruz, Fidel 1926- *ColdWar 2 [port]*
Castro Ruz, Fidel Alejandro 1927- *DcCPCAm*
Castro Ruz, Raul 1931- *ColdWar 2 [port], DcCPCAm*
Castroviejo, S. *WhoScE 91-3*
Castroviejo, Santiago 1946- *WhoWor 93*
Castroviejo Bolibar, Francisco Javier 1940- *WhoScE 91-3*
Castroviejo Bolibar, Santiago 1946- *WhoScE 91-3*
Castrovinci, Cynthia Barnes 1948- *WhoAmW 93*
Castro y Velasco, Antonio Palomino de 1655-1726 *BioIn 17*
Castrucci, George E. *WhoAm 92*
Castrucci, Pietro 1679-1752 *Baker 92*
Casturo, Don James 1942- *WhoE 93*
Casty, Ronald G. 1945- *WhoAm 92*
Caswall Devey, Emily Jane 1954- *WhoAmW 93, WhoEmL 93*
Caswell, Donald Eugene 1948- *WhoWrEP 92*
Caswell, Dorothy Ann Cottrell 1938- *WhoAm 92, WhoAmW 93*
Caswell, Frances Pratt 1929- *WhoAmW 93*
Caswell, Herbert Hall, Jr. 1923- *WhoAm 92*
Caswell, Hollis Leland 1931- *St&PR 93*
Caswell, John Beveridge 1938- *St&PR 93*
Caswell, Kimberly *Law&B 92*
Caswell, Linda Kay 1952- *WhoAmW 93*
Caswell, Lyman Ray 1928- *WhoSSW 93*
Caswell, Paul Hadley 1936- *WhoAm 92*
Caswell, Richard 1729-1789 *HarEnMi*
Caswell, Richard L. *Law&B 92*
Caswell, Robert Douglas 1946- *WhoWor 93*
Caswell, Robert Stearns 1952- *WhoE 93*
Caswell, W.B. 1934- *St&PR 93*
Caswell, W. Cameron 1916- *St&PR 93*
Cata, Alfonso 1937-1990 *BioIn 17*
Catabelle, Jean-Marie Henri 1941- *WhoWor 93*
Catacalos, Rosemary 1944- *DcLB 122 [port]*
Catacosinos, William J. 1930- *St&PR 93*
Catacosinos, William James 1930- *WhoAm 92, WhoE 93*
Catala, Rafael Enrique 1942- *WhoWrEP 92*
Catalan, Manuel 1934- *WhoScE 91-3*
Cataland, James Ronald 1944- *St&PR 93*
Catalani, Alfredo 1854-1893 *Baker 92, IntDcOp, OxDcOp*
Catalani, Angelica 1780-1849 *Baker 92, OxDcOp*
Catalano, Anthony Peter 1946- *St&PR 93*
Catalano, Carl Philip 1953- *WhoEmL 93*
Catalano, Charles Ross 1936- *St&PR 93*
Catalano, Eduardo Fernando 1917- *WhoAm 92, WhoE 93*
Catalano, Jane D. *Law&B 92*
Catalano, Jane Donna *Law&B 92*
Catalano, Jane Donna 1957- *WhoEmL 93*
Catalano, Joseph Michael 1945- *St&PR 93*
Catalano, Louis William, Jr. 1942- *WhoE 93*
Catalano, Michael *Law&B 92*
Catalano, Michael Alfred 1947- *St&PR 93*
Catalano, Paul D. d1991 *BioIn 17*
Catalano, Peter 1961- *WhoE 93*
Catalano, Robert Anthony 1956- *WhoE 93*

Catalano, Vincent Patrick 1935- WhoE 93
Catalanotto, Peter ChlBIID [port]
Catalanotto, Peter 1959- ConAu 138, SmATA 70 [port]
Cataldo, Andrew J. Law&B 92
Cataldo, Anthony Joseph, II 1957- WhoEmL 93
Cataldo, Joseph Michael 1934- WhoAm 92
Cataldo, Louis John, Jr. 1956- WhoSSW 93
Cataldo, Robert J. 1954- St&PR 93
Cataldo, Wallace A. 1950- St&PR 93
Catalfo, Alfred, Jr. 1920- WhoAm 92, WhoE 93, WhoWor 93
Catalfo, Betty Marie 1942- WhoAmW 93, WhoE 93, WhoWor 93
Catalfomo, Philip 1931- WhoAm 92
Catallo, Berna Rose 1936- WhoAmW 93
Catallo, Clarence Guerrino, Jr. 1940- WhoAm 92, WhoWor 93
Catandella, Kenneth F. 1936- WhoE 93
Catanese, Anthony James 1942- WhoAm 92, WhoSSW 93
Catanese, Carmen A. 1942- WhoAm 92
Catanese, Sal 1942- St&PR 93
Catania, Anthony Charles 1936- WhoAm 92, WhoE 93
Catania, Basilio 1926- WhoScE 91-3
Catania, Dorothy J. 1929- St&PR 93
Catania, Joseph A. 1927- St&PR 93
Catania, Lorraine Laura 1942- WhoAm 92
Catania, Robert F. Law&B 92
Catania, Ronald 1945- St&PR 93
Catania, Thomas F., Jr. Law&B 92
Catania, Thomas Francis 1932- St&PR 93
Catania, Vito Charles 1951- WhoE 93
Catanzano, Frank Alexander 1947- WhoEmL 93
Catanzaro, Karen Barbara 1960- WhoEmL 93
Catanzaro, Michael E., Jr. Law&B 92
Catanzaro, Tony WhoAm 92, WhoSSW 93
Catapano, Joseph John 1935- St&PR 93, WhoAm 92
Catarig, Alexandru Teofil 1939- WhoScE 91-4
Catarino, Camilo Jose 1955- WhoEmL 93
Catasus, Jose Magin Perez 1942- WhoSSW 93
Catchapaw, Dorothy Deane 1912- WhoWrEP 92
Catchpole, Lawrence Welton 1952- WhoEmL 93, WhoSSW 93
Catchpole, Robin Michael 1943- WhoWor 93
Cate, Benjamin 1931- BioIn 17
Cate, Benjamin Wilson Upton 1931- WhoAm 92
Cate, Charles H. 1938- St&PR 93
Cate, David Julian 1955- WhoEmL 93
Cate, Dick ChlFicS
Cate, John S. 1948- St&PR 93
Cate, Phillip Dennis 1944- WhoAm 92
Cate, Rex Neil 1958- WhoEmL 93
Cate, Robert Louis 1932- WhoSSW 93
Catechis, Spyros Constantine 1919- WhoWor 93
Catel, Charles-Simon 1773-1830 Baker 92, OxDcOp
Catelani, Angelo 1811-1866 Baker 92
Catell, Robert Barry 1937- St&PR 93, WhoAm 92, WhoE 93
Catelli, Mario 1952- St&PR 93
Catenhusen, Wolf-Michael 1945- WhoScE 91-3
Cateora, Philip Rene 1932- WhoAm 92
Cater, Alice Ruth Wallace 1935- WhoAmW 93, WhoSSW 93, WhoWor 93
Cater, Douglass 1923- WhoAm 92, WhoWrEP 92
Cater, Eugene F. 1940- St&PR 93
Cater, James Thomas 1948- WhoAm 92, WhoEmL 93, WhoSSW 93
Cater, John T. 1935- St&PR 93
Cater, Steven Clyde 1953- WhoEmL 93
Caterino, Linda Claire 1949- WhoAmW 93
Caterino, Ronald F. 1944- St&PR 93
Cates, A. Diane 1954- WhoAmW 93
Cates, Armel Conyers 1943- WhoWor 93
Cates, Charles Brad 1950- WhoEmL 93
Cates, Charles W. 1946- WhoSSW 93
Cates, Clifton Bledsoe 1893-1970 HarEnMi
Cates, Dalton Reede 1933- WhoE 93
Cates, Don Tate 1933- WhoAm 92, WhoSSW 93
Cates, Edward William 1952- WhoWrEP 92
Cates, Emily ScF&FL 92
Cates, George Lewis 1937- WhoAm 92
Cates, Gilbert 1934- ConTFT 10, MiSFD 9, WhoAm 92
Cates, Jennifer A. 1956- St&PR 93
Cates, Jennifer Ann 1956- WhoAmW 93, WhoEmL 93
Cates, Jo Ann 1958- WhoAmW 93
Cates, Joseph 1924- MiSFD 9
Cates, Kathleen Mary 1964- WhoEmL 93
Cates, Lindley Addison 1932- WhoSSW 93
Cates, Lydia Joe 1928- WhoWrEP 92
Cates, M. Stephen 1950- St&PR 93
Cates, MacFarlane Lafferty, Jr. 1927- St&PR 93
Cates, Marla Kaye 1954- WhoAmW 93
Cates, Nelia Barletta de 1932- WhoWor 93
Cates, Phoebe 1964?- ConTFT 10, WhoAm 92
Cates, Phyllis Stork 1921- WhoAmW 93
Cateura, Linda Brandi WhoE 93
Catey, Eric Brian 1962- WhoE 93
Cathcart, Harold Robert 1924- WhoAm 92
Cathcart, Jack Edward 1943- St&PR 93
Cathcart, James A. 1909-1991 BioIn 17
Cathcart, Linda 1947- WhoAm 92
Cathcart, Margaret E. 1945- WhoWrEP 92
Cathcart, Richard 1950- WhoEmL 93
Cathcart, Robert Stephen 1923- WhoAm 92
Cathcart, Silas Strawn 1926- St&PR 93
Cathcart, William Schaw 1755-1843 HarEnMi
Cathelineau, Andre 1950- WhoWor 93
Cathell, David Wayne 1954- St&PR 93
Cather, Donald Warren 1926- WhoAm 92
Cather, James Newton 1931- WhoAm 92
Cather, Willa 1873-1947 AmWomWr 92, BioIn 17, MagSAmL [port], WorLitC [port]
Catherall, Arthur 1906-1980 ConAu 38NR, MajAI [port]
Catherine, Alain Law&B 92
Catherine de Medicis, Queen 1519-1589 BioIn 17
Catherine Of Alexandria OxDcByz
Catherine, of Siena, Saint 1347-1380 BioIn 17
Catherine, of Valois, Queen 1401-1437 BioIn 17
Catherine the Great 1729-1796 OxDcOp
Catherine, the Great, II, Empress of Russia 1729-1796 BioIn 17
Catherinot, Alain 1947- WhoScE 91-2
Catherman, Donna Elaine 1947- WhoEmL 93, WhoWor 93
Cathers, Ken 1951- WhoCanL 92
Catherwood, Frederick 1799-1854 IntDcAn
Cathey, Henry Marcellus 1928- WhoAm 92
Cathey, M. Elizabeth 1946- WhoEmL 93
Cathey, Marsha Pryor 1951- WhoEmL 93
Cathey, Marshall Lester 1941- St&PR 93
Cathey, Mary Ellen Jackson 1926- WhoE 93
Cathey, Sharon Sue Rinn 1940- WhoAmW 93, WhoWor 93
Cathey, Sterling E. Law&B 92
Cathey, Susan Guinette Aldridge 1952- WhoAmW 93
Cathey, Wm. Harve 1939- St&PR 93
Cathie, Richard Harold 1943- WhoWor 93
Cathignol, Dominique WhoScE 91-2
Cathon, Laura E. 1908-1991 BioIn 17
Cathou, Renata Egone 1935- WhoAm 92, WhoAmW 93
Cathy, S. Truett BioIn 17
Catinat, Nicholas 1637-1712 HarEnMi
Cation, Kenneth L. 1940- St&PR 93
Catledge, Turner 1901-1983 DcLB 127 [port], JrnUS
Catlett, Charles Edwin 1949- WhoWor 93
Catlett, Elizabeth BioIn 17
Catlett, Gary 1945- St&PR 93
Catlett, George Roudebush 1917- WhoAm 92
Catlett, James C., Jr. 1957- WhoEmL 93, WhoSSW 93
Catlett, Richard H., Jr. 1921- WhoAm 92
Catlett, Richard Henry, Jr. 1921- St&PR 93
Catlett, Sidney 1910-1951 Baker 92
Catlett, W.H., Jr. 1948- St&PR 93
Catlett, Walter 1889-1960 QDrFCA 92 [port]
Catley, Melanie ScF&FL 92
Catley-Carlson, Margaret 1942- WhoAm 92
Catlin, Avery 1924- WhoAm 92
Catlin, B. Wesley 1917- WhoAm 92, WhoAmW 93
Catlin, Francis Irving 1925- WhoAm 92
Catlin, George 1796-1872 BioIn 17, IntDcAn
Catlin, Harold Harvey 1949- WhoEmL 93
Catlin, Juliana Mikulas 1954- WhoSSW 93
Catling, Darrel 1909-1991 BioIn 17
Catling, Patrick Skene 1925- ScF&FL 92
Cato, Benjamin Ralph, Jr. 1925- WhoSSW 93
Cato, David Edward 1948- WhoSSW 93
Cato, Don MiSFD 9
Cato, Glenn P. St&PR 93
Cato, James R. Law&B 92
Cato, Jett C. 1953- St&PR 93
Cato, Ken BioIn 17
Cato, Marcus Porcius Censorinus 234BC-149BC HarEnMi
Cato, Marcus Porcius Uticensis 95BC-46BC HarEnMi
Cato, Milton 1915- DcCPCAm
Cato, Robert George 1933- WhoE 93
Catoe, Bette Lorrina 1926- WhoAm 92, WhoAmW 93
Catoe, Sandra Clyburn 1937- WhoAmW 93
Catoe, William A. 1964- WhoEmL 93
Catoire, Georgi Lvovitch 1861-1926 Baker 92
Catoline, Pauline Dessie 1937- WhoAmW 93
Caton, Betty Ann 1917- WhoAm 92
Caton, Dewey Jeanne Law&B 92
Caton, Irma Jean BioIn 17
Caton, Jerald Allen 1949- WhoSSW 93
Caton, John Collings 1937- St&PR 93
Caton-Jones, Michael MiSFD 9
Caton-Jones, Michael 1958- ConTFT 10
Catran, Jack 1933- ScF&FL 92
Catravas, George Nicholas 1919- WhoAm 92
Catrini, Elizabeth Ann 1963- WhoAmW 93
Catron, Bob 1934- BioIn 17
Catron, Deborah Ann 1958- WhoEmL 93
Catron, J. Gregory Law&B 92
Catron, John 1786-1865 OxCSupC [port]
Catron, Louis E. WhoWrEP 92
Catron, William C. Law&B 92
Catronio, Ronald Joseph 1951- WhoEmL 93
Catroux, Gerard 1938- WhoScE 91-2
Catsimatidis, John A. 1948- St&PR 93
Catsimatidis, John Andreas 1948- WhoAm 92, WhoEmL 93
Catsoulacos, Panayotis 1935- WhoScE 91-3
Catt, Carrie 1859-1947 GayN
Catt, Carrie Chapman 1859-1947 BioIn 17, PolPar, WomChHR [port]
Catt, John Alfred WhoScE 91-1
Catt, Stephen Richard 1955- WhoE 93
Cattabiani, Eugene John 1927- St&PR 93
Cattafi, Bartolo 1922-1979 DcLB 128
Cattan, Albert 1929- WhoScE 91-2
Cattanach, Robert Edward, Jr. 1949- WhoEmL 93
Cattaneo, Giorgio 1947- WhoWor 93
Cattaneo, Jacquelyn Annette Kammerer 1944- WhoAmW 93
Cattaneo, Jeanne 1928- WhoScE 91-2
Cattani, Debra Ann 1953- WhoEmL 93
Cattani, Jacqueline Ann 1942- WhoUN 92
Cattani, Maryellen B. 1943- WhoAm 92, WhoAmW 93
Cattani, Richard J. 1936- WhoE 93
Cattarulla, Elliot Reynold 1931- St&PR 93, WhoAm 92
Cattaui, Stephane Aslan 1937- WhoWor 93
Cattell, Alan F. 1954- WhoScE 91-1
Cattell, Heather Birkett 1936- WhoAmW 93
Cattell, Hettie Fithian AmWomPl
Cattell, James McKeen 1860-1944 JrnUS
Cattell, Kenneth John WhoScE 91-1
Cattell, Lawrence A. 1947- St&PR 93
Cattell, Psyche 1893-1989 BioIn 17
Cattell, Richard B. 1900-1964 BioIn 17
Catterall, Marlene 1939- WhoAmW 93
Catterson, Francis Joseph 1931- St&PR 93
Catterson, James Michael 1958- WhoE 93
Catterson, Robert Kenneth 1930- St&PR 93
Cattey, James Paul 1935- WhoAm 92
Catti, Michele 1945- WhoScE 91-3
Cattier, Jean 1901-1990 BioIn 17
Cattier, John Francis 1954- WhoEmL 93
Cattin, Carlo Donat 1919-1991 BioIn 17
Cattle, Nancy E. 1959- WhoAmW 93
Catto, Graeme R.D. WhoScE 91-1
Catto, Henry BioIn 17
Catto, Henry Edward 1930- WhoAm 92, WhoWor 93
Catto, Jessica BioIn 17
Catto, Max(well Jeffrey) 1909?-1992 ConAu 137
Catto, William James 1957- WhoEmL 93
Cattoi, Robert Louis 1926- St&PR 93, WhoAm 92
Catton, Bruce 1899-1978 BioIn 17, JrnUS
Catton, Ivan 1934- WhoAm 92
Catton, Jack J. 1920-1990 BioIn 17
Catto of Cairncatto, Stephen Gordon 1923- WhoAm 92
Cattrell, William R. 1948- St&PR 93
Catts, Douglas Byard 1947- WhoEmL 93
Catty, David WhoScE 91-1
Catulus, Gaius Lutatius c. 285BC-c. 230BC HarEnMi
Catulus, Quintus Lutatius c. 142BC-87BC HarEnMi
Catunda, Eunice 1915- Baker 92
Caturano, Carlo 1939- WhoSSW 93
Caturla, Alejandro Garcia 1906-1940 Baker 92
Catuzzi, J. P., Jr. 1938- WhoAm 92
Caty, J. Charles 1940- St&PR 93
Cau, Antoine E. 1947- St&PR 93
Cau, Hoang Dinh 1917- WhoWor 93
Cau, Jean 1925- WhoWor 93
Cau, Pasqualino C. 1934- WhoScE 91-3
Caubere, Paul Jean 1937- WhoScE 91-2
Cauble, Myron L. Law&B 92
Cauchi, Gary Steven 1952- WhoEmL 93
Cauchie, Maurice 1882-1963 Baker 92
Caudano, Roland J.P. 1940- WhoScE 91-2
Caudell, Joy Laraine 1948- WhoSSW 93
Caudella, Edoardo 1841-1924 Baker 92
Caudill, Charlotte 1953- WhoAmW 93
Caudill, David L. 1935- St&PR 93
Caudill, David L. 1937- WhoSSW 93
Caudill, David Stanley 1951- WhoEmL 93
Caudill, Harry M. 1922-1990 BioIn 17
Caudill, Leroy 1954- WhoSSW 93
Caudill, Maureen 1951- WhoAmW 93, WhoEmL 93, WhoWor 93
Caudill, Rebecca 1899-1985 DcAmChF 1960, MajAI [port]
Caudill, Samuel Jefferson 1922- WhoAm 92
Caudill, Terry L. 1947- St&PR 93
Caudill, Terry Lee 1947- WhoEmL 93
Caudill, Vaughn Edward 1952- WhoEmL 93
Caudle, James Gary 1937- St&PR 93
Caudle, Michael Ray 1951- WhoEmL 93
Caudle, Morris Wayne 1942- St&PR 93
Caufield, Francis J. Law&B 92
Caufield, G. Farlin 1927- St&PR 93
Caufield, James D. Law&B 92, St&PR 93
Cauger, A. Scott Law&B 92
Caughlan, Georgeanne Robertson 1916- WhoAm 92, WhoAmW 93
Caughlin, Judith Ann 1941- St&PR 93
Caughlin, Stephenie Jane 1948- WhoEmL 93
Caughman, Bruce BioIn 17
Caughran, William H., Jr. Law&B 92
Caughran, William Hermann, Jr. 1956- WhoEmL 93
Caul, Brian Patrick 1943- WhoWor 93
Caulaincourt, Armand Augustine Louis de, Marquis of 1773-1827 HarEnMi
Caulder, Colline WhoCanL 92
Cauley, Betty K. Law&B 92
Cauley, Betty K. 1951- St&PR 93
Cauley, James R. Law&B 92
Cauley, James Robert 1952- WhoEmL 93
Cauley, John Francis 1932- St&PR 93
Caulfeild, James BioIn 17
Caulfield, Barbara Ann 1947- WhoAm 92
Caulfield, Carlota 1953- WhoWrEP 92
Caulfield, Eileen F. Law&B 92
Caulfield, Henry John WhoAm 92
Caulfield, James Benjamin 1927- WhoAm 92, WhoSSW 93
Caulfield, Joan 1922-1991 AnObit 1991, BioIn 17, News 92
Caulfield, Joan 1943- WhoAmW 93
Caulfield, Matthew Patrick 1936- WhoAm 92
Caulfield, Maxwell 1959- ConTFT 10
Caulfield, Patrick J. Law&B 92
Caulfield, Thomas James 1932- WhoE 93
Caulfield, William E. 1936- St&PR 93
Caulkins, Curtis Henry 1932- St&PR 93
Caulkins, Diana Kay 1948- WhoAmW 93
Caulpetzer, Daniel Bruce 1950- WhoEmL 93
Caum, Sara Jane 1928- WhoE 93
Cauna, Nikolajs 1914- WhoAm 92
Caunes, Antoine de BioIn 17
Caunitz, William J. BioIn 17
Caunt, A.B. WhoScE 91-1
Caunt, J.F. WhoScE 91-1
Caunter, Harry Allen 1935- St&PR 93
Caupin, Jean Henri Georges 1910- WhoWor 93
Caurroy, Eustache du Baker 92
Causby, Jerry Wilburn 1938- St&PR 93
Causett, William ScF&FL 92
Causey, J.P., Jr. Law&B 92
Causey, J.P., Jr. 1943- St&PR 93
Causey, James Robert 1956- WhoEmL 93
Causey, John Paul, Jr. 1943- WhoAm 92
Causey, Marianita 1964- WhoAmW 93
Causey, Robert Louis 1941- WhoAm 92
Caushaj, Philip Fillor 1954- WhoEmL 93
Causley, Charles 1917- BioIn 17
Causley, Charles Stanley 1917- WhoWor 93
Caussade, Georges 1873-1936 Baker 92
Caussanel, Claude 1933- WhoScE 91-2
Causse, Jean-Pierre 1926- WhoWor 93
Causse-Gaven, Christiane M.A. 1941- WhoScE 91-2

Caussignac, Jacques 1945- St&PR 93
Caust-Ellenbogen, Sanford Nathan 1954- WhoEmL 93
Cauthen, Charles Edward, Jr. 1931- WhoAm 92, WhoSSW 93
Cauthen, Deloris Vaughan WhoWor 93
Cauthen, E. Larry 1930- WhoIns 93
Cauthen, Harvey Ellington, Jr. 1949- WhoSSW 93
Cauthen, Irby B., Jr. 1919- ScF&FL 92
Cauthen, Irby Bruce, Jr. 1919- WhoAm 92, WhoSSW 93
Cauthen, Rea Kimbrell, Jr. 1953- WhoEmL 93, WhoSSW 93
Cauthen, Steve 1960- WhoAm 92
Cauthen, Wiley M. 1935- St&PR 93
Cautin, Murray 1941- St&PR 93
Cauvin, Jean 1509-1564 BioIn 17
Cauvin, Jean-Pierre Bernard 1936- WhoSSW 93
Cauzabon, Maurice S., Jr. 1941- St&PR 93
Cava, Michael Patrick 1926- WhoAm 92
Cava, Richard William 1942- St&PR 93
Cavaccio, Giovanni 1556-1626 Baker 92
Cavacini, Lisa Ann 1961- WhoEmL 93
Cavaco Silva, Anibal 1939- BioIn 17, WhoWor 93
Cavada, Abby 1949- WhoE 93
Cavaglieri, Giorgio 1911- WhoAm 92
Cavagnari, Domenico 1876-1966 HarEnMi
Cavagnaro, Richard Ray 1939- St&PR 93
Cavagnol, Richard M. 1942- St&PR 93
Cavagnuolo, Frederick T. Law&B 92
Cavaiani, Mabel S. 1919- WhoWrEP 92
Cavaille-Coll, Aristide 1811-1899 Baker 92
Cavakis, Robert Allan 1947- WhoEmL 93
Cavalcanti, Moema 1943- BioIn 17
Cavalcanti, Walter 1951- St&PR 93
Cavalconte, Charles Carmine 1917- WhoE 93
Cavaleri, Luigi 1940- WhoScE 91-3
Cavalero, George N. d1991 BioIn 17
Cavalet, James Roger 1942- WhoE 93
Cavalie, Gerard 1933- WhoScE 91-2
Cavalier, A.R. BioIn 17
Cavalier, Alain 1931- MiSFD 9
Cavalier, Anthony Ramsden BioIn 17
Cavalier, Arthur BioIn 17
Cavalier, Franziska 1760-1801 Baker 92
Cavalier, John C. 1939- St&PR 93
Cavalier, Margot Oliver Law&B 92
Cavalier, Michael Law&B 92
Cavaliere, Andrew L. 1938- St&PR 93
Cavaliere, Antonino WhoScE 91-3
Cavaliere, Louis Daniel 1947- St&PR 93
Cavaliere, Michael V. 1957- WhoEmL 93
Cavaliere, Paul Joseph 1947- St&PR 93
Cavalieri, Catarina 1760-1801 Baker 92, IntDcOp
Cavalieri, Donald Joseph 1942- WhoE 93
Cavalieri, Emilio de' BioIn 17
Cavalieri, Emilio de' c. 1550-1602 OxDcOp
Cavalieri, Emilio del c. 1550-1602 Baker 92
Cavalieri, Grace 1932- WhoWrEP 92
Cavalieri, Katharina 1760-1801 OxDcOp
Cavalieri, Kathleen 1949- St&PR 93
Cavalieri, Lina 1874-1944 Baker 92, IntDcOp [port], OxDcOp
Cavalieri, Vincent J. Law&B 92
Cavaliero, Glen 1927- ScF&FL 92
Cavallari, Alberto 1927- WhoWor 93
Cavallaro, Ann 1918- BioIn 17
Cavallero, Ugo 1880-1943 HarEnMi
Cavalli (Caletti), Pier Francesco 1602-1676 Baker 92
Cavalli, Francesco 1602-1676 IntDcOp, OxDcOp
Cavalli, Joseph F. 1935- WhoUN 92
Cavallini, Alberto 1938- WhoScE 91-3
Cavallini, Fabio 1949- WhoWor 93
Cavalli-Sforza, Luca Tomaso 1951- WhoUN 92
Cavalli-Sforza, Luigi Luca 1922- WhoAm 92
Cavallo, Domingo WhoWor 93
Cavallo, Enrica 1921- Baker 92
Cavallo, Ernest J. 1933- St&PR 93
Cavallon, Betty Gabler 1918- WhoAm 92, WhoAmW 93, WhoE 93
Cavallon, Michel Francis, III 1936- WhoSSW 93
Cavalucci, Eugene F. Law&B 92
Cavaluzzi, Gerard P. Law&B 92
Cavan, Ann M. 1955- WhoWrEP 92
Cavan, Frederick Rudolph Lambert, Earl of 1865-1946 HarEnMi
Cavan, John Joseph 1936- WhoSSW 93
Cavan, Ruth Shonle 1896- BioIn 17
Cavan, Stephen E. Law&B 92
Cavan, Stephen Edward 1953- St&PR 93
Cavanagh, Carroll John 1943- WhoE 93
Cavanagh, Denis WhoAm 92
Cavanagh, Eduardo 1949- WhoWor 93
Cavanagh, Edward Dean 1949- WhoEmL 93
Cavanagh, Elizabeth d1991 BioIn 17
Cavanagh, Harrison Dwight 1940- WhoAm 92
Cavanagh, Harry Joseph 1923- WhoAm 92
Cavanagh, John Charles 1932- WhoAm 92
Cavanagh, John Edward 1918- WhoAm 92
Cavanagh, John Henry 1955- WhoAm 92
Cavanagh, Michael Francis 1940- WhoAm 92
Cavanagh, Paul Guerard 1948- WhoE 93
Cavanagh, Richard Edward 1946- WhoAm 92, WhoE 93, WhoEmL 93, WhoWor 93
Cavanagh, Ronald Jerome 1940- WhoE 93
Cavanagh, Thomas Edgar 1953- WhoE 93
Cavanagh, William Joseph 1954- St&PR 93
Cavanagh, Wm. E., Jr. 1919- St&PR 93
Cavanah, Frances AmWomPl
Cavanaugh, Dennis Miles 1937- St&PR 93
Cavanaugh, Eric M. Law&B 92
Cavanaugh, Gordon 1928- WhoAm 92
Cavanaugh, James H. St&PR 93
Cavanaugh, James Henry 1937- WhoAm 92
Cavanaugh, James Michael 1949- WhoAm 92
Cavanaugh, James R. Law&B 92
Cavanaugh, James W. Law&B 92
Cavanaugh, John G. 1936- WhoIns 93
Cavanaugh, John Richard 1929- WhoE 93
Cavanaugh, Kathleen Louise Law&B 92
Cavanaugh, Kenneth Clinton 1916- WhoAm 92
Cavanaugh, Louise L. Law&B 92
Cavanaugh, Marie 1953- St&PR 93
Cavanaugh, Mary Crandall 1951- WhoAmW 93
Cavanaugh, Mary L. Law&B 92
Cavanaugh, Maxine Cornell 1931- WhoE 93
Cavanaugh, Niel Christian 1940- St&PR 93
Cavanaugh, Patricia L. 1954- WhoEmL 93
Cavanaugh, Patrick Dennis 1947- WhoEmL 93
Cavanaugh, Paul Francis, Jr. 1955- WhoE 93
Cavanaugh, Paul W. Law&B 92
Cavanaugh, Robert M. 1936- St&PR 93
Cavanaugh, Sara ScF&FL 92
Cavanaugh, Stephen Ward 1946- St&PR 93
Cavanaugh, Susan J. Law&B 92
Cavanaugh, Tom Richard 1923- WhoAm 92
Cavanaugh, Ward Arthur 1930- WhoAm 92
Cavanaugh, Wayne St&PR 93
Cavanaugh, William, III 1939- St&PR 93, WhoAm 92
Cavanaugh, William J. 1932- St&PR 93
Cavaney, Red 1943- WhoAm 92
Cavani, Liliana 1937- MiSFD 9
Cavanna, Betty 1909- DcAmChF 1960, MajAI [port]
Cavano, Lee A. 1950- St&PR 93
Cavaretti, M. Chris 1952- St&PR 93
Cavarretta, Giuseppe 1946- WhoScE 91-3
Cavathas, Constantine 1939- WhoWor 93
Cavazos, Lauro F. 1927- HispAmA
Cavazos, Lauro Fred 1927- BioIn 17, WhoAm 92, WhoE 93, WhoWor 93
Cavazos, Roberto J., Jr. 1943- St&PR 93
Cavazos Mesa, Guillermo 1938- WhoWor 93
Cavazza, Fabio Luca 1927- WhoWor 93
Cavazzoni, Girolamo c. 1520-c. 1577 Baker 92
Cavazzoni, Marco Antonio c. 1490-c. 1570 Baker 92
Cave, Daisy Wilson d1990 BioIn 17
Cave, (John) David 1957- ConAu 138
Cave, George Harold, III 1957- WhoEmL 93
Cave, George Patton 1948- WhoWrEP 92
Cave, Hugh B. 1910- ScF&FL 92
Cave, John B. 1929- St&PR 93
Cave, John Frederick WhoScE 91-1
Cave, Jon Robert 1954- WhoEmL 93
Cave, K.N. 1929- St&PR 93
Cave, Kirk Clark 1957- WhoEmL 93, WhoSSW 93
Cave, Mac Donald 1939- WhoAm 92, WhoSSW 93
Cave, Nick 1957- BioIn 17
Cave, Peter 1940- ScF&FL 92
Cave, Susan Marie 1941- WhoAmW 93
Cave Brown, Anthony ConAu 139
Cavedo, John Rollings 1941- WhoSSW 93
Cavelier, Claude 1935- WhoScE 91-2
Cavell, Daniel A. 1954- WhoEmL 93
Cavell, Edith 1865-1915 DcTwHis
Cavell, John Anthony 1951- WhoEmL 93
Cavell, Michael C. Law&B 92
Cavell, Stanley 1926- WhoAm 92
Cavell, William R. Law&B 92
Cavellier, Thomas Elliot 1949- St&PR 93
Caven, Dean Mitchell 1955- St&PR 93
Caven, Georgia Lee 1952- WhoAmW 93
Caven, Howard S. 1919- St&PR 93
Caven, Victor Clayton 1948- St&PR 93
Cavenaugh, Raymond W., Sr. 1920- St&PR 93
Cavender, Anthony Byrd Law&B 92
Cavender, Patricia Lee 1950- WhoE 93
Cavendish, Margaret 1624?-1674 BioIn 17
Cavendish, Spencer Compton 1833-1908 BioIn 17
Cavendish, Thomas Edgar 1929- WhoAm 92
Cavendish, William Anthony 1952- WhoWor 93
Cavendish, William George Spencer 1790-1858 BioIn 17
Caveney, Philip 1951- ScF&FL 92
Caveney, William Vincent 1926- St&PR 93
Caverly, Gardner A. 1910- WhoAm 92
Caverly, Millis AmWomPl
Cavers-Huff, Dasiea Yvonne 1961- WhoAmW 93
Cavert, Henry Mead 1922- WhoAm 92
Cavert, Twila Lytton 1895-1991 BioIn 17
Cavett, Dick 1936- WhoAm 92
Cavezza, Carmen James 1937- WhoAm 92
Caviano, Robert C. d1992 NewYTBS 92
Cavicchi, Leslie Scott 1954- WhoE 93
Cavicchio, Carolyn C. 1963- WhoE 93
Cavicchioli, Alberto 1955- WhoWor 93
Caviglia, Enrico 1862-1945 HarEnMi
Cavilia, John W. Law&B 92
Cavill, Ronald William 1944- WhoE 93
Cavin, Catherine Jean 1955- WhoAmW 93
Cavin, S.H. Law&B 92
Cavin, Susan Elizabeth 1948- WhoAmW 93, WhoE 93, WhoEmL 93, WhoWor 93
Cavin, William Brooks 1914- WhoAm 92
Cavin, William Pinckney 1925- WhoAm 92
Caviness, Madeline Harrison 1938- WhoAm 92
Caviness, Marie Therese 1942- WhoAmW 93
Cavior, Warren Joseph 1929- WhoAm 92
Cavitt, Glen W. 1935- St&PR 93
Cavlin, S.I. 1944- WhoScE 91-4
Cavnar, Margaret Mary 1945- WhoAmW 93
Cavnar, Samuel Melmon 1925- WhoWor 93
Cavo, Andres 1739-1803 DcMexL
Cavo, Richard C. Law&B 92
Cavonius, C.R. 1932- WhoScE 91-3
Cavonius, Carl Richard 1932- WhoWor 93
Cavos, Alberto 1801-1863 OxDcOp
Cavos, Caterino 1775-1840 OxDcOp
Cavos, Catterino 1775-1840 Baker 92
Cavos, Giovanni OxDcOp
Cavoukian, Raffi 1948- ConAu 136
Caw, Tom BioIn 17
Cawein, Kathrin 1895- WhoAmW 93, WhoWor 93
Cawley, Charles Law&B 92
Cawley, Charles M. WhoWor 93
Cawley, Charles Nash 1937- WhoSSW 93
Cawley, Donald Francis 1929-1990 BioIn 17
Cawley, Edward Philip 1912- WhoAm 92
Cawley, J.C. WhoScE 91-1
Cawley, James M. Law&B 92
Cawley, Jean M. Law&B 92
Cawley, Lance Cooper 1958- WhoE 93
Cawley, Lawrence J. 1934- St&PR 93
Cawley, Lawrence Joseph 1934- WhoAm 92
Cawley, Leo d1991 BioIn 17
Cawley, Marie Law&B 92
Cawley, Robert P. 1933-1991 BioIn 17
Cawley, Thomas Andrew 1956- WhoE 93
Cawley, Timothy James 1955- St&PR 93
Cawley, William Arthur 1925- WhoSSW 93
Cawly, Robert Houston 1950- WhoE 93
Cawood, Elizabeth Jean 1947- WhoEmL 93
Cawood, Harry Edwin, III 1936- St&PR 93
Cawood, Hobart Guy 1935- WhoAm 92
Cawood, James Scott 1956- WhoEmL 93
Caws, Mary Ann 1933- WhoAm 92, WhoAmW 93
Caws, Peter James 1931- WhoAm 92, WhoWrEP 92
Cawsey, David Charles WhoScE 91-1
Cawson, Roderick Anthony WhoScE 91-1
Cawthon, Bill BioIn 17
Cawthon, Charles R. 1912- BioIn 17
Cawthon, Frank H. 1930- WhoSSW 93
Cawthon, Jim BioIn 17
Cawthon, Lanny T. 1949- WhoSSW 93
Cawthon, William Connell 1922- WhoAm 92, WhoWor 93
Cawthon, Zelma Harrison 1911- WhoAmW 93
Cawthorn, James 1929- ScF&FL 92
Cawthorn, Robert Elston 1935- WhoAm 92
Cawthorn, T. Steven 1958- WhoEmL 93
Cawthorne, Kenneth Clifford 1936- WhoAm 92
Cawthorne, Nigel 1951- ConAu 136
Cawthorne, R.J.G. WhoScE 91-1
Caxes, Eugenio 1577-1642 BioIn 17
Cayaldo, Wallace A. 1950- St&PR 93
Cayce, Edgar 1877-1945 BioIn 17
Cayce, Edgar Evans 1918- WhoWrEP 92
Cayce, Hugh Lynn 1907-1982 BioIn 17
Cayco, Simeon Magno 1951- WhoWor 93
Cayetano, Arlene Sangalang 1953- WhoAmW 93
Cayetano, Benjamin Jerome 1939- WhoAm 92
Cayetano, Cecilia Lim 1941- WhoWor 93
Cayetano, Renato Luna 1934- WhoWor 93
Cayford, Nancy Good BioIn 17
Caygill, David Francis 1948- WhoAsAP 91
Cayias, Peter W.G. 1935- St&PR 93
Cayleff, Susan Evelyn 1954- WhoAmW 93, WhoEmL 93
Cayley, Arthur G. 1933- WhoAm 92
Caylor, Dee Jerlyn 1942- WhoAmW 93
Caylor, Marilyn Eleanor WhoSSW 93
Caylor, Rose AmWomPl
Cayne, Bernard Stanley 1924- WhoAm 92, WhoWrEP 92
Cayne, James E. BioIn 17
Cayrol, Jean 1911- BioIn 17
Cayrol, Jean Claude 1933- WhoScE 91-2
Cayton, Horace Roscoe 1903-1970 EncAACR
Cayton, Mary Kupiec 1954- ConAu 137
Cayton, William D'Arcy 1918- St&PR 93
Caywood, Clarke Lawrence 1947- WhoEmL 93
Caywood Beauregard, Janice Eileen 1955- WhoE 93, WhoEmL 93
Caza, Carlton C. 1937- St&PR 93, WhoAm 92
Cazalas, Mary Rebecca Williams 1927- WhoSSW 93
Cazalet, Lisa Anne 1958- WhoAmW 93
Cazalet-Keir, Thelma 1899-1989 BioIn 17
Cazals, Felipe 1937- MiSFD 9
Cazals, Yves Alain Georges 1950- WhoWor 93
Cazan, Matthew John 1912- WhoWor 93
Cazaux, Jacques 1934- WhoScE 91-2
Cazden, Courtney Borden 1925- WhoAm 92
Cazden, Elizabeth 1950- WhoEmL 93
Cazden, Norman 1914-1980 Baker 92
Caze, P.H. 1960- WhoScE 91-2
Cazeau, Charles J. 1931- BioIn 17
Cazeaux, Isabelle Anne Marie 1926- WhoAm 92
Cazedessus, Camille, Jr. ScF&FL 92
Cazenave, Jean-Pierre WhoScE 91-2
Cazes, Jack 1934- WhoAm 92
Cazier, Matthias 1760-1837 BioIn 17
Cazzaniga, Riccardo Angelo 1932- St&PR 93
Cazzola, Gus 1934- SmATA 73
Ce, Marco Cardinal 1925- WhoWor 93
Cearley, Patricia Kay 1949- WhoSSW 93
Cearlock, Dennis Bill 1941- WhoAm 92
Ceausescu, Elena BioIn 17
Ceausescu, Nicolae BioIn 17
Ceausescu, Nicolae 1918-1989 ColdWar 2 [port], DcTwHis
Ceazan, Gary Michael 1942- St&PR 93
Ceballos Maldonado, Jose 1919- DcMexL
Cebollero, Carlos 1927- WhoIns 93
Cebotari, Maria 1910-1949 Baker 92, IntDcOp, OxDcOp
Cebrian Echarri, Juan Luis 1944- WhoWor 93
Cebrik, Melvin Lawrence 1947- WhoEmL 93
Cebula, James Michael 1952- WhoEmL 93
Cebulash, Mel 1937- ScF&FL 92
Cebutaru, Maria 1910-1949 Baker 92
Cecala, Ted T. 1949- St&PR 93
Cecala, Ted Thomas, Jr. 1949- WhoAm 92
Ceccaldi, Jean WhoScE 91-2
Ceccardi, Herman R. 1939- St&PR 93
Ceccato, Aldo 1934- Baker 92
Cecchetti, Giovanni 1922- WhoAm 92
Cecchi, Luciano WhoScE 91-3
Cecchi, Robert Lee d1991 BioIn 17
Cecchini, Robert M. 1960- St&PR 93
Ceccon, Harry Leonard 1930- St&PR 93
Cece, Joseph W. WhoAm 92
Cece, Joseph William BioIn 17
Cecere, Michael Lewis, III 1952- WhoE 93
Cech, John Otto 1944- WhoSSW 93

Cech, Thomas Robert 1947- WhoAm 92, WhoWor 93
Cech, Victoria Shelbourne Brown 1961- WhoAmW 93
Cech, Vladimir 1914- DrEEuF
Ceci, Anthony Thomas 1917- WhoE 93, WhoWor 93
Ceci, Jesse Arthur 1924- WhoAm 92
Ceci, Louis J. 1927- WhoAm 92
Cecich, Donald Edward 1950- WhoAm 92
Cecil, Alex Thomson 1930- WhoE 93
Cecil, Charles Harkless 1945- WhoAm 92
Cecil, David Rolf 1935- WhoAm 92
Cecil, Dorcas Ann 1945- WhoAmW 93
Cecil, John L. Law&B 92
Cecil, John Lamont 1909- St&PR 93, WhoAm 92
Cecil, Loretta A. Law&B 92
Cecil, Martha L. Law&B 92
Cecil, Paula B. 1927- WhoWrEP 92
Cecil, Reed Hallum Law&B 92
Cecil, Richard Thomas 1944- WhoWrEP 92
Cecil, Robert 1563-1612 BioIn 17
Cecil, Robert Arthur Talbot Gascoyne- 1830-1903 BioIn 17
Cecil, Stephen Don 1958- WhoEmL 93
Cecil, William 1520-1598 BioIn 17
Cecin, Antonio J. 1945- St&PR 93
Cedar, Paul Arnold 1938- WhoAm 92, WhoWor 93
Cedarbaum, Miriam Goldman 1929- WhoAm 92, WhoAmW 93, WhoE 93
Cedard, Lise 1929- WhoScE 91-2
Ceddia, Anthony Francis 1944- WhoAm 92, WhoE 93
Ceddia, Jean Hendren Law&B 92
Cedel, Melinda Irene 1957- WhoEmL 93, WhoSSW 93
Cedeno, Cesar Encarnacion 1951- BiDAMSp 1989
Cederbaum, Eugene E. 1942- WhoAm 92
Cederberg, John Edwin 1943- WhoAm 92
Cederblom, Rodney Paul 1949- WhoEmL 93
Cedering, Siv 1939- WhoWrEP 92
Cederlund, Candace Ray 1952- WhoWor 93
Cederstrom, John Andrew 1929- WhoAm 92
Cedoline, Anthony John 1942- WhoWor 93
Cedraschi, Tullio 1938- St&PR 93
Cedrone, Louis Robert, Jr. 1923- WhoAm 92
Cedrone, Marie C. WhoE 93
Ceely, Robert (Paige) 1930- Baker 92
Cefalo, Albert Patrick Law&B 92
Cefalo, Frank P. St&PR 93
Cefalo, Romeo Robert 1949- St&PR 93
Cefalu, Mary Ann 1923- WhoAmW 93
Cefaratti, James P. 1942- St&PR 93
Cefelin, Pavil WhoScE 91-4
Cefis, Adolfo M. 1937- WhoWor 93
Cegielski, Hipolit 1815-1868 PolBiDi
Cegnar, Ronald William 1945- WhoAm 92
Cehanovsky, George 1892-1986 Baker 92
Ceionius OxDcByz
Cejka, Susan BioIn 17
Cekala, Chester Law&B 92
Cekanski, Adam Alexander 1921- WhoWor 93
Cekay, Robert Anthony Law&B 92
Cekorie, Thomas, Jr. St&PR 93
Cela, Camilo Jose 1916- BioIn 17, WhoWor 93
Celan, Paul BioIn 17
Celansky, Ludvik Vitezslav 1870-1931 Baker 92
Celata, Steven Anthony 1957- St&PR 93
Celaya, Gabriel 1911-1991 BioIn 17
Celaya, Haydee 1958- St&PR 93
Celebrezze, Anthony J., Jr. 1941- WhoAm 92
Celebrezze, Steven James 1959- WhoEmL 93
Celebucki, Joseph F. 1945- St&PR 93
Celens, Eduard Anna 1933- WhoScE 91-2
Celentano, Clodoaldo Law&B 92
Celentano, Francis Michael 1928- WhoAm 92
Celentano, Linda Nancy 1958- WhoE 93
Celentano, Thomas Neil 1959- WhoEmL 93
Celenti, Dan Nicholas 1952- WhoE 93
Celenza, Michael Thomas 1946- St&PR 93
Celesia, Gastone Guglielmo 1933- WhoAm 92
Celeste, Christian DcCPCAm
Celeste, Dagmar BioIn 17
Celeste, Lino Joseph 1937- WhoAm 92
Celestine, V, Saint 1215-1296 BioIn 17
Celestine Ujang anak Jilan, Datuk 1947- WhoAsAP 91
Celestino, Gary J. Law&B 92
Celia d1855 BioIn 17
Celibidache, Sergiu 1912- Baker 92
Celigoj, Christian Carl 1946- WhoWor 93
Celine, Louis-Ferdinand 1894-1961 BioIn 17
Celinski, Florian 1924- WhoScE 91-4
Celio, Amelia 1871-1958 BioIn 17
Celis, Frits 1929- Baker 92
Celius, Rolf WhoScE 91-4
Cell, John Whitson 1935- WhoSSW 93
Cella, Beth Ann 1969- WhoE 93
Cella, Christopher L. 1956- St&PR 93
Cella, Francis Raymond 1909- WhoAm 92
Cella, Frank G. 1929- St&PR 93, WhoAm 92
Cella, Frank J. 1939- WhoIns 93
Cellan-Jones, James 1931- MiSFD 9
Cellan-Jones, James Gwynne 1931- WhoAm 92
Celler, Emanuel 1888-1981 JeAmHC
Celler, George K. 1947- WhoE 93
Cellerino, Gian Pietro 1931- WhoScE 91-3
Celletti, Rodolfo 1917- Baker 92
Celli, Bartolome Romulo 1946- WhoEmL 93
Celli, Roberto d1990 BioIn 17
Cellier, Alfred 1844-1891 Baker 92
Celliers, Peter Joubert 1920- WhoE 93
Cellini, William Quirino, Jr. 1951- WhoEmL 93
Cellino, Anna Marie Law&B 92
Cellucci, Argeo Paul 1948- WhoAm 92, WhoE 93
Cellura, Angele Raymond 1932- WhoSSW 93
Celma Serra, Pedro-Juan 1945- WhoScE 91-3
Celnik, Werner E. WhoScE 91-3
Celor, Pierre Louis Joseph Jean 1902-1957 BioIn 17
Celotta, Beverly Kay 1944- WhoE 93
Celton, Henri 1943- WhoUN 92
C.E.M. SmATA 70
Ceman, T. 1931- St&PR 93
Cember, Herman 1924- WhoAm 92
Cember, Jonathan P. Law&B 92
Cember, Susan A. Law&B 92
Cemodanovs, George St&PR 93
Cempel, Czeslaw 1938- WhoScE 91-4
Cenac, Neville DcCPCAm
Cenac, Winston DcCPCAm
Cenarrusa, Pete T. 1917- WhoAm 92
Cenci, Beatrice 1577-1599 BioIn 17
Cenci, Deborah Ann 1959- WhoEmL 93
Cendrars, Blaise 1887-1961 BioIn 17
Cendrero, O. WhoScE 91-3
Cenevski, Kiril 1943- DrEEuF
Ceniceros y Villarreal, Rafael 1855-1933 DcMexL
Cenini, Sergio 1937- WhoScE 91-3
Cenkner, William 1930- WhoAm 92
Cenko, Alexis 1944- WhoE 93
Cenko, Kadri 1951- WhoUN 92
Cennamo, A. Donald Law&B 92
Censabella, Laura Maria 1959- WhoWrEP 92
Censer, Jane Turner 1951- WhoAmW 93
Censits, Richard John 1937- St&PR 93, WhoAm 92
Censor, Walter S. Law&B 92
Centa, William James 1952- WhoEmL 93, WhoSSW 93
Centafont, Richard Alan 1955- WhoE 93
Centanni, Michael A. Law&B 92
Centeio, Jose Couto 1960- WhoE 93, WhoWor 93
Center, Anthony 1949- St&PR 93
Center, David Brian 1942- WhoSSW 93
Center, John William 1946- WhoEmL 93
Center, Leo Ehren 1918- St&PR 93
Center, Ronald 1913-1973 BioIn 17
Center, Stella Stewart 1878-1969 BioIn 17
Center, Stephen B. 1938- St&PR 93
Center, Tony Law&B 92
Center, Tony 1949- WhoEmL 93
Centgraf, Damian Louis 1957- WhoEmL 93
Centineo, Philip A. 1934- St&PR 93
Centlivre, Susanna 1667?-1723 BioIn 17
Centner, Charles William 1915- WhoWor 93
Centrich, F. 1952- WhoScE 91-3
Centrich, Mercedes 1930- WhoScE 91-3
Centumalus, Gnaeus Fulvius c. 255BC-210BC HarEnMi
Cenzer, Douglas Alfred 1947- WhoSSW 93
Cepeda, Michelle A. Law&B 92
Cepeda, Orlando 1937- BioIn 17, HispAmA
Cepeda Ortiz, Edilberto 1946- WhoWor 93
Cepeda Pizarro, Mauricio 1955- WhoWor 93
Cephas, John 1930- BioIn 17
Cepicka, Alexey 1910-1990 BioIn 17
Cepielik, Elizabeth Lindberg 1941- WhoAmW 93
Ceppi, Morales Jose Miguel 1947- WhoUN 92
Ceppos, Jerome Merle 1946- WhoAm 92, WhoEmL 93
Cera, Kenneth Blair 1960- WhoEmL 93
Cera, Lee Marie 1950- WhoAm 92
Cera, Robert Joseph 1962- St&PR 93
Cerago, Carl R. 1946- St&PR 93
Cerami, Anthony 1940- WhoAm 92
Ceramicoli, Carol Frances 1960- WhoEmL 93
Ceranic, Vukosava 1921- WhoScE 91-4
Cerasia, Marcella Lo Castro 1952- WhoE 93
Cerasini, Marc A. 1952- ScF&FL 92
Ceraul, David James 1955- WhoEmL 93
Ceravolo, Anthony J. Law&B 92
Cerchiaro, Lisa Marie 1963- WhoAmW 93
Cerci, Sharon Lee 1942- WhoAmW 93
Cercone, Timothy E. 1965- WhoEmL 93
Cerda, Gabriela WhoWrEP 92
Cerda, Ildefonso 1816-1876 BioIn 17
Cerdas, Jaime DcCPCAm
Cerdonio, Massimo 1941- WhoWor 93
Cere, Ronald Carl 1947- WhoEmL 93, WhoWor 93
Cereceda Hernandez, Mariano 1940- WhoScE 91-3
Cereghino, James Joseph 1937- WhoE 93
Ceremuga, Josef 1930- Baker 92
Ceren, Sandra Levy 1936- WhoAmW 93
Cerenzia, Joseph Anthony 1954- WhoE 93
Cerepnalkovski, Llija 1932- WhoScE 91-4
Cererols, Joan 1618-1676 Baker 92
Ceresara, Sergio WhoScE 91-3
Ceresney, Ian 1938- WhoAm 92
Cerezo, Adolfo 1952- St&PR 93
Cerezo, Carmen C. 1940- HispAmA
Cerezo, Carmen Consuelo 1940- WhoAm 92, WhoAmW 93
Cerezo Arevalo, Marco Vinicio 1942- DcCPCAm
Cerf, Christopher 1941- ScF&FL 92
Cerf, Julie Micou 1957- WhoE 93
Cerf, Vinton Gray 1943- WhoAm 92
Cergol, Gregory Gerard 1959- WhoEmL 93
Cerha, Friedrich 1926- Baker 92, OxDcOp
Cerialis Caesius Rufius, Quintus Petillius c. 30-c. 80 HarEnMi
Ceriani, Gary James 1947- WhoEmL 93
Ceriani, Peter John 1956- WhoEmL 93
Ceribasic, Osman 1928- WhoScE 91-4
Cerini, Costantino Peter 1931- WhoE 93
Cerino, Angela Marie 1950- WhoE 93
Cerio, George A. St&PR 93
Cerjak, Horst H. 1939- WhoScE 91-4
Cerkanowicz, Anthony Edward 1941- WhoE 93
Cerkas, Michael William 1956- WhoEmL 93
Cerkevich, Taras Joseph 1948- WhoSSW 93
Cerletti, Paolo 1929- WhoScE 91-3
Cerlini, Celia L. St&PR 93
Cermak, Anton J. 1873-1933 PolPar
Cermak, Daniel O. 1932- St&PR 93
Cermak, Jack Edward 1922- WhoAm 92
Cermak, Jan 1939- WhoScE 91-4
Cermak, Josef Rudolf Cenek 1924- WhoWor 93
Cermak, Vladimir 1937- WhoScE 91-4
Cerminara, Frank 1948- St&PR 93
Cerna, Christina Monica 1946- WhoE 93
Cerna, Jorge BioIn 17
Cerna, Lucia de BioIn 17
Cerna, Zlata 1905- ScF&FL 92
Cernak, Keith Patrick 1954- WhoWor 93
Cernak, Steven J. Law&B 92
Cernan, Eugene A. 1934- WhoAm 92
Cernek, Jeffrey T. 1958- WhoEmL 93
Cernera, Anthony Joseph 1950- WhoAm 92
Cerni, Horst Max 1935- WhoUN 92
Cerni, Terrence S. Law&B 92
Cernichov, Iakov 1889-1951 BioIn 17
Cernik, Robert Joseph 1954- WhoWor 93
Cernohorsky, Bohuslav Baker 92
Cernovitch, Nicholas 1929- WhoAm 92
Cernuda, Luis 1902-1963 DcMexL
Cernugel, William John 1942- St&PR 93, WhoAm 92
Cernuschi-Frias, Bruno 1952- WhoWor 93
Cerny, Charlene Ann 1947- WhoAm 92
Cerny, Daniel J. 1945- St&PR 93
Cerny, Douglas M. 1958- St&PR 93
Cerny, Elaine Louise 1933- WhoAmW 93
Cerny, Frank Joseph, Jr. 1946- WhoE 93
Cerny, Gerhard 1944- WhoScE 91-3
Cerny, Ivo 1931- WhoScE 91-4
Cerny, Janice Louise 1947- WhoWrEP 92
Cerny, Jeffrey Douglas 1951- WhoEmL 93, WhoSSW 93
Cerny, Jeffrey Joel 1967- St&PR 93
Cerny, Joseph, III 1936- WhoAm 92
Cerny, Joseph Charles 1930- WhoAm 92
Cerny, Judith E. Law&B 92
Cerny, Ladislav 1891-1975 Baker 92
Cerny, Lawrence Charles 1929- WhoE 93
Cerny, Louis Thomas 1942- WhoAm 92
Cerny, Pavel 1946- WhoEmL 93
Cerny, Ronald Neal 1952- WhoE 93
Cerny, Vaclav ScF&FL 92
Cero, Joseph T. 1931- St&PR 93
Cerofolini, Gianfranco 1946- WhoWor 93
Cerone, Domenico Pietro 1566-1625 Baker 92
Cerone, James Francis 1938- WhoWor 93
Cerottini, Jean-Charles WhoScE 91-4
Cerpa, Victor Elber 1955- WhoWor 93
Cerqueira, Maria Teresa 1951- WhoAmW 93
Cerra, Luis R. 1955- WhoE 93
Cerra, Roseanne 1950- WhoAmW 93, WhoEmL 93
Cerrano, Robert Edward 1947- WhoEmL 93
Cerretani, John Louis Law&B 92
Cerretelli, Paolo WhoScE 91-3
Cerretelli, Paolo 1932- WhoScE 91-4
Cerreto, Mary Christine 1951- WhoAmW 93, WhoEmL 93
Cerreto, Scipione 1551-c. 1632 Baker 92
Cerri, Lawrence J. 1923- WhoWrEP 92
Cerrini, S. WhoScE 91-3
Cerrolaza, Miguel Enrique 1957- WhoWor 93
Cerrone, J. 1947- St&PR 93
Cerrone, Jean Baptiste d1991 BioIn 17
Cerrone, Michael Anthony 1933- St&PR 93
Cerrotti, Eugene Don 1944- St&PR 93
Cerruti, Claudio 1940- WhoScE 91-3
Cerruto, Gladys Y. 1929- St&PR 93
Cerruto, Gladys Yarocki 1929- WhoAmW 93
Cerruto, Oscar 1912-1981 SpAmA
Cersosimo, Dominic St&PR 93
Certo, Dominic Nicholas 1950- WhoWrEP 92
Certon, Pierre c. 1510-1572 Baker 92
Cerul, Sandra Mary 1940- WhoE 93
Cerullo, Edward Anthony 1950- St&PR 93
Cerullo, Morris BioIn 17
Cerulus, Frans A. 1927- WhoScE 91-2
Cerutti, Giuseppe 1937- WhoScE 91-3
Cerutty, Percy Wells 1895-1975 BioIn 17
Ceruzzi, Leonard A. Law&B 92
Cerv, Marleen Joy Law&B 92
Cervantes, Jacquelyn Marie 1965- WhoAmW 93
Cervantes (Kawanag), Ignacio 1847-1905 Baker 92
Cervantes, Lorna Dee 1954- HispAmA [port], NotHsAW 93
Cervantes, Maggie 1958- NotHsAW 93
Cervantes, Michael Anthony 1949- WhoEmL 93
Cervantes, Miguel de 1547-1616 MagSWL [port], WorLitC [port]
Cervantes de Salazar, Francisco 1513?-1575 DcMexL
Cervantes Saavedra, Miguel de 1547-1616 HarEnMi, OxDcOp
Cervellero, Paul B. 1942- St&PR 93
Cervellini, Marta Patricia 1958- WhoWor 93
Cerven, Leane English Law&B 92
Cerven, Ludevit 1918- St&PR 93
Cervenka, Exene BioIn 17
Cervenka, Mark A. Law&B 92
Cerveny, Frank Stanley 1933- WhoAm 92
Cerveny, Wenzel Franz 1819-1896 Baker 92
Cervera y Topete, Pascual 1839-1909 HarEnMi
Cervero, Jose M. 1946- WhoScE 91-3
Cervero, Jose Maria 1946- WhoWor 93
Cervetti, Sergio 1940- Baker 92
Cervetto, Giacomo c. 1682-1783 Baker 92
Cervetto, Luigi A. 1940- WhoScE 91-3
Cervi, Gino 1901-1974 IntDcF 2-3
Cervieri, John A., Jr. 1931- St&PR 93
Cervieri, John Anthony, Jr. 1931- WhoE 93
Cervigni, Dino S. 1941- WhoSSW 93
Cervilla, Constance Marlene 1951- WhoAmW 93, WhoWor 93
Cervon, Lawrence John 1922- St&PR 93
Cervone, Michele Bernadette 1964- WhoE 93
Cesa, Michael Peter 1946- WhoE 93
Cesa-Bianchi, Marcello 1926- WhoScE 91-3
Cesaire, Aime BioIn 17
Cesaire, Aime 1913- DcCPCAm
Cesana, Otto 1899-1980 Baker 92
Cesar, Alfredo DcCPCAm
Cesarani, Sal 1941- WhoAm 92
Cesare, Dennis Anthony 1954- WhoE 93
Cesareni, Giovanni 1949- WhoScE 91-3
Cesari, Gaetano 1870-1934 Baker 92
Cesari, Joan Patricia 1955- WhoAmW 93
Cesari, Richard BioIn 17
Cesarik, Joseph M. Law&B 92
Cesario, James Alex 1942- St&PR 93
Cesario, Robert James 1951- WhoEmL 93
Cesarman, Eduardo Vitis 1931- WhoWor 93

Cesarsky, Catherine J. 1943- WhoScE 91-2
Cesarsky, Diego WhoScE 91-2
Cesarz, Joseph Andrew 1941- St&PR 93
Cesarz, Paul Michael 1956- WhoEmL 93
Cesena, Carmen 1947- WhoAmW 93
Cesi, Beniamino 1845-1907 Baker 92
Cesi, Napoleone Baker 92
Cesi, Sigismondo Baker 92
Cesinger, Joan 1936- WhoAmW 93
Ceska, Franz 1936- WhoUN 92
Ceska, Miroslav 1932- WhoWor 93
Ceskova, Eva 1946- WhoScE 91-4
Cesna, Joseph Vito 1932- St&PR 93
Cesnik, James Michael 1935- WhoAm 92
Cespedes, Anthony V. Law&B 92
Cespedes, Augusto 1904- SpAmA
Cespedes, J. Martin 1948- WhoWor 93
Cespedes, Pablo de c. 1538-1608 BioIn 17
Cess, Robert Donald 1933- WhoAm 92
Cessna, Eldon d1992 BioIn 17, NewYTBS 92
Cesso, Stephen Law&B 92
Cesti, Antonio 1623-1669 Baker 92, IntDcOp
Cesti, Pietro 1623?-1669 OxDcOp
Ceszkowski, Daniel David 1954- WhoEmL 93, WhoWor 93
Cetani, Frank R. 1946- St&PR 93
Ceterski, Dorothy 1950- WhoAm 92
Ceterski, John Joseph 1948- WhoEmL 93
Cetin, Hikmet WhoWor 93
Cetina, Gutierre de 1520-1554 DcMexL
Cetinkaya, B. WhoScE 91-4
Cetinsoy, Suzan 1950- WhoScE 91-4
Cetlin, Marshall BioIn 17
Ceto, Nicholas, Jr. 1933- WhoAm 92
Cetola, Thomas Anthony 1933- St&PR 93
Cetron, Marvin Jerome 1930- WhoAm 92, WhoSSW 93
Cetrone, Anthony A. 1928- St&PR 93
Cetshwayo 1827-1884 HarEnMi
Cetta, Anthony Joseph 1949- St&PR 93
Ceva, Horacio 1939- WhoWor 93
Cevallos, Rodrigo Borja 1935- BioIn 17
Cevc, Anica 1926- WhoWor 93
Cevoli, Paul L. Law&B 92
Cey, Ronald Charles 1948- BiDAMSp 1989
Ceyer, Sylvia WhoAmW 93
Ceylan, Salih 1954- WhoScE 91-4
Ceynar, Marvin Emil 1934- WhoWrEP 92
Cezanne, Paul 1839-1906 BioIn 17
Cezar, Corneliu 1937- Baker 92
Cezar, Michael Ellis BioIn 17
Cha, Dong Se 1943- WhoWor 93
Cha, Jaeok 1952- WhoEmL 93
Cha, Se Do 1942- WhoE 93
Chaban, Lawrence Richard 1955- WhoEmL 93
Chaban-Delmas, Jacques 1915- BioIn 17
Chabanel, Martial 1939- WhoScE 91-2
Chabard, Jean-Paul 1959- WhoWor 93
Chabas, J. WhoScE 91-2
Chabe, Alexander Michael 1923- WhoE 93
Chabert, Ivan Ivanitz 1792-1859 BioIn 17
Chabeuf, Noel WhoScE 91-2
Chabloz, Jacques Francois 1936- WhoUN 92
Chabner, Howard L. Law&B 92
Chabon, Michael 1965?- ConAu 139
Chabot, Denys 1945- WhoCanL 92
Chabot, Elliot Charles 1955- WhoEmL 93
Chabot, Gerri Louise 1949- WhoAmW 93
Chabot, Herbert L. 1931- CngDr 91, WhoAm 92
Chabot, Philip Louis, Jr. 1951- WhoAm 92, WhoEmL 93
Chabrias c. 420BC-356BC HarEnMi
Chabrier, Emmanuel 1841-1894 IntDcOp, OxDcOp
Chabrier, (Alexis-) Emmanuel 1841-1894 Baker 92
Chabrier, Patricia Lopaczek 1941- WhoUN 92
Chabrier, Paul E. 1937- WhoUN 92
Chabrillac, Marcel J. 1936- WhoScE 91-2
Chabrol, Claude 1930- BioIn 17, MiSFD 9, WhoWor 93
Chabukiani, Vakhtang 1910-1992 BioIn 17
Chabukiani, Vakhtang Mikhailovich d1992 NewYTBS 92
Chaby, Diane Block 1935- WhoAmW 93
Chace, Hugh R. 1904-1991 BioIn 17
Chace, James BioIn 17
Chace, Todd Robertson 1953- WhoSSW 93
Chace, William Murdough 1938- WhoAm 92, WhoE 93
Chacharis, George 1908- PolPar
Chachere, Diane Cannon 1947- WhoAmW 93
Chacho, Raymond Andrew 1931- St&PR 93
Chachula, Jerzy 1924- WhoScE 91-4
Chachulowa, Jadwiga 1928- WhoScE 91-4, WhoWor 93
Chackes, Kenneth Michael 1949- WhoEmL 93
Chacko, George Kuttickal 1930- WhoAm 92
Chacko, Sunil 1959- WhoE 93
Chacon, Richard Frank 1945- St&PR 93
Chacon Montero, Jose 1948- WhoScE 91-3
Chacowry, Soobasschandra 1944- WhoUN 92
Chacron, Joseph 1936- WhoWor 93
Chadabe, Joel 1938- Baker 92
Chadbourne, Eugene Alexander 1954- WhoSSW 93
Chadbourne, Robert St&PR 93
Chadderdon, John Posey 1965- WhoSSW 93
Chaddock, Paul Henry 1936- St&PR 93
Chadha, Parvinder S. 1955- St&PR 93
Chadick, Gary Robert 1961- WhoEmL 93
Chadirji, Rifat Kamil 1926- WhoWor 93
Chadli, Bendjedid BioIn 17
Chadsey, William Lloyd 1942- St&PR 93
Chadsey, William Lloyd, III 1942- WhoAm 92
Chadurjian, Mark Frank Law&B 92
Chadwick, Alan Frank WhoScE 91-1
Chadwick, Alice AmWomPl
Chadwick, Charles Robb 1923- St&PR 93
Chadwick, Charles William 1912- WhoSSW 93
Chadwick, Derek James 1948- WhoWor 93
Chadwick, Doris DcChlFi
Chadwick, Florence 1918- BioIn 17
Chadwick, Gail Carol 1948- WhoAmW 93
Chadwick, Geoffrey Allan WhoScE 91-1
Chadwick, George Frederick 1930- WhoE 93
Chadwick, George W. BioIn 17
Chadwick, George W(hitefield) 1854-1931 Baker 92
Chadwick, H. Beatty Law&B 92
Chadwick, H. Beatty 1936- St&PR 93, WhoAm 92
Chadwick, Ian W. 1950- WhoWrEP 92
Chadwick, John Edwin 1957- WhoEmL 93
Chadwick, Lynn 1950- WhoE 93
Chadwick, Michael John WhoScE 91-1
Chadwick, Michael John 1934- WhoScE 91-4
Chadwick, Michelle Daniel Law&B 92
Chadwick, Owen 1916- WhoWor 93
Chadwick, Paul ScF&FL 92
Chadwick, Peter WhoScE 91-1
Chadwick, Philip George 1893-1955 ScF&FL 92
Chadwick, Robert 1924- WhoSSW 93, WhoWor 93
Chadwick, Ruth Felicity WhoScE 91-1
Chadwick, Sara Jane Hawks 1942- WhoAmW 93
Chadwick, Sharon Stevens 1951- WhoEmL 93
Chadwick, Wallace Lacy 1897- WhoAm 92, WhoWor 93
Chadwick, William Cornelius, III 1934- WhoSSW 93
Chae, Joon-kee 1929- WhoWor 93
Chaed, Richard T. Law&B 92
Chae Mun Shick 1926- WhoAsAP 91
Chaet, Bernard Robert 1924- WhoAm 92
Chafe, Wallace L. 1927- WhoAm 92
Chafe, William Henry 1942- WhoAm 92
Chafee, Gregory D. Law&B 92
Chafee, John H. 1922- CngDr 91
Chafee, John Hubbard 1922- WhoAm 92, WhoE 93
Chafee, Judith Davidson 1932- WhoAm 92
Chafee, Zechariah, Jr. 1885-1957 OxCSupC
Chafets, Ze'ev 1947?- ConAu 137
Chafets, Zev ConAu 137
Chafetz, Barry Richard 1946- WhoEmL 93
Chafetz, Marc Edward 1953- WhoEmL 93
Chafetz, Marion Claire 1925- WhoWrEP 92
Chafetz, Michael David 1953- WhoSSW 93
Chaffart, Robby Ghislain 1958- WhoE 93, WhoEmL 93
Chaffee, Adna Romanza 1842-1914 CmdGen 1991 [port]
Chaffee, Adna Romanza, Sr. 1842-1914 HarEnMi
Chaffee, Adna Romanza, Jr. 1884-1941 HarEnMi
Chaffee, C. David 1951- WhoWrEP 92
Chaffee, Dennis A. St&PR 93
Chaffee, John Densmore 1952- WhoSSW 93
Chaffee, Kevin St. Clair 1952- WhoE 93, WhoEmL 93, WhoWor 93
Chaffee, Madeline Anne AmWomPl
Chaffee, Nelson R. 1941- St&PR 93
Chaffee, Sheila Marie 1966- WhoAmW 93
Chaffee, Steven Henry 1935- WhoAm 92
Chaffee, Virginia A. Law&B 92
Chaffey, Don 1917-1990 MiSFD 9N
Chaffin, B.E. 1935- St&PR 93
Chaffin, B.W. 1927- WhoIns 93
Chaffin, Bill St&PR 93
Chaffin, Deborah Gayle 1952- WhoAmW 93
Chaffin, Gary 1937- St&PR 93
Chaffin, Gary Roger 1937- WhoAm 92
Chaffin, Julie Eileen 1959- WhoEmL 93
Chaffin, Lillie D. 1925- WhoWrEP 92
Chaffin, Lillie D(orton) 1925- DcAmChF 1960
Chaffin, Mary Law&B 92
Chaffin, Nathaniel 1934- St&PR 93
Chaffin, Richard J. 1932- St&PR 93
Chaffin, Robert C. Law&B 92
Chaffin, Thomas Lafayette 1938- St&PR 93
Chaffin, Wendel T. St&PR 93
Chaffin, William Michael 1947- WhoEmL 93
Chaffinch, Richard A. 1939- St&PR 93
Chafin, Sara Susan 1952- WhoE 93
Chafin, William F. d1992 NewYTBS 92
Chafin, William Vernon, Jr. 1936- WhoAm 92
Chagall, David 1930- WhoAm 92
Chagall, Marc 1887-1985 BioIn 17
Chagami, Michael S. 1952- St&PR 93
Chagas, Judimar Das 1942- WhoUN 92
Chagnon, Andre 1928- WhoAm 92
Chagnon, Jean F. 1949- St&PR 93
Chagnon, Joseph V. 1929- WhoE 93, WhoWor 93
Chagnon, Lucille Tessier 1936- WhoAmW 93
Chagnon, Marcel 1916- St&PR 93
Chagnon, Mary B. Bergen 1946- WhoE 93
Chagwedera, Tansai Ernest 1948- WhoWor 93
Chahid-Nourai, Behrouz J.P. 1938- WhoWor 93
Chahine, Moustafa Toufic 1935- WhoAm 92
Chahine, Youssef BioIn 17
Chahine, Youssef 1926- MiSFD 9
Chai, Alan 1952- St&PR 93
Chai, Foh Chin 1959- WhoWor 93
Chai, Wengang 1949- WhoWor 93
Chai, Winberg 1932- WhoAm 92
Chai Chengwen 1915- BioIn 17
Chaiet, Alan Howard 1943- WhoAm 92
Chaifetz, David Harvey Law&B 92
Chaika, Elaine Ostrach 1934- WhoE 93
Chaika, Gloria Estelle 1945- WhoAmW 93
Chaika, Stephen 1920- St&PR 93
Chaika, Vladimir BioIn 17
Chaiken, Barry Paul 1956- WhoEmL 93
Chaiken, Eugene Barry 1940- St&PR 93
Chaikin, Alyce 1923- WhoE 93
Chaikin, Frances 1926- WhoAmW 93
Chaikin, Joseph 1935- BioIn 17
Chaikin, Sol C. 1918-1991 AnObit 1991, BioIn 17
Chaiklin, Harris WhoE 93
Chaikof, Ellen R. Law&B 92
Chaikovsky Baker 92
Chaikovsky, P.I. 1840-1893 BioIn 17
Chai Ling BioIn 17
Chai Ling c. 1966- ConHero 2 [port]
Chaille-Long, Charles 1842-1917 Expl 93
Chailley, Jacques 1910- Baker 92
Chailly, Luciano 1920- Baker 92, OxDcOp
Chailly, Riccardo 1953- Baker 92, BioIn 17, IntDcOp, OxDcOp
Chaim, Robert Alex 1947- WhoEmL 93, WhoWor 93
Chain, Bobby Lee 1929- WhoSSW 93
Chain, Ernst Boris 1906-1979 BioIn 17
Chairge, Joseph, Jr. 1962- St&PR 93
Chairmen of the Board SoulM
Chairnoff, Hugh 1939- St&PR 93
Chaisson, William T. 1931- St&PR 93
Chait, Arnold 1930- WhoAm 92
Chait, Jon Frederick 1950- WhoAm 92
Chait, Laurence Phillip 1942- WhoE 93
Chait, Lawrence G. 1917- WhoAm 92
Chait, Sallie Hope 1953- WhoEmL 93
Chait, William 1915- WhoAm 92
Chaitin, Anthony 1941- St&PR 93, WhoAm 92
Chaix, Charles 1885-1973 Baker 92
Chaiyasan, Prachuab 1944- WhoAsAP 91
Chaize, Leon Marie 1931- WhoWor 93
Chajes, Julius 1910-1985 Baker 92
Chajet, Clive 1937- WhoAm 92
Chakales, Mary Arakas 1946- WhoAmW 93
Chakava, Henry Miyinzi 1946- WhoWor 93
Chaker, Victor 1934- WhoWor 93
Chakkour, Youssef 1928- HarEnMi
Chako, Nicholas 1910- WhoAm 92
Chakoo, B.L. 1946- ScF&FL 92
Chakovsky, Aleksandr Borisovich 1913- WhoWor 93
Chakrabarti, Arun Kumar 1955- WhoEmL 93
Chakrabarti, Paritosh Mohan 1940- St&PR 93
Chakrabarti, Subrata Kumar 1941- WhoAm 92
Chakrabarty, Ananda Mohan 1938- WhoAm 92, WhoWor 93
Chakraborty, Joana 1934- WhoAmW 93
Chakravarty, Bijoya 1940- WhoAsAP 91
Chakravarty, Indranil 1954- WhoEmL 93, WhoSSW 93
Chakravarty, Sudipto 1951- WhoWor 93
Chakravarty, Sukhamoy 1934-1990 BioIn 17
Chakraverty, Pratima WhoScE 91-1
Chaku, Pran Nath 1942- WhoSSW 93
Chakurov, Eddie Jossif 1951- WhoWor 93
Chalabaev, Almas 1951- WhoScE 91-2
Chalabala, Zdenek 1899-1962 Baker 92, OxDcOp
Chalal, Jo Ann 1954- WhoE 93
Chalandon, Albin 1920- BioIn 17
Chalandon, Fabien Pierre 1953- WhoWor 93
Chalant, Gerard Jean Louis 1949- WhoWor 93
Chalas, John George 1926- St&PR 93
Chalasinska-Macukow, Katarzyna 1946- WhoWor 93
Chalazonitis, Nicolas 1918- WhoScE 91-2
Chalberg-Plunkett, Sherri Linell 1960- WhoAmW 93, WhoEmL 93
Chalek, Sol d1990 BioIn 17
Chalela, Jose F. Law&B 92
Chaletsky, Lawrence A. Law&B 92
Chalfant, C. Dana 1918- St&PR 93
Chalfant, Edward Cole 1937- WhoAm 92
Chalfant, Richard Dewey 1924- WhoE 93
Chalfant, T.W. 1931- St&PR 93
Chalfen, Richard Megson 1942- WhoE 93
Chalfi, Raquel WhoWor 93
Chalfin, Alan I. d1991 BioIn 17
Chalfin, Bernard 1934- St&PR 93
Chalfin, Norman Leonard 1913- WhoWor 93
Chalfin, Samuel 1910- St&PR 93
Chalfin, Susan Rose 1956- WhoAmW 93, WhoSSW 93
Chaliapin, Feodor 1873-1938 BioIn 17
Chaliapin, Feodor, Jr. d1992 NewYTBS 92 [port]
Chaliapin, Feodor (Ivanovich) 1873-1938 Baker 92, IntDcOp [port]
Chaliapin, Fyodor OxDcOp
Chalif, Seymour H. 1927- WhoAm 92
Chalifoux, Michael Thomas 1947- St&PR 93
Chalik, Robert Law&B 92
Chaline, C.H. 1929- WhoScE 91-2
Chalip, Alice Grace 1930- WhoWrEP 92
Chalk, Gary 1952- ScF&FL 92
Chalk, Howard Wolfe 1922- WhoAm 92
Chalk, John Allen 1937- WhoAm 92, WhoSSW 93
Chalk, Phil BioIn 17
Chalk, Rosemary Anne 1948- WhoE 93
Chalk, Vincent BioIn 17
Chalker, Bruce Orrin 1927- St&PR 93
Chalker, Jack L. 1944- ScF&FL 92
Chalker, Robert Phelps 1914- WhoWor 93
Chalker, William Rogers 1920- WhoAm 92
Chalker-Scott, Linda Kay 1957- WhoE 93
Chalkley, Gregrey John 1954- WhoWor 93
Chalkokondyles, Laonikos c. 1423-c. 1490 OxDcByz
Chall, Jeanne Sternlicht 1921- BioIn 17, WhoE 93
Challacombe, Stephen James WhoScE 91-1
Challand, Helen J. BioIn 17
Challe, Maurice 1905-1979 BioIn 17
Challem, Jack Joseph 1950- WhoWrEP 92
Challen, Bernard John 1946- WhoScE 91-1, WhoWor 93
Challender, Stuart d1991 BioIn 17
Challenor, Herschelle Sandra 1938- WhoUN 92
Challinor, David 1920- WhoAm 92
Challis, Brian Christopher WhoScE 91-1
Challis, Lawrence John WhoScE 91-1
Challis, Norma Jean 1934- WhoAmW 93, WhoE 93, WhoWor 93
Challoner, David Reynolds 1935- WhoAm 92
Challoner, Rosemary Regina WhoWrEP 92
Chally, Elizabeth Lorraine Neal 1958- WhoWor 93
Chalmers, Agnes AmWomPl
Chalmers, Alan BioIn 17
Chalmers, Albert J. 1939- WhoScE 91-1
Chalmers, Brian John WhoScE 91-1

Chalmers, Catherine Faye 1959- WhoWrEP 92
Chalmers, David B. 1924- St&PR 93, WhoAm 92
Chalmers, Dianna Jean 1955- WhoAmW 93
Chalmers, Edwin Laurence, Jr. 1928- WhoAm 92
Chalmers, Floyd Sherman 1898- WhoAm 92
Chalmers, Franklin Stevens, Jr. 1928- WhoWor 93
Chalmers, Garet ScF&FL 92
Chalmers, Geoffrey Teale Law&B 92
Chalmers, Geoffrey Teale 1935- WhoE 93
Chalmers, Gordon James 1925- St&PR 93
Chalmers, Iain Geoffrey WhoScE 91-1
Chalmers, Ian Donald WhoScE 91-1
Chalmers, John Harvey, Jr. 1940- WhoSSW 93
Chalmers, Mary AmWomPl
Chalmers, Roberta Teale Swartz 1903- WhoAmW 93
Chalmers, Ruth 1922- WhoE 93
Chalmers, Thomas Clark 1917- WhoAm 92
Chalmin, Jean-Pierre 1944- St&PR 93
Chalnick, Marla Kappen 1949- WhoSSW 93
Chalon, Jean 1935- ConAu 40NR
Chalon, Jonathan William 1960- WhoEmL 93
Chaloner, William Gilbert WhoScE 91-1
Chalsty, John S. 1933- St&PR 93
Chalsty, John Steele 1933- WhoAm 92
Chaltiel, Victor M.G. 1941- St&PR 93
Chalukian, Alberto 1945- WhoWor 93
Chalupecky, Jindrich 1910-1990 BioIn 17
Chamakhi, Mustapha Kameleddine 1942- WhoUN 92
Chamas, Claudia Inez 1967- WhoWor 93
Chamasrour, Joseph Albert 1952- WhoAm 92
Chambaz, E. WhoScE 91-2
Chamber, Thomas L. 1949- St&PR 93
Chamberlain, Adrian Ramond 1929- WhoAm 92
Chamberlain, Anthony George WhoScE 91-1
Chamberlain, Arthur Neville 1869-1940 DcTwHis
Chamberlain, Barbara Greene 1962- WhoAmW 93, WhoEmL 93
Chamberlain, Barbara Jean 1949- WhoAmW 93
Chamberlain, Carl Evered 1945- WhoIns 93
Chamberlain, Charles Ernest 1917- WhoAm 92
Chamberlain, Charles James 1921- WhoAm 92
Chamberlain, Claudia Catherine 1940- St&PR 93
Chamberlain, Claudia J. Law&B 92
Chamberlain, Daniel Robert 1932- WhoAm 92
Chamberlain, David M. 1943- WhoAm 92
Chamberlain, Denise K. Law&B 92
Chamberlain, Diane 1950- WhoAm 92
Chamberlain, Donald William 1905- WhoWrEP 92
Chamberlain, Donna Jon 1937- WhoWrEP 92
Chamberlain, E. Martin 1940- St&PR 93
Chamberlain, Elsie 1910-1991 AnObit 1991
Chamberlain, Ena ConAu 137
Chamberlain, Geoffrey Victor Price WhoScE 91-1
Chamberlain, George Arthur, III 1935- St&PR 93, WhoAm 92
Chamberlain, Gerard Alfred Law&B 92
Chamberlain, Gladys 1890-1978 BioIn 17
Chamberlain, Harriet Feigenbaum 1939- BioIn 17
Chamberlain, Henry Richardson 1859-1911 JrnUS
Chamberlain, Houston Stewart 1855-1927 Baker 92
Chamberlain, Ida Hoyt AmWomPl
Chamberlain, James M. 1947- St&PR 93
Chamberlain, James Robert Law&B 92
Chamberlain, James Robert 1949- WhoEmL 93
Chamberlain, Jill Frances 1954- WhoAmW 93
Chamberlain, Jocelyn O.P. 1932- WhoScE 91-1
Chamberlain, John Angus 1927- BioIn 17, WhoAm 92
Chamberlain, John Rensselaer 1903- WhoAm 92
Chamberlain, Joseph 1836-1914 BioIn 17
Chamberlain, Joseph Austen 1863-1937 DcTwHis
Chamberlain, Joseph Miles 1923- WhoAm 92
Chamberlain, Joseph Wyan 1928- WhoAm 92
Chamberlain, Karen 1942- WhoWrEP 92
Chamberlain, Kathryn Burns Browning 1951- WhoAmW 93
Chamberlain, Kent Clair 1943- WhoWrEP 92
Chamberlain, Lesley 1951- ConAu 137
Chamberlain, Leslie Neville WhoScE 91-1
Chamberlain, Linda Lee 1951- WhoAm 92
Chamberlain, Lindy BioIn 17
Chamberlain, Lois Ann Law&B 92
Chamberlain, Marcella Anne WhoScE 91-1
Chamberlain, Marisha Anne 1952- WhoWrEP 92
Chamberlain, Mary 1947- BioIn 17
Chamberlain, Owen 1920- WhoAm 92, WhoWor 93
Chamberlain, Patricia Ann 1941- WhoAmW 93
Chamberlain, Reca Rene 1961- WhoWor 93
Chamberlain, Richard BioIn 17
Chamberlain, Richard 1935- WhoAm 92
Chamberlain, Richard Gray 1952- WhoWrEP 92
Chamberlain, Robert Glenn 1926- WhoAm 92
Chamberlain, Robert Wayne 1951- WhoE 93
Chamberlain, Samuel F. Law&B 92
Chamberlain, Samuel S. 1815-1916 JrnUS
Chamberlain, Steven Craig 1946- WhoAm 92, WhoEmL 93
Chamberlain, Velma WhoWrEP 92
Chamberlain, Wayne Douglas Law&B 92
Chamberlain, Willard Thomas 1928- WhoAm 92
Chamberlain, William 1903-1969? ScF&FL 92
Chamberlain, William Edwin, Jr. 1951- WhoAm 92
Chamberlain, Wilt 1936- BioIn 17
Chamberlain, Wilton Norman 1936- WhoAm 92
Chamberland, Paul 1939- WhoCanL 92
Chamberlen, Peter 1601-1683 BioIn 17
Chamberlin, Christine A. WhoAm 92
Chamberlin, Gary Dean 1938- WhoSSW 93
Chamberlin, Grace Hilton AmWomPl
Chamberlin, Guy 1894-1967 BioIn 17
Chamberlin, Jo Lund 1954- WhoEmL 93
Chamberlin, John Stephen 1928- WhoAm 92
Chamberlin, Mark Andrew 1962- WhoE 93
Chamberlin, Mary Ellen Law&B 92
Chamberlin, Michael John 1937- WhoAm 92
Chamberlin, Ronald Eugene 1947- St&PR 93
Chamberlin, Terry McBride WhoAm 92
Chamberlin, William Henry 1897-1969 JrnUS
Chambers, Aaron Granville Law&B 92
Chambers, Agnes Mae 1934- WhoAmW 93
Chambers, Aidan 1934- ChlFicS, MajAI [port], ScF&FL 92, SmATA 69 [port]
Chambers, Alan Brent 1948- WhoEmL 93
Chambers, Andrew D. WhoScE 91-1
Chambers, Anne Cox WhoAm 92
Chambers, Arther Eugene 1923- St&PR 93
Chambers, Arthur A. 1922- St&PR 93
Chambers, Brian William 1941- WhoWor 93
Chambers, C. Fred d1989 BioIn 17
Chambers, Carl D. 1934-1989 BioIn 17
Chambers, Carole Ann 1941- WhoAmW 93
Chambers, Carolyn S. 1931- St&PR 93
Chambers, Carolyn Silva 1931- WhoAmW 93
Chambers, Charles C. 1952- WhoSSW 93
Chambers, Curtis Allen 1924- WhoAm 92
Chambers, Dale 1953- WhoEmL 93, WhoSSW 93
Chambers, Daniel Warren 1952- WhoE 93
Chambers, David Edson 1938- St&PR 93
Chambers, David J.G. Law&B 92
Chambers, Dean BioIn 17
Chambers, Donald Arthur 1936- WhoAm 92
Chambers, Dorothy J. Law&B 92
Chambers, Dorothy J. 1950- WhoEmL 93
Chambers, Dorothy Mae 1925- WhoSSW 93
Chambers, Earl Denton 1925- St&PR 93, WhoIns 93
Chambers, Emmett K. St&PR 93
Chambers, Everett 1926- MiSFD 9
Chambers, Faye Marie 1964- WhoSSW 93
Chambers, Frank G. 1916- St&PR 93
Chambers, Frank Morris WhoScE 91-1
Chambers, Fred 1912- WhoAm 92
Chambers, Gene Marion 1926- WhoSSW 93
Chambers, George DcCPCAm
Chambers, George O. d1990 BioIn 17
Chambers, Glenn Darrell 1936- WhoWor 93
Chambers, Gordon BioIn 17
Chambers, Gordon Anthony 1969- WhoE 93
Chambers, H. Richard Law&B 92
Chambers, Harry L. 1932- St&PR 93
Chambers, Henry Carroll 1928- WhoSSW 93
Chambers, Henry George 1956- WhoSSW 93
Chambers, Ian Gordon 1947- WhoUN 92
Chambers, Imogene Klutts 1928- WhoAmW 93, WhoSSW 93
Chambers, J.H.L., II 1927- St&PR 93
Chambers, J. Richard 1930- WhoE 93
Chambers, James Julius 1850-1920 JrnUS
Chambers, Jane 1937-1983 ScF&FL 92
Chambers, Jay Lee 1923- WhoSSW 93
Chambers, Jeffrey B. Law&B 92
Chambers, Jimmie Joe 1951- WhoEmL 93
Chambers, Joan Louise 1937- WhoAm 92
Chambers, John Darby 1939- WhoWrEP 92
Chambers, John Whiteclay, II 1936- ConAu 137
Chambers, Julius 1936- ConBlB 3 [port]
Chambers, Julius LeVonne 1936- WhoAm 92
Chambers, Katherine Tyson 1922- St&PR 93
Chambers, Kenneth Carter 1956- WhoWor 93
Chambers, Kenton Lee 1929- WhoAm 92
Chambers, Lawrence Cleveland 1929- AfrAmBi [port]
Chambers, Leigh Ross 1932- WhoAm 92
Chambers, Letitia Pearl Caroline 1943- WhoE 93
Chambers, Linda Dianne Thompson 1953- WhoAmW 93, WhoSSW 93, WhoWor 93
Chambers, Lois Irene 1935- WhoAmW 93
Chambers, Lon BioIn 17
Chambers, Marcus Rex 1943- WhoWor 93
Chambers, Marsi J. 1969- WhoAmW 93
Chambers, Martha Harrison 1952- WhoAmW 93
Chambers, Martin 1951- See Pretenders, The ConMus 8
Chambers, Mary Anne Beeman 1958- WhoE 93
Chambers, Maurice R. 1916-1990 BioIn 17
Chambers, Merle Catherine 1946- WhoAmW 93
Chambers, Michael Alan 1956- WhoSSW 93
Chambers, Nancy ScF&FL 92
Chambers, Patrick J. 1934- St&PR 93
Chambers, Patrick Joseph, Jr. 1934- WhoAm 92
Chambers, Paula Haver 1947- WhoAmW 93
Chambers, Randy K. 1950- St&PR 93
Chambers, Ray Wayne 1931- WhoSSW 93
Chambers, Richard Dickinson WhoScE 91-1
Chambers, Richard Everett 1931- St&PR 93
Chambers, Richard H. 1935- St&PR 93
Chambers, Richard Lee 1947- WhoAm 92, WhoSSW 93
Chambers, Robert BioIn 17, WhoSSW 93
Chambers, Robert 1802-1871 BioIn 17
Chambers, Robert Hunter, III 1939- WhoAm 92
Chambers, Robert Jeffferson 1930- WhoAm 92
Chambers, Robert W. 1865-1933 ScF&FL 92
Chambers, Robert William 1943- WhoSSW 93, WhoWor 93
Chambers, Robin 1942- ScF&FL 92
Chambers, Rufus A. Law&B 92
Chambers, Russell Raymond 1948- WhoEmL 93
Chambers, Sarah Hillstrom 1938- WhoAmW 93
Chambers, Sarah Jane 1957- WhoAmW 93
Chambers, Stephen A(lexander) Baker 92
Chambers, Stephen L.E. 1956- WhoWor 93
Chambers, Stephen N. 1954- St&PR 93
Chambers, Stephen P. Law&B 92
Chambers, Steven Michael 1960- WhoE 93
Chambers, Theodore D. Law&B 92
Chambers, Theodore D. 1931- St&PR 93
Chambers, Thomas Edward 1934- WhoSSW 93
Chambers, Thomas H. St&PR 93
Chambers, Thomas M. Law&B 92
Chambers, Thomas P. 1942- St&PR 93
Chambers, Tim WhoScE 91-1
Chambers, Tony Edward, Jr. 1951- WhoSSW 93
Chambers, Veronica BioIn 17
Chambers, Walter Ray, Jr. 1931- St&PR 93
Chambers, Whitman 1896-1968 ScF&FL 92
Chambers, Whittaker BioIn 17
Chambers, Whittaker 1901-1961 ColdWar 1 [port], PolPar
Chambers, William c. 1723-1796 BioIn 17
Chambers, William 1800-1883 BioIn 17
Chambers, William Dean Law&B 92
Chambers, William Eldridge 1931- WhoSSW 93
Chambers, William John 1946- St&PR 93
Chambers Family BioIn 17
Chamblee, Wendy Morie 1949- St&PR 93
Chambliss, Alvin BioIn 17
Chambliss, Carroll Christopher 1948- BiDAMSp 1989
Chambliss, Dana Franklin Law&B 92
Chambliss, Jac 1910- St&PR 93
Chambliss, John Davidson 1943- WhoAm 92
Chambliss, Leonard Perryman, Jr. 1949- WhoEmL 93
Chambliss, Linda Christine 1949- WhoEmL 93
Chambliss, William Joseph 1933- WhoAm 92
Chambon, Paul 1939- WhoScE 91-2
Chambon, Pierre BioIn 17
Chambon, Pierre 1931- WhoScE 91-2
Chambonnieres, Jacques Champion c. 1601-1672 Baker 92
Chambord, comte de 1820-1883 BioIn 17
Chambre, Paul L. 1918- WhoAm 92
Chambron, J.E.J. 1929- WhoScE 91-2
Chamby, Gilbert Charles 1930- WhoWor 93
Chamchoum, Georges 1946- MiSFD 9
Chamer, Ryszard 1942- WhoScE 91-4
Chametzky, Barry I. 1961- WhoE 93
Chamfort, Sebastien Roch Nicolas 1740?-1794 BioIn 17
Chaminade, Cecile 1857-1944 BioIn 17
Chaminade, Cecile (Louise Stephanie) 1857-1944 Baker 92
Chamisso, Adelbert von 1781-1838 BioIn 17
Chamlee, Kenneth D. 1952- WhoWrEP 92
Chamness, John Charles 1942- St&PR 93
Chamois, Charles c. 1610-c. 1684 BioIn 17
Chamorro, Carlos Fernando DcCPCAm
Chamorro, Jaime DcCPCAm
Chamorro, Violeta 1929- WhoWor 93
Chamorro, Violeta Barrios de BioIn 17, DcCPCAm
Chamorro, Violeta Barrios de 1929- ColdWar 2 [port]
Chamorro Barrios, Pedro Joaquin, Jr. DcCPCAm
Chamorro Cardenal, Jaime 1934- WhoWor 93
Chamorro Cardenal, Pedro Joaquin 1924-1978 DcCPCAm
Chamorro Cardenal, Xavier DcCPCAm
Chamorro Vargas, Emiliano 1871-1966 DcTwHis
Chamoun, Camille 1900-1987 DcTwHis
Chamoun, Camille Nimer 1900-1987 BioIn 17
Chamoun, Danty d1990 BioIn 17
Champ, Joseph C. 1929- St&PR 93
Champ, Norman B., Jr. 1928- St&PR 93
Champa, Armand BioIn 17
Champagne, Andree 1939- WhoAmW 93
Champagne, Betty June 1949- WhoEmL 93
Champagne, Catherine Margaret 1947- WhoSSW 93
Champagne, Charles F. 1941- St&PR 93
Champagne, Claude (Adonai) 1891-1965 Baker 92
Champagne, Claudia Maria 1956- WhoSSW 93
Champagne, George R. 1953- St&PR 93
Champagne, Guy B. 1928- St&PR 93
Champagne, John 1960- ConGAN
Champagne, John F., Jr. 1952- WhoAm 92
Champagne, Joseph Ernest 1938- WhoAm 92
Champagne, Oliver W.R. Law&B 92
Champagne, Romeo C. Law&B 92
Champagne, Ronald Oscar 1942- WhoAm 92
Champanhet, Francois 1954- WhoScE 91-2
Champe, Pamela Chambers 1945- WhoAmW 93
Champeau, Eugene J. St&PR 93
Champeaux, Junius Joseph, II 1939- WhoAm 92
Champein, Stanislas 1753-1830 Baker 92
Champetier, Yves 1936- WhoScE 91-2

Champfleury 1821-1889 DcLB 119 [port]
Champie, Channing K. ScF&FL 92
Champion, Eleanor D. 1935- St&PR 93
Champion, Elizabeth Hollis 1945- WhoWrEP 92
Champion, Gregg MiSFD 9
Champion, Hale 1922- WhoAm 92
Champion, Herman Daniel, Jr. 1942- WhoSSW 93
Champion, Jacques Baker 92
Champion, Larry Stephen 1932- WhoSSW 93
Champion, Marge 1923- WhoAm 92
Champion, Mary Ellen 1946- WhoEmL 93
Champion, Maxine C. St&PR 93
Champion, Maxine Christina WhoAm 92, WhoAmW 93
Champion, Nathan D. 1857-1892 BioIn 17
Champion, Norma Jean 1933- WhoAmW 93
Champion, Richard Gordon 1931- WhoAm 92
Champion, Robert N. 1933- St&PR 93
Champion, Ronald E. Law&B 92
Champion, Walter Thomas, Jr. 1950- WhoEmL 93
Champion, William J., III Law&B 92
Champion, Wm. David, Jr. 1947- St&PR 93
Championnet, Jean Antoine Etienne 1762-1800 HarEnMi
Champlain, Samuel de c. 1567-1635 HarEnMi
Champlain, Samuel de 1570?-1635 Expl 93 [port]
Champlin, Charles Davenport 1926- WhoAm 92, WhoWrEP 92
Champlin, Edward James 1948- WhoAm 92
Champlin, George Charles 1938- St&PR 93
Champlin, Herbert Alvin 1933- St&PR 93
Champlin, Malcolm McGregor 1911- WhoAm 92
Champlin, Marjorie Weeden 1921- WhoAmW 93
Champlin, Richard H. 1935- St&PR 93, WhoAm 92
Champlin, Rolland S. 1951- St&PR 93
Champlin, Sheila Ann 1946- WhoWrEP 92
Champlin, William Glen 1923- WhoSSW 93
Champnella, Frederic E. Law&B 92
Champney, Margaret AmWomPl
Champney, Paul Arthur 1942- St&PR 93
Champney, Raymond Joseph 1940- WhoSSW 93
Champollion, Jean Francois 1790-1832 BioIn 17
Champourcin, Ernestina de 1905- DcMexL
Champoux, David Harold 1948- WhoE 93
Champy, Maxime O. 1926- WhoScE 91-2
Chamson, Sandra Potkorony 1933- WhoAm 92, WhoAmW 93
Chan, Andrew Mancheong 1957- WhoWor 93
Chan, Anson 1940- WhoAsAP 91
Chan, Benny 1948- St&PR 93
Chan, Bernard Charnwut 1965- WhoWor 93
Chan, Carlyle Hung-lun 1949- WhoEmL 93
Chan, Clara Suet-Phang 1949- WhoE 93, WhoEmL 93
Chan, Curtis Joseph 1953- WhoEmL 93
Chan, D.Y. Law&B 92
Chan, Daniel Chung-Yin 1948- WhoEmL 93
Chan, David K. Law&B 92
Chan, Don A. 1944- St&PR 93
Chan, Donald Pin-Kwan 1937- WhoE 93
Chan, Dwight Kung-Sang 1934- WhoWor 93
Chan, Eddy S.F. 1947- St&PR 93
Chan, Eric Ping-Pang 1952- WhoE 93
Chan, F. Alfonso 1944- WhoUN 92
Chan, George Tze Chung 1952- WhoWor 93
Chan, Gloria So WhoWor 93
Chan, Jack-Kang 1950- WhoE 93
Chan, Jackie 1954- IntDcF 2-3, MiSFD 9
Chan, Jane 1949- WhoAmW 93
Chan, Joan Kawada 1948- WhoAmW 93
Chan, John St&PR 93
Chan, Johnny Kwongchai 1950- WhoEmL 93
Chan, Julius 1939- WhoAsAP 91
Chan, Ka Ku 1935- WhoWor 93
Chan, Lai Kow WhoAm 92
Chan, Lo-Yi Cheung Yuen 1932- WhoAm 92
Chan, Lois Mai 1934- BioIn 17
Chan, Man Hung 1949- WhoWor 93
Chan, Marie Yee 1956- WhoEmL 93
Chan, Michael Chiu-Hon 1961- WhoWor 93
Chan, Ming Kong 1937- WhoWor 93
Chan, Patricia Ping 1953- St&PR 93
Chan, Peter Wing Kwong 1949- WhoEmL 93
Chan, Raymond Honfu 1958- WhoWor 93
Chan, Raymond T. 1955- St&PR 93
Chan, Samuel Kwok Ming 1957- St&PR 93
Chan, Shih Hung 1943- WhoAm 92
Chan, Shu-Park 1929- WhoAm 92
Chan, Simon M.H. 1954- St&PR 93
Chan, Siu 1962- WhoAmW 93
Chan, Steven K.S. 1941- WhoE 93
Chan, Steven Roderick 1959- WhoEmL 93
Chan, Sunney Ignatius 1936- WhoAm 92
Chan, Susan Grace 1958- WhoAmW 93
Chan, Tak-Biu 1961- WhoWor 93
Chan, Tak Hang 1941- WhoAm 92
Chan, Tony Chi-Hung 1954- WhoEmL 93
Chan, W. Y. 1932- WhoAm 92
Chan, Wan Choon 1937- WhoWor 93
Chan, Wing-Chi 1952- WhoE 93
Chan, Wing Ming 1954- WhoWor 93
Chan, Yeon-Hong Hendrick 1955 WhoWor 93
Chan, Yeuk Man Benjamin 1938- WhoWor 93
Chana, Thomas J. 1947- St&PR 93
Chanady, Amaryll Beatrice 1954- ScF&FL 92
Chanak, Adam George Steven 1954- WhoEmL 93
Chanard, Jacques Michel 1939- WhoScE 91-2
Chanatry, Francis WhoE 93
Chance, Britton 1913- WhoAm 92
Chance, Charles 1936- WhoIns 93
Chance, Chris BioIn 17
Chance, Henry Martyn, II 1912- WhoAm 92
Chance, Jane 1945- WhoSSW 93, WhoWrEP 92
Chance, Janet 1885-1953 BioIn 17
Chance, John Newton ScF&FL 92
Chance, Kenneth Bernard 1953- WhoEmL 93
Chance, M. Sue 1942- WhoWrEP 92
Chance, Nancy 1953- WhoAmW 93
Chance, Nolan 1939- BioIn 17
Chance, Paul Bradley 1941- WhoE 93
Chance, Randal Wayne 1950- WhoAm 92
Chance, Steven K. Law&B 92
Chancellor, Ann Laymon ScF&FL 92
Chancellor, Glenn A. 1937- St&PR 93
Chancellor, John 1927- JrnUS
Chancellor, John William 1927- WhoAm 92, WhoE 93
Chancellor, Richard d1556 Expl 93
Chancellor, Rose Ann 1955- WhoAmW 93
Chancellor, William Joseph 1931- WhoAm 92
Chancey, Charles Clifton, III 1955- WhoEmL 93
Chancey, Malcolm Brant 1931- St&PR 93
Chan Choong Tak WhoAsAP 91
Chanco, Maria A. Law&B 92
Chand, Karam 1934- WhoUN 92
Chandek, Lisa M. Law&B 92
Chandelle, Victor J.M. 1933- WhoScE 91-2
Chandio, Bashir Ahmed 1943- WhoWor 93
Chandler, A.B. 1898- PolPar
Chandler, A.B. 1898-1991 AnObit 1991
Chandler, A. Bertram 1912-1984 ScF&FL 92
Chandler, A. Lee 1922- WhoAm 92, WhoSSW 93
Chandler, Albert Benjamin 1898-1991 BioIn 17
Chandler, Alfred Dupont BioIn 17
Chandler, Alfred Dupont, Jr. 1918- WhoAm 92, WhoWor 93
Chandler, Alice 1931- WhoAmW 93
Chandler, Allen E. 1935- AfrAmBi [port]
Chandler, Arthur Bleakley 1926- WhoAm 92
Chandler, Bruce Frederick 1926- WhoWor 93
Chandler, Brue Stanhope, III 1949- WhoSSW 93
Chandler, Bryn 1945- ScF&FL 92
Chandler, Chan 1960- WhoEmL 93
Chandler, Charles Quarles 1926- St&PR 93, WhoAm 92
Chandler, Collis Paul, Jr. 1926- St&PR 93
Chandler, Danny Ricardo 1962- WhoSSW 93
Chandler, David 1944- WhoAm 92
Chandler, David Leon 1937?- ConAu 38NR
Chandler, David Lewis 1926- St&PR 93
Chandler, Dorothy Buffum WhoAmW 93
Chandler, Doug BioIn 17
Chandler, Douglas 1889- BioIn 17
Chandler, E.G. 1905- St&PR 93
Chandler, Edward William 1953- WhoEmL 93
Chandler, Edwin Russell 1932- WhoAm 92
Chandler, Elisabeth Gordon 1913- WhoAm 92, WhoAmW 93, WhoE 93, WhoWor 93
Chandler, Gene 1937- BioIn 17, SoulM
Chandler, George N., II 1938- St&PR 93
Chandler, George P. Law&B 92
Chandler, Glenn ScF&FL 92
Chandler, Happy 1898-1991 BioIn 17
Chandler, Harry 1864-1944 JrnUS
Chandler, Harry Edgar 1920- WhoAm 92
Chandler, Herbert Gray 1925- St&PR 93
Chandler, Hubert Thomas 1933- WhoAm 92
Chandler, Ira Ansel 1953- WhoSSW 93
Chandler, J. Malloy 1946- St&PR 93
Chandler, James Barton 1922- WhoWor 93
Chandler, James Harry, III 1950- WhoSSW 93
Chandler, James John 1932- WhoAm 92
Chandler, James Kenneth 1948- WhoAm 92
Chandler, James Williams 1904- WhoAm 92
Chandler, John 1762-1841 HarEnMi
Chandler, John, Jr. 1920- WhoAm 92
Chandler, John Brandon, Jr. 1939- WhoSSW 93, WhoWor 93
Chandler, John Herrick 1928- WhoAm 92
Chandler, John T. 1932- St&PR 93
Chandler, John Turbeville 1932- WhoSSW 93
Chandler, John Wesley 1923- WhoAm 92
Chandler, Joseph Ripley 1792-1880 JrnUS
Chandler, Judith Anne 1948- WhoEmL 93
Chandler, Julia AmWomPl
Chandler, Katherine M. Law&B 92
Chandler, Kathleen Leone 1932- WhoAmW 93
Chandler, Katrina Pipkins 1955- WhoAmW 93, WhoEmL 93
Chandler, Kay WhoWrEP 92
Chandler, Kenneth A. 1947- WhoAm 92, WhoE 93
Chandler, Kenneth Ashton 1921- WhoE 93
Chandler, Kent, Jr. 1920- WhoAm 92
Chandler, Lana Jean 1954- WhoEmL 93
Chandler, Larry C. 1939- St&PR 93
Chandler, Larry Donald 1948- WhoEmL 93
Chandler, Laurel ScF&FL 92
Chandler, Lawrence Bradford, Jr. 1942- WhoSSW 93, WhoWor 93
Chandler, Leroy 1918- St&PR 93
Chandler, Lewis P., Jr. Law&B 92
Chandler, Lilian F. AmWomPl
Chandler, Linda Hoffner 1947- St&PR 93
Chandler, Linda S(mith) 1929- WhoWrEP 92
Chandler, Marcia Shaw Barnard 1934- WhoAmW 93
Chandler, Margaret 1961- WhoAmW 93
Chandler, Margaret K. 1922-1991 BioIn 17
Chandler, Marguerite Nella 1943- WhoAm 92
Chandler, Marlene Merritt 1949- WhoAmW 93
Chandler, Mary Hsu-Chi Huang 1956- WhoSSW 93
Chandler, Michael David 1959- WhoEmL 93
Chandler, Norbert Francis Law&B 92
Chandler, Norman 1899-1973 DcLB 127 [port]
Chandler, Otis 1927- DcLB 127 [port], JrnUS, St&PR 93, WhoAm 92
Chandler, P. WhoScE 91-1
Chandler, Paul 1921- St&PR 93
Chandler, Paul Anderson 1933- WhoSSW 93
Chandler, Philip 1908- BioIn 17
Chandler, Rachel Eden 1941- WhoE 93
Chandler, Raymond 1888-1959 BioIn 17, MagSAmL [port]
Chandler, Richard H. 1943- St&PR 93
Chandler, Richard Hill 1943- WhoAm 92
Chandler, Richard William 1950- WhoEmL 93
Chandler, Robert Flint, Jr. 1907- WhoAm 92, WhoWor 93
Chandler, Robert Leslie 1948- WhoE 93
Chandler, Rod 1942- CngDr 91
Chandler, Rod Dennis 1942- WhoAm 92
Chandler, Ronald Jay 1949- WhoEmL 93
Chandler, Sadie Arnette 1933- WhoSSW 93
Chandler, Stephen L. 1926- WhoAm 92
Chandler, Theodore Lindy, Jr. 1952- WhoEmL 93
Chandler, Thomas 1954- WhoEmL 93
Chandler, Wallace L. 1926- St&PR 93
Chandler, William Eaton 1835-1917 BioIn 17, JrnUS
Chandler, William Everett 1943- WhoAm 92
Chandler, William H. 1878-1970 BioIn 17
Chandler, William Knox 1933- WhoAm 92
Chandler, Zachariah 1813-1879 BioIn 17, PolPar
Chandley, Ann Chester 1936- WhoWor 93
Chandon, Jean-Louis 1945- WhoWor 93
Chandonnet, Ann Fox 1943- WhoWrEP 92
Chandonnet, Christopher Henry 1961- WhoE 93
Chandonnet, Noel Andrew 1933- St&PR 93
Chandor, Karen Kayser 1950- WhoAmW 93
Chandor, Stebbins Bryant 1933- WhoAm 92
Chandra, Bernard Harish 1944- WhoUN 92
Chandra, Hermanto 1959- WhoWor 93
Chandra, Muralee Nair 1957- WhoWor 93
Chandra, Pankaj Raj 1951- WhoEmL 93, WhoSSW 93
Chandra, Pramod 1930 WhoAm 92
Chandra, Smita 1960- ConAu 138
Chandragupta Maurya d286BC HarEnMi
Chandrani, Prem Kumar Swamidas 1954- WhoWor 93
Chandrasekaran, Balakrishnan 1942- WhoAm 92
Chandrasekaran, Perinkolam Raman 1949- WhoEmL 93, WhoSSW 93
Chandrasekhar, Bellur Sivaramiah 1928- WhoAm 92
Chandrasekhar, Maragatham 1917- WhoAsAP 91
Chandrasekhar, S. WhoScE 91-1
Chandrasekhar, Subrahmanyan 1910- BioIn 17, WhoAm 92, WhoWor 93
Chandra Shekhar, N.L. 1927- WhoAsAP 91
Chandrashekharappa, T.V. 1934- WhoAsAP 91
Chandrasiri Athula, Liyanahetti Ralalage 1942- WhoWor 93
Chandrawati 1928- WhoAsAP 91
Chandy, Kanianthra Mani 1944- WhoAm 92
Chane, George Warren 1910- WhoAm 92
Chanel, Coco 1883-1971 BioIn 17
Chanel, Gabrielle 1883-1971 BioIn 17
Chanen, Jeanne Young 1954- WhoEmL 93
Chanen, Steven Robert 1953- WhoEmL 93, WhoWor 93
Chaney, Courtland Merlyn 1952- WhoSSW 93
Chaney, Don Ray 1937- WhoSSW 93
Chaney, Frederick Michael 1941- WhoAsAP 91
Chaney, James Earl 1943-1964 EncAACR
Chaney, Jean d1991 BioIn 17
Chaney, John BioIn 17
Chaney, John 1932- BiDAMSp 1989
Chaney, John Douglas 1950- WhoEmL 93
Chaney, Ken d1991 BioIn 17
Chaney, Kimberly F. Law&B 92
Chaney, Lon 1883-1930 BioIn 17, IntDcF 2-3 [port]
Chaney, Lon 1906-1973 BioIn 17
Chaney, Martha King 1958- WhoSSW 93
Chaney, Michael Eugene 1935- St&PR 93
Chaney, Michael Thomas 1948- WhoEmL 93
Chaney, Patrice Watson 1953- WhoEmL 93
Chaney, Peggy Velena 1955- WhoWrEP 92
Chaney, Robert J. 1942- St&PR 93
Chaney, Robert Wayne 1947- WhoEmL 93
Chaney, Roy Gene 1947- WhoEmL 93
Chaney, Stephen Gifford 1944- WhoSSW 93
Chaney, Verne Edward, Jr. 1923- WhoAm 92
Chaney, Vincent V. 1913- St&PR 93
Chaney, William Calvin 1952- WhoEmL 93
Chaney, William R. 1932- St&PR 93, WhoE 93
Chanezon, Robert Edouard 1941- WhoWor 93
Chang, Arnold BioIn 17
Chang, Arnold 1954- WhoE 93
Chang, Bianca 1939- WhoE 93
Chang, Caroline Jane 1940- WhoAmW 93
Chang, Charles Shing 1940- WhoWor 93
Chang, Che Tyan 1921- WhoWor 93
Chang, Chia-Lin 1959- WhoE 93, WhoEmL 93
Chang, Chieh 1937- BioIn 17
Chang, Chun 1889-1990 BioIn 17
Chang, Chun-hsing 1927- WhoWor 93
Chang, Chun-Yen 1937- WhoWor 93

Chang, Clarence Dayton 1933- *WhoAm 92*
Chang, Clement 1929- *WhoAsAP 91*
Chang, Craig 1943- *St&PR 93*
Chang, Darwin Ray 1917- *WhoWor 93*
Chang, David Ping-Chung 1929- *St&PR 93, WhoAm 92*
Chang, Deborah S. 1960- *WhoAmW 93*
Chang, Deborah Sook 1960- *WhoEmL 93*
Chang, Ernest Sun-Mei 1950- *WhoEmL 93*
Chang, Feng-chih O. 1941- *WhoWor 93*
Chang, Gary 1953- *ConTFT 10*
Chang, Harry 1916- *St&PR 93*
Chang, Henry Chung-Lien 1941- *WhoAm 92*
Chang, Holly C. *Law&B 92*
Chang, HongJen 1956- *WhoWor 93*
Chang, Hsien-liang 1936- *BioIn 17*
Chang, Hsueh-liang *BioIn 17*
Chang, Iris J. 1935- *St&PR 93*
Chang, Jack Che-man 1941- *WhoAm 92*
Chang, Janice May 1970- *WhoWrEP 92*
Chang, Jason 1942- *WhoWor 93*
Chang, Jenny Wong 1966- *WhoAmW 93*
Chang, Jian Cherng 1939- *WhoWor 93*
Chang, Jim C. I. 1939- *WhoE 93*
Chang, Jo-Anne Marguerite 1960- *St&PR 93*
Chang, John K. 1929- *St&PR 93*
Chang, Joseph Yoon 1952- *WhoE 93*
Chang, Juan-Yuan David 1954- *WhoSSW 93*
Chang, JuJu *BioIn 17*
Chang, Jung 1952- *ConLC 71 [port]*
Chang, K.H. 1945- *WhoScE 91-3*
Chang, Ki-Hong 1934- *WhoWor 93*
Chang, Kwang-Chih 1931- *WhoAm 92*
Chang, Lee 1925- *WhoWor 93*
Chang, Leroy L. 1936- *WhoAm 92*
Chang, Lihchung Patrick 1956- *WhoWor 93*
Chang, Linda Li 1956- *WhoAmW 93*
Chang, Ling Wei 1960- *WhoAmW 93, WhoE 93, WhoEmL 93*
Chang, M.C. 1908-1991 *BioIn 17*
Chang, Margaret (Scrogin) 1941- *SmATA 71 [port]*
Chang, Michael *BioIn 17*
Chang, Michael 1972- *WhoAm 92*
Chang, Min-Chueh 1908-1991 *AnObit 1991, BioIn 17*
Chang, Nat C. *Law&B 92*
Chang, Nelson 1923- *WhoWor 93*
Chang, Nelson Chiuan 1950- *WhoEmL 93*
Chang, Parris Hsu-cheng 1936- *WhoAm 92*
Chang, Patricia Davis 1945- *WhoAm 92, WhoAmW 93*
Chang, Paul Keuk 1913- *WhoE 93*
Chang, Peter 1953- *WhoSSW 93*
Chang, Peter Hon 1941- *St&PR 93*
Chang, Raymond *SmATA 71 [port]*
Chang, Raymond 1955- *St&PR 93*
Chang, Richard Kounai 1940- *WhoE 93*
Chang, Robert Huei 1932- *WhoAm 92*
Chang, Robert Timothy 1958- *WhoAm 92, WhoEmL 93*
Chang, Robin 1951- *St&PR 93, WhoAm 92*
Chang, Rodney Eiu Joon 1945- *WhoWor 93*
Chang, Ronald Chiu Mun 1965- *WhoEmL 93*
Chang, Sheldon Shou Lien 1920- *WhoAm 92*
Chang, Shi-Kuo 1944- *ScF&FL 92, WhoAm 92*
Chang, Shih-Lin 1946- *WhoWor 93*
Chang, Stephen S. 1918- *WhoAm 92*
Chang, Sylvia Tan 1940- *WhoAmW 93*
Chang, Ta-kuang 1955- *WhoEmL 93*
Chang, Tai-Lin 1955- *WhoWor 93*
Chang, Thomas Ming Swi 1933- *WhoAm 92*
Chang, Tsu-Chung 1957- *WhoWor 93*
Chang, Tyrus K.L. 1943- *St&PR 93*
Chang, Weilin Parrish 1947- *WhoAm 92, WhoEmL 93, WhoSSW 93*
Chang, William Shen Chie 1931- *WhoAm 92*
Chang, Winston Wen-tsuen 1939- *WhoE 93*
Chang, Y. Austin *WhoAm 92*
Chang, Yau-Fung Olivia 1963- *WhoEmL 93*
Chang, Yen F. 1949- *St&PR 93*
Chang, Yi-Cheng 1943- *WhoWor 93*
Chang, Yuan 1934- *St&PR 93*
Chang, Yuan-Feng 1928- *WhoAm 92*
Chang Ch'ien d114BC *HarEnMi*
Chang Ch'ien 160?BC-107BC *Expl 93*
Chang Chien-Han 1928- *WhoAsAP 91*
Chang Ching c. 1490-1555 *HarEnMi*
Change *SoulM*
Changeux, Jean-Pierre 1936- *WhoScE 91-2*
Chang Fa-k'uei 1896- *HarEnMi*
Chang Han d207BC *HarEnMi*
Chang-Ho, Bae 1953- *MiSFD 9*
Chang Hsiao-Yen 1941- *WhoAsAP 91*
Chang Hsien-chung 1606-1647 *HarEnMi*
Chang Hsueh-liang 1898- *DcTwHis, HarEnMi*
Chang Hsun 1854-1923 *HarEnMi*
Chang Kyung Woo 1943- *WhoAsAP 91*
Chang-Li, Belle Hsun Ling 1953- *WhoAmW 93*
Chang Lo-hsing d1863 *HarEnMi*
Chang-Mota, Roberto 1935- *WhoWor 93*
Chang Po-Ya 1942- *WhoAsAP 91*
Chang-Rodriguez, Eugenio *WhoWrEP 92*
Chang Shih-ch'eng d1367 *HarEnMi*
Chang Shih-chieh d1279 *HarEnMi*
Chang Suk Wah 1947- *WhoAsAP 91*
Chang Tso-lin 1873-1928 *HarEnMi*
Chang Tsung-ch'ang 1881-1933 *HarEnMi*
Chang Yung Chul 1937- *WhoAsAP 91*
Chanin, Jeffrey T. *Law&B 92*
Chanin, Michael Henry 1943- *WhoAm 92*
Chan Keller, Lilian Man-Yim 1957- *WhoWor 93*
Chanko, Mark S. 1928- *St&PR 93*
Chanler, Margaret 1862-1952 *BioIn 17*
Chanler, Theodore Ward 1902-1961 *Baker 92*
Channel, A.R. *ConAu 38NR, MajAI*
Channell, Carl *BioIn 17*
Channell, Kathy Kopp 1963- *WhoAmW 93*
Channen, S.E. *Law&B 92*
Channer, David A. *Law&B 92*
Channer, Stephen Dyer Stanton 1933- *WhoWor 93*
Channick, Herbert S. 1929- *WhoAm 92*
Channing, Alan Harold 1945- *WhoAm 92*
Channing, Carol 1923- *WhoAm 92, WhoAmW 93*
Channing, Joel *BioIn 17*
Channing, Mark 1879- *ScF&FL 92*
Channing, Stockard *BioIn 17, WhoAm 92*
Channing, Walter *St&PR 93*
Chano, Fouad Georges 1947- *WhoWor 93*
Chanoff, David 1943- *ConAu 138*
Chanoski, Norman Walter 1934- *St&PR 93*
Chanot, Francois 1788-1825 *Baker 92*
Chansky, Norman Morton 1929- *WhoWrEP 92*
Chansler, Jeffrey D. *Law&B 92*
Chant, Davis Ryan 1938- *WhoE 93*
Chant, Dixon S. *WhoAm 92, WhoE 93*
Chant, Dixon S. 1913- *St&PR 93*
Chant, Joy 1945- *ScF&FL 92*
Chantavoine, Jean (Francois Henri) 1877-1952 *Baker 92*
Chantegrelet, Guy 1937- *WhoScE 91-2*
Chantelois, Steve *Law&B 92*
Chantels *SoulM*
Chantereau, J.-C. *WhoScE 91-2*
Chantler, Alan Edwin *WhoScE 91-1*
Chantler, Cyril *WhoScE 91-1*
Chantraine, Alex 1930- *WhoScE 91-4*
Chantres, Gerald Robert 1942- *St&PR 93*
Chantry, Elizabeth Ann 1956- *WhoAmW 93*
Chanussot, Guy 1943- *WhoWor 93*
Chan Wa-Shek 1930- *WhoAsAP 91*
Chany, Charles 1920- *WhoScE 91-2, WhoWor 93*
Chan Yin-Lun 1950- *WhoAsAP 91*
Chao, Bei Tse 1918- *WhoAm 92*
Chao, Cecil *BioIn 17*
Chao, Chih Hsu 1939- *WhoAm 92*
Chao, Chong-Yun 1930- *WhoAm 92*
Chao, Dorothy Chung *Law&B 92*
Chao, Elaine L. *WhoAm 92, WhoAmW 93, WhoE 93*
Chao, James Min-Tzu 1940- *WhoWor 93*
Chao, Jung 1899-1975 *BioIn 17*
Chao, Koung-An 1940- *WhoWor 93*
Chao, Marshall S. 1924- *WhoAm 92*
Chao, Xiuli 1964- *WhoE 93*
Chao, Yuh Jin 1953- *WhoSSW 93*
Chao Chin-Chi 1927- *WhoAsAP 91*
Chao Ch'un fl. c. 1206- *HarEnMi*
Chao Ch'ung kuo 137BC-52BC *HarEnMi*
Chao Hsin fl. c. 123BC- *HarEnMi*
Chao P'o-nu fl. c. 108BC-100BC *HarEnMi*
Chao Shou-Po 1941- *WhoAsAP 91*
Chao T'o dc. 167 *HarEnMi*
Chaoui, Nabil Michel 1950- *WhoEmL 93*
Chap, Hugues *WhoScE 91-2*
Chapa, Elia Kay 1960- *WhoSSW 93*
Chapaa, Kahuuku Karuhanga 1952- *WhoWor 93*
Chapagain, Kirti Raman Bimal 1949- *WhoWor 93*
Chapanis, Alphonse 1917- *WhoAm 92, WhoWor 93*
Chapdelaine, Henri Joseph 1934- *WhoWrEP 92*
Chapdelaine, Perry A. 1925- *ScF&FL 92*
Chapekis, Fred A. 1925- *St&PR 93*
Chapel, Alain 1937-1990 *BioIn 17*
Chapel, Burdette Alan 1941- *St&PR 93*
Chapel, Theron Theodore 1918- *WhoSSW 93*
Chapell, Harry F. 1929- *St&PR 93*
Chapelle, Claire Daniel 1949- *WhoE 93*
Chapelle, Dickey d1965 *BioIn 17*
Chapelle, Pierre 1940- *WhoScE 91-2*
Chapelle, Rene Adrien 1933- *WhoAm 92*
Chapelle, Susan Catherine 1918- *WhoAmW 93*
Chapello, Craig Alan 1956- *WhoEmL 93*
Chapello, Margaret E. *Law&B 92*
Chapeville, Francois 1924- *WhoScE 91-2*
Chapi, Ruperto 1851-1909 *OxDcOp*
Chapi (y Lorente), Ruperto 1851-1909 *Baker 92*
Chapian, Grieg Hovsep 1913- *WhoAm 92*
Chapin, Anna Alice 1880-1920 *AmWomPl*
Chapin, Carolyn Ellen 1934- *WhoAmW 93*
Chapin, Daphne Heath 1935- *WhoE 93*
Chapin, David Chester 1954- *WhoEmL 93*
Chapin, Deborah A. *Law&B 92*
Chapin, Diana Derby 1942- *WhoE 93*
Chapin, Douglas Scott 1922- *WhoE 93*
Chapin, Dwight Allan 1938- *WhoAm 92*
Chapin, Edward W. *Law&B 92*
Chapin, Edward William 1908- *WhoAm 92*
Chapin, Elizabeth Little *AmWomPl*
Chapin, Elliott Lowell 1917- *WhoAm 92*
Chapin, H.N. 1904- *St&PR 93*
Chapin, Harry 1942-1981 *Baker 92*
Chapin, Horace Beecher 1917- *WhoWor 93*
Chapin, Hugh A. 1925- *WhoAm 92*
Chapin, James W. *Law&B 92*
Chapin, Julie K. *Law&B 92*
Chapin, Katherine Garrison 1890-1977 *AmWomPl*
Chapin, Linda Mari 1949- *WhoEmL 93*
Chapin, Lloyd Walter 1937- *WhoSSW 93*
Chapin, Mary Real 1953- *WhoEmL 93*
Chapin, Melville 1918- *St&PR 93, WhoAm 92*
Chapin, R.C. *AmWomPl*
Chapin, Ralph Baldwin 1915- *St&PR 93*
Chapin, Richard 1923- *WhoAm 92*
Chapin, Richard Earl 1925- *WhoAm 92*
Chapin, Roy D., Jr. 1915- *St&PR 93*
Chapin, Roy Dikeman, Jr. 1915- *WhoAm 92*
Chapin, Schuyler G(arrison) 1923- *Baker 92*
Chapin, Schuyler Garrison 1923- *WhoAm 92*
Chapin, Suzanne Phillips 1930- *WhoAm 92, WhoAmW 93, WhoE 93*
Chapin, William S. d1992 *NewYTBS 92 [port]*
Chapiro, Adolphe 1924- *WhoScE 91-2, WhoWor 93*
Chapis, Richard Michael 1943- *St&PR 93*
Chapleo, Adrian Q. *WhoScE 91-1*
Chapleo, Christopher Bourne 1947- *WhoScE 91-1*
Chapley, Nicholas Richard *St&PR 93*
Chaplin, Alice Louise Williams 1887- *AmWomPl*
Chaplin, Ansel Burt 1931- *WhoAm 92, WhoWor 93*
Chaplin, Charles 1889-1977 *MiSFD 9N*
Chaplin, Charlie 1889-1977 *BioIn 17, QDrFCA 92 [port]*
Chaplin, D. Edward 1938- *St&PR 93*
Chaplin, Dora P. d1990 *BioIn 17*
Chaplin, George 1914- *WhoAm 92*
Chaplin, Geraldine 1944- *IntDcF 2-3 [port], WhoAm 92*
Chaplin, Gervase Michael 1936- *St&PR 93, WhoSSW 93*
Chaplin, Herbert S. 1935- *St&PR 93*
Chaplin, Hugh, Jr. 1923- *WhoAm 92*
Chaplin, James Crossan, IV 1933- *WhoAm 92*
Chaplin, John Reginald *WhoScE 91-1*
Chaplin, L(inda) Tarin 1941- *ConAu 40NR*
Chaplin, Lorelei Marie 1954- *WhoEmL 93*
Chaplin, Mark H. 1955- *St&PR 93*
Chaplin, Mark Harlan 1955- *WhoEmL 93*
Chaplin, Mary Ann 1946- *WhoEmL 93*
Chaplin, Oona *BioIn 17*
Chaplin, Oona 1926-1991 *AnObit 1991*
Chaplin, Patrice 1940- *ScF&FL 92*
Chaplin, Robert L. 1930- *St&PR 93*
Chaplin, Sid(ney) 1916-1986 *ConAu 39NR*
Chapline, Ed S. *Law&B 92*
Chaplinski, Stan 1946- *St&PR 93*
Chapman, Alan Jesse 1925- *WhoAm 92*
Chapman, Alfred George, Jr. 1962- *WhoEmL 93*
Chapman, Alger B. 1931- *St&PR 93*
Chapman, Alice Eudora *AmWomPl*
Chapman, Allen Floyd 1930- *WhoE 93, WhoWor 93*
Chapman, Alvah H., Jr. 1921- *St&PR 93*
Chapman, Alvah Herman, Jr. 1921- *WhoAm 92, WhoSSW 93*
Chapman, Andrea 1963- *WhoSSW 93*
Chapman, Andrew 1960- *ScF&FL 92*
Chapman, Antony John *WhoScE 91-1*
Chapman, Antony John 1947- *WhoWor 93*
Chapman, Barbara Della 1952- *WhoEmL 93*
Chapman, Barbara Ellen 1954- *WhoAmW 93*
Chapman, Bernard 1921- *St&PR 93*
Chapman, Brett Robert *Law&B 92*
Chapman, C. Alan 1949- *WhoIns 93*
Chapman, C. Joe 1923- *St&PR 93*
Chapman, Carl Haley 1915-1987 *BioIn 17*
Chapman, Carleton Burke 1915- *WhoAm 92*
Chapman, Carol S. 1956- *WhoSSW 93*
Chapman, Caroline 1818-1876 *BioIn 17*
Chapman, Carolyn 1942- *WhoAmW 93, WhoWor 93*
Chapman, Charles Alan *Law&B 92*
Chapman, Charles Alan 1949- *WhoEmL 93*
Chapman, Charlotte Gower 1902-1982 *IntDcAn*
Chapman, Christine Rose 1957- *WhoWor 93*
Chapman, Christopher Baker *WhoScE 91-1*
Chapman, Christopher Eric 1942- *WhoWor 93*
Chapman, Cindy Lorraine Farr 1952- *WhoWrEP 92*
Chapman, Claire *AmWomPl*
Chapman, Clara Fellows 1944- *WhoE 93*
Chapman, Clodagh 1923- *ScF&FL 92*
Chapman, Conrad Daniel 1933- *St&PR 93*
Chapman, Constance Ann 1935- *WhoWrEP 92*
Chapman, Craig Bruce 1958- *WhoEmL 93, WhoSSW 93*
Chapman, D.D. *ScF&FL 92*
Chapman, David F. 1931- *St&PR 93*
Chapman, David John *WhoScE 91-1*
Chapman, David Lane 1945- *WhoSSW 93*
Chapman, David Lee, II 1943- *St&PR 93*
Chapman, Dennis *WhoScE 91-1*
Chapman, Donald D. 1917- *WhoAm 92*
Chapman, Douglas K. 1928- *St&PR 93*
Chapman, Douglas Kenneth 1928- *WhoAm 92*
Chapman, Edgar L. 1936- *ScF&FL 92*
Chapman, Edward L. 1948- *St&PR 93*
Chapman, Edward William 1925- *WhoAm 92, WhoWor 93*
Chapman, Edwin Karl 1932- *St&PR 93*
Chapman, Ernest F. *Law&B 92*
Chapman, Frederick John 1939- *WhoAm 92*
Chapman, G. Arnold 1917- *WhoAm 92*
Chapman, Gary Ronald 1944- *BioIn 17*
Chapman, George 1559?-1634 *DcLB 121 [port]*
Chapman, George Bunker 1925- *WhoE 93*
Chapman, Gerald T. 1942- *St&PR 93*
Chapman, Gilbert W., Jr. 1933- *WhoAm 92*
Chapman, Graham *BioIn 17*
Chapman, Graham Peter *WhoScE 91-1*
Chapman, Grosvenor 1911- *WhoAm 92*
Chapman, Harry Carrol 1930- *St&PR 93*
Chapman, Hedley Grant Pearson 1949- *WhoAsAP 91*
Chapman, Hedy Luise 1949- *WhoAmW 93*
Chapman, Heidi Goldenberg 1953- *WhoEmL 93*
Chapman, Hope Horan 1954- *WhoAmW 93*
Chapman, Howard Kramer 1918- *St&PR 93*
Chapman, Howard S. *Law&B 92*
Chapman, Howard Stuart 1941- *WhoAm 92*
Chapman, Hugh McMaster 1932- *St&PR 93, WhoAm 92*
Chapman, Irwin *WhoWrEP 92*
Chapman, James Claude 1931- *St&PR 93, WhoAm 92*
Chapman, James Edward 1927- *WhoAm 92*
Chapman, James L. 1945- *WhoAm 92, WhoSSW 93*
Chapman, James L. 1949- *St&PR 93*
Chapman, Janet Carter Goodrich 1922- *WhoAm 92, WhoAmW 93*
Chapman, Jean *DcChlFi*
Chapman, Jeff Crawford 1940- *WhoSSW 93*
Chapman, Jim 1945- *CngDr 91*
Chapman, John 1822-1894 *BioIn 17*
Chapman, John 1947- *ScF&FL 92*
Chapman, John Adkinson 1940- *WhoE 93*
Chapman, John Andrew 1928- *WhoSSW 93*
Chapman, John Arthur 1933- *WhoAm 92*
Chapman, John B. *Law&B 92*
Chapman, John Davol 1934- *WhoAm 92*
Chapman, John Edmon 1931- *WhoAm 92*

Chapman, John Forrest d1991 *BioIn 17*
Chapman, John Haven 1943- *WhoE 93*
Chapman, John M. 1945- *WhoScE 91-2*
Chapman, John N. *WhoScE 91-1*
Chapman, Judith Griffin 1949- *WhoAmW 93, WhoE 93*
Chapman, Karen Louise 1954- *WhoAmW 93*
Chapman, Katharine Linder *AmWomPl*
Chapman, Kathleen Halloran 1937- *WhoAmW 93*
Chapman, Kathryn A. *Law&B 92*
Chapman, Kenneth Stephen 1946- *WhoEmL 93*
Chapman, Laurel Israel *Law&B 92*
Chapman, Laurence Arthur 1949- *WhoAm 92*
Chapman, Lemmie Jerry 1934- *WhoSSW 93*
Chapman, Loren J. 1927- *WhoAm 92*
Chapman, Loring 1929- *WhoAm 92, WhoWor 93*
Chapman, Mark Eugene 1959- *WhoEmL 93*
Chapman, Mary Anderson *Law&B 92*
Chapman, Matthew 1950- *MiSFD 9*
Chapman, Maxinne *AmWomPl*
Chapman, Michael 1935- *MiSFD 9*
Chapman, Michael Edward 1956- *WhoEmL 93*
Chapman, Michael Kent *Law&B 92*
Chapman, Michael William 1937- *WhoAm 92*
Chapman, Nancy D. *Law&B 92*
Chapman, Orville Lamar 1932- *WhoAm 92*
Chapman, Pat 1937- *St&PR 93*
Chapman, Paul K. 1931- *ConAu 139*
Chapman, Paul Lindsey 1943- *WhoE 93*
Chapman, Paul Ray 1937- *St&PR 93*
Chapman, Paula Anne 1960- *WhoAmW 93, WhoEmL 93*
Chapman, Peter Frederick *WhoScE 91-1*
Chapman, Peter Herbert 1953- *WhoAm 92, WhoE 93, WhoEmL 93*
Chapman, Phyllis *AmWomPl*
Chapman, R.M. 1949- *St&PR 93*
Chapman, Ray 1891-1920 *BioIn 17*
Chapman, Raymond Johnson 1891-1920 *BiDAMSp 1989*
Chapman, Reginald Alfred *WhoScE 91-1*
Chapman, Reid Gillis 1920- *WhoAm 92*
Chapman, Richard Alexander 1932- *WhoSSW 93*
Chapman, Richard L. 1928- *St&PR 93*
Chapman, Richard LeRoy 1932- *WhoAm 92*
Chapman, Robert *WhoScE 91-1*
Chapman, Robert Breckinridge, III 1917- *WhoAm 92*
Chapman, Robert Dale 1955- *WhoEmL 93*
Chapman, Robert Foster 1926- *WhoAm 92*
Chapman, Robert Galbraith 1926- *WhoWor 93*
Chapman, Robert H. 1945- *St&PR 93*
Chapman, Robert Hett 1771-1833 *BioIn 17*
Chapman, Robert Lee, III 1946- *WhoEmL 93*
Chapman, Roger William 1949- *WhoWor 93*
Chapman, Ronald Earl 1949- *WhoEmL 93*
Chapman, Ronald Thomas 1933- *WhoE 93, WhoWor 93*
Chapman, Russell Dale 1951- *WhoEmL 93*
Chapman, Samuel Greeley 1929- *WhoAm 92*
Chapman, Sara Simmons 1940- *WhoAm 92, WhoAmW 93*
Chapman, Stephen Bernard *WhoScE 91-1*
Chapman, Terry Glen 1952- *St&PR 93*
Chapman, Thomas F. *WhoIns 93*
Chapman, Tracy *BioIn 17*
Chapman, Tracy 1964- *WhoAm 92, WhoAmW 93*
Chapman, Vera 1898- *ScF&FL 92*
Chapman, Walker *BioIn 17, MajAI*
Chapman, Wes *BioIn 17, WhoAm 92*
Chapman, Wilbur E. 1937- *St&PR 93*
Chapman, William *WhoAm 92*
Chapman, William 1850-1917 *BioIn 17*
Chapman, William Clyde 1944- *WhoSSW 93*
Chapman, William Douglas 1942- *WhoAm 92*
Chapman, William Francis 1925- *WhoWor 93*
Chapman, William Paul 1919- *WhoAm 92*
Chapman, William S., Jr. 1951- *St&PR 93*
Chapnick, Elaine Rae 1939- *WhoAmW 93*
Chappano, Perry Michael 1961- *WhoEmL 93*
Chappel, Bernice M(arie) 1910- *ConAu 37NR*
Chappel, Deborah Kaye 1954- *WhoSSW 93*
Chappelear, Claude Keplar 1937- *St&PR 93*
Chappelear, John M. 1938- *St&PR 93*
Chappelear, Patsy Stallings 1931- *WhoAm 92*
Chappell *Baker 92*
Chappell, Annette M. 1939- *WhoAm 92, WhoAmW 93*
Chappell, Anthony Gordon 1943- *St&PR 93, WhoAm 92*
Chappell, Audrey 1954- *SmATA 72 [port]*
Chappell, Barbara Kelly 1940- *WhoAmW 93*
Chappell, Charles A., Jr. 1924- *St&PR 93*
Chappell, Charles Franklin 1927- *WhoAm 92*
Chappell, Charles Richard 1943- *WhoAm 92*
Chappell, Clovis Gillham, Jr. 1911- *WhoAm 92*
Chappell, Danny Michael 1956- *WhoEmL 93, WhoSSW 93, WhoWor 93*
Chappell, Duncan 1939- *WhoAm 92*
Chappell, Frank W. 1916- *WhoSSW 93*
Chappell, Fred 1936- *BioIn 17, ScF&FL 92, WhoWrEP 92*
Chappell, Fred Davis 1936- *WhoAm 92, WhoSSW 93*
Chappell, Harvey E. d1991 *BioIn 17*
Chappell, John Charles 1935- *WhoAm 92*
Chappell, John Francis 1936- *St&PR 93*
Chappell, Katherine Cheney 1945- *St&PR 93*
Chappell, Marilyn Sue 1959- *WhoAmW 93*
Chappell, Miles Linwood, Jr. 1939- *WhoAm 92*
Chappell, Milton Leroy 1951- *WhoEmL 93*
Chappell, Raymond Edward 1941- *WhoE 93*
Chappell, Robert Earl, Jr. 1936- *St&PR 93, WhoAm 92*
Chappell, Robert Harvey, Jr. 1926- *St&PR 93*
Chappell, Roger Franklin 1951- *WhoSSW 93*
Chappell, S. Arthur 1834-1904 *Baker 92*
Chappell, Shirley Ann 1951- *WhoE 93*
Chappell, T. Stanley d1933 *Baker 92*
Chappell, Thomas M. *BioIn 17*
Chappell, Thomas Patey 1819-1902 *Baker 92*
Chappell, Vere Claiborne 1930- *WhoAm 92*
Chappell, Walter 1925- *WhoAm 92, WhoWor 93*
Chappell, Warren 1904-1991 *BioIn 17, MajAI [port]*
Chappell, Willard Ray 1938- *WhoAm 92*
Chappell, William 1809-1888 *Baker 92*
Chappellet, Cyril 1906-1991 *BioIn 17*
Chappen, Edward Peter 1925- *WhoE 93*
Chappen, Victorine Peter 1920- *WhoAmW 93*
Chapple, Abby 1939- *WhoAmW 93*
Chapple, D. *WhoScE 91-1*
Chapple, Eliot Dismore 1909- *IntDcAn*
Chapple, F. Colleen 1932- *WhoAmW 93*
Chapple, Richard Lynn 1944- *WhoSSW 93*
Chapple, Thomas L. *Law&B 92*
Chapple, Thomas Leslie 1947- *WhoAm 92*
Chapple, Wreford G. d1991 *BioIn 17*
Chappuis, Bob *BioIn 17*
Chappuis, Robert Richard 1923- *BiDAMSp 1989*
Chapront, Jean 1939- *WhoScE 91-2*
Chapuis, Auguste (Paul Jean-Baptiste) 1858-1933 *Baker 92*
Chapuis, Germaine Poinso- 1901-1981 *BioIn 17*
Chapuis, Yves-Louis 1932- *WhoScE 91-2*
Chapuran, Ronald F. *Law&B 92*
Chapus, Edmond d1991 *BioIn 17*
Chaput, Charles J. 1944- *WhoAm 92*
Chaput, Christopher Joseph 1960- *WhoEmL 93*
Char, Carlene 1954- *WhoAmW 93, WhoEmL 93*
Char, Carlene Mae 1954- *WhoWrEP 92*
Char, Daniel S. *Law&B 92*
Char, Paula F. *Law&B 92*
Char, Randall Yau Kunn 1952- *WhoEmL 93*
Char, Rene 1907-1988 *BioIn 17*
Char, Richard Jay 1959- *WhoEmL 93*
Char, Vernon Fook Leong 1934- *WhoAm 92*
Charabati, Victoria France 1954- *WhoE 93*
Charache, Patricia 1929- *WhoE 93*
Charache, Samuel 1930- *WhoAm 92*
Charachon, Robert 1932- *WhoScE 91-2*
Characklis, William Gregory 1941- *WhoAm 92*
Charalambous, John *WhoScE 91-1*
Charalambous, Stefanos 1927- *WhoScE 91-3*
Charalambous, Yiangos 1939- *WhoWor 93*
Charamathieu, Andre Georges 1929- *WhoScE 91-2*
Charania, Barkat 1941- *WhoAm 92, WhoSSW 93*
Charap, John Michael *WhoScE 91-1*
Charap, John Michael 1935- *WhoWor 93*
Charap, Stanley Harvey 1932- *WhoAm 92*
Charatan, Debrah Lee 1957- *WhoEmL 93*
Charatan, Joni Lacks *Law&B 92*
Charatonik, Janusz Jerzy 1934- *WhoWor 93*
Charboneau, Brian Paige 1949- *WhoEmL 93*
Charboneau, William Francis, III 1955- *WhoSSW 93*
Charbonneau, Claudette 1947- *WhoCanL 92*
Charbonneau, Eileen *ScF&FL 92*
Charbonneau, Gil *BioIn 17*
Charbonneau, Jean 1875-1960 *BioIn 17*
Charbonneau, Kevin *BioIn 17*
Charbonneau, Louis 1924- *ScF&FL 92*
Charbonneau, Peter D. 1953- *St&PR 93*
Charbonneau, Richard Joseph 1928- *WhoSSW 93*
Charbonneau, Ruth Dorothy 1929- *WhoAmW 93*
Charbonnier, Jean-Philippe 1921- *BioIn 17*
Charbonnier, Marc 1946- *ScF&FL 92*
Charbonnier, Volker 1939- *WhoAm 92*
Charce, Rene-Charles-Humbert la Tour du Pin Chambly de l 1834-1924 *BioIn 17*
Charcot, Jean-Baptiste 1867-1936 *Expl 93 [port]*
Chard, Chester Stevens 1915- *WhoAm 92*
Chard, John Rouse Merriot 1847-1897 *HarEnMi*
Chard, Roland Turner 1907- *WhoAm 92*
Chard, Timothy *WhoScE 91-1*
Chardak, Sharon R. *Law&B 92*
Chardavoyne, David E. 1948- *St&PR 93*
Chardavoyne, David Edwin 1948- *WhoAm 92, WhoEmL 93*
Chardiet, Bernice Kroll 1930- *WhoAm 92, WhoWor 93*
Chardin, Jean-Baptiste-Simeon 1699-1779 *BioIn 17*
Chardin, Jean-Paul 1939- *WhoUN 92*
Chardin, Pierre Teilhard de *BioIn 17*
Chardon, Michel 1935- *WhoScE 91-2*
Chardot, C. *WhoScE 91-2*
Charef, Mehdi 1952- *MiSFD 9*
Charek, Thomas Jack 1952- *St&PR 93*
Charen, Mona 1957- *WhoAmW 93*
Charendoff, Bruce J. *Law&B 92*
Chareonphongse, Sansern 1937- *WhoWor 93*
Charest, Jean J. 1958- *WhoAm 92*
Charest, Luc 1947- *WhoCanL 92*
Charette, Albert E. *St&PR 93*
Charette, Beverly *ScF&FL 92*
Charette, Norman 1931- *St&PR 93*
Charfoos, Lawrence Selig 1935- *WhoAm 92*
Chargaff, Erwin 1905- *ConAu 39NR, WhoAm 92*
Charif, Hassan Ali 1943- *WhoUN 92*
Charish, Howard Elliott 1945- *WhoE 93*
Charisse, Cyd 1921?- *IntDcF 2-3 [port]*
Charisse, Cyd 1923- *WhoAm 92*
Chariton *OxDcByz*
Charity, David Ellis 1941- *WhoWor 93*
Charity, Neil Mitchell 1915- *WhoWor 93*
Charlap, E. Paul d1991 *BioIn 17*
Charlebois, Jean 1945- *WhoCanL 92*
Charlebois, Jean-Pierre 1949- *St&PR 93*
Charlemagne 742-814 *HarEnMi, OxDcByz*
Charlemagne, Emperor 742-814 *BioIn 17*
Charlemont, Earl of 1728-1799 *BioIn 17*
Charles, Prince of Wales 1948- *BioIn 17*
Charles, I 1600-1649 *HarEnMi*
Charles, I 1887-1922 *DcTwHis*
Charles, I, King of Great Britain 1600-1649 *BioIn 17*
Charles, II, King of France 823-877 *BioIn 17*
Charles, II, King of Great Britain 1630-1685 *BioIn 17*
Charles, IV, Duke of Lorraine and Bar 1604-1675 *HarEnMi*
Charles, V 1338-1380 *HarEnMi*
Charles, V 1500-1558 *HarEnMi*
Charles, V, Duke of Lorraine and Bar 1643-1690 *HarEnMi*
Charles, V, Holy Roman Emperor 1500-1558 *BioIn 17*
Charles, VII 1403-1461 *HarEnMi*
Charles, VIII 1408-1470 *HarEnMi*
Charles, VIII 1470-1498 *HarEnMi*
Charles, XII, King of Sweden 1682-1718 *HarEnMi*
Charles, A. 1930- *WhoAsAP 91*
Charles, Allan G. 1928- *WhoAm 92*
Charles, Arthur Pendrill 1941- *WhoWor 93*
Charles, Arthur William Hessin 1948- *WhoWor 93*
Charles, Bertram 1918- *WhoAm 92*
Charles, Carol Morgan 1931- *WhoAm 92*
Charles, Carolyn Stowell 1921- *WhoAmW 93, WhoSSW 93*
Charles, Cyril *BioIn 17*
Charles, David *ConAu 37NR*
Charles, David Ernest 1948- *WhoAsAP 91*
Charles, Dawn C. 1953- *WhoAmW 93, WhoSSW 93*
Charles, Donald R. *St&PR 93*
Charles, Ernest 1895-1984 *Baker 92*
Charles, Eugenia 1919- *DcCPCAm*
Charles, Faith Harris 1939- *WhoE 93*
Charles, George *DcCPCAm*
Charles, Glen *WhoAm 92*
Charles, Harry 1957- *WhoEmL 93*
Charles, Hubert John 1948- *WhoUN 92*
Charles, Isabel 1926- *WhoAm 92*
Charles, Joel 1914- *WhoSSW 93, WhoWor 93*
Charles, John Andrew *WhoScE 91-1*
Charles, John Franklyn 1937- *WhoSSW 93*
Charles, Judith Korey 1925- *WhoE 93*
Charles, Kevin Edward 1954- *WhoSSW 93*
Charles, Lennox *DcCPCAm*
Charles, Les *WhoAm 92*
Charles, Louis *MajAI*
Charles, Lyn Ellen 1951- *WhoEmL 93*
Charles, Mark Howard *Law&B 92*
Charles, Mary Eugenia 1919- *WhoWor 93*
Charles, Michael Harrison 1952- *WhoE 93*
Charles, Mickey *WhoE 93*
Charles, Nathanael *ConAu 39NR*
Charles, Neil *ScF&FL 92*
Charles, Nicholas J. *MajAI*
Charles, Norma Mae 1940- *WhoCanL 92*
Charles, Norman C. 1937- *WhoE 93*
Charles, Ray *BioIn 17*
Charles, Ray 1930- *Baker 92, CurBio 92 [port], SoulM, WhoAm 92*
Charles, Ray (Robinson) 1930- *AfrAmBi [port]*
Charles, Reid Shaver 1940- *WhoE 93*
Charles, Richard Lloyd 1939- *St&PR 93*
Charles, Robert 1938- *ScF&FL 92*
Charles, Ronald Allan 1944- *WhoWrEP 92*
Charles, Saul *St&PR 93*
Charles, Steven *ScF&FL 92*
Charles Emmanuel, I, Duke of Savoy 1562-1630 *BioIn 17*
Charles Gustavus, X 1622-1660 *HarEnMi*
Charles Louis John 1771-1847 *HarEnMi*
Charles Of Anjou, I 1226-1285 *OxDcByz*
Charles of Valois 1270-1325 *OxDcByz*
Charleson, Ian 1949-1990 *BioIn 17*
Charles Philip Arthur George 1948- *WhoWor 93*
Charlestein, Gary M. 1944- *St&PR 93*
Charles, the Bald 823-877 *BioIn 17*
Charles the Bald, II 823-877 *HarEnMi*
Charles the Great 742-814 *BioIn 17*
Charleston, Robin P. *Law&B 92*
Charles Vasa, IX 1550-1611 *HarEnMi*
Charles Vasa, XI 1655-1697 *HarEnMi*
Charlesworth, Brian 1945- *WhoAm 92*
Charlesworth, Bruce 1950- *BioIn 17*
Charlesworth, Clifford E. 1931-1991 *BioIn 17*
Charlesworth, James Hamilton 1940- *WhoAm 92*
Charlesworth, Maxwell John 1925- *ConAu 40NR*
Charlesworth, Richard Ian 1952- *WhoAsAP 91*
Charlesworth, Sarah *WhoScE 91-1*
Charlesworth, Sarah 1947- *BioIn 17*
Charlesworth, Velma Lillian 1919- *WhoAmW 93*
Charleton, Margaret Ann 1947- *WhoAmW 93*
Charleux, Henri 1924- *WhoScE 91-2*
Charley, Philip J. 1921- *St&PR 93*
Charley, Philip James 1921- *WhoAm 92*
Charlier, Gerard J.W. 1940- *WhoScE 91-2*
Charlier, Jean Pierre 1937- *WhoWor 93*
Charlier, Michel 1944- *WhoScE 91-2*
Charlier, Roger Henri 1921- *WhoAm 92*
Charlip, Remy *BioIn 17*
Charlip, Remy 1929- *MajAI [port]*
Charlot, Martin 1944- *BioIn 17*
Charlotte Augusta, Princess of Great Britain 1796-1817 *BioIn 17*
Charlson, Alan Edward *Law&B 92*
Charlson, Carol Ann 1947- *WhoAmW 93*
Charlson, David Harvey 1947- *WhoAm 92, WhoEmL 93, WhoWor 93*

Charlson, Michael Lloyd 1958- *WhoEmL 93*
Charlton, Audrey Kay 1947- *WhoAmW 93*
Charlton, Betty Jo 1923- *WhoAmW 93*
Charlton, Gordon Taliaferro, Jr. 1923- *WhoAm 92, WhoSSW 93*
Charlton, Graham *WhoScE 91-1*
Charlton, Jesse Melvin, Jr. 1916- *WhoAm 92*
Charlton, John *BioIn 17*
Charlton, John Kipp 1937- *WhoAm 92, WhoWor 93*
Charlton, Stephen *St&PR 93*
Charlton, Tony *BioIn 17*
Charlton, William *ScF&FL 92*
Charlton-Perrin, Geoffrey *WhoAm 92*
Charm, Joel Barry *WhoE 93*
Charm, Leslie 1943- *St&PR 93*
Charmatz, Leslie Howard 1945- *St&PR 93*
Charme, Stuart Zane 1951- *ConAu 137*
Charmpoonod, Suchon 1937- *WhoAsAP 91*
Charms *SoulM*
Charnas, Charles N. *Law&B 92*
Charnas, Michael 1947- *WhoAm 92, WhoEmL 93*
Charnas, Suzy McKee *BioIn 17*
Charnas, Suzy McKee 1939- *ConAu 39NR, ScF&FL 92*
Charnay, Desire 1828-1915 *IntDcAn*
Charnay, Georges J.F. 1944- *WhoScE 91-2*
Charness, Wayne Samuel 1954- *WhoEmL 93*
Charney, Ann *WhoCanL 92*
Charney, David H. 1923- *WhoWrEP 92*
Charney, Elizabeth Ann *BioIn 17*
Charney, Evan 1933- *WhoAm 92*
Charney, Florence R. 1923- *WhoAmW 93, WhoSSW 93*
Charney, Maurice (Myron) 1929- *ConAu 40NR*
Charney, Melvin 1935- *WhoAm 92*
Charney, Shawna Frank *Law&B 92*
Charniak, Eugene 1946- *WhoAm 92*
Charnin, Jade Hobson 1945- *WhoAmW 93, WhoE 93, WhoWor 93*
Charnin, Martin 1934- *ConTFT 10, WhoAm 92*
Charnley, John 1911-1982 *BioIn 17*
Charnley, Mitchell 1898-1991 *BioIn 17*
Charnoff, Scott Dennis 1964- *WhoE 93*
Charny, Charles W. d1992 *NewYTBS 92*
Charochak, Dale Michael 1955- *WhoE 93, WhoEmL 93*
Charocopos, Anthony Nicholaos 1926- *WhoWor 93*
Charola, Asuncion Elena 1942- *HispAmA*
Charollais, Jean Jacques 1934- *WhoScE 91-4*
Charos, Evangelos Nikolaou 1953- *WhoE 93*
Charoulet, E. *WhoScE 91-2*
Charpentier, Celeste Jeannette 1956- *WhoE 93*
Charpentier, Didier Jean 1957- *WhoWor 93*
Charpentier, Francois 1938- *WhoScE 91-2*
Charpentier, Gail Wigutow 1946- *WhoAmW 93, WhoEmL 93, WhoWor 93*
Charpentier, Gustave 1860-1956 *Baker 92, IntDcOp, OxDcOp*
Charpentier, J.M. *WhoScE 91-2*
Charpentier, Jacques 1933- *Baker 92*
Charpentier, Jean-Claude 1939- *WhoScE 91-2*
Charpentier, Keith Lionel 1959- *WhoE 93*
Charpentier, Marc-Antoine c. 1634-1704 *IntDcOp*
Charpentier, Marc-Antoine c. 1645-1704 *Baker 92, OxDcOp*
Charpentier, Raymond (Louis Marie) 1880-1960 *Baker 92*
Charpie, Robert A. 1925- *St&PR 93*
Charques, Dorothy 1899-1976 *ScF&FL 92*
Charrad, Mounira *WhoE 93*
Charren, Peggy 1928- *WhoAm 92, WhoAmW 93*
Charrette, Robert N. *ScF&FL 92*
Charrier, Michael Edward 1945- *WhoAm 92, WhoE 93, WhoWor 93*
Charriere, Isabelle de 1740-1805 *BioIn 17*
Charriere, Jeannine *WhoScE 91-2*
Charriez, Blanca Noelia 1947- *WhoE 93*
Charron, Andre Joseph Charles Pierre 1936- *WhoAm 92*
Charron, Claude *BioIn 17*
Charron, Francois 1952- *WhoCanL 92*
Charron, G. *Law&B 92*
Charron, Kenneth G. *Law&B 92*
Charron, Maureen Joan 1959- *WhoE 93*
Charron, Paul Richard 1942- *WhoAm 92*
Charrow, Cyd Beth 1947- *WhoAmW 93*
Charry, Michael Ronald 1933- *WhoAm 92*
Chartair, Max *ScF&FL 92*
Charteris, Leslie 1907- *ScF&FL 92, WhoAm 92*
Charteris, Richard 1948- *Baker 92*
Charters, Alexander Nathaniel 1916- *WhoAm 92*
Charters, Ann 1936- *WhoAm 92, WhoAmW 93, WhoE 93*
Charters, Ann D. 1936- *WhoWrEP 92*
Charters, David H. 1942- *St&PR 93*
Charters, David Hill 1942- *WhoAm 92*
Charters, David Wilton 1900-1972 *ScF&FL 92*
Chartienitz, Theresa 1965- *WhoAmW 93*
Chartier, Emile 1868-1951 *BioIn 17*
Chartier, Germain Henri 1936- *WhoScE 91-2*
Chartier, Janellen Olsen 1951- *WhoAm 92, WhoAmW 93*
Chartier, Jeffrey David 1956- *WhoEmL 93*
Chartier, Normand 1945- *BioIn 17*
Chartier, Philippe 1937- *WhoScE 91-2*
Chartier, Roger 1945- *ConAu 137*
Chartier, Steven C. 1949- *St&PR 93*
Chartier, Vernon Lee 1939- *WhoAm 92*
Chartock, Hyman 1912- *WhoE 93*
Chartoff, Robert Irwin *WhoAm 92*
Charton, Barbara 1936- *WhoE 93*
Charton, Jean 1924- *St&PR 93*
Charton, Marvin 1931- *WhoAm 92*
Charton-Demeur, Anne 1824-1892 *OxDcOp*
Chartow, Harold 1920- *St&PR 93*
Chartrand, Gabriel *BioIn 17*
Chartrand, J. Claude *WhoIns 93*
Chartrand, Mark Ray 1943- *WhoAm 92, WhoE 93*
Chartrand, Robert Lee 1928- *WhoAm 92*
Charvat, Fedia Rudolf 1931- *St&PR 93*
Charvat, William d1966 *DcLB Y92 [port]*
Charwat, Andrew Franciszek 1925- *WhoAm 92*
Charwat, Arthur Charles 1929- *St&PR 93*
Chary, Mudumbai Srnivas 1934- *WhoE 93*
Charyk, Joseph Vincent 1920- *WhoAm 92*
Charyn, Jerome 1937- *BioIn 17, JeAmFiW, ScF&FL 92*
Charytan, Lynn Robin *Law&B 92*
Charytanski, Jan Zbigniew 1922- *WhoWor 93*
Chasalow, Lewis Craig 1956- *WhoE 93*
Chasan, Barbara *Law&B 92*
Chasanow, Howard Stuart 1937- *WhoAm 92*
Chase, Alan C. 1936- *St&PR 93*
Chase, Alfonso 1945- *SpAmA*
Chase, Alison *WhoAm 92*
Chase, Arnold *BioIn 17*
Chase, Aurin Moody, Jr. 1904- *WhoAm 92*
Chase, Blanche Mary 1948- *WhoEmL 93*
Chase, Carlton *BioIn 17*
Chase, Carol *ScF&FL 92*
Chase, Charley 1893-1940 *MiSFD 9N, QDrFCA 92 [port]*
Chase, Chevy *BioIn 17*
Chase, Chevy 1943- *WhoAm 92*
Chase, Chevy 1944- *QDrFCA 92 [port]*
Chase, Clinton Irvin 1927- *WhoAm 92*
Chase, Cochrane 1932- *WhoAm 92*
Chase, David *MiSFD 9*
Chase, David Edward 1941- *WhoWrEP 92*
Chase, David Marion 1930- *WhoAm 92*
Chase, David T. *BioIn 17*
Chase, Derwood Sumner, Jr. 1931- *WhoSSW 93*
Chase, Doris 1923- *BioIn 17*
Chase, Doris Totten 1923- *WhoAmW 93*
Chase, Edna Woolman 1877-1957 *BioIn 17*
Chase, Elaine Raco 1949- *WhoWrEP 92*
Chase, Elizabeth Coykendall d1992 *BioIn 17, NewYTBS 92*
Chase, Emily *ConAu 136*
Chase, Francis M. 1920- *St&PR 93*
Chase, Franklin Whitner, III 1962- *WhoSSW 93*
Chase, Gary Andrew 1945- *WhoE 93*
Chase, Geoffrey L. *Law&B 92*
Chase, Gilbert 1906- *Baker 92*
Chase, Gilbert 1906-1992 *BioIn 17, ConAu 137, NewYTBS 92*
Chase, Glen *ScF&FL 92*
Chase, Goodwin 1911- *WhoAm 92*
Chase, Gregory J. 1943- *St&PR 93*
Chase, Helen B.R.A. *AmWomPl*
Chase, Helen Louise 1943- *WhoAmW 93*
Chase, Jacoline B. 1953- *WhoEmL 93*
Chase, James Hadley 1906-1985 *ScF&FL 92*
Chase, James Keller 1927- *WhoAm 92*
Chase, Jean Cox 1925- *WhoAmW 93*
Chase, Jeffrey Lake 1954- *WhoSSW 93*
Chase, John David 1920- *WhoAm 92*
Chase, John William 1940- *St&PR 93*
Chase, Keith 1927- *St&PR 93*
Chase, Kelly R. *Law&B 92*
Chase, Leah Feinberg 1938- *WhoAmW 93*
Chase, Lewis 1873-1937 *ScF&FL 92*
Chase, Lincoln *SoulM*
Chase, Linda Arville 1953- *WhoAmW 93, WhoEmL 93*
Chase, Loriene Eck 1934- *WhoAm 92, WhoAmW 93, WhoWor 93*
Chase, Louisa 1951- *BioIn 17*
Chase, Lucia 1897-1986 *BioIn 17*
Chase, Lucius Peter 1902- *WhoAm 92*
Chase, Lynn Edward 1939- *St&PR 93*
Chase, Maria Elaine Garoufalis 1957- *WhoAmW 93*
Chase, Marjorie *AmWomPl*
Chase, Mark Earle 1960- *WhoEmL 93*
Chase, Mary 1907-1981 *ScF&FL 92*
Chase, Merrill Wallace 1905- *WhoAm 92*
Chase, Michael William 1959- *WhoEmL 93, WhoSSW 93*
Chase, Morris 1918- *WhoAm 92, WhoWor 93*
Chase, Naomi Feigelson 1932- *WhoWrEP 92*
Chase, Nicholas *ConAu 136, WhoCanL 92*
Chase, Nicholas Joseph 1913- *WhoAm 92*
Chase, Norman Eli 1926- *WhoAm 92*
Chase, Oscar Gottfried *WhoAm 92*
Chase, Peter R. d1992 *NewYTBS 92*
Chase, Peter R. 1947- *St&PR 93*
Chase, Phyllis A. *St&PR 93*
Chase, Richard 1904-1988 *BioIn 17*
Chase, Richard Hazen 1953- *WhoE 93*
Chase, Richard J. 1922- *St&PR 93*
Chase, Richard Lionel St. Lucian 1933- *WhoAm 92*
Chase, Robert Arthur 1923- *WhoAm 92*
Chase, Robert R. 1948- *ScF&FL 92*
Chase, Salmon P. 1808-1873 *PolPar*
Chase, Salmon Portland 1808-1873 *OxCSupC [port]*
Chase, Samuel 1741-1811 *OxCSupC [port]*
Chase, Samuel Brown 1932- *WhoE 93*
Chase, Saundria Rane *Law&B 92*
Chase, Seymour M. 1924- *WhoAm 92*
Chase, Sharon Sue 1945- *WhoAmW 93*
Chase, Shirley Idelle *Law&B 92*
Chase, Stephen M. *Law&B 92*
Chase, Stuart Alan 1958- *WhoEmL 93*
Chase, Sylvia B. 1938- *WhoAm 92*
Chase, Thomas Newell 1932- *WhoAm 92*
Chase, Victoria Byler 1954- *WhoAmW 93, WhoEmL 93*
Chase, W. Calvin 1854-1921 *EncAACR*
Chase, W. Rowell 1904- *St&PR 93*
Chase, William E. 1931- *WhoWor 93*
Chase, William Howard 1910- *WhoAm 92*
Chase, William Merritt 1849-1916 *BioIn 17*
Chase, William Robert 1951- *WhoEmL 93*
Chase, William Rowell 1904- *WhoAm 92*
Chase, William Thomas, III 1940- *WhoAm 92*
Chasek, Arlene Shatsky 1934- *WhoAmW 93*
Chaseman, Joel 1926- *WhoAm 92*
Chasen, Audrey d1992 *BioIn 17*
Chasen, Barbara *BioIn 17*
Chasen, Edith Andrea 1947- *WhoAmW 93, WhoE 93*
Chasen, Mignon Charney 1911- *WhoE 93*
Chasen, Robert E. 1916- *St&PR 93, WhoAm 92*
Chasen, Sherwin A. 1938- *St&PR 93*
Chasen, Sylvan Herbert 1926- *WhoAm 92*
Chase-Riboud, Barbara Dewayne 1939- *WhoAm 92, WhoAmW 93*
Chaset, Alan Jay 1946- *WhoEmL 93*
Chasey, Jacqueline *Law&B 92*
Chasey, Patrick Ross 1947- *St&PR 93*
Chasin, Charles *Law&B 92*
Chasin, Dana James 1960- *WhoE 93*
Chasin, Holly Kay 1960- *WhoAmW 93*
Chasin, Mark 1942- *WhoE 93*
Chasin, Martin 1938- *WhoE 93*
Chasin, Milton Jack 1919- *St&PR 93*
Chasin, Werner David 1932- *WhoAm 92*
Chasing His Horse *BioIn 17*
Chasins, Abram 1903-1987 *Baker 92*
Chasins, Edward A. 1920- *WhoAm 92*
Chasis, Herbert 1905- *WhoAm 92*
Chaskelson, Marsha Ina 1950- *WhoAm 92, WhoEmL 93*
Chaski, Hilda Cecelia 1951- *WhoAmW 93, WhoEmL 93*
Chaskin, Jay Lionel *Law&B 92*
Chasman, Catherine Sue 1943- *WhoAmW 93*
Chason, Jacob 1915- *WhoAm 92*
Chason, Marie R. *St&PR 93*
Chason, W. Robert 1944- *St&PR 93*
Chassay, Roger Paul, Jr. 1938- *WhoSSW 93, WhoWor 93*
Chasse, David Hendryk 1765-1849 *HarEnMi*
Chasse, Emily Schuder 1953- *WhoAmW 93*
Chasse, John Dennis 1934- *WhoE 93*
Chassery, Claude 1941- *WhoScE 91-2*
Chassman, Leonard Fredric 1935- *WhoAm 92*
Chast, Roz *BioIn 17*
Chast, Roz 1954- *WhoE 93*
Chast, Roz c. 1955- *News 92 [port]*
Chastain, B. Lynn *Law&B 92*
Chastain, Bill H. *Law&B 92*
Chastain, Dorothy Straughan 1950- *WhoAmW 93*
Chastain, Gary P. 1954- *St&PR 93*
Chastain, Larry Kent 1943- *WhoAm 92*
Chastain, Paul Raymond 1934- *St&PR 93*
Chastain, Randall Meads 1945- *WhoAm 92, WhoSSW 93*
Chastain, Sarah Frances 1949- *WhoAmW 93*
Chastain, Sheila McClendon 1948- *WhoEmL 93, WhoSSW 93*
Chastain, William F., Jr. 1946- *St&PR 93*
Chastant, Harold P. 1923- *WhoIns 93*
Chaste, Abimana 1963- *WhoUN 92*
Chaste, Aymar de d1603 *HarEnMi*
Chasteen, Alan Lee 1950- *WhoSSW 93*
Chasteen, James R. *BioIn 17*
Chasteen, Michael Allen 1947- *WhoEmL 93, WhoSSW 93*
Chastel, Andre 1912-1990 *BioIn 17*
Chaston, Ian *WhoScE 91-1*
Chatain, Michel Nicholas Antoine 1927- *WhoScE 91-2*
Chata Noloesca, La *HispAmA*
Chateau, Jacques Marie 1935- *St&PR 93*
Chateau, John-Peter David 1942- *St&PR 93, WhoAm 92*
Chateaubriand, Francois-Rene de 1768-1848 *DcLB 119 [port]*
Chateaurenault, Francois Louis de Rousselet, Marquis of 1637-1716 *HarEnMi*
Chatelain, Carl J. 1932- *St&PR 93*
Chatelet, marquise de 1706-1749 *BioIn 17*
Chatelian, Pierre 1949- *WhoScE 91-2*
Chatelier, Paul Richard 1938- *WhoSSW 93*
Chatellier, Tammy Shealy 1968- *WhoSSW 93*
Chater, Elizabeth 1910- *ScF&FL 92*
Chater, Keith F. *WhoScE 91-1*
Chater, Shirley Sears 1932- *WhoAm 92, WhoAmW 93, WhoSSW 93*
Chatfield, C.J. *WhoScE 91-1*
Chatfield, Cheryl Ann 1946- *WhoAm 92, WhoAmW 93, WhoEmL 93*
Chatfield, David Alan 1939- *St&PR 93*
Chatfield, Mary Van Abshoven *WhoAm 92*
Chatfield, Ruth Christina 1956- *WhoWor 93*
Chatfield-Taylor, Adele 1945- *WhoAmW 93*
Chatham, George Norton 1923- *WhoSSW 93*
Chatham, James Ray 1931- *WhoAm 92*
Chatham, Lois 1928- *WhoSSW 93*
Chatham, Ralph Ernest 1948- *WhoEmL 93*
Chatham, William Pitt 1708-1778 *BioIn 17*
Chatiliez, Etienne *MiSFD 9*
Chatillon, Dominique 1928- *WhoWor 93*
Chatillon, Vaillancourt L. *St&PR 93*
Chatlain, Dean F. 1950- *St&PR 93*
Chatlain, Dean Francis *Law&B 92*
Chatlos, William Edward 1927- *WhoAm 92*
Chatman, James Icelius 1926- *St&PR 93*
Chatman, Stephen (George) 1950- *Baker 92*
Chatman-Johnson, Yvonne Louise *Law&B 92*
Chato, John Clark 1929- *WhoAm 92*
Chato, Joseph Edward 1950- *WhoEmL 93*
Chatoff, Michael Alan 1946- *WhoAm 92, WhoE 93, WhoEmL 93, WhoWor 93*
Chatot, Charles A. 1941- *St&PR 93*
Chatot-Travis, Judee J. 1948- *St&PR 93*
Chatrnuck, Donald W. 1963- *St&PR 93*
Chatroo, Arthur *Law&B 92*
Chatroo, Arthur J. *Law&B 92*
Chatroo, Arthur Jay 1946- *WhoEmL 93*
Chatroop, Louis Carl 1951- *WhoEmL 93*
Chattalas, Michael John 1962- *WhoEmL 93*
Chattaway, Dwight Nelson 1936- *St&PR 93*
Chatterjee, Asima 1917- *WhoAsAP 91*
Chatterjee, Pranab 1936- *WhoAm 92*
Chatterjee, Pronoy K. 1936- *WhoE 93*
Chatterjee, Sisir 1919- *ScF&FL 92*
Chatterjee, Soumitra *IntDcF 2-3 [port]*
Chatterji, Debajyoti 1944- *St&PR 93, WhoAm 92*
Chatterji, Monojit *WhoScE 91-1*
Chatterton, E. Keble 1878-1944 *ScF&FL 92*
Chatterton, Karen Smith 1951- *WhoEmL 93*
Chatterton, N. Jerry 1939- *WhoAm 92*

Chatterton, Raymond Edward 1946- *WhoE 93*
Chatterton, Robert Treat, Jr. 1935- *WhoAm 92*
Chatterton, Roylance Wayne 1921- *WhoWrEP 92*
Chatterton, Sterling Gene 1928- *St&PR 93*
Chatterton, Thomas 1752-1770 *BioIn 17*
Chattin, Gilbert Marshall 1914- *WhoSSW 93, WhoWor 93*
Chattin, Phillip K. *Law&B 92*
Chattler, Zachary Lee 1952- *WhoE 93*
Chatto, Andrew 1840-1913 *BioIn 17*
Chattopadhyay, Sukumar 1950- *WhoWor 93*
Chattopadhyaya, D.P. 1933- *WhoAsAP 91*
Chattoraj, Shib Charan 1924- *WhoWor 93*
Chattree, Mayank 1957- *WhoSSW 93*
Chaturvedi, Bhuvnesh 1928- *WhoAsAP 91*
Chaturvedi, Rama Kant 1933- *WhoE 93*
Chatwin, Bruce *BioIn 17*
Chatwin, Bruce 1940-1989 *MagSWL [port]*
Chatwin, Philip Christopher *WhoScE 91-1*
Chaty, Guy 1934- *WhoScE 91-2*
Chatzkel, Ben 1924- *St&PR 93*
Chatzkel, Larry R. 1952- *St&PR 93*
Chau, Edwin S. *St&PR 93*
Chau, Foo Tim 1948- *WhoWor 93*
Chau, Kwok Wing 1961- *WhoWor 93*
Chaucer, Geoffrey d1400 *BioIn 17*
Chaucer, Geoffrey c. 1340-1400 *OxDcOp*
Chaucer, Geoffrey c. 1343-1400 *MagSWL [port]*
Chaucer Family *BioIn 17*
Chau Cham Son 1932- *WhoAsAP 91*
Chaudhari, Praveen 1937- *WhoAm 92*
Chaudhary, Ahsan Iqbal 1959- *WhoWor 93*
Chaudhary, Ram Prakash 1918- *WhoAsAP 91*
Chaudhary, Shaukat Ali 1931- *WhoWor 93*
Chaudhri, Amin Q. *MiSFD 9*
Chaudhri, Amin Qamar 1942- *WhoWor 93*
Chaudhri, Mohammad Munawar *WhoScE 91-1*
Chaudhry, Mahendra Pal 1942- *WhoAsAP 91*
Chaudhry, Rashid A. 1945- *St&PR 93*
Chaudhuri, Nirad C. 1897- *BioIn 17*
Chaudhuri, Tridib 1911- *WhoAsAP 91*
Chaudry, Irshad Hussain 1945- *WhoWor 93*
Chauff, Eugene Henry 1950- *St&PR 93*
Chauhan, Arun Kumar 1954- *WhoWor 93*
Chauhan, Joseph Hirendra 1922- *WhoWor 93*
Chauhan, Narinder Singh 1952- *WhoE 93*
Chaulieu, Pierre *ConAu 138*
Chauls, Sylvia Jane Whyte 1947- *WhoAmW 93*
Chaun, Frantisek 1921-1981 *Baker 92*
Chauncey, Isaac 1772-1840 *HarEnMi*
Chauncy, Charles 1705-1787 *BioIn 17*
Chauncy, Nan (Cen Beryl Masterman) 1900-1970 *DcChlFi, MajAI [port]*
Chaunu, Pierre Rene 1923- *WhoWor 93*
Chaurette, Normand 1954- *WhoCanL 92*
Chaus, Bernard d1991 *BioIn 17*
Chaus, Petr Grigor'yevich *WhoWor 93*
Chausson, Ernest 1855-1899 *IntDcOp, OxDcOp*
Chausson, (Amedee-) Ernest 1855-1899 *Baker 92*
Chautala, Om Prakash 1935- *WhoAsAP 91*
Chautemps, Camille 1885-1963 *BioIn 17*
Chauve, Pierre Jean 1930- *WhoScE 91-2*
Chauveau, Pierre-Joseph-Olivier 1820-1890 *BioIn 17*
Chauvel, Henry George 1865-1945 *HarEnMi*
Chauvet, Charles-Alexis 1837-1871 *Baker 92*
Chauvette, Claude 1939- *St&PR 93, WhoAm 92*
Chauvin, Andre 1914- *WhoWor 93*
Chauvin, Cy *ScF&FL 92*
Chavan, Shankarrao Bhaorao 1920- *WhoAsAP 91*
Chavane, Bruno Antoine 1942- *WhoUN 92*
Chavarri, Eduardo Lopez 1871-1970 *Baker 92*
Chavarria, Dolores Esparza 1952- *WhoAmW 93*
Chavarria, Ernest Montes, Jr. 1955- *WhoAm 92, WhoEmL 93, WhoSSW 93, WhoWor 93*
Chavasit, Visith 1957- *WhoWor 93*
Chavchavadze, David 1924- *BioIn 17*
Chave, Alan Dana 1953- *WhoE 93*
Chavee, Xavier Noel 1955- *St&PR 93*
Chavel, Francois M. 1946- *WhoIns 93*
Chavera, Ofilia 1948- *St&PR 93*
Chaveriat, Andrew John 1963- *WhoE 93, WhoEmL 93*
Chaves, Aaron D. 1911-1992 *BioIn 17*
Chaves, Christi Cahill 1955- *WhoAmW 93*
Chaves, Damien Edward 1949- *WhoSSW 93*
Chaves, Denis P. 1940- *St&PR 93*
Chaves, Jose A. 1941- *WhoIns 93*
Chaves, Jose Andrade 1941- *St&PR 93*
Chaves, Jose Francisco 1833-1904 *HispAmA*
Chaves, Jose Maria 1922- *WhoAm 92, WhoWor 93*
Chaves, Victorico L. 1932- *WhoAsAP 91*
Chavez, Albert Blas 1952- *WhoWor 93*
Chavez, Angelico 1910- *HispAmA*
Chavez, Cesar 1927- *BioIn 17, HispAmA [port], PolPar*
Chavez, Cesar Estrada 1927- *DcTwHis, WhoAm 92*
Chavez, Cesar Tizoc 1952- *WhoEmL 93*
Chavez, Clementa F. 1952- *WhoWor 93*
Chavez, Denise 1948- *DcLB 122 [port], HispAmA [port], NotHsAW 93*
Chavez, Dennis 1888-1962 *HispAmA*
Chavez, Diane *Law&B 92*
Chavez, Donald J. *Law&B 92*
Chavez, Edward 1917- *HispAmA*
Chavez, Gilberto 1908- *DcMexL*
Chavez, Guillermo D. *Law&B 92*
Chavez, J. Anthony *Law&B 92*
Chavez, Janie Ignacia 1946- *WhoAmW 93, WhoWor 93*
Chavez, John Anthony 1955- *WhoSSW 93*
Chavez, John Richard 1949- *WhoEmL 93, WhoSSW 93*
Chavez, Julio Cesar *BioIn 17*
Chavez, Linda 1947- *NotHsAW 93 [port], WhoAm 92*
Chavez, Lita Lopez *BioIn 17*
Chavez, Robert B. 1946- *St&PR 93*
Chavez, Victor B. 1945- *St&PR 93*
Chavez, Victor Edwin 1930- *WhoAm 92*
Chavez (y Ramirez), Carlos (Antonio de Padua) 1899-1978 *Baker 92*
Chavez-Melo, Skinner d1992 *BioIn 17, NewYTBS 92*
Chavez y Gonzalez, Archbishop *DcCPCAm*
Chavin, Walter 1925- *WhoAm 92*
Chavira, Natividad F. *Law&B 92*
Chavis, Boozoo *BioIn 17*
Chavis, Melvin Lin 1944- *St&PR 93*
Chavis, Wilson *BioIn 17*
Chavis-Mickey, Angela Yelverton 1950- *WhoAm 92, WhoEmL 93*
Chavkin, Wallace 1922- *St&PR 93*
Chavkin, Wendy 1952- *WhoAmW 93, WhoEmL 93*
Chavolla Ramos, Francisco Javier 1946- *WhoAm 92*
Chavoor, Sherm d1992 *NewYTBS 92*
Chavooshian, Marge 1925- *WhoAm 92, WhoAmW 93*
Chavry, Gilbert 1949- *WhoWor 93*
Chawla, Krishan Kumar 1942- *WhoAm 92*
Chawla, Lal Muhammad 1917- *WhoWor 93*
Chawla, Manmohan Singh 1940- *WhoWor 93*
Chawla, Mantosh K. 1946- *St&PR 93*
Chawszczewski, Christopher Mark 1950- *WhoWrEP 92*
Chay, Yee Meng 1956- *WhoWor 93*
Chaya, Henry John, Jr. 1951- *WhoE 93*
Chaya, Stephen D. *Law&B 92*
Chaya-Ngam, Iam 1936- *WhoWor 93*
Chayat, Sherry 1943- *WhoWrEP 92*
Chayefsky, Paddy 1923-1981 *ScF&FL 92*
Chayefsky, Sidney A. *ScF&FL 92*
Chayen, Joseph 1924- *WhoScE 91-1*
Chayes, Abram 1922- *WhoAm 92*
Chayet, Martha 1956- *WhoEmL 93*
Chaykin, Arthur Alan *Law&B 92*
Chaynes, Charles 1925- *Baker 92*
Chayvialle, Jean-Alain 1944- *WhoScE 91-2*
Chazanoff, Jay D. 1945- *St&PR 93*
Chazanoff, Jay David 1945- *WhoAm 92*
Chazen, David Franklin, II 1960- *WhoE 93, WhoEmL 93*
Chazen, Gary David 1951- *St&PR 93*
Chazen, Hartley James 1932- *WhoAm 92*
Chazen, Jerome A. 1927- *St&PR 93, WhoAm 92, WhoE 93*
Chazen, Melvin Leonard 1933- *WhoWor 93*
Chazen, Robert Gordon 1943- *St&PR 93*
Chazov, Yevgeny 1929- *WhoWor 93*
Chbosky, Fred G. 1944- *St&PR 93, WhoAm 92*
Chciuk, Ryszard Marek 1950- *WhoWor 93*
Che, Ming-Zhou 1936- *WhoWor 93*
Che, Tracey Allison 1962- *WhoE 93*
Cheadle, William L. 1927- *St&PR 93*
Cheah, Chow Seng 1953- *WhoWor 93*
Cheah, Jonathon Yoo Chong 1951- *WhoEmL 93*
Cheah, Wi Kwong *WhoWor 93*
Cheairs, M. Norwood *Law&B 92*
Cheaka, Abdou Toure *WhoWor 93*
Cheatham, Benjamin Franklin 1820-1886 *BioIn 17*
Cheatham, Clarence Donald 1923- *WhoSSW 93*
Cheatham, Daniel E. 1949- *WhoEmL 93*
Cheatham, David Todd 1956- *WhoEmL 93*
Cheatham, Gary T. 1937- *St&PR 93*
Cheatham, Geoffrey D. 1941- *St&PR 93*
Cheatham, Glenn Wallace 1934- *WhoAm 92*
Cheatham, Gloria J. *Law&B 92*
Cheatham, Henry Plummer 1857-1935 *BioIn 17*
Cheatham, John Henry, Jr. 1924- *St&PR 93*
Cheatham, John Lawrence, Jr. 1933- *St&PR 93*
Cheatham, Karyn Elizabeth 1943- *WhoWrEP 92*
Cheatham, Mary Lawrence 1930- *WhoSSW 93*
Cheatham, Ollie V. 1945- *St&PR 93*
Cheatham, Richard Reed 1943- *WhoAm 92*
Cheatham, Robert Thomas 1952- *WhoEmL 93, WhoSSW 93*
Cheatham, Robert William 1938- *WhoAm 92*
Cheatham, Valerie Meador 1957- *WhoEmL 93, WhoSSW 93*
Cheatle, Leslie N., Jr. 1940- *St&PR 93*
Cheatwood, Roy Clifton 1946- *WhoEmL 93*
Cheban, David Nikolaevich 1952- *WhoWor 93*
Cheboksarov, N.N. 1907-1980 *IntDcAn*
Chebul, Charles Ray 1954- *WhoEmL 93*
Checa, Eduardo 1959- *WhoWor 93*
Checchi, Al *BioIn 17*
Checchi, Alfred A. 1948- *St&PR 93, WhoAm 92*
Checchi, Vincent V. 1918- *St&PR 93*
Checchi, Vincent Victor 1918- *WhoAm 92, WhoE 93*
Chechele, Tracey Samantha 1965- *WhoAmW 93*
Chechik, H.I. *St&PR 93*
Chechik, Jeremiah S. *MiSFD 9*
Chechile, James S. 1942- *St&PR 93*
Chechowicz, Jozef 1903-1939 *PolBiDi*
Checinski, Sylwester 1930- *DrEEuF*
Checker, Chubby 1941- *Baker 92, BioIn 17, SoulM*
Checketts, Dave 1956- *WhoE 93*
Checketts, David Wayne 1955- *WhoAm 92*
Checkland, Peter Bernard *WhoScE 91-1*
Checklin, Vladimir N. 1941- *WhoE 93*
Checkosky, Anne Catherine 1964- *WhoEmL 93*
Checkovich, Paul J. *Law&B 92*
Checota, Joseph Woodrow 1939- *St&PR 93, WhoAm 92*
Chedgy, David George 1939- *WhoAm 92*
Chedid, Andree *BioIn 17*
Chee, Anthony Ngik Choong 1942- *WhoSSW 93*
Chee, Felix Ping-Ching 1946- *WhoAm 92*
Chee, Percival Hon Yin 1936- *WhoAm 92*
Chee, Shirley 1941- *WhoAmW 93*
Cheech 1946- *WhoAm 92*
Cheech and Chong *QDrFCA 92 [port]*
Cheek, Arthur Lee 1940- *WhoSSW 93*
Cheek, Barbara Lee 1935- *WhoAmW 93*
Cheek, Ben F., III 1936- *St&PR 93*
Cheek, Charles E. *Law&B 92*
Cheek, Dennis William 1955- *WhoE 93, WhoEmL 93*
Cheek, Donna *BioIn 17*
Cheek, Douglas *MiSFD 9*
Cheek, Ed 1948- *WhoSSW 93*
Cheek, Edwin Rives 1928- *WhoSSW 93*
Cheek, Hollis C. 1945- *St&PR 93*
Cheek, James Edward 1932- *WhoAm 92, WhoWor 93*
Cheek, James Howe, III 1942- *WhoAm 92*
Cheek, James Richard 1936- *WhoAm 92, WhoWor 93*
Cheek, Jimmy Geary 1946- *WhoSSW 93*
Cheek, John Henry 1929- *WhoAm 92, WhoSSW 93*
Cheek, John (Taylor) 1948- *Baker 92*
Cheek, King Virgil, Jr. 1937- *WhoAm 92*
Cheek, Leslie, Jr. d1992 *NewYTBS 92*
Cheek, Louis Eugene 1951- *WhoEmL 93*
Cheek, Mary Louise 1942- *WhoAmW 93*
Cheek, Ralph L. 1930- *St&PR 93*
Cheek, Will Tompkins 1943- *WhoSSW 93*
Cheek-Milby, Kathleen 1950- *WhoWor 93*
Cheeks, Maurice Edward 1956- *BiDAMSp 1989, WhoAm 92*
Cheely, Daniel Joseph 1949- *WhoEmL 93*
Cheema, Mohammad Arshad 1955- *WhoWor 93*
Cheema, Mohan Krishan Singh 1936- *WhoE 93*
Cheema, Tariq Javaid 1949- *WhoWor 93*
Cheesbrough, Leon R. 1936- *St&PR 93*
Cheesbrough, Peter H. 1952- *St&PR 93*
Cheeseborough, Chandra *BlkAmWO*
Cheeseman, David John *WhoScE 91-1*
Cheeseman, Douglas Taylor, Jr. 1937- *WhoWor 93*
Cheeseman, Ian Clifford *WhoScE 91-1*
Cheeseman, Valerie Christine 1949- *WhoEmL 93, WhoSSW 93*
Cheeseman, William John 1943- *WhoAm 92*
Cheesman, Evelyn 1881-1969 *Expl 93*
Cheetham, Ann *ScF&FL 92*
Cheetham, David William *WhoScE 91-1*
Cheetham, James 1772-1810 *JrnUS*
Cheever, Allen Williams 1932- *WhoE 93*
Cheever, Daniel Sargent 1916- *WhoAm 92*
Cheever, Esther H. *AmWomPl*
Cheever, John 1912-1982 *BioIn 17, MagSAmL [port], WorLitC [port]*
Cheever, Sharon A. *Law&B 92*
Cheever, Susan *BioIn 17*
Cheffer, Scott Gerard 1964- *WhoAm 92*
Chefitz, Harold Neal 1935- *WhoAm 92*
Cheh, Huk Yuk 1939- *WhoAm 92, WhoWor 93*
Chehab, Fuad 1902?-1973 *BioIn 17*
Cheheyl, R. Stephen *St&PR 93*
Cheidze, Revaz 1926- *DrEEuF*
Cheifetz, Lorna Gale 1953- *WhoAm 92, WhoAmW 93*
Cheifetz, Ralph *Law&B 92*
Cheiffou, Amadou *WhoWor 93*
Cheilas *OxDcByz*
Cheilik, Michael 1937-1990 *BioIn 17*
Cheim, John *BioIn 17*
Cheim, John 1953- *ConAu 138*
Cheimets, Sheila 1936- *WhoE 93*
Chein, Fredrick F. 1935- *WhoAsAP 91*
Cheinstein, Julian Edward 1950- *WhoEmL 93*
Cheit, Earl Frank 1926- *WhoAm 92*
Chekhov, Anton 1860-1904 *MagSWL [port], OxDcOp, WorLitC [port]*
Chekhov, Anton Pavlovich 1860-1904 *BioIn 17*
Chekki, Dan(esh) A(yyappa) 1935- *WhoWrEP 92*
Chelard, Hippolyte 1789-1861 *OxDcOp*
Chelard, Hippolyte-Andre(-Jean)-Baptiste 1789-1861 *Baker 92*
Chelberg, Bruce S. 1934- *St&PR 93*
Chelberg, Bruce Stanley 1934- *WhoAm 92*
Chelberg, Robert Douglas 1938- *WhoAm 92*
Cheldin, Erwin 1931- *St&PR 93*
Chelesnik, Steven Anthony *Law&B 92*
Cheli, Henry Alan 1950- *St&PR 93*
Chelin, Jeffrey D. 1951- *St&PR 93*
Chelin, Steve Clyde 1942- *St&PR 93*
Chelios, Chris *BioIn 17*
Chelius, James Robert 1943- *WhoAm 92, WhoE 93*
Chelius, Maureen O. *Law&B 92*
Chelkowski, August Jan 1927- *WhoScE 91-4*
Chell, Beverly C. 1942- *WhoAm 92, WhoAmW 93*
Chell, K. *WhoScE 91-1*
Chellaiah, Srinivasan 1960- *WhoSSW 93*
Chellappa, Ramalingam 1953- *WhoEmL 93*
Chellas, Brian Farrell 1941- *WhoAm 92*
Chelleri, Fortunato 1686?-1757 *OxDcOp*
Chelleri, Fortunato 1690-1757 *Baker 92*
Chellgren, Paul Wilbur 1943- *St&PR 93, WhoAm 92*
Chellis, Eugene Clifton 1954- *WhoEmL 93*
Chelmonski, Jozef 1849-1914 *PolBiDi*
Chelmsford, Frederick Augustus Thesiger 1827-1905 *HarEnMi*
Chelnov, Anatole d1990 *BioIn 17*
Chelnov, Michael 1947- *WhoEmL 93*
Chelsom, Peter *MiSFD 9*
Chelstrom, Marilyn Ann *WhoAmW 93, WhoWor 93*
Chemerow, David I. 1951- *St&PR 93*
Chemerow, David Irving 1951- *WhoAm 92*
Chemin-Petit, Hans (Helmuth) 1902-1981 *Baker 92*
Chemla, Marius 1927- *WhoScE 91-2*
Chen, Alexander Yu-Kuang 1954- *WhoE 93, WhoEmL 93*
Chen, Alice F. *Law&B 92*
Chen, Alice Tung-Hua 1949- *WhoEmL 93*
Chen, Arbee Liang-Pei 1954- *WhoWor 93*
Chen, Arthur 1949- *WhoWor 93*
Chen, Basilio 1953- *WhoWor 93*
Chen, Bessie B. 1958- *WhoAmW 93*
Chen, Bill Shun-Zer 1941- *St&PR 93, WhoAm 92*

Chen, Carlton S. *Law&B 92*
Chen, Charles Chih-Tsai 1958- *WhoE 93*
Chen, Chi-Tsong 1936- *WhoAm 92*
Chen, Chih-Ying 1951- *WhoWor 93*
Chen, Chin-Tu 1951- *WhoEmL 93*
Chen, Ching-chih 1937- *WhoAmW 93, WhoWrEP 92*
Chen, Ching Jen 1936- *WhoAm 92*
Chen, Chuan Fang 1932- *WhoAm 92*
Chen, Chuanyu Ed 1933- *WhoWor 93*
Chen, Chung Long 1958- *WhoWor 93*
Chen, Concordia Chao *WhoAmW 93, WhoWor 93*
Chen, Daniel Yip Ching 1943- *WhoE 93*
Chen, Davidson Tah-chuen 1942- *WhoE 93*
Chen, De Hui 1940- *WhoWor 93*
Chen, Di 1929- *WhoAm 92*
Chen, Edward Chih-Hung 1954- *WhoE 93*
Chen, Eric *Law&B 92*
Chen, Francis F. 1929- *WhoAm 92*
Chen, Ga-Lane 1953- *WhoEmL 93*
Chen, George A. 1943- *St&PR 93*
Chen, Gong Ning 1939- *WhoWor 93*
Chen, Guan Shang 1919- *WhoE 93*
Chen, Guang-hua 1936- *WhoWor 93*
Chen, Gui-Qiang 1962- *WhoWor 93*
Chen, Guo Liang 1951- *WhoWor 93*
Chen, Hai-chin 1924- *WhoWor 93*
Chen, Han Lin 1932- *WhoWor 93*
Chen, Han-Ping 1949- *WhoWor 93*
Chen, Helen *BioIn 17*
Chen, Helen Wei 1967- *WhoAmW 93*
Chen, Hilo Chao-Hung 1942- *WhoE 93*
Chen, Ho-Hong H. H. 1933- *WhoE 93, WhoWor 93*
Ch'en, Hsueh-Chao 1906- *BioIn 17*
Chen, I-Yu 1946- *WhoAmW 93*
Chen, James H. 1944- *WhoUN 92*
Chen, James Pai-fun 1929- *WhoSSW 93, WhoWor 93*
Chen, Jian Ning 1959- *WhoWor 93*
Chen, Jim Nan 1940- *WhoWor 93*
Chen, Jin 1967- *WhoWor 93*
Chen, Jingliang 1937- *WhoWor 93*
Chen, Joan *BioIn 17*
Chen, John-ren 1936- *WhoWor 93*
Chen, Joseph Tao 1925- *WhoAm 92*
Chen, Jyh-Hong 1951- *WhoE 93*
Chen, Kai-Cheng 1950- *WhoWor 93*
Chen, Kaige *MiSFD 9*
Chen, Kao 1919- *WhoAm 92*
Ch'en, Kenneth Kuan-Sheng 1907- *WhoAm 92*
Chen, Kevin Sangone 1960- *WhoEmL 93*
Chen, Kok-Choo 1947- *WhoEmL 93*
Chen, Kun-Mu 1933- *WhoAm 92*
Ch'en, Li-li 1934- *WhoAm 92*
Chen, Lifu 1899- *BioIn 17*
Chen, Lih-Juann 1946- *WhoWor 93*
Chen, Lihtorng Robert 1952- *WhoE 93, WhoEmL 93*
Chen, Lincoln Chin-ho 1942- *WhoAm 92*
Chen, Linda Tehsing *WhoAmW 93*
Chen, Lung-chu 1935- *WhoWor 93*
Chen, Martha Alter 1944- *WhoAmW 93*
Chen, Michael Chien-Kuo 1955- *WhoE 93*
Chen, Michael Ming 1933- *WhoAm 92*
Chen, Michael Ming-Ming 1961- *WhoEmL 93*
Chen, Michael Shih-ta 1945- *WhoWor 93*
Chen, Min-Chu 1949- *WhoEmL 93, WhoSSW 93, WhoWor 93*
Chen, Ming-Yi 1938- *WhoWor 93*
Chen, Mu-Fa 1946- *WhoWor 93*
Chen, Mu-Tsai 1945- *WhoWor 93*
Chen, Nai Yuen 1926- *WhoAm 92*
Chen, Nan-Xian 1937- *WhoWor 93*
Chen, Peide 1940- *WhoWor 93*
Chen, Peter Pin-Shan 1947- *WhoAm 92, WhoWor 93*
Chen, Peter Wei-Teh 1942- *WhoWor 93*
Chen, Philip Minkang 1944- *WhoAm 92*
Chen, Philip S., Jr. 1932- *WhoAm 92*
Chen, Ping-fan 1917- *WhoAm 92*
Chen, Priscilla B. 1944- *WhoAmW 93*
Chen, Qing Bai 1939- *WhoWor 93*
Chen, Qing Yi 1925- *WhoWor 93*
Chen, Raymond T. 1937- *St&PR 93*
Chen, Richard L. 1938- *St&PR 93*
Chen, Robert Chia-Hua 1946- *WhoE 93*
Chen, Roger Ko-chung 1951- *WhoWor 93*
Chen, Shaozhu 1942- *WhoWor 93*
Chen, Shigiu 1938- *WhoUN 92*
Chen, Shium Andrew 1931- *WhoE 93*
Chen, Shoei-Sheng 1940- *WhoAm 92, WhoWor 93*
Chen, Shu Jin 1939- *WhoWor 93*
Chen, Shuxing 1941- *WhoWor 93*
Chen, Sow-Hsin 1935- *WhoAm 92*
Chen, Steve S. *NewYTBS 92 [port]*
Chen, Steven Kuan-Jen 1958- *WhoEmL 93*
Chen, Stuart Tsau Shiong 1933- *WhoAm 92*
Chen, Ta-Ko *Law&B 92*
Chen, Terry 1951- *St&PR 93*
Chen, Wai-Kai 1936- *WhoAm 92*
Chen, Walter Yi-Chen 1956- *WhoWor 93*
Chen, Wan-Yu 1916- *WhoWor 93*
Chen, Wayne H. 1922- *WhoAm 92*
Chen, Wei-Da 1952- *WhoWor 93*
Chen, Wende 1941- *WhoWor 93*
Chen, Wenxiong 1952- *WhoEmL 93*
Chen, Wesley 1954- *WhoWor 93*
Chen, William Hok-Nin 1950- *WhoEmL 93*
Chen, Yang-Fang 1953- *WhoWor 93*
Chen, Yang-Yuan 1955- *WhoWor 93*
Chen, Yi Yuan 1950- *WhoWor 93*
Chen, Yong-Zhuo 1949- *WhoE 93*
Chen, Yu Why 1910- *WhoE 93*
Chen, Yuan James 1949- *WhoSSW 93*
Chen, Yuan-tsung 1932- *BioIn 17*
Chen, Yubo 1933- *WhoWor 93*
Chen, Yuki Y. Kuo 1930- *WhoAm 92, WhoE 93, WhoWor 93*
Chen, Zao Ping 1925- *WhoWor 93*
Chen, Zhihua 1939- *WhoWor 93*
Chen, Zong Ji 1943- *WhoWor 93*
Chen, Zuchi 1941- *WhoWor 93*
Chen, Zuohuang 1947- *WhoAm 92*
Chenard, Pierre Dominique 1961- *St&PR 93*
Chenault, Hortenius 1910-1990 *BioIn 17*
Chenault, Kenneth I. *BioIn 17*
Chenault, Kenneth I. 1952- *ConBlB 4 [port]*
Chenault, Kenneth Irvine 1951- *WhoAm 92*
Chenault, Robert *MiSFD 9*
Chenault-Woods, Julie *BioIn 17*
Ch'en Ch'eng 1898- *HarEnMi*
Chen Chi 1912- *WhoAm 92, WhoE 93, WhoWor 93*
Ch'en Chiung-ming 1878-1933 *HarEnMi*
Chen Chong *BioIn 17*
Chen Chuan 1934- *WhoAsAP 91*
Chen Darwin 1932- *WhoAsAP 91*
Chen Duxiu 1879-1942 *DcTwHis*
Chene, Jean-J. 1929- *WhoScE 91-4*
Chenel, Laura 1949- *ConEn*
Chenery, Robin 1945- *St&PR 93*
Chenery, Robin 1946- *WhoSSW 93*
Chenevert, Edward Valmore, Jr. 1923- *WhoAm 92*
Chenevert, Norma G. 1947- *WhoAmW 93*
Chenevert, William James 1953- *St&PR 93*
Cheney, Anne Cleveland *AmWomPl*
Cheney, Brainard 1900-1990 *BioIn 17*
Cheney, Carolyn Lynds 1945- *WhoE 93*
Cheney, Cathy L. *Law&B 92*
Cheney, Daniel Lavern 1928- *WhoAm 92*
Cheney, Darwin Leroy 1940- *WhoAm 92*
Cheney, David Willi 1950- *St&PR 93*
Cheney, Dick 1941- *ColdWar 1 [port], WhoAm 92, WhoE 93, WhoWor 93*
Cheney, Eleanora Louise 1923- *WhoAmW 93*
Cheney, Gerald V. 1942- *St&PR 93*
Cheney, Glenn Alan 1951- *WhoEmL 93*
Cheney, Harriet Vaughan 1796-1889 *BioIn 17*
Cheney, James Addison 1927- *WhoAm 92*
Cheney, Janice Louanne 1954- *WhoEmL 93*
Cheney, Lynne V. 1941- *CurBio 92 [port], WhoAm 92, WhoAmW 93*
Cheney, Max W. 1922- *St&PR 93*
Cheney, Meredith 1925- *WhoAm 92*
Cheney, Paul E. 1927- *St&PR 93*
Cheney, Peter A. *St&PR 93*
Cheney, Peter A. 1942- *WhoIns 93*
Cheney, Philip Warren 1935- *WhoE 93*
Cheney, Richard B. *BioIn 17*
Cheney, Richard B. 1941- *CngDr 91, PolPar*
Cheney, Richard Eugene 1921- *WhoAm 92, WhoE 93*
Cheney, Rita Mae 1951- *WhoEmL 93*
Cheney, Russell 1881-1945 *BioIn 17*
Cheney, Theodore Albert 1928- *WhoWrEP 92*
Cheney, Thomas Ward 1914- *WhoAm 92*
Cheney, William A. 1923- *St&PR 93*
Cheney, William J. 1938- *St&PR 93*
Cheng, Alexander Hung-Darh 1952- *WhoE 93*
Cheng, Alexander Lihdar 1956- *WhoE 93*
Cheng, Andrew Francis 1951- *WhoE 93*
Cheng, Ansheng 1938- *WhoWor 93*
Cheng, Carol Wai Yee 1964- *WhoAmW 93*
Cheng, Christopher H.K. 1952- *WhoWor 93*
Cheng, Chu Yuan 1927- *WhoWor 93*
Cheng, Daijie 1936- *WhoWor 93*
Cheng, David Hong 1920- *WhoAm 92*
Cheng, David Hung Sheng 1922- *WhoAm 92*
Cheng, David Ta Ling 1945- *WhoE 93*
Cheng, Edward Hsin-Yi 1955- *WhoE 93*
Cheng, Edward Teh-Chang 1946- *WhoEmL 93*
Cheng, Emily 1953- *WhoE 93*
Cheng, Eugene Yap Giau 1942- *WhoAsAP 91*
Cheng, Franklin Yih 1936- *WhoAm 92*
Cheng, Fred Nai-Chung 1970- *WhoWrEP 92*
Cheng, Fuchang 1933- *WhoWor 93*
Cheng, Herbert Su-Yuen 1929- *WhoAm 92*
Cheng, Hsien Kei 1923- *WhoAm 92*
Cheng, Hwei Hsien 1932- *WhoAm 92*
Cheng, Irene Teresa 1954- *WhoEmL 93*
Cheng, J. S. 1914- *WhoWor 93*
Cheng, J. Weili *Law&B 92*
Cheng, James Kuo-Chiang 1936- *WhoWor 93*
Cheng, Julie J.L. *Law&B 92*
Cheng, Kenneth Tat-Chiu 1954- *WhoEmL 93, WhoSSW 93*
Cheng, Kuang Lu 1919- *WhoAm 92*
Cheng, Linda Y.H. *Law&B 92*
Cheng, Lung 1920- *WhoWor 93*
Cheng, Mei-Fang 1938- *WhoAm 92*
Cheng, Michael Tak-Kin 1938- *WhoAsAP 91*
Cheng, Ming Ming *BioIn 17*
Cheng, Paul Ming-Fun 1936- *WhoAsAP 91*
Cheng, Samson 1934- *WhoWor 93*
Cheng, Scarlet 1953- *WhoWrEP 92*
Cheng, Suan Soon 1953- *WhoWor 93*
Cheng, Szu-Chun 1925- *WhoWor 93*
Cheng, Theresa Y. *Law&B 92*
Cheng, Thomas Clement 1930- *WhoAm 92*
Cheng, Tsen-Chung 1944- *WhoAm 92*
Cheng, Tsung O. 1925- *WhoAm 92*
Cheng, Tung Chao 1931- *St&PR 93*
Cheng, Vic M. 1945- *WhoE 93*
Cheng, Wan-Lee 1945- *WhoAm 92, WhoWor 93*
Cheng, Wilfred David 1948- *WhoEmL 93*
Cheng, Yih-Shyang 1953- *WhoWor 93*
Cheng Ch'eng-kung 1624-1662 *HarEnMi*
Cheng Chih-lung d1661 *HarEnMi*
Cheng Chin c. 1643-1682 *HarEnMi*
Cheng Ho d1451 *HarEnMi*
Cheng Ho 1371-1434? *Expl 93*
Cheng Hon-Kwan 1927- *WhoAsAP 91*
Chen Guangyi 1934- *WhoAsAP 91*
Cheng Weigao 1933- *WhoAsAP 91*
Chenhall, Robert Gene 1923- *WhoAm 92*
Chenhalls, Anne Marie 1929- *WhoAmW 93*
Chen Houpei *BioIn 17*
Chen Huiguang 1938- *WhoAsAP 91*
Chenier, Andre 1762-1794 *BioIn 17*
Chenieux, Jean-Claude 1937- *WhoScE 91-2*
Chenitz, W. Carole 1946-1992 *BioIn 17*
Chenitz-Manley, Carole d1992 *NewYTBS 92*
Chen Jinhua *WhoAsAP 91*
Chen Junsheng 1927- *WhoAsAP 91, WhoWor 93*
Chen Li 1901-1972 *DcTwHis*
Chen Li-An 1937- *WhoAsAP 91, WhoWor 93*
Chen Man Hin, Dennis 1924- *WhoAsAP 91*
Chen Meng-Ling 1934- *WhoAsAP 91*
Chen Min *BioIn 17*
Chen Mingyi 1940- *WhoAsAP 91*
Chen Minzhang 1932- *WhoAsAP 91*
Chen Muhua 1917- *WhoWor 93*
Chen Muhua 1921- *WhoAsAP 91*
Chennault, Anna C. *BioIn 17*
Chennault, Anna Chen 1925- *WhoAm 92, WhoAmW 93, WhoWor 93*
Chennault, Claire Lee 1890-1958 *HarEnMi*
Chenneviere, Daniel *ScF&FL 92*
Chenost, Michel Maurice 1938- *WhoScE 91-2*
Chenot, Jean-Loup 1945- *WhoScE 91-2*
Chenoweth, Daniel Albert 1948- *St&PR 93*
Chenoweth, Dellzell *WhoWrEP 92*
Chenoweth, James M. 1931- *St&PR 93*
Chenoweth, Wilbur 1899-1980 *Baker 92*
Chen Shijun *WhoAsAP 91*
Chen Shing-Ling, Gen. 1924- *WhoAsAP 91*
Chen Shou-Shan 1929- *WhoAsAP 91*
Chensov, Alexandr Georgievich 1947- *WhoWor 93*
Chen Suzhi 1931- *WhoAsAP 91*
Chenu, Marie-Dominique 1895-1990 *BioIn 17*
Chen Xiangmei *BioIn 17*
Chen Xitong *WhoWor 93*
Chen Xitong 1930- *WhoAsAP 91*
Chen Yi 1901-1972 *HarEnMi*
Ch'en Yu d205BC *HarEnMi*
Ch'en Yu-ch'eng 1836-1862 *HarEnMi*
Chen Yujie 1942- *WhoAsAP 91*
Ch'en Yu-liang d1363 *HarEnMi*
Ch'en Yun 1905- *BioIn 17*
Chen Yuying *WhoAsAP 91*
Chen Zhili 1943- *WhoAsAP 91*
Chen Ziming *BioIn 17*
Cheo, Peter Kiong-Liang 1930- *WhoAm 92*
Cheong, Choong Kong 1944- *WhoWor 93*
Cheong, Stephen Kam-Chuen 1941- *WhoAsAP 91*
Chepiga, Pamela Rogers 1949- *WhoAm 92, WhoEmL 93*
Chepow, Steven Barry 1943- *St&PR 93*
Chepucavage, Peter James 1947- *WhoAm 92*
Cher 1946- *BioIn 17, HolBB [port], IntDcF 2-3, News 93-1 [port], WhoAm 92, WhoAmW 93*
Cher, David E. *Law&B 92*
Cheramie, Deany Marie 1964- *WhoSSW 93*
Cheramie, Gail Marie 1953- *WhoAmW 93*
Cherasia, Peter David 1958- *St&PR 93*
Cherberg, John A. 1910-1992 *BioIn 17*
Cherbuliez, Antoine-Elisee 1888-1964 *Baker 92*
Cherbury, Edward Herbert 1583-1648 *BioIn 17*
Cherches, Gisela Blohm *Law&B 92*
Chercover, Murray 1929- *WhoAm 92*
Chereau, Gabriel 1909-1990 *BioIn 17*
Chereau, Patrice *BioIn 17*
Chereau, Patrice 1944- *Baker 92, IntDcOp, OxDcOp, WhoWor 93*
Cherednichenko, Victor Grigoryevich 1945- *WhoWor 93*
Cherem, Barbara Frances 1946- *WhoAm 92*
Cherenkov, Pavel Alexeyevich 1904- *WhoAm 92, WhoWor 93*
Cherenzia, Bradley James 1931- *WhoWor 93*
Cherenzia, Peter Franklin 1937- *St&PR 93*
Cherepanov, Genady Petrovich 1937- *WhoWor 93*
Cherepnin *Baker 92*
Chereskin, Alvin 1928- *WhoAm 92*
Cheresko, Keith A. *Law&B 92*
Cheret, Roger 1939- *WhoWor 93*
Cherian, Jacob 1935- *St&PR 93*
Cherian, Susan 1955- *WhoAmW 93*
Cherici, Coleen Ann 1950- *WhoE 93, WhoEmL 93*
Cherico, Brian M. *Law&B 92*
Cherim, Stan Marshall 1929- *WhoE 93*
Cherin, Stephen J. 1962- *WhoWor 93*
Cherington, Joel *Law&B 92*
Cherins, Robert H. 1940- *St&PR 93*
Cherkaoui, Moulay Ahmed *WhoWor 93*
Cherkasky, Martin 1911- *WhoAm 92*
Cherkasky, Rudy 1928- *St&PR 93*
Cherkassky, Shura *BioIn 17*
Cherkassky, Shura (Alexander Isaakovich) 1911- *Baker 92*
Cherkassov, Nikolai 1903-1966 *IntDcF 2-3*
Cherken, Harry Sarkis, Jr. 1949- *WhoEmL 93*
Cherkes, Joseph Kenneth 1952- *WhoE 93*
Cherksey, Bruce David 1946- *WhoE 93*
Chermak, Gail Donna 1950- *WhoAmW 93, WhoEmL 93*
Chermann, Jean-Claud *WhoScE 91-2*
Chermann, Jean Claude 1939- *WhoWor 93*
Chermayeff, Ivan 1932- *WhoAm 92*
Chern, Jenn-Chuan 1954- *WhoWor 93*
Chern, Ji-Wang 1953- *WhoWor 93*
Chern, Paul 1940- *WhoE 93*
Chern, Shiing-Shen 1911- *WhoAm 92*
Chernack, Stuart E. *Law&B 92*
Chernaik, Judith 1934- *ConAu 39NR*
Chernak, Jerald Lee 1942- *WhoSSW 93, WhoWor 93*
Chernak, John A. 1929- *St&PR 93*
Chernak, Robert A. 1946- *WhoE 93*
Chernay, Gloria Jean 1938- *WhoAmW 93, WhoSSW 93*
Cherne, Leo *BioIn 17*
Chernenko, Konstantin 1911-1985 *ColdWar 2 [port]*
Cherner, Anne *WhoWrEP 92*
Cherner, Joseph *BioIn 17*
Chernesky, Ed *BioIn 17*
Chernesky, Richard John 1939- *WhoAm 92*
Chernetsov, V.N. 1905-1970 *IntDcAn*
Chernev, Melvin 1928- *WhoAm 92*
Cherney, Andrew Knox 1947- *WhoEmL 93*
Cherney, Brian 1942- *Baker 92*
Cherney, Carl D. 1952- *St&PR 93*
Cherney, Elaine Ethel 1929- *WhoAmW 93*
Cherney, James Alan 1948- *WhoAm 92, WhoEmL 93*
Cherniack, Helen Wessel 1911- *WhoAmW 93*
Cherniack, Neil Stanley 1931- *WhoAm 92*
Cherniack, Saul Mark 1917- *WhoAm 92*
Chernichaw, Mark 1946- *WhoAm 92*
Chernick, M.N. *Law&B 92*
Chernick, Michael Louis 1943- *WhoE 93*
Chernick, Sharon Lee 1952- *WhoAmW 93*
Chernick, Steven Roy 1949- *St&PR 93*

Chernik, Barbara Eisenlohr 1938- *WhoAmW 93*
Chernikhov, Iakov Georgievich 1889-1951 *BioIn 17*
Chernikoff, Neil N. 1931- *St&PR 93*
Chernikov, Alexander Antonovich 1949- *WhoWor 93*
Chernikov, Nickolai Sergeevich 1955- *WhoWor 93*
Chernikova, Olga Sergeevna 1957- *WhoWor 93*
Chernin, Fredric David 1939- *St&PR 93, WhoAm 92*
Chernin, Norman Alan *Law&B 92*
Chernin, Peter *WhoAm 92*
Chernin, Russell Scott 1957- *WhoEmL 93*
Chernish, Stanley Michael 1924- *WhoAm 92, WhoWor 93*
Chernivec, Gerald Frank *Law&B 92*
Cherno, Melvin 1929- *WhoAm 92*
Cherno, William Arnold *Law&B 92*
Chernof, David 1935- *WhoAm 92*
Chernoff, Amoz Immanuel 1923- *WhoAm 92*
Chernoff, Carl G. *Law&B 92*
Chernoff, Daniel Paregol 1935- *WhoAm 92*
Chernoff, Edward 1954- *WhoSSW 93*
Chernoff, Eugene M. 1926- *St&PR 93*
Chernoff, Hayley *BioIn 17*
Chernoff, Herman 1923- *WhoAm 92*
Chernoff, Hildegard 1926- *St&PR 93*
Chernoff, Martin 1943- *St&PR 93*
Chernoff, Maxine 1952- *ConAu 136*
Chernoff, Sheryl Stern 1954- *WhoEmL 93*
Chernoff-Pate, Diana 1942- *WhoAmW 93*
Chernomyrdin, Viktor Stepanovich 1938- *NewYTBS 92*
Chernovetz, Douglas Michael 1944- *St&PR 93*
Chernow, David A. 1922- *WhoAm 92*
Chernow, Fred Barnet 1932- *WhoE 93*
Chernow, Jeffrey Scott 1951- *WhoEmL 93*
Chernow, Ron 1949- *WhoAm 92*
Chernow, Stephen A. *Law&B 92*
Cherny, Robert Wallace 1943- *WhoAm 92*
Chernyak, Arkady Alexandrovich 1955- *WhoWor 93*
Chernyak, Zhanna Albertovna 1955- *WhoWor 93*
Chernyayev, Anatoli *BioIn 17*
Chernyshov, Kornely Isidorovich 1946- *WhoWor 93*
Cherokee Bill 1876-1896 *BioIn 17*
Cherokee Bob d1863 *BioIn 17*
Cherol, John A. 1950- *WhoAm 92*
Cheroutes, Michael Louis 1940- *WhoAm 92*
Cherovsky, Erwin Louis 1933- *WhoAm 92*
Cherr, George d1992 *NewYTBS 92*
Cherrick, Henry Morton 1939- *WhoAm 92*
Cherrick, Lorraine Susan *Law&B 92*
Cherrington, Karen G. *Law&B 92*
Cherruault, Yves 1937- *WhoWor 93*
Cherry, Annie M. *AmWomPl*
Cherry, Carolyn *ScF&FL 92*
Cherry, Charles Walter 1939- *St&PR 93*
Cherry, Daniel Ronald 1948- *WhoEmL 93*
Cherry, David A. 1949- *ScF&FL 92*
Cherry, Don(ald) 1936- *Baker 92*
Cherry, Donald G. *Law&B 92*
Cherry, Douglas W. *Law&B 92*
Cherry, Edward Earl 1926- *WhoAm 92*
Cherry, Gordon Emanuel *WhoScE 91-1*
Cherry, Harold 1931- *WhoAm 92*
Cherry, Herman 1909-1992 *BioIn 17, NewYTBS 92*
Cherry, James Alan *Law&B 92*
Cherry, James Donald 1930- *WhoAm 92*
Cherry, James R., Jr. *Law&B 92*
Cherry, James R., Jr. 1938- *St&PR 93*
Cherry, James Wesley, Jr. *Law&B 92*
Cherry, Jeanne Yates 1879- *AmWomPl*
Cherry, Joe Howard 1934- *WhoSSW 93*
Cherry, John *MiSFD 9*
Cherry, John Paul 1941- *WhoE 93*
Cherry, Karen J. 1938- *St&PR 93*
Cherry, Kelly *BioIn 17*
Cherry, Kelly 1940- *WhoWrEP 92*
Cherry, Kenneth F. 1949- *WhoEmL 93*
Cherry, Kenneth W. *St&PR 93*
Cherry, Larry Don 1946- *WhoSSW 93*
Cherry, Linda Lea 1956- *WhoAmW 93*
Cherry, Mack Henry 1947- *WhoEmL 93*
Cherry, Michael Ray 1955- *WhoEmL 93*
Cherry, Paul Stephen 1943- *WhoE 93*
Cherry, Peter Ballard 1947- *St&PR 93, WhoAm 92*
Cherry, Richard John *WhoScE 91-1*
Cherry, Richard L. 1936- *St&PR 93*
Cherry, Robert Earl Patrick 1924- *WhoAm 92*
Cherry, Rona Beatrice 1948- *WhoAm 92, WhoAmW 93*
Cherry, Ronald Lee 1934- *WhoAm 92*
Cherry, Ronald Wilson 1949- *WhoSSW 93*
Cherry, Russel L. *Law&B 92*
Cherry, Sandra Wilson 1941- *WhoAmW 93*
Cherry, Stanley Z. *MiSFD 9*
Cherry, Walter L. 1917- *St&PR 93*
Cherry, Walter Lorain 1917- *WhoAm 92*
Cherry, Wendell *BioIn 17*
Cherry, William Ashley 1924- *WhoAm 92*
Cherryh, C.J. 1942- *BioIn 17, ScF&FL 92, WhoAm 92, WhoAmW 93*
Cherryholmes, James Gilbert 1917- *WhoAm 92*
Cherryman, Myrtle *AmWomPl*
Chersky, Norman L. *Law&B 92*
Chertack, Melvin M. 1923- *WhoAm 92*
Chertos, Cynthia Helene 1950- *WhoAmW 93*
Cherubini, Joseph Charles 1958- *St&PR 93*
Cherubini, Luigi 1760-1842 *IntDcOp [port], OxDcOp*
Cherubini, (Maria) Luigi (Carlo Zenobio Salvatore) 1760-1842 *Baker 92*
Cherubini, Victor Fred 1952- *WhoEmL 93*
Cherundolo, Robert Francis 1941- *St&PR 93*
Cherven, Kenneth Patrick 1959- *WhoEmL 93*
Chervenkov, Vulko 1900-1980 *ColdWar 2*
Chervin, Paul N. 1941- *WhoE 93*
Chervin, Peter C. *St&PR 93*
Chervin, Ronda 1937- *WhoWrEP 92*
Chervin, Sheila A. *Law&B 92*
Chervitz, David Howard 1958- *WhoEmL 93*
Chervokas, John Vincent 1936- *WhoAm 92*
Cherwin, Joel Ira 1942- *WhoE 93*
Chesak, Donna Marie 1942- *WhoAmW 93*
Chesbro, George C. 1940- *ScF&FL 92*
Chesbro, Patricia Rowan 1948- *WhoAmW 93*
Chesbrough, Lindsey Vincent 1949- *St&PR 93*
Chesebro, Kay B. 1930- *St&PR 93*
Chesebro, Robert E., Jr. 1937- *St&PR 93*
Chesen, Carol Rockler 1944- *St&PR 93*
Chesen, Catherine Sue 1953- *WhoAmW 93, WhoEmL 93*
Chesen, Joseph Robert 1933- *WhoUN 92*
Cheshier, Stephen Robert 1940- *WhoAm 92*
Cheshire, Doris Schmidt 1959- *WhoSSW 93*
Cheshire, Edney Brinn 1950- *St&PR 93*
Cheshire, G. Leonard d1992 *NewYTBS 92 [port]*
Cheshire, (Geoffrey) Leonard 1917-1992 *CurBio 92N*
Cheshire, Martin Veale *WhoScE 91-1*
Cheshire, Paul Charles *WhoScE 91-1*
Cheshire, Sandra Kay 1958- *WhoEmL 93*
Cheshire, William Polk 1931- *WhoAm 92*
Chesin, Sorrell Ely 1932- *WhoE 93*
Cheski, Richard Michael 1935- *WhoAm 92*
Chesler, Alan R. *Law&B 92*
Chesler, Carol Ann 1938- *WhoAmW 93*
Chesler, Doris Adelle 1924- *WhoSSW 93*
Chesler, Francine *Law&B 92*
Chesler, Lawrence D. *Law&B 92*
Chesler, Victoria Aimee 1957- *WhoAmW 93*
Chesler-Marsh, Caren Lisa 1963- *WhoAmW 93*
Chesley, Eddie A. 1946- *WhoSSW 93*
Chesley, Karen Alice 1955- *WhoAmW 93*
Chesley, Paul F. 1926- *St&PR 93*
Chesley, Robert 1943-1990 *BioIn 17*
Chesley, Roger D. *Law&B 92*
Chesley, Stanley Morris 1936- *WhoAm 92*
Cheslock, Louis 1898-1981 *Baker 92*
Chesly, Roger *Law&B 92*
Chesman, Michael Richard *Law&B 92*
Chesner, Donald Walter 1944- *WhoSSW 93*
Chesner, Robert W. 1940- *WhoIns 93*
Chesney, David H. 1943- *St&PR 93*
Chesney, Francis Rawdon 1789-1872 *BioIn 17*
Chesney, Lee Roy, Jr. 1920- *WhoAm 92, WhoWor 93*
Chesney, Marion 1936- *ScF&FL 92, WhoAm 92*
Chesney, Patricia Susan 1951- *WhoEmL 93, WhoSSW 93*
Chesney, Russell Wallace 1941- *WhoAm 92*
Chesney, Susan Talmadge 1943- *WhoAmW 93*
Chesnik, Richard *Law&B 92*
Chesnin, Leon 1919- *WhoWor 93*
Chesnoff, Richard Z. 1937- *WhoWor 93*
Chesnoff, Stephen *Law&B 92*
Chesnos, Ronald J. 1944- *St&PR 93*
Chesnut, Carol Fitting 1937- *WhoAm 92, WhoAmW 93*
Chesnut, David Otis, III 1951- *WhoEmL 93*
Chesnut, Donald Blair 1932- *WhoAm 92*
Chesnut, Donald David 1932- *St&PR 93*
Chesnut, Donald Rader, Jr. 1948- *WhoSSW 93*
Chesnut, Edward B., Jr. *WhoE 93*
Chesnut, Franklin Gilmore 1919- *WhoAm 92*
Chesnut, Nondis Lorine 1941- *WhoAmW 93*
Chesnutt, Charles W. 1858-1932 *GayN*
Chesnutt, Charles Waddell 1858-1932 *BioIn 17, BlkAull 92, EncAACR*
Chesnutt, Florence Walker Andrews 1925- *WhoAmW 93*
Chesnutt, Jane 1950- *WhoAmW 93*
Chesnutt, Joy Ann 1948- *WhoAmW 93*
Chesrow, Cathleen Gwen 1947- *WhoWrEP 92*
Chess, Leonard *SoulM*
Chess, Patricia Ann 1953- *WhoAmW 93*
Chess, Richard B. 1953- *St&PR 93*
Chess, Susan H. *Law&B 92*
Chesselet, Roger P. 1926- *WhoScE 91-2*
Chesser, Al H. 1914- *WhoAm 92*
Chesser, Barbara Russell 1941- *WhoWrEP 92*
Chesser, David Michael 1947- *WhoEmL 93*
Chesser, Douglas Stanley 1948- *WhoEmL 93*
Chesser, Kerry Royce 1956- *WhoEmL 93*
Chesser, Michael Joseph 1948- *St&PR 93*
Chessex, Ronald 1929- *WhoScE 91-4*
Chesshire, John Harvey *WhoScE 91-1*
Chessler, Ronald J. 1957- *St&PR 93*
Chessley, Bara *WhoWrEP 92*
Chessman, Rebecca Lee 1945- *WhoAmW 93*
Chesson, Andrew *WhoScE 91-1*
Chesson, Eugene, Jr. 1928- *WhoAm 92*
Chesson, Michael Bedout 1947- *WhoE 93*
Chesson, Wesley Merritt 1927- *St&PR 93*
Chester, Alexander Campbell, III 1947- *WhoAm 92*
Chester, Alfred 1928-1971 *BioIn 17*
Chester, Arthur Noble 1940- *WhoAm 92*
Chester, Barbara 1950- *WhoEmL 93*
Chester, Beverly Dorfman 1953- *WhoSSW 93*
Chester, Buford 1938- *St&PR 93*
Chester, Deborah *ScF&FL 92*
Chester, Douglas Barry 1952- *WhoE 93*
Chester, Douglas C. 1939- *St&PR 93*
Chester, Edward William 1935- *WhoWrEP 92*
Chester, Francis 1936- *WhoSSW 93*
Chester, Geoffrey 1951- *WhoAm 92*
Chester, George M. 1922- *St&PR 93*
Chester, Gerald Edwin *Law&B 92*
Chester, Giraud 1922- *WhoAm 92*
Chester, John Geoffrey 1951- *St&PR 93*
Chester, John Jonas 1920- *WhoAm 92*
Chester, Lemuel Darnell, Jr. *AfrAmBi*
Chester, Lillian Eleanor Hauser 1888- *AmWomPl*
Chester, Malcolm P. *St&PR 93*
Chester, Michael 1928- *ScF&FL 92*
Chester, Milton Rowley 1932- *WhoSSW 93*
Chester, Nia Lane 1945- *WhoAmW 93*
Chester, Norman Charles 1953- *WhoE 93, WhoEmL 93*
Chester, P. Thomas 1947- *St&PR 93*
Chester, Roy *WhoScE 91-1*
Chester, Stephanie Ann 1951- *WhoEmL 93*
Chester, Thomas Jay 1951- *WhoEmL 93*
Chester, Thomas Lee 1949- *WhoEmL 93*
Chester, Timothy J. *WhoAm 92*
Chester, W. Lee 1923- *St&PR 93*
Chester, William L. 1907-1960? *ScF&FL 92*
Chesterfield, Earl of 1694-1773 *BioIn 17*
Chesterfield, John M. 1912- *St&PR 93*
Chesters, Graham *WhoScE 91-1*
Chesterton, G.K. 1874-1936 *BioIn 17, ScF&FL 92*
Chesterton, Gilbert Keith 1874-1936 *BioIn 17*
Chestnov, Robert Eric 1948- *St&PR 93*
Chestnut, Alphonse F. 1917- *WhoSSW 93*
Chestnut, Harold 1917- *WhoAm 92*
Chestnut, J.L., Jr. *BioIn 17*
Chestnut, Jack 1943- *St&PR 93*
Chestnut, Mark E. *St&PR 93*
Chestnut, Randall 1947- *St&PR 93*
Chestnut, Roberta 1940- *WhoAmW 93*
Chestnutt, George Alexander, Jr. 1914- *WhoAm 92*
Chestnutwood, R.L. 1931- *St&PR 93*
Cheston, George Morris 1917- *WhoAm 92*
Cheston, Sheila Carol 1958- *WhoEmL 93*
Cheston, T. Stephen 1941- *WhoSSW 93*
Cheston, Theodore C. 1922- *WhoAm 92*
Cheston, Warren Bruce 1926- *WhoAm 92*
Chestovich, Milan John *Law&B 92*
Cheswick, Richard R. 1924- *St&PR 93*
Chesworth, Edward Thomas 1937- *WhoE 93*
Chetel, Gregory 1950- *WhoEmL 93*
Chetkovich, Michael N. 1916- *WhoAm 92*
Chetkowski, Ryszard Jerzy 1948- *WhoEmL 93*
Chetlin, Sue E. *Law&B 92*
Chetnik, Adam 1880-1967 *IntDcAn*
Chetsanga, Christopher James 1935- *WhoWor 93*
Chetwin, Grace *ScF&FL 92*
Chetwode, Philip Walhouse 1869-1950 *HarEnMi*
Chetwynd, Bridget 1910- *ScF&FL 92*
Chetwynd, Hilary 1929-1990 *BioIn 17*
Chetwynd, Lionel *WhoWor 93*
Chetwynd, Lionel 1940- *ConAu 137, MiSFD 9*
Chetwynd-Hayes, R. 1919- *ScF&FL 92*
Cheung, Alex K.W. 1949- *WhoWor 93*
Cheung, Allan Shi-Chung 1953- *WhoWor 93*
Cheung, Alvin Man Wai 1948- *WhoWor 93*
Cheung, Anthony 1946- *St&PR 93*
Cheung, Benton Yan-Lung 1922- *WhoAsAP 91*
Cheung, David Chi-Kong 1938- *WhoAsAP 91*
Cheung, Jeffrey 1950- *St&PR 93*
Cheung, Judy Hardin 1945- *WhoAmW 93*
Cheung, Kwok-wai 1956- *WhoWor 93*
Cheung, Lung 1947- *WhoWor 93*
Cheung, Raymond Siu-Yuen 1955- *WhoWor 93*
Cheung, Rebecca Mei Kwan 1965- *WhoWor 93*
Cheung, Tak Kee 1955- *WhoEmL 93*
Cheung, To-Yat 1937- *WhoWor 93*
Cheung, Wilkin Wai-Kuen 1941- *WhoWor 93*
Cheung Man-Yee 1946- *WhoAsAP 91*
Chevaillier, Philippe 1939- *WhoScE 91-2*
Cheval, Liz *BioIn 17*
Cheval, Louis Joseph 1932- *WhoWor 93*
Chevaldonne, Pierre Yves 1965- *WhoWor 93*
Chevalier, C. *WhoScE 91-2*
Chevalier, Gilles 1934- *St&PR 93*
Chevalier, Harold F. d1991 *BioIn 17*
Chevalier, Jean 1936- *WhoWor 93*
Chevalier, Maurice 1888-1972 *Baker 92, IntDcF 2-3 [port]*
Chevalier, Paul Edward 1939- *WhoAm 92*
Chevalier, Robert L. 1946- *WhoSSW 93*
Chevalier, Roger Alan 1949- *WhoAm 92*
Chevalier, Samuel Fletcher 1934- *St&PR 93, WhoAm 92*
Chevalier, Sulpice Guillaume 1804-1866 *BioIn 17*
Chevannes, Paul Hayden 1952- *WhoEmL 93*
Chevarier, Alain 1944- *WhoScE 91-2*
Cheve, Emile-Joseph-Maurice 1804-1864 *Baker 92*
Chevenement, Jean-Pierre *BioIn 17*
Chevers, Wilda Anita Yarde *WhoAmW 93*
Cheves, Harry Langdon, Jr. 1924- *WhoSSW 93*
Cheves, Langdon 1776-1857 *PolPar*
Chevillard, (Paul Alexandre) Camille 1859-1923 *Baker 92*
Cheville, Norman Frederick 1934- *WhoAm 92*
Chevins, Anthony Charles 1921- *WhoAm 92*
Chevray, Rene 1937- *WhoAm 92*
Chevreton, M. *WhoScE 91-2*
Chevreuille, Raymond 1901-1976 *Baker 92*
Chevrier, Jean Marc 1916- *WhoAm 92*
Chevrillon, Cyrille Louis 1953- *WhoWor 93*
Chevrillon, Olivier 1929- *WhoWor 93*
Chevron, Jean-Jacques 1933- *WhoUN 92*
Chew, David L. 1952- *St&PR 93*
Chew, Elizabeth 1959- *WhoE 93*
Chew, Frank Stephens 1937- *St&PR 93*
Chew, Geoffrey Foucar 1924- *WhoAm 92*
Chew, James Soong Bill 1961- *WhoEmL 93*
Chew, Julia Diane 1964- *WhoAmW 93*
Chew, Margaret Sarah 1909- *WhoAmW 93*
Chew, Mary Catherine *WhoAm 92*
Chew, Meng-Sang 1954- *WhoSSW 93*
Chew, Pamela Christine 1953- *WhoEmL 93*
Chew, Randall Thornton, III 1926- *WhoSSW 93*
Chew, Ruth 1920- *ScF&FL 92*
Chew, Ruth E. *AmWomPl*
Chew, Tai-Soo 1940- *WhoUN 92*
Chew, William H. *St&PR 93*
Chew Kam Hoy *WhoAsAP 91*
Chewning, Richard Carter 1933- *WhoAm 92*
Chewning, Robert Wills 1929- *WhoAm 92*
Chey, William Yoon 1930- *WhoAm 92*

Cheyer, Thomas Francis 1935- St&PR 93
Cheyette, Irving 1904- WhoWrEP 92
Cheyfitz, Eric ScF&FL 92
Cheyne, Ian St&PR 93
Cheynet, Jean-Pierre 1948- WhoScE 91-2
Cheyney, Arnold B. 1926- WhoWrEP 92
Cheyney, Curtis Paul, III 1942- WhoAm 92, WhoE 93
Cheyney, Harry Stanton 1926- St&PR 93
Che Young Suk 1936- WhoAsAP 91
Cheze, Bernard 1940- WhoScE 91-2
Cheze, Claude 1932- WhoScE 91-2
Cheze, Genevieve 1932- WhoScE 91-2
Chezeau, Jean-Michel 1939- WhoScE 91-2
Chezem, Curtis Gordon 1924- WhoAm 92
Chezy, Helmina von 1783-1856 OxDcOp
Chhabra, A. Law&B 92
Chhieng, Proeung BioIn 17
Chhor, Kylin 1937- WhoUN 92
Chi, Chia-Dann 1936- St&PR 93
Chi, Gou-chung 1946- WhoWor 93
Chi, Lily Mao 1947- WhoAmW 93
Chi, Lotta C. J. Li 1930- WhoAm 92
Chi, Sien 1936- WhoWor 93
Chi, Xian Cheng 1937- WhoUN 92
Chia, Hsin Pao 1920- St&PR 93
Chia, Sandro 1946- BioIn 17
Chia, Siew Whye 1949- WhoWor 93
Chiabrera, Gabriello 1552-1638 OxDcOp
Chiacchierini, Richard Philip 1943- WhoE 93
Chiado, Paul S. 1930- St&PR 93
Chiaffitella, Michael J. 1947- St&PR 93
Chiam, James Shuh-Min 1945- WhoWor 93
Chiancone, Emilia 1938- WhoScE 91-3
Chiang, Madame BioIn 17
Chiang, Albert Chinfa 1946- WhoWor 93
Chiang, Benjamin Bi-Nin 1929- WhoWor 93
Chiang, Cheng-Wen 1943- WhoWor 93
Chiang, Ch'ing 1914-1991 BioIn 17
Chiang, Ching-kuo 1910-1988 BioIn 17
Chiang, Edward Tsung-Ting 1936- WhoE 93
Chiang, George Djia-Chee 1938- WhoE 93
Chiang, Hsiao-wu d1991 BioIn 17
Chiang, Huai Chang 1915- WhoAm 92
Chiang, Hunter H.T. 1935- WhoUN 92
Chiang, Jeff BioIn 17
Chiang, Julie JoLee 1947- WhoAmW 93, WhoEmL 93
Chiang, Kai-shek 1887-1975 BioIn 17
Chiang, Kin Seng 1957- WhoWor 93
Chiang, Mei-ling BioIn 17
Chiang, Peter K. 1941- WhoE 93
Chiang, Shiao-Hung 1929- WhoAm 92
Chiang, Shuching Wang 1946- WhoAmW 93
Chiang, Wen-Li 1946- WhoEmL 93
Chiang Chia-Hsing 1939- WhoAsAP 91
Chiang Ch'ing 1913?-1991 CurBio 92N
Chiang Ching-kuo 1909-1988 DcTwHis
Chiang Kai-shek 1887-1975 ColdWar 2 [port], HarEnMi
Chiang Kai-Shek, Madame 1899- WhoWor 93
Chiantera, Dominic J. Law&B 92
Chiapella, Anne Page 1942- WhoE 93
Chiappa, Francis William 1949- WhoEmL 93
Chiappardi, Stephanie Corp 1953- WhoEmL 93
Chiappe, Jean 1878-1940 BioIn 17
Chiapperini, Patricia Bignoli 1946- WhoAmW 93, WhoE 93, WhoWor 93
Chiappetta, Peter Anthony 1949- WhoAm 92
Chiappini, Umberto 1930- WhoScE 91-3
Chiappo, Leopoldo 1924- WhoWor 93
Chiara, Maria 1939- Baker 92, OxDcOp
Chiara, Ruggero WhoScE 91-3
Chiaradia, Alfredo Vincente 1945- WhoUN 92
Chiaramida, Angeljean 1949- WhoE 93
Chiaramonte, Steven 1956- WhoEmL 93
Chiaramonte, Steven C. 1956- St&PR 93
Chiarella, Denise Gail 1962- WhoAmW 93
Chiarella, Peter Ralph 1932- WhoAm 92
Chiarella, Philip V. 1941- St&PR 93
Chiarelli, Brunetto 1934- WhoScE 91-3
Chiarelli, Joseph 1946- WhoAm 92, WhoE 93, WhoEmL 93, WhoWor 93
Chiarello, Anthony James 1943- St&PR 93
Chiarello, Donald Frederick 1940- WhoAm 92
Chiarenza, Carl 1935- WhoAm 92
Chiarenza, Frank John 1926- WhoAm 92
Chiari, Giuseppe 1926- Baker 92
Chiari, Roberto DcCPCAm
Chiari, Walter 1924-1991 AnObit 1991
Chiarizio, Eric E. Law&B 92
Chiarkas, Nicholas L. WhoAm 92
Chiat, Jay BioIn 17
Chiat, Jay 1931- WhoAm 92
Chiat, Marc BioIn 17
Chiat, Marilyn Joyce 1932- WhoAmW 93
Chiatalas, John L. Law&B 92
Chiau, Ng Nai 1948- WhoWor 93
Chiavario, Nancy Anne 1947- WhoAmW 93
Chiaverini, John Edward 1924- St&PR 93, WhoAm 92, WhoWor 93
Chiazze, Leonard, Jr. 1934- WhoAm 92
Chiba, Akihiro 1934- WhoUN 92
Chiba, Keiko 1948- WhoAsAP 91
Chiba, Kiyoshi 1946- WhoWor 93
Chiba, Milan ScF&FL 92
Chiba, Yoshihiko 1931- WhoWor 93
Chic SoulM
Chicago, Judy 1939- BioIn 17, WhoAm 92, WhoAmW 93, WhoWrEP 92
Chiccarine, Anthony P. 1945- St&PR 93
Chicco, Giacomo Franco 1958- WhoE 93, WhoEmL 93
Chicco, Giuliano Law&B 92
Chichelo, James A. 1958- St&PR 93
Chicherov, V.I. 1907-1957 IntDcAn
Chichester, David Nelson 1945- St&PR 93
Chichester, Francis 1901-1972 BioIn 17
Chichetto, James William WhoWrEP 92
Ch'i Chi-kuang 1528-1587 HarEnMi
Chick, Charles Eugene 1934- St&PR 93
Chick, Edward William George 1932- WhoWor 93
Chick, James P., Jr. 1947- WhoIns 93
Chick, Kenneth E. 1948- St&PR 93
Chick, Victoria BioIn 17
Chickering, F. William 1953- WhoE 93
Chickering, Howard Allen 1942- WhoAm 92, WhoE 93
Chickering, Jonas 1798-1853 Baker 92
Chickering, Lorraine Ellen 1950- WhoSSW 93
Chickering, Thomas E. 1824-1871 Baker 92
Chico, Gregory John 1962- WhoSSW 93
Chicoine, Francis G. 1931- St&PR 93
Chicoine, Jerry L. 1942- St&PR 93
Chicone, Jerry, Jr. 1934- St&PR 93, WhoAm 92
Chicorel, Marietta S. WhoAm 92
Chida, Junaid Hasan 1956- WhoEmL 93
Chidambaram, P. 1945- WhoAsAP 91
Chidambaranathan, Sornampillai 1930- WhoUN 92
Chiddick, Gerald Kevin 1967- WhoE 93
Chiddix, James A. 1945- St&PR 93
Chiddix, James Alan 1945- WhoAm 92
Chidester, Jack Joseph 1958- WhoE 93
Chidester, Otis Holden 1903- WhoAm 92
Chidester, Patricia VerJean WhoAmW 93
Chidley, John S. WhoIns 93
Chidley, William G. 1951- St&PR 93
Chidnese, Patrick N. 1940- WhoSSW 93
Chidzero, Bernard Thomas Gibson 1927- WhoAfr
Chieco, Michael Gerard 1953- WhoEmL 93
Chieco, Pasquale 1948- WhoWor 93
Chieffalo, Mario Victor 1934- WhoWor 93
Chiem, Chi-Yuen 1942- WhoScE 91-2
Chien, Charlene Wang BioIn 17
Ch'ien, Chung-shu 1911- BioIn 17
Chien, Eugene Y.H. 1946- WhoAsAP 91
Chien, Fredrick Fu 1935- WhoWor 93
Chien, Kuei-Ru 1945- WhoWor 93
Chien, Kuei-Yuan 1941- WhoE 93
Chien, Ring-Ling 1952- WhoEmL 93
Chien, Yew-Hu 1951- WhoWor 93
Chien, Yie Wen 1938- WhoWor 93
Chieng, Ching-Chang 1946- WhoWor 93
Chiepe, Gaositwe Keagakwa Tibe 1922- WhoAfr, WhoWor 93
Chierchio, Joe BioIn 17
Chieri, Pericle Adriano Carlo 1905- WhoAm 92
Chierici, Gian Luigi 1926- WhoWor 93
Chiericozzi, Pete R. 1943- St&PR 93
Chiesa, Gabriella 1948- WhoWor 93
Chiesa, John Richard 1924- WhoWrEP 92
Chiesi, Alexander Robert 1937- St&PR 93
Chiet, Arnold 1930- WhoE 93
Chiewsilp, Pimol 1937- WhoWor 93
Chiffons SoulM
Chifley, Joseph Benedict 1885-1951 DcTwHis
Chigan, Evgueni Nicolaevitch 1937- WhoUN 92
Chiger, Jeffrey Stuart 1949- WhoEmL 93, WhoSSW 93
Chigier, Norman 1933- WhoAm 92, WhoWor 93
Chih, Chung-Ying 1916- WhoWor 93
Chi Haotian 1928- WhoAsAP 91
Chihara, Carol Joyce 1941- WhoAmW 93
Chihara, Paul 1938- Baker 92
Chihuly, Dale Patrick 1941- WhoAm 92
Chikafusa, Hirano 1933- WhoWor 93
Chikamatsu, Hiroaki 1926- WhoWor 93
Chikane, Frank 1951- WhoAfr
Chikaoka, Riichiro 1926- WhoAsAP 91
Chikes, Cathy Taylor 1953- WhoAmW 93
Chikichev, Sergei Ilich 1951- WhoWor 93
Chikina, Ekaterina Sergeevna Smirnova- 1893-1979 BioIn 17
Chikofsky, Elliot Jay 1955- WhoE 93, WhoEmL 93
Chikry, Arkady Alexeyevich 1945- WhoWor 93
Chikuse, Yasuko 1943- WhoWor 93
Chikvaidze, Aleksandr Davidovich 1932- WhoWor 93
Chilaka, James Oguike 1942- WhoWor 93
Chiland, Colette 1928- WhoScE 91-2
Chilcote, David Charles 1951- WhoEmL 93
Chilcote, Lugean Lester 1929- WhoAm 92
Chilcote, Ronald H. 1935- WhoWrEP 92
Chilcote, Ronald Hodell 1935- WhoAm 92
Chilcote, Samuel Day, Jr. 1937- WhoAm 92, WhoE 93
Chilcott, Edward Hidinger 1948- WhoEmL 93
Child, Anthony H. 1951- St&PR 93
Child, Arthur J.E. 1910- St&PR 93
Child, Arthur James Edward 1910- WhoAm 92
Child, Charles Gardner 1908-1991 BioIn 17
Child, Curtis d1991 BioIn 17
Child, David Lee 1794-1874 JrnUS
Child, Dennis WhoScE 91-1
Child, Desmond BioIn 17
Child, Edward Taylor 1930- WhoE 93
Child, Frank Clayton 1921- WhoAm 92
Child, Harold L. 1920- St&PR 93
Child, Irvin Long 1915- WhoAm 92, WhoE 93
Child, Jack 1938- WhoE 93
Child, Joan WhoAsAP 91
Child, John WhoScE 91-1
Child, John Sowden, Jr. 1944- WhoE 93, WhoWor 93
Child, Joy Challender 1952- WhoAmW 93
Child, Julia BioIn 17
Child, Julia McWilliams 1912- WhoAm 92, WhoAmW 93
Child, Kent 1951- St&PR 93
Child, Lincoln ScF&FL 92
Child, Lydia Maria Francis 1802-1880 BioIn 17
Child, Tim ScF&FL 92
Child, Vern D. 1944- St&PR 93
Child, William 1606-1697 Baker 92
Childe, David Cyril 1963- WhoEmL 93
Childe, V. Gordon 1892-1957 IntDcAn
Childer, Simon Ian ScF&FL 92
Childerhose, R.J. 1928- ScF&FL 92
Childers, Bruce S. 1938- St&PR 93
Childers, Charles Eugene 1932- WhoAm 92
Childers, Gary Steve 1960- St&PR 93
Childers, James Howard 1942- St&PR 93
Childers, James Monroe, IV 1953- WhoEmL 93
Childers, James Saxon 1899-1965 EncAACR
Childers, John Henry 1930- WhoWor 93
Childers, John Scott 1946- WhoEmL 93
Childers, Malcolm Graeme 1945- BioIn 17
Childers, Norman Franklin 1910- WhoAm 92
Childers, Perry Robert 1932- WhoAm 92, WhoSSW 93, WhoWor 93
Childers, Richard Lee 1930- WhoSSW 93
Childers, Robert Lawson 1948- WhoEmL 93
Childers, Sheri Diane 1954- WhoAmW 93
Childers, Susan Lynn Bohn 1948- WhoAmW 93, WhoEmL 93, WhoWor 93
Childers, Thomas Allen 1940- WhoE 93
Childers, William Edward 1936- WhoSSW 93
Childers, Yildiz Gunduz 1939- WhoWor 93
Childers-Hermann, Judy Kaye 1946- WhoAmW 93, WhoEmL 93, WhoSSW 93
Childres, John C. Law&B 92
Childress, Alice 1920- BioIn 17, BlkAuII 92, ConTFT 10, DcAmChF 1960, MajAI [port], WhoAm 92
Childress, Barry Lee 1941- WhoWor 93
Childress, David T., Jr. 1940- WhoSSW 93
Childress, Evelyn Susan 1951- WhoAmW 93
Childress, Fay Alice 1929- WhoE 93
Childress, James Franklin 1940- WhoAm 92
Childress, James Gary 1947- St&PR 93
Childress, James J. 1942- WhoAm 92
Childress, Jan C. 1954- WhoE 93
Childress, John S. 1932- WhoIns 93
Childress, Kristie Elaine Johnston 1956- WhoAmW 93, WhoEmL 93
Childress, Lana J. St&PR 93
Childress, Mark BioIn 17
Childress, Mark 1957- WhoAm 92
Childress, Raymond Clay, Jr. 1962- WhoAm 92
Childress, Robert Lee 1939- WhoSSW 93
Childress, Scott Julius 1926- WhoAm 92
Childress, Walter Dabney, III 1943- WhoSSW 93
Childress, William Dale 1933- WhoWrEP 92
Childs, Alan WhoScE 91-1
Childs, Barney (Sanford) 1926- Baker 92
Childs, Barton 1916- WhoAm 92
Childs, Billy BioIn 17
Childs, Brevard Springs 1923- WhoAm 92
Childs, Bruce Kenneth 1934- WhoAsAP 91
Childs, Clara AmWomPl
Childs, David M. BioIn 17
Childs, Diana M. 1947- WhoIns 93
Childs, Elizabeth C(atharine) 1954- ConAu 138
Childs, Elizabeth Catharine 1954- WhoAmW 93
Childs, Frank Leighton 1944- St&PR 93
Childs, Gayle Bernard 1907- WhoWor 93
Childs, George L. d1991 BioIn 17
Childs, George William 1829-1894 JrnUS
Childs, Hoyt Abner, Jr. 1945- WhoSSW 93
Childs, Hymen 1938- WhoAm 92
Childs, Irene M. AmWomPl
Childs, J. Mabon 1922- St&PR 93
Childs, James Fielding Lewis 1910- WhoSSW 93
Childs, James William 1935- WhoAm 92
Childs, John David 1939- WhoWor 93
Childs, John F. 1909- St&PR 93
Childs, John Farnsworth 1909- WhoAm 92
Childs, Julie 1950- WhoEmL 93
Childs, Larry Brittain 1952- WhoEmL 93
Childs, Margaret Helen 1951- WhoAmW 93
Childs, Marjorie May Victoria 1918- WhoAm 92
Childs, Marquis 1903- JrnUS
Childs, Marquis William 1903-1990 BioIn 17
Childs, Maryanna 1910- WhoWrEP 92
Childs, Rand Hampton 1949- WhoSSW 93
Childs, Rhonda Louise 1946- WhoAmW 93
Childs, Richard L. MacKenzie BioIn 17
Childs, Ronald Frank 1939- WhoAm 92
Childs, Rosemary Burke 1958- WhoEmL 93
Childs, Sadie L. 1952- WhoAmW 93
Childs, Sheldon Mills 1922- St&PR 93
Childs, Shirle Moone 1936- WhoAmW 93
Childs, Terry A. 1960- WhoWrEP 92
Childs, Thomas 1796-1853 HarEnMi
Childs, Thomas Henry Carr WhoScE 91-1
Childs, Victoria MacKenzie- BioIn 17
Childs, Wylie Jones 1922- WhoAm 92
Chilembwe, John c. 1871-1915 DcTwHis
Chiles, Harry Frazier 1953- WhoEmL 93
Chiles, Lawton BioIn 17
Chiles, Lawton Mainor 1930- WhoAm 92
Chiles, Ross Pershing 1939- WhoSSW 93
Chiles, Stephen Michael 1942- WhoAm 92
Chilesotti, Oscar 1848-1916 Baker 92
Chilgren, Delia M. Law&B 92
Chilian, George William St&PR 93
Chilian, William Joseph 1965- WhoE 93
Chilibeck, Peter J. Law&B 92
Chilingarian, George Varos 1929- WhoAm 92
Chilingirian, Levon 1948- Baker 92
Chi-Lites SoulM
Chilivis, Nickolas Peter 1931- WhoAm 92
Chilleri, Gino Amerigo Law&B 92
Chillida Juantegul, Eduardo 1924- WhoWor 93
Chilly WhoWrEP 92
Chilman, Catherine Earles Street 1914- WhoAm 92
Chilosi, Alberto 1942- WhoWor 93
Chilson, Olin Hatfield 1903- WhoAm 92
Chilson, Rob 1945- ScF&FL 92
Chilton, Alice Pleasance Hunter 1911- WhoWor 93
Chilton, Bradley Stuart, Jr. 1953- WhoEmL 93, WhoSSW 93
Chilton, H. Herman 1863- ScF&FL 92
Chilton, Horace Thomas 1923- WhoAm 92
Chilton, Mary-Dell Matchett 1939- WhoAmW 93
Chilton, Michael Dennis 1942- St&PR 93
Chilton, Nick Ray 1946- St&PR 93
Chilton, Paul 1944- ScF&FL 92
Chilton, Raymond Lee, Jr. 1936- St&PR 93
Chilton, St. John Poindexter 1909- WhoAm 92

Chilton, William David 1954- *WhoWor 93*
Chiluba, Frederick *BioIn 17*
Chiluba, Frederick 1943- *CurBio 92 [port], News 92 [port], -92-3 [port]*
Chiluba, Frederick J. 1943- *WhoAfr*
Chiluba, Frederick Jacob Titus 1943- *WhoWor 93*
Chilver, Henry 1926- *WhoWor 93*
Chilver, Peter 1933- *ConAu 38NR*
Chilvers, Colin 1945- *MiSFD 9*
Chilvers, Derek 1940- *St&PR 93, WhoAm 92*
Chilvers, John James 1924- *St&PR 93*
Chil y Naranjo, Gregorio 1831-1901 *IntDcAn*
Chimaera *MajAI*
Chimel, Robert George 1953- *WhoEmL 93*
Chimenti, Ronald Christopher 1944- *St&PR 93*
Chimento, John F. 1938- *St&PR 93*
Chimera, Paul Robert 1949- *WhoE 93*
Chimerine, Lawrence 1940- *WhoAm 92*
Chimes *SoulM*
Chimes, Philip Richard 1949- *WhoEmL 93*
Chimiak, Andrzej 1932- *WhoScE 91-4*
Chimick, Claire Bessie Reifenheiser 1933- *WhoAmW 93*
Chimoff, Rapheal 1933- *St&PR 93*
Chimples, Constantine George 1948- *St&PR 93*
Chimples, George 1924- *WhoAm 92, WhoE 93, WhoWor 93*
Chimples, Thomas 1959- *St&PR 93*
Chimsky, Mark Evan 1955- *WhoAm 92*
Chimy, Jerome Isidore 1919- *WhoAm 92*
Chin, Aland Kwang-Yu 1950- *WhoWor 93*
Chin, Alexander Foster 1937- *WhoSSW 93*
Chin, Allen E., Sr. 1950- *WhoE 93*
Chin, Alvin Juilin 1953- *WhoE 93*
Chin, Ark G. 1924- *WhoAm 92*
Chin, Bryan Allen 1952- *WhoSSW 93*
Chin, Carolyn Sue 1947- *WhoAm 92*
Chin, Cecilia Hui-Hsin *WhoAm 92*
Chin, Cindy Lai 1957- *WhoAmW 93, WhoEmL 93*
Chin, Cynthia D. *St&PR 93*
Chin, Daryl 1953- *WhoWrEP 92*
Chin, David Chiu Kwan 1949- *WhoE 93*
Chin, Der-Tau 1939- *WhoE 93*
Chin, Ellen Y. 1965- *WhoAmW 93*
Chin, Francis Y. 1950- *St&PR 93*
Chin, Gay *Law&B 92*
Chin, Gilbert Y. 1934-1991 *BioIn 17*
Chin, Gladys M. 1960- *WhoAmW 93*
Chin, Hong Woo 1935- *WhoAm 92, WhoWor 93*
Chin, Hsiao-yi 1921- *WhoAsAP 91*
Chin, James Kee-Hong 1934- *WhoWor 93*
Chin, James Ying 1953- *WhoEmL 93*
Chin, Janet Jue 1930- *WhoAmW 93*
Chin, Janet Sau-Ying 1949- *WhoAmW 93*
Chin, Jeffrey 1953- *WhoE 93*
Chin, John Patrick 1962- *WhoE 93*
Chin, Ken C. *Law&B 92*
Chin, Kenneth 1950- *St&PR 93*
Chin, Kuo-fan 1929- *WhoWor 93*
Chin, Llewellyn Philip 1957- *WhoWor 93*
Chin, Louis 1944- *WhoE 93*
Chin, Lung d1990 *BioIn 17*
Chin, M. Lucie *ScF&FL 92*
Chin, Marilyn Mei Ling 1955- *WhoWrEP 92*
Chin, Mark Stephen 1964- *WhoWor 93*
Ch'in, Michael Kuo-hsing 1921- *WhoWor 93*
Chin, NeeOo Wong 1955- *WhoWor 93*
Chin, P.G. *Law&B 92*
Chin, Penny 1948- *WhoEmL 93*
Chin, Ralph *Law&B 92*
Chin, Robert 1918-1990 *BioIn 17*
Chin, Robert Allen 1950- *WhoEmL 93, WhoSSW 93, WhoWor 93*
Chin, See Keat 1958- *WhoWor 93*
Chin, Sue SooneMarian *WhoAmW 93, WhoWor 93*
Chin, Susan Lee *Law&B 92*
Chin, Susan Wong 1946- *WhoEmL 93*
Chin, Tsai *BioIn 17*
Chin, Vincent Wan-Loy 1961- *WhoWor 93*
Chin, William Waiman 1947- *WhoE 93*
Chinaglia, Leopoldo 1929- *WhoScE 91-3*
Chinard, Francis Pierre 1918- *WhoAm 92*
Chinard, Jeanne *WhoAm 92*
Chincholle, Lucien Henri 1926- *WhoScE 91-2*
Chindemi, Craig Thomas 1959- *WhoSSW 93*
Chinery, Michael 1938- *WhoAm 92*
Chinery-Hesse, Mary Blay 1938- *WhoUN 92*
Ching, Chauncey T.K. 1940- *WhoWrEP 92*
Ching, Chauncey Tai Kin 1940- *WhoAm 92*
Ching, Chiao-Liang Juliana 1955- *WhoWor 93*
Ching, Dorothy K. 1926- *St&PR 93*
Ching, Eric San Hing 1951- *WhoEmL 93*
Ching, Gale Lin Fong 1954- *WhoEmL 93*
Ching, George Ta-Min 1914- *WhoAm 92*
Ching, Hung Wo 1912- *St&PR 93, WhoAm 92*
Ching, Julia 1934- *WhoAmW 93*
Ching, Julia (Chia-yi) 1934- *ConAu 37NR*
Ching, Larry Fong Chow 1912- *WhoWor 93*
Ching, Laureen *WhoWrEP 92*
Ching, Louis Michael 1956- *WhoEmL 93*
Ching, Norman K.Y. 1932- *St&PR 93*
Ching, Philip H. 1931- *St&PR 93, WhoAm 92*
Ching, Raymond Harris- 1939- *BioIn 17*
Ching, Renald 1908- *WhoWor 93*
Ching, Stefanie W. 1966- *WhoWor 93*
Ching, Wesley H. H. 1949- *WhoEmL 93*
Ching, Willard d1992 *BioIn 17*
Ching-Li, Hu *WhoUN 92*
Chiniquy, Charles Paschal Telesphore 1809-1899 *BioIn 17*
Chinitz, Jody Anne Kolb 1953- *WhoAmW 93*
Chink, Alfred Carl 1936- *St&PR 93*
Chinlund, Alicia Lopes 1961- *WhoSSW 93*
Chinn, Donald J. 1938- *St&PR 93*
Chinn, Harold 1965- *WhoE 93*
Chinn, Mike *ScF&FL 92*
Chinn, Peggy Lois 1941- *WhoAmW 93*
Chinn, Rex Arlyn 1935- *WhoWor 93*
Chinn, Robert C. 1916-1991 *BioIn 17*
Chinn, Robert Dudley 1949- *WhoIns 93*
Chinn, Thomas Wayne 1909- *WhoWor 93*
Chinn, Wesley Earl 1946- *St&PR 93*
Chinnappa, K.M. *BioIn 17*
Chinnery, Carl Lloyd 1941- *St&PR 93*
Chinnery, Michael Alistair 1933- *WhoAm 92*
Chinn-Hechter, Mamie May 1951- *WhoAmW 93, WhoEmL 93*
Chinni, Charles Ross 1944- *WhoAm 92*
Chinni, Peter Anthony 1928- *WhoAm 92*
Chinodya, Shimmer 1957- *ConAu 139*
Chinoy, Helen Krich 1922- *WhoAm 92*
Chin-Perez, Cynthia A. *Law&B 92*
Chinsman, Babashola 1944- *WhoUN 92*
Chinta Mohan, Dr. 1954- *WhoAsAP 91*
Chiodi, Charles Karoly 1932- *WhoE 93*
Chiodo, Jacqueline H. 1952- *St&PR 93*
Chiodo, Mary Helen *Law&B 92*
Chiodo, Stephen *MiSFD 9*
Chiodo, Vincent Robert 1955- *WhoE 93*
Chioffi, Joseph Michael *Law&B 92*
Chiogioji, Melvin Hiroaki 1939- *WhoAm 92, WhoE 93*
Chiongbian, James L. 1921- *WhoAsAP 91*
Chioniades, Gregory 124-?-c. 1320 *OxDcByz*
Chiorazzi, Nicholas 1945- *WhoE 93*
Chiosie, Gene *BioIn 17*
Chiou, Win Loung 1938- *WhoWor 93*
Chiovetti, Robert, Jr. 1946- *WhoEmL 93*
Chipande, Alberto *WhoWor 93*
Chipeco, Joaquin M., Jr. 1942- *WhoAsAP 91*
Chipinski, Elizabeth *Law&B 92*
Chipka, Stephen Thomas 1953- *WhoEmL 93, WhoSSW 93*
Chipkevich, Edward Albert, Jr. 1946- *WhoE 93*
Chipman, Debra Decker 1959- *WhoAmW 93*
Chipman, Donald J. d1991 *BioIn 17*
Chipman, Elizabeth A. *AmWomPl*
Chipman, Ernest de Witt 1950- *WhoUN 92*
Chipman, J. *WhoScE 91-1*
Chipman, Jeff 1945- *St&PR 93*
Chipman, John Somerset 1926- *WhoAm 92, WhoWor 93*
Chipman, Marion Walter 1920- *WhoWor 93*
Chipman, Ralph 1945- *WhoUN 92*
Chipman, Susan Elizabeth 1946- *WhoAm 92, WhoAmW 93, WhoEmL 93*
Chipouras, Susan Cathleen Massina 1956- *St&PR 93*
Chipouras, Susan Massina 1956- *WhoEmL 93*
Chipp, Herschel B. d1992 *NewYTBS 92*
Chipp, Herschel B. 1913-1992 *BioIn 17*
Chippendale, Thomas 1749-1822 *BioIn 17*
Chipperfield, Lynn *Law&B 92*
Chirac, Jacques 1932- *BioIn 17*
Chirac, Jacques Rene 1932- *WhoWor 93*
Chiraska, B. S. *ConAu 139*
Chirazi, Marie Therese Antoinette 1945- *WhoWor 93*
Chirban, John Thomas 1951- *WhoE 93*
Chirco, Norman 1961- *St&PR 93*
Chirgwin, Ricardo 1935- *WhoWor 93*
Chirgwin, Thomas D. 1944- *St&PR 93*
Chiriac, Mircea 1919- *Baker 92*
Chiriboga, David Anthony 1941- *WhoSSW 93*
Chirico, Andrea de 1891-1952 *BioIn 17*
Chiricosta, Rick Alan 1956- *WhoEmL 93*
Chirila, J.V. 1923- *WhoScE 91-3*
Chirlian, Paul Michael 1930- *WhoAm 92, WhoE 93*
Chiron, Stuart *Law&B 92*
Chironna, John F. 1930- *WhoAm 92*
Chirovsky, Nicholas Ludomir 1919- *WhoAm 92*
Chirurg, James Thomas, Jr. 1944- *WhoAm 92*
Chisena, Ernest, III 1956- *WhoEmL 93*
Chisenhall, Frank Edward 1949- *WhoWrEP 92*
Chisholm, Alan Oswald Buchanan 1934- *WhoUN 92*
Chisholm, Anthony Hewlings 1939- *WhoWor 93*
Chisholm, Bruce 1952- *WhoWor 93*
Chisholm, Carol Lee 1938- *WhoAm 92, WhoAmW 93, WhoE 93*
Chisholm, Christopher John *WhoScE 91-1*
Chisholm, Colin 1944- *WhoWor 93*
Chisholm, Colin Urquhart *WhoScE 91-1*
Chisholm, Dianne 1953- *ConAu 137*
Chisholm, Donald E. 1938- *St&PR 93, WhoIns 93*
Chisholm, Donald Edward 1938- *WhoAm 92*
Chisholm, Donald Herbert 1917- *WhoAm 92*
Chisholm, Donald William 1953- *WhoEmL 93*
Chisholm, Erik 1904-1965 *Baker 92*
Chisholm, Frank A. 1910- *St&PR 93*
Chisholm, Geoffrey D. *WhoScE 91-1*
Chisholm, J.R. *Law&B 92*
Chisholm, John Stephen Roy *WhoScE 91-1*
Chisholm, Leslie Lee 1900- *WhoSSW 93*
Chisholm, Malcolm Harold 1945- *WhoAm 92*
Chisholm, Margaret Ann d1991 *BioIn 17*
Chisholm, Margaret Elizabeth 1921- *WhoAm 92*
Chisholm, Michael D.I. *WhoScE 91-1*
Chisholm, Sallie Watson 1947- *WhoAmW 93*
Chisholm, Shirley 1924- *BioIn 17, PolPar*
Chisholm, Shirley Anita 1924- *AfrAmBi*
Chisholm, Shirley Anita St. Hill 1924- *EncAACR, WhoAm 92*
Chisholm, Tague Clement 1915- *WhoAm 92*
Chisholm, Tommy *Law&B 92*
Chisholm, Tommy 1941- *St&PR 93, WhoAm 92, WhoSSW 93, WhoWor 93*
Chisholm, William DeWayne 1924- *WhoSSW 93*
Chisholm, William H. 1917- *St&PR 93*
Chisholm, William Hardenbergh 1917- *WhoAm 92*
Chislett, Anne 1942- *WhoCanL 92*
Chislett, Charles J. d1991 *BioIn 17*
Chism, James Arthur 1933- *WhoWor 93*
Chism, John Ross 1954- *WhoE 93*
Chism, Robert W. 1942- *St&PR 93*
Chismar, Constance A. 1950- *WhoAmW 93*
Chismire, Lisa E. *Law&B 92*
Chisner, Michael Brian 1959- *WhoEmL 93*
Chisolm, O. Beirne, Jr. 1928- *St&PR 93*
Chissano, Joaquim Alberto 1939- *BioIn 17, WhoAfr, WhoWor 93*
Chiste, Robert Matthew 1947- *WhoAm 92*
Chistov, Alexander Leonidovich 1954- *WhoWor 93*
Chistov, K.V. 1919- *IntDcAn*
Chistyakov, Gennadii 1945- *WhoWor 93*
Chistyakov, Larisa 1954- *St&PR 93*
Chisum, Bessie Fisher 1945- *WhoSSW 93*
Chisum, Matthew Eual 1953- *WhoSSW 93*
Chiswick, Nancy Rose 1945- *WhoAmW 93*
Chitaia, G.S. 1890-1986 *IntDcAn*
Chitayat, Anwar 1927- *St&PR 93*
Chittenden, Alice *AmWomPl*
Chittenden, Curtis D. 1935- *St&PR 93*
Chittenden, Jean Stahl 1924- *WhoAmW 93*
Chittenden, Margaret 1935- *ScF&FL 92*
Chittenden, Thomas S. *Law&B 92*
Chittenden, William A. 1927- *St&PR 93*
Chittick, David Rupert 1934- *WhoAm 92, WhoE 93*
Chittick, Elizabeth Lancaster 1918- *WhoAm 92*
Chittick, Stanley Woodworth 1941- *St&PR 93*
Chittipeddi, Kumar 1955- *WhoEmL 93*
Chittum, Robert A. *Law&B 92*
Chitty, Arthur Ben, Jr. 1914- *WhoWor 93*
Chitty, Arthur Benjamin, Jr. 1914- *WhoAm 92*
Chitty, Dennis Hubert 1912- *WhoAm 92*
Chitty, Elizabeth Nickinson 1920- *WhoAmW 93, WhoSSW 93, WhoWrEP 92*
Chitty, Gritakumar E. 1939- *WhoUN 92*
Chitty, Royce W. 1943- *St&PR 93*
Chitwood, Benjamin Goodwin 1907-1972 *BioIn 17*
Chitwood, Frank Warren 1933- *St&PR 93*
Chitwood, Harold Otis 1930- *St&PR 93*
Chitwood, James L. *St&PR 93*
Chitwood, James L. 1943- *WhoAm 92*
Chitwood, Julius Richard 1921- *WhoAm 92*
Chitwood, Patricia May 1958- *WhoEmL 93*
Chitwood, Phyllis Ann 1959- *WhoEmL 93*
Chitzanidis, A. *WhoScE 91-3*
Chitzanidis, Anna 1930- *WhoWor 93*
Ch'iu, Chin 1879?-1907 *BioIn 17*
Chiu, David Tak Wai 1945- *WhoAm 92*
Chiu, Hungdah 1936- *WhoAm 92, WhoE 93*
Chiu, Ing-Ming 1952- *WhoEmL 93*
Chiu, Jen-Fu 1940- *WhoE 93*
Chiu, Peter Jiunn-Shyong 1942- *WhoE 93*
Chiu, Tony 1945- *ScF&FL 92*
Chiu, Tsai Fua 1927- *WhoWor 93*
Chiulli, E. Antoinette 1950- *WhoEmL 93*
Chiusano, Charles 1917- *St&PR 93*
Chiusano, Francis 1949- *St&PR 93*
Chivers, Geoffrey Edward *WhoScE 91-1*
Chivers, James Leeds 1939- *WhoE 93*
Chivers, Thomas Holley 1807-1858 *ScF&FL 92*
Chivvis, A. 1954- *St&PR 93*
Ch'ix, Chavela Jvaris *BioIn 17*
Chi Youn Tai 1929- *WhoAsAP 91*
Chizauskas, Cathleen Jo 1954- *WhoAmW 93*
Chizeck, Susan Phyllis 1947- *WhoEmL 93*
Chizen, Harlan J. 1951- *St&PR 93*
Chizhov, Lyudvig A. *BioIn 17*
Chizick, Jerry Lawrence 1948- *St&PR 93, WhoAm 92*
Chizmadia, Stephen Mark 1950- *WhoE 93, WhoEmL 93, WhoWor 93*
Chizmar, Richard T. 1965- *ScF&FL 92*
Chladni, Ernest (Florens Friedrich) 1756-1827 *Baker 92*
Chlan, Caryl Anne 1955- *WhoSSW 93*
Chlapowski, Dezydery 1788-1879 *PolBiDi*
Chlebowska, Krystyna 1933- *WhoUN 92*
Chlebowski, John Francis, Jr. 1945- *St&PR 93, WhoAm 92*
Chlebowski, Roman 1936- *WhoScE 91-4*
Chletsos, Gregory N. *St&PR 93*
Chlique, Pierre 1951- *WhoScE 91-2*
Chllemi, Clifford L. *Law&B 92*
Chlodny, Jozef 1941- *WhoScE 91-4*
Chlopak, Donna Gayle 1950- *WhoAm 92, WhoAmW 93, WhoEmL 93*
Chloupek, Frank James 1935- *St&PR 93*
Chlubna, Osvald 1893-1971 *Baker 92*
Chlumsky, Anna *BioIn 17*
Chlup, Joseph 1928- *St&PR 93*
Chmara, Paul Nicholas 1954- *WhoE 93*
Chmelir, Frank 1946- *St&PR 93*
Chmelir, John David 1949- *WhoEmL 93*
Chmell, Samuel Jay 1952- *WhoEmL 93, WhoWor 93*
Chmely, Robert M. 1934- *St&PR 93*
Chmiel, Horst A. 1940- *WhoScE 91-3*
Chmiel, Joseph Anthony, Jr. 1959- *WhoEmL 93*
Chmiel, Thomas 1944- *St&PR 93*
Chmielarz, Sharon 1940- *SmATA 72 [port]*
Chmielewski, Margaret Ann 1946- *WhoEmL 93*
Chmielewski, Tadeusz 1927- *DrEEuF*
Chmielewski, Wendy E. 1955- *ConAu 139*
Chmielewski, Wit 1938- *WhoScE 91-4, WhoWor 93*
Chmielinski, Edward Alexander 1925- *WhoAm 92, WhoE 93*
Chmielniak, Tadeusz Jan 1941- *WhoScE 91-4*
Chmielnicka, Jadwiga 1925- *WhoScE 91-4*
Chmielnicki, Ferd J. *Law&B 92*
Chmielnik, Henryk 1931- *WhoScE 91-4*
Chmielowski, Adam 1845-1916 *PolBiDi*
Chmielowski, Jerzy 1925- *WhoScE 91-4*
Chmura, Edward 1940- *St&PR 93*
Chmura, Gabriel 1946- *Baker 92, WhoWor 93*
Chmura, John A. 1943- *St&PR 93*
Chmura, Martin W. *Law&B 92*
Chmura, Michael Joseph 1966- *WhoSSW 93*
Chmura, Ronald Mathew 1952- *WhoEmL 93*
Chmurny, William Wayne 1941- *WhoAm 92*
Ch'ng, Soo Ling 1945- *WhoWor 93*
Ch'ng Jit Koon 1934- *WhoAsAP 91*
Cho, Alfred Yi 1937- *WhoAm 92*
Cho, Cheng Tsung 1937- *WhoAm 92*
Cho, Chul Hyung 1955- *WhoWor 93*
Cho, Dong-Hyun 1954- *WhoWor 93*

Cho, Dong-Il Dan 1958- *WhoEmL 93*
Cho, Hi-Ku 1933- *WhoWor 93*
Cho, Hyun Ju 1939- *WhoAm 92*
Cho, Isamu 1895-1945 *HarEnMi*
Cho, Jai Hang 1942- *WhoWor 93*
Cho, Kaho *BioIn 17*
Cho, Kang 1953- *BioIn 17*
Cho, Kwan Soo 1934- *WhoWor 93*
Cho, Lee-Jay 1936- *WhoAm 92*
Cho, Shinil 1951- *WhoEmL 93*
Cho, Soon 1928- *WhoWor 93*
Cho, Sung Hee 1957- *WhoAm 92*
Cho, Sung Yoon 1928- *WhoE 93*
Cho, Young Il 1949- *WhoE 93, WhoEmL 93*
Cho, Young S. 1934- *St&PR 93*
Choain, Jean Georges 1917- *WhoWor 93*
Choate, Alan G. *Law&B 92*
Choate, Alan G. 1939- *St&PR 93*
Choate, Albert George 1947- *WhoE 93*
Choate, Carl 1941- *St&PR 93*
Choate, Dimmitt N. 1943- *St&PR 93*
Choate, Emily Teresa 1953- *WhoEmL 93*
Choate, Eugene 1936- *St&PR 93, WhoIns 93*
Choate, James Brent 1953- *WhoSSW 93*
Choate, Jerry D. 1938- *St&PR 93, WhoIns 93*
Choate, Joseph 1900- *WhoAm 92*
Choate, Joseph Hodges 1832-1917 *OxCSupC*
Choate, M. Rickliffe *Law&B 92*
Choate, Murray Rickliffe, II 1954- *WhoEmL 93*
Choate, Pat *BioIn 17*
Choate, Robert Alden 1912- *WhoAm 92*
Chobanian, Aram Van 1929- *WhoAm 92*
Chobaut, Jean-Claude Charles 1946- *WhoWor 93*
Cho Boo Young 1937- *WhoAsAP 91*
Chobot, John C. *Law&B 92*
Chobot, John Charles 1948- *WhoEmL 93*
Cho Chan-Hyung 1940- *WhoAsAP 91*
Chocholak, Misha *ScF&FL 92*
Chock, Alvin Keali'i 1931- *WhoE 93, WhoWor 93*
Chock, Eric Edward 1950- *WhoWrEP 92*
Chock, Jay Richard 1955- *WhoEmL 93*
Chock, P. Boon 1939- *WhoE 93*
Chocola, J. Christopher *Law&B 92*
Chocron, Yamin 1932- *WhoWor 93*
Choczewski, Bogdan Adam 1935- *WhoWor 93*
Chod, Jerry 1921- *St&PR 93*
Chodakowski, Zorian Dolega *IntDcAn*
Chodan, Dah-Ve *BioIn 17*
Chodorkoff, Bernard 1925- *WhoAm 92*
Chodorow, Marc 1951- *WhoE 93*
Chodorowski, Jan 1918- *WhoScE 91-4*
Chodos, Dale David Jerome 1928- *WhoAm 92*
Chodos, Robert 1946- *ScF&FL 92*
Chodosh, Alan P. 1954- *St&PR 93*
Chodosh, Gary Alan *Law&B 92*
Chodynicki, Stanislaw 1933- *WhoScE 91-4*
Chodynski, Andrzej 1948- *WhoScE 91-4*
Chodzinski, Kazimierz 1861-1919 *PolBiDi*
Choe, Jaigyoung 1953- *WhoWor 93*
Choe, Joseph Jong Kook 1961- *WhoEmL 93*
Choe, Won-Gil 1932- *WhoAm 92*
Choe Jae-Woo 1941- *WhoAsAP 91*
Choguill, Charles Lewis *WhoScE 91-1*
Choguill, Charles Lewis 1941- *WhoWor 93*
Chogyam, Trungpa 1939-1987 *BioIn 17*
Cho Hi Cheol 1929- *WhoAsAP 91*
Cho Hong Gyu 1944- *WhoAsAP 91*
Choi, Byung Ho 1928- *WhoAm 92*
Choi, Chang Ho 1934- *WhoWor 93*
Choi, Chong Ju 1960- *WhoWor 93*
Choi, Chong-Ki 1928- *WhoWor 93*
Choi, Chong Whan 1925- *WhoWor 93*
Choi, Dae Hyun 1932- *WhoWor 93*
Choi, Duk Shin 1914-1989 *BioIn 17*
Choi, Ho 1936- *WhoWor 93*
Choi, Hyungsoo 1958- *WhoWor 93*
Choi, Inn Gui 1947- *WhoSSW 93*
Choi, Jae Hoon 1929- *WhoWor 93*
Choi, Jin-Hak 1928- *WhoWor 93*
Choi, Jong Bum 1954- *WhoWor 93*
Choi, Jongmoo Jay 1945- *WhoE 93*
Choi, Kwang 1947- *WhoWor 93*
Choi, Kwing-So 1953- *WhoWor 93*
Choi, Kyung Kook 1946- *WhoEmL 93*
Choi, Man-Duen 1945- *WhoAm 92*
Choi, Sae Chang 1934- *WhoWor 93*
Choi, Sang-il 1931- *WhoAm 92*
Choi, Sook Nyul *SmATA 73 [port]*
Choi Bong Goo 1941- *WhoAsAP 91*
Choice, Priscilla Kathryn 1939- *WhoAmW 93*
Choi Ee Ho 1935- *WhoAsAP 91*
Choi Gak Kyu 1935- *WhoAsAP 91*
Choi Hyung Woo 1936- *WhoAsAP 91*
Choi Jung Sik 1930- *WhoAsAP 91*
Choi Ki Sun 1946- *WhoAsAP 91*
Choi Mu Ryung 1929- *WhoAsAP 91*
Choi Rak Do 1939- *WhoAsAP 91*
Choiroboskos, George fl. 9th cent.- *OxDcByz*
Choirosphaktes, Leo c. 824-c. 919 *OxDcByz*
Choiseul, Cesar, Duke of 1598-1675 *HarEnMi*
Choi-Su, Park 1947- *MiSFD 9*
Choisy, Claude Gabriel, Marquis of dc. 1795 *HarEnMi*
Choi Woon Ji 1928- *WhoAsAP 91*
Choi Yeoung Keun 1923- *WhoAsAP 91*
Chojnacki, Juliusz Cezary 1943- *WhoScE 91-4*
Chojnacki, Paul Ervin 1950- *WhoEmL 93*
Chojnowska-Liskiewicz, Krystyna 1937- *PolBiDi*
Chokey, James A. *Law&B 92*
Chokshi, Gaurang Navnitlal 1956- *WhoEmL 93*
Choksi, Armeane Murzban 1944- *WhoUN 92*
Choksi, Aroon 1941- *St&PR 93*
Cho Kyoung Mok 1938- *WhoAsAP 91*
"Chola" *ScF&FL 92*
Cholakis, Constantine George 1930- *WhoE 93*
Choldin, Marianna Tax 1942- *WhoAmW 93*
Chole, Richard A. 1944- *WhoAm 92*
Cholewicka, Helena 1848-1883 *PolBiDi*
Cholfin, Bryan *ScF&FL 92*
Cholis, Thomas Joseph 1946- *St&PR 93*
Cholis, Thomas Joseph, Jr. 1946- *WhoEmL 93*
Chollat-Traquet, Claire Mathilde 1944- *WhoUN 92*
Chollet, F. 1957- *WhoScE 91-2*
Chollet, Jean-Louis 1930- *WhoAm 92*
Cholmondeley, Hugh Neville 1940- *WhoUN 92*
Cholnoky, I. John 1958- *WhoIns 93*
Cholnoky, Peter John 1932- *WhoScE 91-4*
Cholodowski, Antonia Marie 1932- *WhoE 93*
Choman, Thomas Bohdan 1959- *WhoE 93*
Cho Man-Hou 1951- *WhoAsAP 91*
Chomatenos, Demetrios dc. 1236 *OxDcByz*
Chomeau, Bernal T. 1931- *St&PR 93*
Chomeau, David D. 1937- *WhoIns 93*
Chomeau, David Douglass 1937- *St&PR 93*
Chomeau, Stuart G. 1955- *St&PR 93*
Chomica, John 1937- *St&PR 93*
Chomiczewska-Mazaraki, Aleksandra 1930- *WhoScE 91-4, WhoWor 93*
Chominski, Jozef Michal 1906- *Baker 92*
Chominski, Pawel Krzysztof 1951- *WhoWor 93*
Chomitz, Morris A. 1925- *St&PR 93*
Choms, Wladyslaw c. 1895-1966 *PolBiDi*
Chomsky, Avram Noam 1928- *WhoAm 92, WhoWor 93, WhoWrEP 92*
Chomsky, Marvin J. 1929- *MiSFD 9, WhoAm 92*
Chomsky, Maryellen *Law&B 92*
Chomsky, Noam *BioIn 17*
Chon, Chun-Su 1942- *WhoWor 93*
Chon, In Chol d1992 *BioIn 17*
Chona, Mathias Mainza 1930- *WhoAfr*
Cho Nam Wook 1934- *WhoAsAP 91*
Chong, Andres 1945- *WhoWor 93*
Chong, Arthur *Law&B 92*
Chong, Bock Weng 1961- *WhoWor 93*
Chong, Carol Chinnon 1949- *WhoSSW 93*
Chong, Christopher Kian 1948- *WhoEmL 93*
Chong, Clayton Elliott 1950- *WhoEmL 93*
Chong, Howard K.O., Jr. 1942- *St&PR 93*
Chong, Lawrence M. 1946- *St&PR 93*
Chong, P.S. *Law&B 92*
Chong, Ping *BioIn 17*
Chong, Rae Dawn *BioIn 17*
Chong, Richard David 1946- *WhoEmL 93*
Chong, Shui-Fong 1954- *WhoE 93, WhoEmL 93*
Chong, Sooi P. 1942- *St&PR 93*
Chong, Sooi Peaw 1942- *WhoAm 92*
Chong, Teik Yean 1961- *WhoWor 93*
Chong, Thomas 1938- *MiSFD 9, WhoAm 92*
Chong, Thomas 1941- *See* Cheech and Chong *QDrFCA 92*
Chong, Vernon 1933- *WhoAm 92*
Chong, Yee Leong 1965- *WhoWor 93*
Chong Keen, Sam 1953- *WhoAsAP 91*
Chong Keng, Tan *WhoAsAP 91*
Choniates, Michael c. 1138-c. 1222 *OxDcByz*
Choniates, Niketas 1155?-1217 *OxDcByz*
Choo, Chunghi 1938- *BioIn 17*
Choo, Yeow Ming 1953- *WhoWor 93*
Chook, Paul Howard 1929- *WhoAm 92*
Chookasian, Lili 1921- *Baker 92*
Chookaszian, Dennis H. 1943- *St&PR 93*
Chookaszian, Dennis Haig 1943- *WhoAm 92, WhoIns 93*
Choomack, Carol Lynn 1947- *WhoAmW 93*
Choonhavan, Chatichai 1922- *WhoWor 93*
Choonhaven, Chatichai 1922- *WhoAsAP 91*
Chop, Max 1862-1929 *Baker 92*
Chope, Robert William 1952- *WhoE 93*
Chopin, Frederic 1810-1849 *BioIn 17*
Chopin, Frederic (-Francois) c. 1810-1849 *Baker 92*
Chopin, Frederick 1810-1849 *PolBiDi [port]*
Chopin, Kate 1850-1904 *AmWomWr 92*
Chopin, Kate 1851-1904 *BioIn 17, GayN, MagSAmL [port]*
Chopin, L. Frank 1942- *WhoAm 92*
Chopin, Nicholas 1771-1844 *PolBiDi*
Chopin, Rene 1885-1953 *BioIn 17*
Chopin, Susan Gardiner 1947- *WhoEmL 93*
Choplin, John M., II 1945- *WhoAm 92*
Chopmaster J. *See* Digital Underground *ConMus 9*
Chopnick, Stephen D. *Law&B 92*
Chopp, Gerald L. 1934- *St&PR 93*
Choppin, Gregory Robert 1927- *WhoAm 92, WhoSSW 93*
Choppin, Purnell Whittington 1929- *WhoAm 92, WhoE 93*
Chopra, Anil Kumar 1941- *WhoAm 92*
Chopra, Joyce 1938- *MiSFD 9*
Chopra, Prom 1949- *WhoUN 92*
Chopra, Sudhir Kumar 1949- *St&PR 93*
Choquet-Bruhat, Yvonne 1923- *WhoWor 93*
Choquette, Keith Alan 1954- *WhoE 93*
Choquette, Paul J., Jr. 1938- *St&PR 93*
Choquette, Philip Wheeler 1930- *WhoAm 92*
Choquette, Pierre 1942- *St&PR 93*
Choquette, Robert 1905- *WhoCanL 92*
Choquette, William H. 1941- *WhoAm 92*
Choquette, William Henry 1941- *St&PR 93*
Chorao, Kay 1936- *SmATA 69 [port]*
Chorao, (Ann Mc)Kay (Sproat) 1936- *MajAI [port]*
Chorazy, Mieczyslaw Rajmund 1925- *WhoScE 91-4*
Chorazy, Sandra Marie 1957- *WhoAmW 93*
Chorba, Dennis Michael *Law&B 92*
Chorengel, Bernd *WhoAm 92*
Chorikios Of Gaza 6th cent.- *OxDcByz*
Chorin, Alexandre Joel 1938- *WhoAm 92*
Chorkendorff, Ib 1955- *WhoScE 91-2*
Chorley, David *BioIn 17*
Chorley, Henry F(othergill) 1808-1872 *Baker 92*
Chorley, Henry Fothergill 1808-1872 *OxDcOp*
Chorley, Jean T. d1992 *NewYTBS 92*
Chorley, Richard John 1927- *WhoWor 93*
Chorley, Roger Richard Edward 1930- *BioIn 17*
Chorlton, David 1948- *WhoWrEP 92*
Chorlton, R.W. 1925- *St&PR 93*
Chormann, Richard F. 1937- *St&PR 93*
Chornesky, Adam Brett 1947- *WhoEmL 93*
Chorney, Harold 1917- *St&PR 93*
Chorney, Theresa Rand 1955- *WhoAmW 93, WhoEmL 93*
Choromokos, James, Jr. 1929- *WhoAm 92*
Choron, Alexandre (Etienne) 1771-1834 *Baker 92*
Choroski, Edmund Peter *Law&B 92*
Chorostecki, Gene Joseph 1933- *WhoE 93*
Chorot, Paloma 1959- *WhoWor 93*
Chorpenning, Charlotte Barrows 1873-1955 *AmWomPl*
Chorpenning, Nancy Ellen 1953- *WhoAm 92*
Chorpita, Fred Michael 1940- *WhoIns 93*
Chortasmenos, John c. 1370-c. 1439 *OxDcByz*
Choruby, Larry Nicholas 1938- *St&PR 93*
Chorzempa, Daniel (Walter) 1944- *Baker 92*
Chorzempa, Martin V. 1936- *St&PR 93*
Cho Se Hyung 1932- *WhoAsAP 91*
Cho Seung Hyung 1935- *WhoAsAP 91*
Cho Soon-Sung 1930- *WhoAsAP 91*
Chosroes, I *OxDcByz*
Chosroes, II d628 *OxDcByz*
Chostner, Chrystal Lea 1963- *WhoAmW 93*
Chosy, John Eugene 1948- *WhoEmL 93*
Chotard, Yvon 1921- *WhoWor 93*
Choteau, Philippe 1934- *WhoScE 91-2*
Chotiner, Barbara Ann 1946- *WhoSSW 93*
Chotiner, Bennett 1941- *WhoE 93*
Chottard, Jean-Claude Camille 1941- *WhoScE 91-2*
Chotzinoff, Samuel 1889-1964 *Baker 92*
Chou, Chung-Kwang 1947- *WhoAm 92*
Chou, Clifford Chi Fong 1940- *WhoAm 92*
Chou, Dean-Yi 1954- *WhoWor 93*
Chou, Erwin C. 1952- *WhoEmL 93*
Chou, Jack Chen 1936- *St&PR 93*
Chou, James Ching-Yung 1959- *WhoEmL 93*
Chou, Kuo-Chen 1938- *WhoWor 93*
Chou, Lih-Hsin 1957- *WhoWor 93*
Chou, Maxine J. 1942- *WhoAm 92*
Chou, Nelson Shih-Toon 1935- *WhoE 93*
Chou, Pei-Chuang 1913- *St&PR 93*
Chou, Raymond H. 1956- *WhoEmL 93*
Chou, Ri-Chee 1961- *WhoEmL 93*
Chou, Shelley Nien-chun 1924- *WhoAm 92*
Chou, Takashi 1934- *WhoWor 93*
Chou, Tein-chen 1953- *WhoWor 93*
Chou, Timothy Chen Kuang 1954- *WhoEmL 93*
Chou, Wen-chung 1923- *WhoAm 92*
Chou, Wushow 1939- *WhoAm 92*
Chou, Youn-Min Amanda *WhoWor 93*
Chou, Yue Hong 1952- *WhoWor 93*
Chouard, Claude-Henri 1931- *WhoScE 91-2*
Choubert, Georges 1946- *WhoScE 91-2*
Choudary, Shaukat Hussain 1958- *WhoWor 93*
Choudhry, Nurun Nabi 1942- *WhoUN 92*
Choudhury, A.B.A. Ghani Khan 1927- *WhoAsAP 91*
Choudhury, A.P. Roy 1929- *St&PR 93*
Choudhury, Abdul Musawwir 1941- *WhoWor 93*
Choudhury, Farook Rasheed 1938- *WhoAsAP 91*
Choudhury, Saifuddin 1952- *WhoAsAP 91*
Choueiri, Youssef M. 1948- *ConAu 136*
Choueri, Chawki Nicholas 1930- *WhoUN 92*
Choufoer, J.H. *WhoScE 91-3*
Chough Yoon Hyung 1933- *WhoAsAP 91*
Chouikh, Mohamed *MiSFD 9*
Chouikha, Mohammed Raouf 1951- *WhoWor 93*
Chouinard, Marc Roger 1957- *St&PR 93*
Chouinard, Richard J. 1932- *St&PR 93, WhoIns 93*
Choukas, Chris Nicholas 1955- *WhoEmL 93*
Choukri, Mohamed 1935- *ConAu 136*
Choukroune, Pierre *WhoScE 91-2*
Chouliaras, A.G. 1920- *WhoScE 91-3*
Choulis, Nicholas H. 1930- *WhoScE 91-3*
Choummali Saignason *WhoWor 93*
Choumnaina, Irene 1291-c. 1355 *OxDcByz*
Choumnos *OxDcByz*
Choumnos, Nikephoros c. 1250?-1327 *OxDcByz*
Choung, Nak Young 1934- *WhoAm 92*
Chouquet, (Adolphe-) Gustave 1819-1886 *Baker 92*
Chouraqui, Elie 1950- *MiSFD 9*
Chouraqui, Eugene 1940- *WhoScE 91-2*
Chou Wen-chung 1923- *Baker 92*
Chovanec, Michael Justin 1968- *WhoE 93*
Chovet, Alain 1947- *WhoScE 91-2*
Chow, Alan Seleung 1944- *WhoSSW 93*
Chow, Amy Ka Pik 1964- *WhoWor 93*
Chow, Anthony Wei-Chik 1941- *WhoAm 92*
Chow, Bettina L. d1992 *NewYTBS 92*
Chow, Charn Ki Kenneth 1953- *WhoWor 93*
Chow, Cyril Chi-Kin 1954- *WhoWor 93*
Chow, Donna Lynne 1945- *WhoAmW 93*
Chow, Eileen Siu-Ha 1951- *WhoWor 93*
Chow, Franklin Szu-Chien 1956- *WhoEmL 93*
Chow, Gregory Chi-Chong 1929- *WhoAm 92*
Chow, John Victor 1942- *St&PR 93*
Chow, Louise Tsi 1943- *WhoAmW 93*
Chow, Michael 1965- *WhoE 93*
Chow, Poo 1934- *WhoAm 92*
Chow, Raymond *BioIn 17*
Chow, Rita Kathleen 1926- *WhoAm 92, WhoAmW 93*
Chow, Robin Denice *Law&B 92*
Chow, Ronald Mei-Tak 1951- *WhoAsAP 91*
Chow, Shirley Chin-Ping 1943- *St&PR 93*
Chow, Shu-Kai 1930- *WhoUN 92*
Chow, Stephen Heung Wing 1954- *WhoWor 93*
Chow, Stephen Yee 1952- *WhoE 93, WhoEmL 93*
Chow, Steven C. *WhoWor 93*
Chow, Tahsin Joseph 1949- *WhoWor 93*
Chow, Tina *BioIn 17*
Chow, Tony H. 1948- *St&PR 93*
Chow, Tse-Tsung 1916- *WhoAm 92, WhoWor 93, WhoWrEP 92*
Chow, Wen Lung 1924- *WhoSSW 93*
Chow, Winston 1946- *WhoEmL 93*
Chow, Ying-Wei 1935- *WhoE 93*
Chow, Yuan Shih 1924- *WhoAm 92*

Chowdhary, Ram Sewak 1927- *WhoAsAP 91*
Chowdhuri, Pritindra 1927- *WhoAm 92, WhoWor 93*
Chowdhury, Abdur Rahim 1953- *WhoEmL 93*
Chowdhury, Anwarul Karim 1947- *WhoUN 92*
Chowdhury, Iqbal Hossain 1945- *WhoAsAP 91*
Chowdhury, Mohammad Rezwanul Huq *WhoAsAP 91*
Chowdhury, Nazrul Islam 1957- *WhoWor 93*
Chowdhury, Renuka 1954- *WhoAsAP 91*
Chowdhury, Sohel Uddin 1965- *WhoWor 93*
Chowen, David E. 1943- *St&PR 93*
Chowings, J.W. 1935- *WhoScE 91-1*
Chow Liang, Selina Shuk-Yee 1945- *WhoAsAP 91*
Chown, David Byron 1953- *St&PR 93*
Chown, Frank D. 1918- *St&PR 93*
Chown, Fred Roger 1950- *St&PR 93*
Chown, Marcus 1959- *ScF&FL 92*
Chowning, John 1934- *Baker 92*
Choy, Christine *MiSFD 9*
Choy, Daniel Shu Jen 1926- *WhoE 93*
Choy, Dean D. *Law&B 92*
Choy, Herbert Young Cho 1916- *WhoAm 92*
Choy, Leona Frances 1925- *WhoWrEP 92*
Choy, Michael K.K. *Law&B 92*
Choy, Tuck Chuen 1954- *WhoWor 93*
Choyce, David Peter 1919- *WhoWor 93*
Choyce, Lesley 1951- *ScF&FL 92, WhoCanL 92*
Choyke, Phyllis May 1921- *WhoWrEP 92*
Choyke, Phyllis May Ford 1921- *WhoAmW 93, WhoWor 93*
Choynacki, Annette 1949- *WhoAmW 93*
Cho Young Jang 1942- *WhoAsAP 91*
Chozen, David Edward 1949- *WhoSSW 93*
Chozick, Henry 1924- *St&PR 93*
Chrabonszczewska, Elzbieta Maria 1944- *WhoWor 93*
Chramostova, Vlasta *BioIn 17*
Chrein, Maxine 1950- *WhoEmL 93*
Chrencik, Frank 1914- *WhoAm 92*
Chretien, Jean *BioIn 17*
Chretien, Joseph-Jacques Jean 1934- *WhoAm 92*
Chretien, Margaret Cecilia 1953- *WhoE 93*
Chretien, Michel 1936- *WhoAm 92*
Chretien, Raymond A.J. 1942- *WhoWor 93*
Chretien de Troyes c. 12th cent.- *CIMLC 10*
Chretign, Paul Bernard 1931- *St&PR 93*
Chrey, Kristine Ann 1951- *WhoEmL 93*
Chrien, Robert Edward 1930- *WhoAm 92*
Chris, Harry Joseph 1938- *WhoWor 93*
Chrisanthopoulos, Peter *BioIn 17, WhoAm 92*
Chriscoe, Christine Faust 1950- *WhoAmW 93*
Chrisjohn, Winona Mae 1934- *St&PR 93*
Chrisler, Joan C. 1953- *WhoAmW 93, WhoE 93*
Chrisman, Bruce Lowell 1943- *WhoAm 92*
Chrisman, Charles Bowles 1921- *WhoIns 93*
Chrisman, Cheryl Lynn 1945- *WhoAm 92*
Chrisman, Diane J. 1937- *WhoAm 92, WhoE 93*
Chrisman, James Joseph 1954- *WhoEmL 93, WhoSSW 93, WhoWor 93*
Chrisman, Marlene Santia 1946- *WhoAmW 93, WhoEmL 93*
Chrisman, Noel D. 1934- *St&PR 93*
Chrismer, Denny L. 1946- *St&PR 93*
Chrismer, Michael Peter 1940- *St&PR 93*
Chrismer, Ronald Michael 1954- *WhoE 93, WhoEmL 93*
Chrisopulos, John 1946- *WhoEmL 93*
Chriss, Diane Altman 1946- *WhoEmL 93*
Christ *BioIn 17*
Christ, Albert Howard 1941- *WhoE 93*
Christ, Carl F. *BioIn 17*
Christ, Catherine Ann 1956- *WhoAmW 93*
Christ, Duane Marland 1932- *WhoE 93*
Christ, Jacob 1926- *WhoWor 93*
Christ, Lillard M. 1932- *St&PR 93*
Christ, Nicholas M. 1951- *St&PR 93*
Christ, Sharon Jeanne 1958- *WhoEmL 93*
Christ, Thomas Warren 1944- *WhoAm 92*
Christakis, Panayiotis A. 1942- *WhoScE 91-3*
Christakos, Sylvia 1946- *WhoAm 92, WhoAmW 93*
Christchild, Ravan *ScF&FL 92*
Christel, Henry Eugene 1945- *St&PR 93*
Christen, Brenda J. 1962- *WhoAmW 93*
Christenberry, Boyd *St&PR 93*
Christenbury, Edward S. *Law&B 92, St&PR 93*
Christenbury, Edward Samuel 1941- *WhoAm 92*
Christenbury, Lynne M. *Law&B 92*
Christenen, Clayton M. 1952- *St&PR 93*
Christenfeld, Stuart H. *Law&B 92*
Christensen, Albert Kent 1927- *WhoAm 92*
Christensen, Albert Sherman 1905- *WhoAm 92*
Christensen, Allen Clare 1935- *WhoWor 93*
Christensen, Allen Thomas 1952- *WhoEmL 93*
Christensen, Anders 1955- *WhoWor 93*
Christensen, Bruce LeRoy 1943- *WhoAm 92*
Christensen, Burke Arthur 1945- *WhoIns 93*
Christensen, Burton Grant 1930- *St&PR 93*
Christensen, Carl Roland 1919- *WhoAm 92*
Christensen, Carl William 1946- *WhoE 93*
Christensen, Charles Brophy 1948- *WhoEmL 93*
Christensen, Chris Dale 1949- *WhoEmL 93*
Christensen, Chris P. 1947- *St&PR 93*
Christensen, Cindy Lee 1958- *WhoAmW 93*
Christensen, Coburn F. 1947- *St&PR 93*
Christensen, Daniel K. 1946- *St&PR 93*
Christensen, David A. 1935- *WhoAm 92*
Christensen, David Allen 1935- *St&PR 93*
Christensen, David C. *Law&B 92*
Christensen, Del S. *Law&B 92*
Christensen, Dennis P. 1943- *St&PR 93*
Christensen, Dieter 1932- *Baker 92*
Christensen, Don A. 1930- *St&PR 93*
Christensen, Donna Radovich 1925- *WhoAmW 93, WhoE 93, WhoWor 93*
Christensen, Douglas A. 1947- *St&PR 93*
Christensen, Ebbe Ahrensburg *WhoScE 91-2*
Christensen, Edward A. *Law&B 92*
Christensen, Eileen Heslin 1959- *WhoAmW 93*
Christensen, Eric L. *Law&B 92*
Christensen, Gail Farrar 1933- *WhoSSW 93*
Christensen, Gary Soren 1937- *St&PR 93*
Christensen, George Curtis 1924- *WhoAm 92*
Christensen, George M. 1921- *St&PR 93*
Christensen, Gerald R. *St&PR 93*
Christensen, Gustav Amstrup 1947- *WhoEmL 93*
Christensen, Halvor Niels 1915- *WhoAm 92*
Christensen, Hanne 1950- *WhoWor 93*
Christensen, Hans 1932- *WhoUN 92*
Christensen, Hans Skov 1945- *WhoWor 93*
Christensen, Heidi Ellen 1966- *WhoAmW 93*
Christensen, Henry, III 1944- *WhoAm 92, WhoE 93, WhoWor 93*
Christensen, Howard Alan 1933- *WhoAm 92*
Christensen, Ib Finn 1940- *WhoScE 91-4*
Christensen, J.V. *WhoScE 91-2*
Christensen, James 1932- *WhoAm 92*
Christensen, Jeannette Louise *Law&B 92*
Christensen, John 1938- *WhoWor 93*
Christensen, John William 1914- *WhoAm 92*
Christensen, Jorgen B. 1932- *St&PR 93*
Christensen, Jorgen Moller *WhoScE 91-2*
Christensen, Julien Martin 1918- *WhoAm 92*
Christensen, Kai 1916- *WhoWor 93*
Christensen, Karen Dorothe 1947- *WhoEmL 93*
Christensen, Karen Kay 1947- *WhoEmL 93*
Christensen, Karen Sue 1958- *WhoEmL 93*
Christensen, Katharine Eleanor 1929- *WhoE 93*
Christensen, Lars 1945- *WhoWor 93*
Christensen, Lee Robert 1932- *St&PR 93*
Christensen, Lillian Langseth- *BioIn 17*
Christensen, Linda *Law&B 92*
Christensen, Lydell Lee 1934- *WhoAm 92*
Christensen, Lynne Ellen 1955- *WhoEmL 93*
Christensen, M. Katherine *St&PR 93*
Christensen, Margaret Jane 1938- *WhoAmW 93, WhoWor 93*
Christensen, Martha 1932- *WhoAm 92*
Christensen, Mayme *AmWomPl*
Christensen, Michael *BioIn 17*
Christensen, Mike Thomas 1949- *WhoSSW 93*
Christensen, Mitchell Allen 1954- *WhoEmL 93*
Christensen, Niels Egede 1943- *WhoWor 93*
Christensen, Nikolas Ivan 1937- *WhoAm 92*
Christensen, Odin Dale 1947- *WhoEmL 93*
Christensen, Ole 1944- *WhoWor 93*
Christensen, Ole Voigt 1937- *WhoScE 91-2*
Christensen, Ole Winther *WhoScE 91-2*
Christensen, Opal Marie 1930- *St&PR 93*
Christensen, Patricia Anne Watkins 1947- *WhoEmL 93*
Christensen, Pattie Suzanne 1967- *WhoAmW 93*
Christensen, Paul 1943- *WhoWrEP 92*
Christensen, Paul Walter, Jr. 1925- *WhoAm 92*
Christensen, Pauline Marie 1939- *WhoAmW 93*
Christensen, Per Rex 1936- *WhoScE 91-2*
Christensen, Ray Richards 1922- *WhoAm 92*
Christensen, Reginald Bernard 1923- *WhoWor 93*
Christensen, Robert A. 1933- *St&PR 93*
Christensen, Rosemary L. 1941- *St&PR 93*
Christensen, Roy E. *St&PR 93*
Christensen, Sally Hayden 1935- *WhoAmW 93*
Christensen, Shara Dawn 1956- *WhoEmL 93, WhoSSW 93*
Christensen, Soren Brogger 1947- *WhoWor 93*
Christensen, Steven Mark 1949- *WhoSSW 93*
Christensen, Svend 1959- *WhoScE 91-2*
Christensen, Terje Bjorn *WhoScE 91-4*
Christensen, Thomas Allen 1939- *St&PR 93*
Christensen, Thomas G. S. d1992 *NewYTBS 92*
Christensen, Thor G. 1936- *St&PR 93*
Christensen, Walter Frederick, Jr. 1949- *WhoE 93*
Christensen, Wendy Ann 1952- *WhoE 93*
Christenson, Bob 1951- *St&PR 93*
Christenson, Charles John 1930- *WhoAm 92*
Christenson, Clifford James 1949- *St&PR 93*
Christenson, Cynthia Lynn 1949- *WhoSSW 93*
Christenson, David M. *Law&B 92*
Christenson, Gordon A. 1932- *WhoAm 92*
Christenson, Grant P. 1951- *St&PR 93*
Christenson, Joseph Charles 1958- *St&PR 93*
Christenson, Le Roy Howard 1948- *WhoAm 92*
Christenson, LeRoy H. 1948- *WhoIns 93*
Christenson, Neil O. 1932- *St&PR 93*
Christenson, Paul J. 1953- *WhoE 93*
Christenson, Philip Lawrence 1947- *WhoAm 92, WhoE 93*
Christenson, Sheryl Hartman 1945- *WhoAmW 93*
Christenson, William Newcome 1925- *WhoAm 92, WhoE 93*
Christer, Anthony Hugh *WhoScE 91-1*
Christgau, Victor Laurence August 1894-1991 *BioIn 17*
Christhilf, Bryson Gill 1918- *St&PR 93*
Christhilf, John Harwood 1946- *WhoEmL 93, WhoSSW 93*
Christiaan *BioIn 17*
Christiaens, Jaak P.A. 1946- *WhoScE 91-2*
Christiaens, Louis Winoc 1935- *WhoUN 92*
Christian, I 1426-1481 *HarEnMi*
Christian, I, Prince of Anhalt-Bernburg 1568-1630 *HarEnMi*
Christian, II 1481-1559 *HarEnMi*
Christian, III 1503-1559 *HarEnMi*
Christian, IV 1577-1648 *HarEnMi*
Christian, V 1646-1699 *HarEnMi*
Christian, Ake 1944- *WhoWor 93*
Christian, Betty Jo 1936- *WhoAm 92*
Christian, Bruce *St&PR 93*
Christian, Carol Pendergast 1948- *WhoWor 93*
Christian, Carolyn Marie *Law&B 92*
Christian, Catherine 1901- *ScF&FL 92*
Christian, Charles Leigh 1926- *WhoAm 92*
Christian, Charlie 1916-1942 *Baker 92, BioIn 17*
Christian, Chester Carsel 1926- *WhoSSW 93*
Christian, David 1948- *BioIn 17*
Christian, David William 1959- *BiDAMSp 1989*
Christian, Dennis W. 1946- *St&PR 93*
Christian, Edward Kieren 1944- *WhoAm 92*
Christian, Edwin Ernest 1953- *WhoE 93*
Christian, Emeline 1909-1984 *ScF&FL 92*
Christian, Ernest Silsbee, Jr. 1937- *WhoAm 92*
Christian, Fletcher 1764-1793 *BioIn 17*
Christian, Frances Eloise *AmWomPl*
Christian, Gary Dale 1937- *WhoAm 92*
Christian, Gary Irvin 1951- *WhoAm 92, WhoWor 93*
Christian, Gene H. 1932- *St&PR 93*
Christian, George Eastland 1927- *WhoAm 92*
Christian, George Lloyd, Jr. 1937- *WhoAm 92*
Christian, Howard Joseph 1923- *WhoE 93*
Christian, James Wayne 1934- *WhoAm 92*
Christian, Jane MacNab 1930- *WhoSSW 93*
Christian, Joe Clark 1934- *WhoAm 92*
Christian, John Catlett, Jr. 1929- *WhoAm 92, WhoSSW 93, WhoWor 93*
Christian, John Edward 1917- *WhoAm 92*
Christian, John Kenton 1927- *WhoAm 92*
Christian, Joseph Ralph 1920- *WhoAm 92*
Christian, Linda 1923- *NotHsAW 93*
Christian, Linda Marie 1949- *WhoAmW 93*
Christian, Lynn Allan *BioIn 17*
Christian, Malcolm M. 1924- *St&PR 93*
Christian, Mary Jo Dinan 1941- *WhoE 93, WhoWor 93*
Christian, Melissa Jo 1958- *WhoAmW 93*
Christian, Melva D. *Law&B 92*
Christian, Michael Beauregard 1964- *WhoE 93*
Christian, Nathaniel *MiSFD 9*
Christian, Nelson Frederick 1949- *WhoAm 92, WhoSSW 93*
Christian, Paula 1953- *WhoWrEP 92*
Christian, Paulette Therese 1947- *WhoEmL 93*
Christian, Peter 1947- *WhoAsAP 91*
Christian, Rebecca Anne 1952- *WhoAmW 93, WhoWrEP 92*
Christian, Rebecca J. *St&PR 93*
Christian, Richard Carlton 1924- *WhoAm 92, WhoWor 93*
Christian, Robert G. 1938- *St&PR 93*
Christian, Robert Henry 1922- *WhoAm 92*
Christian, Roger 1944- *MiSFD 9*
Christian, Roland Carl 1938- *WhoWrEP 92*
Christian, Rudolph, Sr. 1951- *WhoEmL 93*
Christian, Sheridan M. 1933- *AfrAmBi*
Christian, Stephen R. *Law&B 92*
Christian, Suzanne Hall 1935- *WhoAmW 93*
Christian, Thomas Embree 1953- *WhoEmL 93*
Christian, Upton John 1933- *WhoSSW 93*
Christian, W.T. *Law&B 92*
Christian, Will 1871-1897 *BioIn 17*
Christian, William David 1941- *St&PR 93*
Christian, William Gerow, Jr. *Law&B 92*
Christian, Winslow *Law&B 92*
Christian, Winslow 1926- *WhoAm 92*
Christiana, Felix J. 1924- *St&PR 93*
Christiana, Ralph J. 1951- *St&PR 93*
Christian-Michaels, Stephen 1954- *WhoEmL 93*
Christiano, Paul P. 1942- *WhoAm 92*
Christians, Charles Henri Louis 1930- *WhoScE 91-2, WhoWor 93*
Christians, Glenn Arthur 1923- *St&PR 93*
Christiansen, Alan Keith 1946- *WhoEmL 93*
Christiansen, Ann Frances 1955- *WhoAmW 93*
Christiansen, Bent Tolstrup *WhoScE 91-2*
Christiansen, C.M., II 1955- *St&PR 93*
Christiansen, Christian Carl, Jr. 1933- *WhoAm 92*
Christiansen, Donald Barry 1939- *St&PR 93, WhoAm 92*
Christiansen, Donald David 1927- *WhoAm 92*
Christiansen, Fredrik Melius 1871-1955 *Baker 92*
Christiansen, George W. 1915- *St&PR 93*
Christiansen, Ivan W. *Law&B 92*
Christiansen, Jack 1928-1986 *BioIn 17*
Christiansen, James Edward 1930- *WhoSSW 93*
Christiansen, Jean Michele 1941- *WhoAmW 93*
Christiansen, John 1934- *WhoWor 93*
Christiansen, John A. 1941- *St&PR 93*
Christiansen, John Rees 1927- *WhoAm 92*
Christiansen, Kenneth Allen 1924- *WhoAm 92*
Christiansen, Marjorie Miner 1922- *WhoSSW 93*
Christiansen, Marjorie Montrose 1925-1990 *BioIn 17*
Christiansen, Norman Juhl 1923- *WhoAm 92*
Christiansen, Olaf 1901-1984 *Baker 92*

Christiansen, Patricia Ann 1949- WhoAmW 93, WhoEmL 93
Christiansen, Paul J. 1906- St&PR 93
Christiansen, Paul Richard Law&B 92
Christiansen, Philip C. 1922- St&PR 93
Christiansen, Richard Dean 1931- WhoAm 92
Christiansen, Richard Louis 1935- WhoAm 92
Christiansen, Robert E. Law&B 92
Christiansen, Russell 1935- WhoAm 92
Christiansen, Russell Eric 1935- St&PR 93
Christiansen, S. Edward, V 1941- St&PR 93
Christiansen, Steven A. Law&B 92
Christiansen, Susan L. 1952- St&PR 93
Christiansen, Vicky Lynn 1958- WhoEmL 93
Christiansen, Walter Henry 1934- WhoAm 92
Christiansen, William E.S. 1944- St&PR 93
Christianson, Dennis P. Law&B 92
Christianson, Frank L. 1946- St&PR 93
Christianson, James Duane 1952- WhoEmL 93
Christianson, Karen Maria Anna 1949- WhoEmL 93
Christianson, Kevin Earl 1948- WhoWrEP 92
Christianson, Lloyd Fenton 1914- WhoAm 92
Christianson, Marcia LaRaye 1947- WhoAmW 93
Christianson, Peter Robert 1957- WhoEmL 93
Christianson, Roger Gordon 1947- WhoEmL 93
Christianson, Warren George 1921- St&PR 93
Christianson, Willard Erastus 1864-1938 BioIn 17
Christiansson, Carl 1944- WhoScE 91-4
Christias, Christos 1936- WhoScE 91-3
Christie, Agatha 1890-1976 Au&Arts 9 [port], BioIn 17, BritWr S2, MagSWL [port]
Christie, Agatha (Mary Clarissa) 1890-1976 ConAu 37NR
Christie, Albert 1886-1951 MiSFD 9N
Christie, Andrew Dobbie 1922- WhoAm 92
Christie, Andrew George 1936- WhoAm 92
Christie, Bruce WhoScE 91-1
Christie, Cheryl Ann 1964- WhoAmW 93
Christie, Clarence J. 1930- St&PR 93, WhoAm 92
Christie, David G. 1930- St&PR 93
Christie, Donald Melvin, Jr. 1942- WhoE 93
Christie, Douglas 1894- ScF&FL 92
Christie, Edna M. WhoUN 92
Christie, Edward Allen Law&B 92
Christie, Frederick W. Law&B 92
Christie, George 1934- OxDcOp
Christie, George A. 1927- St&PR 93
Christie, George Custis 1934- WhoAm 92
Christie, Hans Frederick 1933- WhoAm 92
Christie, Hugh 1932- St&PR 93
Christie, Jeanne Marie 1944- WhoE 93
Christie, Joanne F. Law&B 92
Christie, John 1882-1962 OxDcOp
Christie, Julie 1940- BioIn 17, WhoAm 92, WhoWor 93
Christie, Julie 1941- IntDcF 2-3 [port]
Christie, Laurence Glenn, Jr. 1930- WhoAm 92
Christie, Lindon Edwin, Jr. 1932- WhoE 93
Christie, Marion Francis 1922- WhoSSW 93
Christie, Mary Lu Law&B 92
Christie, Michael Jae 1956- WhoEmL 93
Christie, Ned 1852-1892 BioIn 17
Christie, Nigel B. 1948- WhoAm 92
Christie, Richard d1992 NewYTBS 92
Christie, Richard East 1918- St&PR 93
Christie, Richard Joel 1962- WhoSSW 93
Christie, Robert Brent 1952- WhoAm 92
Christie, Robert S. 1953- St&PR 93
Christie, Scott Graham 1953- WhoEmL 93
Christie, Thomas Philip 1934- WhoAm 92
Christie, Tod Stephens 1958- WhoEmL 93
Christie, Tom E. 1934- St&PR 93
Christie, W.E. WhoScE 91-1
Christie, Walter Robert 1942- WhoAm 92
Christie, Walter Scott 1922- WhoWor 93
Christie, William 1944- BioIn 17, CurBio 92 [port], OxDcOp
Christie, William (Lincoln) 1944- Baker 92
Christie, Winifred 1882-1965 See Moor, Emanuel 1863-1931 Baker 92
Christiensen, Ole Kopp WhoScE 91-2
Christina, Queen of Sweden 1626-1689 BioIn 17
Christina, Frank ConAu 138
Christina, Teresa ConAu 138
Christine, Dennis Brion, Jr. 1947- WhoEmL 93
Christine, Peter Carroll 1952- WhoE 93
Christine, Virginia Feld 1920- WhoAm 92
Christine, de Pisan c. 1364-c. 1431 BioIn 17
Christison, Muriel Branham WhoSSW 93
Christison, William Henry, III 1936- WhoAm 92
Christ-Janer, Arland Frederick 1922- WhoAm 92
Christman, Arthur Castner, Jr. 1922- WhoAm 92
Christman, Bruce Lee 1955- WhoEmL 93
Christman, Elizabeth A. 1914- WhoWrEP 92
Christman, Henry Max 1932- WhoAm 92, WhoWrEP 92
Christman, Irene Ranck 1918- WhoE 93
Christman, James Edward 1930- WhoAm 92
Christman, John Francis 1924- WhoAm 92
Christman, Kenneth Daniel 1949- WhoEmL 93
Christman, Kenneth W. Law&B 92
Christman, Lawrence Lee 1943- St&PR 93
Christman, Luther Parmalee 1915- WhoAm 92
Christman, Mark H. Law&B 92
Christman, Paul Joseph 1918-1970 BiDAMSp 1989
Christman, Richard Marlo 1950- St&PR 93
Christman, Robert Alan 1955- WhoAm 92
Christman, Ronald A. 1939- St&PR 93
Christmas, George Ronald 1940- WhoAm 92
Christmas, Joseph R. 1940- WhoUN 92
Christmas, Peter WhoScE 91-1
Christmas, R. Bruce 1961- St&PR 93
Christmas, William Anthony 1939- WhoE 93
Christnacht, Alain Michel 1946- WhoWor 93
Christner, David Lee 1949- WhoEmL 93
Christner, Richard Sloan Law&B 92
Christo 1935- News 92 [port], -92-3 [port], WhoAm 92
Christodoros Of Koptos 5th cent.-6th cent. OxDcByz
Christodoulos Of Patmos d1093 OxDcByz
Christodoulou, Aris Peter 1939- WhoAm 92, WhoE 93, WhoWor 93
Christodoulou, C.A. 1942- WhoScE 91-4
Christodoulou, Demetrios 1919- ConAu 136
Christodoulou, Th. WhoScE 91-3
Christoff, Beth Graves 1936- WhoAmW 93
Christoff, Boris 1914- IntDcOp [port], OxDcOp
Christoff, Boris 1919- WhoWor 93
Christoff, Boris (Kirilov) 1914- Baker 92
Christoff, Carl 1936- St&PR 93
Christoff, Dimiter 1933- Baker 92
Christoff, James D. Law&B 92
Christoff, Johann 1785-1870 See Grunbaum, Therese 1791-1876 OxDcOp
Christoffel, Gregory J. Law&B 92
Christoffersen, Arthur Lynn 1946- St&PR 93
Christoffersen, Jorgen 1937- WhoScE 91-2
Christoffersen, Ralph Earl 1937- WhoAm 92
Christofferson, D. Todd Law&B 92
Christofferson, D. Todd 1945- St&PR 93
Christofferson, Kimberlee Killmer 1959- WhoE 93, WhoEmL 93
Christoffersson, John Goran 1945- WhoAm 92
Christofides, Constantine G. 1928- WhoAm 92
Christofides, Nicos WhoScE 91-1
Christofidis, George 1943- St&PR 93
Christofilis, Charles St&PR 93
Christofis, E.C. 1950- WhoScE 91-1
Christoforidis, A. John 1924- WhoAm 92, WhoWor 93
Christoforou, John 1921- BioIn 17
Christol, Carl Quimby 1913- WhoAm 92
Christomos, Timothy M. 1950- St&PR 93
Christopeit, Norbert 1947- WhoWor 93
Christopfel, Steven W. 1951- St&PR 93
Christoph, Doretha J. 1949- St&PR 93
Christoph, Florence A(nna) 1937- ConAu 137
Christoph, Frank Henry, Jr. WhoE 93
Christoph, Peter R(ichard) 1938- ConAu 137
Christoph, Susan Catherine 1960- WhoEmL 93
Christophe, Daniel C. 1951- WhoScE 91-2
Christopher OxDcByz
Christopher fl. 13th cent.- OxDcByz
Christopher, Cena Baile 1907- AmWomPl
Christopher, Cyril (Stanley) 1897-1979 Baker 92
Christopher, Daniel Roy 1947- WhoEmL 93
Christopher, Garland R. 1946- WhoEmL 93
Christopher, George Edwin 1927- St&PR 93
Christopher, Harold 1936- St&PR 93
Christopher, James Roy 1942- WhoE 93
Christopher, James Walker 1930- WhoAm 92
Christopher, Jhon Francis 1949- WhoEmL 93
Christopher, Joe R. 1935- ScF&FL 92
Christopher, Joe Randell 1935- WhoSSW 93
Christopher, John ConAu 37NR, MajAI
Christopher, John 1922- ChlFicS, ScF&FL 92
Christopher, Kevin Scott 1954- St&PR 93
Christopher, Matt 1917- ScF&FL 92
Christopher, Matt(hew F.) 1917- MajAI [port]
Christopher, Matthew Frederick 1917- WhoWrEP 92
Christopher, Maurine Brooks WhoAm 92, WhoWrEP 92
Christopher, Melissa Ruth 1964- WhoAmW 93
Christopher, Ned BioIn 17
Christopher, Paul ScF&FL 92
Christopher, Raymond J. 1945- WhoE 93
Christopher, Renny Teresa 1957- WhoAmW 93
Christopher, Richard Scott 1953- WhoEmL 93
Christopher, Richard T. St&PR 93
Christopher, Robert Allan 1929- WhoAm 92
Christopher, Robert C. 1931- St&PR 93
Christopher, Robert Collins d1992 NewYTBS 92 [port]
Christopher, Robert Collins 1924-1992 ConAu 138
Christopher, Robert Paul 1932- WhoSSW 93
Christopher, Ron d1991 BioIn 17
Christopher, Roy BioIn 17
Christopher, Russell Lewis 1930- WhoAm 92
Christopher, Sharon A. Brown 1944- WhoAm 92, WhoAmW 93
Christopher, Thomas Weldon 1917- WhoAm 92
Christopher, Warren 1925- WhoAm 92
Christopher, Warren Minor 1925- NewYTBS 92 [port]
Christopher, Wilford Scott 1916- WhoAm 92
Christopher, William WhoAm 92
Christopher Lekapenos d931 OxDcByz
Christopher Of Mytilene c. 1000-c. 1050 OxDcByz
Christophers, Enno 1936- WhoScE 91-3
Christophersen, Robert L. 1936- St&PR 93
Christopherson, Cathleen M. 1944- St&PR 93
Christopherson, Karin Agnes 1948- WhoAmW 93
Christopherson, Leroy Omar 1935- WhoWrEP 92
Christopherson, Myrvin Frederick 1939- WhoWor 93
Christopherson, Weston R. 1925- St&PR 93
Christopherson, Weston Robert 1925- WhoAm 92
Christopoulos, Anna Louise 1955- WhoE 93
Christopoulos, Arthur George 1930- St&PR 93
Christopoulos, Christos 1946- WhoWor 93
Christopoulos, Spiros 1960- WhoWor 93
Christoskov, Ljudmil Vladimirov 1936- WhoScE 91-4
Christoskov, Peter 1917- Baker 92
Christou, Jani 1926-1970 Baker 92
Christou, William Michael Law&B 92
Christoulas, Stavros 1937- WhoScE 91-3
Christov, Dobri 1875-1941 Baker 92
Christov, Dragan Spirov 1934- WhoUN 92
Christov, Stefan Georgiev 1910- WhoWor 93
Christoverson, Marcene H. St&PR 93
Christus, Petrus c. 1410-1472 BioIn 17
Christy, Alice AmWomPl
Christy, Arthur Hill 1923- WhoAm 92, WhoWor 93
Christy, Audrey Meyer 1933- WhoAmW 93
Christy, David Hardacker 1955- WhoEmL 93, WhoSSW 93
Christy, Doris 1942- St&PR 93
Christy, Edwin Pearce 1815-1862 Baker 92
Christy, Elizabeth Field AmWomPl
Christy, Gail Law&B 92
Christy, Gary A. 1956- St&PR 93
Christy, James Thomas 1947- WhoE 93
Christy, James Walter 1938- WhoAm 92
Christy, Jim 1945- ConAu 138, WhoCanL 92
Christy, John Gilray 1932- St&PR 93, WhoAm 92
Christy, June 1925-1990 BioIn 17
Christy, Karen Jill 1953- WhoSSW 93
Christy, Kathleen Ann 1941- WhoAmW 93
Christy, Kathleen Ann 1953- WhoEmL 93
Christy, Lawrence Craig 1943- WhoUN 92
Christy, Robert Allen 1956- WhoEmL 93, WhoSSW 93
Christy, Thomas Craig 1952- WhoSSW 93
Christy, William O. 1931- WhoAm 92
Chrome, Lorraine St&PR 93
Chromow, Charles E. Law&B 92
Chromow, Sheri P. 1946- WhoAmW 93
Chromulak, Michael Thomas 1929- St&PR 93
Chromy, James R. 1940- St&PR 93
Chronic, Byron John 1921- WhoAm 92
Chronister, Alan B. ScF&FL 92
Chronister, Gregory Michael 1953- WhoAm 92
Chronister, Jay Lester 1934- WhoSSW 93
Chronister, Richard Bruce WhoSSW 93
Chronister, Stewart E. St&PR 93
Chronley, James Andrew 1930- WhoAm 92
Chrousos, George Panagiotis 1951- WhoE 93
Chrow, Albert E. Law&B 92
Chrucki, Jan 1810-1885 PolBiDi
Chrusciel, Kathleen A. Law&B 92
Chrusciel, Tadeusz Leslaw 1926- WhoScE 91-4
Chruscinska, Elzbieta 1951- WhoWor 93
Chrust, Steven G. 1949- St&PR 93
Chrymko, Margaret Mary 1955- WhoAmW 93
Chrysander, (Karl Franz) Friedrich 1826-1901 Baker 92
Chrysanthopoulos, Themistocles Leonidas 1915- WhoWor 93
Chrysanthos of Madytos c. 1770-1846 Baker 92
Chrysaphes, Manuel fl. c. 1440-1463 OxDcByz
Chrysobalantes, Theophanes fl. 10th cent.- OxDcByz
Chrysoberges OxDcByz
Chrysoberges, Maximos dc. 1410 OxDcByz
Chrysoberges, Nikephoros c. 1160-c. 1213 OxDcByz
Chrysocheir OxDcByz
Chrysokephalos, Makarios c. 1300-1382 OxDcByz
Chrysokokkes, George fl. c. 1335-1350 OxDcByz
Chrysoloras, Demetrios c. 1360-c. 1416 OxDcByz
Chrysoloras, Manuel c. 1350-1415 OxDcByz
Chrysostom, John d407 BioIn 17
Chrysostomos of Oreoi, Bishop 1945- WhoAm 92
Chryssa 1933- WhoAm 92
Chryssafopoulos, Nicholas 1919- WhoAm 92
Chryssanthou-Hushka, Alina Helen 1962- WhoEmL 93
Chryssikos, Telemac N. Law&B 92
Chryssis, George Christopher 1947- St&PR 93, WhoAm 92, WhoE 93, WhoEmL 93
Chryst, Gary 1949- WhoAm 92
Chrystie, Francis N. 1904-1986 BioIn 17
Chrystie, Thomas L. 1933- St&PR 93
Chrystostomos, Konstantinidis 1921- WhoWor 93
Chrzanowski, Edward Francizek 1957- WhoWor 93
Chrzanowski, Ronald P. 1942- St&PR 93
Chrzanowski, Thomas H. 1952- WhoSSW 93
Chrzan-Seelig, Patricia Ann 1954- WhoAmW 93, WhoEmL 93
Chrzavzez, Georges Ladislas 1939- WhoWor 93
Chu, Alexander Hang-Torng 1955- WhoWor 93
Chu, Allen Yum-Ching 1951- WhoWor 93
Chu, Benjamin Thomas Peng-Nien 1932- WhoAm 92, WhoE 93
Chu, C. K. 1927- WhoAm 92
Chu, Chung-Bin 1923- WhoWor 93
Chu, David S. C. 1944- WhoAm 92
Chu, David Yuk 1945- WhoE 93
Chu, Donald Lee 1953- WhoSSW 93
Chu, Esther Briney 1911- WhoAmW 93

Chu, Foo 1921- *WhoE 93*
Chu, Hoi L. 1947- *WhoE 93, WhoEmL 93*
Chu, Huang 1939- *WhoWor 93*
Chu, Jeffrey Chuan 1919- *WhoAm 92*
Chu, John Y. *Law&B 92*
Chu, Johnson Chin Sheng 1918- *WhoAm 92*
Chu, Ka Hou 1954- *WhoWor 93*
Chu, Kuang-Han 1919- *WhoAm 92*
Chu, Li-Chuan 1949- *WhoSSW 93*
Chu, Otto H. *Law&B 92*
Chu, Pak Lim 1940- *WhoWor 93*
Chu, Paul Ching-Wu 1941- *WhoAm 92, WhoSSW 93*
Chu, Petra ten-Doesschate 1942- *ConAu 138*
Chu, Philip Feilong 1949- *WhoSSW 93*
Chu, Richard Chao-Fan 1933- *WhoAm 92, WhoWor 93*
Chu, Robin d1990 *BioIn 17*
Chu, Roderick Gong-Wah 1949- *WhoAm 92, WhoE 93, WhoEmL 93, WhoWor 93*
Chu, Shiu-Kee 1948- *WhoUN 92*
Chu, Steven 1948- *WhoAm 92*
Chu, Tah-Hsiung 1953- *WhoWor 93*
Chu, Tien Hsing 1968- *WhoSSW 93*
Chu, Tony Yeling 1936- *WhoWor 93*
Chu, Tsann Ming 1938- *WhoAm 92*
Chu, Valentin Yuan-ling 1919- *WhoE 93, WhoWor 93*
Chu, Wai-Keong 1964- *WhoWor 93*
Chu, Wen-djang 1914- *WhoAm 92*
Chu, Wesley Wei-Chin 1936- *WhoAm 92*
Chu, Yee-Yeen 1949- *WhoEmL 93*
Chu, Zhong Wu 1923- *WhoWor 93*
Chua, David Sue Hian 1963- *WhoWor 93*
Chua, Evelyn Bautista 1950- *WhoEmL 93*
Chua, Kiat 1962- *WhoE 93*
Chua, Nam-Hai 1944- *WhoAm 92*
Chua, Tommy Dy 1955- *WhoWor 93*
Chua, Virginia 1956- *St&PR 93*
Chua Jui Meng *WhoAsAP 91*
Chuang, Cynthia 1951- *WhoE 93*
Chuang, Frank Shiunn-Jea 1942- *WhoAm 92, WhoWor 93*
Chuang, Shih S. 1940- *St&PR 93*
Chubar'ian, Ogan Stepanovich 1908-1976 *BioIn 17*
Chubb, Hendon 1933- *WhoE 93*
Chubb, Hilkka Aileen 1930- *WhoWrEP 92*
Chubb, James C. *WhoScE 91-1*
Chubb, Percy, III 1934- *St&PR 93, WhoAm 92, WhoIns 93*
Chubb, Stephen Darrow 1944- *WhoAm 92*
Chubb, Talbot Albert 1923- *WhoAm 92*
Chubb, Thomas Caldecot, III *Law&B 92*
Chuber, August Bruce 1922- *St&PR 93*
Chubinsky, Leonard I. *Law&B 92*
Chuchel, Paul B. *WhoIns 93*
Chu Ch'uan-chung 852-912 *HarEnMi*
Chuck, Harry Cousins 1904- *WhoE 93*
Chuck, Walter Goonsun 1920- *WhoAm 92, WhoWor 93*
Chuck D *BioIn 17*
Chuckovits, Charles H. 1912- *BiDAMSp 1989*
Chudacek, Ivo 1932- *WhoScE 91-4*
Chudecki, Zygmunt 1922- *WhoScE 91-4*
Chudek, Miroslaw 1934- *WhoScE 91-4*
Chudgar, Ashok Babulal 1951- *WhoEmL 93*
Chudik, Igor 1935- *WhoScE 91-4*
Chudkowski, Joseph Michael 1939- *St&PR 93*
Chudnoff, Jay 1945- *St&PR 93*
Chudnovsky, Christine Pardo 1958- *WhoEmL 93*
Chudnovsky, D. 1947- *BioIn 17*
Chudnovsky, David 1947- *BioIn 17*
Chudnovsky, G. 1952- *BioIn 17*
Chudnovsky, Gregory 1952- *BioIn 17*
Chudnovsky, Gregory Volfovich 1952- *WhoAm 92*
Chudnow, Byron *MiSFD 9*
Chudnow, Yaffa *ScF&FL 92*
Chudoba, David Thomas 1953- *WhoEmL 93*
Chudobiak, Walter James 1942- *WhoE 93*
Chudomelka, LaMond Richard 1934- *WhoSSW 93*
Chudow, Scott R. 1953- *WhoE 93*
Chudzik, Douglas Walter 1946- *WhoE 93, WhoWor 93*
Chudzikiewicz, Ryszard Jerzy 1923- *WhoScE 91-4*
Chudzinski, Mark Adam 1956- *WhoWor 93*
Chue, Seck Hong 1942- *WhoWor 93*
Chueca, Federico 1846-1908 *Baker 92*
Chueca, Ricardo Silva *Law&B 92*
Chueshov, Igor Dmitrievich 1951- *WhoWor 93*
Chughtai, Abdul Hamid 1948- *WhoWor 93*
Chuha, Maude Fredericka 1927- *WhoAmW 93*
Chuke, Paul Okwudili 1936- *WhoUN 92*
Chukhadjyan, Tigran 1837-1898 *OxDcOp*
Chukovsky, Kornei (Ivanovich) 1882-1969 *MajAI [port]*
Chulack, Lara Teresa 1967- *WhoE 93*
Chulick, Alberta Bjorkman 1951- *WhoEmL 93*
Chuma, James 1850?-1882 *Expl 93 [port]*
Chuma, Koki 1936- *WhoAsAP 91*
Chumacero, Ali 1918- *DcMexL*
Chuman, Dwight 1952- *St&PR 93*
Chuman, Jerilyn Rae 1951- *WhoAmW 93*
Chumas, Constantine 1935- *St&PR 93*
Chumbley, Robert Emmett, III 1944- *WhoSSW 93*
Chumley, Donnie Ann 1942- *WhoAmW 93*
Chumley, Norris Jewett 1956- *WhoEmL 93*
Chumsky, Sandra Evelyn 1934- *WhoAm 92*
Chun, Dai Ho 1905- *WhoWor 93*
Chun, Hon Ming 1960- *WhoE 93*
Chun, Lowell Koon Wa 1944- *WhoWor 93*
Chun, Michael Sing Fong 1944- *St&PR 93*
Chun, Rupert Kaisun 1944- *St&PR 93*
Chun, Se Yong d1991 *BioIn 17*
Chun, Thomas T.W. 1925- *St&PR 93*
Chunchie, Kamel Athon 1886-1953 *BioIn 17*
Chun Doo Hwan 1931- *WhoWor 93*
Chung, Albert Kwok-Kwong 1953- *WhoWor 93*
Chung, Chi Yung 1920- *WhoWor 93*
Chung, Cho Man 1918- *WhoWor 93*
Chung, Connie *BioIn 17, NewYTBS 92 [port]*
Chung, Connie 1946- *WhoE 93*
Chung, Constance 1946- *JrnUS*
Chung, Constance Yu-hwa 1946- *WhoAm 92, WhoAmW 93, WhoE 93*
Chung, Cynthia Norton 1955- *WhoAmW 93, WhoEmL 93*
Chung, Dae Hyun 1934- *WhoWor 93*
Chung, Deborah Duen Ling 1952- *WhoEmL 93*
Chung, Do-Yung 1927- *WhoWor 93*
Chung, Douglas Chu 1951- *WhoWor 93*
Chung, Edward Kooyoung 1931- *WhoAm 92*
Chung, Fan Rong Kung 1949- *WhoEmL 93*
Chung, Fung-Lung 1949- *WhoWor 93*
Chung, George *Law&B 92*
Chung, Hae Woong 1937- *WhoWor 93*
Chung, Harrison Paul 1951- *WhoEmL 93*
Chung, Henry 1902- *BioIn 17*
Chung, Hwan Yung 1927- *WhoWor 93*
Chung, Hyun-Sik 1943- *WhoWor 93*
Chung, Hyungkun 1945- *WhoWor 93*
Chung, Joseph Sang-hoon 1929- *WhoAm 92*
Chung, Ju Yung *BioIn 17*
Chung, Jung Git 1922- *WhoAm 92, WhoE 93*
Chung, Kyung Cho 1921- *WhoAm 92, WhoWor 93*
Chung, Kyung-Wha 1948- *Baker 92, WhoWor 93*
Chung, Myung-Wha 1944- *Baker 92*
Chung, Myung-Whun 1953- *Baker 92, BioIn 17, OxDcOp*
Chung, Paul Myungha 1929- *WhoAm 92*
Chung, Richard S. 1938- *St&PR 93*
Chung, Wai Mun 1932- *St&PR 93*
Chung Chang Wha 1940- *WhoAsAP 91*
Chung Chong-Teck 1936- *WhoAsAP 91*
Chung Dong Ho 1936- *WhoAsAP 91*
Chung Dong Sung 1940- *WhoAsAP 91*
Chung Dong Yun 1938- *WhoAsAP 91*
Chung Hae-Nam 1944- *WhoAsAP 91*
Chung Jey Moon 1938- *WhoAsAP 91*
Chung Jung Hoon 1935- *WhoAsAP 91*
Chung Ki Young 1930- *WhoAsAP 91*
Chung Kyun Hwan 1944- *WhoAsAP 91*
Chung Mong Joon 1953- *WhoAsAP 91*
Chung Pui-Lam 1940- *WhoAsAP 91*
Chung Sang Koo 1926- *WhoAsAP 91*
Chung Sang Yong 1951- *WhoAsAP 91*
Chung Si Bong 1928- *WhoAsAP 91*
Chung Soon Duk 1936- *WhoAsAP 91*
Chung Suk Mo 1930- *WhoAsAP 91*
Chungviwatanant, Smith 1959- *WhoWor 93*
Chung Woong 1929- *WhoAsAP 91*
Chun-Hoon, Lowell Koon Ying 1949- *WhoEmL 93*
Chunn, E. Keith, Jr. *Law&B 92*
Chunn, Leona Hayes 1885- *WhoWrEP 92*
Chun Yong Won 1945- *WhoAsAP 91*
Chupack, Edward A. *Law&B 92*
Chupak, Michael V. 1945- *St&PR 93*
Chupela, Dolores Carole 1952- *WhoAmW 93*
Chupik, Eugene Jerry 1931- *WhoSSW 93*
Chupka, William Andrew 1923- *WhoAm 92*
Chupp, Diana Lynn 1945- *WhoAmW 93*
Chuprinko, John Andrew 1955- *St&PR 93*
Churan, J. Thomas 1940- *St&PR 93*
Churbanov, Vladimir Vladimirovich 1959- *WhoWor 93*
Church, A. Maude 1949- *WhoEmL 93*
Church, Abiah A. 1922- *WhoAm 92*
Church, Alfred J. 1861- *ScF&FL 92*
Church, C. Howard 1904- *WhoAm 92*
Church, Charles *BioIn 17*
Church, David Arthur 1939- *WhoSSW 93*
Church, Douglas M. 1950- *St&PR 93*
Church, Earlyn 1939- *St&PR 93*
Church, Edwin Arnold 1939- *St&PR 93*
Church, Elva Mae 1931- *WhoAmW 93*
Church, Eugene Lent 1925- *WhoAm 92*
Church, F. Forrester *BioIn 17*
Church, Frank 1924-1984 *ColdWar 1 [port]*
Church, Frank Forrester 1948- *WhoAm 92, WhoWor 93*
Church, Frederic Edwin 1826-1900 *BioIn 17*
Church, Gary L. *Law&B 92*
Church, Henry C., Jr. 1905- *St&PR 93*
Church, Herbert Stephen, Jr. 1920- *WhoAm 92*
Church, Irene Zaboly 1947- *WhoAm 92, WhoAmW 93, WhoEmL 93*
Church, Jo Hall 1931- *WhoSSW 93*
Church, John A. 1920- *St&PR 93*
Church, John C. *Law&B 92*
Church, John F., Jr. 1936- *St&PR 93*
Church, John Franklin, Jr. 1936- *WhoAm 92*
Church, John Irwin 1919- *WhoWrEP 92*
Church, John Stewart 1948- *WhoEmL 93*
Church, John Trammell 1917- *St&PR 93, WhoAm 92*
Church, Kathryn Cantey 1954- *WhoE 93*
Church, Margaret B. 1889-1976 *BioIn 17*
Church, Marguerite Stitt 1892-1990 *BioIn 17*
Church, Martha Eleanor 1930- *WhoAm 92, WhoAmW 93*
Church, Mary D. *St&PR 93*
Church, Nancy Jeanne 1950- *WhoEmL 93*
Church, Norris *BioIn 17*
Church, Philip Throop 1931- *WhoAm 92*
Church, Phillip Brent 1960- *WhoE 93*
Church, Ralph 1927- *ScF&FL 92*
Church, Randolph Warner, Jr. 1934- *WhoAm 92*
Church, Richard 1784-1873 *HarEnMi*
Church, Richard 1893-1972 *ScF&FL 92*
Church, Richard Clark 1942- *WhoUN 92*
Church, Richard Dwight 1936- *WhoE 93*
Church, Robert Lindsay 1949- *WhoE 93*
Church, Russell Miller 1930- *WhoAm 92*
Church, Ruth Ellen d1991 *BioIn 17*
Church, Sonia Jane Shutter 1940- *WhoAmW 93*
Church, Stanley E. 1910- *St&PR 93*
Church, Theodore H. 1925- *St&PR 93*
Church, Thomas A. 1933- *St&PR 93*
Church, Thomas Clayton, Jr. 1942- *WhoSSW 93*
Church, Thomas Gale 1940- *St&PR 93*
Church, Thomas Trowbridge 1919- *WhoAm 92*
Church, Virginia Woodson Frame 1880- *AmWomPl*
Church, William Conant 1836-1917 *JrnUS*
Church-Chason, Carolyn Louise 1963- *WhoAmW 93*
Churchhouse, Robert Francis *WhoScE 91-1*
Churchill, Alison B. 1954- *St&PR 93*
Churchill, Anthony Aylward 1938- *WhoUN 92*
Churchill, Armistead 1772-1795 *BioIn 17*
Churchill, Bernardita Reyes 1938- *WhoE 93*
Churchill, Bruce B. 1957- *WhoAm 92*
Churchill, Bruce Barrett 1957- *St&PR 93*
Churchill, Caroline Nichols 1833-1926 *BioIn 17*
Churchill, Caryl *BioIn 17*
Churchill, Caryl 1938- *ConTFT 10*
Churchill, Charles 1731-1764 *BioIn 17*
Churchill, Clementine 1885-1977 *BioIn 17*
Churchill, Daniel Wayne 1947- *WhoEmL 93*
Churchill, Glen D. 1934- *St&PR 93, WhoAm 92*
Churchill, Hildegarde E. *AmWomPl*
Churchill, Hugo M. 1939- *St&PR 93*
Churchill, Jay 1953- *St&PR 93*
Churchill, Jennie 1854-1921 *BioIn 17*
Churchill, Jerry M. 1939- *St&PR 93*
Churchill, Jill *ConAu 39NR*
Churchill, Joan Russell 1931- *WhoE 93*
Churchill, John 1650-1722 *BioIn 17*
Churchill, John William 1931- *WhoE 93*
Churchill, Justina Anne 1963- *WhoAmW 93*
Churchill, Larry Raymond 1945- *WhoAm 92*
Churchill, Mary Carey 1933- *WhoAm 92*
Churchill, Mary Jo *BioIn 17*
Churchill, Neil Center 1927- *WhoAm 92*
Churchill, Phyllis *BioIn 17*
Churchill, Raymond F. *Law&B 92*
Churchill, Robert Craig 1929- *St&PR 93*
Churchill, S. Garton d1992 *NewYTBS 92*
Churchill, Scott Demane 1950- *WhoSSW 93*
Churchill, Stuart Winston 1920- *WhoAm 92*
Churchill, Thomas John 1961- *WhoEmL 93*
Churchill, Timothy Andrew 1948- *WhoE 93*
Churchill, Verne Bartlett 1932- *St&PR 93*
Churchill, Winston 1871-1947 *GayN, PolPar*
Churchill, Winston 1874-1965 *BioIn 17, ConHero 2 [port]*
Churchill, Winston John 1940- *WhoAm 92*
Churchill, Winston Leonard Spencer 1874-1965 *DcTwHis, HarEnMi*
Churchill, Winston S. 1874-1965 *ColdWar 1 [port]*
Churchill, Winston S. 1940- *BioIn 17*
Churchland, Patricia Smith 1943- *WhoAmW 93*
Churchman, Daniel Louis 1960- *WhoSSW 93*
Churchman, David John 1951- *WhoE 93*
Churchman, Norman P. 1910- *St&PR 93*
Churchmuch, Terry *Law&B 92*
Churchward, John *ScF&FL 92*
Churchwell, Edward Bruce 1940- *WhoAm 92*
Churet, Charles Jean A. 1952- *WhoWor 93*
Churg, Jacob 1910- *WhoAm 92, WhoWor 93*
Churinske, Paul Joseph 1948- *St&PR 93*
Churm, Peter 1926- *St&PR 93*
Chused, Andrew Michael 1949- *St&PR 93*
Chused, Paul Leon 1943- *St&PR 93*
Chusid, Martin 1925- *Baker 92*
Chusmir, Janet d1990 *BioIn 17*
Chustek, Roy Stuart 1948- *WhoEmL 93*
Chustz, Harris J. 1915- *St&PR 93*
Chustz, J. Steve *Law&B 92*
Chut, Frank Joseph 1934- *St&PR 93*
Chute, Arthur L. 1945- *St&PR 93*
Chute, Marchette 1909- *WhoAm 92, WhoAmW 93, WhoWrEP 92*
Chute, Marchette Gaylord 1909- *BioIn 17*
Chute, Paul Michael *Law&B 92*
Chute, Robert A. 1938- *St&PR 93*
Chute, Robert M(aurice) 1926- *WhoWrEP 92*
Chute, Robert Maurice 1926- *WhoAm 92*
Chute, Terence Michael 1936- *WhoWor 93*
Chu Teh 1886-1976 *HarEnMi*
Chutes, Brenda *WhoWrEP 92*
Chu Thompson, Jane 1957- *WhoAmW 93*
Chutich, Margaret Helen 1958- *WhoEmL 93*
Chutkow, Jerry Grant 1933- *WhoAm 92*
Chuvin, Arthur E. 1926- *St&PR 93*
Chuwa, Mathias Elikana 1936- *WhoUN 92*
Chu Yung d1449 *HarEnMi*
Chvalovsky, Vaclav 1925- *WhoScE 91-4*
Chvotkin, Alan *Law&B 92*
Chwalek, Bonnie E. *Law&B 92*
Chwalek, C.T. 1943- *St&PR 93*
Chwaliszewski, Robert J. *Law&B 92*
Chwalk, Taras J. 1945- *St&PR 93*
Chwast, Seymour *BioIn 17*
Chwast, Seymour 1931- *WhoAm 92*
Chwaszczewski, Stefan 1935- *WhoScE 91-4*
Chwat, Aleksander *ScF&FL 92*
Chwatsky, Ann 1942- *WhoAmW 93*
Chwiecko, John J. *St&PR 93*
Chybinski, Adolf 1880-1952 *PolBiDi*
Chybinski, Adolf (Eustachy) 1880-1952 *Baker 92*
Chylak, Nestor, Jr. 1922-1982 *BiDAMSp 1989*
Chynoweth, Alan Gerald 1927- *WhoAm 92, WhoWor 93*
Chynoweth, Bradford Grethen 1890-1986 *HarEnMi*
Chynoweth, Rena *BioIn 17*
Chynoweth, Robert Leslie 1941- *WhoAsAP 91*
Chypre, Elizabeth 1938- *WhoAmW 93*
Chytil, Frank 1924- *WhoAm 92*
Chytil, Kurt 1942- *WhoScE 91-4*
Chytilova, Vera 1929- *DrEEuF, MiSFD 9*
Chyu, Ming-Chien 1955- *WhoSSW 93*
Chyung, Chi Han 1933- *WhoWor 93*
Ciabattari, Jane *BioIn 17*
Ciabattari, Jane Dotson 1946- *WhoWrEP 92*
Ciaburri, Joseph Victor 1929- *St&PR 93*
Ciafardini, Edward Peter *Law&B 92*
Ciak, Ann D. 1951- *WhoAmW 93*
Ciak, Brenda Susan 1955- *WhoAmW 93*

Cialdella, Virginia Joanne 1933- *WhoSSW 93*
Cialdini, Enrico 1813-1892 *HarEnMi*
Cialone, Richard Michael 1948- *St&PR 93*
Ciamaga, Gustav 1930- *Baker 92*
Ciampi, Joseph d1991 *BioIn 17*
Ciampi, Mario Joseph 1907- *WhoAm 92*
Ciampi, Vincenzo 1719-1762 *OxDcOp*
Ciamporcero, Alan F. *Law&B 92*
Ciamporcero, Audley A., Jr. *Law&B 92*
Ciancanelli, Gino J. 1950- *St&PR 93*
Cianchette, Alton E. 1930- *St&PR 93*
Cianci, Vincent A., Jr. *BioIn 17*
Cianci, Vincent Albert, Jr. 1941- *WhoAm 92, WhoE 93*
Cianciara, Zdzislaw 1930- *WhoScE 91-4*
Ciancio, Ronald J. *Law&B 92*
Ciancio, Sebastian Gene 1937- *WhoAm 92*
Cianciola, Charles Sal 1933- *WhoAm 92*
Cianciola, Charles Salvatore 1933- *St&PR 93*
Cianciolo, August M. 1936- *WhoAm 92*
Cianciulli, Robert *Law&B 92*
Cianciulli, Robert Philip 1945- *St&PR 93*
Cianelli, Alfred A., Jr. 1930- *St&PR 93*
Cianfarani, Gina 1960- *WhoWrEP 92*
Cianflone, Francis Edward 1930- *WhoSSW 93*
Cianfrocca, Francis 1960- *WhoE 93*
Ciangio, Cynthia M. 1953- *WhoWor 93*
Ciangio, Donna Lenore 1949- *WhoE 93, WhoEmL 93*
Ciani, Samuel Nicholas 1934- *St&PR 93*
Ciani, Suzanne Elizabeth 1946- *WhoEmL 93*
Ciano, Galeazzo 1903-1944 *DcTwHis*
Ciao, Frederick J. *WhoE 93*
Ciappi, Mario Luigi Cardinal 1909- *WhoWor 93*
Ciaramella, Raffaele Joseph 1949- *St&PR 93*
Ciarcia, Debra Ann 1954- *WhoAmW 93*
Ciardi, Giuseppe Francesco 1953- *WhoWor 93*
Ciardi, John 1916-1986 *BioIn 17*
Ciardi, John (Anthony) 1916-1986 *MajAI [port]*
Ciardiello, Ronald J. *Law&B 92*
Ciarlette, David George 1952- *St&PR 93*
Ciarlillo, Marjorie Ann 1940- *WhoAmW 93*
Ciarlo, John Louis 1945- *St&PR 93*
Ciarochi, Sandra Reichert 1943- *WhoSSW 93*
Ciarrocca, Norman *St&PR 93*
Ciarula, Thomas Alan 1948- *WhoE 93, WhoEmL 93*
Ciatto, Debi Lynn 1956- *WhoEmL 93*
Ciaureli, Mihail 1894-1974 *DrEEuF*
Ciavola, Louise Arlene 1933- *WhoWor 93*
Ciavola, Rex George 1931- *WhoWor 93*
Ciavolino, Marco 1956- *WhoEmL 93*
Cibber, Colley 1671-1757 *BioIn 17*
Cibber, Susanna 1714-1766 *OxDcOp*
Cibelli, Ludwig J. 1907-1990 *BioIn 17*
Cibois, Philippe 1941- *WhoScE 91-2*
Ciborowski, Paul John 1943- *WhoE 93*
Ciborowski, Stanislaw 1925- *WhoScE 91-4*
Cibroski, Ronald Bryan 1945- *St&PR 93*
Cibulka, Jiri 1947- *WhoScE 91-4*
Cibulski, Joseph Richard 1941- *WhoSSW 93*
Cic, Milan 1932- *WhoWor 93*
Cicak, Mirko 1940- *WhoScE 91-4*
Cicala, Joseph John 1955- *WhoE 93*
Cicale, Ann Berg 1950- *WhoSSW 93*
Cicalese, Amy Luisa 1954- *WhoEmL 93*
Ciccarelli, John A. 1939- *St&PR 93*
Ciccarone, Antonio 1909-1982 *BioIn 17*
Ciccarone, Richard Anthony 1952- *WhoAm 92, WhoEmL 93*
Cicchetti, Paul W. *Law&B 92*
Cicci, David Allen 1951- *WhoSSW 93*
Cicci, Regina *BioIn 17*
Ciccimarra, Giuseppe 1790-1836 *OxDcOp*
Cicciolina *BioIn 17*
Cicco, Martin John 1955- *St&PR 93*
Ciccolella, Anthony 1959- *WhoEmL 93*
Ciccolella, Catherine Anne 1944- *WhoSSW 93*
Ciccolini, Aldo 1925- *Baker 92*
Ciccone, Anne Panepinto 1943- *WhoAm 92, WhoAmW 93, WhoWor 93*
Ciccone, Christopher G. *BioIn 17*
Ciccone, J. Richard 1943- *WhoAm 92*
Ciccone, Madonna *BioIn 17*
Ciccone, Madonna Louise Veronica 1958- *WhoAm 92, WhoAmW 93*
Ciccone, Marshall John 1947- *St&PR 93, WhoEmL 93*
Ciccone, Patrick Edwin 1944- *WhoAm 92*
Ciccone, Peter M. 1942- *WhoAm 92*
Ciccone, Richard 1940- *WhoAm 92*
Cicconi, Ernest J. *Law&B 92*
Cicconi, Raymond J. 1929- *St&PR 93*
Ciccoritti, Gerard 1956- *MiSFD 9*
Ciccotelli, Teresa T. *Law&B 92*
Ciccotelli, Teresa T. 1951- *St&PR 93*
Cicen, John Randolph 1942- *St&PR 93*
Ciceri, Pierre-Luc-Charles 1782-1868 *IntDcOp, OxDcOp*
Cicero 106BC-43BC *MagSWL [port]*
Cicero, Frank, Jr. 1935- *WhoAm 92*
Cicero, Marcus Tullius 106BC-43BC *BioIn 17*
Cicero, Mary Beth 1953- *WhoEmL 93*
Cicero, Quintus Tullius 102BC-43BC *HarEnMi*
Cicero, Solomon Chadwell 1944- *WhoE 93*
Cicet, Donald James 1940- *WhoSSW 93*
Cich, Frank Anthony *Law&B 92*
Cichacki, Joseph C. 1949- *St&PR 93*
Cichelli, Mario Thomas 1920- *WhoE 93*
Cichoke, Anthony Joseph, Jr. 1931- *WhoWor 93*
Cichon, Joanne M. 1959- *WhoIns 93*
Cichy, Marian 1931- *WhoScE 91-4*
Cicin-Sain, Sime 1921- *WhoScE 91-4*
Ciciora, Walter Stanley 1942- *St&PR 93*
Cicirelli, Bernard William 1932- *St&PR 93*
Cicirelli, Victor George 1926- *WhoAm 92*
Ciclitira, Paul Jonathan 1948- *WhoWor 93*
Cicognini, Giacinto 1606-1651 *OxDcOp*
Cicognini, Giacinto Andrea 1606-1651 *IntDcOp*
Cicognini, Jacopo 1577-1633 *OxDcOp*
Cicolani, Angelo George 1933- *WhoSSW 93*
Ciconia, Jean (Johannes) c. 1335-1411 *Baker 92*
Cid, Joaquin 1941- *WhoWor 93*
Ciechalski, Joseph C. 1946- *WhoSSW 93*
Ciechanover, Joseph 1933- *St&PR 93, WhoAm 92*
Ciechanowicz, Wieslaw 1926- *WhoScE 91-4*
Ciechon, Edward J., Jr. *Law&B 92*
Ciecimirski, L.S. John *Law&B 92*
Cieciorka, Frank *BioIn 17*
Cielinski-Kessler, Audrey Ann 1957- *WhoAmW 93, WhoEmL 93, WhoSSW 93, WhoWor 93*
Cielle, Cynthia Elizabeth 1949- *WhoEmL 93*
Cienava, Debora Mary 1960- *WhoAmW 93*
Cienciala, Anna Maria 1929- *WhoAmW 93*
Ciencin, Scott 1962- *ScF&FL 92*
Cienfuegos, Ferman *DcCPCAm*
Ciepiela, Stephen Joseph 1954- *WhoEmL 93*
Cieplak, Marek 1950- *WhoWor 93*
Cieplinski, Jan 1900-1972 *PolBiDi*
Cieply, Jan 1941- *WhoScE 91-4*
Cier, Ronald J. *Law&B 92*
Ciereszko, Leon Stanley 1917- *WhoAm 92, WhoSSW 93*
Cieri, Anthony J. 1931- *St&PR 93*
Cierniewski, Joseph Walter 1957- *WhoE 93*
Ciesielski, Roman A. 1924- *WhoScE 91-4*
Ciesielski, Thomas G. 1949- *St&PR 93*
Ciesinski, Katherine 1950- *Baker 92*
Ciesinski, Kristine 1952- *Baker 92*
Ciesla, Wojciech A. 1925- *WhoScE 91-4*
Cieslak, Arthur Kazimer 1915- *WhoAm 92*
Cieslak, Kazimierz 1923- *WhoScE 91-4*
Cieslak, Ryszard d1990 *BioIn 17*
Cieslinski, Zbigniew Marian 1930- *WhoScE 91-4*
Cifelli, Barbara Doris 1942- *WhoAmW 93*
Cifelli, John Louis 1923- *WhoAm 92*
Cifelli, Thomas Howard *Law&B 92*
Ciferni, Leon P. *Law&B 92*
Ciferri, Orio 1928- *WhoScE 91-3*
Ciffa, Joseph R. 1950- *WhoE 93*
Cifra, Antonio 1584-1629 *Baker 92*
Cifuentes, Eduardo *WhoUN 92*
Cigarran, Thomas G. *St&PR 93*
Cigna, Arrigo 1932- *WhoScE 91-3*
Cigna, Gina 1900- *Baker 92, IntDcOp, OxDcOp*
Cignarella, Giorgio 1930- *WhoScE 91-3*
Cihaski, Lisa *BioIn 17*
Cihlar, Christine Carol 1948- *WhoAmW 93, WhoEmL 93, WhoWrEP 92*
Cihlar, Frank Phillip 1943- *WhoAm 92*
Cihlar, Jaroslav 1946- *WhoScE 91-4*
Cijan, Rafael Victor 1935- *WhoWor 93*
Cikanek, Harry Arthur, III 1959- *WhoEmL 93, WhoSSW 93*
Cikker, Jan 1911- *OxDcOp*
Cikker, Jan 1911-1989 *Baker 92*
Ciko, John, Jr. *Law&B 92*
Cikovsky, Nicolai, Jr. 1933- *WhoAm 92*
Cilea, Francesco 1866-1950 *Baker 92, IntDcOp, OxDcOp*
Cilella, Salvatore George, Jr. 1941- *WhoAm 92, WhoSSW 93*
Ciletti, Christine Joy 1945- *WhoAmW 93*
Cilfone, Nicholas J. 1950- *St&PR 93*
Ciliberto, Carlo 1923- *WhoWor 93*
Cillario, Carlo Felice 1915- *Baker 92*
Cillario, Carlo Felice 1917- *OxDcOp*
Cillie, Petrus Johannes 1917- *WhoWor 93*
Cillo, Daniel P. *Law&B 92*
Cillo, Larry Joseph 1955- *WhoEmL 93*
Cima, Annalisa 1941- *DcLB 128 [port]*
Cima, Giovanni Paolo d17th cent. *Baker 92*
Cimador 1761-1805 *Baker 92*
Cimadoro, Giovanni Battista 1761-1805 *Baker 92*
Cimara, Pietro 1887-1967 *Baker 92*
Cimarosa, Domenico 1749-1801 *Baker 92, IntDcOp [port], OxDcOp*
Cimasoni, Giorgio 1933- *WhoScE 91-4*
Cimatti, Giovanni Ermanno 1945- *WhoWor 93*
Cimber, Matt *MiSFD 9*
Cimbleris, Borisas 1923- *WhoWor 93*
Ciminero, Gary L. 1943- *St&PR 93*
Cimini, Maria Dolores 1958- *WhoAmW 93, WhoEmL 93*
Cimini, Theresa Ann 1947- *WhoEmL 93*
Cimino, Ann Mary *WhoE 93*
Cimino, Frank Joseph 1947- *WhoEmL 93*
Cimino, James Ernest 1928- *WhoAm 92, WhoWor 93*
Cimino, Joseph Anthony 1934- *WhoAm 92*
Cimino, Michael *BioIn 17*
Cimino, Michael 1943- *MiSFD 9*
Cimino, Michael 1948- *WhoAm 92*
Cimino, Philip A. 1950- *St&PR 93*
Cimino, Richard Dennis 1947- *WhoEmL 93*
Cimino, Stephanie *BioIn 17*
Cimino, Thomas 1935- *St&PR 93, WhoIns 93*
Cimmet, Gerald 1941- *WhoE 93*
Cimochowicz, Diane Marie 1955- *WhoAmW 93*
Cimolino, Marc Christopher 1954- *WhoEmL 93*
Cimons, Marlene 1945- *BioIn 17*
Cimoszko, Bogy Boguslawa 1956- *WhoEmL 93*
Cimpl, David 1958- *St&PR 93*
Cimprich, John Vincent 1949- *WhoSSW 93*
Cimrmancic, Mary Ann 1956- *WhoAmW 93*
Cinader, Arthur *St&PR 93*
Cinader, Bernhard 1919- *WhoAm 92*
Cinader, Emily *BioIn 17*
Cinalli, Joseph P., Jr. 1942- *WhoE 93*
Cinamon, Samuel B. *Law&B 92*
Cinamon, Samuel B. 1923- *St&PR 93*
Cinar, Ahmet 1939- *WhoScE 91-4*
Cinar, Ozden 1940- *WhoScE 91-4*
Cincinnatus, Lucius Quinctius 519?BC-430?BC *HarEnMi*
Cinciotta, Linda Ann 1943- *WhoAmW 93*
Cincotta, Joseph John 1931- *WhoE 93*
Cindrich, Ralph Edward 1949- *WhoE 93*
Cindro, Nikola 1931- *WhoScE 91-4*
Cinel, Dino *BioIn 17*
Cinelli, Francesco 1939- *WhoScE 91-3*
Cingolani, Sergio 1957- *WhoWor 93*
Cini, Anthony Richard 1922- *WhoSSW 93*
Cini, T.J. *St&PR 93*
Cinlar, Erhan 1941- *WhoAm 92*
Cinna, Lucius Cornelius 130BC-84BC *HarEnMi*
Cinnirella, Carmen *AmWomPl*
Cinotti, Alfonse Anthony 1923- *WhoAm 92*
Cinotti, Robert F. 1962- *St&PR 93*
Cinquemani, Joseph Robert 1952- *WhoE 93*
Cinti, David A. 1962- *WhoIns 93*
Cinti-Damoreau, Laure 1801-1863 *Baker 92, OxDcOp*
Cintorino, Richard P. 1936- *St&PR 93*
Cintra, Luis Miguel *BioIn 17*
Cintron, Evelia d1991 *BioIn 17*
Cintron, Guillermo B. 1942- *HispAmA [port]*
Cintron de Frias, Marlene 1951- *NotHsAW 93*
Ciocca, Henry G. *Law&B 92*
Cioccio, Ellen Lacey 1935- *WhoAmW 93*
Cioci, Gerald Robert 1942- *St&PR 93*
Ciociola, Cecilia Mary 1946- *WhoAmW 93*
Cioffi, Frank 1951- *ScF&FL 92*
Cioffi, Margaret *BioIn 17*
Cioffi, Michael Lawrence *Law&B 92*
Cioffi, Michael Lawrence 1953- *WhoWor 93*
Ciofi Degli Atti, Claudio 1940- *WhoScE 91-3*
Ciolek, Erazm 1474-1522 *PolBiDi*
Ciolino, Charles Peter 1955- *WhoEmL 93*
Ciolkosz, Andrzej 1939- *WhoScE 91-4*
Ciolli, Antoinette 1915- *WhoAmW 93, WhoE 93, WhoWor 93*
Cion, Judith A. *Law&B 92*
Cion, Judith Ann 1943- *WhoAm 92*
Cion, Richard M. 1943- *WhoAm 92*
Cioni, Joseph Anthony 1939- *St&PR 93*
Cioni, Renato 1929- *OxDcOp*
Ciopinski, Jan-Bogumil 1938- *WhoWor 93*
Cioroiu, Michael Gelu 1947- *WhoE 93, WhoEmL 93*
Ciortea, Tudor 1903-1982 *Baker 92*
Ciortuz, Iosif 1929- *WhoScE 91-4*
Ciosek, Nancy Carol 1942- *WhoAmW 93*
Ciotti, Christine C. *Law&B 92*
Ciotti, George Anthony 1931- *St&PR 93*
Ciotti, Vikki Ann 1947- *WhoSSW 93*
Ciottone, Richard Thomas *Law&B 92*
Ciottone, Richard Thomas 1945- *St&PR 93*
Cipau, Gabriel R. 1941- *St&PR 93*
Cipcic, Margaret Shoup 1932- *WhoAmW 93*
Cipich, Thomas Hilary 1939- *St&PR 93*
Ciplijauskaite, Birute 1929- *WhoAm 92*
Cipolla, Carlo M(anlio) 1922- *ConAu 39NR*
Cipolla, Dominic 1951- *St&PR 93*
Cipolla, Stephen J. *Law&B 92*
Cipolla, Thomas Alphonse 1950- *WhoEmL 93*
Cipollina, Anthony 1928- *St&PR 93*
Cipollini, Mark Dennis 1951- *St&PR 93*
Cipollini, Romano 1934- *WhoScE 91-3*
Cipollone, Nina Antonia 1953- *WhoEmL 93*
Ciporin, Leone Louise 1960- *WhoEmL 93*
Cipra, Milo 1906-1985 *Baker 92*
Cipriani, A. A. *DcCPCAm*
Cipriani, Curzio 1927- *WhoScE 91-3*
Cipriani, Eugene Nicholas *Law&B 92*
Cipriani, Frank Anthony 1933- *WhoAm 92*
Cipriani, Giovanna *BioIn 17*
Cipriani, Guido Emilio 1956- *St&PR 93*
Cipriani, John F., Sr. 1924- *St&PR 93*
Cipriano, Fred Louis 1944- *St&PR 93*
Cipriano, Gaetano Peter 1956- *St&PR 93*
Cipriano, John Edward *Law&B 92*
Cipriano, Mary Lynn 1947- *WhoAm 92, WhoEmL 93*
Cipriano, Peter A. 1921- *St&PR 93*
Ciprich, Paula Marie *Law&B 92*
Cipro, Victoria Virginia 1929- *WhoAmW 93*
Ciraulo, Stephen Joseph 1960- *WhoEmL 93, WhoWor 93*
Ciravolo, Kate Lommel *Law&B 92*
Circeo, Louis Joseph, Jr. 1934- *WhoAm 92, WhoSSW 93, WhoWor 93*
Cirello, John 1943- *St&PR 93, WhoE 93*
Ciresi, Michael Vincent 1946- *WhoEmL 93, WhoWor 93*
Ciresi, Samuel Michael, Jr. 1965- *WhoEmL 93*
Ciriacy, Edward Walter 1924- *WhoAm 92*
Ciricillo, Rose Casale 1922- *WhoAmW 93*
Ciricillo, Samuel Francis 1920- *St&PR 93*
Ciriclio, Susan E. 1946- *WhoEmL 93*
Cirilius, Marcus *ScF&FL 92*
Cirillo, Carl *BioIn 17*
Cirillo, Gerardo 1942- *WhoWor 93*
Cirillo, John 1943- *St&PR 93*
Cirillo, Patricia Nancy *Law&B 92*
Cirillo, Vivian Linda 1950- *WhoEmL 93*
Cirilo, Amelia Medina 1925- *WhoWor 93*
Cirincion, John C. *Law&B 92*
Cirincion, John C. 1948- *St&PR 93*
Cirincion, Marco Vincent 1938- *WhoE 93*
Cirino, Delia Graham 1929- *WhoWrEP 92*
Cirino, Giulio 1880-1970 *Baker 92*
Cirino, Leonard John 1943- *WhoWrEP 92*
Cirit, Semih 1954- *St&PR 93*
Cirker, Hayward 1917- *WhoAm 92*
Cirlin, Robert Martin *Law&B 92*
Cirne de Toledo, Joaquim Eloi 1950- *WhoWor 93*
Ciroli, J. Vincent, Jr. 1945- *St&PR 93*
Cirolia, Donna Mary 1958- *WhoAmW 93*
Ciroma, Malam Adamu 1934- *WhoAfr*
Cirone, John Christopher *Law&B 92*
Cirrincione, Joseph C. 1936- *St&PR 93*
Cirujano, Santos 1950- *WhoScE 91-3*
Cirulli, Albert Joseph 1929- *St&PR 93*
Cirulli, Vincent 1956- *WhoEmL 93*
Ciruti, Joan Estelle 1930- *WhoAm 92*
Cis, Mark Michael 1950- *WhoIns 93*
Cisaruk, Victorio 1941- *WhoWor 93*
Ciscato, Doriano 1937- *WhoScE 91-3*
Cischke, Susan *BioIn 17*
Cisewski, Fred Louis 1935- *St&PR 93*
Cisic, Milojko S. 1920- *WhoScE 91-4*
Cisler, Dennis Keith 1949- *WhoIns 93*
Cisler, Theresa Ann 1951- *WhoAm 92, WhoAmW 93, WhoEmL 93*
Cisler, Walker Lee *BioIn 17*
Cislo, Jozef Piotr 1931- *WhoScE 91-4*
Cismaru, Pat Klein 1933- *WhoAmW 93*
Cisneros, Antonio 1942-1989 *SpAmA*
Cisneros, Eleanora de 1878-1934 *Baker 92*
Cisneros, Evelyn *BioIn 17*

Cisneros, Evelyn 1955- *NotHsAW 93, WhoAm 92*
Cisneros, Henry G. 1947- *HispAmA, PolPar*
Cisneros, Marc *BioIn 17*
Cisneros, Marc Anthony 1939- *WhoAm 92*
Cisneros, Sandra *BioIn 17*
Cisneros, Sandra 1954- *Au&Arts 9 [port], DcLB 122 [port], IntvWPC 92 [port], NotHsAW 93 [port]*
Cisneros-Alvarez, Francisco Ramon 1956- *WhoWor 93*
Cisneros-Stoianowski, Gerardo 1950- *WhoWor 93*
Ciss, Abdou 1934- *WhoUN 92*
Cisse, Souleymane 1940- *MiSFD 9*
Cissell, James Charles 1940- *WhoAm 92*
Cissey, Ernest Louis Octave Courtot de 1810-1882 *BioIn 17*
Cissik, John Henry 1943- *WhoAm 92*
Cissik, Pamela J. *Law&B 92*
Cissna, William David 1952- *WhoEmL 93*
Cissom, Mary Joan 1941- *WhoWrEP 92*
Cistaro, Peter Anthony 1946- *WhoE 93*
Cistone, Daniel Anthony, Jr. 1947- *St&PR 93*
Cistrunk, Annie Jane 1929- *WhoAmW 93*
Cistue, Luis 1953- *WhoScE 91-3*
Ciszak, Paul Michael 1954- *WhoSSW 93*
Ciszewski, Stanislaw 1865-1930 *IntDcAn*
Citerley, Richard L. 1932- *St&PR 93*
Citino, David John 1947- *WhoWrEP 92*
Citir, Ahmet 1942- *WhoScE 91-4*
Citkowitz, Israel 1909-1974 *Baker 92*
Citrin, Andrew Ted 1961- *WhoEmL 93*
Citrin, Harold L. 1929- *St&PR 93*
Citrin, James Michael 1959- *WhoE 93*
Citrin, Phillip Marshall 1931- *WhoAm 92*
Citrino, Mary Anne 1959- *WhoAmW 93*
Citrino, Robert Joseph 1933- *St&PR 93*
Citro, Joseph *ScF&FL 92*
Citroen, Charles L. 1939- *WhoScE 91-3*
Citron, Beatrice Sally 1929- *WhoAmW 93*
Citron, Burton 1930- *St&PR 93*
Citron, Cynthia Wynne 1934- *WhoAmW 93*
Citron, David B. 1947- *St&PR 93*
Citron, David Sanford 1920- *WhoAm 92*
Citron, Fred *BioIn 17*
Citron, Klaus-Jurgen 1929- *WhoWor 93*
Citron, Minna Wright 1896-1991 *BioIn 17*
Citron, Richard Ira 1944- *WhoAm 92, WhoE 93*
Citron, Thomas H. 1923- *St&PR 93*
Citton, Clare 1959- *WhoEmL 93*
Citty, Brenda Vinson 1959- *WhoEmL 93*
Ciuba, Lynne P. *Law&B 92*
Ciuciura, Leoncjusz 1930- *Baker 92*
Ciuffo, Cynthia Louise 1946- *WhoAmW 93*
Ciulei, Liviu 1923- *DrEEuF*
Ciullo, Peter Anthony 1954- *WhoWrEP 92*
Ciullo, Rosemary *WhoAmW 93*
Ciupka, Richard 1950- *MiSFD 9*
Ciurlionis, Mikolajus Karstantinas 1875-1911 *Baker 92*
Civan, Mortimer M. 1934- *WhoE 93*
Civantos, Francisco 1935- *WhoSSW 93*
Civasaqui, Jose 1916- *WhoWor 93*
Civello, Anthony N. 1944- *St&PR 93*
Civello, Grace M. *St&PR 93*
Civetta, A. *WhoScE 91-4*
Civil, Alan 1929-1989 *Baker 92*
Civiletti, Benjamin R. 1935- *WhoAm 92*
Civili, Patrizio M. 1944- *WhoUN 92*
Civilis, Gaius Julius c. 30-c. 70 *HarEnMi*
Civish, Gayle Ann 1948- *WhoAmW 93*
Cixi 1835-1908 *BioIn 17*
Cixous, Helene 1937- *BioIn 17*
Cizek, Cathy Patrice 1949- *WhoEmL 93*
Cizek, David John 1959- *WhoEmL 93*
Cizek, J. Jan 1925- *WhoScE 91-4*
Cizerle, Mary C. *Law&B 92*
Cizik, Robert *BioIn 17*
Cizik, Robert 1931- *St&PR 93, WhoAm 92, WhoSSW 93, WhoWor 93*
Cizubu, Mbambu W. *Law&B 92*
Claar, John E. 1923- *St&PR 93*
Claassen, Frans Anton 1949- *WhoUN 92*
Claassen, Rachel Diane 1955- *WhoAmW 93*
Claassen, Sharon Elaine 1953- *WhoEmL 93*
Claassens, M.L.M. 1948- *WhoScE 91-3*
Clabaugh, Elmer Eugene, Jr. 1927- *WhoWor 93*
Clabaugh, Henry E. 1942- *St&PR 93*
Clabburn, Robin J.T. 1936- *WhoScE 91-1*
Clabby, William Robert 1931- *St&PR 93, WhoAm 92*
Clabrese, Joseph A. *St&PR 93*
Clack, Jerry 1926- *WhoAm 92, WhoE 93, WhoWor 93*
Cladis, Patricia Elizabeth *WhoE 93*
Claerhout, William A. *Law&B 92*
Claes, Anne 1954- *WhoWor 93*
Claes, Daniel John 1931- *WhoAm 92, WhoWor 93*
Claes, F. *WhoScE 91-2*
Claes, Willy 1938- *WhoWor 93*
Claesens, Hendrik I.H. 1927- *WhoScE 91-2*
Claesges, Axel Walter 1937- *WhoSSW 93*
Claessens, Anton J. *Law&B 92*
Claesson, Arne Lennart 1925- *WhoScE 91-4*
Claesson, E. Ake 1927- *WhoScE 91-4*
Claesson, Per Martin 1957- *WhoScE 91-4*
Claeys, Cor 1951- *WhoWor 93*
Claeys, Roger C. 1924- *WhoScE 91-2*
Claeyssens, Astere E. 1924-1990 *BioIn 17*
Claff, Barbara Joan 1936- *WhoAmW 93*
Claflin, (Alan) Avery 1898-1979 *Baker 92*
Claflin, Janis Ann 1939- *WhoSSW 93*
Claflin, Robert Malden 1921- *WhoAm 92*
Claflin, William 1818-1905 *PolPar*
Clagett, Arthur Frank, Jr. 1916- *WhoAm 92*
Clagett, Brice McAdoo 1933- *WhoAm 92, WhoE 93, WhoWor 93*
Clagett, Diana Wharton Sinkler 1943- *WhoE 93*
Clagett, Donald Carl 1939- *WhoE 93*
Clagett, Galen Ronald 1942- *WhoE 93*
Clagett, John 1916- *ScF&FL 92*
Clagett, Marshall 1916- *WhoAm 92*
Clagett, Robert 1952- *WhoEmL 93*
Clagett, William H., IV 1938- *WhoAm 92*
Clagg, Steve James 1962- *St&PR 93*
Clagg, Thomas L. *Law&B 92*
Clagg, Thomas Lytle 1943- *St&PR 93*
Claggett, Edward R. *Law&B 92*
Claiborn, Stephen Allan 1948- *WhoAm 92*
Claiborne, Billy 1860-1882 *BioIn 17*
Claiborne, Craig *BioIn 17*
Claiborne, Craig 1920- *WhoWrEP 92*
Claiborne, Herbert A., III *Law&B 92*
Claiborne, Jack E. 1931- *WhoE 93*
Claiborne, Janet Mary 1951- *WhoAmW 93*
Claiborne, Jerry David 1928- *BiDAMSp 1989*
Claiborne, John H., III 1946- *St&PR 93*
Claiborne, Josie K. *Law&B 92*
Claiborne, Liz *BioIn 17*
Claiborne, Liz 1929- *WhoAm 92, WhoAmW 93, WhoE 93*
Claiborne, Robert *BioIn 17*
Claiborne, Sybil d1992 *NewYTBS 92*
Claiborne, Sybil 1923- *ScF&FL 92*
Claiborne, Theresa *BioIn 17*
Clair, Carolyn Green 1909- *WhoAm 92, WhoWor 93*
Clair, Ethlyne 1908- *SweetSg B [port]*
Clair, Frank P. d1992 *BioIn 17, NewYTBS 92*
Clair, Jean 1940- *BioIn 17*
Clair, Randall T. *Law&B 92*
Clair, Richard F.X. *Law&B 92*
Clair, William R. *ScF&FL 92*
Claire, Elizabeth 1939- *WhoWrEP 92*
Claire, Fred *WhoAm 92*
Claire, Keith *ScF&FL 92*
Claire, Thomas Andrew 1951- *WhoAm 92, WhoE 93, WhoEmL 93*
Claire, William 1935- *WhoWrEP 92*
Claire, William Francis 1935- *WhoE 93*
Clairemidi, Sonia 1944- *WhoScE 91-2*
Clairjeune, Yuan Saintange 1945- *WhoE 93*
Clairmont, Tracy *BioIn 17*
Clairmont, William Edward 1926- *WhoWor 93*
Claitor, Robert Gregory, Jr. 1959- *St&PR 93*
Claman, Morris Theodore 1928- *St&PR 93*
Clamar, Aphrodite J. 1933- *WhoAm 92, WhoAmW 93*
Clambaneva, James 1942- *WhoWor 93*
Clam-Gallas, Eduard von 1805-1891 *HarEnMi*
Clamme, Marvin Leslie 1953- *WhoEmL 93*
Clammer, Samuel Robert 1936- *St&PR 93*
Clamon, Harleyne Dianne 1940- *WhoAmW 93*
Clamp, John Richard *WhoScE 91-1*
Clampitt, Amy *BioIn 17*
Clampitt, Amy 1920- *CurBio 92 [port]*
Clampitt, Amy Kathleen 1920- *WhoAm 92, WhoAmW 93, WhoWrEP 92*
Clampitt, Martha Redding 1947- *WhoE 93*
Clampitt, Mary O'Briant 1931- *WhoAmW 93, WhoE 93*
Clampitt, Otis Clinton, Jr. 1947- *WhoE 93*
Clancey, Delores Ann 1930- *WhoIns 93*
Clancey, Jennifer 1958- *WhoAmW 93, WhoEmL 93*
Clancey, John P. *BioIn 17, St&PR 93*
Clancy, Anita Domigan 1931- *WhoAmW 93*
Clancy, Cassandra Sue 1949- *WhoAmW 93*
Clancy, David Lawrence *Law&B 92*
Clancy, Donna L. 1943- *WhoIns 93*
Clancy, Edward Bede Cardinal 1923- *WhoWor 93*
Clancy, Elizabeth R. *Law&B 92*
Clancy, George P. 1943- *St&PR 93*
Clancy, James 1955- *St&PR 93*
Clancy, Joan Bennett 1935- *WhoAmW 93*
Clancy, John Joseph 1937- *WhoAm 92*
Clancy, Joseph E. 1930- *St&PR 93*
Clancy, Joseph Patrick 1931- *WhoAm 92*
Clancy, Judith S. *ScF&FL 92*
Clancy, Kathleen Ann 1960- *WhoAmW 93*
Clancy, Kevin J. 1942- *St&PR 93*
Clancy, Leo C. 1932- *St&PR 93*
Clancy, Louis John 1946- *WhoAm 92*
Clancy, Luke 1941- *WhoScE 91-3*
Clancy, Mary Catherine 1948- *WhoAmW 93*
Clancy, Robert A. *Law&B 92*
Clancy, Robert A. 1934- *St&PR 93*
Clancy, Robert James 1949- *St&PR 93*
Clancy, Rockwell F. 1956- *St&PR 93*
Clancy, Steven P. 1956- *WhoWrEP 92*
Clancy, Thomas Gerald 1934- *WhoAm 92*
Clancy, Thomas Hanley 1923- *WhoSSW 93*
Clancy, Thomas L. *ScF&FL 92*
Clancy, Thomas L. 1947- *WhoAm 92*
Clancy, Tom d1990 *BioIn 17*
Clancy, Tom 1947- *Au&Arts 9 [port], BioIn 17, ScF&FL 92*
Clancy, Tom, Jr. 1947- *WhoWrEP 92*
Clanet, Frank E. 1929- *WhoScE 91-2*
Clanon, Thomas Lawrence 1929- *WhoAm 92*
Clanton, Billy 1862-1881 *BioIn 17*
Clanton, Donald B. 1942- *St&PR 93*
Clanton, Ike d1887 *BioIn 17*
Clanton, John Charles 1960- *WhoSSW 93*
Clanton, N.H. d1881 *BioIn 17*
Clanton, Old Man d1881 *BioIn 17*
Clanton, Phineas *BioIn 17*
Clanton, Waverly B., Jr. *Law&B 92*
Clapes, Anthony L. *Law&B 92*
Clapes, Louis d1990 *BioIn 17*
Clapham, John 1908- *Baker 92*
Clapham, Peter B. 1940- *WhoScE 91-1*
Clapisson, Louis 1808-1866 *OxDcOp*
Clapman, Peter C. 1936- *WhoIns 93*
Clapman, Peter Carlyle 1936- *St&PR 93, WhoAm 92*
Clapp, Alan Edward 1963- *WhoSSW 93*
Clapp, Allen Linville 1943- *WhoSSW 93, WhoWor 93*
Clapp, Arnold Basil 1943- *WhoSSW 93*
Clapp, Arthur Warren 1915- *St&PR 93*
Clapp, Benjamin d1990 *BioIn 17*
Clapp, Charles E., II 1923- *CngDr 91*
Clapp, Charles Edward 1930- *WhoAm 92*
Clapp, Christopher Lee 1952- *WhoEmL 93*
Clapp, David D. 1939- *St&PR 93*
Clapp, David Foster 1952- *WhoSSW 93*
Clapp, Dewey Warren 1939- *WhoSSW 93*
Clapp, Earl W. 1926- *St&PR 93*
Clapp, Edwin G. 1918- *St&PR 93*
Clapp, Eugene H., II 1913- *St&PR 93*
Clapp, Eugene Howard, II 1913- *WhoAm 92*
Clapp, James Ford, Jr. 1908- *WhoAm 92*
Clapp, Jeffrey P. 1953- *St&PR 93*
Clapp, John McMahon 1944- *WhoE 93*
Clapp, Joseph Mark 1936- *St&PR 93*
Clapp, Kenneth Wayne 1948- *WhoEmL 93*
Clapp, Lee Irving 1941- *WhoE 93*
Clapp, Malcolme A. 1929- *St&PR 93*
Clapp, Melvin Carl 1933- *St&PR 93, WhoAm 92*
Clapp, Neal Keith 1928- *WhoSSW 93*
Clapp, Patricia 1912- *ConAu 37NR, DcAmChF 1960, MajAI [port]*
Clapp, Philip Greeley 1888-1954 *Baker 92*
Clapp, Richard R. *Law&B 92*
Clapp, Robert 1910-1990 *BioIn 17*
Clapp, Roger Alvin 1909- *WhoAm 92*
Clapp, Roger Edge 1919-1991 *BioIn 17*
Clapp, Roger Howland 1928- *WhoAm 92, WhoSSW 93*
Clapp, William Warland 1826-1891 *JrnUS*
Clapper, Jon C. 1949- *St&PR 93*
Clapper, Lyle Nielsen 1941- *WhoAm 92*
Clapper, Marie Anne 1942- *WhoAm 92*
Clapper, Raymond 1892-1944 *JrnUS*
Clapperton, Hugh 1788-1827 *Expl 93 [port]*
Clapps, Sandra 1948- *St&PR 93*
Claps, Gerard *St&PR 93*
Clapton, Conor 1986-1991 *BioIn 17*
Clapton, Eric *BioIn 17*
Clapton, Eric 1945- *WhoAm 92*
See Also Cream *ConMus 9*
Clapton, Eric (Patrick) 1945- *Baker 92*
Clar, Donna *BioIn 17*
Clar, Harvey *BioIn 17*
Clara, Jose 1878-1958 *BioIn 17*
Claramunt, Ana Maria 1934- *WhoWor 93*
Claramunt, Morrall M. 1941- *St&PR 93*
Clarance, William David 1933- *WhoUN 92*
Clardy, Jon Christel 1943- *WhoAm 92*
Clardy, Thelma Sanders 1955- *WhoAmW 93*
Clare, Christopher Philip *WhoScE 91-1*
Clare, David R. 1925- *St&PR 93*
Clare, Fountain Stewart, III 1936- *WhoSSW 93*
Clare, George 1930- *WhoSSW 93*
Clare, Helen *MajAI*
Clare, John *ScF&FL 92*
Clare, John 1793-1864 *BioIn 17*
Clare, Mariette *ScF&FL 92*
Clare, R.W. *WhoScE 91-1*
Clare, Richard Dexter 1949- *WhoEmL 93*
Clare, Stewart 1913- *WhoAm 92*
Clare, Thomas A. 1920- *St&PR 93*
Claremon, Glenda Ruth 1951- *WhoEmL 93*
Claremont, Chris 1950- *ScF&FL 92*
Clarence, George, Duke of 1449-1478 *HarEnMi*
Clarence and Calvin *SoulM*
Clarendon, Earl of 1609-1674 *BioIn 17*
Clarendon, John Marsden 1946- *WhoE 93, WhoEmL 93*
Clarens, Carlos 1936-1987 *ScF&FL 92*
Clarens, John Gaston 1924- *WhoAm 92*
Clare, of Assisi, Saint 1194-1253 *BioIn 17*
Clareson, Thomas D. 1926- *ScF&FL 92*
Clareson, Thomas D(ean) 1926- *ConAu 39NR*
Claret, Michel 1940- *WhoScE 91-2*
Clarey, Donald Alexander 1950- *WhoAm 92*
Clarey, John Robert 1942- *WhoAm 92*
Clarfield, Gerard Howard 1936- *WhoAm 92*
Clari, Giovanni Carlo Maria 1677-1754 *Baker 92*
Claribel *Baker 92*
Claridge, M.A. *WhoScE 91-1*
Claridge, Michael Frederick *WhoScE 91-1*
Claridge, Richard Allen 1932- *WhoSSW 93, WhoWor 93*
Claridge, Robert H. *Law&B 92*
Clarie, T. Emmet 1913- *WhoAm 92*
Clarity, Timothy Baldwin 1951- *WhoEmL 93*
Clarizio, Josephine Delores 1922- *WhoAm 92*
Clark, Ada *AmWomPl*
Clark, Adam Stormont Sutherland *WhoScE 91-1*
Clark, Alan F. 1931- *St&PR 93*
Clark, Alan F. 1936- *WhoAm 92*
Clark, Alan Kelley 1948- *WhoEmL 93, WhoSSW 93*
Clark, Albert Carl Vernon 1947- *WhoWrEP 92*
Clark, Albert Edwin 1946- *WhoEmL 93*
Clark, Albert William 1922- *WhoWor 93*
Clark, Alfred, Jr. 1936- *WhoAm 92*
Clark, Alfred Samuel 1947- *WhoEmL 93*
Clark, Alice H. *AmWomPl*
Clark, Alice Thompson 1926- *WhoAm 92, WhoAmW 93*
Clark, Allan Richard 1953- *St&PR 93*
Clark, Alson Skinner 1876-1949 *BioIn 17*
Clark, Amy Catherine 1943- *WhoAmW 93*
Clark, Andrea L. *Law&B 92*
Clark, Andrew Francis 1954- *WhoSSW 93*
Clark, Anita Louise 1950- *WhoAm 92*
Clark, Ann Nolan 1896- *MajAI [port], SmATA 16AS [port]*
Clark, Anne Partridge 1949- *WhoAmW 93*
Clark, Arthur Watts 1922- *St&PR 93, WhoAm 92*
Clark, Audrey *AmWomPl*
Clark, Augustus Dayton d1990 *BioIn 17*
Clark, Barry Wayne 1941- *St&PR 93*
Clark, Bernard Francis 1921- *St&PR 93*
Clark, Betty Hudson d1991 *BioIn 17*
Clark, Beverly A. *Law&B 92*
Clark, Beverly Lyon 1948- *ScF&FL 92*
Clark, Billy Pat 1939- *WhoE 93, WhoWor 93*
Clark, Blair Foster *ScF&FL 92*
Clark, Blake 1908- *WhoAm 92*
Clark, Bob 1941- *MiSFD 9*
Clark, Bobby 1888-1960 & McCullough, Paul 1883-1936 *QDrFCA 92 [port]*
Clark, Bonnie Leigh 1961- *WhoEmL 93, WhoSSW 93*
Clark, Brackett David 1940- *St&PR 93*
Clark, Bradford Norman d1990 *BioIn 17*
Clark, Brian R. *St&PR 93*
Clark, Brian Thomas 1951- *WhoEmL 93, WhoWor 93*
Clark, Bruce *MiSFD 9*
Clark, Bruce Arlington, Jr. 1951- *WhoEmL 93*

Clark, Bruce Budge 1918- WhoAm 92
Clark, Bruce Robert 1941- WhoAm 92
Clark, Burton Robert 1921- WhoAm 92
Clark, Byron Standish, II 1959- WhoEmL 93, WhoSSW 93
Clark, C.J. Law&B 92
Clark, Candace A. Law&B 92
Clark, Candy WhoAm 92
Clark, Carl 1927- St&PR 93
Clark, Carol Canda 1947- WhoE 93
Clark, Carol Lois 1948- WhoEmL 93
Clark, Carol M. 1962- St&PR 93
Clark, Carol Morrow 1962- WhoEmL 93
Clark, Carolyn Archer 1944- WhoAm 92, WhoAmW 93, WhoWor 93
Clark, Carolyn Chambers 1941- WhoAmW 93, WhoWrEP 92
Clark, Carolyn Cochran 1941- WhoAm 92, WhoAmW 93
Clark, Carrolle Barber AmWomPl
Clark, Catherine Anthony 1892-1977 ScF&FL 92
Clark, Catherine Anthony (Smith) 1892-1970 DcChlFi
Clark, Cathy Ann 1948- WhoEmL 93
Clark, Champ 1923- WhoWrEP 92
Clark, Chapin DeWitt 1930- WhoAm 92
Clark, Charles 1925- WhoAm 92, WhoSSW 93
Clark, Charles Edward 1949- WhoEmL 93
Clark, Charles Grant WhoScE 91-1
Clark, Charles Joseph 1939- BioIn 17, DcTwHis, WhoAm 92, WhoE 93, WhoWor 93
Clark, Charles Michael Andres 1960- WhoE 93
Clark, Charles Taliferro 1917- WhoAm 92
Clark, Chester Dodge 1938- WhoE 93
Clark, Christine M. 1957- WhoAmW 93
Clark, Christine May 1957- WhoAm 92
Clark, Clarence A. BioIn 17
Clark, Clayton 1912- WhoAm 92
Clark, Clifford Dale 1925- WhoAm 92
Clark, Clifford Edward, Jr. 1941- WhoAm 92
Clark, Clifton Bob 1927- WhoAm 92
Clark, Clinton Anthony 1941- St&PR 93
Clark, Colin 1905-1989 BioIn 17
Clark, Colin Whitcomb 1931- WhoAm 92
Clark, Colleen Kelly 1944- WhoAm 92
Clark, Curt BioIn 17
Clark, Curtis BioIn 17
Clark, Curtis Alan 1955- WhoEmL 93
Clark, Cynthia Law 1946- WhoAmW 93
Clark, Cynthia Lea 1954- WhoAmW 93
Clark, Cynthia Ruth Law&B 92
Clark, Cyrus 1950- St&PR 93
Clark, D. WhoScE 91-1
Clark, D.T. WhoScE 91-1
Clark, Dale ScF&FL 92
Clark, Dale Allen 1922- WhoSSW 93
Clark, Daniel C. 1933- St&PR 93
Clark, Darlene Carol 1944- WhoAmW 93
Clark, Dave J. Law&B 92
Clark, David Crawford 1925- St&PR 93
Clark, David Delano 1924- WhoAm 92
Clark, David H. 1931- St&PR 93
Clark, David Howard 1950- WhoEmL 93
Clark, David J. Law&B 92
Clark, David L. Law&B 92
Clark, David L. 1929- BioIn 17
Clark, David Lee 1887-1956 ScF&FL 92
Clark, David Leigh 1931- WhoAm 92
Clark, David Lewis 1956- WhoEmL 93
Clark, David M. 1940- St&PR 93
Clark, David Michael d1992 BioIn 17
Clark, David Owen 1951- WhoWor 93
Clark, David Randolph 1943- WhoAm 92
Clark, David Rex Law&B 92
Clark, David Ridgley 1920- WhoE 93
Clark, David Robert 1953- WhoEmL 93
Clark, David W., Jr. 1937- St&PR 93
Clark, David Willard 1930- WhoAm 92
Clark, Dayle Meritt 1933- WhoSSW 93
Clark, Dean Kenneth 1941- St&PR 93
Clark, Debra Dawes 1959- WhoAmW 93
Clark, Debra Feiock 1958 WhoAmW 93
Clark, Dee 1938- BioIn 17, SoulM
Clark, Dewey P. 1934- WhoIns 93
Clark, Dianna Lea 1956- WhoAmW 93, WhoEmL 93
Clark, Dick 1928- ColdWar 1, WhoAm 92
Clark, Dick 1929- BioIn 17, WhoAm 92
Clark, Diddo Ruth 1950- WhoEmL 93
Clark, Dixie Dugan 1940- WhoWrEP 92
Clark, Donald B. 1942- St&PR 93
Clark, Donald C. 1931- St&PR 93
Clark, Donald Cameron 1931- WhoAm 92
Clark, Donald Graham-Campbell 1920- WhoE 93
Clark, Donald Judson 1932- WhoE 93
Clark, Donald Malin 1929- WhoAm 92, WhoE 93
Clark, Donald Otis 1934- WhoAm 92, WhoE 93, WhoWor 93
Clark, Donald Robert 1924- WhoAm 92
Clark, Donna E. 1928- St&PR 93
Clark, Dorothy AmWomPl
Clark, Dorothy Van Gelder 1915- St&PR 93
Clark, Doug BioIn 17
Clark, Douglas B. Law&B 92
Clark, Douglas Bernard 1951- WhoEmL 93
Clark, Douglas M. St&PR 93
Clark, Douglas Napier 1944- WhoSSW 93
Clark, Douglas W. ScF&FL 92
Clark, Duane MiSFD 9
Clark, Duncan William 1910- WhoE 93
Clark, Dutch 1906-1978 BioIn 17
Clark, Dwight Edward 1957- BiDAMSp 1989
Clark, E.E. Law&B 92
Clark, E. Payson, Jr. Law&B 92
Clark, E. Roger 1947- St&PR 93
Clark, E. Sharon Law&B 92
Clark, Earl D., Jr. 1923- St&PR 93
Clark, Earnest Hubert, Jr. 1926- St&PR 93, WhoAm 92
Clark, Edgar Sanderford 1933- WhoAm 92
Clark, Edna Allen 1914- WhoAmW 93
Clark, Edward 1888-1962 Baker 92
Clark, Edward 1906- WhoAm 92
Clark, Edward Ferdnand 1921- WhoAm 92
Clark, Edwin Green, Jr. 1940- WhoSSW 93
Clark, Edwin John 1925- St&PR 93
Clark, Eleanor WhoAm 92, WhoAmW 93, WhoWrEP 92
Clark, Elizabeth Adams 1944- WhoSSW 93
Clark, Elizabeth Ann 1950- WhoEmL 93
Clark, Elizabeth Annette 1934- WhoAmW 93
Clark, Elizabeth D. Law&B 92
Clark, Elizabeth Goodwin 1939- WhoAmW 93
Clark, Elliott Earl 1948- WhoEmL 93
Clark, Elliott J., Jr. Law&B 92
Clark, Elmer J. 1919- WhoAm 92
Clark, Eloise Elizabeth 1931- WhoAm 92, WhoAmW 93
Clark, Emily Sears Lodge d1992 BioIn 17, NewYTBS 92
Clark, Emma Chichester 1955- SmATA 69
Clark, Emory Eugene 1931- WhoSSW 93
Clark, Eric Shannon 1963- WhoE 93
Clark, Ernest J. d1992 NewYTBS 92
Clark, Ernest J. 1905-1992 BioIn 17
Clark, Estelle Merryman AmWomPl
Clark, Esther Frances 1929- WhoAm 92
Clark, Etta Ryan Law&B 92
Clark, Eugene Corry 1941- WhoSSW 93
Clark, Eugene Roger 1947- WhoEmL 93
Clark, Eugene V. Law&B 92
Clark, Eugenie 1922- WhoAm 92
Clark, F. Karen Law&B 92
Clark, Faye Louise 1936- WhoAmW 93
Clark, Felicia d1990 BioIn 17
Clark, Francis Charles Law&B 92
Clark, Francis Edward 1851-1927 BioIn 17
Clark, Frank C. MiSFD 9
Clark, Frank R. 1944- St&PR 93
Clark, Frank Rinker, Jr. 1912- WhoAm 92
Clark, Frankie Jo 1948- WhoAmW 93
Clark, Fred 1930- WhoE 93
Clark, Fred Yarbrough 1931- St&PR 93
Clark, Frederick H. Law&B 92
Clark, Frederick R. 1916- St&PR 93
Clark, Frederick Scotson 1840-1883 Baker 92
Clark, G. Bert, Jr. Law&B 92
Clark, G. Peter 1948- WhoEmL 93
Clark, G. Russell 1904-1991 BioIn 17
Clark, Gary C. 1962- WhoAm 92
Clark, Gary L. 1942- St&PR 93
Clark, Gary M. 1935- WhoAm 92
Clark, Gene 1941-1991 AnObit 1991, BioIn 17
See Also Byrds, The ConMus 8
Clark, Geoffrey 1946- WhoEmL 93, WhoSSW 93, WhoWor 93
Clark, George 1932- ConAu 136
Clark, George A. 1929- St&PR 93
Clark, George Bryan 1925- WhoAm 92
Clark, George Edmund Law&B 92
Clark, George Lee 1950- WhoEmL 93
Clark, George M., Jr. 1932- St&PR 93
Clark, George M., Jr. 1947- WhoIns 93
Clark, George Patrick 1955- St&PR 93
Clark, George Roberts 1910- WhoAm 92
Clark, George Rogers 1752-1818 HarEnMi
Clark, George Whipple 1928- WhoAm 92
Clark, Gerald L. 1938- WhoIns 93
Clark, Gilbert Michael 1944- WhoAm 92
Clark, Glen Edward 1943- WhoAm 92
Clark, Glenwood 1926- WhoAm 92
Clark, Gordon Hostetter, Jr. 1947- WhoE 93, WhoEmL 93, WhoWor 93
Clark, Gordon M. 1940- St&PR 93
Clark, Graeme Milbourne 1935- WhoWor 93
Clark, Graham 1941- OxDcOp
Clark, Graham M., Jr. Law&B 92
Clark, Gregory C. Law&B 92
Clark, Gregory C. 1947- St&PR 93
Clark, Gregory Cooper 1947- WhoEmL 93
Clark, Gregory G. Law&B 92
Clark, Greydon MiSFD 9
Clark, Halliday 1918- WhoE 93, WhoWor 93
Clark, Harold F., Jr. 1935- St&PR 93
Clark, Harold Steve 1947- WhoAm 92
Clark, Hebe Hallen AmWomPl
Clark, Helen AmWomPl
Clark, Helen Elizabeth 1950- WhoAsAP 91
Clark, Henry Benjamin, Jr. 1915- WhoAm 92
Clark, Henry G. 1945- St&PR 93
Clark, Herbert Forrester 1943- St&PR 93, WhoAm 92
Clark, Herbert K. 1935- St&PR 93
Clark, Herbert Tryon, Jr. 1913- WhoWor 93
Clark, Holly Jayne 1955- WhoEmL 93
Clark, Howard Longstreth 1916- WhoAm 92
Clark, Howard Longstreth, Jr. 1944- St&PR 93, WhoAm 92
Clark, I. E. 1919- WhoAm 92
Clark, Ian Douglas 1946- WhoAm 92
Clark, J. Michael 1953- BioIn 17
Clark, J. P. 1935- DcLB 117 [port]
Clark, J. Patrick Law&B 92
Clark, J. Peter 1942- St&PR 93
Clark, J(eff) R(ay) 1947- WhoWrEP 92
Clark, J. Thomas WhoAm 92
Clark, Jack 1932- WhoAm 92, WhoSSW 93
Clark, Jack 1955- BioIn 17
Clark, Jack Anthony 1955- BiDAMSp 1989, WhoAm 92
Clark, James ConTFT 10
Clark, James Allen 1948- WhoEmL 93
Clark, James B. MiSFD 9
Clark, James B. 1850-1921 PolPar
Clark, James Benton 1914- WhoAm 92
Clark, James Edward d1991 BioIn 17
Clark, James Edward 1926- WhoAm 92
Clark, James H. 1944- ConEn, St&PR 93
Clark, James Hamel 1960- WhoEmL 93
Clark, James Hanley 1951- WhoWor 93
Clark, James Henry 1931- WhoAm 92
Clark, James Howard 1953- WhoEmL 93
Clark, James Joseph 1957- WhoE 93
Clark, James Milford 1930- WhoAm 92
Clark, James Milo 1944- St&PR 93
Clark, James Norman 1932- St&PR 93, WhoAm 92, WhoIns 93
Clark, James Robert 1943- St&PR 93
Clark, James Robert 1953- WhoEmL 93
Clark, James T. 1940- St&PR 93
Clark, James Whitley 1930- St&PR 93, WhoAm 92
Clark, Jan Stewart Law&B 92
Clark, Jane Angela 1955- WhoAmW 93, WhoEmL 93
Clark, Jane Elizabeth 1946- WhoEmL 93
Clark, Jane Elizabeth Knall 1961- WhoE 93
Clark, Janet Eileen 1940- WhoAmW 93
Clark, Janet Lee 1952- WhoEmL 93
Clark, Janie 1956- ConAu 138
Clark, Jay D. 1936- St&PR 93
Clark, Jeanne Barbara 1948- WhoAmW 93
Clark, Jeffrey Alan 1959- WhoSSW 93
Clark, Jeffrey Charles 1960- WhoEmL 93
Clark, Jeffrey R. Law&B 92
Clark, Jeffrey William 1961- WhoEmL 93, WhoSSW 93
Clark, Jere Walton 1922- WhoE 93
Clark, Jerry A. 1954- WhoE 93
Clark, Jill G. Law&B 92
Clark, Jim BioIn 17
Clark, Jim 1931- ConTFT 10
Clark, Jim Cummings 1841-1895 BioIn 17
Clark, Jimmy WhoSSW 93
Clark, Joan MajAI
Clark, Joan 1934- DcChlFi, ScF&FL 92
Clark, Joan MacDonald 1934- WhoCanL 92
Clark, Joann Ojstersek Law&B 92
Clark, Joanne 1951- St&PR 93
Clark, Joe BioIn 17
Clark, Joe 1939- BioIn 17, WhoAm 92, WhoE 93, WhoWor 93
Clark, Joe Haller 1913- WhoE 93
Clark, John Alden 1923- WhoAm 92
Clark, John Arthur 1920- WhoAm 92
Clark, John Benjamin WhoScE 91-1
Clark, John C., III Law&B 92
Clark, John Clinton, III 1943- St&PR 93
Clark, John Conrad 1913-1990 BioIn 17
Clark, John Desmond 1916- WhoAm 92
Clark, John E. 1943- St&PR 93
Clark, John Elwood 1931- WhoAm 92
Clark, John F. 1920- WhoAm 92, WhoSSW 93
Clark, John Farrell 1927- WhoAm 92
Clark, John Foster 1950- WhoEmL 93
Clark, John H. St&PR 93
Clark, John H., Jr. 1928- WhoAm 92
Clark, John Hallett, III 1918- WhoAm 92
Clark, John Hamilton 1949- WhoEmL 93
Clark, John Holley, III 1918- WhoE 93
Clark, John Hugh 1956- St&PR 93
Clark, John J. 1924- WhoAm 92
Clark, John M. Law&B 92
Clark, John Michael 1953- BioIn 17
Clark, John N., Jr. 1935- St&PR 93
Clark, John P. 1935- St&PR 93
Clark, John Peter, III 1942- WhoAm 92
Clark, John Phelps Law&B 92
Clark, John Phelps 1932- WhoAm 92
Clark, John R. St&PR 93
Clark, John R., III Law&B 92
Clark, John Robert, III 1954- St&PR 93
Clark, John Russell 1927- WhoAm 92
Clark, John Walter, Jr. 1919- WhoAm 92
Clark, John Walter, Jr. 1946- WhoEmL 93
Clark, John Whitcomb 1918- WhoAm 92
Clark, Jonathan Redfield 1958- WhoEmL 93
Clark, Joseph A., III Law&B 92
Clark, Joseph S. 1901-1990 BioIn 17, PolPar
Clark, Joyce Naomi Johnson 1936- WhoAmW 93, WhoSSW 93
Clark, Judith Wells 1943- WhoSSW 93
Clark, Karen 1960- ScF&FL 92
Clark, Karen Elizabeth 1955- WhoAmW 93, WhoEmL 93
Clark, Karen Heath 1944- WhoAmW 93
Clark, Karen Marie 1953- WhoAmW 93, WhoEmL 93, WhoSSW 93
Clark, Karen Sue 1952- WhoEmL 93
Clark, Kathleen Mulhern 1948- WhoAmW 93
Clark, Kay BioIn 17
Clark, Keith Leonard WhoScE 91-1
Clark, Keith T. 1956- St&PR 93
Clark, Kelly BioIn 17
Clark, Kelly 1953- WhoE 93, WhoEmL 93
Clark, Kenneth 1903-1983 BioIn 17
Clark, Kenneth Bancroft 1914- EncAACR, WhoAm 92, WhoE 93
Clark, Kenneth Courtright 1919- WhoAm 92
Clark, Kenneth Edwin 1914- WhoAm 92
Clark, Kenneth J. 1937- St&PR 93
Clark, Kenneth William 1960- WhoWor 93
Clark, Kevin Anthony 1956- WhoE 93, WhoEmL 93
Clark, Kirk A. 1946- St&PR 93
Clark, Larry 1943- WhoAm 92
Clark, Larry Dalton 1942- WhoWor 93
Clark (Latham), Mavis Thorpe 1912?- DcChlFi
Clark, Laurie Jane 1951- WhoAmW 93
Clark, Laverne Harrell 1929- WhoWrEP 92
Clark, Lawrence Gordon MiSFD 9
Clark, Lawrence J. St&PR 93
Clark, Leif Michael 1947- WhoSSW 93
Clark, Leigh ScF&FL 92
Clark, Leonard J., Jr. 1934- St&PR 93
Clark, Leonard P. 1919- St&PR 93
Clark, Leonard Vernon 1938- WhoAm 92
Clark, Lester 1916- St&PR 93
Clark, Letitia Z. 1945- WhoAmW 93
Clark, Linda Wilson 1939- WhoSSW 93
Clark, Lori Ann 1963- WhoSSW 93
Clark, Lotta Alma AmWomPl
Clark, Loyal Frances 1958- WhoAmW 93, WhoWor 93
Clark, Luther John 1941- WhoAm 92
Clark, Lydia Benson 1915- ScF&FL 92
Clark, Lynn C. 1947- WhoIns 93
Clark, M.G. WhoScE 91-1
Clark, M.R. ConAu 37NR, MajAI
Clark, Mamie Phipps 1917-1983 BioIn 17
Clark, Manning 1915-1991 AnObit 1991, BioIn 17
Clark, Margaret Ann 1949- WhoEmL 93
Clark, Margaret G. Law&B 92
Clark, Margaret Goff 1913- WhoWrEP 92
Clark, Margaret June 1941- WhoWor 93
Clark, Margaret Morrison 1942- WhoAmW 93
Clark, Margaret Pruitt 1946- WhoAmW 93
Clark, Margaret Stanley AmWomPl
Clark, Marilyn Hall 1950- St&PR 93
Clark, Mark 1946- ScF&FL 92
Clark, Mark D. Law&B 92
Clark, Mark Edwin 1933- St&PR 93
Clark, Mark Francis 1944- WhoAm 92
Clark, Mark Furman 1940- WhoAm 92
Clark, Mark Lee 1953- WhoEmL 93
Clark, Mark Wayne 1896-1985 HarEnMi
Clark, Martha Ellen Law&B 92
Clark, Martin Michael 1931- St&PR 93
Clark, Marvin R. 1942- St&PR 93
Clark, Mary ScF&FL 92

Clark, Mary Ann 1954- *St&PR 93*
Clark, Mary Ellen *WhoAmW 93*
Clark, Mary Higgins *BioIn 17*
Clark, Mary Higgins 1929- *Au&Arts 10 [port], WhoWrEP 92*
Clark, Mary Higgins 1931- *WhoAm 92, WhoAmW 93*
Clark, Mary Kathleen 1956- *WhoE 93*
Clark, Mary Margaret 1925- *WhoAm 92*
Clark, Mary Twibill *WhoAm 92*
Clark, Mason Alonzo 1921- *WhoWrEP 92*
Clark, Matt *MiSFD 9*
Clark, Matt 1930- *WhoAm 92, WhoWrEP 92*
Clark, Matthew Harvey 1937- *WhoAm 92, WhoE 93*
Clark, Matthew Scott 1962- *WhoE 93*
Clark, Maurice O. *St&PR 93*
Clark, Mavis Thorpe 1909- *ConAu 37NR, MajAI [port]*
Clark, Max Stafford 1941- *BioIn 17*
Clark, Maxine 1949- *WhoAm 92*
Clark, Melville 1850-1918 *Baker 92*
Clark, Melville, Jr. 1921- *WhoAm 92, WhoE 93*
Clark, Melville Antone 1883-1953 *Baker 92*
Clark, Melvin Eugene 1916- *WhoAm 92*
Clark, Merrell Edward, Jr. 1922- *WhoAm 92*
Clark, Merrell Mays 1935- *WhoAm 92, WhoE 93*
Clark, Michael *BioIn 17, ScF&FL 92*
Clark, Michael 1958- *WhoScE 91-1*
Clark, Michael A. *AfrAmBi*
Clark, Michael Earl 1951- *WhoSSW 93*
Clark, Michael Erik 1943- *WhoE 93*
Clark, Michael Joseph 1956- *WhoSSW 93*
Clark, Mitzi Armstrong 1965- *WhoSSW 93*
Clark, Nancy Randall 1938- *WhoAmW 93, WhoE 93*
Clark, Nathaniel Brooks 1956- *WhoSSW 93*
Clark, Noreen Morrison 1943- *WhoAm 92, WhoAmW 93, WhoWor 93*
Clark, Norton Dwight 1932- *WhoE 93*
Clark, Orville Mayo, Jr. 1925- *WhoSSW 93*
Clark, Ouida Ouijella 1949- *WhoSSW 93*
Clark, Pat English 1940- *WhoAm 92*
Clark, Patricia Ann 1936- *WhoAmW 93*
Clark, Patricia J. *Law&B 92*
Clark, Patty Lee *AmWomPl*
Clark, Paul C. *Law&B 92*
Clark, Paul F. 1954- *ConAu 138*
Clark, Paul Frederick 1954- *WhoE 93*
Clark, Paul G. 1922-1991 *BioIn 17*
Clark, Paul N. 1947- *St&PR 93*
Clark, Paul Newton 1947- *WhoEmL 93*
Clark, Paul P. 1956- *St&PR 93*
Clark, Paul Thomas 1954- *WhoEmL 93*
Clark, Paul Wallace 1961- *St&PR 93*
Clark, Pearl Franklin *AmWomPl*
Clark, Peggy 1915- *WhoAm 92*
Clark, Peter Bruce 1928- *WhoAm 92*
Clark, Peter H. 1829-1925 *BioIn 17*
Clark, Peter Humphries 1829-1925 *EncAACR*
Clark, Philip Hart 1938- *WhoE 93*
Clark, Philip Raymond 1930- *WhoAm 92*
Clark, Phyllis 1955- *St&PR 93*
Clark, R. Bradbury 1924- *WhoAm 92, WhoWor 93*
Clark, R. Thomas 1951- *WhoE 93, WhoEmL 93, WhoWor 93*
Clark, Ralph Barlow 1933- *WhoAm 92*
Clark, Ramsey 1927- *BioIn 17, WhoAm 92*
Clark, Randall D. 1948- *St&PR 93*
Clark, Randall Livingston 1943- *WhoAm 92, WhoE 93*
Clark, Raymond Robert d1990 *BioIn 17*
Clark, Raymond Skinner 1913- *St&PR 93, WhoAm 92*
Clark, Reuben Grove, Jr. 1923- *WhoAm 92*
Clark, Rhea Kirby 1930- *WhoSSW 93*
Clark, Rhonda Springer 1955- *WhoAmW 93*
Clark, Richard *MiSFD 9*
Clark, Richard B. 1943- *St&PR 93*
Clark, Richard Dale 1933- *St&PR 93*
Clark, Richard Edward 1947- *WhoEmL 93*
Clark, Richard Larry 1950- *WhoSSW 93*
Clark, Richard Lee 1940- *WhoAm 92, WhoSSW 93*
Clark, Richard M. *Law&B 92*
Clark, Richard McCourt 1937- *WhoAm 92*
Clark, Richard Payne, II 1951- *WhoSSW 93*
Clark, Robert Arthur 1923- *WhoAm 92*
Clark, Robert Henry, Jr. 1941- *St&PR 93, WhoAm 92*
Clark, Robert Jenkins 1913- *WhoE 93*
Clark, Robert King 1934- *WhoAm 92*
Clark, Robert L. *Law&B 92*
Clark, Robert Lloyd, Jr. 1945- *WhoAm 92, WhoSSW 93*
Clark, Robert M., Jr. 1948- *WhoSSW 93, WhoWor 93*
Clark, Robert Newhall 1925- *WhoAm 92*
Clark, Robert Phillips 1921- *WhoAm 92, WhoWor 93*
Clark, Robert Samuel 1931- *WhoSSW 93*
Clark, Robert Sheffield 1934- *WhoAm 92*
Clark, Robert Stuart 1932- *St&PR 93*
Clark, Robert Taylor 1920- *WhoSSW 93*
Clark, Robert W. 1946- *St&PR 93*
Clark, Robert Wesley 1946- *WhoEmL 93*
Clark, Robert William *WhoSSW 93*
Clark, Robin Jon Hawes *WhoScE 91-1*
Clark, Rodney B. 1943- *St&PR 93*
Clark, Roger Arthur 1932- *WhoAm 92*
Clark, Roger Gordon 1937- *WhoAm 92*
Clark, Roger Harrison 1939- *WhoAm 92*
Clark, Roger Lewis 1955- *WhoEmL 93*
Clark, Ron 1933- *MiSFD 9*
Clark, Ron Dean 1947- *WhoAm 92*
Clark, Ronald Brooks 1949- *WhoSSW 93*
Clark, Ronald Dean 1943- *WhoAm 92*
Clark, Ronald George 1928- *WhoWor 93*
Clark, Ronald Hurley 1953- *WhoEmL 93*
Clark, Ronald Keith 1955- *WhoEmL 93*
Clark, Ronald Michael 1947- *WhoAm 92*
Clark, Ronald Ralph 1952- *WhoSSW 93*
Clark, Ronald W. 1916-1987 *ScF&FL 92*
Clark, Rosalyn Davida Pierce 1952- *WhoE 93*
Clark, Ross Bert, II 1932- *WhoAm 92, WhoSSW 93, WhoWor 93*
Clark, Ross Godfrey 1949- *WhoEmL 93*
Clark, Ross Townsend 1956- *WhoEmL 93*
Clark, Roy 1933- *BioIn 17, WhoAm 92*
Clark, Roy (Linwood) 1933- *Baker 92*
Clark, Roy Thomas, Jr. 1922- *WhoSSW 93*
Clark, Russell Gentry 1925- *WhoAm 92*
Clark, Sally 1953- *WhoCanL 92*
Clark, Samuel Delbert 1910- *WhoAm 92*
Clark, Samuel Smith 1932- *WhoAm 92*
Clark, Sandra Helen Becker 1938- *WhoAm 92*
Clark, Sandra Marie 1942- *WhoAmW 93*
Clark, Sara Mott 1915- *WhoAmW 93*
Clark, Sarah Grames *AmWomPl*
Clark, Sarah P. 1959- *St&PR 93*
Clark, Scott Brian *Law&B 92*
Clark, Septima Poinsette 1898-1987 *BioIn 17*
Clark, Seymour G. *Law&B 92*
Clark, Shauna *BioIn 17*
Clark, Sheila *ScF&FL 92*
Clark, Sheldon Brown 1948- *WhoSSW 93*
Clark, Sheryl Lynne 1955- *WhoAmW 93*
Clark, Shirley Reed, Jr. 1932- *St&PR 93*
Clark, Simon *ScF&FL 92*
Clark, Sophie Louise Wepf *AmWomPl*
Clark, Stanford E. 1917- *St&PR 93, WhoAm 92*
Clark, Stanley Lawrence 1943- *WhoAm 92*
Clark, Stephen P. 1923- *WhoAm 92*
Clark, Stephen R. *WhoAm 92*
Clark, Stephen Randolph *Law&B 92*
Clark, Steve 1960-1991 *AnObit 1991, BioIn 17*
Clark, Steven C. 1950- *St&PR 93*
Clark, Susan 1944- *WhoAm 92, WhoAmW 93*
Clark, Susan Dixon 1937- *WhoAmW 93*
Clark, Susan Elaine 1953- *WhoAmW 93*
Clark, Susan Elise 1953- *WhoAmW 93*
Clark, Susan Jane 1953- *WhoEmL 93*
Clark, Susan Louise 1948- *WhoSSW 93*
Clark, Susan M. *Law&B 92*
Clark, Susan Matthews 1950- *WhoAm 92, WhoAmW 93, WhoEmL 93, WhoWor 93*
Clark, Sylvia *St&PR 93*
Clark, T.A. *WhoScE 91-1*
Clark, T.J.H. *WhoScE 91-1*
Clark, Teresa Ellen 1959- *WhoAmW 93*
Clark, Teresa Watkins 1953- *WhoAmW 93*
Clark, Terry Wayne 1950- *St&PR 93*
Clark, Thomas Alonzo 1920- *WhoSSW 93*
Clark, Thomas B. 1942- *St&PR 93*
Clark, Thomas Carlyle 1947- *St&PR 93, WhoAm 92*
Clark, Thomas Clayton *Law&B 92*
Clark, Thomas D. *Law&B 92*
Clark, Thomas Garis 1925- *WhoAm 92*
Clark, Thomas Henry *BioIn 17*
Clark, Thomas Keith 1951- *WhoSSW 93*
Clark, Thomas L. *Law&B 92*
Clark, Thomas Lloyd 1939- *WhoAm 92*
Clark, Thomas R. *St&PR 93*
Clark, Thomas Rolfe *WhoWor 93*
Clark, Thomas Sullivan 1947- *WhoEmL 93*
Clark, Thomas W. *Law&B 92*
Clark, Thomas Willard 1941- *WhoAm 92, WhoWrEP 92*
Clark, Threese Anne 1946- *WhoAmW 93*
Clark, Timothy Alan *Law&B 92*
Clark, Timothy Benjamin Gregory *WhoScE 91-1*
Clark, Timothy John Hayes *WhoScE 91-1*
Clark, Timothy Robert 1949- *WhoWor 93*
Clark, Timothy Warner 1953- *St&PR 93*
Clark, Tobin Keith *Law&B 92*
Clark, Tom *WhoAm 92, WhoE 93*
Clark, Tom Campbell 1899-1977 *OxCSupC [port]*
Clark, Viola Anna 1930- *WhoWrEP 92*
Clark, Virginia Anne 1942- *WhoAmW 93*
Clark, Virginia Lee 1948- *WhoAmW 93*
Clark, Virginia M. 1953- *ScF&FL 92*
Clark, Voris Chester 1930- *St&PR 93*
Clark, W.J.R. *WhoScE 91-1*
Clark, W. Lee 1937- *St&PR 93*
Clark, W. Michael 1950- *St&PR 93*
Clark, W. Richard 1939- *WhoAm 92*
Clark, Walter Burns 1913- *St&PR 93*
Clark, Walter H. 1931- *WhoWrEP 92*
Clark, Wanda 1956- *WhoAmW 93*
Clark, Ward Christopher 1939- *WhoAm 92*
Clark, Wesley C. 1907-1990 *BioIn 17*
Clark, Will *BioIn 17*
Clark, Will 1964- *WhoAm 92*
Clark, William 1770-1838 *BioIn 17, HarEnMi*
Clark, William 1770-1838 *See* Lewis, Meriwether 1774-1809 & Clark, William 1770-1838 *Expl 93*
Clark, William 1916-1985 *ScF&FL 92*
Clark, William, Jr. 1930- *WhoAm 92, WhoWor 93*
Clark, William A. 1839-1925 *GayN*
Clark, William B. 1924- *WhoIns 93*
Clark, William Burton, IV 1947- *WhoSSW 93*
Clark, William Cummin 1948- *WhoAm 92*
Clark, William F. 1922- *St&PR 93*
Clark, William G. 1932- *St&PR 93*
Clark, William G. 1933- *WhoIns 93*
Clark, William George 1924- *WhoAm 92*
Clark, William Hartley 1930- *WhoAm 92*
Clark, William Howard, Jr. 1951- *WhoE 93, WhoEmL 93, WhoWor 93*
Clark, William J. 1923- *St&PR 93, WhoAm 92, WhoIns 93*
Clark, William James 1923- *WhoAm 92*
Clark, William Kalar 1921- *St&PR 93*
Clark, William P. 1921- *St&PR 93*
Clark, William Patrick 1931- *WhoAm 92*
Clark, William Robert *Law&B 92*
Clark, William Robert, Jr. 1951- *WhoEmL 93*
Clark, William Roger 1949- *WhoE 93*
Clark, William Sackett, Jr. 1953- *WhoEmL 93*
Clark, William Stratton 1914- *WhoAm 92*
Clark, Worley H. 1932- *St&PR 93*
Clark, Worley H., Jr. 1932- *WhoAm 92*
Clark-Cole, Brian Howard 1956- *WhoEmL 93*
Clarke, A.F.N. 1948- *ScF&FL 92*
Clarke, Alan 1935-1990 *MiSFD 9N*
Clarke, Alan Douglas 1922- *WhoWor 93*
Clarke, Allan J. 1949- *WhoSSW 93*
Clarke, Allen Bruce 1927- *WhoAm 92*
Clarke, Allen Richard 1957- *WhoEmL 93*
Clarke, Andrew 1949- *WhoScE 91-1*
Clarke, Andrew Gerard 1961- *WhoE 93*
Clarke, Andrew William 1956- *St&PR 93*
Clarke, Anna 1919- *ConAu 39NR*
Clarke, Arthur C. 1917- *BioIn 17, MagSWL [port], ScF&FL 92*
Clarke, Arthur C(harles) 1917- *MajAI [port], SmATA 70 [port]*
Clarke, Arthur Charles 1917- *WhoAm 92, WhoWor 93*
Clarke, Austin 1934- *WhoCanL 92*
Clarke, Austin C. 1934- *ConAu 16AS [port]*
Clarke, Austin C(hesterfield) 1934- *DcLB 125 [port]*
Clarke, B. Devane, Jr. 1929- *St&PR 93*
Clarke, Barby Twelvetrees 1941- *St&PR 93*
Clarke, Benaiah Franklin *AmWomPl*
Clarke, Bobby 1949- *WhoAm 92*
Clarke, Boden *ScF&FL 92*
Clarke, Brian Joseph *Law&B 92*
Clarke, Bryan 1949- *St&PR 93*
Clarke, Bryan Campbel *WhoScE 91-1*
Clarke, Buddy *BioIn 17*
Clarke, C.J. *WhoIns 93*
Clarke, Carter W., Jr. 1926- *St&PR 93*
Clarke, Charles D. 1911-1991 *BioIn 17*
Clarke, Charles Fenton 1916- *WhoAm 92*
Clarke, Charlotte Louise Kirkland 1865-1913 *AmWomPl*
Clarke, Cheryl Ann 1954- *WhoAmW 93*
Clarke, Christopher James Seaton *WhoScE 91-1*
Clarke, Christopher L.A. 1939- *St&PR 93*
Clarke, Clifford Montreville 1925- *WhoAm 92, WhoSSW 93*
Clarke, Cordelia Kay Knight Mazuy 1938- *WhoAm 92*
Clarke, Cynthia Therese 1952- *WhoAm 92*
Clarke, Cyril Astley 1907- *WhoWor 93*
Clarke, Cyril Astley, Sir *WhoScE 91-1*
Clarke, David A. *Law&B 92*
Clarke, David Bruce 1951- *St&PR 93*
Clarke, David H. *St&PR 93*
Clarke, David Marshall 1927- *WhoAm 92*
Clarke, Debra Sieck 1951- *WhoAmW 93*
Clarke, Donald Lancaster 1941- *St&PR 93*
Clarke, Donald Llewelyn *Law&B 92*
Clarke, Ednah Proctor *AmWomPl*
Clarke, Edward Nielsen 1925- *WhoAm 92*
Clarke, Edward Owen, Jr. 1929- *WhoAm 92*
Clarke, Edwin B. 1923- *St&PR 93*
Clarke, Edwin J. 1934- *St&PR 93*
Clarke, Edwin R. 1946- *St&PR 93*
Clarke, Edwin V., Jr. 1925- *St&PR 93*
Clarke, Eileen Clesi 1943- *WhoSSW 93*
Clarke, Elizabeth Ann 1951- *WhoAmW 93*
Clarke, Ella A. *AmWomPl*
Clarke, Eric Thacher 1916- *WhoAm 92*
Clarke, Erwin Bennett 1922- *St&PR 93, WhoAm 92*
Clarke, Eugene C., Jr. 1921- *St&PR 93*
Clarke, Florence Myres 1927- *WhoAmW 93*
Clarke, Frances Elizabeth *AmWomPl*
Clarke, Frank *MiSFD 9*
Clarke, Frank J.J. 1934- *WhoScE 91-1*
Clarke, Frank William 1942- *WhoAm 92*
Clarke, Franklyn Roselle 1926- *WhoAm 92*
Clarke, Frederic B., III 1942- *WhoAm 92*
Clarke, G. Modele *BioIn 17*
Clarke, Garry Evans 1943- *WhoAm 92*
Clarke, Garry Kenneth Connal 1941- *WhoAm 92*
Clarke, Garvey Elliott 1935- *WhoE 93*
Clarke, Gary Kendrick 1939- *WhoAm 92*
Clarke, Gary O. 1936- *St&PR 93*
Clarke, George Elliott 1960- *WhoCanL 92*
Clarke, Gillian *BioIn 17*
Clarke, Glenn W. *St&PR 93*
Clarke, Greta Fields *WhoAmW 93*
Clarke, H. Weston, Jr. 1929- *St&PR 93*
Clarke, (James) Hamilton (Smee) 1840-1912 *Baker 92*
Clarke, Harold Gravely 1927- *WhoAm 92, WhoSSW 93*
Clarke, Helen Archibald 1860-1926 *AmWomPl*
Clarke, Henry de Brunner, Jr. 1933- *St&PR 93*
Clarke, Henry Leland 1907- *Baker 92*
Clarke, Hugh Archibald 1839-1927 *Baker 92*
Clarke, I.F. 1918- *ScF&FL 92*
Clarke, J. Brian 1928- *ScF&FL 92*
Clarke, J. Calvitt, Jr. 1920- *WhoAm 92, WhoSSW 93*
Clarke, J.F.Gates 1905-1990 *BioIn 17*
Clarke, Jack Graeme 1927- *St&PR 93, WhoAm 92*
Clarke, James Kenelm 1941- *MiSFD 9*
Clarke, James P. 1854-1926 *PolPar*
Clarke, James Paton 1808-1877 *Baker 92*
Clarke, James Weston 1937- *WhoAm 92*
Clarke, Jay *ScF&FL 92*
Clarke, Jeremiah c. 1673-1707 *Baker 92*
Clarke, Jeremy 1958- *ScF&FL 92*
Clarke, Jerrold 1942- *WhoE 93*
Clarke, Jimmy Carlton 1967- *WhoE 93*
Clarke, Joan B. 1921- *ScF&FL 92*
Clarke, John 1770-1836 *Baker 92*
Clarke, John 1942- *WhoAm 92*
Clarke, John Clem 1937- *WhoAm 92*
Clarke, John F. *WhoScE 91-1*
Clarke, John Frederick Gates 1905-1990 *BioIn 17*
Clarke, John Hessin 1857-1945 *OxCSupC [port]*
Clarke, John Innes *WhoScE 91-1*
Clarke, John Innes 1929- *WhoWor 93*
Clarke, John K.A. 1931- *WhoScE 91-3*
Clarke, John M. *Law&B 92*
Clarke, John Michael 1941- *St&PR 93*
Clarke, John P. 1930- *St&PR 93*
Clarke, John R. 1913- *WhoWrEP 92*
Clarke, John Robin Paul *WhoScE 91-1*
Clarke, John U. 1952- *St&PR 93*
Clarke, John Vincent, Jr. 1943- *WhoSSW 93*
Clarke, Joseph Andrew *WhoScE 91-1*
Clarke, Joseph Ignatius Constantine 1846-1925 *JrnUS*
Clarke, Karen Elisabeth 1946- *WhoEmL 93*
Clarke, Kathleen 1878-1972 *BioIn 17*
Clarke, Kay Knight 1938- *St&PR 93*
Clarke, Keith E. 1940- *WhoScE 91-1*
Clarke, Kelah Nanette 1956- *WhoE 93*
Clarke, Ken Russell 1944- *WhoAm 92*
Clarke, Kenneth Harry 1940- *WhoWor 93*

Clarke, Kenneth Kingsley 1924- WhoAm 92
Clarke, Kenneth R. 1944- St&PR 93
Clarke, Kenneth Stevens 1931- WhoAm 92
Clarke, Kenny 1914-1985 Baker 92
Clarke, Kevin ScF&FL 92
Clarke, Kevin B. Law&B 92
Clarke, Kit Hansen 1944- WhoAm 92, WhoAmW 93
Clarke, Lambuth McGeehee 1923- WhoAm 92
Clarke, Larry D. 1925- St&PR 93
Clarke, Lee ScF&FL 92
Clarke, Lenny BioIn 17
Clarke, Leslie Earle 1923- St&PR 93
Clarke, Lewis James 1927- WhoAm 92
Clarke, Linda Louise 1952- WhoEmL 93, WhoSSW 93
Clarke, Lindsay 1939- ScF&FL 92
Clarke, Logan, Jr. 1927- St&PR 93, WhoAm 92
Clarke, Lois W. AmWomPl
Clarke, Lynn Marie 1947- WhoAmW 93
Clarke, Mae d1992 NewYTBS 92 [port]
Clarke, Mae 1907- SweetSg C [port]
Clarke, Mae 1910-1992 BioIn 17
Clarke, Malcolm WhoAm 92
Clarke, Margaret WhoScE 91-1
Clarke, Margaret Alice 1942- WhoSSW 93
Clarke, Margaret Courtney- 1949- BioIn 17
Clarke, Marian Williams 1880-1953 BioIn 17
Clarke, Marjorie Jane 1953- WhoAmW 93
Clarke, Martha 1944?- BioIn 17, WhoAm 92
Clarke, Mary Elizabeth 1924- WhoAmW 93
Clarke, Mary Neal 1924- WhoAmW 93
Clarke, Michael WhoScE 91-1
Clarke, Michael 1944- See Byrds, The ConMus 8
Clarke, Michael Bradshaw 1946- St&PR 93, WhoEmL 93
Clarke, Michael L. Law&B 92
Clarke, Milton Charles 1929- WhoAm 92
Clarke, Neil G. 1932- St&PR 93
Clarke, Nicholas Charles 1948- WhoWor 93
Clarke, Norma Jean Kornegay 1947- WhoE 93
Clarke, Oscar Withers 1919- WhoAm 92
Clarke, Patrick E. 1936- St&PR 93
Clarke, Patrick John Law&B 92
Clarke, Pauline 1921- ChlLR 28 [port], MajAI [port], ScF&FL 92
Clarke, Pauline Ann Law&B 92
Clarke, Peter 1936- WhoAm 92
Clarke, Peter Parlee 1943- WhoE 93
Clarke, Philip J. 1939- WhoUN 92
Clarke, Philip R., Jr. 1914- St&PR 93
Clarke, Philip Ream, Jr. 1914- WhoAm 92
Clarke, R.H. WhoScE 91-1
Clarke, Rebecca (Thacher) 1886-1979 Baker 92
Clarke, Richard A. WhoAm 92
Clarke, Richard A. 1930- St&PR 93
Clarke, Richard Alan 1930- WhoAm 92
Clarke, Richard Gerard Law&B 92
Clarke, Richard Lewis 1948- WhoAm 92
Clarke, Richard M. 1931- WhoAm 92
Clarke, Robert ScF&FL 92
Clarke, Robert 1920- BioIn 17
Clarke, Robert Arthur WhoScE 91-1
Clarke, Robert Bradstreet BioIn 17
Clarke, Robert Coningsby 1879-1934 Baker 92
Clarke, Robert Earle 1949- WhoAm 92
Clarke, Robert Emmett 1906- WhoWor 93
Clarke, Robert F. WhoAm 92
Clarke, Robert Fitzgerald 1942- St&PR 93
Clarke, Robert Francis 1915- WhoWor 93
Clarke, Robert Logan 1942- WhoAm 92
Clarke, Robert Thorburn 1945- WhoAm 92
Clarke, Roger Glen 1948- WhoEmL 93
Clarke, Roger John WhoScE 91-1
Clarke, S. Bruce 1940- WhoSSW 93
Clarke, Scott T. 1958- St&PR 93
Clarke, Sheldon 1932- St&PR 93
Clarke, Shirley BioIn 17
Clarke, Shirley 1925- MiSFD 9
Clarke, Shirley Alfretta 1934- St&PR 93
Clarke, Stanley BioIn 17, SoulM
Clarke, Stephan Paul 1945- WhoE 93
Clarke, T.C. 1932- St&PR 93
Clarke, T.E.B. 1907-1989 ScF&FL 92
Clarke, Terence Michael 1937- WhoAm 92
Clarke, Thomas A. 1941- St&PR 93
Clarke, Thomas Crawford 1932- WhoAm 92
Clarke, Thomas D. Law&B 92
Clarke, Thomas F. 1944- St&PR 93
Clarke, Thomas Hal 1914- WhoAm 92
Clarke, Thomas K. 1932- St&PR 93
Clarke, Thomas Lee Law&B 92
Clarke, Timothy A. Law&B 92
Clarke, Urana 1902- WhoAmW 93
Clarke, Violet AmWomPl
Clarke, W. Hall 1927- WhoAm 92
Clarke, Wade P., Jr. Law&B 92
Clarke, Walter Sheldon 1934- WhoAm 92
Clarke, William Burton 1947- WhoEmL 93
Clarke, William J. 1937- St&PR 93, WhoIns 93
Clarke, Wm. A. Lee, III 1949- WhoEmL 93
Clarke-Kudless, Dianne Loch 1951- WhoE 93
Clarken, Elizabeth Ann 1935- WhoAmW 93, WhoE 93
Clarken, Joseph A., Jr. Law&B 92
Clarke-Whitfield, John 1770-1836 Baker 92
Clark-Hurn, Paula Dawne 1952- WhoEmL 93
Clarkin, Donald J. 1929- St&PR 93
Clarkin, Regina J. BioIn 17
Clarkk, Regor ScF&FL 92
Clarkson, Alison Moira BioIn 17
Clarkson, Andrew MacBeth 1937- WhoAm 92
Clarkson, Brian Leonard WhoScE 91-1
Clarkson, Carole Lawrence 1942- WhoAmW 93
Clarkson, Charles 1947- St&PR 93
Clarkson, Christopher Michael Vernon 1948- WhoWor 93
Clarkson, Elisabeth Ann Hudnut 1925- WhoAmW 93
Clarkson, Geoffrey Peniston Elliott 1934- WhoAm 92
Clarkson, George 1772-1804 BioIn 17
Clarkson, Gerard 1772-1793 BioIn 17
Clarkson, Helen 1904- ScF&FL 92
Clarkson, James S. 1842-1918 PolPar
Clarkson, Jocelyn Adrene 1952- WhoAm 92, WhoAmW 93, WhoEmL 93, WhoSSW 93, WhoWor 93
Clarkson, Kenneth Wright 1942- WhoAm 92, WhoWor 93
Clarkson, Lawrence William 1938- WhoAm 92, WhoWor 93
Clarkson, Max B.E. 1922- St&PR 93
Clarkson, Max Boydell Elliott 1922- WhoAm 92
Clarkson, Paul R. 1935- WhoIns 93
Clarkson, Paul Richard 1935- St&PR 93
Clarkson, Robert Noel 1950- WhoEmL 93, WhoWor 93
Clarkson, Ross T. 1922- St&PR 93
Clarkson, Stephen B. Law&B 92
Clarkson, Thomas 1760-1846 BioIn 17
Clarkson, Thomas William 1932- WhoAm 92
Clarkson, Valerie BioIn 17
Clarkson, William Edwin 1925- St&PR 93
Clarkson, William Morris 1954- WhoEmL 93
Clarkson, William Wade 1949- WhoEmL 93, WhoSSW 93
Clarkston, Ronne 1941- WhoAmW 93
Clarner, Walter J. 1947- WhoE 93, WhoEmL 93
Clarnete, Lisette BioIn 17
Clarno, Beverly Ann 1936- WhoAmW 93
Claro, Jaime 1936- St&PR 93, WhoAm 92
Claro, Joe ScF&FL 92
Claro, Jorge C. 1945- WhoUN 92
Claro, Joseph ScF&FL 92
Claro, Silvia Mussi Da Silva 1942- WhoWor 93
Clarren, Sterling Keith 1947- WhoWor 93
Clarricoats, John Bell WhoScE 91-1
Clarson, John P. Law&B 92
Clarus, Max 1852-1916 Baker 92
Clary, A.E. Law&B 92
Clary, Alexia Barbara 1954- WhoAmW 93
Clary, Bradley Grayson 1950- WhoEmL 93
Clary, Charles William, III 1950- WhoSSW 93
Clary, Diana Hunter 1944- WhoAmW 93
Clary, Elsie Ray 1948- WhoAmW 93
Clary, Everett Burton 1921- WhoAm 92
Clary, John G. 1926- St&PR 93
Clary, John J. Law&B 92
Clary, Linda Mixon 1946- WhoEmL 93
Clary, Richard Wayland 1953- WhoAm 92, WhoEmL 93
Clary, Robert 1926- WhoAm 92
Clary, Rosalie Brandon Stanton 1928- WhoAm 92, WhoAmW 93
Clarysse, Albert Mar 1936- WhoWor 93
Clasby, Mark Bower 1943- St&PR 93
Clasen, Robert Burke 1944- WhoAm 92
Clasgens, J.H., II 1924- St&PR 93
Claspell, Margaret Ann 1944- WhoAmW 93
Clasper, Geoffrey S. 1949- St&PR 93
Clasper, Rosemary Kirr Law&B 92
Claspill, James Louis 1946- WhoWor 93
Class, Harold Martin 1932- St&PR 93
Classen, H. Ward Law&B 92
Classen, Hans-Georg 1936- WhoScE 91-3
Classens, Michael John 1955- WhoEmL 93
Classicus, Julius c. 30-c. 70 HarEnMi
Classon, Bruce D. 1932- St&PR 93
Classon, Louise Laurette 1948- WhoWrEP 92
Classon, Rolf A. 1945- St&PR 93
Classon, Rolf Allan 1945- WhoAm 92, WhoWor 93
Claster, Jay B. 1931- St&PR 93
Claster, Mark L. 1952- St&PR 93
Clatanoff, Doris Ann 1932- WhoSSW 93
Clatsoff, William Adam 1940- WhoSSW 93
Claud, Joseph Gillette 1927- St&PR 93, WhoAm 92
Claude, Abram, Jr. 1927- St&PR 93
Claude, Anthony B. 1936- St&PR 93
Claude, Inis Lothair, Jr. 1922- WhoAm 92
Claude, Pierre 1916- WhoWor 93
Claude, Robert W. Law&B 92
Claude, Sylvio 1934- DcCPCAm
Claude, Thomas Eugene 1949- St&PR 93
Claudel, Bernard M. 1932- WhoScE 91-2
Claudel, Camille 1864-1943 BioIn 17
Claudel, Paul 1868-1955 BioIn 17
Claudet, Francis George 1837-1906 BioIn 17
Claudian c. 370-c. 404 OxDcByz
Claudin, M. WhoScE 91-2
Claudin le Jeune Baker 92
Claudio, Dalcidio Moraes 1946- WhoWor 93
Claudius, Emperor of Rome 10BC-54AD BioIn 17
Claudius, Matthias 1740-1815 BioIn 17
Claudius Caudex, Appius c. 307BC-c. 240BC HarEnMi
Claudius Gothicus, II 214-270 HarEnMi
Claudius Pulcher, Publius c. 292BC-c. 248BC HarEnMi
Claudon, Jean-Louis Rene 1950- WhoWor 93
Clauer, Calvin Robert 1910- WhoWor 93
Clauer, Laurel Jane Law&B 92
Clauer, Norbert F. 1941- WhoScE 91-2
Claughton, Edward Napoleon, Jr. 1927- WhoSSW 93
Claughton, Hugh Dawson, Sr. 1928- WhoSSW 93
Claunch, Quinton 1922- SoulM
Claus, C.L. Law&B 92
Claus, Carol Jean 1959- WhoAmW 93
Claus, J. WhoScE 91-3
Claus, Karen Joan 1965- WhoAmW 93, WhoEmL 93
Claus, Marcie Ruth WhoEmL 93
Claus, Paul Honore 1936- WhoUN 92
Claus, Volker 1944- WhoScE 91-3
Clause, Donald John 1930- WhoSSW 93
Clausen, A.W. BioIn 17
Clausen, Alden Winship BioIn 17
Clausen, Alden Winship 1923- WhoAm 92
Clausen, Annamarie 1948- WhoAmW 93
Clausen, Betty Jane Hansen 1925- WhoAmW 93
Clausen, Brenda Ida 1942- WhoAmW 93
Clausen, Bret Mark 1958- WhoEmL 93
Clausen, Christopher N. Law&B 92
Clausen, Claus-Dieter 1937- WhoScE 91-3
Clausen, Dennis M. 1943- ScF&FL 92
Clausen, Edgar Clemens 1951- WhoAm 92, WhoEmL 93, WhoSSW 93
Clausen, George Edward 1929- St&PR 93
Clausen, Hugh Joseph 1926- WhoAm 92
Clausen, Ib Bruun WhoScE 91-2
Clausen, Jerry Lee 1939- WhoAm 92, WhoE 93, WhoWor 93
Clausen, John Adam 1914- WhoAm 92
Clausen, Jorgen WhoScE 91-2
Clausen, Kirk V. 1955- St&PR 93
Clausen, L.G. 1939- St&PR 93
Clausen, Lars 1935- WhoWor 93
Clausen, Peter A. d1991 BioIn 17
Clausen, Robert William 1947- WhoEmL 93
Clausen, Roger H. 1942- St&PR 93
Clausen, Thomas Hans Wilhelm 1950- WhoWor 93
Clausen, Torben 1937- WhoScE 91-2
Clausen, Wendell Vernon 1923- WhoAm 92, WhoWrEP 92
Clausen, William T. Law&B 92
Clauser, Barry Raymond 1953- St&PR 93
Clauser, Donald Roberdeau 1941- WhoAm 92
Clauser, Francis H. 1913- WhoAm 92, WhoWor 93
Clauser, Frederick Dale 1935- St&PR 93
Clausert, Horst 1936- WhoScE 91-3
Clausewitz, Karl Maria von 1780-1831 HarEnMi
Clausewitz, Karl von 1780-1831 BioIn 17
Clausing, Arthur M. 1936- WhoAm 92
Clausman, Gilbert Joseph 1921- WhoAm 92
Clausner, Marlin D., Jr. 1941- St&PR 93
Clauson, Christine Ann 1958- WhoAmW 93
Clauson, Frank Levin, Jr. 1944- WhoE 93
Clauson, Gary Lewis 1952- WhoSSW 93
Clauson, James Wilson 1913- WhoAm 92
Clauson, Peter A. 1955- WhoIns 93
Clauson, Sharyn Ferne 1946- WhoE 93, WhoEmL 93, WhoWor 93
Clauss, Alfred 1906- WhoAm 92
Clauss, C. David 1948- WhoEmL 93
Clauss, Charles J. 1925- St&PR 93, WhoIns 93
Clauss, Peter Otto 1936- WhoWor 93
Clauss, Philip John 1942- St&PR 93
Clauss, Valerie E. 1923- St&PR 93
Clauss, Wayne Francis 1947- WhoE 93
Clauss, Wolfgang 1949- WhoScE 91-3
Claussen, Eileen Barbara 1945- WhoAm 92
Claussen, Eric Walter 1964- WhoE 93
Claussen, John H. Law&B 92
Claussen, Julia 1879-1941 Baker 92
Claussen, Louise Keith 1947- WhoEmL 93, WhoSSW 93
Claussen, W. Hartwig 1931- WhoWor 93
Claustriaux, Jean-Jacques 1948- WhoScE 91-2, WhoWor 93
Claus-Walker, Jacqueline Lucy 1915- WhoAmW 93
Clautice, William Gunther 1937- WhoSSW 93
Clavadetscher, David Jerome 1935- St&PR 93
Clave, Anselmo 1824-1874 BioIn 17
Clavel, Bernard Charles Henri 1923- WhoWor 93
Clavel, Jean 1951- WhoWor 93
Clavell, James BioIn 17
Clavell, James 1924- MiSFD 9, WhoAm 92
Clavell, James 1925- ScF&FL 92
Claveloux, Ronald Louis Law&B 92
Claver, Robert Earl 1928- WhoAm 92
Claver, William F. 1936- WhoAsAP 91
Claverie, Melvin Juice 1960- WhoEmL 93
Clavero, Cesareo 1946- WhoScE 91-3
Clavet, Anthony BioIn 17
Claviere d'Hust, Bernard de BioIn 17
Clavijero, Francisco Javier 1731-1787 DcMexL
Clavijo, Hernando 1950- WhoUN 92
Clavijo, Ruy Gonzalez de d1412 OxDcByz
Clawson, Carol A. 1946- WhoEmL 93
Clawson, Daniel Bruce 1946- St&PR 93
Clawson, David Kay 1927- WhoAm 92
Clawson, Debra A. Law&B 92
Clawson, James Craig 1949- St&PR 93
Clawson, John Addison 1922- WhoAm 92
Clawson, John David 1934- WhoSSW 93
Clawson, John Gibbs 1928- St&PR 93
Clawson, Leanna Lynn 1949- WhoEmL 93
Clawson, Michael Howard 1950- St&PR 93
Clawson, Michael J. 1950- St&PR 93
Clawson, Patrick Lyell 1951- WhoE 93
Clawson, Raymond Walden 1906- WhoWor 93
Clawson, Robert Wayne 1939- WhoAm 92, WhoWor 93
Clawson, Robin Burnham Law&B 92
Clawson, Roxann Eloise 1945- WhoAmW 93, WhoE 93
Clawson, Rudger BioIn 17
Clax, Freda Marie 1959- WhoAmW 93, WhoEmL 93
Claxton, Bradford Wayne 1934- WhoAm 92
Claxton, Harriett Maroy Jones 1930- WhoAmW 93
Claxton, Larry Davis 1946- WhoSSW 93
Claxton, William F. 1914- MiSFD 9
Clay, Aaron Richard 1953- WhoEmL 93
Clay, Alan Bruce Law&B 92
Clay, Albert Greene 1917- WhoAm 92
Clay, Ambrose Whitlock Winston 1941- WhoAm 92
Clay, Andrew Dice BioIn 17, ConAu 138
Clay, Angela Rachelle 1968- WhoSSW 93
Clay, Ben St&PR 93
Clay, Billy Jerrell 1940- St&PR 93
Clay, Cassius 1942- BioIn 17
Clay, Cassius Marcellus 1810-1903 BioIn 17, JrnUS
Clay, Cassius Marcellus 1942- WhoAm 92
Clay, Catesby W. 1923- St&PR 93
Clay, Clifton Ford 1939- WhoWor 93
Clay, David S. 1923- St&PR 93
Clay, Diskin 1938- WhoWrEP 92
Clay, Don BioIn 17
Clay, Don Richard 1937- WhoAm 92
Clay, Elizabeth Robertson 1939- WhoAmW 93
Clay, Frederic (Emes) 1838-1889 Baker 92
Clay, George Harry 1911- WhoAm 92
Clay, Grady Edward 1916- WhoSSW 93

Clay, Harris Aubrey 1911- WhoSSW 93, WhoWor 93
Clay, Henry 1777-1852 BioIn 17, PolPar
Clay, James Franklin 1911- WhoSSW 93
Clay, James Jordan, Jr. 1962- WhoEmL 93
Clay, Jason W. BioIn 17
Clay, John A. 1939- St&PR 93
Clay, John Ernest 1921- WhoAm 92
Clay, John Paul 1910-1991 BioIn 17
Clay, John W., Jr. 1941- WhoAm 92
Clay, John William 1913- WhoAm 92, WhoSSW 93
Clay, Joseph 1764-1811 BioIn 17
Clay, Judy SoulM
Clay, Katherine Coles AmWomPl
Clay, Larry David 1948- St&PR 93
Clay, Lisa A. Law&B 92
Clay, Lucius D. 1897-1978 BioIn 17
Clay, Lucius DuBignon 1897-1978 HarEnMi
Clay, Lyell Buffington 1923- St&PR 93, WhoAm 92
Clay, Margaret Leone 1923- WhoAmW 93
Clay, Marjorie McKeown d1992 BioIn 17, NewYTBS 92
Clay, Orson C. 1930- St&PR 93, WhoAm 92, WhoIns 93, WhoSSW 93
Clay, Otis SoulM
Clay, Otis 1942- BioIn 17
Clay, Paul Eugene, Jr. 1933- WhoSSW 93
Clay, Philip G. 1952- WhoIns 93
Clay, Rudolph AfrAmBi
Clay, Ryburn Glover, Jr. 1928- WhoSSW 93
Clay, W. WhoScE 91-1
Clay, W. Robert 1932- St&PR 93
Clay, Wil 1938- BlkAull 92
Clay, William BioIn 17
Clay, William 1931- CngDr 91
Clay, William Lacy 1931- WhoAm 92
Clay, William Lacy, Jr. 1956- WhoEmL 93
Clay, William Robert 1932- WhoAm 92
Clayborne, Karen McLaurin Law&B 92
Clayburgh, Jill 1944- WhoAm 92
Clayburgh, Jill 1945- IntDcF 2-3
Claycomb, Cecil Keith 1920- WhoAm 92
Clayden, Raymond 1927- St&PR 93
Claydon, Allison BioIn 17
Claydon, Andrew John 1951- WhoSSW 93
Claydon, Charles Thomas 1935- WhoE 93
Claydon, David A. 1935- St&PR 93
Claydon, J.H. 1934- St&PR 93
Clayes, Edith Martin AmWomPl
Clayman, Gary A. 1954- St&PR 93
Clayman, Jacob 1905-1991 BioIn 17
Clayman, Joel A. 1957- St&PR 93
Clayman, Lawrence Alan 1955- WhoE 93
Clayman, Martin J. 1925- St&PR 93
Clayman, Raymond Law&B 92
Claypool, William, III WhoAm 92
Claypoole, Robert Edwin 1936- WhoAm 92
Clayton, Ann Clarissa Law&B 92
Clayton, Barbara Evelyn WhoScE 91-1
Clayton, Bernard BioIn 17
Clayton, Bernard Miles, Jr. 1953- WhoEmL 93
Clayton, Billy Wayne 1928- WhoAm 92
Clayton, Bruce Underhill 1947- St&PR 93
Clayton, Buck 1911-1991 AnObit 1991, BioIn 17
Clayton, Buck (Wilbur Dorsey) 1911- Baker 92
Clayton, Byron Cordell 1957- WhoEmL 93
Clayton, Charles Stelling 1951- WhoE 93
Clayton, Christina E. Law&B 92
Clayton, Constance BioIn 17, WhoAm 92, WhoE 93
Clayton, David Michael Law&B 92
Clayton, David Russell 1943- WhoE 93
Clayton, Donald D. 1935- ScF&FL 92
Clayton, Donald Delbert 1935- WhoAm 92
Clayton, Donald W. 1936- St&PR 93
Clayton, Donna L. Law&B 92
Clayton, Ellen Wright 1952- WhoEmL 93
Clayton, Eva WhoAmW 93
Clayton, Evelyn Williams 1951- WhoAmW 93
Clayton, Frances Elizabeth 1922- WhoAm 92
Clayton, Gene WhoSSW 93
Clayton, Gregory Paul 1949- WhoEmL 93
Clayton, Jack 1921- MiSFD 9, WhoWor 93
Clayton, James BioIn 17
Clayton, James A., Jr. Law&B 92
Clayton, James Edwin 1929- WhoAm 92
Clayton, James N., III Law&B 92
Clayton, Jay 1951- WhoWrEP 92
Clayton, Jay John Bunyan, IV 1951- WhoSSW 93
Clayton, Jo 1939- ScF&FL 92
Clayton, Joan WhoWrEP 92
Clayton, JoAnn Cleveland 1935- WhoE 93
Clayton, Joe Todd 1924- WhoAm 92
Clayton, John BioIn 17
Clayton, John Charles 1924- WhoAm 92
Clayton, John J. 1917- WhoWor 93, WhoWrEP 92
Clayton, John J. 1935- WhoWrEP 92
Clayton, John Middleton, Jr. 1941- WhoE 93
Clayton, Jonathan Alan 1937- WhoAm 92
Clayton, Joseph Coy 1935- St&PR 93
Clayton, Joy May 1947- WhoEmL 93, WhoSSW 93
Clayton, Keith Alan 1957- WhoEmL 93
Clayton, Keith Martin WhoScE 91-1
Clayton, Kenneth P. 1931- St&PR 93
Clayton, Laura Ancelina Law&B 92
Clayton, Laura Ancelina 1960- WhoEmL 93
Clayton, Lawrence 1891-1949 BioIn 17
Clayton, Lawrence (Ray) 1938- ConAu 137, WhoAm 92, WhoSSW 93
Clayton, Margaret Diane 1950- WhoAmW 93
Clayton, Marguerite 1891-1968 SweetSg A [port]
Clayton, Mark Gregory 1961- WhoAm 92
Clayton, Marvin Courtland 1938- WhoSSW 93, WhoWor 93
Clayton, Mary 1954- ConAu 136
Clayton, Mary Jo WhoAm 92
Clayton, Norma Towne 1941- WhoAmW 93
Clayton, Pamela Kay 1959- WhoAmW 93
Clayton, Paula J. Law&B 92
Clayton, Paula Jean 1934- WhoAm 92
Clayton, Preston Copeland 1903- WhoAm 92
Clayton, Randy Joe 1954- WhoEmL 93
Clayton, Rebecca Kilgo 1916- WhoSSW 93
Clayton, Richard R. 1938- St&PR 93
Clayton, Richard Reese 1938- WhoAm 92
Clayton, Robert Hugh 1957- WhoEmL 93
Clayton, Robert Norman 1930- WhoAm 92
Clayton, Ronald S. 1942- St&PR 93
Clayton, Sally Lynn 1946- WhoEmL 93
Clayton, Sheena ScF&FL 92
Clayton, Stephen John 1946- WhoEmL 93
Clayton, Thomas c. 1665-c. 1725 OxDcOp
Clayton, Thomas Michael Law&B 92
Clayton, Tim BioIn 17
Clayton, William E. 1938- WhoAm 92
Clayton, William Edward 1926- St&PR 93
Clayton, William Howard 1927- WhoAm 92
Clayton, William L. 1929- WhoAm 92
Clayton, William Lewis 1930- WhoAm 92
Clayton, Xernona BioIn 17
Clayton, Xernona 1930- AfrAmBi [port], ConBlB 3 [port], WhoAmW 93
Clayton-Greene, Kevin Allen 1952- WhoWor 93
Claytor, Graham, Jr. 1912- WhoE 93
Claytor, Richard Anderson 1927- WhoAm 92
Claytor, Robert B. 1922- St&PR 93
Claytor, Robert Buckner 1922- WhoAm 92
Claywell, Bernard Stephen 1950- WhoSSW 93
Cleage, Pearl BioIn 17
Clear, Albert F., Jr. 1920- WhoAm 92
Clear, John Michael 1948- WhoEmL 93
Clear, Richard 1956- WhoScE 91-3
Clear, Rosemary Elaine 1946- WhoEmL 93
Clear, Val 1915- ScF&FL 92
Clearchus c. 450BC-401BC HarEnMi
Cleare, M.J. WhoScE 91-1
Clearfield, Andrew Mark 1949- WhoAm 92, WhoE 93
Clearfield, Harris Reynold 1933- WhoAm 92
Clearman, Brian (Patrick Joseph) 1941- ConAu 38NR
Clearwater, Scott W. Law&B 92
Cleary, Audrey 1930- WhoAmW 93
Cleary, Beverly BioIn 17
Cleary, Beverly 1916- ChlFicS
Cleary, Beverly Atlee WhoAm 92, WhoAmW 93
Cleary, Beverly (Atlee Bunn) 1916- MajAI [port]
Cleary, Beverly (Bunn) 1916- DcAmChF 1960, DcAmChF 1985
Cleary, David Michael Law&B 92
Cleary, Donald Joseph Law&B 92
Cleary, Edward William 1919- WhoAm 92
Cleary, Francis Charles 1932- St&PR 93
Cleary, Francis Charles, Jr. Law&B 92
Cleary, Frank Joseph 1930- St&PR 93
Cleary, Fritz 1913- WhoAm 92, WhoWor 93
Cleary, James Charles, Jr. 1921- WhoE 93
Cleary, James Roy 1926- WhoAm 92
Cleary, Jean Marie 1964- WhoEmL 93
Cleary, John F. Law&B 92
Cleary, John V. 1901-1990 BioIn 17
Cleary, John Vincent, Jr. 1928- St&PR 93, WhoAm 92
Cleary, John Washington 1911- WhoAm 92
Cleary, Joseph Aloysius, Jr. 1954- St&PR 93
Cleary, Joseph M. 1914- St&PR 93
Cleary, Lynda Woods 1950- WhoAmW 93, WhoEmL 93
Cleary, Manon Catherine 1942- WhoAmW 93, WhoE 93, WhoWor 93
Cleary, Mary Margaret 1955- WhoAmW 93
Cleary, Michael J. Law&B 92
Cleary, Patricia Anne 1954- WhoEmL 93
Cleary, Richard Simon 1956- WhoAm 92
Cleary, Russell George 1933- St&PR 93, WhoAm 92
Cleary, T. Anne 1935-1991 BioIn 17
Cleary, Thomas A. 1925- St&PR 93
Cleary, Thomas John 1939- St&PR 93
Cleary, Timothy B. Law&B 92
Cleary, Timothy Finbar 1925- WhoAm 92
Cleary, William B. 1921- St&PR 93
Cleary, William J., Jr. 1934- BiDAMSp 1989
Cleasby, John LeRoy 1928- WhoAm 92
Cleater, Alice J. AmWomPl
Cleather, Dorothy AmWomPl
Cleaton, Willie BioIn 17
Cleave, Mary L. 1947- WhoAm 92, WhoAmW 93
Cleaveland, David Earl 1944- WhoSSW 93
Cleaveland, John B. 1948- St&PR 93
Cleavelin, Leonard Robert 1957- WhoEmL 93
Cleaver, Bill ConAu 38NR, MajAI
Cleaver, Bill 1920-1981 DcAmChF 1960
Cleaver, Carole Annamay 1934- WhoE 93
Cleaver, Eldridge 1935- BioIn 17, EncAACR, PolPar
Cleaver, Elizabeth 1939-1985 WhoCanL 92
Cleaver, Emanuel BioIn 17
Cleaver, Emanuel 1944- ConBlB 4 [port]
Cleaver, Emanuel, II AfrAmBi
Cleaver, Emanuel, II 1944- WhoAm 92
Cleaver, J.R.A. WhoScE 91-1
Cleaver, Vera 1919- ConAu 38NR, DcAmChF 1960, MajAI [port]
Cleaver, Vera Allen 1919- WhoAm 92, WhoWrEP 92
Cleaver, Wild Bill BioIn 17
Cleaver, William J(oseph) 1920-1981 ConAu 38NR, MajAI [port]
Cleaver, William Lehn 1949- WhoEmL 93
Cleaver, William Pennington 1914- WhoAm 92
Cleaves, Margaret Ann 1946- WhoWrEP 92
Cleaves, Mark Andrew Law&B 92
Cleaves, Peter Shurtleff 1943- WhoAm 92
Cleberg, Harry D. WhoAm 92
Cleburne, Patrick Ronayne 1828-1864 BioIn 17
Clecak, Peter Emmett 1938- WhoAm 92
Clech, Jean Paul Marie 1958- WhoWor 93
Clechet, Paul 1934- WhoScE 91-2
Cleckley, Betty Jane WhoSSW 93
Clede, Emile William, Jr. 1927- WhoWrEP 92
Clee, Jan Evert 1928- WhoAm 92
Cleek, John Earl 1935- WhoWor 93
Cleek, Judy Ann 1948- WhoEmL 93
Cleeland, Peter Robert 1938- WhoAsAP 91
Cleere, Adrienne J. WhoAm 92
Cleese, John BioIn 17
Cleese, John 1939- IntDcF 2-3 [port], QDrFCA 92 [port]
Cleese, John Marwood 1939- WhoAm 92, WhoWor 93
Cleevely, David Douglas 1953- WhoWor 93
Cleff, William Carl 1942- St&PR 93, WhoAm 92
Cleffmann, Gunter 1928- WhoScE 91-3
Clegg, Alan George WhoScE 91-1
Clegg, Alan James 1944- WhoScE 91-1
Clegg, Arthur Bradbury WhoScE 91-1
Clegg, Barbara ScF&FL 92
Clegg, David Benjamin WhoScE 91-1
Clegg, David Louis 1955- WhoEmL 93
Clegg, David William WhoScE 91-1
Clegg, Douglas 1958- ScF&FL 92
Clegg, Edward John WhoScE 91-1
Clegg, Eleanor Rae Law&B 92
Clegg, Johnny BioIn 17
Clegg, Johnny 1953- ConMus 8 [port]
Clegg, Marshall Terrell 1931- St&PR 93
Clegg, Michael BioIn 17
Clegg, Michael Tran 1941- WhoAm 92
Clegg, Milton Lee 1943- St&PR 93
Clegg, Peter Ellis WhoScE 91-1
Clegg, Roger Burton 1955- WhoAm 92
Clegg, Stewart Roger WhoScE 91-1
Clegg, Thomas Boykin 1940- WhoSSW 93
Clegg, Tom MiSFD 9
Clegg, William J., III Law&B 92
Cleghorn, Cheree Briggs 1945- WhoAmW 93, WhoE 93
Cleghorn, G. Dean 1951- WhoSSW 93
Cleghorn, John E. 1941- St&PR 93
Cleghorn, John Edward 1941- WhoAm 92
Cleghorn, Leslie 1941- St&PR 93
Cleghorn, Reese 1930- WhoAm 92, WhoWrEP 92
Clelan, Beverly M. 1939- St&PR 93
Clelan, Gerald B. 1936- St&PR 93
Cleland, Andrew Wallace 1946- WhoE 93, WhoEmL 93
Cleland, Charles Carr 1924- WhoAm 92, WhoSSW 93
Cleland, David C. 1932- St&PR 93
Cleland, Douglas Stewart 1952- WhoEmL 93
Cleland, Edward Gordon 1949- WhoEmL 93
Cleland, Joseph Maxwell 1942- WhoAm 92, WhoSSW 93
Cleland, Philip B. 1945- St&PR 93
Cleland, Robert Erksine 1932- WhoAm 92
Cleland, Robert Hardy 1947- WhoAm 92
Cleland, Robert Lindbergh 1927- WhoAm 92
Cleland, Sherrill 1924- WhoAm 92
Cleland, Sydney Shepherd Law&B 92
Cleland, William Wallace 1930- WhoAm 92
Clelland, Richard Cook 1921- WhoAm 92, WhoE 93
Clelland, Robert Theodore 1943- WhoSSW 93
Clem, Alan Leland 1929- WhoAm 92
Clem, Donald Y. 1926- St&PR 93
Clem, Elizabeth Ann Stumpf 1945- WhoAmW 93
Clem, James Allen 1934- St&PR 93
Clem, John Richard 1938- WhoAm 92
Clem, Lester William 1934- WhoAm 92
Clem, Patricia Mary 1960- WhoAmW 93
Clem, Ralph 1943- ScF&FL 92
Clem, Wendy Lee 1950- WhoWrEP 92
Clemans, Bertha Johanna 1875- AmWomPl
Clemans, Jerald Garrow 1930- St&PR 93
Clemen, John Douglas 1944- WhoE 93
Clemence, Bruce ScF&FL 92
Clemence, Roger Davidson 1936- WhoAm 92
Clemenceau, Georges 1841-1929 BioIn 17
Clemenceau, Georges 1849-1929 DcTwHis
Clemencic, Rene 1928- Baker 92
Clemendor, Anthony Arnold 1933- WhoE 93, WhoWor 93
Clemenhagen, Carol Jane 1954- WhoAm 92
Clemens, Alvin H. St&PR 93
Clemens, Alvin Honey 1937- WhoAm 92
Clemens, Douglas H. 1939- St&PR 93
Clemens, Frank J., Jr. Law&B 92
Clemens, Frank Joseph, Jr. 1940- St&PR 93
Clemens, Hans 1890-1958 Baker 92
Clemens, James R. 1952- St&PR 93
Clemens, Jon K. 1938- St&PR 93
Clemens, Mark George 1950- WhoE 93
Clemens, Mary Etcheverry 1953- St&PR 93
Clemens, Michael John WhoScE 91-1
Clemens, Michael Roland 1948- WhoWor 93
Clemens, Michael Terrence 1950- WhoEmL 93, WhoWor 93
Clemens, P. Blaine 1937- St&PR 93
Clemens, Peter John, III 1943- St&PR 93, WhoAm 92
Clemens, Philip A. 1949- St&PR 93
Clemens, Richard Glenn 1940- WhoAm 92
Clemens, Richard Phillip 1933- St&PR 93
Clemens, Rodgers ScF&FL 92
Clemens, Roger BioIn 17
Clemens, Roger 1962- WhoAm 92
Clemens, Ronald E. 1951- St&PR 93
Clemens, Samuel L. ScF&FL 92
Clemens, Samuel Langhorne GayN
Clemens, Samuel Langhorne 1835-1910 BioIn 17, JrnUS, MajAI [port]
Clemens, Tammy Leah 1958- WhoAmW 93, WhoEmL 93, WhoWor 93
Clemens, Travis G. Law&B 92
Clemens, Walter H. 1928- St&PR 93
Clemens non Papa c. 1510-1555? Baker 92
Clement, III c. 1025-1100 OxDcByz
Clement, V c. 1260-1314 OxDcByz
Clement, VI 1291-1352 OxDcByz
Clement, IX, Pope 1600-1669 BioIn 17
Clement, Aeron 1936?-1989 ScF&FL 92
Clement, Allan M., III 1955- WhoIns 93
Clement, Allan Montgomery, III 1955- St&PR 93
Clement, Alvis Macon 1912- WhoAm 92
Clement, Betsy Kay 1952- WhoEmL 93

Clement, Bob 1943- CngDr 91, WhoAm 92, WhoSSW 93
Clement, Coy 1950- St&PR 93
Clement, Dale E. 1933- St&PR 93
Clement, Dale Eugene 1933- WhoAm 92
Clement, Dallas Brent 1940- WhoWrEP 92
Clement, Daniel G. Law&B 92
Clement, Daniel Roy, III 1943- WhoWor 93
Clement, David Eastman 1936- WhoSSW 93
Clement, David Hale 1909-1991 BioIn 17
Clement, Denis Arthur Law&B 92
Clement, Dick 1937- MiSFD 9
Clement, Donald D. 1929- WhoIns 93
Clement, Edmond 1867-1928 OxDcOp
Clement, Edmond (Frederic-Jean) 1867-1928 Baker 92
Clement, Edward Henry 1843-1920 JrnUS
Clement, F.-M. 1927- WhoScE 91-2
Clement, (Jacques) Felix (Alfred) 1822-1885 Baker 92
Clement, Francois ScF&FL 92
Clement, Franz 1780-1842 Baker 92
Clement, Gregory Vance 1928- WhoWrEP 92
Clement, Hal 1922- BioIn 17, ConAu 16AS [port], ScF&FL 92
Clement, Henry ScF&FL 92
Clement, Henry Joseph, Jr. 1942- St&PR 93, WhoAm 92
Clement, Hope Elizabeth Anna 1930- WhoAm 92
Clement, Howard Wheeler 1917- WhoAm 92
Clement, J. Robert 1944- WhoE 93
Clement, Jacob Baker 92
Clement, Jacquelyn Alma 1943- WhoAmW 93
Clement, James Barney 1945- WhoAm 92
Clement, Janice Faye 1946- WhoAmW 93
Clement, Jean M. 1948- WhoEmL 93
Clement, Jean-Michel 1934- WhoScE 91-2
Clement, John 1932- WhoAm 92
Clement, Joseph Dale 1928- WhoAm 92
Clement, Josephine Dobbs AfrAmBi [port]
Clement, Leslie Joseph, Jr. 1948- WhoEmL 93
Clement, Maude Moore AmWomPl
Clement, Meredith Owen 1926- WhoAm 92
Clement, Patricia Ellen 1951- St&PR 93
Clement, Rene 1913- MiSFD 9
Clement, Rene Jean 1913- WhoWor 93
Clement, Richard F. 1906- St&PR 93
Clement, Richard Francis 1906- WhoAm 92, WhoWor 93
Clement, Robert C. 1952- St&PR 93
Clement, Robert William 1927- WhoAm 92
Clement, Shirley George 1926- WhoAmW 93
Clement, Thomas Earl 1932- WhoAm 92
Clement, William Alexander 1912- WhoAm 92
Clemente, Alice Rodrigues 1934- WhoAmW 93
Clemente, Arthur Clarence 1947- St&PR 93
Clemente, Carmine Domenic 1928- WhoAm 92
Clemente, Celestino 1922- WhoAm 92
Clemente, Constantine Louis Law&B 92
Clemente, Dennis Taylor 1939- St&PR 93
Clemente, Francesco BioIn 17
Clemente, Francesco 1952- News 92 [port]
Clemente, Frank 1945- WhoAm 92
Clemente, Giantelice WhoScE 91-3
Clemente, Holly Anne WhoWor 93
Clemente, Leopold M. 1938- St&PR 93
Clemente, Lilia C. BioIn 17
Clemente, Lilia C. 1941- St&PR 93
Clemente, Mark Andrew 1951- WhoEmL 93
Clemente, Robert Stephen 1956- WhoE 93, WhoEmL 93
Clemente, Roberto 1934-1972 BioIn 17, HispAmA [port]
Clementel, Etienne 1864-1936 BioIn 17
Clementi, Aldo 1925- Baker 92
Clementi, Francesco 1936- WhoScE 91-3
Clementi, Muzio 1752-1832 Baker 92
Clementia 1878- AmWomPl
Clement-O'Brien, Karen 1956- WhoE 93
Clement Of Alexandria c. 150-c. 215 OxDcByz
Clement Of Ohrid OxDcByz
Clements, Alan 1948- WhoWor 93
Clements, Allen, Jr. 1924- WhoWor 93
Clements, Andrea Deason 1961- WhoSSW 93
Clements, Arthur L. 1932- WhoWrEP 92
Clements, Barbara Saunders 1947- WhoAmW 93
Clements, Bernadette Stone 1943- WhoAm 92
Clements, Brian Matthew 1946- WhoAm 92, WhoE 93, WhoWor 93
Clements, Bruce 1931- DcAmChF 1960, WhoAm 92
Clements, Bruce W. St&PR 93
Clements, Bruce W. 1942- WhoIns 93
Clements, Bruce William Law&B 92
Clements, Christopher John 1946- WhoUN 92
Clements, Claudine E. AmWomPl
Clements, Dale Martin 1947- St&PR 93
Clements, David ScF&FL 92
Clements, Donald McKenzie, Jr. Law&B 92
Clements, Donald Ray 1949- WhoEmL 93
Clements, Douglas Harvey 1950- WhoE 93
Clements, Earle C. 1896-1985 PolPar
Clements, Emilia Gonzalez 1944- WhoAm 92
Clements, Ernest Frank 1957- WhoSSW 93
Clements, Fred Preston 1954- WhoWrEP 92
Clements, George BioIn 17
Clements, George Gerald 1939- St&PR 93
Clements, Gregory Neil Law&B 92
Clements, Harold 1932- St&PR 93
Clements, James A. BioIn 17
Clements, James D. Law&B 92
Clements, James David 1931- WhoAm 92, WhoWor 93
Clements, James Franklin 1927- St&PR 93
Clements, Jamie Hager 1957- WhoEmL 93
Clements, John Allen 1923- WhoAm 92
Clements, John B. 1928- St&PR 93
Clements, John Barklie WhoScE 91-1
Clements, John Brian 1928- WhoAm 92
Clements, John David 1938- St&PR 93
Clements, John Robert 1950- WhoEmL 93
Clements, Jonathan David 1963- WhoE 93
Clements, Joyce BioIn 17
Clements, Kevin Anthony 1941- WhoAm 92
Clements, Lynne Fleming 1945- WhoAmW 93, WhoE 93
Clements, Mannen d1887 BioIn 17
Clements, Mannie d1908 BioIn 17
Clements, Maria Gasbarre 1961- WhoEmL 93
Clements, Mark A. ScF&FL 92
Clements, Mary A. 1955- ConAu 136
Clements, Michael Reid 1943- St&PR 93
Clements, Neal Woodson 1926- WhoAm 92
Clements, Patricia Dawn 1940- WhoAmW 93
Clements, Paul Gregory 1955- WhoSSW 93
Clements, Paula Dianne 1947- WhoSSW 93
Clements, R.F. WhoScE 91-1
Clements, Richard Hamer 1926- St&PR 93
Clements, Robert 1932- St&PR 93, WhoAm 92
Clements, Robert John 1912- WhoAm 92
Clements, Ron MiSFD 9
Clements, Stephen A. 1933- St&PR 93
Clements, William Perry, Jr. 1917- WhoAm 92, WhoWor 93
Clements, William Thomas 1947- WhoAm 92
Clements-Jewery, Keith Charles WhoScE 91-1
Clement Smoljatic OxDcByz
Clementson, Judith Ann 1951- WhoE 93
Clemetson, Charles Alan Blake 1923- WhoAm 92
Clemins, Archie Ray 1943- WhoAm 92
Cleminshaw, Frank Foster 1911- WhoAm 92
Clemm, John 1690-1762 Baker 92
Clemm, John, Jr. Baker 92
Clemmens, Albert Jonathan 1953- WhoEmL 93
Clemmer, Leon 1926- WhoE 93
Clemmer, Rhonda Ann 1966- WhoSSW 93
Clemmey, James Q. 1936- St&PR 93
Clemmey, John L., III 1945- St&PR 93
Clemmons, Barry Wayne 1949- WhoEmL 93, WhoSSW 93
Clemmons, David Robert 1947- WhoEmL 93
Clemmons, Gordon L. 1920- St&PR 93
Clemmons, James Glenn 1952- WhoEmL 93
Clemmons, Jane Goodrich 1934- WhoAm 92
Clemon, U. W. 1943- WhoAm 92
Clemons, D. Gradon 1947- St&PR 93
Clemons, Hardy Smith 1933- WhoSSW 93
Clemons, Jane A. 1946- WhoAmW 93
Clemons, John Robert 1948- WhoAm 92
Clemons, Julie Payne 1948- WhoAmW 93, WhoEmL 93
Clemons, Ralph Hardy, Jr. 1926- WhoAm 92
Clemons, Robert Bissell, III 1949- WhoSSW 93
Clemons, V. Gordon St&PR 93
Clemons, Walter 1929- WhoAm 92
Clench, Mary Heimerdinger 1932- WhoSSW 93
Clendaniel, Fontaine Cowan 1951- WhoEmL 93
Clendenen, Bill ScF&FL 92
Clendenen, Ronald L. Law&B 92
Clendenin, Craig Haworth Law&B 92
Clendenin, John L. 1934- St&PR 93, WhoAm 92
Clendenin, John L. 1935- WhoSSW 93
Clendenin, Maria L. St&PR 93
Clendenning, Bonnie Ryon 1945- WhoE 93
Clendenning, William Edmund 1931- WhoAm 92
Clendinen, James Augustus 1910-1991 BioIn 17
Clendinnen, Inga 1934- ConAu 138
Clennan, John Joseph 1951- WhoEmL 93
Clennon, David BioIn 17
Cleombrotus d371BC HarEnMi
Cleomenes, I 540BC-488BC HarEnMi
Cleomenes, III c. 265BC-219BC HarEnMi
Cleon c. 470BC-422BC HarEnMi
Cleonides fl. 2nd cent.- Baker 92
Cleopatra 69?BC-30BC OxDcOp
Cleopatra, Queen of Egypt d30BC BioIn 17
Cleophon c. 460BC-404BC HarEnMi
Clepper, Frank D. 1934- St&PR 93
Clepper, Lee B. 1950- St&PR 93
Clerambault, Cesar Francois Nicolas 1700-1760 See Clerambault, Louis Nicolas 1676-1749 Baker 92
Clerambault, Louis Nicolas 1676-1749 Baker 92
Clerc, Charles 1926- ScF&FL 92
Clerc, J.T. 1934- WhoScE 91-4
Clerc, Jeanne Marie 1954- WhoEmL 93
Clerc, Oliver C., Jr. 1947- St&PR 93
Clercx, Suzanne 1910-1985 Baker 92
Clereau, Pierre fl. 16th cent.- Baker 92
Clerehugh, G. WhoScE 91-1
Clerfayt, Charles Joseph de Croix, Count of 1733-1798 HarEnMi
Clergue, Lucien 1934- BioIn 17
Clergue, Lucien Georges 1934- WhoAm 92, WhoWor 93
Clerice, Justin 1863-1908 Baker 92
Clerico, John A. 1941- St&PR 93
Clerico, John Anthony 1941- WhoAm 92
Clerisme, Joseph Roosevelt 1950- WhoE 93
Clerisseau, Charles Louis 1722-1820 BioIn 17
Clerk, Jayana Jashwantlal 1936- WhoE 93
Clerk, Jean E. Law&B 92
Clerk, John, de Whalale BioIn 17
Clerk, N. W. MajAI
Clerkin, Eugene Patrick 1931- WhoAm 92
Clerkin, Thomas 1950- St&PR 93
Clermont, Kevin Michael 1945- WhoAm 92
Clermont, Yves Wilfrid 1926- WhoAm 92
Clery, Howard BioIn 17
Clery, Jeanne Ann BioIn 17
Clery, Val 1924- ScF&FL 92
Clesi, Bret Alden 1958- WhoEmL 93, WhoSSW 93
Clesi, Frank Joseph 1928- St&PR 93
Cleva, Fausto (Angelo) 1902-1971 Baker 92
Cleve, George 1936- WhoAm 92
Cleve, Halfdan 1879-1951 Baker 92
Cleve, Hartwig K. 1928- WhoScE 91-3
Cleve, Hartwig Karl 1928- WhoWor 93
Cleve, John ConAu 37NR, ScF&FL 92
Cleve-Bannister, Candida 1957- WhoEmL 93
Cleveland, Bernard Fred 1937- WhoSSW 93
Cleveland, C.E. Thomas 1947- St&PR 93
Cleveland, Carl Service, Jr. 1918- WhoWor 93
Cleveland, Ceil Margaret Ellen 1938- WhoWrEP 92
Cleveland, David R. Law&B 92
Cleveland, Donald Leslie 1938- WhoAm 92
Cleveland, Edna Charlotte 1930- WhoAmW 93
Cleveland, Edward Allen 1950- WhoEmL 93
Cleveland, Frances Folsom BioIn 17
Cleveland, Grover 1837-1908 BioIn 17, GayN, PolPar
Cleveland, Harlan 1918- WhoAm 92, WhoWor 93
Cleveland, Helen Storey 1930- WhoAmW 93
Cleveland, Jack 1828-1863 BioIn 17
Cleveland, James BioIn 17
Cleveland, James 1931-1991 AnObit 1991, Baker 92
Cleveland, James Colgate 1920- WhoAm 92
Cleveland, Joan 1932- St&PR 93
Cleveland, John 1613-1658 DcLB 126 [port]
Cleveland, John Edward 1940- St&PR 93
Cleveland, John W. 1949- WhoIns 93
Cleveland, Joseph H. Law&B 92
Cleveland, Kenneth Charles 1933- St&PR 93
Cleveland, Mary Louise 1922- WhoSSW 93
Cleveland, Paul Matthews 1931- WhoAm 92, WhoWor 93
Cleveland, Peggy Rose Richey 1929- WhoAm 92, WhoAmW 93
Cleveland, Peter Watkins 1955- WhoEmL 93
Cleveland, Richard Joseph 1932- WhoAm 92
Cleveland, Robert W. d1990 BioIn 17
Cleveland, Robert W. 1910- St&PR 93
Cleveland, Rose Elizabeth 1846-1918 BioIn 17
Cleveland, Susan Elizabeth 1946- WhoAm 92
Cleveland, Veronica M. 1958- St&PR 93
Cleven, Carol Chapman 1928- WhoAmW 93
Clevenger, Arthur Frank 1928- St&PR 93
Clevenger, Charles 1941- WhoE 93
Clevenger, Ernest A. 1953- St&PR 93
Clevenger, Ernest Allen, III 1953- WhoEmL 93, WhoSSW 93
Clevenger, Jerry L. 1953- WhoEmL 93
Clevenger, Penelope 1940- WhoAmW 93
Clevenger, Raymond C., III 1937- CngDr 91, WhoAm 92, WhoE 93
Clevenger, Robert Vincent 1921- WhoAm 92, WhoWor 93
Clevenger, Rose Weaver AmWomPl
Clevenger, Roy Edward 1953- WhoE 93, WhoEmL 93, WhoWor 93
Clevenger, Sarah 1926- WhoAm 92
Clevenger, Thomas Ramsey 1935- WhoAm 92
Clevenger, William Thomas 1950- WhoEmL 93, WhoSSW 93
Clever, Geraldine 1930- St&PR 93, WhoAm 92
Clever, Linda Hawes WhoAm 92, WhoAmW 93
Clever, Warren Glenn 1918- WhoAm 92
Cleverdon, Walter Irving 1933- St&PR 93
Clevett, Denise Ann 1962- WhoEmL 93
Clew, Harry T. St&PR 93
Clewes, Howard 1912-1988 ScF&FL 92
Clewett, Kenneth Vaughn 1923- WhoAm 92
Clewis, Charlotte Wright Staub 1935- WhoAmW 93
Clewley, Jonathan P. WhoScE 91-1
Clexton, Edward William, Jr. 1937- WhoAm 92
Cliburn, Rildia Bee O'Bryan BioIn 17
Cliburn, Van 1934- Baker 92, BioIn 17, WhoAm 92
Click, David Forrest 1947- WhoEmL 93
Click, John William 1936- WhoAm 92, WhoSSW 93
Clicquot Baker 92
Clicquot, Francois-Henri 1732-1790 Baker 92
Clicquot, Jean-Baptiste 1678-1746 Baker 92
Clicquot, Louis-Alexandre c. 1680-1760 Baker 92
Clicquot, Robert Baker 92
Cliett, Charles Buren 1924- WhoAm 92, WhoSSW 93
Cliff, Jimmy 1948- ConMus 8 [port]
Cliff, John William, Jr. 1949- WhoEmL 93
Cliff, Johnnie Marie 1935- WhoAmW 93, WhoWor 93
Cliff, Judith Anita 1941- WhoAm 92, WhoAmW 93
Cliff, Michelle 1946- ConAu 39NR
Cliff, Ronald Laird 1929- St&PR 93, WhoAm 92
Cliff, Steven Burris 1952- WhoEmL 93, WhoSSW 93
Cliff, Walter Conway 1932- WhoAm 92
Cliffe, Dan Mack 1946- WhoSSW 93
Cliffe, Frederic 1857-1931 Baker 92
Clifford, Ann Tharp 1937- WhoSSW 93
Clifford, Anne 1590-1676 BioIn 17
Clifford, Carmella Marie 1955- WhoE 93
Clifford, Clark 1906- ColdWar 1 [port]
Clifford, Clark M. 1906- BioIn 17, PolPar
Clifford, Clark McAdams 1906- St&PR 93, WhoAm 92, WhoE 93, WhoWor 93
Clifford, Deborah Pickman 1933- ConAu 138
Clifford, Donald Francis, Jr. 1935- WhoAm 92

Clifford, Eamonn Sigerson 1950- *WhoWor 93*
Clifford, Francesca Bishop 1959- *WhoEmL 93*
Clifford, Garry Carroll 1934- *WhoAmW 93*
Clifford, George Orr 1924- *WhoAm 92*
Clifford, Geraldine Marie Joncich 1931- *WhoAm 92, WhoAmW 93*
Clifford, Graeme *MiSFD 9*
Clifford, Helen C. *AmWomPl*
Clifford, J(ohn) Garry 1942- *ConAu 40NR*
Clifford, James Lowry 1901-1978 *BioIn 17*
Clifford, James Michael 1937- *WhoAm 92*
Clifford, John Edmund 1943- *WhoE 93*
Clifford, John Grant *Law&B 92*
Clifford, John Leger 1950- *WhoEmL 93*
Clifford, John Michael 1947- *WhoEmL 93*
Clifford, John Stephen 1951- *WhoE 93*
Clifford, Joseph P. 1943- *WhoAm 92*
Clifford, Kim J. *Law&B 92*
Clifford, Lawrence M. 1935- *WhoAm 92*
Clifford, Lawrence M. 1955- *St&PR 93*
Clifford, Leon Albert 1919- *WhoE 93*
Clifford, Linda *BioIn 17*
Clifford, Lucy Lane d1929 *AmWomPl*
Clifford, Margaret Ellen *AmWomPl*
Clifford, Margaret Louise 1920- *WhoAm 92*
Clifford, Margaret M. 1936- *WhoAmW 93*
Clifford, Maurice Cecil 1920- *WhoAm 92*
Clifford, Nathan 1803-1881 *OxCSupC [port]*
Clifford, Nicholas Rowland 1930- *WhoAm 92*
Clifford, Nigel Robert Leslie 1949- *WhoWor 93*
Clifford, Paul Ingraham 1914- *WhoSSW 93, WhoWor 93*
Clifford, Peter Bulkeley 1931- *WhoE 93*
Clifford, Rachel Mark *SmATA 72*
Clifford, Ralph D. 1954- *WhoEmL 93*
Clifford, Robert Anderson 1957- *WhoEmL 93*
Clifford, Robert L. 1924- *WhoAm 92*
Clifford, Robert William 1937- *WhoAm 92*
Clifford, Sarah 1916-1976 *ScF&FL 92*
Clifford, Sidney, Jr. 1937- *WhoE 93*
Clifford, Steven A. 1942- *St&PR 93*
Clifford, Steven Francis 1943- *WhoAm 92, WhoWor 93*
Clifford, Stewart Burnett 1929- *WhoAm 92, WhoE 93, WhoWor 93*
Clifford, Sylvester 1929- *WhoAm 92*
Clifford, Terry W. 1937- *St&PR 93*
Clifford, Theresa Mary Shea 1934- *WhoAmW 93*
Clifford, Thomas John 1921- *WhoAm 92*
Clifford, Timothy 1946- *BioIn 17, WhoWor 93*
Clifford Rose, Frank 1926- *WhoScE 91-1*
Clifft, Ricky Conway 1950- *WhoSSW 93*
Clift, Elayne G. 1943- *WhoE 93*
Clift, G.W. 1952- *WhoWrEP 92*
Clift, Harlond d1992 *NewYTBS 92*
Clift, Harlond 1912-1992 *BioIn 17*
Clift, Harlond Benton 1912- *BiDAMSp 1989*
Clift, Montgomery 1920-1966 *BioIn 17, IntDcF 2-3 [port]*
Clift, Roland *WhoScE 91-1*
Clift, William Brooks, III 1944- *WhoAm 92*
Clift, William Orrin 1914- *WhoAm 92*
Clifton, Anne Rutenber 1938- *WhoAm 92, WhoAmW 93, WhoE 93*
Clifton, Chester Victor 1913-1991 *BioIn 17*
Clifton, Dan d1897 *BioIn 17*
Clifton, Donald O. 1924- *St&PR 93*
Clifton, Elwyn Martin 1948- *St&PR 93*
Clifton, Ethel *AmWomPl*
Clifton, Flea 1909- *BioIn 17*
Clifton, Harold Ray 1946- *WhoEmL 93*
Clifton, Herman Earl 1909- *BioIn 17*
Clifton, James Albert 1923- *WhoAm 92*
Clifton, John Hill *Law&B 92*
Clifton, John Hill 1946- *St&PR 93*
Clifton, John O. 1947- *St&PR 93*
Clifton, Judy Raelene 1946- *WhoAmW 93*
Clifton, Linda Jane 1940- *WhoAmW 93, WhoWrEP 92*
Clifton, Lucille 1936- *BioIn 17, BlkAull 92, SmATA 69 [port]*
Clifton, (Thelma) Lucille 1936- *MajAI [port]*
Clifton, Marcella Dawn 1956- *WhoAmW 93*
Clifton, Mark A. *BioIn 17*
Clifton, Mark (Irvin) 1906-1963 *ConAu 136, ScF&FL 92*
Clifton, Mary A. Delano *AmWomPl*
Clifton, Merritt Robin 1953- *WhoWrEP 92*
Clifton, Michael Edward 1949- *WhoEmL 93*
Clifton, Nat *BioIn 17*
Clifton, Paul H. 1947- *St&PR 93*
Clifton, Paul Hoot, Jr. 1947- *WhoAm 92*
Clifton, Peter *MiSFD 9*
Clifton, Rachel Keen 1937- *WhoAmW 93*
Clifton, Richard Randall 1950- *WhoEmL 93*
Clifton, Rodney James 1937- *WhoAm 92*
Clifton, Russell B. 1930- *WhoAm 92*
Clifton, Sweetwater *BioIn 17*
Clifton, William Clay *Law&B 92*
Clifton, William Lacy 1920- *St&PR 93*
Cligrow, Edward Thomas, Jr. 1934- *WhoAm 92*
Clijsters, H. 1934- *WhoScE 91-2*
Climan, Richard Elliot 1953- *WhoEmL 93*
Climenko, Jesse 1904- *St&PR 93*
Climenson, Peggy Ann *Law&B 92*
Climer, James Alan 1954- *WhoEmL 93*
Climko, Robert Paul 1953- *WhoEmL 93*
Climo, Lawrence Hanon 1938- *WhoE 93*
Climo, Shirley 1928- *ScF&FL 92*
Climo, Skipton Hill 1868-1937 *HarEnMi*
Clinard, Marshall Barron 1911- *WhoAm 92*
Clinard, Robert Noel 1946- *WhoEmL 93*
Clinch, Harry Anselm 1908- *WhoAm 92*
Clinch, J. Houstoun M., Jr. 1934- *St&PR 93*
Clinch, Paul G. 1947- *WhoScE 91-3*
Clinchy, Richard Alexander, III 1943- *WhoSSW 93*
Clinchy, Walter G. 1911- *St&PR 93*
Cline, Bobby James 1932- *WhoAm 92*
Cline, C. Bob 1946- *St&PR 93*
Cline, C. Terry, Jr. 1935- *ScF&FL 92*
Cline, Carolyn Joan 1941- *WhoAmW 93, WhoWor 93*
Cline, Charles William 1937- *WhoAm 92, WhoWor 93, WhoWrEP 92*
Cline, Clarence Lee 1905- *WhoAm 92*
Cline, Craig Emerson 1951- *WhoEmL 93*
Cline, Darrell Eugene 1962- *WhoEmL 93*
Cline, Denna Lee 1943- *St&PR 93*
Cline, Dorothy May Stammerjohn 1915- *WhoWor 93*
Cline, Edward 1946- *ConAu 40NR*
Cline, Edward Agni 1958- *WhoSSW 93*
Cline, Edward F. 1892-1961 *MiSFD 9N*
Cline, Fred Albert, Jr. 1929- *WhoWor 93*
Cline, Gerald L. *Law&B 92*
Cline, Gibbons Dee 1941- *St&PR 93*
Cline, Glen Edwin 1920- *WhoAm 92*
Cline, Goeffrey Scott *Law&B 92*
Cline, Gregory Paul 1960- *WhoEmL 93*
Cline, Harold Brantley, Jr. 1951- *WhoSSW 93*
Cline, Janice Claire 1945- *WhoE 93*
Cline, Jay A. 1936- *St&PR 93*
Cline, Jess 1941- *St&PR 93*
Cline, John A. *WhoAm 92*
Cline, John Carroll 1955- *WhoE 93*
Cline, Linda 1941- *ScF&FL 92*
Cline, Linda Blair 1950- *WhoAmW 93, WhoEmL 93*
Cline, Marlin George 1909- *WhoE 93*
Cline, Martin Jay 1934- *WhoAm 92*
Cline, Michael Robert 1949- *WhoEmL 93*
Cline, Nancy Lieberman- 1958- *BioIn 17*
Cline, Ned Aubrey 1938- *WhoSSW 93*
Cline, Patricia Dickenson d1991 *BioIn 17*
Cline, Patricia Taylor 1954- *WhoSSW 93*
Cline, Patsy 1932-1963 *Baker 92, BioIn 17*
Cline, Paul Charles 1933- *WhoAm 92*
Cline, Pauline M. 1947- *WhoAmW 93*
Cline, Peter Joseph 1946- *St&PR 93*
Cline, Philip Eugene 1933- *St&PR 93*
Cline, Randall Kent 1948- *WhoE 93*
Cline, Ray Steiner 1918- *WhoAm 92, WhoWor 93*
Cline, Richard Allan 1961- *WhoWrEP 92*
Cline, Richard Gordon 1935- *St&PR 93, WhoAm 92*
Cline, Richard Lee 1942- *St&PR 93, WhoAm 92*
Cline, Robert Stanley 1937- *St&PR 93, WhoAm 92*
Cline, Robert Theodore 1941- *St&PR 93*
Cline, Robert Thomas 1925- *WhoSSW 93, WhoWor 93*
Cline, Roger M. 1935- *St&PR 93*
Cline, Shelia Rhonda 1953- *WhoSSW 93*
Cline, Stewart Martin 1945- *St&PR 93*
Cline, Thomas Farrell 1953- *WhoEmL 93*
Cline, Thomas William 1932- *WhoAm 92*
Cline, Tim 1942- *WhoWrEP 92*
Cline, Van H. *Law&B 92*
Cline, Vivian M. *Law&B 92*
Cline, William Earl 1946- *WhoSSW 93*
Cline, William Richard 1941- *WhoAm 92*
Cline, Wilson Ettason 1914- *WhoWor 93*
Clinefelter, Ruth Elizabeth Wright 1930- *WhoAmW 93*
Clingenpeel, Joanne *BioIn 17*
Clinger, William F., Jr. 1929- *CngDr 91*
Clinger, William Floyd, Jr. 1929- *WhoAm 92, WhoE 93*
Clingerman, Edgar Allen 1934- *St&PR 93*
Clingerman, Edgar Allen, Sr. 1934- *WhoSSW 93*
Clingerman, Roger Brian 1961- *WhoE 93*
Clingman, Stephen Roy 1954- *WhoE 93*
Clingman, William Herbert, Jr. 1929- *WhoSSW 93, WhoWor 93*
Clink, Stephen Henry 1911- *WhoAm 92*
Clinkenbeard, James Howard 1950- *WhoEmL 93, WhoSSW 93*
Clinkenbeard, Pamela Rae 1955- *WhoE 93*
Clinkscale, David Jay 1949- *WhoSSW 93*
Clinkscales, William Abner, Jr. 1928- *WhoAm 92, WhoWor 93*
Clint, R.G. *Law&B 92*
Clinton, Bill 1946- *BioIn 17, NewYTBS 92 [port], News 92 [port], WhoAm 92, WhoEmL 93, WhoSSW 93, WhoWor 93*
Clinton, Cathleen Ann 1950- *WhoEmL 93*
Clinton, Charles A. *WhoIns 93*
Clinton, (Lloyd) D(eWitt) 1946- *ConAu 38NR*
Clinton, Daniel D., Jr. 1930- *St&PR 93*
Clinton, De Witt 1769-1828 *BioIn 17*
Clinton, DeWitt 1769-1828 *PolPar*
Clinton, Dirk *MajAI*
Clinton, Dorothy Randle 1925- *WhoWrEP 92*
Clinton, Edward Fiennes 1512-1585 *HarEnMi*
Clinton, George *BioIn 17*
Clinton, George 1739-1812 *PolPar*
Clinton, George 1940- *SoulM*
Clinton, Gordon Stanley 1920- *WhoAm 92*
Clinton, Henry 1738-1795 *HarEnMi*
Clinton, Hillary *BioIn 17, NewYTBS 92 [port]*
Clinton, Hillary Rodham 1947- *News 93-2 [port], WhoAmW 93, WhoEmL 93*
Clinton, Inez Funk *AmWomPl*
Clinton, J. Hart 1905- *St&PR 93*
Clinton, James 1733-1812 *HarEnMi*
Clinton, James Harmon 1946- *WhoAm 92*
Clinton, Jeff *ScF&FL 92, WhoWrEP 92*
Clinton, Joseph E. 1948- *WhoAm 92*
Clinton, Judith Mary Myers 1945- *WhoAmW 93*
Clinton, Lawrence Paul 1945- *WhoE 93*
Clinton, Lloyd DeWitt 1946- *WhoWrEP 92*
Clinton, Lynne Fox *AmWomPl*
Clinton, Mariann Hancock 1933- *WhoAm 92*
Clinton, Michael *WhoE 93*
Clinton, Richard Lee 1938- *WhoWrEP 92*
Clinton, Richard M. 1941- *WhoAm 92*
Clinton, Ricky John 1954- *WhoE 93*
Clinton, Roger *BioIn 17, NewYTBS 92 [port]*
Clinton, Timothy Edward 1960- *WhoEmL 93*
Clinton, Tracy Peter, Sr. 1948- *WhoEmL 93, WhoSSW 93*
Clinton, William Henry 1769-1846 *HarEnMi*
Clippard, James A. 1942- *St&PR 93*
Clippeleyr, Hans Edward 1957- *WhoWor 93*
Clipper, Terry *BioIn 17*
Clippert, Charles Frederick 1931- *WhoAm 92, WhoWor 93*
Clippinger, Scott 1943- *St&PR 93*
Clipsham, Robert Charles 1955- *WhoWor 93*
Clise, Alfred Hammer 1920- *St&PR 93*
Clisson, Olivier de 1336-1407 *HarEnMi*
Clive, Henry *BioIn 17*
Clive, Kitty 1711-1785 *BioIn 17*
Clive, Robert 1725-1774 *HarEnMi*
Cliver, Dean Otis 1935- *WhoAm 92*
Clizbe, John Anthony 1942- *WhoAm 92, WhoE 93*
Clizer, Herald Kenneth 1932- *St&PR 93*
Cloar, Carroll 1913- *BioIn 17, WhoAm 92*
Cloarec, M. *WhoScE 91-2*
Cloche, Maurice 1907-1990 *BioIn 17*
Clock, Herbert 1890-1979 *ScF&FL 92*
Clock, Kathleen Elizabeth *WhoE 93*
Clocksin, William Frederick *WhoScE 91-1*
Clode, Joao *WhoScE 91-3*
Clodfelter, Daniel Gray 1950- *WhoEmL 93*
Clodfelter, Donald Glen 1933- *St&PR 93*
Clodgo, Phillip David 1946- *WhoSSW 93*
Clodius, Julia Marie 1958- *WhoAmW 93*
Clodius, Leo John 1930- *WhoScE 91-4*
Clodius, Robert LeRoy 1921- *WhoAm 92, WhoWor 93*
Clodius Albinus d197 *HarEnMi*
Clodman, Jo Mira 1954- *St&PR 93, WhoAm 92*
Cloes, Roger Arthur Josef 1956- *WhoWor 93*
Clofine, Henry Lawrence 1940- *St&PR 93*
Clogan, Paul Maurice 1934- *WhoAm 92*
Clogg, Richard Bruce 1949- *WhoEmL 93*
Clogg, William G. 1944- *St&PR 93*
Cloherty, Michael J. 1947- *St&PR 93*
Clohesy, Stephanie J. 1948- *WhoEmL 93*
Cloitre, Heather A. 1941- *St&PR 93*
Cloitre, Louis 1929- *St&PR 93*
Cloitre, Roger 1930- *St&PR 93*
Cloke, Richard 1916- *ScF&FL 92*
Clokey, Art *MiSFD 9*
Clokey, Belle Brown *AmWomPl*
Clokey, Frank R. *Law&B 92*
Clokey, Frank R. 1939- *WhoAm 92*
Clokey, Joseph Waddell 1890-1960 *Baker 92*
Clonch, Leslie Allen, Jr. 1961- *WhoSSW 93, WhoWor 93*
Clond, Michael B. 1961- *St&PR 93*
Cloney, Richard M. 1941- *St&PR 93*
Cloney, Richard Morgan 1941- *WhoAm 92*
Cloninger, Claude Robert 1944- *WhoAm 92, WhoWor 93*
Cloninger, Eugene F. 1941- *St&PR 93*
Cloninger, Kriss, III 1947- *WhoAm 92*
Clonts, George Gary 1940- *WhoSSW 93*
Clonts, Thomas Michael 1942- *St&PR 93*
Cloonan, Clifford B. 1928- *WhoAm 92*
Cloonan, James Brian 1931- *WhoAm 92*
Cloonan, William James 1942- *WhoSSW 93*
Clooney, Rosemary *BioIn 17*
Clooney, Rosemary 1928- *Baker 92, ConMus 9 [port]*
Clooney, Thomas J. 1948- *St&PR 93*
Clopet, Julian *BioIn 17*
Clopine, Marjorie Showers 1914- *WhoAmW 93, WhoSSW 93, WhoWor 93*
Clopine, Sandra Lou 1936- *WhoAmW 93*
Clopton, Beverly Beck *WhoWrEP 92*
Clopton, J.B., Mrs. *AmWomPl*
Clore, Gideon Marius 1955- *WhoEmL 93*
Clorety, Joseph Anthony, III 1942- *St&PR 93, WhoAm 92*
Close, Charles Thomas 1940- *WhoAm 92*
Close, Chuck 1940- *BioIn 17*
Close, David Palmer 1915- *WhoAm 92*
Close, Del *BioIn 17*
Close, Elizabeth Scheu 1912- *WhoAm 92*
Close, Glenn *BioIn 17*
Close, Glenn 1947- *HolBB [port], IntDcF 2-3 [port], WhoAm 92, WhoAmW 93*
Close, Harry Francis 1921- *St&PR 93*
Close, John Robert 1907- *BioIn 17*
Close, Karen Douglass Mott 1951- *WhoE 93*
Close, Karen Elizabeth 1951- *WhoAmW 93*
Close, Melissa Elizabeth 1957- *WhoAmW 93*
Close, Michael John 1943- *WhoAm 92*
Close, Rabbit 1907- *BioIn 17*
Close, Thomas H. *Law&B 92*
Close, Winston Arthur 1906- *WhoAm 92*
Closen, Michael Lee 1949- *WhoAm 92, WhoEmL 93*
Closs, Gerhard d1992 *NewYTBS 92*
Closs, Gerhard 1928-1992 *BioIn 17*
Closser, Patrick Denton 1945- *WhoSSW 93, WhoWor 93*
Closset, Gerard P. 1943- *St&PR 93*
Closset, Gerard Paul 1943- *WhoAm 92, WhoE 93*
Closson, Ernest 1870-1950 *Baker 92*
Closson, John Eugene, Jr. 1947- *WhoEmL 93, WhoWor 93*
Closson, William Deane 1934- *WhoE 93*
Clot, Archlyn Ann 1931- *WhoAmW 93, WhoSSW 93*
Clotfelter, Charles T. 1947- *WhoEmL 93*
Clothier, Birchard Taylor 1936- *St&PR 93*
Clothier, Florence 1903- *AmWomPl*
Clothier, Joanne Nicolai 1951- *WhoE 93*
Clothier, Peter D. 1936- *WhoWrEP 92*
Clothier, Roy A. 1939- *St&PR 93*
Clotworthy, John Harris 1924- *WhoAm 92*
Cloud, A. Doyle, Jr. *Law&B 92*
Cloud, Bruce Benjamin 1920- *St&PR 93*
Cloud, Bruce Benjamin, Sr. 1920- *WhoAm 92*
Cloud, David Eugene 1934- *WhoWrEP 92*
Cloud, Harry E. 1947- *St&PR 93*
Cloud, James Merle 1947- *WhoWor 93*
Cloud, Linda Beal 1937- *WhoAmW 93, WhoSSW 93*
Cloud, Luther Atwood 1920-1991 *BioIn 17*
Cloud, Marina Taylor 1945- *WhoSSW 93*
Cloud, Mark David 1958- *WhoE 93*
Cloud, Peter J. 1942- *St&PR 93*
Cloud, Preston 1912-1991 *BioIn 17*
Cloud, Roger *Law&B 92*
Cloud, Roger Wilcox *Law&B 92*
Cloud, Sanford, Jr. 1944- *St&PR 93*
Cloud, Sharon Lee 1948- *WhoEmL 93*
Cloud, Stanley Wills 1936- *WhoAm 92*
Cloud, Troy *Law&B 92*
Cloud, William Dean *Law&B 92*

Cloud, William Larry 1943- WhoSSW 93
Cloudman, Francis Harold, III 1944- WhoAm 92
Cloudsley, Donald Hugh 1925- WhoAm 92
Cloudsley-Thompson, John Leonard WhoScE 91-1
Cloues, Edward Blanchard, II 1947- St&PR 93
Clough, Anson W. 1936- WhoIns 93
Clough, Arthur Hugh 1819-1861 BioIn 17
Clough, B.W. 1955- ScF&FL 92
Clough, Charles BioIn 17
Clough, Charles E. 1930- St&PR 93
Clough, Charles Elmer 1930- WhoAm 92
Clough, Charles M. 1928- St&PR 93
Clough, Charles Marvin 1928- WhoAm 92
Clough, D.P. WhoScE 91-1
Clough, David Alan 1955- WhoEmL 93
Clough, George James, Jr. 1932- St&PR 93
Clough, Nadine Doerr 1942- WhoAm 92
Clough, Ray William, Jr. 1920- WhoAm 92
Clough, Richard John 1940- St&PR 93
Clough, Robert Lawrence 1957- WhoSSW 93
Clough, Ronald H. 1935- St&PR 93
Clough, S.D.P. 1928- ScF&FL 92
Clough, Scott BioIn 17
Clough, Shepard Bancroft 1901-1990 BioIn 17
Clough, Stanley WhoScE 91-1
Clough, Stephen K. 1953- St&PR 93
Clough-Leighter, Henry 1874-1956 Baker 92
Cloupeau, Michel 1927- WhoScE 91-2
Clous, James M. 1959- WhoEmL 93
Clouse, Charles Hercel 1946- WhoEmL 93
Clouse, Jerome Vincent 1943- St&PR 93
Clouse, John Daniel 1925- WhoWor 93
Clouse, Robert MiSFD 9
Clouse, Robert Wilburn 1937- WhoAm 92
Clouse, Roger R. 1907- St&PR 93
Clouser, Anne Cox 1955- WhoSSW 93
Clouser, Christopher E. 1952- St&PR 93
Clouston, Brendan R. BioIn 17
Clouston, Judith Kay 1940- WhoWrEP 92
Clouston, Ross Neal 1922- WhoAm 92
Clout, Hugh Donald WhoScE 91-1
Clouthier, Manuel DcCPCAm
Cloutier, Carol Lee 1940- WhoAmW 93
Cloutier, Charlotte Berube 1942- WhoE 93
Cloutier, David Edward 1951- WhoWrEP 92
Cloutier, Gilles Georges 1928- WhoAm 92
Cloutier, Guy 1949- WhoCanL 92
Cloutier, James Robert 1947- WhoSSW 93
Cloutier, Madison Joseph 1952- WhoSSW 93
Cloutier, Marius 1945- WhoWor 93
Cloutier, Michelle M. 1948- WhoAmW 93
Cloutier, N. Paul Law&B 92
Cloutier, Richard Robert 1942- St&PR 93
Cloutier, Roger R., II 1953- WhoAm 92
Cloutier-Wojciechowska, Cecile 1930- WhoCanL 92
Clouzot, Henri-Georges 1907-1977 MiSFD 9N
Clover, Anthony David 1938- WhoWor 93
Clover, Gerald T. 1929- St&PR 93
Clover, Michael J. 1947- St&PR 93
Clovers SoulM
Clovis, Albert L. 1935- WhoAm 92
Clovis, Donna Lucille 1957- WhoE 93, WhoEmL 93, WhoWrEP 92
Clovis, James R. 1929- St&PR 93
Clovis, James S. 1937- WhoE 93
Clow, Barbara Hand 1943- WhoWrEP 92
Clow, Timothy James 1960- WhoEmL 93
Cloward, George R. 1935- St&PR 93
Cloward, Richard Andrew 1926- WhoAm 92
Cloward, Steven P. 1947- St&PR 93
Clowdis, Charles Wilburn, Jr. 1944- WhoSSW 93
Clower, Clement Hogbin 1920- WhoSSW 93
Clower, Robert Wayne 1926- WhoAm 92
Clower, William Dewey 1935- WhoAm 92
Clowes, Carolyn 1946- ScF&FL 92
Clowes, Edith W. 1951- WhoAmW 93
Clowes, Garth Anthony 1926- WhoWor 93
Clowney, Shirley Carr 1936- WhoE 93
Clowney, William Clarke 1957- WhoE 93
Clowns SoulM
Cloyd, Sally F. Law&B 92
Clozza, Albert J. d1991 BioIn 17
Clubb, Bruce Edwin 1931- WhoAm 92, WhoWor 93
Clubb, Ian McMaster 1941- St&PR 93
Clubb, Martin L. 1957- St&PR 93
Clubbe, John Louis Edwin 1938- WhoSSW 93
Clubine, Gerald Dean 1939- WhoSSW 93
Clubley, Michael H. 1940- WhoScE 91-1
Cluchey, David Paul 1946- WhoEmL 93
Cluck, Patrick Mitchell 1961- WhoSSW 93
Cluer, John d1728 Baker 92
Cluff, Constance Sockman 1941- WhoE 93
Cluff, E. Dale 1937- WhoAm 92
Cluff, Leighton E. BioIn 17
Cluff, Leighton Eggertsen 1923- WhoAm 92
Cluff, Lloyd Sterling 1933- WhoAm 92
Clugston, Graeme Alistair 1946- WhoUN 92
Clugston, Katharine Thatcher 1892- AmWomPl
Clugston, William H. Law&B 92
Clukey, Wayne P. 1939- St&PR 93
Clum, John Philip 1851-1932 BioIn 17
Clune, Henry W. 1890- WhoWrEP 92
Clune, Robert Bell 1920- WhoAm 92
Clunie, Gordon James Aitken 1932- WhoWor 93
Clunies-Ross, Anthony Ian WhoScE 91-1
Clurman, Richard M. BioIn 17
Clurman, Richard Michael 1924- WhoAm 92, WhoWor 93
Clute, Heidi Grace 1957- WhoAmW 93
Clute, John 1940- ScF&FL 92
Clute, John E. 1934- St&PR 93, WhoAm 92
Clute, Margi 1944- St&PR 93
Clute, Robert Eugene 1924- WhoAm 92
Clutha, Janet Paterson Frame ScF&FL 92
Clutsam, George H(oward) 1866-1951 Baker 92
Clutter, Bertley Allen, III 1942- WhoAm 92
Clutter, Gayle Ann 1945- WhoSSW 93
Clutter, John Allen 1947- WhoEmL 93, WhoSSW 93
Clutter, Mary Elizabeth WhoAm 92, WhoAmW 93
Clutter, R. Marie St&PR 93
Clutter, Randal Robert 1950- WhoSSW 93
Clutterbuck, Alan Ralph 1960- WhoWor 93
Clutterbuck, Howard C. BioIn 17
Clutton-Brock, A. 1868-1924 ScF&FL 92
Clutton-Brock, Arthur 1868-1924 BioIn 17
Clutz, William 1933- WhoAm 92
Cluver, Michael Albert 1942- WhoWor 93
Cluytens, Andre 1905-1967 Baker 92, IntDcOp, OxDcOp
Cluzeau-Mortet, Luis 1889-1957 Baker 92
Clyce, Thomas Ellis 1945- St&PR 93
Clyde, Andy 1892-1967 QDrFCA 92 [port]
Clyde, Craig MiSFD 9
Clyde, Larry Forbes 1941- WhoAm 92
Clyde, Miles Lee 1953- WhoEmL 93
Clyde, Robert W. 1948- St&PR 93
Clyde, Wallace Alexander, Jr. 1929- WhoAm 92
Clymer, Adam BioIn 17
Clymer, Arthur Benjamin 1920- WhoE 93
Clymer, Brian William 1947- WhoAm 92
Clymer, Eleanor 1906- WhoWrEP 92
Clymer, Eleanor (Lowenton) 1906- DcAmChF 1960
Clymer, Ellen Saxe 1930- WhoAmW 93
Clymer, Everett Stuart 1944- St&PR 93
Clymer, Henry 1767-1830 BioIn 17
Clymer, Jane d1985 BioIn 17
Clymer, John 1907-1989 BioIn 17
Clymer, John Marion 1960- WhoEmL 93
Clymer, Meredith 1771-1794 BioIn 17
Clymer, Wayne Kenton 1917- WhoAm 92
Clymo, R.S. WhoScE 91-1
Clynch, Edward John 1942- WhoAm 92
Clyne, James W. 1933- WhoIns 93
Clyne, Patricia Edwards 1935- WhoWrEP 92
Clyne, Terrence John 1947- WhoSSW 93
Clyne, William C. 1909-1991 BioIn 17
Cmar, Janice Butko 1954- WhoAmW 93, WhoEmL 93
Cmarik, Raymond John 1949- WhoSSW 93
Cnong, Sooi Peaw 1942- St&PR 93
Coachman, Alice BioIn 17, BlkAmWO [port]
Coad, Joseph Paul 1946- WhoScE 91-1
Coad, Peter, Jr. 1953- WhoEmL 93
Coady, Philip James, Jr. 1941- WhoAm 92
Coady, William Francis 1940- WhoSSW 93, WhoWor 93
Coady, William John 1939- St&PR 93
Coake, Richard William 1952- St&PR 93
Coaker, James Whitfield 1946- WhoWor 93
Coakley, Davis 1946- WhoScE 91-3
Coakley, James Frederick 1945- WhoE 93
Coakley, Lisabeth H. Law&B 92
Coakley, Robert S. 1931- St&PR 93
Coakley, Thomas Francis 1946- St&PR 93
Coakley, William 1951- St&PR 93
Coakley, William Thomas 1946- WhoEmL 93
Coale, Ansley Johnson 1917- WhoAm 92
Coale, Michael L. Law&B 92
Coale, Samuel 1943- ScF&FL 92
Coale, William 1936- St&PR 93
Coaloa, Demenico 1954- WhoScE 91-3
Coalter, Richard G. Law&B 92
Coan, John Otts, III 1953- WhoSSW 93
Coan, Pamela Elaine 1959- WhoAmW 93, WhoEmL 93
Coan, Richard Morton 1948- WhoEmL 93
Coapstick, Richard P. 1931- St&PR 93
Coar, Richard John 1921- WhoAm 92
Coard, Bernard 1944- DcCPCAm
Coase, Ronald H. BioIn 17
Coase, Ronald Harry 1910- WhoAm 92, WhoWor 93
Coasters SoulM
Coat, Jean 1930- WhoScE 91-2
Coate, D.F.S. 1931- St&PR 93
Coate, David Edward 1955- WhoE 93
Coate, Elaine Kates 1927- WhoAmW 93
Coate, Roland E. 1890-1958 BioIn 17
Coates, Agnes Wintemute 1864-1945 BioIn 17
Coates, Albert 1882-1953 Baker 92, IntDcOp, OxDcOp
Coates, Andrea Law&B 92
Coates, Ann S. WhoSSW 93
Coates, Anna 1958- SmATA 73 [port]
Coates, Anthony Robert Milnes WhoScE 91-1
Coates, Arthur Donwell 1928- WhoE 93
Coates, Bradley Allen 1951- WhoEmL 93
Coates, Carrol F. 1930- WhoE 93
Coates, Charles Lorimer 1940- St&PR 93
Coates, Clarence Leroy, Jr. 1923- WhoAm 92
Coates, David John 1953- WhoEmL 93
Coates, Dianne Kay 1945- WhoAmW 93
Coates, Donald Robert 1922- WhoAm 92
Coates, Edith 1908-1983 OxDcOp
Coates, Edith (Mary) 1908-1983 Baker 92
Coates, Edward Malcolm, III 1966- WhoE 93
Coates, Eleanor Smith 1924- WhoAmW 93
Coates, Eric 1886-1957 Baker 92
Coates, F. Ramsey Law&B 92
Coates, Gardenia Evans 1954- WhoSSW 93
Coates, Glenn Richard 1923- WhoAm 92, WhoWor 93
Coates, Gloria 1938- Baker 92
Coates, Jean-Hubert 1930- WhoScE 91-2
Coates, Jesse 1908- WhoAm 92
Coates, John 1865-1941 Baker 92, OxDcOp
Coates, John 1944- WhoAsAP 91
Coates, John C. 1929- St&PR 93
Coates, John Robert 1961- WhoEmL 93, WhoSSW 93
Coates, Jon P. 1934- St&PR 93
Coates, Joseph Francis 1929- WhoAm 92
Coates, Joseph Gordon 1878-1943 DcTwHis
Coates, Kenneth Sidney 1930- WhoWor 93
Coates, Lewis MiSFD 9
Coates, Maryanne C. Law&B 92
Coates, Paul 1953- ScF&FL 92
Coates, Phyllis 1927- BioIn 17, SweetSg C [port]
Coates, Robert Jay 1922- WhoAm 92
Coates, Robert M. 1897-1973 BioIn 17
Coates, Rodney Frederick William WhoScE 91-1
Coates, Roger Alfred WhoScE 91-1
Coates, Rosemary Ann 1953- WhoSSW 93
Coates, Vincent J. 1925- St&PR 93
Coates, W. Paul 1945- ConAu 136
Coates, Wayne Evan 1947- WhoWor 93
Coatney, Sherry Kay 1960- WhoEmL 93
Coatoam, Gary William 1946- WhoSSW 93
Coats, Andrew Montgomery 1935- WhoAm 92
Coats, Charles F. 1949- WhoEmL 93, WhoSSW 93
Coats, Dan 1943- CngDr 91
Coats, Daniel R. 1943- WhoAm 92
Coats, David Jervis 1924- WhoWor 93
Coats, Douglas J. 1933- St&PR 93
Coats, Douglas James 1933- WhoIns 93
Coats, George Wesley 1936- WhoSSW 93
Coats, Hugh B. 1925- St&PR 93
Coats, James David Law&B 92
Coats, Keith Hal 1934- WhoAm 92
Coats, Michael Edwin 1954- WhoEmL 93
Coats, Nancy L. Law&B 92
Coats, Roy R. 1924- St&PR 93
Coats, Stephen E. 1948- WhoEmL 93
Coats, Warren L. 1942- WhoUN 92
Coats, Wendell John, Jr. 1947- WhoEmL 93
Coats, William Sloan, III 1950- WhoEmL 93, WhoWor 93
Coatsworth, Elizabeth 1893-1986 ScF&FL 92
Coatsworth, Elizabeth (Jane) 1893- DcAmChF 1960
Coatsworth, Elizabeth (Jane) 1893-1986 MajAI [port]
Coba, Robert L. 1954- St&PR 93
Cobain, Kurt
See Nirvana ConMus 8
See Also Nirvana News 92
Cobalt, Martin ConAu 37NR, MajAI, ScF&FL 92
Cobaugh, Stephen Marcus 1955- WhoE 93
Cobb, Allen B. St&PR 93
Cobb, Alonzo Floyd, Jr. 1947- WhoEmL 93
Cobb, Alton B. 1928- WhoAm 92
Cobb, Alton H., Jr. 1954- St&PR 93
Cobb, Andrew Howard WhoScE 91-1
Cobb, Betsy d1991 BioIn 17
Cobb, Calvin Hayes, Jr. 1924- WhoAm 92
Cobb, Carolyn Jane 1943- WhoAmW 93
Cobb, Charles E., Jr. 1936- WhoAm 92, WhoWor 93
Cobb, Charles Kenche 1934- WhoWor 93
Cobb, Christine Marie 1952- WhoEmL 93
Cobb, Dana B. Law&B 92
Cobb, Daniel W., Jr. 1921- WhoAm 92, WhoWor 93
Cobb, Daniel William 1811-1872 BioIn 17
Cobb, David A. 1963- St&PR 93
Cobb, David Keith 1941- WhoE 93
Cobb, Donna Deanne Hill 1943- WhoAm 92
Cobb, Edmund 1892-1974 BioIn 17
Cobb, Elizabeth Bliss Parkinson 1907- WhoAm 92
Cobb, Elizabeth Youngblood d1991 BioIn 17
Cobb, Frank Irving 1869-1923 JrnUS
Cobb, G. Elliott, Jr. 1939- WhoAm 92
Cobb, Gary Dan 1960- WhoSSW 93
Cobb, George C., Mrs. AmWomPl
Cobb, George Hamilton 1911- St&PR 93
Cobb, Geraldyn M. 1931- BioIn 17
Cobb, Henry Nichols 1926- WhoAm 92
Cobb, Henry Pollard 1930- WhoSSW 93
Cobb, Henry Van Zandt 1909- WhoAm 92
Cobb, Howell 1815-1868 PolPar
Cobb, Howell 1922- WhoAm 92, WhoSSW 93
Cobb, Hubbard Hanford 1917- WhoAm 92
Cobb, Irvin S. 1876-1944 ScF&FL 92
Cobb, Irvin Shrewsbury 1876-1944 JrnUS
Cobb, James Richard 1942- St&PR 93, WhoAm 92
Cobb, Jerrie 1931- BioIn 17
Cobb, Jewel Plummer 1924- AfrAmBi, WhoAm 92, WhoAmW 93
Cobb, Jo Ann 1949- WhoAmW 93
Cobb, John A. 1945- St&PR 93
Cobb, John Anthony 1927- WhoAm 92
Cobb, John Blackwell 1904-1966 BiDAMSp 1989
Cobb, John Boswell, Jr. 1925- WhoAm 92
Cobb, John Cecil, Jr. 1927- WhoAm 92, WhoWor 93
Cobb, John W. 1927- St&PR 93
Cobb, Josephine M. AmWomPl
Cobb, Kenneth A. Law&B 92
Cobb, Lee J. 1911?-1976 IntDcF 2-3
Cobb, Lee Solomon 1965- WhoSSW 93
Cobb, Leon Moseley WhoScE 91-1
Cobb, Leslie Davis 1935- St&PR 93, WhoAm 92
Cobb, Lucy M. AmWomPl
Cobb, Margaret Mary 1948- WhoAmW 93, WhoE 93
Cobb, Michael Roy 1945- WhoAsAP 91
Cobb, Miles Alan 1930- WhoAm 92
Cobb, Milton Terry 1949- WhoE 93
Cobb, Nancy (Howard) 1949- ConAu 137
Cobb, Nathan Augustus 1859-1932 BioIn 17
Cobb, Otis Leavill 1941- BioIn 17
Cobb, P.G.W. WhoScE 91-1
Cobb, Patricia Ann 1939- WhoSSW 93
Cobb, Phillip K. Law&B 92
Cobb, Richard 1917- BioIn 17
Cobb, Ronald David 1945- WhoSSW 93
Cobb, Roy C., Jr. Law&B 92
Cobb, Ruth 1914- WhoAm 92
Cobb, Sharon A. 1953- WhoEmL 93
Cobb, Sharon Yvonne 1950- WhoEmL 93
Cobb, Shirley Ann 1936- WhoAmW 93
Cobb, Susan Clason 1953- WhoEmL 93
Cobb, Susan Harrison AmWomPl
Cobb, Terri R. 1934- WhoSSW 93
Cobb, Thomas 1947- ConAu 136
Cobb, Thomas W. 1944- St&PR 93
Cobb, Ty 1886-1961 BioIn 17
Cobb, Ty 1950- WhoEmL 93
Cobb, Verlene P. 1946- St&PR 93
Cobb, Vicki 1938- MajAI [port], SmATA 69 [port]
Cobb, Virginia Horton 1933- WhoAm 92
Cobb, William 1937- WhoWrEP 92
Cobb, William Allen 1947- St&PR 93
Cobb, William Ervin 1947- WhoEmL 93, WhoSSW 93

Cobb, William Montague 1904-1990 *BioIn 17*
Cobbe, Alexander Stanhope 1870-1931 *HarEnMi*
Cobbe, Stuart Malcolm *WhoScE 91-1*
Cobbett, Stuart H. 1948- *St&PR 93*
Cobbett, Walter Willson 1847-1937 *Baker 92*
Cobbett, William 1763-1835 *BioIn 17, JrnUS*
Cobble, Arthur Lee, Jr. 1947- *St&PR 93*
Cobble, James Wikle 1926- *WhoAm 92*
Cobbold, Nicholas Sydney 1934- *WhoWor 93*
Cobbold, Richard Southwell Chevallier 1931- *WhoAm 92*
Cobbs, James Harold 1928- *WhoSSW 93*
Cobbs, John L. *BioIn 17*
Cobbs, John Lewis 1943- *WhoE 93*
Cobbs, Louise Bertram 1947- *WhoEmL 93*
Cobbs, Price Mashaw 1928- *WhoAm 92*
Cobb Smith, Beverly Elizabeth 1962- *WhoAmW 93*
Cobden, Richard 1804-1865 *BioIn 17*
Cobe, Lori 1957- *WhoEmL 93*
Cobelli, Claudio 1946- *WhoScE 91-3, WhoWor 93*
Coben, Daniel Paul 1959- *WhoE 93*
Coben, William Allen 1932- *WhoAm 92*
Cober, Alan E. 1935- *WhoAm 92*
Cober, Richard G. 1928- *St&PR 93*
Coberly, Camden Arthur 1922- *WhoAm 92*
Coberly, Wm. B., Jr. 1908- *St&PR 93*
Cobern, Martin E. 1946- *St&PR 93*
Cobert, Barton Lewis 1950- *WhoE 93*
Cobert, Scott Alan 1955- *WhoSSW 93*
Cobert, Wendy Lynn 1963- *WhoE 93*
Cobery, Thomas John 1946- *St&PR 93*
Cobey, Herbert T. 1917-1986 *ScF&FL 92*
Cobey, James Alexander 1913- *WhoWor 93*
Cobey, Ralph 1909- *WhoAm 92*
Cobey, Susanne 1951- *St&PR 93*
Cobham, Michael John 1927- *St&PR 93*
Cobham, William Emanuel, Jr. 1944- *WhoAm 92*
Cobia, Paula Ivey 1957- *WhoEmL 93*
Cobin, Arthur *BioIn 17*
Coble, Bob *WhoSSW 93*
Coble, Daniel Bruce 1949- *WhoEmL 93, WhoSSW 93*
Coble, David Franklin 1951- *WhoSSW 93*
Coble, Frederick Charles 1961- *WhoEmL 93*
Coble, Howard 1931- *CngDr 91, WhoAm 92, WhoSSW 93*
Coble, Hugh Kenneth 1934- *St&PR 93*
Coble, John C. 1942- *St&PR 93*
Coble, John Dale 1955- *WhoSSW 93*
Coble, Mary Susan 1949- *WhoEmL 93*
Coble, Robert Louis 1928- *WhoAm 92*
Coble, T.C. 1943- *St&PR 93*
Coble, William Carroll 1958- *WhoEmL 93*
Coblentz, Gilbert S. 1949- *St&PR 93*
Coblentz, Stanton A. 1896-1982 *ScF&FL 92*
Coblentz, William Kraemer 1922- *WhoAm 92*
Coblitz, Mark A. 1947- *St&PR 93*
Cobo, Luis Heras *WhoScE 91-3*
Cobos Briceno, Agustin 1945- *WhoWor 93*
Cobson, Corinne *BioIn 17*
Coburn, Anna Mary *Law&B 92*
Coburn, Anthony 1927-1977 *ScF&FL 92*
Coburn, Barry M. 1935- *St&PR 93*
Coburn, Beneta Darliene 1957- *WhoSSW 93*
Coburn, Charles 1877-1961 *IntDcF 2-3 [port]*
Coburn, Donald Lee 1938- *WhoAm 92*
Coburn, Frances Gullett 1919- *WhoAmW 93, WhoSSW 93, WhoWor 93*
Coburn, Harry L. 1934- *WhoAm 92*
Coburn, Howard E. *Law&B 92*
Coburn, James 1928- *BioIn 17, IntDcF 2-3, WhoAm 92*
Coburn, John, Jr. 1941- *WhoE 93*
Coburn, John Bowen 1914- *WhoAm 92*
Coburn, John H. *Law&B 92*
Coburn, Kathleen 1905-1991 *AnObit 1991*
Coburn, Kathryn R. *Law&B 92*
Coburn, Lewis Alan 1940- *WhoAm 92*
Coburn, Marjorie Foster 1939- *WhoAmW 93, WhoWor 93*
Coburn, Richard Joseph 1931- *St&PR 93, WhoAm 92*
Coburn, Robert Craig 1930- *WhoAm 92*
Coburn, Ronald 1948- *St&PR 93*
Coburn, Ronald Murray 1943- *WhoWor 93*
Coburn, Theodore James 1926- *WhoAm 92*
Coburn, Warren B. 1926- *St&PR 93*
Coburn, Warren Baxter 1926- *WhoAm 92*
Cobuzzi, Barbara J. 1955- *WhoEmL 93*
Coca, Imogene 1908- *NotHsAW 93*
Cocanougher, Arthur Benton 1938- *WhoAm 92, WhoSSW 93, WhoWor 93*
Cocanougher, John Everett 1940- *St&PR 93*
Cocanower, Alfred Benjamin 1938- *WhoSSW 93*
Coca-Prados, Jose 1942- *WhoScE 91-3*
Coccagna, Fred Joseph, Jr. 1945- *WhoE 93*
Coccari, Randall C. 1947- *WhoE 93*
Cocchi, Gioacchino c. 1720-c. 1788 *Baker 92, OxDcOp*
Cocchiara, Giuseppe 1904-1965 *IntDcAn*
Coccia, Carlo 1782-1873 *Baker 92, OxDcOp*
Cocciolone, Vincent Scott 1964- *WhoEmL 93*
Cocco, Alex Mark 1952- *WhoE 93*
Cocco, Marie Elizabeth 1956- *WhoAm 92*
Cocconi, Giuseppe 1914- *BioIn 17*
Cocea, Dinu 1929- *DrEEuF*
Coche, Judith Abbe 1942- *WhoAmW 93, WhoE 93*
Cocheci, Vasile 1922- *WhoScE 91-4*
Cochereau, Pierre 1924-1984 *Baker 92*
Cochetti, Roger James 1950- *WhoEmL 93*
Cochin, Arnold Mitchell 1951- *WhoEmL 93*
Cochin, Denys 1851-1922 *BioIn 17*
Cochise d1874 *BioIn 17*
Cochise c. 1812-1874 *HarEnMi*
Cochlaeus 1479-1552 *Baker 92*
Cochnar, Robert John 1939- *WhoAm 92*
Cochran, Ada 1933- *WhoAmW 93*
Cochran, Adam *Law&B 92*
Cochran, Alastair Jack *WhoScE 91-1*
Cochran, Bernard Harvey 1930- *WhoSSW 93*
Cochran, Bill 1942- *WhoSSW 93*
Cochran, Bill 1955- *BioIn 17*
Cochran, Carl Joe *Law&B 92*
Cochran, Carolyn 1934- *WhoAmW 93*
Cochran, Carolyn Collette 1951- *WhoEmL 93*
Cochran, Carolyn L. 1950- *St&PR 93*
Cochran, Clark Jones, Jr. 1949- *WhoEmL 93*
Cochran, Don Wayne 1952- *WhoEmL 93*
Cochran, Douglas E. 1932- *St&PR 93*
Cochran, Douglas Eugene 1932- *WhoAm 92*
Cochran, Earl Vernon 1922- *St&PR 93*
Cochran, Eve Owen *AmWomPl*
Cochran, George Calloway, III 1932- *WhoAm 92, WhoSSW 93, WhoWor 93*
Cochran, George Moffett 1912- *WhoAm 92, WhoWor 93*
Cochran, George Van Brunt 1932- *WhoE 93*
Cochran, Helen Hege 1953- *WhoEmL 93*
Cochran, Howard E. 1938- *St&PR 93*
Cochran, Jacqueline 1910?-1980 *BioIn 17*
Cochran, Jacqueline Louise 1953- *WhoAmW 93, WhoEmL 93*
Cochran, James Alan 1936- *WhoAm 92*
Cochran, James C. *Law&B 92*
Cochran, Jeffery David *Law&B 92*
Cochran, John Arthur 1921- *WhoAm 92*
Cochran, John Charles 1935- *WhoAm 92*
Cochran, John Euell, Jr. 1944- *WhoAm 92*
Cochran, John M. 1936- *St&PR 93*
Cochran, John M., III 1941- *WhoAm 92*
Cochran, John Thomas 1941- *WhoAm 92*
Cochran, Joseph Wesley 1954- *WhoEmL 93, WhoSSW 93*
Cochran, Kendall Pinney 1924- *WhoAm 92*
Cochran, Kenneth L. *Law&B 92*
Cochran, Larry *WhoSSW 93*
Cochran, Les 1935- *WhoAm 92*
Cochran, Leslie Hershel 1939- *WhoAm 92*
Cochran, Lewis W. 1915- *WhoAm 92*
Cochran, Linda G. 1951- *WhoIns 93*
Cochran, Lori Kay *Law&B 92*
Cochran, Mark David *Law&B 92*
Cochran, Maura McNally 1948- *WhoE 93*
Cochran, Molly *ScF&FL 92*
Cochran, Nathan Michael 1957- *WhoE 93*
Cochran, Rebecca Sue 1959- *WhoEmL 93*
Cochran, Richard Michael 1951- *WhoEmL 93*
Cochran, Robert Carter 1932- *WhoSSW 93*
Cochran, Robert Glenn 1919- *WhoAm 92*
Cochran, Ronald Waylon 1941- *WhoWor 93*
Cochran, Sachiko Tomie 1945- *WhoAm 92*
Cochran, Samuel Warren 1921- *WhoSSW 93*
Cochran, Sandra Lynn 1953- *WhoEmL 93*
Cochran, Scott Coryell 1960- *WhoEmL 93*
Cochran, Stacy *MiSFD 9*
Cochran, Stephen Grey 1947- *WhoEmL 93*
Cochran, T. Fletcher 1949- *St&PR 93*
Cochran, Thad 1937- *CngDr 91, WhoAm 92, WhoSSW 93*
Cochran, Wendell 1929- *WhoAm 92*
Cochran, William 1943- *Baker 92*
Cochran, William D. 1930- *St&PR 93*
Cochran, William W., II *Law&B 92*
Cochrane, Alison Lee 1961- *WhoAmW 93*
Cochrane, Andrew R. 1908- *St&PR 93*
Cochrane, Anita L. *Law&B 92*
Cochrane, Betsy Lane *WhoAmW 93*
Cochrane, Edward G. 1954- *St&PR 93*
Cochrane, Edward Grier, II *Law&B 92*
Cochrane, Elizabeth *GayN*
Cochrane, Elizabeth 1867-1922 *BioIn 17, JrnUS*
Cochrane, Francis Douglas 1920- *St&PR 93*
Cochrane, Frederick Pierce 1940- *St&PR 93*
Cochrane, James Louis 1942- *St&PR 93, WhoAm 92, WhoWor 93*
Cochrane, Janet Teresa 1946- *WhoAmW 93*
Cochrane, Jerry Wilson 1934- *St&PR 93*
Cochrane, Katherine Watson 1947- *WhoAmW 93*
Cochrane, Luther Parks 1948- *WhoAm 92*
Cochrane, Michael David 1948- *WhoEmL 93*
Cochrane, Michael Harald 1958- *WhoEmL 93*
Cochrane, Mickey 1903-1962 *BioIn 17*
Cochrane, Pauline Atherton 1929- *WhoAm 92*
Cochrane, Raymond *WhoScE 91-1*
Cochrane, Robert H. 1924- *WhoAm 92*
Cochrane, Ronald Dale 1946- *WhoEmL 93*
Cochrane, Shirley Graves 1925- *WhoWrEP 92*
Cochrane, T.E. 1949- *St&PR 93*
Cochrane, Thomas 1775-1860 *HarEnMi*
Cochrane, Thomas Thurston 1936- *WhoWor 93*
Cochrane, William E. 1926- *ScF&FL 92*
Cochrane, William Henry 1912- *WhoAm 92*
Cocito, Carlo G. 1928- *WhoScE 91-2*
Cociu, Vasile Gh. 1924- *WhoScE 91-4*
Cockayne, Robert Barton 1937- *WhoAm 92*
Cockburn, Bruce 1945- *ConMus 8 [port]*
Cockburn, Eve Gillian 1924- *WhoWor 93*
Cockburn, Forrester *WhoScE 91-1*
Cockburn, Francis C. *ScF&FL 92*
Cockburn, George 1772-1853 *HarEnMi*
Cockburn, John F. 1928- *WhoAm 92*
Cockburn, Joscelyn George *Law&B 92*
Cockburn, Terry *ScF&FL 92*
Cockcroft, George *ScF&FL 92*
Cockcroft, Ronald 1924- *WhoScE 91-4*
Cockcroft, T.G.L. *ScF&FL 92*
Cocke, Charles B. *Law&B 92*
Cocke, Erle, Jr. 1921- *WhoAm 92*
Cocke, James William 1917- *St&PR 93*
Cocke, Norman A. 1945- *St&PR 93*
Cocke, Philip St. George, V 1950- *WhoEmL 93*
Cocke, William Marvin, Jr. 1934- *WhoAm 92, WhoSSW 93*
Cockell, William Arthur, Jr. 1929- *WhoAm 92*
Cocker, Barbara Joan *WhoAm 92, WhoAmW 93*
Cocker, Joe 1944- *Baker 92*
Cocker, Tedd 1941- *WhoE 93*
Cockerell, Christopher 1910- *WhoWor 93*
Cockerham, Columbus Clark 1921- *WhoAm 92*
Cockerham, Donald Lewis 1934- *St&PR 93*
Cockerham, Haven Earl 1947- *St&PR 93*
Cockerham, James Edward 1948- *WhoEmL 93*
Cockerham, Lorris G. 1935- *WhoSSW 93*
Cockerham, Michael Bret 1962- *WhoSSW 93*
Cockerham, Rodney Wayne 1948- *St&PR 93*
Cockerill, John A. 1845-1896 *JrnUS*
Cockett, Abraham T. K. 1928- *WhoAm 92*
Cockfield, Francis Arthur *BioIn 17*
Cocking, Edward Charles Daniel *WhoScE 91-1*
Cocklin, Kim Roland *Law&B 92*
Cocklin, Kim Roland 1951- *St&PR 93, WhoAm 92*
Cocklin, Robert Frank 1919- *WhoAm 92*
Cockman, Anthony George 1939- *WhoWor 93*
Cockman, Richard Lee 1949- *WhoEmL 93, WhoSSW 93*
Cockrell, John T. 1947- *St&PR 93*
Cockrell, Lila May Banks 1922- *WhoAm 92*
Cockrell, Marian 1907-1972 *ScF&FL 92*
Cockrell, Matthew W. *Law&B 92*
Cockrell, Maud *AmWomPl*
Cockrell, Thomas A. 1939- *St&PR 93*
Cockrell, Wilburn Allen 1941- *WhoSSW 93, WhoWor 93*
Cockrell, William Foster, Jr. 1944- *WhoSSW 93*
Cockriel, Russell George, Sr. 1957- *WhoAm 92, WhoEmL 93*
Cockriel, Stephen Eugene 1948- *WhoEmL 93*
Cockrill, Ann T. *Law&B 92*
Cockrum, John E. 1944- *St&PR 93*
Cockrum, Kurt *ScF&FL 92*
Cockrum, William Monroe, III 1937- *WhoAm 92, WhoWor 93*
Cocks *Baker 92*
Cocks, Arthur Lincoln *Baker 92*
Cocks, Franklin Hadley 1941- *WhoAm 92*
Cocks, George Gosson 1919- *WhoAm 92*
Cocks, Robert *Baker 92*
Cocks, Robert MacFarlane *Baker 92*
Cocks, Stroud Lincoln *Baker 92*
Cockshaw, Peter Albert 1934- *WhoE 93*
Cockshott, Carol *Law&B 92*
Cockshott, Gerald Wilfred 1915-1979 *Baker 92*
Cockshutt, Eric Philip 1929- *WhoAm 92*
Cockwell, Jack Lynn 1941- *WhoAm 92, WhoE 93*
Coclers, Leopold 1934- *WhoScE 91-2*
Coclico, Adrianus Petit c. 1500-1563 *Baker 92*
Coco, Charles Edward 1942- *WhoAm 92*
Coco, Lewis Michael 1939- *WhoAm 92*
Coco, Mark Steven 1952- *WhoEmL 93*
Coco, Peter M. 1959- *St&PR 93*
Coco, Samuel B., Jr. 1927- *St&PR 93*
Coco, Samuel Barbin 1927- *WhoAm 92*
Coco, Thomas Michael 1949- *WhoSSW 93*
Cocolis, Peter K. 1942- *St&PR 93*
Cocolis, Peter Konstantine 1942- *WhoSSW 93*
Cocores, James Alexander 1953- *WhoEmL 93*
Cocozza, Anthony J. 1950- *WhoIns 93*
Cocteau, Jean 1889-1963 *BioIn 17, MagSWL [port], MiSFD 9N, OxDcOp, WorLitC [port]*
Cocteau, Jean (Maurice Eugene Clement) 1889-1963 *ConAu 40NR*
Cocuzza, Giuseppe 1930- *WhoScE 91-3*
Coda, John R. 1941- *WhoE 93*
Codaccioni, Jean-Louis 1929- *WhoScE 91-2*
Codd, Geoffrey Allan *WhoScE 91-1*
Codd, Richard Trent, Jr. 1945- *WhoSSW 93*
Coddet, Christian 1949- *WhoWor 93*
Codding, Charles Harold, III 1947- *St&PR 93*
Codding, Frederick Hayden 1938- *WhoAm 92*
Codding, George Arthur, Jr. 1923- *WhoAm 92*
Codding, Hugh Bishop 1917- *St&PR 93*
Coddington, Iqbal Jwaideh 1935- *WhoAmW 93*
Coddington, John I. d1991 *BioIn 17*
Coddington, Joseph, Jr. 1939- *WhoWrEP 92*
Coddington, Robert H. *WhoWrEP 92*
Coddington, Stewart Gould 1940- *WhoE 93*
Coddon, Louis David, II *Law&B 92*
Coddou, Wesley S. *Law&B 92*
Code, James Manley Wayne 1930- *WhoAm 92*
Code, Wayne 1930- *St&PR 93*
Codega, Michael P., II 1953- *WhoE 93*
Codell, David Williams 1951- *St&PR 93*
Codell, J.C., Jr. 1919- *St&PR 93*
Coden, Michael Henri 1947- *St&PR 93, WhoAm 92, WhoE 93, WhoWor 93*
Coderre, Elaine Ann 1947- *WhoAmW 93*
Coderre, James A. 1935- *St&PR 93*
Codey, Lawrence R. 1944- *St&PR 93*
Codi, Joseph L. 1952- *St&PR 93*
Codilla, Gwendolyn Garcia 1955- *WhoWor 93*
Codispoti, Anthony 1946- *St&PR 93, WhoEmL 93*
Codispoti, Joseph Salvatore *Law&B 92*
Codlin, Dennis E. *Law&B 92*
Codman, Charles 1800-1842 *BioIn 17*
Codos, Richard Neil 1955- *St&PR 93*
Codos, William V. 1922- *St&PR 93*
Codraro, Lawrence *Law&B 92*
Codraro, Lawrence Frederick 1926- *St&PR 93*
Codreanu, Corneliu Zelea 1900-1938 *PolBiDi*
Codrescu, Andrei 1946- *BioIn 17, WhoSSW 93, WhoWrEP 92*
Codrington, Edward 1770-1851 *HarEnMi*
Codrington, Robert Henry 1830-1922 *IntDcAn*
Codron, Michael Victor 1930- *WhoWor 93*
Codron, Steven *Law&B 92*
Coducci, Mauro 1440-1504 *BioIn 17*
Codussi, Mauro 1440-1504 *BioIn 17*
Cody, Alan Morrow 1947- *WhoEmL 93*
Cody, Dolores L. *Law&B 92*

Cody, Donna Boult 1954- *WhoAmW 93*
Cody, Edward Bryan 1946- *WhoEmL 93*
Cody, Ginger 1932- *WhoAmW 93*
Cody, Hiram Sedgwick, Jr. 1915- *WhoWor 93*
Cody, Iron Eyes 1915- *WhoAm 92*
Cody, J. Derrill 1938- *WhoAm 92*
Cody, James Marion 1945- *WhoWrEP 92*
Cody, James R. Cronin 1944- *WhoE 93*
Cody, John *BioIn 17*
Cody, John M. 1942- *St&PR 93*
Cody, Mary Bennett *Law&B 92*
Cody, Nancy Cosgrove 1954- *WhoAm 92*
Cody, Raymond G. 1946- *St&PR 93*
Cody, Robert F. *Law&B 92*
Cody, Roger Allen 1944- *WhoE 93*
Cody, Thomas G. *Law&B 92*
Cody, Thomas G. 1929- *St&PR 93*
Cody, Thomas Gerald 1929- *WhoAm 92*
Cody, Thomas Gerald 1941- *WhoAm 92*
Cody, Walter James Michael 1936- *WhoAm 92*
Cody, William Bermond 1949- *WhoSSW 93*
Cody, William F. 1846-1917 *GayN*
Cody, William Frederick 1846-1917 *BioIn 17*
Cody, Wilmer St. Clair 1937- *WhoAm 92*
Cody Brekke, Deirdre *Law&B 92*
Cody-Rice, Edith H. *Law&B 92*
Coe, Benjamin Plaisted 1930- *WhoAm 92*
Coe, Christopher 1954- *ConGAN*
Coe, Christopher Lane 1951- *WhoEmL 93*
Coe, David Lewis 1948- *St&PR 93*
Coe, Dawn *WhoAmW 93*
Coe, Donald Kirk 1934- *WhoAm 92*
Coe, Douglas *ConAu 39NR*
Coe, Elizabeth Beaubien 1919- *WhoSSW 93*
Coe, Frank d1931 *BioIn 17*
Coe, Fredric L. 1936- *WhoAm 92*
Coe, George Frank 1953- *WhoEmL 93*
Coe, George Washington 1856-1941 *BioIn 17*
Coe, Gordon E. *Law&B 92*
Coe, Herring 1907- *WhoAm 92*
Coe, Ilse G. 1911- *WhoAmW 93*
Coe, J.W. 1920- *St&PR 93*
Coe, Jack B. *Law&B 92*
Coe, Joe Ann 1934- *WhoWrEP 92*
Coe, John C. *Law&B 92*
Coe, Keith D. *Law&B 92*
Coe, Kelvin d1992 *NewYTBS 92*
Coe, Linda Marlene Wolfe 1941- *WhoAmW 93*
Coe, Margaret Louise Shaw 1917- *WhoAmW 93, WhoWor 93*
Coe, Marian (Zipperlin) 1931- *WhoWrEP 92*
Coe, Marie E. *AmWomPl*
Coe, Marvin Parnick 1931- *WhoSSW 93*
Coe, Mary Alice 1948- *WhoAmW 93*
Coe, Michael Douglas 1929- *WhoAm 92, WhoE 93*
Coe, N.H. 1923- *St&PR 93*
Coe, Paul E., Jr. 1919- *St&PR 93*
Coe, Paul Francis 1909- *WhoAm 92*
Coe, Paul Michael *Law&B 92*
Coe, Peter Trask 1936- *St&PR 93*
Coe, Philip Haddox d1871 *BioIn 17*
Coe, Robert Campbell 1918- *WhoAm 92*
Coe, Robert Stanford 1919- *WhoAm 92*
Coe, Roger N. *Law&B 92*
Coe, Ross Anton *ScF&FL 92*
Coe, Sebastian *BioIn 17*
Coe, Sue 1951- *BioIn 17*
Coe, Tucker *BioIn 17*
Coe, Ward Baldwin, Jr. 1913- *WhoAm 92*
Coe, William Charles 1930- *WhoAm 92*
Coebergh, Jan Willem 1946- *WhoScE 91-3*
Coedes, George 1886-1969 *IntDcAn*
Coehoorn, Menno van 1641-1704 *HarEnMi*
Coel, Margaret 1937- *ConAu 39NR*
Coelho, Alipio D'Oliveira 1945- *WhoWor 93*
Coelho, Anthony Mendes, Jr. 1947- *WhoEmL 93, WhoSSW 93, WhoWor 93*
Coelho, Helder 1944- *WhoScE 91-3*
Coelho, Helio Teixeira 1941- *WhoWor 93*
Coelho, Joaquim F. da Silva 1943- *WhoScE 91-3*
Coelho, Joseph Richard 1946- *WhoE 93, WhoEmL 93*
Coelho, Pedro Henrique Gouvea 1952- *WhoWor 93*
Coelho, Roland 1926- *WhoScE 91-2*
Coelho, Rui Frederick Wilson 1956- *WhoE 93*
Coelho, Ruy 1891-1986 *Baker 92*
Coelho, Tony 1942- *PolPar, WhoAm 92*
Coelho Alves Correia, Antonio Pedro 1945- *WhoScE 91-3*
Coeling, Laurie Sue *BioIn 17*
Coello, Alonso Sanchez 1531?-1588 *BioIn 17*
Coello, Claudio c. 1630-1693 *BioIn 17*
Coello, Elena Coromoto 1952- *WhoAm 92, WhoEmL 93*
Coeme, Guy 1946- *WhoWor 93*
Coen, Daniel Kennedy 1932- *St&PR 93*
Coen, Daniel Kennedy, Jr. 1932- *WhoAm 92*
Coen, Ethan *BioIn 17*
Coen, Ethan 1958- *WhoAm 92*
See Also Coen, Joel 1955- *News 92*
Coen, Franklin *ScF&FL 92*
Coen, Joel *BioIn 17*
Coen, Joel 1955- *MiSFD 9, News 92 [port], WhoAm 92*
Coen, Lodewijk Karel Celina 1952- *WhoEmL 93*
Coen, Robert Joseph 1923- *WhoAm 92*
Coen, Timothy F. *Law&B 92*
Coene, Edgar T. 1930- *St&PR 93*
Coenen, Dale Stephen 1928- *St&PR 93*
Coenen, Franz 1826-1904 *Baker 92*
Coenen, Johannes (Meinardus) 1824-1899 *Baker 92*
Coenen, Willem 1837-1918 *Baker 92*
Coenson, Barbara Ellen 1956- *WhoEmL 93, WhoSSW 93, WhoWor 93*
Coenus d326BC *HarEnMi*
Coerne, Louis (Adolphe) 1870-1922 *Baker 92*
Coerper, Milo George 1925- *WhoAm 92*
Coerr, Eleanor 1922- *BioIn 17*
Coerr, Eleanor (Beatrice) 1922- *MajAI [port]*
Coers, Donald V. 1941- *ConAu 139*
Coertse, Mimi 1932- *Baker 92*
Coerver, Robert Albert, Jr. 1933- *St&PR 93*
Coes, Kent Day 1910- *WhoAm 92*
Coetzee, J.M. 1940- *BioIn 17, IntLitE, MagSWL [port]*
Coetzee, John M. 1940- *WhoWor 93*
Coeur-Barron, Brent H. *St&PR 93*
Coeur-Bizot, Patrice Raoul 1952- *WhoUN 92*
Coeuroy, Andre 1891-1976 *Baker 92*
Coey, J.M.D. 1945- *WhoScE 91-3*
Cofer, Berdette Henry *WhoWor 93*
Cofer, Charles Norval 1916- *WhoAm 92*
Cofer, David Thornton *Law&B 92*
Cofer, Edwin T. 1946- *St&PR 93*
Cofer, Edwin Tharp *Law&B 92*
Cofer, Gloria Faye *WhoAmW 93*
Cofer, Judith Ortiz 1952- *BioIn 17, HispAmA [port], NotHsAW 93, WhoWrEP 92*
Cofer, Mary Jane 1919- *WhoAmW 93*
Cofer, Patricia K. *Law&B 92*
Coffee, J.R. *Law&B 92*
Coffee, John fl. 1814- *HarEnMi*
Coffee, Joseph Denis, Jr. 1918- *WhoAm 92*
Coffee, Karen Lynn 1956- *WhoEmL 93*
Coffee, Keith E. *BioIn 17*
Coffee, Richard Jerome, II 1954- *WhoEmL 93*
Coffee, Robert M. *Law&B 92*
Coffee, Rudolph, Mrs. *AmWomPl*
Coffee, Virginia Claire 1920- *WhoAmW 93*
Coffelt, Gina Crews 1959- *WhoAmW 93*
Coffen, Richard Wayne 1941- *WhoWrEP 92*
Coffeng, John Adrianus 1948- *WhoWor 93*
Coffey, Brian *ScF&FL 92*
Coffey, Brian 1945- *BioIn 17*
Coffey, C. Shelby *BioIn 17*
Coffey, C. Shelby, III *WhoAm 92*
Coffey, C. Shelby, III 1946- *St&PR 93*
Coffey, Charles d1745 *OxDcOp*
Coffey, Clarence W. 1946- *WhoSSW 93*
Coffey, Daniel Patrick 1954- *WhoEmL 93*
Coffey, David Mario 1949- *WhoEmL 93*
Coffey, Dennis James 1940- *WhoWor 93*
Coffey, Donald Straley 1932- *WhoAm 92*
Coffey, Edward Lyman 1934-1990 *BioIn 17*
Coffey, Frank *ConAu 136*
Coffey, Frank 1947- *ScF&FL 92*
Coffey, Jenness Hall 1951- *WhoE 93, WhoEmL 93*
Coffey, Jim *WhoSSW 93*
Coffey, Joanne Christine 1942- *WhoAmW 93*
Coffey, John Louis 1922- *WhoAm 92*
Coffey, John William 1954- *WhoSSW 93*
Coffey, Joseph Daniel 1938- *WhoAm 92*
Coffey, Joseph Irving 1916- *WhoAm 92*
Coffey, Kathryn Robinson *WhoAmW 93*
Coffey, Kelly Ann 1954- *WhoEmL 93*
Coffey, Kendall Brindley 1952- *WhoEmL 93*
Coffey, Kristine J. Rieck 1942- *St&PR 93*
Coffey, Larry R. 1939- *St&PR 93*
Coffey, Marvin Dale 1930- *WhoAm 92*
Coffey, Matthew B. 1941- *WhoAm 92*
Coffey, Melvin William 1949- *WhoEmL 93*
Coffey, Michael 1926- *ConAu 139*
Coffey, Michael 1936- *St&PR 93*
Coffey, Nancy Ann *WhoAmW 93, WhoWor 93*
Coffey, Patrick Sean 1958- *WhoEmL 93*
Coffey, Paul 1961- *WhoAm 92*
Coffey, Paul B. *Law&B 92*
Coffey, Raymond Richard 1929- *WhoAm 92*
Coffey, Robert Dennis 1950- *WhoEmL 93*
Coffey, Ronald Gibson 1936- *WhoSSW 93*
Coffey, Shelby, III *BioIn 17, WhoAm 92*
Coffey, Thomas Francis, Jr. 1923- *WhoAm 92*
Coffey, Thomas William 1959- *WhoEmL 93*
Coffey, Timothy 1941- *WhoAm 92, WhoE 93*
Coffey, Timothy E. *Law&B 92*
Coffey, Vernon Cornelius, Jr. 1928- *AfrAmBi*
Coffey, Walter J. 1942- *St&PR 93*
Coffey, Wayne Nelson 1950- *WhoSSW 93*
Coffield, Conrad Eugene 1930- *WhoSSW 93*
Coffield, Lloyd Dexter 1937- *St&PR 93*
Coffield, Tom R. 1941- *St&PR 93*
Coffield, Tom R., Jr. *Law&B 92*
Coffill, Marjorie Louise 1917- *WhoAmW 93*
Coffin, Anne Gagnebin 1939- *WhoE 93*
Coffin, Beatriz de Winthuysen 1930- *WhoE 93*
Coffin, Bertha Louise 1919- *WhoAmW 93, WhoWor 93*
Coffin, Charles Carleton 1823-1896 *JrnUS*
Coffin, Charles H. *Law&B 92*
Coffin, David L. 1925- *St&PR 93*
Coffin, David Linwood 1925- *WhoAm 92, WhoE 93*
Coffin, David Robbins 1918- *WhoAm 92*
Coffin, Dean (Fiske) 1911-1992 *ConAu 139*
Coffin, Donald Allen 1948- *WhoEmL 93*
Coffin, Frank Morey 1919- *WhoAm 92*
Coffin, Gertrude Wilson *AmWomPl*
Coffin, Gordon Lee 1938- *WhoAm 92*
Coffin, Harris Alexander, Jr. 1936- *WhoSSW 93*
Coffin, Helen Kingsbury 1907- *WhoAmW 93*
Coffin, John Devereux 1937- *WhoAm 92*
Coffin, John Miller 1944- *WhoE 93*
Coffin, Laurence Edmondston, Jr. 1928- *WhoAm 92*
Coffin, Louis Fussell, Jr. 1917- *WhoAm 92, WhoE 93*
Coffin, Lyn 1943- *WhoWrEP 92*
Coffin, Richard Keith 1940- *WhoAm 92*
Coffin, Tristram 1912- *WhoAm 92, WhoE 93, WhoWor 93*
Coffin, Wayne Philip 1942- *St&PR 93*
Coffing, James Lee 1946- *WhoEmL 93*
Coffinger, Maralin Katharyne 1935- *WhoAmW 93, WhoWor 93*
Coffman, Adelia A. *St&PR 93*
Coffman, Ardis *ScF&FL 92*
Coffman, C.C. *ScF&FL 92*
Coffman, Charles Benjamin 1941- *WhoE 93*
Coffman, Cheryl Clance 1947- *WhoEmL 93*
Coffman, Dallas Whitney 1957- *WhoE 93, WhoEmL 93, WhoWor 93*
Coffman, E. Ronald *Law&B 92*
Coffman, Edward McKenzie 1929- *WhoAm 92*
Coffman, Franklin Edward 1942- *WhoAm 92*
Coffman, James R. 1938- *WhoAm 92*
Coffman, Jay Denton 1928- *WhoAm 92, WhoE 93*
Coffman, Kenneth Morrow 1921- *St&PR 93*
Coffman, Louise M. 1924- *WhoAmW 93*
Coffman, Michael C. 1953- *St&PR 93*
Coffman, Orene Burton 1938- *WhoAmW 93*
Coffman, Phillip Hudson 1936- *WhoAm 92*
Coffman, Robert W. 1939- *St&PR 93*
Coffman, Roy Walter, III 1943- *WhoAm 92*
Coffman, Sandra Jeanne 1945- *WhoAm 92*
Coffman, Stanley Knight, Jr. 1916- *WhoAm 92*
Coffman, Steven D. *BioIn 17*
Coffman, Tom Mills 1942- *WhoSSW 93*
Coffman, Virginia 1914- *ScF&FL 92*
Coffman, Ward Denver, III 1953- *WhoEmL 93*
Coffman, William Eugene 1913- *WhoAm 92*
Coffrin, Albert Wheeler 1919- *WhoAm 92, WhoE 93*
Coffy, Robert Cardinal 1920- *WhoWor 93*
Cofield, Elsie Watson 1924- *WhoAmW 93*
Cofield, Howard John 1926- *WhoAm 92*
Cofield, Philip Thomas 1951- *WhoEmL 93*
Cofino, Manuel 1936-1987 *SpAmA*
Cofrancesco, Donald George 1953- *WhoE 93*
Cogan, Bruce A. *Law&B 92*
Cogan, D.J. 1933- *WhoScE 91-3*
Cogan, David Glendenning 1908- *WhoAm 92*
Cogan, James Richard 1928- *WhoAm 92*
Cogan, John F., Jr. 1926- *St&PR 93*
Cogan, John Francis, Jr. 1926- *WhoAm 92*
Cogan, Kenneth George 1960- *WhoE 93*
Cogan, Mark Charles 1956- *WhoEmL 93*
Cogan, Marshall S. 1937- *WhoAm 92, WhoE 93*
Cogan, Marshall Stuart 1937- *St&PR 93*
Cogan, Philip 1748-1833 *Baker 92*
Cogan, Richard A. *Law&B 92*
Cogan, Robert David 1930- *WhoAm 92*
Cogan, Robert E. 1933- *St&PR 93*
Cogbill, Tommy d1983 *SoulM*
Cogburn, Robert Ray 1935- *WhoSSW 93*
Cogean-Noel, Candice M. *Law&B 92*
Cogell, Elizabeth Cummins *ScF&FL 92*
Coger, Greta Margaret Kay 1934- *WhoSSW 93*
Cogger, Harold Willis 1935- *St&PR 93*
Coggeshall, Calvert 1907-1990 *BioIn 17*
Coggeshall, James Wells 1927- *St&PR 93*
Coggeshall, Janice Reddig 1935- *WhoAmW 93*
Coggeshall, Norman David 1916- *WhoSSW 93, WhoWor 93*
Coggeshall, Randy Lynn 1955- *WhoEmL 93*
Coggeshall, William Turner 1824-1867 *JrnUS*
Coggin, Charlotte Joan 1928- *WhoAm 92, WhoAmW 93*
Coggin, Chris T. 1953- *St&PR 93*
Coggin, James Michael 1952- *WhoEmL 93*
Coggins, Cynthia Anne 1954- *WhoAmW 93*
Coggins, Dana Chandler 1931- *WhoAm 92*
Coggins, Edward Vaughan 1931- *St&PR 93*
Coggins, Freeman Wescoat 1942- *St&PR 93*
Coggins, Homer Dale 1922- *WhoAm 92*
Coggins, John Richard *WhoScE 91-1*
Coggins, Nolan S. 1940- *St&PR 93*
Coggins, Oran Chalmers 1950- *WhoSSW 93*
Coggins, Paul Edward 1951- *WhoEmL 93*
Coggins, Prentiss Mitchell 1948- *WhoSSW 93*
Coggins, R. Stan 1947- *St&PR 93*
Coggins, Wilmer Jesse 1925- *WhoAm 92*
Coggs, G. Spencer *AfrAmBi [port]*
Coggs-Jones, Elizabeth *AfrAmBi [port]*
Coghan, Bob *St&PR 93*
Coghill, George Reid 1942- *WhoWor 93*
Coghill, John Bruce 1925- *WhoAm 92*
Coghill, John P. Jack 1925- *WhoAm 92*
Coghill, Kenneth Alastair 1944- *WhoAsAP 91*
Coghill, Marvin W. 1933- *WhoAm 92, WhoSSW 93*
Coghlan, Alan 1947- *WhoEmL 93*
Coghlan, Anne Eveline 1927- *WhoE 93*
Coghlan, David Buell 1920- *WhoE 93*
Coghlan, Kelly Jack 1952- *WhoEmL 93, WhoSSW 93*
Coghlan, Lida Lavinia 1860- *AmWomPl*
Coghlan, Sharon G. *Law&B 92*
Coghlan, Terence Augustine 1945- *WhoWor 93*
Coghlin, Fitzmaurice, Jr. 1920- *St&PR 93*
Cogliandro, Charles A. 1917- *St&PR 93*
Cogliandro, Charles E. 1953- *St&PR 93*
Cogliandro, Helene Lorraine 1954- *St&PR 93*
Cogliandro, John Anthony 1964- *WhoE 93*
Cogliandro, Robert S. 1951- *St&PR 93*
Coglianese, Fred Anthony 1930- *St&PR 93*
Coglianese, Ralph Edward 1946- *WhoEmL 93*
Cogliano, Michael G. *Law&B 92*
Cognet, Gerard Jean 1941- *WhoScE 91-2*
Cognet, Yves Andre 1950- *WhoWor 93*
Cognetti, Giuseppe 1928- *WhoScE 91-3*
Cogno, Jorge Adrian 1955- *WhoWor 93*
Cograve, John Edwin 1929- *WhoAm 92*
Cogswell, Anthony L. *Law&B 92*
Cogswell, Arnold 1924- *WhoAm 92*
Cogswell, Frederick William 1917- *WhoAm 92, WhoCanL 92, WhoWrEP 92*
Cogswell, Glenn Dale 1922- *WhoAm 92*
Cogswell, John Heyland 1933- *WhoAm 92*
Cogswell, Michael P. *Law&B 92*
Cogswell, Rick 1948- *St&PR 93*

Cogswell, Theodore R. 1918-1987 BioIn 17, ScF&FL 92
Cohalan, Peter Fox 1938- WhoE 93
Cohan, Andrew 1954- St&PR 93
Cohan, Anthony R. ScF&FL 92
Cohan, Anthony Robert 1939- WhoWrEP 92
Cohan, Carole WhoAmW 93
Cohan, Ellen 1945- WhoAmW 93
Cohan, George M(ichael) 1878-1942 Baker 92
Cohan, George Sheldon 1924- WhoAm 92
Cohan, John Robert 1931- WhoAm 92
Cohan, Leon S. Law&B 92
Cohan, Leon Sumner 1929- St&PR 93, WhoAm 92
Cohan, Michael B. Law&B 92
Cohan, Norman H. 1922- St&PR 93
Cohan, Philip L. 1939- WhoAm 92
Cohan, Richard L. 1926- St&PR 93
Cohan, Stanford H. 1929- St&PR 93
Cohan, Thomas Joseph Law&B 92
Cohan, Tony 1939- ScF&FL 92
Cohane, Timothy F. 1952- St&PR 93
Cohea, Melinda Ruth 1961- WhoEmL 93, WhoSSW 93
Coheleach, Guy Joseph WhoAm 92
Cohen, Aaron 1924- WhoSSW 93
Cohen, Aaron 1931- WhoAm 92
Cohen, Aaron M. 1937- WhoAm 92
Cohen, Abby Joseph BioIn 17
Cohen, Abby Joseph 1952- WhoAm 92
Cohen, Abraham Bernard 1922- WhoAm 92
Cohen, Abraham D. 1918- St&PR 93
Cohen, Abraham Ezekiel WhoAm 92, WhoE 93
Cohen, Abraham Ezekiel 1936- St&PR 93
Cohen, Abraham Haft 1900- WhoE 93
Cohen, Abraham J. 1932- WhoAm 92
Cohen, Adam BioIn 17
Cohen, Adele R. 1922- WhoE 93
Cohen, Adrienne Joy WhoSSW 93
Cohen, Ahren L. 1940- St&PR 93
Cohen, Alan Barry 1952- WhoAm 92, WhoE 93
Cohen, Alan Curtis Law&B 92
Cohen, Alan F. Law&B 92
Cohen, Alan Geoffrey 1958- WhoEmL 93
Cohen, Alan Norman 1930- St&PR 93, WhoAm 92
Cohen, Alan Seymour 1926- WhoAm 92
Cohen, Albert 1914- St&PR 93
Cohen, Albert 1929- WhoAm 92
Cohen, Albert D. 1914- St&PR 93
Cohen, Albert Diamond 1914- WhoAm 92
Cohen, Albert J. 1940- St&PR 93
Cohen, Albert Jerome 1940- WhoAm 92
Cohen, Alex 1927- WhoAm 92
Cohen, Alexander H. 1920- WhoAm 92, WhoE 93
Cohen, Alfred G. 1912- St&PR 93
Cohen, Alfred Martin 1941- WhoAm 92
Cohen, Alfredo D. 1924- WhoWor 93
Cohen, Allan 1953- WhoE 93
Cohen, Allan Abraham 1948- WhoSSW 93
Cohen, Allan Richard 1947- WhoAm 92
Cohen, Allan Yale 1939- WhoAm 92
Cohen, Allen 1940- ConAu 139
Cohen, Allen Joseph 1950- St&PR 93
Cohen, Alonzo Clifford, Jr. 1911- WhoSSW 93
Cohen, Alysia 1952- WhoEmL 93
Cohen, Amy 1942- WhoAm 92, WhoE 93
Cohen, Amy S. Law&B 92
Cohen, Andre 1948- St&PR 93
Cohen, Andrea Law&B 92
Cohen, Andrea Harris Law&B 92
Cohen, Andrew Stuart 1930- WhoAm 92
Cohen, Ann Ellen 1949- WhoEmL 93
Cohen, Annette MiSFD 9
Cohen, Anthea 1913- ConAu 40NR
Cohen, Arjeh Marcel 1949- WhoWor 93
Cohen, Arnold 1956- St&PR 93
Cohen, Arnold A. 1914- WhoAm 92
Cohen, Arthur 1919- St&PR 93
Cohen, Arthur 1927- WhoE 93
Cohen, Arthur 1928-1986 BioIn 17
Cohen, Arthur 1945- BioIn 17
Cohen, Arthur A. Law&B 92
Cohen, Arthur A. 1928-1986 JeAmFiW, JeAmHC
Cohen, Arthur Abram 1917- WhoE 93, WhoWor 93
Cohen, Arthur David Law&B 92
Cohen, Arthur Morris 1928- WhoAm 92
Cohen, Audrey C. WhoAmW 93
Cohen, Audrey Gayle Law&B 92
Cohen, Avery S. 1936- St&PR 93
Cohen, Avis H. 1941- BioIn 17
Cohen, B. Stanley 1923- WhoAm 92
Cohen, Barbara 1932- ScF&FL 92
Cohen, Barbara Ann 1958- WhoWrEP 92
Cohen, Barbara Gloria 1952- WhoEmL 93
Cohen, Barbara Kauder d1992 NewYTBS 92
Cohen, Barney ScF&FL 92
Cohen, Barry 1935- WhoAsAP 91
Cohen, Barry David 1952- WhoEmL 93
Cohen, Barry Howard 1949- WhoE 93
Cohen, Ben BioIn 17
Cohen, Benjamin H. 1952- St&PR 93
Cohen, Bennett BioIn 17
Cohen, Bennett J. 1925-1990 BioIn 17
Cohen, Bernard ScF&FL 92
Cohen, Bernard 1929- WhoAm 92
Cohen, Bernard 1947- WhoScE 91-3
Cohen, Bernard B. 1927- WhoE 93
Cohen, Bernard Cecil 1926- WhoAm 92
Cohen, Bernard Leonard 1924- WhoAm 92, WhoE 93
Cohen, Bernard S. 1934- WhoSSW 93
Cohen, Bernard Waley- 1914-1991 BioIn 17
Cohen, Bertram David 1923- WhoAm 92
Cohen, Bertram M. 1931- St&PR 93
Cohen, Brian Jeffrey 1953- WhoEmL 93
Cohen, Bruce Louis 1955- WhoE 93
Cohen, Bruce Michael 1947- WhoAm 92
Cohen, Bruce Preston 1940- WhoSSW 93
Cohen, Burton D. 1940- St&PR 93
Cohen, Burton David Law&B 92
Cohen, Burton David 1940- WhoAm 92
Cohen, Burton Jerome 1933- WhoAm 92
Cohen, Burton Marcus 1925- WhoAm 92, WhoWor 93
Cohen, Byron N. 1940- St&PR 93
Cohen, C.S. St&PR 93
Cohen, Carl Alexander 1952- WhoEmL 93
Cohen, Carla BioIn 17
Cohen, Carla Lynn 1937- WhoAmW 93
Cohen, Carolyn F. Law&B 92
Cohen, Charles Emil 1942- WhoAm 92
Cohen, Charles F. 1945- WhoAm 92
Cohen, Charles J. 1952- WhoAm 92
Cohen, Charles S. Law&B 92
Cohen, Charles Steven Law&B 92
Cohen, Cheryl Diane Durda 1947- WhoAmW 93, WhoEmL 93, WhoWor 93
Cohen, Claire Gorham 1934- St&PR 93
Cohen, Clarence Budd 1925- WhoAm 92
Cohen, Claudia BioIn 17
Cohen, Claudia Beth 1964- WhoAmW 93
Cohen, Cora 1943- WhoAm 92
Cohen, Cynthia Marylyn 1945- WhoAmW 93, WhoWor 93
Cohen, D. David 1940- St&PR 93
Cohen, Dale E. 1954- St&PR 93
Cohen, Damon Boyce 1965- WhoSSW 93
Cohen, Daniel 1936- ScF&FL 92
Cohen, Daniel (E.) 1936- MajAI [port], SmATA 70 [port]
Cohen, Daniel Edward 1936- WhoAm 92
Cohen, Daniel Morris 1930- WhoAm 92
Cohen, David MiSFD 9
Cohen, David 1932- WhoUN 92
Cohen, David 1936- PolPar
Cohen, David E. 1941- St&PR 93
Cohen, David Edward 1950- WhoEmL 93
Cohen, David Harris d1992 NewYTBS 92
Cohen, David Harris 1938- WhoAm 92
Cohen, David J. Law&B 92
Cohen, David J. 1929- St&PR 93
Cohen, David L. Law&B 92
Cohen, David Walter 1926- WhoAm 92
Cohen, David Walter 1947- WhoEmL 93
Cohen, Debra Jo 1957- WhoSSW 93
Cohen, Denise Jodi 1961- WhoAmW 93, WhoEmL 93
Cohen, Diana Louise 1942- WhoAmW 93, WhoE 93
Cohen, Donald Jay 1940- WhoAm 92
Cohen, Donna Eden 1956- WhoAmW 93
Cohen, Dotti 1952- WhoAmW 93
Cohen, Edward 1921- WhoAm 92, WhoWor 93
Cohen, Edward 1954- WhoEmL 93
Cohen, Edward Barth 1949- WhoEmL 93
Cohen, Edward Philip 1932- WhoAm 92
Cohen, Edwin Samuel 1914- WhoAm 92, WhoWor 93
Cohen, Eli MiSFD 9
Cohen, Eli Boyd 1949- WhoEmL 93
Cohen, Eli D. 1926- St&PR 93
Cohen, Eli Edward 1912- WhoAm 92
Cohen, Eliahu 1933- St&PR 93
Cohen, Elizabeth G. 1931- WhoAm 92
Cohen, Ellen B. Law&B 92
Cohen, Elliot D. 1951- ConAu 138
Cohen, Emory M. St&PR 93
Cohen, Etahn M. 1952- WhoEmL 93
Cohen, Eugene Erwin 1917- WhoAm 92
Cohen, Ezechiel Godert David 1923- WhoAm 92
Cohen, Felix A. Law&B 92
Cohen, Felix Asher 1943- St&PR 93, WhoAm 92
Cohen, Florence d1991 BioIn 17
Cohen, Fred 1928- St&PR 93
Cohen, Fred Howard 1948- WhoAm 92
Cohen, Frederick R. Law&B 92
Cohen, Gabriel Murrel 1908- WhoAm 92
Cohen, Gad Jacques 1964- WhoE 93
Cohen, Gary 1948- WhoEmL 93
Cohen, Gary B. Law&B 92
Cohen, Gary Perris 1946- WhoEmL 93
Cohen, Gary S. 1948- WhoEmL 93
Cohen, Gene David 1944- WhoAm 92, WhoWor 93
Cohen, Geoffrey Merrill 1954- WhoE 93, WhoEmL 93
Cohen, George Leon 1930- WhoAm 92
Cohen, Georges N. 1920- WhoScE 91-2
Cohen, Gerald D. St&PR 93
Cohen, Gerry Farmer 1950- WhoEmL 93
Cohen, Gerson David 1924-1991 BioIn 17
Cohen, Geula 1926- BioIn 17
Cohen, Gloria Ernestine 1942- WhoAmW 93, WhoE 93
Cohen, Gordon Seth 1937- St&PR 93
Cohen, Guy 1947- WhoScE 91-2
Cohen, H. Reuben 1921- St&PR 93
Cohen, Harley 1933- WhoAm 92
Cohen, Harold Jeffrey 1947- WhoEmL 93
Cohen, Harriet 1895-1967 Baker 92
Cohen, Harris B. 1921- St&PR 93
Cohen, Harry Law&B 92
Cohen, Harvey Jay 1940- WhoAm 92
Cohen, Harvey Jay 1949- WhoE 93
Cohen, Harvey Martin 1936- WhoE 93
Cohen, Hennig 1919- WhoAm 92
Cohen, Herbert Jesse 1935- WhoAm 92
Cohen, Herman 1894-1990 BioIn 17
Cohen, Herman J. BioIn 17
Cohen, Herman Jay 1932- NewYTBS 92 [port], WhoAm 92
Cohen, Herman Nathan 1949- WhoAm 92, WhoE 93, WhoEmL 93, WhoWor 93
Cohen, Hirsh Joel 1942- WhoAm 92
Cohen, Howard 1927- St&PR 93
Cohen, Howard L. 1941- St&PR 93
Cohen, Howard R. MiSFD 9
Cohen, I. Bernard 1914- BioIn 17
Cohen, I. Roy 1922- St&PR 93
Cohen, Ida Bogin WhoAmW 93
Cohen, Ira H. 1935- WhoWrEP 92
Cohen, Ira Myron 1937- WhoAm 92, WhoE 93
Cohen, Ira Richard 1960- St&PR 93
Cohen, Ira Stanley 1922- WhoAm 92
Cohen, Irving d1991 BioIn 17
Cohen, Irving David 1945- WhoAm 92
Cohen, Irving Elias 1946- WhoAm 92, WhoE 93, WhoWor 93
Cohen, Irving I. 1950- WhoAm 92
Cohen, Irwin 1936- WhoE 93, WhoWor 93
Cohen, Isaac 1940- WhoUN 92
Cohen, Isaac Louis 1948- WhoE 93
Cohen, Isidore 1922- Baker 92
Cohen, Isidore Leonard 1922- WhoAm 92
Cohen, Isidore M. d1991 BioIn 17
Cohen, Israel 1912- St&PR 93, WhoAm 92
Cohen, Jack S. Law&B 92
Cohen, Jack Victor Law&B 92
Cohen, James 1956- ScF&FL 92
Cohen, James A. Law&B 92
Cohen, James A. 1946- St&PR 93
Cohen, James (E.) 1956- ConAu 137
Cohen, James N. Law&B 92
Cohen, James Samuel 1946- WhoEmL 93
Cohen, James Simon 1956- WhoE 93
Cohen, Jamey ScF&FL 92
Cohen, Janis Law&B 92
Cohen, Jay Adam 1962- WhoEmL 93
Cohen, Jay Allen 1951- WhoEmL 93
Cohen, Jay Loring 1953- WhoEmL 93
Cohen, Jay R. 1941- St&PR 93
Cohen, Jay Richard 1941- WhoAm 92
Cohen, Jeffrey Alan 1953- WhoE 93
Cohen, Jeffrey Lewis 1950- WhoEmL 93
Cohen, Jeffrey M. 1940- WhoAm 92
Cohen, Jeffrey Steven 1952- WhoWor 93
Cohen, Jennifer BioIn 17
Cohen, Jeremy 1949- WhoEmL 93
Cohen, Jeri Fried 1956- WhoAmW 93
Cohen, Jerome 1925- WhoAm 92
Cohen, Jerome Bernard 1932- WhoAm 92
Cohen, Jerrold E. d1991 BioIn 17
Cohen, Jerry D. 1948- St&PR 93
Cohen, Joan Lebold 1932- WhoE 93
Cohen, Joan Newman 1934- WhoSSW 93
Cohen, Joel B. 1931- St&PR 93
Cohen, Joel C. WhoAm 92
Cohen, Joel David 1952- WhoEmL 93
Cohen, Joel Ephraim 1944- WhoAm 92
Cohen, Joel (Israel) 1942- Baker 92
Cohen, Joel J. 1938- WhoAm 92
Cohen, Jon ScF&FL 92
Cohen, Jon Stephan 1943- WhoAm 92
Cohen, Jonathan Brewer 1944- WhoAm 92
Cohen, Jonathan L. 1939- St&PR 93
Cohen, Jonathan Little 1939- WhoAm 92
Cohen, Joseph 1926- WhoAm 92, WhoSSW 93
Cohen, Joseph A. 1917- St&PR 93
Cohen, Joseph H. 1921- St&PR 93
Cohen, Joseph M. 1937- St&PR 93
Cohen, Joyce Arnoff 1925- WhoE 93
Cohen, Joyce E. 1937- WhoAmW 93
Cohen, Jozef 1921- WhoAm 92
Cohen, Judith 1945- WhoAmW 93
Cohen, Judith Ann 1953- WhoEmL 93
Cohen, Judith D. Law&B 92
Cohen, Judith Levitt 1948- WhoEmL 93
Cohen, Judith Lynne 1951- WhoEmL 93
Cohen, Judith W. 1937- WhoE 93
Cohen, Judy W. 1954- St&PR 93
Cohen, Jules 1931- WhoAm 92
Cohen, Jules-Emile-David 1835-1901 Baker 92
Cohen, Jules Simon 1937- WhoAm 92
Cohen, Julius George 1921- WhoAm 92
Cohen, Julius Simon 1956- WhoWor 93
Cohen, Karen J. 1949- WhoAmW 93, WhoSSW 93
Cohen, Karl Paley 1913- WhoAm 92
Cohen, Katrina See Turtle Island String Quartet ConMus 9
Cohen, Keith 1945- WhoWrEP 92
Cohen, Kenneth d1990 BioIn 17
Cohen, Kenneth P. Law&B 92
Cohen, Kenneth S. Law&B 92
Cohen, Larry 1941- MiSFD 9
Cohen, Larry Steven 1951- WhoEmL 93
Cohen, Lauren Ann 1949- WhoAm 92
Cohen, Lauren B. Law&B 92
Cohen, Lawrence 1926- WhoAm 92
Cohen, Lawrence Edward 1945- WhoAm 92
Cohen, Lawrence G. Law&B 92
Cohen, Lawrence H. Law&B 92
Cohen, Lawrence N. 1932- St&PR 93, WhoAm 92
Cohen, Lawrence Sorel 1933- WhoAm 92
Cohen, Lee D. 1953- St&PR 93
Cohen, Lee Steven 1959- WhoEmL 93
Cohen, Leeber 1957- WhoE 93
Cohen, Leonard 1925- St&PR 93, WhoAm 92, WhoWor 93
Cohen, Leonard 1934- Baker 92, BioIn 17, WhoAm 92, WhoCanL 92
Cohen, Leonard David 1932- WhoE 93
Cohen, Leonard N. d1992 NewYTBS 92
Cohen, Leonard N. 1920-1992 BioIn 17
Cohen, Leslie Ann 1956- WhoEmL 93
Cohen, Leslie B. 1923- St&PR 93
Cohen, Lewis Cobrain 1947- WhoAm 92, WhoEmL 93
Cohen, Lewis Isaac 1932- WhoAm 92
Cohen, Lewis S. 1947- St&PR 93
Cohen, Lila Beldock 1927- WhoWrEP 92
Cohen, Lizabeth WhoAmW 93
Cohen, Lloyd Robert 1947- WhoEmL 93
Cohen, Lois Jean 1924- WhoE 93
Cohen, Louis d1991 BioIn 17
Cohen, Louis N. 1911- St&PR 93
Cohen, M.E. BioIn 17
Cohen, Malcolm Martin 1937- WhoAm 92
Cohen, Marcy Sharon Law&B 92
Cohen, Marcy Sharon 1954- WhoEmL 93
Cohen, Margaret Ann 1953- WhoEmL 93
Cohen, Margaret Anne 1958- WhoAmW 93
Cohen, Margo Panush 1940- WhoE 93
Cohen, Marion Cantor 1940- WhoE 93
Cohen, Marion Deutsche 1943- WhoWrEP 92
Cohen, Mark Daniel 1951- WhoE 93
Cohen, Mark H. 1932- St&PR 93
Cohen, Mark Herbert 1932- WhoAm 92
Cohen, Mark I. Law&B 92
Cohen, Mark N. 1947- WhoE 93, WhoEmL 93, WhoWor 93
Cohen, Mark Robert 1947- WhoE 93
Cohen, Mark Steven 1948- WhoE 93, WhoEmL 93, WhoWor 93
Cohen, Marlene Lois 1945- WhoAm 92
Cohen, Marlene Zichi 1951- WhoEmL 93
Cohen, Marsha BioIn 17
Cohen, Marsha A. 1952- St&PR 93, WhoIns 93
Cohen, Marsha Nan 1947- WhoAmW 93
Cohen, Marshall WhoAm 92, WhoE 93, WhoWor 93
Cohen, Marshall Harris 1926- WhoAm 92
Cohen, Martin MiSFD 9
Cohen, Martin 1932- St&PR 93, WhoAm 92
Cohen, Martin F. 1939- WhoE 93
Cohen, Martin Gilbert 1938- WhoAm 92
Cohen, Martin R. 1937- St&PR 93
Cohen, Martin S. Law&B 92
Cohen, Marvin Lou 1935- WhoAm 92
Cohen, Marvin William 1936- WhoE 93
Cohen, Mary Ann 1943- CngDr 91, WhoAm 92, WhoAmW 93
Cohen, Mary Ann Adler 1941- WhoAmW 93
Cohen, Matt 1942- ConAu 40NR, WhoCanL 92
Cohen, Matthew 1942- ScF&FL 92
Cohen, Max 1918- WhoWor 93
Cohen, Max Harry 1940- WhoAm 92
Cohen, Maxine Bilsky 1961- WhoEmL 93
Cohen, Maynard Manuel 1920- WhoAm 92
Cohen, Melvin 1926- St&PR 93
Cohen, Melvin Harris 1946- WhoSSW 93
Cohen, Melvin Irwin 1936- WhoAm 92

Cohen, Melvin Joseph 1928- *WhoAm 92*
Cohen, Melvin Lee 1950- *WhoEmL 93, WhoSSW 93*
Cohen, Melvin R. 1911- *WhoAm 92*
Cohen, Melvin S. 1918- *St&PR 93*
Cohen, Melvin S. 1919- *St&PR 93*
Cohen, Melvin Samuel 1918- *WhoAm 92*
Cohen, Melvin Stephen 1919- *WhoAm 92*
Cohen, Melvyn Douglas 1943- *WhoWor 93*
Cohen, Michael 1930- *WhoAm 92*
Cohen, Michael 1939- *WhoAm 92*
Cohen, Michael 1950- *WhoE 93*
Cohen, Michael Alan 1933- *WhoWor 93*
Cohen, Michael Harris 1953- *WhoEmL 93*
Cohen, Michael I. 1935- *WhoAm 92*
Cohen, Michael Norman 1960- *WhoEmL 93*
Cohen, Michael Paul 1947- *WhoEmL 93*
Cohen, Mickey L. 1923- *St&PR 93*
Cohen, Mildred Thaler 1921- *WhoAm 92, WhoE 93*
Cohen, Millard Stuart 1939- *St&PR 93, WhoWor 93*
Cohen, Milton d1991 *BioIn 17*
Cohen, Milton Howard 1911- *WhoAm 92*
Cohen, Milton L. 1928- *St&PR 93*
Cohen, Miriam 1926- *WhoAm 92*
Cohen, Mitchell H. 1904-1991 *BioIn 17*
Cohen, Mitchell Jay 1954- *St&PR 93*
Cohen, Morley M. 1917- *St&PR 93*
Cohen, Morley Mitchell 1917- *WhoAm 92*
Cohen, Morrel Herman 1927- *WhoAm 92*
Cohen, Morris 1911- *WhoAm 92*
Cohen, Morris Leo 1927- *WhoAm 92*
Cohen, Morris Raphael 1880-1947 *BioIn 17, JeAmHC*
Cohen, Morton N. 1921- *ScF&FL 92*
Cohen, Moses Elias 1937- *WhoAm 92*
Cohen, Myer 1907- *WhoAm 92*
Cohen, Myron Leslie 1934- *St&PR 93, WhoAm 92*
Cohen, N. Jerold 1935- *WhoAm 92*
Cohen, Nancy Lin 1957- *WhoEmL 93*
Cohen, Nancy Mahoney *Law&B 92*
Cohen, Neil *MiSFD 9*
Cohen, Neil L. 1961- *St&PR 93*
Cohen, Nicholas 1938- *WhoAm 92, WhoE 93*
Cohen, Noel Lee 1930- *WhoAm 92, WhoE 93*
Cohen, Norm 1936- *WhoAm 92*
Cohen, Norman d1991 *BioIn 17*
Cohen, Norman 1934- *WhoAm 92*
Cohen, Orville Salvator 1922- *St&PR 93*
Cohen, P.J. *WhoScE 91-1*
Cohen, Patrice F. *Law&B 92*
Cohen, Patricia Rose 1946- *WhoAmW 93*
Cohen, Paul d1991 *BioIn 17*
Cohen, Paul 1940- *WhoScE 91-2*
Cohen, Paul M. 1952- *St&PR 93*
Cohen, Perry D. 1946- *WhoE 93, WhoEmL 93*
Cohen, Peter *BioIn 17*
Cohen, Peter Alan 1954- *WhoE 93*
Cohen, Peter Arthur 1951- *WhoSSW 93*
Cohen, Peter Michael *Law&B 92*
Cohen, Philip 1907- *WhoSSW 93*
Cohen, Philip 1931- *WhoAm 92*
Cohen, Philip 1948- *WhoEmL 93*
Cohen, Philip Francis 1911- *WhoAm 92*
Cohen, Philip G(ary) 1954- *ConAu 136*
Cohen, Philip Gary 1950- *WhoEmL 93*
Cohen, Philip Gary 1954- *WhoSSW 93*
Cohen, Philip H. d1992 *NewYTBS 92*
Cohen, Philip Herman 1936- *WhoAm 92*
Cohen, Philip M. *Law&B 92*
Cohen, Philip Pacy 1908- *WhoAm 92*
Cohen, Phillip 1919- *St&PR 93*
Cohen, Phyllis Perkins 1934- *St&PR 93*
Cohen, Ralph 1917- *ConAu 138*
Cohen, Ralph 1919- *WhoAm 92*
Cohen, Ralph H. 1935- *St&PR 93*
Cohen, Randal Lee 1953- *WhoEmL 93*
Cohen, Raymond 1923- *WhoAm 92*
Cohen, Raymond James 1948- *WhoWor 93*
Cohen, Raymond V. *St&PR 93*
Cohen, Reina Joyce 1931- *WhoE 93*
Cohen, Richard *Law&B 92*
Cohen, Richard 1952- *WhoAm 92*
Cohen, Richard 1955- *WhoEmL 93*
Cohen, Richard A. *Law&B 92*
Cohen, Richard Alan *Law&B 92*
Cohen, Richard Allen 1948- *St&PR 93*
Cohen, Richard Gerard 1931- *WhoAm 92*
Cohen, Richard Neil 1953- *WhoEmL 93*
Cohen, Richard Norman 1923- *WhoAm 92*
Cohen, Richard S. *Law&B 92*
Cohen, Richard Steven 1942- *St&PR 93, WhoAm 92*
Cohen, Richard Steven 1955- *WhoE 93*
Cohen, Richard Stockman 1937- *WhoAm 92*
Cohen, Rob 1949- *MiSFD 9*
Cohen, Robert 1932- *WhoE 93*
Cohen, Robert 1957- *WhoEmL 93*
Cohen, Robert Abraham 1909- *WhoAm 92*
Cohen, Robert Avram 1929- *WhoE 93*
Cohen, Robert Bruce *Law&B 92*
Cohen, Robert Donald *WhoScE 91-1*
Cohen, Robert Edward 1947- *WhoAm 92*
Cohen, Robert G. *Law&B 92*
Cohen, Robert Harvey 1928- *St&PR 93*
Cohen, Robert Jay 1942- *WhoSSW 93*
Cohen, Robert L. *Law&B 92*
Cohen, Robert L. 1929- *St&PR 93*
Cohen, Robert L. 1947- *WhoWrEP 92*
Cohen, Robert Leonard 1937- *WhoAm 92*
Cohen, Robert Leonard 1952- *WhoEmL 93*
Cohen, Robert Leslie 1941- *WhoE 93*
Cohen, Robert P. 1927- *St&PR 93*
Cohen, Robert S. 1928- *St&PR 93*
Cohen, Robert Sonne 1923- *WhoAm 92, WhoWor 93*
Cohen, Robert Stephen 1938- *WhoAm 92*
Cohen, Robert Yale, II 1950- *WhoEmL 93*
Cohen, Roberta Sherri 1955- *WhoEmL 93*
Cohen, Robin *WhoScE 91-1*
Cohen, Rochelle Lynn 1963- *WhoE 93*
Cohen, Roger L. 1935- *WhoAm 92*
Cohen, Ron 1956- *WhoEmL 93*
Cohen, Ronald 1930- *WhoAm 92*
Cohen, Ronald Eli 1937- *WhoAm 92*
Cohen, Ronald Jay 1947- *WhoE 93*
Cohen, Ronald Marc 1951- *WhoEmL 93*
Cohen, Ronny Helene 1950- *WhoE 93*
Cohen, Ruben David 1956- *WhoEmL 93, WhoSSW 93*
Cohen, Ruth 1906-1991 *AnObit 1991*
Cohen, Ruth Louisa 1906-1991 *BioIn 17*
Cohen, S. E. *MiSFD 9*
Cohen, Samuel Israel 1933- *WhoE 93, WhoWor 93*
Cohen, Samuel J. 1908-1991 *BioIn 17*
Cohen, Sandon Lee 1960- *WhoEmL 93*
Cohen, Sanford 1938- *St&PR 93*
Cohen, Sanford Charles 1936- *WhoSSW 93*
Cohen, Sanford Irwin 1928- *WhoAm 92, WhoSSW 93*
Cohen, Sanford Ned 1935- *WhoAm 92*
Cohen, Santiago *BioIn 17*
Cohen, Sarah *ScF&FL 92*
Cohen, Saul 1930- *St&PR 93*
Cohen, Saul Bernard 1925- *WhoAm 92*
Cohen, Saul G. 1916- *WhoAm 92*
Cohen, Saul Z. 1926-1992 *BioIn 17*
Cohen, Selma 1930- *WhoAmW 93, WhoWor 93*
Cohen, Selma Jeanne 1920- *WhoAm 92*
Cohen, Seymour 1917- *WhoAm 92*
Cohen, Seymour Jay 1922- *WhoAm 92*
Cohen, Seymour Stanley 1917- *WhoAm 92*
Cohen, Shari Sue 1950- *St&PR 93*
Cohen, Sharon Anne 1956- *WhoWrEP 92*
Cohen, Sheila Forman 1960- *WhoEmL 93*
Cohen, Sheldon Gilbert 1918- *WhoAm 92, WhoE 93*
Cohen, Sheldon Hersh 1934- *WhoAm 92*
Cohen, Sheldon Stanley 1927- *WhoAm 92*
Cohen, Shep 1929- *St&PR 93*
Cohen, Sidney Louis 1926- *St&PR 93*
Cohen, Sidney R. 1920- *St&PR 93*
Cohen, Spencer 1943- *St&PR 93*
Cohen, Stanley 1922- *WhoAm 92, WhoSSW 93, WhoWor 93*
Cohen, Stanley 1937- *WhoAm 92, WhoWor 93*
Cohen, Stanley Allen 1947- *WhoSSW 93*
Cohen, Stanley L. *Law&B 92*
Cohen, Stanley Norman 1935- *WhoAm 92*
Cohen, Stephanie D. *St&PR 93*
Cohen, Stephen A. 1937- *St&PR 93*
Cohen, Stephen Douglas 1944- *WhoWor 93*
Cohen, Stephen F. *BioIn 17*
Cohen, Stephen Frand 1938- *WhoAm 92*
Cohen, Stephen Howard 1938- *WhoAm 92*
Cohen, Stephen Mark 1952- *WhoEmL 93*
Cohen, Stephen Marshall 1929- *WhoAm 92*
Cohen, Stephen Martin 1957- *WhoEmL 93*
Cohen, Stephen Michael 1957- *WhoEmL 93*
Cohen, Stephen Paul *ScF&FL 92*
Cohen, Stephen Philip 1936- *WhoAm 92*
Cohen, Stephen Robert 1950- *WhoEmL 93*
Cohen, Steven 1947- *WhoEmL 93*
Cohen, Steven Aaron *Law&B 92*
Cohen, Steven Arthur 1951- *WhoWor 93*
Cohen, Steven Charles 1947- *WhoEmL 93*
Cohen, Steven L. *Law&B 92*
Cohen, Stewart Eric 1950- *WhoE 93*
Cohen, Stuart R. *Law&B 92*
Cohen, Susan Berk 1942- *WhoAmW 93*
Cohen, Susan H. *ScF&FL 92*
Cohen, Susan Lois 1938- *WhoAm 92*
Cohen, Susan M. 1950- *WhoSSW 93*
Cohen, Sylvan M. 1914- *St&PR 93, WhoAm 92*
Cohen, Ted 1939- *WhoAm 92*
Cohen, Theodore 1929- *WhoE 93*
Cohen, Valerie A. *Law&B 92*
Cohen, Victor *Law&B 92*
Cohen, Victor Andrew *Law&B 92*
Cohen, Wallace M. 1908- *WhoAm 92*
Cohen, Walter Stanley 1936- *WhoAm 92*
Cohen, Warren I. 1934- *WhoAm 92*
Cohen, Wayne Roy 1946- *WhoE 93*
Cohen, William Alan 1937- *WhoAm 92*
Cohen, William Benjamin 1941- *WhoAm 92*
Cohen, William Nathan 1935- *WhoAm 92*
Cohen, William S. 1940- *CngDr 91*
Cohen, William Sebastian 1940- *WhoAm 92, WhoE 93*
Cohen, Yeruham d1991 *BioIn 17*
Cohen-Adad, Roger 1921- *WhoScE 91-2*
Cohen-Berman, Naomi Eileen 1947- *WhoEmL 93*
Cohenca, Jacques 1922- *St&PR 93*
Cohenca, Philip M. 1952- *St&PR 93*
Cohen-Ganouna, Jacques *WhoScE 91-2*
Cohen-Rosenthal, Edward 1952- *WhoE 93*
Cohen-Solal, Annie *BioIn 17*
Cohen-Stratyner, Barbara Naomi 1951- *WhoEmL 93*
Cohen-Tannoudji, Claude 1933- *WhoScE 91-2*
Cohen-Tannoudji, Claude Nessim 1933- *WhoWor 93*
Cohernour, Elizabeth Nelson 1950- *St&PR 93*
Cohick, James Allen, Jr. 1959- *WhoE 93*
Cohill, Maurice Blanchard, Jr. 1929- *WhoAm 92, WhoE 93*
Cohill, Robert Anthony 1939- *St&PR 93*
Cohl, Claudia Hope 1939- *WhoAmW 93*
Cohl, Emile 1857-1938 *BioIn 17*
Cohler, Bertram Joseph 1938- *WhoAm 92*
Cohn, Al(vin Gilbert) 1925-1988 *Baker 92*
Cohn, Andrew Howard 1945- *WhoAm 92*
Cohn, Ann P. *Law&B 92*
Cohn, Arnold N. 1934- *St&PR 93*
Cohn, Arthur 1910- *Baker 92*
Cohn, Bernhard N. d1992 *BioIn 17*
Cohn, Bertram Josiah 1925- *WhoAm 92*
Cohn, Charles *Law&B 92*
Cohn, Cindy A. 1963- *WhoAmW 93*
Cohn, Daniel Ross 1943- *WhoE 93*
Cohn, David Herc 1923- *WhoAm 92*
Cohn, David Valor 1926- *WhoAm 92, WhoWor 93*
Cohn, Derek 1947- *WhoEmL 93*
Cohn, Don Stephen 1950- *WhoEmL 93*
Cohn, Donald A. *Law&B 92*
Cohn, Donald H. 1930- *St&PR 93*
Cohn, Elchanan 1941- *WhoSSW 93*
Cohn, Ellen Sue 1952- *WhoAmW 93*
Cohn, Gary M. *Law&B 92*
Cohn, Gary Michael 1960- *St&PR 93*
Cohn, Gerald Martin 1948- *St&PR 93*
Cohn, Geraldine Lois 1934- *St&PR 93*
Cohn, Harvey 1923- *WhoAm 92*
Cohn, Haskell 1901- *WhoAm 92, WhoWor 93*
Cohn, Heinrich *Baker 92*
Cohn, Herbert B. 1912- *WhoAm 92*
Cohn, Howard 1922- *WhoAm 92*
Cohn, Howard T. 1929- *WhoIns 93*
Cohn, Ian J. 1950- *WhoEmL 93*
Cohn, Isidore, Jr. 1921- *WhoAm 92, WhoSSW 93, WhoWor 93*
Cohn, J. Gunther 1911- *WhoE 93*
Cohn, James (Myron) 1928- *Baker 92*
Cohn, James Ronald 1949- *WhoEmL 93*
Cohn, Jan Kadetsky 1933- *WhoE 93, WhoWrEP 92*
Cohn, Janet Stone 1909- *WhoWrEP 92*
Cohn, Jeanne Terry 1957- *WhoEmL 93*
Cohn, Jess Victor 1908- *WhoAm 92*
Cohn, Jim 1953- *WhoWrEP 92*
Cohn, Joseph David 1937- *WhoE 93*
Cohn, Joshua D. *Law&B 92*
Cohn, Kenneth Doyle 1946- *St&PR 93*
Cohn, Leonard Allan 1929- *St&PR 93, WhoAm 92*
Cohn, Lois Beryl 1955- *WhoAmW 93*
Cohn, Lowell A. 1945- *WhoAm 92*
Cohn, Marianne Winter Miller 1928- *WhoAmW 93, WhoSSW 93, WhoWor 93*
Cohn, Marilyn Barbara 1936- *WhoAmW 93*
Cohn, Marjorie Benedict 1939- *WhoAm 92, WhoAmW 93, WhoWor 93*
Cohn, Martin 1945- *WhoAm 92*
Cohn, Martin David 1925- *St&PR 93*
Cohn, Marvin 1928- *WhoAm 92*
Cohn, Mildred 1913- *WhoAm 92, WhoAmW 93*
Cohn, Milton L. 1915- *St&PR 93*
Cohn, Nathan 1918- *WhoWor 93*
Cohn, Nik 1946- *ScF&FL 92*
Cohn, Norman Stanley 1930- *WhoAm 92*
Cohn, Paul Moritz 1924- *WhoWor 93*
Cohn, Pauletta Palasota *Law&B 92*
Cohn, Racey E. *Law&B 92*
Cohn, Richard Steven 1956- *WhoEmL 93*
Cohn, Robert 1949- *St&PR 93*
Cohn, Robert E. 1945- *WhoAm 92*
Cohn, Robert Mark 1945- *WhoAm 92, WhoE 93*
Cohn, Robert Steven *Law&B 92*
Cohn, Robin Jean 1952- *WhoEmL 93*
Cohn, Ronald Ira 1936- *WhoAm 92*
Cohn, Sam 1929- *WhoAm 92*
Cohn, Samuel Maurice 1915- *WhoAm 92*
Cohn, Sheldon J. *Law&B 92*
Cohn, Sherman Louis 1932- *WhoAm 92*
Cohn, Sidney E. 1908-1991 *BioIn 17*
Cohn, Steven Philip *Law&B 92*
Cohn, Stuart Harris 1950- *WhoE 93*
Cohn, Theodore 1923- *WhoAm 92*
Cohn, Timothy William 1962- *WhoEmL 93*
Cohn, Victor Edward 1919- *WhoAm 92*
Cohn, William Elliott 1951- *WhoEmL 93*
Cohn, Zanvil Alexander 1926- *WhoAm 92*
Cohn-Bendit, Daniel *BioIn 17*
Cohne, Herbert William 1921- *WhoE 93*
Cohn-Haft, Hera Maria 1947- *WhoE 93*
Cohn-Sherbok, Dan 1945- *ConAu 137*
Cohodes, Eli Aaron 1927- *WhoAm 92*
Cohon, Peter 1942- *WhoAm 92*
Cohorn, Ron L. 1943- *WhoSSW 93*
Cohrs, William Robert *Law&B 92*
Cohrt, Poul Tor 1946- *WhoWor 93*
Coia, Robert Salvatore 1944- *WhoE 93*
Coia, Theodore N. 1947- *WhoIns 93*
Coign, Janet Doremus 1963- *WhoSSW 93*
Coign, Robert Walter 1965- *WhoSSW 93*
Coigney, Martha Wadsworth 1933- *WhoAm 92*
Coigney, Rodolphe Lucien 1911- *WhoE 93*
Coil, Charles Ray 1940- *WhoSSW 93*
Coimbra, Jorge Penaranda 1947- *WhoWor 93*
Coin, Sheila Regan 1942- *WhoAmW 93*
Coineau, Yves 1934- *WhoScE 91-2*
Coiner, Maryrose C. 1949- *WhoE 93*
Coins, Wally *ScF&FL 92*
Coirier, Jean 1944- *WhoScE 91-2*
Coirier, Jean Leon 1944- *WhoWor 93*
Coit, Arthur Leon 1934- *WhoWrEP 92*
Coit, Kevin Robert 1957- *WhoSSW 93*
Coit, Lynde Harrison *Law&B 92*
Coit, Margaret Louise 1919- *WhoAm 92*
Coit, Michele Vivian 1954- *WhoAmW 93, WhoEmL 93*
Coit, Richard D. *Law&B 92*
Cojean, Roger 1949- *WhoScE 91-2*
Cojuangco, Jose S., Jr. 1934- *WhoAsAP 91*
Cojuangco Family *BioIn 17*
Coke, Chauncey Eugene *WhoAm 92, WhoWor 93*
Coke, Frank Van Deren 1921- *WhoAm 92*
Coke, Lester Lloyd *BioIn 17*
Coke, Van Deren 1921- *WhoWrEP 92*
Cokelet, Giles Roy 1932- *WhoAm 92*
Coker, Bernard John 1952- *St&PR 93*
Coker, Charles Westfield 1933- *St&PR 93, WhoAm 92, WhoSSW 93*
Coker, Cindy S. 1957- *St&PR 93*
Coker, Donald William 1945- *WhoSSW 93*
Coker, Donna Sue 1957- *WhoEmL 93, WhoSSW 93*
Coker, Gene V. *Law&B 92*
Coker, James Lide 1941- *St&PR 93*
Coker, Richard N. 1947- *St&PR 93*
Coker, Robert Hilton 1947- *WhoAm 92, WhoEmL 93*
Coker, Shirley L. *Law&B 92*
Coker, William R. 1936- *WhoWrEP 92*
Coker, William Sidney 1924- *WhoSSW 93*
Cokliss, Harley 1945- *MiSFD 9*
Col, Jeanne-Marie 1946- *WhoEmL 93*
Col, Martin H. 1951- *St&PR 93*
Colabrese, Gary John 1948- *WhoWor 93*
Colacchio, Judith Maxine 1947- *St&PR 93*
Colacci, Irving Roger 1953- *WhoEmL 93*
Colacecchi, Mary Beth 1961- *WhoAmW 93*
Colacello, Bob 1947- *ConAu 138*
Colacino, Michele 1940- *WhoScE 91-3*
Colacioppo, Tullio Fernando, Jr. 1934- *WhoWor 93*
Colaco, Joseph Phillip 1940- *St&PR 93*
Colacurcio, Daniel V. 1948- *WhoIns 93*
Coladarci, Theodore 1953- *WhoE 93*
Colahan, J. Randolph 1952- *St&PR 93*
Colahan, Patrick Timothy 1948- *WhoSSW 93*
Colahan, Peter D. 1956- *St&PR 93*
Colaianni, Joseph Vincent 1935- *WhoAm 92*
Colaianni, Peter L. 1954- *WhoAm 92*
Colaizzi, John Louis 1938- *WhoAm 92*
Colalucci, Francis Michael 1944- *St&PR 93*
Colamarino, Katrin *Law&B 92*
Colamarino, Katrin Belenky 1951- *WhoAmW 93*

Colamarino, Leonard James 1951- *WhoEmL 93*
Colan, Horia 1926- *WhoScE 91-4*
Colan, Robert *Law&B 92*
Colander, David Charles 1947- *WhoAm 92, WhoEmL 93*
Colander, Valerie Nieman 1955- *ScF&FL 92, WhoWrEP 92*
Colangelo, Jerry John 1939- *WhoAm 92*
Colangelo, Robert d1991 *BioIn 17*
Colangelo, Rocco, Jr. 1964- *WhoE 93*
Colani, Luigi 1928- *BioIn 17*
Colantoni, Alfred D. 1952- *St&PR 93*
Colantoni, Alfred Daniel 1952- *WhoE 93*
Colao, Anthony F. *WhoIns 93*
Colao, Anthony F. 1927- *St&PR 93*
Colao, Ralph F. 1930- *St&PR 93*
Colao, Rudolph Nicholas 1927- *WhoE 93*
Colardyn, Francis Achille 1944- *WhoWor 93*
Colarullo, Louis Anthony 1948- *WhoE 93, WhoEmL 93*
Colas, Alain 1930- *WhoScE 91-2*
Colas, Antonio E. 1928- *HispAmA [port]*
Colas, Antonio Espada 1928- *WhoAm 92*
Colas, Arthur H., Jr. *Law&B 92*
Colas, Bernard Alfred Ignace 1943- *WhoScE 91-2*
Colas, Bernard Henry Francois 1960- *WhoWor 93*
Colas, Emile Jules 1923- *WhoAm 92*
Colasante, Gabriel *St&PR 93*
Colasanti, Fabio 1946- *WhoWor 93*
Colasanto, E.M. 1941- *St&PR 93*
Colasse, Pascal 1649-1709 *Baker 92, OxDcOp*
Colasuonno, Louis Christopher 1948- *WhoAm 92*
Colasurd, Richard Michael 1928- *WhoAm 92*
Colatrella, Carol Ann 1957- *WhoE 93*
Colavecchio, Donald L. 1942- *St&PR 93*
Colavito, Christopher 1955- *St&PR 93*
Colaw, Thomas Allan 1939- *WhoE 93*
Colbacchini, Antonio 1881-1960 *IntDcAn*
Colbeck, Samuel Charles 1940- *WhoE 93*
Colber, Douglas W. *Law&B 92*
Colberg, Malcolm Gunnar 1924- *St&PR 93*
Colberg, Marla Cordell 1963- *WhoAmW 93*
Colberg, Marshall Rudolph 1913- *WhoAm 92*
Colberg, Ralph Eugene 1932- *WhoSSW 93*
Colberg, Thomas Pearsall 1948- *WhoAm 92, WhoWor 93*
Colbert, Alice Taylor 1955- *WhoAmW 93, WhoSSW 93*
Colbert, Annette Darcia 1959- *WhoEmL 93*
Colbert, Celia A. *Law&B 92*
Colbert, Charles Ralph 1921- *WhoAm 92*
Colbert, Chunk d1874 *BioIn 17*
Colbert, Claudette *BioIn 17*
Colbert, Claudette 1903- *WhoAm 92*
Colbert, Claudette 1905- *IntDcF 2-3 [port]*
Colbert, Donald W. 1949- *St&PR 93*
Colbert, Douglas Marc 1948- *WhoE 93*
Colbert, Edwin Harris 1905- *WhoAm 92*
Colbert, Elbert Lynn 1952- *WhoEmL 93*
Colbert, Genie Davis 1944- *WhoAmW 93*
Colbert, Heather Brown 1950- *WhoAm 92, WhoEmL 93*
Colbert, Kevin L. *Law&B 92*
Colbert, Lester Lum 1905- *WhoAm 92*
Colbert, Lester Lum, Jr. 1934- *WhoAm 92*
Colbert, Marc H. *Law&B 92*
Colbert, Marvin Jay 1923- *WhoAm 92*
Colbert, Robert B., Jr. 1921- *WhoAm 92*
Colbert, Stephana I. *Law&B 92*
Colbert, Virgis W. *BioIn 17*
Colborn, Gene Louis 1935- *WhoAm 92, WhoSSW 93*
Colborn, Harry Walter 1921- *WhoAm 92*
Colborn, Patricia Harrison 1952- *WhoAmW 93*
Colborn, Theo E. 1927- *WhoAm 92*
Colborne, John 1778-1863 *HarEnMi*
Colborne, Patricia Becker 1929- *St&PR 93*
Colborne, Paul *Law&B 92*
Colbourn, Andrea Maria *WhoE 93*
Colbourn, Trevor 1927- *WhoSSW 93*
Colbow, Brian R. 1947- *St&PR 93*
Colbran, Isabella 1785-1845 *Baker 92, OxDcOp*
Colburn, Carrie W. *AmWomPl*
Colburn, Craig Paul 1943- *St&PR 93*
Colburn, Gladys La Flamme 1910- *WhoWrEP 92*
Colburn, Henry d1855 *BioIn 17*
Colburn, J. Brian 1943- *St&PR 93*
Colburn, James Edward 1924- *St&PR 93*
Colburn, Jean Hunter 1921- *WhoAmW 93*
Colburn, John Brian *Law&B 92*
Colburn, Julia Katherine Lee 1927- *WhoAmW 93*
Colburn, Kathleen Ann 1950- *WhoAmW 93*
Colburn, Kenneth Hersey 1952- *St&PR 93, WhoAm 92*
Colburn, Larry B. 1944- *WhoIns 93*
Colburn, Philip William 1929- *St&PR 93, WhoAm 92*
Colburn, Richard Dunton 1911- *WhoAm 92, WhoWor 93*
Colburn, Robert Dickinson 1962- *WhoWrEP 92*
Colburn, Steven Edward 1953- *WhoSSW 93*
Colburn, William Edward *Law&B 92*
Colby, Abby M. 1848-1917 *BioIn 17*
Colby, Andrea *Law&B 92*
Colby, Anita 1914-1992 *BioIn 17, NewYTBS 92 [port]*
Colby, Anne *AmWomPl*
Colby, Anne 1946- *WhoAm 92*
Colby, Barbara Diane 1932- *WhoAm 92*
Colby, Barnard L. 1911- *St&PR 93*
Colby, Bob 1959- *St&PR 93*
Colby, Bruce Redfearn 1934- *WhoWor 93*
Colby, Edith Lucille 1917- *WhoWrEP 92*
Colby, Edward 1912 *BioIn 17*
Colby, Eleanor *AmWomPl*
Colby, George Vincent, Jr. 1931- *WhoE 93*
Colby, Gertrude K. *AmWomPl*
Colby, Gretchen *AmWomPl*
Colby, Jonathan Elbridge 1946- *St&PR 93*
Colby, Joy Hakanson *WhoAm 92*
Colby, Kenneth P., Sr. 1908- *WhoIns 93*
Colby, Kenneth Poole 1908- *WhoAm 92*
Colby, Kevin T. *Law&B 92*
Colby, Lewis James, Jr. 1934- *St&PR 93*
Colby, Marion Ida *AmWomPl*
Colby, Mark Steven 1949- *WhoEmL 93*
Colby, Marvelle Seitman 1932- *WhoAmW 93*
Colby, Orrin Tether, Jr. 1940- *St&PR 93*
Colby, Patricia Farley 1958- *WhoAm 92, WhoAmW 93, WhoEmL 93*
Colby, Robert Alan 1920- *WhoAm 92*
Colby, Robert F. *Law&B 92*
Colby, Susan Jill 1961- *WhoAmW 93*
Colby, Virginia Little 1917- *WhoAmW 93*
Colby, William E. *BioIn 17*
Colby, William E. 1920- *ColdWar 1 [port]*
Colby, William Egan 1920- *NewYTBS 92 [port], WhoAm 92*
Colby, William George, Jr. 1939- *WhoAm 92*
Colby-Hall, Alice Mary 1932- *WhoAm 92, WhoAmW 93*
Colchado, Edmundo Moises, Jr. 1954- *WhoE 93*
Colchester, J.E. *WhoScE 91-1*
Colchie, Thomas *ScF&FL 92*
Colclaser, H. Alberta 1911- *WhoAm 92*
Colclough, A.R. 1946- *WhoScE 91-1*
Colclough, Graham *WhoScE 91-1*
Colclough, William F. 1905- *St&PR 93*
Colcock, Charles Jones 1771-1839 *BioIn 17*
Colcord, Herbert Nathaniel 1951- *St&PR 93*
Colcord, Herbert Nathaniel, III 1951- *WhoE 93*
Colcord, Linda Miller 1953- *WhoEmL 93*
Cold, Clarice Mae 1935- *WhoAmW 93*
Coldewey, T.S. 1912- *St&PR 93*
Colding-Jorgensen, Henrik 1944- *Baker 92*
Coldiron, William H. 1916- *WhoAm 92*
Coldren, Diane 1945- *WhoAmW 93*
Coldren, Scott 1964- *St&PR 93*
Coldren, Sharon Louise 1951- *WhoAmW 93*
Coldsmith, Don(ald Charles) 1926- *WhoWrEP 92*
Coldstream, John Nicolas 1927- *WhoWor 93*
Coldstream, William Menzies 1908-1987 *BioIn 17*
Coldwell, Peter Reid 1945- *WhoE 93*
Coldwell, Philip Edward 1922- *BioIn 17, WhoAm 92*
Coldwell, Raymond E. 1941- *St&PR 93*
Coldwell, Stephen O. 1939- *St&PR 93*
Cole, A.C. 1958- *WhoScE 91-1*
Cole, Adrian 1949- *ScF&FL 92*
Cole, Alfred John 1925- *WhoWor 93*
Cole, Alice H. *AmWomPl*
Cole, Allan 1943- *ScF&FL 92*
Cole, Ann Marie 1937- *WhoWrEP 92*
Cole, Anthony F. 1955- *WhoEmL 93*
Cole, Anthony Livingston 1944- *WhoSSW 93*
Cole, Aubrey Louis 1923- *St&PR 93, WhoAm 92, WhoSSW 93*
Cole, Babette *BioIn 17*
Cole, Barbara Ruth 1941- *WhoAm 92*
Cole, Basil 1920- *St&PR 93*
Cole, Benjamin Richason 1916- *WhoAm 92*
Cole, Benjamin Theodore 1921- *WhoAm 92*
Cole, Betsie Anderson 1954- *WhoSSW 93*
Cole, Betty Lou McDonel Shelton 1926- *WhoAmW 93, WhoWor 93*
Cole, Bob 1863-1911 *Baker 92*
Cole, Brady Marshall 1936- *WhoAm 92*
Cole, Brian Douglas 1959- *St&PR 93*
Cole, Brian E. *Law&B 92*
Cole, Brian H. *Law&B 92*
Cole, Brock 1938- *ConAu 136, DcAmChF 1985, MajAI [port], SmATA 72 [port]*
Cole, Bruce Milan 1938- *WhoAm 92*
Cole, Burt 1930- *ScF&FL 92*
Cole, Byron Joseph 1941- *St&PR 93*
Cole, C. Richard 1949- *St&PR 93*
Cole, Carol Anne 1955- *WhoWrEP 92*
Cole, Carole Osborne 1936- *WhoWrEP 92*
Cole, Carolyn Jo 1943- *WhoAm 92*
Cole, Catherine *AmWomPl*
Cole, Cecil S. *WhoAm 92*
Cole, Charlene Helene 1946- *WhoAmW 93*
Cole, Charles Chester, Jr. 1922- *WhoAm 92*
Cole, Charles Dewey, Jr. 1952- *WhoEmL 93*
Cole, Charles Edward 1927- *WhoAm 92*
Cole, Charles F. *Law&B 92*
Cole, Charles Norman 1946- *WhoE 93*
Cole, Charles T., Jr. 1946- *St&PR 93*
Cole, Charles W., Jr. 1935- *WhoAm 92*
Cole, Charles William 1945- *St&PR 93*
Cole, Christopher McKagen *Law&B 92*
Cole, Clarence Russell 1918- *WhoAm 92*
Cole, Clifford Adair 1915- *WhoAm 92*
Cole, Clyde Curtis, Jr. 1932- *WhoAm 92*
Cole, Curtis Allen 1946- *WhoEmL 93*
Cole, Damaris *ScF&FL 92*
Cole, Dandridge *BioIn 17*
Cole, David Andrew 1942- *St&PR 93, WhoAm 92*
Cole, David C. 1936- *St&PR 93*
Cole, David Charles 1948- *WhoE 93*
Cole, David John *Law&B 92*
Cole, David Lee 1947- *WhoIns 93*
Cole, David Winslow 1947- *WhoWor 93*
Cole, Dawn Vroegop 1966- *WhoAmW 93*
Cole, Dayton Thomas 1954- *WhoEmL 93*
Cole, Dean Allen 1952- *WhoWor 93*
Cole, Diane *BioIn 17*
Cole, Diane 1952- *ConAu 138*
Cole, Diane Jackson 1952- *WhoAmW 93*
Cole, Donald Foster 1957- *St&PR 93*
Cole, Donald Willard 1920- *WhoAm 92*
Cole, Douglas 1934- *WhoAm 92, WhoWrEP 92*
Cole, Douglas Leon 1947- *WhoAm 92*
Cole, E(ugene) R(oger) 1930- *WhoWrEP 92*
Cole, E. William *Law&B 92*
Cole, Edna Earle *AmWomPl*
Cole, Edward Logan, Jr. 1953- *WhoE 93*
Cole, Elaine Geneva 1932- *WhoWrEP 92*
Cole, Elbert Lee, Jr. 1940- *WhoE 93*
Cole, Elizabeth *AmWomPl*
Cole, Ellen 1941- *WhoAmW 93*
Cole, Elma Phillipson 1909- *WhoAm 92, WhoAmW 93, WhoE 93, WhoWor 93*
Cole, Eric Alfred Bonner *WhoScE 91-1*
Cole, Ernest d1990 *BioIn 17*
Cole, Ernest George 1940- *WhoE 93*
Cole, Eugene 1933- *St&PR 93*
Cole, Evelyn Marie 1928- *WhoWor 93*
Cole, F.J. 1953- *St&PR 93*
Cole, Fay-Cooper 1881-1961 *IntDcAn*
Cole, Floyd Clinton 1926- *St&PR 93*
Cole, Fran *Law&B 92*
Cole, Frank W. 1925- *St&PR 93*
Cole, Franklin A. 1926- *St&PR 93*
Cole, Galen L. 1925- *St&PR 93*
Cole, Gary *Law&B 92*
Cole, Geoffrey Alexander 1963- *WhoIns 93*
Cole, George 1925- *QDrFCA 92 [port]*
Cole, George David 1925- *WhoAm 92*
Cole, George Watson 1850-1939 *BioIn 17*
Cole, George William 1948- *WhoEmL 93*
Cole, Gerald Albert 1913- *St&PR 93*
Cole, Ginger Sue 1946- *St&PR 93*
Cole, Gordon Bradley 1956- *St&PR 93*
Cole, Gretchen Bornor 1927- *St&PR 93, WhoAmW 93, WhoWor 93*
Cole, Harold E. *Law&B 92*
Cole, Harold Samuel 1916- *WhoE 93*
Cole, Heather E. 1942- *WhoAm 92*
Cole, Helen 1922- *WhoAmW 93*
Cole, Herbert Myrman 1937- *St&PR 93*
Cole, Ida B. *AmWomPl*
Cole, Isaiah Clawson 1940- *WhoAm 92*
Cole, J. Bruce 1941- *St&PR 93*
Cole, J. Gregory 1922- *St&PR 93*
Cole, J. Weldon 1936- *WhoAm 92*
Cole, Jack Eli 1915- *WhoE 93, WhoWor 93*
Cole, James *BioIn 17*
Cole, James Anthony 1945- *WhoSSW 93*
Cole, James D. 1941- *St&PR 93*
Cole, James Mariner, Jr. 1915- *WhoSSW 93*
Cole, James O., Sr. *Law&B 92*
Cole, James Perry 1940- *WhoSSW 93*
Cole, James Robert 1935- *St&PR 93*
Cole, James Woodard, Jr. 1950- *WhoEmL 93*
Cole, Jane Bagby 1931- *WhoAmW 93*
Cole, Janet 1922- *WhoAm 92, WhoAmW 93*
Cole, Jean Hascall 1922- *ConAu 139*
Cole, Jeanette Linda 1952- *WhoE 93*
Cole, Jeff *BioIn 17*
Cole, Jeffrey A. 1941- *WhoAm 92*
Cole, Jeffrey Alan 1941- *St&PR 93*
Cole, Jeffrey Clark 1966- *WhoWor 93*
Cole, Jeffrey Joseph 1954- *WhoEmL 93*
Cole, Jennifer *SmATA 70*
Cole, Jerome Foster 1940- *WhoAm 92, WhoSSW 93*
Cole, Joan Hays 1929- *WhoAmW 93*
Cole, Joanna 1944- *MajAI [port], ScF&FL 92*
Cole, Joe 1938- *St&PR 93*
Cole, John Andrew *Law&B 92*
Cole, John D. 1949- *St&PR 93*
Cole, John Donald 1949- *WhoAm 92, WhoIns 93*
Cole, John Francis 1943- *WhoAm 92*
Cole, John Henry *BioIn 17*
Cole, John L., II 1941- *St&PR 93*
Cole, John Pope, Jr. 1930- *WhoAm 92*
Cole, Johnnetta B. *BioIn 17*
Cole, Johnnetta Betsch 1936- *AfrAmBi, WhoAm 92, WhoAmW 93*
Cole, Jonathan Otis 1925- *WhoAm 92*
Cole, Jonathan Richard 1942- *WhoAm 92*
Cole, Joseph E. 1915- *St&PR 93*
Cole, Joseph Edmund 1915- *WhoAm 92*
Cole, Josephine R. *AmWomPl*
Cole, June Robertson 1931- *WhoAm 92, WhoAmW 93, WhoWor 93*
Cole, Justine *WhoWrEP 92*
Cole, Katherine Ione 1949- *WhoEmL 93*
Cole, Kellie Birdgett Arndt 1964- *WhoAmW 93*
Cole, Kenneth *BioIn 17*
Cole, Kenneth Duane 1932- *WhoAm 92*
Cole, Kenneth R. 1947- *St&PR 93*
Cole, Larry Lee 1941- *WhoWor 93*
Cole, Laurence Anthony 1953- *WhoE 93, WhoWor 93*
Cole, Lawrence Allen, Jr. 1944- *St&PR 93*
Cole, Lawrence Robert 1936- *WhoAm 92*
Cole, Lee *ScF&FL 92*
Cole, Lee Arthur 1953- *WhoEmL 93*
Cole, Leon Monroe 1933- *WhoE 93*
Cole, Leonard Aaron 1933- *WhoAm 92, WhoWor 93*
Cole, Leslie Allen 1945- *WhoSSW 93*
Cole, Lewis George 1931- *WhoAm 92*
Cole, Lloyd 1961- *ConMus 9 [port]*
Cole, Luther Francis 1925- *WhoAm 92, WhoSSW 93*
Cole, M. Dean 1946- *St&PR 93*
Cole, Malvin 1933- *WhoWor 93*
Cole, Margaret Elizabeth 1960- *WhoEmL 93*
Cole, Maria *BioIn 17*
Cole, Marilyn Bush 1945- *WhoAmW 93*
Cole, Max 1937- *WhoAm 92*
Cole, Melvin A. d1992 *NewYTBS 92*
Cole, Michael E. 1913- *St&PR 93*
Cole, Michael R. *Law&B 92*
Cole, Michael Steven 1955- *WhoEmL 93*
Cole, Michelle 1940- *WhoAm 92*
Cole, Michelle Renee 1968- *St&PR 93*
Cole, Mitzi G. *Law&B 92*
Cole, Monroe 1933- *WhoAm 92*
Cole, Murray L. 1922- *St&PR 93*
Cole, Nancy Marion 1949- *WhoAmW 93*
Cole, Nancy Stooksberry 1942- *WhoAm 92*
Cole, Nat 1917-1965 *Baker 92*
Cole, Nat King 1919?-1965 *BioIn 17*
Cole, Natalie *BioIn 17*
Cole, Natalie 1950- *News 92 [port], SoulM*
Cole, Natalie Maria 1950- *WhoAm 92*
Cole, Natalie Robinson 1901-1984 *BioIn 17*
Cole, Neil D., Jr. *St&PR 93*
Cole, Nyla Jessamine 1925- *WhoAm 92, WhoAmW 93*
Cole, Pamela Hartl 1944- *WhoAmW 93*
Cole, Paul K. *Law&B 92*
Cole, Paul Leon 1946- *WhoEmL 93*
Cole, R. Taylor 1905-1991 *BioIn 17*
Cole, Randel Finnell 1950- *WhoEmL 93*
Cole, Richard 1949- *WhoWrEP 92*
Cole, Richard Allen 1939- *St&PR 93*
Cole, Richard Cargill 1926- *WhoAm 92*
Cole, Richard Dennis 1933- *St&PR 93*
Cole, Richard George 1948- *WhoEmL 93*
Cole, Richard John 1926- *WhoAm 92*
Cole, Richard Louis 1946- *WhoAm 92*
Cole, Richard Ray 1942- *WhoAm 92*
Cole, Robert Allen 1952- *WhoEmL 93*
Cole, Robert B. *Law&B 92*
Cole, Robert Bates 1911- *St&PR 93, WhoAm 92*
Cole, Robert Benjamin 1956- *WhoEmL 93*
Cole, Robert Carlton 1937- *WhoE 93*
Cole, Robert G. 1915-1944 *BioIn 17*

Cole, Robert James WhoScE 91-1
Cole, Robert Jeffery 1962- WhoSSW 93
Cole, Robert Taylor 1905-1991 BioIn 17
Cole, Roger David 1924- WhoAm 92
Cole, Roger Jerome 1951- WhoEmL 93
Cole, Ronald L. 1945- St&PR 93
Cole, Rosalie M. 1926- WhoAmW 93, WhoWor 93
Cole, Rossetter Gleason 1866-1952 Baker 92
Cole, Roy M. WhoSSW 93
Cole, Ruby Marie 1929- WhoAmW 93
Cole, Russell Warren 1915- St&PR 93
Cole, Ruth Elena 1918- WhoWrEP 92
Cole, S. WhoScE 91-1
Cole, Samuel Thornton 1932- WhoIns 93
Cole, Sharon F. 1941- WhoAmW 93
Cole, Sharon Kay 1952- WhoAmW 93
Cole, Sherwood Orison 1930- WhoAm 92
Cole, Stephan William 1947- St&PR 93
Cole, Stephen W. 1945- St&PR 93
Cole, Steven Patrick 1960- WhoEmL 93
Cole, Susan Law&B 92
Cole, Susie Cleora WhoAmW 93
Cole, Suzanne C. 1941- WhoSSW 93
Cole, Sylvan, Jr. 1918- WhoAm 92
Cole, Taylor 1905-1991 BioIn 17
Cole, Terri Lynn 1951- WhoAm 92
Cole, Terri Toennisson 1961- WhoAmW 93
Cole, Thomas 1801-1848 BioIn 17
Cole, Thomas Amor 1948- WhoAm 92
Cole, Thomas Gary Law&B 92
Cole, Thomas L. R., III 1958- WhoEmL 93
Cole, Timothy 1938- WhoUN 92
Cole, Timothy P. 1943- WhoSSW 93
Cole, Todd G. 1921- St&PR 93
Cole, Ty Ray 1961- WhoSSW 93
Cole, Ulric 1905- Baker 92
Cole, Vinson WhoAm 92
Cole, Walter G., Jr. Law&B 92
Cole, Warner Booton 1938- St&PR 93
Cole, Warren 1898-1990 BioIn 17
Cole, Wayne Herbert 1947- WhoEmL 93
Cole, Wayne Merritt 1941- St&PR 93
Cole, Wayne Stanley 1922- WhoAm 92
Cole, Wendell Gordon 1914- WhoAm 92
Cole, William Edward 1931- WhoAm 92
Cole, William Howard 1943- WhoSSW 93
Cole, William Kaufman 1914- WhoAm 92
Cole, William Lawren 1926- St&PR 93
Cole, William Randolph 1906-1981 Baker 92
Cole, William (Rossa) 1919- MajAI [port], SmATA 71 [port]
Cole, William W., Jr. Law&B 92
Colebank, Marshall N., Jr. 1942- St&PR 93
Colebrook, Joan BioIn 17
Coleburn, George Wallace 1930- St&PR 93
Colecchia, Francesca Maria WhoAm 92
Colegate, Isabel BioIn 17
Colegrove, Donna F. 1949- WhoAmW 93
Colehamer, Glenn Ludlow 1950- St&PR 93
Cole-Hamilton, David John WhoScE 91-1
Colehan, Barney 1914-1991 AnObit 1991
ColeHuckeba, Paula Jill 1948- WhoAmW 93
Colella, Laura Brigid Law&B 92
Colello, Alan R. 1949- St&PR 93, WhoAm 92
Colello, Daniel R. 1948- WhoIns 93
Colello, Ralph Guy 1942- St&PR 93
Cole Lord, Patriciaann Elizabeth 1958- WhoEmL 93
Coleman, Albert John 1918- WhoAm 92
Coleman, Alex 1949- WhoEmL 93
Coleman, Alfred N. 1930- St&PR 93
Coleman, Alice Mary WhoScE 91-1
Coleman, Allen Markley 1949- WhoEmL 93
Coleman, Almand Rouse 1905- WhoAm 92
Coleman, Amy Joyce WhoSSW 93
Coleman, Angela Marie 1960- WhoAmW 93
Coleman, Anne Kathryn 1950- WhoAmW 93
Coleman, Arlene Florence 1926- WhoAmW 93, WhoWor 93
Coleman, Arlene Hamlett 1946- WhoE 93
Coleman, Barbara Ann 1965- WhoAmW 93
Coleman, Barbara Coleman St&PR 93
Coleman, Barbara Lee Weinstein 1948- WhoAmW 93
Coleman, Barry B.Z. 1931- St&PR 93
Coleman, Beatrice 1916-1990 BioIn 17
Coleman, Benjamin 1673-1747 BioIn 17
Coleman, Bernell 1929- WhoAm 92
Coleman, Bernice Greenbaum 1929- St&PR 93
Coleman, Bessie 1896-1926 BioIn 17
Coleman, Bethany Baldwin 1950- WhoAmW 93
Coleman, Bevelyn A. Law&B 92
Coleman, Beverly Ann 1962- WhoAmW 93
Coleman, Bryan Douglas 1948- WhoEmL 93, WhoSSW 93, WhoWor 93
Coleman, Burlin 1929- St&PR 93
Coleman, C. Norman 1945- WhoAm 92
Coleman, Carla Lynn 1951- WhoSSW 93
Coleman, Carroll 1904-1989 BioIn 17
Coleman, Carter BioIn 17
Coleman, Catherine Amelia 1963- WhoEmL 93
Coleman, Charles Clyde 1937- WhoAm 92
Coleman, Cheryl Anton 1953- WhoAmW 93
Coleman, Christine BioIn 17
Coleman, Christopher Kiernan 1949- WhoSSW 93
Coleman, Clarence William 1909- WhoAm 92, WhoWor 93
Coleman, Clay ScF&FL 92
Coleman, Clive Ian 1948- WhoWor 93
Coleman, Cy WhoAm 92, WhoE 93
Coleman, Cy 1929- Baker 92, BioIn 17
Coleman, D. Jackson 1934- WhoAm 92
Coleman, Dabney 1932- ConTFT 10
Coleman, Dabney W. 1932- WhoAm 92
Coleman, Dale Lynn 1958- WhoWor 93
Coleman, Daniel J. 1932- St&PR 93
Coleman, Darrell Glenn 1953- WhoEmL 93
Coleman, David C. Law&B 92
Coleman, David Cecil 1937- WhoE 93, WhoWor 93
Coleman, David Dennis, II 1957- WhoE 93
Coleman, David Edward 1956- WhoE 93
Coleman, David Manley 1948- WhoEmL 93
Coleman, Dean Joseph 1942- St&PR 93
Coleman, Deborah Ann 1951- WhoEmL 93
Coleman, Deborah Ann 1953- WhoAmW 93
Coleman, Denis Patrick, Jr. 1946- WhoE 93
Coleman, Donald John 1950- St&PR 93
Coleman, Donna M. Law&B 92
Coleman, Dorothy Gabe 1935-1992 ConAu 139
Coleman, Dorothy P. 1954- WhoEmL 93, WhoSSW 93
Coleman, E. Thomas 1943- BioIn 17, CngDr 91, WhoAm 92
Coleman, Earl Maxwell 1916- WhoAm 92
Coleman, Edmund Benedict 1926- WhoAm 92
Coleman, Edward Joseph Law&B 92
Coleman, Eliot BioIn 17
Coleman, Elizabeth 1937- WhoAmW 93
Coleman, Elizabeth J. 1947- WhoAmW 93, WhoEmL 93
Coleman, Ellen Schneid 1943- WhoWrEP 92
Coleman, Eric D. AfrAmBi
Coleman, Eric Norman 1925- WhoWor 93
Coleman, Ernest BioIn 17
Coleman, Ernest Albert 1929- WhoAm 92
Coleman, Ernest Robert, Sr. 1936- St&PR 93
Coleman, F.D.R. 1939- St&PR 93
Coleman, F. Douglas, Mrs. AmWomPl
Coleman, Francis D.R. Law&B 92
Coleman, Francis Xavier, Jr. 1930- St&PR 93, WhoAm 92
Coleman, G.A. John 1945- St&PR 93
Coleman, Gabriella Morris Law&B 92
Coleman, Gary BioIn 17
Coleman, Geoffrey Parker 1956- WhoEmL 93
Coleman, George Edward 1935- WhoAm 92
Coleman, George Michael 1953- WhoEmL 93
Coleman, George T. Law&B 92
Coleman, George Willard 1912- WhoSSW 93
Coleman, Gerald Christopher 1939- WhoAm 92, WhoWor 93
Coleman, Gloria Jean 1952- WhoEmL 93
Coleman, Harold S. d1990 BioIn 17
Coleman, Henry Embry 1768-1837 BioIn 17
Coleman, Henry Thomas 1931- St&PR 93
Coleman, Heyward Hamilton 1943- WhoAm 92
Coleman, Howard S. 1917- WhoAm 92
Coleman, Ivory Claudette 1947- WhoEmL 93
Coleman, J.P. 1914-1991 BioIn 17
Coleman, James Covington 1914- WhoAm 92
Coleman, James Hallett 1936- St&PR 93
Coleman, James Julian 1915- WhoAm 92
Coleman, James Julian, Jr. 1941- WhoSSW 93
Coleman, James Malcolm 1935- WhoAm 92
Coleman, James N. 1931- WhoWrEP 92
Coleman, James Plemon 1914-1991 BioIn 17
Coleman, James S. 1953- St&PR 93
Coleman, James Samuel 1926- BioIn 17, WhoAm 92
Coleman, Jane Candia 1939- ConAu 136, WhoWrEP 92
Coleman, Jane Dwight Dexter 1942- WhoE 93
Coleman, Jason Chandler 1958- WhoEmL 93
Coleman, Jason Gill 1961- WhoEmL 93
Coleman, Jean Black 1925- WhoAmW 93
Coleman, Jeffrey Reaves 1961- WhoSSW 93
Coleman, Joel Clifford 1930- WhoAm 92
Coleman, John Edward WhoScE 91-1
Coleman, John Hewson 1912- WhoAm 92
Coleman, John Jerpel 1932- WhoE 93
Coleman, John Joseph 1937- WhoAm 92, WhoE 93
Coleman, John M. 1947- St&PR 93
Coleman, John Michael Law&B 92
Coleman, John Michael 1949- WhoAm 92, WhoE 93
Coleman, John Royston 1921- St&PR 93, WhoAm 92
Coleman, John Tinsley 1927- St&PR 93
Coleman, John Walter 1938- St&PR 93
Coleman, Jonathan A. 1947- St&PR 93
Coleman, Jonathan (Mark) 1951- ConAu 138, WhoEmL 93, WhoSSW 93
Coleman, Joseph ScF&FL 92
Coleman, Joseph K. d1991 BioIn 17
Coleman, Joseph Michael 1945- WhoAm 92, WhoE 93
Coleman, Katherine Ann WhoAmW 93
Coleman, Kenneth E. Law&B 92
Coleman, Kevin Edwin 1960- WhoE 93
Coleman, Lamar William 1934- WhoAm 92
Coleman, Larry Joseph 1949- WhoEmL 93
Coleman, Lee Sorrels 1949- WhoEmL 93
Coleman, Lester E. 1930- St&PR 93
Coleman, Lester Earl 1930- WhoAm 92
Coleman, Lester L. 1942- St&PR 93
Coleman, Lester Laudy 1911- WhoAm 92
Coleman, Lewis Waldo 1942- St&PR 93
Coleman, Linda Jane 1947- WhoE 93
Coleman, Lisa Ane 1963- WhoEmL 93
Coleman, Lois Tarleton 1930- WhoAmW 93
Coleman, Lonnie ConAu 39NR
Coleman, Lynn Carnell 1954- AfrAmBi [port]
Coleman, Margaret Ann 1959- WhoAmW 93
Coleman, Marion Annalisa 1952- WhoAmW 93
Coleman, Mark J. 1947- St&PR 93
Coleman, Martin M. 1926- WhoSSW 93
Coleman, Martin Stone 1913- WhoAm 92
Coleman, Mary Ann 1928- WhoWrEP 92
Coleman, Mary Stallings WhoAm 92
Coleman, Max Laurence 1942- WhoScE 91-1
Coleman, Melvin Douglas 1948- WhoEmL 93
Coleman, Michael Dortch 1944- WhoSSW 93
Coleman, Michael Murray 1938- WhoAm 92
Coleman, Miles 1931- St&PR 93
Coleman, Morton 1939- WhoAm 92
Coleman, Nancy Braddock 1952- WhoAmW 93
Coleman, Nancy C. WhoWrEP 92
Coleman, Nancy Catherine 1912- WhoAmW 93, WhoE 93, WhoWor 93
Coleman, Nancy Clark 1955- WhoAmW 93, WhoSSW 93
Coleman, Nancy Pees 1955- WhoAm 92, WhoEmL 93
Coleman, Nick BioIn 17
Coleman, Ornette 1930- Baker 92, WhoAm 92
Coleman, Paul David 1927- WhoAm 92, WhoE 93
Coleman, Peter M. 1941- St&PR 93
Coleman, Peter Tali 1919- WhoAm 92
Coleman, R.F. WhoScE 91-1
Coleman, Ralph Edward 1943- WhoAm 92
Coleman, Randall Carisle, III Law&B 92
Coleman, Randall Spencer Law&B 92
Coleman, Randolph G. 1934- St&PR 93
Coleman, Randy Lee 1951- St&PR 93
Coleman, Ray 1937- ConAu 137
Coleman, Rexford Lee 1930- WhoAm 92, WhoWor 93
Coleman, Richard Daly 1932- St&PR 93, WhoIns 93
Coleman, Richard Walter 1922- WhoWor 93
Coleman, Richard William 1935- WhoE 93
Coleman, Robert E. 1925- St&PR 93
Coleman, Robert Griffin 1923- WhoAm 92
Coleman, Robert L. Law&B 92
Coleman, Robert Lee 1929- WhoAm 92
Coleman, Robert Marshall 1925- WhoAm 92
Coleman, Robert Thomas, III Law&B 92
Coleman, Robert Winston 1942- WhoAm 92
Coleman, Rod 1957- St&PR 93
Coleman, Roger Dixon 1915- WhoWor 93
Coleman, Roger Keith BioIn 17
Coleman, Roger Lewis 1945- WhoE 93
Coleman, Roger W. 1929- St&PR 93, WhoAm 92, WhoWor 93
Coleman, Rogers K. 1931- St&PR 93
Coleman, Rogers King 1931- WhoSSW 93
Coleman, Ronald D. 1941- CngDr 91, WhoAm 92, WhoSSW 93
Coleman, Ronald Lee, Sr. 1941- WhoSSW 93
Coleman, Rosa Lee 1916- WhoWrEP 92
Coleman, Roy Melvin 1930- WhoAm 92
Coleman, Sandra Sloan 1943- WhoAm 92
Coleman, Sheldon C. St&PR 93
Coleman, Sherman Smoot 1922- WhoAm 92
Coleman, Sidney Richard 1937- WhoAm 92
Coleman, Stephen 1973- WhoE 93
Coleman, Stephen M. 1911- WhoWrEP 92
Coleman, Steven Eugene 1955- WhoSSW 93
Coleman, Susan Wilson 1953- WhoEmL 93
Coleman, T.W. 1938- St&PR 93
Coleman, Terry N. 1951- St&PR 93
Coleman, Thomas Britt 1952- WhoEmL 93
Coleman, Thomas Young 1949- WhoEmL 93
Coleman, Timothy John 1958- WhoEmL 93
Coleman, Timothy Louis 1946- WhoEmL 93
Coleman, Tom BioIn 17
Coleman, Tom 1943- BioIn 17
Coleman, Vernon ScF&FL 92
Coleman, Victor 1944- WhoCanL 92
Coleman, Vince BioIn 17
Coleman, Vince 1961- WhoAm 92
Coleman, Virgil A. 1950- St&PR 93
Coleman, Wade Hampton, III 1932- WhoAm 92
Coleman, Walter Carpenter, Jr. 1928- St&PR 93
Coleman, Wanda 1946- WhoWrEP 92
Coleman, William 1766-1829 JrnUS
Coleman, William Harvey 1937- WhoE 93
Coleman, William Laurence 1920-1982 ConAu 39NR
Coleman, William Patrick, III 1948- WhoEmL 93
Coleman, William Thaddeus, Jr. 1920- WhoAm 92
Coleman, Wim ScF&FL 92
Coleman, Winifred Ellen 1932- WhoAmW 93
Coleman-Burns, Patricia Wendolyn 1947- WhoAmW 93
Coleman-Johnson, Debra Lynn 1966- WhoAmW 93, WhoEmL 93
Coleman Wood, Krista Ann 1956- WhoAmW 93
Colen, B. D. 1946- WhoAm 92
Colen, Donald Jerome 1917- WhoAm 92
Colen, Frederick Haas 1947- WhoAm 92, WhoE 93
Colenbrander, H.J. 1931- WhoScE 91-3
Coleno, Alain 1936- WhoScE 91-2
Coler, Myron Abraham 1913- WhoAm 92, WhoWor 93
Coleridge, David BioIn 17
Coleridge, Hartley 1796-1849 BioIn 17
Coleridge, Mary Elizabeth 1861-1907 BioIn 17
Coleridge, Samuel Taylor 1772-1834 BioIn 17, MagSWL [port], WorLitC [port]
Coleridge, Sara 1802-1852 BioIn 17
Coleridge-Taylor, Samuel 1875-1912 Baker 92
Coles, Allen BioIn 17
Coles, Allen E. 1927- St&PR 93
Coles, Anna Louise Bailey 1925- WhoAm 92, WhoAmW 93
Coles, Barbara Eugenia 1960- WhoAmW 93
Coles, Bernice BioIn 17
Coles, Bryan Randell WhoScE 91-1
Coles, Charles BioIn 17
Coles, Charles d1992 NewYTBS 92 [port]
Coles, Don WhoCanL 92
Coles, Don 1928- ConAu 38NR
Coles, Donald Earl 1924- WhoAm 92
Coles, Honi BioIn 17
Coles, Honi 1911- WhoAm 92
Coles, Jackie BioIn 17
Coles, James Stacy 1913- St&PR 93

Coles, Jane Hallowell *BioIn 17*
Coles, John David *MiSFD 9*
Coles, Kenneth Allen 1929- *WhoWor 93*
Coles, Kim *BioIn 17*
Coles, Lesley *ScF&FL 92*
Coles, Lewis 1938- *WhoWor 93*
Coles, Michael 1944- *ConEn*
Coles, Mildred *SweetSg C*
Coles, Robert *BioIn 17*
Coles, Robert 1929- *WhoAm 92, WhoE 93, WhoWrEP 92*
Coles, Robert Traynham 1929- *WhoAm 92*
Coles, Wesley Obert, III 1965- *WhoWrEP 92*
Coles, William Henry *WhoAm 92*
Colesar, William Edward, Jr. 1952- *WhoSSW 93*
Colescott, Robert 1925- *BioIn 17*
Colescott, Warrington Wickham 1921- *WhoAm 92*
Cole-Sherman, Sheila 1934- *WhoSSW 93*
Colet, Pete 1964- *WhoWor 93*
Coletta, Johanna Viola 1949- *WhoAmW 93*
Coletta, Patrick J. 1926- *WhoAm 92*
Colette 1873-1954 *BioIn 17, MagSWL [port], ShSCr 10 [port]*
Colette, Claude G.F. 1929- *WhoScE 91-2*
Coletti, Ellen G. *Law&B 92*
Coletti, Filippo 1811-1894 *Baker 92, OxDcOp*
Coletti, John Anthony 1952- *WhoE 93, WhoEmL 93, WhoWor 93*
Coletti, Paul A. *Law&B 92*
Coletti, Paul Anthony 1958- *WhoEmL 93*
Coletti, Theodore A. 1965- *WhoE 93*
Coletto, Peter William 1953- *St&PR 93*
Coley, Betty 1933- *WhoAm 92, WhoSSW 93*
Coley, Bill A. 1929- *St&PR 93*
Coley, Dennis Howard 1945- *St&PR 93*
Coley, Franklin Luke, Jr. 1958- *WhoEmL 93*
Coley, Gwendolyn D. 1941- *WhoSSW 93*
Coley, H. Turner, Jr. 1942- *WhoIns 93*
Coley, Larry David 1957- *St&PR 93*
Coley, Travis Carl 1947- *WhoEmL 93*
Colf, David A. *Law&B 92*
Colfax, Schuyler 1823-1885 *PolPar*
Colfin, Bruce Elliott 1951- *WhoE 93, WhoEmL 93*
Colford, Francis Xavier 1952- *St&PR 93, WhoAm 92*
Colford, Robert Wade 1949- *WhoEmL 93*
Colgan, Charles Joseph 1926- *WhoSSW 93*
Colgan, Charles Thomas 1940- *WhoAm 92*
Colgan, James F. 1935- *St&PR 93*
Colgan, John c. 1582-1658 *BioIn 17*
Colgan, Michael Byrley 1948- *WhoSSW 93*
Colgan, P. Barry 1930- *St&PR 93*
Colgan, Peter David 1933- *St&PR 93*
Colgan, Peter Tristram 1945- *WhoE 93*
Colgan, Sumner 1934- *WhoE 93*
Colgan, William B. 1920- *WhoWrEP 92*
Colgate, Doris Eleanor 1941- *WhoAmW 93, WhoSSW 93*
Colgate, Jessie M. 1950- *WhoAmW 93*
Colgate, Kathleen Bishop 1953- *WhoEmL 93*
Colgate, Stirling Auchincloss 1925- *WhoAm 92*
Colgrass, Michael (Charles) 1932- *Baker 92, WhoAm 92*
Colherty, Karen S. *Law&B 92*
Colhoun, Howard Post 1935- *WhoAm 92*
Colhoun, J.L.A. 1920- *St&PR 93*
Colhour, Donald Bruce 1946- *WhoEmL 93*
Coli, Guido John 1921- *WhoAm 92*
Coli, Robert J. *Law&B 92*
Colica, Carmel *Law&B 92*
Colicelli, Elena Jeanmarie 1950- *WhoAmW 93*
Coligny, Gaspard de, II 1519-1572 *HarEnMi*
Colijn-Hooymans, C.M. 1951- *WhoScE 91-3*
Colin, Ann *MajAI*
Colin, Eduardo 1880-1945 *DcMexL*
Colin, Georgia Talmey *WhoAm 92, WhoAmW 93*
Colin, Jacques *WhoScE 91-2*
Colin, John A. 1914- *St&PR 93*
Colin, Kim Renee 1957- *WhoEmL 93*
Colin, Lawrence 1931- *WhoAm 92*
Colin, Marc-Edouard 1948- *WhoScE 91-2*
Colin, Reginald A.J.A. 1937- *WhoScE 91-2*
Colin, Veronica *ScF&FL 92*
Colina, Jose de la 1934- *DcMexL*
Colin Crespo, Enrique 1960- *WhoWor 93*
Colindress, Jose Roberto 1954- *WhoSSW 93*
Coling, Michael L. 1947- *St&PR 93*
Colini, Filippo 1811-1863 *OxDcOp*
Colino, Richard Ralph 1936- *WhoE 93*
Colip, Greg Russell *Law&B 92*
Colis, George P. 1954- *St&PR 93*
Colish, Marcia Lillian 1937- *WhoAm 92*
Colker, Edward 1927- *WhoAm 92*
Colker, Marvin Leonard 1927- *WhoAm 92*
Coll, Edward Girard, Jr. 1934- *WhoAm 92*
Coll, Helen F. 1921- *WhoAm 92*
Coll, Jesus *BioIn 17*
Coll, John Peter, Jr. 1943- *WhoAm 92*
Coll, Joseph Clement 1881-1921 *ScF&FL 92*
Coll, Lauren Christiane *Law&B 92*
Coll, Patricia W. *Law&B 92*
Coll, Patrick J. *St&PR 93*
Coll, Richard *Law&B 92*
Coll, Stephen Wilson 1958- *WhoAm 92*
Coll, Steve 1958- *ConAu 137*
Coll, William Eugene 1955- *WhoSSW 93*
Colla, Richard A. *MiSFD 9*
Colladay, Robert S. 1940- *WhoAm 92*
Collado, Emilio Gabriel 1910- *WhoAm 92, WhoWor 93*
Collado Alva, Casimiro del 1822-1898 *DcMexL*
Collaer, Paul 1891-1989 *Baker 92, BioIn 17*
Collamore, Edna A. *AmWomPl*
Collamore, Thomas Jones 1959- *WhoAm 92*
Collan, Risto P.J. 1933- *WhoScE 91-4*
Collan, Yrjo U.I. 1941- *WhoScE 91-4*
Collan, Yrjo Urho 1941- *WhoWor 93*
Collande, Constantine von Mitschke- 1884-1956 *BioIn 17*
Collard *Baker 92*
Collard, David Anthony *WhoScE 91-1*
Collard, Jean-Philippe 1948- *Baker 92*
Collard, Joseph Eugene, Jr. 1949- *WhoEmL 93, WhoSSW 93*
Collard, Maurice 1931- *WhoScE 91-2*
Collard, Raymond L. T. 1928- *WhoWor 93*
Collard, Thomas Albert 1942- *WhoE 93*
Collard, Thomas Hardy, Jr. 1927- *WhoSSW 93*
Collares-Pereira, Manual 1951- *WhoScE 91-3*
Collars, Shirley Marie Coffey 1937- *WhoAmW 93*
Collas, Felix E. *ScF&FL 92*
Collas, Juan Garduno, Jr. 1932- *WhoAm 92*
Collas, Phil *ScF&FL 92*
Collatz, Gunter 1932- *WhoScE 91-3*
Collazo, Denice Michelle 1953- *WhoAmW 93*
Collazos, Oscar 1942- *SpAmA*
Collazos Gonzalez, Julio 1955- *WhoWor 93*
Collbohm, Franklin R. 1907-1990 *BioIn 17*
Colle, Bruno *WhoScE 91-3*
Colleary, Kevin M. *Law&B 92*
Collec, Jean-Claude 1959- *WhoWor 93*
Collector, Robert *MiSFD 9*
Collector, Stephen 1951- *ConAu 139*
Colledge, Charles Hopson 1911- *WhoAm 92*
Collee, John Gerald *WhoScE 91-1*
Colleen, Robert Gene 1930- *St&PR 93*
Collen, Desire 1943- *WhoScE 91-2*
Collen, Desire J. 1943- *WhoWor 93*
Collen, Morris Frank 1913- *WhoAm 92, WhoWor 93*
Collen, Robert Philip 1928- *St&PR 93*
Collens, Lewis Morton 1938- *WhoAm 92*
Coller, Gary Hayes 1952- *WhoEmL 93*
Colleran, Kevin 1941- *WhoWor 93*
Colleran, Robert T. *Law&B 92*
Collery, Peter Mitchell 1959- *St&PR 93, WhoEmL 93*
Collery, Philippe 1951- *WhoScE 91-2*
Colles, H(enry) C(ope) 1879-1943 *Baker 92*
Colles, Michael John *WhoScE 91-1*
Collesano, William Joseph 1949- *WhoE 93*
Colless, Jeremy J. 1962- *St&PR 93*
Collet, Henri 1885-1951 *Baker 92*
Collett, Lucy A. *Law&B 92*
Collett, Mary Joan 1926-1991 *BioIn 17*
Collett, Michael G. 1940- *WhoScE 91-1*
Collett, Robert Clement 1928- *St&PR 93*
Collett, Wayne Neville 1941- *WhoAm 92*
Colletta, Patricia R. 1954- *WhoAm 92, WhoAmW 93*
Colletta, Richard A. 1952- *St&PR 93*
Collette, Bruce Baden 1934- *WhoE 93*
Collette, Buddy *BioIn 17*
Collette, Buddy (William Marcell) 1921- *Baker 92*
Collette, Carolyn Penney 1945- *WhoAmW 93*
Collette, Craig D. 1942- *St&PR 93*
Collette, Frances Madelyn 1947- *WhoAmW 93*
Collette, Jean Yves 1946- *WhoCanL 92*
Collette, Kevin J. 1952- *WhoEmL 93*
Collette, Renee Ann 1951- *WhoEmL 93*
Collette, Richard J. 1947- *St&PR 93*
Collette, Roderick Edward 1934- *St&PR 93*
Collette, Susan Harter 1948- *WhoEmL 93*
Collette, W.R. 1920- *St&PR 93*
Colletti, Bruce William 1957- *WhoSSW 93*
Colletti, Francis Anthony, Jr. 1957- *WhoE 93*
Colletti, John J. 1944- *St&PR 93*
Colletti, Paul J. *Law&B 92*
Colletti, Salvatore *Law&B 92*
Colletti-Reina, Marie Goldman *AmWomPl*
Collewijn, Han 1935- *WhoScE 91-3*
Colley, Adrian A. *Law&B 92*
Colley, Carolyn Bernard 1930- *WhoAmW 93*
Colley, Carolyn Virginia 1926- *St&PR 93*
Colley, Charles Bruce 1952- *WhoSSW 93*
Colley, Derek Charles *WhoScE 91-1*
Colley, George Pomeroy 1835-1881 *HarEnMi*
Colley, Howard *WhoScE 91-1*
Colley, John Leonard, Jr. 1930- *WhoAm 92*
Colley, John Richard Thomas *WhoScE 91-1*
Colley, Nathaniel S. 1917-1992 *BioIn 17*
Colley, Nathaniel S., Sr. d1992 *NewYTBS 92*
Colley, Stephen Gallo 1953- *WhoEmL 93*
Colley, Thomas Elbert, Jr. 1928- *WhoSSW 93*
Colli, Bart Joseph 1948- *WhoE 93, WhoEmL 93*
Colliander, Alan C. 1948- *St&PR 93*
Colliander, Douglas C. 1943- *WhoIns 93*
Collias, Elsie Cole 1920- *WhoAm 92*
Colliat, George Henri 1946- *WhoEmL 93*
Collie, Michael (John) 1929- *ConAu 39NR*
Collier, Arthur 1680-1732 *BioIn 17*
Collier, Barbara Lee 1959- *WhoAmW 93*
Collier, Beverly Joanne 1936- *WhoAmW 93*
Collier, Blanton 1906-1983 *BiDAMSp 1989*
Collier, Byron S. *Law&B 92*
Collier, Calvin J. *Law&B 92*
Collier, Charles Arthur, Jr. 1930- *WhoAm 92*
Collier, Christopher 1930- *DcAmChF 1960, MajAI [port], SmATA 70 [port]*
Collier, Clarence Robert 1919- *WhoAm 92*
Collier, Clifford Warthen, Jr. 1927- *WhoAm 92*
Collier, Constance 1878-1955 *AmWomPl*
Collier, Curtis Newton 1933- *WhoSSW 93*
Collier, Cynthia Jean 1957- *WhoEmL 93*
Collier, Daling *BioIn 17*
Collier, David Alan 1947- *WhoEmL 93*
Collier, Diana Gordon 1945- *WhoSSW 93*
Collier, Donald 1911- *IntDcAn*
Collier, Duaine Alden 1950- *WhoE 93*
Collier, Dwight A. 1932- *ScF&FL 92*
Collier, Eartha Welfare 1960- *WhoSSW 93*
Collier, Felton Moreland 1924- *WhoAm 92*
Collier, Gary 1947- *ConAu 138*
Collier, Gaylan Jane 1924- *WhoAm 92, WhoSSW 93*
Collier, George 1738-1795 *HarEnMi*
Collier, Herman Edward, Jr. 1927- *WhoAm 92*
Collier, Holt *BioIn 17*
Collier, James L(incoln) 1928- *SmATA 70 [port]*
Collier, James Lincoln 1928- *DcAmChF 1960, MajAI [port], ScF&FL 92*
Collier, James Warren 1940- *WhoAm 92*
Collier, Jane *WhoWrEP 92*
Collier, Joe C., Jr. 1934- *St&PR 93*
Collier, John 1901-1980 *ScF&FL 92*
Collier, John 1913-1992 *BioIn 17*
Collier, John, Jr. d1992 *NewYTBS 92*
Collier, John Robert 1939- *WhoSSW 93*
Collier, John Thornton 1910- *WhoE 93*
Collier, Judith L. *Law&B 92*
Collier, Ken 1944- *St&PR 93*
Collier, Linda J. 1943- *WhoAmW 93*
Collier, Lois 1919- *SweetSg C [port]*
Collier, Lucille Ann *WhoAm 92*
Collier, Manning Gary 1951- *WhoSSW 93*
Collier, Marie 1926-1971 *Baker 92*
Collier, Marie 1927-1971 *OxDcOp*
Collier, Marsha Ann 1950- *WhoEmL 93*
Collier, Mary fl. 1689-1762 *BioIn 17*
Collier, Maxie Tyron 1945- *WhoE 93*
Collier, Michael 1953- *ConAu 137*
Collier, Michael Thomas 1950- *WhoE 93*
Collier, Mitty *SoulM*
Collier, Mitty 1941- *BioIn 17*
Collier, Oscar 1924- *WhoAm 92*
Collier, Richard Bangs 1918- *WhoWor 93*
Collier, Richard Earl 1927- *WhoSSW 93*
Collier, Robert Daryl 1961- *WhoSSW 93*
Collier, Robert John 1938- *WhoAm 92*
Collier, Robert Joseph 1876-1918 *BioIn 17*
Collier, Rodney M. 1935- *St&PR 93*
Collier, Ron *BioIn 17*
Collier, Ronald 1930- *Baker 92*
Collier, Steven 1942- *BioIn 17*
Collier, Steven D. *Law&B 92*
Collier, Steven Edward 1952- *WhoEmL 93, WhoSSW 93*
Collier, Susan Starr 1939- *WhoAmW 93, WhoE 93*
Collier, Thomas J. 1938- *St&PR 93*
Collier, Tom W. 1948- *WhoEmL 93, WhoWor 93*
Collier, Trudy Jean 1950- *WhoAmW 93*
Collier, William J., II 1953- *WhoEmL 93*
Collier, Zena 1926- *WhoWrEP 92*
Collier-Evans, Demetra Frances 1937- *WhoAm 92, WhoAmW 93*
Colliflower, Kathleen A. 1952- *WhoAmW 93*
Colliflower, Michael A. 1954- *St&PR 93*
Colliflower, Michael Allan *Law&B 92*
Colligan, Douglas *ScF&FL 92*
Colligan, Ian Cunningham *WhoScE 91-1*
Colligan, Jack J. 1929- *St&PR 93*
Colligan, John 1951- *St&PR 93*
Collignon, Jeff 1953- *ConAu 137*
Colligon, John S. *WhoScE 91-1*
Colligon, John Smallwood 1937- *WhoWor 93*
Collin, Arthur Edwin 1929- *WhoAm 92*
Collin, Gerd 1934- *WhoScE 91-3*
Collin, Hans 1913- *WhoWor 93*
Collin, Jacques E.L. 1926- *WhoScE 91-2*
Collin, Jean 1924- *WhoAfr*
Collin, Jean-Pierre 1936- *WhoScE 91-2*
Collin, Richard Harvey 1932- *WhoSSW 93*
Collin, Robert Emanuel 1928- *WhoAm 92*
Collin, Tamara Sue 1963- *WhoAmW 93*
Collin, Thomas James 1949- *WhoEmL 93*
Collina, Kathleen Alice 1938- *WhoAmW 93*
Collin de Blamont, Francois 1690-1760 *Baker 92*
Collin Du Bocage, Arnaud 1951- *WhoWor 93*
Colling, Alfred G. 1937- *St&PR 93*
Colling, David John 1950- *WhoAm 92*
Collingridge, Graham Leon *WhoScE 91-1*
Collings, Albert Frederick 1941- *St&PR 93*
Collings, Celeste Louise 1948- *WhoEmL 93*
Collings, Charles L. 1925- *St&PR 93*
Collings, I. J(illie) *ConAu 38NR*
Collings, Lori Jo 1959- *WhoAmW 93, WhoEmL 93*
Collings, Michael R. 1947- *ScF&FL 92*
Collings, Michael Robert 1947- *WhoWrEP 92*
Collings, Richard James 1946- *WhoE 93*
Collingsworth, William J. *Law&B 92*
Collington, Peter *BioIn 17*
Collingwood, Cuthbert 1748-1810 *HarEnMi*
Collingwood, Lawrance 1887-1982 *OxDcOp*
Collingwood, Lawrance (Arthur) 1887-1982 *Baker 92*
Collingwood, Richard J. 1939- *St&PR 93*
Collins, Adrian Anthony 1937- *WhoAm 92*
Collins, Albert *BioIn 17*
Collins, Albert 1944- *St&PR 93*
Collins, Allen c. 1949- See Lynyrd Skynyrd *ConMus 9*
Collins, Andrew Seymour 1944- *WhoWor 93*
Collins, Angela Gouvis 1956- *WhoAmW 93*
Collins, Anita Marguerite 1947- *WhoAm 92, WhoEmL 93*
Collins, Anne *AmWomPl*
Collins, Anthony (Vincent Benedictus) 1893-1963 *Baker 92*
Collins, Arthur Worth, Jr. 1929- *BiDAMSp 1989*
Collins, Atwood, III 1947- *St&PR 93, WhoAm 92, WhoEmL 93*
Collins, Barbara *BioIn 17*
Collins, Barbara Jo 1958- *WhoEmL 93*
Collins, Barbara-Rose 1939- *CngDr 91, WhoAm 92, WhoAmW 93*
Collins, Ben d1906 *BioIn 17*
Collins, Bert 1934- *St&PR 93, WhoAm 92, WhoIns 93*
Collins, Bertram Aggrey 1930- *WhoUN 92*
Collins, Betty *BioIn 17*
Collins, Bobby *BioIn 17*
Collins, Bonnie *BioIn 17*
Collins, Bootsy 1951- *ConMus 8 [port]*
Collins, Brian John *WhoScE 91-1*
Collins, Bruce D. *Law&B 92*

Collins, Bruce Dennis 1951- *WhoAm 92*
Collins, Candace Brown 1950- *WhoAm 92*
Collins, Cardiss *BioIn 17*
Collins, Cardiss 1931- *AfrAmBi [port], CngDr 91, WhoAm 92, WhoAmW 93*
Collins, Cardiss Robertson 1931- *EncAACR*
Collins, Carl Russell, Jr. 1926- *WhoAm 92*
Collins, Carla Kaye 1966- *WhoSSW 93*
Collins, Carol Malenka *Law&B 92*
Collins, Carter Compton 1925- *WhoAm 92*
Collins, Carvel 1912-1990 *BioIn 17*
Collins, Catherine Clay *WhoAmW 93*
Collins, Catherine Z. *Law&B 92*
Collins, Charles Dillard 1942- *WhoE 93*
Collins, Charles Floyd 1928- *St&PR 93*
Collins, Charles Jesse 1951- *WhoSSW 93*
Collins, Charles M. *ScF&FL 92*
Collins, Charles Peter *Law&B 92*
Collins, Charles R. 1934- *St&PR 93*
Collins, Chris *BioIn 17*
Collins, Christopher Carl 1950- *WhoAm 92, WhoE 93, WhoEmL 93, WhoWor 93*
Collins, Claire Anne 1954- *WhoAmW 93*
Collins, Copp 1914- *WhoAm 92*
Collins, Curtis Allan 1940- *WhoAm 92*
Collins, (Cuthbert) Dale 1897- *DcChlFi*
Collins, Dana J. 1956- *St&PR 93*
Collins, Dana Jon 1956- *WhoEmL 93*
Collins, Daniel F. *Law&B 92*
Collins, Daniel F. 1942- *St&PR 93*
Collins, Daniel Francis 1942- *WhoAm 92*
Collins, Daniel W. 1946- *WhoAm 92, WhoEmL 93*
Collins, Daniel William *Law&B 92*
Collins, David A. *Law&B 92*
Collins, David Browning 1922- *WhoAm 92*
Collins, David Edmond 1934- *WhoAm 92*
Collins, David Raymond 1940- *WhoWrEP 92*
Collins, Denise Louise 1954- *WhoAmW 93*
Collins, Dennis Arthur 1940- *WhoAm 92*
Collins, Dennis Glenn 1944- *WhoWor 93*
Collins, Derryl L. *Law&B 92*
Collins, Diana Josephine 1944- *WhoAm 92*
Collins, Don Cary 1951- *WhoEmL 93*
Collins, Donald Francis 1928- *WhoE 93*
Collins, Donald L. 1918- *St&PR 93*
Collins, Donald Lynn 1952- *St&PR 93*
Collins, Donald Ogden 1934- *WhoAm 92*
Collins, Doug *BioIn 17*
Collins, Douglas Charles 1953- *St&PR 93*
Collins, Douglas Patrick, Jr. 1961- *WhoEmL 93*
Collins, Earlean *WhoAmW 93*
Collins, Eddie 1887-1951 *BioIn 17*
Collins, Eddie Lee 1936- *WhoE 93, WhoWor 93*
Collins, Edith Hopkins 1959- *WhoEmL 93*
Collins, Edmond A. *Law&B 92*
Collins, Edward T. *Law&B 92*
Collins, Edwin B. 1921-1991 *BioIn 17*
Collins, Eileen Louise 1942- *WhoAm 92*
Collins, Eileen Mary 1933- *WhoAmW 93*
Collins, Elgin Bert, Jr. 1955- *WhoSSW 93*
Collins, Elizabeth D. 1957- *St&PR 93*
Collins, Elizabeth M. *Law&B 92*
Collins, Emma Lou 1949- *WhoAmW 93*
Collins, Erik 1938- *WhoE 93*
Collins, Erin Patrick 1962- *WhoE 93*
Collins, Erroll *ScF&FL 92*
Collins, Fleda Mae 1935- *WhoSSW 93*
Collins, Floyd 1890-1925 *BioIn 17*
Collins, Francis *WhoAm 92*
Collins, Francis S. *BioIn 17*
Collins, Francis Winfield 1927- *WhoE 93*
Collins, Frank Charles, Jr. 1927- *WhoAm 92, WhoSSW 93*
Collins, Frank Edwin *Law&B 92*
Collins, Frank Miles 1928- *WhoE 93*
Collins, Gary (Ross) 1934- *WhoWrEP 92*
Collins, George J. 1940- *St&PR 93*
Collins, George Joseph *WhoAm 92*
Collins, George L. d1991 *BioIn 17*
Collins, George Washington 1925-1972 *BioIn 17*
Collins, Gerald Chester 1946- *WhoEmL 93*
Collins, Gerald E. 1924- *St&PR 93*
Collins, Gerard 1938- *WhoWor 93*
Collins, Gerri 1933- *WhoE 93*
Collins, Gilbert *St&PR 93*
Collins, Glenn *BioIn 17*
Collins, Gordon Scott, Jr. 1942- *St&PR 93*
Collins, Gwendolyn Beth 1943- *WhoAmW 93, WhoSSW 93*
Collins, Harker 1924- *St&PR 93, WhoAm 92*
Collins, Harold John, III 1955- *WhoSSW 93*
Collins, Harry David 1931- *WhoWor 93*
Collins, Henry B. 1899-1987 *IntDcAn*
Collins, Henry James, III 1927- *WhoAm 92*
Collins, Henry W. *Law&B 92*
Collins, Herschel Douglas 1928- *WhoAm 92*
Collins, Horace C. *Law&B 92*
Collins, Howard L. *Law&B 92*
Collins, Hubert Rayburn 1927- *St&PR 93*
Collins, Hunt *ConAu 38NR, ScF&FL 92*
Collins, J. Barclay, II *Law&B 92*
Collins, J. Barclay, II 1944- *WhoAm 92*
Collins, J. Christopher *Law&B 92*
Collins, J. Michael 1935- *WhoAm 92, WhoE 93*
Collins, J.P. 1942- *St&PR 93*
Collins, Jack B. d1991 *BioIn 17*
Collins, Jackson 1939- *ScF&FL 92*
Collins, James A. 1926- *St&PR 93*
Collins, James Alexander, II 1944- *WhoAm 92*
Collins, James Arthur 1926- *WhoAm 92*
Collins, James Carstairs 1930- *St&PR 93*
Collins, James Edward 1937- *WhoE 93*
Collins, James Foster 1922- *WhoAm 92*
Collins, James Francis 1943- *WhoWor 93*
Collins, James Harold Lee 1946- *WhoEmL 93*
Collins, James Lawton, Jr. 1917- *WhoAm 92, WhoSSW 93*
Collins, Janet 1923- *BioIn 17*
Collins, Jay Leo 1938- *WhoE 93*
Collins, Jeff *BioIn 17*
Collins, Jeffrey Hamilton 1930- *WhoAm 92*
Collins, Jeremiah James 1931- *St&PR 93*
Collins, Jerry Allan 1936- *WhoAm 92*
Collins, Joan *BioIn 17*
Collins, Joan 1933- *NewYTBS 92 [port]*
Collins, Joan Henrietta 1933- *WhoAm 92, WhoAmW 93, WhoWor 93*
Collins, Joe 1909- *St&PR 93*
Collins, John 1769-1804 *BioIn 17*
Collins, John 1945- *WhoScE 91-3, WhoWor 93*
Collins, John A. d1992 *NewYTBS 92*
Collins, John Alfred 1936- *WhoAm 92*
Collins, John D. *St&PR 93*
Collins, John F. *Law&B 92*
Collins, John Francis 1937- *WhoE 93*
Collins, John Francis 1946- *WhoEmL 93*
Collins, John G. 1936- *St&PR 93*
Collins, John J. 1900-1991 *BioIn 17*
Collins, John Joseph, Jr. 1934- *WhoAm 92*
Collins, John L. *ScF&FL 92*
Collins, John Roger 1941- *St&PR 93, WhoAm 92, WhoSSW 93*
Collins, Joseph Bernard 1953- *WhoEmL 93*
Collins, Joseph J. 1944- *St&PR 93*
Collins, Joseph Jameson 1944- *WhoAm 92*
Collins, Joseph Lawton 1896- *HarEnMi*
Collins, Joseph Lawton 1896-1987 *CmdGen 1991 [port]*
Collins, Joseph M. 1947- *St&PR 93*
Collins, Joseph Thomas 1939- *WhoWrEP 92*
Collins, Joseph V. 1936- *St&PR 93*
Collins, Judy 1939- *BioIn 17*
Collins, Judy (Marjorie) 1939- *Baker 92, WhoAm 92*
Collins, Kathleen *SweetSg B [port]*
Collins, Kathleen A. 1951- *WhoAmW 93*
Collins, Kathleen Elizabeth 1951- *WhoAmW 93, WhoEmL 93*
Collins, Kathleen J. *Law&B 92*
Collins, Kathleen M. *Law&B 92*
Collins, Kenneth Bruce 1939- *WhoAm 92*
Collins, Kenneth J., Jr. 1934- *St&PR 93*
Collins, Kent Howes 1940- *St&PR 93*
Collins, Kevin Joseph 1939- *St&PR 93*
Collins, Larry 1929- *ScF&FL 92, WhoAm 92*
Collins, Larry Wayne 1937- *St&PR 93*
Collins, Len *ScF&FL 92*
Collins, Lena Vestal 1933- *WhoAmW 93*
Collins, Leonard Edward, Jr. *Law&B 92*
Collins, Leroy 1909-1991 *AnObit 1991, BioIn 17, EncAACR*
Collins, Lester Albertson 1914- *WhoAm 92*
Collins, Lillian F. *AmWomPl*
Collins, Lori J. *Law&B 92*
Collins, Louise *AmWomPl*
Collins, Lynn *SoulM*
Collins, Marcus E., Sr. 1927- *WhoAm 92, WhoSSW 93*
Collins, Margaret E.G. *Law&B 92*
Collins, Margaret Helen 1950- *WhoEmL 93*
Collins, Maribeth Wilson 1918- *WhoAm 92*
Collins, Marie *AmWomPl*
Collins, Marjorie Byrd *BioIn 17*
Collins, Mark Steven 1952- *WhoEmL 93*
Collins, Marshall J., Jr. 1941- *St&PR 93*
Collins, Martha 1940- *WhoAmW 93, WhoWrEP 92*
Collins, Martha Layne 1936- *WhoAm 92, WhoAmW 93*
Collins, Marva *BioIn 17*
Collins, Marva 1936- *ConBlB 3 [port]*
Collins, Marva Deloise Nettles 1936- *WhoAmW 93*
Collins, Marva Delores 1936- *AfrAmBi*
Collins, Mary 1846-1920 *BioIn 17*
Collins, Mary 1940- *WhoAm 92, WhoAmW 93*
Collins, Mary Alice 1937- *WhoAmW 93*
Collins, Mary Ann 1938- *WhoAmW 93*
Collins, Mary Anne 1951- *WhoAmW 93*
Collins, Mary Beth 1925- *WhoAmW 93*
Collins, Mary Elizabeth 1949- *WhoAmW 93*
Collins, Mary Elizabeth 1953- *WhoEmL 93, WhoSSW 93*
Collins, Mary Ellen 1949- *WhoAmW 93*
Collins, Mary Ellen Kennedy 1939- *WhoWor 93*
Collins, Mary Jane 1940- *WhoAmW 93*
Collins, Mary Jo 1946- *WhoAmW 93*
Collins, Mary T. *AmWomPl*
Collins, Maureen L. 1938- *St&PR 93*
Collins, Michael *WhoWrEP 92*
Collins, Michael 1890-1922 *BioIn 17, DcTwHis, HarEnMi*
Collins, Michael 1930- *BioIn 17, WhoAm 92, WhoWor 93*
Collins, Michael James 1944- *WhoAm 92*
Collins, Michael P. 1947- *St&PR 93*
Collins, Michael Sean 1951- *WhoEmL 93*
Collins, Michael Wesley 1939- *WhoWor 93*
Collins, Mike *BioIn 17*
Collins, Monica Ann 1951- *WhoAm 92*
Collins, Nancy *BioIn 17*
Collins, Nancy A. 1959- *ScF&FL 92*
Collins, Pat Lowery 1932- *WhoWrEP 92*
Collins, Patricia 1962- *WhoE 93*
Collins, Patricia M. *Law&B 92*
Collins, Paul 1954- *ScF&FL 92*
Collins, Paul J. 1936- *WhoAm 92*
Collins, Paul John 1936- *WhoAm 92, WhoWor 93*
Collins, Pauline 1940- *WhoAm 92, WhoAmW 93*
Collins, Phil *BioIn 17, WhoAm 92*
Collins, Phil(ip) 1951- *Baker 92*
Collins, Philip Reilly 1921- *WhoAm 92*
Collins, Priscilla Bullitt *BioIn 17*
Collins, R. Ken 1946- *WhoSSW 93*
Collins, Ralph Oliver, III *Law&B 92*
Collins, Randall 1941- *ScF&FL 92*
Collins, Ray T. *Law&B 92*
Collins, Raymond C. 1931- *WhoSSW 93*
Collins, Raymond Francis 1935- *WhoWor 93*
Collins, Richard d1991 *BioIn 17*
Collins, Richard B. 1942- *St&PR 93*
Collins, Richard Lawrence 1933- *WhoAm 92*
Collins, Richard Raoul 1936- *WhoAm 92, WhoE 93*
Collins, Richard S. *Law&B 92*
Collins, Richard W. *Law&B 92*
Collins, Richard William 1930- *WhoWor 93*
Collins, Robert *MiSFD 9*
Collins, Robert A. 1929- *ScF&FL 92*
Collins, Robert Allan *Law&B 92*
Collins, Robert Clarkson, II 1949- *WhoEmL 93*
Collins, Robert Edward 1934- *St&PR 93*
Collins, Robert Edward 1949- *WhoE 93*
Collins, Robert Ellwood 1932- *WhoE 93, WhoWor 93*
Collins, Robert Frederick 1931- *WhoAm 92, WhoSSW 93*
Collins, Robert Herschel, Jr. 1935- *St&PR 93*
Collins, Robert Joseph 1927- *WhoAm 92*
Collins, Robert Keith 1947- *WhoEmL 93, WhoSSW 93*
Collins, Robert Lindsay 1946- *WhoAsAP 91*
Collins, Robert Oakley 1933- *WhoAm 92, WhoWrEP 92*
Collins, Rod 1949- *St&PR 93*
Collins, Roderick John *WhoScE 91-1*
Collins, Roger Buckner 1953- *St&PR 93*
Collins, Royal Eugene 1925- *WhoAm 92*
Collins, Russell Ambrose *WhoAm 92*
Collins, Russell M., Jr. 1933- *WhoAm 92*
Collins, Ruth Coffin *AmWomPl*
Collins, S. Ruth 1939- *WhoSSW 93*
Collins, Samuel W., Jr. 1923- *WhoAm 92*
Collins, Sandra Kay 1959- *WhoAmW 93*
Collins, Sarah Helen Boli 1958- *WhoAmW 93, WhoEmL 93*
Collins, Stephen Barksdale 1932- *WhoAm 92*
Collins, Stephen Hugh 1947- *WhoScE 91-1*
Collins, Susan Elizabeth 1959- *WhoAmW 93*
Collins, Susan Margaret 1948- *WhoAmW 93*
Collins, Tai *BioIn 17*
Collins, Terrence T. 1942- *St&PR 93*
Collins, Theodore John *Law&B 92*
Collins, Theodore Joseph 1932- *WhoAm 92*
Collins, Thomas Asa 1921- *WhoAm 92*
Collins, Thomas Joseph 1936- *WhoAm 92*
Collins, Thomas Michael 1934- *WhoE 93*
Collins, Thomas P. *Law&B 92*
Collins, Thomas Stephen 1961- *WhoE 93*
Collins, Traci Wynn 1951- *WhoAmW 93*
Collins, V.H. 1872- *ScF&FL 92*
Collins, Vincent Patrick 1912- *WhoAm 92*
Collins, Vincent Peter 1947- *WhoWor 93*
Collins, Wallace Edmund James, III 1955- *WhoE 93*
Collins, Walter Regis, Jr. 1935- *St&PR 93*
Collins, Warwick *ScF&FL 92*
Collins, Wayne Dale 1951- *WhoAm 92, WhoEmL 93*
Collins, Wayne F. 1941- *St&PR 93*
Collins, Wayne Forrest 1941- *WhoAm 92*
Collins, Wilkie 1824-1889 *BioIn 17, ScF&FL 92*
Collins, William *SoulM*
Collins, William 1721-1759 *BioIn 17*
Collins, William Arthur, III 1943- *WhoSSW 93*
Collins, William C. 1925- *WhoSSW 93*
Collins, William Derek *WhoScE 91-1*
Collins, William Edward 1932- *WhoAm 92*
Collins, William F., Jr. 1924- *WhoAm 92*
Collins, William George, Jr. *Law&B 92*
Collins, William J. *Law&B 92*
Collins, William Leroy 1942- *WhoWor 93*
Collins, William Lewis 1954- *WhoEmL 93*
Collins, William Patrick *WhoScE 91-1*
Collins, William S. *Law&B 92*
Collins, William T. 1917-1992 *BioIn 17*
Collins, William Thomas 1922- *WhoAm 92*
Collins, Winifred Quick *WhoAmW 93, WhoE 93*
Collins-Eiland, Karen Wisler 1949- *WhoAm 92*
Collins-McHugh, Doreen Karen 1966- *WhoAmW 93*
Collinson, Brent Patrick 1952- *WhoEmL 93*
Collinson, Christopher David *WhoScE 91-1*
Collinson, Dale Stanley 1938- *WhoAm 92*
Collinson, John Theodore 1926- *St&PR 93, WhoAm 92*
Collinson, Roger 1936- *ChlFicS*
Collinson, William R. *WhoAm 92*
Collinson-Ghesquiere, Lynn Christine 1946- *WhoEmL 93*
Collins-Scheifele, Lesa Mae 1962- *WhoE 93*
Collins-Weissberg, Barbara Jean 1956- *WhoAmW 93*
Collins-Wright, Robert John 1927- *St&PR 93*
Collis, Charles 1920- *WhoAm 92*
Collis, Kay Lynn 1958- *WhoAmW 93, WhoEmL 93*
Collis, Sidney Robert 1924- *WhoAm 92*
Collishaw, Raymond 1893-1976 *HarEnMi*
Collis-Mele, Nancy Lee 1948- *WhoSSW 93*
Collison, Bayfield Ian 1936- *WhoWor 93*
Collison, Curtis Lee, Jr. 1940- *St&PR 93*
Collison, Robert Lewis 1914-1989 *BioIn 17*
Collman, James Paddock 1932- *WhoAm 92*
Collmer, Robert George 1926- *WhoAm 92*
Collodi, Carlo *MajAI*
Colloff, Roger d1992 *NewYTBS 92*
Colloff, Roger 1946-1992 *BioIn 17*
Colloff, Roger David 1946- *St&PR 93*
Collom, Bette Rae 1937- *WhoAmW 93*
Collomb, Bertrand C. 1942- *St&PR 93*
Collomb, Bertrand Pierre 1942- *WhoAm 92, WhoSSW 93, WhoWor 93*
Collons, Rodger Duane 1935- *WhoAm 92*
Collopy, Christopher Stephen 1952- *WhoEmL 93*
Collor de Mello, Fernando *BioIn 17, NewYTBS 92 [port]*
Collor de Mello, Fernando 1949- *News 92 [port], WhoWor 93*
Colloredo-Mansfeld, Ferdinand 1939- *St&PR 93*
Collot, Claude Louis 1936- *WhoScE 91-2*
Colloton, John William 1931- *WhoAm 92*
Colloton, Patrick G. 1942- *WhoIns 93*
Collum, Dick 1930- *St&PR 93*
Collum, Herbert 1914- *Baker 92*
Collum, Jan *BioIn 17*
Collum, Nancy Jean 1956- *WhoAmW 93*
Collum, Robert Edward 1928- *St&PR 93*
Collum, William Harold 1932- *WhoSSW 93*
Collumb, Peter John 1942- *WhoSSW 93, WhoWor 93*
Collura, Frank John 1947- *WhoSSW 93*

Collura, Mary-Ellen Lang 1949- *DcChlFi*
Collura, Michael J. 1948- *St&PR 93*
Collver, Arthur Edward 1935- *St&PR 93*
Collver, Gary A. *Law&B 92*
Collyer, Charles Ralph 1930- *St&PR 93*
Collyer, Michael 1942- *WhoAm 92*
Collyer, Robert B. 1932- *WhoAm 92*
Collyer, Steven George 1950- *WhoE 93*
Colman, Benjamin 1673-1747 *BioIn 17*
Colman, Charles Kingsbury 1929- *WhoSSW 93*
Colman, Christopher Sean *Law&B 92*
Colman, Emogene Stoddard *AmWomPl*
Colman, George 1732-1794 *BioIn 17*
Colman, George 1762-1836 *BioIn 17*
Colman, Hila *DcAmChF 1960, MajAI [port]*
Colman, James Alan 1949- *St&PR 93*
Colman, John Charles 1927- *St&PR 93*
Colman, Richard Thomas 1935- *WhoE 93*
Colman, Robert Wolf 1935- *WhoAm 92*
Colman, Roberta Fishman *WhoAmW 93, WhoE 93*
Colman, Ronald 1891-1958 *BioIn 17, IntDcF 2-3 [port]*
Colman, Warren *BioIn 17*
Colman, Warren (David) 1944- *ConAu 136*
Colman, Wendy 1950- *WhoAm 92, WhoAmW 93*
Colmano, Germille 1921- *WhoAm 92*
Colmano, Marino Giovanni Augusto 1948- *WhoEmL 93*
Colmcille, Saint 521-597 *BioIn 17*
Colmenares, German 1938-1990 *BioIn 17*
Colmenares, Margarita H. 1957- *NotHsAW 93 [port]*
Colmenares, Margarita Hortensia 1957- *HispAmA*
Colmer, Roy David 1935- *WhoE 93*
Colmery, Harry W., Jr. 1924- *St&PR 93*
Colmery, Joseph P. *BioIn 17*
Colmore, Charles Blayney d1991 *BioIn 17*
Colmore, G. *ScF&FL 92*
Colnes, Martin B. 1927- *St&PR 93*
Colnett, Ronald H. 1929- *WhoAm 92*
Colnon, William Lydon 1928- *WhoAm 92*
Coloane, Francisco 1910- *SpAmA*
Colobrano, Michele Enrico Carafa de *Baker 92*
Colodny, Edwin I. 1926- *EncABHB 8 [port], St&PR 93*
Colodny, Edwin Irving 1926- *WhoAm 92*
Cologne, Knox M., III *Law&B 92*
Colokathis, Jane 1951- *WhoEmL 93*
Colom, Francisco 1927- *WhoScE 91-3*
Colom Argueta, Manuel *DcCPCAm*
Colomar O'Brien, Ana 1938- *NotHsAW 93*
Colomb, Maurice *WhoScE 91-2*
Colomb, P. Kevin *Law&B 92*
Colombani, Paul Michael 1951- *WhoE 93*
Colombetti, Giuliano 1945- *WhoScE 91-3, WhoWor 93*
Colombino, Carlos 1937- *BioIn 17*
Colombo, Agostino *WhoScE 91-3*
Colombo, Antonio 1950- *WhoWor 93*
Colombo, Carol Ann 1960- *WhoEmL 93*
Colombo, Cristoforo *BioIn 17*
Colombo, Emilio 1920- *WhoWor 93*
Colombo, Frank V. 1956- *St&PR 93, WhoAm 92*
Colombo, Furio Marco 1931- *WhoAm 92, WhoWor 93*
Colombo, John Robert 1936- *ScF&FL 92, WhoAm 92, WhoCanL 92, WhoWrEP 92*
Colombo, Judith Woolcock *ScF&FL 92*
Colombo, Lidija 1922- *WhoScE 91-4*
Colombo, Louis John 1947- *WhoEmL 93*
Colombo, Luciano 1960- *WhoWor 93*
Colombo, Pierre 1914- *Baker 92*
Colombo, Roberto *WhoScE 91-3*
Colombo, Umberto P. 1927- *WhoScE 91-3*
Colombo, Umberto Paolo 1927- *WhoWor 93*
Colom-Pastor, Jose F. 1939- *WhoScE 91-3*
Colom Polo, F. *WhoScE 91-3*
Colon, Aly Antonio 1952- *WhoEmL 93*
Colon, Arthur Alan 1947- *WhoEmL 93, WhoSSW 93*
Colon, Benita 1941- *WhoWrEP 92*
Colon, Carlos 1953- *WhoWrEP 92*
Colon, Carlos Wildo 1953- *WhoSSW 93*
Colon, Jesus 1901-1974 *BioIn 17, HispAmA*
Colon, Juan B. Rivera 1940- *St&PR 93*
Colon, Lydia M. 1947- *WhoAmW 93*
Colon, Marie Acosta *NotHsAW 93*
Colon, Michael N.J. *Law&B 92*
Colon, Miriam 1945- *HispAmA, NotHsAW 93*
Colon, Pepe J. *Law&B 92*
Colon, Phyllis Janet 1938- *WhoAmW 93*
Colonel, Sheri L. 1955- *St&PR 93*
Colonel, Sheri Lynn 1955- *WhoAm 92, WhoAmW 93*
Coloney, Wayne Herndon 1925- *WhoAm 92, WhoSSW 93, WhoWor 93*
Colonius, Ray Edward 1935- *St&PR 93*
Colon-Morales, Rafael 1941- *HispAmA*
Colonna, Donatella *BioIn 17*
Colonna, Egidio c. 1243-1316 *BioIn 17*
Colonna, Enzo M. 1943- *St&PR 93*
Colonna, Giovanni 1944- *WhoWor 93*
Colonna, Giovanni Paolo 1637-1695 *Baker 92*
Colonna, Isabel Willett 1961- *WhoAmW 93*
Colonna, Jerry 1904-1986 *QDrFCA 92 [port]*
Colonna, Joseph George 1949- *WhoE 93*
Colonna, Prospero 1452-1523 *HarEnMi*
Colonna, Stefano 1941- *WhoScE 91-3*
Colonna, William Mark 1956- *WhoEmL 93*
Colonne, Edouard 1838-1910 *Baker 92*
Colonnier, Marc Leopold 1930- *WhoAm 92*
Colony-Cokely, Pamela Cameron 1947- *WhoAmW 93, WhoE 93*
Colorado, Antonio Jose 1939- *WhoAm 92*
Colorado, Gabriel *Law&B 92*
Colosi, Thomas Richard 1934- *St&PR 93*
Colosimo, Antonio 1949- *WhoEmL 93*
Colosimo, Robert 1929- *WhoAm 92*
Colosimo, Sandy Marion 1934- *St&PR 93*
Colot, Roseann Marie 1957- *WhoEmL 93*
Colovic, Nikola 1941- *WhoScE 91-4*
Colpaert, Carl *MiSFD 9*
Colquhoun, David *WhoScE 91-1*
Colquitt, Charles G., II 1938- *St&PR 93*
Colsky, Irene Vivian 1929- *WhoAmW 93, WhoSSW 93*
Colson, Charles Wendell 1931- *WhoAm 92, WhoWrEP 92*
Colson, Deborah Anne *Law&B 92*
Colson, Earl M. 1930- *WhoAm 92*
Colson, Elizabeth Florence 1917- *IntDcAn, WhoAm 92, WhoAmW 93*
Colson, Greg *BioIn 17*
Colson, Keith P. 1948- *St&PR 93*
Colson, Steven Douglas 1941- *WhoAm 92*
Colston, Calvin 1940- *St&PR 93*
Colston, Malcolm Arthur 1938- *WhoAsAP 91*
Colston, Michael Joseph *WhoScE 91-1*
Colt, Alexander T. d1990 *BioIn 17*
Colt, Charles Cary d1991 *BioIn 17*
Colt, Edward H. 1956- *St&PR 93*
Colt, Eleanore Phillips 1910- *BioIn 17*
Colt, Martin *ConAu 39NR*
Colt, Samuel 1814-1862 *BioIn 17*
Colt, Zenas M.C. 1946- *St&PR 93*
Coltelli, Laura Rauch 1958- *WhoSSW 93*
Coltellini, Anna *OxDcOp*
Coltellini, Celeste 1760-1828 *Baker 92*
Coltellini, Celeste 1760-1829 *OxDcOp*
Coltellini, Marco 1719-1777 *OxDcOp*
Colten, Harvey Radin 1939- *WhoAm 92*
Colter, Cyrus 1910- *WhoAm 92, WhoWrEP 92*
Colter, John 1774?-1813 *Expl 93*
Colter, Mel Archie 1947- *WhoWor 93*
Colter-Thielemann, Theresa 1965- *WhoAmW 93*
Coltharp, Lurline Hughes 1913- *WhoAmW 93*
Colthart, James M. 1944- *St&PR 93*
Coltman, David A. 1942- *St&PR 93*
Coltman, Edward Jeremiah 1948- *WhoEmL 93*
Coltman, John Wesley 1915- *WhoAm 92*
Coltoff, Beth Jamie 1955- *WhoAm 92, WhoEmL 93*
Colton, Carolyn *Law&B 92*
Colton, Clark Kenneth 1941- *WhoAm 92, WhoE 93*
Colton, David Lem 1943- *WhoAm 92*
Colton, Don Jared 1946- *St&PR 93*
Colton, E.G., Jr. 1929- *St&PR 93*
Colton, Ed Lynn, Jr. 1951- *WhoEmL 93*
Colton, Edward A. *Law&B 92*
Colton, Frank Benjamin 1923- *WhoAm 92*
Colton, Frank W. 1928- *St&PR 93*
Colton, Grant A., Jr. 1940- *St&PR 93*
Colton, Gregg Byron 1953- *St&PR 93*
Colton, Joel 1918- *WhoAm 92, WhoSSW 93*
Colton, John O. *WhoAm 92*
Colton, John P. 1935- *St&PR 93*
Colton, Kendrew H. 1955- *WhoEmL 93*
Colton, Kent W. 1943- *WhoAm 92*
Colton, Nelson Burton 1930- *WhoAm 92*
Colton, Roberta Ann 1957- *WhoEmL 93*
Colton, Roy Charles 1941- *WhoWor 93*
Colton, S. David *Law&B 92*
Colton, Sterling D. *Law&B 92*
Colton, Sterling D. 1929- *St&PR 93*
Colton, Sterling Don 1929- *WhoAm 92*
Colton, Victor Robert 1930- *WhoWor 93*
Coltrain-Sapp, Janice Marie *Law&B 92*
Coltrane, John (William) 1926-1967 *Baker 92*
Coltrane, Robbie 1950- *QDrFCA 92 [port]*
Colucci, Anthony Joseph, III 1958- *WhoEmL 93*
Colum, Padraic 1881-1972 *BioIn 17, MajAI [port]*
Columba, Saint 521-597 *BioIn 17*
Columbo, Lisa *Law&B 92*
Columbus, Chris 1959- *ConTFT 10, MiSFD 9*
Columbus, Christopher *BioIn 17*
Columbus, Christopher 1451-1506 *Expl 93 [port]*
Columbus, Francine Lapan 1950- *WhoEmL 93*
Columbus, John Curtis 1944- *WhoE 93*
Columbus, Phillip J. *BioIn 17*
Columbus, Robert Howard 1952- *WhoEmL 93*
Columella *MajAI*
Colussy, Dan Alfred 1931- *St&PR 93, WhoAm 92*
Colvard, Dean Wallace 1913- *WhoAm 92*
Colvard, Michael d1991 *BioIn 17*
Colvard, Michael David 1954- *WhoEmL 93*
Colvert, Carolyn Fern 1943- *WhoAmW 93*
Colvig, William 1917- *Baker 92*
Colville, David Alexander 1920- *WhoAm 92*
Colville, Kenneth H., Jr. 1923- *St&PR 93*
Colville, William Warner *Law&B 92*
Colville, William Warner 1934- *WhoAm 92*
Colvin, A. Marie 1937- *WhoAmW 93*
Colvin, Amber *BioIn 17*
Colvin, Amelia E. 1957- *WhoAmW 93, WhoEmL 93*
Colvin, Burton Houston 1916- *WhoAm 92*
Colvin, Eleanor Gertrude Scow *WhoAmW 93*
Colvin, Harry Walter, Jr. 1921- *WhoAm 92*
Colvin, Henry McCollough 1940- *WhoAm 92*
Colvin, Herbert, Jr. 1923- *WhoAm 92*
Colvin, Ian 1912-1975 *ScF&FL 92*
Colvin, Iris 1914- *St&PR 93*
Colvin, James *ConAu 38NR*
Colvin, John Kim 1954- *WhoEmL 93*
Colvin, John O. 1946- *CngDr 91*
Colvin, Kenton R. 1944- *St&PR 93*
Colvin, Lloyd Dayton 1915- *St&PR 93*
Colvin, Robert Allan 1952- *WhoEmL 93*
Colvin, Sharon Kay 1947- *WhoAmW 93*
Colvin, Shawn *BioIn 17*
Colvin, Thomas Stuart 1947- *WhoWrEP 92*
Colvin, Walter Bishop 1946- *St&PR 93*
Colvin, William E. 1929- *St&PR 93*
Colvin, William Given 1951- *WhoEmL 93*
Colvin-Phillips, Gayle Ann 1953- *WhoSSW 93*
Colvis, John Paris 1946- *WhoWor 93*
Colwell, Bryan York 1961- *WhoEmL 93, WhoWor 93*
Colwell, Derek John *WhoScE 91-1*
Colwell, Edwin Clinton 1933- *St&PR 93*
Colwell, Eileen *ChlFicS*
Colwell, Elaine Alvina 1947- *WhoSSW 93*
Colwell, Elizabeth Byrne 1928- *WhoAmW 93*
Colwell, Eugene Timothy 1952- *WhoSSW 93*
Colwell, Frances Ione 1924- *WhoSSW 93*
Colwell, Gene Thomas 1937- *WhoSSW 93*
Colwell, Goldie *SweetSg A*
Colwell, Howard Otis 1929- *WhoAm 92*
Colwell, John Amory 1928- *WhoAm 92*
Colwell, John McKenna 1948- *WhoEmL 93*
Colwell, Kent L. 1931- *WhoAm 92*
Colwell, Louise Grieff 1933- *St&PR 93*
Colwell, Richard James 1930- *WhoAm 92*
Colwell, Rita Rossi *WhoAm 92, WhoAmW 93*
Colwell, Scott David 1957- *WhoEmL 93*
Colwell, Teresa M. *Law&B 92*
Colwell, Thomas G. 1930- *St&PR 93*
Colwell, William Maxwell 1931- *WhoSSW 93*
Colwill, Jack Marshall 1932- *WhoAm 92*
Colwill, Ruth Melanie 1956- *WhoE 93*
Colwin, Arthur Lentz 1911- *WhoAm 92*
Colwin, Laurie *BioIn 17*
Colwin, Laurie E. d1992 *NewYTBS 92 [port]*
Colwin, Laurie (E.) 1944-1992 *ConAu 139*
Coly, Lisette 1950- *WhoAmW 93*
Colyar, Ardell Benton 1914- *WhoAm 92*
Colyar, Michael *BioIn 17*
Colyer, Dale Keith 1931- *WhoSSW 93*
Colyer, Sheryl Lynn 1959- *WhoAm 92*
Coma-Canella, Isabel 1948- *WhoWor 93*
Comai, Marzio 1940- *WhoScE 91-3*
Coman, Constantin 1926- *WhoScE 91-4*
Coman, Stelian 1927- *WhoScE 91-4*
Coman, William LeRoy 1948- *WhoE 93, WhoEmL 93*
Comandante Ana Maria *DcCPCAm*
Comandante Cero *DcCPCAm*
Comanduras, Peter Diacoumis 1908-1990 *BioIn 17*
Comaneci, Nadia 1961- *BioIn 17*
Comann, Tyler Kent 1950- *WhoEmL 93*
Comanor, William S. 1937- *WhoAm 92*
Comaroff, Jean 1946- *ConAu 139*
Comaromi, John Phillip 1937-1991 *BioIn 17*
Comas, Juan 1900-1978 *IntDcAn*
Comas Bacardi, Adolfo T. 1944- *WhoAm 92*
Comay, Sholom D. 1937-1991 *BioIn 17*
Comay, Sholom David 1937-1991 *WhoAm 92*
Comba, Trudy *BioIn 17*
Combarieu, Jules (-Leon-Jean) 1859-1916 *Baker 92*
Combarnous, Yves 1947- *WhoScE 91-2*
Combas, Robert 1957- *BioIn 17*
Combe, Bernard Marie-Joel 1947- *WhoWor 93*
Combe, Christopher Bryan 1947- *St&PR 93*
Combe, Daniela Kresic *Law&B 92*
Combe, David Alfred 1942- *WhoAm 92*
Combe, Edouard 1866-1942 *Baker 92*
Combe, Ivan DeBlois 1911- *WhoAm 92*
Combe, John Clifford, Jr. 1939- *WhoAm 92*
Comberg, Dietrich Wilhelm 1928- *WhoWor 93*
Comberg, Hans-Ulrich 1948- *WhoWor 93*
Comberiate, Josephine Bertolini 1917- *WhoWrEP 92*
Combes, Emile 1835-1921 *BioIn 17*
Combes, Justin Louis Emile 1835-1921 *BioIn 17*
Combes, Richard Snyder 1948- *WhoEmL 93*
Combes, Sharon *ScF&FL 92*
Combescot, Charles Pierre 1921- *WhoScE 91-2*
Combest, Craig 1944- *St&PR 93*
Combest, Larry 1945- *CngDr 91*
Combest, Larry Ed 1945- *WhoAm 92, WhoSSW 93*
Combley, Frederick Herbert *WhoScE 91-1*
Combre, Alain Jacques 1944- *WhoScE 91-2*
Combs, Annamaria 1938- *St&PR 93*
Combs, Austin Olin 1917- *WhoWor 93*
Combs, Bert(ram) T(homas) 1911-1991 *CurBio 92N*
Combs, Bert Thomas 1911-1991 *BioIn 17*
Combs, Charles Donald 1952- *WhoEmL 93*
Combs, Charles S. 1940- *St&PR 93*
Combs, Dan Jack 1924- *WhoAm 92, WhoSSW 93*
Combs, David 1934- *ScF&FL 92*
Combs, Deborah Ruby 1952- *WhoAmW 93*
Combs, Don Carlos 1946- *WhoSSW 93*
Combs, Don E. 1934- *WhoIns 93*
Combs, Frederick d1992 *NewYTBS 92*
Combs, George M. 1956- *St&PR 93*
Combs, Gilbert Raynolds 1863-1934 *Baker 92*
Combs, Jack M., Jr. 1949- *St&PR 93*
Combs, James 1941- *ScF&FL 92*
Combs, James Boyd 1942- *St&PR 93*
Combs, James J. *Law&B 92*
Combs, James Milton 1951- *WhoE 93*
Combs, Jo Karen Kobeck 1944- *WhoAm 92, WhoAmW 93*
Combs, John F. 1950- *St&PR 93*
Combs, John Francis 1950- *WhoAm 92*
Combs, John Hayden 1929- *St&PR 93*
Combs, Julius V. 1931- *St&PR 93*
Combs, Leon Lamar 1938- *WhoSSW 93*
Combs, Leslie, II *BioIn 17*
Combs, Linda Jones 1948- *WhoAmW 93, WhoEmL 93, WhoSSW 93*
Combs, Maxine Ruth Solow 1937- *WhoWrEP 92*
Combs, Paul Joseph 1960- *WhoEmL 93, WhoSSW 93*
Combs, Randall Jay 1956- *WhoEmL 93*
Combs, Richard Alex'ander *WhoWrEP 92*
Combs, William David 1938- *WhoSSW 93*
Combs, William G. 1930- *WhoAm 92*
Combs, William George 1930- *St&PR 93*
Combs, William Henry, III 1949- *WhoEmL 93, WhoWor 93*
Combuchen, Sigrid *ConAu 136*
Combuechen, Sigrid 1942- *ConAu 136*
Comchoc, Rudolph A. *WhoAm 92*
Comden, Betty 1915- *Baker 92*
Comden, Betty 1919- *BioIn 17, ConAu 40NR, ConTFT 10, WhoAm 92, WhoAmW 93, WhoE 93*
Come, Daniel 1935- *WhoScE 91-2*
Come, Guy-Marie 1936- *WhoScE 91-2*
Comeau, A.V. *Law&B 92*
Comeau, Andre Victor 1932- *St&PR 93*
Comeau, Anne Bradley 1934- *WhoAmW 93*
Comeau, James Ray, Jr. 1948- *WhoSSW 93*

Comeau, Lorene Anita Emerson 1952- WhoAmW 93, WhoEmL 93
Comeau, Louis Roland 1941- WhoE 93
Comeau, Robert Lee 1947- St&PR 93
Comeaux, John A. 1945- WhoSSW 93
Comeaux, Joyce Lynne 1951- St&PR 93
Comeaux, Katharine Jeanne 1949- WhoAmW 93
Comeau Yager, Kimberly Kay 1954- WhoWrEP 92
Comegys, Walker Brockton 1929- WhoAm 92
Comella, Philip L. Law&B 92
Comellas, Luis 1950- WhoScE 91-3
Comelli, Adelaide OxDcOp
Comen, Ronald Gary 1942- WhoE 93
Comen, Steven J. 1941- WhoAm 92
Comencini, Luigi 1916- MiSFD 9
Comenitz, Elliot 1925- St&PR 93
Comenitz, Louis 1916- St&PR 93
Comer, Braxton Bragg, II 1951- WhoEmL 93, WhoSSW 93, WhoWor 93
Comer, Clarence C. 1948- St&PR 93, WhoAm 92, WhoSSW 93
Comer, Dan K. 1947- WhoE 93
Comer, Debra Ruth 1960- WhoAmW 93
Comer, Donald, III 1938- WhoAm 92
Comer, Evan Philip 1927- WhoAm 92
Comer, Gary C. 1927- WhoAm 92
Comer, James P. BioIn 17
Comer, James Pierpont 1934- St&PR 93, WhoAm 92
Comer, John Edward 1938- St&PR 93
Comer, John Fletcher, Jr. 1946- WhoEmL 93
Comer, Kelvie Cureton 1946- WhoEmL 93
Comer, M. Margaret 1942- WhoE 93
Comer, Michael Francis 1946- WhoAm 92
Comer, Miriam M. d1990 BioIn 17
Comer, Nathan Lawrence 1923- WhoAm 92, WhoE 93, WhoWor 93
Comer, Owen A. 1933- St&PR 93
Comer, Robert BioIn 17, WhoIns 93
Comer, Suzanne d1990 BioIn 17
Comerford, Francis R. 1933- WhoScE 91-3
Comerford, John Anthony Law&B 92
Comerford, Philip M. 1931- St&PR 93
Comerford, Philip Michael 1931- WhoE 93
Comerford, Sherna ScF&FL 92
Comerford, Thomas M. Law&B 92
Comerford, Vanessa R. Law&B 92
Comers, Russell D. 1939- St&PR 93
Comes, Franz Josef 1928- WhoScE 91-3
Comes, Juan Bautista c. 1582-1643 Baker 92
Comesgrias, Jacqueline Law&B 92
Comet, Catherine WhoAm 92, WhoAmW 93
Comettant, (Jean-Pierre-) Oscar 1819-1898 Baker 92
Comey, Bernice E. AmWomPl
Comey, Dale Raymond 1941- WhoAm 92
Comey, Dennis Francis, III 1955- St&PR 93
Comey, J. Martin 1934- St&PR 93, WhoAm 92
Comey, James Hugh 1947- WhoWrEP 92
Comfort, Alex 1920- ScF&FL 92
Comfort, Alexander 1920- WhoAm 92
Comfort, Daniel 1950- ScF&FL 92
Comfort, Florence Crocker AmWomPl
Comfort, Hartley B. 1909- St&PR 93
Comfort, Iris 1917- ScF&FL 92
Comfort, Priscilla Maria 1947- WhoAmW 93, WhoEmL 93
Comfort, Ted Paul 1950- St&PR 93
Comfort, William Twyman, Jr. 1937- WhoAm 92
Comfort, William Wistar 1933- WhoAm 92
Comine, Lawrence, Jr. 1939- St&PR 93
Comings, David Edward 1935- WhoAm 92
Comings, William Daniel, Jr. 1938- WhoAm 92
Comini, Alessandra 1934- WhoAm 92
Comins, Frederic Marshall, Jr. 1948- St&PR 93
Cominsky, Lynn Ruth 1953- WhoEmL 93
Comis, Robert Leo 1945- WhoE 93
Comisar, Chris Farah-Lynn 1952- WhoEmL 93
Comiskey, Donald George 1943- WhoE 93
Comiskey, James August 1926- WhoAm 92
Comiskey, Michael Peter 1948- WhoEmL 93
Comisky, Marvin 1918- WhoAm 92
Comissiona, Sergiu 1928- Baker 92, WhoAm 92, WhoWor 93
Comitas, Lambros 1927- WhoAm 92
Comito, Carmelo Ciro 1949- St&PR 93
Comito, John William 1961- WhoE 93
Comizio-Assante, Delva Maria 1964- WhoE 93
Comizzoli, Robert Benedict 1940- WhoE 93
Commack, William E. 1929- St&PR 93
Commack, William Earl 1929- WhoAm 92
Commager, Henry Steele 1902- BioIn 17
Commando Jammo Jet 1955- WhoEmL 93, WhoSSW 93
Commelin, Anna Olcott AmWomPl
Commelin, M. WhoScE 91-2
Comment, Denis X. St&PR 93
Commer, Eric Alan 1955- WhoEmL 93
Commer, Franz 1813-1887 Baker 92
Commerford, Kathleen Anne 1951- WhoAm 92, WhoEmL 93
Commes, Thomas Allen 1942- St&PR 93
Commins, Daniel Edwin 1940- WhoWor 93
Commins, Dorothy BioIn 17
Commins, Ernest Altman 1946- WhoEmL 93
Commins, James Alton 1927- St&PR 93
Commins, Lori Helen 1955- WhoAmW 93
Commins, Michael William 1948- WhoWrEP 92
Commire, Anne WhoAm 92, WhoWrEP 92
Commito, Albert Joseph 1953- St&PR 93
Commito, Richard William 1951- WhoWor 93
Commito, Thomas F. 1948- St&PR 93
Commodores SoulM
Common, Frank Breadon, Jr. 1920- St&PR 93, WhoWor 93
Commoner, Barry 1917- BioIn 17, PolPar, WhoAm 92
Commons, Donald William Law&B 92
Commons, Donald William 1951- WhoEmL 93
Commons, Ella Brown Downey AmWomPl
Commons, John R. 1862-1945 BioIn 17
Comnena, Anna ConAu 139
Comnenus, Manuel Eroticus dc. 1050 HarEnMi
Comninou, Maria 1947- WhoEmL 93
Como, Francis W. 1931- St&PR 93
Como, James T. ScF&FL 92
Como, Joseph Paul 1949- WhoEmL 93
Como, Perry 1912- Baker 92
Como, Perry 1913- BioIn 17, WhoAm 92
Como, Ronald A. 1935- St&PR 93
Comola, James Paul 1931- WhoAm 92, WhoSSW 93
Comolli, Roberto 1929- WhoScE 91-3
Comollo, Thomas C. 1947- St&PR 93
Comotto, Robert Paul 1948- WhoEmL 93
Compagna, Robert E. 1953- St&PR 93
Compagnon, Antoine Marcel 1950- WhoE 93
Compagnon, Jean George Andre 1916- WhoWor 93
Compaignolle, Jean 1926- WhoScE 91-2
Compaore, Blaise BioIn 17, WhoWor 93
Compaore, Blaise 1950- WhoAfr
Comparin, Robert Anton 1928- WhoAm 92
Compean, Michael David 1952- WhoEmL 93
Comper, F.A. 1945- St&PR 93
Compere, Loyset c. 1450-1518 Baker 92
Compiseno, Deborah Loraine 1956- WhoEmL 93
Compitello, Malcolm Alan 1946- ConAu 136
Complak, Krystian Antoni 1949- WhoWor 93
Comporti, Mario 1935- WhoScE 91-3
Compson, Betty 1897-1974 SweetSg B [port]
Compton, Ann Woodruff 1947- WhoAm 92, WhoAmW 93
Compton, Arthur Holly 1892-1962 BioIn 17
Compton, Asbury Christian 1929- WhoAm 92, WhoSSW 93
Compton, Charles B. 1926- St&PR 93
Compton, Charles Daniel 1915- WhoAm 92
Compton, D.G. 1930- ScF&FL 92
Compton, Dale Leonard 1935- WhoAm 92
Compton, David Bruce 1952- WhoEmL 93, WhoWor 93
Compton, David Orville, Jr. 1959- WhoSSW 93
Compton, George Lough 1928- St&PR 93
Compton, George William, Jr. 1965- WhoE 93
Compton, James F. 1940- St&PR 93
Compton, John 1926- DcCPCAm
Compton, John George 1926- WhoWor 93
Compton, John Joseph 1928- WhoSSW 93
Compton, John Robinson 1923- WhoAm 92
Compton, Joseph E. 1925- St&PR 93
Compton, Joyce SweetSg C [port]
Compton, Lana Sue 1955- WhoAmW 93
Compton, Laurence B. 1925- St&PR 93
Compton, Mary Beatrice Brown 1923- WhoAmW 93
Compton, Mary Murdock 1827-1915 BioIn 17
Compton, Norma Haynes 1924- WhoAm 92, WhoSSW 93
Compton, Olin Randall 1925- WhoAm 92
Compton, Ralph Theodore, Jr. 1935- WhoAm 92
Compton, Raymond Hayden 1927- St&PR 93
Compton, Richard MiSFD 9
Compton, Robert C. 1947- St&PR 93
Compton, Robert G. St&PR 93
Compton, Robert H. WhoAm 92
Compton, Robert Harold Law&B 92
Compton, Ronald E. 1933- WhoAm 92
Compton, Ronald Edward 1933- WhoIns 93
Compton, Sara ScF&FL 92
Compton, Shannon Leigh 1953- WhoAm 92
Compton, Spencer ScF&FL 92
Compton, Susan LaNell 1917- WhoAmW 93, WhoSSW 93, WhoWor 93
Compton, W. Dale 1929- WhoAm 92
Compton, Walter Ames 1911-1990 BioIn 17
Compton, Walter K. Law&B 92
Compton-Burnett, I. 1884-1969 BioIn 17
Compton-Burnett, Ivy 1884-1969 BioIn 17
Compton-Rickett, Arthur 1869-1937 ScF&FL 92
Compton-Rickett, Joseph 1847-1919 ScF&FL 92
Comras, Jay 1934- St&PR 93
Comras, Rema 1936- WhoAm 92, WhoSSW 93
Comras, Rosemary 1940- St&PR 93
Comrie, Allan 1919- St&PR 93
Comrie, John W. Law&B 92
Comrie, Keith Brian 1939- WhoAm 92
Comrie, Sandra Melton 1940- WhoAmW 93
Comstock, Anthony 1844-1915 BioIn 17, GayN
Comstock, C.B. 1930- St&PR 93
Comstock, Dale Robert 1934- WhoAm 92
Comstock, Donald W. 1928- St&PR 93
Comstock, Edwin Fisk, III 1952- WhoSSW 93
Comstock, Fanny Amanda 1854- AmWomPl
Comstock, Glen David 1945- WhoAm 92
Comstock, James William 1946- WhoEmL 93
Comstock, Jarrod ScF&FL 92
Comstock, Keith BioIn 17
Comstock, Merrilee Ann 1956- WhoAmW 93
Comstock, R. Warren Law&B 92
Comstock, Ralph J., Jr. 1917- St&PR 93
Comstock, Robert Donald, Jr. 1921- WhoSSW 93
Comstock, Robert Francis 1936- WhoE 93, WhoWor 93
Comstock, Robert Ray 1927- WhoAm 92
Comstock, Rollie Walter 1930- WhoAm 92
Comstock, Stephen Edward Law&B 92
Comte, William H. 1953- WhoEmL 93, WhoSSW 93
Comte-Bellot, Genevieve 1929- WhoScE 91-2
Comtois, George Spencer 1940- WhoE 93
Comtois, L. Pierre Law&B 92
Comtois, Pierre 1943- St&PR 93
Comtois, Robert Raymond 1947- St&PR 93
Comyn, James 1921- BioIn 17
Comyn, John WhoScE 91-1
Comyns, Barbara BioIn 17
Comyns, Barbara 1909-1992 ScF&FL 92
Con, Alexis 1957- St&PR 93
Cona, Michelle Teresa 1951- WhoAmW 93
Conabee, Earl Edward 1937- St&PR 93
Conable, Barber B., Jr. 1923- St&PR 93
Conaboy, Richard Paul 1925- WhoE 93
Conacher, Desmond John 1918- WhoAm 92
Conafay, Stephen Rogers 1943- WhoAm 92
Conaghan, Thomas B. 1950- St&PR 93
Conalty, Michael L. 1920- WhoScE 91-3
Conan, Laure 1845-1924 BioIn 17
Conan, Louis 1931- WhoScE 91-2
Conan, Robert James, Jr. 1924- WhoAm 92
Conanan, Mila P. d1990 BioIn 17
Conant, Allah B., Jr. 1939- WhoAm 92
Conant, Barton C. 1928- St&PR 93
Conant, Colleen Christner 1947- WhoAm 92, WhoAmW 93
Conant, Donald Edward Law&B 92
Conant, G.E. 1945- St&PR 93
Conant, Herbert D. 1924- WhoAm 92
Conant, Howard Rosset 1924- WhoAm 92
Conant, Howard Somers 1921- WhoAm 92
Conant, Isabella Howe Fiske 1874- AmWomPl
Conant, James B. 1893-1978 ColdWar 1 [port]
Conant, L. Victor 1946- St&PR 93
Conant, Michael 1924- ConAu 138
Conant, Miriam Bernheim 1931- WhoAm 92
Conant, Ralph Gordon, Jr. 1929- St&PR 93
Conant, Robert Scott 1928- WhoAm 92
Conant, Roger Scott 1950- WhoE 93
Conant, Shari 1947- WhoAmW 93, WhoEmL 93
Conant, Steven George 1949- WhoEmL 93
Conant, Susan ConAu 139
Conard, Diane Joy 1959- WhoAm 92
Conard, Elsie G. 1929- St&PR 93
Conard, Frederick Underwood, Jr. 1918- WhoAm 92
Conard, Jacques F.M. 1931- WhoScE 91-2
Conard, John Joseph 1921- WhoAm 92
Conard, Paul Lee 1933- WhoE 93
Conard, Spencer D. Law&B 92
Conard, Virgil Warren 1921- WhoSSW 93, WhoWor 93
Conarroe, Joel Osborne 1934- WhoAm 92
Conarty, Murray Rogers 1963- WhoE 93
Conary, David Arlan 1937- WhoAm 92, WhoWor 93
Conaton, Michael Joseph 1933- St&PR 93, WhoAm 92
Conaway, J.C. ScF&FL 92
Conaway, J. Michal 1948- St&PR 93
Conaway, James 1941- BioIn 17
Conaway, Jane Ellen 1941- WhoAmW 93
Conaway, Orrin Bryte 1918- WhoAm 92
Conaway, Stephan Wayne 1947- WhoWor 93
Conboy, Kenneth 1938- WhoAm 92, WhoE 93
Conboy, Thomas F., III 1955- St&PR 93
Concaison, John Silva 1963- WhoWrEP 92
Concannon, Richard James 1933- WhoAm 92
Concar, John R. 1937- St&PR 93
Concaret, Jacques 1930- WhoScE 91-2
Conceicao, Mauro Costa Law&B 92
Concepcion, Dave 1948- HispAmA [port]
Concepcion, Hermogenes D., Jr. 1920- WhoAsAP 91
Concepcion, Jose V., Jr. 1931- WhoAsAP 91
Concepcion, Luis O. Law&B 92
Concha, Dianna F. 1955- St&PR 93
Conchon, Georges 1925-1990 BioIn 17
Concialini, Vittorio 1937- WhoScE 91-3
Concilio, Joseph R. d1990 BioIn 17
Concilio, M. Alphonsa 1932- WhoE 93
Concone, (Paolo) Giuseppe (Gioacchino) 1801-1861 Baker 92
Conconi, Diana Alexis 1962- WhoE 93
Concordia, Charles 1908- WhoAm 92
Condal-Bosch, Lluis 1925- WhoScE 91-3
Condax, Kate Delano 1945- WhoE 93
Condayan, John 1933- WhoAm 92
Conde, Alice 1946- WhoAm 92, WhoAmW 93
Conde, Antonio 1939- WhoWor 93
Conde, Carmen 1907- BioIn 17
Conde, Henri de Bourbon, II, Prince de 1588-1646 HarEnMi
Conde, Jose Benvenuto 1954- WhoWor 93
Conde, Louis de Bourbon, II, Prince of 1621-1686 HarEnMi
Conde, Mario BioIn 17
Conde, Maryse 1937- BioIn 17
Conde, Nicholas ScF&FL 92
Conde, P. Henri L. 1930- WhoScE 91-4
Conde, Phillip ScF&FL 92
Condello, Russell Anthony 1958- WhoEmL 93
Condello, Victor F. 1918-1991 BioIn 17
Conder, Charles 1868-1909 BioIn 17
Conder, Robert Lake, Jr. 1950- WhoSSW 93
Conder, Robert M. 1930- St&PR 93
Conder, Thomas Joseph Law&B 92
Condict, Aaron 1765-1851 BioIn 17
Condict, Edgar Rhodes 1940- WhoAm 92, WhoE 93, WhoWor 93
Condict, Ira 1764-1811 BioIn 17
Condict, Wayne Arthur Law&B 92
Condie, Carol Joy 1931- WhoAm 92
Condie, Isabel AmWomPl
Condie, Robert Stevens 1950- WhoEmL 93
Condie, Thomas M.J. 1929- St&PR 93
Condino, Debra E. Law&B 92
Condino, Rosemary 1949- WhoAmW 93
Condis y Troyano, Francisco Lazaro 1940- WhoWor 93
Condit, Carl Wilbur 1914- WhoAm 92
Condit, David P. Law&B 92
Condit, Doris Elizabeth WhoAm 92
Condit, Douglas Dodd, Jr. 1945- WhoE 93
Condit, Gary A. CngDr 91

Condit, Gary A. 1948- *WhoAm 92*
Condit, Linda F. 1947- *St&PR 93*
Condit, Linda Faulkner 1947- *WhoAm 92*
Condit, Madeleine Kay Bryant 1941- *WhoAmW 93*
Condit, Philip Murray 1941- *WhoAm 92*
Condit, Tom *ScF&FL 92*
Condit, William H. *BioIn 17*
Condo, James Robert 1952- *WhoEmL 93*
Condom, Pierre Philippe 1941- *WhoWor 93*
Condon, Ann E. *Law&B 92*
Condon, Breen O. *Law&B 92*
Condon, Daniel Deal 1956- *St&PR 93*
Condon, David Bruce 1949- *WhoEmL 93*
Condon, Deborah Rene 1955- *WhoAmW 93*
Condon, Eddie 1905-1973 *Baker 92*
Condon, Edward John, Jr. 1940- *WhoAm 92*
Condon, Francis Edward 1919- *WhoAm 92*
Condon, Frederick Hughes *Law&B 92*
Condon, Frederick Hughes 1934- *St&PR 93*
Condon, G.J. 1947- *St&PR 93*
Condon, George Edward 1916- *WhoAm 92*
Condon, Gregory C. 1948- *St&PR 93*
Condon, James Edward 1950- *St&PR 93*
Condon, James Michael 1914- *WhoSSW 93*
Condon, Joseph F. 1925- *St&PR 93, WhoAm 92*
Condon, Kevin R. *Law&B 92*
Condon, Richard *BioIn 17*
Condon, Richard 1915- *ScF&FL 92*
Condon, Richard Bernard, Jr. 1955- *WhoEmL 93*
Condon, Richard Thomas 1915- *WhoAm 92*
Condon, Robert Edward 1929- *WhoAm 92*
Condon, Robert Lewis 1937- *St&PR 93*
Condon, Ronald L. 1940- *St&PR 93*
Condon, Ronald Reginald 1947- *WhoWor 93*
Condon, Thomas Brian 1942- *WhoE 93*
Condon, Thomas J. 1930- *WhoAm 92*
Condon, Thomas J. 1945- *St&PR 93*
Condon, Verner Holmes, Jr. 1926- *WhoAm 92*
Condon, William *MiSFD 9*
Condon, William P. 1937- *St&PR 93*
Condos, Frank *BioIn 17*
Condos, James Alexander 1959- *WhoEmL 93*
Condos, Nick *BioIn 17*
Condos, Steve 1918-1990 *BioIn 17*
Condra, Allen Lee 1950- *WhoEmL 93, WhoWor 93*
Condran, Cynthia Marie 1953- *WhoAmW 93, WhoEmL 93, WhoWor 93*
Condray, Ansel Lynn 1942- *St&PR 93*
Condray, Bruno G. 1921- *ScF&FL 92*
Condrell, Constance Alexander 1937- *WhoAmW 93*
Condren, James L. *Law&B 92*
Condrill, Jo Ellaresa 1935- *WhoAm 92, WhoAmW 93*
Condron, Kevin E. *Law&B 92*
Condron, William A. d1992 *BioIn 17*
Condron, William A., Jr. d1992 *NewYTBS 92*
Condry, Dorothea June 1935- *WhoWrEP 92*
Condry, Robert Stewart 1941- *WhoAm 92*
Condy, Sylvia Robbins 1931- *WhoAmW 93*
Cone, Bernice *AmWomPl*
Cone, Carl Bruce 1916- *WhoAm 92*
Cone, Cynthia Abbott 1934- *WhoAmW 93*
Cone, David *BioIn 17*
Cone, David Brian 1963- *WhoAm 92*
Cone, Deborah Lynn 1957- *WhoAmW 93*
Cone, Edward Christopher 1937- *WhoE 93*
Cone, Edward T(oner) 1917- *Baker 92*
Cone, Edward Toner 1917- *WhoAm 92*
Cone, Frances McFadden 1938- *WhoAmW 93*
Cone, Frederick Hayes *Law&B 92*
Cone, Gregory A. *Law&B 92*
Cone, James H. *BioIn 17*
Cone, James H. 1938- *ConBlB 3 [port]*
Cone, James Hal 1938- *WhoAm 92*
Cone, Joseph Jay 1955- *WhoAm 92*
Cone, Julian, Jr. 1944- *WhoSSW 93*
Cone, Karen Elizabeth Croft 1961- *WhoEmL 93*
Cone, Max R. 1939- *St&PR 93*
Cone, Molly Lamken 1918- *ConAu 37NR, DcAmChF 1960*
Cone, Robert E. *St&PR 93*
Cone, Robert Edward 1943- *WhoE 93*
Cone, Ruby *WhoWrEP 92*
Cone, Spencer Burtis 1910- *WhoAm 92*
Cone, Stephen *BioIn 17*
Cone, Stephen Michael *Law&B 92*
Cone, Steven Scott 1940- *WhoSSW 93*
Cone, Sydney M., III 1930- *WhoAm 92*
Cone, Thomas Conrad 1948- *WhoEmL 93, WhoSSW 93*
Cone, Thomas Edward, Jr. 1915- *WhoE 93*
Cone, Tom 1947- *WhoCanL 92*
Cone, Virgie Horne Hyman 1912- *WhoAmW 93*
Cone, William W. 1952- *WhoSSW 93*
Coneglio, Vince 1950- *St&PR 93*
Conejero, Manuel Angel 1943- *WhoWor 93*
Coneliano, Robert 1952- *WhoWor 93*
Conerly, Charles Albert, Jr. 1921- *BiDAMSp 1989*
Conerly, Dorothy F. 1933- *St&PR 93*
Conerly, R.P. 1924- *St&PR 93*
Conerly, Richard Pugh 1924- *WhoAm 92*
Conerly-Perks, Erlene Brinson 1938- *WhoAmW 93*
Conert, Hans Joachim 1929- *WhoScE 91-3*
Concsa, A.P. *WhoScE 91-2*
Conese, Eugene P. *St&PR 93*
Conestabile, Frank Rocco 1956- *WhoE 93*
Conetti, Sergio 1944- *WhoAm 92*
Coneway, Steve 1946- *St&PR 93*
Coney, Aims C., Jr. 1929- *WhoAm 92*
Coney, Carole Anne 1944- *WhoAmW 93*
Coney, Michael *BioIn 17*
Coney, Michael 1932- *ScF&FL 92*
Coney, Michael E. *Law&B 92*
Coneys, Robert T. *St&PR 93*
Confalone, Pat Nicholas 1945- *WhoE 93*
Confalonieri, Giulio 1896-1972 *Baker 92*
Confer, Ogden William 1945- *St&PR 93*
Confer, Thomas A. 1951- *St&PR 93*
Conford, Ellen *BioIn 17*
Conford, Ellen 1942- *Au&Arts 10 [port], MajAI [port], ScF&FL 92*
Conforte, Joe *BioIn 17*
Conforti, Evandro 1947- *WhoWor 93*
Conforti, Giovanni Luca c. 1560- *Baker 92*
Conforti, Joanne 1944- *WhoAm 92*
Conforti, John J. 1934- *St&PR 93*
Conforti, Michael Peter 1945- *WhoAm 92*
Conforto, Giovanni Luca c. 1560- *Baker 92*
Conforto, Nicola 1718-c. 1788 *OxDcOp*
Conforto, Tracie Ruiz- *BioIn 17*
Conforzi, Ignaco 1885- *BioIn 17*
Confrey, Zez 1895-1971 *Baker 92*
Confucius *BioIn 17*
Confusione, Michael Joseph 1947- *WhoE 93*
Congalton, Christopher William 1946- *WhoEmL 93*
Congalton, Susan Tichenor 1946- *WhoAm 92*
Congdon, David S. *St&PR 93*
Congdon, Jay Stewart 1951- *WhoEmL 93*
Congdon, John Rhodes 1933- *WhoAm 92*
Congdon, Kristin G. 1948- *ConAu 138*
Congdon, Marsha B. 1947- *St&PR 93, WhoAm 92*
Congdon, Raymond J. 1927- *St&PR 93*
Congdon, Sarah-Braeme 1952- *WhoAmW 93, WhoEmL 93*
Congdon, Thomas B., Jr. 1931- *WhoAm 92*
Congedo, Carol Zinn 1950- *WhoAmW 93*
Congel, Frank Joseph 1943- *WhoAm 92*
Conger, Bob Vernon 1938- *WhoAm 92*
Conger, Clement Ellis 1912- *WhoAm 92*
Conger, Cynthia Lynne 1948- *WhoAmW 93*
Conger, Daniel J. *St&PR 93*
Conger, Franklin Barker 1929- *WhoAm 92*
Conger, Harry M. 1930- *St&PR 93*
Conger, Harry Milton 1930- *WhoAm 92*
Conger, John Janeway 1921- *WhoAm 92*
Conger, Kenneth William 1936- *St&PR 93*
Conger, Kyril B. 1913- *WhoAm 92*
Conger, Lesley *WhoWrEP 92*
Conger, Lucinda Dickinson 1941- *BioIn 17*
Conger, Margaret Lynch *AmWomPl*
Conger, Stephen Halsey 1927- *St&PR 93, WhoAm 92*
Conger, Sue Ann 1947- *WhoEmL 93*
Conger, Syndy M. 1942- *ScF&FL 92*
Conger, Virginia Louise 1945- *WhoSSW 93*
Conger, William Frame 1937- *WhoAm 92*
Congleton, Joseph Patrick 1947- *WhoEmL 93*
Congleton, Laura Helen 1962- *WhoAmW 93*
Congleton, Robert B. 1924- *St&PR 93*
Congleton, William Harold 1922- *St&PR 93*
Congrains, Enrique 1932- *SpAmA*
Congreve, Giles *ConAu 39NR*
Congreve, William 1670-1729 *BioIn 17, LitC 21 [port], MagSWL [port], WorLitC [port]*
Congreve, William 1772-1828 *HarEnMi*
Conhagen, Alfred *St&PR 93*
Conheim, Martha Morton *AmWomPl*
Conia, Jean-Marie 1921- *WhoScE 91-2*
Coniaris, Jeffrey J. *Law&B 92*
Conibear, Shirley A. 1946- *St&PR 93*
Conibear, Shirley Ann 1946- *WhoAm 92, WhoEmL 93*
Conidi, Daniel Joseph 1957- *WhoEmL 93, WhoWor 93*
Coniff Kane, Marguerite 1948- *WhoE 93*
Conigilaro, Phyllis Ann 1932- *WhoAmW 93, WhoE 93*
Conigliaro, Laura Claire 1945- *WhoAmW 93*
Conigliaro, Tony *BioIn 17*
Coniglio, Thomas W. 1949- *St&PR 93*
Coniglione, Roy 1938- *St&PR 93*
Conine, Ernest 1925- *WhoAm 92*
Conine, Thomas Edmund, Jr. 1951- *WhoWor 93*
Coningham, Arthur 1895-1948 *BioIn 17, HarEnMi*
Coningham, William 1815-1884 *BioIn 17*
Conino, Joseph Aloysius 1920- *WhoSSW 93, WhoWor 93*
Conis, Thomas *Law&B 92*
Conix, Andre Jan 1925- *WhoWor 93*
Conk, Richard Vincent 1947- *St&PR 93*
Conkey, Sharyn Yanoshak 1945- *WhoWrEP 92*
Conkin, Paul Keith 1929- *WhoAm 92*
Conkle, Daniel Oliver 1953- *WhoEmL 93*
Conkle, Donald Steven 1948- *WhoWrEP 92*
Conkle, Henry 1917- *WhoSSW 93*
Conklin, Andrew S. 1961- *BioIn 17*
Conklin, Anna Immaculata G. 1951- *WhoAmW 93*
Conklin, C. Amy 1965- *WhoE 93*
Conklin, Charles D. 1938- *WhoIns 93*
Conklin, Charles Russell 1922- *St&PR 93*
Conklin, Chester 1888-1971 *QDrFCA 92 [port]*
Conklin, David Arnold 1930- *St&PR 93, WhoAm 92, WhoWor 93*
Conklin, David J. 1950- *St&PR 93*
Conklin, Diane L. 1953- *St&PR 93*
Conklin, Donald David 1944- *WhoE 93*
Conklin, Donald Ransford 1936- *WhoAm 92, WhoE 93*
Conklin, George Melville 1921- *WhoAm 92*
Conklin, George T., Jr. 1914- *St&PR 93*
Conklin, Gerald T. *Law&B 92*
Conklin, Gerald Thomas 1935- *WhoIns 93*
Conklin, Gordon Leroy 1927- *WhoAm 92*
Conklin, Harold Colyer 1926- *WhoAm 92*
Conklin, Hugh Randolph 1911- *WhoAm 92*
Conklin, Jack Lariviere 1942- *WhoE 93*
Conklin, James LaRue 1922- *St&PR 93*
Conklin, Jean Annette 1939- *WhoAmW 93*
Conklin, Jeffrey Marshall *Law&B 92*
Conklin, John Evan 1943- *WhoAm 92*
Conklin, John Roger 1933- *St&PR 93, WhoWor 93*
Conklin, Kenneth Edward 1939- *WhoAm 92*
Conklin, Marie Yvonne 1954- *WhoSSW 93*
Conklin, Patricia Alice Harlan 1934- *WhoAmW 93*
Conklin, Randall R. *Law&B 92*
Conklin, Richard E. 1946- *St&PR 93*
Conklin, Richard J. 1945- *St&PR 93*
Conklin, Ronald 1942- *St&PR 93*
Conklin, Susan Jane 1950- *WhoAm 92, WhoAmW 93, WhoEmL 93*
Conklin, Thomas J. 1946- *St&PR 93, WhoAm 92*
Conklin, Thomas William 1938- *WhoAm 92*
Conklin, William Spencer 1940- *St&PR 93*
Conklin, William T. d1990 *BioIn 17*
Conklin-Andreski, Barbara Jeanne-Anne 1959- *WhoEmL 93*
Conkling, Roger Linton 1917- *WhoAm 92*
Conkling, Roscoe 1828-1888 *PolPar*
Conkling, Roscoe 1829-1888 *OxCSupC*
Conkov, Stoyan 1939- *WhoScE 91-4*
Conkwright, John M. 1944- *St&PR 93*
Conlan, Edward Francis, Jr. 1939- *WhoE 93*
Conlan, Gary D. 1936- *St&PR 93*
Conlan, Terrence J. 1940- *St&PR 93*
Conland, Stephen 1916- *WhoAm 92*
Conlee, Cecil D. 1936- *St&PR 93*
Conley, Arthur 1946- *SoulM*
Conley, Carolynn Lee *WhoSSW 93*
Conley, Carroll Lockard 1915- *WhoAm 92*
Conley, Chip *BioIn 17*
Conley, Christopher John 1946- *WhoEmL 93*
Conley, Clare Dean 1929- *WhoAm 92*
Conley, David N. *St&PR 93*
Conley, David R. 1944- *St&PR 93*
Conley, David T. *Law&B 92*
Conley, Diana Mae 1942- *WhoAmW 93*
Conley, Edward Vincent, Jr. 1940- *WhoWor 93*
Conley, Eugene 1908-1981 *Baker 92*
Conley, Eugene Allen 1925- *WhoAm 92*
Conley, Frances *BioIn 17*
Conley, Gary I. 1948- *St&PR 93*
Conley, Gene Raymond 1952- *WhoEmL 93*
Conley, George Michael 1949- *St&PR 93*
Conley, Henry Q. *Law&B 92*
Conley, Jack Francis 1933- *St&PR 93*
Conley, James Daniel 1928- *WhoAm 92*
Conley, Jerry Lynn 1946- *WhoEmL 93, WhoSSW 93*
Conley, John Michael 1953- *WhoSSW 93*
Conley, Joseph H. *St&PR 93*
Conley, Joseph Howard 1941- *WhoAm 92*
Conley, Joseph Milton *Law&B 92*
Conley, Karyne Jones *AfrAmBi [port]*
Conley, Katherine Logan 1911- *WhoSSW 93*
Conley, Linda Susan 1953- *WhoAmW 93*
Conley, Lloyd B. *Law&B 92*
Conley, Margaret Elizabeth 1960- *WhoEmL 93*
Conley, Mariita Arosemena 1951- *WhoEmL 93*
Conley, Martha R. *Law&B 92*
Conley, Michael *Law&B 92*
Conley, Michael Clark 1938- *St&PR 93*
Conley, Nancy MacConnell 1959- *WhoEmL 93*
Conley, Ned Leroy 1925- *WhoAm 92, WhoSSW 93, WhoWor 93*
Conley, Paul A., Jr. *Law&B 92*
Conley, Philip James, Jr. 1927- *WhoAm 92*
Conley, Raymond Leslie 1923- *WhoSSW 93*
Conley, Richard Michael 1910- *St&PR 93*
Conley, Richard Michael 1943- *St&PR 93*
Conley, Steven W. 1952- *St&PR 93*
Conley, Susan Jane 1941- *WhoSSW 93*
Conley, Theresa R. 1956- *WhoAmW 93*
Conley, Tim *Law&B 92*
Conley, Tom Clark 1943- *WhoAm 92*
Conley, Walter Leslie 1941- *St&PR 93*
Conley-Pitchell, Anne M. *Law&B 92*
Conlin, Alfred Thomas 1921- *WhoAm 92*
Conlin, James Francis 1949- *WhoE 93*
Conlin, James Joseph 1921- *WhoWor 93*
Conlin, James M. *Law&B 92*
Conlin, Joanne 1955- *WhoEmL 93*
Conlin, Joseph R. 1940- *ConAu 40NR*
Conlin, Kellie Ann 1964- *WhoEmL 93*
Conlin, Olive Westberry 1943- *WhoAmW 93*
Conlin, Roxanne Barton 1944- *WhoAm 92, WhoAmW 93*
Conlin, Thomas Byrd 1944- *WhoAm 92*
Conlin, Thomas William 1949- *St&PR 93*
Conlin, William P. 1933- *St&PR 93*
Conlin, William Patrick 1933- *WhoAm 92*
Conlogue, Jon Alan 1959- *WhoE 93*
Conlogue, William Paul 1963- *WhoWrEP 92*
Conlon, Brian Thomas 1958- *WhoE 93*
Conlon, Harry B., Jr. 1935- *WhoAm 92*
Conlon, James *BioIn 17*
Conlon, James 1950- *Baker 92*
Conlon, James Joseph 1950- *WhoAm 92*
Conlon, John A. 1944- *St&PR 93*
Conlon, John Joseph 1945- *WhoE 93*
Conlon, Joseph 1937- *St&PR 93*
Conlon, Joseph R. *WhoIns 93*
Conlon, Kathryn Ann 1958- *WhoAmW 93*
Conlon, Michael William 1946- *WhoAm 92*
Conlon, Patrick J. *Law&B 92*
Conlon, Peter John, Jr. 1951- *WhoEmL 93, WhoSSW 93*
Conlon, Richard 1951- *St&PR 93*
Conlon, Suzanne B. 1939- *WhoAm 92, WhoAmW 93*
Conlon, T.W. *WhoScE 91-1*
Conlon, Thomas James 1935- *WhoAm 92*
Conlon, William Martin 1953- *WhoEmL 93*
Conlon-McKenna, Marita 1956- *SmATA 71 [port]*
Conly, Frank 1930- *WhoIns 93*
Conly, Jane Leslie *ScF&FL 92*
Conly, John Franklin 1933- *WhoAm 92*
Conly, Robert *ScF&FL 92*
Conly, Robert Leslie 1918-1973 *MajAI [port]*
Conlyn, Alexander E. *Law&B 92*
Conmy, George Frank 1955- *WhoE 93*
Conmy, Patrick A. 1934- *WhoAm 92*
Conmy, Peter Thomas 1901- *WhoAm 92*
Conn, A.C. 1947- *St&PR 93*
Conn, Arthur Leonard 1913- *WhoAm 92*
Conn, Carol 1952- *WhoEmL 93, WhoWrEP 92*
Conn, Christopher 1948- *WhoWrEP 92*
Conn, Eric Edward 1923- *WhoAm 92*

Conn, Hadley Lewis, Jr. 1921- *WhoAm 92, WhoWor 93*
Conn, Harold O. 1925- *WhoAm 92*
Conn, Jacob Harry 1904-1990 *BioIn 17*
Conn, Jan 1952- *WhoCanL 92*
Conn, Jerome W. 1907- *WhoAm 92*
Conn, Joseph Bert 1950- *WhoEmL 93*
Conn, Paul Harding, Jr. 1955- *WhoEmL 93, WhoSSW 93*
Conn, Paul Kohler 1929- *WhoE 93*
Conn, Phoebe 1941- *ScF&FL 92*
Conn, Rex Boland, Jr. 1927- *WhoAm 92, WhoE 93, WhoWor 93*
Conn, Richard 1960- *St&PR 93*
Conn, Robert William 1942- *WhoAm 92*
Conn, Sandra Jean 1944- *WhoAmW 93*
Conn, Thomas Finley 1939- *WhoSSW 93*
Conn, Walter Eugene 1940- *WhoE 93*
Connable, Alfred Barnes 1904- *WhoAm 92*
Connally, Ernest Allen 1921- *WhoAm 92*
Connally, John B., Jr. *BioIn 17*
Connally, John B., Jr. 1917- *PolPar*
Connally, Michael W. 1957- *WhoEmL 93*
Connan, Jacques Marcel Rene 1940- *WhoWor 93*
Connard, Carroll Schaeffer *Law&B 92*
Connare, William Graham 1911- *WhoAm 92*
Connaughton, Charles Arthur 1908-1989 *BioIn 17*
Connaway, Robert Wallace 1956- *WhoSSW 93*
Conneely, John 1944- *St&PR 93*
Connell, Alastair McCrae 1929- *WhoAm 92*
Connell, Bruce A. *Law&B 92*
Connell, Clyde 1900- *BioIn 17*
Connell, Daniel W. 1948- *St&PR 93*
Connell, Diane Jacobs 1951- *WhoAmW 93*
Connell, Elizabeth 1946- *OxDcOp*
Connell, Eugene C. 1954- *WhoIns 93*
Connell, Evan S. 1924- *BioIn 17*
Connell, Evan S(helby), Jr. 1924- *ConAu 39NR*
Connell, Evan Shelby, Jr. 1924- *WhoAm 92, WhoWrEP 92*
Connell, George Edward 1930- *WhoAm 92*
Connell, Grover 1918- *WhoAm 92*
Connell, Harriet N. *AmWomPl*
Connell, Hugh P. 1931- *St&PR 93*
Connell, Jane 1925- *BioIn 17*
Connell, Janet Southall 1943- *WhoSSW 93*
Connell, Janice T. 1939- *WhoAmW 93*
Connell, Jim O. *Law&B 92*
Connell, John Gibbs, Jr. 1914- *WhoAm 92*
Connell, Joseph Edward 1930- *St&PR 93, WhoAm 92*
Connell, Karl 1924- *St&PR 93*
Connell, Kathleen Sullivan 1937- *WhoAm 92, WhoAmW 93, WhoE 93*
Connell, Louise Fox *AmWomPl*
Connell, Mary A. 1948- *WhoAmW 93*
Connell, Michael James 1958- *WhoEmL 93*
Connell, Michael T. *Law&B 92*
Connell, Peter John *Law&B 92*
Connell, Philip F. 1924- *St&PR 93*
Connell, Philip Francis 1924- *WhoAm 92*
Connell, Shirley Hudgins 1946- *WhoAmW 93, WhoE 93, WhoEmL 93*
Connell, Ted 1946- *WhoAm 92*
Connell, Terry 1950- *WhoAm 92*
Connell, Thomas A. 1947- *St&PR 93*
Connell, Thomas G.G. 1961- *St&PR 93*
Connell, Wilfred 1937- *St&PR 93*
Connell, William D. 1955- *WhoAm 92*
Connell, William Francis 1938- *WhoAm 92, WhoE 93*
Connell-Tatum, Elizabeth Bishop 1925- *WhoAm 92*
Connelly, Alan F. *Law&B 92*
Connelly, Albert R. 1908- *WhoAm 92*
Connelly, Alwine *Law&B 92*
Connelly, Anne *Law&B 92*
Connelly, Bridget 1941- *WhoAmW 93*
Connelly, Carolyn Thomas 1941- *WhoAmW 93*
Connelly, Chuck 1955- *WhoE 93*
Connelly, Colin Charles 1956- *WhoEmL 93*
Connelly, Daniel F. 1939- *St&PR 93*
Connelly, Donald P. 1939- *St&PR 93*
Connelly, Donald Preston 1939- *WhoAm 92*
Connelly, Donald Webb 1930- *WhoAm 92*
Connelly, Elizabeth Ann 1928- *WhoAmW 93*
Connelly, Elizabeth K. 1956- *St&PR 93*
Connelly, Eric 1910- *St&PR 93*
Connelly, James *Law&B 92*
Connelly, Jennifer *BioIn 17*
Connelly, Joan M. *Law&B 92*
Connelly, John Dooley 1946- *WhoEmL 93*
Connelly, John E. *BioIn 17*
Connelly, John E., Jr. 1904- *St&PR 93*
Connelly, John Edward 1934- *WhoE 93*
Connelly, John F. 1905-1990 *BioIn 17*
Connelly, John J. 1946- *St&PR 93*
Connelly, John Joseph 1925- *WhoE 93*
Connelly, John Matthew 1942- *St&PR 93, WhoAm 92*
Connelly, John Robert, Jr. 1936- *WhoE 93*
Connelly, John Thomas 1952- *WhoE 93*
Connelly, Karen 1969- *WhoCanL 92*
Connelly, Kimberly A. *Law&B 92*
Connelly, Linda McLean 1950- *WhoEmL 93*
Connelly, Mark 1951- *ScF&FL 92*
Connelly, Martin J. 1931- *St&PR 93*
Connelly, Michael Christopher *Law&B 92*
Connelly, Michael J. 1952- *St&PR 93*
Connelly, Owen Sergeson 1929- *WhoSSW 93*
Connelly, P. Kevin 1950- *WhoEmL 93*
Connelly, Patricia Lorraine 1948- *WhoAmW 93, WhoEmL 93*
Connelly, Rebecca L. *Law&B 92*
Connelly, Robert Bourke 1935- *WhoWrEP 92*
Connelly, Robert John 1960- *WhoE 93*
Connelly, Robert Joseph 1939- *WhoSSW 93*
Connelly, Robert L., Jr. *Law&B 92*
Connelly, Sally S. 1953- *St&PR 93*
Connelly, Sharon Rudolph 1940- *WhoAm 92*
Connelly, Thomas J. *Law&B 92*
Connelly, Thomas Lawrence *BioIn 17*
Connelly, William Howard 1920- *WhoAm 92*
Connelly, William Joseph 1954- *WhoEmL 93*
Connelly-Sistovaris, Anne-Francoise 1959- *WhoWor 93*
Conner, Bruce 1933- *BioIn 17*
Conner, Casey d1990 *BioIn 17*
Conner, Charlotte Evans 1950- *WhoSSW 93*
Conner, Cindy Dixon 1951- *WhoWrEP 92*
Conner, David Allen 1939- *WhoAm 92*
Conner, Don R. 1949- *WhoWrEP 92*
Conner, Donald Gene 1936- *St&PR 93*
Conner, Donald Matthew 1951- *WhoEmL 93*
Conner, Finis 1943- *ConEn, WhoAm 92*
Conner, Finis F. 1943- *St&PR 93*
Conner, Frederick William 1909- *WhoSSW 93*
Conner, Gay Arterburn 1962- *WhoEmL 93*
Conner, Holly Reid 1951- *WhoE 93*
Conner, Jack I. 1944- *St&PR 93*
Conner, James Arnel 1940- *St&PR 93*
Conner, James Edward 1927- *WhoAm 92*
Conner, James John, III 1939- *WhoE 93*
Conner, Janet Chestelynn 1953- *WhoAm 92*
Conner, Jeanette Jones 1934- *WhoAmW 93, WhoSSW 93*
Conner, Jeanne Williams 1930- *WhoAmW 93*
Conner, Jeff *ScF&FL 92*
Conner, Jimmie Hoyt 1937- *WhoSSW 93*
Conner, John Davis 1911- *WhoAm 92*
Conner, John Richard 1961- *WhoEmL 93*
Conner, John Wayne 1919- *WhoAm 92*
Conner, Judy Sue 1947- *WhoEmL 93*
Conner, Karen Jean 1941- *WhoAmW 93*
Conner, Kathryn Gamble 1959- *WhoEmL 93*
Conner, Keith Cameron 1960- *WhoSSW 93*
Conner, Lea *Law&B 92*
Conner, Leland Lavon 1930- *WhoWor 93*
Conner, Linda Adcock 1959- *WhoEmL 93*
Conner, Lindsay Andrew 1956- *WhoEmL 93*
Conner, Lynda Marie 1962- *WhoEmL 93*
Conner, Michael *Law&B 92*
Conner, Michael 1951- *ScF&FL 92*
Conner, Mike *ScF&FL 92*
Conner, Nancy Helen 1965- *WhoAmW 93*
Conner, Phillip Lee 1953- *WhoEmL 93*
Conner, Robert L. 1927-1990 *BioIn 17*
Conner, Sandra Lynn *WhoAmW 93*
Conner, Steve 1960- *BioIn 17*
Conner, Stewart Edmund 1941- *WhoSSW 93*
Conner, Susan *BioIn 17*
Conner, Timothy James 1954- *WhoEmL 93*
Conner, Troy Blaine, Jr. 1926- *WhoAm 92*
Conner, Wallace J. 1933- *St&PR 93*
Conner, William Curtis 1920- *WhoAm 92*
Conner, William Joseph, Jr. 1923- *St&PR 93*
Conner, William P. 1941- *St&PR 93*
Connerade, Jean-Patrick *WhoScE 91-1*
Connerly, Dianna Jean 1947- *WhoAmW 93*
Conners, Bernard F. 1926- *ScF&FL 92*
Conners, Gary H. 1936- *St&PR 93*
Conners, Ibra Lockwood 1894-1988 *BioIn 17*
Conners, James *WhoE 93*
Conners, John B. 1945- *WhoIns 93*
Conners, John Brendan 1945- *St&PR 93, WhoAm 92*
Conners, John Reed 1954- *WhoEmL 93*
Conners, Keith J. 1948- *WhoEmL 93*
Conners, Terrance Edward 1954- *WhoSSW 93*
Conners, William Patrick 1938- *St&PR 93*
Connery, Carol Jean 1948- *WhoAmW 93*
Connery, Robert Howe 1907- *WhoAm 92*
Connery, Sean *BioIn 17*
Connery, Sean 1930- *ConTFT 10, IntDcF 2-3 [port], WhoAm 92, WhoWor 93*
Connery, Timothy Philip *WhoScE 91-1*
Connett, Cathy Colleen 1956- *WhoAmW 93*
Conney, Allan Howard 1930- *WhoAm 92*
Connick, Charles Milo 1917- *WhoAm 92*
Connick, Clifford Stewart 1957- *WhoWor 93*
Connick, Harry, Jr. *BioIn 17*
Connick, Harry, Jr. 1968- *WhoAm 92*
Connick, Robert Elwell 1917- *WhoAm 92*
Conniff, Ray 1916- *Baker 92, WhoAm 92*
Connochie, Robert Gordon 1941- *St&PR 93*
Connola, Donald Pascal, Jr. 1948- *WhoE 93*
Connole, William Roger 1922-1991 *BioIn 17*
Connolly, Arthur G. 1905- *St&PR 93*
Connolly, Arthur Guild 1905- *WhoAm 92*
Connolly, Billy *BioIn 17*
Connolly, Brian E. 1945- *St&PR 93*
Connolly, Brian Michael 1949- *WhoAm 92*
Connolly, Catherine Theresa 1957- *WhoAmW 93*
Connolly, Charles H. 1934- *St&PR 93*
Connolly, Christopher James 1961- *WhoSSW 93*
Connolly, Coleman M. *Law&B 92*
Connolly, Connie Christine 1947- *WhoAmW 93, WhoEmL 93*
Connolly, Cyril 1903-1974 *BioIn 17*
Connolly, David I. 1934- *St&PR 93, WhoAm 92*
Connolly, David Miles 1939- *WhoAsAP 91*
Connolly, David Paul 1936- *WhoE 93*
Connolly, Donna Marie 1953- *WhoEmL 93*
Connolly, Eileen *ScF&FL 92*
Connolly, Elma Troutman 1931- *WhoE 93, WhoWor 93*
Connolly, Eugene B., Jr. 1932- *WhoAm 92*
Connolly, Eugene Bernard, Jr. 1932- *St&PR 93*
Connolly, George P. 1917- *St&PR 93*
Connolly, Gerald Edward 1943- *WhoAm 92*
Connolly, H. Andrew 1945- *St&PR 93*
Connolly, Harold Vincent 1931- *BiDAMSp 1989*
Connolly, J. Wray 1934- *St&PR 93, WhoAm 92*
Connolly, James 1868-1916 *BioIn 17*
Connolly, James M. 1942- *St&PR 93*
Connolly, James P. *Law&B 92*
Connolly, Jane Terrell 1942- *WhoAmW 93*
Connolly, Janna L. 1956- *St&PR 93*
Connolly, John *BioIn 17*
Connolly, John Earle 1923- *WhoAm 92, WhoWor 93*
Connolly, John J. 1939- *St&PR 93*
Connolly, John Joseph 1940- *WhoAm 92*
Connolly, John Matthew 1943- *WhoE 93*
Connolly, John R. d1992 *NewYTBS 92*
Connolly, John Stephen 1936- *WhoAm 92*
Connolly, Joseph Francis, II 1944- *WhoSSW 93, WhoWor 93*
Connolly, Julian Welch 1949- *WhoSSW 93*
Connolly, Justin (Riveagh) 1933- *Baker 92*
Connolly, K. Thomas 1940- *WhoWor 93*
Connolly, Kathy Ann Schultz 1952- *WhoEmL 93*
Connolly, L. William 1923- *WhoAm 92*
Connolly, Lynda Murphy 1948- *WhoE 93*
Connolly, Mark 1955- *St&PR 93*
Connolly, Martin F. 1949- *WhoEmL 93*
Connolly, Matthew B., Jr. 1941- *WhoAm 92*
Connolly, Maureen *BioIn 17*
Connolly, Maureen Ann 1958- *WhoEmL 93*
Connolly, Michael Eugene Henry *WhoScE 91-1*
Connolly, Michael Joseph 1947- *WhoAm 92, WhoE 93*
Connolly, Michael Thomas 1959- *WhoSSW 93*
Connolly, Patrick J. *Law&B 92*
Connolly, Peggy 1951- *WhoAmW 93*
Connolly, Peter *Law&B 92*
Connolly, Peter D. *Law&B 92*
Connolly, Roberta Sue 1947- *WhoAmW 93*
Connolly, Ronald C. 1932- *St&PR 93*
Connolly, Ronald Cavanagh 1932- *WhoAm 92*
Connolly, S(ean) J. 1951- *ConAu 138*
Connolly, Sarah Whetstone 1944- *WhoE 93*
Connolly, Stephen J., III 1920- *St&PR 93*
Connolly, Stephen John, IV 1949- *St&PR 93*
Connolly, Thomas A. 1899-1991 *BioIn 17*
Connolly, Thomas Edward 1942- *WhoE 93, WhoWor 93*
Connolly, Thomas Joseph 1922- *WhoAm 92*
Connolly, Thomas Joseph 1957- *WhoWor 93*
Connolly, Walter Justin, Jr. *BioIn 17*
Connolly, Walter Justin, Jr. 1928- *St&PR 93*
Connolly, William Declan 1943- *WhoUN 92*
Connolly, William Gerard 1937- *WhoAm 92, WhoE 93*
Connolly, William Joseph 1929- *St&PR 93*
Connolly-O'Neill, Barrie Jane 1943- *WhoAmW 93, WhoWor 93*
Connon, Bryan (James Milne) 1927- *ConAu 137*
Connor, Bull 1897-1973 *BioIn 17*
Connor, Constance Gibson Wehrman 1935- *WhoAmW 93*
Connor, David Edmund 1925- *WhoAm 92*
Connor, David J. 1942- *St&PR 93*
Connor, David John 1953- *WhoWor 93*
Connor, David Michael 1935- *WhoE 93*
Connor, Geoffrey Michael 1946- *St&PR 93, WhoAm 92*
Connor, Geoffrey Warren 1946- *WhoE 93*
Connor, George 1925- *BioIn 17*
Connor, J.A. *WhoScE 91-1*
Connor, J. Robert 1927- *WhoAm 92, WhoWrEP 92*
Connor, Jack A. 1923- *St&PR 93*
Connor, James Edward, Jr. 1924- *WhoAm 92*
Connor, James Lewis, III *Law&B 92*
Connor, James Michael *WhoScE 91-1*
Connor, James Richard 1928- *WhoAm 92*
Connor, James W. 1926- *St&PR 93*
Connor, John Edwin 1959- *WhoWrEP 92*
Connor, John Joseph *Law&B 92*
Connor, John M. 1952- *St&PR 93*
Connor, John Patrick *Law&B 92*
Connor, John Thomas 1914- *WhoAm 92*
Connor, John Thomas, Jr. 1941- *WhoAm 92*
Connor, John Thorp, II 1944- *WhoAm 92*
Connor, Jonathan Nigel Lynton 1944- *WhoWor 93*
Connor, Jonathan Peter 1949- *WhoEmL 93*
Connor, Joseph Andrew 1952- *WhoEmL 93*
Connor, Joseph E. 1931- *WhoAm 92*
Connor, Kenneth 1918- *QDrFCA 92 [port]*
Connor, Kevin 1940- *MiSFD 9*
Connor, Margo 1943- *WhoAmW 93*
Connor, Marie Stella 1918- *WhoAm 92*
Connor, Martin J., Jr. 1933- *St&PR 93*
Connor, P.E. 1820-1891 *BioIn 17*
Connor, Patrick Edward 1820-1891 *BioIn 17*
Connor, Paul Eugene 1921- *WhoE 93, WhoWor 93*
Connor, Peter Y. *Law&B 92*
Connor, Ralph 1860-1937 *BioIn 17*
Connor, Richard Hallowell 1946- *St&PR 93*
Connor, Robert Patrick 1948- *WhoAm 92*
Connor, Robert T. 1919- *WhoE 93*
Connor, Roger 1857-1931 *BioIn 17*
Connor, Seymour Vaughan 1923- *WhoAm 92, WhoWrEP 92*
Connor, Sheila B. *Law&B 92*
Connor, Sidney Gregg 1947- *WhoEmL 93*
Connor, Theophilus Eugene 1897-1973 *BioIn 17*
Connor, Thomas Byrne 1921- *WhoAm 92*
Connor, Thomas G. 1938- *St&PR 93*
Connor, Tony 1930- *WhoWrEP 92*
Connor, Walter Fischer 1938- *St&PR 93*
Connor, Walter Robert 1934- *WhoAm 92*
Connor, Wilda 1947- *WhoAmW 93, WhoEmL 93*
Connor, William Elliott 1921- *WhoAm 92*
Connors, Basil J. 1927- *St&PR 93*
Connors, Catherine Louise 1960- *WhoEmL 93*
Connors, Chuck d1992 *NewYTBS 92 [port]*
Connors, Chuck Kevin Joseph 1921- *WhoAm 92*
Connors, Cornelia Kathleen 1958- *WhoEmL 93*

Connors, Dennis Michael 1943- WhoAm 92
Connors, Donald Louis 1936- WhoAm 92
Connors, Dorsey WhoAm 92, WhoAmW 93
Connors, Edward Anthony 1940- WhoE 93
Connors, Edward Joseph 1929- WhoAm 92
Connors, Eugene Kenneth 1946- WhoAm 92
Connors, James Patrick 1952- WhoEmL 93
Connors, James T. 1935- St&PR 93, WhoAm 92
Connors, Jean Merrifield 1931- WhoAmW 93
Connors, Jimmy 1952- BioIn 17, WhoAm 92, WhoWor 93
Connors, John A. 1928- St&PR 93
Connors, John Francis 1958- WhoE 93
Connors, John Michael, Jr. 1942- WhoAm 92
Connors, John Patrick d1989 BioIn 17
Connors, Joseph Aloysius, III 1946- WhoEmL 93, WhoSSW 93, WhoWor 93
Connors, Joseph C. Law&B 92
Connors, Kathryn Dughi 1947- WhoAmW 93
Connors, Kenneth Antonio 1932- WhoAm 92
Connors, Leo G. 1927- St&PR 93
Connors, Leo Gerard 1927- WhoAm 92
Connors, Mary Eileen 1953- WhoAm 92, WhoAmW 93
Connors, Mary Jean 1952- St&PR 93
Connors, Mary Jo Reilly 1958- WhoAmW 93
Connors, Maureen Stotler 1955- WhoAmW 93
Connors, Michele Perrott 1952- WhoSSW 93
Connors, Mike 1925- WhoAm 92
Connors, Richard James 1931- St&PR 93
Connors, Robert Leo 1940- WhoE 93
Connors, Stompin' Tom BioIn 17
Connors, Thomas BioIn 17
Connors, Thomas Anthony WhoScE 91-1
Connors, Thomas E. 1929- WhoWrEP 92
Connors, Thomas Edward 1929- WhoE 93
Connors, Thomas H. 1959- WhoEmL 93
Connors, Timothy John 1947- St&PR 93
Connors, Tom BioIn 17
Connors, Tom A. 1934- WhoScE 91-1
Connors, Toni Louise 1941- WhoAmW 93
Connors, W.F. 1940- St&PR 93
Connors, William J. Law&B 92
Connuck, Paul Dennis 1951- WhoEmL 93
Conoby, Joseph Francis 1930- WhoE 93, WhoWor 93
Conole, Clement Vincent 1908- WhoAm 92, WhoWor 93
Conole, Richard Clement 1936- WhoWor 93
Conoley, Gillian 1955- WhoWrEP 92
Conoley, Joann Shipman 1931- WhoWor 93
Conolly, Brian W. WhoScE 91-1
Conolly, R.N. 1913- St&PR 93
Conomikes, George Spero 1925- WhoWor 93
Conomy, John Paul 1938- WhoAm 92
Conon c. 440BC-390BC HarEnMi
Conor, William 1881-1968 BioIn 17
Conoscenti, Craig Stephen 1955- WhoE 93
Conoscenti, Thomas C. 1945- St&PR 93, WhoAm 92
Conour, William Frederick 1947- WhoEmL 93
Conover, Arthur Verner, III 1942- St&PR 93
Conover, Brooks William, III 1959- WhoEmL 93
Conover, Charles Todd 1939- WhoAm 92
Conover, Chris ChIBIID [port]
Conover, Harvey 1925- WhoAm 92
Conover, Jean AmWomPl
Conover, Jerry Neil 1950- WhoEmL 93
Conover, Julia A. Law&B 92
Conover, Lloyd Hillyard 1923- WhoE 93
Conover, Mona Lee 1929- WhoAmW 93
Conover, Neal G. St&PR 93
Conover, Nellie Coburn 1921- WhoAmW 93
Conover, Raymond Arthur 1950- WhoEmL 93
Conover, Robert A. WhoIns 93
Conover, Robert Fremont 1920- WhoAm 92, WhoE 93
Conover, Robert Warren 1937- WhoWor 93
Conover, Sanford BioIn 17
Conover, Sarah Miller 1965- WhoAmW 93
Conover, Val Vagts 1930- WhoAmW 93
Conover, Wendy Lee 1961- WhoAmW 93
Conover, William Jay 1936- WhoAm 92, WhoWor 93
Conover, Willis 1920- ScF&FL 92
Conquest, Joan 1883?-1941 ScF&FL 92
Conquest, Loveday Loyce 1948- WhoAmW 93
Conquest, Richard Lee 1949- St&PR 93
Conquest, Robert Acworth 1917- WhoAm 92
Conrad, III 1093-1152 OxDcByz
Conrad, Allan ScF&FL 92
Conrad, Andree 1945- WhoSSW 93
Conrad, Barbara Kay 1946- WhoAmW 93
Conrad, Barnaby, Jr. 1922- ScF&FL 92
Conrad, Barry Bruce 1940- WhoSSW 93
Conrad, Bruce Phillips 1943- WhoE 93
Conrad, Carlton J. 1922- St&PR 93
Conrad, Cecilia Ann 1955- WhoAmW 93
Conrad, Conrad A. 1946- WhoAm 92, WhoE 93
Conrad, Constance Hoevel 1948- St&PR 93
Conrad, David Edward 1941- St&PR 93
Conrad, David Paul 1946- WhoEmL 93, WhoSSW 93, WhoWor 93
Conrad, Donald Glover 1930- WhoAm 92
Conrad, Doris Lenore 1928- WhoAmW 93
Conrad, Dorol 1956- BioIn 17
Conrad, Earl 1912-1986 ScF&FL 92
Conrad, Edward Craig 1958- WhoEmL 93
Conrad, Edward Ezra 1927- WhoAm 92
Conrad, Flavius Leslie, Jr. 1920- WhoSSW 93
Conrad, Frank 1874-1941 BioIn 17
Conrad, Gail Joanne 1953- WhoAmW 93
Conrad, George John 1943- WhoE 93
Conrad, Gerald Paul 1932- WhoWor 93
Conrad, Harold BioIn 17
Conrad, Harold Theodore 1934- WhoSSW 93, WhoWor 93
Conrad, Harry Lester, Jr. 1917- St&PR 93
Conrad, Jane A. 1935- WhoAmW 93
Conrad, Jeffrey Carter Law&B 92
Conrad, John R. 1915- St&PR 93, WhoAm 92
Conrad, John Regis 1955- WhoEmL 93
Conrad, Joseph 1857-1924 BioIn 17, MagSWL [port], WorLitC [port]
Conrad, Joseph Korzeniowski 1857-1924 PolBiDi
Conrad, Kathryn Jo 1956- WhoAmW 93, WhoEmL 93
Conrad, Kenneth Allen 1946- WhoE 93, WhoEmL 93
Conrad, Kent 1948- BioIn 17, CngDr 91, WhoAm 92
Conrad, Larry 1935-1990 BioIn 17
Conrad, Larry Wayne 1961- WhoEmL 93
Conrad, Laura Ann 1951- WhoSSW 93
Conrad, Laurie Margaret 1946- WhoEmL 93
Conrad, Lori Lynn 1963- WhoEmL 93
Conrad, Marcel Edward 1928- WhoAm 92, WhoSSW 93
Conrad, Marcia Hart 1939- WhoAmW 93
Conrad, Mark A. Law&B 92
Conrad, Nancy Lu 1927- WhoAmW 93
Conrad, Natalie Teresa 1953- WhoAm 92
Conrad, Norman Lee Law&B 92
Conrad, Osmond 1936- St&PR 93, WhoAm 92
Conrad, Pam 1947- BioIn 17, DcAmChF 1985, MajAI [port], ScF&FL 92, WhoAm 92
Conrad, Patricia Ann 1955- WhoAmW 93
Conrad, Paul ScF&FL 92
Conrad, Paul Edward 1956- WhoAm 92, WhoEmL 93
Conrad, Paul Ernest 1927- WhoAm 92
Conrad, Paul (Francis) 1924- ConAu 38NR, WhoAm 92
Conrad, Peter BioIn 17
Conrad, Peter 1945- ConAu 139
Conrad, Phillip Gordon 1957- WhoEmL 93
Conrad, Richard Philip Law&B 92
Conrad, Robert 1935- MiSFD 9, WhoAm 92
Conrad, Robert Allen Law&B 92
Conrad, Robert E. 1949- St&PR 93
Conrad, Robert M. BioIn 17
Conrad, Rupert 1907-1979 BioIn 17
Conrad, Sally Y. WhoAmW 93
Conrad, Susan Lynne 1948- WhoAmW 93
Conrad, Sybil 1927- WhoAmW 93
Conrad, Terry Lee 1954- WhoE 93
Conrad, Terry Lynn 1947- WhoE 93
Conrad, Thomas Robert 1940- WhoE 93
Conrad, William 1920- MiSFD 9, WhoAm 92
Conrad, William Charles 1936- St&PR 93
Conrades, George Henry 1939- WhoAm 92
Conradi, August 1821-1873 Baker 92
Conradi, Eugene Paul 1929- St&PR 93
Conradi, Johann Georg d1699 OxDcOp
Conrad Of Montferrat d1192 OxDcByz
Conrad Regan, Terri Jo 1961- WhoAmW 93, WhoEmL 93
Conrads, Robert J. 1947- St&PR 93
Conrads, Robert John 1947- WhoAm 92
Conradsen, Cliff D. 1941- St&PR 93
Conradsen, Knut 1945- WhoScE 91-2
Conrad von Hotzendorf, Franz 1852-1925 DcTwHis
Conrad Von Hotzendorf, Franz Xavier Josef 1852-1925 HarEnMi
Conran, Mary 1957- St&PR 93
Conran, Sebastian BioIn 17
Conran, Shirley BioIn 17
Conrat, Richard Fraenkel WhoAm 92
Conrath, Barney Jay 1935- WhoE 93
Conrey, Theron Albert 1948- WhoEmL 93
Conried, Hans 1917-1982 QDrFCA 92 [port]
Conried, Heinrich 1848-1909 Baker 92, OxDcOp
Conroe, Henry Gerald 1946- WhoEmL 93
Conron, John Phelan 1921- WhoAm 92, WhoWor 93
Conron, Shana Law&B 92
Conrow, James Willard 1952- WhoAm 92
Conroy, Cathryn Devan 1954- WhoWrEP 92
Conroy, David J. 1929- St&PR 93
Conroy, David James 1918- WhoAm 92
Conroy, David Loram 1946- WhoE 93
Conroy, Dennis Patrick 1945- WhoE 93
Conroy, Donald Patrick 1945- WhoAm 92, WhoWrEP 92
Conroy, Edmund John Law&B 92
Conroy, Frank 1936- BioIn 17
Conroy, Georgetta Ann 1946- WhoAmW 93
Conroy, (Francis) Hilary 1919- ConAu 39NR
Conroy, Jack 1899-1990 BioIn 17
Conroy, Janet M. 1931- WhoAmW 93
Conroy, Jeanne S. Law&B 92
Conroy, John 1951- ConAu 136
Conroy, Michael J. 1941- St&PR 93
Conroy, Pat BioIn 17
Conroy, Pat 1945- ConLC 74 [port], WhoAm 92
Conroy, Patrick F. 1957- St&PR 93
Conroy, Richard Alan 1944- WhoSSW 93
Conroy, Richard T.W.L. 1933- WhoScE 91-3
Conroy, Robert John 1953- WhoEmL 93
Conroy, Robert Warren 1938- WhoAm 92
Conroy, Roberta A. Law&B 92
Conroy, Sarah Booth 1927- WhoAm 92
Conroy, Stephen Martin 1959- WhoEmL 93
Conroy, Tamara Boks WhoE 93
Conroy, Thomas Francis 1938- St&PR 93, WhoAm 92
Conroy, William Eugene 1933- St&PR 93
Conroy, Williams Eugene 1933- WhoIns 93
Conroyd, Danielle St&PR 93
Conroy-LaCivita, Diane Catherine 1965- WhoE 93
Conry, Thomas Francis 1942- WhoAm 92
Cons, Emma 1837-1912 BioIn 17
Consagra, Pietro 1920- WhoWor 93
Consagra, Sophie Chandler 1927- WhoAm 92
Consalvi, Simon Alberto 1927- WhoAm 92, WhoWor 93
Consdorf, Arnold P. BioIn 17
Consdorf, Frank 1936- St&PR 93
Conser, Lucille 1951- WhoAmW 93
Consese, Eugene Paul 1929- St&PR 93
Consey, Kevin Edward 1952- WhoAm 92
Consider, Ellen Marie 1961- WhoAmW 93
Considine, Frank W. 1921- St&PR 93
Considine, Frank William 1921- WhoAm 92
Considine, John Joseph 1941- WhoAm 92
Considine, John R. 1950- St&PR 93
Considine, Joseph Byrne 1961- WhoE 93
Considine, Michael Anthony 1953- St&PR 93
Considine, Richard 1933- St&PR 93
Considine, Shaun 1940- ConAu 137
Considine, Susan M. 1958- St&PR 93
Considine, Susan Mary 1958- WhoAmW 93, WhoEmL 93
Considine, Timothy James 1953- WhoE 93
Consiglio, Louis V. 1934- St&PR 93
Consilio, Barbara Ann 1938- WhoAmW 93
Console, F.M. 1924- St&PR 93
Console, Frank Milton 1924- WhoAm 92
Consoli, Marc-Antonio 1941- Baker 92, WhoAm 92
Consolino, Joseph d1991 BioIn 17
Consolo, Silvana 1935- WhoScE 91-3
Consolver, Carol A. Law&B 92
Consolver, Kay Ellen Law&B 92
Consor, Jennette Estelle 1948- WhoSSW 93
Constable, Elinor Greer 1934- WhoAm 92, WhoAmW 93
Constable, Robert Lee 1942- WhoE 93
Constable, William G. 1950- St&PR 93
Constan, Louis Leonard 1947- WhoEmL 93
Constance, Barbara Ann 1945- WhoAmW 93
Constance, Mervyn 1950- WhoWor 93
Constance, Thomas Ernest 1936- WhoAm 92
Constandy, John Peter 1924- WhoAm 92
Constans, I c. 323-350 OxDcByz
Constans, II 630-668 OxDcByz
Constans, Henry Philip, Jr. 1928- WhoSSW 93
Constans, J. 1943- WhoScE 91-2
Constans, Jean Antoine Ernest 1833-1913 BioIn 17
Constant, Benjamin 1767-1830 BioIn 17
Constant, Clinton 1912- WhoAm 92
Constant (de Rebecque), (Henri) Benjamin 1767-1830 DcLB 119 [port]
Constant, Franz 1910- Baker 92
Constant, Joseph 1956- WhoEmL 93
Constant, Maria Law&B 92
Constant, Marius 1925- Baker 92
Constant, Rene Joseph Pierre 1926- WhoScE 91-2
Constant, William David 1954- WhoEmL 93, WhoSSW 93
Constantin, Daniel 1940- WhoWor 93
Constantin, James Alford 1922- WhoAm 92
Constantinau, Walea Lokelani 1962- WhoEmL 93
Constantine OxDcByz
Constantine d411 HarEnMi
Constantine c. 859-879 OxDcByz
Constantine, I c. 282-337 HarEnMi
Constantine, I, Emperor of Rome d337 BioIn 17
Constantine, II 317-340 OxDcByz
Constantine, II 1940- DcTwHis
Constantine, III d411 OxDcByz
Constantine, IV c. 650-685 OxDcByz
Constantine, V 718-775 OxDcByz
Constantine, VI 771-c. 805 OxDcByz
Constantine, VIII 960?-1028 OxDcByz
Constantine, Doreen 1953- WhoAmW 93
Constantine, Eddie 1917- IntDcF 2-3
Constantine, Jan Friedman 1948- WhoAm 92, WhoAmW 93
Constantine, Jean M. WhoWrEP 92
Constantine, K. C. 1934- ConAu 138
Constantine, Murray ScF&FL 92
Constantine, Storm 1956- ScF&FL 92
Constantine Bereng Seeiso 1938- WhoWor 93
Constantine Bodin d1101? OxDcByz
Constantine Copronymus, V 718-775 HarEnMi
Constantine Doukas, X c. 1006-1067 OxDcByz
Constantine Dragas d1395 OxDcByz
Constantine Laskaris OxDcByz
Constantine Leichoudes, III c. 1000- OxDcByz
Constantine Monomachos, IX c. 1000-1055 OxDcByz
Constantine Of Kerkyra OxDcByz
Constantine Of Rhodes c. 870-c. 931 OxDcByz
Constantine Of Sicily 9th cent.- OxDcByz
Constantine Palaiologos, XI 1405-1453 OxDcByz
Constantine Paleologos, XI 1404-1453 HarEnMi
Constantine Pogonatus, IV c. 652-685 HarEnMi
Constantine Porphyrogennetos, VII 905-959 OxDcByz [port]
Constantinescu, Corneliu 1929- WhoWor 93
Constantinescu, Dan 1931- Baker 92
Constantinescu, Paul 1909-1963 Baker 92
Constantinescu, Romulus WhoScE 91-4
Constantinescu, Virgiliu-Niculae G. 1931- WhoWor 93
Constantine The Great, I 273?-337 OxDcByz [port]
Constantine The Jew dc. 886 OxDcByz
Constantine The Philosopher 826?-869 OxDcByz
Constantine Tich OxDcByz
Constantini, JoAnn M. 1948- WhoAmW 93
Constantini, Louis Orlando 1948- WhoEmL 93
Constantinides, Anthony George WhoScE 91-1
Constantinides, Dinos Demetrios 1929- WhoAm 92
Constantinides, Ellen 1946- St&PR 93
Constantinides, Spiros Minas 1932- WhoE 93
Constantino, Carol L. 1948- St&PR 93
Constantino, Gary James 1954- WhoE 93
Constantino, Gregory J. Law&B 92
Constantino-Bana, Rose Eva 1940- WhoAmW 93, WhoWor 93
Constantinou, Antis Michael 1928- WhoScE 91-4

Constantinou, Clay 1951- *WhoE 93*
Constantinou, Grigoris 1950- *WhoWor 93*
Constantin-Weyer, Maurice 1881-1964 *BioIn 17*
Constantius, I d306 *HarEnMi*
Constantius, II 317-361 *HarEnMi, OxDcByz*
Constantius, III d421 *HarEnMi*
Constantius Chlorus c. 250-306 *OxDcByz*
Constenla, Manuel 1941- *WhoUN 92*
Conston, Henry S. 1928- *St&PR 93*
Conston, Henry Siegismund 1928- *WhoAm 92*
Conston, Marcia 1956- *WhoAmW 93*
Conston, Stanley Ross 1958- *WhoEmL 93*
Conta, Bart Joseph 1914- *WhoAm 92*
Contag, Kimberly Elizabeth 1958- *WhoSSW 93*
Contamine, Philippe 1932- *WhoWor 93*
Contardi, Evaldo 1915- *St&PR 93*
Conte, Albert 1932- *St&PR 93*
Conte, Anthony C. 1945- *St&PR 93*
Conte, Christine W. *Law&B 92*
Conte, Edward Le *ScF&FL 92*
Conte, Frederick Henry 1951- *St&PR 93*
Conte, Gian Biagio 1941- *ConAu 136*
Conte, James W. 1928- *St&PR 93*
Conte, Jean 1938- *WhoScE 91-2*
Conte, Jean Jacques 1938- *WhoWor 93*
Conte, John Michael 1951- *WhoE 93*
Conte, Joseph John, II 1932- *WhoAm 92*
Conte, Lansana 1944- *WhoWor 93*
Conte, Lansana c. 1945- *WhoAfr*
Conte, Maryanne Micchelli 1959- *WhoAmW 93*
Conte, Richard Nicholas 1918- *WhoAm 92*
Conte, Robert Francis 1942- *St&PR 93*
Conte, Sal *ScF&FL 92*
Conte, Samuel Daniel 1917- *WhoAm 92*
Conte, Sarah Rodwick 1965- *WhoAmW 93*
Conte, Silvio O. 1921-1991 *BioIn 17*
Conte-Grand, Alfredo Horacio 1939- *WhoUN 92*
Conteh, Abdulai Osman 1945- *WhoAfr*
Contenti, John Anthony 1948- *St&PR 93*
Contento, William G. 1947- *ScF&FL 92*
Conterato, Bruno Paul 1920- *WhoAm 92*
Conteris, Hiber 1933- *SpAmA*
Contestabile, John Michael 1956- *WhoE 93*
Conti, Adam Jerome 1949- *WhoEmL 93*
Conti, Armand de Bourbon, Prince of 1629-1666 *HarEnMi*
Conti, Bill 1942- *WhoAm 92*
Conti, Carl Joseph 1937- *St&PR 93*
Conti, Carlo 1796-1868 *Baker 92*
Conti, Christopher David 1963- *WhoSSW 93*
Conti, Daniel Joseph 1949- *WhoEmL 93*
Conti, David John 1951- *WhoAm 92*
Conti, Doreen Marie 1964- *WhoAmW 93*
Conti, Francesco 1681-1732 *OxDcOp*
Conti, Francesco Bartolomeo 1681-1732 *Baker 92*
Conti, Franco *WhoScE 91-3*
Conti, Fred A. 1941- *St&PR 93*
Conti, Gioacchino 1714-1761 *Baker 92*
Conti, Haroldo 1925-1976 *SpAmA*
Conti, Isabella 1942- *WhoAm 92*
Conti, James Joseph 1930- *WhoAm 92*
Conti, Louis Thomas Moore 1949- *WhoEmL 93*
Conti, Luigi Giacomo 1928- *WhoWor 93*
Conti, Maurizio *WhoScE 91-3*
Conti, Michael 1956- *St&PR 93*
Conti, Paul Thomas 1945- *St&PR 93*
Conti, Peter Selby 1934- *WhoAm 92*
Conti, Tom 1941- *ConTFT 10, WhoAm 92, WhoWor 93*
Conti, Vincent Roy 1943- *WhoSSW 93*
Conti, Walter *BioIn 17*
Conticchio, Linda Anne 1953- *WhoAmW 93, WhoEmL 93*
Contie, Leroy John, Jr. 1920- *WhoAm 92*
Conti-Guglia, John 1937-
See Conti-Guglia, Richard 1937- *Baker 92*
Contiguglia, Joseph Justin 1948- *WhoEmL 93, WhoSSW 93*
Conti-Guglia, Richard 1937- *Baker 92*
Contilli, Gino 1907-1978 *Baker 92*
Contini, Cesare Augustus 1907-1990 *BioIn 17*
Contini, Edgardo d1990 *BioIn 17*
Contini, Osvaldo 1931- *St&PR 93*
Contino, Vincent Nicholas 1952- *WhoEmL 93*
Contner, James A. *MiSFD 9*
Contney, John Joseph 1932- *WhoAm 92, WhoWor 93*
Contominas, Dimitris 1939- *WhoWor 93*
Contopoulos, George 1928- *WhoScE 91-3, WhoWor 93*
Contos, Larry D. 1940- *St&PR 93, WhoAm 92*
Contours *SoulM*
Contrada, Joseph Guy 1950- *St&PR 93*
Contrades, Stanley Ka'inoa 1963- *WhoWor 93*
Contreni, John Joseph, Jr. 1944- *WhoAm 92*
Contreras, Cesar Augusto 1957- *WhoSSW 93*
Contreras, Joseph J. 1941- *St&PR 93*
Contreras, Pedro de Moya *BioIn 17*
Contreras, Priscilla *Law&B 92*
Contursi, Paul 1953- *WhoWrEP 92*
Contzen, J.-P. *WhoScE 91-3*
Contzen, Jean-Pierre 1935- *WhoScE 91-2*
Conus, Georgi (Eduardovich) 1862-1933 *Baker 92*
Conus, Julius 1869-1942 *Baker 92*
Conus, Sergei 1902- *Baker 92*
Conversano, Henry M. 1931- *St&PR 93*
Converse, Charles (Crozat) 1832-1918 *Baker 92*
Converse, Daniel K. *Law&B 92*
Converse, Florence 1871- *AmWomPl*
Converse, Frank H. d1889 *ScF&FL 92*
Converse, Frederick 1871-1940 *OxDcOp*
Converse, Frederick Shepherd 1871-1940 *Baker 92*
Converse, George Marquis 1940- *WhoSSW 93*
Converse, James Clarence 1942- *WhoAm 92*
Converse, Mary Parker *AmWomPl*
Converse, Philip Ernest 1928- *WhoAm 92*
Converse, William Rawson Mackenzie 1937- *WhoAm 92*
Converti, Vincenzo 1925- *WhoAm 92*
Convertino, Victor Anthony 1949- *WhoAm 92*
Convertito, Bill *ScF&FL 92*
Convery, Liam P. 1937- *WhoScE 91-3*
Convey, Cecil G. 1934- *St&PR 93*
Conviser, Richard James 1938- *WhoAm 92*
Convisser, Theodora S. *Law&B 92*
Convisser, Theodora S. 1947- *St&PR 93*
Convy, Bert *BioIn 17*
Convy, Bert 1934-1991 *AnObit 1991, ConTFT 10, News 92*
Convy, Richard John 1954- *St&PR 93*
Conway, Alice E. *Law&B 92*
Conway, Alice Frances 1907- *WhoWrEP 92*
Conway, Alvin James 1925- *WhoAm 92*
Conway, Brenda *BioIn 17*
Conway, Brian P. *Law&B 92*
Conway, Charles Francis 1931- *St&PR 93*
Conway, Clayton R. 1942- *St&PR 93*
Conway, Daniel E. 1940- *WhoUN 92*
Conway, David Antony 1941- *WhoAm 92*
Conway, David J. 1954- *St&PR 93*
Conway, Donald Ernest *WhoScE 91-1*
Conway, Donald L. *Law&B 92*
Conway, Duncan Arthur *WhoScE 91-1*
Conway, Dwight Colbur 1930- *WhoAm 92*
Conway, E. Virgil 1929- *St&PR 93, WhoAm 92*
Conway, Ellen *Law&B 92*
Conway, Gerald W. 1937- *St&PR 93*
Conway, Gerard F. 1952- *ScF&FL 92*
Conway, Gregory Charles 1941- *St&PR 93*
Conway, H.L. 1937- *WhoScE 91-1*
Conway, Hobart McKinley, Jr. 1920- *WhoAm 92*
Conway, Jack 1887-1952 *MiSFD 9N*
Conway, James Arthur 1933- *WhoE 93*
Conway, James Donald 1946- *WhoSSW 93*
Conway, James F., Jr. *WhoAm 92*
Conway, James F., Jr. 1924- *St&PR 93*
Conway, James Francis 1939- *WhoUN 92*
Conway, James L. 1950- *MiSFD 9*
Conway, James Valentine Patrick 1917- *WhoAm 92*
Conway, Jill K. 1934- *BioIn 17*
Conway, Jill Kathryn Ker 1934- *WhoAm 92, WhoAmW 93*
Conway, Jim 1932- *ConAu 39NR*
Conway, Joan I. 1949- *St&PR 93*
Conway, John *WhoScE 91-1*
Conway, John E. 1934- *WhoAm 92*
Conway, John K. *Law&B 92*
Conway, John K. 1953- *St&PR 93*
Conway, John Keating *Law&B 92*
Conway, John L. 1932- *St&PR 93*
Conway, John R. 1952- *WhoWrEP 92*
Conway, John S. 1929- *WhoAm 92*
Conway, John Thomas 1924- *WhoAm 92*
Conway, Junior *BioIn 17*
Conway, Karen 1959- *WhoEmL 93*
Conway, Katharine St. John 1867-1950 *BioIn 17*
Conway, Kevin 1942- *MiSFD 9, WhoAm 92*
Conway, Kevin G. 1948- *St&PR 93*
Conway, Kevin John 1951- *WhoEmL 93*
Conway, Laura *ScF&FL 92*
Conway, Leonard F. *St&PR 93*
Conway, Louise Dicken 1909- *WhoAmW 93*
Conway, Lynn Ann 1938- *WhoAm 92, WhoAmW 93*
Conway, Megan Louise 1953- *WhoSSW 93*
Conway, Michael A. 1947- *WhoIns 93*
Conway, Michael Anthony 1947- *WhoAm 92*
Conway, Michael J. 1945- *St&PR 93*
Conway, Michael Marion 1942- *WhoAm 92*
Conway, Mike *WhoScE 91-4*
Conway, Nancy A. 1941- *St&PR 93*
Conway, Neil James, III 1950- *WhoEmL 93*
Conway, Norman *ScF&FL 92*
Conway, Olive *AmWomPl*
Conway, Peter P. 1936- *WhoIns 93*
Conway, Richard Ashley 1931- *WhoAm 92*
Conway, Richard Francis 1954- *WhoE 93*
Conway, Richard James, Jr. 1952- *WhoEmL 93*
Conway, Richard Walter 1931- *WhoAm 92*
Conway, Rita M. 1953- *WhoEmL 93*
Conway, Robert A. 1927- *St&PR 93*
Conway, Robert Alfred 1927- *WhoAm 92*
Conway, Robert E. 1954- *WhoAm 92*
Conway, Robert George, Jr. 1951- *WhoEmL 93*
Conway, Robert M. *Law&B 92*
Conway, Robert P. 1946- *WhoAm 92*
Conway, Ronald J. 1944- *St&PR 93*
Conway, Sally 1934- *ConAu 39NR*
Conway, Sharon *BioIn 17*
Conway, Shawn Christopher 1956- *WhoWor 93*
Conway, Stephen J. 1938- *St&PR 93*
Conway, Suzanne Tillery 1956- *WhoAmW 93*
Conway, Teresa M. *Law&B 92*
Conway, Thomas 1733-c. 1800 *HarEnMi*
Conway, Thomas A. 1910- *St&PR 93*
Conway, Thomas A. 1942- *WhoAm 92*
Conway, Thomas James 1913- *WhoAm 92*
Conway, Tim 1933- *WhoAm 92*
Conway, Tom 1904-1967 *BioIn 17*
Conway, Troy *ConAu 39NR*
Conway, William Augustine 1948- *WhoEmL 93*
Conway, William Augustus 1789-1828 *BioIn 17*
Conway, William Edward 1927- *St&PR 93*
Conway, William Judson 1947- *WhoEmL 93*
Conway de Macario, Everly 1939- *WhoE 93*
Conwell, Brian 1958- *St&PR 93*
Conwell, Esther Marly 1922- *WhoAm 92, WhoAmW 93*
Conwell, Michael James 1946- *WhoEmL 93, WhoSSW 93*
Conwell, Russell Herman 1843-1925 *BioIn 17*
Conwell, Sharon Louise 1958- *WhoAmW 93*
Conwell, Theresa Gallo 1947- *WhoAmW 93*
Conwill, Joseph Dillard 1954- *WhoE 93*
Conwill, William Louis 1946- *WhoSSW 93*
Conyard, Shirley Jean 1940- *WhoAmW 93*
Conyers, Abda Johnson, III 1944- *WhoSSW 93*
Conyers, Jean Louise 1932- *WhoAmW 93*
Conyers, John 1929- *BioIn 17*
Conyers, John, Jr. *AfrAmBi [port]*
Conyers, John, Jr. 1929- *CngDr 91, ConBlB 4 [port], WhoAm 92*
Conyers, John G. *BioIn 17*
Conyngham, Barry 1944- *Baker 92*
Conza, Anthony P. *St&PR 93*
Conzelman, Jimmy 1898-1970 *BioIn 17*
Conzelman, Nancy C. *Law&B 92*
Coo, Robert Gaston 1941- *St&PR 93*
Cooder, Ry 1947- *WhoAm 92*
Cooder, Ry(land Peter) 1947- *Baker 92*
Coodley, Alfred Edgar 1922- *WhoAm 92*
Cooey, William Randolph 1942- *WhoSSW 93*
Coogan, Keith *BioIn 17*
Coogan, Keith 1970?- *ConTFT 10*
Coogan, Keith R. *St&PR 93*
Coogan, Michael David 1942- *WhoE 93*
Coogan, Patrick Donlan *Law&B 92*
Coogan, Paul M. *St&PR 93*
Coogan, Philip Shields 1938- *WhoAm 92, WhoSSW 93*
Coogan, Robyn Kay Ankney 1951- *WhoEmL 93*
Coogan Seltzer, Deborah 1963- *WhoAmW 93*
Coogle, Joseph Moore, Jr. 1933- *St&PR 93, WhoAm 92*
Cook, A.B. *St&PR 93*
Cook, A. Jerome 1941- *St&PR 93*
Cook, A. Philip, Jr. 1944- *St&PR 93*
Cook, Addison Gilbert 1933- *WhoAm 92*
Cook, Alan Hugh 1922- *WhoWor 93*
Cook, Alan Hugh, Sir *WhoScE 91-1*
Cook, Albert S(paulding) 1925- *ConAu 37NR*
Cook, Albert Spaulding 1925- *WhoAm 92, WhoWrEP 92*
Cook, Albert Thomas Thornton, Jr. 1940- *WhoWor 93*
Cook, Alexander Burns 1924- *WhoWor 93*
Cook, Alice Carter 1868- *AmWomPl*
Cook, Alva Judith Lynne 1950- *WhoAmW 93*
Cook, Anda Suna 1935- *WhoAmW 93*
Cook, Angela Denise 1963- *WhoAmW 93*
Cook, Ann Jennalie 1934- *WhoAm 92*
Cook, Anne Welsh 1948- *WhoEmL 93*
Cook, Annie
See Goossens, Eugene 1867-1958 *OxDcOp*
Cook, Annie d1952 *BioIn 17*
Cook, Annis Jane 1946- *WhoAmW 93*
Cook, Anthony John Raine 1963- *WhoE 93*
Cook, Anthony M. 1939- *St&PR 93*
Cook, April Joy 1953- *WhoEmL 93*
Cook, Arthur L. 1926- *St&PR 93*
Cook, Audella 1948- *WhoEmL 93*
Cook, Barbara Ann 1947- *WhoEmL 93*
Cook, Barry L. 1949- *St&PR 93*
Cook, Bart R. 1950- *WhoAm 92*
Cook, Bedford d1992 *BioIn 17*
Cook, Benjamin Hopson 1926- *WhoAm 92*
Cook, Beth Marie 1933- *WhoAm 92, WhoAmW 93*
Cook, Bette Walker Philpott 1941- *WhoAmW 93*
Cook, Betty *BioIn 17*
Cook, Blanche McLane 1901- *WhoAm 92*
Cook, Blanche Wiesen 1941- *WhoAm 92*
Cook, Bob 1948- *WhoE 93*
Cook, Boyd McCoy 1930- *St&PR 93*
Cook, Brian Thomas 1961- *WhoSSW 93*
Cook, Bruce *MiSFD 9*
Cook, Bruce Dennis 1937- *WhoWor 93*
Cook, Bryson Leitch 1948- *WhoAm 92, WhoEmL 93*
Cook, Burleigh Don 1932- *St&PR 93*
Cook, C. Edgar 1936- *St&PR 93*
Cook, Camille Wright *WhoAm 92*
Cook, Carl J. 1927- *St&PR 93*
Cook, Carole *BioIn 17*
Cook, Chandler Lewis 1937- *WhoE 93*
Cook, Charles A. *Law&B 92*
Cook, Charles Addison 1952- *St&PR 93*
Cook, Charles Beckwith, Jr. 1929- *WhoAm 92*
Cook, Charles Caruthers 1932- *St&PR 93*
Cook, Charles Davenport 1919- *WhoAm 92*
Cook, Charles David 1924- *WhoAm 92*
Cook, Charles Edward, Jr. 1953- *WhoEmL 93*
Cook, Charles Emerson 1926- *WhoAm 92*
Cook, Charles Francis 1941- *WhoAm 92*
Cook, Charles J. 1917- *St&PR 93*
Cook, Charles Leo, Jr. *Law&B 92*
Cook, Charles Wilkerson, Jr. 1934- *St&PR 93, WhoAm 92, WhoSSW 93*
Cook, Charles William 1927- *WhoAm 92*
Cook, Charlotte Dasher 1948- *WhoEmL 93*
Cook, Charlyn A. 1948- *St&PR 93*
Cook, Chauncey William Wallace 1909- *WhoAm 92*
Cook, Christopher Capen 1932- *WhoAm 92*
Cook, Christopher David Kentish 1933- *WhoScE 91-4*
Cook, Clarence Edgar 1936- *WhoAm 92*
Cook, Clarence Sharp 1918- *WhoAm 92*
Cook, Colin Burford 1927- *WhoWor 93*
Cook, Connie Sue 1951- *WhoEmL 93*
Cook, Cookie d1991 *BioIn 17*
Cook, Corona Rayle *AmWomPl*
Cook, Daniel Walter 1945- *WhoSSW 93*
Cook, David 1940?- *ScF&FL 92*
Cook, David Alastair 1942- *WhoAm 92*
Cook, David C. *Law&B 92*
Cook, David Charles, III 1912- *WhoWrEP 92*
Cook, David G. 1938- *St&PR 93*
Cook, David Lee 1952- *WhoEmL 93*
Cook, David Sheldon 1921- *St&PR 93*
Cook, David Sherman 1952- *WhoEmL 93*
Cook, Deanna Wickline 1940- *WhoAmW 93*
Cook, Dennis L. *Law&B 92*
Cook, Desmond C. 1949- *WhoEmL 93, WhoSSW 93*
Cook, Don 1920- *WhoAm 92*
Cook, Donald *BioIn 17*
Cook, Donald E. 1928- *WhoAm 92*
Cook, Donald E. 1931- *St&PR 93*
Cook, Donald Eugene 1935- *WhoSSW 93, WhoWor 93*
Cook, Donald H. 1930- *St&PR 93*
Cook, Donald Jean 1920- *WhoAm 92*
Cook, Donald Michael 1953- *WhoE 93*
Cook, Donald Wilfred 1938- *WhoSSW 93*
Cook, Donna Phillips 1964- *WhoSSW 93*

Cook, Doris Marie 1924- *WhoAm 92, WhoAmW 93, WhoSSW 93, WhoWor 93*
Cook, Douglas Neilson 1929- *WhoAm 92*
Cook, Douglas Todd 1965- *WhoSSW 93*
Cook, Dwight Ray 1951- *WhoEmL 93*
Cook, Edward Joseph 1925- *WhoAm 92*
Cook, Edward Willingham 1922- *WhoAm 92, WhoSSW 93*
Cook, Eileen Marie 1950- *WhoWrEP 92*
Cook, Eliza 1856-1947 *BioIn 17*
Cook, Eric L. 1963- *WhoAm 92*
Cook, Ernest Ewart 1926- *St&PR 93*
Cook, Ernest T., Jr. 1935- *WhoAm 92*
Cook, Erwin A. *Law&B 92*
Cook, Estelle *AmWomPl*
Cook, Eugene Augustus 1938- *WhoAm 92, WhoSSW 93, WhoWor 93*
Cook, Eugene E. 1922- *St&PR 93*
Cook, Eung-Do 1935- *WhoAm 92*
Cook, Faye 1933- *St&PR 93*
Cook, Fielder *WhoAm 92*
Cook, Fielder 1923- *MiSFD 9*
Cook, Frances A. *AmWomPl*
Cook, Frances D. 1945- *WhoAm 92, WhoAmW 93, WhoWor 93*
Cook, Francis Edward 1916- *St&PR 93*
Cook, Frank Xavier, Jr. 1940- *WhoE 93*
Cook, Fred *ScF&FL 92*
Cook, Fred James 1911- *WhoAm 92*
Cook, Fred S. 1915- *WhoWrEP 92*
Cook, Frederick Albert 1865-1940 *BioIn 17, Expl 93 [port]*
Cook, G. Jeffrey *Law&B 92*
Cook, G. Mark *Law&B 92*
Cook, Gail Fairman 1937- *WhoAm 92*
Cook, Galen Bruce 1930- *WhoSSW 93*
Cook, Gary M. 1942- *St&PR 93*
Cook, Gary Raymond 1950- *WhoAm 92, WhoSSW 93*
Cook, Gayland Braun 1952- *WhoAm 92*
Cook, Gayle Freeman 1949- *WhoEmL 93*
Cook, Gene Paul 1945- *St&PR 93*
Cook, Geoffrey Arthur 1946- *WhoWrEP 92*
Cook, Geoffrey Bernard *WhoScE 91-1*
Cook, George Edward 1938- *WhoAm 92*
Cook, George Henry, Jr. 1951- *WhoAm 92, WhoEmL 93*
Cook, George Patrick *Law&B 92*
Cook, George Valentine 1927- *WhoAm 92*
Cook, George Wallace Foster 1919- *WhoAm 92*
Cook, Gerald 1937- *WhoAm 92*
Cook, Gillian Elizabeth 1934- *WhoSSW 93*
Cook, Glen 1944- *ScF&FL 92*
Cook, Glen Andre 1954- *WhoEmL 93*
Cook, Glyn M. *Law&B 92*
Cook, Gordon F. 1927- *WhoSSW 93*
Cook, Gregory M. 1942- *WhoCanL 92*
Cook, Harold Dale 1924- *WhoAm 92*
Cook, Harold Rodney 1944- *WhoWor 93*
Cook, Harry Clayton, Jr. 1935- *WhoAm 92, WhoWor 93*
Cook, Harvey Carlisle 1936- *WhoE 93*
Cook, Herbert Frederick 1868-1939 *BioIn 17*
Cook, Herbert S. 1915- *St&PR 93*
Cook, Herman d1992 *NewYTBS 92*
Cook, Howard Lawrence 1925- *WhoE 93*
Cook, Hugh 1956- *ScF&FL 92*
Cook, Hugh Craig, Jr. 1948- *WhoSSW 93*
Cook, J. Christopher *Law&B 92*
Cook, J.R. *Law&B 92*
Cook, J. Stuart 1945- *WhoScE 91-1*
Cook, Jack H. 1939- *St&PR 93*
Cook, Jackson G. 1908-1991 *BioIn 17*
Cook, James 1728-1779 *BioIn 17, Expl 93 [port]*
Cook, James 1926- *WhoAm 92, WhoWrEP 92*
Cook, James D. 1933- *St&PR 93*
Cook, James Donald 1934- *WhoSSW 93*
Cook, James Harrison 1942- *WhoE 93*
Cook, James Harry 1959- *WhoEmL 93*
Cook, James Ivan 1925- *WhoAm 92*
Cook, James J. *Law&B 92*
Cook, James R. *ScF&FL 92*
Cook, James Stuart 1943- *St&PR 93*
Cook, James Winfield Clinton 1908- *WhoWor 93*
Cook, Jan 1939- *WhoAm 92*
Cook, Jane Kathleen Alexandra *WhoScE 91-1*
Cook, Janet Donella 1941- *WhoAmW 93*
Cook, Jay Michael 1942- *WhoAm 92, WhoWor 93*
Cook, Jeannine Harriss 1929- *WhoAmW 93*
Cook, Jeannine Salvo 1929- *WhoE 93*
Cook, Jeffrey Ross 1934- *WhoAm 92*
Cook, Joe Edward *Law&B 92*
Cook, John Alfred 1930- *WhoAm 92*
Cook, John Alvin 1952- *WhoEmL 93*
Cook, John F. *Law&B 92*
Cook, John Laird 1941- *St&PR 93*
Cook, John R. 1943- *WhoIns 93*
Cook, John Rowell *BioIn 17*
Cook, John Rowland 1941- *St&PR 93, WhoAm 92*
Cook, John W. 1939- *St&PR 93*
Cook, John William 1929- *WhoSSW 93*
Cook, Jonathan Boyd 1942- *WhoE 93*
Cook, Joseph 1838-1901 *BioIn 17*
Cook, Joseph C., Jr. 1942- *St&PR 93*
Cook, Joseph D. 1951- *St&PR 93*
Cook, Joseph J., II *Law&B 92*
Cook, Joseph Leslie 1952- *WhoEmL 93*
Cook, Joseph R. *Law&B 92*
Cook, Juanita Kimbell 1948- *WhoAmW 93, WhoEmL 93, WhoSSW 93*
Cook, Judith Helen 1942- *WhoE 93*
Cook, Julian Abele, Jr. 1930- *WhoAm 92*
Cook, Junior 1934-1992 *BioIn 17*
Cook, Kathleen Ann 1946- *WhoEmL 93*
Cook, Kathleen Thomas 1960- *WhoAmW 93*
Cook, Kathryn Ella 1945- *WhoAmW 93*
Cook, Kenneth *Law&B 92*
Cook, Kenneth J. 1936- *St&PR 93*
Cook, Kenneth L. 1934- *WhoIns 93*
Cook, Kenneth Ray 1953- *WhoSSW 93*
Cook, Kenneth Totman 1950- *WhoEmL 93*
Cook, Kristen E. *Law&B 92*
Cook, L.H.J. *WhoScE 91-1*
Cook, Larry Wayne 1934- *WhoSSW 93*
Cook, Leah Marie 1966- *WhoE 93*
Cook, LeAnn Cecilia 1950- *WhoEmL 93*
Cook, Leonard Clarence 1936- *WhoAm 92*
Cook, LeRoy Franklin, Jr. 1931- *WhoE 93*
Cook, Linda Jean 1957- *WhoAmW 93*
Cook, Linda Sue 1950- *WhoAmW 93*
Cook, Lisa Dannielle 1962- *WhoAmW 93*
Cook, Lisa Marie 1965- *WhoSSW 93*
Cook, Lodwrick M. *BioIn 17*
Cook, Lodwrick Monroe 1928- *St&PR 93, WhoAm 92, WhoWor 93*
Cook, Lois Anna 1924- *WhoAmW 93*
Cook, Luella B. 1890-1976 *BioIn 17*
Cook, Lyle Edwards 1918- *WhoAm 92, WhoSSW 93*
Cook, Lyn 1918- *WhoCanL 92*
Cook, Lynda 1948- *St&PR 93*
Cook, Marian Alice 1928- *WhoAm 92*
Cook, Marjorie Ellen 1942- *WhoAmW 93*
Cook, Marjorie Ruth Cochrane 1920- *WhoWrEP 92*
Cook, Mary Frances 1962- *WhoEmL 93*
Cook, Mary Margaret 1944- *WhoAmW 93*
Cook, Mary Rozella 1936- *WhoAm 92*
Cook, Maurice Gayle 1931- *WhoAm 92*
Cook, Melvin 1929- *St&PR 93*
Cook, Melvin Garfield 1940- *WhoAm 92*
Cook, Michael 1933- *WhoCanL 92*
Cook, Michael Allan 1940- *WhoAm 92*
Cook, Michael Anthony 1956- *WhoE 93, WhoEmL 93*
Cook, Michael Blanchard 1942- *WhoAm 92*
Cook, Michael Colin Foskett *WhoScE 91-1*
Cook, Michael L. 1929-1988 *ScF&FL 92*
Cook, Michael Lewis 1944- *WhoAm 92*
Cook, Michael Lyles 1946- *WhoEmL 93*
Cook, Michael Stephen, Sr. 1951- *WhoEmL 93*
Cook, Mildred Emily *AmWomPl*
Cook, Morreece Elaine 1946- *WhoEmL 93*
Cook, Nancy Anne 1953- *WhoEmL 93*
Cook, Nancy W. 1936- *WhoAmW 93*
Cook, Neville George Wood 1938- *WhoAm 92*
Cook, Owen T. 1926- *St&PR 93*
Cook, P.J. *WhoScE 91-1*
Cook, Pat Moffitt 1956- *WhoEmL 93*
Cook, Patrick Joseph 1954- *WhoSSW 93*
Cook, Paul 1950- *ScF&FL 92*
Cook, Paul Christopher 1953- *WhoEmL 93*
Cook, Paul J. 1958- *St&PR 93*
Cook, Paul M. *WhoAm 92*
Cook, Paul Maxwell 1924- *St&PR 93*
Cook, Peggy Jo 1931- *WhoSSW 93*
Cook, Peggy Rae *Law&B 92*
Cook, Peter *BioIn 17*
Cook, Peter 1937- *QDrFCA 92 [port]*
Cook, Peter 1943- *WhoAsAP 91*
Cook, Peter Bigelow 1939- *WhoE 93*
Cook, Peter G. d1992 *NewYTBS 92*
Cook, Petronelle *ScF&FL 92*
Cook, Petronelle Marguerite Mary 1925- *WhoWrEP 92*
Cook, Philip George 1957- *WhoE 93*
Cook, Philip J. *MiSFD 9*
Cook, Philip Jackson 1946- *WhoEmL 93*
Cook, Ralph 1946- *WhoE 93*
Cook, Richard A. 1921- *St&PR 93*
Cook, Richard A. 1937- *St&PR 93*
Cook, Richard Allen *Law&B 92*
Cook, Richard Borreson 1937- *WhoAm 92*
Cook, Richard Burton 1944- *WhoE 93*
Cook, Richard F., Jr. 1951- *St&PR 93*
Cook, Richard K. 1931- *St&PR 93*
Cook, Richard Kelsey 1931- *WhoAm 92*
Cook, Richard L. 1935- *St&PR 93*
Cook, Richard Wallace 1907- *WhoAm 92*
Cook, Rick 1944- *ScF&FL 92*
Cook, Robert A. 1912-1991 *BioIn 17*
Cook, Robert C. 1947- *St&PR 93*
Cook, Robert Carter 1898-1991 *BioIn 17*
Cook, Robert Crossland 1947- *WhoEmL 93*
Cook, Robert Donald 1929- *St&PR 93, WhoAm 92*
Cook, Robert Douglas *Law&B 92*
Cook, Robert Edgar 1941- *St&PR 93*
Cook, Robert Edward 1943- *WhoSSW 93*
Cook, Robert Edward 1946- *WhoAm 92*
Cook, Robert George 1953- *WhoE 93*
Cook, Robert John 1951- *WhoEmL 93*
Cook, Robert John 1954- *WhoEmL 93*
Cook, Robert Lee, Jr. 1928- *St&PR 93*
Cook, Robert Richard *Law&B 92*
Cook, Robert S. 1935- *St&PR 93*
Cook, Robert Sherman 1954- *WhoEmL 93*
Cook, Robin 1940- *BioIn 17, ScF&FL 92, WhoAm 92*
Cook, Roderick d1990 *BioIn 17*
Cook, Rodney Mims, Jr. *BioIn 17*
Cook, Rosemarie Scotti 1943- *WhoSSW 93*
Cook, Roy *MajAI*
Cook, Roy Rodney 1951- *WhoSSW 93*
Cook, Ruby *AmWomPl*
Cook, Ruth Ellen 1929- *WhoAmW 93*
Cook, Sam B. 1922- *WhoAm 92*
Cook, Sam Bryan 1951- *WhoEmL 93*
Cook, Samuel DuBois 1928- *WhoAm 92*
Cook, Samuel Ronald 1924- *St&PR 93*
Cook, Scott *BioIn 17*
Cook, Sharon Sue 1947- *WhoAmW 93*
Cook, Stanton R. 1925- *WhoAm 92*
Cook, Stephani 1944- *WhoWrEP 92*
Cook, Stephen Anthony 1962- *WhoSSW 93*
Cook, Stephen Arthur 1939- *WhoAm 92*
Cook, Stephen Bernard 1947- *WhoAm 92, WhoEmL 93*
Cook, Stephen Champlin 1915- *WhoWor 93*
Cook, Stephen Hubbard 1960- *WhoEmL 93*
Cook, Stephen John 1948- *WhoWor 93*
Cook, Steven 1957- *WhoEmL 93*
Cook, Steven R. 1955- *WhoAm 92*
Cook, Steven Robert 1955- *St&PR 93*
Cook, Stuart Donald 1936- *WhoAm 92*
Cook, Susan Farwell 1953- *WhoAmW 93, WhoEmL 93, WhoWor 93*
Cook, Sybilla Avery 1930- *WhoAmW 93*
Cook, Sylvia *BioIn 17*
Cook, Tad Edward 1955- *St&PR 93*
Cook, Tara *BioIn 17*
Cook, Terry Lee 1955- *WhoEmL 93*
Cook, Thalis T. *BioIn 17*
Cook, Thomas Edward *Law&B 92*
Cook, Thomas Henry 1915- *St&PR 93*
Cook, Thomas Herbert 1936- *WhoE 93*
Cook, Thomas Nelson, Jr. 1956- *WhoEmL 93*
Cook, Timothy M. d1991 *BioIn 17*
Cook, Todd McClure 1962- *WhoSSW 93*
Cook, Tom L. 1950- *St&PR 93*
Cook, Tony Stanley 1960- *WhoE 93*
Cook, Victor Joseph, Jr. 1938- *WhoAm 92, WhoSSW 93*
Cook, W.G.A. *WhoScE 91-1*
Cook, W. Paul 1881-1948 *ScF&FL 92*
Cook, Walter Gresham 1927- *St&PR 93*
Cook, Walter R. 1954- *St&PR 93*
Cook, Walter Roudley 1954- *WhoAm 92*
Cook, Warren A. *BioIn 17*
Cook, Will Marion 1869-1944 *Baker 92*
Cook, Willa McGuire *BioIn 17*
Cook, William Campbell 1923- *St&PR 93*
Cook, William Craig 1955- *WhoWor 93*
Cook, William Holmes 1920- *CngDr 91*
Cook, William Howard 1924- *WhoAm 92*
Cook, William J. *Law&B 92*
Cook, William Leslie, Jr. 1949- *WhoEmL 93*
Cook, William S. d1992 *NewYTBS 92 [port]*
Cook, William Wilber 1921- *WhoAm 92*
Cooke, A. Curts 1936- *WhoAm 92*
Cooke, A. Goodwin d1991 *BioIn 17*
Cooke, Alan 1935- *MiSFD 9*
Cooke, Albert Curts 1960- *WhoE 93, WhoEmL 93*
Cooke, Alfred Alistair 1908- *BioIn 17, WhoAm 92*
Cooke, Alistair 1908- *BioIn 17*
Cooke, Ann *MajAI*
Cooke, Arnold 1906- *Baker 92*
Cooke, Audrey *WhoWrEP 92*
Cooke, Barbara Ayres 1936- *WhoAmW 93*
Cooke, Benjamin 1734-1793 *Baker 92*
Cooke, Bette Louise 1929- *WhoAmW 93*
Cooke, Brian Arthur *WhoScE 91-1*
Cooke, C. Roy 1947- *St&PR 93*
Cooke, Carlton Lee, Jr. 1944- *WhoAm 92, WhoSSW 93*
Cooke, Catherine 1963- *ScF&FL 92*
Cooke, Chester W. 1943- *St&PR 93*
Cooke, Claude Everett, Jr. 1929- *WhoSSW 93*
Cooke, Constance Blandy 1935- *WhoAm 92, WhoAmW 93*
Cooke, Constance Cottin *AmWomPl*
Cooke, Danny Frank 1948- *St&PR 93*
Cooke, David Alan 1942- *WhoScE 91-1*
Cooke, David Ohlmer 1920- *WhoAm 92*
Cooke, David P. *Law&B 92*
Cooke, Deryck 1919-1976 *Baker 92*
Cooke, Donald Alan 1953- *WhoE 93*
Cooke, Donald E. 1916-1985 *ScF&FL 92*
Cooke, Edith Mary *WhoScE 91-1*
Cooke, Edward William 1921- *WhoAm 92*
Cooke, Eileen Delores 1928- *WhoAm 92*
Cooke, Fred Charles 1915- *WhoSSW 93*
Cooke, George A., Jr. *Law&B 92*
Cooke, Gillian Lewis 1935- *WhoAm 92*
Cooke, Gloria Grayson 1939- *WhoAmW 93*
Cooke, Gordon *BioIn 17*
Cooke, Gordon Richard 1945- *WhoAm 92*
Cooke, Hazel Watts *AmWomPl*
Cooke, Henry 1788-1868 *BioIn 17*
Cooke, Henry David 1825-1881 *IrnUS*
Cooke, Herbert Basil Sutton 1915- *WhoAm 92*
Cooke, Holland 1950- *WhoEmL 93*
Cooke, Howard 1915- *WhoWor 93*
Cooke, Ian Douglas *WhoScE 91-1*
Cooke, Jack Kent 1912- *BioIn 17, WhoAm 92, WhoE 93*
Cooke, Jacob Ernest 1924- *WhoAm 92*
Cooke, James Francis 1875-1960 *Baker 92*
Cooke, John Estes *MajAI*
Cooke, John Franklin 1946- *WhoIns 93*
Cooke, John Peyton 1967- *ScF&FL 92*
Cooke, Jonathan *WhoScE 91-1*
Cooke, Joseph Peter 1947- *WhoAm 92*
Cooke, Katherine Marjul *BioIn 17*
Cooke, Kenneth 1932- *WhoAm 92*
Cooke, Lawrence Henry 1914- *WhoAm 92, WhoWor 93*
Cooke, Lloyd Miller 1916- *WhoAm 92*
Cooke, Louise Rene 1953- *WhoScE 91-1*
Cooke, Margaret Robb 1944- *WhoAmW 93*
Cooke, Marian G. 1923- *St&PR 93*
Cooke, Marjorie Benton 1876-1920 *AmWomPl*
Cooke, Mary A. 1944- *WhoAm 92, WhoAmW 93*
Cooke, Merritt Todd 1920- *WhoAm 92*
Cooke, Michael *ScF&FL 92*
Cooke, Michael G. *BioIn 17*
Cooke, Michael J. 1943- *WhoScE 91-1*
Cooke, Morris Dawes, Jr. 1954- *WhoEmL 93*
Cooke, P. *WhoScE 91-1*
Cooke, Paul Phillips 1917- *WhoE 93*
Cooke, Philip St. George 1809-1895 *HarEnMi*
Cooke, Robert 1768-1814 *See* Cooke, Benjamin 1734-1793 *Baker 92*
Cooke, Robert Edmond 1920- *WhoAm 92*
Cooke, Robert John 1923- *WhoAm 92, WhoWor 93*
Cooke, Robert William 1935- *WhoAm 92*
Cooke, Robin Brunskill 1926- *WhoWor 93*
Cooke, Rodney D. 1949- *WhoScE 91-1*
Cooke, Roger Anthony 1948- *St&PR 93, WhoAm 92*
Cooke, Roger Lee 1942- *WhoE 93*
Cooke, Ronald Urwick *WhoScE 91-1*
Cooke, Sam 1931-1964 *Baker 92, SoulM*
Cooke, Sara Mullin Graff 1935- *WhoAm 92, WhoAmW 93*
Cooke, Sarah Belle 1910- *WhoAmW 93*
Cooke, Suzanne Gamsby 1945- *WhoSSW 93*
Cooke, Terence F. 1935- *St&PR 93*
Cooke, Terence James 1921-1983 *BioIn 17*
Cooke, Terence Stuart 1946- *St&PR 93*
Cooke, Theodore Frederic, Jr. 1913- *WhoAm 92*
Cooke, Theresa Robson 1942- *WhoAmW 93*
Cooke, Thomas (Simpson) 1782-1848 *Baker 92*
Cooke, Thornton, II 1928- *WhoIns 93*
Cooke, Timothy Mirfield 1942- *WhoWor 93*
Cooke, Tom 1782-1848 *OxDcOp*
Cooke, Walta Pippen 1940- *WhoSSW 93*
Cooke, William Donald 1918- *WhoAm 92*
Cooke, William Peter 1932- *WhoWor 93*
Cooker, Philip George 1942- *WhoSSW 93*
Cookies *SoulM*
Cook-Lynn, Elizabeth 1930- *WhoWrEP 92*
Cook Passalaqua, Pamela Rae Leuthold 1947- *WhoAmW 93*
Cooksey, David Carl 1944- *St&PR 93*
Cooksey, Helen Sperry 1947- *WhoAmW 93*

Cooksey, Joe B. 1946- *St&PR 93*
Cooksey, Patricia Joen *WhoAmW 93*
Cooksey, Vance Sterling 1960- *WhoSSW 93*
Cooksey, Virginia Epting 1949- *WhoEmL 93, WhoSSW 93*
Cookson, Alan Howard 1939- *WhoAm 92*
Cookson, Albert Ernest 1921- *WhoAm 92*
Cookson, Barry David *WhoScE 91-1*
Cookson, Catherine *BioIn 17*
Cookson, Catherine 1906- *ScF&FL 92*
Cookson, Catherine Ann 1906- *WhoAm 92*
Cookson, Grace Elizabeth 1948- *WhoEmL 93*
Cookson, Jane 1939- *WhoAmW 93*
Cookson, John Simmons 1944- *St&PR 93*
Cookson, Robert *BioIn 17*
Cookson, Tony *MiSFD 9*
Cookus, Gerald 1938- *WhoE 93*
Cool, Gary Paul 1963- *St&PR 93*
Cool, Judd R. 1935- *St&PR 93*
Cool, Kim Patmore 1940- *WhoAmW 93*
Coolahan, James Edward, Jr. 1950- *WhoE 93*
Coolbaugh, Ronald Charles 1944- *WhoAm 92*
Coolbrith, Ina 1842-1928 *GayN*
Coolbroth, Frederick James 1951- *WhoEmL 93*
Coole, W.W. *ConAu 37NR*
Coole, William R. *Law&B 92*
Coolen, P.A. *Law&B 92*
Cooler, Amanda Jeffers 1955- *WhoWrEP 92*
Cooler, Whey 1960- *WhoE 93*
Cooles, Philip Edward 1953- *WhoWor 93*
Cooley, Andrew Lyman 1934- *WhoAm 92, WhoWor 93*
Cooley, Ann Marlowe 1951- *WhoWor 93*
Cooley, Arthur Maxwell 1951- *St&PR 93*
Cooley, Croyden d1917 *BioIn 17*
Cooley, Cynthia F. *BioIn 17*
Cooley, Daniel F. *Law&B 92*
Cooley, Dennis *WhoCanL 92*
Cooley, Denton Arthur 1920- *WhoAm 92*
Cooley, Donna Jean 1961- *WhoAmW 93*
Cooley, Edward Hanes 1922- *St&PR 93*
Cooley, Frank J. *Law&B 92*
Cooley, George Farmer 1931- *St&PR 93*
Cooley, Gordon Miles *Law&B 92*
Cooley, Harold Eugene 1929- *St&PR 93*
Cooley, Hilary Elizabeth 1953- *WhoAmW 93, WhoEmL 93*
Cooley, Howard Dager 1934- *WhoAm 92*
Cooley, Ivory Lee 1951- *WhoE 93, WhoEmL 93*
Cooley, Jackson M. *Law&B 92*
Cooley, James Franklin 1926- *WhoSSW 93*
Cooley, James Lawrence 1938- *WhoE 93*
Cooley, James William 1926- *WhoAm 92*
Cooley, John R. 1937- *WhoWrEP 92*
Cooley, Julia *AmWomPl*
Cooley, Kathleen Shannon 1939- *WhoAm 92*
Cooley, Ken *Law&B 92*
Cooley, Lawrence Sachse 1948- *WhoEmL 93*
Cooley, Leland Frederick 1909- *WhoWor 93*
Cooley, Louise Ellen 1948- *WhoEmL 93*
Cooley, Peter 1940- *BioIn 17*
Cooley, Peter John 1940- *WhoWrEP 92*
Cooley, R.H. 1924- *St&PR 93*
Cooley, Raymond H. 1914-1947 *BioIn 17*
Cooley, Richard P. *BioIn 17*
Cooley, Richard Pierce 1923- *St&PR 93*
Cooley, Robert Earl 1930- *WhoAm 92*
Cooley, Robert Holmes 1944- *St&PR 93*
Cooley, Robert James 1929- *St&PR 93*
Cooley, Roger B. 1940- *St&PR 93*
Cooley, Samuel P. 1931- *St&PR 93*
Cooley, Scott d1876 *BioIn 17*
Cooley, Sidney Elizabeth Ann 1953- *WhoAmW 93*
Cooley, "Spade" (Donnell Clyde) 1910-1969 *Baker 92*
Cooley, Thomas McIntyre 1824-1898 *OxCSupC*
Cooley, Warren W. 1922- *St&PR 93*
Cooley, Wils LaHugh 1942- *WhoSSW 93*
Coolican, Thomas Francis *Law&B 92*
Coolidge, Calvin 1872-1933 *BioIn 17, PolPar*
Coolidge, David A., Jr. 1956- *WhoEmL 93*
Coolidge, Edwin Channing 1925- *WhoAm 92*
Coolidge, Elizabeth (Penn) Sprague 1864-1953 *Baker 92*
Coolidge, Gloria Geary 1948- *WhoE 93*
Coolidge, Grace Anna Goodhue 1879-1957 *BioIn 17*
Coolidge, Harold Lane 1933- *St&PR 93*
Coolidge, Jane Toy *AmWomPl*
Coolidge, Kenneth Byron 1936- *St&PR 93*
Coolidge, Lawrence 1936- *St&PR 93*
Coolidge, Martha *BioIn 17*
Coolidge, Martha 1946- *MiSFD 9, WhoAmW 93*
Coolidge, Martha Henderson 1925- *WhoAmW 93*
Coolidge, Mary Elizabeth Burroughs Roberts Smith 1860-1945 *BioIn 17*
Coolidge, Nathaniel Silsbee 1939- *St&PR 93*
Coolidge, Olivia 1908- *ScF&FL 92*
Coolidge, Olivia E(nsor) 1908- *MajAI [port]*
Coolidge, Olivia (Ensor) 1908- *DcAmChF 1960*
Coolidge, Rita 1945- *WhoAm 92*
Coolidge, Ruth Burleigh Dame 1880- *AmWomPl*
Coolidge, Susan *AmWomPl*
Coolidge, Thomas Richards 1934- *St&PR 93*
Cooling, James Edward *WhoScE 91-1*
Cooling, Wendy *BioIn 17*
Cools, Alta Marie 1941- *WhoWrEP 92*
Cools, Andre 1927-1991 *BioIn 17*
Cools, Eugene 1877-1936 *Baker 92*
Coomans, August V. 1936- *WhoScE 91-2*
Coombe, George W. 1925- *St&PR 93*
Coombe, George William, Jr. 1925- *WhoAm 92*
Coombe, Jack D. 1922- *WhoWrEP 92*
Coombe, V. Anderson 1926- *St&PR 93, WhoAm 92*
Coombes, Raoul Charles 1949- *WhoWor 93*
Coombes, Raoul Charles Dalmedo Stuart *WhoScE 91-1*
Coombes, Robert Law 1929- *St&PR 93*
Coombes Goodman, Ann Adair 1963- *WhoAmW 93*
Coombs, Bradley Maxwell 1953- *St&PR 93*
Coombs, C'Ceal Phelps *WhoAmW 93*
Coombs, Charles I. 1914- *SmATA 15AS [port]*
Coombs, Charles I(ra) 1914- *MajAI [port]*
Coombs, Chick *MajAI*
Coombs, Douglas Saxon 1924- *WhoWor 93*
Coombs, Graham H. *WhoScE 91-1*
Coombs, J. Curtis 1939- *St&PR 93*
Coombs, John Wendell 1905- *WhoAm 92*
Coombs, Judith Munroe 1947- *WhoAmW 93*
Coombs, Maurice Martin 1929- *WhoScE 91-1*
Coombs, Patricia 1926- *MajAI [port]*
Coombs, Philip H(all) 1915- *WhoWrEP 92*
Coombs, Robert Holman 1934- *WhoAm 92*
Coombs, Robert Royster Amos *WhoScE 91-1*
Coombs, Walter Paul 1920- *WhoAm 92*
Coombs, William Fremont, Jr. 1934- *WhoSSW 93*
Coomer, Joe 1958- *WhoWrEP 92*
Coomes, Marguerite Wilton 1942- *WhoAmW 93, WhoE 93*
Coon, Carleton Stevens 1904-1981 *IntDcAn*
Coon, Charles Edward 1933- *St&PR 93, WhoAm 92*
Coon, Daren Ross 1953- *WhoEmL 93*
Coon, Gerald Lynn *Law&B 92*
Coon, J. Frederick 1951- *WhoIns 93*
Coon, Julian Barham 1939- *St&PR 93, WhoAm 92*
Coon, Kenneth Charles 1950- *St&PR 93*
Coon, Merlin J. 1912-1956 *ScF&FL 92*
Coon, Miles Anthony 1938- *St&PR 93*
Coon, Minor Jesser 1921- *WhoAm 92*
Coon, Penny K. 1959- *WhoAmW 93*
Coon, Saundra Kay 1943- *WhoAmW 93*
Coon, Susan 1945- *ScF&FL 92*
Coon, Thomas 1945- *St&PR 93*
Coon, Thomas Gary 1957- *WhoE 93*
Coon, W.E. 1927- *St&PR 93*
Coonan, Liam S. *Law&B 92*
Cooner, William Hollis 1927- *WhoSSW 93*
Cooney, Barbara *ChlBIID [port]*
Cooney, Barbara 1917- *ConAu 37NR, MajAI [port], WhoAm 92, WhoAmW 93*
Cooney, Bernard Cornelius 1934- *WhoAsAP 91*
Cooney, Caroline B. 1947- *ConAu 37NR, MajAI [port], ScF&FL 92*
Cooney, Charles Leland 1944- *WhoAm 92*
Cooney, Christine Joyce 1954- *WhoAmW 93*
Cooney, Daniel P. *Law&B 92*
Cooney, David Francis 1954- *WhoEmL 93, WhoSSW 93, WhoWor 93*
Cooney, David M. 1930- *St&PR 93*
Cooney, David Martin 1930- *WhoAm 92*
Cooney, Diane *WhoAm 92*
Cooney, Edward Crandal, Jr. *Law&B 92*
Cooney, Edward J. *Law&B 92*
Cooney, Ellen 1948- *WhoWrEP 92*
Cooney, Eugene Joseph 1948- *WhoEmL 93*
Cooney, Gary M. 1951- *St&PR 93*
Cooney, James Patrick, Jr. 1933- *WhoAm 92*
Cooney, Jimmy 1894-1991 *BioIn 17*
Cooney, Joan Ganz 1929- *St&PR 93, WhoAm 92, WhoAmW 93*
Cooney, John F., Jr. *Law&B 92*
Cooney, John Gerard 1952- *WhoEmL 93*
Cooney, John Gordon 1930- *WhoAm 92, WhoE 93, WhoWor 93*
Cooney, John Thomas 1927- *WhoAm 92*
Cooney, Judith Lifshitz 1956- *WhoE 93*
Cooney, Kevin Packard 1952- *St&PR 93*
Cooney, Lenore *WhoAm 92, WhoAmW 93, WhoE 93*
Cooney, Lynn Futch 1961- *WhoEmL 93*
Cooney, Margaret M. 1965- *St&PR 93*
Cooney, Mike 1954- *WhoAm 92*
Cooney, Miriam P. 1925- *WhoAmW 93*
Cooney, Patricia Ruth *WhoAmW 93, WhoE 93, WhoWor 93*
Cooney, Patrick John 1952- *WhoSSW 93*
Cooney, Patrick Ronald 1934- *WhoAm 92*
Cooney, Robert J. *Law&B 92*
Cooney, Robert Lincoln 1934- *St&PR 93*
Cooney, Thomas J. *Law&B 92*
Cooney, Thomas M. 1926- *St&PR 93*
Cooney, Thomas Michael 1926- *WhoAm 92*
Cooney, William F. *Law&B 92*
Cooney, Wilson Charles 1934- *WhoIns 93*
Coonfield, Ed 1941- *WhoWrEP 92*
Coonjohn, Jeffrey J. *BioIn 17*
Coonridge, Nancy Joan 1947- *WhoAmW 93*
Coonrod, Delberta Hollaway 1937- *WhoAmW 93*
Coonrod, Linda Jeanette 1953- *WhoAmW 93*
Coonrod, Richard Allen 1931- *St&PR 93, WhoAm 92*
Coons, Ann M. *Law&B 92*
Coons, David W. *Law&B 92*
Coons, Eldo Jess, Jr. 1924- *WhoWor 93*
Coons, Helen Louise 1958- *WhoAmW 93, WhoE 93*
Coons, James William 1957- *St&PR 93*
Coons, Marion M. 1915- *St&PR 93*
Coons, Ronald Edward 1936- *WhoAm 92, WhoE 93*
Coons, Theodore W. 1950- *St&PR 93*
Coontz, Kathleen Read *AmWomPl*
Coontz, Morris Stephen 1946- *WhoEmL 93*
Coontz, Otto 1946- *ScF&FL 92*
Coop, Frederick Robert 1914- *WhoAm 92*
Coopee, Thomas L. 1946- *St&PR 93*
Cooper, Alan Samuel 1942- *WhoAm 92*
Cooper, Alice 1945?- *ConMus 8 [port]*
Cooper, Allan John 1954- *WhoCanL 92*
Cooper, Allen David 1942- *WhoAm 92*
Cooper, Amy Levin 1945- *WhoAm 92*
Cooper, Andrew Rutledge 1951- *WhoSSW 93*
Cooper, Anna D. *AmWomPl*
Cooper, Anna Julia 1858?-1964 *AmWomWr 92*
Cooper, Anthony Ashley 1671-1713 *BioIn 17*
Cooper, April Helen 1951- *WhoAm 92, WhoEmL 93*
Cooper, Arnold Michael 1923- *WhoAm 92, WhoE 93*
Cooper, Arthur Irving 1922- *WhoAm 92*
Cooper, Arthur Martin 1937- *WhoAm 92, WhoWrEP 92*
Cooper, Arthur Wells 1931- *WhoAm 92*
Cooper, B. Anne *WhoIns 93*
Cooper, B.J. *WhoScE 91-1*
Cooper, B. Jay 1950- *WhoAm 92*
Cooper, B(rian) Lee 1942- *ConAu 40NR*
Cooper, Barbara Jo 1945- *WhoE 93*
Cooper, Barbara Mary 1949- *WhoWrEP 92*
Cooper, Barry John 1932- *WhoUN 92*
Cooper, Barry Stuart 1943- *WhoWor 93*
Cooper, Benita Ann 1944- *WhoAm 92*
Cooper, Bernard 1951- *BioIn 17*
Cooper, Bernard Richard 1936- *WhoAm 92*
Cooper, Billy J. *Law&B 92*
Cooper, Billy Norman 1937- *WhoWrEP 92*
Cooper, Brown 1957- *WhoSSW 93*
Cooper, C.B. *WhoScE 91-1*
Cooper, C. Everett *ScF&FL 92*
Cooper, C.F. *WhoScE 91-1*
Cooper, Calvin Gordon 1925- *St&PR 93*
Cooper, Camille Sutro 1946- *St&PR 93*
Cooper, Carol Diane 1953- *WhoAm 92, WhoAmW 93, WhoEmL 93*
Cooper, Carol Joan 1938- *WhoAm 92, WhoE 93*
Cooper, Caroline Ann 1943- *WhoAmW 93*
Cooper, Carolyn Helen *WhoAmW 93*
Cooper, Cary D. 1942- *St&PR 93*
Cooper, Cary L. *WhoScE 91-1*
Cooper, Cary Wayne 1939- *WhoAm 92*
Cooper, Charles B. 1938- *St&PR 93*
Cooper, Charles Byron 1938- *WhoAm 92*
Cooper, Charles Donald 1932- *WhoAm 92, WhoSSW 93*
Cooper, Charles Edward 1933- *WhoAm 92, WhoWor 93*
Cooper, Charles G. 1928- *St&PR 93, WhoAm 92*
Cooper, Charles Gerson 1932- *WhoAm 92, WhoE 93*
Cooper, Charles Gordon 1927- *WhoAm 92*
Cooper, Charles Grafton 1927- *WhoAm 92*
Cooper, Charles Howard 1920- *WhoAm 92*
Cooper, Charles Jasper 1929- *WhoAm 92*
Cooper, Charles Justin 1952- *WhoAm 92*
Cooper, Charles Kneeland, III 1953- *WhoSSW 93*
Cooper, Charles Leonard 1936- *WhoE 93*
Cooper, Charlotte B. 1941- *St&PR 93*
Cooper, Chester Lawrence 1917- *WhoE 93, WhoWor 93*
Cooper, Christopher B. 1958- *St&PR 93*
Cooper, Clara Etta 1868- *AmWomPl*
Cooper, Clare 1935- *ScF&FL 92*
Cooper, Clare Dunlap 1938- *WhoAm 92*
Cooper, Colette Frances *Law&B 92*
Cooper, Colin 1926- *ScF&FL 92*
Cooper, Corinne 1952- *WhoEmL 93*
Cooper, Cynthia Lee 1964- *WhoEmL 93*
Cooper, D.B. *BioIn 17*
Cooper, D.H. *WhoScE 91-1*
Cooper, D.J. *WhoScE 91-1*
Cooper, Dalton *St&PR 93*
Cooper, Daniel 1931- *WhoAm 92, WhoWor 93*
Cooper, Daniel Eugene 1947- *WhoSSW 93*
Cooper, Daniel J. 1926- *St&PR 93*
Cooper, Daniel John 1956- *WhoE 93*
Cooper, Daryle Dean 1936- *St&PR 93*
Cooper, David B., Jr. 1956- *St&PR 93*
Cooper, David Booth, Jr. 1956- *WhoAm 92*
Cooper, David Clayton 1943- *WhoE 93*
Cooper, David D. 1948- *ConAu 137*
Cooper, David Lee 1949- *WhoSSW 93*
Cooper, David R. 1942- *St&PR 93*
Cooper, David Samuel 1955- *WhoEmL 93*
Cooper, Dayton Charles, Jr. 1947- *WhoEmL 93*
Cooper, Deborah Robinson 1958- *WhoEmL 93*
Cooper, Dennis 1953- *ConGAN*
Cooper, Dennis Lamar 1941- *WhoE 93*
Cooper, Diana 1892-1986 *BioIn 17*
Cooper, Dolores Ann 1935- *WhoAmW 93*
Cooper, Don L. *Law&B 92*
Cooper, Donald 1927- *St&PR 93*
Cooper, Donald Lee 1928- *WhoAm 92*
Cooper, Donald M. 1939- *St&PR 93*
Cooper, Donna Campbell 1942- *WhoSSW 93*
Cooper, Doris Jean 1934- *WhoAmW 93*
Cooper, Dorothy Summers 1918- *WhoAmW 93*
Cooper, Douglas 1911-1984 *BioIn 17*
Cooper, Douglas K. *Law&B 92*
Cooper, Douglass William 1956- *WhoE 93, WhoEmL 93*
Cooper, E. Camron 1939- *WhoAm 92*
Cooper, Edgar S. *WhoWrEP 92*
Cooper, Edmund 1926-1982 *ScF&FL 92*
Cooper, Edward Hayes 1941- *WhoAm 92*
Cooper, Edwin Lowell 1936- *WhoAm 92*
Cooper, Effie Ann 1937- *WhoAmW 93*
Cooper, Elizabeth Marie 1954- *WhoAmW 93, WhoEmL 93*
Cooper, Ellen *BioIn 17*
Cooper, Emil 1877-1960 *OxDcOp*
Cooper, Emil (Albertovich) 1877-1960 *Baker 92*
Cooper, Eugene Bruce 1933- *WhoAm 92*
Cooper, Evelyn Yvonne 1949- *WhoSSW 93*
Cooper, Floyd Donald, II 1956- *BlkAull 92*
Cooper, Francis Loren 1919- *WhoAm 92*
Cooper, Frank Evans 1928- *WhoAm 92*
Cooper, Franklin Seaney 1908- *WhoAm 92*
Cooper, Fred 1936- *St&PR 93*
Cooper, Frederick Eansor 1942- *WhoAm 92*
Cooper, Fritz Alexander 1951- *WhoSSW 93*
Cooper, G. John 1939- *St&PR 93*
Cooper, Garrett Wayne 1952- *WhoEmL 93*
Cooper, Gary 1901-1961 *BioIn 17, IntDcF 2-3 [port]*
Cooper, Gary Keith 1954- *WhoEmL 93*
Cooper, George Brinton 1916- *WhoAm 92*
Cooper, George David 1935- *WhoE 93*
Cooper, George Emery 1916- *WhoAm 92*
Cooper, George Robert 1921- *WhoAm 92*

Cooper, George Wilson 1927- St&PR 93
Cooper, Gershon N. 1949- St&PR 93
Cooper, Gladys L. 1951- St&PR 93
Cooper, Gloria 1931- WhoAm 92
Cooper, Gordon Mayo 1925- St&PR 93, WhoAm 92
Cooper, Graeme John 1937- WhoWor 93
Cooper, Grant B. 1903-1990 BioIn 17
Cooper, H. Jackie 1939- St&PR 93
Cooper, H. Lee 1938- St&PR 93
Cooper, Hal 1923- MiSFD 9, WhoAm 92
Cooper, Hal Dean 1934- WhoAm 92
Cooper, Harris 1937- St&PR 93
Cooper, Henry S.F. 1933- BioIn 17
Cooper, Hester Rebecca 1948- WhoWor 93
Cooper, Holly Beth 1958- WhoAmW 93
Cooper, Howard 1934- WhoE 93
Cooper, Howard Norvin 1922- WhoE 93
Cooper, Hughes ScF&FL 92
Cooper, Ian WhoScE 91-1
Cooper, Ilene BioIn 17
Cooper, Ilene Linda 1948- WhoAm 92
Cooper, Irmgard Marie 1946- WhoEmL 93
Cooper, Irving Ben 1902- WhoAm 92, WhoE 93
Cooper, J. California BioIn 17
Cooper, J. Kent Law&B 92
Cooper, Jack M. 1939- St&PR 93
Cooper, Jack Ross 1924- WhoAm 92
Cooper, Jackie 1921- IntDcF 2-3 [port]
Cooper, Jackie 1922- MiSFD 9, WhoAm 92
Cooper, Jacqueline Marie 1947- WhoEmL 93
Cooper, Jacquelyn Barber 1940- WhoAmW 93
Cooper, James Albert, Jr. 1946- WhoAm 92
Cooper, James C. 1935- St&PR 93
Cooper, James David 1948- WhoEmL 93
Cooper, James Fenimore 1789-1851 BioIn 17, MagSAmL [port]
Cooper, James Hayes Shofner 1954- WhoAm 92, WhoSSW 93
Cooper, James Henry Law&B 92
Cooper, James Lee 1952- WhoSSW 93
Cooper, James M., Jr. 1941- St&PR 93, WhoIns 93
Cooper, James Michael 1939- WhoAm 92
Cooper, James Richard 1943- WhoAm 92
Cooper, James William 1943- WhoE 93
Cooper, Jane Leslie 1948- WhoAmW 93
Cooper, Jane Todd 1943- WhoAm 92
Cooper, Janis C. BioIn 17
Cooper, Janis C. 1947- St&PR 93
Cooper, Janis Campbell 1947- WhoAmW 93
Cooper, Jay Leslie 1929- WhoAm 92
Cooper, Jean Saralee 1946- WhoAm 92, WhoAmW 93
Cooper, Jeanne BioIn 17
Cooper, Jeffrey 1950- ScF&FL 92, WhoEmL 93
Cooper, Jeffrey B. 1950- WhoWrEP 92
Cooper, Jeffrey Stuart 1947- WhoE 93, WhoEmL 93
Cooper, Jerome A. 1913- WhoAm 92
Cooper, Jerome Maurice 1930- WhoAm 92, WhoSSW 93
Cooper, Jerrold Stephen 1942- WhoAm 92
Cooper, Jerry Lee, Jr. 1963- WhoEmL 93
Cooper, Jewel Carol 1949- WhoAmW 93
Cooper, Jim 1954- CngDr 91
Cooper, JoAnn Sobkowiak 1945- WhoAmW 93
Cooper, Joel 1953- & Tomson, Michael 1954- ConEn
Cooper, John A., Jr. 1938- St&PR 93
Cooper, John Allen Dicks 1918- WhoAm 92
Cooper, John Arnold 1917- WhoWor 93
Cooper, John Byrne, Jr. 1942- WhoSSW 93, WhoWor 93
Cooper, John Charles 1933- WhoWrEP 92
Cooper, John Edward WhoScE 91-1
Cooper, John Edward 1929- WhoWor 93
Cooper, John Ireland 1955- WhoEmL 93
Cooper, John J. 1924- St&PR 93
Cooper, John Joseph 1924- WhoAm 92
Cooper, John L. 1937- St&PR 93
Cooper, John Miller 1912- BioIn 17
Cooper, John Milton, Jr. 1940- WhoAm 92
Cooper, John Montgomery 1881-1949 IntDcAn
Cooper, John Paul WhoE 93
Cooper, John R. ScF&FL 92
Cooper, John Sherman BioIn 17
Cooper, John Sherman 1901-1991 AnObit 1991
Cooper, Jordan D. Law&B 92
Cooper, Joseph 1933- WhoAm 92, WhoWor 93
Cooper, Joseph V. 1920- St&PR 93
Cooper, Josephine Smith 1945- WhoAm 92
Cooper, Judith WhoWrEP 92
Cooper, Karen Elizabeth Mauser 1955- WhoEmL 93
Cooper, Kathleen Anne Law&B 92
Cooper, Kathleen Bell 1945- WhoAm 92
Cooper, Kathy Nelle 1956- WhoWrEP 92
Cooper, Kay 1941- ConAu 37NR
Cooper, Keith Harvey 1936- WhoAm 92
Cooper, Ken Errol 1939- WhoAm 92
Cooper, Kenneth 1941- Baker 92
Cooper, Kenneth Banks 1923- WhoAm 92
Cooper, Kenneth Carlton 1948- WhoEmL 93, WhoWrEP 92
Cooper, Kenneth J. Law&B 92
Cooper, Kenneth Stanley 1948- WhoEmL 93, WhoSSW 93
Cooper, Kent 1880-1965 JrnUS
Cooper, Kent D. 1952- St&PR 93
Cooper, Kim M. Law&B 92
Cooper, Kristina Marie 1955- WhoAm 92
Cooper, Lance Eugene 1943- St&PR 93
Cooper, Larry B. 1943- St&PR 93
Cooper, Larry Preston 1936- St&PR 93
Cooper, Laurie A. 1952- WhoEmL 93
Cooper, Lawrence Allen 1948- WhoEmL 93, WhoSSW 93
Cooper, Lee J. 1946- St&PR 93
Cooper, Lena Frances 1875-1961 BioIn 17
Cooper, Leon 1929- St&PR 93
Cooper, Leon Melvin 1924- WhoAm 92, WhoWor 93
Cooper, Leon N. 1930- St&PR 93, WhoAm 92, WhoE 93, WhoWor 93
Cooper, Leroy Gordon, Jr. 1927- WhoAm 92
Cooper, Linda Faye 1945- WhoSSW 93
Cooper, Linda Frances 1961- WhoEmL 93
Cooper, Linda G. Law&B 92
Cooper, Linda Groomes 1954- WhoEmL 93
Cooper, Lisa Ivy 1961- WhoEmL 93
Cooper, Lois Blount 1939- WhoAmW 93
Cooper, Louis Zucker 1931- WhoE 93
Cooper, Louise 1952- ScF&FL 92
Cooper, Louise Field d1992 NewYTBS 92
Cooper, Louise Field 1905- WhoAm 92
Cooper, Louise Field 1905-1992 ConAu 139
Cooper, Malcolm E. St&PR 93
Cooper, Margaret C. ScF&FL 92
Cooper, Margaret Leslie 1950- WhoEmL 93
Cooper, Margery Wilkens 1947- WhoEmL 93
Cooper, Marilyn P. 1943- WhoAmW 93
Cooper, Marilyn R. 1934- WhoAm 92
Cooper, Mario BioIn 17
Cooper, Mario 1905- WhoAm 92, WhoWor 93
Cooper, Mark Arthur 1949- WhoE 93
Cooper, Marlene S. Law&B 92
Cooper, Marsh Alexander 1912- St&PR 93, WhoAm 92
Cooper, Martha Rose 1956- WhoEmL 93
Cooper, Martin 1928- WhoAm 92
Cooper, Martin (Du Pre) 1910-1986 Baker 92
Cooper, Martin Michael 1941- St&PR 93
Cooper, Marvin Arthur 1933- St&PR 93
Cooper, Marvin Meyer 1931- WhoE 93
Cooper, Mary Adrienne 1927- WhoAm 92, WhoAmW 93
Cooper, Mary Anita 1942- WhoAmW 93
Cooper, Mary Campbell 1940- WhoAmW 93
Cooper, Mary Louise 1950- WhoSSW 93
Cooper, Maury M. 1944- St&PR 93
Cooper, Max 1884-1959 OxDcOp
Cooper, Max Dale 1933- WhoAm 92
Cooper, Merian C. 1893-1973 MiSFD 9N
Cooper, Merri-Ann 1946- WhoAm 92, WhoE 93, WhoEmL 93
Cooper, Michael Allen 1936- St&PR 93
Cooper, Michael Anthony 1936- WhoAm 92
Cooper, Michael Hymie 1938- WhoWor 93
Cooper, Michael J. 1953- WhoEmL 93
Cooper, Michael James 1951- WhoWor 93
Cooper, Michael R. 1946- St&PR 93, WhoE 93
Cooper, Milton 1929- St&PR 93, WhoAm 92
Cooper, Miriam Denness AmWomPl
Cooper, Mitchell Barry 1948- WhoEmL 93
Cooper, Morton 1917- St&PR 93
Cooper, Morton Cecil 1914-1958 BiDAMSp 1989
Cooper, Murray W. 1932- St&PR 93
Cooper, Nathan 1946- St&PR 93
Cooper, Neil 1950- St&PR 93
Cooper, Neil Louis 1930- WhoWor 93
Cooper, Nelson BioIn 17
Cooper, Norman 1931- WhoAm 92
Cooper, Norman John 1950- WhoEmL 93
Cooper, Norman Streich 1920- WhoAm 92
Cooper, Norton J. 1931- St&PR 93, WhoAm 92, WhoWor 93
Cooper, Pamela Ann 1959- WhoEmL 93
Cooper, Pamela Mary 1950- St&PR 93
Cooper, Parley J. 1937- ScF&FL 92
Cooper, Patricia Ann 1949- WhoEmL 93
Cooper, Patricia Dawkins 1944- WhoAmW 93
Cooper, Patricia Gorman 1946- WhoEmL 93
Cooper, Patricia Jacqueline 1958- WhoEmL 93
Cooper, Paul 1926- Baker 92, WhoAm 92
Cooper, Paul Douglas 1941- WhoAm 92
Cooper, Paula 1938- WhoAm 92
Cooper, Paulette BioIn 17
Cooper, Paulette Marcia 1942- WhoAm 92, WhoE 93, WhoWrEP 92
Cooper, Penny 1918- ConAu 137
Cooper, Peter 1791-1883 PolPar
Cooper, Peter Dirr 1940- St&PR 93
Cooper, Peter H. MiSFD 9
Cooper, Peter L. 1949- ScF&FL 92
Cooper, R.A. St&PR 93
Cooper, R. Belvin 1923- WhoIns 93
Cooper, R. Jack 1933- WhoSSW 93
Cooper, R. John Law&B 92
Cooper, R. John, III 1942- WhoAm 92
Cooper, Rachel Bremer 1950- WhoAmW 93
Cooper, Ralph d1992 NewYTBS 92 [port]
Cooper, Randall L. 1951- St&PR 93
Cooper, Rebecca 1957- WhoAmW 93
Cooper, Reginald Rudyard 1932- WhoAm 92
Cooper, Rene Victor 1924- WhoSSW 93
Cooper, Rhonda Helene 1950- WhoEmL 93
Cooper, Richard ScF&FL 92
Cooper, Richard A. Law&B 92
Cooper, Richard A. 1927- St&PR 93
Cooper, Richard Alan 1936- WhoAm 92
Cooper, Richard Alan 1953- WhoEmL 93
Cooper, Richard Clyde 1951- WhoSSW 93
Cooper, Richard Earl 1947- WhoEmL 93
Cooper, Richard F. Law&B 92
Cooper, Richard F. 1951- St&PR 93
Cooper, Richard Lee 1946- WhoAm 92, WhoE 93
Cooper, Richard Melvin 1942- WhoAm 92
Cooper, Richard Newell 1934- WhoAm 92
Cooper, Rick ScF&FL 92
Cooper, Robert A. 1926- St&PR 93
Cooper, Robert Alfred 1938- WhoE 93
Cooper, Robert Arthur, Jr. 1932-1992 WhoAm 92
Cooper, Robert C. Law&B 92
Cooper, Robert Elbert 1920- WhoAm 92
Cooper, Robert Gordon 1953- WhoEmL 93
Cooper, Robert H. 1925- WhoAm 92
Cooper, Robert Harold 1925- St&PR 93
Cooper, Robert Rodney 1938- WhoE 93
Cooper, Robert S. 1932- BioIn 17
Cooper, Robert Shanklin 1932- WhoAm 92
Cooper, Robert Vernon, Jr. 1954- WhoEmL 93, WhoSSW 93
Cooper, Rochella 1933- WhoAmW 93
Cooper, Roger Frank 1944- WhoAm 92
Cooper, Roger Merlin 1943- WhoAm 92
Cooper, Roy G. Law&B 92
Cooper, Rubin Seymour 1946- WhoEmL 93
Cooper, Russell 1918- St&PR 93
Cooper, Ruthie Mae 1948- WhoEmL 93
Cooper, Samuel 1798-1876 HarEnMi
Cooper, Sandra L. ScF&FL 92
Cooper, Sandra Lenore 1934- WhoWrEP 92
Cooper, Sharon Elizabeth 1951- WhoE 93
Cooper, Sharon Marsha 1944- WhoAmW 93
Cooper, Sharon Skille 1941- WhoAmW 93
Cooper, Sheldon Mark 1942- WhoE 93
Cooper, Shiela Perfect 1957- WhoEmL 93
Cooper, Sidney 1920- St&PR 93
Cooper, Sonni 1934- ScF&FL 92
Cooper, Stephen Herbert 1939- WhoAm 92
Cooper, Stephen Randolph 1950- WhoWor 93
Cooper, Steve Neil 1944- WhoE 93
Cooper, Steven Gary Law&B 92
Cooper, Stuart 1942- MiSFD 9
Cooper, Stuart Leonard 1941- WhoAm 92
Cooper, Susan 1935- BioIn 17, ScF&FL 92
Cooper, Susan Eileen 1960- WhoAmW 93
Cooper, Susan (Mary) 1935- ConAu 37NR, DcAmChF 1960, MajAI [port]
Cooper, Susan Rogers 1947- ConAu 136
Cooper, Terry Lane 1946- WhoEmL 93
Cooper, Theodore 1928- St&PR 93, WhoAm 92
Cooper, Thomas A. 1936- WhoAm 92
Cooper, Thomas Louis 1938- WhoAm 92
Cooper, Thomas Luther 1917- WhoAm 92
Cooper, Thomas M. 1945- St&PR 93
Cooper, Todd 1951- St&PR 93
Cooper, Tom ScF&FL 92
Cooper, Tommye 1938- WhoUN 92
Cooper, W. Ronald Law&B 92
Cooper, Wallace J. 1926- WhoAm 92
Cooper, Ward R. Law&B 92
Cooper, Warren Ernest 1933- WhoAsAP 91, WhoWor 93
Cooper, Warren S. 1922- St&PR 93
Cooper, Wendy E. 1950- WhoIns 93
Cooper, Wendy Fein 1946- WhoEmL 93
Cooper, William Allen 1943- WhoAm 92
Cooper, William Edward 1930- St&PR 93
Cooper, William Eugene 1924- WhoAm 92
Cooper, William Ewing, Jr. 1929- WhoAm 92
Cooper, William James 1945- WhoSSW 93
Cooper, William James, Jr. 1940- WhoAm 92
Cooper, William Lee 1925- WhoSSW 93
Cooper, William Marion 1919- WhoAm 92
Cooper, William Secord 1935- WhoAm 92
Cooper, William Thomas 1938- WhoE 93
Cooper, William Walker 1915-1991 BiDAMSp 1989
Cooper-Lewter, Marcia Jean 1959- WhoAmW 93, WhoEmL 93
Cooperman, Alvin WhoWor 93
Cooperman, Barry S. 1941- WhoAm 92
Cooperman, Bruce 1937- St&PR 93
Cooperman, Gene David 1952- WhoE 93
Cooperman, Hasye 1909- WhoWrEP 92
Cooperman, Jack M. 1921- WhoE 93
Cooperman, Leon G. 1943- St&PR 93, WhoAm 92
Cooperman, Lewis J. 1936- St&PR 93
Cooperman, Saul 1934- WhoAm 92
Cooperrider, Tom Smith 1927- WhoAm 92
Cooper-Scott, Nedra Denise 1953- WhoEmL 93
Coopersmith, Barry 1946- St&PR 93
Coopersmith, Georgia Ann 1950- WhoEmL 93
Coopersmith, Jeffrey Alan 1946- St&PR 93, WhoEmL 93
Coopersmith, Martin Joseph 1940- St&PR 93
Coopersmith, Shirley Ann 1944- WhoAmW 93
Cooperstein, Alice Ruth 1925- WhoAmW 93
Cooperstein, Martin 1924- St&PR 93
Cooperstein, Sherwin Jerome 1923- WhoAm 92
Coor, Lattie Finch 1936- WhoAm 92
Coordes, Duane Allen Law&B 92
Coore, David 1925- WhoWor 93
Coors, Jeffrey H. 1945- WhoAm 92
Coors, Joseph BioIn 17
Coors, Joseph 1917- WhoAm 92
Coors, Peter H. BioIn 17
Coors, Peter Hanson 1946- WhoAm 92
Coors, William K. BioIn 17
Coors, William K. 1916- St&PR 93, WhoAm 92
Coortenaar, Egbert Meauwszoom c. 1610-1665 HarEnMi
Coorts, Gerald Duane 1932- WhoAm 92
Coosemans, J.T.A. 1943- WhoScE 91-2
Coosemans, Marc H.C. 1953- WhoScE 91-2
Coote, Adrian James 1945- St&PR 93
Coote, Eyre 1728-1783 HarEnMi
Coote, John Haven WhoScE 91-1
Cooter, Dale A. 1948- WhoEmL 93
Coots, Daniel Jay 1951- St&PR 93
Coots, Frank Shepherd, III 1949- WhoE 93
Coover, David B. 1932- St&PR 93
Coover, Harry Wesley 1919- WhoAm 92
Coover, Harry Wesley, Jr. 1919- St&PR 93
Coover, James B(urrell) 1925- Baker 92, WhoWrEP 92
Coover, Paula Louise Henry 1947- WhoAmW 93
Coover, Robert BioIn 17
Coover, Robert 1932- ScF&FL 92
Coover, Robert (Lowell) 1932- ConAu 37NR
Coover-Clark, Carol 1955- WhoAm 92, WhoAmW 93, WhoEmL 93
Coovert, C.E. 1950- St&PR 93
Coovert, Dale Lee 1948- WhoSSW 93
Coox, Alvin David 1924- WhoAm 92
Copa, Kathleen Therese 1955- WhoAm 92, WhoAmW 93, WhoEmL 93
Copacino, William Charles 1950- St&PR 93
Copage, Eric V. BioIn 17
Copage, Marc BioIn 17
Copas, John Brian WhoScE 91-1
Copass, Don Perry 1934- WhoSSW 93
Cope, Alfred Haines 1912- WhoE 93, WhoWor 93
Cope, Brenda Louise 1956- WhoEmL 93
Cope, David Edge 1948- WhoWrEP 92

Cope, David (Howell) 1941- Baker 92
Cope, Harold Cary 1918- WhoAm 92
Cope, James Dudley 1932- WhoAm 92, WhoE 93
Cope, James Wilson 1947- WhoSSW 93
Cope, John 1688-1760 HarEnMi
Cope, John Robert 1942- WhoAm 92, WhoE 93, WhoWor 93
Cope, Juanita Violet 1963- WhoAmW 93
Cope, Kenneth Wayne 1924- WhoAm 92
Cope, Kevin Lee 1957- WhoEmL 93
Cope, Larry R. Law&B 92
Cope, Lewis 1934- WhoAm 92
Cope, Randolph Howard, Jr. 1927- WhoAm 92
Cope, Roger W. 1945- St&PR 93
Cope, Teresa Suzanne 1958- WhoAmW 93
Cope, William Scott 1948- St&PR 93
Copeau, Jacques 1879-1949 BioIn 17
Copel, Ken 1962- WhoEmL 93
Copelan, John Jefferson, Jr. 1951- WhoEmL 93
Copelan, Mildred Louise 1925- WhoAmW 93
Copeland, Adrian Dennis 1928- WhoAm 92
Copeland, Alice Rivers 1950- WhoAmW 93
Copeland, Alvin Charles 1944- WhoAm 92
Copeland, Ann WhoCanL 92
Copeland, Anne Pitcairn 1951- WhoAm 92, WhoE 93, WhoEmL 93
Copeland, Barry Lee Law&B 92
Copeland, Carolyn Abigail 1931- WhoAmW 93
Copeland, Charles Herbert 1931- WhoSSW 93
Copeland, Charles Townsend 1860-1952 GayN
Copeland, Conrad Grant 1924- St&PR 93
Copeland, Darrel William 1944- WhoWor 93
Copeland, Darryl Wade 1936- WhoAm 92
Copeland, David A. Law&B 92
Copeland, Donald Eugene 1912- WhoAm 92
Copeland, Douglas Wallace, Jr. 1952- WhoEmL 93
Copeland, Edward Jerome 1933- WhoAm 92
Copeland, Edward Meadors, III 1937- WhoAm 92
Copeland, Elaine Wilson 1944- WhoAmW 93
Copeland, Eric A., Jr. 1936- St&PR 93
Copeland, Eugene Leroy 1939- WhoAm 92
Copeland, Floyd Dean 1939- WhoAm 92
Copeland, Gary A. 1952- ConAu 138
Copeland, George d1991 BioIn 17
Copeland, Gilbert Eugene 1941- WhoSSW 93
Copeland, Glen Reid Law&B 92
Copeland, Henry Jefferson, Jr. 1936- WhoAm 92
Copeland, Hunter Armstrong 1918- WhoAm 92
Copeland, J. Carl Law&B 92
Copeland, James N. Law&B 92
Copeland, Jana Renea Parson 1958- WhoAmW 93
Copeland, Jane Conyers 1941- WhoAmW 93
Copeland, Jennie Freeman 1879- AmWomPl
Copeland, Jerre Leigh 1951- WhoSSW 93
Copeland, Joan Miller WhoAm 92
Copeland, John Alexander, III 1941- WhoAm 92
Copeland, John Wesley 1935- St&PR 93, WhoAm 92
Copeland, Keith Lamont 1946- WhoEmL 93
Copeland, Lila 1922- WhoAm 92
Copeland, Lillian 1904-1964 BiDAMSp 1989
Copeland, Lori ScF&FL 92
Copeland, Manton, III 1958- St&PR 93
Copeland, Mary Jo BioIn 17
Copeland, Miles BioIn 17
Copeland, Miles 1913-1991 AnObit 1991
Copeland, Miles Alexander 1934- WhoAm 92
Copeland, Morris Albert 1895-1989 BioIn 17
Copeland, Peter 1957- ConAu 139
Copeland, Peter A. Law&B 92
Copeland, Reese Bowen Law&B 92
Copeland, Rita Lynette 1960- WhoE 93
Copeland, Robert Bodine 1938- WhoAm 92
Copeland, Robert Glenn 1941- WhoAm 92
Copeland, Robert Marshall 1945- WhoE 93
Copeland, Robert Tayloe 1947- WhoEmL 93
Copeland, Ronald Max WhoAm 92
Copeland, Sally C. Law&B 92
Copeland, Suzanne Johnson WhoAmW 93, WhoWor 93
Copeland, Tatiana Brandt WhoAmW 93
Copeland, Terrilyn Denise 1954- WhoAm 92, WhoEmL 93
Copeland, Thomas C., III 1940- St&PR 93
Copeland, Vicki Renae 1959- WhoEmL 93
Copeland, Victor G. Law&B 92
Copeland, Walter E. 1926- St&PR 93
Copeland, William Edgar 1920- WhoAm 92
Copeland, William George 1926- St&PR 93
Copeland, William John 1918- WhoAm 92
Copeman, Darwin G. 1950- St&PR 93
Copeman, Herbert Arthur 1923- WhoWor 93
Copeman, Mary Jeanette 1951- WhoAmW 93
Copenhaver, Brian Paul 1942- WhoAm 92
Copenhaver, Charles Leonard, III Law&B 92
Copenhaver, Eleanor AmWomPl
Copenhaver, John Thomas, Jr. 1925- WhoSSW 93
Copenhaver, Laura Scherer AmWomPl
Copenhaver, Marion Lamson 1925- WhoAmW 93
Copenhaver, William Pierce 1924- St&PR 93
Coperari, Giovanni Baker 92
Copernicus, Nicholas 1473-1543 PolBiDi [port]
Copernicus, Nicolaus 1473-1543 BioIn 17
Copes, Marvin Lee 1938- WhoAm 92, WhoSSW 93
Copestakes, Vesta 1949- WhoEmL 93
Copi, Irving Marmer 1917- WhoAm 92
Copin, Charis Wagner 1949- St&PR 93
Copinschi, Georges 1933- WhoScE 91-2
Coplan, Daniel Jonathan 1955- WhoEmL 93
Coplan, Norman Allan 1919- WhoAm 92
Coplan, Stan 1955- St&PR 93
Copland, Aaron 1900-1990 Baker 92, BioIn 17, JeAmHC, OxDcOp
Copland, Aaron 1900-1991 IntDcOp [port]
Copland, Elizabeth Ann 1951- WhoAm 92
Copland, Thomas Alexander 1952- WhoScE 91-1
Coplans, John Rivers 1920- WhoAm 92
Cople, William James, III 1955- WhoEmL 93
Copler, Judith Ann 1951- WhoEmL 93
Copley, Alfred L. d1992 NewYTBS 92 [port]
Copley, Alfred L. 1910-1992 BioIn 17
Copley, Cynthia Sue 1957- WhoAmW 93
Copley, David C. WhoAm 92
Copley, Helen K. 1922- St&PR 93
Copley, Helen Kinney 1922- WhoAm 92, WhoAmW 93
Copley, John 1933- IntDcOp, OxDcOp
Copley, John Michael Harold 1933- WhoWor 93
Copley, M. WhoScE 91-1
Copley, Stephen Michael 1936- WhoAm 92
Copley, Steven M. 1936- BioIn 17
Copley, William McKinley, III 1943- WhoSSW 93
Coplin, Haskell R. d1992 NewYTBS 92
Coplin, Mark David 1928- WhoAm 92
Coplin, William David WhoAm 92
Coplon, Ronald H. 1935- St&PR 93
Copmann, Elizabeth AmWomPl
Copp, DeWitt S. ScF&FL 92
Copp, Douglas Harold 1915- WhoAm 92
Copp, Earle Morse, III 1955- WhoEmL 93
Copp, Emmanuel Anthony 1945- WhoAm 92
Copp, James Harris 1925- WhoAm 92
Copp, Robert Mecca 1949- WhoE 93
Copp, Webster T. Law&B 92
Coppa, Francis Law&B 92
Coppard, Audrey 1931- ScF&FL 92
Coppe, Albert Leon 1911- WhoWor 93
Coppedge, Robert Locke 1958- WhoEmL 93
Coppee, Georges Henri 1940- WhoUN 92
Coppel, Alfred 1921- ScF&FL 92, WhoAm 92
Coppenger, Anne Patton 1950- WhoSSW 93
Coppenrath, Robert A.M. 1928- St&PR 93
Coppens, Claude A(lbert) 1936- Baker 92
Coppens, Patrick John 1952- St&PR 93
Coppens, Philip 1930- WhoAm 92
Coppens, Thomas Adriaan 1923- WhoE 93, WhoWor 93
Coppens, Yves Jean Edouard 1934- WhoScE 91-2
Copper, Basil 1924- ScF&FL 92
Copper, John Franklin 1940- WhoAm 92, WhoSSW 93, WhoWor 93
Copper, Robert Arnold de Vignier 1938- WhoE 93
Copperfield, David 1956- CurBio 92 [port], WhoAm 92
Copperman, Stuart Morton 1935- WhoAm 92, WhoWor 93
Coppernoll, Sue 1933- WhoAmW 93
Copperud, Roy H(erman) 1915-1991 ConAu 136
Copperud, Roy Herman 1915-1991 BioIn 17
Coppet, Edward J. de 1855-1916 Baker 92
Coppi, Fausto BioIn 17
Coppie, Comer Swift 1932- St&PR 93, WhoAm 92
Coppiellie, Raymond Lawrence Law&B 92
Copping, Allen Anthony 1927- WhoAm 92, WhoSSW 93
Copping, Craig P. 1943- St&PR 93
Copping, Robert Edward 1932- St&PR 93
Coppinger, Raymond Parke 1937- WhoAm 92
Coppini, Paolo Arturo 1934- WhoUN 92
Coppins, Brian John 1949- WhoScE 91-1
Copple, Christine D. 1950- St&PR 93
Copple, J.R. 1955- St&PR 93
Copple, Michael Andrew 1951- WhoEmL 93
Copple, Robert Francis 1955- WhoEmL 93
Copple, William Perry 1916- WhoAm 92
Copplestone, David Wesley 1952- WhoE 93
Coppock, David M. 1942- St&PR 93
Coppock, Paul C. Law&B 92
Coppock, Paul C. 1950- St&PR 93
Coppola, Albert Anthony 1933- St&PR 93
Coppola, Anthony 1935- WhoAm 92
Coppola, August 1934- WhoAm 92
Coppola, Carl St&PR 93
Coppola, Carlo 1938- WhoWrEP 92
Coppola, Carmine 1910-1991 AnObit 1991, BioIn 17, ConTFT 10
Coppola, Christopher MiSFD 9
Coppola, Elaine Marie 1947- WhoAmW 93
Coppola, Eleanor BioIn 17
Coppola, Eugene A. 1938- WhoAm 92
Coppola, Francis Ford 1939- BioIn 17, ConAu 40NR, MiSFD 9, WhoAm 92
Coppola, Grace J. Law&B 92
Coppola, Heidi S. Law&B 92
Coppola, Jean Frances 1964- WhoEmL 93
Coppola, Lawrence 1958- WhoE 93
Coppola, Piero 1888-1971 Baker 92
Coppola, Pietro Antonio 1793-1877 Baker 92
Coppola, Sofia BioIn 17
Coppola, Steven A. Law&B 92
Coppoletti, John H. 1942- St&PR 93
Coppotelli, H. Catherina 1944- WhoAm 92, WhoSSW 93
Copps, Sheila 1952- BioIn 17
Copps, Sheila Maureen 1952- WhoAmW 93
Copps, Thomas Richard 1939- St&PR 93
Coprario, Giovanni c. 1575-1626 Baker 92
Copsetta, Norman George 1932- WhoWor 93
Copsey, Reed Dennis 1956- WhoEmL 93
Copulsky, Lewis 1958- WhoEmL 93
Coquard, Arthur (-Joseph) 1846-1910 Baker 92
Coque, Roger Gabriel Armand 1923- WhoScE 91-2
Coquerelle, Michel 1932- WhoScE 91-3
Coquery, Jean-Marie 1937- WhoScE 91-2
Coquilla, Beatriz Hordista 1948- WhoAm 92, WhoEmL 93
Coquillette, Lorene 1933- St&PR 93
Coquillette, William Hollis 1949- WhoEmL 93
Coquillette-Dean, Daniel Robert 1944- WhoAm 92, WhoE 93, WhoWor 93
Cora, C. Peter St&PR 93
Cora, Lee Frank 1931- St&PR 93
Corabi, Joseph Michael 1952- WhoEmL 93
Corace, Joseph Russell 1953- WhoAm 92
Corace, William Ross Carle 1940- St&PR 93
Coradini, Angioletta WhoScE 91-3
Corah, Norman Lewis 1933- WhoE 93
Corak, William Sydney 1922- WhoE 93
Cora Lee SmATA 72
Coralie SmATA 72
Corallo, Karen C. Law&B 92
Coram, Edward Clinton 1947- WhoAm 92, WhoE 93, WhoEmL 93
Coran, Arnold Gerald 1938- WhoAm 92
Coraor, John Edward 1955- WhoAm 92, WhoE 93
Corasanti, Eugene R. 1930- St&PR 93
Corathers, Lorna Joan 1931- WhoAmW 93
Coratti, John Edward 1950- WhoE 93
Corazon, Alberto 1942- BioIn 17
Corazzini, Arthur John 1939- WhoAm 92
Corb, Michael Murphey- BioIn 17
Corbalis, Judith ChlFicS
Corbally, John Edward 1924- WhoAm 92
Corban, Karen Elliott 1954- WhoSSW 93
Corbat, Emerson William, Jr. 1948- WhoEmL 93
Corbat, Sara S. Law&B 92
Corbato, Charles Edward 1932- WhoAm 92
Corbato, Fernando Jose 1926- BioIn 17, WhoAm 92
Corbel, Michael John WhoScE 91-1
Corben, Herbert Charles 1914- WhoAm 92
Corben, Roberta Joy WhoAmW 93
Corber, Billy G. Law&B 92
Corber, Robert Jack 1926- WhoE 93, WhoWor 93
Corber, Robert Jack, I 1926- WhoAm 92
Corberand, Joel X. 1943- WhoScE 91-2
Corbet, David Lewis 1953- St&PR 93, WhoE 93
Corbet, Donald Lee 1959- WhoEmL 93
Corbet, Hugh WhoScE 91-1
Corbet, Nancy Jane Law&B 92
Corbet, Philip Steven WhoScE 91-1
Corbet, Robert 1948- WhoWor 93
Corbet, Timothy Boyd 1948- St&PR 93
Corbett, Bruce Loring 1955- St&PR 93
Corbett, Charlene Miranda 1967- WhoAmW 93
Corbett, Daniel Ray 1959- WhoWor 93
Corbett, Elizabeth Frances 1887- AmWomPl
Corbett, Frank Joseph 1917- WhoAm 92
Corbett, Fred ScF&FL 92
Corbett, Gentleman Jim 1866-1933 BioIn 17
Corbett, Gerard F. 1950- St&PR 93
Corbett, Gerard Francis 1950- WhoE 93, WhoEmL 93
Corbett, Gloria Ann WhoSSW 93
Corbett, Harold John 1927- St&PR 93
Corbett, Howard Lewis 1924- St&PR 93
Corbett, Idna Maritza 1960- WhoAmW 93, WhoEmL 93
Corbett, J. Elliott 1920- St&PR 93
Corbett, J.O. 1945- St&PR 93
Corbett, Jack Elliott 1920- WhoAm 92, WhoE 93, WhoWor 93
Corbett, James d1958? ScF&FL 92
Corbett, James J. 1866-1933 GayN
Corbett, James John 1866-1933 BioIn 17
Corbett, James Michael 1927- WhoIns 93
Corbett, James Otho 1945- WhoSSW 93
Corbett, James William 1928- WhoAm 92
Corbett, Jim 1875-1955 BioIn 17
Corbett, Joan Dufner 1928- WhoAmW 93
Corbett, John BioIn 17
Corbett, John A. d1992 NewYTBS 92
Corbett, John Dudley 1926- WhoAm 92
Corbett, John Frank 1935- St&PR 93
Corbett, John Richard 1928- St&PR 93
Corbett, Jonathan Martin 1956- WhoWor 93
Corbett, Joseph Edward 1921- St&PR 93
Corbett, Kathleen Watson 1933- WhoAmW 93
Corbett, Keith Bernard 1956- St&PR 93
Corbett, Larry R. 1945- St&PR 93
Corbett, Leon H., Jr. 1937- WhoAm 92
Corbett, Lionel ScF&FL 92
Corbett, Michael Alan 1951- St&PR 93
Corbett, Michael Derrik 1929- WhoWor 93
Corbett, Michael Karl 1947- WhoUN 92
Corbett, Michael McGregor 1923- WhoWor 93
Corbett, Peter Frank 1959- WhoE 93, WhoEmL 93
Corbett, Peter G. Law&B 92
Corbett, Raymond R. d1992 NewYTBS 92 [port]
Corbett, Richard 1582-1635 DcLB 121 [port]
Corbett, Richard Alexander 1948- WhoE 93
Corbett, Richard Edward 1949- WhoE 93
Corbett, Roger L. 1931- St&PR 93
Corbett, Roger Lee 1931- WhoAm 92
Corbett, Ronnie 1930- QDrFCA 92 [port]
Corbett, Roy Gilman 1932- WhoE 93
Corbett, Scott 1913- DcAmChF 1960, MajAI [port], ScF&FL 92
Corbett, (Winfield) Scott 1913- WhoWrEP 92
Corbett, Suzanne Elaine 1953- WhoAmW 93, WhoEmL 93
Corbett, Thomas John 1951- WhoEmL 93
Corbett, Thomas Wingett, Jr. 1949- WhoAm 92
Corbett, W.J. 1938- ScF&FL 92
Corbett, W(illiam) J(esse) 1938- ConAu 137, MajAI [port]
Corbett, William John 1937- WhoAm 92
Corbett, William Thomas, Jr. Law&B 92
Corbett, William Thomas, Jr. 1960- WhoEmL 93
Corbett Ashby, Margery Irene 1882-1981 BioIn 17

Corbiau, Gerard MiSFD 9
Corbin, Barry 1940- ConTFT 10, WhoAm 92
Corbin, David Randolph 1956- WhoEmL 93
Corbin, Donald L. 1938- WhoAm 92, WhoSSW 93
Corbin, Everett Jimmy 1932- WhoSSW 93
Corbin, Herbert Leonard 1940- St&PR 93, WhoAm 92
Corbin, John 1920- WhoSSW 93
Corbin, John B(oyd) 1935- WhoWrEP 92
Corbin, John Stephen 1946- WhoEmL 93
Corbin, Kendall Brooks 1907- WhoAm 92
Corbin, Krestine Margaret 1937- WhoAmW 93, WhoWor 93
Corbin, Lauren Lee 1959- WhoEmL 93
Corbin, Patrick F. Law&B 92
Corbin, Richard J. 1939- St&PR 93
Corbin, Robert Edward 1935- St&PR 93
Corbin, Robert Keith 1928- WhoAm 92
Corbin, Rori Cooper 1951- WhoAm 92, WhoAmW 93
Corbin, Scott Douglas 1950- WhoSSW 93
Corbin, Sol Neil 1927- WhoAm 92
Corbin, William 1916- DcAmChF 1960
Corbin, William Lewis 1935- St&PR 93
Corbin, William S. 1945- St&PR 93
Corbishley, David Edward 1946- St&PR 93
Corbishley, Douglas A. 1936- St&PR 93
Corbitt, Deborah Davidson 1951- WhoAmW 93
Corbman, Eric Stuart 1952- WhoEmL 93
Corbo, Alan Gerald 1927- St&PR 93
Corbo, Angela Marie 1958- WhoAmW 93
Corboy, James John 1929- St&PR 93
Corboy, Philip Harnett 1924- WhoAm 92
Corboz, Michel (-Jules) 1934- Baker 92
Corbridge, D. Bruce Law&B 92
Corbridge, James Noel, Jr. 1934- WhoAm 92
Corbridge, Richard M. 1932- St&PR 93
Corbucci, Sergio 1927-1990 MiSFD 9N
Corbulo, Gnaeus Domitius d67 HarEnMi
Corby, Adam ScF&FL 92
Corby, Brian 1929- WhoWor 93
Corby, Dan ConAu 38NR, MajAI
Corby, Francis M., Jr. 1944- St&PR 93
Corby, Francis Michael, Jr. 1944- WhoAm 92
Corby, Michael ScF&FL 92
Corby, Michael Charles 1960- WhoEmL 93
Corby, Nancy Hawkins 1937- WhoAmW 93
Corces, Loretta Cueto 1943- WhoSSW 93
Corcia, John T. 1945- St&PR 93
Corcione-Navarre, Joy Marie 1960- WhoAmW 93
Corcoran, Andrew Patrick, Jr. 1948- WhoEmL 93
Corcoran, Barbara 1911- DcAmChF 1960
Corcoran, Barbara Asenath 1911- WhoAm 92
Corcoran, Bernadette Ellen 1947- WhoE 93
Corcoran, Bill MiSFD 9
Corcoran, C. Timothy, III 1945- WhoSSW 93
Corcoran, Carol Ann 1968- WhoAmW 93
Corcoran, Chris K. 1951- St&PR 93
Corcoran, David 1947- WhoAm 92
Corcoran, David Howard 1942- St&PR 93
Corcoran, David M. 1903-1990 BioIn 17
Corcoran, Edward M. Law&B 92
Corcoran, Eileen Lynch 1917- WhoAm 92
Corcoran, Eugene Francis 1916- WhoAm 92, WhoSSW 93
Corcoran, J. Walter 1938- St&PR 93, WhoE 93
Corcoran, James C. 1926- St&PR 93, WhoAm 92
Corcoran, James Martin, Jr. 1932- WhoAm 92
Corcoran, James Thomas 1929- St&PR 93
Corcoran, Janet C. Law&B 92
Corcoran, John BioIn 17
Corcoran, John 1937- WhoAm 92
Corcoran, John Joseph 1920- WhoAm 92
Corcoran, Mary Barbara 1924- WhoAm 92
Corcoran, Maureen Elizabeth 1944- WhoAm 92
Corcoran, Michael Patrick 1957- WhoEmL 93
Corcoran, Miriam Denise 1938- WhoAmW 93
Corcoran, Paul John 1934- WhoAm 92
Corcoran, Robert Lee, Jr. 1944- WhoAm 92
Corcoran, Ruth F. 1910-1991 BioIn 17
Corcoran, Thomas G. 1900-1981 PolPar
Corcoran, Thomas Joseph 1920- WhoAm 92
Corcoran, Thomas M. 1955- St&PR 93
Cord, Alex 1933- WhoAm 92
Cord, Barry Kieselstein- BioIn 17
Cord, E. L. 1894-1974 EncABHB 8 [port]
Cord, Joseph Anthony 1956- WhoEmL 93
Cord, Steven B. 1928- WhoE 93
Cordaro, Matthew C. 1943- St&PR 93
Cordaro, Matthew Charles 1943- WhoAm 92
Cordaro, Michael J. 1958- St&PR 93
Cordaro, Tom Anthony 1954- WhoE 93
Cordasco, Alfred F. Law&B 92
Cordasco, Francesco 1920- WhoAm 92, WhoWrEP 92
Corday, Amy Beth Law&B 92
Corday, Barbara 1944- WhoAmW 93
Corday, Mara 1932- SweetSg D
Corddry, Paul Imlay 1936- St&PR 93, WhoAm 92
Corde, Eleanor AmWomPl
Cordeiro, Joseph Cardinal 1918- WhoWor 93
Cordeiro Ferreira, Nuno Tornelli 1926- WhoScE 91-3
Cordek, Lawrence Donald 1946- St&PR 93
Cordell, Alfred H. 1928- St&PR 93
Cordell, Edwin B. 1958- St&PR 93
Cordell, Francis Merritt 1932- WhoWor 93
Cordell, H. Ken BioIn 17
Cordell, Joe B. 1927- St&PR 93
Cordell, LaDoris Hazzard 1949- WhoEmL 93
Cordell, Martin Lewis 1950- WhoEmL 93
Cordell, Robert James 1917- WhoAm 92, WhoSSW 93
Cordell, Ronald Eugene 1949- WhoSSW 93
Cordell, Steven Mark 1955- WhoEmL 93
Cordell, Tom BioIn 17
Cordell, William H., Jr. Law&B 92
Corden, Warner Max 1927- WhoAm 92
Corder, Billie Farmer 1934- WhoAmW 93, WhoSSW 93
Corder, Clinton Nicholas 1941- WhoWor 93
Corder, Eddie Charles 1949- St&PR 93
Corder, Frederick 1852-1932 Baker 92, OxDcOp
Corder, Paul 1879-1942 Baker 92
Corderi, Victoria BioIn 17
Corderi, Victoria 1957- NotHsAW 93
Corderman, John Printz 1942- WhoAm 92
Cordero, Angel BioIn 17
Cordero, Angel 1942- HispAmA, NewYTBS 92 [port]
Cordero, Angel T., Jr. 1942- WhoAm 92
Cordero, David Law&B 92
Cordero, Julio 1923- HispAmA
Cordero, Mortimer Florendo 1964- WhoWor 93
Cordero, Roque 1917- Baker 92
Cordero, Salvador 1876-1951 DcMexL
Cordero Martin, Jose Antonio WhoScE 91-3
Corderre, Emile 1893-1970 BioIn 17
Cordery, Antony John 1951- WhoWor 93
Cordes, Alexander Charles 1925- WhoAm 92
Cordes, Clifford Frederick, III 1946- WhoEmL 93
Cordes, Donald L. Law&B 92
Cordes, Donald Wesley 1917- WhoAm 92
Cordes, Eugene Harold 1936- WhoAm 92
Cordes, G.W. WhoScE 91-1
Cordes, James F. 1940- St&PR 93
Cordes, Larry Dean 1957- WhoSSW 93
Cordes, Loverne Christian 1927- WhoAm 92
Cordes, Mary Kenrick 1933- WhoAm 92, WhoAmW 93
Cordes, Omar Martin 1954- WhoWor 93
Cordier, Ralph W. 1902-1990 BioIn 17
Cordier, William K. 1927- St&PR 93
Cording, Edward James 1937- WhoAm 92
Cordingley, John Stuart 1953- WhoEmL 93
Cordingley, Mary Jeanette Bowles 1918- WhoAm 92, WhoAmW 93, WhoWor 93
Cordingley, William Andrew 1917- WhoAm 92
Cordis, Maria 1929- WhoAm 92
Cordner, Jacqueline Willingham 1922- WhoWrEP 92
Cordoba, Gonsalvo Fernandez de 1585-1635 HarEnMi
Cordon, Frank Joseph 1925- St&PR 93
Cordon, Glenda Sue 1943- WhoAmW 93
Cordon, Jenean C. 1943- St&PR 93
Cordon, Norman 1904-1964 Baker 92
Cordonnier, Daniel J. 1937- WhoScE 91-2
Cordonnier, Daniel Jacques 1937- WhoWor 93
Cordova, Ernest Leroy 1950- WhoEmL 93
Cordova, France Anne-Dominic 1947- WhoAm 92
Cordova, Karen Sue 1951- WhoAmW 93
Cordova, Luis 1908- DcMexL
Cordova, Maria Asuncion 1941- WhoAmW 93
Cordova Rivas, Rafael DcCPCAm
Cordova y Vazquez, Ana 1967- WhoWor 93
Cordover, Ronald H. 1943- St&PR 93
Cordover, Ronald Harvey 1943- WhoAm 92
Cordovez, Diego 1935- WhoWor 93
Cordray, Richard Lynn 1952- WhoEmL 93
Cordrey, Richard Stephen 1933- WhoAm 92
Cordts, Harold J. BioIn 17
Cordts, Paul Roger 1958- WhoE 93
Cordy, David P. 1953- St&PR 93
Cordy, Ida AmWomPl
Cordy, Jean-Marie A. 1946- WhoScE 91-2
Core, Lyndell Douglas 1956- WhoSSW 93
Core, Mary Carolyn W. Parsons 1949- WhoAm 92, WhoAmW 93, WhoEmL 93
Corea, Chick BioIn 17
Corea, Chick 1941- WhoAm 92
Corea, "Chick" (Armando Anthony) 1941- Baker 92
Corea, Luigi 1939- WhoWor 93
Corea, Nicholas 1943- MiSFD 9
Corea, Roger C. 1943- St&PR 93
Corell, Mildred AmWomPl
Corell, Robert W. 1934- BioIn 17
Corell, Robert Walden 1934- WhoAm 92
Corella, Jose 1944- WhoScE 91-3
Corelli, Arcangelo 1653-1713 Baker 92
Corelli, Franco 1921- IntDcOp [port], OxDcOp
Corelli, Franco (Dario) 1921- Baker 92
Corelli, John Charles 1930- WhoAm 92
Coren, Arthur 1933- St&PR 93
Coren, Lance Scott 1949- WhoEmL 93
Coren, Stanley 1942- ConAu 137
Corena, Fernando 1916-1984 Baker 92, IntDcOp, OxDcOp
Corenblith, Clifton Wayne Law&B 92
Coreth, Joseph Herman 1937- WhoAm 92, WhoE 93
Corette, John E. 1908- WhoAm 92
Corey, Brian F. Law&B 92
Corey, Donald Lee 1932- St&PR 93, WhoAm 92
Corey, Elias J. BioIn 17
Corey, Elias James 1928- WhoAm 92, WhoE 93, WhoWor 93
Corey, Elizabeth BioIn 17
Corey, Gordon Richard 1914- WhoAm 92
Corey, Jeff 1914- WhoAm 92
Corey, Jim d1950? BioIn 17
Corey, John C. 1947- St&PR 93
Corey, John Charles 1947- WhoEmL 93
Corey, John R. 1946- WhoE 93
Corey, Kenneth Edward 1938- WhoAm 92
Corey, Leslie Norman, Jr. 1949- WhoEmL 93
Corey, Melinda Ann 1957- WhoEmL 93
Corey, Melody Lane WhoE 93
Corey, Orlin Russell 1926- WhoAm 92
Corey, Paul Frederick 1903- WhoAm 92
Corey, Richard James 1945- WhoSSW 93
Corey, Ronald 1938- WhoAm 92
Corey, Stephen Dale 1948- WhoWrEP 92
Corey, Steven d1991 BioIn 17
Corfield, George C. WhoScE 91-1
Corfman, Stanley Luccock 1953- WhoEmL 93
Corfmat, Francois Lucien 1945- WhoUN 92
Corgan, Margaret M. 1936- WhoAmW 93
Corhan, Kenneth P. Law&B 92
Cori, Carl Thomas 1936- St&PR 93
Cori, Gregory Salvatore 1925- WhoAm 92, WhoWor 93
Cori, Ronald Joseph 1956- WhoE 93
Coria, Miguel Angel 1937- Baker 92
Coriaty, George Michael 1933- WhoE 93
Coriden, Michael Warner Law&B 92
Coriden, Michael Warner 1948- WhoEmL 93
Coriell, Lewis Lemon 1911- WhoAm 92
Coriell, Vernell 1918-1987 ScF&FL 92
Corigliano, John 1901-1975 Baker 92
Corigliano, John 1938- BioIn 17
Corigliano, John (Paul) 1938- Baker 92, WhoAm 92
Corina, D.L. WhoScE 91-1
Corinaldi, Austin 1921- WhoAm 92
Corinth, Lovis 1858-1925 BioIn 17
Corinthios, Michael Jean George 1941- WhoAm 92
Corippus dc. 567 OxDcByz
Corish, A.T. WhoScE 91-1
Corish, Brendan 1919-1990 BioIn 17
Cork, D. Bradley 1950- St&PR 93
Cork, Dennis Bradley 1950- WhoEmL 93
Cork, Donald Burl 1949- WhoEmL 93
Cork, Edwin Kendall WhoAm 92
Cork, Herbert V. 1933- St&PR 93
Cork, Holly BioIn 17
Cork, Holly A. 1966- WhoAmW 93
Cork, John Robert 1947- St&PR 93
Cork, Kenneth 1913-1991 AnObit 1991
Cork, Linda Katherine 1936- WhoAm 92, WhoAmW 93
Corke, Lawrence William 1951- St&PR 93
Corker, Charles Edward 1917- WhoAm 92
Corker, Frank Thomas 1935- WhoSSW 93
Corker, R. Stephen 1941- St&PR 93
Corkern, Carl Bruce 1961- St&PR 93
Corkern, Wilton Claude, Jr. 1946- WhoE 93
Corkery, Christopher Jane 1946- WhoWrEP 92
Corkery, F. Daniel Law&B 92
Corkery, James Caldwell 1925- WhoAm 92
Corkhill, Arlene Finatti 1946- St&PR 93
Corkidi, Rafael 1930- MiSFD 9
Corkill, Charles P. Law&B 92
Corkin, Cary J. 1951- St&PR 93
Corkins, Gary Charles 1935- St&PR 93
Corkran, Donald Allen 1937- WhoAm 92
Corle, Frederic William, II 1945- WhoE 93
Corle, James T. Law&B 92
Corless, Harry 1928- WhoAm 92
Corless, James J. 1927- St&PR 93
Corlett, Mary Lee 1957- ConAu 139
Corlett, William 1938- ScF&FL 92
Corlew, Charles R. 1957- St&PR 93
Corley, Arnett Browne, Jr. 1942- WhoSSW 93
Corley, Bruce E. 1926- St&PR 93
Corley, Carol A. 1948- St&PR 93
Corley, Edwin 1931-1981 ScF&FL 92
Corley, Elizabeth A. 1955- WhoAmW 93
Corley, Emery L. Law&B 92
Corley, Farrell Wayne 1949- WhoE 93
Corley, James 1947- ScF&FL 92
Corley, Jean Arnette Leister 1944- WhoAmW 93
Corley, Leslie M. 1946- WhoAm 92, WhoE 93
Corley, Linda Gail 1947- WhoEmL 93
Corley, Pat 1930- WhoAm 92
Corley, Patricia Lynde 1931- WhoSSW 93
Corley, William Edward 1942- WhoAm 92
Corley, William Gene 1935- WhoAm 92
Corley, William Harold 1961- WhoSSW 93
Corley, William J. 1953- St&PR 93
Corlieto, Martin, III 1954- WhoEmL 93, WhoSSW 93
Corliss, George F. Law&B 92
Corliss, George Henry 1817-1888 BioIn 17
Corliss, John Ozro 1922- WhoAm 92
Corliss, Ken T. 1949- St&PR 93
Corliss, Richard Nelson 1944- WhoAm 92
Corliss, Robert WhoAm 92
Corliss, William R(oger) 1926- ConAu 37NR
Corll, Vivian Morgan 1940- WhoWrEP 92
Cormac, C.D. WhoWrEP 92
Cormack, Allan MacLeod 1924- WhoAm 92, WhoE 93, WhoWor 93
Cormack, D. WhoScE 91-1
Cormack, Maribelle 1902-1984 ScF&FL 92
Cormack, Robert George Hall 1904- WhoAm 92
Cormack, Robert J. 1946- ConAu 139
Corman, Avery BioIn 17
Corman, Avery 1935- ScF&FL 92, WhoAm 92, WhoWrEP 92
Corman, Cid 1924- WhoAm 92, WhoWrEP 92
Corman, Elliot St&PR 93
Corman, Eugene Harold 1927- WhoAm 92
Corman, Jack Bernard 1926- WhoSSW 93
Corman, Julie Ellen St&PR 93
Corman, Karen Marie 1962- WhoEmL 93
Corman, Marc H. Law&B 92
Corman, Roger BioIn 17
Corman, Roger 1926- MiSFD 9
Corman, Roger William 1926- WhoAm 92
Corman, Samuel St&PR 93
Corman, William Franklin 1916- St&PR 93
Cormanick, Rosa-Maria 1946- WhoWor 93
Cormey, John R. 1947- St&PR 93
Cormia, Frank Howard 1936- WhoSSW 93
Cormia, Robert L. 1935- St&PR 93
Cormie, Donald Mercer 1922- WhoAm 92, WhoWor 93
Cormier, Andrew M. St&PR 93
Cormier, Bruce Matthew Law&B 92
Cormier, Claudia K. Law&B 92
Cormier, Elizabeth Ferguson 1925- WhoSSW 93
Cormier, Jean G. 1941- WhoAm 92
Cormier, Robert BioIn 17
Cormier, Robert 1925- DcAmChF 1960, MagSAmL [port], ScF&FL 92
Cormier, Robert (Edmund) 1925- DcAmChF 1985, MajAI [port], WhoAm 92, WhoWrEP 92
Cormier, Robert Joseph 1941- WhoE 93
Cormy, Gerard WhoScE 91-2
Cormy, Gerard 1935- WhoScE 91-2

Corn, Alfred 1943- *DcLB 120 [port]*
Corn, Alfred DeWitt 1943- *WhoAm 92, WhoWrEP 92*
Corn, Amy Crean *Law&B 92*
Corn, Bennett Julian 1944- *WhoAm 92*
Corn, Jack W. 1929- *WhoE 93*
Corn, James Rickman 1956- *WhoSSW 93*
Corn, John W. 1955- *St&PR 93*
Corn, Joseph Edward, Jr. 1932- *WhoAm 92*
Corn, Joseph J. *ScF&FL 92*
Corn, Julius Alfred 1931- *St&PR 93*
Corn, Larry R. 1941- *St&PR 93*
Corn, Leslie Joan 1949- *WhoAm 92*
Corn, Lovick Pierce 1922- *St&PR 93*
Corn, Mary Louise Johnston 1948- *WhoSSW 93*
Corn, Michael A. *Law&B 92*
Corn, Milton 1928- *WhoAm 92*
Corn, Morton 1933- *WhoAm 92, WhoE 93*
Corn, Pauline Gordon 1931- *St&PR 93*
Corna, Louis J. *Law&B 92*
Corna, Mark Steven 1949- *WhoEmL 93*
Cornacchio, Joseph Vincent 1934- *WhoAm 92*
Cornacchio, Peter Anthony 1941- *St&PR 93*
Cornatzer, William Eugene 1918- *WhoAm 92*
Cornblath, Marvin 1925- *WhoAm 92*
Cornblatt, Max 1906- *WhoAm 92*
Cornbleet, Aileen Gail Hirsch 1946- *WhoAmW 93*
Cornblit, Oscar Enrique 1927- *WhoWor 93*
Cornea, Aurel 1933- *WhoWor 93*
Corneau, Maude S. *AmWomPl*
Cornebise, Alfred E(mile) 1929- *ConAu 38NR*
Corneglio, Donald Lewis *Law&B 92*
Corneille, Pierre 1606-1684 *MagSWL [port], OxDcOp*
Cornejo, Cesar E. 1949- *St&PR 93*
Cornelio, Albert C. 1930- *St&PR 93, WhoIns 93*
Cornelio, Albert Carmen 1930- *WhoAm 92*
Cornelio, Charles C. *Law&B 92*
Cornelio, Ferdinando 1938- *WhoScE 91-3*
Cornelis, Eric Rene 1960- *WhoWor 93*
Cornelis, Evert 1884-1931 *Baker 92*
Cornelis, Frans Charles 1957- *WhoWor 93*
Cornelis, Johannes 1922- *WhoWor 93*
Cornelis, Pieter Arsene 1927- *WhoWor 93*
Cornelisen, Ann 1926- *BioIn 17*
Cornelison, Albert O., Jr. *Law&B 92*
Cornelison, Daniel *Law&B 92*
Cornelison, David Richard 1957- *St&PR 93*
Cornelison, Floyd Shovington, Jr. 1918- *WhoAm 92*
Cornelison, John Michael 1967- *WhoSSW 93*
Cornelissen-Guillaume, Germaine Gabriell 1949- *WhoEmL 93*
Corneliu, Rauta I. 1928- *WhoScE 91-4*
Corneliu, Sabetay I. 1944- *WhoScE 91-4*
Cornelius, Carter 1948-1991 *BioIn 17*
Cornelius, Charles B.R. *Law&B 92*
Cornelius, Cynthia Jeanne 1952- *WhoE 93*
Cornelius, D.F. *WhoScE 91-1*
Cornelius, Dennis Alfred 1942- *St&PR 93*
Cornelius, Don *BioIn 17*
Cornelius, Don 1936- *ConBlB 4 [port]*
Cornelius, Gordon A. 1928- *St&PR 93*
Cornelius, H. Thomas 1933- *St&PR 93*
Cornelius, James Alfred 1936- *WhoAm 92*
Cornelius, James M. 1943- *St&PR 93*
Cornelius, Janet Duitsman 1938- *WhoAmW 93*
Cornelius, Kay Oldham 1933- *WhoWrEP 92*
Cornelius, Kenneth Cremer, Jr. 1944- *WhoAm 92*
Cornelius, Lester Ernest 1953- *WhoE 93, WhoEmL 93*
Cornelius, Linda Louise 1953- *WhoAm 92, WhoAmW 93*
Cornelius, Michael A. *Law&B 92*
Cornelius, Paul K. 1955- *WhoSSW 93*
Cornelius, Peter 1824-1874 *Baker 92, IntDcOp, OxDcOp*
Cornelius, Peter 1865-1934 *Baker 92*
Cornelius, Richard Dean 1947- *WhoE 93*
Cornelius, Sara M. 1941- *St&PR 93*
Cornelius, Virginia H. 1922- *St&PR 93*
Cornelius, Walter Felix 1922- *WhoSSW 93*
Cornelius, William Edward 1931- *St&PR 93, WhoAm 92*
Corneliussen, Pal 1964- *WhoE 93*
Corneliys Petersen, Lauritz Peter 1865-1934 *Baker 92*
Cornell, A. Jefferson 1941- *WhoWrEP 92*
Cornell, Alan 1929- *WhoE 93*
Cornell, Anton S. 1932- *St&PR 93*
Cornell, Carl Allin 1938- *WhoAm 92*
Cornell, Corwin David 1924- *WhoAm 92*
Cornell, Edgar 1918- *St&PR 93*
Cornell, Elizabeth *AmWomPl*
Cornell, Eugenia Ann 1943- *WhoAmW 93*
Cornell, Fred C. 1867-1921 *ScF&FL 92*
Cornell, George Ware, Jr. 1950- *WhoEmL 93*
Cornell, George Washington, II 1920- *WhoAm 92*
Cornell, Harry M. 1928- *St&PR 93*
Cornell, Howard Vernon 1947- *WhoE 93, WhoEmL 93*
Cornell, Ian Beaumont 1960- *WhoEmL 93*
Cornell, James H. *Law&B 92*
Cornell, James Mark 1953- *WhoEmL 93*
Cornell, John 1941- *MiSFD 9*
Cornell, John William 1929- *WhoE 93*
Cornell, Jorge Eduardo 1949- *WhoWor 93*
Cornell, Joseph 1903-1972 *BioIn 17*
Cornell, Karen Holley *Law&B 92*
Cornell, Keith Arthur 1957- *WhoE 93*
Cornell, Lawrence Everett 1933- *WhoE 93*
Cornell, M.K. 1936- *St&PR 93*
Cornell, Michael V. 1955- *St&PR 93*
Cornell, Minnie Jo 1926- *St&PR 93*
Cornell, Nancy Trinka 1954- *WhoEmL 93*
Cornell, Paul *ScF&FL 92*
Cornell, Paul Grant 1918- *WhoAm 92*
Cornell, Paul Harold 1952- *WhoEmL 93*
Cornell, Peter Joseph 1952- *WhoEmL 93*
Cornell, Peter McCaul 1926- *WhoAm 92*
Cornell, Ralph Lawrence, Jr. 1951- *WhoE 93, WhoEmL 93*
Cornell, Rhonda Holmes 1951- *WhoEmL 93, WhoSSW 93*
Cornell, Richard Garth 1930- *WhoAm 92*
Cornell, Robert Arthur 1936- *WhoAm 92, WhoWor 93*
Cornell, Susan E. 1948- *St&PR 93*
Cornell, Sylvia Ryce 1941- *WhoSSW 93*
Cornell, Tanis Jill 1953- *WhoEmL 93*
Cornell, Theodore Elmer 1949- *WhoEmL 93*
Cornell, Thomas Browne 1937- *WhoAm 92*
Cornell, William Daniel 1919- *WhoAm 92*
Cornell-Ohl, Susan 1955- *WhoAmW 93*
Cornell-Ohlman, Joanne Hutchison 1956- *WhoAmW 93*
Cornelsen, Paul F. 1923- *St&PR 93*
Cornelsen, Paul Frederick 1923- *WhoWor 93*
Cornelsen, Rufus 1914- *WhoAm 92*
Cornelson, George Henry 1931- *WhoAm 92*
Cornely, Paul Bertau 1906- *WhoAm 92*
Corner, Bruce E. 1949- *St&PR 93*
Corner, Ian Eric *WhoScE 91-1*
Corner, Michael A. 1933- *WhoScE 91-3*
Corner, Philip (Lionel) 1933- *Baker 92*
Corner, Richard Scott 1959- *WhoSSW 93*
Corner, William Derek 1923- *WhoWor 93*
Cornes, David Langford 1944- *WhoWor 93*
Cornet, Antonio Gaudi y 1852-1926 *BioIn 17*
Cornet, Daniel 1937- *WhoScE 91-2*
Cornet, Edward P. 1948- *St&PR 93*
Cornet, Jean-Claude Michel 1944- *St&PR 93*
Cornett, Dan E. 1949- *St&PR 93*
Cornett, Deborah K. *Law&B 92*
Cornett, Gregg 1954- *WhoSSW 93*
Cornett, Joe Delayne 1935- *WhoSSW 93*
Cornett, John David 1958- *St&PR 93*
Cornett, Laureen Elizabeth 1946- *WhoAmW 93, WhoEmL 93*
Cornett, Lawrence Eugene 1951- *WhoSSW 93*
Cornett, Lewis LaVerne 1938- *WhoSSW 93*
Cornett, Lloyd Harvey, Jr. 1930- *WhoAm 92, WhoSSW 93*
Cornett, Richard Orin 1913- *WhoAm 92*
Cornett, Robert 1952- *ScF&FL 92*
Cornett, Robert Mack 1939- *St&PR 93*
Cornett, William Forrest, Jr. 1919- *WhoAm 92*
Cornette, James Lawson 1935- *WhoAm 92*
Cornette, William Magnus 1945- *WhoAm 92*
Cornette de Saint-Cyr, Bernard 1944- *WhoWor 93*
Corney, Gerald Walter *WhoScE 91-1*
Cornez, Gerald H. 1946- *WhoAm 92, WhoEmL 93*
Cornfeld, Dave Louis 1921- *WhoAm 92*
Cornfeld, Richard Steven 1950- *WhoEmL 93*
Cornfield, Hubert 1929- *MiSFD 9*
Cornfield, Melvin 1927- *WhoAm 92*
Cornford, James *WhoScE 91-1*
Cornforth, John Warcup *WhoScE 91-1*
Cornforth, John Warcup 1917- *WhoAm 92, WhoWor 93*
Corngold, Stanley Alan 1934- *WhoAm 92*
Cornia, Giovanni Andrea 1947- *WhoUN 92*
Cornick, Glenn 1947- See Jethro Tull *ConMus 8*
Cornick, Walter Francis 1926- *St&PR 93*
Cornille, David P. *Law&B 92*
Corning, Erastus, II 1909-1983 *PolPar*
Corning, Joy Cole 1932- *WhoAm 92, WhoAmW 93*
Corning, Nathan E. 1931- *St&PR 93*
Cornish, Donovan Eugene 1930- *St&PR 93*
Cornish, Edward Seymour 1927- *WhoAm 92, WhoE 93, WhoWor 93, WhoWrEP 92*
Cornish, Elizabeth Turverey 1919- *WhoAmW 93*
Cornish, Frederick Hector John *WhoScE 91-1*
Cornish, Geoffrey St. John 1914- *WhoAm 92*
Cornish, J.P. *WhoScE 91-1*
Cornish, Jeannette Carter 1946- *WhoEmL 93*
Cornish, John Philip *WhoScE 91-1*
Cornish, Larry Brian 1946- *St&PR 93*
Cornish, Mary Taylor *AmWomPl*
Cornish, Sam 1935- *BioIn 17, BlkAull 92*
Cornish, Scott Charles 1960- *WhoEmL 93*
Cornis-Pope, Marcel Horatiu 1946- *WhoSSW 93*
Cornman, Guy Leslie, Jr. 1923- *WhoSSW 93*
Corno, Lyn 1950- *WhoE 93*
Corno di Bassetto *OxDcOp*
Cornog, Robert Andrew 1940- *St&PR 93*
Cornuelle, Herbert Cumming 1920- *WhoAm 92*
Cornum, Rhonda (Leah Scott) 1954- *ConAu 139*
Cornwall, Barry 1787-1874 *BioIn 17*
Cornwall, Deborah J. 1946- *St&PR 93*
Cornwall, Deborah Joyce 1946- *WhoAm 92, WhoAmW 93, WhoE 93, WhoEmL 93*
Cornwall, Ian W. 1909- *ScF&FL 92*
Cornwall, J. Michael 1935- *St&PR 93*
Cornwall, John *BioIn 17*
Cornwall, John 1928- *ConAu 37NR*
Cornwall, John Michael 1934- *WhoAm 92*
Cornwall, Robert Maynard 1921- *St&PR 93*
Cornwallis, Charles 1738-1805 *HarEnMi*
Cornwallis, William 1744-1819 *HarEnMi*
Cornwell, Barbara E.L. *Law&B 92*
Cornwell, Betty Ann 1954- *St&PR 93*
Cornwell, Charles Daniel 1924- *WhoAm 92*
Cornwell, David George 1927- *WhoAm 92*
Cornwell, David John Moore 1931- *BioIn 17, WhoWor 93*
Cornwell, Don 1948- *BioIn 17*
Cornwell, Gibbons Gray, III 1933- *WhoAm 92*
Cornwell, Gilbert Darwyn 1943- *St&PR 93*
Cornwell, Ilene Jones 1942- *WhoAmW 93, WhoWrEP 92*
Cornwell, Jerald Moyer 1928- *WhoAm 92*
Cornwell, Keith John *WhoScE 91-1*
Cornwell, Neil 1942- *ScF&FL 92*
Cornwell, Patricia Daniels *BioIn 17*
Cornwell, Stephen *MiSFD 9*
Cornwell, Sue *ScF&FL 92*
Cornwell, Trevor 1964- *WhoE 93*
Cornwell, W. Don *St&PR 93*
Cornwell, William David *Law&B 92*
Cornyn, John *WhoSSW 93*
Cornyn-Selby, Alyce P. 1946- *WhoWrEP 92*
Cornyn-Selby, Alyce Patricia 1946- *WhoEmL 93*
Corogin, John Solon 1925- *St&PR 93*
Corogin, Peter J. 1956- *St&PR 93*
Corominas, Jordi 1952- *WhoScE 91-3*
Coron, Hannah *ScF&FL 92*
Corona, Bert 1918- *HispAmA*
Coronado, Alejandro Gamaliel 1950- *WhoSSW 93*
Coronado, Eduardo *DcCPCAm*
Coronado, Elaine 1959- *NotHsAW 93*
Coronado, Francisco Vazquez de 1510?-1554 *Expl 93 [port]*
Coronado, Jose R. 1932- *HispAmA [port]*
Coronado, Jose Ricardo 1932- *WhoAm 92, WhoSSW 93*
Coronado, Shirley Jeanne 1948- *WhoEmL 93*
Coronado, William J. 1953- *St&PR 93*
Coronaro, Gellio (Benvenuto) 1863-1916 *Baker 92*
Coronas, Jose J. *St&PR 93*
Coronati, J. Richard *St&PR 93*
Coronel Urtecho, Jose 1906- *SpAmA*
Coroniti, Ferdinand Vincent 1943- *WhoAm 92*
Corotis, Ross Barry 1945- *WhoAm 92*
Corpi, Lucha 1945- *NotHsAW 93*
Corporon, John Robert 1929- *WhoAm 92*
Corr, Christine Ellen 1953- *WhoAmW 93*
Corr, Edwin Gharst 1934- *WhoAm 92*
Corr, Eugene *MiSFD 9*
Corr, Fitzhugh Lee 1934- *WhoAm 92*
Corr, Gary Alan 1948- *WhoAm 92*
Corr, James E., III *BioIn 17*
Corr, James Vanis 1922- *WhoAm 92*
Corr, Michael William 1940- *WhoWor 93*
Corr, Robert Mark 1948- *WhoEmL 93*
Corrada, Manuel Corrada 1953- *WhoWor 93*
Corrada del Rio, Baltasar 1935- *DcCPCAm*
Corradini, Corrado 1947- *WhoScE 91-3*
Corradini, Deedee *WhoAmW 93*
Corradino, Le Roy Michael 1932- *St&PR 93*
Corrado, Anthony Joseph, Jr. 1957- *WhoE 93*
Corrado, Fred 1940- *St&PR 93, WhoAm 92*
Corral, Edward A. 1931- *HispAmA*
Corrales, Oralia Lillie 1940- *NotHsAW 93*
Corrales, Patrick 1941- *WhoAm 92*
Corrales, William Alfred 1928- *WhoSSW 93*
Corrall, J.C. *WhoScE 91-1*
Corrallo, Carl Anthony *Law&B 92*
Corrao, Darren Joseph *Law&B 92*
Corrao, Jo Ann 1953- *WhoAmW 93*
Corrao, Richard Gaetano 1946- *WhoE 93*
Correa, Charles M. 1930- *WhoWor 93*
Correa, Craig Arthur 1959- *WhoE 93*
Correa, Diva Diniz 1918- *WhoWor 93*
Correa, Gustavo 1914- *WhoAm 92*
Correa, Jose Lucio de Araujo 1942- *WhoWor 93*
Correa, Richard A. *Law&B 92*
Correa de Arauxo, Francisco c. 1576-1654 *Baker 92*
Correa de Azevedo, Luis Heitor 1905- *Baker 92*
Correa Monge, Francisco Javier 1960- *WhoWor 93*
Correa-Prado, Bernardo 1943- *WhoWor 93*
Correa-Villasenor, Adolfo 1946- *WhoE 93, WhoEmL 93*
Correa Zapata, Dolores 1853-1924 *DcMexL*
Corredor, Livia Margarita 1960- *WhoEmL 93*
Correge, Deborah A. *Law&B 92*
Correggio c. 1489-1534 *BioIn 17*
Correia, Alberto Abrantes 1956- *WhoE 93, WhoEmL 93*
Correia, Ana Maria Ramalho *WhoScE 91-3*
Correia, Antone 1945- *St&PR 93*
Correia, Armand S. 1946- *St&PR 93*
Correia, Claudine Maria 1954- *WhoE 93*
Correia, John Arthur 1945- *WhoE 93*
Correia, John Furia 1939- *WhoE 93*
Correia, Jose Henrique Rocha Dias 1958- *WhoWor 93*
Correia De Ramalho Carlos, C.A. 1937- *WhoScE 91-3*
Correjolles, Gerald Lee *St&PR 93*
Correll, Alston Dayton, Jr. 1941- *WhoAm 92, WhoSSW 93*
Correll, Charles *MiSFD 9*
Correll, Gary Robert 1953- *WhoSSW 93*
Correll, Helen Butts 1907- *WhoAm 92, WhoAmW 93*
Correll, Joanna Rae 1948- *WhoEmL 93*
Correll, John Thomas 1939- *WhoAm 92*
Correll, Richard *MiSFD 9*
Corren, Grace *ScF&FL 92*
Correnti, John D. 1947- *St&PR 93*
Correnti, John David 1947- *WhoAm 92, WhoEmL 93, WhoSSW 93*
Correra, Francis X. 1938- *St&PR 93*
Correrini, Franco 1959- *WhoWor 93*
Correro, Anthony James, III 1941- *WhoAm 92, WhoSSW 93*
Corressel, Robert Henry 1947- *WhoE 93*
Corretjer, Juan Antonio 1908-1985 *SpAmA*
Corrette, Michel 1709-1795 *Baker 92*
Correy, Lee *ScF&FL 92*
Correze, Jacques 1912-1991 *BioIn 17*
Corri, Charles 1861-1941 *OxDcOp*
Corri, Domenico 1744-1825 *Baker 92*
Corri, Domenico 1746-1825 *OxDcOp*
Corri, Ghita 1869?-1937 *OxDcOp*
Corri, Haydn 1785-1860 See Corri, Domenico 1744-1825 *Baker 92*
Corri, Haydn Jun 1845-1876 *OxDcOp*
Corri, Henry 1822-1888 *OxDcOp*
Corri, Montague 1784-1849 See Corri, Domenico 1744-1825 *Baker 92*
Corri, Patrick Anthony 1820-1876 *OxDcOp*
Corri, Sophia Giustina 1775-c. 1828 *OxDcOp*
Corrick, Ann Marjorie *WhoAm 92*
Corrick, James A. 1913- *ScF&FL 92*
Corridori, Anthony Joseph 1961- *WhoE 93*

Corridori, Franco WhoScE 91-3
Corri Dussek, Sophia Giustina 1775-c. 1828
See Corri, Domenico 1744-1825 Baker 92
Corrie, Craig R. 1946- St&PR 93
Corrie, Craig Royal WhoIns 93
Corrie, John Roy 1945- St&PR 93
Corrie, Stephan James 1943- WhoUN 92
Corriere, Joseph N., Jr. 1937- WhoAm 92
Corrigall, Don Joseph 1929- St&PR 93
Corrigan, Alfred E. Law&B 92
Corrigan, Ann Phillips Law&B 92
Corrigan, Charles Lawrence 1936- WhoWor 93
Corrigan, Daniel Joseph 1947- WhoAm 92
Corrigan, Dennis A. 1937- St&PR 93
Corrigan, E. Gerald 1941- St&PR 93
Corrigan, Edward Thomas, Jr. Law&B 92
Corrigan, Edward William 1925- St&PR 93
Corrigan, Fredric H. 1914- WhoAm 92
Corrigan, Harold 1927- St&PR 93
Corrigan, Harold Cauldwell 1927- WhoAm 92
Corrigan, Helen Gonzalez 1922- WhoAmW 93
Corrigan, James Henry, Jr. 1926- St&PR 93, WhoAm 92
Corrigan, James John, Jr. 1935- WhoAm 92
Corrigan, John D., Jr. Law&B 92
Corrigan, John Edward 1931- WhoAm 92
Corrigan, John Edward, Jr. 1922- WhoAm 92
Corrigan, John Edward, III 1953- WhoE 93
Corrigan, John Thomas 1936- WhoWrEP 92
Corrigan, Joseph Thomas 1942- St&PR 93
Corrigan, Leo F., Jr. 1925- St&PR 93
Corrigan, Leslie S. Law&B 92
Corrigan, Lorna Sue 1956- WhoAmW 93
Corrigan, Lynda Dyann 1949- WhoAmW 93, WhoEmL 93, WhoSSW 93, WhoWor 93
Corrigan, Michael Edward 1955- WhoAm 92
Corrigan, Michael Joseph 1951- St&PR 93
Corrigan, Richard Lawrence 1940- St&PR 93
Corrigan, Robert A. BioIn 17
Corrigan, Robert Anthony 1935- WhoAm 92, WhoWor 93
Corrigan, Robert Emmett 1920- WhoWor 93
Corrigan, Robert Foster 1914- WhoAm 92
Corrigan, Robert Willoughby 1927- WhoAm 92
Corrigan, Theresa 1949- ScF&FL 92
Corrigan, Timothy Patrick Pennington Blake 1957- WhoWor 93
Corrigan, Wilfred James 1938- St&PR 93
Corrigan, William Thomas 1921- WhoAm 92
Corrigan-Bastuk, Therese Anne 1962- WhoAmW 93
Corrigan-Maguire, Mairead 1944- WhoWor 93
Corrin, Bryan WhoScE 91-1
Corrin, Sara & Corrin, Stephen ChlFicS
Corrin, Sara 1918- ScF&FL 92
Corrin, Stephen ScF&FL 92
Corrin, Stephen
See Corrin, Sara & Corrin, Stephen ChlFicS
Corrington, John William 1932- WhoWrEP 92
Corrington, Richard Fitch 1931- St&PR 93
Corriol, Jacques H. 1920- WhoScE 91-2
Corri-Paltoni, Fanny 1795?-c. 1833 OxDcOp
Corripio Ahumada, Ernesto 1919- WhoSSW 93
Corripio Ahumada, Ernesto Cardinal 1919- WhoWor 93
Corrodi, James A. Law&B 92
Corrody, Carol Ann 1957- WhoWrEP 92
Corrons Rodriguez, Antonio 1941- WhoScE 91-3
Corroon, Robert F. 1922- St&PR 93, WhoIns 93
Corrothers, Helen Gladys 1937- WhoAmW 93
Corry, Andrew Francis 1922- WhoAm 92
Corry, Bernard A. WhoScE 91-1
Corry, Carl WhoAm 92
Corry, Charles A. BioIn 17
Corry, Charles Albert 1932- St&PR 93, WhoAm 92, WhoE 93
Corry, Emmett Brother WhoAm 92, WhoE 93
Corry, James Michael 1947- WhoE 93, WhoEmL 93
Corry, John BioIn 17
Corry, Kathryn Mary 1948- WhoEmL 93
Corry, Lawrence Lee 1939- St&PR 93, WhoAm 92
Corry, Mark BioIn 17
Corry, Megan Jacobs 1958- WhoAmW 93
Corry, Robert John 1934- WhoAm 92
Cors, Allan D. 1936- St&PR 93
Cors, Francois 1948- WhoScE 91-2
Corsa, Cheryl Hoffman 1951- WhoAmW 93
Corsa, Helen Storm 1915- WhoAm 92
Corsano Leopizzi, Stefano 1928- WhoScE 91-3
Corsaro, Frank Andrew 1924- IntDcOp, WhoAm 92
Corsaro, Robert Dominic 1944- WhoE 93
Corsbie, Shirley Arnold 1963- WhoAmW 93
Corse, John Doggett Law&B 92
Corse, John Doggett 1924- WhoAm 92
Corse, Mary AmWomPl
Corse, Richard Michael 1946- WhoWor 93
Corselli, Andrew Law&B 92
Corselli, Francesco c. 1702-1778 Baker 92, OxDcOp
Corsello, Florence St&PR 93
Corser, David Hewson 1930- WhoAm 92
Corseri, Gary Steven 1946- WhoWrEP 92
Corset, Jacques WhoScE 91-2
Corset, Jacques 1935- WhoScE 91-2
Corsi, Achille 1840-1906 OxDcOp
Corsi, Deborah Eranda 1953- WhoWrEP 92
Corsi, Emilia 1870-1927 OxDcOp
Corsi, Giovanni 1822-1890 OxDcOp
Corsi, Giuseppe 1630-1690 Baker 92
Corsi, Jacopo 1560-1602 Baker 92
Corsi, Jacopo 1561-1601 OxDcOp
Corsi, Philip Donald 1928- WhoAm 92
Corsi, Pietro 1937- WhoWrEP 92
Corsiglia, Louis A. 1932- St&PR 93
Corsini, Andrew Cameron 1935- St&PR 93
Corsini, Carlo WhoScE 91-3
Corsini, Raymond Joseph 1914- WhoAm 92, WhoWrEP 92
Corso, Giuseppe Baker 92
Corso, Gregory BioIn 17
Corso, Gregory Nunzio 1930- WhoAm 92, WhoWrEP 92
Corso, Joseph R. 1908-1990 BioIn 17
Corson, Dale Raymond 1914- WhoAm 92
Corson, Don Edward 1956- WhoEmL 93
Corson, Dorthy Scheide 1927- St&PR 93
Corson, James Robert 1945- St&PR 93
Corson, John Arthur 1940- St&PR 93
Corson, John Jay 1905-1990 BioIn 17
Corson, Kenneth S. Law&B 92
Corson, Richard Howell 1931- WhoSSW 93
Corson, Robert W. 1946- St&PR 93
Corson, Thomas H. 1927- St&PR 93
Corson, Thomas Harold 1927- WhoAm 92
Corstanje, Brahm J. Law&B 92
Cort, Bud MiSFD 9
Cort, Diana 1934- WhoAmW 93
Cort, Kenneth J. 1941- St&PR 93
Cort, Ned ConAu 137
Cort, Robert BioIn 17
Cort, Winifred Mitchell 1917- WhoAm 92
Cortada, James N. 1914- WhoAm 92
Cortada, Rafael Leon 1934- WhoAm 92
Cortambert, Louis Richard 1808-1881 JrnUS
Cortazar, Julio 1914-1984 BioIn 17, ScF&FL 92, SpAmA
Cortazzi, (Henry Arthur) Hugh 1924- ConAu 39NR
Corte, Andrea della Baker 92
Corte, Jean-Francois 1951- WhoScE 91-2
Corte, Lawrence J. Law&B 92
Corte, Lawrence Julius 1954- WhoEmL 93
Corteccia, Francesco Bernardo 1502-1571 Baker 92
Cortell, Jason Merrill 1936- WhoE 93
Cortelyou, George B. 1862-1940 PolPar
Cortelyou, George Bruce 1862-1940 BioIn 17
Corten, Irina H. 1941- ConAu 137
Cortera, Martha P. 1938- NotHsAW 93 [port]
Corte-Real, Gaspar 1455?-1501 & Corte-Real, Miguel 1450?-1502 Expl 93
Corte-Real, J.A.M. 1942- WhoScE 91-3
Corte-Real, Miguel 1450?-1502
See Corte-Real, Gaspar 1455?-1501 & Corte-Real, Miguel 1450?-1502 Expl 93
Cortes, Antonio 1937- WhoScE 91-3
Cortes, Carlos E. 1934- HispAmA [port]
Cortes, Doris Janice 1956- WhoAmW 93
Cortes, Ernesto BioIn 17
Cortes, Hernan 1485-1547 BioIn 17, Expl 93 [port], HarEnMi
Cortes, Julio 1924- WhoSSW 93
Cortes, Leon DcCPCAm
Cortes, Marcos Henrique Camillo 1935- WhoWor 93
Cortes, Ramiro 1933-1984 Baker 92
Cortes, Robert 1955- WhoEmL 93
Cortes, William Patrick 1955- WhoEmL 93
Cortese, Alfred William, Jr. 1937- WhoAm 92, WhoWor 93
Cortese, Anthony D. BioIn 17
Cortese, Armand Ferdinand 1932- WhoE 93
Cortese, Diane C. Law&B 92
Cortese, Jorge Daniel 1957- WhoEmL 93
Cortese, Joseph Samuel, II 1955- WhoEmL 93
Cortese, Luigi 1899-1976 Baker 92
Cortese, Richard Anthony 1942- WhoAm 92
Cortes-Hwang, Adriana 1928- WhoE 93
Cortesi, Francesco 1826-1904 Baker 92
Cortesi, Lawrence WhoWrEP 92
Cortesi, Sergio WhoScE 91-4
Cortez, Edwin Michael 1951- WhoAm 92
Cortez, Mauro BioIn 17
Cortez, Ricardo 1899-1977 BioIn 17
Corthell, Jon R. Law&B 92
Corti, Axel 1933- MiSFD 9
Corti, Robert J. 1949- St&PR 93
Corticelli, Bruno 1921- WhoScE 91-3
Cortina, Anibal Jose Law&B 92
Cortina, Rodolfo J. 1946- HispAmA [port]
Cortinez, Veronica 1958- WhoEmL 93, WhoWor 93
Cortinovis, Dan 1947- WhoWrEP 92
Cortis, Antonio 1891-1952 Baker 92
Cortis, Louise AmWomPl
Cortissoz, Paul 1924-1991 BioIn 17
Cortner, Jean Alexander 1930- WhoAm 92
Cortney, David E. 1958- St&PR 93
Corto, Diana Maria WhoAmW 93
Cortolezis, Fritz 1878-1934 Baker 92
Cortopassi, Sandy J. Law&B 92
Cortor, Eldzier 1916- WhoAm 92
Cortot, Alfred (Denis) 1877-1962 Baker 92
Cortrera, Richard A. 1945- St&PR 93
Cortright, Barbara Jean 1927- WhoAmW 93
Cortright, Inga Ann 1949- WhoAmW 93, WhoWor 93
Cortright, Louise Vera 1938- WhoAmW 93
Cortrubas, Ileana 1939- OxDcOp
Corts, Paul Richard 1943- WhoAm 92, WhoSSW 93
Corts, Thomas Edward 1941- WhoAm 92, WhoSSW 93
Cortsen, Henry A. 1941- St&PR 93
Corum, B. H. 1933- WhoAm 92
Corum, Bill 1918- St&PR 93
Corum, James S(terling) 1953- ConAu 139
Corum, William R. Law&B 92
Corum, Wm. M. 1942- St&PR 93
Corva, Angelo Francis 1948- WhoE 93
Corvalan, Hugo Antonio 1942- WhoUN 92
Corvi, Corrado 1928- WhoScE 91-3
Corvilain, Jacques A.J. 1923- WhoScE 91-2
Corvin, Carl Dean Law&B 92
Corvino, Frank Anthony 1949- WhoE 93, WhoEmL 93
Corvino, Joseph J. 1951- St&PR 93
Corvo, Max BioIn 17
Corvo, Nicolangelo 1950- WhoEmL 93
Corvol, P. WhoScE 91-2
Corvol, Pierre 1941- WhoScE 91-2
Corwell, Ann Elizabeth WhoAmW 93
Corwin, Arthur B. 1956- St&PR 93
Corwin, Bert Clark 1930- WhoAm 92, WhoWor 93
Corwin, Bruce Charles 1963- WhoEmL 93
Corwin, Douglas Henry 1958- St&PR 93
Corwin, Edward Samuel 1878-1963 OxCSupC
Corwin, Frederic W., Jr. 1947- St&PR 93
Corwin, Hal Michael 1953- WhoEmL 93
Corwin, Joyce Elizabeth Stedman WhoAmW 93, WhoWor 93
Corwin, Judith Marie 1953- WhoAmW 93
Corwin, Jules Arthur 1946- WhoUN 92
Corwin, Laura J. Law&B 92
Corwin, Laura J. 1945- WhoAm 92
Corwin, Norman 1910- WhoAm 92
Corwin, Philip Seth 1950- WhoEmL 93
Corwin, Phillip 1936- WhoUN 92
Corwin, Rex 1935- St&PR 93
Corwin, Richard L. 1952- St&PR 93
Corwin, Ronald G(ary) 1932- WhoWrEP 92
Corwin, Scott L. 1958- St&PR 93
Corwin, Scott Laurence 1958- WhoEmL 93
Corwin, Sherman Phillip 1917- WhoAm 92
Corwin, Stanley C. Law&B 92
Corwin, Stanley Joel 1938- WhoAm 92
Corwin, Thomas Michael 1952- WhoEmL 93
Corwin, Vera-Anne Versfelt WhoAmW 93
Corwin, Walter Horton 1924- St&PR 93
Corwin, William 1908- WhoSSW 93, WhoWor 93
Corwine, David B. Law&B 92
Corwine, David Brooks 1937- St&PR 93
Cory, Anita Jessamine 1911- WhoAmW 93
Cory, Barbara Ellen 1951- WhoEmL 93
Cory, Charles Robinson 1955- WhoAm 92
Cory, Charlotte 1956- ConAu 137
Cory, Gordon Lee 1939- St&PR 93
Cory, James d1978 BioIn 17
Cory, Jeffrey 1945- WhoE 93
Cory, Jim 1953- WhoWrEP 92
Cory, Lee Troutman Law&B 92
Cory, Lee Troutman 1956- WhoAm 92
Cory, Pamela Mitchell 1962- WhoEmL 93
Cory, Paul Russell 1926- WhoAm 92
Cory, Ronald Joseph 1932- St&PR 93
Cory, Susan Elizabeth 1953- WhoEmL 93
Cory, Timothy Robert 1961- WhoEmL 93
Cory, Vivian ScF&FL 92
Cory, Walt Dennie 1934- WhoSSW 93
Cory, William Eugene 1927- WhoAm 92
Corydon, Bent ScF&FL 92
Corydon, George Patrick 1948- St&PR 93
Coryell, Kenneth M. Law&B 92
Coryell, Roger Charles 1916- WhoAm 92
Cory-Slechta, Deborah Ann 1950- WhoE 93
Corzilius, Max W. 1924- St&PR 93
Corzine, Jon Stevens 1947- WhoAm 92
Corzo, Jaime Alfonso 1951- WhoWor 93
Cosand, Joseph Parker, Jr. 1914- WhoAm 92
Cosar, Dominique Suzanne Law&B 92
Cosby, Anna Pearl BioIn 17
Cosby, Bill QDrFCA 92
Cosby, Bill 1937- BioIn 17, WhoAm 92, WhoE 93, WhoWrEP 92
Cosby, Clair Golihew 1944- WhoWrEP 92
Cosby, Donald J. Law&B 92
Cosby, Erinn BioIn 17
Cosby, John T. St&PR 93
Cosby, William F. 1939- St&PR 93
Cosby, William H., Jr. 1937- MiSFD 9
Cosby, William Henry, Jr. 1937- AfrAmBi
Coscarelli, Don 1954- MiSFD 9
Coscas, Gabriel Josue 1931- WhoWor 93
Cosden, William E., Jr. Law&B 92
Cosell, Howard 1918- WhoAm 92
Cosentino, Louis C. 1944- St&PR 93
Cosentino, Marlene Franklin Law&B 92
Cosenza, Arthur George 1924- WhoAm 92, WhoSSW 93
Cosenza, Joseph M. d1991 BioIn 17
Cosenza, Vincent John 1962- WhoE 93, WhoEmL 93
Coseo, David Paul 1936- WhoE 93
Coser, Lewis Alfred 1913- WhoAm 92
Coser, Rose Laub 1916- BioIn 17
Coseteng, Anna Dominique M.L. 1952- WhoAsAP 91
Cosford, P.R. St&PR 93
Cosgrave, Liam 1920- DcTwHis
Cosgrave, William Thomas 1880-1965 DcTwHis
Cosgriff, John P. Law&B 92
Cosgriff, Stuart Worcester 1917- WhoAm 92, WhoWor 93
Cosgrove, Beatrice Mary 1917- WhoAmW 93
Cosgrove, Emmet Lawrence 1948- WhoEmL 93
Cosgrove, Erin E. 1957- St&PR 93
Cosgrove, Howard Edward, Jr. 1943- WhoAm 92
Cosgrove, John Patrick 1918- WhoAm 92
Cosgrove, Joseph D. Law&B 92
Cosgrove, Joseph William 1947- WhoEmL 93
Cosgrove, Kathleen Ann 1958- St&PR 93
Cosgrove, Maryellen Smith 1948- WhoSSW 93
Cosgrove, Terence Joseph 1957- WhoEmL 93
Cosic, Dobrica 1921- ConAu 138
Cosier, Richard A. 1947- WhoAm 92
Cosio Pascal, Enrique 1941- WhoUN 92
Coskran, Kathleen 1943- ConAu 139
Coskun, Hudaver 1950- WhoScE 91-4
Coslet, Bruce N. 1946- WhoAm 92
Coslet, Dorothy Gawne 1924- WhoWrEP 92
Coslett, Charles Reynolds 1952- WhoEmL 93
Cosley, Jerry W. 1935- St&PR 93
Coslow, Richard David 1942- WhoAm 92, WhoE 93
Cosma, Viorel 1923- Baker 92
Cosman, Ian d1990 BioIn 17
Cosman, Jeffrey M. 1951- St&PR 93
Cosmas, George James 1929- WhoSSW 93
Cosmatos, Alexandros 1927- WhoScE 91-3
Cosmatos, George Pan 1941- MiSFD 9
Cosmetatos, George Phocas 1938- WhoWor 93
Cosmi, Ermelando Vinicio 1937- WhoWor 93

Cosmographer of Ravenna 7th cent.BC- *OxDcByz*
Cosner, Charles Kinian, Jr. 1950- *WhoEmL 93*
Cosner, Jerry Lee 1936- *St&PR 93*
Cosner, Melvin 1929- *St&PR 93*
Cosner, Shaaron 1940- *ConAu 38NR*
Cosner, Shaaron Louise 1940- *WhoWrEP 92*
Cosovic, Rade 1936- *WhoScE 91-4*
Cosper, William Huston 1948- *St&PR 93*
Cospolich, James Donald 1944- *St&PR 93*
Coss, Frank d1990 *BioIn 17*
Coss, Herbert David 1934- *St&PR 93*
Coss, John Edward 1947- *WhoEmL 93*
Cossa, Dominic 1935- *Baker 92*
Cossa, Dominic Frank 1935- *WhoAm 92*
Cosse, R. Paul 1956- *WhoEmL 93, WhoSSW 93, WhoWor 93*
Cosse, Steven A. *Law&B 92*
Cossette, Pierre *WhoAm 92*
Cossetto, Emil 1918- *Baker 92*
Cossi, Lidia A. *Law&B 92*
Cossi, Olga *BioIn 17*
Cossiga, Francesco 1928- *WhoWor 93*
Cossins, Edwin Albert 1937- *WhoAm 92*
Cossitt, James Henry 1957- *WhoEmL 93*
Cossman, Joanne Patricia Tully 1949- *WhoEmL 93*
Cossmann, Bernhard 1822-1910 *Baker 92*
Cossons, Neil 1939- *WhoWor 93*
Cossotto, Fiorenza 1935- *Baker 92, OxDcOp, WhoAm 92, WhoWor 93*
Cossutta, Carlo 1932- *Baker 92, IntDcOp, OxDcOp*
Cost, James Peter 1923- *WhoAm 92*
Cost, John Joseph 1934- *WhoAm 92*
Cost, Thomas *MiSFD 9*
Costa, Alberto 1951- *WhoScE 91-3*
Costa, Antoinette Geraldine 1956- *WhoAmW 93*
Costa, Catherine M. *Law&B 92*
Costa, Ciulio F. 1939- *WhoScE 91-3*
Costa, Dominic P. *Law&B 92*
Costa, Don 1925-1983 *Baker 92*
Costa, Donna Marie 1955- *WhoAmW 93*
Costa, Erminio 1924- *WhoAm 92, WhoE 93*
Costa, Ernest Fiorenzo 1926- *WhoAm 92*
Costa, Fernando 1953- *WhoEmL 93*
Costa, G.M. *WhoScE 91-3*
Costa, Gilberto Jose Ferreira 1948- *WhoWor 93*
Costa, Giovanni 1930- *WhoScE 91-3*
Costa, Gustavo 1930- *WhoAm 92*
Costa, Helen Marie 1951- *WhoWrEP 92*
Costa, Jaunita 1948- *St&PR 93*
Costa, John Joseph 1922- *St&PR 93*
Costa, Judith Ann 1928- *WhoAmW 93*
Costa, Judith Bloomquist 1954- *WhoAmW 93*
Costa, Kathy 1933- *WhoAmW 93*
Costa, Lucio Guido 1954- *WhoEmL 93*
Costa, Luis Chaves da 1952- *WhoWor 93*
Costa, Manuel Antone 1933- *WhoSSW 93*
Costa, Mary *WhoAmW 93*
Costa, Mary 1932- *Baker 92*
Costa, Max *WhoScE 91-2*
Costa, Michael 1808-1884 *OxDcOp*
Costa, Michael (Andrew Agnus) 1806-1884 *Baker 92*
Costa, Pat Vincent 1943- *St&PR 93, WhoAm 92*
Costa, Paul I. 1933- *WhoScE 91-2*
Costa, Richard Hauer 1921- *ScF&FL 92*
Costa, Robert Richard 1928- *WhoAm 92*
Costa, Santo Joseph *Law&B 92*
Costa, Thomas E. *Law&B 92*
Costa, Victor Charles 1935- *WhoAm 92*
Costa Aguiar, Joao Baptista da 1947- *BioIn 17*
Costabel, Martin 1948- *WhoWor 93*
Costabel, Pierre 1912-1989 *BioIn 17*
Costacurta, Angelo 1941- *WhoScE 91-3*
Costa du Rels, Adolfo 1887-1980 *SpAmA*
Costa Ferreira, Jose d1991 *BioIn 17*
Costa-Gaudiosi, Roberta Frances 1952- *WhoEmL 93*
Costa-Gavras *MiSFD 9*
Costagliola, Francesco 1917- *WhoE 93, WhoWor 93*
Costagliola, John 1962- *St&PR 93*
Costagliola, Robert J. *Law&B 92*
Costaguta, Attilio Arrigo 1946- *WhoUN 92*
Costain, Michael Douglas 1954- *WhoSSW 93*
Costain, Robert George 1939- *St&PR 93*
Costakis, George 1912-1990 *BioIn 17*
Costa Lopes, Martinho da d1991 *BioIn 17*
Costa-Lopez, Jose 1936- *WhoScE 91-3*
Costa Mendez, Nicanor 1922-1992 *NewYTBS 92*
Costantini, Alfiero 1918- *WhoScE 91-3*
Costantini, Anthony Joseph *Law&B 92*
Costantini, Antonio 1938- *WhoWor 93*
Costantini, Humberto *BioIn 17*
Costantini, Humberto 1924-1987 *SpAmA*
Costantini, Lana Ellen 1955- *WhoEmL 93*
Costantini, William P. *Law&B 92*
Costantini, William Paul 1947- *St&PR 93*
Costantino, Giuseppe 1937- *WhoE 93*
Costantino, Lorine Protzman 1921- *WhoAmW 93*
Costantino, Mark A. 1920-1990 *BioIn 17*
Costanza, Angelo Anthony 1926- *St&PR 93*
Costanza, Margaret Midge 1932- *WhoAm 92*
Costanza, Tony *BioIn 17*
Costanzi, Giovanni Battista 1704-1778 *OxDcOp*
Costanzo, Frank T. 1948- *St&PR 93*
Costanzo, Hilda Alba *WhoAm 92*
Costanzo, Nanci Joy 1947- *WhoAmW 93*
Costanzo, Richard Michael 1947- *WhoSSW 93*
Costanzo, W. Kenneth 1952- *St&PR 93*
Costa-Pierce, Barry Allen 1954- *WhoWor 93*
Costar, Deborah Jeanne 1958- *WhoAmW 93*
Costas, Bob *NewYTBS 92 [port]*
Costas, Bob 1952- *WhoAm 92*
Costas, Menelaos *WhoScE 91-1*
Costas, Peter Louis 1931- *WhoE 93*
Costas, Robert Quinlan 1952- *WhoAm 92, WhoE 93*
Costea, Ileana 1947- *WhoWor 93*
Costea, Nicolas Vincent 1927- *WhoAm 92*
Coste-Floret, Paul 1911-1979 *BioIn 17*
Costela, Angel 1947- *WhoWor 93*
Costeley, Guillaume c. 1531-1606 *Baker 92*
Costellese, Linda E. Grace 1950- *WhoAm 92*
Costello, A.M. *St&PR 93*
Costello, Albert J. 1935- *St&PR 93*
Costello, Albert Joseph 1935- *WhoAm 92, WhoE 93*
Costello, Allan John 1956- *St&PR 93*
Costello, Amelia Fusco 1946- *WhoE 93, WhoEmL 93*
Costello, Arthur N. 1924- *St&PR 93*
Costello, Charles Francis, Jr. *Law&B 92*
Costello, Charles H. 1907- *St&PR 93*
Costello, Cheryl A. *Law&B 92*
Costello, Christine Ann 1958- *WhoAm 92*
Costello, Cynthia Ann 1952- *WhoE 93, WhoEmL 93*
Costello, Daniel Brian 1950- *WhoEmL 93*
Costello, Daniel Walter 1930- *WhoAm 92*
Costello, David L. 1951- *St&PR 93*
Costello, Dawn Elizabeth Barnes 1940- *WhoAmW 93*
Costello, Dolores 1905-1979 *IntDcF 2-3*
Costello, Dorothy Stassun *Law&B 92*
Costello, Dorothy Stassun 1954- *St&PR 93*
Costello, Eileen Marie 1949- *WhoEmL 93*
Costello, Elvis 1954- *Baker 92, WhoAm 92*
Costello, George B. *Law&B 92*
Costello, Gerald Michael 1931- *WhoAm 92*
Costello, J. Robert 1918- *St&PR 93*
Costello, James A. *Law&B 92*
Costello, James Joseph 1930- *St&PR 93, WhoAm 92*
Costello, James Paul 1953- *WhoEmL 93*
Costello, Jerry *BioIn 17*
Costello, Jerry F. 1949- *CngDr 91, WhoAm 92*
Costello, John B. 1936- *St&PR 93*
Costello, John Francis *Law&B 92*
Costello, John Francis, Jr. 1935- *WhoAm 92*
Costello, John H., III 1947- *WhoAm 92, WhoEmL 93, WhoWor 93*
Costello, John K. *Law&B 92*
Costello, John Michael, Jr. 1961- *WhoEmL 93*
Costello, John Richard 1954- *WhoEmL 93*
Costello, John Robert 1942- *WhoAm 92, WhoWor 93*
Costello, John Robert 1947- *WhoEmL 93, WhoSSW 93*
Costello, Joseph *St&PR 93*
Costello, Joseph Ball 1953- *St&PR 93*
Costello, Joseph Mark, III 1940- *WhoAm 92*
Costello, Joseph Oren *Law&B 92*
Costello, Lou *IntDcF 2-3*
Costello, Lou d1959 *BioIn 17*
Costello, Lou 1906-1959 *See* Abbott, Bud 1895-1974 *IntDcF 2-3*
Costello, Lou 1906-1959 *See* Abbott, Bud 1895-1974 & Costello, Lou 1906-1959 *QDrFCA 92*
Costello, Margaret Claire 1956- *WhoAmW 93*
Costello, Marilyn C. *WhoAm 92*
Costello, Mark *Law&B 92*
Costello, Mark Gregory 1960- *WhoEmL 93*
Costello, Matthew J. 1948- *ScF&FL 92*
Costello, Maurice 1877-1950 *IntDcF 2-3*
Costello, Michael J. *Law&B 92*
Costello, Michael Joseph 1952- *WhoEmL 93*
Costello, Pat d1990 *BioIn 17*
Costello, Patrick Raymond 1948- *St&PR 93*
Costello, Peter 1946- *ScF&FL 92*
Costello, Richard H. *Law&B 92*
Costello, Richard Neumann 1943- *WhoAm 92*
Costello, Robert Ersil *Law&B 92*
Costello, Robert L. 1951- *St&PR 93*
Costello, Robert Michael 1940- *WhoE 93*
Costello, Russell Hill 1904- *WhoAm 92*
Costello, Sean *ScF&FL 92*
Costello, Thomas Joseph 1929- *WhoAm 92*
Costello, Thomas M., Jr. *Law&B 92*
Costello, Thomas Murray 1950- *WhoAm 92*
Costello, Thomas Patrick 1931- *St&PR 93, WhoAm 92*
Costello, Timothy James *Law&B 92*
Costelloe, Brian E. *WhoScE 91-1*
Costenbader, Charles Michael 1935- *WhoE 93*
Costenoble, Philostene *ConAu 40NR*
Coster, Wendy Jane 1948- *WhoAmW 93*
Costermans, J. 1935- *WhoScE 91-2*
Costes, Alain *WhoScE 91-2*
Costes, Alain 1939- *WhoScE 91-2*
Costes, Claude Roger 1933- *WhoScE 91-2*
Costes, Nicholas Constantine 1926- *WhoAm 92*
Costet, Jean 1927- *WhoScE 91-2*
Costi, Jack 1946- *St&PR 93*
Costie, Candy *BioIn 17*
Costigan, Alexander James 1944- *St&PR 93*
Costigan, Constance Frances 1935- *WhoAm 92*
Costigan, Edward John 1914- *WhoAm 92, WhoWor 93*
Costigan, Giovanni 1905-1990 *BioIn 17*
Costigan, John Mark *Law&B 92*
Costigan, John Mark 1942- *St&PR 93, WhoAm 92*
Costigan, William D., Jr. *Law&B 92*
Costikyan, Edward Nazar 1924- *WhoAm 92*
Costikyan, Granger 1907- *St&PR 93*
Costikyan, Greg 1959- *ScF&FL 92, WhoE 93*
Costikyan-Waite, Janet F. 1955- *WhoIns 93*
Costilla, Miguel Hidalgo y 1753-1811 *BioIn 17*
Costin, Eugene 1935- *St&PR 93*
Costin, George Miron 1934- *WhoScE 91-4*
Costin, J. Laurence 1941- *St&PR 93*
Costin, Michael Craig 1947- *St&PR 93*
Costle, Douglas Michael 1939- *WhoE 93*
Costley, Bill 1942- *WhoWrEP 92*
Costley, Gary Edward 1943- *St&PR 93, WhoAm 92*
Costley, Jennifer L. 1956- *WhoEmL 93*
Costlow, Curt C. 1942- *St&PR 93*
Costner, Kevin *BioIn 17*
Costner, Kevin 1955- *HolBB [port], IntDcF 2-3 [port], MiSFD 9, WhoAm 92*
Coston, Ann Sorg d1991 *BioIn 17*
Coston, James E. 1955- *WhoEmL 93*
Costonis, Maureen Needham 1938- *WhoSSW 93*
Costopoulos, Eve *Law&B 92*
Costopoulos, Stelios 1932- *WhoScE 91-3*
Costrell, Louis 1915- *WhoAm 92*
Costrell, Robert Michael 1950- *WhoEmL 93*
Cosulich, Paolo Ulisse 1916- *WhoWor 93*
Cosway, Richard 1742-1821 *BioIn 17*
Cosway, Richard 1917- *WhoAm 92*
Cot, Pierre 1895-1977 *BioIn 17*
Cota, A. James 1947- *St&PR 93*
Cota, John Francis 1924- *WhoAm 92*
Cota-Cardenas, Margarita 1941- *DcLB 122 [port]*
Cotanch, Stephen Robert 1947- *WhoSSW 93*
Cotand, Gilbert 1934- *WhoUN 92*
Cotant, Marilyn Jean 1950- *WhoEmL 93*
Cotapos (Baeza), Acario 1889-1969 *Baker 92*
Cotchett, Joseph Winters 1939- *WhoAm 92, WhoWor 93*
Cote, Charles R. 1960- *St&PR 93*
Cote, Denis 1954- *ScF&FL 92, WhoCanL 92*
Cote, Henri G. 1914- *St&PR 93*
Cote, Jean-Eudes 1942- *St&PR 93*
Cote, Joseph A.C. 1939- *St&PR 93*
Cote, Louise Roseann 1959- *WhoAm 92, WhoAmW 93, WhoEmL 93*
Cote, Normand *WhoCanL 92*
Cote, Paul O. 1941- *St&PR 93*
Cote, Pierre 1926- *St&PR 93, WhoAm 92*
Cote, Ralph Warren 1927- *WhoWor 93*
Cote, Richard Norman 1945- *WhoSSW 93*
Cote, Rick 1946- *St&PR 93*
Cote, Robert Andrew 1958- *WhoEmL 93*
Cote, Roger Burton 1949- *WhoEmL 93*
Cote, Sally Spilker 1946- *WhoEmL 93*
Cote, Stephen M. 1955- *St&PR 93*
Cote, William Alfred 1942- *St&PR 93*
Cotek, Pavel 1922- *Baker 92*
Cotelingam, James Dwarkanath 1941- *WhoE 93*
Cotellessa, Robert Francis 1923- *WhoAm 92*
Cote-O'Hara, Jocelyne M. 1945- *St&PR 93*
Cotey, David E. *Law&B 92*
Cotham, John T. 1951- *St&PR 93*
Cotherman, Audrey Mathews 1930- *WhoAmW 93*
Cothern, Stanley C. 1942- *St&PR 93*
Cothorn, John Arthur 1939- *WhoAm 92*
Cothran, Anne Jennette 1952- *WhoAmW 93*
Cothran, Bettina Kluth 1952- *WhoEmL 93, WhoSSW 93*
Cothran, Jack T. *Law&B 92*
Cothran, Tilman Christopher 1918- *WhoAm 92*
Cothran, William T. 1946- *St&PR 93*
Cothren, J.W. 1947- *St&PR 93*
Cothren, Michael Watt 1951- *WhoE 93*
Cothren, Phillis Ann McKiddy 1948- *WhoAmW 93*
Coti, Ralph 1952- *WhoE 93*
Coticchia, Michael Louis *Law&B 92*
Cotier, Ralph 1936- *WhoE 93*
Cotignola, Desiree Rose 1959- *WhoE 93*
Cotignola, Joyce V. *Law&B 92*
Cotillon, Pierre 1933- *WhoScE 91-2*
Cotlar, Morton 1928- *WhoAm 92*
Cotler, Jay 1951- *St&PR 93*
Cotler, Joanna 1954- *WhoAm 92*
Cotler, Joseph D. d1990 *BioIn 17*
Cotler, Leslie B. 1938- *St&PR 93*
Cotler, Marvin Aaron 1932- *WhoE 93*
Cotlov, Jerry L. 1951- *St&PR 93*
Cotlov, Jerry Louis 1951- *WhoEmL 93*
Cotman, Danna Jenine 1968- *WhoAmW 93*
Cotman, John Martin Matthew 1953- *WhoEmL 93*
Cotner, C. Beth 1952- *St&PR 93*
Cotner, Carol Beth 1952- *WhoEmL 93*
Cotner, Kathleen Yvonne 1963- *WhoEmL 93*
Cotner, Mary Y. 1952- *St&PR 93*
Cotner, Roger Garner 1952- *WhoEmL 93*
Cotney, Carol Ann 1957- *WhoAmW 93*
Cotogni, Antonio 1831-1918 *Baker 92, OxDcOp*
Coton, Carlos David 1950- *WhoEmL 93, WhoSSW 93*
Coton, Luis Donovan 1947- *WhoEmL 93*
Cotros, Charles H. 1937- *WhoAm 92*
Cotrubas, Ileana *WhoAm 92, WhoWor 93*
Cotrubas, Ileana 1939- *Baker 92, IntDcOp*
Cotruvo, Joseph Alfred 1942- *WhoAm 92, WhoE 93*
Cotsen, Lloyd E. 1929- *BioIn 17, St&PR 93*
Cotsonas, Nicholas John, Jr. 1919- *WhoAm 92*
Cotsonis, Theodore 1956- *WhoWor 93*
Cotsworth, J.B. 1925- *St&PR 93*
Cott, Jonathan 1942- *ScF&FL 92*
Cott, Joseph H. *Law&B 92*
Cotta, Joe M. 1906- *St&PR 93*
Cottam, Grant 1918- *WhoAm 92*
Cottam, Keith M. 1941- *WhoAm 92*
Cottarelci, Carlo 1954- *WhoUN 92*
Cotte, Gerard 1929- *WhoScE 91-2*
Cotten, Catheryn Deon 1952- *WhoAmW 93, WhoEmL 93*
Cotten, Joseph *WhoAm 92*
Cotten, Joseph 1905- *IntDcF 2-3 [port]*
Cotten, Martha Lanier 1928- *WhoAmW 93*
Cotten, Samuel Richard 1946- *WhoAm 92*
Cotten-Huston, Annie Laura 1923- *WhoAmW 93, WhoE 93*
Cottenie, A.H. 1919- *WhoScE 91-2*
Cotter, Berchmans Paul, Jr. 1937- *WhoAm 92*
Cotter, Clifton Joseph 1926- *St&PR 93*
Cotter, Daniel A. 1934- *St&PR 93, WhoAm 92*
Cotter, Donald R. d1991 *BioIn 17*
Cotter, Douglas Adrian 1943- *WhoE 93*
Cotter, E. Robert 1951- *St&PR 93*
Cotter, Ernest Robert, III 1951- *WhoAm 92*
Cotter, Gary William 1947- *WhoEmL 93*
Cotter, George Edward 1918- *WhoAm 92*
Cotter, H. Barton 1940- *WhoIns 93*
Cotter, James Michael 1942- *WhoAm 92, WhoE 93, WhoWor 93*
Cotter, John *ScF&FL 92*
Cotter, John d1991 *BioIn 17*
Cotter, John Burley 1946- *WhoSSW 93*
Cotter, John Lambert 1911- *IntDcAn*
Cotter, Joseph Francis 1927- *WhoAm 92*
Cotter, Mary Carole *Law&B 92*

Cotter, Patricia M. Law&B 92
Cotter, Paul Barry, Jr. 1949- WhoE 93
Cotter, Richard J. 1928- St&PR 93
Cotter, Susan Mary 1943- WhoAmW 93
Cotter, Thomas Michael Law&B 92
Cotter, Veronica Irene 1949- WhoAmW 93
Cotter, Vincent P. 1927- St&PR 93
Cotter, Vincent Paul 1927- WhoAm 92
Cotter, William Dennis Law&B 92
Cotter, William Donald 1921- WhoAm 92
Cotter, William Joseph 1921- WhoAm 92
Cotter, William Joseph 1952- WhoEmL 93
Cotter, William Reckling 1936- WhoAm 92
Cotterill, Carl Hayden 1918- WhoAm 92
Cotterill, David Lee 1937- St&PR 93, WhoAm 92
Cotterill, Rodney Michael John 1933- WhoScE 91-2
Cotterill, Sarah L. 1948- WhoWrEP 92
Cotterman, William Woods 1935- WhoSSW 93
Cotterrell, David WhoScE 91-1
Cotti, Flavio WhoScE 91-4
Cotti, Flavio 1939- WhoWor 93
Cotti, Gianfranco 1929- WhoWor 93
Cottick, William Law&B 92
Cottin, Sophie 1770-1807 BioIn 17
Cotting, James Charles 1933- St&PR 93, WhoAm 92, WhoWor 93
Cottingham, James P. 1943- St&PR 93
Cottingham, Marion Scott 1948- WhoWor 93
Cottingham, Mary Patricia 1930- WhoAmW 93
Cottingham, Stephen Kent 1951- WhoEmL 93, WhoSSW 93
Cottingham, Susan Marie 1950- WhoEmL 93
Cottingham, William B. 1933- St&PR 93
Cottingham, William Bryan, Jr. 1946- WhoEmL 93
Cottington, Linda Renee 1948- WhoAmW 93, WhoEmL 93
Cottle, Anne Elizabeth 1966- WhoAmW 93
Cottle, Doris Janell 1940- WhoAmW 93
Cottle, Gail 1951- St&PR 93
Cottle, James Garlon, Jr. 1952- WhoSSW 93
Cottle, John V. Law&B 92
Cottle, John V. 1936- St&PR 93
Cottle, Robert Duquemin 1935- WhoAm 92, WhoE 93
Cottle, Susan Kara 1961- WhoAmW 93
Cottle, William Andrew 1941- WhoE 93
Cotton, Albert E. 1939- St&PR 93
Cotton, Aylett Borel 1913- WhoAm 92
Cotton, Bruce C. 1931- St&PR 93
Cotton, Bruce Conway 1931- WhoAm 92
Cotton, Carolina SweetSg C [port]
Cotton, Donald ScF&FL 92
Cotton, Donald Lloyd 1914- St&PR 93
Cotton, Dorothy Foreman WhoAm 92
Cotton, Douglas L. 1940- St&PR 93
Cotton, Eddie d1990 BioIn 17
Cotton, Eileen Giuffre 1947- WhoAmW 93
Cotton, Eugene 1914- WhoAm 92
Cotton, Frank Albert 1930- WhoAm 92
Cotton, Gary Douglas 1940- St&PR 93
Cotton, James 1938- WhoAm 92
Cotton, James A. Law&B 92
Cotton, Jane Law&B 92
Cotton, Jean-Pierre Aime 1941- WhoWor 93
Cotton, John Baker 92
Cotton, John 1584-1652 BioIn 17
Cotton, John 1938- WhoAm 92
Cotton, Jose Edmondson ScF&FL 92
Cotton, Julie A. Law&B 92
Cotton, Raymond WhoScE 91-1
Cotton, Richard Law&B 92
Cotton, Richard 1944- WhoAm 92
Cotton, Stapleton 1773-1865 HarEnMi
Cotton, Vincent John, Jr. 1957- WhoEmL 93
Cotton, William Robert 1931- WhoAm 92
Cottone, Benedict Peter 1909- WhoAm 92
Cottone, Francis John 1929- WhoE 93
Cottone, James Anthony 1947- WhoEmL 93
Cottongame, Charlotte Brock 1947- WhoEmL 93
Cottonis, Johannis Baker 92
Cottony, Herman Vladimir 1909- WhoAm 92
Cottrau, Giulio 1831-1916
See Cottrau, Teodoro 1827-1879 Baker 92
Cottrau, Guglielmo Louis 1797-1847
See Cottrau, Teodoro 1827-1879 Baker 92
Cottrau, Teodoro 1827-1879 Baker 92
Cottrell, Alan BioIn 17
Cottrell, Arthur J. Law&B 92
Cottrell, Comer J. 1931- St&PR 93
Cottrell, Comer J., Jr. 1931- AfrAmBi [port]
Cottrell, Donald P. 1902-1991 BioIn 17
Cottrell, Donrita Y. Law&B 92
Cottrell, Frank S. 1942- St&PR 93
Cottrell, Frank Stewart Law&B 92
Cottrell, Frank Stewart 1942- WhoAm 92
Cottrell, G. Walton 1939- WhoAm 92
Cottrell, Glen Alfred WhoScE 91-1
Cottrell, J. Thomas, Jr. 1925- St&PR 93
Cottrell, James Edward 1933- St&PR 93
Cottrell, Jane R. Law&B 92
Cottrell, Janet Ann 1943- WhoAmW 93
Cottrell, Jeannette Elizabeth 1923- WhoAmW 93
Cottrell, Mary-Patricia Tross 1934- WhoAm 92, WhoAmW 93
Cottrell, Paul 1951- WhoEmL 93
Cottrell, Wilbert Curtis, Jr. 1933- St&PR 93
Cottrill, Tim 1958- ScF&FL 92
Cotts, Cynthia L. 1958- WhoWrEP 92
Cotts, Robert Milo 1927- WhoE 93
Cottu, Jean-Paul 1939- WhoScE 91-2
Cotumaccio, Philip Walter 1948- St&PR 93
Coty, Francois 1874-1934 BioIn 17
Coty, Rene 1882-1962 BioIn 17
Couch, B. Joyce 1954- WhoAmW 93
Couch, Darius S. 1822-1897 HarEnMi
Couch, George Walter, III 1947- WhoEmL 93
Couch, Harvey Crowley, III 1936- WhoAm 92
Couch, J. O. Terrell 1920- WhoAm 92
Couch, James Houston 1919- WhoAm 92
Couch, James Russell 1901-1991 BioIn 17
Couch, James Russell, Jr. 1939- WhoAm 92
Couch, Janeen Melvina 1954- WhoAmW 93
Couch, Jesse Wadsworth 1921- WhoAm 92
Couch, John Charles 1939- St&PR 93, WhoAm 92
Couch, Johnson 1943- St&PR 93
Couch, Margaret Wheland 1941- WhoAm 92, WhoSSW 93
Couch, Michael Jaye 1952- St&PR 93
Couch, Richard W. d1991 BioIn 17
Couch, Robert Barnard 1930- WhoAm 92
Couch, Robert Chesley 1930- WhoSSW 93
Couch, Robert Franklin 1947- WhoE 93
Couch, Robin Dale Law&B 92
Couch, Tommy SoulM
Couch, William Garrant, Jr. 1952- WhoE 93
Couchman, Donald Louis 1931- St&PR 93
Couchman, Peter Robert 1947- WhoE 93
Couchman, Robert George James 1937- WhoAm 92
Couchoud-Gregori, Milagros 1944- WhoScE 91-3
Coucouzis, Demetrios A. 1911- WhoAm 92
Coudanne, Hubert 1924- WhoScE 91-2
Coudenhove-Kalergi, R.N. von 1894-1972 DcTwHis
Couderc WhoScE 91-2
Coudert, Allison Moore d1991 BioIn 17
Coudert, Ferdinand Wilmerding 1909- WhoAm 92
Coudert, Jean-Michel A. 1953- WhoScE 91-2
Coudert, Rene John 1936- WhoE 93
Coudert, Victor Raphael, Jr. 1926- WhoAm 92, WhoE 93
Coudray, Jean-Marc ConAu 138
Coudray, Michel WhoScE 91-2
Coudriet, Charles Edward 1946- St&PR 93, WhoAm 92, WhoE 93
Coudurier, Diane L. Law&B 92
Coues, W. Pearce St&PR 93
Coufal, Franz Anton 1927- WhoWor 93
Coufal, Ronald Louis 1952- WhoSSW 93
Couffer, Jack MiSFD 9
Couffer, Jack 1924- ScF&FL 92
Couffin, Callixte 1922- WhoScE 91-2
Cougar, John 1951- WhoAm 92
Couger, James Daniel 1929- WhoAm 92
Coughlan, Brendan 1940- WhoScE 91-3
Coughlan, Gary Patrick 1944- St&PR 93, WhoAm 92
Coughlan, John Appleby 1929- WhoAm 92
Coughlan, Joseph D. Law&B 92
Coughlan, Kenneth Lewis 1940- WhoAm 92
Coughlan, Michael P. 1940- WhoScE 91-3
Coughlan, Patrick Campbell 1940- WhoAm 92
Coughlan, Raymond T. 1936- St&PR 93
Coughlan, (John) Robert 1914- WhoWrEP 92
Coughlan, William David 1946- WhoAm 92, WhoEmL 93
Coughlin, Barring 1913- WhoAm 92
Coughlin, Caroline Mary 1944- WhoAmW 93, WhoE 93
Coughlin, Charles E. 1891-1979 PolPar
Coughlin, Colleen 1962- WhoEmL 93
Coughlin, Daniel J. 1940- St&PR 93
Coughlin, Francis Raymond, Jr. 1927- WhoAm 92, WhoE 93
Coughlin, Jack 1932- WhoAm 92
Coughlin, James P. St&PR 93
Coughlin, James Porter 1938- St&PR 93
Coughlin, Joseph P. 1934- St&PR 93
Coughlin, Lawrence CngDr 91
Coughlin, Lawrence 1929- WhoAm 92, WhoE 93
Coughlin, Magdalen 1930- WhoAm 92
Coughlin, Paul A. 1954- St&PR 93
Coughlin, Peter Joseph 1952- WhoE 93, WhoEmL 93
Coughlin, Sabrina M. Law&B 92
Coughlin, T(homas) Glen 1958- ConAu 136
Coughlin, Terrance J. 1948- WhoEmL 93
Coughlin, Thomas Joseph 1943- WhoAm 92
Coughlin, Thomas Martin 1949- St&PR 93
Coughlin, Thomas Patrick 1954- WhoEmL 93
Coughlin, Thomas Stanley 1942- St&PR 93
Coughlin, Timothy Crathorne 1942- WhoAm 92
Coughlin, Vincent J., Jr. Law&B 92
Coughlin, William J(eremiah) 1929?-1992 ConAu 139
Coughlin-Wilkins, Kathleen M. A. T. 1953- WhoAmW 93
Coughlon, Tim 1951- St&PR 93
Coughman, Susan BioIn 17
Coughran, Bruce Edward 1955- WhoEmL 93
Coughran, Jeffrey Adams 1955- WhoSSW 93
Coughran, Tom Bristol 1906- WhoAm 92, WhoWor 93
Cougill, Roscoe McDaniel 1941- WhoAm 92
Couillard, Reynald St&PR 93
Coukart, Edward A. 1943- St&PR 93
Coukis, Peter George 1955- WhoE 93
Coulbeck, Bryan WhoScE 91-1
Coulbourn, Thomas Edgar 1940- St&PR 93
Couliano, I.P. ScF&FL 92
Coulier, David BioIn 17
Coulier, Patrick 1958- WhoWor 93
Coull, Alexander WhoScE 91-1
Coulman, George Albert 1930- WhoAm 92
Coulomb, Philippe Jean 1941- WhoScE 91-2
Coulomb, Pierre 1929- WhoScE 91-2
Coulombe, Andre Normand 1953- WhoEmL 93
Coulombe, Cecile 1925- St&PR 93
Coulombe, Lynn Catherine 1956- WhoE 93
Coulombe, Raymond R. 1924- St&PR 93
Coulon, Daniel 1945- WhoScE 91-2
Coulon, Gerard 1950- WhoScE 91-2
Coulon, Michel J.-P. 1942- WhoScE 91-2
Coulouris, George F. WhoScE 91-1
Coulson, Donna Sackett 1949- WhoWrEP 92
Coulson, Edmund BioIn 17
Coulson, J. Philip 1949- WhoIns 93
Coulson, Jack Richard 1931- WhoE 93
Coulson, Jimmie T.G. 1933- St&PR 93
Coulson, John Selden 1915- WhoAm 92
Coulson, Juanita 1933- ScF&FL 92
Coulson, Kinsell Leroy 1916- WhoAm 92
Coulson, Lesley BioIn 17
Coulson, Patricia Bunker 1942- WhoAm 92
Coulson, R.J. WhoScE 91-4
Coulson, Robert 1924- St&PR 93, WhoAm 92, WhoE 93
Coulson, Robert 1928- ScF&FL 92
Coulson, Roland Armstrong 1915- WhoSSW 93
Coulson, Tracy Noreen 1957- WhoEmL 93
Coulson, William R. 1933- BioIn 17
Coulson, William Roy 1949- WhoEmL 93
Coulson, Zoe Elizabeth 1932- St&PR 93, WhoAmW 93
Coult, John H. Law&B 92
Coultas, James C. 1921- St&PR 93, WhoAm 92
Coulter, Andrew I. Law&B 92
Coulter, Barbara Clare 1950- WhoEmL 93
Coulter, Calvin Warren Law&B 92
Coulter, Carleton, III 1932- WhoSSW 93
Coulter, Catherine ConAu 139
Coulter, Charles Roy 1940- WhoAm 92
Coulter, Deborah Ann 1952- WhoEmL 93
Coulter, Don Allen 1940- WhoWor 93
Coulter, Edith Isham AmWomPl
Coulter, Elizabeth Jackson 1919- WhoAm 92, WhoAmW 93, WhoWor 93
Coulter, Harris L. 1932- ConAu 136
Coulter, Jack Benson, Jr. 1947- WhoEmL 93, WhoSSW 93
Coulter, James Bennett 1920- WhoAm 92
Coulter, John Breitling 1891- HarEnMi
Coulter, John Breitling, III 1941- WhoSSW 93, WhoWor 93
Coulter, John Richard 1930- WhoAsAP 91
Coulter, Jon E. 1958- St&PR 93
Coulter, Julia Holloway 1963- WhoSSW 93
Coulter, Kyle Jane 1937- WhoAmW 93
Coulter, Murray Whitfield 1932- WhoSSW 93
Coulter, Myron Lee 1929- WhoAm 92, WhoSSW 93
Coulter, N(orman) Arthur, Jr. 1920- WhoWrEP 92
Coulter, Norman Arthur, Jr. 1920- WhoAm 92
Coulter, Paul David Todd 1938- WhoAm 92
Coulter, Paul L. Law&B 92
Coulter, Philip Wylie 1938- WhoAm 92
Coulter, Richard 1827?-1908 BioIn 17
Coulter, Thomas Henry 1911- St&PR 93
Coulter, William Alexander 1849-1936 BioIn 17
Coulter, William Goddard 1928- WhoE 93
Coulter, William John 1934- St&PR 93
Coulter Family BioIn 17
Coulthard, Jean BioIn 17
Coulthard, Jean 1908- Baker 92
Coulton, Babette Norreen 1938- WhoAmW 93
Coulton, Martha Jean Glasscoe 1927- WhoAmW 93
Coultrap-McQuin, Susan (M.) 1947- ConAu 137
Coultry, Barbara A. 1945- WhoWrEP 92
Coumoulos, Demetrios George 1937- WhoWor 93
Counceller, John 1946- St&PR 93
Counce-Nicklas, Sheila Jean 1927- WhoAm 92
Council, Brenda J. Law&B 92
Counen, Michael N. 1929- St&PR 93
Counihan, Darlyn Joyce 1948- WhoAmW 93
Counihan, Timothy B. 1923- WhoScE 91-3
Counsel, June 1926- ChlFicS, ConAu 138, SmATA 70
Counsell, Dennis A. 1930- St&PR 93
Counsell, Paul Stone 1936- St&PR 93
Counsell, Raymond Ernest 1930- WhoAm 92
Counselman, Charles C., Jr. 1916- WhoIns 93
Counselman, Charles Claude, III 1943- WhoAm 92
Counselman, Eleanor Frey 1946- WhoEmL 93
Counselman, Mary Elizabeth 1911- ScF&FL 92
Counsil, William G. 1937- St&PR 93
Counsil, William Glenn 1937- WhoAm 92
Counsilman, Doc BioIn 17
Counsilman, James Edward 1920- WhoAm 92
Count de T'Serclaes, Wenceslas Jacques 1924- WhoWor 93
Countermine, Donald 1938- St&PR 93
Countryman, Dayton Wendell 1918- WhoAm 92
Countryman, Edward Francis 1944- WhoAm 92
Countryman, Ellen Witt 1951- WhoAmW 93
Countryman, Gary Lee 1939- St&PR 93, WhoAm 92, WhoIns 93
Countryman, John Russell 1933- WhoAm 92
Countryman, Keith R. 1951- St&PR 93
Countryman, May Ella 1882- AmWomPl
Countryman, Richard Alva 1926- WhoWor 93
Countryman, Vern 1917- WhoAm 92
Counts, Catherine Ann 1962- WhoAmW 93
Counts, James Curtis 1915- WhoAm 92
Counts, Justice Fuller 1941- St&PR 93
Counts, Mary Lou 1933- WhoSSW 93
Counts, Stanley Thomas 1926- WhoAm 92
Counts, Thomas James 1957- WhoSSW 93
Counts, Wayne Boyd 1936- WhoSSW 93
Couot, Jacques 1937- WhoScE 91-2
Coupe, James Warnick 1949- WhoEmL 93
Coupe, John Donald 1931- WhoAm 92
Coupe, Rodger, Jr. 1947- WhoEmL 93
Couper, Richard W. 1922- St&PR 93
Couper, Richard Watrous 1922- WhoAm 92
Couper, Stephen ConAu 138, ScF&FL 92
Couper, William 1947- WhoAm 92
Couperin Baker 92

Couperin, Armand-Louis 1727-1789 *Baker 92*
Couperin, Celeste 1793-1860 *See* Couperin, Gervais-Francois 1759-1826 *Baker 92*
Couperin, Charles *Baker 92*
Couperin, Charles 1638-1679 *Baker 92*
Couperin, Francois c. 1631-c. 1708 *Baker 92*
Couperin, Francois 1668-1733 *Baker 92, BioIn 17*
Couperin, Gervais-Francois 1759-1826 *Baker 92*
Couperin, Louis c. 1626-1661 *Baker 92*
Couperin, Marguerite-Antoinette 1705-1778 *See* Couperin, Francois 1668-1733 *Baker 92*
Couperin, Marie-Madeleine 1690-1742 *See* Couperin, Francois 1668-1733 *Baker 92*
Couperin, Nicolas 1680-1748 *Baker 92*
Couperin, Pierre-Louis 1755-1789 *Baker 92*
Coupland, Douglas *BioIn 17, WhoCanL 92*
Coupland, George Michael *WhoScE 91-1*
Couples, Fred *BioIn 17*
Couples, Fred 1959- *WhoAm 92*
Cour, Niels la 1944- *Baker 92*
Courage, Alexander 1938- *ConTFT 10*
Couranjou, Jean 1932- *WhoScE 91-2*
Courant, Ernest David 1920- *WhoAm 92*
Couraud, Marcel 1912-1986 *Baker 92*
Courbet, Gustave 1819-1877 *BioIn 17*
Courboin, Charles (Marie) 1884-1973 *Baker 92*
Courbon, Pierre Alain 1963- *WhoWor 93*
Courchene, Ernest E., Jr. 1932- *St&PR 93*
Courcy, D. *Law&B 92*
Coureil, Pierre M. 1953- *St&PR 93*
Courey, Michael Herbert 1947- *WhoEmL 93, WhoSSW 93*
Courey, Norman Leon 1942- *WhoE 93*
Courgeau, Daniel 1937- *WhoScE 91-2*
Couri, Bradford B. *Law&B 92*
Couri, John A. 1941- *WhoAm 92*
Couric, Katherine 1957- *WhoAm 92, WhoAmW 93, WhoE 93*
Couric, Katie *BioIn 17*
Courier, Jim *BioIn 17, NewYTBS 92 [port]*
Courier, Jim 1970- *News 93-2 [port], WhoAm 92*
Courington, Chella 1947- *WhoSSW 93*
Courington, Jerry D. 1945- *St&PR 93*
Courjon, Jean Antoine 1918- *WhoScE 91-2*
Courlander, Harold 1908- *ConAu 40NR, ScF&FL 92*
Cournoyea, Nellie 1940- *WhoAmW 93*
Cournoyer, Barry Roger 1947- *WhoEmL 93*
Cournoyer, R.O. 1933- *St&PR 93*
Courot, Michel 1932- *WhoScE 91-2*
Courouble, M. 1930- *WhoScE 91-2*
Courreges, Andre 1923- *BioIn 17*
Courrier, Kathleen K. 1949- *WhoE 93*
Courrier, Yves Gilbert 1946- *WhoUN 92*
Courriere, Philippe 1942- *WhoScE 91-2*
Cours, John Dave 1934- *WhoAm 92*
Coursaget, Pierre Louis 1947- *WhoWor 93*
Courseille, Christian 1945- *WhoWor 93*
Coursen, Christopher Dennison 1948- *WhoE 93*
Coursen, H.R. 1932- *WhoWrEP 92*
Courshon, Arthur Howard 1921- *St&PR 93, WhoAm 92*
Courshon, Carol Biel 1923- *WhoAm 92*
Courson, John Edward 1944- *WhoSSW 93*
Courson, Marna B. P. 1951- *WhoAmW 93*
Courson, Timothy Howard *Law&B 92*
Court, Allen Henry 1942- *WhoWor 93*
Court, Arnold 1914- *WhoWor 93*
Court, Hazel 1926- *BioIn 17*
Court, Janet Holmes a *BioIn 17*
Court, John C. 1942- *St&PR 93*
Court, Kathryn Diana 1948- *WhoAm 92*
Court, Leonard 1947- *WhoAm 92, WhoEmL 93, WhoSSW 93*
Court, Margaret 1942- *BioIn 17*
Court, Robert Holmes a *BioIn 17*
Court, Wesli *WhoWrEP 92*
Courtade, Judy Louise 1951- *St&PR 93*
Courtemanche, Albert Douglas 1929- *WhoAm 92*
Courtemanche, Leo Maurice 1959- *WhoE 93, WhoEmL 93*
Courtenay, Bryce 1933- *ConAu 138*
Courtenay, Harry *DcCPCAm*
Courtenay, Irene Doris 1920- *WhoAmW 93, WhoE 93, WhoWor 93*
Courtenay, William James 1935- *WhoAm 92*
Courter, Amy S. 1961- *WhoEmL 93*
Courter, Jack E. 1933- *St&PR 93*
Courter, James A. *BioIn 17*
Courter, James A. 1936- *St&PR 93*
Courter, James Andrew *Law&B 92*
Courter, James Andrew 1936- *WhoAm 92*
Courter, Jeanne Lynn 1953- *WhoE 93, WhoEmL 93*
Courter, William R. 1930- *St&PR 93*
Courtet, Joseph-Jean 1930- *WhoScE 91-2*
Courtice, Brian William 1950- *WhoAsAP 91*
Courtice, Thomas Barr 1943- *WhoAm 92*
Courtier, S.H. 1904-1974 *ScF&FL 92*
Courtieu, Andre-Louis 1925- *WhoWor 93*
Courtieu, Andre Louis M. 1925- *WhoScE 91-2*
Courtillot, Vincent 1948- *WhoScE 91-2*
Courtiss, Eugene Howard 1930- *WhoAm 92*
Courtland, Jerome 1926- *MiSFD 9*
Courtneidge, Cicely 1893-1980 *QDrFCA 92 [port]*
Courtney, Barbara Wood 1929- *WhoAmW 93*
Courtney, Charles Edward 1936- *WhoAm 92*
Courtney, David Richard 1953- *WhoEmL 93*
Courtney, Dayle *ConAu 40NR, ScF&FL 92, WhoWrEP 92*
Courtney, Diane Trossello 1951- *WhoEmL 93*
Courtney, Donald E. 1930- *St&PR 93*
Courtney, Edward 1932- *WhoAm 92*
Courtney, Eugene W. 1936- *St&PR 93*
Courtney, Eugene Whitmal 1936- *WhoAm 92*
Courtney, Gladys Atkins 1930- *WhoAm 92*
Courtney, Howard Perry 1911- *WhoAm 92*
Courtney, James Edmond 1931- *St&PR 93, WhoAm 92*
Courtney, James McNiven 1940- *WhoWor 93*
Courtney, James Patrick, Jr. 1952- *WhoSSW 93*
Courtney, John Watson 1956- *WhoSSW 93*
Courtney, Kathleen 1878-1974 *BioIn 17*
Courtney, Kevin *Law&B 92*
Courtney, Max A. 1946- *St&PR 93*
Courtney, Michael 1954- *WhoScE 91-1*
Courtney, R.G. *WhoScE 91-1*
Courtney, Richard Augustus 1953- *WhoEmL 93*
Courtney, Robin S. 1927- *St&PR 93*
Courtney, Rosemary 1961- *WhoEmL 93*
Courtney, Ruth Englehardt *Law&B 92*
Courtney, Suzan Lee 1947- *WhoE 93, WhoEmL 93*
Courtney, Thomas Joseph *Law&B 92*
Courtney, Victoria Black 1943- *WhoAmW 93*
Courtney, Vincent *ScF&FL 92*
Courtney, Wayne 1953- *St&PR 93*
Courtney, William Francis 1914- *WhoAm 92*
Courtney, William V. *Law&B 92*
Courtney-Clarke, Margaret 1949- *BioIn 17*
Courtois, B. *WhoScE 91-2*
Courtois, Bernard *Law&B 92*
Courtois, Bernard P. 1948- *WhoScE 91-2*
Courtois, Edmond Jacques 1920- *St&PR 93, WhoAm 92*
Courtois, Horst 1926- *WhoScE 91-3*
Courtois, Jean fl. 16th cent.- *Baker 92*
Courtois, Yves *WhoScE 91-2*
Courtois, Yves 1940- *WhoScE 91-2*
Courtot, Pierre 1932- *WhoScE 91-2*
Courtright, Elliott George *Law&B 92*
Courtright, Timothy Isaiah 1848-1887 *BioIn 17*
Courtsal, Donald Preston 1929- *WhoAm 92*
Courville, Leon 1945- *St&PR 93*
Courvoisier, Georges Rene 1946- *WhoWor 93*
Courvoisier, Karl 1846-1908 *Baker 92*
Courvoisier, Walter 1875-1931 *Baker 92*
Coury, Ameel Sam 1936- *WhoSSW 93*
Coury, John, Jr. 1921- *WhoAm 92*
Coury, Maxime 1925- *WhoWor 93*
Couse, Blake Thomas 1928- *St&PR 93*
Couse, Eanger Irving 1866-1936 *BioIn 17*
Cousens, R.H. *WhoScE 91-1*
Couser, Griffith Thomas 1946- *WhoE 93*
Couser, William Griffith 1939- *WhoAm 92*
Cousin, Jean-Paul 1948- *St&PR 93*
Cousin, M.T. 1932- *WhoScE 91-2*
Cousin, Maribeth Anne 1949- *WhoAm 92, WhoEmL 93*
Cousin, Rebecca Elizabeth 1932- *WhoWor 93*
Cousineau, Marian 1944- *WhoAmW 93*
Cousineau, Pierre 1948- *WhoEmL 93*
Cousino, Gerald A. 1928- *St&PR 93*
Cousino, Ralph Emmett 1932- *St&PR 93*
Cousins, David 1959- *St&PR 93*
Cousins, David Arthur *Law&B 92*
Cousins, George H. 1952- *St&PR 93*
Cousins, Linda 1946- *WhoWrEP 92*
Cousins, Lucy *BioIn 17*
Cousins, Margaret 1905- *WhoAm 92*
Cousins, Morison Stuart 1934- *WhoAm 92*
Cousins, Norman *BioIn 17*
Cousins, Norman 1915- *JrnUS*
Cousins, Peter Charles 1955- *WhoSSW 93*
Cousins, Robert John 1941- *WhoAm 92, WhoWor 93*
Cousins, Robin 1957- *BioIn 17*
Cousins, Ruth Hubbard *WhoSSW 93*
Cousins, Thomas G. 1931- *St&PR 93*
Cousins, William, Jr. *AfrAmBi [port]*
Cousins, William M., Jr. 1924- *St&PR 93*
Cousland, Charles Patrick 1930- *St&PR 93*
Coussemaker, (Charles-) Edmond (-Henri) de 1805-1876 *Baker 92*
Coussement, A. 1939- *WhoScE 91-2*
Coussement, Romain J.P. 1935- *WhoScE 91-2*
Cousteau, J.Y. *WhoScE 91-4*
Cousteau, Jacques 1910- *ConHero 2 [port]*
Cousteau, Jacques(-Yves) 1910- *Expl 93 [port]*
Cousteau, Jacques Yves *BioIn 17*
Cousteau, Jacques-Yves 1910- *WhoAm 92, WhoWor 93*
Cousteau, Simone d1990 *BioIn 17*
Cousy, Bob 1928- *BioIn 17*
Cousy, Bob Joseph 1928- *WhoAm 92*
Coutard, Christian Edmond 1945- *WhoWor 93*
Coutard, Raoul 1924- *MiSFD 9*
Coutin, Florence 1922- *St&PR 93*
Coutin, Ronald Steven 1949- *St&PR 93*
Coutinho, Antonio M.P.B. do A.T. 1946- *WhoScE 91-4*
Coutinho, Roeland Arnold 1946- *WhoWor 93*
Couto, C. Douglass 1950- *WhoEmL 93*
Couto, Joao Manuel 1949- *WhoWor 93*
Couto, Jose Bernardo 1803-1862 *DcMexL*
Couto, Nancy Vieira 1942- *ConAu 136*
Couto, Robert 1946- *St&PR 93*
Coutras, Angelo Anest *Law&B 92*
Coutrot, Philippe 1941- *WhoScE 91-2*
Couts, Shirley Ashley 1943- *WhoWrEP 92*
Coutsouradis, Dimitri 1929- *WhoScE 91-2*
Coutts, Frederick 1899- *BioIn 17*
Coutts, Gene Michael 1949- *WhoEmL 93*
Coutts, Gordon d1937 *BioIn 17*
Coutts, John R. 1936- *St&PR 93*
Coutts, John Wallace 1923- *WhoAm 92*
Coutts, Lawrence Robert 1948- *WhoEmL 93*
Coutts, Ronald Thomson 1931- *WhoAm 92*
Coutu, Joseph Henry 1932- *St&PR 93*
Couture, Charles E. 1940- *St&PR 93*
Couture, Christin 1951- *SmATA 73 [port]*
Couture, Jean G. 1924- *WhoAm 92*
Couture, Jean Guy 1929- *WhoAm 92*
Couture, Maurice 1926- *WhoAm 92*
Couture, Robert E. 1921- *St&PR 93*
Couture, Ronald David 1944- *WhoAm 92*
Couturie, Bill *MiSFD 9*
Couturier, Lance Cornelius 1948- *WhoE 93*
Couturier, Naomi Hewitt- *BioIn 17*
Couturier, Robert *BioIn 17*
Couturier, Ronald Lee 1949- *WhoAm 92, WhoEmL 93, WhoWor 93*
Couve de Murville, Maurice 1907- *BioIn 17*
Couvillion, Linda Carol 1951- *WhoAmW 93*
Couvillon, Tucker H., III *Law&B 92*
Covachev, Valery Christov 1955- *WhoWor 93*
Coval-Apel, Naomi Miller *WhoAm 92, WhoAmW 93*
Covalt, Robert B. *St&PR 93*
Covalt, Robert Byron 1931- *WhoAm 92*
Covan, James Parker 1940- *WhoSSW 93*
Covan, Willie 1897-1989 *BioIn 17*
Covault, Carolyn *Law&B 92*
Covault, Lloyd R., Jr. 1928- *WhoAm 92, WhoWor 93*
Covay, Don 1938- *SoulM*
Cove, David John *WhoScE 91-1*
Cove, Jeffrey A. 1946- *St&PR 93*
Covell, Andrea M. *Law&B 92*
Covell, Christopher Greene 1947- *WhoE 93*
Covell, Ian *ScF&FL 92*
Covell, Lyman David 1922- *St&PR 93*
Covell, Richard *ScF&FL 92*
Covell, Richard B. 1929- *St&PR 93*
Covell, Richard Bertram 1929- *WhoAm 92*
Covelli, Joy Allene 1941- *WhoAmW 93*
Covelli, Ralph 1921- *St&PR 93*
Covello, Aldo 1935- *WhoWor 93*
Covello, Alfred Vincent 1933- *WhoAm 92*
Covello, Gina Rae 1966- *WhoAmW 93*
Covello, Philip J. 1954- *St&PR 93*
Coven, Berdeen 1941- *WhoAm 92, WhoAmW 93*
Coveney, Richard Marean 1933- *St&PR 93*
Covenko, Howard Louis 1942- *St&PR 93*
Coventry, Lynne Margaret 1964- *WhoWor 93*
Cover, Albert David 1947- *WhoEmL 93*
Cover, Arthur Byron 1950- *ScF&FL 92*
Cover, David Joseph 1962- *WhoE 93*
Cover, David M. *Law&B 92*
Cover, E. McIntosh *Law&B 92*
Cover, E. McIntosh 1933- *St&PR 93*
Cover, Franklin Edward 1928- *WhoAm 92*
Cover, Fred W. 1942- *St&PR 93*
Cover, James P. *ScF&FL 92*
Cover, Nelson *BioIn 17*
Cover, Norman Bernard 1935- *WhoSSW 93*
Cover, Thomas M. 1938- *WhoAm 92*
Cover, William A. 1930- *St&PR 93*
Coverdale, Glen E. 1930- *St&PR 93*
Coverdale, Glen Eugene 1930- *WhoAm 92*
Coverly, Robert 1864-1944 *Baker 92*
Coverston, David Yost 1920- *WhoWrEP 92*
Covert, Calvin C. 1924- *St&PR 93, WhoAm 92*
Covert, Eugene Edzards 1926- *WhoAm 92, WhoE 93*
Covert, Gerald H. 1939- *St&PR 93*
Covert, Michael Henri 1949- *WhoAm 92*
Covert, Robert John 1938- *St&PR 93*
Covert, Roberta Marsha 1950- *WhoEmL 93*
Covert, Thomas C. 1934- *St&PR 93*
Covert-Vail, Lucinda *BioIn 17*
Covey, Charles William 1918- *WhoAm 92*
Covey, Cyclone 1922- *WhoAm 92, WhoSSW 93*
Covey, F. Don 1934- *St&PR 93, WhoAm 92*
Covey, Frank Michael, Jr. 1932- *WhoAm 92*
Covey, Harold D. 1930- *St&PR 93, WhoIns 93*
Covey, Harold Dean 1930- *WhoAm 92*
Covey, Norma Scott 1924- *WhoAmW 93*
Covey, Ronald H. 1932- *St&PR 93*
Covey, Ronald H., Jr. 1956- *St&PR 93*
Covey, Ronald P. 1929-1990 *BioIn 17*
Covey, Sean *BioIn 17*
Covey, Sharon Arlene 1941- *WhoSSW 93*
Covey, Steven K. *Law&B 92*
Covey, William Roderic 1929- *St&PR 93*
Covi, Lino 1926- *WhoE 93*
Coviello, Robert Frank 1941- *WhoE 93*
Covil, James P. 1952- *St&PR 93*
Covilhao, Pero da 1450-1545 *Expl 93*
Covill, Keith, Sr. 1948- *WhoE 93*
Coville, Bruce 1950- *ScF&FL 92, WhoWrEP 92*
Coville, Peter Francis 1944- *WhoWor 93*
Covin, Elizabeth Gwinn 1963- *WhoAmW 93*
Covin, Theron Michael 1947- *WhoEmL 93, WhoSSW 93*
Covina, Gina 1952- *WhoWrEP 92*
Covington, Alice Lucille 1955- *WhoEmL 93*
Covington, Ann K. 1942- *WhoAm 92, WhoAmW 93*
Covington, Arthur Kenneth *WhoScE 91-1*
Covington, C.A., Jr. *Law&B 92*
Covington, Calvin Blackwell 1955- *WhoEmL 93*
Covington, Charles J. 1914- *WhoWor 93*
Covington, Clarence Allen 1917- *St&PR 93*
Covington, Dennis *BioIn 17*
Covington, Dianna Lynn 1948- *WhoAmW 93*
Covington, Don Kingsley, Jr. 1920- *St&PR 93*
Covington, Duncan Seay 1949- *St&PR 93*
Covington, Gail Lynn 1950- *WhoEmL 93*
Covington, George M. 1935- *St&PR 93*
Covington, George Morse 1942- *WhoAm 92*
Covington, J. Harriss 1920- *St&PR 93*
Covington, Loran D. 1929- *St&PR 93*
Covington, Oscar Brandford, Jr. 1932- *St&PR 93*
Covington, Patricia Ann 1946- *WhoAmW 93, WhoEmL 93*
Covington, Robert E. 1921- *St&PR 93*
Covington, Robert Newman 1936- *WhoAm 92*
Covington, Stephanie Stewart 1942- *WhoAmW 93*
Covington, Valerie Ann 1953- *WhoSSW 93*
Covington, Virginia Seay 1915- *St&PR 93*
Covington, William Clyde, Jr. 1932- *WhoAm 92*
Covington, Zellah Wall *AmWomPl*
Covington-Kent, Dawna Marie 1948- *WhoAmW 93, WhoEmL 93*
Covino, Benjamin G. 1930-1991 *BioIn 17*
Covino, Charles P. 1923- *St&PR 93*
Covino, Charles Peter 1923- *WhoAm 92*

Covino, Michael WhoWrEP 92
Covitch, Michael Judah 1949- WhoEmL 93
Covitz, Carl D. 1939- WhoAm 92
Covone, James Michael 1948- WhoAm 92, WhoEmL 93
Cowal, Sally Grooms 1944- WhoAmW 93
Cowan, Andrew Glenn 1951- WhoEmL 93
Cowan, Barton Zalman 1934- WhoAm 92, WhoE 93
Cowan, Charles Douglas 1950- St&PR 93
Cowan, Charles G. Law&B 92
Cowan, Charles Gibbs 1928- St&PR 93, WhoAm 92
Cowan, Dale ScF&FL 92
Cowan, David M. Law&B 92
Cowan, Dwaine Oliver 1935- WhoAm 92
Cowan, Edward 1933- WhoAm 92
Cowan, Fairman Chaffee 1915- WhoAm 92
Cowan, Frederic Joseph 1945- WhoAm 92, WhoSSW 93, WhoWor 93
Cowan, George Arthur 1920- WhoAm 92
Cowan, George Sheppard Marshall, Jr. 1938- WhoSSW 93
Cowan, Henry Jacob 1919- WhoWor 93
Cowan, Homer H., Jr. Law&B 92
Cowan, Homer H., Jr. 1923- St&PR 93, WhoIns 93
Cowan, Ian J. 1952- WhoScE 91-3
Cowan, Irving 1932- WhoAm 92
Cowan, J. Milton 1907- WhoAm 92
Cowan, Jack William 1940- WhoSSW 93
Cowan, James 1870-1943 ScF&FL 92
Cowan, James C. 1927- WhoSSW 93
Cowan, James (Granville) 1942- ConAu 139
Cowan, James Spencer 1952- WhoAm 92
Cowan, Janice 1941- WhoCanL 92
Cowan, Jerry Louis 1927- WhoAm 92
Cowan, John WhoScE 91-1
Cowan, John Mack 1944- WhoSSW 93
Cowan, Lester d1990 BioIn 17
Cowan, Marcia K. Law&B 92
Cowan, Mark Douglas 1949- WhoAm 92
Cowan, Mary Katherine Otahal 1957- WhoAmW 93
Cowan, Nancy Sue 1949- WhoSSW 93
Cowan, Paul BioIn 17
Cowan, R. WhoScE 91-1
Cowan, Ralph Wolfe 1931- WhoAm 92
Cowan, Richard 1957- WhoAm 92
Cowan, Richard Wayne 1942- St&PR 93
Cowan, Robert Jenkins 1937- WhoAm 92
Cowan, Robert Vern 1939- St&PR 93
Cowan, Sada 1883-1943 AmWomPl
Cowan, Sally Law&B 92
Cowan, Stanley Earl 1918-1991 BioIn 17
Cowan, Stuart DuBois 1917- WhoAm 92
Cowan, Stuart Marshall 1932- WhoWor 93
Cowan, Susan Alison 1959- WhoAmW 93
Cowan, Susan Kaufman 1959- WhoEmL 93
Cowan, Theo 1917-1991 AnObit 1991
Cowan, Thomas David 1957- WhoEmL 93, WhoSSW 93, WhoWor 93
Cowan, Timothy Scott 1950- St&PR 93
Cowan, Wallace Law&B 92
Cowan, Wallace Edgar 1924- St&PR 93, WhoAm 92
Cowan, Walter G., Jr. Law&B 92
Cowan, Warren J. WhoAm 92
Cowan, William Maxwell 1931- WhoAm 92
Coward, Carroll L. 1957- St&PR 93
Coward, Henry 1849-1944 Baker 92
Coward, John Mortimer d1991 BioIn 17
Coward, Michael Peter WhoScE 91-1
Coward, Noel BioIn 17
Coward, Noel 1899-1973 Baker 92, BritWr S2, OxDcOp
Cowart, Bill Frank 1932- WhoAm 92
Cowart, David 1947- ScF&FL 92
Cowart, David Guyland 1947- WhoSSW 93
Cowart, Elgin Courtland, Jr. 1923- WhoAm 92
Cowart, Jack 1945- WhoAm 92
Cowart, Jess R. 1923- St&PR 93
Cowart, Patricia E. Law&B 92
Cowart, Richard Merrill 1951- WhoEmL 93
Cowart, Thomas David 1953- WhoAm 92, WhoEmL 93, WhoSSW 93
Cowasjee, Saros WhoCanL 92
Cowburn, David Alan 1945- WhoE 93
Cowden, Bess Sherman AmWomPl
Cowden, Carrie A. AmWomPl
Cowden, Chester Lyle 1917- WhoWor 93
Cowden, Constance L. Law&B 92
Cowden, Robert Laughlin 1933- WhoAm 92
Cowden, Roger Rehm Law&B 92
Cowderoy, James Anthony Frank 1960- WhoEmL 93
Cowdery, Charles Kendrick 1951- WhoEmL 93
Cowdery, R. Joe 1952- St&PR 93
Cowdin, Maria Vita 1961- WhoAmW 93
Cowdin, Timothy O. Law&B 92
Cowdrey, Albert Edward 1933- WhoAm 92
Cowdry, Rex William 1947- WhoAm 92, WhoEmL 93
Cowee, John Widmer 1918- WhoAm 92
Cowell, Adrian MiSFD 9
Cowell, Allan Tyler, Jr. 1950- WhoEmL 93
Cowell, Casey G. St&PR 93
Cowell, Ensign Jay 1941- St&PR 93
Cowell, Frances Irene 1953- WhoWor 93
Cowell, Gary R. 1940- St&PR 93
Cowell, Henry 1897-1965 BioIn 17
Cowell, Henry (Dixon) 1897-1965 Baker 92
Cowell, Marion A., Jr. Law&B 92
Cowell, Marion A., Jr. 1934- St&PR 93
Cowell, Marion Aubrey, Jr. 1934- WhoAm 92
Cowell, Steven S. 1949- St&PR 93
Cowell, Susan BioIn 17
Cowen, Bruce D. 1953- St&PR 93
Cowen, Daniel C. 1927- St&PR 93
Cowen, David Elias 1957- WhoEmL 93
Cowen, Emory L. BioIn 17
Cowen, Emory L. 1926- WhoAm 92
Cowen, Eugene Sherman 1925- WhoAm 92
Cowen, Frederic 1852-1935 OxDcOp
Cowen, Frederic (Hymen) 1852-1935 Baker 92
Cowen, Ida 1898- BioIn 17
Cowen, James L. Law&B 92
Cowen, Jill Bernice 1943- WhoE 93
Cowen, Joseph Hamilton 1943- WhoSSW 93
Cowen, Michael Bruce 1939- WhoSSW 93
Cowen, Nathaniel 1900-1989 BioIn 17
Cowen, Philip R. BioIn 17
Cowen, Philip R. 1942- St&PR 93
Cowen, Philip Richard 1942- WhoE 93
Cowen, Raymond A. 1934- WhoScE 91-1
Cowen, Robert E. 1930- WhoAm 92, WhoE 93
Cowen, Robert Henry 1915- WhoAm 92
Cowen, Robert Nathan 1948- St&PR 93, WhoAm 92
Cowen, Roy Chadwell, Jr. 1930- WhoAm 92
Cowen, Wilson 1905- CngDr 91, WhoAm 92
Cowen, Zelman 1919- WhoWor 93
Cowens, David William 1948- WhoAm 92
Cowern, Nicholas Edward Benedict 1953- WhoWor 93
Cowern, Roger W. ScF&FL 92
Cowett, Richard Michael 1942- WhoE 93
Cowey, Alan WhoScE 91-1
Cowger, Alfred R., Jr. Law&B 92
Cowgill, F. Brooks 1932- St&PR 93
Cowgill, Frank Brooks 1932- WhoAm 92
Cowgill, Mary Lu 1932- WhoAmW 93
Cowgill, Ursula Moser 1927- WhoAm 92, WhoAmW 93
Cowher, Bill 1957- WhoAm 92, WhoE 93
Cowher, Salene Juanita 1953- WhoSSW 93
Cowherd, Edwin R. 1921- St&PR 93
Cowhig, Michael Thomas 1947- St&PR 93
Cowhill, William Joseph 1928- WhoAm 92
Cowie, Al T. St&PR 93
Cowie, Bruce Edgar 1938- WhoAm 92
Cowie, Catherine Christine 1953- WhoAm 92, WhoAmW 93
Cowie, Donald 1911- ScF&FL 92
Cowie, Edward 1943- Baker 92
Cowie, Geoff Law&B 92
Cowie, John McKenzie Grant WhoScE 91-1
Cowie, John McKenzie Grant 1933- WhoWor 93
Cowie, Lennox Lauchlan 1950- WhoAm 92
Cowie, William Henry, Jr. 1931- WhoAm 92
Cowin, Daniel d1992 NewYTBS 92
Cowin, Daniel 1921- St&PR 93
Cowin, Daniel 1922-1992 BioIn 17
Cowin, John J. 1928- St&PR 93
Cowin, Stephen Corteen 1934- WhoAm 92
Cowin, William T. 1901-1991 BioIn 17
Cowing, Walter Lishman 1926- WhoAm 92
Cowings, John Sherman 1943- AfrAmBi
Cowl, Gorham A. 1935- St&PR 93
Cowl, Jane 1883?-1950 AmWomPl
Cowlard, Keith Arthur WhoScE 91-1
Cowles, Ann Littlefield 1933- WhoAmW 93
Cowles, Charles 1941- WhoAm 92
Cowles, Chauncey D. 1911- WhoIns 93
Cowles, David Lyle 1955- WhoEmL 93
Cowles, Donald Thurston Law&B 92
Cowles, Edwin 1825-1890 JrnUS
Cowles, Fleur BioIn 17, WhoAm 92
Cowles, Florence A. AmWomPl
Cowles, Frederick I. 1900-1949 ScF&FL 92
Cowles, Frederick Oliver Law&B 92
Cowles, Frederick Oliver 1937- WhoAm 92, WhoE 93
Cowles, Gardner 1861-1946 JrnUS
Cowles, Gardner A., Jr. 1903-1985 DcLB 127 [port]
Cowles, Harold Andrews, Jr. 1924- WhoAm 92
Cowles, Joe Richard 1941- WhoAm 92
Cowles, John, Jr. 1929- WhoAm 92
Cowles, John N. 1950- St&PR 93
Cowles, LeRoy Eugene 1880-1957 BioIn 17
Cowles, Milly 1932- WhoAm 92, WhoAmW 93
Cowles, Neill Jacobi, III 1961- WhoEmL 93
Cowles, Roger William 1945- WhoAm 92, WhoE 93, WhoWor 93
Cowles, William H., III BioIn 17
Cowles, William H., III d1992 NewYTBS 92
Cowley, Alastair Glenn 1959- WhoWor 93
Cowley, Elmer 1939- St&PR 93
Cowley, Hannah Parkhouse 1743-1809 BioIn 17
Cowley, John Maxwell 1923- WhoAm 92
Cowley, John W. 1946- WhoIns 93
Cowley, John Wade 1946- St&PR 93
Cowley, Joseph Gilbert 1923- WhoWrEP 92
Cowley, (Cassia) Joy (Summers) 1936- DcChlFi
Cowley, Malcolm 1898-1989 BioIn 17
Cowley, R. Adams 1917-1991 BioIn 17
Cowley, Roger Arthur WhoScE 91-1
Cowley, Roger Arthur 1939- WhoWor 93
Cowley, Samuel P. Law&B 92
Cowley, Samuel P. 1934- St&PR 93
Cowley, Stanley William Herbert WhoScE 91-1
Cowley, Stewart ScF&FL 92
Cowley, William Eugene 1909- WhoAm 92
Cowling, Denny Patrick 1954- WhoEmL 93, WhoSSW 93
Cowling, Keith BioIn 17
Cowlishaw, Mary Lou 1932- WhoAmW 93
Cowman, Harold Arthur 1931- St&PR 93
Cownie, George Lawrence Law&B 92
Cownie, John Bowler 1940- WhoAm 92
Cownie, William Garry Law&B 92
Cowper, Richard 1926- ScF&FL 92
Cowper, Stephen Cambreleng 1938- WhoAm 92
Cowper, William 1731-1800 BioIn 17
Cowper, William Henry Law&B 92
Cowperthwaite, David ScF&FL 92
Cowperthwaite, John Milton, Jr. 1912- WhoE 93
Cowsen, Art, Sr. BioIn 17
Cowsen, Art, Jr. BioIn 17
Cowser, Danny Lee 1948- WhoEmL 93
Cowsill, Barbara 1929-1985 BioIn 17
Cowsill, Barry 1955- BioIn 17
Cowsill, Bill 1948- BioIn 17
Cowsill, Bob 1950- BioIn 17
Cowsill, John 1960- BioIn 17
Cowsill, Paul 1952- BioIn 17
Cowsill, Susan 1960- BioIn 17
Cowx, Ian Graham 1952- WhoWor 93
Cox, Albert Harrington, Jr. 1932- WhoAm 92
Cox, Albert R., Jr. 1946- St&PR 93
Cox, Albert Reginald 1928- WhoAm 92
Cox, Alex 1954- ConTFT 10, MiSFD 9
Cox, Allan J. 1937- WhoAm 92
Cox, Alma Tenney 1919- WhoSSW 93
Cox, Alvin Earl 1918- WhoAm 92
Cox, Andrew Brian 1950- WhoEmL 93
Cox, Andrew Hood 1917- WhoAm 92
Cox, Andrew J. 1941- St&PR 93
Cox, Andrew Paul, Jr. 1937- WhoSSW 93
Cox, Andrew William WhoScE 91-1
Cox, Andy 1956-
See English Beat, The ConMus 9
See Also Fine Young Cannibals SoulM
Cox, Angela Birch Law&B 92
Cox, Ann Bruger WhoAm 92
Cox, Anna Lee 1931- WhoAmW 93
Cox, Anthony BioIn 17
Cox, Anthony R. 1938- WhoScE 91-1
Cox, Antony Dawson WhoScE 91-1
Cox, Archibald 1912- WhoAm 92
Cox, Archibald, Jr. 1940- St&PR 93, WhoAm 92
Cox, Barbara Claire 1939- WhoSSW 93
Cox, Barbara Gresbach 1932- WhoAmW 93, WhoSSW 93
Cox, Barbara J. Law&B 92
Cox, Barry 1931- BioIn 17
Cox, Berry Gordon 1923- WhoSSW 93
Cox, Bert G. 1920- St&PR 93
Cox, Beverly Elaine 1945- WhoAmW 93
Cox, Bob 1936- BioIn 17
Cox, Bobby 1941- WhoAm 92
Cox, Bobby L., Jr. St&PR 93
Cox, Bradley 1941- WhoSSW 93
Cox, Brenda Gale 1948- WhoEmL 93
Cox, Brian 1946- BioIn 17
Cox, Britton Parks 1957- WhoEmL 93
Cox, Carol Annette 1935- WhoAmW 93
Cox, Carol M. 1942- St&PR 93
Cox, Carol Moore 1946- WhoWrEP 92
Cox, Chapman Beecher 1940- WhoAm 92
Cox, Charles C. 1945- WhoAm 92
Cox, Charles Daniel, III 1946- St&PR 93
Cox, Charles Ernest, Jr. 1929- St&PR 93
Cox, Charles Robert 1942- St&PR 93
Cox, Charles Shipley 1922- WhoAm 92
Cox, Cheryl Craft 1948- WhoAmW 93, WhoSSW 93
Cox, Christopher BioIn 17
Cox, Christopher 1944- WhoE 93
Cox, Christopher 1952- CngDr 91, WhoAm 92
Cox, Christopher Barry 1931- WhoWor 93
Cox, Clair Edward, II 1933- WhoAm 92
Cox, Clark 1943- WhoSSW 93
Cox, Clifton B. 1916- St&PR 93
Cox, Craig M. 1956- St&PR 93
Cox, Cynthia Lee 1960- WhoEmL 93
Cox, D.J. WhoScE 91-1
Cox, Daniel Thomas 1946- WhoIns 93
Cox, David 1924- WhoWor 93
Cox, David Brummal 1940- WhoAm 92
Cox, David Buchtel 1927- St&PR 93
Cox, David C. 1937- St&PR 93
Cox, David Carson 1937- WhoAm 92
Cox, David Eugene 1949- WhoEmL 93
Cox, David Jackson 1934- WhoAm 92
Cox, David S. 1942- WhoIns 93
Cox, David Walter 1951- WhoEmL 93
Cox, Dennis Christian 1947- WhoEmL 93
Cox, Dennis Edwin 1948- WhoEmL 93
Cox, Diana Caryl Carswell 1945- WhoAmW 93
Cox, Diane Steiger 1948- WhoE 93
Cox, Donald Clyde 1937- WhoAm 92, WhoWor 93
Cox, Donna BioIn 17
Cox, Douglas L. 1945- St&PR 93
Cox, Douglas Lynn 1945- WhoAm 92
Cox, E. Morris 1903- St&PR 93
Cox, Ebbie Lee 1927- WhoAm 92
Cox, Edward Charles 1937- WhoAm 92
Cox, Elizabeth 1953- ConAu 136
Cox, Emmett Ripley 1935- WhoAm 92, WhoSSW 93
Cox, Eric Frederick 1932- WhoE 93, WhoWor 93
Cox, Ernest S. 1929- St&PR 93
Cox, Ethel Louise AmWomPl
Cox, Exum Morris 1903- WhoAm 92
Cox, F. Kim 1952- St&PR 93
Cox, Frank D. 1932- WhoSSW 93
Cox, Fred B. 1934- St&PR 93
Cox, Frederick Moreland 1928- WhoAm 92
Cox, G.L. St&PR 93
Cox, Garen Law&B 92
Cox, Gary Forrest 1949- WhoEmL 93
Cox, Gary H. 1947- St&PR 93
Cox, Gary Robert 1953- WhoEmL 93
Cox, Gary W(alter) 1955- ConAu 139
Cox, Gene Spracher 1921- WhoAm 92
Cox, Geoffrey WhoScE 91-1
Cox, George d1990 BioIn 17
Cox, George A. 1923- St&PR 93
Cox, George B. 1853-1916 PolPar
Cox, Gerald Everett 1932- St&PR 93
Cox, Geraldine Vang 1944- WhoAm 92
Cox, Gerard Anthony WhoE 93
Cox, Gilbert Edwin 1917- WhoAm 92
Cox, Glen N. 1903-1991 BioIn 17
Cox, Glenn Andrew 1929- St&PR 93
Cox, Glenn Andrew, Jr. 1929- WhoAm 92, WhoSSW 93
Cox, Greg 1959- ScF&FL 92
Cox, Grover Arnold 1933- WhoAm 92
Cox, Harry Seymour 1923- WhoAm 92
Cox, Harvey Gallagher BioIn 17
Cox, Headley Morris, Jr. 1916- WhoAm 92, WhoSSW 93
Cox, Helen Kem Carstarphen 1922- WhoAmW 93
Cox, Helen Parks 1949- WhoEmL 93
Cox, Henry 1935- WhoAm 92
Cox, Henry Reid 1956- WhoEmL 93
Cox, Herbert Bartle 1944- WhoAm 92
Cox, Herbert Bartle 1944- St&PR 93
Cox, Hollis Utah 1944- WhoAm 92
Cox, Houston Abraham, Jr. 1918- WhoSSW 93
Cox, Howard Allan 1954- WhoSSW 93
Cox, Howard Ellis, Jr. 1944- WhoAm 92, WhoWor 93
Cox, Hubert E. Law&B 92
Cox, J. Randolph 1936- ScF&FL 92
Cox, J. Tom 1929- St&PR 93
Cox, J. William 1928- WhoAm 92
Cox, James Andrew 1942- WhoWrEP 92
Cox, James Carl, Jr. 1919- WhoWor 93
Cox, James D. 1943- WhoAm 92

Cox, James Darrell 1950- *WhoSSW 93*
Cox, James David 1945- *WhoAm 92*
Cox, James M. 1870-1957 *PolPar*
Cox, James McMahon 1903-1974 *DcLB 127 [port]*
Cox, James Melville 1925- *WhoAm 92*
Cox, James Middleton 1870-1957 *DcLB 127 [port], JrnUS*
Cox, James Oliver, III 1946- *WhoAm 92*
Cox, James Randall 1950- *WhoEmL 93*
Cox, James S. 1946- *St&PR 93*
Cox, James Sidney 1950- *WhoEmL 93*
Cox, James Talley 1921- *WhoAm 92*
Cox, James William 1937- *WhoAm 92*
Cox, Janet Lorraine 1957- *WhoAmW 93*
Cox, Janis Faye 1958- *WhoAmW 93*
Cox, Jean 1922- *Baker 92, OxDcOp*
Cox, Jeffery G. 1947- *St&PR 93*
Cox, Jerome Rockhold, Jr. 1925- *WhoAm 92*
Cox, Jerry 1943- *St&PR 93*
Cox, Jessie Lynn 1929- *St&PR 93*
Cox, Jo-Ann M. d1990 *BioIn 17*
Cox, Joan 1942- *ScF&FL 92*
Cox, Joan Alaire 1956- *WhoAmW 93*
Cox, Joanne Furtek 1947- *WhoEmL 93*
Cox, Joe Bruce 1939- *WhoAm 92*
Cox, Joe Mansfield, II 1958- *WhoE 93*
Cox, John 1935- *IntDcOp, OxDcOp*
Cox, John 1946- *WhoWor 93*
Cox, John Carroll 1933- *St&PR 93*
Cox, John David 1954- *WhoSSW 93*
Cox, John F. *BioIn 17*
Cox, John Francis 1929- *WhoAm 92*
Cox, John R. *Law&B 92*
Cox, John R. 1944- *St&PR 93*
Cox, John Thomas 1921- *WhoSSW 93*
Cox, John Thomas, Jr. 1943- *WhoSSW 93*
Cox, John W., Jr. 1947- *CngDr 91, WhoAm 92*
Cox, Joseph King 1950- *WhoEmL 93*
Cox, Joseph Mason Andrew 1930- *WhoWrEP 92*
Cox, Joseph Merrells, II 1949- *WhoEmL 93*
Cox, Joseph William 1937- *WhoAm 92*
Cox, Joy Dean 1940- *WhoAmW 93, WhoWor 93*
Cox, Joyce Stegall 1957- *WhoEmL 93*
Cox, Judith Hild 1938- *WhoAmW 93*
Cox, Justin Brantlin (Jack) 1934- *WhoWrEP 92*
Cox, Karen Sue 1953- *WhoEmL 93*
Cox, Kathleen A. *Law&B 92*
Cox, Kathryn Cullen 1943- *WhoAmW 93*
Cox, Kathy L. *Law&B 92*
Cox, Kellie Breanna 1963- *WhoAmW 93*
Cox, Kenneth Allen 1916- *WhoAm 92*
Cox, Kenneth K. 1952- *St&PR 93*
Cox, Kenneth Mitchell *Law&B 92*
Cox, Kermitt L. 1943- *St&PR 93*
Cox, Kevin *AfrAmBi [port]*
Cox, Larry Duane 1955- *WhoEmL 93*
Cox, Laura Joan 1959- *WhoEmL 93, WhoSSW 93*
Cox, Laurence A., Jr. 1939- *St&PR 93*
Cox, Lawrence 1950- *St&PR 93*
Cox, Lawrence Henry 1947- *WhoEmL 93*
Cox, Lee Ann 1956- *WhoAmW 93*
Cox, Leona Dixon *BioIn 17*
Cox, Lester Lee 1922- *St&PR 93, WhoAm 92*
Cox, Lewis Franklin 1949- *WhoEmL 93, WhoWor 93*
Cox, Linda Blankenship 1952- *WhoAmW 93*
Cox, Lisa Colette 1958- *WhoSSW 93*
Cox, Lisa Czirjak 1958- *WhoAmW 93, WhoEmL 93*
Cox, Luther 1901- *ScF&FL 92*
Cox, Lynn Evans 1957- *St&PR 93*
Cox, Mabel Crampton *AmWomPl*
Cox, Marie-Therese Henriette 1925-1991 *ConAu 136*
Cox, Marjorie Milham 1960- *WhoAmW 93*
Cox, Mark Dale 1950- *WhoSSW 93*
Cox, Mark Stanley 1953- *WhoEmL 93, WhoSSW 93*
Cox, Marsden Haigh, III 1950- *WhoEmL 93*
Cox, Marshall 1932- *WhoAm 92*
Cox, Marshall G. 1935- *St&PR 93*
Cox, Marvin M., Jr. 1953- *St&PR 93*
Cox, Marvin Melvin, Jr. 1953- *WhoEmL 93*
Cox, Mary Blanche 1945- *WhoAmW 93, WhoE 93*
Cox, Mary E. 1937- *WhoAmW 93*
Cox, Mary Lathrop 1930- *WhoE 93*
Cox, Mary Linda 1946- *WhoAmW 93*
Cox, Maurice A. *St&PR 93*
Cox, Maurice G. 1940- *WhoScE 91-1*
Cox, Melvin Monroe 1947- *WhoEmL 93*
Cox, Michael 1933- *WhoScE 91-1, WhoWor 93*
Cox, Michael 1948- *ScF&FL 92*
Cox, Michael Walter 1942- *St&PR 93*
Cox, Mitchel Neal 1956- *WhoAm 92*
Cox, Molly *ConAu 136*
Cox, Molly 1925-1991 *AnObit 1991*
Cox, Myron Keith 1926- *WhoWor 93*
Cox, Nancy Burney *AmWomPl*
Cox, Nell *MiSFD 9*
Cox, Nelson Anthony, Jr. 1943- *WhoSSW 93*
Cox, Norman Lee 1947- *WhoEmL 93*
Cox, Owen D. 1910-1990 *BioIn 17*
Cox, Patricia Bale *ScF&FL 92*
Cox, Patrick W. 1953- *St&PR 93*
Cox, Paul 1940- *MiSFD 9*
Cox, Paul L. 1946- *WhoEmL 93*
Cox, Percy Zachariah 1864-1937 *DcTwHis*
Cox, Peter H. *WhoScE 91-3*
Cox, Peter W. 1937- *St&PR 93*
Cox, Rachel Dunaway 1904- *WhoAmW 93, WhoE 93*
Cox, Randal M. 1955- *WhoSSW 93*
Cox, Raymond 1954- *St&PR 93*
Cox, Raymond E. 1955- *St&PR 93*
Cox, Raymond H. 1926- *St&PR 93*
Cox, Raymond Whitten, III 1949- *WhoEmL 93*
Cox, Reavis d1992 *NewYTBS 92*
Cox, Reavis 1900-1992 *ConAu 139*
Cox, Richard 1931- *ScF&FL 92*
Cox, Richard Garner 1928- *WhoSSW 93*
Cox, Richard George 1903-1990 *BioIn 17*
Cox, Richard Horton 1920- *WhoAm 92*
Cox, Richard Joseph 1929- *WhoAm 92*
Cox, Rita Agler 1951- *WhoAmW 93, WhoEmL 93, WhoSSW 93*
Cox, Robert 1931- *WhoE 93*
Cox, Robert Andrew 1963- *WhoEmL 93*
Cox, Robert E. *BioIn 17*
Cox, Robert G. 1941- *St&PR 93*
Cox, Robert Gene 1929- *WhoAm 92, WhoWor 93*
Cox, Robert H. 1940- *St&PR 93*
Cox, Robert Hames 1923- *WhoWor 93*
Cox, Robert Joe 1941- *WhoSSW 93*
Cox, Robert L. 1930- *WhoAm 92*
Cox, Robert L., III *Law&B 92*
Cox, Robert Lewis 1947- *WhoSSW 93*
Cox, Robert M., Jr. 1945- *WhoAm 92*
Cox, Robert Osborne 1917- *WhoAm 92*
Cox, Robert Sayre, Jr. 1925- *WhoAm 92*
Cox, Robert Thornton 1953- *WhoE 93*
Cox, Robert W. 1945- *WhoSSW 93*
Cox, Rody Powell 1926- *WhoAm 92*
Cox, Roger *WhoScE 91-1*
Cox, Roger Frazier 1939- *WhoAm 92*
Cox, Roger Lindsay 1931- *WhoE 93*
Cox, Roger Stephen 1957- *WhoEmL 93*
Cox, Ronald Baker 1943- *WhoAm 92*
Cox, Ronald Frederick 1946- *WhoEmL 93*
Cox, Ronald O. 1938- *St&PR 93*
Cox, Samuel S. 1824-1889 *PolPar*
Cox, Stephen 1966- *ScF&FL 92*
Cox, Steven Allen 1944- *St&PR 93*
Cox, Terrence Guy 1956- *WhoE 93, WhoEmL 93, WhoWor 93*
Cox, Terry Allen 1939- *WhoAm 92*
Cox, Thomas K. *Law&B 92*
Cox, Thomas P. 1954- *St&PR 93*
Cox, Thomas R. 1951- *St&PR 93*
Cox, Thomas Rodford *WhoScE 91-1*
Cox, Timothy C. 1946- *WhoEmL 93*
Cox, Timothy Martin *WhoScE 91-1*
Cox, Toni Harris 1961- *WhoSSW 93*
Cox, Traci Alane 1961- *WhoEmL 93*
Cox, Valerie Kay 1962- *WhoSSW 93*
Cox, Verne E. 1930- *St&PR 93*
Cox, Vincent Daniel 1932- *St&PR 93*
Cox, Walter Maddox 1932- *St&PR 93*
Cox, Walter Thompson, III 1942- *CngDr 91, WhoAm 92, WhoE 93*
Cox, Warren Jacob 1935- *WhoAm 92*
Cox, Whitson William 1921- *WhoAm 92*
Cox, Wilford Donald 1925- *WhoAm 92*
Cox, William *ScF&FL 92*
Cox, William Albert, Jr. 1927- *WhoSSW 93*
Cox, William Andrew 1925- *WhoAm 92, WhoSSW 93, WhoWor 93*
Cox, William Bruce 1951- *WhoSSW 93*
Cox, William Huff 1939- *WhoSSW 93*
Cox, William Jackson 1921- *WhoAm 92*
Cox, William Jay 1947- *WhoEmL 93*
Cox, William K. 1950- *St&PR 93*
Cox, William Martin 1922- *WhoE 93, WhoWor 93*
Cox, William Plummer 1915- *WhoAm 92*
Cox, William Trevor 1928- *ConAu 37NR, WhoWor 93*
Cox, William Walter 1947- *WhoSSW 93*
Cox, Willis Franklin 1927- *WhoWrEP 92*
Cox, Winston H. 1941- *St&PR 93, WhoAm 92, WhoE 93*
Coxall, David Oxford 1943- *WhoWor 93*
Cox-Ash, Martha Elizabeth 1955- *WhoAmW 93*
Coxe, Clovis *AmWomPl*
Coxe, Donald *BioIn 17*
Coxe, Gordon L. 1937- *St&PR 93*
Coxe, Molly 1959- *ConAu 137, SmATA 69 [port]*
Coxe, Thomas Chatterton, III 1930- *St&PR 93*
Coxeter, Harold Scott Macdonald 1907- *WhoAm 92*
Coxey, Jacob Sechler 1854-1951 *GayN*
Coxon, Anthony Peter Macmillan *WhoScE 91-1*
Cox-Pursley, Carol Sue 1951- *WhoSSW 93, WhoWor 93*
Coxwell, Melvin Rogers 1929- *St&PR 93*
Coy, Arvel Jean 1951- *WhoEmL 93*
Coy, Cameron D. *Law&B 92*
Coy, David Lavar 1951- *WhoWrEP 92*
Coy, Delphine Harris *AmWomPl*
Coy, Elba Boone 1924- *WhoSSW 93*
Coy, Frank *BioIn 17*
Coy, M. L. 1922- *WhoSSW 93*
Coy, Patricia Ann 1952- *WhoAmW 93, WhoEmL 93*
Coy, Thomas Richard 1948- *WhoEmL 93*
Coy, Timothy Kirk 1958- *WhoEmL 93*
Coyer, Anthony Joseph, Jr. 1955- *St&PR 93*
Coyle, Bernard Hugh, Jr. 1951- *St&PR 93*
Coyle, Brian d1991 *BioIn 17*
Coyle, Clara V. *AmWomPl*
Coyle, Dennis P. 1938- *St&PR 93*
Coyle, Donald Walton 1922- *WhoSSW 93*
Coyle, Edward John 1956- *WhoEmL 93*
Coyle, Elizabeth Alling 1959- *WhoEmL 93*
Coyle, Harold W. 1952- *ScF&FL 92*
Coyle, Mara Genevieve 1961- *WhoE 93, WhoEmL 93*
Coyle, Marie Bridget 1935- *WhoAm 92, WhoAmW 93*
Coyle, Martin A. *Law&B 92*
Coyle, Martin Adolphus 1941- *St&PR 93*
Coyle, Martin Adolphus, Jr. 1941- *WhoAm 92*
Coyle, Michael Anthony 1946- *St&PR 93*
Coyle, Neva 1943- *ConAu 138*
Coyle, Peter James 1937- *WhoWor 93*
Coyle, Rhonda May 1957- *WhoEmL 93*
Coyle, Richard Jay 1948- *St&PR 93*
Coyle, Robert Everett 1930- *WhoAm 92*
Coyle, Stephen C. 1945- *St&PR 93*
Coyle, Wallace *ScF&FL 92*
Coyle, William 1917- *ScF&FL 92, WhoAm 92, WhoSSW 93*
Coym, Peter 1942- *WhoAm 92*
Coyne, Charles Cole 1948- *WhoE 93*
Coyne, Edward James, Jr. 1953- *WhoSSW 93*
Coyne, Frank J. 1948- *WhoAm 92*
Coyne, George V. *WhoScE 91-3*
Coyne, James K. 1946- *St&PR 93*
Coyne, James O. 1928- *WhoIns 93*
Coyne, Jamie 1971- *BioIn 17*
Coyne, John 1937- *ScF&FL 92*
Coyne, John Thomas 1927- *St&PR 93*
Coyne, Joseph Gillick 1934- *WhoAm 92*
Coyne, Karen Ann 1948- *St&PR 93*
Coyne, Lisa Ann 1952- *WhoEmL 93*
Coyne, M. Jeanne 1926- *WhoAmW 93*
Coyne, Marilyn Aldrich 1939- *WhoSSW 93*
Coyne, Nancy *BioIn 17*
Coyne, Patrick Ivan 1944- *WhoAm 92*
Coyne, Peter R. 1953- *St&PR 93*
Coyne, Raymond Michael *Law&B 92*
Coyne, Richard 1926-1990 *BioIn 17*
Coyne, Sarah Theresa 1941- *WhoAmW 93*
Coyne, Terry H. *Law&B 92*
Coyne, Thomas Joseph 1933- *WhoAm 92*
Coyne, Thomas R. 1926- *St&PR 93*
Coyne, William J. 1936- *CngDr 91*
Coyne, William Joseph 1936- *WhoAm 92, WhoE 93*
Coyner, C.P. 1942- *St&PR 93*
Coyner, Randolph Stratton 1944- *WhoSSW 93*
Coyner, Russell R. 1932- *St&PR 93*
Coyote, Peter 1942- *WhoAm 92*
Coyro, William F. 1943- *St&PR 93*
Cozad, James W. *BioIn 17*
Cozad, James W. 1927- *St&PR 93, WhoAm 92*
Cozad, John Condon 1944- *WhoAm 92*
Cozamanis, Steve C. *Law&B 92*
Cozan, Lee *WhoAm 92*
Cozart, John Roger 1955- *WhoEmL 93, WhoWor 93*
Cozart, Richard Michael *Law&B 92*
Cozen, Sidney 1924- *St&PR 93*
Cozens, Roger A. 1950- *St&PR 93*
Cozon, Jean-Noel 1944- *WhoSSW 93*
Cozort, Amber Lynne 1963- *WhoEmL 93*
Cozy, Carl A. 1930- *St&PR 93*
Cozza, Patrick A. 1955- *St&PR 93*
Cozzarelli, Francis Anthony 1933- *WhoE 93*
Cozzarelli, Isabelle Mary 1961- *WhoAmW 93*
Cozzens, James Gould 1903-1978 *BioIn 17*
Cozzens, Winifred *AmWomPl*
Cozzi, Aldo John *Law&B 92*
Cozzi, Hugo Louis 1934- *WhoAm 92*
Cozzi, Julia E. 1954- *WhoEmL 93*
Cozzi, Luigi *MiSFD 9*
Cozzi, Paul D.J. *Law&B 92*
Cozzi, Ronald Lee 1943- *WhoE 93*
Cozzolino, Salvatore James 1924- *St&PR 93*
Cozzone, Alain J. 1942- *WhoScE 91-2*
Cozzone, Patrick J. 1945- *WhoScE 91-2*
Cprek, Kent Gordon 1953- *WhoEmL 93*
Crabb, Barbara Brandriff 1939- *WhoAmW 93*
Crabb, Carol Ann 1944- *WhoWor 93*
Crabb, Jennifer H. *Law&B 92*
Crabb, Kenneth Wayne 1950- *WhoEmL 93*
Crabb, Trevor Arthur *WhoScE 91-1*
Crabbe, Armand (Charles) 1883-1947 *Baker 92*
Crabbe, Buster 1908-1983 *IntDcF 2-3 [port]*
Crabbe, Chris Wallace- *BioIn 17*
Crabbe, George 1754-1832 *BioIn 17*
Crabbe, Jean 1927- *WhoScE 91-2, WhoWor 93*
Crabbe, John Crozier 1914- *WhoAm 92*
Crabbe, Katharyn W. 1945- *ScF&FL 92*
Crabbs, Roger Alan 1928- *WhoAm 92*
Crabiel, J. Edward d1992 *NewYTBS 92 [port]*
Crable, John A. *Law&B 92*
Crable, Richard Ellsworth 1947- *WhoAm 92*
Crabtree, Andrea Yvette 1958- *WhoAmW 93, WhoEmL 93*
Crabtree, Beverly June 1937- *WhoAm 92*
Crabtree, Bill Preston 1952- *WhoEmL 93*
Crabtree, Bruce Ibester, Jr. 1923- *St&PR 93*
Crabtree, Bruce Isbester, Jr. 1923- *WhoAm 92*
Crabtree, Harold L. 1935- *St&PR 93*
Crabtree, I. Bruce, Jr. 1923- *St&PR 93*
Crabtree, Jack Turner 1936- *WhoAm 92*
Crabtree, Joel J. 1938- *St&PR 93*
Crabtree, John Henry, Jr. 1925- *WhoAm 92*
Crabtree, John Michael 1949- *WhoSSW 93*
Crabtree, Judith 1928- *BioIn 17*
Crabtree, Larry Alston 1943- *St&PR 93*
Crabtree, Lotta 1847-1924 *BioIn 17*
Crabtree, Mattie *AmWomPl*
Crabtree, Ray S. 1935- *WhoIns 93*
Crabtree, Richard Alan 1946- *St&PR 93*
Crabtree, Robert Howard 1948- *WhoE 93*
Crabtree, William 1905-1991 *BioIn 17*
Cracas, Ronald John *Law&B 92*
Cracco, Roger Quinlan 1934- *WhoAm 92*
Crace, Jim 1946- *ScF&FL 92*
Crace, John C. 1887-1968 *HarEnMi*
Crackel, Theodore Joseph 1938- *WhoAm 92*
Cracraft, Ivan Wayne 1933- *St&PR 93*
Craddock, Campbell 1930- *WhoAm 92*
Craddock, Frank Wootters 1928- *St&PR 93*
Craddock, J.T. 1963- *St&PR 93*
Craddock, James Hill 1960- *WhoWor 93*
Craddock, Mark C. 1949- *St&PR 93*
Craddock, Muriel Annie 1948- *WhoWor 93*
Craddock, Patricia Bland 1938- *WhoSSW 93*
Crader, Rebecca Jane 1951- *WhoWrEP 92*
Cradock, Christopher George Francis Maurice 1862-1914 *HarEnMi*
Crafoord, Ralph J. 1936- *WhoScE 91-4*
Craft, Alice May 1947- *WhoEmL 93*
Craft, C. Douglas 1953- *WhoEmL 93*
Craft, Carolyn Martin 1942- *WhoAmW 93, WhoSSW 93*
Craft, Cheri Carroll 1961- *WhoAmW 93*
Craft, David William 1952- *WhoAm 92, WhoEmL 93*
Craft, Diane 1955- *WhoE 93*
Craft, Donald Bruce 1935- *WhoAm 92*
Craft, Douglas Durwood 1924- *WhoAm 92*
Craft, Edmund Coleman 1939- *St&PR 93, WhoAm 92*
Craft, George Sullivan 1947- *WhoEmL 93*
Craft, Harold Dumont, Jr. 1938- *WhoAm 92*
Craft, Jack Johnson 1930- *St&PR 93*
Craft, James H. 1945- *WhoSSW 93*
Craft, James Pressley, Jr. 1913- *WhoSSW 93*
Craft, Jerome Walter 1932- *WhoSSW 93*
Craft, Joseph W., III *WhoAm 92*
Craft, Kinuko 1940- *BioIn 17*
Craft, Marjorie *BioIn 17*
Craft, Randal Robert, Jr. 1941- *WhoAm 92*
Craft, Rebecca A. *Law&B 92*
Craft, Richard Earl 1947- *WhoEmL 93*
Craft, Robbie Wright 1951- *WhoEmL 93*
Craft, Robert Homan 1906- *WhoAm 92*
Craft, Robert (Lawson) 1923- *Baker 92*
Craft, Robert M. *Law&B 92*
Craft, Robert Merrill 1958- *WhoEmL 93*

Crafton, Andrew Allen 1957- *WhoEmL 93*
Crafton, Donald (Clayton) 1947- *ConAu 138*
Crafton, Richard Douglas 1932- *WhoAm 92*
Crafts, John Smith 1927- *St&PR 93*
Cragen, Donald E. 1930- *St&PR 93*
Cragen, John P. 1950- *St&PR 93*
Crager, Bruce Lee 1952- *WhoEmL 93*
Cragg, Anthony Louis Talbot 1956- *WhoWor 93*
Cragg, Ernest Elliott 1927- *WhoAm 92, WhoE 93*
Cragg, Laurence Harold 1912- *WhoAm 92*
Cragg, Tony *BioIn 17*
Craggs, Carolyn *WhoScE 91-1*
Craghead, James Douglas 1950- *WhoWor 93*
Cragin, Michael Dennis 1947- *WhoEmL 93*
Cragon, Harvey George 1929- *WhoAm 92*
Crahan, Jack Bertsch 1923- *St&PR 93, WhoAm 92*
Crahay, Roland 1915- *WhoWor 93*
Crahen, Daniel Edward 1944- *WhoE 93*
Craib, Kenneth Bryden 1938- *WhoAm 92*
Craib, Ralph G(rant) 1925- *ConAu 136*
Craib, Ralph Grant 1925- *WhoAm 92*
Craig *BioIn 17*
Craig, A. *WhoScE 91-1*
Craig, Alan Daniel 1935- *WhoE 93*
Craig, Albert Morton 1927- *WhoAm 92*
Craig, Alexander Joseph, III *Law&B 92*
Craig, Alexander Robert 1941- *St&PR 93*
Craig, Alisa *ConAu 40NR*
Craig, Amanda 1959- *ConAu 137*
Craig, Andrew *Law&B 92*
Craig, Andrew Billings, III 1931- *St&PR 93*
Craig, Angela Heitert 1956- *WhoEmL 93, WhoSSW 93*
Craig, Anna Maynard 1944- *WhoAmW 93*
Craig, Anne Abbot Throop 1869- *AmWomPl*
Craig, Ben H. 1921- *St&PR 93*
Craig, Brenda Susan 1953- *WhoAmW 93*
Craig, Brian *ScF&FL 92*
Craig, Charles Grant 1957- *WhoEmL 93*
Craig, Charles Raymond 1940- *St&PR 93*
Craig, Charles Samuel 1943- *WhoAm 92, WhoE 93*
Craig, Christopher Patrick 1952- *WhoSSW 93*
Craig, Curtis L. *Law&B 92*
Craig, Curtis Lee 1955- *WhoSSW 93*
Craig, Dana Michael 1950- *WhoEmL 93*
Craig, Daniel H. 1811-1895 *JrnUS*
Craig, David 1932- *ConAu 37NR*
Craig, David Clarke 1955- *WhoEmL 93, WhoSSW 93*
Craig, David Jeoffrey 1925- *WhoAm 92*
Craig, David W. 1925- *WhoAm 92*
Craig, Douglas Warren 1942- *WhoE 93*
Craig, E. Wilson 1930- *St&PR 93*
Craig, Edith 1869-1947 *BioIn 17*
Craig, Edward A. *Law&B 92*
Craig, Edward Armstrong, III 1934- *WhoAm 92*
Craig, Edward Gordon 1872-1966 *IntDcOp, OxDcOp*
Craig, Elaine 1958- *WhoEmL 93*
Craig, Floyd William 1933- *St&PR 93*
Craig, G(illian) M(ary) 1949- *ConAu 139*
Craig, Gail Heidbreder 1941- *WhoWor 93*
Craig, Gavin P. *Law&B 92*
Craig, Gene Martin 1957- *WhoE 93*
Craig, George *WhoAm 92*
Craig, George Brownlee, Jr. 1930- *WhoAm 92*
Craig, George Dennis 1936- *WhoSSW 93*
Craig, George N. d1992 *NewYTBS 92*
Craig, Glendon Brooks 1933- *WhoAm 92*
Craig, Gordon Alexander 1913- *WhoAm 92*
Craig, Grace E. *AmWomPl*
Craig, Gregory Lewis 1961- *WhoEmL 93*
Craig, Harald Franklin 1930- *WhoAm 92*
Craig, Harmon *BioIn 17*
Craig, Harmon 1926- *WhoAm 92*
Craig, Hurshel Eugene 1932- *WhoWor 93*
Craig, James 1871-1940 *BioIn 17*
Craig, James Donald 1944- *WhoSSW 93*
Craig, James Duhadway 1943- *WhoWrEP 92*
Craig, James Gordon 1951- *WhoEmL 93*
Craig, James Lynn 1933- *St&PR 93, WhoAm 92, WhoWor 93*
Craig, James Robert 1913- *WhoWor 93*
Craig, James Roland 1940- *WhoSSW 93*
Craig, James William 1921- *WhoAm 92*
Craig, Jean 1937- *BioIn 17, WhoAm 92, WhoAmW 93*
Craig, Jeanne Anne 1936- *WhoAmW 93*
Craig, Jenny *BioIn 17*
Craig, Joe *BioIn 17*
Craig, John G. 1942- *St&PR 93*
Craig, John Gilbert, Jr. 1933- *WhoAm 92*
Craig, John Grant 1942- *WhoAm 92*
Craig, John Tucker 1926- *WhoE 93*
Craig, Judith 1937- *WhoAmW 93*
Craig, Judith Margaret 1946- *WhoAmW 93*
Craig, Karen Lynn 1959- *WhoAmW 93*
Craig, Kenneth Denton 1937- *WhoAm 92*
Craig, L. Clifford 1938- *WhoAm 92*
Craig, Larry E. *BioIn 17*
Craig, Larry E. 1945- *CngDr 91*
Craig, Larry Edwin 1945- *WhoAm 92*
Craig, Leslie R. 1950- *St&PR 93*
Craig, Lexie Ferrell 1921- *WhoAm 92, WhoWor 93*
Craig, M.S. 1923-1991 *BioIn 17*
Craig, Malcolm Everett 1930- *WhoAm 92*
Craig, Malcolm Jay 1962- *WhoSSW 93*
Craig, Malin 1875-1945 *CmdGen 1991 [port]*
Craig, Margaret Berol d1992 *BioIn 17, NewYTBS 92*
Craig, Margaret Wilcox 1934- *WhoAmW 93*
Craig, Martha Ann 1952- *WhoEmL 93*
Craig, Mary Francis 1923-1991 *BioIn 17*
Craig, Mary Francis Shura 1923- *WhoWrEP 92*
Craig, Maurice James 1919- *BioIn 17*
Craig, Norman Lee *Law&B 92*
Craig, P. James 1925- *WhoIns 93*
Craig, Paul Max, Jr. 1921- *WhoAm 92*
Craig, Peter John 1959- *WhoEmL 93*
Craig, Peter Stebbins 1928- *WhoE 93, WhoWor 93*
Craig, Philip Joel 1949- *WhoE 93*
Craig, Randolph *ScF&FL 92*
Craig, Richard James 1959- *WhoE 93, WhoEmL 93*
Craig, Robert 1921- *ScF&FL 92*
Craig, Robert D. 1955- *St&PR 93*
Craig, Robert George 1923- *WhoAm 92*
Craig, Robert James 1958- *WhoEmL 93*
Craig, Robert Mark, III *Law&B 92*
Craig, Robert McMeekin 1926- *WhoSSW 93*
Craig, Robert Michael 1944- *WhoSSW 93*
Craig, Robert Sanderson 1932- *St&PR 93*
Craig, Roger 1960- *AfrAmBi*
Craig, Roger A. *Law&B 92*
Craig, Roger Lee 1930- *WhoAm 92*
Craig, Rufus Hagood *Law&B 92*
Craig, Sandra Noel 1954- *WhoEmL 93*
Craig, Sid *St&PR 93*
Craig, Stephen Wright 1932- *WhoAm 92*
Craig, Stuart N. 1942- *WhoAm 92*
Craig, Susan L. *Law&B 92*
Craig, Thomas Franklin 1943- *WhoSSW 93*
Craig, Walter M., Jr. *Law&B 92*
Craig, William C. 1939- *St&PR 93*
Craig, William E. *Law&B 92*
Craig, William Francis 1931- *St&PR 93, WhoAm 92*
Craig, William Glenn 1952- *WhoE 93*
Craig, William Ooley 1931- *WhoE 93*
Craig, Winchell McKendree 1930- *WhoWor 93*
Craigavon, Viscount 1871-1940 *BioIn 17*
Craige, Betty Jean 1946- *ConAu 40NR, WhoSSW 93*
Craige, Danny Dwaine 1946- *WhoSSW 93*
Craige, Ernest 1918- *WhoAm 92*
Craighead, Frank Cooper, Jr. 1916- *WhoAm 92*
Craighead, Ian Alexander *WhoScE 91-1*
Craighead, Rodkey 1916- *WhoAm 92*
Craighill, Nancy Theresa 1962- *WhoAmW 93*
Craigie, David 1908- *ScF&FL 92*
Craigie, Dorothy M. *ScF&FL 92*
Craigie, Pearl Mary Teresa Richards 1867-1906 *AmWomPl*
Craiglow, James Hawkins 1941- *WhoE 93*
Craigmile, David F. 1928- *St&PR 93*
Craigmile, Jeffrey S. *Law&B 92*
Craigo, Gordon Earl 1951- *WhoEmL 93*
Craigs, Anne F. *St&PR 93*
Craig-Wentworth, Marion, Mrs. *AmWomPl*
Craik, Alexander Duncan Davidson *WhoScE 91-1*
Craik, Charles Scott 1954- *WhoEmL 93*
Craik, Dinah Maria (Mulock) 1826-1887 *MajAI [port]*
Craik, Dinah Mulock 1826-1887 *NinCLC 38 [port]*
Craik, Gary Charles 1949- *WhoSSW 93*
Craik, Philip Lee 1952- *WhoEmL 93, WhoSSW 93*
Crain, Alan R., Jr. *Law&B 92*
Crain, Bluford Walter, Jr. 1914- *WhoAm 92*
Crain, Cullen Malone 1920- *WhoAm 92*
Crain, Darrell Clayton, Jr. 1910- *WhoE 93*
Crain, F. Carter *Law&B 92*
Crain, Frances Utterback 1914- *WhoSSW 93*
Crain, G.D. 1885-1973 *BioIn 17*
Crain, Gertrude Ramsay *WhoAm 92, WhoAmW 93*
Crain, Irving Jay 1914- *WhoAm 92*
Crain, James Francis 1931- *St&PR 93, WhoAm 92*
Crain, James T., Jr. 1937- *St&PR 93*
Crain, James Walter 1949- *WhoEmL 93*
Crain, John Walter 1944- *WhoAm 92, WhoSSW 93*
Crain, Keith Evans 1941- *WhoAm 92*
Crain, Lacy E. 1910- *St&PR 93*
Crain, Margie Lynn 1912- *St&PR 93*
Crain, Morris E. 1924-1945 *BioIn 17*
Crain, Nancy L. 1953- *WhoAmW 93, WhoEmL 93*
Crain, Rance *WhoAm 92*
Crain, Stanley Wilson 1925- *St&PR 93*
Crain, Stephen Lee 1948- *WhoEmL 93*
Crain, Theodore Scott, Jr. 1955- *WhoE 93*
Crain, William 1949- *MiSFD 9*
Crain, William Edwin 1929- *WhoAm 92*
Crain, William Henry 1917- *WhoAm 92, WhoSSW 93*
Craine, Edith Janice 1881- *AmWomPl*
Craine, Thomas Knowlton 1942- *WhoAm 92*
Crainer, Herchel Americus, III 1955- *WhoEmL 93*
Crair-Schleger, Stacey Ess 1961- *WhoE 93*
Crais, Arthur A., Jr. *Law&B 92*
Crais, Thomas Floyd, Jr. 1943- *WhoWor 93*
Crakes, Gary Michael 1953- *WhoE 93, WhoEmL 93*
Crall, Hugh C. *Law&B 92*
Crall, James Monroe 1914- *WhoAm 92*
Crall, Michael J. 1943- *St&PR 93*
Cram, Donald J. 1919- *BioIn 17*
Cram, Donald James 1919- *WhoAm 92, WhoWor 93, WhoWrEP 92*
Cram, Douglas M. *Law&B 92, WhoAm 92*
Cram, Eva J. *Law&B 92*
Cram, Ira Higgins, Jr. 1929- *St&PR 93*
Cram, Judith M. *Law&B 92*
Cram, Lawrence Edward 1948- *WhoWor 93*
Cram, Mildred 1889-1985 *ScF&FL 92*
Cram, Phillip J. 1943- *St&PR 93*
Cram, Ralph Adams 1863-1942 *ModArCr 3 [port], ScF&FL 92, TwCLC 45 [port]*
Cram, Reginald Maurice 1914- *WhoAm 92*
Cram, William John *WhoScE 91-1*
Cramarossa, Francesco *WhoScE 91-3*
Cramb, Rosemary *AmWomPl*
Cramblett, Henry Gaylord 1929- *WhoAm 92*
Cramblit, Miggie E. *Law&B 92*
Cramblit, Miggie Ellen *Law&B 92*
Cramer, Albert *WhoWor 93*
Cramer, Alfred Bartlett, III 1932- *WhoSSW 93*
Cramer, Bernhard 1930- *WhoScE 91-3*
Cramer, Bertrand 1934- *WhoScE 91-4*
Cramer, Betty F. 1920- *WhoAm 92*
Cramer, Bud 1947- *BioIn 17, CngDr 91, WhoAm 92*
Cramer, Catherine Patricia *WhoE 93*
Cramer, Conrad Charles 1927- *St&PR 93*
Cramer, Dale Lewis 1924- *WhoAm 92*
Cramer, Doc 1905-1990 *BioIn 17*
Cramer, Donald C. *Law&B 92*
Cramer, Edward Morton 1925- *WhoAm 92*
Cramer, Elliot Myron 1933- *WhoSSW 93*
Cramer, Friedrich 1923- *WhoScE 91-3*
Cramer, Gerald 1916-1991 *BioIn 17*
Cramer, H. Eugene 1932- *St&PR 93*
Cramer, Harold 1927- *WhoAm 92*
Cramer, Howard Ross 1925- *WhoAm 92, WhoWor 93*
Cramer, Jacob 1705-1770 *See* Cramer, Wilhelm c. 1746-1799 *Baker 92*
Cramer, Jacqueline Marian 1951- *WhoWor 93*
Cramer, James Perry 1947- *WhoAm 92, WhoE 93*
Cramer, Jennifer Mary 1964- *WhoAmW 93*
Cramer, Johann Baptist 1771-1858 *Baker 92*
Cramer, John 1934- *ScF&FL 92*
Cramer, John Sanderson 1942- *WhoE 93*
Cramer, John Scott 1930- *WhoAm 92*
Cramer, Kathryn 1962- *ScF&FL 92*
Cramer, Kirby L. 1936- *St&PR 93*
Cramer, Klaus Jurgen 1932- *WhoScE 91-3*
Cramer, Laura Schwarz 1925- *WhoSSW 93*
Cramer, Lee H. 1945- *St&PR 93, WhoE 93*
Cramer, Marian H. 1934- *WhoWrEP 92*
Cramer, Marjorie 1941- *WhoAm 92*
Cramer, Mark Clifton 1954- *WhoEmL 93*
Cramer, Maurice Browning 1910-1990 *ScF&FL 92*
Cramer, Michael William 1924- *WhoWor 93*
Cramer, Morgan Joseph, Jr. 1906- *WhoAm 92*
Cramer, Owen Carver 1941- *WhoAm 92*
Cramer, Paul 1944- *St&PR 93*
Cramer, Richard Charles 1932- *WhoAm 92*
Cramer, Richard F., Jr. 1947- *St&PR 93*
Cramer, Robert E., Jr. 1947- *WhoSSW 93*
Cramer, Robert Eli 1919- *WhoAm 92*
Cramer, Robert Vern 1933- *WhoAm 92*
Cramer, Roger 1905-1990 *BioIn 17*
Cramer, Roxanne Herrick 1934- *WhoAmW 93*
Cramer, Scott Steven *Law&B 92*
Cramer, Stanley Howard 1933- *WhoAm 92*
Cramer, Steven Edward 1945- *WhoWor 93*
Cramer, Walter Haynes 1928- *WhoAm 92*
Cramer, Wilhelm c. 1746-1799 *Baker 92*
Cramer, William Anthony 1938- *WhoAm 92*
Cramer, William F. 1923- *WhoAm 92*
Cramer, William Mitchell 1948- *WhoEmL 93*
Cramers, Carel A.M.G. 1935- *WhoScE 91-3*
Cramm, D.C. 1925- *St&PR 93*
Cramp, Donald Arthur 1936- *WhoAm 92*
Cramp, Lori Angell 1955- *WhoEmL 93*
Cramp, Rosemary Jean *WhoScE 91-1*
Crampin, Michael *WhoScE 91-1*
Crampton, John Philip 1941- *WhoAm 92*
Crampton, Julian Moray *WhoScE 91-1*
Crampton, Luke 1959- *ConAu 139*
Crampton, Scott Paul 1913- *WhoAm 92*
Crampton, Stuart Jessup Bigelow 1936- *WhoAm 92*
Crampton, William DeVer 1920- *WhoAm 92*
Cramton, Charles Davis 1955- *WhoEmL 93*
Cramton, Roger Conant 1929- *WhoAm 92*
Crancer, Alfred, III 1958- *WhoSSW 93*
Crancer, Lester Allen, Jr. 1932- *St&PR 93*
Cranch, William 1769-1855 *OxCSupC*
Crandal, Jack *WhoWrEP 92*
Crandall, Alissa Joy 1954- *WhoEmL 93*
Crandall, Arlene Bernadette 1956- *WhoE 93, WhoEmL 93*
Crandall, Brad d1991 *BioIn 17*
Crandall, Charles Jordan 1958- *WhoWrEP 92*
Crandall, Dale Eugene 1944- *St&PR 93*
Crandall, Drew Martin 1955- *WhoEmL 93*
Crandall, Edward David 1938- *WhoAm 92*
Crandall, Emily S. *Law&B 92*
Crandall, George T. 1947- *St&PR 93*
Crandall, Gilbert Albert 1915- *WhoWrEP 92*
Crandall, Ira Carlton 1931- *WhoAm 92*
Crandall, Irene Jean *AmWomPl*
Crandall, John Karl 1931- *WhoWrEP 92*
Crandall, John Lynn 1927- *St&PR 93, WhoWor 93*
Crandall, Lee Walter 1913- *WhoAm 92*
Crandall, Nancy Lee 1940- *WhoAmW 93*
Crandall, Nelson David, III 1954- *WhoEmL 93*
Crandall, Norma Rand *WhoWrEP 92*
Crandall, Prudence 1803-1890 *BioIn 17*
Crandall, Richard G. 1946- *St&PR 93*
Crandall, Richard L. 1943- *St&PR 93*
Crandall, Robert 1935- *CurBio 92 [port]*
Crandall, Robert L. *BioIn 17*
Crandall, Robert L. 1935- *EncABHB 8 [port], News 92 [port]*
Crandall, Robert Lloyd 1935- *St&PR 93, WhoAm 92, WhoSSW 93*
Crandall, Robert Mason 1928- *St&PR 93, WhoE 93*
Crandall, Robert W. 1940- *BioIn 17*
Crandall, Roderick Pendleton 1948- *WhoEmL 93*
Crandall, Sonia Jane 1952- *WhoAmW 93, WhoEmL 93, WhoWor 93*
Crandall, Stephen Alan *Law&B 92*
Crandall, Stephen Harry 1920- *WhoAm 92*
Crandall, Victoria d1990 *BioIn 17*
Crandall, Vine, III 1943- *St&PR 93*
Crandall, Walter Ellis 1916- *WhoAm 92*
Crandell, Bill *BioIn 17*
Crandell, J. Wayne 1933- *St&PR 93*
Crandell, Jodie Leigh 1959- *WhoAmW 93*
Crandell, John Underhill d1991 *BioIn 17*
Crandell, Kenneth James 1957- *WhoEmL 93, WhoSSW 93, WhoWor 93*
Crandlemere, Robert Wayne 1947- *WhoE 93*
Crandles, George Marshal 1917- *WhoAm 92*
Crandon, John Howland 1912- *WhoAm 92, WhoWor 93*

Crane, A. Reynolds 1908-1990 *BioIn 17*
Crane, Adrian *BioIn 17*
Crane, Andrew B. 1946- *WhoAm 92*
Crane, Andrew Marion 1946- *St&PR 93*
Crane, Angus Edgar 1955- *WhoEmL 93*
Crane, Ann Robinson 1930- *WhoE 93*
Crane, Anne M. 1934- *WhoAmW 93*
Crane, Barbara Bachmann 1928- *WhoAm 92*
Crane, Barbara Joyce 1934- *WhoAm 92, WhoWrEP 92*
Crane, Benjamin Field 1929- *WhoAm 92*
Crane, Bob 1929-1978 *BioIn 17*
Crane, Bonnie Loyd 1930- *WhoE 93*
Crane, Burton *WhoWrEP 92*
Crane, C.J. 1946- *St&PR 93*
Crane, Caroline 1930- *ScF&FL 92*
Crane, Charles F. 1949- *St&PR 93*
Crane, Charles Russell, Jr. 1928- *WhoSSW 93*
Crane, Charlotte 1951- *WhoEmL 93*
Crane, Cora Howarth Stewart Taylor 1868-1910 *BioIn 17*
Crane, David *Law&B 92*
Crane, David Mark 1948- *WhoEmL 93*
Crane, David S. 1954- *St&PR 93*
Crane, Diana Marilyn 1933- *WhoE 93*
Crane, Donald F., Jr. *Law&B 92*
Crane, Douglas Allen 1949- *WhoEmL 93*
Crane, Dwight Burdick 1937- *WhoAm 92*
Crane, Edward H. *Law&B 92*
Crane, Edward Harrison, III 1944- *WhoAm 92*
Crane, Edward J. 1928- *EncABHB 8 [port]*
Crane, Edward M. *WhoE 93*
Crane, Eileen Cunningham 1935- *WhoAmW 93*
Crane, Eleanor Maud *AmWomPl*
Crane, Elizabeth Green *AmWomPl*
Crane, Faye 1947- *WhoEmL 93*
Crane, Francis George 1916- *St&PR 93*
Crane, Frederick A. d1991 *BioIn 17*
Crane, Frederick G., Jr. d1992 *NewYTBS 92*
Crane, Gary Wade 1957- *WhoEmL 93, WhoSSW 93*
Crane, Gerald William 1938- *St&PR 93*
Crane, Glenda Paulette 1946- *WhoAmW 93*
Crane, Hal R. *Law&B 92*
Crane, Harold Elroy, Jr. 1930- *WhoSSW 93*
Crane, Hart 1899-1932 *BioIn 17, MagSAmL [port], WorLitC [port]*
Crane, Hewitt David 1927- *WhoAm 92*
Crane, Horace Richard 1907- *WhoAm 92*
Crane, Howard C. 1937- *St&PR 93*
Crane, Irving Donald 1913- *WhoAm 92*
Crane, Isaac Watts 1773-1856 *BioIn 17*
Crane, James 1877-1974 *BioIn 17*
Crane, Jameson 1926- *St&PR 93, WhoAm 92*
Crane, Jim d1881 *BioIn 17*
Crane, John D. *Law&B 92*
Crane, John K. 1942- *ScF&FL 92*
Crane, John Murdoch, Jr. *Law&B 92*
Crane, John William 1940- *WhoE 93*
Crane, Jonathan Townley 1953- *WhoSSW 93*
Crane, Julia Gorham 1925- *WhoAm 92*
Crane, Julian Coburn 1918- *WhoAm 92*
Crane, Kathleen Dorothy 1918- *WhoAmW 93*
Crane, Keenan Durkin 1944- *WhoAmW 93*
Crane, L. Patrick, Jr. *Law&B 92*
Crane, Laura Jane 1941- *WhoAm 92, WhoE 93*
Crane, Leo Stanley 1915- *WhoAm 92*
Crane, Lillie *ScF&FL 92*
Crane, Louis Arthur 1922- *WhoAm 92*
Crane, Mabel H. *AmWomPl*
Crane, Margaret Ann 1940- *WhoAmW 93*
Crane, Marilyn N. 1930- *WhoSSW 93*
Crane, Mark 1930- *WhoAm 92*
Crane, Martin *ScF&FL 92*
Crane, Mary L. 1919- *St&PR 93*
Crane, Michael Patrick 1948- *WhoAm 92*
Crane, Michael T. 1960- *St&PR 93*
Crane, Nancy Jean *Law&B 92*
Crane, Neal D. 1916- *St&PR 93*
Crane, Neal Dahlberg 1916- *WhoAm 92*
Crane, Peter *MiSFD 9*
Crane, Philip M. 1930- *CngDr 91*
Crane, Philip Miller 1930- *WhoAm 92*
Crane, Ray 1923- *St&PR 93*
Crane, Regina Ann 1961- *WhoAmW 93, WhoEmL 93*
Crane, Richard 1918-1969 *BioIn 17*
Crane, Richard Clement 1925- *WhoAm 92*
Crane, Robert *ConAu 136, -37NR*
Crane, Robert 1908-1990 *ScF&FL 92*
Crane, Robert Carl 1938- *St&PR 93*
Crane, Robert Kendall 1935- *WhoAm 92*
Crane, Robert Myrl 1941- *WhoSSW 93*
Crane, Robert Sellers, Jr. 1922- *St&PR 93, WhoAm 92*
Crane, Robyn Lillibridge *Law&B 92*
Crane, Ronald Lawrence *Law&B 92*
Crane, Ronald Salmon 1886-1967 *BioIn 17*
Crane, Simon Robert Peter 1952- *WhoWor 93*
Crane, Stephen 1871-1900 *BioIn 17, GayN, JrnUS, MagSAmL [port], WorLitC [port]*
Crane, Stephen Andrew 1945- *St&PR 93, WhoAm 92*
Crane, Stephen Blake 1955- *WhoAm 92*
Crane, Stephen D. 1951- *St&PR 93*
Crane, Stephen Joel 1946- *WhoEmL 93*
Crane, Terese Ann 1947- *WhoEmL 93*
Crane, Walter 1845-1915 *MajAI [port]*
Crane, Winthrop Murray 1910- *St&PR 93*
Cranefield, Paul Frederic 1925- *WhoAm 92*
Craner, Lorne Whitney *WhoAm 92*
Crane-Robinson, Colyn *WhoScE 91-1*
Cranford, Brenda S. 1957- *St&PR 93*
Cranford, Henry Lee 1928- *St&PR 93*
Cranford, J. Wayne 1933- *St&PR 93, WhoAm 92*
Cranford, Jack Allen 1939- *WhoSSW 93*
Cranford, James Blease 1950- *WhoEmL 93, WhoSSW 93*
Cranford, Luke 1939- *St&PR 93*
Cranford, Page DeRonde 1935- *St&PR 93, WhoAm 92*
Cranford, Peter G. *BioIn 17*
Cranford, Rebecca Jo 1962- *WhoAmW 93*
Cranford, Steven Leon 1951- *WhoEmL 93*
Cranford, Wilson Hessburg, Jr. 1916- *WhoE 93*
Crang, Richard Francis Earl 1936- *WhoAm 92*
Crangle, Joseph F. 1932- *PolPar*
Crangle, Robert Dale 1943- *St&PR 93*
Crangle, Victoria Lynn 1966- *WhoAmW 93*
Cranin, Marilyn Sunners 1932- *WhoAm 92, WhoAmW 93*
Cranis, Peter F. 1962- *WhoSSW 93*
Crank, J. David 1954- *St&PR 93*
Crank, Mildred *AmWomPl*
Crank, Ruth Elizabeth 1938- *WhoAmW 93*
Cranley, Martin Joseph 1924- *WhoScE 91-3*
Cranmer, David Charles 1954- *WhoEmL 93*
Cranmer, James Paul 1938- *St&PR 93*
Cranmer, Sheridan M. *Law&B 92*
Cranmer, Thomas William 1951- *WhoEmL 93*
Cranmore, Robert 1927- *WhoSSW 93*
Crann, Gordon Parker 1952- *WhoWor 93*
Cranna, Rick Lee 1956- *WhoEmL 93*
Crannell, David J. 1947- *St&PR 93*
Crannell, Melvin Y., Jr. 1948- *WhoIns 93*
Crannell, Richard 1953- *St&PR 93*
Cranney, Marilyn Kanrek *Law&B 92*
Cranney, Marilyn Kanrek 1949- *WhoAmW 93, WhoE 93, WhoWor 93*
Cranois, Nicole Simone 1949- *WhoWor 93*
Cranshaw, Stanley *ConAu 136, MajAI*
Cranston, Alan *BioIn 17*
Cranston, Alan 1914- *CngDr 91, WhoAm 92*
Cranston, Caroline Wood 1925- *WhoAmW 93, WhoWor 93*
Cranston, John Montgomery 1909- *WhoAm 92*
Cranston, John Welch 1931- *WhoSSW 93*
Cranston, Maurice William 1920- *WhoWor 93*
Cranston, Meg *BioIn 17*
Cranston, W.I. 1928- *WhoScE 91-1*
Cranton, Nina Renee 1949- *WhoEmL 93*
Crants, D. Robert, Jr. 1944- *St&PR 93*
Crants, Doctor Robert, Jr. 1944- *WhoWor 93*
Crantz, Frank Richard 1948- *WhoSSW 93*
Cranwell, John Philips 1904- *ScF&FL 92*
Cranwell, Peter A. *WhoScE 91-1*
Cranz, Alwin 1834-1923 *Baker 92*
Cranz, August *Baker 92*
Cranz, August Heinrich 1789-1870 *Baker 92*
Cranz, Edmund Pendleton *Law&B 92*
Cranz, Oskar d1929 *Baker 92*
Craon, Diane Beauvau- *BioIn 17*
Crapo, Sheila Anne 1951- *WhoAmW 93, WhoEmL 93*
Crary, Alice *AmWomPl*
Crary, Bess J. *AmWomPl*
Crary, Mildred Rodgers 1925- *WhoWrEP 92*
Crary, Miner Dunham, Jr. 1920- *WhoAm 92*
Crary, Sharon Anne 1953- *WhoE 93*
Cras, Jean Emile Paul 1879-1932 *Baker 92*
Crase, Darrell *BioIn 17*
Crase, Douglas 1944- *WhoWrEP 92*
Crasemann, Bernd 1922- *WhoAm 92*
Crashaw, Richard 1612?-1649 *DcLB 126*
Crashaw, Richard 1613?-1649 *BioIn 17*
Craske, Margaret d1990 *BioIn 17*
Crass, Franz 1928- *Baker 92*
Crass, James E., IV 1940- *St&PR 93*
Crass, Linda J. *St&PR 93*
Crassus, Marcus Licinius c. 115BC-53BC *HarEnMi*
Crassus, Publius Licinius c. 85BC-53BC *HarEnMi*
Crassweller, Robert Michael 1954- *WhoE 93*
Crasto, Justin M. 1947- *St&PR 93*
Craswell, Ellen 1932- *WhoAmW 93*
Crate, Stephen Church 1952- *WhoE 93, WhoEmL 93, WhoWor 93*
Crater, Glenn Douglas 1942- *WhoSSW 93*
Craterus c. 370BC-321BC *HarEnMi*
Craton, Joseph Michael 1946- *WhoEmL 93*
Craton, Roger P. 1932- *St&PR 93*
Craufurd, Robert 1764-1812 *HarEnMi*
Craugh, Carolyn 1929- *WhoSSW 93*
Craugh, Joseph P., Jr. 1934- *St&PR 93*
Craugh, Joseph Patrick, Jr. *Law&B 92*
Craugh, Joseph Patrick, Jr. 1934- *WhoAm 92, WhoE 93*
Craun Brown, Tammy Lee 1963- *WhoAmW 93*
Cravatts, Richard Louis 1949- *WhoEmL 93*
Craven, David L. *Law&B 92*
Craven, David L. 1953- *St&PR 93*
Craven, David Leigh 1953- *WhoEmL 93*
Craven, Debbie Lynn 1954- *WhoAmW 93*
Craven, Donald Neil 1924- *WhoAm 92*
Craven, Edward d1991 *BioIn 17*
Craven, Frank J. 1939- *St&PR 93*
Craven, Grover Oliver, Jr. 1943- *WhoSSW 93*
Craven, John M. 1948- *St&PR 93*
Craven, John Michael 1948- *WhoEmL 93*
Craven, John Pinna 1924- *WhoAm 92*
Craven, John W. 1927- *St&PR 93*
Craven, Keith J. 1935- *St&PR 93*
Craven, Pamela F. *Law&B 92*
Craven, Robert H. 1922- *St&PR 93*
Craven, Roberta Jill 1962- *WhoSSW 93*
Craven, Robin Gray 1948- *WhoSSW 93*
Craven, Roy Curtis, Jr. 1924- *WhoAm 92*
Craven, Wes 1949- *MiSFD 9*
Craven, Wes(ley Earl) 1939- *ConAu 137*
Craven, William 1606-1697 *BioIn 17*
Craven, William W. *BioIn 17*
Craven, William Wallace 1935- *St&PR 93*
Cravens, Ben 1868-1950 *BioIn 17*
Cravens, Gwyneth *ScF&FL 92*
Cravens, Hartley Dodge 1935- *WhoIns 93*
Cravens, Kathryn d1991 *BioIn 17*
Cravens, Malcolm 1907- *WhoIns 93*
Cravens, Raymond Lewis 1930- *WhoAm 92*
Cravens, Richard J. *Law&B 92*
Cravens, William Lewis 1947- *WhoEmL 93*
Craver, Adelaide Austell 1942- *St&PR 93*
Craver, Carrol Mickey 1924- *St&PR 93*
Craver, Donald H. 1935- *WhoE 93*
Craver, James Bernard 1943- *St&PR 93, WhoAm 92*
Craver, Larry Dean 1950- *WhoEmL 93*
Craver, Margret 1907- *BioIn 17*
Craver, Theodore F. *Law&B 92*
Cravero, Kathleen Ann *WhoUN 92*
Cravey, Robin T. 1951- *WhoWrEP 92*
Cravez, Glenn Edward 1957- *WhoEmL 93*
Cravioto, Alfonso 1883-1955 *DcMexL*
Craviotto, Darlene Susan 1950- *WhoEmL 93*
Craw, Demas T. d1942 *BioIn 17*
Craw, Freeman *WhoAm 92*
Craw, Lillian J. *AmWomPl*
Crawford, Albert Gene 1950- *WhoE 93*
Crawford, Alex *WhoScE 91-1*
Crawford, Ashton 1958- *WhoEmL 93*
Crawford, Austin Albert 1920- *St&PR 93*
Crawford, Barrett Lynn 1951- *WhoEmL 93*
Crawford, Betty Anne *ScF&FL 92*
Crawford, Betty Lee 1925- *WhoAmW 93*
Crawford, Brinton 1944- *St&PR 93*
Crawford, Broderick 1911-1986 *IntDcF 2-3*
Crawford, Bruce *BioIn 17*
Crawford, Bruce 1929- *St&PR 93*
Crawford, Bruce D. 1952- *St&PR 93*
Crawford, Bruce Edgar 1929- *WhoAm 92*
Crawford, Bryce Low, Jr. 1914- *WhoAm 92*
Crawford, Burnett Hayden 1922- *WhoAm 92, WhoSSW 93, WhoWor 93*
Crawford, Caren Lee 1954- *WhoEmL 93*
Crawford, Carl Benson 1923- *WhoAm 92*
Crawford, Charles M. 1951- *St&PR 93*
Crawford, Charles McNeil 1918- *WhoAm 92*
Crawford, Charles Merle 1924- *WhoAm 92*
Crawford, Charles P. 1953- *St&PR 93*
Crawford, Christopher Miller 1942- *St&PR 93*
Crawford, Cindy *BioIn 17*
Crawford, Craig 1953- *St&PR 93*
Crawford, Cynthia Elaine 1957- *WhoAmW 93*
Crawford, Cynthia Richard 1959- *WhoAmW 93*
Crawford, Daniel Eldon 1939- *St&PR 93*
Crawford, Daniel J. 1942- *ConAu 136*
Crawford, Daniel L. 1944- *St&PR 93*
Crawford, David Coleman 1930- *WhoAm 92*
Crawford, Dewey Byers 1941- *WhoAm 92*
Crawford, Don D. 1936- *St&PR 93*
Crawford, Donald Wesley 1938- *WhoAm 92*
Crawford, E.H. 1925- *St&PR 93*
Crawford, E. Stanley d1992 *NewYTBS 92*
Crawford, Earl Boyd 1906- *WhoAm 92*
Crawford, Ed. d1873 *BioIn 17*
Crawford, Edward Hamon 1925- *WhoIns 93*
Crawford, Elouise S. 1949- *WhoAmW 93, WhoEmL 93*
Crawford, F. Marion 1854-1909 *GayN, ScF&FL 92*
Crawford, Frederic Mull 1930- *WhoSSW 93*
Crawford, Frederick William 1931- *WhoWor 93*
Crawford, G. Irene *Law&B 92*
Crawford, Gary William 1953- *ScF&FL 92, WhoWrEP 92*
Crawford, Harold Bernard 1934- *WhoAm 92*
Crawford, Helen Hurt 1939- *WhoSSW 93*
Crawford, Howard A. 1917- *St&PR 93*
Crawford, Howard Allen 1917- *WhoAm 92*
Crawford, Hunt Dorn, Jr. 1948- *WhoE 93*
Crawford, Iain Lindsay 1953- *WhoSSW 93*
Crawford, Ira S. 1937- *St&PR 93*
Crawford, Isabella Valancy 1850-1887 *BioIn 17*
Crawford, Jack *BioIn 17*
Crawford, Jack 1908-1991 *AnObit 1991, BioIn 17*
Crawford, James *ScF&FL 92*
Crawford, James D. 1950- *St&PR 93*
Crawford, James Douglas 1932- *WhoAm 92*
Crawford, James L. 1935- *St&PR 93*
Crawford, James Richard 1948- *WhoWor 93*
Crawford, James Weldon 1927- *WhoAm 92*
Crawford, Jay Bruce 1946- *WhoE 93*
Crawford, Jean Andre 1941- *WhoAmW 93*
Crawford, Jean Gray 1924- *St&PR 93*
Crawford, Jeffrey A. *Law&B 92*
Crawford, Jennifer Eastman *Law&B 92*
Crawford, Jennifer Lynn 1956- *WhoEmL 93*
Crawford, Jerry N. 1937- *St&PR 93*
Crawford, Joan 1908-1977 *BioIn 17, IntDcF 2-3 [port]*
Crawford, Joe Allen 1961- *WhoWrEP 92*
Crawford, John Edward 1924- *WhoAm 92*
Crawford, John F. 1940- *WhoWrEP 92*
Crawford, John Littlefield, III 1943- *WhoSSW 93*
Crawford, John M. *Law&B 92*
Crawford, John M., Jr. *BioIn 17*
Crawford, John Milton, Jr. 1939- *WhoSSW 93*
Crawford, John T. *WhoIns 93*
Crawford, John William 1936- *WhoWrEP 92*
Crawford, Johnny *BioIn 17*
Crawford, Judith Ann 1952- *WhoAmW 93*
Crawford, Judith L. 1945- *St&PR 93*
Crawford, Kathleen *Law&B 92*
Crawford, Keith Edward 1953- *St&PR 93*
Crawford, Kelly Griffith 1951- *WhoEmL 93*
Crawford, Kenneth Charles 1918- *WhoAm 92*
Crawford, Kevin Scott 1957- *WhoEmL 93*
Crawford, Larry S. 1944- *WhoSSW 93*
Crawford, Lester Mills, Jr. 1938- *WhoAm 92*
Crawford, Lewis Cleaver 1925- *WhoAm 92*
Crawford, Lewis O. 1943- *St&PR 93*
Crawford, Linda Sibery 1947- *WhoAmW 93, WhoE 93, WhoEmL 93*
Crawford, Lionel *WhoScE 91-1*
Crawford, Loretta 1944- *WhoAmW 93*
Crawford, Lucy A. 1947- *WhoIns 93*
Crawford, Lucy Clark 1957- *WhoAmW 93*
Crawford, Lynn S. 1940- *St&PR 93*
Crawford, Maria Luisa 1939- *WhoAm 92*
Crawford, Mark Alan 1956- *WhoEmL 93*
Crawford, Mary B. 1949- *WhoAmW 93*
Crawford, Mary Catherine 1947- *WhoAsAP 91*
Crawford, Mary E. 1942- *WhoE 93*

Crawford, Mary Janet 1946- *WhoAmW 93*
Crawford, Mary Louise Perri *WhoAmW 93*
Crawford, Mary Mead 1957- *WhoAm 92*
Crawford, Meredith Pullen 1910- *WhoAm 92*
Crawford, Michael *BioIn 17*
Crawford, Michael 1942- *CurBio 92 [port]*
Crawford, Michael Thomas 1946- *St&PR 93*
Crawford, Michael Wayne 1962- *WhoSSW 93*
Crawford, Muriel Laura *WhoAm 92, WhoAmW 93*
Crawford, Myron Lloyd 1938- *WhoAm 92*
Crawford, Nancy Corrine 1938- *WhoE 93*
Crawford, Nanette Jayne *Law&B 92*
Crawford, Ned *ScF&FL 92*
Crawford, Norman Crane, Jr. 1930- *WhoAm 92*
Crawford, Pamela E. 1950- *WhoEmL 93*
Crawford, Pamela Gail 1960- *WhoSSW 93*
Crawford, Peggy 1917- *WhoAmW 93*
Crawford, Peter Baker 1939- *St&PR 93*
Crawford, Peter S. 1945- *WhoAm 92*
Crawford, Purdy *Law&B 92, WhoAm 92*
Crawford, Randy *BioIn 17*
Crawford, Randy 1952- *SoulM*
Crawford, Randy Charles 1952- *St&PR 93*
Crawford, Raymond Maxwell, Jr. 1933- *WhoAm 92*
Crawford, Richard 1935- *WhoAm 92*
Crawford, Richard A. 1930- *St&PR 93*
Crawford, Richard Bradway 1933- *WhoAm 92*
Crawford, Richard Eben, Jr. 1930- *WhoWor 93*
Crawford, Richard G. 1926- *St&PR 93*
Crawford, Richard Jay 1947- *WhoE 93*
Crawford, Robert George 1943- *WhoAm 92*
Crawford, Robert J. *Law&B 92*
Crawford, Robert James *WhoScE 91-1*
Crawford, Robert Lawrence *Law&B 92*
Crawford, Robert MacGregor Martyn *WhoScE 91-1*
Crawford, Robert (McArthur) 1899-1961 *Baker 92*
Crawford, Robert S. 1914- *St&PR 93*
Crawford, Robin V. *Law&B 92*
Crawford, Roger Brentley 1951- *WhoWor 93*
Crawford, Roy Edgington, III 1938- *WhoAm 92*
Crawford, Ruth 1901-1953 *BioIn 17*
Crawford, Ruth Porter 1901-1953 *Baker 92*
Crawford, Sally Sue 1944- *WhoAmW 93*
Crawford, Sam 1880-1968 *BioIn 17*
Crawford, Samuel Johnson 1835-1913 *BioIn 17*
Crawford, Sarah Carter 1938- *WhoAmW 93*
Crawford, Shirley Ann 1933- *WhoE 93*
Crawford, Stanley *BioIn 17*
Crawford, Stanley E., Jr. *Law&B 92*
Crawford, Stanley Edward 1932- *St&PR 93*
Crawford, Steven Riley 1952- *St&PR 93*
Crawford, Stuart Michael *WhoScE 91-1*
Crawford, Susan Jean 1947- *WhoAm 92, WhoAmW 93*
Crawford, Susan N. Young *WhoAm 92*
Crawford, Suzanne C. *Law&B 92*
Crawford, Sylvia Booth 1937- *WhoAmW 93*
Crawford, T.E. 1940- *St&PR 93*
Crawford, Thomas Joey 1955- *St&PR 93*
Crawford, Tom *BioIn 17*
Crawford, Vernon E. 1946- *ConAu 136*
Crawford, Wahoo 1880-1968 *BioIn 17*
Crawford, Wayne *MiSFD 9*
Crawford, Wayne 1946- *WhoSSW 93*
Crawford, William A. 1936- *AfrAmBi*
Crawford, William Basil, Jr. 1941- *WhoAm 92*
Crawford, William David 1947- *WhoE 93*
Crawford, William F. 1911- *WhoAm 92*
Crawford, William H. 1772-1834 *PolPar*
Crawford, William L. 1911-1984 *ScF&FL 92*
Crawford, William Rex, Jr. 1928- *WhoAm 92*
Crawford, William Richard 1936- *WhoAm 92*
Crawford, William W. 1928- *St&PR 93*
Crawford, William Walsh 1927- *WhoAm 92*
Crawford-Cabral, Joao 1929- *WhoScE 91-3*
Crawford-Mason, Clare Wootten 1936- *WhoAm 92*
Crawley, Ernest 1869-1924 *IntDcAn*
Crawley, Fenton *ScF&FL 92*
Crawley, Jacqueline Nina 1950- *WhoAm 92, WhoAmW 93*
Crawley, James B. 1926- *St&PR 93*
Crawley, John Boevey 1946- *WhoAm 92, WhoE 93*
Crawley, John Cornelius William *WhoScE 91-1*
Crawley, John L. *Law&B 92*
Crawley, Marie Therese *WhoScE 91-1*
Crawley, Peter J. *Law&B 92*
Crawley, Robert Allen 1950- *WhoEmL 93*
Crawley, Robert Evans 1937- *St&PR 93*
Crawley, Thomas Michael 1963- *WhoEmL 93*
Crawley, Tony 1938- *ScF&FL 92*
Crawshaw, Alwyn 1934- *WhoWor 93*
Crawshaw, Ralph 1921- *WhoAm 92*
Craxi, Bettino 1934- *WhoWor 93*
Cray, Brian E. *Law&B 92*
Cray, Cloud Lanor, Jr. 1922- *St&PR 93, WhoAm 92, WhoWor 93*
Cray, Ed(ward) 1933- *ConAu 37NR*
Cray, Robert *BioIn 17*
Cray, Robert 1953- *ConMus 8 [port], SoulM, WhoAm 92*
Cray, Seymour *BioIn 17*
Cray, Seymour R. 1925- *WhoAm 92*
Cray, William C. *Law&B 92*
Craycraft, Carl LeRoy 1935- *WhoWor 93*
Craycroft, Joseph L., Jr. 1937- *St&PR 93*
Crayder, Teresa *MajAI*
Crayencour, Marguerite De *BioIn 17, ScF&FL 92*
Crayne, Larry R. *Law&B 92*
Craypo, Charles 1936- *WhoAm 92*
Craythorne, Norman William Brian 1931- *WhoAm 92*
Crayton, Render 1933- *St&PR 93*
Craze, Anthony 1944- *ScF&FL 92*
Crazy Gang, The *IntDcF 2-3 [port]*
Crazy Horse c. 1849-1877 *HarEnMi*
Crazzolara, Pasquale 1884-1976 *IntDcAn*
Creadick, Wayne Samuel, Jr. 1962- *WhoEmL 93*
Creagan, Clarence Wayne 1929- *St&PR 93, WhoAm 92*
Creagan, Robert Joseph 1919- *WhoAm 92*
Creager, Joe Scott 1929- *WhoAm 92*
Creager, Maureen 1931- *WhoWrEP 92*
Creagh, Richard P. 1946- *St&PR 93*
Creagh-Dexter, Linda Truitt 1941- *WhoAmW 93*
Creal, Richard Charles 1930- *WhoAm 92*
Cream *ConMus 9 [port]*
Creamer, Andrew G. 1929- *St&PR 93*
Creamer, Claude Wendell 1936- *St&PR 93*
Creamer, David E. 1947- *St&PR 93*
Creamer, Jack Major 1954- *WhoEmL 93, WhoSSW 93*
Creamer, James J. 1928- *St&PR 93*
Creamer, Jose Emilio *Law&B 92*
Creamer, Linda Edith 1954- *WhoAm 92, WhoAmW 93*
Creamer, Nelson Glenn 1959- *WhoE 93*
Creamer, Robert 1958- *St&PR 93*
Creamer, Robert W. 1922- *BiDAMSp 1989*
Creamer, Thomas F. 1917- *St&PR 93*
Creamer, William Henry, III 1927- *WhoAm 92*
Crean, John Anthony *Law&B 92*
Crean, John C. 1925- *St&PR 93*
Crean, John Gale 1910- *St&PR 93, WhoAm 92*
Crean, Peter Anthony 1953- *WhoWor 93*
Crean, Simon 1949- *WhoAsAP 91*
Crean, Susan 1945- *WhoCanL 92*
Creany, Cathleen Annette 1950- *WhoAm 92*
Creasey, David Edward 1944- *WhoE 93*
Creasey, David John *WhoScE 91-1*
Creasey, Frederick A. 1950- *St&PR 93*
Creasey, John 1908-1973 *BioIn 17, ScF&FL 92*
Creasey, William Alfred 1933- *WhoE 93*
Creasia, Donald Anthony 1937- *WhoWor 93*
Creasman, William Paul 1952- *St&PR 93, WhoEmL 93*
Creasman, William Thomas 1934- *WhoAm 92*
Creason, John Paul 1942- *WhoAm 92*
Creason, Karen Kay 1943- *WhoAmW 93*
Creason, Kenneth Claude 1940- *St&PR 93*
Creasor, A.R. 1944- *St&PR 93*
Creasy, Colin Frederick Maurice *WhoScE 91-1*
Creasy, Paul W. *Law&B 92*
Creasy, Wayne *St&PR 93*
Creatore, Giuseppe 1871-1952 *Baker 92*
Creatore, Luigi *SoulM*
Creatore, Paul William 1941- *St&PR 93*
Creaturo, Barbara *BioIn 17*
Creaven, Patrick Joseph 1933- *WhoAm 92*
Crecelius, Daniel 1937- *ConAu 139*
Crecelius, Sylvia Ann 1942- *WhoAmW 93*
Crecine, John Patrick 1939- *WhoAm 92, WhoSSW 93, WhoWor 93*
Crecquillon, Thomas c. 1480-1557 *Baker 92*
Crede, Robert Henry 1915- *WhoAm 92*
Credico, John D. 1926- *St&PR 93*
Credit, Samuel L. 1940- *St&PR 93*
Cree, George d1992 *BioIn 17, NewYTBS 92*
Creech, Fulton Hunter 1929- *WhoAm 92*
Creech, Hugh John 1910- *WhoAm 92*
Creech, Jay Heyward 1956- *WhoEmL 93*
Creech, John Lewis 1920- *WhoAm 92*
Creech, Wilbur Lyman 1927- *WhoAm 92*
Creech, William Ayden 1925- *WhoSSW 93*
Creecy, Adrien Felicia 1962- *WhoAmW 93*
Creed, Nellie Anne 1955- *WhoWrEP 92*
Creed, Robert Payson, Sr. 1925- *WhoAm 92*
Creed, Thomas G. 1933- *WhoAm 92*
Creed, Thomas Gary 1933- *St&PR 93*
Creed, Thomas Wayne 1943- *WhoSSW 93, WhoWor 93*
Creedon, Janice Leigh 1939- *WhoAmW 93*
Creedon, John J. 1924- *St&PR 93, WhoAm 92*
Creedon, Richard O. *Law&B 92*
Creedon, William Henry 1938- *St&PR 93*
Creedy, David Peter 1951- *WhoScE 91-1*
Creef, Sarah *BioIn 17*
Creegan, John B. 1910-1990 *BioIn 17*
Creegan, Kevin Paul 1950- *WhoE 93*
Creegan, Robert Francis 1915- *WhoAm 92*
Creeger, Allan D. 1921- *St&PR 93*
Creeger, Lawrence Allan 1947- *St&PR 93*
Creek, Geoffrey 1946- *WhoWor 93*
Creek, Phillip G. 1952- *St&PR 93*
Creekmore, Anne Filosa 1957- *WhoAmW 93*
Creekmore, Marion Virgil, Jr. 1939- *WhoAm 92, WhoWor 93*
Creekmore, William Brown 1959- *WhoEmL 93, WhoSSW 93*
Creel, Alexandra Gardiner d1990 *BioIn 17*
Creel, Austin Bowman 1929- *WhoAm 92*
Creel, Carol *Law&B 92*
Creel, Dana Shannon 1912- *WhoAm 92*
Creel, David Russel 1949- *WhoEmL 93*
Creel, Diane C. 1948- *St&PR 93*
Creel, Frank Warner 1941- *WhoE 93*
Creel, George 1876-1953 *JrnUS*
Creel, George C. 1934- *St&PR 93*
Creel, James Randall 1904-1990 *BioIn 17*
Creel, Luther Edward, III 1937- *WhoAm 92*
Creel, Michael Allen 1953- *WhoEmL 93*
Creel, Roger Ellis 1933- *St&PR 93*
Creeley, Robert 1926- *BioIn 17, MagSAmL [port]*
Creeley, Robert White 1926- *WhoAm 92, WhoWrEP 92*
Creelman, James 1859-1915 *JrnUS*
Creelman, Marjorie Broer 1908- *WhoAmW 93*
Creelman, Wayne Lewis 1951- *WhoEmL 93*
Creenan, Katherine Heras 1945- *WhoAmW 93, WhoE 93*
Creenspan, Louis 1931- *St&PR 93*
Creer, Carl R. 1942- *St&PR 93*
Creer, Philip Douglas 1903- *WhoAm 92*
Creese, Elwin H. 1931- *St&PR 93*
Creese, Irene *ScF&FL 92*
Creevey, Caroline Alathea Stickney 1843-1920 *AmWomPl*
Creevey, Lucy Ellsworth 1940- *WhoE 93*
Creevy, Donald Charles 1936- *WhoAm 92*
Creevy, Edward T. 1950- *St&PR 93*
Creffield, Dennis 1931- *BioIn 17*
Cregan, John B. 1930- *WhoIns 93*
Cregan, John Barry 1930- *St&PR 93*
Cregan, John P. 1937- *St&PR 93*
Cregar, Douglas E. 1943- *St&PR 93*
Cregger, Morris M. 1939- *St&PR 93*
Creggy, Stuart 1939- *WhoWor 93*
Cregier, Don M(esick) 1930- *WhoWrEP 92*
Crehan, Joseph Edward 1938- *WhoAm 92*
Crehan, Michael Joseph 1954- *St&PR 93*
Crehan, Susan K. *Law&B 92*
Crehore, Charles Aaron *Law&B 92*
Crehore, Tom Oliver *BioIn 17*
Creidler, Barbara Jean 1968- *WhoAmW 93*
Creigh, Thomas, Jr. 1912- *WhoAm 92*
Creighton, Beatrice *AmWomPl*
Creighton, Dale Edward 1934- *St&PR 93, WhoAm 92*
Creighton, David O'Nell 1938- *St&PR 93*
Creighton, Douglas George 1923- *WhoE 93*
Creighton, Edward 1932- *St&PR 93*
Creighton, Helen 1899-1989 *BioIn 17*
Creighton, Joanne Vanish 1942- *WhoAmW 93*
Creighton, John Douglas 1928- *WhoAm 92*
Creighton, John W., Jr. 1932- *St&PR 93, WhoAm 92*
Creighton, Jon L. *Law&B 92*
Creighton, Joseph R. *Law&B 92*
Creighton, Lee *ScF&FL 92*
Creighton, Neal 1930- *WhoAm 92*
Creim, William Benjamin 1954- *WhoEmL 93*
Cremaschi, Dario 1941- *WhoScE 91-3*
Cremaschi, Domenico 1929- *WhoScE 91-3*
Cremazie, Octave 1827-1879 *BioIn 17*
Creme, Lol *MiSFD 9*
Cremer, Christoph G.M. 1944- *WhoScE 91-3*
Cremer, Leon Earl 1945- *WhoE 93*
Cremer, Mabelle A. 1927- *WhoAm 92*
Cremer, Michel C.A. 1933- *WhoScE 91-2*
Cremer, Richard Eldon 1928- *WhoWor 93*
Cremer, Victoriano 1908- *BioIn 17*
Cremers, Armin Bernd 1946- *WhoWor 93*
Cremers, Clifford John 1933- *WhoAm 92*
Cremieux, Andree 1938- *WhoScE 91-2*
Cremin, Lawrence Arthur 1925-1990 *BioIn 17*
Cremins, William Daniel 1939- *WhoWor 93*
Cremlyn, Richard James William *WhoScE 91-1*
Cremona, Vincent Anthony 1925- *WhoAm 92*
Cremoux, Catherine *Law&B 92*
Crenna, James Alan 1950- *St&PR 93, WhoEmL 93*
Crenna, Richard 1926- *MiSFD 9*
Crenna, Richard 1927- *WhoAm 92*
Crenne, Helisenne de c. 1510-c. 1560 *BioIn 17*
Crenshaw, Albert Burford 1942- *WhoAm 92*
Crenshaw, Barbara House 1925- *WhoSSW 93*
Crenshaw, Ben 1952- *WhoAm 92*
Crenshaw, Ben Daniel 1952- *BiDAMSp 1989*
Crenshaw, Carlton Boyd 1945- *St&PR 93*
Crenshaw, Claudia Regan 1951- *WhoAm 92, WhoAmW 93, WhoEmL 93*
Crenshaw, Elizabeth Wells 1948- *WhoEmL 93*
Crenshaw, Francis Nelson 1922- *WhoAm 92*
Crenshaw, Gordon L. 1922- *St&PR 93*
Crenshaw, Gordon Lee 1922- *WhoAm 92*
Crenshaw, Iris Marie 1955- *WhoAmW 93*
Crenshaw, Jack W. 1934- *WhoSSW 93*
Crenshaw, James Faulkner 1911- *WhoSSW 93*
Crenshaw, Jan Carol 1945- *WhoSSW 93*
Crenshaw, Jere Walton 1950- *WhoSSW 93*
Crenshaw, John Lewis *Law&B 92*
Crenshaw, Kevin Mills 1960- *WhoEmL 93*
Crenshaw, Kristina 1943- *WhoSSW 93*
Crenshaw, Marion Carlyle, Jr. 1931- *WhoAm 92*
Crenshaw, Marva Louise 1951- *WhoAmW 93*
Crenshaw, Patricia Shryack 1941- *WhoAmW 93*
Crenshaw, Sally Ann 1945- *WhoAmW 93*
Crenshaw, Scott 1966- *WhoSSW 93*
Crenson, Matthew Allen 1943- *WhoAm 92*
Crenwelge, Dayton R. 1937- *St&PR 93*
Creo, Matthew J., Jr. 1929- *St&PR 93*
Creo, Robert Angelo 1952- *WhoEmL 93*
Crepaldi, Gaetano 1931- *WhoScE 91-3*
Crepeau, Michel 1930- *BioIn 17*
Crepeau, Richard Charles 1941- *WhoSSW 93*
Crepet, William Louis 1946- *WhoAm 92*
Creppel, Claire Binet 1936- *WhoAmW 93*
Crequi, Charles de Blanchefort de Canaples de, I 1578-1638 *HarEnMi*
Crequi, Francois de Bonne, II, Marquis of 1629-1687 *HarEnMi*
Crequillon, Thomas c. 1480-1557 *Baker 92*
Cerand, Mary J. 1933- *St&PR 93*
Crernejewski, Larry Craig 1949- *St&PR 93*
Cresap, Charles Nash 1919- *WhoE 93*
Crescentini, Girolamo 1762-1846 *Baker 92, OxDcOp*
Crescenzi, Vittorio 1932- *WhoScE 91-3*
Crescenzo, Peter Joseph 1923- *St&PR 93*
Crescimanno, Francesco Giulio *WhoScE 91-3*
Creser, William 1844-1933 *Baker 92*
Cresimore, James Leonard 1928- *WhoWor 93*
Creson, Lenore Sapinsley 1940- *St&PR 93*
Creson, Thomas Kyle, Jr. 1931- *WhoSSW 93*
Crespi, Irving 1926- *WhoAm 92*
Crespi, Tony D. 1955- *WhoE 93*
Crespi-Gonzalez, M. Alicia 1928- *WhoScE 91-3*
Crespin, Leslie 1947- *BioIn 17*
Crespin, Regine *WhoAm 92*

Crespin, Regine 1927- *Baker 92, IntDcOp, OxDcOp*
Crespo, Cynthia Ann 1952- *St&PR 93*
Crespo, Enrique Baron *BioIn 17*
Crespo, Vitor 1932- *WhoWor 93*
Crespo Casares, Alfredo Eduardo 1927- *WhoWor 93*
Crespy, Melissa Fonya 1959- *WhoAmW 93*
Cress, Cecile Colleen 1914- *WhoAmW 93*
Cress, Floyd Cyril 1920- *WhoWrEP 92*
Cress, George Ayers 1921- *WhoAm 92*
Cress, George H. 1936- *St&PR 93*
Cress, Kevin Bruce 1957- *WhoE 93*
Cress, Sally 1954- *St&PR 93*
Cresse, Richard Staunton 1928- *St&PR 93*
Cression, Louisa Keay *Law&B 92*
Cressionnie, Lucien Leon, III 1961- *WhoSSW 93*
Cressman, Edward Howard 1945- *St&PR 93*
Cressman, Frank C. 1933- *St&PR 93*
Cresson, David Homer, Jr. 1955- *WhoWor 93*
Cresson, Edith 1934- *BioIn 17, News 92 [port], WhoWor 93*
Cresswell, Catherine A. 1957- *St&PR 93*
Cresswell, Helen 1934- *ChlFicS, ConAu 37NR, MajAI [port], ScF&FL 92*
Cresswell, Peter R. 1935- *St&PR 93*
Cresswell, Ronald M. 1934- *St&PR 93*
Cressy, Peter Hollon 1941- *WhoAm 92*
Crestin, Jean-Pierre 1942- *WhoScE 91-2*
Creston, Paul 1906-1985 *Baker 92*
Creswell, Charles Alexander 1952- *WhoSSW 93*
Creswell, Dorothy Anne 1943- *WhoAmW 93, WhoWor 93*
Creswell, K.A.C. 1879-1974 *BioIn 17*
Creswell, Keppel Archibald Cameron 1879-1974 *BioIn 17*
Creta, Gavril 1923- *WhoScE 91-4*
Cretella, Tina Kincaid 1959- *WhoAmW 93*
Creteur, Rudolph 1945- *St&PR 93*
Cretin, Shan 1946- *WhoEmL 93*
Cretsinger, Ann *Law&B 92*
Crette, Jean-Paul 1929- *WhoScE 91-2*
Cretu, Gheorghe 1936- *WhoScE 91-4*
Cretu, Ion 1933- *WhoScE 91-4*
Cretzmeyer, Stacy Megan 1959- *WhoWrEP 92*
Creusy, Colette 1943- *WhoScE 91-2*
Creutz, Carol 1944- *WhoAmW 93*
Creutz, Edward Chester 1913- *WhoAm 92*
Creutz, Michael John 1944- *WhoE 93*
Creutzberg, D. 1930- *WhoScE 91-3*
Creutzfeldt, Otto-Detlev 1927- *WhoScE 91-3*
Creutzfeldt, Werner Otto Carl 1924- *WhoScE 91-3*
Creutzinger, Janice Kaye Terry 1954- *WhoSSW 93*
Creutzmann, Harry F. 1943- *St&PR 93, WhoIns 93*
Crevaux, Jules 1847-1883 *Expl 93*
Crevel, Rene 1900-1935 *BioIn 17*
Creveling, Cyrus Robbins 1930- *WhoE 93*
Crevelt, Dwight Eugene 1957- *WhoEmL 93*
Crever, Robert 1936- *St&PR 93*
Crevier, Guy *St&PR 93*
Crevier, Roger L. 1939- *St&PR 93*
Creviston, Robert Louis 1940- *St&PR 93*
Crevoiserat, Patricia Jill 1955- *WhoAmW 93, WhoE 93, WhoEmL 93*
Crew, Helen Coale 1866-1941 *AmWomPl*
Crew, John Neal 1954- *St&PR 93*
Crew, Kermit Ray 1952- *WhoEmL 93*
Crew, Linda 1951- *SmATA 71 [port]*
Crew, Louie 1936- *WhoAm 92*
Crew, Richard Marion 1949- *St&PR 93*
Crew, Spencer 1949- *WhoAm 92*
Crewdson, John 1945- *BioIn 17*
Crewdson, John Mark 1945- *WhoAm 92, WhoE 93*
Crewe, Albert Victor 1927- *WhoAm 92*
Crewe, Nancy Moe 1939- *WhoAmW 93*
Crewe, Trenton Guy, Jr. 1950- *WhoEmL 93*
Crews, Albert E. 1932- *WhoIns 93*
Crews, Catherine *AmWomPl*
Crews, Clyde F. 1944- *ConAu 38NR*
Crews, Donald *BioIn 17, ChlBIID [port]*
Crews, Donald 1938- *BlkAuII 92, MajAI [port]*
Crews, Donald R. *Law&B 92*
Crews, Donald R. 1943- *St&PR 93*
Crews, Frederick Campbell 1933- *WhoAm 92, WhoWrEP 92*
Crews, Fulton T. 1949- *WhoAm 92*
Crews, Harry 1935- *BioIn 17*
Crews, Harry Eugene 1935- *WhoAm 92, WhoWrEP 92*
Crews, Jane Bell 1947- *WhoAmW 93*
Crews, John Eric 1946- *WhoEmL 93, WhoWor 93*
Crews, John Russell 1956- *St&PR 93*
Crews, Judith Carol 1948- *WhoEmL 93*
Crews, Kenneth Donald 1955- *WhoEmL 93*
Crews, Lucile 1888-1972 *Baker 92*
Crews, Paul David *BioIn 17*
Crews, Richard Douglas 1951- *WhoEmL 93*
Crews, Rita Frencella 1952- *WhoAmW 93*
Crews, Robert C., II *Law&B 92*
Crews, William Edwin *Law&B 92*
Crews, William Odell, Jr. 1936- *WhoAm 92*
Crewse, Douglas Owen 1951- *WhoSSW 93*
Crewse, Leonard Lee 1934- *St&PR 93*
Crewson, Lawrence Joel 1934- *St&PR 93*
Crewson, Walter F.J. 1938- *St&PR 93*
Creydt, Tugeborg Wanda 1933- *WhoUN 92*
Creyf, Hubert 1945- *WhoScE 91-2*
Criares, Nicholas James 1934- *WhoE 93*
Cribb, G.S. *WhoScE 91-1*
Cribb, Jeffery E. 1925- *St&PR 93*
Cribb, Peter Harold 1931- *WhoAm 92*
Cribb, Robert (Bridson) 1957- *ConAu 137*
Cribb, Walter Raymond 1949- *WhoAm 92*
Cribbet, John Edward 1918- *WhoAm 92, WhoWor 93*
Cribbins, Bernard 1928- *QDrFCA 92 [port]*
Cribbs, Claire Linton 1912-1985 *BiDAMSp 1989*
Cribbs, Harold *BioIn 17*
Cribiore, Alberto 1945- *WhoAm 92*
Cricco-Lizza, Roberta 1952- *WhoEmL 93*
Crice, Douglas B. 1941- *St&PR 93*
Crichfield, Douglas 1943- *St&PR 93*
Crichley, Lynne *WhoWrEP 92*
Crichlow, Ernest 1914- *BlkAuII 92*
Crichlow, Timothy Nathaniel 1946- *WhoUN 92*
Crichton, Charles 1910- *BioIn 17, MiSFD 9*
Crichton, Dorothy *AmWomPl*
Crichton, John H. 1920- *St&PR 93*
Crichton, John Michael 1942- *WhoAm 92, WhoWrEP 92*
Crichton, Kimberly *Law&B 92*
Crichton, Michael 1942- *Au&Arts 10 [port], BioIn 17, MiSFD 9, ScF&FL 92*
Crichton, (John) Michael 1942- *ConAu 40NR*
Crichton, Neil 1932- *ScF&FL 92*
Crichton, Robert Renfrew 1941- *WhoScE 91-2*
Crichton, Robin 1940- *ConAu 139*
Crichton, Roni Michele *Law&B 92*
Crichton, Theodore P. 1927- *St&PR 93*
Crichton-Browne, Noel Ashley 1944- *WhoAsAP 91*
Crick, Bernard 1929- *ScF&FL 92*
Crick, Francis Harry Compton 1916- *WhoAm 92, WhoWor 93*
Crider, Allen Billy *ScF&FL 92*
Crider, Andrew Blake 1936- *WhoAm 92, WhoE 93*
Crider, Charles J. *Law&B 92*
Crider, David S. 1948- *St&PR 93*
Crider, Hoyt 1924- *WhoWor 93*
Crider, Irene Perritt 1921- *WhoAmW 93, WhoSSW 93, WhoWor 93*
Crider, Jean Marie 1963- *WhoE 93*
Crider, Karen K. *Law&B 92*
Crider, Rudyard Lee 1942- *WhoE 93*
Crider, Stephen W. 1939- *St&PR 93*
Crider, Stephen Wayne 1939- *WhoAm 92*
Cridlin, W.G., Jr. 1946- *St&PR 93*
Criep, Leo H. d1992 *NewYTBS 92*
Criger, Nancy S. 1951- *WhoAmW 93, WhoEmL 93*
Crigger, Debra Linda 1960- *WhoSSW 93*
Crigger, Gary B. 1946- *St&PR 93*
Crigger, Martha Susan 1947- *WhoAmW 93*
Crighton, David G. *WhoScE 91-1*
Crigler, B. Waugh 1948- *WhoEmL 93*
Crigler, T. P. 1933- *WhoAm 92*
Crile, George, Jr. 1907- *WhoAm 92*
Crile, George, Jr. 1907-1992 *NewYTBS 92 [port]*
Crile, Susan 1942- *WhoAm 92, WhoAmW 93*
Crilley, Joseph James 1920- *WhoE 93*
Crilly, John P. *Law&B 92*
Crilly, Karen Ann 1963- *WhoAmW 93*
Crim, Alonzo A. 1928- *BioIn 17, WhoAm 92*
Crim, Jack C. 1930- *St&PR 93, WhoAm 92*
Crim, Joseph Calvin *Law&B 92*
Crim, R. Sidney 1942- *St&PR 93*
Crim, Reuben Sidney 1942- *WhoAm 92, WhoSSW 93*
Crim, Walter R. *Law&B 92*
Crimella, Casimiro 1942- *WhoScE 91-3*
Crimi, Alfred DiGiorgio 1900- *WhoAm 92*
Crimi, Giulio 1885-1939 *Baker 92, OxDcOp*
Criminale, William Oliver, Jr. 1933- *WhoAm 92*
Crimlisk, Jane Therese 1945- *WhoE 93*
Crimmins, Agnes Louise *AmWomPl*
Crimmins, Alfred Stephen, Jr. 1934- *WhoAm 92*
Crimmins, Eileen M. *Law&B 92*
Crimmins, John Blaine, Jr. 1928- *St&PR 93*
Crimmins, Philip Patrick 1930- *WhoAm 92*
Crimmins, Robert John 1938- *WhoAm 92*
Crimmins, Ryan 1960- *St&PR 93*
Crimmins, Sean T. *Law&B 92*
Crimmins, Sean T. 1945- *St&PR 93*
Crimmins, Sean Thomas 1945- *WhoAm 92*
Crimmins, William Gerard *Law&B 92*
Crinella, Francis Michael 1936- *WhoAm 92*
Criner, Douglas E. 1942- *St&PR 93*
Criner, John Lawrence 1960- *WhoWrEP 92*
Cringan, Mary E. 1955- *WhoAmW 93*
Crinion, Gregory Paul 1959- *WhoEmL 93*
Criniti, Mary Pauline 1931- *WhoWrEP 92*
Crinnion, David Martin 1949- *WhoWor 93*
Crinnion, James Patrick 1927- *WhoSSW 93*
Crino, Marjanne Helen 1933- *WhoAm 92, WhoAmW 93*
Cripe, David Lyle 1952- *WhoEmL 93*
Cripe, Nicholas McKinney 1913- *WhoAm 92*
Cripe, Richard L. 1958- *St&PR 93*
Cripe, Wyland Snyder 1921- *WhoAm 92*
Crippen, Robert L. 1937- *BioIn 17*
Crippen, Robert Laurel 1937- *WhoAm 92*
Crippin, Byron Miles, Jr. 1928- *WhoAm 92*
Cripps, Alice Keenen *AmWomPl*
Cripps, Howard D. 1932- *St&PR 93*
Cripps, Richard Stafford 1889-1952 *DcTwHis*
Criqui, William Edmund 1922- *WhoAm 92*
Crisa, John Baptist 1927- *St&PR 93*
Crisafulli, Frank, Jr. 1940- *St&PR 93, WhoIns 93*
Crisafulli, Stephen W. 1940- *St&PR 93*
Crisalli, Anthony P. 1929- *St&PR 93*
Crisalli, Joel R. 1948- *St&PR 93, WhoIns 93*
Crisan, John T. *Law&B 92*
Crisan, Ovidiu 1938- *WhoScE 91-4*
Crisanti, John A. 1940- *St&PR 93*
Crisanto, Teresa 1929- *WhoScE 91-3*
Crisci, John C. 1938- *WhoIns 93*
Crisci, Mathew G. 1941- *WhoAm 92*
Criscillis, Paul A., Jr. 1949- *St&PR 93*
Criscoe, Arthur Hugh 1939- *WhoSSW 93, WhoWor 93*
Criscuolo, Jack J. *St&PR 93*
Criscuolo, Louis d1991 *BioIn 17*
Criscuolo, Rodolfo E. 1935- *WhoIns 93*
Criscuolo, Wendy Laura 1949- *WhoAmW 93, WhoEmL 93*
Crise, Richard 1925- *St&PR 93*
Crise, Robert 1929- *St&PR 93*
Criser, Marshall M. 1928- *St&PR 93, WhoAm 92, WhoSSW 93*
Crisler, Charles Robert 1948- *WhoEmL 93*
Crisler, Ted *Law&B 92*
Crisman, Mary Frances Borden 1919- *WhoAm 92, WhoAmW 93*
Crisman, Ruth 1914- *SmATA 73 [port]*
Crisman, Thomas Lynn 1941- *WhoAm 92*
Crismond, Linda F. 1943- *BioIn 17*
Crismond, Linda Fry 1943- *WhoAm 92*
Crisona, George Joseph, Jr. 1949- *WhoE 93*
Crisona, James Joseph 1907- *WhoAm 92*
Crisostomo, Manny *WhoAm 92*
Crisp, Arthur Hamilton *WhoScE 91-1*
Crisp, Carolyn Ann 1962- *WhoSSW 93*
Crisp, Charles F. 1845-1896 *PolPar*
Crisp, David James 1946- *St&PR 93*
Crisp, David Trevor *WhoScE 91-1*
Crisp, Donald 1880-1974 *IntDcF 2-3*
Crisp, Donald 1882-1974 *BioIn 17*
Crisp, Elizabeth Amanda 1922- *WhoAm 92*
Crisp, Nancy Lee 1961- *WhoAmW 93*
Crisp, Polly Lenore 1952- *WhoEmL 93, WhoSSW 93*
Crisp, Quentin 1908- *BioIn 17, ScF&FL 92*
Crisp, Terry Arthur 1943- *WhoSSW 93*
Crisp, Victor Harry Charles *WhoScE 91-1*
Crispen, Jennifer Leigh 1945- *WhoAmW 93*
Crispi, Michele Marie 1962- *WhoAmW 93*
Crispien, Kai-Peter 1964- *WhoWor 93*
Crispin, A.C. 1950- *ScF&FL 92*
Crispin, Andre Arthur 1923- *St&PR 93, WhoAm 92*
Crispin, James Hewes 1915- *WhoWor 93*
Crispin, Kathleen Margaret 1945- *WhoAmW 93*
Crispin, Mildred Swift *WhoAm 92, WhoAmW 93*
Crispin, Robert W. 1946- *WhoIns 93*
Crispin, Robert William 1946- *WhoAm 92*
Crispo, Lawrence Walter 1934- *WhoAm 92*
Crispus c. 305-326 *OxDcByz*
Crispus, Flavius Julius c. 303-326 *HarEnMi*
Criss, Charles Kenneth 1932- *WhoSSW 93*
Criss, Darlene June 1931- *WhoAmW 93, WhoWor 93*
Criss, Francis 1901-1973 *BioIn 17*
Criss, Peter *BioIn 17*
Criss, Roger H. *Law&B 92*
Criss, Steven Eugene 1954- *WhoSSW 93*
Criss, William Sotelo 1949- *WhoEmL 93*
Crissinger, Daniel Richard 1860-1942 *BioIn 17*
Crissinger, Karen Denise 1956- *WhoAm 92, WhoEmL 93*
Crissman, James Hudson 1937- *WhoAm 92*
Crist, B. Vincent 1953- *WhoWor 93*
Crist, Bainbridge 1883-1969 *Baker 92*
Crist, Brigitte H. *Law&B 92*
Crist, Christine Myers 1924- *WhoAmW 93, WhoE 93*
Crist, Darlene Trew 1954- *WhoE 93*
Crist, Gertrude H. *WhoWor 93*
Crist, James Joseph 1961- *WhoSSW 93*
Crist, Judith 1922- *WhoAm 92, WhoAmW 93*
Crist, M. Grace 1957- *WhoE 93*
Crist, Mary Jane 1946- *WhoAmW 93*
Crist, Robert A. *St&PR 93*
Crist, William Miles 1943- *WhoAm 92*
Cristal, Edward G. 1935- *WhoAm 92*
Cristal, Linda 1935- *HispAmA*
Cristaldi, Franco d1992 *NewYTBS 92 [port]*
Criste, Jessie Gertrude *AmWomPl*
Cristecscu, Nicolae Dan 1929- *WhoScE 91-4*
Cristella, Arleen Karima 1941- *WhoE 93*
Cristello, Michael 1931- *St&PR 93*
Cristiani, Alfredo *BioIn 17*
Cristiani, Alfredo 1947- *WhoWor 93*
Cristiani, Katherine K. *Law&B 92*
Cristiani, Luca Giovanni 1957- *WhoWor 93*
Cristiani Burkard, Alfredo 1947- *DcCPCAm*
Cristiano, Joseph P. 1940- *St&PR 93*
Cristiano, Marilyn Jean 1954- *WhoEmL 93*
Cristiano, Paul Anthony, Jr. 1955- *St&PR 93*
Cristillo, Louis Francis d1959 *BioIn 17*
Cristina, Donna M. *WhoAmW 93, WhoEmL 93*
Cristini, Angela *WhoE 93*
Cristini, Angela Louise 1948- *WhoEmL 93*
Cristofalo, Vincent Joseph 1933- *WhoAm 92*
Cristofano, Daniel J. *St&PR 93*
Cristofer, Michael 1945- *WhoAm 92*
Cristoferi, Graziella *WhoScE 91-3*
Cristoforeanu, Florica 1887-1960 *Baker 92*
Cristofori, Bartolomeo 1655-1731 *Baker 92*
Cristofori, Fernando *WhoScE 91-3*
Cristol, Stanley Jerome 1916- *WhoAm 92*
Cristoloveanu, Sorin 1949- *WhoScE 91-2*
Cristus, Petrus 1410-1472 *BioIn 17*
Criswell, Charles Harrison 1943- *WhoWor 93*
Criswell, Eleanor Camp 1938- *WhoAmW 93*
Criswell, Eleanor Lee 1950- *WhoSSW 93*
Criswell, Kimberly Ann 1957- *WhoAmW 93, WhoEmL 93*
Criswell, Paul Lindsay 1954- *WhoEmL 93*
Criswell, Sharon L. *Law&B 92*
Criswell, W.A. 1909- *BioIn 17*
Criswell, Wallie A. 1909- *BioIn 17*
Critchell, Brian John 1953- *St&PR 93*
Critchell, Simon James 1946- *WhoAm 92*
Critcher, Larry Lee 1947- *WhoSSW 93*
Critchett, David Loren 1935- *St&PR 93*
Critchett, Ferd Brian 1926- *St&PR 93*
Critchfield, Jack B. 1933- *WhoAm 92*
Critchfield, Jack Barron 1933- *St&PR 93, WhoSSW 93*
Critchfield, Nancy H. 1960- *St&PR 93*
Critchfield, Richard (Patrick) 1931- *ConAu 40NR, WhoAm 92*
Critchley, D. Ellen 1948- *WhoEmL 93*
Critchley, Frank *WhoScE 91-1*
Critchlow, B. Vaughn 1927- *WhoAm 92*

Critchlow, Charles Howard 1950- WhoEmL 93
Critchlow, Dale Leverne 1932- WhoAm 92
Critchlow, Patricia C. d1990 BioIn 17
Critchlow, Susan Melissa 1950- WhoEmL 93, WhoWor 93
Critelli, Catherine A. Law&B 92
Critelli, Catherine Ann 1956- WhoEmL 93
Critelli, Cheryl Munyon Law&B 92
Critelli, Frank 1929- St&PR 93
Critelli, Michael J. Law&B 92
Critelli, Paul Joseph 1949- WhoEmL 93
Crites, Dorothy Adele 1919- WhoWrEP 92
Crites, Lucile 1885- AmWomPl
Crites, Omar Don, Jr. 1928- WhoAm 92, WhoSSW 93
Crites, Richard Ray 1952- WhoEmL 93, WhoWor 93
Crites, William Dean Law&B 92
Critolaus d146BC HarEnMi
Critoph, Eugene 1929- WhoAm 92
Critten, Donald Louis WhoScE 91-1
Critten, Stephen H. ScF&FL 92
Crittenden, Eugene Dwight, Jr. 1927- WhoAm 92
Crittenden, Gary 1953- WhoE 93
Crittenden, Gazaway Lamar 1918- WhoAm 92
Crittenden, George Bibb 1812-1880 BioIn 17, HarEnMi
Crittenden, Jack 1928- St&PR 93
Crittenden, James Arthur 1956- WhoWor 93
Crittenden, John Alan Law&B 92
Crittenden, John Jordan 1787-1863 OxCSupC
Crittenden, Leianne S. Law&B 92
Crittenden, Mary Rita 1928- WhoAmW 93
Crittenden, Sophie Marie 1926- WhoAmW 93
Crittenden, Steven Alan 1961- WhoEmL 93
Crittenden, Thomas Leonidas 1819-1893 HarEnMi
Crittenden, Toya Cynthia 1958- WhoWrEP 92
Crittenden, Victoria Lynn 1956- WhoEmL 93
Crittendon, Robert Russell 1930- St&PR 93
Critto, Sara 1946- WhoWor 93
Critz, Boyd Ridley, III Law&B 92
Critz, Richard Laurens 1922- WhoAm 92
Critzer, Rex L. 1947- St&PR 93
Critzer, Rex Laird 1947- WhoIns 93
Critzer, William Ernest 1934- WhoAm 92
Crivella, Arthur R. 1956- St&PR 93
Crivellari, Lucio 1950- WhoScE 91-3
Crivelli, Giovanni Battista d1652 Baker 92
Crivelli, Joseph Louis 1947- WhoAm 92
Crivellone, Angelo Anthony 1919- St&PR 93
Crivellone, Ernest L. 1956- St&PR 93
Crklis, Jerzy 1936- WhoScE 91-4
Crncich, Tony Joseph 1930- St&PR 93, WhoAm 92
Crnic, Linda Smith 1948- WhoEmL 93
Crnojevic, Zdravko 1933- WhoScE 91-4
Croak, Henry St&PR 93
Croan, Robert James 1937- WhoE 93
Croasdale, Bill BioIn 17
Croatti, Aldo A. 1917- St&PR 93
Croatti, Cynthia M. St&PR 93
Crobaugh, Emma Adelia 1903- WhoWrEP 92
Croccel, Lucien Jean 1930- WhoScE 91-2
Crocco, John Anthony 1934- WhoAm 92, WhoE 93
Crocco, Kyle ScF&FL 92
Croce, Arlene Louise 1934- WhoAm 92, WhoAmW 93
Croce, Giovanni c. 1557-1609 Baker 92
Croce, Jim 1942-1973 Baker 92
Croce, Richard 1948- St&PR 93
Crochet, Gregory Randolph 1957- WhoEmL 93
Crochet, Laura Browning 1953- WhoEmL 93
Crochet, Marcel J. 1938- WhoScE 91-2
Crochet, Marcel Jules 1938- WhoWor 93
Crochiere, Ronald Eldon WhoAm 92
Crochon, Michel 1946- WhoScE 91-2
Crociata, Francis J. 1948- WhoE 93
Crocitto, Peter 1957- St&PR 93
Crocker, Alan Godfrey WhoScE 91-1
Crocker, Albert John WhoScE 91-1
Crocker, Bristol B. 1926- St&PR 93
Crocker, Bruce E. 1942- St&PR 93
Crocker, C. Lamar 1950- WhoSSW 93
Crocker, Charles 1822-1888 GayN
Crocker, Chester A. BioIn 17
Crocker, Chester Arthur 1941- WhoAm 92, WhoE 93
Crocker, David R. Law&B 92
Crocker, Edgar 1930- St&PR 93
Crocker, Frederick Greeley, Jr. 1937- St&PR 93, WhoAm 92
Crocker, Gary Lamar 1951- St&PR 93, WhoEmL 93
Crocker, Jack J. 1924- St&PR 93
Crocker, James A. St&PR 93
Crocker, Jane Lopes 1946- WhoAmW 93, WhoE 93
Crocker, Keith F.S. Law&B 92
Crocker, Kenneth Franklin 1950- WhoEmL 93
Crocker, Malcolm John 1938- WhoAm 92
Crocker, Ray Dean 1949- WhoEmL 93
Crocker, Richard L(incoln) 1927- Baker 92
Crocker, Ryan BioIn 17
Crocker, Ryan C. 1949- WhoAm 92, WhoWor 93
Crocker, Sewall BioIn 17
Crocker, Thomas P. 1960- St&PR 93
Crockett, Arthur H. 1917- St&PR 93
Crockett, Arthur J. d1990 BioIn 17
Crockett, Betty 1936- St&PR 93
Crockett, Bruce Larmour 1944- WhoAm 92
Crockett, Clyll Webb 1934- WhoAm 92
Crockett, David 1786-1836 PolPar
Crockett, Davy DcAmChF 1960
Crockett, Davy 1786-1836 BioIn 17
Crockett, Ethel Stacy 1915- WhoAm 92
Crockett, G.L. 1929-1967 BioIn 17
Crockett, George W., Jr. BioIn 17
Crockett, George W., Jr. 1909- AfrAmBi [port]
Crockett, James Grover, III 1937- WhoAm 92
Crockett, John Cayce 1948- St&PR 93
Crockett, Linda ScF&FL 92
Crockett, Lori Lee 1963- WhoWrEP 92
Crockett, Marlene Elizabeth 1955- WhoAmW 93
Crockett, Mortimer Crane 1919- St&PR 93
Crockett, Phyllis Darlene 1950- WhoAmW 93
Crockett, Reed G. 1935- St&PR 93
Crockett, Rex Jerold 1940- St&PR 93
Crockett, Richard Hayden 1947- WhoE 93
Crockett, Robert York 1962- WhoEmL 93
Crockett, Sharon Patricia 1963- St&PR 93
Crockett, Susan Joan 1944- WhoAmW 93
Crockett-Blassingame, Linda Kathleen 1948- WhoEmL 93
Crockford, Robert David 1948- St&PR 93
Croco, Jack 1925- St&PR 93
Crocono, Barbara Ann 1957- WhoAmW 93
Croes, Betico 1938-1986 DcCPCAm
Croes, Henri-Jacques de 1705-1786 Baker 92
Croes, Keith John 1952- WhoWrEP 92
Croes, Robert Allen 1948- WhoE 93
Croesus fl. c. 560BC-546BC HarEnMi
Crofford, Emily BioIn 17
Crofford, Harry R. 1921- St&PR 93
Crofford, Helen Lois 1932- WhoAmW 93
Crofford, Oscar Bledsoe, Jr. 1930- WhoAm 92
Crofford, Tom R. 1951- St&PR 93
Croft, Anthony Joseph WhoScE 91-1
Croft, Caroline Jane 1947- WhoAm 92
Croft, David WhoScE 91-1
Croft, Desmond Nicholas 1931- WhoWor 93
Croft, Elaine M. 1947- St&PR 93
Croft, Giles Laurence 1957- WhoWor 93
Croft, Gregory E. Law&B 92
Croft, Harry Allen 1943- WhoAm 92
Croft, James Edwin 1929- WhoSSW 93
Croft, John W. Law&B 92
Croft, P. Howard, Jr. 1927- St&PR 93
Croft, Paddy ConTFT 10
Croft, Roxanne Gayle Fralley 1947- WhoAmW 93, WhoE 93
Croft, William 1678-1727 Baker 92
Croft, William Crosswell 1918- St&PR 93, WhoAm 92
Crofts, Antony Richard 1940- WhoAm 92
Crofts, Lisa Christine 1955- WhoAmW 93
Crofts, Robert D. Law&B 92
Crofts, William ConAu 137
Crofts, William 1678-1727 Baker 92
Crogan, Neva Lynne 1957- WhoEmL 93
Croghan, Antony ScF&FL 92
Croghan, Dennis Michael 1956- WhoWor 93
Croghan, Gary Alan 1954- WhoE 93, WhoEmL 93
Crohain, A. WhoScE 91-2
Crohn, Frank T. 1924- WhoIns 93
Crohn, Max Henry, Jr. 1934- WhoAm 92
Crois, John Henry 1946- WhoEmL 93, WhoWor 93
Croissiaux, Michel G. 1928- WhoScE 91-2
Croix, Louise Speers d1992 BioIn 17
Croizat, Pierre D. 1940- WhoIns 93
Croke, Jerome P. Law&B 92
Croke, Jerome Patrick 1933- St&PR 93
Croke, Prudence 1926- WhoE 93
Croke, Thomas Michael, IV 1952- WhoEmL 93
Croker, John Wilson 1780-1857 BioIn 17
Croker, Richard F. 1841-1922 GayN
Croll, David 1900-1991 BioIn 17
Croll, James George Arthur WhoScE 91-1
Croll, Mark W. Law&B 92
Croll, Robert Frederick 1934- WhoWor 93
Croll, S.W. 1949- St&PR 93
Croly, David Goodman 1829-1889 JrnUS
Croly, Herbert 1869-1930 PolPar
Croly, Herbert David 1869-1930 BioIn 17, JrnUS
Croly, Jane Cunningham 1829-1901 JrnUS
Crom, Debora L. St&PR 93
Crom, James Oliver 1933- WhoAm 92
Crom, Thomas Le Roy, III 1955- WhoEmL 93
Cromack, Margot Schlegel 1952- WhoAmW 93
Cromartie, Eric Ross 1955- WhoEmL 93
Cromartie, Eugene Rufus 1936- AfrAmBi
Cromartie, John L. 1941- BioIn 17
Cromartie, Lynn Prendergast Law&B 92
Cromartie, Warren BioIn 17
Cromartie, William James 1913- WhoAm 92
Cromarty, Andrew David 1959- WhoWor 93
Crombie, Donald MiSFD 9
Crombie, Douglass Darnill 1924- WhoAm 92
Crombie, Leslie WhoScE 91-1
Cromeens, Gail Young 1948- St&PR 93
Cromer, Earl of 1918-1991 BioIn 17
Cromer, Lord 1918-1991 AnObit 1991
Cromer, Benjamin Dean 1954- WhoEmL 93
Cromer, Jenny Lu 1954- WhoEmL 93
Cromer, Mary Joan 1932- WhoAmW 93
Cromie, Judith E. 1943- St&PR 93
Cromie, Judith Elaine 1943- WhoIns 93
Cromie, Peter E. 1920- St&PR 93
Cromley, Allan Wray 1922- WhoAm 92
Cromley, Jon Lowell 1934- WhoWor 93
Cromley, Raymond Avolon 1910- WhoAm 92, WhoWor 93
Cromme, Ludwig Josef 1951- WhoWor 93
Crommelynck, Fernand 1885-1970 ConLC 75 [port]
Crompton, Anne 1930- ScF&FL 92
Crompton, Anne Eliot 1930- SmATA 73 [port]
Crompton, Arnold 1914- WhoWor 93
Crompton, David William Thomasson WhoScE 91-1
Crompton, Don 1935?-1983 ScF&FL 92
Crompton, Louis William 1925- WhoAm 92
Crompton, Richard fl. 1573-1599 BioIn 17
Crompton, Thomas Charles 1953- WhoEmL 93
Cromwell, Adelaide M. 1919- WhoAm 92
Cromwell, Douglas Henry 1950- St&PR 93
Cromwell, Edwin Boykin 1909- WhoAm 92
Cromwell, Florence Stevens 1922- WhoAm 92, WhoAmW 93
Cromwell, James H.R. 1898-1990 BioIn 17
Cromwell, Jarvis d1992 NewYTBS 92 [port]
Cromwell, Jarvis 1896-1992 BioIn 17
Cromwell, John 1888-1979 MiSFD 9N
Cromwell, John L. 1940- St&PR 93
Cromwell, Oliver 1599-1658 BioIn 17, HarEnMi
Cromwell, Oliver Dean 1950- WhoAm 92, WhoEmL 93, WhoWor 93
Cromwell, Roxane Dean 1956- WhoEmL 93
Cromwell, Rue LeVelle 1928- WhoAm 92
Cromwell, Sharon Lee 1947- WhoWrEP 92
Cromwell, Terry Alan 1938- WhoSSW 93
Cron, Edward Leroy 1937- St&PR 93
Cron, Ferdinand BioIn 17
Cron, Jennifer Lynne 1956- WhoEmL 93
Cronan, Douglas P. 1956- St&PR 93
Cronan, Kathleen Michele 1953- WhoEmL 93
Cronan, Thomas L., III Law&B 92
Cronan, Thomas Leo, III 1959- WhoEmL 93
Cronas, Peter Chris 1945- WhoE 93
Cronau, Rebecca Lynn 1962- WhoAmW 93, WhoEmL 93
Cronauer, Adrian 1938- WhoE 93
Cronbach, Lee Joseph 1916- WhoAm 92
Cronbach, Robert M. 1908- WhoAm 92, WhoE 93
Cronberg, Stig 1935- WhoScE 91-4, WhoWor 93
Crone, Dana BioIn 17
Crone, John Porter WhoAm 92
Crone, Joni ScF&FL 92
Crone, Richard Allan 1947- WhoEmL 93
Crone, Richard Irving 1909- WhoAm 92
Crone, Richard Kenneth 1957- WhoEmL 93
Cronemiller, Philip Douglas 1918- WhoAm 92
Cronen, Arthur Clark 1946- WhoEmL 93
Cronen, Linda Margaret 1960- WhoAmW 93
Cronenberg, Albert H. d1991 BioIn 17
Cronenberg, David BioIn 17
Cronenberg, David 1943- ConAu 138, CurBio 92 [port], MiSFD 9, News 92 [port], -92-3 [port], WhoWor 93
Cronenberger, Jo Helen 1939- WhoAmW 93
Cronenwett, Jack LeMoyne 1946- WhoE 93
Cronenworth, Charles Douglas 1921- WhoAm 92
Croney, J. Kenneth Law&B 92
Croney, J. Kenneth 1942- St&PR 93, WhoAm 92
Cronhjort, Bjorn Torvald 1934- WhoWor 93
Cronholm, Lois S. 1930- WhoAm 92
Cronin, Ambrose M., III 1930- St&PR 93
Cronin, Anthony 1926- ConAu 137
Cronin, Bernard ScF&FL 92
Cronin, Blaise WhoScE 91-1
Cronin, Bonnie Kathryn Lamb 1941- WhoAm 92
Cronin, Catherine Mary 1948- WhoAmW 93
Cronin, Christopher H. 1928- WhoScE 91-1
Cronin, Daniel Anthony 1927- WhoAm 92
Cronin, Daniel P. Law&B 92
Cronin, Dennis M., Jr. Law&B 92
Cronin, Eugene F., Jr. 1940- St&PR 93
Cronin, Francis J. St&PR 93
Cronin, Gerard Thomas 1947- WhoSSW 93
Cronin, James J. 1945- St&PR 93
Cronin, James Watson 1931- WhoAm 92, WhoWor 93
Cronin, Jeremiah P. 1943- St&PR 93
Cronin, Jeremiah Patrick 1943- WhoAm 92
Cronin, John BioIn 17
Cronin, John Garrett 1936- St&PR 93
Cronin, John P. Law&B 92
Cronin, John Welsch 1944- St&PR 93
Cronin, Joseph F. 1936- St&PR 93
Cronin, Margaret M. Law&B 92
Cronin, Michael F. Law&B 92
Cronin, Michael J. Law&B 92
Cronin, Patti Adrienne Wright 1943- WhoAmW 93
Cronin, Paul William 1938- WhoAm 92
Cronin, Paula Lee 1943- WhoAmW 93
Cronin, Philip Mark 1932- WhoAm 92
Cronin, Philip Sullivan 1962- WhoWor 93
Cronin, Raymond Valentine 1924- WhoAm 92
Cronin, Robert Francis Patrick 1926- WhoAm 92
Cronin, Robert Lawrence 1936- WhoAm 92
Cronin, Timothy Cornelius, III 1927- WhoAm 92
Cronin, Timothy N. Law&B 92
Cronin, Timothy X. BioIn 17
Cronin, Timothy Xavier 1924- St&PR 93
Cronin, Vena BioIn 17
Croninger, George Julian 1905- St&PR 93
Cronin Seligson, Karen 1956- WhoAmW 93
Cronise, Joan Gregg 1945- WhoAmW 93
Cronje, Pieter Arnoldus c. 1835-1911 HarEnMi
Cronk, Alfred Edward 1915- WhoSSW 93
Cronk, Caspar 1935- WhoWor 93
Cronk, Daniel T. Law&B 92
Cronk, E.G., Mrs. AmWomPl
Cronk, Katharine Scherer 1877- AmWomPl
Cronkhite, James Vernor Law&B 92
Cronkhite, Leland James 1933- WhoAm 92
Cronkhite, Leonard Wolsey, Jr. 1919- WhoAm 92
Cronkite, Eugene Pitcher 1914- WhoAm 92
Cronkite, Lawrence S. 1948- St&PR 93
Cronkite, Walter BioIn 17
Cronkite, Walter 1916- JrnUS, WhoAm 92, WhoE 93
Cronkite, Walter (Leland, Jr.) 1916- ConAu 37NR
Cronn, Dagmar Rais 1946- WhoEmL 93
Cronon, Edmund David, Jr. 1924- WhoAm 92
Cronon, William 1954- WhoAm 92, WhoEmL 93
Cronquist, Arthur d1992 NewYTBS 92 [port]

Cronquist, Arthur 1919-1992 *BioIn 17*
Cronson, Harry Marvin 1937- *WhoAm 92*
Cronson, Robert Granville 1924- *WhoAm 92*
Cronstein, Ralph 1918- *St&PR 93*
Cronstrom, Runo 1935- *WhoScE 91-4*
Cronyn, Hume *BioIn 17*
Cronyn, Hume 1911- *WhoAm 92*
Cronyn, J.B. 1920- *St&PR 93*
Cronyn, Marshall William 1919- *WhoAm 92*
Croog, Robert Dean *Law&B 92*
Croog, Roslyn Deborah 1942- *WhoSSW 93*
Crook, Compton N. *ScF&FL 92*
Crook, David S. 1954- *St&PR 93*
Crook, Donald Martin *Law&B 92*
Crook, Donald Martin 1947- *St&PR 93, WhoAm 92, WhoEmL 93*
Crook, Elizabeth 1959- *BioIn 17*
Crook, General 1945- *BioIn 17*
Crook, George 1828-1890 *BioIn 17*
Crook, George 1829-1890 *GayN, HarEnMi*
Crook, Hal *BioIn 17*
Crook, J.A.F. *WhoScE 91-1*
Crook, J.A.F. 1936- *St&PR 93*
Crook, Robert Lacey 1929- *WhoSSW 93*
Crook, Robert Wayne 1936- *WhoAm 92*
Crook, Roy M. 1945- *St&PR 93*
Crook, Sean Paul 1953- *WhoEmL 93*
Crook, Sharon Marie 1965- *WhoEmL 93*
Crook, Stephen Richard 1963- *WhoEmL 93, WhoWor 93*
Crook, Tressa Helen 1956- *WhoEmL 93*
Crookall, John Roland *WhoScE 91-1*
Crooke, Edward A. 1938- *WhoE 93*
Crooke, Rosanne Muzyka 1955- *WhoAmW 93, WhoEmL 93*
Crooke, Stanley Thomas 1945- *St&PR 93, WhoAm 92, WhoWor 93*
Crooke, Steven F. *Law&B 92*
Crooke, Theresa Whitt *WhoSSW 93*
Crooker, Barbara 1945- *WhoWrEP 92*
Crooker, John H., Jr. 1914- *WhoAm 92*
Crookes, Harold R. *Law&B 92*
Crookes, John Norman *WhoScE 91-1*
Crookes, Joyce Fuda 1941- *WhoWrEP 92*
Crooks, Bruce Philip 1944- *WhoAm 92*
Crooks, Christopher P. *Law&B 92*
Crooks, David William *Law&B 92*
Crooks, Edwin William 1919- *WhoAm 92*
Crooks, Marjorie Wilson *AmWomPl*
Crooks, Peter Anthony 1942- *WhoSSW 93*
Crooks, Philomene *AmWomPl*
Crooks, Richard (Alexander) 1900-1972 *Baker 92*
Crookshanks, Michael Donald 1938- *St&PR 93*
Croom, Frederick Hailey 1941- *WhoAm 92, WhoSSW 93*
Croom, Jacques H. *Law&B 92*
Croom, John Henry 1932- *St&PR 93*
Croom, John Henry, III 1932- *WhoAm 92, WhoE 93*
Croom, Wanda Joyce 1944- *WhoAmW 93*
Croome, Derek John *WhoScE 91-1*
Croome, John Minturn 1933- *WhoUN 92*
Crooy, Pierre 1935- *WhoWor 93*
Cropper, M. Elizabeth *WhoE 93*
Cropper, P.J. *WhoScE 91-1*
Cropper, Rebecca Lynn 1957- *WhoEmL 93*
Cropper, Stephen L. 1950- *St&PR 93*
Cropper, Steve 1941- *SoulM*
Cropper, Susan Peggy 1941- *WhoAm 92, WhoAmW 93, WhoE 93*
Cropper, William A. 1939- *St&PR 93, WhoAm 92*
Cropsey, Jeffrey D. 1942- *St&PR 93*
Cropsey, Joseph 1919- *WhoAm 92*
Crorey, David J. 1945- *St&PR 93*
Cros, Christian *WhoScE 91-2*
Cros, Edmond Georges 1931- *WhoWor 93*
Cros, Jean *WhoScE 91-2*
Crosa, Adolfo Jose 1941- *WhoUN 92*
Crosa, Peter James 1951- *WhoSSW 93*
Crosbie, Alfred Linden 1942- *WhoAm 92*
Crosbie, John Carnell *BioIn 17*
Crosbie, John Carnell 1931- *WhoAm 92, WhoE 93, WhoWor 93*
Crosbie, John S(haver) 1920- *WhoWrEP 92*
Crosbie, Lester Lyle 1945- *St&PR 93*
Crosbie, Sylvia Kowitt 1938- *WhoAmW 93*
Crosbie, Vincent B. 1955- *St&PR 93*
Crosby, Alfred Worcester 1931- *WhoAm 92*
Crosby, Amy *BioIn 17*
Crosby, B.P. 1938- *St&PR 93*
Crosby, Bing 1901-1977 *Baker 92, IntDcF 2-3 [port]*
Crosby, Bing 1904-1977 *BioIn 17*
Crosby, Bob 1913- *Baker 92*
Crosby, Charles Julian 1945- *WhoSSW 93*
Crosby, David 1941- See Byrds, The *ConMus 8*
Crosby, David P. 1940- *St&PR 93*
Crosby, Dennis 1935-1991 *BioIn 17*
Crosby, Faye Jacqueline 1947- *WhoEmL 93*
Crosby, Fred McClellan 1928- *WhoAm 92*
Crosby, Gary L. *Law&B 92*
Crosby, George S. 1927- *St&PR 93*
Crosby, Gertrude Nicholson 1931- *WhoSSW 93*
Crosby, Glenn Arthur 1928- *WhoAm 92*
Crosby, Gordon E., Jr. 1920- *St&PR 93, WhoIns 93*
Crosby, Gordon Eugene, Jr. 1920- *WhoE 93*
Crosby, Harry C. Jr. *ScF&FL 92*
Crosby, Howard J. d1991 *BioIn 17*
Crosby, James Earl 1935- *WhoSSW 93*
Crosby, Joan Carew 1934- *WhoAm 92*
Crosby, John 1912-1991 *BioIn 17*
Crosby, John Bartlett 1947- *WhoEmL 93*
Crosby, John Griffith 1943- *WhoAm 92, WhoE 93*
Crosby, John (O'Hea) 1926- *Baker 92, WhoAm 92*
Crosby, LaVon Kehoe Stuart 1924- *WhoAmW 93*
Crosby, Lindsay 1938-1989 *BioIn 17*
Crosby, Lindsey L. 1948- *St&PR 93*
Crosby, Nickey Aaron, Sr. 1936- *WhoAm 92*
Crosby, Norman Lawrence 1927- *WhoAm 92*
Crosby, Philip B. *BioIn 17*
Crosby, Philip B. 1926- *St&PR 93*
Crosby, Philip Bayard 1926- *WhoAm 92*
Crosby, Ralph D. 1947- *St&PR 93*
Crosby, Ralph Wolf 1933- *WhoE 93*
Crosby, Richard A. 1930- *St&PR 93*
Crosby, Richard John 1934- *St&PR 93*
Crosby, Russell Udellius 1951- *WhoE 93*
Crosby, Scott Alan 1955- *St&PR 93*
Crosby, Susan 1945- *WhoAmW 93*
Crosby, Thomas Anthony 1947- *WhoE 93*
Crosby, Thomas M., Jr. 1938- *St&PR 93*
Crosby, Vivian *AmWomPl*
Crosby Metzger, Lisa M. 1960- *WhoWrEP 92*
Crose, Gayle L. *Law&B 92*
Crosen, Robert Glenn, Jr. 1931- *WhoIns 93*
Croser, Mary Doreen 1944- *WhoAm 92, WhoAmW 93*
Croset, Michel Roger 1945- *WhoWor 93*
Croshal, Kathleen Klotz 1947- *WhoAmW 93*
Crosher, Geoffrey *ScF&FL 92*
Crosier, Pamela G. *Law&B 92*
Crosignani, Bruno 1938- *WhoWor 93*
Crosland, Alan 1894-1936 *MiSFD 9N*
Crosland, Charles Anthony Raven 1918-1977 *DcTwHis*
Crosland, Edward Burton, Sr. 1912- *WhoAm 92*
Crosland, John, Jr. 1928- *St&PR 93, WhoAm 92*
Crosland, Philip Crawford 1943- *St&PR 93, WhoAm 92*
Crosman, Gregory Paul 1950- *WhoEmL 93*
Crosnier, Jean-Claude 1936- *WhoScE 91-2*
Croson, Donald C. 1936- *St&PR 93*
Croson, Eric Alan 1948- *St&PR 93*
Cross, Alexander Dennis 1932- *St&PR 93, WhoAm 92*
Cross, Alfred Ernest 1861-1932 *BioIn 17*
Cross, Allan Joseph 1944- *WhoE 93*
Cross, Aureal Theophilus 1916- *WhoAm 92*
Cross, Betty Felt 1920- *WhoAmW 93, WhoWor 93*
Cross, Burton B. 1940- *St&PR 93*
Cross, Carroll N. 1903- *St&PR 93*
Cross, Charles A. *Law&B 92*
Cross, Charles W. *Law&B 92*
Cross, Charlotte Lord 1941- *WhoAmW 93*
Cross, Christopher 1951- *WhoAm 92*
Cross, Christopher T. 1940- *WhoAm 92*
Cross, Clyde Cleveland 1918- *WhoAm 92*
Cross, Dale L. 1947- *St&PR 93*
Cross, Dan S. *Law&B 92*
Cross, David *ScF&FL 92*
Cross, Deborah *BioIn 17*
Cross, Deborah Ann 1957- *WhoSSW 93*
Cross, Dewain Kingsley 1937- *St&PR 93, WhoAm 92*
Cross, Dolores *BioIn 17*
Cross, Dolores Evelyn 1938- *WhoAm 92, WhoAmW 93*
Cross, Doris Leah 1939- *WhoAmW 93*
Cross, Dorothy Abigail 1924- *WhoAmW 93*
Cross, Earle Albright 1925- *WhoSSW 93*
Cross, Eason, Jr. 1925- *WhoAm 92*
Cross, Elmo Garnett, Jr. 1942- *WhoSSW 93*
Cross, Elsa 1946- *SpAmA*
Cross, Eric L. 1943- *St&PR 93*
Cross, Frank Moore, Jr. 1921- *WhoAm 92, WhoWrEP 92*
Cross, Gary D. 1933- *St&PR 93*
Cross, George Alan Martin 1942- *WhoAm 92*
Cross, George Lynn 1905- *WhoAm 92*
Cross, George R. 1923- *WhoAm 92*
Cross, George S. 1949- *St&PR 93*
Cross, Gilbert B. 1939- *BioIn 17, ScF&FL 92*
Cross, Gillian 1945- *ChlLR 28 [port], ScF&FL 92*
Cross, Gillian (Clare) 1945- *ChlFicS, ConAu 38NR, MajAI [port], SmATA 71 [port]*
Cross, Glenn Griffin 1923- *St&PR 93*
Cross, Glenn Laban 1941- *WhoWor 93*
Cross, Harold Zane 1941- *WhoWor 93*
Cross, Harry Maybury 1913- *WhoAm 92*
Cross, Ian J.T. *Law&B 92*
Cross, Irvie Keil 1917- *WhoAm 92*
Cross, James 1916- *WhoAm 92*
Cross, James E. *St&PR 93*
Cross, James E. 1921- *St&PR 93*
Cross, James Millard 1945- *WhoWor 93*
Cross, James Paul 1954- *WhoEmL 93*
Cross, Janis Moore 1929- *WhoAmW 93*
Cross, Jayne Roberta 1953- *WhoAmW 93*
Cross, Jeannette Bickner *Law&B 92*
Cross, Jeffrey D. *Law&B 92*
Cross, Jennifer Mary 1932- *WhoAm 92*
Cross, Joan 1900- *Baker 92, OxDcOp*
Cross, John Douglas 1944- *WhoSSW 93*
Cross, John R. 1936- *St&PR 93*
Cross, John R. 1948- *WhoScE 91-3*
Cross, John William 1943- *WhoE 93*
Cross, June Victoria 1954- *WhoAm 92*
Cross, Junius Bracy, Jr. 1953- *WhoEmL 93*
Cross, Kathleen *BioIn 17*
Cross, Laura Elizabeth *WhoE 93, WhoWor 93*
Cross, Leah Dawn 1946- *WhoEmL 93*
Cross, Leland Briggs, Jr. 1930- *WhoAm 92*
Cross, Lisa C. *Law&B 92*
Cross, Lois Ann 1958- *WhoAmW 93*
Cross, Lowell (Merlin) 1938- *Baker 92*
Cross, M. Lucille 1923- *St&PR 93*
Cross, Manfred Douglas 1929- *WhoAsAP 91*
Cross, Margaret Bessie *AmWomPl*
Cross, Marilyn 1942- *WhoWor 93*
Cross, Mark *WhoScE 91-1*
Cross, Mary Ann Evans 1819-1880 *BioIn 17*
Cross, Mary Frances 1956- *WhoWrEP 92*
Cross, Nigel 1942- *ConAu 38NR*
Cross, Nigel George *WhoScE 91-1*
Cross, O. Dee 1948- *St&PR 93*
Cross, Patsy Lynn Wylie 1950- *WhoEmL 93*
Cross, Paul Anthony *WhoScE 91-1*
Cross, Paul Thomas 1962- *St&PR 93*
Cross, Philip Domingo 1951- *WhoUN 92*
Cross, Philip Sidney 1922- *St&PR 93*
Cross, Ralph Emerson 1910- *WhoAm 92*
Cross, Raymond Edward 1922- *St&PR 93*
Cross, Rex D. 1922- *St&PR 93*
Cross, Richard E. 1910- *St&PR 93*
Cross, Richard Eugene 1910- *WhoAm 92*
Cross, Richard John 1929- *WhoAm 92*
Cross, Richard Vernon 1935- *St&PR 93, WhoAm 92*
Cross, Robert Clark 1939- *WhoAm 92*
Cross, Robert Curtis *Law&B 92*
Cross, Robert Edward 1942- *WhoSSW 93*
Cross, Robert Roy 1935- *WhoIns 93*
Cross, Robert William 1937- *St&PR 93*
Cross, Robin 1948- *ScF&FL 92*
Cross, Ronald 1929- *Baker 92, WhoE 93, WhoWor 93*
Cross, Ronald Anthony 1937- *ScF&FL 92, WhoWrEP 92*
Cross, Ros *BioIn 17*
Cross, Russell S., Jr. 1930- *St&PR 93*
Cross, Ryan N. *Law&B 92*
Cross, Samuel S. 1919- *WhoAm 92*
Cross, Sandra Lee 1946- *WhoEmL 93*
Cross, Shelley Ann 1948- *WhoEmL 93*
Cross, Steven Jasper 1954- *WhoEmL 93*
Cross, Susan Lee 1960- *WhoAmW 93, WhoEmL 93*
Cross, Theodore Lamont 1924- *WhoAm 92, WhoWor 93*
Cross, Thomas *WhoScE 91-1*
Cross, Thomas A. 1957- *St&PR 93*
Cross, Thomas Gary 1947- *WhoE 93, WhoWor 93*
Cross, Timothy D. 1947- *WhoSSW 93*
Cross, Victoria 1868-1952? *ScF&FL 92*
Cross, Virginia Rose 1950- *WhoEmL 93*
Cross, Wilbur J. 1942- *St&PR 93*
Cross, Wilbur L. 1862-1948 *PolPar*
Cross, William Lee 1936- *WhoIns 93*
Cross, William Redmond, Jr. 1917- *WhoAm 92*
Crossan, Donald Franklin 1926- *WhoE 93*
Crossan, Geordie John 1959- *WhoEmL 93*
Crossa-Raynaud, Patrice Henry 1922- *WhoScE 91-2*
Crosse, Gordon 1937- *Baker 92, IntDcOp, OxDcOp*
Crosse, St. George *BioIn 17*
Crossen, Frank Marvin 1923- *St&PR 93*
Crossen, Henry M. 1921- *St&PR 93*
Crossen, John Jacob 1932- *WhoSSW 93*
Crossen, Kendell Foster 1910-1981 *ScF&FL 92*
Crossen, Margaret Lee 1958- *WhoEmL 93*
Crossen, Mark S. 1948- *St&PR 93*
Crossett, Kevin Stephen 1960- *WhoE 93, WhoEmL 93*
Crossett, R.N. *WhoScE 91-1*
Crossfield, Albert Scott 1921- *WhoAm 92*
Crossland, Bernard 1923- *WhoWor 93*
Crossland, Harriet Kent 1902- *WhoAm 92*
Crossland, Martin Dale 1953- *WhoAm 92*
Crossland, Richard Irving, Jr. 1948- *WhoEmL 93*
Crossland, Roger Lee *Law&B 92*
Crossland, Sue Dell 1933- *WhoAmW 93*
Crossley, Ada (Jessica) 1874-1929 *Baker 92*
Crossley, Francis Rendel Erskine 1915- *WhoE 93*
Crossley, Frank Alphonso 1925- *WhoAm 92*
Crossley, Gary Exley 1951- *WhoE 93, WhoEmL 93*
Crossley, Guy Alexander 1966- *WhoSSW 93*
Crossley, Linda Susan 1950- *WhoAmW 93, WhoEmL 93*
Crossley, Lytton F. 1935- *St&PR 93*
Crossley, Paul (Christopher Richard) 1944- *Baker 92*
Crossley, Peter Anthony 1939- *WhoSSW 93*
Crossley, Ralph Clifton, Jr. 1945- *WhoSSW 93*
Crossley, Randolph Allin 1904- *WhoAm 92*
Crossley, Robert 1945- *ScF&FL 92*
Crossley-Holland, Kevin (John William) 1941- *ChlFicS, MajAI*
Crossley-Holland, Peter 1916- *Baker 92*
Crossman, A.R. *WhoScE 91-1*
Crossman, Edgar O., II 1930- *St&PR 93*
Crossman, Patrick F. 1931- *St&PR 93*
Crossman, R.H.S. 1907-1974 *BioIn 17*
Crossman, Richard Howard Stafford 1907-1974 *BioIn 17, DcTwHis*
Crossman, William Warren 1946- *WhoE 93*
Crossman, William Whittard 1927- *WhoAm 92*
Crossno, Charles Lee 1956- *WhoEmL 93*
Crossno, Jerry Lee 1936- *WhoSSW 93*
Crosson, David Earl 1948- *WhoAm 92*
Crosson, Frank 1943- *St&PR 93*
Crosson, Frederick James 1926- *WhoAm 92*
Crosswhite, Dan Elsworth 1944- *WhoE 93*
Crosswhite, Ilona Trastorff *Law&B 92*
Crosswhite, Randal Neal 1953- *St&PR 93*
Crostack, Horst-Artur 1945- *WhoScE 91-3*
Crosthwait, D. Lloyd, Jr. 1942- *St&PR 93*
Crosthwait, Ruth Agnes 1925- *WhoSSW 93*
Croswell, Edgar DeWitt 1913-1990 *BioIn 17*
Croswell, Edwin 1797-1871 *JrnUS*
Crotch, William 1775-1847 *Baker 92*
Croteau, Julie *BioIn 17*
Croteau, Maureen Elizabeth 1949- *WhoAmW 93*
Croteau, Robert Francis 1950- *St&PR 93*
Crothers, Derrick Samuel Frederick *WhoScE 91-1*
Crothers, Donald Morris 1937- *WhoAm 92*
Crothers, J.H. *WhoScE 91-1*
Crothers, Rachel 1870?-1958 *AmWomPl*
Crotin, Lionel Elliott *Law&B 92*
Crotta, Annette Gunter 1930- *WhoSSW 93*
Crotts, Glenn David 1953- *WhoEmL 93, WhoSSW 93*
Crotts, Jodi Lynette 1965- *WhoAmW 93*
Crotty, John Joseph, Jr. 1934- *St&PR 93*
Crotty, Leo William 1927- *St&PR 93*
Crotty, Michael F. 1947- *WhoEmL 93*
Crotty, Peter J. d1992 *NewYTBS 92 [port]*
Crotty, Peter J. 1910-1992 *BioIn 17*
Crotty, Wayne E. 1913- *St&PR 93*
Crotty, William 1936- *WhoAm 92*
Crotty, William H. 1947- *St&PR 93*
Crotty, William M. 1937- *St&PR 93*
Crouch, Andrae 1942- *ConMus 9 [port]*
Crouch, Betty Louise 1930- *WhoAmW 93*
Crouch, Bill W. 1947- *St&PR 93*
Crouch, Brenda Lee 1961- *WhoAmW 93*
Crouch, Cedric Vincent 1967- *WhoE 93*
Crouch, Constance Waite 1941- *WhoAmW 93*
Crouch, Eldon L. 1948- *St&PR 93*
Crouch, Frederick Nicholls 1808-1896 *Baker 92*
Crouch, Gary Clinton 1956- *WhoEmL 93*

Crouch, Gary L. 1941- *St&PR 93*
Crouch, Helen Olive 1925- *WhoAm 92*
Crouch, James Michael 1949- *WhoEmL 93*
Crouch, Jennifer Elaine 1952- *WhoEmL 93*
Crouch, John H. *Law&B 92*
Crouch, Joyce Greer 1925- *WhoAmW 93*
Crouch, Les 1946- *St&PR 93*
Crouch, Mabel *AmWomPl*
Crouch, Richard W. 1950- *WhoSSW 93*
Croudace, I.W. *WhoScE 91-1*
Crough, Daniel Francis 1936- *WhoAm 92, WhoE 93*
Crough, Maura P. *Law&B 92*
Crouigneau, Francoise 1944- *WhoWor 93*
Crounse, Avery *MiSFD 9*
Crounse, George P. 1912- *St&PR 93*
Crouse, Anne D. *ScF&FL 92*
Crouse, Clifford F. 1918- *St&PR 93*
Crouse, Edwin R. 1920- *St&PR 93*
Crouse, Farrell Rondall 1932- *WhoAm 92*
Crouse, James Robert 1949- *WhoEmL 93*
Crouse, Jere W. *BioIn 17*
Crouse, Joseph Robert 1946- *WhoAm 92*
Crouse, Karen Jean 1962- *WhoWrEP 92*
Crouse, Lindsay 1948- *WhoAm 92, WhoAmW 93*
Crouse, Lloyd Roseville 1918- *WhoAm 92, WhoE 93*
Crouse, Mary Therese *Law&B 92*
Crouse, Philip Charles 1951- *WhoSSW 93*
Crouse, R. Daniel *Law&B 92*
Crouse, Richard Paul 1939- *St&PR 93*
Crouse, Roger Leslie 1944- *WhoE 93*
Crout, David Herbert George *WhoScE 91-1*
Crout, John J. 1937- *WhoE 93, WhoIns 93*
Crout, John Richard 1929- *WhoAm 92*
Crout, Teresa Elizabeth Kochmar 1945- *WhoWrEP 92*
Croutch, Leslie A. 1915-1969 *ScF&FL 92*
Crouter, Richard Earl 1937- *WhoAm 92*
Crouthamel, Michael R. 1956- *St&PR 93*
Crouzet, Jean 1934- *WhoScE 91-2*
Crouzet, Y. *WhoScE 91-2*
Crovini, Luigi R. 1937- *WhoScE 91-3*
Crovitz, Charles K. 1953- *St&PR 93, WhoAm 92*
Crovitz, Louis Gordon 1958- *WhoEmL 93*
Crovo, Frank Anthony, Jr. 1930- *St&PR 93*
Crow, Barry L. 1943- *St&PR 93*
Crow, Betty Lee 1929- *St&PR 93*
Crow, C. Gary 1936- *St&PR 93*
Crow, Carl Arnold, Jr. 1951- *WhoEmL 93, WhoSSW 93*
Crow, Charles Delmar 1945- *WhoSSW 93*
Crow, Charles L. 1940- *ScF&FL 92*
Crow, David Richard *WhoScE 91-1*
Crow, Edwin Louis 1916- *WhoAm 92*
Crow, Elizabeth 1946- *St&PR 93*
Crow, Elizabeth Smith *WhoAm 92*
Crow, Harold Eugene 1933- *WhoAm 92, WhoWor 93*
Crow, James *BioIn 17*
Crow, James Franklin 1916- *WhoAm 92*
Crow, James Sylvester 1915- *WhoAm 92*
Crow, Joe Miles 1954- *St&PR 93*
Crow, John Armstrong 1906- *WhoAm 92*
Crow, John William 1937- *WhoAm 92, WhoWor 93*
Crow, Leslie Ellen 1954- *WhoEmL 93*
Crow, Lynne Campbell Smith 1942- *WhoAmW 93*
Crow, Martha Foote 1854-1924 *AmWomPl*
Crow, Mary 1933- *ConAu 138*
Crow, Mary Lynn 1934- *WhoSSW 93*
Crow, Nancy Rebecca 1948- *WhoEmL 93*
Crow, Neil Edward 1926- *WhoAm 92*
Crow, Paul Abernathy, Jr. 1931- *WhoAm 92, WhoWor 93*
Crow, Richard Ronald 1915- *St&PR 93*
Crow, Richard Thomas 1939- *WhoAm 92, WhoSSW 93*
Crow, Rosemary Anne 1934- *WhoScE 91-1*
Crow, Samuel Alfred, II 1950- *WhoSSW 93*
Crow, Stephen Martin 1942- *WhoSSW 93*
Crow, Thomas James 1945- *WhoSSW 93*
Crow, Timothy John *WhoScE 91-1*
Crow, Trammell *BioIn 17*
Crow, Trammell 1914- *St&PR 93*
Crow, Warren B., III 1930- *St&PR 93*
Crowcroft, Jon Andrew 1957- *WhoWor 93*
Crowcroft, Peter 1922- *ScF&FL 92*
Crowder, Albert M., Jr. *Law&B 92*
Crowder, Barbara Lynn 1956- *WhoAmW 93, WhoEmL 93*
Crowder, Bonnie Walton 1916- *WhoAmW 93, WhoSSW 93*
Crowder, Charles B. *Law&B 92*
Crowder, Fay *ScF&FL 92*
Crowder, Helen L. 1928- *St&PR 93*
Crowder, Henry Alvin 1953- *WhoSSW 93*
Crowder, Herbert 1925- *ScF&FL 92*
Crowder, Jack *ConTFT 10*
Crowder, James Caswell 1941- *St&PR 93*
Crowder, James Landon *Law&B 92*
Crowder, Julian Anthony 1950- *WhoSSW 93*
Crowder, Martha Linda 1951- *WhoAmW 93*
Crowder, Miles Keeney 1943- *WhoSSW 93*
Crowder, Moncure Gravatt 1940- *St&PR 93*
Crowder, Nathion F. *Law&B 92*
Crowder, Robert G. 1939- *ConAu 138*
Crowder, Shirley *BioIn 17, BlkAmWO*
Crowder, Todd William 1962- *WhoSSW 93*
Crowdus, Clark 1949- *WhoEmL 93*
Crowdus, Gary Alan 1945- *WhoWrEP 92*
Crowe, Byron A. *St&PR 93*
Crowe, Cameron 1957- *MiSFD 9*
Crowe, Christopher *MiSFD 9*
Crowe, Daniel L. 1947- *St&PR 93*
Crowe, Devon George 1948- *WhoSSW 93*
Crowe, Dewey E., II 1947- *WhoSSW 93*
Crowe, Hal Scott 1953- *WhoSSW 93*
Crowe, James J. *Law&B 92*
Crowe, James Joseph 1935- *St&PR 93*
Crowe, John *WhoWrEP 92*
Crowe, John Carl 1937- *St&PR 93*
Crowe, John E. *Law&B 92*
Crowe, John T. 1938- *WhoWor 93*
Crowe, Joseph Francis 1938- *St&PR 93*
Crowe, Malcolm Kenneth *WhoScE 91-1*
Crowe, Martin A. *St&PR 93*
Crowe, Martin Joseph, III 1930- *St&PR 93*
Crowe, Patrick J. 1944- *WhoIns 93*
Crowe, Patrick James 1944- *St&PR 93*
Crowe, Robert Alan 1950- *WhoEmL 93*
Crowe, Ronald Girardeau 1932- *WhoWrEP 92*
Crowe, Thomas Kealey 1957- *WhoEmL 93*
Crowe, Victoria 1945- *BioIn 17*
Crowe, Virginia Mary 1933- *WhoE 93*
Crowe, Vivienne *Law&B 92*
Crowe, W.R. 1925- *St&PR 93*
Crowe, William J. 1925- *BioIn 17*
Crowe, William J., Jr. *Law&B 92*
Crowe-Hagans, Natonia 1955- *WhoAmW 93*
Crowell, Anne *AmWomPl*
Crowell, Caleb 1932- *St&PR 93*
Crowell, Carol Ann 1958- *WhoAmW 93*
Crowell, Charles *Law&B 92*
Crowell, Charles Byron 1943- *St&PR 93*
Crowell, Donald R., II *Law&B 92*
Crowell, Douglas John 1954- *St&PR 93*
Crowell, J.B. 1933- *St&PR 93*
Crowell, J.L. 1916- *St&PR 93*
Crowell, James Douglas *Law&B 92*
Crowell, John David 1944- *WhoWor 93*
Crowell, Kay Upton 1947- *WhoSSW 93*
Crowell, Kenneth Wayne 1939- *WhoSSW 93*
Crowell, Lorenzo Mayo 1943- *WhoSSW 93*
Crowell, Nancy Melzer 1948- *WhoEmL 93*
Crowell, Ohmer O. 1924- *St&PR 93*
Crowell, Raymond E. 1926- *St&PR 93*
Crowell, Richard Lane 1930- *WhoE 93*
Crowell, Robert L. 1909- *BioIn 17*
Crowell, Rodney 1950- *ConMus 8 [port]*
Crowell, Ronald Keith 1948- *St&PR 93*
Crowell, Wayne Franklin 1937- *St&PR 93*
Crowers, Richard T. 1923- *St&PR 93*
Crowfield, Christopher *MajAI*
Crowl, Gary Michael 1955- *WhoEmL 93*
Crowl, Kent L. *Law&B 92*
Crowl, Richard R. *Law&B 92*
Crowley, Aleister 1875-1947 *BioIn 17, ScF&FL 92*
Crowley, Carol Dee 1931- *WhoWrEP 92*
Crowley, Catherine M. *Law&B 92*
Crowley, Claudia O. *Law&B 92*
Crowley, Denis Mark 1922- *St&PR 93*
Crowley, Dennis W. 1941- *WhoE 93*
Crowley, Diane 1939- *WhoAm 92*
Crowley, E.J. 1938- *St&PR 93*
Crowley, Edward A. *ScF&FL 92*
Crowley, Edward Denis 1926- *St&PR 93*
Crowley, Elizabeth Marlene 1940- *WhoAmW 93*
Crowley, Ellen Teresa 1943- *St&PR 93*
Crowley, Frances L., Jr. *Law&B 92*
Crowley, Francis E. 1934- *St&PR 93*
Crowley, Francis L. *Law&B 92*
Crowley, Francis L., Jr. 1931- *St&PR 93*
Crowley, Frank W. 1929- *WhoScE 91-1*
Crowley, George J. 1939- *St&PR 93*
Crowley, Gerald S. *Law&B 92*
Crowley, Gregory George *Law&B 92*
Crowley, James Farrell 1946- *WhoAm 92*
Crowley, James M. *Law&B 92*
Crowley, James M. 1942- *WhoIns 93*
Crowley, James T. 1943- *WhoAm 92*
Crowley, James Worthington *Law&B 92*
Crowley, James Worthington 1930- *St&PR 93, WhoAm 92, WhoSSW 93*
Crowley, Janeen Lou 1954- *WhoAmW 93*
Crowley, Jennie M. *Law&B 92*
Crowley, Jerome J., Jr. 1939- *St&PR 93*
Crowley, Jerome Joseph, Jr. 1939- *WhoAm 92*
Crowley, John *BioIn 17*
Crowley, John 1942- *ScF&FL 92*
Crowley, John J. 1932- *St&PR 93*
Crowley, John Joseph, Jr. 1928- *WhoAm 92*
Crowley, John P. 1924- *St&PR 93*
Crowley, John Robert 1929- *WhoWor 93*
Crowley, John Schaft 1923- *St&PR 93*
Crowley, John William 1945- *WhoAm 92*
Crowley, Joseph Michael 1940- *WhoAm 92*
Crowley, Joseph Neil 1933- *WhoAm 92*
Crowley, Joseph Paul 1944- *St&PR 93*
Crowley, Kathleen 1931- *SweetSg D [port]*
Crowley, Keith L. 1934- *St&PR 93*
Crowley, Kevin David 1958- *WhoEmL 93*
Crowley, Kevin John 1956- *WhoE 93*
Crowley, Leonard James 1921- *WhoAm 92*
Crowley, Lisa A. *St&PR 93*
Crowley, Margaret Colleen 1960- *WhoAmW 93*
Crowley, Michael Anthony 1958- *WhoSSW 93*
Crowley, Nicholas Pearse 1949- *WhoEmL 93*
Crowley, Patrick J. 1941- *St&PR 93*
Crowley, Philip Patrick *Law&B 92*
Crowley, Phillip O. *Law&B 92*
Crowley, Richard d1992 *NewYTBS 92*
Crowley, Richard M. 1935- *St&PR 93*
Crowley, Richard Martyn 1931- *St&PR 93*
Crowley, Robert Dale 1948- *St&PR 93*
Crowley, Rosemary Anne 1938- *WhoAsAP 91*
Crowley, Sharon Burke 1945- *WhoE 93*
Crowley, Steven R. *Law&B 92*
Crowley, Thomas A. d1991 *BioIn 17*
Crowley, Thomas Joseph 1930- *St&PR 93*
Crowley, William Francis, Jr. 1943- *WhoAm 92*
Crowley-Long, Kathleen 1958- *WhoEmL 93*
Crowling, Patrick McGuire, Jr. 1942- *WhoSSW 93*
Crowll, John Lee 1954- *WhoEmL 93, WhoSSW 93*
Crown, Arie Steven 1952- *St&PR 93*
Crown, Barry Michael 1943- *WhoSSW 93*
Crown, David Allan 1928- *WhoAm 92, WhoSSW 93*
Crown, Frederick Smith, Jr. 1949- *WhoEmL 93*
Crown, Henry 1896-1990 *BioIn 17*
Crown, Judith Ann 1952- *WhoE 93*
Crown, Lester 1925- *St&PR 93, WhoAm 92*
Crown, Nancy Elizabeth 1955- *WhoAmW 93, WhoEmL 93*
Crown, William Harry 1954- *WhoE 93*
Crowninshield, Frank 1872-1947 *BioIn 17*
Crownover, James Darragh 1929- *St&PR 93*
Crowns *SoulM*
Crowson, Gatha Ann 1938- *WhoAmW 93*
Crowson, James L. 1938- *St&PR 93*
Crowson, James Lawrence *Law&B 92*
Crowson, Robert E., Jr. 1947- *St&PR 93*
Crowston, Wallace Bruce Stewart 1934- *WhoAm 92*
Crowther, (Francis) Bosley 1905-1981 *ConAu 38NR*
Crowther, Derek *WhoScE 91-1*
Crowther, George L. *St&PR 93*
Crowther, George Rodney, III 1927- *WhoE 93, WhoWor 93*
Crowther, H. David 1930- *WhoAm 92*
Crowther, James E. 1930- *St&PR 93*
Crowther, James Earl 1930- *WhoAm 92*
Crowther, Julia Ann 1935- *WhoAmW 93*
Crowther, Mark Edward 1951- *WhoScE 91-1*
Crowther, Richard Layton 1910- *WhoAm 92*
Crowther, Samuel 1806?-1891 *BioIn 17*
Crowther, Samuel Adjai 1811-1892 *Expl 93*
Crowther-Alwyn, Peter 1944- *WhoWor 93*
Croxdale, Judith Lee 1941- *WhoAmW 93*
Croxford, Lynne Louise 1947- *WhoAmW 93*
Croxton, Frederick E. 1899-1991 *BioIn 17*
Croxton, Frederick Emory 1923- *WhoAm 92*
Croy, Dick 1943- *MiSFD 9*
Croyle, Barbara Ann 1949- *WhoAmW 93*
Croyle, R.G. *Law&B 92*
Croyle, Thomas J. 1949- *St&PR 93*
Croyle, William R. 1920- *St&PR 93*
Crozatier, Bertrand *WhoScE 91-2*
Crozemarie, Jacques *BioIn 17*
Crozer, Robert P. 1947- *WhoAm 92*
Crozier, Catharine 1914- *Baker 92*
Crozier, Eric 1914- *OxDcOp*
Crozier, Francis 1796-1848 *BioIn 17*
Crozier, Lorna 1948- *WhoCanL 92*
Crozier, Nancy Joyce 1933- *WhoAmW 93*
Crozier, Ouida G. 1947- *WhoWrEP 92*
Crozier, Prudence Slitor 1940- *WhoAmW 93*
Crozier, Scott A. *Law&B 92*
Crozier, W.W. 1956- *WhoScE 91-1*
Crozier, William Marshall, Jr. 1932- *St&PR 93, WhoAm 92*
Cruce, Andrew C. *St&PR 93*
Cruchaud, Andre 1928- *WhoScE 91-4*
Cruden, Joan Patricia 1951- *WhoEmL 93*
Cruden, John Charles 1946- *WhoEmL 93*
Crudu, Ion 1927- *WhoScE 91-4*
Cruess, Leigh Saunders 1958- *WhoEmL 93*
Cruess, Richard Leigh 1929- *WhoAm 92*
Cruft, Edgar Frank 1933- *St&PR 93, WhoAm 92*
Cruger, F. Christopher 1935- *St&PR 93, WhoWor 93*
Cruger, G. *WhoScE 91-3*
Cruger, Johann 1598-1662 *Baker 92*
Cruger, Julie *ScF&FL 92*
Cruger, Julie Grinnell Storrow d1920 *AmWomPl*
Cruger, Michael H. 1945- *St&PR 93*
Crugnale, Joseph *St&PR 93*
Cruice, William James 1937- *WhoE 93*
Cruickshank, Alexander Middleton 1919- *WhoAm 92*
Cruickshank, Durward William John *WhoScE 91-1*
Cruickshank, James Stanley 1946- *St&PR 93*
Cruickshank, Michael James 1929- *WhoAm 92, WhoWor 93*
Cruickshank, Walter R. 1946- *St&PR 93*
Cruickshank, William M(ellon) 1915-1992 *ConAu 139*
Cruickshank, William Mellon 1915- *WhoAm 92*
Cruikshank, David C. 1946- *WhoIns 93*
Cruikshank, John W., III 1933- *WhoAm 92*
Cruikshank, Paul D. *Law&B 92*
Cruikshank, Robert Lane 1936- *WhoAm 92*
Cruikshank, Ronald George *Law&B 92*
Cruikshank, Thomas Henry 1931- *St&PR 93, WhoAm 92, WhoSSW 93*
Cruikshank, Warren Lott 1916- *WhoAm 92*
Cruise, John R. 1941- *St&PR 93*
Cruise, Tom *BioIn 17*
Cruise, Tom 1962- *IntDcF 2-3, WhoAm 92*
Crull, Timm F. *BioIn 17*
Crum, Albert Byrd 1931- *WhoAm 92, WhoE 93, WhoWor 93*
Crum, Chester L., Jr. *St&PR 93*
Crum, Denny Edwin 1937- *WhoAm 92, WhoSSW 93*
Crum, Floyd Maxilas 1922- *WhoSSW 93*
Crum, Fred C., Jr. 1944- *St&PR 93*
Crum, George Francis, Jr. 1926- *WhoAm 92*
Crum, George Thomas 1942- *WhoSSW 93*
Crum, Henry Hayne 1914- *WhoSSW 93*
Crum, James Francis 1934- *WhoAm 92*
Crum, James Merrill 1912- *WhoWor 93*
Crum, John Kistler 1936- *WhoAm 92*
Crum, Kay Marilyn 1934- *WhoAmW 93*
Crum, Lawrence Lee 1933- *WhoAm 92*
Crum, Maurice *BioIn 17*
Crum, Nancy Ann 1960- *WhoAmW 93*
Crum, Susan Wey 1957- *WhoE 93*
Crumb, George *BioIn 17*
Crumb, George Henry 1929- *WhoAm 92*
Crumb, George (Henry, Jr.) 1929- *Baker 92*
Crumb, Owen Joseph 1925- *WhoAm 92*
Crumbaugh, James Charles 1912- *WhoSSW 93*
Crumbaugh, Lee Forrest 1947- *WhoAm 92*
Crumbley, Donald Larry 1941- *WhoAm 92*
Crumbley, Elizabeth Boothe 1949- *WhoSSW 93*
Crumbley, Esther Helen Kendrick 1928- *WhoAmW 93, WhoSSW 93, WhoWor 93*
Crumbliss, Alvin Lee 1942- *WhoAm 92*
Crumbo, Minisa 1942- *WhoAm 92*
Crumb-Wolfe, Brenda Jean 1962- *WhoAmW 93, WhoEmL 93*
Crume, Vic *ScF&FL 92*
Crumley, Beth Bailey 1962- *WhoEmL 93, WhoSSW 93*
Crumley, Bruce L. 1948- *St&PR 93*
Crumley, James 1939- *WhoWrEP 92*
Crumley, James Harold 1953- *WhoAm 92*
Crumley, James Robert, Jr. 1925- *WhoAm 92, WhoSSW 93*
Crumley, John Walter 1944- *WhoSSW 93, WhoWor 93*
Crumley, Laura Lee 1949- *WhoWor 93*
Crumley, Roger Lee 1941- *WhoAm 92*

Crumlin, Rosemary Anne 1932- WhoWor 93
Crumlish, James C. d1992 BioIn 17
Crumlish, James Patrick 1944- St&PR 93
Crummell, Alexander 1819-1898 BioIn 17, EncAACR
Crummer, Murray Thomas, Jr. 1922- WhoAm 92
Crummette, Hugh David 1937- St&PR 93
Crummey, Robert Owen 1936- WhoAm 92
Crummins, Agnes L. AmWomPl
Crump, Carla Jean 1953- WhoAmW 93
Crump, Charles H. 1926- WhoWrEP 92
Crump, Charles Metcalf 1913- WhoAm 92, WhoSSW 93
Crump, Deryk Patrick WhoScE 91-1
Crump, Diana Lynne 1950- WhoAmW 93
Crump, Edward 1874-1954 PolPar
Crump, Elizabeth Burford 1937- St&PR 93
Crump, Freida Boyd 1950- WhoAmW 93
Crump, G. Lindsay 1922- St&PR 93
Crump, Galbraith Miller 1929- WhoAm 92
Crump, Gerald Franklin 1935- WhoWor 93
Crump, Harold Craft 1931- St&PR 93
Crump, Irving 1887-1979 ScF&FL 92
Crump, James Gleason 1930- St&PR 93
Crump, James Noble 1908- St&PR 93
Crump, Judy Gail 1955- WhoWrEP 92
Crump, Larry Cameron 1948- WhoEmL 93
Crump, Mary Nola 1919- St&PR 93
Crump, R.E., Mrs. AmWomPl
Crump, R.G. WhoScE 91-1
Crump, Ronald Cordell 1951- WhoEmL 93
Crump, Spencer WhoAm 92
Crump, Stuart Faulkner, Jr. 1945- WhoSSW 93
Crump, Thomas Fletcher 1956- St&PR 93, WhoAm 92
Crumpacker, Carol Ann 1958- WhoAmW 93
Crumpacker, Jack R. Law&B 92
Crump-Crossling, Monica Inez 1960- WhoAmW 93
Crumpler, Donna Burt 1950- WhoSSW 93
Crumpley, Wayne E. 1943- St&PR 93
Crumpton, Charles Whitmarsh 1946- WhoEmL 93
Crumpton, M.J. WhoScE 91-1
Crunelle, Melissa Lynn 1963- WhoAmW 93
Crupi, Lisa L. Law&B 92
Crupi, Thomas James 1946- WhoEmL 93
Crusaders SoulM
Cruse, C. Lansford 1956- St&PR 93
Cruse, Donald, Jr. 1932- St&PR 93
Cruse, Emily E. 1952- WhoEmL 93
Cruse, Fredrich James 1947- WhoEmL 93
Cruse, Irma Belle Russell 1911- WhoAmW 93, WhoSSW 93, WhoWor 93
Cruse, Irma Russell 1911- WhoWrEP 92
Cruse, Julius Major, Jr. 1937- WhoAm 92, WhoSSW 93, WhoWor 93
Cruse, R.L. 1932- St&PR 93
Crusell, Bernhard Henrik 1775-1838 Baker 92
Cruser, George E. 1930- St&PR 93
Crusham, Michael S. 1950- St&PR 93
Cruso, Solomon 1887-1977 ScF&FL 92
Crusol, Jean 1943- DcCPCAm
Crusto, Mitchell Ferdinand WhoAm 92
Crusz, Rienzi WhoCanL 92
Crutcher, Bettye SoulM
Crutcher, Chris 1946- Au&Arts 9 [port], BioIn 17, ChlLR 28 [port]
Crutcher, Chris(topher C.) 1946- MajAI [port]
Crutcher, Christopher C. 1946- WhoWrEP 92
Crutcher, Dimetrec Artez 1964- WhoSSW 93
Crutcher, Harold Trabue, Jr. 1938- WhoAm 92
Crutcher, John William 1916- WhoAm 92
Crutcher, Lawrence McVickar 1942- St&PR 93
Crutcher, Michael B. Law&B 92
Crutcher, Michael B. 1944- St&PR 93
Crutcher, Michael Bayard 1944- WhoAm 92
Crutcher, William C., III Law&B 92
Crutchfield, Alexander 1958- WhoWor 93
Crutchfield, Charles Calvin, Jr. 1948- WhoEmL 93
Crutchfield, Charles H. 1912- St&PR 93
Crutchfield, Edward Elliott 1941- BioIn 17
Crutchfield, Edward Elliott, Jr. 1941- St&PR 93, WhoSSW 93
Crutchfield, Gary A. 1950- St&PR 93
Crutchfield, James Andrew 1938- WhoWrEP 92
Crutchfield, Sam Shaw, Jr. 1934- WhoAm 92
Crutchfield, William Richard 1932- WhoAm 92
Crutchley, Carolynn Adele 1951- WhoAmW 93, WhoEmL 93
Crutchley, Victor Alexander Charles 1893-1986 HarEnMi
Crute, Beverly Jean WhoAmW 93
Cruthird, Robert Lee 1944- WhoWor 93
Cruthirds, Elizabeth Rennix 1952- WhoAmW 93, WhoEmL 93, WhoSSW 93
Crutsinger, Robert Keane 1930- St&PR 93, WhoAm 92
Crutzen, Yves Robert 1950- WhoWor 93
Cruvelli, Sofia 1826-1907 OxDcOp
Cruvellier, Paul WhoScE 91-2
Cruver, Suzanne Lee 1942- WhoAmW 93
Crux, Lauren BioIn 17
Cruysberghs, Paul Franciscus 1944- WhoWor 93
Cruz, Albert Raymond 1933- WhoE 93
Cruz, Alejandro BioIn 17
Cruz, Anthony Pinho 1955- WhoEmL 93
Cruz, Benjamin Joseph Franquez 1951- WhoAm 92
Cruz, Brandon BioIn 17
Cruz, Celia 1924- Baker 92
Cruz, Celia 1929?- NotHsAW 93 [port]
Cruz, Daniel da ScF&FL 92
Cruz, Deanna Law&B 92
Cruz, Florentino d1882 BioIn 17
Cruz, Ivo 1901-1985 Baker 92
Cruz, J. Mirabeau WhoScE 91-3
Cruz, Jorge Augusto B. 1939- WhoWor 93
Cruz, Jose BioIn 17
Cruz, Jose 1947- BiDAMSp 1989
Cruz, Jose Antonio Tavares 1936- WhoWor 93
Cruz, Jose Bejar, Jr. 1932- WhoAm 92
Cruz, Juana Ines de la 1651-1695 BioIn 17, DcMexL
Cruz, Nicky BioIn 17
Cruz, Norma Oropesa 1943- WhoAm 92
Cruz, R.D., Jr. Law&B 92
Cruz, Ralph 1935- St&PR 93
Cruz, Ramon Ernesto DcCPCAm
Cruz, Ricardo A. 1950- St&PR 93
Cruz, Ricardo Cortez 1964- ConAu 139
Cruz, Salvador de la 1922-1979 DcMexL
Cruz, Victor Hernandez 1949- BioIn 17, ConAu 17AS [port], HispAmA [port]
Cruzado, Antonio 1940- WhoWor 93
Cruzan, Clarah Catherine 1913- WhoSSW 93
Cruzan, Nancy BioIn 17
Cruz Aponte, Ramon Aristides 1927- WhoAm 92
Cruz-Cuebas, Blanca 1939- WhoSSW 93
Cruz-Diez, Carlos 1923- WhoWor 93
Cruze, Alvin M. 1939- St&PR 93, WhoAm 92
Cruze, James 1884-1942 MiSFD 9N
Cruze, Kenneth 1927- WhoE 93
Cruzeiro, Ana Bela Ferreira 1957- WhoWor 93
Cruze Silva, J. WhoScE 91-3
Cruz Fabres, Rafael Gonzalo 1941- WhoWor 93
Cruz Kronfly, Fernando 1943- SpAmA
Cruz-Pinto, J.J.C. 1948- WhoScE 91-3
Cruz-Pinto, Jose Joaquim C. 1948- WhoWor 93
Cruz Porras, Arturo Jose 1923- DcCPCAm
Cruz-Romo, Gilda WhoAm 92
Cruz-Romo, Gilda 20th cent.- HispAmA
Cruz-Romo, Gilda 1940- Baker 92
Cruz-Saco, Maria Amparo 1957- WhoWor 93
Cruz-Saenz, Michele Frances Schiavone de 1949- WhoAmW 93
Cruz-Serrano, Alejandro Reynaldo 1947- WhoWor 93
Cruz Tenbrook, Catherine Stannie 1960- WhoEmL 93
Cruz-Velez, David Francisco 1951- WhoSSW 93
Cryer, Eugene Edward 1935- WhoAm 92, WhoSSW 93, WhoWor 93
Cryer, Gretchen 1935- WhoAm 92
Cryer, Jon BioIn 17
Cryer, Theodore Hudson 1946- WhoE 93
Crymble, John Frederick 1916- WhoWor 93
Crymes, Ronald Jack 1935- WhoSSW 93
Crynes, Billy Lee 1938- WhoAm 92
Crypton, Dr. 1956- ScF&FL 92
Crystal, Allan A. 1929- St&PR 93
Crystal, Billy BioIn 17
Crystal, Billy 1947?- ConTFT 10, HolBB [port], QDrFCA 92 [port], WhoAm 92
Crystal, Billy 1948- MiSFD 9
Crystal, Boris 1931- WhoAm 92, WhoWor 93
Crystal, Graef S. BioIn 17, NewYTBS 92
Crystal, Graef Slater 1934- WhoAm 92
Crystal, James William 1937- WhoAm 92, WhoE 93, WhoWor 93
Crystal, Joel Frome Law&B 92
Crystal, Lester Martin 1934- WhoAm 92
Crystal, Robert Abraham 1956- WhoE 93, WhoEmL 93
Crystal, Sam 1927- St&PR 93
Crystall, Ellen 1950- WhoAmW 93
Crystals SoulM
Cryz, Stanley J. 1953- WhoScE 91-4
Crzellitzer, Franz 1905-1979 Baker 92
Csaba, Bela 1931- WhoScE 91-4
Csaba, G. 1929- WhoScE 91-4
Csaba, Imre Ferenc 1926- WhoScE 91-4
Csabalik, Gyula 1930- WhoScE 91-4
Csaky, Adrian BioIn 17
Csaky, Irena BioIn 17
Csanady, Gabriel Tibor 1925- WhoAm 92
Csanady, Miklos 1937- WhoScE 91-4
Csango, Peter Andras 1942- WhoWor 93
Csanyi, Laszlo J. 1927- WhoScE 91-4
Csaposs, Jean Fox 1931- WhoAmW 93
Csavinszky, Peter John 1931- WhoAm 92
Cseko, Louis L., Jr. 1950- St&PR 93
Cselenyi, Jozsef 1936- WhoScE 91-4
Csellak, Linda Marie 1960- WhoAmW 93
Cselotei, Laszlo 1925- WhoScE 91-4
Csemez, Attila 1945- WhoScE 91-4
Csencsits, Christopher Joseph WhoE 93
Csendes, Ernest 1926- WhoWor 93
Csermely, Jeno 1938- WhoScE 91-4
Csermely, Thomas John 1931- WhoE 93
Csernai, Laszlo Pal 1949- WhoWor 93
Csernay, Laszlo 1931- WhoScE 91-4
Csernovicz, Barbara Ann 1933- WhoAmW 93
Cserr, Helen FitzGerald 1937- WhoE 93
Cserr, Robert 1936- WhoAm 92
Cserveny, Vilmos 1951- WhoUN 92
Csia, Susan Rebecca Law&B 92
Csia, Susan Rebecca 1945- WhoAm 92, WhoAmW 93
Csiba, Arpad 1928- WhoScE 91-4
Csibi, Sandor 1927- WhoScE 91-4
Csikai, Gyula 1930- WhoScE 91-4, WhoWor 93
Csikos, Rezso 1930- WhoScE 91-4
Csikszentmihalyi, Mihaly 1934- WhoAm 92
Csiky, Boldizsar 1937- Baker 92
Csillik, Bertalan 1927- WhoScE 91-4
Csirik, Janos 1946- WhoWor 93
Csizmazia, Zoltan 1937- WhoScE 91-4
Csokas, Janos 1918- WhoScE 91-4
Csomor, Sandor 1919- WhoScE 91-4
Csonka, Larry BioIn 17
Csoori, Sandor 1930- BioIn 17
Csorba, Sandor 1929- WhoScE 91-4
Csordas, Gabor d1992 BioIn 17
Csorgo, Miklos 1932- WhoAm 92
Csukas, Istvan 1936- BioIn 17
Csurgay, Arpad I. 1936- WhoScE 91-4
Csuri, Charles A. BioIn 17
Ctesibius fl. 246BC-221BC Baker 92
Ctyroky, Jiri 1946- WhoScE 91-4
Cua, Antonio S. 1932- WhoAm 92
Cuadra, Carlos Albert 1925- WhoAm 92
Cuadra, Jose de la 1903-1941 SpAmA
Cuadra, Julio Cesar 1946- WhoEmL 93
Cuadra, Pablo Antonio DcCPCAm
Cuadra, Pablo Antonio 1912- SpAmA
Cuajao, Tracy Lee 1953- WhoWor 93
Cuaron, Alicia 1939- NotHsAW 93
Cuartero, Jesus 1946- WhoScE 91-3
Cuatrecasas, Pedro Martin 1936- WhoAm 92, WhoWor 93
Cuban, Larry BioIn 17
Cubas, Jose Manuel 1930- WhoE 93
Cubbage, Frederick Willis 1951- WhoSSW 93
Cubbage, Thomas Leon, II Law&B 92
Cubberley, Robert R. 1948- St&PR 93
Cubberley, William Charles 1945- WhoE 93
Cubbin, James C. Law&B 92
Cubbon, Robert C.P. 1936- WhoScE 91-1
Cube BioIn 17
Cuber, Ronnie BioIn 17
Cuberes, Juan 1952- WhoWor 93
Cuberli, Lella BioIn 17
Cuberli, Lella 1950- OxDcOp
Cubillo, Enrique BioIn 17
Cubine, Margaret Virginia 1919- WhoSSW 93
Cubiotti, Gaetano 1939- WhoScE 91-3
Cubita, Peter Naylor 1957- WhoEmL 93
Cubitt, George ScF&FL 92
Cubitt, Iain 1947- WhoScE 91-1
Cuboni, Giuseppe G. 1939- WhoUN 92
Cuccaro, Ronald Anthony 1944- WhoE 93
Cucci, Cesare Eleuterio 1925- WhoAm 92
Cucci, Louis Anthony 1943- WhoE 93
Cuccinelli, Kenneth T. 1945- St&PR 93
Cucciniello, Dawn Grace 1949- WhoAmW 93
Cucco, Salvatore Nicholas 1948- St&PR 93
Cucco, Ulisse P. 1929- WhoAm 92
Cuchna, Ronald J. Law&B 92
Cucin, Robert Louis 1946- WhoEmL 93
Cucinotta, Philip L. St&PR 93
Cucinotta, Victor Michael 1949- St&PR 93
Cucksey, John Davenport 1934- St&PR 93
Cuclin, Dimitrie 1885-1978 Baker 92
Cucuz, Ron St&PR 93
Cuda, Vincent, Jr. 1956- WhoSSW 93
Cudahy, Michael J. St&PR 93
Cudahy, Richard D. 1926- WhoAm 92
Cudak, Gail Linda Law&B 92
Cudd, Margaret Amelia 1953- WhoWor 93
Cuddeback, James Edward 1934- St&PR 93
Cuddeback, Thomas Joel, Jr. 1926- WhoWor 93
Cuddehe, Judith Link 1961- WhoAmW 93, WhoEmL 93
Cuddihy, Robert V., Jr. 1959- St&PR 93
Cuddihy, Robert Vincent, Jr. 1959- WhoE 93, WhoEmL 93
Cuddon, J.A. 1928- ScF&FL 92
Cuddy, Daniel Hon 1921- WhoAm 92
Cuddy, John C. Law&B 92
Cuddy, John David Arnold 1945- WhoUN 92
Cuddy, Lucy Alsanson AmWomPl
Cude, Bobby Lee 1925- WhoSSW 93
Cude, Reginald Hodgin 1936- WhoAm 92
Cudlip, Charles Thomas 1940- WhoAm 92, WhoE 93
Cudlip, David R. 1933- ScF&FL 92
Cudlip, Jack Merlin 1924- St&PR 93
Cudmore, Angela AmWomPl
Cudmore, Bob 1945- WhoE 93
Cudmore, Laurence E. WhoAm 92
Cudnohufsky, Walter Lee 1940- WhoE 93
Cudworth, Allen L. 1929- WhoAm 92
Cudworth, Charles (Cyril Leonard) 1908-1977 Baker 92
Cudworth, Marsha Elizabeth 1947- WhoWrEP 92
Cudworth, Raymond P. 1938- St&PR 93
Cue, Nelson 1941- WhoWor 93
Cuellar, Enrique Roberto 1955- WhoEmL 93
Cuellar, Gilbert, Jr. HispAmA [port]
Cuellar, Gilbert, Jr. 1954- WhoAm 92
Cuellar, Javier Perez de BioIn 17
Cuellar, John A. Law&B 92
Cuellar, John A. 1945- St&PR 93
Cuellar, Jose Tomas de 1830-1894 DcMexL
Cuellar, Miguel Angel Santana 1937- BiDAMSp 1989
Cuellar, Virginia Adrien 1967- WhoSSW 93
Cuello, Augusto Claudio Guillermo 1939- WhoAm 92
Cuenca, Agustin 1850-1884 DcMexL
Cuenco, Antonio V. 1936- WhoAsAP 91
Cuendet, Antoine 1926- WhoScE 91-4
Cuenod, Hugues 1902- IntDcOp, OxDcOp
Cuenod, Hugues (-Adhemar) 1902- Baker 92
Cuenod, Michel R. 1933- WhoScE 91-4
Cuentas-Zavala, Jose Carlos 1945- WhoUN 92
Cueny, Burke William 1959- WhoEmL 93
Cuer, Michel Charles 1947- WhoWor 93
Cuero, Delphina c.1900- BioIn 17
Cuervo, Asela M. Law&B 92
Cuervo, Felix J. d1992 NewYTBS 92 [port]
Cuesta, Gregorio Garcia de la 1744-1811 HarEnMi
Cuesta, Jorge 1903-1942 DcMexL
Cuesta, Tony d1992 NewYTBS 92
Cuesta Rodriguez, Jairo Antonio 1952- WhoWor 93
Cuetara, Dulce Maria 1954- WhoSSW 93
Cuetara, Paul Savage 1947- WhoE 93
Cueva, Juan de la 1543?-1610 DcMexL
Cuevas, David 1947- WhoSSW 93
Cuevas, Jose Luis 1934- BioIn 17, WhoAm 92
Cuevas, Manuel BioIn 17
Cuevas, Milton Joseph 1934- WhoAm 92
Cuevas, Pedro WhoWor 93
Cuevas, Rosemary 1958- WhoEmL 93
Cuevas de Dolmetsch, Angela 1942- WhoWor 93
Cuff, Dennis James 1942- St&PR 93
Cuff, Douglas George 1961- WhoWrEP 92
Cuff, Robert G., Jr. Law&B 92
Cuff, William 1942- St&PR 93
Cuffari, Richard 1925-1978 BioIn 17, MajAI [port]
Cuffe, Stafford Sigesmund 1949- WhoEmL 93
Cuffin, B. Neil 1941- WhoE 93
Cugat, Xavier 1900-1990 Baker 92, BioIn 17
Cugiani, Corrado WhoScE 91-3
Cugiani, Marco WhoScE 91-3
Cugley, Ian (Robert) 1945- Baker 92
Cugnon, Joseph 1944- WhoScE 91-2
Cugurra, Franco 1923- WhoScE 91-3
Cuhaj, George Stephen 1960- WhoE 93

Cuhraj, Grigorij 1921- DrEEuF
Cui, Bao Tong 1960- WhoWor 93
Cui, Cesar 1835-1918 OxDcOp
Cui, Cesar (Antonovich) 1835-1918 Baker 92
Cuil de Stratclut, Alecsandr 1931- WhoWor 93
Cui Naifu 1929- WhoAsAP 91
Cuisia, Jose 1944- WhoAsAP 91
Cuisia, Jose L., Jr. BioIn 17
Cuisia, Jose L., Jr. 1944- WhoWor 93
Cuisinaud, Guy Eugene Antoine 1939- WhoScE 91-2
Cukier, Rona 1951- St&PR 93
Cukor, George 1899-1983 BioIn 17, MiSFD 9N
Cukor, Peter 1936- WhoAm 92
Culache, Domnica WhoScE 91-4
Culb, Dorothy E. 1938- WhoAmW 93
Culberg, Paul S. 1942- St&PR 93
Culberson, James Lee 1941- WhoSSW 93
Culberson, James M., Jr. BioIn 17
Culberson, James M., Jr. 1928- St&PR 93
Culberson, John Andrew 1947- WhoEmL 93
Culberson, Robert Allan 1935- St&PR 93
Culberson, Robert Neil 1938- WhoSSW 93
Culberson, William Louis 1929- WhoAm 92
Culbert, Kenneth Edward 1948- WhoE 93
Culbertson, Alexander 1809-1879 BioIn 17
Culbertson, Dooley Ewell 1936- St&PR 93, WhoAm 92
Culbertson, Frances Mitchell 1921- WhoAm 92, WhoAmW 93
Culbertson, Jack A. BioIn 17
Culbertson, James Francis, Jr. 1949- St&PR 93
Culbertson, Janet Lynn 1932- WhoAm 92
Culbertson, John Mathew 1921- WhoAm 92
Culbertson, Judi C. 1941- WhoE 93
Culbertson, Katheryn Campbell 1920- WhoAm 92
Culbertson, Philip Edgar 1925- WhoAm 92
Culbreath, Hugh Lee, Jr. 1921- St&PR 93
Culbreath, Myrna 1938- ScF&FL 92
Culbreth, Arnold Arthur, Jr. 1934- St&PR 93
Culbreth, Thomas B. 1937- WhoIns 93
Culby, Keene Ray 1931- St&PR 93
Culer, Louis 1925- WhoWor 93
Culhane, Floyd C. 1945- St&PR 93
Culhane, James Edward 1941- WhoAm 92
Culhane, James F. 1930- St&PR 93
Culhane, John Joseph Law&B 92
Culhane, John Leonard WhoScE 91-1
Culhane, John William 1934- WhoAm 92, WhoE 93
Culhane, Shamus 1908- ConTFT 10, WhoAm 92
Culianu, I.P. 1950-1991 ScF&FL 92
Culianu, Ioan P. BioIn 17
Culick, Fred Ellsworth Clow 1933- WhoAm 92
Culin, Walter Georg 1930- St&PR 93
Culkin, Elizabeth Anne 1950- WhoEmL 93
Culkin, Macaulay BioIn 17
Culkin, Macaulay 1980?- ConTFT 10
Cull, Chris Alan 1947- WhoEmL 93
Cull, Robert Robinette 1912- WhoAm 92
Cull, William Judson Law&B 92
Cullari, Salvatore Santino 1952- WhoE 93
Cullen, Arlene Hope 1957- WhoAmW 93
Cullen, Bill 1920-1990 BioIn 17
Cullen, Brian ScF&FL 92
Cullen, Brian C. 1952- St&PR 93
Cullen, Brian Dennis 1940- St&PR 93
Cullen, Charles David 1951- WhoEmL 93
Cullen, Charles Thomas 1940- WhoAm 92
Cullen, Cornelius W. Law&B 92
Cullen, Countee 1903-1946 BioIn 17, BlkAuII 92, EncAACR
Cullen, Donna Marie 1953- WhoEmL 93
Cullen, Frederick Landis 1947- St&PR 93, WhoAm 92
Cullen, Gail Frederick 1940- St&PR 93
Cullen, Gavin Anthony WhoScE 91-1
Cullen, Gerard Lyons 1943- WhoSSW 93
Cullen, J. Russell, Jr. 1939- St&PR 93
Cullen, Jack Sydney George Bud 1927- WhoAm 92
Cullen, James Barrie 1939- WhoWor 93
Cullen, James Donald 1947- WhoEmL 93
Cullen, James Douglas 1945- WhoAm 92
Cullen, James G. 1942- WhoAm 92
Cullen, James John, Jr. Law&B 92
Cullen, James Patrick 1944- WhoAm 92, WhoE 93
Cullen, James Thaddeus, Jr. 1935- WhoAm 92
Cullen, Jean V. ScF&FL 92
Cullen, John M. Law&B 92
Cullen, Joseph W. 1936-1990 BioIn 17
Cullen, Linda Jo Krozser 1955- WhoAmW 93, WhoEmL 93
Cullen, Lynn 1948- WhoEmL 93
Cullen, Margaret 1924- WhoWrEP 92
Cullen, Marygael 1951- WhoEmL 93
Cullen, Matthew William Law&B 92
Cullen, Michael A. 1961- St&PR 93
Cullen, Michael James WhoScE 91-1
Cullen, Michael John 1941- WhoScE 91-3
Cullen, Michael John 1945- WhoAsAP 91
Cullen, Mike Law&B 92
Cullen, Pamela Cheryl 1959- WhoAmW 93
Cullen, R. Gerard 1929- WhoScE 91-3
Cullen, Scott St&PR 93
Cullen, Seamus ScF&FL 92
Cullen, Stephen Leonard, Jr. 1940- WhoE 93
Cullen, Terrance Michael 1953- WhoEmL 93
Cullen, Vincent Albert 1934- WhoE 93
Cullen, William P. 1954- WhoIns 93
Cullenbine, Clair Stephens 1905- WhoAm 92
Cullenbine, Roy 1915-1991 BioIn 17
Cullens, Annie Laurie AmWomPl
Cullens, Williams Scott 1930- St&PR 93
Culler, Arthur Dwight 1917- WhoAm 92
Culler, Eugene R. 1938- St&PR 93, WhoAm 92
Culler, Joe Henry 1928- St&PR 93
Culler, Jonathan Dwight 1944- WhoAm 92, WhoWrEP 92
Culler, Robert Ransom 1950- WhoSSW 93
Culler, Robert W. 1933- St&PR 93
Cullers, D. Kent BioIn 17
Cullers, James J. 1930- St&PR 93
Cullers, Jeffery Bryan 1957- WhoEmL 93
Cullers, Marian BioIn 17
Cullers, Mark Eugene 1958- WhoEmL 93
Cullerton, William J. BioIn 17
Culleton, James E. 1941- St&PR 93
Culley, Grant Burdette, Jr. 1921- St&PR 93
Culley, James Spencer 1950- WhoSSW 93
Culley, John Henry 1947- WhoEmL 93
Culley-Foster, Anthony Robert 1947- WhoE 93, WhoEmL 93
Culliford, Pierre 1928-1992 NewYTBS 92 [port]
Culliford, Sydney B. 1932- St&PR 93
Culligan, Brian Keith 1959- WhoSSW 93
Culligan, Jane Teresa 1933- WhoE 93
Culligan, John W. 1916- St&PR 93
Culligan, John William 1916- WhoAm 92
Cullimore, Kelvyn Henry, Jr. 1956- St&PR 93
Cullina, William Michael 1921- WhoAm 92
Cullinan, Elizabeth 1933- WhoWrEP 92
Cullinan, Richard 1923- St&PR 93
Cullinan, Thomas ScF&FL 92
Cullinan, Thomas William 1951- WhoEmL 93, WhoSSW 93
Cullinane, Daniel C., Jr. St&PR 93
Cullinane, Joe St&PR 93
Cullinane, Joe 1927- WhoSSW 93
Cullinane, Julia G. Law&B 92
Cullingford, Hatice Sadan 1945- WhoAmW 93
Cullingham, Mark 1941- MiSFD 9
Cullings, Robert E. 1938- St&PR 93
Cullingworth, L. Ross 1939- St&PR 93
Cullingworth, Larry Ross 1939- WhoAm 92, WhoE 93
Cullingworth, N.J. ScF&FL 92
Cullis, Charles Fowler WhoScE 91-1
Cullis, Christopher Ashley 1945- WhoAm 92
Cullis, Christopher Paul 1956- St&PR 93
Cullis, Elizabeth M. AmWomPl
Cullis, Ford Miller 1919- St&PR 93
Cullison, Irene Margaret AmWomPl
Cullison, William E. 1935- St&PR 93
Cullison, William Lester 1931- WhoAm 92
Culliton, Edward F. 1941- St&PR 93
Cullity, John Patrick 1928- WhoE 93
Cullman, Edgar M. 1918- St&PR 93
Cullman, Edgar M., Jr. 1946- WhoAm 92
Cullman, Hugh 1923- WhoAm 92
Cullman, Joseph F., III 1912- St&PR 93
Cullman, Lewis B. 1919- St&PR 93
Cullman, W. Arthur d1992 NewYTBS 92
Cullo, Leonard A., Jr. Law&B 92
Cullom, Hale Ellicott 1935- St&PR 93
Cullom, Paul C., Jr. Law&B 92
Cullom, Shelby M. 1829-1914 PolPar
Cullom, William Otis 1932- WhoAm 92, WhoSSW 93, WhoWor 93
Cullop, Edythe K. 1925- St&PR 93
Cullotta, Betty Antionette 1928- WhoAmW 93
Cullum, Gay Nelle 1952- WhoEmL 93
Cullum, John Michael 1959- WhoEmL 93
Cullum, Robert B., Jr. 1948- WhoAm 92
Cully, Kathleen G. Law&B 92
Cully, Russell A. 1900-1990 BioIn 17
Culm, Gerald P. Law&B 92
Culman, John Kelley 1927- St&PR 93
Culmer, Cara Lee 1949- WhoEmL 93
Culmer, Marjorie Mehne 1912- WhoAm 92
Culmone, Jody Robinson 1936- WhoAmW 93
Culotta, Denise Fern 1958- WhoAmW 93
Culp, Amy Martin 1964- WhoAmW 93
Culp, Charles Allen 1930- WhoAm 92
Culp, Cliff Thomas 1952- WhoEmL 93
Culp, Clyde E., III 1942- WhoAm 92
Culp, Edward Ronald 1947- WhoEmL 93
Culp, Even Asher 1952- WhoEmL 93, WhoSSW 93
Culp, George Hart 1938- WhoAm 92, WhoSSW 93
Culp, Gordon Louis 1939- WhoAm 92
Culp, Iris Land 1960- WhoEmL 93, WhoSSW 93
Culp, James Stanley 1935- St&PR 93
Culp, Joe Carl 1933- WhoAm 92, WhoSSW 93
Culp, John Stephen 1947- WhoEmL 93
Culp, Judy Lee 1943- WhoSSW 93
Culp, Julia 1880-1970 Baker 92
Culp, King K. Law&B 92
Culp, Margaret Juanita 1928- WhoAmW 93
Culp, Marvin Edward 1948- WhoEmL 93, WhoSSW 93
Culp, Michael 1952- WhoAm 92, WhoE 93
Culp, Mildred Louise 1949- WhoAm 92, WhoEmL 93
Culp, Robert 1930- MiSFD 9, WhoAm 92
Culp, Robert George, III 1946- St&PR 93
Culp, Stephanie (Anne) 1947- ConAu 136
Culp, Terry P. 1946- St&PR 93
Culp, W.S. 1949- St&PR 93
Culp, William Maurice ScF&FL 92
Culp, William Newton 1923- WhoAm 92
Culpepper, Dennis Wayne 1940- St&PR 93
Culpepper, Jerri Lea 1958- WhoAmW 93, WhoEmL 93
Culpepper, Leon 1937- St&PR 93
Culpepper-Smith, Lena 1934- WhoIns 93
Culshaw, Brian WhoScE 91-1
Culshaw, John (Royds) 1924-1980 Baker 92
Culter, John Dougherty 1937- WhoWor 93
Culton, Sarah Alexander 1927- WhoAmW 93
Cultra, George A. 1915- St&PR 93
Cultra, John W. 1945- St&PR 93
Culvahouse, Arthur Boggess, Jr. 1948- WhoAm 92, WhoEmL 93
Culver, (David) Andrew 1953- Baker 92
Culver, C. Wayne Law&B 92
Culver, Charles George 1937- WhoAm 92
Culver, Curtis N. Law&B 92
Culver, Dan Louis 1957- WhoEmL 93, WhoSSW 93, WhoWor 93
Culver, David M. 1924- St&PR 93
Culver, Edward H. 1918- St&PR 93
Culver, Edward Holland 1918- WhoAm 92
Culver, Ernest Wayne 1938- WhoE 93, WhoWor 93
Culver, Florence Morrow 1915- WhoAmW 93
Culver, James Calvin 1944- WhoAm 92
Culver, John Eskridge 1932- St&PR 93, WhoAm 92
Culver, John Handy, III 1959- WhoEmL 93
Culver, Kirsten BioIn 17
Culver, Larry G. St&PR 93
Culver, Linda S. 1953- St&PR 93
Culver, Robert Elroy 1926- WhoAm 92
Culver, Robert J. 1937- St&PR 93
Culver, Steven Michael 1956- WhoSSW 93
Culver, Timothy J. BioIn 17
Culver, Walter Julius 1937- WhoAm 92
Culverhouse, E. Allen BioIn 17
Culverhouse, Hugh Franklin 1919- WhoAm 92, WhoSSW 93
Culverhouse, Joy McCann 1920- WhoAm 92
Culverhouse, Thomas Anthony 1964- WhoSSW 93
Culvern, Julian Brewer 1919- WhoSSW 93
Culverwell, Albert Henry 1913- WhoAm 92
Culverwell, Ronald LeRoy 1936- St&PR 93
Culverwell, Rosemary Jean 1934- WhoAmW 93
Culviner, William H. Law&B 92
Culwell, Charles Louis 1927- WhoAm 92
Culwell, Curtis L. 1954- WhoSSW 93
Culwick, James C. 1845-1907 Baker 92
Culyer, Anthony J. WhoScE 91-1
Cumbaa, Stephen 1947- SmATA 72 [port]
Cumber, Carol Jane 1956- WhoEmL 93
Cumberland, Patrick James Law&B 92
Cumberland, Richard 1732-1811 BioIn 17
Cumberland, William Augustus, Duke of 1721-1765 HarEnMi
Cumberworth, Starling 1915-1985 Baker 92
Cumbest, Elvis Mark 1953- WhoEmL 93
Cumbo, Lawrence James, Jr. 1947- WhoWor 93
Cumbow, Robert C. 1946- ScF&FL 92
Cumbow, Robert Charles 1946- WhoEmL 93
Cumby, Dorothy Elizabeth 1956- WhoEmL 93
Cumby, Trevor Roy WhoScE 91-1
Cumello, Charles BioIn 17
Cumerford, William Richard 1916- WhoAm 92, WhoSSW 93
Cuming, Christopher Bernard WhoScE 91-1
Cuming, David Brumpton 1932- St&PR 93
Cuming, George Scott 1915- WhoAm 92
Cuming, Pamela Jane 1944- WhoAmW 93
Cumings, Edwin Harlan 1933- WhoE 93, WhoWor 93
Cumins, Mark BioIn 17
Cumiskey, Colin Edward 1942- St&PR 93
Cummer, William Jackson 1922- WhoAm 92
Cummerford, John E. Law&B 92
Cummerton, Joan Marie 1931- WhoAmW 93
Cummin, Alfred Samuel 1924- St&PR 93, WhoAm 92, WhoE 93, WhoWor 93
Cumming, David 1943- WhoAm 92
Cumming, David Robert, Jr. 1927- WhoAm 92
Cumming, David T. 1943- St&PR 93
Cumming, Donald A. 1937- St&PR 93
Cumming, Douglas G. 1938- St&PR 93
Cumming, Elizabeth (Skeoch) 1948- ConAu 137
Cumming, Glen Edward 1936- WhoAm 92, WhoWor 93
Cumming, Ian M. 1940- WhoAm 92
Cumming, Ian MacNeill 1940- St&PR 93
Cumming, Janice Dorothy 1953- WhoAmW 93
Cumming, John Battin 1936- St&PR 93
Cumming, L.W. 1930- St&PR 93
Cumming, Margaret M. Law&B 92
Cumming, Patricia Arens 1932- WhoWrEP 92
Cumming, Peter 1951- WhoCanL 92
Cumming, Robert 1935- WhoWrEP 92
Cumming, Robert 1945- BioIn 17
Cumming, Robert Emil 1933- WhoAm 92
Cumming, Robert Henry WhoScE 91-1
Cumming, Robert Hugh 1943- WhoAm 92
Cumming, Thomas Alexander 1937- WhoAm 92
Cumming, Virgil H. 1945- WhoIns 93
Cummings, Alan G. Law&B 92
Cummings, Amos Jay 1841-1902 JrnUS
Cummings, Andrew M. St&PR 93
Cummings, Angela BioIn 17
Cummings, Ann WhoWrEP 92
Cummings, Barton 1946- WhoEmL 93
Cummings, Betty Sue 1918- DcAmChF 1960, WhoWrEP 92
Cummings, Beverly A. 1953- St&PR 93
Cummings, Brian Thomas 1945- WhoAm 92
Cummings, Byron 1860-1954 IntDcAn
Cummings, C. Bradley 1953- St&PR 93
Cummings, Charles Edgeworth, Jr. 1946- St&PR 93
Cummings, Charles Rogers 1930- WhoAm 92
Cummings, Charles William 1935- WhoAm 92
Cummings, Conrad Milton 1933- WhoSSW 93
Cummings, Constance WhoAm 92, WhoAmW 93
Cummings, Constance 1910- BioIn 17
Cummings, David George ScF&FL 92
Cummings, David K. 1941- WhoIns 93
Cummings, David William 1937- WhoAm 92
Cummings, E.E. 1894-1962 BioIn 17, MagSAmL [port], PoeCrit 5 [port], WorLitC [port]
Cummings, Edward Estlin 1894-1962 BioIn 17
Cummings, Edward J., Jr. Law&B 92
Cummings, Edward L. 1948- St&PR 93
Cummings, Eileen Bass 1945- WhoSSW 93
Cummings, Erika Helga WhoAmW 93
Cummings, Erwin Karl 1954- WhoEmL 93
Cummings, Francis Joseph 1948- WhoSSW 93
Cummings, Frank 1929- WhoAm 92, WhoE 93, WhoWor 93
Cummings, Frederick J. 1933-1990 BioIn 17
Cummings, Gary D. 1950- St&PR 93

Cummings, Gary David 1950- *WhoE 93*
Cummings, George Elrick d1991 *BioIn 17*
Cummings, Glenn D. 1934- *St&PR 93*
Cummings, Helen Margaret 1933- *WhoAmW 93*
Cummings, Homer S. 1870-1956 *PolPar*
Cummings, Homer Stille 1870-1956 *BioIn 17*
Cummings, Howard *MiSFD 9*
Cummings, Howard D. 1948- *WhoEmL 93*
Cummings, Irving 1888-1959 *MiSFD 9N*
Cummings, James B. *Law&B 92*
Cummings, Jean 1930- *WhoWrEP 92*
Cummings, Jill Ann 1958- *WhoAmW 93*
Cummings, Joe 1952- *ConAu 137*
Cummings, John F. 1950- *St&PR 93*
Cummings, John R. *Law&B 92*
Cummings, John Rodgers 1933- *St&PR 93*
Cummings, Josephine Anna 1949- *WhoAm 92, WhoAmW 93*
Cummings, Larry E. 1952- *St&PR 93*
Cummings, Larry Lee 1937- *WhoAm 92*
Cummings, Lawrence B. *St&PR 93*
Cummings, Lee Philip 1945- *St&PR 93*
Cummings, Louise L. G. *AmWomPl*
Cummings, M.A. 1914- *ScF&FL 92*
Cummings, Martin Marc 1920- *WhoAm 92*
Cummings, Mary Dappert 1922- *WhoAmW 93*
Cummings, Merilyn Lloy 1939- *WhoAmW 93, WhoWor 93*
Cummings, Michael S. 1943- *ScF&FL 92*
Cummings, Monette 1914- *ConAu 40NR*
Cummings, Nancy Boucot 1927- *WhoAm 92, WhoE 93*
Cummings, Nathan 1896-1985 *BioIn 17*
Cummings, Nicholas A. *St&PR 93*
Cummings, Nicholas Andrew 1924- *WhoAm 92, WhoWor 93*
Cummings, Pat *ChlBIID [port]*
Cummings, Pat 1950- *MajAI [port]*
Cummings, Pat Marie 1950- *BlkAuII 92, SmATA 71 [port]*
Cummings, Patrick Henry 1941- *WhoSSW 93*
Cummings, Paul 1933- *WhoE 93*
Cummings, Rachel Rice *Law&B 92*
Cummings, Ralph Waldo, Jr. 1938- *WhoE 93*
Cummings, Ray 1887-1957 *ScF&FL 92*
Cummings, Richard Howe 1921- *St&PR 93*
Cummings, Rita 1950- *WhoEmL 93*
Cummings, Robert 1910-1990 *BioIn 17*
Cummings, Robert Eugene 1940- *WhoSSW 93*
Cummings, Robert Lawrence, Jr. 1959- *WhoE 93*
Cummings, Rose Beheler 1959- *WhoEmL 93*
Cummings, Sam *BioIn 17*
Cummings, Sam R. 1944- *WhoSSW 93*
Cummings, Samuel M. d1882 *BioIn 17*
Cummings, Sandra Bielawa 1961- *WhoEmL 93*
Cummings, Spangler 1936- *WhoWor 93*
Cummings, Stephen Thomas 1954- *WhoEmL 93*
Cummings, Thomas Gerald 1944- *WhoAm 92*
Cummings, Thomas L., III 1954- *St&PR 93*
Cummings, Timothy W. *Law&B 92*
Cummings, Victor 1925- *WhoAm 92*
Cummings, Victoria 1956- *WhoAmW 93*
Cummings, W(illiam) H(ayman) 1831-1915 *Baker 92*
Cummings, Walter J. 1916- *WhoAm 92*
Cummings, Wesley Ralph 1950- *WhoSSW 93*
Cummings, William F. 1945- *St&PR 93*
Cummings, William Kenneth 1943- *WhoE 93*
Cummins, Albert B. 1850-1926 *PolPar*
Cummins, Cecil Stratford 1918- *WhoSSW 93*
Cummins, Delmer Duane 1935- *WhoAm 92*
Cummins, Elizabeth 1939- *ScF&FL 92*
Cummins, Gary Steven 1950- *WhoE 93*
Cummins, Georgette Jaber 1931- *WhoE 93*
Cummins, Herman Zachary 1933- *WhoAm 92*
Cummins, Hugh *DcCPCAm*
Cummins, James *MiSFD 9*
Cummins, James Dale 1929- *WhoAm 92, WhoWor 93*
Cummins, James Duane 1945- *WhoSSW 93*
Cummins, John David 1946- *WhoAm 92*
Cummins, John J. *Law&B 92*
Cummins, John Stephen 1928- *WhoAm 92*
Cummins, Joseph Hervey 1916- *WhoAm 92*
Cummins, Julie Ann 1939- *WhoE 93*
Cummins, Karen Muir 1959- *WhoAmW 93*
Cummins, Kenneth Burdette 1911- *WhoAm 92*
Cummins, Kenneth Copeland *Law&B 92*
Cummins, Kenneth Copeland 1943- *St&PR 93, WhoAm 92*
Cummins, Marjorie Whited 1906- *WhoAmW 93*
Cummins, Mary Katherine 1947- *WhoAmW 93*
Cummins, Nancyellen Heckeroth 1948- *WhoAmW 93, WhoEmL 93*
Cummins, Patricia Willett 1948- *WhoAmW 93*
Cummins, Peter *WhoScE 91-1*
Cummins, Peter W. 1937- *St&PR 93*
Cummins, Richard J. *Law&B 92*
Cummins, Robert L. 1926- *St&PR 93*
Cummins, Shirley Jean 1948- *WhoAm 92, WhoEmL 93*
Cummins, Susan Amy 1957- *WhoEmL 93*
Cummins, Walter Merrill 1936- *WhoE 93, WhoWrEP 92*
Cummins, William M. *St&PR 93*
Cummis, Clive Sanford 1928- *WhoAm 92*
Cummiskey, J. Kenneth 1928- *WhoAm 92*
Cumo, Maurizio 1939- *WhoScE 91-3*
Cumpston, Graham Neil 1935- *WhoWor 93*
Cumpsty, Nicholas A. *WhoScE 91-1*
Cunard, Grace 1893-1967 *SweetSg A [port]*
Cunat, Pascual 1933- *WhoScE 91-3*
Cundall, Joseph 1818-1895 *BioIn 17*
Cundari, Dominick L. *St&PR 93*
Cundell, Edric 1893-1961 *Baker 92*
Cundey, Paul Edward, Jr. 1936- *WhoSSW 93*
Cundiff, Edward William 1919- *WhoAm 92*
Cundiff, James Nelson *Law&B 92*
Cundiff, James Nelson 1954- *WhoEmL 93*
Cundiff, James Robert *Law&B 92*
Cundiff, Paul Arthur 1909- *WhoAm 92*
Cundiff, Susan K. *Law&B 92*
Cundiff, William Earl 1945- *WhoWor 93*
Cundy, Richard M. 1949- *St&PR 93*
Cundy, S.L. *WhoScE 91-1*
Cundy, Vic Arnold 1950- *WhoAm 92, WhoEmL 93, WhoSSW 93*
Cunegunda 1224-1292 *PolBiDi*
Cuneo, Albert A. d1991 *BioIn 17*
Cuneo, Dennis C. *Law&B 92*
Cuneo, Dennis Clifford 1950- *WhoWor 93*
Cuneo, Jack A. 1947- *St&PR 93*
Cuneo, John Andrew, Jr. 1929- *WhoE 93*
Cuneo, John F. 1931- *St&PR 93*
Cunetto, Dominic Joseph 1932- *WhoSSW 93*
Cuney, Norris Wright 1846-1896 *EncAACR*
Cuney, William Waring 1906-1976 *EncAACR*
Cuney-Hare, Maud 1874-1936 *AmWomPl*
Cunha, Caio Marcio 1950- *WhoWor 93*
Cunha, Denise Anne 1956- *WhoAmW 93*
Cunha, George Daniel Martin 1911- *BioIn 17*
Cunha, George Martin 1911- *WhoSSW 93, WhoWor 93*
Cunha, Mark Geoffrey 1955- *WhoEmL 93*
Cunha, Robert E. *Law&B 92*
Cunha, Timothy Martin 1951- *St&PR 93*
Cunha, Tony Joseph 1916- *WhoAm 92*
Cunha-Vaz, Jose Guilherme Fernandes 1938- *WhoWor 93*
Cunico, Gianni *Law&B 92*
Cunietti, Mariano 1921- *WhoScE 91-3*
Cunin, John Raymond 1924- *St&PR 93*
Cuninghame-Green, Raymond Albert *WhoScE 91-1*
Cunion, Earl Eugene 1927- *St&PR 93*
Cunliffe, Charles H. 1930- *St&PR 93*
Cunliffe, E. *WhoScE 91-1*
Cunliffe, Frederick Routh, III 1946- *WhoEmL 93*
Cunliffe, Marcus 1922-1990 *BioIn 17*
Cunnane, James Joseph 1938- *St&PR 93, WhoAm 92*
Cunnane, Patricia S. 1946- *WhoAmW 93*
Cunnane, Thomas A. *Law&B 92*
Cunneen, Charles T. 1928- *St&PR 93*
Cunneen, Joseph 1923- *WhoWrEP 92*
Cunneen, Michael James 1944- *St&PR 93*
Cunneen, Thomas Michael *St&PR 93*
Cunniff, Gregory Nixon 1947- *WhoEmL 93*
Cunniff, Melvin d1990 *BioIn 17*
Cunniff, Patrick Francis 1933- *WhoAm 92*
Cunniffe, Terence R. 1946- *St&PR 93*
Cunningham, Alan Gordon 1887-1983 *HarEnMi*
Cunningham, Alan T. 1942- *St&PR 93*
Cunningham, Alice Jeanne 1937- *WhoAmW 93*
Cunningham, Allan 1784-1842 *DcLB 116 [port]*
Cunningham, Allan 1791-1839 *Expl 93*
Cunningham, Andrew Browne 1883-1963 *DcTwHis, HarEnMi*
Cunningham, Ann Marie 1947- *WhoE 93*
Cunningham, Arthur 1928- *Baker 92*
Cunningham, Arthur Francis 1922- *WhoAm 92*
Cunningham, Atlee Marion, Jr. 1938- *WhoAm 92, WhoSSW 93, WhoWor 93*
Cunningham, Barry Thomas 1939- *WhoAsAP 91*
Cunningham, Bill *BioIn 17*
Cunningham, Billy 1943- *WhoAm 92*
Cunningham, Bob Dale 1935- *St&PR 93*
Cunningham, Bruce Arthur 1940- *WhoAm 92*
Cunningham, Cathy *ScF&FL 92*
Cunningham, Charles Baker 1941- *St&PR 93*
Cunningham, Charles Baker, III 1941- *WhoAm 92*
Cunningham, Charles J., Jr. *St&PR 93*
Cunningham, Charles Joseph, Jr. 1932- *WhoAm 92*
Cunningham, Chester *ScF&FL 92*
Cunningham, Chet 1928- *ScF&FL 92*
Cunningham, Christine *Law&B 92*
Cunningham, Clair Monroe, Jr. 1935- *WhoSSW 93*
Cunningham, Clark Edward 1934- *WhoAm 92*
Cunningham, Craig R. 1959- *St&PR 93*
Cunningham, Dale Everett 1927- *St&PR 93*
Cunningham, Dale V. *Law&B 92*
Cunningham, Darla *Law&B 92*
Cunningham, Darla K. *Law&B 92*
Cunningham, David Jowett 1925- *St&PR 93*
Cunningham, Deborah Lynn 1954- *WhoWrEP 92*
Cunningham, Dennis Dean 1939- *WhoAm 92*
Cunningham, Donna Rae 1942- *WhoWrEP 92*
Cunningham, Dorothy Jane 1927- *WhoAm 92*
Cunningham, Dwayne *BioIn 17*
Cunningham, E. Bruce *Law&B 92*
Cunningham, E.V. *WhoWrEP 92*
Cunningham, Earlene Brown 1930- *WhoE 93*
Cunningham, Edward Henry 1869-1930 *BioIn 17*
Cunningham, Edward Joseph 1938- *St&PR 93*
Cunningham, Edward Patrick 1934- *WhoScE 91-3, WhoUN 92*
Cunningham, Elaine *ScF&FL 92*
Cunningham, Emmett Thomas, Jr. 1960- *WhoAm 92*
Cunningham, Eric Ladell 1965- *WhoSSW 93*
Cunningham, Francis Joseph *WhoScE 91-1*
Cunningham, Frank R. 1937- *ConAu 137*
Cunningham, G. Kevin *Law&B 92*
Cunningham, Gail Blair 1950- *WhoAmW 93*
Cunningham, Gary Lee 1948- *WhoEmL 93*
Cunningham, George Francis John 1956- *WhoWor 93*
Cunningham, George Gray 1951- *WhoEmL 93, WhoSSW 93*
Cunningham, George Woody 1930- *WhoAm 92*
Cunningham, Glenn Clarence 1912- *WhoAm 92*
Cunningham, Gordon R. *Law&B 92*
Cunningham, Gordon Ross 1944- *WhoWor 93*
Cunningham, Guy H. *Law&B 92*
Cunningham, Harry B. d1992 *NewYTBS 92 [port]*
Cunningham, Harry Blair 1907- *BioIn 17*
Cunningham, Hervey Leigh 1945- *WhoSSW 93*
Cunningham, Isabella Clara Mantovani 1942- *WhoAm 92, WhoSSW 93*
Cunningham, J. Thalia 1953- *WhoEmL 93*
Cunningham, Jack 1939- *BioIn 17*
Cunningham, Jack R. *Law&B 92*
Cunningham, Jack Wayne 1962- *WhoSSW 93*
Cunningham, Jacqueline Lemme 1941- *WhoAmW 93*
Cunningham, James A. 1945- *St&PR 93*
Cunningham, James Everett 1923- *St&PR 93, WhoAm 92*
Cunningham, James Gerald 1930- *St&PR 93*
Cunningham, James Gerald, Jr. 1930- *WhoAm 92*
Cunningham, James Joseph 1949- *WhoEmL 93*
Cunningham, James Lee 1936- *WhoAm 92*
Cunningham, Janet Lynnette 1955- *WhoAmW 93*
Cunningham, Jean Wooden *Law&B 92*
Cunningham, Jean Wooden 1946- *WhoAmW 93*
Cunningham, Jeffrey Milton 1952- *WhoAm 92*
Cunningham, Jere 1943- *ScF&FL 92*
Cunningham, Jerry Joe 1946- *St&PR 93*
Cunningham, Joel Luther 1944- *WhoAm 92, WhoE 93*
Cunningham, John 1932- *ConTFT 10*
Cunningham, John David 1953- *WhoEmL 93*
Cunningham, John Elliott 1956- *WhoSSW 93*
Cunningham, John Fabian 1928- *WhoAm 92*
Cunningham, John Henry Dacres 1885-1962 *HarEnMi*
Cunningham, John James 1941- *WhoE 93*
Cunningham, John O. *Law&B 92*
Cunningham, Joseph 1931- *WhoScE 91-3*
Cunningham, Joseph Francis, Jr. 1924- *WhoAm 92*
Cunningham, Joseph John, Jr. 1949- *WhoEmL 93*
Cunningham, Joseph Oliver 1918- *St&PR 93*
Cunningham, Julia W(oolfolk) 1916- *DcAmChF 1960*
Cunningham, Julia (Woolfolk) 1916- *MajAI [port], WhoAm 92, WhoWrEP 92*
Cunningham, Karen Ann 1954- *WhoE 93*
Cunningham, Karon Lynette 1950- *WhoEmL 93*
Cunningham, Keith 1939- *ConAu 139*
Cunningham, Keith Allen, II 1948- *St&PR 93, WhoE 93*
Cunningham, Kenneth R. 1945- *St&PR 93*
Cunningham, Kevin F. *Law&B 92*
Cunningham, Kirk B. 1943- *WhoIns 93*
Cunningham, Larry Hugh 1944- *St&PR 93, WhoAm 92*
Cunningham, Larry J. 1944- *WhoAm 92*
Cunningham, Laura *BioIn 17*
Cunningham, Laura 1947- *WhoEmL 93*
Cunningham, Lawrence David 1936- *WhoSSW 93*
Cunningham, Leon William 1927- *WhoAm 92, WhoSSW 93*
Cunningham, Linda Jane 1940- *WhoAmW 93*
Cunningham, Linda Louise 1939- *WhoAmW 93*
Cunningham, Linda S. 1951- *St&PR 93*
Cunningham, Lorinne Mitchell 1909- *WhoAmW 93*
Cunningham, Lucille Walker 1926- *WhoSSW 93*
Cunningham, Luvern L. *BioIn 17*
Cunningham, M.C., II *Law&B 92*
Cunningham, Madeleine White 1946- *WhoAmW 93, WhoSSW 93*
Cunningham, Marcia Lynn 1955- *WhoWrEP 92*
Cunningham, Marilyn *ScF&FL 92*
Cunningham, Marion *BioIn 17*
Cunningham, Mark Douglas 1951- *WhoSSW 93*
Cunningham, Mark Eric 1962- *WhoEmL 93*
Cunningham, Mark Francis 1959- *WhoE 93*
Cunningham, Mark James 1955- *WhoWor 93*
Cunningham, Mary Elizabeth *BioIn 17*
Cunningham, Mary Elizabeth 1931- *WhoAm 92*
Cunningham, Matthew Zachary 1961- *WhoEmL 93, WhoSSW 93*
Cunningham, Merce *BioIn 17, WhoAm 92, WhoE 93*
Cunningham, Michael 1952- *BioIn 17, ConAu 136, ConGAN*
Cunningham, Michael W. 1948- *St&PR 93*
Cunningham, Michael Wayne 1948- *WhoAm 92*
Cunningham, Murray Hunt, Jr. 1942- *WhoAm 92, WhoE 93, WhoWor 93*
Cunningham, Myron Keith *Law&B 92*
Cunningham, Neil Lewis 1924- *St&PR 93, WhoAm 92*
Cunningham, Nina Strickler *WhoEmL 93*
Cunningham, Norman Francis *WhoScE 91-1*
Cunningham, Pam 1957- *BioIn 17*
Cunningham, Patricia Marr 1943- *WhoSSW 93*
Cunningham, Patrick 1943- *St&PR 93*
Cunningham, Patrick Colm 1933- *WhoScE 91-3*
Cunningham, Patrick Joseph 1943- *WhoAm 92*
Cunningham, Patrick Joseph, III 1950- *WhoEmL 93*
Cunningham, Paul Johnston 1928- *WhoSSW 93*
Cunningham, Paul Raymond Goldwyn 1949- *WhoEmL 93, WhoSSW 93*

Cunningham, Pierce Edward 1934- WhoAm 92
Cunningham, R. John 1926- WhoAm 92
Cunningham, R. Walter 1932- WhoAm 92
Cunningham, Randall BioIn 17
Cunningham, Randall 1941- CngDr 91
Cunningham, Randall 1963- AfrAmBi, WhoAm 92, WhoE 93
Cunningham, Randy 1941- BioIn 17, WhoAm 92
Cunningham, Raymond Clement 1931- WhoAm 92
Cunningham, Rebecca Commans 1956- St&PR 93
Cunningham, Richard B. 1932- ScF&FL 92
Cunningham, Richard Dave Law&B 92
Cunningham, Richard J. Law&B 92
Cunningham, Robert Cyril 1914- WhoAm 92
Cunningham, Robert D. Law&B 92
Cunningham, Robert Henry 1945- St&PR 93
Cunningham, Robert M(aris), Jr. 1909-1992 ConAu 137
Cunningham, Robert Morton 1907- WhoAm 92
Cunningham, Robert Shannon, Jr. 1958- WhoEmL 93
Cunningham, Robert Thomas Law&B 92
Cunningham, Roger L. 1914- St&PR 93
Cunningham, Ronald 1942- St&PR 93
Cunningham, Rosemary Thomas 1957- WhoAmW 93, WhoSSW 93
Cunningham, Russell McWhorter, III 1941- St&PR 93
Cunningham, Sam Roland 1951- WhoSSW 93
Cunningham, Scott 1956- ScF&FL 92
Cunningham, Scott Alan 1957- WhoSSW 93
Cunningham, Sean S. 1941- MiSFD 9
Cunningham, Sherron Gatlin 1954- WhoAmW 93
Cunningham, Simon John 1948- WhoUN 92
Cunningham, Sue Carol 1940- WhoAmW 93
Cunningham, Susanna Lee 1943- WhoAmW 93
Cunningham, T. Jefferson, III 1942- St&PR 93
Cunningham, Thom W. 1943- WhoE 93
Cunningham, Thomas Earle, Jr. 1950- WhoEmL 93
Cunningham, Tom d1992 NewYTBS 92
Cunningham, Tom Alan 1946- WhoAm 92
Cunningham, Trudy Bender 1943- WhoAmW 93
Cunningham, Walter Jack 1917- WhoAm 92
Cunningham, William AfrAmBi
Cunningham, William Francis, Jr. 1931- WhoAm 92
Cunningham, William Gerard 1933- St&PR 93
Cunningham, William Henry 1930- WhoAm 92
Cunningham, William Hughes 1944- WhoAm 92, WhoSSW 93, WhoWor 93
Cunningham, Woodrow M. Law&B 92
Cunningham-Agee, Mary BioIn 17
Cunningham-Dunlop, G. Richard 1932- St&PR 93
Cunninghame Graham, R.B. 1852-1936 BioIn 17
Cunninghame Graham, Robert Bontine 1852-1936 BioIn 17
Cunningham-Rundles, Charlotte 1943- WhoE 93
Cunnington, Adrian C. 1960- WhoScE 91-1
Cunnion, Doris Sorg 1919- St&PR 93
Cunnold, Derek Martin 1940- WhoSSW 93
Cunnyngham, Jon 1935- WhoAm 92
Cunnyngham, Maxine Brown 1949- WhoEmL 93
Cuntz, Joachim Johannes Richard 1948- WhoWor 93
Cuny, Alain 1908- IntDcF 2-3
Cuny, Bernard 1932- WhoWor 93
Cunyus, George Law&B 92
Cunyus, George Marvin 1930- St&PR 93, WhoAm 92
Cunyus, John Grady 1962- WhoSSW 93
Cun Zheng, Wang 1936- WhoWor 93
Cuoco, Daniel A. Law&B 92
Cuoco, Daniel A. 1937- St&PR 93
Cuomo, Andrea 1954- WhoWor 93
Cuomo, Andrew BioIn 17
Cuomo, George (Michael) 1929- WhoWrEP 92
Cuomo, Kerry Kennedy BioIn 17
Cuomo, Mario BioIn 17
Cuomo, Mario 1932- News 92 [port]
Cuomo, Mario M. 1932- PolPar
Cuomo, Mario Matthew 1932- ConAu 40NR, WhoAm 92, WhoE 93, WhoWor 93
Cuomo, Ralph Albert 1925- St&PR 93
Cuozzo, Donald H. Law&B 92
Cuozzo, Steven David 1950- WhoAm 92
Cupak, Kresimir 1922- WhoScE 91-4
Cupelli, Redino James Law&B 92
Cupelo, William F. Law&B 92
Cupero, Kelly McFarland Law&B 92
Cupery, Robert Rink 1944- WhoWor 93
Cupiccia, Louis A. 1928- St&PR 93
Cupka, Brian J. Law&B 92
Cupp, Cecil Watson, III 1952- WhoSSW 93
Cupp, David Foster 1938- WhoAm 92
Cupp, Dolores 1937- WhoAmW 93
Cupp, John S., Jr. 1950- WhoEmL 93
Cupp, Samuel B. 1945- WhoIns 93
Cupp, Stephen G. St&PR 93
Cupp, William Franklyn 1939- St&PR 93
Cuppleditch, David 1946- ConAu 38NR
Cupples, Andrew M. 1951- St&PR 93
Cupples, Janet Cummings 1942- WhoAmW 93
Cupples, John Eustace 1944- WhoE 93
Cuppy, Elizabeth Overstreet AmWomPl
Cuppy, George Joseph 1869-1922 BiDAMSp 1989
Cuq, Francois 1954- WhoScE 91-2
Curati-Alasonatti, Walter 1943- WhoWor 93
Curato, Randy Joseph 1958- WhoEmL 93
Curatola, Dorothy Margaret 1938- St&PR 93
Curatolo, Alphonse Frank 1936- WhoAm 92
Curatolo, Joseph Gerard Law&B 92
Curatolo, Paolo 1950- WhoWor 93
Curazzato, Ronald Samuel 1955- WhoE 93
Curb, Michael Charles 1944- WhoAm 92
Curbelo, Joseph Michael 1965- WhoSSW 93
Curboy, Robert Edward 1928- WhoSSW 93
Curcaneanu, Stefan 1939- WhoScE 91-4
Curchod, Francois 1943- WhoUN 92
Curchoe, Carl A. 1944- WhoE 93
Curci, Giuseppe 1808-1877 Baker 92
Curcio, Christopher Frank 1950- WhoEmL 93, WhoWor 93
Curcio, Cynthia Davies 1947- WhoE 93, WhoEmL 93
Curcio, Frances Rena 1951- WhoEmL 93
Curcio, John Baptist 1934- St&PR 93
Curcuru, Felix 1947- WhoIns 93
Curcuru, Felix C. 1947- St&PR 93
Curd, Ed BioIn 17
Curd, Howard R. 1939- St&PR 93
Curdy, Harold M. 1947- St&PR 93
Cure, Carol Campbell 1944- WhoAmW 93
Cure, DeAnn Kay 1955- WhoAmW 93
Cure, Ira Steven 1954- WhoEmL 93
Cure, William Leroy 1944- WhoSSW 93
Cureton, Bryant Lewis 1938- WhoAm 92
Cureton, Elva Sawyer AmWomPl
Cureton, Thomas K., Jr. d1992 NewYTBS 92
Curfman, David Ralph 1942- WhoE 93, WhoWor 93
Curfman, Lawrence Everett 1909- WhoAm 92
Curfman, Wayne Corbet 1949- WhoSSW 93
Curi, Kriton 1942- WhoScE 91-4
Curiale, Salvatore R. 1945- WhoIns 93
Curie, Eve 1904- WhoAmW 93, WhoWor 93
Curie, Frederic Joliot- 1900-1958 BioIn 17
Curie, Irene Joliot- 1897-1956 BioIn 17
Curie, Maria Sklodowska 1867-1934 PolBiDi [port]
Curie, Marie 1867-1934 BioIn 17, ConHero 2 [port]
Curiel, Herman F. 1934- WhoSSW 93
Curiel, Imma Jacinta 1960- WhoE 93
Curien, Hubert BioIn 17
Curien, Hubert 1924- WhoScE 91-2, WhoWor 93
Curig Roberts, T.C. WhoScE 91-1
Curio, Gaius Scribonius c. 90BC-49BC HarEnMi
Curio, O.E. Eberhard 1932- WhoScE 91-3
Curioli, Paul D. 1948- WhoIns 93
Curkendall, Brenda Irene 1954- WhoAmW 93, WhoEmL 93
Curko, Kathleen Ann 1950- WhoE 93
Curl, A. Delmour 1925- St&PR 93
Curl, Blake, Jr. 1940- St&PR 93
Curl, Donald Walter 1935- WhoSSW 93
Curl, Gregory Lynn 1948- St&PR 93
Curl, James Stevens WhoScE 91-1
Curl, Richard L. 1932- St&PR 93
Curl, Robert Floyd, Jr. 1933- WhoAm 92
Curl, Samuel Everett 1937- WhoAm 92, WhoSSW 93
Curl, Steven M. 1954- St&PR 93
Curl, Thomas Leonard 1948- WhoSSW 93
Curl, Vincent Stuart 1947- WhoE 93
Curle, Robin Lea 1950- WhoAmW 93, WhoEmL 93
Curlee, Dorothy Sumner 1921- WhoSSW 93
Curlee, Steven A. Law&B 92
Curlee, Steven A. 1951- St&PR 93
Curler, Jeffrey H. 1950- St&PR 93
Curless, Carroll D. 1938- St&PR 93
Curless, Larry 1931- St&PR 93
Curless, Larry Dean 1931- WhoAm 92
Curlett, Howard D. 1945- St&PR 93
Curley, Anne L. 1953- St&PR 93
Curley, Arthur 1938- WhoAm 92, WhoE 93
Curley, Chris ScF&FL 92
Curley, Daniel BioIn 17
Curley, Denis Michael 1947- St&PR 93
Curley, Dwight G. 1936- St&PR 93
Curley, Edwin Munson 1937- WhoAm 92
Curley, Frank Donald 1929- St&PR 93
Curley, James Michael 1874-1958 PolPar
Curley, James O. 1941- St&PR 93
Curley, John E., Jr. WhoAm 92
Curley, John Francis, Jr. 1939- St&PR 93, WhoAm 92, WhoE 93, WhoWor 93
Curley, John H. Law&B 92
Curley, John J. 1938- St&PR 93, WhoAm 92, WhoE 93, WhoSSW 93
Curley, Judith Marie 1949- WhoE 93
Curley, Michael Edward 1947- WhoAm 92
Curley, Pauline c. 1895- SweetSg B [port]
Curley, Robert M. 1947- St&PR 93
Curley, Sarah Sharer WhoAmW 93
Curley, Stephen Joseph 1947- WhoSSW 93
Curley, Thomas 1948- WhoAm 92
Curley, Thomas F. 1925- WhoWrEP 92
Curley, Thomas J., Jr. 1957- WhoEmL 93
Curley, Walter J.P. 1922- St&PR 93
Curley, Walter Joseph Patrick, Jr. 1922- WhoAm 92, WhoWor 93
Curlin, Barbara Price 1924- St&PR 93
Curlin, Jack V. 1917- St&PR 93
Curll, Bruce d1991 BioIn 17
Curll, Daniel B., III 1942- St&PR 93
Curlook, Walter 1929- St&PR 93, WhoAm 92, WhoE 93
Curlovich, John ScF&FL 92
Curnin, Thomas Francis 1933- WhoAm 92
Curnow, Robert Nicholas WhoScE 91-1
Curnutt, Esther Clark 1935- WhoSSW 93
Curnutt, Ronald Colin 1947- WhoEmL 93
Curnutte, Mark William 1954- WhoAm 92, WhoEmL 93, WhoSSW 93
Curoe, Bernadine Mary 1930- WhoAmW 93
Curoe, Michael R. Law&B 92
Curol, Helen Ruth 1944- WhoAmW 93, WhoSSW 93
Curott, David Richard 1937- WhoSSW 93
Curotto, Ricky Joseph Law&B 92
Curp, John H. Law&B 92
Curran, Alvin 1938- Baker 92
Curran, Barbara Adell 1928- WhoAm 92
Curran, Barbara Sanson 1955- St&PR 93, WhoEmL 93
Curran, Bruce Malcolm 1948- WhoWor 93
Curran, Catherine Moore Law&B 92
Curran, Charles Edward 1934- WhoSSW 93, WhoWrEP 92
Curran, Charles Eschman, III 1946- St&PR 93
Curran, Connie 1947- WhoWor 93
Curran, D. Patrick 1944- St&PR 93
Curran, Daniel J. 1950- ConAu 139
Curran, Darryl Joseph 1935- WhoAm 92
Curran, David Bernard, Jr. 1959- WhoSSW 93
Curran, Dennis Law&B 92
Curran, Dolores BioIn 17
Curran, Donald C. BioIn 17
Curran, Donald Charles 1933- WhoAm 92
Curran, Dorothy Elizabeth 1952- WhoEmL 93
Curran, Edward Owen d1990 BioIn 17
Curran, Frank d1992 NewYTBS 92
Curran, Frank Earl 1912- WhoAm 92
Curran, Frank J. St&PR 93
Curran, George William, III 1953- WhoEmL 93
Curran, Guernsey, III 1931- St&PR 93
Curran, Harold Thomas 1935- St&PR 93
Curran, J. Joseph, Jr. 1931- WhoAm 92, WhoE 93
Curran, James WhoScE 91-1
Curran, James F. 1932- St&PR 93
Curran, Janet S. 1953- WhoEmL 93
Curran, John J. 1931- WhoE 93
Curran, John Jude 1953- WhoE 93
Curran, John P. 1930- St&PR 93
Curran, John W. Law&B 92
Curran, Johnny Walter 1952- WhoEmL 93
Curran, Judith Ellen 1953- WhoE 93
Curran, Kevin J. 1945- St&PR 93
Curran, Lawrence T. Law&B 92
Curran, M. Christina 1962- WhoEmL 93
Curran, Madeline Mc Grath 1947- WhoWrEP 92
Curran, Mark A. 1954- St&PR 93
Curran, Mary Ellen Law&B 92
Curran, Michael Walter 1935- WhoAm 92, WhoWor 93
Curran, Paul James WhoScE 91-1
Curran, Paul Saether 1960- WhoEmL 93
Curran, Robert Allen 1938- St&PR 93
Curran, Robert Bruce 1948- WhoEmL 93
Curran, Robert W. 1927- St&PR 93
Curran, Ronald 1938- ScF&FL 92
Curran, Samuel Crowe 1912- WhoWor 93
Curran, Thomas A. 1957- St&PR 93
Curran, Tim BioIn 17
Curran, Ward Schenk 1935- WhoAm 92
Curran, William Edward 1938- St&PR 93
Curran, William Edward 1948- WhoAm 92
Curran, William F. 1948- St&PR 93
Curran, William Patrick, III 1953- WhoEmL 93
Currell, Brian Robert WhoScE 91-1
Currelley, Lorraine 1951- WhoAmW 93, WhoWrEP 92
Curren, Francis H. 1923- St&PR 93
Curren, Terence MiSFD 9
Currence, Richard Morrison 1938- St&PR 93
Currens, Daniel R. Law&B 92
Current, Gene Paul 1935- St&PR 93
Current, Richard Allen 1952- WhoWor 93
Current, Richard Nelson 1912- WhoAm 92
Curreri, Anthony J. 1937- St&PR 93
Curreri-Alibrandi, Gaetano 1927- WhoE 93
Currey, Agneta BioIn 17
Currey, Brownlee BioIn 17
Currey, John Donald WhoScE 91-1
Currey, L.W. 1942- ScF&FL 92
Currey, Patricia Lou 1954- WhoE 93
Currey, Richard 1949- WhoWrEP 92
Currey, Thomas Arthur 1933- WhoSSW 93
Curria, Carol Jean 1963- WhoEmL 93
Currid, Cheryl Clarke 1950- WhoAmW 93, WhoEmL 93, WhoSSW 93
Currie, Barbara Flynn 1940- WhoAmW 93
Currie, Bruce 1911- WhoAm 92
Currie, Charles Peter 1924- St&PR 93
Currie, Clifford William Herbert 1918- WhoAm 92, WhoWor 93
Currie, Constance Mershon 1950- WhoAmW 93
Currie, Dean Winn 1947- WhoEmL 93
Currie, Diana Mary St&PR 93
Currie, Earl James 1939- St&PR 93, WhoAm 92
Currie, Gilbert A. St&PR 93
Currie, Glenn Kenneth 1943- WhoAm 92
Currie, Jackie L. AfrAmBi [port]
Currie, James Angus 1919- St&PR 93
Currie, James B. Law&B 92
Currie, Jane Moore 1953- WhoEmL 93, WhoSSW 93
Currie, John Craig 1945- WhoWor 93
Currie, John L. 1955- St&PR 93
Currie, John Thornton 1928- WhoAm 92
Currie, Kenneth Max 1947- WhoE 93
Currie, Lauchlin Bernard BioIn 17
Currie, Lawrence Charles WhoScE 91-1
Currie, Leonard James 1913- WhoAm 92
Currie, Madeline Ashburn 1922- WhoAmW 93
Currie, Malcolm Roderick 1927- St&PR 93, WhoAm 92
Currie, Michael Robert 1952- WhoEmL 93
Currie, Neal J. 1929- St&PR 93
Currie, Norman T. 1928- St&PR 93
Currie, Norman Thorne 1928- WhoAm 92
Currie, Richard Alan 1941- WhoE 93
Currie, Richard James 1937- WhoWor 93
Currie, Robert BioIn 17
Currie, Robert 1937- WhoCanL 92
Currie, Robert 1959- WhoE 93
Currie, Robert Andrew Law&B 92
Currie, Robert John Law&B 92
Currie, Robert Raymond 1921- WhoE 93
Currie, Steven Ray 1954- WhoE 93
Currie, W.M. 1934- WhoScE 91-1
Currier, Barry Arthur 1946- WhoEmL 93, WhoSSW 93
Currier, Benjamin Atkinson 1933- St&PR 93, WhoIns 93
Currier, Frederick Plumer 1923- WhoAm 92
Currier, Jeffrey L. 1940- WhoAm 92
Currier, Jeffrey Lee 1940- St&PR 93
Currier, Meriel 1954- St&PR 93
Currier, Richard Agnew 1940- St&PR 93
Currier, Robert David 1925- WhoAm 92, WhoWor 93
Currier, Ruth BioIn 17

Currier, Ruth 1926- *WhoAm 92*
Currier, Susan Anne 1949- *WhoAmW 93*
Currier, Teresa K.D. *Law&B 92*
Currin, George Spencer 1936- *St&PR 93*
Currin, Julie Amarie 1960- *WhoEmL 93*
Currin, Margaret Person 1950- *WhoAm 92, WhoAmW 93*
Currin, Richard N. *St&PR 93*
Curris, Constantine William 1940- *WhoAm 92*
Currivan, Jean *BioIn 17*
Curry, Alan C. 1933- *St&PR 93, WhoIns 93*
Curry, Alan Chester 1933- *WhoAm 92*
Curry, Alton Frank 1933- *WhoAm 92*
Curry, Ann (Gabrielle) 1934- *SmATA 72 [port]*
Curry, Anna Anthony *AfrAmBi*
Curry, Arthur Mansfield 1866-1953 *Baker 92*
Curry, Beatrice Chesrown 1932- *WhoAmW 93*
Curry, Bernard Francis 1918- *WhoAm 92*
Curry, Bill *BioIn 17*
Curry, Catharine Terrill 1950- *WhoEmL 93, WhoSSW 93*
Curry, Chris 1957?- *ScF&FL 92*
Curry, Daniel A. *Law&B 92*
Curry, Daniel Arthur 1937- *WhoAm 92*
Curry, Daniel R. *Law&B 92*
Curry, David Lee 1942- *WhoWrEP 92*
Curry, Diane Breeding 1944- *WhoAmW 93*
Curry, Donald Robert 1943- *WhoWor 93*
Curry, Duncan Steele 1940- *St&PR 93*
Curry, Edward Thomas, Jr. 1926- *WhoSSW 93*
Curry, Elizabeth R. 1934- *WhoWrEP 92*
Curry, Ellen Rose 1943- *WhoAmW 93*
Curry, Francis John 1911- *WhoAm 92*
Curry, Francis R. 1910- *St&PR 93*
Curry, G(len) David 1948- *ConAu 136*
Curry, Gayle Lynn 1962- *WhoSSW 93*
Curry, George 1871-1900 *BioIn 17*
Curry, George Edward 1947- *WhoAm 92*
Curry, Graeme *ScF&FL 92*
Curry, Graham 1940-1990 *BioIn 17*
Curry, Hugh Robert 1948- *WhoSSW 93*
Curry, Jack *WhoAm 92*
Curry, James Edwin 1950- *WhoEmL 93*
Curry, James P. 1942- *WhoScE 91-3*
Curry, James Trueman, Jr. 1936- *WhoAm 92*
Curry, Jane L(ouise) 1932- *MajAI [port]*
Curry, Jane Louise 1932- *DcAmChF 1960, ScF&FL 92, WhoAm 92, WhoWrEP 92*
Curry, Jerry Ralph 1932- *WhoAm 92*
Curry, John 1949- *BioIn 17*
Curry, John Anthony, Jr. 1934- *WhoAm 92, WhoE 93*
Curry, John Charles *Law&B 92*
Curry, John Joseph 1936- *WhoAm 92*
Curry, John Michael 1942- *WhoAm 92, WhoE 93*
Curry, John Patrick 1934- *WhoWor 93*
Curry, Julia 1964- *WhoAmW 93*
Curry, Kathleen 1953- *WhoEmL 93*
Curry, Kathleen Bridget 1931- *WhoAmW 93*
Curry, Kelly E. 1955- *St&PR 93*
Curry, Kelly Edwin 1955- *WhoAm 92, WhoEmL 93*
Curry, Kid c. 1867-c. 1910 *BioIn 17*
Curry, Leyla Cambel 1953- *WhoEmL 93*
Curry, Lillian *BioIn 17*
Curry, Mary Earle Lowry 1917- *WhoWrEP 92*
Curry, Mary Grace 1947- *WhoEmL 93*
Curry, Michael Paul 1952- *WhoEmL 93*
Curry, Nancy Ellen 1931- *WhoAm 92*
Curry, Norval Herbert 1914- *WhoAm 92*
Curry, Paul F. *Law&B 92*
Curry, Paula Clare 1958- *WhoAmW 93*
Curry, Peter L. *Law&B 92*
Curry, Richard A. 1926- *St&PR 93*
Curry, Richard Orr 1931- *WhoAm 92, WhoE 93*
Curry, Robert A. 1931- *St&PR 93*
Curry, Robert E., Jr. 1963- *St&PR 93*
Curry, Robert Lee 1923- *WhoAm 92*
Curry, Robert Michael 1947- *WhoEmL 93*
Curry, Ruth A. *WhoIns 93*
Curry, Sarah Jefferis *AmWomPl*
Curry, Stephen Martindale *WhoSSW 93*
Curry, Thomas Fortson 1926- *WhoAm 92*
Curry, Tim 1946- *BioIn 17*
Curry, Toni Griffin 1938- *WhoAmW 93*
Curry, William Charles 1942- *St&PR 93*
Curry, William Thomas, Jr. 1947- *WhoEmL 93*
Curry-Lindahl, Kai *BioIn 17*
Curschmann, Karl Friedrich 1805-1841 *Baker 92*
Curschmann, Michael Johann Hendrik 1936- *WhoAm 92*
Curson, Charles Randolph *Law&B 92*
Curson, Theodore 1935- *WhoAm 92*
Curt, Denise morris 1936- *WhoAmW 93*
Curtain, Antonette McIntosh 1948- *WhoEmL 93*
Curtas, William Warren 1947- *St&PR 93*
Curteis, Ian 1935- *ConTFT 10*
Curteis, Ian Bayley 1935- *WhoWor 93*
Curthoys, Norman P. 1944- *WhoAm 92*
Curti, Franz 1854-1898 *Baker 92*
Curti, Merle Eugene 1897- *WhoAm 92*
Curties, Henry 1860- *ScF&FL 92*
Curtin, Alma Cardell d1938 *BioIn 17*
Curtin, Andrew Gregg 1815-1894 *BioIn 17*
Curtin, Brian Joseph 1921- *WhoAm 92, WhoWor 93*
Curtin, Catherine Marie 1951- *WhoAmW 93*
Curtin, Christopher James 1951- *WhoEmL 93*
Curtin, Daniel M. *Law&B 92*
Curtin, David Stephen 1955- *WhoAm 92*
Curtin, David Yarrow 1920- *WhoAm 92*
Curtin, Deane 1951- *ConAu 138*
Curtin, Doreen T. *WhoAmW 93, WhoE 93*
Curtin, Francis Michael 1951- *WhoE 93*
Curtin, Gary Lee 1943- *WhoAm 92*
Curtin, Gene Lawrence 1948- *WhoEmL 93*
Curtin, J. Lawrence 1939- *St&PR 93*
Curtin, James B. 1929- *St&PR 93*
Curtin, James Bernard 1929- *WhoAm 92*
Curtin, Jane *BioIn 17*
Curtin, Jane Therese 1947- *WhoAm 92, WhoAmW 93*
Curtin, Jeremiah 1835-1906 *BioIn 17*
Curtin, Joe Lawrence 1950- *WhoEmL 93*
Curtin, John D., Jr. 1932- *St&PR 93*
Curtin, John Dorian, Jr. 1932- *WhoAm 92*
Curtin, John Joseph 1885-1945 *DcTwHis*
Curtin, John Joseph, Jr. 1933- *WhoAm 92*
Curtin, John V. *Law&B 92*
Curtin, John William 1922- *WhoAm 92*
Curtin, Kathleen K. *Law&B 92*
Curtin, Leah Louise 1942- *WhoAm 92, WhoAmW 93, WhoWor 93*
Curtin, Phyllis *BioIn 17, WhoAm 92*
Curtin, Phyllis 1921- *IntDcOp*
Curtin, Phyllis 1922- *Baker 92, OxDcOp*
Curtin, Richard B. 1940- *St&PR 93*
Curtin, Richard Daniel 1915- *WhoAm 92, WhoWor 93*
Curtin, Tom d1976 *BioIn 17*
Curtin, Virginia Marie 1958- *WhoAmW 93*
Curtis, Adam Sebastian *WhoScE 91-1*
Curtis, Adam Sebastian Genevieve 1934- *WhoWor 93*
Curtis, Agnes Beryl *AmWomPl*
Curtis, Alan 1937- *St&PR 93*
Curtis, Alan (Stanley) 1934- *Baker 92*
Curtis, Albert Bradley, II 1957- *WhoEmL 93, WhoSSW 93*
Curtis, Alton Kenneth 1939- *WhoE 93, WhoWor 93*
Curtis, Alva Marsh 1911- *WhoAm 92, WhoAmW 93, WhoWor 93*
Curtis, Anita Louise 1936- *WhoAmW 93*
Curtis, Anthony 1926- *ConAu 40NR*
Curtis, Arnold Bennett 1940- *WhoAm 92*
Curtis, Benjamin Robbins 1809-1874 *OxCSupC [port]*
Curtis, Byrd Collins 1926- *WhoAm 92*
Curtis, C(hristopher) Michael 1934- *ConAu 136*
Curtis, Carl Thomas 1905- *WhoAm 92*
Curtis, Charles 1860-1936 *PolPar*
Curtis, Charles David *WhoScE 91-1*
Curtis, Charles Edward 1931- *WhoAm 92*
Curtis, Charles G. 1933- *St&PR 93*
Curtis, Charles Melvin 1926- *St&PR 93*
Curtis, Chester Harris 1913- *WhoAm 92*
Curtis, Christopher Dean 1961- *WhoEmL 93*
Curtis, Clark Britten 1951- *WhoEmL 93, WhoWor 93*
Curtis, Cyrus 1850-1933 *JrnUS*
Curtis, Cyrus Hermann Kotzschmar 1850-1933 *BioIn 17*
Curtis, Dan 1928- *ConTFT 10, MiSFD 9*
Curtis, David *Law&B 92*
Curtis, Deloris Yvonne 1945- *WhoAmW 93*
Curtis, Dianne 1949- *WhoEmL 93*
Curtis, Don K. 1949- *St&PR 93*
Curtis, Donald James 1941- *WhoAm 92*
Curtis, Doris M. 1914-1991 *BioIn 17*
Curtis, Douglas *MiSFD 9*
Curtis, Douglas B. 1933- *St&PR 93*
Curtis, Douglas Homer 1934- *WhoAm 92*
Curtis, Edward Joseph, Jr. 1942- *WhoE 93*
Curtis, Edward S. 1868-1952 *BioIn 17*
Curtis, Edward Sheriff 1868-1952 *IntDcAn*
Curtis, Elizabeth Alden 1878- *AmWomPl*
Curtis, Elizabeth Van Olinda *AmWomPl*
Curtis, Francis Henry 1934- *WhoE 93*
Curtis, Frank J. *Law&B 92*
Curtis, Frank R. 1946- *WhoAm 92*
Curtis, Gayle Lynne 1955- *WhoEmL 93*
Curtis, George Edward 1942- *St&PR 93*
Curtis, George W. 1824-1892 *PolPar*
Curtis, George William 1824-1892 *JrnUS*
Curtis, Grant Bradley 1948- *WhoSSW 93*
Curtis, Gregory Dyer 1947- *WhoAm 92, WhoE 93, WhoEmL 93*
Curtis, Guy H., III 1936- *WhoAm 92*
Curtis, H. Lamar, Jr. *Law&B 92*
Curtis, H.W. *WhoScE 91-1*
Curtis, Hallie Vea 1930- *WhoWrEP 92*
Curtis, Helen Margaret *WhoScE 91-1*
Curtis, Ivan L. 1928- *St&PR 93*
Curtis, J.-L. 1917- *ScF&FL 92*
Curtis, Jack 1922- *ScF&FL 92*
Curtis, James Austin 1927- *WhoAm 92*
Curtis, James B. *Law&B 92*
Curtis, James L. 1922- *WhoAm 92, WhoE 93*
Curtis, James Michael 1943- *BiDAMSp 1989*
Curtis, James Richard 1953- *WhoEmL 93*
Curtis, James Robert 1905- *St&PR 93*
Curtis, James Robert, Sr. 1905- *WhoWor 93*
Curtis, James Theodore 1923- *WhoE 93, WhoWor 93*
Curtis, Jamie Lee *BioIn 17*
Curtis, Jamie Lee 1958- *HolBB [port], IntDcF 2-3 [port], WhoAm 92*
Curtis, Jan J. *Law&B 92*
Curtis, Jane Wingfield 1941- *WhoAmW 93*
Curtis, Jean Trawick *WhoAm 92*
Curtis, Jeff Bain 1953- *WhoEmL 93*
Curtis, Jennifer L. 1949- *St&PR 93*
Curtis, Jesse William, Jr. 1905- *WhoAm 92*
Curtis, Joan *AmWomPl*
Curtis, John Harold 1937- *WhoSSW 93*
Curtis, John McDonald 1951- *WhoWor 93*
Curtis, John Philip 1953- *WhoWor 93*
Curtis, Karen Janann 1947- *WhoEmL 93*
Curtis, Karla Lauren 1956- *WhoAmW 93, WhoEmL 93*
Curtis, Kelly *BioIn 17*
Curtis, Ken 1916-1991 *BioIn 17, ConTFT 10*
Curtis, Kenneth M. 1931- *PolPar, WhoE 93*
Curtis, Kenneth Stewart 1925- *WhoAm 92*
Curtis, Kevin A. 1951- *St&PR 93*
Curtis, Kipp Allen 1953- *WhoEmL 93*
Curtis, Lamont William 1937- *St&PR 93*
Curtis, Lawrence Henry 1958- *WhoE 93, WhoWor 93*
Curtis, Lewis E., III 1941- *WhoAm 92*
Curtis, Lewis G. 1934- *WhoAm 92*
Curtis, Linda Lee 1950- *WhoWrEP 92*
Curtis, Loretta O'Ellen 1937- *WhoAmW 93*
Curtis, Marcia 1931- *WhoAm 92*
Curtis, Margaret 1883-1965 *BiDAMSp 1989*
Curtis, Mark Hubert 1920- *WhoAm 92*
Curtis, Mary Ellen 1946- *WhoAm 92, WhoAmW 93*
Curtis, Mary Louise 1928- *WhoAmW 93*
Curtis, Mary Pacifico 1953- *WhoAmW 93*
Curtis, Michael A. *Law&B 92*
Curtis, Michael Raymond 1923- *WhoWrEP 92*
Curtis, Monica 1892- *ScF&FL 92*
Curtis, Natalie 1875-1921 *Baker 92, IntDcAn*
Curtis, Nevius Minot 1929- *St&PR 93, WhoAm 92*
Curtis, Orlie Lindsey, Jr. 1934- *WhoAm 92*
Curtis, Paul 1889-1943 *BioIn 17*
Curtis, Penny Johnson 1957- *WhoEmL 93*
Curtis, Peter *ScF&FL 92*
Curtis, Peter Campbell John 1929- *WhoWor 93*
Curtis, Philip *BioIn 17*
Curtis, Philip 1920- *ChlFicS, ScF&FL 92*
Curtis, Philip C. 1907- *WhoAm 92, WhoWor 93*
Curtis, Philip Chadsey, Jr. 1928- *WhoAm 92*
Curtis, Philip James 1918- *WhoAm 92*
Curtis, Richard 1937- *ScF&FL 92*
Curtis, Richard Anson 1926- *St&PR 93*
Curtis, Richard B. 1931- *St&PR 93*
Curtis, Richard Earl 1930- *WhoAm 92*
Curtis, Robert Joseph 1945- *WhoAm 92*
Curtis, Robert Kern 1940- *WhoE 93*
Curtis, Roger William 1910- *WhoAm 92*
Curtis, Samuel Ryan 1805-1866 *HarEnMi*
Curtis, Sheldon *Law&B 92*
Curtis, Sheldon 1932- *St&PR 93, WhoAm 92*
Curtis, Shelley S. *Law&B 92*
Curtis, Sherry Lynn 1954- *WhoEmL 93*
Curtis, Staton Russell 1921- *WhoAm 92*
Curtis, Steven Alan 1954- *WhoEmL 93*
Curtis, Ted 1937- *St&PR 93*
Curtis, Thomas Newton 1947- *WhoSSW 93*
Curtis, Thompson 1941- *St&PR 93*
Curtis, Tony 1925- *IntDcF 2-3 [port], WhoAm 92*
Curtis, V. Kay *Law&B 92*
Curtis, Willbur N., Jr. 1933- *St&PR 93*
Curtis, William 1953- *St&PR 93*
Curtis, William Edgar 1914- *WhoAm 92*
Curtis, William Eleroy 1850-1911 *JrnUS*
Curtis, William Hall 1915- *WhoAm 92*
Curtiss, Alice A. *Law&B 92*
Curtiss, Charles Francis 1921- *WhoAm 92*
Curtiss, Elden F. 1932- *WhoAm 92*
Curtiss, Glenn Hammond 1878-1930 *BioIn 17*
Curtiss, Howard Crosby, Jr. 1930- *WhoAm 92*
Curtiss, James C. *Law&B 92*
Curtiss, Jeffrey Eugene 1948- *St&PR 93, WhoEmL 93*
Curtiss, Joseph Toy d1992 *NewYTBS 92*
Curtiss, Mina 1896-1985 *Baker 92*
Curtiss, Roy, III 1934- *WhoAm 92*
Curtiss, Thomas, Jr. 1941- *WhoAm 92*
Curtiss, Trumbull Cary 1940- *WhoAm 92*
Curtis-Smith, Curtis O(tto) B(ismarck) 1941- *Baker 92*
Curtiz, Michael 1888-1962 *BioIn 17, MiSFD 9N*
Curtler, William Terry 1943- *WhoSSW 93*
Curto, G.M. 1925- *WhoScE 91-3*
Curtright, Norman C. *Law&B 92*
Curts, Harold Layne 1957- *WhoEmL 93*
Curval, Philippe 1929- *ScF&FL 92*
Curwen, John 1816-1880 *Baker 92*
Curwen, John Spencer 1847-1916 *Baker 92*
Curwen, Randall William 1946- *WhoAm 92*
Curwin, Jon *WhoScE 91-1*
Curwin, Ronald 1930- *St&PR 93*
Curzan, Myron P. 1940- *WhoIns 93*
Curzan, Myron Paul 1940- *WhoAm 92, WhoWor 93*
Curzio, Elaine Mary 1947- *WhoEmL 93*
Curzio, Francis Xavier 1944- *WhoAm 92*
Curzon, Clifford (Michael) 1907-1982 *Baker 92*
Curzon, Daniel *WhoWrEP 92*
Curzon, Daniel 1938- *ConGAN*
Curzon, David 1941- *ConAu 137, WhoUN 92*
Curzon, George Nathaniel 1859-1925 *BioIn 17, DcTwHis*
Curzon, Gerald *WhoScE 91-1*
Curzon, (Emmanuel-) Henri (-Parent) de 1861-1942 *Baker 92*
Curzon, Martin Edward John *WhoScE 91-1*
Curzon, Sarah Anne 1833-1898 *BioIn 17*
Curzon, Susan Carol 1947- *WhoAm 92, WhoAmW 93, WhoEmL 93*
Cusack, Cyril 1910- *IntDcF 2-3 [port]*
Cusack, Cyril James 1910- *WhoWor 93*
Cusack, Donald James 1926- *St&PR 93*
Cusack, Frank *ScF&FL 92*
Cusack, Gerald William 1939- *St&PR 93*
Cusack, Jack 1890-1973 *BiDAMSp 1989*
Cusack, James Campbell 1936- *St&PR 93*
Cusack, John *BioIn 17*
Cusack, John 1966- *WhoAm 92*
Cusack, John Thomas 1935- *WhoAm 92*
Cusack, Lauric J. *Law&B 92*
Cusack, Michael 1847-1906 *BioIn 17*
Cusack, Michael Joseph 1928- *WhoAm 92*
Cusack, Thomas Joseph 1938- *WhoAm 92, WhoE 93*
Cusano, Anthony John 1950- *WhoE 93, WhoEmL 93*
Cusano, Cristino 1941- *WhoAm 92*
Cusano, Mary A. *Law&B 92*
Cusanza, Darlene Guerrera 1959- *WhoAmW 93*
Cuschieri, Alfred *WhoScE 91-1*
Cuschieri, Joseph M. 1957- *BioIn 17*
Cuscuna, Michael *BioIn 17*
Cuse, Carlton 1959- *WhoEmL 93*
Cusens, Anthony Ralph *WhoScE 91-1*
Cusenza, Vito P. 1930- *St&PR 93*
Cush, Geoffrey 1956- *ScF&FL 92*
Cushing, Caleb 1800-1879 *OxCSupC*
Cushing, Catherine Chisholm *AmWomPl*
Cushing, David Albert, II 1960- *WhoEmL 93*
Cushing, Eliza Lanesford 1794-1886 *BioIn 17*
Cushing, Frank Hamilton 1857-1900 *BioIn 17, IntDcAn*
Cushing, Frederic Sanford 1920- *WhoAm 92*
Cushing, Gail Elaine 1954- *WhoSSW 93*
Cushing, Harry Cooke, IV *WhoAm 92*
Cushing, James E., Jr. *Law&B 92*
Cushing, John J. *St&PR 93*
Cushing, Kay Smith 1944- *WhoAmW 93, WhoE 93*
Cushing, M. G. *AmWomPl*
Cushing, Mary T. *Law&B 92*
Cushing, Olivia Donaldson *AmWomPl*
Cushing, Peter 1913- *BioIn 17, IntDcF 2-3 [port], ScF&FL 92*

Cushing, Peter Wilton 1913- WhoWor 93
Cushing, Richard W. 1914- St&PR 93
Cushing, Robert Hunter 1953- WhoAm 92
Cushing, Steven 1948- WhoAm 92, WhoEmL 93
Cushing, Susan Rochelle 1955- WhoAmW 93
Cushing, William 1732-1810 OxCSupC [port]
Cushing, William Barker 1842-1874 HarEnMi
Cushman, Aaron D. 1924- WhoAm 92
Cushman, Allerton, Jr. 1936- St&PR 93
Cushman, Carol Ann 1945- WhoAmW 93
Cushman, David Wayne 1939- WhoAm 92
Cushman, Doug BioIn 17
Cushman, Edward L. 1914- WhoAm 92
Cushman, H.C. Law&B 92
Cushman, Helen Merle Baker WhoAm 92
Cushman, John Holloway 1921- WhoAm 92
Cushman, John S. Law&B 92
Cushman, Laura Ann 1958- WhoEmL 93
Cushman, Margaret Jane 1948- WhoEmL 93
Cushman, Mary Susan Livingstone 1932- WhoSSW 93
Cushman, Paul 1930- WhoAm 92
Cushman, Pauline BioIn 17
Cushman, Robert Earl 1913- WhoAm 92
Cushman, Robert Everton, Jr. 1914-1985 HarEnMi
Cushman, Robert Fairchild 1918- WhoAm 92
Cushman, Robert W. St&PR 93
Cushman, Sharon Bloomberg 1953- WhoAmW 93
Cushman, Timothy James 1958- WhoEmL 93
Cushman, William Chandler 1948- WhoSSW 93
Cushmore, Carole Lee WhoAm 92, WhoAmW 93
Cushwa, Charles Benton, III 1934- St&PR 93
Cushwa, William Wallace 1937- St&PR 93, WhoAm 92
Cusic, Donald F. 1948- WhoEmL 93
Cusick, J. Ambler 1961- WhoE 93
Cusick, John C. BioIn 17
Cusick, Ralph A., Jr. 1934- St&PR 93, WhoAm 92
Cusick, Richie BioIn 17
Cusick, Richie Tankersley 1952- ScF&FL 92
Cusick, Stephen Kent Law&B 92
Cusick, Thomas A. 1944- St&PR 93, WhoAm 92
Cusimano, Adeline Mary 1939- WhoE 93
Cusimano, Charles V. St&PR 93
Cusimano, Frank N., III Law&B 92
Cusins, William (George) 1833-1893 Baker 92
Cussac, Max 1940- WhoScE 91-2
Cussans, George William WhoScE 91-1
Cussen, G. WhoScE 91-3
Cussen, June 1944- WhoWrEP 92
Cussler, Clive BioIn 17
Cussler, Clive 1931- ScF&FL 92
Cussler, Clive Eric 1931- WhoAm 92
Cusson, Anne-Marie Law&B 92
Cusson-Cobb, Jody Marie 1957- WhoEmL 93
Custance, D.A. 1942- St&PR 93
Custer, Arthur 1923- Baker 92
Custer, Barbara Ann Law&B 92
Custer, Benjamin Scott, Jr. 1937- WhoAm 92
Custer, Charles Francis 1928- WhoAm 92
Custer, Elizabeth Bacon 1842-1933 BioIn 17
Custer, George Armstrong d1991 BioIn 17
Custer, George Armstrong 1839-1876 BioIn 17, HarEnMi
Custer, John Charles 1934- WhoAm 92, WhoE 93
Custer, Quessnal Stewart, Jr. 1931- WhoSSW 93
Custer, Richard Lewis Payzant 1940- WhoE 93
Custer, Robert L. 1927-1990 BioIn 17
Custine, Astolphe, marquis de 1790-1847 BioIn 17
Custis, Daniel Parke 1710-1757 BioIn 17
Custis, Donald L. 1917- BioIn 17
Custis, John 1678-1749 BioIn 17
Cusumano, Gary M. 1943- St&PR 93
Cusumano, James Anthony 1942- WhoAm 92, WhoWor 93
Cutbush, James D. 1947- St&PR 93
Cutchins, C.A., III 1923- St&PR 93
Cutchins, Clifford Armstrong, III 1923- WhoAm 92
Cutchins, Clifford Armstrong, IV Law&B 92
Cutchins, Clifford Armstrong, IV 1948- St&PR 93, WhoAm 92, WhoEmL 93
Cutchins, Malcolm Armstrong 1935- WhoSSW 93
Cutcliff, Lee S. Law&B 92
Cuthbert, Alan William WhoScE 91-1
Cuthbert, Robert Allen WhoAm 92
Cuthbertson, Betsy Alice 1952- WhoEmL 93
Cuthbertson, David P. 1900-1989 BioIn 17
Cuthbertson, John Brown 1929- St&PR 93
Cuthbertson, Keith WhoScE 91-1
Cuthbertson, Richard W. 1935- St&PR 93
Cuthbertson, William D., Jr. 1920- St&PR 93
Cuthrell, Carl Edward 1934- WhoAm 92
Cuthrell, Faith Baldwin 1893-1978 AmWomPl
Cuti, Anthony J. 1945- St&PR 93
Cutileiro Indias, Maria Amelia 1928- WhoScE 91-3
Cutilletta, Thomas Paul 1943- St&PR 93, WhoAm 92
Cutkosky, Richard Edwin 1928- WhoAm 92
Cutland, Nigel John WhoScE 91-1
Cutler, Alexander MacDonald 1951- St&PR 93, WhoAm 92
Cutler, Andrew Hall 1956- WhoEmL 93
Cutler, Arnold Robert 1908- WhoAm 92, WhoE 93
Cutler, Barry Jay 1943- WhoAm 92
Cutler, Benjamin M., II 1944- WhoIns 93
Cutler, Bernard Joseph 1924- WhoAm 92
Cutler, Beth Fisher 1960- WhoAmW 93
Cutler, Beverly 1950- WhoAmW 93
Cutler, Bruce 1930- WhoWrEP 92
Cutler, Cassius Chapin 1914- WhoAm 92
Cutler, Charles Russell 1924- WhoAm 92
Cutler, Christopher Ashton 1950- St&PR 93
Cutler, David 1956- ConAu 137
Cutler, David F. 1939- WhoScE 91-1
Cutler, Devorah Ann 1952- WhoEmL 93
Cutler, Douglas E. Law&B 92
Cutler, Edward I. 1913- WhoAm 92
Cutler, Everette Wayne 1938- WhoSSW 93
Cutler, F. Sanford d1990 BioIn 17
Cutler, Frank Charles 1949- WhoEmL 93
Cutler, Harris O. Law&B 92
Cutler, Henry Stephen 1824-1902 Baker 92
Cutler, Howard Armstrong 1918- WhoAm 92
Cutler, James J. 1954- St&PR 93
Cutler, Jane 1936- WhoWrEP 92
Cutler, Jay B. 1930- WhoE 93
Cutler, Jay M. Law&B 92
Cutler, John Charles 1915- WhoAm 92
Cutler, Kathryne Alyce Law&B 92
Cutler, Kenneth B. 1932- St&PR 93
Cutler, Kenneth Burnett Law&B 92
Cutler, Kenneth Burnett 1932- WhoAm 92
Cutler, L. Norton, Jr. Law&B 92
Cutler, Laurence Stephan 1940- WhoAm 92
Cutler, Leonard Samuel 1928- WhoAm 92
Cutler, Leslie Stuart 1943- WhoE 93
Cutler, Linda L. Law&B 92
Cutler, Lloyd Norton 1917- WhoAm 92
Cutler, Mark Owen 1947- WhoEmL 93
Cutler, Mary AmWomPl
Cutler, Mary Morrison 1939- WhoAmW 93
Cutler, Mitchell R. d1990 BioIn 17
Cutler, Morene Parten 1911- WhoAm 92, WhoAmW 93
Cutler, Rhoda WhoAm 92, WhoE 93
Cutler, Richard J. 1931- St&PR 93
Cutler, Richard Jay Law&B 92
Cutler, Richard M. 1920- St&PR 93
Cutler, Richard Steven 1953- WhoEmL 93
Cutler, Richard Woolsey 1917- WhoAm 92
Cutler, Robert H. 1918- WhoAm 92
Cutler, Robert Porter 1917- WhoAm 92
Cutler, Robert Steven 1962- WhoE 93
Cutler, Robert Ward 1905- WhoAm 92
Cutler, Roland 1938- ScF&FL 92
Cutler, Ron ScF&FL 92
Cutler, Ronnie WhoE 93
Cutler, Ruth Ellen Lemon 1928- WhoAmW 93
Cutler, Stan 1925- ConAu 137
Cutler, Stephen D. 1936- St&PR 93
Cutler, Stephen Joel 1943- WhoAm 92
Cutler, Suzanne 1939- St&PR 93
Cutler, Ted 1941- St&PR 93
Cutler, Theodore John 1941- WhoAm 92
Cutler, Thomas Kelvin 1959- WhoSSW 93
Cutler, Timothy Rookwood 1931- St&PR 93
Cutler, Walter Leon 1931- WhoAm 92
Cutler, Winnifred B(erg) 1944- ConAu 40NR
Cutler, Winnifred Berg 1944- WhoAmW 93
Cutlip, Gary C. 1942- St&PR 93
Cutlip, James D. Law&B 92
Cutlip, Randall Brower 1916- WhoAm 92, WhoWor 93
Cutlip, Scott Munson 1915- WhoAm 92, WhoSSW 93
Cutlip, Thomas A. 1941- St&PR 93
Cutmore, Ross Herbert James 1929- WhoAm 92
Cutrell, Benjamin Elwood 1923- WhoAm 92
Cutrell, Charles C., III Law&B 92
Cutrer, Hebron D. 1938- St&PR 93
Cutri, William J. 1949- St&PR 93
Cutrie, Sherri Ann 1948- WhoAmW 93
Cutright, Susan Law&B 92
Cutright, William Marcus 1952- WhoEmL 93
Cutrone, Lee David 1947- St&PR 93
Cutrone, Lee J. 1948- St&PR 93
Cutrone, Luigi Cutrone 1950- WhoWor 93
Cutrubus, Christina Nina 1934- WhoAmW 93
Cutshall, Jon Tyler 1964- WhoSSW 93
Cutshaw, Kenneth Andrew 1953- WhoAm 92, WhoEmL 93
Cutt, W. Towrie 1898-1981 ScF&FL 92
Cuttat, Jacques A. 1943- WhoUN 92
Cutter, Charles Richard, III 1924- WhoAm 92
Cutter, Curtis Carly 1928- WhoWor 93
Cutter, David L. 1929- St&PR 93
Cutter, David L. 1941- WhoE 93
Cutter, David L., Jr. 1952- St&PR 93
Cutter, David Lee 1929- WhoAm 92
Cutter, Dennis A. 1941- St&PR 93
Cutter, Dennis M. 1945- St&PR 93
Cutter, Donald Brackett 1931- St&PR 93
Cutter, Edward A. Law&B 92
Cutter, Edward A. 1939- St&PR 93
Cutter, Edward Jerome Law&B 92
Cutter, John Michael 1952- WhoEmL 93
Cutter, Lawrence D. Law&B 92
Cutter, Margaret Mead 1953- WhoWrEP 92
Cutter, Portia Lynette 1938- WhoAmW 93
Cutter, Ralph Frederick 1955- WhoWrEP 92
Cutter, Richard Ammi 1902- WhoAm 92
Cutter, Richard Dean 1934- WhoSSW 93
Cutting, Arolyn Caverly AmWomPl
Cutting, Bronson M. 1888-1935 PolPar
Cutting, Christine Joan 1943- WhoAmW 93
Cutting, Evan Jay Law&B 92
Cutting, Heyward 1921- WhoAm 92
Cutting, Judie Dawne 1960- WhoAmW 93
Cutting, Mary Stewart Doubleday 1851-1924 AmWomPl
Cutting, Pat G. 1930- WhoWrEP 92
Cutting, Robert A. 1946- St&PR 93
Cutting, Robert Thomas 1929- WhoAm 92
Cuttino, Charles Lynum, III 1940- WhoSSW 93
Cuttino, John Edward 1957- WhoEmL 93
Cuttle, Tracy Donald 1908- WhoAm 92
Cuttner, Craig Davis 1955- WhoEmL 93
Cutts, Beau 1946- WhoSSW 93
Cutts, Charles Eugene 1914- WhoAm 92
Cutts, William Gibson, Jr. 1938- WhoSSW 93
Cutugno, Leonard F. 1952- WhoAm 92, WhoE 93
Cuvillier, Charles (Louis Paul) 1877-1955 Baker 92
Cuvillier, Philippe 1930- WhoWor 93
Cuyler, Louise (Elvira) 1908- Baker 92
Cuypers, Frank 1961- WhoWor 93
Cuyt, Annie Antoinette Michel 1956- WhoWor 93
Cuyvers, Luc 1954- WhoEmL 93
Cuzick, Jack M. 1948- WhoScE 91-1
Cuzin, Francois WhoScE 91-2
Cuzzetto, Charles Edward 1954- WhoEmL 93
Cuzzocrea, Dominic David 1945- St&PR 93
Cuzzoni, Francesca c. 1698-1770 IntDcOp [port], OxDcOp
Cuzzoni, Francesca c. 1700-1770 Baker 92
Cuzzort, Belva AmWomPl
Cuzzort, R.P. 1926- WhoWrEP 92
Cuzzort, Ray Paul 1926- WhoAm 92
Cvak, Zdenek 1949- WhoScE 91-4
Cvarch, John A. Law&B 92
Cvekic, Vojin 1925- WhoScE 91-4
Cvelbar, Anthony W. 1943- St&PR 93
Cvengros, William D. 1948- WhoIns 93
Cvensros, Katherine Anne 1961- WhoAmW 93
Cvetkovic, Dimitrije WhoScE 91-4
Cvetkovic, Miodrag 1923- WhoScE 91-4
Cvetnic, Slavko 1929- WhoScE 91-4
Cvijanovic, Alex 1923- WhoAm 92
Cvjetkovic, Bogdan 1941- WhoScE 91-4
Cweiber, Bruce Edward Law&B 92
Cwenarski, Waldemar 1926-1953 PolBiDi
Cwik, Margaret Elizabeth 1946- WhoAmW 93
Cwik, Wayne S. 1947- WhoIns 93
Cwiklinski, Claude 1944- WhoScE 91-2
Cwirka, Karen J. Law&B 92
Cwyner, George J.J. 1949- St&PR 93
Cybis, Boleslaw 1895-1958 PolBiDi
Cybis, Jan 1897-1972 PolBiDi
Cybulski, Joanne Karen 1950- WhoAm 92
Cybulski, Zbigniew 1927-1967 IntDcF 2-3
Cybulski, Zbigniew 1928-1967 PolBiDi
Cybyk, Bohdan Zynowij 1961- WhoE 93
Cyccone, Louis Anthony 1956- WhoEmL 93, WhoWor 93
Cyert, Richard Michael 1921- WhoAm 92, WhoWor 93
Cyganiewicz, Stanislaw 1881-1967 PolBiDi
Cyganski, Andrzej 1927- WhoScE 91-4
Cyklis, Jerzy Edward 1936- WhoWor 93
Cylke, Frank Kurt 1932- WhoAm 92
Cylwicki, Albert 1932- ConAu 38NR
Cymbala, Robert J. 1937- St&PR 93
Cymbala, Robert Joseph 1937- WhoAm 92
Cymbalak, Rodney BioIn 17
Cymborowski, Bronislaw 1939- WhoScE 91-4
Cymet, Tyler Childs 1963- WhoWrEP 92
Cymone, Andre SoulM
Cymrot, Mark Alan 1947- WhoEmL 93
Cyn, T. G. 1948- WhoAm 92
Cynader, Max Sigmund 1947- WhoAm 92
Cynar, Sandra Jean 1941- WhoAmW 93, WhoWor 93
Cynegius Maternus d388 OxDcByz
Cynkar, Maribeth 1951- WhoEmL 93
Cynkin, Thomas Michael 1958- WhoEmL 93
Cyperski, Nancy Lynn Law&B 92
Cypert, Jimmy Dean 1934- WhoAm 92
Cypher, Robert Leonard 1938- St&PR 93
Cypher, Thomas W. 1944- WhoE 93
Cypher, Victor Joseph 1938- St&PR 93
Cyphers, Edward J. 1946- St&PR 93
Cyphers, Stanley P. 1944- St&PR 93
Cyphert, Frederick Ralph 1928- WhoAm 92
Cypress, Conrad Sigmond 1927- St&PR 93
Cypress, F.G. 1928- St&PR 93
Cyprian OxDcByz
Cyprus, N.S. St&PR 93
Cyr, Alan Joseph 1947- WhoEmL 93
Cyr, Arthur 1945- WhoAm 92, WhoWor 93
Cyr, Conrad Keefe 1931- WhoAm 92, WhoE 93
Cyr, Ellen M. d1920 AmWomPl
Cyr, Ellie R. 1942- WhoAmW 93
Cyr, J.V. Raymond 1934- St&PR 93, WhoAm 92, WhoWor 93
Cyr, Maurice J. 1932- St&PR 93
Cyr, Susan E. Law&B 92
Cyran, Frederic Bruce 1955- WhoSSW 93
Cyran, William John 1954- WhoSSW 93
Cyrankiewicz, Jozef 1911-1989 PolBiDi
Cyranoski, David L. 1943- St&PR 93
Cyriacus Of Ancona c. 1391-c. 1455 OxDcByz
Cyril OxDcByz
Cyril c. 313- OxDcByz
Cyril 378-444 OxDcByz
Cyril, III OxDcByz
Cyril Of Skythopolis c. 525-c. 559 OxDcByz
Cyril Of Turov OxDcByz
Cyril Phileotes c. 1015-1110? OxDcByz
Cyrot, M. 1939- WhoScE 91-2
Cyrot-Lackmann, Francoise 1940- WhoScE 91-2
Cyrus, King of Persia d529BC BioIn 17
Cyrus, Billy Ray c. 1961- News 93-1 [port]
Cyrus, Kenneth M. Law&B 92, WhoAm 92
Cyrus, Kenneth M. 1938- St&PR 93
Cyrus, Teriece Dyer 1912- WhoAmW 93
Cyrus, Virginia Joan 1939- WhoAmW 93
Cysarz, Jan M. 1931- St&PR 93
Cysewski, Gerald R. 1949- St&PR 93
Cytowic, Richard Edmund 1952- WhoAm 92
Cytraus, Aldona Ona 1947- WhoEmL 93
Cytryn, Jack 1916- St&PR 93
Cywinska, Izabella BioIn 17
Cywinski, Zbigniew 1929- WhoScE 91-4
Czabalay, Lenke 1927- WhoScE 91-4
Czacka, Roza 1876-1961 PolBiDi
Czacki, Tadeusz 1765-1813 PolBiDi
Czaja, Ludwik 1935- WhoScE 91-4
Czaja, Mary Ann 1943- WhoAmW 93
Czajka, James Vincent 1950- WhoE 93, WhoEmL 93
Czajkouski, Francis D. 1937- St&PR 93
Czajkowski, Eva Anna 1961- WhoAmW 93, WhoEmL 93, WhoWor 93
Czajkowski, Frank Henry Law&B 92
Czajkowski, Gerard 1944- WhoScE 91-4

Czajkowski, Joseph J. *Law&B 92*
Czajkowski, Michal 1804-1876 *PolBiDi*
Czajkowski, Przemyslaw Lucjan Kazimierz Krzysztof 1949- *WhoWor 93*
Czajkowski, Stanislaw 1878-1954 *PolBiDi*
Czako, Jozsef 1923- *WhoScE 91-4*
Czamarski, Janusz S. 1934- *WhoUN 92*
Czander, Walter W. 1931- *St&PR 93*
Czapka, Thomas J. 1947- *St&PR 93*
Czaplewski, Karen Marie 1947- *WhoEmL 93*
Czaplewski, Lawrence Michael *Law&B 92*
Czaplinski, Czeslaw *BioIn 17*
Czaplinski, Kazimierz 1926- *WhoScE 91-4*
Czaplinski, Waclaw Bogdan 1923- *WhoScE 91-4*
Czapnik, Sheldon Jacob 1947- *WhoE 93*
Czapor, Edward P. *WhoAm 92*
Czarlinsky, Randall Gregg 1954- *WhoEmL 93, WhoWor 93*
Czarnecki, Alan Joseph 1951- *WhoEmL 93*
Czarnecki, Caroline MaryAnne 1929- *WhoAm 92, WhoAmW 93*
Czarnecki, Eugene Bielen 1947- *WhoWor 93*
Czarnecki, Gerald Milton 1940- *WhoAm 92*
Czarnecki, Kazimierz 1939- *WhoScE 91-4*
Czarnecki, Richard Edward 1931- *WhoAm 92*
Czarnecki, Roman 1940- *WhoScE 91-4*
Czarnecky, David Joseph 1943- *St&PR 93*
Czarnezki, Joseph John 1954- *WhoEmL 93*
Czarniecki, Myron James, III 1948- *WhoAm 92, WhoEmL 93*
Czarniecki, Stefan 1599-1665 *PolBiDi*
Czarnik, Marvin Ray 1932- *WhoAm 92*
Czarnocki, Adam 1784-1825 *IntDcAn*
Czarnowski, Stefan Zygmunt 1879-1937 *IntDcAn*
Czarra, Edgar F., Jr. 1928- *WhoAm 92*
Czartolomny, Piotr Antoni 1946- *WhoEmL 93*
Czartoryska, Izabela Elzbieta 1746-1835 *PolBiDi*
Czartoryska, Marcelline 1817-1894 *PolBiDi*
Czartoryski, Adam Jerzy 1770-1861 *PolBiDi*
Czartoryski, Adam Kazimierz 1734-1823 *PolBiDi*
Czebatul, Anthony A. *ScF&FL 92*
Czech, Bronislaw 1908-1944 *PolBiDi*
Czech, Grover E. 1942- *WhoIns 93*
Czech, Michael Paul 1945- *WhoAm 92*
Czechowicz, Kazimierz 1926- *WhoScE 91-4*
Czechowicz, Szymon 1689-1755 *PolBiDi*
Czechowski, Mary Ann 1942- *WhoAmW 93*
Czeczuga, Bazyli 1930- *WhoScE 91-4*
Czegledi, Bela 1930- *WhoScE 91-4*
Czekanowska, Anna 1929- *Baker 92*
Czekanowski, Aleksander Piotr 1833-1876 *PolBiDi*
Czekanowski, Jan 1882-1965 *IntDcAn, PolBiDi*
Czelakowski, Janusz Michal 1949- *WhoWor 93*
Czelnai, Rudolf 1932- *WhoUN 92*
Czelusniak, Vernon Lee 1956- *WhoSSW 93*
Czembor, Henryk Jerzy 1941- *WhoScE 91-4*
Czemerda, Linda Ann 1964- *WhoEmL 93*
Czepiel, Thomas P. 1932- *St&PR 93*
Czerepak, Andrew J. *Law&B 92*
Czermak, Wilhelm 1889-1953 *IntDcAn*
Czermanski, Zdzislaw 1896-1970 *PolBiDi*
Czerniec, Timothy Henry 1947- *WhoSSW 93*
Czerniecki, Marion Andre *WhoCanL 92*
Czernilofsky, Armin Peter 1945- *WhoWor 93*
Czernin, Ottokar, Count von 1872-1932 *DcTwHis*
Czerny, Carl 1791-1857 *Baker 92*
Czerski, Zdzislaw 1926- *WhoScE 91-4*
Czerwenka, Oskar 1924- *Baker 92*
Czerwinski, Edward Joseph 1929- *WhoAm 92, WhoWor 93*
Czerwinski, Henry Richard 1933- *St&PR 93, WhoAm 92*
Czerwinski, Patricia Peterson 1948- *WhoAmW 93*
Czerwonka, Joseph John 1956- *WhoEmL 93*
Czerwonko, Jerzy 1936- *WhoScE 91-4*
Czeschin, Betsie Ross 1959- *WhoAmW 93*
Czeswik, Frederick Randall 1946- *WhoEmL 93*
Czibere, Tibor 1930- *WhoScE 91-4*
Czibulka, Alphons 1842-1894 *Baker 92*
Czichos, Horst 1937- *WhoScE 91-3*
Cziffra, Gyorgy 1921- *Baker 92*
Czigany, Sebestyen 1932- *WhoScE 91-4*
Czigner, Jeno 1937- *WhoScE 91-4*
Czihak, Gerhard 1928- *WhoScE 91-4*
Czin, Felicia Tedeschi 1950- *WhoAmW 93, WhoEmL 93*
Czin, Jerry Wolf 1938- *WhoE 93*
Czinkota, Michael Rudolf 1951- *WhoE 93*
Czinner, Paul 1890-1972 *MiSFD 9N*
Czirbik, Rudolf Joseph 1953- *WhoWor 93*
Czirr, Ruth Patrice 1954- *WhoEmL 93, WhoSSW 93*
Czitrom, Anne Veronica 1947- *WhoAmW 93*
Czlonkowska, Anna 1943- *WhoScE 91-4*
Czlonkowski, Andrzej 1943- *WhoScE 91-4*
Czochanska, Jagna 1928- *WhoScE 91-4*
Czochralska, Barbara 1938- *WhoScE 91-4*
Czolgosz, Leon F. 1873-1901 *PolBiDi*
Czopek, Juliusz 1922- *WhoScE 91-4*
Czuba, Roman 1928- *WhoScE 91-4*
Czubak, Antoni 1928- *WhoScE 91-4*
Czubek, Jan Andrzej 1935- *WhoScE 91-4*
Czuj, Chester Francis, Jr. 1955- *WhoE 93, WhoEmL 93*
Czukay, Holger 1938- *Baker 92*
Czukor, Balint 1938- *WhoScE 91-4*
Czulowski, Ann Marie Plubell 1950- *WhoAmW 93*
Czuszak, Janis Marie 1956- *WhoAmW 93, WhoEmL 93*
Czygan, Franz-Christian 1934- *WhoScE 91-3*
Czynczyk, Alojzy 1933- *WhoScE 91-4*
Czyz, Henryk 1923- *Baker 92*
Czyz, Wieslaw Stanislaw 1927- *WhoWor 93*
Czyzewski, Tytus 1880-1945 *PolBiDi*

D

Daab-Krzykowski, Andre 1949- *WhoEmL 93*
Daaga, Makandal *DcCPCAm*
Daalder, Renee *MiSFD 9*
Daan, Niels 1942- *WhoScE 91-3*
Daane, J. Dewey 1918- *BioIn 17*
Daane, James Dewey 1918- *WhoAm 92*
Daane, Mary Ann 1932- *WhoAm 92*
Dabac, Toso 1907-1970 *BioIn 17*
Dabadie, Henri-Bernard 1797-1853 *OxDcOp*
Dabagia, Lee Warren 1937- *St&PR 93*
Dabah, Haim 1951- *WhoAm 92, WhoE 93*
Dabah, Isaac 1958- *WhoAm 92*
Dabah, Morris 1925- *WhoAm 92, WhoE 93*
D'Abate, Janina Monica 1921- *WhoAmW 93, WhoE 93*
D'Abate, JoAnn Therese 1946- *WhoEmL 93*
Dabatenos *OxDcByz*
Dabbagh, Mohamed Abdul-Hay 1932- *WhoWor 93*
Dabbiere, David Kevin *Law&B 92*
D'Abbieri, Philip 1938- *St&PR 93*
Dabbs, Doris *AmWomPl*
Dabbs, Henry Erven 1932- *WhoAm 92*
Dabbs, Jeanne Kernodle McCluer 1922- *WhoAmW 93*
Dabbs, Loretta *BioIn 17*
Dabbs, Robert Lowell 1937- *St&PR 93*
Dabby, Sabah Salman 1946- *St&PR 93, WhoAm 92, WhoWor 93*
Dabek, R.A. *Law&B 92*
Dabelsteen, Erik 1941- *WhoScE 91-2*
Daberko, David A. 1945- *St&PR 93, WhoAm 92*
Dabescat, Olivier *BioIn 17*
Dabholkar, Uttam Gunawant 1941- *WhoUN 92*
Dabich, Eli, Jr. 1939- *WhoAm 92, WhoIns 93*
Dabill, Phillip Alvin 1942- *WhoAm 92*
Dabinovic, Bozo Anthony 1924- *WhoWor 93*
Dabir-Alai, Parviz 1955- *WhoWor 93*
Dabner, Jack Duane 1930- *WhoWor 93*
Dabney, Donna Callander *Law&B 92*
Dabney, Frances S. *AmWomPl*
Dabney, Fred E., II 1937- *WhoIns 93*
Dabney, Hovey Slayton 1923- *WhoAm 92*
Dabney, Julia Parker 1850- *AmWomPl*
Dabney, Madeleine E. *Law&B 92*
Dabney, Marilyn Carol 1956- *WhoAmW 93*
Dabney, Seth Mason, III 1918- *WhoAm 92*
Dabney, Thomasina Elaine 1964- *WhoAmW 93*
Dabney, Virginia Bell 1919- *BioIn 17, ConAu 139*
Dabney, Virginius 1901- *WhoAm 92*
Dabney, Watson Barr 1923- *WhoAm 92*
Dabney, William Kroehle 1933- *WhoAm 92*
D'Abo, Olivia *BioIn 17*
Daboni, Luciano 1920- *WhoWor 93*
Daboval, Wendy F. *Law&B 92*
d'Aboville, Benoit 1942- *WhoWor 93*
Dabrowska, Maria 1889-1965 *PolBiDi*
Dabrowska, Renata 1936- *WhoScE 91-4*
Dabrowski, Adam Miroslaw 1953- *WhoWor 93*
Dabrowski, Edward John 1957- *WhoEmL 93, WhoWor 93*
Dabrowski, Edward Michael 1944- *St&PR 93*
Dabrowski, Jan Henryk 1755-1818 *PolBiDi*
Dabrowski, Joseph Michael 1933- *St&PR 93*
Dabrowski, Miroslav *WhoScE 91-4*
Dabrowski, Richard C. 1947- *St&PR 93*
Dabrowski, Robert Albert 1938- *St&PR 93*
Dabrowski, Robyn *BioIn 17*
Dabrowski, Ryszard 1924- *WhoScE 91-4*
Dabrowski, Stanislaw 1922- *WhoScE 91-4*
Dabry, Jean d1990 *BioIn 17*
Dabul, Barbara Lohman 1942- *WhoAmW 93*
Dabydeen, Cyril *WhoCanL 92*
Daccach, Alberto Elias 1930- *WhoWor 93*
D'Accone, Frank A(nthony) 1931- *Baker 92*
D'Accone, Frank Anthony 1931- *WhoAm 92*
Daccord, Roger 1940- *WhoScE 91-4*
Dacey, Brian Francis 1951- *WhoE 93*
Dacey, Eileen M. 1948- *WhoAmW 93*
Dacey, George Clement 1921- *WhoAm 92*
Dacey, Judith Elaine 1946- *WhoEmL 93*
Dacey, Kathleen Ryan *WhoAm 92*
Dacey, Michael F. *WhoAm 92*
Dacey, Michael R. *Law&B 92*
Dacey, Philip *BioIn 17*
Dacey, Philip 1939- *ConAu 17AS [port]*
Dacey, (John) Philip 1939- *WhoWrEP 92*
Dach, Leslie Alan 1954- *WhoAm 92, WhoE 93*
Dache, Lilly d1989 *BioIn 17*
Dachev, Bogdan 1927- *WhoScE 91-4*
Dachner, Bernardo 1941- *WhoWor 93*
Dachniwsky, Orest B. *Law&B 92*
Dachowski, Lawrence William 1935- *WhoSSW 93*
Dachowski, Peter Richard 1948- *St&PR 93, WhoAm 92, WhoEmL 93*
Dachs, Joachim 1930- *WhoScE 91-3*
Dachs, Joseph 1825-1896 *Baker 92*
Dachs, Louis L. *Law&B 92*
Dachtler, Jilene Rae 1961- *WhoAmW 93*
Dachy, Marc E. 1952- *WhoWor 93*
Dacier, Paul T. *Law&B 92*
Daciuk, Myron Michael 1919- *WhoAm 92*
Dack, Simon 1908- *WhoAm 92, WhoE 93*
Dackawich, S. John 1926- *WhoAm 92*
Dackow, Orest Taras 1936- *St&PR 93, WhoAm 92, WhoWor 93*
Dackow, Sandra Katherine 1951- *WhoEmL 93*
Da Costa, Ana M. 1957- *WhoEmL 93*
da Costa, Carlos Eduardo Rodrigues 1936- *WhoUN 92*
Dacosta, David H. 1950- *St&PR 93*
DaCosta, Edward Hoban 1918- *WhoAm 92*
Da Costa, Jose Barbosa 1954- *WhoWor 93*
Da Costa, Manuel Pinto 1937- *WhoAfr*
da Costa, Margaret Anne 1941- *WhoAmW 93*
Da Costa, Morton 1914-1989 *MiSFD 9N*
da Costa, Newton Carneiro Affonso 1929- *WhoWor 93*
Da Costa, Pires *WhoScE 91-3*
Da Costa Lopes, Martinho d1991 *BioIn 17*
Dacre, Jack Craven *WhoE 93*
Dacri, Stephen Robert 1952- *WhoEmL 93*
da Cruz, Daniel 1921-1991 *ScF&FL 92*
Dacy, John F. 1949- *St&PR 93*
Dada, Hector *DcCPCAm*
Dadaglio, Luigi d1990 *BioIn 17*
D'Adamo, Dominic Frank 1947- *St&PR 93*
D'Adamo, Martha Mosko 1957- *WhoAmW 93*
Dadamo, Vincent Michael *Law&B 92*
Dadamo, Vincent Michael 1948- *St&PR 93*
Dadd, Ronald Frederick 1943- *St&PR 93*
D'Adda, Carlo 1937- *WhoWor 93*
Daddario, Emilio Quincy 1918- *WhoAm 92*
D'addea, Nunzio 1938- *WhoScE 91-3*
D'Addetta, Amy A. *Law&B 92*
Daddiego, Vincent *BioIn 17*
Daddino, Anthony Francis 1940- *St&PR 93*
Daddona, Joseph S. 1933- *WhoE 93*
Daddona, Patricia Ann 1960- *WhoWrEP 92*
Dadds, Harry Leon, II 1950- *WhoEmL 93*
Dadds, Jerry 1939- *BioIn 17*
Daddy-O *BioIn 17*
Dade, Francis Langhorne c. 1793-1835 *HarEnMi*
Dade, Malcolm G. 1931- *St&PR 93*
Dadelsen, Georg von 1918- *Baker 92*
Dadey, Debbie *ScF&FL 92*
Dadey, Debbie 1959- *SmATA 73 [port]*
Dadey, Debra S. *ScF&FL 92*
Dadez, Edward William 1956- *WhoE 93*
Dadic, Ivan 1943- *WhoScE 91-4*
Dadisman, Joseph Carrol 1934- *WhoAm 92, WhoSSW 93*
Dadley, Arlene Jeanne 1941- *WhoAm 92, WhoAmW 93*
Dadlez, Ryszard 1931- *WhoScE 91-4*
Dadmun, Frances May 1875- *AmWomPl*
Dado, Diane Valentina 1952- *WhoEmL 93*
d'Adolf, Stuart Victor 1925- *WhoAm 92*
Dadoune, Jean-Pierre 1935- *WhoScE 91-2*
Dadourian, Dadour d1990 *BioIn 17*
Dadowski, Francis Jerome, Jr. 1942- *St&PR 93*
Dadrian, Vahakn Norair 1926- *WhoAm 92*
Dady, Eric L. *Law&B 92*
Daehlen, Kaare 1926- *WhoUN 92*
Daehnick, Wilfried W. 1928- *WhoE 93*
Daele, Jacques Joseph 1947- *WhoWor 93*
Daelemans, Jan 1935- *WhoScE 91-2*
Daelhousen, Scott Glenn 1950- *WhoE 93*
Daem, Edmun A. *St&PR 93*
Daemen, Frans J.M. 1935- *WhoScE 91-3*
Daenzer, Bernard John 1916- *St&PR 93, WhoAm 92, WhoIns 93*
Daering, Duane Howard 1929- *St&PR 93*
Daerr, Richard L., Jr. 1944- *St&PR 93*
Daerr, Richard Leo, Jr. 1944- *WhoAm 92*
Daes, Erica Irene 1925- *WhoUN 92*
Daeschner, Charles William, Jr. 1920- *WhoAm 92*
Daeschner, Richard Wilbur 1917- *WhoAm 92*
Dafa, Xhezair 1940- *DrEEuF*
DaFano, Marc 1926- *St&PR 93*
Dafermos, Constantine Michael 1941- *WhoAm 92*
Dafermos, Stella 1940-1990 *BioIn 17*
Daffer, Stephanie Lee 1952- *WhoEmL 93*
Daffin, Carol Farwell 1953- *WhoWor 93*
Daffner, Gregg 1954- *WhoEmL 93*
Daffner, Hugo 1882-1936 *Baker 92*
Daffos, Fernand Alain 1947- *WhoWor 93*
Daffron, Mary Foley 1965- *WhoAmW 93*
Daffron, MaryEllen 1946- *WhoAm 92, WhoEmL 93*
Dafoe, Christopher Randy 1962- *WhoE 93*
Dafoe, Willem *BioIn 17*
Dafoe, Willem 1955- *HolBB [port], WhoAm 92*
DaFoe, William Alfred 1917- *WhoSSW 93*
Da Fonseca, Glenda *Law&B 92*
DaFonseca, Raul Rasteiro *Law&B 92*
Dafora, Asadata 1890-1965 *BioIn 17*
Daft, Jack Robert 1929- *WhoAm 92*
Daftary, Farhad 1938- *ConAu 136*
Daga, Andrew William 1957- *St&PR 93, WhoE 93*
Daga, Arun *BioIn 17*
Daga, Meryl Ann 1963- *St&PR 93*
Dagalea, Antonio Jamiro 1941- *WhoWor 93*
da Gama, Vasco 1460?-1524 *Expl 93 [port]*
Dagavarian-Bonar, Debra Aghavni 1952- *WhoE 93*
Dagdag, Faustino 1949- *St&PR 93*
Dagdagan, Venus 1959- *WhoAmW 93*
Dagdeviren, Emre 1946- *WhoWor 93*
Dagenais, Don Frederick 1951- *WhoEmL 93*
Dagenais, Marcel Gilles 1935- *WhoAm 92*
Dagenais, Michel Hubert *St&PR 93*
Dagenais, Sandra Lee 1958- *WhoEmL 93*
Dagenhart, Larry Jones 1932- *WhoAm 92*
Dager, Michael B. 1943- *St&PR 93*
Dagerskog, Magnus *WhoScE 91-4*
Dagg, Tom 1930- *St&PR 93*
Dagger, Thomas G. *Law&B 92*
Dagger, William Carson 1949- *WhoEmL 93*
Dagget, James R. *BioIn 17*
Daggett, Andrea Stuhlman 1952- *WhoEmL 93*
Daggett, Beverly Clark 1945- *WhoAmW 93*
Daggett, Robert Sherman 1930- *WhoAm 92, WhoWor 93*
Daggs, Sheila Denise White 1956- *WhoAmW 93*
Dagher, Azar Peter 1960- *WhoE 93*
Dagher, Louise L. *Law&B 92*
Daghlian, John Edward 1946- *WhoE 93, WhoEmL 93*
Dagit, Charles Edward, Jr. 1943- *WhoAm 92*
Dagless, Erik Leslie *WhoScE 91-1*
Dagley, Larry Jack 1948- *St&PR 93, WhoAm 92*
Daglian, John Peter 1946- *WhoEmL 93*
Dagmar *ScF&FL 92*
Dagmar, Peter *ScF&FL 92*
Dagna, Lawrence R. 1950- *St&PR 93*
Dagnan, Gary R. 1946- *WhoSSW 93*
Dagnan, Owen Gregory 1939- *St&PR 93*
Dagnelie, Pierre J.A. 1933- *WhoScE 91-2*
D'Agnese, Helen Jean 1922- *WhoAm 92, WhoAmW 93*

D'Agnese, John Joseph 1920- WhoSSW 93
Dagnol, Jules N. ScF&FL 92
Dagnon, James Bernard 1940- St&PR 93, WhoAm 92
Dagon, Alfred Josiah 1930- WhoSSW 93
Dagorn, Jean-Charles Y. 1946- WhoScE 91-2
D'Agostino, Anthony Carmen 1939- WhoE 93
D'Agostino, Anthony M. 1957- St&PR 93
D'Agostino, Arthur D. 1948- St&PR 93
D'Agostino, Beatrice Ruth 1938- WhoAmW 93
D'Agostino, Daniel 1947- St&PR 93
D'Agostino, Don E. 1942- St&PR 93
D'Agostino, Douglas 1952- St&PR 93
D'Agostino, James Samuel, Jr. 1946- WhoAm 92, WhoIns 93
D'Agostino, Joseph Salvatore 1928- WhoE 93
Dagostino, Ken A. 1929- St&PR 93
D'Agostino, Mae A. 1954- WhoE 93, WhoEmL 93
D'Agostino, Matthew Paul 1948- WhoE 93
D'Agostino, Paul Alan 1944- WhoSSW 93
D'Agostino, Ralph Benedict 1940- WhoAm 92, WhoE 93, WhoWor 93
D'Agostino, Richard Daniel 1957- WhoEmL 93
D'Agostino, Rondi H. 1946- St&PR 93
D'Agostino, Salvatore Anthony 1956- St&PR 93
D'Agostino, Stephen I. 1933- St&PR 93, WhoAm 92
D'Agostino, Vito Julius 1933- St&PR 93
Dagover, Lil 1897?-1980 IntDcF 2-3 [port]
Dagsoz, Alpin Kemal 1935- WhoScE 91-4
Dague, Paul David 1931- St&PR 93
Daguerre, Louis 1787-1851 OxDcOp
Dagum, Camilo 1925- WhoWor 93
Dagys, Marc Christopher 1955- St&PR 93
Dahan, G. WhoScE 91-2
Dahan, Jose S. 1937- WhoScE 91-2
Dahan, Rene St&PR 93
Dahbany, Avivah 1951- WhoE 93
Dahill, E. Kevin 1947- St&PR 93
DaHinden, Dean Richard 1939- St&PR 93
Dahinden, Justus 1925- WhoWor 93
Dahiya, Jai Bhagwan 1956- WhoWor 93
Dahiya, Rajbir Singh 1940- WhoWor 93
Dahl, Andrew Wilbur 1943- WhoWor 93
Dahl, Arlene 1928- WhoAm 92, WhoAmW 93, WhoE 93, WhoWor 93
Dahl, Arthur Ernest 1916- WhoAm 92
Dahl, Arthur Lyon 1942- WhoUN 92
Dahl, Bard 1926- WhoWrEP 92
Dahl, Bernt Olle 1950- WhoWor 93
Dahl, Bren Bennington 1954- WhoAm 92, WhoAmW 93
Dahl, Chester George 1946- St&PR 93
Dahl, Christopher Curtis 1946- WhoE 93
Dahl, Christopher T. 1943- WhoAm 92
Dahl, Cindy Anne 1964- WhoAmW 93
Dahl, Curtis 1920- WhoAm 92
Dahl, Dwight D. 1952- St&PR 93
Dahl, Eugene R. 1924- St&PR 93
Dahl, Gardar Godfrey, Jr. 1946- WhoEmL 93
Dahl, Garyt W. 1955- St&PR 93
Dahl, Gregory C. 1948- WhoEmL 93, WhoUN 92
Dahl, H. Wayne WhoAm 92
Dahl, Harry Martin 1926- WhoSSW 93
Dahl, Harry Waldemar 1927- WhoAm 92
Dahl, Hilbert Douglas 1942- WhoAm 92
Dahl, Ingolf 1912-1970 Baker 92
Dahl, Jeffrey Alan 1953- WhoEmL 93
Dahl, John MiSFD 9
Dahl, John Anton 1922- WhoAm 92
Dahl, Jorgen 1925- WhoScE 91-2
Dahl, Joyle Cochran 1935- WhoAm 92
Dahl, Kenn T. 1958- St&PR 93
Dahl, Kenneth P. Law&B 92
Dahl, Lawrence Frederick 1929- WhoAm 92
Dahl, Marilyn Gail 1946- WhoEmL 93, WhoSSW 93
Dahl, Martin Astor 1933- WhoIns 93
Dahl, Michael Stephen 1955- WhoEmL 93
Dahl, Nancy Marie 1960- WhoEmL 93
Dahl, Ottar 1924- WhoWor 93
Dahl, Otto 1940- WhoScE 91-2
Dahl, Ragnvald BioIn 17
Dahl, Reynold Paul 1924- WhoAm 92
Dahl, Roald BioIn 17
Dahl, Roald 1916-1990 ChlFicS, ConAu 37NR, MajAI [port], ScF&FL 92, SmATA 73 [port]
Dahl, Robert Alan 1915- BioIn 17, WhoAm 92
Dahl, Robert R. 1923- St&PR 93
Dahl, Stephen Michael Law&B 92
Dahl, Susan M. Law&B 92
Dahl, Torger N. Law&B 92
Dahl, Tyrus Vance, Jr. 1949- WhoEmL 93, WhoSSW 93
Dahl, Viking 1895-1945 Baker 92
Dahl, Winfried 1928- WhoScE 91-3
Dahlbeck, Eva 1920- IntDcF 2-3
Dahlberg, Albert 1908- WhoAm 92, WhoWor 93
Dahlberg, Albert Edward 1938- WhoAm 92
Dahlberg, Alfred William 1940- WhoSSW 93
Dahlberg, Alfred William, III 1940- St&PR 93
Dahlberg, Arnold R. 1923- St&PR 93
Dahlberg, Burton Francis 1932- WhoAm 92
Dahlberg, Carl Fredrick, Jr. 1936- WhoSSW 93
Dahlberg, Edward 1900-1977 BioIn 17
Dahlberg, John E. 1947- St&PR 93
Dahlberg, Joyce Karen 1943- WhoWrEP 92
Dahlberg, Kenneth H. BioIn 17
Dahlberg, Marvin H. 1942- St&PR 93
Dahlberg, Peter Black 1952- St&PR 93
Dahlberg, Richard E. 1939- St&PR 93
Dahlberg, Rlene H. 1925- WhoWrEP 92
Dahlberg, William Stewart 1956- St&PR 93
Dahlbom, J. Richard 1918- WhoScE 91-4
Dahlborg, Ulf WhoScE 91-4
Dahle, Daniel John 1958- WhoEmL 93
Dahle, Hans K. 1939- WhoScE 91-4
Dahle, Karen 1945- WhoAmW 93
Dahle, Raymond Keith 1941- St&PR 93
Dahlem, Maurice Jacob 1912- WhoAm 92
Dahlen, Richard Gordon Law&B 92
Dahlen, Roger Wayne 1935- WhoE 93
Dahlenburg, Lyle Marion 1935- WhoAm 92
Dahlenburg, William Lyle 1959- WhoSSW 93
Dahler, John Spillers 1930- WhoAm 92
Dahlgren, Carl Herman Per 1929- WhoAm 92
Dahlgren, Charles Marshall, Jr. 1950- St&PR 93
Dahlgren, Christine Kenyon 1949- WhoEmL 93
Dahlgren, Dan Lee 1949- WhoEmL 93
Dahlgren, Diana 1957- WhoAmW 93
Dahlgren, Hans 1948- WhoWor 93
Dahlgren, John Adolphus Bernard 1809-1870 HarEnMi
Dahlgren, Ulric 1842-1864 HarEnMi
Dahlgrun, Volker 1936- WhoWor 93
Dahl-Hansen, Tom 1946- WhoUN 92
Dahlhaus, Carl 1928-1989 Baker 92, OxDcOp
Dahlie, Paul Norman 1940- St&PR 93
Dahlin, Bob MiSFD 9
Dahlin, Donald Clifford 1941- WhoAm 92
Dahlin, Robert Nelson 1942- WhoWor 93
Dahling, Daniel Fred 1957- WhoEmL 93
Dahling, E. Gunter 1931- WhoIns 93
Dahling, Gerald Vernon Law&B 92
Dahling, Gerald Vernon 1947- WhoEmL 93
Dahlinger, Randolph 1953- WhoEmL 93
Dahlke, Deborah Jean 1950- WhoAmW 93
Dahlke, Donald W. 1930- St&PR 93
Dahlke, Mary Ellen 1941- WhoAmW 93
Dahlke, Walter Emil 1910- WhoAm 92
Dahlke, Wayne T. 1941- St&PR 93
Dahlke, Wayne Theodore 1941- WhoAm 92
Dahlman, Barbro Elsa 1946- WhoEmL 93
Dahlman, Jeffrey Stuart Law&B 92
Dahlman, Ola 1939- WhoScE 91-4
Dahlman, Steven Ray 1961- WhoEmL 93
Dahlmann, David S. 1949- St&PR 93
Dahlmann, J. WhoScE 91-3
Dahlquist, John Terrence 1930- WhoSSW 93
Dahlstroem, H. Norbert 1936- WhoAm 92
Dahlstroem, Kjell-Ake 1941- WhoWor 93
Dahlstrom, Annica B. 1941- WhoScE 91-4
Dahlstrom, Donald Albert 1920- WhoAm 92
Dahlstrom, Earl C(arl) 1914-1992 ConAu 139
Dahlstrom, Hans Albert 1920- WhoWor 93
Dahlstrom, William Grant 1922- WhoAm 92
Dahltorp, Bruce L. 1937- St&PR 93
Dahl-Wolfe, Louise BioIn 17
Dahly, John H. 1940- St&PR 93
Dahm, Alfons George 1942- WhoE 93
Dahmen, Hans Dieter 1936- WhoScE 91-3
Dahmen, Wolfgang Anton 1949- WhoWor 93
Dahmer, E. Joe 1943- St&PR 93
Dahmer, Edward C. 1941- St&PR 93
Dahmer, Jeffrey BioIn 17
Dahmer, Vernon Ferdinand 1908-1966 EncAACR
Dahms, Heinrich 1954- MiSFD 9
Dahms, Janet H. 1919- WhoWrEP 92
Dahms, Walter 1887-1973 Baker 92
Dahms, William J. 1943- St&PR 93
Dahn, Hans 1919- WhoScE 91-4, WhoWor 93
Dahnke, Keith Francis 1947- WhoEmL 93
Dahod, Aarif Mansur 1952- WhoEmL 93
Dahood, Michael K. 1947- St&PR 93
Dahrendorf, Ralf Gustav 1929- WhoWor 93
Dai, Li 1895-1946 BioIn 17
Dai, Peter Kuang-Hsun 1934- WhoWor 93
Dai, Tianmin 1931- WhoWor 93
Dai, Wen S. St&PR 93
Daibagya, Bhubaneshwor Prasad 1932- WhoUN 92
Daichendt, Gary James 1951- St&PR 93
Daiches, David 1912- WhoWor 93
Dai-Chul Chyung 1945- WhoAsAP 91
Daicoff, Cathy L. 1955- St&PR 93
Daidola, John Chris 1947- WhoEmL 93
Daidone, Donald 1942- WhoE 93
Daidone, Lewis Eugene 1957- WhoE 93, WhoEmL 93, WhoWor 93
Daie, Jaleh 1948- WhoEmL 93, WhoWor 93
Daigle, David James 1935- St&PR 93
Daigle, Lennet Joseph, Jr. 1948- WhoEmL 93, WhoSSW 93
Daigle, Pierre Varmon 1923- WhoWrEP 92
Daigle, Richard Charles 1955- WhoSSW 93
Daigle, Steven R. 1953- St&PR 93
Daigle, Valerie I. Law&B 92
Daigle, Wilfred C. 1926- St&PR 93
Daignault, Ronald A. Law&B 92
Daigneault, Diane Sue 1955- WhoAmW 93
Daigneault, Marilyn Yvonne 1935- WhoAmW 93
Daigo, Tadashige 1891-1947 HarEnMi
Daigon, Ruth 1933- WhoWrEP 92
Daigre, Jean Francois BioIn 17
Daigre, Jean-Francois d1992 NewYTBS 92
Daikuhara, Yashushi 1937- WhoWor 93
Dail, C.C. 1851-1902 ScF&FL 92
Dail, Herman Graham 1945- WhoWor 93
Dail, Hilda Lee 1920- WhoAm 92, WhoAmW 93, WhoSSW 93, WhoWor 93
Dail, Joseph Garner, Jr. 1932- WhoAm 92
Dail, Patricia Keyes 1967- WhoE 93
Dailacis, Diane D. 1939- WhoIns 93
Daileda, David Allen 1949- WhoAm 92
Dailey, Ann Armstrong- BioIn 17
Dailey, Benjamin Peter 1919- WhoAm 92
Dailey, Bonnie Christine Law&B 92
Dailey, Cass 1915-1975 QDrFCA 92 [port]
Dailey, Charles Martel 1953- WhoEmL 93, WhoSSW 93
Dailey, Coleen Hall 1955- WhoAmW 93
Dailey, Cornelius Edwin, Jr. 1959- WhoEmL 93
Dailey, Daniel Owen 1947- WhoAm 92
Dailey, Donald Earl 1914- WhoAm 92
Dailey, Edward J. Law&B 92
Dailey, George R. 1943- St&PR 93
Dailey, George Randolph 1943- WhoIns 93
Dailey, Harry Alva 1950- WhoSSW 93
Dailey, Irene 1920- WhoAm 92
Dailey, Irene Eleanor 1952- WhoAmW 93
Dailey, Janet BioIn 17
Dailey, Janet 1944- WhoAm 92, WhoAmW 93, WhoWrEP 92
Dailey, Janet (Ann) 1944- ConAu 39NR
Dailey, John Revell 1934- WhoAm 92
Dailey, Joyce Cullinan Law&B 92
Dailey, Lee Kenneth 1940- WhoE 93
Dailey, Marion Vincent AmWomPl
Dailey, Paul L. 1956- St&PR 93
Dailey, Peter Heath 1930- WhoAm 92
Dailey, Peter J. Law&B 92
Dailey, Priscilla Fieder 1947- WhoE 93
Dailey, Richard R. 1928- WhoAm 92
Dailey, Robert M. 1929- St&PR 93
Dailey, Roger F. 1940- St&PR 93
Dailey, Thomas E. 1932- St&PR 93
Dailey, Thomas F. Law&B 92
Dailey, Thomas Hammond WhoE 93
Dailey, Thomas M. Law&B 92
Dailey, Victoria Ann 1945- WhoE 93
Dailey-Coletta, Jeanne 1959- WhoAmW 93
D'Ailly, Pierre 1350-1420? BioIn 17
Daily, Alphabell AmWomPl
Daily, Eileen M. Law&B 92
Daily, Ellen Wilmoth Matthews 1949- WhoAmW 93, WhoEmL 93
Daily, Fay Kenoyer 1911- WhoAmW 93
Daily, Francis Willson 1920- WhoSSW 93
Daily, Frank Jerome 1942- WhoAm 92
Daily, James L., Jr. 1929- WhoAm 92
Daily, Jeanette Marie 1965- WhoEmL 93
Daily, Louis 1919- WhoSSW 93, WhoWor 93
Daily, Lowell Robert 1927- WhoAm 92
Daily, Steven R. Law&B 92
Daily, Thomas V. 1927- WhoAm 92, WhoE 93
Daily, Thomas Vincent Law&B 92
Daim bin Zainuddin, Dato' Paduka Abdul 1938- WhoAsAP 91
Daim Zainuddin BioIn 17
Dain, Sandia Elizabeth 1955- WhoEmL 93
Daines, J.T. Law&B 92
Daingerfield, Richard P. Law&B 92
Dainton, Frederick Sydney 1914- WhoWor 93
Dainty, Jack 1919- BioIn 17
Dainwood, James Darwin 1955- WhoEmL 93, WhoSSW 93
Dais, Calvin BioIn 17
Daisak, Stephen Theodore 1957- WhoE 93
Daise, Anita Louise 1958- WhoAmW 93
Daisey, Edward Lora 1936- St&PR 93
Daisley, Roy William WhoScE 91-1
Daisley, William Prescott 1935- WhoAm 92
Daitch, Sheldon 1948- WhoEmL 93
Daiute, Colette Agnes 1948- WhoE 93
D'Aiutolo, Diane Virginia 1959- WhoEmL 93
Dajani, Mahmoud T. 1932- St&PR 93
Dajani, Taher 1933- WhoUN 92
Dajay, Julgen Rivera 1956- WhoWor 93
Dajniak, Henryk 1924- WhoScE 91-4
Dakan, Norman E. 1926- WhoAm 92
Dakay, Alan R. 1952- WhoIns 93
Dake, Marcia Allene 1923- WhoAm 92
Dakers, Elaine K. ScF&FL 92
Dakin, Arthur Hazard 1905- WhoE 93
Dakin, Christine Whitney 1949- WhoAm 92
Dakin, Donald J. Law&B 92
Dakin, Margaret AmWomPl
Dakin, Mary Meier 1956- WhoAmW 93, WhoEmL 93
Dakin, Robert F. Law&B 92
Dakin, Susan Faith 1950- WhoAmW 93
Dakin, William G. Law&B 92
Dakov, Mako 1920- WhoScE 91-4
Dal, Erik 1922- WhoWor 93
Dal', V.I. 1801-1872 IntDcAn
Daladier, Edouard 1884-1970 BioIn 17, DcTwHis
Dalage, Jean d1992 NewYTBS 92
Dalager, Jon Karl 1956- WhoEmL 93
Dalai Lama 1935- ConHero 2 [port], WhoWor 93
Dalai Lama, XIV 1935- BioIn 17
Dalassene, Anna c. 1025-1100? OxDcByz
Dalassenos OxDcByz
Dalayrac, Nicolas(-Marie) 1753-1809 Baker 92
Dalayrac, Nicolas-Marie 1753-1809 OxDcOp
Dalbak, Verlyn M. 1942- St&PR 93
Dalbeck, Elizabeth Ann 1959- WhoEmL 93
Dalbeck, Richard Bruce 1929- WhoAm 92
Dalberg, Johann Friedrich Hugo 1760-1812 Baker 92
D'Albergaria, Nancy Keck 1956- WhoEmL 93
d'Albert, Eugen 1864-1932 IntDcOp
D'Albert, Eugene Baker 92
D'Albertis, Luigi Maria 1841-1901 Expl 93, IntDcAn
D'Albert-Lake, Virginia BioIn 17
Dalbor, Edmund 1869-1926 PolBiDi
Dalby, Alan J. 1937- St&PR 93
Dalby, Alan James 1937- WhoAm 92
Dalby, Richard 1949- ScF&FL 92
Dalcanton, Carol Laduke Law&B 92
Dalcq, Roger Olivier 1928- WhoWor 93
Dalcroze, Emile Jaques Baker 92
Dalcroze, Emile Jaques- 1865-1950 BioIn 17
Dalderup, Louise Maria 1925- WhoWor 93
Dale, (Mary) Alzina Stone 1931- ConAu 38NR
Dale, B.G. WhoScE 91-1
Dale, Benjamin (James) 1885-1943 Baker 92
Dale, Beverly Ann 1942- WhoAmW 93
Dale, Brenda Stephens 1942- WhoAmW 93
Dale, Charlene Boothe 1942- WhoAmW 93, WhoE 93
Dale, Charlie 1881-1971 See Smith, Joe 1884-1980 & Dale, Charlie 1881-1971 QDrFCA 92
Dale, Chris 1949- St&PR 93
Dale, Clamma 1948- Baker 92
Dale, Dave Fowler 1916- St&PR 93
Dale, David C. 1940- WhoAm 92
Dale, David S. Law&B 92
Dale, Dianna Cocuzza 1952- WhoE 93
Dale, Douglas Don 1950- WhoEmL 93
Dale, Erwin Randolph 1915- WhoAm 92
Dale, Floyd D. ScF&FL 92
Dale, Francis Lykins 1921- WhoAm 92
Dale, Gary E. St&PR 93
Dale, George E. ConAu 137, MajAI

Dale, Gretchen *AmWomPl*
Dale, Harvey Philip 1937- *WhoAm 92*
Dale, Iain Leonard 1940- *WhoWor 93*
Dale, James Alan 1943- *WhoWor 93*
Dale, James Alexander 1942- *WhoE 93*
Dale, James C. *Law&B 92*
Dale, James Michael 1948- *WhoAm 92*
Dale, Jim *QDrFCA 92 [port]*
Dale, Jim 1935- *WhoAm 92*
Dale, John D. 1916- *St&PR 93*
Dale, John Denny 1916- *WhoAm 92*
Dale, John Egerton *WhoScE 91-1*
Dale, John M. 1936- *St&PR 93*
Dale, John T., Jr. *Law&B 92*
Dale, Judy Ries 1944- *WhoAmW 93, WhoSSW 93*
Dale, Larry H. 1946- *St&PR 93*
Dale, Larry Huston 1946- *WhoAm 92*
Dale, Leon Andrew 1921- *WhoAm 92, WhoWor 93*
Dale, Madeline Houston McWhinney 1922- *WhoAm 92, WhoE 93*
Dale, Mae *WhoWrEP 92*
Dale, Martin Albert 1932- *WhoAm 92*
Dale, Paul Ross 1915- *WhoWor 93*
Dale, Penny 1954- *ConAu 138, SmATA 70 [port]*
Dale, Peter Fearnley *WhoScE 91-1*
Dale, Peter (John) 1938- *ConAu 39NR*
Dale, Rebecca Van Hamm *AmWomPl*
Dale, Richard *BioIn 17*
Dale, Richard L. 1950- *St&PR 93*
Dale, Richard Ray 1958- *WhoAm 92*
Dale, Richard T. 1927- *St&PR 93*
Dale, Robert Francis 1949- *WhoE 93*
Dale, Robert Gordon 1920- *WhoAm 92*
Dale, Ronald L. 1950- *St&PR 93*
Dale, Stephen Glenn 1955- *WhoEmL 93*
Dale, Theresa Lee Hollingsworth 1958- *WhoAmW 93*
Dale, Theresa Marie 1957- *WhoEmL 93*
Dale, V. Inez 1946- *WhoAmW 93*
Dale, Veronica *WhoWrEP 92*
Dale, Wesley John 1921- *WhoAm 92*
Dale, William Brown 1924- *WhoAm 92*
Dale, William C., Jr. *Law&B 92*
Dalecio, Leslie Anthony 1940- *St&PR 93*
Dalecke, Brenda Joy 1958- *WhoAmW 93*
Dale-Harris, Rosalind *ScF&FL 92*
D'Alembert, Jean le Rond *Baker 92*
D'Alembert, Jean Le Rond 1717-1783 *BioIn 17*
D'Alemberte, Talbot Sandy 1933- *WhoAm 92*
Dalen, James Eugene 1932- *WhoAm 92*
Dalen, Zale 1947- *MiSFD 9*
D'Alene, Alixandria Frances 1951- *WhoAmW 93, WhoEmL 93*
Dales, David G. *Law&B 92*
Dales, George F. 1927-1992 *BioIn 17*
Dales, George F., Jr. d1992 *NewYTBS 92*
Dales, Harold Garth *WhoScE 91-1*
Dales, Richard Clark 1926- *WhoAm 92*
Dales, Rodney Phillips *WhoScE 91-1*
Dales, Samuel 1927- *WhoAm 92*
D'Alessandri, Richard John *Law&B 92*
D'Alessandris, Paul David 1965- *WhoE 93*
D'Alessandro, Daniel Anthony 1949- *WhoEmL 93*
D'Alessandro, David Francis 1951- *WhoAm 92*
D'Alessandro, Dominic 1947- *St&PR 93*
D'Alessandro, Ralph *Law&B 92*
D'Alessandro, Richard William 1948- *WhoEmL 93*
Dalessio, A.J. 1933- *St&PR 93*
Dalessio, Donald John 1931- *WhoAm 92*
D'Alessio, Edward Patrick 1958- *WhoEmL 93*
D'Alessio, Frederick D. *St&PR 93*
D'Alessio, Jacqueline Ann 1943- *WhoAmW 93*
d'Alessio, Jon W. 1946- *St&PR 93*
D'Alessio, Lauran S. *Law&B 92*
D'Alessio, Natalie Marino 1951- *WhoAmW 93, WhoE 93, WhoEmL 93*
D'Alessio, Richard M. 1955- *St&PR 93*
Daleuski, Edward Joseph 1931- *WhoSSW 93*
D'Alexander, William Joseph 1927- *WhoAm 92*
Daley, Arthur James 1916- *WhoAm 92*
Daley, Arthur Stuart 1908- *WhoAm 92, WhoWor 93*
Daley, Brian 1947- *ScF&FL 92*
Daley, Brian Francis *WhoScE 91-1*
Daley, C. Michael 1936- *St&PR 93*
Daley, Charles G. 1910-1990 *BioIn 17*
Daley, Donald F. *Law&B 92*
Daley, Donald O. 1934- *St&PR 93*
Daley, Donald Oscar 1934- *WhoAm 92*
Daley, Dorian Estelle *Law&B 92*
Daley, James A. 1927- *St&PR 93*
Daley, James P. *Law&B 92*
Daley, James R. 1944- *St&PR 93*
Daley, John 1948- *WhoWrEP 92*
Daley, John F. 1939- *St&PR 93*
Daley, John Patrick 1958- *WhoWor 93*
Daley, Leslie G. 1947- *St&PR 93*
Daley, Linda B. *St&PR 93*
Daley, Pamela *Law&B 92*
Daley, Paul Patrick 1941- *WhoAm 92*
Daley, Richard J. 1902-1976 *BioIn 17, PolPar*
Daley, Richard M. *BioIn 17*
Daley, Richard M. 1942- *CurBio 92 [port]*
Daley, Richard Michael 1942- *WhoAm 92*
Daley, Robert *BioIn 17*
Daley, Robert Edward 1939- *St&PR 93, WhoAm 92*
Daley, Robert Emmett 1933- *WhoAm 92*
Daley, Robert James, Jr. 1953- *St&PR 93*
Daley, Robert W. *Law&B 92*
Daley, Ronald Duane 1950- *WhoSSW 93*
Daley, Royston Tuttle 1929- *St&PR 93, WhoAm 92*
Daley, Susan J. 1959- *WhoEmL 93*
Daley, Tammy Kay *Law&B 92*
Daley, Thomas Francis *Law&B 92*
Daley, Tom 1947- *MiSFD 9*
Daley, Victor N. 1943- *St&PR 93*
Daley, Victor Neil 1943- *WhoIns 93*
Daley, William P. 1925- *BioIn 17*
Dal Farra, Ricardo 1957- *Baker 92*
Dalfes, Abdi 1921- *WhoScE 91-4*
D'Alfonsi, Saturno J. 1932- *St&PR 93*
D'Alfonso, Antonio 1953- *WhoCanL 92*
D'Alfonso, Gina Marie 1961- *WhoEmL 93*
Dalgarno, Alexander 1928- *WhoAm 92*
Dalgetty, Ian *WhoScE 91-1*
Dalgetty, J. William *Law&B 92*
Dalgliesh, Alice 1893-1979 *MajAI [port]*
Dalglish, Lucy Ann 1959- *WhoAmW 93*
Dalgoutte, D. *WhoScE 91-1*
Dalhart, Vernon 1883-1948 *Baker 92*
D'Alheim, Marie *Baker 92*
Dalhouse, Warner Norris 1934- *St&PR 93, WhoAm 92, WhoSSW 93*
Dali, 'Abd al'Aziz al- *WhoWor 93*
Dali, Salvador 1904-1989 *BioIn 17*
Dalia, Vesta Mayo 1932- *WhoAmW 93*
Dalichau, Harald G.J. 1934- *WhoScE 91-3*
Dalimonte, Anthony Wayne *Law&B 92*
Dalin, Sergei *BioIn 17*
Dalinka, Murray Kenneth 1938- *WhoAm 92*
Dalio, Marcel 1900-1983 *IntDcF 2-3 [port]*
Dalis, Irene 1925- *Baker 92, WhoAm 92*
D'Alisa, Rose 1948- *WhoAm 92*
Dalitz, Richard Henry *WhoScE 91-1*
Dalitzky, Martha Okun 1932- *WhoE 93*
D'Alkaine, Carlos Ventura 1935- *WhoWor 93*
Dalke, Barbara Helen 1946- *WhoSSW 93*
Dalke, Constance Olivia Logan 1950- *WhoEmL 93*
Dalke, Robert Lynn 1945- *WhoAm 92*
Dalkeith, Lena *AmWomPl*
Dalkey, Kara 1953- *ScF&FL 92*
Dalkoff, Morris Sidney 1948- *WhoEmL 93*
Dall, Curtis B. d1991 *BioIn 17*
Dall, Frank Patrick 1943- *WhoUN 92*
Dall, Jes J. 1921- *St&PR 93*
Dall, Peter Andrew 1951- *WhoEmL 93, WhoSSW 93, WhoWor 93*
Dall, William H. 1845-1927 *IntDcAn*
Dall'Abaco, Evaristo Felice *Baker 92*
Dall'Abaco, Joseph *Baker 92*
Dall'acqua, Francesco 1936- *WhoScE 91-3*
Dallacqua, Joseph Eugene 1954- *WhoSSW 93*
Dal Lago, Frank E. 1927- *St&PR 93*
Dallal, Alberto 1936- *DcMexL*
Dallal, Salim S. 1940- *St&PR 93*
Dalla Lana, Mary E. *Law&B 92*
Dallapiccola, Bruno 1941- *WhoScE 91-3*
Dallapiccola, Luigi 1904-1975 *Baker 92, IntDcOp, OxDcOp*
Dallaporta, Gianfranco 1940- *WhoScE 91-3*
Dallapozza, Adolf 1940- *Baker 92*
Dallara, Bruce D. 1942- *St&PR 93*
Dallara, Mark J. *Law&B 92*
Dalla Rizza, Gilda 1892-1975 *Baker 92, OxDcOp*
Dallas, Alexander James 1759-1817 *OxCSupC*
Dallas, Donald Edward, Jr. 1931- *WhoE 93*
Dallas, George M. 1792-1864 *PolPar*
Dallas, George Sherman 1956- *St&PR 93*
Dallas, Kate Weaver *AmWomPl*
Dallas, Marguerite *AmWomPl*
Dallas, Mike Dale 1961- *WhoSSW 93*
Dallas, Peter August 1935- *St&PR 93*
Dallas, Ruth 1919- *DcChlFi*
Dallas, Thomas Abraham 1923- *WhoAm 92*
Dallas, William Moffit, Jr. 1949- *WhoAm 92*
Dalla-Vicenza, Mario J. 1938- *St&PR 93*
Dalla-Vicenza, Mario Joseph 1938- *WhoAm 92*
Dalla Viola, Alfonso c. 1508-c. 1573 *Baker 92*
Dalla Viola, Francesco d1568 *Baker 92*
Dalla-Vorgia, Panagiota 1944- *WhoWor 93*
Dallek, Robert *BioIn 17*
Dallek, Robert 1934- *WhoAm 92*
Dalle Molle, Daniel 1950- *St&PR 93*
DallePezze, John Raymond 1943- *WhoAm 92*
Daller, W.E. *St&PR 93*
Daller, Walter E., Jr. 1939- *WhoAm 92*
Dallery, Jacques Andre 1951- *WhoEmL 93*
D'Allest, Frederic 1940- *BioIn 17*
Dallett, Janet Osborn 1933- *WhoAmW 93*
Dalley, Bill *BioIn 17*
Dalley, George Albert 1941- *WhoAm 92*
Dalley, Joseph Winthrop A. 1918- *WhoAm 92*
Dalli, John Saviour 1948- *WhoWor 93*
Dallin, Alexander 1924- *WhoAm 92*
Dallin, Vittoria *AmWomPl*
Dallis, Herbert 1930- *St&PR 93*
Dallis, Nicholas 1911-1991 *AnObit 1991*
Dallis, Nick 1911-1991 *BioIn 17*
Dallison, Frank Keith 1940- *WhoE 93*
Dallison, Ken 1933- *BioIn 17*
Dallman, Elaine Gay *WhoWrEP 92*
Dallman, Paul Jerald 1939- *WhoAm 92*
Dallman, Peter Richard 1929- *WhoAm 92*
Dallmann, Daniel F. 1942- *WhoAm 92*
Dallmann-Schaper, Mary Louise 1951- *WhoAmW 93, WhoEmL 93*
Dallmayr, Winfried Reinhard 1928- *WhoAm 92*
Dallmeier, Francisco 1953- *HispAmA [port]*
Dallmer, Howie 1922-1991 *BioIn 17*
Dallmeyer, Craig E. 1941- *St&PR 93*
Dallmeyer, Dorothy Marie 1923- *WhoAmW 93*
Dallmeyer, Mary Dorinda Gilmore 1952- *WhoEmL 93, WhoSSW 93*
Dallmeyer, R. Ford *Law&B 92*
Dall'o, Marie-Raphaelle *Law&B 92*
Dallob, Naomi Clare *Law&B 92*
dall'Occa, Sophie 1807-1863 *See* Schoberlechner, Franz 1797-1843 *Baker 92*
Dallos, Lisa Kay 1961- *WhoAmW 93, WhoE 93*
Dallos, Peter John 1934- *WhoAm 92*
Dallos, Robert E. d1991 *BioIn 17*
Dallosto, Philip S. *Law&B 92*
Dalloway, Marie 1945- *WhoWrEP 92*
Dally, James William 1929- *WhoAm 92*
Dalman, Gisli Conrad 1917- *WhoAm 92*
Dalman, Pirjo Vuokko 1953- *WhoScE 91-4*
Dalmas, John 1926- *ScF&FL 92*
Dalmaso, Roseann *Law&B 92*
Dalmasso, Antoine 1937- *WhoScE 91-2*
Dal Monte, Toti 1893-1975 *Baker 92, IntDcOp [port], OxDcOp*
Dalmores, Charles 1871-1939 *Baker 92, OxDcOp*
Dalmy, Adam M. *Law&B 92*
D'Alo, Frederick Anthony 1949- *WhoE 93*
D'Aloia, G. Peter 1945- *St&PR 93*
Daloisio, Alfonso, Jr. 1953- *St&PR 93*
D'Aloisio, Virginia Marie 1951- *WhoAmW 93*
Dalos, Gyorgy 1943- *ScF&FL 92*.
Daloze, D.A. 1940- *WhoScE 91-2*
Dalpino, Ida Jane 1936- *WhoAmW 93*
Dal Pont, Jean-Pierre 1937- *St&PR 93*
Dalquist, Dorothy Margerite 1925- *St&PR 93*
Dalquist, H. David 1918- *St&PR 93*
Dal-Re, Rafael 1927- *WhoScE 91-3*
Dalrymple, Angus 1937- *WhoCanL 92*
Dalrymple, Donald Wylie 1947- *WhoEmL 93*
Dalrymple, Eric Gordon 1940- *St&PR 93*
Dalrymple, Gary Brent 1937- *WhoAm 92*
Dalrymple, Gerald Richard 1907-1962 *BiDAMSp 1989*
Dalrymple, Gordon Bennett 1924- *WhoAm 92*
Dalrymple, Jean Van Kirk 1902- *WhoAm 92, WhoAmW 93*
Dalrymple, John Kern 1954- *WhoAm 92*
Dalrymple, Leona 1884- *AmWomPl*
Dalrymple, Margaret Fisher *WhoAm 92, WhoAmW 93*
Dalrymple, Ronald Gerald 1949- *WhoWrEP 92*
Dalrymple, Ted Lawrence 1932- *St&PR 93*
Dalrymple, Thomas Lawrence 1921- *WhoAm 92*
Dal Santo, Diane 1949- *WhoAmW 93*
DalSanto, Robert J. 1955- *St&PR 93*
Dalsin, T.J. 1940- *St&PR 93*
Dalston, Jeptha William 1931- *WhoAm 92*
Daltas, Arthur John 1945- *WhoAm 92*
d'Altena, Arnaud *ScF&FL 92*
Dalto, Michael 1956- *WhoE 93*
Dalton, Albert B. *Law&B 92*
Dalton, Annie 1948?- *ScF&FL 92*
Dalton, Arthur Joseph 1936- *WhoE 93*
Dalton, Ben S. 1943- *St&PR 93*
Dalton, Billy *BioIn 17*
Dalton, Brian *BioIn 17*
Dalton, Caryl 1949- *WhoEmL 93*
Dalton, Charles D. *Law&B 92*
Dalton, Christopher John 1956- *St&PR 93*
Dalton, Claudette Ellis Harloe 1947- *WhoAmW 93, WhoEmL 93*
Dalton, Daniel Joseph 1949- *WhoE 93*
Dalton, David L. 1948- *St&PR 93*
Dalton, Dennis Gilmore 1938- *WhoAm 92*
Dalton, Dick N. 1937- *St&PR 93*
Dalton, Dick Newton 1937- *WhoAm 92*
Dalton, Dorothy 1915- *WhoWrEP 92*
Dalton, Douglas 1929- *WhoAm 92*
Dalton, Emmett 1871-1937 *BioIn 17*
Dalton, Gratton 1862?-1892 *BioIn 17*
Dalton, H.R.S. 1835- *ScF&FL 92*
Dalton, Harry 1928- *WhoAm 92*
Dalton, Howard *WhoScE 91-1*
Dalton, Howard E. 1937- *St&PR 93*
Dalton, Howard Edward 1937- *WhoAm 92*
Dalton, James Edward 1930- *WhoAm 92*
Dalton, James F. *Law&B 92*
Dalton, James F. 1950- *St&PR 93*
Dalton, James Joseph, II 1941- *WhoSSW 93*
Dalton, Jennifer Faye 1959- *WhoEmL 93, WhoSSW 93*
Dalton, John Charles 1931- *WhoAm 92*
Dalton, John J. *ScF&FL 92*
Dalton, John Jay T. *Law&B 92*
Dalton, Larry Raymond 1945- *WhoAm 92*
Dalton, Louisiana 1936- *WhoWrEP 92*
Dalton, Margaret Anne 1951- *WhoEmL 93*
Dalton, Parks H. 1929- *St&PR 93*
Dalton, Patrick James 1949- *WhoE 93*
Dalton, Phyllis Irene 1909- *WhoAmW 93, WhoWor 93*
Dalton, Pleasant Hunter, III 1948- *St&PR 93*
Dalton, Priscilla *ConAu 39NR*
Dalton, Robert 1867-1892 *BioIn 17*
Dalton, Robert Isaac, Jr. 1921- *WhoSSW 93*
Dalton, Roger M. 1936- *St&PR 93*
Dalton, Roque *DcCPCAm*
Dalton, Roque 1935-1975 *SpAmA*
Dalton, Ruth Margaret 1926- *WhoAmW 93*
Dalton, Sean *ScF&FL 92*
Dalton, Ted 1901-1989 *BioIn 17*
Dalton, Thomas Francis 1928- *WhoE 93*
Dalton, William 1866-1895 *BioIn 17*
Dalton, William Lee 1949- *WhoEmL 93*
Dalton, William Matthews 1922- *St&PR 93, WhoAm 92*
Daltrey, Roger 1944- *WhoAm 92*
D'Alusio, John V. 1955- *St&PR 93*
Dalva, Robert 1942- *MiSFD 9*
Dalven, Joseph 1899-1990 *BioIn 17*
Dalven, Rae d1992 *NewYTBS 92*
Dalven, Rae 1904-1992 *ConAu 139*
Dalvimare, Pierre 1772-1839 *Baker 92*
d'Alvimare, (Martin-)Pierre *Baker 92*
Daly, Augustin 1838-1899 *GayN*
Daly, Barrett Bond *Law&B 92*
Daly, Barrett Bond 1954- *WhoEmL 93*
Daly, Benedict Dudley Thomas, Jr. 1939- *WhoAm 92*
Daly, Bob 1936- *ConTFT 10*
Daly, Brian Kevin 1960- *WhoEmL 93*
Daly, Brian Patrick 1961- *WhoEmL 93*
Daly, Cahal Brendan Cardinal 1917- *WhoWor 93*
Daly, Carroll John 1889-1958 *ScF&FL 92*
Daly, Charles Joseph 1933- *WhoAm 92*
Daly, Charles Patrick 1930- *WhoAm 92*
Daly, Charles Ulick 1927- *WhoAm 92, WhoE 93*
Daly, Cheryl 1947- *WhoAmW 93*
Daly, Christopher Thomas 1955- *WhoEmL 93*
Daly, Chuck *BioIn 17*
Daly, David G. 1936- *St&PR 93*
Daly, David T. *Law&B 92*
Daly, David Tapman *Law&B 92*
Daly, Denis J. 1940- *St&PR 93*
Daly, Denis Jon 1940- *WhoAm 92*
Daly, Dennis Francis 1948- *WhoE 93*
Daly, Donald Francis 1928- *WhoWor 93*
Daly, Edward H., Jr. 1952- *WhoIns 93*
Daly, Edward J. 1922-1984 *EncABHB 8 [port]*
Daly, Edwin A. 1917- *St&PR 93*
Daly, Eleanor Theresa 1929- *St&PR 93*
Daly, Elizabeth *Law&B 92*
Daly, Ita 1945- *ConAu 136*
Daly, James Joseph 1921- *WhoAm 92*
Daly, James M. 1935- *St&PR 93*
Daly, James Michael, III 1958- *WhoEmL 93*

Daly, James William 1931- WhoAm 92
Daly, Janet Morgan 1937- WhoAmW 93, WhoWrEP 92
Daly, Janice P. 1950- St&PR 93
Daly, Jim MajAI
Daly, Jim 1940- BioIn 17
Daly, Joe Ann Godown 1924- WhoAm 92
Daly, John BioIn 17, NewYTBS 92 [port]
Daly, John 1966- WhoAm 92
Daly, John Augustine 1952- WhoSSW 93
Daly, John Charles 1914-1991 BioIn 17
Daly, John Dennis 1936- St&PR 93, WhoAm 92
Daly, John M. Law&B 92
Daly, John Neal 1937- WhoAm 92
Daly, John P. Law&B 92
Daly, John Patrick 1932- St&PR 93
Daly, John Paul 1939- WhoAm 92
Daly, Joseph Leo 1942- WhoAm 92, WhoWor 93
Daly, Joseph R. 1918- St&PR 93
Daly, Julian Law&B 92
Daly, Julian 1929- St&PR 93
Daly, Karen Kocurek 1962- WhoSSW 93
Daly, Kenna I. Law&B 92
Daly, Leo Anthony 1917- BioIn 17
Daly, Marcus 1841-1900 GayN
Daly, Mary BioIn 17
Daly, Mary 1943- WhoAmW 93
Daly, Mary F. WhoAmW 93
Daly, Maureen 1921- ConAu 37NR, MajAI [port]
Daly, Michael BioIn 17
Daly, Michael C. 1948- St&PR 93
Daly, Michael de Burgh WhoScE 91-1
Daly, Michael J. 1924- BioIn 17
Daly, Michael Joseph 1942- WhoAm 92
Daly, Nancy Jane 1932- WhoAmW 93, WhoWor 93
Daly, Nancy Rosenfeld 1959- WhoAmW 93
Daly, Nicholas 1946- MajAI [port]
Daly, Nicolas Jean 1947- WhoScE 91-2
Daly, Niki MajAI
Daly, Patricia A. Law&B 92
Daly, Patricia Marie 1963- WhoEmL 93
Daly, Patricia Skinner d1991 BioIn 17
Daly, Patrick E. Law&B 92
Daly, Peter WhoScE 91-1
Daly, R.A., Jr. 1914- St&PR 93
Daly, Richard Farrell 1926- St&PR 93
Daly, Robert Anthony 1936- WhoAm 92
Daly, Robert Ward 1932- WhoAm 92
Daly, Ronald BioIn 17
Daly, Ruth Agnes 1958- WhoAmW 93
Daly, S.K. Law&B 92
Daly, Saralyn R. 1924- WhoWrEP 92
Daly, Simeon Philip John 1922- WhoAm 92
Daly, Stephen J. Law&B 92
Daly, Susan Elizabeth S. 1939- WhoAm 92, WhoAmW 93
Daly, Susan Loftus 1951- WhoEmL 93
Daly, Thomas F. Law&B 92
Daly, Thomas Francis Gilroy 1931- WhoAm 92, WhoE 93
Daly, Thomas Milton 1946- St&PR 93
Daly, Tyne BioIn 17
Daly, Tyne 1946- CurBio 92 [port]
Daly, Tyne 1947- WhoAm 92, WhoAmW 93
Daly, Wally K. ScF&FL 92
Daly, Walter Joseph 1930- WhoAm 92
Daly, William F. 1942- St&PR 93
Daly, William Gerald 1924- WhoAm 92
Daly, William James 1917- WhoAm 92
Daly, William Joseph 1928- WhoAm 92
Daly, William P. 1931- St&PR 93
Dalyai, Stephen Attila 1938- St&PR 93
Dalzell, Fred Briggs 1922- WhoAm 92
Dalzell, Helen Dexter 1941- WhoAmW 93
Dalzell, Jeffrey Alexander 1956- WhoSSW 93, WhoWor 93
Dalzell, Robert Fenton, Jr. 1937- WhoAm 92
Dalzell, Robert James, Jr. 1928- St&PR 93
Dalzell, Steven William 1958- St&PR 93
Dalziel, Charles Meredith, Jr. 1956- WhoEmL 93
Dalziel, Robert David 1934- WhoAm 92
D'Alzon, Emmanuel Marie Joseph Maurice 1810-1880 BioIn 17
Dam, Hans 1945- WhoWor 93
Dam, Kenneth W. 1932- WhoAm 92
Damadian, Raymond 1936- St&PR 93
Daman, Ernest Ludwig 1923- WhoAm 92
Daman, F.J. WhoScE 91-2
Daman, Harlan Richard 1941- WhoE 93, WhoWor 93
Daman, Hortense BioIn 17
Damanti, Patrick J. Law&B 92
Damas, J.A.M. 1944- WhoScE 91-2
Damas, Philippe Georges 1950- WhoWor 93
Damase, Jean-Michel 1928- Baker 92, OxDcOp
Damashek, Philip Michael 1940- WhoWor 93
Damasio, Antonio R. 1944- WhoAm 92
Damaska, Mirjan Radovan 1931- WhoAm 92
Damaskenos, Peter fl. c. 1156-1157 OxDcByz
Damaskios c. 460-c. 538 OxDcByz
D'Amato, Alfonse BioIn 17
D'Amato, Alfonse M. 1937- CngDr 91, WhoAm 92, WhoE 93
D'Amato, Aniello 1958- WhoWor 93
D'Amato, Anthony 1937- WhoAm 92
D'Amato, Anthony Roger 1931- WhoAm 92, WhoWor 93
D'Amato, Anthony S. 1930- St&PR 93, WhoAm 92, WhoE 93
Damato, Carol 1932- St&PR 93
D'Amato, Cus BioIn 17
Damato, David Joseph 1953- WhoEmL 93, WhoSSW 93
D'Amato, Domenico Donald 1911- WhoAm 92
D'Amato, Ellen Ann Law&B 92
D'Amato, Francesco 1916- WhoWor 93
D'Amato, Frederick M. 1954- St&PR 93
D'Amato, Janice M. Law&B 92
Damato, Kathryn Leathem 1948- WhoAmW 93
Damato, Mark 1955- St&PR 93
D'Amato, Michael Angelo 1953- WhoE 93
Damato, Nicholas 1922- St&PR 93
D'Amato, Rosemary 1956- WhoE 93
D'Amato, Salvatore F. 1928- St&PR 93
DaMatta, Roberto Augusto 1936- WhoAm 92
Damay, Pierre 1942- WhoScE 91-2
Damaz, Paul F. 1917- WhoAm 92
Damberg, Bo Ivar Berndt 1937- WhoWor 93
Dambois, Maurice 1889-1969 Baker 92
D'Amboise, Christopher BioIn 17
d'Amboise, Christopher 1960- WhoAm 92, WhoE 93
D'Amboise, Jacques BioIn 17
D'Ambrisi, Joseph Vincent 1928- WhoAm 92
Dambroff, Nathan d1991 BioIn 17
D'Ambrose, Alphonse Eugene 1932- WhoSSW 93
D'Ambrosia, Richard E. St&PR 93
D'Ambrosia, Robert Dominick 1938- WhoAm 92
D'Ambrosio, Blanche Fada Grawe 1926- WhoAmW 93
D'Ambrosio, Charles A. 1932- WhoWrEP 92
D'Ambrosio, Charles Anthony, Sr. 1932- WhoAm 92
D'Ambrosio, Eugene Joseph 1921- WhoAm 92
D'Ambrosio, Franc BioIn 17
D'Ambrosio, Joseph Anthony 1954- WhoE 93
d'Ambrosio, Madeleine B. 1950- WhoAm 92
D'Ambrosio, Vinnie-Marie WhoWrEP 92
Dambroth, M. WhoScE 91-3
Dambska, Maria 1925- WhoScE 91-4
Damcke, Berthold 1812-1875 Baker 92
Dame, David Allan 1931- WhoSSW 93
Dame, Edna Genevieve Otto 1906- WhoWrEP 92
Dame, Enid 1943- WhoWrEP 92
Dame, Richard Franklin 1941- WhoSSW 93
Dame, Samuel 1917- WhoE 93
Dame, William Page, III 1940- WhoAm 92, WhoE 93, WhoWor 93
D'Amelio, Antonietta 1960- WhoAmW 93
D'Amelio, Dan 1927- ScF&FL 92
Damerini, Adelmo 1880-1976 Baker 92
Dameron, Charles Law&B 92
Dameron, J. Lasley 1925- ScF&FL 92
Dameron, John Lasley 1925- WhoSSW 93
Dameron, Larry Wright 1949- WhoEmL 93
Dameron, Rodger Scott 1951- WhoSSW 93
Dameron, "Tadd" 1917-1965 Baker 92
Dameron, Thomas Barker, Jr. 1924- WhoAm 92
Damerow, Gail Jane 1944- WhoWrEP 92
Damerow, Mae Wright 1956- WhoAmW 93, WhoEmL 93
Damerst, Lisa Yvonne 1958- WhoAmW 93
Dames, Joan Foster 1934- WhoAm 92
Dameshek, Harold Lee 1937- WhoAm 92, WhoE 93
Damgaci, Eray 1947- WhoScE 91-4
Damgard, John Michael 1939- WhoAm 92
Damian, Carol G. 1939- WhoAmW 93
Damian, Guillermo Rustia 1925- WhoWor 93
Damian, I. Ioan 1922- WhoScE 91-4
Damian, James Robert 1947- WhoEmL 93
Damian, Walter Edward 1940- St&PR 93
Damianakes, Stephanie AmWomPl
Damiani, Damiano 1922- MiSFD 9
Damiano, Chris W. 1930- St&PR 93
Damiano, Robert 1936- St&PR 93
Damianos, Sylvester 1933- WhoAm 92
D'Amico, Andrew John 1942- WhoAm 92
D'Amico, Darlene Marie 1955- WhoAmW 93
Damico, Debra Lynn 1956- WhoAmW 93, WhoEmL 93
D'Amico, Esteban L. 1935- St&PR 93
D'Amico, Frank N. 1934- St&PR 93
Damico, James Anthony 1932- WhoSSW 93
D'Amico, James P. 1945- St&PR 93
D'Amico, John Anthony, Sr. 1931- St&PR 93
D'Amico, Joseph Allen 1962- WhoEmL 93, WhoSSW 93, WhoWor 93
D'Amico, Joseph Thomas 1930- St&PR 93
D'Amico, Karl D. 1956- St&PR 93
D'Amico, Louis Edward 1922- St&PR 93
D'Amico, Mary Barbara 1940- WhoE 93
Damico, Nicholas Peter 1937- WhoE 93
D'Amico, Paul M. 1947- St&PR 93
D'Amico, Richard J. Law&B 92
Damico, Sandra Bowman 1941- WhoAmW 93
D'Amico, Theodore 1954- St&PR 93
D'Amico, Thomas F. 1948- WhoE 93
Damien, Father 1840-1889 BioIn 17
Damilas, Neilos dc. 1417 OxDcByz
Damjanov, Ivan 1941- WhoE 93
Damjanovich, Sandor 1936- WhoScE 91-4
Damm, B. WhoScE 91-3
Damm, James E. 1946- St&PR 93
Damm, Reinhard 1943- WhoWor 93
Damm, Werner 1952- WhoScE 91-3
Damman, James Joseph, Jr. 1958- WhoWor 93
D'Ammassa, Don 1946- ScF&FL 92
D'Ammassa, Donald Eugene 1946- St&PR 93
Dammel, Cathryn Vergobbi Law&B 92
Dammerman, Dennis Dean 1945- St&PR 93, WhoAm 92
Dammers, Steven Willem 1942- WhoAm 92
Dammeyer, Robert P. 1948- St&PR 93
Dammeyer, Rod F. 1940- St&PR 93
Dammeyer, Rodney Foster 1940- WhoAm 92
Dammin, Gustave J. 1911-1991 BioIn 17
Damminger, Maryanne Margaret 1949- WhoE 93
Dammon, James R. 1943- St&PR 93
Damon, Constance Tiffany WhoWrEP 92
Damon, E. Kent 1918- St&PR 93
Damon, Edmund Holcombe 1929- St&PR 93, WhoAm 92
Damon, Ethel Moseley 1883- AmWomPl
Damon, Gene 1933- WhoAmW 93
Damon, John D(rew) 1926- WhoWrEP 92
Damon, Laura Provost 1938- WhoAmW 93
Damon, Ralph S. 1897-1956 EncABHB 8 [port]
Damon, Valerie Hubbard 1945- WhoWrEP 92
Damon, William Van Buren 1944- WhoAm 92
Damon, William Winchell 1943- WhoAm 92
Damone, Vic 1928- Baker 92
Damonte, James C. 1949- WhoIns 93
Damonte, James Charles 1949- St&PR 93
Damoose, George Lynn 1938- WhoAm 92
Damor, Somjibhai 1938- WhoAsAP 91
Damora, Robert Matthew WhoAm 92
D'Amore, Anthony Allan Law&B 92
D'Amore, Joseph R. Law&B 92
D'Amore, Shirley Marie 1959- WhoAmW 93
D'Amore, Victor 1943- WhoE 93
Damoreau, Laure Cinti- Baker 92
Da Mota, Clarice Novaes 1943- WhoWor 93
Damoth, Gene Richard 1953- WhoEmL 93
Da Motta, Jose Vianna Baker 92
DaMotta, Lorraine 1957- WhoEmL 93
DaMoude, Denise Ann 1953- WhoEmL 93
D'Amour, Charles Louis 1953- WhoAm 92
D'Amour, Claire Marie 1956- WhoAmW 93, WhoE 93, WhoEmL 93
D'Amour, Donald H. 1943- St&PR 93
D'Amour, Gerald E. 1920- St&PR 93
Damov, Daniel 1927- St&PR 93
Dampeer, John Lyell 1916- WhoAm 92
Dampier, Frederick Walter 1941- WhoE 93
Dampier, William 1651-1715 Expl 93
Dam Quang Trung WhoWor 93
Damrell, C. Bruce 1932- St&PR 93
Damri, Kersi Phiroze 1951- WhoEmL 93
Damron, Kay 1954- WhoEmL 93, WhoSSW 93
Damron, Virginia Lee 1937- WhoAmW 93
Damrong, Rajanubhab 1862-1943 IntDcAn
Damrosch, Douglas Stanton 1915-1991 BioIn 17
Damrosch, Frank 1859-1937 OxDcOp
Damrosch, Frank (Heino) 1859-1937 Baker 92
Damrosch, Gretchen AmWomPl
Damrosch, Leopold 1832-1885 Baker 92, IntDcOp, OxDcOp
Damrosch, Shirley Patchel WhoAmW 93
Damrosch, Walter 1862-1950 OxDcOp
Damrosch, Walter (Johannes) 1862-1950 Baker 92
Damrow, Donald E. 1934- St&PR 93
Dams, Christopher Henry 1934- St&PR 93
Damsbo 1947- WhoScE 91-2
Damsbo, Ann Marie 1931- WhoAm 92, WhoAmW 93
Damsbo, Ole 1947- WhoWor 93
Damschroder, Michael E. 1952- St&PR 93
Damse, Jozef 1789-1852 OxDcOp
Damsel, Richard A. 1942- WhoAm 92
Damsgaard, Kell Marsh 1949- WhoAm 92
Damski, Mel 1946- MiSFD 9
Damsky, Kenneth L. 1946- St&PR 93
Damsleth, Eivind 1947- WhoScE 91-4
Damson, Barrie M. 1936- St&PR 93
Damson, Barrie Morton 1936- WhoAm 92
Damsteegt, Don Calvin 1946- WhoEmL 93
Damstra, Donald D. 1946- St&PR 93
Damstrom, Harvey J. Law&B 92
Damtoft, Janet Russell 1922- WhoSSW 93
Damtoft, Walter Atkinson 1922- WhoAm 92
Damuck, Walter Edward, Jr. 1949- WhoE 93
Damusis, Adolfas 1908- WhoAm 92
Damuth, John Erwin 1942- WhoSSW 93
Damynov, George Borisov 1927- WhoScE 91-4
Dan, Ikuma 1924- Baker 92
Dan, Satendra Nan WhoAsAP 91
Dan, Thein 1934- WhoUN 92
Dan, Uri 1937- ScF&FL 92
Dana, Bill 1924- BioIn 17
Dana, Charles A. 1819-1897 JrnUS
Dana, Donald Marion, Jr. 1937- WhoSSW 93
Dana, Edward Runkle 1919- WhoAm 92
Dana, Frank Mitchell 1942- WhoAm 92, WhoE 93
Dana, Jayne WhoWrEP 92
Dana, Jerilyn Denise 1949- WhoAm 92
Dana, John Cotton 1856-1929 BioIn 17
Dana, Lauren Elizabeth 1950- WhoAm 92, WhoEmL 93
Dana, Leo I. BioIn 17
Dana, Marie Immaculee 1931- WhoAmW 93
Dana, Michael Ray 1947- WhoEmL 93
Dana, Napoleon Jackson Tecumseh 1822-1905 BioIn 17
Dana, Randall M. 1945- WhoAm 92
Dana, Richard E. 1944- St&PR 93
Dana, William Henry 1846-1916 Baker 92
Danahar, David C. 1941- WhoE 93
Danaher, James William 1929- WhoAm 92
Danaher, John G. 1952- St&PR 93
Danaher, Mallory Millett 1939- WhoWor 93
Danaher, Maria Greco Law&B 92
Danaher, Susan Marie 1957- WhoEmL 93
Danahy, James Patrick 1944- WhoAm 92, WhoSSW 93
Danather, John A. 1899-1990 BioIn 17
Danatos, Michael Ross 1954- WhoE 93
Danatos, Steven C. Law&B 92
Danbe, Jules 1840-1905 Baker 92
Danberg, James Edward 1927- WhoE 93
Danberg, Norman A. ScF&FL 92
Danbom, Stephen Herring 1944- WhoSSW 93
Danburg, Debra 1951- WhoAmW 93
Danburg, Jerome Samuel 1940- WhoSSW 93
Danbury, Richard S., III 1936- WhoE 93
Danby, Kenneth Edison 1940- WhoAm 92
Danby, Mary 1941- ScF&FL 92
Danby, Mary (Heather) 1941- ConAu 39NR
Dance, Francis Esburn Xavier 1929- WhoAm 92
Dance, Gloria Fenderson 1932- WhoAm 92
Dance, James Walter 1951- WhoE 93
Dance, Maurice Eugene 1923- WhoAm 92
Dance, Warren C. Law&B 92
Dancer, Donald R. Law&B 92
Dancer, Doug Winston 1941- St&PR 93
Dancer, John T. 1928- St&PR 93
Dancer, S.N. WhoScE 91-1
Dancer, Winston C. 1917- St&PR 93
Dancewicz, John Edward 1949- WhoAm 92, WhoEmL 93
Dancey, Charles Lohman 1916- WhoAm 92
Danchet, Antoine 1671-1740 OxDcOp

Danckers, Andreas Michael *Law&B 92*
Danckert, Werner 1900-1970 *Baker 92*
Danckerts, Ghiselin c. 1510-1565? *Baker 92*
Dancla, Arnaud Phillipe 1819-1862 *Baker 92*
Dancla, (Jean Baptiste) Charles 1817-1907 *Baker 92*
Dancla, (Jean Pierre) Leopold 1822-1895 *Baker 92*
Danco, Leon A. 1923- *St&PR 93*
Danco, Leon Antoine 1923- *WhoAm 92*
Danco, Linda Marie 1961- *WhoEmL 93*
Danco, Suzanne 1911- *Baker 92, IntDcOp, OxDcOp*
D'Ancona, Alessandro 1835-1914 *IntDcAn*
Dancy, John Albert 1936- *WhoAm 92*
Dancy, Joseph Richard *Law&B 92*
Dancy, Linda Smith 1947- *WhoEmL 93*
Dancy, Patrick J. 1971- *BioIn 17*
Danczak-Ginalska, Zofia 1926- *WhoScE 91-4*
Dandara, Liviu 1933- *Baker 92*
Dandavate, Madhu 1924- *WhoAsAP 91*
Dandelot, Georges (Edouard) 1895-1975 *Baker 92*
Dandler, Jorge E. 1940- *WhoUN 92*
Dandliker, Rene 1939- *WhoScE 91-4*
Dando, A. Jeffrey 1938- *WhoAm 92*
Dando, Brian Clifford 1935- *WhoUN 92*
Dando, George William 1935- *WhoE 93*
Dandolo, Andreas 1306-1354 *OxDcByz*
Dandolo, Enrico c. 1107-1205 *OxDcByz*
Dandolo, Enrico c. 1120-1205 *HarEnMi*
Dandolo, Nicolo c. 1515-1570 *HarEnMi*
Dandora, Nathu R. 1942- *St&PR 93*
Dandoy, Maxima Antonio *WhoAm 92*
Dandoy, Suzanne Eggleston 1935- *WhoAm 92, WhoAmW 93*
D'Andrade, Hugh Alfred 1938- *St&PR 93, WhoAm 92*
Dandrea, Carmine 1929- *WhoWrEP 92*
D'Andrea, Carol Dorothy 1959- *WhoE 93*
D'Andrea, Francis Joseph 1933- *St&PR 93*
D'Andrea, Lucio Anthony 1933- *WhoUN 92*
D'Andrea, Mark 1960- *WhoSSW 93, WhoWor 93*
Dandridge, Dorothy 1922-1965 *ConBlB 3 [port]*
Dandridge, Dorothy 1923-1965 *IntDcF 2-3 [port]*
Dandridge, Rita Bernice *WhoSSW 93*
Dandridge, Robert 1947- *BiDAMSp 1989*
Dandridge, William Shelton 1914- *WhoSSW 93, WhoWor 93*
Dandrieu, Jean Francois 1682-1738 *Baker 92*
Dandrieux, Edouard Pierre Olivier 1941- *WhoWor 93*
Dandrifosse, Guy A.L.J. 1940- *WhoScE 91-2*
Dandy, Roscoe Greer 1946- *WhoE 93, WhoWor 93*
Dandzin 1947- *WhoAsAP 91*
Dane, B. *WhoScE 91-3*
Dane, Beth-Ann Sandler 1958- *WhoEmL 93*
Dane, Christopher *ScF&FL 92*
Dane, Christopher J. 1952- *WhoEmL 93*
Dane, Clemence 1888-1965 *ScF&FL 92*
Dane, Karl 1886-1934 & Arthur, George K. 1899- *QDrFCA 92 [port]*
Dane, Kate Nelson 1952- *WhoEmL 93*
Dane, Lawrence 1937- *MiSFD 9*
Dane, Leila Finlay 1936- *WhoAm 92*
Dane, Mark *ConAu 39NR*
Dane, Maxwell 1906- *St&PR 93, WhoAm 92*
Dane, Peter D. 1947- *St&PR 93*
Dane, Stephen Mark 1956- *WhoEmL 93*
Daneau, Nicolas 1866-1944 *Baker 92*
Daneau, Suzanne 1901-1971 *See* Daneau, Nicolas 1866-1944 *Baker 92*
Daneholt, P. Bertil E. 1940- *WhoScE 91-4*
Daneholt, Per Bertil Edvard 1940- *WhoWor 93*
Danek, Jeffrey Charles *Law&B 92*
Danek, Marita McKenna 1942- *WhoAmW 93*
Danel, David B. 1959- *St&PR 93*
Danel, Jean-Baptiste 1947- *WhoE 93*
Danelija, Georgij 1930- *DrEEuF*
Danelis c. 820-c. 890 *OxDcByz*
Daneliuc, Mircea 1943- *DrEEuF*
Danello, Timothy Francis *Law&B 92*
Danello, Timothy Francis 1956- *WhoE 93*
Danells, Daniel F. *Law&B 92*
Danelski, David Joseph 1930- *WhoAm 92*
Danenberg, Harold 1930- *WhoAm 92*
Danenhauer, Sid David 1942- *St&PR 93*
Daner, William E., Jr. *Law&B 92*
Daneri, Robert W. *Law&B 92*
Danes, Gibson A. d1992 *NewYTBS 92*
Danesh, Abol Hassan 1952- *WhoE 93*
Danesi, Pier Roberto 1938- *WhoUN 92*
Danev, Stoyan 1932- *WhoWor 93*
Danford, Ardath Anne 1930- *WhoAm 92*
Danford, Richard Otto 1938- *WhoE 93*
Danford, Robert Edward 1947- *WhoEmL 93*
Danford, Thaddus S. 1956- *WhoEmL 93*
Danforth, Arthur Edwards 1925- *WhoAm 92, WhoE 93, WhoWor 93*
Danforth, David Newton, Jr. 1942- *WhoE 93, WhoWor 93*
Danforth, Elliot, Jr. 1933- *WhoAm 92*
Danforth, John C. *BioIn 17*
Danforth, John C. 1936- *CngDr 91, CurBio 92 [port]*
Danforth, John Claggett 1936- *WhoAm 92, WhoWor 93*
Danforth, Linda Mangold 1944- *WhoAmW 93*
Danforth, Louis F. 1913- *St&PR 93*
Danforth, Louis Fremont 1913- *WhoAm 92*
Danforth, Robert Wallace 1931- *St&PR 93*
Danforth, William Henry 1926- *WhoAm 92, WhoWor 93*
Dang, Ba Van 1944- *WhoUN 92*
Dang, Marvin S.C. 1954- *WhoEmL 93*
Dang, Minh Ngoc 1958- *WhoEmL 93*
Dang, T. Lam *Law&B 92*
Dang, Thong Quoc 1959- *WhoE 93*
D'Angeli, Miriam Toigo- d1990 *BioIn 17*
D'Angelico, John 1905-1964 *BioIn 17*
D'Angelico, Michael John 1943- *WhoAm 92*
Dangelmaier, Wilhelm *WhoScE 91-3*
D'Angelo, Anthony William 1960- *WhoE 93*
D'Angelo, Beverly *WhoAm 92*
D'Angelo, Carmen 1949- *WhoIns 93*
D'Angelo, Carr *ScF&FL 92*
Dangelo, Charles H. 1950- *WhoIns 93*
D'Angelo, Christopher Scott 1953- *WhoEmL 93*
D'Angelo, Dolores Amidon 1947- *WhoE 93*
D'Angelo, Elmer Mauro 1922- *St&PR 93*
D'Angelo, Ernest Eustachio 1944- *WhoE 93*
D'Angelo, John P. 1937- *St&PR 93*
D'Angelo, Joseph Francis 1930- *WhoAm 92*
D'Angelo, Nicholas 1937- *St&PR 93*
Dangelo, Norman A. 1940- *St&PR 93*
D'Angelo, Rita Yvonne 1928- *WhoE 93*
D'Angelo, Robert William 1932- *WhoAm 92*
D'Angelo, Ronald Holmes 1933- *WhoE 93*
Dangerfield, Richard Scott *Law&B 92*
Dangerfield, Rodney 1921- *QDrFCA 92 [port]*
Dangerfield, Rodney 1922- *WhoAm 92*
D'Angeri, Anna 1853-1907 *OxDcOp*
Danginis, Vassilis Aristidis 1960- *WhoE 93*
D'Angio, Giulio John 1922- *WhoAm 92*
Dangiade, Ruth Ellen 1940- *WhoAmW 93*
Dangler, Richard Reiss 1940- *WhoAm 92*
D'Angola, Patrick M. 1952- *St&PR 93*
Dangoor, David Ezra Ramsi 1949- *WhoAm 92*
Dangremond, David W. 1952- *WhoAm 92*
Danguy, Andre J.C. 1944- *WhoScE 91-2*
Dang Van, Ky 1941- *WhoScE 91-2*
Dangwa, Samuel M. 1935- *WhoAsAP 91*
Danhauser, Adolphe-Leopold 1835-1896 *Baker 92*
Danica, Elly *BioIn 17*
Danican, Michel c. 1600-1659 *See* Philidor *Baker 92*
Danicki, Eugene J. 1942- *WhoScE 91-4*
Daniel *BioIn 17*
Daniel, Albert Lynn 1951- *WhoSSW 93*
Daniel, Albro Dickinson 1943- *St&PR 93*
Daniel, Arlie Verl 1943- *WhoSSW 93*
Daniel, Beth *BioIn 17*
Daniel, Beth 1956- *WhoAm 92, WhoAmW 93*
Daniel, Carlton Ralph, III 1952- *WhoEmL 93, WhoSSW 93*
Daniel, Carol Gene 1945- *WhoE 93*
Daniel, Cathy Brooks 1946- *WhoEmL 93, WhoSSW 93*
Daniel, Charles Dwelle, Jr. 1925- *WhoAm 92*
Daniel, Charles Henry Olive 1836-1919 *BioIn 17*
Daniel, Christopher Hobart 1958- *WhoEmL 93*
Daniel, Clarence H. 1917- *St&PR 93*
Daniel, Colin *ScF&FL 92*
Daniel, Daniel Salman 1934- *WhoE 93*
Daniel, Darden Edwards *Law&B 92*
Daniel, David Logan 1906- *WhoAm 92*
Daniel, David Ronald 1930- *WhoAm 92*
Daniel, Donald Knight 1946- *St&PR 93*
Daniel, E. Clifton 1912- *JrnUS*
Daniel, E. Ralph 1928- *St&PR 93*
Daniel, Edward Bart 1955- *WhoAm 92*
Daniel, Elaine Marie 1963- *WhoAmW 93*
Daniel, Elbert Clifton 1912- *WhoAm 92*
Daniel, Eleanor Sauer 1917- *WhoAmW 93, WhoE 93*
Daniel, Elmer Leon 1936- *St&PR 93*
Daniel, Eugene Lee 1941- *WhoAm 92*
Daniel, Frances Kay 1944- *WhoAmW 93*
Daniel, G. *Law&B 92*
Daniel, Gary Wayne 1948- *WhoEmL 93*
Daniel, Gerard Lucian 1927- *WhoAm 92, WhoE 93, WhoWor 93*
Daniel, Hardie William 1933- *WhoWrEP 92*
Daniel, Henry 1936-1919 *BioIn 17*
Daniel, Herbert Gustav Karl 1926- *WhoScE 91-3*
Daniel, Ilene Charles 1944- *WhoAmW 93*
Daniel', IUlii 1925-1988 *ScF&FL 92*
Daniel, James 1916- *WhoAm 92*
Daniel, James Allen 1953- *WhoEmL 93*
Daniel, James Edward 1955- *WhoEmL 93*
Daniel, James Richard 1940- *WhoSSW 93*
Daniel, James Richard 1947- *WhoAm 92, WhoEmL 93*
Daniel, Jermaine d1991 *BioIn 17*
Daniel, Joan Lisa 1966- *WhoSSW 93*
Daniel, John C. d1992 *NewYTBS 92*
Daniel, John M. 1825-1865 *JrnUS*
Daniel, John Sagar 1942- *WhoAm 92*
Daniel, John Schrimsher 1947- *WhoEmL 93*
Daniel, Jonathan L. *Law&B 92*
Daniel, Jonathan Russell 1961- *WhoE 93*
Daniel, Kenneth Rule 1913- *WhoAm 92, WhoWor 93*
Daniel, Leon 1931- *WhoAm 92*
Daniel, Lorne 1953- *WhoCanL 92*
Daniel, Marilyn S. *Law&B 92*
Daniel, Mark 1954- *ScF&FL 92*
Daniel, Mark D. 1950- *St&PR 93*
Daniel, Mark R. *Law&B 92*
Daniel, Marva Jeane 1943- *WhoAmW 93*
Daniel, Marvin Valerius 1946- *WhoEmL 93*
Daniel, Max 1891-1963 *BioIn 17*
Daniel, Minna 1898- *Baker 92*
Daniel, Oliver 1911-1990 *Baker 92, BioIn 17*
Daniel, Paul 1959- *OxDcOp*
Daniel, Peter Vivian 1784-1860 *OxCSupC [port]*
Daniel, Raoul Charles 1937- *WhoScE 91-4*
Daniel, Raymond John 1942- *St&PR 93*
Daniel, Raymond Martin 1957- *WhoEmL 93, WhoSSW 93*
Daniel, Reginald Scott 1949- *WhoSSW 93*
Daniel, Richard H. 1946- *St&PR 93*
Daniel, Richard I. 1926- *St&PR 93*
Daniel, Richard Nicholas 1935- *St&PR 93, WhoAm 92, WhoE 93*
Daniel, Robert E. 1939- *St&PR 93*
Daniel, Robert Edwin 1906- *WhoAm 92*
Daniel, Robert L. 1926- *St&PR 93*
Daniel, Robert Michael 1947- *WhoAm 92*
Daniel, Robert Williams, Jr. 1936- *WhoAm 92*
Daniel, Rod *MiSFD 9*
Daniel, Royal Thomas, III 1956- *WhoEmL 93*
Daniel, Salvador 1831-1871 *Baker 92*
Daniel, Simeon 1934- *DcCPCAm, WhoWor 93*
Daniel, Stephen C. *Law&B 92*
Daniel, Stephen Hartley 1950- *WhoSSW 93*
Daniel, Stephen James 1943- *WhoE 93*
Daniel, T. D. 1939- *WhoSSW 93*
Daniel, Teresa A. *Law&B 92*
Daniel, Teresa Ann 1957- *WhoEmL 93*
Daniel, Thomas J. 1956- *St&PR 93*
Daniel, Victor James, Jr. 1916- *WhoAm 92*
Daniel, Wilbon Harrison 1922- *WhoSSW 93*
Daniel, William Bryan 1949- *WhoSSW 93*
Daniel, William Marvin 1949- *St&PR 93*
Daniel, William Verner 1928- *St&PR 93*
Daniel, Yuli *ScF&FL 92*
Danielak, Christopher 1959- *St&PR 93*
Daniel-Dreyfus, Susan B. Russe 1940- *WhoAmW 93, WhoE 93, WhoWor 93*
Daniele, Barbara E. *Law&B 92*
Daniele, Graciela 1939- *ConTFT 10, NotHsAW 93*
Daniele, Joan O'Donnell 1958- *WhoAmW 93*
Daniele, Joseph A. 1938- *St&PR 93*
Danieli, Roberto *WhoScE 91-3*
Danielian, Arthur Calvin 1935- *WhoAm 92*
Daniell, Ellen 1947- *WhoEmL 93*
Daniell, Henry 1894-1963 *BioIn 17*
Daniell, Herman Burch 1929- *WhoAm 92*
Daniell, Jere Rogers 1932- *WhoAm 92*
Daniell, Mark Haynes 1955- *WhoWor 93*
Daniell, Rebecca Louraine 1964- *WhoAmW 93*
Daniell, Robert F. 1933- *WhoAm 92, WhoE 93, WhoWor 93*
Daniell, Robert Fisher 1933- *St&PR 93*
Daniell, Warren Fisher, Jr. 1926- *St&PR 93*
Daniel-Lesur *Baker 92*
Daniel-Lesur, Jean Yves 1908- *WhoWor 93*
Daniel Of Sketis dc. 576 *OxDcByz*
Danielou, Alain 1907- *Baker 92*
Daniels, Albert Peet 1914- *St&PR 93*
Daniels, Alfred Harvey 1912- *WhoAm 92*
Daniels, Alrie McNiff 1962- *WhoAmW 93*
Daniels, Arlene Kaplan 1930- *WhoAm 92, WhoAmW 93*
Daniels, Barbara 1946- *Baker 92*
Daniels, Barbara Joyce 1945- *WhoE 93*
Daniels, Bebe 1901-1961 *IntDcF 2-3 [port]*
Daniels, Bebe 1901-1971 *QDrFCA 92 [port]*
Daniels, Bill 1920- *St&PR 93*
Daniels, Calvin L. 1936- *St&PR 93*
Daniels, Carlton *BioIn 17*
Daniels, Cecil Edwin, III 1961- *WhoE 93*
Daniels, Celia Annette 1958- *WhoWrEP 92*
Daniels, Charic Michelle *Law&B 92*
Daniels, Charles E. *Law&B 92*
Daniels, Charles Joseph, III 1941- *WhoE 93*
Daniels, Charlie 1936- *Baker 92, ConAu 138, WhoAm 92*
Daniels, Christine C. *Law&B 92*
Daniels, Cindy Lou 1959- *WhoAmW 93, WhoEmL 93, WhoSSW 93, WhoWor 93*
Daniels, Clemon, Jr. 1937- *BiDAMSp 1989*
Daniels, Cora Lynn 1852- *ScF&FL 92*
Daniels, David Mark 1959- *St&PR 93*
Daniels, David P. 1954- *St&PR 93*
Daniels, Dean Wallace 1938- *WhoSSW 93*
Daniels, Deborah J. *WhoAm 92, WhoAmW 93*
Daniels, Diana M. *Law&B 92, WhoAm 92, WhoAmW 93*
Daniels, Diana M. 1949- *St&PR 93*
Daniels, Doral Lee 1925- *WhoWor 93*
Daniels, Doria Lynn 1951- *WhoEmL 93*
Daniels, Dorothy 1915- *ScF&FL 92*
Daniels, Douglas H. *Law&B 92*
Daniels, Douglas Lee 1956- *WhoSSW 93*
Daniels, Eddie *BioIn 17, WhoAm 92*
Daniels, Edmond 1953- *WhoE 93*
Daniels, Elizabeth Adams 1920- *WhoAm 92*
Daniels, Erik 1927- *WhoScE 91-4*
Daniels, Erik William 1954- *WhoEmL 93*
Daniels, Faith *BioIn 17*
Daniels, Frank Arthur, Jr. 1931- *WhoAm 92*
Daniels, Frank Emmett 1963- *WhoEmL 93*
Daniels, Frank W. 1934- *St&PR 93*
Daniels, George Benjamin 1953- *WhoEmL 93*
Daniels, George Frank *Law&B 92*
Daniels, George Goetz 1925- *WhoWrEP 92*
Daniels, George P. *Law&B 92*
Daniels, Gladys Roberta Steinman 1912- *WhoWrEP 92*
Daniels, Glenda Ann 1959- *WhoAmW 93*
Daniels, Glenn J. *Law&B 92*
Daniels, Guy *BioIn 17*
Daniels, Hope Mary 1947- *WhoWrEP 92*
Daniels, Isabel *BlkAmWO [port]*
Daniels, Isabel 1937- *BioIn 17*
Daniels, Jack 1936- *BioIn 17*
Daniels, James Douglas 1935- *WhoSSW 93*
Daniels, James Maurice 1924- *WhoAm 92*
Daniels, James Walter 1945- *WhoAm 92*
Daniels, Janet DeLuca 1939- *WhoE 93*
Daniels, Jeff *BioIn 17, WhoAm 92*
Daniels, Jeff 1955- *HolBB [port]*
Daniels, Jeffrey Irwin 1951- *WhoEmL 93*
Daniels, Jennifer 1957- *WhoE 93*
Daniels, Jeremy Lynn 1941- *St&PR 93*
Daniels, Jim 1956- *DcLB 120 [port], WhoWrEP 92*
Daniels, Joanne P. 1947- *WhoE 93*
Daniels, John Clifford 1936- *BioIn 17, WhoAm 92*
Daniels, John Dean 1949- *WhoEmL 93*
Daniels, John H. 1921- *St&PR 93*
Daniels, John Hancock 1921- *WhoAm 92*
Daniels, John Mark 1958- *WhoEmL 93*
Daniels, John Maynard 1935- *WhoE 93*
Daniels, John Peter 1937- *WhoAm 92*
Daniels, John Scott 1955- *WhoSSW 93*
Daniels, Jonathan 1902-1981 *JrnUS, ScF&FL 92*
Daniels, Jonathan B. d1990 *BioIn 17*
Daniels, Jonathan Myrick 1939-1965 *EncAACR*
Daniels, Jonathan (Worth) 1902-1981 *DcLB 127 [port], EncAACR*
Daniels, Joseph Anton 1940- *St&PR 93*
Daniels, Joseph Jerard 1953- *WhoE 93*

Daniels, Josephus 1862-1948 *JrnUS*
Daniels, Kathryn Lee 1952- *WhoAmW 93*
Daniels, Keith Allen 1956- *WhoWrEP 92*
Daniels, Kurt R. 1954- *WhoWor 93*
Daniels, Lee S. 1925- *St&PR 93*
Daniels, Legree *BioIn 17*
Daniels, Les 1943- *ScF&FL 92*
Daniels, Lloyd *BioIn 17*
Daniels, M.A. 1946- *St&PR 93*
Daniels, Mabel Wheeler 1878-1971 *Baker 92*
Daniels, Madeline Marie 1948- *WhoAmW 93, WhoE 93, WhoWrEP 92*
Daniels, Malcolm L. 1926- *St&PR 93*
Daniels, Marc d1989 *MiSFD 9N*
Daniels, Max 1927- *ScF&FL 92*
Daniels, Melvin Joe 1944- *BiDAMSp 1989*
Daniels, Michael Alan 1946- *WhoWor 93*
Daniels, Michael John *WhoScE 91-1*
Daniels, Michael Paul 1930- *WhoAm 92*
Daniels, Molly *WhoWrEP 92*
Daniels, Molly Ann 1932- *WhoAmW 93*
Daniels, Myra Janco *WhoAm 92*
Daniels, Norman 1942- *WhoAm 92, WhoWrEP 92*
Daniels, Norman A. 1906- *ScF&FL 92*
Daniels, Norman W. 1939- *St&PR 93*
Daniels, Peter George *WhoScE 91-1*
Daniels, Peter Walters *WhoScE 91-1*
Daniels, Philip 1924- *ScF&FL 92*
Daniels, Phyllis H. 1951- *WhoAmW 93*
Daniels, Raymond DeWitt 1928- *WhoSSW 93*
Daniels, Rebecca Joye 1961- *WhoEmL 93*
Daniels, Ritchie
See Delfonics *SoulM*
Daniels, Robert Alan 1944- *WhoAm 92, WhoE 93*
Daniels, Robert Sanford 1927- *WhoAm 92, WhoSSW 93*
Daniels, Robert Vincent 1926- *WhoAm 92*
Daniels, Rochelle J. *Law&B 92*
Daniels, Rona *Law&B 92*
Daniels, Roy G. 1928- *WhoIns 93*
Daniels, Roy Gwynne 1928- *St&PR 93*
Daniels, Sadie d1991 *BioIn 17*
Daniels, Sandra Tawes 1944- *WhoAmW 93*
Daniels, Sandy Lee 1958- *WhoEmL 93*
Daniels, Shirley *Law&B 92*
Daniels, Stanley L. 1937- *WhoAm 92*
Daniels, Stephen M. 1947- *WhoAm 92*
Daniels, Thaddeus Lee 1951- *WhoSSW 93*
Daniels, Tricia 1961- *WhoEmL 93*
Daniels, Virginia Annamae 1907- *WhoWrEP 92*
Daniels, Wilbur 1923- *WhoAm 92, WhoE 93*
Daniels, William Albert 1937- *WhoE 93*
Daniels, William Burton 1930- *WhoAm 92, WhoE 93*
Daniels, William Carlton, Jr. 1920- *WhoAm 92*
Daniels, William D. *BioIn 17*
Daniels, William David 1927- *WhoAm 92*
Daniels, William Dohn 1949- *St&PR 93*
Daniels, William James 1940- *WhoE 93*
Daniels, William Lewis 1944- *WhoAm 92*
Daniels, Yvonne *BioIn 17*
Danielsen, Clifford R. 1949- *St&PR 93*
Danielsen, Harland Allen 1964- *WhoEmL 93*
Danielson, Craig *WhoAm 92*
Danielson, Donald C. 1919- *St&PR 93*
Danielson, Elizabeth Kay 1949- *WhoEmL 93*
Danielson, Gary R. 1953- *WhoEmL 93*
Danielson, Gilbert L. 1946- *St&PR 93*
Danielson, Gordon Kenneth, Jr. 1931- *WhoAm 92*
Danielson, Henry *ScF&FL 92*
Danielson, James R. *Law&B 92*
Danielson, Jerry Craig 1953- *WhoEmL 93*
Danielson, Kenneth Leroy 1950- *St&PR 93*
Danielson, Leon Charles 1945- *St&PR 93*
Danielson, Patricia Rochelle Frank 1941- *WhoAmW 93*
Danielson, Sybil Lentner *AmWomPl*
Danielson, Ursel Rehding 1935- *WhoE 93*
Danielson, Wayne Allen 1929- *WhoAm 92*
Danielsson, Henry *WhoScE 91-4*
Danielsson-Tham, Marie-Louise 1947- *WhoScE 91-4*
Daniel The Stylite 409-493 *OxDcByz*
Daniil, II c. 1270-1337 *OxDcByz*
Daniil Igumen 12th cent.- *OxDcByz*
Danilaev, Peter Grigor-evich 1945- *WhoWor 93*
Danilek, Donald J. 1937- *WhoAm 92*
Danilewicz-Stysiak, Zofia 1922- *WhoScE 91-4*
Danilov, Victor Joseph 1924- *WhoAm 92*
Danilova, Alexandra *WhoAm 92*
Danilow, Deborah Marie 1947- *WhoAmW 93*
Danilowicz, Delores Ann 1935- *WhoAm 92*
Danilowicz, L. Paul 1936- *St&PR 93*
Danilson, David Ray 1954- *WhoEmL 93*
Danin, Mary Ann 1928- *WhoAm 92*
Danino, Roberto 1951- *WhoWor 93*
Danis, Julie Marie 1955- *WhoEmL 93*
Danis, Marcel 1943- *WhoE 93*
Danis, Peter G., Jr. 1932- *St&PR 93, WhoAm 92*
Danis, Richard Ralph 1943- *St&PR 93*
Danis, Richard Ralph, Sr. 1943- *WhoAm 92*
Danis, Roy Steven 1956- *WhoE 93*
Danish, Roy Bertram 1919- *WhoAm 92*
Danishefsky, Isidore 1923- *WhoAm 92*
Danisman, Mustafa Cihat 1947- *WhoWor 93*
Danismendids *OxDcByz*
Daniszewska, Malgorzata *BioIn 17*
Daniszewski, Joseph J. 1941- *St&PR 93*
Danitz, Marilynn Patricia *WhoAm 92, WhoAmW 93, WhoE 93, WhoWor 93*
Danjczek, David William 1951- *WhoWor 93*
Danjczek, William Emil 1913- *WhoWor 93*
Danjou, Jean-Louis-Felix 1812-1866 *Baker 92*
Dank, Gloria Rand 1955- *ScF&FL 92*
Dank, Leonard Dewey 1929- *WhoAm 92*
Dank, Milton 1920- *ScF&FL 92*
Dankanyin, R.J. 1934- *St&PR 93*
Dankanyin, Robert John 1934- *WhoAm 92*
Danker, Frederick J. 1923- *St&PR 93*
Danker, Mervyn Kenneth 1944- *WhoE 93*
Dankers, Norbert M.J.A. 1947- *WhoScE 91-3*
Dankevich, Konstantin 1905-1984 *Baker 92*
Dankin, Alexander Harry 1916- *St&PR 93*
Dankin, Peter Alfred 1942- *St&PR 93*
Dankmeyer, T. Rognald *Law&B 92*
Dankmeyer, Theodore Rognald 1938- *St&PR 93*
Dankner, Jay Warren 1949- *WhoEmL 93*
Danko, Barbara Daly 1953- *WhoAmW 93, WhoEmL 93*
Danko, George M. 1927- *St&PR 93*
Danko, Harold 1947- *WhoEmL 93*
Danko, Joseph Christopher 1927- *WhoAm 92*
Danko, Joseph O., Jr. 1926- *St&PR 93*
Danko, Patricia St. John 1944- *WhoAmW 93, WhoSSW 93, WhoWor 93*
Danko, Rick 1943-
See Band, The *ConMus 9*
Danko, William David 1952- *WhoE 93, WhoEmL 93*
Danks, H(art) P(ease) 1834-1903 *Baker 92*
Dankworth, Charles Henry 1950- *WhoEmL 93*
Dankworth, Clementina Dinah 1927- *WhoAm 92, WhoAmW 93*
Dankworth, John (Philip William) 1927- *Baker 92*
Danky, James Philip 1947- *WhoWrEP 92*
Danley, Richard Earl, Jr. *Law&B 92*
Danly, Donald Robert 1923- *WhoAm 92*
Dann, Colin 1943- *ScF&FL 92*
Dann, Colin (Michael) 1943- *ChlFicS*
Dann, Diane Furman *Law&B 92*
Dann, Dorothy *St&PR 93*
Dann, Emily 1932- *WhoAmW 93*
Dann, Jack *BioIn 17*
Dann, Jack 1945- *ScF&FL 92*
Dann, Jack M. 1945- *WhoWrEP 92*
Dann, Jeanne Van Buren 1949- *ScF&FL 92*
Dann, Max 1955- *BioIn 17*
Dann, Norman 1927- *St&PR 93*
Dann, Rosemary Weinstein 1948- *WhoEmL 93*
Dann, Sam 1918- *ScF&FL 92*
Dann, Theodore E. 1917- *St&PR 93*
D'Anna, Angelo Nino 1924- *St&PR 93*
D'Anna, Anthony S. 1926- *St&PR 93*
Danna, Carl 1930- *WhoWrEP 92*
D'Anna, Carmen Vito 1920- *WhoAm 92*
D'Anna, Claude 1945- *MiSFD 9*
Danna, Jo J. *WhoAm 92*
Danna, Robert 1951- *WhoEmL 93*
Danna, Theresa Mary 1958- *WhoAmW 93*
Dannay, Frederic 1905-1982 *BioIn 17, ConAu 39NR*
Danneberg, Kenneth I. 1927- *St&PR 93*
Danneel, Ilse 1931- *WhoScE 91-3*
Danneels, Godfried Cardinal 1933- *WhoWor 93*
Dannehold, Sandra A. *Law&B 92*
Dannelly, C. Eugene 1940- *St&PR 93*
Dannemeyer, William E. 1929- *CngDr 91*
Dannemeyer, William Edwin 1929- *WhoAm 92*
Dannenbaum, Mildred *AmWomPl*
Dannenbaum, Paul O. 1916- *St&PR 93*
Dannenberg, Arthur Milton, Jr. 1923- *WhoAm 92, WhoE 93*
Dannenberg, Martin Ernest 1915- *WhoAm 92*
Dannenbring, Fredo 1926- *WhoUN 92*
Dannenmann, Otto Karl 1915- *WhoWrEP 92*
Danner, Blythe 1944- *BioIn 17*
Danner, Blythe Katharine 1944- *WhoAm 92*
Danner, Bobby Charles 1930- *St&PR 93*
Danner, Dean W. 1950- *St&PR 93*
Danner, Dean Wilson 1950- *WhoEmL 93*
Danner, Donald G. 1944- *St&PR 93*
Danner, Ernie L. *St&PR 93*
Danner, George W. *St&PR 93*
Danner, John Joseph, Jr. 1940- *WhoSSW 93*
Danner, Lawrence Melville 1949- *WhoEmL 93, WhoSSW 93*
Danner, Pamela Jean 1962- *WhoE 93*
Danner, Patsy Ann 1934- *WhoAm 92, WhoAmW 93*
Danner, Paul Kruger, III 1957- *WhoWor 93*
Danner, Richard Allen 1947- *WhoAm 92*
Danner, Robert P. 1924- *St&PR 93*
Danner, Sharon Kay 1946- *WhoAmW 93*
Danner, Siegfried 1942- *WhoWor 93*
Danner, William B. *Law&B 92*
Dannhauser, Robert K. *Law&B 92*
Dannheisser, Werner d1992 *BioIn 17, NewYTBS 92*
D'Anniballe, Priscilla Lucille 1950- *WhoAmW 93, WhoEmL 93*
Dannible, Anthony Frank 1947- *WhoE 93*
Dannible, Carmin D. 1929- *St&PR 93*
Dannis-Applegate, Fern Sue 1953- *WhoEmL 93*
Dannreuther, Edward (George) 1844-1905 *Baker 92*
Dannreuther, Gustav 1853-1923 *Baker 92*
Dannreuther, John West 1948- *St&PR 93*
D'Annunzio, Gabriele 1863-1938 *BioIn 17, DcTwHis, OxDcOp*
Danny-Roberts, Lisa *Law&B 92*
Dano, Keld 1936- *WhoScE 91-2*
Dano, Paul Kenneth 1935- *St&PR 93*
Danoff, I. Michael 1940- *WhoAm 92*
Danoff, Stuart S. 1933- *WhoWor 93*
Danoff-Kraus, Pamela Sue 1946- *WhoAmW 93, WhoEmL 93*
Danon, Giuliana M. *Law&B 92*
Danon, Giuliana Maria 1957- *WhoEmL 93*
Danon, Oskar 1913- *Baker 92, OxDcOp*
Danos, Robert McClure 1929- *St&PR 93, WhoAm 92*
Danosi, Kimberly A. *Law&B 92*
Danowski, Edward Frank 1911- *BiDAMSp 1989*
Danquah, Joseph Boakye 1895-1965 *DcTwHis*
Dans, Alvin G. 1951- *WhoAsAP 91*
Dansak, Daniel Albert 1943- *WhoSSW 93*
Dansby, Eunice Lillith 1927- *WhoWor 93*
Dansby, John Walter 1944- *St&PR 93, WhoAm 92, WhoSSW 93*
Dansby, Robert F. 1940- *St&PR 93*
Danscher, Gorm 1938- *WhoScE 91-2*
Dansen, Robert C. 1916- *St&PR 93*
Danser, Bonita Kay 1949- *WhoAmW 93, WhoEmL 93*
Danser, Eduard 1937- *WhoWor 93*
Danser, Harold Wesley, III 1945- *WhoWor 93*
Dansereau, Fred Edward, Jr. 1946- *WhoE 93*
Dansereau, Pierre 1911- *WhoAm 92*
Danska, Herbert *MiSFD 9*
Danski, Jon F. 1952- *St&PR 93*
Danskin, Wesley Robert 1952- *WhoEmL 93*
Dansler, Oscar *BioIn 17*
Danson, Stephen Michael 1943- *WhoAm 92*
Danson, Ted *BioIn 17*
Danson, Ted 1947?- *HolBB [port], WhoAm 92*
Dant, Alan Hale 1935- *WhoSSW 93*
Dant, Brenda Sue 1945- *WhoAmW 93*
Dante, Harris Loy 1912- *WhoAm 92*
Dante, Joe *BioIn 17, MiSFD 9*
Dante, Nicholas 1942?-1991 *BioIn 17*
Dante, Robert David 1953- *WhoWrEP 92*
Dante, Ronald 1920- *WhoWor 93*
Dante Alighieri 1265-1321 *BioIn 17, MagSWL [port], OxDcOp*
Danthanarayana, W. 1936- *WhoWor 93*
Dantin, Louis 1865-1945 *BioIn 17*
Dantini, Julie Ann 1947- *WhoE 93*
Dantley, Adrian *BioIn 17*
Danto, Arthur Coleman 1924- *BioIn 17, WhoAm 92, WhoWrEP 92*
Danton, Joseph Periam 1908- *WhoAm 92*
Danton, Ray d1992 *NewYTBS 92 [port]*
Danton, Ray 1931-1992 *BioIn 17, MiSFD 9N*
Danton, Rebecca *WhoWrEP 92*
Dantone, Jerry B. 1942- *St&PR 93*
Dantone, Joseph John, Jr. 1942- *WhoAm 92*
Dantone, William Bryan 1951- *WhoSSW 93*
D'Antoni, Philip 1929- *MiSFD 9*
D'Antonio, James Joseph 1959- *WhoEmL 93*
D'Antonio, Robert Vincent, Jr. 1962- *WhoE 93*
D'Antonio, Thomas Samuel 1957- *WhoEmL 93*
D'Antonio, William Vincent 1926- *WhoAm 92*
Dantsin, Eugene 1951- *WhoWor 93*
D'Antuono, D.J. 1943- *St&PR 93*
Dantyszek, Jan 1485-1548 *PolBiDi*
Dantz, William R. *ScF&FL 92*
Dantzig, George Bernard 1914- *WhoAm 92*
Dantzig, Rudi Van 1933- *WhoWor 93*
Dantzler, Duane 1954- *St&PR 93*
Dantzler, John William, Jr. 1953- *WhoEmL 93*
Dantzler, Kelley Diane 1959- *WhoEmL 93*
Dantzler-Wolfe, Dolores Jane 1941- *WhoSSW 93*
Danus, Richard *MiSFD 9*
Danuser, Jerry *St&PR 93*
Danvers, Dennis 1947- *ConLC 70 [port], ScF&FL 92*
Danyluk, Paul R. 1937- *St&PR 93*
Danysz, Andrzej 1924- *WhoScE 91-4*
Danz, Christian Klaus 1944- *WhoWor 93*
Danza, Anne C. *Law&B 92*
Danza, Tony 1951- *HolBB [port], WhoAm 92*
Danzberger, Alexander Harris 1932- *WhoAm 92*
Danzer, Sylvia Joy 1944- *WhoAmW 93*
Danzi, Franz (Ignaz) 1763-1826 *Baker 92*
Danzi, Robert F. 1954- *WhoWor 93*
Danzig, Aaron Leon 1913- *WhoAm 92*
Danzig, Allen E. *Law&B 92*
Danzig, Allen Edward 1956- *WhoEmL 93*
Danzig, Allen J. *Law&B 92*
Danzig, Frederick Paul 1925- *WhoAm 92*
Danzig, Jerome Alan 1913- *WhoAm 92*
Danzig, Lisa 1958- *St&PR 93, WhoEmL 93*
Danzig, Richard Jeffrey 1944- *WhoAm 92*
Danzig, Robert James 1932- *WhoAm 92*
Danzig, Sarah H. Palfrey 1912- *WhoAm 92*
Danzig, Sarah Palfrey *BioIn 17*
Danzig, Sheila Ring 1948- *WhoAmW 93, WhoEmL 93, WhoSSW 93*
Danzig, William Harold 1947- *WhoEmL 93, WhoSSW 93, WhoWor 93*
Danziger, Fred 1946- *BioIn 17*
Danziger, Frederick Michael 1940- *St&PR 93*
Danziger, Gertrude *St&PR 93*
Danziger, Gertrude Seelig 1919- *WhoAmW 93*
Danziger, Glenn Norman 1930- *WhoAm 92*
Danziger, Gustaf *ScF&FL 92*
Danziger, Howard 1941- *St&PR 93*
Danziger, James 1953- *BioIn 17*
Danziger, James Norris 1945- *WhoAm 92*
Danziger, Jerry 1924- *WhoAm 92*
Danziger, Joan 1934- *WhoAm 92*
Danziger, Louis 1923- *WhoAm 92*
Danziger, Martin Breitel 1931- *WhoAm 92*
Danziger, Michael Roy 1954- *WhoEmL 93*
Danziger, Paula 1944- *BioIn 17, ConAu 37NR, MajAI [port], ScF&FL 92*
Danziger, Richard Ira 1956- *St&PR 93*
Danziger, Richard Martin 1938- *WhoE 93*
Danziger, Sidney 1903-1991 *BioIn 17*
Danziger, Terry Leblang 1933- *WhoSSW 93*
Danzin, Charles Marie 1944- *WhoWor 93*
Danzis, Colin Michael 1938- *WhoWor 93*
Danzis, Jo-Ann Fine 1941- *WhoAmW 93, WhoWor 93*
Danzis, Michele Kelly 1951- *WhoAmW 93*
Danzis, Rose Marie *WhoAm 92*
Danzl, Daniel Frank 1950- *WhoWor 93*
Dao, Huu Tuong 1930- *WhoUN 92*
Daolio, Sergio *WhoScE 91-3*
Daou, M'pe David 1936- *WhoUN 92*
Daoud, Abraham Joseph, IV 1957- *WhoEmL 93, WhoSSW 93*
Daoud, Iyadh Selman 1944- *WhoScE 91-1*
Daoud, Mohamed 1947- *WhoEmL 93*
Daoud, Soliman Mohamed 1934- *WhoWor 93*
Daoudy, Adib *WhoUN 92*
Daoust, Donald Roger 1935- *St&PR 93, WhoAm 92*
Daoust, Hubert 1928- *WhoAm 92*

D'Aoust, Jean-Jacques 1924- WhoSSW 93
Daoust, Jean-Paul 1946- WhoCanL 92
Daoust, Raymond George 1932- WhoE 93
Da-Oz, Ram 1929- Baker 92
Da Parma, Claire Elizabeth 1945- WhoAmW 93
Dapaz Strout, Lilia 1930- WhoSSW 93
Daphinoff, Dimiter Michael 1950- WhoWor 93
Daphne BioIn 17
Daphnis, Nassos 1914- WhoAm 92
Daphnopates, Theodore dc. 961 OxDcByz
Dapice, Ronald R. 1937- WhoAm 92
Dapier, Mark E. Law&B 92
D'Apolito, David Joseph 1955- WhoE 93
Da Ponte, Lorenzo 1749-1838 Baker 92, IntDcOp [port], OxDcOp
Dapples, Edward Charles 1906- WhoAm 92
D'Appolonia, David J. 1944- St&PR 93
Dapron, Elmer Joseph, Jr. 1925- WhoWor 93
Dapuzzo, Peter James 1941- St&PR 93, WhoAm 92
Daquin, Louis-Claude 1694-1772 Baker 92
D'Aquino, Iva Toguri BioIn 17
d'Aquino, Thomas 1940- WhoAm 92, WhoWor 93
D'Aquisto, James 1935- BioIn 17
Dar, Karamat Hussain 1941- WhoWor 93
Dar, Mueen Ud-Din 1947- WhoWor 93
Darabont, Frank MiSFD 9
Darack, Arthur J. 1918- ConAu 37NR, WhoAm 92, WhoWrEP 92
Daragan, Thomas 1946- St&PR 93
Daragan, Thomas W. 1946- WhoAm 92
Darany, Michael Anthony 1946- WhoEmL 93
Daranyi, Catherine N. Law&B 92
D'Aranyi, Jelly Baker 92
Darazidi, James Joseph 1949- St&PR 93
Darazsdi, James Joseph 1949- WhoAm 92
Darbellay, Charly 1943- WhoScE 91-4
Darbelnet, Jean Louis 1904- WhoWrEP 92
d'Arbeloff, George Vladimir 1945- St&PR 93
D'Arblay, Frances Burney 1752-1840 BioIn 17
Darbo, Bakary Bunja 1946- WhoWor 93
Darby, Artemas Keitt, III 1947- WhoSSW 93
Darby, Catherine 1935- ScF&FL 92
Darby, Douglas Alan 1946- St&PR 93
Darby, Edwin Wheeler 1922- WhoAm 92
Darby, Elton H. 1918- St&PR 93
Darby, Elton H., Jr. 1961- St&PR 93
Darby, Gene ConAu 39NR
Darby, Graham K. 1942- WhoScE 91-1
Darby, Helen T. AmWomPl
Darby, Jay Rodney 1953- WhoEmL 93, WhoWor 93
Darby, Jean 1921- BioIn 17
Darby, Jean (Kegley) 1921- ConAu 39NR
Darby, Jerome S. 1950- St&PR 93
Darby, John Kenneth WhoScE 91-1
Darby, John O. R. 1930- WhoWor 93
Darby, Joseph Branch, Jr. 1925- WhoAm 92
Darby, Joseph Jasper, III 1942- WhoSSW 93, WhoWor 93
Darby, Ken d1992 NewYTBS 92
Darby, Kenneth Lorin 1909-1992 BioIn 17
Darby, Kenneth M. 1946- St&PR 93
Darby, Lyndan ScF&FL 92
Darby, Michael 1944- ConAu 38NR
Darby, Michael A. Law&B 92
Darby, Michael Rucker 1945- WhoAm 92
Darby, Michele Leonardi 1949- WhoEmL 93, WhoSSW 93
Darby, Stephen John, Jr. 1933- St&PR 93
D'Arby, Terence Trent 1962- SoulM
Darby, Todd 1962- St&PR 93
Darbyshire, John Frederick WhoScE 91-1
D'Arcangelo, Allan Matthew 1930- WhoAm 92
D'Arcangelo, Marcia Diane 1945- WhoAmW 93, WhoE 93
Darcemont, Michel WhoScE 91-2
D'Archambeau, Iwan Baker 92
Darclee, Hariclea 1860-1939 Baker 92, OxDcOp
Darclee, Ion Hartulary- 1886-1969 OxDcOp
D'Arco, Joseph A. Law&B 92
D'Arcy, Adelyse Marie 1934- WhoAmW 93
Darcy, Denise Ann Law&B 92
Darcy, George Robert 1920- WhoAm 92
D'Arcy, Gerald Paul 1933- WhoAm 92
D'Arcy, John Michael 1932- WhoAm 92
Darcy, Keith Thomas 1948- WhoE 93, WhoEmL 93
D'Arcy, Peter A. d1991 BioIn 17
Darcy, Robert 1910-1967 Baker 92
D'Arcy, Rosemary V. 1944- WhoAmW 93
D'Arcy, Scotti d1990 BioIn 17
D'Arcy, Thomas Joseph 1933- WhoSSW 93
Dardas, Charles L. 1953- St&PR 93
Dardeck, Kathryn Lee 1951- WhoAmW 93
Darden, Celia Odom 1963- WhoAmW 93
Darden, Dawn Leigh 1963- WhoEmL 93
Darden, Edwin Speight, Sr. 1920- WhoAm 92
Darden, George 1943- CngDr 91
Darden, George Washington, III 1943- WhoAm 92, WhoSSW 93
Darden, Jeannie May 1940- WhoAmW 93
Darden, John F. 1946- WhoIns 93
Darden, Joseph S., Jr. BioIn 17
Darden, Joseph Samuel, Jr. 1925- WhoE 93
Darden, Lindley 1945- WhoAmW 93
Darden, Margaret 1955- WhoE 93
Darden, Michael P. Law&B 92
Darden, Norman BioIn 17
Darden, Severn Teackle WhoAm 92
Darden, William E. 1916- St&PR 93
Darden, William Horace 1923- CngDr 91
Darden, William Howard, Jr. 1937- WhoAm 92, WhoSSW 93
Darden-Gettys, Gloria Ann WhoAmW 93
Dardenne, Guy WhoScE 91-2
Dardes, Jack Andrew 1946- WhoEmL 93
Dardi, Robert John Law&B 92
Dardick, Kenneth Regen 1946- WhoAm 92
Dardick, Leon M. 1926- St&PR 93
Dardik, Irving BioIn 17
Dardis, Stan K. 1949- St&PR 93
Dardis, Thomas A. 1926- ScF&FL 92
Dardon, Gisela 1934- WhoAmW 93
Dare, L.G. WhoScE 91-1
Dare, Thomas A. Law&B 92
Dareff, Hal 1920- WhoAm 92, WhoWrEP 92
Darehshori, Nader F. 1936- St&PR 93
Darehshori, Nader Farhang 1936- WhoAm 92, WhoE 93
Darel, Florence BioIn 17
Darga, Helene M. St&PR 93
Darga, Jerome Paul 1944- St&PR 93
Dargahi-Noubary, Gholamreza 1946- WhoE 93
Dargan, Mary Palmer Kelley 1954- WhoWor 93
Dargan, Olive Tilford 1869-1968 AmWomPl
Dargan, William 1799-1867 BioIn 17
Dargaud, Georges d1990 BioIn 17
D'Argenteuil, Paul ScF&FL 92
Darger, Stanford Parley 1920- St&PR 93
Dargie, James Donald 1943- WhoUN 92
Dargis, Jean Anthony 1931- WhoE 93
D'Argnac, Jesse WhoWrEP 92
Dargomizhsky, Alexander 1813-1869 IntDcOp
Dargomyzhsky, Alexander 1813-1869 OxDcOp
Dargomyzhsky, Alexander (Sergeievich) 1813-1869 Baker 92
Darian, Ralph 1925- St&PR 93
Darias, Alicia 1949- WhoAmW 93
Darien, Steven Martin 1942- St&PR 93, WhoAm 92, WhoE 93
Darin, Bobby 1936-1973 Baker 92
Darin, Frank Victor John 1930- WhoWor 93
Dario, Ruben 1867-1916 BioIn 17
Darion, Joe 1917- WhoAm 92
Darish, Allan Law&B 92
D'Arista, Jane Webb 1932- WhoAmW 93, WhoE 93
Darius, King of Persia 548?BC-486?BC BioIn 17
Darjany, John C. 1948- St&PR 93
Darjany, John Charles 1948- WhoEmL 93
Dark, Alvin Ralph 1922- WhoAm 92
Dark, James 1917- ScF&FL 92
Dark, Jon ScF&FL 92
Dark, Larry ScF&FL 92
Dark, Larry 1959- ConAu 136
Dark, Lawrence C. ScF&FL 92
Dark, Philip John Crosskey 1918- WhoAm 92
Darke, Harold (Edwin) 1888-1976 Baker 92
Darke, James ScF&FL 92
Darke, Marjorie 1929- ScF&FL 92
Darke, Richard Francis 1943- WhoAm 92
Darke, Roy Anthony WhoScE 91-1
Darken, Marjorie Alice 1915- WhoSSW 93
Darken, Teresa Joan Joyce 1961- WhoAmW 93
Darker, John W. 1932- St&PR 93
Darkey, Kermit Louis 1930- WhoWor 93
Darkfeather, Mona SweetSg A
Darkovich, Sharon Marie 1949- WhoAmW 93
Darlan, Francois 1881-1942 BioIn 17
Darlan, Jean Louis Xavier Francois 1881-1942 DcTwHis
Darland, Nancy Ann Wilson 1958- WhoEmL 93
Darlaston, Brian John LeTellier 1932- WhoWor 93
D'Arles, Henri 1870-1930 BioIn 17
Darley, George 1795-1846 BioIn 17
Darley, Jeffrey S. 1958- St&PR 93
Darley, John McConnon 1938- WhoAm 92
Darley, Paul C. 1963- St&PR 93
Darley, William Joseph 1928- St&PR 93
Darling, Bruce M. 1958- St&PR 93
Darling, Cheryl MacLeod 1949- WhoAmW 93
Darling, Clifford 1922- WhoWor 93
Darling, David J. BioIn 17
Darling, David J. 1953- ConAu 138
Darling, Donald C. 1952- St&PR 93
Darling, Effie Evelyn 1910- WhoWrEP 92
Darling, Elaine Elizabeth WhoAsAP 91
Darling, Ella AmWomPl
Darling, Erik 1933- See Weavers, The ConMus 8
Darling, Frank Clayton 1925- WhoAm 92
Darling, George Bapst, Jr. 1905- WhoAm 92
Darling, Gwendolyn 1961- WhoAmW 93
Darling, Jay Norwood 1876-1962 JrnUS
Darling, Joan 1935- MiSFD 9
Darling, John Albert 1937- St&PR 93
Darling, John Dallas 1944- St&PR 93
Darling, John Rothburn, Jr. 1937- WhoAm 92, WhoSSW 93, WhoWor 93
Darling, Lois MacIntyre 1917-1989 BioIn 17, ConAu 38NR, MajAI [port]
Darling, Louis, Jr. 1916-1970 ConAu 38NR, MajAI [port]
Darling, Mark Paul 1949- St&PR 93
Darling, Paul Gifford 1916-1990 BioIn 17
Darling, Ralph Clement 1927- WhoAm 92
Darling, Richard Harrison 1925- St&PR 93
Darling, Robert Edward 1937- WhoAm 92
Darling, Robert F. Law&B 92
Darling, Sandra BioIn 17
Darling, Scott Edward 1949- WhoEmL 93, WhoWor 93
Darling, Scott Martin 1953- St&PR 93
Darling, Stephen Edward 1949- WhoEmL 93
Darling, Sturgis W. 1932- St&PR 93
Darling, Tom 1917- St&PR 93
Darling, William Ritchie 1933- WhoWrEP 92
Darlinger, Copper 1954- WhoEmL 93
Darlington, Anne Charlotte AmWomPl
Darlington, Dorothy Sillcox 1952- WhoAmW 93
Darlington, Henry, Jr. 1925- WhoE 93, WhoWor 93
Darlington, J. WhoScE 91-1
Darlington, Jared Lloyd 1933- WhoWor 93
Darlington, Lloyd F. 1945- St&PR 93
Darlington, Oscar Gilpin 1909- WhoAm 92
Darlington, Richard Benjamin 1937- WhoAm 92
Darlington, Thomas B. 1924- St&PR 93
Darlington, W.D. 1932- St&PR 93
Darlot, Andre 1919- WhoScE 91-2
Darlow, David MiSFD 9
Darlow, Julia Donovan 1941- WhoAm 92
Darlow, Mark Howard 1941- St&PR 93
Darlow, Sheldon Jay 1935- St&PR 93
Darlton, Clark ScF&FL 92
Darman, A. David Law&B 92
Darman, Richard BioIn 17
Darman, Richard Gordon 1943- WhoAm 92, WhoE 93
Darmanian, Denise G. 1957- St&PR 93
Darmer, Harold Leonard 1923- WhoSSW 93
Darmojuwono, Justin Cardinal 1914- WhoWor 93
Darmon, Robert L. 1925- St&PR 93
D'Arms, Edward F. 1904-1991 BioIn 17
D'Arms, John Haughton 1934- WhoAm 92
Darmstadter, Howard M. Law&B 92
Darmstandler, Harry Max 1922- WhoAm 92
Darnall, Dennis Wayne 1941- WhoAm 92
Darnall, John H., Jr. 1944- St&PR 93
Darnall, Marcy Bradshaw, III Law&B 92
Darnall, Michael Steven 1947- St&PR 93
Darnall, Robert J. WhoAm 92
Darnall, Roberta Morrow 1949- WhoEmL 93
Darnall, Thomas S., Jr. 1936- St&PR 93
Darnand, Joseph 1897-1945 BioIn 17
Darnay, Arsen 1936- ScF&FL 92
Darneille, Wallace Lambert 1951- WhoEmL 93
Darnell, James Oral 1955- WhoEmL 93
Darnell, Leonard Robert 1957- WhoEmL 93, WhoWor 93
Darnell, Linda 1923-1965 BioIn 17, IntDcF 2-3
Darnell, Merris Zon WhoAmW 93
Darnell, Michael WhoScE 91-1
Darnell, Quinton L. 1928- St&PR 93
Darnell, R. William 1956- St&PR 93
Darnell, Riley Carlisle 1940- WhoSSW 93
Darnell, Robert William 1956- WhoEmL 93
Darnell, Sara Law&B 92
Darnell, Stephen E. Law&B 92
Darnell, Susan Pritchard 1946- WhoEmL 93
Darnes-Kaiser, Dorothy Carolyn 1935- WhoAmW 93
Darney, Philip Dempsey 1943- WhoAm 92
Darnhofer-Demar, Benno 1939- WhoScE 91-3
Darnton, (Philip) Christian 1905-1981 Baker 92
Darnton, Geoffrey 1948- WhoWor 93
Darnton, Robert BioIn 17
Darnton-Hill, Ian 1946- WhoUN 92
Daroff, Robert Barry 1936- WhoAm 92
Darold, Jane M. Law&B 92
da Roza, Victoria Cecilia 1945- WhoAmW 93
D'Arpino, Tony 1951- WhoWrEP 92
Darr, Alan Phipps 1948- WhoAm 92
Darr, Alice Louise 1951- WhoEmL 93
Darr, Ann Russell 1920- WhoWrEP 92
Darr, Barbara Harman 1927- WhoAmW 93
Darr, James E., Jr. Law&B 92
Darr, John 1951- St&PR 93, WhoEmL 93
Darr, Milton Freeman, Jr. 1921- WhoAm 92
Darr, Robert Charles 1937- St&PR 93
Darr, Walter Robert 1956- WhoE 93
Darr, William M. Law&B 92
Darrach, Orlin Ward 1928- St&PR 93
Darragh, Cavan J. 1916- St&PR 93
Darragh, James Hilton 1924- WhoAm 92
Darragh, John K. BioIn 17
Darragh, John K. 1929- St&PR 93
Darrah, Joan WhoAmW 93
Darrah, Katherine Simpson WhoAmW 93
Darrah, Larry Lynn 1943- WhoAm 92
Darrah, William Culp 1909-1989 BioIn 17
Darre, Bernard John 1939- St&PR 93
Darre, Jeanne-Marie 1905- Baker 92
Darrell, Edward BioIn 17
Darrell, Evelyn Boyden WhoAmW 93
Darrell, George Albert 1931- WhoAm 92
Darrell, Gilbert DcCPCAm
Darrell, Norris, Jr. 1929- WhoAm 92
Darrell, R(obert) D(onaldson) 1903-1988 Baker 92
Darren, James 1936- MiSFD 9
Darretta, John Lawrence 1938- WhoE 93
Darrid, William d1992 NewYTBS 92
Darrieux, Danielle 1917- IntDcF 2-3 [port]
Darrigan, Robert Joseph, Jr. 1958- WhoE 93, WhoEmL 93
D'Arrigo, Joseph Law&B 92
Darroll, Sally SmATA 72
Darrone, Donald William 1916- WhoAm 92
Darrow, Carroll L. Law&B 92
Darrow, Clarence 1857-1938 BioIn 17, ConHero 2 [port]
Darrow, Henry 1933- HispAmA
Darrow, Katherine Prager 1943- WhoAmW 93
Darrow, Paul ScF&FL 92
Darrow, Robert Arthur 1911- WhoAm 92
Darrow, Terri Lynn 1955- WhoAmW 93, WhoWrEP 92
Darrow, William Richard 1939- WhoAm 92, WhoE 93, WhoWor 93
Darsey, Betty Jean 1931- WhoAmW 93
Darsieres, Camille 1932- DcCPCAm
Darsky, Julius 1907- WhoWor 93
Darsky, Richard H. 1941- St&PR 93
Darsono, Charles Lukman 1930- WhoWor 93
Darst, David High 1943- WhoSSW 93
Darst, David Martin 1947- WhoAm 92, WhoE 93, WhoEmL 93
Dart, Anthony Michael 1947- WhoWor 93
Dart, Charles Edward 1915- WhoAm 92
Dart, E.C. WhoScE 91-1
Dart, Jack Calhoon 1912- St&PR 93, WhoE 93
Dart, Joanna Pousette- BioIn 17
Dart, John Robert 1925- WhoE 93
Dart, John Seward 1936- WhoAm 92
Dart, Justin, Jr. 1930- WhoAm 92
Dart, Raymond A. 1893-1988 IntDcAn
Dart, Richard Pousette- 1916- BioIn 17
Dart, Rollin B. 1925- St&PR 93
Dart, (Robert) Thurston 1921-1971 Baker 92
D'Artagnan, Pierre de Montesquiou 1645-1725 HarEnMi
Darter, Jeffrey Allen 1958- WhoEmL 93
Darter, Steven Mark 1949- WhoEmL 93
Dartez, Franklin 1934- WhoAm 92
Dartez, Louis Avery 1925- WhoSSW 93

Dartiguenave, Alain M. 1952- *WhoWor 93*
Dartiguenave, Michele 1939- *WhoScE 91-2*
Darting, Edith Anne 1945- *WhoAmW 93*
D'Artois Chambord, Henri-Charles-Ferdinand-Marie-Dieudonne 1820-1883 *BioIn 17*
Dartt, Roger Wallace 1941- *St&PR 93*
Daruni, Sam K. *St&PR 93*
Darusenkov, Oleg Tijonovich 1932- *WhoWor 93*
Darvarova, Elmira *WhoAm 92*
Darvas, Endre Peter 1946- *WhoEmL 93*
Darvas, Gabor 1911-1985 *Baker 92*
Darvas, Gyorgy *WhoScE 91-4*
Darver, Gerald B. 1944- *St&PR 93*
Darvick, Martin I. *Law&B 92*
Darville, Robert Henry, III 1953- *WhoSSW 93*
Darvill-Evans, Peter *ScF&FL 92*
Darwell, Jane 1879-1967 *IntDcF 2-3*
Darwin, Allen Charles 1948- *St&PR 93*
Darwin, Charles 1809-1882 *BioIn 17, Expl 93 [port]*
Darwin, Christopher John *WhoScE 91-1*
Darwin, Erasmus 1731-1802 *BioIn 17*
Darwin, Gary Robert 1952- *St&PR 93*
Darwin, John Walter 1953- *WhoEmL 93, WhoSSW 93*
Darwin, Natalie W. 1923- *St&PR 93*
Darwin, Sidney 1915- *St&PR 93*
Dary, David Archie 1934- *WhoAm 92*
Daryanani, Raj 1961- *WhoEmL 93*
Darzins, Emils 1875-1910 *Baker 92*
Das, Anadi Charan 1935- *WhoAsAP 91*
Das, Jibanananda 1899-1954 *BioIn 17*
Das, Kalyan 1956- *WhoEmL 93, WhoWor 93*
Das, Manjusri 1946- *WhoAm 92*
Das, Manoj 1934- *ScF&FL 92*
Das, Pradip Kumar 1951- *WhoE 93, WhoWor 93*
Das, Rathin C. 1948- *WhoAm 92*
Das, Samir Kumar 1939- *WhoWor 93*
Das, Suman Kumar 1944- *WhoWor 93*
Das, Suranjan 1954- *ConAu 139*
Das, T. K. 1938- *WhoE 93, WhoWor 93*
D'Asalena, Helene *AmWomPl*
Dasburg, John H. 1943- *St&PR 93*
Dascenzo, Doug *BioIn 17*
Daschbach, James M. 1932- *WhoAm 92*
Dascher, Paul Edward 1942- *WhoAm 92*
Daschle, Thomas A. 1947- *CngDr 91*
Daschle, Thomas Andrew 1947- *WhoAm 92*
Daseking, Edith *AmWomPl*
Dasent, George Webbe 1817-1896 *BioIn 17*
Daser, Ludwig c. 1525-1589 *Baker 92*
Das Gupta, Gurudas 1936- *WhoAsAP 91*
Dasgupta, Ranjit Kumar *WhoWor 93*
Dash, Barry Harold 1931- *St&PR 93, WhoE 93*
Dash, George E. 1950- *St&PR 93*
Dash, Julie *BioIn 17, MiSFD 9, NewYTBS 92 [port]*
Dash, Julie 1952?- *ConBlB 4 [port]*
Dash, Leon DeCosta, Jr. 1944- *WhoAm 92*
Dash, Marcus J. 1944- *St&PR 93*
Dash, Robert Warren 1931- *WhoE 93*
Dash, Samuel 1925- *WhoAm 92*
Dash, Thomas R. d1991 *BioIn 17*
Dashef, Stephen Sewell 1941- *WhoAm 92*
Dashefsky, Arnold Martin 1942- *WhoE 93*
Dashen, Roger Frederick 1938- *WhoAm 92*
Dasher, Michael Joseph 1949- *St&PR 93*
Dasher, Richard Taliaferro 1933- *WhoSSW 93*
Dashiell, George Easley 1924- *St&PR 93*
Dashiell, Pamela Moran *Law&B 92*
Dashow, James (Hilyer) 1944- *Baker 92*
Da Silva, Alexandre *WhoScE 91-3*
Da Silva, Fernando M. *Law&B 92*
Da Silva, Jose Antonio T. Lopes 1963- *WhoWor 93*
Da Silva, Lydia Louise 1948- *WhoAmW 93*
DaSilva, Mark Edward 1955- *WhoEmL 93*
Da Silva, Reginaldo 1950- *WhoWor 93*
Da Silva Correa, Carlos Maria Martins 1936- *WhoScE 91-3*
Daskal, Robert H. 1941- *St&PR 93*
Daskal, Steven Edward 1956- *WhoSSW 93*
Dasmann, Raymond Fredric 1919- *WhoAm 92*
Dass, Dean A. 1955- *WhoEmL 93*
Dassanowsky-Harris, Robert 1956- *WhoWrEP 92*
Dassanowsky-Harris, Robert von 1956- *WhoEmL 93*
DasSarma, Basudeb 1923- *WhoAm 92*
Dassas, Alain Patrick 1946- *WhoWor 93*
Dassault, Marcel 1892-1986 *BioIn 17*
Dassen, Willem Rene Marie 1953- *WhoWor 93*
Dassenko, Paul Edward 1951- *WhoEmL 93*
Dasser, Ludwig *Baker 92*
D'Assia, Enrico *BioIn 17*
Dassin, Jules 1911- *MiSFD 9*
Dassios, George 1946- *WhoScE 91-3*
Dassios, George Theodore 1946- *WhoWor 93*
Dassler, A. Fred 1936- *WhoWor 93*
Dasso, Jerome Joseph 1929- *WhoAm 92, WhoWor 93*
Dasso, William J. *Law&B 92*
Dassori, Frederic Davis, Jr. 1942- *WhoAm 92*
D'Asta, Nicholas A. 1953- *St&PR 93*
Daste, Betsy Louise 1950- *WhoAmW 93*
Dasti, Joseph G. 1932- *St&PR 93*
Dastidar, Pranab 1933- *WhoUN 92*
D'Astier de la Vigerie, Emmanuel 1900-1969 *BioIn 17*
D'Astolfo, Frank Joseph 1943- *WhoE 93*
Dastoll, Donald Anthony 1950- *WhoE 93*
Dastuge-Hannetelle, Michele *WhoScE 91-2*
Dastvar, Hassan *BioIn 17*
Daszynski, Ignacy 1860-1936 *PolBiDi*
Daszynski, Janusz 1922- *WhoScE 91-4*
Dat, Phan Huu 1928- *WhoWor 93*
Data, Joann Lucille 1944- *WhoAm 92*
Datars, William Ross 1932- *WhoAm 92*
Date, Elaine Satomi 1957- *WhoEmL 93*
Date, Etsuro 1950- *WhoWor 93*
Date, Masamune 1566-1636 *HarEnMi*
Date, Toshihiro 1931- *WhoWor 93*
Dater, Elizabeth B. *WhoAm 92*
Dater, Judy Lichtenfeld 1941- *WhoAm 92*
Dates, Lois Ann 1952- *WhoE 93, WhoEmL 93*
Datesh, James R. 1955- *St&PR 93*
Datesh, John Nicholas 1950- *ScF&FL 92*
Dathe, Robert F. 1951- *St&PR 93*
Dati, James Donald 1958- *WhoEmL 93*
Datiles, Manuel Bernaldes, III 1951- *WhoE 93, WhoEmL 93, WhoWor 93*
Datin, Xavier 1964- *WhoWor 93*
Datka, Jerzy 1942- *WhoScE 91-4*
Datlow, Ellen 1949- *ScF&FL 92*
Datoo, Bashir Ahmed 1941- *St&PR 93*
Datri, Tamara Jo 1960- *WhoEmL 93*
Datskovsky, Boris Abramovich 1960- *WhoE 93*
Datt, Krishna *WhoAsAP 91*
Datta, Arup Kumar *DcChlFi*
Datta, Prasanta Kumar *WhoScE 91-1*
Datta, Ranajit Kumar 1933- *WhoE 93*
Datta, Subhendu Kumar 1936- *WhoAm 92*
Dattee, Francois Edme 1939- *WhoScE 91-2*
Dattilo, Anton Michael 1953- *WhoEmL 93*
Dattilo, Joseph T. *Law&B 92*
Dattilo, Nicholas C. *WhoAm 92*
Dattilo, Nicholas C. 1932- *WhoE 93*
Dattilo, Thomas A. *WhoAm 92*
Dattilo, Vincent Joseph 1967- *WhoE 93, WhoEmL 93*
Dattner, Benjamin *BioIn 17*
Dattner, John William 1948- *WhoIns 93*
Datuin, Angelena Lucretia Shelton 1961- *WhoSSW 93*
Datz, Israel Mortimer 1928- *WhoAm 92*
Dau, John J. 1926- *St&PR 93*
Daub, Albert Walter 1931- *WhoAm 92, WhoE 93*
Daub, Cindy S. 1944- *WhoAmW 93*
Daub, Gerald Jacob 1953- *WhoEmL 93*
Daub, Hal 1941- *WhoAm 92*
Daub, Jorg F. 1940- *WhoScE 91-3*
Daub, Matthew Forrest 1951- *WhoE 93*
Daub, Richard Paul 1946- *WhoEmL 93*
Daub, Suzanne Marie 1960- *WhoAmW 93*
Daubechies, Ingrid 1954- *WhoAmW 93*
Daubel, James Francis 1941- *St&PR 93*
Dauben, Joseph Warren 1944- *WhoE 93*
Dauben, William Garfield 1919- *WhoAm 92*
Daubenas, Jean Dorothy Tenbrinck *WhoAmW 93*
Daubenspeck, Albert Warren 1951- *St&PR 93*
Daubenspeck, Robert Donley 1926- *WhoAm 92*
Daubenspeck, William L. *Law&B 92*
Dauber, Arthur George 1943- *St&PR 93*
Dauber, Kenneth Marc 1945- *ConAu 37NR*
Daubert, Scott David 1959- *WhoE 93*
Daublaine et Callinet *Baker 92*
Daubs, Michael Steven 1943- *St&PR 93*
D'Aubuisson, Roberto *BioIn 17*
D'aubuisson, Roberto 1943-1992 *CurBio 92N, NewYTBS 92 [port]*
D'Aubuisson Arrieta, Roberto 1943- *DcCPCAm*
Dauca, Michel 1947- *WhoScE 91-2*
Dauch, Richard Eugene 1942- *St&PR 93*
Dauchez, Pierre Guislain 1958- *WhoWor 93*
Daucsavage, Bruce L. 1952- *St&PR 93*
Daud, Ben H. 1939- *St&PR 93*
Daud, David 1954- *ScF&FL 92*
Daud, Munawar 1954- *WhoWor 93*
Daud, Sulaiman Haji 1934- *WhoAsAP 91*
Daudel, Raymond 1920- *WhoScE 91-2*
Daudet, Alphonse 1840-1897 *DcLB 123 [port], OxDcOp*
Daudet, Leon 1867-1942 *BioIn 17*
Dauer, Donald Dean 1936- *WhoAm 92*
Dauer, Edward Arnold 1944- *WhoAm 92*
Dauer, Francis Watanabe 1939- *WhoAm 92*
Dauernheim, Mel A. d1990 *BioIn 17*
Daufin, Evie-Kaiulani 1960- *WhoAmW 93, WhoEmL 93*
Daufin, Georges 1941- *WhoScE 91-2*
Daughaday, William Hamilton 1918- *WhoAm 92*
Daughdrill, James Harold, Jr. 1934- *WhoAm 92*
Daughdrill, Kay Hairston 1942- *WhoAmW 93*
Daughenbaugh, Randall J. 1948- *St&PR 93*
Daughenbaugh, Randall Jay 1948- *WhoAm 92, WhoEmL 93*
Daughenbaugh, Terry L. 1939- *WhoE 93*
Daugherty, Alfred Clark 1923- *St&PR 93, WhoAm 92*
Daugherty, Bettye Dillingham 1936- *WhoAmW 93*
Daugherty, Billy Joe 1923- *WhoAm 92*
Daugherty, Bradley Lee 1965- *WhoAm 92*
Daugherty, Charles A. 1917- *St&PR 93*
Daugherty, Charles James *BioIn 17*
Daugherty, David Martin, Jr. 1951- *WhoEmL 93*
Daugherty, Donald Finley *Law&B 92*
Daugherty, Edward L., Jr. *Law&B 92*
Daugherty, Edward Payson 1956- *WhoEmL 93*
Daugherty, Frederick Alvin 1914- *WhoAm 92*
Daugherty, Gerald E. 1936- *St&PR 93*
Daugherty, Harry M. 1860-1941 *PolPar*
Daugherty, Herschel *MiSFD 9*
Daugherty, Jack Edward 1947- *WhoEmL 93, WhoSSW 93*
Daugherty, James A. *Law&B 92*
Daugherty, James (Henry) 1889-1974 *MajAI [port]*
Daugherty, Jean Marie 1931- *WhoSSW 93*
Daugherty, Jerry Robert 1956- *WhoSSW 93*
Daugherty, Joe *BioIn 17*
Daugherty, John Wayne 1946- *WhoEmL 93*
Daugherty, Linda Hagaman 1940- *WhoAmW 93*
Daugherty, Louis E. 1946- *St&PR 93*
Daugherty, Martha Jane 1928- *WhoSSW 93*
Daugherty, Michael 1954- *Baker 92*
Daugherty, Michael Dennis 1948- *WhoEmL 93*
Daugherty, R.C. 1950- *St&PR 93*
Daugherty, Raymond Edward 1946- *St&PR 93*
Daugherty, Richard Bernard 1915- *WhoAm 92*
Daugherty, Robert A. 1936- *St&PR 93*
Daugherty, Robert Melvin, Jr. 1934- *WhoAm 92*
Daugherty, Robert Michael 1949- *WhoAm 92, WhoEmL 93*
Daugherty, Ron D. *Law&B 92*
Daugherty, Roy 1870-1924 *BioIn 17*
Daugherty, Sonia V. M. *AmWomPl*
Daugherty, Tim S. 1942- *St&PR 93*
Daugherty, William L. 1927- *St&PR 93*
Daughton, Christian Gaaei 1948- *WhoEmL 93*
Daughton, Donald 1932- *WhoAm 92, WhoWor 93*
Daughton, Robert Michael 1949- *St&PR 93*
Daughtrey, Martha Craig 1942- *WhoAm 92, WhoAmW 93, WhoSSW 93*
Daughtrey, Max E. 1947- *St&PR 93*
Daughtrey, Tana J. *Law&B 92*
Daughtrey, William T. 1952- *St&PR 93*
Daughtry, DeWitt Cornell 1914- *WhoAm 92*
Daughtry, Earlie Mitchell 1952- *WhoAmW 93*
Daughtry, Sue Barden 1947- *WhoSSW 93*
Daugs, Edward Herold 1931- *St&PR 93*
D'Augusta, Alfred M. 1941- *St&PR 93, WhoAm 92*
D'Augustine, Robert 1947- *WhoE 93*
Daujare Torres, Felix 1920- *DcMexL*
Dauk, Regis A. 1941- *St&PR 93*
Daukshus, A. Joseph 1948- *WhoE 93*
D'Aulaire, Edgar Parin 1898-1986 *BioIn 17, MajAI [port]*
D'Aulaire, Ingri 1904-1980 *BioIn 17*
d'Aulaire, Ingri (Mortenson Parin) 1904-1980 *MajAI*
Dauler, L. Van V., Jr. 1943- *St&PR 93, WhoAm 92, WhoE 93*
D'Aulnoy, Madame 1650?-1705 *BioIn 17*
Daulton, David Coleman 1937- *St&PR 93, WhoAm 92*
Daum, Bryan Edwin 1949- *WhoEmL 93*
Daum, Conrad Henry 1943- *WhoSSW 93*
Daum, David Ernest 1939- *St&PR 93, WhoAm 92*
Daum, John H. 1907- *St&PR 93*
Daum, Kenneth Arno 1931- *St&PR 93*
Daum, Nancy Lee 1957- *WhoEmL 93*
Daum, Robert Charles 1952- *WhoEmL 93*
Daumas Ladouce, Pablo 1908- *WhoWor 93*
Daume, Daphne Marie 1924- *WhoAmW 93*
Daun, Mary Agnes 1945- *WhoAmW 93*
Daune, Michel *WhoScE 91-2*
Dauney, William 1800-1843 *Baker 92*
Daunt, Joan Otto 1931- *WhoSSW 93*
Daunt, Jon 1951- *WhoWrEP 92*
Dauphin, Sue 1928- *WhoWrEP 92*
Dauphinais, George Arthur 1918 *WhoAm 92*
Dauphine, Andre 1942- *WhoScE 91-2*
Dauprat, Louis-Francois 1781-1868 *Baker 92*
Daure, Bernard *WhoUN 92*
Dauriac, Lionel (-Alexandre) 1847-1923 *Baker 92*
Daurio, Karen Andrea 1962- *WhoAmW 93, WhoEmL 93*
D'Aurora, James Joseph 1949- *WhoEmL 93*
Daus, Anita Dacpano 1935- *WhoAmW 93*
Dauscher, Kenneth R. 1943- *WhoIns 93*
Dauser, Kimberly Ann 1947- *WhoAmW 93, WhoEmL 93*
Dauser, Steven Kent 1952- *WhoSSW 93*
Dauses, Joseph E. 1950- *St&PR 93*
Dausman, George Erwin *WhoAm 92*
Daussant, Jean 1932- *WhoScE 91-2*
Dausset, Jean 1916- *WhoAm 92, WhoWor 93*
Daussman, Grover Frederick 1919- *WhoAm 92, WhoSSW 93, WhoWor 93*
Daussoigne-Mehul, Louis-Joseph 1790-1875 *Baker 92*
Dauster, William Charles 1956- *WhoE 93*
Dauster, William Gary 1957- *WhoE 93, WhoEmL 93*
Daut, Steven William 1951- *WhoEmL 93*
Dautel, Charles Shreve 1923- *WhoAm 92*
Dauterman, Carl Christian 1908-1989 *BioIn 17*
Dauterman, Steven Lynn 1954- *WhoEmL 93*
Dauth, Frances Kutcher 1941- *WhoAm 92*
Dautremont, James H. *Law&B 92*
Dauverchain, Jean 1932- *WhoScE 91-2*
Dauvergne, Antoine 1713-1797 *Baker 92, OxDcOp*
Dauzat, Samuel Varner 1942- *WhoSSW 93*
Dauzier, Louis 1923- *WhoScE 91-2*
Dauzier, Pierre 1939- *WhoWor 93*
Davalos, Balbino 1866-1951 *DcMexL*
Davalos, Juan Carlos 1887-1959 *SpAmA*
Davalos, Marcelino 1871-1923 *DcMexL*
Davant, Charles, III 1946- *WhoSSW 93*
Davant, James Waring 1917- *WhoAm 92*
D'Avanzo, Barbara T. *Law&B 92*
Da Vanzo, Joan Elizabeth 1953- *WhoAmW 93*
Davaux, Jean-Baptiste 1742-1822 *Baker 92*
Davda, Paresh Jayantilal 1949- *St&PR 93*
Dave, Raju S. 1958- *WhoE 93, WhoEmL 93*
D'Avella, John C. 1948- *St&PR 93*
Davelli, Sal 1939- *St&PR 93*
Daveluy, Paule 1919- *WhoCanL 92*
Davenant, William 1606-1668 *DcLB 126 [port], OxDcOp*
Davenel, George Francis 1914- *WhoE 93*
Davenport, Alan Garnett 1932- *WhoAm 92*
Davenport, Anthony Peter 1955- *WhoWor 93*
Davenport, Arnold L. *BioIn 17*
Davenport, Barry M. 1947- *St&PR 93*
Davenport, Cal H. 1929- *WhoSSW 93*
Davenport, Carolyn Wesley 1952- *WhoEmL 93*
Davenport, Charles Benedict 1866-1944 *BioIn 17*
Davenport, Chester 1940- *WhoAm 92*
Davenport, David 1950- *WhoAm 92*
Davenport, David Charles 1948- *WhoSSW 93*
Davenport, David G. *Law&B 92*
Davenport, Dona Lee 1931- *WhoAm 92*
Davenport, Edwin C. 1940- *St&PR 93*
Davenport, Ernest Harold 1917- *WhoAm 92*

Davenport, Fountain St. Clair 1914- *WhoSSW 93*
Davenport, Francis William 1847-1925 *Baker 92*
Davenport, Gerald B. *Law&B 92*
Davenport, Guy Mattison 1927- *WhoWrEP 92*
Davenport, Guy Mattison, Jr. 1927- *WhoAm 92*
Davenport, Gwen 1910- *WhoAm 92, WhoWrEP 92*
Davenport, Horace Willard 1912- *WhoAm 92*
Davenport, Howard *ScF&FL 92*
Davenport, James 1716-1757 *BioIn 17*
Davenport, James Harold *WhoScE 91-1*
Davenport, John 1597-1670 *BioIn 17*
Davenport, John L. *Law&B 92*
Davenport, John T. 1930- *St&PR 93*
Davenport, Joseph Dale 1931- *WhoSSW 93*
Davenport, Judith Ann 1944- *WhoAmW 93*
Davenport, Karen Odom 1953- *WhoWrEP 92*
Davenport, Kay 1950- *St&PR 93*
Davenport, Lawrence Franklin 1944- *WhoAm 92*
Davenport, Lee L. 1915- *St&PR 93*
Davenport, Linda G. 1949- *St&PR 93*
Davenport, Manuel Manson 1929- *WhoAm 92*
Davenport, Marcia 1903- *BioIn 17*
Davenport, Michael G. *St&PR 93*
Davenport, Michael R.C. *Law&B 92*
Davenport, Norma Elaine *Law&B 92*
Davenport, Novetah H. d1992 *NewYTBS 92*
Davenport, Pamela Beaver 1948- *WhoAmW 93*
Davenport, Patricia Marie 1948- *WhoEmL 93*
Davenport, Paul *WhoAm 92*
Davenport, Paul S., Jr. 1941- *St&PR 93*
Davenport, Robert Newton *Law&B 92*
Davenport, Robert Raymond *WhoScE 91-1*
Davenport, Roger 1946- *ScF&FL 92*
Davenport, Sally Ann 1935- *St&PR 93*
Davenport, W. Bennett 1931- *WhoIns 93*
Davenport, Wilbur Bayley, Jr. 1920- *WhoAm 92*
Davenport, William Kirk *Law&B 92*
Davenport, William Kirk 1928- *St&PR 93*
Davenson, Wendy H. 1943- *WhoE 93*
Daventry, Leonard 1915- *ScF&FL 92*
Daver, Edul Minoo 1944- *St&PR 93*
Daves, Delmer 1904-1977 *MiSFD 9N*
Daves, George 1867-1888 *BioIn 17*
Daves, Glenn Doyle, Jr. 1936- *WhoAm 92*
Daves, Priscilla Eugenia 1948- *WhoSSW 93*
Daves, Suanne Melanie 1959- *WhoAmW 93*
Davey, Bruce James 1927- *St&PR 93, WhoAm 92*
Davey, Charles Bingham 1928- *WhoAm 92*
Davey, Clark William 1928- *St&PR 93, WhoAm 92, WhoE 93, WhoWor 93*
Davey, Frank 1940- *WhoCanL 92*
Davey, Janet Calonge 1956- *WhoWrEP 92*
Davey, Janet Christopherson 1928- *WhoAmW 93*
Davey, John 1937- *ScF&FL 92*
Davey, Kenneth George 1932- *WhoAm 92*
Davey, Kenneth Jackson *WhoScE 91-1*
Davey, Lycurgus Michael 1918- *WhoAm 92*
Davey, Robert Charles 1938- *WhoAm 92*
Davi, Antonio E. 1924- *St&PR 93*
Davi, Horace Jean 1945- *WhoWor 93*
Daviau, Allen *WhoAm 92*
Daviau, Allen 1942- *ConTFT 10*
Davico, Vincenzo 1889-1969 *Baker 92*
David, King of Israel *BioIn 17*
David, IV, The Restorer *OxDcByz*
David, A.R. *ConAu 37NR*
David, A(nn) Rosalie 1946- *ConAu 37NR*
David, Ann Anita 1910- *WhoAmW 93*
David, Ann Marie 1964- *WhoAmW 93*
David, Bruce Edward 1952- *WhoWrEP 92*
David, Bruce Kent 1947- *WhoEmL 93*
David, Catherine Anne 1963- *WhoAmW 93, WhoEmL 93*
David, Clive 1934- *WhoAm 92*
David, Diana Lee 1952- *WhoAmW 93*
David, Edgeworth 1858-1934 *BioIn 17*
David, Edward Joseph 1942- *WhoE 93*
David, Elizabeth d1992 *NewYTBS 92 [port]*
David, Elizabeth 1913-1992 *BioIn 17*
David, Emily *AmWomPl*
David, Felicien 1810-1876 *BioIn 17, OxDcOp*
David, Felicien (-Cesar) 1810-1876 *Baker 92*
David, Ferdinand 1810-1873 *Baker 92*
David, Gabriel Samuel 1951- *WhoEmL 93*
David, Gabrielle 1947- *WhoEmL 93*
David, George *Law&B 92*
David, George Alfred Lawrence 1942- *WhoAm 92*
David, Giacomo 1750-1830 *Baker 92, OxDcOp*
David, Gilbert 1946- *WhoCanL 92*
David, Giovanni 1790-1864 *Baker 92, OxDcOp*
David, Giuseppina 1821-1907 *OxDcOp*
David, Gyula 1913-1977 *Baker 92*
David, Hal *WhoAm 92*
David, Hal 1921- *Baker 92*
David, Hans T(heodor) 1902-1967 *Baker 92*
David, Herbert Aron 1925- *WhoAm 92*
David, Jack E. 1937- *St&PR 93*
David, Jack W. 1943- *St&PR 93*
David, Jacklin Kim 1960- *WhoAmW 93*
David, Jacques-Louis 1748-1825 *BioIn 17*
David, James Milton 1942- *St&PR 93*
David, Jean-Frederic 1928- *WhoScE 91-2*
David, Jean Robert 1931- *WhoScE 91-2*
David, Johann Nepomuk 1895-1977 *Baker 92*
David, John Robert 1947- *St&PR 93*
David, Jose 1913- *Baker 92*
David, Joseph Ben- *BioIn 17*
David, Karl Heinrich 1884-1951 *Baker 92*
David, Larry Fay 1949- *WhoSSW 93*
David, Leon 1867-1962 *Baker 92*
David, Leon Thomas 1901- *WhoWor 93*
David, Leona T. 1930- *St&PR 93*
David, Leonard A. *Law&B 92*
David, Lolita *ConTFT 10*
David, Lynn Allen 1948- *WhoEmL 93*
David, Mack 1912- *Baker 92*
David, Madeleine Paul- 1908-1989 *BioIn 17*
David, Marjorie 1950- *ScF&FL 92*
David, Martha Lena Huffaker 1925- *WhoAmW 93*
David, Martin A. 1939- *WhoWrEP 92*
David, Martin Heidenhain 1935- *WhoAm 92*
David, Mary Sue 1930- *WhoAmW 93, WhoSSW 93*
David, Melvin J. 1915- *St&PR 93*
David, Michel Louis 1945- *WhoAm 92*
David, Miles 1926- *WhoAm 92*
David, Miriam Lang 1945- *WhoAm 92*
David, Neal O. 1950- *St&PR 93*
David, Nora Ratcliff 1913- *BioIn 17*
David, Pamela Ray 1954- *WhoSSW 93*
David, Paul Theodore 1906- *WhoAm 92*
David, Peter 1956- *ScF&FL 92*
David, Philip 1931- *St&PR 93, WhoWor 93*
David, Rene 1949- *WhoScE 91-2*
David, Richard Francis 1938- *WhoAm 92*
David, Richard H. 1931- *St&PR 93*
David, Robert Paine 1939- *WhoE 93*
David, Ronald Albert 1951- *WhoEmL 93*
David, Rosalie *ConAu 37NR*
David, Samuel 1836-1895 *Baker 92*
David, Shirley Hart 1949- *WhoEmL 93*
David, Stephen Paul 1957- *WhoEmL 93*
David, Steven Howard *Law&B 92*
David, Theresa 1959- *WhoEmL 93*
David, Thomas Christian 1925- *Baker 92*
David, Thomas Meredith 1941- *WhoAm 92*
David, Vicente C. 1930- *WhoWor 93*
David, Winifred M. *AmWomPl*
David d'Angers, Pierre-Jean 1788-1856 *BioIn 17*
Davidenko, Alexander 1899-1934 *Baker 92*
Davidescu, Velicica 1936- *WhoScE 91-4*
Davidesz, Janos 1929- *WhoScE 91-4*
Davidge, Anne Marjorie 1957- *WhoE 93*
Davidge, Robert Cunninghame, Jr. 1942- *WhoAm 92*
Davidian, Janice Ann 1932- *WhoAmW 93*
Davidian, Tim N. 1946- *St&PR 93*
Davidio, Joseph A. *Law&B 92*
David Komnenos d1212 *OxDcByz*
David Komnenos, I c. 1407-1463 *OxDcByz*
David-Neel, Alexandra 1868-1969 *BioIn 17, Expl 93 [port]*
David Nolan, Catherine S. 1957- *St&PR 93*
Davidoff, E. Martin 1952- *WhoE 93*
Davidoff, Howard 1956- *WhoEmL 93*
Davidoff, Michail 1940- *WhoScE 91-4*
Davidoff, Robert George 1926- *St&PR 93*
Davidoff, Roger 1949- *WhoEmL 93*
David of Mytilene 716-783? *OxDcByz*
David Of Tayk'/Tao d1000 *OxDcByz*
David Of Thessalonike c. 450-c. 540 *OxDcByz*
Davidon, William Cooper 1927- *WhoE 93, WhoWor 93*
Davidov, Carl 1838-1889 *Baker 92*
Davidov, Johann Todorov 1949- *WhoWor 93*
Davidov, Louis Philip 1953- *WhoE 93*
Davidov, M. *WhoScE 91-1*
Davidov, Stepan Ivanovich 1777-1825 *Baker 92*
Davidovich, Bella 1928- *Baker 92, WhoAm 92, WhoAmW 93*
Davidovich, Lolita *BioIn 17*
Davidovich, Lolita 1961?- *ConTFT 10*
Davidovits, Paul 1935- *WhoE 93*
Davidovsky, Mario 1934- *Baker 92, WhoAm 92*
Davidow, Glenn Robert 1958- *WhoEmL 93*
Davidow, Harry M. *Law&B 92*
Davidow, Joseph Russell 1955- *WhoE 93*
Davidow, Robert 1947- *WhoAm 92, WhoEmL 93*
Davidow, Stanley *St&PR 93*
Davidow, William Henry 1935- *St&PR 93*
Davidowitz, Sherman 1927- *St&PR 93*
Davids, Glenn Corey 1951- *WhoEmL 93*
Davids, Hollace Goodman 1947- *WhoEmL 93*
Davids, Norman 1918- *WhoAm 92*
Davids, Peter 1944- *WhoScE 91-3*
Davids, Robert Norman 1938- *WhoWor 93*
Davidse, Gerard John, II 1953- *WhoEmL 93*
Davidson, A.N. 1930- *WhoIns 93*
Davidson, Abraham A. 1935- *WhoAm 92*
Davidson, Ada Clark 1882- *AmWomPl*
Davidson, Adam *BioIn 17*
Davidson, Alan 1943- *ScF&FL 92*
Davidson, Alan H. 1952- *WhoScE 91-1*
Davidson, Alan John 1938- *St&PR 93*
Davidson, Alberta 1957- *WhoAmW 93*
Davidson, Alexander 1934- *WhoUN 92*
Davidson, Alexander George *WhoScE 91-1*
Davidson, Alexander Kent 1935- *WhoAm 92*
Davidson, Alexander Turnbull 1947- *St&PR 93*
Davidson, Alfred Edward 1911- *WhoAm 92*
Davidson, Allain G., Jr. 1943- *St&PR 93*
Davidson, Angela *ScF&FL 92*
Davidson, Ann D. *Law&B 92*
Davidson, Anne Stowell *Law&B 92*
Davidson, Anne Stowell 1949- *WhoAmW 93*
Davidson, Arnold Edward 1936- *WhoSSW 93*
Davidson, Avram 1923- *BioIn 17, ScF&FL 92*
Davidson, Barbara Taylor 1920- *WhoAmW 93*
Davidson, Barry Daniel 1960- *WhoE 93*
Davidson, Barry Rodney 1943- *WhoSSW 93*
Davidson, Ben d1991 *BioIn 17*
Davidson, Bill 1918- *WhoWor 93*
Davidson, Boaz 1943- *MiSFD 9*
Davidson, Bonnie Jean 1941- *WhoWor 93*
Davidson, Bruce Merrill 1924- *WhoAm 92*
Davidson, Carl B. 1933- *WhoAm 92*
Davidson, Carl Barry 1933- *St&PR 93*
Davidson, Cathy N. 1949- *ScF&FL 92*
Davidson, Cathy Notari 1949- *WhoAm 92*
Davidson, Chalmers Gaston 1907- *WhoAm 92, WhoWrEP 92*
Davidson, Chandler 1936- *WhoSSW 93*
Davidson, Charles H. *BioIn 17*
Davidson, Charles Sprecher 1910- *WhoAm 92*
Davidson, Charles T. 1940- *St&PR 93*
Davidson, Cheryl Adair 1949- *St&PR 93*
Davidson, Cliff Ian 1950- *WhoE 93*
Davidson, Colin Henry 1928- *WhoAm 92*
Davidson, Craig J. 1954-1991 *BioIn 17*
Davidson, Crow Girard 1910- *WhoAm 92*
Davidson, Cynthia Gay 1960- *WhoAmW 93*
Davidson, Dalwyn Robert 1918- *WhoAm 92*
Davidson, Dan Eugene 1944- *WhoE 93*
Davidson, Daniel Everett 1949- *WhoEmL 93*
Davidson, Daniel Joseph 1958- *St&PR 93*
Davidson, David Edward, Jr. 1935- *WhoUN 92*
Davidson, David Scott 1925- *WhoAm 92*
Davidson, Dennis Keith 1941- *St&PR 93*
Davidson, Diane *Law&B 92*
Davidson, Donald 1917- *BioIn 17*
Davidson, Donald 1921- *St&PR 93*
Davidson, Donald H. d1991 *BioIn 17*
Davidson, Donald Herbert 1917- *WhoAm 92*
Davidson, Donald William 1938- *WhoAm 92, WhoE 93*
Davidson, Douglas A. 1936- *WhoAm 92*
Davidson, Douglas Alvin 1936- *St&PR 93*
Davidson, Douglas G. *Law&B 92*
Davidson, Duncan Lewis Watt *WhoScE 91-1*
Davidson, Duncan Mowbray 1953- *WhoEmL 93*
Davidson, Earnest Jefferson 1946- *WhoSSW 93*
Davidson, Edmund B. 1936- *St&PR 93*
Davidson, Edward H. 1912- *ScF&FL 92*
Davidson, Edward W., Jr. 1937- *St&PR 93*
Davidson, Eleanor Gaddis *AmWomPl*
Davidson, Eric Harris 1937- *WhoAm 92*
Davidson, Ernest Roy 1936- *WhoAm 92*
Davidson, Eugene Abraham 1930- *WhoAm 92*
Davidson, Eugene Arthur 1902- *WhoAm 92*
Davidson, Ezra C., Jr. 1933- *WhoAm 92, WhoWor 93*
Davidson, Francoise 1925- *WhoScE 91-2*
Davidson, Frank Geoffrey 1920- *WhoWor 93*
Davidson, Frank P(aul) 1918- *ConAu 40NR*
Davidson, Frank Paul 1918- *WhoE 93*
Davidson, Frederic McShan 1941- *WhoAm 92*
Davidson, Gail S. 1941- *WhoAm 92*
Davidson, Gail S. 1943- *WhoAmW 93*
Davidson, Garrison Holt 1904-1992 *NewYTBS 92*
Davidson, Gary 1946- *St&PR 93*
Davidson, Gary Edward 1959- *WhoEmL 93*
Davidson, George A., Jr. 1938- *St&PR 93*
Davidson, George Forrester 1909- *WhoAm 92*
Davidson, George H. 1944- *St&PR 93*
Davidson, Gerry *BioIn 17*
Davidson, Glen Everette 1925- *St&PR 93*
Davidson, Glen Harris 1941- *WhoAm 92, WhoSSW 93*
Davidson, Gordon 1933- *MiSFD 9, WhoAm 92*
Davidson, Gordon Byron 1926- *WhoAm 92*
Davidson, Gordon Chambers 1927- *St&PR 93*
Davidson, Grace Evelyn 1920- *WhoAmW 93*
Davidson, H. Justin 1930- *St&PR 93*
Davidson, Harry Lee 1956- *WhoEmL 93*
Davidson, Herbert Alan 1932- *WhoAm 92*
Davidson, Herbert M. Tippen, Jr. 1925- *WhoAm 92*
Davidson, Herbert S. 1922- *St&PR 93*
Davidson, Howard Steven 1955- *St&PR 93*
Davidson, Ian Bruce 1931- *St&PR 93*
Davidson, Jack Leroy 1927- *WhoAm 92*
Davidson, James Arthur 1946- *WhoEmL 93*
Davidson, James E. 1957- *St&PR 93*
Davidson, James P. *Law&B 92*
Davidson, Janet Toll 1939- *WhoAmW 93*
Davidson, Jaye *NewYTBS 92 [port]*
Davidson, Jean Dail 1930- *WhoAmW 93*
Davidson, Jeannie 1938- *WhoWor 93*
Davidson, Jeff Alan 1961- *WhoE 93*
Davidson, Jeffery H. 1946- *St&PR 93*
Davidson, Jeffrey H. 1952- *WhoEmL 93*
Davidson, Jeffrey Owen *Law&B 92*
Davidson, Jo 1883-1952 *BioIn 17*
Davidson, Joan Gather 1934- *WhoAmW 93*
Davidson, Joan K. 1927- *St&PR 93*
Davidson, Joan Rebecca Lipson 1940- *WhoE 93*
Davidson, Joel E. *Law&B 92*
Davidson, John 1857-1909 *BioIn 17*
Davidson, John 1916- *WhoAm 92*
Davidson, John Frank *WhoScE 91-1*
Davidson, John Herbert 1938- *St&PR 93*
Davidson, John Kenneth, Sr. 1939- *WhoAm 92, WhoWor 93*
Davidson, John Pirnie 1924- *WhoAm 92*
Davidson, John Robert 1947- *WhoEmL 93, WhoWor 93*
Davidson, Joy Elaine 1940- *WhoAm 92*
Davidson, Judith Ann 1947- *WhoE 93*
Davidson, Juli 1960- *WhoAmW 93, WhoEmL 93, WhoWor 93*
Davidson, Karen Green 1960- *WhoAmW 93*
Davidson, Karen Sue 1950- *WhoAmW 93, WhoEmL 93, WhoWor 93*
Davidson, Kenneth Eugene 1951- *WhoEmL 93*
Davidson, Kevin D. 1953- *St&PR 93*
Davidson, Lacinda Susan 1958- *WhoAm 92*
Davidson, Larry 1960- *WhoE 93*
Davidson, Lillian *AmWomPl*
Davidson, Lionel 1922- *ScF&FL 92*
Davidson, Louis E. *Law&B 92*
Davidson, Louise T. 1931- *WhoAmW 93*
Davidson, Lyle 1938- *Baker 92*
Davidson, Lynda S. 1934- *St&PR 93*
Davidson, Marc Leon 1954- *St&PR 93, WhoSSW 93*
Davidson, Marcella Schools 1952- *WhoAmW 93, WhoEmL 93*
Davidson, Marie Diane 1924- *WhoAmW 93*
Davidson, Marilyn Hanrahan 1930- *WhoAmW 93*
Davidson, Marion Lamont *AmWomPl*

Davidson, Mark 1940- *ConAu 138*
Davidson, Mark Rogers 1962- *WhoSSW 93*
Davidson, Mark Steven 1959- *WhoSSW 93*
Davidson, Martin 1939- *ConTFT 10, MiSFD 9*
Davidson, Mary Frances Logue 1958- *WhoAmW 93*
Davidson, Mary Richmond *AmWomPl*
Davidson, Mary S. 1940- *BioIn 17*
Davidson, Mary Theresa 1952- *WhoAmW 93*
Davidson, Maureen Kathryn 1951- *WhoSSW 93*
Davidson, Max 1955- *ConAu 139*
Davidson, Mayer B. 1935- *WhoAm 92*
Davidson, Megan *Law&B 92*
Davidson, Melvin L. 1936- *St&PR 93*
Davidson, Michael *ConAu 38NR, ScF&FL 92*
Davidson, Michael 1940- *WhoAm 92*
Davidson, Michael J. *Law&B 92*
Davidson, Michael Samuel 1938- *WhoE 93*
Davidson, Michael W. *Law&B 92*
Davidson, Michael Walker 1947- *WhoAm 92*
Davidson, Michael William *Law&B 92*
Davidson, Miles E. *Law&B 92*
Davidson, Nancy Elaine 1946- *WhoAmW 93*
Davidson, Neil 1941- *WhoWor 93*
Davidson, Noreen Hanna 1950- *WhoAmW 93*
Davidson, Norman Ralph 1916- *WhoAm 92*
Davidson, O. Wesley 1903-1991 *BioIn 17*
Davidson, P. Marques 1939- *St&PR 93*
Davidson, Park R. 1934- *St&PR 93*
Davidson, Paul *BioIn 17*
Davidson, Paul James *WhoScE 91-1*
Davidson, Paul Michael 1941- *WhoE 93*
Davidson, Peggy Eileen 1947- *WhoAmW 93*
Davidson, Philip D. 1931- *St&PR 93*
Davidson, Phillip B. 1915- *BioIn 17*
Davidson, Phillip T. 1925- *St&PR 93*
Davidson, Ralph Kirby 1921- *WhoAm 92*
Davidson, Ralph Parsons 1927- *St&PR 93, WhoAm 92*
Davidson, Randall W. *BioIn 17*
Davidson, Randolph L. 1955- *St&PR 93*
Davidson, Richard Alan 1946- *WhoWor 93*
Davidson, Richard D. 1948- *St&PR 93*
Davidson, Richard J. *BioIn 17*
Davidson, Richard John 1954- *St&PR 93*
Davidson, Richard K. 1942- *St&PR 93, WhoAm 92*
Davidson, Robert A. 1947- *St&PR 93*
Davidson, Robert Bruce 1945- *WhoAm 92*
Davidson, Robert Church 1932- *WhoSSW 93*
Davidson, Robert K. *ScF&FL 92*
Davidson, Robert Laurenson Dashiell 1909- *WhoAm 92*
Davidson, Robert Lee, III 1923- *WhoWrEP 92*
Davidson, Robert Michael 1941- *WhoE 93*
Davidson, Robert Stephen *WhoScE 91-1*
Davidson, Roger Harry 1936- *WhoAm 92, WhoE 93*
Davidson, Ronald Adolphe 1935- *WhoUN 92*
Davidson, Ronald Crosby 1941- *WhoAm 92*
Davidson, Rosalie *BioIn 17*
Davidson, Roy Grady, Jr. 1922- *WhoSSW 93*
Davidson, Sandra Lee Dresman 1947- *WhoEmL 93*
Davidson, Sigmund Edward 1922- *St&PR 93*
Davidson, Simon David 1927- *St&PR 93*
Davidson, Steven C. 1953- *St&PR 93*
Davidson, Steven J. 1950- *WhoE 93*
Davidson, Suzanne M. *Law&B 92*
Davidson, Thomas Ferguson 1930- *WhoWor 93*
Davidson, Thomas Maxwell 1937- *St&PR 93, WhoAm 92*
Davidson, Thomas N. 1939- *St&PR 93*
Davidson, Thomas Noel 1939- *WhoAm 92*
Davidson, Tina 1952- *Baker 92*
Davidson, Tommy *BioIn 17*
Davidson, Wayne A. 1931- *WhoAm 92*
Davidson, William Francis 1968- *WhoE 93*
Davidson, William G. *BioIn 17*
Davidson, William M. 1921- *WhoAm 92*
Davidson, William Ward, III 1940- *WhoWor 93*
Davidson-Moore, Kathy Louise 1949- *WhoAmW 93*
David The Philosopher 6th cent.- *OxDcByz*
David-Weill, Michel Alexandre 1932- *WhoAm 92*
Davie, Bruce Fenwick 1936- *WhoE 93*
Davie, Donald *BioIn 17*
Davie, Donald Alfred 1922- *WhoAm 92*
Davie, Frank *AfrAmBi [port]*
Davie, Joseph Myrten 1939- *WhoAm 92*
Davie, Malcolm Henderson 1918- *WhoE 93, WhoWor 93*
Davier, Michel 1942- *WhoScE 91-2*
Davies, A.J.E. 1939- *WhoScE 91-1*
Davies, A.J.S. *WhoScE 91-1*
Davies, Alfred Robert 1933- *WhoAm 92*
Davies, Alison Gwen *WhoScE 91-1*
Davies, Alma *WhoE 93*
Davies, Alwyn George *WhoScE 91-1*
Davies, Alwyn George 1926- *WhoWor 93*
Davies, Andrew 1936- *ScF&FL 92*
Davies, Andrew (Wynford) 1936- *ChlFicS*
Davies, Anthony Christopher *WhoScE 91-1*
Davies, Anthony Edmund Josephs Adrian 1965- *WhoE 93*
Davies, Anthony James *WhoScE 91-1*
Davies, Beaumont John *WhoScE 91-1*
Davies, Ben(jamin) Grey 1858-1943 *Baker 92*
Davies, Benjamin Trevor *WhoScE 91-1*
Davies, Bob 1920-1990 *BioIn 17*
Davies, Brian E. *WhoScE 91-1*
Davies, Brian Michael *WhoWor 93*
Davies, Bryan Allen 1955- *WhoE 93*
Davies, C.J. David 1936- *St&PR 93*
Davies, Carol Ann 1951- *WhoAmW 93*
Davies, Cecilia 1756?-1836 *OxDcOp*
Davies, Charles R. *Law&B 92*
Davies, Charles Travers d1990 *BioIn 17*
Davies, Christopher J. 1959- *WhoEmL 93*
Davies, Cyril Thomas Mervyn *WhoScE 91-1*
Davies, D. Keith 1934- *WhoScE 91-1*
Davies, Daniel R. 1911- *WhoAm 92*
Davies, David *BioIn 17*
Davies, David Brian 1950- *WhoIns 93*
Davies, David George 1928- *WhoAm 92*
Davies, David Keith 1940- *WhoAm 92, WhoWor 93*
Davies, David Llewellyn 1941- *WhoE 93*
Davies, David Rees *Law&B 92*
Davies, David Roy *WhoScE 91-1*
Davies, Dennis Russell 1944- *Baker 92, WhoAm 92*
Davies, Diane Marie 1952- *WhoEmL 93*
Davies, Douglas Lowell *Law&B 92*
Davies, Douglas R. *Law&B 92*
Davies, Duane Alan 1953- *St&PR 93*
Davies, Edward Brian *WhoScE 91-1*
Davies, Edward James 1933- *St&PR 93*
Davies, Elizabeth Ann 1961- *WhoE 93*
Davies, Elizabeth Ursula 1958- *WhoWor 93*
Davies, Eurfil Rhys *WhoScE 91-1*
Davies, Evan Thomas 1919- *St&PR 93*
Davies, F.L. *WhoScE 91-1*
Davies, Fanny 1861-1934 *Baker 92*
Davies, G.H. *St&PR 93*
Davies, Gareth 1930- *BioIn 17*
Davies, Gareth John 1944- *WhoAm 92*
Davies, Geoffrey 1942- *WhoE 93*
Davies, George *BioIn 17*
Davies, Gerald Andrew 1957- *WhoWrEP 92*
Davies, Glyn A.O. *WhoScE 91-1*
Davies, Graham John 1953- *St&PR 93*
Davies, Graham Michael 1943- *WhoWor 93*
Davies, Gregory Lane 1951- *WhoEmL 93*
Davies, Guy *BioIn 17*
Davies, Gwen Ffrangcon- 1891-1992 *BioIn 17*
Davies, H.S. *WhoScE 91-1*
Davies, Horton Marlais 1916- *WhoAm 92*
Davies, Howard Edmundson *WhoScE 91-1*
Davies, Howard John 1951- *WhoWor 93*
Davies, Hugh Marlais 1948- *WhoAm 92*
Davies, Hugh (Seymour) 1943- *Baker 92*
Davies, Hugh Sykes 1909-1984 *ScF&FL 92*
Davies, (Edward) Hunter 1936- *ChlFicS*
Davies, Huw C. 1944- *WhoScE 91-4*
Davies, J(ohn) D(avid) 1957- *ConAu 139*
Davies, Jack L. 1923- *St&PR 93*
Davies, James John *WhoScE 91-1*
Davies, James Jump 1941- *WhoSSW 93*
Davies, James Scott 1958- *WhoEmL 93*
Davies, Jane Badger 1913- *WhoAm 92, WhoAmW 93, WhoE 93*
Davies, Jeffrey William *WhoScE 91-1*
Davies, Jennifer (Eileen) 1950- *ConAu 139*
Davies, Jo Ann 1948- *WhoE 93*
Davies, Joan *ScF&FL 92*
Davies, John *MiSFD 9*
Davies, John 1934- *MiSFD 9*
Davies, John Arthur 1927- *WhoAm 92*
Davies, John Brian *WhoScE 91-1*
Davies, John Dale 1927- *St&PR 93, WhoAm 92*
Davies, John E. 1936- *St&PR 93*
Davies, John Edward 1936- *WhoAm 92*
Davies, John Eric *WhoScE 91-1*
Davies, John G. 1929- *WhoAm 92*
Davies, John H. 1936- *St&PR 93*
Davies, John Howard *WhoScE 91-1*
Davies, John Michael *WhoScE 91-1*
Davies, John Michael 1939- *WhoWor 93*
Davies, John William 1934- *WhoScE 91-1*
Davies, Kent Richard 1947- *WhoWrEP 92*
Davies, L.P. 1914- *ScF&FL 92*
Davies, Laura J. *Law&B 92*
Davies, Lee A. 1950- *St&PR 93*
Davies, Loma G. 1934- *ConAu 137*
Davies, Marcus Owen 1928- *St&PR 93*
Davies, Maria Thompson *AmWomPl*
Davies, Marilyn Anne 1949- *WhoEmL 93*
Davies, Marion 1897-1961 *BioIn 17, IntDcF 2-3 [port]*
Davies, Mary Carolyn *AmWomPl*
Davies, Meredith 1922- *Baker 92*
Davies, Michael John *WhoScE 91-1*
Davies, Michael L. *St&PR 93*
Davies, Michael Norman *Law&B 92*
Davies, Michael Norman Arden 1932- *WhoAm 92*
Davies, Myrta Little 1888- *AmWomPl*
Davies, Neville *WhoScE 91-1*
Davies, Nicholas E. 1926-1991 *BioIn 17*
Davies, Nick 1953- *ConAu 136*
Davies, Ogden R. 1913- *St&PR 93*
Davies, P.T. *WhoScE 91-1*
Davies, Paul 1946- *ScF&FL 92*
Davies, Paul Lewis, Jr. 1930- *WhoAm 92*
Davies, Paul R. *WhoIns 93*
Davies, Pete 1959- *ScF&FL 92*
Davies, Peter John 1940- *WhoAm 92*
Davies, Peter Maxwell 1934- *Baker 92, IntDcOp, OxDcOp, WhoWor 93*
Davies, Peter Owen Alfred Lawe *WhoScE 91-1*
Davies, Philip Andrew 1962- *WhoWor 93*
Davies, Philip H. *Law&B 92*
Davies, Philip John 1948- *ScF&FL 92*
Davies, Phillip Anthony *WhoScE 91-1*
Davies, R. Scott 1944- *WhoAm 92*
Davies, Ray *MiSFD 9*
Davies, Raymond Douglas 1944- *WhoAm 92*
Davies, Richard B. *WhoScE 91-1*
Davies, Richard Owen 1931- *WhoE 93*
Davies, Richard Warren *Law&B 92*
Davies, Richard Warren 1946- *St&PR 93*
Davies, Robert *WhoScE 91-1*
Davies, Robert 1935- *WhoWor 93*
Davies, Robert 1940- *St&PR 93*
Davies, Robert Abel, III 1935- *WhoAm 92*
Davies, Robert Allan 1928- *WhoWrEP 92*
Davies, Robert B. d1990 *BioIn 17*
Davies, Robert Ernest 1919- *WhoAm 92*
Davies, Robert Evan 1931- *St&PR 93*
Davies, Robert Thomas 1954- *WhoWor 93*
Davies, Robertson 1913- *BioIn 17, ConLC 75 [port], IntLitE, MagSWL [port], ScF&FL 92, WhoAm 92, WhoCanL 92, WhoWrEP 92, WorLitC [port]*
Davies, Ronald F. 1932- *St&PR 93*
Davies, Ronald Wynn 1941- *WhoAm 92*
Davies, Rupert Eric 1909- *ConAu 39NR*
Davies, Ryland 1943- *Baker 92, OxDcOp*
Davies, S. Connally 1961- *WhoAmW 93*
Davies, Sally Kevill *ConAu 138*
Davies, Simon William 1957- *WhoWor 93*
Davies, Sonja M.L. 1923- *WhoAsAP 91*
Davies, Stephen William *WhoScE 91-1*
Davies, Sue *BioIn 17*
Davies, Suzan *ScF&FL 92*
Davies, Suzanne Kaye 1940- *St&PR 93*
Davies, Terence *MiSFD 9*
Davies, Theodore Peter 1928- *WhoAm 92*
Davies, Thomas *ScF&FL 92*
Davies, Thomas D. 1914-1991 *BioIn 17*
Davies, Thomas Mockett, Jr. 1940- *WhoAm 92*
Davies, Thomas Summers 1909?-1989 *BioIn 17*
Davies, Thomas William 1946- *WhoSSW 93*
Davies, Todd E. *Law&B 92*
Davies, Tom *ScF&FL 92*
Davies, Tudor 1892-1958 *Baker 92, OxDcOp*
Davies, Tudor Thomas 1938- *WhoAm 92*
Davies, W.X. *ScF&FL 92*
Davies, Walford 1869-1941 *Baker 92*
Davies, Wayne *BioIn 17*
Davies, Wendy Jeanne 1965- *WhoAmW 93*
Davies, Wilfred 1929- *ScF&FL 92*
Davies, William D., Jr. 1928- *WhoAm 92*
Davies, William E. 1917-1990 *BioIn 17*
Davies, William J. 1947- *St&PR 93*
Davies, William Robert 1942- *WhoE 93*
Davies, William Robertson 1913- *BioIn 17*
Davies-McNair, Jane 1922- *WhoAmW 93, WhoWor 93*
Davies of Hereford, John 1565?-1618 *DcLB 121 [port]*
Davies-Owen, Shirley 1937- *WhoWrEP 92*
Davies-Sekle, Michael P. *Law&B 92*
D'Avignon, R. Joseph *Law&B 92*
Davila, Elisa 1944- *WhoAmW 93*
Davila, Jacques *BioIn 17*
Davila, Maria Amparo 1928- *DcMexL*
Davila, Ramon 1953- *WhoWor 93*
Davila, Robert R. *BioIn 17*
Davila, William S. 1931- *WhoAm 92*
Davin, James Manson 1945- *St&PR 93*
Davin, James Martin 1958- *WhoEmL 93, WhoSSW 93*
Davin, Nicholas Flood 1840?-1901 *BioIn 17*
Da Vinci, Leonardo 1452-1519 *BioIn 17*
Davini, Vittorio 1921- *WhoScE 91-3*
Davinic, Prvoslav 1938- *WhoUN 92*
D'Avino, Rick *Law&B 92*
Davio, Joseph A. 1951- *St&PR 93*
Davion, Ethel Johnson 1948- *WhoAmW 93, WhoEmL 93*
Davis, A. Arthur 1928- *WhoAm 92*
Davis, A. Dano 1945- *St&PR 93, WhoSSW 93*
Davis, A. Jann 1941- *WhoWrEP 92*
Davis, Al *BioIn 17*
Davis, Alan C. *Law&B 92*
Davis, Alan J. 1925- *BioIn 17*
Davis, Albert 1923- *St&PR 93*
Davis, Albert Belisle 1947- *ConAu 138*
Davis, Alfred Lewis 1941- *WhoSSW 93*
Davis, Algenita Scott *BioIn 17, Law&B 92*
Davis, Allan S. 1926- *St&PR 93*
Davis, Allen 1929- *WhoAm 92*
Davis, Allen, III 1929- *WhoWrEP 92*
Davis, Allen Freeman 1931- *WhoAm 92, WhoE 93*
Davis, Alline Elizabeth d1991 *BioIn 17*
Davis, (William) Allison 1902-1983 *EncAACR*
Davis, Altovise *BioIn 17*
Davis, Alvin H. 1928- *WhoSSW 93*
Davis, Andre LeRoy 1965- *WhoE 93*
Davis, Andrew *MiSFD 9*
Davis, Andrew 1944- *OxDcOp, WhoWor 93*
Davis, Andrew (Frank) 1944- *Baker 92, WhoAm 92, WhoE 93*
Davis, Andrew Hambley, Jr. 1937- *WhoE 93*
Davis, Angela 1944- *EncAACR*
Davis, Angela Diane *Law&B 92*
Davis, Angela Yvonne 1944- *BioIn 17*
Davis, Ann 1946- *ConAu 137*
Davis, Ann B. 1926- *BioIn 17*
Davis, Ann-Marie 1951- *WhoWrEP 92*
Davis, Anna Marie 1946- *WhoAm 92, WhoEmL 93*
Davis, Anthony *BioIn 17*
Davis, Anthony 1951- *Baker 92*
Davis, Anthony Michael John 1939- *WhoSSW 93*
Davis, Arthur David *WhoAm 92*
Davis, Arthur Horace 1917- *WhoAm 92*
Davis, Audrey Elizabeth 1957- *WhoSSW 93*
Davis, B. J. *MiSFD 9*
Davis, B. Susan 1957- *WhoAmW 93*
Davis, Barbara B. 1931- *St&PR 93*
Davis, Barbara Jean *Law&B 92*
Davis, Barbara Jean Siemens 1931- *WhoAmW 93*
Davis, Barbara Lynn 1957- *WhoAmW 93*
Davis, Barbara Mae 1926- *WhoAmW 93*
Davis, Barry *WhoScE 91-1*
Davis, Barry K. *BioIn 17*
Davis, Barry Randolph 1956- *WhoEmL 93*
Davis, Bart 1950- *ScF&FL 92*
Davis, Bart McKay 1955- *St&PR 93*
Davis, Barton Bolling *Law&B 92*
Davis, Ben Hill, Jr. 1944- *WhoSSW 93*
Davis, Benjamin O. 1880-1970 *BioIn 17*
Davis, Benjamin O., Sr. 1877-1970 *ConBlB 4 [port]*
Davis, Benjamin O., Sr. 1880-1970 *EncAACR [port]*
Davis, Benjamin O., Jr. *BioIn 17*
Davis, Benjamin Oliver, Jr. 1912- *AfrAmBi*
Davis, Bennie Luke 1928- *WhoAm 92*
Davis, Bernard David 1916- *WhoAm 92*
Davis, Berta 1942- *WhoAmW 93*
Davis, Bertram George 1919- *WhoAm 92*
Davis, Bertram Hylton 1918- *WhoAm 92, WhoSSW 93*
Davis, Bette 1908-1989 *BioIn 17, IntDcF 2-3 [port]*
Davis, Betty Byrd Harrington 1936- *WhoAmW 93*
Davis, Betty Jean Bourbonia 1931- *WhoAmW 93*
Davis, Billie Johnston 1933- *WhoWor 93*
Davis, Billy 1937- *BioIn 17*
Davis, Bonni G. 1957- *St&PR 93*
Davis, Bonnie B. 1926- *St&PR 93*

Davis, Bonnie Christell 1949- *WhoEmL 93*
Davis, Bonnie Jean 1957- *WhoAmW 93*
Davis, Brad 1949-1991 *AnObit 1991, BioIn 17, ConTFT 10*
Davis, Brenda Molen 1956- *WhoAmW 93*
Davis, Brian 1925-1988 *ScF&FL 92*
Davis, Brian Howell *Law&B 92*
Davis, Britt Duane 1933- *St&PR 93*
Davis, Britton Anthony 1936- *WhoAm 92*
Davis, Bruce Allen 1948- *WhoEmL 93*
Davis, Bruce F. 1958- *St&PR 93*
Davis, Bruce Henry 1948- *WhoEmL 93*
Davis, Bruce Livingston, Jr. 1929- *WhoAm 92*
Davis, Bruce Warren 1947- *WhoEmL 93*
Davis, Burl Edward 1930- *WhoAm 92*
Davis, Cabell Seal, Jr. 1926- *WhoAm 92*
Davis, Calla Lea 1944- *WhoSSW 93*
Davis, Calvin De Armond 1927- *WhoAm 92*
Davis, Candace P. *Law&B 92*
Davis, Carl 1934- *BioIn 17*
Davis, Carl George 1937- *WhoAm 92*
Davis, Carle E. 1920- *WhoAm 92*
Davis, Carlton *BioIn 17*
Davis, Carol A. *Law&B 92*
Davis, Carol Ann 1957- *St&PR 93*
Davis, Carol Lyn 1953- *WhoAmW 93*
Davis, Carole Joan 1942- *WhoAm 92*
Davis, Carolyn 1960- *WhoSSW 93*
Davis, Carolyn Kahle 1932- *WhoAm 92, WhoAmW 93*
Davis, Carolyn Sue 1954- *WhoEmL 93*
Davis, Carroll Douglas 1949- *WhoSSW 93*
Davis, Catherine Agnes 1933- *WhoAmW 93*
Davis, Cecile I.G. 1939- *WhoUN 92*
Davis, Chandler 1926- *WhoAm 92*
Davis, Charisse Maria 1952- *WhoEmL 93*
Davis, Charles 1939- *BioIn 17*
Davis, Charles Carroll 1911- *WhoAm 92*
Davis, Charles E., Sr. 1933- *St&PR 93*
Davis, Charles Edward 1928- *St&PR 93*
Davis, Charles Edwin 1940- *WhoSSW 93*
Davis, Charles F. 1949- *St&PR 93*
Davis, Charles Francis, Jr. 1908- *WhoAm 92*
Davis, Charles H. *Law&B 92*
Davis, Charles Hargis 1938- *WhoAm 92*
Davis, Charles Henry 1807-1877 *HarEnMi*
Davis, Charles Howard, II 1944- *WhoE 93*
Davis, Charles L. 1960- *St&PR 93*
Davis, Charles Patrick 1945- *WhoSSW 93*
Davis, Charles Raymond 1945- *WhoSSW 93*
Davis, Charles T. 1945- *St&PR 93*
Davis, Charles Thomas, III 1939- *WhoSSW 93*
Davis, Charles Till 1929- *WhoAm 92*
Davis, Charles W. *Law&B 92*
Davis, Charles W. 1917-1991 *BioIn 17*
Davis, Charles William 1948- *WhoEmL 93, WhoSSW 93*
Davis, Cherie Lynn *WhoAmW 93*
Davis, Cheryl D. 1959- *St&PR 93*
Davis, Cheryl Lee *Law&B 92*
Davis, Chester Charles 1887-1975 *BioIn 17*
Davis, Chester P., Jr. 1922- *St&PR 93*
Davis, Chester R., Jr. 1930- *WhoAm 92, WhoWor 93*
Davis, Chip *WhoAm 92*
Davis, Christina Ann 1965- *WhoAmW 93*
Davis, Christina Linda 1940- *WhoE 93*
Davis, Christine Noelle 1955- *WhoAmW 93*
Davis, Christopher 1928- *WhoWrEP 92*
Davis, Christopher 1951?- *ConGAN*
Davis, Christopher Lee 1950- *WhoEmL 93*
Davis, Christopher Lyth 1949- *WhoE 93*
Davis, Christopher Moody 1948- *WhoEmL 93*
Davis, Christopher Patrick 1954- *WhoEmL 93*
Davis, Cindy Ann 1955- *WhoSSW 93*
Davis, Clark Bryant, Jr. 1964- *WhoE 93*
Davis, Claud Neal 1936- *WhoSSW 93*
Davis, Claude-Leonard 1944- *WhoSSW 93*
Davis, Claudia Christine Hill 1944- *WhoAmW 93*
Davis, Clayton Arthur Larsh 1955- *WhoEmL 93*
Davis, Clifton *BioIn 17*
Davis, Clive *SoulM*
Davis, Clive 1932- *BioIn 17*
Davis, Clive Jay 1934- *WhoAm 92, WhoE 93*
Davis, Clyde Robert *Law&B 92*
Davis, Coleen Cockerill 1930- *WhoAmW 93*
Davis, Colette *Law&B 92*
Davis, Colin 1927- *IntDcOp, OxDcOp*
Davis, Colin Peter *BioIn 17*
Davis, Colin (Rex) 1927- *Baker 92, WhoWor 93*
Davis, Constance Haranin 1947- *WhoAmW 93*
Davis, Courtland Harwell, Jr. 1921- *WhoAm 92*
Davis, Craig Alphin 1940- *St&PR 93*
Davis, Cullen *BioIn 17*
Davis, Curtis Carroll 1916- *WhoE 93*
Davis, Curtis Wheeler 1928-1986 *ConAu 136*
Davis, Cynthia D'Ascenzo 1953- *WhoEmL 93*
Davis, Cynthia Jeanne 1948- *WhoEmL 93*
Davis, D. Bruce 1943- *WhoAm 92*
Davis, Daisy Sidney 1944- *WhoAmW 93*
Davis, Dale Allen 1955- *WhoEmL 93, WhoSSW 93*
Davis, Daniel J. *Law&B 92*
Davis, Dannie Earl 1949- *WhoSSW 93*
Davis, Danny 1925- *WhoAm 92*
Davis, Darrell J. *Law&B 92*
Davis, Darrell L. 1939- *WhoSSW 93, WhoWor 93*
Davis, Dave McAlister 1937- *WhoSSW 93, WhoWor 93*
Davis, David 1815-1886 *OxCSupC [port], PolPar*
Davis, David 1927- *WhoAm 92*
Davis, David Brion 1927- *WhoAm 92*
Davis, David F. 1934- *St&PR 93*
Davis, David George 1945- *WhoAm 92*
Davis, David James 1938- *WhoWor 93*
Davis, David MacFarland 1926- *WhoAm 92, WhoWor 93*
Davis, David McCall 1946- *WhoSSW 93*
Davis, David Oliver 1933- *WhoAm 92*
Davis, Dean M. *Law&B 92*
Davis, Deane Chandler 1900-1990 *BioIn 17*
Davis, Deborah Anne 1955- *WhoSSW 93*
Davis, Deborah Cecilia 1952- *WhoAmW 93*
Davis, Deborah DuBois *Law&B 92*
Davis, Deborah Lee 1956- *WhoAmW 93*
Davis, Deborah Lynn 1948- *WhoEmL 93*
Davis, Deborah Sullivan *Law&B 92*
Davis, Deforest P., Jr. 1943- *St&PR 93*
Davis, Delmont A. 1935- *St&PR 93*
Davis, Delmont Alvin, Jr. 1935- *WhoAm 92*
Davis, Dempsie Augustus 1929- *WhoSSW 93*
Davis, Denise Lucille 1959- *WhoAmW 93*
Davis, Desmond 1928- *MiSFD 9*
Davis, Devra Lee *BioIn 17*
Davis, Diana Fagan *WhoWor 93*
Davis, Dianne Louise 1940- *WhoAmW 93*
Davis, Dinah Hamilton *Law&B 92*
Davis, Dix F. 1937- *St&PR 93*
Davis, Don *ScF&FL 92*
Davis, Don Clarence 1943- *WhoSSW 93*
Davis, Don H. *BioIn 17*
Davis, Don K. 1945- *St&PR 93*
Davis, Don Ray 1924- *WhoAm 92, WhoWor 93*
Davis, Donald d1992 *BioIn 17, NewYTBS 92*
Davis, Donald 1928- *ConTFT 10*
Davis, Donald Alan 1939- *WhoAm 92*
Davis, Donald E. 1956- *St&PR 93*
Davis, Donald Eugene 1931- *WhoSSW 93*
Davis, Donald George 1943- *WhoE 93*
Davis, Donald Gordon, Jr. 1939- *WhoAm 92, WhoWrEP 92*
Davis, Donald Jack 1938- *WhoSSW 93*
Davis, Donald Marc 1952- *WhoEmL 93*
Davis, Donald Marshall 1924- *St&PR 93*
Davis, Donald Ray 1934- *WhoAm 92*
Davis, Donald W. 1921- *St&PR 93*
Davis, Donna 1960- *WhoEmL 93*
Davis, Donna M. 1961- *St&PR 93*
Davis, Dorinne Sue Taylor Lovas 1949- *WhoAm 92, WhoAmW 93*
Davis, Doris McGinty 1922- *WhoSSW 93*
Davis, Dorothy Marie *AmWomPl*
Davis, Dorothy Salisbury 1916- *WhoAm 92*
Davis, Doryne Shari 1960- *WhoE 93, WhoEmL 93*
Davis, Douglas Charles 1949- *St&PR 93*
Davis, Douglas Matthew 1933- *WhoAm 92*
Davis, Douglas Richard 1944- *St&PR 93*
Davis, Drew Melvin 1947- *WhoE 93*
Davis, Duane Lee 1950- *WhoEmL 93*
Davis, Dwight 1948- *WhoAm 92*
Davis, Dwight E. 1944- *WhoIns 93*
Davis, Dwight John 1953- *WhoEmL 93*
Davis, E.K. 1937- *BioIn 17*
Davis, E. Marcus 1951- *WhoEmL 93*
Davis, Earl Clifford 1945- *St&PR 93*
Davis, Earl James 1934- *WhoAm 92*
Davis, Earon Scott 1950- *WhoEmL 93*
Davis, Eddie 1921-1986 *Baker 92*
Davis, Eddie Joe 1945- *WhoSSW 93*
Davis, Edgar E. 1941- *St&PR 93*
Davis, Edgar Glenn 1931- *St&PR 93, WhoAm 92, WhoWor 93*
Davis, Edith Kunhardt 1937- *BioIn 17*
Davis, Edna Clark *AmWomPl*
Davis, Edward B. 1927- *St&PR 93*
Davis, Edward Bertrand 1933- *WhoAm 92*
Davis, Edward Bradford 1953- *WhoE 93*
Davis, Edward Braxton, III 1938- *WhoSSW 93*
Davis, Edward Joseph, Jr. 1930- *WhoWrEP 92*
Davis, Edward Mott 1918- *WhoAm 92, WhoSSW 93*
Davis, Edward N. 1927- *St&PR 93*
Davis, Edward William *WhoScE 91-1*
Davis, Edward Wilson 1935- *WhoAm 92*
Davis, Edwin L. *St&PR 93*
Davis, Eleanor J. 1941- *WhoAmW 93*
Davis, Eleanor Lauria 1923- *WhoAmW 93*
Davis, Elisa Elaine 1963- *WhoAmW 93*
Davis, Elise Miller 1915- *WhoAmW 93*
Davis, Elizabeth Ann 1955- *WhoEmL 93*
Davis, Elizabeth Hawk 1945- *WhoSSW 93*
Davis, Elizabeth Mary 1948- *WhoAm 92*
Davis, Ella Jane Peebles 1945- *WhoSSW 93*
Davis, Elmer 1890-1958 *BioIn 17*
Davis, Elmer Holmes 1890-1958 *JrnUS*
Davis, Elmo Wright, Jr. 1946- *WhoEmL 93*
Davis, Emery Stephen 1940- *WhoAm 92, WhoSSW 93*
Davis, Emily 1944- *WhoIns 93*
Davis, Emma-Jo Levey 1932- *WhoAm 92*
Davis, Emma R. 1944- *WhoAmW 93*
Davis, Eric *BioIn 17*
Davis, Eric Clark 1952- *WhoEmL 93*
Davis, Eric Keith 1962- *WhoAm 92*
Davis, Erroll Brown, Jr. *BioIn 17*
Davis, Erroll Brown, Jr. 1944- *St&PR 93, WhoAm 92*
Davis, Evan Anderson 1944- *WhoAm 92*
Davis, Evelyn Y. *WhoAm 92*
Davis, Evelyn Yvonne *WhoWor 93*
Davis, Everett M. 1934- *WhoE 93*
Davis, Ferd Leary, Jr. 1941- *WhoAm 92, WhoSSW 93*
Davis, Finis E. 1911- *WhoAm 92, WhoWor 93*
Davis, Florea Jean 1953- *WhoEmL 93*
Davis, Florence A. 1955- *WhoAmW 93*
Davis, Florence Ann *Law&B 92*
Davis, Foster B., Jr. 1917- *St&PR 93*
Davis, Frances Kay 1952- *WhoAmW 93, WhoEmL 93*
Davis, Frances M. 1925- *WhoAm 92*
Davis, Francis *BioIn 17*
Davis, Francis Keith 1928- *WhoAm 92*
Davis, Francis Raymond 1920- *WhoE 93*
Davis, Francis W. 1905- *St&PR 93*
Davis, Frank B. 1928- *WhoAm 92*
Davis, Frank Edward 1956- *WhoEmL 93*
Davis, Frank N. 1925- *St&PR 93*
Davis, Frank Tradewell, Jr. 1938- *WhoAm 92, WhoWor 93*
Davis, Franklin Taravhonty 1964- *WhoE 93*
Davis, Fred C. 1928- *St&PR 93*
Davis, Fred Donald, Jr. 1959- *WhoSSW 93*
Davis, Fred Swanton, Jr. 1922- *St&PR 93*
Davis, Frederick C. 1902-1977 *ScF&FL 92*
Davis, G. Lynn *St&PR 93*
Davis, Gail 1924- *SweetSg C [port]*
Davis, Gail Yvette 1953- *WhoEmL 93*
Davis, Gale Elwood 1909- *WhoAm 92*
Davis, Gary 1896-1972 *BioIn 17*
Davis, Gary E. 1938- *WhoUN 92*
Davis, Gary Lynn 1949- *WhoEmL 93*
Davis, Geena *BioIn 17, WhoAm 92, WhoAmW 93*
Davis, Geena 1957- *ConTFT 10, News 92 [port]*
Davis, Gene 1938- *BioIn 17*
Davis, George *St&PR 93, WhoIns 93*
Davis, George A. 1928- *St&PR 93*
Davis, George Donald 1942- *WhoAm 92*
Davis, George Edward 1928- *WhoAm 92, WhoSSW 93, WhoWor 93*
Davis, George Hightower 1944- *WhoE 93*
Davis, George Holmes 1936- *St&PR 93*
Davis, George Kelso 1910- *WhoAm 92*
Davis, George Linn 1934- *WhoAm 92*
Davis, George Lynn 1940- *WhoAm 92*
Davis, George Osmond 1957- *WhoEmL 93*
Davis, George Wilmot 1933- *WhoAm 92*
Davis, Georgene Webber 1900- *AmWomPl*
Davis, Gerald Glenn 1950- *WhoEmL 93*
Davis, Gerald Hinkle 1930- *WhoSSW 93*
Davis, Gerald Titus 1932- *WhoAm 92*
Davis, Gerry 1931-1991 *ScF&FL 92*
Davis, Gilbert S. 1924- *St&PR 93*
Davis, Gladys Rockmore 1901-1967 *BioIn 17*
Davis, Glen Edward 1956- *WhoE 93*
Davis, Glenn E. *Law&B 92*
Davis, Glenn Edward *Law&B 92*
Davis, Gordon Richard Fuerst 1925- *WhoAm 92*
Davis, Graeme *ScF&FL 92*
Davis, Grania 1943- *ConAu 39NR, ScF&FL 92*
Davis, Gregory S. *Law&B 92*
Davis, Gregory Todd 1959- *WhoWrEP 92*
Davis, Guillett Gervaise, III 1932- *St&PR 93*
Davis, Gwen 1936- *ScF&FL 92*
Davis, Gwenda Rosetta 1950- *WhoAmW 93*
Davis, H. Alan 1932- *WhoSSW 93*
Davis, H. Brian *Law&B 92*
Davis, Hal *BioIn 17*
Davis, Hal Scott 1957- *WhoEmL 93*
Davis, Hallowell 1896-1992 *NewYTBS 92*
Davis, Hamilton G. *Law&B 92*
Davis, Harley Cleo 1941- *WhoAm 92*
Davis, Harlow M. 1927- *St&PR 93*
Davis, Harold 1950- *WhoAm 92, WhoEmL 93*
Davis, Harold 1953- *WhoEmL 93*
Davis, Harold A. 1902-1955 *ScF&FL 92*
Davis, Harold L. 1924- *St&PR 93*
Davis, Harold Truscott 1895- *WhoAm 92*
Davis, Harold William 1929- *St&PR 93*
Davis, Harry E. *BioIn 17*
Davis, Harry H. 1873-1947 *BiDAMSp 1989*
Davis, Harry L. 1927- *St&PR 93*
Davis, Harry Lee, Jr. 1952- *WhoEmL 93*
Davis, Harry Lendall 1937- *WhoAm 92*
Davis, Harry P. *Law&B 92*
Davis, Harry Rex 1921- *WhoAm 92*
Davis, Harry Scott, Jr. 1943- *St&PR 93, WhoAm 92*
Davis, Harry Stephen 1952- *WhoE 93*
Davis, Hartwell 1906- *WhoAm 92*
Davis, Hayden E. *Law&B 92*
Davis, Hayden E. 1933- *St&PR 93*
Davis, Hazel K. 1941- *ScF&FL 92*
Davis, Helen Gordon 1924- *WhoAmW 93, WhoSSW 93*
Davis, Helen Messick 1955- *WhoAmW 93*
Davis, Helen Nancy Matson 1905- *WhoAmW 93, WhoWor 93*
Davis, Helen White 1939- *WhoE 93*
Davis, Henry Barnard, Jr. 1923- *WhoWor 93*
Davis, Henry G. 1823-1916 *PolPar*
Davis, Henry Jefferson, Jr. 1929- *WhoAm 92*
Davis, Herbert *Law&B 92*
Davis, Herbert Lowell 1933- *St&PR 93, WhoAm 92*
Davis, Herbert Owen 1935- *WhoAm 92*
Davis, Herbert W. 1927- *St&PR 93*
Davis, Hiram Logan 1943- *WhoAm 92*
Davis, Hope Hale 1903- *WhoWrEP 92*
Davis, Horance Gibbs, Jr. 1924- *WhoAm 92*
Davis, Howard d1992 *NewYTBS 92*
Davis, Howard C., Jr. 1932- *St&PR 93*
Davis, Howard Ted 1937- *WhoAm 92*
Davis, I. G., Jr. 1924- *WhoAm 92*
Davis, Ian Robert *WhoScE 91-1*
Davis, Iris *BlkAmWO*
Davis, Irvin 1926- *St&PR 93, WhoWrEP 92*
Davis, Ivan 1932- *Baker 92*
Davis, J.A. 1821-1855 *BioIn 17*
Davis, J. Madison 1951- *ScF&FL 92*
Davis, J(ames) Madison, Jr. 1951- *WhoWrEP 92*
Davis, J. Michael *Law&B 92*
Davis, J. Michael 1947- *WhoAm 92*
Davis, J. Morton 1929- *St&PR 93, WhoAm 92*
Davis, J. Steve 1945- *WhoAm 92*
Davis, Jack 1916-1991 *BioIn 17*
Davis, Jack C. 1938- *St&PR 93, WhoAm 92*
Davis, Jack H. *Law&B 92*
Davis, Jack J. 1938- *WhoAm 92*
Davis, Jackie *BioIn 17*
Davis, Jacqueline Eda 1944- *WhoAmW 93*
Davis, Jacquelyn Kay 1950- *WhoAm 92, WhoEmL 93*
Davis, James *ScF&FL 92*
Davis, James d1992 *NewYTBS 92*
Davis, James Allan 1953- *WhoAm 92*
Davis, James B. 1950- *St&PR 93*
Davis, James C., Jr. *Law&B 92*
Davis, James Carl 1945- *WhoE 93, WhoWor 93*
Davis, James Clarke 1951- *WhoEmL 93*
Davis, James E. 1907- *St&PR 93*
Davis, James E. 1934- *ScF&FL 92*
Davis, James Edward 1921- *St&PR 93*
Davis, James Evans 1918- *WhoAm 92, WhoSSW 93, WhoWor 93*
Davis, James F. *Law&B 92*
Davis, James Gordon *Law&B 92*
Davis, James Harold 1943- *WhoAm 92*
Davis, James Henry 1932- *WhoAm 92*
Davis, James Hornor, III 1928- *WhoAm 92*
Davis, James Hornor, IV 1953- *WhoAm 92*
Davis, James Howard 1955- *WhoEmL 93*

Davis, James Hubbard *Law&B 92*
Davis, James John 1946- *WhoAm 92*
Davis, James K. *AfrAmBi*
Davis, James L. 1927- *WhoAm 92*
Davis, James Luther 1924- *WhoAm 92*
Davis, James M. 1936- *St&PR 93*
Davis, James Michael, Jr. 1954- *WhoE 93*
Davis, James Minor, Jr. 1936- *WhoAm 92*
Davis, James Norman 1939- *WhoAm 92*
Davis, James Othello 1916- *WhoAm 92*
Davis, James P. *St&PR 93*
Davis, James Paxton 1925- *WhoWrEP 92*
Davis, James Richard 1939- *WhoAm 92*
Davis, James Robert 1945- *WhoAm 92*
Davis, James Royce 1938- *WhoSSW 93*
Davis, James Verlin 1935- *WhoAm 92*
Davis, Jan 1943- *WhoAmW 93*
Davis, Jane Ellen 1943- *WhoAmW 93*
Davis, Jane G. *Law&B 92*
Davis, Jane Strauss 1944- *WhoAmW 93, WhoWor 93*
Davis, Janet 1951- *St&PR 93*
Davis, Jasper Claud 1920- *St&PR 93*
Davis, Jay *ScF&FL 92, St&PR 93*
Davis, Jean McArthur 1924- *St&PR 93*
Davis, Jeanine Marie 1955- *WhoEmL 93*
Davis, Jeannine M. *Law&B 92*
Davis, Jeannine M. 1948- *St&PR 93*
Davis, Jefferson 1808-1889 *BioIn 17, HarEnMi, PolPar*
Davis, Jefferson Clark, Jr. 1931- *WhoSSW 93*
Davis, Jefferson Columbus 1828-1879 *HarEnMi*
Davis, Jefferson J. 1913- *St&PR 93*
Davis, Jeffrey C. *Law&B 92*
Davis, Jeffrey L. *Law&B 92*
Davis, Jenny (Schneider) 1953- *DcAmChF 1985*
Davis, Jeraldine B. *Law&B 92*
Davis, Jeremy Matthew 1953- *WhoEmL 93*
Davis, Jerrold Calvin 1926- *WhoAm 92*
Davis, Jerry d1991 *BioIn 17*
Davis, Jerry A. 1962- *St&PR 93*
Davis, Jerry Bernard 1932- *WhoE 93*
Davis, Jerry Ray 1938- *WhoAm 92*
Davis, Jess W. *Law&B 92*
Davis, Jill Renee 1963- *WhoAmW 93*
Davis, Jimmie Dan 1940- *WhoAm 92*
Davis, Jo Culbertson 1937- *WhoSSW 93*
Davis, Joan 1907-1961 *QDrFCA 92 [port]*
Davis, JoAn 1947- *WhoAmW 93, WhoEmL 93*
Davis, Joanne Fatse *Law&B 92*
Davis, Joanne Johnson King Herring *BioIn 17*
Davis, Joanne King Herring *WhoAmW 93, WhoSSW 93*
Davis, Jodie 1959- *ConAu 139*
Davis, Joe Lee 1906-1974 *ScF&FL 92*
Davis, Joe Louis 1943- *St&PR 93*
Davis, Joel 1934- *St&PR 93, WhoAm 92*
Davis, Joel Anthony 1948- *WhoE 93, WhoEmL 93*
Davis, Joel Foster 1953- *WhoEmL 93*
Davis, Joel L. 1942- *WhoSSW 93*
Davis, John *BioIn 17, WhoScE 91-1*
Davis, John 1550-1605 *Expl 93*
Davis, John A., III *Law&B 92*
Davis, John Adams, Jr. 1944- *WhoE 93, WhoWor 93*
Davis, John Allen *WhoScE 91-1*
Davis, John Byron 1922- *WhoAm 92, WhoWrEP 92*
Davis, John Chandler Bancroft 1822-1907 *OxCSupC*
Davis, John Charles 1943- *WhoAm 92*
Davis, John Christopher 1944- *WhoAm 92*
Davis, John David 1867-1942 *Baker 92*
Davis, John E. 1942- *St&PR 93*
Davis, John Edward *WhoWor 93*
Davis, John Edward 1913-1990 *BioIn 17*
Davis, John Edward 1942- *WhoAm 92*
Davis, John Eugene 1948- *WhoE 93*
Davis, John F. d1990 *BioIn 17*
Davis, John H. 1927- *WhoAm 92*
Davis, John H. 1929- *ConAu 40NR*
Davis, John Herschel 1924- *WhoAm 92*
Davis, John I. 1917- *St&PR 93*
Davis, John J., III *Law&B 92*
Davis, John James 1936- *WhoAm 92*
Davis, John Joseph 1942- *St&PR 93*
Davis, John K. 1940- *St&PR 93*
Davis, John Kennerly, Jr. 1945- *WhoAm 92*
Davis, John Louis, II 1934- *WhoSSW 93*
Davis, John M. 1935- *St&PR 93*
Davis, John MacDougall 1914- *WhoAm 92*
Davis, John Marcell 1933- *WhoAm 92*
Davis, John Mason 1935- *WhoAm 92*
Davis, John Michael 1948- *WhoEmL 93*
Davis, John P. *St&PR 93*
Davis, John P. 1905-1973 *EncAACR*
Davis, John Phillips, Jr. 1925- *WhoAm 92*
Davis, John Roger, Jr. 1927- *WhoAm 92, WhoWor 93*
Davis, John Rowland 1927- *WhoAm 92*
Davis, John Sidney 1942- *WhoAm 92*
Davis, John Staige, IV 1931- *WhoAm 92*
Davis, John Stuart *Law&B 92*
Davis, John W. 1799-1859 *PolPar*
Davis, John Wesley 1873-1955 *PolPar*
Davis, John William 1873-1955 *BioIn 17, OxCSupC*
Davis, John William 1926- *WhoAm 92*
Davis, Jolene Bryant 1942- *WhoAmW 93, WhoWor 93*
Davis, Jon Edward 1952- *WhoWrEP 92*
Davis, Jonathan McMillan 1871-1943 *BioIn 17*
Davis, Joseph E. d1870 *BioIn 17*
Davis, Joseph Edward 1926- *WhoAm 92*
Davis, Joseph Frank 1939- *St&PR 93*
Davis, Joseph H., III *Law&B 92*
Davis, Joseph Lloyd 1927- *WhoAm 92*
Davis, Joseph S. 1930- *St&PR 93*
Davis, Joseph Samuel 1930- *WhoAm 92*
Davis, Josephine Dunbar 1942- *WhoAmW 93*
Davis, Joy Lee 1931- *WhoAmW 93*
Davis, Joy Lynn Edwards 1945- *WhoAmW 93, WhoWrEP 92*
Davis, Joyce Nannette 1958- *WhoEmL 93*
Davis, Juanita Johnson 1942- *WhoE 93*
Davis, Judith Carol 1949- *WhoAmW 93*
Davis, Judith M. *Law&B 92*
Davis, Judy Ann 1942- *WhoAmW 93*
Davis, Julia B. *Law&B 92*
Davis, Julia McBroom 1930- *WhoAm 92, WhoAmW 93*
Davis, Julia Snow 1964- *WhoAmW 93*
Davis, Julian Mason, Jr. 1935- *WhoAm 92*
Davis, Julie Lynn 1956- *WhoEmL 93*
Davis, Julie Mann 1960- *WhoEmL 93*
Davis, Karen 1952- *WhoIns 93*
Davis, Karen Elaine 1957- *WhoAmW 93*
Davis, Karen Padgett 1942- *WhoAm 92, WhoAmW 93*
Davis, Katharine Bement 1860-1935 *BioIn 17*
Davis, Katharine Cleland 1907-1991 *WhoAmW 93*
Davis, Katherine Wengen 1953- *WhoSSW 93*
Davis, Kathleen Ann 1948- *WhoAmW 93*
Davis, Kathleen Ann 1955- *WhoAm 92, WhoEmL 93*
Davis, Kathleen Sue 1950- *WhoAmW 93*
Davis, Kathlene Elizabeth 1939- *WhoWor 93*
Davis, Kathlyne Mary Elizabeth 1954- *WhoAmW 93, WhoEmL 93*
Davis, Kathryn Ward 1949- *WhoAmW 93*
Davis, Kathryn Wasserman 1907- *WhoAm 92*
Davis, Kay 1950- *WhoAm 92*
Davis, Kaye Pearce 1953- *WhoAmW 93*
Davis, Kaye Unger 1953- *St&PR 93*
Davis, Keith E. *Law&B 92*
Davis, Keith Eugene 1936- *WhoAm 92*
Davis, Keith Irwin 1952- *WhoEmL 93*
Davis, Kenneth *WhoScE 91-1*
Davis, Kenneth A. *Law&B 92*
Davis, Kenneth A. 1949- *WhoAm 92*
Davis, Kenneth Boone, Jr. 1947- *WhoEmL 93*
Davis, Kenneth C. *ConAu 139*
Davis, Kenneth Dudley 1958- *WhoEmL 93*
Davis, Kenneth Earl 1937- *WhoSSW 93*
Davis, Kenneth Ira 1941- *WhoE 93*
Davis, Kenneth Sidney 1912- *WhoAm 92*
Davis, Kenneth Stephen *WhoScE 91-1*
Davis, Kerry Lee 1954- *WhoEmL 93*
Davis, Kevin Adam 1962- *WhoWrEP 92*
Davis, Kevin R. 1945- *WhoWrEP 92*
Davis, Kevin T. 1958- *St&PR 93*
Davis, Kim McAlister 1958- *WhoAmW 93*
Davis, Kingsley 1908- *WhoAm 92*
Davis, Kristin Woodford 1944- *WhoAmW 93*
Davis, L. Clifford 1925- *AfrAmBi*
Davis, LaNay Flint 1933- *WhoAmW 93*
Davis, Lance Alan 1939- *WhoAm 92*
Davis, Lance Edwin 1928- *WhoAm 92*
Davis, Lane *BioIn 17*
Davis, Larry Michael 1947- *WhoEmL 93, WhoWor 93*
Davis, Latham Windsor 1942- *WhoAm 92*
Davis, Laura Ann 1959- *WhoEmL 93*
Davis, Laura Anne 1966- *WhoSSW 93*
Davis, Laura Arlene 1935- *WhoAm 92, WhoAmW 93*
Davis, Laura Beth 1960- *WhoAmW 93*
Davis, Laura L. *Law&B 92*
Davis, Laurence Laird 1915- *WhoAm 92*
Davis, Lawrence C. 1935- *WhoIns 93*
Davis, Lawrence Edward 1947- *WhoEmL 93*
Davis, Lawrence Stanley 1925- *St&PR 93*
Davis, Lawrence William 1935- *WhoE 93*
Davis, Lee Edward 1966- *WhoEmL 93*
Davis, Lennard J. 1949- *BioIn 17, ConAu 39NR, WhoEmL 93*
Davis, Leon 1918- *WhoSSW 93*
Davis, Leon J. 1906-1992 *NewYTBS 92 [port]*
Davis, Leonard 1919- *WhoAm 92*
Davis, Leonard A. *Law&B 92*
Davis, Leonard Ellsworth 1948- *WhoEmL 93*
Davis, Leonard McCutchan 1919- *WhoAm 92*
Davis, Leslie *SmATA 72*
Davis, Leslie 1924- *WhoSSW 93*
Davis, Leslie J. *Law&B 92*
Davis, Leslie Shannon 1963- *WhoAmW 93*
Davis, Leverett, Jr. 1914- *WhoAm 92*
Davis, Lila Ross 1941- *WhoAmW 93*
Davis, Lillie *AmWomPl*
Davis, Linda Jacobs 1955- *WhoAmW 93, WhoEmL 93*
Davis, Linda Prewett 1946- *WhoEmL 93*
Davis, Linda Susan *Law&B 92*
Davis, Lionel Edward *WhoScE 91-1*
Davis, Lloyd Edward 1929- *WhoAm 92*
Davis, Lonnie *Law&B 92*
Davis, Lorraine Jensen 1924- *WhoAm 92*
Davis, Lou Bryant 1955- *WhoEmL 93*
Davis, Louie R. 1927- *St&PR 93*
Davis, Louise Spiers 1911- *WhoAmW 93*
Davis, Lucille *AmWomPl*
Davis, Lucy Tolbert *WhoAmW 93*
Davis, Luther 1921- *WhoAm 92*
Davis, Luther, Jr. 1922- *WhoAm 92*
Davis, Lydia 1947- *ConAu 139*
Davis, Lyle E. 1927- *St&PR 93*
Davis, Lyn E. 1911- *St&PR 93*
Davis, Lynn Harry 1949- *WhoE 93, WhoEmL 93, WhoWor 93*
Davis, M. G. 1930- *WhoSSW 93*
Davis, M. Gail 1951- *WhoSSW 93*
Davis, Mac 1942- *Baker 92, WhoAm 92*
Davis, Maceo Nathaniel 1948- *WhoAm 92, WhoE 93, WhoEmL 93*
Davis, Maggie *ScF&FL 92*
Davis, Mamie 1940- *BioIn 17*
Davis, Maralee G. *WhoWrEP 92*
Davis, Marc *BioIn 17*
Davis, Marc 1947- *WhoAm 92*
Davis, Marc I. 1934- *WhoWrEP 92*
Davis, Marcia Rae *Law&B 92*
Davis, Marcia Welch 1949- *WhoEmL 93*
Davis, Margaret A. 1952- *WhoWrEP 92*
Davis, Margaret Bryan 1931- *WhoAm 92, WhoAmW 93*
Davis, Marguerite R. 1941- *St&PR 93*
Davis, Maria Antiona 1929- *WhoAmW 93*
Davis, Maria Teresa 1961- *WhoSSW 93*
Davis, Marie Hermenia 1929- *WhoAmW 93*
Davis, Marijane Rountree 1952- *WhoSSW 93*
Davis, Marilyn Tamaren *Law&B 92*
Davis, Marilynn A. *BioIn 17*
Davis, Marilynn A. 1952- *WhoAm 92, WhoAmW 93*
Davis, Marjorie H. *AmWomPl*
Davis, Marjorie R. *AmWomPl*
Davis, Mark *ScF&FL 92, WhoAm 92*
Davis, Mark Herbert Ainsworth *WhoScE 91-1*
Davis, Mark Hezekiah, Jr. 1948- *WhoWor 93*
Davis, Mark Jefferson 1954- *WhoEmL 93*
Davis, Mark L. *Law&B 92*
Davis, Mark M. *WhoAm 92*
Davis, Mark R. 1950- *WhoAm 92*
Davis, Mark Randall 1955- *WhoAm 92*
Davis, Mark Thomas 1959- *WhoEmL 93*
Davis, Marsha Ross 1952- *WhoEmL 93*
Davis, Martha Algenita Scott 1950- *WhoAm 92, WhoEmL 93*
Davis, Martha Ann 1958- *WhoSSW 93*
Davis, Martha Whitfield 1959- *WhoAmW 93*
Davis, Martin S. *BioIn 17*
Davis, Martin S. 1927- *St&PR 93, WhoAm 92*
Davis, Marvin *BioIn 17*
Davis, Mary *SoulM*
Davis, Mary A. *AmWomPl*
Davis, Mary Evalyn *AmWomPl*
Davis, Mary Evelyn Moore 1852-1909 *AmWomPl*
Davis, Mary Helen 1949- *WhoAmW 93, WhoEmL 93*
Davis, Mary Josephine 1947- *WhoEmL 93*
Davis, Mary Louise 1942- *WhoAmW 93, WhoSSW 93*
Davis, Matthew Livingston 1773-1850 *JrnUS*
Davis, Mattie Belle Edwards 1910- *WhoAm 92, WhoWor 93*
Davis, Melinda Hauser 1937- *WhoAmW 93*
Davis, Melodie M. 1951- *BioIn 17*
Davis, Melvin Clayton 1929- *St&PR 93*
Davis, Michael *Law&B 92*
Davis, Michael 1943- *See* MC5, The *ConMus 9*
Davis, Michael A. *Law&B 92*
Davis, Michael A. 1950- *St&PR 93*
Davis, Michael Allan 1941- *WhoE 93*
Davis, Michael John Earls 1952- *WhoWor 93*
Davis, Michael Peter 1947- *WhoE 93*
Davis, Michael Richard 1942- *WhoWor 93*
Davis, Michael Riley *Law&B 92*
Davis, Michael S. 1947- *WhoEmL 93*
Davis, Michael Todd 1963- *WhoSSW 93*
Davis, Michael William 1949- *WhoEmL 93*
Davis, Mike 1959- *BioIn 17*
Davis, Miles *BioIn 17*
Davis, Miles 1926-1991 *AnObit 1991, ConBlB 4 [port], News 92*
Davis, Miles (Dewey, III) 1926- *Baker 92*
Davis, Milton Wickers, Jr. 1923- *WhoAm 92*
Davis, Minnie Delores 1945- *WhoAm 92*
Davis, Monique D. *AfrAmBi*
Davis, Monique D. 1936- *WhoAmW 93*
Davis, Monte Vincent 1923- *WhoAm 92*
Davis, Morris Schuyler 1919- *WhoAm 92, WhoSSW 93*
Davis, Morton David 1930- *WhoE 93*
Davis, Moshe 1916- *WhoAm 92*
Davis, Muller 1935- *WhoAm 92, WhoWor 93*
Davis, N. Jan 1953- *WhoAmW 93*
Davis, Nancy Broome 1941- *WhoAmW 93*
Davis, Nancy Davis 1945- *WhoAmW 93*
Davis, Nancy E. 1948- *WhoAm 92*
Davis, Nancy Jane 1947- *WhoEmL 93*
Davis, Nancy L. *Law&B 92*
Davis, Natalie Zemon 1928- *BioIn 17, WhoAm 92, WhoAmW 93*
Davis, Nathan Tate 1937- *WhoAm 92*
Davis, Nelle *BioIn 17*
Davis, Nelle 1958- *SmATA 73*
Davis, Nicholas 1965- *ConAu 136*
Davis, Nicholas Homans Clark 1938- *WhoAm 92*
Davis, Nick *ConAu 136*
Davis, Nick 1965- *BioIn 17*
Davis, Norah Deakin 1941- *WhoAmW 93*
Davis, Norman 1913-1989 *BioIn 17*
Davis, Norman Edward 1935- *WhoWor 93*
Davis, O. L., Jr. 1928- *WhoAm 92, WhoSSW 93*
Davis, Orlin Ray 1937- *WhoAm 92*
Davis, Orval C. 1920- *St&PR 93*
Davis, Ossie 1917- *BioIn 17, BlkAuII 92, MiSFD 9, WhoAm 92, WhoE 93*
Davis, Otto Anderson 1934- *WhoAm 92*
Davis, Owen *WhoScE 91-1*
Davis, P. Craig 1958- *WhoEmL 93*
Davis, Pamela Bowes 1949- *WhoEmL 93*
Davis, Pamela Eileen 1956- *WhoAmW 93*
Davis, Pamela Sue Howard 1959- *WhoSSW 93*
Davis, Patricia A. 1939- *St&PR 93*
Davis, Patricia Mahoney 1957- *WhoAmW 93*
Davis, Patrick Andrew 1965- *WhoSSW 93*
Davis, Patrick Reese 1935- *St&PR 93*
Davis, Patti *BioIn 17*
Davis, Paul *Law&B 92*
Davis, Paul F. 1932- *WhoScE 91-1*
Davis, Paul Francis 1947- *WhoEmL 93, WhoSSW 93*
Davis, Paul Joseph 1937- *WhoAm 92*
Davis, Paul Michael 1940- *WhoSSW 93*
Davis, Paul W. *Law&B 92*
Davis, Paul Woodall 1927- *WhoSSW 93*
Davis, Paulette Jean Turner 1946- *WhoAmW 93*
Davis, Paxton 1925- *WhoAm 92*
Davis, Peggy Cooper 1943- *WhoAmW 93*
Davis, Peggy Hamlette 1940- *WhoAmW 93*
Davis, Perry John 1932- *WhoAm 92*
Davis, Peter *MiSFD 9*
Davis, Peter Bennett 1942- *St&PR 93*
Davis, Peter Frank 1937- *WhoAm 92*
Davis, Peter Werner *Law&B 92*
Davis, Phil *ScF&FL 92*
Davis, Philip 1952- *WhoEmL 93*
Davis, Philip J. *St&PR 93*
Davis, Philip J. 1923- *WhoAm 92*
Davis, Philip P. 1938- *St&PR 93*
Davis, Phillip Eugene 1933- *WhoSSW 93*
Davis, Phillip Howard 1946- *WhoEmL 93, WhoSSW 93*
Davis, Phillip Samuel 1953- *AfrAmBi [port]*
Davis, Phyllis Ann 1963- *WhoAmW 93*
Davis, Phyllis Burke 1931- *St&PR 93, WhoAm 92, WhoAmW 93*
Davis, Preston Homer 1913- *St&PR 93*
Davis, R.A. *Law&B 92*
Davis, R. Kent 1956- *WhoEmL 93*
Davis, R.L., Sr. *Law&B 92*
Davis, R. Steven, II *Law&B 92*

Davis, Rachel Lee Mostert 1952- *WhoAmW 93, WhoEmL 93, WhoSSW 93*
Davis, Ralph Austin *Law&B 92*
Davis, Ralph E. 1919- *WhoAm 92*
Davis, Ralph Manning 1926- *St&PR 93*
Davis, Randall A. *Law&B 92*
Davis, Randall Eugene 1947- *WhoE 93*
Davis, Randall Paul 1956- *WhoWrEP 92*
Davis, Randy L. 1950- *WhoWor 93*
Davis, Ray *BioIn 17*
Davis, Ray C. 1941- *St&PR 93, WhoAm 92*
Davis, Raymond, Jr. 1914- *WhoAm 92*
Davis, Rebecca Harding 1831-1910 *AmWomWr 92, GayN*
Davis, Rebecca Jean *Law&B 92*
Davis, Regina Lois Goodman 1952- *WhoSSW 93*
Davis, Reginald *WhoScE 91-1*
Davis, Rex Darwin 1924- *WhoE 93*
Davis, Rex Lloyd 1929- *WhoAm 92, WhoIns 93*
Davis, Rhysa Meryt 1948- *WhoEmL 93*
Davis, Richard 1930- *WhoAm 92*
Davis, Richard 1945- *ScF&FL 92*
Davis, Richard B. *Law&B 92*
Davis, Richard Bradley 1926- *WhoAm 92*
Davis, Richard Bruce 1940- *WhoAm 92*
Davis, Richard Francis 1936- *WhoAm 92*
Davis, Richard Harding 1864-1916 *GayN, JrnUS*
Davis, Richard J. *Law&B 92*
Davis, Richard Joel 1946- *WhoAm 92*
Davis, Richard Jones, Jr. 1950- *WhoSSW 93*
Davis, Richard L. 1949- *WhoEmL 93*
Davis, Richard Macomber 1929- *WhoAm 92*
Davis, Richard Malone 1918- *WhoAm 92*
Davis, Richard Owen 1949- *WhoEmL 93*
Davis, Richard R. *Law&B 92*
Davis, Richard Ralph 1936- *WhoAm 92*
Davis, Richard Rodney 1944- *WhoAm 92*
Davis, Richard Thomas 1947- *BioIn 17*
Davis, Richard Whitlock 1935- *WhoAm 92*
Davis, Rick *BioIn 17*
Davis, Robert Aldine 1928- *WhoAm 92*
Davis, Robert Carlton 1944- *WhoAm 92*
Davis, Robert E. 1942- *St&PR 93*
Davis, Robert Edward 1931- *WhoAm 92*
Davis, Robert Edwin 1931- *St&PR 93, WhoAm 92*
Davis, Robert Harry 1927- *WhoAm 92*
Davis, Robert Hunter *WhoScE 91-1*
Davis, Robert J. 1896-1991 *BioIn 17*
Davis, Robert James 1929- *WhoE 93*
Davis, Robert Jocelyn 1951- *WhoAm 92, WhoEmL 93*
Davis, Robert Leach 1924- *WhoAm 92*
Davis, Robert Lee 1937- *St&PR 93*
Davis, Robert Lewis *Law&B 92*
Davis, Robert Louis 1927- *WhoAm 92*
Davis, Robert M. 1923- *St&PR 93*
Davis, Robert M. 1947- *St&PR 93*
Davis, Robert Murray 1934- *WhoSSW 93*
Davis, Robert Nason 1938- *WhoAm 92*
Davis, Robert Nelson, Jr. *Law&B 92*
Davis, Robert Nelson, Jr. 1948- *WhoEmL 93*
Davis, Robert Paul 1926- *WhoAm 92*
Davis, Robert Phillip 1941- *St&PR 93*
Davis, Robert S. 1914- *St&PR 93*
Davis, Robert Spink 1919- *St&PR 93*
Davis, Robert Stanley 1945- *WhoSSW 93*
Davis, Robert Thomas 1927- *St&PR 93*
Davis, Robert W. 1932- *CngDr 91*
Davis, Robert William 1932- *WhoAm 92*
Davis, Robin Ray 1948- *WhoSSW 93*
Davis, Rod 1946- *WhoWrEP 92*
Davis, Roderick William 1936- *St&PR 93, WhoAm 92*
Davis, Roger Edwin 1928- *WhoAm 92*
Davis, Roger Kenneth 1937- *St&PR 93*
Davis, Roger William 1949- *WhoIns 93*
Davis, Roland Hayes 1927- *WhoE 93*
Davis, Roman T.H. 1961- *St&PR 93*
Davis, Ronald 1937- *WhoAm 92*
Davis, Ronald Clark 1943- *St&PR 93*
Davis, Ronald Farlandi, Jr. 1946- *WhoEmL 93*
Davis, Ronald L. 1937- *St&PR 93*
Davis, Ronald Wayne 1941- *WhoAm 92*
Davis, Ronald Wayne 1954- *WhoWrEP 92*
Davis, Ronnette M. 1948- *WhoEmL 93*
Davis, Ronnie Dale 1957- *WhoEmL 93*
Davis, Rose Lee 1944- *WhoAmW 93*
Davis, Ross Dane 1919- *WhoAm 92*
Davis, Roy Walton, Jr. 1930- *WhoAm 92, WhoSSW 93*
Davis, Russell E. 1944- *St&PR 93*
Davis, Ruth C. 1943- *WhoAmW 93, WhoWor 93*
Davis, Ruth Helen *AmWomPl*
Davis, Ruth Lenore 1910- *WhoAmW 93*
Davis, Ruth Margaret 1928- *WhoSSW 93, WhoWor 93*
Davis, Ruthann M. *Law&B 92*
Davis, S. Gareth 1921- *WhoE 93*
Davis, St. Clair O. *Law&B 92*
Davis, Sam A., II 1948- *St&PR 93*
Davis, Sam H. 1921- *St&PR 93*
Davis, Sammy, Jr. *BioIn 17*
Davis, Sammy, Jr. 1925-1990 *Baker 92*
Davis, Samuel 1931- *WhoAm 92*
Davis, Samuel Bernhard 1942- *St&PR 93, WhoAm 92*
Davis, Sandra H. 1942- *St&PR 93*
Davis, Sara Lea 1951- *WhoAm 92, WhoAmW 93, WhoWor 93*
Davis, Sarah Irwin 1923- *WhoSSW 93, WhoWrEP 92*
Davis, Scott Jonathan 1952- *WhoAm 92, WhoEmL 93*
Davis, Scott Livingston 1941- *WhoAm 92*
Davis, Seth Richard 1954- *WhoEmL 93*
Davis, Sharon *Law&B 92*
Davis, Sharon Keeping 1954- *WhoAmW 93*
Davis, Sharon Marshall 1952- *WhoSSW 93*
Davis, Shelby Cullom 1909- *WhoAm 92*
Davis, Shelby M.C. 1937- *St&PR 93, WhoAm 92*
Davis, Shirley Escott 1930- *WhoAmW 93*
Davis, Shirley Harriet 1922- *WhoSSW 93*
Davis, Shirley Smith 1953- *WhoAmW 93*
Davis, Shoshana Tikva 1950- *WhoE 93*
Davis, Sid 1927- *WhoAm 92*
Davis, Sonia *WhoWrEP 92*
Davis, Sonia H. 1883-1972 *ScF&FL 92*
Davis, Sonya Meyers *Law&B 92*
Davis, Stacia G. 1958- *St&PR 93*
Davis, Stafford Grise 1924- *WhoSSW 93*
Davis, Stanley Nelson 1924- *WhoAm 92*
Davis, Stanley Stewart *WhoScE 91-1*
Davis, Stephen Alan 1946- *WhoWrEP 92*
Davis, Stephen Allen 1947- *WhoEmL 93*
Davis, Stephen B. *Law&B 92*
Davis, Stephen Edward 1925- *St&PR 93, WhoAm 92*
Davis, Stephen Edward Folwell 1964- *WhoE 93*
Davis, Stephen F. *BioIn 17*
Davis, Stephen Howard 1939- *WhoAm 92*
Davis, Stephen John 1945- *WhoAm 92*
Davis, Stephen Marshall 1955- *WhoE 93*
Davis, Stephen Oliver 1942- *WhoE 93*
Davis, Stephen Robert 1923- *WhoAm 92*
Davis, Stephen W. 1953- *WhoWrEP 92*
Davis, Steve L. *St&PR 93*
Davis, Stewart 1918- *St&PR 93*
Davis, Stewart Thorpe 1951- *WhoEmL 93, WhoSSW 93, WhoWor 93*
Davis, Stuart 1892-1964 *BioIn 17*
Davis, Stuart 1916- *St&PR 93*
Davis, Susan Emily 1951- *WhoAm 92*
Davis, Susan Frances 1939- *WhoAmW 93*
Davis, Susan Gloria 1957- *WhoAmW 93, WhoEmL 93*
Davis, Susan Jean *WhoWrEP 92*
Davis, Susan Lynn 1958- *WhoAmW 93*
Davis, Susan Smith 1943- *WhoE 93*
Davis, Suzanne Gould 1947- *WhoAmW 93, WhoEmL 93*
Davis, Suzy 1936- *WhoAmW 93*
Davis, Sybil Alicia 1954- *WhoAm 92, WhoEmL 93*
Davis, Sybil Lou 1918- *WhoAmW 93*
Davis, T. Cullen *BioIn 17*
Davis, T. Eleanor 1960- *WhoEmL 93*
Davis, Tamara Jean 1964- *WhoE 93*
Davis, Tamara Petrosian 1945- *St&PR 93*
Davis, Tamra *MiSFD 9*
Davis, Tamra Kathleen 1958- *WhoEmL 93*
Davis, Teresa 1950- *See* Emotions *SoulM*
Davis, Terrel Ellis *Law&B 92*
Davis, Terry Michael 1957- *WhoWrEP 92*
Davis, Thomas Charles 1938- *WhoE 93*
Davis, Thomas Edward 1932- *St&PR 93*
Davis, Thomas F. *Law&B 92*
Davis, Thomas Gene 1936- *WhoE 93*
Davis, Thomas H. 1918- *EncABHB 8 [port], St&PR 93*
Davis, Thomas Henry 1918- *WhoAm 92*
Davis, Thomas J. d1990 *BioIn 17*
Davis, Thomas Jerome 1946- *WhoEmL 93*
Davis, Thomas M., III *Law&B 92*
Davis, Thomas Osborne 1814-1845 *BioIn 17*
Davis, Thomas Robin MacLeod 1947- *WhoWor 93*
Davis, Thomas William 1927- *St&PR 93*
Davis, Thomas William 1946- *WhoAm 92*
Davis, Thunderbird d1992 *BioIn 17*
Davis, Tim Douglas 1956- *WhoEmL 93*
Davis, Timothy John 1954- *WhoEmL 93*
Davis, Timothy M. *St&PR 93*
Davis, Tina Ann 1962- *WhoSSW 93*
Davis, Tom Ivey, II 1946- *WhoEmL 93, WhoSSW 93*
Davis, Tony *ScF&FL 92*
Davis, True 1919- *WhoAm 92*
Davis, Tyrone 1938- *BioIn 17, SoulM*
Davis, Veronica A. 1959- *WhoAmW 93, WhoEmL 93*
Davis, Vickie Beene 1951- *WhoAmW 93*
Davis, Vincent 1930- *WhoAm 92, WhoWor 93*
Davis, Virginia *WhoAmW 93*
Davis, W. L. *WhoAm 92*
Davis, Walter 1912- *WhoWrEP 92*
Davis, Walter 1932-1990 *BioIn 17*
Davis, Walter Bond 1930- *WhoE 93*
Davis, Walter Jackson, Jr. 1936- *AfrAmBi [port]*
Davis, Walter Paul 1956- *BiDAMSp 1989*
Davis, Walter Stanley 1928- *WhoE 93*
Davis, Walter Stewart 1924- *St&PR 93, WhoAm 92*
Davis, Walter William *Law&B 92*
Davis, Wanda Rose 1937- *WhoAmW 93*
Davis, Wayne Alton 1931- *WhoAm 92*
Davis, Wayne Harry 1930- *WhoSSW 93*
Davis, Wendell, Jr. 1933- *WhoAm 92*
Davis, Wesley LeRoy 1943- *WhoWor 93*
Davis, William Albert 1946- *WhoAm 92, WhoSSW 93*
Davis, William Arthur 1932- *WhoAm 92*
Davis, William Charles 1948- *WhoSSW 93*
Davis, William Columbus 1910- *WhoAm 92, WhoWor 93*
Davis, William Doyle 1931- *WhoAm 92*
Davis, William E. 1942- *St&PR 93*
Davis, William Eugene 1921- *WhoAm 92*
Davis, William Eugene 1929- *WhoAm 92, WhoSSW 93*
Davis, William Eugene 1936- *WhoAm 92*
Davis, William F. 1946- *St&PR 93*
Davis, William Grenville 1929- *WhoAm 92*
Davis, William H. 1922-1991 *BioIn 17*
Davis, William Harry 1925- *WhoAm 92*
Davis, William Howard 1951- *WhoEmL 93*
Davis, William J. *Law&B 92*
Davis, William James *Law&B 92*
Davis, William John *Law&B 92*
Davis, William K. 1926- *St&PR 93*
Davis, William Kruger 1926- *WhoE 93*
Davis, William M. 1940- *St&PR 93*
Davis, William Maxie, Jr. 1932- *WhoSSW 93, WhoWor 93*
Davis, William Pearce *Law&B 92*
Davis, William Robert 1929- *WhoAm 92*
Davis, William Robert, Sr. 1949- *WhoEmL 93*
Davis, William Russell 1955- *WhoSSW 93*
Davis, William Stanley 1922- *St&PR 93*
Davis, William Terry 1954- *WhoWor 93*
Davis, William Virgil 1940- *WhoSSW 93, WhoWrEP 92*
Davis, William Walter 1946- *WhoSSW 93*
Davis, William Wayne *Law&B 92*
Davis, William Wootton, Jr. 1933- *WhoSSW 93*
Davis, Willie *BioIn 17*
Davis, Winston C. 1932- *St&PR 93*
Davis, Winthrop Fisk 1942- *St&PR 93*
Davis, Wyatt 1931- *St&PR 93*
Davis, Wylie Herman 1919- *WhoAm 92*
Davis, Yvonne D. 1947- *WhoAmW 93, WhoEmL 93*
Davis, Yvonne Singleton 1952- *WhoAmW 93*
Davis Aspinwall, Gail Ann 1959- *WhoWrEP 92*
Davis-Ek, Mary Ione 1942- *WhoAmW 93*
Davis-Fuller, Ethlyn Anita 1944- *WhoE 93*
Davis-Grossman, Carol Gail 1952- *WhoAm 92*
Davis-Harris, Jeannette G. *AfrAmBi [port]*
Davis-Imhof, Nancy Louise 1940- *WhoAmW 93*
Davison, A(rchibald) T(hompson) 1883-1961 *Baker 92*
Davison, Alan Nelson *WhoScE 91-1*
Davison, Arthur d1992 *NewYTBS 92*
Davison, Arthur Lee 1936- *WhoAm 92*
Davison, Beatrice Gesina 1906- *WhoAmW 93*
Davison, Beaumont 1929- *WhoAm 92*
Davison, Bill 1906-1989 *BioIn 17*
Davison, Bruce *BioIn 17*
Davison, Calvin 1932- *WhoAm 92*
Davison, Charles Hamilton 1926- *WhoAm 92, WhoE 93*
Davison, Charles Hamilton, Jr. 1959- *St&PR 93*
Davison, Daniel P. 1925- *St&PR 93*
Davison, Daniel Pomeroy 1925- *WhoAm 92*
Davison, Douglas S. 1946- *St&PR 93*
Davison, Edward Joseph 1938- *WhoAm 92*
Davison, Endicott Peabody 1923- *WhoAm 92*
Davison, Frank Dalby 1893-1970 *DcChlFi*
Davison, Frederic Ellis 1917- *AfrAmBi*
Davison, Frederick Corbet 1929- *WhoAm 92*
Davison, George Frederick, Jr. 1950- *WhoEmL 93*
Davison, Glenn Alan 1963- *WhoE 93*
Davison, Helen Irene 1926- *WhoAmW 93, WhoWor 93*
Davison, J(ames) W(illiam) 1813-1885 *Baker 92*
Davison, James Eric 1953- *WhoE 93*
Davison, Jean *ScF&FL 92*
Davison, John Herbert 1930- *WhoAm 92*
Davison, Jon 1949- *ConTFT 10*
Davison, Kenneth Edwin 1924- *WhoAm 92*
Davison, Kenneth Lewis 1935- *WhoAm 92*
Davison, Kerry *Law&B 92*
Davison, Kyle S. 1961- *St&PR 93*
Davison, Kyle Scott 1961- *WhoAm 92*
Davison, Luella May 1922- *WhoAmW 93*
Davison, Mark Roberts 1949- *WhoWor 93*
Davison, Maxine Baker 1912- *St&PR 93*
Davison, Nancy Reynolds 1944- *WhoAm 92*
Davison, Patricia Louise 1951- *WhoAmW 93*
Davison, Paul Sioussa 1955- *WhoEmL 93, WhoSSW 93*
Davison, Peter 1948- *WhoEmL 93*
Davison, Peter 1951- *ScF&FL 92*
Davison, Peter Fitzgerald 1927- *WhoAm 92*
Davison, Peter Hubert 1928- *WhoAm 92, WhoWrEP 92*
Davison, Richard 1937- *WhoAm 92*
Davison, Robert Manning 1937- *St&PR 93*
Davison, Roderic Hollett 1916- *WhoAm 92*
Davison, Selvan 1912-1990 *BioIn 17*
Davison, Stanley Martin 1928- *St&PR 93*
Davison, Thomas Cornell Barringer 1948- *WhoEmL 93*
Davison, Victoria Dillon 1949- *WhoSSW 93*
Davison, Wild Bill 1906-1989 *BioIn 17*
Davison, William (Edward) 1906-1989 *Baker 92*
Davisson, Lee David 1936- *WhoAm 92*
Davisson, Ralph M. *Law&B 92, St&PR 93*
Davisson, Teresa Lynn 1964- *WhoAmW 93*
Davisson, Timothy P. *Law&B 92*
Davisson, Vanessa Teresa 1958- *WhoEmL 93*
Davisson, William I. 1929-1989 *BioIn 17*
Davisson, William Sears 1946- *WhoE 93*
Davis-Willis, Norma E. 1939- *St&PR 93*
Davlin, Michael C. 1955- *St&PR 93, WhoIns 93*
Davlin, Michael Charles *Law&B 92*
D'avout, G.A. *WhoScE 91-3*
Davout, Louis Nicolas 1770-1823 *HarEnMi*
Davrou, Claude 1947- *WhoScE 91-2*
Davtyan, Ohannes Karapety 1911- *WhoWor 93*
Davy, George Francis *Law&B 92*
Davy, Gloria 1931- *Baker 92*
Davy, John 1763-1824 *Baker 92*
Davy, Nadine Irene 1958- *WhoEmL 93*
Davy, Philip Sheridan 1915- *WhoAm 92*
Davy, Richard Gordon, Jr. 1948- *St&PR 93*
Davy, Samuel Jackson 1922- *St&PR 93*
Davy, Thomas *BioIn 17*
Davydov, Oleg Viktorovich 1962- *WhoWor 93*
Davydov, Stepan 1777-1825 *OxDcOp*
Daw, Harold John 1926- *WhoAm 92*
Daw, Lenore E. *WhoAmW 93*
Daw, Marjorie 1902- *SweetSg B [port]*
Dawalt, Kenneth Francis 1911- *WhoAm 92*
Daw Aung San Suu Kyi 1945- *WhoWor 93*
Dawbarn, H.D., Jr. 1942- *St&PR 93*
Dawbarn, Henry Dunlop 1915- *St&PR 93*
Dawber, John Graham *WhoScE 91-1*
Dawber, Martin *WhoScE 91-1*
Dawber, Pam *BioIn 17, WhoAm 92*
Dawe, David H. 1945- *St&PR 93*
Dawe, Rebecca L. 1944- *St&PR 93*
Dawe, Theodore G. 1949- *St&PR 93*
Dawes, Carol J. 1931- *WhoAm 92*
Dawes, Charles G. 1865-1951 *PolPar*
Dawes, David Ford 1909- *WhoWor 93*
Dawes, Douglas Charles 1952- *WhoEmL 93*
Dawes, Edwin Alfred *WhoScE 91-1*
Dawes, Geoffrey Sharman 1918- *WhoAm 92*
Dawes, Jerome Martin 1947- *St&PR 93*
Dawes, Jo Robinson 1959- *WhoAmW 93*
Dawes, Lyell Clark 1931- *WhoE 93*
Dawes, Michael Graham 1938- *WhoWor 93*
Dawes, Michael V. 1944- *St&PR 93*

Dawes, Peter Graham 1948- *WhoWor 93*
Dawes, Robert Leo 1945- *WhoSSW 93*
Dawes, Robert Taylor 1904- *St&PR 93*
Dawes, Robyn Mason 1936- *WhoAm 92*
Dawes, Sharon Scavia 1949- *WhoAmW 93*
Dawes, Stephen Graham *WhoScE 91-1*
Dawid, Igor Bert 1935- *WhoAm 92*
Dawidowicz, Lucy S. *BioIn 17*
Dawidowicz, Samuel 1951- *St&PR 93*
Dawidziak, Mark 1956- *ScF&FL 92*
Dawis, Rene V. 1928- *WhoAm 92*
Dawkins, Cecil 1927- *WhoWrEP 92*
Dawkins, David Michael 1948- *WhoEmL 93, WhoSSW 93*
Dawkins, Diantha Dee 1942- *WhoSSW 93*
Dawkins, Jerome E. *Law&B 92*
Dawkins, John Sydney *WhoWor 93*
Dawkins, John Sydney 1947- *WhoAsAP 91*
Dawkins, John Vernon *WhoScE 91-1*
Dawkins, Johnny *BioIn 17*
Dawkins, Katherine Penelope 1962- *WhoAmW 93*
Dawkins, Margot Morris 1954- *WhoAmW 93*
Dawkins, Marva Phyllis 1948- *WhoAm 92, WhoAmW 93, WhoEmL 93*
Dawkins, Maurice Anderson 1921- *WhoAm 92*
Dawkins, Vickie Lynn 1960- *WhoWrEP 92*
Dawkins, Wayne Jesse 1955- *WhoE 93*
Dawkins, William Boyd 1837-1929 *BioIn 17*
Dawkins, William James 1948- *St&PR 93*
Dawkins, William Lee, Jr. 1960- *WhoEmL 93*
Dawley, Alan Charles 1943- *WhoE 93*
Dawley, Eloise K. *AmWomPl*
Dawley, J. Searle d1950 *MiSFD 9N*
Dawley, John P. 1929- *St&PR 93*
Dawley, Patricia K. 1937- *WhoAm 92*
Dawn, Clarence Ernest 1918- *WhoAm 92*
Dawn, Deborah *WhoAm 92*
Dawn, Frederic Samuel 1916- *WhoWor 93*
Dawn, Marva J. 1948- *ConAu 139*
Dawood, Mushtaq Husain 1941- *WhoWor 93*
Dawood, Qazi Mohammad 1961- *WhoEmL 93*
Dawood Al-Azdi, Abdullah Bin Hussain 1931- *WhoWor 93*
Daws, Andrew Michael Bennett 1943- *WhoWor 93*
Daws, Jerry Wayne 1944- *St&PR 93*
Dawson, Adrian 1948- *St&PR 93*
Dawson, Allen Daniel 1955- *St&PR 93*
Dawson, Andre *BioIn 17*
Dawson, Andre Fernando 1954- *WhoAm 92*
Dawson, Anthony M. 1930- *MiSFD 9*
Dawson, Arthur Wayne 1946- *WhoSSW 93*
Dawson, Barbara Jean 1957- *WhoEmL 93*
Dawson, Bonnie Jean 1955- *WhoWrEP 92*
Dawson, Brian Robert 1947- *WhoWor 93*
Dawson, Carol Gene 1937- *WhoAm 92, WhoAmW 93*
Dawson, Charles D. *Law&B 92*
Dawson, Cindy Lou 1958- *WhoAmW 93*
Dawson, Craig Gayden 1954- *WhoEmL 93*
Dawson, David George 1947- *St&PR 93*
Dawson, Dawn Paige 1956- *WhoAmW 93*
Dawson, Deborah L. *BioIn 17*
Dawson, Dennis R. *Law&B 92*
Dawson, Dennis R. 1948- *St&PR 93*
Dawson, Dennis Ray 1948- *WhoAm 92, WhoEmL 93*
Dawson, Donald Andrew 1937- *WhoAm 92*
Dawson, Donald C. 1937- *St&PR 93*
Dawson, Earl Bliss 1930- *WhoSSW 93*
Dawson, Edmund R. *Law&B 92*
Dawson, Edward Joseph 1944- *WhoWor 93*
Dawson, Elida Webb d1975 *BioIn 17*
Dawson, Elizabeth Elaine 1956- *WhoAmW 93*
Dawson, Fielding 1930- *ScF&FL 92*
Dawson, Forbes 1860- *ScF&FL 92*
Dawson, Francis Hugh *WhoScE 91-1*
Dawson, Francis Washington 1840-1889 *JrnUS*
Dawson, George Amos 1924- *WhoWrEP 92*
Dawson, George Glenn 1925- *WhoAm 92*
Dawson, Gerald Lee 1933- *WhoSSW 93*
Dawson, Harace G., III *Law&B 92*
Dawson, Helen Payne 1909- *WhoAmW 93*
Dawson, Horace Greeley, Jr. 1926- *WhoAm 92*
Dawson, Howard 1953- *WhoEmL 93*
Dawson, Howard A., Jr. 1922- *CngDr 91*
Dawson, Howard Athalone, Jr. 1922- *WhoAm 92*
Dawson, James A. 1937- *St&PR 93*
Dawson, James Ambrose 1937- *WhoAm 92*
Dawson, James Reginald *WhoScE 91-1*
Dawson, Jeanne R. *Law&B 92*
Dawson, Joanne B. 1950- *WhoAmW 93*
Dawson, John *WhoScE 91-1*
Dawson, John 1946- *BioIn 17*
Dawson, John Alan *WhoScE 91-1*
Dawson, John Barker *WhoScE 91-1*
Dawson, John Frederick 1930- *WhoAm 92*
Dawson, John Harold 1950- *WhoSSW 93*
Dawson, John Huger, Jr. 1943- *St&PR 93*
Dawson, John Joseph 1947- *WhoAm 92*
Dawson, John Lewis 1945- *WhoWor 93*
Dawson, John Myrick 1930- *WhoAm 92*
Dawson, John Scott 1953- *WhoEmL 93*
Dawson, John Wyndham 1928- *WhoWor 93*
Dawson, Kenneth L. d1992 *BioIn 17, NewYTBS 92 [port]*
Dawson, Larry Alan *Law&B 92*
Dawson, Leland Bradley 1950- *WhoEmL 93*
Dawson, Len 1935- *BioIn 17*
Dawson, Les *ScF&FL 92*
Dawson, Lewis Edward 1933- *WhoSSW 93*
Dawson, Linda Smith 1945- *WhoAmW 93*
Dawson, M. Taylor, Jr. 1929- *St&PR 93*
Dawson, Malinda Catherine 1961- *WhoAmW 93*
Dawson, Mary Martha 1908- *WhoWrEP 92*
Dawson, Mary Ruth 1931- *WhoAm 92*
Dawson, Mimi 1944- *WhoAm 92*
Dawson, Nelson Lloyd 1939- *WhoSSW 93*
Dawson, O. Douglas 1944- *St&PR 93*
Dawson, Peter John 1928- *WhoSSW 93*
Dawson, Petrina R. *Law&B 92*
Dawson, R.B. *Law&B 92*
Dawson, Ray Fields 1911- *WhoAm 92*
Dawson, Rhett 1943- *WhoAm 92*
Dawson, Rhett B. *Law&B 92*
Dawson, Rhett Brewer 1943- *St&PR 93*
Dawson, Richard *WhoAm 92*
Dawson, Richard James 1936- *WhoUN 92*
Dawson, Richard T. *Law&B 92*
Dawson, Richard T. 1945- *St&PR 93*
Dawson, Richard Thomas 1931- *WhoWor 93*
Dawson, Richard Thomas 1945- *WhoAm 92*
Dawson, Robert C. 1923- *St&PR 93*
Dawson, Robert Earle 1923- *WhoAm 92*
Dawson, Robert Edward, Sr. 1918- *WhoAm 92*
Dawson, Robert Kent 1946- *WhoAm 92*
Dawson, Robert Kevin 1953- *WhoEmL 93*
Dawson, Robert Oscar 1939- *WhoAm 92*
Dawson, Robert Victor 1939- *St&PR 93*
Dawson, Samuel Cooper, Jr. 1909- *WhoAm 92, WhoWor 93*
Dawson, Samuel H. 1942-1991 *BioIn 17*
Dawson, Sandra *WhoScE 91-1*
Dawson, Saranne *ScF&FL 92*
Dawson, Shannon M. 1953- *WhoAmW 93*
Dawson, Sheryl W. *Law&B 92*
Dawson, Stephen Edwin 1949- *WhoEmL 93*
Dawson, Stephen Everette 1946- *WhoEmL 93*
Dawson, Stuart Owen 1935- *WhoAm 92*
Dawson, Suzanne S. 1941- *WhoAmW 93*
Dawson, Ted 1951- *Baker 92*
Dawson, Thomas Cleland, II 1948- *WhoAm 92*
Dawson, Thomas Wayne 1947- *WhoEmL 93, WhoSSW 93*
Dawson, Timothy S. *Law&B 92*
Dawson, Todd *Law&B 92*
Dawson, Wallace Douglas, Jr. 1931- *WhoAm 92*
Dawson, Walter Francis *Law&B 92*
Dawson, Wilfred Thomas 1928- *WhoAm 92, WhoSSW 93*
Dawson, William 1901-1990 *BioIn 17*
Dawson, William J. 1963- *St&PR 93*
Dawson, William James, Jr. 1930- *WhoAm 92*
Dawson, William Johnson, Jr. 1925- *WhoSSW 93*
Dawson, William Levi 1886-1970 *BioIn 17*
Dawson, William Levi 1898-1990 *Baker 92*
Dawson, William Levi 1899-1990 *BioIn 17*
Dawson, William Ryan 1927- *WhoAm 92*
Dawson, William Stone 1917- *WhoWor 93*
Dawson, William Thomas 1938- *St&PR 93*
Dawson-August, Annie Lee 1953- *WhoEmL 93*
Dawson-Sauser, Nancy Edith 1940- *WhoAmW 93*
Day, A. Grove 1904- *ScF&FL 92*
Day, Alexandra *BioIn 17, ConAu 136*
Day, Ann *WhoAmW 93*
Day, Anne Glendenning White Parker 1926- *WhoAmW 93*
Day, Anne Marjorie 1875- *AmWomPl*
Day, Anthony 1933- *WhoAm 92*
Day, Arthur Grove 1904- *WhoAm 92*
Day, Audrey *WhoWrEP 92*
Day, Barnie K. 1952- *St&PR 93*
Day, Benjamin Henry 1810-1889 *JrnUS*
Day, Beth (Feagles) 1924- *ConAu 40NR*
Day, Beverly Karen 1959- *WhoAmW 93*
Day, Bobby d1990 *BioIn 17*
Day, Bobby 1932-1990 *SoulM*
Day, Brad 1963- *WhoWor 93*
Day, Bradford M. 1916- *ScF&FL 92*
Day, Bruce W. 1945- *St&PR 93*
Day, Castle Nason 1933- *St&PR 93, WhoAm 92*
Day, Cecil LeRoy 1922- *WhoAm 92*
Day, Charles Roger, Jr. 1947- *WhoAm 92*
Day, Charles Russell 1860-1900 *Baker 92*
Day, Chet *ScF&FL 92*
Day, Chon 1907- *WhoAm 92*
Day, Christian Charles 1946- *WhoEmL 93*
Day, Clarence 1901-1990 *BioIn 17*
Day, Colin Leslie 1944- *WhoAm 92*
Day, Daniel Edgar 1913- *WhoAm 92*
Day, David 1947- *DcChlFi, ScF&FL 92, WhoCanL 92*
Day, David Owen 1958- *WhoSSW 93*
Day, Delbert Edwin 1936- *WhoAm 92*
Day, Dennis G. *Law&B 92*
Day, Donald 1895-1966 *BioIn 17*
Day, Donald 1899-1991 *BioIn 17*
Day, Donald B. 1909-1978 *ScF&FL 92*
Day, Donald Joseph 1929- *WhoWor 93*
Day, Donald Lee 1947- *WhoEmL 93*
Day, Donald Morfoot 1954- *WhoEmL 93*
Day, Donald Richard *Law&B 92*
Day, Donald Sheldon 1924- *WhoAm 92*
Day, Doris 1924- *IntDcF 2-3 [port], WhoAm 92*
Day, Dorothy 1897-1980 *BioIn 17, JrnUS*
Day, Dorothy G. 1930- *St&PR 93*
Day, Edith Eleanor *AmWomPl*
Day, Edward C. 1932- *SmATA 72*
Day, Edward Francis, Jr. 1946- *WhoEmL 93, WhoWor 93*
Day, Edward Roy, III 1958- *WhoSSW 93*
Day, Emerson 1913- *WhoAm 92*
Day, Ernest *MiSFD 9*
Day, Eugene Davis, Sr. 1925- *WhoAm 92*
Day, Francisco 1907- *WhoWor 93*
Day, Frank E. 1918- *WhoAm 92*
Day, Frank Parker 1881-1950 *BioIn 17*
Day, G.J. *BioIn 17*
Day, Gale Unger 1946- *WhoUN 92*
Day, Gary T. *Law&B 92*
Day, George C. *Law&B 92*
Day, George E. *BioIn 17*
Day, George R. 1950- *WhoAm 92, WhoWrEP 92*
Day, Graham J. *BioIn 17*
Day, Gregg Alan 1952- *WhoEmL 93*
Day, Holliday T. 1936- *ConAu 137*
Day, Howard Wilman 1942- *WhoAm 92*
Day, Irving Meade, III 1938- *WhoE 93*
Day, J.K. Mackendree *Law&B 92*
Day, James *BioIn 17*
Day, James Edward 1914- *WhoAm 92*
Day, James Edward 1940- *St&PR 93*
Day, James H. 1927-1990 *BioIn 17*
Day, James L. 1932- *St&PR 93*
Day, James Meredith 1955- *WhoE 93*
Day, James Milton 1931- *WhoAm 92*
Day, James Todd 1948- *WhoSSW 93*
Day, Jane Ann 1946- *WhoAmW 93*
Day, Janice Eldredge 1919- *WhoAmW 93*
Day, Jennie D. *WhoAmW 93*
Day, Jennifer Carolyn 1966- *WhoAmW 93*
Day, Joel M. 1941- *St&PR 93*
Day, John *MiSFD 9*
Day, John A. 1949- *WhoScE 91-1*
Day, John Alan 1945- *WhoAm 92*
Day, John Arthur 1956- *WhoEmL 93, WhoSSW 93*
Day, John Baldwin *Law&B 92*
Day, John Denton 1942- *WhoWor 93*
Day, John Francis 1920- *WhoAm 92*
Day, John Franklin 1928- *WhoAm 92*
Day, John Michael 1945- *WhoE 93*
Day, John Shuey 1949- *WhoSSW 93*
Day, John Sidney 1917- *WhoAm 92*
Day, John W. 1933- *WhoAm 92*
Day, Jonny Mac 1946- *St&PR 93*
Day, Joseph Dennis 1942- *WhoAm 92*
Day, Kyle 1959- *WhoEmL 93*
Day, Larry D. 1944- *St&PR 93*
Day, Larry Douglas 1944- *WhoAm 92*
Day, Lawrence Elwood 1947- *WhoEmL 93*
Day, Lawrence Eric 1941- *WhoAm 92*
Day, LeRoy Edward 1925- *WhoAm 92*
Day, Lewis Rodman 1915-1990 *BioIn 17*
Day, Lila *WhoWrEP 92*
Day, Lillian 1893-1991 *BioIn 17*
Day, Lorraine *BioIn 17*
Day, Lucille Elizabeth 1947- *WhoAmW 93, WhoEmL 93*
Day, Lyndon R. *WhoScE 91-1*
Day, Marceline 1907?- *SweetSg B [port]*
Day, Margaret Ranft *Law&B 92*
Day, Mary Carol *WhoAmW 93*
Day, Mary Jane Thomas 1927- *WhoAm 92, WhoAmW 93*
Day, Marylouise Muldoon *WhoAmW 93*
Day, Maurice Jerome 1913- *St&PR 93, WhoAm 92*
Day, Melvin Sherman 1923- *WhoAm 92*
Day, Michael H. 1949- *St&PR 93*
Day, Michelle *Law&B 92*
Day, Mildred Leake 1929- *WhoSSW 93*
Day, Nancy I. 1944- *St&PR 93*
Day, Nicholas Edward *WhoScE 91-1*
Day, Pamela Triplett *Law&B 92*
Day, Paul Richard 1922- *WhoAm 92*
Day, Paul William *Law&B 92*
Day, Peggy Jean 1946- *WhoAmW 93*
Day, Peter *WhoScE 91-1*
Day, Peter R. *Law&B 92*
Day, Peter Rodney 1928- *WhoE 93*
Day, Peter William 1944- *WhoSSW 93*
Day, Pomeroy 1906- *WhoAm 92*
Day, Richard B. *BioIn 17*
Day, Richard Cortez 1927- *WhoWrEP 92*
Day, Richard Curtis 1934- *St&PR 93*
Day, Richard Elledge 1939- *WhoWor 93*
Day, Richard Putnam 1930- *St&PR 93, WhoAm 92, WhoIns 93*
Day, Rob *BioIn 17*
Day, Robert 1922- *MiSFD 9*
Day, Robert Androus 1924- *WhoAm 92*
Day, Robert Charles 1934- *WhoUN 92*
Day, Robert Edgar 1919- *WhoAm 92*
Day, Robert Jennings 1925- *St&PR 93*
Day, Robert L. *Law&B 92*
Day, Robert Michael 1950- *WhoSSW 93*
Day, Robert Winsor 1930- *WhoAm 92*
Day, Roland Bernard 1919- *WhoAm 92*
Day, Ronald Elwin 1933- *WhoE 93, WhoWor 93*
Day, Russell Clover 1943- *WhoE 93*
Day, Samuel H. *BioIn 17*
Day, Sharon Hoelscher 1952- *WhoEmL 93*
Day, Sharon S. 1956- *WhoSSW 93*
Day, Stacey Biswas 1927- *WhoAm 92, WhoE 93, WhoWor 93*
Day, Stephen Martin 1931- *WhoAm 92*
Day, Steven J. *BioIn 17*
Day, Suzanne Marie 1953- *WhoAmW 93, WhoEmL 93*
Day, Thomas Brennock 1932- *WhoAm 92*
Day, Thomas Gerard 1956- *WhoSSW 93*
Day, Thomas Kevin 1946- *WhoWor 93*
Day, Timothy T. 1937- *St&PR 93*
Day, Tod Eugene 1964- *WhoEmL 93*
Day, Todd *BioIn 17*
Day, Victor R. *Law&B 92*
Day, Wayne Allan 1955- *WhoEmL 93, WhoSSW 93*
Day, Weston S. 1945- *WhoIns 93*
Day, William *WhoScE 91-1*
Day, William Alan 1942- *WhoWor 93*
Day, William Homer 1934- *WhoE 93*
Day, William Hudson 1937- *WhoAm 92*
Day, William Patrick 1950- *ScF&FL 92*
Day, William Rufus 1849-1923 *OxCSupC [port]*
Day, Willie S. 1947- *St&PR 93*
Day, Wynne Gregory 1954- *WhoEmL 93*
Dayal, Virendra 1935- *WhoUN 92*
Dayala, Haji Farooq 1948- *WhoEmL 93*
Dayan, Anthony David *WhoScE 91-1*
Dayan, Jacob 1944- *St&PR 93*
Dayan, Joan 1949- *ScF&FL 92*
Dayan, Josee *MiSFD 9*
Dayan, Moshe 1915-1981 *BioIn 17, DcTwHis, HarEnMi*
Dayan, Nissim 1946- *MiSFD 9*
Dayan, Rodney S. 1933- *WhoAm 92, WhoE 93*
Dayananda, Mysore Ananthamurthy 1934- *WhoAm 92*
Dayananda, Palahela Withana Arachiag 1940- *WhoWor 93*
Dayananda Sarasvati, Swami 1824-1883 *BioIn 17*
Dayanghirang, Enrico G. 1955- *WhoAsAP 91*
Dayani, John Hassan, Sr. 1947- *WhoEmL 93*
Dayday, Henry *WhoAm 92*
Dayharsh, Virginia Fiengo 1942- *WhoAmW 93*
Dayhoff, Jocelyn Rausch 1956- *WhoEmL 93*
Dayhoff, Ruth Elizabeth 1952- *WhoAmW 93*
Day Lewis, C. 1904-1972 *BioIn 17*
Day Lewis, Cecil 1904-1972 *BioIn 17*
Day-Lewis, Daniel *BioIn 17*
Day Lewis, Daniel 1957- *IntDcF 2-3 [port]*
Day-Meyers, Linda Lee 1939- *WhoAmW 93*
Dayne, Taylor *BioIn 17*
Dayton, Bruce Mc Lean 1934- *WhoIns 93*

Dayton, Deane Kraybill 1949- *WhoSSW 93*
Dayton, Douglas J. 1924- *St&PR 93*
Dayton, Helena Smith *AmWomPl*
Dayton, Irene Catherine 1922- *WhoWrEP 92*
Dayton, Jonathan 1760-1824 *PolPar*
Dayton, Katharine *AmWomPl*
Dayton, Lyman *MiSFD 9*
Dayton, Martin 1944- *WhoSSW 93*
Dayton, Richard Lee 1934- *WhoAm 92*
Dayton, S. Grey, Jr. 1921- *St&PR 93*
Dayton, Samuel Grey, Jr. 1921- *WhoAm 92*
Dayton, William L. 1807-1864 *PolPar*
Daywalt, Daniel G. 1957- *St&PR 93*
Daywalt, Daniel Gray 1957- *WhoE 93*
Daywalt, Lorrie 1959- *St&PR 93*
Daza, Raul A. 1935- *WhoAsAP 91*
Daze, D. Timothy *Law&B 92*
Daze, David Timothy 1949- *WhoEmL 93*
Daze, Michel A. *Law&B 92*
Dazey, William Boyd 1915- *WhoAm 92, WhoWor 93*
D'Azzo, John Joachim 1919- *WhoAm 92*
D'Costa, Opyll *Law&B 92*
Dea, David Young Fong 1924- *WhoWor 93*
Dea, Donald Don 1954- *WhoE 93, WhoEmL 93*
Dea, Iain Cunningham Mutter 1943- *WhoScE 91-1, WhoWor 93*
Dea, Margaret Mary 1946- *WhoAmW 93*
Dea, Phoebe Kin-Kin 1946- *WhoEmL 93*
Deacon, David Emmerson 1949- *WhoAm 92*
Deacon, Donald M. 1920- *St&PR 93*
Deacon, John H. *Law&B 92*
Deacon, Paul Septimus 1922- *WhoAm 92*
Deacon, Robert H. 1926- *St&PR 93*
Deacon, Ruth E. *BioIn 17*
Deacon, Sandra Faye 1950- *WhoSSW 93*
Deacon, Sharon Rae 1942- *WhoAmW 93*
de Acosta, Alejandro Daniel 1941- *WhoAm 92*
Deacy, Thomas Edward, Jr. 1918- *WhoAm 92*
Deaderick, Jimmy R. 1947- *WhoAm 92*
Deadman, Leonard John 1932- *WhoAm 92*
Deadrich, Paul Eddy 1925- *WhoWor 93*
Deadrick, Diana Lyn 1957- *WhoAmW 93*
Deagon, Ann 1930- *WhoWrEP 92*
de Aguiar, Geraldo Nogueira 1949- *St&PR 93*
Deahl, James 1945- *WhoCanL 92*
De Ahna, Heinrich Karl Hermann 1835-1892 *Baker 92*
Deak, Csaba 1932- *Baker 92*
Deak, Franklin Harry *Law&B 92*
Deak, Istvan 1926- *WhoAm 92*
Deak, Peter 1952- *WhoWor 93*
Deak, Richard A. *Law&B 92*
Deak, Tibor 1935- *WhoScE 91-4*
Deakin, Alfred 1856-1919 *DcTwHis*
Deakin, Edward B. 1943- *WhoAm 92*
Deakin, Edwin 1838-1923 *BioIn 17*
Deakins, John *ScF&FL 92*
Deakins, John David 1942- *St&PR 93, WhoAm 92*
Deakins, Warren Whitney 1938- *St&PR 93*
Deal, Bruce Elmer 1927- *WhoAm 92*
Deal, Ernest L., Jr. 1929- *St&PR 93*
Deal, Ernest Linwood, Jr. 1929- *WhoAm 92, WhoSSW 93*
Deal, G. Ralph 1940- *St&PR 93*
Deal, George A. 1914- *St&PR 93*
Deal, George Edgar 1920- *WhoAm 92, WhoWor 93*
Deal, Grady Abee 1944- *St&PR 93*
Deal, J. Thomas *Law&B 92*
Deal, James A. *St&PR 93*
Deal, John Milton 1906- *WhoSSW 93*
Deal, Joseph Maurice 1947- *WhoAm 92*
Deal, Luisa 1943- *WhoAmW 93*
Deal, Mary E. *Law&B 92*
Deal, Pony d1882 *BioIn 17*
Deal, Richard Allen 1929- *St&PR 93*
Deal, Shirley Mae Herd 1935- *WhoWrEP 92*
Deal, Susan Strayer 1948- *WhoWrEP 92*
Deal, Thomas B. *Law&B 92*
Deal, Timothy 1940- *WhoAm 92*
Dealessandro, Joseph P. 1930- *St&PR 93*
DeAlessandro, Joseph Paul 1930- *WhoAm 92*
Dealexandris, Robert A. 1941- *St&PR 93*
Dealey, Joseph MacDonald, Jr. 1947- *WhoEmL 93, WhoSSW 93*
Dealey, Samuel D. 1906-1944 *BioIn 17*
De Almeida, Antonio Castro Mendes 1934- *WhoWor 93*
DeAlmeida, Cynthia Koledo 1959- *WhoAm 92*
De Alwis, Susantha 1932- *WhoWor 93*
Dealy, Catherine Ann 1949- *WhoAmW 93*
Dealy, James J. 1935- *St&PR 93*
Dealy, John Francis 1939- *WhoAm 92*
Dealy, John Michael 1937- *WhoAm 92*
Deam, Carol Pearce 1959- *WhoAmW 93*
De Amaral, Olga Ceballos *BioIn 17*
Deam-Daves, Barbara Joan 1940- *WhoAmW 93*
Deamer, Dulcie 1890-1972 *ScF&FL 92*
De Amicis, Anna Lucia c. 1733-1816 *Baker 92*
De Amicis, Antonio Domenico c. 1716- *OxDcOp*
De Amicis Buonsollazzi, Anna Lucia c. 1733-1816 *OxDcOp*
Deamouchet, Leonard *Law&B 92*
Dean, Alan Loren 1918- *WhoAm 92*
Dean, Andrea Oppenheimer 1935- *WhoAm 92*
Dean, Anthony Marion 1944- *WhoE 93*
Dean, Anthony Taylor 1945- *St&PR 93*
Dean, Beale 1922- *WhoAm 92, WhoSSW 93*
Dean, Betty Marlene 1941- *WhoAmW 93*
Dean, Billie Eason 1966- *WhoSSW 93*
Dean, Bruce Campbell 1958- *WhoEmL 93*
Dean, Burton Victor 1924- *WhoAm 92*
Dean, Carl L. 1927- *St&PR 93*
Dean, Carl W. 1946- *St&PR 93*
Dean, Carolynn Leslie 1952- *WhoEmL 93*
Dean, Charles Henry, Jr. 1925- *WhoAm 92*
Dean, Charles Thomas 1918- *WhoAm 92*
Dean, Christopher *BioIn 17*
Dean, Clifford A. *Law&B 92*
Dean, Cynthia Bailey 1956- *WhoWrEP 92*
Dean, Daffy 1913-1981 *BioIn 17*
Dean, David 1942- *St&PR 93*
Dean, David Jerome 1948- *WhoEmL 93*
Dean, Dearest 1911- *WhoAm 92, WhoAmW 93*
Dean, Denis Allen 1942- *WhoSSW 93*
Dean, Dennis R(ichard) 1938- *ConAu 137*
Dean, Dewey Hobson, Jr. 1920- *St&PR 93*
Dean, Diane D. 1949- *WhoE 93*
Dean, Dizzy 1911-1974 *BioIn 17*
Dean, Don R. 1941- *St&PR 93*
Dean, Donna Joyce 1947- *WhoEmL 93*
Dean, Dora 1872?-1950 *BioIn 17*
Dean, E. Joseph 1949- *WhoEmL 93*
Dean, Edwin Becton 1940- *WhoSSW 93, WhoWor 93*
Dean, Elizabeth M. 1948- *WhoEmL 93*
Dean, Eloise Earle *AmWomPl*
Dean, Frances *AmWomPl*
Dean, Frances Childers 1930- *WhoAm 92*
Dean, Francis Hill 1922- *WhoAm 92*
Dean, Frederick B. 1927- *St&PR 93*
Dean, Frederick Bernard 1927- *WhoAm 92*
Dean, Gary Neal 1953- *WhoSSW 93*
Dean, Geoffrey 1940- *WhoAm 92*
Dean, George Alden 1929- *WhoAm 92*
Dean, Harold Leon 1950- *WhoSSW 93*
Dean, Harry Todrick 1947- *St&PR 93*
Dean, Hollis R. 1926- *WhoSSW 93*
Dean, Howard 1948- *WhoAm 92, WhoE 93, WhoWor 93*
Dean, Howard Brush 1921- *WhoAm 92*
Dean, Howard M. 1937- *St&PR 93*
Dean, Howard M., Jr. 1937- *WhoAm 92*
Dean, Jack Pearce 1931- *WhoAm 92*
Dean, Jaclynn Lee 1947- *WhoEmL 93*
Dean, Jacquelyn Marie 1954- *WhoAmW 93*
Dean, James 1931-1955 *BioIn 17, IntDcF 2-3 [port]*
Dean, James B. 1941- *WhoAm 92*
Dean, James Edward 1944- *WhoSSW 93*
Dean, James Leroy 1942- *WhoE 93*
Dean, James Wendell 1948- *WhoEmL 93*
Dean, Jeffrey David 1960- *WhoE 93*
Dean, Jerome F. 1953- *WhoAm 92*
Dean, Jerry Robert 1935- *St&PR 93*
Dean, Jimmy 1928- *St&PR 93, WhoAm 92*
Dean, Jimmy Ray 1928- *BioIn 17*
Dean, John Aurie 1921- *WhoAm 92, WhoWor 93*
Dean, John Drury *Law&B 92*
Dean, John Gunther 1926- *WhoAm 92*
Dean, John Martin 1958- *WhoSSW 93*
Dean, John Stanley 1939- *St&PR 93*
Dean, John Wilson, Jr. 1918- *WhoAm 92*
Dean, Jonathan *Law&B 92*
Dean, Karen Abbey 1962- *WhoSSW 93*
Dean, Kenneson Gene 1948- *WhoEmL 93*
Dean, Kenneth H. 1939- *St&PR 93*
Dean, Laura 1945- *WhoAm 92, WhoAmW 93*
Dean, Laura Hansen 1951- *WhoEmL 93*
Dean, Lawrence W. 1943- *St&PR 93*
Dean, Lena Carson *AmWomPl*
Dean, Leslie Alan 1940- *WhoE 93*
Dean, Lisa *ScF&FL 92*
Dean, Lydia Margaret Carter 1919- *WhoAm 92, WhoAmW 93, WhoWor 93*
Dean, Lynda G. 1945- *St&PR 93*
Dean, Lynn 1923- *St&PR 93*
Dean, Margia *SweetSg D [port]*
Dean, Margo 1927- *WhoAm 92, WhoSSW 93*
Dean, Martyn *ScF&FL 92*
Dean, Mary Elizabeth 1947- *WhoEmL 93*
Dean, Michael Francis *WhoScE 91-1*
Dean, Michael M. 1933- *WhoAm 92*
Dean, Michael Patrick 1946- *WhoEmL 93*
Dean, Monica F. 1950- *WhoAmW 93*
Dean, Nathan Wesley 1941- *WhoE 93*
Dean, Norman E. 1943- *St&PR 93*
Dean, Pamela 1953- *ScF&FL 92*
Dean, Paul Dee 1913-1981 *BioIn 17*
Dean, Paul John 1941- *WhoAm 92, WhoWrEP 92*
Dean, Paul Regis 1918- *WhoAm 92*
Dean, Peter 1941- *WhoAm 92, WhoE 93*
Dean, Philip Michael *WhoScE 91-1*
Dean, R.R. *WhoScE 91-1*
Dean, Randy L. *Law&B 92*
Dean, Richard Anthony 1935- *St&PR 93*
Dean, Richard Whaley 1942- *St&PR 93*
Dean, Robert Berridge 1913- *WhoWor 93*
Dean, Robert Bruce 1949- *WhoE 93, WhoEmL 93*
Dean, Robert Charles 1903- *WhoAm 92*
Dean, Robert Charles, Jr. 1928- *WhoAm 92*
Dean, Robert Franklin 1942- *WhoSSW 93*
Dean, Robert Scott 1955- *WhoEmL 93*
Dean, Robert Walter, Jr. 1950- *WhoEmL 93*
Dean, Roger 1944- *ScF&FL 92*
Dean, Roger Thornton 1948- *WhoWor 93*
Dean, Ruth Josephine 1902- *WhoE 93*
Dean, Sandra Harrison 1945- *WhoAmW 93*
Dean, Sidney Walter, Jr. 1905- *WhoAm 92*
Dean, Stafford (Roderick) 1937- *Baker 92*
Dean, Stanley Rochelle 1908- *WhoAm 92*
Dean, Stephen Odell 1936- *WhoAm 92, WhoE 93*
Dean, T.W.R. *WhoScE 91-1*
Dean, Thomas G. 1967- *WhoE 93*
Dean, Thomas H. 1928- *St&PR 93*
Dean, Thomas Scott 1924- *WhoAm 92*
Dean, Vernon Keller d1984 *BioIn 17*
Dean, Vicky Charlene 1949- *WhoAmW 93*
Dean, Walter *BioIn 17*
Dean, Walter L. 1927- *St&PR 93*
Dean, Walter Nelson 1919- *WhoAm 92*
Dean, Walter Wood *Law&B 92*
Dean, Warren Michael 1944- *St&PR 93*
Dean, William Evans 1930- *St&PR 93, WhoAm 92*
Dean, William George 1921- *WhoAm 92*
Dean, William H. 1910-1952 *BioIn 17*
Dean, William L. 1926- *St&PR 93*
Dean, William Shirley 1947- *WhoEmL 93*
Dean, Winton (Basil) 1916- *Baker 92*
DeAnda, James 1925- *HispAmA, WhoSSW 93*
Dean-Daniel, Alice Elaine 1941- *WhoAmW 93*
de Andino, Jean-Pierre Martinez 1946- *WhoEmL 93*
de Andrade, Jose Luiz Coelho *Law&B 92*
de Andrade, Mario *ScF&FL 92*
De Andrade, Mario 1928-1990 *BioIn 17*
De Andres Sanz, Miguel Pedro 1926- *WhoScE 91-3*
Deane, Buddy 1924- *WhoSSW 93*
Deane, Daniel J. 1956- *St&PR 93*
Deane, Derrick Peter 1944- *WhoUN 92*
Deane, Dora *AmWomPl*
Deane, Edwin G. 1928- *St&PR 93*
Deane, Elaine 1958- *WhoEmL 93*
Deane, Frederick, Jr. 1926- *St&PR 93, WhoAm 92*
Deane, Herbert Andrew 1921-1991 *BioIn 17*
Deane, James Garner 1923- *WhoAm 92, WhoWor 93, WhoWrEP 92*
Deane, James R. *Law&B 92*
Deane, James R. 1935- *St&PR 93*
Deane, James Richard 1935- *WhoAm 92*
Deane, John Herbert 1952- *WhoE 93, WhoEmL 93*
Deane, Joseph R. 1926- *St&PR 93*
Deane, Lyttleton Nicholas 1954- *WhoEmL 93*
Deane, Marjorie Wilson 1950- *WhoAmW 93*
Deane, Matthew P. d1991 *BioIn 17*
Deane, Sally Jan 1948- *WhoAmW 93, WhoEmL 93*
Deane, Seamus Francis 1940- *WhoWor 93*
Deane, Terry Allan 1952- *St&PR 93*
Deane, Thomas Andersen 1921- *WhoAm 92*
Deane, William John 1938- *St&PR 93*
Deaner, R. Milton 1924- *WhoAm 92*
de Angeli, Marguerite (Lofft) 1889-1987 *MajAI [port]*
De Angelis, Barbara *BioIn 17*
De Angelis, Barbara (Ann) 1951- *ConAu 139*
De Angelis, Costanzo Maria 1924- *WhoScE 91-3*
De Angelis, Deborah Ann Ayars 1948- *WhoAmW 93*
DeAngelis, John A. 1913- *St&PR 93*
De Angelis, John Louis, Jr. *Law&B 92*
DeAngelis, John Louis, Jr. 1951- *WhoEmL 93, WhoSSW 93*
DeAngelis, Lorraine Theresa 1960- *WhoEmL 93*
DeAngelis, Margaret Scalza 1936- *WhoAmW 93, WhoWor 93*
De Angelis, Milo 1951- *DcLB 128*
De Angelis, Nazzareno 1881-1962 *Baker 92, OxDcOp*
De Angelis, Pasquale Luigi 1948- *WhoWor 93*
DeAngelis, Peter 1929- *St&PR 93*
DeAngelis, Robert Neal 1942- *WhoSSW 93*
DeAngelis, Susan Penny 1950- *WhoAmW 93, WhoEmL 93*
DeAngelo, Gina Marie 1963- *WhoAmW 93*
Deangelo, John 1928- *St&PR 93*
DeAngelo, Joseph A. 1944- *St&PR 93*
DeAngelus, Ronald Patrick 1935- *WhoE 93*
Deanin, Rudolph Dreskin 1921- *WhoE 93*
Dean-McCarthy, Pamela Roslyn Kahikina 1959- *WhoAmW 93*
Deans, Glenn Norfleet 1947- *WhoE 93*
Deans, Janice P. 1958- *WhoEmL 93*
Deans, John E. *Law&B 92*
Deans, John E. 1946- *St&PR 93*
Deans, Jonathan *BioIn 17*
Deans, Marie *BioIn 17*
Deans, Norman Dickson *WhoScE 91-1*
Deans, Penny Candace 1952- *WhoAmW 93*
Deans, Stanley Gordon 1951- *WhoWor 93*
Deans, Thomas Seymour 1946- *WhoEmL 93*
De Antoni, Edward Paul 1941- *WhoAm 92*
De Antonio, Emile *BioIn 17*
De Antonio, Emile 1920-1989 *MiSFD 9N*
DeAntonis, G.W., Jr. 1940- *St&PR 93*
Dean-Zubritsky, Cynthia Marian 1950- *WhoAm 92, WhoAmW 93, WhoE 93, WhoEmL 93*
Dear, David Ollie 1941- *St&PR 93*
Dear, Ian 1935- *ScF&FL 92*
Dear, Robert Ernest Arthur 1933- *WhoAm 92*
Dear, William *MiSFD 9*
De Aragon, RaGena Cheri 1952- *WhoEmL 93*
Dearborn, Bruce B. 1949- *St&PR 93*
Dearborn, Donald Edward 1939- *WhoE 93*
Dearborn, Henry 1751-1829 *CmdGen 1991 [port], HarEnMi*
Dearborn, Laura *WhoAmW 93*
Dearborn, Maureen Markt 1948- *WhoAmW 93*
De Arcangelis, Giuseppe 1962- *WhoWor 93*
Dearden, Basil 1911-1971 *MiSFD 9N*
Dearden, Douglas E. 1921- *St&PR 93*
Dearden, James 1949- *ConAu 136, ConTFT 10, MiSFD 9*
Dearden, John Christopher *WhoScE 91-1*
Dearden, William Edgar Chambers 1922- *St&PR 93, WhoAm 92*
Deardorf, David A. 1937- *WhoAm 92*
Deardorf, David Allen 1937- *St&PR 93*
Deardorff, Linda Ann 1953- *WhoAmW 93*
Deardorff, Michael Kent 1949- *WhoIns 93*
Deardourff, John *See* Bailey, Douglas & Deardourff, John *PolPar*
Deardourff, John D. 1933- *WhoAm 92*
Deare, Jennifer Laurie 1952- *WhoEmL 93*
de Arellano, Diana Ramirez *NotHsAW 93*
Dearen, Patrick 1951- *ScF&FL 92*
Dearie, Raymond J. 1944- *WhoAm 92, WhoE 93*
Dearing, David A. 1948- *St&PR 93*
Dearing, Deborah Carter 1957- *WhoEmL 93*
Dearing, Dennis A. *Law&B 92*
Dearing, Judy *BioIn 17*
Dearing, Reinhard Josef 1947- *WhoEmL 93, WhoSSW 93*
Dearing, Victoria Suzanne 1948- *WhoSSW 93*
Dearing, Vinton Adams 1920- *WhoAm 92, WhoWrEP 92*
Dearman, Henry Hursell 1934- *WhoAm 92*
DeArman, Richard L. 1947- *St&PR 93*
De Armas, Frederick Alfred 1945- *WhoAm 92*
De Armas, Jorge Benito 1931- *St&PR 93*
De Armas, Mario S. 1943- *WhoWor 93*
DeArment, George S. 1913- *St&PR 93*
De Arment, Roderick Allen 1948- *WhoAm 92*

DeArment, William Almon 1915- *St&PR 93*
De Arment, William S. 1947- *St&PR 93*
DeArmond, Dale 1914- *ConAu 138*
DeArmond, Dale Burlison *ConAu 138*
DeArmond, Dale Burlison 1914- *SmATA 70 [port]*
De Armond, Lizzie *AmWomPl*
Dearmore, Thomas Lee 1927- *WhoAm 92*
Dearstyne, Bruce William 1944- *WhoE 93*
Dearstyne, Kenneth Edgar, Jr. 1959- *St&PR 93*
de Arteaga-Morgan, Ivette 1931- *WhoAmW 93*
Dearth, Jeffrey L. 1950- *WhoAm 92, WhoE 93*
Dearth, William Benton, III 1950- *St&PR 93*
Deary, Roy Grant, Jr. 1930- *St&PR 93*
Deas, David 1771- *BioIn 17*
Deas, Henry 1770-1846 *BioIn 17*
Deas, Richard Ryder, III 1927- *WhoSSW 93*
Dease, Ann Wilks 1938- *WhoSSW 93*
Deason, Edward Joseph 1955- *WhoEmL 93, WhoWor 93*
Deason, George T. *Law&B 92*
Deason, Glen Albert 1941- *WhoSSW 93*
De Asua, Luis 1962- *WhoWor 93*
Deasy, Cornelius Michael 1918- *WhoAm 92*
Deasy, Frank *MiSFD 9*
Deasy, Kevin 1953- *WhoEmL 93*
Deasy, Patrick B. 1941- *WhoScE 91-3*
Deasy, Patrick G. 1938- *St&PR 93*
Deasy, Rickard Hugh 1948- *WhoWor 93*
Deasy, Theresa 1958- *WhoAmW 93*
Deasy, William John 1937- *St&PR 93, WhoAm 92*
Deat, Marcel 1894-1955 *BioIn 17*
Deat, Michel Jean 1944- *WhoScE 91-2*
Deatherage, Bill Guy 1951- *WhoSSW 93*
Deatherage, Martha Martin *WhoSSW 93*
Deatly, Richard Henry 1928- *St&PR 93*
Deatly, William N. 1958- *St&PR 93*
Deaton, Angus Stewart 1945- *WhoAm 92*
Deaton, Betty J. *Law&B 92*
Deaton, Bobby Charles 1936- *WhoSSW 93*
Deaton, David Lee 1954- *WhoSSW 93*
Deaton, Fae Adams 1932- *WhoWor 93*
Deaton, Frank A. 1925- *St&PR 93*
Deaton, Michael Paul 1951- *WhoEmL 93*
Deaton, Tammie Lynn 1964- *WhoAmW 93*
Deaton, Wendy Susan 1941- *WhoAmW 93*
Deats, Paul Edwin 1946- *WhoEmL 93*
Deats, Paul Kindred, Jr. 1918- *WhoAm 92*
Deavenport, Earnest W., Jr. *St&PR 93*
Deaver, Darwin Holloway 1914- *WhoAm 92*
Deaver, Gerald R. *Law&B 92*
Deaver, Jeffrey Wilds 1950- *ScF&FL 92*
Deaver, Julie Reece *BioIn 17*
Deaver, Julie Reece 1953- *ConAu 37NR*
Deaver, Michael Keith 1938- *WhoAm 92*
Deaver, Nancy *SweetSg B*
Deaver, Phillip Lester 1952- *WhoEmL 93*
Deavers, James Frederick 1947- *WhoSSW 93*
Deavers, Karl A. 1934- *St&PR 93*
Deavers, Karl Alan 1934- *WhoAm 92*
Deaves, D.M. 1950- *WhoScE 91-1*
De Aviles, Pedro Menendez 1519-1574 *BioIn 17*
De Aza, Salvador 1933- *WhoScE 91-3*
Deb, Arun Kumar 1936- *St&PR 93*
Deb, Krishna K. 1936- *WhoSSW 93*
Deb, Sanjay Kumar 1938- *WhoE 93*
de Baca Gilbert, Fabiola Cabeza *NotHsAW 93*
Debache, Herve 1945- *WhoWor 93*
De Backer, Guy G. 1944- *WhoScE 91-2*
De Backer, Louis W. 1937- *WhoScE 91-2*
DeBacker, Michael L. *Law&B 92*
Debaes, Bernard G. 1951- *WhoScE 91-2*
De Baets, Marc Hubert 1950- *WhoWor 93*
Debain, Alexandre-Francois 1809-1877 *Baker 92*
DeBakey, Lois *WhoAm 92, WhoSSW 93, WhoWor 93*
DeBakey, Michael Ellis 1908- *WhoAm 92, WhoSSW 93, WhoWor 93*
DeBakey, Selma *WhoAm 92, WhoSSW 93, WhoWor 93*
Debal, Swami Puja *ScF&FL 92*
De Balboa, Vasco Nunez 1475-1519 *BioIn 17*
de Baliol, Alexander *ScF&FL 92*
de Balzac, Honore *ScF&FL 92*
DeBane, Pierre 1938- *WhoAm 92*
De Banfield, Graziella *BioIn 17*
De Banfield, Raffaello 1922- *BioIn 17*
De Bankole, Isaach *BioIn 17*
Debany, Christine 1950- *WhoAmW 93*
deBarbadillo, John Joseph 1942- *WhoAm 92*
De Barbancon, Diane d1566 *BioIn 17*
De Barbentane, P.C. *WhoScE 91-2*
De Barbieri, Mary Ann 1945- *WhoAmW 93*
De Barbieri, Roy Louis 1947- *WhoEmL 93*
Debard, Deniel Lee 1954- *St&PR 93*
De Bardeleben, Arthur 1918- *WhoAm 92, WhoWor 93*
DeBardeleben, John Thomas, Jr. 1926- *WhoAm 92*
DeBardeleben, Marian Zalis 1946- *WhoEmL 93*
De Bardeleben, Mary Christine 1881- *AmWomPl*
DeBardeleben, Prince, Jr. 1924- *St&PR 93*
DeBarge *SoulM*
De Barriault, Lee 1952- *WhoEmL 93, WhoSSW 93*
De Barros, J. Frias *WhoScE 91-3*
DeBartolo, Edward J. 1946- *BioIn 17*
DeBartolo, Edward J., Sr. *BioIn 17*
DeBartolo, Edward J., Sr. 1919- *WhoAm 92, WhoE 93*
DeBartolo, Edward John, Jr. 1946- *WhoAm 92*
DeBartolo, Jack, Jr. 1938- *WhoAm 92*
deBary, William Theodore 1919- *ConAu 37NR, WhoAm 92*
Debas, Haile T. 1937- *WhoAm 92*
De Bassini, Achille 1819-1881 *OxDcOp*
De Bassini, Alberto 1847- *OxDcOp*
DeBat, Donald Joseph 1944- *WhoAm 92*
De Batist, Rene 1932- *WhoScE 91-2*
DeBauche, William James 1956- *WhoEmL 93*
Debb, Larry 1955- *St&PR 93*
Debbeler, John Michael 1955- *WhoEmL 93*
Debe, A. Joseph 1927- *St&PR 93*
deBear, Richard Stephen 1933- *WhoWor 93*
De Beauce, Thierry *BioIn 17*
De Beaufort, Francois 1936- *WhoScE 91-2*
De Beauvoir, Simone 1908-1986 *BioIn 17*
De Begnis, Giuseppe 1793-1849 *OxDcOp*
de Begnis, Giuseppina 1800-1853 *OxDcOp*
De Beistegui, Carlos *BioIn 17*
Debeljkovic, Dragutin 1950- *WhoScE 91-4*
DeBella, Louis J. *Law&B 92*
de Bellaigue, Eric 1931- *WhoAm 92*
De Bello, John *MiSFD 9*
Debendictis, Nicholas Joseph *Law&B 92*
De Benedetti, Carlo *BioIn 17, NewYTBS 92 [port]*
DeBenedetti, Carlo 1934- *WhoWor 93*
De Benedetti, Enzo Enrico 1935- *St&PR 93*
Debenedetti, Patrick John 1952- *WhoEmL 93*
De Benedictis, Dario 1918- *WhoAm 92*
DeBenedictis, Karen *Law&B 92*
DeBenedictis, Leonard C. 1940- *St&PR 93*
Debenham, Peter 1951- *St&PR 93*
De Benko, Eugene 1917- *WhoAm 92*
De Benoist, Alain 1943- *BioIn 17*
Debenport, Don 1934- *St&PR 93*
DeBerg, Steve *BioIn 17*
DeBerge, Gary A. 1947- *St&PR 93*
Debergh, Pierre C.A. 1944- *WhoScE 91-2*
Debergh, Pierre Carlos 1944- *WhoWor 93*
De Bernardi, Riccardo 1947- *WhoScE 91-3*
de Bernieres, Louis 1954- *ScF&FL 92*
DeBerry, Virginia Joyce *BioIn 17*
De Bersaques, Jean 1931- *WhoScE 91-2*
Debertin, Klaus 1933- *WhoScE 91-3*
de Bethune, Guy Jacques 1934- *WhoWor 93*
Debets, G.F. 1905-1969 *IntDcAn*
Debevere, J.M.J. 1942- *WhoScE 91-2*
Debevoise, Dickinson Richards 1924- *WhoAm 92, WhoE 93*
Debevoise, Eli Whitney 1899-1990 *BioIn 17*
Debevoise, Thomas McElrath 1929- *WhoAm 92*
Debeyssey, Mark Sammer 1966- *WhoWor 93*
DeBiagi, Anna Lillian 1930- *WhoAmW 93*
De Biase, John Francis 1952- *WhoE 93*
Debiasi, Giovanni Battista 1928- *WhoScE 91-3*
DeBiasi, Ralph Michael 1920- *St&PR 93*
de Biasi, Ronaldo Sergio 1943- *WhoWor 93*
Debicki, Andrew P(eter) 1934- *ConAu 37NR*
Debicki, Andrew Peter 1934- *WhoAm 92*
Debiec, Barbara 1923- *WhoScE 91-4*
Debien, Gabriel 1906-1990 *BioIn 17*
De Bievre, Paul Jan 1933- *WhoWor 93*
de Bilderling, Pierre 1950- *WhoWor 93*
Debin, George J. 1945- *St&PR 93*
De Binder, Todd C. 1931- *St&PR 93*
DeBitetto, Robert John *Law&B 92*
DeBlanc, Jeff 1919- *BioIn 17*
Deblasi, Gerald A. *Law&B 92*
De Blasi, Tony 1933- *WhoAm 92*
Deblasio, Ernest F. 1926- *St&PR 93*
DeBlasio, Michael P. 1937- *St&PR 93*
De Blasio, Michael Peter 1937- *WhoAm 92*
DeBlasis, Celeste Ninette 1946- *WhoE 93*
DeBlasis, Donna Maria 1946- *WhoAmW 93, WhoE 93, WhoEmL 93*
de Blasis, James Michael 1931- *WhoAm 92*
Deble, Lluis 1923- *WhoWor 93*
De Bleecker, Jan Leon Emiel 1961- *WhoWor 93*
Debler, Stephen W. *St&PR 93*
DeBlieck, Marilyn Jean 1943- *WhoAmW 93*
DeBlieu, Ivan Knowlton 1919- *WhoWor 93*
de Blij, Harm Jan 1935- *WhoAm 92*
Deblock, Glenn 1949- *St&PR 93*
De Blocq Van Kuffeler, John Philip 1949- *WhoWor 93*
De Blois, Roland Matthew 1958- *WhoSSW 93*
deBlonk, Donald M. 1941- *St&PR 93*
Debo, Angie 1890-1988 *BioIn 17, ConAu 40NR*
Debo, David Ray 1955- *WhoE 93*
Debo, Vincent J. 1940- *St&PR 93*
Debo, Vincent Joseph 1940- *WhoAm 92*
De Board, Janeen Sloan 1953- *WhoWrEP 92*
DeBock, Florent Alphonse 1924- *WhoAm 92*
De Bock, Theodorus F.D.H. 1962- *WhoWor 93*
de Bodman, J. 1943- *WhoWor 93*
De Boeck, Auguste 1865-1937 *Baker 92*
DeBoer, Bruce R. *Law&B 92*
DeBoer, Bruce R. 1953- *St&PR 93*
Deboer, Dave M. 1951- *St&PR 93*
DeBoer, George Edward 1944- *WhoE 93*
De Boer, Gerben F. 1935- *WhoScE 91-3*
de Boer, Hans Alfred 1925- *WhoWor 93*
De Boer, John F. 1942- *St&PR 93*
De Boer, Jorrit 1930- *WhoScE 91-3*
DeBoer, Kathryn Anne 1960- *WhoEmL 93*
De Boer, Klaas S. 1941- *WhoScE 91-3*
De Boer, Pieter Cornelis Tobias 1930- *WhoAm 92, WhoE 93*
DeBois, James A. *Law&B 92*
DeBois, James Adolphus 1929- *St&PR 93, WhoAm 92*
Debois, Jean M.P. 1934- *WhoWor 93*
De Boissezon, Birgit *WhoScE 91-2*
de Bold, Adolfo J. 1942- *WhoAm 92*
DeBold, Joseph Francis 1947- *WhoE 93*
DeBolt, Adriana *ScF&FL 92*
DeBolt, Gary Paul 1951- *WhoE 93*
de Bolt, Joe 1939- *ScF&FL 92*
de Bolt, Joseph W. *ScF&FL 92*
DeBolt, Richard Howard 1926- *St&PR 93*
Debondt, Jan Hendrik Maria 1961- *WhoWor 93*
Deboni, Roberto Luigi 1955- *WhoWor 93*
DeBoni, Walter 1946- *St&PR 93*
De Bonis, Louis 1934- *WhoScE 91-2*
De Bono, Edward 1933- *BioIn 17*
de Bont, Otto K.M. 1945- *WhoIns 93*
De Boodt, Marcel F.L.P. 1926- *WhoScE 91-2*
de Boor, Carl 1937- *WhoAm 92*
De Boorder, Tjeerd 1930- *WhoScE 91-3*
Deborah *BioIn 17*
De Borchgrave, Arnaud *BioIn 17*
de Borchgrave, Arnaud 1926- *ScF&FL 92, WhoAm 92, WhoE 93, WhoWor 93*
Debord, Donald Edward 1933- *St&PR 93*
deBord, Linda Lorene 1946- *WhoEmL 93*
DeBord, Mary Beth *Law&B 92*
De Borger, Raymond L.N. 1931- *WhoScE 91-2*
De Borgona, Juan fl. 1495-1533 *BioIn 17*
De Borst, Rene 1958- *WhoWor 93*
de Bosio, Gianfranco 1924- *MiSFD 9*
de Bosschere, Jean *ScF&FL 92*
Debost, Denis Charles 1929- *WhoWor 93*
De Botton, Gilbert *BioIn 17*
Debouche, Chales L.L.M. 1948- *WhoScE 91-2*
Debouche, Charles L.L.M. 1948- *WhoScE 91-2*
De Bougainville, Louis Antoine 1729-1811 *BioIn 17*
Debourge, M.J.-C. *WhoScE 91-1*
Debow, Jay 1932- *St&PR 93*
DeBow, Jay Howard Camden 1932- *WhoAm 92*
DeBra, Daniel B. 1930- *WhoAm 92*
De Brabander, D.L.M. 1947- *WhoScE 91-2*
De Brabander, Hubert F. 1946- *WhoScE 91-2*
De Brabander, Louis F.C. 1932- *WhoScE 91-2*
De Braganca, John 1912-1991 *BioIn 17*
de Braganca, Miguel 1951- *WhoE 93*
DeBragga, Robert d1990 *BioIn 17*
de Branges de Bourcia, Louis 1932- *WhoWor 93*
Debras, Christian 1939- *WhoScE 91-2*
Debray, Quentin 1944- *WhoScE 91-2*
Debray, Regis *BioIn 17, DcCPCAm*
Debray, Rosine 1936- *WhoScE 91-2*
Debre, Michel 1912- *BioIn 17*
Debrecht, Donald Robert 1946- *St&PR 93*
Debreczeni, Elemer 1936- *WhoScE 91-4*
Debreczeny, Paul 1932- *WhoAm 92, WhoSSW 93*
De Bremaecker, Jean-Claude 1923- *WhoAm 92*
Debrenne, Francoise M. 1932- *WhoScE 91-2*
De Bretteville, Sheila Levrant *BioIn 17*
Debreu, Gerard *BioIn 17*
Debreu, Gerard 1921- *WhoAm 92, WhoWor 93*
De Breuck, William A. 1933- *WhoScE 91-2*
Debrey, Adele F. 1924- *St&PR 93*
Debrey, Andrew Dale 1922- *St&PR 93*
Debrey, Drew Stephen 1953- *St&PR 93*
De Brier, Donald Paul 1940- *WhoAm 92*
Debro, Julius 1931- *WhoAm 92*
de Broca, Philippe 1933- *MiSFD 9*
De Broglie, Jacques Victor Albert 1821-1901 *BioIn 17*
Debrot, Peter 1960- *WhoE 93, WhoEmL 93*
De Brouwere, Vincent Jacques 1953- *WhoUN 92*
Debrovner, Steven H. *WhoIns 93*
DeBrow, Mical E. 1954- *WhoEmL 93*
DeBrower, Louise Margaret 1944- *WhoAmW 93*
Debruge, Pierre Joseph 1949- *WhoSSW 93*
De Bruhl, Arthur Marshall 1935- *WhoAm 92*
De Bruijn, Chris Henry 1946- *WhoWor 93*
De Bruin, David Lee 1955- *WhoEmL 93*
De Bruin, Jerome Edward 1941- *WhoWrEP 92*
DeBruin, Peter Jerry *Law&B 92*
DeBrule, William J. 1930- *WhoSSW 93*
DeBruler, Roger O. 1934- *WhoAm 92*
DeBrun, Sally Elizabeth 1935- *WhoAmW 93*
de Brun, Shauna Doyle 1956- *WhoAmW 93, WhoEmL 93*
DeBrunner, Gerald Joseph 1937- *WhoAm 92*
Debrunner, Hermann *WhoScE 91-4*
Debrunner, Peter George 1931- *WhoAm 92*
DeBruycker, Jane Crystal 1936- *WhoAmW 93*
Debruyckere, Marcel 1931- *WhoScE 91-2*
De Bruyn, Peter Paul Henry 1910- *WhoAm 92*
De Bruyn, Robert Lee 1934- *WhoWrEP 92*
De Bruyne, Eric A.J. 1939- *WhoScE 91-2*
de Bruyne, Yves *Law&B 92*
de Bruyn Kops, Julian 1908- *WhoAm 92*
Debs, Barbara Knowles 1931- *WhoAm 92, WhoAmW 93, WhoE 93, WhoWor 93*
Debs, Eugene V. 1855-1926 *BioIn 17, GayN, PolPar*
Debs, Eugene V(ictor) 1855-1926 *DcTwHis*
Debs, Richard A. 1930- *St&PR 93, WhoAm 92, WhoWor 93*
Debuhr, Ted 1947- *St&PR 93*
De Bulhoes, Otavio Gouveia 1906-1990 *BioIn 17*
DeBunda, Salvatore Michael 1943- *WhoAm 92*
De'Buondelmonti, Cristoforo fl. 1420- *BioIn 17*
DeBuono, Laureen *Law&B 92, St&PR 93*
de Burciaga, Cecilia Preciado *NotHsAW 93*
De Burgh, Hubert d1243 *BioIn 17*
De Burgos, Julia 1916-1953 *BioIn 17*
de Burlo, Comegys Russell, Jr. *WhoAm 92, WhoWor 93*
Debus, Allen George 1926- *WhoAm 92*
Debus, Eleanor Viola 1920- *WhoAmW 93*
Debus, Kurt H. 1908-1983 *BioIn 17*
DeBusk, Manuel Conrad 1914- *WhoAm 92*
DeBusschere, David Albert 1949- *WhoAm 92*
DeBusschop, Yolande Ursula *Law&B 92*
DeBussey, Robert Chancellor 1944- *St&PR 93*
De Bussieres, Arthur 1887-1913 *BioIn 17*
Debussy, Claude 1862-1918 *BioIn 17, IntDcOp [port], OxDcOp*
Debussy, (Achille-)Claude 1862-1918 *Baker 92*
deButts, Robert Edward Lee 1927- *St&PR 93, WhoAm 92*
de Buys, Harry Duggan, Jr. 1941- *WhoSSW 93*

deBuys, William Eno, Jr. 1949- *ConAu 136*
Deby, Idriss *WhoWor 93*
Deby, Idriss 1956- *WhoAfr*
DeCabia, Francis Carmen 1941- *WhoE 93*
Decadt, Jan 1914- *Baker 92*
De Cadt, Roger Jerome Henri Cornelius 1927- *WhoWor 93*
De Caillavet, Gaston Arman 1869-1915 *BioIn 17*
Decaminada, Joseph P. *Law&B 92*
Decaminada, Joseph P. 1935- *St&PR 93, WhoIns 93*
Decaminada, Joseph Pio 1935- *WhoAm 92*
de Camp, Catherine Crook 1907- *ScF&FL 92*
DeCamp, Graydon 1934- *WhoAm 92*
De Camp, L. Sprague 1907- *BioIn 17, ScF&FL 92*
De Camp, L(yon) Sprague 1907- *WhoWrEP 92*
De Camp, Lyon Sprague 1907- *BioIn 17*
DeCamp, Rosemary Shirley 1910- *WhoAm 92*
DeCampli-Stewart, Mary L. *BioIn 17*
DeCamps, Charles Michael 1950- *WhoEmL 93*
Decamps, Henri 1935- *WhoScE 91-2*
de Cani, John Stapley 1924- *WhoAm 92*
DeCanio, Salvatore Michael, Jr. 1953- *WhoEmL 93*
Decanski *OxDcByz*
de Capitani, Alberto 1942- *WhoE 93*
De Caranza, Ernest fl. c. 1850-1863 *BioIn 17*
DeCarava, Roy 1919- *BioIn 17*
DeCarava, Roy R. 1919- *WhoAm 92*
De Carbonera, Mercedes Cabello 1845-1909 *BioIn 17*
De Carbonnel, Francois Eric 1946- *St&PR 93*
De Cardenas, Nora C. *Law&B 92*
Decareau, Eugene Francis 1929- *St&PR 93*
DeCarli, Ralph Peter 1958- *WhoEmL 93*
De Carlo, Donald T. *Law&B 92*
De Carlo, Leonard Dominick 1939- *WhoWrEP 92*
DeCarlo, Michael 1960- *WhoEmL 93*
De Carlo, Yvonne 1922?- *BioIn 17, IntDcF 2-3 [port], SweetSg D [port]*
Decarnin, Camilla *ScF&FL 92*
De Caro, Angelo 1943- *St&PR 93*
De Caro, Giuseppe G.A. 1932- *WhoScE 91-3*
DeCaro, John Cecil 1923- *WhoSSW 93*
De Caro, Laurence Thomas 1945- *WhoE 93*
Decarpigny, Jean-Noel 1948- *WhoScE 91-2*
De Carvalho, A.J. Coelho *WhoScE 91-3*
De Carvalho, Apolonio 1913- *BioIn 17*
De Carvalho, Delfin *WhoScE 91-3*
Decary, Robert 1944- *WhoE 93*
Decassou, Dominique *WhoScE 91-2*
De Castella, Robert *BioIn 17*
De Castelnau, Noel Marie Joseph Edouard de Curieres 1851-1944 *BioIn 17*
De Castries, Christian 1902-1991 *BioIn 17*
de Castro, Adolphe 1859-1959 *ScF&FL 92*
deCastro, Donald John 1930- *St&PR 93*
de Castro, Edson D. 1938- *St&PR 93*
de Castro, Hugo Daniel 1935- *WhoAm 92*
De Castro, J. Temudo *WhoScE 91-3*
Decastro, Stephen Alan 1956- *St&PR 93*
DeCato, Clifford Miles 1940- *WhoE 93*
Decator, Carl J. 1949- *WhoE 93*
Decatur, Stephen 1779-1820 *HarEnMi*
De Caunes, Antoine *BioIn 17*
De Caussin, Adrian X. 1935- *St&PR 93*
Decaux, Abel 1869-1943 *Baker 92*
Decazes, Louis Charles Elie 1819-1886 *BioIn 17*
Deccio, David M. 1946- *St&PR 93*
Decebalus c. 40-106 *HarEnMi*
De Cecco, Raymond Joseph 1924- *St&PR 93*
De Celles, Charles Edouard 1942- *WhoWor 93*
De Cerna, Lucia *BioIn 17*
de Cervens, Jeanne *Law&B 92*
Decesare, James C. 1931- *St&PR 93*
Decesare, James Louis *Law&B 92*
DeCesare, Jeanne Anne 1949- *WhoAmW 93*
DeCesare, Nicholas *Law&B 92*
DeCesaro, Arthur F. 1948- *St&PR 93*
de Cespedes, President *DcCPCAm*
De Cespedes, Pablo c. 1538-1608 *BioIn 17*
DeCew, Judith Wagner 1948- *WhoE 93*
DeChaine, Dean Dennis 1936- *WhoAm 92*
De Chamorro, Violeta Barrios *BioIn 17*
de Champlain, Vera Chopak 1928- *WhoAm 92, WhoAmW 93*
Dechamps, Yves J.J. 1936- *WhoScE 91-2*
DeChancie, John 1946- *ScF&FL 92*
DeChant, Joseph Michael 1958- *WhoSSW 93*
Dechant, Virgil C. 1930- *WhoAm 92*
Dechar, Peter Henry 1942- *WhoAm 92*
DeCharles, Diana Marie 1956- *WhoAmW 93*
De Charriere, Isabelle 1740-1805 *BioIn 17*
de Chastelain, Alfred John Gardyne Drummond 1937- *WhoAm 92*
De Chastelain, John *BioIn 17*
Dechene, James Charles 1953- *WhoAm 92, WhoEmL 93*
Dechene, Joseph Fernand 1959- *WhoEmL 93*
Dechene, Lucy Irene 1950- *WhoAmW 93*
Dechenne, James Allen 1943- *WhoSSW 93*
Decher, Rudolf 1927- *WhoAm 92, WhoSSW 93*
Decherd, Robert William 1951- *St&PR 93, WhoAm 92, WhoSSW 93*
de Chernatony, Leslie 1953- *WhoWor 93*
De Cherney, Alan Hersh 1942- *WhoAm 92, WhoE 93*
Dechert, Joseph P. 1916- *St&PR 93*
Dechery, Bertrand F. 1950- *St&PR 93*
Dechevrens, Antoine 1840-1912 *Baker 92*
Dechi, Daniel Salomon 1959- *WhoE 93*
De Chirico, Andrea 1891-1952 *BioIn 17*
De Chirico, Giorgio 1888-1978 *BioIn 17*
Dechmann, Manfred 1942- *WhoWor 93*
Dechnik, James Edward 1946- *St&PR 93*
Dechow, Friedrich L. von d1776 *HarEnMi*
Dechristopher, Joseph L. 1936- *St&PR 93*
Dechter, Bradley Graham 1956- *WhoWor 93*
Deci, Edward L(ewis) 1942- *ConAu 39NR*
Deci, Edward Lewis 1942- *WhoAm 92, WhoE 93*
Deci, Mary D. 1947- *St&PR 93*
Deciccio, Donald R. 1934- *St&PR 93*
De Cicco, Andrew *Law&B 92*
DeCicco, Anne Lommel 1950- *WhoAmW 93*
DeCicco, James 1946- *St&PR 93*
De Cicco Brothers *BioIn 17*
Decio, Arthur J. 1931- *St&PR 93*
Decio, Arthur Julius 1930- *WhoAm 92*
De Cissey, Ernest Louis Octave Courtot 1810-1882 *BioIn 17*
Decius *OxDcByz*
Decius, Gaius Messius Quintus Traianus c. 201-251 *HarEnMi*
deCiutiis, Alfred Charles Maria 1945- *WhoAm 92, WhoWor 93*
Deck, James David, Sr. 1930- *WhoSSW 93*
Deck, Joseph Francis 1907- *WhoAm 92*
Deckelbaum, Nelson 1928- *WhoAm 92*
Decker, Alfred M. 1925- *WhoScE 91-2*
Decker, Allan F. 1929- *St&PR 93*
Decker, Alonzo Galloway, Jr. 1908- *St&PR 93*
Decker, Andrew *BioIn 17*
Decker, Bernard Martin 1904- *WhoAm 92*
Decker, C. Lawrence 1940- *St&PR 93*
Decker, Carol Arne 1946- *WhoAmW 93*
Decker, Carolyn Richards 1936- *WhoAmW 93*
Decker, Charles David 1945- *WhoAm 92*
Decker, Charles L. *WhoAm 92*
Decker, Charles Richard 1937- *WhoAm 92*
Decker, Christian 1940- *WhoScE 91-2*
Decker, David G. 1917-1990 *BioIn 17*
Decker, Edward W., Jr. 1952- *St&PR 93*
Decker, Edwin Albert 1929- *St&PR 93*
Decker, Elizabeth Anne 1952- *WhoAmW 93*
Decker, Erwin Louis 1925- *St&PR 93*
Decker, Frank N., Jr. *Law&B 92*
Decker, Franz-Paul 1923- *Baker 92*
Decker, Frederic C. 1916-1991 *BioIn 17*
Decker, Gary Arden 1942- *WhoE 93*
Decker, George Henry 1902-1980 *CmdGen 1991 [port]*
Decker, Gilbert Felton 1937- *WhoAm 92*
Decker, Gregory Allen 1951- *WhoEmL 93*
Decker, Hannah Shulman 1937- *WhoAm 92, WhoSSW 93*
Decker, Hans Wilhelm 1929- *WhoAm 92*
Decker, Harold James *Law&B 92*
Decker, Howard Elwood 1922- *St&PR 93*
Decker, Iris *AmWomPl*
Decker, Jake *ScF&FL 92*
Decker, James Harrison, Jr. 1948- *WhoEmL 93*
Decker, James Thomas 1944- *WhoWor 93*
Decker, Jeffrey Lee 1962- *WhoEmL 93*
Decker, Jerome L. 1948- *St&PR 93*
Decker, Joey 1955- *WhoEmL 93*
Decker, John B. 1927- *St&PR 93*
Decker, John Laws 1921- *WhoAm 92*
Decker, John Louis 1946- *WhoEmL 93*
Decker, John Robert 1952- *WhoEmL 93*
Decker, John William 1948- *WhoEmL 93*
Decker, Josephine I. 1933- *WhoAmW 93*
Decker, Judith Elaine 1940- *WhoAmW 93*
Decker, Karl F.A. 1925- *WhoScE 91-3*
Decker, Karrie Lynn 1956- *WhoEmL 93*
Decker, Ken Clark *Law&B 92*
Decker, Kurt Hans 1946- *WhoEmL 93*
Decker, Lisa M. *Law&B 92*
Decker, Martha Ilene 1954- *WhoWrEP 92*
Decker, Mary *BioIn 17*
Decker, Mary A. *AmWomPl*
Decker, Mary Clare *Law&B 92*
Decker, Mary Clare 1948- *St&PR 93*
Decker, Mary Locher 1936- *WhoWrEP 92*
Decker, Mary Lucia 1956- *WhoAmW 93*
Decker, MaryClare *Law&B 92*
Decker, Michael Bryan 1949- *St&PR 93*
Decker, Michael Lynn 1953- *WhoEmL 93*
Decker, Norman Edward *Law&B 92*
Decker, Peter William 1919- *WhoWor 93*
Decker, Randy L. *Law&B 92*
Decker, Raymond Frank 1930- *WhoAm 92*
Decker, Richard K. 1913- *St&PR 93*
Decker, Richard Knore 1913- *WhoAm 92*
Decker, Robert Owen 1927- *WhoE 93*
Decker, Susan Janet 1944- *WhoSSW 93*
Decker, Thomas Andrew *Law&B 92*
Decker, Thomas Andrew 1946- *St&PR 93, WhoAm 92*
Decker, Virginia Ann 1942- *WhoWrEP 92*
Decker, W. Patrick *St&PR 93*
Decker, Wayne *BioIn 17*
Decker, Wayne Leroy 1922- *WhoAm 92*
Decker, Willard Lee 1929- *St&PR 93*
Deckers, Tom M.J.P. *WhoScE 91-2*
Decker Slaney, Mary Teresa 1958- *WhoAm 92, WhoAmW 93*
Deckert, Dair Susan *Law&B 92*
Deckert, Myrna Jean 1936- *WhoAmW 93*
Deckert, Ralph E. 1952- *St&PR 93*
Deckert, Robert Allen 1935- *WhoWrEP 92*
Decker-Ward, James Gordon 1943- *St&PR 93*
Deckinger, Elliott Lawrence 1917- *WhoAm 92*
Deckmym, Lucas *Law&B 92*
Deckov, Dicko Varbanov 1925- *WhoScE 91-4*
Deckro, John P. *St&PR 93*
De Claviere d'Hust, Bernard *BioIn 17*
Decle, Denis Christopher 1951- *WhoE 93*
De Cleene, Trevor Albert 1933- *WhoAsAP 91*
Decleir, Walter Lodewijk 1937- *WhoScE 91-2*
Decleire, Marc H.H. 1933- *WhoScE 91-2*
Declemente, Donna Marie 1958- *WhoEmL 93*
DeClements, Barthe 1920- *ScF&FL 92, SmATA 71 [port], WhoWrEP 92*
Declerck, Robert 1946- *WhoWor 93*
De Clerck, Rudolphe Jacques 1939- *WhoScE 91-2*
De Clercq, Erik Desire Alice 1941- *WhoScE 91-2*
De Clercq, Marcel L.J.J. 1946- *WhoScE 91-2*
Declercq, Peter Emiel 1956- *WhoScE 91-2*
DeCles, Jon 1941- *ScF&FL 92*
Declue, Stephen S. 1944- *St&PR 93*
DeCock, Jennifer Elizabeth 1965- *WhoE 93*
DeColaines, Don William, III 1947- *WhoSSW 93*
Decomps, Bernard *WhoScE 91-2*
DeCon, Maude *AmWomPl*
De Conceicao, Alda Bandeira Tavares Vas *WhoWor 93*
DeConcini, Dennis *BioIn 17*
DeConcini, Dennis 1937- *CngDr 91, CurBio 92 [port], WhoAm 92*
DeCongelio, Frank Joseph 1948- *St&PR 93*
Deconninck, Gaston 1924- *WhoScE 91-2*
de Conte, Sieur Louis *MajAI*
DeCook, Richard Cyril 1942- *WhoAm 92*
Decor, Jean-Pierre 1943- *WhoScE 91-2*
de Cordoba, Pedro 1881-1950 *HispAmA*
de Cordova, Arturo 1908-1973 *HispAmA*
De Cordova, Fred *BioIn 17*
de Cordova, Frederick Timmins 1910- *WhoAm 92*
De Cormier-Shekerjian, Regina *WhoWrEP 92*
De Cormis, Louis C. 1936- *WhoScE 91-2*
DeCorso, Nicholas *Law&B 92*
De Corte, Erik Willy Alberic 1941- *WhoWor 93*
DeCosse, Sheila Flynn 1935- *WhoAmW 93*
De Costa, Edwin J. 1906- *WhoAm 92*
DeCosta, Peter F. *WhoE 93, WhoWor 93*
Decoste, Paul *St&PR 93*
DeCoste, Reginald *BioIn 17*
De Coster, Barbara Lou 1932- *WhoAmW 93*
De Coster, Cyrus Cole 1914- *WhoAm 92*
DeCoster, Dorothy A. *St&PR 93*
Decoster, Leonard L. 1921- *St&PR 93*
DeCoteau, Ann M. 1946- *St&PR 93*
DeCoteau, David *MiSFD 9*
DeCotis, Deborah Anne 1952- *WhoAmW 93*
De Cotret, Robert Rene 1944- *WhoAm 92, WhoE 93*
de Cou, Emil *WhoAm 92*
Decourcelle, Gerard Raymond 1942- *St&PR 93*
De Courcy, John W. 1918- *WhoScE 91-3*
DeCourcy, Kim Gary 1948- *St&PR 93*
DeCoursey, John P. *Law&B 92*
DeCoursey, Paul Alex 1946- *WhoEmL 93*
De Coursey, Robert Wurts 1927- *WhoE 93*
De Court, Bruce Wayne 1953- *WhoE 93*
Decourtray, Albert Cardinal 1923- *WhoWor 93*
Decoust, Michel 1936- *Baker 92*
de Coux, Janet 1904- *WhoAm 92*
Decowski, Piotr 1940- *WhoScE 91-4*
De Craene, Jacques Maria 1929- *WhoWor 93*
Decrane, Alfred Charles, Jr. 1931- *St&PR 93, WhoAm 92, WhoE 93, WhoWor 93*
De Crane, Victor C. 1932- *St&PR 93*
De Crayencour, Marguerite *BioIn 17, ScF&FL 92*
Decreau, Pierrette M.E. 1944- *WhoScE 91-2*
De Creeft, Jose 1884-1982 *BioIn 17*
De Crenne, Helisenne c. 1510-c. 1560 *BioIn 17*
DeCresce, Joseph P. *Law&B 92*
De Crescentis, James 1948- *WhoWrEP 92*
DeCrescenzo, Jame Melisse 1955- *WhoEmL 93, WhoSSW 93*
Decreus, Camille 1876-1939 *Baker 92*
De Crevoisier, Philippe 1941- *WhoScE 91-2*
DeCristoforo, Michael John 1932- *St&PR 93*
Decristoforo, Thomas P. 1957- *St&PR 93*
Decroix, Marc 1926- *WhoScE 91-2*
DeCrosta, Edward Francis, Jr. 1926- *WhoE 93*
DeCrosta, Susan Elyse 1956- *WhoAmW 93, WhoE 93, WhoEmL 93*
Decroux, Etienne *BioIn 17*
DeCrow, Karen 1937- *ConAu 37NR, WhoAm 92, WhoAmW 93, WhoWrEP 92*
Decsenyi, Janos 1927- *Baker 92*
Decsey, Ernst (Heinrich Franz) 1870-1941 *Baker 92*
Decsy, Zoltan 1945- *WhoScE 91-4*
Decter, Marcia H. *Law&B 92*
Decter, Midge 1927- *WhoAm 92, WhoWrEP 92*
DeCubellis, Robert 1946- *WhoEmL 93*
De Cuevas, George 1886-1961 *BioIn 17*
DeCuir, Alfred Frederick, Jr. 1950- *WhoSSW 93*
De Curtis, David Samuel 1930- *WhoAm 92*
De Cusatis, Casimer Maurice 1964- *WhoWor 93*
DeCusatis, Fred S. 1953- *St&PR 93*
De Custine, Astolphe 1790-1847 *BioIn 17*
De Cuyper, Jacques Anatole 1929- *WhoWor 93*
Decuypere, Jaak Albert 1943- *WhoScE 91-2*
Decyk, Roxanne Jean 1952- *St&PR 93, WhoAmW 93*
Deddens, James Carroll 1928- *St&PR 93*
Dede, Brenda Sanders 1948- *WhoAmW 93*
DeDe, Spiro 1945- *WhoWor 93*
Dedeaux, Raoul Martial 1915- *BiDAMSp 1989*
de Decker, Anne-Catherine 1958- *WhoWor 93*
Dedecker, Linda Marie 1953- *WhoEmL 93*
Dedecker, Paul Jean 1921- *WhoWor 93*
Dedek, Miroslav *WhoScE 91-4*
De Dell, Gary Jerome *WhoE 93*
Deden, Ann Elizabeth 1948- *WhoAmW 93*
De Deo, Joseph E. 1937- *St&PR 93, WhoAm 92*
Dederer, James W., Jr. *Law&B 92*
Dederer, James Wadsworth 1946- *St&PR 93*
Dederer, John Morgan 1951- *ConAu 136*
Dederer, Michael Eugene 1932- *WhoAm 92*
Dederich-Pejovich, Susan Russell 1951- *WhoAm 92*
Dederick, Robert Gogan 1929- *WhoAm 92*
Dederick, Ronald Osburn 1935- *WhoAm 92*
Dedert, Nancy Ann 1941- *St&PR 93*
Dedert, Steven Ray 1953- *WhoEmL 93*
Dedijer, Vladimir 1914-1990 *BioIn 17*
Dedini, Eldon Lawrence 1921- *WhoAm 92*
De Dios, Manuel *BioIn 17*
Dedler, Rochus 1779-1822 *Baker 92*

Dedman, Bertram Cottingham 1914- *WhoAm 92*
Dedman, Malcolm John 1948- *WhoWor 93*
Dedman, Robert Henry 1926- *WhoAm 92*
Dedmon, Donald Newton 1931- *WhoSSW 93*
Dedo, Dorothy Junell Turner 1920- *WhoAmW 93*
Dedomenico, Vincent Michael 1915- *St&PR 93*
DeDominicis, Henry Ken 1947- *WhoSSW 93*
Dedona, Francis A. 1924- *St&PR 93*
DeDona, Francis Alfred 1924- *WhoWor 93*
DeDonato, David Michael 1947- *WhoEmL 93, WhoSSW 93*
DeDonato, Donald Michael 1952- *WhoEmL 93*
Dedonder, R. *WhoScE 91-2*
Dedrick, John Rockwell 1939- *St&PR 93*
Dedrick, Kenneth C. 1947- *St&PR 93*
de Duve, Christian Rene 1917- *WhoAm 92, WhoWor 93*
Dee, James Digiacomo *Law&B 92*
Dee, John *ScF&FL 92*
Dee, John 1527-1608 *LitC 20 [port]*
Dee, Raymond C. 1942- *St&PR 93*
Dee, Raymond Charles 1942- *WhoE 93*
Dee, Robert F. 1924- *St&PR 93*
Dee, Roger 1914- *ScF&FL 92*
Dee, Ron 1957- *ScF&FL 92*
Dee, Ruby *BioIn 17, WhoAm 92, WhoAmW 93*
Dee, Ruby 1923- *BlkAull 92*
Dee, Rusty 1952- *BioIn 17*
Dee, Sandra 1942- *BioIn 17*
Dee, Sylvia 1914-1967 *ScF&FL 92*
Dee, Thomas D., II 1920- *St&PR 93*
Dee, Vivien 1944- *WhoAmW 93*
Deeb, Gary (James) 1945- *ConAu 138*
Deecken, George Christian 1922- *WhoAm 92*
Deed, Martha Louise 1941- *WhoAmW 93*
Deeds, Robert Creigh 1958- *WhoEmL 93*
Deedwania, Prakash Chandra 1948- *WhoEmL 93*
Deedy, John Gerard, Jr. 1923- *WhoAm 92, WhoWrEP 92*
Deedy, Joyce 1928- *WhoWrEP 92*
Deee-Lite *ConMus 9 [port], SoulM*
Deegan, David J. *Law&B 92*
Deegan, Denis James 1954- *St&PR 93*
Deegan, Dennis M. *St&PR 93*
Deegan, Derek James 1940- *St&PR 93, WhoAm 92*
Deegan, Donald James 1962- *St&PR 93*
Deegan, E. Gregory, III 1948- *WhoE 93*
Deegan, Gail 1946- *St&PR 93*
Deegan, Gene Austin 1936- *WhoAm 92*
Deegan, John, Jr. 1944- *WhoAm 92*
Deegan, John Edward, Jr. 1936- *St&PR 93*
Deegan, Nan Marie 1952- *WhoEmL 93*
Deegear, James Otis, III 1948- *WhoEmL 93*
Deegen, Eckehard 1941- *WhoScE 91-3*
Deegen, Uwe Frederick 1948- *WhoSSW 93*
Deehan, William J. 1952- *St&PR 93*
Deeik, Khalil George 1937- *WhoWor 93*
Deeken, Julian Francis d1991 *BioIn 17*
Deeks, William George 1933- *WhoAm 92*
Deel, Daryl Wayne 1953- *St&PR 93*
Deel, Frances Quinn 1939- *WhoAm 92, WhoAmW 93*
Deel, Rebecca Lynne 1964- *WhoAmW 93*
Deeley, Edward Joseph 1956- *WhoE 93, WhoWor 93*
Deeley, Thomas J. *WhoScE 91-1*
de Elorza, John 1919- *St&PR 93*
Deelstra, Hendrik Andries 1938- *WhoScE 91-2*
Deem, George 1932- *WhoAm 92*
Deem, Howard H. 1926- *St&PR 93*
Deemer, Bill 1945- *WhoWrEP 92*
Deems, Nyal David 1948- *WhoEmL 93*
Deems, Richard E. 1913- *St&PR 93*
Deems, Richard Emmet 1913- *WhoAm 92*
Deen, Edith Alderman 1905- *WhoAm 92*
Deen, Harold Eugene 1926- *WhoE 93*
Deen, James Rylee *Law&B 92*
Deen, Sayyed Misbah *WhoScE 91-1*
Deen, Sayyed Misbah 1938- *WhoWor 93*
Deen, Susan Silverstein 1946- *WhoAmW 93*
Deen, Thomas Blackburn 1928- *WhoAm 92*
Deene 1942- *WhoAmW 93*
Deener, Larry Colby 1950- *WhoEmL 93*
Deeny, Michael Charles 1957- *WhoEmL 93*
Deep, Ira Washington 1927- *WhoAm 92*
Deephouse, Christopher Vaughn 1954- *WhoE 93*
Deepwell, Andre H. *St&PR 93*
Deer, Donald M. 1932- *St&PR 93*
Deer, James W. 1917- *St&PR 93*
Deer, James Willis 1917- *WhoAm 92, WhoE 93, WhoWor 93*
Deer, Richard Elliott 1932- *WhoAm 92*
Deere, Cyril Thomas 1924- *WhoAm 92*
Deere, John 1804-1886 *BioIn 17*
Deering, Allan B. 1934- *St&PR 93*
Deering, Allan Brooks 1934- *WhoAm 92*
Deering, Fred A. 1928- *St&PR 93, WhoIns 93*
Deering, Fred Arthur 1928- *WhoAm 92*
Deering, John R. 1936- *St&PR 93*
Deering, Joseph William 1940- *St&PR 93*
Deering, Mabel Clare Craft 1872- *AmWomPl*
Deering, Richard c. 1580-1630 *Baker 92*
Deering, Ronald Franklin 1929- *WhoSSW 93, WhoWor 93*
Deering, William Dougless 1933- *WhoSSW 93*
Deerson, Bruce A. *Law&B 92*
Dees, C. Stanley 1938- *WhoAm 92*
Dees, Julian Worth 1933- *WhoAm 92*
Dees, Lynne 1954- *WhoAm 92*
Dees, Morris *BioIn 17*
Dees, Morris 1936- *News 92 [port]*
Dees, Morris Seligman, Jr. 1936- *WhoAm 92, WhoSSW 93*
Dees, Richard Lee 1955- *WhoEmL 93*
Dees, Rick *BioIn 17*
Dees, Sam *SoulM*
Dees, Sandra Kay Martin 1944- *WhoAm 92, WhoAmW 93, WhoSSW 93*
Dees, Stephen P. *Law&B 92*
Dees, Stephen P. 1943- *St&PR 93*
Dees, Stephen Phillip 1943- *WhoAm 92*
Dees, Susan Coons 1909- *WhoAmW 93*
Dees, Tom Moore 1931- *WhoSSW 93*
Dees, William Hunter 1955- *WhoSSW 93*
De Escamilla, Luis Tristan 1586?-1624 *BioIn 17*
Deese, David Fred 1947- *WhoEmL 93*
Deese, James Earle 1921- *WhoAm 92*
Deese, James LaMotte 1944- *WhoAm 92*
Deeter, Bernard S. 1924- *St&PR 93*
Deeths, Lenore Clair 1940- *WhoAmW 93*
Deetjen, Peter H. 1932- *WhoScE 91-4*
Deets, Dwain Aaron 1939- *WhoAm 92*
Deets, Floyd H. 1929- *St&PR 93*
Deets, Horace 1938- *WhoAm 92*
DeFabis, Mike 1932- *St&PR 93*
DeFabritiis, Oliviero (Carlo) 1902-1982 *Baker 92*
Defago, Genevieve Jeanne 1942- *WhoScE 91-4*
DeFalco, Anthony Joseph 1936- *St&PR 93*
DeFalco, Frank Damian 1934- *WhoAm 92*
DeFanti, Michael Peter 1942- *WhoAm 92*
De Faria, Alexandre 1941- *WhoUN 92*
Defauw, Desire 1885-1960 *Baker 92*
de Fay, Olivier Louis Michel 1960- *WhoWor 93*
DeFazio, Antoinette Carmela *WhoAmW 93*
DeFazio, Frank 1925- *St&PR 93*
DeFazio, Lynette Stevens 1930- *WhoAmW 93, WhoWor 93*
DeFazio, Peter A. 1947- *CngDr 91, WhoAm 92*
Defebaugh, James Elliott, IV *Law&B 92*
de Feghe, Willem 1687-c. 1757 *Baker 92*
de Feldman, Susanna Redondo *NotHsAW 93*
DeFelice, Cynthia C. *ScF&FL 92*
DeFelice, Dennis Joseph 1949- *WhoEmL 93*
DeFelice, Eugene Anthony 1927- *WhoAm 92*
De Felice, Fortune Barthelmy 1723-1789 *BioIn 17*
De Felice, James 1940- *WhoCanL 92*
DeFelice, Jonathan Peter 1947- *WhoAm 92*
DeFelice, Linda 1952- *WhoAmW 93*
DeFelice, Lois Anne 1950- *WhoEmL 93*
De Felipe Anton, M.R. 1934- *WhoScE 91-3*
de Felitta, Frank 1921- *MiSFD 9, ScF&FL 92*
De Felitta, Frank Paul *WhoAm 92*
De Fels, Marie-Laure *BioIn 17*
Defenbaugh, Richard Eugene 1946- *WhoAm 92, WhoEmL 93, WhoSSW 93*
Defendini, Maria Leria 1960- *WhoWor 93*
Defendorf, Charles E. 1912- *St&PR 93*
Defensor-Santiago, Miriam *BioIn 17*
Defeo, John E. 1946- *St&PR 93*
DeFeo, John Eugene 1946- *WhoAm 92*
DeFeo, Ralph R. *Law&B 92*
DeFeo, William Thomas, Jr. 1927- *WhoE 93*
De Ferrari, Gabriella 1941- *WhoAm 92*
De Ferrari, Gian Antonio 1928- *St&PR 93*
De Ferrari, Gianfranco *WhoScE 91-3*
De Fesch, Willem 1687-c. 1757 *Baker 92*
Defesche, Charles Leon 1948- *St&PR 93*
Defeyter, David W. 1954- *St&PR 93*
Deffe, Cindy Maitland 1959- *WhoAmW 93*
Defferre, Gaston 1910-1986 *BioIn 17*
Deffes, Pierre-Louis 1819-1900 *Baker 92*
Deffner, Virginia d1991 *BioIn 17*
Defibaugh, Patricia J. 1946- *St&PR 93*
De Fiellettaz Goethart, Rene L. 1940- *WhoScE 91-3*
DeFife, Susan Williams 1961- *WhoAmW 93, WhoEmL 93*
De Figueiredo, Desmond Peter 1938- *St&PR 93*
de Filippis, Lisa M. *Law&B 92*
DeFilippo, Allan John 1946- *St&PR 93*
De Filippo, Eduardo 1900-1984 *BioIn 17*
DeFilippo, Kathleen Byrne 1943- *WhoE 93*
Defilippo, Robert C. 1952- *St&PR 93*
DeFina, Vincent R. *Law&B 92*
Define, William Thomas 1941- *WhoAm 92*
DeFiore, Joseph C., Jr. 1938- *WhoSSW 93*
De Flers, Robert 1872-1927 *BioIn 17*
Defleur, Lois B. 1936- *WhoAm 92, WhoAmW 93, WhoE 93*
DeFleur, Melvin Lawrence 1923- *WhoAm 92*
Defliese, Philip Leroy 1915- *WhoAm 92*
Deflorez, Suzanne Humphreys 1915- *St&PR 93*
DeFlorio, Mary Lucy *WhoAmW 93*
deFluiter, Mary-Louise Edna 1956- *WhoAmW 93*
Defoe, Daniel 1660-1731 *MagSWL [port], MajAI [port], WorLitC [port]*
Defoe, Daniel 1661?-1731 *BioIn 17*
De Foe, John E. 1946- *St&PR 93*
De Folter, Leo C. 1941- *St&PR 93*
Defonseca, Maurice Joseph 1940- *WhoWor 93*
De Fontaine, Felix Gregory 1834-1896 *JrnUS*
Defontenay, C.I. 1814-1856 *ScF&FL 92*
de Fonville, Paul Bliss 1923- *WhoWor 93*
Defoor, Jerry W. 1952- *St&PR 93*
DeFoor, John Allen 1961- *WhoEmL 93*
Defoor, Nathan Dwight 1952- *WhoSSW 93, WhoWor 93*
Deford, Frank 1938- *BiDAMSp 1989, WhoAm 92*
DeFord, Harry A., II *Law&B 92*
De Ford, Sara Whitcraft 1916- *WhoWrEP 92*
Deford, Thomas McAdams 1942- *WhoWor 93*
DeForest, Albert J., III 1940- *St&PR 93*
De Forest, James Vincent 1926- *St&PR 93*
De Forest, Marian 1864-1935 *AmWomPl*
DeForest, Orrin *BioIn 17*
De Forest, Roy 1930- *BioIn 17*
De Forest, Sherwood Searle 1921- *WhoAm 92*
De Forest, Thomas M. *Law&B 92*
DeForest, Walter Pattison, III 1944- *WhoAm 92, WhoE 93, WhoWor 93*
DeForge, William J. 1940- *WhoIns 93*
de Fortis, Paul *ScF&FL 92*
Defossez, Rene 1905-1988 *Baker 92*
DeFotis, Constance 1951- *WhoAmW 93*
De Foucauld, Charles-Eugene 1858-1916 *BioIn 17*
De Fouquet, Jacques 1927- *WhoScE 91-2*
De Fouw, Eugene Allen 1941- *St&PR 93*
De Fraja Frangipane, Eugenio 1928- *WhoScE 91-3*
Defrance, Harry Anthony 1929- *St&PR 93*
Defrance, Newilda 1944- *St&PR 93*
DeFranceaux, George W. 1913- *St&PR 93*
DeFrances, Leroy A. 1928- *St&PR 93*
De Francesco, Joey *BioIn 17*
De Francesco, John Blaze, Jr. 1936- *WhoAm 92*
de Francesco, John Kenneth 1932- *WhoE 93*
DeFrancesco, Mark L. 1962- *St&PR 93*
DeFrancesco, Raymond P. 1960- *St&PR 93*
de Franchi, Antonio Dante Napoleone 1921- *WhoWor 93*
DeFrancis, Suellen Maria 1946- *WhoAmW 93, WhoE 93, WhoEmL 93*
DeFrancisci, Teresa Cafarelli *BioIn 17*
De Franciscis, Pietro 1919- *WhoScE 91-3*
De Francisco, Darlene Suzanne 1959- *WhoAmW 93*
de Francisco Blanco, Miguel A. 1939- *WhoUN 92*
De Franco, "Buddy" (Boniface Ferdinand Leonardo) 1923- *Baker 92*
Defranco, James, Jr. *Law&B 92*
Defranco, Salvatore 1924- *St&PR 93*
De Frank, Vincent 1915- *WhoAm 92*
DeFrantz, Anita *BioIn 17*
DeFrees, Douglas John 1952- *WhoEmL 93*
DeFrees, John Stallard 1938- *WhoSSW 93*
Defrees, Madeline *BioIn 17*
Defrees, Madeline 1919- *WhoWrEP 92*
DeFrehn, John Allen 1948- *WhoSSW 93*
Defreitas, Robert Frederick 1924- *St&PR 93*
De Freycinet, Charles Louis de Saulces 1828-1923 *BioIn 17*
de Frias, Marlene Cintron *NotHsAW 93*
De Fries, John Clarence 1934- *WhoAm 92*
De Frietas, Vieira *WhoScE 91-3*
De Frondeville, Bertrand Lambert 1934- *WhoE 93, WhoWor 93*
De Fry, Cyril Trevor 1947- *WhoWor 93*
De Fuentes, Fernando 1895-1952 *MiSFD 9N*
De Funes, Louis 1908-1983 *QDrFCA 92 [port]*
De Gaay Fortman, Bastiaan 1937- *WhoWor 93*
De Gaeta, Albert M. *St&PR 93*
De Gaeta, Edythe C. *St&PR 93*
De Gaetani, Barbara Ann 1934- *St&PR 93, WhoAmW 93*
DeGaetani, Jan(ice) 1933-1989 *Baker 92*
De Gaetano, Dominic A. 1939- *St&PR 93*
De Gaetano, Giovanni 1943- *WhoScE 91-3*
de Gail, Patrick 1936- *St&PR 93*
De Galan, Leo 1937- *WhoScE 91-3*
Degan, Robert Anderson 1939- *St&PR 93*
Degand, Pierre *WhoScE 91-2*
De Gara, Paul F. 1902-1991 *BioIn 17*
DeGaris, Roger *ScF&FL 92*
DeGarmo, Chris *BioIn 17*
DeGarmo, Chris c. 1965- *See* Queensryche *ConMus 8*
Degarmo, George 1938- *St&PR 93*
DeGarmo, Lindley Grant 1953- *WhoEmL 93*
DeGarmo, Robert M. 1945- *St&PR 93*
Degas, Edgar 1834-1917 *BioIn 17, ModArCr 3 [port]*
Degas, Hilaire Germain Edgar 1834-1917 *BioIn 17*
De Gasperi, Alcide 1881-1954 *DcTwHis*
De Gasperis, Paolo *WhoScE 91-3*
Degast, Hilaire G. 1928- *St&PR 93*
De Gaster, Zachary 1926- *WhoAm 92*
Degatano, Anthony Thomas 1950- *WhoE 93*
DeGaugh-Gross, Jackie L. 1951- *WhoEmL 93*
De Gaulle, Charles 1890-1970 *BioIn 17, ColdWar 1 [port]*
De Gaulle, Charles Andre Joseph Marie 1890-1970 *DcTwHis*
Degauque, Pierre 1946- *WhoScE 91-2*
deGavre, Robert T. 1940- *St&PR 93*
deGavre, Robert Thompson 1940- *WhoAm 92*
De Geer, Lars-Erik Gerard 1945- *WhoWor 93*
De Geest, Gerrit 1960- *WhoWor 93*
Degeest, Willy Andre 1943- *WhoWor 93*
Degen, Bernard John, II 1937- *WhoAm 92*
Degen, Bruce 1945- *BioIn 17*
Degen, Helmut 1911- *Baker 92*
Degen, Rolf 1926- *WhoScE 91-3*
De Genaro, Jennie Jennings 1932- *WhoWrEP 92*
Degener, Curtis Don 1930- *St&PR 93*
Degenford, James Edward 1938- *WhoAm 92*
Degenhardt, Robert A. 1943- *St&PR 93*
Degenhardt, Robert Allan 1943- *WhoAm 92*
Degenhart, Paul V. 1946- *St&PR 93*
Degenkolb, Henry John 1913-1989 *BioIn 17*
De Gennaro, Richard 1926- *WhoAm 92*
De Gennes, Pierre-Gilles 1932- *WhoScE 91-2, WhoWor 93*
Degens, T(uti) *DcAmChF 1960*
Degenszejn, Debora 1959- *WhoAmW 93*
DeGeorge, Francis Donald 1929- *WhoAm 92*
DeGeorge, Lawrence J. 1916- *St&PR 93*
De George, Lawrence Joseph 1916- *WhoAm 92*
De George, Richard T(homas) 1933- *ConAu 39NR*
De George, Richard Thomas 1933- *WhoAm 92*
Deger, Robert John, Jr. 1943- *WhoSSW 93*
Degeratu, Cornelia Virginia 1936- *WhoScE 91-4*
de Gerenday, Laci Anthony 1911- *WhoAm 92*
Degerstedt, Ross Maurice 1958- *WhoEmL 93*
De Geus, Aart J. *St&PR 93*
DeGeus, Wendell Ray 1948- *WhoEmL 93*
Degeyter, Pierre 1848-1932 *Baker 92*
Degheele, Danny 1941- *WhoScE 91-2*
DeGhetto, Kenneth Anselm 1924- *WhoAm 92*
Deghy, Guy (Stephen) 1912-1992 *ConAu 137*
De Gier, A. 1944- *WhoScE 91-3*
Degioanni, Henri *St&PR 93*
Degiorgio, Vittorio 1939- *WhoScE 91-3*

De Giorgis, Marcello A. 1930- *St&PR 93*
DeGiovanni, Jack Robert, Jr. 1960- *WhoEmL 93*
DeGiovanni-Donnelly, Rosalie Frances 1926- *WhoAm 92*
De Girardin, Delphine 1804-1855 *BioIn 17*
DeGiusti, Dominic Lawrence 1911- *WhoAm 92*
De Givenchy, Hubert James Marcel Taffin 1927- *WhoAm 92, WhoWor 93*
Degkwitz, Eva Gertrud 1926- *WhoScE 91-3*
Degkwitz, Rudolf 1920- *WhoScE 91-3*
Degler, Carl Neumann 1921- *WhoAm 92*
Degli Antoni, Giovanni 1935- *WhoScE 91-3*
Deglise, Xavier 1941- *WhoScE 91-2*
Degnan, Elizabeth Josephine 1927- *WhoAmW 93*
Degnan, Herbert Raymond 1921- *WhoAm 92*
Degnan, James J. 1932- *St&PR 93*
Degnan, John J. *Law&B 92*
Degnan, John Michael 1948- *WhoEmL 93*
Degnan, Joseph 1955- *WhoAm 92*
Degnan, Kim Ellen 1956- *WhoWor 93*
Degnan, Martin J. *Law&B 92*
Degnan, Robert A. 1930- *St&PR 93*
Degnan, Terrance J. *Law&B 92*
Degnan, Thomas Leonard 1909- *WhoAm 92*
Degner, Erich Wolf 1858-1908 *Baker 92*
Degner, Robert Louis 1942- *WhoSSW 93*
De Goede, Hendrik 1948- *WhoWor 93*
De Goff, Victoria Joan 1945- *WhoAmW 93*
DeGolier, Laura Prange 1945- *WhoAmW 93*
De Goncourt, Edmond 1822-1896 *BioIn 17*
De Goncourt, Jules 1830-1870 *BioIn 17*
DeGonia, Mary Elise 1954- *WhoAmW 93, WhoEmL 93*
Degos, Laurent 1945- *WhoScE 91-2*
De Gournay, Marie le Jars d1645 *BioIn 17*
De Graaf, L.A. 1936- *WhoScE 91-3*
De Graaff, Christopher Stuart 1951- *WhoWor 93*
DeGrace, Charles A.H. 1926- *St&PR 93*
De Graciansky, Pierre-Charles 1935- *WhoScE 91-2*
Degrada, Francesco 1940- *Baker 92*
Degraff, David Charles 1954- *WhoE 93, WhoWor 93*
DeGraff, Jill Katherine 1965- *WhoAmW 93*
Degraff, Robin L. *St&PR 93*
De Graffenreidt, James H., Jr. *Law&B 92*
de Graffenried, Velda Mae Camp *WhoAmW 93*
De Graffigny, Francoise d'Issembourg d'Happoncourt 1695-1758 *BioIn 17*
de Graft, Joe 1924-1978 *DcLB 117 [port]*
de Gramont, Sanche *ScF&FL 92*
DeGrande, Gary Christopher 1949- *WhoE 93*
DeGrandi, Donna M. *Law&B 92*
DeGrandi, Joseph Anthony 1927- *WhoAm 92*
de Grandi, Juan Carlos 1941- *WhoUN 92*
De Grandi, Pierre 1941- *WhoScE 91-4*
DeGrandis, Donald J. *Law&B 92*
DeGrandis, Donald James 1948- *WhoAm 92*
de Grandpre, Albert Jean 1921- *St&PR 93, WhoAm 92, WhoWor 93*
De Grandval, Marie 1830-1907 *BioIn 17*
DeGrange, Mary Whitcomb d1990 *BioIn 17*
De Grassi, Alex 1953- *Baker 92*
de Gravelles, William Decatur, Jr. 1928- *WhoAm 92*
De Graw, Darrel Garvin 1934- *WhoSSW 93*
deGrazia, Bruce Clinton *Law&B 92*
De Grazia, Joseph d1991 *BioIn 17*
De Grazia, Loretta Theresa 1955- *WhoAmW 93*
de Grazia, Sebastian 1917- *WhoAm 92, WhoE 93*
Degre, Miklos 1936- *WhoScE 91-4*
Degreef, H.J. 1940- *WhoScE 91-2*
Degregorie, Robert P. *Law&B 92*
Degregorio, Michael A. 1954- *St&PR 93*
DeGregorio, Tony *BioIn 17*
De Gregory, Alfred D. 1941- *St&PR 93*
DeGregory, Alfred Dean 1941- *WhoAm 92*
De Greiff, Monica *BioIn 17*
Degremont, Antoine *WhoScE 91-4*
Degremont, Francois 1937- *WhoScE 91-2*
de Grey, Roger 1918- *WhoWor 93*
DeGrilla, Robert J. 1942- *WhoSSW 93*
DeGroat, William Chesney 1938- *WhoAm 92, WhoE 93*
DeGroff, Ralph Lynn, Jr. 1936- *WhoAm 92, WhoE 93*
De Grolier, Eric 1911- *BioIn 17*
De Groodt-Lasseel, Marie H.A. 1914- *WhoScE 91-2*
DeGroot, George Paul 1933- *St&PR 93*
De Groot, Huub Johannes Maria 1958- *WhoWor 93*
De Groot, John 1941- *St&PR 93, WhoAm 92*
de Groot, Klaas 1940- *WhoWor 93*
Degroot, Leslie Jacob 1928- *WhoAm 92*
De Groot, Mart J.H. 1938- *WhoScE 91-1*
De Groot, Martin Jan Hugo 1938- *WhoWor 93*
De Groot, S.J. 1937- *WhoScE 91-3*
de Groot, Stephen F. 1961- *WhoEmL 93*
De Groote, Alexandre G. 1958- *WhoWor 93*
De Groote, Bruno Philippe 1957- *WhoWor 93*
De Groote, Georges 1936- *WhoScE 91-2*
De Groote, Jan 1925- *WhoScE 91-2*
De Groote-Striano, Maryanne *Law&B 92*
DeGross, Pierce Edward, III 1964- *WhoE 93*
De Grouchy, Jean *WhoScE 91-2*
deGruchy, Kenneth Ackerman, Jr. 1954- *WhoEmL 93*
De Grummond, Lena Young d1989 *BioIn 17*
DeGruson, Eugene Henry 1932- *WhoAm 92*
De Gruson, Gene 1932- *WhoWrEP 92*
Degtiarev, Stepan (Anikievich) 1766-1813 *Baker 92*
Degtyarev, Alexander Igorevich 1962- *WhoWor 93*
De Gubernatis, Angelo 1840-1913 *IntDcAn*
Deguchi, Alicia Tai 1963- *WhoAmW 93*
Degueffe, Taffara 1926- *WhoWor 93*
DeGuere, Philip *MiSFD 9*
De Guide, Richard 1909-1962 *Baker 92*
De Guiran, Georges 1931- *WhoScE 91-2*
Deguire, Kathryn Silber 1932- *WhoAmW 93*
DeGuire, Margaret Ann 1950- *WhoAmW 93*
de Guitaut, Guillaume *Law&B 92*
DeGulis, Albert Joseph 1934- *St&PR 93*
DeGuzman, Edmundo Maningat 1942- *WhoWor 93*
de Guzman, Gregorio Tercero, Jr. 1936- *WhoWor 93*
De Guzman, Helena *AmWomPl*
De Guzman, Nicanor G., Jr. 1932- *WhoAsAP 91*
de Guzman, Rodolfo A. 1948- *WhoUN 92*
DeHaan, Christel 1942- *WhoAmW 93*
De Haan, H. 1944- *WhoScE 91-3*
DeHaan, Norman Richard 1927-1990 *BioIn 17*
de Haan, Tom *ScF&FL 92*
De Haan-Puls, Joyce Elaine 1941- *WhoAmW 93*
DeHaas, John Neff, Jr. 1926- *WhoAm 92*
De Haen, Hartwig 1941- *WhoUN 92*
Dehaene, Jean-Luc 1940- *WhoWor 93*
de Haenen, Remy 1916- *DcCPCAm*
Dehahn, Julia *ConAu 139*
De Hamel, Joan (Littledale Pollock) 1924- *DcChlFi*
Dehan, Kelly Marie 1961- *St&PR 93*
Deharde, John Robert 1962- *WhoSSW 93*
De Haro, Andres 1925- *WhoWor 93*
De Hart, Allen *BioIn 17*
DeHart, David Glenn 1958- *WhoEmL 93*
De Hart, Harold C. 1938- *St&PR 93*
DeHart, James French, Jr. 1961- *WhoEmL 93*
DeHart, James Louis 1946- *WhoEmL 93*
De Hart, Jane Sherron *WhoAmW 93*
DeHart, Robert Charles 1917- *WhoAm 92*
DeHart, Robert L. 1933- *St&PR 93*
DeHart, Ronald David 1948- *WhoE 93*
de Hartog, Jan 1914- *ScF&FL 92, WhoAm 92, WhoWor 93*
Deharveng, Jean Michel *WhoScE 91-2*
DeHaven, Kenneth Le Moyne 1913- *WhoWor 93*
de Haven, Tom 1949- *ScF&FL 92, SmATA 72 [port], WhoWrEP 92*
De Havilland, Olivia 1916- *IntDcF 2-3 [port]*
de Havilland, Olivia Mary 1916- *WhoAm 92*
DeHay, Jerry Marvin 1939- *WhoSSW 93*
DeHay, John Carlisle, Jr. 1922- *WhoAm 92*
DeHayes, Daniel Wesley 1941- *WhoAm 92*
De Heer, Arend Robert Eduard 1950- *WhoWor 93*
De Heer, Hendrik Jan 1931- *WhoWor 93*
De Heer, Rolf *MiSFD 9*
de Hegedus, Coloman 1942- *St&PR 93*
Dehejia, Makarand V. 1934- *St&PR 93*
Dehejia, Vidya 1942- *ConAu 136*
De Hemptinne, Xavier A. 1932- *WhoScE 91-2*
Dehennin, Herman 1929- *WhoAm 92*
De Henriquez, Salome Urena 1850-1897 *BioIn 17*
De Herrera, Francisco c. 1576-1656 *BioIn 17*
De Herrera, Francisco 1622-1685 *BioIn 17*
Deheuvels, Paul Rene Louis 1948- *WhoWor 93*
Deheuvels, Rene 1923- *WhoWor 93*
Dehlendorf, Robert O., II 1931- *St&PR 93*
Dehlinger, Peter 1917- *WhoAm 92*
Dehmelt, Hans *BioIn 17*
Dehmelt, Hans Georg 1922- *WhoAm 92, WhoWor 93*
Dehmer, Carlos 1949- *WhoEmL 93*
Dehmler, Mari Lynch 1953- *WhoWrEP 92*
Dehmlow, Eckehard Volker 1933- *WhoWor 93*
Dehmlow, Louis H.T. 1927- *St&PR 93*
Dehmlow, Louis Henry Theodore, III 1927- *WhoAm 92*
Dehmlow, Nancy 1952- *St&PR 93*
Dehmlow, Nancy Jean 1952- *WhoAmW 93*
Dehn, James Theodore 1930- *WhoE 93*
Dehn, Joseph William, Jr. 1928- *WhoAm 92*
Dehn, Paula Faye 1951- *WhoEmL 93*
Dehn, Siegfried (Wilhelm) 1799-1858 *Baker 92*
Dehner, Ann Therese 1950- *WhoAmW 93*
Dehner, Dorothy *WhoAm 92*
Dehner, John 1915-1992 *ConTFT 10*
Dehnert, Charles Walter 1944- *WhoSSW 93*
Dehon, Piere R.M. 1946- *WhoScE 91-2*
De Hont, Raymond Joseph 1954- *St&PR 93*
DeHoogh, Noreen Beth 1943- *WhoAmW 93*
DeHope, Edward Kim 1952- *WhoEmL 93*
DeHority, Edward Havens, Jr. 1930- *WhoAm 92*
Dehousse, Martin Eugene 1920- *WhoWor 93*
Dehousse, Nicolas Maurice 1930- *WhoScE 91-2*
DeHovitz, Jack Alan 1952- *WhoE 93*
de Hoyos, Angela 1945?- *NotHsAW 93 [port]*
de Hoyos, Debora 1953- *NotHsAW 93*
de Hoyos, Debora M. 1953- *WhoAmW 93*
De Huff, Elsie *AmWomPl*
Dei, Sharon 1936- *WhoAmW 93*
Dei-Anang, Kofi Kumi 1940- *WhoWor 93*
De Ibanez, Sara 1909-1971 *BioIn 17*
De Ibarbourou, Juana 1895-1979 *BioIn 17*
Deibel, David C. 1950- *St&PR 93*
Deibel, Jerome P. 1924- *St&PR 93*
Deibel, Mildred Inez 1929- *WhoAmW 93*
Deibel, Robert F., Jr. 1917- *St&PR 93*
Deiber, Julio Alcides 1945- *WhoWor 93*
Deibert, David Daniel 1958- *St&PR 93*
Deibert, Donald George *Law&B 92*
Deibler, John B. 1943- *St&PR 93*
Deibler, Marie Phillips *WhoAmW 93, WhoWor 93*
Deibler, Portia G. 1951- *St&PR 93*
Deibler, William Edwin 1932- *WhoAm 92, WhoE 93*
Deicher, Helmuth R.G. 1929- *WhoScE 91-3*
Deichman, Erica 1914- *BioIn 17*
Deichman, Kjeld 1901-1963 *BioIn 17*
Deichmann, Dick H. 1928- *St&PR 93*
Deichmann, Frederick William 1942- *WhoIns 93*
Deichmann, Helmut *St&PR 93*
Deieso, Donald Allan 1949- *WhoAm 92*
Deighan, Thomas E. 1932- *St&PR 93*
Deighan, Thomas Michael *Law&B 92*
Deighton, Len 1929- *BioIn 17, ScF&FL 92, WhoAm 92, WhoWor 93*
Deighton, Leonard C. *ScF&FL 92*
Deihl, Richard Harry 1928- *St&PR 93, WhoAm 92*
Deihl, Richard T. *Law&B 92*
Deikel, Theodore 1935- *St&PR 93*
Deily, Ann Beth 1948- *WhoE 93*
Deily, James H. 1946- *St&PR 93*
Deily, James Richard 1921- *St&PR 93*
Deily, Linnet F. *St&PR 93*
Deimel, Mark *MiSFD 9*
Deimer, Lorena Ruth Murrill 1926- *WhoWrEP 92*
Deimling, George F. 1945- *St&PR 93*
Deiner, John B. 1940- *WhoIns 93*
Deinert, J.C. *St&PR 93*
Deininger, James Paul 1950- *WhoEmL 93*
Deinken, John J. *Law&B 92*
Deiotte, Margaret Williams Tukey 1952- *WhoAmW 93, WhoEmL 93*
Deis, Carl 1883-1960 *Baker 92*
dei Santi, Anna
See Andreozzi, Gaetano 1755-1826 *OxDcOp*
Deisch, Phillip Scott *Law&B 92*
Deisenhofer, Johann 1943- *WhoAm 92, WhoSSW 93, WhoWor 93*
Deisenroth, Clinton Wilbur 1941- *WhoAm 92*
Deiseroth, Hans-Jorg 1945- *WhoScE 91-3*
Deisler, Paul Frederick, Jr. 1926- *WhoAm 92*
Deissler, Mary A. 1955- *WhoAm 92*
Deissler, Robert George 1921- *WhoAm 92, WhoWor 93*
Deist, Wilhelm 1931- *ConAu 136*
Deister, Irwin Frederick, Jr. 1929- *St&PR 93*
Deitch, Arline Douglis 1922- *WhoAm 92*
Deitch, David A. *Law&B 92*
Deitch, Donna 1945- *MiSFD 9*
Deitch, Gerald E. *Law&B 92*
Deitch, Ira 1942- *WhoE 93*
Deitch, James Michael 1954- *WhoE 93, WhoEmL 93*
Deitch, Jeffrey *BioIn 17*
Deitch, Marc W. 1942- *St&PR 93*
Deitch, Marsha Pilchik *Law&B 92*
Deitch, Stephen Howard 1945- *WhoE 93*
Deitch, Stewart 1941- *St&PR 93*
Deitcher, Herbert 1933- *St&PR 93, WhoAm 92*
Deitchle, Gerald W. 1951- *St&PR 93*
Deitchle, Gerald Wayne 1951- *WhoAm 92*
Deiters, Hermann (Clemens Otto) 1833-1907 *Baker 92*
Deiters, Joan Adele 1934- *WhoAm 92, WhoE 93*
Deitrick, Frances I. 1962- *ConAu 137*
Deitrick, George Albert, III 1946- *WhoE 93*
Deitrick, William Edgar 1944- *WhoAm 92*
Deits, Mary Patricia 1936- *WhoAmW 93*
Deitsch, Marian Mimi 1933- *WhoAmW 93*
Deitz, Herbert J. 1908-1991 *BioIn 17*
Deitz, Lewis Levering 1944- *WhoSSW 93*
Deitz, Paula 1938- *WhoAm 92*
Deitz, Robert David 1926- *St&PR 93*
Deitz, Susan Rose 1934- *WhoAmW 93*
Deitz, Thomas F. *ScF&FL 92*
Deitz, Tom 1952- *ScF&FL 92*
Deitzler, Harry G. 1951- *WhoWor 93*
Deiz, Mercedes F. 1917- *AfrAmBi [port]*
DeJacimo, Alexandria Welzien 1951- *WhoEmL 93*
DeJaco, Frani B. *Law&B 92*
de Jaegher, Francois Ed 1951- *WhoWor 93*
De Jaffa, Kathleen H.B. *AmWomPl*
de Jager, Cornelis 1921- *WhoWor 93*
Dejagers, Dorothy *AmWomPl*
de Janvry, Alain 1939- *WhoAm 92*
DeJarnatt, Steve *MiSFD 9*
DeJarnette, Bettye Harper 1936- *WhoAmW 93*
DeJarnette, Edmund 1938- *WhoAm 92, WhoWor 93*
De Jary, J.J. *St&PR 93*
De Jesus, Maria Leonora Vasquez 1950- *WhoWor 93*
De Jesus, Nydia Rosa 1930- *WhoAm 92*
deJesus-Burgos, Sylvia Teresa 1941- *WhoAmW 93*
Dejmek, Kazimierz 1924- *PolBiDi, WhoWor 93*
DeJohn, Charles Andrew 1945- *WhoSSW 93*
De Johnette, Jack 1942- *WhoAm 92*
Dejoie, Louis, II 1928- *DcCPCAm*
Dejoncker, Theodore 1894-1964 *Baker 92*
De Jong, Arthur Jay 1934- *WhoAm 92*
De Jong, Ate *MiSFD 9*
De Jong, Conrad J(ohn) 1934- *Baker 92*
De Jong, David John 1951- *WhoEmL 93*
DeJong, David Neil 1963- *WhoE 93*
De Jong, David Samuel 1951- *WhoE 93, WhoEmL 93, WhoWor 93*
De Jong, Dola 1911- *DcAmChF 1960*
DeJong, Gerben 1946- *WhoAm 92, WhoE 93, WhoEmL 93*
De Jong, J. 1943- *WhoScE 91-3*
De Jong, Jan Willem 1942- *WhoScE 91-3*
De Jong, Joan Arius Henricus 1936- *WhoWor 93*
De Jong, Marinus *Baker 92*
Dejong, Meindert 1906- *ChlFicS, DcAmChF 1960*
DeJong, Meindert 1906-1991 *AnObit 1991, BioIn 17, MajAI [port]*
de Jong, Michael 1962- *WhoSSW 93*
De Jong, Norman Klay 1930- *St&PR 93*
De Jong, Paul T.V.M. 1942- *WhoScE 91-3*
De Jong, Robert Duris 1945- *WhoWrEP 92*
DeJong, Russell N. 1907-1990 *BioIn 17*
DeJonge, David Earl 1959- *WhoEmL 93*
De Jonge, Jan Benjamin 1936- *WhoScE 91-3*
De Jonge, Johannes Wietse G. 1939- *WhoWor 93*
DeJonge, Sophia L. *Law&B 92*
De Jongh, Adriaan *Law&B 92*
Dejongh, J. Paul *Law&B 92*
De Jongh, James Laurence 1942- *WhoWrEP 92*

Dejonghe, Leon J.A. 1946- *WhoScE 91-2*
DeJonghe, Thomas G. *Law&B 92*
De Joria, John Paul Jones *BioIn 17*
Dejours, P. *WhoScE 91-2*
De Juanes, Juan d1579 *BioIn 17*
De Julio, Sergio 1939- *WhoScE 91-3*
De Justo, Mario 1940- *WhoWor 93*
DeKam, Emilee *BioIn 17*
Dekanic Ozegovic, Darinka 1943- *WhoScE 91-4*
Dekaris, Dragan 1936- *WhoScE 91-4*
DeKay, Dennis Alan 1952- *WhoEmL 93*
de Kazinczy, Ferenc Andor 1929- *WhoWor 93*
Dekazos, Elias Demetrios 1920- *WhoSSW 93*
De Keersmaecker, Roger F.J. 1948- *WhoScE 91-2*
De Kempener, Pieter 1503-c. 1580 *BioIn 17*
Dekens, Alexander Leon Jean 1953- *WhoWor 93*
de Kerautem, Yves 1948- *WhoWor 93*
De Kerchove, Gerald 1946- *St&PR 93*
De Kerillis, Henri 1889-1958 *BioIn 17*
DeKeyser, James C. 1937- *St&PR 93*
Dekeyser, P. *WhoScE 91-2*
Dekeyser, Raf 1939- *WhoScE 91-2*
DeKeyser, William Richard, Jr. 1948- *WhoEmL 93*
Dekeyser, Willy Clement 1910- *WhoWor 93*
Dekhuijzen, H.M. 1930- *WhoScE 91-3*
deKieffer, Donald Eulette 1945- *WhoAm 92*
De Kimpe, Norbert 1948- *WhoScE 91-2*
De Kinder, Jan Karel Maria 1965- *WhoWor 93*
Dekker, Adrianus Jacobus 1918- *WhoWor 93*
Dekker, Carl *WhoWrEP 92*
Dekker, Eugene Earl 1927- *WhoAm 92*
Dekker, Fred 1959- *MiSFD 9*
Dekker, George Gilbert 1934- *WhoAm 92*
Dekker, Harriett Gromb 1942- *WhoAm 92*
Dekker, Howard R. 1920- *St&PR 93*
Dekker, Jerry Allen 1954- *St&PR 93*
Dekker, Johan 1925- *WhoScE 91-3*
Dekker, Marcel 1931- *WhoAm 92*
Dekker, Maurits 1899- *WhoAm 92*
Dekker, P.H.M. 1948- *WhoScE 91-3*
Dekker, Willem 1938- *WhoWor 93*
Dekker, Wisse 1924- *WhoAm 92*
Dekkers, J.J. 1951- *WhoScE 91-3*
Dekko, Thomas L. 1927- *St&PR 93*
De Klerk, Frederik Willem *BioIn 17*
DeKlerk, Frederik Willem 1936- *WhoAfr, WhoWor 93*
De Klerk, Fredrik Willem 1936- *DcTwHis*
De Klerk, G.J.M. 1952- *WhoScE 91-3*
Dekmejian, Richard Hrair 1933- *WhoAm 92*
De Kock, Josse 1933- *WhoWor 93*
de Koff, John Peter 1954- *WhoEmL 93*
Dekom, Peter James 1946- *WhoAm 92*
De Koning, Jan 1924- *WhoScE 91-3*
De Kool, Marthijn 1957- *WhoWor 93*
De Kooning, Lisa *BioIn 17*
De Kooning, Willem 1904- *BioIn 17, WhoAm 92*
De Korne, David J. 1956- *St&PR 93*
De Korne, Jack E. 1947- *St&PR 93*
Dekorsi, Ann Elizabeth 1947- *WhoAmW 93*
DeKosky, Steven Trent 1947- *WhoE 93*
de Koster, Henri Johan 1914- *WhoWor 93*
Dekoster, Paul R. *Law&B 92*
DeKoven, Reginald, III 1948- *WhoAm 92*
De Koven, (Henry Louis) Reginald 1859-1920 *Baker 92*
De Kovner-Mayer, Barbara 1938- *WhoWrEP 92*
De Koyer, Edward *St&PR 93*
De Kresz, Geza 1882-1959 *BioIn 17*
De Kresz, Norah 1882-1960 *BioIn 17*
de Kruif, Jack H. 1921- *WhoAm 92*
DeKruif, Paul 1890-1971 *JrnUS*
Dekster, Boris Veniamin 1938- *WhoWor 93*
Dektyarev, Israil Munevich 1940- *WhoWor 93*
Dela, Maurice 1919-1978 *Baker 92*
de Laat, Joannes Adrianus Petrus Maria 1955- *WhoWor 93*
De Laat, S.W. *WhoScE 91-3*
de la Bandera, Elna Marie 1936- *WhoE 93, WhoWor 93*
DelaBarre Powers, Nancy May 1941- *WhoAmW 93*
De La Beckwith, Byron *BioIn 17*
de la Bedoyere, Quentin Michael 1934- *WhoWor 93*
Delaborde, Elie (Miriam) 1839-1913 *Baker 92*
Delabre, Kevin Michael 1952- *WhoEmL 93*
De La Casiniere, Alain 1942- *WhoScE 91-2*
Delacato, Carl Henry 1923- *WhoAm 92*
Delacey, Deborah Hartwell 1952- *WhoAmW 93*
de Lacharriere, Olivier Roger 1953- *WhoWor 93*
de la Colina, Rafael 1898- *WhoAm 92*
Delacorte, George T. 1893-1991 *AnObit 1991*
Delacorte, George T. 1894-1991 *BioIn 17*
Delacote, Jacques 1942- *Baker 92*
Delacour, Yves Jean Claude Marie 1943- *WhoWor 93*
De La Court, F.H. *WhoScE 91-3*
Dela Cruz, Jose Santos 1948- *WhoAm 92, WhoEmL 93, WhoWor 93*
De la Cruz, Juana Ines 1651-1695 *BioIn 17*
De La Cruz, Mariano Villaroman, Jr. 1928- *WhoWor 93*
De La Cuadra, Humberto Enrique 1938- *WhoWor 93*
De La Cueva, Julio Jose Iglesias 1943- *WhoWor 93*
de la Espriella, Ricardo *DcCPCAm*
De La Falaise, Loulou *BioIn 17*
De La Falaise, Lucie *BioIn 17*
Delafield, E.M. 1890-1943 *BioIn 17*
De La Fressange, Ines *BioIn 17*
Delafuente, Jacqueline D. *Law&B 92*
Delagardelle, Norma Jean 1934- *St&PR 93*
De La Garza, Alexander 1929-1992 *BioIn 17*
de la Garza, E. 1927- *CngDr 91, HispAmA [port]*
De La Garza, Edward *Law&B 92*
de la Garza, Eligio 1927- *WhoAm 92*
de la Garza, Eligio Kika 1927- *WhoSSW 93*
De La Garza, Eloise Young 1951- *WhoAmW 93*
de la Garza, Rodolfo 1942- *HispAmA*
Delage, Carol Anne 1958- *WhoEmL 93*
Delage, Jean d1992 *BioIn 17*
Delage, Maurice (Charles) 1879-1961 *Baker 92*
Delagrave, Yves *St&PR 93*
de la Guardia, Antonio *DcCPCAm*
de la Guardia, Mario Francisco 1936- *WhoAm 92*
de la Gueronniere, Raphael *WhoE 93*
de la Guerra Ord, Angustias 1815-1890 *NotHsAW 93*
De la Guerre, Elisabeth Claude Jacquet 1659-1729 *BioIn 17*
de La Guierce, Eric George 1950- *WhoWor 93*
Del Aguila, Ralph W. 1939- *St&PR 93*
de Laguna, Frederica 1906- *WhoAm 92, WhoAmW 93*
de la Haba, Gabriel Luis 1926- *WhoE 93*
Delahanty, Ed 1867-1903 *BioIn 17*
Delahaye, Guy 1888-1969 *BioIn 17*
Delahaye, Jean-Paul Roland 1952- *WhoWor 93*
Delahaye, Michael 1946- *ScF&FL 92*
De La Haye, R. *WhoScE 91-1*
Delahoussaye, Mary Katherine 1956- *WhoAmW 93*
De La Hoya, Oscar *BioIn 17*
Delahunty, Joseph Lawrence 1935- *WhoE 93*
Delahunty, Michael Leo d1990 *BioIn 17*
De La Iglesia, Felix Alberto 1939- *WhoAm 92*
Delain, Nancy Baum 1956- *WhoE 93*
DeLaine, Tina Marie 1962- *WhoSSW 93*
Delaire, Jean 1923- *WhoScE 91-2*
deLaittre, John d1992 *NewYTBS 92 [port]*
De Laittre, John 1907-1992 *BioIn 17*
Delakas, Daniel Liudviko 1921- *WhoAm 92*
Delakova, Katya d1991 *BioIn 17*
Delalande, Michel-Richard 1657-1726 *Baker 92*
De la Lastra, Albert 1936- *St&PR 93*
DeLalio, George M. 1929- *St&PR 93*
Delalio, Louis D. 1926- *St&PR 93*
Delalio, Marilyn 1928- *St&PR 93*
de la Llave, Rafael 1957- *WhoEmL 93, WhoSSW 93*
Delaloye, Bernard 1928- *WhoWor 93*
Delaloye, John Francis 1945- *WhoIns 93*
De la Madrid Hurtado, Miguel 1934- *DcCPCAm, WhoWor 93*
Delamare, Francois 1938- *WhoScE 91-2*
De La Mare, Roger Francois *WhoScE 91-1*
de la Mare, Walter 1873-1956 *WorLitC [port]*
de la Mare, Walter (John) 1873-1956 *ConAu 137, MajAI [port]*
De Lamarter, Eric 1880-1953 *Baker 92*
DeLamater, James Newton 1912- *WhoAm 92*
Delamater, Jerome Herbert 1943- *WhoE 93*
DeLaMater, Robert Griffin 1959- *WhoEmL 93*
Delambert, Guy M., III *Law&B 92*
DeLambo, Robert J. *Law&B 92*
DeLamielleure, Joseph Michael 1951- *BiDAMSp 1989*
de Lamirande, Claire 1929- *WhoCanL 92*
Delamont, Gordon (Arthur) 1918-1981 *Baker 92*
De la Mora, Annabelle *Law&B 92*
de la Mora, Pablo 1951- *WhoWor 93*
de la Mota, Juan 1950- *St&PR 93*
De La Mota Gomez-Acebo, Juan 1950- *WhoWor 93*
de la Motte, Dean Ells 1961- *WhoSSW 93*
Delamuraz, Jean-Pascal 1936- *WhoWor 93*
De Lancey, John Oliver Lang 1951- *WhoEmL 93*
DeLancey, Teresa Hammack 1954- *WhoEmL 93*
De Lancie, John (Sherwood) 1921- *Baker 92*
Deland, Michael R. *BioIn 17*
Deland, Michael Reeves 1941- *WhoAm 92*
De Land, Michelle Karen 1954- *WhoWrEP 92*
Deland, Raymond John 1927-1991 *BioIn 17*
Delaney, Andrew 1920- *WhoSSW 93, WhoWor 93*
Delaney, C. Timothy 1957- *WhoEmL 93*
Delaney, Caldwell *WhoAm 92*
Delaney, Cornelius Francis 1938- *WhoAm 92*
Delaney, Edward Leopold 1885-1972 *BioIn 17*
Delaney, Edward Norman 1927- *WhoAm 92, WhoE 93, WhoWor 93*
Delaney, Eleanor Cecilia Coughlin *WhoAmW 93, WhoWor 93*
Delaney, George Joseph 1936- *St&PR 93*
Delaney, Gina *WhoWrEP 92*
Delaney, Harold 1919- *WhoE 93*
Delaney, John Adrian 1956- *WhoEmL 93*
Delaney, John Francis 1938- *WhoAm 92*
Delaney, John Martin, Jr. 1956- *WhoEmL 93*
Delaney, John P. 1913-1990 *BioIn 17*
Delaney, Joseph 1904-1991 *BioIn 17*
Delaney, Joseph H. 1932- *ScF&FL 92*
Delaney, Joseph P. 1934- *WhoAm 92, WhoSSW 93*
Delaney, Karoline Ann 1965- *WhoAmW 93*
Delaney, Laurence *ScF&FL 92*
Delaney, Lawrence John 1935- *WhoAm 92*
Delaney, Lisa June 1965- *WhoAmW 93*
Delaney, Marion Patricia 1952- *WhoEmL 93*
Delaney, Mark Steven 1952- *WhoEmL 93, WhoSSW 93*
Delaney, Marshall *WhoCanL 92*
Delaney, Mary Jane *Law&B 92*
Delaney, Michael *ScF&FL 92*
Delaney, Nancy Jo 1941- *WhoAmW 93, WhoE 93*
Delaney, Patrick E. 1953- *St&PR 93*
Delaney, Patrick James 1940- *WhoAm 92*
Delaney, Paul 1933- *BioIn 17*
Delaney, Philip Alfred 1928- *St&PR 93, WhoAm 92*
Delaney, Richard James 1946- *WhoAm 92*
Delaney, Richard Peter *Law&B 92*
Delaney, Robert Finley 1925- *WhoWor 93*
DeLaney, Robert J., Jr. 1931- *St&PR 93*
Delaney, Robert (Mills) 1903-1956 *Baker 92*
Delaney, Robert Patrick 1961- *WhoE 93, WhoEmL 93*
Delaney, Robert Richard, Jr. 1954- *WhoEmL 93*
Delaney, Robert V. 1934- *St&PR 93*
Delaney, Robert Vernon 1936- *WhoAm 92*
Delaney, Robert Vincent 1934- *WhoAm 92*
Delaney, Robert William 1929- *St&PR 93*
Delaney, Shelagh 1939- *BioIn 17*
Delaney, Terry W. 1949- *WhoEmL 93*
Delaney, Thomas Caldwell, Jr. 1918- *WhoAm 92*
Delaney, Thomas Francis 1948- *WhoE 93*
Delaney, Thomas P. 1934- *St&PR 93*
Delaney, William F., Jr. *WhoIns 93*
Delaney, William Francis, Jr. *WhoAm 92*
Delaney, William Timothy 1937- *St&PR 93*
DeLaney Adams, Donna Marie 1952- *WhoEmL 93*
Delanney, Susana D. *Law&B 92*
Delannoy, Jean 1908- *MiSFD 9*
Delannoy, Marcel 1898-1962 *Baker 92*
Delano, Dana Porter 1960- *St&PR 93*
Delano, Edith Barnard *AmWomPl*
Delano, Frederic Adrian 1863-1953 *BioIn 17*
Delano, Gerard Curtis 1890-1972 *BioIn 17*
Delano, Jonathan William 1949- *WhoEmL 93*
Delano, Lester Almy, Jr. 1928- *WhoAm 92*
Delano, Marcia Patricia 1939- *WhoAmW 93*
Delano, Robert Barnes, Jr. 1956- *WhoEmL 93*
Delano, Ruth B. *AmWomPl*
Delano, Victor 1919- *WhoAm 92*
Delano, William Adams 1874-1960 *BioIn 17*
De La Noe, Jerome L. 1941- *WhoScE 91-2*
De Lanoy, Charles James 1956- *WhoEmL 93*
Delany, Clarissa Scott 1901-1927 *AmWomPl*
Delany, Dana *BioIn 17, WhoAm 92, WhoAmW 93*
Delany, Dana 1956- *ConTFT 10*
Delany, Edward L. *WhoAm 92*
Delany, Hubert T. 1901-1990 *BioIn 17*
Delany, Logan D., Jr. 1949- *St&PR 93*
Delany, Logan Drummond, Jr. 1949- *WhoAm 92, WhoEmL 93*
Delany, Martin Robinson 1812-1885 *BioIn 17, EncAACR*
Delany, Samuel R. *BioIn 17*
Delany, Samuel R. 1942- *ConGAN, MagSAmL [port], ScF&FL 92*
Delap, J. Q., Jr. 1948- *WhoEmL 93, WhoSSW 93*
Delap, James Harve 1930- *WhoSSW 93*
Delap, Richard 1942-1987 *ScF&FL 92*
Delap, Tony 1927- *WhoAm 92*
Delapalme, Alain 1930- *WhoScE 91-2*
De la Parra, Teresa 1890-1936 *BioIn 17*
de la Pava, Fabio *Law&B 92*
de La Pena, George 1956- *WhoAm 92*
De La Pena Fuentes, Rosendo 1947- *WhoWor 93*
Delapenha, Linda Bunn 1942- *WhoAmW 93*
Delaperouse, Marc *Law&B 92*
Delapeyre, Edward *WhoScE 91-1*
de la Piedra, Jorge 1923- *WhoSSW 93*
Delaplain, Laura Zuleme 1955- *WhoAmW 93*
de la Plante, Walter Sowerby 1915- *WhoE 93*
De la Poer, Charles William Beresford 1846-1919 *BioIn 17*
Delaporte, Francois Louis 1941- *ConAu 137*
DeLapp, Albert Ashley, II 1931- *WhoAm 92*
DeLapp, Tina Davis 1946- *WhoAmW 93*
Delappe, Irving Pierce 1915- *WhoAm 92*
De Lara, Annette Laurie 1956- *WhoAmW 93*
De Lara, Isidore 1858-1935 *Baker 92, OxDcOp*
de la Ree, Gereaux *ScF&FL 92*
de la Ree, Gerry 1924- *ScF&FL 92*
De la Renta, Oscar *BioIn 17*
de la Renta, Oscar 1932- *WhoAm 92, WhoE 93*
De La Rey, Jacobus Hercules 1847-1914 *HarEnMi*
Delarge, Jacques E. 1938- *WhoScE 91-2*
De Large, Robert Carlos 1842-1874 *BioIn 17*
DeLargy, Elisabeth S. *Law&B 92*
Delaro, Hattie *AmWomPl*
Delaro, Selina *ScF&FL 92*
De La Rocha Corzo, Julio Cesar 1957- *WhoWor 93*
De La Roche, Hubert 1925- *WhoScE 91-2*
De la Roche, Mazo 1879-1961 *BioIn 17*
De La Rocque, Francois 1886?-1946 *BioIn 17*
DeLaRonde, Barbara Joan 1953- *WhoAmW 93*
DeLaRosa, Denise Maria 1954- *WhoAmW 93, WhoEmL 93, WhoWor 93*
De La Rosa, Edna Elnore 1918- *WhoWrEP 92*
De la Rosa, Javier *BioIn 17*
de Larosiere, Jacques 1929- *WhoWor 93*
de Larrabeiti, Michael *ScF&FL 92*
de Larrocha, Alicia 1923- *WhoAm 92, WhoAmW 93, WhoWor 93*
De La Rubia, Javier 1954- *WhoWor 93*
De La Rue, Richard Michael *WhoScE 91-1*
De La Ruelle, Marc 1943- *WhoWor 93*
Delarue-Mardrus, Lucie d1945 *BioIn 17*
Delaryd, Bengt 1929- *WhoWor 93*
De Lasa, Jose M. *Law&B 92*
de Lasa, Jose M. 1941- *WhoAm 92*
De las Casas, Bartolome 1474-1566 *BioIn 17*
de la Sena, Cesar Arana 1955- *WhoWor 93*
De La Serna, Vicente L. *WhoAsAP 91*
de las Heras, Gonzalo 1940- *WhoAm 92*
de Lastours, Aymar 1929- *WhoWor 93*
de La Taille, Michel Francois 1940- *WhoUN 92*

de la Teja, Elpidio Leoncio 1943- *WhoE 93*
de la Torre, Alberto Clemente 1944- *WhoWor 93*
De La Torre, Consuelo 1937- *WhoScE 91-3*
DeLaTorre, Phillip Eugene 1953- *WhoEmL 93*
De La Torre, Teofilo Arguello 1938- *WhoWor 93*
Delatour, Claude 1941- *WhoScE 91-2*
Delatour, Paul M.F. 1939- *WhoScE 91-2*
de Lattre, Andre Marie Joseph 1923- *WhoWor 93*
Delatush, Edith G. *ScF&FL 92*
Delauder, William B. *WhoAm 92*
DeLauer, Richard 1918-1990 *BioIn 17*
DeLaughter, Bobby *BioIn 17*
DeLaughter, Thomas Glenn 1948- *WhoEmL 93*
Delaunay, Jean 1942- *WhoScE 91-2*
Delaunay, Sonia 1885-1979 *BioIn 17*
Delaune, (Jewel) Lynn (De Grummond) *WhoWrEP 92*
De Launey, Wallace Edward 1928- *WhoWor 93*
Delaunois, Luc M. 1947- *WhoScE 91-2*
DeLaura, David Joseph 1930- *WhoAm 92, WhoE 93, WhoWrEP 92*
DeLaura, Michael Anthony 1960- *WhoEmL 93, WhoSSW 93*
De Laurentiis, Dino *BioIn 17*
De Laurentiis, Dino 1919- *WhoAm 92, WhoWor 93*
Delaurentis, Anthony Joseph *Law&B 92*
Delaurentis, Anthony Joseph 1946- *St&PR 93*
De Laurentis, Louise Budde 1920- *WhoWrEP 92*
de Laurentis, Sarah *Law&B 92*
DeLauro, Albert A. 1946- *St&PR 93*
DeLauro, Rosa *WhoAm 92, WhoAmW 93, WhoE 93*
DeLauro, Rosa L. 1943- *CngDr 91*
de Lauture, Herve 1924- *WhoWor 93*
De Lavallade, Carmen *BioIn 17*
De La Varre, Andre *WhoE 93*
Delaveau, Pierre 1921- *WhoScE 91-2*
de La Vega, Dianne Winifred DeMarinis *WhoAmW 93*
De la Vega, Garcilaso 1539-1616 *BioIn 17*
DeLaVergne, Susan Perez 1961- *WhoAmW 93*
De La Viesca, Rosa *WhoScE 91-3*
Delawie, Homer Torrence 1927- *WhoAm 92*
DeLay, Dorothy 1917- *Baker 92, WhoAm 92, WhoAmW 93*
Delay, Eugene Raymond 1948- *WhoEmL 93*
De Lay, Robert Francis 1919- *WhoAm 92*
Delay, Robert P. 1934- *St&PR 93*
DeLay, Thomas D. 1947- *WhoAm 92, WhoSSW 93*
DeLay, Tom 1947- *CngDr 91*
Delaye, Bruno 1952- *WhoWor 93*
Delaye, J.H. 1933- *WhoScE 91-2*
De Layo, Leonard Joseph 1921- *WhoAm 92*
Del Balzo, Joseph Michael 1936- *WhoAm 92*
Del Balzo, Mary Domenica *Law&B 92*
Delbanco, Nicholas F. 1942- *WhoWrEP 92*
Delbanco, Thomas Lewis 1939- *WhoAm 92*
Del Barco, Lucy Salamanca d1989 *BioIn 17*
Del Barrio, Eduardo *BioIn 17*
Delbeke, Frans T.M.C. 1945- *WhoScE 91-2*
Del Bel, Paul Thomas 1949- *WhoEmL 93*
Del Bello, Bernard N. *Law&B 92*
Del Bello, Bernard Nicholas 1935- *St&PR 93*
Del Bene, Adriana Gabrieli *IntDcOp*
Del Biaggio, Elio 1964- *WhoWor 93*
Delbianco, E. *Law&B 92*
Del Bo, Massimo 1925- *WhoWor 93*
Del Bono, Elizabeth Anne 1951- *WhoEmL 93*
Del Borgo, Nancy W. 1946- *WhoE 93*
Del Borgo, Nancy Withington 1946- *WhoAmW 93*
Delcambre, Darnelle LaDouceur 1942- *WhoSSW 93*
Delcamp, Natalie Lowey 1923- *WhoSSW 93*
Del Campo, Carlos Humberto 1940- *WhoWor 93*
Del Campo, Sergio Enrique 1952- *WhoWor 93*
Del Caro, Adrian 1952- *ConAu 137*
Delcaro, Lucio G. 1937- *WhoScE 91-3*
Del Casal, Mauro Pereira 1934- *WhoWor 93*
Delcasse, Theophile 1852-1923 *BioIn 17*
Del Castillo, Adelaida 1952- *NotHsAW 93*
del Castillo, Carlos Ernesto 1959- *WhoSSW 93*
del Castillo, Graciania 1951- *WhoUN 92*
Del Castillo, Jaime 1951- *WhoWor 93*
del Castillo, Jeanne Louise Taillac 1933- *WhoAmW 93*
del Castillo, Ricardo A. 1946- *WhoSSW 93*
Del Castillo y Saavedra, Antonio 1603-1667 *BioIn 17*
Delchambre, Rudy Alois 1959- *WhoWor 93*
Delchamps, Alfred F., III *Law&B 92*
Delchamps, O.H., Jr. 1933- *St&PR 93*
Delchamps, Randolph 1943- *St&PR 93*
Del Chiaro, Mario Aldo 1925- *WhoAm 92*
Del Colliano, Gerard Anthony 1946- *WhoE 93*
del Corral, Milagros 1945- *WhoUN 92*
Del Cotto, Steven Joseph *Law&B 92*
Delcour, J. *WhoScE 91-3*
Delcour, Jan A. 1956- *WhoScE 91-2*
Delcourt, Christian C. T. 1948- *WhoWor 93*
Delcroix, Jean-Loup 1924- *WhoScE 91-2*
Delcroix, Leo Franciscus Wilhelmina 1949- *WhoWor 93*
Delcroix, Leon Charles 1880-1938 *Baker 92*
Delcroix, Michel 1946- *WhoScE 91-2*
Delden, Lex van 1919-1988 *Baker 92*
Deldevez, Edouard(-Marie-Ernest) 1817-1897 *Baker 92*
Del Duca, Rita 1933- *WhoAmW 93*
Del Duce, Gregory J. 1942- *St&PR 93*
Dele, Dorothy A. *WhoWrEP 92*
Delea, Martha Anne *Law&B 92*
Deleanu, Maurice 1920- *WhoScE 91-4*
Deleault, Robert R. 1951- *St&PR 93*
De Leceta, Juan 1911-1991 *BioIn 17*
de Ledebur, Juan Carlos 1954- *WhoEmL 93, WhoSSW 93*
Deledicque, Alain-Georges 1944- *WhoWor 93*
Deleeck, Herman 1928- *WhoWor 93*
De Leenheer, Andre Prudent 1941- *WhoScE 91-2, WhoWor 93*
Deleers, Michel 1951- *WhoWor 93*
De Leeuw, David E. *St&PR 93*
de Leeuw, Frank 1930- *WhoAm 92*
Delehant, Joseph H. *Law&B 92*
Delehant, Joseph Henry 1950- *WhoEmL 93*
Delehant, Raymond Leonard 1937- *WhoE 93, WhoWor 93*
Delehanty, Edward John 1929- *WhoAm 92*
Delehanty, Garrett James, Jr. *Law&B 92*
Delehanty, Jeanne M. *Law&B 92*
Delehanty, Peter Michael 1954- *WhoEmL 93*
Delehaunty, James Francis *Law&B 92*
Delelio, James D. *Law&B 92*
Delella, Diane M. 1951- *St&PR 93*
De Lellis, Keith 1955- *BioIn 17*
Deleloye, Michel Francois 1936- *WhoScE 91-4*
de Lemos, Antonio Jose Monteiro 1953- *WhoWor 93*
de Lemos, Ruth Geisler 1907- *WhoE 93*
de Lemos, Sheila Victoria 1949- *WhoAm 92*
Delen, Nafiz 1941- *WhoScE 91-4*
De Leo, Dennis Michael 1939- *St&PR 93*
DeLeo, Maryann 1952- *WhoAmW 93*
De Leon, Albert Vernon *Law&B 92*
De Leon, Argeo Rodriguez 1938- *WhoScE 91-3*
de Leon, Arthur Ariel *WhoSSW 93*
DeLeon, Arthur Eugene 1942- *WhoWor 93*
de Leon, Carmen Maria 1956- *WhoEmL 93, WhoSSW 93*
De Leon, Daniel 1852-1910 *PolPar*
DeLeon, David Camden 1816-1872 *BioIn 17*
De Leon, Fernando Don *St&PR 93*
de Leon, John Louis 1962- *WhoSSW 93, WhoWor 93*
de Leon, Lidia Maria 1957- *WhoAm 92, WhoAmW 93*
De Leon, Lucrecia 1568- *BioIn 17*
DeLeon, Marcus *MiSFD 9*
DeLeon, Morris Jack 1941- *WhoSSW 93*
DeLeon, Patrick H. 1943- *BioIn 17*
Deleon, Patrick Henry 1943- *WhoAm 92*
DeLeon, Robert Louis 1954- *WhoE 93*
DeLeone, Carmon 1942- *WhoAm 92*
de Leone, Francesco (Bartolomeo) 1887-1948 *Baker 92*
Deleon Guerrero, Lorenzo Iglesias Larry *WhoWor 93*
De Leon-Polanco, Jorge Andres 1958- *WhoWor 93*
De L'Epine, Margherita *OxDcOp*
DeLerno, Joseph 1924- *St&PR 93*
Deleroi, Werner Hermann Emil 1933- *WhoWor 93*
Delerue, Georges d1992 *NewYTBS 92*
Delerue, Georges 1924-1992 *BioIn 17*
Delescluze, Louis Charles 1809-1871 *BioIn 17*
De Lespinasse, Julie 1732-1776 *BioIn 17*
De L'Espine, Dominique *WhoCanL 92*
Delessert, Etienne 1941- *ConAu 37NR, MajAI [port]*
Delessert, Jacquine *ConAu 139*
Delessio-Neubauer, Elizabeth Mary 1950- *WhoAmW 93*
del'Estrac, Jean-Claude Gervais Raoul 1948- *WhoWor 93*
Deletant, Dennis 1946- *BioIn 17*
Deleuran, Aage 1925- *WhoWor 93*
Deleuze, Olivier *WhoScE 91-2*
Delevan, Sybil Marie 1950- *WhoAmW 93*
Delevie, Harold Jacob 1931- *WhoAm 92*
Delevoryas, Theodore 1929- *WhoAm 92*
De Ley, Jozef 1924- *WhoScE 91-2*
Deleze, Jean Bernard 1931- *WhoScE 91-2*
Delfano, M.M. *WhoWrEP 92*
DelFavero-Campbell, Patricia Graciela 1957- *WhoEmL 93*
Delfiner, Joel Steven 1952- *WhoE 93*
Delfiner, Michael *St&PR 93*
Delfini, Claudio 1947- *WhoScE 91-3*
Delfino, Astrid Diann 1966- *WhoAmW 93, WhoE 93*
Delfino, Joseph John 1941- *WhoSSW 93*
Delfino, Michelangelo 1950- *WhoEmL 93*
Delfino, Richard 1938- *St&PR 93*
Delfmann, Stephanie 1960- *BioIn 17*
Delfonics *SoulM*
Delfont, Bernard 1909- *WhoWor 93*
DelForge, Gary Lynn 1953- *WhoSSW 93*
Del Forno, Anton 1950- *WhoEmL 93*
Del Fosse, Claude Marie 1940- *WhoSSW 93*
Delfosse, Gilles C. 1929- *WhoScE 91-2*
Del Franco, Ray Joseph 1945- *St&PR 93*
Delfyette, Raymond 1955- *WhoE 93*
Delgadillo, Luis (Abraham) 1887-1961 *Baker 92*
Delgado, Abelardo 1931- *HispAmA [port]*
Delgado, Cesar Aurelio 1933- *WhoWor 93*
Delgado, Eric Dirk 1963- *WhoSSW 93*
Delgado, James P. 1958- *ConAu 136*
Delgado, Jane L. 1953- *NotHsAW 93 [port]*
Delgado, Juan B. 1868-1929 *DcMexL*
Delgado, Lenore R. 1948- *WhoEmL 93*
Delgado, Mercedes Caridad 1962- *WhoAmW 93*
Delgado, Natalia 1953- *WhoEmL 93*
Delgado, Rafael 1853-1914 *DcMexL*
Delgado, Tomas Edwin, Sr. 1948- *WhoEmL 93*
Delgado-Barrio, Gerardo 1946- *WhoWor 93*
Delgado-Penin, Jose A. 1942- *WhoScE 91-3*
Delgado Rubio, Alfonso 1944- *WhoScE 91-3*
Del Ghingaro, Virgil B. 1931- *St&PR 93*
DelGiudice, Katherine Marie *Law&B 92*
Delgiudice, Michael J. 1943- *St&PR 93*
Del Giudice, Vincent James 1921- *WhoWor 93*
Delgorio, Frances Ann 1954- *WhoAmW 93, WhoEmL 93*
del Greco, Francesco 1923- *WhoAm 92*
Delgrego, Andrew A. 1942- *St&PR 93*
Del Guercio, James P. *Law&B 92*
Del Guercio, Louis Richard Maurice 1929- *WhoAm 92, WhoWor 93*
Del Guerra, Alberto 1944- *WhoWor 93*
Del Guidice, Debra Ann 1954- *WhoAmW 93*
Delhaes, P. *WhoScE 91-2*
Delhalle, Joseph Armand Ghislain 1946- *WhoScE 91-2*
Delhaye, Alain Jacques 1936- *St&PR 93*
Delhaye, Jean R. 1921- *WhoScE 91-2*
Delhaye, Michel 1929- *WhoScE 91-2*
Delhey, Duncan C. *Law&B 92*
DelHomme, Beverly Ann 1954- *WhoEmL 93*
Delia, Albert Arrigo 1960- *WhoEmL 93, WhoSSW 93*
D'Elia, Anthony d1990 *BioIn 17*
D'Elia, Bill *MiSFD 9*
Delia, Francis *MiSFD 9*
Delia, Frank S. *Law&B 92*
D'Elia, Gerardo Antonio, Jr. 1942- *WhoE 93*
D'Elia, Giacomo 1934- *WhoScE 91-4*
D'Elia, James Joseph 1954- *WhoE 93*
Delia, Jesse Graves 1944- *WhoAm 92*
D'Elia, Nicholas 1959- *WhoEmL 93*
Deliac, Eric Pierre 1956- *WhoScE 91-2*
Delianides, George 1931- *St&PR 93*
DeLiberato, Robert Vincent 1955- *St&PR 93*
DeLibero, Mary Smellie 1950- *WhoAmW 93, WhoEmL 93*
Delibes, Leo 1836-1891 *IntDcOp, OxDcOp*
Delibes, (Clement-Philibert-)Leo 1836-1891 *Baker 92*
Delibes, Miguel *BioIn 17*
Delibes Castro, Miguel 1947- *WhoScE 91-3*
Delich, John M. 1930- *WhoAm 92*
Deliege, Denise A. 1938- *WhoScE 91-2*
Delienne, Jacquelyn E. 1947- *WhoEmL 93*
Delight, Cherry *ScF&FL 92*
Deligiorgis, Stavros G. 1933- *WhoAm 92*
Deligne, Pierre 1926- *WhoWor 93*
Deligne, Pierre R. 1944- *WhoAm 92*
DeLigter, Robert d1991 *BioIn 17*
Delilah *BioIn 17*
De Lilla, Celina S. 1934- *WhoWrEP 92*
DeLillo, Don *BioIn 17*
DeLillo, Don 1936- *MagSAmL [port], ScF&FL 92, WhoAm 92*
De Lima, Oscar Ferreira 1952- *WhoWor 93*
de Lima, Paulo-Tarso Flecha 1933- *WhoWor 93*
Delima, Richard F. *Law&B 92*
deLima, Richard Ford 1930- *St&PR 93, WhoAm 92*
De Lima, Sigrid 1921- *WhoWrEP 92*
de Limantour, Clarice B. 1918- *WhoE 93*
Delimar, Natasa 1940- *WhoScE 91-4*
deLinde, Mark Terry 1956- *WhoEmL 93*
Delins, Emils 1921- *WhoWor 93*
de Lint, Charles 1951- *ScF&FL 92*
De Lio, Anthony Peter 1928- *WhoWor 93*
DeLio, Richard Michael 1948- *WhoAm 92, WhoE 93*
Delio, Richard Peter 1943- *St&PR 93*
DeLio, Thomas 1951- *Baker 92*
DeLisi, Charles 1941- *WhoAm 92*
Delisi, Dianne White 1943- *WhoAmW 93*
De Lisi, Joanne *WhoEmL 93*
Delisi, Vincent J. 1931- *St&PR 93*
De Lisio, Stephen Scott 1937- *WhoAm 92*
DeLisle, Gaudry 1943- *St&PR 93*
Delisle, Guy *Law&B 92*
Delisle, James Robert 1953- *WhoEmL 93*
Delisle, Roseline *BioIn 17*
de Lisle, Suzanne Turner 1948- *WhoEmL 93*
Delisle, Victor A. 1927- *St&PR 93*
de L'Isle Adam, Auguste Villiers *ScF&FL 92*
Deliso, Joseph J., Sr. 1909- *St&PR 93*
de Lisser, H. G. 1878-1944 *DcLB 117 [port]*
Delissio, John F. 1930- *St&PR 93*
Deliu, Gheorghe 1939- *WhoScE 91-4*
Delius, Frederick 1862-1934 *Baker 92, IntDcOp, OxDcOp*
Delivanis, Dimitrios John 1909- *WhoWor 93*
Deliyannis, Constantine Christos 1938- *WhoE 93, WhoWor 93*
DeLizasoain, Patricia Maria 1962- *WhoAmW 93*
Delizee, A.F. *WhoScE 91-2*
Deljan, Peter dc. 1041 *OxDcByz*
del Junco, Tirso 20th cent.- *HispAmA*
Delk, Ira Edwin 1930- *St&PR 93*
Delker, David Glen 1952- *WhoEmL 93*
Dell, Christine Marie 1963- *WhoEmL 93*
Dell, Claudia 1910- *SweetSg C [port]*
Dell, David Donald 1953- *WhoEmL 93*
Dell, Donald Lundy 1938- *WhoE 93*
Dell, Donna Marie *Law&B 92*
Dell, Ernest Robert 1928- *WhoAm 92, WhoE 93, WhoWor 93*
Dell, Frances G. d1991 *BioIn 17*
Dell, Harold K. 1943- *St&PR 93*
Dell, Jeffrey 1899-1985? *ScF&FL 92*
Dell, Kevin J. *Law&B 92*
Dell, Michael *BioIn 17*
Dell, Michael 1965- *ConEn*
Dell, Michael John 1954- *WhoEmL 93*
Dell, Michael S. 1965- *St&PR 93, WhoSSW 93*
Dell, Myrna 1924- *SweetSg D [port]*
Dell, R. *WhoScE 91-1*
Dell, Ralph Bishop 1935- *WhoAm 92, WhoE 93*
Dell, Robert Christopher 1950- *WhoAm 92, WhoE 93, WhoWor 93*
Dell, Robert E. 1935- *St&PR 93*
Dell, Sidney 1918-1990 *BioIn 17*
Dell, Stephen O. *St&PR 93*
Dell, Stephen Owen 1944- *WhoE 93*
Dell, W. Frank 1945- *St&PR 93*
Dell, Warren Frank, II 1945- *WhoE 93*
Dell, Willie Jones 1930- *WhoSSW 93*
Della Casa, Carlo 1941- *WhoScE 91-3*
Della Casa, Lisa 1919- *Baker 92, IntDcOp [port], OxDcOp*
Della Ciaia, Azzolino Bernardino 1671-1755 *Baker 92*
Della Corte, Andrea 1883-1968 *Baker 92*
Della Corte, Francesco 1930- *WhoWor 93*
Della Croce, Norberto 1926- *WhoScE 91-3*
Della Femina, Jerry 1936- *BioIn 17, WhoAm 92*
Della Franco, Thomas J. 1952- *St&PR 93*
Della-Giustina, Daniel *BioIn 17*
Dell'Aglio, Frank James 1954- *St&PR 93*

Del Vecchio Family 18th cent.-19th cent. *BioIn 17*
Delventhal, Bruce Warren 1949- *WhoE 93*
Delventhal, Jerald Alan 1953- *WhoEmL 93*
Delventhal, Thomas M. *Law&B 92*
Delves, Barrington *WhoScE 91-1*
Delves, L.M. *WhoScE 91-1*
Delvigne, Gerard Ate Leon 1942- *WhoWor 93*
Delvincourt, Claude 1888-1954 *Baker 92*
Delving, Michael *ConAu 39NR, MajAI*
Delvingt, W. 1938- *WhoScE 91-2*
Delwiche, Lyle D. 1934- *St&PR 93*
Dely, Steven 1943- *St&PR 93, WhoAm 92*
De Lyrot, Alain Herve 1926- *WhoAm 92*
Delz, Christoph 1950- *Baker 92*
Delz, William Ronald 1932- *WhoAm 92*
Delza-Munson, Elizabeth *WhoAm 92*
Delzell, Charles Floyd 1920- *WhoSSW 93*
Delzio, Frank 1925- *WhoWor 93*
Delzotto, Angelo N. *St&PR 93*
Delzotto, Elvio *St&PR 93*
de Macedo, Carlyle Guerra 1937- *WhoE 93, WhoUN 92*
De MacMahon, Marie Edme Patrice Maurice 1808-1893 *BioIn 17*
DeMael, Jacques Jean 1964- *WhoWor 93*
De Maertelaer, Viviane 1946- *WhoScE 91-2*
DeMaet, K.L. 1926- *St&PR 93*
De Maeyer, Leo C.M. 1927- *WhoScE 91-3*
Demaeyer, Thomas R. 1942- *St&PR 93*
Demaille, A. *WhoScE 91-2*
Demaille, J. *WhoScE 91-2*
De Maille, Leon Scott 1963- *WhoE 93*
Demain, Dominique Jacques 1935- *WhoWor 93*
De Main, John 1944- *WhoAm 92*
De Main, John (Lee) 1944- *Baker 92*
DeMaio, Dorothy J. 1927- *WhoAm 92, WhoAmW 93*
De Maio, James Michael 1961- *WhoE 93*
De Maio, M.C. Susan 1958- *St&PR 93*
De Maio, Marie Rose 1940- *WhoE 93*
deMaio, Michele T. 1953- *WhoAm 92*
Demaitre, Edmund d1991 *BioIn 17*
Demaitre, Edmund 1906-1991 *ScF&FL 92*
De Maiziere, Lothar 1940- *BioIn 17*
Demakes, John N. 1945- *St&PR 93*
Demakes, Nicholas Euthymios 1910- *St&PR 93*
Demakis, Louise Ward 1935- *WhoE 93*
De Man, Paul *BioIn 17*
Demange, Michel Andre 1944- *WhoScE 91-2*
Demangeot, P. *WhoScE 91-2*
Demantius, (Johannes) Christoph 1567-1643 *Baker 92*
D'Emanuele, Mary Ann 1934- *WhoAmW 93*
de Mar, Leoda Miller 1929- *WhoAm 92, WhoAmW 93, WhoE 93*
Demarais, Nancy Lee 1966- *WhoAmW 93*
Demarais, Yves Didier 1943- *WhoWor 93*
Demaray, Donald E(ugene) 1926- *ConAu 37NR*
Demaray, Elizabeth S. 1952- *St&PR 93*
Demaray, Ronald Benjamin 1959- *WhoEmL 93*
Demarchi, Ernest Nicholas 1939- *WhoAm 92, WhoWor 93*
DeMarco, Anita Joyce 1933- *WhoAmW 93*
DeMarco, Annemarie Bridgeman 1960- *WhoAmW 93*
De Marco, Carlo 1929- *WhoScE 91-3*
Demarco, Duncan G.W. *Law&B 92*
DeMarco, Gino Paul 1961- *WhoEmL 93*
de Marco, Guido 1931- *WhoWor 93*
DeMarco, John J., Jr. *St&PR 93*
De Marco, Michael Joseph 1960- *WhoE 93*
DeMarco, Nancy Jean 1946- *WhoSSW 93*
De Marco, Natalie Anne 1961- *WhoAmW 93*
DeMarco, Peter Anthony 1961- *WhoE 93*
DeMarco, Ralph John 1924- *WhoWor 93*
DeMarco, Robert Thomas 1950- *WhoAm 92*
DeMarco, Roland R. 1910- *WhoAm 92, WhoE 93, WhoWor 93*
DeMarco, Thomas Andrew, III 1948- *WhoE 93*
De Marco, Thomas Joseph 1942- *WhoAm 92*
DeMarco, Toni Marie 1957- *WhoAmW 93*
Demarcq, Gerard Jean Henry 1931- *WhoScE 91-2*
Demard, Francois 1940- *WhoScE 91-2*
Demaree, Gaston Rene 1940- *WhoScE 91-2*
Demaree, Robert Glenn 1920- *WhoSSW 93*
Demaree, Rosalyn Voige 1954- *WhoAmW 93*
Demarest, Clifford J. 1932- *St&PR 93*
Demarest, Daniel Anthony 1924- *WhoAm 92*
Demarest, David *Law&B 92*
Demarest, David Franklin, Jr. 1951- *WhoAm 92*
Demarest, David N. *NewYTBS 92 [port]*
Demarest, Philip S. 1936- *St&PR 93*
Demarest, Richard *BioIn 17*
Demarest, Sylvia M. 1944- *WhoAm 92*
De Marffy, Annick Marie 1944- *WhoUN 92*
De Margerie, Emmanuel 1924-1991 *BioIn 17*
de Margerie, Jean-M. 1927- *WhoAm 92*
De Margerie, Roland 1899-1990 *BioIn 17*
de Margitay, Gedeon 1924- *WhoE 93, WhoWor 93*
DeMaria, Alfred Anthony, Jr. 1952- *WhoEmL 93*
De Maria, Anthony John 1931- *WhoAm 92*
DeMaria, Anthony Nicholas 1943- *WhoAm 92*
Demaria, Carl *St&PR 93*
DeMaria, Dennis Michael 1946- *WhoEmL 93*
De Maria, Giovanni 1931- *WhoScE 91-3*
DeMaria, Jean Dominici 1938- *WhoE 93*
Demaria, John L. 1936- *St&PR 93*
DeMaria, Joseph Angelo 1957- *WhoEmL 93*
DeMaria, Michael Brant 1962- *WhoSSW 93*
DeMaria, Peter James 1934- *St&PR 93, WhoAm 92*
DeMaria, Theodora Roseanne 1963- *WhoAmW 93*
Demaria, Thomas Patrick 1960- *WhoE 93*
Demaria, Walter 1935- *WhoAm 92*
Demaria-Pesce, Victor Hugo 1951- *WhoWor 93*
DeMarie, Linda Esther 1960- *WhoE 93*
DeMarinis, Paul 1948- *Baker 92*
DeMarinis, Rick 1934- *BioIn 17, ScF&FL 92*
De Marino, Donald Nicholson 1945- *WhoAm 92, WhoE 93*
de Marino, Lawrence 1943- *ScF&FL 92*
Demaris, Ovid 1919- *WhoAm 92, WhoWrEP 92*
DeMark, Eugene F. 1947- *WhoE 93*
DeMark, Richard Reid 1925- *WhoAm 92*
DeMarle, Richard H. 1951- *St&PR 93*
de Marneffe, Barbara Rowe 1929- *WhoAmW 93*
de Marneffe, Francis 1924- *WhoAm 92, WhoSSW 93*
Demarquez, Suzanne 1899-1965 *Baker 92*
Demarquilly, Camille 1934- *WhoScE 91-2*
Demarr, Jean A. *Law&B 92*
De Marr, Mary Jean 1932- *WhoAm 92, WhoAmW 93*
de Marrais, Herbert J. 1928- *St&PR 93*
DeMars, Bruce *WhoAm 92*
De Mars, Caron Emerson 1955- *WhoAmW 93, WhoEmL 93*
De Mars, Dan Richard 1943- *St&PR 93*
DeMars, Richard B. 1918- *St&PR 93*
Demar-Salad, Geraldine 1929- *WhoAmW 93*
De Marsily, Ghislain 1939- *WhoScE 91-2*
Demarthe, Jean-Michel 1945- *WhoScE 91-2*
DeMartin, Charles P. *St&PR 93*
DeMartin, Charles Peter 1952- *WhoEmL 93*
De Martini, Alfred E. 1916- *WhoE 93*
De Martini, Alfred Eugene 1916- *St&PR 93*
DeMartini, Richard Michael 1952- *WhoAm 92*
Demartini, Robert John 1919- *St&PR 93, WhoAm 92*
DeMartino, Anthony Gabriel 1931- *WhoAm 92*
De Martino, Ernesto 1908-1965 *IntDcAn*
De Martino, John A. 1939- *St&PR 93*
DeMartino, Linda Klinc 1961- *WhoEmL 93*
de Marzio, Alfredo 1940- *WhoAm 92*
De Marzo, C. *WhoScE 91-3*
Demas, Thomas Theodore 1942- *St&PR 93*
Demas, William 1929- *DcCPCAm*
Demas, William Gilbert 1929- *WhoWor 93*
Demas, William N. 1937- *St&PR 93*
DeMasi, Jack Bernard 1946- *WhoEmL 93, WhoWrEP 92*
Demasi, Walter Mario Rosario 1926- *WhoWor 93*
Demaske, Susan J. *Law&B 92*
DeMaso, David Ray 1949- *WhoE 93, WhoEmL 93*
DeMaso, Jeffrey Anthony 1964- *WhoE 93*
Demaso, L. William 1941- *St&PR 93*
De Massa, Jessie G. *WhoAmW 93*
De Mastry, John A. 1930- *WhoSSW 93*
Demastus, Melodye Rose 1958- *St&PR 93*
Demattei, Angelo F. 1926- *St&PR 93*
DeMatteis, Thomas James 1962- *WhoE 93*
Dematteo, Albert 1932- *St&PR 93*
DeMatteo, Gloria Jean 1943- *WhoAmW 93*
Dematteo, Madelyn M. *Law&B 92*
DeMatteo, Madelyn M. 1948- *St&PR 93*
deMatties, Nicholas Frank 1939- *WhoAm 92*
de Maupassant, Guy *ScF&FL 92*
de Mauriac, Caroline Marie 1959- *WhoEmL 93*
deMause, Lloyd 1931- *WhoAm 92*
DeMay, Helen Louise 1927- *WhoAmW 93*
DeMay, Karl F. 1922- *St&PR 93*
De May, Robert Lee 1946- *WhoEmL 93*
DeMay, Thomas James *Law&B 92*
Demazeau, Gerard Maurice 1943- *WhoScE 91-2*
Demb, Ada 1948- *ConAu 138*
Dembach, Wilfried *Law&B 92*
Dembczynski, Jerzy 1943- *WhoScE 91-4*
Dembe, Cheryl Louise 1946- *WhoAmW 93*
Dembeck, Louise E. *Law&B 92*
Dembeck, Mary Grace 1931- *WhoAm 92, WhoE 93, WhoWor 93*
Dember, William Norton 1928- *WhoAm 92*
Dembicki, Eugeniusz Wieslaw 1929- *WhoScE 91-4*
Dembicks, Andrew E. 1941- *St&PR 93*
Dembinski, Henryk 1791-1864 *PolBiDi*
Dembinski, Stanislaw T. 1933- *WhoScE 91-4*
Dembitsky, Valery Mikhailovich 1949- *WhoWor 93*
Dembitz, Maria Bark *Law&B 92*
Dembling, Paul Gerald 1920- *WhoAm 92*
Demblowski, Denis Anthony *Law&B 92*
Dembner, S. Arthur 1920-1990 *BioIn 17*
Dembo, L.S. 1929- *ScF&FL 92*
Dembo, Lawrence Sanford 1929- *WhoAm 92*
Dembo, Richard 1948- *MiSFD 9*
Dembofsky, Thomas Joseph 1927- *WhoAm 92*
Dembour, Philippe 1952- *WhoWor 93*
Dembow, David E. 1925- *St&PR 93*
Dembowski, Edward 1822-1846 *PolBiDi*
Dembowski, Frederick Lester 1948- *WhoE 93, WhoEmL 93*
Dembowski, Peter Florian 1925- *WhoAm 92*
Dembroski, George Steven 1934- *WhoAm 92*
Dembry, George E. 1929- *St&PR 93*
Dembski, Stephen Michael 1949- *WhoEmL 93*
Demby, Betty J. *WhoWrEP 92*
Demby, Karen Bowks 1958- *WhoEmL 93*
Demchenko, Alexander Petrovych 1944- *WhoWor 93*
Demchuk, Bob *MiSFD 9*
De Medeiros, Maria *BioIn 17*
De' Medici, Lorenzo 1449-1492 *BioIn 17*
De Medicis, Catherine, Queen 1519-1589 *BioIn 17*
Demedts, Maurits G.P. 1941- *WhoScE 91-2*
De Meester, Paul J.A. 1935- *WhoScE 91-2*
De Meester, Paul Jozef August 1935- *WhoWor 93*
de Meijer, Robert Johan 1940- *WhoWor 93*
De Meijere, Armin 1939- *WhoScE 91-3*
DeMeis, Richard Anthony 1945- *WhoE 93*
De Mejo, Oscar 1911-1992 *BioIn 17*
Demek, Jaromir 1930- *WhoScE 91-4*
Demel, Gerald F. 1941- *St&PR 93*
Demel, Sol 1933- *St&PR 93*
DeMelio, Joseph John 1930- *St&PR 93, WhoAm 92*
DeMello, Austin Eastwood 1939- *WhoWor 93*
Demello, Louise Ann 1948- *WhoE 93*
de Mello-Franco, Affonso Arinos 1930- *WhoWor 93*
De Melo Neto, Joao Cabral 1920- *BioIn 17*
De Mena, Juan Pascual *BioIn 17*
De Mendelssohn, Peter 1909-1982 *ScF&FL 92*
Demenge, Pierre 1941- *WhoScE 91-2*
DeMenil, Dominique 1908- *WhoAm 92*
DeMent, Caren Winifred 1965- *WhoAmW 93*
Dement, Gridley 1919- *St&PR 93*
DeMent, James Alderson, Jr. 1947- *WhoEmL 93*
Dement, Jay M. 1951- *St&PR 93*
DeMent, K.R. *Law&B 92*
Dement, Thomas Anthony 1950- *St&PR 93*
Dement, William Charles 1928- *WhoAm 92*
Dementhon, Alain 1933- *WhoWor 93*
Dementis, Katharine Hopkins 1922- *WhoE 93*
Demento, Sandra Jo 1956- *WhoEmL 93*
Demeny, Desiderius 1871-1937 *Baker 92*
DeMeo, Donald A. *St&PR 93*
De Meo, Emilia M. *Law&B 92*
Demer, Ronald 1937- *St&PR 93*
Demeranville, Mark Irving 1952- *WhoEmL 93*
Demerath, Nicholas Jay, III 1936- *WhoAm 92*
DeMerchant, Beth 1957- *WhoWor 93*
Demerdash, Nabeel Aly Omar 1943- *WhoAm 92*
Demere, Robert H. 1924- *St&PR 93*
Demerec, Milislav 1895-1966 *BioIn 17*
De Mere-Dwyer, Leona 1928- *WhoSSW 93*
Demerest, Ada Rose *AmWomPl*
DeMerit, Susan C. 1950- *WhoAmW 93*
De Meritt, Bromley 1935- *St&PR 93*
DeMerritt, Ted C. 1932- *St&PR 93*
Demers, Andrea Nancy 1965- *WhoE 93*
Demers, Jacques 1944- *WhoAm 92*
DeMers, Judy Lee 1944- *WhoAmW 93*
Demers, Patricia 1946- *ScF&FL 92*
Demers, Paul Rene 1937- *WhoE 93*
Demers, Raymond 1937- *St&PR 93*
Demers, Walter V., Jr. 1928- *St&PR 93*
Demerson, Elisha L. 1951- *AfrAmBi [port]*
Demerson, Gordon E. 1930- *St&PR 93*
Demery, Barbara Carol Bell 1947- *WhoAmW 93*
Demessieux, Jeanne 1921-1968 *Baker 92*
De Mestral, Georges d1990 *BioIn 17*
de Mestre, Neville John 1938- *WhoWor 93*
Demeter, Jean Ellen 1947- *WhoAmW 93*
Demeter, John C. *Law&B 92*
Demeter, Nancy Ford 1957- *WhoAmW 93*
Demeter, Steven 1947- *WhoE 93*
Demetra, Tula Alexandra 1958- *WhoEmL 93*
Demetre, S. Gordon 1943- *St&PR 93*
Demetreon, Daiboune Elayne 1945- *WhoAmW 93*
Demetrescu, Mihai Constantin 1929- *WhoWor 93*
Demetriadi, Peter Michael 1953- *WhoWor 93*
Demetrio, Thomas A. 1947- *WhoAm 92*
Demetrion, James Thomas 1930- *WhoAm 92, WhoE 93*
Demetrion, Jim J. 1926- *St&PR 93*
Demetrios *OxDcByz*
Demetrios, Eames *MiSFD 9*
Demetrios Angelos Doukas c. 1220- *OxDcByz*
Demetrios Of Lampe fl. 116-?- *OxDcByz*
Demetrios Of Thessalonike *OxDcByz*
Demetrios Palaiologos c. 1407-1470 *OxDcByz*
Demetriou, Charles Arthur 1941- *WhoSSW 93*
Demetriou, Ioannes Constantine 1956- *WhoWor 93*
Demetriou, Kristin *BioIn 17*
Demetriou, Michael 1927- *WhoE 93*
Demetrius, II c. 276BC-229BC *HarEnMi*
Demetrius Poliorcetes, I 336BC-283BC *HarEnMi*
Demetropoulos, Andreas 1938- *WhoScE 91-4*
Demetrovics, Janos 1946- *WhoScE 91-4*
Demetry, James Steve 1936- *WhoAm 92*
Demetter, Richard A. 1940- *St&PR 93*
DeMetz, Kathleen Susan 1952- *WhoEmL 93*
Demetz, Peter 1922- *WhoAm 92*
De Meuse, Donald H. 1936- *St&PR 93*
De Meuse, Donald Howard 1936- *WhoAm 92*
Demeusy, John W. 1955- *WhoIns 93*
De Meuter, F. *WhoScE 91-2*
De Meyer, Kristin 1951- *WhoScE 91-2*
De Meyer, Roger 1927- *WhoScE 91-2*
De Meza, Anabel T. 1938- *WhoAmW 93*
De Meza, David *WhoScE 91-1*
Demharter, Cheryl Ann Marie 1955- *WhoWor 93*
Demi *MajAI*
Demi 1942- *BioIn 17*
Demian, Barbu Adrian 1940- *WhoSSW 93*
Demian, Wilhelm 1910- *Baker 92*
Demianczyk, Pamela J. 1949- *WhoE 93*
Demianski, Marek 1939- *WhoWor 93*
DeMichele, Michael Francis 1949- *St&PR 93*
De Michele, O. Mark 1934- *St&PR 93, WhoAm 92*
DeMichele, Robert Michael 1944- *St&PR 93, WhoAm 92*
De Michelis, Gianni *BioIn 17*
De Michelis, Gianni 1940- *WhoWor 93*
DeMichiei, Robert Allen 1964- *WhoE 93*
De Micoli, Salvatore 1939- *WhoAm 92, WhoWor 93*

Demidov, Serguei Sergueevitch 1942- *WhoWor 93*
Demidovich, Stephen F. 1939- *St&PR 93*
Demidowicz, Zenon 1953- *WhoWor 93*
Demiene, William L. 1932- *St&PR 93*
DeMieri, Joseph L. 1940- *WhoAm 92*
De Miguel Anasagasti, Pedro L. 1946- *WhoScE 91-3*
Demijohn, Thom *MajAI*
DeMik, Anita Lorraine 1945- *WhoAmW 93*
De Mik, Gerrit 1942- *WhoScE 91-3*
Demik, Roger Lynn *Law&B 92*
Demildt, Andre Charles 1933- *WhoScE 91-2*
D'Emilia, Robert F. *Law&B 92*
De Mille, Agnes *BioIn 17, WhoAm 92, WhoAmW 93*
De Mille, Anna *BioIn 17*
De Mille, Beatrice *AmWomPl*
De Mille, Cecil B. 1881-1959 *BioIn 17, MiSFD 9N*
De Mille, James 1833-1880 *BioIn 17*
DeMille, Katherine 1911- *SweetSg C*
DeMille, Nelson 1943- *ScF&FL 92*
De Mille, Nelson Richard 1943- *WhoE 93, WhoWor 93, WhoWrEP 92*
De Mille, William Churchill 1878-1955 *BioIn 17*
Demilliere, Bernard Henri Joseph 1931- *WhoWor 93*
DeMillion, Julianne 1955- *WhoAmW 93*
DeMillo, Richard A. 1947- *WhoAm 92*
De Milt, Aida Rodman 1871- *AmWomPl*
Demilt, Kenneth E. 1924- *St&PR 93*
De Milt, William A. 1941- *St&PR 93*
De Milto, Lori 1960- *WhoEmL 93*
Deming, Alison Hawthorne 1946- *WhoWrEP 92*
Deming, Claiborne Payne *Law&B 92*
Deming, David Lawson 1943- *WhoAm 92*
Deming, Donald Livingston 1924- *WhoAm 92, WhoWor 93*
Deming, Frank Stout 1927- *WhoAm 92*
Deming, Frederick Lewis 1912- *WhoAm 92*
Deming, Ira Michael 1958- *WhoE 93*
Deming, Mary Janes Beard 1946- *WhoEmL 93*
Deming, Norma Helen *AmWomPl*
Deming, Richard *ScF&FL 92*
Deming, Robert H. *St&PR 93*
Deming, Robert Herschel 1934- *WhoAm 92*
Deming, Thomas Edward 1954- *WhoEmL 93*
Deming, W. Edwards *BioIn 17*
Deming, W. Edwards 1900- *News 92 [port]*
Deming, William Edwards *WhoAm 92*
Deming, Willis Riley *Law&B 92*
Deming, Willis Riley 1914- *St&PR 93, WhoAm 92*
Demir, Ramsey *St&PR 93*
Demir, Remzi 1944- *WhoScE 91-4*
Demiray, Hilmi D. 1942- *WhoScE 91-4*
Demirel, Suleyman 1924- *BioIn 17, WhoWor 93*
Demirjian, Gerald Jerier 1932- *St&PR 93*
Demiroglu, Mehmet Cem'i 1928- *WhoWor 93*
Demiroren, Sabri 1937- *WhoScE 91-4*
Demis, D. Joseph *WhoE 93*
De Mita, Francis Anthony 1927- *WhoE 93*
DeMitchell, Terri Ann 1953- *WhoAmW 93*
Demitros, Kathleen Lawler *BioIn 17*
Demitz, Carol K. *Law&B 92*
Demjanjuk, John *BioIn 17*
Demko, Jonathan Alexander 1957- *WhoSSW 93*
Demko, Paul, Jr. 1944- *St&PR 93*
Demko, Thomas A. *Law&B 92*
Demkovich, Paul Bryan 1956- *WhoEmL 93*
Demler, Frederick Russel 1953- *WhoAm 92, WhoEmL 93*
Demler, Linda Kass 1954- *WhoEmL 93*
Demler, Marvin Christian 1909- *WhoE 93*
Demling, Robert Hugh 1943- *WhoAm 92*
Demme, Jonathan *BioIn 17*
Demme, Jonathan 1944- *MiSFD 9, News 92 [port], WhoAm 92*
Demmer, Paul G. 1927- *St&PR 93*
Demmer, Richard A. 1931- *St&PR 93*
Demmer, William R. 1933- *St&PR 93*
Demmer, William Roy 1933- *WhoAm 92*
Demmin, Lester Franz 1929- *WhoSSW 93*
Demmler, Albert William, Jr. 1929- *WhoE 93*
Demmler, Eugene F. 1936- *St&PR 93*
Demmler, John Henry 1932- *WhoAm 92*
Demmler, Ralph Henry 1904- *WhoAm 92*
Demner, Henryk *BioIn 17*
De Moerloose, Prosper H.M. 1923- *WhoScE 91-2*
Demoff, Samuel Louis 1909- *WhoAm 92*
Demoge, Paul Hugh Leon 1925- *WhoScE 91-2*
Demokan, Muhtesem Suleyman 1948- *WhoWor 93*
Demol, Leo *WhoScE 91-2*
De Mol, Pierre 1825-1899 *Baker 92*
Demond, Joan *WhoAm 92*
Demond, Walter Eugene 1947- *WhoEmL 93*
Demone, Henry *WhoAm 92*
DeMone, Robert Stephen 1932- *WhoAm 92*
De Money, Fred William 1919- *WhoAm 92*
Demont, Edwin G. 1942- *St&PR 93*
Demont, Jason P. *Law&B 92*
De Montaigne, Michel 1533-1592 *BioIn 17*
De Montalembert, Charles Forbes 1810-1870 *BioIn 17*
de Montalembert, Marc Rene 1940- *WhoUN 92*
De Montbrial, Thierry 1943- *WhoWor 93*
DeMonte, Claudia Ann 1947- *WhoAm 92*
DeMonte, Cynthia Maria 1956- *WhoAmW 93*
De Montebello, Philippe *BioIn 17*
de Montebello, Philippe Lannes 1936- *WhoAm 92, WhoWor 93*
de Montferrand, Bernard de Faubournet 1945- *WhoWor 93*
De Montfort, Simon 1208?-1265 *BioIn 17*
De Montherlant, Henry *BioIn 17*
DeMontier, Paulette LaPointe 1948- *WhoAm 92*
De Montigny, Louvigny 1876-1955 *BioIn 17*
De Monzie, Anatole 1876-1947 *BioIn 17*
De Moor, Bart L.R. 1960- *WhoWor 93*
Demopulos, Chris 1924- *WhoAm 92*
de Mora, Stephen John 1954- *WhoWor 93*
De Moraes, Waldemar 1937- *WhoUN 92*
De Morales, Luis c. 1509-1586 *BioIn 17*
DeMore, Jane Elyse 1950- *WhoAm 92*
Demorest, Joan Florence 1947- *WhoEmL 93*
Demorest, Mark Stuart 1957- *WhoEmL 93*
Demorest, Robert L. 1945- *St&PR 93*
De Mori, Renato 1941- *WhoAm 92*
De Mornay, Rebecca *BioIn 17*
De Mornay, Rebecca 1961- *WhoAm 92*
DeMoro, Pierre *MiSFD 9*
de Morsella, Guy Christopher 1926- *WhoWor 93*
Demorsky, Susan Anne *WhoSSW 93*
Demortier, Guy F.A. 1937- *WhoScE 91-2, WhoWor 93*
Demos, Jean 1919- *WhoScE 91-2*
Demos, Jeffrey Charles 1954- *WhoEmL 93*
Demos, John *Law&B 92*
Demos, John 1931- *St&PR 93*
Demos, John Putnam 1937- *ConAu 137, WhoAm 92*
Demos, Victoria Camille 1959- *WhoEmL 93*
De Moss, Darrell L. *Law&B 92*
De Moss, Deborah Lynne 1960- *WhoEmL 93*
DeMoss, Dinah L. 1952- *WhoAmW 93*
DeMoss, Emmett Roland, Jr. 1936- *St&PR 93*
DeMoss, Harold R., Jr. 1930- *WhoAm 92, WhoSSW 93*
Demoss, J.E. 1941- *St&PR 93*
DeMoss, Jon W. 1947- *WhoAm 92*
DeMoss, Kathryn E. 1932- *St&PR 93*
De Moss, Lisa Sewell *Law&B 92*
De Moss, Robert George 1928- *WhoAm 92*
DeMoss, Robert Lee 1926- *WhoSSW 93*
DeMoss, Ronald D. *Law&B 92*
Demosthenes 382BC-322BC *OxDcByz*
Demosthenes, (I) d413BC *HarEnMi*
Demosthenes, (II) 384?BC-322BC *HarEnMi*
Demott, Benjamin Hailer 1924- *WhoWrEP 92*
Demott, Deborah Ann 1948- *WhoAm 92*
De Mott, Marjorie *AmWomPl*
DeMott, Roberta Phillips 1942- *WhoAmW 93*
DeMotto, Benjamin Albert 1933- *St&PR 93*
Demougeot, (Jeanne Marguerite) Marcelle (Decorne) 1871-1931 *Baker 92*
DeMoulas, Telemachus A. 1923- *WhoAm 92*
DeMoulin, Raymond H. *St&PR 93*
De Moura, Patricia Brown 1948- *WhoE 93*
De Mourgues, Louis *WhoScE 91-2*
Demouth, Robin Madison *Law&B 92*
Demouth, Robin Madison 1939- *WhoAm 92*
deMoville, David Brent 1952- *WhoEmL 93*
De Moya y Contreras, Pedro *BioIn 17*
Demps, Patricia Redd *Law&B 92*
Dempsey, Al *ScF&FL 92*
Dempsey, Bernard Shanley 1929- *St&PR 93*
Dempsey, Brian P. 1937- *St&PR 93*
Dempsey, Carolyn B. 1937- *WhoAmW 93*
Dempsey, Daniel *BioIn 17*
Dempsey, Daniel Thomas 1953- *WhoE 93*
Dempsey, David N. *St&PR 93*
Dempsey, Edward 1944- *WhoAm 92*
Dempsey, Edward J. *Law&B 92*
Dempsey, Gail Rolader 1949- *WhoEmL 93*
Dempsey, Guy C., Jr. *Law&B 92*
Dempsey, Henry *ScF&FL 92*
Dempsey, Howard Stanley 1939- *WhoAm 92*
Dempsey, Jack 1895-1983 *BioIn 17*
Dempsey, James Howard, Jr. 1916- *WhoAm 92*
Dempsey, James J. 1963- *St&PR 93*
Dempsey, James Raymon 1921- *St&PR 93, WhoAm 92*
Dempsey, James W. *Law&B 92*
Dempsey, Jerry Edward 1932- *St&PR 93, WhoAm 92, WhoWor 93*
Dempsey, Joanne d1990 *BioIn 17*
Dempsey, John C. 1914- *St&PR 93*
Dempsey, John Cornelius 1914- *WhoAm 92*
Dempsey, John E. 1941- *St&PR 93*
Dempsey, John M., Jr. 1928- *St&PR 93*
Dempsey, Julian Ned 1942- *WhoAm 92*
Dempsey, Lee Edward 1962- *WhoSSW 93*
Dempsey, Levon Franklin 1934- *St&PR 93*
Dempsey, Louis F. 1926- *St&PR 93*
Dempsey, Louis Francis, III 1926- *WhoAm 92*
Dempsey, Mary Lu 1940- *WhoAmW 93*
Dempsey, Michael James 1957- *WhoEmL 93*
Dempsey, Owen Andre 1957- *WhoE 93*
Dempsey, Pamela Jean 1951- *WhoAmW 93*
Dempsey, Patrick *BioIn 17*
Dempsey, Phillip M. *Law&B 92*
Dempsey, Raymond Leo, Jr. 1949- *WhoE 93*
Dempsey, Sean E. *Law&B 92*
Dempsey, Stanley 1939- *St&PR 93*
Dempsey, Stephen Brian 1921- *St&PR 93*
Dempsey, Thomas A. *Law&B 92*
Dempsey, Thomas L. 1926- *St&PR 93*
Dempsey, Timothy Michael 1939- *WhoAm 92*
Dempsey, Wallace Guy *Law&B 92*
Dempsey, Wallace Guy 1925- *St&PR 93*
Dempsey, William H. 1925- *St&PR 93*
Dempsey-Polan, Laura 1950- *WhoAmW 93*
Dempster, Barry *WhoCanL 92*
Dempster, Curt 1938- *WhoE 93*
Dempster, George Roby 1887-1964 *BioIn 17*
Dempster, J.P. *WhoScE 91-1*
Dempster, Lauramay Tinsley 1905- *WhoAm 92*
Dempster, Richard Vreeland 1928- *WhoAm 92*
Dempster, Stuart (Ross) 1936- *Baker 92*
Dempwolff, Otto 1871-1938 *IntDcAn*
Demsetz, Harold 1930- *WhoAm 92*
Demsey, David Blackstone 1955- *WhoE 93*
Demske, James Michael 1922- *WhoAm 92*
DeMueller, Lucia 1937- *WhoAmW 93*
de Mul, Erick Eduard 1943- *WhoUN 92*
DeMunbrun, Julie D. *Law&B 92*
De Munck, Jan Casper 1962- *WhoWor 93*
De Munoz, Ines Mendoza d1990 *BioIn 17*
De Muro, David A. *Law&B 92*
DeMuro, Paul Robert 1954- *WhoEmL 93*
Demus, Jorg (Wolfgang) 1928- *Baker 92*
Demus, Lee Anne 1959- *WhoEmL 93*
Demus, Leslie M. *Law&B 92*
Demusz, Waldemar Henryk 1959- *St&PR 93*
Demusz, Walter 1933- *St&PR 93*
DeMuth, Christopher Clay 1946- *WhoAm 92*
DeMuth, David Peter 1945- *St&PR 93*
Demuth, Dennis Milton 1945- *WhoSSW 93*
DeMuth, Donald Lynn 1951- *WhoE 93*
Demuth, Hans-Ulrich 1953- *WhoWor 93*
De Muth, Laurence W., Jr. *Law&B 92*
DeMuth, Laurence Wheeler, Jr. *WhoAm 92*
Demuth, Laurence Wheeler, Jr. 1928- *St&PR 93*
Demuth, Leopold 1861-1910 *Baker 92*
Demuth, Marvin L. 1930- *St&PR 93*
Demuth, Norman 1898-1968 *Baker 92*
Demuyt, Don J. 1943- *St&PR 93*
Demy, Jacques 1931-1990 *BioIn 17, ConTFT 10, MiSFD 9N*
Demyan, David Blake 1947- *WhoE 93*
Demyanov, Vladimir Fedorovich 1938- *WhoWor 93*
Den, Hideo 1923- *WhoAsAP 91*
Dena, James 1947- *St&PR 93*
Denaburg, Charles Robert 1935- *WhoAm 92, WhoSSW 93*
Denaerde, Stefan *ScF&FL 92*
de Nagy, Tibor Julius 1910- *WhoAm 92*
Denahan, Joseph Anthony 1936- *St&PR 93, WhoAm 92*
Denard, Roslyn 1924- *St&PR 93*
Denardi, William M. 1933- *St&PR 93*
Denari, Neil M. 1957- *BioIn 17*
Denaro, Anthony Thomas 1929- *WhoE 93*
Denaro, Charles T. 1953- *St&PR 93*
Denaro, Charles Thomas *Law&B 92*
Denaro, Charles Thomas 1953- *WhoEmL 93*
Denaro, Gregory 1954- *WhoAm 92, WhoEmL 93, WhoSSW 93*
De Natale, Andrew Peter 1950- *WhoEmL 93*
DeNault, John B. 1919- *St&PR 93*
De Naut, James Eric 1940- *St&PR 93*
De Navarrete, Juan Fernandez c. 1526-1579 *BioIn 17*
Den Besten, Ronald Wayne 1948- *St&PR 93*
Den Biggelaar, Johan C. M. 1951- *WhoWor 93*
Denbo, Donald K. *Law&B 92*
Den Boer, David Hendrik *Law&B 92*
Den Boer, M.H. 1940- *WhoScE 91-3*
Denbow, Anthony Mark 1956- *WhoWor 93*
Denbow, Donald Michael 1953- *WhoSSW 93*
Den Braber, Joyce Elaine 1947- *St&PR 93*
den Breejen, Jan-Dirk 1963- *WhoWor 93*
Denburg, Dorian S. *Law&B 92*
Denburg, Dorian Sue 1954- *WhoEmL 93*
Denburg, Dorothy Urman 1949- *WhoE 93*
Denburg, Sheldon 1925- *St&PR 93*
Denby, David *WhoE 93*
Denby, Edwin 1903-1983 *BioIn 17*
Denby, Edwin (Orr) 1903-1983 *ConAu 138*
Denby, Emily D. *AmWomPl*
Dence, Edward William, Jr. 1938- *WhoAm 92*
Dence, Michael Robert 1931- *WhoAm 92*
Dench, Judith Olivia 1934- *WhoWor 93*
Denchev, Rumen Georgiev 1960- *WhoWor 93*
Dencik, Peter 1943- *WhoWor 93*
Dencke, Jeremiah 1725-1795 *Baker 92*
Dencker, Peter Anthony 1947- *WhoE 93*
Denckhoff, Robert H., Jr. 1940- *St&PR 93*
Dendurent, Sharon Drwall 1945- *WhoAmW 93*
Dendy, Cheryl Golasinski *Law&B 92*
Dendy, F.M. 1956- *WhoScE 91-1*
Dendy, Philip Palin *WhoScE 91-1*
De Neal, Gary Robert 1944- *WhoWrEP 92*
De Neal, Judy Kay 1947- *WhoWrEP 92*
Deneau, Ronald Arthur 1938- *WhoE 93*
Deneen, Daniel Guy 1957- *WhoEmL 93*
Denef, Carl 1941- *WhoScE 91-2*
Denegall, John Palmer, Jr. 1959- *WhoE 93, WhoEmL 93*
Denegre, George 1923- *St&PR 93, WhoAm 92*
Denegre, Stanhope Bayne-Jones 1952- *WhoEmL 93*
Denegre-Tosun, Louise *Law&B 92*
Denegre-Tosun, Louise 1958- *WhoEmL 93*
Denegri, Guillermo Maria 1956- *WhoWor 93*
Denehy, Robert Corneilius 1931- *St&PR 93*
Denek, Kazimierz 1932- *WhoWor 93*
Deneka, Charles W. 1944- *St&PR 93*
Denekamp, Juliana 1943- *WhoScE 91-1*
Deneken, Gerhard 1963- *WhoScE 91-2*
Denempont, Geoffrey Louis *Law&B 92*
Denenberg, Charlotte G. 1947- *St&PR 93*
Denenberg, Ed 1937- *St&PR 93*
Denenberg, Herbert Sidney 1929- *WhoAm 92, WhoIns 93*
Denenberg, Jeffrey Neil 1943- *St&PR 93*
Denenberg, Victor Hugo 1925- *WhoAm 92*
Denenholz, Judy Rimelspach *Law&B 92*
Deneny, Sean Francis 1951- *WhoE 93*
Denereaz, Alexandre 1875-1947 *Baker 92*
Denerstein, Ezra J. d1992 *BioIn 17, NewYTBS 92*
Denerstein, Ezra J. 1918- *St&PR 93*
Denes, Agnes C. 1938- *WhoAm 92*
Denes, Alex Eugene 1947- *WhoEmL 93*
Denes, Josef 1939- *WhoScE 91-4*
Denes, Magda *WhoE 93*
de Nesnera, Alexander Peter 1957- *WhoE 93*
de Neufville, Lawrence Eustace 1913- *WhoE 93*
de Neufville, Richard Lawrence 1939- *WhoAm 92, WhoWor 93*
Deneuve, Catherine *BioIn 17*

Deneuve, Catherine 1943- *IntDcF 2-3 [port], WhoAm 92, WhoWor 93*
Denev, Stefan Angelov 1954- *WhoWor 93*
Denev, Stoyan 1928- *WhoScE 91-4*
Denevan, William Maxfield 1931- *WhoAm 92*
De Neve, Roland E.A. 1927- *WhoScE 91-2*
Denevi, Marco 1922- *SpAmA*
DeNevi, Mary Kathryn 1954- *WhoAmW 93*
Deney, Richard L. 1949- *St&PR 93*
Denfeld, Louis Emil 1891-1972 *HarEnMi*
Deng, Julong 1933- *WhoWor 93*
Deng, Pio Yukwan d1991 *BioIn 17*
Deng, Xiao Hua 1953- *ConAu 139*
Deng, Xiaoping 1904- *BioIn 17*
Deng, Zike 1938- *WhoWor 93*
Dengel, Dennis Michael 1949- *WhoE 93*
Denger, George Robert 1966- *WhoE 93*
Deng Hongxun *WhoAsAP 91*
Dengler, Horst C. *Law&B 92*
Dengler, Robert Anthony 1947- *WhoWor 93*
Dengremont, Maurice 1866-1893 *Baker 92*
Dengrove, Ida Libby 1918- *WhoAmW 93*
Deng Xiaoping 1904- *ColdWar 2 [port], DcTwHis, WhoAsAP 91, WhoWor 93*
Deng Yingchao 1904-1992 *NewYTBS 92*
Denhaan, George Gerard 1947- *St&PR 93*
Denham, Caroline Virginia 1937- *WhoSSW 93*
Denham, Carolyn Hunter 1945- *WhoAmW 93*
Denham, Frederick Ronald 1929- *WhoAm 92*
Denham, John 1615-1669 *DcLB 126 [port]*
Denham, Michael James *WhoScE 91-1*
Denham, Patricia Eileen Keller 1952- *WhoEmL 93*
Denham, Robert Dayton 1938- *WhoSSW 93*
Denham, Robert E. *BioIn 17, Law&B 92*
Denham, Robert Edwin 1945- *WhoAm 92*
Denham, Rodney Russell 1939- *WhoWor 93*
Denham, Vernon Robert, Jr. 1948- *WhoEmL 93, WhoSSW 93*
Denhardt, David Tilton 1939- *WhoAm 92, WhoE 93*
Denhart, Gun 1945- *WhoAmW 93*
Denhof, Miki *WhoAm 92*
Den Hollander, F.C. 1941- *WhoScE 91-3*
Denholm, Diana B. 1944- *WhoSSW 93*
Denic, Srdjan 1952- *WhoE 93*
De Nicola, Peter Francis 1954- *WhoE 93, WhoEmL 93*
Denicolo, Pamela Maureen *WhoScE 91-1*
Denielou, Guy 1923- *WhoScE 91-2*
Denig, Stephen Joseph 1948- *WhoEmL 93*
Denig, William Francis 1953- *WhoE 93*
Denigan, Susan Marie 1957- *WhoEmL 93*
Denikin, Anton Ivanovich 1872-1947 *BioIn 17, DcTwHis*
DeNino, Mark Justin 1953- *WhoE 93*
Denio, Dale William 1947- *St&PR 93*
Denious, Robert Wilbur 1936- *WhoAm 92*
Denious, Sharon Marie 1941- *WhoAmW 93*
De Niro, Robert 1943- *ConTFT 10, IntDcF 2-3 [port]*
De Niro, Robert 1945?- *BioIn 17, WhoAm 92*
Denis, Bernard 1934- *WhoScE 91-2*
Denis, Bernard Leon 1932- *WhoWor 93*
Denis, Christiane *Law&B 92*
Denis, Claire *MiSFD 9*
Denis, Didier 1947- *Baker 92*
Denis, Francois A. 1941- *WhoScE 91-2*
Denis, Herman 1935- *WhoScE 91-2*
Denis, Herman Alfred 1935- *WhoScE 91-2*
Denis, Jean-Pierre *MiSFD 9*
Denis, John *ScF&FL 92*
Denis, L.J. 1933- *WhoScE 91-2*
Denis, Paul-Yves 1932- *WhoAm 92*
Denisco, John Anthony 1948- *WhoAm 92*
DeNisco, S.G. 1918- *St&PR 93*
Denise, Robert Phillips 1936- *WhoAm 92*
Denise, Theodore Cullom 1919- *WhoAm 92*
Denise Lange, Monica 1951- *WhoEmL 93*
Denis'evskii, Nickolai Alekseevich 1958- *WhoWor 93*
Denish, Darrell L. 1957- *St&PR 93*
Denisoff, R. Serge 1939- *WhoAm 92*
Denison, Dan L. *Law&B 92*
Denison, Dan Leyland 1939- *St&PR 93*
Denison, David Maurice 1933- *WhoScE 91-1*
Denison, Edward F. d1992 *NewYTBS 92*
Denison, Edward Fulton 1915- *WhoAm 92*
Denison, Emily Herey *AmWomPl*
Denison, Floyd G. 1943- *St&PR 93, WhoIns 93*
Denison, Floyd Gene 1943- *WhoAm 92*
Denison, Glen H. 1924- *St&PR 93*
Denison, John B. 1940- *St&PR 93*
Denison, John G. 1945- *St&PR 93*
Denison, Mary Boney 1956- *WhoEmL 93*
Denison, Merrill 1893-1975 *BioIn 17*
Denison, Richard Eugene 1932- *WhoE 93*
Denison, Susan S. 1946- *WhoAmW 93*
Denison, Thomas Renau 1960- *WhoEmL 93*
Denison, Toni Angela 1954- *WhoAmW 93*
Denison, William Rae 1937- *WhoSSW 93*
Denisov, Dmitri Abram 1945- *WhoWor 93*
Denisov, Edison 1929- *Baker 92*
De Nitto, Nicholas John *Law&B 92*
Denitz, Peter Jonathan 1954- *WhoEmL 93*
Denitz, Ronald P. *Law&B 92*
Denius, Franklin Wofford 1925- *St&PR 93*
Deniz, Esref 1930- *WhoScE 91-4*
Denk, Frederick *Law&B 92*
Denk, Viktor 1930- *WhoScE 91-3*
Denke, Paul Herman 1916- *WhoWor 93*
Denker, David D. 1915-1992 *BioIn 17*
Denker, Hans-Werner 1941- *WhoScE 91-3*
Denker, Henry 1912- *WhoAm 92, WhoWor 93*
Denker, Randall Elizabeth 1950- *WhoEmL 93*
Denker, Susan A. 1948- *WhoE 93, WhoEmL 93*
Denkowski, Zdzislaw 1940- *WhoScE 91-4*
Denlea, Leo E., Jr. 1932- *St&PR 93*
Denlea, Leo Edward, Jr. 1932- *WhoAm 92*
Denlinger, Edgar Jacob 1939- *WhoAm 92*
Denlinger, John Kenneth 1942- *WhoAm 92*
Denlinger, William Watson 1924- *WhoSSW 93*
Denman, Catherine Cheryl 1958- *WhoAmW 93*
Denman, Charles Frank 1934- *WhoAm 92*
Denman, Gertrude Mary 1884-1954 *BioIn 17*
Denman, Joe C., Jr. 1923- *St&PR 93*
Denman, Joe Carter, Jr. 1923- *WhoAm 92*
Denman, John Clinton, Jr. *Law&B 92*
Denman, Margaret Love 1940- *WhoAmW 93*
Denman, Nicholas Werner 1946- *WhoEmL 93*
Denman, William Foster 1929- *WhoAm 92*
Denmark, Bernhardt 1917- *WhoAm 92*
Denmark, Florence L. *BioIn 17*
Denmark, Stanley Jay 1927- *WhoE 93*
Denn, Cyril Joseph 1948- *WhoEmL 93, WhoWor 93*
Denn, Morton Mace 1939- *WhoAm 92*
Dennard, Cleveland L. d1992 *NewYTBS 92*
Dennard, Cleveland Leon 1929- *WhoAm 92*
Dennard, Robert Heath 1932- *WhoAm 92*
Dennee, Charles (Frederick) 1863-1946 *Baker 92*
Denneen, John Paul 1940- *WhoAm 92*
Denne-Hinnov, Gerd Boel 1954- *WhoWor 93*
Dennehy, Brian *BioIn 17*
Dennehy, Brian 1939- *WhoAm 92*
Dennehy, Daniel Paul 1938- *St&PR 93*
Dennen, Grace Atherton 1874- *AmWomPl*
Denneny, James Clinton, Jr. 1924- *WhoAm 92*
Denner, Melvin Walter 1933- *WhoAm 92*
Dennerlein, Barbara *BioIn 17*
Dennery, Moise Waldhorn 1915- *WhoAm 92*
Dennett, Daniel Clement 1942- *WhoAm 92*
Dennett, Ellen Loughrin 1960- *WhoAmW 93, WhoEmL 93*
Denney, Arthur Hugh 1916- *WhoAm 92*
Denney, Charles Eugene 1951- *WhoEmL 93*
Denney, George Covert, Jr. 1921- *WhoAm 92*
Denney, Laura Falin 1948- *WhoEmL 93, WhoSSW 93*
Denney, Nancy Wadsworth 1944- *WhoAmW 93*
Denney, Ralph J. *Law&B 92*
Denney, William Francis 1933- *St&PR 93*
Dennie, Deborah Thomas 1939- *WhoSSW 93, WhoWor 93*
Dennie, Joseph 1768-1812 *JrnUS*
Dennies, Sandra Lee 1951- *WhoAmW 93, WhoE 93, WhoEmL 93*
Dennin, Nancy Taylor 1960- *WhoEmL 93*
Dennin, Robert Aloysius, Jr. 1951- *WhoE 93*
Denning, Eileen Bonar 1944- *WhoAmW 93*
Denning, Hazel May 1907- *WhoAmW 93*
Denning, Paul F. 1942- *St&PR 93*
Denning, Peter James 1942- *WhoAm 92*
Denning, Richard Lynn 1947- *St&PR 93*
Denning, Troy 1958- *ScF&FL 92*
Denninger, Douglas E. *Law&B 92*
Dennis, Aaron Seth 1938- *St&PR 93*
Dennis, Amel J. 1954- *St&PR 93*
Dennis, Anthony James *Law&B 92*
Dennis, Barbara Ann 1950- *WhoE 93*
Dennis, Barry William 1942- *WhoE 93*
Dennis, Beatrice Markley 1956- *WhoEmL 93*
Dennis, Benjamin Franklin, III 1942- *WhoE 93*
Dennis, Betty Jo 1935- *WhoAmW 93*
Dennis, Bobby Gene 1938- *WhoSSW 93*
Dennis, Brian Christopher 1952- *WhoEmL 93*
Dennis, Carlos *Law&B 92*
Dennis, Carol L. 1938- *ScF&FL 92*
Dennis, Chandler, Jr. *BioIn 17*
Dennis, Charles Erwin, Jr. 1925- *WhoE 93*
Dennis, Charles L., III 1947- *St&PR 93*
Dennis, Charles Leslie, II *Law&B 92*
Dennis, Charles Newton 1942- *WhoSSW 93*
Dennis, Clarence 1909- *WhoAm 92*
Dennis, Clifford E. 1891-1979 *ScF&FL 92*
Dennis, Colin 1946- *WhoScE 91-1*
Dennis, Cornelious 1956- *WhoSSW 93*
Dennis, David William 1959- *WhoEmL 93*
Dennis, Davis 1940- *EncAACR*
Dennis, Donald Daly 1928- *WhoAm 92*
Dennis, Doneldon Michael 1948- *WhoEmL 93*
Dennis, Donna Jean 1937- *WhoE 93*
Dennis, Dorothy *WhoWor 93*
Dennis, Earlene *BiDAMSp 1989*
Dennis, Eugene 1904-1961 *PolPar*
Dennis, Evie *BlkAmWO*
Dennis, Frank George, Jr. 1932- *WhoAm 92*
Dennis, Gary Owen 1946- *WhoEmL 93*
Dennis, Gerald S. *Law&B 92*
Dennis, Ian 1952- *ScF&FL 92*
Dennis, India Rae 1952- *WhoAmW 93*
Dennis, Ivanette Jones 1940- *WhoWrEP 92*
Dennis, Jack Bonnell 1931- *WhoAm 92*
Dennis, James Leon 1936- *WhoAm 92, WhoSSW 93*
Dennis, James Michael 1940- *St&PR 93*
Dennis, Jeffrey Mark *Law&B 92*
Dennis, John 1657-1734 *BioIn 17*
Dennis, John A. 1930- *WhoScE 91-1*
Dennis, John Alan 1930- *WhoWor 93*
Dennis, John Emory, Jr. 1939- *WhoAm 92*
Dennis, John Murray 1923- *WhoE 93*
Dennis, John S. 1935- *St&PR 93*
Dennis, K.C. *ScF&FL 92*
Dennis, Lorraine Bradt 1921- *WhoE 93*
Dennis, Marilyn J. 1945- *St&PR 93*
Dennis, N. 1929- *WhoAsAP 91*
Dennis, Nicholas John 1950- *St&PR 93*
Dennis, Nigel 1912-1989 *BioIn 17*
Dennis, Pamela *BioIn 17*
Dennis, Patricia Diaz *NotHsAW 93*
Dennis, Patrick Harley 1932- *WhoAm 92*
Dennis, R.B. *WhoScE 91-1*
Dennis, Ralph E. 1925- *St&PR 93*
Dennis, Richard Alan 1946- *WhoSSW 93*
Dennis, Richard Irwin 1934- *St&PR 93, WhoAm 92*
Dennis, Robert 1933- *WhoAm 92*
Dennis, Robert A. 1948- *St&PR 93*
Dennis, Robert C. 1915-1983 *ScF&FL 92*
Dennis, Robert Franklin 1939- *WhoSSW 93*
Dennis, Robert G. 1927- *St&PR 93*
Dennis, Robert N. 1936- *St&PR 93*
Dennis, Roger Wilson 1902- *WhoE 93*
Dennis, (Mary) Ruth 1907- *WhoWrEP 92*
Dennis, Rutledge Melvin 1939- *WhoSSW 93*
Dennis, Samuel Sibley, III 1910- *WhoAm 92*
Dennis, Sandy 1937-1992 *BioIn 17, ConTFT 10, CurBio 92N, NewYTBS 92 [port], News 92*
Dennis, Sharina Marie 1963- *WhoEmL 93*
Dennis, Stephen Neal 1943- *WhoE 93*
Dennis, Steven Pellowe 1960- *WhoAm 92, WhoEmL 93*
Dennis, Suzanne Marie 1951- *WhoAmW 93*
Dennis, Walter Decoster 1932- *WhoAm 92*
Dennis, Ward Brainerd 1922- *WhoAm 92*
Dennis, Ward H. d1992 *NewYTBS 92 [port]*
Dennis, Ward Haldan 1938- *WhoAm 92*
Dennis, Wayne Allen 1941- *WhoWor 93*
Dennis, Wesley 1903-1966 *MajAI [port]*
Dennis, William Robert 1955- *WhoEmL 93*
Dennish, George William, III 1945- *WhoAm 92*
Dennis-Hollis, Robbie Smagula 1957- *WhoAmW 93, WhoEmL 93*
Dennison, A. Michael 1941- *WhoUN 92*
Dennison, Allen Mansfield 1952- *WhoE 93, WhoEmL 93*
Dennison, Brian Kenneth 1949- *WhoEmL 93*
Dennison, Byron Lee 1930- *WhoAm 92*
Dennison, Charles Stuart 1918- *WhoAm 92*
Dennison, David Short, Jr. 1918- *WhoAm 92*
Dennison, Edward S. 1941- *St&PR 93*
Dennison, George Marshel 1935- *WhoAm 92*
Dennison, John *Law&B 92*
Dennison, John Manley 1934- *WhoAm 92*
Dennison, Milo *ScF&FL 92*
Dennison, Nellie M. *AmWomPl*
Dennison, Ramona Pollan 1938- *WhoSSW 93*
Dennison, Richard W. 1945- *St&PR 93*
Dennison, Sally Elizabeth 1946- *WhoWrEP 92*
Dennison, Stanley Scott 1920- *WhoAm 92, WhoWor 93*
Dennison, Theresa Marie 1965- *WhoEmL 93*
Denniston, Brackett Badger, III 1947- *WhoEmL 93*
Denniston, George 1917- *St&PR 93*
Denniston, Marjorie McGeorge 1913- *WhoAmW 93, WhoE 93*
Denniston, Pamela Boggs 1948- *WhoAmW 93*
Denno, Dale J. *Law&B 92*
Denny, Brewster Castberg 1924- *WhoAm 92*
Denny, Charles Morton, Jr. 1931- *St&PR 93*
Denny, David Ray 1949- *WhoEmL 93, WhoSSW 93*
Denny, Floyd Wolfe, Jr. 1923- *WhoAm 92*
Denny, J. William 1935- *St&PR 93*
Denny, James McCahill 1932- *St&PR 93*
Denny, John Lawrence 1920-1990 *BioIn 17*
Denny, Judith Ann 1946- *WhoEmL 93*
Denny, Leon A., Jr. 1930- *St&PR 93*
Denny, Mark Cozzens 1957- *WhoEmL 93*
Denny, Norman D. d1990 *BioIn 17*
Denny, Paul Cecil 1935- *WhoSSW 93*
Denny, Reginald 1891-1967 *BioIn 17*
Denny, Richard Alden, Jr. 1931- *WhoAm 92*
Denny, Thomas Albert 1933- *WhoSSW 93*
Denny, William D(ouglas) 1910-1980 *Baker 92*
Denny, William E. 1937- *St&PR 93*
Denny-James, Mary Craver 1948- *WhoAmW 93*
De No, Rafael Lorente 1902-1990 *BioIn 17*
DeNoma, Bernard Louis 1925- *St&PR 93*
Denomme, James Lane *Law&B 92*
Denomme, Robert Thomas 1930- *WhoAm 92*
Denomme, Thomas Gerald 1939- *St&PR 93*
Denommee, Denis G. 1953- *St&PR 93*
Denomy, Robert William *Law&B 92*
de Nonancourt, Bernard Marie 1920- *WhoWor 93*
Denoon, Clarence England, Jr. 1915- *WhoAm 92, WhoE 93*
Denoon, David Baugh Holden 1945- *WhoAm 92, WhoWor 93*
Denoon, Lennox *DcCPCAm*
Denooyer, LeRoy L. *Law&B 92*
Denoroy, Luc 1952- *WhoScE 91-2*
Denoth, Franco 1935- *WhoScE 91-3*
Den Otter, Cornelis Johannes 1935- *WhoWor 93*
Den Otter, Willem 1938- *WhoScE 91-3*
DeNoux, O'Neil 1950- *ScF&FL 92*
De Noux, O'Neill *ScF&FL 92*
Denov, Sam 1923- *WhoAm 92*
DeNovo, John August 1916- *WhoAm 92*
DeNoyer, Georgia Ann 1948- *WhoAmW 93, WhoEmL 93*
Densberger, Stephen James 1950- *St&PR 93*
Denschlag, Johannes Otto 1937- *WhoScE 91-3, WhoWor 93*
Densen, Paul Maximillian 1913- *WhoAm 92*
Densen, Peter M. 1942- *St&PR 93*
Densen-Gerber, Judianne 1934- *WhoAm 92*
Densham, Pen 1947- *MiSFD 9*
Denslow, Cecilia P. *AmWomPl*
Denslow, Deborah Pierson 1947- *WhoAmW 93, WhoE 93, WhoEmL 93, WhoWor 93*
Denslow, Sharon Phillips 1947- *BioIn 17, ConAu 136*
Densmore, Ann 1941- *WhoAmW 93*
Densmore, Frances 1867-1957 *Baker 92*
Densmore, John *BioIn 17*
Densmore, John 1944- *ConAu 136*
Densmore, William Phillips 1924- *WhoAm 92*

Denson, Alexander Bunn 1936- WhoSSW 93
Denson, Bruce P. 1938- St&PR 93
Denson, Joe Russell 1930- WhoE 93
Denson, John Eley 1937- St&PR 93
Denson, Mary Craig 1922- WhoAmW 93
Denson, Michael 1956- WhoEmL 93
Denson, Mort 1933- St&PR 93
Denson, Raymond 1941- St&PR 93
Denson, William F., III Law&B 92
Denson, William Frank, III 1943- St&PR 93, WhoAm 92, WhoWor 93
Denson-Law, Wanda K. Law&B 92
Denson-Low, Wanda K. BioIn 17, WhoAmW 93
Dent, Barbara A. Law&B 92
Dent, Bucky 1951- BioIn 17
Dent, E.J. 1876-1957 OxDcOp
Dent, Edward Eugene 1948- WhoEmL 93, WhoSSW 93
Dent, Edward J(oseph) 1876-1957 Baker 92
Dent, Ernest DuBose, Jr. 1927- WhoWor 93
Dent, Frederick Baily 1922- St&PR 93, WhoAm 92
Dent, George 1756-1813 PolPar
Dent, James Jay 1947- WhoEmL 93
Dent, Lawrence M. 1939- St&PR 93
Dent, Lester 1904-1959 BioIn 17
Dent, Lester 1905-1959 ScF&FL 92
Dent, Paul R. 1922- St&PR 93
Dent, Richard Lamar 1960- WhoAm 92
Dent, Sharon Pierce 1948- WhoAmW 93
Dent, Thompson S. St&PR 93
Dent, V. Edward 1918- WhoAm 92
Dentai, Andrew Gomperz 1942- WhoE 93
Dentatus, Manius Curius c. 333BC-270BC HarEnMi
Dente, Barbara BioIn 17
Den Tex, P. WhoScE 91-3
Dentice, Jeanne Lynn 1960- WhoAmW 93
Dentice, Thomas Santo 1939- WhoAm 92
Dentinger, Stephen WhoWrEP 92
Dentiste, Paul George 1930- WhoAm 92, WhoSSW 93
Dentler, Robert Arnold 1928- WhoAm 92
Denton, Aubrey E. 1952- WhoSSW 93
Denton, Betty 1946- WhoAmW 93
Denton, Bradley 1958- ScF&FL 92
Denton, Charles Mandaville 1924- WhoAm 92
Denton, Charles Mandaville 1957- WhoEmL 93
Denton, Christine T. 1956- St&PR 93
Denton, Clara Janetta Fort AmWomPl
Denton, D. Keith 1948- WhoAm 92
Denton, David Alan 1951- WhoEmL 93
Denton, David Edward 1935- WhoAm 92
Denton, Don G. 1939- St&PR 93
Denton, Donald Dean WhoSSW 93
Denton, Eleanor AmWomPl
Denton, Frank Marion 1935- St&PR 93
Denton, George H. 1929- St&PR 93
Denton, Harold Ray 1937- WhoAm 92
Denton, Jere Michael 1947- St&PR 93, WhoEmL 93
Denton, Jerome F. 1951- St&PR 93
Denton, Joe D. 1924- St&PR 93
Denton, John D. WhoScE 91-1
Denton, John Joseph 1915- WhoAm 92
Denton, Kady MacDonald BioIn 17
Denton, Karl Robert 1959- WhoEmL 93, WhoWor 93
Denton, Keith G. 1945- WhoE 93
Denton, Laurie R. 1951- WhoAm 92, WhoEmL 93
Denton, Melinda Fay 1944- WhoAmW 93
Denton, Michael J. Law&B 92
Denton, Michael John 1956- WhoEmL 93
Denton, Ray Douglas 1937- WhoWor 93
Denton, Richard A. 1914- St&PR 93
Denton, Richard Michael WhoScE 91-1
Denton, Richard Todd 1932- WhoAm 92
Denton, Robert Albert, Jr. 1939- WhoAm 92
Denton, Robert Randall 1950- St&PR 93
Denton, Robert William 1944- WhoSSW 93
Denton, Russell L. 1944- St&PR 93
Denton, Sidney Benny 1928- St&PR 93
Denton, Thomas Wade 1952- WhoEmL 93
Denton, Wayne K. 1939- St&PR 93
Denton, William C. Law&B 92
Denton, William R. 1930- St&PR 93
D'Entremont, Alice BioIn 17
D'Entremont, Edward Joseph 1954- WhoEmL 93
Dentz, Jeffrey W. 1948- St&PR 93
Dentz, Paul Albert, Jr. 1936- WhoE 93
Dentzer, William Thompson, Jr. 1929- St&PR 93
DeNuccio, Raymond Adolph 1933- St&PR 93, WhoAm 92
De Nuce De Lamothe, Michel E. 1936- WhoScE 91-2
Denum, Gretchen H. Law&B 92
DeNunzio, Ralph D. 1931- St&PR 93
DeNunzio, Ralph Dwight 1931- WhoAm 92
De-Nur, Amnon 1926- St&PR 93
DeNuzzio, Albert S. 1921- St&PR 93
DeNuzzo, Rinaldo Vincent 1922- WhoAm 92, WhoWor 93
Denver, Andrew Malcolm 1947- WhoE 93
Denver, Daniel Joseph 1944- WhoSSW 93
Denver, Eileen Ann 1942- WhoAm 92
Denver, James William 1817-1892 BioIn 17
Denver, John BioIn 17
Denver, John 1942- Baker 92
Denver, John 1943- WhoAm 92
Denvers, Robert BioIn 17
Denvir, James Peter, III 1950- WhoEmL 93
Denyer, Nicholas (Charles) 1955- ConAu 136
Denyer, Peter B. WhoScE 91-1
Denyer, Stephen Robert Noble 1955- WhoWor 93
Denyes, James Richard 1948- WhoSSW 93
Denysyk, Bohdan 1947- WhoAm 92, WhoE 93, WhoEmL 93, WhoWor 93
Denza, Luigi 1846-1922 Baker 92
Denzel, Justin 1917- ScF&FL 92
Denzer, Richard G. d1992 NewYTBS 92 [port]
Denzer, Richard G. 1911-1992 BioIn 17
Denzler, Hans Rudolf WhoScE 91-4
Denzler, Robert 1892-1972 Baker 92, OxDcOp
Deo, Naresh C. 1951- St&PR 93
Deo, Narsingh 1936- WhoAm 92
Deodato, Giovanni 1946- WhoUN 92
Deodato, Ruggero MiSFD 9
De Oliveira, Arlinda Franco WhoScE 91-3
De Oliveira, Manoel 1908- MiSFD 9
De Oliveira, Roberto Cardoso BioIn 17
De Oliveira, Sergio J. 1945- WhoWor 93
De Oliveira Rodrigues, B.N. WhoScE 91-3
De Oliveira Salazar, Antonio 1889-1970 BioIn 17
DeOllos, Ione Yvonne 1951- WhoAmW 93
D'Eon, Leonard Joseph 1929- WhoWrEP 92
Deon, Michel 1919- ConAu 37NR
De Onate, Juan fl. 1595-1622 BioIn 17
Deones, Jack E. 1931- St&PR 93, WhoAm 92
Deora, Murli Sitaram 1937- WhoAsAP 91
De Orellana, Francisco dc. 1546 BioIn 17
Deori, Omem Moyong 1943- WhoAsAP 91
Deorio, Anthony Joseph 1945- WhoWor 93
DeOrio, David James 1959- WhoE 93, WhoEmL 93
DeOrio, George Louis 1945- WhoE 93
De Ortega, Francisco BioIn 17
DeOtte, Robert Eugene, Jr. 1949- WhoSSW 93
Deoul, Neal 1931- WhoE 93, WhoWor 93
de Ovalle, Pilar ScF&FL 92
de Pablo, Juan Carlos 1943- WhoWor 93
DePace, Nicholas Louis 1953- WhoE 93
De Padirac, M.R. WhoScE 91-2
Depadt, Gerard 1938- WhoScE 91-2
De Paepe, Christian Auguste Joseph Raoul 1938- WhoWor 93
DePalma, Anthony G. d1992 BioIn 17, NewYTBS 92
De Palma, Anthony Robert 1952- WhoWrEP 92
De Palma, Brian BioIn 17
De Palma, Brian 1940- MiSFD 9
De Palma, Brian Russell 1940- WhoAm 92
DePalma, Diane Marie 1952- WhoAmW 93
De Palma, Frank 1957- MiSFD 9
DePalma, Philip Nicholas, Jr. 1947- WhoEmL 93
DePalma, Ralph George 1931- WhoAm 92, WhoE 93
Depalo, Armand M. 1949- St&PR 93
de Palo, Armand Michael 1949- WhoEmL 93
DePamphilis, Melvin Louis 1943- WhoE 93
DePaola, Dominick Philip 1942- WhoAm 92
De Paola, Thomas Anthony 1934- BioIn 17, ConAu 37NR, MajAI [port]
dePaola, Tomie ChlBIID [port], ConAu 37NR, MajAI
De Paola, Tomie 1934- BioIn 17, SmATA 15AS [port]
DePaoli, Geri Mary 1941- WhoAm 92, WhoAmW 93
dePaolis, Potito Umberto 1925- WhoWor 93
De Paolis, Rosemary 1962- WhoWrEP 92
DePaolo, Donald James 1951- WhoAm 92
De Paolo, Joseph John St&PR 93
dePaolo, Ronald Francis 1938- WhoAm 92
De Pape, Robert 1935- WhoScE 91-2
de Papp, Elise Wachenfeld 1933- WhoAm 92
Depardieu, Gerard BioIn 17
Depardieu, Gerard 1948- IntDcF 2-3 [port], WhoWor 93
De Pas, Penney 1951- WhoEmL 93
Depasqua, Louis Paul 1938- St&PR 93
Depasqua, Robert J. St&PR 93
De Pasquale, John Anthony 1942- WhoAm 92
de Pasquale, Joseph 1919- WhoAm 92
Depasquale, N.H. 1941- St&PR 93
DePasquale, Peter Gerard 1955- WhoE 93
de Pasquale, R.H. 1905- St&PR 93
DePasquale, Robert Joseph 1953- WhoE 93
DePass, William K. 1956- St&PR 93
De Passe, Derrel Blauvelt 1950- WhoAmW 93
De Passe, Suzanne BioIn 17, WhoAm 92, WhoAmW 93
DePatie, David H. 1930- ConTFT 10
DePatie, David Hudson 1930- WhoAm 92
Depaul, Carol S. Law&B 92
de Paul, Don ScF&FL 92
de Paul, Edith 1921-1991 ScF&FL 92
Depaul, John D. 1931- St&PR 93
Depaul, Louis A. Law&B 92
DePaulis, Palmer Anthony 1945- WhoAm 92
De Paulo, Joseph Raymond, Jr. 1946- WhoEmL 93
De Pauw, Carlo WhoScE 91-2
De Pauw, Gommar Albert 1918- WhoAm 92, WhoWor 93
De Pauw, Linda Grant 1940- WhoAm 92
De Pauw, Niels 1944- WhoScE 91-2
De'Pazzi, Ellen E. 1915- WhoWrEP 92
De Pedro, Hilario L., III WhoAsAP 91
Depelchin, A.A.J.G. 1925- WhoScE 91-2
De Pellegrin, M.L. 1938- St&PR 93
Depelteau, Daniel Alfred 1951- WhoWor 93
Depenbrock, Manfred 1929- WhoScE 91-3
De Pencier, Michael BioIn 17
De Peralta, Enriqueta 1940- WhoAmW 93
De Pereda, Antonio c. 1599-c. 1678 BioIn 17
DePersio, Richard John 1949- WhoEmL 93
Depetris, R.A. 1942- St&PR 93
DePetris, Susan Abrahams 1946- WhoE 93
DePew, Carol Ann 1962- WhoEmL 93
Depew, Charles G. 1930- St&PR 93
Depew, Charles Gardner 1930- WhoAm 92
Depew, Jeffrey Scott 1955- WhoEmL 93, WhoWor 93
DePew, Marie Kathryn 1928- WhoAmW 93
DePew, William Earl 1948- WhoWor 93
De Peyer, David WhoScE 91-1
De Peyer, Gervase (Alan) 1926- Baker 92
Depeyrot, Michel Yves-Louis 1940- WhoWor 93
dePeyster, Frederic Augustus 1914- WhoAm 92
De Pfyffer, Andre 1928- WhoWor 93
Dephillips, Paul S. 1939- WhoIns 93
Dephtereof, D.L. Law&B 92
Dephtereos, David L. 1954- WhoAm 92
de Picciotto, Maurice Law&B 92
DePiero, Raymond 1957- WhoEmL 93
Depierre, Alain 1940- WhoScE 91-2
DePietro, Joseph 1897-1990 BioIn 17
DePillars, Murry Norman 1938- WhoSSW 93
de Pina, Arsenio Daniel Fermino 1935- WhoUN 92
Depkovich, Francis John 1924- WhoAm 92
De Planque, Johan Henrick Willem 1950- WhoWor 93
Deplazes, Gion Duri 1951- WhoWor 93
Depledge, Michael Harold 1954- WhoWor 93
De Ploey, Jan G.L. 1937- WhoScE 91-2
De Pol, John 1913- WhoAm 92
de Polignac, Jeanne 1945- St&PR 93
de Polnay, Peter 1906-1984 ScF&FL 92
Deponai, Pierre Lamont Law&B 92
De Pont, Jan Joep H.H.M. 1942- WhoScE 91-3
DePonte, Kathleen Ann 1954- WhoSSW 93
De Ponti, O.M.B. WhoScE 91-3
DePorter, Diane BioIn 17
Deportes, Charles Henri 1930- WhoScE 91-2
De Portu, Goffredo 1950- WhoScE 91-3
De Portugal Alvarez, Jose 1934- WhoScE 91-3
De Posada, Joachim Arturo 1947- WhoWor 93
Depp, Johnny BioIn 17
Depp, Johnny 1963- ConTFT 10, WhoAm 92
Depp, Richard, III 1938- WhoAm 92
Deppe, Henry A. 1920- WhoAm 92, WhoWor 93
Deppe, Ludwig 1828-1890 Baker 92
Deppe, Scott Allen 1953- WhoE 93
Deppe, Steven L. 1948- St&PR 93
Deppen, Pauline Sargent BioIn 17
Deppenbrock, Bonnie L. Law&B 92
Depperschmidt, Thomas Orlando 1935- WhoAm 92
de Pre, Jean-Anne ConAu 39NR
DePree, D.J. 1891-1990 BioIn 17
DePree, Dirk Jan 1891-1990 BioIn 17
De Pree, Max O. 1924- WhoAm 92
De Pree, Willard Ames 1928- WhoAm 92
DePreist, James 1936- BioIn 17
DePreist, James (Anderson) 1936- Baker 92, WhoAm 92
Depres, Robert WhoAm 92
de Presno, Odd 1944- WhoWor 93
De Pressense, Francis Dehaut 1853-1914 BioIn 17
Depreux, Edouard 1898-1981 BioIn 17
Deprez, Deborah Ann 1952- WhoAmW 93
DePrez, Gene 1940- St&PR 93
DePrez, Gene Edward 1940- WhoE 93
De Prez, James Anthony 1935- St&PR 93
De Priest, Oscar 1871-1951 BioIn 17
DePriest, Oscar Stanton 1871-1951 EncAACR [port]
Depriest, Ted 1948- St&PR 93
DePrima, Anthony E. 1939- St&PR 93
Deprit, Andre Albert 1926- WhoAm 92
Deptula, George S. 1942- St&PR 93
Deptula, Nancy Monteith 1928- WhoE 93
De Pue, Elva AmWomPl
DePue, Josephine Helen 1948- WhoAmW 93, WhoEmL 93
Depuit, Thomas Harry 1950- St&PR 93
Depukat, Thaddeus Stanley 1936- WhoWor 93
Deputat, Julian 1935- WhoScE 91-4
Deputy, Byard Sanford 1929- WhoAm 92
Deputy, Stephen N. 1951- St&PR 93
DePuy, Brenda Jane 1946- WhoAmW 93
De Puy, Carlos Domingo 1952- WhoWor 93
DePuy, Charles Herbert 1927- WhoAm 92
DePuy, William D. Law&B 92
Depuydt, Frans 1939- WhoScE 91-2
De Puydt, Marcel 1855-1940 IntDcAn
DeQuattro, George Robert 1942- St&PR 93
DeQuattro, Vincent Louis 1933- WhoAm 92
deQuay, Laurence 1958- WhoSSW 93
Dequeant, Donald James 1952- WhoSSW 93
de Queiroz, Eca ScF&FL 92
Dequeker, Jan 1934- WhoScE 91-2
De Quille, Dan 1829-1898 BioIn 17
De Quincey, Thomas 1785-1859 BioIn 17
Der, James J., Jr. 1959- WhoEmL 93
Dera, Jerzy 1933- WhoScE 91-4
De Raad, Bastiaan 1931- WhoScE 91-4
De Radzitzky D'Ostrowick, Pierre M.J.G. 1927- WhoScE 91-2
Derago, Anthony Francis 1928- St&PR 93
Derain, Andre 1880-1954 BioIn 17
DeRaleau, Steven James 1951- WhoIns 93
DeRamus, Betty Jean 1941- WhoAm 92
Deramus, William N. 1915-1989 BioIn 17
DeRan, Timothy Michael 1951- WhoEmL 93
Derand, Tore 1937- WhoScE 91-4
De Ranitz, F.J. WhoScE 91-3
De Ranter, Camiel J. 1937- WhoScE 91-2
Derapelian, Dorothy 1955- WhoE 93
de Rath, Suzanne Marie 1963- WhoAmW 93
De Rautlin De La Roy, Yves M. 1925- WhoScE 91-2
Deray, Jacques 1929- MiSFD 9
Derber, Dana M. 1955- WhoEmL 93
Derbes, Albert Joseph, III 1940- WhoSSW 93
Derbes, Daniel William 1930- St&PR 93, WhoAm 92
Derbort, John Joseph 1959- WhoE 93
Derby, Cheryl Ann 1946- WhoAmW 93
Derby, Ernest Stephen 1938- WhoAm 92
Derby, George Horatio 1823-1861 BioIn 17
Derby, John Montague 1966- WhoAm 92
Derby, John Montague, Sr. 1940- WhoAm 92
Derby, Peter Jared 1940- WhoWor 93
Derby, Robert James 1931- WhoAm 92
D'Erchia, Peter John 1951- St&PR 93
Derchin, Dary Ingham 1941- WhoWor 93
Derchin, Michael Wayne 1942- WhoAm 92, WhoE 93
Derda, Adolf G. 1930- St&PR 93
Derdenger, Patrick 1946- WhoAm 92, WhoEmL 93, WhoWor 93

Derdzinski, Kenneth Joseph 1929- *St&PR 93*
Dere, Jean 1886-1970 *Baker 92*
DeReamer, Martha Laing 1953- *WhoSSW 93*
De Regge, Peter P.M.H. 1944- *WhoScE 91-2*
De Regge, Peter Paul 1944- *WhoWor 93*
De Regniers, Beatrice Schenk *BioIn 17*
de Regniers, Beatrice Schenk (Freedman) 1914- *MajAI [port]*
Deregowski, Jan Bronislaw *WhoScE 91-1*
Derek, John 1926- *MiSFD 9*
Derek, Susan Jean 1954- *WhoAmW 93*
Derelian, Doris Virginia 1945- *WhoAmW 93*
DeRemee, Richard Arthur 1933- *WhoAm 92*
Deremeik-Newcott, Mary Anne 1952- *WhoAmW 93*
Deremer, Richard Lynn *Law&B 92*
Deren, Donald David 1949- *WhoEmL 93*
Deren, Edward Alison 1951- *WhoEmL 93*
Deren, Maya 1917-1961 *BioIn 17*
De Rensis, Raffaello 1879-1970 *Baker 92*
De Renzi, Ennio 1924- *WhoScE 91-3*
DeRenzo, Evan Gaines 1951- *WhoE 93*
De Repentigny, Isabelle *Law&B 92*
Deres, Janos 1938- *WhoScE 91-4*
Deresiewicz, Herbert 1925- *WhoAm 92*
Dereske, Jo *ScF&FL 92*
Dereske, Jo 1947- *SmATA 72 [port]*
De Reszke, Edouard 1853-1917 *Baker 92, IntDcOp, OxDcOp, PolBiDi*
De Reszke, Jean 1850-1925 *Baker 92, OxDcOp, PolBiDi*
De Reszke, Jean 1850-1935 *IntDcOp [port]*
De Reszke, Josephine 1855-1891 *Baker 92, OxDcOp, PolBiDi*
Dereszynski, Jeffrey 1959- *St&PR 93*
De Reuck, K. Marjorie *WhoScE 91-1*
Dereux, Jean-F. 1927- *WhoScE 91-2*
de Reyniac, Maurice Druon *ScF&FL 92*
Derfelt, Grant William 1932- *St&PR 93*
Derfler, Leslie 1933- *WhoSSW 93*
Dergarabedian, Paul 1922- *WhoAm 92*
Derge, David Richard 1928- *WhoAm 92*
Derge, Klaus Fritz 1937- *St&PR 93*
Dergenc, Slobodan 1924- *WhoScE 91-4*
Derham, Anthony R. d1990 *BioIn 17*
Derham, C.J. *WhoScE 91-1*
de Rham, Casimir, Jr. 1924- *WhoAm 92*
De Rham, David P. 1931- *St&PR 93*
Derham, Matthew Joseph 1928- *WhoWrEP 92*
Derham, Richard Andrew 1940- *WhoAm 92*
Der Harootian, Khoren 1909- *WhoAm 92*
Der-Houssikian, Haig 1938- *WhoAm 92*
Der Hovanessian, Diana *WhoWrEP 92*
Der Hovanessian, Diana 1934- *WhoWor 93*
Deria, Abdullahi 1934- *WhoUN 92*
Deriabin, Peter S. d1992 *NewYTBS 92*
de Ribaupierre, Francois Olivier 1939- *WhoWor 93*
De Ribera, Fernando Enriquez y Afan 1583-1637 *BioIn 17*
De Ribera, Jusepe 1591-1652 *BioIn 17*
De Ribere, Lisa *BioIn 17*
Deric, Arthur J. 1926- *WhoIns 93*
DeRicco, Lawrence Albert 1923- *WhoAm 92*
Derickson, Holly Grehan Hill 1953- *WhoSSW 93*
Derickson, John Garner 1913- *WhoSSW 93*
de Rico, Ul 1944- *ScF&FL 92*
De Ridder, Johannes J. 1941- *WhoScE 91-3*
De Ridder, Nicolaas A. 1924- *WhoScE 91-3*
De Riemer, Daniel Louis 1950- *WhoEmL 93, WhoSSW 93*
De Rienzo, William Thomson 1955- *WhoSSW 93*
Derieux, Maurice *WhoScE 91-2*
DeRiggi, Raymond Joseph 1948- *St&PR 93*
De Rijke, D. *WhoScE 91-3*
Derin, Greg David 1954- *WhoEmL 93*
Dering, Richard *Baker 92*
Derion, Toniann 1954- *WhoAmW 93*
de Rios, Marlene Dobkin 1939- *WhoAmW 93*
Derise, Nellie Louise 1937- *WhoSSW 93*
De Rise, Raymond John, Jr. *Law&B 92*
De Risi, Dwight Carlton 1947- *WhoE 93*
De Riso, Thomas Neil 1946- *WhoE 93*
DeRita, Frank Edward 1952- *WhoEmL 93*
de Rivas, Carmela Foderaro 1920- *WhoAm 92*
De Rivera, Pilar Primo d1991 *BioIn 17*
Derivis, Henri Etienne 1780-1856 *Baker 92, OxDcOp*
Derivis, Prosper 1808-1880 *Baker 92, OxDcOp*
Derkach, Boris Eugenievich 1958- *WhoWor 93*
Derkach, Vladimir Alexandrovich 1950- *WhoWor 93*
Derkacht, Gregory D. 1947- *St&PR 93*
Derke, Hanns Joachim 1957- *WhoE 93*
Derksen, Sandra Kay 1953- *WhoSSW 93*
Derlacki, Eugene Lubin 1913- *WhoAm 92*
D'Erlanger, Frederic *OxDcOp*
Derleth, August 1909-1971 *ScF&FL 92*
Derleth, August William 1909-1971 *BioIn 17*
Derloshon, Jack H. 1929- *St&PR 93*
Derman, Andrew B. *Law&B 92*
Derman, Andrew Brad 1954- *WhoEmL 93*
Derman, Cyrus 1925- *WhoAm 92*
Derman, Martha *ScF&FL 92*
Dermer, Zigmund L. *Law&B 92*
Dermid, Robert Aaron 1951- *WhoEmL 93, WhoSSW 93*
Dermietzel, Rolf Ernst 1943- *WhoScE 91-3*
Dermine, Jean Marie 1953- *WhoWor 93*
Derminer, Robert 1944-1991 *BioIn 17*
Dermody, Vincent J. d1992 *BioIn 17, NewYTBS 92*
Dermokaites *OxDcByz*
Dermota, Anton 1910-1989 *Baker 92, IntDcOp, OxDcOp*
Dern, Bruce 1936- *BioIn 17, IntDcF 2-3 [port]*
Dern, Bruce MacLeish 1936- *WhoAm 92*
Dern, Laura *BioIn 17*
Dern, Laura 1966- *WhoAm 92*
Dern, Laura 1967?- *ConTFT 10, CurBio 92 [port], News 92 [port], -92-3 [port]*
Der Nersessian, Sirarpie 1896-1989 *BioIn 17*
Dernesch, Helga 1939- *Baker 92, IntDcOp, OxDcOp*
Deroanne, Claude Leon 1944- *WhoScE 91-2*
De Robeck, John Michael 1862-1928 *HarEnMi*
De Robertis, Edward M. 1947- *WhoScE 91-4*
DeRoburt, Hammer d1992 *NewYTBS 92*
De Rocco, Andrew Gabriel 1929- *WhoAm 92*
Deroche, E.H. 1947- *St&PR 93*
Deroche, John Walter 1932- *St&PR 93*
De Rochebouet, Gaetan de Grimaudet 1813-1899 *BioIn 17*
de Rocquigny, Herve-Francois 1951- *WhoWor 93*
DeRodes, Robert P. 1950- *WhoIns 93*
deRoeck, Pascal *Law&B 92*
Deroeck, Walter A. 1942- *St&PR 93*
de Roe Devon, The Marchioness 1934- *WhoAmW 93*
De Roelas, Juan c. 1560-1625 *BioIn 17*
De Roes, Nanda Yvonne 1945- *WhoAm 92*
DeRoest, Leon Douglas 1949- *WhoEmL 93*
De Rogatis, Pascual 1880-1980 *Baker 92*
De Rohm, Jean-Jacques *Law&B 92*
Derom, Fritz 1927- *WhoScE 91-2*
DeRoma, Leonard James 1953- *WhoAm 92*
DeRoma, Nicholas J. *Law&B 92*
Derome, Daniel *WhoCanL 92*
Derome, Jacques Florian 1941- *WhoAm 92*
Derome, John R.M. 1947- *WhoScE 91-4*
De Romilly, Jacqueline *BioIn 17*
Deron, Stein Tristan 1937- *WhoUN 92*
de Ronceray, Hubert 1932- *DcCPCAm*
Deronzier, Alain 1947- *WhoScE 91-2*
De Roo, Remi Joseph 1924- *WhoAm 92*
De Rooij, Dirk G. 1942- *WhoScE 91-3*
De Roos, Juanita G. *Law&B 92*
deRosa, Dee *SmATA 70 [port]*
Derosa, Donald John 1943- *St&PR 93*
Derosa, Francis J. *Law&B 92*
De Rosa, John-Paul *Law&B 92*
DeRosa, Mary Catherine 1952- *WhoEmL 93*
DeRosa, Patti Jean 1946- *WhoAmW 93*
DeRose, Anne Margarette 1932- *WhoAmW 93*
De Rose, Louis John 1952- *WhoE 93, WhoEmL 93*
De Rose, Mary Frances 1957- *WhoAmW 93*
De Rose, Peter 1900-1953 *Baker 92*
De Rose, Peter Louis 1947- *WhoEmL 93*
De Rose, Sandra Michele *WhoAmW 93*
DeRosier, Arthur Henry, Jr. 1931- *WhoAm 92*
Derosier, David John 1939- *WhoAm 92*
Derosier, H. Peter 1934- *St&PR 93*
Deross, Thomas C. 1946- *St&PR 93*
De Rothschild, Guy *BioIn 17*
De Rothschild, Julian Remy-Maximilian 1964- *WhoWrEP 92*
De Rothschild, Marie-Helene *BioIn 17*
Derouane, Eric G.J. 1944- *WhoScE 91-2*
DeRouchey, Beverly Jean 1958- *WhoE 93*
Derouin, Raymond E. 1937- *St&PR 93*
Deroulede, Paul 1846-1914 *BioIn 17*
Derounian, Arthur 1909-1991 *BioIn 17*
Derounian, Steven Boghos 1918- *WhoAm 92*
Derow, Peter Alfred 1940- *WhoAm 92*
DeRoy, Cathy *Law&B 92*
Deroy, Jean-Marc Roger 1948- *WhoUN 92*
DeRoy, M. Rita 1939- *WhoAmW 93*
Derpinghaus, Patrick James 1955- *WhoEmL 93*
Derr, Harold James, Jr. 1927- *St&PR 93*
Derr, Jack 1927- *St&PR 93*
Derr, John Frederick 1936- *St&PR 93*
Derr, Kenneth T. *WhoAm 92, WhoWor 93*
Derr, Kenneth Tindall 1936- *St&PR 93*
Derr, Lee E. 1948- *WhoEmL 93*
Derr, Mark David 1951- *WhoEmL 93*
Derr, Richard d1992 *NewYTBS 92 [port]*
Derr, Richard 1917-1992 *BioIn 17*
Derr, Richard Edward 1933- *WhoAm 92*
Derr, Richard L. *Law&B 92*
Derr, Teresa Marie 1953- *WhoEmL 93*
Derr, Thomas Burchard 1929- *WhoWor 93*
Derr, Thomas Sieger 1931- *WhoE 93*
Derr, Vernon Ellsworth 1921- *WhoAm 92*
Derrey, Robert Fairbairn 1931- *St&PR 93*
Derrick, Alice Meade 1944- *WhoAmW 93*
Derrick, Anthony 1953- *WhoWor 93*
Derrick, Butler C., Jr. 1936- *CngDr 91*
Derrick, Butler Carson, Jr. 1936- *WhoAm 92, WhoSSW 93*
Derrick, Charles Warren, Jr. 1935- *WhoAm 92*
Derrick, Gary Wayne 1953- *WhoEmL 93*
Derrick, Graham Holbrook 1934- *WhoWor 93*
Derrick, Jack Holley 1947- *WhoEmL 93*
Derrick, James V., Jr. 1945- *St&PR 93*
Derrick, Jim *Law&B 92*
Derrick, John Edward 1930- *St&PR 93*
Derrick, John M., Jr. 1940- *St&PR 93*
Derrick, Karlton L. 1960- *WhoE 93*
Derrick, Lionel *ScF&FL 92*
Derrick, Malcolm 1933- *WhoAm 92*
Derrick, Michael Lionel 1957- *WhoEmL 93*
Derrick, Noah E. 1889- *BioIn 17*
Derrick, Peter John *WhoScE 91-1*
Derrick, Robert Parker 1931- *WhoAm 92*
Derrick, Tyree C., Jr. *Law&B 92*
Derrickson, Denise Ann 1956- *WhoSSW 93*
Derrickson, William Borden 1940- *St&PR 93, WhoAm 92, WhoWor 93*
Derrick-White, Elizabeth 1940- *WhoAmW 93, WhoWor 93*
D'Errico, Diane Fava 1946- *WhoE 93*
Derricotte, Toi M. 1941- *WhoWrEP 92*
Derrida, Jacques *BioIn 17*
Derrida, Jacques 1930- *WhoWor 93*
Derrig, Andrea Marie 1953- *WhoEmL 93*
Derrig, Deidre B. *Law&B 92*
Derrig, Joanne Morrissey *Law&B 92*
Derrota, Luis Humberto *Law&B 92*
Derrough, Lee A. 1944- *St&PR 93*
Derrough, Neil E. 1936- *WhoAm 92*
Derrow, David D. 1923- *St&PR 93*
Derry, Charles 1951- *ScF&FL 92*
Derry, John Leonard 1950- *WhoSSW 93*
Derry, Lisa Anne 1953- *WhoAmW 93*
Derry, Patricia Marie 1952- *WhoAmW 93*
Derry, R. Michael 1937- *St&PR 93, WhoAm 92*
Derry, Ronald L. *St&PR 93*
Derry, William J. 1951- *St&PR 93*
Derryberry, Andy Lynn 1952- *WhoEmL 93*
Derryberry, Phillip Eugene 1952- *St&PR 93*
Derry Down Derry *MajAI*
Dersch, John 1923- *St&PR 93*
Dersh, Jerome 1928- *WhoE 93*
Dersh, Rhoda E. 1934- *WhoAm 92, WhoAmW 93, WhoE 93*
Dersham, Timothy Orson 1952- *WhoSSW 93*
Dershowitz, Alan c. 1938- *News 92 [port]*
Dershowitz, Alan M. *BioIn 17*
Dershowitz, Alan Morton 1938- *WhoAm 92*
Dershowitz, Morris *Law&B 92*
Derthick, Lawrence G., Sr. d1992 *NewYTBS 92*
Derthick, Martha Ann 1933- *WhoAm 92*
Dertien, Donald Charles 1936- *WhoWor 93*
Dertien, James LeRoy 1942- *WhoAm 92*
Dertouzos, Michael Leonidas 1936- *WhoAm 92*
DeRubertis, Patricia Sandra 1950- *WhoAmW 93, WhoEmL 93*
Deruddere, Dominique 1957- *MiSFD 9*
De Ruiter, Hans 1956- *St&PR 93*
Derus, Patricia Irene 1947- *WhoEmL 93*
Derus, Stephen J. 1943- *St&PR 93*
Derusha, Gerald F. 1937- *St&PR 93*
Derusha, William Charles 1950- *St&PR 93*
deRuyter, Carol Ann 1948- *WhoEmL 93*
Deruyttere, Andre Emiel August 1925- *WhoScE 91-2*
Dervaes, Claudine Lucienne 1954- *WhoEmL 93*
Dervan, Edward Cunningham 1947- *St&PR 93*
Dervan, Peter Brendan 1945- *WhoAm 92*
Dervaux, Pierre 1917- *Baker 92*
Dervin, Brenda Louise 1938- *WhoAm 92*
Dervis, Kemal 1949- *WhoUN 92*
Dervisoglu, Ahmet 1935- *WhoScE 91-4*
Derwent, R.G. *WhoScE 91-1*
Derwin, Jordan 1931- *WhoE 93*
Derwinski, Edward J. *BioIn 17*
Derwinski, Edward J. 1926- *CngDr 91*
Derwinski, Edward Joseph 1926- *WhoAm 92, WhoE 93, WhoWor 93*
Der-Yeghiayan, Samuel 1952- *WhoEmL 93*
De Rysky, Salvatore 1921- *WhoScE 91-3*
Derzai, Matthew 1928- *WhoWor 93*
Derzaw, Richard Lawrence *Law&B 92*
Derzhavets, Boris Abramovich 1956- *WhoWor 93*
Derzon, Gordon M. 1934- *WhoAm 92*
Derzon, Robert Alan 1930- *WhoAm 92*
De Saavedra, Ruben d1990 *BioIn 17*
De Sabata, Coleta 1935- *WhoScE 91-4*
De Sabata, Victor 1892-1967 *Baker 92, IntDcOp, OxDcOp*
De Sable, Jean Baptiste Pointe 1745?-1818 *BioIn 17*
de Sa e Silva, Elizabeth Anne 1931- *WhoAmW 93*
Desafey, Thomas 1930- *St&PR 93*
Desai, Anita 1935- *IntvWPC 92 [port]*
Desai, Anita 1937- *BioIn 17, DcChlFi, IntLitE*
Desai, Barin G. 1933- *WhoE 93*
Desai, Bharat I. 1935- *St&PR 93*
Desai, Cawas Jal 1938- *St&PR 93, WhoAm 92, WhoE 93*
Desai, Hemant Kishore 1962- *WhoE 93*
Desai, Jagesh 1926- *WhoAsAP 91*
Desai, Kiran A. 1948- *WhoEmL 93*
Desai, Meghnad *BioIn 17*
Desai, Meghnad Jagdischandra 1940- *WhoWor 93*
Desai, Morarji Ranchhodji 1896- *DcTwHis*
Desai, Nitin 1941- *WhoUN 92*
Desai, Rohit Mojilal 1938- *WhoAm 92*
Desai, Vishakha N. 1949- *WhoAm 92, WhoAmW 93*
De Saint-Aubin, Gabriel Jacques 1724-1780 *BioIn 17*
de Saint-Aubin, Horace *ScF&FL 92*
De Saint-Exupery, Antoine 1900-1944 *BioIn 17*
De St. Jorre, Danielle Marie-Madeline 1941- *WhoWor 93*
De St. Paer, Jerry M. 1942- *St&PR 93*
de Saint Phalle, Francois 1946- *St&PR 93, WhoAm 92*
de Saint Phalle, Pierre Claude 1948- *WhoAm 92*
De Saint Phalle, Therese 1930- *WhoWrEP 92*
de Saint Phalle, Thibaut 1918- *WhoAm 92*
De Saint Pierre, Michel 1916-1987 *BioIn 17*
deSaint Victor, Diane *Law&B 92*
Desaix De Veygoux, Louis Charles Antoine 1768-1800 *HarEnMi*
De Salis, Jean Rodolphe 1901- *BioIn 17*
DeSalle, James L. 1946- *St&PR 93*
De Salva, Salvatore Joseph 1924- *WhoAm 92, WhoWor 93*
DeSalvo, Deborah Lynn 1954- *WhoAmW 93*
Desa-Matos, Marta Teresa 1950- *WhoEmL 93*
De San, Yves 1945- *WhoUN 92*
De Sana, Jimmy 1950-1990 *BioIn 17*
DeSanctis, Carmine Edward 1935- *WhoSSW 93*
DeSanctis, Richard 1956- *St&PR 93*
DeSanctis, Roman William 1930- *WhoAm 92*
De Sanctis, Vincent 1941- *WhoE 93*
De San Martin, Jose 1778?-1850 *BioIn 17*
De Santa Anna, Antonio Lopez 1794?-1876 *BioIn 17*
Desante, William F. 1955- *St&PR 93*
Desanti, Carole J. 1958- *St&PR 93*
DeSanti, Frederick D. 1950- *St&PR 93*
DeSanti, Richard J. *Law&B 92*
De Santis, Anthony 1914- *WhoAm 92*
DeSantis, Donald Anthony 1950- *WhoAm 92*
DeSantis, Frank Joseph, Jr. 1958- *WhoAm 92*
De Santis, Larry 1929- *WhoAm 92*
DeSantis, Lynette S. *Law&B 92*

DeSantis, Nunzio P. 1951- *St&PR 93*
De Santis, P. 1935- *WhoScE 91-3*
De Santis, Vincent Paul 1916- *WhoAm 92*
De Santo, Charles P(asquale) 1923- *ConAu 139*
De Santo, Donald James 1942- *WhoE 93, WhoWor 93*
DeSanto, Gerarda Marie 1955- *WhoAm 92*
DeSanto, Michael Francis 1949- *WhoE 93*
DeSanto, Sugar Pie 1935- *BioIn 17*
DeSanto, Sugarpie *SoulM*
de Santos, Robin King 1958- *WhoEmL 93*
Desanty, James R. 1934- *St&PR 93*
DeSapio, Carmine 1908- *PolPar*
DeSapio, Gerard Joseph 1954- *WhoEmL 93*
DeSarno, Judith Martin 1944- *WhoE 93*
Desarzens, Victor 1908-1986 *Baker 92*
DeSassure, Charles 1961- *WhoEmL 93*
Desaugiers, Marc-Antoine 1742-1793 *OxDcOp*
Desaugiers, Marc Antoine Madeleine 1772-1827 *OxDcOp*
Desaulniers, Andre 1941- *St&PR 93*
Desaulniers, Gonzalve 1863-1934 *BioIn 17*
Desaulniers, Lorraine 1941- *St&PR 93*
Desaulniers, Marc Joseph 1951- *WhoEmL 93*
Desaulniers, Marcel Andre 1945- *WhoSSW 93*
Desaulniers, Yvon J. 1936- *St&PR 93*
Desautelle, William Peter 1939- *St&PR 93, WhoAm 92*
Desautels, Claude 1941- *St&PR 93*
Desautels, Ernest J. *Law&B 92*
De Sayn-Wittgenstein, Carolyne 1819-1887 *BioIn 17*
Desbarats, Peter Hullett 1933- *WhoAm 92*
Des Barres, Michael *BioIn 17*
Desberg, Daniel 1925- *WhoSSW 93*
DesBois, L. Cameron *Law&B 92*
Des Bois, Louis Cameron 1931- *St&PR 93*
Desbordes-Valmore, Marceline 1786-1859 *BioIn 17*
Desbrandes, Robert 1924- *WhoAm 92, WhoWor 93*
Descamps, Eugene 1922- *BioIn 17*
Descamps, Johan Jozef Arthur 1951- *WhoWor 93*
Descartes, Rene 1596-1650 *BioIn 17, LitC 20 [port]*
DeScenna, Linda 1949- *ConTFT 10*
DeScenza, Joseph W. *BioIn 17*
Desch, Carl William 1915- *WhoAm 92*
Desch, Robert T. 1945- *St&PR 93*
Desch, Theodore Edward 1931- *WhoAm 92*
Deschacht, Johan Paul 1959- *WhoWor 93*
Deschaine, Barbara Ralph 1930- *WhoAmW 93*
Deschambault, Danielle Eileen 1947- *WhoAmW 93*
Deschamp, Gloria J. 1949- *WhoAmW 93*
Deschamps, Gary W. 1951- *WhoEmL 93*
Deschamps, Jean-Pierre 1941- *WhoScE 91-2*
Des Champs, Nicholas Howard 1937- *St&PR 93*
Deschamps, Roland 1932- *WhoScE 91-2*
Deschamps-Jehin, Blanche 1859-1923 *OxDcOp*
Deschamps-Jehin, (Marie-)Blanche 1857-1923 *Baker 92*
Deschanel, Caleb 1941- *BioIn 17*
Deschanel, Caleb 1944- *MiSFD 9, WhoAm 92*
Deschanel, Paul Eugene Louis 1856-1922 *BioIn 17*
Deschaux, Pierre Antoine 1943- *WhoScE 91-2*
Deschene, Kevin *BioIn 17*
Deschenie, Tina *BioIn 17*
De Schepper, J.K.L. 1940- *WhoScE 91-2*
De Schepper, Paul Julien 1929- *WhoScE 91-2*
De Schoutheete, Philippe 1932- *WhoWor 93*
De Schryver, Frans Carl 1939- *WhoScE 91-2*
DeSchutter, Richard U. 1940- *WhoAm 92*
Descoins, Charles Eugene 1935- *WhoScE 91-2*
Descombes, Donald R. 1932- *WhoIns 93*
Descombes, Vincent 1943- *ConAu 136*
Descomps, Bernard 1937- *WhoScE 91-2*
Descoteaux, Carol J. 1948- *WhoAmW 93*
Descotes, Gerard 1933- *WhoScE 91-2*
De Scudery, Madeleine 1607-1701 *BioIn 17*
Desderi, Ettore 1892-1974 *Baker 92*
Desdier, Steven Ross 1952- *WhoEmL 93*
de Sedle, Michele Lorraine 1962- *WhoAmW 93*
de Seguin des Hons, Luc Donald 1919- *WhoWor 93*
De Segurola, Andres 1873-1953 *BioIn 17*
De Segurola, Andres 1874-1953 *Baker 92*
de Seingalt, Giacomo Casanova *ScF&FL 92*
de Selding, Edward Bertrand 1926- *WhoAm 92*
DeSello, Eugene Te 1961- *WhoE 93*
De Selm, Henry Rawie 1924- *WhoSSW 93*
De Selys, Michel 1938- *St&PR 93*
DeSena, Alphonse Thomas 1947- *WhoAm 92*
de Sena, Jorge *ScF&FL 92*
Desenberg, Carol Ann 1952- *WhoAmW 93*
Desens, Richard Emil 1941- *St&PR 93*
De Senti, William L. 1916- *St&PR 93*
Deseo, Lydia May Glover 1898- *AmWomPl*
Deser, Stanley 1931- *WhoAm 92*
de Serres, Frederick Joseph 1929- *WhoAm 92*
Deserres, Roger 1914- *St&PR 93*
Desert, Francois-Xavier 1960- *WhoWor 93*
Desertl, Luigi 1915 *WhoWor 93*
DeSesa, Michael Anthony 1927- *WhoAm 92*
Desesquelles, Jean 1936- *WhoScE 91-2*
Des Forets, Louis Rene 1918- *BioIn 17*
Desforges, Bruno 1925- *St&PR 93*
Desforges, Jane Fay 1921- *WhoAm 92, WhoAmW 93*
Des Forges, Robert 1935- *St&PR 93*
Desfosses, Louis Robert 1937- *WhoE 93*
des Gachons, Gilles Peyrot 1959- *WhoE 93*
DesGrey, Arthur H. d1991 *BioIn 17*
Desgrez, Alex 1929- *WhoScE 91-2*
Deshaies, Kenneth Joseph 1946- *WhoEmL 93*
De Shane, William Wesley 1938- *St&PR 93*
Desharnais, Richard R. *Law&B 92*
DeShaw, Donald *Law&B 92*
Deshayes, Prosper-Didier d1815 *OxDcOp*
DeShazer, Mary Kirk 1949- *WhoSSW 93*
De Shazor, Ashley Dunn 1919- *WhoAm 92*
Desherow, James Dartmouth 1940- *St&PR 93*
DeShetler, Kenneth Edward 1928- *St&PR 93, WhoIns 93*
Deshevov, Vladimir 1889-1955 *Baker 92*
Deshmukh, Shankarrao Narayanrao 1913- *WhoAsAP 91*
Deshmukh, Sudhir G. *Law&B 92*
Deshong, John Kirk 1953- *WhoE 93*
Deshpande, Chris 1950- *ConAu 137, SmATA 69*
Deshpande, Nilendra Ganesh 1938- *WhoAm 92*
Deshpande, Rohit 1951- *WhoEmL 93*
Deshpande, Vijay Dattatraya 1949- *WhoEmL 93*
Deshusses, Jacques 1932- *WhoScE 91-4*
Desi, Illes 1931- *WhoScE 91-4*
De Sica, Vittorio 1902-1974 *MiSFD 9N*
Desideri, Ippolito 1684-1733 *Expl 93*
Desiderio, Carmen Gerald 1952- *St&PR 93*
Desiderio, Dominic Morse, Jr. 1941- *WhoAm 92*
Desiderio, Michelle 1964- *WhoAmW 93*
Desieno, John Anthony 1949- *WhoEmL 93*
Desilets, Brian Henry 1927- *WhoE 93*
Desilets, Marian Horgan *Law&B 92*
Desilets, Pierre Andre 1961- *WhoE 93*
Desilets, Roland B., Jr. *Law&B 92*
de Silva, Alvaro 1949- *ConAu 138*
De Silva, Archangela Maria *Law&B 92*
de Silva, Colin *WhoAm 92*
de Silva, Diane Marie 1952- *WhoAmW 93*
de Silva, Ginige Tennyson Francis 1937- *WhoWor 93*
De Silva, Hakkini Ames Piyadasa 1925- *WhoWor 93*
De Silva, Merl 1935- *WhoWor 93*
De Silva, Mervyn Dominic 1930- *WhoWor 93*
DeSilvia, Christine Hunt 1944- *WhoAmW 93*
DeSimone, Angela Rose 1947- *WhoAmW 93*
De Simone, Daniel V. 1930- *WhoAm 92*
DeSimone, Glenn J. 1947- *WhoAm 92*
deSimone, Jack A. 1920- *St&PR 93*
De Simone, James William 1932- *St&PR 93*
DeSimone, Livio Diego 1936- *St&PR 93, WhoAm 92*
DeSimone, Tom *MiSFD 9*
De Simone, Virginia Carey 1930- *WhoE 93*
Desind, Philip 1910- *WhoE 93*
Desio, Abel Oscar 1949- *WhoWor 93*
DeSio, Anthony 1930- *ConEn*
De Sio, Anthony W. 1930- *St&PR 93*
Desio, Peter John 1938- *WhoE 93*
De Sio, Robert J. 1934- *St&PR 93*
DeSiome, Livio D. 1936- *WhoAm 92*
De Sipio, George 1925- *WhoAm 92*
DeSisto, Elizabeth Agnes 1954- *WhoAmW 93, WhoEmL 93*
Desjardins, Alice 1934- *WhoE 93*
Desjardins, Chantal *Law&B 92*
Desjardins, Christopher J. *Law&B 92*
Desjardins, Christopher John 1948- *St&PR 93*
Desjardins, Claude 1938- *WhoAm 92*
Desjardins, Guy 1961- *St&PR 93*
Desjardins, Marie Catherine Hortense d1683 *BioIn 17*
Desjardins, Pierre 1941- *WhoAm 92*
Desjardins, Raoul 1933- *WhoAm 92*
Desjardins, Robert James 1937- *St&PR 93*
Desjarlais, Erika Else 1934- *WhoAm 92, WhoAmW 93*
Desjarlais, John 1953- *ScF&FL 92, SmATA 71 [port]*
Desjarlais, John Joseph 1953- *WhoEmL 93*
Desjeux, Jehan-Francois 1940- *WhoScE 91-2*
Deskins, Wilbur Eugene 1927- *WhoAm 92*
Deskur, Andre-Marie 1924- *PolBiDi*
Deskur, Andrzej Maria Cardinal 1924- *WhoWor 93*
Deslandres, Adolphe-Edouard-Marie 1840-1911 *Baker 92*
Desloge, George Burdeau 1924- *St&PR 93*
Desloge, Louis, Jr. 1922- *St&PR 93*
Desloge, Taylor S. 1921- *St&PR 93*
Desloge, Theodore P., Jr. 1939- *St&PR 93*
Deslongchamps, Pierre 1938- *WhoAm 92*
Desmaison, J.G. 1944- *WhoScE 91-2*
Desmarais, Charles Joseph 1949- *WhoAm 92*
Desmarais, Gerald Francis 1952- *WhoE 93*
Desmarais, James 1956- *WhoE 93*
Des Marais, Louise Mercier 1923- *WhoWrEP 92*
Desmarais, Maurice 1946- *WhoAm 92, WhoEmL 93*
Desmarais, Naureen Gertrude 1944- *WhoE 93*
Desmarais, Paul 1927- *WhoAm 92*
Des Marais, Paul (Emile) 1920- *Baker 92*
Desmarais, Paul Guy *BioIn 17*
Desmarais, Paul Guy 1927- *St&PR 93*
Des Marais, Pierre, II 1934- *St&PR 93, WhoAm 92*
Desmarescaux, Philippe 1938- *WhoAm 92*
Desmarets, Henri 1661-1741 *Baker 92*
Desmarets, Henry 1661-1741 *OxDcOp*
DesMarteau, Darryl Dwayne 1940- *WhoAm 92*
Desmed, A. *WhoScE 91-2*
De Smet, J. *WhoScE 91-2*
Desmet, Johan R.M. 1953- *WhoScE 91-2*
de Smet, Lorraine May 1928- *WhoE 93*
Desmet, Valeer Julien 1931- *WhoScE 91-2*
DeSmidt, Robert J. 1947- *St&PR 93*
De Smith, Rod 1925- *St&PR 93*
Desmond, Daniel Joseph 1942- *St&PR 93*
Desmond, JoAnn 1947- *WhoAmW 93*
Desmond, John J., III *Law&B 92*
Desmond, John Jacob 1922- *WhoAm 92*
Desmond, John S. 1944- *St&PR 93*
Desmond, Kathleen Mae 1940- *WhoAmW 93*
Desmond, Leslie R. *Law&B 92*
Desmond, Mark L. 1958- *St&PR 93*
Desmond, Paul 1924-1977 *Baker 92, BioIn 17*
Desmond, Richard L. 1937- *St&PR 93*
Desmond, Richard Michael 1934- *St&PR 93*
Desmond, Shaw 1877-1960 *ScF&FL 92*
Desmond, Thomas Edward 1931- *St&PR 93*
Desmond, Walter Thomas, Jr. 1953- *WhoWrEP 92*
Desmond, William 1878-1949 *BioIn 17*
Desmond, William James 1951- *WhoE 93*
Desmono, John R. 1944- *St&PR 93*
De Smul, Pierre Hector 1959- *WhoEmL 93*
Desnick, Robert John 1943- *WhoAm 92, WhoWor 93*
Desnoes, Peter Blaise *WhoAm 92*
Desnos, Jacques 1922- *WhoScE 91-2*
DeSobe, Gerald Joseph 1948- *WhoSSW 93*
Desocio, Walter Gerard *Law&B 92*
Desoer, Charles Auguste 1926- *WhoAm 92*
de Soet, J. F. A. *WhoAm 92*
De Soete, G.G. *WhoScE 91-3*
De Sofi, Oliver Julius 1929- *WhoSSW 93*
Desoize, Bernard 1946- *WhoScE 91-2*
De Sola, Ralph 1908- *WhoAm 92*
De Solis, Frank W. 1950- *St&PR 93*
De Solla Price, Derek 1922-1983 *BioIn 17*
De Sombre, Robert Magnus 1915-1991 *BioIn 17*
De Somogyi, Joseph *BioIn 17*
Desonia, Clinton D. d1990 *BioIn 17*
DeSoo, F. Kenneth 1931- *St&PR 93*
DeSorbo, Lawrence A. 1931- *St&PR 93*
Desormiere, Roger 1898-1963 *Baker 92, OxDcOp*
de Soto, Alvaro 1943- *WhoUN 92*
Desoto, Clinton Burgel 1931- *WhoAm 92*
De Soto, Hernando *BioIn 17*
De Soto, Hernando c. 1500-1542 *BioIn 17, Expl 93 [port]*
DeSoto, Pete 1939- *St&PR 93, WhoAm 92*
De Soto, Rosana 1950?- *NotHsAW 93*
de Soto, Simon 1925- *WhoAm 92*
De Souny, Leonie *AmWomPl*
de Sousa, David James 1943- *WhoE 93*
De Sousa, Flavio Pereira 1944- *WhoWor 93*
DeSousa, Karen Evans 1953- *WhoEmL 93*
De Sousa, Rui C. 1934- *WhoScE 91-4*
De Souter, Paul Dominique Desire 1944- *WhoWor 93*
de Souza, Dudley *ScF&FL 92*
de Souza, Janes Angelo 1933- *WhoUN 92*
de Souza e Silva, Edmundo Albuquerque 1952- *WhoWor 93*
DeSpain, Becky Ann 1948- *WhoAmW 93*
Despain, Dezra *ScF&FL 92*
DeSpain, Ronald Leroy 1940- *WhoSSW 93*
DeSpain, Sara Ellen 1949- *WhoEmL 93*
Despars, G. *Law&B 92*
Despenser, Hugh le d1326 *HarEnMi*
Despenser, Hugh le 1261-1326 *HarEnMi*
D'Esperey, Louis Felix Marie Francois Franchet 1856-1942 *BioIn 17*
Despiau, Charles 1874-1946 *BioIn 17*
Desplaces, Andree M. 1934- *WhoScE 91-2*
de Spoelberch, Guillaume 1933- *WhoWor 93*
Despommier, Dickson Donald 1940- *WhoAm 92*
Despont, Thierry W. *BioIn 17*
Despot, Shirley Ann 1932- *WhoAmW 93*
Despotakis, Constantine A. *Law&B 92*
Despres, Leo Arthur 1932- *WhoAm 92*
Despres, Leon Mathis 1908- *WhoAm 92*
Despres, Robert 1924- *WhoAm 92*
Despres, Robert Leon 1940- *WhoE 93*
Des Prez, Josquin c. 1440-1521 *Baker 92*
Desprez, Louis-Jean 1742-1804 *OxDcOp*
Despujols, Jacques J. 1925- *WhoScE 91-2*
des Rioux, Deena Victoria Coty 1941- *WhoAm 92*
Desroche, Jerold J. 1937- *St&PR 93*
Desrochers, Clemence 1933- *WhoCanL 92*
DesRochers, Gerard Camille 1922- *WhoE 93*
Desrochers, L. 1941- *St&PR 93*
Des Roches, Antoine 1924- *WhoAm 92*
DesRoches, Diane Blanche 1947- *WhoEmL 93, WhoWrEP 92*
Desrosier, Thomas J. *Law&B 92*
DesRosiers, Deniseh L. *Law&B 92*
Des Rosiers, Elaine Virginia 1930- *WhoAmW 93*
Desrosiers, Marc Frederic 1956- *WhoE 93*
Desrosiers, Robert *BioIn 17*
DesRosiers, Roger I. 1935- *WhoAm 92*
Desrosiers, Ronald Charles 1948- *WhoE 93*
Desrousseaux, Alexandre Marie 1861-1955 *BioIn 17*
Dessalines, Jean Jacques c. 1746-1806 *HarEnMi*
Dessart, Francis 1948- *WhoWor 93*
Dessart, Michel Alexandre 1938- *WhoUN 92*
Dessaso, Deborah Ann 1952- *WhoAmW 93*
Dessau, Bernhard 1861-1923 *Baker 92*
Dessau, Erling 1934- *WhoUN 92*
Dessau, Paul 1894-1979 *Baker 92, OxDcOp*
Dessau, Randy Scot 1959- *WhoEmL 93*
Dessauer, Carin 1963- *WhoAmW 93, WhoEmL 93, WhoWor 93*
Dessauer, Herbert Clay 1921- *WhoSSW 93*
Dessauer, John Hans 1905- *WhoAm 92, WhoWor 93*
Dessauer, John Phillip 1936- *WhoE 93*
Dessauer, Josef 1798-1876 *Baker 92, OxDcOp*
Dessauer, Rolf 1926- *WhoE 93*
Dessaulles, Louis-Antoine 1819-1895 *BioIn 17*
Dessaux, Odile 1939- *WhoScE 91-2*
Desse, Jean 1943- *WhoScE 91-2*
Desseine, Jean 1929- *WhoScE 91-2*
Dessel, Arnold M. 1921- *St&PR 93*
Dessel, Arnold Martin 1921- *WhoE 93*
Desselberger, Ulrich *WhoScE 91-1*
Dessem, R. Lawrence 1951- *WhoEmL 93*
Dessen, Edgar Lee 1917- *St&PR 93*
Dessen, Stanley B. 1938- *St&PR 93*
Dessen, Stanley Benjamin 1938- *WhoAm 92, WhoWor 93*

Desser, Maxwell Milton *WhoAm 92*
Dessert, Lynn Marie 1960- *WhoEmL 93*
Dessi-Fulgheri, Francesco 1943- *WhoScE 91-3*
Dessler, Alexander Jack 1928- *WhoAm 92, WhoSSW 93*
Dessler, Gary S. 1942- *WhoSSW 93*
Dessner, Allan 1938- *WhoE 93*
Dessoff, Margarethe 1874-1944 *Baker 92*
Dessoff, Otto 1835-1892 *Baker 92*
Dessonville, Loren Edward 1953- *WhoEmL 93*
Desta, Fisseha *WhoAfr*
De Stael, Nicolas 1914-1955 *BioIn 17*
de Stains, Ian 1948- *WhoWor 93*
D'Este, Mary Ernestine 1941- *WhoAmW 93*
deStefano, Anthony *ScF&FL 92*
De Stefano, Francesco 1933- *WhoScE 91-3*
De Stefano, John J. *WhoIns 93*
DeStefano, John J. 1932- *St&PR 93*
De Stefano, John Joseph 1949- *WhoWor 93*
DeStefano, Joseph Louis 1943- *WhoE 93*
DeStefano, Luigi Gaetano 1948- *WhoWor 93*
DeStefano, Michael Thomas 1946- *St&PR 93*
DeStefano, Rhonda *Law&B 92*
De Stempel, Susan *BioIn 17*
deStevens, George 1924- *WhoAm 92*
Destinn, Emmy 1878-1930 *Baker 92, IntDcOp [port], OxDcOp*
Destino, Ralph, Jr. 1936- *WhoAm 92*
Destler, I. Mac 1939- *WhoAm 92*
Destouches, Andre 1672?-1749 *OxDcOp*
Destouches, Andre-Cardinal 1672-1749 *Baker 92*
Destouches, Charles Rene Dominique Gochet, Chevalier de fl. c. 1781- *HarEnMi*
Destouches, Franz Seraph von 1772-1844 *OxDcOp*
Destouches, Franz (Seraph) von 1772-1844 *Baker 92*
Destouches, Henri-Louis 1894-1961 *BioIn 17*
Destranges, Louis (Augustin Etienne Rouille) 1863-1915 *Baker 92*
Destree, Ouvier H.J. 1943- *WhoScE 91-3*
Destro, Robert Anthony 1950- *WhoEmL 93*
de Stwolinski, Gail Rounce Boyd 1921- *WhoAm 92*
De Surville, Renaud *WhoWor 93*
DeSutter Family *BioIn 17*
de Suze, Jacques Christophe 1944- *WhoSSW 93*
Desvaux, Martin Patrick *WhoScE 91-1*
De Swart, Henricus Cornelius Maria 1944- *WhoWor 93*
Deswert, Jules *Baker 92*
Desy, Luc O. *St&PR 93*
de Szigethy, James Ridgway 1953- *WhoE 93*
de Takacsy, Nicholas Benedict 1939- *WhoAm 92*
DeTar, DeLos F. 1920- *WhoSSW 93*
DeTata, Richard Anthony 1931- *St&PR 93*
Detchon, Bryan Reid 1948- *WhoAm 92*
Detels, Roger 1936- *WhoAm 92*
De Tencin, Claudine Alexandrine Guerin 1682-1749 *BioIn 17*
Deter, Robert Edward 1944- *St&PR 93*
De Teran, Lisa St. Aubin 1953- *BioIn 17*
Deterding, James Martin 1928- *St&PR 93*
Deterding, Mark Walter 1959- *St&PR 93, WhoEmL 93*
Deterling, Ralph Alden, Jr. 1917- *WhoAm 92*
Determan, James R. 1934- *St&PR 93*
Determan, John David 1933- *WhoAm 92*
Deters, Arthur H. 1937- *WhoIns 93*
Deters, James Raymond 1937- *St&PR 93, WhoAm 92*
Detert, James W. 1959- *St&PR 93*
Detert-Moriarty, Judith Anne 1952- *WhoAmW 93, WhoEmL 93*
Deteso, John Salvatore 1956- *WhoSSW 93*
Detgen, John Peter 1939- *St&PR 93*
De-The, Guy 1930- *WhoScE 91-2*
Dethero, J. Hambright 1932- *WhoAm 92*
de Thibault de Boesinghe, Leopold Baron 1943- *WhoWor 93*
Dethier, Edouard 1886-1962 *Baker 92*
Dethier, Gaston-Marie 1875-1958 *Baker 92*
Dethier, Vincent Gaston 1915- *WhoAm 92*
Dethlefsen, George Russell, Jr. 1948- *St&PR 93*
Dethlefsen, V. *WhoScE 91-3*
Dethloff, Henry Clay 1934- *WhoAm 92*
DeThomas, Bruno Michel Pierre 1945- *WhoWor 93*
DeThomasis, Louis 1940- *WhoAm 92*
Dethoor, Jean-Marc 1941- *WhoUN 92*
Dethy, Ray Charles 1928- *WhoAm 92*
de Timmes, Graeme *ScF&FL 92*
de Timms, Graeme *ScF&FL 92*
Detine, Padre *ConAu 37NR, MajAI*
Detjen, David Wheeler 1948- *WhoEmL 93*
Detlefsen, Arthur Louis, Jr. 1936- *WhoE 93*
Detlefsen, Guy-Robert 1919- *WhoAm 92*
Detmar-Pines, Gina Louise 1949- *WhoAmW 93, WhoE 93, WhoEmL 93*
Detmer, Don Eugene 1939- *WhoAm 92*
Detmer, Ty *BioIn 17*
De Tocqueville, Alexis *BioIn 17*
De Togores, Josep 1893-1970 *BioIn 17*
de Toledo, Catherine Holt 1954- *WhoEmL 93*
Detolve, Ethel June *St&PR 93*
Detoni, Dubravko 1937- *Baker 92*
de Tonnancour, Paul Roger Godefroy 1926- *WhoAm 92*
de Tornyay, Rheba 1926- *WhoAm 92, WhoAmW 93*
deTorres, Manuel Ramon 1924- *St&PR 93*
De Toth, Andre 1910- *MiSFD 9*
De Tounens, Orelie-Antoine 1825-1878 *BioIn 17*
DeTour, Michele Ellen *Law&B 92*
DeTour, Walter F. 1933- *St&PR 93*
De Toytot, Arnaud 1962- *St&PR 93*
Detra, Ralph William 1925- *St&PR 93, WhoAm 92*
Detrano, John Michael 1927- *WhoAm 92*
Detraz, Claude 1938- *WhoScE 91-2*
Detre, Katherine Maria 1926- *WhoAm 92*
Detre, L. 1874-1939 *ScF&FL 92*
Detre, L. 1906-1974 *ScF&FL 92*
Detre, Thomas 1924- *WhoAm 92*
De Treaux, Tamara d1990 *BioIn 17*
Detrekoi, Akos 1939- *WhoScE 91-4*
Detremmerie, Jan Karel 1958- *WhoWor 93*
Detrick, Richard William 1933- *St&PR 93*
Detrick, Thomas H. 1934- *St&PR 93*
Detroit Emeralds *SoulM*
Detroit Spinners *SoulM*
Detroux, Louis Jules 1921- *WhoScE 91-2*
DeTroye, Jeff Eliot 1955- *WhoEmL 93*
Detsch, Donald D. 1947- *WhoEmL 93*
Dett, R(obert) Nathaniel 1882-1943 *Baker 92*
Dettbarn, Wolf-Dietrich 1928- *WhoAm 92*
Dettelbach, Iona Schaffer 1935- *WhoAmW 93*
Detter, Helmut 1939- *WhoScE 91-4*
Detter, Marshall Lee 1932- *St&PR 93*
Dettinger, Garth Bryant 1921- *WhoAm 92*
Dettinger, Warren W. 1954- *St&PR 93*
Dettinger, Warren Walter *Law&B 92*
Dettinger, Warren Walter 1954- *WhoAm 92, WhoEmL 93*
Dettlaff, Theodore H. 1930- *St&PR 93*
Dettli, Luzius 1923- *WhoScE 91-4*
Dettloff, Donna Jean 1939- *WhoAmW 93*
Dettman, Bruce *ScF&FL 92*
Dettmann, Terry Robert 1947- *WhoEmL 93*
Dettmer, Robert G. 1931- *St&PR 93*
Dettmer, Robert Gerhart 1931- *WhoAm 92*
Dettmering, William O'Neal, Jr. 1948- *WhoEmL 93*
Dettore, Raymond James 1943- *St&PR 93*
Detuno, Joseph Edward 1931- *WhoAm 92*
De Turk, Frederick Walter 1928- *WhoAm 92*
DeTurk, Pamela Elizabeth 1946- *WhoEmL 93*
De Turner, Clorinda Matto 1852-1909 *BioIn 17*
Detweiler, David Kenneth 1919- *WhoAm 92, WhoE 93*
Detweiler, Donald 1947- *St&PR 93*
Detweiler, Mearde David 1920- *St&PR 93*
Detweiler, Robert Chester 1938- *WhoAm 92*
Detwiler, David Alan 1950- *WhoE 93*
Detwiler, Donald Scaife 1933- *WhoWor 93*
Detwiler, George E. *St&PR 93*
Detwiler, Harold E. 1930- *WhoIns 93*
Detwiler, Nancy Baird 1941- *WhoAmW 93*
Detwiler, Paul I., Jr. 1933- *St&PR 93*
Detwiler, Peter M. 1928- *St&PR 93*
Detwiler, Peter Mead 1928- *WhoAm 92*
Detwiler, Ralph Paul 1955- *WhoEmL 93*
Detwiler, Susan Margaret 1953- *WhoEmL 93*
Detz, Joan Marie 1951- *WhoWrEP 92*
Deuble, John H. 1930- *WhoIns 93*
Deuble, Stephen G. 1947- *St&PR 93*
Deubler, Donald L. 1946- *St&PR 93*
Deubner, Franz-Ludwig 1934- *WhoScE 91-3*
Deuchler, Philip George 1927- *WhoAm 92*
Deudon, Charles-Henri 1832-1914 *BioIn 17*
Deuel, Kenneth Harrington 1929- *WhoSSW 93*
Deuflhard, Peter *WhoScE 91-3*
D'Eugenio, David P. 1957- *WhoEmL 93*
Deuker, Carl *ScF&FL 92*
Deukmejian, George 1928- *WhoAm 92, WhoWor 93*
De Ulloa, Francisco Noguerol 16th cent.- *BioIn 17*
Deumlich, Reinhard 1940- *WhoWor 93*
Deupree, Marvin Mattox 1917- *St&PR 93, WhoAm 92*
Deupree, Michael Harold 1946- *WhoEmL 93*
Deupree, Ralph Todd 1958- *WhoSSW 93*
DeuPree, Robert Marshall 1912- *WhoWor 93*
Deur, Lynne A. 1941- *WhoWrEP 92*
Deuring, Stuart R. *Law&B 92*
Deuschle, Kurt Walter 1923- *WhoAm 92*
Deuschle, Mark John 1959- *St&PR 93*
Deuse, Jochen *Law&B 92*
Deuser, Charles William, II *Law&B 92*
Deuss, Jean *WhoAm 92, WhoAmW 93*
Deutch, Howard *MiSFD 9*
Deutch, Howard E. *Law&B 92*
Deutch, John Mark 1938- *WhoAm 92*
Deutchman, Ira J. 1953- *St&PR 93*
Deutekom, Cristina 1932- *Baker 92*
Deutman, August F. 1939- *WhoScE 91-3*
Deutsch, Armand 1913- *BioIn 17*
Deutsch, Barry E. *Law&B 92*
Deutsch, Claude David 1936- *WhoWor 93*
Deutsch, Cynthia Jane 1946- *WhoEmL 93*
Deutsch, David 1952- *WhoEmL 93*
Deutsch, Diana 1938- *Baker 92*
Deutsch, Edward J. 1922- *St&PR 93*
Deutsch, Emanuel 1829-1873 *BioIn 17*
Deutsch, Ernst 1883?-1938 *BioIn 17*
Deutsch, Florence Elayne Goodill 1923- *WhoAmW 93*
Deutsch, Helen d1992 *NewYTBS 92*
Deutsch, Helen 1906-1992 *BioIn 17, ConAu 137*
Deutsch, Helene 1884-1982 *BioIn 17*
Deutsch, Howard Jay 1946- *WhoE 93*
Deutsch, Hunting Folger 1952- *St&PR 93*
Deutsch, James Bernard 1948- *WhoAm 92, WhoEmL 93*
Deutsch, Jeremy J. *Law&B 92*
Deutsch, John Ludwig 1938- *WhoE 93*
Deutsch, Judith 1929- *WhoE 93*
Deutsch, Judith Sharon 1953- *WhoEmL 93*
Deutsch, Judith Sloan 1947- *WhoAm 92*
Deutsch, Karl W. d1992 *NewYTBS 92*
Deutsch, Karl W(olfgang) 1912-1992 *ConAu 139*
Deutsch, Karl Wolfgang 1912- *WhoAm 92*
Deutsch, Lee Kevin *Law&B 92*
Deutsch, Marshall Emanuel 1921- *WhoAm 92, WhoE 93*
Deutsch, Martin Bernard Joseph 1931- *WhoAm 92*
Deutsch, Max 1892-1982 *Baker 92*
Deutsch, Norman 1927- *WhoE 93*
Deutsch, Otto Erich 1883-1967 *Baker 92*
Deutsch, Randolph W. *Law&B 92*
Deutsch, Reinhard Erich 1936- *WhoWor 93*
Deutsch, Robert V. 1959- *WhoIns 93*
Deutsch, Robert William 1924- *WhoAm 92*
Deutsch, Sarah B. *Law&B 92*
Deutsch, Sid 1918- *WhoAm 92*
Deutsch, Stanley 1930- *WhoAm 92, WhoE 93*
Deutsch, Thomas Alan 1954- *WhoEmL 93*
Deutsch, Thomas Frederick 1932- *WhoAm 92*
Deutsch, William Emil 1926- *WhoAm 92*
Deutscher, Allan 1940- *St&PR 93*
Deutscher, Rebecca Ann 1954- *St&PR 93*
Deutscher, Tamara d1990 *BioIn 17*
Deutschman, Deborah *ScF&FL 92*
Deutz, Natalie Rubinstein *WhoAmW 93*
Deux-Ponts, Christian de Forbach, Count of 1752-1813 *HarEnMi*
Dev, Santosh Mohan 1934- *WhoAsAP 91*
Dev, Vasu 1933- *WhoAm 92*
Devai, Gyorgy 1942- *WhoScE 91-4*
Devajee, Ved *WhoCanL 92*
De Valdes Leal, Juan 1622-1690 *BioIn 17*
De Valera, Eamon 1882-1975 *DcTwHis*
De Valera, Eamonn 1882-1975 *BioIn 17*
De Valincour, Jean Baptiste Henri du Trousset 1653-1730 *BioIn 17*
Devall, Richard Alvin 1947- *WhoSSW 93*
de Valois, Geoffrey Herrick 1954- *WhoEmL 93*
De Valpine, Jean England 1921- *St&PR 93*
Devan, Margaret Brice 1929- *WhoAmW 93*
Devanand, Davangere Prahalad 1955- *WhoE 93, WhoEmL 93*
Devane, Denis James 1938- *WhoAm 92, WhoSSW 93*
Devane, Milton Phillips 1929- *St&PR 93*
Devane, William 1939- *WhoAm 92*
DeVaney, Cynthia Ann 1947- *WhoAmW 93*
Devaney, Dominic Joseph 1939- *St&PR 93*
Devaney, Everett M. 1948- *WhoAm 92*
Devaney, John Francis 1946- *WhoAm 92*
Devaney, Michelle Cobb 1963- *WhoEmL 93*
Devaney, Robert James, Jr. 1942- *WhoWor 93*
Devanney, Joseph J. *Law&B 92*
Devanney, Kevin A. *Law&B 92*
Devanney, William T., Jr. 1955- *St&PR 93*
Devanny, Louise Bell 1939- *WhoEmL 93*
Devant, David 1868-1941 *BioIn 17*
Devantier, Paul W. 1946- *WhoAm 92*
Devarajan, B. 1936- *WhoAsAP 91*
Devard-Kemp, Jean *AfrAmBi*
De Vargas, Luis 1505-1557 *BioIn 17*
De Vargas, Pedro *BioIn 17*
DeVaris, Jeannette Mary 1947- *WhoAm 92, WhoAmW 93, WhoEmL 93*
De Varis, Panayotis Eric 1932- *WhoAm 92*
de Varon, Lorna Cooke 1921- *WhoAm 92*
De Varona, Donna *BioIn 17*
De Varona, Esperanza Bravo 1929- *WhoSSW 93*
de Varona, Manuel Antonio 1908-1992 *NewYTBS 92*
DeVarso, James F. *Law&B 92*
DeVarso, James F. 1948- *St&PR 93, WhoIns 93*
de Vasconcelos, Luiz 1945- *WhoWor 93*
De Vauban, Sebastien Le Prestre 1633-1707 *BioIn 17*
de Vaucouleurs, Gerard Henri 1918- *WhoAm 92*
Devaud, Judith Anne 1943- *WhoAmW 93*
DeVaughn, Christopher Michael 1966- *WhoSSW 93*
De Vaughn, Deborah A. 1955- *WhoEmL 93*
De Vaul, Richard Allan 1940- *WhoAm 92*
Devault, David V. 1954- *St&PR 93*
De Vault, George H. 1907- *St&PR 93*
De Vault, Sharon L. *Law&B 92*
De Vault, Virgil Thomas 1901- *WhoAm 92*
DeVault, William Leonard 1950- *WhoSSW 93*
de Vaux, Peter Fordney 1944- *WhoAm 92*
Devcic, Natko 1914- *Baker 92*
Deve, Claire *BioIn 17*
Deveau, Jack Thomas 1927- *St&PR 93*
Deveau, Nancy Louise Walsh 1944- *WhoAmW 93*
Deveaux, Alexis 1948- *BlkAull 92*
DeVeaux, Dawn Della 1962- *WhoAmW 93*
Devecchi, Juan-Luis 1932- *WhoUN 92*
Deveen, John *Law&B 92*
De Veer, J. *WhoScE 91-3*
Deveer, Robert K. 1946- *St&PR 93*
deVeer, Robert K., Jr. 1946- *WhoAm 92, WhoE 93, WhoEmL 93*
De Vegt, Christian 1936- *WhoScE 91-3*
Devejian, Albert G. 1929- *St&PR 93*
De Vekey, Robert Claude *WhoScE 91-1*
De Velasco, Maria Mercedes 1949- *WhoE 93*
Devell, Lennart *WhoScE 91-4*
Devellano, James Charles 1943- *WhoAm 92*
Devellis, Raymond J. *Law&B 92*
Devendorf, David S. 1935- *St&PR 93*
Devendorf, Don *BioIn 17*
De Venecia, Jose C., Jr. 1936- *WhoAsAP 91*
Deveney, John L. 1921- *St&PR 93*
Deveney, Marie Regina 1951- *WhoAmW 93*
Devening, R. Randolph 1942- *St&PR 93*
Devening, Robert Randolph 1942- *WhoAm 92*
Devenish, Ross *MiSFD 9*
DeVenny, Lillian Nickell *WhoSSW 93*
Devenport, Emily *ScF&FL 92*
Devenport, Roger J. 1919- *WhoAm 92*
Devens, Paul 1931- *WhoAm 92*
Deveny, Thomas A., III *Law&B 92*
De Venzio, Huck 1947- *WhoEmL 93*
Dever, James A. 1911- *St&PR 93*
Dever, James L. 1927- *St&PR 93*
Dever, Jeffrey Lloyd 1953- *WhoEmL 93*
Dever, Joe 1956- *ScF&FL 92*
Dever, William Emmett 1862-1929 *BioIn 17*
De Vera Fernandez, Manuel Ignacio 1949- *WhoEmL 93*
Deveraux, Jude *ScF&FL 92*
De Verdier, Carl-Henric A.D. 1924- *WhoScE 91-4*
De Vere, Mary Ainge *AmWomPl*

de Vere, V.C. 1931- *ScF&FL 92*
Devereaux, J. Peter 1956- *WhoEmL 93*
Devereaux, James Oliver 1927- *St&PR 93*
Devereaux, Marilyn 1941- *St&PR 93*
Devereaux, Wanda Davis 1946- *WhoAmW 93, WhoEmL 93*
Deverell, Rex 1941- *WhoCanL 92*
Deverell, William H. 1937- *WhoCanL 92*
Devereux, Frances *WhoAm 92*
Devereux, James P. 1903- *HarEnMi*
Devereux, John Robert 1946- *WhoAsAP 91*
Devereux, Lane Gustafson 1950- *WhoAmW 93*
Devereux, Lawrence Hackett 1929- *WhoAm 92*
Devereux, Mark Jonathan 1956- *WhoWor 93*
Devereux, Mary d1914 *AmWomPl*
Devereux, Owen Francis 1937- *WhoAm 92, WhoE 93*
Devereux, Richard Blyton 1945- *WhoE 93*
Devereux, Timothy Edward 1932- *St&PR 93, WhoAm 92*
Deverka, Louis T. 1932- *St&PR 93*
De Vernal, Francois 1933- *WhoCanL 92*
Devers, Darryl Trimble 1955- *WhoEmL 93*
Devers, Gail *WhoAmW 93*
Devers, Jacob Loucks 1887-1979 *HarEnMi*
Devers, Peter Dix *Law&B 92*
DeVerter, Elizabeth Scott *Law&B 92*
Devery, Kieran M. 1937- *St&PR 93*
Deveshwar, Yogesh Chander 1947- *WhoWor 93*
Devesi, Baddeley 1941- *WhoAsAP 91, WhoWor 93*
de Vet, Charles V. 1911- *ScF&FL 92*
DeVette, John Ben 1957- *WhoWor 93*
Deveughele, Michel 1948- *WhoScE 91-2*
Devi, Lal 1914- *WhoAsAP 91*
Devi, Ramadhar 1937- *WhoUN 92*
Devide, Zvonimir 1921- *WhoScE 91-4*
De Vido, Alfredo Eduardo 1932- *WhoAm 92*
Devienne, Francois 1759-1803 *Baker 92*
Devigne, Karen Cooke 1943- *WhoAmW 93, WhoSSW 93, WhoWor 93*
DeVilbiss, Jonathan Frederick 1961- *WhoSSW 93*
De Villa, Renato S. 1935- *WhoWor 93*
De Ville, Chris Moore 1956- *WhoSSW 93*
Deville, Michel 1931- *MiSFD 9*
DeVille, Paul Vincent 1908- *St&PR 93*
deVille, Vicki Lynne 1950- *WhoEmL 93*
De Villedieu, Madame d1683 *BioIn 17*
de Villenfagne de Vogelsanck, Jean 1949- *WhoWor 93*
Devillers, Michel Maurice 1958- *WhoWor 93*
Devillers, Raymond Edmond R. 1945- *WhoScE 91-2*
DeVillier, Guy Joseph 1966- *WhoSSW 93*
de Villiers, Henri Paul 1925- *WhoWor 93*
de Villiers, Nelson Adalberto 1949- *WhoAm 92*
Devin, Edward J. 1937- *St&PR 93*
Devin, Flanna *ScF&FL 92*
Devin, John J. *St&PR 93*
Devin, Lee 1938- *WhoAm 92*
Devinatz, Allen 1922- *WhoAm 92*
De Vincenzo, Doris Kremsdorf 1923- *WhoE 93*
De Vincenzo, Richard Anthony 1947- *St&PR 93*
De Vinck, Jose M. 1912- *WhoWrEP 92*
Devine, Aubrey Alvin 1897-1981 *BiDAMSp 1989*
DeVine, B. Mack 1945- *WhoAm 92*
Devine, Brian Kiernan 1942- *WhoAm 92*
Devine, Charles Arthur 1965- *WhoE 93*
DeVine, Charles Donald 1943- *St&PR 93*
Devine, Charles Joseph, Jr. 1923- *WhoAm 92*
Devine, Charles V., Jr. 1948- *WhoEmL 93*
Devine, David F. 1929- *St&PR 93*
Devine, David Francis 1929- *WhoIns 93*
Devine, Don R. *Law&B 92*
Devine, Donald J. 1937- *WhoAm 92*
Devine, Donald R. 1941- *St&PR 93*
Devine, Donn 1929- *WhoE 93, WhoWor 93*
Devine, Earl L. *Law&B 92*
DeVine, Edmond Francis 1916- *WhoAm 92, WhoWor 93*
Devine, Elaine T. 1924- *St&PR 93*
Devine, (Mary) Elizabeth 1938- *ConAu 38NR*
Devine, Frank A. 1946- *St&PR 93*
Devine, Frank James 1922- *WhoSSW 93*
Devine, George J. *Law&B 92*
Devine, Grant 1944- *WhoAm 92*
Devine, Hugh James, Jr. 1938- *St&PR 93*
Devine, J. Martin *Law&B 92*
Devine, James F. *Law&B 92*
Devine, James Francis 1935- *WhoSSW 93*
Devine, James Joseph 1926- *WhoE 93*
Devine, James Richard 1948- *WhoEmL 93*
Devine, Janet *St&PR 93*
De Vine, John Bernard 1920- *WhoAm 92*
Devine, John M. 1944- *WhoAm 92*
Devine, John W. d1992 *NewYTBS 92*
Devine, John W. 1928-1992 *BioIn 17*
Devine, Joseph W. 1944- *St&PR 93*
Devine, Katherine 1951- *WhoAmW 93, WhoEmL 93, WhoWor 93*
Devine, Laura Faye 1947- *WhoSSW 93*
DeVine, Lawrence 1935- *WhoAm 92*
Devine, Loretta *ConTFT 10*
Devine, Michael Buxton 1953- *WhoEmL 93*
Devine, Michael Joseph 1952- *WhoEmL 93, WhoSSW 93*
Devine, Richard Kevin 1959- *WhoEmL 93, WhoSSW 93*
Devine, Richard William 1938- *St&PR 93*
Devine, Roderick Anthony Blunden 1944- *WhoWor 93*
Devine, Sean Fearon 1950- *St&PR 93*
Devine, Shane 1926- *WhoAm 92, WhoE 93*
Devine, Sharon Jean *Law&B 92*
Devine, T(homas) M(artin) 1945- *ConAu 136*
Devine, Thomas Edward *WhoAm 92*
Devine, Thomas Francis d1990 *BioIn 17*
Devine, Thomas Gerard 1928- *WhoE 93*
Devine, W. John 1940- *St&PR 93, WhoAm 92*
Devine, William Douglas 1962- *WhoEmL 93, WhoSSW 93*
Devine, William H. 1937- *St&PR 93*
Devine, Yolanda Jay 1962- *WhoSSW 93*
DeViney, Elizabeth Catherine 1943- *WhoAm 92, WhoAmW 93*
Deviney, Marvin Lee, Jr. 1929- *WhoAm 92, WhoSSW 93, WhoWor 93*
de Vink, Lodewijk J. R. 1945- *WhoAm 92*
Devinney, Timothy Michael 1956- *WhoEmL 93*
DeVino, James F. *Law&B 92*
Devino, William Stanley 1926- *WhoAm 92*
Devins, Robert Sylvester 1949- *WhoEmL 93*
DeVirgilio, Charles Joseph *Law&B 92*
De Viri, Anne *WhoWrEP 92*
DeVise, Pierre Romain 1924- *WhoAm 92*
de Visscher, Francois Marie 1953- *WhoE 93, WhoEmL 93, WhoWor 93*
De Vita, Joseph Stephen 1941- *St&PR 93, WhoIns 93*
De Vita, Sharon Louise 1950- *WhoWrEP 92*
DeVita, Vincent Theodore, Jr. 1935- *WhoAm 92*
DeVitis, Joseph Liberatore 1945- *WhoE 93*
DeVito, Albert Kenneth 1919- *WhoE 93*
De Vito, Danny *BioIn 17*
DeVito, Danny 1944- *MiSFD 9, QDrFCA 92 [port]*
Devito, Danny Michael 1944- *WhoAm 92*
DeVito, Donato Enrico 1955- *WhoE 93*
DeVito, Francis Joseph 1938- *WhoAm 92*
De Vito, Gioconda 1907- *Baker 92*
De Vito, Joseph Anthony 1938- *WhoWrEP 92*
DeVito, Karen Smith 1953- *WhoEmL 93*
DeVito, Karla *BioIn 17*
De Vito, Lodovico 1926- *WhoWor 93*
DeVito, Mathias J. 1930- *St&PR 93*
DeVito, Mathias Joseph 1930- *WhoAm 92, WhoE 93*
DeVito, Michael A. 1924- *WhoE 93*
DeVito, Michael John 1957- *St&PR 93*
DeVito, Paul Leonard 1953- *WhoE 93*
DeVito, Richard Anthony 1940- *WhoAm 92*
Devito, Robert A. 1937- *St&PR 93*
DeVito-Gross, Nancy 1951- *WhoAmW 93*
De Vitry D'Avaucourt, Arnaud 1926- *WhoWor 93*
Devitt, Craig Vincent 1943- *St&PR 93*
Devitt, Edward James 1911- *WhoAm 92*
de Vivies, Patrice Philippe 1952- *WhoE 93*
DeVivo, Ange 1925- *WhoAmW 93, WhoSSW 93, WhoWor 93*
De Vivo, Darryl Claude 1937- *WhoAm 92*
DeVivo, Sal J. 1937- *WhoAm 92*
De Vizia, Ann Marie Ruth 1945- *WhoE 93*
De Vlaminck, Maurice 1876-1958 *BioIn 17*
Devlesaver, Philippe Louis 1938- *WhoWor 93*
Devlieger, Louis F. *St&PR 93*
De Vlieger, Marinus 1920- *WhoScE 91-3*
Devlin, Anne 1778?-1851 *BioIn 17*
Devlin, Barbara Jo 1947- *WhoEmL 93*
Devlin, Barry Columba 1926- *WhoScE 91-3*
Devlin, Bernadette 1947- *BioIn 17*
Devlin, Cathy Crowell 1962- *WhoSSW 93*
Devlin, Diana (Mary) 1941- *ConAu 37NR*
Devlin, Dominick 1942- *WhoUN 92*
Devlin, Edward *BioIn 17*
Devlin, Elise Seibert 1954- *WhoE 93*
Devlin, Francis J. *Law&B 92*
Devlin, Francis James 1943- *WhoSSW 93*
Devlin, Gerald M. 1930- *WhoIns 93*
Devlin, Greg Martin 1950- *WhoEmL 93*
Devlin, Harry 1918- *ConAu 37NR, MajAI [port]*
Devlin, J.G. 1907-1991 *AnObit 1991*
Devlin, J. Richard 1950- *St&PR 93*
Devlin, James K. 1938- *St&PR 93*
Devlin, James Richard *Law&B 92*
Devlin, James Richard 1950- *WhoAm 92*
Devlin, Jean Theresa 1947- *WhoAmW 93, WhoWor 93*
Devlin, John Byrne 1951- *St&PR 93*
Devlin, Joseph 1871-1934 *BioIn 17*
Devlin, Joseph Aloysius 1932- *St&PR 93*
Devlin, Michael (Coles) 1942- *Baker 92, WhoAm 92*
Devlin, Michael Patrick 1950- *WhoEmL 93*
Devlin, Patrick Arthur d1992 *NewYTBS 92 [port]*
Devlin, Patrick (Arthur) 1905-1992 *ConAu 138*
Devlin, Paul Leo 1939- *WhoE 93*
Devlin, Ray 1926- *WhoAsAP 91*
Devlin, Robert 1947- *WhoUN 92*
Devlin, Robert Manning 1941- *St&PR 93, WhoAm 92*
Devlin, Robert Martin 1931- *WhoE 93*
Devlin, Terrence E. *Law&B 92*
Devlin, Thomas McKeown 1929- *WhoAm 92*
Devlin, Wende 1918- *ConAu 37NR*
Devlin, (Dorothy) Wende 1918- *MajAI [port]*
Devlin, Willard R. 1949- *St&PR 93*
Devney, Darcy C(ampion) 1960- *ConAu 138*
Devney, John Leo 1938- *WhoAm 92*
De Vocht, Lodewijk 1887-1977 *Baker 92*
Devoe, Chuck 1943- *WhoSSW 93*
De Voe, David R. *Law&B 92*
Devoe, James Kent 1937- *St&PR 93, WhoAm 92*
DeVoe, Joanne McMahon 1943- *WhoE 93*
DeVogt, John Frederick 1930- *WhoAm 92*
Devoid, Katharine Bancroft *Law&B 92*
Devol, Kenneth Stowe 1929- *WhoAm 92*
DeVol, Luana 1942- *WhoWor 93*
DeVon, Albert J., Jr. 1947- *WhoIns 93*
Devon, Gary *ScF&FL 92*
Devon, Richard 1931- *BioIn 17*
Devon, Wesley S., Jr. 1961- *St&PR 93*
Devon, Wesley Scott 1939- *St&PR 93*
Devona, Thomas C. 1905- *St&PR 93*
Devons, Samuel 1914- *WhoAm 92*
Devons, Sonia 1974- *SmATA 72 [port]*
Devonshire, Duke of 1790-1858 *BioIn 17*
Devonshire, Duke of 1833-1908 *BioIn 17*
Devonshire, Alan Lee *WhoScE 91-1*
Devonshuk, Joseph Edward 1955- *WhoEmL 93*
De Voogd, Nicolaas 1939- *WhoScE 91-3*
DeVore, Carl Brent 1940- *WhoAm 92*
DeVore, Daun Aline 1955- *WhoEmL 93*
DeVore, Gilbert 1918- *St&PR 93*
DeVore, Howard 1925- *ScF&FL 92*
Devore, Hugh d1992 *NewYTBS 92*
Devore, John Edwin 1940- *St&PR 93*
DeVore, Jon Eugene 1945- *WhoSSW 93*
De Vore, Mary Alice 1940- *WhoWrEP 92*
DeVore, Paul Cameron 1932- *WhoAm 92*
De Vore, Paul Warren 1926- *WhoAm 92*
De Vore, Sheryl Lynn 1956- *WhoWrEP 92*
DeVore, William D. 1936- *St&PR 93*
Devorkin, Joseph d1990 *BioIn 17*
de Vos, Luk *ScF&FL 92*
Devos, Paul 1943- *WhoScE 91-2*
de Vos, Peter Jon 1938- *WhoAm 92, WhoWor 93*
Devos, Pierre E.M.B. 1941- *WhoScE 91-2*
DeVos, Richard M. 1926- *BioIn 17, St&PR 93*
DeVos, Richard Marvin 1926- *WhoAm 92*
DeVos, Richard Marvin, Jr. 1955- *WhoAm 92*
DeVoss, James Thomas 1916- *WhoAm 92*
de Vos van Steenwijk, Alwine Antoinette 1921- *WhoUN 92*
Devoto, Howard c. 1957- *See* Buzzcocks, The *ConMus 9*
DeVoto, Mark (Bernard) 1940- *Baker 92*
De Voto, Richard H. 1934- *St&PR 93*
Devoto, W. Wesley 1949- *St&PR 93*
Devoy, John 1842-1928 *JrnUS*
Devreese, Frederic 1929- *Baker 92*
Devreese, Godefroid 1893-1972 *Baker 92*
Devreese, Jozef T. 1937- *WhoScE 91-2*
Devreotes, Peter Nicholas 1948- *WhoE 93*
Devrient, Eduard 1801-1877 *OxDcOp*
Devrient, Eduard (Philipp) 1801-1877 *Baker 92*
De Vries, Ben H. 1936- *St&PR 93*
DeVries, Beverly Mae 1935- *WhoAmW 93*
De Vries, C. 1924- *WhoScE 91-3*
deVries, David *MiSFD 9*
Devries, David 1881-1934 *OxDcOp*
DeVries, Ellen Jan 1931- *WhoWor 93*
Devries, Fides 1850-1941? *OxDcOp*
DeVries, Glenn Fredrick 1952- *WhoEmL 93*
De Vries, Hans W. 1944- *WhoScE 91-3*
Devries, Hermann 1858-1949 *OxDcOp*
DeVries, J.D. 1936- *St&PR 93*
de Vries, Jacobus E. 1934- *WhoAm 92, WhoE 93, WhoWor 93*
De Vries, Jacques Alexandre 1952- *St&PR 93*
Devries, James H. *Law&B 92*
Devries, James Howard 1932- *St&PR 93*
De Vries, Jan E. 1944- *WhoScE 91-2*
Devries, Jeanne c. 1849- *OxDcOp*
DeVries, Joe E.R. *St&PR 93*
DeVries, John d1992 *NewYTBS 92*
De Vries, John 1915-1992 *BioIn 17*
De Vries, Kenneth Lawrence 1933- *WhoAm 92*
de Vries, Lois Jean 1946- *WhoEmL 93*
de Vries, Margaret Garritsen 1922- *WhoAm 92*
DeVries, Marvin Frank 1937- *WhoAm 92*
DeVries, Mary Elaine 1950- *WhoAmW 93*
Devries, Maurice 1854-1919 *OxDcOp*
deVries, Nicholas 1953- *WhoEmL 93*
De Vries, Peter *BioIn 17*
De Vries, Peter 1910- *WhoAm 92, WhoWrEP 92*
De Vries, Peter J.M. 1941- *St&PR 93*
De Vries, Peter Michael Johannes Maria 1962- *WhoWor 93*
DeVries, Raymond E., Jr. *St&PR 93*
De Vries, Rene R.P. 1946- *WhoWor 93*
de Vries, Rimmer 1929- *WhoAm 92*
DeVries, Robert Charles 1922- *WhoE 93*
Devries, Robert K. *Law&B 92*
DeVries, Robert K. 1932- *WhoAm 92*
de Vries, Rosa Van Os 1828-1889 *OxDcOp*
De Vries, Walter Dale 1929- *WhoSSW 93*
DeVries, William Castle 1943- *WhoAm 92*
Devriese, L.A. 1941- *WhoScE 91-2*
De Vries Reilingh, Oscar Gerard 1943- *WhoUN 92*
Devroe, Jan Raoul 1931- *WhoWor 93*
De Vroey, Charles J.A.H. 1937- *WhoScE 91-2*
Devroye, Theodore-Joseph 1804-1873 *Baker 92*
De Vuyst, A. *WhoScE 91-3*
Devyatykh, Grigory Grigorievich 1918- *WhoWor 93*
DeVylder, Edgar Paul, Jr. *Law&B 92*
DeVylder, Edgar Paul, Jr. 1945- *WhoE 93*
Dew, Cecil Coleman 1930- *St&PR 93*
Dew, Charles Burgess 1937- *WhoAm 92*
Dew, Donald F. 1924- *St&PR 93*
Dew, Hartwell Coleman 1953- *WhoIns 93*
Dew, Joan King 1932- *WhoWor 93*
Dew, Kathi Rattin 1950- *WhoEmL 93*
Dew, Linda Sue 1956- *WhoAmW 93*
Dew, Louise E. 1871- *AmWomPl*
Dew, Mary Amanda 1955- *WhoEmL 93*
Dew, Peter Michael *WhoScE 91-1*
Dew, William Waldo, Jr. 1935- *WhoAm 92*
Dewaal, Gary A. *Law&B 92*
De Waal, H. 1935- *WhoScE 91-3*
De Waal, Ian C. Smith 1950- *WhoE 93*
De Waal, K.J.A. *WhoScE 91-3*
De Waart, Edo 1941- *BioIn 17, WhoAm 92, WhoWor 93*
de Waart, Tina Jannette 1961- *WhoAmW 93*
De Wachter, Frans 1939- *WhoWor 93*
De Wachter, Rupert 1937- *WhoScE 91-2*
DeWaele, Richard M. *Law&B 92*
DeWalch, Donald P. 1933- *St&PR 93*
Dewald, Anna Lucille *WhoAmW 93*
DeWald, Ernest James 1946- *WhoSSW 93*
DeWald, Horace Albert 1922- *WhoE 93*
Dewald, Howard Dean 1958- *WhoEmL 93*
Dewald, John 1947- *St&PR 93*
Dewald, John Edward *Law&B 92*
DeWald, John Edward 1946- *WhoEmL 93*
Dewald, Maureen *Law&B 92*
Dewald, Paul Adolph 1920- *WhoAm 92*
De Waldner, Lulu *BioIn 17*
DeWall, Richard Allison 1926- *WhoAm 92*
De Walle, F.B. *WhoScE 91-3*
Dewalt, Mark Douglas 1951- *WhoEmL 93*
Dewan, Binoy Kumar 1925- *WhoAsAP 91*
Dewan, Mantosh Jaimani 1951- *WhoEmL 93*
Dewan, Margaret W. *Law&B 92*
Dewan, Shashi Bhushan 1941- *WhoAm 92*
De Wan-Carlson, Anna Theresa 1949- *WhoE 93*
De Wandeleer, Patrick Jules 1949- *WhoWor 93*
Dewane, John Richard 1934- *WhoWor 93*
Dewar, Alan M. *WhoScE 91-1*
Dewar, James McEwen 1943- *WhoWor 93*

Dewar, Michael James Steuart 1918- *WhoAm 92*
Dewar, Norman E. 1930- *St&PR 93*
Dewar, Norman Ellison 1930- *WhoAm 92*
de Warren, Robert *WhoWor 93*
Dewart, Edward Hartley 1828-1903 *BioIn 17*
Dewart, Gilbert 1932- *BioIn 17*
Dewa Shigeto 1856-1930 *HarEnMi*
DeWaters, Clarke 1931- *WhoIns 93*
De Waziers, Fernand 1954- *St&PR 93*
Dewberry, Betty Bauman 1930- *WhoAmW 93, WhoSSW 93*
Dewberry, Claire DeArment 1937- *WhoAmW 93*
Dewberry, J. Terry 1943- *St&PR 93*
Dewberry, James A. 1941- *St&PR 93*
Dewbre, J.W. *Law&B 92*
Dewbre, J.W. 1933- *WhoIns 93*
Dewdney, A.K. 1941- *ScF&FL 92*
Dewdney, Christopher 1951- *WhoCanL 92*
Dewdney, John Christopher *WhoScE 91-1*
Dewdney, Selwyn 1909-1979 *BioIn 17*
De Weck, Alain L. 1928- *WhoScE 91-4*
Deweerd, Terrence Bruce 1942- *St&PR 93*
De Weerdt, Jackie Lynn 1951- *St&PR 93*
Dewees, Cheryl *Law&B 92*
DeWees, Darwin Dallas 1940- *St&PR 93*
Dewees, Donald Charles 1931- *WhoAm 92, WhoE 93*
Dewees, John Garrett 1951- *St&PR 93*
Deweese, Charles William 1944- *WhoSSW 93*
DeWeese, Gene 1934- *ScF&FL 92*
DeWeese, James Arville 1925- *WhoAm 92, WhoE 93*
DeWeese, Jean *ScF&FL 92*
DeWeese, Marion Spencer 1915- *WhoAm 92*
DeWeese, Thomas E. *ScF&FL 92*
Dewell, Michael 1931- *WhoAm 92*
De Wendel, Francois 1874-1949 *BioIn 17*
Dewerdt, Francis 1937- *WhoScE 91-2*
DeWerth, Gordon Henry 1939- *WhoAm 92*
Dewese, Mohandas *BioIn 17*
De Westbrook, Cicero *WhoWrEP 92*
De Wet, Christiaan Rudolph 1854-1922 *HarEnMi*
de Wetter, Herman Peter 1920- *WhoAm 92*
De Wever, Alain 1946- *WhoScE 91-2*
Dewey, Adrian Christopher *Law&B 92*
Dewey, Anne Elizabeth Marie 1951- *WhoAmW 93, WhoEmL 93*
Dewey, Ariane 1937- *WhoWrEP 92*
Dewey, Barbara 1923- *WhoWrEP 92*
Dewey, Barbara Lynn 1947- *WhoEmL 93*
Dewey, Bradley, III 1943- *WhoAm 92*
Dewey, Clarence Forbes 1935- *WhoE 93*
Dewey, Craig Douglas 1950- *WhoWor 93*
Dewey, David Lawrence 1952- *WhoEmL 93*
Dewey, Donald Odell 1930- *WhoAm 92*
Dewey, Donald William 1933- *WhoAm 92, WhoWor 93, WhoWrEP 92*
Dewey, Edward Allen 1932- *WhoAm 92*
Dewey, Gene Lawrence 1938- *WhoAm 92*
Dewey, George 1837-1917 *GayN, HarEnMi*
Dewey, George W. 1923- *St&PR 93*
Dewey, Jane M. *Law&B 92*
Dewey, John 1859-1952 *BioIn 17, GayN*
Dewey, John Byron 1950- *WhoEmL 93*
Dewey, John F. 1937- *WhoWor 93*
Dewey, John Frederick *WhoScE 91-1*
Dewey, John Russell 1953- *WhoEmL 93*
Dewey, Joseph 1957- *ScF&FL 92*
Dewey, Linda Sue 1955- *WhoEmL 93*
Dewey, Martha *AmWomPl*
Dewey, Pat Parker 1923- *WhoAmW 93, WhoE 93, WhoSSW 93*
Dewey, Patrick R. 1949- *ScF&FL 92*
Dewey, Phelps 1928- *WhoAm 92*
Dewey, Robert J. 1935- *St&PR 93*
Dewey, Robert Manson, Jr. 1931- *WhoAm 92*
Dewey, Ronald L. 1939- *St&PR 93*
Dewey, Thomas E. 1902-1971 *PolPar*
Dewey, Thomas E. 1944- *St&PR 93*
Dewey, Thomas E., Jr. 1932- *St&PR 93*
Dewez, Brigitte M. *Law&B 92*
Dewhirst, Eric Charles 1951- *St&PR 93*
Dewhurst, Blanca Maria Peres 1944- *WhoAmW 93*
Dewhurst, Charles Kurt 1948- *WhoAm 92*
Dewhurst, Colleen *BioIn 17*
Dewhurst, Colleen 1924-1991 *News 92*
Dewhurst, Colleen 1926-1991 *AnObit 1991*
Dewhurst, David George *WhoScE 91-1*
Dewhurst, Francis *WhoScE 91-1*
Dewhurst, Peter *BioIn 17*
Dewhurst, Stephen B. 1942- *WhoAm 92*
Dewhurst, William George 1926- *WhoAm 92*
De Wied, David 1925- *WhoScE 91-3*
De Wilde, David Allen 1934- *St&PR 93*
deWilde, David Michael 1940- *WhoAm 92, WhoWor 93*
DeWilde, Dick *Law&B 92*
DeWind, Adrian William, Jr. 1943- *WhoE 93*
de Windt, Edward Mandell 1921- *WhoSSW 93*
DeWine, R. Michael 1947- *WhoAm 92*
Dewing, Merlin Eugene 1934- *WhoAm 92*
Dewing, Robert Thomas 1953- *WhoEmL 93*
DeWint, Christian 1771-1803 *BioIn 17*
DeWinter, Charles Mark 1941- *St&PR 93*
deWir, Harriet 1948- *WhoAm 92*
DeWire, Fred C. 1934- *St&PR 93*
DeWire, John W. 1916-1990 *BioIn 17*
De Wisdelaere, Chris *WhoScE 91-2*
De Wissoca, Francois *St&PR 93*
De Wit, Cornelis Teunis 1924- *WhoScE 91-3*
de Wit, Dirk G. 1938- *WhoUN 92*
deWit, Roland 1930- *WhoE 93*
De Wit, Willem 1948- *WhoScE 91-3*
De Witt, Bryce Seligman 1923- *WhoAm 92*
DeWitt, Calvin B. 1935- *ConAu 136*
DeWitt, Charles E., Jr. *Law&B 92*
DeWitt, Dennis Carroll 1945- *St&PR 93*
Dewitt, Diane Crume 1961- *WhoAmW 93*
DeWitt, Elizabeth Kathleen 1947- *WhoEmL 93*
De Witt, Eugene A. 1943- *WhoAm 92*
Dewitt, Frank J. 1929- *St&PR 93*
Dewitt, Harry Morton 1920- *WhoE 93, WhoWor 93*
Dewitt, John David 1943- *WhoSSW 93*
DeWitt, John Hibbett, Jr. 1906- *WhoAm 92*
DeWitt, Karen Lee 1963- *WhoAmW 93*
Dewitt, Katherine Louise 1948- *WhoEmL 93*
DeWitt, Kimber 1956- *WhoEmL 93*
DeWitt, Lew 1938-1990 *BioIn 17*
DeWitt, Lew C. 1938-1990 *See* Statler Brothers, The *ConMus 8*
Dewitt, Linda Ross 1951- *WhoEmL 93*
DeWitt, Mary Schiller 1948- *WhoAmW 93, WhoEmL 93*
DeWitt, Richard John, Jr. 1947- *WhoSSW 93*
Dewitt, Thomas H. *Law&B 92*
DeWitt, Thomas Jay 1947- *St&PR 93*
Dewitt, Walter Newton 1937- *St&PR 93*
De Witt, William Gerald 1937- *WhoAm 92*
De Witt-Morette, Cecile 1922- *WhoAm 92*
Dewitz, Jean Laura 1946- *WhoEmL 93*
Dewitz, Robert Donald 1934- *St&PR 93*
de Wolf, David Alter 1934- *WhoAm 92, WhoSSW 93*
DeWolf, John *Law&B 92*
DeWolf, Louise Henry *AmWomPl*
Dewolf, Ted 1946- *St&PR 93*
De Wolfe, Billy 1907-1974 *QDrFCA 92 [port]*
De Wolfe, Elsie 1865-1950 *BioIn 17*
Dewolfe, Gregory S. *Law&B 92*
DeWolfe, John Chauncey, Jr. 1913- *WhoAm 92*
de Wolff, Frederik Albert 1944- *WhoWor 93*
De Wolff, Louis 1929- *WhoSSW 93*
Dewolff, Maurice K. *Law&B 92*
Dewolff, Maurice Konrad 1941- *St&PR 93, WhoAm 92*
DeWoody, Barbara McKenna 1966- *WhoE 93*
Dewoskin, Irvin S. 1909- *St&PR 93*
De Wreede, Clarice Evans 1928- *WhoAmW 93*
Dews, Anne Wakefield 1943- *WhoSSW 93*
Dews, Peter Booth 1922- *WhoAm 92*
Dews, Stanley John *WhoScE 91-1*
Dewsbury, Donald Allen 1939- *WhoAm 92, WhoSSW 93*
Dewsnap, David Graham 1961- *WhoSSW 93*
Dewson, Mary W. 1874-1962 *PolPar*
De Wulf, Henri-Charles 1937- *WhoScE 91-2*
De Wulf, Kathryn Colleen 1959- *WhoWrEP 92*
DeWyer, Gary Alton 1940- *St&PR 93*
De Wyn Gaert, Laura Lane *WhoAmW 93, WhoE 93, WhoWor 93*
Dexheimer, John H. 1925- *St&PR 93*
Dexippus, Publius Herennius c. 210-276 *HarEnMi*
Dextar, Baron of 1934- *WhoWor 93*
Dexter, Anthony 1919- *BioIn 17*
Dexter, Carmen *ScF&FL 92*
Dexter, Catherine *ScF&FL 92*
Dexter, Charles Virgil 1940- *St&PR 93*
Dexter, Dallas-Lee 1950- *WhoAmW 93*
Dexter, Dean Joseph 1948- *WhoEmL 93*
Dexter, Deirdre O'Neil Elizabeth 1956- *WhoAmW 93, WhoEmL 93*
Dexter, Donald Harvey 1928- *WhoAm 92*
Dexter, Frederick Jay 1947- *WhoE 93*
Dexter, Helen Louise 1908- *WhoWor 93*
Dexter, Jerry D. (Hal Wayne) 1947- *WhoWrEP 92*
Dexter, Joan d1990 *BioIn 17*
Dexter, John 1925- *OxDcOp*
Dexter, John 1925-1990 *BioIn 17, ConTFT 10, IntDcOp*
Dexter, John 1935-1990 *MiSFD 9N*
Dexter, Lewis 1910- *WhoAm 92*
Dexter, Maury 1927- *MiSFD 9*
Dexter, Pete 1943- *BioIn 17*
Dexter, Peter Edward 1945- *WhoUN 92*
Dexter, Susan 1955- *ScF&FL 92*
Dexter, Theodore Henry 1923- *WhoAm 92*
Dey, Carol Ruth 1943- *WhoAmW 93*
Dey, Jeffrey R. *Law&B 92*
Dey, Joe 1907-1991 *BioIn 17*
Dey, Krishno 1944- *WhoUN 92*
Dey, Marlene Melchiorre 1952- *WhoE 93*
Dey, Richard Dennis 1948- *WhoEmL 93, WhoSSW 93*
Dey, Susan 1952- *WhoAm 92*
Deyal, Anthony Sookdeo 1945- *WhoWor 93*
Deyer, Kirk Donald 1947- *St&PR 93*
Deyo, Asta Nygren 1898-1953 *See* Deyo, Felix 1888-1959 *Baker 92*
Deyo, David D., Jr. 1962- *ScF&FL 92*
Deyo, Felix 1888-1959 *Baker 92*
Deyo, Mary Forster 1857-1947 *See* Deyo, Felix 1888-1959 *Baker 92*
Deyo, Russell Carter *Law&B 92*
Deyo, Ruth Lynda 1884-1960 *Baker 92*
Deyo, Steve 1949- *WhoEmL 93, WhoSSW 93*
Deyo, Steven Mark 1957- *WhoWrEP 92*
Deyo, Tanya Varie *Law&B 92*
Deyoe, Alan Maurice, Jr. 1927- *WhoAm 92*
Deyoe-Chiullan, Rita Maxine 1947- *WhoEmL 93, WhoSSW 93*
De Yong, Joe 1894-1975 *BioIn 17*
Deyoreo, Sal 1925- *St&PR 93*
DeYoung, Billie Schaefer 1936- *WhoSSW 93*
DeYoung, David Ralph 1945- *St&PR 93*
De Young, David Spencer 1940- *WhoAm 92*
De Young, E. Donald *St&PR 93*
DeYoung, E. Donald 1940- *WhoSSW 93*
DeYoung, Joel J. *Law&B 92*
de Young, M. H., Jr. 1849-1925 *JrnUS*
De Young, Stephen Paul 1953- *St&PR 93, WhoEmL 93*
Deyoung, Vince G. *Law&B 92*
DeYoung, Yvonne Marie 1951- *WhoAmW 93*
Deyrolle *WhoScE 91-2*
Deysher, Paul Evans 1923- *WhoE 93*
Deyton, Camilla Hill 1952- *WhoAmW 93*
de Zagon, Monique S. 1944- *WhoAmW 93*
De Zanger, Jan F. 1932-1991 *BioIn 17*
Dezede, Nicolas c. 1740-1792 *OxDcOp*
Dezede, Nicolas c. 1742-1792 *Baker 92*
De Zeeuw, A. *WhoScE 91-3*
De Zeeuw, Dick 1924- *WhoScE 91-3*
Dezelic, Gjuro 1935- *WhoScE 91-4*
Dezell, James E. 1933- *St&PR 93*
Dezell, James Elton, Jr. 1933- *WhoAm 92*
Dezern, Kay Langley 1945- *WhoSSW 93*
De Zespedes, Vicente Manuel *BioIn 17*
Dezhnev, Semyon Ivanovich 1605?-1673? *Expl 93*
DeZinno, Benjamin N. 1924-1992 *BioIn 17*
DeZinno, Benjamin N., Jr. d1992 *NewYTBS 92*
Dezort, Jacquelyn L. 1950- *St&PR 93*
Dezort, Jacquelyn Louise Link 1950- *WhoAm 92, WhoAmW 93*
De Zurbaran, Francisco 1598-1664 *BioIn 17*
Dezure, Thomas J. *Law&B 92*
De Zwirek, Phillip J. 1937- *St&PR 93*
Dezza, Paolo Cardinal 1901- *WhoWor 93*
D'Gabriel, Carlos Leonardo 1930- *WhoSSW 93, WhoWor 93*
Dgetluck, Nancy 1961- *WhoAmW 93*
D'Haene, Rafael 1943- *Baker 92*
D'Haeze, Thomas M. *St&PR 93*
Dhahab, Abu'l fl. c. 1772- *HarEnMi*
Dhainaut, Andre 1936- *WhoScE 91-2*
Dhakkar, Ahmed Botan 1935- *WhoUN 92*
D'Hallvin, Jean-Claude *WhoScE 91-2*
Dhamelincourt, Paul Andre 1944- *WhoScE 91-2*
Dhammarungruang, Jajjai 1949- *WhoWor 93*
Dhamo, Kristaq 1933- *DrEEuF*
Dhanabalan, Suppiah 1937- *WhoAsAP 91, WhoWor 93*
Dhanani, Alnoor H.K.J. 1955- *St&PR 93*
Dhanapala, Jayantha *WhoUN 92*
Dhanawardena, Attygala Dematanpitiya 1940- *WhoWor 93*
Dhandwar, Tarsem Singh *BioIn 17*
Dhanjal, Surjeet Singh 1923- *WhoSSW 93*
Dharam Pal 1934- *WhoAsAP 91*
Dharlo, Rinchen 1948- *WhoE 93*
D'Harnoncourt, Anne *BioIn 17, WhoAm 92, WhoE 93*
Dharsono, H.R. *BioIn 17*
Dhawan, Vivek 1961- *WhoWor 93*
Dhein, Richard *St&PR 93*
Dhein, Richard D. 1953- *WhoE 93*
Dhermy, Didier *WhoScE 91-2*
Dhesi, Autar Singh 1936- *WhoWor 93*
d'Heurle, Francois Max 1925- *WhoAm 92*
Dhillon, Harwant Singh 1929- *WhoUN 92*
Dhindsa, Ragwinder Kaur 1937- *WhoE 93*
Dhir, Krishna Swaroop 1944- *WhoSSW 93*
Dhiravamsa 1935- *BioIn 17*
D'Hoedt, Henri-Georges 1885-1936 *Baker 92*
Dhombres, J.G. 1942- *WhoScE 91-2*
Dhombres, Jean Guy 1942- *WhoWor 93*
Dhondt, Annie V.J. 1942- *WhoScE 91-2*
D'Hondt, Jean-Loup Lucien 1943- *WhoScE 91-2*
Dhondt, Steven Thomas 1944- *WhoE 93, WhoWor 93*
Dhondt, Urbain 1930- *WhoWor 93*
Dhondy, Farrukh *BioIn 17*
Dhondy, Farrukh 1944- *MajAI*
D'Hoore, Marc Johan 1940- *WhoWor 93*
Dho Young Shim 1949- *WhoAsAP 91*
Dhuey, John Anthony *Law&B 92*
Dhungel, Dwarika Nath 1945- *WhoWor 93*
Dhungel, Ishwor 1963- *WhoWor 93*
Dhu-Nuwas d525 *OxDcByz*
Dhusiya, Sohan Lal 1923- *WhoAsAP 91*
Diabatenos *OxDcByz*
Diabelli, Anton 1781-1858 *Baker 92*
Diaco, Michael Anthony 1953- *WhoEmL 93*
Diaconis, Persi W. 1945- *WhoAm 92*
Di Addezzio, Frederick John, Jr. 1947- *WhoEmL 93*
Diadochos c. 400-c. 486 *OxDcByz*
Diaghilev, Serge *OxDcOp*
Diaghilev, Serge 1872-1929 *BioIn 17*
Diaghilev, Sergei (Pavlovich) 1872-1929 *Baker 92*
Diagne, Blaise 1872-1932 *DcTwHis*
DiAiso, Robert Joseph 1940- *WhoAm 92, WhoE 93*
Dial, Denise Lorraine 1957- *WhoAmW 93*
Dial, Frederick Clark 1950- *St&PR 93*
Dial, Jack Grady 1947- *WhoSSW 93*
Dial, Michael Curtis 1941- *St&PR 93*
Dial, Nathaniel Victor 1938- *WhoWor 93*
Dial, Oliver Eugene 1922- *WhoAm 92*
Dial, Ronald Owen 1950- *WhoEmL 93*
Dial, Teresa A. *BioIn 17, St&PR 93*
Dial, Vic *BioIn 17*
Dial, William Henry 1907- *WhoAm 92*
Dialdriver, Emily *WhoSSW 93*
Dialer, Kurt R. 1920- *WhoScE 91-3*
Dialer, Kurt Rudolf 1920- *WhoWor 93*
Diallo, Abdoul Aziz 1953- *WhoWor 93*
Diallo, Abdourahmane *WhoWor 93*
Diallo, Aliou M. 1939- *WhoUN 92*
Diallo, Djibril 1953- *WhoUN 92*
Diallo, Hama Arba 1939- *WhoUN 92*
Diallo, Hamidou Hassane *WhoWor 93*
Diallo, Harouna Matienga 1944- *WhoUN 92*
Diallo, Issa *WhoUN 92*
Diallo, Youssoupha 1938- *WhoUN 92*
Diaman, N.A. 1936- *ScF&FL 92, WhoWrEP 92*
Diamand, Peter 1913- *OxDcOp*
Diamandis, Peter G. 1931- *WhoAm 92*
Diamandis, Stephanos 1947- *WhoScE 91-3*
Diamandopoulos, Peter 1928- *WhoAm 92, WhoWor 93*
Diamant, Alfred 1917- *WhoAm 92*
Diamant, Anita *WhoAm 92*
Diamant, Barbara Greenstein 1932- *WhoAm 92*
Diamant, Bertil 1930- *WhoScE 91-2*
Diamant, Gregory Eric 1949- *WhoEmL 93*
Diamant, Michael Harlan 1946- *WhoEmL 93*
Diamante, John Matthew 1940- *WhoE 93*
Diamond, Abel Joseph 1932- *WhoAm 92, WhoWor 93*
Diamond, Adele Dorothy 1952- *WhoAmW 93*
Diamond, Alisa R. 1962- *St&PR 93*
Diamond, Alisa Robin 1962- *WhoEmL 93*
Diamond, Ann Berkman 1951- *WhoEmL 93*
Diamond, Ann Cynthia 1947- *WhoEmL 93*
Diamond, Arthur Mansfield, Jr. 1953- *WhoEmL 93*
Diamond, Bernard L. 1912-1990 *BioIn 17*
Diamond, Bruce Irwin 1945- *WhoSSW 93*
Diamond, Christopher Shaun 1946- *St&PR 93*

Diamond, Cora Ann 1937- *WhoAm 92*
Diamond, David A. 1955- *St&PR 93*
Diamond, David Joseph 1940- *WhoE 93*
Diamond, David (Leo) 1915- *Baker 92, WhoAm 92*
Diamond, Deborah Lynn 1950- *WhoAmW 93*
Diamond, Diana Louise 1937- *WhoWor 93*
Diamond, Donna 1950- *MajAI [port], SmATA 69 [port]*
Diamond, Donna Gail *Law&B 92*
Diamond, Edward Jay 1948- *WhoE 93*
Diamond, Elayne Fern 1945- *WhoE 93*
Diamond, Elliot 1952- *WhoE 93*
Diamond, Elyse *WhoWrEP 92*
Diamond, Eugene Christopher 1952- *WhoEmL 93*
Diamond, Fred I. 1925- *WhoAm 92*
Diamond, Freda *WhoAm 92*
Diamond, G. William 1945- *WhoAm 92, WhoE 93*
Diamond, George A. 1923-1991 *BioIn 17*
Diamond, Graham 1945- *ScF&FL 92*
Diamond, Gustave 1928- *WhoAm 92, WhoE 93*
Diamond, Harley David 1959- *WhoEmL 93*
Diamond, Harold Fred 1960- *St&PR 93*
Diamond, Harvey Jerome 1928- *WhoSSW 93, WhoWor 93*
Diamond, Herbert S. 1938- *WhoE 93*
Diamond, Hindi 1934- *WhoAmW 93*
Diamond, Howard 1941- *St&PR 93*
Diamond, Irene 1910- *WhoAm 92*
Diamond, Irving T. *WhoAm 92*
Diamond, Irwin 1923- *St&PR 93*
Diamond, Isadore 1918- *St&PR 93*
Diamond, Jacqueline *ScF&FL 92*
Diamond, James Edward, Jr. 1946- *WhoAm 92*
Diamond, James R. 1945- *St&PR 93*
Diamond, James William 1939- *St&PR 93*
Diamond, Jane Sydney 1952- *WhoEmL 93*
Diamond, Jared Mason 1937- *WhoAm 92*
Diamond, Jay Harrison 1951- *WhoEmL 93*
Diamond, Jeffrey Brian 1950- *WhoEmL 93*
Diamond, John P. 1936- *St&PR 93*
Diamond, Joni Lynn 1956- *WhoWor 93*
Diamond, Josef 1907- *St&PR 93*
Diamond, Kim S. 1965- *St&PR 93*
Diamond, Lee Gregory 1946- *WhoEmL 93*
Diamond, Leonard 1927- *St&PR 93*
Diamond, M. Jerome 1942- *WhoAm 92*
Diamond, Malcolm Luria 1924- *WhoAm 92*
Diamond, Manuelle Suzanne 1939- *WhoUN 92*
Diamond, Marc 1944- *WhoCanL 92*
Diamond, Maria Sophia 1958- *WhoEmL 93*
Diamond, Marian Cleeves *BioIn 17*
Diamond, Marian Cleeves 1926- *WhoAm 92*
Diamond, Mark *Law&B 92*
Diamond, Matthew Philip 1951- *WhoAm 92*
Diamond, Mike c. 1966- See Beastie Boys, The *ConMus 8*
Diamond, Neil (Leslie) 1941- *Baker 92, WhoAm 92*
Diamond, Norman 1914- *WhoAm 92*
Diamond, Olivia Harriet 1947- *WhoWrEP 92*
Diamond, Pamela Ann 1963- *WhoEmL 93*
Diamond, Pamela Shaffer 1948- *WhoE 93*
Diamond, Paul 1933- *WhoUN 92*
Diamond, Paul Steven 1953- *WhoEmL 93*
Diamond, Philip Ernest 1925- *WhoAm 92*
Diamond, Richard John 1941- *St&PR 93, WhoAm 92*
Diamond, Richard Scott 1960- *WhoE 93, WhoWor 93*
Diamond, Robert Francis 1951- *WhoEmL 93*
Diamond, Robert Jocke 1950- *WhoEmL 93*
Diamond, Robert S. 1939- *St&PR 93*
Diamond, Robert Stephen 1939- *WhoAm 92*
Diamond, Russell W. 1956- *St&PR 93*
Diamond, Sander 1942- *ScF&FL 92*
Diamond, Seymour 1925- *WhoAm 92*
Diamond, Shari Seidman 1947- *WhoEmL 93*
Diamond, Sidney 1929- *WhoAm 92*
Diamond, Sidney R. d1992 *BioIn 17, NewYTBS 92*
Diamond, Sigmund 1920- *WhoAm 92*
Diamond, Stanley *BioIn 17*
Diamond, Stanley Jay 1927- *WhoAm 92*
Diamond, Stuart *BioIn 17*
Diamond, Stuart 1948- *WhoAm 92*
Diamond, Susan Zee 1949- *WhoAmW 93*
Diamond, Suzanne Barbara 1941- *WhoE 93*
Diamond, William J. 1937- *WhoAm 92*
Diamond Marc, J. 1960- *WhoIns 93*
Diamondstein, Nelson Lee 1950- *WhoEmL 93*
Diamondstone, Lawrence 1928- *St&PR 93, WhoE 93, WhoWor 93*
Diamonstein, Arthur A. 1930- *St&PR 93*
Diamonstein, Richard Gartner 1957- *St&PR 93*
Diamonstein-Spielvogel, Barbaralee *WhoAm 92*
Diana, Princess 1961- *WhoWor 93*
Diana, Princess of Wales 1961- *BioIn 17, News 93-1 [port]*
DiAna, DiAna *BioIn 17*
Diana, John Nicholas 1930- *WhoAm 92, WhoWor 93*
Diana, Joseph A. 1924- *WhoAm 92*
Diana, Ronald S. *Law&B 92*
Dianalan, Nhazrudin Dimakuta *WhoWor 93*
Dianalan, Omar M. 1931- *WhoAsAP 91*
Dianda, Hilda 1925- *Baker 92*
Diangi, Carmella 1920- *St&PR 93*
Diani, Elaine S. *Law&B 92*
Dianich, Michael B., Sr. 1942- *St&PR 93*
Dianin, Sergei 1888-1968 *Baker 92*
Dianis, Walter Joseph 1918- *WhoAm 92*
Dianiska, G.P. 1938- *St&PR 93*
Dianov, Anton 1882-1939 *Baker 92*
Dianzani, Mario Umberto 1925- *WhoScE 91-3*
Diaper, John *ScF&FL 92*
Diar, Prakash 1956- *ConAu 137*
Diare, Youssouf 1940- *WhoUN 92*
Dias, Bartolomeu 1450?-1500 *Expl 93 [port]*
Dias, Ron 1937- *SmATA 71 [port]*
Diasparra, Frank *BioIn 17*
Diassi, Patrick A. 1926- *St&PR 93*
Diaz, A. Michel 1945- *WhoWor 93*
Diaz, Adolfo *DcCPCAm*
Diaz, Agustin *DcCPCAm*
Diaz, Agustin 1936- *St&PR 93*
Diaz, Alberto 1942- *WhoWor 93*
Diaz, Alek 1944- *WhoAm 92*
Diaz, Antonio Rufino 1935- *St&PR 93*
Diaz, Armando 1861-1928 *HarEnMi*
Diaz, Clifton Stanley 1949- *WhoE 93*
Diaz (de la Pena), Eugene (-Emile) 1837-1901 *Baker 92*
Diaz, Domingo *DcCPCAm*
Diaz, Enrique *DcCPCAm*
Diaz, Enrique Perez 1939- *WhoWor 93*
Diaz, Fernando Gustavo 1946- *WhoEmL 93, WhoWor 93*
Diaz, Frank Edward 1942- *St&PR 93*
Diaz, Gerald Joseph, Jr. 1952- *WhoEmL 93*
Diaz, Gonzalo *BioIn 17*
Diaz, H. Joseph 1930- *St&PR 93*
Diaz, Henry Frank 1948- *HispAmA*
Diaz, Jean Michael 1949- *WhoE 93*
Diaz, Jesus 1941- *SpAmA*
Diaz, Jose Aspillera 1941- *WhoWor 93*
Diaz, Jose-Luis 1943- *WhoWor 93*
Diaz, Jose Pedro 1921- *SpAmA*
Diaz, Joseph 1950- *WhoScE 91-3*
Diaz, Justino 1940- *Baker 92, WhoAm 92*
Diaz, Luis Florentino 1946- *WhoEmL 93*
Diaz, Mauricio *DcCPCAm*
Diaz, Michael Harlan 1966- *WhoE 93*
Diaz, Michel 1945- *WhoScE 91-2*
Diaz, Nils Juan 1938- *WhoWor 93*
Diaz, Orfelina Rosa 1962- *WhoE 93*
Diaz, Pedro J. 1937- *WhoIns 93*
Diaz, Porfirio *DcCPCAm*
Diaz, Rafael Octavio 1949- *WhoSSW 93*
Diaz, Raisa Evangelina 1949- *WhoWor 93*
Diaz, Ramon Valero 1918- *WhoAm 92*
Diaz, Raul 1957- *WhoSSW 93*
Diaz, Rene Michel 1961- *WhoEmL 93*
Diaz, Robert Edward 1945- *WhoSSW 93*
Diaz, Roberto *DcCPCAm*
Diaz, Roberto 1951- *WhoSSW 93*
Diaz, Sharon 1946- *WhoAmW 93, WhoEmL 93*
Diaz, William Adams 1945- *WhoAm 92*
Diaz-Alejandro, Carlos Frederico 1937-1985 *BioIn 17*
Diaz-Arrastia, George Ravelo 1959- *WhoEmL 93*
Diaz Arrivillaga, Efrain *DcCPCAm*
Diaz Bartlett, Tomas 1919-1957 *DcMexL*
Diaz Calleja, Ricardo 1947- *WhoWor 93*
Diaz Casanueva, Humberto d1992 *NewYTBS 92*
Diaz-Casanueva, Humberto 1907- *SpAmA*
Diaz Castillo, Roberto 1931- *WhoWor 93*
Diaz-Coller, Carlos 1916- *WhoAm 92*
Diaz Covarrubias, Juan 1837-1859 *DcMexL*
Diaz-Cruz, Jorge Hatuey 1914- *WhoSSW 93*
Diaz del Castillo, Bernal 1492?-1584? *DcMexL*
Diaz Dennis, Patricia 1946- *NotHsAW 93 [port]*
Diaz Dufoo, Carlos 1861-1941 *DcMexL*
Diaz-Kintz, Margarita 1949- *WhoAmW 93*
Diaz Lozano, Argentina 1912- *SpAmA*
Diaz Martinez, Manuel 1936- *SpAmA*
Diaz Miron, Salvador 1853-1928 *DcMexL*
Diaz-Oliver, Remedios 1938- *NotHsAW 93 [port]*
Diaz Ordaz, Gustavo 1911-1979 *DcCPCAm*
Diaz Pena, Mateo 1925- *WhoScE 91-3*
Diaz-Piedrahita, Santiago 1944- *WhoWor 93*
Diaz Sanchez, Ramon 1903-1968 *SpAmA*
Diaz Serrano, Jorge *DcCPCAm*
Diaz-Soares, Francisco Jose 1938- *WhoWor 93*
Diaz Valcarcel, Emilio 1929- *SpAmA*
Diaz Vargas, Alejandro 1944- *St&PR 93*
Diaz Vela, Luis Humberto 1953- *WhoWor 93*
Diaz-Verson, Salvador 1951- *St&PR 93*
Diaz-Verson, Salvador, Jr. 1951- *WhoAm 92, WhoSSW 93, WhoWor 93*
Diaz y de Ovando, Clementina 1920- *DcMexL*
Diaz-Zubieta, Agustin 1936- *WhoWor 93*
Di Bacco, Richard David 1940- *WhoE 93*
Dibal, Diedre Ann 1951- *WhoAmW 93*
Dibango, Manu *BioIn 17*
DiBartolomeo, Diane Lynn 1956- *WhoEmL 93*
Dibb, David Walter 1943- *WhoAm 92, WhoSSW 93*
Dibba, Sherif Mustapha 1937- *WhoAfr*
Dibbern, H.C. *WhoScE 91-2*
Dibble, Birney 1925- *ScF&FL 92*
Dibble, David B. 1931- *St&PR 93*
Dibble, Francis Daniel, Jr. 1947- *WhoEmL 93*
Dibble, Gladys Gage d1991 *BioIn 17*
Dibble, Gordon Lynch 1928- *WhoAm 92*
Dibble, James Birney 1925- *WhoWrEP 92*
Dibble, James R. *BioIn 17*
Dibble, Kenneth 1945- *WhoWor 93*
Dibble, Nancy *ScF&FL 92*
Dibble, Rob *BioIn 17*
Dibble, Suzanne Gerdy 1939- *St&PR 93*
Dibdin, Charles 1745-1814 *Baker 92, OxDcOp*
Dibdin, Henry Edward 1813-1866 See Dibdin, Charles 1745-1814 *Baker 92*
Dibell, Ansen 1942- *ScF&FL 92*
DiBella, Anne Marie 1963- *WhoSSW 93*
Di Bella, Joseph *Law&B 92*
DiBella, Joseph Carmen 1950- *WhoEmL 93*
DiBella, Joseph Patrick 1940- *St&PR 93*
DiBella, Lucy Leola 1951- *WhoEmL 93*
DiBella, Rosanne Henry 1960- *WhoAmW 93*
Dibello, Lucille *Law&B 92*
DiBenedetti, Paul E. R. 1937- *WhoE 93*
Di Benedetto, Al, III 1943- *St&PR 93*
DiBenedetto, Anthony Thomas 1933- *WhoAm 92*
Di Benedetto, Antonio 1922-1986 *SpAmA*
DiBenedetto, Paul J. 1949- *St&PR 93*
DiBerardinis, Louis Joseph 1947- *WhoE 93*
DiBerardino, Marie Antoinette 1926- *WhoAm 92, WhoAmW 93, WhoE 93*
Dibernardi, John Joseph, Jr. *Law&B 92*
Dibert, Rosalie A. *BioIn 17*
Dibert, William R. 1938- *St&PR 93*
DiBiaggio, John 1932- *WhoAm 92, WhoWor 93*
Dibianca, Joseph P. 1954- *WhoAm 92*
Di Biase, Angelo *BioIn 17*
DiBiase, Michael 1957- *WhoEmL 93*
DiBiasio, Daniel Anthony *WhoE 93*
DiBiasio, Linda April 1944- *WhoAmW 93*
DiBlasi, John Peter 1955- *WhoEmL 93*
DiBlasi, Philip James 1954- *WhoWor 93*
Dible, William Trotter 1925- *St&PR 93*
Dibner, David 1927- *WhoAm 92*
Dibner, David R. 1926- *St&PR 93*
Dibner, David Robert 1926- *WhoAm 92*
Dibner, Martin d1992 *NewYTBS 92*
Dibner, Martin 1911- *WhoWrEP 92*
Dibner, Martin 1911-1992 *BioIn 17, ConAu 136*
DiBona, Charles Joseph 1932- *WhoAm 92*
di Bonaventura, Anthony *Baker 92*
di Bonaventura, Mario *Baker 92*
Dibrell, Louis Nelson, III 1945- *St&PR 93, WhoAm 92*
Dibrita, Anthony J. 1940- *St&PR 93*
Dibrov, Boris Fedorovich 1952- *WhoWor 93*
Dibui, W.J. 1943- *St&PR 93*
Dibuono, Anthony J. *Law&B 92*
diBuono, Anthony Joseph 1930- *St&PR 93, WhoAm 92*
DiCamillo, Debra Allen 1957- *WhoAmW 93, WhoEmL 93*
DiCamillo, Gary Thomas 1950- *WhoAm 92, WhoEmL 93*
Dicanio, Frank 1916- *St&PR 93*
Di Capua, Eduardo 1864-1917 *Baker 92*
DiCara, Costante John 1927- *WhoSSW 93*
DiCara, Lawrence S. 1949- *WhoEmL 93*
DiCarlantonio, Martin *ScF&FL 92*
DiCarlo, Dominick L. 1928- *CngDr 91, WhoAm 92, WhoE 93*
DiCarlo, Edward Francis William 1953- *WhoE 93*
DiCarlo, Louis Michael 1903- *WhoAm 92, WhoWor 93*
DiCarlo, Susanne Helen 1956- *WhoAmW 93, WhoEmL 93*
Di Castri, F. *WhoScE 91-2*
Dicello, John Francis, Jr. 1938- *WhoAm 92, WhoE 93, WhoWor 93*
Di Celso, Pietro Mazziotti *WhoScE 91-3*
Dicembre, Anna Louise 1955- *WhoSSW 93*
di Cenzo, Colin Domenic 1923- *WhoAm 92*
Dicerto, Anthony R. 1941- *St&PR 93*
Di Certo, Joseph 1933- *BioIn 17*
Di Cesare, Dominick *St&PR 93*
Dichev, Todor Petkov 1938- *WhoUN 92*
Dichgans, Johannes 1938- *WhoScE 91-3*
Dichiara, Armand 1943- *St&PR 93*
Di Chiara, Gaetano 1945- *WhoWor 93*
DiChiara, Robert *ScF&FL 92*
Di Chiera, David 1937- *WhoAm 92*
Dichter, Anna 1913- *St&PR 93*
Dichter, Barry Joel 1950- *WhoAm 92, WhoE 93, WhoEmL 93*
Dichter, Cipa 1944- See Dichter, Misha 1945- *Baker 92*
Dichter, Ernest *BioIn 17*
Dichter, Ernest 1907-1991 *CurBio 92N*
Dichter, Misha 1945- *Baker 92, WhoAm 92, WhoE 93*
DiCiaccio, John F. 1949- *St&PR 93*
DiCianni, Joe 1946- *WhoEmL 93*
DiCicco, Nicholas J., Jr. 1932- *St&PR 93*
Di Cicco, Pier Giorgio 1949- *WhoCanL 92*
DiCicco, Susan Ailene 1959- *WhoEmL 93*
DiCillo, Tom *MiSFD 9*
DiCindio, Linda Anne 1955- *WhoAmW 93*
DiCioccio, Joseph John 1955- *WhoE 93*
Dick, A.B. 1856-1934 *GayN*
Dick, Alain E.R. 1939- *WhoUN 92*
Dick, Aurora Claudette 1946- *WhoAmW 93*
Dick, Barbara Ann 1935- *St&PR 93*
Dick, Bernard F. 1935- *ScF&FL 92*
Dick, Bertram Gale, Jr. 1926- *WhoAm 92*
Dick, Carol June 1963- *WhoAmW 93*
Dick, Carol L. 1942- *WhoAmW 93*
Dick, Curtis *WhoAm 92*
Dick, David Andrew Thomas *WhoScE 91-1*
Dick, David L. *Law&B 92*
Dick, Dennis Eugene 1939- *St&PR 93*
Dick, Donald Albert 1933- *St&PR 93*
Dick, Douglas Patrick 1953- *St&PR 93*
Dick, Emanuel 1915- *St&PR 93*
Dick, Erik Remi 1950- *WhoWor 93*
Dick, Harold L. 1943- *WhoAm 92*
Dick, Heather Lynn 1969- *WhoAmW 93*
Dick, Heather M. *WhoScE 91-1*
Dick, Henry Henry 1922- *WhoAm 92*
Dick, Jerry Wayne 1947- *St&PR 93*
Dick, Jill *BioIn 17*
Dick, John R. 1936- *St&PR 93*
Dick, Joseph M. 1941- *St&PR 93*
Dick, Katherine Restaino 1937- *WhoE 93*
Dick, Kay 1915- *ScF&FL 92*
Dick, Kenneth John 1950- *WhoEmL 93*
Dick, Louise Lattomus 1937- *WhoSSW 93*
Dick, Marcel 1898- *Baker 92*
Dick, Martin 1939- *St&PR 93*
Dick, Nigel *MiSFD 9*
Dick, Patricia A. 1929- *WhoAmW 93, WhoWor 93*
Dick, Paul Wyatt 1940- *WhoAm 92*
Dick, Philip K. *BioIn 17*
Dick, Philip K. 1928-1982 *ConLC 72 [port], MagSAmL [port], ScF&FL 92*
Dick, Raymond Dale 1930- *WhoAm 92*
Dick, Richard Irwin 1935- *WhoAm 92*
Dick, Stacy S. 1956- *St&PR 93, WhoAm 92*
Dick, Stephen Lewis 1951- *WhoEmL 93*
Dick, Stephen W. 1949- *St&PR 93*
Dick, Susan Marie 1940- *WhoAmW 93*
Dick, Thomas Michael 1955- *WhoEmL 93, WhoSSW 93*
Dick, William J. *Law&B 92*
Dick, Wolfgang F. *WhoScE 91-3*
Dickason, James Frank 1922- *WhoAm 92*
Dickason, John Hamilton 1931- *WhoAm 92*
Dickason, L. King, Jr. 1942- *St&PR 93*
Dickason, Richard R. 1946- *St&PR 93*
Dicke, Arnold A. 1942- *WhoIns 93*
Dicke, Arnold Arthur 1942- *St&PR 93*
Dicke, Candice Edwards 1949- *WhoAm 92*
Dicke, James Frederick, II 1945- *WhoAm 92*
Dicke, Patricia Ann *Law&B 92*

Dickstein, Simone Andrea 1957- WhoEmL 93
Dick the Bruiser d1991 BioIn 17
DiClaudio, Richard Alexander 1959- WhoE 93
DiClemente, John Law&B 92
Di Cocco, G. WhoScE 91-3
DiColo, Robert Louis 1958- WhoE 93
Di Como, Michael Paul 1948- St&PR 93
Dicorcia, Edward T. 1930- St&PR 93
Di Cosimo, Joanne Violet 1953- WhoAm 92
DiCosola, Lois Ann 1935- WhoE 93
DiCostanzo, Geraldine 1938- St&PR 93
DiCresce, Gary Peter 1946- WhoE 93
DiCroce, Deborah Marie 1952- WhoEmL 93, WhoSSW 93
Dicterow, Glenn Eugene 1948- WhoAm 92
Dictrow, Joel P. Law&B 92
Dicus, Clarence Howard, Jr. 1921- WhoAm 92
Dicus, John Carmack 1933- WhoAm 92
Dicus, Stephen Howard 1948- WhoEmL 93
Diczok, Paul D. Law&B 92
Diczok, Paul D. 1943- St&PR 93
Didat, Emma Bell 1939- WhoAmW 93
Didat, Louisa Law&B 92
Didden, George A., Jr. 1909- St&PR 93
Didden, George A., III 1945- St&PR 93
Diddens, Albert Nomdo 1928- WhoWor 93
Diddle, Deborah Kay 1949- WhoWrEP 92
Diddley, Bo 1928- Baker 92, SoulM
Didenko, Viktor 1954- WhoWor 93
Diderot, Denis 1713-1784 Baker 92, BioIn 17, OxDcOp
Didieo, James 1949- St&PR 93, WhoAm 92
Didier, Marcelo 1937- WhoWor 93
Didier, Philippe 1947- WhoScE 91-2
DiDio, Liberato John Alphonse 1920- WhoAm 92
Didion, Dale A. 1957- WhoE 93
Didion, Doug 1949- St&PR 93
Didion, Gilbert 1921- St&PR 93
Didion, Joan BioIn 17
Didion, Joan 1934- MagSAmL [port], WhoAm 92, WhoAmW 93, WhoWor 93, WhoWrEP 92
Didius Julianus, Marcus d193 HarEnMi
Didlake, Ralph Hunter, Jr. 1953- WhoSSW 93
Di Domenica, Robert 1927- Baker 92
Di Domenica, Robert Anthony 1927- WhoAm 92
DiDomenico, Mauro, Jr. 1937- WhoAm 92
DiDomizio, Robert Anthony, Jr. 1955- WhoE 93, WhoEmL 93
Didona, David Joseph 1947- WhoSSW 93
Didonato, Ann M. Law&B 92
DiDonato, Edward Joseph WhoE 93
Di Donato, Louis Michael 1946- WhoEmL 93
Di Donato, Pietro 1911-1992 BioIn 17, ConAu 136, NewYTBS 92 [port]
Didrick, Robert M. Law&B 92
Didriksen, Caleb H., III 1955- WhoEmL 93
Didrikson, Babe 1911-1956 BioIn 17
Didur, Adam 1874-1946 OxDcOp, PolBiDi
Didur, Adamo 1874-1946 Baker 92
Didur, Jill Renee 1961- WhoEmL 93
Didus, Terry G. Law&B 92
Didway, Christine Duncan 1967- WhoAmW 93
Didymos The Blind c. 313-c. 398 OxDcByz
Didymus, Chalcenterus (Of the Brazen Guts) fl. c. 80BC-10BC Baker 92
Didzerekis, Paul Patrick 1939- WhoWor 93
Die, Ann Marie Hayes 1944- WhoAmW 93
Dieb, Dennis Rodney 1942- St&PR 93
Dieball, Scott Alan Law&B 92
Diebel, Donald Ray 1947- WhoSSW 93, WhoWrEP 92
Diebel, William 1905- St&PR 93
Diebenkorn, Richard 1922- NewYTBS 92 [port]
Diebenkorn, Richard Clifford, Jr. 1922- WhoAm 92
Diebold, Foster Frank 1932- WhoAm 92, WhoE 93
Diebold, Gerald J. 1943- WhoAm 92
Diebold, Jacques-Jose 1932- WhoScE 91-2
Diebold, John 1926- WhoAm 92
Diebold, John Mark 1957- WhoSSW 93
Diebold, Kenneth M. 1950- St&PR 93
Diebold, Raymond Joseph 1940- St&PR 93
Dieck, Daniel William 1951- WhoEmL 93
Dieck, E. Leopold 1940- WhoWor 93
Dieck, William Wallace Sandford 1924- WhoE 93
Diecke, Friedrich Paul Julius 1927- WhoAm 92
Dieckmann, Ed(ward), Jr. 1920- WhoWrEP 92
Dieckmann, Karl W. 1928- St&PR 93
Dieckmann, O. Karl 1913- St&PR 93
Dieckmann, Wallace C. 1943- St&PR 93
Diederich, Anne Marie 1943- WhoAmW 93
Diederich, Daniel Kevin 1957- WhoEmL 93
Diederich, Hunt 1884-1953 BioIn 17
Diederich, John William 1929- St&PR 93, WhoAm 92, WhoSSW 93, WhoWor 93
Diederich, Mathias J. Law&B 92
Diederich, R. David 1942- St&PR 93
Diederichs, John Kuensting 1921- WhoAm 92, WhoWor 93
Diedrich, Richard Joseph 1936- WhoSSW 93
Diedrick, Arthur Hill, Jr. 1937- St&PR 93
Diedrick, George Vernon 1936- St&PR 93
Diefenbach, Thomas A. St&PR 93
Diefenbach, Viron Leroy 1922- WhoAm 92
Diefenbaker, John George BioIn 17
Diefenbaker, John George 1895-1979 DcTwHis
Diefenderfer, Caren 1952- WhoAmW 93
Diefenderfer, William Martin, III 1945- WhoAm 92
Diefendorf, Arthur Ashley 1935- St&PR 93
Dieffenbach, Jon Michael 1948- WhoEmL 93
Diegel, Donald Wayne 1953- WhoEmL 93
Diego, Eliseo 1920- SpAmA
Diego, Wycliffe DcCPCAm
Diegues, Carlos 1940- MiSFD 9
Dieguez, Carmen 1952- WhoAmW 93
Dieguez, Richard Peter 1960- WhoEmL 93
Diehl, Alden Edgar 1931- St&PR 93
Diehl, Ann Marie 1938- WhoE 93
Diehl, Daniel Lee 1948- WhoE 93
Diehl, Deborah Hilda 1951- WhoEmL 93
Diehl, Digby Robert 1940- WhoAm 92
Diehl, Dolores 1927- WhoAmW 93
Diehl, George A. d1991 BioIn 17
Diehl, Gerald George 1916- WhoAm 92
Diehl, Harrison Lueders, Jr. 1935- St&PR 93
Diehl, Johannes Friedrich 1929- WhoScE 91-3
Diehl, Karen Ann 1951- WhoAmW 93
Diehl, Keith Kenneth 1952- St&PR 93
Diehl, L.H., Jr. 1919- St&PR 93
Diehl, L.H., III 1953- St&PR 93
Diehl, Lauren Traynor 1955- WhoEmL 93
Diehl, Lesley Ann 1943- WhoAm 92
Diehl, Mark Emory 1951- WhoEmL 93
Diehl, Richard E. 1941- St&PR 93
Diehl, Richard Kurth 1935- WhoAm 92
Diehl, Richard Lee 1928- St&PR 93
Diehl, Roland 1944- WhoScE 91-3
Diehl, Russell R. 1946- St&PR 93
Diehl, Sarah J. Law&B 92
Diehl, Stephen Anthony 1942- WhoAm 92
Diehl, Timothy Jerel 1949- WhoEmL 93, WhoWor 93
Diehl, Walter F. d1991 BioIn 17
Diehl, Walter Francis, Jr. Law&B 92
Diehl, Walter Francis, Jr. 1935- St&PR 93
Diehm, James Warren 1944- WhoAm 92
Diehm, Russell Charles 1946- WhoEmL 93
Diehr, Beverly Hunt 1954- WhoEmL 93
Diekamp, Ulrich 1941- WhoWor 93
Diekema, Anthony J. 1933- WhoAm 92
Diekemper, Gregory Robert 1958- St&PR 93
Diekemper, Joe St&PR 93
Dieker, Lawrence L. Law&B 92
Diekmann, Andreas 1951- WhoWor 93
Diekmann, Gilmore Frederick, Jr. 1946- WhoEmL 93
Diekmann, Godfrey BioIn 17
Diekmann, Hans 1931- WhoScE 91-3
Diekmann, Nancy Kassak 1952- WhoAmW 93
Diel, Delores Kay 1953- WhoEmL 93
Diels, Jean-Pierre Frederic 1949- St&PR 93
Diels, L. WhoScE 91-2
Diem, Glenda J. Law&B 92
Diem, Ngo Dinh 1901-1963 ColdWar 2 [port], DcTwHis
Diemar, Robert Emery, Jr. 1942- WhoAm 92
Diemberger, Kurt BioIn 17
Diemecke, Enrique Arturo 1952- WhoAm 92
Diemente, Damon L. WhoE 93
Diemer, Arthur William 1925- WhoSSW 93
Diemer, Emma Lou 1927- Baker 92, WhoAm 92
Diemer, Kenneth J. 1956- St&PR 93
Diemer, Louis (-Joseph) 1843-1919 Baker 92
Diemer, Nils Henrik 1944- WhoScE 91-2
Diemling, A. WhoScE 91-4
Diemont, W.H. 1944- WhoScE 91-3
Diemoz, Dennis K. Law&B 92
Diemunsch, Jean WhoScE 91-2
Diendere, Gilbert 1959- WhoAfr
Diene, Doudou 1941- WhoUN 92
Diener, Bert 1915- WhoAm 92
Diener, Betty Jane 1940- WhoAm 92, WhoE 93
Diener, Erwin 1932- WhoAm 92
Diener, Jerry L. St&PR 93
Diener, Robert L.B. 1948- St&PR 93
Diener, Royce 1918- WhoAm 92
Diener, Terry 1949- St&PR 93
Diener, Theodor Otto 1921- WhoAm 92, WhoWor 93
Diener, Urban Lowell 1921- WhoSSW 93
Diener, William P. Law&B 92
Diener, William Paul 1941- WhoAm 92
Dienes, John R. 1946- St&PR 93
Dienes, Sari 1898-1992 BioIn 17, NewYTBS 92
Dienesch, Marie-Madeleine 1914- BioIn 17
Dienst, Henry W. 1935- St&PR 93
Dienstag, Eleanor Foa WhoE 93
Dienstag, Jules Leonard 1946- WhoE 93
Dienstbier, Dan L. 1940- WhoAm 92
Dienstbier, Jiri 1937- WhoWor 93
Dienstbier, Zdenek 1926- WhoScE 91-4
Diepenbrock, Alphons (Johannes Maria) 1862-1921 Baker 92
Diepenbroick-Gruter, Hartwig Freiherr von 1931- WhoScE 91-3
Dieperbrock, James St&PR 93
Diepholz, David Lester 1962- WhoEmL 93
Dieppe, Paul Adrian WhoScE 91-1
Dier, Kelly E. 1949- St&PR 93
Dierauf, Leslie Ann 1948- WhoAm 92, WhoAmW 93
Dierckman, Nicholas Bernard 1951- WhoEmL 93
Diercks, Chester William, Jr. 1926- WhoAm 92
Diercks, Frederick Otto 1912- WhoAm 92, WhoSSW 93, WhoWor 93
Diercks, Robert John 1941- WhoAm 92
Diercks, Walter Elmer 1945- WhoAm 92
Dierdorf, Daniel Lee 1949- WhoAm 92
Dierdorff, John Ainsworth 1928- WhoAm 92
Diereky de Casterle, Emmanuel 1946- WhoUN 92
Dieren, Bernard van 1887-1936 Baker 92
Dierich, Manfred WhoScE 91-4
Dierickx, Willy Rene 1942- WhoScE 91-2
Dieringer, Cindy Sue 1949- WhoEmL 93
Dierkens, Jean Charles 1926- WhoScE 91-2
Dierks, Henry T. 1931- St&PR 93
Dierks, John H. 1963- St&PR 93
Dierks, Richard Ernest 1934- WhoAm 92, WhoSSW 93
Dierks, Terry A. 1946- St&PR 93
Dierman, Gerald F. 1942- St&PR 93
Dierna, Joseph Biagio 1959- WhoEmL 93
Diernisse, Villy 1928- WhoWrEP 92
Diers, Donna Kaye 1938- WhoAm 92
Diers, Hank H. 1931- WhoAm 92
Diers, Michael Everett 1961- WhoEmL 93
Diers, Yves 1937- WhoWor 93
Diersen, David John 1948- WhoEmL 93
Diersen, Karen Annette 1950- WhoEmL 93
Diersen, Michael Larry 1954- WhoEmL 93
Diersing, Robert Joseph 1949- WhoSSW 93
Dierssen, Klaus 1948- WhoScE 91-3
Dies, Bruce F. 1939- St&PR 93
Dies, Douglas Hilton 1913- WhoAm 92
Dies, Martin 1900-1972 BioIn 17
Dies, Rose Ann 1958- St&PR 93
Diesch, Stanley La Verne 1925- WhoAm 92
Dieschbourg, Edward J. 1955- St&PR 93
Diesel, John P. 1926- St&PR 93
Diesel, Leota AmWomPl
Diesel, Paul M. 1944- St&PR 93
Diesem, Charles David 1921- WhoAm 92
Diesem, John Lawrence 1941- WhoAm 92
Dieskau, Dietrich Fischer- 1925- BioIn 17
Diestelkamp, Dawn Lea 1954- WhoAmW 93
Diesveld, Rene Johannes 1945- WhoWor 93
Diet, Edmond-Marie 1854-1924 Baker 92
Dietch, Henry Xerxes 1913- WhoAm 92
Dietch, Robert 1938- St&PR 93
Dietel, Gregory Louis 1948- St&PR 93
Dietel, James Edwin 1941- WhoE 93
Dietel, Norman J. 1911-1990 BioIn 17
Dietel, William Moore 1927- WhoAm 92
Dieter, Alice Hunt 1928- WhoAmW 93
Dieter, Allen Charles 1942- St&PR 93
Dieter, Christian Ludwig 1757-1822 OxDcOp
Dieter, F. Robert 1930- St&PR 93
Dieter, George E., Jr. 1928- WhoAm 92
Dieter, Joseph Marshall, Jr. 1951- WhoEmL 93
Dieter, Raymond Andrew, Jr. 1934- WhoAm 92
Dieter, Richard Charles 1952- WhoE 93, WhoEmL 93
Dieter, William G., Jr. 1942- St&PR 93
Dieter, William J. 1939- St&PR 93
Dieterich, Douglas Thomas 1951- WhoE 93, WhoEmL 93
Dieterich, Michael Karl 1942- WhoWor 93
Dieterich, Sixtus c. 1493-1548 Baker 92
Dieterich, Wolfgang 1942- WhoScE 91-3
Dieterle, Donald Lyle 1908- WhoAm 92
Dieterle, William 1893-1972 MiSFD 9N
Dietert, Rodney Reynolds 1951- WhoE 93
Diethelm, Arnold Gillespie 1932- WhoAm 92
Diether, Jack 1919-1987 Baker 92
Diethorn, Gregory Andrew 1946- WhoEmL 93
Diethrich, Edward Bronson 1935- WhoAm 92
Diethrich, Robert 1942- WhoScE 91-2
Dietl, Eduard 1890-1944 HarEnMi
Dietl, Jozef 1804-1878 PolBiDi
Dietl, Tomasz 1950- WhoWor 93
Dietlinde, Agnes Juliane 1928- WhoSSW 93
Dietmeyer, Donald Leo 1932- WhoAm 92
Dietrich, Alan D. Law&B 92
Dietrich, Alan D. 1950- St&PR 93
Dietrich, Albert (Hermann) 1829-1908 Baker 92
Dietrich, Bruce Leinbach 1937- WhoAm 92, WhoE 93
Dietrich, Bruce Neal 1956- WhoEmL 93
Dietrich, Christian Peter 1944- St&PR 93
Dietrich, Frank Karl 1944- WhoSSW 93
Dietrich, George Charles 1927- WhoAm 92
Dietrich, Glenn St&PR 93
Dietrich, Harley Harrison, Jr. 1951- WhoSSW 93
Dietrich, Helmut 1952- WhoScE 91-3
Dietrich, John Hassler, II 1951- WhoEmL 93
Dietrich, Josef 1892-1966 HarEnMi
Dietrich, Joseph Jacob 1932- WhoAm 92
Dietrich, Klaus M. 1934- WhoScE 91-3
Dietrich, Kurt E. 1951- St&PR 93
Dietrich, Laura Jordan 1952- WhoAm 92
Dietrich, Marek Stanislaw 1934- WhoScE 91-4
Dietrich, Marian Law&B 92
Dietrich, Marion C. 1922- St&PR 93
Dietrich, Marlene 1901?- IntDcF 2-3 [port]
Dietrich, Marlene 1901-1992 BioIn 17, ConTFT 10, CurBio 92N, NewYTBS 92 [port], News 92
Dietrich, Martha Jane 1916- WhoAm 92, WhoAmW 93
Dietrich, Maryrose Clark 1952- WhoAmW 93, WhoEmL 93
Dietrich, Nancy Bishop 1946- St&PR 93
Dietrich, Paul George 1949- WhoAm 92
Dietrich, Peter W. 1939- St&PR 93
Dietrich, Renee Long 1937- WhoAmW 93, WhoE 93
Dietrich, Richard Farr 1936- WhoSSW 93
Dietrich, Richard Vincent 1924- WhoAm 92
Dietrich, Robert Anthony 1933- WhoAm 92
Dietrich, Sepp 1892-1966 BioIn 17
Dietrich, Sixtus c. 1493-1548 Baker 92
Dietrich, Suzanne Claire 1937- WhoAmW 93
Dietrich, Thomas W. Law&B 92
Dietrich, William Alan 1951- WhoAm 92
Dietrich, William Colman 1949- St&PR 93
Dietrich, William Gale 1925- WhoAm 92
Dietrich, Wolf 1940- WhoWor 93
Dietrick, Laurabelle AmWomPl
Dietsch, Alfred John 1931- St&PR 93, WhoAm 92
Dietsch, Louis 1808-1865 OxDcOp
Dietsch, (Pierre-)Louis(-Philippe) 1808-1865 Baker 92
Dietsch, Phil BioIn 17
Dietz, Albert George Henry 1908- WhoAm 92
Dietz, Allen 1951- WhoEmL 93
Dietz, Arthur Townsend 1923- WhoSSW 93, WhoWor 93
Dietz, Charlton Law&B 92
Dietz, Charlton Henry 1931- St&PR 93, WhoAm 92
Dietz, Deborah Jean 1958- WhoAmW 93
Dietz, Dennis A. Law&B 92
Dietz, Donald Elmore, III 1946- St&PR 93, WhoAm 92
Dietz, Donald William 1935- St&PR 93

Dietz, Earl Daniel 1928- WhoAm 92
Dietz, Frank Herbert 1940- WhoSSW 93
Dietz, Gail Annette 1953- WhoAmW 93
Dietz, George Robert 1931- St&PR 93
Dietz, Gunter 1928- WhoScE 91-3
Dietz, Howard 1896-1983 Baker 92
Dietz, J. Randolph 1951- WhoEmL 93
Dietz, Janis Camille 1950- WhoAmW 93
Dietz, Jess Clay 1914- WhoSSW 93
Dietz, John A. Law&B 92
Dietz, John Raphael 1912- WhoAm 92
Dietz, Klaus 1940- WhoScE 91-3
Dietz, Linda C. 1952- St&PR 93
Dietz, Margaret Jane 1924- WhoAmW 93
Dietz, Max 1857-1928 Baker 92
Dietz, Milton S. 1931- St&PR 93, WhoAm 92
Dietz, Olof Willy 1927- WhoScE 91-3
Dietz, Peter 1939- WhoScE 91-3
Dietz, R. WhoScE 91-1
Dietz, Reinhold Henry, Jr. 1933- WhoSSW 93
Dietz, Robert Barron 1942- WhoE 93
Dietz, Robert Sinclair 1914- WhoAm 92
Dietz, Russell Scott 1963- WhoWor 93
Dietz, Ruth d1991 BioIn 17
Dietz, Scott Douglas 1965- WhoE 93
Dietz, Stephen E. Law&B 92
Dietz, Stephen I. 1934- WhoIns 93
Dietz, Steven Wayne Law&B 92
Dietz, Timothy Jon 1955- St&PR 93
Dietz, William C. 1945- ScF&FL 92
Dietz, William Harry 1944- WhoE 93
Dietz, William Ronald 1942- WhoAm 92
Dietze, Dayrel Elizabeth 1961- WhoAmW 93
Dietze, Gottfried 1922- WhoAm 92
Dietze, Gunther 1936- WhoScE 91-3
Dietze, Joachim 1931- WhoWor 93
Dietze, John L. Law&B 92
Dietzel, Jorg 1961- WhoWor 93
Dietzman, Leslie WhoAm 92
Dieudonne, Florence Carpenter 1850- ScF&FL 92
Dieupart, Charles Francois c. 1670-c. 1740 Baker 92
Dieuzaide, Jean Yan 1921- WhoWor 93
Dievler, David Harold 1929- St&PR 93
Diez, Jose Alberto 1956- WhoWor 93
Diez, Jose L. 1938- WhoScE 91-3
Diez, Ricardo J. 1946- WhoAm 92
Diez-Canedo, Enrique 1879-1944 DcMexL
Diez-Canseco, Jose 1904-1949 SpAmA
Diez-Roche, Jose T. 1934- WhoScE 91-3
DiFate, Vincent 1945- ScF&FL 92
Di Ferdinand, Rosalie Chillemi 1955- WhoE 93, WhoEmL 93
Diffenbaugh, John Nicholas 1954- WhoEmL 93, WhoSSW 93
Diffendaffer, Gary Lee 1946- WhoEmL 93
Diffendal, Anne P. 1943- WhoAm 92
Diffenderfer, Robert Charles 1936- St&PR 93
Diffin, Edward Wilson, Jr. Law&B 92
Diffine, Linda Carol 1944- WhoAmW 93
Diffrient, Niels 1928- WhoAm 92
DiFilippo, Fernando, Jr. 1948- WhoAm 92
DiFilippo, Nando 1948- St&PR 93
DiFillippo, Anthony Francis 1927- St&PR 93, WhoAm 92
DiFiore, Albert Angelo 1939- WhoE 93
DiFiore, Michael 1949- St&PR 93
Difley, R. William 1942- St&PR 93
DiFoggio, Rocco 1952- WhoSSW 93
DiForio, James P., Jr. 1951- WhoIns 93
Diforio, Robert G. 1940- WhoAm 92
Diforio, Robert George 1940- St&PR 93
Di Franco, Anthony M. 1945- WhoWrEP 92
Di Franco, Loretta Elizabeth 1942- WhoAm 92
Di Furia, Arthur Joseph 1933- St&PR 93
DiGangi, Frank Edward 1917- WhoAm 92
Digby, Anne 1935- SmATA 72 [port]
Digby, Anne 1942?- ScF&FL 92
Digby, Lyle Martin 1943- St&PR 93
Digby, Peter John 1943- WhoScE 91-4
DiGello, Michele M. Law&B 92
DiGennaro, Robert C. 1947- St&PR 93
Di Geronimo, Diane Mary 1946- WhoSSW 93
DiGeronimo, Joseph 1944- St&PR 93
Digeser, Andreas Johannes 1925- WhoWor 93
DiGesu, Mary St&PR 93
Digges, Deborah Lea 1950- WhoWrEP 92
Digges, Dudley Perkins 1918- WhoAm 92
Digges, John Joseph 1932- St&PR 93
Digges, Sam Cook 1916-1990 BioIn 17
Diggins, Peter Sheehan 1938- WhoAm 92
Diggle, Peter John WhoScE 91-1
Diggle, Steve
See Buzzcocks, The ConMus 9
Diggs, Charles 1922- BioIn 17
Diggs, Charles C., Jr. 1922- EncAACR
Diggs, Charles Clayton 1947- WhoEmL 93
Diggs, Elizabeth Francis 1939- WhoWrEP 92
Diggs, Ellen Irene 1906- BioIn 17
Diggs, James Clarence Law&B 92
Diggs, Jesse Frank 1917- WhoAm 92
Diggs, Linda Staser 1955- WhoAmW 93
Diggs, Matthew O., Jr. 1933- St&PR 93
Diggs, Matthew O'Brien, Jr. 1933- WhoAm 92
Diggs, Phyllis Allen 1926- WhoAmW 93
Diggs, Walter Edward 1936- St&PR 93
Diggs, Walter Edward, Jr. 1936- WhoAm 92
Diggs, Walter Whitley 1932- WhoSSW 93
Digia, Robert M. 1924- St&PR 93
DiGiacomo, Anna Catherine 1967- WhoEmL 93
DiGiacomo, David Robert 1952- WhoEmL 93
DiGiacomo, Enzo BioIn 17
DiGiacomo, Joseph BioIn 17
Digiacomo, Joseph A. 1935- St&PR 93
Di Giacomo, Thomas Anthony 1941- WhoAm 92, WhoE 93, WhoWor 93
DiGiamarino, Marian Eleanor 1947- WhoAmW 93
DiGiampaolo, Ellen Ruth 1948- WhoAmW 93
DiGiannantonio, Edmond Philip BioIn 17
DiGidio, Mark David Law&B 92
Di Gioia, Anthony Michael, Jr. 1934- WhoAm 92
Di Giorgio, Robert 1911-1991 BioIn 17
DiGiovachino, John 1955- WhoE 93
DiGiovanna, Joseph Thomas 1927- St&PR 93
DiGiovanna, Leonard Dominick 1955- WhoE 93
Di Giovanni, Anthony 1919- WhoAm 92
DiGiovanni, Eleanor Elma 1944- WhoAmW 93, WhoE 93, WhoWor 93
Di Giovanni, Eric Paul 1965- WhoEmL 93
DiGiovanni, Hugo J. 1912- St&PR 93
DiGiovanni, Joan Fimbel 1935- WhoAmW 93, WhoE 93
DiGiovanni, Larry Joseph 1948- WhoE 93, WhoEmL 93
DiGiovanni, Leonard Jerome 1928- WhoE 93
Digital Underground ConMus 9 [port]
Di Giuseppe, Enrico 1932- Baker 92
DiGiuseppe, N. Louis 1943- St&PR 93
Di Giusto, Walter 1949- St&PR 93
Dignac, Geny 1932- WhoAm 92
Dignam, Erin MiSFD 9
Dignam, Mark 1909-1989 ConTFT 10
Dignam, Robert Joseph 1925- WhoAm 92
Dignam, William Joseph 1920- WhoAm 92
Dignan, Peter J. 1951- St&PR 93
Dignan, Thomas Gregory, Jr. 1940- WhoAm 92, WhoE 93, WhoWor 93
D'Ignazio, Fred 1949- ScF&FL 92
Digney, Beryl R. St&PR 93
Digney, James Brian 1946- St&PR 93, WhoIns 93
Di Gregorio, Albert J. 1921- St&PR 93
Digregorio, Charlotte Antonia 1953- WhoWrEP 92
Digregorio, Michael Anthony 1954- St&PR 93
Di Gregorio, Vincent 1928- St&PR 93
Di Guardo, Joseph A. St&PR 93
Diguisto, Carlo A. 1947- St&PR 93
Digulla, Katy Jo 1958- WhoAmW 93
Dihel, Donald Loran 1955- WhoSSW 93
Dihigo, Martin HispAmA
di Jeso, Fernando 1931- WhoWor 93
Dijk, Jan van 1918- Baker 92
Dijkema, Kees S. 1949- WhoScE 91-3
Dijkhuis, Christian G.M. 1936- WhoScE 91-3
Dijkman, J.H. 1933- WhoScE 91-3
Dijksman, Evert Albertus 1931- WhoWor 93
Dijkstra, A. WhoScE 91-3
Dijkstra, Albert J. 1939- WhoScE 91-?
Dijkstra, Edsger Wybe 1930- WhoAm 92
Dijkstra, J. 1938- WhoScE 91-3
Dijkstra, W. WhoScE 91-2
Di Julio, Joseph Michael 1923- St&PR 93
Dik, Susan Lee 1956- WhoEmL 93
Dike, Alexander T. Law&B 92
Dike, Karen Doyle Law&B 92
Dike, Margaret Hopcraft 1921- WhoAmW 93
Dike, Richard Joe 1944- WhoSSW 93
Dikeman, Michael Lee 1949- St&PR 93
Dikeman, Ralph J. 1927- St&PR 93
Diker, Charles Michael 1934- St&PR 93
Dikko, Umaru Abdurrahman 1936- WhoAfr
Dikmen, Ned F. WhoWrEP 92
Dikranjan, Dikran Nishan 1950- WhoWor 93
Dikstein, Shabtay 1931- WhoWor 93
Diktas, Christos James 1955- WhoEmL 93
Dikty, Judy ScF&FL 92
Dikty, Julian May 1931- BioIn 17
Dikty, Thaddeus 1920-1991 ScF&FL 92
Diktys Of Crete OxDcByz
Di Lampedusa, Giuseppe Tomasi 1896-1957 BioIn 17
Dilanian, Zaven Khristoforovich 1903-1990 BioIn 17
Dilatush, Robert E., Jr. 1929- St&PR 93
Di Laura, Kenneth Anthony 1945- St&PR 93
Dilbeck, Walter J. d1991 BioIn 17
Dilcher, David Leonard 1936- WhoAm 92
Dilda, Dennis d1886 BioIn 17
Dilday, William H. 1937- BioIn 17
Di Lella, Alexander Anthony 1929- WhoAm 92
Dilella, James Theodore 1951- St&PR 93
DiLemmo, Ralph Pasquale 1956- WhoE 93
Dilenbeck, John ScF&FL 92
Dilenschneider, Robert Louis 1943- St&PR 93, WhoAm 92
Dileo, Frank BioIn 17
Di Leo, Mario MiSFD 9
DiLeo, Peter George 1953- WhoE 93
DiLeonardi, Joan Wall 1935- WhoAmW 93
Dileone, Carmel Montano 1926- WhoE 93
Di Leone, Helaine 1945- WhoSSW 93
Dilg, Robert Fred, Jr. 1958- St&PR 93
Dilgard, Robert Carl 1932- St&PR 93
Dilger, Joseph Patrick 1948- WhoEmL 93
DiLiberto, John Gerard 1950- St&PR 93
DiLiello, Danny Damiano 1950- St&PR 93
Di Liello, Salvatore 1958- WhoEmL 93
DiLillo, Leonard Michael 1935- WhoAm 92
Dilks, Park Bankert, Jr. 1928- WhoAm 92
Dilks, S.N. WhoScE 91-1
Dill, Bobby 1920-1991 BioIn 17
Dill, Bonnie Thornton BioIn 17
Dill, Carlton Jerome 1960- WhoWor 93
Dill, Charles A. 1939- St&PR 93
Dill, Charles Anthony 1939- WhoAm 92
Dill, Charles William 1952- WhoSSW 93
Dill, Craig H. 1958- WhoSSW 93
Dill, Edith Palliser 1925- WhoWrEP 92
Dill, Ellen Renee 1949- WhoAmW 93, WhoEmL 93, WhoWor 93
Dill, Ellis Harold 1932- WhoAm 92
Dill, Everett Charles Law&B 92
Dill, Frederick Hayes 1932- WhoAm 92
Dill, James R. Law&B 92
Dill, John Francis 1934- St&PR 93, WhoAm 92
Dill, John J. 1939- St&PR 93
Dill, John Junior 1939- WhoAm 92
Dill, John R. BioIn 17
Dill, Karole Edwyna 1961- WhoEmL 93
Dill, Kenneth Austin 1947- WhoWor 93
Dill, Laddie John 1943- WhoAm 92
Dill, M. Reese, Jr. 1937- WhoE 93
Dill, Mary Alyson 1951- WhoEmL 93, WhoSSW 93
Dill, Maurice Earl 1948- WhoAm 92
Dill, Michael W. Law&B 92
Dill, Michele Andrus WhoWrEP 92
Dill, Peter Joseph Law&B 92
Dill, Richard Everett 1952- WhoEmL 93
Dill, Robert Clifton 1943- St&PR 93
Dill, Virginia S. 1938- WhoAm 92
Dill, William Allen 1918- WhoE 93
Dill, William Joseph 1935- WhoAm 92
Dill, William Rankin 1930- WhoAm 92
Dillaber, Philip Arthur 1922- WhoAm 92, WhoE 93, WhoWor 93
Dillahunty, Leslie Edmon 1947- St&PR 93
Dillamore, Ian L. WhoScE 91-1
Dillamore, Ian Leslie 1938- WhoWor 93
Dillard, Annie BioIn 17, NewYTBS 92 [port]
Dillard, Annie 1945- MagSAmL [port], WhoAm 92, WhoAmW 93, WhoWrEP 92
Dillard, David Brownrigg 1935- WhoAm 92
Dillard, David Hugh 1923- WhoAm 92
Dillard, Dean Innes 1947- WhoWor 93
Dillard, Dennis Alexander 1950- St&PR 93, WhoSSW 93
Dillard, Dudley 1913-1991 WhoAm 92
Dillard, Dudley D. BioIn 17
Dillard, Emil Lee 1921- WhoWrEP 92
Dillard, Gary Eugene 1938- WhoSSW 93
Dillard, Godfrey Joseph 1948- WhoEmL 93
Dillard, J.M. 1954- ScF&FL 92
Dillard, J. Michael 1951- WhoSSW 93
Dillard, Jill Richards 1955- WhoAmW 93
Dillard, Joan Helen 1951- WhoAm 92, WhoAmW 93
Dillard, John Martin 1945- WhoWor 93
Dillard, John Robert 1955- WhoEmL 93
Dillard, Maria Antoinette 1955- WhoAmW 93
Dillard, Marilyn Dianne 1940- WhoAmW 93, WhoWor 93
Dillard, Max Murray 1935- St&PR 93
Dillard, Nancy Rose 1950- WhoAmW 93, WhoE 93, WhoEmL 93, WhoWor 93
Dillard, R.H.W. 1937- ScF&FL 92
Dillard, Richard Henry Wilde 1937- WhoAm 92
Dillard, Robert Carl 1931- St&PR 93
Dillard, Robert G. 1931- St&PR 93
Dillard, Robert Lionel, Jr. 1913- WhoAm 92
Dillard, Rodney Jefferson 1939- WhoAm 92, WhoSSW 93
Dillard, Ronda Lenser WhoAmW 93
Dillard, Teresa Mary 1956- WhoSSW 93
Dillard, W. Thomas 1941- WhoAm 92
Dillard, William 1914- St&PR 93, WhoAm 92
Dillard, William, II 1945- WhoSSW 93
Dillard, William T. 1914- WhoAm 92, WhoSSW 93
Dillard-McGeoch, M. Anne 1950- WhoEmL 93
Dillaway, Robert Beacham 1924- WhoAm 92, WhoSSW 93
Dillaye, Blanche d1931 AmWomPl
Dille, Deborah Lynn Law&B 92
Dille, Earl Kaye 1927- St&PR 93, WhoAm 92
Dille, Flint 1955- ScF&FL 92
Dille, Guy 1929- St&PR 93
Dille, John Flint, Jr. 1913- WhoAm 92
Dille, John Robert 1931- WhoAm 92
Dille, Kenneth Leroy 1925- WhoE 93
Dille, Roland Paul 1924- WhoAm 92
Dillehay, David Rogers 1936- WhoSSW 93
Dillehay, Pamela Ann 1957- WhoAmW 93
Dillemans, Roger H. 1932- WhoWor 93
Dillen, John Thomas 1930- St&PR 93
Dillenberger, John 1918- ConAu 38NR, WhoAm 92
Diller, Angela 1877-1968 Baker 92
Diller, Barry BioIn 17
Diller, Barry 1942- WhoAm 92
Diller, Burgoyne 1906-1965 BioIn 17
Diller, Charles Herbert, Jr. 1945- St&PR 93, WhoAm 92
Diller, John C. WhoAm 92
Diller, Kathleen L. Law&B 92
Diller, Phyllis 1917- BioIn 17, QDrFCA 92 [port], WhoAm 92, WhoWrEP 92
Diller, Ralph L. Law&B 92
Diller, Thomas Eugene 1950- WhoSSW 93
Dilles, Denis Louis Aline 1955- WhoWor 93
Dillett, Gregory C. 1943- St&PR 93
Dilley, Barbara Jean 1938- WhoAmW 93
Dilley, David Wayne 1963- WhoWrEP 92
Dilley, Margarita K. 1957- St&PR 93
Dilley, Margarita Knoepffler 1957- WhoAmW 93
Dilley, Nancy Hiatt 1954- WhoAmW 93
Dilley, Peggy 1935- St&PR 93
Dilley, Thomas Robert 1953- WhoEmL 93
Dilliard, Irving 1904- JrnUS
Dillin, John Woodward, Jr. 1936- WhoAm 92
Dilling, Horst 1933- WhoScE 91-3
Dilling, Kirkpatrick Wallwick 1920- WhoAm 92, WhoWor 93
Dilling, Mildred 1894-1982 Baker 92
Dilling, Roger Oliver 1934- WhoSSW 93
Dillingham, Charles, III 1942- WhoAm 92
Dillingham, Daniel Jay 1958- WhoWrEP 92
Dillingham, John Allen 1939- WhoAm 92
Dillingham, Marjorie Carter 1915- WhoAmW 93
Dillingham, Robert Bulger 1932- WhoAm 92
Dillingham, William Byron 1930- WhoAm 92, WhoSSW 93
Dilling-Ostrowska, Ewa 1934- WhoScE 91-4
Dillion, Theresa Lee 1948- WhoEmL 93
Dillione, Michelle T. Law&B 92
Dilliplaine, Wayne F. 1942- St&PR 93
Dillman, Bradford 1930- ConTFT 10, WhoAm 92
Dillman, Grant 1918- WhoAm 92
Dillman, Joseph John Thomas 1941- WhoE 93
Dillman, Kristin Wicker 1953- WhoAmW 93, WhoEmL 93
Dillman, Leon Gracen 1932- WhoSSW 93
Dillman, Robert John 1941- WhoSSW 93
Dillmann, August 1823-1894 IntDcAn
Dillmann, Edward B. 1935- St&PR 93
Dillmann, Nancy Cameron 1947- WhoWrEP 92
Dillon, Andrew Joseph 1947- WhoEmL 93
Dillon, Barbara Ladene 1935- WhoSSW 93
Dillon, Bradley Eugene Law&B 92
Dillon, Carol Jane 1951- WhoAmW 93

Dillon, Charles T.G. 1926- *WhoScE 91-3*
Dillon, Clarence Douglas 1909- *WhoAm 92*
Dillon, Clifford Brien 1921- *WhoAm 92*
Dillon, David B. 1951- *St&PR 93*
Dillon, David Brian 1951- *WhoAm 92*
Dillon, Debra Jean 1952- *WhoWrEP 92*
Dillon, Diane *BioIn 17, Law&B 92*
Dillon, Diane 1933- *ScF&FL 92*
Dillon, Diane (Claire) 1933- *MajAI [port]*
Dillon, Don *BioIn 17*
Dillon, Donald Francis 1940- *St&PR 93*
Dillon, Donald Ward 1936- *WhoAm 92*
Dillon, Dorothy *BioIn 17*
Dillon, Eilis 1920- *ConAu 38NR, MajAI [port]*
Dillon, Fannie Charles 1881-1947 *Baker 92*
Dillon, Francis Richard 1939- *WhoAm 92*
Dillon, G. Michael 1938- *St&PR 93*
Dillon, Gary G. 1934- *St&PR 93*
Dillon, Gary Gene 1934- *WhoAm 92*
Dillon, George C. 1922- *St&PR 93*
Dillon, Glenn Mark 1958- *St&PR 93*
Dillon, Gregory Russell 1922- *St&PR 93, WhoAm 92*
Dillon, Helen *BioIn 17*
Dillon, Henri 1912-1954 *Baker 92*
Dillon, James Charles 1951- *WhoE 93*
Dillon, James Joseph 1948- *WhoEmL 93*
Dillon, James Lee 1928- *St&PR 93, WhoAm 92*
Dillon, James M. 1933- *WhoAm 92*
Dillon, James McNulty 1933- *St&PR 93*
Dillon, Jeffrey Warren 1959- *St&PR 93*
Dillon, Jesse A. *Law&B 92*
Dillon, John 1923- *ScF&FL 92*
Dillon, John 1923-1991 *BioIn 17*
Dillon, John Andrew 1954- *WhoE 93, WhoEmL 93*
Dillon, John C. 1919- *St&PR 93*
Dillon, John C., III 1920- *St&PR 93*
Dillon, John H. 1938- *St&PR 93*
Dillon, John Robert 1941- *St&PR 93*
Dillon, John Robert, III 1941- *WhoAm 92*
Dillon, John T. 1938- *St&PR 93, WhoAm 92*
Dillon, Joy 1942- *WhoSSW 93*
Dillon, Judy Reep 1944- *WhoAmW 93*
Dillon, Karl Douglas *St&PR 93*
Dillon, Kate Rose *AmWomPl*
Dillon, Kathleen Margaret Gereaux 1957- *WhoAmW 93, WhoEmL 93*
Dillon, Kathryn Sullivan 1953- *WhoSSW 93*
Dillon, Keith Gregory 1946- *WhoEmL 93*
Dillon, Kevin Patrick 1954- *WhoSSW 93*
Dillon, Leo 1933- *BioIn 17, BlkAull 92, MajAI, ScF&FL 92*
Dillon, Lionel *ScF&FL 92*
Dillon, Matt *BioIn 17*
Dillon, Matt 1964- *IntDcF 2-3 [port], News 92 [port], WhoAm 92*
Dillon, Melinda 1939- *ConTFT 10*
Dillon, Merton Lynn 1924- *WhoAm 92*
Dillon, Michael F. d1991 *BioIn 17*
Dillon, Millicent 1925- *WhoWrEP 92*
Dillon, Nancy 1954?- *BioIn 17*
Dillon, Neal Winfield 1925- *WhoAm 92*
Dillon, Oscar Wendell, Jr. 1928- *WhoAm 92*
Dillon, Patricia Anne 1948- *WhoAmW 93*
Dillon, Paul Sanford 1943- *WhoAm 92*
Dillon, Paul Wilson 1926- *WhoAm 92*
Dillon, Peter C. *ScF&FL 92*
Dillon, Ralph I. *St&PR 93*
Dillon, Ray William 1954- *WhoEmL 93, WhoSSW 93*
Dillon, Richard Hugh 1924- *WhoAm 92, WhoWrEP 92*
Dillon, Robert Morton 1923- *WhoAm 92*
Dillon, Robert Sherwood 1929- *WhoE 93*
Dillon, Robert W. *Law&B 92*
Dillon, Susan Rosenthal *BioIn 17*
Dillon, Terry 1948- *St&PR 93*
Dillon, Thomas Joseph *Law&B 92*
Dillon, Thomas Ray 1948- *WhoEmL 93*
Dillon, Veronica *Law&B 92*
Dillon, William Joseph 1938- *WhoE 93*
Dillon, Wilton Sterling 1923- *WhoAm 92*
Dillon-Malone, Basil 1947- *WhoE 93*
Dillon-McHugh, Cathleen Theresa 1951- *WhoE 93*
Dillow, Jeffrey C. *ScF&FL 92*
Dillow, John David 1946- *WhoEmL 93*
Dillport, Janet Files 1951- *WhoEmL 93*
Dills, Carol Ingle 1953- *WhoSSW 93*
Dills, James Arlof 1930- *WhoAm 92*
Dills, James Carl 1954- *WhoEmL 93*
Dillworth, Robert J. *Law&B 92*
Di Lorenzo, Aldo *WhoScE 91-3*
DiLorenzo, Frank R. 1965- *WhoE 93*
DiLorenzo, Gary P. 1956- *St&PR 93*
Di Lorenzo, John F., Jr. *Law&B 92*
DiLorenzo, John F., Jr. 1940- *St&PR 93*
Di Lorenzo, John Florio, Jr. 1940- *WhoAm 92*
DiLorenzo, Joseph L. *WhoAm 92*
Di Lorenzo, Kris M. 1950- *WhoE 93*
DiLorenzo, Louis Patrick 1952- *WhoEmL 93*
DiLorenzo, Sherri Ann 1963- *WhoAmW 93*
di Lorenzo Badia, Giulio 1928- *WhoUN 92*
DiLoreto, Ann Marie 1953- *WhoEmL 93*
DiLoreto, Joanne Marie 1963- *WhoAmW 93*
DiLouis, Anthony 1945- *St&PR 93*
Dils, Henry H., Jr. 1914- *St&PR 93*
Dils, Raymond R. *WhoScE 91-1*
Dilsaver, Paul 1949- *ScF&FL 92*
Dilsizian, Rick Charles 1946- *WhoEmL 93*
Dilts, David Michael 1950- *WhoAm 92*
Dilts, Mervin Robert 1938- *WhoAm 92*
Dilts, Michael C. 1956- *St&PR 93*
DiLuco, Dora 1922- *St&PR 93*
DiLuco, Eugene 1919- *St&PR 93*
DiLuglio, Domenic Raymond 1920- *WhoE 93*
Di Lullo, Charles S. 1938- *WhoIns 93*
DiLuzio, Adrian Louis 1946- *WhoE 93*
Diluzio, C.B. 1955- *St&PR 93*
DiLuzio, C. Bruce *Law&B 92*
Di Luzio, Vittorio Tito 1939- *WhoWor 93*
Dilworth, Ann E. 1947- *St&PR 93*
Dilworth, Ann Evans 1947- *WhoAm 92, WhoEmL 93*
Dilworth, Billy D. 1934- *WhoSSW 93*
Dilworth, David A. 1934- *ConAu 136*
Dilworth, Edwin Earle 1914- *WhoAm 92*
Dilworth, James Weldon 1928- *WhoAm 92*
Dilworth, Jonathan Robin *WhoScE 91-1*
Dilworth, Joseph Richardson 1916- *WhoAm 92, WhoWor 93*
Dilworth, Richardson 1898-1974 *PolPar*
Dilworth, Robert Lexow 1936- *WhoAm 92*
Dilworth, Stephen James 1959- *WhoEmL 93, WhoWor 93*
Dima, Gheorghe 1847-1925 *Baker 92*
Dima, Ioan 1934- *WhoScE 91-4*
Dima, Nicholas *BioIn 17*
Dimaggio, Dennis *WhoIns 93*
DiMaggio, Dominic Paul 1917- *BiDAMSp 1989*
DiMaggio, Dominic Paul, Jr. 1950- *St&PR 93*
DiMaggio, Frank Louis 1929- *WhoAm 92*
DiMaggio, Joe *BioIn 17*
Di Maggio, Joseph Paul 1914- *WhoAm 92*
Di Maiolo, Vincent, Jr. *Law&B 92*
Dimaiti, Mary C. *Law&B 92*
Dimant, Jacob 1947- *WhoE 93, WhoWor 93*
Di Mantova, Walter Dario 1958- *WhoEmL 93*
Dimaporo, Abdullah D. *WhoAsAP 91*
Dimaporo, Mohamed Ali B. 1918- *WhoAsAP 91*
DiMarco, Anthony 1947- *WhoE 93*
Di Marco, Piergiulio 1942- *WhoScE 91-3*
Di Marco, Stefano 1957- *WhoScE 91-3*
Dimare, Leonard E. *Law&B 92*
Di Maria, Charles C. 1923- *St&PR 93*
Di Maria, Valerie Theresa 1957- *WhoAm 92, WhoAmW 93*
Di Marino, Fulvio 1935- *WhoScE 91-3*
Dimarogonas, Andrew D. 1938- *WhoScE 91-3*
Di Martino, Joseph S. 1943- *St&PR 93*
DiMartino, Rita 1937- *NotHsAW 93*
Dimarzio, Dennis A. 1943- *WhoIns 93*
DiMarzio, Rick 1948- *St&PR 93*
Di Mascio, John Philip 1944- *WhoE 93*
DiMascio, William Michael 1943- *WhoE 93*
Dimas de Melo Pimenta, Emanuel 1957- *Baker 92*
Di Massa, Ernani Vincenzo, Jr. 1947- *WhoEmL 93*
DiMatteo, Dominick, Jr. 1918- *WhoAm 92*
DiMatteo, John R. 1931- *WhoE 93*
DiMatteo, Philip Stephen 1947- *WhoEmL 93*
Di Mauro, Concetto d1991 *BioIn 17*
DiMauro, Patrick Samuel 1949- *WhoE 93*
Dimbleby, David 1938- *WhoWor 93*
DiMeglio, Ralph 1926- *St&PR 93*
Dimen, Muriel Vera 1942- *WhoAm 92*
Dimenstein, Catherine *ScF&FL 92*
Dimeny, Imre 1922- *WhoScE 91-4*
Di Meo, Dominick 1927- *WhoAm 92, WhoE 93*
DiMeo, James Stephen 1954- *WhoE 93*
Dimeo, R. Steven 1945- *WhoWrEP 92*
Dimic, Viktor *WhoScE 91-4*
DiMicco, Wendy Ann 1948- *WhoEmL 93*
Dimiceli, Vincent J. 1918- *WhoWor 93*
Dimich, William Michael 1931- *St&PR 93*
DiMichele, Leonard Vincent 1952- *WhoSSW 93*
Di Michele, Mary 1949- *BioIn 17, WhoCanL 92*
Dimick, Alan Robert 1932- *WhoSSW 93*
Dimick, Elisabeth *AmWomPl*
Dimick, Walter S. 1950- *WhoEmL 93*
Dimiev, Stancho Genchev 1932- *WhoWor 93*
Diminnie, Carol B. 1945- *WhoAmW 93*
Diminnie, Charles Richard 1944- *WhoE 93*
Diminno, Frank S. *St&PR 93*
Dimino, Alfonso 1920- *St&PR 93*
Di Mino, Andre Anthony 1955- *St&PR 93, WhoE 93, WhoEmL 93*
Dimino, Franklin Joseph 1933- *St&PR 93*
Dimino, Joseph Carl *Law&B 92*
Dimino, Sylvia Theresa 1955- *WhoAmW 93, WhoEmL 93*
Dimitracopoulos, George 1940- *WhoScE 91-3*
Dimitras, Panayote Elias 1953- *WhoWor 93*
Dimitri, Lyubomir 1934- *WhoScE 91-3*
Di Mitri, Piero 1933- *WhoAm 92*
Dimitriadis, Andre C. 1940- *WhoAm 92*
Dimitrijevic, Braco 1948- *BioIn 17*
Dimitrijevic, Milorad 1926- *WhoScE 91-4*
Dimitrijevic Apis, Dragutin T. 1876-1917 *BioIn 17*
Dimitrios, I *BioIn 17*
Dimitrios, I 1914-1991 *AnObit 1991*
Dimitriou, Theodore 1926- *St&PR 93, WhoAm 92*
Dimitroff, Ivan 1931- *WhoScE 91-4*
Dimitrov, Boyan Nedyalkov 1943- *WhoWor 93*
Dimitrov, Georgi 1882-1949 *ColdWar 2 [port], DcTwHis*
Dimitrov, Philip Dimitrov 1955- *WhoWor 93*
Dimitrov, Vladimir Dimov 1942- *WhoWor 93*
Dimitrova, Ghena 1940- *OxDcOp*
Dimitrova, Ghena 1941- *Baker 92*
Dimitry, Charles Patton 1837-1910 *JrnUS*
Dimitry, Edward S. *Law&B 92*
Dimitry, John Randolph 1929- *WhoAm 92*
Dimitry, Theodore George 1937- *WhoAm 92*
Dimler, George Richard 1931- *WhoWrEP 92*
Dimling, David Stanton 1932- *WhoAm 92*
Dimling, John A. 1938- *St&PR 93*
Dimling, John Arthur 1938- *WhoAm 92*
Dimma, William Andrew 1928- *St&PR 93, WhoAm 92*
Dimmick, Carolyn Reaber 1929- *WhoAm 92, WhoAmW 93*
Dimmick, Charles William 1940- *WhoAm 92*
Dimmig, Bruce David 1956- *WhoE 93*
Dimmitt, Cornelia 1938- *WhoAmW 93*
Dimmitt, Lawrence A. *Law&B 92*
Dimmitt, Simon Burn 1956- *WhoWor 93*
Dimmock, John Oliver 1936- *WhoAm 92*
Dimmock, Nigel John *WhoScE 91-1*
Dimock, Marshall E(dward) 1903-1991 *ConAu 136*
Dimock, Marshall Edward 1903-1991 *BioIn 17*
Dimock, Rodney Claude 1946- *St&PR 93*
Dimoff, Roy 1959- *St&PR 93*
Dimon, James 1956- *St&PR 93, WhoAm 92*
Dimon, John E. 1916- *St&PR 93*
Dimond, Alan Theodore 1943- *WhoAm 92*
Dimond, Albert Eugene 1914-1972 *BioIn 17*
Dimond, Albert Kenneth 1923- *St&PR 93*
Dimond, Douglas A. *Law&B 92*
Dimond, Edmunds Grey 1918- *WhoAm 92*
Dimond, Jeffrey John 1952- *WhoEmL 93*
Dimond, Robert Edward 1936- *WhoAm 92*
Dimond, Roberta Ralston 1940- *WhoAmW 93*
Dimond, Thomas 1916- *WhoE 93*
Dimondstein, Boris 1891-1973 *ScF&FL 92*
Dimos, John Nicholas *Law&B 92*
Dimotakis, Paul Nicholas 1928- *WhoScE 91-3*
Dimoulas, William N. 1943- *St&PR 93*
Dimov, Bojidar 1935- *Baker 92*
Dimov, Dimo Ivanov 1929- *WhoScE 91-4*
Dimov, Ivan 1926- *WhoScE 91-4*
Dimov, Ivan 1927- *Baker 92*
D'Imperio, Connie Boling 1946- *WhoAmW 93*
Dimsdale, Joel Edward 1947- *WhoEmL 93*
Dimsey, Peter S. P. *WhoAm 92*
Dimson, Irving d1992 *BioIn 17*
DiMucci, Monica 1964- *WhoAmW 93*
DiMucci, Susan *BioIn 17*
Di Muccio, Mary Jo 1930- *WhoAm 92*
Di Muccio, Robert A. 1957- *WhoIns 93*
Di Muro, Adolfo 1939- *WhoScE 91-3*
Di Muro, Joseph V. *Law&B 92*
Di Murska, Ilma 1836-1889 *OxDcOp*
Dinaburg, Mary Ellen 1954- *WhoAm 92*
Dinal, J.G. *Law&B 92*
Dinale, Margherita Silvi 1928- *WhoAmW 93*
Dinan, Donald Robert 1949- *WhoEmL 93*
Dinan, James C. *Law&B 92*
Dinan, James Gerard 1959- *WhoE 93*
Dinan, Patrick Alan 1950- *WhoEmL 93*
Di Napoli, Augusto *WhoScE 91-3*
Dinapoli, Leonard F., Jr. *Law&B 92*
DiNapoli, Patrick Anthony 1942- *St&PR 93*
Dinapoli, Thomas John 1943- *St&PR 93*
Dinar, Sami *BioIn 17*
Dinardi, Peter L. 1952- *St&PR 93*
DiNardo, Bruno *Law&B 92*
DiNardo, Christopher *Law&B 92*
Dinardo, Marilynn 1937- *WhoWrEP 92*
DiNardo, Tom 1964- *WhoEmL 93*
DiNatale, Paul Peter 1951- *WhoEmL 93*
Dinauer, Thomas A. 1925- *St&PR 93*
Dinbgo, Wu *ScF&FL 92*
Dinc, Ural 1937- *WhoScE 91-4*
D'Incalci, Maurizio 1952- *WhoScE 91-3*
Dince, Robert R. *BioIn 17*
Dincer, Hamdi Mustafa 1940- *WhoScE 91-4*
Dincer, Salih 1947- *WhoScE 91-4*
Dinces, Franklin Gary 1958- *WhoEmL 93*
Dinculeanu, Nicolae 1925- *WhoAm 92*
Dindesky, Viliam 1925- *WhoScE 91-4*
Dindorf, Joseph Lee 1940- *St&PR 93*
D'Indy, Vincent *Baker 92, OxDcOp*
d'Indy, Vincent 1851-1931 *IntDcOp*
Dine, James 1935- *BioIn 17*
Dine, Jim 1935- *BioIn 17, WhoAm 92*
Dine, Richard 1958- *WhoE 93*
Dineen, Daniel Thomas 1948- *St&PR 93*
Dineen, J. Walter 1936-1990 *BioIn 17*
Dineen, John K. 1928- *WhoAm 92*
Dineen, Robert J. 1929- *St&PR 93*
Dineen, William Patrick Bill 1932- *WhoAm 92*
Dinel, Richard Henry 1942- *WhoWor 93*
Dineley, David Lawrence *WhoScE 91-1*
Dinella, Roger Walsh *Law&B 92*
Dinelli, Mel d1991 *BioIn 17*
Diner, Wilma Canada 1926- *WhoAm 92*
Dinerstein, Norman (Myron) 1937-1982 *Baker 92*
Dinerstein, Robert David 1953- *WhoEmL 93*
Dinescu, Mircea 1950- *BioIn 17*
Dinesen, Bo 1947- *WhoWor 93*
Dinesen, Isak 1885-1962 *BioIn 17*
DiNetta, Dianne Connell 1951- *WhoEmL 93*
Ding, Chen 1919- *WhoE 93, WhoWor 93*
Ding, Decheng 1943- *WhoWor 93*
Ding, Er-Sheng 1928- *WhoWor 93*
Ding, Hai 1969- *WhoWor 93*
Ding, Hua 1960- *WhoWor 93*
Ding, Jianping 1957- *WhoWor 93*
Ding, K.H. *BioIn 17*
Ding, Ren 1939- *WhoWor 93*
Ding, Xing Fu 1945- *WhoWor 93*
Ding, Yuanhong 1931- *WhoWor 93*
Dingel, James D. *Law&B 92*
Dingell, John D. *BioIn 17*
Dingell, John D. 1926- *CngDr 91*
Dingell, John David, Jr. 1926- *WhoAm 92*
Dinger, Paul L. *Law&B 92*
Dinger, William Sadlier 1941- *St&PR 93*
Dinges, Richard Allen 1945- *WhoE 93, WhoWor 93*
Dingfelder, Tammi Lee 1965- *WhoE 93*
Ding Guan'gen 1929- *WhoAsAP 91*
Ding Guangxun *BioIn 17*
Ding Henggao 1931- *WhoAsAP 91*
Dingiswayo c. 1770-1818 *HarEnMi*
Dingle, Donna Victoria 1952- *WhoWrEP 92*
Dingle, Doreen Mary 1956- *WhoAmW 93*
Dingle, John Reginald 1921-1989 *BioIn 17*
Dingle, John T. 1927- *WhoScE 91-1*
Dingle, M.G.W. *WhoScE 91-1*
Dingle, Margaret Concetta Spargo 1918- *WhoAmW 93*
Dingle, Percy Arnold 1962- *WhoE 93*
Dingle, Susan 1950- *WhoEmL 93*
Ding Ling 1904-1986 *BioIn 17*
Dingman, Avon Marie 1962- *WhoAmW 93*
Dingman, Dennis Keith 1945- *St&PR 93*
Dingman, James Daniel 1954- *WhoEmL 93*
Dingman, Janet Simpson 1940- *WhoSSW 93*
Dingman, M. Howard 1925- *St&PR 93*
Dingman, Mark R. 1949- *St&PR 93*
Dingman, Martha L. *AmWomPl*
Dingman, Maurice J. 1914- *WhoAm 92*
Dingman, Michael Bruce 1950- *WhoEmL 93*
Dingman, Michael David 1931- *St&PR 93, WhoAm 92*
Dingman, Robert John 1941- *St&PR 93*

Dingman, Robert Lewis 1931- *WhoSSW 93*
Dingman, Robert Walter 1926- *WhoAm 92*
Dingman, Sheila Elaine 1965- *WhoEmL 93*
Dings, Jan Anna Maria 1961- *WhoWor 93*
Dings, John Linton 1937- *St&PR 93*
Ding Tingmo 1936- *WhoAsAP 91*
Dingus, David Hamilton 1948- *St&PR 93*
Dingus, Michael H.R. 1948- *St&PR 93*
Dingwall, Craig David *Law&B 92*
Dingwell, David W. 1936- *St&PR 93*
Dinh, Nguyen Thi 1920-1992 *NewYTBS 92*
Dinh, Nguyen Thi, Madame 1920- *DcTwHis*
Dinh, Xavier 1929- *WhoUN 92*
Dinhaupt, Francis Valentine 1907-1991 *BioIn 17*
Dinhut, Patrice *WhoAm 92*
Dini, John F. 1951- *St&PR 93*
Dini, Joseph J. 1941- *WhoE 93*
Dinic, Carl Joseph 1903- *WhoE 93*
Di Nicola, Albert 1917- *WhoWrEP 92*
Dinicola, John W. *Law&B 92*
DiNicola, John W. 1938- *St&PR 93*
Dinicu, Grigoras 1889-1949 *Baker 92*
Dinielli, Nicholas 1930- *St&PR 93*
Di Niro, John J. 1945- *St&PR 93*
Dinitz, Simon 1926- *WhoAm 92*
Dinius, E. Lowell *Law&B 92*
Diniz, Francisco Antonio Martins 1945- *WhoWor 93*
Dinizulu, Nana Yao Opare d1991 *BioIn 17*
Dinkard, Lawrence W. *St&PR 93*
Dinkel, John George 1944- *WhoAm 92*
Dinkel, Thomas A. 1928- *St&PR 93*
Dinkelspiel, John R. 1935- *St&PR 93*
Dinkelspiel, Paul Gaines 1935- *WhoAm 92*
Dinkelspiel, Ulf Adolf Roger 1939- *WhoWor 93*
Dinkes, Marc 1954- *WhoE 93*
Dinkespiler, Jean-Albert 1927- *WhoScE 91-2*
Dinkins, Benjamin Alan *Law&B 92*
Dinkins, Carol Eggert 1945- *WhoAm 92, WhoAmW 93*
Dinkins, David 1927- *BioIn 17, ConBlB 4 [port]*
Dinkins, David N. *AfrAmBi [port]*
Dinkins, David N. 1927- *WhoAm 92, WhoE 93*
Dinkins, Joyce *BioIn 17*
Dinkins, Richard Stailley 1944- *WhoSSW 93*
Dinkins, Thomas Allen, III 1946- *WhoEmL 93*
Dinkins, William H. d1991 *BioIn 17*
Dinklage, Lillian Brandon 1937- *WhoE 93*
Dinklocker, Christina Marie 1952- *WhoAmW 93*
Dinman, Bertram David 1925- *WhoAm 92*
Dinn, Jerome R. *St&PR 93*
Dinn, John P. *Law&B 92*
Dinnage, James D. *Law&B 92*
Dinneen, Betty 1929- *BioIn 17*
Dinneen, George F. d1991 *BioIn 17*
Dinneen, Gerald Paul 1924- *WhoAm 92*
Dinneen, J. Robert 1941- *St&PR 93*
Dinneen, James Francis 1915- *WhoAm 92*
Dinneen, William Henry 1876-1955 *BiDAMSp 1989*
Dinner, Dara Lisa *Law&B 92*
Dinner, Janice Marie 1957- *WhoEmL 93*
Dinner, Michael *BioIn 17, MiSFD 9*
Dinnerstein, Dorothy d1992 *NewYTBS 92*
Dinnerstein, Harvey 1928- *WhoAm 92*
Dinnerstein, Leonard 1934- *WhoAm 92*
Dinnerstein, Lois 1932- *WhoE 93*
Dinnerstein, Michael 1960- *WhoEmL 93*
Dinnerstein, Myra 1934- *WhoAmW 93*
Dinnerstein, Simon Abraham 1943- *WhoE 93*
Dinniman, Andrew Eric 1944- *WhoE 93*
Dinning, Woodford Wyndham, Jr. 1954- *WhoEmL 93*
Dinnocenzo, Deborah Anne 1964- *WhoEmL 93*
D'Innocenzo, Phillis 1942- *St&PR 93*
Dinon, Richard A. 1944- *St&PR 93*
Dinopoulos, Odisseas 1927- *WhoScE 91-3*
Dinorscia, Joseph 1929- *St&PR 93*
Dinos, Nicholas 1934- *WhoAm 92*
Dinoso, Vicente Pescador, Jr. 1936- *WhoAm 92*
Dinov, Ventzislav Rangelov 1930- *WhoScE 91-4*
DiNovo, Theresa Christine 1958- *WhoEmL 93*
Dinowitz, Debra L. *Law&B 92*
Dinsch, F. Lawrence 1938- *St&PR 93*
Dinse, Curt W. 1958- *St&PR 93*
Dinse, John Merrell 1925- *WhoAm 92*
Dinsmoor, James Arthur 1921- *WhoAm 92*
Dinsmore, David Allen 1951- *WhoEmL 93*
Dinsmore, Gordon Griffith 1917- *WhoAm 92*
Dinsmore, Mary C. *AmWomPl*
Dinsmore, Philip Wade 1942- *WhoAm 92*
Dinsmore, Roberta Joan Maier 1934- *WhoAmW 93, WhoE 93*
Dinsmore, Ronald E. 1926- *St&PR 93*
Dinsmore, Stephen R. *Law&B 92*
Dinsmore, Thomas Hall 1953- *St&PR 93*
Dinsmore, Wiley 1934- *WhoAm 92*
Dinstber, George Charles 1966- *WhoE 93*
Dinstel, Edward R. 1954- *WhoIns 93*
Dinstl, Karl *WhoScE 91-4*
Dintaman, James L. 1943- *St&PR 93*
Dintenfass, Julius 1910- *WhoE 93*
Dintenfass, Mark 1941- *WhoWrEP 92*
Dinter, Harald Josef 1956- *WhoWor 93*
DiNucci, Judy Christenson 1935- *WhoAmW 93*
Dinuzulu 1868-1913 *HarEnMi*
Dinvaut, Jeanne Margaret 1940- *WhoAmW 93*
Dinwiddie, George L., Jr. 1924- *St&PR 93*
Dinwiddie, Heather Leah 1953- *WhoE 93*
Dinwiddie, John Alexander 1931- *St&PR 93*
Dinwiddle, George 1958- *St&PR 93*
Dinwiddy, J.R. 1939-1990 *BioIn 17*
Dinwiddy, John Rowland 1939-1990 *BioIn 17*
Dinya, Laszlo 1949- *WhoScE 91-4*
Diocletian c. 250-c. 313 *HarEnMi, OxDcByz*
Diocletian, Emperor of Rome 245?-313? *BioIn 17*
Diodene, Alonzo Nelson 1941- *WhoSSW 93*
Diodoros dc. 394 *OxDcByz*
Diodorov, Boris *BioIn 17*
Diogenes *OxDcByz*
Dioguardi, Michael Joseph 1943- *St&PR 93*
Dioguardi, Raymond Thomas 1955- *St&PR 93*
Diohep, John Lewis 1933- *St&PR 93*
Diomede, Matthew 1940- *WhoWrEP 92*
Dion, Arnold Silva 1939- *WhoE 93*
Dion, Celine *BioIn 17*
Dion, Jean-Michel Robert 1950- *WhoWor 93*
Dion, Marc Ronald, Sr. *Law&B 92*
Dion, Peter *ConAu 137*
Dion, Philip J. 1944- *St&PR 93*
Dion, Philip M. 1950- *St&PR 93*
Dion, Robert 1942- *St&PR 93*
Dion, Robert L. 1932- *St&PR 93, WhoIns 93*
Dion, Ronald P. 1936- *St&PR 93*
Dionne, Gerald Francis 1935- *WhoWor 93*
Dionne, James J. 1951- *St&PR 93*
Dionne, Joseph L. 1933- *St&PR 93*
Dionne, Joseph Lewis 1933- *WhoAm 92, WhoE 93*
Dionou, Fidele Tanor 1948- *WhoUN 92*
Dionysios Of Tell Mahre d845 *OxDcByz*
Dionysios The Areopagite *OxDcByz*
Dionysios The Areopagite, Pseudo- fl. c. 500- *OxDcByz*
Dionysios Thrax c. 170BC-c. 90BC *OxDcByz*
Dionysiou, Demetrios 1939- *WhoWor 93*
Dionysius Exiguus fl. c. 500-c. 550 *OxDcByz*
Dionysius the Elder c. 432BC-367BC *HarEnMi*
Diop, Birago 1906-1989 *BioIn 17, BlkAull 92*
Diop, Cheikh Anta 1923-1986 *ConBlB 4 [port]*
Dior, Christian 1905-1957 *BioIn 17*
D'Iorio, Margaret Jean 1943- *WhoAmW 93*
Diorio, Margaret Toarello *WhoWrEP 92*
Diorio, Mary Ann Lucia 1945- *WhoE 93*
DiOrio, Robert Michael 1947- *WhoEmL 93*
Dios, Manuel Unanue de *BioIn 17*
Dioskorides fl. c. 65- *OxDcByz*
Dioskoros d454 *OxDcByz*
Dioskoros Of Aphrodito dc. 585 *OxDcByz*
Dioso, Leocadio Fernandez, Jr. 1941- *WhoUN 92*
Diot, Bernard *WhoScE 91-2*
Diotalevi, Robert Nicholas 1959- *WhoEmL 93*
Diotte, Alfred P. 1925- *St&PR 93*
Diotte, Alfred Peter 1925- *WhoAm 92*
Diouf, Abdou 1935- *ConBlB 3 [port], WhoAfr, WhoWor 93*
Diouf, Bouna Semou 1947- *WhoUN 92*
Diouf, Jacques 1938- *WhoUN 92*
Di Paglia, Raymond 1929- *St&PR 93*
Di Palma, Joseph Alphonse 1931- *WhoWor 93*
DiPalma, Joseph Rupert 1916- *WhoAm 92*
di Palma, Salvatore 1942- *WhoUN 92*
DiPalma, Susan *St&PR 93*
Di Paola, Robert *WhoScE 91-2*
Di Paola, Robert Arnold 1933- *WhoE 93*
Di Paola, Robert B. *Law&B 92*
Di Paolo, Joseph Amadeo 1924- *WhoE 93*
Di Paolo, Joseph Amedeo 1924- *WhoAm 92*
Di Paolo, Nicholas P. 1941- *WhoAm 92*
DiPaolo, Peter Thomas 1937- *WhoSSW 93*
Dipasqua, Lucy Ann 1927- *WhoAmW 93*
Di Pasquale, Emanuel Paul 1943- *WhoE 93, WhoWrEP 92*
Di Pasquale, Gene 1932- *WhoE 93*
Di Pasquale, Pasquale, Jr. 1928- *WhoAm 92*
Dipasquale, Thomas James *Law&B 92*
DiPego, Gerald 1941- *ScF&FL 92*
DiPentima, Renato Anthony 1941- *WhoAm 92*
DiPerna, Karen Ann 1956- *WhoE 93*
DiPerna, Paula 1949- *WhoEmL 93*
DiPersio, Vincent *MiSFD 9*
Diphusa, Patty *ConTFT 10*
DiPiazza, Michael Charles 1953- *WhoEmL 93*
DiPiero, Andrew Edward, Jr. 1952- *WhoEmL 93*
Di Piero, W(illiam) S. 1945- *ConAu 138*
DiPierro, Karen P. 1964- *WhoAmW 93*
DiPierro, Patrick M. 1940- *St&PR 93*
DiPietro, Janice Diane 1957- *WhoEmL 93*
Dipietro, John J. *St&PR 93*
DiPietro, Ralph Anthony 1942- *WhoAm 92*
Di Pietro, Robert Joseph 1932-1991 *ConAu 136*
Di Placido, Joseph Martin 1957- *WhoE 93*
DiPlacido, Lisa Ann 1967- *WhoAmW 93*
Diplas, Panayiotis 1954- *WhoSSW 93*
Diplock, Anthony Tytherleigh *WhoScE 91-1*
Diplock, Anthony Tytherleigh 1935- *WhoWor 93*
Diplovatatzes *OxDcByz*
DiPolvere, Edward John 1929- *WhoE 93*
Dippel, (Johann) Andreas 1866-1932 *Baker 92*
Dipple, William M. 1923- *St&PR 93*
Dippo, Cathryn Suzette 1947- *WhoEmL 93*
D'Ippolito, Anthony 1962- *WhoEmL 93*
Dippy, George Bradner, III 1934- *WhoAm 92*
Di Prima, Diane 1934- *WhoWrEP 92*
DiPrima, Joseph F. *Law&B 92*
Di Prima, Stephanie Marie 1952- *WhoEmL 93*
Di Primo, Marie Ann 1952- *WhoAmW 93, WhoEmL 93*
Diprova, Robert A. *St&PR 93*
Dirac, Paul Adrien Maurice 1902-1984 *BioIn 17*
Diracles, James Constantine 1948- *WhoEmL 93*
Diracles, John Michael, Jr. 1944- *St&PR 93, WhoAm 92*
Dircks, Robert J. 1927- *St&PR 93*
Dircks, William Joseph 1929- *WhoUN 92*
Director, Stephen William 1943- *WhoAm 92, WhoWor 93*
Direen, Harry George, Jr. 1955- *WhoEmL 93*
Direnfeld, Lorne Kenneth 1949- *WhoEmL 93*
DiRenzo, Gordon James 1934- *WhoAm 92*
DiResta, James John 1952- *WhoE 93*
Dirheimer, Guy 1931- *WhoScE 91-2*
Diria, Ahmed Hassan 1937- *WhoAfr*
Diria, Hassan Ahmed *WhoWor 93*
Dirico, Henry 1927- *St&PR 93*
Di Rienzo, Frederick J. 1948- *WhoIns 93*
DiRienzo, Joseph Michael 1950- *WhoE 93*
DiRienzo, Orlando N. 1933- *St&PR 93*
Dirik, Joseph Paul 1956- *St&PR 93*
Dirkes, Dan *Law&B 92*
Dirkin, Shirley Barbara Anne 1959- *WhoWor 93*
Dirks, Bruce Lane 1950- *WhoSSW 93*
Dirks, Dennis J. 1948- *St&PR 93*
Dirks, John Alan *Law&B 92*
Dirks, John Herbert 1933- *WhoAm 92*
Dirks, Kenneth Ray 1925- *WhoAm 92*
Dirks, Lee Edward 1935- *WhoAm 92*
Dirks, Leslie Chant 1936- *WhoAm 92*
Dirks, Rudolph 1877-1968 *BioIn 17*
Dirks, Vickie Ellen 1953- *WhoAmW 93, WhoEmL 93*
Dirksen, Everett McKinley 1896-1969 *BioIn 17, PolPar*
Dirksen, Gordon F. 1943- *St&PR 93*
Dirksen, Linda K. *Law&B 92*
Dirksen, Richard Wayne 1921- *WhoAm 92*
Dirksing, John Walter 1941- *St&PR 93*
Dirkzwager, Arie 1930- *WhoWor 93*
Dirlam, John *MiSFD 9*
Dirmeier, Michael Dennis 1950- *WhoE 93, WhoEmL 93*
Diro, Ted R. 1944- *WhoAsAP 91*
Di Roberto, Federico 1935- *WhoWor 93*
Di Roberto, Samuel Joseph 1937- *WhoE 93*
DiRocco, John J., Jr. *Law&B 92*
DiRocco, Joseph A. 1950- *St&PR 93*
Di Rosa, Herve 1959- *BioIn 17*
Dirr, Peter J. 1941- *WhoE 93*
Dirrane, Brian Michael 1945- *St&PR 93*
Dirring, Joanne Carlton 1947- *WhoSSW 93*
Dirring, William Andrew 1946- *WhoEmL 93, WhoSSW 93*
Dirsken, Geoff *BioIn 17*
Dirst, Stephanie Lemke 1942- *WhoAmW 93*
Diruta, Girolamo c. 1554-1610 *Baker 92*
Dirvin, Gerald Vincent 1937- *St&PR 93, WhoAm 92*
DiSaia, Philip John 1937- *WhoWor 93*
DiSalle, Mark *MiSFD 9*
DiSalvo, Anthony Joseph 1950- *WhoE 93*
Di Salvo, Arthur Francis 1932- *WhoAm 92, WhoSSW 93*
DiSalvo, Frank Paul 1946- *WhoEmL 93*
DiSalvo, Jacqueline 1943- *ConAu 139*
Di Salvo, Jacqueline Anne 1943- *WhoE 93*
DiSalvo, Joanne P. *WhoE 93*
DiSalvo, Louis Henry 1940- *WhoWor 93*
Di Salvo, Nicholas Armand 1920- *WhoAm 92*
DiSalvo, Phyllis Rita 1933- *WhoAmW 93*
DiSalvo, Raymond d1990 *BioIn 17*
Disalvo, Richard S. *Law&B 92*
Disanayake, Bandula Asoka 1944- *WhoWor 93*
DiSandro, Edmond A. 1932- *WhoE 93*
DiSanti, Alexander Donald 1958- *WhoEmL 93*
Di Santo, Grace Johanne DeMarco 1924- *WhoAm 92, WhoAmW 93*
Di Santo, Laura M. *Law&B 92*
DiSarro, Frances Joanne *Law&B 92*
Disbrow, Janet Alice 1946- *WhoEmL 93*
Disbrow, Michael Ray 1959- *WhoEmL 93, WhoWor 93*
Disbrow, Richard E. 1930- *St&PR 93*
Disbrow, Richard Edwin 1930- *WhoAm 92*
Discenza, Peter V. *Law&B 92*
Disch, Fred Kenneth 1945- *WhoSSW 93*
Disch, Thomas M. *BioIn 17*
Disch, Thomas M. 1940- *ScF&FL 92, SmATA 15AS [port]*
Disch, Thomas M(ichael) 1940- *MajAI [port]*
Disch, Thomas Michael 1940- *WhoAm 92*
Disch, Tom *MajAI*
Discher, David P. *Law&B 92*
Dischinger, Terry Gilbert 1940- *BiDAMSp 1989*
Dischler, Tena Mary 1949- *WhoAmW 93*
Dischner, Donald D. 1932- *St&PR 93*
Di Sciascio, Eve Francesca 1954- *WhoWrEP 92*
DiSciullo, Alan Michael *Law&B 92*
DiSciullo, Alan Michael 1950- *WhoEmL 93*
DiSciullo, William James 1946- *St&PR 93*
Discoe, Patricia Andel *Law&B 92*
Dise, J.C. 1920- *St&PR 93*
Dise, P.R. 1949- *St&PR 93*
Disen, Erling *WhoScE 91-4*
Disenso, Daniel Richard 1944- *St&PR 93*
DiSerio, Frank Joseph 1931- *WhoAm 92*
Disharoon, Barbara Schaeffer 1946- *WhoAmW 93*
Disharoon, Leslie Benjamin 1932- *WhoAm 92*
Disher, J. William 1933- *St&PR 93*
Disheroon, Fred Russell 1931- *WhoE 93*
Dishman, Leonard I. 1920- *WhoAm 92*
Dishman, Michael Ray 1959- *WhoSSW 93*
Dishman, Timothy Alan 1958- *WhoSSW 93*
Dishy, Bob *WhoAm 92*
Dishypatos, David dc. 1347 *OxDcByz*
Dishypatos, Manuel fl. 13th cent.- *OxDcByz*
Disick, Renee 1941- *WhoAmW 93*
Di Silverio, F. 1937- *WhoScE 91-3*
DiSilvestro, Roger L. 1949- *ScF&FL 92*
Di Silvio, Giampaolo 1938- *WhoScE 91-3*
Disimine, Pat 1962- *BioIn 17*
Disinger, John Franklin 1930- *WhoAm 92*
Disinger, Roland Thomas 1953- *WhoEmL 93*
DiSipio, Fred 1927- *BioIn 17*
Diskant, Gregory L. 1948- *WhoEmL 93*
Diski, Jenny 1947- *ConAu 138*
Diskin, Lahna F. 1932- *ScF&FL 92*
Disle, Michel 1934- *WhoWor 93*
Disley, Lance E. 1938- *St&PR 93*
Dismuke, Fred Wynne, Jr. 1937- *St&PR 93*

DiSmukes, Carol Jaehne 1938- *WhoAmW 93*
Disney, Anthea *NewYTBS 92 [port]*
Disney, Anthea 1944- *WhoAm 92*
Disney, J. 1940- *WhoScE 91-1*
Disney, Michael George 1955- *WhoEmL 93*
Disney, Michael John *WhoScE 91-1*
Disney, Roy Edward 1930- *WhoAm 92*
Disney, Walt 1901-1966 *BioIn 17*
Dison, Jack Everitt 1944- *WhoSSW 93*
Dispeker, Thea *WhoAm 92*
Dispenza, Robet Gerard 1946- *St&PR 93*
Di Spigna, Tony 1943- *WhoAm 92*
Di Spigno, Guy Joseph 1948- *WhoWor 93*
Disque, Carol Sue 1951- *WhoEmL 93*
Disraeli, Benjamin 1804-1881 *BioIn 17, NinCLC 39 [port]*
Disraeli, Isaac 1766-1848 *BioIn 17*
Dissen, Walter C. *Law&B 92*
Dissette, Alyce Marie 1952- *WhoEmL 93*
Dissette, G. Keith 1944- *St&PR 93*
DiStasio, James Shannon 1947- *WhoAm 92*
Di Stasio, Lynne E. *Law&B 92*
Di Stasio, Richard P. 1954- *St&PR 93*
Distaso, Salvatore 1937- *WhoWor 93*
DiStaso, Stephen Anthony 1956- *WhoE 93*
Disteche, Albert E.H.J. 1922- *WhoScE 91-2*
DiStefano, Alan A. 1945- *St&PR 93*
Di Stefano, Anthony Ferdinand 1945- *WhoAm 92*
DiStefano, Francis Glenn 1945- *WhoSSW 93*
Di Stefano, Giuseppe 1921- *Baker 92, IntDcOp, OxDcOp*
DiStefano, Joseph Robert 1938- *St&PR 93*
Distel, Karla Jean 1965- *WhoAmW 93*
Distelhorst, Craig Tipton 1941- *WhoSSW 93, WhoWor 93*
Distelhorst, Garis Fred 1942- *WhoAm 92*
Distenfeld, Yvonne S. *Law&B 92*
Distenfeld, Yvonne S. 1956- *St&PR 93*
Distler, Hugo 1908-1942 *Baker 92*
Distler, Theodore A. 1898-1991 *BioIn 17*
Distler, William Francis 1917- *WhoAm 92*
Distler, William Joseph 1942- *St&PR 93*
Diston, David George 1932- *St&PR 93*
Di Suvero, Mark 1933- *WhoAm 92*
D'Italia, Russell V. *Law&B 92*
Di Tata, Juan Carlos 1953- *WhoUN 92*
Ditchek, Brian Michael 1951- *WhoE 93*
Ditchfield, Allan W. 1937- *St&PR 93*
Ditchoff, Pamela Jane 1950- *WhoWrEP 92*
Di Tella, Guido 1931- *WhoWor 93*
DiTeresa, Matthew J. 1939- *St&PR 93*
Di Teresi, Emanuel J. 1945- *St&PR 93*
Ditka, Michael Keller 1939- *WhoAm 92*
Ditka, Mike 1939- *BioIn 17*
Ditkof, Martin L. *Law&B 92*
Ditlevsen, Ove Dalager 1935- *WhoScE 91-2*
Ditlow, Clarence M., III *BioIn 17*
Ditmore, Dana C. 1940- *St&PR 93*
Dito, John Allen 1935- *WhoAm 92*
DiTomaso, Gino 1940- *St&PR 93*
Di Tomaso, Nick *St&PR 93*
DiTonno, Daniel Christian 1951- *WhoEmL 93*
Ditonto, Douglas P. *Law&B 92*
DiTorrice, Guy Louis 1952- *WhoEmL 93*
Ditrapani, G. 1950- *St&PR 93*
D'Itri, Frank Michael 1933- *WhoAm 92*
di Troppenburg, Ulderico *ScF&FL 92*
Ditsler, John William *Law&B 92*
Ditson, Charles *Baker 92*
Ditson, Oliver 1811-1888 *Baker 92*
Dittberner, Gerald John 1941- *WhoSSW 93*
Dittenhafer, Brian Douglas 1942- *St&PR 93, WhoAm 92*
Ditter, John William, Jr. 1921- *WhoAm 92*
Ditterline, John R. 1950- *St&PR 93*
Ditters, Karl 1739-1799 *Baker 92*
Dittersdorf, Karl Ditters von 1739-1799 *Baker 92, OxDcOp*
Dittert, J. Lee, Jr. 1931- *WhoAm 92*
Dittert, Lewis William 1934- *WhoAm 92*
Dittes, James Edward 1926- *WhoAm 92*
Dittgen, Herbert 1956- *WhoWor 93*
Dittman, Duane Arthur 1924- *WhoAm 92*
Dittman, Mark Allen 1950- *WhoEmL 93*
Dittman, Stevan Craig 1949- *WhoEmL 93*
Dittmann, Reidar 1922- *WhoAm 92*
Dittmar, Helga 1960- *WhoWor 93*
Dittmar, Susan Jane 1952- *WhoAmW 93*
Dittmeier, Thomas Edwin 1944- *WhoAm 92*
Dittmer, Charlene Suzanne *Law&B 92*
Dittmer, Clark Martin 1936- *WhoAm 92*
Dittmer, Stevan W. 1952- *WhoWrEP 92*
Ditto, Arthur Harry 1941- *St&PR 93*
Ditto, Daniel Thomas 1954- *WhoEmL 93*
Ditto, Kane 1944- *WhoAm 92, WhoSSW 93*
Ditto, Michael E. 1943- *St&PR 93*
Dittrich, Denise Marie 1960- *WhoAmW 93*
Dittrich, Gregory Duane 1960- *WhoEmL 93*
Dittrich, Jaroslav 1947- *WhoScE 91-4*
Dittrich, John Edward 1931- *WhoSSW 93*
Dittrich, Joseph H. 1924- *St&PR 93*
Dittrich, Klaus Robert 1950- *WhoWor 93*
Dittrich, Paul-Heinz 1930- *Baker 92*
Dittrich, Raymond Joseph 1932- *WhoAm 92*
Dittrich, Raymond Robert 1949- *St&PR 93*
Dittrich, Robert J. 1931- *St&PR 93*
Dittrich, Thomas Stayton 1954- *WhoEmL 93*
DiTullo, Michael Joseph 1952- *WhoE 93*
Ditz, John Adams 1921-1991 *BioIn 17*
Ditzel, Paul Calvin 1926- *WhoWrEP 92*
Ditzler, Daniel Edwin 1955- *WhoWrEP 92*
Ditzler, Robert Lisle 1931- *St&PR 93*
Diubaldo, Robert F. *Law&B 92*
DiUlio, Albert Joseph 1943- *WhoAm 92*
Diuro, Ray *St&PR 93*
Divac, Vlade *BioIn 17*
Divalerio, Richard M. *Law&B 92*
DiValerio, Richard Michael 1930- *St&PR 93*
Divall, Robert Keith 1923- *St&PR 93*
Divelbiss, Terry L. 1947- *St&PR 93*
Dively, John A., Jr. 1958- *WhoEmL 93*
DiVenuto, John Paul 1940- *WhoE 93*
Diver, William 1921- *WhoAm 92*
Divers, R. Thomas *St&PR 93*
Divich, Duane G. 1937- *WhoIns 93*
Divilio, Louis Thomas 1949- *WhoE 93*
Divin, Rolland Glen 1947- *WhoAm 92*
DiVincenti, Marie 1924- *WhoAmW 93*
Divine, Arthur D. 1904-1987 *ScF&FL 92*
Divine, B. Lees 1937- *St&PR 93*
Divine, Father c. 1882-1965 *DcTwHis*
Divine, M.J. *BioIn 17*
Divine, Major J. *BioIn 17*
Divine, Robert Alexander 1929- *WhoAm 92*
Divine, William Robinson 1915- *WhoAm 92*
Diviney, Jim *ScF&FL 92*
Diviney, Shirl *ScF&FL 92*
Divins, Dana L. *Law&B 92*
Divis, Deborah B. *Law&B 92*
Divita, Phillip S. *St&PR 93*
Divitis, Antonius 1475?-1526? *Baker 92*
Divitis de Ryche, Antonius 1475?-1526? *Baker 92*
Divitis le Riche, Antonius c. 1475?-1526? *Baker 92*
DiVito, Anthony 1931- *St&PR 93*
Divito, Vincent 1959- *St&PR 93*
Divok, Mario J. *WhoWrEP 92*
DiVono, Sharman *ScF&FL 92*
Diwan, Joyce Johnson 1940- *WhoE 93*
Diwan, Romesh Kumar 1933- *WhoAm 92*
Diwoky, Roy John 1910- *WhoAm 92*
Dix, Annee *AmWomPl*
Dix, Beulah Marie 1876-1970 *AmWomPl*
Dix, Christopher Scovell 1948- *St&PR 93*
Dix, David Wayne 1954- *WhoEmL 93*
Dix, Dorothea Lynde 1802-1887 *BioIn 17*
Dix, Doug Lee 1949- *St&PR 93*
Dix, Douglas Shields 1960- *WhoWor 93*
Dix, Fred Andrew, Jr. 1931- *WhoAm 92*
Dix, Gerald Bennett *WhoScE 91-1*
Dix, Harold G. *Law&B 92*
Dix, Linda Skidmore 1948- *WhoEmL 93*
Dix, Otto 1891-1969 *BioIn 17*
Dix, Richard 1894-1949 *BioIn 17*
Dix, Rollin Cumming 1936- *WhoAm 92*
Dix, Ronald Lee 1951- *St&PR 93*
Dix, Stephen David *Law&B 92*
Dix, William Kenneth *Law&B 92*
Dix, William S. 1910-1978 *BioIn 17*
Dixie, May *AmWomPl*
Dixie Cups *SoulM*
Dixie Flyers *SoulM*
Dixit, Anita S. 1946- *St&PR 93*
Dixit, Bal 1939- *St&PR 93*
Dixit, Balwant Narayan 1933- *WhoAm 92*
Dixit, Ganesh Datta 1935- *WhoWor 93*
Dixit, Kaivalya Mahendra 1942- *St&PR 93*
Dixon, Alan J. *BioIn 17*
Dixon, Alan J. 1927- *CngDr 91*
Dixon, Alan John 1927- *WhoAm 92*
Dixon, Allen N., III *Law&B 92*
Dixon, Allen Walter 1948- *WhoE 93*
Dixon, Andrew Derart 1925- *WhoAm 92*
Dixon, Andrew Douglas 1958- *WhoE 93, WhoEmL 93*
Dixon, Andrew Lee, Jr. 1942- *WhoAm 92, WhoE 93*
Dixon, Annemarie Anderson 1962- *WhoEmL 93*
Dixon, Anthony 1947- *WhoE 93*
Dixon, Anthony Frederick George *WhoScE 91-1*
Dixon, Armendia Pierce 1937- *WhoE 93, WhoWor 93*
Dixon, Belinda Roberta 1961- *WhoAmW 93*
Dixon, Billy Gene 1935- *WhoAm 92*
Dixon, Bonnie Lynn 1955- *WhoEmL 93*
Dixon, Brendan M. *Law&B 92*
Dixon, Charles Douglas *Law&B 92*
Dixon, Chris *ScF&FL 92*
Dixon, Dabney White 1949- *WhoEmL 93*
Dixon, Dean 1915-1976 *Baker 92*
Dixon, Diane *BlkAmWO*
Dixon, Diane B. 1951- *St&PR 93*
Dixon, Don *BioIn 17*
Dixon, Donald D. 1935- *St&PR 93*
Dixon, Donald Riley, II 1946- *WhoAm 92*
Dixon, Dougal 1947- *ScF&FL 92*
Dixon, Elizabeth Gruse 1927- *WhoE 93*
Dixon, Fitz Eugene, Jr. 1923- *WhoAm 92*
Dixon, Frank James 1920- *WhoAm 92*
Dixon, Frank James 1951- *WhoEmL 93*
Dixon, Frank M. 1892-1965 *PolPar*
Dixon, Franklin W. *ConAu 37NR, MajAI, ScF&FL 92*
Dixon, Franklin W. 1862-1930 *BioIn 17*
Dixon, G. Lowell *Law&B 92*
Dixon, George Francis, Jr. 1918- *WhoAm 92*
Dixon, George Hall 1920- *St&PR 93*
Dixon, George Lane, Jr. 1928- *WhoAm 92*
Dixon, Glenn T. 1943- *St&PR 93*
Dixon, Gordon *WhoScE 91-1*
Dixon, Gordon Henry 1930- *WhoAm 92*
Dixon, Guy E. 1920- *St&PR 93*
Dixon, Guy Edwin, III 1946- *St&PR 93*
Dixon, H. Diane *Law&B 92*
Dixon, Harvey Lewis 1927- *WhoAm 92*
Dixon, Hewritt d1992 *NewYTBS 92*
Dixon, Hubert George 1937- *WhoUN 92*
Dixon, Irl Graham 1950- *WhoEmL 93*
Dixon, Irma Muse *AfrAmBi*
Dixon, Irma Muse 1952- *WhoAmW 93*
Dixon, Ivan 1931- *MiSFD 9*
Dixon, J. Michael *Law&B 92*
Dixon, Jacqueline 1949- *WhoAmW 93, WhoEmL 93*
Dixon, James *ScF&FL 92*
Dixon, James 1928- *Baker 92*
Dixon, James Andrew, Jr. 1951- *WhoAm 92, WhoEmL 93*
Dixon, James J. *Law&B 92*
Dixon, Jay R. 1938- *St&PR 93*
Dixon, Jeane *WhoAm 92, WhoWor 93, WhoWrEP 92*
Dixon, Jeanne *ScF&FL 92*
Dixon, Joe Boris 1930- *WhoAm 92*
Dixon, John Edward 1946- *WhoWor 93*
Dixon, John Fulton 1946- *WhoEmL 93*
Dixon, John Matthews 1942- *WhoSSW 93*
Dixon, John Morris 1933- *WhoAm 92*
Dixon, John Richard *WhoScE 91-1*
Dixon, John Spencer 1957- *WhoEmL 93, WhoSSW 93*
Dixon, John Wesley, Jr. 1919- *WhoAm 92*
Dixon, Joseph M. 1867-1934 *PolPar*
Dixon, Joseph Moore 1910- *WhoSSW 93*
Dixon, Judy Earlene 1950- *WhoSSW 93*
Dixon, Julian C. *AfrAmBi [port]*
Dixon, Julian C. 1934- *BioIn 17, CngDr 91*
Dixon, Julian Carey 1934- *WhoAm 92*
Dixon, Kelvin Norman 1959- *WhoE 93*
Dixon, Ken *MiSFD 9*
Dixon, L. Allyn *Law&B 92*
Dixon, Langford 1915- *WhoCanL 92*
Dixon, Larry Dean 1942- *WhoSSW 93*
Dixon, Lawrence Paul 1938- *WhoE 93*
Dixon, Leon *BioIn 17*
Dixon, Linda Diane 1960- *WhoEmL 93*
Dixon, Lisa Gillian 1955- *WhoEmL 93*
Dixon, Louis Frederick 1928- *WhoAm 92*
Dixon, Louis M. *WhoAm 92*
Dixon, Luther *SoulM*
Dixon, M. Ellen *Law&B 92*
Dixon, Marcus K. 1945- *St&PR 93*
Dixon, Melvin d1992 *NewYTBS 92*
Dixon, Melvin 1950- *BioIn 17*
Dixon, Melvin 1950-1992 *ConGAN*
Dixon, Melvin (W.) 1950-1992 *ConAu 139*
Dixon, Michael Albert 1948- *WhoEmL 93*
Dixon, Michael Wayne 1942- *WhoWor 93*
Dixon, Nancy *Law&B 92*
Dixon, Norman Rex 1932- *WhoAm 92*
Dixon, Norval W. 1931- *St&PR 93*
Dixon, Patricia Jane 1949- *WhoAmW 93*
Dixon, Paul Edward 1944- *WhoAm 92*
Dixon, Peter Bower *WhoScE 91-1*
Dixon, Phillip Ray, Sr. 1949- *WhoEmL 93*
Dixon, Richard Alan 1965- *WhoSSW 93*
Dixon, Richard Allan 1946- *WhoSSW 93*
Dixon, Richard C. 1929- *St&PR 93*
Dixon, Richard Cressie 1929- *WhoAm 92*
Dixon, Richard D. *Law&B 92*
Dixon, Richard Newland *WhoScE 91-1*
Dixon, Richard Newland 1930- *WhoWor 93*
Dixon, Richard T. 1925- *St&PR 93*
Dixon, Richard Wayne 1936- *WhoAm 92*
Dixon, Robert F. 1948- *WhoE 93*
Dixon, Robert James 1920- *WhoAm 92*
Dixon, Roger *ScF&FL 92*
Dixon, Roland B. 1875-1934 *IntDcAn*
Dixon, Ronney Theodore 1954- *WhoEmL 93*
Dixon, Rosina Berry 1942- *WhoE 93*
Dixon, Sandra Alice 1954- *WhoAmW 93*
Dixon, Sharon Pratt *BioIn 17*
Dixon, Sharon Pratt 1944- *AfrAmBi*
Dixon, Sheila D. 1948- *St&PR 93*
Dixon, Shirley Juanita 1935- *WhoAmW 93, WhoWor 93*
Dixon, Stephen *BioIn 17*
Dixon, Stephen 1936- *ConAu 40NR, WhoWrEP 92*
Dixon, Steven Mitchell *Law&B 92*
Dixon, Stewart Strawn 1930- *WhoAm 92*
Dixon, Susan Diane 1954- *WhoAmW 93*
Dixon, Terry Phillip 1946- *WhoEmL 93, WhoSSW 93*
Dixon, Thomas *ScF&FL 92*
Dixon, Thomas F. *Law&B 92*
Dixon, Thomas Francis 1916- *WhoAm 92*
Dixon, Thomas Lloyd 1957- *WhoEmL 93*
Dixon, Tod O. 1939- *St&PR 93*
Dixon, Tracy A. 1941- *St&PR 93*
Dixon, Vincent W. 1942- *St&PR 93*
Dixon, Wendell L. 1923- *St&PR 93*
Dixon, Wesley Moon, Jr. 1927- *St&PR 93*
Dixon, Wheeler 1950- *MiSFD 9*
Dixon, Wilfrid Joseph *WhoAm 92*
Dixon, William *ScF&FL 92*
Dixon, William Cornelius 1904- *WhoAm 92*
Dixon, William L. 1931- *St&PR 93*
Dixon, William Orlan 1957- *WhoEmL 93*
Dixon, William Robert 1917- *WhoAm 92*
Dixon, William Robert 1925- *WhoAm 92*
Dixon, Willie *BioIn 17*
Dixon, Willie 1915-1992 *ConBlB 4 [port], CurBio 92N, NewYTBS 92 [port]*
Dixon, Wylie 1936- *BioIn 17*
Dixon-Fyle, Samuel Randolph 1932- *WhoUN 92*
Dixson, Robert Morgan 1948- *St&PR 93*
Diz, Adolfo Cesar 1931- *WhoWor 93*
Diz, Harry Richard 1947- *St&PR 93*
Dizard, Wilson Paul, Jr. 1922- *WhoAm 92*
Dizard, Wilson Paul, III 1953- *WhoE 93*
Dizdar, Marijan A. 1943- *St&PR 93*
Dizengremel, Pierre 1948- *WhoScE 91-2*
Dizer, John T., Jr. 1921- *ScF&FL 92*
Dizer, Muammer 1924- *WhoScE 91-4*
DiZerega, James G. *Law&B 92*
di Zerega, Thomas William 1927- *WhoAm 92*
Dizi, Francois-Joseph 1780-1847 *Baker 92*
Dizikes, Pamela Brown *Law&B 92*
Djakov, Lubomir 1928- *WhoScE 91-4*
Djakovic, Ljubomir M. 1926- *WhoScE 91-4*
Djalatta, Loretta Jean 1943- *WhoAmW 93*
Djambazov, Pirin Vasilev 1928- *WhoScE 91-4*
DJang, Arthur H.K. 1925- *WhoE 93*
D'Javid, Ismail Faridoon 1908- *WhoWor 93*
Djebar, Assia 1936- *BioIn 17*
Djeddah, Richard Nissim *WhoE 93*
Djerassi, Carl *BioIn 17*
Djerassi, Carl 1923- *WhoAm 92*
Djerassi, Isaac 1925- *WhoAm 92*
Djerejian, Edward Peter 1939- *WhoWor 93*
Djerejian, Robert A. 1931- *St&PR 93*
Djidingar, Dono-Ngardoum (Michel) 1928- *WhoAfr*
Djilas, Aleksa 1953- *ConAu 139*
Djilas, Milovan 1911- *BioIn 17, ColdWar 2 [port], DcTwHis*
Djindjihashvili, Nodar *BioIn 17*
Djiwandono, J. Soedradjad 1938- *WhoAsAP 91*
Djogo, Djibril Negue 1932- *WhoAfr*
Djohar, Said Mohamed *WhoWor 93*
Djohar, Said Mohammed 1918- *WhoAfr*
Djokic, Georgije 1949- *WhoAm 92*
Djokic, Michelle *BioIn 17*
Djola, Badja *ConTFT 10*
Djordjevic, Bojan 1937- *WhoScE 91-4*
Djordjevic, Cirila 1926- *WhoAm 92*
Djordjevic, Dimitrije 1922- *WhoAm 92*
Djordjevic, Jovan 1922- *WhoScE 91-4*
Djordjevic, Miodrag Borislav 1919- *WhoWor 93*
Djordjevic, Mladomir 1924- *DrEEuF*
Djordjevic, Vladan D. 1938- *WhoScE 91-4*
Djordjevich, Michael 1936- *St&PR 93, WhoAm 92*
Djulgerov, Georgi 1943- *DrEEuF*
Djurdjevic, Djurdje 1928- *WhoScE 91-4*
Djurhuus, Jorgen 1955- *WhoScE 91-2*
Djuric, Dusan 1926- *WhoScE 91-4*
Djurickovic-Tuvic, Jelisaveta B. 1948- *WhoUN 92*
Djurovic, Robert 1958- *WhoEmL 93*

Dlab, Vlastimil 1932- *WhoAm 92, WhoWor 93*
Dlabac, Bohumir Jan 1758-1820 *Baker 92*
Dlabacz, Gottfried Johann 1758-1820 *Baker 92*
Dlamini, Barnabas Sibusiso 1942- *WhoAfr*
Dlamini, Bhekimpi Alpheus 1924- *WhoAfr*
Dlamini, Mfanasibili 1939- *WhoAfr*
Dlamini, Obed *WhoAfr*
Dlamini, Obed Mfanyana 1937- *WhoWor 93*
Dlamini, Sotsha Ernest 1940- *WhoAfr*
Dlamini, Timothy Lutfo Lucky 1952- *WhoUN 92, WhoWor 93*
Dlamini, Veleleni Virginia 1947- *WhoWor 93*
D'Lauro, Frank Andrew, Jr. 1940- *St&PR 93, WhoE 93*
Dlesk, George 1914- *WhoAm 92*
Dlipasquier, Alfredo 1939- *WhoScE 91-3*
Dlouhy, Phillip E. 1941- *St&PR 93*
Dlouhy, Phillip Edward 1941- *WhoAm 92*
D'Lower, Del 1912- *WhoE 93*
Dlubak, Zbigniew 1921- *WhoWor 93*
Dlugi, Alexander Michael 1952- *WhoEmL 93*
Dlugoff, Marc Alan 1955- *WhoE 93, WhoEmL 93*
Dlugolenski, Ella M. 1951- *St&PR 93*
Dlugoraj, Wojciech c. 1550-c. 1619 *PolBiDi*
Dlugosz, Jan 1415-1480 *PolBiDi*
Dlugosz, Robert Walter 1952- *St&PR 93*
Dlugoszewski, Lucia 1931- *Baker 92*
Dlugoszewski-Wieniawa, Boleslaw 1881-1942 *PolBiDi*
Dlugy, Alexander 1941- *WhoE 93*
Dluhy, Deborah Haigh 1940- *WhoAmW 93, WhoE 93*
Dlutman, Roselyn C. *Law&B 92*
D'Mato, Patrick M. 1938- *St&PR 93*
Dmitrichev, Timour F. 1937- *WhoUN 92*
Dmochowski-Saunders, Henry 1810-1863 *PolBiDi*
Dmowski, Roman 1864-1939 *PolBiDi*
Dmytryk, Edward 1908- *MiSFD 9*
Dmytryk, John James 1955- *WhoSSW 93*
Dmytryshyn, Basil 1925- *WhoAm 92, WhoWor 93*
Dneprov, Anatoly 1919-1975 *BioIn 17*
D.N.J. *ScF&FL 92*
Doak, Kenneth Worley 1916- *WhoE 93*
Doak, Robert A., Jr. 1928- *St&PR 93*
Doak, Ron Kent 1937- *WhoSSW 93*
Doak, Sheila Jean *St&PR 93*
Doak, William Leopold 1891-1954 *BiDAMSp 1989*
Doamaral, Diogo Freitas 1941- *WhoWor 93*
Do Amaral, Ilidio *WhoScE 91-3*
Doan, Charles Austin 1896-1990 *BioIn 17*
Doan, Cortland Charles 1926- *WhoAm 92*
Doan, Gloria *BioIn 17*
Doan, James Edward 1953- *WhoSSW 93*
Doan, James Nelson *Law&B 92*
Doan, Kirk Hugh 1953- *WhoEmL 93*
Doan, Patricia Nan 1930- *WhoSSW 93*
Doan, Peter Leisenring 1955- *WhoEmL 93*
Doan, Tuan Anh 1961- *WhoEmL 93*
Doane, David Green 1921- *WhoAm 92*
Doane, Helen Mitzi 1952- *WhoAmW 93*
Doane, Marcia E. *Law&B 92*
Doane, Roseanne Marie 1950- *WhoEmL 93*
Doane, Samuel Wallace 1956- *WhoSSW 93*
Doane, William H(oward) 1832-1915 *Baker 92*
Doar, John M. 1921- *EncAACR*
Doat, Jacqueline *WhoScE 91-2*
Dobaj, Edward *WhoScE 91-4*
Doban, Robert Charles 1924- *St&PR 93*
Dobb, Maurice Herbert 1900-1976 *BioIn 17*
Dobbel, Rodger Francis 1934- *WhoWor 93*
Dobbelaere, Karel Marie Theophiel Cornel 1933- *WhoWor 93*
Dobber, Johannes 1866-1921 *Baker 92*
Dobberpuhl, William E. *Law&B 92*
Dobbert, Daniel Joseph 1946- *WhoEmL 93*
Dobbert, Dean Roger 1954- *WhoEmL 93*
Dobbie, Dorothy 1945- *WhoAmW 93*
Dobbie, George Herbert 1918- *St&PR 93, WhoAm 92*
Dobbin, Craig L. 1935- *St&PR 93*
Dobbin, Edmund J. *WhoAm 92*
Dobbin, Edmund J. 1935- *WhoE 93*
Dobbin, Muriel *ScF&FL 92*
Dobbin, Murray 1945- *ConAu 139*
Dobbins, Cassandra Lynn 1958- *WhoAmW 93*
Dobbins, James Francis, Jr. 1942- *WhoAm 92*
Dobbins, James Joseph 1924- *WhoAm 92*
Dobbins, John Joseph 1940- *St&PR 93*
Dobbins, John Potter 1914- *WhoWor 93*
Dobbins, Judith *BioIn 17*
Dobbins, Robert Newton 1904- *WhoE 93*
Dobbins, Sharon Kay 1955- *WhoE 93*
Dobbs, Andrew James 1960- *WhoEmL 93*
Dobbs, Betty Jo Teeter 1930- *WhoAmW 93*
Dobbs, Charles Edward 1949- *WhoEmL 93*
Dobbs, Curtis Edward 1941- *WhoSSW 93*
Dobbs, Dan Byron 1932- *WhoAm 92*
Dobbs, Donald Edwin 1931- *St&PR 93*
Dobbs, Dorothy 1945- *WhoIns 93*
Dobbs, Edwin Roland *WhoScE 91-1*
Dobbs, Edwin Roland 1924- *WhoWor 93*
Dobbs, Frank Q. *MiSFD 9*
Dobbs, Frank Wilbur 1932- *WhoAm 92*
Dobbs, George Albert 1943- *WhoSSW 93*
Dobbs, Gregory Allan 1946- *WhoAm 92*
Dobbs, James C. 1944- *St&PR 93*
Dobbs, James Charles *Law&B 92*
Dobbs, John Barnes 1931- *WhoAm 92*
Dobbs, Kildare Robert 1923- *WhoCanL 92*
Dobbs, Mattiwilda 1925- *Baker 92*
Dobbs, Michael 1950- *ScF&FL 92*
Dobbs, Michael Sean 1950- *WhoAm 92*
Dobbs, Patricia Jean 1938- *WhoAmW 93*
Dobbs, Robert E. 1953- *St&PR 93*
Dobbs, Rosalyne Brown 1933- *WhoWrEP 92*
Dobbs, Warren 1950- *WhoE 93*
Dobbyn, Colm J. *Law&B 92*
Dobbyn, Edward T., Jr. 1916- *St&PR 93*
Dobbyn, Jerome W. 1942- *St&PR 93*
Dobda, Deborah Joan 1949- *WhoAmW 93*
Dobe, Carl F. *Law&B 92*
Dobeck, Robert B. *Law&B 92*
Dobeck, Robert Bradley 1954- *WhoEmL 93*
Dobeck, Timothy G. 1961- *WhoEmL 93*
Dobelis, Inge Nachman 1933- *WhoAmW 93*
Dobell, Byron *BioIn 17*
Dobell, Byron Maxwell 1927- *WhoAm 92, WhoWrEP 92*
Dobell, Charles Macpherson 1869-1954 *HarEnMi*
Dobell, (Eleanor) Mercy *WhoWrEP 92*
Dober, Terry L. 1956- *St&PR 93*
Dobereiner, Jurgen 1923- *WhoWor 93*
Doberenz, Alexander R. 1936- *WhoAm 92, WhoE 93*
Doberneck, Raymond C. 1932- *WhoAm 92*
Doberstein, Audrey K. 1932- *WhoAmW 93*
Doberstein, Carole Jean 1957- *St&PR 93*
Dobes, James Michael 1953- *WhoSSW 93*
Dobes, William Lamar, Jr. 1943- *WhoWor 93*
Dobey, James Kenneth 1919- *WhoAm 92*
Dobias, Vaclav 1909-1978 *Baker 92*
Dobiasova, Milada 1934- *WhoScE 91-4*
Dobie, James Donald Mathieson 1927- *WhoAsAP 91*
Dobie, Robert E. 1948- *St&PR 93*
Dobie, Shirley Imogene 1930- *WhoAmW 93*
Dobilas, John J. 1946- *St&PR 93*
Dobilas, Ronald John 1942- *St&PR 93*
Dobin, Michael H. 1949- *WhoAm 92, WhoEmL 93*
Dobin, Rubin R. 1915-1990 *BioIn 17*
Dobin, Solomon S. d1990 *BioIn 17*
Dobis, Joan Pauline 1944- *WhoAmW 93*
Dobkin, David Paul 1948- *WhoAm 92*
Dobkin, Irving Bern 1918- *WhoAm 92, WhoWor 93*
Dobkin, James Allen 1940- *WhoAm 92*
Dobkin, John Howard 1942- *WhoAm 92*
Dobkin, Kaye 1945- *ScF&FL 92*
Dobkin, Marjorie Housepian 1923- *ScF&FL 92*
Dobler, Bruce Garside 1939- *WhoE 93*
Dobler, Donald William 1927- *WhoAm 92*
Dobler, James B. *Law&B 92*
Dobler, Merri Louise Bailey 1956- *WhoWrEP 92*
Doblin, Alfred 1878-1957 *BioIn 17*
Doblin, Stephen Alan 1945- *WhoSSW 93*
Dobmaier, Walter *WhoScE 91-3*
Dobner, T. *WhoScE 91-4*
Dobo, William 1935- *St&PR 93*
Dobos, Albert Michael 1942- *St&PR 93*
Dobos, Donald Jack 1948- *St&PR 93*
Dobos, Kalman 1931- *Baker 92*
Dobosz, Debbie *BioIn 17*
Dobozy, Attila 1939- *WhoScE 91-4*
Dobraczynski, Jan 1910- *WhoWor 93*
Dobran, James M. *Law&B 92*
Dobranski, Bernard 1939- *WhoAm 92*
Dobratz, Betty Ann 1947- *WhoEmL 93*
Dobrescu, Dumitru 1927- *WhoScE 91-4*
Dobrev, Dobromir 1918- *WhoScE 91-4*
Dobrev, Petar 1928- *WhoScE 91-4*
Dobrev, Vladimir Krastev 1946- *WhoWor 93*
Dobreva, Anitsa M. 1926- *WhoScE 91-4*
Dobriansky, Lev Eugene 1918- *WhoAm 92, WhoWor 93*
Dobriansky, Paula Jon 1955- *WhoAm 92, WhoAmW 93*
Dobrich, Fulvio V. 1947- *St&PR 93*
Dobrijevic, Stevo 1932- *WhoWor 93*
Dobrin, Arthur Barry 1943- *WhoWrEP 92*
Dobrin, Bernard Robert 1937- *WhoAm 92*
Dobrinski, Gail Vicki Margaret 1946- *WhoAmW 93*
Dobrinsky, Herbert Colman 1933- *WhoE 93*
Dobrjanskyj, Danylo Borys 1956- *WhoEmL 93*
Dobroczoni, Adam 1944- *WhoScE 91-4*
Dobrokhotov, Boris Petrovitch 1939- *WhoUN 92*
Dobromir Chrysos dc. 1201 *OxDcByz*
Dobronic, Antun 1878-1955 *Baker 92*
Dobrossy, Lajos 1934- *WhoUN 92*
Dobrotica dc. 1387 *OxDcByz*
Dobroven, Issay 1891-1953 *OxDcOp*
Dobrovolny, Jerry Stanley 1922- *WhoAm 92*
Dobrovsky, Lubos 1932- *WhoWor 93*
Dobrow, Harvey Robert 1942- *WhoE 93*
Dobrow, Marvin Paul 1934- *WhoE 93*
Dobrowen, Issay (Alexandrovich) 1891-1953 *Baker 92*
Dobrowolny, Marino 1940- *WhoScE 91-3*
Dobrowolski, Andrzej 1921-1990 *Baker 92*
Dobrowolski, James Phillip 1955- *WhoAm 92*
Dobrowolski, Kathleen 1954- *WhoAmW 93, WhoE 93, WhoEmL 93*
Dobrowolski, Kazimierz 1894-1987 *IntDcAn*
Dobrowolski, Kazimierz A. 1931- *WhoScE 91-4*
Dobrowolski, Krzysztof Bohdan 1943- *WhoWor 93*
Dobrozemsky, Rudolf Wilhelm 1939- *WhoWor 93*
Dobrski, Julian 1812-1886 *PolBiDi*
Dobrucki, Wladyslaw Karol 1918- *WhoWor 93*
Dobry, Stanley Thomas 1948- *WhoEmL 93*
Dobry, Sylvia Hearn 1938- *WhoWor 93*
Dobryszycka, Wanda Maria 1921- *WhoScE 91-4*
Dobrzanska, Irena-Maria 1933- *WhoScE 91-4*
Dobrzanski, Anthony 1944- *PolBiDi*
Dobrzycka, Maria 1928- *WhoScE 91-4*
Dobrzynski, Bronislaw See Dobrzynski, Ignacy Felix 1807-1867 *Baker 92*
Dobrzynski, Ignacy 1779-1841 See Dobrzynski, Ignacy Felix 1807-1867 *Baker 92*
Dobrzynski, Ignacy Feliks 1807-1867 *PolBiDi*
Dobrzynski, Ignacy Felix 1807-1867 *Baker 92*
Dobschensky, Carolyn Sue 1943- *WhoAmW 93*
Dobsevage, Alvin Philip 1922- *WhoE 93, WhoWor 93*
Dobson, Alan 1928- *WhoAm 92*
Dobson, Alan P. 1951- *ConAu 139*
Dobson, Allen 1943- *WhoAm 92*
Dobson, Brian 1934- *St&PR 93*
Dobson, Bridget McColl Hursley 1938- *WhoAm 92, WhoAmW 93, WhoWor 93*
Dobson, Clarence A. 1921- *St&PR 93*
Dobson, Donald Alfred 1928- *WhoAm 92*
Dobson, Gavin Richard 1951- *WhoEmL 93*
Dobson, Geoffrey M. 1937- *St&PR 93*
Dobson, Geoffrey Martin 1937- *WhoAm 92*
Dobson, Geoffrey Robert 1940- *WhoScE 91-1*
Dobson, Hilary 1948- *WhoWor 93*
Dobson, James C. 1936- *BioIn 17*
Dobson, James Gordon, Jr. 1942- *WhoE 93*
Dobson, John Edward *WhoScE 91-1*
Dobson, John McCullough 1940- *WhoAm 92*
Dobson, John Robert 1930- *St&PR 93*
Dobson, John Vincent *WhoScE 91-1*
Dobson, Kathi A. 1958- *WhoEmL 93*
Dobson, Kevin 1943- *WhoAm 92*
Dobson, Kevin James *MiSFD 9*
Dobson, Margaret 1931- *ScF&FL 92*
Dobson, Mark Michael 1948- *WhoEmL 93*
Dobson, Michael W. 1946- *St&PR 93*
Dobson, Peter *BioIn 17*
Dobson, Richard Lawrence 1928- *WhoAm 92*
Dobson, Robert Albertus, III 1938- *WhoWor 93*
Dobson, Robert Albertus, IV 1957- *WhoSSW 93*
Dobson, Roger *ScF&FL 92*
Dobson, Stuart Halstead 1935- *St&PR 93*
Dobson, Susann Douglas 1949- *WhoEmL 93*
Dobson, Terrance James 1940- *St&PR 93, WhoAm 92*
Dobson, Warren Theodore, II 1958- *WhoEmL 93*
Doby, E. Joseph, Jr. *St&PR 93*
Doby, Larry *BioIn 17*
Doby, Raymond 1923- *WhoE 93*
Dobyns, Jerome Middleton 1926- *St&PR 93*
Dobyns, Lloyd Allen 1936- *WhoAm 92*
Dobyns, Nancy Annette 1956- *WhoEmL 93*
Dobyns, Norman L. 1933- *St&PR 93*
Dobyns, Stephen 1941- *BioIn 17*
Dobzhansky, Theodosius Grigorievich 1900-1975 *BioIn 17*
doCarmo, Winston G. 1942- *St&PR 93*
Doche, Joseph-Denis 1766-1825 *Baker 92*
Docherty, Brian *ScF&FL 92*
Doc Howard 1830-1864 *BioIn 17*
Docimo, Rocco 1928- *WhoScE 91-3*
Dock, Deborah L. 1955- *St&PR 93*
Dock, Marie-Claude 1932- *WhoUN 92*
Dock, William 1898-1990 *BioIn 17*
Dock, Yvonne Denise 1960- *WhoAmW 93*
Docken, Edsel Ardean, Sr. 1928- *WhoE 93*
Dockendorf, Denise D. 1953- *WhoIns 93*
Dockendorff, Robert Lawrence 1930- *WhoE 93*
Docker, Ralph J. 1929- *St&PR 93*
Dockery, Daniel P. *Law&B 92*
Dockery, Herbert Donald 1954- *WhoEmL 93, WhoSSW 93*
Dockery, Robert J. *Law&B 92*
Dockery, Ronald Carl 1948- *WhoEmL 93*
Dockett, Sonya Denise *Law&B 92*
Dockhorn, Robert John 1934- *WhoAm 92*
Docking, George 1904-1964 *BioIn 17*
Docking, Robert 1925-1983 *BioIn 17*
Docking, Thomas Robert 1954- *WhoAm 92*
Dockman, Darlene Joyce 1949- *WhoAmW 93*
Dockray, Graham J. *WhoScE 91-1*
Dockray, Graham John 1946- *WhoWor 93*
Dockry, Kathleen A. *Law&B 92*
Dockser, William Barnet 1937- *St&PR 93, WhoAm 92*
Dockson, Robert Ray 1917- *St&PR 93, WhoAm 92*
Dockstader, Robert Allin *Law&B 92*
Docktor-Smith, Mary Ann 1957- *WhoAmW 93*
Docter, Charles Alfred 1931- *WhoAm 92*
Docter, Glenn Joseph 1949- *St&PR 93*
Docter, Lloyd W. 1954- *St&PR 93*
Doctor John 1941- *SoulM*
Doctoroff, Martin Myles 1933- *WhoAm 92*
Doctorow, E.L. 1931- *BioIn 17, MagSAmL [port]*
Doctorow, Edgar Lawrence 1931- *WhoAm 92, WhoWrEP 92*
Dod, Bruce Douglas 1941- *WhoSSW 93*
Dod, Charlotte 1871-1960 *BioIn 17*
Dodak, Lewis 1946- *WhoAm 92*
Dodaro, John Carl 1951- *WhoE 93*
Dodd, A.E. *WhoScE 91-1*
Dodd, Anna Bowman Blake 1855- *AmWomPl*
Dodd, Anne Wescott 1940- *WhoWrEP 92*
Dodd, Carol Elizabeth 1925- *WhoSSW 93*
Dodd, Catherine Elizabeth 1939- *St&PR 93*
Dodd, Charles Gardner 1915- *WhoAm 92*
Dodd, Charles M. *St&PR 93*
Dodd, Christopher J. 1944- *CngDr 91, WhoAm 92, WhoE 93*
Dodd, Darlene Mae 1935- *WhoAmW 93*
Dodd, David Anthony 1960- *WhoSSW 93*
Dodd, Deborah Jane 1947- *WhoEmL 93*
Dodd, Dixie Lee 1939- *WhoAmW 93*
Dodd, Donald Bradford 1940- *WhoWrEP 92*
Dodd, Edward Benton 1902-1991 *BioIn 17*
Dodd, Edwin Dillon 1919- *St&PR 93, WhoAm 92*
Dodd, Emmeline Irwin 1939- *WhoSSW 93*
Dodd, Francis Townsend 1899-1973 *HarEnMi*
Dodd, Gary Wayne 1958- *WhoEmL 93*
Dodd, Gerald Dewey, Jr. 1922- *WhoAm 92*
Dodd, Glenn W. 1938- *St&PR 93*
Dodd, Howell Eugene, Jr. 1910- *St&PR 93*
Dodd, Jack Gordon, Jr. 1926- *WhoAm 92*
Dodd, James Bruce *Law&B 92*
Dodd, James Charles 1923- *WhoAm 92*
Dodd, James Robert 1934- *WhoAm 92*
Dodd, Jeanne Dolores *Law&B 92*
Dodd, Jerry Lee *Law&B 92*
Dodd, Joe David 1920- *WhoWor 93*
Dodd, John Francis 1931- *St&PR 93*

Dodd, John P. d1991 *BioIn 17*
Dodd, Keith L. 1925- *St&PR 93*
Dodd, L.G. 1940- *St&PR 93*
Dodd, Lawrence Roe 1944- *WhoSSW 93*
Dodd, Lionel G. 1940- *WhoAm 92*
Dodd, Lisa Britt 1960- *WhoAmW 93*
Dodd, Lois 1927- *BioIn 17*
Dodd, Lowell A. 1938- *St&PR 93*
Dodd, Marie Walters 1936- *St&PR 93*
Dodd, Martha Eccles 1908-1990 *BioIn 17*
Dodd, Martin H. *Law&B 92*
Dodd, Michael F. 1938- *WhoIns 93*
Dodd, Michael Joseph 1952- *WhoEmL 93*
Dodd, Mike *BioIn 17*
Dodd, Monroe *WhoAm 92*
Dodd, Morgan Cary 1951- *WhoE 93*
Dodd, Nellie C. *AmWomPl*
Dodd, Patty *BioIn 17*
Dodd, Peter 1956- *WhoScE 91-3*
Dodd, Peter Frederic 1946- *WhoE 93, WhoEmL 93*
Dodd, Robert Bruce 1921- *WhoAm 92*
Dodd, Roger James 1951- *WhoEmL 93*
Dodd, Sara Mae Palmer *WhoE 93*
Dodd, Terry Gene 1938- *WhoSSW 93*
Dodd, Thomas J. 1907-1971 *PolPar*
Dodd, Virginia Marilyn 1950- *WhoAm 92, WhoAmW 93, WhoEmL 93*
Dodderidge, Esme 1916- *ScF&FL 92*
Dodderidge, Richard William 1926- *WhoAm 92*
Dodds, Brad *St&PR 93*
Dodds, Brenda Kay 1961- *WhoEmL 93*
Dodds, C. William 1926- *St&PR 93*
Dodds, Catherine Elizabeth 1955- *WhoAmW 93*
Dodds, Claudette La Vonn 1947- *WhoEmL 93*
Dodds, Frances Alison 1950- *WhoEmL 93*
Dodds, Frederick Joseph, III *Law&B 92*
Dodds, Gerald Cribbs 1932- *St&PR 93*
Dodds, Joan *St&PR 93*
Dodds, Johnny 1892-1940 *Baker 92, BioIn 17*
Dodds, Michael Bruce 1952- *WhoEmL 93*
Dodds, Rebecca 1950- *WhoEmL 93, WhoSSW 93*
Dodds, Robert F. *Law&B 92*
Dodds, Robert James, Jr. 1916- *WhoAm 92*
Dodds, Robert James, III 1943- *WhoAm 92*
Dodds, Russell E. *St&PR 93*
Dodds, Warren 1898-1959 *Baker 92*
Dodds, Wayne S. 1916- *St&PR 93*
Dodds, William Robert, Jr. 1952- *St&PR 93*
Doddy, Reginald Nathaniel 1952- *WhoEmL 93*
Dodell, Neal David *Law&B 92*
Dodenhoff, Helen Jean 1938- *WhoAmW 93*
Doderer, Minnette Frerichs 1923- *WhoAmW 93*
Doderlein, Jan M. 1932- *WhoScE 91-4*
Dodez, James Stewart 1958- *St&PR 93*
Dodge, Anne-Laurence 1950- *WhoAmW 93*
Dodge, Arnold J. 1920- *St&PR 93*
Dodge, Arthur Bryon, Jr. 1923- *St&PR 93*
Dodge, Arthur Byron, Jr. 1923- *WhoWor 93*
Dodge, Calvert Renaul 1921- *WhoE 93*
Dodge, Carroll William 1895-1988 *BioIn 17*
Dodge, Charles (Malcolm) 1942- *Baker 92, WhoAm 92*
Dodge, Cleveland Earl, Jr. 1922- *WhoAm 92*
Dodge, Cole P. 1946- *WhoUN 92*
Dodge, Consuelo 1942- *WhoWrEP 92*
Dodge, Donald William 1928- *WhoE 93*
Dodge, Douglas Daniel 1933- *St&PR 93*
Dodge, Douglas Walker 1932- *WhoAm 92*
Dodge, Earl Farwell 1932- *WhoAm 92*
Dodge, Ellen Elizabeth 1932- *WhoE 93*
Dodge, Flora Begelow *AmWomPl*
Dodge, Franklin Tiffany 1936- *WhoSSW 93*
Dodge, Fremont *ConAu 37NR*
Dodge, George Alan 1957- *WhoEmL 93*
Dodge, Grenville Mellon 1831-1916 *HarEnMi*
Dodge, Harlan B. 1919- *St&PR 93*
Dodge, Jacob Richards 1823-1902 *JrnUS*
Dodge, Jeffrey Carl 1953- *WhoEmL 93*
Dodge, Jim *ScF&FL 92*
Dodge, John Ashton *WhoScE 91-1*
Dodge, John David *WhoScE 91-1*
Dodge, Joseph Jeffers 1917- *WhoSSW 93*
Dodge, Mark S. 1946- *St&PR 93*
Dodge, Martin Clark 1942- *WhoE 93*
Dodge, Mary Abigail 1833-1896 *BioIn 17*
Dodge, Mary Louise *ScF&FL 92*
Dodge, Mary Mapes 1830-1905 *BioIn 17*
Dodge, Mary (Elizabeth) Mapes 1831?-1905 *ConAu 137, MajAI [port]*
Dodge, May Hewes *AmWomPl*
Dodge, Michael J. *Law&B 92, ScF&FL 92*
Dodge, N.S., Jr. *St&PR 93*
Dodge, Nancy Noble 1957- *WhoEmL 93*
Dodge, Peter Hampton 1929- *WhoAm 92*
Dodge, Philip Rogers 1923- *WhoAm 92*
Dodge, Ralph Edward 1936- *WhoSSW 93*
Dodge, Robert Earl 1945- *WhoE 93*
Dodge, Theodore Ayrault 1911- *WhoWor 93*
Dodge, William Douglas 1937- *WhoAm 92*
Dodgen, Harold Warren 1921- *WhoAm 92*
Dodgion, Lee A. 1935- *St&PR 93*
Dodgson, Charles Lutwidge 1832-1898 *BioIn 17, MajAI [port]*
Dodgson, Stephen (Cuthbert Vivian) 1924- *Baker 92*
Dodington, Sven H. d1992 *NewYTBS 92*
Dodington, Sven H. 1912-1992 *BioIn 17*
Dodohara, Jean Noton 1934- *WhoAmW 93*
Dodrill, Dale W. 1944- *St&PR 93*
Dodro, Robert Stephen 1949- *St&PR 93*
Dods, Mary Diana *BioIn 17*
Dods, Walter Arthur, Jr. 1941- *St&PR 93, WhoAm 92*
Dodsley, Robert 1703-1764 *BioIn 17*
Dodson, Bertha M. *Law&B 92*
Dodson, Billy 1944- *St&PR 93*
Dodson, Catherine E. Brown 1948- *WhoEmL 93*
Dodson, Christine 1935- *WhoUN 92*
Dodson, Christopher J. *Law&B 92*
Dodson, D. Keith 1943- *WhoAm 92, WhoWor 93*
Dodson, Daniel Boone 1918-1991 *BioIn 17*
Dodson, Daryl Theodore 1934- *WhoAm 92, WhoWor 93*
Dodson, David Louis 1955- *WhoSSW 93*
Dodson, David Scott 1942- *WhoSSW 93*
Dodson, Debbi Lewis 1947- *WhoAmW 93*
Dodson, Donald Mills 1937- *St&PR 93, WhoAm 92*
Dodson, Elaine 1944- *WhoAmW 93*
Dodson, Fitzhugh 1923- *ScF&FL 92*
Dodson, George Guy *WhoScE 91-1*
Dodson, George W. 1937- *WhoSSW 93*
Dodson, Helen Zrake 1954- *WhoEmL 93*
Dodson, James B. *Law&B 92*
Dodson, James Graham 1949- *St&PR 93*
Dodson, John *WhoScE 91-1*
Dodson, John Edward 1952- *St&PR 93*
Dodson, Judith Lynne 1947- *WhoAmW 93*
Dodson, Linda S. 1952- *WhoAm 92, WhoAmW 93, WhoEmL 93*
Dodson, Oscar Henry 1905- *WhoAm 92, WhoWor 93*
Dodson, Owen 1914-1983 *BioIn 17*
Dodson, Paulette Rennalls *Law&B 92*
Dodson, Raymond Guerrant 1947- *WhoEmL 93*
Dodson, Samuel Robinette, III 1943- *WhoAm 92*
Dodson, Sharon Doris 1952- *WhoAmW 93*
Dodson, Thomas Andrew 1949- *St&PR 93*
Dodson, Vernon Nathan 1923- *WhoAm 92*
Doe, Bruce Roger 1931- *WhoAm 92*
Doe, Lubin 1946- *WhoUN 92*
Doe, Patricia Louise 1948- *WhoE 93, WhoEmL 93*
Doe, Richard Philip 1926- *WhoAm 92*
Doe, Samuel Kanyon *BioIn 17*
Doe, Weldon W., Jr. 1918- *St&PR 93*
Doebbeling, Minda Kay 1942- *WhoAmW 93*
Doebler, Curt 1896-1970 *Baker 92*
Doebler, James Carl 1939- *WhoAm 92*
Doebler, Leland Kent 1947- *WhoEmL 93, WhoSSW 93*
Doebler, Paul Dickerson 1930- *WhoAm 92*
Doede, John Henry 1937- *St&PR 93, WhoAm 92*
Doehr, Ruth Nadine 1932- *WhoAmW 93*
Doehring, Richard Clayton 1936- *St&PR 93*
Doel, Kenneth John 1948- *St&PR 93, WhoAm 92*
Doel, Timothy Richard *WhoScE 91-1*
Doelitzsch, Dennis F. 1947- *WhoEmL 93*
Doelker, Eric 1944- *WhoScE 91-4*
Doell, Aubrey Clarence 1918- *St&PR 93*
Doell, Mary Rae 1940- *St&PR 93*
Doellinger, Steve 1949- *St&PR 93*
Doelp, Florinda Donato 1936- *St&PR 93*
Doelp, Paul Robert 1934- *St&PR 93*
Doelz, Melvin Louis 1918- *WhoAm 92*
D'Oench, Russell *St&PR 93*
D'Oench, Russell Grace, Jr. 1927- *WhoE 93, WhoWor 93*
D'Oench, Woodbridge Adams 1931- *St&PR 93*
Doenecke, Carol Anne 1942- *WhoAm 92*
Doenecke, Justus Drew *WhoSSW 93*
Doenges, Byron Frederick 1922- *WhoAm 92*
Doenges, Norman Arthur 1926- *WhoAm 92*
Doenges, Rudolph Conrad 1930- *WhoAm 92*
Doenhoff, Albert von 1880-1940 *Baker 92*
Doenitz, Karl 1891-1980 *DcTwHis*
Doepke, Katherine Louise Guldberg 1921- *WhoAmW 93*
Doepkens, Frederick Henry 1958- *WhoE 93*
Doeppenschmidt, William *Law&B 92*
Doeppner, Thomas Walter 1920- *WhoAm 92, WhoWor 93*
Doerfel, Helmut 1928- *WhoScE 91-3*
Doerfer, Gerhard 1920- *WhoWor 93*
Doerfer, John Charles d1992 *NewYTBS 92 [port]*
Doerfer, John Charles 1904-1992 *BioIn 17*
Doerfler, Andrew Charles 1952- *WhoSSW 93*
Doerfler, Leo G. 1919- *WhoAm 92*
Doerfler, Leonard Anthony 1954- *WhoE 93*
Doerfler, Ronald John 1941- *St&PR 93, WhoAm 92*
Doerfler, Thomas Eugene 1937- *WhoE 93*
Doerfler, Trina Allegre 1956- *WhoAmW 93*
Doerfler, Walter Hans 1933- *WhoScE 91-3*
Doerflinger, Marlys Irene 1943- *WhoAmW 93*
Doerger, Gerald Lawrence 1944- *St&PR 93*
Doerhoff, Dale Charles 1946- *WhoEmL 93*
Doering, Alan Norbert 1940- *WhoE 93*
Doering, Charles Rogers 1956- *WhoEmL 93*
Doering, James Dean 1936- *St&PR 93*
Doering, Mark Allen 1947- *WhoEmL 93*
Doering, William von Eggers 1917- *WhoAm 92*
Doermann, Humphrey 1930- *WhoAm 92*
Doermann, Paul Edmund 1926- *WhoAm 92*
Doermer, Richard T. 1922- *St&PR 93*
Doernberger, William Le Claire 1951- *St&PR 93*
Doerper, John Erwin 1943- *WhoWor 93*
Doerr, Christopher Lee 1949- *St&PR 93*
Doerr, Edd 1930- *ScF&FL 92*
Doerr, Harriet *BioIn 17*
Doerr, R. Chris 1946- *St&PR 93*
Doerr, Ronald H. 1940- *St&PR 93*
Doerr, Thomas Michael *Law&B 92*
Doerr, Veronica M. *WhoE 93*
Doerries, Eric W. *Law&B 92*
Doerries, Reinhard Rene 1934- *WhoAm 92*
Doersam, Charles Henry, Jr. 1921- *WhoE 93*
Doersam, Charles Henry, III 1957- *WhoE 93, WhoEmL 93*
Doersch, Richard C. *Law&B 92*
Doerschuk, Jeanclaire Oakes 1925- *WhoAmW 93*
Doesburg, Jan van 1931- *WhoScE 91-3*
Doescher, William Frederick 1937- *St&PR 93*
Doetsch, Douglas Allen 1957- *WhoEmL 93*
Doetsch, Karl Maximilian 1941- *WhoSSW 93*
Doettling, Robert L. 1937- *St&PR 93*
Doettling, Robert Lester 1937- *WhoAm 92*
Doflein, Erich 1900-1977 *Baker 92*
Doft, Alan 1933- *St&PR 93*
Doft, Avrom I. 1938- *St&PR 93*
Dogali, Jo M. *Law&B 92*
Dogali, Jo Marie 1949- *WhoEmL 93*
Dogan, Zeki M. 1924- *WhoScE 91-4*
Dogancay, Burhan C. 1929- *WhoAm 92*
Doganis, Rigas *WhoScE 91-1*
Dogbe, Yves-Emmanuel 1939- *WhoWor 93*
Dogbolt, Barnaby 1906- *ScF&FL 92*
Dogger, Allen J. 1947- *WhoEmL 93, WhoSSW 93*
Doggett, Aubrey Clayton, Jr. 1928- *WhoAm 92*
Doggett, Lloyd 1946- *WhoAm 92, WhoSSW 93*
Doggett, Ron E. 1934- *St&PR 93*
Doggette, David H. 1954- *St&PR 93*
Doggrell, Henry Patton 1948- *WhoEmL 93*
Dogoloff, Lee Israel 1939- *WhoAm 92*
Dogramaci, Ihsan *WhoScE 91-4*
Dohahue, Judith L. 1950- *St&PR 93*
Dohanian, Diran Kavork 1931- *WhoAm 92*
Dohanos, Stevan *BioIn 17*
Doheny, Donald Aloysius 1924- *WhoAm 92, WhoWor 93*
Doheny, Edward L. 1856-1935 *BioIn 17*
Doheny, Margaret A. *AmWomPl*
Doheny, Sharon Virginia 1968- *WhoAmW 93*
Doherty, Barbara 1931- *WhoAm 92, WhoAmW 93*
Doherty, Berlie 1943- *ChlFicS, MajAI [port], ScF&FL 92, SmATA 72 [port], -16AS [port]*
Doherty, Bernard J. *Law&B 92*
Doherty, Catherine de Hueck 1900- *BioIn 17*
Doherty, Charles Vincent 1933- *WhoAm 92*
Doherty, Christopher J. *Law&B 92*
Doherty, Daniel Edward 1952- *WhoE 93*
Doherty, Daniel Eugene *Law&B 92*
Doherty, Deena G. *Law&B 92*
Doherty, Donald Patrick *Law&B 92*
Doherty, Donna Kathryn 1948- *WhoAm 92*
Doherty, Edward Denvir 1935- *St&PR 93*
Doherty, Edward James 1950- *WhoEmL 93*
Doherty, Edward Woods d1992 *NewYTBS 92*
Doherty, Edward Woods 1914-1992 *BioIn 17*
Doherty, Eileen Claire 1946- *St&PR 93*
Doherty, Eileen Patricia 1952- *WhoEmL 93*
Doherty, Elizabeth Rose 1958 *WhoAmW 93*
Doherty, Evelyn Marie 1941- *WhoAmW 93, WhoE 93*
Doherty, George M. 1942- *St&PR 93*
Doherty, Gerald Dean 1937- *St&PR 93*
Doherty, Gerald Thomas 1929- *WhoWor 93*
Doherty, Harry Patrick 1942- *WhoAm 92*
Doherty, Henry Joseph 1933- *WhoAm 92*
Doherty, Herbert Joseph, Jr. 1926- *WhoAm 92*
Doherty, James Edward, III 1923- *WhoAm 92*
Doherty, James Francis, Jr. *Law&B 92*
Doherty, James J. 1935- *St&PR 93*
Doherty, Joe *BioIn 17*
Doherty, John 1798?-1854 *BioIn 17*
Doherty, John L. 1934- *WhoE 93*
Doherty, John Patrick 1947- *WhoWrEP 92*
Doherty, Joseph J. 1933- *St&PR 93*
Doherty, Karen Ann 1952- *WhoAmW 93, WhoEmL 93*
Doherty, Katherine Mann 1951- *WhoE 93*
Doherty, Kelly Sean 1956- *St&PR 93*
Doherty, Leonard E. 1940- *St&PR 93*
Doherty, Leonard Edward 1940- *WhoAm 92*
Doherty, M. Stephen *BioIn 17*
Doherty, M. Stephen 1948- *WhoAm 92*
Doherty, Margaret Ann 1952- *WhoAmW 93, WhoEmL 93*
Doherty, Mary Kay *Law&B 92*
Doherty, Mary Margaret 1960- *WhoAmW 93*
Doherty, Maureen A. *Law&B 92*
Doherty, Michel George 1930- *WhoAm 92, WhoAmW 93, WhoSSW 93*
Doherty, Nan 1956- *WhoAmW 93*
Doherty, Patricia Ann 1959- *WhoE 93, WhoEmL 93*
Doherty, Patricia M. 1951- *St&PR 93*
Doherty, Paul Edward 1937- *St&PR 93*
Doherty, Peter Charles 1940- *WhoAm 92*
Doherty, Rebecca Feeney 1952- *WhoAmW 93*
Doherty, Richard J. 1953- *St&PR 93*
Doherty, Richard M. *Law&B 92*
Doherty, Robert Cunningham 1930- *WhoAm 92*
Doherty, Robert Francis, Jr. 1954- *WhoE 93*
Doherty, Shannen *BioIn 17*
Doherty, Theresa Fuhr 1964- *WhoAmW 93*
Doherty, Thomas 1935- *WhoAm 92*
Doherty, Thomas A. 1938- *St&PR 93*
Doherty, Thomas Joseph 1933- *WhoAm 92, WhoWor 93*
Doherty, William Thomas, Jr. 1923- *WhoAm 92*
Dohihara, Kenji 1883-1948 *HarEnMi*
Dohla, Johann Conrad 1750-1820 *BioIn 17*
Dohler, Gottfried Heinrich 1938- *WhoWor 93*
Dohler, Theodor (von) 1814-1856 *Baker 92*
Dohm, Volker 1943- *WhoScE 91-3*
Dohmen, Erwin John 1927- *St&PR 93*
Dohmen, John F. 1955- *St&PR 93*
Dohmen, Robert Charles 1951- *St&PR 93*
Dohn, Betty Kirksey 1939- *St&PR 93*
Dohnal, David E. *Law&B 92*
Dohnal, David Edward 1937- *St&PR 93*
Dohnal, William Edward 1912- *WhoSSW 93, WhoWor 93*
Dohnanyi, Christoph von 1929- *Baker 92, OxDcOp*
Dohnanyi, Ernst von 1877-1960 *Baker 92*

Dohner, Barry Craig 1952- *WhoEmL 93*
Dohner, John P. 1936- *St&PR 93*
Dohrenwend, Bruce Philip 1927- *WhoAm 92*
Dohrenwend, Sandra Blackman Masterman 1935- *WhoAmW 93*
Dohrmann, Bernd 1942- *WhoScE 91-3*
Dohrmann, R.W. 1942- *St&PR 93*
Dohrmann, Richard John 1932- *WhoSSW 93*
Dohrmann, Richard Martin 1947- *WhoEmL 93*
Dohrmann, Russell William 1942- *WhoAm 92*
Dohrn, Madelyn *WhoWrEP 92*
Dohy, Janos 1934- *WhoScE 91-4*
Doi, Akoka *WhoWor 93*
Doi, Akoka 1951- *WhoAsAP 91*
Doi, Dorothy Mitsue 1934- *WhoAmW 93*
Doi, James Isao 1923- *WhoAm 92*
Doi, Kathryn 1960- *WhoEmL 93*
Doi, Lois 1951- *WhoEmL 93*
Doi, Mary Ellen 1933- *WhoAm 92*
Doi, Masayuki 1933- *WhoWor 93*
Doi, Ryuichi 1939- *WhoAsAP 91*
Doi, Stanley Toshio 1935- *St&PR 93*
Doi, Takako 1928- *BioIn 17, CurBio 92 [port], WhoAsAP 91*
Doi, Yoshihara 1947- *WhoWor 93*
Doidge, J.L. *Law&B 92*
Doig, Agnes M. *AmWomPl*
Doig, Beverly Irene 1936- *WhoAmW 93*
Doig, Ivan 1939- *WhoAm 92*
Doig, James Conroy 1929- *WhoSSW 93*
Doig, Jameson Wallace 1933- *WhoAm 92*
Doig, Raymond Allen 1936- *St&PR 93*
Doigan, Lloyd D. *Law&B 92*
Doin, David M. 1955- *St&PR 93*
Doire, Rene 1879-1959 *Baker 92*
Doiron, Donald F. 1943- *St&PR 93*
Doisneau, Robert 1912- *BioIn 17*
Doisneau, Robert Sylvain 1912- *WhoWor 93*
Doje Cering 1939- *WhoAsAP 91*
Dojka, Edwin Sigmund 1924- *WhoAm 92, WhoE 93*
Dojny, Richard Francis 1940- *WhoAm 92*
Doka, Kenneth J. 1948- *WhoE 93*
Doke, Marshall J., Jr. 1934- *WhoAm 92*
Dokeianos *OxDcByz*
Dokeianos, John fl. 15th cent.- *OxDcByz*
Doken, Mustafa Timur 1947- *WhoScE 91-4*
Dokmeci, Ismet 1942- *WhoScE 91-4*
Dokmeci, M. Cengiz 1936- *WhoScE 91-4*
Dokopoulos, Petros 1939- *WhoScE 91-3*
Dokoudovsky, Nina Ludmila 1947- *WhoAmW 93, WhoEmL 93*
Dokoupil, Jiri Georg 1954- *BioIn 17*
Dokshitcher, Timofei 1921- *Baker 92*
Doktor, Paul (Karl) 1919-1989 *Baker 92*
Doku, Hristo Chris 1928- *WhoAm 92*
Dokulil, Martin T. 1943- *WhoScE 91-4*
Dokurno, Anthony David 1957- *WhoE 93, WhoEmL 93, WhoWor 93*
Dolak, Anna E. *Law&B 92*
Dolak, David E. 1944- *St&PR 93*
Dolak, David John 1945- *St&PR 93*
Dolak, Terence Martin 1951- *WhoAm 92, WhoE 93*
Dolan, Allison Fish 1954- *WhoAmW 93*
Dolan, Barbara *BioIn 17*
Dolan, Beverly Franklin 1927- *St&PR 93*
Dolan, Bill *ScF&FL 92*
Dolan, Brian Patrick 1955- *St&PR 93*
Dolan, Charles F. 1926- *St&PR 93*
Dolan, Charles Francis 1926- *WhoAm 92*
Dolan, Clifford Wilson 1930- *St&PR 93*
Dolan, Daniel A. *Law&B 92*
Dolan, Dennis Joseph 1946- *WhoEmL 93, WhoSSW 93*
Dolan, Dorothy Rose 1912- *WhoAmW 93*
Dolan, Edward Corcoran 1952- *WhoE 93*
Dolan, Edward Francis 1924- *WhoAm 92*
Dolan, Eugene Thomas 1930- *WhoE 93*
Dolan, G. Keith 1927- *WhoWrEP 92*
Dolan, Gary C. *Law&B 92*
Dolan, Harold Ernest 1926- *WhoSSW 93*
Dolan, Helen M. 1937- *St&PR 93*
Dolan, James Daniel 1956- *WhoSSW 93*
Dolan, James Francis 1930- *WhoAm 92*
Dolan, James Patrick 1949- *WhoEmL 93*
Dolan, James T., Jr. 1926- *WhoAm 92*
Dolan, James V. *Law&B 92*
Dolan, James Vincent 1938- *WhoAm 92*
Dolan, Janet M. *BioIn 17*
Dolan, Janet Marie *Law&B 92*
Dolan, John E. 1923- *WhoAm 92*
Dolan, John J. 1956- *St&PR 93*
Dolan, John Jude 1956- *WhoEmL 93*
Dolan, John Patrick 1935- *WhoE 93, WhoWor 93*
Dolan, John Ralph 1926- *WhoAm 92*
Dolan, Joseph J. *St&PR 93*
Dolan, Kevin Joseph 1944- *WhoAm 92*
Dolan, Kevin L. 1937- *St&PR 93*
Dolan, Kevin Leo 1937- *WhoAm 92*
Dolan, Leigh Ann *Law&B 92*
Dolan, Lenore K. *AmWomPl*
Dolan, Louis Robert 1937- *St&PR 93*
Dolan, Louise Ann 1950- *WhoAm 92, WhoAmW 93*
Dolan, Mark V. *Law&B 92*
Dolan, Maryanne McLorn 1924- *WhoAmW 93*
Dolan, Michael G. 1949- *St&PR 93*
Dolan, Michael John 1958- *WhoE 93*
Dolan, Michael P. *Law&B 92*
Dolan, Michael William 1942- *WhoAm 92*
Dolan, Mick 1951- *WhoEmL 93*
Dolan, Paul 1929- *St&PR 93*
Dolan, Peter Brown 1939- *WhoAm 92*
Dolan, Peter Robert 1956- *WhoAm 92, WhoEmL 93*
Dolan, Raymond Bernard 1923- *WhoAm 92*
Dolan, Richard Edwin 1933- *St&PR 93*
Dolan, Robert Glennon 1939- *St&PR 93*
Dolan, Robert Glennon, Jr. 1939- *WhoAm 92*
Dolan, Robert Lee 1943- *St&PR 93, WhoIns 93*
Dolan, Robyn Kay 1964- *WhoAmW 93*
Dolan, Ronald J. 1947- *St&PR 93*
Dolan, Ronald John *Law&B 92*
Dolan, Ronald Vincent 1942- *St&PR 93, WhoAm 92*
Dolan, Sarah Ann 1933- *WhoAmW 93*
Dolan, Terrence Raymond 1940- *WhoAm 92*
Dolan, Therese Ann 1946- *WhoAmW 93*
Dolan, Thomas Ironside 1927- *St&PR 93, WhoAm 92*
Dolan, Thomas Joseph 1943- *WhoAm 92*
Dolan, Timothy J. *Law&B 92*
Dolan, Timothy J. 1954- *St&PR 93*
Dolan, William David, Jr. 1913- *WhoAm 92*
Dolan, William F. 1933- *St&PR 93*
Dolan, William G. 1927- *St&PR 93*
Dolan, William P. 1953- *St&PR 93*
Dolan, William R. 1945- *WhoIns 93*
Dolan, William S.C. 1911-1991 *BioIn 17*
Dolan, William Thomas 1937- *St&PR 93*
Doland, Jack 1928-1991 *BioIn 17*
Doland, Judy Ann 1940- *WhoAmW 93*
Dolansky, Janet Lynn 1963- *WhoAmW 93*
Dolapchiev, Luben Bl. 1939- *WhoScE 91-4*
Dolata, Albert *Law&B 92*
Dolben, David Howland 1935- *St&PR 93*
Dolber, Wendy 1949- *St&PR 93*
Dolberg, Steve *St&PR 93*
Dolby, Alan Ernest *WhoScE 91-1*
Dolby, Cheryl Sue 1945- *WhoAmW 93*
Dolby, Ray Milton 1933- *WhoAm 92*
Dolce, Carl John 1928- *WhoAm 92*
Dolce, Domenico *BioIn 17*
Dolch, Norman Allen 1947- *WhoEmL 93, WhoSSW 93*
Dolch, William Lee 1925- *WhoAm 92*
Dold, Albrecht 1928- *WhoScE 91-3*
Dold, Albrecht Egon 1928- *WhoWor 93*
Dold, Catherine Anne 1957- *WhoWrEP 92*
Dold, Gaylord 1947- *ConAu 139*
Dolder, Kenneth Thomas *WhoScE 91-1*
Dolder, V. *WhoScE 91-4*
Dolderer, Alan 1958- *WhoEmL 93*
Dole, Arthur Alexander 1917- *WhoAm 92*
Dole, Burton Andrew, Jr. 1937- *St&PR 93*
Dole, Elizabeth Hanford 1936- *BioIn 17, WhoAm 92, WhoAmW 93, WhoE 93, WhoWor 93*
Dole, Jody *BioIn 17*
Dole, Karen Faye 1951- *WhoAmW 93*
Dole, Malcolm 1903-1990 *BioIn 17*
Dole, Richard 1945- *WhoSSW 93*
Dole, Richard Fairfax, Jr. 1936- *WhoAm 92*
Dole, Robert 1923- *CngDr 91*
Dole, Robert J. *PolPar*
Dole, Robert J. 1923- *BioIn 17, WhoAm 92*
Dole, Robert Paul 1923- *St&PR 93, WhoAm 92*
Dole, Vincent Paul 1913- *WhoAm 92*
Dole, Vincent Paul, III 1944- *WhoE 93, WhoWor 93*
Doleac, Charles Bartholomew 1947- *WhoAm 92, WhoE 93, WhoEmL 93, WhoWor 93*
Dolecki, Lawrence L. *Law&B 92*
Dolega, Roger *St&PR 93*
Dolega-Kamienski *Baker 92*
Dolejs, Petr 1952- *WhoScE 91-4*
Doleman, Christopher John 1961- *WhoAm 92*
Dolena, James E. *BioIn 17*
Dolensek, Emil P. d1990 *BioIn 17*
Dolenz, Ami *BioIn 17*
Dolenz, Mickey 1945- *WhoAm 92*
Doler, Daniel C. 1926- *St&PR 93*
Doles, Johann Friedrich 1715-1797 *Baker 92*
Doleschall, Sandor 1936- *WhoScE 91-4*
Doley, Harold Emanuel, Jr. 1947- *WhoAm 92*
Doley, Helena Cobette 1946- *WhoAmW 93*
Dolezal, Dale Francis 1936- *WhoE 93, WhoWor 93*
Dolezal, Leo Thomas 1944- *WhoSSW 93*
Dolezalek, Hans 1912- *WhoSSW 93*
Dolezalek, Jan Emanuel 1780-1858 *Baker 92*
Dolezelova-Velingerova, Milena 1932- *WhoWrEP 92*
Dolezsai, Karoly 1924- *WhoScE 91-4*
Dolfato, Giovanni V. *Law&B 92*
Dolge, Alfred Karl 1926- *St&PR 93*
Dolgen, Jonathan L. *WhoAm 92*
Dolger, Jonathan 1938- *WhoAm 92, WhoWrEP 92*
Dolgikh, B.O. 1904-1971 *IntDcAn*
Dolgikh, Sergey Nickolaevich 1966- *WhoWor 93*
Dolgin, Ann B. *WhoAmW 93*
Dolgin, Bernard 1924- *St&PR 93*
Dolgin, Martin 1919- *WhoAm 92*
Dolgin, Steve Alan 1949- *St&PR 93*
Dolgin, Stuart 1936- *St&PR 93*
Dolgoff, Eugene J. 1950- *St&PR 93*
Dolgoff, Sam 1902-1990 *BioIn 17*
Dolgov, Vyacheslav Ivanovich 1937- *WhoWor 93*
Dolgow, Samuel Robert *Law&B 92*
Dolgushin, Nikita 1938- *BioIn 17*
Dolich, Andrew Bruce 1947- *WhoAm 92, WhoEmL 93*
Dolich, Ira Richard 1935- *St&PR 93*
D'Olieslager, Willem M.J. 1939- *WhoScE 91-2*
Dolin, Albert Harry 1913- *WhoAm 92*
Dolin, Michelle Cynthia 1952- *WhoEmL 93*
Dolin, Mitchell F. 1956- *WhoEmL 93*
Dolin, Samuel (Joseph) 1917- *Baker 92, WhoAm 92*
Dolinich, Christine 1950- *WhoAmW 93*
Dolinka, Bertalan 1932- *WhoScE 91-4*
Dolique, Jean-Michel 1930- *WhoScE 91-2*
Dolis, John 1945- *WhoE 93*
Dolive, Earl 1917- *WhoAm 92*
Doll, Craig Allen 1948- *WhoE 93*
Doll, Eugenia Delarova d1990 *BioIn 17*
Doll, Henri-Georges d1991 *BioIn 17*
Doll, Jimmie Dave 1945- *WhoE 93*
Doll, Lynne Marie 1961- *WhoAm 92*
Doll, Mary Aswell 1940- *WhoSSW 93*
Doll, Maurice Edward, Jr. 1956- *WhoEmL 93*
Doll, Patricia Marie 1960- *WhoE 93, WhoEmL 93*
Doll, Richard 1912- *WhoScE 91-1*
Doll, William Elder, Jr. 1931- *WhoSSW 93*
Dollahite, David Curtis 1958- *WhoEmL 93, WhoSSW 93*
Dollar, Beverly Marie *Law&B 92*
Dollar, Matt 1972- *BioIn 17*
Dollar, T. Roby 1938- *St&PR 93*
Dollar, Thomas Roby, Jr. 1938- *WhoSSW 93*
Dollard, Mark Cantwell d1991 *BioIn 17*
Dollard, Michael Joseph 1939- *WhoE 93*
Dollard, Virginia Marie 1952- *WhoE 93, WhoEmL 93*
Dolle, Ann B. *Law&B 92*
Dolle, Raymond F. 1952- *ConAu 136*
Dollen, Charles Joseph 1926- *WhoWrEP 92*
Dollerup, Cay 1939- *ScF&FL 92*
Dollerup, Erik Cay Krebs 1939- *WhoWor 93*
Dollerup, Robert Fin Krebs 1942- *WhoWor 93*
Dollery, Colin Terence 1931- *WhoScE 91-1*
Dollet, Michel 1949- *WhoScE 91-2*
Dollfus, Audouin 1924- *WhoScE 91-2*
Dollfuss, Engelbert 1892-1934 *DcTwHis*
Dollich, Ira R. 1935- *St&PR 93*
Dollinger, Joel I. 1942- *St&PR 93*
Dollinger, Peter 1944- *WhoScE 91-4*
Dollins, James C. *St&PR 93*
Dollison, Dwight G. 1943- *St&PR 93*
Dollison, Dwight Guy 1943- *WhoAm 92*
Dolliver, James Morgan 1924- *WhoAm 92*
Dolliver, Robert Henry 1934- *WhoAm 92*
Dollman, Friedrich 1876-1944 *HarEnMi*
Dollner, Karl *ScF&FL 92*
d'Ollone, Max(imilien-Paul-Marie-Felix) 1875-1959 *Baker 92*
Dollson, H. C., Mrs. *AmWomPl*
Dolly, John Patrick 1942- *WhoAm 92*
Dollyhigh, Randy Monroe 1956- *WhoSSW 93*
Dolman, John Phillips, Jr. 1944- *WhoAm 92*
Dolmans, N.G.M. *WhoScE 91-3*
Dolmatch, Theodore Bieley 1924- *WhoAm 92*
Dolmath, Stephen J. *Law&B 92*
Dolmazon, J.M. 1946- *WhoScE 91-2*
Dolmetsch, (Eugene) Arnold 1858-1940 *Baker 92*
Dolmetsch, Carl Frederick 1911- *Baker 92*
Dolmetsch, Carl Richard, (Jr.) 1924- *WhoSSW 93*
Dolmetsch, Christopher Lee 1950- *WhoSSW 93*
Dolney, James Kenneth 1950- *WhoSSW 93*
Dolnick, David Benjamin 1950- *WhoEmL 93*
Dolny, Warren Stuart 1928- *WhoE 93*
Dolores, Juan 1880-1948 *IntDcAn*
Dolorico, Julio Estrellado 1912- *WhoWor 93*
Dolowitz, David Augustus 1913- *WhoWor 93*
Dolowy, Krysztof 1949- *WhoWor 93*
Dolph, Charles Laurie 1918- *WhoAm 92*
Dolph, Robert Norman 1925- *WhoAm 92*
Dolph, Wilbert Emery 1923- *WhoAm 92*
Dolphin, David 1940- *St&PR 93*
Dolphin, James 1949- *St&PR 93*
Dolphin, John Leo 1924- *St&PR 93*
Dolphin, Reginald C. *ScF&FL 92*
Dolphin, Rex *ScF&FL 92*
Dolphy, Eric (Allan) 1928-1964 *Baker 92*
Dolsingh, Michael R. 1952- *WhoWor 93*
Dolson, Charles H. d1992 *NewYTBS 92*
Dolson, Donald 1937- *St&PR 93*
Dolson, Franklin Robert 1933- *WhoAm 92*
Doluisio, James Thomas 1935- *WhoAm 92*
Dolujanoff, Emma 1922- *DcMexL*
Dolukhanova, Zara 1918- *Baker 92, OxDcOp*
Dolz, J. 1949- *WhoScE 91-3*
Dom, John A. 1941- *St&PR 93*
Dom, Rene J. 1940- *WhoScE 91-2*
Domac, Dragutin Charles 1940- *WhoWrEP 92*
Domachowski, Zygfryd 1939- *WhoScE 91-4*
Domagala, Richard Edward 1947- *WhoAm 92, WhoE 93*
Domagalski, Michael Ralph 1950- *WhoEmL 93*
Doman, Daniel John *Law&B 92*
Doman, David Alan *ScF&FL 92*
Doman, Janet Joy 1948- *WhoAm 92*
Doman, Linda Eileen 1961- *WhoAmW 93*
Doman, Margaret Horn 1946- *WhoAmW 93*
Doman, Nicholas R. 1913- *WhoAm 92*
Domange, Albert, Mme. *Baker 92*
Domanico, Robert A. 1948- *WhoIns 93*
Domaniewski, Boleslaus 1857-1925 *Baker 92*
Domaniewski, Boleslaw 1857-1925 *PolBiDi*
Domaninska, Libuse 1924- *Baker 92*
Domanska, Janina *BioIn 17, MajAI [port]*
Domanski, Donald 1950- *WhoCanL 92*
Domansky, Hanus 1944- *Baker 92*
Domantay, Norlito Valdez 1946- *WhoAm 92*
Domanus, Jozef 1919- *WhoScE 91-2*
Domany, Eytan 1947- *WhoWor 93*
Domar, Evsey D. *BioIn 17*
Domar, Evsey David 1914- *WhoAm 92*
Domaradzki, Jerzy *MiSFD 9*
Domaradzki, Jerzy 1943- *DrEEuF*
Domaradzki, Theodore Felix 1910- *WhoAm 92, WhoWrEP 92*
Domarkas, Ionas 1934- *Baker 92*
Domatilla, John 1936- *ScF&FL 92*
Dombeck, Harold Arthur 1941- *WhoE 93*
Dombeck, John Conrad 1939- *St&PR 93*
Dombeck, Thomas Walter 1945- *WhoSSW 93*
Dombek, Curtis Michael 1958- *WhoEmL 93*
Dombovari, Janos 1929- *WhoScE 91-4*
Dombro, Richard 1927- *WhoSSW 93*
Dombro, Roy Sandor 1933- *WhoSSW 93*
Dombroski, Patricia Newman 1953- *WhoAmW 93*
Dombrowski, Anne Wesseling 1948- *WhoAmW 93, WhoEmL 93*
Dombrowski, Charles F. 1954- *St&PR 93*
Dombrowski, David 1956- *WhoAm 92, WhoE 93*
Dombrowski, David Michael 1959- *WhoEmL 93*
Dombrowski, Eugene Joseph 1931- *St&PR 93*
Dombrowski, Frank Paul, Jr. 1943- *WhoE 93*
Dombrowski, Michael G. *Law&B 92*
Dombrowski, Mitchell Paul 1953- *WhoEmL 93*
Dombrowski, Norman *WhoScE 91-1*
Dombrowski, Raymond Edward, Jr. *Law&B 92*
Domcke, Wolfgang 1948- *WhoScE 91-3*
Dome, Lawrence Arthur 1946- *WhoEmL 93*
Domeier, David J. 1953- *St&PR 93*
Domeier, David John 1953- *WhoAm 92*

Domek, Richard Charles, Jr. 1945- WhoSSW 93
Domel, Neal David 1963- WhoSSW 93
Domen, Haruo 1930- WhoWor 93
Domenchina, Juan Jose 1898-1959 DcMexL
Domenech i Montaner, Lluis 1850-1923 BioIn 17
Domenici, Pete 1932- WhoAm 92
Domenici, Pete V. 1932- CngDr 91
Domentijan c. 1210-c. 1264 OxDcByz
Domeny, Rose Marie 1941- WhoAmW 93
Domer, Floyd Ray 1931- WhoAm 92
Domer, Judith Elaine 1939- WhoAmW 93
Domer, Ronald G. 1935- St&PR 93
Domeracki, Walter Arthur 1939- St&PR 93
Domes, Jurgen Otto 1932- WhoWor 93
Domeyko, Ignacy 1802-1889 PolBiDi
Domgraf-Fassbaender, Willi 1897-1978 OxDcOp
Domgraf-Fassbander, Willi 1897-1978 Baker 92
Domi, Tahir NewYTBS 92 [port]
Domi, Tie BioIn 17
Domigan, Stephen K. BioIn 17
Domin, Bruce R. St&PR 93
Domingo, Damian c. 1790-1832 BioIn 17
Domingo, Estrella Tina 1965- WhoAmW 93
Domingo, Llorenc 1956- WhoScE 91-3
Domingo, Placido BioIn 17
Domingo, Placido 1941- Baker 92, IntDcOp [port], News 93-2 [port], OxDcOp, WhoAm 92, WhoWor 93
Domingo, Sharon Patterson Law&B 92
Domingo, Simplicio B., Jr. 1934- WhoAsAP 91
Domingos, Henry 1934- WhoE 93
Domingue, Emery 1926- WhoAm 92
Domingue, Gerald James 1937- WhoAm 92
Domingue, Nicole Zuber 1932- WhoAm 92
Domingues, Oralia 1928- Baker 92
Dominguez, Cari M. 1949- HispAmA [port]
Dominguez, Demetrio 1948- WhoWor 93
Dominguez, Eddie 1957- BioIn 17
Dominguez, Jorge I. 1945- HispAmA
Dominguez, Jorge Ignacio 1945- WhoAm 92
Dominguez, Kathryn Mary 1960- WhoEmL 93
Dominguez, Manuel 1960- WhoEmL 93
Dominguez, Rene O. 1943- St&PR 93
Dominguez, Steven 1942- St&PR 93
Dominguez, Sylvia Maida 1935- DcLB 122 [port]
Dominguez, Victor S. 1935- WhoAsAP 91
Dominguez, Virginia Rosa 1952- WhoEmL 93
Dominguez Abascal, Jaime 1951- WhoScE 91-3
Dominguez-Mayoral, Rodrigo 1947- WhoEmL 93, WhoSSW 93
Dominguez Ortega, Luis 1941- WhoWor 93
Dominiak, George M. 1955- WhoEmL 93
Dominiak, Geraldine Florence 1934- WhoAm 92, WhoSSW 93
Dominianni, Emilio Anthony 1931- St&PR 93
Dominic, Zoe BioIn 17
Dominiceti, Cesare 1821-1888 Baker 92
Dominick, David DeWitt 1937- WhoAm 92
Dominick, Fred Adam 1925- St&PR 93
Dominick, Paul Allen 1954- WhoEmL 93
Dominie, Albert Duane 1943- St&PR 93
Dominik, Jack Edward 1924- WhoAm 92
Dominique, Daniel Roy 1918- WhoIns 93
Dominique, Lise Marie 1956- WhoEmL 93
Dominique, Paul A. 1947- WhoE 93
Domino, Anthony Joseph, Jr. 1962- WhoE 93
Domino, Edward Felix 1924- WhoAm 92
Domino, Eric 1949- BioIn 17
Domino, Fats 1928- SoulM, WhoAm 92
Domino, "Fats" (Antoine, Jr.) 1928- Baker 92
Domino, Gilbert George 1926- St&PR 93
Domino, John ConAu 139, SmATA 72
Dominoes SoulM
Dominowski, Roger Lynn 1939- WhoWrEP 92
Dominy, Michele Denise 1953- WhoAmW 93
Domis, Raymond C. 1944- St&PR 93
Domitian 51-96 HarEnMi
Domitianos c. 550-602 OxDcByz
Domitius Alexander OxDcByz
Domjan, Joseph 1907- WhoAm 92
Domjan, Laszlo Karoly 1947- WhoEmL 93, WhoWor 93
Domka, Florian Ludwik 1932- WhoWor 93
Domke, Kerry Lynn 1950- St&PR 93, WhoEmL 93
Domm, Alice 1954- WhoAmW 93
Dommel, Darlene Hurst 1940- WhoAmW 93
Dommen, Arthur John 1934- WhoAm 92
Dommen, Edward Charles 1938- WhoUN 92
Dommer, Luke A., Sr. d1992 NewYTBS 92
Dommermuth, William Peter WhoAm 92, WhoWor 93
Dommick, Catherine Anderson 1929- WhoAmW 93
Domokos, Gabor 1933- WhoAm 92
Domokos, Gyorgy 1931- WhoScE 91-4
Domonkos, Patricia Mahoney 1949- WhoAmW 93
Domonkos, Sandor 1931- WhoScE 91-4
Domoto, Akiko 1932- WhoAsAP 91
Dompierre, Judith Evlyn 1957- WhoE 93
Domres, Terry A. 1943- St&PR 93
Domroe, William E. 1945- St&PR 93
Domros, Manfred Rudi 1940- WhoScE 91-3
Doms, Keith 1920- WhoAm 92
Domsa, Julietta 1948- WhoScE 91-4
Domsa, S.B. 1945- WhoScE 91-4
Domsch, David 1945- St&PR 93
Domsch, Klaus H. 1926- WhoScE 91-3
Domsic, Dennis Michael 1949- WhoEmL 93
Domun, Zafrullah 1953- WhoWor 93
Do Muoi 1911- WhoWor 93
Domzal, David A. Law&B 92
Domzalski, Kenneth Stanley 1949- WhoEmL 93
Domzella, Janet 1935- WhoE 93
Don, Arthur 1953- WhoEmL 93
Don, Ian ScF&FL 92
Don, James K. 1936- St&PR 93
Don, Michael H. 1956- St&PR 93
Don, Richard 1929- St&PR 93
Donabedian, Avedis 1919- WhoAm 92
Donabedian, Bairj ScF&FL 92
Donachy, Shirley Ann 1946- WhoAmW 93
Donadio, Babette L. Law&B 92
Donadio, Leonard E. 1928- St&PR 93
Donadio, Mark C. Law&B 92
Donadio, Mary M. 1954- St&PR 93
Donadio, Robert Nicholas 1935- WhoAm 92
Dona-Fologo, Laurent 1939- WhoAfr
Donagan, Alan 1925-1991 BioIn 17
Donaghue, John Ames 1937- St&PR 93
Donaghy, Debra Ann 1957- WhoAmW 93, WhoEmL 93
Donaghy, Emily AmWomPl
Donaghy, Henry James 1930- WhoAm 92
Donaghy, James Edison 1934- St&PR 93
Donaghy, Patrick Christopher 1933- St&PR 93, WhoAm 92
Donaghy, Raymond Madiford Peardon 1910-1991 BioIn 17
Donagi, Ron 1956- WhoE 93
Donahoe, David Lawrence 1949- WhoAm 92
Donahoe, Thomas P. 1950- St&PR 93
Donahoo, Melvin Lawrence 1930- WhoE 93
Donahue, Barbara Lynn Sean 1956- WhoAmW 93
Donahue, Bernard A. Law&B 92
Donahue, C. Richard 1931- WhoE 93
Donahue, Charlotte Mary 1954- WhoAmW 93, WhoE 93, WhoEmL 93, WhoWor 93
Donahue, Daniel J. 1933- St&PR 93
Donahue, Daniel William 1942- WhoAm 92
Donahue, Deirdre Elizabeth Law&B 92
Donahue, Dennis Donald 1940- WhoWor 93
Donahue, Donald Jordan 1924- WhoAm 92
Donahue, Donald P. 1917- St&PR 93
Donahue, Douglas Aidan, Jr. 1951- WhoAm 92
Donahue, Elinor 1937- WhoAm 92
Donahue, Hayden Hackney 1912- WhoAm 92
Donahue, Irving James, Jr. 1922- St&PR 93
Donahue, Jack 1917-1991 BioIn 17
Donahue, Jayne Keirn 1953- WhoEmL 93
Donahue, Jeff BioIn 17
Donahue, John A. Law&B 92
Donahue, John Donald 1937- St&PR 93
Donahue, John F. 1924- St&PR 93, WhoE 93
Donahue, John F. 1936- WhoE 93, WhoIns 93
Donahue, John Joseph 1931- WhoE 93
Donahue, John McFall 1924- WhoAm 92
Donahue, John Michael 1952- WhoEmL 93
Donahue, John P. Law&B 92
Donahue, Judith Linnea 1950- WhoEmL 93
Donahue, Kenneth Joseph 1950- St&PR 93
Donahue, Laura Kent 1949- WhoAmW 93
Donahue, Lauri Michele 1961- WhoEmL 93
Donahue, Leslie D. Law&B 92
Donahue, Mary Elizabeth 1968- WhoAmW 93
Donahue, Mary Rosenberg 1932- WhoAmW 93, WhoE 93
Donahue, Michael James 1953- WhoEmL 93
Donahue, Michael Joseph 1947- WhoEmL 93
Donahue, Michael Richard 1949- WhoEmL 93
Donahue, Mitch BioIn 17
Donahue, Patricia Toothaker 1922- WhoSSW 93
Donahue, Peggy Jo Ruetsch 1955- WhoAmW 93
Donahue, Phil BioIn 17
Donahue, Phil 1935- WhoAm 92
Donahue, Richard J. St&PR 93
Donahue, Robert F. St&PR 93
Donahue, Suzanne Mary 1956- WhoAm 92
Donahue, Terrance Michael 1944- BiDAMSp 1989
Donahue, Thomas Michael 1921- WhoAm 92, WhoWor 93
Donahue, Thomas P. Law&B 92
Donahue, Thomas Reilly 1928- WhoAm 92
Donahue, Timothy Patrick 1955- WhoSSW 93
Donahue, William E. 1957- St&PR 93
Donahue, William J. 1950- St&PR 93
Donahugh, Robert Hayden 1930- WhoAm 92
Donais, Gary W. Law&B 92
Donais, Gary W. 1952- St&PR 93
Donais, Gary Warren 1952- WhoAm 92
Donaker, John C. 1943- St&PR 93
Donald, Aida DiPace 1930- WhoAm 92, WhoAmW 93
Donald, Alexander Grant 1928- WhoAm 92, WhoSSW 93
Donald, Andrew L. Law&B 92
Donald, Atley d1992 NewYTBS 92
Donald, Charlie Holman 1937- WhoSSW 93
Donald, David Herbert 1920- WhoAm 92, WhoE 93
Donald, Dorothy AmWomPl
Donald, Eric Paul 1930- WhoAm 92
Donald, Jack C. 1934- St&PR 93, WhoAm 92
Donald, James 1948- ScF&FL 92
Donald, James L. 1931- WhoAm 92
Donald, James Lee 1931- St&PR 93
Donald, James Maitland 1961- WhoE 93
Donald, James Robert 1933- WhoAm 92
Donald, Joe Kennan 1942- St&PR 93
Donald, John W. 1955- St&PR 93
Donald, Karen E. Law&B 92
Donald, Larry Watson 1945- WhoAm 92
Donald, Merlin 1939- ConAu 137
Donald, Milton Louis 1946- WhoEmL 93
Donald, Norman Henderson, III 1937- WhoAm 92
Donald, Paul Aubrey 1929- WhoAm 92
Donald, Peter (Harry) 1962- ConAu 137
Donald, Robert Graham 1943- WhoAm 92
Donald, Roger Thomas 1936- WhoE 93
Donald, William Roger 1938- WhoWor 93
Donald, Williamson P. Law&B 92
Donalda, Pauline 1882-1970 Baker 92, OxDcOp
Donaldson, Alan Stuart 1958- WhoEmL 93
Donaldson, Alexander Ivan WhoScE 91-1
Donaldson, Bryna ConAu 136
Donaldson, Coleman duPont 1922- WhoAm 92
Donaldson, Cynthia Brandt 1960- WhoAmW 93
Donaldson, D.J. ScF&FL 92
Donaldson, Daniel Reed 1940- St&PR 93
Donaldson, Darcy Miller 1953- WhoAmW 93
Donaldson, David Howard, Jr. 1951- WhoEmL 93
Donaldson, David Marbury 1938- WhoAm 92
Donaldson, David Robert 1945- St&PR 93
Donaldson, Donald Ray 1940- St&PR 93
Donaldson, Edward Mossop 1939- WhoAm 92
Donaldson, Eric Leonhart 1960- WhoEmL 93
Donaldson, Frank A. 1919-1991 BioIn 17
Donaldson, Frank W. 1921- WhoAm 92
Donaldson, Fred Lee, Jr. 1946- WhoE 93
Donaldson, Gordon BioIn 17
Donaldson, Gordon Bryce WhoScE 91-1
Donaldson, Harvey A. 1883-1972 BioIn 17
Donaldson, Howard Meyer 1952- WhoAm 92
Donaldson, Iain Malcolm Lane WhoScE 91-1
Donaldson, James Adrian 1930- WhoAm 92
Donaldson, James Oswell, III 1942- WhoE 93
Donaldson, Jeff Richardson 1932- WhoAm 92
Donaldson, John 1894-1970 BiDAMSp 1989
Donaldson, John 1928- WhoAm 92
Donaldson, John Anthony Law&B 92
Donaldson, John Anthony 1938- St&PR 93, WhoAm 92
Donaldson, John B. Law&B 92
Donaldson, John Cecil, Jr. 1933- WhoAm 92, WhoE 93, WhoWor 93
Donaldson, John Dallas WhoScE 91-1
Donaldson, John Edward, Jr. 1945- St&PR 93
Donaldson, John H. St&PR 93
Donaldson, John Scott BioIn 17
Donaldson, Kenneth 1950- WhoScE 91-1
Donaldson, Kenneth Lee 1957- WhoSSW 93
Donaldson, Lauren R. 1903- WhoAm 92
Donaldson, Mary Kendrick 1937- WhoAmW 93
Donaldson, Maureen 1946- BioIn 17
Donaldson, Merle Richard 1920- WhoAm 92
Donaldson, Richard Miesse 1929- WhoAm 92
Donaldson, Robert Herschel 1943- WhoAm 92, WhoSSW 93
Donaldson, Robert Macartney, Jr. 1927- WhoAm 92
Donaldson, Roger 1945- ConTFT 10, MiSFD 9
Donaldson, Ruth Louise 1909- WhoAmW 93
Donaldson, Samuel Andrew 1934- JrnUS, WhoAm 92
Donaldson, Scott BioIn 17
Donaldson, Scott 1928- WhoAm 92
Donaldson, Simon Kirwan WhoScE 91-1
Donaldson, Stephen R. 1947- ScF&FL 92
Donaldson, Stephen Reeder 1947- WhoAm 92, WhoWrEP 92
Donaldson, Thomas 1943- WhoIns 93
Donaldson, Thomas 1945- ConAu 139, WhoE 93
Donaldson, Timothy J. Law&B 92
Donaldson, William BioIn 17
Donaldson, William B. Law&B 92
Donaldson, William H. 1931- St&PR 93
Donaldson, William Henry 1931- WhoAm 92, WhoE 93
Donaldson, William V. d1991 BioIn 17
Donaldson, Willis Lyle 1915- WhoAm 92, WhoWor 93
Donaldson-Evans, Mary Prudhomme 1943- WhoE 93
Donangelo, Raul Jose 1947- WhoWor 93
Donars, Paul W. 1932- St&PR 93
do Nascimento, Alexander Cardinal 1925- WhoWor 93
Do Nascimento, Isaias Goncalves BioIn 17
Donat, Alexander d1983 BioIn 17
Donat, Robert 1905-1958 IntDcF 2-3
Donat, Thomas C. 1952- St&PR 93
Donat, Walter Kennedy 1954- WhoEmL 93
Donat Cattin, Carlo 1919-1991 BioIn 17
Donatelli, Dee 1955- WhoAmW 93
Donatelli, Luciano Pietro 1947- WhoWor 93
Donath, Alfred 1932- WhoScE 91-4
Donath, Clarence Edgar 1912- WhoE 93
Donath, David Alan 1951- WhoEmL 93
Donath, Fred Arthur 1931- WhoAm 92
Donath, Helen 1940- Baker 92, OxDcOp
Donath, Robert E. 1945- WhoWrEP 92
Donath, Therese BioIn 17
Donath, Therese 1928- WhoAm 92, WhoAmW 93, WhoWor 93
Donath, Tibor 1926- WhoScE 91-4
Donathan, Robert F. 1951- St&PR 93
Donati, Baldassare c. 1527-c. 1603 Baker 92
Donati, Dale A. 1953- St&PR 93
Donati, Enrico 1909- BioIn 17, WhoAm 92
Donati, Gian Carlo 1929- WhoWor 93
Donati, Ignazio c. 1575-1638 Baker 92
Donati, Maria Benedetta 1944- WhoScE 91-3
Donati, Pino 1907-1975 Baker 92
Donati, Robert Mario 1934- WhoAm 92, WhoWor 93
Donatiello, Nicholas E. 1934- St&PR 93
Donato, Alfred Virgil 1917- WhoE 93
Donato, Anthony 1909- Baker 92
Donato, Baldassare c. 1527-c. 1603 Baker 92
Donato, Frank J. 1945- St&PR 93
Donato, Luigi WhoScE 91-3

Donato, Marilyn Ranada 1940- WhoSSW 93
Donato, Michael A. BioIn 17
Donato, Nola 1955- WhoEmL 93
Donato, Samuel Joseph 1941- St&PR 93
Donatoni, Franco 1927- Baker 92, WhoWor 93
Donaubauer, Edwin WhoScE 91-4
Donaudy, Stefano 1879-1925 Baker 92
Donavan, Douglas A. 1949- St&PR 93
Donavel, David Frank 1946- WhoWrEP 92
Donawho, Karen 1955- WhoAmW 93
Donawick, William Joseph 1940- WhoE 93
Donay, Natalie d1991 BioIn 17
Donayre, Jose C.A. 1933- WhoUN 92
Donbavand, James Joseph, Jr. 1947- WhoEmL 93
Doncaster, Hilary Louise 1960- WhoE 93
Donch, Karl 1915- Baker 92
Donchak, Andrew F. 1951- St&PR 93, WhoAm 92
Donches, Stephen G. 1945- St&PR 93
Donchess, Barbara M. 1922- WhoWrEP 92
Donchev, Peter Vassilev 1939- WhoScE 91-4
Donchian, Richard D. 1905- St&PR 93
Donchian, Richard Davoud 1905- WhoAm 92
Donckers, Richard H. 1950- St&PR 93
Dondanville, Jeffrey W. Law&B 92
Dondanville, John Wallace 1937- WhoAm 92
Dondanville, Leo John, Jr. 1930- St&PR 93
Dondas, Nicholas Manuel 1939- WhoAsAP 91
Dondero, James Law&B 92
Donders, Joseph Gerard 1929- WhoE 93
Dondes, Robert Jonathan 1960- WhoE 93, WhoEmL 93
Done, D.L. WhoScE 91-1
Done, George Taylor Sutton WhoScE 91-1
Donegan, Ann Marie 1961- WhoAmW 93
Donegan, Carolyn May 1937- WhoE 93
Donegan, Charles Edward 1933- WhoAm 92
Donegan, Dorothy BioIn 17
Donegan, Horace W(illiam) B(aden) 1900-1991 CurBio 92N
Donegan, Horace William Baden 1900-1991 BioIn 17
Donegan, James Edward 1945- St&PR 93
Donegan, James Edward 1959- WhoEmL 93
Donegan, James Michael Law&B 92
Donegan, Patricia Morris 1953- WhoSSW 93
Donegan, Robert E. 1953- St&PR 93
Donegan, Thomas James 1907- WhoAm 92
Donehue, John Douglas 1928- WhoAm 92, WhoSSW 93
Donelan, Francis P. Law&B 92
Donelan, Francis P. 1939- St&PR 93
Donelan, Francis Patrick 1939- WhoAm 92
Donelan, William Joseph 1946- WhoAm 92
Donelian, Armen 1950- WhoEmL 93
Donelian, Khatchik O. d1991 BioIn 17
Donell, Donald Ray 1929- St&PR 93
Donelli, Gianfranco 1943- WhoScE 91-3
Donelson, Angie Fields Cantrell Merritt 1914- WhoAmW 93, WhoWor 93
Donelson, David C. Law&B 92
Donelson, Irene W. 1913- WhoAmW 93
Donelson, John Everett 1943- WhoAm 92
Donelson, Kenneth L. 1927- WhoWrEP 92
Donelson, Scott Eugene 1968- WhoE 93
Donely, George Anthony Thomas, III 1934- WhoE 93, WhoWor 93
Donen, Stanley 1924- MiSFD 9
Donenfeld, Kenneth Jay 1946- WhoAm 92
Donenfeld, Michael Simon 1933- St&PR 93
Doner, Frederick Nathan 1943- WhoAm 92
Doner, Gary William 1951- WhoEmL 93
Doner, John Robert 1942- WhoSSW 93
Doner, Wilfred B. 1914-1990 BioIn 17
Donetti, Arturo Guido 1941- WhoWor 93
Donev, Petr 1926- DrEEuF
Donewirth, Donald Jack 1927- St&PR 93
Doney, B.J. 1950- St&PR 93
Doney, Judith Karen 1942- WhoAmW 93, WhoSSW 93, WhoWor 93
Doney, Kimberley A. St&PR 93
Doney, Willis Frederick 1925- WhoAm 92
Don Francisco BioIn 17
Donfrid, Johannes 1585-1650 Baker 92
Donfried, Karl Paul 1940- WhoAm 92
Dong, Alvin Lim 1955- WhoE 93, WhoEmL 93, WhoWor 93
Dong, Deok-mo 1925- WhoWor 93
Dong, Eugene 1932- ScF&FL 92
Dong, Fang Zhong 1915- WhoWor 93
Dong, Fu-Reng 1927- WhoWor 93
Dong, Guang Chang 1928- WhoWor 93
Dong, Xiu-yu 1941- WhoWor 93
Dong, Zhengxiang 1933- WhoWor 93
Dongarra, Jack 1950- WhoSSW 93
Donge, Bernard 1935- WhoWor 93
Dongen, Kees van 1877-1968 BioIn 17
Donghi, Antonio 1897-1963 BioIn 17
Dong Jichang 1930- WhoAsAP 91
Dong Jiping 1940- BioIn 17
Dong Suh, Bark 1929- WhoWor 93
Dong Zhanlin 1923- WhoAsAP 91
Donham, Daniel R. St&PR 93
Donham, Philip d1990 BioIn 17
Donham, Russell G. 1944- St&PR 93
Donheiser, Walter Joseph 1927- WhoWor 93
Donhoffer, Dieter K. 1939- WhoScE 91-4
Doni, Antonio Francesco 1513-1574 Baker 92
Doni, Giovanni Battista 1594-1647 Baker 92
Doni, Giovanni Battista 1595?-1647 OxDcOp
Donicht, James Douglas 1938- St&PR 93
Donicht, Joyce Mae 1949- WhoEmL 93
Doniger, Walter 1917- MiSFD 9
Doniger, Wendy 1940- WhoAm 92
Doninger, John Albert Law&B 92
Doninger, Joseph Eugene 1939- St&PR 93, WhoAm 92
Donington, Robert BioIn 17
Donington, Robert 1907-1990 Baker 92, OxDcOp
Donini, Gerald P. 1941- St&PR 93
Donini, Ippolito Giuseppe 1929- WhoScE 91-3
Doniol-Valcroze, Jacques 1920-1989 BioIn 17
Doniphan, Alexander William 1808-1887 HarEnMi
Donis, Miles 1936-1979 ScF&FL 92
Donisthorpe, Christine Ann 1932- WhoAmW 93
Donitz, Karl 1891-1980 BioIn 17, HarEnMi
Donitz, Ursula 1917- BioIn 17
Donivan, Douglas L. 1947- St&PR 93
Donizetti, Alfredo 1867-1921 Baker 92
Donizetti, Gaetano 1797-1848 IntDcOp [port], OxDcOp
Donizetti, (Domenico) Gaetano (Maria) 1797-1848 Baker 92
Donizetti, Giuseppe 1788-1856 Baker 92
Donizetti, Mario 1932- WhoWor 93
Donker, Richard Bruce 1950- WhoWor 93
Donkervoet, Richard Cornelius 1930- WhoAm 92
Donlan, Dan M. 1935- WhoAm 92
Donleavy, J.P. 1926- BioIn 17
Donleavy, James Patrick 1926- BioIn 17, WhoAm 92
Donlevy, John Dearden 1933- WhoAm 92
Donley, Alice Marie AmWomPl
Donley, Corrine Russell 1936- WhoAmW 93
Donley, Edward 1921- St&PR 93, WhoAm 92
Donley, G.L. 1937- St&PR 93
Donley, Glenda Jane 1954- WhoEmL 93
Donley, James Walton 1934- WhoAm 92
Donley, Joseph Francis 1952- WhoEmL 93
Donley, Michael Bruce 1952- WhoAm 92
Donley, Peggy O'Neill Law&B 92
Donley, Richard D. 1930- St&PR 93
Donley, Roger Thomas 1937- St&PR 93
Donley, Rosemary WhoAm 92
Donley, Russell Lee, III 1939- WhoAm 92
Donley, Terrance Kanear 1929- St&PR 93
Donlick, Daniel Kalena 1941- WhoE 93
Donlin, Terence James 1931- St&PR 93
Donlin-Smith, Colleen M. 1961- WhoE 93
Donlon, J.P. 1948- WhoEmL 93
Donlon, James Peter 1957- WhoEmL 93, WhoSSW 93
Donlon, John J. Law&B 92
Donlon, Joseph Thomas 1929- St&PR 93
Donlon, William J. 1930- St&PR 93
Donlon, William Joseph 1930- WhoAm 92, WhoE 93
Donn, Steven Mark 1949- WhoEmL 93
Donnachie, Alexander WhoScE 91-1
Donnahoe, Alan S. 1916- St&PR 93
Donnahoe, Alan Stanley 1916- WhoAm 92
Donnald, Joann O'Melveny 1935- WhoAmW 93
Donnally, Patricia Broderick 1955- WhoAmW 93, WhoWor 93
Donnally, Robert Andrew Law&B 92
Donnan, Gregory Douglas 1952- WhoEmL 93
Donn-Byrne, Dorothea Cadogan AmWomPl
Donne, Antonius Johannes Herman 1956- WhoWor 93
Donne, John 1572-1631 BioIn 17, DcLB 121 [port], MagSWL [port], WorLitC [port]
Donnell, Barry B. 1939- St&PR 93
Donnell, Brian James 1955- WhoEmL 93
Donnell, Bruce Bolton 1946- WhoE 93, WhoEmL 93
Donnell, David 1939- WhoCanL 92
Donnell, Edward S. 1919- St&PR 93
Donnell, Harold Eugene, Jr. 1935- WhoAm 92
Donnell, Jeff 1921-1985 SweetSg C
Donnell, John Randolph 1912- WhoAm 92
Donnell, Joseph Stover, III 1932- WhoAm 92
Donnell, Mildred Webster 1951- WhoEmL 93
Donnell, Randy Stephen 1952- WhoSSW 93
Donnell, Susan ConAu 137
Donnell, William Franklin 1933- WhoSSW 93
Donnella, Michael A. Law&B 92
Donnella, Michael Andre 1954- WhoEmL 93
Donnellan, Andrew B., Jr. Law&B 92
Donnellan, Andrew B., Jr. 1952- St&PR 93
Donnellan, Gerard J. Law&B 92
Donnellan, Lynda A. 1957- WhoWrEP 92
Donnelley, Gaylord d1992 NewYTBS 92 [port]
Donnelley, Gaylord 1910- WhoAm 92
Donnelley, Gaylord 1910-1992 BioIn 17
Donnelley, James Russell 1935- St&PR 93, WhoAm 92
Donnelly, Barbara Schettler 1933- WhoAm 92, WhoAmW 93, WhoSSW 93, WhoWor 93
Donnelly, Brian J. Law&B 92
Donnelly, Brian J. 1946- CngDr 91, WhoAm 92
Donnelly, Charles Lawthers, Jr. 1929- WhoAm 92
Donnelly, Charles R. 1947- St&PR 93
Donnelly, Charles Robert 1921- WhoAm 92
Donnelly, David H. 1932- St&PR 93
Donnelly, Dorothy 1880-1928 AmWomPl
Donnelly, Edwin Harold 1947- WhoEmL 93, WhoSSW 93
Donnelly, Gerard K. 1933- St&PR 93
Donnelly, Gerard Kevin 1933- WhoAm 92, WhoWor 93
Donnelly, Gerard Thomas 1954- WhoAm 92
Donnelly, Harrison James 1930- WhoE 93
Donnelly, Ignatius 1831-1901 GayN, PolPar
Donnelly, James C. 1945- St&PR 93
Donnelly, James Charles 1945- WhoAm 92
Donnelly, James S. 1913-1989 BioIn 17
Donnelly, Joan Mary 1945- WhoAmW 93
Donnelly, Joe ScF&FL 92
Donnelly, Joe 1950- ConAu 139
Donnelly, John 1914- WhoAm 92
Donnelly, John A. Law&B 92
Donnelly, John Casgrain 1953- St&PR 93
Donnelly, John E. Law&B 92
Donnelly, John F. 1947- St&PR 93
Donnelly, John Francis 1929- WhoAm 92
Donnelly, John James, III 1954- WhoE 93, WhoWor 93
Donnelly, Joseph Dennis Law&B 92
Donnelly, Joseph L. 1924- St&PR 93
Donnelly, Joseph Lennon 1929- St&PR 93, WhoAm 92
Donnelly, Joseph Michael 1942- St&PR 93
Donnelly, Kathleen Ann 1947- WhoAmW 93
Donnelly, Kathleen Ann 1951- WhoEmL 93
Donnelly, Kevin W. Law&B 92
Donnelly, Kevin W. 1954- St&PR 93
Donnelly, Kevin William 1954- WhoAm 92
Donnelly, Liam WhoScE 91-3
Donnelly, Lloyd W. 1927- WhoAm 92
Donnelly, Lori Ann 1963- WhoEmL 93
Donnelly, Lynne Carol 1955- WhoAmW 93
Donnelly, Margarita BioIn 17
Donnelly, Margarita Patricia 1942- WhoWrEP 92
Donnelly, Marian Card 1923- WhoAmW 93
Donnelly, Marilyn Lewis 1942- WhoAmW 93
Donnelly, Mary Elizabeth 1951- WhoAmW 93
Donnelly, Michael Joseph 1951- WhoEmL 93, WhoSSW 93
Donnelly, Michael Timothy 1950- WhoEmL 93
Donnelly, Patrick C. 1956- WhoE 93
Donnelly, Peter James WhoScE 91-1
Donnelly, Peter Matthew Law&B 92
Donnelly, Richard BioIn 17
Donnelly, Robert Edward 1940- St&PR 93
Donnelly, Robert True 1924- WhoAm 92
Donnelly, Roger Cedric 1933- WhoSSW 93
Donnelly, Russell James 1930- WhoAm 92, WhoWor 93
Donnelly, Thomas J. 1925- St&PR 93
Donnelly, Thomas J. 1930- St&PR 93
Donnelly, Thomas Joseph 1925- WhoAm 92
Donnelly, Timothy J. 1952- St&PR 93
Donnelly, Timothy John Law&B 92
Donnelly, Tom MiSFD 9
Donnelly, William G. Law&B 92
Donnelly-Barrett, Shannon Kathleen 1956- WhoAmW 93
Donnem, Roland William 1929- WhoAm 92
Donnem, Sarah Lund 1936- WhoAmW 93, WhoWor 93
Donnenwirth, Carol 1930- WhoAmW 93
Donner, Clive 1926- MiSFD 9
Donner, Henrik Otto 1939- Baker 92
Donner, Joakim Jalmar 1926- WhoScE 91-4
Donner, John R. Law&B 92
Donner, Jorn 1933- MiSFD 9
Donner, Jorn Johan 1933- WhoWor 93
Donner, Kai Otto 1922- WhoScE 91-4
Donner, Kenneth 1915- St&PR 93
Donner, Martin W. 1920-1992 BioIn 17
Donner, Pamela Klock 1963- WhoAmW 93
Donner, Richard WhoAm 92
Donner, Richard 1939- MiSFD 9
Donner, William Troutman 1921- WhoE 93
Donnerstein, Edward Irving 1945- WhoAm 92
Donneson, Seena Sand WhoAm 92
Donnet, Jean-Baptiste 1923- WhoScE 91-2, WhoWor 93
Donnici, Peter Joseph 1939- WhoWor 93
Donnison, David WhoScE 91-1
Donnola, Carlos Alberto 1942- WhoWor 93
Donofrio, Beverly BioIn 17
D'Onofrio, Dominic Anthony 1944- WhoE 93
Donofrio, Frederick Allen 1942- St&PR 93
Donofrio, Joseph R. 1946- St&PR 93
D'Onofrio, Mary Ann 1933- WhoWor 93
D'Onofrio, Michael F. 1952- St&PR 93
Donofrio, Peter Daniel 1950- WhoEmL 93, WhoSSW 93
Donofrio, Richard Michael 1938- St&PR 93
Donofrio, William Arthur 1951- WhoEmL 93
Donoghue, Denis BioIn 17
Donoghue, Grace Koo 1921- WhoAmW 93
Donoghue, J. WhoScE 91-3
Donoghue, John BioIn 17
Donoghue, John F. 1928- WhoAm 92, WhoSSW 93
Donoghue, John Francis 1950- WhoE 93
Donoghue, John J. WhoAm 92
Donoghue, Larry M. Law&B 92
Donoghue, Mary Agnes MiSFD 9
Donoghue, Mildred Ransdorf WhoAm 92, WhoAmW 93
Donoghue, William E(lliott) 1941- ConAu 39NR
Donoghue, William Thomas 1932- WhoSSW 93
Donoho, Burnett W. 1939- St&PR 93
Donohoe, Amanda BioIn 17
Donohoe, Edward F. 1907- St&PR 93
Donohoe, James Aloysius, III 1945- WhoAm 92
Donohoe, Jerome F. Law&B 92
Donohoe, Jerome F. 1939- St&PR 93
Donohoe, Jerome Francis 1939- WhoAm 92
Donohoe, John P. Law&B 92
Donohoe, Kevin Gerard 1948- St&PR 93
Donohoe, Leonard Charles 1928- St&PR 93
Donohoe, Peter (Howard) 1953- Baker 92
Donohue, Carroll John 1917- WhoAm 92, WhoWor 93
Donohue, Cheryl Forzley Law&B 92
Donohue, David Lee 1950- WhoAm 92
Donohue, David Patrick 1931- WhoSSW 93
Donohue, Delaine R. 1931- St&PR 93
Donohue, Edith M. 1938- WhoAmW 93, WhoSSW 93
Donohue, Elizabeth Anne 1961- WhoEmL 93
Donohue, George L. 1944- St&PR 93, WhoAm 92
Donohue, Gerald Joseph, Jr. 1959- WhoEmL 93
Donohue, Irene Mary WhoWrEP 92
Donohue, J.R. 1935- St&PR 93

Donohue, Jack 1908-1984 MiSFD 9N
Donohue, Jerry P. 1937- St&PR 93
Donohue, John Barry, Jr. Law&B 92
Donohue, John F. 1956- St&PR 93
Donohue, John F., III 1949- WhoIns 93
Donohue, John J., Jr. Law&B 92
Donohue, Marc David 1951- WhoAm 92
Donohue, Margaret Anne 1953- WhoEmL 93
Donohue, Patricia Carol 1946- WhoAmW 93, WhoEmL 93
Donohue, Patrick A. 1950- St&PR 93
Donohue, Richard Harney 1950- WhoEmL 93
Donohue, Robert F. Law&B 92
Donohue, Robert F. 1943- St&PR 93
Donohue, Sheila M. Law&B 92
Donohue, Terence 1946- WhoEmL 93
Donohue, Therese Brady 1937- WhoAmW 93
Donohue, Thomas Patrick Law&B 92
Donohue, Trevor ScF&FL 92
Donohue, William T. Law&B 92
Donohue-Babiak, Amy Lorraine 1961- WhoEmL 93
Donohugh, Donald Lee 1924- WhoWor 93
Donor, Mary Elizabeth 1938- WhoAmW 93
Donoso, Jose BioIn 17
Donoso, Jose 1924- ScF&FL 92, SpAmA, WhoWor 93
Donoso Pareja, Miguel 1931- SpAmA
Donostia, Jose Antonio de 1886-1956 Baker 92
Donov, Victor 1931- WhoScE 91-4
Donovan 1943- Baker 92
Donovan 1946- ConMus 9 [port]
Donovan, Alan Barton 1937- WhoAm 92
Donovan, Alice AmWomPl
Donovan, Allen Francis 1914- WhoAm 92
Donovan, Arthur J. BioIn 17
Donovan, Bernadette Marie 1936- WhoAmW 93
Donovan, Brian Joseph 1953- WhoWor 93
Donovan, Bruce Elliot 1937- WhoAm 92
Donovan, Carolyn Sue 1954- WhoAmW 93
Donovan, Carrie BioIn 17
Donovan, Christine S. BioIn 17
Donovan, Dalvin E. 1923- St&PR 93
Donovan, Daniel J. 1958- WhoIns 93
Donovan, Deborah Carolyn 1951- WhoEmL 93
Donovan, Denis Miller 1946- WhoSSW 93
Donovan, Diane C. 1956- WhoWrEP 92
Donovan, Dianne Francys 1948- WhoAm 92
Donovan, Donal J. 1951- WhoUN 92
Donovan, Donna Mae 1952- WhoAm 92, WhoAmW 93, WhoE 93
Donovan, Donna Marie 1945- WhoAmW 93
Donovan, Doran Warren 1941- St&PR 93
Donovan, Edythe W. d1991 BioIn 17
Donovan, Ellen L. 1950- WhoAmW 93
Donovan, Eugene J., Jr. 1935- St&PR 93
Donovan, Frances R. 1880-1965 BioIn 17
Donovan, George Joseph 1935- WhoAm 92
Donovan, Gerald Alton 1925- WhoAm 92
Donovan, Gregory Edward 1950- WhoWrEP 92
Donovan, Hedley BioIn 17
Donovan, Herbert Alcorn, Jr. 1931- WhoAm 92
Donovan, James D. 1955- St&PR 93
Donovan, James H. 1923-1990 BioIn 17
Donovan, James Joseph, III 1954- WhoEmL 93
Donovan, James Patrick 1945- WhoAm 92
Donovan, James Robert 1932- WhoAm 92
Donovan, Jane Ellen 1957- WhoAmW 93, WhoEmL 93
Donovan, Jerome Francis 1936- WhoAm 92
Donovan, Jerome J. d1991 BioIn 17
Donovan, John BioIn 17
Donovan, John d1992 NewYTBS 92
Donovan, John 1928- DcAmChF 1960, ScF&FL 92
Donovan, John 1928-1992 ConAu 137, MajAI, SmATA 72 [port]
Donovan, John Francis 1946- WhoE 93
Donovan, John Joseph, Jr. 1916- WhoWor 93
Donovan, John S. Law&B 92
Donovan, John V. 1924- St&PR 93
Donovan, Joseph Richard, Jr. 1951- WhoE 93
Donovan, Kathleen A. Law&B 92
Donovan, Kathleen Owen 1931- WhoWor 93
Donovan, Laurence d1950? ScF&FL 92
Donovan, Lowava Denise 1958- WhoAmW 93, WhoEmL 93
Donovan, Lynley Kay 1962- WhoAmW 93, WhoEmL 93
Donovan, Madeline Frances 1926- WhoAmW 93
Donovan, Margaret 1950- WhoAmW 93, WhoEmL 93
Donovan, Marie Phillips WhoAmW 93, WhoWor 93
Donovan, Mark 1960- WhoWrEP 92
Donovan, Martin MiSFD 9
Donovan, Mary Frances 1935- WhoWor 93
Donovan, Mary Marcia 1936- WhoAmW 93
Donovan, Maryann 1960- WhoE 93
Donovan, Michael BioIn 17
Donovan, Michael Dennis 1959- WhoEmL 93
Donovan, Michael L. BioIn 17
Donovan, Michelle Regan 1944- WhoAmW 93
Donovan, Nancy St&PR 93
Donovan, Nancy S. 1951- WhoAm 92
Donovan, Patricia Hasselhorn 1927- WhoAmW 93
Donovan, Paul BioIn 17
Donovan, Paul 1947- WhoAm 92
Donovan, Paul 1954- MiSFD 9
Donovan, Paul V. 1924- WhoAm 92
Donovan, Peter Morse 1943- WhoE 93
Donovan, Richard Edward 1952- WhoEmL 93
Donovan, Richard Frank 1891-1970 Baker 92
Donovan, Richard Paul 1941- St&PR 93
Donovan, Richard Zell 1952- WhoE 93
Donovan, Robert Alan 1921- WhoAm 92
Donovan, Robert Emmet 1952- WhoEmL 93
Donovan, Robert John WhoScE 91-1
Donovan, Robert John 1912- WhoAm 92
Donovan, Robert John 1941- WhoWor 93
Donovan, Robert Joseph 1923- WhoE 93
Donovan, Robert Orovan 1914- WhoWrEP 92
Donovan, Stephen Patrick, Jr. 1941- St&PR 93
Donovan, Thomas A. 1952- St&PR 93
Donovan, Thomas Roy 1937- WhoAm 92
Donovan, Timothy Matthew Law&B 92
Donovan, Tom MiSFD 9
Donovan, Walter Edgar 1926- WhoAm 92
Dons, J.J.M. 1946- WhoScE 91-3
Donsker, Monroe D. 1924-1991 BioIn 17
Donskoj, Mark 1901-1981 DrEEuF
Donson, Cyril 1919-1986 ScF&FL 92
Dont, Jakob 1815-1888 Baker 92
Dont, Joseph Valentin 1776-1833 Baker 92
Donwen, William John 1936- St&PR 93
Donzelli, Domenico 1790-1873 OxDcOp
Donziger, Michael 1932- St&PR 93
Doob, Joseph Leo 1910- WhoAm 92
Doob, Leonard William 1909- WhoAm 92
Doochin, Jerald H. 1931- St&PR 93
Doochin, Michael David 1953- St&PR 93, WhoEmL 93, WhoSSW 93
Doochin, Robert S. 1940- St&PR 93
Doodan, Michael M. Law&B 92
Doody, Agnes G. WhoE 93
Doody, Alton Frederick 1934- WhoWor 93
Doody, Barbara Pettett 1938- WhoSSW 93
Doody, Daniel John 1952- St&PR 93
Doody, Daniel Patrick 1952- WhoE 93
Doody, J. Robert 1930- St&PR 93
Doody, James J., III Law&B 92
Doody, John Edward 1925- WhoSSW 93
Doody, John Robert 1930- WhoAm 92
Doody, Louis Clarence, Jr. 1940- WhoSSW 93, WhoWor 93
Doody, Margaret Anne 1939- WhoAm 92
Doogan, James Law&B 92
Dooge, James Clement Ignatius 1922- WhoWor 93
Doogs, Carol Wallace Kaki 1941- WhoAm 92
Doohan, Mary Elizabeth Law&B 92
Dooher, Terry Law&B 92
Dooher, Thomas Jerome 1935- St&PR 93
Doo Kingue, Michel 1934- WhoUN 92
Dool, Bonnie Dell 1941- WhoAmW 93
Doolen, Paul Dwight 1905-1990 BioIn 17
Dooley, Allan C(harles) 1943- ConAu 138
Dooley, Ann Elizabeth 1952- WhoAm 92
Dooley, Arch Richard 1925- WhoAm 92
Dooley, Calvin 1954- WhoAm 92
Dooley, Calvin M., Jr. 1954- CngDr 91
Dooley, Carol June 1955- WhoSSW 93
Dooley, Charles Richard 1913- St&PR 93
Dooley, Clyde Gerard 1953- WhoSSW 93
Dooley, Dan 1948- WhoIns 93
Dooley, Daniel Anthony 1959- WhoEmL 93
Dooley, Delmer John 1920- WhoAm 92
Dooley, Dennis 1942- ScF&FL 92
Dooley, Donald John 1921- WhoAm 92
Dooley, Douglas John 1955- WhoWor 93
Dooley, Edmund Robert 1940- St&PR 93
Dooley, George Elijah 1918- WhoAm 92
Dooley, Jo Ann Catherine 1930- WhoAmW 93
Dooley, Joseph T. 1944- WhoIns 93
Dooley, Lawrence W. 1944- St&PR 93
Dooley, Mary Agnes 1923- WhoAmW 93
Dooley, Maura 1957- ConAu 139
Dooley, Michael P. 1944- WhoUN 92
Dooley, Patrick Kiaran 1942- WhoAm 92
Dooley, Richard Gordon 1929- St&PR 93
Dooley, Robert St&PR 93
Dooley, Roger B(urke) 1920- WhoWrEP 92
Dooley, Ruby Wells 1931- WhoSSW 93
Dooley, Sue Ann WhoAmW 93
Dooley, Timothy Michael 1959- WhoEmL 93
Dooley, Tom 1927-1961 ConHero 2 [port]
Dooley, Vince 1932- BioIn 17
Dooley, William (Edward) 1932- Baker 92
Doolin, Bill 1858-1896 BioIn 17
Doolin, Earl d1992 BioIn 17
Doolin, Earl Bernard d1992 NewYTBS 92
Doolin, John B. 1918- WhoAm 92
Dooling, Brian Thomas 1965- WhoE 93
Dooling, D.M. d1991 BioIn 17
Dooling, Eugene Michael 1953- St&PR 93
Dooling, Richard (Patrick) 1954- ConAu 139
Doolittle, Bev BioIn 17
Doolittle, Diane Lewis 1959- WhoEmL 93
Doolittle, Duane S. 1912-1991 BioIn 17
Doolittle, Hilda 1886-1961 AmWomPl, BioIn 17
Doolittle, James Harold 1896- BioIn 17, HarEnMi
Doolittle, Jesse William, Jr. 1929- WhoAm 92
Doolittle, John T. 1950- CngDr 91
Doolittle, John Taylor 1950- WhoAm 92
Doolittle, Kenneth K. Law&B 92
Doolittle, Robert Ellsworth 1936- WhoSSW 93
Doolittle, Robert Frederick 1902- WhoAm 92
Doolittle, Russell Francis 1931- WhoAm 92
Doolittle, Sidney Newing 1934- St&PR 93, WhoAm 92
Doolittle, William Hotchkiss 1929- WhoAm 92
Dooly, Nancy Anne 1944- WhoAmW 93
Dooly, Weyman I., Jr. 1932- St&PR 93
Doom, Don Neil 1949- WhoEmL 93
Dooms-Goossens, Anne E. 1950- WhoScE 91-2
Doon, John Anthony 1935- WhoE 93
Doon, Roger Hugh 1938- WhoIns 93
Doonan, Shawn 1940- WhoScE 91-3
Doonan, Simon BioIn 17
Doone, Michele Marie 1942- WhoAmW 93
Dooner, Darlene Pruett 1954- WhoSSW 93
Dooner, John Joseph, Jr. 1948- WhoAm 92
Dooner, Peter Samuel, Jr. 1929- St&PR 93
Door, Anton 1833-1919 Baker 92
Doores, Brad L. Law&B 92
Doores, Brad L. 1950- St&PR 93
Doorey, Andrew 1952- WhoE 93
Doorley, Michael G. 1955- St&PR 93
Doorley, Thomas Lawrence, III 1944- WhoAm 92
Doorslaer, Georges van 1864-1940 Baker 92
Dooskin, Herbert P. 1941- St&PR 93, WhoAm 92
Doo-Yong, Lee 1942- MiSFD 9
Dopazo, Cesar 1943- WhoWor 93
Dopchie, Henri A. 1925- WhoScE 91-2
Dopf, Glenn William 1953- WhoEmL 93
Dopheide, Fred J. 1924- WhoIns 93
Dopkins, Leonard A. 1929- St&PR 93
Doplicher, Fabio 1938- DcLB 128 [port]
Dopp, Dietrich 1937- WhoScE 91-3, WhoWor 93
Dopp, Katherine Elizabeth 1863- AmWomPl
Doppelt, Earl H. Law&B 92, WhoAm 92
Dopper, Cornelis 1870-1939 Baker 92
Dopper, J.H. WhoScE 91-3
Doppler, Arpad 1857-1927 Baker 92
Doppler, (Albert) Franz (Ferenc) 1821-1883 Baker 92
Doppler, Karl 1825-1900 Baker 92
Doppstadt, William K. 1932- St&PR 93
Doptis, Jean Sanders 1945- WhoAmW 93
Dor, Pierre J.L. 1926- WhoScE 91-2
Dor, Yoram 1945- St&PR 93, WhoAm 92
Dora, Joan Teresa 1935- WhoAmW 93
Dorado, Marianne Gaertner 1956- WhoEmL 93
Dorado, Raymond J. Law&B 92
Dorain, Paul Brendel 1926- WhoE 93
Doran, A.J. BioIn 17
Doran, Ann 1911- SweetSg D [port]
Doran, Barbara Lee 1953- WhoEmL 93
Doran, Benjamin Thomas 1955- WhoEmL 93
Doran, Charles Edward 1928- WhoAm 92
Doran, David A. 1941- St&PR 93
Doran, Diane BioIn 17
Doran, Doris Jeanne 1932- WhoSSW 93
Doran, Felix, III 1924- St&PR 93
Doran, Gillian Frances 1949- WhoWor 93
Doran, Hugh H., Jr. Law&B 92
Doran, James Edward WhoScE 91-1
Doran, James Martin 1933- WhoAm 92
Doran, Kenneth John 1950- WhoEmL 93
Doran, Marie AmWomPl
Doran, Martha Lawrence 1956- WhoSSW 93
Doran, Matt (Higgins) 1921- Baker 92
Doran, Michael Howard 1957- WhoEmL 93
Doran, Patricia Ann 1948- WhoAmW 93
Doran, Robert Stuart 1937- WhoSSW 93, WhoWor 93
Doran, Russell Del 1957- St&PR 93
Doran, Sandra Jansak Law&B 92
Doran, Verna Hattie 1917- WhoAmW 93
Doran, William M. 1940- St&PR 93
Dorantes, Andres DcAmChF 1960
Dorati, Antal 1906-1988 Baker 92, OxDcOp
Dorato, Peter 1932- WhoAm 92
Doray, Andrea Wesley 1956- WhoAmW 93, WhoEmL 93, WhoWrEP 92
Doray, Anna Kalenak 1935- WhoAmW 93
D'Orazio, Sante BioIn 17
Dorcas, William Gary 1949- WhoWor 93
Dorchester, John D. BioIn 17
Dorcsi, Mathias WhoScE 91-4
Dorcy, Mary 1950- ScF&FL 92
Dordal, Erl 1927- WhoAm 92
Dordelman, William Forsyth 1940- WhoAm 92
Dordor, Patrice 1946- WhoWor 93
Dore, Bonny Ellen 1947- WhoAm 92, WhoWor 93
Dore, Fred Hudson 1925- WhoAm 92
Dore, J. Elliot 1954- St&PR 93
Dore, James F. 1946- St&PR 93
Dore, James Francis 1946- WhoAm 92, WhoSSW 93
Dore, Janet 1950- WhoEmL 93
Dore, Jean WhoAm 92, WhoE 93
Dore, Jean-Francois Alain Joseph 1940- WhoScE 91-2
Dore, Patricia M. Law&B 92
Dore, Stephen Edward, Jr. 1918- WhoAm 92
Doremus, Elizabeth Johnson Ward AmWomPl
Doremus, John C., Jr. 1931- WhoAm 92
Doremus, John Clinton, Jr. 1931- St&PR 93
Doremus, Ogden 1921- WhoAm 92
Doremus, Robert Heward 1928- WhoAm 92, WhoE 93
Doren, Carl Van ScF&FL 92
Doren, Henry Julius Thaddeus 1929- WhoE 93
Doren, Konstantin (Corky) 1956- WhoWrEP 92
Doren, Marion Walker 1928- DcAmChF 1985
Doren, Neall Evan 1961- WhoEmL 93
Dorenfeld, Alan S. 1945- St&PR 93
Dorenfeld, Alan Steven 1945- WhoE 93
Dorenwendt, Klaus 1936- WhoScE 91-3
Dorer, Frances ScF&FL 92
Dorer, Fred Harold 1936- WhoAm 92
Dorer, Michael A. 1952- St&PR 93
Dorer, Nancy ScF&FL 92
Dorer, William R. 1924- St&PR 93
Dorer, William R., Jr. Law&B 92
Doret, Gustave 1866-1943 Baker 92
Dorey, Anthony Peter WhoScE 91-1
Dorey, Cheryl Kathleen 1944- WhoAmW 93
Dorey, R.F. WhoScE 91-1
Dorf, Fran 1953- ConAu 138
Dorf, James J. 1946- St&PR 93
Dorf, Jerome 1936- St&PR 93, WhoAm 92
Dorf, Martin Edward 1944- WhoE 93
Dorf, Philip WhoAm 92
Dorf, Richard Carl 1933- WhoAm 92
Dorf, Robert L. 1949- WhoAm 92
Dorff, Ervin K. 1932- St&PR 93
Dorff, Joseph Ruppert 1936- St&PR 93
Dorff, Philip Henri, Jr. 1949- WhoEmL 93
Dorffel, Alfred 1821-1905 Baker 92
Dorffling, Karl 1935- WhoScE 91-3
Dorfi, Klaus G. 1942- St&PR 93, WhoIns 93
Dorflinger, Max F. 1938- St&PR 93
Dorflinger, Peter Glen Law&B 92
Dorflinger, Peter Glen 1951- St&PR 93
Dorfman, Allen Bernard 1930- WhoAm 92, WhoWor 93
Dorfman, Andrea Randall 1959- WhoAmW 93
Dorfman, Ariel 1942- ScF&FL 92, SpAmA
Dorfman, Don 1931- St&PR 93
Dorfman, Henry S. 1922- WhoAm 92
Dorfman, Howard Lewis Law&B 92
Dorfman, Isaiah S. 1907- WhoAm 92
Dorfman, Jacques MiSFD 9

Dorfman, John Charles 1925- *WhoAm 92*
Dorfman, Joseph 1904-1991 *BioIn 17*
Dorfman, Lorraine M. 1952- *WhoAmW 93*
Dorfman, Mark Stanley 1945- *WhoSSW 93*
Dorfman, Paul Michael 1939- *St&PR 93*
Dorfman, Steven David 1935- *WhoAm 92*
Dorfman, Wilfred d1992 *NewYTBS 92*
Dorfman, Wilfred 1909-1992 *BioIn 17*
Dorfmann, Ania 1899-1984 *Baker 92*
Dorfmont, Linda Bernice 1947- *WhoEmL 93*
Dorfmuller, Thomas *WhoScE 91-3*
Dorfzaun, Eve Inge 1935- *WhoUN 92*
Dorgan, Byron L. 1942- *CngDr 91*
Dorgan, Byron Leslie 1942- *WhoAm 92*
Dorgan, John Joseph 1923- *St&PR 93*
Dorgan, Richard Joseph 1939- *St&PR 93*
Dorgeres, Henri Auguste d'Halluin 1897-1985 *BioIn 17*
Dorgon 1612-1650 *HarEnMi*
Doria, Andrea 1466-1560 *HarEnMi*
Doria, Anthony Notarnicola 1927- *WhoAm 92, WhoWor 93*
Doria, Charles *WhoWrEP 92*
Doria, Clara *Baker 92*
Doria, Cynthia A. *Law&B 92*
Doria, Giacomo 1840-1913 *IntDcAn*
Doria, Nito 1931- *WhoWor 93*
Doria, Sante Joseph 1927- *St&PR 93*
Doria, Vincent Mark 1947- *ConAu 138*
Dorian, Edward S., Sr. *St&PR 93*
Dorian, Edward S., Jr. 1954- *St&PR 93*
Dorian, Frederick 1902-1991 *Baker 92, BioIn 17*
Dorian, Harry A. 1928- *St&PR 93*
Dorian, Harry Aram 1928- *WhoAm 92*
Dorian, Nancy Currier 1936- *WhoAm 92*
Dorian, Nancy Marilyn 1933- *WhoAmW 93*
Dorian, Patricia Neal 1954- *WhoAmW 93*
Dorin, Barry P. *St&PR 93*
Dorin, Bernard J. 1929- *WhoWor 93*
Dorin, William Joseph 1950- *WhoEmL 93*
Doring, Ernest Nicholas 1877-1955 *Baker 92*
Doring, Heinrich 1834-1916 *Baker 92*
Doring, Wolfgang 1934- *WhoScE 91-3*
Dorinson, Joseph *WhoE 93*
Dorio, Marc Anthony 1944- *WhoE 93*
Dorio, Martin Matthew 1945- *WhoWor 93*
Dorion, Robert Charles 1926- *WhoSSW 93, WhoWor 93*
Doriot, Georges Frederic 1899-1987 *BioIn 17*
Doriot, Jacques 1898-1945 *BioIn 17*
Dorioz, Jean-Marcel 1953- *WhoScE 91-2*
Doris Ann 1917- *WhoAm 92*
Dority, Douglas H. 1938- *WhoAm 92*
Dority, John Jerome 1953- *St&PR 93*
Dorius, Kermit Parrish 1926- *WhoAm 92*
Dorius, Richard Gordon, Jr. 1942- *St&PR 93*
Dorjes, Jurgen F. 1936- *WhoScE 91-3*
Dorji, Paljor Jigmi 1943- *WhoUN 92*
Dorkey, Charles Edward, III 1948- *WhoE 93*
Dorkin, Frederic Eugene *Law&B 92*
Dorkin, Frederic Eugene 1932- *WhoAm 92*
Dorl-Adams, Donna Marie 1948- *WhoEmL 93*
Dorland, Byrl Brown 1915- *WhoAmW 93*
Dorland, Dodge Oatwell 1948- *WhoAm 92, WhoE 93, WhoEmL 93*
Dorland, Frank Norton 1914- *WhoWor 93*
Dorland, Gilbert Meding 1912- *St&PR 93*
Dorland, John Howard 1940- *WhoSSW 93*
Dorland, William A. *Law&B 92*
Dorleac, Francoise 1942-1967 *BioIn 17*
Dorliak, Xenia 1882-1945 *OxDcOp*
Dorman, Albert A. 1926- *St&PR 93, WhoAm 92*
Dorman, Charles William 1948- *WhoSSW 93*
Dorman, Craig Emery *BioIn 17*
Dorman, Craig Emery 1940- *WhoAm 92*
Dorman, Finck 1901- *WhoSSW 93*
Dorman, Gerald Charles 1937- *WhoAm 92*
Dorman, Gerald Huntington 1931- *St&PR 93*
Dorman, Hattie Lawrence 1932- *WhoAmW 93*
Dorman, James 1928- *WhoSSW 93*
Dorman, Joe B. *Law&B 92*
Dorman, John Frederick 1928- *WhoAm 92*
Dorman, Karen Gail 1952- *WhoEmL 93*
Dorman, Linneaus Cuthbert 1935- *WhoAm 92*
Dorman, Lyn 1953- *WhoE 93*
Dorman, Rex Lee 1934- *St&PR 93, WhoAm 92*
Dorman, Richard Frederick, Jr. 1944- *WhoAm 92*
Dorman, Richard W. 1948- *WhoIns 93*
Dorman, Robert Joseph 1929- *St&PR 93*
Dorman, Sonya 1924- *BioIn 17, ScF&FL 92*
Dorman, Thomas 1914- *ScF&FL 92*
Dorman, Yosef Naine d1990 *BioIn 17*
Dormann, Henry O. 1932- *WhoAm 92, WhoE 93*
Dormann, J.L. 1933- *WhoScE 91-2*
Dormer, Kenneth John 1944- *WhoSSW 93*
D'Ormesson, Jean 1925- *WhoWor 93*
Dorminey, David Harley 1941- *St&PR 93*
Dorminey, Elizabeth Kline 1956- *WhoAmW 93*
Dorminey, Henry Clayton, Jr. 1949- *WhoEmL 93*
Dormire, John Carl 1931- *St&PR 93*
Dormitzer, Henry, II 1935- *WhoAm 92*
Dorn, Alexander (Julius Paul) 1833-1901 *Baker 92*
Dorn, Charles Meeker 1927- *WhoAm 92, WhoSSW 93*
Dorn, David Norman 1944- *WhoE 93*
Dorn, Dolores *WhoAm 92*
Dorn, Edward Harvey 1952- *WhoEmL 93*
Dorn, Edward Merton 1929- *WhoAm 92*
Dorn, Ernest F., Jr. 1932- *St&PR 93*
Dorn, Frank *ScF&FL 92*
Dorn, Heinrich 1804-1892 *OxDcOp*
Dorn, Heinrich (Ludwig Egmont) 1800-1892 *Baker 92*
Dorn, James Andrew 1945- *WhoAm 92*
Dorn, Jennifer Lynn 1950- *WhoAm 92, WhoAmW 93*
Dorn, Joseph L. 1915- *St&PR 93*
Dorn, Nancy Patricia 1958- *WhoAmW 93*
Dorn, Paul Carter *Law&B 92*
Dorn, Philip Brian 1947- *WhoEmL 93, WhoSSW 93*
Dorn, Robert Murray 1921- *WhoAm 92*
Dorn, Roosevelt F. 1935- *WhoWor 93*
Dorn, Samuel O. 1946- *WhoEmL 93, WhoSSW 93*
Dorn, Sue Bricker 1934- *WhoE 93*
Dorn, Wanda Faye 1945- *WhoAm 92*
Dorn, William Jennings Bryan 1916- *WhoAm 92*
Dorn, William L. 1948- *St&PR 93*
Dorna, Richard C. *Law&B 92*
Dornan, Candace Butler 1952- *WhoEmL 93*
Dornan, Dorothy R. *Law&B 92*
Dornan, Earle McClean *Law&B 92*
Dornan, Robert K. 1933- *CngDr 91*
Dornan, Robert Kenneth 1933- *WhoAm 92*
Dornbaum, Michael L. *Law&B 92*
Dornburgh, William Walter 1931- *St&PR 93, WhoAm 92*
Dornbusch, Arthur A., II *Law&B 92*
Dornbusch, Arthur A., II 1943- *St&PR 93, WhoAm 92*
Dornbusch, Joan Louise Falquet 1932- *WhoWrEP 92*
Dornbusch, Rudiger 1942- *WhoAm 92*
Dornbusch, Sanford Maurice 1926- *WhoAm 92*
Dornbush, Charles F. 1947- *St&PR 93*
Dornbush, Darwin Cecil 1930- *St&PR 93*
Dornbush, Kirk T. 1933- *St&PR 93*
Dorne, Arthur 1917- *WhoAm 92*
Dorneman, Penny Lee Harding 1957- *WhoAmW 93*
Dorner, Barbara Emilia 1945- *WhoAmW 93, WhoE 93*
Dorner, Bruno 1936- *WhoScE 91-2*
Dorner, Clifford O. 1933- *St&PR 93*
Dorner, Peter Paul 1925- *WhoAm 92*
Dor-Ner, Zvi Richard 1941- *WhoE 93*
Dorner-Andelora, Sharon Agnes Haddon 1943- *WhoAmW 93*
Dornfeld, James L. 1954- *St&PR 93*
Dornfeld, James Lee 1954- *WhoIns 93*
Dornfest, Burton Saul 1930- *WhoE 93*
Dornfest, Stanley 1939- *WhoE 93*
Dornhelm, Robert *MiSFD 9*
Dornic, Ivan Dusan 1939- *WhoE 93*
Dorning, John Joseph 1938- *WhoAm 92, WhoSSW 93*
Dornsife, H.W. 1915- *St&PR 93*
Dornsife, Samuel Jonathan 1916- *WhoE 93*
Doro, Marion Elizabeth 1928- *WhoAm 92, WhoAmW 93*
Dorobiala, John Vincent 1931- *St&PR 93*
Dorochenko, Peter 1627-1698 *HarEnMi*
Dorocke, Lawrence Francis 1946- *WhoEmL 93*
Doroghazi, Stephen Joseph, Jr. *Law&B 92*
Dorogovtsev, Anatoliy Yakovlevich 1935- *WhoWor 93*
Doron, Mary Ellen 1946- *WhoAmW 93*
Doron, Roland 1921- *WhoScE 91-2*
Doronila, Amando Ermitano 1928- *WhoWor 93*
Doronina, Tatyana Vasiliyevna 1933- *WhoWor 93*
Doroschak, John Z. 1928- *WhoWor 93*
Doroski, Diane *BioIn 17*
Dorotheos *OxDcByz*
Dorotheos Of Gaza c. 500-560? *OxDcByz*
Dorotheos Of Monemvasia *OxDcByz*
Dorough, H. Wyman 1936- *WhoAm 92*
Dorough, Tracey Leigh 1963- *WhoEmL 93*
Dorow, Stuart Allen 1940- *WhoSSW 93*
Dorpat, Theodore Lorenz 1925- *WhoAm 92*
Dorr, Adriana *BioIn 17*
Dorr, Darwin Alfred 1940- *WhoSSW 93*
Dorr, Douglas David 1963- *WhoE 93*
Dorr, Jackson G. *WhoWrEP 92*
Dorr, James Suhrer 1941- *WhoWrEP 92*
Dorr, Rheta Childe 1866-1948 *JrnUS*
Dorr, Rick *BioIn 17*
Dorr, Sidney J. *St&PR 93*
Dorr, Thomas W. 1805-1854 *PolPar*
Dorrance, G. Morris, Jr. 1922- *St&PR 93*
Dorrance, George Morris, Jr. 1922- *WhoAm 92*
Dorrance, John T. 1873-1930 *BioIn 17*
Dorre, Pamela *ScF&FL 92*
Dorrian, Catherine Anne 1960- *WhoWor 93*
Dorrian, Krista Bean *Law&B 92*
Dorrian, Krista Bean 1956- *St&PR 93*
Dorrie, Doris 1955- *MiSFD 9*
Dorrier, Lindsay Gordon, Jr. 1943- *WhoSSW 93*
Dorries, Mark Alan 1962- *WhoSSW 93*
Dorrill, William Franklin 1931- *WhoAm 92, WhoWor 93*
Dorrington, K. *WhoScE 91-1*
Dorris, Albert Francis 1936- *WhoAm 92*
Dorris, Michael *BioIn 17*
Dorris, Michael Anthony 1945- *WhoAm 92, WhoE 93*
Dorris, Reynold Abel d1991 *BioIn 17*
Dorritie, John F. 1934-1991 *BioIn 17*
Dorros, Irwin 1929- *WhoAm 92*
Dorros, Kenneth M. 1959- *St&PR 93*
Dors, Diana 1931-1984 *IntDcF 2-3 [port]*
Dorsch, Charles R. 1931- *St&PR 93*
Dorsch, Raymond Michael, III 1956- *WhoE 93*
Dorsel, Andreas Nikolaus 1958- *WhoWor 93*
Dorsen, David Milton 1935- *WhoWor 93*
Dorsen, Harriette *Law&B 92*
Dorsen, Helen *AmWomPl*
Dorsen, Norman 1930- *WhoAm 92*
Dorset, Earl of 1591-1652 *BioIn 17*
Dorset, Earl of 1638?-1706 *BioIn 17*
Dorsett, Anthony Drew 1954- *WhoAm 92*
Dorsett, C. Powers *Law&B 92*
Dorsett, Charles Irvin 1945- *WhoSSW 93, WhoWor 93*
Dorsett, John Russel 1950- *St&PR 93*
Dorsett, John Russel, III 1950- *WhoAm 92*
Dorsett, Joseph J. 1929- *St&PR 93*
Dorsett, Judith Adele 1944- *WhoWrEP 92*
Dorsett, Kattie Grays 1932- *AfrAmBi*
Dorsett, Martha Janette 1943- *WhoWrEP 92*
Dorsett, Mary Janeen 1943- *WhoWrEP 92*
Dorsett, Patricia Jean Poole 1935- *WhoAmW 93*
Dorsett, Wayne Arnold 1941- *WhoSSW 93*
Dorsey, Albert Rich, Jr. 1921- *St&PR 93*
Dorsey, Benjamin 1924- *St&PR 93*
Dorsey, Benjamin H. *Law&B 92*
Dorsey, Bernard William *Law&B 92*
Dorsey, Candas Jane 1952- *ScF&FL 92*
Dorsey, David I. 1941- *St&PR 93*
Dorsey, Debra Schneider 1962- *WhoAmW 93*
Dorsey, Dennis Basil 1912- *WhoSSW 93*
Dorsey, Dolores Florence 1928- *WhoAm 92*
Dorsey, Donald Merrill 1953- *WhoEmL 93*
Dorsey, Eugene Carroll 1927- *WhoAm 92*
Dorsey, Frank James 1930- *St&PR 93, WhoAm 92*
Dorsey, George A. 1868-1931 *IntDcAn*
Dorsey, Gilbert L. *WhoAm 92*
Dorsey, Gray Lankford 1918- *WhoAm 92*
Dorsey, Helen Danner 1928- *WhoAm 92*
Dorsey, Ivory *AfrAmBi [port]*
Dorsey, James Francis, Jr. 1934- *WhoAm 92*
Dorsey, James Owen 1848-1895 *IntDcAn*
Dorsey, James Wilkinson, Jr. 1953- *WhoWrEP 92*
Dorsey, Jimmy 1904-1957 *Baker 92*
See Also Dorsey Brothers, The *ConMus 8*
Dorsey, John F. *Law&B 92*
Dorsey, John J. 1911-1990 *BioIn 17*
Dorsey, John Russell 1938- *WhoAm 92*
Dorsey, John Wesley, Jr. 1936- *WhoAm 92*
Dorsey, Kent *BioIn 17*
Dorsey, Laurens 1925- *WhoAm 92*
Dorsey, Lee 1926-1986 *SoulM*
Dorsey, Maurice Wayne 1947- *WhoE 93*
Dorsey, Norbert M. 1929- *WhoAm 92, WhoSSW 93*
Dorsey, Peter 1922- *WhoAm 92*
Dorsey, Peter Collins 1931- *WhoAm 92, WhoE 93*
Dorsey, Rhoda Mary 1927- *WhoAm 92, WhoAmW 93*
Dorsey, Richard P., III 1959- *WhoEmL 93*
Dorsey, Robert Francis 1947- *St&PR 93*
Dorsey, Robert Thomas, II 1952- *WhoSSW 93*
Dorsey, Thomas A(ndrew) 1899- *Baker 92*
Dorsey, Thomas Edward 1946- *WhoE 93*
Dorsey, Tommy 1905-1956 *Baker 92*
See Also Dorsey Brothers, The *ConMus 8* ,
Dorsey, Vanessa Evelyn 1967- *WhoAmW 93*
Dorsey, Vickie Cheek *Law&B 92*
Dorsey, William Oscar Parks, III 1948- *WhoEmL 93*
Dorsey Brothers, The *ConMus 8 [port]*
Dorsey-Hudson, Hattie 1939- *WhoAmW 93*
Dorsilien, Jacques *DcCPCAm*
Dorsinville, Roger d1992 *NewYTBS 92*
Dorsinville, Roger 1911-1992 *BioIn 17*
Dorskind, Albert A. 1922- *St&PR 93*
Dorson, Richard M. 1916-1981 *IntDcAn*
Dorst, Jean P. 1924- *WhoScE 91-2*
Dorst, Jean Pierre 1924- *WhoWor 93*
Dorst, John Phillips 1926- *WhoAm 92*
Dorst, Tankred 1925- *DcLB 124 [port]*
Dort, Dean Russell, II *Law&B 92*
Dort, Dennis John *Law&B 92*
Dort, Diana Marie 1961- *WhoAmW 93*
Dortbudak, Nukhet 1942- *WhoScE 91-4*
Dortch, Carl Raymond 1914- *WhoAm 92*
Dortch, Charlene Denise 1954- *St&PR 93*
Dortch, H. Wayne 1931- *St&PR 93, WhoIns 93*
Dortch, Helen *AmWomPl*
Dorticos Torrado, Osvaldo 1919- *DcCPCAm*
Dorton, David Lynn 1955- *WhoEmL 93*
Dorton, Louise 1936- *WhoAmW 93*
D'Ortona, Paul d1992 *NewYTBS 92*
Dorus-Gras, Julie 1805-1896 *OxDcOp*
Dorval, Romeo E. 1924- *St&PR 93*
D'Orville, Hans 1949- *WhoE 93, WhoUN 92*
Dorvillier, William Joseph 1908- *WhoAm 92, WhoWor 93*
D'Orvilliers, Anne Lillian 1953- *WhoAmW 93*
Dorward, Judith A. 1941- *WhoAmW 93*
Dorward, W. Wilson 1948- *WhoEmL 93*
Dorwart, Bonnie Brice 1942- *WhoAmW 93*
Dorwart, Harold Laird 1902- *WhoE 93*
Dorwart, Mary Lucille 1948- *WhoEmL 93*
Dorwart, Paul Gregg 1944- *St&PR 93*
Dorwart, Robert Alan 1947- *WhoE 93, WhoEmL 93*
Dos, Serge Jacques 1934- *WhoWor 93*
Dosa, J. Rick *Law&B 92*
Dosanjh, Darshan Singh 1921- *WhoAm 92, WhoE 93*
Dosch, Rosemary 1938- *WhoAmW 93*
Doscher, Dennis Allen 1940- *St&PR 93*
Dosdall, Thomas Edward 1930- *St&PR 93*
Dose, Klaus 1928- *WhoScE 91-3, WhoWor 93*
Dose, Volker 1940- *WhoScE 91-3*
Dosedel, James Anthony 1951- *WhoWrEP 92*
Dosen, Susan Gail 1951- *WhoAmW 93, WhoEmL 93*
Doser, Diane Irene 1956- *WhoAmW 93*
Dosh, Steven Allan 1950- *WhoEmL 93*
Dosher, John Rodney 1936- *WhoAm 92*
Doshi, Bipin 1939- *St&PR 93*
Doshi, Jitendra Bhagwandas 1946- *WhoEmL 93*
Dosio, Ernest J. 1950- *St&PR 93*
Dosio, John F. 1930- *St&PR 93*
Doskey, John Stanley 1927- *WhoWrEP 92*
Doskocil, Larry 1932- *WhoAm 92*
Dosland, William Buehler 1927- *St&PR 93, WhoAm 92*
Dosluoglu, Nebahat 1937- *WhoScE 91-4*
Dos Passos, John *BioIn 17*
Dos Passos, John 1896-1970 *MagSAmL [port], WorLitC [port]*
Dospil-Julian, Margaret Louise 1958- *WhoEmL 93*
Doss, Alan C. 1945- *WhoUN 92*
Doss, Desmond *BioIn 17*
Doss, Diana Lynn 1957- *WhoEmL 93*
Doss, Dianne Moore 1940- *WhoSSW 93*
Doss, Donald James 1952- *WhoEmL 93*
Doss, Lawrence Paul 1927- *WhoAm 92*
Doss, Manfred O. 1935- *WhoScE 91-3*
Doss, Marion Kenneth *Law&B 92*
Doss, Michael Peter 1944- *WhoE 93*
Doss, Richard William 1942- *St&PR 93*
Dos Santos, Alexandre Jose Maria Cardinal 1924- *WhoWor 93*

Dos Santos, Jose Eduardo 1942- BioIn 17, WhoAfr, WhoWor 93
dos Santos, Joyce Audy 1949- ConAu 136
Dos Santos, Marcelino 1931- WhoAfr
Dos Santos, Nelson Pereira 1928- MiSFD 9
Dos Santos, Sergio Machado WhoScE 91-3
Dossenbach, William R. 1943- St&PR 93
Dossetor, John Beamish 1925- WhoAm 92
Dossett, Walter B., Jr. 1927- St&PR 93
Dossett, Walter Brown, Jr. 1927- WhoSSW 93
Dossey, Richard L. 1937- WhoAm 92
Dossick, Renee Law&B 92
Dossin, Diane Patrice Law&B 92
Dossin, Ernest Joseph, III 1941- WhoE 93
Dossor, Howard F. ScF&FL 92
Doss-Quinby, Eglal 1953- WhoE 93
Dostal, Hermann 1874-1930 See Dostal, Nico 1895-1981 Baker 92
Dostal, Miloslav 1947- WhoScE 91-4
Dostal, Nico 1895-1981 Baker 92
Dostal, Raymond F. 1943- St&PR 93, WhoIns 93
Dostal, Robert Alan 1943- St&PR 93
Dostart, Paul Joseph 1951- WhoEmL 93
Doster, Daniel Harris 1934- WhoSSW 93
Doster, Gayl William 1938- St&PR 93
Doster, Joseph C. 1928- WhoAm 92, WhoSSW 93
Doster, Joseph Michael 1954- WhoSSW 93
Doster, Robert Thomas 1927- WhoSSW 93
Doster, Rodney Lynn 1940- WhoSSW 93
Doster, Stephen Michael 1959- WhoSSW 93
Doster, William Woods 1950- WhoSSW 93
Doster-Jones, Leslie 1954- WhoSSW 93
Dosti, Hasan d1991 BioIn 17
Dostoevski, Fyodor 1821-1881 MagSWL [port]
Dostoevskii, Fedor Mikhailovich 1821-1881 BioIn 17
Dostoomian, Ashod S. 1932- St&PR 93
Dostou, Christine Anne 1968- WhoAmW 93
Dostou, Steven 1921- St&PR 93
Dostoyevsky, Fyodor 1821-1881 BioIn 17, OxDcOp, WorLitC [port]
Doswald, Herman Kenneth 1932- WhoAm 92
Dotan, Shimon 1949- MiSFD 9
Doten, Edith Kinney AmWomPl
Dothan, Yossef BioIn 17
Doti, Lynne Pierson 1948- ConAu 137
Doto, Joseph Francis 1943- St&PR 93
Doto, Paul Jerome 1917- WhoE 93, WhoWor 93
Dotreppe, Jean-Claude 1945- WhoScE 91-2
Dotson, David Casto 1934- St&PR 93
Dotson, Donald L. 1938- WhoAm 92
Dotson, Francis BioIn 17
Dotson, George Stephen 1940- St&PR 93, WhoAm 92, WhoSSW 93
Dotson, Jarine Ann 1953- St&PR 93
Dotson, John Louis, Jr. 1937- WhoAm 92
Dotson, Raymond Paul 1933- WhoWrEP 92
Dotson, Robert C. Law&B 92
Dotson, Robert Charles 1946- WhoAm 92, WhoEmL 93
Dotson, Robert J. Law&B 92
Dotson, Robert Lee 1924- WhoSSW 93
Dotson, Rodger A. 1948- St&PR 93
Dotson, Terry Lee 1950- St&PR 93
Dott, Jackson York 1958- St&PR 93
Dott, Robert Henry, Jr. 1929- WhoAm 92
Dott, Wolfgang 1949- WhoScE 91-3
Dottin, Olivier WhoScE 91-2
Dottori, Frank BioIn 17
Dotts, M. Franklin 1929- WhoSSW 93
Dotu, Jose Antonio 1935- WhoWor 93
Doty, Carl K. 1931- St&PR 93, WhoAm 92
Doty, Carolyn House 1941- WhoWrEP 92
Doty, Cecile C. d1991 BioIn 17
Doty, Charles Stewart 1928- WhoAm 92
Doty, Christine Marie Law&B 92
Doty, David Singleton 1929- WhoAm 92
Doty, David Wesley 1950- WhoSSW 93
Doty, Della Corrine 1945- WhoAmW 93
Doty, Donald D. 1928- St&PR 93, WhoAm 92
Doty, Douglas A. Law&B 92
Doty, George E. 1918- St&PR 93
Doty, Georgette Lynn 1956- WhoAmW 93
Doty, Gordon Leroy 1931- WhoAm 92
Doty, Gresdna Ann 1931- WhoSSW 93
Doty, Huberta M. 1904- St&PR 93
Doty, James Edward 1922- WhoAm 92
Doty, James Robert 1940- WhoAm 92
Doty, Jean Slaughter 1924- ScF&FL 92
Doty, Marlene Joan 1955- WhoE 93
Doty, Matthew Emerson 1959- WhoE 93, WhoEmL 93
Doty, Natalie Johnston 1939- WhoAmW 93
Doty, Philip Edward 1943- WhoAm 92
Doty, Robert M. 1933-1992 NewYTBS 92
Doty, Robert Walter 1942- WhoAm 92
Doty, Robert William 1920- WhoAm 92
Doty, Rod Law&B 92
Doty, Roger F. 1934- St&PR 93
Doty, Ruth 1947- WhoWrEP 92
Doty, Virginia Mary Law&B 92
Doty, Walter L. BioIn 17
Doty, William D'Orville 1920- WhoE 93
Dotzauer, Earl G. 1931- St&PR 93
Dotzauer, (Justus Johann) Friedrich 1783-1860 Baker 92
Douaire, Daniel Lawlor 1934- St&PR 93
Douaud, Andre 1943- WhoScE 91-2
Doub, William Offutt 1931- WhoAm 92, WhoWor 93
Doubek, Fayola Marie 1952- WhoEmL 93
Doubell, R.D. 1945- WhoWor 93
Douben, Peter E.T. 1956- WhoScE 91-3
Double, John Anthony WhoScE 91-1
Doubleday, Abner 1819-1893 HarEnMi
Doubleday, Nelson WhoAm 92
Doubleday, William Alan 1951- WhoEmL 93
Doubledee, Deanna Gail 1958- WhoAmW 93
Doubledee, Sara Lynn 1946- WhoEmL 93
Doubler, Kenneth Francis 1946- WhoEmL 93
Doubles, James 1941- St&PR 93
Doubles, Michael J. 1945- St&PR 93
Doubrava, Jaroslav 1909-1960 Baker 92
Doubrovine, Alexandre V. 1944- WhoUN 92
Doubrovsky, Serge 1928- ConAu 136
Doubtfire, Dianne (Abrams) 1918- ConAu 39NR
Douce, Marjorie Esther 1932- WhoSSW 93
Douce, Patrice 1942- WhoAm 92
Douce, Wayne Richard 1928- WhoAm 92
Doucet, Clive WhoCanL 92
Doucet, Gerald 1943- WhoWor 93
Doucet, J.P.M.G. 1919- WhoScE 91-2
Doucet, Marlon Joseph 1957- WhoSSW 93
Doucet, Michael 1951- ConMus 8 [port]
Doucette, Daniel Robert 1949- St&PR 93
Doucette, David Robert 1946- WhoE 93, WhoWor 93
Doucette, Edward I. 1929- St&PR 93
Doucette, Hubert Joseph 1930- St&PR 93
Doucette, James W. 1951- St&PR 93
Doucette, Joseph J. 1929- St&PR 93
Doucette, Mary-Alyce 1924- WhoAmW 93, WhoE 93
Doucette, Paul Bernard 1946- WhoSSW 93
Doucette, Stephen Gordon Law&B 92
Doucette-Ashman, Linda June Law&B 92
Douchkess, Donald N. Law&B 92
Douctre, Gaylene Pandolfi 1943- WhoAmW 93
Doud, Deborah S. Law&B 92
Doud, Donald Joseph 1940- St&PR 93
Doud, Jeff WhoAm 92
Doud, Robert Hugh Law&B 92
Doud, Robert Skinner 1931- St&PR 93
Doud, Wallace C. 1925- WhoAm 92
Doud, William F. 1935- St&PR 93
Doudera, Gerard Emil 1932- WhoE 93
Doudna, Donald J. 1949- St&PR 93
Doudna, Dorothy Williams 1930- WhoAmW 93
Doudnikoff, Gregory M. Law&B 92
Douds, H. James 1930- WhoIns 93
Dougal, Arwin Adelbert 1926- WhoAm 92
Dougall, Lily 1858-1923 BioIn 17
Dougan, Deborah Rae 1952- WhoSSW 93
Dougan, Paul Marriott 1938- St&PR 93
Dougan, Pauline Virginia 1928- St&PR 93
Dougan, Robert Ormes 1904- WhoAm 92
Dougan, Virginia L. 1958- St&PR 93
Dougard, Ronald Joseph 1945- WhoE 93
Doug E. Fresh BioIn 17
Doughan, James 1933- St&PR 93
Dougher, Colleen Marie 1962- WhoWrEP 92
Dougherty, Betsey Olenick 1950- WhoAm 92, WhoEmL 93
Dougherty, Carolann Jackson 1957- WhoEmL 93
Dougherty, Cathy West 1956- WhoE 93
Dougherty, Celius (Hudson) 1902-1986 Baker 92
Dougherty, Charles John 1949- WhoAm 92
Dougherty, Charles Joseph 1919- WhoAm 92
Dougherty, Charles Thomas 1918- WhoSSW 93
Dougherty, Dana Dean Lesley WhoAmW 93
Dougherty, David J. 1936- St&PR 93
Dougherty, Dennis Law&B 92
Dougherty, Dennis A. 1952- WhoEmL 93
Dougherty, Douglas Wayne 1943- WhoAm 92
Dougherty, Elmer Lloyd, Jr. 1930- WhoAm 92
Dougherty, F. Jay 1950- WhoEmL 93
Dougherty, Flavian 1923-1990 BioIn 17
Dougherty, Geoffrey WhoScE 91-1
Dougherty, H.W. 1916- St&PR 93
Dougherty, James 1926- WhoAm 92, WhoE 93, WhoWor 93
Dougherty, James B., Jr. 1955- WhoEmL 93
Dougherty, James Douglas 1936- St&PR 93
Dougherty, James Henry 1936- St&PR 93
Dougherty, James Joseph 1951- WhoEmL 93
Dougherty, James T. Law&B 92
Dougherty, James Thomas 1935- WhoAm 92
Dougherty, Jay Edwin 1959- WhoWrEP 92
Dougherty, Joann H. Law&B 92
Dougherty, John Law&B 92
Dougherty, John Chrysostom, III 1915- WhoAm 92, WhoSSW 93, WhoWor 93
Dougherty, John Edward Law&B 92
Dougherty, John F. 1912- St&PR 93
Dougherty, John James 1924- WhoAm 92
Dougherty, John Michael 1953- WhoSSW 93
Dougherty, Joseph Charles 1934- WhoSSW 93
Dougherty, Joseph P. d1990 BioIn 17
Dougherty, Jude Patrick 1930- WhoAm 92, WhoE 93
Dougherty, June Eileen 1929- WhoAmW 93
Dougherty, Kathleen ScF&FL 92
Dougherty, Linda Marie 1957- WhoSSW 93
Dougherty, Linda Watson 1944- WhoAmW 93
Dougherty, Mary Lisbeth 1965- WhoAmW 93
Dougherty, Michael Robert 1958- St&PR 93
Dougherty, Molly Ireland 1949- WhoAmW 93, WhoEmL 93
Dougherty, Philip H. 1923-1988 BioIn 17
Dougherty, Rae Ann 1955- WhoSSW 93
Dougherty, Raymond Edward 1942- WhoE 93
Dougherty, Richard Hamlen 1952- WhoEmL 93, WhoWor 93
Dougherty, Richard M. BioIn 17
Dougherty, Richard Martin 1935- WhoAm 92
Dougherty, Robert Anthony 1928- WhoAm 92
Dougherty, Robert James 1923- WhoSSW 93
Dougherty, Robert Ward 1945- St&PR 93
Dougherty, Ronald Jary 1936- St&PR 93
Dougherty, Russell Elliott 1920- St&PR 93, WhoAm 92
Dougherty, Samuel Allen 1917- WhoWrEP 92
Dougherty, Sherilyne Earnest 1950- WhoAmW 93, WhoEmL 93
Dougherty, Thomas Paul, Jr. 1948- WhoEmL 93
Dougherty, Ursel Thielbeule 1942- WhoAmW 93, WhoWor 93
Dougherty, William ScF&FL 92
Dougherty, William Howard, Jr. 1930- WhoAm 92
Doughten, Russ BioIn 17
Doughtie, Katharine Kinard AmWomPl
Doughty, Bob 1938- St&PR 93
Doughty, Charles Montagu 1843-1926 Expl 93 [port]
Doughty, Dennis O. 1956- St&PR 93
Doughty, George Franklin 1946- WhoAm 92
Doughty, H. Cort, Jr. Law&B 92
Doughty, John 1754-1826 CmdGen 1991 [port]
Doughty, Julian Orus 1933- WhoSSW 93
Doughty, Marilou Altland 1955- WhoAmW 93, WhoEmL 93
Doughty, Michael Dean 1947- WhoEmL 93
Doughty, Robert Allen 1945- WhoAm 92
Douglas, Aaron 1898-1979 EncAACR
Douglas, Andrew 1932- WhoAm 92
Douglas, Archibald c. 1369-1424 HarEnMi
Douglas, Archibald 1929- St&PR 93
Douglas, Barry 1960- Baker 92
Douglas, Ben Harold WhoSSW 93
Douglas, Betty Jo 1940- WhoAmW 93
Douglas, Bill BioIn 17
Douglas, Bill d1991 MiSFD 9N
Douglas, Bill 1937-1991 AnObit 1991
Douglas, Brandon 1968- BioIn 17
Douglas, Bruce Lee 1925- WhoAm 92
Douglas, Bryce 1924- WhoAm 92
Douglas, Buster BioIn 17
Douglas, Carlyle C. d1992 NewYTBS 92
Douglas, Carole Nelson 1944- ScF&FL 92, SmATA 73 [port]
Douglas, Carolyn Jory 1953- WhoE 93
Douglas, Carolyn Temple 1934- WhoAmW 93
Douglas, Charles Albert 1946- WhoEmL 93, WhoSSW 93
Douglas, Charles Francis 1930- WhoAm 92
Douglas, Clarence James, Jr. 1924- WhoSSW 93
Douglas, Clifford Eric 1958- WhoEmL 93
Douglas, Clive (Martin) 1903-1977 Baker 92
Douglas, Cynthia Lynn 1952- WhoAm 92
Douglas, Daniel Roger 1954- St&PR 93
Douglas, Denzil DcCPCAm
Douglas, Diane M. 1957- WhoAmW 93
Douglas, Donald Dean 1944- WhoE 93
Douglas, Donald Wills 1892-1981 BioIn 17
Douglas, Dorothy C. 1944- St&PR 93
Douglas, Douglas 1948- St&PR 93
Douglas, Drake ScF&FL 92
Douglas, Dwight Charles 1949- WhoEmL 93
Douglas, Dwight Oliver 1941- WhoAm 92
Douglas, Eileen 1946- WhoAm 92, WhoAmW 93
Douglas, Ellen BioIn 17, ConAu 39NR
Douglas, Ellen 1921- ConLC 73 [port]
Douglas, Emily Taft 1899- BioIn 17
Douglas, Frank Fair 1945- WhoAm 92
Douglas, Fred Robert 1924- WhoAm 92
Douglas, Fred Walter 1949- WhoE 93
Douglas, Frederick John 1928- WhoAm 92
Douglas, G. Archibald d1992 NewYTBS 92
Douglas, G. Archibald 1910-1992 BioIn 17
Douglas, Garry ScF&FL 92
Douglas, Gary 1945- WhoWor 93
Douglas, Gary Michael 1954- WhoEmL 93
Douglas, Gavin 1475?-1522 LitC 20
Douglas, Gordon 1909- MiSFD 9
Douglas, Gordon Watkins 1921- WhoAm 92
Douglas, Gregory A. WhoWrEP 92
Douglas, Gregory A. 1913- ScF&FL 92
Douglas, Helen Gahagan 1900-1980 BioIn 17, PolPar
Douglas, Herbert P., Jr. BioIn 17
Douglas, Herbert Paul, Jr. 1922- WhoWor 93
Douglas, Iain ScF&FL 92
Douglas, Ian WhoScE 91-1
Douglas, Ian 1936- WhoWor 93
Douglas, Isodore AmWomPl
Douglas, J. Paul Law&B 92
Douglas, James BioIn 17
Douglas, James Buster WhoAm 92
Douglas, James Holley 1951- WhoAm 92, WhoE 93
Douglas, James McM. ConAu 40NR
Douglas, James Merrill 1933- WhoE 93
Douglas, James W. 1951- St&PR 93
Douglas, Jane Yellowlees 1962- WhoWor 93
Douglas, Jocelyn Fielding 1927- WhoAm 92
Douglas, John B. 1953- St&PR 93
Douglas, John B., III Law&B 92
Douglas, John Breed, III 1953- WhoAm 92
Douglas, John H. 1941- St&PR 93
Douglas, John Hoffmann 1920- WhoE 93, WhoWor 93
Douglas, John W. 1944- WhoIns 93
Douglas, Joseph Pickens, III 1946- WhoEmL 93
Douglas, Josephine St&PR 93
Douglas, Judy Carol 1948- WhoAmW 93
Douglas, Kathleen Mary Harrigan 1950- WhoSSW 93
Douglas, Kenneth 1922- St&PR 93
Douglas, Kenneth Dale 1943- WhoSSW 93
Douglas, Kenneth Jay 1922- WhoAm 92
Douglas, Kenneth Thomas WhoScE 91-1
Douglas, Kirk 1916- BioIn 17, ConAu 138, IntDcF 2-3 [port], MiSFD 9
Douglas, Kirk 1918- WhoAm 92
Douglas, Lalette 1931- WhoWrEP 92
Douglas, Larry B. Law&B 92
Douglas, Laura Lynn 1960- WhoE 93
Douglas, Lauren Wright 1947- ScF&FL 92
Douglas, Lee WhoWrEP 92
Douglas, Lee 1951- WhoEmL 93
Douglas, Leslie 1914- St&PR 93, WhoAm 92
Douglas, Leslie Gay 1949- St&PR 93
Douglas, Lindsey Russell 1950- WhoSSW 93
Douglas, Lloyd C. 1877-1951 BioIn 17
Douglas, Lloyd Evans 1951- WhoEmL 93

Douglas, Marilyn Eileen 1941- *WhoE 93*
Douglas, Marion Joan 1940- *WhoAmW 93*
Douglas, Marjory Stoneman *BioIn 17*
Douglas, Marjory Stoneman 1890- *News 93-1 [port]*
Douglas, Mary Tew 1921- *WhoAm 92*
Douglas, Melvyn 1901-1981 *BioIn 17, IntDcF 2-3*
Douglas, Michael *BioIn 17, ConAu 40NR*
Douglas, Michael 1940- *DcCPCAm*
Douglas, Michael 1944- *IntDcF 2-3 [port]*
Douglas, Michael Kirk 1944- *WhoAm 92*
Douglas, Michael R. *Law&B 92*
Douglas, Michael Thomas 1961- *WhoE 93*
Douglas, Nancy W. 1958- *St&PR 93*
Douglas, O. 1878-1948 *BioIn 17*
Douglas, Patricia Jeanne 1939- *WhoE 93*
Douglas, Paul H. 1892-1976 *PolPar*
Douglas, Paul Hofmann 1947- *WhoE 93*
Douglas, Paul I. *Law&B 92*
Douglas, Paul W. 1926- *St&PR 93*
Douglas, Paul Wolff 1926- *WhoWor 93*
Douglas, Peggy Z. d1992 *NewYTBS 92 [port]*
Douglas, Penelope Alice 1952- *WhoAmW 93*
Douglas, Peter *MiSFD 9*
Douglas, R. Lee, Jr. *St&PR 93*
Douglas, Robert Ellis 1919- *WhoAm 92*
Douglas, Robert Gordon, Jr. 1934- *WhoAm 92*
Douglas, Robert Ramsay 1944- *WhoWor 93*
Douglas, Roger Owen 1937- *WhoAsAP 91*
Douglas, Ronald George 1938- *WhoAm 92*
Douglas, Ronald L. 1954- *St&PR 93*
Douglas, Rosie 1942- *DcCPCAm*
Douglas, Roxanne Grace 1951- *WhoAmW 93*
Douglas, Scott S. *Law&B 92*
Douglas, Stephen A. 1813-1861 *PolPar*
Douglas, Stephen Lane 1952- *WhoEmL 93, WhoSSW 93*
Douglas, Stewart N. *Law&B 92*
Douglas, Sue McKnight 1939- *WhoSSW 93*
Douglas, Susan 1946- *WhoAmW 93, WhoEmL 93, WhoWor 93*
Douglas, Teresa Lynn 1956- *WhoAmW 93*
Douglas, Thomas Edward 1937- *St&PR 93*
Douglas, Thomas Harrelson, III 1936- *St&PR 93*
Douglas, Thomas O'Neal 1935- *St&PR 93, WhoAm 92*
Douglas, Tommy Charles 1946- *WhoSSW 93*
Douglas, Wade *WhoWrEP 92*
Douglas, Walter Sholto *BioIn 17*
Douglas, William C., Jr. 1955- *St&PR 93*
Douglas, William Ernest 1930- *WhoAm 92*
Douglas, William John 1938- *St&PR 93*
Douglas, William O. 1898-1980 *BioIn 17*
Douglas, William Orville 1898-1980 *OxCSupC [port]*
Douglas, William Randolph 1921- *WhoAm 92*
Douglas-Hamilton, Margaret M. *St&PR 93*
Douglas-Home, Alec 1903- *ColdWar 1 [port]*
Douglas-Home, Alexander Frederick 1903- *DcTwHis*
Douglas-Home, Elizabeth Alington d1990 *BioIn 17*
Douglas Home, William *ConAu 139*
Douglas-Home, William d1992 *NewYTBS 92 [port]*
Douglass, A.E. 1867-1962 *IntDcAn*
Douglass, Andrew Ian 1943- *St&PR 93, WhoAm 92*
Douglass, Bruce E. 1917- *WhoAm 92*
Douglass, Carl Dean 1925- *WhoAm 92*
Douglass, Carol Suzanne 1955- *WhoSSW 93*
Douglass, Don Nelson 1947- *WhoEmL 93*
Douglass, Edward Trent, Jr. 1906- *WhoSSW 93*
Douglass, Ellsworth *ScF&FL 92*
Douglass, Emily Beth 1966- *WhoSSW 93*
Douglass, Enid Hart 1926- *WhoAmW 93*
Douglass, Frederick 1817?-1895 *BioIn 17, GayN, JrnUS, WorLitC [port]*
Douglass, Frederick 1818-1895 *AmWr S3, EncAACR [port], PolPar*
Douglass, Harry Robert 1937- *WhoAm 92, WhoWor 93*
Douglass, Irwin Bruce 1904- *WhoE 93*
Douglass, Jackson Fred 1940- *WhoE 93*
Douglass, James Frederick 1934- *WhoSSW 93*
Douglass, Jane Dempsey 1933- *WhoAm 92*
Douglass, Jeanette E. *AmWomPl*
Douglass, John Jay 1922- *WhoAm 92, WhoSSW 93*
Douglass, John Michael 1939- *WhoAm 92*
Douglass, Karen Denise *WhoAmW 93*
Douglass, Keith *ScF&FL 92*
Douglass, Kimberly Plaster 1960- *WhoEmL 93, WhoSSW 93*
Douglass, Kingman 1923- *St&PR 93*
Douglass, Melvin Isadore 1948- *WhoAm 92, WhoE 93*
Douglass, Phillip Alan 1962- *WhoSSW 93*
Douglass, Ramona Elizabeth 1949- *WhoEmL 93, WhoWor 93*
Douglass, Robert Duncan 1941- *WhoE 93*
Douglass, Robert Joseph, Jr. 1951- *WhoEmL 93, WhoWor 93*
Douglass, Robert Royal 1931- *St&PR 93, WhoAm 92, WhoE 93*
Douglass, Sam Preston 1932- *St&PR 93*
Douglass, Susan Daniel 1959- *WhoEmL 93*
Douglass, Wilford David 1927- *WhoSSW 93*
Douglass, William D. 1937- *St&PR 93*
Douglass, William James, Jr. 1932- *WhoE 93*
Douglas-Williams, Kordice Majella *Law&B 92*
Douglis, Avron 1918- *WhoAm 92*
Douglis, Marjie *ScF&FL 92*
Douhet, Giulio 1869-1930 *HarEnMi*
Doukas *OxDcByz*
Doukas c. 1400-1462? *OxDcByz*
Doukas, Andronikos dc. 910 *OxDcByz*
Doukas, Constantine d913 *OxDcByz*
Doukas, Constantine c. 1074-c. 1095 *OxDcByz*
Doukas, Georgette Ann 1947- *WhoSSW 93*
Doukas, John dc. 1088 *OxDcByz*
Doukas, John D. 1953- *WhoScE 91-3*
Doulah, Mohammed Seraj 1936- *WhoWor 93*
Doulis, Thomas John 1931- *WhoWrEP 92*
Doull, John 1922- *WhoAm 92*
Doulos, Charles James 1935- *St&PR 93*
Doulton, Charles William 1923- *St&PR 93, WhoAm 92*
Douma, Harry Hein 1933- *WhoWor 93*
Douma, Jacob Hendrick 1912- *WhoAm 92*
Doumani, George Alexander 1929- *WhoE 93*
Doumar, Albert George 1935- *WhoE 93*
Doumar, Robert George 1930- *WhoSSW 93*
Doumas, Basil Thomas 1930- *WhoWor 93*
Doumas, Gena Kathleen 1963- *WhoAmW 93*
Doumas, Michael P. 1944- *St&PR 93*
Doumato, Lamia 1947- *WhoEmL 93*
Doumenge, F. *WhoScE 91-4*
Doumenge, Francois 1926- *WhoScE 91-4*
Doumer, Paul 1857-1932 *BioIn 17*
Doumergue, Gaston 1863-1937 *BioIn 17*
Doumet, Juan Foad 1945- *WhoWor 93*
Doumlele, John A., Jr. 1946- *St&PR 93*
Doumlele, Ruth Hailey 1925- *WhoAmW 93, WhoSSW 93, WhoWor 93*
Dounias, Minos 1900-1962 *Baker 92*
Dounis, Demetrius Constantine 1886-1954 *Baker 92*
Doupe, G.E. Craig *Law&B 92*
Dourado, Autran 1926- *BioIn 17*
Dourlen, Victor (-Charles-Paul) 1780-1864 *Baker 92*
Dourlet, Ernest Francis 1924- *St&PR 93*
Dourley, Brian M. *Law&B 92*
Dourney, Martin W. 1944- *WhoIns 93*
Dourney, Wilma M. 1943- *St&PR 93*
Dournovo, Pierre Alexandre 1945- *WhoWor 93*
Dourojeanni, Axel Charles 1942- *WhoUN 92*
Douskey, Franz Thomas 1941- *WhoE 93, WhoWrEP 92*
Douskey, Theresa Kathryn 1938- *WhoAmW 93*
Doussinault, Gerard 1942- *WhoScE 91-2*
Dout, Anne Jacqueline 1955- *WhoAm 92, WhoEmL 93*
Douthat, James Evans 1946- *WhoAm 92*
Doutheau, A. *WhoScE 91-2*
Douthitt, Claude Alton 1928- *St&PR 93*
Douthitt, Shirley Ann 1947- *WhoAmW 93*
Douthwaite, Clifford *WhoScE 91-1*
Douthwaite, Graham 1913- *WhoWrEP 92*
Doutremepuich, C. P. 1949- *WhoWor 93*
Doutt, Richard Leroy 1916- *WhoAm 92*
Douty, Lucy Evelyn 1951- *WhoAmW 93, WhoEmL 93*
Douvan, Elizabeth 1926- *WhoAm 92*
Douville, Arthur John 1945- *St&PR 93*
Douville, Jean 1943- *St&PR 93*
Douwes, Adrianus Cornelis 1940- *WhoWor 93*
Douxchamps, Francis *WhoScE 91-2*
Douzou, Pierre 1926- *WhoScE 91-2*
Doval, Carlos Alberto 1947- *WhoWor 93*
DoVale, Antonio Joseph, Jr. 1954- *WhoE 93, WhoWor 93*
Dovalina, Mario A., Jr. 1954- *St&PR 93*
Dovalina, Mario Alonzo 1924- *St&PR 93*
Do Valle, Cyro Eyer 1937- *WhoWor 93*
Dove, Bruce Alan 1958- *WhoE 93*
Dove, Bruce Lee *Law&B 92*
Dove, Christopher Collier 1948- *St&PR 93*
Dove, Colin *WhoScE 91-1*
Dove, Edward Stellwagen, III 1952- *WhoEmL 93*
Dove, Gloria Ann 1948- *WhoAmW 93*
Dove, Grant Alonza 1928- *WhoAm 92*
Dove, Herbert Paul, Jr. 1944- *WhoSSW 93*
Dove, Jeffrey Austin 1959- *WhoEmL 93*
Dove, Kathleen Meg Lindemann 1953- *WhoAmW 93*
Dove, Kenley Royce 1936- *WhoE 93*
Dove, Kenneth John 1935- *St&PR 93*
Dove, Michael John *WhoScE 91-1*
Dove, Richard Allan 1958- *WhoEmL 93*
Dove, Ricky Joe 1955- *WhoEmL 93, WhoSSW 93*
Dove, Rita *BioIn 17*
Dove, Rita 1952- *PoeCrit 6 [port]*
Dove, Rita (Frances) 1952- *DcLB 120 [port], WhoAm 92, WhoAmW 93, WhoWrEP 92*
Dove, Thomas Gene 1926- *St&PR 93*
Dove, William E. 1937- *St&PR 93*
Dovells *SoulM*
Dover, Carl Bellman 1941- *WhoE 93*
Dover, Clarence Joseph 1919- *WhoAm 92, WhoWor 93*
Dover, James Burrell 1927- *WhoAm 92*
Dover, Kenneth James 1920- *WhoWor 93*
Dover, William Duncan *WhoScE 91-1*
Doverspike, William Fred 1951- *WhoSSW 93*
Dovey, Brian H. *St&PR 93*
Dovey, Brian Hugh 1941- *WhoAm 92*
Doviak, Richard James 1933- *WhoAm 92*
Dovids, Gerhard Wilhelm 1963- *WhoWor 93*
Dovima d1990 *BioIn 17*
Dovish, Chuck 1954- *WhoEmL 93*
Dovland, Harald 1941- *WhoScE 91-4*
Dovlatov, Sergei *BioIn 17*
Dovorany, Richard J. 1946- *St&PR 93*
Dovring, Folke 1916- *WhoWor 93*
Dovring, Karin Elsa Ingeborg 1919- *WhoAm 92, WhoAmW 93, WhoWor 93*
Dovzhenko, Alexander Petrovich 1894-1956 *MiSFD 9N*
Dow, Alexander Carmichael *WhoScE 91-1*
Dow, Avard Morton, Sr. 1916- *St&PR 93*
Dow, Barry Park 1961- *WhoEmL 93*
Dow, Charles Henry 1851-1902 *BioIn 17*
Dow, Daniel Gould 1930- *WhoAm 92*
Dow, Daniel Peter 1959- *WhoSSW 93*
Dow, Donald C. d1990 *BioIn 17*
Dow, Edward *St&PR 93*
Dow, Frederick Warren 1917- *WhoAm 92*
Dow, Herbert Henry 1866-1930 *GayN*
Dow, Herbert Henry 1927- *WhoAm 92*
Dow, Janet Henson 1928- *WhoAmW 93*
Dow, Jean Louise 1955- *WhoAmW 93, WhoEmL 93*
Dow, Kenneth J. *Law&B 92*
Dow, Kevin 1956- *St&PR 93*
Dow, Les d1896 *BioIn 17*
Dow, Leslie Wright 1938- *WhoAmW 93*
Dow, Lois Weyman 1942- *WhoAm 92, WhoAmW 93, WhoWor 93*
Dow, Lorenzo 1777-1834 *BioIn 17*
Dow, Mary Alexis 1949- *WhoAmW 93, WhoEmL 93*
Dow, Michael Craig 1947- *WhoAm 92, WhoSSW 93*
Dow, Michael McDonald 1936- *WhoE 93*
Dow, Peter Anthony 1933- *St&PR 93, WhoAm 92*
Dow, Peter Burton 1932- *St&PR 93*
Dow, Teresa Elmerick 1957- *WhoEmL 93, WhoSSW 93*
Dow, Thomas Alva 1945- *WhoSSW 93*
Dow, Tony Fares 1947- *WhoEmL 93*
Dow, Wilbur Egerton 1906-1991 *BioIn 17*
Dow, William Gould 1895- *WhoAm 92, WhoWor 93*
Dowben, Carla Lurie 1932- *WhoAmW 93*
Dowben, Robert Morris 1927- *WhoAm 92*
Dowbenko, Rostyslaw 1927- *WhoE 93*
Dowbenko, Uri 1951- *WhoWrEP 92*
Dowcett, James Michael 1949- *WhoEmL 93*
Dowd, A. Joseph 1929- *St&PR 93*
Dowd, Andrew Joseph *Law&B 92*
Dowd, Andrew Joseph 1929- *WhoAm 92*
Dowd, David D., Jr. 1929- *WhoAm 92*
Dowd, David Joseph 1924- *WhoAm 92*
Dowd, Diane 1953- *WhoWor 93*
Dowd, Edward J. 1934- *St&PR 93*
Dowd, Elizabeth Ann 1964- *WhoAmW 93*
Dowd, Frances Smardo 1947- *WhoEmL 93, WhoSSW 93*
Dowd, Harriet R. 1950- *St&PR 93*
Dowd, J. Richard 1956- *St&PR 93*
Dowd, James *Law&B 92*
Dowd, James Edward 1922- *St&PR 93*
Dowd, James F. 1941- *WhoIns 93*
Dowd, Janice Lee 1948- *WhoAmW 93, WhoEmL 93*
Dowd, Jeffrey Marc 1948- *St&PR 93*
Dowd, John Michael, Jr. 1935- *St&PR 93*
Dowd, John Robert Arthur 1940- *WhoAsAP 91*
Dowd, Joseph A. 1929- *St&PR 93*
Dowd, Karen *Law&B 92*
Dowd, Kenneth Lowell, Jr. 1940- *WhoAm 92*
Dowd, Kevin Michael 1961- *WhoEmL 93*
Dowd, Kevin P. 1948- *St&PR 93*
Dowd, Matthew Joseph *Law&B 92*
Dowd, Maureen *BioIn 17*
Dowd, Michael *BioIn 17*
Dowd, Michael Edward 1934- *St&PR 93*
Dowd, Morgan Daniel 1933- *WhoAm 92*
Dowd, Nancy *MiSFD 9*
Dowd, Peter Alan 1946- *WhoWor 93*
Dowd, Peter Jerome 1942- *WhoAm 92*
Dowd, Sallie Proctor 1950- *WhoAmW 93*
Dowd, Steven M. *Law&B 92*
Dowd, Thomas P. *Law&B 92*
Dowd, Tom *ScF&FL 92*
Dowd, Tom 1925- *SoulM*
Dowdall, Janice L. *Law&B 92*
Dowdall, Jean A. 1942- *WhoE 93*
DowDell, Del *ScF&FL 92*
Dowdell, Dorothy Florence 1910- *WhoAm 92*
Dowdell, Rodger B. 1949- *St&PR 93*
Dowden, Albert R. *Law&B 92*
Dowden, Albert Ricker 1941- *St&PR 93, WhoAm 92, WhoE 93, WhoWor 93*
Dowden, Carroll Vincent 1933- *WhoAm 92*
Dowden, Charles Wingate 1955- *St&PR 93, WhoSSW 93*
Dowden, James C. 1939- *St&PR 93*
Dowden, Kaviraj George 1932- *WhoWrEP 92*
Dowden, Richard Michael 1954- *WhoEmL 93*
Dowden, Thomas Clark 1935- *WhoSSW 93, WhoWor 93*
Dowdey, Kathleen 1949- *MiSFD 9*
Dowding, Clara M. 1928- *St&PR 93*
Dowding, Henry Wallace 1888?-1967? *ScF&FL 92*
Dowding, Hugh Caswall Tremenheere 1882-1970 *DcTwHis, HarEnMi*
Dowding Duncan, Maria Lavonne 1954- *WhoEmL 93*
Dowdle, James C. *BioIn 17*
Dowdle, John Robert 1938- *St&PR 93*
Dowdle, Patrick Dennis 1948- *WhoEmL 93, WhoWor 93*
Dowdle, Walter Reid 1930- *WhoAm 92*
Dowds, Allan Alva 1931- *WhoSSW 93*
Dowds, John Joseph 1938- *WhoAm 92*
Dowdy, Clifford Albert 1950- *WhoSSW 93*
Dowdy, Frances Rose 1944- *WhoAmW 93*
Dowdy, James T. 1960- *St&PR 93*
Dowdy, John Vernard 1912- *WhoSSW 93*
Dowdy, John Wesley 1912- *WhoAm 92*
Dowdy, Mrs. Regera *MajAI, SmATA 70*
Dowdy, Robert A. *Law&B 92*
Dowdy, Ronald Raymond 1944- *WhoAm 92*
Dowdy, Timothy Wayne *Law&B 92*
Dowdye, Edward Henry, Jr. 1943- *WhoE 93*
Dowell, Alvis L. 1936- *St&PR 93*
Dowell, Anthony 1943- *BioIn 17*
Dowell, Anthony James 1943- *WhoAm 92, WhoWor 93*
Dowell, Arthur Maultsby 1944- *WhoSSW 93*
Dowell, Bill 1932- *St&PR 93*
Dowell, Boyd Max 1934- *WhoSSW 93*
Dowell, Earl Hugh 1937- *WhoAm 92*
Dowell, Flonnie 1947- *WhoEmL 93*
Dowell, James 1942- *St&PR 93*
Dowell, John Derek *WhoScE 91-1*
Dowell, Michael Brendan 1942- *WhoAm 92*
Dowell, Richard Patrick 1934- *WhoSSW 93*
Dowell, Robert Vernon 1947- *WhoEmL 93*
Dowell, Tommie Jean 1943- *WhoAmW 93*
Dowen, Thomas, Jr. 1931- *St&PR 93*
Dower, J. W. *ConAu 137*
Dower, John W(illiam) 1938- *ConAu 137*
Dower, Robert John *WhoScE 91-1*
Dowey, James L. 1949- *St&PR 93*
Dowgiallo, Zygmunt 1926- *WhoScE 91-4, WhoWor 93*
Dowgiewicz, Michael John 1952- *WhoEmL 93*
Dowhen, Garrick Storm 1945- *WhoWor 93*
Dowis, Lenore 1934- *WhoAmW 93, WhoE 93*
Dowiyogo, Bernard 1946- *WhoAsAP 91, WhoWor 93*
Dowland, Deborah A. 1967- *WhoSSW 93*

Dowland, John 1563-1626 *Baker 92*
Dowland, Robert 1591-1641 *Baker 92*
Dowley, Joel Edward 1952- *WhoEmL 93*
Dowlin, Kenneth Everett 1941- *WhoAm 92*
Dowling, Adele Neill *AmWomPl*
Dowling, Carolyn Henderson 1943- *WhoWor 93*
Dowling, David 1950- *ScF&FL 92*
Dowling, Edward Thomas 1938- *WhoAm 92, WhoE 93*
Dowling, Jacques MacCuiston 1906- *WhoAm 92, WhoAmW 93, WhoWor 93*
Dowling, James Hamilton 1931- *WhoAm 92, WhoE 93*
Dowling, James Knox 1934- *WhoSSW 93*
Dowling, James Stephen 1951- *WhoWrEP 92*
Dowling, John Elliott 1935- *WhoAm 92*
Dowling, John James, III *Law&B 92*
Dowling, Jonathan Patrick 1955- *WhoSSW 93*
Dowling, Joseph Albert 1926- *WhoAm 92*
Dowling, Joseph P. *Law&B 92*
Dowling, Joseph Patrick 1961- *WhoWor 93*
Dowling, Kevin *ScF&FL 92*
Dowling, Marie Augustine 1924- *WhoE 93*
Dowling, Mildred *AmWomPl*
Dowling, Nadine Valery 1947- *WhoEmL 93*
Dowling, Nancy Hill *Law&B 92*
Dowling, Patrick Joseph *WhoScE 91-1*
Dowling, Richard Cornell 1950- *WhoEmL 93*
Dowling, Robert Murray 1932- *WhoAm 92*
Dowling, Roderick A. 1940- *St&PR 93*
Dowling, Roderick Anthony 1940- *WhoAm 92*
Dowling, Terry 1948- *ScF&FL 92*
Dowling, Thomas Allan 1941- *WhoAm 92*
Dowling, Thomas F. 1951- *St&PR 93*
Dowling, Virginia M. *Law&B 92*
Down, Carl V. *Law&B 92*
Down, H.J. *WhoScE 91-1*
Down, John Frederick 1946- *WhoEmL 93*
Down, Lesley-Anne *BioIn 17*
Down, Wendy Margaret 1947- *WhoWor 93*
Downard, Bob Hanson 1946- *WhoEmL 93*
Downard, Rita Ellen *Law&B 92*
Downarowicz, Olgierd 1931- *WhoScE 91-4*
Downe, W. E. *Law&B 92*
Downen, David Earl 1940- *St&PR 93, WhoAm 92*
Downen, Richard V. 1951- *St&PR 93*
Downer, Alexander John Gosse 1951- *WhoAsAP 91*
Downer, Ann 1960- *ScF&FL 92*
Downer, Elizabeth Ann *Law&B 92*
Downer, Eugene Debs, Jr. 1939- *WhoAm 92*
Downer, Lee Alan 1941- *WhoAm 92*
Downer, Michael J. *Law&B 92*
Downer, Richard Fenton 1940- *WhoSSW 93*
Downer, William Clark 1936- *St&PR 93*
Downes, Diane Louise 1950- *WhoAmW 93*
Downes, Edward 1924- *OxDcOp*
Downes, Edward O(lin) D(avenport) 1911- *Baker 92*
Downes, Edward Olin Davenport 1911- *WhoAm 92*
Downes, Edward (Thomas) 1924- *Baker 92*
Downes, Geoff
See Yes *ConMus 8*
Downes, Gregory 1939- *St&PR 93*
Downes, L.M. 1957- *St&PR 93*
Downes, Laurence M. 1957- *WhoAm 92*
Downes, (Edwin) Olin 1886-1955 *Baker 92*
Downes, Rackstraw *BioIn 17*
Downes, Rackstraw 1939- *WhoAm 92*
Downes, Ralph (William) 1904- *Baker 92*
Downes, Robert Eugene 1942- *St&PR 93*
Downes, Roger Patrick *Law&B 92*
Downes, Terry L. 1945- *St&PR 93*
Downes, Tony William Edwin 1941- *WhoScE 91-1*
Downes, Victoria Ann 1964- *WhoE 93*
Downey, Arthur Harold, Jr. 1938- *WhoAm 92*
Downey, Bernard L. 1923- *St&PR 93*
Downey, Brian William 1960- *WhoEmL 93*
Downey, Daniel Granville, Jr. 1947- *St&PR 93*
Downey, Deoborah Ann 1958- *WhoAmW 93, WhoEmL 93, WhoWor 93*
Downey, Douglas Worth 1929- *St&PR 93*
Downey, Edmund *ScF&FL 92*
Downey, Ellen *WhoAm 92*
Downey, Eric *WhoScE 91-1*
Downey, Fairfax 1893-1990 *BioIn 17*
Downey, Frederick Fish 1948- *St&PR 93*
Downey, H. Fred 1939- *WhoSSW 93*
Downey, J. Patrick 1944- *St&PR 93*
Downey, Jack *ScF&FL 92*
Downey, James 1939- *WhoAm 92*
Downey, James Russell, Jr. 1948- *St&PR 93*
Downey, James S. *Law&B 92*
Downey, Jane Marie 1950- *WhoAmW 93*
Downey, Jean Ann 1928- *St&PR 93*
Downey, Joan Carol 1931- *WhoAmW 93*
Downey, John Alexander 1930- *WhoAm 92, WhoE 93*
Downey, John Charles 1926- *WhoAm 92*
Downey, John Harold 1956- *WhoEmL 93*
Downey, John P. *Law&B 92*
Downey, John R. *Law&B 92*
Downey, John Redmond 1950- *WhoEmL 93*
Downey, John (Wilham) 1927- *Baker 92, WhoAm 92*
Downey, Juan Antonio 1940- *WhoAm 92*
Downey, June Etta 1875-1932 *AmWomPl*
Downey, Kenneth W. *Law&B 92*
Downey, Laurence J. 1950- *St&PR 93*
Downey, Lowell 1937- *St&PR 93*
Downey, Michael W. 1952- *WhoEmL 93*
Downey, Mortimer Leo, III 1936- *WhoAm 92*
Downey, Patrick D. 1943- *St&PR 93*
Downey, Paul Anthony 1939- *WhoAm 92*
Downey, R. M. *Law&B 92*
Downey, Richard Ralph 1934- *WhoAm 92*
Downey, Richard Stephen 1953- *WhoSSW 93*
Downey, Richard T. *St&PR 93*
Downey, Robert *Law&B 92*
Downey, Robert 1936- *MiSFD 9*
Downey, Robert, Jr. *BioIn 17*
Downey, Rodney Graham 1957- *WhoWor 93*
Downey, Roma *BioIn 17*
Downey, Thomas J. 1949- *CngDr 91*
Downey, Thomas Joseph 1949- *WhoAm 92, WhoE 93*
Downey, William Hugh 1945- *St&PR 93*
Downey, William John 1927- *St&PR 93*
Downham, David Yorston 1939- *WhoWor 93*
Downham, Michael Thomas 1948- *St&PR 93*
Downie, Gary *ScF&FL 92*
Downie, Jill 1938- *ScF&FL 92*
Downie, John Allan *WhoScE 91-1*
Downie, John F. *Law&B 92*
Downie, John Francis 1934- *St&PR 93, WhoAm 92*
Downie, Leonard 1942- *BioIn 17*
Downie, Leonard, Jr. 1942- *WhoAm 92, WhoE 93, WhoWrEP 92*
Downie, Mary Alice 1934- *WhoCanL 92*
Downie, Robert Charles 1947- *St&PR 93*
Downie, Robert Silcock 1933- *WhoWor 93*
Downie, Sandra Carroll 1939- *WhoAmW 93*
Downie, Thomas Moore 1936- *St&PR 93*
Downie, Timothy J. 1942- *St&PR 93*
Downing, A.L. 1926- *WhoScE 91-1*
Downing, Big Al 1940- *SoulM*
Downing, Brian Jay 1950- *BiDAMSp 1989*
Downing, Brian T. 1947- *St&PR 93*
Downing, Brian Thomas 1947- *WhoAm 92*
Downing, Cheryl Marie 1946- *WhoAmW 93*
Downing, Damien *WhoScE 91-1*
Downing, David 1946- *ScF&FL 92*
Downing, Forrest W. *WhoIns 93*
Downing, Forrest William 1949- *WhoAm 92, WhoE 93*
Downing, George Walter 1924- *St&PR 93*
Downing, Gordon R. *Law&B 92*
Downing, Graham 1954- *ConAu 136*
Downing, Harry F. 1937- *St&PR 93*
Downing, James Stuart *Law&B 92*
Downing, Jeffrey Melvin 1948- *St&PR 93*
Downing, Joan Forman 1934- *WhoAm 92*
Downing, John A. 1916- *St&PR 93*
Downing, John Edward 1937- *WhoSSW 93*
Downing, Liz *BioIn 17*
Downing, Margaret Mary 1952- *WhoAmW 93*
Downing, Mary Brigetta 1938- *WhoWrEP 92*
Downing, Michael Bernard 1958- *WhoE 93*
Downing, Morris 1942- *St&PR 93*
Downing, Noel *ConAu 138*
Downing, Paul A. 1925- *St&PR 93*
Downing, Paula E. 1951- *ConAu 136, ScF&FL 92*
Downing, Peggy 1924- *ScF&FL 92*
Downing, Peggy Ann 1957- *WhoAmW 93*
Downing, Robert Edward 1949- *WhoSSW 93*
Downing, Robert F. *Law&B 92*
Downing, Robert George *Law&B 92*
Downing, Robin Wilson 1962- *WhoAmW 93, WhoE 93, WhoEmL 93*
Downing, Wayne Allan 1940- *WhoAm 92*
Downing, Will *BioIn 17, SoulM*
Downing, William Edward 1940- *St&PR 93*
Downing, William Myron 1907- *WhoE 93*
Downs, Anthony 1930- *St&PR 93, WhoAm 92*
Downs, Anthony John 1936- *WhoWor 93*
Downs, Bobby Lee *BioIn 17*
Downs, Cathy 1924?-1976 *SweetSg C*
Downs, Charity Ann 1943- *WhoAmW 93*
Downs, Charles Robert 1950- *WhoUN 92*
Downs, Chris *BioIn 17*
Downs, Clark Evans 1946- *WhoAm 92*
Downs, David Lane 1961- *WhoSSW 93*
Downs, David R. 1937- *St&PR 93*
Downs, Diarmuid 1922- *WhoWor 93*
Downs, Douglas J. 1955- *St&PR 93*
Downs, Ernest Charles *BioIn 17*
Downs, Florella McIntyre 1921- *WhoAmW 93*
Downs, Gerry *ScF&FL 92*
Downs, Gregory Thomas 1952- *WhoSSW 93*
Downs, Harry 1932- *St&PR 93, WhoAm 92*
Downs, Hartley Harrison, III 1949- *WhoEmL 93, WhoWor 93*
Downs, Hugh *BioIn 17*
Downs, Hugh Malcolm 1921- *WhoAm 92*
Downs, Hugh Malcolm 1922- *JrnUS*
Downs, James H. 1927- *St&PR 93*
Downs, James L. 1940- *St&PR 93*
Downs, James R. 1944- *St&PR 93*
Downs, James William 1927- *WhoE 93*
Downs, Jerral Wayne 1943- *St&PR 93*
Downs, Jon Franklin 1938- *WhoSSW 93, WhoWor 93*
Downs, Kathleen Anne 1951- *WhoAmW 93, WhoEmL 93*
Downs, Kenneth T. d1991 *BioIn 17*
Downs, Larry R. 1949- *St&PR 93*
Downs, Linn Hedwig 1954- *WhoEmL 93*
Downs, Mel 1933- *St&PR 93*
Downs, Melanie 1957- *WhoAmW 93*
Downs, Michael John 1941- *WhoScE 91-1*
Downs, Michael Patrick 1940- *WhoAm 92*
Downs, Natasha *BioIn 17*
Downs, Richard Scott 1947- *St&PR 93*
Downs, Robert B. 1903-1991 *BioIn 17*
Downs, Robert C.S. 1937- *WhoWrEP 92*
Downs, Robert Jack 1923- *WhoSSW 93*
Downs, Robert John, Jr. 1936- *St&PR 93*
Downs, Ryan A. 1944- *St&PR 93*
Downs, Sally Gibson- *ScF&FL 92*
Downs, Steven Edward 1960- *WhoE 93, WhoWor 93*
Downs, Thomas Michael 1943- *WhoAm 92*
Downs, Wilbur George 1913-1991 *BioIn 17*
Downsbrough, Bruce Owen 1953- *WhoEmL 93*
Downum, Bob L. 1950- *St&PR 93*
Downum, Lawrence Morgan, Jr. 1939- *St&PR 93*
Dowrick, Stephanie *ScF&FL 92*
Dows, David Alan 1928- *WhoAm 92*
Dowse, Granton Hall, Jr. 1911- *St&PR 93*
Dowsett, Charles James Frank 1924- *WhoWor 93*
Dowsett, Connie M. 1955- *St&PR 93*
Dowsett, Mark Graeme *WhoScE 91-1*
Dowsett, Patrick W. 1946- *St&PR 93*
Dowsett, Robert Chipman 1929- *St&PR 93, WhoAm 92, WhoIns 93*
Dowsett, William J. 1918- *St&PR 93*
Dowson, Duncan *WhoScE 91-1*
Dowst, Somerby Rohrer 1926-1990 *BioIn 17*
Dowty, Leonard d1991 *BioIn 17*
Dox, Ida 1927- *WhoE 93*
Doxey, William 1935- *ScF&FL 92*
Doxopatres, John fl. 11th cent.- *OxDcByz*
Doxopatres, Neilos fl. 12th cent.- *OxDcByz*
Doxsee, Lawrence Edward 1934- *WhoAm 92*
Doye, Peter Karl 1927- *WhoWor 93*
Doyen, Albert 1882-1935 *Baker 92*
Doyer, Leo F. 1945- *St&PR 93*
Doyle, Alfred Alan 1964- *WhoEmL 93*
Doyle, Arthur Conan 1859-1930 *BioIn 17, BritWr S2, MagSWL [port], ScF&FL 92, WorLitC [port]*
Doyle, Arthur J. 1923- *St&PR 93*
Doyle, Arthur James 1923- *WhoAm 92*
Doyle, Brett Colby 1958- *WhoSSW 93*
Doyle, Brian *BioIn 17*
Doyle, Brian 1935- *DcChlFi, MajAI [port], SmATA 16AS [port], WhoCanL 92*
Doyle, Brian Bowles 1941- *WhoE 93*
Doyle, Brian Francis Xavier 1962- *WhoSSW 93*
Doyle, Brian King 1957- *St&PR 93*
Doyle, Brooks S., Jr. *Law&B 92*
Doyle, Charles *WhoCanL 92*
Doyle, Charles Andrew 1937- *St&PR 93*
Doyle, Charles Thomas 1934- *WhoSSW 93*
Doyle, Christine *Law&B 92*
Doyle, Christine A. *Law&B 92*
Doyle, Christopher John *WhoScE 91-1*
Doyle, Christopher R. *Law&B 92*
Doyle, Clare Hooper *Law&B 92*
Doyle, Conan 1859-1930 *BioIn 17*
Doyle, Constance Talcott Johnston 1945- *WhoAmW 93*
Doyle, Daniel A. 1958- *St&PR 93*
Doyle, David Allen 1959- *WhoEmL 93, WhoSSW 93*
Doyle, David Anthony 1947- *WhoWor 93*
Doyle, David Perrie 1960- *WhoEmL 93*
Doyle, David Wilson 1954- *WhoWor 93*
Doyle, Debra 1952- *ScF&FL 92*
Doyle, Diana Lee 1963- *WhoAmW 93*
Doyle, Diana M. *WhoAmW 93*
Doyle, Donald Earl 1930- *St&PR 93*
Doyle, Edward Murphy *Law&B 92*
Doyle, Eileen Marie 1953- *WhoE 93*
Doyle, Eleanor Janosek *Law&B 92*
Doyle, Esther Marion 1910- *WhoAmW 93*
Doyle, Eugenie Fleri 1921- *WhoAm 92*
Doyle, Eva Curlee 1961- *WhoE 93*
Doyle, Fiona Mary 1956- *WhoAmW 93*
Doyle, Francis C. 1906- *St&PR 93*
Doyle, Frank Lawrence 1926- *WhoAm 92, WhoSSW 93*
Doyle, Frank P. 1931- *St&PR 93*
Doyle, Frederick Joseph 1920- *WhoAm 92*
Doyle, George Edward 1948- *St&PR 93*
Doyle, Gerard Francis 1942- *WhoAm 92*
Doyle, Gerard S., Jr. *Law&B 92*
Doyle, Gerry 1946- *WhoScE 91-3*
Doyle, Helen MacKnight 1873-1957 *BioIn 17*
Doyle, Irene Elizabeth 1920- *WhoAmW 93*
Doyle, Jack 1953- *WhoEmL 93*
Doyle, Jack E. 1936- *St&PR 93*
Doyle, Jacqueline 1951- *WhoAmW 93*
Doyle, James A. 1947- *St&PR 93*
Doyle, James Aloysius 1921- *WhoAm 92*
Doyle, James Edward 1945- *WhoAm 92*
Doyle, James F. 1952- *St&PR 93*
Doyle, James J. *Law&B 92*
Doyle, James J., Jr. *Law&B 92*
Doyle, James Stephen 1935- *WhoSSW 93*
Doyle, James Thomas 1933- *St&PR 93, WhoAm 92*
Doyle, Janet Marie 1956- *WhoAmW 93*
Doyle, Jay d1990 *BioIn 17*
Doyle, Jennifer 1952- *WhoAmW 93*
Doyle, Jennifer Lydia 1953- *WhoAmW 93*
Doyle, John 1955- *St&PR 93*
Doyle, John A. 1944- *St&PR 93*
Doyle, John Laurence 1931- *WhoAm 92*
Doyle, John Lawrence 1939- *WhoAm 92*
Doyle, John Leonard *Law&B 92*
Doyle, John Peter 1942- *WhoIns 93*
Doyle, John Robert, Jr. 1910- *WhoAm 92, WhoSSW 93, WhoWor 93*
Doyle, John Thomas 1943- *WhoE 93*
Doyle, Joseph Anthony 1920- *WhoAm 92, WhoE 93*
Doyle, Joseph Theobald 1918- *WhoAm 92*
Doyle, Joyce Ann 1937- *WhoAm 92, WhoAmW 93*
Doyle, Judith Stovall 1940- *WhoAmW 93*
Doyle, Judith Warner 1943- *WhoAm 92*
Doyle, Justin Emmett 1935- *WhoAm 92*
Doyle, Katherine Lee Lee 1932- *WhoAm 92*
Doyle, Kevin F. 1934- *St&PR 93*
Doyle, Kevin John 1943- *WhoAm 92, WhoE 93*
Doyle, Kevin M. *Law&B 92*
Doyle, King 1922- *St&PR 93*
Doyle, L.F. Boker 1931- *St&PR 93, WhoAm 92*
Doyle, Lawrence Sawyer 1943- *St&PR 93*
Doyle, Lynn 1873-1961 *BioIn 17*
Doyle, Margaret M. *Law&B 92*
Doyle, Marjorie W. *Law&B 92*
Doyle, Marty *BioIn 17*
Doyle, Mary Elizabeth *Law&B 92*
Doyle, Mary Ellen 1932- *WhoSSW 93*
Doyle, Mathias Francis 1933- *WhoAm 92*
Doyle, Maureen Ryan 1951- *WhoAmW 93*
Doyle, Michael Anthony 1937- *WhoAm 92*
Doyle, Michael David *Law&B 92*
Doyle, Michael Francis 1951- *WhoE 93, WhoEmL 93*
Doyle, Michael J. *Law&B 92*
Doyle, Michael O'Brien 1948- *WhoEmL 93, WhoSSW 93*
Doyle, Mike 1928- *WhoCanL 92*
Doyle, Mills Henry, III 1958- *WhoEmL 93*
Doyle, Morris McKnight 1909- *WhoAm 92*
Doyle, Owen Paul 1925- *St&PR 93*
Doyle, P. Jill 1955- *WhoAmW 93, WhoEmL 93*
Doyle, Patricia A. 1942- *WhoAmW 93*
Doyle, Patrick John 1926- *WhoAm 92*

Doyle, Patrick L. 1929- *St&PR 93*
Doyle, Patrick Lee 1929- *WhoAm 92*
Doyle, Paul A. 1925- *WhoWrEP 92*
Doyle, Peter *WhoScE 91-1*
Doyle, Peter C. *Law&B 92*
Doyle, Peter Thomas 1928- *St&PR 93*
Doyle, Regina 1907-1931 *SweetSg B*
Doyle, Richard James 1923- *WhoAm 92*
Doyle, Robert Gerard 1950- *WhoE 93*
Doyle, Roland M. 1930- *St&PR 93*
Doyle, Sheila Marie 1958- *WhoEmL 93*
Doyle, Stephen Patrick 1946- *St&PR 93*
Doyle, Susan *Law&B 92*
Doyle, Terence Nicholas 1936- *WhoAm 92*
Doyle, Theresa Lipari 1957- *WhoAmW 93*
Doyle, Thomas James, III 1935- *St&PR 93*
Doyle, Wilfred Emmett 1913- *WhoAm 92*
Doyle, William Jay, II 1928- *WhoWor 93*
Doyle, William Lynn 1941- *WhoSSW 93*
Doyle, William Stowell 1944- *WhoAm 92, WhoWor 93*
Doyle, William Thomas 1925- *WhoAm 92*
Doyle Place, Lori L. *Law&B 92*
D'Oyly Carte, Richard *Baker 92*
Doyon, Dominique 1932- *WhoScE 91-2*
Doyon, Michael 1960- *St&PR 93*
Doza, Lawrence O. 1938- *St&PR 93, WhoAm 92*
Dozier, Ann Marie 1954- *WhoEmL 93*
Dozier, Brent A. *WhoWrEP 92*
Dozier, Bruce Emmitt *Law&B 92*
Dozier, Bruce Emmitt 1948- *WhoEmL 93*
Dozier, D.J. *BioIn 17*
Dozier, David Charles, Jr. 1938- *WhoAm 92*
Dozier, Edward P. 1916-1971 *IntDcAn*
Dozier, Eugenie Louise 1905- *WhoAmW 93*
Dozier, Glenn J. 1950- *St&PR 93*
Dozier, Glenn Joseph 1950- *WhoAm 92, WhoEmL 93*
Dozier, Graham Pinson, III 1932- *St&PR 93*
Dozier, Irene 1936- *WhoAmW 93*
Dozier, James Lee 1931- *WhoAm 92*
Dozier, Lamont *SoulM*
Dozier, Lamont 1941- *Baker 92, BioIn 17*
See Also Holland, Dozier & Holland *SoulM*
Dozier, O. Kemp 1929- *WhoAm 92*
Dozier, Ollin Kemp 1929- *St&PR 93*
Dozier, Russell William, Jr. 1927- *WhoSSW 93*
Dozier, Thomas Jefferson 1954- *WhoEmL 93*
Dozier, William 1908-1991 *BioIn 17, ConTFT 10*
Dozier, William Everett, Jr. 1922- *WhoAm 92*
Dozinel, Paul *WhoScE 91-2*
Dozois, Gardner 1947- *ScF&FL 92*
Dozoretz, Jerry 1947- *WhoEmL 93*
d'Providence, Rossi 1939- *WhoE 93*
Dr. A.
ConAu 137
MajAI, SmATA 69
Draa, Horace Vincent, III *Law&B 92*
Draayer, Jerry P. 1942- *WhoAm 92*
Draba, Roman A. 1953- *St&PR 93*
Drabanski, Emily Ann 1952- *WhoAmW 93*
Drabb, Michael J. 1933- *St&PR 93*
Drabble, Bernard James 1925- *WhoAm 92*
Drabble, Margaret 1939- *BioIn 17, MagSWL [port], WhoAm 92, WhoWor 93*
Drabek, Douglas Dean Doug 1962- *WhoAm 92*
Drabek, Jan 1935- *WhoCanL 92*
Drabek, Thomas E(dward) 1940- *ConAu 37NR*
Drabiak, Jerome D. *Law&B 92*
Drabinsky, Garth 1948- *BioIn 17*
Drabkin, Irving L. 1920- *St&PR 93*
Drabkin, Murray 1928- *WhoAm 92*
Drabkin, Stephen H. 1946- *St&PR 93*
Drabowicz, Barbara Linnea 1953- *WhoEmL 93*
Drach, George Wisse 1935- *WhoAm 92*
Drach, John Charles 1939- *WhoAm 92*
Drach, Michel 1930-1990 *BioIn 17*
Drachkovitch, Milorad M. 1921- *WhoAm 92*
Drachler, Norman 1912- *WhoAm 92*
Drachman, Daniel Bruce 1932- *WhoAm 92*
Drachman, David Alexander 1932- *WhoAm 92*
Drachman, Harold 1926- *St&PR 93*
Drachman, Sally Spaid 1931- *WhoAmW 93*
Drachnik, Catherine Meldyn 1924- *WhoWor 93*
Drack, Paul E. 1928- *WhoAm 92*
Drack, Paul Edward 1928- *St&PR 93*
Drackert, Harry d1990 *BioIn 17*
Dracula 1431-1476 *BioIn 17*
Draddy, Vincent de Paul 1907-1990 *BioIn 17*
Draeger, Jerald 1951- *St&PR 93*
Draeger, Kenneth W. 1940- *WhoE 93*
Draeger, Wayne Harold 1946- *St&PR 93, WhoAm 92*
Draegert, David A. *Law&B 92*
Draeseke, Felix (August Bernhard) 1835-1913 *Baker 92*
Draetta, Ugo *Law&B 92*
Draffin, Cyril William, Jr. 1950- *St&PR 93*
Drag, Michelle Mary 1963- *WhoEmL 93*
Draga, Gheorghe 1935- *Baker 92*
Dragan, Gleb 1920- *WhoScE 91-4*
Dragan, Ioan 1925- *WhoScE 91-4*
Dragan, Mircea 1932- *DrEEuF*
Draganescu, Mihai 1929- *WhoWor 93, WhoScE 91-4*
Draganescu, Nicolae 1927- *WhoScE 91-4*
Draganik, Bohdan 1937- *WhoScE 91-3*
Dragas *OxDcByz*
Dragaun, Heinz G. 1943- *WhoScE 91-4*
Drage, Michelle Susan 1965- *WhoEmL 93*
Drage, Starla Rae 1932- *WhoAmW 93*
Drager, Bertha Ours 1905- *WhoSSW 93*
Drager, Hans-Heinz 1909-1968 *Baker 92*
Drager, Nick 1949- *WhoUN 92, WhoWor 93*
Drager, Victoria Rae 1947- *WhoSSW 93*
Dragesund, Olav 1926- *WhoScE 91-4*
Dragg, Stephen S. *St&PR 93*
Draghi, Antonio c. 1634-1700 *Baker 92, OxDcOp*
Draghi, Giovanni Battista c. 1640-1708 *Baker 92, OxDcOp*
Draghici, Ion 1945- *WhoScE 91-4*
Dragic, Dusan Petar 1938- *WhoUN 92*
Dragin, Bert L. *MiSFD 9*
Dragisic, John 1940- *St&PR 93*
Dragland, Stan 1942- *WhoCanL 92*
Dragna, Nick Charles 1938- *WhoAm 92*
Drago, Joseph 1950- *St&PR 93*
Drago, Robert John 1958- *WhoE 93*
Drago, Russell Stephen 1928- *WhoAm 92*
Dragoi, Sabin V(asile) 1894-1968 *Baker 92*
Dragoiu, John A. 1947- *St&PR 93*
Dragojchev, Chavdar Colin 1925- *WhoScE 91-4*
Dragomir, Silvian Aurel 1943- *WhoScE 91-4*
Dragon, Carmen 1914-1984 *Baker 92*
Dragon, Daryl 1942- *Baker 92*
Dragon, Elizabeth Alice 1948- *WhoE 93, WhoEmL 93*
Dragon, Perry L. 1949- *St&PR 93*
Dragon, Renato P. *WhoAsAP 91*
Dragon, William, Jr. 1942- *WhoAm 92*
Dragone, Allan R. 1926- *St&PR 93, WhoAm 92, WhoE 93*
Dragonetti, Domenico (Carlo Maria) 1763-1846 *Baker 92*
Dragoni, Walter 1945- *WhoScE 91-3, WhoWor 93*
Dragonwagon, Crescent 1952- *MajAI [port], WhoAm 92, WhoEmL 93*
Dragoo, John William 1949- *WhoEmL 93*
Dragoti, Stan 1932- *MiSFD 9*
Dragoumis, Paul 1934- *St&PR 93, WhoAm 92*
Dragoun, Otokar 1937- *WhoScE 91-4*
Dragsted, Jens R. 1938- *WhoScE 91-2*
Dragt, Alexander James 1936- *WhoAm 92, WhoE 93*
Dragulev, Vassil 1945- *WhoUN 92*
Dragunas, Ruta M. *Law&B 92*
Draheim, Edward Ray 1927- *St&PR 93*
Draheim, Jennifer Ellen 1961- *WhoAmW 93*
Drahmann, Theodore 1926- *WhoAm 92*
Drahos, Istvan 1931- *WhoScE 91-4*
Drahos, Leslie Ann 1942- *WhoWrEP 92*
Drahos, Nicholas 1918- *BiDAMSp 1989*
Drahota, Zdenek 1932- *WhoScE 91-4*
Drain, Albert Sterling 1925- *WhoAm 92*
Drain, Diane Louise 1951- *WhoEmL 93*
Drain, Elaine Marie 1965- *WhoAmW 93*
Drain, George Warren 1932- *WhoSSW 93*
Drain, John F. 1932- *St&PR 93*
Drain, Lee 1925- *WhoAm 92*
Drain, Matthew P. *Law&B 92*
Drain, Randall Gordon *Law&B 92*
Draine, Betsy 1945- *ScF&FL 92*
Draisma, Jacob 1925- *WhoScE 91-3*
Drake, Albert Estern 1927- *WhoAm 92*
Drake, Alexander W. 1843-1916 *ScF&FL 92*
Drake, Alfred 1914-1992 *CurBio 92N*
Drake, Alfred C. d1992 *NewYTBS 92 [port]*
Drake, Alison *ScF&FL 92*
Drake, Asa *ScF&FL 92*
Drake, Barbara 1876-1963 *BioIn 17*
Drake, Charles D. *WhoScE 91-1*
Drake, Charles George 1920- *WhoAm 92*
Drake, Charles Richard 1924- *St&PR 93*
Drake, Charles Whitney 1926- *WhoAm 92*
Drake, Charlie 1925- *QDrFCA 92 [port]*
Drake, Cheryl Susan 1950- *WhoEmL 93*
Drake, Christine Spata 1946- *WhoWrEP 92*
Drake, Clara B. *AmWomPl*
Drake, David 1945- *ScF&FL 92*
Drake, David (Allen) 1945- *ConAu 38NR, WhoWrEP 92*
Drake, David Ralph 1949- *WhoSSW 93*
Drake, David Rice 1946- *WhoEmL 93*
Drake, Donald Charles 1935- *WhoAm 92*
Drake, Dorothy Louise 1953- *WhoAmW 93*
Drake, Douglas James 1948- *WhoEmL 93*
Drake, Earl R(oss) 1865-1916 *Baker 92*
Drake, Edwin Perry *Law&B 92*
Drake, Elisabeth Mertz 1936- *WhoAm 92, WhoAmW 93*
Drake, Emily H. *AmWomPl*
Drake, Eric Searfoss 1948- *WhoEmL 93*
Drake, Fabia 1904-1990 *BioIn 17*
Drake, Francis 1540?-1596 *BioIn 17*
Drake, Francis 1543-1596 *Expl 93 [port]*
Drake, Francis E., Jr. 1915- *St&PR 93*
Drake, Frank Donald 1930- *BioIn 17, WhoAm 92*
Drake, Franklin G. 1928- *St&PR 93*
Drake, Gary Kent 1950- *WhoEmL 93*
Drake, George A. *BioIn 17*
Drake, George Albert 1934- *WhoAm 92*
Drake, Gordon William Frederic 1943- *WhoAm 92*
Drake, Grace L. 1926- *WhoAmW 93*
Drake, Gregory S. *Law&B 92*
Drake, H.B. 1894- *ScF&FL 92*
Drake, H.L. *ScF&FL 92*
Drake, Harrington 1919- *St&PR 93, WhoAm 92*
Drake, Hudson Billings 1935- *WhoAm 92*
Drake, James R. *MiSFD 9*
Drake, Janet Marie 1952- *WhoAmW 93*
Drake, Jessica 1956- *WhoWor 93*
Drake, John 1927- *St&PR 93*
Drake, John Walter 1932- *WhoAm 92*
Drake, John Warren 1930- *WhoAm 92*
Drake, Kingsley Dimitri 1937- *WhoAm 92*
Drake, Larry *WhoAm 92*
Drake, Linda Kay 1957- *WhoAmW 93, WhoEmL 93, WhoWor 93*
Drake, Linda S. *Law&B 92*
Drake, Lorin James 1953- *WhoSSW 93*
Drake, Lucius Charles, Jr. 1946- *WhoEmL 93*
Drake, Lynn Annette 1949- *WhoAm 92*
Drake, Mary E. *Law&B 92*
Drake, Mary Frances 1934- *WhoAmW 93*
Drake, Michael L. 1936- *St&PR 93*
Drake, Michael W. 1953- *St&PR 93*
Drake, Michael Wayne 1953- *WhoEmL 93*
Drake, Miriam Anna 1936- *WhoAm 92, WhoSSW 93*
Drake, Morgan *ScF&FL 92*
Drake, Nicholas *WhoWrEP 92*
Drake, Pamela O'Bryant 1957- *WhoEmL 93*
Drake, Patricia Evelyn 1946- *WhoAmW 93*
Drake, Paul Steven *Law&B 92*
Drake, Philip Meurer 1925- *WhoAm 92*
Drake, Richard *BioIn 17*
Drake, Richard Allen 1959- *WhoSSW 93*
Drake, Robert 1930- *BioIn 17*
Drake, Robert 1938- *St&PR 93*
Drake, Robert B. 1913- *St&PR 93*
Drake, Robert Young, Jr. 1930- *WhoSSW 93*
Drake, Rodman Leland 1943- *St&PR 93, WhoAm 92, WhoWor 93*
Drake, Ruth K. *AmWomPl*
Drake, St. Clair 1911-1990 *BioIn 17, EncAACR, IntDcAn*
Drake, Sarah Frances Ashford 1943- *WhoAmW 93, WhoWor 93*
Drake, Stanley Albert 1921- *WhoAm 92*
Drake, Stanley Joseph 1916- *WhoSSW 93*
Drake, Stephen Douglas 1947- *WhoSSW 93*
Drake, Stillman 1910- *WhoAm 92*
Drake, (Bryant) Stillman 1910- *ConAu 40NR*
Drake, Sylvia *WhoWrEP 92*
Drake, Sylvie 1930- *WhoAm 92*
Drake, Teddy Millington- *BioIn 17*
Drake, Vaughn Paris, Jr. 1918- *WhoSSW 93*
Drake, Whitney 1942- *St&PR 93*
Drake, William E. *Law&B 92*
Drake, William E. 1939- *St&PR 93*
Drake, William Everett 1939- *WhoAm 92*
Drake, William Frank, Jr. 1932- *St&PR 93, WhoAm 92*
Drakeman, Donald Lee 1953- *WhoAm 92, WhoEmL 93*
Drakos, Charles Peter 1945- *WhoAm 92*
Drakos, Irene Sasso 1932- *WhoAm 92, WhoAmW 93*
Drakulic, Slavenka *BioIn 17*
Dramatics *SoulM*
Drame, Tieble *WhoWor 93*
Dramis, Francesco 1938- *WhoWor 93*
Drane, Edwin Byrd 1949- *WhoEmL 93*
Drane, Walter Harding 1915- *WhoAm 92*
Draney, Cyril L. 1939- *St&PR 93*
Drang, Diane Edelson 1951- *WhoAmW 93*
Dranginis, Peter J., Jr. *Law&B 92*
Dranginis, Peter J., Jr. 1944- *St&PR 93*
Drangosch, Ernesto 1882-1925 *Baker 92*
Dranias, Dean Anthony 1936- *WhoAm 92*
Dranishnikov, Alexander Nikolaevich 1958- *WhoWor 93*
Dranishnikov, Vladimir 1893-1939 *Baker 92*
Dranow, John Theodore 1948- *WhoEmL 93, WhoWrEP 92*
Dransfeld, Klaus 1926- *WhoScE 91-3*
Dransfield, Jane 1875-1975 *AmWomPl*
Drantz, Veronica Ellen 1943- *WhoAmW 93*
Drap, Albert Joseph, Jr. 1949- *WhoSSW 93*
Drapeau, Donald Francis 1932- *St&PR 93*
Drapeau, Phillip David 1938- *St&PR 93, WhoAm 92*
Draper, Brice M. 1937- *St&PR 93*
Draper, Cecil Vanoy 1940- *St&PR 93*
Draper, Colin J. 1924- *St&PR 93*
Draper, Daniel Clay 1920- *WhoAm 92*
Draper, Delbert M., III *Law&B 92*
Draper, E. Linn, Jr. 1942- *St&PR 93, WhoAm 92, WhoSSW 93*
Draper, Earle Sumner 1893- *WhoAm 92*
Draper, Edgar 1926- *WhoAm 92*
Draper, Eileen Marie Adams 1954- *WhoWrEP 92*
Draper, Ernest Gallaudet 1885-1954 *BioIn 17*
Draper, Frances E. 1956- *St&PR 93*
Draper, Frances M. 1947- *St&PR 93*
Draper, Frances Murphy 1947- *WhoAmW 93, WhoEmL 93*
Draper, Gary James 1957- *WhoEmL 93*
Draper, Gerald John *WhoScE 91-1*
Draper, Heidi d1992 *BioIn 17*
Draper, James David 1943- *WhoAm 92*
Draper, James Ross 1938- *St&PR 93*
Draper, James Wilson 1926- *WhoAm 92*
Draper, Jerry Lee 1939- *WhoSSW 93*
Draper, John Clayton 1945- *WhoAm 92*
Draper, John H., III 1939- *St&PR 93*
Draper, Line Bloom *WhoAm 92, WhoSSW 93, WhoWor 93*
Draper, Mary Lytton *WhoAmW 93, WhoE 93*
Draper, Norman Richard 1931- *WhoAm 92*
Draper, Paul 1909- *BioIn 17*
Draper, Paul Richard *WhoScE 91-1*
Draper, Polly *BioIn 17*
Draper, Robert Eugene 1936- *St&PR 93*
Draper, Simon Robert 1945- *WhoScE 91-1*
Draper, Theodore 1912- *WhoAm 92*
Draper, Verden Rolland 1916- *WhoAm 92*
Draper, W.H. 1946- *St&PR 93*
Draper, William David 1949- *WhoEmL 93, WhoSSW 93*
Draper, William F. 1912- *BioIn 17*
Draper, William Franklin 1912- *WhoAm 92*
Draper, William H., III 1928- *WhoUN 92*
Draper, William Henry, III 1928- *WhoAm 92*
Drapkin, Arnold Howard 1931- *WhoAm 92*
Drasar, Bohumil Sawdon *WhoScE 91-1*
Drasco, Dennis J. 1948- *WhoEmL 93*
Drasin, Resa T. *Law&B 92*
Draskovic, Boro 1935- *DrEEuF*
Draskovich, Zlatana Jennie 1948- *WhoAmW 93*
Drasner, Fred *WhoE 93*
Drattell, Eric Marc 1958- *WhoEmL 93*
Draucker, Claire Burke 1955- *WhoEmL 93*
Draude, Thomas Valentine 1940- *WhoAm 92*
Drauden, Gail 1948- *WhoEmL 93*
Draudt, Donald A. 1925- *St&PR 93*
Draudt, Richard J. 1948- *St&PR 93*
Draughon, Scott Wilson 1952- *WhoEmL 93*
Draughon, Terry Wayne 1947- *St&PR 93*
Draughon, Walter D., Jr. 1925- *WhoSSW 93*
Dravecky, Dave *BioIn 17*
Dravecky, Dave 1956- *News 92 [port]*
Draves, William August 1917- *WhoWrEP 92*
Drawbaugh, Roy Eugene 1930- *St&PR 93*
Drawe, Patricia Smith *Law&B 92*
Drawert, James George 1941- *St&PR 93*
Dray, Donald Dean 1954- *St&PR 93*
Dray, F. *WhoScE 91-2*
Dray, Mark S. 1943- *WhoSSW 93*

Dray, Valerie Eliza 1945- *WhoE 93*
Dray, William Herbert 1921- *WhoAm 92, WhoWrEP 92*
Drayer, Calvin Searle, Jr. 1939- *WhoE 93*
Drayer, Cynthia *WhoAm 92*
Drayer, Frank 1926- *St&PR 93*
Drayer, Jan Ignatius 1946- *WhoE 93*
Drayer, Lonnie R. *Law&B 92*
Drayton, Harold Alexander 1929- *WhoSSW 93*
Drayton, Michael 1563-1631 *DcLB 121 [port]*
Drayton, William *See* Public Enemy *News 92*
Drayton, William 1943- *WhoAm 92*
Drayton, William Henry 1742-1779 *BioIn 17*
Drazan, Anthony *MiSFD 9*
Drazan, P.J. *WhoScE 91-3*
Drazancic, Ante 1928- *WhoScE 91-4*
Drazen, Erica L. 1946- *St&PR 93*
Drazen, Jeffrey Mark 1946- *WhoE 93*
Drazin, Lisa 1953- *WhoAmW 93*
Drazin, Philip Gerald *WhoScE 91-1*
Drdla, Franz 1868-1944 *Baker 92*
Dreadstone, Carl *ScF&FL 92*
Dreager, Jacqueline *BioIn 17*
D'Realo, Duke *WhoWrEP 92*
Dreasler, Brady William 1956- *WhoEmL 93*
Drebbel, Cornelis c. 1572-1633 *BioIn 17*
Dreben, Burton Spencer 1927- *WhoAm 92*
Dreben, Raya Spiegel 1927- *WhoAm 92*
Dreben, Samuel 1878-1925 *BioIn 17*
Drebing, Barbara Gail 1955- *WhoEmL 93*
Dreblow, Darlene DeMarie 1952- *WhoEmL 93*
Drebsky, Dennis Jay 1946- *WhoAm 92*
Drebtchinsky, Julio 1930- *WhoWor 93*
Drebus, Richard William 1924- *WhoAm 92, WhoWor 93*
Drechsel, Edwin Jared 1914- *WhoAm 92*
Drechsler, Dorothy Roberta 1949- *WhoAmW 93*
Drechsler, Joseph 1782-1852 *Baker 92*
Drechsler, Karl 1800-1873 *Baker 92*
Drechsler, Michael 1923- *WhoScE 91-2*
Drechsler, Randall Richard 1945- *WhoWor 93*
Drechsler, Richard Ernest 1934- *St&PR 93*
Drechsler-Parks, Deborah Marie 1952- *WhoEmL 93*
Dreckshage, Brian Jeffrey 1955- *WhoSSW 93*
Dreeben, Octavine Lopez 1886- *AmWomPl*
Drees, Patricia Sue 1958- *WhoAmW 93*
Drees, Ralph A. *BioIn 17*
Dreeskamp, Herbert 1929- *WhoScE 91-3*
Dreesman, Robert 1947-1987 *BioIn 17*
Dreesman Family *BioIn 17*
Dreger, Dwight Elliot 1957- *St&PR 93*
Dreger, Jonathan M. *Law&B 92*
Dreger, Jonathan M. 1947- *St&PR 93*
Dregne, Harold Ernest 1916- *WhoAm 92*
Dreher, Caroline Hyde *AmWomPl*
Dreher, Donald Dean 1949- *St&PR 93*
Dreher, Karen C. 1929- *WhoUN 92*
Dreher, Mariam Jean *WhoE 93*
Dreher, Nancy C. 1942- *WhoAmW 93*
Dreher, Otmar 1940- *St&PR 93*
Dreher, P. Michael 1934- *St&PR 93*
Dreher, Sarah 1937- *ScF&FL 92*
Drehkoff, W. Dennis *Law&B 92*
Drehmer, Vernon J. *St&PR 93*
Dreibelbis, Eric Paul 1952- *WhoEmL 93*
Dreibholz, Frederick John 1955- *WhoE 93*
Dreiblatt, David J. 1937- *WhoUN 92*
Dreicer, Nancy 1949- *St&PR 93*
Dreier, David 1952- *CngDr 91*
Dreier, David Timothy 1952- *WhoAm 92*
Dreier, Mark Edward 1952- *WhoEmL 93*
Dreier, Per 1929- *Baker 92*
Dreier, R. Chad 1947- *St&PR 93*
Dreifke, Gerald Edmond 1918- *WhoAm 92*
Dreifus, David 1952- *WhoEmL 93*
Dreifus, Jean-Jacques 1936- *WhoScE 91-4*
Dreifuss, Arthur 1908- *MiSFD 9*
Dreifuss, Fritz Emanuel 1926- *WhoAm 92*
Dreifuss, Kurt 1897-1991 *ScF&FL 92*
Dreikausen, Margret 1937- *WhoE 93*
Dreiling, David A. 1918-1991 *BioIn 17*
Dreiling, Harry R. 1921- *St&PR 93*
Dreiling, Lynda S. 1947- *St&PR 93*
Dreiling, Robert Kilian *Law&B 92*
Dreilinger, Charles Lewis 1945- *WhoAm 92*
Dreilinger, Lloyd A. *Law&B 92*
Dreim, Lisa K. *Law&B 92*
Dreimanis, Aleksis 1914- *WhoAm 92*
Dreimann, Leonhard 1948- *St&PR 93*
Dreisbach, John Gustave 1939- *WhoWor 93*
Dreiser, Theodore 1871-1945 *BioIn 17, GayN, JrnUS, MagSAmL [port], WorLitC [port]*
Dreiss, L. Jack 1948- *WhoAm 92*
Dreissinger, Michelle Hartal- 1961- *BioIn 17*
Dreitler, Joseph R. *Law&B 92*
Dreizen, Alison M. 1952- *WhoAmW 93*
Dreizler, Gisela Mott- 1941- *BioIn 17*
Dreizler, Reiner Martin 1936- *WhoScE 91-3*
Drejsl, Radim 1923-1953 *Baker 92*
Drelich, Iris M. 1951- *WhoSSW 93*
Drell, Jill Leslie *Law&B 92*
Drell, Leonard B. 1919- *St&PR 93*
Drell, Sidney David 1926- *WhoAm 92*
Drell, William 1922- *WhoAm 92*
Drellich, Karen Kinney 1942- *WhoWrEP 92*
Drells *SoulM*
Dreman, David Nasaniel 1936- *WhoAm 92, WhoE 93*
Drendel, Mark *BioIn 17*
Drenik, Douglas Jay 1943- *St&PR 93*
Drenik, Gary William 1950- *WhoEmL 93*
Drennan, George Eldon 1921- *WhoAm 92*
Drennan, Janice S. 1950- *WhoWrEP 92*
Drennan, Marie *AmWomPl*
Drennan, Michael Eldon 1946- *WhoEmL 93*
Drennan, Paul 1949- *ScF&FL 92*
Drennan, William Anthony 1960- *WhoEmL 93*
Drennan, William D. 1935- *WhoE 93*
Drennen, Felix M., III 1951- *St&PR 93*
Drennen, John C. 1947- *St&PR 93*
Drennen, Marcia Simonton 1915- *WhoWrEP 92*
Drennen, William Miller 1914- *CngDr 91, WhoAm 92*
Drennen, William Miller, Jr. 1942- *WhoAm 92, WhoSSW 93*
Drenning, Gary Lynn 1954- *WhoSSW 93*
Drennon, Cindy-Jo Simmons 1956- *WhoEmL 93*
Drensek, Robert Arthur 1961- *WhoSSW 93*
Drenth, Dieter Johan Diederik 1935- *WhoScE 91-3*
Drenth, Jan 1925- *WhoScE 91-3*
Drenth, P.J.D. *WhoScE 91-3*
Drenth, Pieter Johan Diederk 1935- *WhoWor 93*
Drenz, Charles Francis 1930- *WhoAm 92*
Drepper, Kraft 1921- *WhoScE 91-3*
Dresbach, David Philip 1947- *WhoEmL 93*
Dresbach, Mary Louise 1950- *WhoAmW 93*
Dresch, Fred H. *MiSFD 9*
Dresch, John A. 1941- *St&PR 93*
Dresch, Stephen Paul 1943- *WhoAm 92*
Drescher, Henrik *ChlBIID [port]*
Drescher, Henrik 1955- *BioIn 17, MajAI [port]*
Drescher, Joseph Gerard 1940- *St&PR 93*
Drescher, Judith Altman 1946- *WhoAm 92, WhoAmW 93, WhoSSW 93*
Drescher, Mary *AmWomPl*
Drescher, Seymour 1934- *WhoAm 92*
Dreschhoff, Gisela Auguste Marie 1938- *WhoAm 92*
Dreschler, Wouter Albert 1953- *WhoWor 93*
Dresden, Marc Henri 1938-1990 *BioIn 17*
Dresden, Sem 1881-1957 *Baker 92*
Dresdow, Mary A. 1943- *St&PR 93*
Dresel, Otto 1826-1890 *Baker 92*
Dresen, Lothar 1939- *WhoScE 91-3*
Dresher, James T. 1919- *St&PR 93*
Dresher, Paul (Joseph) 1951- *Baker 92, WhoEmL 93*
Dresher, William Henry 1930- *WhoAm 92*
Dresing, Robert K. 1935- *WhoAm 92*
Dreska, John P. 1938- *WhoAm 92*
Dreskin, Jeanet Steckler 1921- *WhoWor 93*
Dresmal, James Eugene 1939- *St&PR 93, WhoIns 93*
Dresner, Bruce Michael 1948- *WhoWor 93*
Dresner, Mara Susan 1961- *WhoEmL 93*
Dresner, Thomas Leland 1948- *WhoEmL 93*
Dress, Joe Anthony 1923- *St&PR 93*
Dress, Susan Hildebrant 1948- *WhoE 93*
Dresse, Albert E.V. *WhoScE 91-2*
Dressel, Barry 1947- *WhoAm 92*
Dressel, Diane Lisette 1955- *WhoAm 92, WhoAmW 93, WhoEmL 93*
Dressel, Erwin 1909-1972 *Baker 92*
Dressel, Henry Francis 1914- *WhoE 93*
Dressel, Roy Robert 1923- *WhoAm 92*
Dresselhaus, Mildred Spiewak 1930- *WhoAm 92, WhoAmW 93*
Dressen, Charles Walter 1898-1966 *BiDAMSp 1989*
Dressendofer, Jo-Anne 1960- *WhoAmW 93, WhoEmL 93*
Dresser, Christopher 1834-1904 *BioIn 17*
Dresser, David W. *St&PR 93*
Dresser, Jesse Dale 1906- *WhoAm 92*
Dresser, Linda Ann 1948- *WhoAmW 93*
Dresser, Norine 1931- *ScF&FL 92*
Dresser, Paul A., Jr. 1942- *St&PR 93*
Dresser, Paul Alton, Jr. 1942- *WhoAm 92*
Dresser, (John) Paul, (Jr.) 1858-1906 *Baker 92*
Dresser, Robert L. 1925- *St&PR 93*
Dresser, Roblyn Lafferty 1957- *WhoEmL 93*
Dresser, Thomas L. 1949- *St&PR 93*
Dresser, W. Donald *Law&B 92*
Dresser, W. Donald 1947- *WhoAm 92*
Dresser, William Donald 1947- *St&PR 93*
Dressing, Julie Stumpe 1957- *WhoEmL 93*
Dressler, Alan *BioIn 17*
Dressler, Brenda Joyce 1943- *WhoAmW 93*
Dressler, David Charles 1928- *St&PR 93, WhoAm 92*
Dressler, Frederic Michael 1941- *St&PR 93*
Dressler, Gallus 1533-c. 1584 *Baker 92*
Dressler, Kurt 1929- *WhoScE 91-4, WhoWor 93*
Dressler, Marie 1869-1934 *IntDcF 2-3 [port], QDrFCA 92 [port]*
Dressler, Marshall Leonard 1934- *St&PR 93*
Dressler, Michael Barry 1950- *WhoEmL 93*
Dressler, Robert 1925- *WhoAm 92*
Dressler, Robert A. 1945- *WhoAm 92*
Dressman, Michael Rowan 1946- *WhoSSW 93*
Dressner, Howard Roy 1919- *WhoAm 92*
Dressner, Paul Robert 1955- *WhoEmL 93, WhoSSW 93*
Dressner, Robert G. *Law&B 92*
Drettner, Olof Borje 1926- *WhoScE 91-4*
Dreux, Joan Albert 1951- *WhoEmL 93*
Drevemo, Stig A. 1943- *WhoScE 91-4*
Drevemo, Stig Alfred 1943- *WhoWor 93*
Drevenkar, Vlasta 1949- *WhoScE 91-4*
Drevenstedt, Jean 1927- *WhoAmW 93*
Dreves, Guido Maria 1854-1909 *Baker 92*
Drevitson, Neil *BioIn 17*
Drew, Bernard A. 1950- *ScF&FL 92*
Drew, Charles Richard 1904-1950 *BioIn 17, EncAACR*
Drew, Clifford James 1943- *WhoAm 92*
Drew, Debra Rae 1952- *WhoAmW 93*
Drew, Derek C. 1956- *WhoWrEP 92*
Drew, Di 1948- *MiSFD 9*
Drew, Donald Allen 1945- *WhoAm 92*
Drew, Elizabeth *BioIn 17*
Drew, Elizabeth 1935- *JrnUS, WhoAm 92, WhoAmW 93*
Drew, Elizabeth Heineman 1940- *WhoAm 92*
Drew, Ellen 1915- *SweetSg D*
Drew, Ernest Harold 1937- *St&PR 93, WhoAm 92*
Drew, Fraser Bragg Robert 1913- *WhoAm 92*
Drew, George 1943- *WhoWrEP 92*
Drew, Gerald John 1939- *WhoIns 93*
Drew, Horace Rainsford, Jr. 1918- *WhoAm 92, WhoSSW 93*
Drew, James 1929- *Baker 92*
Drew, James Mulcro 1929- *WhoAm 92*
Drew, Jane Beverly 1911- *WhoWor 93*
Drew, K. *WhoAmW 93, WhoWor 93*
Drew, Katherine Fischer 1923- *WhoAm 92*
Drew, Patti 1944- *BioIn 17*
Drew, Paul 1935- *WhoAm 92, WhoWor 93*
Drew, Russell Cooper 1931- *WhoAm 92*
Drew, Stephen Richard 1949- *WhoEmL 93*
Drew, Teresa L. *Law&B 92*
Drew, Walter H. 1935- *St&PR 93*
Drew, Walter Harlow 1935- *WhoAm 92*
Drew, Wayland 1932- *ScF&FL 92*
Drew, William Arthur 1929- *WhoSSW 93*
Drew, William James *Law&B 92*
Drewe, Robert (Duncan) 1943- *ConAu 138*
Drewek, Joann F. *St&PR 93*
Drewer, Milton Lee, Jr. 1923- *WhoAm 92*
Drewery, Ida Mae Moore 1927- *WhoAmW 93*
Drewes, Charles E. 1941- *St&PR 93*
Drewes, Lester Richard 1943- *WhoAm 92*
Drewett, A. Keith 1946- *St&PR 93*
Drewniak, Michael J. 1926- *St&PR 93*
Drewnowski, Jan 1908- *WhoWor 93*
Drewry, David J. 1947- *WhoScE 91-1*
Drewry, David John 1947- *WhoWor 93*
Drewry, Guy Carleton 1901- *WhoWrEP 92*
Drewry, Guy Carleton 1901-1991 *ConLC 70*
Drews, Jurgen 1933- *WhoScE 91-4*
Drews, K.L. Gerhart 1925- *WhoScE 91-3*
Drews, Mark William 1960- *WhoEmL 93*
Drews, Paul 1934- *WhoScE 91-3*
Drewsen, Alan Charles *Law&B 92*
Drewsen, Edmond Titus, Jr. 1932- *WhoAm 92*
Drexel, Constance 1894-1956 *BioIn 17*
Drexel, Dagmar 1953- *BioIn 17*
Drexel, Max 1914- *BioIn 17*
Drexel, William R. *Law&B 92*
Drexhage, karl Heinz 1934- *WhoScE 91-3, WhoWor 93*
Drexler, Bradley Mark 1960- *WhoEmL 93*
Drexler, Clyde *BioIn 17*
Drexler, Clyde 1962- *ConBlB 4 [port], News 92 [port], WhoAm 92*
Drexler, Deborah Lynn 1957- *WhoEmL 93*
Drexler, Edwin Smith 1952- *WhoE 93*
Drexler, Fred 1915- *WhoAm 92*
Drexler, Helmut 1951- *WhoWor 93*
Drexler, Jerome 1927- *St&PR 93*
Drexler, Joanne Lee 1944- *WhoAmW 93, WhoE 93, WhoWor 93*
Drexler, K. Eric *BioIn 17*
Drexler, Kim Eric 1955- *WhoEmL 93*
Drexler, Lloyd A. 1918- *St&PR 93*
Drexler, Mark Andrew 1953- *WhoEmL 93*
Drexler, Mary Sanford 1954- *WhoAmW 93, WhoEmL 93, WhoWor 93*
Drexler, Michael David *BioIn 17*
Drexler, Michael David 1938- *WhoAm 92, WhoE 93*
Drexler, Millard S. 1944- *WhoAm 92*
Drexler, Richard Allan 1947- *St&PR 93, WhoAm 92*
Drexler, Ruth *Law&B 92*
Drey, Norman W., Jr. *Law&B 92*
Dreyer, Barbara Jean 1938- *St&PR 93*
Dreyer, Carl Theodor 1889-1968 *MiSFD 9N*
Dreyer, D.J. 1954- *St&PR 93*
Dreyer, Franklin Delano 1936- *St&PR 93*
Dreyer, James A. 1946- *St&PR 93*
Dreyer, Jerome Lee 1930- *WhoAm 92*
Dreyer, Johann Melchior 1747-1824 *Baker 92*
Dreyer, Randolph Eugene 1957- *WhoE 93*
Dreyer, Robert H. 1937- *St&PR 93*
Dreyer, Steven James 1958- *St&PR 93*
Dreyer, Terence D. *Law&B 92*
Dreyer, Wolfgang E. 1920- *WhoScE 91-3*
Dreyfus, Alfred 1859-1935 *BioIn 17, HarEnMi*
Dreyfus, Alfred Stanley 1921- *WhoAm 92*
Dreyfus, Donald *Law&B 92*
Dreyfus, George 1928- *Baker 92*
Dreyfus, George Joseph 1920- *WhoAm 92*
Dreyfus, Howard Marlow 1942- *WhoIns 93*
Dreyfus, Marc George 1926- *WhoE 93*
Dreyfus, Pierre 1907- *BioIn 17*
Dreyfus, Richard B. *Law&B 92*
Dreyfus, Richard Baeck 1958- *WhoEmL 93*
Dreyfus, Robert Louis- *BioIn 17*
Dreyfuss, Ernst 1910?-1976? *ScF&FL 92*
Dreyfuss, Jeramie *BioIn 17*
Dreyfuss, John Alan 1933- *WhoAm 92*
Dreyfuss, Lawrence J. *Law&B 92*
Dreyfuss, Nancy Matis 1954- *WhoAm 92, WhoAmW 93*
Dreyfuss, Norman *St&PR 93*
Dreyfuss, Richard 1947- *BioIn 17, HolBB [port], IntDcF 2-3 [port]*
Dreyfuss, Richard Stephan 1947- *WhoAm 92*
Dreyling, Robert H. 1943- *WhoE 93*
Dreyschock, Alexander 1818-1869 *Baker 92*
Dreyschock, Felix 1860-1906 *Baker 92*
Dreyschock, Raimund 1824-1869 *Baker 92*
Dreyspool, Anthony Alan *Law&B 92*
Dreyzehner, John Joseph 1963- *WhoSSW 93*
Drezdzon, William Lawrence 1934- *WhoWor 93*
Drezner, Stephen M. 1937- *St&PR 93, WhoAm 92*
Dreznes, John Joseph *St&PR 93*
Driberg, Jack Herbert 1888-1946 *IntDcAn*
Driberg, Tom 1905-1976 *BioIn 17*
Drickamer, Harry George 1918- *BioIn 17, WhoAm 92*
Drickey, Steven L. *Law&B 92*
Driebe, Edward K. 1916- *St&PR 93*
Driebe, Mary R. 1921- *St&PR 93*
Driebeek, Patrick *Law&B 92*
Drieberg, Denver Chris 1955- *WhoEmL 93*
Drieberg, Friedrich von 1780-1856 *Baker 92*
Drieberg, Keith Lambert 1952- *WhoEmL 93*
Driedger, Florence Gay 1933- *WhoAm 92*
Driedonks, Ad.G.M. 1947- *WhoScE 91-3*
Driegert, Robert S. 1942- *St&PR 93*
Driehaus, Robert J. 1928- *St&PR 93, WhoIns 93*

Driehuys, Leonardus Bastiaan 1932- *WhoAm 92*
Drielsma, Willem Frans Carel 1919- *WhoE 93*
Dries, Alice Emerita 1920- *WhoSSW 93*
Dries, Kathleen Marie 1946- *WhoAmW 93*
Driese, Edward Clark 1933- *St&PR 93*
Driessel, A. Berkley 1937- *WhoWrEP 92*
Driessen, Klaus Werner 1948- *WhoSSW 93*
Driessens, Ferdinand C.M. 1937- *WhoScE 91-3*
Driessler, Johannes 1921- *Baker 92*
Drieu La Rochelle, Pierre 1893-1945 *BioIn 17*
Driffill, Edward John *WhoScE 91-1*
Drifte, Reinhard *WhoScE 91-1*
Drifters *SoulM*
Driftmier, Richard Prentice 1948- *WhoEmL 93*
Driggers, Sharon Rowlett 1946- *WhoSSW 93*
Driggers, Stephen A. 1922- *St&PR 93*
Driggs, Allan F. 1951- *St&PR 93*
Driggs, Charles Mulford 1924- *WhoAm 92*
Driggs, David M. 1953- *WhoEmL 93*
Driggs, Elsie 1895-1992 *NewYTBS 92*
Driggs, Gary H. 1934- *St&PR 93*
Driggs, Margaret 1909- *WhoWor 93*
Drigo, Riccardo 1846-1930 *Baker 92*
Driker, Eugene 1937- *WhoAm 92*
Driks, Jordan J. *Law&B 92*
Drilleau, Jean-Francois *WhoScE 91-2*
Driller, Henry Charles 1956- *WhoSSW 93*
Drillich, Lisa G. *Law&B 92*
Drillman, Paula *WhoAm 92, WhoAmW 93*
Drimmer, Frederick *BioIn 17*
Drimmer, Melvin 1934- *WhoAm 92*
Drimys *OxDcByz*
Drinan, Robert F. *BioIn 17*
Drinan, Robert Frederick 1920- *WhoAm 92, WhoE 93*
Drinan, Ronald J. *Law&B 92*
Dring, Lorri Ann 1959- *WhoAmW 93*
Dring, Madeleine 1923-1977 *Baker 92*
Drings, Peter H.W. 1939- *WhoWor 93*
Drinkard, Lawrence W. 1939- *St&PR 93*
Drinkard, Michael *BioIn 17*
Drinker, Elizabeth Sandwith 1735?-1807 *BioIn 17*
Drinker, Henry S(andwith, Jr.) 1880-1965 *Baker 92*
Drinker, Sophie (Lewis) 1888-1967 *See* Drinker, Henry S(andwith, Jr.) 1880-1965 *Baker 92*
Drinko, John *Law&B 92*
Drinko, John Deaver 1921- *WhoAm 92, WhoWor 93*
Drinkwaard, Abraham C. 1926- *WhoScE 91-3*
Drinkward, Cecil William 1927- *St&PR 93*
Drinkwater, Herbert R. *WhoAm 92*
Drinkwater, J.M. 1945- *St&PR 93*
Drinkwater, Terrell C. 1908-1985 *EncABHB 8 [port]*
Drinkwine, Edward Allen 1946- *WhoEmL 93*
Drinnan, Alan John 1932- *WhoAm 92*
Drinnon, Doris Jean 1930- *WhoWrEP 92*
Drinnon, Elizabeth McCants 1925- *WhoWrEP 92*
Drinnon, Richard 1925- *WhoAm 92*
Dripchak, David Alan 1955- *WhoE 93*
Driscoll, Brigid *WhoAmW 93*
Driscoll, Christianne 1952- *WhoWor 93*
Driscoll, Clara 1881-1945 *AmWomPl*
Driscoll, Constance Fitzgerald 1926- *WhoAmW 93, WhoE 93*
Driscoll, Edward Carroll 1929- *WhoAm 92*
Driscoll, Edward Carroll, Jr. 1952- *St&PR 93*
Driscoll, Garrett Bates 1932- *WhoSSW 93*
Driscoll, Gary Graham *Law&B 92*
Driscoll, Genevieve Bosson 1937- *WhoAmW 93*
Driscoll, Gertrude Porter 1898- *AmWomPl*
Driscoll, Glen Robert 1920- *WhoAm 92*
Driscoll, Jack 1946- *WhoWrEP 92*
Driscoll, James G. 1932- *St&PR 93*
Driscoll, James Michael 1939- *WhoAm 92*
Driscoll, Jeanne Marie 1956- *WhoEmL 93*
Driscoll, Jeanne Watson 1949- *WhoEmL 93*
Driscoll, John Brian 1946- *WhoAm 92*
Driscoll, John Gerard 1933- *WhoE 93*
Driscoll, John H. d1990 *BioIn 17*
Driscoll, John Patrick 1935- *St&PR 93*
Driscoll, John R. 1950- *St&PR 93*
Driscoll, John S. 1934- *WhoAm 92, WhoE 93*
Driscoll, Katherine E. *Law&B 92*
Driscoll, Kelly Q. *Law&B 92*
Driscoll, Kimberlee M. *Law&B 92*
Driscoll, Lee F., Jr. 1926- *St&PR 93*
Driscoll, Lee Francis, Jr. 1926- *WhoAm 92*
Driscoll, Linda 1959- *St&PR 93*
Driscoll, Louise 1875- *AmWomPl*
Driscoll, Marjorie *AmWomPl*
Driscoll, Mary Harris 1928- *WhoWrEP 92*
Driscoll, Michael D. *Law&B 92*
Driscoll, Paddy 1896-1968 *BioIn 17*
Driscoll, Patricia Anne 1955- *WhoEmL 93*
Driscoll, Richard K. 1922- *St&PR 93*
Driscoll, Richard Michael Christopher *WhoScE 91-1*
Driscoll, Robert *Law&B 92*
Driscoll, Robert Eugene 1949- *WhoAm 92, WhoE 93, WhoEmL 93*
Driscoll, Robert S. 1947- *St&PR 93*
Driscoll, Thomas F. 1925- *St&PR 93*
Driscoll, Thomas J. *Law&B 92*
Driscoll, William B. 1926- *St&PR 93*
Driscoll, William Michael 1929- *WhoAm 92*
Driskill, John R. 1934- *WhoIns 93*
Driskill, John Ray 1934- *WhoAm 92*
Driskill, Kevin 1957- *WhoSSW 93*
Drisko, Elliot Hillman 1917- *WhoAm 92*
Driss, Nour Eddine 1945- *WhoUN 92*
Drissell, Norman Earl 1928- *WhoAm 92*
Dritsas, George Vassilios 1940- *WhoWor 93*
Driveness, Glen A. *Law&B 92*
Driver, Bev *BioIn 17*
Driver, C. Stephen 1936- *WhoE 93*
Driver, Elwood T. d1992 *NewYTBS 92*
Driver, Elwood T. 1921-1992 *BioIn 17*
Driver, Elwood Thomas 1921- *WhoE 93*
Driver, Frank L., III 1930- *St&PR 93*
Driver, Glenda Jewel 1951- *WhoEmL 93*
Driver, Harold E. 1907- *IntDcAn*
Driver, Joe L. 1946- *WhoEmL 93*
Driver, John *ScF&FL 92*
Driver, Lottie Elizabeth 1918- *WhoAm 92*
Driver, Richard Ellis, Jr. 1926- *WhoE 93*
Driver, Robert Baylor, Jr. 1942- *WhoAm 92*
Driver, Rodney David 1932- *WhoE 93, WhoWor 93*
Driver, Sara 1956- *MiSFD 9*
Driver, Sharon Humphreys 1949- *WhoAmW 93, WhoE 93, WhoEmL 93*
Driver, Spruell, Jr. *Law&B 92*
Driver, Tom Faw 1925- *WhoAm 92*
Driver, William Raymond, Jr. 1907- *St&PR 93, WhoAm 92*
Dr. Mcloughlin *DcAmChF 1960*
Drnovsek, Janez 1950- *WhoWor 93*
Drobashevsky, Vladimir 1929- *WhoE 93*
Drobile, James Albert 1927- *WhoAm 92*
Drobinski, Roger J. 1951- *WhoIns 93*
Drobis, David R. *WhoAm 92*
Drobisch, Moritz Wilhelm 1802-1896 *Baker 92*
Drobner, Ann Rose 1963- *WhoAmW 93*
Drobner, Boleslaw 1883-1968 *PolBiDi*
Drobnick, Jack Anthony 1940- *St&PR 93*
Drobnjak, Djordje 1934- *WhoScE 91-4*
Drobnjak, Predrag 1924- *WhoScE 91-4*
Drobny, Dennis P. 1945- *WhoSSW 93*
Drobny, Josef 1938- *WhoScE 91-4*
Drobotukhina, Julia Vladimirovna 1966- *WhoWor 93*
Droege, Arthur J. 1948- *St&PR 93*
Droege, John D.L. 1933- *St&PR 93*
Droege, Marie Therese 1961- *WhoEmL 93*
Droege, Peter Friedrich Valentin 1952- *WhoE 93*
Droegemueller, William 1934- *WhoAm 92*
Droeger, William H. d1991 *BioIn 17*
Droegkamp, Janis Mildred 1946- *WhoEmL 93*
Droegmueller, Lee *WhoAm 92*
Droescher, Michael Johannes 1949- *WhoWor 93*
Droeshout, Martin 1601-c. 1650 *BioIn 17*
Drogalis, Robert Michael 1960- *St&PR 93*
Droge, Wulf 1939- *WhoScE 91-3*
Drogendijk, A.C. 1932- *WhoScE 91-3*
Drogin, Marsha *BioIn 17*
Droguett, Carlos 1912- *SpAmA*
Drohan, Thomas H. 1936- *WhoAm 92*
Drohan, William Michael 1954- *WhoEmL 93*
Droitcour, Howard 1908- *St&PR 93*
Droke, Rose Mary 1935- *WhoSSW 93*
Drolet, Robert *Law&B 92*
Droll, Helen Marie 1940- *WhoSSW 93*
Droll, Marian Clarke 1931- *WhoAm 92*
Droll, Ronald William 1950- *WhoEmL 93*
Droller, Deborah S. *Law&B 92*
Drollet, Dag *BioIn 17*
Drollinger, John, Jr. 1924- *St&PR 93*
Drollinger, John M. 1946- *WhoEmL 93*
Drollinger, Lisabeth Marie 1963- *WhoAmW 93*
Drombetta, Larry *St&PR 93*
Dromer, Jean Philippe 1929- *WhoWor 93*
Droms, William George 1944- *WhoAm 92, WhoE 93, WhoWor 93*
Dronamraju, Satya Narayana 1933- *WhoAsAP 91*
Dronke, Ernst 1822-1891 *BioIn 17*
Drood, Eugene E. 1929- *St&PR 93*
Drook, Gary G. 1945- *St&PR 93*
Drootin, Ivan 1947- *St&PR 93*
Dropkin, Robert F. 1941- *St&PR 93*
Droppleman, John Joseph *Law&B 92*
Dropsy, Gerard E. 1927- *WhoScE 91-2*
Drosche, Richard Rydell 1952- *WhoSSW 93*
Droschler, Eve *BioIn 17*
Drosdick, Claire K. *Law&B 92*
Drosdick, John G. 1943- *St&PR 93*
Drosdoff, Daniel Aaron 1941- *WhoAm 92*
Drosopoulos, Sakis 1944- *WhoScE 91-3*
Dross, Cornelius William 1915- *WhoSSW 93*
Dross, Karl P. 1933- *WhoScE 91-3*
Drossman, Douglas Arnold 1946- *WhoSSW 93*
Drossman, Jay Lewis 1932- *WhoE 93*
Drost, Cristina Llorente 1934- *WhoAmW 93*
Drost, Marianne 1950- *St&PR 93, WhoAm 92, WhoAmW 93, WhoEmL 93*
Droste, Donald Casper *Law&B 92*
Droste, Flip Gerrit 1928- *WhoWor 93*
Droste, Jean Rasmusen 1941- *WhoAmW 93*
Droste, Keith Joseph 1933- *St&PR 93*
Droste, Manfred F. 1956- *WhoWor 93*
Drost-Hansen, Walter 1925- *WhoSSW 93*
Drotar, Blase Thomas, Jr. 1959- *WhoE 93*
Drotar, Paul Peter 1946- *St&PR 93*
Drotning, John Evan 1932- *WhoAm 92*
Drotos, Patrick Volker 1954- *WhoWor 93*
Drouet, Gilbert F. 1932- *WhoScE 91-4*
Drouet, Louis Francois-Philippe 1792-1873 *Baker 92*
Drouet d'Erlon, Jean Baptiste 1765-1844 *HarEnMi*
Drought, Brian Dennis 1943- *St&PR 93*
Drouilh, Suzanne 1932- *WhoUN 92*
Drouilhet, Paul Raymond, Jr. 1933- *WhoAm 92*
Drouillard, Jerome Raphael *Law&B 92*
Drouin, Marie Josee *BioIn 17*
Droukas, Ann Hantis 1923- *WhoAmW 93*
Droullard, Steven Maurice 1951- *WhoEmL 93*
Drown, Merle 1943- *WhoWrEP 92*
Drowota, Frank F., III 1938- *WhoSSW 93*
Droz, Bernard 1930- *WhoScE 91-4*
Droz, Henry 1926- *WhoAm 92*
Droz, Kenneth Mark 1957- *WhoEmL 93*
Drozd, Andrew Peter 1947- *WhoEmL 93*
Drozd, Leon F. *Law&B 92*
Drozd, Yuri Anatolyevich 1944- *WhoWor 93*
Drozda, Helen Dorothy 1924- *WhoAm 92*
Drozdis, Marie Trese 1939- *WhoAmW 93*
Drozdov, Anatol 1883-1950 *Baker 92*
Drozdov, Mark 1963- *WhoEmL 93*
Drozdov, Vladimir 1882-1960 *See* Drozdov, Anatol 1883-1950 *Baker 92*
Drozdowicz, Carol Elaine 1933- *WhoSSW 93*
Drozdowski, Bronislaw 1928- *WhoScE 91-4*
Drozdowski, Jan 1857-1918 *Baker 92*
Drozdowski, Stanley Michael 1938- *St&PR 93*
Drozdziel, Marion John 1924- *WhoE 93*
Drozeski, Leo Cornelius, Jr. 1940- *St&PR 93*
Dr. Seuss *BioIn 17, MajAI*
Dru, Joanne 1923- *SweetSg D [port]*
Drubel, James Michel 1931- *St&PR 93*
Druce, Howard Martin 1953- *WhoEmL 93*
Druck, James Burton 1941- *WhoAm 92*
Druck, Kalman Breschel 1914- *WhoAm 92, WhoSSW 93*
Druck, Marilyn A. *Law&B 92*
Druck, Mark *WhoAm 92*
Drucker, Andrea Holtzman *Law&B 92*
Drucker, Daniel Charles 1918- *WhoAm 92, WhoSSW 93*
Drucker, Deborah Ferdman 1952- *WhoAmW 93*
Drucker, Jacquelin F. *WhoAmW 93*
Drucker, Jakob Richard 1946- *WhoE 93, WhoEmL 93*
Drucker, Joseph 1922- *St&PR 93*
Drucker, Kenneth A. 1945- *St&PR 93*
Drucker, Kenneth Glenn 1962- *St&PR 93*
Drucker, Melvin Bruce 1927- *WhoSSW 93*
Drucker, Mindy M. 1957- *WhoAmW 93*
Drucker, Mort 1929- *WhoAm 92, WhoE 93*
Drucker, Myra R. 1948- *WhoAm 92*
Drucker, Nathan J. 1949- *St&PR 93*
Drucker, Norman 1938- *St&PR 93*
Drucker, Peter F. 1909- *News 92 [port], -92-3 [port]*
Drucker, Peter Ferdinand 1909- *BioIn 17, WhoAm 92, WhoWor 93*
Drucker, Philip 1911-1982 *IntDcAn*
Drucker, Ronald Walter 1941- *WhoAm 92*
Drucker, William Richard 1922- *WhoAm 92*
Druckman, Jacob (Raphael) 1928- *Baker 92, WhoAm 92*
Druckman, Margaret Smith 1937- *WhoAmW 93*
Druckman, Nancy *BioIn 17*
Drudge, Junior Harold 1922- *WhoAm 92*
Drudi, John Louis 1935- *WhoWor 93*
Drudy, Patrick 1943- *WhoAm 92*
Drueke, Tilman *WhoScE 91-2*
Druen, W. Sidney *Law&B 92*
Druen, W. Sidney 1942- *St&PR 93*
Druen, William Sidney 1942- *WhoAm 92*
Druesedow, Jean Ruth Lawrence 1942- *WhoAm 92*
Druet, Cheslav 1926- *WhoScE 91-4*
Druet, Philippe *WhoScE 91-2*
Drugan, Cornelius Bernard 1946- *WhoEmL 93*
Druick, Douglas Wesley 1945- *WhoAm 92*
Druker, Henry Leo 1953- *WhoAm 92, WhoE 93*
Druker, Scott Douglas 1955- *WhoEmL 93*
Drukker, Austin C. 1934- *St&PR 93*
Drukker, Jan 1936- *WhoScE 91-3*
Drulard, Frederick F. 1940- *St&PR 93*
Drum, Alice 1935- *WhoAmW 93, WhoE 93*
Drum, Jack D. *Law&B 92*
Drum, Joan Marie McFarland 1932- *WhoAmW 93*
Drum, Joan Mc Farland 1932- *WhoWrEP 92*
Drumetz, Michel Jean Camille 1928- *WhoWor 93*
Drumheller, Dan Parkes 1948- *St&PR 93*
Drumheller, George Jesse 1933- *WhoWor 93*
Drumheller, Linda Beth 1947- *WhoEmL 93*
Drumheller, Philip M. 1953- *St&PR 93*
Drumheller, Ronald L. *Law&B 92*
Drumm, Chris 1949- *ScF&FL 92, WhoWrEP 92*
Drumm, D.B. *ScF&FL 92*
Drumm, Gregory William 1965- *WhoE 93*
Drumm, Philip Russell 1932- *WhoWor 93*
Drumm, Raymond F. 1933- *St&PR 93*
Drummer, Donald Raymond 1941- *St&PR 93, WhoAm 92*
Drummer, Dorothy Jean 1949- *WhoEmL 93*
Drummer, Larry *BioIn 17*
Drummond, C. Shireen *Law&B 92*
Drummond, Carol Cramer 1933- *WhoAmW 93, WhoWor 93*
Drummond, David Joseph 1957- *WhoEmL 93*
Drummond, Doris Wiggins 1938- *WhoAm 92*
Drummond, Frank G. d1991 *BioIn 17*
Drummond, Gerard K. 1937- *St&PR 93*
Drummond, Gerard Kasper 1937- *WhoAm 92*
Drummond, James Everman 1932- *WhoAm 92*
Drummond, James Henry 1946- *WhoEmL 93*
Drummond, Jeffrey N. *Law&B 92*
Drummond, Joanne 1962- *WhoAmW 93*
Drummond, John A. 1929- *WhoAm 92*
Drummond, Marshall Edward 1941- *WhoAm 92*
Drummond, Michael *BioIn 17*
Drummond, Pamela Johnson 1946- *WhoEmL 93, WhoSSW 93*
Drummond, Robert Kendig 1939- *WhoAm 92*
Drummond, Sally Hazelet 1924- *WhoAm 92*
Drummond, Walter *MajAI*
Drummond, William Henry 1854-1907 *BioIn 17*
Drummond, Winslow 1933- *WhoAm 92*
Drummond of Hawthornden, William 1585-1649 *DcLB 121 [port]*
Drumont, Edouard Adolphe 1844-1917 *BioIn 17*
Drumright, Donald A. *Law&B 92*
Drungole, Paula Elaine 1963- *WhoEmL 93*
Druon, Maurice 1918- *ScF&FL 92*
Drupka, S. *WhoScE 91-4*
Drury, Allen 1918- *JrnUS, ScF&FL 92*
Drury, Allen Stuart 1918- *WhoAm 92, WhoWrEP 92*
Drury, Amber *BioIn 17*
Drury, Daniel Patrick 1936- *St&PR 93*
Drury, David *MiSFD 9*
Drury, David J. 1944- *WhoIns 93*
Drury, Edward A. *Law&B 92*
Drury, Edward Anthony 1953- *St&PR 93*
Drury, Finvola d1991 *BioIn 17*
Drury, Francis T. 1947- *St&PR 93*
Drury, James 1934- *BioIn 17*
Drury, James Colin *WhoScE 91-1*

Drury, John E. 1944- WhoAm 92, WhoSSW 93
Drury, L. Wayne 1951- St&PR 93
Drury, Leon Arthur, III 1944- WhoE 93
Drury, Leonard Leroy 1928- WhoAm 92
Drury, Luke O'Connor 1953- WhoScE 91-3
Drury, Lynn Easley 1958- WhoAmW 93
Drury, Michael Ivo 1920- WhoScE 91-3
Drury, Regina Rose 1951- WhoEmL 93
Drury, Richard B. 1949- St&PR 93
Drury, Roger W(olcott) 1914- DcAmChF 1960
Drury, Sally 1960- ConAu 139
Drury, Stephen 1955- Baker 92
Drury, Susanne Schroeder 1942- WhoAmW 93
Drury, Walter Lee 1934- St&PR 93
Drury, William Holland d1992 NewYTBS 92
Drury, William Holland 1921-1992 BioIn 17
Drury Gane, Margaret 1926- WhoCanL 92
Drusin, Lewis Martin 1939- WhoE 93
Druss, Joseph George d1992 NewYTBS 92
Drusus, Nero Claudius 38BC-9BC HarEnMi
Drutz, David Jules 1938- WhoE 93
Druvenga, Gordon Dale 1956- WhoEmL 93
Druxman, Michael Barnett 1941- ConAu 37NR
Drvota, Mojmir 1923- WhoAm 92
Dry, Frank Thomas WhoScE 91-1
Dry, Morris E. 1896-1990 BioIn 17
Dryburgh, Bruce Sinclair 1943- St&PR 93, WhoAm 92
Dryden, Charles 1860-1931 BiDAMSp 1989
Dryden, David Charles 1947- WhoWor 93
Dryden, Ernst 1883?-1938 BioIn 17
Dryden, John 1631-1700 BioIn 17, DramC 3 [port], LitC 21 [port], MagSWL [port], OxDcOp, WorLitC [port]
Dryden, Martin Francis, Jr. 1915- WhoAm 92
Dryden, Martin Glen 1944- WhoSSW 93
Dryden, Mary Elizabeth 1949- WhoAmW 93
Dryden, Phillis Kay Law&B 92
Dryden, Phyllis Kay 1947- St&PR 93, WhoAm 92
Dryden, Robert Charles 1936- St&PR 93, WhoAm 92
Dryden, Robert Edward Law&B 92
Dryden, Robert Eugene 1927- WhoAm 92
Dryden, Robert L. 1933- St&PR 93
Dryden, Robert R. Law&B 92
Drye, Richard Arthur, Jr. 1950- WhoEmL 93, WhoSSW 93
Drye, William James 1939- WhoE 93
Dryer, Douglas Poole 1915- WhoAm 92, WhoWrEP 92
Dryer, Fred 1946- BioIn 17
Dryer, Mark Law&B 92
Dryer, Moira d1992 NewYTBS 92
Dryer, Moira 1957-1992 BioIn 17
Dryer, Moira Jane 1957- WhoE 93
Dryer, Murray 1925- WhoAm 92
Dryer, Stephen J. 1942- St&PR 93
Dryfoos, Donald d1992 NewYTBS 92
Dryfoos, Nancy 1918-1991 BioIn 17
Dryfoos, Nancy Proskauer WhoAm 92
Drygas, Hilmar Gerhard 1937- WhoWor 93
Drygulski, John Stanley 1949- WhoE 93
Dryhurst, Glenn 1939- WhoAm 92
Dryja-Swierski, Karen Ann 1954- WhoE 93
Drykerman, Dan 1948- St&PR 93
Drykos, William Ronald 1939- St&PR 93
Drylie, Christine Marie 1966- WhoAmW 93
Drymalski, Raymond Hibner 1936- WhoAm 92
Drynan, Margaret Isobel 1915- WhoAmW 93
Dryovage, Mary Margaret 1954- WhoEmL 93
Drysdale, Donald Scott 1936- WhoAm 92
Drysdale, (George John) Learmont 1866-1909 Baker 92
Drysdale, Lee MiSFD 9
Drysdale, Russell 1912-1981 BioIn 17
Drzewiecki, Stefan 1844-1938 PolBiDi
Drzewiecki, Tadeusz Maria 1943- WhoAm 92
Drzewiecki, Zbigniew 1890-1971 Baker 92
Drzymala, Jan 1949- WhoScE 91-4
Drzymala, Zygmunt 1936- WhoScE 91-4
Drzymalski, Elizabeth Anne Hooper 1960- WhoAmW 93
D'Sa-Correia, Ivy Janet 1966- WhoAmW 93
Dsika, E.L., Jr. 1946- St&PR 93
D'Souza, Anthony Frank 1929- WhoAm 92
D'Spain, Suzanne Lancaster 1947- WhoSSW 93
Du, Gonghuan 1934- WhoWor 93
Du, Honghua 1962- WhoE 93
Du, Julie Yi-Fang Tsai 1937- WhoAm 92
Du, Xingyuan 1931- WhoUN 92
Du, Ying Tzyong 1947- St&PR 93
Dua, Patrick 1949- WhoWor 93
Du Aime, Albert ScF&FL 92
Duall, John William 1928- St&PR 93, WhoAm 92
Duan, Haibao 1956- WhoWor 93
Duan, Kui-Chen 1934- WhoWor 93
Duane, Daniel Joseph 1946- St&PR 93
Duane, Diane 1952- ScF&FL 92
Duane, Diane (Elizabeth) 1952- ConAu 139, DcAmChF 1985
Duane, Jean Marie 1957- WhoAmW 93
Duane, Joseph M. Law&B 92
Duane, Morris d1992 NewYTBS 92
Duane, Robert Edward 1928- St&PR 93
Duane, Thomas David 1917- WhoAm 92
Duane, William 1760-1835 JrnUS
Duangploy, Orapin 1946- WhoEmL 93, WhoSSW 93
Duangwisuthi, Surasak 1949- WhoWor 93
Duarte, Armando da Costa 1952- WhoScE 91-3
Duarte, Cristobal G. 1929- WhoWor 93
Duarte, Elvino Dias 1933- WhoScE 91-3
Duarte, Frank 1965- WhoE 93
Duarte (Fuentes), Jose Napoleon 1925-1990 ConAu 137
Duarte, Jose Napoleon BioIn 17
Duarte, Jose Napoleon 1926-1990 DcCPCAm
Duarte, Patricia 1938- WhoAmW 93, WhoE 93
Duarte, Ramon Gonzalez 1948- WhoWor 93
Duarte, Roberto Jose 1938- WhoSSW 93
Duarte-Ramos, Herminio 1936- WhoScE 91-3
Duato, Jose Francisco 1958- WhoWor 93
Duatti, Adriano 1952- WhoScE 91-3
Duax, William Leo 1939- WhoAm 92, WhoE 93
Dub, Anthony V. 1949- St&PR 93, WhoAm 92
Duba, Roger Ernest 1938- St&PR 93
Duback, Steven Rahr 1944- St&PR 93, WhoAm 92
Dubai, Matthew Michael 1953- WhoE 93
Du Bain, Myron 1923- WhoAm 92
Dubanevich, Arlene 1950- ConAu 40NR
Dubanevich, Keith Scott 1957- WhoEmL 93
Du Bar, Jules Ramon 1923- WhoAm 92
Dubas, Lynda Ann 1951- WhoAmW 93
Dubas, Pierre 1924- WhoScE 91-4
Dubay, Christopher F. Law&B 92
DuBay, Daniel Joseph Alexander 1949- WhoEmL 93
Dubay, Eugene N. 1948- St&PR 93
Dubay, Roger L. Law&B 92
DuBay, Sandra 1954- ScF&FL 92
Dubay, Stephen Newton 1941- WhoSSW 93
Dubbelday, Pieter Steven 1928- WhoSSW 93
Dubberly, Ronald Alvah 1942- WhoAm 92, WhoSSW 93
Dubbers, Dietrich Jochen 1943- WhoWor 93
Dubbert, Patricia Marie 1947- WhoAm 92, WhoEmL 93
Dubbey, John Michael 1934- WhoWor 93
Dubbins, Don 1929-1991 BioIn 17
Dubble, Curtis William 1922- WhoAm 92
Dubble, Roger L. 1937- St&PR 93
Dubbs, Chris ScF&FL 92
Dubbs, Robert Morton 1943- St&PR 93, WhoAm 92
Dubcek, Aleksander 1921-1992 ColdWar 2 [port]
Dubcek, Alexander BioIn 17
Dubcek, Alexander 1921- DcTwHis, WhoWor 93
Dubcek, Alexander 1921-1992 NewYTBS 92 [port]
Dube, Daniel 1908- St&PR 93
Dube, James L. 1949- St&PR 93
Dube, Lawrence Edward, Jr. 1948- WhoEmL 93
Dube, Louise-Martin Law&B 92
Dube, Marcel 1930- BioIn 17, WhoCanL 92
Dube, Miriam St&PR 93
Dube, Noreen Mary 1941- WhoE 93, WhoWor 93
Dube, Oscar 1940- St&PR 93
Dube, Peter 1958- St&PR 93
Dube, Rajesh 1952- WhoE 93
Dube, Richard Lawrence 1950- WhoE 93
Dube, Robert Donald 1941- St&PR 93
Dube, Thomas Msebe 1938- WhoUN 92
Dubeau, Robert C. 1934- St&PR 93
Dubedout, Hubert 1922-1986 BioIn 17
Dubelaar, Thea 1947- BioIn 17
Dubensky, Arcady 1890-1966 Baker 92
Duberg, John Edward 1917- WhoAm 92, WhoSSW 93, WhoWor 93
DuBerger, J. Law&B 92
Duberman, Lewis Donald 1940- St&PR 93
Duberman, Martin B. BioIn 17
Duberstein, Aaron D. d1991 BioIn 17
Duberstein, Barbara Fern 1958- St&PR 93
Duberstein, Helen Laura 1926- WhoWrEP 92
Dubertret, Louis WhoScE 91-2
Dubes, George Richard 1926- WhoAm 92
Dubes, Michael J. 1942- St&PR 93, WhoAm 92
Dubes, Richard Charles 1934- WhoAm 92
Dubester, Michael Steven 1947- St&PR 93
Dubester, Robert Gary 1951- St&PR 93
Dubey, Bindeshwari 1921- WhoAsAP 91
Dubey, Jitender Prakash 1938- WhoAm 92
Dubey, Satya Deva 1930- WhoAm 92, WhoE 93, WhoWor 93
Dubey, Stephen Arthur 1947- WhoEmL 93
Dubi, Leonard A. BioIn 17
Dubie, Norman 1945- BioIn 17
Dubie, Norman (Evans) 1945- DcLB 120 [port]
Dubief, Jean 1903- WhoWor 93
Dubiel, Thomas Wieslaw 1929- WhoWor 93
Du Biez, Oudard d1551 BioIn 17
Dubigeon, Serge 1941- WhoScE 91-2
Dubilier, Martin H. BioIn 17
Dubin, Alan 1954- WhoE 93
Dubin, Alvin 1950- WhoAm 92
Dubin, Anne BioIn 17
Dubin, Arthur Detmers 1923- WhoAm 92
Dubin, Charles Leonard 1921- WhoAm 92, WhoE 93
Dubin, Charles S. 1919- MiSFD 9
Dubin, E. Beverly 1945- WhoWor 93
Dubin, Ellen Fenton 1953- WhoAmW 93, WhoEmL 93, WhoWor 93
Dubin, Howard Victor 1938- WhoAm 92
Dubin, James Michael 1946- WhoAm 92
Dubin, Jay MiSFD 9
Dubin, Joseph William 1948- WhoE 93, WhoEmL 93, WhoWor 93
Dubin, Leonard 1934- WhoAm 92
Dubin, Mark William 1942- WhoAm 92
Dubin, Martin David 1927- WhoAm 92
Dubin, Mel 1923- St&PR 93
Dubin, Michael 1943- WhoAm 92, WhoE 93, WhoWor 93
Dubin, Michael J. 1938- ConAu 137
Dubin, Morton Donald 1931- WhoAm 92
Dubin, Norman Harold 1942- WhoE 93
Dubin, Seth Harris 1933- WhoAm 92
Dubin, Stephen V. Law&B 92
Dubin, Stephen V. 1938- St&PR 93
Dubina, Joel Fredrick 1947- WhoAm 92, WhoSSW 93
Dubinin, Nikolai Petrovich 1907- WhoWor 93
Dubinski, Gerald Z., Sr. 1928- St&PR 93
Dubinskii, Anatolii Valentinovich 1948- WhoWor 93
Dubinskii, Rostislav BioIn 17
Dubinsky, John P. 1943- St&PR 93
Dubis, Charles Stanley 1948- WhoEmL 93
Dublanc, Jean Marc 1954- St&PR 93
Duble, Ethel Mokhiber 1956- WhoEmL 93
Duble, Harold G. 1938- WhoIns 93
Duble, Harold Grover 1938- St&PR 93
Dublin, Elvie Wilson 1937- WhoAmW 93
Dublin, Frederick Raymond 1945- WhoE 93
Dublin, Louis Israel 1882-1969 BioIn 17
Dublin, Thomas David 1912- WhoAm 92
Dubner, Anne Louise 1954- WhoSSW 93
Dubner, Ronald 1934- WhoAm 92
Dubnick, Bernard 1928- WhoAm 92
Dubnov, Simon 1860-1941 BioIn 17
Dubnov, William Lyle 1951- WhoE 93
Dubnow, Simon 1860-1941 BioIn 17
Duboff, Robert Samuel 1948- WhoAm 92, WhoEmL 93
Duboff, Samuel J. Law&B 92
Dubofsky, Melvyn 1934- ConAu 37NR
Dubois, Alain 1955- WhoE 93, WhoEmL 93, WhoWor 93
DuBois, Alan Beekman 1935- WhoAm 92
DuBois, Arthur Brooks 1923- WhoAm 92, WhoE 93, WhoWor 93
Du Bois, Barbara Rattray 1926- WhoWrEP 92
Dubois, Bernard 1935- WhoScE 91-2
Dubois, Bernard Claude 1947- St&PR 93
Dubois, Christine 1956- WhoWrEP 92
DuBois, Cora 1903-1991 IntDcAn
Du Bois, Cora Alice 1903-1991 BioIn 17
Dubois, D. ScF&FL 92
Dubois, Duane R. Law&B 92
Dubois, Duane R. 1934- WhoIns 93
Du Bois, E. WhoScE 91-1
DuBois, Ellen Carol 1947- ConAu 136
Dubois, Eugene 1858-1940 IntDcAn
DuBois, Gaylord 1899- ScF&FL 92
DuBois, Gazell Macy 1929- WhoWor 93
Dubois, George E. 1951- St&PR 93
DuBois, Howard J. 1936- St&PR 93
Dubois, J.P. 1949- WhoScE 91-2
Dubois, Jacques E. 1921- St&PR 93
Dubois, Jacques E., Jr. 1949- St&PR 93
Dubois, Jacques O.J. 1931- WhoScE 91-2
DuBois, Jan Ely 1931- WhoAm 92, WhoE 93
Dubois, Jean-Antoine 1766-1848 IntDcAn
DuBois, Jean Gabriel 1926- WhoWor 93
Dubois, Jean-Marie 1950- WhoWor 93
Dubois, Joseph A. 1936- WhoScE 91-2
Dubois, Leon 1859-1935 Baker 92
DuBois, Louis H. 1930- St&PR 93
DuBois, Mark Benjamin 1955- WhoEmL 93
DuBois, Michel Marie 1943- WhoWor 93
Dubois, Pascalc Helene Law&B 92
Dubois, Paul 1934- WhoScE 91-2
Du Bois, Paul Zinkhan 1936- WhoAm 92
Du Bois, Philip Hunter 1903- WhoAm 92, WhoWor 93
Dubois, Pierre-Max 1930- Baker 92
DuBois, Raymond F. d1992 NewYTBS 92
DuBois, Raymond F. 1915-1992 BioIn 17
Dubois, Rene-Daniel 1955- WhoCanL 92
Dubois, Rhoda Nicole Alexandra 1953- WhoEmL 93
du Bois, Robert Stuart 1951- WhoEmL 93
Du Bois, Shirley Graham AmWomPl
Du Bois, Shirley Graham 1906-1977 BioIn 17
Dubois, Stephen Cairfield 1940- WhoAsAP 91
DuBois, Theodora 1890-1986 ScF&FL 92
Du Bois, Theodora Mc Cormick 1890- AmWomPl
Dubois, Theodore 1837-1924 Baker 92
Du Bois, W.E.B. 1868-1963 BioIn 17, ConBlB 3 [port], ConHero 2 [port], GayN, JrnUS, PolPar, WorLitC [port]
Du Bois, William Edward Burghardt 1868-1963 BioIn 17, DcTwHis, EncAACR [port]
du Bois, William Pene MajAI
Du Bois, William Pene 1916- BioIn 17, DcAmChF 1960
Du Boise, Kim Rees 1953- WhoEmL 93, WhoSSW 93
Dubos, Rene Jules 1901-1982 BioIn 17
DuBose, Carol Ann 1954- WhoEmL 93
DuBose, Carroll Jones 1937- St&PR 93
DuBose, Charles Wilson 1949- WhoEmL 93
Du Bose, Guy S. 1954- St&PR 93
DuBose, Guy Steven Law&B 92
DuBose, Hugh Hammond 1922- WhoSSW 93
Dubose, Reagan Layne, Jr. 1932- St&PR 93
Dubourdieu, Saumarez 1717-1812 BioIn 17
Dubourg, Olivier Jean 1952- WhoWor 93
DuBoux, Patricia Jane 1956- WhoAmW 93, WhoEmL 93
Dubov, Larry Herbert 1936- St&PR 93
Dubov, Spencer Floyd 1935- WhoE 93
Dubovsky, Mortimer H. 1914-1991 BioIn 17
Dubow, Arthur Myron 1933- WhoAm 92
Dubow, Marla E. Law&B 92
Dubow, Paul J. Law&B 92
Dubow, Susan Diane 1948- WhoEmL 93
Dubowski, Cathy East ScF&FL 92
Dubowsky, Steven 1942- WhoAm 92
Dubowy, Burton Stephen 1939- St&PR 93
DuBreuil, Elizabeth L. ScF&FL 92
Dubreuil, Etienne 1950- St&PR 93
DuBreuil, Linda 1924-1980 ScF&FL 92
DuBridge, Lee Alvin 1901- WhoAm 92
Dubridge, Richard A. 1933- St&PR 93
DuBrin, Andrew John 1935- WhoAm 92
Dubrish, Douglas Martin 1953- WhoEmL 93
Dubro, Alec Charles 1944- WhoE 93
Dubroux, Daniele MiSFD 9
Dubrovay, Laszlo 1943- Baker 92
Dubrovin, Vivian BioIn 17
Dubrovin, Vivian 1931- ConAu 40NR
Dubrow, Gary Steven Law&B 92
Dubrow, Hilliard 1911-1991 BioIn 17
Dubrow, Louis A. 1947- St&PR 93
Dubrow, Marsha Ann 1948- WhoEmL 93
DuBrul, Stephen M., Jr. 1929- St&PR 93
Dubrule, Paul Jean-Marie 1934- WhoWor 93
Dubs, Patrick Christian 1947- WhoAm 92
Dubsky, Paul Joseph 1964- WhoSSW 93
Dubsky, Robert F. 1945- St&PR 93
Dubson, Jean Carol 1932- WhoAmW 93
Dubuc, Andre 1945- WhoAm 92
Dubuc, Carroll Edward 1933- WhoAm 92, WhoE 93
Dubuc, Jacques A. 1930- St&PR 93
Dubuc, Mary Ellen 1950- WhoAmW 93, WhoEmL 93
Dubuc, Serge 1939- WhoAm 92
Dubuffet, Jean 1901-1985 BioIn 17

Dubuisson, B. 1945- *WhoScE 91-2*
Dubuisson, Eleanor *AmWomPl*
Dubuque, Alexander 1812-1898 *Baker 92*
Dubuque, Cheryl Anne 1952- *WhoWrEP 92*
Dubus, Andre 1936- *BioIn 17*
Dubuss, Robert Francis 1935- *St&PR 93*
Duby, Paul Bernard 1947- *WhoEmL 93*
Dubynin, Viktor d1992 *NewYTBS 92*
Duc, Gabriel 1932- *WhoScE 91-4*
Duca, Alfred Milton 1920- *WhoAm 92*
Duca, Carmine A. *St&PR 93*
Duca, James F. *Law&B 92*
Du Camp, Maxime 1822-1894 *BioIn 17*
Du Cange, Charles Du Fresne 1610-1688 *Baker 92*
Ducanis, Alex Julius 1931- *WhoAm 92, WhoWor 93*
Ducas, Charles George 1959- *WhoSSW 93*
Ducas, John J. d1990 *BioIn 17*
Du Castel, Francois 1924- *WhoScE 91-2*
Ducatelle, R.V.A. 1955- *WhoScE 91-2*
Du Caurroy, Francois-Eustache 1549-1609 *Baker 92*
Duce, Graciela E. 1944- *WhoUN 92*
Duceman, Mark Eugene 1960- *WhoEmL 93*
Ducey, Pat *Law&B 92*
Duch, Benedictus c. 1490-1544 *Baker 92*
Duch, Edward K. 1949- *St&PR 93*
Duch, Edward Karl, Jr. 1949- *WhoAm 92*
Duch, Gregory S. 1951- *St&PR 93*
Duch, William Kingsley 1947- *WhoE 93*
Duchacek, Ivo *ScF&FL 92*
Du Chaillu, Paul 1831?-1903 *Expl 93 [port]*
Duchamp, Gaston 1875-1963 *BioIn 17*
Duchamp, L. Timmel *ScF&FL 92*
Duchamp, Marcel 1887-1968 *BioIn 17, ModArCr 3 [port]*
DuChanois, Lee Scott 1961- *St&PR 93*
Ducharme, Joseph Rudolph Pierre 1956- *WhoWor 93*
DuCharme, Paul *BioIn 17*
Ducharme, Rejean *BioIn 17*
Ducharme, Rejean 1941- *ConLC 74 [port], WhoCanL 92*
Ducharme, Roger Charles 1942- *St&PR 93*
Duch Colell, Juan 1920- *DcMexL*
Duchemin, Jean Pascal 1945- *WhoScE 91-2*
Duchen, Leo Wilfred *WhoScE 91-1*
Duchene, Dominique 1941- *WhoScE 91-2*
Duchene-Marullaz, Pierre 1921- *WhoScE 91-2*
Duchesnay, Isabelle *BioIn 17*
Duchesnay, Paul *BioIn 17*
Duchesne, Christiane 1949- *WhoCanL 92*
Duchesne, Jean-Clair M.C. 1937- *WhoScE 91-2*
Duchesne, Kay Ellen 1942- *WhoAmW 93*
Duchet, Roger 1906-1981 *BioIn 17*
Duchin, Peter Oelrichs 1937- *WhoAm 92*
Duch Martorell, Cesar 1950- *WhoWor 93*
Duchossois, Richard L. 1921- *St&PR 93*
Duchossois, Richard Louis 1921- *WhoAm 92*
Duchowny, Irv Allan 1949- *St&PR 93*
Duchowny, Jack 1920- *St&PR 93*
Duchowny, Roger *MiSFD 9*
Duchting, Werner 1933- *WhoScE 91-3*
Ducich, Dan 1951- *St&PR 93*
Ducie, Charles Jon, Jr. 1935- *St&PR 93*
Ducimetiere, Pierre *WhoScE 91-2*
Ducis, Benedictus c. 1490-1544 *Baker 92*
Duck, Edward W. 1927- *WhoScE 91-3*
Duck, June Moody 1947- *WhoEmL 93*
Duck, Michael 1945- *WhoWor 93*
Duck, Stephen 1705-1756 *BioIn 17*
Duck, William G. *Law&B 92*
Ducke, Kenneth F. 1943- *St&PR 93*
Ducken, Lynn K. *St&PR 93*
Duckenfield, Thomas d1992 *NewYTBS 92*
Duckenfield, Thomas A. 1935- *St&PR 93*
Ducker, Bruce 1938- *WhoAm 92*
Duckers, Ronald Lee 1935- *WhoSSW 93*
Duckers, Sarah Ann 1961- *WhoAmW 93*
Duckert, Audrey Rosalind 1927- *WhoAm 92*
Duckett, Ann Lorraine 1951- *WhoEmL 93*
Duckett, Jeffrey Graham *WhoScE 91-1*
Duckett, Joan 1934- *WhoAmW 93*
Duckett, Karen I. *AfrAmBi [port]*
Duckett, Karen Irene 1947- *WhoEmL 93, WhoSSW 93*
Duckles, Sue Piper 1946- *WhoAmW 93, WhoEmL 93*
Duckles, Vincent 1913-1985 *BioIn 17*
Duckles, Vincent H(arris) 1913-1985 *Baker 92*
Duckworth, Carol Kay 1941- *WhoAmW 93*
Duckworth, Elwood P. 1942- *St&PR 93*
Duckworth, Guy 1923- *WhoAm 92*
Duckworth, Kevin Jerome 1964- *WhoAm 92*
Duckworth, Kim Pelto 1956- *WhoAmW 93*
Duckworth, Lynn Allison 1948- *WhoEmL 93*
Duckworth, Paula Oliver 1940- *WhoSSW 93*
Duckworth, Robert Vincent 1938- *WhoIns 93*
Duckworth, Rosemary Ellen 1949- *WhoAmW 93*
Duckworth, Ruth 1919- *BioIn 17*
Duckworth, Tara Ann 1956- *WhoAmW 93*
Duckworth, W.E. *WhoScE 91-1*
Duckworth, W. Joseph 1948- *WhoEmL 93*
Duckworth, Walter Donald 1935- *WhoAm 92*
Duckworth, William Capell, III 1953- *WhoE 93*
Duckworth, William (Ervin) 1943- *Baker 92*
Duckworth, Winston Howard 1918- *WhoAm 92*
Duclerc, Charles Theodore Eugene 1812- *BioIn 17*
Duclon, Warren Eugene 1924- *St&PR 93*
DuClos, Danielle *BioIn 17*
DuClos, Deanna *BioIn 17*
Duclos, Jacques 1896-1975 *BioIn 17*
Duclos, Keith Francis 1959- *WhoEmL 93*
Ducloux, Walter 1913- *Baker 92*
Ducloy, Martial 1945- *WhoScE 91-2*
Ducom, Jean 1938- *WhoScE 91-2*
Ducommun, Edmond G. 1918- *St&PR 93*
Ducornet, Rikki 1943- *WhoCanL 92*
Ducos, Jean 1926- *WhoScE 91-2*
Ducos, Jean Bernard 1926- *WhoWor 93*
Ducot, Jean 1754- *BioIn 17*
Ducote, Dean Barton 1964- *WhoSSW 93*
Ducote, Marjorie Ellen 1938- *WhoAm 92*
DuCran, Claudette Deloris 1941- *WhoAmW 93*
Ducret, Lucette 1948- *WhoEmL 93, WhoWor 93*
Ducreux, Pierre 1921- *WhoScE 91-2*
Du Cros, Eric Teissier *WhoScE 91-2*
Ducros, Pierre Y. 1939- *WhoAm 92*
Ducrot, Guy-Georges 1926- *WhoScE 91-2*
Ducruet, Daniel *BioIn 17*
Ducuing, Jacques 1932- *WhoScE 91-2*
Ducy, Patricia Cornelia 1945- *WhoSSW 93*
Duczek, Richard L. 1942- *St&PR 93*
Duczmal, Karol W. 1930- *WhoScE 91-4*
Duda, Edwin 1928- *WhoSSW 93*
Duda, Longin 1922- *WhoScE 91-4*
Duda, Michael J. 1946- *St&PR 93*
Duda, Miloslav 1941- *WhoScE 91-4*
Duda, Patricia Mary 1949- *WhoAmW 93*
Duda, Richard J. *Law&B 92*
Duda, Richard Oswald 1936- *WhoAm 92*
Duda, Roman 1935- *WhoWor 93*
Duda, Ronald P. 1942- *St&PR 93*
Duda, Seweryn J. 1933- *WhoScE 91-3*
Duda, Zenon Michael 1955- *WhoEmL 93*
Dudack, Gail M. 1948- *St&PR 93*
Dudack, Gail Marie 1948- *WhoAm 92*
Dudarew-Ossetynski, Leonidas 1912-1989 *PolBiDi*
Dudarova, Veronika 1916- *Baker 92*
Dudas, Louis Anthony 1935- *St&PR 93*
Dudash, C. Michael *BioIn 17*
Dudash, Charles Michael 1952- *WhoE 93*
Dudash, Linda Christine *WhoAmW 93*
Duddeck, Heinz 1928- *WhoScE 91-3*
Dudden, Arthur Power 1921- *WhoAm 92*
Duddles, Charles W. 1940- *St&PR 93*
Duddles, Charles Weller 1940- *WhoAm 92*
Duddy, Philip G. 1947- *St&PR 93*
Dude, Cornelia E. *Law&B 92*
Dudeck, Joachim W. 1932- *WhoScE 91-3*
Dudeck, Michel A. 1945- *WhoScE 91-2*
Du Deffand, Marie Anne de Vichy-Chamrond 1697-1780 *BioIn 17*
Dudek, Anthony Edward 1953- *WhoEmL 93*
Dudek, Felicia Anne 1947- *WhoAmW 93, WhoEmL 93*
Dudek, Henry Thomas 1929- *WhoE 93, WhoWor 93*
Dudek, Julian 1935- *WhoScE 91-4*
Dudek, Louis 1918- *WhoCanL 92*
Dudek, Richard Albert 1926- *WhoAm 92*
Dudek, Stephanie Zuperko 1921- *WhoAm 92*
Dudek, Wieslaw Aleksander 1953- *WhoWor 93*
Dudek, William Michael 1956- *St&PR 93*
Duder, Tessa *DcChlFi*
Duderstadt, James Johnson 1942- *WhoAm 92, WhoWor 93*
Duderstadt, Janet F. *Law&B 92*
Dudevant, Amantine Lucile Aurore Dupin 1804-1876 *BioIn 17*
Du De Voire, Diana Elizabeth 1953- *WhoAmW 93*
Dudewicz, Edward John 1942- *WhoAm 92*
Dudey, Norman D. 1937- *St&PR 93*
Dudgeon, Edna 1913- *WhoAmW 93*
Dudgeon, Robert Ellis 1820-1904 *ScF&FL 92*
Dudgeon, Stephen Murray 1949- *St&PR 93*
Dudich, Endre 1934- *WhoScE 91-2, -91-4, WhoUN 92*
Dudich, John T. d1991 *BioIn 17*
Dudick, Michael Joseph 1917- *WhoAm 92, WhoE 93*
Dudics-Dean, Susan Elaine 1950- *WhoAmW 93, WhoEmL 93*
Dudik, Rollie M. 1935- *WhoWor 93*
Dudits, Denes 1943- *WhoScE 91-4*
Dudkiewicz, Jan 1931- *WhoWor 93*
Dudko, Stanislaw Jan 1946- *WhoScE 91-4*
Dudley, Alden Woodbury, Jr. 1937- *WhoSSW 93*
Dudley, Alfred E. *St&PR 93*
Dudley, Alfred Edward 1928- *WhoE 93*
Dudley, Beverly Jean Kemp 1941- *WhoAmW 93*
Dudley, Bill 1921?- *BioIn 17*
Dudley, Bobby G. 1928- *WhoWrEP 92*
Dudley, Debra C. 1955- *St&PR 93*
Dudley, Dennis W. 1951- *St&PR 93*
Dudley, Elizabeth Hymer 1937- *WhoAmW 93*
Dudley, Gail Jean 1950- *WhoSSW 93*
Dudley, George Austin 1914- *WhoAm 92*
Dudley, George Ellsworth 1922- *WhoAm 92*
Dudley, John Wesley, Jr. 1957- *WhoEmL 93*
Dudley, Kenneth Eugene 1937- *St&PR 93*
Dudley, Linda Jean 1946- *WhoEmL 93*
Dudley, Lonnie LeRoy 1948- *WhoWor 93*
Dudley, Mark R. 1958- *St&PR 93*
Dudley, Mark Ziegler *Law&B 92*
Dudley, Martha Ann 1952- *WhoAmW 93*
Dudley, Michael James 1960- *WhoEmL 93*
Dudley, Paul V. 1926- *WhoAm 92*
Dudley, Peggy Loucelle 1943- *WhoWrEP 92*
Dudley, Richard Mansfield 1938- *WhoAm 92*
Dudley, Robert 1532?-1588 *BioIn 17*
Dudley, Robert Hamilton 1933- *WhoSSW 93*
Dudley, Robert Thane 1916- *St&PR 93*
Dudley, Robert W. *Law&B 92*
Dudley, Terence *ScF&FL 92*
Dudley, Terri Crawford 1929- *WhoE 93*
Dudley, Wayne Carroll 1930- *St&PR 93*
Dudley, Wilbur George 1946- *WhoEmL 93, WhoSSW 93*
Dudley, William Craig 1948- *WhoEmL 93*
Dudley, William J. 1920- *St&PR 93*
Dudley-Smith, Trevor *ScF&FL 92*
Dudman, Bryan L. 1956- *St&PR 93*
Dudman, Martha Tod 1952- *WhoAmW 93*
Dudman, Richard Beebe 1918- *WhoAm 92*
Dudnick, Carol Lee *Law&B 92*
Dudnick, Solis 1922- *St&PR 93*
Dudovicz, Walter 1956- *St&PR 93*
Dudow, Slatan 1903-1963 *DrEEuF*
Dudrick, Stanley John 1935- *WhoAm 92*
Duduit, James Michael 1954- *WhoEmL 93*
Dudziak, Edward Daniel 1941- *St&PR 93*
Dudziak, Walter Francis 1923- *WhoAm 92*
Dudzick, Thomas Francis 1950- *WhoE 93*
Dudzik, Kenneth Richard 1949- *WhoE 93*
Dudzik, Mary Theresa 1860-1918 *PolBiDi*
Dudzinski, Jerzy Antoni 1947- *WhoWor 93*
Due, Jean Margaret 1921- *WhoAm 92*
Due, John Fitzgerald 1915- *WhoAm 92*
Due, Linnea A. 1948- *BioIn 17*
Dueber, Charles LeRoy 1945- *St&PR 93*
Dueck, John 1941- *WhoAm 92*
Duecker, Heyman Clarke 1929- *WhoAm 92*
Duecker, Robert Sheldon 1926- *WhoAm 92*
Duecker, Stephen Allen 1948- *WhoEmL 93*
Duecy, Charles Michael 1912- *WhoAm 92*
Duell, Daniel Paul 1952- *WhoAm 92*
Duell, Randall d1992 *NewYTBS 92*
Duelli, Peter 1945- *WhoScE 91-4*
Duemer, Joseph 1951- *WhoWrEP 92*
Duemling, Robert Werner 1929- *WhoAm 92*
Duenas, Cristobal Camacho 1920- *WhoAm 92*
Duenas, Guadalupe 1920- *DcMexL*
Duenas, Martha Loza 1942- *WhoUN 92*
Duenk, Lester Gerald 1927- *WhoSSW 93*
Duenkelsbuehler, Ilrike Oudee 1959- *WhoWor 93*
Duenser, Mark William *Law&B 92*
Duenser, Ruth Edwards *Law&B 92*
Duensing, G. *WhoScE 91-3*
Duensing, James Arlin 1959- *WhoEmL 93*
Duenzl, Hans 1943- *St&PR 93*
Due Pedersen, Torben 1935- *WhoScE 91-2*
Duer, Caroline King 1865- *AmWomPl*
Duer, David Edward 1954- *WhoWrEP 92*
Duer, Ellen Ann Dagon 1936- *WhoAmW 93, WhoE 93*
Duer, Thomas C. *WhoAm 92*
Duer, Thomas Charles 1936- *St&PR 93*
Duerden, Brian Ion *WhoScE 91-1*
Duerden, Brian Ion 1948- *WhoWor 93*
Duerden, John H. 1941- *WhoE 93*
Duerinck, Louis T. 1929- *WhoAm 92*
Duerksen, Christopher James 1948- *WhoEmL 93*
Duerksen, Dean Fariss 1931- *WhoSSW 93*
Duerksen, Deanne Adene 1944- *WhoAmW 93*
Duerksen, Erwin 1923- *WhoAm 92*
Duerksen, George Louis 1934- *WhoAm 92*
Duerksen, Gregory J. 1957- *St&PR 93*
Duerr, Dianne Marie 1945- *WhoAmW 93, WhoE 93*
Duerr, Herman George 1931- *WhoAm 92*
Duerr, J. Stephen 1943- *St&PR 93*
Duerr, Mary Jane 1955- *WhoEmL 93*
Duerr, Paula Cumming 1929- *WhoWrEP 92*
Duerr, Werner Albert 1934- *WhoE 93*
Duerre, John Arden 1930- *WhoAm 92*
Duerst, Susan Lee 1948- *WhoAmW 93*
Dues, Theodore Roosevelt, Jr. 1953- *WhoEmL 93, WhoSSW 93, WhoWor 93*
Duesdieker, George Steven *Law&B 92*
Duesenberg, Richard William *Law&B 92*
Duesenberg, Richard William 1930- *St&PR 93, WhoAm 92*
Duesenberg, Robert H. *Law&B 92*
Duesenberg, Robert H. 1930- *St&PR 93, WhoAm 92*
Duesterberg, Thomas J. 1950- *WhoAm 92*
Duet, Kendrick Joseph 1953- *WhoEmL 93*
Dueweke, Donald Gordon 1944- *St&PR 93*
Duewel, Klaus 1935- *WhoWor 93*
Duewer, Elizabeth Ann 1937- *WhoAmW 93*
Dufallo, Richard (John) 1933- *Baker 92*
Dufault, Joseph Ernest Nephtali *MajAI*
Dufault, Roseanna Lewis 1954- *ConAu 138*
Dufaure, Jean-Pierre 1935- *WhoScE 91-2*
Dufaure, Jules Armand Stanislas 1798-1881 *BioIn 17*
Dufay, Guillaume c. 1400-1474 *Baker 92*
Dufek, Jaroslav 1934- *WhoScE 91-4*
Dufendach, Carl William 1953- *WhoEmL 93*
Dufer, J. 1947- *WhoScE 91-2*
Duff, Alexander Roy *WhoScE 91-1*
Duff, Allen Jerome, Jr. 1947- *WhoEmL 93, WhoSSW 93*
Duff, Brian Barnett 1930- *WhoAm 92*
Duff, Cathleen Cushing 1950- *WhoAmW 93*
Duff, Daniel Vincent 1916- *WhoAm 92*
Duff, David Arnold 1958- *WhoSSW 93*
Duff, Donald D. 1928- *St&PR 93*
Duff, Dorothy Manley *AmWomPl*
Duff, Duane R. 1940- *St&PR 93*
Duff, Ernest Arthur 1929- *WhoAm 92, WhoSSW 93*
Duff, Frank 1889-1980 *BioIn 17*
Duff, George Alexander 1931- *WhoAm 92*
Duff, George Edwin 1912- *St&PR 93*
Duff, Howard 1913-1990 *BioIn 17*
Duff, James George 1938- *St&PR 93, WhoAm 92*
Duff, James Henderson 1883-1969 *BioIn 17*
Duff, James Henry 1943- *WhoAm 92, WhoE 93*
Duff, James I. 1931- *WhoIns 93*
Duff, John Ewing 1943- *WhoAm 92*
Duff, John Francis 1946- *WhoAm 92*
Duff, Michael John Benjamin *WhoScE 91-1*
Duff, Philip Nicholas 1957- *St&PR 93*
Duff, Ronald G. *St&PR 93*
Duff, Ronald G. 1936- *WhoAm 92*
Duff, Steven W. 1953- *St&PR 93*
Duff, Thomas Michael 1947- *St&PR 93*
Duff, William Grierson 1936- *WhoAm 92, WhoSSW 93, WhoWor 93*
Duff, William Leroy, Jr. 1938- *WhoAm 92*
Duffee, Daniel J., Jr. 1918- *St&PR 93*
Duffee, Keene Delahay Embrey 1962- *WhoAmW 93*
Duffee, Richard Anthony 1930- *St&PR 93*
Duffell, James Roger *WhoScE 91-1*
Duffell, Peter John *MiSFD 9*
Duffell, Peter Royson 1939- *WhoAsAP 91*
Duffens, Robert Eugene 1924- *St&PR 93*
Duffett, Benton Samuel, Jr. 1936- *WhoSSW 93*
Duffett, John C. 1927- *St&PR 93*
Duffey, Dick 1917- *WhoE 93*
Duffey, H. Lyle 1922- *St&PR 93*

Duffey, Joseph Daniel 1932- *WhoAm 92, WhoE 93*
Duffey, Michael S. 1954- *St&PR 93*
Duffey, Robert Joseph, II 1945- *St&PR 93*
Duffey, William H. *Law&B 92*
Duffey, William Norman 1946- *St&PR 93*
Duffey, William Simon, Jr. 1952- *WhoEmL 93*
Duffie, Edward R., Jr. 1929- *St&PR 93*
Duffie, Gerald Stover 1932- *WhoSSW 93*
Duffie, John Atwater 1925- *WhoAm 92*
Duffie, Tommie C. 1929- *St&PR 93*
Duffie, Virgil Whatley, Jr. 1935- *WhoAm 92*
Duffield, Don Forrest 1935- *St&PR 93*
Duffield, Edward H. *Law&B 92*
Duffield, Thomas A. *Law&B 92*
Duffield, Thomas Andrew 1925- *St&PR 93*
Duffin, Brian James 1955- *WhoWor 93*
Duffin, Michael B. 1948- *St&PR 93*
Duffin, Richard James 1909- *WhoAm 92*
Duffin, Robert *Law&B 92*
Duffus, C.M. *WhoScE 91-1*
Duffus, James Robert *Law&B 92*
Duffus, John Henderson *WhoScE 91-1*
Duffus, Roy A. 1923- *St&PR 93*
Duffy, Ann-Marie K. 1959- *WhoAmW 93*
Duffy, Brian J. 1941- *WhoIns 93*
Duffy, Brian William 1951- *St&PR 93*
Duffy, Bruce *BioIn 17*
Duffy, Bruce Cary 1938- *St&PR 93*
Duffy, Charles Gavan 1816-1903 *BioIn 17*
Duffy, Charles R. 1947- *St&PR 93*
Duffy, Dave 1948- *St&PR 93*
Duffy, David Livingstone 1957- *WhoWor 93*
Duffy, Deborah M. *Law&B 92*
Duffy, Dennis 1938- *WhoCanL 92*
Duffy, Earl Gavin 1926- *WhoAm 92*
Duffy, Edmund Charles 1942- *WhoAm 92*
Duffy, Edward F. 1949- *St&PR 93*
Duffy, Elaine Marie 1954- *WhoAm 92*
Duffy, F. Maureen *Law&B 92*
Duffy, Francis Martin, Jr. 1949- *WhoEmL 93*
Duffy, Francis Ramon 1915- *WhoAm 92*
Duffy, Gary Wayne 1950- *WhoEmL 93*
Duffy, Grace Landis 1949- *WhoAmW 93*
Duffy, Henry A. 1934- *EncABHB 8 [port]*
Duffy, Hugh Brian 1954- *St&PR 93*
Duffy, J. O'Neill 1926- *St&PR 93*
Duffy, Jacques Wayne 1922- *WhoAm 92*
Duffy, James F. *Law&B 92*
Duffy, James F. 1949- *St&PR 93*
Duffy, James Henry 1934- *WhoAm 92*
Duffy, Jerome L. 1936- *St&PR 93*
Duffy, John 1915- *WhoAm 92*
Duffy, John Charles 1934- *WhoAm 92, WhoWor 93*
Duffy, John F. *Law&B 92*
Duffy, John Joseph 1931- *WhoAm 92, WhoSSW 93*
Duffy, John Leonard 1947- *WhoEmL 93*
Duffy, Joseph W. *Law&B 92*
Duffy, Julia *BioIn 17*
Duffy, Julia 1951- *WhoAm 92*
Duffy, Kent Haviland 1951- *WhoEmL 93*
Duffy, Kevin 1943- *St&PR 93*
Duffy, Kevin Francis *Law&B 92*
Duffy, Kevin Thomas 1933- *WhoAm 92, WhoE 93*
Duffy, La Verne d1992 *NewYTBS 92*
Duffy, Lawrence Kevin 1948- *WhoWor 93*
Duffy, Malachy James, II 1951- *WhoAm 92*
Duffy, Margaret 1942- *ConAu 139*
Duffy, Martin Edward 1940- *WhoE 93, WhoWor 93*
Duffy, Martin H. 1951- *St&PR 93*
Duffy, Maureen 1933- *BioIn 17, ScF&FL 92*
Duffy, Michael J. *Law&B 92*
Duffy, Michael John 1938- *WhoAsAP 91*
Duffy, Nancy Keogh 1947- *WhoAmW 93*
Duffy, Nicole *WhoAm 92*
Duffy, Pamela Jean 1954- *WhoAmW 93*
Duffy, Patricia Mary 1955- *WhoEmL 93*
Duffy, Patrick *BioIn 17*
Duffy, Patrick 1949- *WhoAm 92*
Duffy, Paul Gerald 1930- *St&PR 93*
Duffy, Richard A. 1928- *St&PR 93*
Duffy, Robert Aloysius 1921- *WhoAm 92, WhoE 93*
Duffy, Robert Thomas 1949- *WhoEmL 93*
Duffy, Robert Townsend 1926- *WhoSSW 93*
Duffy, Robert William 1939- *WhoUN 92*
Duffy, Roseanne R. *Law&B 92*
Duffy, Russell E. *St&PR 93*
Duffy, Sally M. 1953- *WhoAmW 93*
Duffy, Stephen W. *Law&B 92*
Duffy, Thomas Brogan 1953- *St&PR 93*
Duffy, Thomas Edward 1947- *WhoAm 92*
Duffy, Thomas F. *BioIn 17*
Duffy, Thomas James 1934- *WhoWor 93*
Duffy, Thomas Michael *Law&B 92*
Duffy, Thomas Patrick 1937- *St&PR 93*
Duffy, Thomas Patrick 1957- *WhoSSW 93*
Duffy, W. Leslie 1939- *WhoAm 92*
Duffy, William J. *St&PR 93*
Duffy, William Joseph, Jr. 1946- *WhoEmL 93*
Duffy, William Smith 1946- *St&PR 93*
Duffy, Yvonne Helen Patricia 1964- *WhoWrEP 92*
Duflos de Saint-Amand, Hubert 1936- *WhoWor 93*
Duflot, Marcelle 1928- *WhoScE 91-2*
Dufner, Max 1920- *WhoAm 92*
Dufoix, Georgina 1943- *BioIn 17*
DuFord, Sally Trew 1934- *WhoSSW 93*
Dufour, Darlene 1944- *WhoWrEP 92*
Dufour, E. James 1934- *St&PR 93*
Dufour, Gilles *BioIn 17*
Dufour, Gregory Andre 1960- *WhoEmL 93*
Dufour, Paul V. 1939- *St&PR 93*
Dufour, Rene Andre 1949- *WhoE 93*
DuFour, Richard William, Jr. 1940- *WhoAm 92*
Dufour, Val 1927- *WhoAm 92*
Dufourcq, Norbert 1904-1990 *Baker 92*
Dufranne, Hector 1870-1951 *OxDcOp*
Dufranne, Hector (Robert) 1870-1951 *Baker 92*
Dufresne, Armand Alphee, Jr. 1909- *WhoAm 92*
Dufresne, Dewayne J. 1930- *St&PR 93*
duFresne, Elizabeth Jamison 1942- *WhoAm 92*
Dufresne, Guy 1915- *WhoCanL 92*
Dufresne, Guy Georges 1941- *WhoAm 92*
Dufresne, Isabelle 1935- *ConAu 136*
Dufresne, Jerilyn Clare 1947- *WhoEmL 93*
Dufresne, John 1948- *ConAu 139*
Duft, Patricia Hitt *Law&B 92*
Duftschmid, Klaus E. 1937- *WhoScE 91-4*
Dufty, James Wellons 1940- *WhoSSW 93*
Dufy, Raoul 1877-1953 *BioIn 17, ModArCr 3 [port]*
Dug, David Chow Lip *St&PR 93*
Dugal, Louis Paul 1911- *WhoAm 92*
Dugan, Alan *BioIn 17*
Dugan, Charles Clark 1921- *WhoSSW 93*
Dugan, Charles Francis, II 1939- *WhoAm 92*
Dugan, Charles P. *Law&B 92*
Dugan, Denis K. 1939- *St&PR 93*
Dugan, Dennis *MiSFD 9*
Dugan, Dixie *WhoWrEP 92*
Dugan, Edward F. 1934- *St&PR 93*
Dugan, Edward Francis 1934- *WhoAm 92*
Dugan, Ellen R. *Law&B 92*
Dugan, Francis Robert 1927- *St&PR 93*
Dugan, Franjo 1874-1948 *Baker 92*
Dugan, Gerard A. 1945- *WhoIns 93*
Dugan, Jack *ConAu 40NR*
Dugan, James Francis, III 1943- *WhoSSW 93*
Dugan, James R. *Law&B 92*
Dugan, James Richard, Jr. *Law&B 92*
Dugan, John James, Jr. 1940- *St&PR 93*
Dugan, John Leslie, Jr. 1921- *WhoAm 92*
Dugan, John Michael 1909- *WhoAm 92*
Dugan, John Raymond, Jr. 1948- *WhoEmL 93*
Dugan, Kevin M. *Law&B 92*
Dugan, Luan M. 1952- *WhoAmW 93, WhoEmL 93*
Dugan, M. Diane 1955- *WhoAmW 93*
Dugan, Mary E. *St&PR 93*
Dugan, Michael *MiSFD 9*
Dugan, Michael J. 1937- *WhoAm 92*
Dugan, Michael Kevin 1940- *WhoAm 92*
Dugan, Natalie Martin 1938- *WhoAmW 93*
Dugan, Patrick Raymond 1931- *WhoAm 92*
Dugan, Patrick William *Law&B 92*
Dugan, Patrick William 1952- *St&PR 93*
Dugan, Raymond C. 1930- *St&PR 93*
Dugan, Robert Michael 1953- *WhoEmL 93*
Dugan, Robert Perry, Jr. 1932- *WhoAm 92*
Dugan, Sean Francis Xavier 1951- *WhoEmL 93*
Dugan, Thomas Allen 1925- *St&PR 93*
Dugan, Thomas E. *Law&B 92*
Dugan, William Edward d1991 *BioIn 17*
Dugard, Jaycee *BioIn 17*
Dugas, Edward *Law&B 92*
Dugas, Lester J., Jr. 1924- *St&PR 93*
Dugas, Louis, Jr. 1928- *WhoAm 92*
Dugas, Lynn Hudson *Law&B 92*
Dugas, Marcel 1883-1947 *BioIn 17*
Dugas, Michael *Law&B 92*
Dugas, Rene Louis, Sr. 1909- *WhoE 93*
Dugazon, Louise 1755-1821 *OxDcOp*
Dugazon, Louise (Rosalie) 1755-1821 *Baker 92*
Dugdale, George *WhoScE 91-1*
Dugdale, John Sydney 1922- *WhoWor 93*
Dugdale, Raymond J. 1949- *St&PR 93*
Dugdale, William d1868 *BioIn 17*
Duggan, Arthur William *WhoScE 91-1*
Duggan, Carol Cook 1946- *WhoAmW 93, WhoSSW 93*
Duggan, Charles Perkins 1922- *St&PR 93*
Duggan, Dennis Michael 1927- *WhoAm 92*
Duggan, Edward James 1931- *St&PR 93, WhoE 93*
Duggan, Edward Patrick 1945- *WhoE 93*
Duggan, Ervin S. *BioIn 17*
Duggan, Ervin S. 1939- *WhoAm 92*
Duggan, Eugene Joseph 1933- *WhoE 93*
Duggan, J. Richard *Law&B 92*
Duggan, James Edgar 1961- *WhoEmL 93*
Duggan, James H. 1935- *St&PR 93, WhoAm 92, WhoSSW 93*
Duggan, James Roy 1916- *St&PR 93, WhoAm 92*
Duggan, Jeremiah J. *Law&B 92*
Duggan, John C. *Law&B 92*
Duggan, John Patrick 1952- *WhoEmL 93*
Duggan, Joseph Francis 1817-1900 *Baker 92*
Duggan, Kevin 1944- *WhoSSW 93*
Duggan, Mary Kathleen 1926- *WhoAmW 93*
Duggan, Mary Kathryn 1964- *WhoAmW 93*
Duggan, Maurice (Noel) 1922-1974 *DcChlFi*
Duggan, Patrick James 1933- *WhoAm 92*
Duggan, Patrick O'Neill 1953- *WhoEmL 93*
Duggan, Peter James 1946- *St&PR 93*
Duggan, Robert E. 1939- *St&PR 93*
Duggan, Robert Maurice 1939- *WhoE 93*
Duggan, Terance Vincent *WhoScE 91-1*
Duggan, Thomas Michael 1950- *WhoEmL 93*
Duggan, Thomas Patrick 1946- *WhoEmL 93*
Dugger, Edwin Ellsworth 1940- *WhoAm 92*
Dugger, John Leland *Law&B 92*
Dugger, Julia Burns 1942- *WhoWrEP 92*
Dugger, Mari Michelle *Law&B 92*
Dugger, Morse 1942- *St&PR 93*
Dugger, Ronnie E. 1930- *WhoAm 92, WhoWrEP 92*
Duggin, Lorraine Jean 1941- *WhoWrEP 92*
Duggins, G. Thomas 1945- *WhoSSW 93*
Duggleby, Brian David 1952- *WhoEmL 93*
Dughi, Robert Louis *Law&B 92*
Dugle, William M. 1942- *St&PR 93*
Dugmore, C.W. 1910-1990 *BioIn 17*
Dugmore, Clifford William 1910-1990 *BioIn 17*
Dugmore, Edward 1915- *WhoAm 92, WhoE 93*
Dugmore, Kent C. *Law&B 92*
Dugoff, Howard Jay 1936- *WhoAm 92*
Dugoni, Arthur A. 1925- *WhoAm 92*
Duguay, Christian *MiSFD 9*
Duguay, Raoul 1939- *WhoCanL 92*
du Guerny, Jacques M. 1941- *WhoUN 92*
Du Guillet, Pernette 1520?-1545 *BioIn 17*
Dugundji, John 1925- *WhoAm 92, WhoE 93*
Dugwell, Denis Richmond *WhoScE 91-1*
DuHadway, Thomas d1991 *BioIn 17*
Duhaime, Arthur Joseph, III 1951- *WhoE 93*
Duhaime, Lloyd P. *Law&B 92*
Duhaime, Ricky Edward 1953- *WhoEmL 93, WhoSSW 93*
Duhalde, Eduardo *WhoWor 93*
Duhamel, Antoine 1925- *Baker 92*
Duhamel, Georges 1884-1966 *BioIn 17*
Duhamel, Jean-Francois 1942- *WhoScE 91-2*
Duhamel, Monique Julianne 1966- *WhoAmW 93, WhoWrEP 92*
Duhamel, Pierre Albert 1920- *WhoAm 92*
Duhamel, Raymond Conrad 1942- *WhoE 93*
Duhamel Duffy, Helene Marie 1962- *WhoAmW 93*
Duhe, John Malcolm, Jr. 1933- *WhoAm 92, WhoSSW 93*
Duhem, Pierre Maurice Marie 1861-1916 *BioIn 17*
Duhig, Michael J. *Law&B 92*
Duhl, David M. 1953- *WhoSSW 93*
Duhl, Leonard 1926- *WhoAm 92*
Duhl, Michael Foster 1944- *WhoAm 92*
Duhl, Stuart 1940- *St&PR 93*
Duhm, Kenneth David 1952- *WhoEmL 93*
Duhme, Carol McCarthy 1917- *WhoWor 93*
Duhme, Herman Richard, Jr. 1914- *WhoAm 92*
Duhmke, Eckhart 1942- *WhoWor 93*
Duhms, Martin 1947- *St&PR 93*
Duhnke, Robert Emmet, Jr. 1935- *WhoWor 93*
Duhot, Francois Marcel 1934- *WhoWor 93*
Duhr, Allen W. 1938- *St&PR 93*
Duiffoprugcar, Gaspar 1514-1571 *Baker 92*
Duigan, John *MiSFD 9*
Duigon, Lee *ScF&FL 92*
Duijves, Klaas A. 1948- *WhoScE 91-3*
Duijvestijn, A.J.W. 1927- *WhoScE 91-3*
Duilius, Gaius c. 300BC-c. 225BC *HarEnMi*
Duin, G.J. *WhoScE 91-3*
Duinker, Jan C. 1934- *WhoScE 91-3*
Duiverman, C.J. *WhoScE 91-3*
Dujardin, E.C. 1932- *WhoScE 91-2*
Dujardin, Edouard 1861-1949 *DcLB 123 [port]*
Dujardin de Calonne, Andre Bernard 1942- *WhoWor 93*
Duka, Ivo 1913-1988 *ScF&FL 92*
Dukakis, Kitty *BioIn 17*
Dukakis, Michael *BioIn 17*
Dukakis, Michael S. 1933- *PolPar*
Dukakis, Michael Stanley 1933- *WhoAm 92, WhoE 93*
Dukakis, Olympia *BioIn 17*
Dukakis, Olympia 1931- *WhoAm 92, WhoAmW 93*
Dukas, Nicholas George 1947- *WhoEmL 93*
Dukas, Paul 1865-1935 *Baker 92, IntDcOp, OxDcOp*
Dukas, Peter 1919- *WhoAm 92*
Duke, A. W., Jr. 1931- *WhoAm 92*
Duke, Angier Biddle 1915- *WhoAm 92, WhoWor 93*
Duke, Anthony D., Jr. 1942- *St&PR 93*
Duke, Anthony Drexel 1918- *WhoAm 92*
Duke, Bernie 1927- *St&PR 93*
Duke, Bill *BioIn 17, ConTFT 10, MiSFD 9*
Duke, Bill 1943- *ConBlB 3 [port]*
Duke, Charles Bryan 1938- *WhoAm 92*
Duke, Charles J. 1949- *St&PR 93*
Duke, Charles M. 1935- *BioIn 17*
Duke, Charles Richard 1940- *WhoE 93*
Duke, Clifford Frank 1953- *WhoEmL 93, WhoSSW 93*
Duke, Daryl *MiSFD 9*
Duke, David *BioIn 17*
Duke, David Allen 1935- *St&PR 93, WhoAm 92*
Duke, David Carroll 1932- *St&PR 93*
Duke, Denis M. *Law&B 92*
Duke, Donald Norman 1929- *WhoAm 92*
Duke, Doris *SoulM*
Duke, Doris 1912- *BioIn 17*
Duke, Edward J. 1939- *WhoScE 91-3*
Duke, Ellen Kay 1952- *WhoAmW 93, WhoEmL 93*
Duke, Emanuel 1916- *WhoAm 92*
Duke, Gary James 1947- *WhoEmL 93, WhoSSW 93*
Duke, Gary Philip 1957- *WhoEmL 93*
Duke, Geoff *BioIn 17*
Duke, George 1946- *SoulM*
Duke, George Wesley 1953- *WhoE 93*
Duke, Harold Benjamin, Jr. 1922- *St&PR 93, WhoAm 92*
Duke, J. Dale 1938- *WhoIns 93*
Duke, James *St&PR 93*
Duke, James Alan 1929- *WhoAm 92*
Duke, Jesse W. 1927- *St&PR 93*
Duke, John Wayne 1943- *St&PR 93*
Duke, John (Woods) 1899-1984 *Baker 92*
Duke, Judith Silverman 1934- *WhoAmW 93*
Duke, Karen Kay *Law&B 92*
Duke, Kenneth Jason 1957- *WhoEmL 93*
Duke, Kevin E. *Law&B 92*
Duke, Leslie Allen 1946- *WhoSSW 93*
Duke, Linda Ruth Warren 1945- *WhoAmW 93, WhoSSW 93*
Duke, Lois Lovelace 1935- *WhoSSW 93*
Duke, Madeleine 1919- *ScF&FL 92*
Duke, Martin 1930- *ConAu 138*
Duke, Mathilde Weaver 1911- *WhoWrEP 92*
Duke, Michael B. 1935- *WhoSSW 93*
Duke, Michael Charles 1956- *WhoE 93*
Duke, Michael S. 1940- *ConAu 136*
Duke, Patty *BioIn 17*
Duke, Patty 1946- *WhoAm 92, WhoAmW 93*
Duke, Paul Robert 1929- *WhoAm 92*
Duke, Randolph *BioIn 17*
Duke, Robert D. *Law&B 92*
Duke, Robert Dominick 1928- *St&PR 93, WhoAm 92*
Duke, Robin Chandler Tippett 1923- *WhoAmW 93*
Duke, Ron 1949- *St&PR 93*
Duke, Sophie Marie 1945- *WhoAmW 93*
Duke, Steven Barry 1934- *WhoAm 92*
Duke, Susanna Neale *Law&B 92*
Duke, Timothy R. 1951- *St&PR 93*
Duke, Tracy L. 1960- *WhoEmL 93*
Duke, Vernon *Baker 92*
Duke, Will *ConAu 37NR*
Duke, William Meng d1992 *NewYTBS 92 [port]*

Dukek, Nancy Bowman 1916- *WhoAmW 93*
Dukelsky, Vladimir 1903-1969 *Baker 92*
Duker, Denis Craig *Law&B 92*
Duker, Nahum Johanan 1942- *WhoE 93*
Dukert, Betty Cole 1927- *WhoAm 92*
Dukes, David Coleman 1945- *WhoAm 92*
Dukes, James Otis 1946- *WhoEmL 93*
Dukes, Jimmy Ward 1941- *WhoSSW 93*
Dukes, Joan 1947- *WhoAmW 93*
Dukes, John P. *Law&B 92*
Dukes, Rebecca Weathers 1934- *WhoAmW 93, WhoE 93*
Dukes, Tamara Downham 1962- *WhoAmW 93*
Dukes, William W., Jr. 1917- *St&PR 93*
Dukes, Yvonne B. *St&PR 93*
Dukic, Dusan 1923- *WhoScE 91-4*
Dukler, Abraham Emanuel 1925- *WhoAm 92*
Dukoff, Robert Charles 1918- *WhoSSW 93*
Dukor, Peter *WhoScE 91-4*
Dukore, Bernard Frank 1931- *WhoAm 92*
Dukowitz, James Albert 1945- *WhoSSW 93*
Dula, Gloria Elisabeth 1958- *WhoEmL 93, WhoSSW 93*
Dula, Norman Lee 1924- *St&PR 93*
Dula, Rosa Lucile Noell 1914- *WhoAmW 93*
Dula, William A. 1932- *St&PR 93*
Dulai, Surjit Singh *WhoAm 92*
Dulak, Norman C. *Law&B 92*
Dulan, Harold Andrew 1911- *WhoAm 92*
Dulaney, Carol J. *Law&B 92*
Dulaney, Frank Alan 1929- *St&PR 93*
Dulaney, Richard Alvin 1948- *WhoEmL 93*
DuLaney, Tanya Lea 1958- *WhoAmW 93*
Dulanski, Gary Michael 1955- *WhoE 93*
Dulany, Charles Reihl 1934- *St&PR 93*
Dulany, Elizabeth Gjelsness 1931- *WhoAm 92, WhoAmW 93*
Dulany, Franklin Reed, Jr. 1931- *St&PR 93*
Dulany, William Bevard 1927- *St&PR 93, WhoAm 92*
DuLaurence, Henry J. 1905-1991 *BioIn 17*
DuLaux, Russell Frederick 1918- *WhoE 93*
Dulbecco, Renato 1914- *WhoAm 92, WhoWor 93*
Dulberg, Andrea I. *Law&B 92*
Dulchinos, Peter 1935- *WhoE 93*
Dulcken, Ferdinand Quentin 1837-1901 *Baker 92*
Dulcken, Luise 1811-1850 *Baker 92*
Dulcu, George 1940- *WhoScE 91-4*
Duley, John Alexander *WhoScE 91-1*
Dulfer, Candy *BioIn 17*
Dulfer, R.V. *WhoScE 91-3*
Dulich, Philipp 1562-1631 *Baker 92*
Dulichius, Philipp 1562-1631 *Baker 92*
Dulick, David J. *Law&B 92*
Dulieu, Hubert Louis 1935- *WhoScE 91-2*
Dulik, Arthur, Jr. 1946- *St&PR 93*
Dulik, Edward A. 1947- *St&PR 93*
Dulin, Thomas N. 1949- *WhoEmL 93*
Dulin, William A. 1949- *WhoEmL 93*
Duling, Brian Russell 1937- *WhoAm 92*
Duling, Paul 1916- *WhoWrEP 92*
Duling, Richard E. 1933- *St&PR 93*
Dulka, Joseph John 1951- *WhoE 93*
Dull, Charles W. 1940- *St&PR 93, WhoIns 93*
Dull, Christine *BioIn 17*
Dull, Dallas Kevin 1961- *WhoEmL 93, WhoSSW 93*
Dull, John E. *Law&B 92*
Dull, Ralph *BioIn 17*
Dull, William Martin 1924- *WhoAm 92*
Dullaghan, Matthew Peter 1957- *WhoEmL 93*
Dullea, Charles W. *WhoAm 92*
Dullea, Keir 1936- *WhoAm 92*
Dullens, H.F.J. 1947- *WhoScE 91-3*
Dulles, Allen 1893-1969 *ColdWar 1 [port]*
Dulles, Avery 1918- *WhoAm 92*
Dulles, Eleanor Lansing 1895- *WhoAm 92*
Dulles, Frederick Hendrik *Law&B 92*
Dulles, John Foster 1888-1959 *BioIn 17, ColdWar 1 [port], DcTwHis, PolPar*
Dullinger, Dennis R. *Law&B 92*
Dullum, Mervin E. 1922- *St&PR 93*
Dully, Frank Edward, Jr. 1932- *WhoWor 93*
Du Locle, Camille 1832-1903 *OxDcOp*
Du Locle, Camille Theophile Germain du Commun 1832-1903 *Baker 92*
Dulog, Lothar 1929- *WhoScE 91-3*
Dulog, Lothar Georg 1929- *WhoWor 93*
Dulon, Friedrich Ludwig 1769-1826 *Baker 92*
Duls, Louisa *AmWomPl*
Dultz, Ron William 1943- *WhoWrEP 92*
Dulude, Alain *Law&B 92*
Dulude, Donald O. 1928- *St&PR 93*
Dulude, Donald Owen 1928- *WhoAm 92*
Dulude, Richard 1933- *St&PR 93, WhoAm 92*
Duma, Richard Joseph 1933- *WhoAm 92*
Dumaine, Deborah Louise 1948- *WhoE 93*
Dumaine, F.C. 1902- *St&PR 93, WhoAm 92*
Dumaine, Pierre *BioIn 17*
DuMaine, R. Pierre 1931- *WhoAm 92*
du Maine, Wayne *NewYTBS 92 [port]*
Dumais, John Martin 1949- *WhoE 93*
Dumais, Lucien *BioIn 17*
Dumais, Mario 1941- *St&PR 93*
Duman, Maximilian G. 1906-1990 *BioIn 17*
Dumar, John W. 1945- *St&PR 93*
Dumaresq, John Edward 1913- *WhoAm 92*
Dumars, Joe, III 1963- *WhoAm 92*
Dumas, Alexandre 1802-1870 *BioIn 17, OxDcOp, WorLitC [port]*
Dumas, Alexandre 1824-1895 *BioIn 17, OxDcOp*
Dumas, Alexandre (Davy de la Pailleterie) 1802-1870 *DcLB 119 [port]*
Dumas, Benny T. *Law&B 92*
Dumas, Claudia J. *Law&B 92*
Dumas, Claudia Jean 1959- *WhoAmW 93, WhoEmL 93*
Dumas, Dale H. *St&PR 93*
Dumas, Jeffrey Mack *Law&B 92*
Dumas, Linda Jean 1959- *WhoEmL 93*
Dumas, Neil Stephen 1940- *WhoSSW 93*
Dumas, Patricia Morgan 1927- *WhoAmW 93*
Dumas, Rhetaugh Etheldra Graves 1928- *WhoAmW 93*
Dumas, Roland *BioIn 17*
Dumas, Roland 1922- *WhoWor 93*
Dumas, Thomas Alexandre 1762-1806 *BioIn 17*
Dumas-Hermes, Jean-Louis *BioIn 17*
Du Maurier, Daphne 1907-1989 *BioIn 17, ScF&FL 92*
Dumbacher, Robert *St&PR 93*
Dumbaugh, George David 1930- *St&PR 93*
Dumbaugh, John David 1949- *WhoSSW 93*
Dumbauld, Edward 1905- *WhoE 93*
Dumbleton, Mike 1948- *SmATA 73 [port]*
Dumbrajs, Olgierd 1942- *WhoWor 93*
Dumbuya, Ahmed R. *WhoWor 93*
Dumelin, Bruce Clayton 1948- *St&PR 93*
Dumelow, J. *WhoScE 91-1*
Dumencil, Josephine Alcantara 1964- *WhoWor 93*
Dumeny, Marcel J. *Law&B 92*
Dumeny, Marcel Jacque 1950- *St&PR 93, WhoAm 92, WhoEmL 93*
Dumesnil, Carla Davis 1946- *WhoEmL 93*
Dumesnil, Eugene Frederick, Jr. 1924- *St&PR 93*
Dumesnil, Maurice 1886-1974 *Baker 92*
Dumesnil, Rene (Alphonse Adolphe) 1879-1967 *Baker 92*
du Mesnil de Rochemont, Rudolf 1944- *WhoWor 93*
Du Mesnil Du Buisson, Francois 1925- *WhoScE 91-2*
Dumett, Clement Wallace, Jr. 1927- *WhoAm 92*
Dumezil, Georges 1898-1986 *IntDcAn*
Dumin, David Joseph 1935- *WhoSSW 93*
Dumit, Thomas A. *Law&B 92*
Dumitrescu, Natalia 1915- *BioIn 17*
Dumitrescu, Domnita *WhoAmW 93*
Dumitrescu, Gheorghe 1914- *Baker 92*
Dumitrescu, Ion 1913- *Baker 92*
Dumitrescu, Sorin *BioIn 17*
Dumitrescu, Traian 1922- *WhoScE 91-4*
Dumke, William Edner 1930- *St&PR 93*
Dumm, Demetrius Robert 1923- *WhoAm 92*
Dumm, Frances Edwina 1893-1990 *BioIn 17*
Dummer, George *BioIn 17*
Dummett, Clifton Orrin 1919- *WhoAm 92*
Dummett, Michael Anthony Eardley 1925- *WhoWor 93*
Dumnire, Ronald Warren 1937- *St&PR 93*
Dumond, John William *Law&B 92*
Dumonet, Andre A. 1930- *St&PR 93, WhoWor 93*
DuMont, Alfred Neven- 1927- *BioIn 17*
Dumont, Allan Eliot 1924- *WhoAm 92*
Dumont, Andre *WhoScE 91-2*
DuMont, Bruce *WhoAm 92*
Dumont, Clark Peter 1955- *WhoE 93*
Du Mont, Dolph Joseph 1927- *WhoSSW 93*
Dumont, Edward Abdo 1961- *WhoSSW 93*
Dumont, Eleanora d1897 *BioIn 17*
Du Mont, Henri 1610-1684 *Baker 92*
Dumont, Jacques 1927- *WhoScE 91-2*
Dumont, Jacques E. 1931- *WhoScE 91-2*
Dumont, Johan Joseph 1935- *WhoWor 93*
Dumont, Judith Owen *Law&B 92*
Dumont, Louis 1911- *IntDcAn*
Dumont, Margaret 1889-1965 *IntDcF 2-3, QDrFCA 92 [port]*
Dumont, Pierre Alphonse M. 1928- *WhoScE 91-2*
Dumont, Rene 1904- *BioIn 17*
Dumont, Richard George 1940- *WhoE 93*
Du Mont, Robert James, Sr. 1942- *WhoE 93*
Du Mont, Rosemary Ruhig 1947- *WhoAm 92*
Dumont, Sandra Jean 1955- *WhoAmW 93, WhoEmL 93*
Dumont, Wayne 1914-1992 *BioIn 17*
Dumont, Wayne, Jr. 1914-1992 *NewYTBS 92 [port]*
Du Mont, Wolf-Walter 1945- *WhoScE 91-3*
Dumont, Yves Jean-Marie 1950- *WhoWor 93*
Dumont d'Urville, Jules-Sebastien-Cesar 1790-1842 *Expl 93 [port]*
Dumont du Voitel, Roland Jean 1947- *WhoWor 93*
Dumortier, Francois-Xavier 1948- *WhoWor 93*
Dumouchel, J. Robert 1936- *WhoWrEP 92*
DuMoulin, Diana Cristaudo 1939- *WhoAmW 93*
Dumoulin, Jacques 1942- *St&PR 93*
Dumouriez, Charles Francois du Perrier 1739-1823 *HarEnMi*
Du Mouza, Jean 1948- *WhoScE 91-2*
Dumovich, Loretta 1930- *WhoAm 92*
Dumpas, M. Stevens 1937- *St&PR 93*
Dun, Peter *WhoScE 91-1*
Dunagan, Dianne Efurd 1943- *WhoSSW 93*
Dunagan, J. Conrad 1914- *WhoSSW 93*
Dunagan, John Charles 1942- *WhoE 93*
Dunagan, Walter Benton 1937- *WhoSSW 93*
Dunaif, Alexandra Louise 1957- *WhoEmL 93*
Dunajski, Zbigniew 1936- *WhoScE 91-4*
Dunand, Jean 1877-1942 *BioIn 17*
Dunant, Christiane 1917-1991 *BioIn 17*
Dunant, Henri 1828-1910 *BioIn 17*
Dunant, Yves 1937- *WhoScE 91-4*
Dunathan, Harmon Craig 1932- *WhoAm 92*
Dunavan, Ilena Abrams 1938- *WhoAmW 93*
Dunaway, Carl L. *St&PR 93*
Dunaway, David King 1948- *ScF&FL 92*
Dunaway, Donald L. 1937- *St&PR 93*
Dunaway, Donald Lucius 1937- *WhoAm 92*
Dunaway, Faye *BioIn 17*
Dunaway, Faye 1941- *IntDcF 2-3 [port], WhoAm 92, WhoAmW 93*
Dunaway, Hettie Jane *AmWomPl*
Dunaway, Victor Allan 1928- *WhoAm 92*
Dunaway, Wayland Fuller 1912- *St&PR 93*
Dunaway, William Burns 1939- *St&PR 93*
Dunaway, William Preston 1936- *WhoSSW 93*
Dunayevskaya, Alla 1920- *WhoAm 92*
Dunayevsky, Isaak 1900-1955 *Baker 92*
Dunbar, Anne Cynthia 1938- *WhoE 93*
Dunbar, Anthony P. *Law&B 92*
Dunbar, Bonnie J. 1949- *WhoAmW 93*
Dunbar, Brian Jay d1991 *BioIn 17*
Dunbar, Bruce C. 1949- *St&PR 93*
Dunbar, Charles Edward, III 1926- *WhoAm 92*
Dunbar, Charles Franklin 1937- *WhoWor 93*
Dunbar, Childs E., III *Law&B 92*
Dunbar, David Wesley 1952- *WhoEmL 93, WhoSSW 93*
Dunbar, Dirk R. 1954- *St&PR 93*
Dunbar, Dorothy M. d1991 *BioIn 17*
Dunbar, Edward Caswell 1925- *St&PR 93*
Dunbar, Frank Rollin 1953- *WhoAm 92*
Dunbar, Holly Jean 1960- *WhoAmW 93, WhoEmL 93*
Dunbar, Jacob Ross, III 1952- *WhoEmL 93, WhoSSW 93*
Dunbar, James Anthony *WhoScE 91-1*
Dunbar, James V., Jr. 1937- *WhoAm 92*
Dunbar, Jill H. 1949- *WhoE 93, WhoEmL 93*
Dunbar, Joan Mary 1931- *WhoE 93*
Dunbar, John Burton 1929- *WhoAm 92*
Dunbar, John Raine 1911- *WhoAm 92*
Dunbar, Joyce *ScF&FL 92*
Dunbar, Leslie Wallace 1921- *WhoAm 92*
Dunbar, Maxwell John 1914- *WhoAm 92*
Dunbar, Natalie Marie 1961- *WhoAmW 93*
Dunbar, Olivia Howard 1873- *AmWomPl*
Dunbar, Paul Laurence 1872-1906 *BioIn 17, BlkAull 92, EncAACR, GayN, MagSAmL [port], PoeCrit 5 [port], WorLitC [port]*
Dunbar, Prescott Nelson 1942- *WhoSSW 93*
Dunbar, Richard Paul 1951- *WhoEmL 93, WhoWor 93*
Dunbar, Robert *ScF&FL 92*
Dunbar, Robert J. 1948- *St&PR 93*
Dunbar, W. Rudolph 1907-1988 *Baker 92*
Dunbar, Wallace 1931- *St&PR 93*
Dunbar, Wallace Huntington 1931- *WhoAm 92*
Dunbar, William 1460?-1530? *LitC 20*
Dunbar-Nelson, Alice Moore 1875-1935 *BioIn 17*
Dunbar-Nelson, Alice Ruth Moore 1875-1935 *AmWomPl*
Dunbavin, Philip Richard 1953- *WhoWor 93*
Dunbobbin, Brian Roy 1951- *WhoE 93*
Duncalf, Deryck 1926- *WhoAm 92*
Duncan, A. Baker 1927- *St&PR 93, WhoAm 92*
Duncan, Alan Eugene 1951- *WhoEmL 93*
Duncan, Alastair 1942- *ConAu 40NR*
Duncan, Alastair Robert Campbell 1915- *WhoAm 92*
Duncan, Andrew Rodway 1950- *WhoSSW 93*
Duncan, Antonia O. *St&PR 93*
Duncan, Barbara 1882-1965 *BioIn 17*
Duncan, Budd Lee 1936- *WhoSSW 93*
Duncan, Buell Gard, Jr. 1928- *St&PR 93*
Duncan, Carol Spindler 1942- *WhoE 93*
Duncan, Charles Clifford 1907- *WhoAm 92, WhoWor 93*
Duncan, Charles Howard 1924- *WhoAm 92*
Duncan, Charles Lee 1939- *WhoAm 92*
Duncan, Charles Tignor 1924- *WhoAm 92*
Duncan, Charles William, Jr. 1926- *WhoAm 92*
Duncan, Christopher John *WhoScE 91-1*
Duncan, Claudia Louise 1955- *WhoAmW 93, WhoEmL 93, WhoSSW 93*
Duncan, Constance Catharine 1948- *WhoE 93*
Duncan, Craig *WhoScE 91-1*
Duncan, Cynthia Kay 1952- *WhoSSW 93*
Duncan, D. K. *DcCPCAm*
Duncan, Daniel Lee 1956- *WhoEmL 93*
Duncan, Daniel Ward 1956- *WhoEmL 93*
Duncan, Dave 1933- *ScF&FL 92*
Duncan, David Douglas 1916- *WhoAm 92*
Duncan, David J. *ScF&FL 92*
Duncan, David S. 1958- *St&PR 93*
Duncan, Donald Pendleton 1916- *WhoAm 92*
Duncan, Donald William 1932- *WhoAm 92*
Duncan, Douglas Ronald, Jr. 1962- *WhoSSW 93*
Duncan, Elizabeth Charlotte 1919- *WhoAm 92, WhoAmW 93, WhoWor 93*
Duncan, Erica Joan 1953- *WhoE 93*
Duncan, Ernest R. d1990 *BioIn 17*
Duncan, Frances 1877- *AmWomPl*
Duncan, Frances Murphy 1920- *WhoAmW 93*
Duncan, (Sandy) Frances (Mary) 1942- *ConAu 37NR*
Duncan, Francis 1922- *WhoAm 92*
Duncan, George H. 1931- *WhoAm 92*
Duncan, George Ronald 1923- *WhoIns 93*
Duncan, Gordon Stuart 1933- *St&PR 93*
Duncan, Hearst Randolph 1905- *WhoAm 92*
Duncan, Irma Wagner 1912- *WhoAmW 93*
Duncan, Isadora 1878-1927 *BioIn 17*
Duncan, J. Ann 1940-1989 *BioIn 17*
Duncan, J. Russell *St&PR 93*
Duncan, Jack G. 1939- *WhoE 93*
Duncan, James Daniel 1941- *St&PR 93*
Duncan, James Elton *St&PR 93*
Duncan, James H., Jr. 1947- *WhoEmL 93*
Duncan, James Herbert C. 1925- *St&PR 93*
Duncan, James Lindsay *WhoScE 91-1*
Duncan, James Ward 1963- *WhoEmL 93*
Duncan, Jody *ScF&FL 92*
Duncan, John Bonner 1910- *WhoAm 92*
Duncan, John C. 1920- *St&PR 93, WhoAm 92*
Duncan, John Dean, Jr. 1950- *WhoAm 92*
Duncan, John H. *WhoAm 92*
Duncan, John J., Jr. 1947- *CngDr 91, WhoAm 92, WhoSSW 93*
Duncan, John Lapsley 1933- *WhoAm 92*
Duncan, John R., Jr. *Law&B 92*
Duncan, John Wiley 1947- *WhoEmL 93*
Duncan, John Willie Kwamina 1933- *WhoUN 92*
Duncan, Jon Allan 1954- *WhoEmL 93*
Duncan, Joseph Thomas David 1933- *WhoWor 93*
Duncan, Joseph Wayman 1936- *St&PR 93, WhoAm 92*
Duncan, Joyce Louise 1946- *WhoAmW 93*
Duncan, Judith Farley 1941- *WhoAmW 93*

Duncan, Julia K. MajAI
Duncan, Julie SweetSg C
Duncan, K.P. 1924- WhoScE 91-1
Duncan, Keith Duncan WhoScE 91-1
Duncan, Kenne d1972 BioIn 17
Duncan, Kenneth V. 1938- St&PR 93
Duncan, Kirk ScF&FL 92
Duncan, L. B. AmWomPl
Duncan, Larry Thomas 1951- WhoSSW 93
Duncan, Lisa Ann 1962- WhoAmW 93
Duncan, Lois 1934- ChlLR 29 [port], DcAmChF 1960, DcAmChF 1985, MajAI [port], ScF&FL 92
Duncan, Lonnie Ernest 1929- St&PR 93
Duncan, Mallory B. Law&B 92
Duncan, Marcus Homer, III 1941- WhoSSW 93
Duncan, Margaret Caroline 1930- WhoAm 92
Duncan, Mark William 1954- WhoWor 93
Duncan, Matthew 1785-1844 JrnUS
Duncan, Maurice Greer 1928- WhoSSW 93
Duncan, Melba Frances Hurd WhoAmW 93
Duncan, Michael Jeffrey 1959- WhoEmL 93
Duncan, Michael P. Law&B 92
Duncan, Norman 1871-1916 BioIn 17
Duncan, Patrick MiSFD 9
Duncan, Patrick 1948- WhoScE 91-2
Duncan, Paul R. Law&B 92
Duncan, Paul R. 1940- St&PR 93
Duncan, Peter 1945- WhoAsAP 91
Duncan, Peter A. 1942- St&PR 93
Duncan, Phillip K. 1951- St&PR 93
Duncan, Phillip Marshall 1954- WhoEmL 93, WhoSSW 93
Duncan, Pope Alexander 1920- WhoAm 92, WhoSSW 93
Duncan, R. Michael 1931-1991 BioIn 17
Duncan, Raymond Glenn 1952- WhoEmL 93
Duncan, Richard 1913- WhoAm 92
Duncan, Richard Fred 1951- WhoEmL 93
Duncan, Richard Fredrick, Jr. 1947- WhoEmL 93
Duncan, Richard Hurley 1944- WhoSSW 93
Duncan, Richard Marc Law&B 92
Duncan, Robert 1919-1988 MagSAmL [port]
Duncan, Robert Bannerman 1942- WhoAm 92
Duncan, Robert Clifton 1923- WhoAm 92
Duncan, Robert D. 1939- St&PR 93
Duncan, Robert Edward 1919-1988 BioIn 17
Duncan, Robert Eugene 1938- WhoSSW 93
Duncan, Robert L. 1927- ScF&FL 92
Duncan, Robert L. 1942- St&PR 93
Duncan, Robert Michael 1951- WhoSSW 93
Duncan, Ronald 1914-1982 ScF&FL 92
Duncan, Rosslyn K. 1952- St&PR 93
Duncan, Russell Cushman, III 1947- WhoEmL 93
Duncan, Ruth WhoScE 91-1
Duncan, Sandy BioIn 17
Duncan, Sandy 1946- WhoAm 92
Duncan, Sandy Frances 1942- WhoCanL 92
Duncan, Sara Jeannette 1861-1922 BioIn 17
Duncan, Sarah L. AmWomPl
Duncan, Starkey Davis, Jr. 1935- WhoAm 92
Duncan, Stephen Mack 1941- WhoAm 92
Duncan, Steven Andrew 1947- St&PR 93
Duncan, Sylvia Lorena 1949- WhoAmW 93
Duncan, Tanya Faye 1959- WhoAmW 93
Duncan, Thelma Myrtle 1902- AmWomPl
Duncan, Thomas Alton 1942- WhoAm 92
Duncan, Thomas Michael Cavanaugh 1962- WhoEmL 93
Duncan, Timothy Brian 1950- WhoEmL 93
Duncan, Todd BioIn 17
Duncan, Virgil D. 1920- St&PR 93
Duncan, W.R. St&PR 93
Duncan, Wallace Lee 1956- WhoEmL 93
Duncan, William 1879-1961 BioIn 17
Duncan, William Anthony 1940- WhoWor 93
Duncan, William Edmondstoune 1866-1920 Baker 92
Duncan, William M. 1939- St&PR 93
Duncan, William Millen 1939- WhoAm 92, WhoE 93
Duncan, Winifred AmWomPl
Duncanson, Harry Richard 1947- WhoEmL 93, WhoSSW 93
Duncanson, William A. Law&B 92
Duncker, Dora 1855-1915 AmWomPl
Duncker, Hans-Rainer 1933- WhoScE 91-3
Duncombe, Henry L. 1914-1990 BioIn 17
Duncombe, Raynor Bailey 1942- WhoE 93
Duncombe, Raynor Lockwood 1917- WhoAm 92, WhoWor 93
Duncovich, Richard M. 1933- St&PR 93
Duncumb, P. WhoScE 91-1
Dundas, Anthony J. 1946- St&PR 93
Dundas, Philip Blair, Jr. 1948- WhoAm 92, WhoE 93
Dundee, Angelo BioIn 17
Dundee, Harold Abraham 1924- WhoSSW 93
Dunderfelt, Stig Goran 1929- WhoWor 93
Dundes, Alan 1934- WhoAm 92
Dundes, Jules 1913- WhoAm 92
Dundes, Lester BioIn 17
Dundish, Harold Ian 1946- St&PR 93
Dundon, James A. Law&B 92
Dundon, Margo Elaine 1950- WhoAm 92, WhoAmW 93
Dundon, Robert Walden 1932- WhoWor 93
Dundon, Susan BioIn 17
Dundy, Richard Alan 1945- WhoE 93
Dune, Steve Charles 1931- St&PR 93, WhoAm 92, WhoWor 93
Dunea, George 1933- WhoAm 92
Dunetz, Lora E. WhoWrEP 92
Dunfee, David Edward 1952- St&PR 93
Dunfee, Earl William 1934- St&PR 93
Dunfee, Thomas Wylie 1941- WhoAm 92
Dunfey, Robert John, Jr. 1951- WhoEmL 93
Dunfey, William Leo 1926-1991 BioIn 17
Dunford, E.D. BioIn 17
Dunford, Robert A. Law&B 92
Dunford, Robert A. 1931- St&PR 93, WhoAm 92, WhoWor 93
Dungan, Laurel Jane 1963- WhoAmW 93
Dungan, Malcolm Thon 1922- WhoAm 92
Dungan, Martha Jan 1954- WhoSSW 93
Dungan, Ronald S. 1939- St&PR 93
Dungan, Ronald Samuel 1939- WhoAm 92
Dungan, Vicki Lou 1951- WhoEmL 93
Dungan, William Joseph, Jr. 1956- WhoEmL 93, WhoSSW 93
D'Unger, Giselle C. AmWomPl
Dungey, Gordon S. 1926- St&PR 93
Dungey, Joan Marie 1944- WhoWrEP 92
Dungworth, Donald L. 1931- WhoAm 92
Dunham, Alice Clarke 1905- WhoAmW 93
Dunham, Allison d1992 NewYTBS 92
Dunham, Ansel Charles WhoScE 91-1
Dunham, Audian D. 1941- WhoAm 92
Dunham, Benjamin Starr 1944- WhoAm 92
Dunham, Bernadette Margaret 1950- WhoAmW 93
Dunham, Charles A. BioIn 17
Dunham, Christine WhoAm 92
Dunham, Corydon Busnell 1927- WhoAm 92
Dunham, D. Ross 1928- WhoAm 92
Dunham, David Barr 1953- WhoSSW 93
Dunham, Donald Carl 1908- WhoAm 92
Dunham, Frank G., Jr. 1930- WhoIns 93
Dunham, Frank L. 1940- WhoAm 92
Dunham, Frederick St&PR 93
Dunham, Gregory Mark 1958- WhoSSW 93
Dunham, Henry Morton 1853-1929 Baker 92
Dunham, James Ira 1942- St&PR 93
Dunham, Joanne Krok 1957- WhoEmL 93
Dunham, John E. St&PR 93
Dunham, Katherine BioIn 17
Dunham, Katherine 1910?- ConBlB 4 [port]
Dunham, Katherine 1912- IntDcAn
Dunham, (Bertha) Mabel 1881-1957 DcChlFi
Dunham, Meggin Marie 1956- WhoAmW 93, WhoEmL 93
Dunham, Mikel 1948- ConAu 138
Dunham, Philip Bigelow 1937- WhoAm 92, WhoE 93
Dunham, Portia Playfair d1990 BioIn 17
Dunham, Rick 1959- BioIn 17
Dunham, Robert S. 1906-1991 BioIn 17
Dunham, Selena L. 1952- WhoAmW 93
Dunham, Sherrie Ann 1949- WhoWrEP 92
Dunham, Spurgeon M. d1991 BioIn 17
Dunham-Cragg, Melissa Kay 1956- WhoEmL 93
Dunhill, Robert 1929- St&PR 93
Dunhill, Robert H. 1929- WhoAm 92
Dunhill, Thomas (Frederick) 1877-1946 Baker 92
Duni, Egidio Romualdo 1708?-1775 OxDcOp
Duni, Egidio (Romualdo) 1709-1775 Baker 92
Dunican, John James 1932- St&PR 93
Dunigan, Dennis Wayne 1952- WhoEmL 93, WhoWor 93
Dunigan, Michael W. Law&B 92
Dunikowski, Stanislaw 1925- WhoScE 91-4
Dunikowski, Xawery 1875-1964 PolBiDi
Dunin, Martin Von 1774-1842 PolBiDi
Dunin-Karwicka, Teresa 1931- WhoWor 93
Dunin-Wasowicz, Edward 1951- WhoEmL 93
Dunipace, Ian Douglas 1939- WhoAm 92
Dunitz, Jay BioIn 17
Duniway, John Mason 1942- WhoAm 92
Dunk, Jeanne M. Law&B 92
Dunk, Thomas W. 1955- ConAu 139
Dunkel, Arthur 1932- WhoUN 92, WhoWor 93
Dunkel, Florence Vaccarello 1942- WhoAm 92, WhoAmW 93
Dunkel, James Michael 1949- St&PR 93
Dunkel, Nancy Ann 1955- WhoAmW 93
Dunkel, Tom Richard 1950- WhoWrEP 92
Dunkelberg, James Graham 1959- WhoSSW 93
Dunkelberger, Rosemarie 1926- WhoE 93
Dunker, Robert F. 1931- St&PR 93
Dunker, Robert Ferdinand 1931- WhoIns 93
Dunkerley, Eve Law&B 92
Dunkerley, William 1942- WhoE 93
Dunkerson, Dennis L. 1947- St&PR 93, WhoIns 93
Dunkin, Ellen R. Law&B 92
Dunkirk, Alan B. 1947- St&PR 93
Dunklau, Rupert Louis 1927- WhoAm 92
Dunkle, Eleanor C. 1941- St&PR 93
Dunkle, Joseph Lee 1943- WhoWor 93
Dunkle, Sidney Warren 1940- WhoSSW 93
Dunkle, William F. 1942- St&PR 93
Dunklebarger, Eddie L. 1954- St&PR 93
Dunkley, Ferdinand (Luis) 1869-1956 Baker 92
Dunkley, S.H. Law&B 92
Dunko, M.G. Law&B 92
Dunlap, Bruce 1945- St&PR 93
Dunlap, Charles Lee 1943- WhoAm 92
Dunlap, Charles Leonard Law&B 92
Dunlap, Connie 1924- WhoAm 92
Dunlap, Connie Sue Zimmerman 1952- WhoEmL 93
Dunlap, David Houston 1947- WhoEmL 93
Dunlap, Doris Elaine 1926- WhoAmW 93
Dunlap, Douglas R. 1948- St&PR 93
Dunlap, E. T. 1914- WhoAm 92
Dunlap, Ellen S. 1951- WhoAm 92, WhoAmW 93
Dunlap, F. Thomas 1951- St&PR 93
Dunlap, F. Thomas, Jr. Law&B 92
Dunlap, F. Thomas, Jr. 1951- WhoAm 92
Dunlap, Frederick C. 1859-1902 BiDAMSp 1989
Dunlap, G.A. 1925- St&PR 93
Dunlap, George H. 1906-1991 BioIn 17
Dunlap, Gerard Willard 1956- WhoE 93
Dunlap, Henrietta F. AmWomPl
Dunlap, Henry Francis 1916- WhoSSW 93
Dunlap, Jack BioIn 17
Dunlap, James Lapham 1937- St&PR 93, WhoAm 92
Dunlap, Jane Reber 1932- St&PR 93
Dunlap, Joe Everett 1930- WhoWrEP 92
Dunlap, John 1747-1812 JrnUS
Dunlap, Joseph 1913-1984? ScF&FL 92
Dunlap, Kathleen Powers 1958- WhoAmW 93, WhoEmL 93
Dunlap, Linda Louise 1954- WhoEmL 93
Dunlap, Paul D. 1930- St&PR 93, WhoAm 92
Dunlap, Philip Glenn 1940- WhoE 93
Dunlap, Philip Stanley 1918- WhoAm 92, WhoE 93
Dunlap, Robert Bruce 1942- WhoSSW 93
Dunlap, Robert H. Law&B 92
Dunlap, Rufus Thornwell, Jr. 1931- WhoSSW 93
Dunlap, Stanton Parks 1934- WhoSSW 93
Dunlap, Troy BioIn 17
Dunlap, William Crawford 1918- WhoAm 92
Dunlap, William D. 1938- St&PR 93
Dunlap, William Gray 1937- WhoSSW 93
Dunlavey, Nicholas Robert WhoScE 91-1
Dunlea, Nancy D. AmWomPl
Dunleavy, Gareth Winthrop 1923- WhoAm 92
Dunleavy, Janet Egleson 1928- WhoWrEP 92
Dunleavy, Janet Frank Egleson 1928- WhoAm 92
Dunleavy, Kristie Lyn 1957- WhoEmL 93
Dunleavy, Mary Ann 1956- WhoAmW 93
Dunleavy, Mike WhoAm 92
Dunleavy, Nancy B. 1936- WhoAmW 93
Dunleavy, Patricia Elizabeth 1955- WhoAmW 93, WhoE 93
Dunleavy, Richard Michael 1933- WhoAm 92
Dunleavy, Steve BioIn 17
Dunleavy, Thomas J. 1938- St&PR 93
Dunlevy, Jerome Michael 1926- St&PR 93
Dunlevy, Marion B. 1930- WhoWrEP 92
Dunlevy, Ralph Donald 1925- St&PR 93
Dunlevy, Richard J. 1934- St&PR 93
Dunlevy, William Gregory 1955- WhoSSW 93
Dunlop, Bruce Robert 1953- WhoE 93
Dunlop, David John 1941- WhoAm 92
Dunlop, Eileen 1938- ScF&FL 92
Dunlop, Eileen (Rhona) 1938- MajAI [port]
Dunlop, Frank 1927- WhoWor 93
Dunlop, George Rodgers 1906- WhoAm 92
Dunlop, Isobel 1901-1975 Baker 92
Dunlop, James Joseph 1934- WhoE 93
Dunlop, John WhoScE 91-1
Dunlop, John Barrett 1942- WhoAm 92
Dunlop, John Thomas 1914- WhoAm 92, WhoE 93
Dunlop, Nicholas James 1956- WhoWor 93
Dunlop, Robert G. 1909- St&PR 93
Dunlop, Robert Galbraith 1909- WhoAm 92
Dunlop, Robert Hugh 1929- WhoAm 92
Dunlop, William 1792-1848 BioIn 17
Dunman, Leonard Joe, III 1952- WhoEmL 93, WhoSSW 93
Dunmeyer, Sarah Louise Fisher 1935- WhoAmW 93
Dunmire, Ethel M. AmWomPl
Dunmire, Philip L. 1946- St&PR 93
Dunmire, Ronald W. 1937- St&PR 93
Dunmire, Ronald Warren 1937- WhoAm 92
Dunmire, Virginia J. Law&B 92
Dunmire, William Werden 1930- WhoAm 92
Dunmore, Brian Lynn Law&B 92
Dunmore, John Murray, Earl of 1732-1809 HarEnMi
Dunmore, Spencer 1928- ScF&FL 92, WhoCanL 92
Dunn, A. Dale 1923- St&PR 93
Dunn, Adolphus William 1922- WhoSSW 93
Dunn, Alan Michael 1953- WhoAm 92
Dunn, Alexander Simpson 1927- WhoWor 93
Dunn, Andrew Diedrich 1959- WhoE 93
Dunn, Andrew Fletcher 1922- WhoAm 92
Dunn, Arnold Samuel 1929- WhoAm 92
Dunn, Arthur J. 1933- St&PR 93
Dunn, Barbara A. Law&B 92
Dunn, Bernice Marie 1934- WhoAmW 93
Dunn, Bonnie Brill 1953- WhoAm 92, WhoAmW 93, WhoEmL 93
Dunn, Bruce A. 1931- St&PR 93
Dunn, Bruce Edward 1951- WhoWrEP 92
Dunn, Bruce Sidney 1948- WhoAm 92
Dunn, Charles DeWitt 1945- WhoAm 92
Dunn, Charles R. 1930- WhoAm 92
Dunn, Charles T. 1930- St&PR 93
Dunn, Charles William 1915- WhoAm 92, WhoE 93
Dunn, Charleta Jessie 1927- WhoSSW 93
Dunn, Christopher Leslie 1953- WhoE 93
Dunn, Clark Allan 1901- WhoAm 92
Dunn, David 1943- St&PR 93
Dunn, David E. 1935- WhoAm 92
Dunn, David J. 1930- St&PR 93
Dunn, David Joseph 1930- WhoAm 92
Dunn, David N. 1940- WhoIns 93
Dunn, David Nelson 1940- St&PR 93
Dunn, David S. 1943- St&PR 93
Dunn, Dawn 1958- ScF&FL 92
Dunn, Dean Alan 1954- WhoSSW 93
Dunn, Deborah Dechellis 1960- WhoAmW 93, WhoEmL 93
Dunn, Delmer Delano 1941- WhoAm 92
Dunn, Dennis ScF&FL 92
Dunn, Donald 1941- SoulM
Dunn, Donald Allen 1925- WhoAm 92
Dunn, Donald M. 1903- St&PR 93
Dunn, Douglas BioIn 17
Dunn, E. Paul 1953- St&PR 93
Dunn, Edward K., Jr. 1935- WhoAm 92
Dunn, Elizabeth T. Law&B 92
Dunn, Ellen Marie 1958- WhoAmW 93
Dunn, Elsie 1893-1963 BioIn 17
Dunn, Elwood 1906- WhoAm 92
Dunn, Evans, Jr. 1932- St&PR 93
Dunn, Fannie Wyche 1879- AmWomPl
Dunn, Floyd 1924- WhoAm 92
Dunn, Geoffrey 1903- OxDcOp
Dunn, George B. Law&B 92
Dunn, George J. Law&B 92
Dunn, George J. 1935- St&PR 93, WhoAm 92
Dunn, Gerald A. 1934- St&PR 93
Dunn, Gertrude 1884-1926 ScF&FL 92
Dunn, Gloria 1939- WhoAmW 93
Dunn, Grace Veronica WhoAmW 93, WhoE 93, WhoWor 93
Dunn, H. Stewart, Jr. 1929- WhoAm 92
Dunn, Hampton 1916- WhoWrEP 92
Dunn, Harry David 1954- St&PR 93

Dunn, Henry Hampton 1916- *WhoAm 92, WhoSSW 93, WhoWor 93*
Dunn, Horton, Jr. 1929- *WhoAm 92, WhoWor 93*
Dunn, Howard James 1931- *St&PR 93*
Dunn, Jackson Thomas, Jr. *Law&B 92*
Dunn, James Alan 1933- *WhoE 93*
Dunn, James Edward, Jr. 1947- *WhoEmL 93*
Dunn, James Ewing 1937- *WhoSSW 93*
Dunn, James Joseph 1920- *WhoAm 92*
Dunn, James Melvin 1948- *WhoEmL 93*
Dunn, James Milton 1932- *WhoE 93*
Dunn, James P., Jr. 1936- *St&PR 93*
Dunn, James Philip 1884-1936 *Baker 92*
Dunn, James Robert 1921- *WhoAm 92*
Dunn, Jason M. *Law&B 92*
Dunn, Jeffrey Allyn 1955- *WhoEmL 93*
Dunn, Jeffrey Marc 1946- *WhoEmL 93*
Dunn, Jeffrey William 1947- *WhoEmL 93*
Dunn, Jennifer Blackburn 1941- *WhoAmW 93*
Dunn, Jerry Camarillo, Jr. 1947- *WhoEmL 93*
Dunn, Jerry R. 1935- *St&PR 93*
Dunn, Jim Edward 1948- *WhoEmL 93, WhoSSW 93*
Dunn, John 1866-1940 *Baker 92*
Dunn, John Benjamin 1948- *WhoEmL 93*
Dunn, John David 1945- *St&PR 93*
Dunn, John Joseph 1872-1928 *BiDAMSp 1989*
Dunn, John Petri 1878-1931 *Baker 92*
Dunn, John R. 1934- *St&PR 93*
Dunn, John Samuel 1954- *WhoSSW 93*
Dunn, John W. 1944- *St&PR 93*
Dunn, Jon Michael 1941- *WhoAm 92*
Dunn, Jonah Marshall 1913- *WhoWrEP 92*
Dunn, Joseph Charles 1938- *WhoSSW 93*
Dunn, Joseph Franklin 1936- *WhoSSW 93*
Dunn, Judy Agner 1945- *WhoAmW 93*
Dunn, Julia 1953- *WhoWrEP 92*
Dunn, Katherine 1945- *ConLC 71 [port], ScF&FL 92*
Dunn, Keith Mervin 1959- *WhoEmL 93*
Dunn, Kendra Lee 1952- *WhoSSW 93*
Dunn, Kenneth Ralph 1958- *WhoE 93*
Dunn, L.E. *Law&B 92*
Dunn, Larry A. 1945- *St&PR 93*
Dunn, Leon A., Jr. 1938- *St&PR 93*
Dunn, Leslie Clarence 1893-1974 *BioIn 17*
Dunn, Linda Kay 1947- *WhoAm 92, WhoAmW 93*
Dunn, Linwood G. 1904- *BioIn 17*
Dunn, Lloyd W. d1991 *BioIn 17*
Dunn, Lydia 1940- *WhoAsAP 91*
Dunn, M. Catherine 1934- *WhoAm 92, WhoAmW 93*
Dunn, Margaret Ann 1953- *WhoAmW 93*
Dunn, Margaret Mary Coyne 1909- *WhoAmW 93*
Dunn, Mark Rodney 1956- *WhoE 93*
Dunn, Marvin Irvin 1927- *WhoAm 92*
Dunn, Mary E. *Law&B 92*
Dunn, Mary Elizabeth 1954- *WhoEmL 93, WhoSSW 93*
Dunn, Mary Jarratt 1942- *WhoAm 92*
Dunn, Mary Lois 1930- *DcAmChF 1960*
Dunn, Mary Maples *BioIn 17*
Dunn, Mary Maples 1931- *WhoAm 92, WhoAmW 93*
Dunn, Matthew Joseph 1958- *WhoEmL 93*
Dunn, Maureen H. *Law&B 92*
Dunn, Melvin B. 1936- *WhoIns 93*
Dunn, Melvin Bernard 1936- *St&PR 93, WhoAm 92*
Dunn, Michael Brown 1954- *WhoEmL 93*
Dunn, Mignon *WhoAm 92*
Dunn, Mignon 1931- *Baker 92*
Dunn, Morris Douglas 1944- *WhoAm 92*
Dunn, Norman S. 1921- *St&PR 93*
Dunn, Norman Samuel 1921- *WhoAm 92*
Dunn, Parker Southerland 1910- *WhoAm 92*
Dunn, Patrice Marie 1956- *WhoEmL 93*
Dunn, Patricia d1990 *BioIn 17*
Dunn, Patricia Ann 1942- *WhoAmW 93*
Dunn, Patricia Dixon 1946- *WhoAmW 93*
Dunn, Paul Francis, Jr. 1958- *WhoE 93*
Dunn, Pauline *ScF&FL 92*
Dunn, Peter *WhoScE 91-1*
Dunn, Peter 1946- *WhoIns 93*
Dunn, Peter L. 1945- *St&PR 93*
Dunn, Philip *ScF&FL 92*
Dunn, R.P. *St&PR 93*
Dunn, Randy Edwin 1954- *WhoEmL 93*
Dunn, Ray Aloysius, III 1948- *WhoE 93*
Dunn, Raymond Elmer, Jr. 1956- *WhoEmL 93*
Dunn, Rebecca Diane 1948- *WhoAmW 93, WhoEmL 93*
Dunn, Richard Johann *BioIn 17*
Dunn, Richard John 1938- *WhoAm 92*
Dunn, R Richard John 1938- *WhoAm 92*
Dunn, Robert Alex 1946- *St&PR 93*
Dunn, Robert Andrew *Law&B 92*
Dunn, Robert C. *St&PR 93*
Dunn, Robert Hayes, Jr. 1927- *St&PR 93*
Dunn, Robert Vincent 1929- *St&PR 93, WhoAm 92*
Dunn, Roger Terry 1946- *WhoEmL 93*
Dunn, Ronald 1937- *WhoScE 91-1*
Dunn, Ronald Holland 1937- *WhoSSW 93, WhoWor 93*
Dunn, Ronald Leslie 1954- *WhoEmL 93*
Dunn, Roy J. 1946- *WhoAm 92*
Dunn, Saul 1946- *ScF&FL 92*
Dunn, Sharon 1946- *St&PR 93*
Dunn, Stephen 1939- *BioIn 17*
Dunn, Stephen Elliott 1939- *WhoWrEP 92*
Dunn, Stephen Michael 1950- *WhoEmL 93*
Dunn, Susan 1954- *WhoAm 92, WhoAmW 93*
Dunn, Susan Carole 1956- *WhoE 93*
Dunn, Susan Rhea 1946- *WhoE 93, WhoEmL 93*
Dunn, Susan Stevens *Law&B 92*
Dunn, Suzan McVay 1953- *WhoAmW 93*
Dunn, Teresa Ann 1950- *WhoEmL 93*
Dunn, Thomas (Burt) 1925- *Baker 92*
Dunn, Thomas G. 1921- *WhoAm 92*
Dunn, Thomas P. 1940- *ScF&FL 92*
Dunn, Timothy Charles 1948- *St&PR 93*
Dunn, Vicki Lynn 1949- *WhoAm 92*
Dunn, W.C. *Law&B 92*
Dunn, W. Carleton 1932- *WhoIns 93*
Dunn, Walter Scott, Jr. 1928- *WhoAm 92*
Dunn, Warren H. 1934- *St&PR 93*
Dunn, Warren Howard 1934- *WhoAm 92*
Dunn, Wendell Earl, III 1945- *WhoAm 92*
Dunn, Wesley Brankley 1951- *WhoEmL 93*
Dunn, Wesley John 1924- *WhoAm 92*
Dunn, William B. d1896 *BioIn 17*
Dunn, William Bruna, III 1947- *WhoAm 92, WhoSSW 93*
Dunn, William J. d1992 *NewYTBS 92*
Dunn, William J. 1906-1992 *ConAu 139*
Dunn, William L. *BioIn 17*
Dunn, William M.S. 1931- *St&PR 93*
Dunn, William Randolph 1935- *St&PR 93*
Dunn, William Warren 1936- *St&PR 93*
Dunn, Wilson *BioIn 17*
Dunnagan, Steven Alan 1954- *WhoSSW 93*
Dunnahoo, Terry 1927- *WhoAm 92*
Dunne, Christopher E. *Law&B 92*
Dunne, Dana Philip C. 1963- *WhoE 93*
Dunne, Diane C. *WhoE 93, WhoWor 93*
Dunne, Finley P. d1991 *BioIn 17*
Dunne, Finley Peter 1867-1936 *BioIn 17, GayN, JrnUS*
Dunne, Francis H. *Law&B 92*
Dunne, Irene 1898?-1990 *IntDcF 2-3*
Dunne, Irene 1901?-1990 *ConTFT 10*
Dunne, Irene 1904-1990 *BioIn 17*
Dunne, James Arthur 1934- *WhoAm 92, WhoWor 93*
Dunne, James E. 1949- *St&PR 93*
Dunne, James L. 1940- *St&PR 93*
Dunne, James Robert 1929- *WhoSSW 93*
Dunne, Jeanette 1952- *SmATA 72 [port]*
Dunne, John Gregory 1932- *WhoAm 92, WhoWrEP 92*
Dunne, John Joseph *WhoScE 91-1*
Dunne, John R. *BioIn 17*
Dunne, John Richard 1930- *WhoAm 92*
Dunne, Katherine A. *Law&B 92*
Dunne, Keith J. 1959- *St&PR 93*
Dunne, Marie *MajAI*
Dunne, Peter Francis 1954- *WhoAsAP 91*
Dunne, Philip 1908-1992 *BioIn 17, NewYTBS 92*
Dunne, Phillip 1908-1992 *ConAu 137*
Dunne, Phillip George 1934- *St&PR 93*
Dunne, R. 1936- *WhoScE 91-3*
Dunne, Richard d1990 *BioIn 17*
Dunne, Thomas 1943- *WhoAm 92*
Dunne, Thomas Gregory 1930- *WhoAm 92*
Dunne, Thomas L. 1946- *ScF&FL 92*
Dunne, Thomas Leo 1946- *WhoAm 92*
Dunne, Thomas P. 1943- *St&PR 93*
Dunne, Timothy R. *Law&B 92*
Dunnegan, Jeannine Clare 1963- *WhoAmW 93*
Dunnell, Robert Chester 1942- *WhoAm 92*
Dunnery, John Anthony 1957- *WhoEmL 93*
Dunnet, George Mackenzie *WhoScE 91-1*
Dunnett, Stephen Bruce 1950- *WhoWor 93*
Dunnette, Marvin Dale 1926- *WhoAm 92*
Dunnigan, Brian Leigh 1949- *WhoEmL 93*
Dunnigan, Frank Joseph 1914-1990 *BioIn 17*
Dunnigan, T. Kevin 1938- *WhoAm 92, WhoE 93*
Dunnigan, Thomas Kevin 1938- *St&PR 93*
Dunnihoo, Dale Russell 1928- *WhoAm 92, WhoSSW 93, WhoWrEP 92*
Dunnill, Peter *WhoScE 91-1*
Dunning, Ann Marie 1942- *WhoAm 92*
Dunning, Brad 1957- *ScF&FL 92*
Dunning, Ethel Flo 1935- *WhoWrEP 92*
Dunning, Frank Barry 1945- *WhoSSW 93*
Dunning, Herbert Neal 1923- *WhoAm 92*
Dunning, James L. 1938- *St&PR 93*
Dunning, James Morse 1904-1991 *BioIn 17*
Dunning, John Harry *WhoScE 91-1*
Dunning, John Harry 1927- *WhoWor 93*
Dunning, Joseph S. *BioIn 17*
Dunning, Lawrence 1931- *WhoWrEP 92*
Dunning, Luella M. *AmWomPl*
Dunning, Ronald Richard 1942- *WhoE 93*
Dunning, Thomas Earl 1944- *WhoAm 92*
Dunninger, Joseph 1892-1975 *BioIn 17*
Dunnington, Walter Grey, Jr. 1927- *WhoAm 92, WhoWor 93*
Dunnock, Mildred 1900-1991 *BioIn 17, ConTFT 10*
Dunnock, Mildred 1901-1991 *AnObit 1991*
Dunoff, Richard 1952- *WhoEmL 93*
Dunoyer, Philippe 1930- *St&PR 93, WhoAm 92*
Dunphy, Donald Arthur 1909- *BiDAMSp 1989*
Dunphy, Edward Joseph 1930- *St&PR 93*
Dunphy, Harry 1940- *WhoWor 93*
Dunphy, Jack *BioIn 17*
Dunphy, Jack d1992 *NewYTBS 92*
Dunphy, Jack 1914-1992 *ConAu 137*
Dunphy, John Patrick 1932- *St&PR 93*
Dunphy, Maureen Ann 1949- *WhoAmW 93, WhoEmL 93*
Dunphy, Rose Marie 1943- *WhoAmW 93*
Dunphy, T.J. Dermot 1932- *St&PR 93*
Dunsany, Lord 1878-1957 *ScF&FL 92*
Dunseath, Robert *St&PR 93*
Dunsire, Andrew *WhoScE 91-1*
Dunsire, P. Kenneth 1932- *St&PR 93*
Dunsire, Peter Kenneth 1932- *WhoAm 92*
Dunsky, Menahem 1930- *WhoAm 92*
Dunsmore, Ian Robert *WhoScE 91-1*
Dunsmore, Mark R. 1957- *St&PR 93*
Dunsmore, Rosemary *BioIn 17*
Dunsmore, Walter *St&PR 93*
Dunson, William Albert 1941- *WhoAm 92*
Duns Scotus, John c. 1266-1308 *BioIn 17*
Dunst, Laurence David 1941- *WhoAm 92*
Dunstable, John c. 1390-1453 *Baker 92*
Dunstan, Daniel G. 1944- *St&PR 93*
Dunstan, Garland Herrington, Jr. 1957- *WhoEmL 93, WhoSSW 93*
Dunstan, I. *WhoScE 91-2*
Dunstan, Larry Kenneth 1948- *WhoEmL 93*
Dunstan, Michael Richard 1953- *WhoEmL 93*
Dunstan, Russ Frank 1953- *WhoE 93*
Dunstaple, John c. 1390-1453 *Baker 92*
Dunster, Henry 1609?-1659 *BioIn 17*
Dunster, Ron Allan 1940- *St&PR 93*
Dunstone, Janet Pamela 1950- *WhoWor 93*
Dunstone, William Henry 1930- *St&PR 93*
Dunsworth, Deborah Ellen 1948- *WhoAmW 93*
Dunteman, George Henry 1935- *WhoAm 92*
Dunton, Edith Kellogg 1875- *AmWomPl*
Dunton, James Gerald 1899- *WhoSSW 93*
Dunton, James Kegebein 1938- *St&PR 93*
Dunton, Loren *BioIn 17*
Dunton, Susan Beth 1955- *WhoAmW 93*
Dunton, W. Herbert 1878-1936 *BioIn 17*
Dunwell, J.L. 1939- *St&PR 93*
Dunwich, Gerina 1959- *WhoEmL 93, WhoWor 93*
Dunwiddie, Charlotte 1907- *BioIn 17, WhoAm 92, WhoAmW 93*
Dunwody, Kenneth Webster, Jr. 1926- *St&PR 93*
Dunwoody, James *WhoScE 91-1*
Dunwoody, Kenneth Reed 1953- *WhoAm 92, WhoWrEP 92*
Dunwoody, Robert Cecil 1933- *St&PR 93*
Dunworth, Gerald J. 1911-1991 *BioIn 17*
Dunworth, John 1924- *WhoAm 92*
Duong, Anh *BioIn 17*
Duong, Nghiep Bao 1935- *WhoWor 93*
Duong, Thieu 1936- *WhoE 93*
DuPagne, Nestor L. 1922- *WhoWor 93*
Dupanloup, Felix Antoine Philibert 1802-1878 *BioIn 17*
Duparc, Elisabeth d1778? *OxDcOp*
Duparc, (Marie-Eugene) Henri 1848-1933 *Baker 92*
Du Pasquier, Shelby Robert 1960- *WhoWor 93*
Dupavillion, Marc *BioIn 17*
Dupaya, Tito M. 1922- *WhoAsAP 91*
Du Pen, Everett George 1912- *WhoAm 92*
Duper, Mark Super 1959- *WhoAm 92*
Duperdu, Raymond Jacques Antoine 1926- *WhoScE 91-2*
Duperreault, Brian 1947- *St&PR 93*
Duperron, Alexandrine 1808-1872
See Duprez, Gilbert 1806-1896 *OxDcOp*
Dupey, Michele Mary 1953- *WhoAmW 93, WhoEmL 93*
Duphiney, Bonnie Lee 1950- *WhoAmW 93*
Dupies, Donald Albert 1934- *WhoAm 92*
Dupin, Henri 1923- *WhoScE 91-2*
Dupin, Paul 1865-1949 *Baker 92*
Dupis, Andre 1939- *WhoScE 91-2*
Duplaga, Edward Kazimierz *Law&B 92*
Duplant, Max Stephanie 1956- *WhoEmL 93*
Duplantier, Adrian Guy 1929- *WhoSSW 93*
Duplantier, David L. *Law&B 92*
Duplantier Rhea, Beatrice Marie Charlotte 1942- *WhoSSW 93*
Duplechan, Larry 1956- *ConGAN*
DuPlessis, Barend Jacobus 1940- *WhoAfr, WhoWor 93*
Duplessis, Guy 1947- *St&PR 93*
DuPlessis, Rachel Blau 1941- *ConAu 139*
Duplessis, Suzanne 1940- *WhoAmW 93*
Duplessy, Jean-Claude *WhoScE 91-2*
Duplissey, Donnie R. *Law&B 92*
DuPois, Sidney Joseph 1936- *WhoSSW 93*
Dupong, William Gregg 1911- *WhoE 93, WhoWor 93*
Du Pont, Alfred I. 1864-1935 *BioIn 17*
Dupont, Andrew Joseph, Jr. 1941- *St&PR 93*
Dupont, Augustus I. *Law&B 92*
duPont, Augustus Irenee 1951- *WhoAm 92*
Dupont, Barbara Jean 1946- *WhoE 93*
Dupont, Colyer Lee 1957- *WhoEmL 93, WhoWor 93*
Dupont, Daniel Georges Valere 1931- *WhoWor 93*
du Pont, Denise *ScF&FL 92*
du Pont, Diane *ScF&FL 92*
Dupont, E.A. 1891-1956 *MiSFD 9N*
Dupont, Edouard Francois 1841-1911 *IntDcAn*
Dupont, Edouard Frederic- 1902- *BioIn 17*
duPont, Edward Bradford 1934- *St&PR 93*
Dupont, Edward Charles, Jr. 1950- *WhoE 93*
du Pont, Eleuthere I. 1921- *St&PR 93*
Dupont, Gabriel 1878-1914 *Baker 92*
DuPont, Herbert Lancashire 1938- *WhoAm 92*
Dupont, Inge *ScF&FL 92*
Dupont, Jacqueline 1934- *WhoAm 92*
Dupont, Jacques Pierre 1929- *WhoWor 93*
DuPont, James A. 1947- *St&PR 93*
DuPont, James Maxime d1991 *BioIn 17*
Du Pont, James Richard 1937- *St&PR 93*
Dupont, Jean *St&PR 93*
Dupont, Joanne Meralda 1948- *WhoAmW 93*
Dupont, Johanne *Law&B 92*
DuPont, John Joseph 1930- *WhoAm 92*
Dupont, Judith (Eva Maria) 1925- *ConAu 136*
DuPont, Lorrie Anne 1956- *WhoAm 92*
DuPont, Michael Richard 1961- *WhoEmL 93*
DuPont, Michel Paul 1933- *WhoWor 93*
Dupont, Pierre 1821-1870 *Baker 92*
Du Pont, Pierre S. 1870-1954 *BioIn 17*
Du Pont, Pierre Samuel, IV 1935- *WhoAm 92*
Dupont, Ralph Paul 1929- *WhoAm 92*
du Pont, Richard C. 1911-1943 *EncABHB 8 [port]*
DuPont, Robert Louis, Jr. 1936- *WhoAm 92*
Du Pont, Samuel Francis 1803-1865 *HarEnMi*
DuPont, Stephen Carter 1958- *WhoAm 92*
Dupont, Todd F. 1942- *WhoAm 92*
Dupont, Walter F. 1933- *St&PR 93*
Duport, Jean-Louis 1749-1819 *Baker 92*
Duport, Jean-Pierre 1741-1818 *Baker 92*
Duportail, Louis Lebeque de Presle 1743-1802 *HarEnMi*
Dupouey, Pierre Yves 1929- *WhoScE 91-2*
Dupper, Larry Lin 1953- *WhoEmL 93*
Duppstadt, Marlyn Henry 1947- *WhoAm 92, WhoEmL 93*
Duprato, Jules-Laurent 1827-1892 *Baker 92*
Dupre, A. 1930- *WhoScE 91-2*
Dupre, Douglas Frank 1943- *WhoSSW 93*
Dupre, Durward D. *Law&B 92*
Dupre, Francis H. 1932- *St&PR 93*
DuPre, Jacqueline 1945-1987 *Baker 92, BioIn 17*
Dupre, Judith Ann Neil 1945- *WhoAmW 93*
Dupre, Louis *ConAu 39NR, WhoAm 92*
Dupre, Marcel 1886-1971 *Baker 92*
Dupre, Martha Ann *Law&B 92*
Dupre, Patricia Dianne 1957- *WhoE 93, WhoEmL 93*
Dupree, Anderson Hunter 1921- *WhoAm 92*

Dupree, Andrea K. 1939- *BioIn 17*
Dupree, Andrew Lane, Sr. 1956- *WhoEmL 93, WhoWor 93*
Dupree, Champion Jack d1992 *NewYTBS 92*
Dupree, Champion Jack 1910-1992 *BioIn 17*
Dupree, Charles 1934- *St&PR 93*
DuPree, Clifford H. R. 1950- *WhoAm 92, WhoEmL 93*
Dupree, David H. 1959- *WhoEmL 93*
Dupree, Debra Vitali 1955- *WhoAmW 93*
Dupree, F. Gene 1935- *St&PR 93*
Dupree, Franklin Taylor, Jr. 1913- *WhoAm 92*
Dupree, Joseph E. 1950- *St&PR 93*
Dupree, R. *WhoScE 91-1*
Dupree, Richard Wayne 1946- *St&PR 93*
Dupree, Sandra Kay 1956- *WhoEmL 93*
DuPree, Sherry Sherrod 1946- *WhoSSW 93*
Dupree, Thomas Andrew 1950- *WhoE 93*
Dupree, Tom E., Jr. *St&PR 93*
Dupree, William E., Jr. 1922- *St&PR 93*
DuPree-Martin, Jean 1950- *WhoEmL 93, WhoSSW 93*
Duprey, Jean 1947- *WhoWor 93*
Duprey, Richard 1929- *ScF&FL 92*
Duprey, Thomas Donald 1951- *WhoEmL 93*
Duprey, Wilson Gilliland 1924- *WhoAm 92*
Duprez, Caroline Vandenheuval- 1832-1875 *OxDcOp*
Duprez, Gilbert 1806-1896 *OxDcOp*
Duprez, Gilbert (-Louis) 1806-1896 *Baker 92*
Duprez, Gilbert-Louis 1806-1896 *IntDcOp [port]*
DuPriest, Douglas Millhollen 1951- *WhoEmL 93*
Dupuch, Etienne, Jr. 1931- *WhoWor 93*
Dupuis, Albert 1877-1967 *Baker 92*
Dupuis, Claude 1927- *WhoScE 91-2*
Dupuis, Gerard Adrien 1937- *St&PR 93*
Dupuis, Gilbert 1947- *WhoCanL 92*
Dupuis, Mary 1937- *WhoAmW 93*
Dupuis, Olga Ann 1961- *WhoAmW 93*
Dupuis, P. Blake 1953- *St&PR 93*
Dupuis, Paul H. *Law&B 92*
Dupuis, Pierre 1944- *WhoAm 92*
Dupuis, Russell Dean 1947- *WhoAm 92*
Dupuis, Sylvain 1856-1931 *Baker 92*
Dupuis, Sylvio Louis 1934- *WhoAm 92, WhoE 93, WhoWor 93*
Dupuis, Victor Lionel 1934- *WhoAm 92*
Du Puis, Walter Gus 1932- *St&PR 93*
Dupuy, Ben *DcCPCAm*
Dupuy, Charles Alexandre 1851-1923 *BioIn 17*
Dupuy, Claude 1944- *WhoScE 91-2*
Dupuy, Frank Russell, Jr. 1907- *WhoAm 92*
Dupuy, Howard Moore, Jr. 1929- *WhoAm 92*
Dupuy, Jean *WhoScE 91-2*
Dupuy, John B. 1919- *St&PR 93*
Dupuy, Ralph Anthony 1925- *St&PR 93*
Dupuy, T(revor) N(evitt) 1916- *ConAu 40NR*
Dupuy, Trevor Nevitt 1916- *WhoAm 92*
Duquaine, William Raymond 1937- *St&PR 93*
Duque, Carlos *DcCPCAm*
Duquenoy, Albert 1946- *WhoScE 91-2*
Duquenoy, Linda Irene 1960- *WhoAmW 93*
Duquette, David Joseph 1939- *WhoE 93*
Duquette, Diane Rhea 1951- *WhoAmW 93*
Duquette, Donald Norman 1947- *WhoAm 92*
Duquette, Donald Richard 1954- *St&PR 93*
Duquette, Jean-Pierre 1939- *WhoAm 92*
Duquette, Joseph E., III 1944- *WhoSSW 93*
Duquette, Roderick Daniel 1956- *WhoEmL 93*
Duquette, Tony *BioIn 17*
Dur, Philip Alphonse 1944- *WhoAm 92*
Dur, Philip Francis 1914- *WhoAm 92*
Durachko, Michael Joseph 1955- *WhoWrEP 92*
Durack, David Tulloch 1944- *WhoAm 92*
Durack, Peter Drew 1926- *WhoAsAP 91*
Durai, Deivan 1955- *WhoEmL 93*
Durairaj, G. 1949- *WhoWor 93*
Duraiswamy, Viji D. *Law&B 92*
Dural, Stanley *BioIn 17*
Durall, Keith Leighton 1928- *St&PR 93*
Duran, Andrew J. 1932- *St&PR 93*
Duran, Ilan 1959- *WhoEmL 93*
Duran, Lois J. *Law&B 92*
Duran, Lois Janine 1952- *WhoEmL 93*
Duran, Luis 1932- *WhoScE 91-3*
Duran, Manuel 1925- *DcMexL*
Duran, Michael Carl 1953- *WhoEmL 93, WhoWor 93*
Duran, Natividad Perez 1946- *WhoWrEP 92*
Duran, Paul *MiSFD 9*
Duran, Roberto 1951- *HispAmA [port]*
Duran Ache, Armando *WhoWor 93*
Duran Ballen, Sixto *WhoWor 93*
Durance, Diane Frances 1958- *WhoAmW 93*
Durand, Bernice Black 1942- *WhoAmW 93*
Durand, Catherine Louise 1948- *WhoAmW 93, WhoEmL 93*
Durand, Edward N. *Law&B 92*
Durand, Emile 1830-1903 *Baker 92*
Durand, Francis 1935- *WhoScE 91-2*
Durand, Harrison F. 1903- *St&PR 93*
Durand, Jacques *WhoScE 91-1*
Durand, Jacques 1865-1928 *Baker 92*
Durand, Jacques 1928- *WhoWor 93*
Durand, Jose d1990 *BioIn 17*
Durand, Lucile 1930- *BioIn 17*
Durand, Marie-Auguste 1830-1909 *Baker 92*
Durand, P. *WhoScE 91-2*
Durand, Patrick Y. 1944- *WhoScE 91-2*
Durand, Philippe 1947- *WhoScE 91-2*
Durand, Ralph Scott 1933- *St&PR 93*
Durand, Roger 1933- *WhoScE 91-2*
Durand, Rudy *MiSFD 9*
Durand, Sydnie Mae 1934- *WhoAmW 93*
Durando, Paul 1944- *St&PR 93*
Duran-Downing, Luis H. 1945- *WhoUN 92*
Durang, Christopher 1949- *BioIn 17*
Durano, Ramon D., III 1948- *WhoAsAP 91*
Duran Rosado, Esteban 1905- *DcMexL*
Durant, Connie *BioIn 17*
Durant, Francois V.A.M. 1939- *WhoScE 91-2*
Durant, Frederick C., III 1916- *ScF&FL 92*
Durant, Frederick Clark, III 1916- *WhoAm 92*
Durant, Graham John 1934- *WhoAm 92*
Durant, John H. 1923- *St&PR 93*
Durant, John R. 1935- *St&PR 93*
Durant, John Ridgeway 1930- *WhoAm 92*
Durant, Linda Sue 1950- *WhoE 93*
Durant, Marc 1947- *WhoEmL 93*
Durant, Martin A., III 1948- *St&PR 93*
Durant, Paul D., II 1931- *St&PR 93*
Durant, Peter Montgomery 1950- *WhoEmL 93*
Durant, Richard K. *Law&B 92*
Durant, Rochelle Lynne *Law&B 92*
Durant, William James 1885-1981 *BioIn 17*
Durante, Francesco 1684-1755 *Baker 92, OxDcOp*
Durante, Jimmy 1893-1980 *Baker 92, BioIn 17, IntDcF 2-3 [port], QDrFCA 92 [port]*
Durante, Robert Francis 1962- *St&PR 93*
Duranty, Walter 1884-1957 *BioIn 17, JrnUS*
Duras, duchesse de 1777-1828 *BioIn 17*
Duras, Marguerite 1914- *BioIn 17, MiSFD 9, WhoWor 93*
Durastanti, Margherita fl. 1700-1734 *OxDcOp*
Duray-Bito, Siegfried Peter 1957- *WhoEmL 93*
Durazo, Maria Elena 1954?- *NotHsAW 93*
Durazo Moreno, Arturo *DcCPCAm*
Durazzo, Giacomo 1717-1794 *OxDcOp*
Durazzo, Ricardo Doria 1963- *WhoWor 93*
Durbaum, Hans-Jurgen 1925- *WhoScE 91-3*
Durbec, Martin R. 1943- *St&PR 93*
Durbetaki, N. John 1955- *WhoEmL 93*
Durbetaki, Pandeli 1928- *WhoAm 92, WhoSSW 93*
Durbin, Daniel B. 1946- *WhoEmL 93*
Durbin, Deanna 1921- *IntDcF 2-3 [port]*
Durbin, Donald Dean 1928- *St&PR 93*
Durbin, Enoch Job 1922- *WhoAm 92*
Durbin, Evan Frank Mottram 1906-1948 *BioIn 17*
Durbin, James *WhoScE 91-1*
Durbin, Lynne M. *Law&B 92*
Durbin, M. Rosamond 1952- *St&PR 93*
Durbin, Raymond C. *Law&B 92*
Durbin, Richard J. 1944- *CngDr 91*
Durbin, Richard Joseph 1944- *WhoAm 92*
Durbin, Richard Louis, Sr. 1928- *WhoAm 92, WhoSSW 93*
Durbin, Richard Louis, Jr. 1955- *WhoAm 92*
Durbin, Robert Cain 1931- *WhoAm 92*
Durbin, Robert Francis 1936- *St&PR 93*
Durbin, Rosamond 1952- *WhoAmW 93, WhoEmL 93*
Durbin, Timothy Terrell 1957- *WhoEmL 93*
Durboraw, Wayne A. 1944- *St&PR 93*
Durcan, Paul 1944- *ConLC 70 [port]*
Durchholz, Dale Leroy 1948- *WhoEmL 93*
Durchholz, Patricia 1933- *WhoWor 93*
Durck, Craig Harold 1953- *WhoEmL 93*
Durda, Daniel Joseph 1948- *WhoWor 93*
Durdahl, Carol Lavaun 1933- *WhoAmW 93*
Durden, Charles Dennis 1930- *WhoAm 92*
Durden, Christopher John 1940- *WhoAm 92*
Durden, Donna McDonald 1955- *WhoSSW 93*
Durden, Lois Mills *St&PR 93*
Durden, Robert Franklin 1925- *WhoAm 92*
Du Reau, Charles 1964- *WhoWor 93*
Dureau, Milton Maurice, Jr. 1952- *WhoEmL 93*
Duregger, Karen Marie 1952- *WhoAmW 93*
Dureich, Patricia S. 1942- *WhoAmW 93*
Durein, Joseph F. 1912- *St&PR 93*
Durek, Thomas Andrew 1929- *WhoE 93, WhoSSW 93, WhoWor 93*
Durell, Ann 1930- *BioIn 17, ConAu 136, WhoAm 92*
Durell, Jack 1928- *WhoAm 92, WhoE 93*
Duren, Barry Ross 1957- *WhoEmL 93, WhoSSW 93*
Duren, David Loren 1951- *WhoEmL 93*
Duren, Mark Williams *Law&B 92*
Duren, Peter Larkin 1935- *WhoAm 92*
Durenberger, Dave 1934- *CngDr 91*
Durenberger, David *BioIn 17*
Durenberger, David Ferdinand 1934- *WhoAm 92*
Durer, Albrecht 1471-1528 *BioIn 17*
Durette, Andrew F. 1942- *St&PR 93*
Durette, Philippe Lionel 1944- *WhoE 93*
Durey, Louis (Edmond) 1888-1979 *Baker 92*
Durey, Philippe Jean Marcel 1953- *WhoWor 93*
Dureza, Jesus G. 1947- *WhoAsAP 91*
Durfee, Amy Lee McElheny 1954- *WhoEmL 93*
Durfee, Dick W. *St&PR 93*
Durfee, Glenn Russell 1947- *WhoEmL 93*
Durfee, Harold Allen 1920- *WhoAm 92*
Durfee, Herbert Ashley, Jr. 1924- *WhoE 93*
Durfee, Louis, Jr. 1923- *St&PR 93*
Durfee, Sally E. *Law&B 92*
Durfee, Waite D., Jr. 1920- *St&PR 93*
Durfey, John Howard *Law&B 92*
Durfey, Robert Walker 1925- *WhoAm 92*
Durffe, Francis L. 1935- *St&PR 93*
Durflinger, Elizabeth Ward 1912- *WhoAmW 93*
Durfort, Claire de 1777-1828 *BioIn 17*
Durgin, Diane *Law&B 92*
Durgin, Diane 1946- *St&PR 93, WhoAm 92, WhoAmW 93*
Durgin, Don 1924- *St&PR 93*
Durgin, Frank Albert, Jr. 1923- *WhoAm 92*
Durgin, Leslie *BioIn 17*
Durgin, Scott 1961- *WhoE 93*
Durham, Alden *DcCPCAm*
Durham, Ashley Grey 1959- *WhoE 93, WhoEmL 93*
Durham, Barbara 1942- *WhoAm 92, WhoAmW 93*
Durham, Bill George 1943- *WhoSSW 93*
Durham, Carolyn Richardson 1947- *WhoEmL 93*
Durham, Charles William 1917- *St&PR 93*
Durham, Christine Meaders 1945- *WhoAm 92, WhoAmW 93*
Durham, Clarence R. 1930- *St&PR 93*
Durham, Daniel Cassell 1959- *WhoEmL 93, WhoSSW 93*
Durham, David L. *St&PR 93*
Durham, Davis Godfrey 1914- *WhoAm 92*
Durham, Eddie 1906-1987 *Baker 92*
Durham, Ernestine 1951- *WhoEmL 93*
Durham, Frank Edington 1935- *WhoSSW 93*
Durham, G. Robert 1929- *St&PR 93*
Durham, Guy *ScF&FL 92*
Durham, Guy Floyd 1937- *WhoE 93*
Durham, Helen 1893-1932 *AmWomPl*
Durham, Henry Francis 1923- *St&PR 93*
Durham, James Geoffrey 1951- *WhoEmL 93*
Durham, James Michael 1945- *WhoE 93*
Durham, James Michael, Sr. 1937- *WhoWor 93*
Durham, James W. *Law&B 92*
Durham, James W. 1937- *St&PR 93, WhoAm 92*
Durham, Jeanette Randall 1945- *WhoE 93*
Durham, Kenneth Joe 1953- *WhoEmL 93*
Durham, Kenneth M. 1953- *WhoWrEP 92*
Durham, Lee B., Jr. 1930- *St&PR 93*
Durham, Marilyn Jean (Wall) 1930- *WhoWrEP 92*
Durham, Mary Edith 1863-1944 *IntDcAn*
Durham, Michael J. 1951- *St&PR 93*
Durham, Michael Jonathan 1951- *WhoAm 92, WhoEmL 93*
Durham, Norman Nevill 1927- *WhoAm 92*
Durham, Richard Monroe 1954- *WhoEmL 93*
Durham, Robert Lewis 1912- *WhoAm 92*
Durham, Sharon Feeney 1951- *WhoAmW 93, WhoEmL 93, WhoWor 93*
Durham, Susan B. *WhoAmW 93*
Durham, Thomas Wesley 1952- *WhoSSW 93*
Durham, Tina Marie 1953- *WhoE 93*
Durham, Todd *MiSFD 9*
Durham, William 1937- *WhoE 93*
Durham, William Andrew 1956- *WhoEmL 93*
Durham, William Emory, Jr. 1931- *St&PR 93*
Durham, William L. 1928- *St&PR 93*
Durham, William Lloyd 1928- *WhoAm 92*
Durica, A. James 1947- *St&PR 93*
Duricko, Michael W. 1944- *St&PR 93*
Duricko, Michael William 1944- *WhoAm 92*
Durie, Alistair *ScF&FL 92*
Durie, Jack Frederick, Jr. 1944- *WhoSSW 93*
Duriez, Colin *ScF&FL 92*
Durig, Douglas Tybor 1961- *WhoSSW 93*
Durigon, Michel Louis 1942- *WhoWor 93*
Durin, George Warren 1957- *St&PR 93*
Durina, Michael F. 1954- *St&PR 93*
During, Ebba 1937- *WhoScE 91-4*
During, Marcel H. 1925- *St&PR 93*
Durinzi, Dominic 1952- *St&PR 93*
DuRivage, Donald Jay 1927- *St&PR 93*
Durk, Marion G. 1947- *St&PR 93*
Durkan, Michael Joseph 1925- *WhoAm 92*
Durkee, Daniel Edward 1964- *WhoE 93*
Durkee, George Allen *BioIn 17*
Durkee, Jackson Leland 1922- *WhoAm 92*
Durkee, Michael C. 1938- *St&PR 93*
Durkee, Sarah Bruce 1955- *WhoAm 92*
Durkee, William Robert 1923- *WhoAm 92*
Durkes, Richard Warren 1950- *St&PR 93*
Durkin, Charles Joseph, Jr. 1943- *St&PR 93*
Durkin, Diane Barbara 1960- *WhoEmL 93*
Durkin, Dorothy Angela 1945- *WhoAmW 93, WhoE 93*
Durkin, Douglas 1884-1967 *ScF&FL 92*
Durkin, James A. *Law&B 92*
Durkin, Lisa Marie 1957- *WhoEmL 93*
Durkin, Marguerite 1958- *St&PR 93*
Durkin, Martin Anthony, Jr. 1957- *WhoEmL 93*
Durkin, Martin Timothy 1949- *WhoIns 93*
Durkin, Philip Jay 1946- *WhoSSW 93*
Durko, Zsolt 1934- *Baker 92*
Durlach, Christopher Lee 1951- *WhoEmL 93*
Durlacher, Paul Dominic 1951- *St&PR 93*
Durland, Jack Raymond 1916- *WhoAm 92*
Durland, Leslie L. 1947- *St&PR 93*
Durlet, Emmanuel 1893-1977 *Baker 92*
Durlik, Ireneusz 1931- *WhoScE 91-4*
Durling, C. Correll 1952- *St&PR 93*
Durme, Jef van *Baker 92*
Durmer, William Howard 1940- *St&PR 93*
Durn, Raymond Joseph 1925- *WhoAm 92*
Durnbaugh, Donald Floyd 1927- *WhoAm 92*
Durney, Harry A. 1924- *St&PR 93*
Durney, Lawrence John, III 1948- *WhoEmL 93*
Durney, Michael Cavalier 1943- *WhoAm 92*
Durnford, James Henry 1915- *St&PR 93*
Durnin, John *WhoScE 91-1*
Durnin, Richard Gerry 1920- *WhoE 93*
Durning, Charles *BioIn 17*
Durning, Charles 1923- *WhoAm 92*
Durno, John D. 1936- *St&PR 93*
Duroc-Danner, Bernard J. 1953- *St&PR 93*
Durocher, Cort Louis 1946- *WhoAm 92*
Durocher, Daniel Leonard 1948- *WhoEmL 93*
Durocher, Jeanne Marie 1951- *WhoEmL 93*
Durocher, Leo 1905-1991 *AnObit 1991, BioIn 17, News 92*
Duron, Mary Salinias *NotHsAW 93*
Duron, Michel 1967- *WhoWor 93*
Duroni, Charles E. *Law&B 92*
Duroni, Charles E. 1933- *St&PR 93*
Duroni, Charles Eugene 1933- *WhoAm 92*
Duros, Karen Witte *Law&B 92*
DuRose, Richard Arthur 1937- *WhoAm 92*

DuRose, Stanley Charles, Jr. 1923- *WhoAm 92*
Durosko, Jeffrey Scott 1959- *WhoEmL 93*
Durosko, Philip J. 1927- *St&PR 93*
Durr, Alfred 1918- *Baker 92*
Durr, Clifford *BioIn 17*
Durr, Clifford J. 1899-1975 *EncAACR*
Durr, Frank Richard 1927- *WhoSSW 93*
Durr, Hans-Peter 1929- *WhoScE 91-3*
Durr, Heinz Gunter 1934- *WhoWor 93*
Durr, Janis Joy 1947- *WhoEmL 93*
Durr, Kent Skelton 1941- *WhoWor 93*
Durr, Robert Joseph 1932- *WhoAm 92*
Durr, Virginia Foster 1903- *EncAACR*
Durrani, Arif *BioIn 17*
Durrani, Sajjad Haidar 1928- *WhoAm 92, WhoE 93*
Durrani, Shiraz Khan 1967- *WhoWor 93*
Durrani, Tariq Salim *WhoScE 91-1*
Durrant, Dan Martin 1933- *WhoAm 92*
Durrant, Geoffrey Hugh 1913- *WhoAm 92*
Durrant, John 1949- *WhoWor 93*
Durrant, Michael John *WhoScE 91-1*
Durrant, Shawn *BioIn 17*
Durrell, Gerald Malcolm 1925- *BioIn 17, WhoAm 92, WhoWor 93*
Durrell, Jim *WhoAm 92*
Durrell, Lawrence *BioIn 17*
Durrell, Lawrence 1912-1990 *ScF&FL 92*
Durrell, Lawrence (George) 1912-1990 *ConAu 40NR*
Durrenberger, William John 1917- *WhoAm 92*
Durrence, James Larry 1939- *WhoSSW 93*
Durrence, Julia Leigh 1962- *WhoAmW 93*
Durrenmatt, Friedrich *BioIn 17*
Durrenmatt, Friedrich 1921-1990 *DcLB 124 [port]*
Durrett, George Mann 1917- *St&PR 93*
Durrett, James Frazer, Jr. 1931- *WhoAm 92*
Durrett, Richard Lamar 1939- *St&PR 93*
Durrieu, Guy 1931- *WhoScE 91-2*
Durrigl, Theodor 1926- *WhoScE 91-4*
Durrner, Ruprecht Johannes Julius 1810-1859 *Baker 92*
Dursin, Henry L. 1921- *St&PR 93*
Dursin, Henry Louis 1921- *WhoAm 92, WhoE 93*
Durslag, Melvin 1921- *WhoAm 92*
Durso, Edwin M. *Law&B 92*
Durso, Joseph A. 1928- *St&PR 93*
D'Urso, Joseph Paul 1943- *WhoAm 92*
Durso, Peter Joseph 1954- *WhoE 93*
Durst, Eric *WhoAm 92*
Durst, Michael Charles 1954- *WhoE 93*
Durst, Steven F. 1941- *St&PR 93*
Dursteler, J. Glade 1938- *St&PR 93*
Durstenfeld, Robert M. 1955- *WhoEmL 93*
Durston, Anthony John 1944- *WhoScE 91-3*
Durufle, Maurice 1902-1986 *Baker 92*
Durum, Daryl Eugene 1940- *St&PR 93, WhoIns 93*
Durup, Henri 1930- *WhoScE 91-2*
Durve, Mohan Jagannath 1948- *WhoEmL 93*
Durwood, Edward D. 1950- *WhoAm 92*
Durwood, Stanley H. 1920- *WhoAm 92*
Durwood, Thomas *ScF&FL 92*
Dury, Ronald E. 1950- *St&PR 93*
Duryea, Dan 1907-1968 *IntDcF 2-3*
Duryea, Jayne Ellen 1954- *WhoSSW 93*
Duryea, Ladd 1930- *St&PR 93, WhoSSW 93*
Duryea, Perry Belmont, Jr. 1921- *WhoAm 92*
Duryee, Harold Taylor 1930- *WhoAm 92*
Dusan *OxDcByz*
Dusansky, Richard 1942- *WhoAm 92*
Dusar, Lutgart M. 1950- *WhoWor 93*
Du Sault, Philip Ames 1937- *WhoAm 92*
Duscha, Julius Carl 1924- *WhoAm 92*
Duscha, Lloyd Arthur 1925- *WhoAm 92*
Duschatko, William L. 1944- *St&PR 93*
Dusek, Frank Arthur 1946- *WhoEmL 93*
Dusek, Franz 1731-1799 *Baker 92*
Dusek, Karel 1930- *WhoScE 91-4*
Dusel, Robert George 1942- *WhoE 93*
Dusell, Roy Robert 1941- *St&PR 93*
Dusenberry, Philip Bernard 1936- *WhoAm 92, WhoE 93*
Dusenbery, Walter Condit 1939- *WhoAm 92*
Dusenbury, John D. *Law&B 92*
Dusenbury, Linda Anne 1959- *WhoE 93, WhoEmL 93*
Du Shane, James William 1912- *WhoAm 92*
DuShane, Phyllis Miller 1924- *WhoAmW 93*
Dushkin, Harvey Brent 1948- *St&PR 93*
Dushkin, Samuel 1891-1976 *Baker 92*
Dusik, Franz 1731-1799 *Baker 92*
Dusik, Johann Ladislaus (Ludwig) 1760-1812 *Baker 92*
Dusio, Penelope A. 1943- *St&PR 93*
Dusky, Lorraine *BioIn 17*
Dusmet de Smours, Luigi 1926- *WhoWor 93*
DuSold, Elizabeth L. *Law&B 92*
Dusold, Laurence Richard 1944- *WhoE 93, WhoWor 93*
Dussardier, Michel 1925- *WhoScE 91-2*
Dussauchoy, Alain E. 1942- *WhoScE 91-2*
Dussault, Marilyn Black 1943- *WhoAmW 93*
Dussault, Richard E. 1927- *St&PR 93*
Dussault, William Leonard Ernest 1947- *WhoEmL 93*
D'Usseau, Arnaud 1916-1990 *BioIn 17*
Dusseau, Deborah Kay 1952- *WhoAmW 93*
Dusseau, Nancy Steustall *Law&B 92*
Dusseault, Arthur W. 1938- *St&PR 93*
Dusseault, C. Dean 1938- *WhoAm 92*
Dusseault, Norman Paul 1930- *St&PR 93*
Dussek, Franz 1731-1799 *Baker 92*
Dussek, Johann Ladislaus (Ludwig) 1760-1812 *Baker 92*
Dussek, Sophia *OxDcOp*
Dusserre, Liliane 1932- *WhoScE 91-2*
Dusserre, Liliane Denise France 1932- *WhoScE 91-2*
Dussert, Claudine V. 1942- *WhoE 93*
Dussik, Johann Ladislaus (Ludwig) 1760-1812 *Baker 92*
Dussman, Judith Ann 1947- *WhoEmL 93*
Duster, Christopher Clayton 1957- *WhoEmL 93*
Dusthimer, Thomas Lee 1934- *St&PR 93*
Dustin, Cedric Herbert, Jr. 1925- *St&PR 93*
Dustin, Pierre 1914- *WhoScE 91-2*
Dustman, Jack 1922- *St&PR 93*
Dustman, Wayne John *Law&B 92*
Dusuki bin Haji Ahmad, Dato' Haji 1944- *WhoAsAP 91*
Duszynski, Donald Walter 1943- *WhoAm 92*
Duszynski, Richard James 1957- *St&PR 93*
Dutcher, Flora Mae 1908- *WhoAmW 93*
Dutcher, Janice Jean Phillips 1950- *WhoWor 93*
Dutcher, Joseph A. 1949- *St&PR 93*
Dutcher Thornton, Alice Marilyn 1934- *WhoAmW 93*
Duthie, Mary Eva *AmWomPl*
Duthilleul, Anne *WhoScE 91-2*
Du Thinh, Kien 1947- *WhoScE 91-2*
Duthler, Julius 1921- *St&PR 93*
Duthler, Reed Allen *Law&B 92*
Dutia, B.P. *WhoScE 91-3*
Dutia, Bhupendra Padmasinh 1927- *WhoUN 92*
Dutia, Suren G. 1942- *St&PR 93*
Dutil, Jayne Anne 1947- *WhoAmW 93*
Dutil, Marcel E. 1942- *WhoAm 92*
Dutil, P. *WhoScE 91-2*
Dutile, Fernand Neville 1940- *WhoAm 92*
Dutile, Richard R. 1937- *St&PR 93*
Dutile, Trudy G. 1939- *St&PR 93*
Dutilleux, Henri 1916- *Baker 92*
Duti Yang Teramat Mulia Raja Nazrin Shah 1956- *WhoAsAP 91*
Dutka, Andrew Joseph 1951- *WhoE 93, WhoEmL 93*
Dutkiewicz, Daniel *WhoScE 91-4*
Dutmers, James E. 1943- *St&PR 93*
Du Toit, Charles *BioIn 17*
Dutoit, Charles 1936- *WhoAm 92, WhoE 93*
Dutoit, Charles (Edouard) 1936- *Baker 92*
Dutra, Eurico Gaspar 1885-1974 *DcTwHis*
Dutra, Lisa Ann 1968- *WhoSSW 93*
Du Tremblay, Francois-Joseph le Clerc 1577-1638 *BioIn 17*
Dutrisac, Maurice G. 1948- *St&PR 93*
Dutro, John Thomas, Jr. 1923- *WhoAm 92*
Dutruel, F. *WhoScE 91-2*
Dutson, Brent Rogers 1950- *St&PR 93*
Dutt, Hank 1952-
See Kronos Quartet, The *News 93-1*
Dutt, James Lee 1925- *St&PR 93*
Dutt, John R. *Law&B 92*
Dutta, Ajit Singh 1944- *WhoE 93*
Dutta, Arup Kumar 1946- *DcChlFi*
Dutta, Niloy K. 1953- *WhoAm 92*
Dutta, Prabhat Kumar, II 1940- *WhoWrEP 92*
Dutta, Rono J. 1951- *St&PR 93*
Duttenhoeffer, Diana Lee 1956- *WhoAmW 93*
Dutter, Andrew Allen 1964- *WhoAm 92*
Dutterer, Dennis A. *Law&B 92*
Dutton, Carey June *Law&B 92*
Dutton, Charles S. *BioIn 17*
Dutton, Charles S. 1951- *ConBlB 4 [port]*
Dutton, Christopher L. *Law&B 92*
Dutton, Christopher L. 1948- *St&PR 93*
Dutton, Clarence Benjamin 1917- *WhoAm 92*
Dutton, Dan M. 1947- *St&PR 93*
Dutton, Diana Cheryl 1944- *WhoAm 92, WhoAmW 93*
Dutton, Doug E. 1942- *St&PR 93*
Dutton, Emma Bartlett *AmWomPl*
Dutton, F. Mitchell *Law&B 92*
Dutton, Frank Elroy 1946- *WhoEmL 93, WhoSSW 93, WhoWor 93*
Dutton, Gardiner S. 1931- *St&PR 93*
Dutton, Geoffrey 1936- *St&PR 93*
Dutton, George E. 1913- *St&PR 93*
Dutton, Guy G. S. *WhoAm 92*
Dutton, Jack *WhoScE 91-1*
Dutton, Jeanne Marie *Law&B 92*
Dutton, John Altnow 1936- *WhoAm 92*
Dutton, John B. 1945- *St&PR 93*
Dutton, John Coatsworth 1918- *WhoAm 92*
Dutton, John Edgar 1924- *WhoAm 92*
Dutton, Jonathan Joseph 1942- *WhoSSW 93*
Dutton, Kenneth *WhoScE 91-1*
Dutton, Leland S. 1905-1991 *BioIn 17*
Dutton, Lois Ann 1939- *WhoAmW 93*
Dutton, Lynn B. *Law&B 92*
Dutton, Paul 1943- *WhoCanL 92*
Dutton, Robert Edward, Jr. 1924- *WhoAm 92*
Dutton, Robert Newell 1941- *WhoSSW 93*
Dutton, Roderic William *WhoScE 91-1*
Dutton, Rosalyn Sotile 1948- *WhoAmW 93*
Dutton, Susan Scott 1957- *WhoEmL 93*
Dutton, Tom 1952- *WhoEmL 93*
Dutton, Wilmer Coffman, Jr. 1920- *WhoAm 92*
Dutu, Stefan 1924- *WhoScE 91-4*
Duty, Daniel Morgan, III *Law&B 92*
Duty, J. Bruce 1951- *St&PR 93*
Duty, Michael Shannon 1948- *St&PR 93*
Duursma, Egbert Klaas 1929- *WhoScE 91-3*
Duus, Fritz 1941- *WhoScE 91-2*
Duus, Peter 1908- *WhoWor 93*
Duus, Peter 1933- *WhoAm 92*
Duva, Donna Marie 1956- *WhoEmL 93, WhoWor 93*
Duva, Lou *BioIn 17*
Duva, Philip 1945- *St&PR 93, WhoAm 92*
Duval, Albert Frank 1920- *WhoAm 92*
Duval, Barbara Mary 1956- *WhoAmW 93*
Duval, Barry Eugene 1959- *WhoAm 92, WhoSSW 93*
Duval, Charles Gaetan 1930- *WhoAfr*
Duval, Daniel Webster 1936- *WhoAm 92*
Duval, David Paul 1945- *St&PR 93*
Duval, Denise 1921- *Baker 92, OxDcOp*
Duval, Gaetan 1930- *WhoWor 93*
Duval, Jeanne fl. 1845- *BioIn 17*
Duval, John Tabb 1940- *WhoWrEP 92*
Duval, Leon-Etienne Cardinal 1903- *WhoWor 93*
Duval, Leonard Anthony 1921- *WhoWor 93*
Duval, Mark E. *Law&B 92*
Duval, Mary Virginia 1850- *AmWomPl*
Duval, Michael Raoul 1938- *WhoAm 92*
Duval, Raymond A. 1933- *St&PR 93*
Duval, Raymond Alfred 1933- *WhoE 93*
Duval, Regis J. 1939- *WhoUN 92*
Duval, Robert *Law&B 92*
Duval, Ruth *BioIn 17*
DuVal, Thomas Howard 1813-1880 *BioIn 17*
Duval, Virginia Hensley 1948- *WhoAmW 93*
Duval-Beaupere, G. 1928- *WhoScE 91-2*
Duvaldestin, Philippe 1942- *WhoScE 91-2*
Duvalier, Francois 1907-1971 *BioIn 17, DcCPCAm, DcTwHis*
Duvalier, Jean-Claude *BioIn 17*
Duvalier, Jean-Claude 1951- *DcCPCAm*
Duvall, Arndt John, III 1931- *WhoAm 92*
Duvall, Bernice Bettum 1948- *WhoE 93*
Duvall, Camille *BioIn 17*
Duvall, Charles D. 1939- *St&PR 93*
Duvall, Charles Patton 1936- *WhoE 93*
Duvall, Cheryl Pepmeier 1957- *WhoAmW 93*
Duvall, Fannie Eliza 1861?-1934 *BioIn 17*
Duvall, Gabriel 1752-1844 *OxCSupC [port]*
DuVall, Jack 1946- *WhoSSW 93, WhoWor 93*
Duvall, Jean M. *Law&B 92*
Duvall, John Edward 1947- *WhoEmL 93*
Duvall, Lawrence Del 1942- *WhoIns 93*
Duvall, Lawrence Delbert 1942- *WhoE 93*
DuVall, Lorraine 1925- *WhoAmW 93*
Duvall, Mark N. *Law&B 92*
Duvall, Paul Hamilton 1947- *WhoEmL 93*
Duvall, Robert *BioIn 17*
Duvall, Robert 1931- *IntDcF 2-3 [port], MiSFD 9, WhoAm 92*
Duvall, Shelley *BioIn 17*
Duvall, Shelley 1949- *WhoAm 92, WhoAmW 93*
Duvall-Itjen, Phyllis 1951- *WhoAmW 93*
Duvall-Kellar, Donna Susann 1951- *WhoEmL 93*
Duvar, Ivan E.H. 1939- *St&PR 93*
Duvar, Ivan Ernest Hunter 1939- *WhoAm 92, WhoWor 93*
Duvar, John Hunter- 1821-1899 *BioIn 17*
Duve, C. de *WhoScE 91-2*
Duverger, Maurice 1917- *PolPar*
Duvernay, Terrence R. *BioIn 17*
DuVernet, Elizabeth E. *AmWomPl*
Duverneuil, Germain Edme 1935- *WhoScE 91-2*
Duvernoy, Charles 1776-1845 *Baker 92*
Duvernoy, Frederic Nicolas 1765-1838 *Baker 92*
Duvernoy, Henri-Louis-Charles 1820-1906 *Baker 92*
Duvernoy, Victor-Alphonse 1842-1907 *Baker 92*
Duveyrier, Henri 1840-1892 *Expl 93*
Duvick, Donald Nelson 1924- *WhoAm 92*
Duvin, Robert Phillip 1937- *WhoAm 92*
Duvivier, Julien 1896-1967 *MiSFD 9N*
DuVivier, Katharine Keyes 1953- *WhoEmL 93*
Duvivier, Roger 1945- *WhoE 93*
Duvo, Mechelle Louise 1962- *WhoAmW 93, WhoEmL 93*
Duvoisin, Roger Antoine 1904-1980 *MajAI [port]*
Duvoisin, Roger Clair 1927- *WhoE 93*
Duvosel, Lieven 1877-1956 *Baker 92*
Duwabane, Gai 1948- *WhoAsAP 91*
Duwe, Brian Miles 1941- *WhoSSW 93*
Duwe, John 1941- *St&PR 93*
Duwel, Dieter 1928- *WhoScE 91-3*
Duwes, Giles d1535 *BioIn 17*
Dux, Claire 1885-1967 *Baker 92*
Dux, Pierre 1908-1990 *BioIn 17*
Duxbury, Geoffrey *WhoScE 91-1*
Duynstee, Anthony Ernst Mary 1920- *WhoWor 93*
Duysens, Daniel 1944- *WhoUN 92*
Duytschaver, Linda Lyvonne 1949- *WhoEmL 93*
Du Yuesheng 1887-1951 *BioIn 17*
Duyverman, C.J. 1933- *WhoScE 91-3*
Duzan, James Robert *Law&B 92*
Duzan, S.A. 1941- *St&PR 93*
Duzan, Stephen Andrew 1941- *WhoAm 92*
Duzhin, Sergei Vassilievich 1956- *WhoWor 93*
Dvarionas, Balis 1904-1972 *Baker 92*
Dveirin, Jack L. 1958- *WhoEmL 93*
Dvoichenko-Markov, Demetrius 1921- *WhoWor 93*
Dvoor, Deborah Ann 1959- *WhoEmL 93*
Dvoracek, Jiri 1928- *Baker 92*
Dvorak, Allen Dale 1943- *WhoAm 92*
Dvorak, Antonin 1841-1904 *BioIn 17, IntDcOp, OxDcOp*
Dvorak, Antonin (Leopold) 1841-1904 *Baker 92*
Dvorak, Craig R. *St&PR 93*
Dvorak, Daniel F. 1954- *St&PR 93*
Dvorak, Donald Allen 1933- *St&PR 93*
Dvorak, Harold F. 1937- *WhoAm 92*
Dvorak, Jane Ann 1955- *WhoEmL 93*
Dvorak, Joseph J. *Law&B 92*
Dvorak, Ray P. 1931- *WhoWor 93*
Dvorak, Rudolf 1932- *WhoScE 91-4*
Dvorak, Stanley Joseph 1935- *St&PR 93*
Dvorak, Vaclav 1931- *WhoScE 91-4*
Dvorakova, Ludmila 1923- *Baker 92*
Dvorchak, Dennis 1940- *St&PR 93*
Dvorchak, Thomas Edward 1933- *St&PR 93, WhoAm 92*
Dvores, Neil 1949- *St&PR 93*
Dvorkin, Daniel 1969- *ScF&FL 92*
Dvorkin, David 1943- *ScF&FL 92*
Dvorsky, Peter 1951- *Baker 92, OxDcOp*
Dwan, Allan 1885-1981 *MiSFD 9N*
Dwan, Dennis Edwin 1958- *WhoEmL 93*
Dwan, Dorothy *SweetSg B [port]*
Dwan, William Edward 1941- *St&PR 93*
Dwarica, Leonard Alexander *Law&B 92*
Dwass, Meyer 1923- *WhoAm 92*
Dweck, Susan 1943- *WhoAmW 93*
Dwek, Cyril S. 1936- *WhoAm 92*
Dwek, Raymond A. *BioIn 17*
Dwek, Raymond Allen *WhoScE 91-1*
Dweller, Cliff 1953- *WhoE 93*
Dwernicki, Jozef 1778-1857 *PolBiDi*
Dwiggins, Claudius William, Jr. 1933- *WhoSSW 93*
Dwiggins, Don 1913-1988 *BioIn 17*
Dwiggins, Elmer *ScF&FL 92*
Dwight, Donald Rathbun 1931- *St&PR 93, WhoAm 92*
Dwight, Harvey Alpheus 1928- *WhoE 93*
Dwight, James Scutt, Jr. 1934- *WhoAm 92*
Dwight, John Sullivan 1813-1893 *Baker 92*
Dwight, Mabel 1876-1955 *BioIn 17*
Dwight, Olivia *WhoWrEP 92*
Dwight, Reginald Kenneth 1947- *WhoAm 92*
Dwight, Theodore 1764-1846 *JrnUS*
Dwight, Timothy 1752-1817 *BioIn 17*
Dwight, William, Jr. 1929- *WhoAm 92*

Dwinell, James Fisher 1939- *St&PR 93*
Dwinell, Ralph M. 1894-1978 *ScF&FL 92*
Dwinnell, R.M. 1894- *ScF&FL 92*
Dwivedi, Surendra Nath 1945- *WhoAm 92*
Dwojak, Stanislaw Marian 1930- *WhoScE 91-4*
Dwon, Larry 1913- *WhoAm 92*
Dworetsky, Samuel H. *Law&B 92*
Dworetzky, Murray 1917- *WhoAm 92, WhoE 93*
Dworin, Jeffrey Zolla 1950- *St&PR 93*
Dwork, Joel *Law&B 92*
Dwork, Melvin *BioIn 17*
Dworkin, Andrea *BioIn 17*
Dworkin, Andrea 1946- *ConAu 39NR*
Dworkin, Howard Jerry 1932- *WhoAm 92*
Dworkin, Howard S. *Law&B 92*
Dworkin, James Barnet 1948- *WhoAm 92*
Dworkin, Martin 1927- *WhoAm 92*
Dworkin, Michael Leonard 1947- *WhoEmL 93*
Dworkin, Ronald Myles 1931- *WhoAm 92*
Dworkin, Samuel Franklin 1933- *WhoAm 92*
Dworkin, Sidney 1921- *St&PR 93*
Dworski, Bernard M. *Law&B 92*
Dworsky, Clara Weiner 1918- *WhoAmW 93*
Dworsky, Daniel Leonard 1927- *WhoAm 92*
Dworsky, Leonard B. 1915- *WhoAm 92*
Dwyer, Andrew T. 1948- *WhoAm 92, WhoE 93*
Dwyer, Andrew Thompson 1948- *St&PR 93*
Dwyer, Ann Elizabeth 1953- *WhoAm 92, WhoEmL 93*
Dwyer, Bernard J. 1921- *CngDr 91*
Dwyer, Bernard James 1921- *WhoAm 92, WhoE 93*
Dwyer, Brian Michael 1940- *St&PR 93*
Dwyer, Catherine T. *Law&B 92*
Dwyer, Charles Breen 1952- *WhoE 93*
Dwyer, Daniel P. 1959- *St&PR 93*
Dwyer, Darrell James 1946- *WhoEmL 93*
Dwyer, Dennis D. 1943- *WhoWor 93*
Dwyer, Dennis Grant 1947- *WhoSSW 93*
Dwyer, Dennis J. *Law&B 92*
Dwyer, Dennis Richard 1943- *St&PR 93*
Dwyer, Diane Marie 1958- *WhoEmL 93*
Dwyer, Doriot Anthony *WhoAmW 93*
Dwyer, Ethel Theresa 1931- *WhoAmW 93*
Dwyer, Florence Price 1902-1976 *BioIn 17*
Dwyer, Francis Gerard 1931- *WhoE 93*
Dwyer, Gary Joseph 1958- *WhoEmL 93*
Dwyer, Gerald Paul, Jr. 1947- *WhoEmL 93*
Dwyer, Gregg A. *Law&B 92*
Dwyer, Gregg Allan 1943- *St&PR 93*
Dwyer, Gregory Allen 1951- *WhoSSW 93*
Dwyer, Herbert Edward 1940- *WhoE 93*
Dwyer, James Francis 1874-1952 *ScF&FL 92*
Dwyer, James Gormley 1913- *St&PR 93*
Dwyer, James J. d1991 *BioIn 17*
Dwyer, James L. 1932- *St&PR 93*
Dwyer, James Richard 1949- *WhoEmL 93*
Dwyer, James Robert 1947- *WhoEmL 93*
Dwyer, Jim 1957- *WhoAm 92*
Dwyer, Johanna Todd 1938- *WhoE 93*
Dwyer, John *MiSFD 9*
Dwyer, John Denis 1927- *St&PR 93*
Dwyer, John J. 1955- *St&PR 93*
Dwyer, Joseph P. 1956- *St&PR 93*
Dwyer, K.R. 1945- *BioIn 17*
Dwyer, Maria D. *Law&B 92*
Dwyer, Mary Elizabeth 1946- *WhoAmW 93*
Dwyer, Maureen Quinn 1947- *WhoIns 93*
Dwyer, Michael John *WhoScE 91-1*
Dwyer, Michael Thomas 1945- *St&PR 93*
Dwyer, Michelle Maureen *Law&B 92*
Dwyer, Nancy Jean 1945- *WhoWrEP 92*
Dwyer, P. Clarke 1932- *St&PR 93*
Dwyer, Patrick C. 1939- *St&PR 93*
Dwyer, Robert Francis 1911- *St&PR 93*
Dwyer, Robert Francis, Jr. 1936- *St&PR 93*
Dwyer, Roberta M. 1960- *WhoAmW 93*
Dwyer, Terence Michael 1948- *WhoWor 93*
Dwyer, Terrence *St&PR 93*
Dwyer, Virginia Alice 1921- *WhoAm 92*
Dwyer, Virginia Anne 1962- *WhoAmW 93*
Dwyer, William Kenney, Jr. *Law&B 92*
Dwyer, William L. 1929- *WhoAm 92*
Dwyer-Dobbin, Mary Alice 1942- *WhoAmW 93*
Dwyre, William Patrick 1944- *WhoAm 92*
Dyaczynska-Herman, Anna L. 1933- *WhoScE 91-4*
Dyagilev, Sergey 1872-1929 *OxDcOp*
D'yakonov, Eugenii Georgievich 1935- *WhoWor 93*
Dyakowski, Anthony 1948- *St&PR 93*
Dyal, H. Kaye *MiSFD 9*
Dyal, Thomas Leroy 1931- *St&PR 93*
Dyal, William M., Jr. 1928- *WhoAm 92*
Dyar, Julia Traylor 1925- *WhoAmW 93*
Dyar, Kathryn Wilkin 1945- *WhoAm 92*
Dyar, Stephen Craig 1961- *WhoSSW 93*
Dyar, William Heller 1918- *WhoSSW 93*
Dybeck, Alfred Charles 1928- *WhoAm 92*
Dybeck, Dennis Joseph 1940- *WhoWrEP 92*
Dybek, Stuart 1942- *ConAu 39NR*
Dybek, Stuart John 1942- *WhoWrEP 92*
Dybell, Elizabeth Anne Sledden 1958- *WhoAmW 93, WhoEmL 93*
Dybern, Bernt I. 1928- *WhoScE 91-4*
Dybiec, Linda J. 1944- *St&PR 93*
Dybing, Erik 1943- *WhoScE 91-4*
Dybkaer, Rene 1926- *WhoScE 91-2, WhoWor 93*
Dybowski, Benedykt Tadeusz 1833-1930 *PolBiDi*
Dyche, David Bennett, Jr. 1932- *WhoAm 92*
Dyche, Kathie Louise 1949- *WhoAmW 93*
Dyche, Lewis Lindsay 1857-1915 *BioIn 17*
Dyches, Barry 1938- *St&PR 93*
Dyck, Andrew Roy 1947- *WhoAm 92*
Dyck, Anthonie van 1599-1641 *BioIn 17*
Dyck, Arthur James 1932- *WhoAm 92*
Dyck, E.F. 1939- *WhoCanL 92*
Dyck, George 1937- *WhoAm 92*
Dyck, Manfred F. 1935- *St&PR 93*
Dyck, Paul 1917- *BioIn 17*
Dyck, Walter Peter 1935- *WhoAm 92*
Dycke, Ignatz Sahula- *ScF&FL 92*
Dyckman, Thomas Richard 1932- *WhoAm 92*
Dyczek, Carl J. *Law&B 92*
Dye, Alan Page 1946- *WhoEmL 93*
Dye, Bradford Johnson, Jr. 1933- *WhoAm 92, WhoWor 93*
Dye, C.D. *St&PR 93*
Dye, Cecil Marion 1940- *WhoE 93*
Dye, Charity 1849- *AmWomPl*
Dye, Clifford W. 1930- *St&PR 93*
Dye, David Alan 1956- *WhoE 93*
Dye, David Ray 1951- *WhoEmL 93*
Dye, Edward R. *Law&B 92*
Dye, Florence *SweetSg A*
Dye, Frank John 1942- *WhoE 93*
Dye, Glenn W. 1921- *WhoE 93*
Dye, Hugh B. *Law&B 92*
Dye, James Louis 1927- *WhoAm 92*
Dye, Kenneth M. *BioIn 17*
Dye, Kimberly Anderson 1961- *WhoEmL 93*
Dye, Michael Edward 1954- *WhoSSW 93*
Dye, Molly Ball 1951- *WhoAmW 93, WhoEmL 93*
Dye, Myron L. 1954- *WhoIns 93*
Dye, Myrtice Willis *WhoSSW 93*
Dye, Pat *BioIn 17*
Dye, Patrick Fain 1939- *BiDAMSp 1989, WhoAm 92*
Dye, Rob 1964- *BioIn 17*
Dye, Robert C. 1943- *St&PR 93*
Dye, Robert M. 1947- *St&PR 93*
Dye, Roger Herbert *WhoScE 91-1*
Dye, Ron 1962- *BioIn 17*
Dye, Sherman 1915- *WhoAm 92*
Dye, Thomas Alfred 1954- *WhoEmL 93*
Dye, Thomas Roy 1935- *WhoAm 92*
Dye, William David 1961- *WhoSSW 93*
Dyekman, Gregory Chris 1955- *WhoEmL 93*
Dyen, Isidore 1913- *WhoAm 92*
Dyer, Alexander P. 1932- *St&PR 93*
Dyer, Alexander Patrick 1932- *WhoAm 92*
Dyer, Alfred *ScF&FL 92*
Dyer, Alice Mildred 1929- *WhoAm 92, WhoAmW 93*
Dyer, Allen Ralph 1944- *WhoAm 92*
Dyer, Arlene Thelma 1942- *WhoAmW 93*
Dyer, Betsey Dexter 1954- *WhoAmW 93*
Dyer, Betty Tauber *Law&B 92*
Dyer, Charles *BioIn 17*
Dyer, Charles Arnold 1940- *WhoWor 93*
Dyer, Charles H. *Law&B 92*
Dyer, Charles Herbert 1949- *WhoEmL 93*
Dyer, Christopher *BioIn 17*
Dyer, Cromwell Adair, Jr. 1932- *WhoWor 93*
Dyer, Cynthia Myers 1955- *WhoAmW 93, WhoEmL 93*
Dyer, Dale *BioIn 17*
Dyer, Darrell Dean 1933- *St&PR 93*
Dyer, David Paul 1956- *WhoEmL 93*
Dyer, David William 1910- *WhoAm 92, WhoSSW 93*
Dyer, Doris Anne 1944- *WhoAmW 93*
Dyer, Ellen Marie 1954- *WhoAmW 93*
Dyer, Esther R. 1950- *WhoE 93*
Dyer, Frederick Charles 1918- *WhoAm 92, WhoE 93*
Dyer, George 1755-1841 *BioIn 17*
Dyer, Geraldine Ann 1921- *WhoAm 92, WhoAmW 93, WhoWor 93*
Dyer, Goudyloch Erwin 1919- *WhoAm 92*
Dyer, Gregory Clark 1947- *WhoEmL 93*
Dyer, Ira 1925- *WhoAm 92*
Dyer, J. Lawson 1908- *St&PR 93*
Dyer, James M. 1950- *St&PR 93*
Dyer, James Mason, Jr. 1928- *St&PR 93*
Dyer, James Simpson 1943- *WhoAm 92*
Dyer, Jaye F. 1927- *St&PR 93*
Dyer, Jaye Floyd 1927- *WhoAm 92*
Dyer, John 1700?-1758 *BioIn 17*
Dyer, John Martin 1920- *WhoAm 92, WhoSSW 93*
Dyer, Joseph Edward 1924- *St&PR 93*
Dyer, Joseph R. *Law&B 92*
Dyer, Kevin James 1941- *WhoSSW 93*
Dyer, Kevin L. 1946- *St&PR 93*
Dyer, Leon 1807-1883 *BioIn 17*
Dyer, Lois Pratt 1946- *WhoAmW 93*
Dyer, Louise 1890-1962 *Baker 92*
Dyer, Lyndall Ellen 1936- *St&PR 93*
Dyer, Margaret Ellen 1951- *WhoAmW 93*
Dyer, Michael John *WhoScE 91-1*
Dyer, Nancy Joe *WhoSSW 93*
Dyer, Peter Edward *WhoScE 91-1*
Dyer, Raymond Wayne 1946- *St&PR 93*
Dyer, Richard E. 1942- *St&PR 93*
Dyer, Richard Sanders, Sr. 1929- *St&PR 93*
Dyer, Robert Campbell 1913- *WhoAm 92*
Dyer, Robert Francis, Jr. 1926- *WhoAm 92, WhoE 93*
Dyer, Samuel Edwin 1925- *WhoAm 92*
Dyer, Sarah Kappas 1935- *WhoAmW 93*
Dyer, Stephen Edward 1946- *St&PR 93*
Dyer, T(homas) A(llan) 1947- *DcAmChF 1960*
Dyer, Tina Marie 1948- *WhoAmW 93*
Dyer, Travis N. 1939- *WhoAm 92*
Dyer, Victor D. 1934- *St&PR 93*
Dyer, Walter Sullivan, III 1957- *WhoEmL 93, WhoWor 93*
Dyer, Wayne 1940- *ScF&FL 92*
Dyer, Wayne Walter 1940- *WhoAm 92*
Dyer, William A., Jr. 1902- *St&PR 93*
Dyer, William Allan, Jr. 1902- *WhoAm 92*
Dyer, William Frederick 1949- *WhoE 93*
Dyer-Bennet, Pamela *ScF&FL 92*
Dyer-Bennet, Richard 1913- *Baker 92*
Dyer-Bennet, Richard 1913-1991 *BioIn 17, CurBio 92N*
Dyer-Smith, Howard Edward 1952- *St&PR 93*
Dyer-Weissman, Margaret Bellis 1942- *WhoAmW 93*
Dyess, Bobby Dale 1935- *WhoAm 92, WhoSSW 93*
Dygard, Thomas J. 1931- *SmATA 15AS [port]*
Dygas, Ignacy 1881-1947 *PolBiDi*
Dygasinski, Adolf 1839-1902 *PolBiDi*
Dygat, Stanislaw 1914-1978 *PolBiDi*
Dygert, Dave L. 1943- *St&PR 93*
Dyhouse, Henry Norval 1945- *WhoAm 92*
Dyhr-Nielsen, Mogens *WhoScE 91-2*
Dyk, Bob d1991 *BioIn 17*
Dyk, George Van 1943- *St&PR 93*
Dyk, Timothy Belcher 1937- *WhoAm 92*
Dyke, Charles William 1935- *WhoAm 92*
Dyke, Douglas M. 1942- *St&PR 93*
Dyke, James T. 1937- *St&PR 93*
Dyke, James Trester 1937- *WhoAm 92*
Dyke, John Malcolm *WhoScE 91-1*
Dyke, Kermit Robert 1947- *St&PR 93*
Dyke, Philip Peter George *WhoScE 91-1*
Dyke, Philip Peter George 1948- *WhoWor 93*
Dyke, Robert *MiSFD 9*
Dyke, Vernon A. *St&PR 93*
Dyke, William H. *Law&B 92*
Dykema, Henry L. 1939- *WhoAm 92*
Dykema, Jeffrey Lynn 1950- *St&PR 93*
Dykema, John Russel 1918- *WhoAm 92*
Dykema, Peter (William) 1873-1951 *Baker 92*
Dyken, Mark Lewis 1928- *WhoAm 92*
Dykes, Archie Reece 1931- *St&PR 93, WhoAm 92*
Dykes, Aubrey H. *WhoSSW 93*
Dykes, Bill G. 1947- *WhoEmL 93, WhoSSW 93*
Dykes, C. Allen 1949- *St&PR 93*
Dykes, Clifford Earl, Jr. 1941- *WhoSSW 93*
Dykes, Dale David 1945-1990 *BioIn 17*
Dykes, Eva Beatrice 1893- *BioIn 17*
Dykes, Iva Ree 1942- *WhoWrEP 92*
Dykes, Jack *ConAu 37NR*
Dykes, James Edgar 1919- *WhoAm 92*
Dykes, Jefferson Chenowth 1900-1989 *BioIn 17*
Dykes, John Bacchus 1823-1876 *Baker 92*
Dykes, John Henry 1934- *St&PR 93*
Dykes, John Henry, Jr. 1934- *WhoAm 92*
Dykes, Julius A. 1943- *St&PR 93*
Dykes, Nancy Haun 1934- *WhoAmW 93*
Dykes, Robert F. *Law&B 92*
Dykes, Robert R.B. 1949- *St&PR 93*
Dykes, Virginia Chandler 1930- *WhoAm 92, WhoAmW 93*
Dykes, Vivian 1898-1943 *BioIn 17*
Dykewoman, Elana *ScF&FL 92*
Dykhouse, David B. 1948- *St&PR 93*
Dykhouse, David Jay 1936- *WhoAm 92*
Dykhouse, David Wayne 1949- *WhoEmL 93*
Dykhta, Vladimir Alexandrovitch 1949- *WhoWor 93*
Dykhuisen, Gerald Arthur 1946- *WhoSSW 93*
Dykla, Edward George 1933- *WhoAm 92*
Dykman, Charlene Ann 1948- *WhoSSW 93*
Dykstra, Daniel D. 1955- *WhoEmL 93*
Dykstra, Daniel James 1916- *WhoAm 92*
Dykstra, David A. 1960- *St&PR 93*
Dykstra, David Allen 1938- *WhoWor 93*
Dykstra, David Charles 1941- *WhoAm 92*
Dykstra, David Laurie 1946- *WhoE 93*
Dykstra, Doward William 1933- *St&PR 93*
Dykstra, Edie M. 1954- *WhoAmW 93*
Dykstra, Gregg A. *Law&B 92*
Dykstra, Len 1963- *BioIn 17*
Dykstra, Mary Elizabeth 1939- *WhoAm 92*
Dykstra, Paul Hopkins 1943- *WhoAm 92*
Dykstra, Robert T. 1918- *St&PR 93*
Dykstra, Thomas Karl 1935- *WhoE 93*
Dykstra, Vergil Homer 1925- *WhoAm 92*
Dykstra, William Dwight 1927- *WhoWor 93*
Dykstra, William Henry 1928- *St&PR 93, WhoAm 92*
Dylag, Michal 1938- *WhoScE 91-4*
Dylan, Bob 1941- *Baker 92, BioIn 17, MiSFD 9, WhoAm 92*
Dy Liacco, Tomas Enciso 1920- *WhoAm 92*
Dym, Clive Lionel 1942- *WhoAm 92*
Dymacek, Wayne Marshall 1952- *WhoSSW 93*
Dymally, Mervyn M. *BioIn 17*
Dymally, Mervyn M. 1926- *AfrAmBi [port], CngDr 91*
Dymally, Mervyn Malcolm 1926- *WhoAm 92*
Dymarczyk, Walter S. 1948- *St&PR 93*
Dymarkowski, Daniel W. *Law&B 92*
Dymecki, Jerzy Marian 1926- *WhoScE 91-4*
Dymek, James S. *St&PR 93*
Dyment, John J. 1933- *St&PR 93*
Dyment, John Joseph 1933- *WhoAm 92*
Dyment, Paul George 1935- *WhoAm 92*
Dymicky, Michael 1920- *WhoE 93*
Dymiotis, Petros Georgiou 1940- *WhoWor 93*
Dymond, Barbara Louise 1956- *WhoAmW 93*
Dymond, Lewis Wandell 1920- *WhoAm 92*
Dymond, Robert Christopher John 1939- *WhoAm 92*
Dynan, Mark James 1957- *WhoEmL 93*
Dynek, Sigred *Law&B 92*
Dynna, Harold Olaf 1935- *St&PR 93*
Dynowski, Witold 1903-1986 *IntDcAn*
Dyomin, Sviatoslav 1941- *WhoUN 92*
Dyott, Richard Burnaby 1924- *WhoAm 92*
Dypvik, Henning 1950- *WhoScE 91-4*
Dyrcz, Andrzej 1933- *WhoScE 91-4*
Dyregrov, Michael 1931- *WhoWor 93*
Dyrek, Krystyna 1930- *WhoScE 91-4*
Dyrmundsson, Olafur R. 1944- *WhoScE 91-4*
Dyro, Frances Mary Agnes 1941- *WhoAmW 93*
Dyroff, Helge 1935- *WhoScE 91-3*
Dyrstad, Joanell M. 1942- *WhoAm 92, WhoAmW 93*
Dyrud, Jarl Edvard 1921- *WhoAm 92*
Dysart, Benjamin Clay, III 1940- *WhoAm 92*
Dysart, Chloe *AmWomPl*
Dysart, Joel Alyn 1940- *WhoAm 92*
Dysart, Mitchell David 1956- *WhoEmL 93*
Dysart, Richard A. 1929- *WhoAm 92*
Dysart, Robert Lewis 1956- *WhoEmL 93*
Dysinger, Paul William 1927- *WhoAm 92*
Dyson, Allan Judge 1942- *WhoAm 92*
Dyson, Arthur *BioIn 17*
Dyson, Arthur Thomas 1940- *St&PR 93*
Dyson, Brian G. 1935- *St&PR 93, WhoAm 92, WhoSSW 93*
Dyson, Charles H. 1909- *St&PR 93*
Dyson, David Arnold 1951- *WhoSSW 93*
Dyson, David P. *Law&B 92*
Dyson, Esther 1951- *WhoAm 92*
Dyson, Freeman J. 1923- *BioIn 17*
Dyson, Freeman John 1923- *WhoAm 92*
Dyson, George 1883-1964 *Baker 92*
Dyson, James David *Law&B 92*
Dyson, John Edgar David *WhoScE 91-1*
Dyson, Kenneth H.F. *WhoScE 91-1*
Dyson, Paul Robert 1960- *WhoWor 93*
Dyson, Raymond Clegg 1902- *WhoAm 92, WhoWor 93*
Dyson, Robert Graham *WhoScE 91-1*
Dyson, Robert Harris 1927- *WhoAm 92*
Dyson, Ronnie *BioIn 17*
Dyson, Sue J. 1956- *WhoScE 91-1*

Dyson, Walter Raymond 1937- *WhoScE 91-1*
Dysort, Patricia *Law&B 92*
Dystel, Jane Dee 1945- *WhoAm 92*
Dystel, Oscar 1912- *WhoAm 92*
Dyte, Kerry Don *Law&B 92*
Dytell, Rita Scher 1943- *WhoAmW 93*
Dyvig, Peter P. 1934- *WhoAm 92, WhoWor 93*
Dywan, Jeffery Joseph 1949- *WhoEmL 93*
Dyyon, Frazier 1946- *WhoAm 92*
Dzakpasu, Cornelius K. 1944- *WhoUN 92*
Dzapo, Vlado 1939- *WhoScE 91-3*
Dzbenski, Tadeusz H. 1938- *WhoScE 91-4*
Dzegelenok, Alexander (Mikhailovich) 1891-1969 *Baker 92*
Dzenitis, Talis *Law&B 92*
Dzervens, Pamela Vilma 1956- *WhoAmW 93*
Dzerzhinskii, Feliks Edmundovich 1877-1926 *BioIn 17*
Dzerzhinsky, Felix Edmundovich 1877-1926 *DcTwHis*
Dzerzhinsky, Ivan 1909-1978 *Baker 92, OxDcOp*
Dzhaparidze, Giorgie 1961- *WhoWor 93*
Dziak, Regina Marcelline 1951- *WhoAmW 93*
Dziardziel, Henry 1946- *WhoWor 93*
Dziech, Andrzej 1946- *WhoScE 91-4*
Dziedziak, Bryan John 1958- *WhoEmL 93*
Dziedzic, Gene 1945- *WhoSSW 93*
Dziegielewski, Greg *Law&B 92*
Dzielak, Richard Anthony 1943- *St&PR 93*
Dziembaj, Roman 1941- *WhoScE 91-4*
Dziembowski, Wojciech A. 1940- *WhoScE 91-4*
Dziemianowicz, Stefan R. 1957- *ScF&FL 92*
Dzienia, Stanislaw 1934- *WhoScE 91-4*
Dzierozynski, Francis 1779-1850 *PolBiDi*
Dzierza, Wieslaw 1934- *WhoScE 91-4*
Dzierzanowski, Michal 1725-1808 *PolBiDi*
Dzierzon, Jan 1811-1906 *PolBiDi*
Dzierzynski, Feliks E. 1877-1926 *PolBiDi*
Dzierzynski, Jean 1946- *WhoAmW 93*
Dziewanowska, Zofia Elizabeth 1939- *WhoWor 93*
Dziewanowski, Kazimierz 1930- *WhoWor 93*
Dziewanowski, Marian Kamil 1913- *WhoAm 92*
Dzieweczynski, Gregory John 1951- *WhoEmL 93*
Dziewulski, Wladyslaw 1878-1962 *PolBiDi*
Dziljanov, L. *WhoScE 91-4*
Dzisiak, John F. *Law&B 92*
Dziuba, Henry Frank 1918- *WhoAm 92*
Dziubla, Robert W. 1952- *WhoAm 92*
Dziurzynski, Bogdan 1948- *St&PR 93*
Dzodin, Harvey Cary 1947- *WhoAm 92, WhoEmL 93*
Dzuback, Mary Ann 1950- *ConAu 138*
Dzubera, Patricia 1951- *WhoEmL 93*
Dzugan, Miki E. 1944- *WhoAmW 93*
Dzurec, Richard L. 1928- *St&PR 93*
D'Zurilla, William Thomas 1953- *WhoSSW 93*

E

E., Sheila 1958?- *NotHsAW 93*
E, Sheila 1959- *SoulM*
Each, Thomas C. 1932- *St&PR 93*
Eachus, Joseph Jackson 1911- *WhoAm 92*
Eacott, James H., Jr. 1923- *St&PR 93*
Eacott, James Henry, III 1948- *St&PR 93*
Eaddy, Wildon Brooks 1933- *St&PR 93*
Eade, George James 1921- *St&PR 93, WhoAm 92*
Eade, Lucy Gaye 1948- *WhoEmL 93*
Eadens, Barry Lynn 1952- *WhoEmL 93*
Eades, Cynda L. *Law&B 92*
Eades, James Beverly, Jr. 1923- *WhoAm 92*
Eades, Ronald Wayne 1948- *WhoEmL 93*
Eadie, Douglas Browning 1944- *WhoSSW 93*
Eadie, John William 1935- *WhoAm 92*
Eadie, Margaret Louise Larson *WhoAmW 93*
Eadie, Ronald E. 1931- *WhoAm 92*
Eadington, Joan 1926- *ChlFicS*
Eads, Darwin Leroy 1949- *WhoE 93*
Eads, George Curtis 1942- *WhoAm 92*
Eads, Lyle Willis 1916- *WhoSSW 93, WhoWor 93*
Eads, M. Adela 1920- *WhoAmW 93, WhoE 93*
Eads, Ora Wilbert 1914- *WhoAm 92*
Eads, Ronald Preston 1948- *WhoEmL 93, WhoSSW 93, WhoWor 93*
Eady, Carol Murphy 1918- *WhoAm 92*
Eady, Cornelius Robert 1954- *WhoWrEP 92*
Eady, Lydia Davis 1958- *WhoAmW 93, WhoWor 93*
Eady, Robert Roy *WhoScE 91-1*
Eady, Robin Anthony Jeffery *WhoScE 91-1*
Eagan, Claire Veronica 1950- *WhoEmL 93*
Eagan, Dennis P. *Law&B 92*
Eagan, Emmett E., Jr. *Law&B 92*
Eagan, John 1925-1987 *BioIn 17*
Eagan, Marie T. 1952- *WhoAmW 93, WhoE 93*
Eagan, Sherman G. 1942- *WhoAm 92*
Eagar, Patrick *BioIn 17*
Eagar, William Dees 1942- *WhoSSW 93*
Eagel, Seymour 1927- *St&PR 93*
Eager, Carolyn Hall 1945- *WhoAmW 93*
Eager, Edward (McMaken) 1911-1964 *DcAmChF 1960, MajAI [port]*
Eager, George Sidney, Jr. 1915- *WhoAm 92, WhoE 93*
Eager, Karen Andrews 1949- *WhoAmW 93*
Eager, Margaret Maclaren *AmWomPl*
Eager, Robert Donald 1950- *WhoWor 93*
Eager, Robert W., Jr. 1944- *WhoIns 93*
Eager, Stephen J. 1927- *St&PR 93*
Eager, William E. 1946- *St&PR 93*
Eager, William Earl 1946- *WhoAm 92*
Eagle, Arnold d1992 *NewYTBS 92*
Eagle, Charles A. 1936- *St&PR 93*
Eagle, Ellen 1953- *BioIn 17*
Eagle, Harry d1992 *NewYTBS 92 [port]*
Eagle, Jack 1926- *WhoE 93*
Eagle, Jerry Lee *Law&B 92*
Eagle, John M. *St&PR 93*
Eagle, Kathleen 1947- *WhoWrEP 92*
Eagle, Kevin Dale 1954- *St&PR 93*
Eagleburger, Debrah Jean 1948- *WhoEmL 93*
Eagleburger, Lawrence S. *BioIn 17*
Eagleburger, Lawrence S. 1930- *CngDr 91, CurBio 92 [port]*
Eagleburger, Lawrence Sidney 1930- *WhoWor 93*
Eagles, Charles W. 1946- *ConAu 138*
Eagles, Douglas Alan 1943- *WhoE 93*
Eagles, Lee N. 1947- *St&PR 93*
Eagles, Lee Neild 1947- *WhoE 93*
Eagles, Sidney Smith, Jr. 1939- *WhoAm 92*
Eagles, Stuart Ernest 1929- *WhoAm 92*
Eagleson, Alan 1933- *BioIn 17*
Eagleson, David 1943- *St&PR 93*
Eagleson, Nancy Robinson 1936- *WhoAmW 93*
Eagleson, Peter Sturges 1928- *WhoAm 92*
Eagleson, William Boal, Jr. 1925- *WhoAm 92*
Eagleson, William James 1937- *St&PR 93*
Eaglet, Robert Danton 1934- *WhoAm 92, WhoE 93*
Eagleton, Beth Bernadette 1950- *WhoEmL 93*
Eagleton, Robert Don 1937- *WhoAm 92*
Eagleton, Terry 1943- *BioIn 17*
Eagleton, Thomas F. 1929- *PolPar*
Eagleton, William Lester, Jr. 1926- *WhoAm 92*
Eaglin, Ronald George 1940- *WhoAm 92, WhoSSW 93*
Eaglstein, William Howard 1940- *WhoAm 92*
Eagly, Alice Hendrickson 1938- *WhoAm 92*
Eagon, Carrie Wilson 1920- *WhoAmW 93*
Eaione, Joseph Henry 1949- *WhoEmL 93*
Eakeley, Douglas Scott 1946- *WhoEmL 93*
Eaken, Bruce Webb *Law&B 92*
Eaker, Charles William 1949- *WhoEmL 93, WhoSSW 93*
Eaker, Ira 1922- *WhoAm 92*
Eaker, Ira Clarence 1896-1987 *HarEnMi*
Eaker, John H. *Law&B 92*
Eaker, Kenneth August 1952- *St&PR 93*
Eaker, Sherry Ellen 1949- *WhoEmL 93*
Eakes, John Ashley 1953- *WhoE 93*
Eakin, Barbara Ann 1921- *WhoAmW 93*
Eakin, David McClellan 1950- *WhoEmL 93*
Eakin, Margaretta Morgan 1941- *WhoWor 93*
Eakin, Richard Ronald 1938- *WhoAm 92, WhoSSW 93*
Eakin, Robert Earl 1938- *WhoSSW 93*
Eakin, Thomas Capper 1933- *WhoAm 92*
Eakin, Thomas Robert 1954- *St&PR 93*
Eakin, Tom S., Jr. 1927- *St&PR 93*
Eakin, Tom Scott, Jr. 1927- *WhoAm 92*
Eakin, William Wayne 1949- *WhoEmL 93*
Eakins, Hazel Kelly 1936- *WhoAmW 93*
Eakins, Kenneth E. 1935- *St&PR 93*
Eakins, Patricia 1942- *WhoWrEP 92*
Eakins, Thomas 1844-1916 *BioIn 17, GayN*
Eakins, Wayne 1926- *WhoE 93*
Eakins, William *ScF&FL 92*
Eakins, William Shannon 1951- *WhoEmL 93*
Eakle, Arlene H. 1936- *WhoAm 92*
Eakman, Florence E. *AmWomPl*
Eales, John Geoffrey 1937- *WhoAm 92*
Eales, V. Richard 1936- *St&PR 93*
Ealy, Carleton Cato 1957- *St&PR 93*
Ealy, Jonathan Bruce 1960- *WhoEmL 93*
Ealy, Lawrence Orr 1915- *WhoAm 92, WhoWor 93*
Eamer, Richard K. 1928- *St&PR 93*
Eames, Emma 1865-1952 *IntDcOp [port], OxDcOp*
Eames, Emma (Hayden) 1865-1952 *Baker 92*
Eames, G. Clifton 1927- *St&PR 93*
Eames, Henry Purmort 1872-1950 *Baker 92*
Eames, John Heagan 1900- *WhoAm 92*
Eames, Ray *BioIn 17*
Eames, Wilmer Ballou 1914- *WhoAm 92*
Eanes, Edward David 1934- *WhoE 93*
Eanes, Jim Roger 1936- *WhoSSW 93*
Eanes, John Philp, Jr. 1947- *WhoSSW 93*
Eanes, Joseph Cabel, Jr. 1935- *St&PR 93, WhoAm 92, WhoIns 93*
Eanes, Michael Bailey 1941- *St&PR 93*
Eanes, Wanda Marie 1958- *WhoEmL 93, WhoSSW 93*
Eannace, Carol Joan 1953- *WhoSSW 93*
Eannello, Dominick Michael 1932- *WhoE 93*
Eannes, Gil fl. 15th cent.- *Expl 93*
Eardley-Wilmot, Brian 1939- *WhoWor 93*
Eareckson, Joni *BioIn 17*
Earhart, Amelia 1897-1937 *DcTwHis*
Earhart, Amelia 1898-1937 *BioIn 17, Expl 93 [port]*
Earhart, Bill d1896 *BioIn 17*
Earhart, Donald M. 1944- *St&PR 93*
Earhart, Donald Marion 1944- *WhoAm 92*
Earhart, Eileen Magie 1928- *WhoAm 92*
Earhart, J. Troy *WhoAm 92*
Earhart, Will 1871-1960 *Baker 92*
Earl, Anthony Scully 1936- *WhoAm 92*
Earl, Bill *BioIn 17*
Earl, Charles Reginald Arnold *WhoScE 91-1*
Earl, Christopher Francis *WhoScE 91-1*
Earl, Don Charles 1925- *WhoSSW 93*
Earl, Jack F. 1936- *St&PR 93*
Earl, John Richard 1934- *WhoIns 93*
Earl, Johnny 1965- *BioIn 17*
Earl, Leigh *BioIn 17*
Earl, Lewis Harold 1918- *WhoAm 92*
Earl, Lisa Maija 1960- *WhoAmW 93*
Earl, Maureen 1944- *ConAu 137*
Earl, Peter M. 1949- *St&PR 93*
Earl, Robert *BioIn 17*
Earl, William John 1950- *WhoEmL 93*
Earle, Arthur Percival 1922- *St&PR 93, WhoAm 92*
Earle, Arthur Scott 1924- *WhoAm 92*
Earle, Clifford John, Jr. 1935- *WhoAm 92*
Earle, Darrien *BioIn 17*
Earle, David Jeffrey *Law&B 92*
Earle, David P., III *Law&B 92*
Earle, David Prince, Jr. 1910- *WhoAm 92*
Earle, Dorothy Kirchener *AmWomPl*
Earle, Douglas Vandyke 1955- *St&PR 93*
Earle, Elizabeth Deutsch 1937- *WhoAmW 93*
Earle, Eyvind *BioIn 17*
Earle, George Howard 1890-1974 *BioIn 17*
Earle, Georgia *AmWomPl*
Earle, Harry Woodward 1924- *St&PR 93, WhoAm 92*
Earle, Hubert Potter 1918- *St&PR 93*
Earle, John 1601?-1665 *BioIn 17*
Earle, Kenneth Martin 1919- *WhoAm 92*
Earle, Nathaniel Cabot 1952- *WhoE 93*
Earle, Ralph, II 1928- *WhoAm 92*
Earle, Sylvia A. 1935- *BioIn 17, CurBio 92 [port]*
Earle, Sylvia Alice 1935- *WhoAm 92, WhoAmW 93*
Earle, Victor M. *Law&B 92*
Earle, Victor Montagne, III 1933- *WhoAm 92*
Earle, William *MajAI*
Earles, Dorothy Robertson 1946- *WhoAm 92*
Earles, Richard Lee 1952- *St&PR 93*
Earles, Stanley William Edward *WhoScE 91-1*
Earles, Stanley William Edward 1929- *WhoWor 93*
Earley, Anthony F. 1949- *St&PR 93*
Earley, Anthony F., Jr. *Law&B 92*
Earley, Anthony Francis, Jr. 1949- *WhoAm 92, WhoE 93*
Earley, Daniel L. 1942- *St&PR 93*
Earley, Edward Joseph, Jr. 1952- *WhoEmL 93*
Earley, Joseph Emmet 1932- *WhoE 93*
Earley, Joseph Francis 1924- *St&PR 93*
Earley, Kathleen Sanders 1946- *WhoAmW 93*
Earley, Laurence Elliott 1931- *WhoAm 92*
Earley, Miriam Lee 1878- *AmWomPl*
Earley, Robert Horn 1948- *St&PR 93*
Earley, William Guthrie 1941- *St&PR 93*
Earlie, Willie 1947- *WhoSSW 93*
Earl-Jean *SoulM*
Earll, Jerry Miller 1928- *WhoAm 92*
Earl of Dunsmere, Baron Horan of Antwerp 1950- *WhoWor 93*
Earlougher, Robert Charles, Sr. 1914- *WhoAm 92, WhoSSW 93*
Earls, Bill *ScF&FL 92*
Earls, Clifford Dewight 1935- *St&PR 93*
Earls, David M. 1952- *St&PR 93*
Earls, H. Clayton *ScF&FL 92*
Earls, Hugh C. *Law&B 92*
Earls, Irene Anne *WhoAmW 93, WhoSSW 93, WhoWor 93*
Earls, Priscilla Sue 1945- *St&PR 93*
Earls, William *ScF&FL 92*
Early, Bert Hylton 1922- *WhoAm 92, WhoWor 93*
Early, Deloreese Patricia 1931- *WhoAm 92*
Early, Glen Alan 1948- *WhoSSW 93*
Early, Jack Dent 1929- *WhoAm 92*
Early, Jack Gavin, Jr. 1953- *WhoEmL 93*
Early, Jack Jones 1925- *St&PR 93, WhoAm 92*
Early, James Michael 1922- *WhoAm 92*
Early, Jim Lee 1933- *WhoSSW 93*
Early, Johnnie L. 1949- *WhoSSW 93*
Early, Jon *MajAI*
Early, Joseph D. 1933- *CngDr 91*
Early, Joseph Daniel 1933- *WhoAm 92, WhoE 93*

Early, Jubal Anderson 1816-1894 *BioIn 17*
Early, Margaret 1951- *SmATA 72 [port]*
Early, Margaret Henderson 1952- *WhoEmL 93*
Early, Martin W. 1929- *St&PR 93*
Early, Mary Beth 1949- *WhoAmW 93, WhoE 93*
Early, Norman S., Jr. 1945- *AfrAmBi [port]*
Early, Patrick Joseph 1933- *WhoAm 92*
Early, Richard M. *Law&B 92*
Early, Robert Joseph 1936- *WhoAm 92*
Early, Scott E. *Law&B 92*
Early, Stephen Barry 1945- *St&PR 93*
Early, Thomas *Law&B 92*
Early, William Bernard 1936- *St&PR 93*
Early, William James 1921- *WhoAm 92*
Earner, George Edward 1930- *WhoE 93, WhoWor 93*
Earner, William Anthony, Jr. 1941- *WhoAm 92*
Earnest, Jack E. 1928- *St&PR 93*
Earnest, Jack Edward 1928- *WhoAm 92*
Earnest, William *St&PR 93*
Earnhardt, Dale *BioIn 17, WhoAm 92*
Earnhardt, Edward 1938- *St&PR 93*
Earnhardt, Ralph Dale 1952- *BiDAMSp 1989*
Earnhart, Mark Warren 1955- *WhoEmL 93*
Earnshaw, Brian 1924- *ScF&FL 92*
Earnshaw, John Christopher *WhoScE 91-1*
Earnshaw, Thomas L. 1954- *St&PR 93*
Earp, James Francy 1935- *WhoSSW 93*
Earp, Josephine Marcus 1862-1944 *BioIn 17*
Earp, Morgan 1851-1882 *BioIn 17*
Earp, Virgil 1843-1906? *BioIn 17*
Earp, Warren 1855-1900 *BioIn 17*
Earp, Wyatt 1848-1929 *BioIn 17, GayN*
Earth, Wind & Fire *SoulM*
Earwicker, Martin John 1948- *WhoScE 91-1*
Earwood, Dale C. *Law&B 92*
Earwood-Smith, Glenda Faye 1953- *WhoAmW 93*
Easdale, Brian 1909- *Baker 92*
Easdon, Don 1947- *WhoAm 92*
Easey, John Frederick 1940- *WhoUN 92*
Eash, Joseph J. 1938- *WhoAm 92*
Eash, Maurice James 1928- *WhoE 93*
Easley, Betty 1929- *WhoAmW 93*
Easley, Cheryl Eileen 1946- *WhoAmW 93*
Easley, Christa Birgit 1941- *WhoAmW 93*
Easley, David 1952- *WhoAm 92, WhoE 93*
Easley, Dick L. 1935- *St&PR 93*
Easley, John Allen, Jr. 1922- *WhoAm 92*
Easley, Loyce Anna 1918- *WhoAmW 93*
Easley, Mack 1916- *WhoAm 92*
Easley, Marjorie A. *St&PR 93*
Easley, Marjorie Mae 1935- *WhoAmW 93*
Easley, Matthew S. 1956- *St&PR 93*
Easley, Patsy Fletcher 1931- *WhoAm 92, WhoAmW 93, WhoSSW 93*
Easley, Waverly 1925- *St&PR 93*
Easlick, David Kenneth 1921- *WhoAm 92*
Easmon, Charles Syrett Farrell *WhoScE 91-1*
Easmon, John Farrell 1856-1900 *BioIn 17*
Easo, Jacob 1951- *WhoSSW 93*
Eason, Clifton W. 1943- *St&PR 93*
Eason, Forrest K. 1940- *St&PR 93*
Eason, James Oscar 1947- *St&PR 93*
Eason, Jimmie Jerome 1940- *St&PR 93*
Eason, Kathleen S. 1954- *WhoAmW 93*
Eason, Mitchell R. 1935- *St&PR 93*
Eason, Randolph Arthur 1946- *St&PR 93*
Eason, Richard Odell 1956- *WhoE 93*
Eason, Robert *WhoScE 91-1*
Eason, Robert Gaston 1924- *WhoAm 92*
Eason, Thomas K. 1911- *St&PR 93*
Eason, William Everette, Jr. 1943- *WhoAm 92*
Easson, William McAlpine 1931- *WhoAm 92*
East, Catherine Shipe 1916- *WhoSSW 93*
East, Charles 1924- *WhoWrEP 92*
East, Charles E., Jr. 1949- *WhoEmL 93, WhoSSW 93*
East, Charles Robert 1936- *WhoIns 93*
East, Darrell 1956- *St&PR 93*
East, David J. 1927- *St&PR 93*
East, Ernest Earl 1942- *St&PR 93*
East, F. Howard 1937- *St&PR 93*
East, Frank Howard 1937- *WhoAm 92*
East, Jack Milton 1950- *WhoSSW 93*
East, John Delos 1945- *St&PR 93*
East, June 1926- *WhoScE 91-1*
East, Marjorie *BioIn 17*
East, Maurice Alden 1941- *WhoAm 92*
East, Paul 1946- *WhoWor 93*
East, Paul Clayton 1946- *WhoAsAP 91*
East, Robin Alexander *WhoScE 91-1*
East, Robin Alexander 1935- *WhoWor 93*
East, Sarah *BioIn 17*
East, Stephen John 1958- *WhoWor 93*
East, Thomas c. 1535-1608 *Baker 92*
Eastaway, Robert 1962- *ConAu 139*
Eastburn, Jeannette Rose 1916- *WhoAmW 93, WhoWor 93*
Eastburn, Robert, Jr. *Law&B 92*
Eastburn, Ronald W. 1949- *St&PR 93*
Eastby, Allen Gerhard 1946- *WhoWrEP 92*
Easte, Thomas c. 1535-1608 *Baker 92*
Eastep, Larry Gene 1938- *WhoWor 93*
Easter, David Eugene, II 1950- *WhoWor 93*
Easter, John W. 1946- *WhoIns 93*
Easter, Luke *BioIn 17*
Easter, Stephen Sherman, Jr. 1938- *WhoAm 92*
Easter, Steven Wycliffe 1941- *St&PR 93*
Easterbrook, Frank H. 1948- *ConAu 138*
Easterbrook, Frank Hoover 1948- *WhoAm 92*
Easterbrook, James Arthur 1923- *WhoAm 92*
Easterbrook, Kenneth Brian 1935- *WhoAm 92*
Easterday, Bernard Carlyle 1929- *WhoAm 92*
Easterday, Debra Scott *Law&B 92*
Easterday, Gene E. 1930- *St&PR 93*
Easterday, Jack Kahl 1932- *St&PR 93*
Easterday, Linda Lee 1950- *WhoAmW 93*
Easterday, Richard Lee 1938- *St&PR 93, WhoAm 92*
Easterday, Thomas Vernon *Law&B 92*
Easterlin, Donald J. 1942- *St&PR 93*
Easterlin, Donald Jacob, III 1942- *WhoAm 92*
Easterlin, John Howard 1962- *WhoEmL 93*
Easterlin, Richard Ainley 1926- *WhoAm 92*
Easterling, Charles Armo 1920- *WhoSSW 93*
Easterling, Cynthia SoRelle 1953- *WhoEmL 93*
Easterling, William Ewart, Jr. 1930- *WhoAm 92*
Easterly, Clark 1926- *St&PR 93*
Easterly, David Eugene 1942- *WhoAm 92*
Easterly, Thomas B. 1947- *St&PR 93*
Easterly, William B. 1959- *St&PR 93*
Easterman, Daniel 1949- *ScF&FL 92*
Easterung, Kenneth 1933- *WhoScE 91-4*
Easterwood, Janice Carol 1956- *WhoAmW 93*
Eastes, JoAnn Ferrare 1928- *WhoAmW 93*
Eastham, Alan Walter, Jr. 1951- *WhoAm 92*
Eastham, Dennis M. 1946- *St&PR 93*
Eastham, Dennis Michael 1946- *WhoAm 92*
Eastham, James Saxon *Law&B 92*
Eastham, John F. 1952- *St&PR 93*
Eastham, Thomas 1923- *WhoAm 92*
Eastin, Carol Prior 1941- *WhoAmW 93*
Eastin, Keith E. 1940- *WhoAm 92*
Eastlake, William Derry 1917- *WhoAm 92, WhoWrEP 92*
Eastland, James O. 1904-1986 *PolPar*
Eastland, Woods Eugene 1945- *St&PR 93*
Eastlick, John Taylor 1912-1990 *BioIn 17*
Eastline, Richard Leonard 1926- *St&PR 93*
Eastman, Albert Theodore 1928- *WhoAm 92*
Eastman, Allan 1950- *MiSFD 9*
Eastman, Ben Robert 1959- *WhoSSW 93*
Eastman, Benjamin Bangs 1911- *BiDAMSp 1989*
Eastman, Carol Mary 1941- *WhoAm 92*
Eastman, Caroline Merriam 1946- *WhoAm 92, WhoEmL 93*
Eastman, Carolyn Ann 1946- *WhoAmW 93, WhoEmL 93*
Eastman, Carolyn Bertha 1933- *WhoAmW 93*
Eastman, Charles *MiSFD 9*
Eastman, Charles 1858-1939 *GayN*
Eastman, Charles Gamage 1816-1860 *JrnUS*
Eastman, Creswell John *St&PR 93*
Eastman, Crystal 1881-1928 *BioIn 17*
Eastman, Dean Eric 1940- *WhoAm 92*
Eastman, Elaine Goodale 1863-1953 *AmWomPl*
Eastman, Forest David 1950- *WhoEmL 93*
Eastman, George 1854-1932 *Baker 92, BioIn 17, GayN*
Eastman, George D. 1912-1991 *BioIn 17*
Eastman, Glen Preston 1948- *WhoEmL 93*
Eastman, Harland Horace 1929- *WhoAm 92*
Eastman, Harry Claude MacColl 1923- *WhoAm 92*
Eastman, Ida Rauh *AmWomPl*
Eastman, James Michael 1936- *St&PR 93*
Eastman, Janet *SweetSg A*
Eastman, Janet Louise 1957- *WhoEmL 93*
Eastman, John *BioIn 17*
Eastman, John Garratt 1941- *WhoWor 93*
Eastman, John Richard 1917- *WhoAm 92*
Eastman, Joseph M. 1941- *St&PR 93*
Eastman, Lee V. 1910-1991 *BioIn 17*
Eastman, Leonard 1936- *St&PR 93*
Eastman, Lester C. 1918- *St&PR 93*
Eastman, Lester Fuess 1928- *WhoAm 92*
Eastman, Lucius Root d1991 *BioIn 17*
Eastman, Lynn Alfred 1948- *WhoEmL 93*
Eastman, Max 1883-1969 *BioIn 17*
Eastman, P. Dwight 1917- *St&PR 93*
Eastman, Ronald E. *BioIn 17*
Eastman, William Don 1931- *WhoAm 92*
Eastment, George T., III 1945- *St&PR 93*
Eastment, Thomas James 1950- *WhoAm 92, WhoE 93, WhoEmL 93*
Easton, Agnes *ScF&FL 92*
Easton, Bradd Steven *Law&B 92*
Easton, Carol 1932- *ConAu 39NR*
Easton, Carol Lee 1939- *WhoAmW 93*
Easton, David 1917- *BioIn 17*
Easton, Edward 1940- *ScF&FL 92*
Easton, Florence 1882-1955 *OxDcOp*
Easton, Florence (Gertrude) 1882-1955 *Baker 92*
Easton, Geoffrey *WhoScE 91-1*
Easton, Glenn Hanson, Jr. *WhoAm 92, WhoWor 93*
Easton, Jane 1918- *ConAu 138*
Easton, Jill Johanna 1949- *WhoEmL 93*
Easton, John Edward 1935- *WhoAm 92*
Easton, John Jay, Jr. 1943- *WhoAm 92*
Easton, Keith E. *Law&B 92*
Easton, Kelly Mark 1963- *WhoEmL 93, WhoSSW 93*
Easton, M. Coleman 1942- *ScF&FL 92*
Easton, Michelle 1950- *WhoAm 92, WhoAmW 93*
Easton, Nina Jane 1958- *WhoAmW 93*
Easton, Robert Andrew 1945- *WhoSSW 93*
Easton, Robert G. *Law&B 92*
Easton, Robert J. 1943- *St&PR 93*
Easton, Robert Morrell, Jr. 1954- *WhoSSW 93*
Easton, Robert Olney 1915- *WhoAm 92, WhoWor 93*
Easton, Robert William Simpson 1922- *BioIn 17*
Easton, Sheena 1959- *WhoAmW 93*
Easton, Stanley 1919- *St&PR 93*
Easton, Stephen Douglas 1958- *WhoEmL 93*
Easton, Susan Mellin *Law&B 92*
Easton, Susan Shearer 1950- *WhoSSW 93*
Easton, Thomas A. 1944- *ScF&FL 92*
Easton, Thomas Atwood 1944- *WhoE 93*
Easton, William Heyden 1916- *WhoAm 92*
Easton-Hafkenschiel, Cynthia Ruth 1949- *WhoEmL 93*
Eastridge, Michael Dwayne 1956- *WhoSSW 93*
Eastvold, Paul Dean 1948- *WhoEmL 93*
Eastwick-Field, Nikolas 1944- *St&PR 93*
Eastwood, Clint *BioIn 17*
Eastwood, Clint 1930?- *IntDcF 2-3 [port], MiSFD 9, WhoAm 92, WhoWor 93*
Eastwood, Dana Alan 1947- *WhoE 93, WhoEmL 93*
Eastwood, DeLyle 1932- *WhoAm 92*
Eastwood, Douglas William 1918- *WhoAm 92*
Eastwood, Geoffrey Rowland *WhoScE 91-1*
Eastwood, Peter 1939- *St&PR 93*
Eastwood, William Scott 1942- *St&PR 93*
Easty, David *WhoScE 91-1*
Eatherly, Walter Pasold 1923- *WhoSSW 93*
Eatinger, Robert Joseph, Jr. 1957- *WhoEmL 93*
Eatock Taylor, W. Rodney *WhoScE 91-1*
Eaton, Alan Noel 1931- *WhoWor 93*
Eaton, Allen Ober 1910- *WhoAm 92*
Eaton, Alvin Ralph 1920- *WhoAm 92, WhoWor 93*
Eaton, Ann Berrien 1960- *WhoEmL 93*
Eaton, Ben 1963- *St&PR 93*
Eaton, Berrien Clark 1919- *WhoAm 92, WhoWor 93*
Eaton, Candace Johnson 1952- *WhoE 93*
Eaton, Charles Edward 1916- *WhoAm 92, WhoWrEP 92*
Eaton, Clara Barbour 1930- *WhoAm 92*
Eaton, Claudia *Law&B 92*
Eaton, Conrad Paul 1941- *WhoAm 92*
Eaton, Craig Loren *Law&B 92*
Eaton, David Edgar *WhoScE 91-1*
Eaton, Deborah Hayward 1946- *WhoWor 93*
Eaton, Dorla Dean 1929- *WhoAmW 93*
Eaton, E.P., Jr. 1923- *St&PR 93*
Eaton, Edgar Philip, Jr. 1923- *WhoAm 92, WhoE 93, WhoWor 93*
Eaton, Edmund Denis, Jr. 1951- *WhoE 93*
Eaton, Edna Dorothy 1938- *WhoAmW 93*
Eaton, Edwin H., Jr. 1938- *St&PR 93*
Eaton, Edwin Harvey, Jr. 1938- *WhoAm 92*
Eaton, Emma Florence *AmWomPl*
Eaton, Frederick G. d1992 *NewYTBS 92*
Eaton, Frederick Howard 1933- *St&PR 93, WhoAm 92*
Eaton, Gareth Richard 1940- *WhoAm 92*
Eaton, George Benjamin 1958- *WhoE 93, WhoEmL 93*
Eaton, George L. *ConAu 37NR*
Eaton, Gerald Manley *Law&B 92*
Eaton, Gordon Pryor 1929- *WhoAm 92, WhoWor 93*
Eaton, Haven McCrillis 1926- *St&PR 93*
Eaton, Henry Felix 1925- *WhoAm 92*
Eaton, Henry Taft 1918- *WhoWor 93*
Eaton, Janet Clarice 1941- *WhoAmW 93*
Eaton, Jeanette 1886-1968 *MajAI [port]*
Eaton, Joe Oscar 1920- *WhoAm 92*
Eaton, John 1935- *IntDcOp*
Eaton, John A. 1925- *St&PR 93*
Eaton, John C. 1935- *WhoAm 92*
Eaton, John (Charles) 1935- *Baker 92*
Eaton, John H. 1945- *St&PR 93*
Eaton, John Henry 1790-1856 *PolPar*
Eaton, John LeRoy 1939- *WhoSSW 93*
Eaton, John Stanley 1932- *St&PR 93*
Eaton, John Walton Tristram 1964- *WhoWor 93*
Eaton, Joseph W. 1919- *WhoAm 92*
Eaton, Karl F. 1925- *St&PR 93*
Eaton, Kim Diane 1956- *WhoEmL 93*
Eaton, L. Daniel 1940- *WhoWor 93*
Eaton, Larry Ralph 1944- *WhoAm 92*
Eaton, Leonard James, Jr. 1934- *St&PR 93, WhoAm 92*
Eaton, Leonard Kimball 1922- *WhoAm 92*
Eaton, Lewis Swift 1919- *St&PR 93, WhoAm 92*
Eaton, Mable E. *AmWomPl*
Eaton, Malachy Michael 1960- *WhoWor 93*
Eaton, Margaret Ann 1953- *WhoAmW 93, WhoEmL 93*
Eaton, Mark R. 1952- *St&PR 93*
Eaton, Mark Rayner 1952- *WhoAm 92*
Eaton, Martha Bacher 1935- *WhoAmW 93*
Eaton, Merrill Thomas 1920- *WhoAm 92*
Eaton, Nancy L. 1943- *WhoAm 92, WhoAmW 93*
Eaton, Pauline 1935- *WhoAm 92, WhoAmW 93*
Eaton, Quaintance *BioIn 17*
Eaton, Quaintance d1992 *NewYTBS 92*
Eaton, Richard Bozman, Jr. 1931- *WhoSSW 93*
Eaton, Richard Gillette 1929- *WhoWor 93*
Eaton, Richard J. 1936- *St&PR 93*
Eaton, Robert Charles 1946- *WhoWrEP 92*
Eaton, Robert Edward Lee 1909- *WhoWor 93*
Eaton, Robert J. *BioIn 17*
Eaton, Robert J. 1940- *NewYTBS 92*
Eaton, Robert James 1908- *WhoWor 93*
Eaton, Robert James 1940- *St&PR 93, WhoAm 92*
Eaton, Rodney Arthur *WhoScE 91-1*
Eaton, Sandra Shaw 1946- *WhoEmL 93*
Eaton, Theodore A. 1950- *St&PR 93, WhoIns 93*
Eaton, Thomas B. 1930- *St&PR 93*
Eaton, Thomas Clark 1952- *WhoEmL 93, WhoWor 93*
Eaton, W. Thompson 1938- *St&PR 93*
Eaton, William Charles 1927- *WhoAm 92*
Eaton, William Lawrence 1946- *WhoEmL 93*
Eaton, William Lee 1947- *WhoEmL 93*
Eatwell, John *BioIn 17*
Eaves, Allen Charles Edward 1941- *WhoAm 92*
Eaves, G. Lorraine *Law&B 92*
Eaves, George Newton 1935- *WhoAm 92*
Eaves, James Edwin 1953- *WhoE 93*
Eaves, Laurence *WhoScE 91-1*
Eaves, Lucile 1869-1953 *BioIn 17*
Eaves, Maria Perry *WhoAmW 93*
Eaves, Morris Emery 1944- *WhoAm 92*
Eaves, Patricia Ann 1959- *St&PR 93*
Eaves, Ronald Weldon 1937- *WhoAm 92*
Eayrs, James George 1926- *WhoAm 92*
Ebacher, David C. 1942- *St&PR 93*
Ebacher, Roger 1936- *WhoAm 92*
Ebagezio, Valter 1958- *WhoWor 93*
Ebagosti, Andre 1945- *WhoWor 93*
Eban, Abba 1915- *WhoWor 93*
Eban, Abba Solomon 1915- *DcTwHis*
Ebanks, Benson 1935- *DcCPCAm*
Ebanks, Marlon Udel 1967- *WhoE 93*
Ebara, Ryuichiro 1942- *WhoWor 93*
Ebarb, William Lawrence 1950- *WhoEmL 93*
Ebaugh, Frank Wright 1901- *WhoSSW 93, WhoWor 93*
Ebaugh, Franklin G. 1921-1990 *BioIn 17*

Ebaugh, Helen Rose 1942- *WhoAm 92*
Ebb, Fred 1936- *WhoE 93*
Ebb, Nina Zdenka 1923- *WhoWor 93*
Ebb, Sophie B. *AmWomPl*
Ebben, James A. *WhoAm 92*
Ebben, Joyce Marie 1952- *WhoEmL 93*
Ebbers, Larry Harold 1941- *WhoAm 92*
Ebbers, Laura Kay 1954- *WhoEmL 93*
Ebbert, Arthur, Jr. 1922- *WhoAm 92*
Ebbert, Donald C. 1921- *St&PR 93*
Ebbert, Martin B., Jr. 1939- *St&PR 93*
Ebbert, Robert 1910- *St&PR 93*
Ebbesen, Peter 1936- *WhoScE 91-2*
Ebbesen, Samuel Emanuel 1938- *AfrAmBi [port]*
Ebbing, Darrell Delmar 1933- *WhoAm 92*
Ebbitt, Kenneth Cooper 1908- *WhoAm 92*
Ebbitt, Kenneth Cooper, Jr. 1941- *WhoAm 92*
Ebbs, George Heberling, Jr. 1942- *WhoAm 92, WhoE 93*
Ebbs, Susan Lancet 1943- *WhoAmW 93*
Ebeid, Evon M. *Law&B 92*
Ebeid, Farouk Ali 1935- *WhoUN 92*
Ebeid, Russell Joseph 1940- *St&PR 93*
Ebejer, Francis 1925- *ConAu 40NR*
Ebejer, George 1940- *WhoWor 93*
Ebel, Arnold 1883-1963 *Baker 92*
Ebel, Charles William 1951- *WhoWrEP 92*
Ebel, David M. 1940- *WhoAm 92*
Ebel, Friedrich 1944- *WhoWor 93*
Ebel, Jack E. *Law&B 92*
Ebel, Jean-Pierre *WhoScE 91-2*
Ebel, Marvin Emerson 1930- *WhoAm 92*
Ebeling, Werner 1936- *WhoScE 91-3*
Ebell, Cecil Walter 1947- *WhoEmL 93*
Ebelt, George Michael 1964- *WhoSSW 93*
Ebeltoft, Gary L. 1949- *St&PR 93*
Eben, James R. *Law&B 92*
Eben, Lois Ellen 1922- *WhoWrEP 92*
Eben, Petr 1929- *Baker 92*
Ebenberger, Hermann K. 1918- *WhoScE 91-4*
Ebener, Brian Scott 1961- *WhoEmL 93*
Ebenholtz, Jean Miriam 1934- *WhoAmW 93*
Ebenholtz, Larry 1942- *St&PR 93*
Ebenholtz, Sheldon Marshal 1932- *WhoE 93*
Ebenstein, Jerome S. *Law&B 92*
Eber, Herbert Wolfgang 1928- *WhoAm 92, WhoSSW 93*
Eber, Martha Christine d1991 *BioIn 17*
Eber, Michel 1943- *WhoWor 93*
Eberdt, Mary Gertrude 1932- *WhoWrEP 92*
Eberhard, John Paul 1927- *WhoAm 92*
Eberhard, Wolfram 1909-1989 *BioIn 17*
Eberhardt, H. Alfred 1924- *St&PR 93*
Eberhardt, Jerrold Lee 1941- *St&PR 93*
Eberhardt, Siegfried 1883-1960 *Baker 92*
Eberhardt, Thom *MiSFD 9*
Eberhardt, Wayne R. *Law&B 92*
Eberhart, Allan Charles 1961- *WhoE 93*
Eberhart, David L. *St&PR 93*
Eberhart, John C. *BioIn 17*
Eberhart, Jonathan *BioIn 17*
Eberhart, Mary Ann Petesie 1940- *WhoAm 92, WhoSSW 93*
Eberhart, Max E. *Law&B 92*
Eberhart, Nelle Richmond McCurdy 1871-1944 *AmWomPl*
Eberhart, Richard 1904- *BioIn 17, WhoAm 92, WhoWrEP 92*
Eberhart, Robert Clyde 1937- *WhoAm 92*
Eberhart, Robert James 1930- *WhoE 93*
Eberhart, Steve A. 1931- *WhoAm 92*
Eberhart, Steven Wesley 1952- *WhoEmL 93*
Eberius, Wayne Richard 1944- *WhoSSW 93*
Eberl, Anton (Franz Josef) 1765-1807 *Baker 92*
Eberl, Edward G. 1951- *St&PR 93*
Eberl, Rudolf 1923- *WhoScE 91-4*
Eberle, Charles Edward 1928- *WhoAm 92, WhoSSW 93*
Eberle, Johann Ernst 1702-1762 *Baker 92*
Eberle, Kathy M. 1966- *WhoEmL 93*
Eberle, Laurie Ann 1953- *WhoE 93*
Eberle, Merab *AmWomPl*
Eberle, Peter H. 1942- *St&PR 93*
Eberle, Robert Frank 1946- *St&PR 93*
Eberle, Robert William 1931- *WhoAm 92*
Eberle, Sandra Ann 1949- *WhoAmW 93*
Eberle, Todd Bailey 1946- *WhoEmL 93, WhoSSW 93*
Eberle, William Denman 1923- *WhoAm 92, WhoE 93*
Eberlein, Patricia James 1925- *WhoAm 92*
Eberlein, Patrick Barry 1944- *WhoSSW 93*
Eberley, Helen-Kay 1947- *WhoAm 92, WhoEmL 93*
Eberlin, Johann Ernst 1702-1762 *Baker 92*
Eberling, Edward Robert J. 1967- *WhoEmL 93*
Eberly, David Michael 1947- *WhoE 93*
Eberly, Harry Landis 1924- *WhoAm 92*
Eberly, Lisa R. 1964- *WhoAmW 93*
Eberly, Nancy Susan 1957- *WhoAmW 93*
Eberly, Robert Edward 1918- *St&PR 93, WhoAm 92*
Ebers, John c. 1785-c. 1830 *OxDcOp*
Ebersberger, Arthur Darryl 1946- *WhoE 93, WhoEmL 93*
Ebersol, Dick *BioIn 17*
Ebersole, George D. 1936- *St&PR 93*
Ebersole, Mark Chester 1921- *WhoAm 92*
Ebersole, Patricia Sue 1952- *WhoAmW 93, WhoEmL 93*
Eberson, John c. 1875-1954 *BioIn 17*
Eberson, Lennart E. 1933- *WhoScE 91-4*
Eberspacher, E. C. 1949- *WhoEmL 93*
Eberspacher, Jurgen 1943- *WhoScE 91-3*
Eberspacher, Nelson Ernest 1925- *WhoWrEP 92*
Eberstadt, Fernanda 1960- *ConAu 136*
Eberstadt, Frederick 1926- *WhoE 93*
Eberstadt, Nicholas Nash 1955- *WhoEmL 93*
Eberstadt, Rudolph, Jr. 1923- *St&PR 93*
Eberstein, Arthur 1928- *WhoAm 92*
Ebert, Alan M. 1935- *WhoE 93*
Ebert, Barry Austin 1945- *St&PR 93*
Ebert, Carl 1887-1980 *IntDcOp, OxDcOp*
Ebert, (Anton) Carl 1887-1980 *Baker 92*
Ebert, Carol Anne 1945- *St&PR 93*
Ebert, Charles H. V. 1924- *WhoAm 92*
Ebert, Darlene Marie 1951- *WhoEmL 93*
Ebert, Douglas *BioIn 17*
Ebert, Douglas Edmund 1945- *St&PR 93, WhoAm 92, WhoSSW 93*
Ebert, Friedrich 1871-1925 *DcTwHis*
Ebert, G. Donald 1932- *St&PR 93*
Ebert, Gotthold 1925- *WhoScE 91-3*
Ebert, Henry 1929- *St&PR 93*
Ebert, Herbert A. 1928- *St&PR 93*
Ebert, James David 1921- *WhoAm 92, WhoWor 93*
Ebert, James Ian 1948- *WhoEmL 93*
Ebert, James Joel 1940- *St&PR 93*
Ebert, Karl Michael 1948- *WhoAm 92*
Ebert, Larry Paul 1952- *WhoEmL 93*
Ebert, Paul Allen 1932- *WhoAm 92*
Ebert, Peter 1918- *OxDcOp*
Ebert, Peter deC. 1942- *St&PR 93*
Ebert, Reinhold 1945- *WhoWor 93*
Ebert, Richard Vincent 1912- *WhoAm 92*
Ebert, Robert Alvin 1915- *WhoAm 92*
Ebert, Robert Higgins 1914- *WhoAm 92*
Ebert, Roger Joseph 1942- *WhoAm 92, WhoWrEP 92*
Ebert, Terry Harold 1946- *WhoE 93*
Ebert, Valerie Anne 1959- *WhoAmW 93*
Eberts, Michael Albert 1955- *WhoWrEP 92*
Eberwein, Barton Douglas 1951- *WhoEmL 93*
Eberwein, Carl 1786-1868 *Baker 92, OxDcOp*
Eberwein, Carol Ann Shiebeck 1942- *WhoAmW 93*
Eberwein, Thomas Charles 1948- *WhoEmL 93*
Eberwein, Traugott 1775-1831 *OxDcOp*
Eberwein, Traugott (Maximilian) 1775-1831 *Baker 92*
Ebetino, Frank Hallock 1956- *WhoEmL 93*
Ebetino, James M. *Law&B 92*
Ebie, William D. 1942- *WhoAm 92*
Ebin, Robert Felix 1940- *WhoAm 92*
Ebing, Winfried Kurt 1930- *WhoScE 91-3*
Ebinger, Mary Ritzman 1929- *WhoE 93*
Ebinger, Thomas Ernst 1962- *WhoWor 93*
Ebisawa, Yoshinobu 1961- *WhoWor 93*
Ebitz, Elizabeth Kelly 1950- *WhoAmW 93*
Eble, John Nelson 1951- *WhoEmL 93*
Eble, Martin J. *St&PR 93*
Eblen, George Thomas 1936- *WhoAm 92*
Eblen, Jack Ericson 1936- *WhoE 93*
Eblin, Scott Stewart 1961- *WhoSSW 93*
Ebner, Alan M. 1939- *St&PR 93*
Ebner, Guido E. 1931- *WhoScE 91-4*
Ebner, Kurt Ewald 1931- *WhoAm 92*
Ebner, Martin *BioIn 17*
Ebner, Paul Jeffrey 1957- *St&PR 93*
Ebner, Randall Miles *Law&B 92*
Ebner, Reinhold *WhoScE 91-4*
Ebner-Eschenbach, Marie von 1830-1916 *BioIn 17*
Ebnet, Paul John 1955- *WhoEmL 93*
Eboue, Felix 1884-1944 *BioIn 17, DcTwHis*
Ebrahim, Shaheen Brian John *WhoScE 91-1*
Ebrahimi, Fereshteh 1951- *WhoEmL 93*
Ebrahimzadeh, Alex *St&PR 93*
Ebrahimzadeh, Shideh Delrahim 1962- *WhoEmL 93*
Ebright, George W. 1939- *St&PR 93*
Ebright, George Watson 1938- *WhoAm 92*
Ebright, Mitchell A. *Law&B 92*
Ebright, Mitchell A. 1943- *St&PR 93*
Ebrom, Ralph P. 1943- *St&PR 93*
Ebsen, Buddy 1908- *BioIn 17, WhoAm 92*
Ebsen, Vilma 1911- *BioIn 17*
Ebsworth, Evelyn Algernon Valentine 1933- *WhoWor 93*
Ebtinger, Rene Pierre Charles 1928- *WhoScE 91-2*
Ebu, Allen Marai 1953- *WhoAsAP 91*
Eby, Cecil DeGrotte 1927- *WhoAm 92, WhoWrEP 92*
Eby, Clare Virginia 1959- *WhoE 93*
Eby, John Robert 1935- *St&PR 93*
Eby, Martin K., Jr. 1934- *St&PR 93*
Eby, Martin Keller, Jr. 1934- *WhoAm 92*
Ecabert, Peter Leo 1948- *WhoEmL 93*
Eca de Queiroz *ScF&FL 92*
Ecare, Desire 1939- *MiSFD 9*
Eccard, Johannes 1553-1611 *Baker 92*
Eccard, Walter Thomas 1946- *WhoAm 92*
Eccarius, J.G. *ScF&FL 92*
Eccher, Alberto *WhoScE 91-3*
Eccher Dall'eco, Alberto 1937- *WhoScE 91-3*
Eccles, Viscountess 1912- *WhoAm 92*
Eccles, Andrew *BioIn 17*
Eccles, H. Peter *Law&B 92*
Eccles, Harry 1942- *WhoWor 93*
Eccles, Henry 1640?-1711 *Baker 92*
Eccles, Henry 1675?-1735? *Baker 92*
Eccles, John c. 1668-1735 *Baker 92, OxDcOp*
Eccles, John Carew 1903- *WhoAm 92, WhoWor 93*
Eccles, John Edward 1932- *St&PR 93*
Eccles, Margot Lacy 1935- *St&PR 93*
Eccles, Marriner S. 1890-1977 *BioIn 17*
Eccles, Ronald *WhoScE 91-1*
Eccles, Solomon c. 1617-1682 *Baker 92*
Eccles, Solomon 1640?-1710 *Baker 92*
Eccles, Spencer Fox 1934- *St&PR 93*
Eccles, Stephen David 1938- *WhoUN 92*
Eccles, W.H.T. *ScF&FL 92*
Eccleston, Thomas Robert 1948- *St&PR 93*
Eccleston, William *WhoScE 91-1*
Ecevit, Bulent 1925- *BioIn 17, WhoWor 93*
Echaniz, Jose 1905-1969 *Baker 92*
Echard, Laurence 1670?-1730 *BioIn 17*
Echegaray, Jose 1832-1916 *BioIn 17*
Echement, John R. 1935- *St&PR 93, WhoAm 92*
Echenique, Pedro Miguel *WhoWor 93*
Echerd, John Hartly *Law&B 92*
Echeruo, Michael Joseph Chukwudalu 1937- *WhoE 93*
Echevarria, Alvarado Ana H. *WhoSSW 93*
Echevarria, Margarita *Law&B 92*
Echevarria, Margarita 1951- *WhoAmW 93*
Echevarria, Nicolas *MiSFD 9*
Echeverria Alvarez, Luis 1922- *DcCPCAm, DcTwHis*
Echeverria del Prado, Vicente 1898- *DcMexL*
Echezarreta, Arnoldo Francisco 1953- *WhoWor 93*
Echikson, Richard 1929- *WhoE 93*
Echlin, Bernard Joseph 1918- *WhoAm 92*
EchoHawk, Larry 1948- *WhoAm 92*
Echols, Dorothy 1955- *WhoE 93*
Echols, George E. 1884-1990 *BioIn 17*
Echols, Harrison 1933- *WhoAm 92*
Echols, Ivor Tatum 1919- *WhoAmW 93*
Echols, Margaret Ann *Law&B 92*
Echols, Margaret J. 1938- *St&PR 93*
Echols, Mary Evelyn 1915- *WhoAm 92*
Echols, Mary Louise Brown 1906- *WhoAmW 93*
Echols, Mary Tuck 1925- *WhoAmW 93*
Echols, Robert Wootten, Jr. 1928- *St&PR 93*
Echols, Thomas Matthew 1925- *St&PR 93*
Echsner, Stephen Herre 1954- *WhoEmL 93*
Echtenkamp, Mike G. 1934- *St&PR 93*
Eck, Charles Paul 1956- *WhoEmL 93*
Eck, Dennis K. *St&PR 93*
Eck, Dorothy Fritz 1924- *WhoAmW 93*
Eck, Franklin Edward 1923- *St&PR 93*
Eck, James John 1946- *St&PR 93*
Eck, Joseph E. 1939- *St&PR 93*
Eck, Kenneth Christopher 1960- *WhoE 93, WhoWor 93*
Eck, Kenneth Frank 1917- *WhoSSW 93*
Eck, R. Paul *Law&B 92*
Eck, Richard Allan 1945- *St&PR 93*
Eck, Robert Edwin 1938- *WhoAm 92*
Eck, Robert J. *Law&B 92*
Eck, Ronald Warren 1949- *WhoEmL 93, WhoSSW 93*
Eck, Theresa Ann 1941- *WhoAmW 93*
Eckam, Robert C. 1926- *St&PR 93*
Eckard, Johann Gottfried 1735-1809 *Baker 92*
Eckard, Ralph Edgar 1927- *WhoSSW 93*
Eckardt, Arthur Roy 1918- *WhoAm 92*
Eckardt, Carl R. 1931- *WhoE 93*
Eckardt, Gladys Evangeline 1912- *WhoAmW 93*
Eckardt, Hans 1905-1969 *Baker 92*
Eckardt, Johann Gottfried 1735-1809 *Baker 92*
Eckardt, Michael Jon 1943- *WhoE 93*
Eckardt, Richard William 1938- *WhoAm 92*
Eckart, Christian 1959- *WhoE 93*
Eckart, Dennis E. 1950- *CngDr 91*
Eckart, Dennis Edward 1950- *WhoAm 92*
Eckart, Jean *BioIn 17*
Eckart, Johann Gottfried 1735-1809 *Baker 92*
Eckart, William *BioIn 17*
Eckaus, Richard Samuel 1926- *WhoAm 92*
Eckaus, Theodore M. 1922- *St&PR 93*
Eckblad, Finn-Egil 1923- *WhoScE 91-4, WhoWor 93*
Eckbo, Garrett 1910- *BioIn 17, WhoAm 92*
Eckbreth, Kelly Anne 1967- *WhoE 93*
Eckdahl, Donald Edward 1924- *WhoAm 92*
Ecke, Hermann 1927- *WhoScE 91-3*
Ecke, Paul d1991 *BioIn 17*
Eckebrecht, Betty Marie 1958- *WhoEmL 93*
Eckel, Catherine Coleman 1953- *WhoAmW 93*
Eckel, Eugene Joseph 1924- *WhoAm 92*
Eckel, James A. 1943- *St&PR 93*
Eckel, Michael John 1961- *WhoEmL 93*
Eckel, Peter Dwight 1966- *WhoE 93*
Eckelbarger, Donald Eugene 1933- *WhoAm 92*
Eckelberger, James Elton 1938- *WhoAm 92*
Eckelberry, John Evans 1933- *St&PR 93*
Eckelberry, Stephen *MiSFD 9*
Eckelman, Richard Joel 1951- *WhoEmL 93*
Eckelmann, Frank Donald 1929- *WhoAm 92*
Eckels, Mary Elizabeth 1948- *WhoAmW 93*
Eckelson, Robert Alan 1947- *WhoEmL 93, WhoSSW 93*
Eckelt, Johann Valentin 1673-1732 *Baker 92*
Eckenfelder, William Wesley, Jr. 1926- *WhoAm 92, WhoSSW 93*
Eckenfels, James Francis 1956- *St&PR 93*
Eckenhoff, Edward Alvin 1943- *WhoWor 93*
Eckenhoff, James Edward 1915- *WhoAm 92*
Eckenrode, Brian Allen 1959- *WhoSSW 93*
Eckenrode, J. Thaddeus 1958- *WhoEmL 93*
Ecker, Allan B. 1921- *St&PR 93*
Ecker, Allan Benjamin 1921- *WhoAm 92*
Ecker, Carol Adele 1940- *WhoAm 92*
Ecker, H. Allen 1935- *WhoAm 92*
Ecker, Howard J. 1953- *St&PR 93*
Ecker, Jerome Albert 1919- *WhoSSW 93*
Ecker, Jonathan 1946- *WhoEmL 93*
Ecker, Leroy Gordon 1942- *WhoE 93*
Ecker, Paul Gerard 1919- *WhoE 93*
Eckerberg, (Axel) Sixten (Lennart) 1909- *Baker 92*
Eckerle, David Edward 1943- *St&PR 93*
Eckerling, Stanley *St&PR 93*
Eckerman, Dale H., Jr. 1940- *St&PR 93*
Eckerman, David Alan 1939- *WhoSSW 93*
Eckerman, Jerome 1925- *WhoAm 92*
Eckermann, Gerald Carlton 1934- *WhoWor 93*
Eckersley, Dennis Lee 1954- *BiDAMSp 1989, WhoAm 92*
Eckersley, John Alan 1945- *St&PR 93*
Eckersley, Norman C. 1924- *St&PR 93*
Eckersley, Norman Chadwick 1924- *WhoAm 92*
Eckerson, Nancy Fiedler 1940- *WhoAm 92*
Eckert, Alfred Carl, III 1948- *WhoAm 92*
Eckert, Allan W. 1931- *DcAmChF 1960, ScF&FL 92, WhoAm 92*
Eckert, Arlene Gail 1956- *WhoAmW 93, WhoE 93*
Eckert, Carter H. 1942- *St&PR 93*
Eckert, Charles Alan 1938- *WhoAm 92*
Eckert, David D. 1948- *St&PR 93*
Eckert, David K. d1992 *NewYTBS 92*
Eckert, David Page 1957- *WhoE 93*
Eckert, Ernst R. G. 1904- *WhoAm 92*
Eckert, Geraldine Gonzales 1948- *WhoAmW 93*
Eckert, Hans 1947- *WhoWor 93*
Eckert, Horst 1931- *ConAu 38NR, MajAI [port], SmATA 72 [port]*
Eckert, Jean Patricia 1935- *WhoAmW 93*
Eckert, John P. 1933- *St&PR 93*
Eckert, Karl (Anton Florian) 1820-1879 *Baker 92*
Eckert, Marlene MacNeal 1952- *WhoEmL 93*

Eckert, Michael Joseph 1947- *WhoAm 92, WhoEmL 93, WhoSSW 93*
Eckert, Opal Effie 1905- *WhoAmW 93*
Eckert, Ralph J. 1929- *WhoIns 93*
Eckert, Reagan Al 1950- *St&PR 93*
Eckert, Rinde 1951- *Baker 92*
Eckert, Roger Earl 1926- *WhoAm 92*
Eckert, Stephen Paul 1955- *WhoEmL 93*
Eckert, Theodor 1924- *WhoScE 91-3*
Eckert, William Terry 1948- *WhoE 93, WhoEmL 93*
Eckert, Yates P. 1929- *St&PR 93*
Eckert, Yates Peter 1929- *WhoE 93*
Eckert-Burton, Suzanne Mary 1960- *WhoEmL 93*
Eckerty, R. David 1946- *St&PR 93*
Eckes, Alfred Edward, Jr. 1942- *WhoAm 92*
Eckford, Eugenia *BioIn 17*
Eckhard, Jacob 1757-1833 *Baker 92*
Eckhardt, August Gottlieb 1917- *WhoAm 92*
Eckhardt, Bruce N. 1949- *WhoAm 92, WhoEmL 93*
Eckhardt, Caroline Davis 1942- *WhoAm 92*
Eckhardt, Celia Morris *ConAu 138*
Eckhardt, Craig Jon 1940- *WhoAm 92*
Eckhardt, Donald D. 1929- *St&PR 93*
Eckhardt, Donald Henry 1932- *WhoE 93*
Eckhardt, Donard D. *Law&B 92*
Eckhardt, Juliane 1946- *WhoWor 93*
Eckhardt, Richard Dale 1918- *WhoAm 92*
Eckhardt, Robert Fuess 1949- *WhoSSW 93*
Eckhardt, Sandor 1927- *WhoScE 91-4*
Eckhardt, Terri *BioIn 17*
Eckhardt, Ulrich Albert 1939- *WhoWor 93*
Eckhardt-Gramatte, S(ophie)-C(armen) 1899-1974 *Baker 92*
Eckhart, Meister c. 1260-c. 1327 *ClMLC 9*
Eckhart, James McKinley 1931- *St&PR 93*
Eckhart, Morris Lee Roy 1948- *WhoEmL 93*
Eckhart, Myron, Jr. 1923- *WhoAm 92*
Eckhart, Walter 1938- *WhoAm 92*
Eckhaus, Eleanor Annette 1956- *WhoAmW 93*
Eckhaus, Jay Elliot 1944- *WhoAm 92, WhoE 93*
Eckhoff, Carl D. 1933- *WhoAm 92*
Eckhoff, Kathleen Louise 1946- *WhoAmW 93*
Eckhoff, Rosalee 1930- *WhoAmW 93*
Eckhold, Scott Reed 1953- *WhoEmL 93*
Eckholm, William Arthur 1951- *St&PR 93*
Eckis, Thomas M. 1948- *St&PR 93*
Eckland, Diane Marie 1958- *WhoEmL 93*
Eckland, Jeff Howard 1957- *WhoEmL 93*
Ecklar, George Patrick 1951- *WhoEmL 93*
Ecklar, Julia 1964- *ScF&FL 92*
Eckler, A. Ross 1901-1991 *BioIn 17*
Eckler, John Alfred 1913- *WhoAm 92*
Eckler, Norman S. *St&PR 93*
Eckler, Todd Harrison 1967- *WhoE 93*
Eckles, William F. 1933- *St&PR 93*
Eckley, Alicia Kathryn 1959- *WhoAmW 93, WhoEmL 93*
Eckley, Gerald Boice 1926- *St&PR 93*
Eckley, James Robert 1947- *WhoEmL 93*
Eckley, Robert Spence 1921- *WhoAm 92*
Eckley, Wilton Earl, Jr. 1929- *WhoAm 92*
Ecklin, Robert L. 1938- *St&PR 93*
Ecklin, Robert Luther 1938- *WhoE 93, WhoWor 93*
Ecklund, Dennis Edward 1960- *WhoSSW 93*
Ecklund, Harry Vincent 1908- *WhoWrEP 92*
Ecklund, N. Russell 1934- *St&PR 93*
Eckmair, Frank Cornwall 1930- *WhoE 93*
Eckman, David Walter 1942- *WhoAm 92*
Eckman, Fern Marja *WhoAm 92*
Eckman, George 1919- *WhoE 93*
Eckman, John W. 1919- *St&PR 93*
Eckman, John Whiley 1919- *WhoAm 92, WhoWor 93*
Eckmann, Harold A. 1922- *St&PR 93*
Eckmann, Jean-Pierre 1944- *WhoScE 91-4*
Eckmann, Jeffrey A. 1952- *St&PR 93*
Eckmiller, Rolf Eberhard 1942- *WhoWor 93*
Eckoldt, Klaus Otto 1929- *WhoWor 93*
Eckols, Thomas Aud *Law&B 92*
Eckols, Thomas Aud 1950- *WhoEmL 93*
Eckroat, Larry R. 1941- *WhoE 93*
Eckstam-Ames, Kathryn Ann 1956- *WhoEmL 93*
Eckstein, Abbe 1965- *BioIn 17*
Eckstein, Donald A. *Law&B 92*
Eckstein, Edmund Charles 1944- *WhoE 93*
Eckstein, Harry 1924- *WhoAm 92*
Eckstein, Heiner 1942- *WhoWor 93*
Eckstein, James 1937- *St&PR 93*
Eckstein, Jerome 1925- *WhoAm 92*
Eckstein, John William 1923- *WhoAm 92*
Eckstein, Kerry W. *Law&B 92*
Eckstein, Marie 1917- *St&PR 93*
Eckstein, Marlene R. 1948- *WhoAm 92, WhoEmL 93*
Eckstein, Mary Ellen 1953- *WhoAmW 93, WhoEmL 93*
Eckstein, Michael Gilbert 1947- *WhoEmL 93*
Eckstein, Michael Lehman 1954- *WhoEmL 93*
Eckstein, Pavel 1911- *Baker 92*
Eckstine, Billy *BioIn 17*
Eckstine, Billy 1914- *Baker 92, WhoAm 92*
Eckstrand, Katherine Lynn 1954- *WhoAmW 93*
Eckstrom, Michael *ScF&FL 92*
Eckstut, Michael Kauder 1952- *St&PR 93, WhoEmL 93*
Eckstut, Stanton 1942- *WhoAm 92*
Eckton, Mary Louise 1932- *WhoE 93*
Eckweiler, Karl T. *Law&B 92*
Ecleo, Glenda B. 1937- *WhoAsAP 91*
Eco, Umberto *BioIn 17*
Eco, Umberto 1932- *ScF&FL 92, WhoWor 93*
Economaki, Chris *St&PR 93*
Economaki, Chris Constantine 1920- *WhoAm 92*
Economides, Nicholas George 1949- *WhoSSW 93*
Economides, Peter Achilles 1953- *WhoWor 93*
Economides, Soterios 1940- *WhoScE 91-4*
Economopoulos, Alexander Panagiotis 1944- *WhoWor 93*
Economopoulos, John N. 1926- *WhoScE 91-3*
Economopoulos, Nicholas Theodore 1949- *WhoE 93*
Economos, Christina Demetra 1965- *WhoAmW 93*
Economos, George Louis 1932- *St&PR 93*
Economou, Eleftherios N. 1940- *WhoScE 91-3*
Economou, Eleftherios Nickolas 1940- *WhoWor 93*
Economou, George 1934- *ConAu 38NR, WhoWrEP 92*
Economou, George Aristotle 1923- *St&PR 93*
Economou, George Demetrios 1934- *WhoSSW 93*
Economou, Steve George 1922- *WhoAm 92*
Economou-Pease, Bessie Carasoulas 1933- *WhoE 93*
Economy, James 1929- *WhoAm 92*
Ecorcheville, Jules (Armand Joseph) 1872-1915 *Baker 92*
Ecordian, G. *ScF&FL 92*
Ecroyd, Lawrence Gerald 1918- *WhoAm 92*
Ecton, Donna R. 1947- *WhoAm 92, WhoAmW 93*
Eda, Satsuki 1941- *WhoAsAP 91*
Edan, Mark 1950- *WhoEmL 93*
Eda-Pierre, Christiane 1932- *Baker 92, OxDcOp*
Edberg, Bengt G.T. 1929- *WhoScE 91-4*
Edberg, Peter *Law&B 92*
Edberg, Rolf Filip 1912- *WhoWor 93*
Edberg, Stefan *BioIn 17*
Edberg, Stefan 1966- *WhoAm 92*
Edbril, Donna E. *Law&B 92*
Edde, Donald Y. 1939- *St&PR 93*
Edde, Howard Jasper 1937- *WhoAm 92*
Eddinger, Gerald W. 1930- *St&PR 93*
Eddings, David 1931- *ScF&FL 92*
Eddings, Dennis W. 1938- *ScF&FL 92*
Eddings, James Dean 1956- *WhoSSW 93*
Eddington, Arthur Stanley 1882-1944 *BioIn 17*
Eddington, Edward C. 1944- *St&PR 93*
Eddington, Thomas L. 1960- *WhoE 93, WhoEmL 93*
Eddins, Debbie Ann 1957- *WhoSSW 93*
Eddins, James William, Jr. 1944- *WhoSSW 93*
Eddis, Jerry 1941- *St&PR 93*
Eddis, Nicola Joy Lindsay 1954- *WhoWor 93*
Eddison, Elizabeth Bole 1928- *WhoAm 92, WhoAmW 93, WhoE 93*
Eddison, John Corbin 1919- *WhoAm 92, WhoE 93*
Eddison, Jonathan B. *Law&B 92*
Eddison, Jonathan Bole 1952- *WhoEmL 93*
Eddison, Robert 1908-1991 *AnObit 1991*
Eddleman, Clyde D. d1992 *NewYTBS 92*
Eddleman, Cora Janice Bufford 1941- *WhoSSW 93*
Eddleman, Floyd Eugene 1930- *WhoSSW 93*
Eddleman, J. Dalton *WhoWrEP 92*
Eddleman, Wallace A. *Law&B 92*
Eddleman, William Roseman 1913- *WhoAm 92*
Eddo, James Ekundayo 1936- *WhoWor 93*
Eddowes, Elizabeth Anne 1931- *WhoAmW 93, WhoSSW 93*
Edds, Kenneth Tiffany 1945- *WhoE 93*
Eddy, A.A. *WhoScE 91-1*
Eddy, C.M., Jr. 1896-1967 *ScF&FL 92*
Eddy, Charles Alan 1948- *WhoEmL 93, WhoWor 93*
Eddy, Charles Phillips 1941- *WhoAm 92*
Eddy, Charles Russell, Jr. 1940- *St&PR 93*
Eddy, (Hiram) Clarence 1851-1937 *Baker 92*
Eddy, Colette Ann 1950- *WhoAmW 93*
Eddy, Darlene Mathis 1937- *WhoAm 92*
Eddy, David Latimer 1936- *St&PR 93, WhoAm 92*
Eddy, Don 1944- *WhoAm 92*
Eddy, Donald Davis 1929- *WhoAm 92*
Eddy, Duane 1938- *ConMus 9 [port]*
Eddy, Edward Blaine 1928- *WhoSSW 93*
Eddy, Edward Danforth 1921- *WhoAm 92*
Eddy, Edward Mitchell 1940- *WhoSSW 93*
Eddy, Elsbeth Marie 1934- *WhoE 93*
Eddy, Esther Dewitz 1926- *WhoAm 92*
Eddy, Helen Jerome d1990 *BioIn 17*
Eddy, James Richard 1955- *WhoSSW 93*
Eddy, Jane Marie 1955- *St&PR 93*
Eddy, John Joseph 1933- *WhoAm 92*
Eddy, John S. 1933- *St&PR 93*
Eddy, Latimar B. 1937- *St&PR 93*
Eddy, Latimer Ballou 1937- *WhoAm 92*
Eddy, Linda Joan 1949- *WhoEmL 93*
Eddy, Lori Mason *Law&B 92*
Eddy, Margaret d1990 *BioIn 17*
Eddy, Mary Baker 1821-1910 *BioIn 17, GayN, JrnUS*
Eddy, Muriel E. 1896-1978 *ScF&FL 92*
Eddy, Nancy Burns 1937- *WhoE 93*
Eddy, Nelson 1901-1967 *Baker 92*
Eddy, Nelson 1907-1967 *IntDcF 2-3*
Eddy, Paul H. *Law&B 92*
Eddy, Roger Graham 1940- *WhoWor 93*
Eddy, Thomas Alexander 1930- *St&PR 93*
Eddy, Wallace Leslie 1964- *WhoE 93*
Ede, Jim *BioIn 17*
Ede, Joyce Kinlaw 1936- *WhoAmW 93*
Edebo, Ralph Bertil 1932- *WhoWor 93*
Edeki, Joyce O. *Law&B 92*
Edel, Abraham 1908- *WhoAm 92, WhoE 93*
Edel, Doris Rita 1936- *WhoWor 93*
Edel, Edwin E. 1932- *WhoAm 92*
Edel, Joseph Leon 1907- *BioIn 17*
Edel, Kathleen 1944- *WhoAmW 93*
Edel, Leon 1907- *BioIn 17, WhoAm 92*
Edel, (Joseph) Leon 1907- *WhoWrEP 92*
Edel, Matthew *BioIn 17*
Edel, Uli 1947- *MiSFD 9*
Edel, Wilbur 1915- *ConAu 138*
Edelbaum, Philip R. 1936- *WhoE 93*
Edelcup, Norman S. 1935- *St&PR 93*
Edelcup, Norman Scott 1935- *WhoAm 92*
Edelen, Buddy 1937- *BioIn 17*
Edelfelt, Jonathan D. *Law&B 92*
Edelglass, Stephen Mark 1935- *WhoE 93*
Edelin, Ramona Hoage *WhoAmW 93*
Edeline, Francis 1930- *WhoScE 91-2*
Edeline, Jean Jacques 1939- *WhoUN 92*
Edell, Dennis *BioIn 17*
Edell, Dunnan D. 1955- *St&PR 93*
Edell, Joseph E. 1927- *St&PR 93*
Edell, William Steven 1953- *WhoEmL 93*
Edelman, Alan Irwin 1958- *WhoE 93, WhoEmL 93, WhoWor 93*
Edelman, Allan 1933- *St&PR 93*
Edelman, Alvin 1916- *WhoAm 92*
Edelman, Andrew 1947- *St&PR 93*
Edelman, Anton 1940- *WhoScE 91-3*
Edelman, Arthur Jay 1925- *WhoAm 92*
Edelman, Asher B. *BioIn 17*
Edelman, Asher Barry 1939- *WhoAm 92*
Edelman, Daniel Amos 1954- *WhoEmL 93*
Edelman, Daniel J. 1920- *St&PR 93*
Edelman, Daniel Joseph 1920- *WhoAm 92*
Edelman, Debra Zarlin *Law&B 92*
Edelman, Elaine *WhoWrEP 92*
Edelman, Elizabeth A. *Law&B 92*
Edelman, Eugene *BioIn 17*
Edelman, Fredric Mark 1958- *WhoEmL 93, WhoWor 93*
Edelman, Gerald Maurice 1929- *WhoAm 92, WhoWor 93*
Edelman, Harold 1923- *WhoAm 92*
Edelman, Harry Rollings, III 1928- *WhoAm 92, WhoE 93*
Edelman, Harry Rollings, IV 1955- *WhoE 93*
Edelman, Hendrik 1937- *WhoAm 92*
Edelman, Irving *St&PR 93*
Edelman, Isidore Samuel 1920- *WhoAm 92*
Edelman, Joel 1931- *WhoAm 92*
Edelman, Judith Hochberg 1923- *WhoAm 92, WhoAmW 93*
Edelman, Jules *St&PR 93*
Edelman, Lawrence Conrad *Law&B 92*
Edelman, Louise 1954- *ConEn*
Edelman, Louise B. *St&PR 93*
Edelman, Marek 1921- *PolBiDi*
Edelman, Marian Wright *BioIn 17, NewYTBS 92 [port]*
Edelman, Marian Wright 1939- *AfrAmBi [port], CurBio 92 [port], WhoAm 92, WhoAmW 93*
Edelman, Mark Leslie 1943- *WhoAm 92*
Edelman, Martin 1939- *WhoE 93*
Edelman, Martin Philip 1940- *WhoAm 92*
Edelman, Murray Richard 1939- *St&PR 93*
Edelman, Norman H. 1937- *WhoAm 92*
Edelman, Paul Sterling 1926- *WhoAm 92*
Edelman, Peter Benjamin 1938- *WhoAm 92*
Edelman, Regina *BioIn 17*
Edelman, Renee *BioIn 17*
Edelman, Richard Winston 1954- *WhoE 93*
Edelman, Robert 1942- *WhoE 93*
Edelman, Samuel 1952- *ConEn*
Edelman, Samuel L. *St&PR 93*
Edelman, Scott 1955- *ScF&FL 92*
Edelman, Steven M. 1955- *St&PR 93*
Edelman, Stuart Edward 1947- *WhoEmL 93*
Edelman, Thomas Jeffery 1951- *St&PR 93, WhoAm 92*
Edelmann, Anton Sebastian 1952- *WhoWor 93*
Edelmann, Carolyn Foote 1937- *WhoE 93*
Edelmann, Chester Monroe, Jr. 1930- *WhoAm 92*
Edelmann, Frank Thomas 1954- *WhoWor 93*
Edelmann, Jean-Frederic 1749-1794 *Baker 92*
Edelmann, Joel Scott 1958- *WhoEmL 93*
Edelmann, Otto 1917- *OxDcOp*
Edelmann, Otto (Karl) 1917- *Baker 92*
Edelmann, Sergei 1960- *Baker 92*
Edelschick, Daniel Frederick 1944- *St&PR 93*
Edelson, Alan Martin 1937- *WhoAm 92, WhoE 93*
Edelson, Allan J. 1942- *St&PR 93*
Edelson, Burton Irving 1926- *WhoAm 92*
Edelson, David 1927- *WhoSSW 93*
Edelson, Edward 1932- *ScF&FL 92*
Edelson, Edward H. 1947- *WhoE 93*
Edelson, Gilbert Seymour 1928- *WhoAm 92*
Edelson, Ira J. 1946- *WhoAm 92*
Edelson, Marshall 1928- *WhoAm 92*
Edelson, Mary Beth *WhoAmW 93*
Edelson, Morris 1937- *WhoWrEP 92*
Edelson, Paul Jeffrey 1943- *WhoE 93*
Edelson, Stanley 1931- *St&PR 93*
Edelson, Zelda Sarah Toll 1929- *WhoAmW 93*
Edelstein, Alan Shane 1936- *WhoE 93*
Edelstein, Barry Allen 1945- *WhoSSW 93*
Edelstein, David Northon 1910- *WhoAm 92*
Edelstein, Gerald A. *Law&B 92*
Edelstein, Haskell *Law&B 92*
Edelstein, Haskell 1933- *WhoAm 92*
Edelstein, Jason Zelig 1930- *WhoE 93*
Edelstein, Jerome Melvin 1924- *WhoAm 92*
Edelstein, Lewis M. 1934- *St&PR 93*
Edelstein, Pam *BioIn 17*
Edelstein, Raymond Lewis 1954- *WhoEmL 93*
Edelstein, Robert M. d1991 *BioIn 17*
Edelstein, Rose Marie 1935- *WhoAmW 93*
Edelstein, Ruben 1918- *St&PR 93*
Edelstein, Scott 1954- *ScF&FL 92*
Edelstein, Scott Samuel 1954- *WhoWrEP 92*
Edelstein, Sergej Leonid 1954- *WhoWor 93*
Edelstein, Stuart 1941- *WhoScE 91-4*
Edelstein, Teri J. 1951- *WhoAm 92, WhoAmW 93*
Edelstein, Tilden G. 1931- *WhoAm 92*
Edelstenne, Charles 1938- *WhoWor 93*
Edelstone, Gordon 1927- *St&PR 93*
Eden, Anthony 1897-1977 *BioIn 17, ColdWar 1 [port]*
Eden, Barbara *BioIn 17*
Eden, Barbara Janiece 1951- *WhoAm 92, WhoEmL 93*
Eden, Barbara Jean *WhoAm 92*
Eden, Bruce Douglas 1961- *WhoE 93*
Eden, Colin *WhoScE 91-1*
Eden, Diane Burn *BioIn 17*
Eden, Florence Brown 1916- *WhoAmW 93, WhoSSW 93, WhoWor 93*
Eden, Glenda Lee 1959- *WhoWrEP 92*
Eden, James Gary 1950- *WhoAm 92*
Eden, Lee Smythe 1937- *WhoAm 92*
Eden, Murray 1920- *WhoAm 92*
Eden, Nathan E. 1944- *WhoSSW 93, WhoWor 93*

Eden, Richard Carl 1939- *WhoAm 92*
Eden, Richard John *WhoScE 91-1*
Eden, Robert Anthony 1897-1977 *DcTwHis*
Eden, Ronald William 1931- *St&PR 93, WhoAm 92*
Eden, Steven M. *Law&B 92*
Eden-Fetzer, Dianne Toni 1946- *WhoAmW 93*
Edenfield, Berry Avant 1934- *WhoAm 92, WhoSSW 93*
Edenfield, James C. *St&PR 93*
Edenfield, Mary Ann 1945- *WhoSSW 93*
Edenfield, Virginia Anne 1949- *WhoEmL 93*
Edens, Alric 1914-1990 *BioIn 17*
Edens, Donald Keith 1928- *WhoAm 92*
Edens, Frank Wesley 1946- *WhoSSW 93*
Edens, Gary Denton 1942- *St&PR 93, WhoAm 92*
Edens, Jerry Jeanne 1943- *WhoSSW 93*
Edens, P. Clifton 1930- *St&PR 93*
Edens, Richard Woodward 1928- *WhoIns 93*
Edens, Samuel Vinson 1930- *St&PR 93*
Edens, Stephanie Rene 1965- *WhoAmW 93*
Edenshaw, Charles c. 1839-1920 *BioIn 17*
Eder, George Jackson 1900- *WhoAm 92*
Eder, Gernot 1929- *WhoScE 91-4*
Eder, Helmut 1916- *Baker 92*
Eder, Howard Abram 1917- *WhoAm 92*
Eder, James A. 1945- *St&PR 93*
Eder, James Andrew *Law&B 92*
Eder, Otto J. 1936- *WhoScE 91-4*
Eder, Paula Ruth 1943- *WhoE 93*
Eder, Richard Gray 1932- *WhoAm 92, WhoE 93*
Eder, Stephen K. 1952- *St&PR 93*
Ederer, Ronald Frank 1943- *WhoAm 92*
Ederer-Schwartz, Jane 1939- *WhoAm 92*
Ederle, Douglas Richard 1962- *WhoE 93, WhoEmL 93*
Ederle, Gertrude 1906- *BioIn 17*
Ederma, Arvo Bruno 1928- *WhoE 93*
Eder-Rieder, Maria Anna 1950- *WhoWor 93*
Edersheim, Maurits E. 1918- *St&PR 93*
Edersheim, Maurits Ernst 1918- *WhoAm 92*
Edes, Benjamin 1732-1803 *JrnUS*
Edes, Nik Bruce 1943- *WhoAm 92, WhoSSW 93*
Edey, Dianne N. 1943- *St&PR 93*
Edey, Maitland A. d1992 *NewYTBS 92 [port]*
Edey, Maitland A(rmstrong) 1910-1992 *ConAu 137, SmATA 71*
Edey, Maitland Armstrong 1910-1992 *BioIn 17*
Edgar, Allan G. 1934- *St&PR 93*
Edgar, Alvis, Jr. 1929- *WhoAm 92*
Edgar, Archer L. 1938- *WhoIns 93*
Edgar, David *BioIn 17*
Edgar, Gordon Russell 1948- *St&PR 93*
Edgar, Harold Simmons Hull 1942- *WhoAm 92*
Edgar, James Macmillan, Jr. 1936- *WhoAm 92*
Edgar, Janelle Diane Ward 1955- *WhoEmL 93*
Edgar, Jim 1946- *WhoAm 92, WhoWor 93*
Edgar, Ken 1925- *ScF&FL 92*
Edgar, Kimberly Sue 1964- *WhoEmL 93*
Edgar, Martin B. *Law&B 92*
Edgar, Mary S. *AmWomPl*
Edgar, Michael Howell 1954- *WhoSSW 93*
Edgar, Robert Allan 1940- *WhoAm 92*
Edgar, Ruth R. 1930- *WhoAmW 93*
Edgar, Thomas Flynn 1945- *WhoAm 92*
Edgar, Vicki Louise 1954- *WhoAmW 93*
Edgar, Walter Bellingrath 1943- *WhoAm 92*
Edgar, William 1938- *WhoScE 91-1*
Edgar, William John 1933- *WhoAm 92*
Edgar, William Michael *WhoScE 91-1*
Edge, Bruce A. *St&PR 93*
Edge, Charles Geoffrey 1920- *WhoAm 92*
Edge, Donald Joseph 1955- *WhoEmL 93*
Edge, Findley Bartow 1916- *WhoAm 92*
Edge, G.M. *WhoScE 91-1*
Edge, Harold Lee 1933- *WhoAm 92*
Edge, James Edward 1948- *WhoWor 93*
Edge, Kenneth Eugene 1945- *St&PR 93*
Edge, Lawrence Lott 1945- *St&PR 93*
Edge, Norris Lagrand 1931- *St&PR 93*
Edge, Ronald Dovaston 1929- *WhoAm 92*
Edge, Stephen Martin 1950- *WhoWor 93*
Edgehouse, Gregory J. *Law&B 92*
Edgell, Annias Waitman, III 1950- *WhoEmL 93*
Edgell, Robert Louis 1922-1991 *BioIn 17*
Edgemon, Roy T., Jr. 1934- *WhoSSW 93*
Edger, R.J. 1946- *St&PR 93*
Edgerly, James Robert *Law&B 92*
Edgerly, Len 1950- *St&PR 93*
Edgerly, William S. 1927- *St&PR 93*
Edgerly, William Skelton 1927- *WhoAm 92*
Edgerton, Brenda E. 1949- *St&PR 93*
Edgerton, Brenda Evans 1949- *WhoAm 92, WhoAmW 93*
Edgerton, Charles N. 1944- *St&PR 93*
Edgerton, David 1959- *ConAu 138*
Edgerton, David Allison 1940- *St&PR 93*
Edgerton, David George 1950- *WhoEmL 93*
Edgerton, Debra *BioIn 17*
Edgerton, Harold Eugene 1903-1990 *BioIn 17*
Edgerton, Harriet *AmWomPl*
Edgerton, J. Howard 1908- *St&PR 93*
Edgerton, Mills Fox, Jr. 1931- *WhoAm 92*
Edgerton, Milton Thomas, Jr. 1921- *WhoAm 92*
Edgerton, Rebecca Jane 1953- *WhoAmW 93*
Edgerton, Richard 1911- *WhoSSW 93, WhoWor 93*
Edgerton, Robert B. 1953- *WhoEmL 93*
Edgerton, Teresa 1949- *ScF&FL 92*
Edgerton, William B. 1914- *WhoAm 92*
Edgerton, Winfield Dow 1924- *WhoAm 92*
Edgett, Steven Dennis 1948- *WhoEmL 93*
Edgett, William Maloy 1927- *WhoAm 92*
Edgeworth, Alan C. 1945- *St&PR 93*
Edgeworth, Maria 1767-1849 *BioIn 17*
Edgeworth, Maria 1768-1849 *DcLB 116 [port]*
Edgeworth, Robert Joseph 1947- *WhoAm 92, WhoEmL 93, WhoSSW 93*
Edgington, Lloyd V. 1927-1989 *BioIn 17*
Edgington, Ruth 1911-1990 *BioIn 17*
Edgington, Theresa Marie *WhoAmW 93*
Edginton, Helen Marion 1883- *AmWomPl*
Edginton, John Arthur 1935- *WhoAm 92*
Edgreen, Robert J. 1946- *WhoE 93, WhoEmL 93*
Edgren, Gretchen Grondahl 1931- *WhoAmW 93*
Edgren, Gustaf Adolf *WhoUN 92*
Edgson, George A. *St&PR 93*
Edholm, Katherine Glassey 1957- *WhoAmW 93*
Edholm, Paul R. 1926- *WhoScE 91-4*
Edholm, Rand Alan 1955- *WhoEmL 93*
Edidin, Michael Aaron 1939- *WhoAm 92*
Edie, Carlene Jennifer 1955- *WhoAmW 93*
Edie, Leslie C. 1914-1990 *BioIn 17*
Edie, Mark Douglas *Law&B 92*
Ediger, Lewis W. 1931- *St&PR 93*
Ediger, Nicholas Martin 1928- *WhoAm 92*
Ediger, Robert Ike 1937- *WhoAm 92*
Edin, Karl-Axel 1937- *WhoScE 91-4*
Edinburgh, Philip, Duke of 1921- *BioIn 17*
Edinger, Charles B. 1934- *WhoE 93*
Edinger, Fred 1936- *WhoAm 92*
Edinger, J. Raymond 1914- *St&PR 93*
Edinger, Keith M. 1931- *St&PR 93*
Edinger, Lewis Joachim 1922- *WhoAm 92*
Edinger, Lois Virginia 1925- *WhoAm 92*
Edinger, Ronald W. *St&PR 93*
Edington, Minnie A.G. *AmWomPl*
Edington, Robert Van 1935- *WhoAm 92*
Edison, Allen Ray 1926- *WhoAm 92*
Edison, Bernard Alan 1928- *St&PR 93, WhoAm 92*
Edison, Glenn *Law&B 92*
Edison, Hali Jean 1953- *WhoAmW 93, WhoEmL 93*
Edison, Julian I. 1929- *WhoAm 92*
Edison, Robert G. 1928- *St&PR 93*
Edison, Theodore *MajAI*
Edison, Theodore M. d1992 *NewYTBS 92*
Edison, Thomas A. 1847-1931 *BioIn 17, GayN*
Edkins, Charles L. 1949- *St&PR 93*
Edkins, William D. 1952- *St&PR 93*
Edland, Elisabeth *AmWomPl*
Edler, Richard Bruce 1943- *WhoAm 92*
Edler, Robert Weber 1936- *WhoAm 92*
Edley, Christopher F. 1928- *BioIn 17*
Edlich, Richard French 1939- *WhoAm 92*
Edlich, Stephen 1944-1989 *BioIn 17*
Edlin, Gerald Elwyn 1946- *WhoSSW 93*
Edling, Sally Ann 1960- *WhoAmW 93*
Edlin-Marlowe, Sara 1943- *WhoAmW 93*
Edlmann Abbate, Maria Laura 1933- *WhoScE 91-3*
Edloe, Leonard Levi 1947- *WhoEmL 93, WhoSSW 93*
Edlosi, Mario *WhoWrEP 92*
Edlow, Jeremy Barth 1960- *WhoE 93*
Edlow, Kenneth Lewis 1941- *St&PR 93, WhoAm 92*
Edlow, Robert Blair 1946- *St&PR 93*
Edlund, Bo 1936- *WhoScE 91-4*
Edlund, Lars 1922- *Baker 92*
Edlund, Milton Carl 1924- *WhoAm 92, WhoSSW 93*
Edlund, Sven Gunnar 1946- *WhoScE 91-4*
Edly, Alan John 1935- *St&PR 93*
Edman, Janet Lee 1956- *WhoEmL 93*
Edman, Jeff Daniel 1952- *WhoEmL 93*
Edman, John Richard 1927- *WhoAm 92*
Edman, K.A. Paul 1926- *WhoScE 91-4*
Edmands, Donald Newton, Jr. 1944- *WhoSSW 93*
Edmands, Susan Banks 1944- *WhoAmW 93*
Edmark, David Stanley 1951- *WhoSSW 93*
Edminster, Steven Allen 1931- *WhoUN 92*
Edmisten, Charles E. 1929- *St&PR 93*
Edmisten, Rufus Ligh 1941- *WhoAm 92, WhoSSW 93*
Edmister, Richard R. *Law&B 92*
Edmister, Richard Riley 1939- *St&PR 93, WhoAm 92*
Edmiston, David Crockett, Jr. 1930- *St&PR 93*
Edmiston, Marilyn 1934- *WhoAmW 93, WhoSSW 93*
Edmiston, Mark Morton 1943- *WhoAm 92, WhoE 93*
Edmiston, Robert Bruce 1962- *St&PR 93*
Edmiston, Ronald Lee 1946- *WhoE 93, WhoEmL 93*
Edmiston, Theresa F. 1950- *WhoAmW 93*
Edmond, Lauris 1924- *BioIn 17*
Edmonds, Albert J. 1942- *AfrAmBi*
Edmonds, Andrea Magdelene 1944- *WhoE 93*
Edmonds, Andrew Nicola 1955- *WhoWor 93*
Edmonds, Anne Carey 1924- *WhoAm 92*
Edmonds, David A. 1938- *St&PR 93*
Edmonds, David Carson 1937- *WhoWrEP 92*
Edmonds, David G. 1934- *St&PR 93*
Edmonds, Don *MiSFD 9*
Edmonds, Ernest Allan *WhoScE 91-1*
Edmonds, Gill *ScF&FL 92*
Edmonds, Harry 1891-1989 *ScF&FL 92*
Edmonds, Helen Woods *ScF&FL 92*
Edmonds, James D., Jr. 1939- *WhoSSW 93*
Edmonds, Kenny *BioIn 17*
Edmonds, Mary Patricia 1922- *WhoAm 92*
Edmonds, Michael Darnell 1960- *WhoEmL 93, WhoSSW 93*
Edmonds, Norman Douglas 1938- *AfrAmBi*
Edmonds, Walter 1938- *WhoE 93*
Edmonds, Walter D. 1903- *ScF&FL 92*
Edmonds, Walter D(umaux) 1903- *MajAI [port]*
Edmonds, Walter Dumaux 1903- *DcAmChF 1960, WhoAm 92*
Edmonds, William Fleming 1923- *St&PR 93, WhoAm 92*
Edmonds Mumford, Deborah Ann *Law&B 92*
Edmondson, Barbara Jean 1945- *WhoAmW 93*
Edmondson, Belle 1840-1873 *BioIn 17*
Edmondson, Frank K. 1912- *WhoAm 92*
Edmondson, G.C. 1922- *ScF&FL 92*
Edmondson, George Alan, Jr. 1955- *WhoSSW 93*
Edmondson, George Bradley 1959- *WhoE 93*
Edmondson, Harold Elbert 1930- *St&PR 93*
Edmondson, Jack Bernhard 1927- *St&PR 93*
Edmondson, James Larry 1947- *WhoAm 92, WhoSSW 93*
Edmondson, James W. 1930- *WhoIns 93*
Edmondson, James William 1930- *St&PR 93, WhoAm 92*
Edmondson, John Richard 1927- *WhoAm 92*
Edmondson, Keith Henry 1924- *WhoAm 92*
Edmondson, Linda Louise 1947- *WhoAmW 93*
Edmondson, Wallace Thomas 1916- *WhoAm 92*
Edmondson, William Brockway 1927- *WhoAm 92*
Edmondson y Cotton, Jose *ScF&FL 92*
Edmonson, Karen Marie 1957- *WhoAmW 93*
Edmonson, Lowell Russell, Jr. 1936- *St&PR 93*
Edmonson, Munro Sterling 1924- *WhoAm 92, WhoSSW 93*
Edmonson, Nancy Jane 1942- *WhoAmW 93*
Edmonson, Richard Lewis *Law&B 92*
Edmonson, Susan Marie 1958- *WhoEmL 93*
Edmonson, Thomas L., Jr. 1934- *WhoSSW 93*
Edmonston, William Edward, Jr. 1931- *WhoAm 92*
Edmund, Alexander Gordon 1924- *WhoSSW 93*
Edmund, Robert M. 1948- *St&PR 93*
Edmund, Sean *MajAI*
Edmunds, David Eric *WhoScE 91-1*
Edmunds, Douglas Andrew 1948- *WhoEmL 93*
Edmunds, George F. 1828-1919 *PolPar*
Edmunds, Jane Clara 1922- *WhoAm 92*
Edmunds, Jeffrey Garth 1953- *WhoEmL 93*
Edmunds, John 1913-1986 *Baker 92*
Edmunds, John C. *St&PR 93*
Edmunds, Joseph Edsel 1935- *WhoAm 92*
Edmunds, Lowell 1938- *WhoAm 92*
Edmunds, Malcolm *WhoScE 91-1*
Edmunds, Wyndham Michael 1941- *WhoWor 93*
Edmundson, Lisa Becker 1959- *WhoAmW 93*
Edney, Leon A. Bud *WhoAm 92*
Edney, William Milton 1925- *St&PR 93*
Edqvist, Lars-Erik 1942- *WhoScE 91-4*
Edrei, Michael 1942- *WhoAm 92*
Edrington, Frank Roberts, II *Law&B 92*
Edrington, Jack B. *Law&B 92*
Edrington, Jack Brown 1943- *St&PR 93*
Edrington, Teresa R. *Law&B 92*
Edris, C. Lawrence 1942- *St&PR 93*
Edris, Charles Lawrence 1942- *WhoAm 92*
Edris, Dwight Pierce 1946- *St&PR 93*
Edris, James Alan 1944- *WhoE 93*
Edsall, Howard Linn 1904- *WhoE 93, WhoWor 93*
Edsall, John Tileston 1902- *WhoAm 92, WhoE 93*
Edsall, Thomas Byrne 1941- *WhoAm 92, WhoE 93*
Edson, Bernard d1992 *BioIn 17*
Edson, Charles Louis 1934- *WhoAm 92*
Edson, David W. *Law&B 92*
Edson, Eugene Hirsh 1924- *St&PR 93*
Edson, J.T. 1928- *ScF&FL 92*
Edson, Kay L. 1946- *St&PR 93*
Edson, Kay Louise 1946- *WhoE 93*
Edson, Kent E. 1942- *St&PR 93*
Edson, Lewis 1748-1820 *Baker 92*
Edson, Marian Louise 1940- *WhoAmW 93*
Edson, Martha Janet 1933- *St&PR 93*
Edson, Ralph A. 1929- *St&PR 93*
Edson, William Alden 1912- *WhoAm 92*
Edson, William Arthur 1951- *WhoEmL 93*
Edson-Shermeyer, Mary Christine 1959- *WhoEmL 93*
Edstrom, Anders 1938- *WhoScE 91-4*
Edstrom, Eric Wayne 1950- *St&PR 93*
Edstrom, John Olof 1926- *WhoScE 91-4*
Edstrom, Karin Gunilla 1934- *WhoUN 92*
Edstrom, Liva 1876-1971 *See* Jarnefelt, (Edvard) Armas 1869-1958 *Baker 92*
Edvina, Louise 1878-1948 *OxDcOp*
Edvinsson, Johan Henrik Leif 1946- *WhoWor 93*
Edvinsson, Lars I.H. 1947- *WhoScE 91-4*
Edwall, Lennart 1931- *WhoScE 91-4*
Edward, Duke of Windsor 1894-1972 *BioIn 17*
Edward, Prince of Great Britain 1964- *BioIn 17*
Edward, I 1239-1307 *HarEnMi*
Edward, II 1284-1327 *HarEnMi*
Edward, III 1312-1377 *HarEnMi*
Edward, IV 1442-1483 *HarEnMi*
Edward, VII, King of Great Britain 1841-1910 *BioIn 17*
Edward, VIII 1894-1972 *DcTwHis*
Edward, VIII, King of Great Britain 1894-1972 *BioIn 17*
Edward, David Andrew 1962- *WhoEmL 93, WhoSSW 93*
Edward, John Thomas 1919- *WhoAm 92*
Edward, Nickolas W. 1928- *St&PR 93*
Edward, Norman Stewart *WhoScE 91-1*
Edward Albert, Prince of Wales 1894-1972 *BioIn 17*
Edwards, Al *AfrAmBi [port]*
Edwards, Albert Glen 1907-1973 *BioIn 17*
Edwards, Alexander 1767?-1811 *BioIn 17*
Edwards, Alfred Leroy 1920- *WhoAm 92*
Edwards, Allison Jean 1953- *WhoSSW 93*
Edwards, Allison Regina 1955- *WhoE 93*
Edwards, Amy E. *Law&B 92*
Edwards, Ann Louise Corbin 1949- *WhoAmW 93*
Edwards, Anne 1927- *ScF&FL 92*
Edwards, Anne-Marie 1932- *ConAu 38NR*
Edwards, Archie 1918- *BioIn 17*
Edwards, Arthur Anderson 1926- *WhoAm 92*
Edwards, Audrey 1947- *BlkAull 92*
Edwards, Barry Reese 1956- *WhoE 93*
Edwards, Ben 1950- *BioIn 17*
Edwards, Benjamin Franklin, III 1931- *St&PR 93, WhoAm 92*
Edwards, Bernard 1952- *SoulM*

Edwards, Bert Tvedt 1937- *WhoAm 92, WhoE 93*
Edwards, Betty Jo 1950- *WhoAmW 93*
Edwards, Blake 1922- *MiSFD 9, WhoAm 92*
Edwards, Bob 1947- *News 93-2 [port], WhoAm 92, WhoE 93*
Edwards, Bobby G. 1948- *St&PR 93*
Edwards, Brenda Faye 1945- *WhoSSW 93*
Edwards, Bruce L. 1952- *ScF&FL 92*
Edwards, Bruce Lynn 1948- *WhoEmL 93*
Edwards, Bryna L. *Law&B 92*
Edwards, C. Webb 1947- *St&PR 93*
Edwards, Calvin Wayne 1954- *WhoEmL 93, WhoSSW 93*
Edwards, Carl E., Jr. *Law&B 92*
Edwards, Carl Normand 1943- *WhoE 93*
Edwards, Carlos D. *Law&B 92*
Edwards, Carol A. *Law&B 92*
Edwards, Carol Lynn 1950- *WhoAmW 93*
Edwards, Carole A. 1954- *WhoEmL 93*
Edwards, Catharin Karen 1949- *WhoSSW 93*
Edwards, Catharine Patricia 1955- *WhoAmW 93*
Edwards, Catherine d1990 *BioIn 17*
Edwards, Charlene Whitney 1948- *WhoEmL 93*
Edwards, Charles 1925- *WhoAm 92, WhoSSW 93*
Edwards, Charles C., Jr. 1947- *St&PR 93*
Edwards, Charles Elvin, Jr. 1953- *WhoEmL 93*
Edwards, Charles Harris Wesley 1951- *WhoEmL 93*
Edwards, Charles Lloyd 1940- *WhoAm 92*
Edwards, Charles Merriwell 1941- *WhoE 93*
Edwards, Charles Mundy, III 1935- *WhoWor 93*
Edwards, Chet *WhoAm 92*
Edwards, Chet 1951- *CngDr 91*
Edwards, Christine A. *Law&B 92*
Edwards, Christine A. 1952- *WhoAm 92*
Edwards, Christine Utley 1951- *WhoEmL 93*
Edwards, Christopher Bryan *WhoScE 91-1*
Edwards, Christopher Watkin 1942- *WhoWor 93*
Edwards, Clara 1887-1974 *Baker 92*
Edwards, Claudia J. 1943- *ScF&FL 92*
Edwards, Claudia Jane 1943- *WhoWrEP 92*
Edwards, Cliff 1895-1971 *BioIn 17*
Edwards, Clifford Murray 1952- *WhoE 93, WhoEmL 93*
Edwards, Connie Lynn 1946- *WhoEmL 93*
Edwards, Craig K. *Law&B 92*
Edwards, Craig Richard *Law&B 92*
Edwards, Daniel Walden 1950- *WhoEmL 93, WhoWor 93*
Edwards, David *Law&B 92*
Edwards, David 1945?- *ScF&FL 92*
Edwards, David Charles 1937- *WhoAm 92*
Edwards, David H. 1922-1992 *BioIn 17*
Edwards, David H., Jr. d1992 *NewYTBS 92*
Edwards, David Hugh *WhoScE 91-1*
Edwards, David Iwan *WhoScE 91-1*
Edwards, David J. *St&PR 93*
Edwards, David Murray *WhoScE 91-1*
Edwards, David Northrop 1923- *WhoSSW 93*
Edwards, David R. *Law&B 92*
Edwards, David Sheridan 1941- *St&PR 93*
Edwards, David Teify *WhoScE 91-1*
Edwards, David Thomas 1944- *WhoWor 93*
Edwards, David VanDeusen 1941- *WhoSSW 93*
Edwards, Dawn Ann 1956- *WhoE 93, WhoEmL 93*
Edwards, Deborah Joy 1951- *WhoEmL 93*
Edwards, Deborah L. *Law&B 92*
Edwards, Deborah Leah 1957- *WhoAmW 93*
Edwards, Del Mount 1953- *WhoEmL 93, WhoSSW 93, WhoWor 93*
Edwards, Denise Althea Michelle 1965- *WhoEmL 93*
Edwards, Dennis 1943- *SoulM*
Edwards, Dennis 1952- *St&PR 93*
Edwards, Devin Shawn 1963- *WhoSSW 93*
Edwards, Diane Elaine 1959- *WhoE 93*
Edwards, Don *CngDr 91*
Edwards, Don 1915- *WhoAm 92*
Edwards, Don Earl *St&PR 93*
Edwards, Donald James 1952- *WhoEmL 93*
Edwards, Donald Mervin 1938- *WhoAm 92*
Edwards, Donna Reed 1955- *WhoEmL 93*
Edwards, Doris Porter 1962- *WhoEmL 93*
Edwards, Dorothy 1914-1982 *ChlFicS, ScF&FL 92*
Edwards, Douglas 1917-1990 *BioIn 17*
Edwards, Douglas Alan 1959- *WhoWor 93*
Edwards, Douglas W. *Law&B 92*
Edwards, Dwayne Dee 1948- *WhoEmL 93*
Edwards, E. Everett 1937- *St&PR 93*
Edwards, Earnest Jonathan 1938- *St&PR 93*
Edwards, Eddie *BioIn 17*
Edwards, Eddie d1990 *BioIn 17*
Edwards, Edith Y. 1919- *St&PR 93*
Edwards, Edward W. 1943- *St&PR 93*
Edwards, Edwin W. *BioIn 17*
Edwards, Edwin Washington 1927- *WhoAm 92*
Edwards, Elaine Schwartzenburg 1929- *BioIn 17*
Edwards, Eleanor Cecile 1940- *WhoAmW 93*
Edwards, Eleanor Mattiasich 1938- *WhoAmW 93*
Edwards, Elizabeth A. 1951- *St&PR 93*
Edwards, Elizabeth Robinson 1907-1990 *BioIn 17*
Edwards, Ellis Duncan 1947- *WhoAm 92*
Edwards, Eric Alan 1953- *WhoEmL 93*
Edwards, Eric Vaughan 1946- *WhoWor 93*
Edwards, Ernest Preston 1919- *WhoAm 92*
Edwards, Esther *WhoAm 92*
Edwards, Frances Sue 1933- *WhoAmW 93*
Edwards, Francis Charles 1947- *WhoE 93*
Edwards, Francis Gordon 1924- *St&PR 93*
Edwards, Franklin R. 1937- *WhoAm 92*
Edwards, Frederick Harold 1965- *WhoSSW 93*
Edwards, Gawain 1901-1987 *ScF&FL 92*
Edwards, Gene 1932- *ScF&FL 92*
Edwards, Geoffrey Hartley 1936- *WhoAm 92, WhoSSW 93*
Edwards, George Alva 1916- *WhoAm 92*
Edwards, George Danny 1951- *St&PR 93*
Edwards, George Kent 1939- *WhoAm 92*
Edwards, George W. 1939- *St&PR 93*
Edwards, George W., Jr. 1939- *WhoAm 92*
Edwards, Gilbert Franklin 1915- *WhoAm 92*
Edwards, Glenn Allen 1934- *St&PR 93*
Edwards, Glenn Thomas 1931- *WhoAm 92*
Edwards, Gregory J. 1944- *St&PR 93*
Edwards, Guy H. 1939- *St&PR 93*
Edwards, H.L. *Law&B 92*
Edwards, Haden William 1952- *St&PR 93*
Edwards, Harold Mills 1930- *WhoAm 92*
Edwards, Harold Mortimer 1936- *WhoAm 92*
Edwards, Harry *BioIn 17*
Edwards, Harry 1942- *EncAACR*
Edwards, Harry LaFoy 1936- *WhoSSW 93, WhoWor 93*
Edwards, Harry Raymond 1927- *WhoAsAP 91*
Edwards, Harry T. 1940- *CngDr 91, WhoAm 92, WhoE 93*
Edwards, Helen Jean 1937- *WhoWrEP 92*
Edwards, Helen Jex *Law&B 92*
Edwards, Helen Thom 1936- *WhoAm 92*
Edwards, Henry *ScF&FL 92*
Edwards, Henry Percival 1939- *WhoAm 92*
Edwards, Hilton 1903-1982 *BioIn 17*
Edwards, Horace Burton 1925- *WhoAm 92*
Edwards, Howard Dawson 1923- *WhoAm 92*
Edwards, Howard L. 1931- *St&PR 93*
Edwards, Howard Lee 1931- *WhoAm 92*
Edwards, Ian 1956- *WhoScE 91-1*
Edwards, Ian Keith 1926- *WhoAm 92*
Edwards, Ian Kenneth 1953- *WhoEmL 93, WhoSSW 93*
Edwards, India d1990 *BioIn 17*
Edwards, India 1895-1990 *PolPar*
Edwards, Iola Darlene *WhoE 93*
Edwards, Ivana Michaela 1946- *WhoWrEP 92*
Edwards, J.M.B. 1935- *WhoWrEP 92*
Edwards, Jack *WhoScE 91-1*
Edwards, Jack 1928- *WhoAm 92*
Edwards, Jack A. 1948- *WhoEmL 93*
Edwards, Jack P. 1945- *WhoAm 92*
Edwards, James Benjamin 1935- *WhoSSW 93*
Edwards, James Burnsides 1949- *WhoSSW 93*
Edwards, James Burrows *BioIn 17*
Edwards, James Burrows 1927- *WhoAm 92, WhoSSW 93*
Edwards, James Clifford 1930- *WhoAm 92*
Edwards, James Cook 1923- *WhoAm 92*
Edwards, James Dallas, III 1937- *WhoWor 93*
Edwards, James Edwin 1914- *WhoSSW 93*
Edwards, James Griffith *WhoScE 91-1*
Edwards, James Kennedy 1943- *WhoAm 92*
Edwards, James Lynn 1952- *WhoAm 92, WhoEmL 93*
Edwards, James Malone 1931- *WhoAm 92*
Edwards, James O. 1943- *St&PR 93*
Edwards, James Owen 1943- *WhoAm 92*
Edwards, James R. *Law&B 92*
Edwards, James Richard 1951- *WhoEmL 93*
Edwards, James Scott 1945- *St&PR 93*
Edwards, Jane Elizabeth 1932- *WhoWrEP 92*
Edwards, Jay Thomas 1931- *WhoAm 92*
Edwards, Jean Butler 1950- *WhoE 93*
Edwards, Jeffrey Rex 1959- *WhoSSW 93*
Edwards, Jere Lee 1949- *WhoSSW 93*
Edwards, Jerome 1912- *WhoAm 92*
Edwards, Jesse Efrem 1911- *WhoAm 92*
Edwards, Jesse G. 1926- *St&PR 93*
Edwards, Jim *BioIn 17*
Edwards, Jimmie M. *Law&B 92*
Edwards, Jimmy 1920-1988 *QDrFCA 92 [port]*
Edwards, JoAnn Louise 1955- *WhoE 93*
Edwards, John *ScF&FL 92*
Edwards, John Blodgett 1938- *WhoAm 92*
Edwards, John Brooks *WhoScE 91-1*
Edwards, John Charles *WhoWrEP 92*
Edwards, John Charles 1941- *St&PR 93*
Edwards, John Coates 1934- *WhoWor 93*
Edwards, John Duncan 1953- *WhoEmL 93*
Edwards, John E. 1930- *St&PR 93*
Edwards, John Hamilton 1922- *WhoAm 92*
Edwards, John Hilton *WhoScE 91-1*
Edwards, John Kenneth 1944- *St&PR 93*
Edwards, John Lewis 1946- *WhoSSW 93*
Edwards, John P. 1942- *St&PR 93*
Edwards, John Ralph 1937- *WhoAm 92, WhoE 93*
Edwards, John Saul 1943- *WhoSSW 93*
Edwards, John Steven 1952- *WhoWor 93*
Edwards, John Stuart 1931- *WhoAm 92*
Edwards, John Wesley, Jr. 1933- *WhoWor 93*
Edwards, John White *WhoAm 92*
Edwards, John Womer 1958- *WhoEmL 93*
Edwards, Jonathan 1703-1758 *BioIn 17*
Edwards, Jonathan 1745-1801 *BioIn 17*
Edwards, Jonathan Hayes 1949- *WhoEmL 93*
Edwards, Jorge 1931- *SpAmA*
Edwards, Joseph Castro 1909- *WhoAm 92*
Edwards, Judith Elizabeth 1933- *WhoAmW 93*
Edwards, Julia *MajAI*
Edwards, Julia Spalding 1920- *WhoAm 92*
Edwards, Julian 1855-1910 *Baker 92*
Edwards, Julie *BioIn 17*
Edwards, June *WhoCanL 92*
Edwards, K.C. *ScF&FL 92*
Edwards, Karen *BioIn 17*
Edwards, Kathleen S. *Law&B 92*
Edwards, Kathryn Inez 1947- *WhoAmW 93, WhoEmL 93*
Edwards, Kathryn Louise 1947- *WhoAm 92*
Edwards, Kenneth 1917- *WhoAm 92*
Edwards, Kenneth Anthony 1939- *WhoUN 92*
Edwards, Kenneth J., Jr. 1952- *St&PR 93*
Edwards, Kenneth Neil 1932- *WhoWor 93*
Edwards, Kent Martin 1948- *WhoSSW 93*
Edwards, Kevin Dale 1957- *WhoWrEP 92*
Edwards, Kirk Lewis 1950- *WhoWor 93*
Edwards, L. Ward 1936- *St&PR 93*
Edwards, Lacy Lee, Jr. 1941- *WhoAm 92*
Edwards, Larry A. 1935- *WhoAm 92*
Edwards, Larry David 1937- *WhoAm 92, WhoWor 93*
Edwards, Larry Glenn 1945- *WhoE 93*
Edwards, Laurie Ellen 1951- *WhoAmW 93*
Edwards, Leila 1937- *WhoAmW 93*
Edwards, Leroy 1914-1971 *BiDAMSp 1989*
Edwards, Les *ScF&FL 92*
Edwards, Lillian Brown 1921- *St&PR 93*
Edwards, Lillie Johnson 1952- *WhoEmL 93*
Edwards, Linda A. *AfrAmBi [port]*
Edwards, Linda Ann 1944- *WhoWrEP 92*
Edwards, Lisa *BioIn 17*
Edwards, Lisa Michele 1956- *WhoAmW 93*
Edwards, Louis Ward, Jr. 1936- *WhoAm 92*
Edwards, Lydia Justice 1937- *WhoAm 92, WhoAmW 93*
Edwards, Lynn *WhoWrEP 92*
Edwards, M.E. 1947- *St&PR 93*
Edwards, Malcolm 1949- *ScF&FL 92*
Edwards, Marc T. 1949- *WhoE 93*
Edwards, Margaret McRae 1931- *WhoAmW 93*
Edwards, Marguerite Ruth 1960- *WhoAmW 93*
Edwards, Marie A. *ScF&FL 92*
Edwards, Marie Babare *WhoAmW 93*
Edwards, Marjorie H. 1930- *St&PR 93*
Edwards, Mark Brownlow 1939- *WhoSSW 93*
Edwards, Mark E. *Law&B 92*
Edwards, Mark H. *Law&B 92*
Edwards, Martin H. 1931- *St&PR 93*
Edwards, (Kenneth) Martin 1955- *ConAu 137*
Edwards, Marvin Earle 1943- *WhoAm 92, WhoSSW 93*
Edwards, Marvin Raymond 1921- *WhoSSW 93*
Edwards, Mary 1949- *WhoEmL 93*
Edwards, McKinley C. 1942- *St&PR 93*
Edwards, Michael David 1955- *WhoEmL 93*
Edwards, Michael J. *St&PR 93*
Edwards, Michael Paul 1950- *WhoWor 93*
Edwards, Michelle 1955- *ConAu 138, SmATA 70 [port]*
Edwards, Michelle LaVerne 1960- *WhoAmW 93*
Edwards, Mickey 1937- *BioIn 17, CngDr 91, WhoAm 92, WhoSSW 93*
Edwards, Mike *BioIn 17*
Edwards, Monte R. *Law&B 92*
Edwards, Nancy Radcliffe 1942- *WhoSSW 93*
Edwards, Nicholas *ScF&FL 92*
Edwards, Nicholas d1992 *BioIn 17, NewYTBS 92*
Edwards, Nicky 1958- *ScF&FL 92*
Edwards, Norman Arthur *WhoScE 91-1*
Edwards, Otis Carl, Jr. 1928- *WhoAm 92*
Edwards, P.E. *WhoWrEP 92*
Edwards, Page Lawrence, Jr. 1941- *WhoAm 92*
Edwards, Patrick Ross 1940- *WhoAm 92*
Edwards, Paul *ScF&FL 92*
Edwards, Paul Beverly 1915- *WhoSSW 93*
Edwards, Paul Geoffrey 1926-1992 *ConAu 137*
Edwards, Paul Kerr *WhoScE 91-1*
Edwards, Penny 1929- *SweetSg C [port]*
Edwards, Peter 1946- *ScF&FL 92*
Edwards, Peter S., Jr. 1921- *St&PR 93*
Edwards, Peter Stuart Allenby 1948- *WhoWor 93*
Edwards, Philip Yonge 1957- *St&PR 93*
Edwards, Phillip Milton 1933- *WhoE 93, WhoWor 93*
Edwards, Phyllis Ann 1947- *WhoEmL 93*
Edwards, Phyllis Mae 1921- *WhoAmW 93, WhoWor 93*
Edwards, Presley W. 1904- *St&PR 93*
Edwards, R. LaVell 1930- *BiDAMSp 1989*
Edwards, Ralph M. 1933- *WhoAm 92*
Edwards, Randall Hamilton 1961- *WhoEmL 93*
Edwards, Ray Conway 1913- *St&PR 93, WhoWor 93*
Edwards, Ray Dean 1932- *St&PR 93*
Edwards, Rayburn F. 1940- *St&PR 93*
Edwards, Redick 1947- *St&PR 93*
Edwards, Renee Camille 1961- *WhoAmW 93, WhoEmL 93, WhoWor 93*
Edwards, Rex Lanier, Jr. *Law&B 92*
Edwards, Richard 1524-1566 *Baker 92*
Edwards, Richard A. 1957- *St&PR 93*
Edwards, Richard Alan 1938- *WhoAm 92*
Edwards, Richard Alan 1957- *WhoEmL 93*
Edwards, Richard Ambrose 1922- *WhoAm 92*
Edwards, Richard Charles 1948- *WhoEmL 93*
Edwards, Richard Humphrey Tudor *WhoScE 91-1*
Edwards, Richard LeRoy 1943- *WhoAm 92*
Edwards, Richard Lester 1928- *St&PR 93*
Edwards, Richard Thomas 1941- *WhoSSW 93*
Edwards, Rob 1963- *WhoEmL 93*
Edwards, Robert Anthony *Law&B 92*
Edwards, Robert Edmund 1926- *WhoWor 93*
Edwards, Robert Hazard 1935- *WhoAm 92*
Edwards, Robert J. *Law&B 92*
Edwards, Robert John 1951- *St&PR 93*
Edwards, Robert Nelson 1946- *St&PR 93*
Edwards, Robert Roy 1947- *WhoAm 92*
Edwards, Robert S. 1927- *St&PR 93*
Edwards, Robert Valentino 1940- *WhoAm 92*
Edwards, Roger P. 1933- *St&PR 93*
Edwards, Ron W. *WhoScE 91-1*
Edwards, Ronald F. 1950- *WhoSSW 93*
Edwards, Ronald Fredrick 1945- *WhoAsAP 91*
Edwards, Ross 1943- *Baker 92*

Edwards, Roy Anderson, III 1945- *WhoAm 92*
Edwards, Russell 1909-1991 *BioIn 17*
Edwards, Ryan Hayes *WhoAm 92*
Edwards, S. Albert 1946- *WhoEmL 93*
Edwards, Sallie Ann Nelson 1836-1922 *BioIn 17*
Edwards, Sally 1947- *BioIn 17*
Edwards, Sam *WhoScE 91-1*
Edwards, Samuel Frederick 1928- *WhoWor 93*
Edwards, Sara Lee 1942- *WhoSSW 93*
Edwards, Scott Samuel, Jr. 1915- *WhoSSW 93*
Edwards, Sebastian 1953- *WhoAm 92*
Edwards, Sian *WhoWor 93*
Edwards, Sian 1959- *OxDcOp*
Edwards, Stanley Ewart 1921- *St&PR 93*
Edwards, Stephen Charles *WhoScE 91-1*
Edwards, Stephen E. 1944- *St&PR 93*
Edwards, Stephen Jeffrey *WhoScE 91-1*
Edwards, Steve 1930- *WhoSSW 93*
Edwards, Steve 1946- *WhoEmL 93*
Edwards, Steven Alan 1956- *WhoEmL 93*
Edwards, Susan L. *Law&B 92*
Edwards, Sylvia Lorene 1946- *WhoEmL 93*
Edwards, Tamara Gordon *Law&B 92*
Edwards, Theodore R. 1925- *St&PR 93*
Edwards, Theodore Unaldo 1934- *WhoE 93*
Edwards, Thomas Ashton 1960- *WhoE 93, WhoEmL 93, WhoWor 93*
Edwards, Thomas Blaine 1947- *WhoEmL 93*
Edwards, Thomas Henry, Jr. 1918- *WhoSSW 93*
Edwards, Thomas Robert, Jr. 1928- *WhoAm 92*
Edwards, Tom *BioIn 17*
Edwards, Tracy A. 1957- *St&PR 93*
Edwards, Turk 1907-1973 *BioIn 17*
Edwards, Valerie Anne 1949- *St&PR 93*
Edwards, Victor Henry 1940- *WhoAm 92, WhoSSW 93*
Edwards, Vincent 1928- *MiSFD 9*
Edwards, Virginia Davis 1927- *WhoAmW 93*
Edwards, Wallace Winfield 1922- *WhoAm 92*
Edwards, Walter Meayers 1908- *WhoAm 92*
Edwards, Ward Dennis 1927- *WhoAm 92*
Edwards, Warren *BioIn 17*
Edwards, Wayne Forrest 1934- *WhoAm 92*
Edwards, Wendell Edward 1937- *WhoSSW 93*
Edwards, Wilbur Shields 1916- *WhoAm 92*
Edwards, William Brundige, III 1942- *WhoSSW 93*
Edwards, William C., Jr. 1930- *St&PR 93*
Edwards, William F. 1946- *St&PR 93*
Edwards, William Foster 1946- *WhoAm 92*
Edwards, William I., III 1931- *St&PR 93*
Edwards, William J. 1939- *St&PR 93*
Edwards, William James 1869- *BioIn 17*
Edwards, William James 1915- *WhoAm 92, WhoWor 93*
Edwards, William L. 1931- *St&PR 93*
Edwards, William N. 1929- *WhoIns 93*
Edwards, William Newton 1929- *St&PR 93, WhoE 93*
Edwards, William Rowland, Jr. 1942- *WhoSSW 93*
Edwards, William Sterling, III 1920- *WhoAm 92*
Edwards, William Terrell, Jr. 1927- *WhoSSW 93*
Edwards, William Thomas, Jr. 1956- *WhoEmL 93*
Edwardsen, John Christian *Law&B 92*
Edwardson, J.A. *WhoScE 91-1*
Edwardson, John Albert, Jr. 1949- *St&PR 93, WhoAm 92*
Edward the Black Prince 1330-1376 *HarEnMi*
Edwin, Ellen Owens 1953- *WhoAmW 93*
Edzard, Christine *MiSFD 9*
Eeden, Jean-Baptiste van den 1842-1917 *Baker 92*
Eek, Luis 1932- *WhoWor 93*
Eek, Nathaniel Sisson 1927- *WhoAm 92*
Eekman, Thomas Adam 1923- *WhoAm 92*
Eelkema, Robert Cameron 1930- *WhoAm 92*
Eells, Chris Allen 1955- *WhoEmL 93*
Eells, Cushing 1810-1893 *BioIn 17*
Eells, Gwen J. *Law&B 92*
Eells, James 1926- *WhoWor 93*
Eells, Myron 1843-1907 *IntDcAn*
Eells, Richard 1917- *WhoAm 92, WhoWor 93*
Eells, Richard Sedric Fox d1992 *NewYTBS 92*
Eells, William Hastings 1924- *WhoAm 92*
Eenink, A.H. *WhoScE 91-3*
Eenmaa, Ivi V. *BioIn 17*
Eenshuistra, J. *WhoScE 91-3*
Eerde, John A. Van *ScF&FL 92*
Eerdmans, Johannes d1990 *BioIn 17*
Eerkens, Cornelis 1937- *WhoScE 91-2*
Eernisse, Errol Peter 1940- *WhoAm 92*
Eerola, Lasse Olavi 1950- *WhoWor 93*
Eerola, Osmo Tapio 1956- *WhoWor 93*
Efaw, Cary R. 1949- *WhoE 93, WhoEmL 93*
Efe, Kemal 1953- *WhoSSW 93*
Eff, Thomas Allan *Law&B 92*
Effel, Laura *Law&B 92*
Effenberger, Franz Xaver 1930- *WhoScE 91-3, WhoWor 93*
Effenberger, John A. 1934- *St&PR 93*
Effert, Sven 1922- *WhoScE 91-3*
Effimoff, Igor 1946- *St&PR 93*
Effinger, Cecil 1914-1990 *Baker 92, BioIn 17*
Effinger, George Alec 1947- *ScF&FL 92*
Effinger, Harold J. 1952- *WhoEmL 93*
Effinger, Jerry Lee *Law&B 92*
Effinger, Wm. L. 1943- *St&PR 93*
Effren, Gary Ross 1956- *WhoEmL 93*
Effros, Robert C. 1933- *WhoUN 92*
Efi, Tupua Tamasese Tupuola 1939- *WhoAsAP 91*
Efimov, Igor' *ScF&FL 92*
Efimov, Igor Markovich 1937- *WhoE 93*
Efland, Simpson Lindsay 1913- *WhoSSW 93, WhoWor 93*
Efner, Howard Franklyn 1944- *WhoSSW 93*
Efnor, Richard Merrill 1949- *WhoEmL 93*
Eforo, John Francis 1930- *WhoAm 92*
Efron, Arthur 1931- *WhoWrEP 92*
Efron, Bradley 1938- *WhoAm 92*
Efron, Meryl Joy 1957- *WhoAmW 93*
Efron, Robert 1927- *WhoAm 92*
Efron, Samuel 1915- *WhoAm 92, WhoE 93, WhoWor 93*
Efros, Ellen Ann 1950- *WhoAmW 93, WhoEmL 93*
Efros, Evdokiia 1861-1943 *BioIn 17*
Efros, Norbert 1930- *St&PR 93*
Efroymson, Daniel R. 1941- *St&PR 93*
Efstathiou, George Petros 1955- *WhoWor 93*
Efthimiades, Michael Constantine 1958- *WhoE 93*
Efthimiou, Milton Basil 1935- *WhoE 93*
Efthymiatos, Denis 1941- *WhoScE 91-3*
Efthymiou, Paul N. 1945- *WhoScE 91-3*
Eftink, Jeffrey Joseph 1956- *WhoEmL 93*
Egami, Takeshi 1945- *WhoE 93*
Egan, Ann L. 1932- *WhoAmW 93*
Egan, Bruce Anthony 1939- *St&PR 93*
Egan, Cara M. *BioIn 17*
Egan, Charles Joseph, Jr. *Law&B 92*
Egan, Charles Joseph, Jr. 1932- *WhoAm 92*
Egan, Charles M. 1936- *St&PR 93*
Egan, Daniel Francis 1915- *WhoAm 92*
Egan, Donald G. 1961- *St&PR 93*
Egan, Doris *ScF&FL 92*
Egan, Edward F. 1919- *St&PR 93*
Egan, Edward M. 1932- *WhoAm 92, WhoE 93*
Egan, Eileen Elizabeth *WhoAmW 93*
Egan, Eileen Mary *WhoAmW 93*
Egan, Ferol 1923- *WhoWrEP 92*
Egan, Frank T. 1933- *WhoAm 92*
Egan, Gerald F. 1947- *St&PR 93*
Egan, Greg 1961- *ScF&FL 92*
Egan, Harold A., Jr. 1926- *St&PR 93*
Egan, Harvey D. *BioIn 17*
Egan, James Clayton 1956- *WhoEmL 93*
Egan, James J. *Law&B 92*
Egan, James J., Jr. 1939- *St&PR 93*
Egan, Jocelyn Ann 1962- *WhoEmL 93*
Egan, John *BioIn 17*
Egan, John Francis 1944- *WhoAm 92*
Egan, John Frederick 1935- *St&PR 93, WhoAm 92, WhoE 93, WhoWor 93*
Egan, John J. 1916- *BioIn 17*
Egan, John M. *WhoAm 92*
Egan, John T. *Law&B 92*
Egan, John T. d1990 *BioIn 17*
Egan, John T. 1927- *St&PR 93*
Egan, John Tinnerman 1948- *WhoEmL 93*
Egan, John V. 1934- *St&PR 93*
Egan, John W. 1939- *St&PR 93*
Egan, Joseph Edward 1936- *St&PR 93*
Egan, Joseph John 1940- *WhoE 93*
Egan, Joseph Richard 1954- *WhoEmL 93*
Egan, Kevin *ScF&FL 92*
Egan, Kevin James 1950- *WhoEmL 93*
Egan, Leo A. *Law&B 92*
Egan, Leonard Joseph 1945- *St&PR 93*
Egan, Louise *ScF&FL 92*
Egan, M. Sylvia 1930- *WhoAmW 93*
Egan, Mark H. *Law&B 92*
Egan, Mark Seamus 1963- *WhoWor 93*
Egan, Mary E. *Law&B 92*
Egan, Michael Joseph 1926- *WhoAm 92*
Egan, P. David *Law&B 92*
Egan, Patricia Geithman 1947- *WhoEmL 93*
Egan, Paul E. *Law&B 92*
Egan, Richard B. *Law&B 92*
Egan, Richard Burke 1931- *St&PR 93*
Egan, Richard Leo 1917- *WhoAm 92*
Egan, Robert 1945- *ScF&FL 92*
Egan, Robert J. *Law&B 92*
Egan, Robert M. d1990 *BioIn 17*
Egan, Robert Thomas 1952- *WhoEmL 93*
Egan, Robert Wheeler 1943- *WhoE 93*
Egan, Roger Edward 1921- *WhoAm 92, WhoWor 93*
Egan, Roger Neal 1943- *St&PR 93*
Egan, Rory Bernard 1942- *WhoAm 92*
Egan, Shirley Anne *WhoAm 92, WhoAmW 93*
Egan, Sylvia 1930- *WhoAm 92*
Egan, Thomas J. 1944- *St&PR 93*
Egan, Thomas P., Jr. *Law&B 92*
Egan, Vincent Joseph 1921- *WhoAm 92*
Egan, William Joseph 1956- *WhoE 93*
Egan, William M. 1929- *St&PR 93*
Egart, William V. 1939- *St&PR 93*
Egatz, Laura Ann Brugos 1942- *WhoAmW 93*
Egbert, Caroline S. *Law&B 92*
Egbert, Emerson Charles 1924- *WhoAm 92*
Egbert, John Clarence 1938- *St&PR 93*
Egbert, Richard Cook 1927- *WhoAm 92*
Egbert, Robert Baldwin 1916-1991 *BioIn 17*
Egbert, Robert Iman 1950- *WhoAm 92*
Egbufor, Emmanuel Michael Ukadike 1941- *WhoE 93*
Egdahl, Richard Harrison 1926- *WhoAm 92*
Ege, H. Ray 1937- *St&PR 93*
Egee, Michel 1939- *WhoScE 91-2*
Egekvist, W. Soren 1918- *WhoAm 92*
Egel, Christoph 1962- *WhoWor 93*
Egeland, Haakon G. 1921- *St&PR 93*
Egeler, William George 1954- *WhoE 93*
Egelstaff, Peter Alfred 1925- *WhoAm 92*
Egelston, Diane Carroll 1955- *WhoEmL 93*
Egelston, Jimmie Don 1941- *WhoWrEP 92*
Egelston, Robert Burnley 1930- *St&PR 93*
Egelston, Roberta Riethmiller 1946- *WhoAmW 93*
Egen, Richard Bell 1938- *St&PR 93*
Egenolff, Christian 1502-1555 *Baker 92*
Egensteiner, Donald Thomas 1932- *WhoAm 92*
Eger, Edmond I., II 1930- *WhoAm 92*
Eger, Felix Martin 1936- *WhoE 93*
Eger, John B. 1940- *St&PR 93*
Eger, Joseph 1925- *WhoAm 92*
Egerer, Frigyes 1936- *WhoScE 91-4*
Egermeier, Elsie E. 1890-1986 *BioIn 17*
Egert, Bruce 1955- *WhoEmL 93*
Egerton, Anne H. *Law&B 92*
Egerton, Arthur 1923- *St&PR 93*
Egerton, Emily O'Leary 1964- *WhoAmW 93*
Egerton, George 1859-1945 *BioIn 17*
Egerton, John Walden 1935- *WhoWrEP 92*
Eggan, Andrew Michael 1949- *WhoEmL 93*
Eggan, Fred 1906-1991 *IntDcAn*
Eggan, Fred R. 1906-1991 *BioIn 17*
Eggar, Samantha 1939- *WhoAm 92*
Egge, Klaus 1906-1979 *Baker 92*
Eggebrecht, Hans Heinrich 1919- *Baker 92*
Egged, Molly M. 1950- *St&PR 93*
Eggen, Arne 1881-1955 *Baker 92*
Eggen, Erik 1877-1957 *Baker 92*
Eggen, John Albert, Jr. 1934- *WhoAm 92*
Eggen, Olin Jeuck 1919- *WhoAm 92*
Eggen, Patricia Ann 1940- *St&PR 93*
Eggenberger, Andrew Jon 1938- *WhoE 93*
Eggenschwiler, James E., Jr. *Law&B 92*
Egger, Albert E. 1911- *St&PR 93*
Egger, Carl Thomas 1937- *St&PR 93*
Egger, Egon 1943- *WhoScE 91-3*
Egger, George E. 1905- *St&PR 93*
Egger, Josef Wilhelm 1949- *WhoScE 91-4*
Egger, Joseph Patrick 1948- *WhoEmL 93*
Egger, Roscoe L., Jr. 1920- *WhoAm 92*
Egger, Stephen Edwin 1942- *St&PR 93*
Egger, Susan Davis 1958- *St&PR 93*
Eggerding, Herbert F., Jr. 1937- *St&PR 93*
Eggermont, Ephrem A.J. 1930- *WhoScE 91-2*
Eggermont, Jos 1942- *WhoScE 91-3*
Eggers, Alfred J., Jr. 1922- *WhoAm 92*
Eggers, Alfred John, Jr. 1922- *WhoWor 93*
Eggers, Cecilia Demovich 1942- *WhoAmW 93*
Eggers, David Frank, Jr. 1922- *WhoAm 92*
Eggers, Ernest Russell 1931- *WhoAm 92, WhoWor 93*
Eggers, George William Nordholtz, Jr. 1929- *WhoAm 92*
Eggers, Hans J. 1927- *WhoScE 91-3*
Eggers, Hans Joachim 1927- *WhoWor 93*
Eggers, Idamarie Rasmussen 1925- *WhoAmW 93*
Eggers, James Wesley 1925- *WhoWor 93*
Eggers, Joan Frances 1934- *WhoAmW 93*
Eggers, Kerry 1953- *ConAu 137*
Eggers, Klaus W.H. 1922- *WhoScE 91-3*
Eggers, Mark Lee 1956- *St&PR 93, WhoEmL 93*
Eggers, Paul Walter 1919- *WhoAm 92, WhoWor 93*
Eggers, Valdemar Kay Henrik 1929- *WhoWor 93*
Eggers, William J., III 1939- *WhoWor 93*
Eggert, Alan R. 1949- *St&PR 93*
Eggert, Denise Ann 1957- *WhoSSW 93*
Eggert, Edward F. 1939- *St&PR 93*
Eggert, Elizabeth Parmelee *Law&B 92*
Eggert, Gerald Gordon 1926- *WhoAm 92, WhoE 93*
Eggert, Lilly Tegge *AmWomPl*
Eggert, Paul Richard 1954- *WhoEmL 93*
Eggert, Richard 1933- *St&PR 93*
Eggert, Robert J. 1913- *St&PR 93*
Eggert, Robert John, Sr. 1913- *WhoAm 92, WhoWor 93*
Eggert, Russell Raymond 1948- *WhoAm 92, WhoWor 93*
Eggert, Theodore Philip 1929- *WhoAm 92*
Eggerth, Marta 1912- *See* Kiepura, Jan 1902-1966 *OxDcOp*
Eggertsen, Claude Andrew 1909- *WhoAm 92*
Eggertsen, Paul Fred 1925- *WhoAm 92*
Eggertson, Gary V. *St&PR 93*
Egghard, Julius 1834-1867 *Baker 92*
Egghe, Leo Camiel 1952- *WhoWor 93*
Eggiman, Fritz *WhoScE 91-4*
Eggimann, Harry Luis 1953- *WhoWor 93*
Egginton, Geoffrey Twining 1940- *WhoAm 92*
Eggler, David Hewitt 1940- *WhoE 93*
Eggleson, Karen Jean 1961- *WhoAmW 93*
Eggleston, Alan Earl 1949- *WhoWrEP 92*
Eggleston, Alan P. 1953- *St&PR 93*
Eggleston, Carmen Rita 1956- *WhoAmW 93*
Eggleston, Claud Hunt, III 1954- *WhoEmL 93*
Eggleston, David Robert 1951- *St&PR 93*
Eggleston, George Cary 1839-1911 *JrnUS*
Eggleston, George Dudley 1936- *WhoSSW 93*
Eggleston, George T. 1906-1990 *BioIn 17*
Eggleston, John *BioIn 17*
Eggleston, Kent Lee 1936- *St&PR 93*
Eggleston, Lawrence William *WhoScE 91-1*
Eggleston, R. Dale *Law&B 92*
Eggleston, Robert Dale 1949- *WhoEmL 93*
Eggleston, Tom I. *St&PR 93*
Eggleston, Wilfrid 1901-1986 *BioIn 17*
Eggleston-Wehr, Sylvia Elaine Johnson 1940- *WhoE 93*
Eggleton, Arthur C. *WhoAm 92, WhoE 93*
Eggleton, Phillip G. 1950- *St&PR 93*
Eggli, Donald F. 1932- *St&PR 93*
Eghbal, Morad 1952- *WhoE 93*
Egide, James Allen 1934- *St&PR 93*
Egidi, Arthur 1859-1943 *Baker 92*
Egidi, Claudio 1914- *WhoScE 91-3*
Egidio Colonna c. 1243-1316 *BioIn 17*
Egielski, Richard *ChlBIID [port]*
Egielski, Richard 1952- *MajAI [port], WhoAm 92*
Eginton, Charles Theodore 1914- *WhoAm 92*
Eginton, Warren William 1924- *WhoAm 92, WhoE 93*
Egizii, Mary Jo *Law&B 92*
Egk, Werner 1901- *OxDcOp*
Egk, Werner 1901-1983 *Baker 92, IntDcOp [port]*
Egle, Davis Max 1939- *WhoAm 92*
Eglee, Charles Hamilton 1951- *WhoEmL 93*
Egler, Frederick Norton 1922- *WhoAm 92*
Egleson, Jan *MiSFD 9*
Egleton, Clive 1927- *ScF&FL 92*
Egley, Loren Edward 1931- *St&PR 93*
Egley, Thomas M. 1946- *St&PR 93*
Egli, Dorrit *BioIn 17*
Egli, Ida Rae 1946- *ConAu 137*
Egli, Johann Heinrich 1742-1810 *Baker 92*
Eglinton, Geoffrey *WhoScE 91-1*
Eglinton, William Matthew *WhoAm 92*
Egloff, Julius, III 1946- *WhoWor 93*
Eglow, Michael E. 1956- *WhoE 93*
Eglowstein, Howard 1934- *St&PR 93*
Egly, Dewayne 1950- *St&PR 93*
Egmond, Max von 1936- *Baker 92*
Egmont, Lamoral, Count of 1522-1568 *HarEnMi*

Egmont, Nina Hodjash 1941- *WhoUN 92*
Egnatchik, Michael Richard *Law&B 92*
Egnatinsky, Jack 1941- *WhoE 93*
Egnatius, Gellius d295BC *HarEnMi*
Egner, Betty Jane 1951- *WhoAmW 93*
Egner, Donald Otto 1928- *WhoE 93*
Egner, John David 1957- *WhoEmL 93*
Egner, Thorbjorn 1912-1990? *BioIn 17*
Egnew, Thomas Romine 1947- *WhoEmL 93*
Egnor-Brown, Rose Marie *WhoWrEP 92*
Ego-Aguirre, Ernesto 1928- *WhoE 93*
Egoff, Sheila A. 1918- *ScF&FL 92*
Egol, Andrew Barry 1950- *WhoSSW 93*
Egolf, Donald R. 1928-1990 *BioIn 17*
Egolf, Paula Moore 1944- *WhoAmW 93*
Egorov, Jurij 1920-1982 *DrEEuF*
Egorov, Youri 1954-1988 *Baker 92*
Egorov, Yuri Vladimirovich 1938- *WhoWor 93*
Egorushkin, Andrey Albertovich 1960- *WhoWor 93*
Egoyan, Atom 1960- *MiSFD 9*
Egremont, Michael *ScF&FL 92*
Egsmose, Tage 1922- *WhoScE 91-2*
Eguchi, Hidekazu 1929- *WhoWor 93*
Eguchi, Kazuo 1937- *WhoAsAP 91*
Eguchi, Michael Steven 1947- *WhoEmL 93*
Eguchi, Tetsuo 1921- *WhoWor 93*
Eguchi, Yasu *BioIn 17*
Eguchi, Yasu 1938- *WhoAm 92*
Eguez, Ivan 1944- *SpAmA*
Eguiara y Eguren, Juan Jose de 1696-1763 *DcMexL*
Eguiluz, Luis Ignacio 1943- *WhoScE 91-3*
Eguren, Gustavo 1925- *SpAmA*
Eguren, Jose Maria 1874-1942 *SpAmA*
Egypt, Ophelia Settle 1903-1984 *BlkAuII 92*
Ehas, Joan T. *Law&B 92*
Ehgartner, George Joseph, Jr. 1962- *WhoEmL 93*
Ehhalt, Dieter Hans 1935- *WhoScE 91-3*
Ehinger, Albert Louis, Jr. 1927- *WhoAm 92, WhoE 93*
Ehinger, Berndt E.J. 1937- *WhoScE 91-4*
Ehinger, Charles E. 1928- *St&PR 93*
Ehinger, Charles Edward 1928- *WhoAm 92*
Ehle, Jay Sutton *Law&B 92*
Ehle, Jay Sutton 1950- *WhoEmL 93*
Ehle, John 1925- *BioIn 17, WhoWrEP 92*
Ehle, John Marsden, Jr. 1925- *WhoAm 92*
Ehle, Joseph S. *St&PR 93*
Ehlen, Judy 1944- *WhoSSW 93*
Ehler, Herbert 1958- *WhoWor 93*
Ehler, R(ichard) L. 1930- *ConAu 137*
Ehler, Richard Lee 1930- *WhoWrEP 92*
Ehlerman, Paul Michael 1938- *St&PR 93, WhoAm 92*
Ehlers, Alice (Pauly) 1887-1981 *Baker 92*
Ehlers, Carl 1944- *WhoScE 91-4*
Ehlers, Charles H. 1930- *St&PR 93*
Ehlers, Eleanor May Collier 1920- *WhoAmW 93*
Ehlers, Gregory Allen, Sr. 1947- *WhoEmL 93*
Ehlers, J. *WhoScE 91-3*
Ehlers, James LeRoy 1950- *WhoWor 93*
Ehlers, Kathryn Hawes 1931- *WhoAm 92*
Ehlers, Lyle M. 1947- *St&PR 93*
Ehlers, Michael Gene 1951- *WhoEmL 93*
Ehlers, Niels 1938- *WhoScE 91-2*
Ehlers, P. *WhoScE 91-3*
Ehlers, W. *WhoScE 91-3*
Ehlers, Walter D. *BioIn 17*
Ehlers, Walter George 1933- *WhoAm 92*
Ehlers, William A. 1921- *St&PR 93*
Ehlers, William Henry 1950- *WhoE 93*
Ehlert, Fay *AmWomPl*
Ehlert, Lois *ChlBIID [port]*
Ehlert, Lois 1934- *BioIn 17, ChlLR 28 [port], SmATA 69*
Ehlert, Lois (Jane) 1934- *ConAu 137, MajAI [port]*
Ehlert, Louis 1825-1884 *Baker 92*
Ehlert, Marilyn Ann 1947- *WhoAmW 93*
Ehlert, Mary Anne 1950- *WhoEmL 93*
Ehley, Scott William 1955- *WhoEmL 93*
Ehlinger, Ladd P. 1940- *WhoSSW 93*
Ehlotzky, Fritz 1929- *WhoScE 91-4*
Ehly, Ehren M. *ScF&FL 92*
Ehly, Moreen *ScF&FL 92*
Ehm, Phillip D. 1932- *WhoAm 92*
Ehman, Michael Frederick 1945- *WhoE 93*
Ehmann, Anthony Valentine 1935- *WhoWor 93*
Ehmann, Carl William 1942- *St&PR 93, WhoAm 92*
Ehmann, David Benedict 1937- *St&PR 93*
Ehmann, Frank A. 1933- *St&PR 93, WhoAm 92*
Ehmann, Nancy Gallagher 1932- *WhoSSW 93*
Ehmann, Wilhelm 1904-1989 *Baker 92*
Ehmann, William Donald 1931- *WhoAm 92, WhoSSW 93*
Ehmer, Marjy Arduina Niccoll 1927- *WhoE 93*
Ehmke, Gilbert F. 1959- *St&PR 93*
Ehnholm, Christian 1939- *WhoScE 91-4*
Ehntholt, Daniel James 1945- *WhoE 93*
Ehpremidis, Charalambos 1927- *WhoScE 91-3*
Ehramjian, Vartkes Hagop 1932- *WhoAm 92*
Ehre, Edward 1905-1990 *BioIn 17*
Ehre, Victor Tyndall 1913- *St&PR 93, WhoAm 92*
Ehren, Charles Alexander, Jr. 1932- *WhoAm 92*
Ehren, Dennis Randolph 1950- *WhoEmL 93*
Ehren, James Bernard 1946- *St&PR 93*
Ehrenberg, Carl (Emil Theodor) 1878-1962 *Baker 92*
Ehrenberg, Edward 1930- *St&PR 93, WhoAm 92*
Ehrenberg, Miriam Colbert 1930- *WhoE 93*
Ehrenberg, Robert John 1953- *WhoEmL 93*
Ehrenburg, Ann Eleanor 1943- *WhoAmW 93*
Ehrendorfer, Friedrich 1927- *WhoScE 91-4*
Ehrenfeld, David *ScF&FL 92*
Ehrenfeld, David William 1938- *WhoAm 92*
Ehrenfeld, John Henry 1917- *WhoAm 92*
Ehrenfeld, John Roos 1931- *WhoE 93*
Ehrenfeld, Phyllis Rhoda 1932- *WhoE 93*
Ehrenfried, Albert D. 1922- *St&PR 93*
Ehrenhaft, Johann Leo 1915- *WhoAm 92*
Ehrenhaft, Peter David 1933- *WhoAm 92*
Ehrenkrantz, David 1952- *WhoE 93*
Ehrenkranz, Gil *Law&B 92*
Ehrenkranz, Shirley Malakoff 1920- *WhoAm 92, WhoAmW 93*
Ehrenpreis, Diane Carlberg 1957- *WhoAmW 93*
Ehrenpreis, Seymour 1927- *WhoAm 92*
Ehrenreich, Barbara *BioIn 17*
Ehrenreich, Barbara 1941- *ConAu 37NR, WhoAm 92*
Ehrenreich, Henry 1928- *WhoAm 92*
Ehrensberger, Charles J. 1923- *St&PR 93*
Ehrensberger, Ray 1904- *WhoAm 92*
Ehrenstein, Gottried W. 1937- *WhoScE 91-3*
Ehrenstrom, James William 1936- *St&PR 93*
Ehrensvard, Karl August 1745-1800 *HarEnMi*
Ehrenwerth, David Harry 1947- *WhoEmL 93*
Ehresman, Paula Suzette 1951- *WhoAmW 93*
Ehrgood, Pauline Anne Worrilow 1924- *WhoAmW 93*
Ehrgood, Thomas A., Jr. *Law&B 92*
Ehrhardt, Dietmar 1951- *WhoWor 93*
Ehrhardt, Eleanor *ScF&FL 92*
Ehrhardt, Laurence White 1940- *St&PR 93*
Ehrhardt, Robert W. 1942- *St&PR 93*
Ehrhardt, Thomas Andrew 1961- *WhoEmL 93*
Ehrhart, Carl Yarkers 1918- *WhoAm 92*
Ehrhart, Daniel Diehl 1929- *St&PR 93*
Ehrhart, Laura Gerdes 1962- *WhoAmW 93*
Ehrhart, William Daniel 1948- *WhoWrEP 92*
Ehrhorn, Richard William 1934- *WhoAm 92*
Ehrich, Fredric F. 1928- *WhoAm 92*
Ehrich, Marion 1945- *WhoSSW 93*
Ehrich, Wulf 1926- *WhoScE 91-3*
Ehrig, Hartmut 1944- *WhoWor 93*
Ehringer, Ann Graham 1938- *WhoAmW 93*
Ehrlacher, Alain 1952- *WhoScE 91-2*
Ehrle, Roy W. 1928- *WhoIns 93*
Ehrlenspiel, Klaus 1930- *WhoScE 91-3*
Ehrler, H. Whit 1941- *St&PR 93*
Ehrlich, Abel 1915- *Baker 92*
Ehrlich, Alvin McIntyre 1950- *WhoEmL 93*
Ehrlich, Amy 1942- *BioIn 17, WhoAm 92*
Ehrlich, Ava 1950- *WhoAmW 93*
Ehrlich, Bernard Herbert 1927- *WhoAm 92*
Ehrlich, Burtt R. 1939- *St&PR 93*
Ehrlich, Charles Edward 1969- *WhoE 93*
Ehrlich, Clarence Eugene 1938- *WhoAm 92*
Ehrlich, Clifford John 1938- *St&PR 93, WhoAm 92*
Ehrlich, Daniel Jacob 1951- *WhoAm 92*
Ehrlich, Danuta 1931- *WhoAmW 93*
Ehrlich, Donald J. *St&PR 93*
Ehrlich, Douglas D. *Law&B 92*
Ehrlich, Elma C. *AmWomPl*
Ehrlich, Evelyn Joan 1950- *WhoEmL 93*
Ehrlich, Everett Michael 1950- *St&PR 93, WhoAm 92*
Ehrlich, Frederick 1932- *WhoWor 93*
Ehrlich, George Edward 1928- *WhoAm 92, WhoE 93*
Ehrlich, Geraldine Elizabeth 1939- *WhoAmW 93, WhoWor 93*
Ehrlich, Gert 1926- *WhoAm 92*
Ehrlich, Gertrude 1923- *WhoAm 92*
Ehrlich, Grant Conklin 1916- *WhoAm 92*
Ehrlich, (Karl) Heinrich (Alfred) 1822-1899 *Baker 92*
Ehrlich, Henry Louis *Law&B 92*
Ehrlich, Ida Lublenski 1886- *AmWomPl*
Ehrlich, Ira Robert 1926- *WhoAm 92*
Ehrlich, Jerrold I. *Law&B 92*
Ehrlich, Karen Lynn *Law&B 92*
Ehrlich, Kenneth Craig 1943- *WhoSSW 93*
Ehrlich, Kingston W. 1914- *St&PR 93*
Ehrlich, Margaret Elizabeth Gorley 1950- *WhoAmW 93*
Ehrlich, Max 1909-1983 *ScF&FL 92*
Ehrlich, Morton 1934- *WhoAm 92*
Ehrlich, Nathan d1991 *BioIn 17*
Ehrlich, Paul 1923- *WhoAm 92*
Ehrlich, Paul Ewing 1948- *WhoSSW 93*
Ehrlich, Paul R. *BioIn 17*
Ehrlich, Paul Ralph 1932- *WhoAm 92*
Ehrlich, Phyllis L. 1952- *WhoAmW 93*
Ehrlich, Raymond 1918- *WhoAm 92*
Ehrlich, Richard 1924- *WhoAm 92*
Ehrlich, Robert R. 1908- *St&PR 93*
Ehrlich, Robert Stark 1940- *WhoE 93*
Ehrlich, Saul Paul, Jr. 1932- *WhoAm 92*
Ehrlich, Stephen Jeffrey 1943- *WhoSSW 93*
Ehrlich, Thomas 1934- *WhoAm 92, WhoWor 93*
Ehrlich, Vivian Fenster 1942- *WhoAm 92*
Ehrlicher, Thomas G. 1947- *St&PR 93*
Ehrlichman, Howard 1944- *WhoE 93*
Ehrlichman, John Daniel 1925- *WhoAm 92, WhoWrEP 92*
Ehrling, Robert Francis 1939- *St&PR 93*
Ehrling, Sixten 1918- *WhoAm 92, WhoE 93*
Ehrling, (Evert) Sixten 1918- *Baker 92*
Ehrman, Joachim Benedict 1929- *WhoAm 92*
Ehrman, Joseph S. 1931- *WhoAm 92*
Ehrman, Lee 1935- *WhoAm 92, WhoAmW 93*
Ehrman, Madeline Elizabeth 1942- *WhoAmW 93*
Ehrman, Samuel K. 1943- *St&PR 93*
Ehrmann, Alexander 1926- *St&PR 93*
Ehrmann, Bess *AmWomPl*
Ehrmann, Thomas William 1935- *WhoAm 92*
Ehrnrooth, Robert Goran 1939- *WhoWor 93*
Ehrnschwender, Arthur R. 1922- *St&PR 93*
Ehrnschwender, Arthur Robert 1922- *WhoAm 92*
Ehrnst, Craig Francis 1964- *WhoEmL 93*
Ei, Susan Michelle 1952- *WhoEmL 93*
Eibel, Andrew H. 1950- *WhoE 93*
Eiben, Robert Michael 1922- *WhoAm 92*
Eibenschutz, Jose 1872-1952 *Baker 92*
Eiberger, Carl Frederick 1931- *WhoAm 92*
Eibl-Eibesfeldt, Irenaus 1928- *WhoScE 91-3, WhoWor 93*
Eich, Eckart 1938- *WhoScE 91-3*
Eich, Gunter 1907-1972 *DcLB 124 [port]*
Eich, Margaret Holder 1948- *WhoEmL 93, WhoSSW 93*
Eich, Ronald B. 1948- *St&PR 93*
Eichacker, George 1930- *St&PR 93*
Eichbauer, Paul R. *Law&B 92*
Eichberg, Joseph 1906- *St&PR 93*
Eichberg, Julius 1824-1893 *Baker 92*
Eichborn, Hermann 1847-1918 *Baker 92*
Eichel, Beverly Anne 1946- *WhoAmW 93*
Eichel, Leslie P. *AmWomPl*
Eichel, Paul Martin 1932- *St&PR 93*
Eichel, Roger Madison 1948- *St&PR 93*
Eichelberger, Brittany *BioIn 17*
Eichelberger, Charles Bell 1934- *WhoAm 92*
Eichelberger, Ethyl *BioIn 17*
Eichelberger, Martin *BioIn 17*
Eichelberger, R. Tony 1940- *WhoE 93*
Eichelberger, Robert John 1921- *WhoAm 92*
Eichelberger, Robert Lawrence 1886-1961 *HarEnMi*
Eichelman, Burr Simmons, Jr. 1943- *WhoAm 92, WhoE 93*
Eichelman, Sarah Moreman 1952- *WhoEmL 93, WhoSSW 93*
Eichenbaum, Andrew Charles 1962- *St&PR 93*
Eichenbaum, Bernard 1924- *St&PR 93*
Eichenberg, Fritz 1901-1990 *BioIn 17, MajAI [port]*
Eichenberger, Gerhard 1939- *WhoScE 91-4*
Eichenberger, Mark d1991 *BioIn 17*
Eichendorff, Joseph, Freiherr von 1788-1857 *BioIn 17*
Eichenfield, Samuel 1937- *St&PR 93*
Eichenlaub, Janet M. *Law&B 92*
Eichenwald, Heinz Felix 1926- *WhoAm 92*
Eicher, Carol Susan 1958- *WhoAmW 93*
Eicher, George John 1916- *WhoAm 92*
Eicher, Joanne Bubolz 1930- *WhoAm 92*
Eicher, Lawrence Dean 1938- *WhoUN 92*
Eicher, Roma Jean 1942- *WhoWor 93*
Eichfeld, Timothy Joseph 1946- *WhoEmL 93*
Eichheim, Henry 1870-1942 *Baker 92*
Eichhold, Louis B. 1943- *St&PR 93*
Eichholz, Geoffrey Gunther 1920- *WhoAm 92*
Eichhorn, Arthur David 1953- *WhoEmL 93*
Eichhorn, Bradford Reese 1954- *WhoEmL 93*
Eichhorn, Frederick Foltz, Jr. 1930- *WhoAm 92*
Eichhorn, Gerhard Walter 1925- *WhoScE 91-3*
Eichhorn, Gunther Louis 1927- *WhoAm 92*
Eichhorn, Heinrich Karl 1927- *WhoAm 92, WhoSSW 93*
Eichhorn, Jurgen 1942- *WhoWor 93*
Eichhorn, Kurt (Peter) 1908- *Baker 92*
Eichhorn, Siegfried 1923- *WhoScE 91-3*
Eichinger, Marilynne H. *WhoAm 92, WhoAmW 93*
Eichleay, John William, Jr. 1946- *St&PR 93*
Eichler, Frank Martin *Law&B 92*
Eichler, Franklin Roosevelt 1933- *St&PR 93, WhoAm 92*
Eichler, Fred Sheldon 1948- *St&PR 93*
Eichler, John Alfred *Law&B 92*
Eichler, Jurgen 1942- *WhoWor 93*
Eichler, Ralph Alexander 1947- *WhoWor 93*
Eichler, Richard Samuel 1931- *St&PR 93*
Eichler, Thomas P. 1944- *WhoAm 92*
Eichler, Tyrrell Burton, Jr. 1934- *St&PR 93*
Eichling, Mary Tourond 1947- *WhoAmW 93, WhoEmL 93*
Eichman, Dale Bruce 1953- *WhoEmL 93*
Eichman, Russell John 1936- *St&PR 93*
Eichmann, Adolf 1906-1962 *BioIn 17*
Eichmann, Grace Shull *AmWomPl*
Eichmann, Karl Adolf 1906-1962 *DcTwHis*
Eichmann, Klaus 1939- *WhoScE 91-3*
Eichner, Alfred S. 1937-1988 *BioIn 17*
Eichner, Barbara J. d1991 *BioIn 17*
Eichner, Ernst (Dieterich Adolph) 1740-1777 *Baker 92*
Eichner, F. Karl 1926- *WhoScE 91-3*
Eichner, Hans 1921- *WhoAm 92*
Eichner, Henry M. 1910-1971 *ScF&FL 92*
Eichner, Ira A. 1931- *St&PR 93*
Eichner, L. John 1921- *St&PR 93*
Eichner, Patrick Ramsey 1960- *WhoE 93*
Eichold, Samuel 1916- *WhoAm 92*
Eichorn, Hermann von 1848-1918 *HarEnMi*
Eichorn, John F.G., Jr. 1924- *St&PR 93*
Eichorn, John Frederick Gerard, Jr. 1924- *WhoAm 92*
Eichorst, Terry Alan 1948- *WhoSSW 93*
Eichstadt, Craig Martin 1951- *WhoEmL 93*
Eichstadt, Frank Thomas 1956- *WhoSSW 93*
Eichstadt, Hermann Werner 1948- *WhoWor 93*
Eick, James E. 1937- *WhoIns 93*
Eickelberg, W. Warren Barbour 1925- *WhoE 93*
Eickhoff, Dennis R. 1944- *St&PR 93*
Eickhoff, Dennis Raymond 1944- *WhoAm 92*
Eickhoff, Ekkehard 1927- *WhoWor 93*
Eickhoff, Harold Walter 1928- *WhoAm 92, WhoE 93*
Eickhoff, Janie *BioIn 17*
Eickhoff, Leo E., Jr. *Law&B 92*
Eickhoff, Theodore Carl 1931- *WhoAm 92*
Eickleberg, John Edwin 1944- *WhoAm 92*
Eickman, Jennifer Lynn 1946- *WhoAmW 93*
Eickmann, Kenneth Elmer 1945- *WhoAm 92*
Eickoff, Margaret Kathyrn 1939- *WhoE 93*
Eid, Gordon L. *Law&B 92*
Eid, Steven Allen 1950- *WhoEmL 93*
Eid, Yousef Raffoul 1945- *WhoWor 93*
Eide, Craig Donald 1949- *WhoEmL 93*
Eide, Geir Egil 1951- *WhoWor 93*
Eide, Marlene 1932- *WhoAmW 93*

Eide, Melvin O. 1930- *St&PR 93*
Eide, Michael L. *St&PR 93*
Eide, Randolph S. *Law&B 92*
Eidelhoch, Lester Philip 1932- *WhoE 93*
Eidell, Ronald George 1944- *WhoAm 92*
Eidelman, David Robert 1944- *St&PR 93*
Eidelman, Gene 1958- *WhoEmL 93*
Eidelson, Sam 1920- *St&PR 93*
Eidenire, Charles William 1939- *WhoSSW 93*
Eidenshink, Carla Kay 1959- *WhoEmL 93*
Eidlin, Fred Howard 1942- *WhoWor 93*
Eidsmoe, John 1945- *ConAu 40NR*
Eidsmoe, Pamela Kaye *Law&B 92*
Eidson, Louise Beaulieu 1959- *WhoAmW 93*
Eidson, Thomas E. 1944- *WhoAm 92*
Eidson, Walter J., Jr. *Law&B 92*
Eidson, William Whelan 1935- *WhoAm 92*
Eidt, C.M., Jr. 1935- *St&PR 93*
Eidt, Clarence Martin, Jr. 1935- *WhoAm 92*
Eidus, Robert 1948- *WhoEmL 93*
Eielson, Jorge Eduardo 1924- *SpAmA*
Eiesland, Mark Leon 1952- *WhoEmL 93*
Eiferman, Sharon Rees 1948- *WhoWrEP 92*
Eifert, Donald A. 1929- *WhoIns 93*
Eiff, Hansjoerg Hugo 1933- *WhoWor 93*
Eiffert, Jack Warden 1921- *St&PR 93*
Eiffler-Orton, Carol Ann 1948- *WhoEmL 93*
Eifler, Carl Frederick 1906- *WhoWor 93*
Eifler, Carl Morgan 1948- *St&PR 93*
Eifrig, David Eric 1935- *WhoAm 92*
Eig, Lisa Wendy 1959- *WhoAmW 93*
Eig, Norman 1941- *WhoAm 92*
Eige, Lillian E. 1915- *BioIn 17*
Eige, (Elizabeth) Lillian 1915- *ConAu 136*
Eigel, Edwin George, Jr. 1932- *WhoAm 92*
Eigel, Marcia Duffy 1936- *WhoAmW 93*
Eigen, Barbara Helen 1945- *WhoAmW 93*
Eigen, Howard 1942- *WhoAm 92*
Eigen, Manfred 1927- *WhoAm 92, WhoScE 91-3, WhoWor 93*
Eigen, Michael 1936- *ConAu 39NR, WhoE 93*
Eigenberger, Gerhart 1939- *WhoScE 91-3*
Eiger, Richard William 1933- *WhoAm 92, WhoE 93*
Eighmey, Douglas Joseph, Jr. 1946- *WhoAm 92, WhoEmL 93, WhoSSW 93*
Eigl, Christian 1943- *WhoUN 92*
Eigler, Donald M. *BioIn 17*
Eigles, William P. *Law&B 92*
Eigner, William Whitling 1959- *WhoEmL 93*
Eigo, Joe 1957- *BioIn 17*
Eigsti, Roger Harry 1942- *St&PR 93, WhoAm 92*
Eihusen, Virgil R. 1930- *WhoAm 92*
Eijken, Jan Albert van *Baker 92*
Eijkman, E.G.J. 1928- *WhoScE 91-3*
Eijkman, Paul Felix Willibrord 1962- *WhoWor 93*
Eijsvoogel, V.P. *WhoScE 91-3*
Eike, Linda 1943- *St&PR 93*
Eikel, Werner 1928- *BioIn 17*
Eikelberger, Rand Jaffrey 1947- *St&PR 93*
Eikenberry, Arthur Raymond 1920- *WhoWor 93, WhoWrEP 92*
Eikenberry, Ching Yuan 1947- *WhoAmW 93, WhoEmL 93, WhoWor 93*
Eikenberry, Jill *BioIn 17*
Eikenberry, Jill 1947- *WhoAm 92*
Eikenberry, Kenneth Otto 1932- *WhoAm 92*
Eikenberry, Michael J. 1941- *St&PR 93*
Eikeri, Oddvar 1936- *WhoScE 91-4*
Eikermann, Ruth Ann 1921- *WhoAmW 93*
Eil, Charles 1946- *WhoE 93*
Eiland, Finn 1947- *WhoScE 91-2*
Eiland, Gary Wayne 1951- *WhoEmL 93*
Eilbeck, John Christopher *WhoScE 91-1*
Eilber, Warren S. 1927- *St&PR 93*
Eilbracht, Lee Paul 1924- *WhoAm 92*
Eilen, Howard Scott 1954- *WhoEmL 93*
Eilenberg, Lawrence Ira 1947- *WhoWor 93*
Eilenberg, Matthew L. 1958- *WhoEmL 93*
Eilenberg, Samuel 1913- *WhoAm 92*
Eilenberger, Bruce F. 1947- *St&PR 93*
Eilenberger, Gert 1936- *WhoScE 91-3*
Eilenfeldt, Cecelia Rae 1953- *WhoSSW 93*
Eiler, G. Roger 1944- *WhoIns 93*
Eiler, James W. 1951- *St&PR 93*
Eilerman, Betty Jean 1942- *WhoAmW 93, WhoWor 93*
Eilers, Albert 1830-1896 *Baker 92*
Eilers, Robert *ScF&FL 92*
Eilers, Robert Paul 1949- *WhoE 93*
Eilers, Sally 1908-1978 *SweetSg C [port]*
Eilers, Warner William 1936- *St&PR 93*
Eilertsen, Anita 1950- *WhoAmW 93*
Eils, Richard George 1937- *St&PR 93, WhoAm 92*
Eilts, Hermann Frederick 1922- *WhoAm 92*
Eilts, Karin Lynn 1956- *WhoWrEP 92*
Eilts, Michael Dean 1959- *WhoSSW 93*
Eilts, Susanne Elizabeth 1955- *WhoAmW 93*
Eimer, Gerhard Werner Karl 1928- *WhoWor 93*
Eimert, (Eugen Otto) Herbert 1897-1972 *Baker 92*
Eimicke, Robert C. *Law&B 92*
Eimicke, Victor William 1925- *WhoAm 92, WhoE 93*
Eimon, Perry Leroy 1933- *WhoE 93*
Ein, Daniel 1938- *WhoE 93*
Ein, Melvin Bennett 1932- *WhoAm 92*
Einaga, Hisahiko 1936- *WhoWor 93*
Einaga, Yoshiyuki 1945- *WhoWor 93*
Einarsson, Bo Gustaf 1939- *WhoWor 93*
Einarsson, Eythor 1929- *WhoScE 91-4*
Einarsson, Gretar 1940- *WhoScE 91-4*
Einarsson, Stig G. 1940- *WhoScE 91-4*
Einasto, Jaan 1929- *WhoWor 93*
Einaudi, Marco Tullio 1939- *WhoAm 92*
Einbender, Alvin H. 1929- *WhoAm 92*
Einbender, Alvin Herbert 1929- *St&PR 93*
Einbond, Bernard Lionel 1937- *WhoWrEP 92*
Einbrodt, Hans Joachim 1927- *WhoScE 91-3*
Einck, Dean Robert 1957- *WhoEmL 93*
Einem, Gottfried von 1918- *Baker 92, IntDcOp, OxDcOp*
Einem, Karl von 1853-1934 *HarEnMi*
Einer-Jensen, Niels 1936- *WhoUN 92*
Einfalt, Linda Mary 1950- *WhoAmW 93*
Einhorn, Alan S. *Law&B 92*
Einhorn, David Allen 1961- *WhoE 93, WhoEmL 93, WhoWor 93*
Einhorn, Edward Martin 1936- *WhoAm 92*
Einhorn, Eric John 1948- *WhoAm 92*
Einhorn, Harold *Law&B 92*
Einhorn, Harold 1929- *WhoE 93*
Einhorn, Lawrence Henry 1942- *WhoAm 92*
Einhorn, Marcel *St&PR 93*
Einhorn, Steven Gary 1948- *WhoAm 92*
Einiger, Carol Blum 1949- *WhoAm 92*
Einiger, Roger William 1947- *St&PR 93*
Einoder, Camille Elizabeth 1937- *WhoAmW 93*
Einschlag, Michael Barry *Law&B 92*
Einsfalt, Melinda D. 1961- *WhoAmW 93*
Einspanier, Laura Ann *Law&B 92*
Einspruch, Burton Cyril 1935- *WhoWor 93*
Einspruch, Norman Gerald 1932- *WhoAm 92, WhoSSW 93*
Einstein, Albert 1879-1955 *BioIn 17, ConHero 2 [port], DcTwHis, JeAmHC*
Einstein, Albert 1947- *ConAu 37NR*
Einstein, Alfred 1880-1952 *Baker 92*
Einstein, Arthur William, Jr. 1933- *WhoAm 92*
Einstein, Clifford Jay 1939- *WhoAm 92*
Einstein, Jaime *Law&B 92*
Einstein, Karl d1991 *BioIn 17*
Einstein, Margery A. 1943- *WhoAm 92*
Einstein, Robert *Law&B 92*
Einstein, Stephen Jan 1945- *WhoWor 93*
Einstein, Ted d1992 *NewYTBS 92*
Einstein, Theodore Lee 1947- *WhoE 93*
Einstein, Xavier *ScF&FL 92*
Einstein-Maric, Mileva 1875-1948 *BioIn 17*
Einsweiler, Robert Charles 1929- *WhoAm 92, WhoWor 93*
Einzig, Barbara Ellen 1951- *WhoWrEP 92*
Eipper, Michael G. 1950- *St&PR 93*
Eirich, Frederick Roland 1905- *WhoAm 92*
Eiriksdottir, Karolina 1951- *Baker 92*
Eisaman, Josiah Reamer, III 1924- *WhoAm 92*
Eisberg, James Stephen 1938- *St&PR 93*
Eisberg, Robert Martin 1928- *WhoAm 92*
Eisch, John Joseph 1930- *WhoAm 92, WhoE 93*
Eischeid, Theodore Joseph 1950- *St&PR 93*
Eischen, Michael Hugh 1931- *WhoAm 92*
Eisdell, Anton Hubert Mortimer 1945- *WhoWor 93*
Eisdorfer, Carl 1930- *WhoAm 92*
Eisel, Jean Ellen 1946- *WhoAmW 93*
Eisele, Edward Harrison, III 1941- *WhoAm 92*
Eisele, Garnett Thomas 1923- *WhoAm 92, WhoSSW 93*
Eisele, John Allan 1929- *WhoWor 93*
Eisele, John Evans 1940- *WhoSSW 93*
Eisele, John William 1952- *WhoSSW 93*
Eisele, Robert Henry 1948- *WhoEmL 93*
Eisele, William David 1927- *WhoSSW 93*
Eiselen, Elizabeth *BioIn 17*
Eiseley, Loren C. 1907-1977 *BioIn 17, IntDcAn*
Eiselstein, June 1949- *WhoAmW 93*
Eiseman, Alan J. *St&PR 93*
Eiseman, Barbara Ann 1955- *St&PR 93*
Eiseman, Neal Martin 1955- *WhoEmL 93*
Eisemann, Alexander, Jr. 1924- *St&PR 93*
Eisen, Armand 1952- *ScF&FL 92*
Eisen, Edwin Otto 1940- *WhoSSW 93*
Eisen, Frederick 1930- *WhoAm 92*
Eisen, Gary D. *Law&B 92*
Eisen, Harold M. 1932- *St&PR 93*
Eisen, Henry 1921- *WhoAm 92*
Eisen, Herman Nathaniel 1918- *WhoAm 92*
Eisen, Irving M. 1927- *St&PR 93*
Eisen, Jay Loeb 1957- *St&PR 93*
Eisen, Lawrence Edward 1944- *St&PR 93*
Eisen, Leonard 1934- *St&PR 93, WhoAm 92*
Eisen, Marlene Ruth 1931- *WhoAmW 93*
Eisen, Morton d1990 *BioIn 17*
Eisen, Rebecca Dianne 1949- *WhoEmL 93*
Eisen, Roland 1941- *WhoWor 93*
Eisen, Ruth Ilene *Law&B 92*
Eisen, Steven Jeffrey 1958- *WhoEmL 93*
Eisen, Stuart Terry 1952- *WhoE 93*
Eisenacher, Craig E. 1947- *St&PR 93, WhoIns 93*
Eisenbarth, Gary L. 1947- *WhoIns 93*
Eisenbarth, Gary Lee 1947- *St&PR 93*
Eisenbeis, Robert A. 1941- *WhoAm 92*
Eisenbeiss, William Curran 1942- *St&PR 93*
Eisenberg, Adi 1935- *WhoAm 92*
Eisenberg, Alan 1935- *WhoAm 92*
Eisenberg, Alan David 1942- *WhoE 93*
Eisenberg, Alan I. 1950- *St&PR 93*
Eisenberg, Albert Joel 1925- *St&PR 93*
Eisenberg, Amy Marcie 1956- *WhoEmL 93*
Eisenberg, Anne Mendel 1942- *WhoE 93*
Eisenberg, Arlene *ConAu 139*
Eisenberg, Barbara Anne K. 1945- *WhoAm 92*
Eisenberg, Barbara K. *Law&B 92*
Eisenberg, Bertram William 1930- *WhoE 93*
Eisenberg, Carola 1917- *WhoAmW 93*
Eisenberg, Daniel Bruce 1946- *WhoSSW 93*
Eisenberg, David Henry 1936- *St&PR 93, WhoAm 92*
Eisenberg, David M. *Law&B 92*
Eisenberg, David M. 1950- *St&PR 93*
Eisenberg, David Samuel 1939- *WhoAm 92*
Eisenberg, Dorothy 1929- *WhoAmW 93*
Eisenberg, George Henry Gilbert, Jr. 1940- *WhoE 93*
Eisenberg, George T. 1926- *St&PR 93*
Eisenberg, Harry Victor 1945- *WhoSSW 93*
Eisenberg, Harve 1935- *St&PR 93*
Eisenberg, Harvey Ellis 1949- *WhoEmL 93*
Eisenberg, Howard Bruce 1946- *WhoEmL 93*
Eisenberg, Howard Edward 1946- *WhoE 93, WhoWor 93*
Eisenberg, James 1930- *St&PR 93*
Eisenberg, Jeffrey S. 1958- *WhoEmL 93*
Eisenberg, Joe Davidson 1920- *St&PR 93*
Eisenberg, John Meyer 1946- *WhoAm 92*
Eisenberg, Joseph Martin 1944- *WhoE 93, WhoWor 93*
Eisenberg, Karen Sue Byer 1954- *WhoAmW 93, WhoEmL 93*
Eisenberg, Larry H. 1952- *WhoEmL 93*
Eisenberg, Lawrence B. *ScF&FL 92*
Eisenberg, Lee B. 1946- *WhoAm 92, WhoE 93*
Eisenberg, Leon 1922- *WhoAm 92*
Eisenberg, Lewis M. *BioIn 17*
Eisenberg, Manuel 1946- *ScF&FL 92*
Eisenberg, Marlene McGregor *Law&B 92*
Eisenberg, Marvin 1922- *WhoAm 92*
Eisenberg, Maurice 1900-1972 *Baker 92*
Eisenberg, Melvin 1929- *St&PR 93*
Eisenberg, Melvin A. 1934- *WhoAm 92*
Eisenberg, Meyer 1931- *WhoAm 92*
Eisenberg, Morris 1921- *WhoAm 92*
Eisenberg, Murray 1939- *WhoE 93*
Eisenberg, Peter A. 1932- *St&PR 93*
Eisenberg, Philip *Law&B 92*
Eisenberg, Philip Guy *Law&B 92*
Eisenberg, R. Neal 1936- *WhoE 93, WhoWor 93*
Eisenberg, Richard K. 1944- *St&PR 93*
Eisenberg, Richard M. 1942- *WhoAm 92*
Eisenberg, Richard S. 1943- *WhoAm 92*
Eisenberg, Robert Shin 1942- *WhoAm 92*
Eisenberg, Robin Ledgin 1951- *WhoAmW 93, WhoEmL 93*
Eisenberg, Ronald Lee 1941- *St&PR 93*
Eisenberg, Ruth F. 1927- *WhoAmW 93*
Eisenberg, Sonja Miriam 1926- *WhoAm 92, WhoAmW 93*
Eisenberg, Stanley d1990 *BioIn 17*
Eisenberg, Steven Allen 1947- *St&PR 93*
Eisenberg, Steven Dale 1958- *WhoEmL 93*
Eisenberg, Steven E. 1958- *St&PR 93*
Eisenberg, Theodore 1947- *WhoAm 92*
Eisenberg, Viviane *Law&B 92*
Eisenberger, Gary D. 1934- *St&PR 93*
Eisenberger, Mario Alfredo 1949- *WhoE 93, WhoEmL 93*
Eisenberger, Robert Alan 1958- *WhoEmL 93*
Eisenberger, Severin 1879-1945 *Baker 92*
Eisenbraun, Doreen Karen 1942- *WhoAmW 93*
Eisenbraun, Eric Charles 1955- *WhoEmL 93*
Eisenbraun, Robert Alfred 1928- *St&PR 93*
Eisenbud, David 1947- *WhoE 93*
Eisenbud, Merril *BioIn 17*
Eisenbud, Merril 1915- *WhoAm 92*
Eisendrath, Blanche Goodman *AmWomPl*
Eisendrath, Charles *BioIn 17*
Eisendrath, Henri B. 1939- *WhoScE 91-2*
Eisenhardt, Roy 1939- *WhoAm 92*
Eisenhart, Blake H. 1952- *St&PR 93*
Eisenhart, Edna Jane 1922- *WhoAmW 93*
Eisenhart, Margaret Ann 1950- *WhoAmW 93*
Eisenhart, Martin P. *St&PR 93*
Eisenhart, S. Forry, Jr. 1950- *St&PR 93*
Eisenhauer, Linda Ann 1937- *WhoAmW 93*
Eisenhauer, Steven M. *Law&B 92*
Eisenhauer, Thomas Walter 1936- *St&PR 93*
Eisenhauer, Wayne Harold 1949- *WhoEmL 93*
Eisenhauer, William Joseph 1934- *St&PR 93*
Eisenhower, Dwight D. *DcCPCAm*
Eisenhower, Dwight D. 1890-1969 *BioIn 17, ColdWar 1 [port], PolPar*
Eisenhower, Dwight David 1890-1969 *CmdGen 1991 [port], DcTwHis, HarEnMi*
Eisenhower, Jean Ann 1952- *WhoEmL 93*
Eisenhower, John S.D. 1922- *BioIn 17*
Eisenhower, John Sheldon Doud 1922- *WhoAm 92*
Eisenhower, Mamie Doud 1896-1979 *BioIn 17*
Eisenhower, Susan *BioIn 17*
Eisenkramer, Charles C. 1937- *St&PR 93*
Eisenlohr, David L. 1954- *St&PR 93*
Eisenlohr, Mike J. 1955- *St&PR 93*
Eisenman, Alvin 1921- *WhoAm 92*
Eisenman, Peter 1932- *BioIn 17, News 92 [port]*
Eisenman, Peter David 1932- *WhoAm 92*
Eisenman, Russell 1940- *WhoSSW 93*
Eisenman, Selma Tamber d1991 *BioIn 17*
Eisenman, Steven Alexis *Law&B 92*
Eisenman, Trudy Fox 1940- *WhoAm 92, WhoAmW 93*
Eisenmann, I. Roberto, Jr. 1937- *WhoWor 93*
Eisenmann, James R. 1941- *St&PR 93*
Eisenmann, Josef 1928- *WhoWor 93*
Eisenmann, Olivier Daphnis 1940- *WhoWor 93*
Eisenmann, Roberto *BioIn 17*
Eisenmenger, Robert Waltz 1926- *St&PR 93*
Eisenpreis, Alfred 1924- *WhoAm 92*
Eisenreich, David L. 1943- *St&PR 93*
Eisenreich, Gunther Alfred 1933- *WhoWor 93*
Eisenschiml, Nancy *Law&B 92*
Eisenshtat, Sidney Herbert 1914- *WhoAm 92*
Eisenstadt, Abraham S. 1920- *WhoAm 92*
Eisenstadt, Arlene Ellen 1954- *WhoEmL 93*
Eisenstadt, Debbie Miriam 1951- *WhoEmL 93*
Eisenstadt, G. Michael 1928- *WhoAm 92, WhoWor 93*
Eisenstadt, Jill *BioIn 17*
Eisenstadt, Pauline Doreen Bauman 1938- *WhoAmW 93*
Eisenstadt, Raymond 1921- *WhoE 93*
Eisenstadt, Samuel 1922- *St&PR 93*
Eisenstaedt, Alfred *BioIn 17*
Eisenstaedt, Alfred 1898- *ModArCr 3 [port], WhoAm 92*
Eisenstaedt, Richard M. *Law&B 92*
Eisenstat, Albert A. 1930- *St&PR 93, WhoAm 92*
Eisenstein, Bruce Allan 1941- *WhoAm 92*
Eisenstein, Elizabeth Lewisohn 1923- *WhoAm 92*
Eisenstein, Hester 1940- *ConAu 137*
Eisenstein, Ira 1906- *JeAmHC*
Eisenstein, Laurence Jay 1960- *WhoEmL 93*
Eisenstein, Lois Peel *Law&B 92*

Eisenstein, Michael 1950- WhoEmL 93, WhoWor 93
Eisenstein, Naomi 1938- WhoAmW 93
Eisenstein, Paul Allan 1953- WhoWrEP 92
Eisenstein, Phyllis 1946- ScF&FL 92
Eisenstein, Sam 1936- WhoSSW 93
Eisenstein, Sergei 1898-1948 BioIn 17, MiSFD 9N
Eisenstein, Stephen Michael Fels WhoScE 91-1
Eisenstein, Theodore Donald 1930- WhoE 93, WhoWor 93
Eisenstein, Toby K. 1942- WhoAm 92
Eisenstodt, Joan L. BioIn 17
Eisenthal, Kenneth B. 1933- WhoAm 92
Eisenzimmer, Betty Wenner 1939- WhoAmW 93
Eiser, John Richard WhoScE 91-1
Eiserer, Leonard Albert Carl 1916- WhoAm 92, WhoE 93, WhoWor 93
Eiserer, Paul Emmanuel 1912- WhoSSW 93
Eiserling, Frederick Allen 1938- WhoAm 92
Eisert, Debra Claire 1952- WhoAm 92, WhoEmL 93
Eisert, Edward Gaver 1948- WhoEmL 93
Eisfeld, Theodor(e) 1816-1882 Baker 92
Eisinger, Peter Kendall 1942- WhoAm 92
Eisinger, Robert Peter 1929- WhoE 93
Eisler, Ann Olmsted 1954- WhoEmL 93
Eisler, Benita 1937- ConAu 136
Eisler, Colin Tobias 1931- WhoAm 92
Eisler, David 1955-1992 BioIn 17, NewYTBS 92 [port]
Eisler, Hanns 1898-1962 Baker 92
Eisler, Paul 1875-1951 Baker 92
Eisler, Paul 1907- BioIn 17
Eisler, Ronald 1932- WhoE 93
Eisler, Steven ScF&FL 92
Eisler, Susan Krawetz 1946- St&PR 93, WhoAm 92, WhoAmW 93
Eisley, Anthony 1925- BioIn 17
Eisma, Will (Leendert) 1929- Baker 92
Eisman, Esther 1950- WhoEmL 93
Eisman, Wayne Brook 1948- WhoE 93
Eismont, Diane S. Law&B 92
Eismont, Diane S. 1944- St&PR 93, WhoAm 92
Eisner, Alan M. 1939- St&PR 93
Eisner, Alan S. 1948- WhoAm 92, WhoE 93
Eisner, Alfred 1932- WhoE 93
Eisner, Carole Swid 1937- WhoE 93
Eisner, Elliot W. BioIn 17
Eisner, Georg Michael 1930- WhoWor 93
Eisner, Harvey Brian 1958- WhoEmL 93
Eisner, Henry W. 1920- St&PR 93
Eisner, Henry Wolfgang 1920- WhoAm 92
Eisner, Howard 1935- WhoAm 92, WhoE 93
Eisner, Janet Margaret 1940- WhoAm 92, WhoAmW 93
Eisner, Joel 1959- ScF&FL 92
Eisner, Joseph 1929- WhoE 93
Eisner, Leonard d1991 BioIn 17
Eisner, Lisa BioIn 17
Eisner, Michael 1942- BioIn 17
Eisner, Michael C. 1939- St&PR 93
Eisner, Michael D. 1942- ConTFT 10, St&PR 93
Eisner, Michael Dammann 1942- WhoAm 92, WhoWor 93
Eisner, Peter Norman 1950- WhoAm 92
Eisner, Robert 1922- WhoAm 92
Eisner, Seth A. Law&B 92
Eisner, Susanne Glock 1950- WhoEmL 93
Eisner, Thomas BioIn 17
Eisner, Thomas 1929- WhoAm 92
Eisner, Will 1917- WhoAm 92
Eisner, William Law&B 92
Eiss, David H. 1942- St&PR 93
Eissenstat, Eric Spencer 1958- WhoEmL 93
Eissler, Veda Alicia 1960- WhoAmW 93, WhoEmL 93
Eisuke, Ono 1935- WhoWor 93
Eiswerth, Barry Neil 1942- WhoAm 92
Eiszner, James R. 1927-1990 BioIn 17
Eiszner, James Richard, Jr. 1953- WhoEmL 93
Eitan, Raphael 1926- WhoWor 93
Eitan, Raphael 1929- BioIn 17
Eitel, Eric Vaughn 1964- WhoE 93
Eitel, John A., Jr. Law&B 92
Eitel, Karl Emil 1928- St&PR 93, WhoAm 92
Eiten, Geoffrey Joel 1950- WhoEmL 93
Eitler, Esteban 1913-1960 Baker 92
Eitner, Lorenz Edwin Alfred 1919- WhoAm 92
Eitner, Robert 1832-1905 Baker 92
Eitreim, Anthony C. Law&B 92
Eitz, Carl (Andreas) 1848-1924 Baker 92
Eitze, William Osborne 1961- St&PR 93
Eitzen, David Stanley 1934- WhoAm 92
Eizenberg, Michael 1947- WhoE 93
Eizenstat, Stuart E. 1943- WhoAm 92
Eizou, Yokoyama 1929- WhoWor 93
Ejima, Shusaku 1941- WhoWor 93
Ejiogu, Charles Nwanna 1934- WhoUN 92
Ejsmond, Julian 1892-1930 PolBiDi
Ejsymont, Jan 1934- WhoScE 91-4
Ejzak, Paul J. 1945- St&PR 93
Ek, Alan Ryan 1942- WhoAm 92
Ek, Brian Roy 1952- WhoE 93
Ek, Corneille S. 1926- WhoScE 91-2
Ek, Francine Antoinette 1927- WhoAmW 93
Ek, (Fritz) Gunnar (Rudolf) 1900-1981 Baker 92
Ek, Nils 1924- WhoScE 91-4
Ekandem, Dominic Ignatius Cardinal 1917- WhoWor 93
Ekberg, Anita 1931- BioIn 17
Ekberg, Carl Edwin, Jr. 1920- WhoAm 92
Ekberg, Delores June 1939- WhoWrEP 92
Ekberg, Jan G. 1940- WhoScE 91-4
Ekberg, Kent Francis 1947- WhoEmL 93
Ekblom, Harry Edward 1928- WhoAm 92
Ekdahl, Hans Gisel 1943- WhoWor 93
Ekdahl, Jon N. Law&B 92
Ekdale, Allan Anton 1946- WhoEmL 93
Eke, Istvan 1947- WhoScE 91-4
Ekedahl, David D. 1930- WhoAm 92
Ekedahl, James George 1946- St&PR 93
Ekeland, Arne Erling 1942- WhoWor 93
Ekeland, Brian J. 1959- WhoE 93
Ekelman, Daniel Louis 1926- WhoAm 92
Ekelof, Gunnar 1907-1968 BioIn 17
Ekelof, Tord Johan Carl 1945- WhoWor 93
Ekelund, Leif WhoScE 91-4
Ekenstierna, Harvey Scott 1935- WhoWor 93
Eker, Dorothy 1925- WhoWrEP 92
Ekern, Carl 1954-1990 BioIn 17
Ekern, George P. Law&B 92
Ekern, George Patrick 1931- St&PR 93, WhoAm 92
Ekernas, Sven Anders 1945- WhoAm 92
Ekesbo, Ingvar WhoScE 91-4
Ekeus, Rolf 1935- NewYTBS 92 [port]
Ekholm, Gordon F. 1909-1987 IntDcAn
Ekier, Jan (Stanislaw) 1913- Baker 92
Ekimov, Vyacheslav BioIn 17
Ekins, William George 1956- St&PR 93
Ekkers, C.L. WhoScE 91-3
Ekland, Britt 1942- BioIn 17
Ekland, Kirk Martin 1966- WhoSSW 93
Ekle, Thomas Charles 1951- St&PR 93, WhoEmL 93
Eklof, Svea Christine 1951- WhoAm 92
Eklund, Claudia Rieth 1951- WhoEmL 93
Eklund, Dan E. 1940- WhoScE 91-4
Eklund, Dean Robert 1957- WhoSSW 93
Eklund, Donald Arthur 1929- WhoAm 92
Eklund, Donald Bruce 1944- St&PR 93
Eklund, George J. 1943- St&PR 93
Eklund, Gordon 1945- BioIn 17, ScF&FL 92
Eklund, Gordon Stewart 1945- WhoWrEP 92
Eklund, Hans 1927- Baker 92
Eklund, K. Krister 1932- WhoScE 91-4
Eklund, Louis E., Jr. 1931- St&PR 93
Eklund, Maria Law&B 92
Eklund, Paul Joseph 1963- WhoEmL 93
Eklund, Reginald Ronald 1940- St&PR 93
Eklund, Robert Dunn 1953- WhoEmL 93
Eklund, Wayne O. d1991 BioIn 17
Ekman, Gershon Law&B 92
Ekman, Karl 1869-1947 Baker 92
Ekman, Lea Ann 1946- WhoEmL 93
Ekman, Linda AmWomPl
Ekman, Patricia Law&B 92
Ekman, Richard 1945- WhoAm 92
Ekman, Thomas Arthur 1957- WhoEmL 93
Ekong, Etim Samuel 1953- WhoE 93, WhoEmL 93
Ekra, Rene Vangha 1953- WhoWor 93
Ekrom, Roy Herbert 1929- WhoAm 92
Ekspong, A.G. 1922- WhoScE 91-4
Ekstract, Richard Evan 1931- WhoAm 92
Ekstrand, Bo 1949- WhoScE 91-4
Ekstrand, Bruce Rowland 1940- WhoAm 92
Ekstrand, Margaret Elizabeth 1952- WhoEmL 93
Ekstrom, Katina Bartsokas 1929- WhoAmW 93
Ekstrom, Molly Anne 1929- WhoWrEP 92
Ekstrom, Parmenia Migel 1908-1989 BioIn 17
Ekstrom, Robert Carl 1917- WhoWor 93
Ekstrom, Ruth Burt 1931- WhoAm 92, WhoAmW 93
Ekstrom, Walter F. 1927- WhoAm 92
Ekstrom, Walter F. 1937- St&PR 93
Ekstrom, William Ferdinand 1912- WhoAm 92
Ekuan, Kenji BioIn 17
Ekushov, Arkadiy Ivanovich 1956- WhoWor 93
Ekwensi, Cyprian 1921- BioIn 17, DcChlFi
Ekwensi, Cyprian (Odiatu Duaka) 1921- DcLB 117 [port]
Ekwueme, Alex Ifeanyichukwu 1932- WhoAfr
El, Yusuf Ali 1948- WhoWrEP 92
Ela, Erik 1957- WhoEmL 93
El-Achkar, Issam 1962- WhoE 93
Elad, Emanuel 1935- WhoAm 92
Elafros, Bernard 1927- St&PR 93
El-Agraa, Ali M. 1941- WhoWor 93
Elakovich, Stella Daisy 1945- WhoAmW 93
Elam, Albert Garland, II 1955- WhoEmL 93
Elam, Andrew Gregory, II 1932- WhoSSW 93
Elam, Fred Eldon 1937- WhoAm 92
Elam, Gene G. 1939- St&PR 93
Elam, Harper Johnston, III 1926- WhoAm 92
Elam, Jack Gordon 1921- WhoSSW 93
Elam, Joe 1931- St&PR 93
Elam, John Carlton 1924- WhoAm 92
Elam, Leslie Albert 1938- WhoAm 92, WhoE 93
Elam, Stanley Munson BioIn 17
Elam, W. Dale 1948- St&PR 93
Elamin, Abdelaziz 1955- WhoWor 93
Elangasekere, Chittaranjan Tilaksiri 1940- WhoWor 93
Elango, Mart 1936- WhoWor 93
El-Ansary, Adel Ibrahim 1941- WhoAm 92
El Araby, Kadri M. Gharib 1931- WhoUN 92
Elaraby, Nabil A. 1935- WhoUN 92
Elath, Eliahu 1903-1990 BioIn 17
El-Ayashy, Mamdouh Mahmoud 1954- WhoWor 93
Elayyan, Abdullah Ali 1946- WhoWor 93
Elbaek Jensen, Peder 1940- WhoScE 91-2
El-Banhawy, Mohamed Said 1935- WhoWor 93
Elbaradei, Mohamed Mostafa 1942- WhoUN 92
Elbaum, Charles 1926- WhoAm 92
Elbaz, Edgard Aaron 1937- WhoScE 91-2
El-Baz, Farouk BioIn 17
Elbee, Miss ConAu 139
Elbein, Richard Craig 1958- WhoSSW 93
Elberg, Dale Allen 1950- St&PR 93
Elberg, Darryl Gerald 1944- WhoAm 92
Elberg, Mitchell Law&B 92
Elberg, Sanford Samuel 1913- WhoAm 92
Elberger, Andrea June 1952- WhoSSW 93
Elberry, Zainab Abdelhaliem 1948- WhoEmL 93
Elberson, Elwood L. 1918- St&PR 93
Elberson, Robert E. 1928- St&PR 93
Elbert, Donnie SoulM
Elbert, James Peak 1937- WhoSSW 93
Elbert, Joanna M. WhoAmW 93
Elbert, Lisa Marie 1958- WhoEmL 93
Elbert, Thomas Rudolf WhoWor 93
Elbert, Tomas 1949- WhoScE 91-4
Elbery, Kathleen Marie 1959- WhoAmW 93, WhoEmL 93
Elbilia, Bruce David 1958- St&PR 93
Elbing, Alvar Oliver 1928- WhoWor 93
Elbing, Carol Jeppson 1930- WhoWor 93
Elbir, Suheyl WhoScE 91-4
Elble, Rodger Jacob 1948- WhoEmL 93
Elbling, Irving Nelson 1920- WhoE 93
Elbow, Gary Stewart 1938- WhoSSW 93
Elbow, Peter 1935- WhoE 93
Elboz, Stephen ScF&FL 92
Elbracht, Dietrich H. 1934- WhoScE 91-3
Elcar, Dana BioIn 17
Elchaar, Gerard J. 1960- St&PR 93
El Chiati, Ahmed Z. Law&B 92
El Chino BioIn 17
Elchynski, Theodore Frank 1936- St&PR 93
Elcock, W.B., Jr. 1920- St&PR 93
Elconin, Michael Henry 1953- WhoEmL 93
Elconin, Robert M. Law&B 92
El-Dabh, Halim (Abdul Messieh) 1921- Baker 92
El-Dajani, Shukri Zaki 1936- WhoUN 92
Eldeiry, Bahig Riad P.E. 1944- WhoE 93
Elden, Douglas L. 1947- WhoEmL 93
Elden, Gary Michael 1944- WhoAm 92
Elden, Joyce Lynne 1958- WhoEmL 93
Elden, Richard E. Law&B 92
Elder, Alfred Stratton 1936- WhoSSW 93
Elder, Bessie Ruth 1935- WhoSSW 93
Elder, David W. WhoIns 93
Elder, Douglas P. 1951- St&PR 93
Elder, Douglas Paul 1951- WhoEmL 93
Elder, Eldon 1921- WhoAm 92
Elder, Fred Kingsley, Jr. 1921- WhoAm 92
Elder, Frederick Arthur 1945- WhoAm 92
Elder, Gary Michael 1939- WhoWrEP 92
Elder, Jack Arnold 1949- WhoAsAP 91
Elder, James Carl 1947- WhoSSW 93, WhoWor 93
Elder, James H., Jr. 1924- St&PR 93
Elder, Jean Katherine 1941- WhoAm 92, WhoAmW 93
Elder, Joan Elizabeth 1954- WhoEmL 93
Elder, John Blanton 1926- WhoSSW 93
Elder, John Howard, Jr. 1920- WhoSSW 93
Elder, John N. 1930- St&PR 93
Elder, John Richard 1948- St&PR 93
Elder, Joseph Walter 1930- WhoAm 92
Elder, Karl Curtis 1948- WhoWrEP 92
Elder, Lee BioIn 17
Elder, Leon WhoWrEP 92
Elder, M.A. 1926- St&PR 93
Elder, Marjorie Jeanne 1921- WhoAmW 93
Elder, Mark 1947- OxDcOp
Elder, Mark (Philip) 1947- Baker 92, WhoAm 92, WhoE 93, WhoWor 93
Elder, Michael 1931- ScF&FL 92
Elder, Murdoch George WhoScE 91-1
Elder, Paul G. 1917- St&PR 93
Elder, Philip 1949- St&PR 93
Elder, Rex Alfred 1917- WhoAm 92
Elder, Richard A. Law&B 92
Elder, Robert L. 1946- St&PR 93
Elder, Robert Laurie 1938- WhoAm 92
Elder, Robert Lee 1934- WhoAm 92
Elder, Robin Lee WhoScE 91-1
Elder, Rose BioIn 17
Elder, Samuel Adams 1929- WhoAm 92
Elder, Stewart Taylor 1917- WhoAm 92
Elder, T.L. 1938- St&PR 93
Elder, Thomas Martin 1946- WhoSSW 93
Elder, William John 1929- WhoIns 93
Elderdice, Dorothy AmWomPl
Elderen, E. van 1932- WhoScE 91-3
Elderfield, John 1943- WhoAm 92
Elderkin, Charles Edwin 1930- WhoAm 92
Elderkin, Dana Vance 1955- WhoEmL 93
Elderkin, Edwin Judge 1932- WhoAm 92
Elderkin, Helaine Grace Law&B 92
Elders, M. Joycelyn 1933- WhoAm 92
Elders, Robert K. 1941- St&PR 93
Eldershaw, M. Barnard 1897-1987 ScF&FL 92
Elderton, Richard John 1942- WhoWor 93
Elding, Lars Ivar 1936- WhoScE 91-4
Eldon, Ethan Cawthorne 1938- WhoE 93
Eldred, Annmarie 1962- St&PR 93
Eldred, Gerald Marcus 1934- WhoAm 92
Eldred, Jeffrey Laine 1956- WhoEmL 93
Eldred, Jill Ann 1961- WhoAmW 93
Eldred, Kenneth McKechnie 1929- St&PR 93, WhoAm 92
Eldred, Mumford BioIn 17
Eldred, N.A. WhoScE 91-1
Eldred, Nigel WhoScE 91-1
Eldred, Nina R. Law&B 92
Eldred, Willard G. 1928- St&PR 93
Eldredge, Bruce Beard 1952- WhoAm 92
Eldredge, Charles Child, III 1944- WhoAm 92
Eldredge, George Badge 1950- WhoSSW 93
Eldredge, H. Wentworth 1909-1991 BioIn 17
Eldredge, John M. 1954- St&PR 93
Eldredge, Niles BioIn 17, WhoAm 92
Eldredge, Peter W. BioIn 17, WhoAm 92
Eldredge, Todd 1971?- BioIn 17
Eldredge, William Augustus, Jr. 1925- WhoAm 92
Eldredge-Thompson, Linda Gaile 1959- WhoSSW 93
Eldridge, Charles Arthur 1949- WhoEmL 93
Eldridge, David Carlton 1949- WhoAm 92
Eldridge, Douglas Hilton 1916- WhoAm 92
Eldridge, Erwin James, III 1952- WhoEmL 93
Eldridge, Ethel J. AmWomPl
Eldridge, Florence M. AmWomPl
Eldridge, George Thomas, Jr. 1942- St&PR 93
Eldridge, James F. 1946- St&PR 93, WhoIns 93
Eldridge, James Francis 1946- WhoAm 92, WhoEmL 93
Eldridge, James Gordon 1925- WhoScE 91-1
Eldridge, Joan AmWomPl
Eldridge, John Charles 1955- WhoSSW 93
Eldridge, John Cole 1933- WhoAm 92
Eldridge, Larry 1932- WhoAm 92
Eldridge, Maxine Jew 1941- WhoAmW 93
Eldridge, Paul 1888-1982 ScF&FL 92
Eldridge, Peter B. Law&B 92
Eldridge, Richard Clement 1937- WhoE 93
Eldridge, Richard Mark 1951- WhoEmL 93
Eldridge, Robert Coulter 1917- WhoSSW 93

Eldridge, Robert J. 1944- *St&PR 93*
Eldridge, Roger *ScF&FL 92*
Eldridge, Roy 1911-1989 *BioIn 17, ConMus 9 [port]*
Eldridge, (David) Roy 1911-1989 *Baker 92*
Eldridge, Sandra Renee 1956- *WhoAmW 93*
Eldridge, Sarah B. *AmWomPl*
El-Duweini, Aadel Khalaf 1945- *WhoWor 93*
Eleanor, Queen 1122?-1204 *BioIn 17*
Eleanor, of Aquitaine 1122?-1204 *BioIn 17*
Eleazar Ben Ya'ir *DcAmChF 1960*
Elefant, Bernard 1946- *St&PR 93*
Elefante, Jeffrey Paul *Law&B 92*
Eleftheriades, Andreas Nicos 1956- *WhoWor 93*
Elegant, Lucien 1938- *WhoScE 91-2*
Elegant, Robert Sampson 1928- *WhoAm 92*
El-Eid, Ghassan Ezzat 1952- *WhoE 93*
Elek, Judit 1937- *DrEEuF*
Elena, Antonio 1931- *WhoScE 91-3*
Elenich, Phyllis Marie 1934- *WhoAmW 93*
Elenkov, Dimitar Georgiev 1919- *WhoScE 91-4*
Elequin, Cleto, Jr. 1933- *WhoWor 93*
El-Erian, Mohamed Ali 1958- *WhoUN 92*
El-Erian, Tahani Said 1939- *WhoUN 92*
Elers, Karl E. 1938- *St&PR 93*
Elers, Karl Emerson 1938- *WhoAm 92*
Elesboam c. 500-c. 540 *OxDcByz*
Eleta, Carlos *DcCPCAm*
Eleta A., Fernando 1921- *WhoWor 93*
Elevitch, Morton D. 1925- *WhoWrEP 92*
Eley, Barry Michael *WhoScE 91-1*
Eley, Lynn W. 1925- *WhoAm 92*
Eley, Randall Robbi 1952- *WhoEmL 93, WhoSSW 93*
Eley, Thomas Wendell 1953- *WhoE 93*
Elfant, Noel *Law&B 92*
El-Fattal, Dia-Allah 1927- *WhoUN 92*
El-Fayoumy, Joanne Quinn 1930- *WhoAmW 93*
Elfenbein, Mickey 1947- *St&PR 93*
Elferdink, Terry Lee 1947- *WhoEmL 93*
Elfers, Lawrence Anthony 1938- *St&PR 93*
Elfers, William 1918- *St&PR 93, WhoAm 92*
Elfert, Donald Lee 1933- *WhoSSW 93*
Elfin, Mel 1929- *WhoAm 92, WhoE 93*
Elflandsson, Galad 1951- *ScF&FL 92*
Elflein, Kenneth John 1952- *WhoEmL 93*
Elfman, Blossom 1925- *ConAu 39NR, ScF&FL 92*
Elfman, Danny *BioIn 17, WhoAm 92*
Elfman, Danny 1953?- *ConMus 9 [port], ConTFT 10*
Elfman, Eric Michael 1954- *WhoE 93, WhoEmL 93*
Elfman, Robert *MiSFD 9*
Elfner, Albert H., III 1944- *St&PR 93*
Elfner, Albert Henry, III 1944- *WhoAm 92*
Elford, Catherine Williams 1951- *WhoAmW 93*
Elfring, Robert Lowell 1921- *WhoIns 93*
Elfstrom, Dorothy Lillian Bettencourt *WhoAm 92*
Elfstrom, Robert *MiSFD 9*
Elftmann, Joel A. 1940- *St&PR 93*
Elfvin, Lars-Gosta 1929- *WhoScE 91-4*
Elfving, Robin Gustaf 1956- *WhoWor 93*
Elg, Darren Allen 1953- *St&PR 93*
Elgar, Edward 1857-1934 *OxDcOp*
Elgar, Edward (William) 1857-1934 *Baker 92*
Elgart, Larry Joseph 1922- *WhoAm 92*
Elgart, Mervyn L. 1933- *WhoAm 92*
Elgass, James A. *Law&B 92*
Elgavish, Ada 1946- *WhoAmW 93, WhoEmL 93*
Elgee, D.J. 1943- *St&PR 93*
Elgee, Neil Johnson 1926- *WhoAm 92*
Elger, William Robert, Jr. 1950- *WhoEmL 93*
Elgersma, Doekle Marten 1937- *WhoScE 91-3*
El-Gewely, M. Raafat 1942- *WhoWor 93*
Elgin, Don D. 1944- *ScF&FL 92*
Elgin, John Tom 1940- *WhoE 93*
Elgin, John Warren 1943- *St&PR 93*
Elgin, Renee Kay 1953- *WhoEmL 93*
Elgin, Ron Alan 1941- *WhoAm 92*
Elgin, Suzette Haden 1936- *ScF&FL 92*
El-Gindi, Peter 1942- *St&PR 93*
Elgins *SoulM*
Elgort, Robert *BioIn 17*
El Greco 1541-1614 *BioIn 17*
Elguero, Francisco 1856-1932 *DcMexL*
El Hadi, Benzerroug 1949- *WhoUN 92*
El Hage, Hicham 1930- *WhoUN 92*
el Hajjam, Mohammed ben Chaib 1940- *ConAu 38NR*
el-Hajjan, Mohammed *ScF&FL 92*
El-Halees, Yousef Abdul Khaliq 1936- *WhoWor 93*
El-Hamalaway, Mohamed-Younis Abd-El-Sami 1947- *WhoWor 93*
El Hatri, Mohamed 1954- *WhoWor 93*
El-Heneidi, Roushdi 1935- *WhoUN 92*
El-Husban, Tayseer Khalaf 1955- *WhoWor 93*
Elia, Michele 1945- *WhoWor 93*
Eliachar, Haim S. d1990 *BioIn 17*
Eliade, Mircea 1907-1986 *BioIn 17, ScF&FL 92*
Eliahu, Mordechai 1928- *WhoWor 93*
Elias *BioIn 17, OxDcByz*
Elias, I c. 430-518 *OxDcByz*
Elias, Abigail 1952- *WhoEmL 93*
Elias, Albert J. 1920- *ScF&FL 92*
Elias, Alfonso de 1902-1984 *Baker 92*
Elias, David 1925- *St&PR 93*
Elias, Diana Linda 1955- *WhoEmL 93*
Elias, Donald Francis 1949- *WhoE 93*
Elias, Eliane *BioIn 17*
Elias, Ellen Lee 1950- *WhoAmW 93*
Elias, Ellen Victoria 1959- *WhoAmW 93*
Elias, Fred 1913- *St&PR 93*
Elias, Giacomo 1937- *WhoScE 91-3*
Elias, Harold John 1920- *WhoAm 92*
Elias, Harry *BioIn 17*
Elias, John W. 1940- *WhoAm 92*
Elias, Julius Anthony 1925- *WhoAm 92*
Elias, Linda Ann 1945- *WhoAmW 93*
Elias, Manuel Jorge de 1939- *Baker 92*
Elias, Paul S. 1926- *St&PR 93, WhoAm 92*
Elias, Peter 1923- *WhoAm 92, WhoE 93*
Elias, Peter Stefan 1919- *WhoScE 91-3*
Elias, Philip David *Law&B 92*
Elias, Rosalind 1930- *Baker 92, IntDcOp*
Elias, Rosalind 1931- *WhoAm 92*
Elias, Russell Joseph 1960- *WhoEmL 93*
Elias, Salomon *Baker 92*
Elias, Samuel J. 1919- *St&PR 93*
Elias, Samy E. G. 1930- *WhoAm 92*
Elias, Sarah Davis 1934- *WhoAmW 93*
Elias, T.O. 1914-1991 *BioIn 17*
Elias, Taslim Olawale 1914-1991 *AnObit 1991, BioIn 17*
Elias, Thomas Ittan 1947- *WhoEmL 93*
Elias, Thomas Sam 1942- *WhoAm 92*
Elias, Ziad Malek 1934- *WhoAm 92*
Elias bar Shinaya 975-c. 1049 *OxDcByz*
Elias Bastarrachea, Fernando Alberto 1956- *WhoWor 93*
Eliasberg, Jan *MiSFD 9*
Eliasberg, Jay 1919- *St&PR 93*
Eliasberg, Louis, Jr. 1929- *St&PR 93*
Eliasch, Harald M. 1923- *WhoWor 93*
Eliasek, Thomas Gary 1951- *St&PR 93*
Elias Ekdikos fl. 11th cent.?- *OxDcByz*
Eliasen, Reine *WhoWrEP 92*
Elias-Ivicic, Deborah Ruth 1955- *WhoAmW 93*
Elias Of Alexandria *OxDcByz*
Eliason, Bonnie Mae 1947- *WhoAmW 93*
Eliason, Edward Best 1940- *St&PR 93, WhoIns 93*
Eliason, Leslie Carol 1959- *WhoAmW 93*
Eliason, Robert Gordon 1959- *WhoE 93*
Eliasoph, Joan *WhoAmW 93*
Eliasoph, Philip *WhoE 93*
Eliassen, Jon Eric 1947- *WhoAm 92*
Eliassen, Rolf 1911- *WhoAm 92*
Eliasson, Anders 1947- *Baker 92*
Eliasson, Ann-Charlotte Elisabet 1953- *WhoWor 93*
Eliasson, Jan Kenneth 1940- *WhoUN 92*
Eliasson, Leif Sture Rudolf 1939- *WhoWor 93*
Eliasson, Lennart 1925- *WhoScE 91-4*
Eliasson, Uno H. 1939- *WhoScE 91-4*
Elias Speleotes 864?-960 *OxDcByz*
Eliastam, Michael 1944- *WhoE 93*
Elias The Younger 823?-903 *OxDcByz*
Elick, Catherine Lilly 1953- *WhoWrEP 92*
Elicker, Gordon Leonard 1940- *WhoAm 92*
Elicker, Paul H. 1923- *St&PR 93*
Elie, Jean Andre 1943- *WhoAm 92*
Eliel, Ernest Ludwig 1921- *BioIn 17, WhoAm 92*
Eliel, Stefan E. 1936- *St&PR 93*
Elien, Mona Marie 1932- *WhoAmW 93, WhoWor 93*
Eliezer, Shalom 1940- *WhoWor 93*
Elijah *BioIn 17*
Elijah ben Solomon 1720-1797 *BioIn 17*
Elijah Muhammad *EncAACR*
Elijah Muhammad 1897-1975 *BioIn 17*
Elikann, Lawrence 1923- *MiSFD 9*
Elikann, Lawrence S. 1923- *WhoAm 92*
Elimimian, Isaac Irabor 1948- *WhoWor 93*
Elin, Ronald John 1939- *WhoAm 92, WhoE 93*
Elinski, Karen M. *Law&B 92*
Elinson, Henry David 1935- *WhoWor 93*
Elinson, Jack 1917- *WhoAm 92*
Elion, Gary D. *St&PR 93*
Elion, Gertrude Belle 1918- *BioIn 17, WhoAm 92, WhoAmW 93, WhoSSW 93, WhoWor 93*
Elion, Glenn R. 1948- *St&PR 93*
Elion, Herbert A. 1923- *WhoAm 92, WhoWor 93*
Elion, Herbert Aaron 1923- *St&PR 93*
Eliot, Abigail Adams 1892-1992 *NewYTBS 92*
Eliot, Alexander 1919- *WhoAm 92*
Eliot, Annie *AmWomPl*
Eliot, Charles William John 1928- *WhoAm 92*
Eliot, Charlotte Champe Stearns 1843-1929 *AmWomPl*
Eliot, Dan *MajAI*
Eliot, Ethel Cook 1890-1972 *ScF&FL 92*
Eliot, George 1819-1880 *BioIn 17, MagSWL [port], WorLitC [port]*
Eliot, Jill Luise 1937- *WhoAmW 93, WhoWor 93*
Eliot, John 1604-1690 *BioIn 17*
Eliot, John 1933- *WhoE 93*
Eliot, Lucy Carter 1913- *WhoAm 92, WhoAmW 93, WhoE 93, WhoWor 93*
Eliot, Marc *ScF&FL 92*
Eliot, Robert Salim 1929- *WhoAm 92*
Eliot, T.S. 1888-1965 *BioIn 17, MagSAmL [port], MagSWL [port], PoeCrit 5 [port], WorLitC [port]*
Eliot, Theodore Lyman, Jr. 1928- *WhoAm 92*
Eliot, Theodore Quentin 1954- *WhoEmL 93*
Eliot, Thomas H(opkinson) 1907-1991 *CurBio 92N*
Eliot, Thomas Hopkinson 1907-1991 *BioIn 17*
Eliot, Thomas Stearns 1888-1965 *BioIn 17, DcTwHis*
Elipe, Antonio 1957- *WhoWor 93*
Elis, Jiri 1930- *WhoScE 91-4*
Elis, Morrie d1992 *BioIn 17, NewYTBS 92*
Elisabeth The Thaumaturge fl. 5th cent.- *OxDcByz*
Elisar, Patricia Garside 1934- *WhoAm 92*
Eliscu, Frank 1912- *WhoAm 92*
Elise *OxDcByz*
Elish, Dan 1960- *BioIn 17, ConAu 136*
Elish, Herbert *St&PR 93*
Elish, Herbert 1933- *WhoAm 92, WhoSSW 93*
Elisha, Walter Y. *St&PR 93*
Elisha, Walter Y. 1932- *WhoAm 92, WhoSSW 93*
Elissa, Raja Issa 1922- *WhoWor 93*
Elitzik, Paul 1945- *WhoWrEP 92*
Elitzur, Moshe 1944- *WhoSSW 93*
Elium, Don 1954- *ConAu 139*
Elium, Jeanne (Ann) 1947- *ConAu 138*
Elizabeth, Queen 1900- *BioIn 17*
Elizabeth, I, Queen of England 1533-1603 *BioIn 17*
Elizabeth, II 1926- *DcTwHis, WhoAsAP 91, WhoWor 93*
Elizabeth, II, Her Majesty 1926- *WhoAm 92*
Elizabeth, II, Queen of Great Britain 1926- *BioIn 17*
Elizabeth Angela Marguerite 1900- *WhoWor 93*
Elizabeth of the Trinity, Sister 1880-1906 *BioIn 17*
Elizaga, Noel Bendoy 1961- *WhoWor 93*
Elizalde, Federico 1908-1979 *Baker 92*
Elizondo, Ann Mock 1957- *WhoEmL 93*
Elizondo, Edelmiro Bonifacio 1946- *WhoEmL 93*
Elizondo, Eduardo Luis 1935- *WhoE 93*
Elizondo, Hector 1936- *BioIn 17, CurBio 92 [port], WhoAm 92*
Elizondo, Rita 1953- *NotHsAW 93 [port]*
Elizondo, Salvador 1932- *DcMexL, SpAmA*
Elizza, Elise 1870-1926 *Baker 92*
Elk, Ger van 1941- *BioIn 17*
Elk, Seymour Benjamin 1932- *WhoE 93*
Elkan, Harold A. *Law&B 92*
Elkan, Harold S. 1943- *St&PR 93*
Elkan, Henri 1897-1980 *Baker 92*
Elkan, Walter *WhoScE 91-1*
Elkan-Moore, Brooke 1951- *WhoE 93*
Elkebrokk, B. 1954- *WhoScE 91-4*
Elkeiy, Mahmoud Mohamed 1936- *WhoUN 92*
Elkerton, Stanley D. 1946- *St&PR 93*
Elkes, Terrence Allen 1934- *WhoAm 92*
El Khadem, Hassan S. 1923- *WhoAm 92, WhoWor 93*
Elkhadem, Saad Eldin Amin 1932- *WhoAm 92*
El-Khalil, Khazem d1990 *BioIn 17*
Elkhansa, Ali Mahmoud 1957- *WhoSSW 93*
El Khazen, Amine 1941- *WhoUN 92*
El-Khoury, Ishaya Toufic 1951- *WhoUN 92*
Elkies, Anita 1924- *St&PR 93*
Elkies, Leonard 1924- *St&PR 93*
Elkies, William 1949- *St&PR 93*
Elkin, A.P. 1891-1979 *IntDcAn*
Elkin, Marsha *ScF&FL 92*
Elkin, Milton 1916- *WhoAm 92*
Elkin, Robert H. 1945- *St&PR 93*
Elkin, Stanley 1930- *BioIn 17, JeAmFiW, ScF&FL 92*
Elkin, Stanley Lawrence 1930- *WhoAm 92, WhoWrEP 92*
Elkind, David 1931- *WhoAm 92*
Elkind, Jerome Bernard 1939- *WhoWor 93*
Elkind, Mort William 1925- *WhoE 93*
Elkind, Mortimer Murray 1922- *WhoAm 92*
Elkington, John Hunter *WhoScE 91-1*
Elkins, Anita Louise 1965- *WhoAmW 93*
Elkins, Charles 1940- *ScF&FL 92*
Elkins, Chris Charles 1929- *St&PR 93*
Elkins, David J. 1941- *WhoAm 92*
Elkins, Donald Marcum 1940- *WhoAm 92*
Elkins, Doug *BioIn 17*
Elkins, Fait *BioIn 17*
Elkins, Francis Clark 1923- *WhoAm 92*
Elkins, Frank Callihan 1939-1966 *BioIn 17*
Elkins, George W. 1899- *St&PR 93*
Elkins, Glen Ray 1933- *WhoAm 92*
Elkins, Hillard 1929- *WhoAm 92*
Elkins, James A., Jr. 1919- *St&PR 93*
Elkins, James Anderson, Jr. 1919- *WhoAm 92, WhoSSW 93, WhoWor 93*
Elkins, James Anderson, III 1952- *WhoEmL 93, WhoSSW 93*
Elkins, Judith Molinar 1935- *WhoAmW 93*
Elkins, Kate Felton 1862-1934 *BioIn 17*
Elkins, Ken Joe 1937- *WhoAm 92*
Elkins, Kenneth Joe *BioIn 17*
Elkins, Lincoln Feltch 1918- *WhoAm 92*
Elkins, Lizabeth Jean 1952- *WhoAmW 93*
Elkins, Lloyd Edwin, Sr. 1912- *WhoAm 92*
Elkins, Merry Catherine 1948- *WhoWrEP 92*
Elkins, Robert N. 1943- *WhoE 93*
Elkins, Scott *St&PR 93*
Elkins, Stanley Maurice 1925- *WhoAm 92*
Elkins, Stephen B. 1841-1911 *PolPar*
Elkins, Stephen G. *Law&B 92*
Elkins, Steven Paul 1949- *WhoEmL 93*
Elkins, Wilson Homer 1908- *WhoE 93*
Elkjaer, H.P. 1927- *WhoScE 91-2*
Elkman, Stanley 1922- *WhoAm 92*
Elko, Nicholas T. 1909-1991 *BioIn 17*
El Kodsi, Baroukh 1923- *WhoE 93*
Elkouri, Frank 1921- *WhoAm 92*
El Koutri, Abdelkader 1952- *WhoWor 93*
Elkow, Susan Lynne 1955- *WhoAmW 93*
Elkowitz, Lloyd Kent 1936- *WhoE 93, WhoWor 93*
Elks, Hazel Hulbert 1916- *WhoAm 92*
Elks, William Chester, Jr. 1952- *WhoSSW 93*
Elkus, Albert (Israel) 1884-1962 *Baker 92*
Elkus, Howard F. 1938- *St&PR 93*
Elkus, Howard Felix 1938- *WhoAm 92*
Elkus, Jonathan (Britton) 1931- *Baker 92*
Elkus, Philip 1926- *St&PR 93*
Elkus, Richard J. 1910- *WhoAm 92*
Elkus, Richard J., Jr. 1935- *WhoAm 92*
Ell, Peter J. *WhoScE 91-1*
Ella, John 1802-1888 *Baker 92*
Ella, Vincent G. *St&PR 93*
Ellacuria, Ignacio d1989 *BioIn 17*
Ellard, Bret Lewis 1958- *WhoSSW 93*
Ellard, Henry *BioIn 17*
Ellard, Stanley Mark 1953- *WhoEmL 93*
Ellard, Timothy Daniel 1934- *St&PR 93*
Ellaway, Peter Harry *WhoScE 91-1*
Ellberg, Ernst (Henrik) 1868-1948 *Baker 92*
Ellcessor, Steven J. 1952- *St&PR 93*
Ellcessor, Steven James *Law&B 92*
Ellebrecht, Mark Gerard 1954- *WhoAm 92*
Elledge, Ella Kay 1962- *WhoAmW 93*
Elledge, F. Judy *Law&B 92*
Elledge, Jim 1950- *ConAu 39NR*
Elledge, Karen Sue *Law&B 92*
Elledge, Larry Francis 1941- *WhoAm 92*
Elledge, Richard Douglas 1941- *St&PR 93*
Elledge, Scott Bowen 1914- *WhoAm 92, WhoWrEP 92*
Ellefsen, Earle Reginald 1944- *WhoE 93*
Ellefson, Dave
See Megadeth *ConMus 9*
Ellefson, James C. 1951- *WhoEmL 93*
Ellefson, Judy Fay 1958- *WhoAmW 93*
Ellefson, Karen Ann 1943- *WhoSSW 93*
Ellegood, Donald Russell 1924- *WhoAm 92*
Elleinstein, Jean 1927- *BioIn 17*
Elleithy, Khaled Mohamed 1960- *WhoWor 93*
Elleman, Lawrence Robert 1940- *WhoAm 92*

Ellemann-Jensen, Uffe 1941- *WhoWor 93*
Ellen, Jaye *ConAu 38NR, MajAI*
Ellen, Roberta Doris 1944- *St&PR 93*
Ellenberg, William J., II *Law&B 92*
Ellenberger, Connie Louise 1959- *WhoAmW 93*
Ellenberger, Diane Marie 1946- *WhoAmW 93*
Ellenberger, Jack Stuart 1930- *WhoAm 92*
Ellenberger, Lee C. 1915-1990 *BioIn 17*
Ellenbogen, Charles 1939- *WhoSSW 93*
Ellenbogen, George 1934- *WhoAm 92*
Ellenbogen, Joan 1954- *WhoAmW 93*
Ellenbogen, Leon 1927- *WhoAm 92*
Ellenbogen, Linda L. 1948-1992 *BioIn 17*
Ellenbogen, Milton Joseph 1935- *WhoAm 92, WhoWrEP 92*
Ellenbogen, Tina Rochelle 1952- *WhoAm 92*
Ellenbogen Handelsman, Joan 1954- *WhoEmL 93*
Ellenbroek, Albertus Antonius 1958- *WhoWor 93*
Ellenbrook, Edward Charles 1938- *WhoSSW 93*
Ellender, Allen J. 1891-1972 *PolPar*
Ellendorff, Franz *WhoScE 91-3*
Ellenoff, Theodore 1924- *St&PR 93*
Ellenshaw, Harrison *MiSFD 9*
Ellentuch, Leonard I. 1938- *St&PR 93*
Ellenwood, Clayton John 1930- *St&PR 93*
Ellenwood, W. Ray 1939- *WhoCanL 92*
Ellenzweig, Allen Bruce 1950- *WhoEmL 93*
Eller, Brenda Ann 1959- *WhoAmW 93, WhoEmL 93*
Eller, Bruno 1936- *St&PR 93*
Eller, Carl *AfrAmBi [port]*
Eller, Charles Manning 1929- *St&PR 93*
Eller, Evelyn Rosenbaum 1933- *WhoE 93*
Eller, Heino 1887-1970 *Baker 92*
Eller, James E. 1931- *St&PR 93*
Eller, Leona Zigler 1910- *WhoAmW 93*
Eller, Leslie Robert 1949- *WhoEmL 93*
Eller, Louis 1820-1862 *Baker 92*
Eller, Scott *WhoWrEP 92*
Eller, Terry K. *Law&B 92*
Eller, William 1921- *WhoE 93*
Eller, William Whitney, Jr. 1933- *St&PR 93*
Ellerbe, Harry d1992 *NewYTBS 92*
Ellerbe, James M. *Law&B 92*
Ellerbee, Linda *BioIn 17*
Ellerbee, Linda 1944- *WhoAm 92, WhoAmW 93*
Ellerbrock, Charles Henry *Law&B 92*
Ellerbrook, Niel Cochran 1948- *St&PR 93, WhoAm 92*
Ellerby, Alfred McKay 1911- *St&PR 93*
Ellerby, John H. 1939- *St&PR 93*
Ellerd, Gary L. 1950- *St&PR 93*
Ellerhorst, William J. 1929- *St&PR 93*
Ellerin, Albert A. 1915- *St&PR 93*
Ellerin, Charles 1918- *St&PR 93*
Ellerman, Anna *ScF&FL 92*
Ellermann, Donald R. *Law&B 92*
Ellern, William B. 1933- *ScF&FL 92*
Ellerton, J.J. 1944- *St&PR 93*
Ellerton, John Lodge 1801-1873 *Baker 92*
Eller-Whittington, Paula Sue 1962- *WhoAmW 93*
Ellery, John Blaise 1920- *WhoAm 92, WhoWor 93*
Ellestad, David Elver 1940- *St&PR 93*
Ellett, Alan Sidney 1930- *St&PR 93, WhoAm 92*
Ellett, J. David, Jr. *Law&B 92*
Ellett, Jeryl Lynn 1953- *WhoSSW 93*
Ellett, John David, II 1966- *WhoE 93*
Elleven, Raymond A. 1951- *WhoEmL 93*
Elleviou, Jean 1769-1842 *OxDcOp*
Elleviou, (Pierre-) Jean (-Baptiste-Francois) 1769-1842 *Baker 92*
Ellfeldt, Howard James 1937- *WhoAm 92*
Elli, Neal P. 1956- *St&PR 93*
Ellickson, Robert Chester 1941- *WhoAm 92*
Ellicott, Aimee Gibson 1959- *WhoAmW 93*
Ellicott, John LeMoyne 1929- *WhoAm 92*
Ellig, Bruce Robert 1936- *St&PR 93, WhoAm 92, WhoE 93, WhoWor 93*
Elligett, Raymond Thomas, Jr. 1953- *WhoEmL 93*
Elliman, David *BioIn 17*
Elliman, Donald *WhoAm 92*
Ellin, Marvin 1923- *WhoAm 92*
Ellin, Stanley *BioIn 17*
Elling, Catharinus 1858-1942 *Baker 92*
Elling, Folmer 1940- *WhoScE 91-2*
Ellingboe, John K. *Law&B 92*
Ellingboe, John Keith 1950- *WhoAm 92, WhoEmL 93*
Ellingboe, Karen Lee 1957- *WhoEmL 93*
Ellinger, Steven 1952- *WhoEmL 93*
Ellinghaus, William M. 1922- *WhoAm 92*
Ellingsberg, Donald J. *Law&B 92*
Ellingsen, Kenneth J. 1956- *St&PR 93*
Ellingsen, Knut 1938- *WhoScE 91-4*
Ellingsen, Olav 1941- *WhoWor 93*
Ellingson, David P. 1944- *WhoIns 93*
Ellingson, Diane *BioIn 17*
Ellingson, John Rostad 1938- *St&PR 93*
Ellingson, Richard A. 1936- *St&PR 93*
Ellingson, Sheri Ann 1959- *WhoAmW 93*
Ellington, B. Kevin 1938- *St&PR 93*
Ellington, Buford 1907-1972 *BioIn 17*
Ellington, Charles Ronald 1941- *WhoAm 92*
Ellington, Duke 1899-1974 *BioIn 17, ConHero 2 [port]*
Ellington, "Duke" (Edward Kennedy) 1899-1974 *Baker 92*
Ellington, Edward Leonard 1877-1967 *BioIn 17*
Ellington, Jesse Thompson, Jr. 1931- *St&PR 93*
Ellington, John David 1935- *WhoAm 92, WhoSSW 93*
Ellington, Mercer Kennedy 1919- *WhoAm 92*
Ellington, Robert Allan 1946- *WhoAm 92*
Ellingwood, Bruce Russell 1944- *WhoAm 92*
Ellinor, Robert Allen 1939- *St&PR 93*
Ellinwood, Everett Hews, Jr. 1934- *WhoAm 92*
Ellinwood, Leonard (Webster) 1905- *Baker 92*
Elliot, Bruce *WhoWrEP 92*
Elliot, David Clephan 1917- *WhoAm 92*
Elliot, David Hawksley 1936- *WhoAm 92*
Elliot, Douglas Gene 1941- *WhoSSW 93, WhoWor 93*
Elliot, Elisa Louise 1956- *WhoEmL 93*
Elliot, Frances 1820-1898 *ScF&FL 92*
Elliot, Gordon Henry 1948- *WhoWor 93*
Elliot, Graham 1960- *WhoAm 92*
Elliot, James Ludlow 1943- *WhoAm 92*
Elliot, Jared 1928- *WhoAm 92*
Elliot, Jeffrey M. 1947- *ScF&FL 92, WhoAm 92, WhoWrEP 92*
Elliot, Jesse Duncan 1782-1845 *BioIn 17*
Elliot, Jim 1927-1956 *BioIn 17*
Elliot, Joe Oliver 1923- *WhoE 93*
Elliot, John H. 1927- *St&PR 93*
Elliot, John T. *WhoAm 92*
Elliot, Kate *WhoCanL 92*
Elliot, Michael Blake 1952- *WhoEmL 93*
Elliot, Ralph Gregory 1936- *WhoAm 92, WhoE 93*
Elliot, Ramey Robert 1949- *WhoEmL 93*
Elliot, Robert M. 1923- *St&PR 93, WhoAm 92*
Elliot, Russell *BioIn 17*
Elliot, Sean Michael 1968- *BiDAMSp 1989*
Elliot, Simon 1912- *WhoWor 93*
Elliot, Stephen d1992 *NewYTBS 92*
Elliot, Stephen Charles 1954- *WhoSSW 93*
Elliot, Willard Somers 1926- *WhoAm 92*
Elliot, William Cater 1961- *WhoEmL 93*
Elliot, William Davis 1946- *St&PR 93*
Elliott, A. Randle 1914-1990 *BioIn 17*
Elliott, A. Wright *WhoAm 92*
Elliott, A. Wright 1935- *St&PR 93*
Elliott, Alison Goddard *BioIn 17*
Elliott, Arlen R. 1928- *St&PR 93*
Elliott, Arthur James 1941- *WhoAm 92*
Elliott, Benjamin Paul 1920- *WhoAm 92*
Elliott, Betty F. *WhoAmW 93*
Elliott, Bill 1955- *WhoAm 92*
Elliott, Bob 1923- *BioIn 17*
Elliott, Brady Gifford 1943- *WhoSSW 93, WhoWor 93*
Elliott, Brig 1954- *WhoEmL 93*
Elliott, Bruce 1914-1973 *ScF&FL 92*
Elliott, Burton *WhoAm 92*
Elliott, Byron Kauffman 1899- *WhoAm 92, WhoE 93, WhoWor 93*
Elliott, C.L. 1910- *St&PR 93*
Elliott, C. Sidney *St&PR 93*
Elliott, Campbell Walter 1913- *St&PR 93*
Elliott, Candice K. 1949- *WhoAmW 93, WhoE 93, WhoEmL 93*
Elliott, Carl *BioIn 17*
Elliott, Carl Hartley 1922- *WhoAm 92*
Elliott, Carol Harris 1950- *WhoAm 92, WhoEmL 93*
Elliott, Catherine Stewart 1954- *WhoAmW 93*
Elliott, Charles 1951- *ConAu 138*
Elliott, Charles A. 1933- *St&PR 93*
Elliott, Charles C. *Law&B 92*
Elliott, Charles Harold 1948- *WhoEmL 93*
Elliott, Charles Martin *WhoScE 91-1*
Elliott, Charles W. 1932- *St&PR 93, WhoAm 92*
Elliott, Charles William 1953- *WhoEmL 93*
Elliott, Chris *BioIn 17*
Elliott, Christopher James 1952- *WhoScE 91-1*
Elliott, Clare W. 1925- *WhoSSW 93*
Elliott, Clark A. 1941- *ConAu 137*
Elliott, Corinne Adelaide *WhoWrEP 92*
Elliott, Corinne Adelaide 1927- *WhoAmW 93*
Elliott, Cynthia Louise 1963- *WhoSSW 93*
Elliott, D.J. 1929- *WhoScE 91-1*
Elliott, D. Stephen 1949- *St&PR 93*
Elliott, D. William 1925- *WhoIns 93*
Elliott, Daniel R., Jr. *Law&B 92*
Elliott, Daniel Robert, Jr. 1939- *St&PR 93, WhoAm 92*
Elliott, Daniel Whitacre 1922- *WhoAm 92*
Elliott, Darrell Kenneth 1952- *WhoWor 93*
Elliott, David Anthony *WhoScE 91-1*
Elliott, David Duncan, III 1930- *WhoAm 92*
Elliott, David H. 1929- *St&PR 93*
Elliott, David H. 1941- *WhoAm 92*
Elliott, David LeRoy 1932- *WhoAm 92*
Elliott, David Mark 1959- *St&PR 93*
Elliott, David R. 1943- *St&PR 93*
Elliott, Denholm d1992 *NewYTBS 92 [port]*
Elliott, Denholm 1922- *IntDcF 2-3 [port]*
Elliott, Denholm 1922-1992 *News 93-2*
Elliott, Denholm Mitchell 1922- *WhoAm 92*
Elliott, Deni 1953- *WhoE 93*
Elliott, Dennis Dawson 1945- *WhoE 93*
Elliott, Diana Marie 1952- *WhoAmW 93, WhoEmL 93*
Elliott, Don *MajAI*
Elliott, Donald Harrison 1932- *WhoAm 92*
Elliott, Doreen 1941- *WhoSSW 93*
Elliott, Dorothy Gale 1948- *WhoAmW 93*
Elliott, Ebenezer 1781-1849 *BioIn 17*
Elliott, Eddie Mayes 1938- *WhoAm 92*
Elliott, Edna Young 1946- *WhoEmL 93*
Elliott, Edward 1915- *WhoAm 92*
Elliott, Edward Procter 1916- *WhoAm 92*
Elliott, Edwin Donald, Jr. 1948- *WhoAm 92, WhoEmL 93*
Elliott, Edwin Oliver, Jr. 1954- *WhoEmL 93*
Elliott, Edwin Powers, Jr. 1947- *WhoWrEP 92*
Elliott, Elaine Sally 1951- *WhoAmW 93*
Elliott, Eleanor Thomas 1926- *WhoAm 92*
Elliott, Ellen Pigage 1943- *WhoAmW 93*
Elliott, Elton T. *ScF&FL 92*
Elliott, Emerson John 1933- *WhoAm 92*
Elliott, Emory Bernard 1942- *WhoAm 92*
Elliott, Frank Nelson 1926- *WhoAm 92*
Elliott, Frank S. 1942- *St&PR 93*
Elliott, Frank Wallace 1930- *WhoAm 92, WhoSSW 93, WhoWor 93*
Elliott, Gary T. 1957- *St&PR 93*
Elliott, George Alexander 1901-1988 *BioIn 17*
Elliott, George Arthur 1945- *WhoAm 92*
Elliott, George Edward Peter *WhoScE 91-1*
Elliott, George P. 1918-1980 *ScF&FL 92*
Elliott, George Thomas 1956- *WhoSSW 93*
Elliott, Gerald Frank *WhoScE 91-1*
Elliott, Gordon Jefferson 1928- *WhoWor 93*
Elliott, Gordon Ray 1916- *WhoWor 93*
Elliott, Grover Sager 1940- *St&PR 93, WhoAm 92*
Elliott, Harry 1945- *WhoAm 92*
Elliott, Hayward Lee 1916- *St&PR 93*
Elliott, Hettie 1865-1926 *ScF&FL 92*
Elliott, Howard *WhoScE 91-3*
Elliott, Howard, Jr. 1933- *WhoAm 92*
Elliott, Hugh 1912-1989 *BioIn 17*
Elliott, Inger McCabe *BioIn 17*
Elliott, Inger McCabe 1933- *WhoWor 93*
Elliott, J. Jean *Law&B 92*
Elliott, J. Steve 1940- *St&PR 93*
Elliott, James Heyer 1924- *WhoAm 92*
Elliott, James Philip *WhoScE 91-1*
Elliott, James R. 1941- *St&PR 93*
Elliott, James Robert 1910- *WhoAm 92*
Elliott, James V. *Law&B 92*
Elliott, James Ward 1954- *WhoEmL 93*
Elliott, James William, Jr. 1950- *WhoWor 93*
Elliott, Janice 1931- *ScF&FL 92*
Elliott, Jannean *ScF&FL 92*
Elliott, Jean Ann 1933- *WhoAmW 93, WhoSSW 93*
Elliott, Joan Elizabeth 1945- *WhoE 93*
Elliott, Joe *BioIn 17*
Elliott, John d1992 *NewYTBS 92*
Elliott, John 1896-1992 *BioIn 17*
Elliott, John, Jr. 1921- *WhoAm 92*
Elliott, John Cain, Jr. 1950- *WhoEmL 93, WhoSSW 93*
Elliott, John Dorman 1941- *WhoWor 93*
Elliott, John F. 1958- *St&PR 93*
Elliott, John Fayi 1939- *WhoUN 92*
Elliott, John Franklin 1915- *WhoSSW 93, WhoWor 93*
Elliott, John Gibson 1908- *WhoWrEP 92*
Elliott, John Gregory 1948- *WhoEmL 93*
Elliott, John Huxtable *BioIn 17*
Elliott, John J. 1935- *St&PR 93*
Elliott, John Michael 1941- *WhoAm 92*
Elliott, John W. 1944- *St&PR 93*
Elliott, Jon Victor 1954- *WhoEmL 93*
Elliott, Joseph Gordon, Jr. 1914- *WhoAm 92*
Elliott, Jumbo *BioIn 17*
Elliott, K. Charles 1924- *St&PR 93*
Elliott, Kathleen Adele 1956- *WhoAmW 93*
Elliott, Kathleen Margaret 1947- *St&PR 93*
Elliott, Kenneth *WhoScE 91-1*
Elliott, Lang 1950- *MiSFD 9*
Elliott, Larry Marcus 1942- *WhoSSW 93*
Elliott, Larry Paul 1931- *WhoAm 92*
Elliott, Lawrence 1924- *WhoAm 92, WhoWrEP 92*
Elliott, Lee Ann *WhoAm 92, WhoAmW 93*
Elliott, Lee Ann 1923- *WhoAm 92, WhoWor 93*
Elliott, Letha Elaine Cranford 1936- *WhoAmW 93*
Elliott, Linnea Constance 1948- *WhoAmW 93*
Elliott, Lois Lawrence 1931- *WhoAm 92, WhoAmW 93*
Elliott, Margaret Johnson 1913- *WhoWrEP 92*
Elliott, Mary E. *AmWomPl*
Elliott, Mary Elizabeth *Law&B 92*
Elliott, Mary Ellen 1956- *WhoAmW 93*
Elliott, Maud Howe 1854-1948 *AmWomPl*
Elliott, Maurice Wallner 1939- *WhoAm 92*
Elliott, Meena L. *Law&B 92*
Elliott, Michael 1924- *WhoScE 91-1*
Elliott, Michael M. 1940- *St&PR 93*
Elliott, Mitchell Lee 1958- *WhoWor 93*
Elliott, Nathan *ScF&FL 92*
Elliott, Osborn *BioIn 17*
Elliott, Osborn 1924- *WhoAm 92*
Elliott, Owen Basil 1922- *WhoSSW 93*
Elliott, Paul 1950- *Baker 92*
Elliott, Peggy Gordon 1937- *WhoAm 92, WhoAmW 93*
Elliott, Pete Christopher *Law&B 92*
Elliott, Peter *BioIn 17*
Elliott, Peter David 1946- *WhoWor 93*
Elliott, Peter R. 1926- *WhoAm 92*
Elliott, Piers Gavin 1956- *St&PR 93*
Elliott, R. Fraser 1921- *St&PR 93*
Elliott, R. Keith 1942- *St&PR 93, WhoAm 92*
Elliott, R. Lance 1943- *WhoAm 92*
Elliott, Richard *ScF&FL 92*
Elliott, Richard Francis 1946- *St&PR 93*
Elliott, Richard Gene 1948- *WhoEmL 93*
Elliott, Richard Gibbons, Jr. 1940- *WhoAm 92*
Elliott, Richard H. 1957- *St&PR 93*
Elliott, Rita Lynn 1950- *WhoAmW 93*
Elliott, Robbins Leonard 1920- *WhoAm 92*
Elliott, Robert B. 1923- *WhoAm 92*
Elliott, Robert Brown 1842-1884 *BioIn 17*
Elliott, Robert Burl 1919- *WhoSSW 93*
Elliott, Robert J. 1936- *St&PR 93*
Elliott, Robert John 1934- *WhoAm 92*
Elliott, Robert M. 1923- *St&PR 93*
Elliott, Robert M., Jr. 1923- *WhoAm 92, WhoSSW 93*
Elliott, Robert R. *Law&B 92*
Elliott, Roger James *WhoScE 91-1*
Elliott, Roger James 1928- *WhoWor 93*
Elliott, Ronald Paul 1958- *WhoEmL 93*
Elliott, Rosalie Dawn 1961- *WhoAmW 93*
Elliott, Rosalie Story *Law&B 92*
Elliott, Roxanne Snelling 1954- *WhoWor 93*
Elliott, Roy Fraser 1921- *WhoAm 92*
Elliott, Sam 1944- *WhoAm 92*
Elliott, Stephen Alan 1951- *St&PR 93*
Elliott, Stephen R. 1949- *St&PR 93*
Elliott, Stuart Jay 1952- *WhoE 93*
Elliott, Sumner Locke *BioIn 17*
Elliott, Sumner Locke 1917- *WhoWrEP 92*
Elliott, Sumner Locke 1917-1991 *AnObit 1991, ConTFT 10, ScF&FL 92*
Elliott, Susan Auguste 1951- *WhoAmW 93*
Elliott, Tedi Spencer *Law&B 92*
Elliott, Thomas Arthur 1917- *WhoSSW 93*
Elliott, Thomas G. *BioIn 17*
Elliott, Thomas Lawrence 1940- *St&PR 93*
Elliott, Thomas Michael 1942- *WhoAm 92, WhoE 93, WhoWor 93*
Elliott, Thomas Morrow 1939- *WhoWrEP 92*
Elliott, Tim 1948- *WhoAm 92*
Elliott, Timothy Raymond 1956- *WhoSSW 93*
Elliott, Tom *ScF&FL 92*
Elliott, Vickie F. 1956- *WhoEmL 93*
Elliott, Walter Albert 1926- *WhoWor 93*
Elliott, William 1920- *BioIn 17*
Elliott, William B. 1944- *St&PR 93*
Elliott, William C. 1955- *BiDAMSp 1989*

Elliott, William Ditto 1930- *WhoE 93*
Elliott, William H. 1932- *St&PR 93*
Elliott, William Hall 1932- *WhoAm 92*
Elliott, William Harrison 1941- *WhoSSW 93*
Elliott, William Homer, Jr. 1918- *WhoAm 92*
Elliott, William M. 1903-1990 *BioIn 17*
Elliott, William M. 1922- *St&PR 93*
Elliott, William McBurney 1922- *WhoAm 92*
Elliott, William Paul 1928- *WhoE 93*
Elliott, William Robert 1944- *St&PR 93*
Elliott, Yancey Caldonia, Jr. 1935- *St&PR 93*
Elliott-Smith, Paul Henry 1919- *WhoAm 92*
Elliott-Watson, Doris Jean 1932- *WhoAm 92, WhoWor 93*
Ellis, Albert 1913- *ConAu 40NR, WhoAm 92*
Ellis, Albert C. 1947- *ScF&FL 92*
Ellis, Alexander J(ohn) 1814-1890 *Baker 92*
Ellis, Alice Thomas *BioIn 17*
Ellis, Alpheus Lee 1906- *St&PR 93*
Ellis, Amabel Williams- *ScF&FL 92*
Ellis, Andrew Jackson, Jr. 1930- *WhoWor 93*
Ellis, Andrew Warwick *WhoScE 91-1*
Ellis, Anne 1875-1938 *BioIn 17*
Ellis, Anne Elizabeth 1945- *WhoAm 92, WhoAmW 93, WhoE 93, WhoWor 93*
Ellis, Arthur Baron 1951- *WhoAm 92*
Ellis, Arthur H. 1902-1990 *BioIn 17*
Ellis, Arthur Stanwood 1926- *St&PR 93*
Ellis, Barbara W. 1953- *ConAu 139*
Ellis, Barbara Williams 1953- *WhoWrEP 92*
Ellis, Bernard J. 1926- *WhoE 93*
Ellis, Bernice *WhoAmW 93, WhoE 93, WhoWor 93*
Ellis, Bernice Allred 1932- *WhoAmW 93, WhoSSW 93*
Ellis, Brenda Lee 1965- *WhoAmW 93*
Ellis, Brent 1946- *Baker 92*
Ellis, Bret Easton *BioIn 17*
Ellis, Bret Easton 1964- *ConLC 71 [port], WhoAm 92*
Ellis, C. Douglas 1923- *WhoWrEP 92*
Ellis, Calvert N. 1904- *WhoAm 92*
Ellis, Carol 1946- *ScF&FL 92*
Ellis, Charles Bernard 1941- *WhoWor 93*
Ellis, Charles C. 1919-1990 *BioIn 17*
Ellis, Charles R. 1935- *St&PR 93*
Ellis, Charles Richard 1935- *WhoAm 92, WhoE 93*
Ellis, Charles Warren 1927- *WhoE 93*
Ellis, Cheryl Bonini 1951- *WhoAm 92, WhoEmL 93*
Ellis, Christopher L. *St&PR 93*
Ellis, Cynthia Ann 1955- *WhoAmW 93*
Ellis, Cynthia Elaine 1954- *WhoEmL 93*
Ellis, D.E. *ScF&FL 92*
Ellis, D. Rose Angela 1939- *WhoWrEP 92*
Ellis, Daniel Sumner 1913- *WhoE 93*
Ellis, David George *Law&B 92*
Ellis, David Maldwyn 1914- *WhoAm 92*
Ellis, David W. 1923- *St&PR 93*
Ellis, David Wertz 1936- *WhoAm 92, WhoE 93*
Ellis, Deborah Hicks 1952- *WhoEmL 93*
Ellis, Delbert R. 1932- *St&PR 93*
Ellis, Denise Taylor 1946- *WhoEmL 93*
Ellis, Dock *BioIn 17*
Ellis, Don(ald Johnson) 1934-1978 *Baker 92*
Ellis, Donald Edwin 1939- *WhoAm 92*
Ellis, Donald Lee 1950- *WhoEmL 93*
Ellis, Dorsey Daniel, Jr. 1938- *WhoAm 92*
Ellis, Douglas E. 1946- *St&PR 93*
Ellis, E. *WhoScE 91-1*
Ellis, Earl J. 1936- *St&PR 93*
Ellis, Edith 1876-1960 *AmWomPl*
Ellis, Edith Mary Oldham Lees 1861-1916 *BioIn 17*
Ellis, Edward d1992 *BioIn 17*
Ellis, Edward B. 1937- *St&PR 93*
Ellis, Edward Steven 1950- *WhoE 93*
Ellis, Ella Thorp 1928- *WhoWrEP 92*
Ellis, Ellen Wilkins 1962- *WhoE 93*
Ellis, Elliot Frederic 1929- *WhoAm 92*
Ellis, Elmo Israel 1918- *WhoAm 92*
Ellis, Elwood Addison, III 1947- *WhoAm 92*
Ellis, Emmett 1940- *BioIn 17*
Ellis, Emory Nelson, Jr. 1929- *WhoAm 92*
Ellis, Eugenia Victoria 1953- *WhoAmW 93*
Ellis, Eva Lillian 1920- *WhoAm 92, WhoAmW 93, WhoWor 93*
Ellis, Evelyn 1948- *ConAu 138*
Ellis, Frank B. 1931- *WhoScE 91-1*
Ellis, Frank Hale 1916- *WhoAm 92*
Ellis, Franklin Henry, Jr. 1920- *WhoAm 92*
Ellis, Fred K. 1939- *WhoIns 93*
Ellis, Fred Wilson 1914- *WhoAm 92*
Ellis, Frederick Startridge 1830-1901 *BioIn 17*
Ellis, Gary Michael 1952- *WhoEmL 93*
Ellis, George Burkhardt 1939- *WhoSSW 93*
Ellis, George Edward 1934- *WhoWrEP 92*
Ellis, George Edwin, Jr. 1921- *WhoWor 93*
Ellis, George Fitzallen, Jr. 1923- *WhoAm 92*
Ellis, George Francis Rayner 1939- *WhoWor 93*
Ellis, George Hathaway 1920- *WhoAm 92*
Ellis, George Richard 1937- *WhoAm 92*
Ellis, Georgiann 1947- *WhoAmW 93, WhoEmL 93*
Ellis, Giles Lambert, Jr. 1942- *St&PR 93*
Ellis, Glen Edward, Jr. 1960- *WhoEmL 93, WhoSSW 93*
Ellis, Gordon L. 1947- *St&PR 93*
Ellis, Grace Carol 1935- *WhoAmW 93*
Ellis, Grover, Jr. 1920- *WhoAm 92*
Ellis, Hadyn Douglas *WhoScE 91-1*
Ellis, Harold Bernard 1917- *WhoAm 92*
Ellis, Harry E. 1938- *St&PR 93*
Ellis, Harvey 1852-1904 *BioIn 17*
Ellis, Havelock 1859-1939 *BioIn 17*
Ellis, Henry C. 1927- *BioIn 17*
Ellis, Henry M. 1929- *St&PR 93*
Ellis, Herb 1921- *BioIn 17*
Ellis, Herb 1938- *St&PR 93*
Ellis, Herbert Lee 1912- *WhoE 93*
Ellis, Herbert Wayne 1948- *WhoEmL 93*
Ellis, Howard S. d1992 *NewYTBS 92*
Ellis, Howard S(ylvester) 1898-1992 *ConAu 137*
Ellis, Howard Sylvester 1898-1992 *BioIn 17*
Ellis, Howard W(oodrow) 1914- *ConAu 38NR*
Ellis, Howard Woodrow 1914- *WhoAm 92*
Ellis, J.R.S. 1944- *WhoScE 91-1*
Ellis, J.V. *St&PR 93*
Ellis, James B. 1940- *St&PR 93*
Ellis, James C. *Law&B 92*
Ellis, James D. *Law&B 92, St&PR 93*
Ellis, James D. 1943- *WhoAm 92*
Ellis, James David 1948- *WhoEmL 93*
Ellis, James Henry 1933- *WhoWor 93*
Ellis, James Jolly 1937- *WhoSSW 93*
Ellis, James Reed 1921- *WhoAm 92*
Ellis, James Van Norwood 1951- *WhoSSW 93*
Ellis, James Watson 1927- *WhoAm 92, WhoSSW 93*
Ellis, Jeanette Christine 1962- *WhoEmL 93*
Ellis, Jeffrey L. 1949- *WhoSSW 93*
Ellis, Jeffrey Warren 1947- *WhoEmL 93*
Ellis, Jeremy K. 1936- *St&PR 93*
Ellis, Jerry L. 1947- *WhoWrEP 92*
Ellis, Joan Sayre 1949- *WhoAmW 93*
Ellis, Joanne Hammonds 1946- *WhoEmL 93*
Ellis, John 1912- *St&PR 93*
Ellis, John 1929- *WhoAm 92, WhoE 93*
Ellis, John B. 1924- *St&PR 93*
Ellis, John Bryan *WhoScE 91-1*
Ellis, John David 1949- *WhoEmL 93*
Ellis, John Martin 1936- *WhoAm 92*
Ellis, John R. *Law&B 92*
Ellis, John Taylor 1920- *WhoAm 92, WhoE 93*
Ellis, John Tracy d1992 *NewYTBS 92 [port]*
Ellis, John Tracy 1905- *BioIn 17*
Ellis, John Tracy 1905-1992 *ConAu 139*
Ellis, John W. 1928- *St&PR 93, WhoAm 92*
Ellis, Jon Brantley, III 1950- *WhoSSW 93*
Ellis, Jonathan Richard 1946- *WhoWor 93*
Ellis, Joseph N. 1928- *St&PR 93*
Ellis, Joseph Newlin 1928- *WhoAm 92*
Ellis, Joyce K. 1950- *WhoWrEP 92*
Ellis, Julie *ScF&FL 92*
Ellis, Julie H. *Law&B 92*
Ellis, Karen Lynn 1960- *WhoAmW 93*
Ellis, Kate Ferguson 1938- *ScF&FL 92*
Ellis, Kate Florence *AmWomPl*
Ellis, Kent 1921- *WhoAm 92*
Ellis, Kevin V. *Law&B 92*
Ellis, Kim *BioIn 17*
Ellis, Lawrence Dobson 1932-1988 *WhoWor 93*
Ellis, Leigh 1959- *ScF&FL 92*
Ellis, Linda Diane 1952- *WhoAmW 93*
Ellis, Linda Gaye Adams 1943- *WhoAmW 93*
Ellis, Lonnie Calvert 1945- *WhoSSW 93*
Ellis, Loren Elizabeth 1953- *WhoE 93*
Ellis, Lynn Webster 1928- *WhoAm 92*
Ellis, Marie Stacker *AmWomPl*
Ellis, Martha McCracken 1952- *WhoAmW 93*
Ellis, Mary Dianne 1952- *WhoAmW 93*
Ellis, Mary Ila 1950- *St&PR 93*
Ellis, Mary Louise 1943- *WhoAm 92*
Ellis, Melody Genneane 1952- *WhoEmL 93*
Ellis, Michael *WhoScE 91-1*
Ellis, Michael 1917- *WhoAm 92*
Ellis, Michael David 1952- *WhoSSW 93*
Ellis, Michael Hudson 1944- *WhoWor 93*
Ellis, Myron A. 1908-1991 *BioIn 17*
Ellis, Nan Jane 1956- *WhoEmL 93, WhoSSW 93*
Ellis, Newton Cass 1934- *WhoAm 92*
Ellis, Novalyne Price 1908- *ScF&FL 92*
Ellis, Patrick 1928- *WhoAm 92, WhoE 93*
Ellis, Peter Berresford *ScF&FL 92*
Ellis, Peter Hudson 1944- *WhoAm 92*
Ellis, Philip C., Jr. *Law&B 92*
Ellis, Phillip A. 1950- *St&PR 93*
Ellis, R.J. 1949- *ScF&FL 92*
Ellis, Raymond Clinton, Jr. 1921- *WhoE 93, WhoWor 93*
Ellis, Reed *ScF&FL 92*
Ellis, Reginald John *WhoScE 91-1*
Ellis, Richard Emanuel 1937- *WhoE 93*
Ellis, Richard Salisbury *WhoScE 91-1*
Ellis, Robert A. *BioIn 17*
Ellis, Robert Bryan, Jr. 1957- *WhoEmL 93*
Ellis, Robert Charles 1954- *WhoEmL 93*
Ellis, Robert E. 1903- *EncABHB 8 [port]*
Ellis, Robert Griswold 1908- *WhoAm 92, WhoWor 93*
Ellis, Robert James 1943- *St&PR 93*
Ellis, Robert Jeffry 1935- *WhoSSW 93*
Ellis, Robert Lee 1949- *WhoEmL 93*
Ellis, Robert Malcolm 1922- *WhoAm 92*
Ellis, Robert W. *Law&B 92*
Ellis, Robert William 1939- *WhoAm 92*
Ellis, Rodney D. 1950- *St&PR 93*
Ellis, Rodney Glenn 1954- *WhoSSW 93*
Ellis, Ronald Kevin 1953- *WhoEmL 93*
Ellis, Rose Allen *Law&B 92*
Ellis, Rosemary Clark 1954- *WhoAmW 93*
Ellis, Roswell P. 1934- *WhoIns 93*
Ellis, Rudolph Lawrence 1911- *WhoAm 92*
Ellis, Ruth 1926-1955 *BioIn 17*
Ellis, S.M. *ScF&FL 92*
Ellis, Sarah 1952- *BioIn 17*
Ellis, Shirley 1941- *SoulM*
Ellis, Spencer Percy 1923- *WhoAm 92*
Ellis, Stacey Martin 1951- *WhoEmL 93, WhoSSW 93*
Ellis, Susan Gottenberg 1949- *WhoAmW 93, WhoSSW 93*
Ellis, Sydney 1917- *WhoAm 92*
Ellis, T. Mullett 1850-1919 *ScF&FL 92*
Ellis, Ted Ellsworth 1927- *WhoAm 92*
Ellis, Terry *ScF&FL 92*
Ellis, Thelma C. 1936- *St&PR 93*
Ellis, Thomas Selby, III 1940- *WhoAm 92, WhoSSW 93*
Ellis, Tracey *BioIn 17*
Ellis, Vanessa Howard *Law&B 92*
Ellis, Veronica F. 1950- *BlkAull 92*
Ellis, Vivian Elizabeth *WhoAmW 93*
Ellis, W. Frank 1952- *WhoE 93*
Ellis, Walter M. 1943- *ConAu 137*
Ellis, Weldon Thompson, Jr. 1909- *WhoWor 93*
Ellis, William A. 1946- *WhoScE 91-1*
Ellis, William B. 1940- *St&PR 93*
Ellis, William Ben 1940- *WhoAm 92*
Ellis, William Edward, Jr. 1948- *St&PR 93*
Ellis, William Elliott 1940- *WhoSSW 93*
Ellis, William Grenville 1940- *WhoWor 93*
Ellis, William Harold 1925- *WhoAm 92*
Ellis, William L., Jr. *Law&B 92*
Ellis, William Leigh 1908-1990 *BioIn 17*
Ellis, William Thomas *Law&B 92*
Ellis, Willis Hill 1927- *WhoAm 92*
Ellis Crawford Taylor, Emily 1898- *WhoWrEP 92*
Ellison, Alan *WhoScE 91-1*
Ellison, Alton Lynn, Jr. 1950- *WhoEmL 93, WhoSSW 93*
Ellison, Carl 1951- *AfrAmBi*
Ellison, Charles L. 1950- *St&PR 93*
Ellison, Clara Anna 1958- *WhoAmW 93*
Ellison, Claude R. 1916- *St&PR 93*
Ellison, Craig William 1944- *WhoE 93*
Ellison, Cyril Lee 1916- *WhoAm 92*
Ellison, E. Graham *WhoScE 91-1*
Ellison, Elaine 1926- *WhoAmW 93*
Ellison, Ellen Wells 1934- *WhoSSW 93*
Ellison, Eugene Curtis 1949- *WhoAm 92*
Ellison, Floyd Earl, Jr. 1934- *St&PR 93*
Ellison, Gerald Alexander 1910-1992 *ConAu 139*
Ellison, Greg H. 1946- *WhoIns 93*
Ellison, Harlan *BioIn 17*
Ellison, Harlan 1934- *ScF&FL 92*
Ellison, Harlan Jay 1934- *WhoAm 92, WhoWrEP 92*
Ellison, Herbert Jay 1929- *WhoAm 92*
Ellison, James Oliver 1929- *WhoSSW 93*
Ellison, Jeffrey L. 1948- *St&PR 93*
Ellison, Joseph *MiSFD 9*
Ellison, Katherine Esther 1957- *WhoAmW 93*
Ellison, Katherine Ruffner White 1941- *WhoE 93*
Ellison, Kerry *BioIn 17*
Ellison, Lawrence J. 1944- *WhoAm 92*
Ellison, Lawrence Joseph 1944- *St&PR 93*
Ellison, Lorin Bruce 1932- *WhoAm 92*
Ellison, Lorraine *SoulM*
Ellison, Luther Frederick 1925- *St&PR 93, WhoWor 93*
Ellison, Martha French 1926- *St&PR 93*
Ellison, Michael Harris *Law&B 92*
Ellison, Michael S. 1939- *St&PR 93*
Ellison, Peter K. 1942- *St&PR 93*
Ellison, Ralph *BioIn 17*
Ellison, Ralph 1914- *EncAACR, MagSAmL [port], WorLitC [port]*
Ellison, Ralph Waldo 1914- *WhoAm 92*
Ellison, Richard H. 1949- *St&PR 93*
Ellison, Richard Perham 1930- *St&PR 93*
Ellison, Robert Gordon 1916- *WhoAm 92*
Ellison, Rudd C. 1944- *St&PR 93*
Ellison, Samuel Porter, Jr. 1914- *WhoAm 92*
Ellison, Sarah Higbie 1915- *WhoE 93*
Ellison, Siobhan Patricia 1952- *WhoAmW 93*
Ellison, Solon Arthur 1922- *WhoAm 92*
Ellison, Stephen Gil *Law&B 92*
Ellison, Thorleif 1902- *WhoSSW 93, WhoWor 93*
Ellison, William 1927- *St&PR 93*
Ellis-Vant, Karen McGee 1950- *WhoEmL 93*
Ellman, Elaine *BioIn 17*
Ellman, Roger Arnold 1952- *WhoEmL 93*
Ellmann, Douglas Stanley 1956- *WhoEmL 93*
Ellmann, Richard 1918-1987 *BioIn 17*
Ellmann, Sheila Frenkel 1931- *WhoAmW 93, WhoWor 93*
Ellmann, William Marshall 1921- *WhoAm 92*
Ellmyer, Virginia Ruth 1958- *WhoEmL 93*
Ellner, Carolyn Lipton 1932- *WhoAm 92*
Ellner, Paul D. 1925- *WhoAm 92*
Ellrod, Frederick Edward, III 1953- *WhoEmL 93*
Ellrodt, Robert Jean Louis 1922- *WhoWor 93*
Ellroy, James *BioIn 17*
Ellroy, James 1948- *ConAu 138*
Ellsasser, Michael Gordon 1934- *WhoSSW 93*
Ellsberg, Daniel 1931- *ColdWar 1 [port]*
Ellsberg, Edward 1891-1983 *BioIn 17*
Ellsen, Isabel *BioIn 17*
Ellspermann, Stanley C. 1942- *St&PR 93*
Ellstein, Carol Gail 1951- *WhoAmW 93*
Ellstrom, Olof W., Jr. 1946- *St&PR 93*
Ellstrom-Calder, Annette 1952- *WhoAmW 93, WhoEmL 93*
Ellsworth, Arthur W. 1934- *St&PR 93*
Ellsworth, Arthur Whitney 1936- *WhoAm 92*
Ellsworth, Cynthia Ann 1950- *WhoEmL 93*
Ellsworth, Dick 1940- *BioIn 17*
Ellsworth, Duncan S., Jr. 1928- *St&PR 93*
Ellsworth, Duncan Steuart, Jr. 1928- *WhoAm 92*
Ellsworth, Frank L. 1943- *WhoAm 92*
Ellsworth, Jane Dewey d1991 *BioIn 17*
Ellsworth, John E. 1904- *St&PR 93*
Ellsworth, Joseph Cordon 1955- *WhoEmL 93, WhoSSW 93*
Ellsworth, Larry Paul *Law&B 92*
Ellsworth, Lincoln 1880-1951 *BioIn 17, Expl 93 [port]*
Ellsworth, Lucius Fuller 1941- *WhoAm 92*
Ellsworth, Mary Ellen Tressel 1940- *WhoAmW 93*
Ellsworth, Michael J. 1943- *St&PR 93*
Ellsworth, Myrna Ruth 1948- *WhoWor 93*
Ellsworth, Oliver 1745-1807 *OxCSupC [port], PolPar*
Ellsworth, Robert Fred 1926- *WhoAm 92*
Ellsworth, Robert Malcolm 1928- *WhoAm 92*
Ellsworth, Samuel George 1916- *WhoAm 92*
Ellsworth, Stoughton Lathrop 1927- *St&PR 93*
Ellsworth, Thomas A. 1938- *St&PR 93*
Ellwanger, C. Scott 1947- *St&PR 93, WhoIns 93*
Ellwanger, J. David 1937- *WhoAm 92*
Ellwanger, Mike 1925- *WhoAm 92*
Ellwein, Michael D. *Law&B 92*
Ellwein, Rebecca Anne 1952- *WhoAmW 93*
Ellwood, Derek Clifford *WhoScE 91-1*
Ellwood, Gracia Fay 1938- *ScF&FL 92*
Ellwood, Paul Murdock, Jr. 1926- *WhoAm 92*
Ellwood, Scott 1936- *WhoAm 92*

Ellwood, Terrence J. *Law&B 92*
Ellwood-Filkins, Lea Beatrice 1955- *WhoEmL 93*
Elly, Robert Arthur 1934- *St&PR 93*
Ellzey, Randal Edmond 1958- *WhoEmL 93*
Elm, Clayton B. 1928- *St&PR 93*
Elm, Kaspar Joseph 1929- *WhoWor 93*
Elm, Kevin Lee 1959- *WhoSSW 93*
Elmachat, Ridha 1941- *WhoWor 93*
El-Magd, Essam A. 1941- *WhoScE 91-3*
Elmaghraby, Salah Eldin 1927- *WhoAm 92*
El-Mahdi, Anas Morsi 1935- *WhoAm 92*
El Mahdi, Galal Mohamed Rasheed 1935- *WhoWor 93*
El Mahdi, Sadiq 1936- *BioIn 17*
Elmaleh, Joseph 1938- *St&PR 93, WhoWor 93*
Elmaleh, Lou *St&PR 93*
Elman, Gerry Jay 1942- *WhoAm 92, WhoWor 93*
Elman, Mischa 1891-1967 *Baker 92, BioIn 17*
Elman, Naomi Geist *WhoAmW 93*
Elman, Philip 1918- *WhoAm 92*
Elman, Richard 1934- *JeAmFiW, WhoWrEP 92*
Elman, Robert 1930- *WhoE 93*
Elmasry, Mohamed Ibrahim 1943- *WhoAm 92*
Elmburg, John Robert 1941- *St&PR 93*
Elmegreen, Debra Anne Meloy 1952- *WhoAmW 93, WhoEmL 93*
Elmen, James W. 1932- *St&PR 93*
Elmen, Robert C. 1930- *St&PR 93*
Elmendorf, William Welcome 1912- *WhoAm 92*
Elmendorff, Karl 1891-1962 *OxDcOp*
Elmendorff, Karl (Eduard Maria) 1891-1962 *Baker 92*
Elmer, Bernard E. 1927- *St&PR 93*
Elmer, Brian Christian 1936- *WhoAm 92*
Elmer, Doris Eileen 1936- *WhoSSW 93*
Elmer, Jean Radley 1946- *WhoAm 92, WhoAmW 93*
Elmer, Marilyn Ann 1931- *WhoSSW 93*
Elmer, Thomas J. 1948- *WhoIns 93*
Elmer, William Morris 1915- *WhoAm 92*
Elmes, David Gordon 1942- *WhoAm 92*
Elmes, Graham Wakely *WhoScE 91-1*
Elmets, Craig Allan 1949- *WhoEmL 93*
Elmets, Harry Barnard 1920- *WhoAm 92*
El Midani, Munzer Sami 1930- *WhoUN 92*
Elmiligy, Ismail A. 1937- *St&PR 93*
el-Miniawy, Wahib Fahmy 1933- *WhoWor 93*
Elmlinger, Paul Joseph *Law&B 92*
Elmo, Cloe 1910-1962 *Baker 92*
Elmont, Maxine *WhoE 93*
Elmore, Andrew Monteverde 1952- *WhoE 93*
Elmore, Bruce J. 1950- *St&PR 93*
Elmore, Cecelia Anne 1936- *WhoAmW 93*
Elmore, E. Whitehead *Law&B 92*
Elmore, Edward Whitehead 1938- *St&PR 93, WhoAm 92*
Elmore, Ernest 1901-1957 *ScF&FL 92*
Elmore, Eugene L. 1931- *St&PR 93*
Elmore, Geraldine Catharine 1936- *WhoAmW 93, WhoWor 93*
Elmore, James Bernard 1949- *WhoWrEP 92*
Elmore, James Walter 1917- *WhoAm 92*
Elmore, Mark Alan 1950- *WhoEmL 93*
Elmore, Matthew Bret 1951- *WhoEmL 93*
Elmore, Robert Hall 1913-1985 *Baker 92*
Elmore, Roscoe C. *Law&B 92*
Elmore, Stancliff Churchill 1921- *WhoAm 92, WhoWor 93*
Elmore, Stephen A., Sr. 1952- *St&PR 93*
Elmore, Thomas Stephen 1952- *WhoSSW 93*
Elmore, Walter A. 1925- *WhoAm 92*
Elmquist, H. Richard *Law&B 92*
Elms, James Cornelius, IV 1916- *WhoAm 92, WhoWor 93*
Elms, Ruth *AmWomPl*
Elmslie, Kenward Gray 1929- *WhoAm 92*
El Naggar, Mohamed Nour Eldin Ismail 1938- *WhoUN 92*
El-Najdawi, Eva 1950- *WhoEmL 93*
El-Nozahi, Ahmed Mohamed 1940- *WhoWor 93*
Elo, Arpad E. d1992 *NewYTBS 92 [port]*
Elofson, Nancy Meyer 1923- *WhoAmW 93*
Elofsson, Rolf 1930- *WhoScE 91-4*
Elomaa, Kari Olavi 1932- *WhoWor 93*
Elonen, Paavo Lauri 1936- *WhoScE 91-4*
Elong Mansul, Clarence 1940- *WhoAsAP 91*
Elorduy, Francisco Gil *Law&B 92*
Elorriaga, John A. 1923- *St&PR 93*
Elous, Marv *ScF&FL 92*
Elovainio, Liisa Inkeri *WhoScE 91-4*
Elowitch, Abraham B. 1917- *St&PR 93*
Elowitch, Stanley J. 1942- *St&PR 93*
Eloy, Jean-Claude 1938- *Baker 92*
Eloy, Marie-Rose *WhoScE 91-2*
Elphinstone, Margaret 1948- *ScF&FL 92*
Elpidios *OxDcByz*
Elpios The Roman *OxDcByz*
Elrick, George S. 1921- *ScF&FL 92*
Elrick, Stephen Thomas 1945- *St&PR 93*
Elrod, Ben Moody 1930- *WhoAm 92*
Elrod, Eugene Richard 1949- *WhoAm 92, WhoE 93, WhoEmL 93*
Elrod, Harold Glenn 1918- *WhoAm 92*
Elrod, James Gordon 1965- *WhoSSW 93*
Elrod, James Lake, Jr. 1954- *St&PR 93, WhoAm 92*
Elrod, John William 1940- *WhoAm 92*
Elrod, Kenneth A. 1936- *St&PR 93*
Elrod, Linda Diane Henry 1947- *WhoEmL 93*
Elrod, P.N. *ScF&FL 92*
Elrod, Richard Bryan 1949- *WhoEmL 93*
Elrod, Richard L. 1935- *St&PR 93*
Elrod, Robert Grant 1940- *WhoAm 92*
Elrod, Taylor Larue, Jr. 1933- *St&PR 93*
El-Saadawi, Nawal *BioIn 17*
El Sabeh, Hani A. 1944- *St&PR 93*
Elsaesser, Folkmar 1942- *WhoScE 91-3*
Elsaesser, Robert James 1926- *WhoAm 92*
El Saffar, Ruth Snodgrass 1941- *WhoAm 92, WhoAmW 93*
Elsammak, Ibahim 1923- *St&PR 93*
Elsas, Louis Jacob, II 1937- *WhoAm 92*
Elsasser, Albert B(ertrand) 1918- *WhoWrEP 92*
Elsasser, Hans Friedrich 1929- *WhoScE 91-3*
Elsasser, Walter M. 1904-1991 *BioIn 17*
El-Sayed, Hosney Hussein 1925- *WhoWor 93*
Elsayed, Khalil Mohamad 1950- *WhoEmL 93*
El-Sayed, Mostafa Amr 1933- *WhoAm 92*
Elsberg, John William 1945- *WhoWrEP 92*
Elsberg, Stuart Michael 1939- *WhoAm 92*
Elsberry, Nancy Lee 1938- *WhoAmW 93*
Elsberry, Susan Davis 1953- *WhoEmL 93*
Elsbree, John Francis 1912- *WhoAm 92*
Elsbree, Willard S. 1897-1991 *BioIn 17*
Elschek, Oskar 1931- *Baker 92*
Elschenbroich, Christoph Heinrich Edwin 1939- *WhoWor 93*
Elschner, Bruno R. 1924- *WhoScE 91-3*
Elschner, Johannes 1949- *WhoWor 93*
Elsdoerfer, Ronald Waldemar 1949- *St&PR 93*
Elsdon, Margaret Buchanan 1949- *WhoAmW 93*
Else, Chas W. 1911- *St&PR 93*
Else, Willis Irl 1931- *St&PR 93, WhoAm 92*
Elsea, Deborah Lorraine 1965- *WhoAmW 93*
Elsea, Frederick J., III *St&PR 93*
Elsen, Albert Edward 1927- *WhoAm 92*
Elsen, J.F. 1925- *St&PR 93*
Elsen, Lowell Neff *Law&B 92*
Elsen, Pierre M.M. 1940- *WhoScE 91-2*
Elsen, Sheldon Howard 1928- *WhoAm 92, WhoE 93*
Elsener, G. Dale 1951- *WhoEmL 93*
Elser, Donna Louise 1955- *WhoSSW 93*
Elser, John Robert 1912- *WhoE 93*
Elser, Massimo Fielding 1962- *WhoWor 93*
Elser, Nancy C. 1942- *WhoAmW 93*
Elsesser, James R. *WhoAm 92*
Elsesser, James Richard 1944- *St&PR 93*
Elsey, George McKee 1918- *WhoAm 92*
Elsey, John H. 1945- *St&PR 93, WhoIns 93*
Elsey, Myrtle Giard *AmWomPl*
Elsey, William Martin 1953- *WhoSSW 93*
El-Shafei, Omran Abdel-Salam 1925- *WhoUN 92*
El-Shater, Safaa *ScF&FL 92*
el-Shati, Bint *WhoWor 93*
Elshennawy, Ahmad Kamal 1952- *WhoSSW 93*
Elsila, David August 1939- *WhoAm 92*
Elsing, Siegfried Hermann 1950- *WhoWor 93*
Elsinger, Carolyn d1991 *BioIn 17*
Elsinger, George R. 1934- *St&PR 93*
Elsinger, Verna *AmWomPl*
Elsman, James Leonard, Jr. 1936- *WhoAm 92*
Elsmark, Ivan 1938- *WhoUN 92*
Elsna, Hebe *ScF&FL 92*
Elsner, James A. 1946- *St&PR 93, WhoWor 93*
Elsner, Joseph (Anton Franciskus) 1769-1854 *Baker 92*
Elsner, Jozef 1769-1854 *OxDcOp*
Elsner, Jozef Ksawery 1769-1854 *PolBiDi*
Elsner, Jurg 1946- *WhoWor 93*
Elsner, Larry 1930-1990 *BioIn 17*
Elsner, Paul C. *Law&B 92*
Elsner, Sidney Edgar 1919- *WhoAm 92*
El-Solh, Abdel-Mawla Omar 1938- *WhoUN 92*
Elsom, Clint Gary 1946- *WhoEmL 93*
Elson, Alex 1905- *WhoAm 92*
Elson, Arthur 1873-1940 *Baker 92*
Elson, B.M. *WhoScE 91-1*
Elson, Charles 1909- *WhoAm 92*
Elson, Charles Myer 1959- *WhoEmL 93*
Elson, Edward Elliott 1934- *WhoAm 92, WhoSSW 93, WhoWor 93*
Elson, Edward Lee Roy 1906- *WhoAm 92*
Elson, Gerald L. *St&PR 93*
Elson, Gerald W. 1922- *St&PR 93*
Elson, Jenny *ScF&FL 92*
Elson, Louis (Charles) 1848-1920 *Baker 92*
Elson, Robert 1904-1981 *BiDAMSp 1989*
Elson, Suzanne Goodman 1937- *WhoAmW 93*
Elsperman, Robert Pauly 1936- *St&PR 93*
Elstad, Ann Austin 1952- *WhoSSW 93*
Elstad, Leonard Marvin 1899-1990 *BioIn 17*
Elste, Charles E. 1941- *St&PR 93*
Elstein, Stephen Edgar 1932- *St&PR 93*
Elster, Allen DeVaney 1954- *WhoSSW 93*
Elster, Leon 1926- *St&PR 93*
Elster, Marc A. *Law&B 92*
Elster, Richard Sanford 1939- *WhoAm 92*
Elster, Robert James, Jr. 1952- *WhoE 93*
Elster, Samuel Kase 1922- *WhoAm 92*
Elstner, Richard Chesney 1924- *WhoAm 92*
Elston, Andrew Stephen 1951- *WhoEmL 93*
Elston, Arnold 1907-1971 *Baker 92*
Elston, D.J. *WhoScE 91-1*
Elston, Jay W. *Law&B 92*
Elston, Jeremy *WhoScE 91-1*
Elston, Joseph Buell, II 1938- *St&PR 93, WhoAm 92*
Elston, Judith Ann *Law&B 92*
Elston, Lloyd Warren 1926- *WhoAm 92*
Elston, Peter 1927- *WhoIns 93*
Elston, Ralph Beckman 1937- *St&PR 93*
Elston, Walter Frank 1944- *WhoSSW 93*
Elston, William Steger 1940- *WhoAm 92*
Elston, William T. *Law&B 92*
Elstow, William *WhoScE 91-1*
Elstun, Esther Nies *WhoAmW 93*
El-Swaify, Samir Aly 1937- *WhoAm 92*
Elsworth, Derek 1958- *WhoE 93*
Elsworth, Roscoe V. d1990 *BioIn 17*
El-Tahan, Mona 1950- *WhoWor 93*
Elterich, Joachim Gustav 1930- *WhoAm 92*
Elterich, John *Law&B 92*
Elthon, Donald Lee 1952- *WhoEmL 93, WhoSSW 93*
Elting, Everett E. 1936- *WhoAm 92*
Elting, Victor, III *Law&B 92*
Elting, Victor, III 1938- *St&PR 93*
Eltinge, Lamont 1926- *WhoAm 92*
Eltman, Elizabeth Theresa 1941- *WhoAmW 93*
Elto, Patrick William 1947- *WhoEmL 93*
Elton, Ben 1959- *ScF&FL 92*
Elton, Bruce Ferriday 1937- *St&PR 93*
Elton, Charles S. 1900-1991 *BioIn 17*
Elton, Geoffrey Rudolph 1921- *WhoWor 93*
Elton, Lewis *WhoScE 91-1*
Elton, Lewis Richard Benjamin 1923- *WhoWor 93*
Elton, Michael John 1933- *WhoWor 93*
Elton, Milan Lee 1940- *St&PR 93*
Elton, Wallace Wesley 1907-1991 *BioIn 17*
Elton, William R. 1921- *WhoE 93, WhoWor 93*
El-Tour, Anna 1886-1954 *Baker 92*
El'tsin, Boris Nikolaevich *BioIn 17*
El-Turk, Said Nejam 1946- *WhoWor 93*
Eltz, Katharine Elizabeth 1952- *WhoAmW 93*
Elverum, Gerard William, Jr. 1927- *WhoAm 92, WhoWor 93*
Elverum, H.D. 1925- *St&PR 93*
Elvey, George (Job) 1816-1893 *Baker 92*
Elvey, Stephen 1805-1860 *Baker 92*
El Vez 1961- *BioIn 17*
Elvin, Peter Wayne 1955- *WhoE 93, WhoEmL 93*
Elvin, Sten 1940- *WhoScE 91-4*
Elvira, Pablo 1937- *Baker 92*
Elvira Munoz, Jose Luis 1946- *WhoScE 91-3*
Elvius, Aina Margareta 1917- *WhoWor 93*
Elvove, Carl X. 1919- *St&PR 93*
El Wardini, Edward 1940- *WhoUN 92*
Elwart, Antoine (-Aimable-Elie) 1808-1877 *Baker 92*
Elwart, Nancy M. 1939- *WhoAmW 93*
Elwart, Ralph J. *Law&B 92*
Elway, John *BioIn 17*
Elway, John Albert 1960- *WhoAm 92*
Elwell, Celia Candace 1954- *WhoEmL 93*
Elwell, Ellen C. 1945- *WhoAmW 93*
Elwell, Herbert 1898-1974 *Baker 92*
Elwell, Howard Andrew 1940- *WhoSSW 93*
Elwer, Ronald R. 1953- *St&PR 93*
Elwes, Cary *BioIn 17*
Elwes, Christina Oxenberg- *BioIn 17*
Elwes, Damian *BioIn 17*
Elwes, Gervase (Cary) 1866-1921 *Baker 92*
Elwes, Mary *AmWomPl*
Elwin, Eric Ross *Law&B 92*
Elwin, Eric Ross 1957- *St&PR 93*
Elwin, James William, Jr. 1950- *WhoEmL 93*
Elwin, Verrier 1902-1964 *IntDcAn*
Elwood, Brian Clay 1958- *WhoEmL 93*
Elwood, Clark Dale *Law&B 92*
Elwood, David Michael 1935- *WhoAm 92*
Elwood, H. Philip 1946- *WhoEmL 93*
Elwood, P.C. *WhoScE 91-1*
Elwood, Patricia 1941- *WhoE 93*
Elwood, Roger 1943- *ScF&FL 92*
Elwood, Thomas H. *Law&B 92*
Elwood, William Edward 1943- *WhoE 93*
Elwork, Amiram 1949- *WhoE 93*
Elworthy, Kenneth David *WhoScE 91-1*
Elwyn, Lizzie May *AmWomPl*
Ely, Betty Jo 1947- *WhoEmL 93*
Ely, Blanche T. *AmWomPl*
Ely, Bruce Peter 1955- *WhoEmL 93*
Ely, David 1927- *ScF&FL 92*
Ely, Donald Jean 1935- *WhoE 93, WhoWor 93*
Ely, Donald Paul 1930- *WhoE 93*
Ely, Duncan Cairnes 1951- *WhoSSW 93*
Ely, Edward Marshall, II 1948- *St&PR 93*
Ely, Elizabeth Wickenberg 1953- *WhoSSW 93*
Ely, JoAnn Denice 1951- *WhoAmW 93, WhoEmL 93*
Ely, Joe *BioIn 17*
Ely, Joseph Buell, II 1938- *St&PR 93, WhoAm 92*
Ely, Lockhart *St&PR 93*
Ely, Myron C. *Law&B 92*
Ely, Northcutt 1903- *WhoAm 92*
Ely, Paul Coughanour, Jr. 1932- *WhoAm 92*
Ely, Robert Eugene 1949- *WhoEmL 93*
Ely, Robert Pollock, Jr. 1930- *WhoAm 92*
Ely, Robert Thomas 1946- *WhoEmL 93*
Ely, Scott 1944- *ScF&FL 92*
Ely, Scott Rex 1961- *BioIn 17*
Ely, Timothy B. 1948- *St&PR 93*
Ely, Timothy Clyde 1949- *WhoE 93*
Ely, William H.H. 1943- *St&PR 93*
Elya, John Adel 1928- *WhoAm 92*
Elyakime, Bernard 1949- *WhoScE 91-2*
Elyasiani, Elyas 1949- *WhoEmL 93*
Elyea, Michael K. 1953- *St&PR 93*
Elyn, Mark 1932- *WhoAm 92*
Ely-Raphel, Nancy 1937- *WhoAmW 93*
Elyse, Joy *WhoWrEP 92*
Elytes, Odysseus 1911- *BioIn 17*
Elytis, Odysseus 1911- *WhoWor 93*
El'Zabar, Kahil *BioIn 17*
El-Zanati, Abdel Ghani A. 1934- *WhoUN 92*
Elzas, Maurice S. 1934- *WhoScE 91-3*
Elzay, Richard Paul 1931- *WhoAm 92*
El Zayat, Elhamy Mostafa 1942- *WhoWor 93*
Elzer, Ruth Marie 1966- *WhoAmW 93*
Elzinga, Donald Jack 1939- *WhoAm 92*
Elzinga, Peter 1944- *WhoAm 92*
Elznic, Tom *St&PR 93*
Ema, Yasuo 1945- *WhoE 93, WhoWor 93*
Emad, Jamal 1931- *WhoE 93*
Emal, James G. 1947- *WhoEmL 93*
Emami, Shirin *Law&B 92*
Eman, Evelyn 1949- *WhoEmL 93*
Eman, Henny 1948- *DcCPCAm*
Emans, Robert LeRoy 1934- *WhoAm 92*
Emanuel, Ezekiel J(onathan) 1957- *ConAu 139*
Emanuel, Herbert L. 1930- *WhoIns 93*
Emanuel, Herbert Leon 1930- *WhoAm 92*
Emanuel, Irvin 1926- *WhoAm 92*
Emanuel, James A. *BioIn 17*
Emanuel, James Steven 1949- *WhoE 93*
Emanuel, Myron 1920- *WhoWor 93*
Emanuel, Peter M. *Law&B 92*
Emanuel, Stephanie 1949- *St&PR 93*
Emanuel, Victor *ScF&FL 92*
Emanuel, William Joseph 1938- *WhoAm 92*
Emanuele, Jack Anthony 1931- *St&PR 93*
Emanuele, Luciano 1948- *WhoEmL 93*
Emanuele, R. Martin 1954- *St&PR 93*
Emanuelson, James Robert 1931- *St&PR 93, WhoAm 92, WhoIns 93*
Emanuelson, Karen Sue 1959- *WhoEmL 93*
Emanuelson, Richard Gilsey 1954- *WhoE 93*
Embel, Philemon Teiel 1962- *WhoAsAP 91*
Ember, A.A. *WhoScE 91-1*
Ember, Carol R. 1943- *WhoE 93*
Ember, Howard 1952- *St&PR 93*
Ember, Melvin Lawrence 1933- *WhoAm 92*

Emberg, Kelly BioIn 17
Emberg, Ronald Robert 1950- WhoSSW 93
Emberger, Andre 1926- WhoScE 91-2
Emberley, Barbara A(nne) 1932- MajAI [port], SmATA 70 [port]
Emberley, Ed(ward Randolph) 1931- MajAI [port], SmATA 70 [port]
Embery, Graham WhoScE 91-1
Embiricos, Epaminondas George 1943- WhoWor 93
Emblad, Hans W. 1938- WhoUN 92
Embler, Stephen Frank 1952- St&PR 93
Embleton, Tom William 1918- WhoAm 92, WhoWor 93
Embleton, Tony Frederick Wallace 1929- WhoAm 92
Embody, Daniel Robert 1914- WhoAm 92, WhoE 93, WhoWor 93
Embody, Daniel Robert, Jr. 1954- WhoEmL 93, WhoSSW 93
Embree, Ainslie Thomas 1921- WhoAm 92
Embree, James Ray 1949- WhoEmL 93, WhoSSW 93, WhoWor 93
Embree, John Fee 1908-1950 IntDcAn
Embree, Norman R. 1943- St&PR 93
Embrey, Cathy Graham 1956- WhoEmL 93
Embrey, John Derek 1945- WhoWor 93
Embrey, Robert Edward 1942- WhoIns 93
Embry, Dianne C. 1932- WhoAm 92
Embry, James Alden, II 1936- WhoSSW 93
Embry, Judith Carol 1950- WhoSSW 93
Embry, Michael Heard 1951- WhoEmL 93
Embry, Stephen Creston 1949- WhoE 93, WhoEmL 93
Embry, Susan Fleming 1954- WhoAmW 93
Embry, T. Eric 1921-1992 BioIn 17, NewYTBS 92
Embry, Wayne Richard 1937- WhoAm 92
Embury, Edward C. d1990 BioIn 17
Emch, Gerard Gustav 1936- WhoAm 92, WhoSSW 93
Emch-Deriaz, Antoinette Suzanne 1935- WhoSSW 93
Emecheta, Buchi BioIn 17
Emecheta, Buchi 1944- BlkAuII 92, IntLitE, IntvWPC 92 [port], ScF&FL 92
Emecheta, (Florence Onye) Buchi 1944- DcLB 117 [port]
Emeigh, Donald A., Jr. 1954- WhoIns 93
Emeigh Hart, Susan Gail 1957- WhoAmW 93
Emek, Sharon Helene 1945- WhoAmW 93
Emel, Erdal 1958- WhoScE 91-4
Emeleus, Karl George 1901-1989 BioIn 17
Emely, Charles Harry 1943- WhoWor 93
Emen, Michael S. Law&B 92
Emen, Michael Stuart 1950- St&PR 93
Emendorfer, Dieter 1927- WhoScE 91-3
Emeneau, Murray Barnson 1904- IntDcAn
Emenhiser, Jedon Allen 1933- WhoAm 92
Emerich, Donald Warren 1920- WhoAm 92, WhoSSW 93
Emerick, James Edwin 1945- St&PR 93
Emerick, Paul d1991 BioIn 17
Emerick, Robert Twite 1950- WhoE 93
Emerine, Wendell Roger 1939- St&PR 93
Emering, Edward John 1945- WhoWor 93
Emering, Sandra Ann 1949- WhoAmW 93
Emerling, Carol Frances 1930- WhoAm 92
Emerling, Carol G. 1930- St&PR 93
Emerling, Stanley Justin 1926- WhoSSW 93
Emerson, Alice B. MajAI
Emerson, Alice Frey 1931- WhoAm 92, WhoAmW 93, WhoE 93
Emerson, Andi 1932- WhoE 93
Emerson, Andrew C. Law&B 92
Emerson, Andrew C. 1929- St&PR 93
Emerson, Andrew Craig 1929- WhoAm 92
Emerson, Ann Parker 1925- WhoAm 92, WhoAmW 93
Emerson, Anne Devereux 1946- WhoAm 92, WhoEmL 93
Emerson, Bill BioIn 17
Emerson, Bill 1938- CngDr 91
Emerson, Billy 1925- BioIn 17
Emerson, Cae Alexius 1950- WhoEmL 93
Emerson, Catharine Law&B 92
Emerson, Christel Law&B 92
Emerson, D.C. WhoScE 91-1
Emerson, Daniel Everett 1924- St&PR 93, WhoAm 92
Emerson, Danny G. 1947- St&PR 93
Emerson, David Frederick 1926- WhoAm 92
Emerson, Diane Marie 1953- WhoEmL 93
Emerson, Duane E. 1937- WhoAm 92
Emerson, Edward James 1942- WhoAm 92
Emerson, Everett H. 1925- BioIn 17
Emerson, Everett Harvey 1925- WhoSSW 93, WhoWrEP 92
Emerson, Forrest M. Law&B 92
Emerson, Frederick George 1933- St&PR 93, WhoAm 92
Emerson, Gloria BioIn 17
Emerson, Horace Mann, III 1914- WhoAm 92
Emerson, James Larry 1938- WhoSSW 93
Emerson, James Timothy 1952- WhoEmL 93
Emerson, John Roy 1949- WhoEmL 93
Emerson, Kary Cadmus 1918- WhoAm 92
Emerson, Kathy Lynn BioIn 17
Emerson, Kathy Lynn 1947- WhoWrEP 92
Emerson, Luther Orlando 1820-1915 Baker 92
Emerson, Mark WhoWrEP 92
Emerson, Mark Forbush 1947- WhoEmL 93
Emerson, Michael W. Law&B 92
Emerson, Paul Carlton 1923- WhoAm 92
Emerson, Ralph Waldo 1803-1882 BioIn 17, MagSAmL [port], NinCLC 38 [port], WorLitC [port]
Emerson, Randall Allen 1948- St&PR 93
Emerson, Robert Kennerly, Sr. 1922- WhoAm 92
Emerson, Rose 1945- WhoAmW 93
Emerson, Ru 1944- ScF&FL 92, SmATA 70 [port]
Emerson, S. Jonathan 1929- WhoAm 92
Emerson, Steven A. 1954- WhoE 93
Emerson, Susan 1947- WhoAmW 93
Emerson, Thomas Edward, Jr. 1935- WhoAm 92
Emerson, Thomas Irwin 1907-1991 BioIn 17
Emerson, Vivian John 1937- WhoScE 91-1
Emerson, Walter Caruth 1912- WhoAm 92, WhoWor 93
Emerson, William 1938- WhoAm 92
Emerson, William Allen 1921- WhoAm 92
Emerson, William Harry 1928- St&PR 93, WhoAm 92
Emerson, William Keith 1925- WhoAm 92, WhoE 93
Emerson, William R. WhoAm 92, WhoE 93
Emerson-Davies, Dede 1933- WhoUN 92
Emert, John P. Law&B 92
Emert, Joseph Stewart 1953- WhoSSW 93
Emerton, Robert Walter, III Law&B 92
Emery, Alden Hayes, Jr. 1925- WhoAm 92
Emery, C.L., Jr. 1909- St&PR 93
Emery, Christine Vientiane 1957- WhoEmL 93
Emery, Clayton 1953- ScF&FL 92
Emery, Dallas Truett John 1925- St&PR 93
Emery, Dick 1917-1983 QDrFCA 92 [port]
Emery, Earl Eugene 1931- St&PR 93
Emery, Edith ScF&FL 92
Emery, Edwin 1914- WhoAm 92, WhoWor 93
Emery, Ernest C., Jr. 1945- St&PR 93
Emery, Howard Ivan, Jr. 1932- WhoE 93
Emery, Inez AmWomPl
Emery, James W. St&PR 93
Emery, Jane Leslie 1951- WhoAmW 93
Emery, John Colvin, Jr. 1924- St&PR 93
Emery, Jonathan W. Law&B 92
Emery, Karen J. Law&B 92
Emery, Kenneth Orris 1914- WhoAm 92
Emery, Lavinia 1944- St&PR 93
Emery, Lee Patrick 1938- St&PR 93
Emery, Lynnda Joyce 1953- WhoEmL 93
Emery, Marcia Rose 1937- WhoAm 92
Emery, Mark H. 1953- St&PR 93
Emery, Michael B. 1938- WhoAm 92
Emery, Oren Dale 1927- WhoAm 92
Emery, Paul Emile 1922- WhoAm 92, WhoWor 93
Emery, Paul R. Law&B 92
Emery, Philip H., Jr. 1934- St&PR 93
Emery, Priscilla 1952- WhoEmL 93
Emery, Ralph BioIn 17
Emery, Renata Martin 1960- WhoSSW 93
Emery, Robert Firestone 1927- WhoAm 92, WhoE 93
Emery, Robert J. 1937- St&PR 93
Emery, Ronald Howard 1944- St&PR 93
Emery, Sherman Raymond 1924- WhoAm 92
Emery, Sidney W., Jr. 1946- St&PR 93
Emery, Stephen Albert 1841-1891 Baker 92
Emery, Sue 1920- WhoAm 92
Emery, Susan Woodruff 1923- WhoAmW 93
Emery, Vince 1951- WhoEmL 93
Emery, Virginia Olga Beattie 1938- WhoAmW 93
Emery, Walter 1909-1974 Baker 92
Emery, Walter C. 1918- St&PR 93
Emerzian, Harry BioIn 17
Emes, Ian 1949- MiSFD 9
Emge, Kirk J. Law&B 92
Emi, Gregory M. Law&B 92
Emick, William John 1931- WhoSSW 93, WhoWor 93
Emig, Christian C. 1941- WhoScE 91-2
Emig, Evelyn AmWomPl
Emigh, Donald C. 1927- St&PR 93
Emile, Jean 1934- WhoScE 91-2
Emiliani, Andrea 1931- WhoWor 93
Emiliani, Cesare 1922- WhoAm 92
Emiliani, Vittorio 1935- WhoWor 93
Emilio, Marguerite AmWomPl
Emilson, C. Herbert 1929- St&PR 93
Emily, Dolores Jean 1952- WhoWrEP 92
Emin, Gevorg 1919- BioIn 17
Emini, Emilio Anthony 1953- WhoE 93
Eminovici, Angela 1937- WhoScE 91-4
Emin Pasha 1840-1892 Expl 93 [port]
Eminyan, Maurice 1922- WhoWor 93
Emison, James W. 1930- WhoAm 92
Emken, Robert Allan 1929- WhoAm 92
Emken, Robert Allan, Jr. Law&B 92
Emlen, Stephen Thompson 1940- WhoAm 92
Emler, Donald Gilbert 1939- WhoSSW 93
Emler, Jay Scott 1949- WhoEmL 93
Emlet, Harry Elsworth, Jr. 1927- St&PR 93
Emlet, Phyllis Joyce C. 1937- WhoAmW 93
Emley, Miles Lovelace Brereton 1949- WhoWor 93
Emley, Suzanne Elaine 1949- WhoEmL 93
Emling, Jay 1955- St&PR 93
Emmanouel, Dimitrios Spyridon 1940- WhoWor 93
Emmanouilides, George Christos 1926- WhoAm 92
Emmanuel, Arghiri 1911- WhoWor 93
Emmanuel, Jean Clifford 1941- WhoUN 92
Emmanuel, Jorge Agustin 1954- WhoWor 93
Emmanuel, Maurice 1862-1938 Baker 92, OxDcOp
Emmanuel, Michel George 1918- WhoAm 92
Emmanuel Philibert, Duke of Savoy 1528-1580 HarEnMi
Emme, Eugene M. 1919-1985 ScF&FL 92
Emmel, John Edward 1952- WhoSSW 93
Emmeluth, Bruce Palmer 1940- WhoAm 92
Emmen, Dennis R. 1933- St&PR 93, WhoAm 92
Emmenegger, Franz Peter 1935- WhoScE 91-4
Emmens, David P. Law&B 92
Emmens, David Peck 1948- St&PR 93
Emmens, Robert G. d1992 BioIn 17, NewYTBS 92
Emmer, Barbara Louise 1947- WhoAmW 93
Emmer, Bradford Noel 1949- WhoEmL 93
Emmer, David M. 1954- WhoEmL 93
Emmer, Edward Z. 1946- St&PR 93
Emmer, John Richard 1940- St&PR 93
Emmer, Philip I. 1928- St&PR 93
Emmerich, Andre 1924- WhoAm 92
Emmerich, Donald BioIn 17
Emmerich, Elsbeth BioIn 17
Emmerich, Francisco Guilherme 1956- WhoWor 93
Emmerich, John Patrick 1940- WhoE 93
Emmerich, Karol Denise 1948- St&PR 93, WhoAm 92, WhoAmW 93
Emmerich, Klaus Rudolf 1928- WhoWor 93
Emmerich, Myron H. 1929- St&PR 93
Emmerich, Roland MiSFD 9
Emmerich, Walter 1929- WhoAm 92
Emmerich, Werner Sigmund 1921- WhoAm 92
Emmerij, Louis WhoScE 91-2
Emmerling, Mary Ellisor BioIn 17
Emmerling, Paul E. 1933- St&PR 93
Emmerman, Michael N. 1945- St&PR 93, WhoAm 92
Emmermann, Rolf F.K. 1940- WhoScE 91-3
Emmerson, Bryan Thomas 1929- WhoWor 93
Emmerson, J.O. 1920- St&PR 93
Emmerson, John Gregory 1950- St&PR 93
Emmerson, John Lynn 1933- WhoAm 92
Emmerson, Peter Tunley WhoScE 91-1
Emmerson, Virginia Dillon 1929- St&PR 93
Emmert, Amor Charles, Jr. 1925- St&PR 93
Emmert, Gayle Evans 1938- St&PR 93
Emmert, Gilbert Arthur 1938- WhoAm 92
Emmert, John C., Jr. 1958- St&PR 93
Emmert, Richard Eugene 1929- WhoAm 92
Emmert, Roy G. 1958- St&PR 93
Emmert, Steven Michael Law&B 92
Emmerton, Anton ScF&FL 92
Emmerton, W. James Law&B 92
Emmerton, William James 1947- WhoAm 92
Emmet, Christopher Temple 1943- St&PR 93
Emmet, Robert 1778-1803 BioIn 17
Emmet, Timothy Goodsmith 1958- WhoEmL 93
Emmet-Miller, Maureen Law&B 92
Emmett, Daniel Decatur 1815-1904 Baker 92
Emmett, Edward Martin 1949- WhoAm 92
Emmett, Frederick Joseph, Jr. 1945- WhoAm 92
Emmett, James R. Law&B 92
Emmett, Martin F.C. 1934- BioIn 17
Emmett, Martin Frederick C. 1934- St&PR 93
Emmett, Martin Frederick Cheere 1934- WhoAm 92, WhoE 93
Emmett, Meredith WhoSSW 93
Emmett, Michael 1945- WhoSSW 93
Emmett, Robert Addis, III 1943- WhoAm 92
Emmett, Walter Charles 1925- WhoSSW 93
Emmi, Michael J. 1942- St&PR 93
Emmich, Otto von 1848-1915 HarEnMi
Emmiyan, Robert 1965- BioIn 17
Emmons, B.R. Law&B 92
Emmons, Charles Wayne 1952- WhoEmL 93
Emmons, Christopher W. 1955- St&PR 93
Emmons, Delia McQuade 1947- St&PR 93
Emmons, Donn 1910- WhoAm 92
Emmons, Guy W. 1947- St&PR 93
Emmons, Howard Wilson 1912- WhoAm 92
Emmons, Joanne 1934- WhoAmW 93
Emmons, Julia Voorhees 1941- WhoAmW 93
Emmons, Larry R. 1930- St&PR 93
Emmons, Marcia Faykus Law&B 92
Emmons, Marguerite Atteberry 1949- WhoWrEP 92
Emmons, Myra AmWomPl
Emmons, Nathanael 1745-1840 BioIn 17
Emmons, Olin Neill 1917- St&PR 93
Emmons, Raymond Allen 1950- St&PR 93
Emmons, Robert Duncan 1932- WhoAm 92
Emmons, Steven L. Law&B 92
Emmons, Walter Franklin 1928- St&PR 93
Emmons, William Monroe, III 1959- WhoEmL 93
Emmott, Bill ConAu 136
Emmott, William John 1956- ConAu 136
Emmrich, Frank 1949- WhoScE 91-3
Emms, Josepha Murray AmWomPl
Emms, William ScF&FL 92
Emney, Fred 1900-1980 QDrFCA 92 [port]
Emond, Edouard 1936- St&PR 93
Emond, Leonard David 1928- WhoE 93
Emond, Lionel Joseph 1932- WhoAm 92, WhoE 93
Emonds, Joseph Embley 1940- WhoAm 92
Emord, Jonathan Walker 1961- WhoEmL 93
Emorey, Howard O. 1928- St&PR 93
Emorey, Howard Omer 1928- WhoAm 92
Emori, Richard Ichiro 1924- WhoWor 93
Emory, Alan Steuer 1922- WhoE 93
Emory, Emerson 1925- WhoWor 93
Emory, John Druse 1938- St&PR 93
Emory, Kenneth Pike 1897- IntDcAn
Emory, Linda B. 1938- WhoIns 93
Emory, Malcolm BioIn 17
Emory, Martha Keller 1949- WhoEmL 93
Emory, Meade 1931- WhoAm 92
Emory, Samuel Thomas 1933- WhoSSW 93
Emory, Sonny BioIn 17
Emory, Thomas M., Jr. 1940- St&PR 93
Emotions SoulM
Empel, Wojciech Bernard 1932- WhoScE 91-4
Empelmann, Thomas 1962- WhoWor 93
Emperado, Mercedes Lopez 1941- WhoAm 92
Emperor Akihito 1933- WhoWor 93
Emplit, Raymond Henry 1948- WhoEmL 93
Empson, Cheryl Diane 1962- WhoAmW 93
Empson, William 1906-1984 BioIn 17, BritWr S2
Emptoz, H. WhoScE 91-2
Emr, Stephen Thomas 1946- St&PR 93
Emre, Yunus d1320? BioIn 17
Emrealp, Sadun Hasan 1954- WhoWor 93
Emrich, Dieter 1929- WhoScE 91-3
Emrich, Edmund Michael 1956- WhoEmL 93
Emrich, William Julius 1925- St&PR 93

Emrich, William Julius, Jr. 1951- *WhoSSW 93*
Emrick, Charles Robert, Jr. 1929- *WhoAm 92*
Emrick, Mark Gregory 1959- *St&PR 93*
Emrick, Robert D. 1941- *St&PR 93*
Emrick, Terry Lamar 1935- *WhoAm 92*
Emry, Dean Edwin 1952- *WhoEmL 93*
Emry, Douglas Kriss 1938- *WhoWrEP 92*
Emsheimer, Ernst 1904-1989 *BioIn 17*
Emsheimer, Ernst 1905- *Baker 92*
Emshwiller, Carol 1921- *ScF&FL 92*
Emshwiller, Carol Fries 1921- *WhoWrEP 92*
Emshwiller, Ed 1925-1990 *BioIn 17*
Emshwiller, Peter R. 1959- *ScF&FL 92*
Emson, Harry Edmund 1927- *WhoAm 92*
Emtman, Steve *BioIn 17*
Emtsev, Mikhail 1930- *ScF&FL 92*
Enacovici, George 1891-1965 *Baker 92*
Enanche, Radu 1950- *WhoScE 91-4*
Enander, Hilma Lewis *AmWomPl*
Enander, Jan-Sture *WhoScE 91-4*
Enantiophanes *OxDcByz*
Enari, T.M. *WhoScE 91-3*
Enari, Tor-Magnus 1928- *WhoScE 91-4, WhoWor 93*
Enarson, Harold L. 1919- *WhoAm 92*
Enberg, David *BioIn 17*
Enberg, Denis Alan *WhoWor 93*
Enberg, Dick *WhoAm 92*
Enberg, Henry Winfield 1940- *WhoE 93, WhoWor 93*
Enborg, Kenneth D. *Law&B 92*
Encarnacao, Jose L. *WhoScE 91-3*
Encarnacion, Jose, Jr. 1928- *WhoWor 93*
Encchev, Encho Athanassov 1921- *WhoScE 91-4*
Encel, Sol *ConAu 37NR*
Encel, Solomon 1925- *ConAu 37NR*
Enchanters *SoulM*
Enchev, Encho Athanasov 1921- *WhoWor 93*
Enchi, Fumiko 1905-1986 *BioIn 17*
Encina, Juan del 1468-1529? *Baker 92*
Encinas, Dionisio *DcCPCAm*
Encinas, Gary P. *Law&B 92*
Encinas, Jaime Fernando 1948- *WhoE 93*
Enck, Henry Synder 1942- *WhoE 93*
Enck, John Edward d1980 *ScF&FL 92*
Enckhausen, Heinrich Friedrich 1799-1885 *Baker 92*
Encle, Warren Charles 1948- *St&PR 93*
End, Henry 1915- *WhoAm 92, WhoWor 93*
End, John Michael 1946- *WhoEmL 93*
End, Ralph P. *Law&B 92*
End, Ralph P. 1938- *St&PR 93*
End, William Thomas 1947- *WhoAm 92*
Endacott, James H. *Law&B 92*
Endara, Guillermo *BioIn 17, WhoWor 93*
Endara Galimany, Guillermo 1936- *DcCPCAm*
Ende, Michael *BioIn 17*
Ende, Michael 1929- *ScF&FL 92*
Ende, Michael (Andreas Helmuth) 1929- *MajAI [port]*
Endejan, Judith A. *Law&B 92*
Endelman, Sharon Jean 1948- *WhoEmL 93*
Endemann, Carl T. 1902- *WhoWrEP 92*
Ender, Clara Adams- *BioIn 17*
Ender, Jon T. 1942- *St&PR 93*
Ender, Jon Terry 1942- *WhoAm 92*
Ender, Kornelia 1958- *BioIn 17*
Enderby, J. *WhoScE 91-2*
Enderby, John Edwin *WhoScE 91-1*
Enderle, Judith 1941- *ScF&FL 92*
Enderle, Judith (Ann) Ross 1941- *WhoWrEP 92*
Enderlein, Rolf 1936- *WhoScE 91-3*
Enderlin, Lee 1951- *WhoWrEP 92*
Enders, Allen Coffin 1928- *WhoAm 92*
Enders, Elizabeth McGuire 1939- *WhoE 93*
Enders, John F. 1897-1985 *BioIn 17*
Enders, Robert *MiSFD 9*
Endersby, Clive *WhoCanL 92*
Endewelt, Jack 1935- *BioIn 17*
Endfield, Cy 1914-1983 *MiSFD 9N*
Endicott, Frank S. 1904-1990 *BioIn 17*
Endicott, Gene Thomas 1959- *WhoEmL 93*
Endicott, John *Law&B 92*
Endicott, Sarah Ann 1956- *WhoAmW 93*
Endicott, William F. 1935- *WhoAm 92*
Endieveri, Anthony Frank 1939- *WhoE 93, WhoWor 93*
Endl, Gerald L. 1915-1944 *BioIn 17*
Endler, Franz *WhoScE 91-4*
Endler, James A. *Law&B 92*
Endler, Norman Solomon 1931- *WhoAm 92*
Endley, Ronald Ian Charles 1951- *WhoWor 93*
Endo, Hajime 1950- *WhoWor 93*
Endo, Kaname 1915- *WhoAsAP 91*
Endo, Kazuyoshi 1943- *WhoAsAP 91*
Endo, Noboru 1929- *WhoAsAP 91*
Endo, Otohiko 1947- *WhoAsAP 91*
Endo, Shusaku 1923- *BioIn 17, WhoWor 93*
Endo, Takehiko 1938- *WhoAsAP 91*
Endo, Tetsuya 1935- *WhoUN 92*
Endo, Yukihiko 1957- *WhoWor 93*
Endom, Phillip D. *Law&B 92*
Endore, Gita 1944- *WhoWrEP 92*
Endrenyi, Ferenc 1946- *WhoScE 91-4*
Endrenyi, Janos 1927- *WhoAm 92*
Endres, Albert Philipp 1932- *WhoWor 93*
Endres, Alfred Rudolf 1950- *WhoWor 93*
Endres, Ernst Wolfgang 1943- *St&PR 93*
Endres, Kathleen Lillian 1949- *WhoAmW 93*
Endres, Stefan J. 1957- *WhoWor 93*
Endres, Stephen Michael 1950- *St&PR 93*
Endresen, Endre, Jr. 1925- *St&PR 93*
Endress, Jay Wayne 1960- *WhoEmL 93*
Endress, Peter Karl 1942- *WhoScE 91-4*
Endress, Rudolf Helmut 1941- *WhoScE 91-3*
Endries, John Michael 1942- *St&PR 93, WhoAm 92, WhoE 93*
Endries, Robert N. *Law&B 92*
Endrikat, Klaus 1939- *BioIn 17*
Endriss, James Wagner 1933- *WhoSSW 93*
Endriss, Marilyn Jean 1953- *WhoAmW 93*
Endroczi, Elemer 1927- *WhoScE 91-4*
Endruweit, Gunter 1939- *WhoWor 93*
Endsley, Ferral Lee 1958- *WhoSSW 93*
Endsley, Gregory Howard 1949- *WhoEmL 93*
Endsley, Meredith *Law&B 92*
Endweiss, Patricia Conger 1948- *WhoAmW 93*
Endy, Melvin Becker, Jr. 1938- *WhoAm 92*
Endyke, Debra Joan 1955- *WhoEmL 93*
Endyke, Mary Louise 1960- *WhoE 93*
Enebuske, Sarah Folsom *AmWomPl*
Enegess, David Norman 1946- *WhoWor 93*
Enegren, Bradley 1947- *St&PR 93*
Enell, John Warren 1919- *WhoAm 92*
Enelow, Allen Jay 1922- *WhoAm 92*
Enemar, E. Anders V. 1926- *WhoScE 91-4*
Enenkel, Wolfgang *WhoScE 91-4*
Eneroth, Peter *WhoScE 91-4*
Enersen, Burnham 1905- *WhoAm 92*
Enesco, Georges 1881-1955 *Baker 92*
Enescu, George 1881-1955 *Baker 92, BioIn 17, OxDcOp*
Enfantino, Peter *ScF&FL 92*
Enfield, Donald Michael 1945- *WhoWor 93*
Enfield, Franklin D. 1933- *WhoAm 92*
Eng, Anne Chin 1950- *WhoAmW 93*
Eng, Gloria 1951- *St&PR 93*
Eng, Ingrid Ong Lee 1962- *WhoAmW 93, WhoEmL 93*
Eng, Kenneth Y. 1950- *WhoE 93*
Eng, Lawrence Fook 1931- *WhoAm 92*
Eng, Mamie 1954- *WhoEmL 93*
Eng, Michael J. *Law&B 92*
Eng, Patricia Siang Cher *Law&B 92*
Eng, Peter d1991 *BioIn 17*
Eng, Steve 1940- *WhoSSW 93, WhoWrEP 92*
Engberg, Nancy Jean *Law&B 92*
Engberg, Ole Hieronymus 1922- *WhoWor 93*
Engberg, Robert Eugene 1937- *St&PR 93*
Engblom, Goran *WhoUN 92*
Engbretson, Peter Curtis 1939- *WhoE 93*
Engdahl, Richard Alan 1941- *WhoSSW 93*
Engdahl, Richard Bott 1914- *WhoAm 92*
Engdahl, Sylvia Louise 1933- *DcAmChF 1960, MajAI [port], ScF&FL 92*
Engdahl, Walter A. *Law&B 92*
Engebrecht, Patricia Ann 1935- *WhoE 93*
Engebretson, Charles K. 1950- *St&PR 93*
Engebretson, David 1964- *ScF&FL 92*
Engebretson, David J. 1951- *St&PR 93*
Engebretson, Douglas Kenneth 1946- *WhoAm 92*
Engebretson, Milton Benjamin 1920- *WhoAm 92*
Engebritson, Scott J. 1958- *WhoIns 93*
Engel, Alan 1941- *ScF&FL 92*
Engel, Albert Joseph 1924- *WhoAm 92*
Engel, Alfred Julius 1927- *WhoAm 92*
Engel, Allan D. *Law&B 92*
Engel, Andi *MiSFD 9*
Engel, Andrew George 1930- *WhoAm 92*
Engel, Barbara Marcus 1946- *WhoEmL 93*
Engel, Bernard Theodore 1928- *WhoAm 92*
Engel, Brian Evan 1951- *WhoEmL 93*
Engel, Brian K. 1956- *WhoIns 93*
Engel, Bruce L. 1940- *ConEn*
Engel, Carl 1818-1882 *Baker 92*
Engel, Carl 1883-1944 *Baker 92, BioIn 17*
Engel, Charlene Stant 1946- *WhoEmL 93*
Engel, Charles Robert 1922- *WhoAm 92, WhoWor 93*
Engel, David Anthony 1951- *WhoEmL 93*
Engel, David Donald 1937- *St&PR 93*
Engel, David Hermann 1816-1877 *Baker 92*
Engel, David Lewis 1947- *WhoEmL 93*
Engel, David M. 1947- *St&PR 93*
Engel, David S. 1944- *St&PR 93*
Engel, David Wayne 1956- *WhoEmL 93*
Engel, Diana 1947- *ConAu 138, SmATA 70 [port]*
Engel, Dinah Bogart *Law&B 92*
Engel, Edward John 1948- *St&PR 93*
Engel, Eliot L. 1947- *CngDr 91, WhoAm 92, WhoE 93*
Engel, Frances Holiday 1915- *WhoAmW 93*
Engel, Frederik 1924- *St&PR 93*
Engel, Gabriel 1892-1952 *Baker 92*
Engel, George Larry 1947- *WhoEmL 93*
Engel, George Libman 1913- *WhoAm 92*
Engel, Gustav 1931- *WhoScE 91-3*
Engel, Hans 1894-1970 *Baker 92*
Engel, Herman A., Jr. 1915- *St&PR 93*
Engel, Howard 1931- *WhoCanL 92*
Engel, Irving H. 1909- *St&PR 93*
Engel, James Harry 1946- *WhoSSW 93*
Engel, James Joseph 1934- *St&PR 93*
Engel, James Marc 1956- *WhoE 93*
Engel, Jerome, Jr. 1938- *WhoWor 93*
Engel, Joan Marcia 1946- *WhoAmW 93, WhoEmL 93*
Engel, Joel 1868-1927 *Baker 92*
Engel, Joel 1952- *ScF&FL 92*
Engel, Joel Stanley 1936- *WhoAm 92*
Engel, John Charles 1955- *WhoEmL 93*
Engel, John Jacob 1936- *WhoAm 92, WhoE 93*
Engel, John Jay 1941- *WhoAm 92*
Engel, Joyce H. 1927- *St&PR 93*
Engel, Juergen Kurt 1945- *WhoWor 93*
Engel, Jurgen 1935- *WhoScE 91-4*
Engel, Karl 1923- *Baker 92*
Engel, Keith Curtiss 1948- *St&PR 93*
Engel, Lawrence Edward 1943- *WhoIns 93*
Engel, Lehman 1910-1982 *Baker 92*
Engel, Leonard W. 1936- *WhoE 93*
Engel, Linda Jeanne 1949- *St&PR 93, WhoEmL 93*
Engel, Lon 1959- *WhoEmL 93*
Engel, Marcy *Law&B 92*
Engel, Marian 1933-1985 *WhoCanL 92*
Engel, Melissa Hale 1956- *WhoEmL 93*
Engel, Monroe 1921- *WhoWrEP 92*
Engel, Nina Stawski 1955- *WhoAmW 93*
Engel, Pamela Marie 1956- *WhoEmL 93*
Engel, Paul Bernard 1926- *WhoAm 92*
Engel, Philip L. 1940- *St&PR 93*
Engel, Ralph 1934- *WhoAm 92*
Engel, Ralph Manuel 1944- *WhoAm 92*
Engel, Ronald Richard 1936- *St&PR 93, WhoIns 93*
Engel, Theodore *ScF&FL 92*
Engel, Thomas 1942- *WhoAm 92*
Engel, Victor Boynton 1914- *WhoWor 93*
Engel, William R. 1930- *WhoIns 93*
Engel, Zbigniew 1933- *WhoScE 91-4*
Engel-Arieli, Susan Lee 1954- *WhoAmW 93, WhoEmL 93, WhoWor 93*
Engelbach, David 1946- *MiSFD 9*
Engelbardt, Robert Miles 1931- *St&PR 93, WhoAm 92*
Engelbart, Doug *BioIn 17*
Engelberg, Alan D. *ScF&FL 92*
Engelberg, Edward 1929- *WhoE 93*
Engelberg, Elaine A. 1930- *WhoAmW 93*
Engelberg, Stephen Paul 1958- *WhoAm 92*
Engelberger, John K. 1930- *St&PR 93*
Engelberger, Joseph F. *BioIn 17*
Engelberger, Joseph F. 1925- *St&PR 93*
Engelberger, Joseph Frederick 1925- *WhoAm 92*
Engelberger, William V. 1938- *St&PR 93*
Engelbert, Arthur Ferdinand 1903- *WhoAm 92*
Engelbrecht, Christiaan Mauritz 1943- *WhoWor 93*
Engelbrecht, Mary Lou 1954- *WhoEmL 93*
Engelbrecht, Richard Stevens 1926- *WhoAm 92*
Engelbrecht, Robert Martin 1923-1991 *BioIn 17*
Engelbrecht, Rudolf 1928- *WhoAm 92*
Engelbrecht, William Robert 1949- *St&PR 93*
Engelbright, Curtis Lee 1928- *WhoSSW 93*
Engeleiter, Gerald H. 1951- *St&PR 93*
Engeleiter, Susan Shannon 1952- *WhoAm 92*
Engeler, Erwin 1930- *WhoWor 93*
Engeler, William Ernest 1928- *WhoAm 92*
Engelfriet, Cornelis Paulus 1927- *WhoScE 91-3*
Engelhard, Diane Mary 1964- *WhoEmL 93*
Engelhard, George, Jr. 1953- *WhoSSW 93*
Engelhardt, Albert George 1935- *WhoAm 92, WhoSSW 93*
Engelhardt, Cynthia Allison 1950- *WhoEmL 93*
Engelhardt, Dean Lee 1940- *St&PR 93, WhoAm 92*
Engelhardt, G.H. 1930- *WhoScE 91-3*
Engelhardt, H(ugo) Tristram, Jr. 1941- *ConAu 139*
Engelhardt, Hugo Tristram, Jr. 1941- *WhoAm 92, WhoWor 93*
Engelhardt, John Hugo 1946- *WhoEmL 93, WhoSSW 93*
Engelhardt, Knut P. *Law&B 92*
Engelhardt, LeRoy A. 1924- *WhoAm 92*
Engelhardt, Robert Joseph 1941- *St&PR 93*
Engelhardt, Rolf-Udo 1935- *WhoWor 93*
Engelhardt, Sara Lawrence 1943- *WhoAm 92*
Engelhardt, Susan Gay 1943- *WhoSSW 93*
Engelhardt, Thomas Alexander 1930- *WhoAm 92*
Engelhardt, Wolfgang von 1932- *WhoScE 91-3*
Engelhart, Joanne 1948- *WhoAmW 93*
Engelhart, Kenneth G. *Law&B 92*
Engelhart, Michael Anthony 1945- *WhoAm 92*
Engelke, Jane Lewis *BioIn 17*
Engelkes, Donald J. 1938- *WhoIns 93*
Engelkes, Donald John 1938- *St&PR 93, WhoAm 92*
Engelking, Henry Mark 1949- *WhoEmL 93*
Engell, Hans-Jurgen *WhoScE 91-3*
Engell, James Theodore 1951- *WhoE 93*
Engell, John Emil 1944- *WhoScE 91-2*
Engelmaier, Werner 1939- *WhoE 93*
Engelman, Arthur 1930- *WhoE 93*
Engelman, Charles Edward 1935- *St&PR 93*
Engelman, Donald Bertam 1948- *WhoEmL 93*
Engelman, Donald Max 1941- *WhoAm 92*
Engelman, Irwin *St&PR 93*
Engelman, Karl 1933- *WhoAm 92*
Engelman, Melvin Alkon 1921- *WhoAm 92, WhoWor 93*
Engelman, Richard A. *Law&B 92*
Engelman, Robert S. 1912- *WhoAm 92*
Engelman, Susan Phyllis 1948- *WhoAm 92, WhoAmW 93*
Engelmann, Charles V. 1931- *WhoScE 91-2*
Engelmann, F. *WhoScE 91-3*
Engelmann, Hans Ulrich 1921- *Baker 92*
Engelmann, Larry *BioIn 17*
Engelmann, Lothar Klaus 1926- *WhoAm 92*
Engelmann, Rudolf Jacob 1930- *WhoAm 92*
Engels, Frank A. 1936- *St&PR 93*
Engels, Friedrich 1820-1895 *BioIn 17*
Engels, Lawrence Arthur 1933- *St&PR 93*
Engels, Thomas Joseph 1958- *WhoEmL 93*
Engels, Walter D. d1992 *BioIn 17, NewYTBS 92*
Engels-Adams, Kathleen M. 1943- *St&PR 93*
Engelson, David 1920- *St&PR 93*
Engelson, Erik T. *St&PR 93*
Engelson, Joyce *BioIn 17*
Engemann, Robert B. 1949- *St&PR 93*
Engen, D. Travis 1944- *St&PR 93*
Engen, Donald Travis 1944- *WhoAm 92*
Enger, Carl Christian 1929- *WhoSSW 93*
Enger, Edward Henry, Jr. 1930- *WhoE 93*
Enger, Linda May 1955- *WhoEmL 93*
Enger, Walter Melvin 1914- *WhoAm 92*
Engerer, Brigitte 1952- *Baker 92*
Engerman, Stanley Lewis 1936- *WhoAm 92, WhoE 93*
Engerrand, Doris Dieskow 1925- *WhoAmW 93, WhoSSW 93*
Engerrand, Kenneth G. 1952- *WhoWor 93*
Engers, Scott J. *Law&B 92*
Engesser, Donald Gilbert 1927- *WhoE 93*
Engfeldt, Lars-Goran 1944- *WhoUN 92*
Enggaard, Knud 1929- *WhoWor 93*
Enggass, Robert 1921- *WhoAm 92*
Engh, M.J. 1933- *ScF&FL 92*
Engh, Thorvald Abel 1934- *WhoScE 91-4*
Enghien, Francois de Bourbon, Count of 1519-1546 *HarEnMi*
Engholm, Mary Korstad Mueller 1918- *WhoAmW 93, WhoWor 93*
Enginol, Turan B. 1933- *WhoScE 91-4*
Englade, Ken *BioIn 17*
England, Anthony Wayne 1942- *WhoAm 92*
England, Arthur Jay, Jr. 1932- *WhoAm 92*
England, Brenda 1940- *WhoAmW 93*
England, C. McDonald 1916- *St&PR 93*

England, Claire Agricola 1948- WhoAmW 93
England, Dan Benjamin 1955- WhoEmL 93, WhoSSW 93
England, Daniel Eugene 1947- St&PR 93
England, Dean Daniels 1954- St&PR 93
England, Edward 1937- St&PR 93
England, Eugene Knight 1919- St&PR 93
England, Gary Alan WhoSSW 93
England, Gary L. 1958- St&PR 93
England, George F. 1938- St&PR 93
England, Howard 1935- St&PR 93
England, J.K. Robert 1948- WhoUN 92
England, Jack Ray 1921- St&PR 93
England, James ScF&FL 92
England, John F.L. 1936- St&PR 93
England, Jonathan S. 1913- St&PR 93
England, Jonnie Lee 1949- WhoAmW 93, WhoSSW 93
England, Joseph Walker 1940- St&PR 93, WhoAm 92
England, Linda BioIn 17
England, Lynne Lipton 1949- WhoAmW 93, WhoEmL 93, WhoSSW 93, WhoWor 93
England, Mary Jane BioIn 17
England, Richard 1920- St&PR 93, WhoE 93
England, Roland 1940- WhoWor 93
England, Ruth Catherine 1955- WhoAm 92
England, Stephen James 1951- WhoEmL 93
England, Wendy ScF&FL 92
Englander, Elliot Jordan 1931- St&PR 93
Englander, Joseph 1908- St&PR 93
Englander, Kenneth Harold 1939- St&PR 93
Englander, Paula Tyo 1951- WhoAmW 93
Englander, Robert L. 1933- St&PR 93
Englander, Roger Leslie 1926- WhoAm 92
Englander, Tom 1946- WhoEmL 93, WhoSSW 93
Englar, John D. Law&B 92
Englar, John David 1947- St&PR 93
Englard, Sara Fae 1959- WhoEmL 93
Engle, Carole Ruth 1952- WhoEmL 93, WhoSSW 93
Engle, Donald Edward 1927- WhoAm 92, WhoWor 93
Engle, Ed 1950- BioIn 17
Engle, Gary 1947- ScF&FL 92
Engle, Gary P. 1952- St&PR 93
Engle, Harold Martin 1914- WhoAm 92
Engle, Jacob Lenhart, Jr. 1937- WhoSSW 93
Engle, James Bruce 1919- WhoAm 92
Engle, James Wayne 1951- WhoWor 93
Engle, Janet Patricia 1959- WhoEmL 93
Engle, Jeannette Cranfill 1941- WhoAmW 93
Engle, John David, Jr. 1922- WhoSSW 93
Engle, Lewis Hole 1948- WhoSSW 93
Engle, Mary Allen English 1922- WhoAm 92
Engle, Paul 1908-1991 AnObit 1991, BioIn 17
Engle, Phillip Raymond 1940- WhoAm 92
Engle, Ralph Landis, Jr. 1920- WhoAm 92
Engle, Richard Carlyle 1934- St&PR 93, WhoAm 92
Engle, Richard Mallory 1933- WhoE 93
Engle, Sandra Louise 1949- WhoEmL 93
Engle, William John 1948- WhoSSW 93
Engledow, Jack Lee 1931- WhoAm 92
Englehart, Joan Anne 1940- WhoAmW 93, WhoWor 93
Englehart, John BioIn 17
Englehart, Stephen ScF&FL 92
Englehart, Theodore M. 1920- St&PR 93
Englehaupt, William Myles 1918- WhoAm 92
Englehaupt, William Myles, III 1954- WhoEmL 93
Engleman, Charles Edward 1911- WhoSSW 93
Engleman, Dennis Eugene 1948- WhoEmL 93, WhoSSW 93
Engleman, Donald James Law&B 92
Engleman, Donald James 1947- St&PR 93, WhoAm 92
Engleman, Ephraim Philip 1911- WhoAm 92
Engleman, Gene E. 1911- St&PR 93
Englemann, Glenn M. Law&B 92
Englemann, John H. Law&B 92
Engler, Brian David 1947- WhoSSW 93
Engler, Frederick Ernst 1928- St&PR 93
Engler, George Nichols 1944- WhoAm 92
Engler, Hans Philipp 1953- WhoEmL 93
Engler, Joaquim J. de C. 1942- WhoWor 93
Engler, John BioIn 17
Engler, John Mathias 1948- WhoAm 92
Engler, Marky Ann 1956- WhoEmL 93
Engler, Robert 1922- WhoAm 92
Engler, Siegfried 1931- WhoScE 91-3
Engler, W. Joseph, Jr. Law&B 92
Engler, W. Joseph, Jr. 1940- St&PR 93, WhoAm 92
Engler, William Dean, Jr. 1936- St&PR 93
Englert, Giuseppe Giorgio 1927- Baker 92
Englert, Joseph S., Jr. Law&B 92
Englert, Roy Theodore 1922- WhoAm 92
Englert, Wolf Dieter 1942- WhoScE 91-3
Englerth, Rebecca Ann 1942- WhoAmW 93
Engles, Charles R. 1947- St&PR 93
Engles, David 1946- WhoIns 93
Engles, John L., Jr. 1937- WhoAm 92
Englesbe, Andrew Joseph 1950- WhoIns 93
Englesmith, Tejas 1941- WhoAm 92
Engling, Richard 1952- ScF&FL 92
Engling, Robert John 1945- St&PR 93, WhoAm 92
English, Arthur Vernon 1946- WhoEmL 93
English, Bill BioIn 17
English, Bruce Vaughan 1921- WhoAm 92, WhoSSW 93
English, Charles Brand 1924- WhoAm 92
English, Charles Royal 1938- WhoWor 93
English, Cindy Marie 1957- WhoEmL 93
English, Clarence R. AfrAmBi [port]
English, Clifford, Jr. 1940- WhoIns 93
English, Curtis Riegel 1934- WhoE 93
English, Dale Lowell 1956- WhoEmL 93
English, Darryl Law&B 92
English, David 1792-1856 BioIn 17
English, David 1839-1862 BioIn 17
English, David Floyd 1948- WhoE 93, WhoEmL 93
English, Diane BioIn 17, WhoAmW 93
English, Donald Marvin 1951- WhoEmL 93
English, Edna Soraghan 1938- St&PR 93
English, Elizabeth Ann 1962- WhoEmL 93
English, Elizabeth Stacy 1959- WhoAmW 93, WhoEmL 93
English, Ellen Darlene 1952- WhoEmL 93
English, Eva Uber 1925- WhoAmW 93
English, Floyd Leroy 1934- St&PR 93, WhoAm 92
English, Glenn 1940- CngDr 91, WhoAm 92, WhoSSW 93
English, Granville 1895-1968 Baker 92
English, H.R. WhoScE 91-1
English, Jack R. 1930- St&PR 93
English, James Dunston 1941- St&PR 93
English, James Fairfield, Jr. 1927- WhoAm 92
English, James Hilton, Jr. 1919- WhoE 93
English, James Jones, II 1927- WhoSSW 93
English, Jean 1937- ScF&FL 92
English, John Wesley 1940- WhoWrEP 92
English, John Winfield 1933- WhoE 93
English, Joseph R. 1931- St&PR 93
English, Karan 1939- WhoAmW 93
English, Kevin W. 1953- St&PR 93
English, Lawrence Gregory 1948- St&PR 93
English, Lawrence William 1942- St&PR 93, WhoAm 92
English, Lynne Law&B 92
English, Mark G. Law&B 92
English, Maureen S. Law&B 92
English, Nicholas Conover 1912- WhoAm 92
English, Paul Ward 1936- WhoAm 92
English, Richard Allyn 1936- WhoAm 92
English, Richard D. 1948- WhoAm 92, WhoEmL 93
English, Richard George 1946- WhoSSW 93
English, Richard Walter d1990 BioIn 17
English, Robert Joseph 1932- WhoAm 92
English, Ruth Ann Cowder 1948- WhoAmW 93, WhoSSW 93
English, Ruth Hill 1904- WhoAmW 93
English, Stanley Fraser 1935- St&PR 93
English, Thomas Francis Law&B 92
English, Thomas James 1942- WhoAm 92
English, Walter 1904- St&PR 93
English, Wannell T. 1940- St&PR 93
English, Wilke Denton 1949- WhoEmL 93
English, William deShay 1924- WhoAm 92
English, William Hazen 1929- WhoAm 92
English, William N. 1950- St&PR 93
English, Woodruff Jones 1909- WhoAm 92
English, Zeborah Anita 1951- WhoEmL 93
English Beat, The ConMus 9 [port]
Englund, Einar (Sven) 1916- Baker 92
Englund, Gage Bush 1931- WhoAm 92
Englund, George 1926- MiSFD 9
Englund, Gunnar Martin 1940- WhoWor 93
Englund, John Arthur 1926- WhoAm 92
Englund, Lizbeth A. Law&B 92
Englund, Paul Theodore 1938- WhoAm 92
Englund, Philip J. Law&B 92
Englund, Richard 1931-1991 BioIn 17
Englund, Robert BioIn 17
Englund, Robert 1931- MiSFD 9
Englund, Robert Derr 1947- St&PR 93
Engman, Arnold 1949- St&PR 93
Engman, James William 1948- WhoSSW 93
Engman, John Robert Law&B 92
Engman, John Robert 1949- WhoWrEP 92
Engman, Lewis August 1936- WhoAm 92
Engmann, Douglas Joe 1947- WhoEmL 93
Engoren, Sampson Seymour 1929- WhoAm 92
Engoron, Edward David 1946- WhoEmL 93, WhoWor 93
Engquist, Bjorn Erik 1945- WhoScE 91-4
Engqvist, Mikael Law&B 92
Engstrand, U.E. Lennart 1942- WhoScE 91-4
Engstrom, Arne V. 1920- WhoScE 91-4
Engstrom, Arne Vilhelm 1920- WhoWor 93
Engstrom, Betsy L. ScF&FL 92
Engstrom, Bjorn Greger 1951- WhoWor 93
Engstrom, Donald James 1948- WhoEmL 93
Engstrom, Elizabeth 1951- ScF&FL 92
Engstrom, Eric Gustaf 1942- WhoAm 92
Engstrom, Fredrik 1939- WhoScE 91-2
Engstrom, Leonard Ernest Law&B 92
Engstrom, Mark W. Law&B 92
Engstrom, Mark William 1955- WhoEmL 93
Engstrom, N.A. Lorentz 1931- WhoScE 91-4
Engstrom, N. Daniel 1928- St&PR 93
Engum, Eric Stanley 1949- WhoSSW 93
Engvall, Lars Olof 1931- WhoUN 92
Engvalson, Kinley Irving 1956- WhoEmL 93
Enichen, Robert C. 1948- St&PR 93
Enin, Aanaa Naanna 1939- WhoAfr
Enis, Ben M(elvin) 1942- WhoWrEP 92
Enix, Agnes Lucille 1933- WhoAm 92
Enjalbert, Patrice WhoScE 91-2
Enkegaard, Torben 1936- WhoScE 91-2
Enkvist, Nils Erik August 1925- WhoWor 93
Enloe, Cortez Ferdinand, Jr. 1910- WhoAm 92, WhoWor 93
Enloe, Cynthia H(olden) 1938- ConAu 39NR
Enloe, Margaret McIntyre Law&B 92
Enloe, Mary A. AmWomPl
Enloe, Robert Ted, III 1938- WhoAm 92, WhoSSW 93
Enloe, Ted 1938- St&PR 93
Enlow, Donald Hugh 1927- WhoAm 92
Enlow, Fred Clark 1940- WhoAm 92
Enlow, Larry Daniel 1947- St&PR 93
Enlow, Ralph Eugene 1950- WhoSSW 93
Enlow, Rick Lynn 1956- WhoSSW 93
Enlund, E. Stanley 1917- St&PR 93
Enlund, Nils E.S. 1946- WhoScE 91-4
Enna, August 1859-1939 OxDcOp
Enna, August (Emil) 1859-1939 Baker 92
Enna, Salvatore Joseph 1944- WhoAm 92
Enna, Stephen Alexander 1946- St&PR 93
Ennals, Martin 1927-1991 AnObit 1991, BioIn 17
Enneking, Ronald Leo 1953- WhoE 93
Enneli, Sebahat 1949- WhoScE 91-4
Ennest, John William 1942- St&PR 93, WhoAm 92
Ennevaara, Mikko Kyosti 1946- WhoWor 93
Enney, James Crowe 1930- WhoAm 92
Enney, Victoria L. Law&B 92
Ennis, Billy Mack 1938- St&PR 93
Ennis, Brian R. St&PR 93
Ennis, Catherine 1937- ScF&FL 92
Ennis, Charles R. 1932- St&PR 93
Ennis, Charles Roe Law&B 92
Ennis, Charles Roe 1932- WhoAm 92
Ennis, Edgar William, Jr. 1945- WhoAm 92
Ennis, Floyd R. 1928- St&PR 93
Ennis, Frank E. 1943- St&PR 93
Ennis, George Elliott 1933- WhoSSW 93
Ennis, Herbert Leo 1932- WhoE 93
Ennis, Joseph BioIn 17
Ennis, Lamar Wallache 1954- WhoWrEP 92
Ennis, Leslie Frederick 1933- St&PR 93, WhoWor 93
Ennis, Louis Joseph 1929- WhoE 93
Ennis, Michael Don 1953- St&PR 93
Ennis, Michael Stanislaus 1929- WhoWor 93
Ennis, Thomas Michael 1931- WhoAm 92, WhoWor 93
Enns, Mark Kynaston 1931- WhoAm 92
Enns, Rodrick John 1955- WhoEmL 93
Eno, Brian 1940- ConMus 8 [port]
Eno, Brian 1948- Baker 92, WhoAm 92
Eno, Gerard Francis 1946- St&PR 93
Eno, Paul Frederick 1953- WhoE 93
Enoch, Charles A. 1951- WhoWor 93
Enoch, Charles Johnson 1917- St&PR 93
Enoch, Herbert Zvi 1933- WhoWor 93
Enoch, Jay Martin 1929- WhoAm 92
Enoch, Leslie Blythe 1942- St&PR 93
Enoch, Leslie Blythe, II Law&B 92
Enoch, Leslie Blythe, II 1942- WhoSSW 93
Enol'Skii, Victor Zelikovich 1945- WhoWor 93
Enomoto, Takeaki 1836-1908 HarEnMi
Enos, Chris 1944- WhoE 93
Enos, Gregory Joseph WhoE 93
Enos, Mindy 1962- WhoAmW 93
Enos, Paul 1934- WhoAm 92
Enos, Paul R. 1931- WhoIns 93
Enos, Paul Richard 1931- St&PR 93
Enos, Randall 1936- WhoAm 92
Enos, Robert Warren 1932- St&PR 93
Enos, Theresa Jarnagin WhoAmW 93
Enouen, William Albert 1928- St&PR 93, WhoAm 92
Enous, Karen B. 1942- WhoAmW 93
Enquist, Irving Fridtjof 1920- WhoAm 92
Enquist, Lynn William 1945- WhoE 93
Enrico, Ferorelli 1941- WhoE 93
Enrico, Robert 1931- MiSFD 9
Enrico, Roger A. WhoAm 92
Enright, Arthur Joseph 1932- WhoE 93
Enright, Cynthia Lee 1950- WhoAmW 93
Enright, D.J. 1920- BioIn 17
Enright, Dan d1992 NewYTBS 92 [port]
Enright, Daniel BioIn 17
Enright, Dennis Joseph 1920- BioIn 17
Enright, Elizabeth 1909-1968 DcAmChF 1960, MajAI [port]
Enright, James Peter 1941- St&PR 93
Enright, Jeremiah Francis 1929- WhoUN 92
Enright, John Kevin Law&B 92
Enright, Michael J(ohn) 1958- ConAu 139
Enright, Michael Joseph 1955- WhoSSW 93
Enright, Nancy Helen 1955- WhoAmW 93
Enright, Ray 1896-1965 MiSFD 9N
Enright, Robert S. 1946- St&PR 93
Enright, Stephanie Veselich 1929- WhoAmW 93, WhoWor 93
Enright, Vincent D. 1943- St&PR 93
Enright, William Benner 1925- WhoAm 92
Enright, William Fairleigh, Jr. 1920- WhoAm 92
Enrile, Juan Ponce 1924- WhoAsAP 91
Enriques, Edward R. 1940- St&PR 93
Enrique Y Tarancon, Vicente Cardinal 1907- WhoWor 93
Enriquez, Carola Rupert 1954- WhoAm 92, WhoAmW 93
Enriquez, Manuel 1926- Baker 92
Enriquez, Miguel Angel 1943- WhoUN 92
Enriquez, Rene d1990 BioIn 17
Enriquez de Valderrabano, Enrique fl. 16th cent.- Baker 92
Enroth, Theresa Louise 1925- WhoWrEP 92
Enroth-Cugell, Christina Alma Elisabeth 1919- WhoAm 92
Ensch, Thomas John 1938- WhoAm 92
Ense, Karl August Varnhagen von 1785-1858 BioIn 17
Ense, Rahel Varnhagen von 1771-1833 BioIn 17
Ensenat, Donald Burnham 1946- WhoEmL 93
Ensenat, Louis Albert 1916- WhoSSW 93
Enser, Syed Ali 1949- WhoWor 93
Enser, William A. 1944- St&PR 93
Ensey, Michael A. 1941- St&PR 93
Ensign, D. Brent 1956- St&PR 93
Ensign, Gregory Moore Law&B 92
Ensign, John H. 1939- St&PR 93
Ensign, Nancy Udelson 1950- WhoAmW 93
Ensign, Peter Lowe 1949- St&PR 93
Ensign, Richard L. 1925- St&PR 93
Ensign, Richard Papworth 1919- WhoAm 92
Ensign, William Lloyd 1928- WhoAm 92
Ensigner, I.J. 1942- St&PR 93
Ensikat, Klaus 1937- BioIn 17
Ensing, A. 1930- WhoScE 91-3
Enslen, Richard Alan 1931- WhoAm 92
Ensley, Evangeline ScF&FL 92
Ensley, George H. 1927- WhoIns 93
Ensley, Rodney Gene 1934- St&PR 93, WhoIns 93
Enslin, Theodore Vernon 1925- WhoAm 92, WhoWrEP 92
Enslinger, Gary Lee 1952- WhoEmL 93
Enslow, Ridley M., Jr. 1926- St&PR 93
Enslow, Ridley Madison, Jr. 1926- WhoAm 92
Enslow, Sam 1946- ConAu 136, WhoEmL 93, WhoSSW 93
Ensminger, Luther Glenn 1919- WhoAm 92

Ensminger, Marion Eugene 1908- *WhoAm 92*
Ensminger, Ronald Jay 1943- *WhoE 93*
Ensor, Allison Rash 1935- *WhoSSW 93*
Ensor, Gary Albert 1956- *WhoEmL 93*
Ensor, Patricia Lee 1959- *WhoEmL 93*
Ensor, Peter John 1930- *WhoWor 93*
Ensor, Richard Joseph 1953- *WhoE 93*
Ensslin, Robert Frank, Jr. 1928- *WhoAm 92*
Enstice, Wayne 1943- *ConAu 139*
Enstine, Raymond Wilton, Jr. 1946- *WhoE 93, WhoEmL 93, WhoWor 93*
Enstrom, James Eugene 1943- *WhoAm 92*
Enstrom, Robert 1946- *ScF&FL 92*
Entel, Melvin Allen 1944- *St&PR 93*
Enteman, Willard Finley 1936- *WhoAm 92*
Entenberg, Herbert 1934- *St&PR 93*
Entenman, Alfred M., Jr. 1921- *St&PR 93*
Enters, Laurel Maguire 1939- *WhoAmW 93*
Entes, Judith 1951- *WhoAmW 93, WhoE 93*
Enthoven, Adolf Jan Henri 1928- *WhoSSW 93*
Enthoven, (Henri) Emile 1903-1950 *Baker 92*
Entian, Karl-Dieter 1952- *WhoWor 93*
Entin, Frederic *BioIn 17*
Entin, Jonathan Lowe 1947- *WhoEmL 93*
Entine, Joseph Howard 1927- *WhoE 93*
Entine, Lynn Bergmann 1947- *WhoEmL 93*
Entmacher, Paul Sidney 1924- *WhoAm 92*
Entman, Barbara Sue 1954- *WhoAmW 93*
Entman, Mark Lawrence 1938- *WhoSSW 93*
Entner, Paul Dwight 1947- *WhoEmL 93*
Entorf, Richard Carl 1929- *WhoAm 92*
Entrecasteaux, Joseph-Antoine Raymond Bruni d' 1739-1793 *Expl 93*
Entrekin, Charles Edward, Jr. 1941- *WhoWrEP 92*
Entremont, Philippe 1934- *Baker 92, WhoAm 92, WhoWor 93*
Entwisle, Doris Roberts 1924- *WhoAm 92*
Entwistle, Andrew John 1959- *WhoEmL 93*
Entwistle, Gordon Thomas 1942- *St&PR 93*
Entwistle, James Tobit 1944- *WhoIns 93*
Entwistle, Noel (James) 1936- *ConAu 39NR*
Entzminger, John Nelson, Jr. 1936- *WhoAm 92, WhoSSW 93*
Entzminger, Robert Lee 1948- *WhoSSW 93*
Enver Bey 1881-1922 *DcTwHis*
Enverga, Wilfrido L. 1941- *WhoAsAP 91*
Enveri fl. 15th cent.- *OxDcByz*
Enver Pasha 1881-1922 *HarEnMi*
Enya c. 1962- *News 92 [port], -92-3 [port]*
Enyeart, Curtis W. *Law&B 92*
Enyeart, James L. 1943- *WhoAm 92, WhoE 93*
Enyedi, Gyorgy 1930- *WhoScE 91-4*
Enyedi, Ildiko *MiSFD 9*
Enyedy, Gustav, Jr. 1924- *WhoAm 92*
Enz, Cathy Ann 1956- *WhoE 93*
Enz, Charles Paul 1925- *WhoScE 91-4*
Enzenauer, Robert William 1953- *WhoEmL 93*
Enzensberger, Hans Magnus *BioIn 17*
Enzensberger, Hans Magnus 1929- *WhoWor 93*
Enzer, Norbert Beverley 1930- *WhoAm 92*
Eoh, Dang 1947- *WhoWor 93*
Eori, Teresia 1940- *WhoScE 91-4*
Eotvos, Peter 1944- *Baker 92*
Epale, Priso Horace 1959- *WhoE 93*
Eparchius Avitus c. 395-457? *OxDcByz*
Epel, David 1937- *WhoAm 92*
Epel, Joseph H. 1945- *St&PR 93*
Epel, Lidia Marmurek 1941- *WhoAmW 93*
Epelstein, Vjacheslav 1944- *WhoWor 93*
Epes, Travis F. *Law&B 92*
Ephland, John Russell 1952- *WhoAm 92*
Ephraim *OxDcByz*
Ephraim fl. 13th cent.-14th cent. *OxDcByz*
Ephraim, Charles 1924- *WhoAm 92*
Ephraim, Donald Morley 1932- *WhoAm 92*
Ephraim, Gary *St&PR 93*
Ephraim, Max, Jr. 1918- *WhoAm 92*
Ephremides, Anthony 1943- *WhoAm 92*
Ephrem The Syrian c. 306-373 *OxDcByz*
Ephron, Amy 1955- *ConAu 138*
Ephron, Delia *BioIn 17*
Ephron, Henry d1992 *NewYTBS 92*
Ephron, Henry 1911?-1992 *ConAu 139*
Ephron, Henry 1912-1992 *News 93-2*
Ephron, Nora *BioIn 17*
Ephron, Nora 1941- *ConAu 39NR, MiSFD 9, News 92 [port], -92-3 [port], WhoAm 92, WhoAmW 93, WhoE 93*
Epich, Raymond John 1931- *St&PR 93*
Epifanij Premudryj dc. 1420 *OxDcByz*
Epifano, Robert J. 1933- *St&PR 93*
Epinay, marquise d' 1726-1783 *BioIn 17*
Epine, Margherita de l' c. 1683-1746 *OxDcOp*
Epiphanios c. 315-403 *OxDcByz*
Epiphanios Hagiopolites fl. 8th cent.-9th cent. *OxDcByz*
Epler, Doris M. 1928- *SmATA 73 [port]*
Epler, Jerry L. *WhoIns 93*
Epley, H. Robert, III 1941- *WhoSSW 93*
Epley, Lewis Everett, Jr. 1936- *WhoAm 92*
Epley, Marion Jay 1907- *WhoAm 92, WhoWor 93*
Epley, Michael G. 1945- *St&PR 93*
Epley, Thomas Kerfoot, III 1947- *WhoEmL 93*
Epley-Shuck, Barbara Jeanne 1936- *WhoWrEP 92*
Epling, Richard Louis 1951- *WhoEmL 93*
Epling, Scot Anthony 1962- *WhoSSW 93*
Epner, Donald Bruce 1927- *St&PR 93*
Epner, Marcia Gornick 1933- *WhoSSW 93*
Epner, Paul Lawrence 1950- *WhoEmL 93*
Epner, Steven Arthur *WhoAm 92*
Epp, Anita Louise 1953- *WhoAmW 93*
Epp, Arthur Jacob 1939- *WhoAm 92, WhoE 93*
Epp, Eldon Jay 1930- *WhoAm 92*
Epp, Mary Elizabeth 1941- *WhoAmW 93, WhoWor 93*
Epp, William H. 1929- *St&PR 93*
Eppard, Rose Chasanov 1945- *WhoAmW 93*
Eppelheimer, Linda Louise 1949- *WhoAmW 93*
Eppen, Gary Dean 1936- *WhoAm 92*
Epper, Karl F. 1937- *St&PR 93*
Epperson, Barbara 1921- *WhoSSW 93, WhoWor 93*
Epperson, D. Mike 1944- *St&PR 93*
Epperson, David Ernest 1935- *WhoAm 92*
Epperson, Eleanor Louise 1916- *WhoWor 93*
Epperson, Eric Robert 1949- *WhoEmL 93*
Epperson, Jean Warner 1919- *WhoSSW 93*
Epperson, Jerry *ScF&FL 92*
Epperson, Joel Rodman 1945- *WhoSSW 93, WhoWor 93*
Epperson, Kraettli Quynton 1949- *WhoEmL 93*
Epperson, Margaret Farrar 1922- *WhoAmW 93*
Epperson, Vaughn Elmo 1917- *WhoWor 93*
Eppert, Carl 1882-1961 *Baker 92*
Eppes, Richard d1801 *BioIn 17*
Eppes, Thomas Evans 1952- *WhoAm 92*
Eppes, William David *WhoWrEP 92*
Eppich, John L. 1934- *St&PR 93*
Eppig, Aileen 1951- *WhoE 93*
Eppink, Andreas 1946- *WhoWor 93*
Epple, Dennis Norbert 1946- *WhoAm 92*
Epple, Kat 1952- *WhoEmL 93*
Eppler, Cecilia Maria 1951- *WhoEmL 93*
Eppler, David M. 1950- *St&PR 93*
Eppler, James Dale 1926- *WhoSSW 93*
Eppler, Jerome Cannon 1924- *WhoAm 92*
Eppler, Laura Sharon 1961- *WhoE 93*
Eppler, Richard Andrew 1934- *WhoE 93*
Eppley, Frances Fielden 1921- *WhoAmW 93, WhoSSW 93*
Eppley, Jennifer Ann 1967- *WhoE 93*
Eppley, Perley E. *St&PR 93*
Eppley, Roland Raymond, Jr. 1932- *WhoAm 92, WhoE 93*
Eppley, Ronald L. 1943- *St&PR 93*
Eppley, Stephen Clyde 1949- *WhoAm 92*
Eppner, Gerald Allen 1939- *WhoAm 92, WhoWor 93*
Epps, Augustus Charles 1916- *WhoAm 92*
Epps, Charles H., Jr. 1930- *WhoAm 92*
Epps, James Haws, III 1936- *WhoSSW 93*
Epps, James Vernon 1928- *WhoIns 93*
Epps, Joseph D., Jr. *Law&B 92*
Epps, Kurt Emil 1948- *WhoE 93*
Epps, O. Carey, Jr. *Law&B 92*
Epps, Richard Lee, Sr. 1952- *WhoEmL 93, WhoSSW 93*
Epps, Roselyn Elizabeth Payne 1930- *WhoAm 92, WhoAmW 93, WhoWor 93*
Epps, Susie Rebecca Smith 1951- *WhoEmL 93, WhoSSW 93*
Epps, Thad Deemer 1931- *WhoSSW 93*
Epps, William David 1951- *WhoWrEP 92*
Eppstein, Richard Tuteur 1947- *WhoEmL 93*
Ep'rem Mcire d11th cent. *OxDcByz*
Epright, Charles John 1932- *WhoSSW 93*
Eprile, Tony *BioIn 17*
Epstein, Abraham 1892-1942 *JeAmHC*
Epstein, Abraham H. 1926- *WhoAm 92*
Epstein, Alice Hopper *BioIn 17*
Epstein, Allan Cane 1937- *St&PR 93*
Epstein, Alvin 1925- *WhoAm 92*
Epstein, Arthur Joseph 1945- *WhoAm 92*
Epstein, Arthur William 1923- *WhoAm 92*
Epstein, Barbara 1929- *WhoAm 92, WhoAmW 93*
Epstein, Barbara Oberhard 1927- *WhoAmW 93*
Epstein, Barry R. 1942- *WhoAm 92*
Epstein, Beryl (M. Williams) 1910- *ConAu 39NR*
Epstein, Charles Joseph 1933- *WhoAm 92*
Epstein, Charles M. 1920- *St&PR 93*
Epstein, Clifford L. 1945- *St&PR 93*
Epstein, Cynthia Fuchs *WhoAm 92*
Epstein, Dan *St&PR 93*
Epstein, Daniel Mark 1948- *WhoAm 92, WhoWrEP 92*
Epstein, David 1935- *WhoAm 92*
Epstein, David Bernard Alper *WhoScE 91-1*
Epstein, David Gustav 1943- *WhoAm 92*
Epstein, David Lee 1947- *WhoEmL 93*
Epstein, David M(ayer) 1930- *Baker 92*
Epstein, David Mayer 1930- *WhoAm 92*
Epstein, David Norton 1930- *WhoSSW 93*
Epstein, David S. d1992 *NewYTBS 92*
Epstein, Edward *St&PR 93*
Epstein, Edward S. 1931- *WhoAm 92*
Epstein, Ellen Sue 1948- *WhoAmW 93*
Epstein, Emanuel 1916- *WhoAm 92*
Epstein, Franklin Harold 1924- *WhoAm 92*
Epstein, Fred 1937- *BioIn 17*
Epstein, Frederick Bennett 1953- *WhoSSW 93*
Epstein, Gary Marvin 1946- *WhoAm 92, WhoEmL 93*
Epstein, George 1934- *WhoSSW 93*
Epstein, Gilbert Michael 1942- *St&PR 93*
Epstein, Helen 1947- *BioIn 17*
Epstein, Henry David 1927- *St&PR 93, WhoAm 92*
Epstein, Henry Fredric 1944- *WhoSSW 93*
Epstein, Howard M. *Law&B 92*
Epstein, Ida Sylvia 1937- *WhoAmW 93*
Epstein, Irving Robert 1945- *WhoAm 92*
Epstein, Jacob 1880-1959 *BioIn 17, PolBiDi*
Epstein, Jane L. 1954- *St&PR 93*
Epstein, Jason *BioIn 17*
Epstein, Jason 1928- *WhoAm 92*
Epstein, Jaye Mark 1950- *WhoEmL 93, WhoSSW 93*
Epstein, Jeffrey E. 1956- *St&PR 93*
Epstein, Jeffrey Emanuel 1956- *WhoAm 92*
Epstein, Jeffrey Mark 1951- *WhoE 93, WhoEmL 93*
Epstein, Jeremiah Fain 1924- *WhoAm 92*
Epstein, Jerome Michael 1943- *WhoAm 92*
Epstein, Joel L. 1946- *St&PR 93*
Epstein, John Howard 1926- *WhoAm 92*
Epstein, Jon d1990 *BioIn 17*
Epstein, Jonathan Akiba 1963- *WhoEmL 93*
Epstein, Jose D. 1924- *St&PR 93*
Epstein, Joseph *BioIn 17*
Epstein, Joseph 1917- *WhoAm 92, WhoE 93*
Epstein, Joseph 1937- *WhoAm 92, WhoWrEP 92*
Epstein, Joseph Hugo, Jr. 1931- *WhoSSW 93*
Epstein, Joshua 1940- *WhoSSW 93*
Epstein, Julius 1832-1926 *Baker 92*
Epstein, Julius J. 1909- *WhoAm 92*
Epstein, Kenneth 1942- *St&PR 93*
Epstein, Kenneth Richard 1948- *WhoEmL 93*
Epstein, Kenneth Robert 1942- *WhoAm 92*
Epstein, Larry J. 1957- *St&PR 93*
Epstein, Laura 1914- *WhoAm 92*
Epstein, Lawrence Jeffrey 1946- *WhoEmL 93*
Epstein, Lee Joan 1958- *WhoEmL 93*
Epstein, Leon Joseph 1917- *WhoAm 92*
Epstein, Leslie Donald 1938- *WhoWrEP 92*
Epstein, Lionel Charles 1924- *WhoAm 92*
Epstein, Louis 1901-1991 *BioIn 17*
Epstein, Louis R. 1926- *St&PR 93*
Epstein, Louis Ralph 1926- *WhoAm 92*
Epstein, Marc N. *Law&B 92*
Epstein, Marcelo *MiSFD 9*
Epstein, Margaret Lynn *Law&B 92*
Epstein, Marvin M. 1928- *St&PR 93*
Epstein, Matthew *WhoWor 93*
Epstein, Max d1990 *BioIn 17*
Epstein, Max 1925- *WhoAm 92*
Epstein, Melvin 1938- *WhoAm 92*
Epstein, Michael Alan 1954- *WhoAm 92, WhoEmL 93*
Epstein, Michael Frank 1941- *WhoE 93*
Epstein, Michael Lee 1958- *WhoSSW 93*
Epstein, Mikhail Naumovich 1950- *WhoE 93*
Epstein, Murray 1937- *WhoSSW 93*
Epstein, Patricia N. *Law&B 92*
Epstein, Paul Mark 1946- *WhoE 93*
Epstein, Philip Barry 1947- *WhoEmL 93*
Epstein, Rachelle *BioIn 17*
Epstein, Ralph Alan 1939- *WhoE 93*
Epstein, Raymond 1918- *St&PR 93, WhoAm 92*
Epstein, Richard 1869-1919 *Baker 92*
Epstein, Richard A. 1943- *WhoAm 92*
Epstein, Richard H. 1929- *WhoScE 91-4*
Epstein, Richard J. 1944- *St&PR 93*
Epstein, Rick *BioIn 17*
Epstein, Robert *MiSFD 9*
Epstein, Robert Alan 1952- *St&PR 93*
Epstein, Robert Harry 1958- *WhoEmL 93*
Epstein, Robert Marvin 1928- *WhoAm 92*
Epstein, Samuel 1909- *ConAu 39NR*
Epstein, Samuel 1919- *WhoAm 92*
Epstein, Samuel Abraham 1956- *WhoSSW 93*
Epstein, Samuel D. 1946- *WhoEmL 93, WhoSSW 93*
Epstein, Samuel David 1946- *St&PR 93*
Epstein, Sandra Gail 1939- *WhoE 93*
Epstein, Selma 1927- *WhoAm 92, WhoAmW 93*
Epstein, Seymour 1917- *WhoWrEP 92*
Epstein, Sherwin Lewis 1930- *WhoWor 93*
Epstein, Sidney 1920- *WhoAm 92*
Epstein, Sidney 1923- *St&PR 93, WhoAm 92*
Epstein, Simon Jules 1934- *WhoAm 92*
Epstein, Steven *BioIn 17*
Epstein, Steven 1949- *WhoEmL 93*
Epstein, Thomas 1957- *St&PR 93*
Epstein, Valerie Wyber *Law&B 92*
Epstein, William 1931- *WhoAm 92*
Epstein, William 1948- *WhoEmL 93*
Epstein, William A. 1909-1990 *BioIn 17*
Epstein, William H. *Law&B 92*
Epstein, William Louis 1925- *WhoAm 92*
Epstein, William Stuart 1940- *WhoAm 92*
Epstein, Wilma Geller 1946- *WhoAmW 93*
Epstein, Wolfgang 1931- *WhoAm 92*
Epting, C. Christopher *WhoAm 92*
Epting, Cynthia Renee 1959- *WhoEmL 93*
Epting, Ruth Elaine F. *Law&B 92*
Epton, Delmar 1934- *St&PR 93*
Epton, Roger *WhoScE 91-1*
Epton, Ronda Arli Lynn 1951- *WhoE 93*
Equale, Paul *BioIn 17*
Equiluz, Kurt 1929- *Baker 92*
Eraklis, Angelo John 1933- *WhoE 93*
Eramo, John Jeffrey 1954- *WhoEmL 93*
Erard, Barbara Hughes 1955- *WhoAmW 93*
Erard, Pierre 1794-1865 *See* Erard, Sebastien 1752-1831 *Baker 92*
Erard, Sebastien 1752-1831 *Baker 92*
Erasmus, Anthony *Law&B 92*
Erasmus, Charles John 1921- *WhoAm 92*
Erasmus, Desiderius 1466?-1536 *BioIn 17*
Erasmus, John J. 1924- *St&PR 93*
Erath, George Snider 1927- *St&PR 93*
Erath, Sally Grace Marie 1927- *WhoE 93*
Eratosthenes c. 276BC-c. 194BC *Baker 92*
Erazmus, Walter Thomas 1947- *St&PR 93, WhoEmL 93*
Erb, Dennis Joseph 1952- *WhoE 93*
Erb, Donald 1927- *WhoAm 92*
Erb, Donald (James) 1927- *Baker 92*
Erb, Fred A. 1923- *St&PR 93*
Erb, Frederick Geist, III 1950- *WhoWor 93*
Erb, John Lawrence 1877-1950 *Baker 92*
Erb, Karl 1877-1958 *Baker 92, OxDcOp*
Erb, Karl Albert 1942- *WhoWor 93*
Erb, Marie Joseph 1858-1944 *Baker 92*
Erb, Richard D. 1941- *WhoUN 92*
Erb, Richard Louis Lundin 1929- *WhoAm 92, WhoWor 93*
Erb, Robert Allan 1932- *WhoAm 92*
Erb, Wolfgang 1936- *WhoScE 91-3*
Erba, Luciano 1922- *DcLB 128*
Erbach, Christian c. 1568-1635 *Baker 92*
Erbe, Gary Thomas 1944- *WhoE 93*
Erbe, Joan 1926- *WhoE 93*
Erbe, Jonathan Richard 1968- *WhoE 93*
Erbe, Stuart A. 1935- *St&PR 93*
Erbeck, Robert Nelson 1948- *WhoEmL 93*
Erbel, Raimund 1948- *WhoWor 93*
Erben, Heinrich Karl 1921- *WhoScE 91-3*
Erben, Ralph 1931- *St&PR 93*
Erber, Les N. 1945- *St&PR 93*
Erber, Robert, Jr. 1931- *St&PR 93*
Erber, Thomas 1930- *WhoAm 92*
Erbersdobler, Helmut F. 1937- *WhoScE 91-3*
Erbes, William Tracy 1948- *WhoEmL 93*
Erbse, Heimo 1924- *Baker 92*
Erbsen, Claude Ernest 1938- *St&PR 93, WhoAm 92*

Erbst, Fred Paul 1931- St&PR 93
Erbstein, Keith Sandy 1946- WhoEmL 93
Erbstoesser, Eugene Law&B 92
Erburu, Robert F. 1930- St&PR 93, WhoAm 92
Ercan, Ahmet 1948- WhoScE 91-4
Ercan, Yucel 1943- WhoScE 91-4
Erce, Ignacio, III 1964- WhoWor 93
Erchempert fl. 9th cent.- OxDcByz
Ercis, Ahmet 1952- WhoScE 91-4
Erck, Jerome F. 1939- St&PR 93
Erck, Theodore Augustus, Jr. 1949- WhoAm 92, WhoEmL 93, WhoWor 93
Ercklentz, Alexander Tonio 1936- WhoAm 92
Ercklentz, Enno W., Jr. 1931- St&PR 93
Ercklentz, Enno Wilhelm, Jr. 1931- WhoAm 92
Ercolano, Thomas Francis 1944- St&PR 93
Ercole, Joseph R. 1965- WhoE 93
Erdahl, Leland Odell 1928- St&PR 93
Erdberg, Mindel Ruth 1916- WhoAmW 93
Erdei, Peter 1928- WhoScE 91-4
Erdel, Bert Paul 1943- WhoAm 92, WhoE 93
Erdelack, Wayne F. Law&B 92
Erdeljac, Daniel Joseph 1932- WhoAm 92
Erdeljac, Laurie Ann 1968- WhoAmW 93
Erdeljan, Aleksandar 1950- St&PR 93
Erdely, Stephen Lajos 1921- WhoAm 92
Erdelyi, Erzsebet 1932- WhoScE 91-4
Erdelyi, Miklos 1928- Baker 92
Erden, Abdulkadir 1948- WhoScE 91-4
Erden, Ferit 1930- WhoScE 91-4
Erden, Sybil Isolde 1950- WhoAm 92, WhoAmW 93
Erdenechuluun, Luvsangiin 1948- WhoUN 92
Erdentug, Nermin 1917- IntDcAn
Erdheim, Allen 1943- WhoE 93
Erdle, Jack A. St&PR 93
Erdle, Norma St&PR 93
Erdlen, Susan Marie Victoria 1961- WhoAmW 93, WhoEmL 93
Erdley, Dennis Robert Law&B 92
Erdman, Barbara 1936- WhoAm 92, WhoAmW 93
Erdman, Carl L. N. 1915- WhoAm 92
Erdman, Carroll M. 1941- St&PR 93
Erdman, Cindy Susan 1957- WhoEmL 93
Erdman, Daniel Gig 1955- WhoEmL 93
Erdman, David Vorse 1911- WhoE 93
Erdman, Donald Seward 1919- WhoWrEP 92
Erdman, Florence Waring AmWomPl
Erdman, Harold Richard, Jr. 1930- St&PR 93
Erdman, Howard Loyd 1935- WhoAm 92
Erdman, James Patrick d1991 BioIn 17
Erdman, Joseph 1935- WhoAm 92
Erdman, Leon R. 1950- St&PR 93
Erdman, Lowell Paul 1926- WhoAm 92
Erdman, Pamela Ann 1962- WhoAmW 93
Erdman, Paul 1932- ScF&FL 92
Erdman, Paul Emil 1932- WhoAm 92
Erdman, Robert L. 1927- BioIn 17
Erdman, William Albert Law&B 92
Erdmann, Eduard 1896-1958 Baker 92
Erdmann, Edward Alexander, III 1947- St&PR 93
Erdmann, Robert Joseph 1937- WhoWrEP 92
Erdmann, Volker A. 1941- WhoScE 91-3
Erdmann, William Louis 1928- St&PR 93
Erdmannsdoerfer, Helmut 1950- WhoWor 93
Erdmannsdorfer, Max von 1848-1905 Baker 92
Erdos, Andre 1941- WhoUN 92, WhoWor 93
Erdos, Ervin George 1922- WhoAm 92
Erdos, Marianne Eva WhoAmW 93
Erdos, Paul 1930- WhoScE 91-4
Erdos, Reni 1941- WhoAmW 93
Erdreich, Ben 1938- CngDr 91
Erdreich, Ben Leader 1938 WhoAm 92, WhoSSW 93
Erdrich, Karen Louise 1954- WhoAm 92, WhoAmW 93, WhoE 93
Erdrich, Louise BioIn 17
Erdrich, Louise 1954- AmWomWr 92, Au&Arts 10 [port], MagSAmL [port]
Erdtman, Holger 1902-1989 BioIn 17
Erebara, Gezim 1928- DrEEuF
Erede, Alberto 1908- Baker 92
Erede, Alberto 1909- OxDcOp
Ereira, Alan 1943- ConAu 137
Eremin, Oleg WhoScE 91-1
Erenberg, Eve Braun 1907- St&PR 93
Erenrich, Evelyn Schwartz 1946- WhoE 93
Erens, Jay Allan 1935- WhoAm 92
Erensen, George B. Law&B 92
Erensen, George B. 1944- St&PR 93
Erenstoft, David L. 1942- St&PR 93
Erera, Laurence E. 1940- St&PR 93
Erfani, Shervin 1948- WhoE 93, WhoEmL 93, WhoWor 93
Erfft, Kenneth Reynders 1908- WhoSSW 93
Ergas, Elizabeth ScF&FL 92
Ergas, Enrique 1938- WhoAm 92
Ergas, Jean-Pierre M. 1939- St&PR 93
Ergas, Jean-Pierre Maurice 1939- WhoAm 92
Ergene, A. WhoScE 91-4
Ergenzinger, Peter Jurgen 1937- WhoWor 93
Ergmann, Raoul d1990 BioIn 17
Ergunay, O. WhoScE 91-4
Erhard, Ludwig 1897-1977 ColdWar 1 [port], DcTwHis
Erhard, Werner BioIn 17
Erhard, Werner 1935- WhoAm 92
Erhardt, Edward Richard 1957- WhoAm 92
Erhardt, Henri S. 1943- St&PR 93
Erhardt, Otto 1888-1971 Baker 92, OxDcOp
Erhardt, Warren Richard 1924- WhoAm 92
Erhart, Charles H. 1925- St&PR 93
Erhart, James Nelson 1953- WhoEmL 93
Erhmann, Alex BioIn 17
Eribon, Didier 1953- ConAu 138
Eric B. c. 1965- & Rakim c. 1968- ConMus 9 [port]
Erice, Victor 1940- MiSFD 9
Erichsen, Stian 1921- WhoScE 91-4
Erichsen-Hubbard, Isabel Janice 1935- WhoAmW 93
Erick, Miriam A. 1948- WhoWrEP 92
Ericksen, Gordon d1991 BioIn 17
Ericksen, Rick L. 1948- WhoSSW 93
Ericksen, Robert L. St&PR 93
Ericksen, Wayne R. 1936- St&PR 93
Erickson, Alan Eric 1928- WhoAm 92
Erickson, Andrew M. 1939- WhoIns 93
Erickson, Arthur 1924- BioIn 17
Erickson, Arthur Charles 1924- WhoAm 92, WhoWor 93
Erickson, Barden 1930- St&PR 93
Erickson, Barry Kenneth 1952- WhoEmL 93
Erickson, Bill 1951- St&PR 93
Erickson, Bob 1942- BioIn 17
Erickson, Brian F. 1936- St&PR 93
Erickson, Brian James 1950- WhoEmL 93, WhoSSW 93
Erickson, C. Leonard 1912- St&PR 93
Erickson, Carey d1990 BioIn 17
Erickson, Charles B. 1932- St&PR 93
Erickson, Charles Burton 1932- WhoAm 92
Erickson, Charles E. Law&B 92
Erickson, Charles Edward 1947- WhoAm 92, WhoE 93, WhoIns 93
Erickson, David Belnap 1951- WhoEmL 93
Erickson, David Bruce 1947- WhoEmL 93
Erickson, David Burdette 1950- WhoWrEP 92
Erickson, David Erick 1950- WhoEmL 93
Erickson, David L. 1948- St&PR 93
Erickson, David Martin 1953- WhoWor 93
Erickson, Dennis D. 1938- St&PR 93
Erickson, Dennis Duane 1938- WhoAm 92
Erickson, Diane Quinn 1959- WhoEmL 93
Erickson, Don d1989 BioIn 17
Erickson, Donna Mary WhoWrEP 92
Erickson, Douglas E. Law&B 92
Erickson, Edward Leonard 1946- WhoE 93
Erickson, Frank William 1923- WhoAm 92
Erickson, Gail 1934- WhoAmW 93
Erickson, Gail M. Law&B 92
Erickson, Garwood Elliott 1946- WhoEmL 93
Erickson, Gerald Meyer 1927- WhoAm 92
Erickson, Gordon R. Law&B 92
Erickson, Gordon Richard 1928- St&PR 93
Erickson, Gregory Kevin 1953- WhoIns 93
Erickson, Ingrid Geijer 1967- WhoE 93
Erickson, Jackie Mahi Law&B 92
Erickson, James Paul 1929- WhoAm 92
Erickson, James Warren 1935- St&PR 93
Erickson, Jeanne Marie Peterson Law&B 92
Erickson, Joel M. Law&B 92
Erickson, John David 1933- St&PR 93
Erickson, John Duff 1933- WhoAm 92
Erickson, John R. 1943- ConAu 138, SmATA 70
Erickson, Julia Ann 1958- WhoE 93
Erickson, Karen Louise 1939- WhoAmW 93, WhoE 93
Erickson, Kent Vincent 1948- St&PR 93
Erickson, Kim L. 1951- WhoEmL 93
Erickson, L.E. 1925- St&PR 93
Erickson, Lance Karl 1946- WhoSSW 93
Erickson, Larry 1936- St&PR 93
Erickson, Laura Lynn 1951- WhoAmW 93
Erickson, Lawrence Wilhelm 1915- WhoAm 92
Erickson, Lea Ella 1947- WhoAmW 93
Erickson, Leland John 1951- WhoEmL 93
Erickson, Lennart G. 1914- St&PR 93
Erickson, LeRoy Alexander 1921- WhoAm 92
Erickson, Linda Rae 1948- WhoAmW 93, WhoEmL 93
Erickson, Lloyd E. Law&B 92
Erickson, Luther Eugene 1933- WhoAm 92
Erickson, Margaret Kathryn 1954- WhoAmW 93
Erickson, Mark Refell 1949- St&PR 93
Erickson, Nancy Joan 1947- WhoE 93
Erickson, Nancy Salome 1945- WhoAmW 93
Erickson, Neil Le Roy, II 1951- WhoWrEP 92
Erickson, Paul ScF&FL 92
Erickson, Paul Joseph, Jr. 1953- WhoEmL 93
Erickson, Philip Lee Law&B 92
Erickson, Philip Torry 1934- St&PR 93
Erickson, Phillip A. Law&B 92
Erickson, Phillip A. 1941- St&PR 93
Erickson, Ralph Ernest 1928- WhoAm 92
Erickson, Ralph O. 1914- WhoAm 92
Erickson, Raymond Leroy 1925- WhoAm 92, WhoE 93
Erickson, Refell Leon 1912- St&PR 93
Erickson, Richard Ames 1923- WhoAm 92
Erickson, Richard Beau 1952- WhoEmL 93, WhoWor 93
Erickson, Richard L. 1942- WhoAm 92
Erickson, Richard Theodore 1932- St&PR 93, WhoAm 92
Erickson, Robert 1917- Baker 92
Erickson, Robert Andrew 1953- WhoE 93
Erickson, Robert D. 1943- St&PR 93
Erickson, Robert Daniel 1943- WhoAm 92
Erickson, Robert L. Law&B 92
Erickson, Robert L. 1929- WhoAm 92
Erickson, Robert Lewis 1929- St&PR 93
Erickson, Rodney L. 1931- St&PR 93
Erickson, Roger E. Law&B 92
Erickson, Roland Axel 1913- WhoAm 92
Erickson, Ronald Kent 1938- WhoE 93
Erickson, Roy Frederick, Jr. 1928- WhoAm 92
Erickson, Roy L. Law&B 92
Erickson, Roy Lydeen 1923- WhoAm 92
Erickson, Sandra Lynne 1959- WhoAmW 93
Erickson, Scott Lee 1959- WhoEmL 93
Erickson, Stephen M. ScF&FL 92
Erickson, Steve 1950- ScF&FL 92
Erickson, Steven W. Law&B 92
Erickson, Tamara Jo 1954- St&PR 93
Erickson, Thomas J. 1954- WhoIns 93
Erickson, Thomas Sherman WhoAm 92
Erickson, Todd T. Law&B 92
Erickson, Victor B. St&PR 93
Erickson, Virginia Bemmels 1948- WhoEmL 93
Erickson, Walter Bruce 1938- WhoAm 92
Erickson, William Hurt 1924- WhoAm 92
Erickstad, Ralph John 1922- WhoAm 92
Ericson, Alvin Charles 1955- WhoE 93, WhoEmL 93, WhoWor 93
Ericson, Elizabeth S. BioIn 17
Ericson, Eric 1918- Baker 92
Ericson, Eric 1925- ScF&FL 92
Ericson, Hans Christer BioIn 17
Ericson, Helen Irene Peterson 1903- WhoAmW 93
Ericson, James Donald 1935- St&PR 93, WhoAm 92
Ericson, John M., Jr. 1942- St&PR 93
Ericson, Jon Meyer 1928- WhoAm 92
Ericson, Kaj L. 1944- WhoScE 91-4
Ericson, Leif E. 1941- WhoScE 91-4
Ericson, Magda 1929- WhoScE 91-2
Ericson, Roger D. Law&B 92
Ericson, Roger D. 1934- St&PR 93
Ericson, Roger Delwin 1934- WhoAm 92, WhoSSW 93
Ericson, Ruth Ann WhoAm 92, WhoAmW 93, WhoSSW 93
Ericson, Thomas 1942- WhoScE 91-4
Ericsson, John BioIn 17
Ericsson, S. Torsten 1938- WhoScE 91-4
Ericsson, Sven Torsten 1938- WhoWor 93
Ericsson, Tore 1943- WhoWor 93
Erie, Gretchen Ann 1945- WhoAmW 93
Erigena, John Scotus c. 810-c. 877 Baker 92, BioIn 17
Erik (the Red) 950?-1004? Expl 93
Eriks, Mark C. Law&B 92
Eriksen, Charles Walter 1923- WhoAm 92
Eriksen, Dennis A. 1939- St&PR 93
Eriksen, Gary L. 1943- WhoE 93
Eriksen, Gordon MiSFD 9
Eriksen, Otto Louis 1930- WhoAm 92
Eriksen, Poul Jakob 1925- WhoWor 93
Eriksen, Rolf F. 1942- St&PR 93
Eriksen, Stein BioIn 17
Erikson, Erik H. 1902- BioIn 17
Erikson, Erik Homburger 1902- WhoAm 92
Erikson, George Emil 1920- WhoAm 92, WhoWor 93
Erikson, George William Law&B 92
Erikson, George William 1941- St&PR 93
Erikson, J. Lance 1943- St&PR 93, WhoAm 92
Erikson, Joan M. BioIn 17
Erikson, Kai 1931- WhoAm 92
Erikson, Paul Maverick 1961- WhoSSW 93
Erikson, Phyllis A. Law&B 92
Erikson, Raymond Leo 1936- WhoAm 92
Erikson, Robert Warren 1945- St&PR 93
Erikson, Sheldon R. 1941- St&PR 93, WhoAm 92
Erikson, Uno E. 1930- WhoScE 91-4
Eriksson, Anders F. 1951- WhoScE 91-4
Eriksson, E. Gosta 1935- WhoScE 91-4
Eriksson, Erik A., Jr. Law&B 92
Eriksson, Erik Alexander, Jr. 1953- WhoEmL 93
Eriksson, Folke Samuel 1927- WhoWor 93
Eriksson, Gosta E. 1935- WhoScE 91-4
Eriksson, Jarl-Thure 1944- WhoScE 91-4
Eriksson, John Law&B 92
Eriksson, Larry John 1945- St&PR 93, WhoAm 92
Eriksson, Lars-Ove Gunnar 1946- WhoWor 93
Eriksson, Leif 97-?-1020? Expl 93
Eriksson, Ronald J. 1942- St&PR 93
Eriksson, Tage R. 1926- WhoScE 91-4
Eriksson-Capes, Barbara Jean 1956- WhoAmW 93
Erill, Sergio 1938- WhoWor 93
Erim, Kenan T. BioIn 17
Erimoglu, Cevdet 1922- WhoScE 91-4
Erion, Carol Elizabeth 1943- WhoAmW 93
Erisman, Fred Raymond 1937- WhoAm 92, WhoSSW 93
Erismann, Th. WhoScE 91-4
Erismann, Werner 1956- WhoWor 93
Eriugena, John Scotus c. 810-c. 877 BioIn 17
Erjala, Matti Kalle Oskari 1946- WhoScE 91-4
Erjefalt, Lennart 1939- WhoScE 91-4
Erk, Adam Wilhelm 1779-1820 See Erk, Ludwig (Christian) 1807-1883 Baker 92
Erk, Ludwig (Christian) 1807-1883 Baker 92
Erkam, Erdogan 1931- WhoScE 91-4
Erkan, Onur 1939- WhoScE 91-4
Erkan, Semih 1951- WhoScE 91-4
Erkan, Yavuz 1939- WhoScE 91-4
Erkel, Elek 1843-1893 See Erkel, Franz 1810-1893 Baker 92
Erkel, Ferenc 1810-1893 IntDcOp [port], OxDcOp
Erkel, Franz 1810-1893 Baker 92
Erkel, Gyula 1842-1909 See Erkel, Franz 1810-1893 Baker 92
Erkel, Laszlo 1844-1896 See Erkel, Franz 1810-1893 Baker 92
Erkel, Sandor 1846-1900 See Erkel, Franz 1810-1893 Baker 92
Erkelens, Dirk Willem 1941- WhoWor 93
Erkelenz, William F. Law&B 92
Erkenbrack, Stephen Kenneth 1952- WhoEmL 93
Erker, Barbara A. Law&B 92
Erker, Charles F. 1955- St&PR 93
Erkilla, Jack R. Law&B 92
Erkin, Ulvi Cemal 1906-1972 Baker 92
Erkinaro, Eino Kalervo 1934- WhoScE 91-4
Erkkila, Barbara Howell 1918- WhoWrEP 92
Erkkila, Dan d1992 NewYTBS 92
Erkkila, Kathleen Liisa 1947- WhoAmW 93
Erl, Gerhard Hans 1947- St&PR 93
Erla, Karen 1942- WhoAm 92, WhoE 93
Erlander, Sven 1934- WhoScE 91-4
Erlander, Sven Bertil 1934- WhoWor 93
Erlander, Tage F. 1901-1985 BioIn 17
Erlander, Tage Fritiof 1901-1985 DcTwHis
Erlandson, David Alan 1936- WhoAm 92
Erlandsson, Ragnar 1951- WhoWor 93
Erlanger, Bernard Ferdinand 1923- WhoAm 92
Erlanger, Brandee d1991 BioIn 17
Erlanger, Camille 1863-1919 Baker 92
Erlanger, David Kenneth 1953- St&PR 93
Erlanger, Ellen 1950- ScF&FL 92
Erlanger, Francois Rodolphe d' 1872-1932 Baker 92

Erlanger, Frederic d' 1868-1943 *Baker 92, OxDcOp*
Erlanger, Steven Jay 1952- *WhoAm 92*
Erlanson, Deborah McFarlin 1943- *WhoAmW 93*
Erlebach, Philipp Heinrich 1657-1714 *Baker 92*
Erlebacher, Albert 1932- *WhoAm 92*
Erlebacher, Arlene Cernik 1946- *WhoAm 92, WhoAmW 93*
Erlenbach, Gary L. 1945- *St&PR 93*
Erlenborn, John Neal 1927- *WhoAm 92*
Erlendsdottir, Gudrun 1936- *WhoWor 93*
Erlenmeyer-Kimling, L. *WhoAm 92, WhoE 93*
Erler, Fred C. 1945- *St&PR 93, WhoAm 92*
Erlewine, Richard H. 1914- *St&PR 93*
Erlich, Henryk 1882-1942? *BioIn 17*
Erlich, Louis W. 1913- *St&PR 93*
Erlich, Richard D. 1943- *ScF&FL 92*
Erlich, Richard Henry 1949- *WhoEmL 93*
Erlich, Victor 1914- *WhoAm 92*
Erlichman, Stanton Roy 1939- *WhoSSW 93*
Erlichson, Miriam 1948- *WhoAmW 93*
Erlicht, Lewis Howard 1939- *WhoAm 92*
Erlick, Everett Howard 1921- *WhoAm 92*
Erlick, Lance E. 1951- *WhoEmL 93*
Erlinge, G. Sam E. 1928- *WhoScE 91-4*
Erlinger, Serge 1938- *WhoScE 91-2*
Erlingsson, Leif Erling Gunnar 1958- *WhoWor 93*
Erlmann, Veit 1951- *ConAu 139*
Erma, Reino Mauri 1922- *WhoWor 93*
Ermakov, Voldemar 1936- *WhoUN 92*
Erman, Bill 1930- *BioIn 17*
Erman, John *MiSFD 9*
Erman, John 1935- *ConTFT 10, WhoAm 92*
Erman, Peter 1937- *WhoScE 91-4*
Erman, Peter Paul 1937- *WhoWor 93*
Ermatinger, Erhart 1900-1966 *Baker 92*
Ermel, Frederick C. 1942- *St&PR 93*
Ermenc, Joseph John 1912- *WhoAm 92*
Ermer, James 1942- *WhoAm 92*
Ermer, Marilyn *Law&B 92*
Ermida-Uriarte, Oscar 1949- *WhoUN 92*
Ermisch, Armin 1935- *WhoScE 91-3*
Ermler, Fridrih 1898-1967 *DrEEuF*
Ermshar, Linda Charline 1943- *WhoAmW 93*
Ermutlu, Ilhan Mehmet 1927- *WhoSSW 93*
Ern, Hartmut 1935- *WhoScE 91-3*
Ernenwein, Raymond Joseph 1941- *WhoE 93*
Ernesaks, Gustav 1908- *Baker 92*
Ernest, Albert D., Jr. *St&PR 93*
Ernest, Albert Devery, Jr. 1930- *WhoAm 92*
Ernest, Paul 1944- *WhoWor 93*
Ernest, Richard B. 1934- *St&PR 93*
Ernest, Robert Charles 1924- *St&PR 93*
Ernest, Shirley Ann 1936- *WhoAmW 93*
Ernesti, Hans P. 1936- *St&PR 93*
Erni, Hans 1909- *WhoWor 93*
Ernsbarger, Rebecca Faye 1949- *WhoAmW 93*
Ernsberger, Donald Craig 1947- *WhoEmL 93*
Ernst, Alfred 1860-1898 *Baker 92*
Ernst, Alice Henson *AmWomPl*
Ernst, Calvin Bradley 1934- *WhoAm 92*
Ernst, Chad E. 1933- *St&PR 93*
Ernst, Chadwick Ellsworth 1933- *WhoWor 93*
Ernst, Charles Stephen *Law&B 92*
Ernst, Chester Nelson 1948- *WhoEmL 93*
Ernst, Christina Miller 1949- *St&PR 93*
Ernst, Daniel Pearson 1931- *WhoWor 93*
Ernst, Donald Martin 1938- *St&PR 93*
Ernst, Douglas Ray 1950- *WhoEmL 93*
Ernst, Edward Willis 1924- *WhoAm 92*
Ernst, Elizabeth McGeachy 1936- *WhoAmW 93, WhoSSW 93*
Ernst, Gerd Hans 1926- *St&PR 93*
Ernst, Heinrich Wilhelm 1814-1865 *Baker 92*
Ernst, Janet Lee 1955- *WhoAmW 93, WhoEmL 93, WhoSSW 93*
Ernst, Jean 1926- *WhoScE 91-2*
Ernst, Jessie *AmWomPl*
Ernst, John Louis 1932- *WhoAm 92*
Ernst, Kathryn F. 1942- *ScF&FL 92*
Ernst, Kathryn Fitzgerald 1942- *WhoE 93*
Ernst, Laura Waters 1953- *WhoE 93*
Ernst, Lois Geraci 1933- *WhoAm 92*
Ernst, Marcia McCrory 1961- *WhoEmL 93*
Ernst, Mark A. 1958- *St&PR 93*
Ernst, Max 1891-1976 *BioIn 17*
Ernst, Morris Leopold 1888-1976 *OxCSupC*
Ernst, Norman Frank, Jr. 1942- *WhoIns 93*
Ernst, Paul 1866-1933 *DcLB 118 [port]*
Ernst, Paul 1899-1985 *ScF&FL 92*
Ernst, Paul William 1939- *St&PR 93*
Ernst, Philip d1991 *BioIn 17*
Ernst, Ricardo 1959- *WhoE 93*
Ernst, Richard Dale 1951- *WhoEmL 93*
Ernst, Richard R. 1933- *WhoScE 91-4*
Ernst, Richard Robert 1933- *WhoWor 93*
Ernst, Roger 1924- *WhoAm 92*
Ernst, Roger Charles 1914- *WhoAm 92*
Ernst, Stephen K. *Law&B 92*
Ernst, Thomas Albert 1941- *St&PR 93*
Ernst, Timothy Scott *Law&B 92*
Ernst, Wallace Gary 1931- *WhoAm 92*
Ernst, Wolfgang 1930- *WhoScE 91-3*
Ernster, Deszo 1898-1981 *Baker 92*
Ernster, Jacquelyn 1939- *WhoAmW 93*
Ernsthaft, William *Law&B 92*
Ernsting, Eugene C. 1928- *St&PR 93*
Ernsting, Walter 1920- *ScF&FL 92*
Ernstthal, Henry L. 1940- *WhoAm 92*
Eroglu, Hasan 1956- *WhoEmL 93*
Erokan, Dennis William 1950- *WhoAm 92, WhoEmL 93*
Erol, Nurhan 1940- *WhoScE 91-4*
Erol, Oguz Abdulkerim 1926- *WhoScE 91-4*
Eromin, Frederick W. *Law&B 92*
Eron, Leonard David 1920- *WhoAm 92*
Eron, Madeline Marcus 1919- *WhoAmW 93*
Eronen, Matti Juhani 1944- *WhoWor 93*
Eros, Peter 1932- *Baker 92*
Erosh, William Daniel 1956- *St&PR 93, WhoAm 92, WhoEmL 93*
Erpenbeck, Mary-Lou Brockett 1961- *WhoWrEP 92*
Erpf, Hermann (Robert) 1891-1969 *Baker 92*
Erps, Jack H. *Law&B 92*
Errera, Maria Antoinette 1947- *WhoAmW 93*
Errera, Maurice Leo 1914- *WhoScE 91-2*
Errera, Samuel Joseph 1926- *WhoE 93*
Errickson, Barbara Bauer 1944- *WhoAmW 93*
Errico, Michael Edward 1920- *St&PR 93*
Erro, Luis Enrique 1897-1955 *DcMexL*
Errol, Leon 1881-1951 *QDrFCA 92 [port]*
Ersek, Bruce Andrew 1938- *St&PR 93*
Ersek, Gregory Joseph Mark 1956- *WhoEmL 93, WhoSSW 93, WhoWor 93*
Ersek, Robert Allen 1938- *WhoAm 92*
Ersgaard, Ole Kristian 1948- *WhoWor 93*
Ershad, Hossain Mohammad 1930- *WhoAsAP 91*
Ershad, Hussain Mohammad *BioIn 17*
Ershler, William Baldwin 1949- *WhoAm 92*
Ershoff, Benjamin H. 1914-1989 *BioIn 17*
Ershov, Ivan 1867-1943 *OxDcOp*
Ershov, Ivan (Vasilievich) 1867-1943 *Baker 92*
Ershow-Levenberg, Linda S. 1954- *WhoEmL 93*
Erskine, Barbara 1944- *ScF&FL 92*
Erskine, Chester 1905-1986 *MiSFD 9N*
Erskine, Dennis Wayne 1948- *WhoEmL 93*
Erskine, Douglas *ScF&FL 92*
Erskine, George *ScF&FL 92*
Erskine, James Lorenzo 1942- *WhoAm 92*
Erskine, Jeffrey Allan 1960- *WhoEmL 93*
Erskine, John 1879-1951 *Baker 92, BioIn 17*
Erskine, John Morse 1920- *WhoAm 92, WhoWor 93*
Erskine, Laurie Yorke 1894- *AmWomPl*
Erskine, Paul Anderson 1926- *St&PR 93*
Erskine, Ralph 1914- *WhoWor 93*
Erskine, Terry Michael 1943- *St&PR 93*
Erskine, Thomas 1788-1870 *BioIn 17*
Erskine, Thomas L. 1939- *ScF&FL 92*
Erslev, Allan Jacob 1919- *WhoAm 92*
Ersoy, S. Yalcin 1938- *WhoScE 91-4*
Ersoy, Ugur 1932- *WhoScE 91-4*
Ersoz, Clara Jean 1937- *WhoAmW 93*
Erspamer, Michael Stephen 1949- *WhoWor 93*
Erstad, Leon Robert 1947- *WhoEmL 93, WhoWor 93*
Ersted, Ruth Marion 1904-1990 *BioIn 17*
Erstling, Christopher Michael 1947- *WhoE 93, WhoEmL 93*
Ertas, Ismet 1932- *WhoScE 91-4*
Erte 1892-1990 *BioIn 17*
Ertegun, Ahmet *SoulM*
Ertegun, Ahmet M. *BioIn 17*
Ertegun, Ahmet Munir 1923- *WhoAm 92*
Ertegun, Mica *BioIn 17*
Ertel, Allen Edward 1936- *WhoAm 92*
Ertel, Gary Arthur 1954- *WhoEmL 93*
Ertel, Inta Janners 1932- *WhoAm 92*
Ertel, John Charles, IV *St&PR 93*
Ertel, Mark Edward 1958- *WhoSSW 93*
Ertel, (Jean) Paul 1865-1933 *Baker 92*
Ertelt, Henry Robinson *Law&B 92*
Ertem, Atila 1954- *WhoScE 91-4*
Erthein, Marc Bartholdy 1930- *St&PR 93*
Ertl, Gerhard 1936- *WhoScE 91-3, WhoWor 93*
Ertl, Gunter 1940- *WhoWor 93*
Ertl, James Louis 1931- *St&PR 93*
Ertl, Richard D. 1939- *St&PR 93*
Ertugrul, Hursit *WhoScE 91-4*
Ertugrul, Mehmet 1954- *WhoScE 91-4*
Ertuna, Cengiz 1943- *WhoUN 92*
Ertur, Omer S. 1944- *WhoUN 92*
Ertz, Carol Ann Ryan 1955- *WhoEmL 93*
Ertz, Colleen Lillian 1939- *WhoAmW 93*
Ertz, Susan 1894-1985 *ScF&FL 92*
Erumsele, Andrew Akhigbe 1944- *WhoE 93, WhoWor 93*
Erundina, Luiza *BioIn 17*
Erven, Eric Lynn 1965- *WhoEmL 93*
Ervin, Bernice Ledbetter 1958- *WhoAmW 93*
Ervin, Billy Maxwell 1933- *WhoE 93, WhoWor 93*
Ervin, Cathy Ann *Law&B 92*
Ervin, Connie Yvonne 1954- *WhoAmW 93*
Ervin, Donald Neal 1931- *St&PR 93*
Ervin, Douglas Lee *Law&B 92*
Ervin, Gina Renee 1956- *WhoAmW 93*
Ervin, Joseph A. 1947- *St&PR 93*
Ervin, Klon Randol 1941- *St&PR 93*
Ervin, Margaret Howie 1924- *WhoAmW 93*
Ervin, Naomi Estalee 1942- *WhoAmW 93*
Ervin, Patrick Franklin 1946- *WhoEmL 93*
Ervin, Robert Marvin 1917- *WhoAm 92*
Ervin, Russell T. 1897-1990 *BioIn 17*
Ervin, Samuel James, III 1926- *WhoAm 92, WhoSSW 93*
Ervin, Scott Alan 1964- *WhoSSW 93*
Ervin, Susan Chadwick 1951- *WhoEmL 93*
Ervin, Thomas E. d1992 *NewYTBS 92*
Ervin, Thomas E. 1911-1992 *BioIn 17*
Ervin, Thomas Marion 1953- *WhoEmL 93*
Ervine, St. John G. 1883-1971 *BioIn 17*
Erving, Claude Moore, Jr. 1952- *WhoWor 93*
Erving, Julius Winfield 1950- *WhoAm 92*
Erving, Julius Winfield, II 1950- *AfrAmBi*
Ervolino, Joanne Marie 1959- *WhoAmW 93, WhoEmL 93*
Ervynck, Gontran Jozef 1935- *WhoWor 93*
Erwin, Alan R. *ScF&FL 92*
Erwin, Betty K. *DcAmChF 1960*
Erwin, Chesley Para, Jr. 1953- *WhoEmL 93*
Erwin, Clyde Vernon, Jr. *Law&B 92*
Erwin, Dell Coats 1936- *WhoE 93*
Erwin, Donald Carroll 1920- *WhoAm 92*
Erwin, Douglas Homer 1954- *WhoEmL 93*
Erwin, Elmer Louis 1926- *WhoAm 92*
Erwin, Emily Ann 1953- *WhoAmW 93*
Erwin, Frank W. 1931- *St&PR 93*
Erwin, Frank William 1931- *WhoAm 92*
Erwin, Frederick Joseph 1925- *WhoE 93*
Erwin, Henry *BioIn 17*
Erwin, Joseph Arnold 1956- *WhoEmL 93*
Erwin, Judith Ann 1939- *WhoAm 92, WhoAmW 93*
Erwin, Katherine A. *Law&B 92*
Erwin, Larry E. 1938- *St&PR 93*
Erwin, Martin Craig *Law&B 92*
Erwin, Martin Nesbitt 1938- *WhoAm 92*
Erwin, Maurice George 1937- *St&PR 93*
Erwin, Morton *Law&B 92*
Erwin, Richard C. 1923- *WhoAm 92*
Erwin, Richard Cannon 1923- *WhoSSW 93*
Erwin, Robert C. 1914- *WhoSSW 93*
Erwin, Robert Dean 1949- *St&PR 93*
Erwin, Robert Lester 1953- *WhoAm 92*
Erwin, Robert P., Jr. *Law&B 92*
Erwin, Steven P. 1943- *St&PR 93*
Erwin, Sue Carlanne 1950- *WhoEmL 93*
Erwin, Thomas Dary 1950- *WhoEmL 93, WhoSSW 93*
Erwin, Thomas K. 1950- *St&PR 93*
Erwin-Cook, Nancy Elizabeth 1949- *WhoAmW 93*
Erwine, Donald T. 1945- *St&PR 93*
Erwitt, Elliott 1928- *BioIn 17*
Erwitt, Elliott Romano 1928- *WhoAm 92*
Erxleben, William Charles 1942- *WhoAm 92*
Erz, Wolfgang 1936- *WhoScE 91-3*
Erzinger, Dennis Eugene, Sr. 1951- *WhoEmL 93, WhoWor 93*
Esak, J. Ronald 1944- *St&PR 93*
Esaki, Howard Yuji 1953- *WhoE 93*
Esaki, Leo 1925- *WhoAm 92, WhoE 93, WhoWor 93*
Esaki, Masumi 1915- *WhoAsAP 91*
Esakof, Rosalind 1932- *WhoAmW 93*
Esakov, Janice H. 1951- *WhoEmL 93*
E. Santos, Faria *WhoScE 91-3*
Esanu, Vladimir 1928- *WhoScE 91-4*
Esarey, Melvin M. 1910- *WhoWrEP 92*
Esasky, Nick *BioIn 17*
Esau, Abraham 1865?-1901 *BioIn 17*
Esau, Katherine 1898- *WhoAmW 93*
Esaw, James Reginald 1956- *WhoEmL 93*
Esayag, Mery 1935- *WhoWor 93*
Esbensen, Barbara Juster *BioIn 17*
Esbensen, Barbara Juster 1925- *WhoWrEP 92*
Esbenshade, Kathryn Mitchell 1955- *WhoAmW 93, WhoEmL 93*
Esbitt, William 1910-1991 *BioIn 17*
Escala, Carmen 1947- *WhoScE 91-3*
Escalante, Anibal *DcCPCAm*
Escalante, Jaime *BioIn 17*
Escalante, Jaime 1930- *HispAmA [port]*
Escalante, Juan Antonio 1633-1669 *BioIn 17*
Escalante, Judson Robert 1930- *WhoE 93*
Escalante-Ramirez, Vladimir 1958- *WhoWor 93*
Escaler, Narcisa de Leon 1944- *WhoUN 92*
Escalera, Karen Weiner 1944- *WhoAmW 93*
Escalet, Frank Diaz 1930- *WhoE 93*
Escalona, Beatriz 1903-1980 *HispAmA*
Escalon Delgado, Clara Sue 1952- *WhoAmW 93, WhoEmL 93*
Escamilla 1586?-1624 *BioIn 17*
Escandell, Noemi 1936- *WhoWrEP 92*
Escarraz, Enrique, III 1944- *WhoSSW 93*
Esce, Susan Nan 1961- *WhoEmL 93*
Esch, Karen Eileen 1943- *WhoE 93*
Esch, Robert Ernst 1932- *St&PR 93, WhoAm 92*
Esch, Robert Morley 1940- *WhoSSW 93*
Esch, Robin Ernest 1930- *WhoAm 92*
Eschbach, Jesse Ernest 1920- *WhoAm 92, WhoSSW 93*
Eschbach, Joseph Wetherill 1933- *WhoAm 92*
Escheikh, Abdelhamid 1935- *WhoWor 93*
Eschelbach, Claire John 1929- *ScF&FL 92*
Eschen, Siegfried 1945- *WhoScE 91-3*
Eschenbach, Christoph 1940- *Baker 92, WhoAm 92, WhoSSW 93, WhoWor 93*
Eschenbach, Karen 1961- *WhoAmW 93*
Eschenbach, Marie von Ebner- 1830-1916 *BioIn 17*
Eschenbacher, Larry Watts 1965- *WhoEmL 93*
Eschenbrenner, Gunther Paul 1925- *WhoAm 92*
Eschenburg, Johann Joachim 1743-1820 *BioIn 17*
Eschenlohr, John W. 1936- *St&PR 93*
Eschenmoser, Albert 1925- *WhoScE 91-4, WhoWor 93*
Eschenroeder, Alan Quade 1933- *WhoAm 92, WhoWor 93*
Escher, Arthur 1928- *WhoScE 91-4*
Escher, Rudolf (George) 1912-1980 *Baker 92*
Eschert, Erwin R. *St&PR 93*
Eschete, Mary Louise 1949- *WhoAmW 93, WhoEmL 93*
Eschig, Max(imilian) 1872-1927 *Baker 92*
Eschino, Robert P. 1940- *St&PR 93*
Eschke, Karl-Richard 1939- *WhoScE 91-3*
Eschmann, Johann Karl 1826-1882 *Baker 92*
Eschmeyer, William Neil 1939- *WhoAm 92*
Eschwege, Eveline M. 1936- *WhoScE 91-2*
Eschweiler, Peter Quintus 1932- *WhoE 93*
Escobar, Esperanza 1947- *WhoSSW 93*
Escobar, Frank Joseph 1941- *WhoSSW 93*
Escobar, Javier I. 1943- *HispAmA*
Escobar, Javier Ignacio 1943- *WhoAm 92*
Escobar, Luis Antonio 1925- *Baker 92*
Escobar, Manuel G., Jr. 1953- *WhoEmL 93*
Escobar, Maria J. 1947- *WhoAmW 93*
Escobar, Marisol *NotHsAW 93, WhoAm 92, WhoAmW 93*
Escobar, Pablo *BioIn 17*
Escobar, Sixto 1913- *HispAmA [port]*
Escobar-Budge, Roberto 1926- *Baker 92*
Escobar Chavez, Cesar Enrique 1948- *WhoWor 93*
Escobar Galindo, David 1943- *SpAmA*
Escobedo, Bartolome de c. 1500-1563 *Baker 92*
Escobedo, Ernest 1948- *WhoEmL 93, WhoSSW 93*
Escobedo, Federico 1874-1949 *DcMexL*
Escobillo, Evangeline Crisostomo 1954- *WhoWor 93*
Escoffier, Auguste 1847-1935 *BioIn 17*
Escolar, Carmen Cecilia 1965- *WhoUN 92*
Escoriaza, Carmen Maria 1947- *WhoSSW 93*
Escot, Pozzi (Olga) 1931- *Baker 92*
Escott, Lloyd Harrison 1948- *St&PR 93*
Escott, Shoolah Hope 1952- *WhoAmW 93, WhoEmL 93*
Escott-Russell, Sundra E. 1954- *AfrAmBi*
Escousse, A.E. 1935- *WhoScE 91-2*
Escousse, Andre 1935- *WhoScE 91-2*
Escribano, Joseph M. 1954- *St&PR 93*

Escribano, Marisa 1950- *WhoAmW 93*
Escribano-Alberca, Ignacio 1928- *WhoWor 93*
Escribano Saenz, Albino *Law&B 92*
Escriva de Balaguer y Albas, Jose Maria 1902-1975 *BioIn 17*
Escudero, J.L. 1948- *WhoScE 91-3*
Escudero, Jose 1934- *WhoUN 92*
Escudero, Salvador H., III 1942- *WhoAsAP 91*
Escudier, Leon 1816-1881 *Baker 92*
Escudier, Marie (-Pierre-Yves) 1809-1880 *See* Escudier, Leon 1816-1881 *Baker 92*
Esculier, Jacques 1959- *St&PR 93*
Esdaile, Earl Charles 1954- *WhoSSW 93*
Esdorn, Horst 1925- *WhoScE 91-3*
Esdorn, Richard L., III 1945- *St&PR 93*
Esecson, Robert M. 1950- *WhoE 93*
Esenberg, Franklyn 1933- *St&PR 93*
Esen Taiji Khasa d1452 *HarEnMi*
Esfahani, Farhad 1961- *WhoSSW 93*
Esfandiary, Mary S. 1929- *WhoAmW 93, WhoWor 93*
Esguerra, Angel Mendoza, III *WhoWor 93*
Esh, Dalia Regina 1950- *WhoAmW 93, WhoEmL 93*
Eshagian, Joseph 1951- *WhoEmL 93*
Esham, Richard Henry 1942- *WhoSSW 93*
Eshbach, Brenda Lee 1959- *WhoSSW 93*
Eshbach, Lloyd Arthur 1910- *ScF&FL 92*
Eshbach, William Wallace 1917- *WhoAm 92*
Eshelbrenner, Gary C. 1942- *St&PR 93*
Eshelman, David Richard 1949- *WhoEmL 93*
Eshelman, George C. 1952- *St&PR 93*
Eshelman, Lester P. *St&PR 93*
Eshelman, William Robert 1921- *JrnUS, WhoAm 92*
Eshelman Singleton, Dawn 1951- *St&PR 93*
Esher, Brian R. 1948- *St&PR 93*
Esher, Brian Richard 1948- *WhoAm 92*
Esherick, Joseph 1914- *WhoAm 92*
Eshkol, Levi 1895-1969 *BioIn 17, ColdWar 2 [port], DcTwHis*
Eshleman, Clayton 1935- *WhoWrEP 92*
Eshleman, Dennis Newcomer 1954- *WhoEmL 93*
Eshleman, Donald E. 1944- *St&PR 93*
Eshleman, J. Richard 1930- *St&PR 93*
Eshleman, James J. 1953- *St&PR 93*
Eshleman, Lloyd Wendell 1902-1949 *ScF&FL 92*
Eshleman, Silas Kendrick, III 1928- *WhoAm 92, WhoE 93*
Esho, Hideki 1947- *WhoWor 93*
Eshoo, Anna Georges 1942- *WhoAmW 93*
Eshoo, Barbara Anne Rudolph 1946- *WhoAmW 93, WhoE 93, WhoEmL 93*
Eshoo, Robert Pius 1926- *WhoE 93*
Eshpai, Andrei 1925- *Baker 92*
Eshpai, Yakov 1890-1963 *Baker 92*
Esiason, Boomer 1961- *WhoAm 92*
Eskandarian, Edward 1936- *St&PR 93, WhoAm 92, WhoE 93*
Eskeland, Trond 1942- *WhoScE 91-4*
Eskell, Camille A. 1954- *WhoE 93*
Eskenasy, Alexandre 1918- *WhoScE 91-4*
Eskenazi, Maxine Solomon 1951- *WhoWor 93*
Esker, Lori *BioIn 17*
Eskesen, Bennet Hallum (Hal), Jr. 1947- *WhoWrEP 92*
Eskesen, Morten 1926- *WhoWor 93*
Eskesen, Ruth Ellen 1939- *WhoAmW 93*
Eskew, Carolyn Preslar 1942- *WhoAmW 93*
Eskew, Cathleen Cheek 1953- *WhoEmL 93*
Eskew, Rhea Taliaferro 1923- *WhoAm 92*
Eskew, Ron Wayne 1951- *WhoE 93*
Eskijian, Nancy L. *Law&B 92*
Eskil, Ragna B. *AmWomPl*
Eskildsen, Morten 1939- *WhoScE 91-2*
Eskilson, Eskil T. 1905- *St&PR 93*
Eskilson, Thomas Talbot 1942- *St&PR 93*
Eskin, Jeffrey Laurence 1952- *WhoEmL 93*
Eskind, Norman Jo Andrew 1955- *WhoEmL 93*
Eskoff, Richard Joseph 1936- *St&PR 93*
Eskola, Antti Aarre 1934- *WhoWor 93*
Eskola, Lauri *WhoScE 91-4*
Eskola, Tarmo Juhani 1945- *WhoWor 93*
Eskow, Mary Ann 1946- *St&PR 93*
Eskowitz, Leonard Irving 1948- *WhoE 93*
Eskridge, James Arthur 1942- *St&PR 93*
Eskridge, John I. 1940- *St&PR 93*
Eskridge, Joni Kay 1956- *WhoEmL 93*
Eskridge, Wayne 1942- *St&PR 93*
Eskuri, Neil *WhoAm 92*
Eslami, Habib 1952- *WhoSSW 93*
Eslami, Hossein Hojatol 1927- *WhoAm 92*
Eslava (y Elizondo), (Miguel) Hilarion 1807-1878 *Baker 92*
Esler, Anthony 1934- *ScF&FL 92*
Esler, Anthony James 1934- *WhoAm 92, WhoSSW 93, WhoWrEP 92*
Esler, John Kenneth 1933- *WhoAm 92*
Esler, W. R. 1926- *WhoAm 92*
Esler, William Christopher 1951- *WhoWrEP 92*
Esler, William R. 1926- *St&PR 93*
Eslick, Annette *Law&B 92*
Eslick, Willa McCord Blake 1878-1961 *BioIn 17*
Eslyn, Robert N. 1923- *St&PR 93*
Esmaeili Khatir, Nazia 1962- *WhoWor 93*
Esman, Aaron H. 1924- *WhoAm 92*
Esman, Rosa Mencher 1927- *WhoAm 92, WhoE 93*
Esme *BioIn 17*
Esmon, Charles Thomas 1947- *WhoSSW 93*
Esmond, Jack Bailey 1943- *WhoSSW 93*
Esmond, Jill 1908-1990 *BioIn 17*
Esmond, Sidney 1893- *ScF&FL 92*
Esnault, Helene Irene 1953- *WhoWor 93*
Esnouf, C. 1942- *WhoScE 91-2*
Esnouf, Catherine 1956- *WhoScE 91-2*
Esoldi, Vincent Carmine 1947- *WhoE 93*
Espada, Martin 1957- *BioIn 17*
Espaillat, Rhina Polonia 1932- *WhoWrEP 92*
Espaldon, Ernesto Mercader 1926- *WhoAm 92*
Espanca, Florbela 1894-1930 *BioIn 17*
Esparza, Jose 1945- *WhoUN 92*
Esparza, Moctezuma 20th cent.- *HispAmA [port]*
Espe, David Ronald 1955- *WhoE 93, WhoEmL 93*
Espe, James Elliott *Law&B 92*
Espejo, Beatriz 1939- *DcMexL*
Espejo, Pierre Marc *Law&B 92*
Espelage, John J. 1938- *St&PR 93*
Espeland, Lynn L. *Law&B 92*
Espenhain, Flemming Carl 1947- *WhoScE 91-2*
Espenlaub, Charles Fredrick, Jr. 1935- *St&PR 93*
Espenschied, Lenne E. *Law&B 92*
Espenshade, Edward Bowman, Jr. 1910- *WhoAm 92*
Esper, William Joseph 1932- *WhoE 93*
Esperian, Kallen Rose 1961- *WhoAm 92*
Espersen, Gert 1922- *WhoScE 91-2*
Esperseth, Maurice H. 1925- *St&PR 93*
Espert, Nuria *MiSFD 9*
Espert Soro, Francisco Vicente 1935- *WhoUN 92*
Espey, Frances McDowell 1951- *WhoSSW 93*
Espi, Jose 1942- *WhoWor 93*
Espie, Colin Alexander *WhoScE 91-1*
Espina Salguero, Gustavo *WhoWor 93*
Espinasse, Jacques 1937- *WhoScE 91-2*
Espinasse, Jacques Paul 1943- *WhoWor 93*
Espino, Fern Ruby *WhoAmW 93*
Espinola, Francisco 1901-1973 *SpAmA*
Espino-Ramirez, Rosa Maria 1964- *WhoAmW 93*
Espinosa, Daniel 1955- *WhoWor 93*
Espinosa, Francisco C. 1936- *St&PR 93*
Espinosa, Guillermo 1905-1990 *Baker 92*
Espinosa, Margo Denzine 1928- *WhoAmW 93*
Espinosa, Moises R. 1933- *WhoAsAP 91*
Espinosa, Paul 1950- *HispAmA*
Espinosa, Tito R. 1943- *WhoAsAP 91*
Espinosa Altamirano, Horacio 1931- *DcMexL*
Espinosa Ramon, Renan Alfonso 1947- *WhoWor 93*
Espinoza, Jose Oltio 1932- *WhoUN 92*
Espinoza, Luis Rolan 1943- *WhoSSW 93*
Espinoza, Mario Antonio 1962- *WhoSSW 93*
Espla (y Triay), Oscar 1886-1976 *Baker 92*
Esplugas, Celia Catalina *WhoAmW 93*
Espmark, Yngve O. 1933- *WhoScE 91-4*
Esposito, Albert Charles 1912- *WhoAm 92*
Esposito, Andrea Marie 1957- *St&PR 93*
Esposito, Anthony F. 1935- *St&PR 93*
Esposito, Anthony Morris 1952- *WhoEmL 93*
Esposito, Bonnie Lou 1947- *WhoAmW 93, WhoEmL 93*
Esposito, Bruce John 1941- *WhoE 93*
Esposito, Charles Joseph 1964- *WhoE 93*
Esposito, Cheryl Lynne 1964- *WhoE 93*
Esposito, Dennis Harry 1947- *WhoEmL 93*
Esposito, Donna J. 1954- *WhoWrEP 92*
Esposito, Donna Jordon 1961- *WhoAmW 93*
Esposito, Eugene Henry 1940- *St&PR 93*
Esposito, Giancarlo *BioIn 17*
Esposito, Giovanni 1934- *WhoScE 91-3*
Esposito, John *St&PR 93*
Esposito, John Charles 1926- *WhoE 93*
Esposito, Joseph C. 1950- *WhoEmL 93*
Esposito, Joseph E. *Law&B 92*
Esposito, Joseph J. 1951- *St&PR 93*
Esposito, Joseph John 1951- *WhoAm 92, WhoE 93*
Esposito, Larry Wayne 1951- *BioIn 17, WhoEmL 93*
Esposito, Meade H. 1907- *PolPar*
Esposito, Michael 1956- *St&PR 93*
Esposito, Michael A. 1956- *St&PR 93*
Esposito, Michael F. *Law&B 92*
Esposito, Michael P., Jr. 1939- *St&PR 93*
Esposito, Michael Patrick, Jr. 1939- *WhoAm 92, WhoE 93*
Esposito, Michael Wayne 1968- *WhoSSW 93*
Esposito, Michele 1855-1929 *Baker 92*
Esposito, Paulette 1945- *WhoAmW 93*
Esposito, Philip Anthony 1942- *WhoSSW 93*
Esposito, Raffaele 1932- *WhoWor 93*
Esposito, Robert Louis 1935- *St&PR 93*
Esposito, Rochelle Easton 1941- *WhoAm 92*
Esposito, Thomas R. 1946- *St&PR 93*
Esposito, Vincent 1957- *WhoE 93, WhoEmL 93, WhoWor 93*
Espoy, Henry Marti 1917- *WhoAm 92*
Espronceda, Jose de 1808-1842 *NinCLC 39 [port]*
Espy, Charles Clifford 1910- *WhoAm 92*
Espy, Herbert Hastings 1931- *WhoE 93*
Espy, Isaac Pugh 1939- *WhoSSW 93*
Espy, James William 1948- *WhoWor 93*
Espy, Marrin Lilley 1931- *WhoSSW 93*
Espy, Mary Susan 1952- *St&PR 93, WhoAmW 93*
Espy, Michael *BioIn 17*
Espy, Mike 1953- *CngDr 91, WhoAm 92, WhoSSW 93*
Espy, Paul Dacy 1941- *WhoSSW 93*
Espy, Reynette Coats 1960- *WhoEmL 93*
Espy, Willard R. 1910- *WhoWrEP 92*
Espy, Willard Richardson 1910- *WhoAm 92*
Esquibel, Edward Valdez 1928- *WhoSSW 93*
Esquinazi, Pablo David 1956- *WhoWor 93*
Esquirol, John H. *Law&B 92*
Esquiroz, Margarita 1945- *NotHsAW 93*
Esquival-Heinemann, Barbara Paula 1946- *WhoSSW 93*
Esquivel, Agerico Liwag 1932- *WhoAm 92*
Esquivel, Alan de Souza 1946- *WhoWor 93*
Esquivel, Giselle Beatriz 1950- *WhoEmL 93*
Esquivel, John M. *Law&B 92*
Esquivel, Manuel 1940- *DcCPCAm*
Esquivel, Rita 1932- *NotHsAW 93 [port]*
Esquivel, Roderick *DcCPCAm*
Esquivel, Ruben E. 1943- *St&PR 93*
Esrey, William T. *NewYTBS 92 [port]*
Esrey, William Todd 1940- *St&PR 93, WhoAm 92, WhoWor 93*
Esry, Donald Howard 1940- *WhoSSW 93*
Essa, Lisa Beth 1955- *WhoAmW 93*
Essaafi, M'Hamed 1930- *WhoUN 92*
Essam, John *WhoScE 91-1*
Essayan, Charles H. 1928- *St&PR 93*
Essenberg, Jack R. 1938- *St&PR 93*
Essenberg, Margaret Kottke 1943- *WhoSSW 93*
Essenwanger, Oskar Maximilian Karl 1920- *WhoSSW 93*
Esser, Aristide Henri 1930- *WhoAm 92, WhoE 93, WhoWor 93*
Esser, Carl Eric 1942- *WhoAm 92*
Esser, Frank V. 1939- *St&PR 93*
Esser, Frank Vincent 1939- *WhoAm 92*
Esser, George Francis 1955- *WhoEmL 93*
Esser, Heinrich 1818-1872 *Baker 92*
Esser, Karl 1924- *WhoWor 93*
Esser, Kevin 1953- *ScF&FL 92*
Esserman, Dean *BioIn 17*
Essert, Gary d1992 *NewYTBS 92*
Essex, Earl of 1631-1683 *BioIn 17*
Essex, Francis Xavier 1931- *WhoSSW 93*
Essex, Harry J. 1915- *WhoAm 92*
Essex, Joseph Michael 1947- *WhoAm 92*
Essex, Judson Paul 1936- *WhoSSW 93*
Essex, Lewis W. 1932- *St&PR 93*
Essex, Myron Elmer 1939- *WhoAm 92, WhoE 93, WhoWor 93*
Essex, Robert Devereux, Earl of 1591-1646 *HarEnMi*
Essex, Rosamund 1900-1985 *ScF&FL 92*
Essex, Stephen S. 1955- *St&PR 93*
Essex, Wanda Elizabeth 1925- *WhoAmW 93*
Essex, William *ScF&FL 92*
Essian, Jim *BioIn 17*
Essick, Robert Newman 1942- *WhoAm 92*
Essick, Samuel Coleman 1920- *St&PR 93*
Essien, Joyce Dian Kirkland 1945- *WhoSSW 93*
Essig, Kathleen Susan 1956- *WhoAmW 93*
Essig, Mark G. 1957- *St&PR 93*
Essig, Mitchell Neil 1950- *WhoEmL 93*
Essig, Nancy Claire 1939- *WhoAm 92, WhoSSW 93*
Essig, Philip Martin 1939- *St&PR 93*
Essimengane, Simon 1930- *WhoAfr*
Essin, Emmett Mohammed, Jr. 1920- *WhoSSW 93*
Essinger, Giles F. 1934- *St&PR 93*
Essington, Diane Marie 1951- *WhoAmW 93*
Essipoff, Anna 1851-1914 *Baker 92*
Essipova, Anna 1851-1914 *Baker 92*
Esslin, Martin *BioIn 17*
Esslinger, Charlene Marie Dobbs 1945- *WhoAmW 93*
Esslinger, John Thomas 1943- *WhoE 93*
Esslinger, Margaret Frances Lipscomb 1925- *WhoSSW 93*
Esslinger, Nell Daniel 1903- *WhoAmW 93*
Esslinger, Paul 1928- *WhoScE 91-3*
Esslinger, Tamra Jo 1959- *WhoEmL 93*
Essman, Alyn 1932- *WhoAm 92*
Essman, Alyn V. 1932- *St&PR 93*
Essman, Douglas Jay 1956- *WhoEmL 93*
Essman, Janet Lynn 1963- *WhoAmW 93*
Essman, Pansy Ellen 1918- *WhoAmW 93*
Essman, Robert Norvel 1937- *WhoE 93*
Essmyer, Michael Martin 1949- *WhoEmL 93, WhoSSW 93*
Essock, Cyd Pauline 1956- *WhoWrEP 92*
Esson, J. Douglas 1940- *St&PR 93*
Esson, Robert 1944- *St&PR 93*
Essrig, C. Lee *Law&B 92*
Essrig, Harry 1912- *BioIn 17*
Esstman, Michael Brady 1946- *St&PR 93*
Esswein, Arthur Joseph 1947- *WhoE 93*
Esswood, Paul (Lawrence Vincent) 1942- *Baker 92*
Essy, Amara 1943- *WhoWor 93*
Estabo, Tranquellano *BioIn 17*
Estabrook, Alison 1951- *WhoAmW 93, WhoEmL 93*
Estabrook, Anne L. *AmWomPl*
Estabrook, Reed 1944- *WhoAm 92*
Estabrook, Robert Harley 1918- *WhoAm 92*
Estabrook, Ronald Winfield 1926- *WhoAm 92*
Estabrook, Steven H. *Law&B 92*
Estabrooks, G.H. 1895-1973 *ScF&FL 92*
Estadieu, B. *WhoScE 91-2*
Estaing, Charles Hector Theodat d' 1729-1794 *HarEnMi*
Estaing, Valery Giscard d' 1926- *BioIn 17*
Estall, John R. *Law&B 92*
Estall, Robert Charles *WhoScE 91-1*
Estang, Luc 1911-1992 *ConAu 139*
Estanislao, Oscar Desiderio 1959- *WhoWor 93*
Este, Isabella d' 1474-1539 *BioIn 17*
Esteban, Julio 1906-1987 *Baker 92*
Esteban, Mariano 1944- *WhoE 93*
Estebe y Grimau, Pablo c. 1730-1794 *Baker 92*
Estefan, Emilio *BioIn 17*
Estefan, Gloria *BioIn 17*
Estefan, Gloria 1958- *NotHsAW 93 [port]*
Estefan, Gloria Maria 1957- *WhoAm 92*
Estell, Dora Lucile 1930- *WhoAmW 93*
Estenson, Noel Keith 1938- *St&PR 93*
Estep, Carolyn Benjamin 1947- *WhoWrEP 92*
Estep, Ida W. *Law&B 92*
Estep, Janet Olson 1956- *WhoEmL 93*
Estep, Ronald Eugene 1951- *WhoEmL 93*
Estep, Sarah Virginia 1926- *WhoE 93, WhoWor 93*
Estep-Johnston, Megan Alexander 1957- *WhoAmW 93*
Esterbauer, Hermann 1936- *WhoScE 91-4*
Esterbrook, Elizabeth *WhoWrEP 92*
Estergren, Eric D. 1944- *St&PR 93*
Esterhai, John Louis 1920- *St&PR 93, WhoAm 92*
Esterhazy, Johannes Graf *Law&B 92*
Esterline, Shirley Jeanne 1936- *WhoAmW 93*
Esterly, David 1944- *BioIn 17*
Esterly, Juliet King Bindt 1912- *WhoAmW 93*
Esterly, Nancy Burton 1935- *WhoAm 92*
Esterman, Benjamin 1906- *WhoE 93*
Esterman, Jill L. *Law&B 92*
Esterow, David J. 1928- *St&PR 93*
Esterow, Milton 1928- *WhoAm 92, WhoE 93*
Esterquest, Peter 1946- *St&PR 93*
Esters, Donald J. 1939- *WhoE 93*
Estersohn, Harold Sydney 1927- *WhoE 93*
Esterson, Larry L. 1916- *St&PR 93, WhoE 93*
Estervig, Howard Raymond 1947- *WhoEmL 93*
Estes, Alexandra Haeger 1949- *St&PR 93*
Estes, Carl Lewis, II 1936- *WhoAm 92, WhoSSW 93, WhoWor 93*
Estes, Carroll Lynn 1938- *WhoAm 92*
Estes, Charles Byron 1946- *WhoEmL 93*

Estes, Clarissa Pinkola 1943- *NotHsAW 93 [port]*
Estes, David Charles 1950- *WhoEmL 93, WhoSSW 93*
Estes, Edward Harvey, Jr. 1925- *WhoAm 92*
Estes, Edward Richard, Jr. 1925- *WhoSSW 93*
Estes, Elaine 1950- *WhoAmW 93, WhoSSW 93*
Estes, Elaine Rose Graham 1931- *WhoAm 92*
Estes, Eleanor 1906- *DcAmChF 1960*
Estes, Eleanor 1906-1988 *ScF&FL 92*
Estes, Eleanor (Ruth) 1906-1988 *MajAI [port]*
Estes, Frank W. *Law&B 92*
Estes, Gerald Walter 1928- *WhoAm 92*
Estes, Harper 1956- *WhoEmL 93*
Estes, Jacob Thomas, Jr. 1944- *WhoSSW 93, WhoWor 93*
Estes, Jon Carleton 1944- *St&PR 93*
Estes, Joseph O. 1927- *St&PR 93*
Estes, Joseph Richard 1925- *WhoSSW 93*
Estes, Joseph Worth 1934- *WhoE 93*
Estes, Kenneth Edward *Law&B 92*
Estes, Linton H., Jr. 1920- *St&PR 93*
Estes, Lola Caroline 1959- *WhoAmW 93*
Estes, Moreau Pinckney, IV 1917- *WhoSSW 93, WhoWor 93*
Estes, Rebecca 1953- *WhoAmW 93*
Estes, Richard 1932- *WhoAm 92*
Estes, Richard 1936- *BioIn 17*
Estes, Rose *ScF&FL 92*
Estes, Royce J. *Law&B 92*
Estes, Royce Joe 1944- *WhoAm 92*
Estes, Simon (Lamont) 1938- *Baker 92, WhoAm 92*
Estes, Sylvia D. 1951- *St&PR 93*
Estes, Tanya 1959- *St&PR 93*
Estes, William Kaye 1919- *WhoAm 92*
Esteva, Jose Maria 1818-1904 *DcMexL*
Esteva Fabregat, Claudio 1918- *IntDcAn*
Estevan d1539 *BioIn 17*
Estevanico 1500?-1539 *Expl 93*
Esteve, Daniel 1941- *WhoScE 91-2*
Esteves, Sandra Maria 1948- *BioIn 17, NotHsAW 93*
Esteve y Grimau, Pablo c. 1730-1794 *Baker 92*
Estevez, Antonio 1916-1988 *Baker 92*
Estevez, Emilio 1962- *ConTFT 10, HispAmA, MiSFD 9, WhoAm 92*
Estevez, Emilio 1963- *BioIn 17*
Estevez, Ramon 1940- *WhoAm 92*
Estey, Audree Phipps 1910- *WhoAm 92, WhoAmW 93*
Estey, Dale *ScF&FL 92*
Estey, John Sherman 1926- *St&PR 93*
Estey, Willard Zebedee 1919- *WhoAm 92*
Esther, Queen of Persia *BioIn 17*
Estibal, Georges *WhoScE 91-2*
Estill, James C. *St&PR 93*
Estill, John Staples, Jr. 1919- *WhoSSW 93*
Estill, Robert Whitridge 1927- *WhoAm 92, WhoSSW 93*
Estin, Hans Howard 1928- *St&PR 93, WhoAm 92*
Estinel, Marina 1942- *WhoUN 92*
Estin-Klein, Libbyada 1937- *WhoAmW 93*
Estis, Dennis Arnold 1947- *WhoEmL 93*
Estleman, Loren D. *BioIn 17*
Estleman, Loren D. 1952- *ScF&FL 92*
Estler, Claus-Jurgen 1930- *WhoScE 91-3*
Estol, Conrado D.J. 1931- *WhoWor 93*
Estoril, Jean *MajAI*
Estrada, Anthony J. *St&PR 93*
Estrada, Candelario J. *St&PR 93*
Estrada, Carlos 1909-1970 *Baker 92*
Estrada, David Robert 1944- *WhoSSW 93*
Estrada, Garcia Juan Agustin 1895-1961 *Baker 92*
Estrada, Genaro 1887-1937 *DcMexL*
Estrada, Jacquelyn Ann 1946- *WhoEmL 93*
Estrada, Josefina 1957- *DcMexL*
Estrada, Joseph Ejercito 1937- *WhoAsAP 91*
Estrada, Joseph Marcelo Ejercito 1937- *WhoWor 93*
Estrada, Julio 1943- *Baker 92*
Estrada, Miguel *Law&B 92*
Estrada, Miguel Francisco *BioIn 17*
Estrada, Mike, Jr. 1959- *WhoE 93*
Estrada, Patricia *ScF&FL 92*
Estrada, Rodney Joseph 1937- *St&PR 93, WhoAm 92*
Estrada, Victoria Ocampo de 1891-1979 *BioIn 17*
Estrada Palma, Tomas *DcCPCAm*
Estrazulas, Enrique 1942- *SpAmA*
Estrees, Francois Annibal d' 1572-1670 *HarEnMi*
Estreicher, Karol 1827-1908 *PolBiDi*
Estreicher, Karol 1906-1984 *PolBiDi*
Estreicher, Samuel 1948- *WhoEmL 93*
Estrella, Conrado B., Jr. 1943- *WhoAsAP 91*
Estrella, Conrado M., III 1960- *WhoAsAP 91*
Estrella, Ernesto T. 1926- *WhoAsAP 91*
Estrella, William A. 1953- *St&PR 93*
Estren, Mark James 1948- *St&PR 93, WhoAm 92*
Estrich, Susan Rachel 1952- *WhoAm 92*
Estridge, Robin *ScF&FL 92*
Estridge, Ronald B. 1937- *WhoAm 92*
Estrin, Barry *Law&B 92*
Estrin, Dianne G. *Law&B 92*
Estrin, Elizabeth Gougam 1912-1992 *BioIn 17*
Estrin, Eric Charles 1953- *WhoEmL 93*
Estrin, Gerald 1921- *WhoAm 92*
Estrin, Herbert Alvin 1925- *WhoAm 92*
Estrin, Herman A. 1915- *WhoWrEP 92*
Estrin, Herman Albert 1915- *WhoAm 92*
Estrin, Kari 1954- *WhoEmL 93*
Estrin, Mitchell Stewart 1956- *WhoEmL 93*
Estrin, Norman Frederick 1939- *WhoE 93*
Estrin, Richard William 1932- *WhoAm 92*
Estrin, Thelma Austern 1924- *WhoAm 92*
Estrup, Peder Jan 1931- *WhoAm 92*
Estuar, Fiorello R. *WhoAsAP 91*
Estus, Boyd 1941- *WhoE 93*
Estwing, Norman E. 1921- *St&PR 93*
Esty, David Cameron 1932- *WhoAm 92*
Esty, John C., Jr. *BioIn 17*
Esty, John Cushing, Jr. 1928- *WhoAm 92*
Esvelt, Becky Miller 1952- *WhoAmW 93*
Eswein, Bruce James, II 1951- *WhoAm 92, WhoE 93, WhoEmL 93*
Esworthy, Helen Feaga 1950- *WhoE 93*
Etaix, Pierre 1928- *QDrFCA 92 [port]*
Etampes, duchesse d' 1508-1580 *BioIn 17*
Etchecopar, Robert Daniel 1905-1990 *BioIn 17*
Etchegaray, Roger Cardinal 1922- *WhoWor 93*
Etchelecu, Albert D. 1937- *St&PR 93*
Etchelecu, Albert Dominic 1937- *WhoAm 92*
Etchemendy, Jeanne Marie 1959- *WhoEmL 93*
Etchemendy, Nancy 1952- *ScF&FL 92*
Etchen, Rebecca Sue 1954- *WhoAmW 93*
Etcher, Anne Margaret 1962- *WhoAmW 93*
Etcheson, Warren Wade 1920- *WhoAm 92*
Etcheverry, Bernard 1921- *St&PR 93*
Etcheverry, Bertrand 1900-1960 *OxDcOp*
Etcheverry, Henri-Bertrand 1900-1960 *Baker 92*
Etchison, Dennis 1943- *ScF&FL 92*
Eteriano, Hugo c. 1110-1182 *OxDcByz*
Etessami, Rambod 1960- *WhoEmL 93*
Etevenon, Pierre R. 1935- *WhoScE 91-2*
Etgen, Charles D. 1928- *St&PR 93*
Ethan, Carol Baehr 1920- *WhoAm 92*
Ethans, Harry 1952- *St&PR 93*
Ethelbald d757 *HarEnMi*
Ethelbald, (II) d860 *HarEnMi*
Ethelbert d865 *HarEnMi*
Ethelfirth d616 *HarEnMi*
Ethell, Jeffrey L(ance) 1947- *ConAu 39NR*
Ethelred, II c. 968-1016 *HarEnMi*
Ethelred of Wessex, I d871 *HarEnMi*
Ethelwold fl. 900- *HarEnMi*
Ethelwulf d860 *HarEnMi*
Etheredge, Charles E. 1937- *St&PR 93*
Etheredge, Forest DeRoyce 1929- *WhoAm 92*
Etheredge, Robert Foster 1920- *WhoAm 92*
Etheredge, William Marion 1947- *WhoSSW 93*
Etheridge, Anna Blair *BioIn 17*
Etheridge, Claire Ellen 1931- *WhoAmW 93*
Etheridge, J. Wayne 1946- *St&PR 93*
Etheridge, Jack Paul 1927- *WhoAm 92*
Etheridge, James Edward, Jr. 1929- *WhoAm 92*
Etheridge, Jeff D., Jr. 1949- *St&PR 93*
Etheridge, Melissa *WhoAm 92*
Etherington, Amy R. *Law&B 92*
Etherington, Edwin D. 1924- *St&PR 93*
Etherington, Edwin Deacon 1924- *WhoAm 92*
Etherington, Frank 1945- *WhoCanL 92*
Etherington, Geoffrey 1928- *St&PR 93*
Etherington, Jim *St&PR 93*
Etherington, Norman 1941- *ScF&FL 92*
Etherington, Roger B. 1923- *St&PR 93*
Etherington, Roger Bennett 1923-1990 *BioIn 17*
Etherton, Bud 1930- *WhoE 93*
Ethier, Marietta M. *Law&B 92*
Ethier-Blais, Jean 1925- *WhoCanL 92*
Ethington, James W. 1917- *St&PR 93*
Ethington, Raymond Lindsay 1929- *WhoAm 92*
Ethridge, Doris Irene 1933- *WhoSSW 93*
Ethridge, Edwin Clark 1950- *WhoEmL 93*
Ethridge, J.B. 1941- *St&PR 93*
Ethridge, James Merritt 1921- *WhoAm 92*
Ethridge, Larry Clayton 1946- *WhoEmL 93*
Ethridge, Mark Foster, Sr. 1896-1981 *DcLB 127 [port]*
Ethridge, Mark Foster, III 1949- *WhoAm 92*
Ethridge, Max Michael 1949- *WhoSSW 93*
Ethridge, Robert Wylie 1940- *WhoSSW 93*
Etienne, C.F. 1928- *WhoScE 91-3*
Etienne, Dirk *St&PR 93*
Etienne, Eugene 1844-1921 *BioIn 17*
Etienne, Jerzy 1938- *WhoScE 91-4*
Etienne, Maurice 1933- *WhoScE 91-2*
Etievant, P.X. 1950- *WhoScE 91-2*
Etikerentse, Godfrey *Law&B 92*
Etkin, Anne 1923- *ScF&FL 92*
Etkind, Efim Grigorievich 1918- *WhoWor 93*
Etler, Alvin 1913-1973 *Baker 92*
Etling, Howard F. 1914- *St&PR 93*
Etling, John Charles 1935- *WhoAm 92, WhoIns 93*
Etling, Russell Hull 1955- *WhoAm 92*
Etling, Terry Douglas 1943- *WhoWor 93*
Etlinger, Joseph D. 1946- *WhoAm 92, WhoE 93*
Etnier, Elizabeth d1991 *BioIn 17*
Eto, Jun 1932- *WhoWor 93*
Eto, Seichiro 1941- *WhoAsAP 91*
Eto, Seiichi 1947- *WhoAsAP 91*
Eto, Susumu 1936- *St&PR 93*
Eto, Toshiya 1927- *Baker 92*
Etourneau, Jean *WhoScE 91-2*
Etowski, Earl John, Jr. 1942- *St&PR 93*
Etra, Jonathan 1952-1991 *BioIn 17, ScF&FL 92*
Etra, Richard H. 1948- *St&PR 93*
Etrillard, Gilles 1957- *WhoWor 93*
Etris, Denise Eileen 1950- *WhoAmW 93*
Etris, Samuel Franklin 1922- *WhoAm 92*
Ets, Marie Hall 1893-1984 *MajAI [port]*
Etskovitz, Fredric Jon 1954- *WhoE 93*
Etsou-Nzabi-Bamungwabi, Frederic Cardinal 1930- *WhoWor 93*
Etsuo, Niki 1939- *WhoWor 93*
Ett, Kaspar 1788-1847 *Baker 92*
Ettel, Anna Marie *Law&B 92*
Ettelson, Charles David 1952- *WhoEmL 93*
Ettenberg, Michael 1943- *WhoAm 92*
Ettenberg, Morris 1916-1991 *BioIn 17*
Ettensohn, Frank Robert 1947- *WhoAm 92, WhoEmL 93, WhoSSW 93*
Ettensohn, Richard L. *Law&B 92*
Ettenson, Mel W. 1933- *St&PR 93*
Etter, Dave 1928- *BioIn 17, WhoWrEP 92*
Etter, David Pearson 1928- *WhoAm 92*
Etter, George, IV 1940- *St&PR 93*
Etter, Howard Lee 1931- *WhoE 93*
Etter, Laszlo 1940- *WhoScE 91-4*
Etter, Paul Courtney 1947- *WhoE 93*
Etter, Robert M. 1932- *St&PR 93*
Etter, Robert Miller 1932- *WhoAm 92*
Etter, Steven Milton 1946- *WhoAm 92*
Etter, Thomas C. *Law&B 92*
Etter, Thomas Clifton, Jr. 1938- *WhoE 93*
Etter, William D. 1940- *St&PR 93*
Etterlin, Frido von Senger und 1891-1963 *BioIn 17*
Ettin, Frank L. *Law&B 92*
Ettinger, Clifford d1990 *BioIn 17*
Ettinger, Jeffrey M. *Law&B 92*
Ettinger, Joseph Alan 1931- *WhoWor 93*
Ettinger, Lawrence Jay 1947- *WhoAm 92*
Ettinger, Max (Markus Wolf) 1874-1951 *Baker 92*
Ettinger, Milton Gene 1930- *WhoAm 92*
Ettinger, Mort 1924- *WhoWor 93*
Ettinger, Patrice *Law&B 92*
Ettinger, Richard Prentice 1922- *WhoAm 92*
Ettinger, William A. *Law&B 92*
Ettinghoff, Tracy H. 1953- *WhoEmL 93*
Ettl, Wolfgang Johann 1955- *WhoWor 93*
Ettlich, William F. 1936- *WhoAm 92*
Ettlin, Robert A. 1946- *WhoScE 91-4*
Ettlinger, Leopold D. 1913-1989 *BioIn 17*
Ettlinger, Ralph d1992 *NewYTBS 92*
Ettlinger, Stephen Ralph 1949- *WhoE 93*
Ettre, Leslie Stephen 1922- *WhoAm 92*
Ettrick, Marco Antonio 1945- *WhoE 93, WhoWor 93*
Etz, Lois Kapelsohn 1944- *WhoAmW 93*
Etzel, Alan Emery 1946- *WhoWor 93*
Etzel, James Edward 1929- *WhoAm 92*
Etzel, Kathleen Byron 1960- *WhoE 93*
Etzenbach, John William 1957- *WhoEmL 93*
Etzioni, Amitai *BioIn 17*
Etzioni, Amitai Werner 1929- *WhoAm 92*
Etzkorn, K. Peter *WhoAm 92*
Etzweiler, William David 1935- *St&PR 93*
Etzwiler, Donnell Dencil 1927- *WhoAm 92*
Etzwiler, Nancy Grey *Law&B 92*
Eu, March Kong Fong 1922- *WhoAm 92, WhoAmW 93*
Euba, Femi 1941- *WhoSSW 93*
Eubank, Carol Anne 1948- *WhoAmW 93*
Eubank, Emerson Etheridge, IV 1957- *WhoSSW 93*
Eubank, J. Thomas 1930- *WhoAm 92*
Eubank, Michele Doreen 1963- *WhoAmW 93*
Eubank, Ray H. 1927- *St&PR 93*
Eubank, Ray Henry 1927- *WhoSSW 93*
Eubank, Sandra K. 1958- *WhoEmL 93*
Eubanks, Eugene Emerson 1939- *WhoAm 92*
Eubanks, Gary Leroy, Sr. 1933- *WhoSSW 93*
Eubanks, Jackie Karen *WhoWrEP 92*
Eubanks, James Medric 1931- *St&PR 93*
Eubanks, Michael A. *Law&B 92*
Eubanks, Omer Lafayette 1956- *WhoSSW 93*
Eubanks, Philip D. 1953- *St&PR 93*
Eubanks, Robin S. *Law&B 92*
Eubanks, Ronald W. 1946- *WhoEmL 93, WhoSSW 93*
Eubanks, Terri Ann Ferrell 1962- *WhoSSW 93*
Eubanks-Pope, Sharon G. 1943- *WhoAmW 93*
Euclid 300BC- *Baker 92*
Euclid fl. c. 300BC- *OxDcByz*
Eudaly, Nathan Hoyt, Jr. 1955- *WhoEmL 93*
Eudenbach, Grace Caine 1936- *WhoE 93*
Eudokia *OxDcByz*
Eudokia Ingerina c. 840-882? *OxDcByz*
Eudokia Makrembolitissa dc. 1078 *OxDcByz*
Eudokimos 807-840 *OxDcByz*
Eudoxia d404 *OxDcByz*
Eudy, Judy B. 1949- *WhoAmW 93*
Eugene, Prince of Savoy-Carignan 1663-1736 *HarEnMi*
Eugene, Christie 1928- *St&PR 93*
Eugene, Gregoire 1925- *DcCPCAm*
Eugeneianos, Niketas fl. 12th cent.- *OxDcByz*
Eugenie, Princess of York 1990- *BioIn 17*
Eugenikos, John c. 1394-c. 1454 *OxDcByz*
Eugenikos, Manuel *OxDcByz*
Eugenikos, Mark 1394?-1445 *OxDcByz*
Eugenios *OxDcByz*
Eugenios of Palermo c. 1130-c. 1203 *OxDcByz*
Eugenius d394 *OxDcByz*
Eugenius, III d1153 *OxDcByz*
Eugenius, IV c. 1383-1447 *OxDcByz*
Eugenius Vulgarius fl. c. 900- *OxDcByz*
Eugippius dc. 533 *OxDcByz*
Eugster, Ernest 1950- *WhoWor 93*
Eugster, Jack Wilson 1945- *St&PR 93, WhoAm 92*
Euille, William Darnell 1950- *WhoE 93*
Eul, Hermann Josef 1959- *WhoWor 93*
Eulalios *OxDcByz*
Eulau, Heinz 1915- *BioIn 17, WhoAm 92*
Eule, Julian Nathan 1949- *WhoAm 92, WhoEmL 93*
Eulenburg, Ernst (Emil Alexander) 1847-1926 *Baker 92*
Eulenburg, Kurt 1879-1982 *Baker 92*
Eulenburg-Hertefeld, Philipp, Furst zu 1847-1921 *BioIn 17*
Euler, Aline *WhoAmW 93, WhoE 93*
Euler, Franz, III 1943- *St&PR 93*
Euler, Leonhard 1707-1783 *Baker 92*
Eulert, Don(ald Dean) 1935- *ConAu 40NR*
Eulert, Jochen 1943- *WhoScE 91-3*
Euller, Steven Carl *Law&B 92*
Eulo, Elena Yates *ScF&FL 92*
Eulo, Ken 1939- *ScF&FL 92*
Eumenes c. 362BC-316BC *HarEnMi*
Eumenes, I d241BC *HarEnMi*
Eunapios of Sardis 345?-c. 414 *OxDcByz*
Eunomios c. 335-c. 394 *OxDcByz*
Eunpu, Deborah Lee 1952- *WhoEmL 93*
Euper, Veronica Barbara *Law&B 92*
Euphemia of Chalcedon d303 *OxDcByz*
Euphrosyne Doukaina Kamatera fl. c. 1169-1210 *OxDcByz*
Eure, Geraldine R. *Law&B 92*
Eure, Mary Ferebee *Law&B 92*
Eurich, Nell 1919- *WhoAm 92*
Eurich, Thomas R. 1946- *St&PR 93*
Euripides 480BC-406BC *OxDcByz*
Euripides c. 485BC-406BC *MagSWL [port]*
Euro, Heikki 1940- *WhoWor 93*
Eurola, Seppo 1930- *WhoScE 91-4*
Europe, James Reese 1881-1919 *Baker 92, EncAACR*
Eury, Lynn Wade 1937- *St&PR 93, WhoAm 92, WhoSSW 93*
Eurybiades fl. c. 480BC- *HarEnMi*
Eusden, John Dykstra 1922- *WhoAm 92*
Eusebi, Vincenzo 1943- *WhoScE 91-3*
Eusebio, Robert 1949- *St&PR 93*
Eusebio, Thomas Clifton 1952- *St&PR 93*

Eusebios *OxDcByz*
Eusebios of Caesarea c. 260-339? *OxDcByz*
Eusebios of Emesa c. 300-359 *OxDcByz*
Eusebios of Nikomedeia dc. 342 *OxDcByz*
Eustace, Frank James 1934- *WhoIns 93*
Eustace, Peter 1936- *WhoScE 91-3*
Eustache, Jean 1938-1981 *MiSFD 9N*
Eustathios *OxDcByz*
Eustathios of Antioch dc. 337 *OxDcByz*
Eustathios of Epiphaneia dc. 505 *OxDcByz*
Eustathios of Thessalonike c. 1115-1195? *OxDcByz*
Euster, Joanne Reed 1936- *WhoAm 92, WhoAmW 93*
Eustice, Francis Joseph 1951- *WhoAm 92, WhoEmL 93*
Eustice, James Samuel 1932- *WhoAm 92*
Eustice, Russell Clifford 1919- *WhoAm 92*
Eustis, Albert Anthony 1921- *WhoAm 92*
Eustis, Robert Henry 1920- *WhoAm 92*
Eustis, Truman W., III *Law&B 92*
Eustratios *OxDcByz*
Eustratios dc. 602 *OxDcByz*
Eustratios of Nicaea fl. c. 1100- *OxDcByz*
Euteneuer, Ursula Brigitte 1949- *WhoAm 92*
Eutherios dc. 434 *OxDcByz*
Euthymios c. 834-917 *OxDcByz*
Euthymios of Akmonia fl. 11th cent.- *OxDcByz*
Euthymios of Sardis 754-831 *OxDcByz*
Euthymios the Great 376?-473 *OxDcByz*
Euthymios the Iberian 955?-1028 *OxDcByz*
Euthymios the Younger 823?-898 *OxDcByz*
Euthymiou, Paraskevi Constantin 1923- *WhoWor 93*
Euthymtou, Paraskevi 1923- *WhoWor 93*
Euting, Ernst 1874-1925 *Baker 92*
Eutokios c. 480- *OxDcByz*
Eutropios d399 *OxDcByz*
Eutropius 4th cent.- *OxDcByz*
Eutsler, Mark Leslie 1958- *WhoEmL 93*
Eutsler, Therese Anne 1959- *WhoEmL 93*
Eutyches c. 370-c. 451 *OxDcByz*
Eutychios fl. c. 728-751 *OxDcByz*
Eutychios 512- *OxDcByz*
Eutychios of Alexandria 877-940 *OxDcByz*
Euwe, Machgielis 1901-1981 *BioIn 17*
Euwe, Max 1901-1981 *BioIn 17*
Euzeby, Jacques Achille 1920- *WhoScE 91-2*
Eva, Biro 1929- *WhoScE 91-4*
Evagrios Pontikos c. 345-399 *OxDcByz*
Evagrios Scholastikos c. 536-c. 594 *OxDcByz*
Evagues, Katherine Ann 1948- *WhoAmW 93, WhoEmL 93*
Evan, J. Edward 1943- *St&PR 93*
Evan, William Martin 1922- *WhoAm 92*
Evanbar, B.H. *WhoWrEP 92*
Evander, Gerry Mitchell *Law&B 92*
Evangelist, Frank E. *St&PR 93*
Evangelista, Donato A. *Law&B 92*
Evangelista, Donato A. 1932- *St&PR 93, WhoAm 92*
Evangelista, Jesus Soriano 1946- *WhoE 93, WhoEmL 93*
Evangelista, Linda *BioIn 17*
Evangelista, Thomas Anthony 1951- *WhoE 93*
Evangelista-Cua, Junie 1945- *WhoAsAP 91*
Evangelisti, Franco 1926-1980 *Baker 92*
Evangelou, Spiros Nikolaos 1954- *WhoWor 93*
Evanhoe, Clara May 1908- *WhoAmW 93*
Evanick, Robert Joseph 1952- *St&PR 93*
Evanoff, Carolyn Yvonne 1955- *WhoAmW 93*
Evanoff, George C. 1931- *St&PR 93, WhoAm 92*
Evanoff, Michael B. *St&PR 93*
Evanoff, Sara Ronkin 1953- *WhoAmW 93*
Evans, Abigail Rian 1937- *WhoE 93*
Evans, Adeline Marie Lemelle 1939- *WhoAm 92*
Evans, Alan William *WhoScE 91-1*
Evans, Albert Leslie, Jr. 1939- *St&PR 93*
Evans, Alfred Lee, Jr. 1940- *WhoAm 92*
Evans, Alfred Spring 1917- *WhoAm 92, WhoE 93*
Evans, Alice Mc Donald 1940- *WhoWrEP 92*
Evans, Anna Cape *AmWomPl*
Evans, Anne 1939- *Baker 92*
Evans, Anne 1941- *OxDcOp*
Evans, Anthony Howard 1936- *WhoAm 92*
Evans, Anthony Maurice 1948- *WhoAm 92*
Evans, Arthur B. 1946- *ScF&FL 92*
Evans, Arthur R. 1939- *St&PR 93*
Evans, Audrey Elizabeth 1925- *WhoAm 92*
Evans, Austin James 1920- *WhoAm 92*
Evans, B. Ray 1943- *St&PR 93*
Evans, Barry George *WhoScE 91-1*
Evans, Barry John 1948- *WhoWor 93*
Evans, Barton, Jr. 1947- *St&PR 93, WhoAm 92*
Evans, Benjamin Hampton 1926- *WhoAm 92*
Evans, Bernard William 1934- *WhoAm 92*
Evans, Bill 1920- *WhoAm 92*
Evans, Bill 1921-1985 *ScF&FL 92*
Evans, Bill 1929-1980 *Baker 92*
Evans, Bill 1940- *WhoAm 92*
Evans, Blackwell Bugg 1927- *WhoAm 92*
Evans, Bob 1930- *BioIn 17*
Evans, Bob Overton 1927- *WhoAm 92*
Evans, Bradley Keith 1954- *WhoSSW 93*
Evans, Brian Joseph *Law&B 92*
Evans, Britt 1946- *St&PR 93, WhoAm 92*
Evans, Bruce A. *MiSFD 9*
Evans, Bruce A. 1946- *ConTFT 10*
Evans, Bruce Dwight 1934- *WhoAm 92*
Evans, Bruce Haselton 1939- *WhoAm 92*
Evans, Bruce Max 1937- *WhoAm 92*
Evans, C.R. *WhoScE 91-1*
Evans, Carlos Elbert 1951- *St&PR 93*
Evans, Carol Ann Butler 1938- *WhoSSW 93*
Evans, Carole Lynn 1956- *WhoEmL 93*
Evans, Catherine Gulley 1950- *WhoSSW 93*
Evans, Catherine Veronica 1962- *WhoAmW 93*
Evans, Charles 1850-1935 *BioIn 17*
Evans, Charles Albert 1912- *WhoAm 92*
Evans, Charles C. 1943- *St&PR 93*
Evans, Charles Hawes, Jr. 1940- *WhoAm 92*
Evans, Charles Wayne, II 1929- *WhoSSW 93*
Evans, Charlie Anderson 1945- *WhoE 93*
Evans, Charlotte Mortimer 1933- *WhoAmW 93*
Evans, Chester *St&PR 93*
Evans, Chris *BioIn 17*
Evans, Chris 1951- *ScF&FL 92*
Evans, Christopher 1931-1979 *ScF&FL 92*
Evans, Christopher C. 1946- *St&PR 93*
Evans, Clifford Jessie 1923- *WhoAm 92, WhoWor 93*
Evans, Constance Faye 1949- *WhoAmW 93*
Evans, Craig 1949- *WhoE 93, WhoEmL 93, WhoWor 93*
Evans, Craig H. *Law&B 92*
Evans, Craig N. 1947- *St&PR 93*
Evans, D.A. *WhoScE 91-1*
Evans, D.F. *WhoScE 91-1*
Evans, Dale 1912- *SweetSg C [port]*
Evans, Dale (Frances Octavia) 1912- *Baker 92*
Evans, Damon 1950- *ConTFT 10*
Evans, Daniel Arthur 1948- *WhoE 93*
Evans, Daniel B. 1945- *St&PR 93*
Evans, Daniel Budd 1952- *WhoEmL 93*
Evans, Daniel E. 1936- *St&PR 93*
Evans, Daniel Fraley 1922- *WhoAm 92*
Evans, Daniel Jackson 1925- *WhoAm 92*
Evans, Daniel Warren 1956- *WhoEmL 93*
Evans, Darrell Wayne 1947- *BiDAMSp 1989*
Evans, David *WhoScE 91-1*
Evans, David 1951- *WhoScE 91-1*
Evans, David Alan 1952- *St&PR 93*
Evans, David Allan 1940- *WhoWrEP 92*
Evans, David Andreoff 1948- *WhoE 93*
Evans, David (Emlyn) 1843-1913 *Baker 92*
Evans, David Emrys *WhoScE 91-1*
Evans, David J.D. 1944- *St&PR 93*
Evans, David John *WhoScE 91-1*
Evans, David John 1937- *WhoWor 93*
Evans, David L. 1948- *St&PR 93*
Evans, David Livingston 1948- *St&PR 93*
Evans, David Lynn 1954- *WhoEmL 93, WhoSSW 93*
Evans, David P. *WhoScE 91-1*
Evans, David R(ichard) 1940- *ConAu 39NR*
Evans, David Stanley 1916- *WhoAm 92, WhoSSW 93*
Evans, David Vincent *WhoScE 91-1*
Evans, David Wesley 1954- *WhoSSW 93*
Evans, David William *WhoScE 91-1*
Evans, David William 1956- *St&PR 93*
Evans, Debbie Jo 1966- *WhoEmL 93*
Evans, Della J. *AmWomPl*
Evans, Denis James 1951- *WhoWor 93*
Evans, Dennis Hyde 1939- *WhoAm 92*
Evans, Diane M. *Law&B 92*
Evans, Dik *ScF&FL 92*
Evans, Donald David 1952- *WhoSSW 93*
Evans, Donald Dwight 1927- *WhoWrEP 92*
Evans, Donald Foster 1949- *WhoWor 93*
Evans, Donald Frank 1952- *WhoE 93*
Evans, Donald Fredrick 1945- *WhoSSW 93*
Evans, Donald John 1926- *St&PR 93, WhoAm 92*
Evans, Donald Leroy *BioIn 17*
Evans, Donald Louis 1946- *St&PR 93*
Evans, Donna Irene 1951- *WhoE 93, WhoEmL 93*
Evans, Douglas Hayward 1950- *WhoEmL 93*
Evans, Douglas McCullough 1925- *WhoAm 92*
Evans, Douglas Raymond 1945- *St&PR 93*
Evans, Dwight Michael 1951- *BiDAMSp 1989*
Evans, E. Estyn 1905-1989 *BioIn 17*
Evans, E. Susan *Law&B 92*
Evans, E. Susan 1945- *St&PR 93*
Evans, Earl Alison, Jr. 1910- *WhoAm 92, WhoWor 93*
Evans, Edith 1888-1976 *BioIn 17, IntDcF 2-3 [port]*
Evans, Edward Frank *WhoScE 91-1*
Evans, Edward Nathaniel, II 1940- *St&PR 93*
Evans, Edward Parker 1942- *WhoAm 92*
Evans, Edwin, Sr. 1844-1923 *Baker 92*
Evans, Edwin, Jr. 1874-1945 *Baker 92*
Evans, Edwin Charles 1910- *WhoAm 92*
Evans, Edwin Curtis 1917- *WhoAm 92*
Evans, Elizabeth Ann West 1933- *WhoAmW 93*
Evans, Elizabeth Carpenter 1911- *WhoE 93*
Evans, Elizabeth Hendrick Causey 1920- *WhoSSW 93*
Evans, Elizabeth Hilary *WhoScE 91-1*
Evans, Ellis Dale 1934- *WhoAm 92*
Evans, Elmer Ellsworth 1921- *St&PR 93*
Evans, Elton E. 1932- *St&PR 93*
Evans, Eric Bertram 1949- *WhoSSW 93*
Evans, Eric C. 1952- *St&PR 93*
Evans, Eric Charles 1952- *WhoEmL 93*
Evans, Ernest E. d1944 *BioIn 17*
Evans, Ernest Pipkin, Jr. 1944- *WhoE 93*
Evans, Ernestine D. 1927- *NotHsAW 93*
Evans, Ersel Arthur 1922- *WhoAm 92*
Evans, Essi H. 1950- *WhoE 93*
Evans, Ethan C. *Law&B 92*
Evans, Evelyn M. 1955- *St&PR 93*
Evans, Farris 1925- *St&PR 93*
Evans, Florence Wilkinson *AmWomPl*
Evans, Floy Wood *BioIn 17*
Evans, Frances Billinge *AmWomPl*
Evans, Francis Cope 1914- *WhoAm 92*
Evans, Frank *Law&B 92*
Evans, Franklin Bachelder 1922- *WhoAm 92*
Evans, Fred 1889-1951 *QDrFCA 92 [port]*
Evans, Fred John *WhoScE 91-1*
Evans, Frederick Earl 1948- *WhoSSW 93*
Evans, G. Robert 1931- *St&PR 93*
Evans, Garen Lee 1946- *WhoEmL 93, WhoSSW 93*
Evans, Gareth 1944- *WhoWor 93*
Evans, Gareth John 1944- *WhoAsAP 91*
Evans, Gary Cone 1957- *WhoEmL 93*
Evans, Gary Lee 1944- *WhoAm 92*
Evans, Geneva Marie Coleman 1938- *WhoAmW 93*
Evans, George Edward Charles 1930- *WhoE 93*
Evans, George Ewart 1909-1988 *BioIn 17*
Evans, George Henry 1805-1856 *JrnUS*
Evans, George Monroe 1947- *St&PR 93*
Evans, George Robert, Jr. 1931- *WhoAm 92*
Evans, George W. *Law&B 92*
Evans, George Walton, Jr. 1954- *WhoEmL 93*
Evans, Geraint 1922- *OxDcOp*
Evans, Geraint 1922-1992 *IntDcOp [port], NewYTBS 92 [port]*
Evans, Geraint (Llewellyn) 1922- *Baker 92, WhoAm 92*
Evans, Gerald 1910- *ScF&FL 92*
Evans, (Ian Ernest) Gil(more Green) 1912-1988 *Baker 92*
Evans, Gladys La Due *AmWomPl*
Evans, Godfrey B. *Law&B 92*
Evans, Godfrey B. 1954- *St&PR 93*
Evans, Gordon Richard *WhoScE 91-1*
Evans, Greg 1947- *SmATA 73 [port]*
Evans, Gregory Thomas 1913- *WhoAm 92*
Evans, Grose 1916- *WhoAm 92*
Evans, Gwilym O. 1924- *WhoScE 91-3*
Evans, Gwyn 1899-1938 *ScF&FL 92*
Evans, H. Dean 1929- *WhoAm 92*
Evans, Handel E. *St&PR 93*
Evans, Harold *BioIn 17*
Evans, Harold Edward 1927- *St&PR 93, WhoAm 92*
Evans, Harold G. 1944- *WhoAm 92*
Evans, Harold J. 1921- *WhoAm 92*
Evans, Harold Matthew 1928- *WhoWrEP 92*
Evans, Harry Kent 1935- *WhoAm 92*
Evans, Helena Phillips *AmWomPl*
Evans, Henry John *WhoScE 91-1*
Evans, Henry R. 1938- *St&PR 93*
Evans, Hilary 1929- *ScF&FL 92*
Evans, Hiram Kraig 1953- *WhoEmL 93*
Evans, Howard Ensign 1919- *WhoAm 92*
Evans, Howard McTyiere 1927- *St&PR 93*
Evans, Howell McKendree 1926- *St&PR 93*
Evans, Hubert 1892-1986 *BioIn 17, WhoCanL 92*
Evans, Hubert Roy *WhoScE 91-1*
Evans, Hugh E. 1934- *WhoAm 92*
Evans, I.H.N. 1886-1957 *IntDcAn*
Evans, Ian *ScF&FL 92*
Evans, J. Harvey d1992 *NewYTBS 92*
Evans, J.M. *WhoScE 91-1*
Evans, J. Mark *Law&B 92*
Evans, Jack W. 1922- *St&PR 93*
Evans, James Craig *Law&B 92*
Evans, James E. *Law&B 92*
Evans, James E. 1946- *WhoAm 92*
Evans, James Edmund 1946- *St&PR 93*
Evans, James Edward 1933- *St&PR 93*
Evans, James Edward 1946- *WhoSSW 93*
Evans, James H. 1920- *St&PR 93*
Evans, James H. 1934- *WhoIns 93*
Evans, James Harold 1939- *WhoAm 92, WhoSSW 93*
Evans, James Hart *Law&B 92*
Evans, James Hurlburt 1920- *WhoAm 92*
Evans, James Roose- *BioIn 17*
Evans, James Stanley 1921- *St&PR 93, WhoAm 92*
Evans, James Warren 1938- *WhoSSW 93*
Evans, James William 1943- *WhoAm 92*
Evans, Jane 1944- *WhoAm 92, WhoAmW 93*
Evans, Janet *BioIn 17, NewYTBS 92 [port]*
Evans, Janet 1971- *BiDAMSp 1989, WhoAmW 93*
Evans, Janet Ann 1936- *WhoAmW 93*
Evans, Janice Weston 1946- *WhoEmL 93*
Evans, Jay Bruce 1964- *WhoSSW 93*
Evans, Jerry *BioIn 17*
Evans, Jerry B. 1928- *St&PR 93*
Evans, Jerry Lee 1931- *WhoAm 92*
Evans, Jerry Norman *WhoAm 92*
Evans, Jesse E. *BioIn 17*
Evans, Jessie 1853- *BioIn 17*
Evans, Jo Burt 1928- *WhoAmW 93, WhoSSW 93*
Evans, Joan Whitehead *Law&B 92*
Evans, Jodie 1954- *WhoEmL 93*
Evans, Joel Raymond 1948- *WhoE 93, WhoEmL 93*
Evans, Johannes Sanao 1927- *WhoSSW 93, WhoWor 93*
Evans, John *WhoScE 91-1*
Evans, John 1814-1897 *BioIn 17*
Evans, John 1932- *WhoAm 92*
Evans, John A. 1928- *WhoScE 91-3*
Evans, John Allan 1949- *WhoWor 93*
Evans, John Allen *Law&B 92*
Evans, John B. *Law&B 92*
Evans, John Bradley 1947- *WhoWor 93*
Evans, John Byron 1947- *WhoEmL 93*
Evans, John C., Sr. 1930- *St&PR 93*
Evans, John Colin 1945- *WhoWor 93*
Evans, John Davies 1925- *WhoWor 93*
Evans, John Derby 1944- *WhoWor 93*
Evans, John Dows 1930- *St&PR 93*
Evans, John Dwight *Law&B 92*
Evans, John Erik 1927- *WhoAm 92, WhoIns 93*
Evans, John Harvey 1914- *WhoAm 92*
Evans, John J. 1955- *St&PR 93*
Evans, John James 1923- *WhoAm 92*
Evans, John K. *BioIn 17*
Evans, John L. d1992 *NewYTBS 92*
Evans, John Maurice 1936- *WhoAm 92*
Evans, John Mervin 1949- *WhoEmL 93*
Evans, John Miles *Law&B 92*
Evans, John Millard 1918- *WhoE 93*
Evans, John Robert 1929- *WhoAm 92*
Evans, John Vaughan 1933- *St&PR 93, WhoAm 92*
Evans, John W. *Law&B 92*
Evans, Johnny Glenn 1950- *WhoEmL 93*
Evans, Jon Hugh 1934- *WhoSSW 93*
Evans, Joni *BioIn 17*
Evans, Joni 1942- *WhoAm 92*
Evans, Judith M. 1962- *WhoE 93*
Evans, Judy Anne 1940- *WhoAmW 93*
Evans, Julian 1946- *WhoScE 91-1*
Evans, Karen 1958- *WhoEmL 93*
Evans, Karen Marilyn *WhoScE 91-1*
Evans, Karl Dean, Jr. 1963- *WhoSSW 93*
Evans, Katharine Krieger 1952- *WhoEmL 93*
Evans, Katherine Jeannine 1958- *St&PR 93*
Evans, Kenneth Eugene 1948- *St&PR 93*
Evans, L.K. 1928- *St&PR 93*
Evans, Landon 1936- *St&PR 93*
Evans, Lane 1951- *CngDr 91, WhoAm 92*
Evans, Larry Fredric 1947- *WhoWrEP 92*
Evans, Larry Melvyn 1932- *WhoAm 92*

Evans, Larry W. *Law&B 92*
Evans, Lawrence Boyd 1934- *WhoAm 92*
Evans, Lawrence E. *Law&B 92*
Evans, Lawrence Jack, Jr. 1921- *WhoWor 93*
Evans, Lawrence Watt *ScF&FL 92*
Evans, Lena N. 1962- *St&PR 93*
Evans, Leslie R. 1934- *St&PR 93*
Evans, Linda 1942- *BioIn 17, WhoAm 92, WhoAmW 93*
Evans, Linda Niemann 1948- *WhoAmW 93*
Evans, Lisa Upchurch 1964- *WhoAmW 93*
Evans, Lisbeth Clark 1952- *St&PR 93*
Evans, Lloyd I. 1927- *St&PR 93*
Evans, Lois Logan 1937- *WhoAm 92, WhoAmW 93*
Evans, Loren Kenneth 1928- *WhoAm 92*
Evans, Louise *WhoAm 92, WhoAmW 93, WhoWor 93*
Evans, Luther Harris 1902-1981 *BioIn 17*
Evans, Lynne Smith 1947- *WhoAm 92*
Evans, Lynwood J. *Law&B 92*
Evans, M. Ann *ScF&FL 92*
Evans, Mandy Bouic 1941- *WhoWrEP 92*
Evans, Margaret *AmWomPl*
Evans, Margaret A. 1924- *WhoAmW 93*
Evans, Margaret Ann *Law&B 92*
Evans, Margarita Sawatzky 1930- *WhoAmW 93*
Evans, Mari *WhoWrEP 92*
Evans, Mari 1926- *BlkAull 92*
Evans, Maribeth R. *Law&B 92*
Evans, Mark David 1958- *WhoE 93*
Evans, Mark David J. 1955- *WhoEmL 93*
Evans, Mark Ira 1952- *WhoEmL 93*
Evans, Martha Noel 1939- *WhoAmW 93*
Evans, Martyn John 1953- *WhoWor 93*
Evans, Mary Ann *ScF&FL 92*
Evans, Mary Ellen 1961- *WhoAmW 93*
Evans, Mary Johnston 1930- *WhoAm 92, WhoAmW 93*
Evans, Max Jay 1943- *WhoAm 92*
Evans, Max T. 1924- *St&PR 93*
Evans, May Garrettson 1866-1947 *ScF&FL 92*
Evans, Melvin 1917-1984 *DcCPCAm*
Evans, Melvin H. 1917-1984 *BioIn 17*
Evans, Melvin I. *BioIn 17*
Evans, Michael Bryan *WhoScE 91-1*
Evans, Michael Charles Whitmore *WhoScE 91-1*
Evans, Michael Dean 1953- *WhoEmL 93*
Evans, Michael L. 1949- *WhoSSW 93*
Evans, Michael P. 1953- *St&PR 93*
Evans, Michael W. *St&PR 93*
Evans, Michelle 1963- *WhoE 93*
Evans, Muriel 1911- *SweetSg C [port]*
Evans, Nancy 1915- *OxDcOp*
Evans, Nancy 1950- *BioIn 17, WhoAm 92*
Evans, Nathan George 1824-1868 *HarEnMi*
Evans, Nicola E. 1953- *WhoScE 91-1*
Evans, Nolly Seymour 1927- *WhoAm 92*
Evans, P. Diane 1949- *WhoAmW 93*
Evans, Pamela Roye 1957- *WhoAmW 93, WhoEmL 93*
Evans, Patrick James 1950- *WhoE 93*
Evans, Paul 1950- *WhoE 93*
Evans, Paul M. 1954- *WhoEmL 93*
Evans, Pauline D. 1922- *WhoAmW 93*
Evans, Peter Darvill- *ScF&FL 92*
Evans, Peter David *WhoScE 91-1*
Evans, Peter Kenneth 1935- *WhoAm 92*
Evans, Peter Yoshio 1925- *WhoE 93*
Evans, Philip Ian Peter *WhoScE 91-1*
Evans, Philip Jay 1951- *WhoEmL 93*
Evans, Philip Morgan 1933- *WhoAm 92*
Evans, R. Daniel 1944- *WhoE 93*
Evans, R. Gareth *Law&B 92*
Evans, Ralph Aiken 1924- *WhoAm 92, WhoSSW 93*
Evans, Rand Boyd 1942- *WhoSSW 93*
Evans, Raymond F., Jr. 1944- *WhoIns 93*
Evans, Rebecca Alexandria 1962- *WhoEmL 93*
Evans, Rebecca Wetherford 1954- *WhoSSW 93*
Evans, Richard Aloysius 1923- *WhoAm 92*
Evans, Richard Andrew 1940- *St&PR 93*
Evans, Richard Gale, Jr. 1932- *St&PR 93*
Evans, Richard Gwilym *Law&B 92*
Evans, Richard J. 1947- *ConAu 138*
Evans, Richard John 1956- *WhoE 93*
Evans, Richard Milner 1946- *WhoSSW 93*
Evans, Richard Wayne 1942- *WhoSSW 93*
Evans, Robert, Jr. 1932- *WhoAm 92, WhoE 93*
Evans, Robert A. 1952- *St&PR 93*
Evans, Robert B. *Law&B 92*
Evans, Robert Beverley 1906- *St&PR 93*
Evans, Robert Brown 1912- *WhoSSW 93*
Evans, Robert Carey 1955- *WhoE 93*
Evans, Robert D. 1947- *St&PR 93*
Evans, Robert E. 1940- *St&PR 93*
Evans, Robert George, Jr. 1953- *WhoEmL 93, WhoWor 93*
Evans, Robert J. 1930- *WhoAm 92*
Evans, Robert James 1914- *WhoAm 92*
Evans, Robert Michael 1953- *St&PR 93*
Evans, Robert O. 1919- *ScF&FL 92*
Evans, Robert S. 1935- *WhoAsAP 91*
Evans, Robert Sheldon 1944- *St&PR 93, WhoE 93*
Evans, Robert Stacy 1946- *WhoE 93*
Evans, Robert Vincent 1958- *WhoWor 93*
Evans, Robley D. 1957- *St&PR 93*
Evans, Robley Dunglison 1907- *WhoAm 92, WhoWor 93*
Evans, Roger *WhoScE 91-1*
Evans, Roger 1951- *WhoAm 92, WhoEmL 93, WhoWor 93*
Evans, Ronald A. 1940- *St&PR 93*
Evans, Ronald Allen 1940- *WhoAm 92*
Evans, Ronald D. 1944- *St&PR 93*
Evans, Ronald E. 1933-1990 *BioIn 17*
Evans, Ronald E. 1938- *St&PR 93*
Evans, Ronald H. *Law&B 92*
Evans, Ronald K. *Law&B 92*
Evans, Rose Mary 1928- *WhoWrEP 92*
Evans, Rosemary Hall 1925- *WhoAmW 93, WhoWor 93*
Evans, Ross S. *Law&B 92*
Evans, Rowland 1921- & Novak, Robert 1931- *JrnUS*
Evans, Rowland, Jr. 1921- *WhoAm 92*
Evans, Roxanne Romack 1952- *WhoSSW 93*
Evans, Rudolph Martin 1890-1956 *BioIn 17*
Evans, Russell Wyndham *WhoScE 91-1*
Evans, Ruth Anne *Law&B 92*
Evans, Ruth Anne 1944- *WhoAmW 93*
Evans, S. Clark 1938- *St&PR 93*
Evans, Sandra Bernice 1955- *WhoEmL 93*
Evans, Sandra J. *Law&B 92*
Evans, Sandra Wheeler 1934- *WhoAmW 93*
Evans, Sharon L. *Law&B 92*
Evans, Sharon L. 1947- *WhoAmW 93*
Evans, Stanley Robert 1955- *WhoEmL 93*
Evans, Stephen James Weston *WhoScE 91-1*
Evans, Stephen M. 1941- *St&PR 93*
Evans, Steven C. *Law&B 92*
Evans, Stuart 1934- *BioIn 17*
Evans, Susan Hedling 1946- *WhoEmL 93*
Evans, Suzanne Marie 1953- *WhoAmW 93, WhoEmL 93*
Evans, Suzy *Law&B 92*
Evans, Terri Lynne 1963- *WhoE 93*
Evans, Terry *BioIn 17*
Evans, Thelma Jean Mathis 1944- *WhoAm 92, WhoAmW 93*
Evans, Thomas Chives Newton 1947- *WhoAm 92, WhoE 93, WhoEmL 93*
Evans, Thomas Denny *Law&B 92*
Evans, Thomas E. 1944- *St&PR 93*
Evans, Thomas Grady *WhoSSW 93*
Evans, Thomas Ladd 1945- *WhoSSW 93*
Evans, Thomas Mellon 1910- *St&PR 93*
Evans, Thomas Passmore 1921- *WhoSSW 93*
Evans, Thomas William 1930- *WhoAm 92*
Evans, Timothy Monroe 1945- *St&PR 93*
Evans, Todd Edwin 1947- *WhoEmL 93*
Evans, Todd Robert 1960- *WhoE 93*
Evans, Tommy Nicholas 1922- *WhoAm 92*
Evans, Travis G. 1933- *St&PR 93*
Evans, Trevor *WhoScE 91-1*
Evans, Trevor Heiser 1909- *WhoAm 92*
Evans, Trevor John 1947- *WhoScE 91-1*
Evans, Van Michael 1916- *WhoAm 92*
Evans, Vickie Lynn 1947- *WhoAmW 93*
Evans, Victor M. 1939- *St&PR 93*
Evans, Victor Miles 1939- *WhoAm 92*
Evans, Victoria Regina 1963- *WhoAmW 93*
Evans, Walter Cope 1948- *WhoEmL 93*
Evans, William Charles 1924- *WhoWor 93*
Evans, William Davidson, Jr. 1943- *WhoE 93*
Evans, William Desmond *WhoScE 91-1*
Evans, William Desmond 1940- *WhoWor 93*
Evans, William Earl, Jr. 1956- *WhoEmL 93, WhoSSW 93*
Evans, William Ellis 1952- *WhoEmL 93*
Evans, William Frederick 1957- *WhoAm 92*
Evans, William H. *ScF&FL 92*
Evans, William Halla 1950- *WhoEmL 93*
Evans, William James 1928- *WhoAm 92*
Evans, William John 1924- *St&PR 93*
Evans, William L. 1934- *St&PR 93*
Evans, William Lee 1924- *WhoAm 92*
Evans, William O. 1935- *St&PR 93*
Evans, William Thomas *WhoScE 91-1*
Evans, William Thomas 1941- *WhoWor 93*
Evans, William Wilson 1932- *WhoAm 92*
Evans, Winthrop Shattuck 1939- *WhoWor 93*
Evans-Freke, Stephen Ralfe 1952- *WhoAm 92, WhoWor 93*
Evans Kelly, Christine 1952- *St&PR 93*
Evans Lombe, Peter Michael 1933- *WhoWor 93*
Evanson, Barbara Jean 1944- *WhoAmW 93*
Evanson, John Malcolm *WhoScE 91-1*
Evanson, Paul John 1941- *WhoAm 92*
Evans-Pritchard, E.E. 1902-1973 *IntDcAn*
Evans-Rogers, Debbie Lynn 1963- *WhoAmW 93*
Evans-Silman, Jill Marie 1961- *WhoAmW 93*
Evan-Wong, Sue 1947- *WhoWor 93*
Evard, John E., Jr. 1946- *St&PR 93*
Evaristos fl. 10th cent.- *OxDcByz*
Evarts, Caren Goodin 1942- *WhoE 93*
Evarts, Charles McCollister 1931- *WhoAm 92*
Evarts, Hal G. 1915- *DcAmChF 1960*
Evarts, Hal G., Jr. 1915- *ScF&FL 92*
Evarts, Harry Franklin 1928- *St&PR 93*
Evarts, M. Richard 1920- *St&PR 93*
Evarts, R.C. 1890-1972 *ScF&FL 92*
Evarts, William Maxwell, Jr. 1925- *WhoAm 92*
Evashwick, Connie Joann 1949- *WhoAmW 93, WhoEmL 93*
Evason, Kenneth L. 1949- *St&PR 93*
Evatt, Herbert Vere 1894-1965 *DcTwHis*
Evdokimova, Eva 1948- *WhoAm 92, WhoWor 93*
Eve *BioIn 17*
Eve, Rodney Ellis 1947- *St&PR 93*
Eveans, Richard Wesley 1960- *WhoEmL 93*
Evearitt, Gregory Alan *Law&B 92*
Evearitt, Timothy Cedric 1942- *WhoSSW 93*
Eveillard, Elizabeth Mugar 1947- *St&PR 93*
Eveland, Charles Leonard 1927- *WhoSSW 93*
Eveland, Georgette Anne 1945- *WhoE 93*
Eveland, Winsor G. 1938- *St&PR 93*
Eveleigh, Virgil William 1931- *WhoAm 92*
Eveleth, Janet Stidman 1950- *WhoWrEP 92*
Evelev, Martin S. *Law&B 92*
Evelyn, Douglas Everett 1941- *WhoAm 92*
Evelyn, Gwyneth 1925- *WhoAm 92*
Even, Francis Alphonse 1920- *WhoAm 92*
Even, James A. *WhoIns 93*
Even, Robert Lawrence 1932- *WhoAm 92*
Evenchik, Lynn Robin 1956- *WhoE 93, WhoEmL 93*
Evenden, Dawn Eva 1934- *WhoWor 93*
Eveno, Moach *BioIn 17*
Evens, Martha Walton 1935- *WhoAmW 93*
Evens, Michelle Jeanette 1964- *WhoAmW 93*
Evens, Ronald Gene 1939- *WhoAm 92*
Evensen, David 1955- *St&PR 93*
Evensen, Jens 1917- *WhoUN 92, WhoWor 93*
Even-Shemuel, Yehuda 1886-1976 *BioIn 17*
Evenson, Darrick *BioIn 17*
Evenson, Frederick Donald 1928- *St&PR 93*
Evenson, Merle Armin 1934- *WhoAm 92*
Evenson, Michael Donald 1961- *WhoSSW 93*
Evenson, Russell Allen 1947- *St&PR 93, WhoEmL 93*
Everakes, Howard C. *Law&B 92*
Everard, Alfred Colin 1930- *WhoUN 92*
Everbach, Erich E. *Law&B 92*
Everbach, O. George *Law&B 92*
Everbach, Otto George 1938- *WhoAm 92, WhoWor 93*
Everdale, John *WhoIns 93*
Everdell, William 1915- *WhoAm 92*
Everdell, William Romeyn 1941- *WhoAm 92*
Everding, August 1928- *IntDcOp, OxDcOp*
Everduim, Melinde-Louise (Lindy-Lou) *Law&B 92*
Evered, Donna R. 1955- *WhoEmL 93*
Everest, Alan Samuel 1937- *WhoUN 92*
Everest, George 1790-1866 *BioIn 17*
Everest, Richard James 1939- *St&PR 93*
Everett, Betty 1939- *BioIn 17, SoulM*
Everett, Bradley Paul 1947- *WhoEmL 93*
Everett, Bruce Edgar 1948- *WhoEmL 93*
Everett, C. Curtis 1930- *WhoAm 92*
Everett, Carl Bell 1947- *WhoEmL 93*
Everett, Curtis Lammar 1921- *St&PR 93*
Everett, Daniel Charles 1942- *WhoE 93*
Everett, Deborah Stuart 1951- *WhoAmW 93*
Everett, Donna Raney 1939- *WhoAmW 93, WhoSSW 93*
Everett, Dorothy A. 1917- *St&PR 93*
Everett, Durward R., Jr. 1925- *WhoAm 92*
Everett, Edith 1875- *AmWomPl*
Everett, Graham 1947- *WhoE 93, WhoWrEP 92*
Everett, H.D. 1851-1923 *ScF&FL 92*
Everett, Hobart Ray, Jr. 1949- *WhoWor 93*
Everett, James LeGrand, III 1926- *St&PR 93, WhoAm 92*
Everett, James William, Jr. 1957- *WhoE 93*
Everett, Jeffrey C. *Law&B 92*
Everett, Jim *BioIn 17*
Everett, Joann Marie 1950- *WhoWrEP 92*
Everett, John Howard 1948- *WhoSSW 93*
Everett, John R. d1992 *NewYTBS 92 [port]*
Everett, John Richard *Law&B 92*
Everett, John Rutherford 1918-1992 *BioIn 17*
Everett, Jonathan Jubal 1950- *WhoEmL 93*
Everett, Karen J. 1926- *WhoWor 93*
Everett, Kathrine Robinson d1992 *BioIn 17, NewYTBS 92 [port]*
Everett, Kenneth Deane 1955- *WhoEmL 93*
Everett, Laurie Ann 1956- *WhoEmL 93*
Everett, Lee Allen *Law&B 92*
Everett, Leolyn Louise 1888- *AmWomPl*
Everett, Lorne G. 1943- *St&PR 93*
Everett, Lou Ann 1953- *WhoAmW 93*
Everett, Mark Allen 1928- *WhoAm 92*
Everett, Mary Elizabeth 1929- *WhoAmW 93*
Everett, Melinda Brown 1946- *WhoE 93*
Everett, Michael 1949- *St&PR 93*
Everett, Michael Grayson 1954- *WhoEmL 93*
Everett, Michael Thomas 1949- *WhoAm 92*
Everett, Mike 1948- *WhoSSW 93*
Everett, Nancy E. *Law&B 92*
Everett, Pamela Irene 1947- *WhoAmW 93, WhoEmL 93, WhoWor 93*
Everett, Patricia Robertson 1957- *WhoE 93*
Everett, Percival 1937- *ScF&FL 92*
Everett, Reynolds Melville, Jr. 1946- *WhoEmL 93*
Everett, Robert R. 1921- *St&PR 93*
Everett, Robert W. *Law&B 92*
Everett, Robinson O. 1928- *CngDr 91*
Everett, Robinson Oscar 1928- *WhoAm 92*
Everett, S.W. *WhoWrEP 92*
Everett, Torrey, Mrs. *AmWomPl*
Everett, Walter Howell 1934- *WhoE 93*
Everett, Warren Sylvester 1910- *WhoAm 92, WhoWor 93*
Everett, Wendy Ann 1950- *WhoE 93*
Everett, William Carter *Law&B 92*
Everett, William Hume, III 1936- *St&PR 93*
Everett, Woodrow Wilson 1937- *WhoAm 92, WhoWor 93*
Everette, Cora *AmWomPl*
Everette, Sharon Esther McLeod 1949- *WhoEmL 93*
Everette, Tony L. 1945- *St&PR 93*
Everett-Volgy, Sandra Sue 1946- *WhoAmW 93, WhoEmL 93*
Evergettis, Barry P. 1936- *St&PR 93*
Evergood, Philip 1901-1973 *BioIn 17*
Everhard, Martin E. 1933- *WhoE 93*
Everhart, Edgar S. 1912- *St&PR 93*
Everhart, Leon Eugene 1928- *WhoWor 93*
Everhart, Rex 1920- *WhoAm 92*
Everhart, Robert Phillip 1936- *WhoWrEP 92*
Everhart, Sally Marie 1952- *WhoE 93*
Everhart, Thomas Eugene 1932- *WhoAm 92, WhoWor 93*
Everill, Richard Harold 1942- *WhoWor 93*
Everingham, Ann Jacobson 1933- *WhoAmW 93*
Everingham, Donald E. 1947- *St&PR 93*
Everingham, Lyle J. 1926- *St&PR 93*
Everingham, Philip B. 1948- *St&PR 93*
Everist, Norma Cook 1938- *WhoAmW 93*
Everitt, Alice Lubin 1936- *WhoAmW 93*
Everitt, Brian Sidney 1944- *WhoWor 93*
Everitt, Charles P. 1931- *St&PR 93*
Everitt, E. Glenn, Jr. 1944- *St&PR 93*
Everitt, George Bain 1914- *WhoAm 92*
Everitt, Robert Henry 1939- *St&PR 93*
Everitt, William Norrie *WhoScE 91-1*
Everitt, William Norrie 1924- *WhoWor 93*
Everling, Friedrich Gustav 1927- *WhoWor 93*
Everling, Lawrence J. 1941- *St&PR 93*
Everling, Ulrich 1925- *WhoWor 93*
Everly, Bradley S. 1951- *St&PR 93*
Everly, Don *BioIn 17*
Everly, Don 1937- *Baker 92*
Everly, George Stotelmyer, Jr. 1950- *WhoEmL 93*

Everly, Margaret Evelyn 1935- *WhoAmW 93*
Everly, Phil *BioIn 17*
Everly, Phil 1939- *See* Everly, Don 1937- *Baker 92*
Everly, William 1967- *WhoE 93*
Everman, C. Robert 1936- *St&PR 93*
Everman, Paul Dawson 1932- *St&PR 93*
Everman, Welch D. 1946- *ScF&FL 92*
Evernden, Margery Elizabeth 1916- *WhoWrEP 92*
Evers, Anne Bigelow 1954- *WhoAmW 93*
Evers, B. *WhoScE 91-3*
Evers, Ben H. 1937- *WhoScE 91-3*
Evers, Bradley W. *Law&B 92*
Evers, Bradley Wayne 1955- *St&PR 93*
Evers, Charles 1922- *PolPar*
Evers, Charles K. 1928- *St&PR 93*
Evers, D.J. *WhoScE 91-3*
Evers, Emily R. 1950- *St&PR 93*
Evers, Hoot 1921-1991 *BioIn 17*
Evers, James Charles 1922- *EncAACR*
Evers, Judith Ann 1939- *WhoAmW 93*
Evers, Kate 1948- *St&PR 93*
Evers, L(eonard) H(erbert) 1926- *DcChlFi*
Evers, Mark Anthony 1953- *St&PR 93*
Evers, Martin Louis 1957- *WhoE 93*
Evers, Medgar d1963 *NewYTBS 92 [port]*
Evers, Medgar 1925-1963 *ConBlB 3 [port]*
Evers, Medgar W. 1925-1963 *EncAACR*
Evers, Medgar Wiley 1925-1963 *BioIn 17*
Evers, Michael Bennett 1946- *WhoSSW 93*
Evers, Myrlie *BioIn 17*
Evers, R. Elizabeth *Law&B 92*
Evers, R. Michael *ScF&FL 92*
Evers, Sean Robert 1949- *WhoE 93*
Evers, Sharon Lee 1951- *WhoAmW 93*
Evers, William Louis 1906- *WhoAm 92*
Eversley, Frederick John 1941- *WhoAm 92*
Eversole, William Cromwell 1934- *St&PR 93*
Everson, Brenda Faye 1948- *WhoAmW 93*
Everson, Christine Ariail 1947- *WhoEmL 93*
Everson, Corinna *BioIn 17*
Everson, Dale M. 1931- *St&PR 93*
Everson, David B., Jr. 1954- *St&PR 93*
Everson, Diane Louise 1953- *WhoAmW 93*
Everson, Elaine E. 1957- *St&PR 93*
Everson, George A., Jr. 1943- *St&PR 93*
Everson, John 1956- *St&PR 93*
Everson, Kirke B., Jr. 1920- *St&PR 93*
Everson, Leonard Charles 1923- *WhoAm 92*
Everson, Nina Marie Brode 1949- *WhoAmW 93*
Everson, Ronald G. 1903- *WhoCanL 92*
Everson, William 1912- *BioIn 17*
Everson, William K. 1929- *ScF&FL 92*
Everson, William Oliver 1912- *WhoAm 92*
Evers-Szostak, Mary Lee 1958- *WhoSSW 93*
Eversull, Jack Wilson 1942- *St&PR 93*
Evert, Chris *BioIn 17*
Evert, Christine Marie 1954- *WhoAm 92, WhoAmW 93, WhoWor 93*
Evert, James F. *Law&B 92*
Evert, Patricia Ann 1962- *WhoEmL 93*
Evert, Teresa Diane 1957- *WhoE 93*
Everton, Marta Ve 1926- *WhoAm 92, WhoAmW 93*
Everts, Connor 1926- *WhoAm 92*
Everts, Daan W. 1941- *WhoUN 92*
Everts, Edward H. 1951- *St&PR 93*
Everts, Geldolph Adriaan 1944- *WhoUN 92*
Everts, R. Alain *ScF&FL 92*
Everts, Todd 1966- *WhoE 93*
Evertsz, Juancho *DcCPCAm*
Every, Martin Gaither 1939- *St&PR 93*
Every, Philip Cochrane *WhoCanL 92*
Every, Richard W. 1942- *St&PR 93*
Every, Russel B. 1924- *St&PR 93*
Eves, Jeffrey Parvin 1946- *St&PR 93*
Eves, Judith Allen 1938- *WhoAmW 93*
Eves, Margaret Elizabeth 1957- *WhoWor 93*
Evett, Robert 1922-1975 *Baker 92*
Evetts, Mark Alan 1956- *WhoSSW 93*
Evey, Lois Reed 1925- *WhoE 93*
Evigan, Greg *WhoAm 92*
Evilsizor, Marvin Rex 1937- *WhoSSW 93*
Evilsizor, William Chris 1960- *WhoE 93*
Evin, Jacques 1937- *WhoScE 91-2*
Evinger, Suzann 1947- *WhoAmW 93*
Evins, Dan 1935- *St&PR 93*
Evins, David d1991 *BioIn 17*
Evins, John C. 1912- *St&PR 93*
Evitt, William Robert 1923- *WhoAm 92*
Evleth, Earl M. 1931- *WhoScE 91-2*
Evleth, Earl Mansfield 1931- *WhoWor 93*
Evliya Celebi 1611-1684 *OxDcByz*
Evnin, Anthony Basil 1941- *WhoAm 92*
Evoss, Suzanne *Law&B 92*
Evoy, John Joseph 1911- *WhoAm 92*
Evoy, William Harrington 1938- *WhoSSW 93*
Evrard, Guy H. 1943- *WhoScE 91-2*
Evrard, Janice Marie 1959- *WhoAmW 93*
Evrard, Roger P. 1934- *WhoScE 91-2*
Evren, Lisa A. *Law&B 92*
Evrenos d1417 *OxDcByz*
Evseyev, Sergei 1893-1956 *Baker 92*
Evslin, Bernard 1922- *ScF&FL 92*
Evstatiev, Dimiter Konstantinov 1943- *WhoScE 91-4*
Evstigneev, Valeri Pavlovich 1939- *WhoUN 92*
Evteev, Sveneld Alexandrovich 1932- *WhoUN 92*
Evtimij of Turnovo c. 132-?-c. 1400 *OxDcByz*
Evvard, John Marcus 1884-1948 *BioIn 17*
Ewald, Barry J. 1944- *St&PR 93*
Ewald, Camille *BioIn 17*
Ewald, Elin Lake 1940- *WhoE 93*
Ewald, Gunter 1929- *WhoWor 93*
Ewald, Henry Theodore, Jr. 1924- *WhoWor 93*
Ewald, Kitty Marie 1956- *WhoAmW 93*
Ewald, Klaus C. 1941- *WhoScE 91-3*
Ewald, Paul William 1953- *WhoE 93*
Ewald, Rex Alan 1951- *WhoEmL 93*
Ewald, Robert Frederick 1924- *WhoIns 93*
Ewald, Robert H. 1947- *WhoAm 92*
Ewald, Victor 1860-1935 *Baker 92*
Ewald, William Bragg, Jr. 1925- *WhoAm 92*
Ewald, Zinaida 1894-1942 *See* Ewald, Victor 1860-1935 *Baker 92*
Ewaldz, Donald Baird 1933- *St&PR 93*
Ewalt, Henry *Law&B 92*
Ewan, George Thomson 1927- *WhoAm 92*
Ewan, James 1949- *St&PR 93, WhoEmL 93*
Ewan, Joseph Andorfer 1909- *WhoAm 92, WhoWor 93*
Ewart, Ann 1957- *WhoEmL 93*
Ewart, Carole Von Kamp 1938- *WhoAmW 93*
Ewart, Gavin *BioIn 17*
Ewart, James B. *St&PR 93*
Ewart, Roberta Marie 1959- *WhoEmL 93*
Ewart, Scott L. *Law&B 92*
Ewart-Biggs, Baroness d1992 *NewYTBS 92*
Ewasko, Bernard Anthony 1934- *St&PR 93*
Ewbank, Thomas Peters 1943- *St&PR 93*
Ewbank, Walter F(rederick) 1918- *ConAu 38NR*
Ewbank, Weeb 1907- *BioIn 17*
Ewell, A. Ben, Jr. 1941- *WhoWor 93*
Ewell, Barbara Claire 1947- *WhoSSW 93*
Ewell, Charles Muse 1937- *WhoAm 92*
Ewell, Eric Richard 1962- *WhoE 93*
Ewell, Harold Norwood 1918- *BiDAMSp 1989*
Ewell, Miranda Juan 1948- *WhoAm 92*
Ewell, Patricia B. d1992 *NewYTBS 92*
Ewell, Richard Stoddert 1817-1872 *HarEnMi*
Ewell, Tom 1909- *QDrFCA 92 [port]*
Ewell, Vincent F., Jr. *Law&B 92*
Ewell, Vincent Fletcher, Jr. 1943- *St&PR 93, WhoAm 92*
Ewen, David 1907-1985 *Baker 92*
Ewen, David Paul 1944- *WhoWor 93*
Ewen, Harold Irving 1922- *WhoAm 92, WhoWor 93*
Ewen, Robert B. 1940- *WhoSSW 93*
Ewen, Robert W. 1931- *St&PR 93*
Ewer, John Patrick 1944- *WhoWor 93*
Ewers, Anne *WhoAmW 93*
Ewers, Hanns Heinz 1871-1943 *ScF&FL 92*
Ewers, John Canfield 1909- *WhoAm 92, WhoWor 93*
Ewers, Patricia O'Donnell 1935- *WhoAm 92, WhoAmW 93, WhoE 93*
Ewers, R. Darrell 1933- *St&PR 93, WhoAm 92*
Ewers, Robert E. *Law&B 92*
Ewert, Brita Louise 1929- *WhoWor 93*
Ewert, Heinrich H. 1855-1934 *BioIn 17*
Ewert, Janina 1938- *WhoWor 93*
Ewert, Jorg-Peter 1938- *WhoScE 91-3*
Ewert, William G. *Law&B 92*
Ewerz, Cynthia Buchanan 1940- *WhoAmW 93*
Ewh, Debra Ann 1965- *WhoAmW 93*
Ewick, Charles Ray 1937- *WhoAm 92*
Ewig, Carl F. d1990 *BioIn 17*
Ewigleben, Donald C. *Law&B 92*
Ewing, Andrew Graham 1957- *WhoE 93*
Ewing, Bayard 1916- *St&PR 93*
Ewing, Bayard 1916-1991 *BioIn 17*
Ewing, Benjamin Baugh 1924- *WhoAm 92*
Ewing, Bernie Edward 1944- *WhoAm 92*
Ewing, Bessie d1966 *BioIn 17*
Ewing, Blair Gordon 1933- *WhoE 93*
Ewing, Channing Lester 1927- *WhoAm 92*
Ewing, Charles d1927 *BioIn 17*
Ewing, Charles Patrick 1949- *WhoEmL 93*
Ewing, Colin W. *Law&B 92*
Ewing, Crystal Anne 1966- *WhoAmW 93*
Ewing, David Leon 1941- *WhoE 93*
Ewing, David Walkley 1923- *WhoAm 92*
Ewing, Dessa Crawford 1941- *WhoE 93*
Ewing, Dianne L. *Law&B 92*
Ewing, Donald L. 1946- *St&PR 93*
Ewing, Eddie Ruth 1928- *St&PR 93*
Ewing, Edgar Louis 1913- *WhoAm 92*
Ewing, Edwin S., Jr. 1924- *WhoIns 93*
Ewing, Frank Crockett 1951- *WhoE 93*
Ewing, Frank Marion 1915- *WhoAm 92*
Ewing, George H. 1925- *WhoAm 92*
Ewing, George Wilmeth 1923- *WhoSSW 93*
Ewing, Gerad C. 1951- *St&PR 93*
Ewing, Gordon A. d1990 *BioIn 17*
Ewing, Jack 1945- *WhoWrEP 92*
Ewing, James D. 1917- *St&PR 93*
Ewing, Jeanne Bunderson 1933- *WhoWrEP 92*
Ewing, Jeannie Pendleton *AmWomPl*
Ewing, Jerry L. 1930- *St&PR 93*
Ewing, John Isaac 1924- *WhoAm 92*
Ewing, John Kirby 1923- *WhoSSW 93*
Ewing, Juliana Horatia 1841-1885 *BioIn 17*
Ewing, Kenneth Patrick Ky 1964- *WhoE 93*
Ewing, Ky Pepper, Jr. 1935- *WhoAm 92*
Ewing, Laurence Lee 1943- *WhoAm 92*
Ewing, Louis H. 1908-1983 *BioIn 17*
Ewing, Lynn M., Jr. 1930- *St&PR 93*
Ewing, Lynn Moore, Jr. 1930- *WhoAm 92*
Ewing, Malcolm C. *Law&B 92*
Ewing, Margaret *AmWomPl*
Ewing, Maria *BioIn 17*
Ewing, Maria 1950- *IntDcOp [port], OxDcOp*
Ewing, Maria Louise *WhoAm 92*
Ewing, Maria (Louise) 1950- *Baker 92*
Ewing, Mark Jerome 1950- *St&PR 93*
Ewing, Martin S. 1945- *WhoE 93*
Ewing, Michael Delvin 1951- *WhoEmL 93*
Ewing, Nanine Ruth 1950- *WhoEmL 93, WhoSSW 93*
Ewing, Patrick *BioIn 17*
Ewing, Patrick 1962- *WhoAm 92*
Ewing, Randy Lee 1958- *WhoSSW 93*
Ewing, Raymond C. 1936- *WhoAm 92*
Ewing, Richard Edward 1946- *WhoWor 93*
Ewing, Richard Tucker 1918- *WhoAm 92*
Ewing, Robert 1922- *WhoAm 92, WhoE 93, WhoWor 93*
Ewing, Robert Clark 1957- *WhoEmL 93*
Ewing, Robert Paul 1925- *St&PR 93*
Ewing, Samuel Daniel, Jr. 1938- *WhoAm 92*
Ewing, Sidney Alton 1934- *WhoAm 92*
Ewing, Sondra Darlene 1948- *WhoWrEP 92*
Ewing, Stephen E. 1944- *WhoAm 92*
Ewing, Tess *WhoWrEP 92*
Ewing, Thomas W. 1935- *BioIn 17, WhoAm 92*
Ewing, Valerie Margaret 1951- *WhoAmW 93*
Ewing, Vernon Richard 1948- *WhoEmL 93*
Ewing, Wayne T. 1933- *St&PR 93*
Ewing, Wayne Turner 1933- *WhoAm 92*
Ewing, William, Jr. 1912- *St&PR 93*
Ewing, William Henszey 1939- *WhoE 93*
Ewing, William Hickman, Jr. 1942- *WhoAm 92*
Ewing-Chow, John 1943- *WhoWor 93*
Ewins, David John *WhoScE 91-1*
Ewins, Maxie Staedtler 1936- *WhoAm 92*
Ewins, P.D. *WhoScE 91-1*
Ewoldt, Craig R. 1949- *St&PR 93*
Ewry, Fred *St&PR 93*
Ewy, Gordon Allen 1933- *WhoAm 92*
Ex, Mitchell Craig *Law&B 92*
Exan, Eve K. *Law&B 92*
Exbrayat, Joseph 1933- *WhoScE 91-2*
Excellent, Matilda *ConAu 37NR*
Excestre, William fl. c. 1390-1410 *Baker 92*
Exciters *SoulM*
Exel, Ruy Filho 1956- *WhoWor 93*
Exelbert, Lois Love 1948- *WhoEmL 93*
Exelbert, Michael Mark 1948- *WhoSSW 93*
Exendine, Albert Andrew 1884-1973 *BiDAMSp 1989*
Eximeno (y Pujades), Antonio 1729-1808 *Baker 92*
Exley, Charles E., Jr. 1929- *St&PR 93*
Exley, Charles Errol, Jr. 1929- *WhoAm 92*
Exley, Frederick 1929-1992 *CurBio 92N*
Exley, Frederick E. d1992 *NewYTBS 92 [port]*
Exley, Frederick (Earl) 1929-1992 *ConAu 138*
Exley, Mark King 1953- *WhoEmL 93*
Exline, John Kevin 1957- *WhoEmL 93*
Exline, Robert W. 1932- *St&PR 93*
Exner, Judith *BioIn 17*
Exner, Walter 1911- *WhoWor 93*
Exner-Clayton, Katherine J. 1949- *St&PR 93*
Exon, J. James 1921- *CngDr 91*
Exon, John James 1921- *WhoAm 92*
Expert, (Isidore Norbert) Henry 1863-1952 *Baker 92*
Extermann, Pierre 1936- *WhoScE 91-4*
Exton, John M. d1990 *BioIn 17*
Exum, Helen McDonald 1924- *St&PR 93*
Exum, James Gooden, Jr. 1935- *WhoAm 92, WhoSSW 93*
Exume, Claude 1949- *WhoWor 93*
Exupery, Antoine de Saint- 1900-1944 *BioIn 17*
Eyadema, Etienne Gnassingbe 1937- *WhoAfr, WhoWor 93*
Eyberg, Donald Theodore, Jr. 1944- *WhoAm 92*
Eyberg, Sheila Maxine 1944- *WhoSSW 93*
Eybler, Joseph Leopold, Edler von 1765-1846 *Baker 92*
Eychner, David C. *Law&B 92*
Eyck, Jan van c. 1390-1441 *BioIn 17*
Eyckmans, Luc A.F. 1930- *WhoScE 91-2*
Eyckmans, Luc Alphonse Francois 1930- *WhoWor 93*
Eyde, Louis J. 1932- *St&PR 93*
Eyde, Ted H. *BioIn 17*
Eydgahi, Ali Mohammadzadeh 1957- *WhoE 93*
Eyen, Jerome *ConTFT 10*
Eyen, Tom 1940-1991 *BioIn 17*
Eyen, Tom 1941-1991 *AnObit 1991, ConLC 70, ConTFT 10*
Eyer, John Geoffrey 1944- *St&PR 93*
Eyerer, Daphne Margaret Berta 1953- *WhoAmW 93, WhoE 93*
Eyerer, Peter 1941- *WhoScE 91-3*
Eyerly, Jeannette (Hyde) 1908- *DcAmChF 1960*
Eyerman, Irwin R. 1944- *St&PR 93*
Eyerman, Linda Kathleen 1948- *WhoEmL 93*
Eyerman, Thomas Jude 1939- *WhoAm 92*
Eyers, John *ScF&FL 92*
Eyestone *WhoWrEP 92*
Eyestone, Ed. *BioIn 17*
Eyken, Jan Albert van 1823-1868 *Baker 92*
Eykhoff, Pieter 1929- *WhoScE 91-3, WhoWor 93*
Eylenbosch, Willy Jan 1937- *WhoWor 93*
Eyler, Donald Neil 1931- *St&PR 93*
Eyler, Larry *BioIn 17*
Eyler, Steven Howard 1952- *WhoSSW 93*
Eyles, Allen 1941- *ScF&FL 92*
Eyles, Marianne McGregor 1957- *St&PR 93*
Eyles, Thomas H. 1936- *St&PR 93*
Eyman, Earl Duane 1925- *WhoAm 92*
Eyman, Richard H. 1930- *St&PR 93*
Eyman, Richard Harrison 1930- *WhoAm 92*
Eyman, Richard Kenneth 1931- *WhoAm 92*
Eymieu, Henry 1860-1931 *Baker 92*
Eynard, Italo 1932- *WhoScE 91-3, WhoWor 93*
Eynon, Richard Ries 1947- *St&PR 93*
Eynon, Stuart B. 1922- *St&PR 93*
Eyo, Clement I.B. 1944- *WhoE 93*
Eyraud, F. *WhoScE 91-2*
Eyraud, L. *WhoScE 91-2*
Eyre, Brian Leonard *WhoScE 91-1*
Eyre, D. *WhoScE 91-1*
Eyre, Edward John 1815-1901 *Expl 93 [port]*
Eyre, Frank 1910-1988 *BioIn 17*
Eyre, Ivan 1935- *WhoAm 92*
Eyre, Pamela Catherine 1948- *WhoAmW 93, WhoEmL 93*
Eyre, Richard *MiSFD 9*
Eyre, Richard 1943- *BioIn 17*
Eyre, Richard John, III 1940- *St&PR 93*
Eyre, Stephen Carstairs 1922- *St&PR 93*
Eyre, William H., Jr. 1951- *WhoIns 93*
Eyres, Brian D. *Law&B 92*
Eysel, Ulf T. 1944- *WhoScE 91-3*
Eysenck, Hans Jurgen 1916- *WhoWor 93*
Eysenck, Michael William *WhoScE 91-1*
Eyser, Eberhard 1932- *Baker 92*
Eyskens, Mark 1933- *WhoWor 93*
Eysler, Edmund 1874-1949 *Baker 92*
Eysman, Harvey A. 1939- *WhoWrEP 92*
Eyssen, Hendrik J.M. 1930- *WhoScE 91-2*
Eysteinsson, Astradur 1957- *WhoWor 93*
Eyster, Franklin S. 1941- *St&PR 93*
Eyster, Franklin S., II *Law&B 92*
Eyster, Franklin Spangler, II 1941- *WhoAm 92*
Eyster, Mary Elaine 1935- *WhoAm 92*
Eytchison, Ronald Marvin 1936- *WhoAm 92*
Eytinge, Rose 1835-1911 *AmWomPl*
Eyton, Bessie 1890- *SweetSg A [port]*
Eyton, J. Trevor *Law&B 92*

Eyton, R.T. *St&PR 93*
Eza, John C. 1947- *St&PR 93*
Ezaki, Kenjiro 1926- *Baker 92*
'Ezana *OxDcByz*
Ezarik, David B. *Law&B 92*
Ezawa, Hiroshi 1932- *WhoWor 93*
Ezawa, Yuichi 1939- *WhoWor 93*
Ezekiel *BioIn 17*
Ezell, Annette Schram 1940- *WhoAmW 93*
Ezell, Carolyn Woltz 1949- *WhoWrEP 92*
Ezell, Edward Clinton 1939- *WhoE 93*
Ezell, Kenneth Pettey, Jr. 1949- *WhoEmL 93*
Ezell, Kerry Moore 1935- *St&PR 93*
Ezell, Margaret Prather 1951- *WhoEmL 93, WhoSSW 93*
Ezell, Ruth Anne 1947- *WhoEmL 93*
Ezell, William Bruce, Jr. 1941- *WhoE 93*
Ezelle, Robert Eugene 1927- *WhoAm 92*
Ezenkwele, Andrew Agochukwu Chukwudike 1932- *WhoUN 92*
Ezer, Stephen M. 1944- *St&PR 93*
Ezerski, Ronald E. 1946- *St&PR 93*
Ezersky, Lauren Elise 1954- *WhoE 93*
Ezersky, William Martin 1951- *WhoEmL 93*
Ezeyza-Alvear, Carlos Willy 1930- *WhoWor 93*
Ezhaya, Joseph Bernard 1943- *WhoE 93*
Ezin, Jean-Pierre Onvehoun 1944- *WhoWor 93*
Ezor, Sheldon D. 1924- *St&PR 93*
Ezra *BioIn 17*
Ezra, David A. 1947- *WhoAm 92*
Ezrin, Alvin 1940- *St&PR 93*
Ezzamel, Mahmoud A.M. *WhoScE 91-1*

F

Faaola, Nuu *BioIn 17*
Faarup, Poul 1933- *WhoScE 91-2*
Faatz, Jeanne Ryan 1941- *WhoAmW 93*
Fabana Asin, Felipe 1962- *WhoWor 93*
Fabares, Shelley *BioIn 17, WhoAm 92*
Fabaron, Jean-Pierre 1928- *WhoScE 91-2*
Fabbri, Augusto 1939- *WhoScE 91-3*
Fabbri, Brian John 1944- *WhoAm 92*
Fabbri, Bruno 1945- *WhoScE 91-3*
Fabbri, Gianfranco 1929- *WhoScE 91-3*
Fabbri, Ottavio *MiSFD 9*
Fabbri, William Paul 1955- *WhoE 93*
Fabbrini, Sergio 1949- *WhoWor 93*
Fabbris, Roberto 1943- *WhoWor 93*
Fabel, Robin Francis Abbott 1934- *WhoSSW 93*
Fabel, Warren L. 1933- *St&PR 93, WhoIns 93*
Fabens, Andrew Lawrie, III 1942- *WhoAm 92*
Faber, Adele 1928- *ConAu 37NR, WhoAm 92*
Faber, Alexander W. d1992 *BioIn 17*
Faber, Christian *MiSFD 9*
Faber, Eberhard 1936- *St&PR 93*
Faber, Elmer L. 1913- *St&PR 93*
Faber, Fred S., Jr. 1924- *St&PR 93*
Faber, Georges 1926- *WhoWor 93*
Faber, Heije 1907- *ConAu 139*
Faber, Heinrich c. 1500-1552 *Baker 92*
Faber, Horace B., Jr. 1931- *St&PR 93*
Faber, Inez M. *ScF&FL 92*
Faber, Inez Mc Alister 1897- *WhoWrEP 92*
Faber, John Henry 1918- *WhoAm 92*
Faber, Louis Steven *Law&B 92*
Faber, Mark E. *Law&B 92*
Faber, Michael Warren 1943- *WhoAm 92*
Faber, Milton David 1909- *St&PR 93*
Faber, Neil 1938- *WhoAm 92*
Faber, Peter Lewis 1938- *WhoAm 92*
Faber, Ronald Carl 1961- *WhoSSW 93*
Faber, Sandra M. *BioIn 17*
Faber, Sandra Moore 1944- *WhoAm 92*
Faber, Susan Gail 1960- *WhoE 93*
Faber, Vickie Lynn 1967- *WhoEmL 93*
Faber, William Joseph 1950- *WhoEmL 93*
Faber-Castell, Anton-Wolfgang, Graf von *BioIn 17*
Faber-Castell, Mary Elizabeth von, Grafin *BioIn 17*
Faberge, Peter Carl 1846-1920 *BioIn 17*
Fabert, Jacques 1925- *WhoE 93*
Fab Five Freddy 1958?- *BioIn 17*
Fabi, Bernard *St&PR 93*
Fabian, Csaba Bela 1941- *WhoWor 93*
Fabian, Dick *BioIn 17*
Fabian, F.G., Jr. 1915- *St&PR 93*
Fabian, G. Leslie 1927- *St&PR 93*
Fabian, Jeanne 1946- *WhoAmW 93, WhoEmL 93*
Fabian, Jerome Francis 1943- *WhoE 93*
Fabian, John Andrew 1934- *St&PR 93*
Fabian, John M. *WhoAm 92*
Fabian, John McCreary 1939- *St&PR 93, WhoSSW 93*
Fabian, Joseph Vincent 1948- *WhoEmL 93*
Fabian, Judith A. 1947- *St&PR 93*
Fabian, Juraj F. 1935- *WhoScE 91-4*
Fabian, Larry Louis 1940- *WhoAm 92*
Fabian, Leonard William 1923- *WhoAm 92*
Fabian, Louis James 1955- *WhoE 93*
Fabian, Michael William 1931- *WhoE 93*
Fabian, Stephen E. 1930- *ScF&FL 92*
Fabian, Tibor 1934- *WhoScE 91-4*
Fabiani, Claudio 1945- *WhoWor 93*
Fabiani, Dante C. 1917- *St&PR 93*
Fabiani, Dante Carl 1917- *WhoAm 92*
Fabiani, Mario J. 1923- *St&PR 93*
Fabiano, Roberta Mary *WhoE 93, WhoEmL 93*
Fabiano, Vincent L. *Law&B 92*
Fabian-Strelkow, Deborah 1961- *WhoAmW 93*
Fabiaschi, Michael Anthony 1955- *St&PR 93*
Fabic, M. Margaret *Law&B 92*
Fabick, Joseph G. 1927- *St&PR 93*
Fabietti, Victor Armando 1920- *WhoE 93, WhoWor 93*
Fabilli, Mary 1914- *WhoWrEP 92*
Fabini, (Felix) Eduardo 1882-1950 *Baker 92*
Fabio, Adriane Vella 1961- *WhoAmW 93*
Fabish, Thomas John 1938- *WhoE 93*
Fabius, Laurent *BioIn 17*
Fabius Maximus Verrucosus, Quintus c. 266BC-203BC *HarEnMi*
Fabos, Suzanna *Law&B 92*
Fabra, Paul Andre 1927- *WhoWor 93*
Fabray, Nanette 1920- *BioIn 17*
Fabre, Fred Ruffin 1939- *WhoSSW 93*
Fabre, J.W. *WhoScE 91-1*
Fabre, Jean Henri Casimir 1823-1915 *BioIn 17*
Fabre, Michel J(acques) 1933- *ConAu 37NR*
Fabre, Raoul Francois 1925- *WhoWor 93*
Fabre, Raymund Cruz 1960- *WhoWor 93*
Fabre, Robert 1915- *BioIn 17*
Fabre, Susan Doyle *Law&B 92*
Fabrega Enfedaque, Albert 1951- *WhoWor 93*
Fabrega P., Jorge 1922- *WhoWor 93*
Fabretti Costantino, Antonio 1941- *WhoScE 91-3*
Fabri, Annibale Pio 1697-1760 *Baker 92, OxDcOp*
Fabri, Zoltan 1917- *DrEEuF, MiSFD 9*
Fabricand, Burton Paul 1923- *WhoAm 92*
Fabricant, Arthur E. 1935- *WhoAm 92*
Fabricant, Catherine Grenci 1919- *WhoE 93*
Fabricant, Solomon 1906-1989 *BioIn 17*
Fabricius, Johann Albert 1668-1736 *Baker 92*
Fabricius, Jorgen C.F.S. 1920- *WhoScE 91-2*
Fabricius, Richard Neil 1928- *WhoE 93*
Fabricius, Sara 1880-1974 *BioIn 17*
Fabricius, Werner 1633-1679 *Baker 92*
Fabrick, Howard David 1938- *WhoAm 92*
Fabries, J. *WhoScE 91-2*
Fabrikant, Craig Steven 1952- *WhoEmL 93, WhoWor 93*
Fabrikant, Irving X. d1990 *BioIn 17*
Fabris, James A. 1938- *WhoAm 92*
Fabrizi, Aldo 1905-1990 *BioIn 17, IntDcF 2-3 [port]*
Fabrizi, Jennifer Mary 1960- *WhoAmW 93*
Fabrizi, Vincenzo 1764-c. 1812 *OxDcOp*
Fabrizio, Gerald James 1962- *WhoEmL 93*
Fabrizio, Margaret Mary 1954- *WhoEmL 93*
Fabrizio, Shelia Ann Hughes 1955- *WhoAmW 93*
Fabrizio, Tuula Irja 1931- *WhoE 93*
Fabrizius, Peter *ConAu 40NR*
Fabros, Roberto Tancinco 1950- *WhoE 93, WhoEmL 93*
Fabry, Gyorgy 1927- *WhoScE 91-4*
Fabry, Laszlo Georg 1947- *WhoWor 93*
Fabry, Paul Andrew *WhoSSW 93*
Fabry, Thomas Lester 1937- *WhoE 93*
Fabrycky, Wolter Joseph 1932- *WhoAm 92*
Fabrycy, Mark Zdzislaw 1922- *WhoAm 92*
Fabyan, Scott Spooner 1962- *WhoE 93*
Faccenda, Philip John 1929- *WhoAm 92*
Facchini, Diane M. 1963- *St&PR 93*
Facciano, Pauline Rose 1959- *WhoEmL 93*
Faccinto, Victor Paul 1945- *WhoAm 92*
Faccio, Chiarina 1846-1923 *OxDcOp*
Faccio, Franco 1840-1891 *Baker 92, IntDcOp, OxDcOp*
Facciotto, Gianni 1956- *WhoScE 91-3*
Faccone, Dominic M. 1947- *St&PR 93*
Face, Roy 1928- *BioIn 17*
Face, Wayne Bruce 1942- *WhoE 93*
Facenda, Albert Joseph 1947- *St&PR 93*
Facer, Eric Fouts 1953- *WhoEmL 93*
Facey, D.J. *WhoScE 91-1*
Facey, John Abbott 1926- *St&PR 93, WhoIns 93*
Facey, John Abbott, III 1950- *WhoEmL 93*
Fachada, Ederito Paul 1929- *WhoE 93*
Faches, William George 1928- *WhoAm 92*
Fachet, Jozsef 1935- *WhoScE 91-4*
Fachiri, Adila 1886-1962 *Baker 92*
Fachnie, Hugh Douglas 1952- *WhoE 93, WhoEmL 93*
Facione, Peter Arthur 1944- *WhoAm 92*
Fackelman, Robert H. 1906- *St&PR 93*
Facklam, Margery (Metz) 1927- *WhoWrEP 92*
Fackler, Benjamine Lloyd 1926- *WhoAm 92*
Fackler, Edwin John 1927- *St&PR 93*
Fackler, John Paul, Jr. 1934- *WhoAm 92*
Fackler, Martin Luther 1933- *WhoAm 92*
Fackler, Walter David 1921- *WhoAm 92*
Facos, James 1924- *WhoWrEP 92*
Facsar, Imre 1939- *WhoScE 91-4*
Factor, Davis 1902-1991 *BioIn 17*
Factor, Mallory 1950- *St&PR 93*
Factor, Max, III 1945- *WhoAm 92*
Factor, Ruth P. *Law&B 92*
Factor, Sidney 1916- *St&PR 93*
Factoran, Fulgencio S. 1943- *WhoAsAP 91*
Faculak, Mary Helen 1960- *WhoWrEP 92*
Facundo, Jose R. *BioIn 17*
Facundo, Jose R. 1938- *WhoWor 93*
Facundus dc. 571 *OxDcByz*
Facusse, Miguel *DcCPCAm*
Fadden, Delmar McLean 1941- *WhoWor 93*
Fadden, John P. d1990 *BioIn 17*
Faddis, Jon *BioIn 17*
Fadel, Kim A. *Law&B 92*
Fadeley, Edward Norman 1929- *WhoAm 92*
Fadem, Lloyd Robert 1951- *WhoEmL 93, WhoSSW 93*
Fader, Daniel Nelson 1930- *WhoAm 92*
Fader, Ellen Strahs 1952- *St&PR 93, WhoAm 92*
Fader, Peter Radd 1955- *St&PR 93*
Fader, Seymour Jeremiah 1923- *WhoE 93, WhoWor 93*
Fader, Shirley Sloan *WhoAm 92, WhoAmW 93, WhoE 93, WhoWor 93*
Fader, William B. 1931- *St&PR 93*
Faderman, Lillian 1940- *ConAu 37NR*
Fadiman, Clifton *WhoAm 92*
Fadley, Ann Miller 1933- *WhoSSW 93*
Fadool, George Joseph 1959- *St&PR 93*
Fadum, Ralph Eigil 1912- *WhoAm 92*
Fadyn, Joseph Nicholas 1947- *WhoEmL 93, WhoSSW 93*
Fadzil Che Wan, Dato' Toh Muda Abdullah 1945- *WhoAsAP 91*
Faeber, Harry W. d1990 *BioIn 17*
Faeder, Gustav S. 1921- *WhoWrEP 92*
Faehnle, Robert Kirkwood 1949- *WhoEmL 93*
Faelli, Alide 1935- *WhoScE 91-3*
Faelten, Carl 1846-1925 *Baker 92*
Faelten, Reinhold 1856-1949 *Baker 92*
Faensen, Hubert-Heinz 1928- *WhoWor 93*
Faenza, Roberto *MiSFD 9*
Faerber, Donald Bartley 1935- *WhoWrEP 92*
Faerber, Jorg 1929- *Baker 92*
Faerber, Tom Harold 1930- *St&PR 93*
Faerden, Kirstin 1949- *WhoScE 91-4*
Faessler, Shirley *WhoCanL 92*
Faeth, Gerard Michael 1936- *WhoAm 92*
Fafian, Joseph, Jr. 1939- *WhoAm 92, WhoIns 93*
Fafinski, Stanley d1990 *BioIn 17*
Fagal, Virginia Mae 1917- *WhoAmW 93*
Fagaly, William Arthur 1938- *WhoAm 92*
Fagan, Cary 1957- *ConAu 136*
Fagan, Clifford B. 1911- *BiDAMSp 1989*
Fagan, Edward F. d1992 *BioIn 17*
Fagan, Eleanora 1915-1959 *BioIn 17*
Fagan, Gail G. *Law&B 92*
Fagan, Garth *BioIn 17*
Fagan, Gideon 1904-1980 *Baker 92*
Fagan, James F. 1948- *St&PR 93*
Fagan, James Reynolds 1931- *St&PR 93*
Fagan, Jane Dixon 1957- *WhoAmW 93*
Fagan, Jeffrey A. 1951- *St&PR 93*
Fagan, Joan M. *Law&B 92*
Fagan, John E. *Law&B 92*
Fagan, John Ernest 1949- *WhoEmL 93*
Fagan, John Paul 1930- *WhoAm 92*
Fagan, Joseph D. *Law&B 92*
Fagan, Joseph Francis, III 1941- *WhoAm 92*
Fagan, Julie Miriam 1953- *WhoE 93*
Fagan, Kate J. 1951- *WhoEmL 93*
Fagan, Keith H. *Law&B 92*
Fagan, Kenneth F. *Law&B 92*
Fagan, Kevin *BioIn 17*
Fagan, Kevin Joseph 1954- *WhoE 93*
Fagan, Michael Glennon 1949- *WhoEmL 93*
Fagan, Peter F. 1944- *St&PR 93*
Fagan, Peter Thomas *Law&B 92*
Fagan, Peter Thomas 1948- *WhoEmL 93*
Fagan, Sheila M. 1956- *WhoAmW 93*
Fagan, Timothy Robert 1955- *WhoEmL 93*

Fagan, Wayne Irwin 1943- *WhoAm 92, WhoSSW 93*
Fagan, William E. 1945- *St&PR 93*
Fagan, William Francis 1941- *St&PR 93*
Fagan, William Lawrence 1927- *WhoWor 93*
Fagan, William Thomas, Jr. 1923- *WhoE 93*
Fagans, Karl P. 1942- *St&PR 93*
Fagbemi, Stephen Fola 1953- *WhoE 93*
Fageer, Abdul Ghaffar Mohammed 1947- *WhoWor 93*
Fagen, David G. *Law&B 92*
Fagen, Richard Rees 1933- *WhoAm 92, WhoWrEP 92*
Fagenson, Don *BioIn 17*
Fager, Charles Anthony 1924- *WhoAm 92*
Fager, Charles Eugene 1942- *WhoSSW 93*
Fager, Jay B. 1947- *St&PR 93*
Fagerberg, Roger Richard 1935- *WhoAm 92, WhoWor 93*
Fagerhol, Magne Kristoffer 1935- *WhoWor 93*
Fagerholm, Nils-Erik 1928- *WhoScE 91-4*
Fagerlund, Eric 1926- *St&PR 93*
Fagerlund, Sven Goran 1937- *WhoScE 91-4*
Fagersten, Barbara Jeanne 1924- *WhoAmW 93*
Fagerstone, Dennis E. 1949- *St&PR 93*
Fagerstrom, Torbjorn K.B. 1944- *WhoScE 91-4*
Faget, Maxime A. 1921- *BioIn 17*
Fagg, Carolyn Sue 1952- *WhoAmW 93*
Fagg, Gary T. 1948- *St&PR 93*
Fagg, Gary Thomas 1948- *WhoIns 93*
Fagg, George Gardner 1934- *WhoAm 92*
Fagg, Larry Ermel 1949- *WhoEmL 93*
Fagg, Lawrence Wellburn 1923- *WhoE 93*
Fagg, Martha A. 1957- *WhoEmL 93*
Fagg, Susan Darlene Richardson 1947- *WhoAmW 93*
Fagg, William Harrison 1924- *WhoE 93*
Faggard, Phoebe 1956- *WhoEmL 93*
Faggiano, Pompilio Massimo 1956- *WhoWor 93*
Faggin, Federico 1941- *WhoAm 92*
Faggioli, Justin Mark 1951- *WhoEmL 93*
Faggioli, Michelangelo 1666-1733 *OxDcOp*
Faggs, Heriwentha Mae *BiDAMSp 1989*
Faggs, Mae *BlkAmWO [port]*
Faggs, Mae 1932- *BioIn 17*
Fagher, Olof Erik Birger 1942- *WhoWor 93*
Fagin, Charles Thomas 1939- *St&PR 93*
Fagin, Claire Mintzer *WhoAm 92, WhoAmW 93*
Fagin, David Kyle 1938- *WhoAm 92*
Fagin, Henry 1913- *WhoAm 92*
Fagin, Mary *AmWomPl*
Fagin, Nathan Bryllion 1888-1972 *ScF&FL 92*
Fagin, Richard 1935- *WhoAm 92*
Faglia, Giovanni 1930- *WhoScE 91-3*
Fagnani, Francis *WhoScE 91-2*
Fagnani, Francis 1943- *WhoScE 91-2*
Fago, Elizabeth Marie 1950- *WhoEmL 93, WhoSSW 93*
Fago, Lorenzo 1704-1793
See Fago, (Francesco) Nicola 1677-1745 *Baker 92*
Fago, (Francesco) Nicola 1677-1745 *Baker 92*
Fagot, Joseph Burdell 1917- *WhoAm 92*
Fagot, Robert Frederick 1921- *WhoAm 92*
Fagoth, Steadman *DcCPCAm*
Fagothey, Austin 1901-1975 *BioIn 17*
Fagundes, Joseph Marvin, III 1953- *WhoEmL 93*
Fagundes Telles, Lygia *ScF&FL 92*
Fagundo, Ana Maria 1938- *WhoAm 92*
Faguni Ram, Dr. 1945- *WhoAsAP 91*
Fahad Ibn Abdul Aziz 1920- *WhoWor 93*
Fahd, King of Saudi Arabia 1922- *BioIn 17*
Faherty, Kevin M. 1943- *WhoE 93*
Faherty, Mike *BioIn 17*
Fahey, Colleen Elizabeth 1950- *St&PR 93*
Fahey, James D. *Law&B 92*
Fahey, James Edward 1953- *WhoE 93, WhoWor 93*
Fahey, James J. d1991 *BioIn 17*
Fahey, Jeff *ConTFT 10*
Fahey, Joseph Francis, Jr. 1925- *WhoAm 92*
Fahey, Patricia Anne 1957- *WhoE 93, WhoEmL 93*
Fahey, Peter Matthew 1946- *WhoAm 92*
Fahey, Sandra Justice 1948- *WhoSSW 93*
Fahien, Leonard August 1934- *WhoAm 92*
Fahim, Ayshe 1960- *WhoEmL 93*
Fahimi, H. Dariush 1933- *WhoScE 91-3, WhoWor 93*
Fahl, John 1936- *St&PR 93*
Fahlbeck, Reinhold Hans 1938- *WhoWor 93*
Fahlberg, John *St&PR 93*
Fahlen, Per 1947- *WhoScE 91-4*
Fahlgren, H. Smoot 1930- *St&PR 93*
Fahlgren, Herbert Smoot 1930- *WhoAm 92*
Fahlman, Anders G. 1937- *WhoScE 91-4*
Fahlund, Michael Jay 1949- *WhoE 93, WhoEmL 93*
Fahmy, Ibrahim Mounir 1943- *WhoE 93*
Fahn, Jay 1949- *WhoEmL 93*
Fahn, Stanley 1933- *WhoAm 92*
Fahner, Harold Thomas 1940- *WhoSSW 93, WhoWor 93*
Fahner, Tyrone C. 1942- *WhoAm 92*
Fahnestock, Jean Howe 1930- *WhoAmW 93*
Fahnestock, Margaret 1952- *WhoEmL 93*
Fahr, Hans Jorg 1939- *WhoScE 91-3*
Fahr, Wolfgang Otto 1926- *WhoWor 93*
Fahrbach, Philipp 1815-1885 *Baker 92*
Fahrenfort, J.J. 1885-1975 *IntDcAn*
Fahrenkopf, Frank J., Jr. 1939- *PolPar*
Fahrenkopf, Frank Joseph, Jr. 1939- *WhoAm 92*
Fahrenkrog, G.A. *WhoScE 91-3*
Fahrenwald, William Edward 1955- *WhoEmL 93*
Fahringer, Catherine Hewson 1922- *WhoAm 92*
Fahrlander, Henry William, Jr. 1934- *WhoSSW 93*
Fahrnbruch, Dale E. 1924- *WhoAm 92*
Fahrner, James J. 1951- *St&PR 93*
Fahs, James Kenneth 1947- *St&PR 93*
Fa-Hsien 374?-462? *Expl 93*
Fahy, Charles Laurence 1947- *WhoAm 92, WhoEmL 93, WhoSSW 93, WhoWor 93*
Fahy, Christopher 1937- *ScF&FL 92*
Fahy, Daniel P. *Law&B 92*
Fahy, Nancy Lee 1946- *WhoAmW 93, WhoEmL 93*
Fahy, Thomas James 1936- *WhoScE 91-3*
Fai, Tamara 1947- *WhoWor 93*
Fai'atoa, Ben Gale 1944- *WhoAsAP 91*
Faidutti, Bernard 1936- *WhoScE 91-4*
Faig, Kenneth W., Jr. *ScF&FL 92*
Faigen, Ivan M. 1926- *St&PR 93*
Faignant, John Paul 1953- *WhoEmL 93*
Faignient, Noe c. 1540-c. 1595 *Baker 92*
Fail, James M. *BioIn 17*
Fail, Joseph D. *St&PR 93*
Failey, George Leo 1928- *St&PR 93*
Failey, George Leo, Jr. 1928- *WhoAm 92*
Failing, Craig Adam 1961- *WhoEmL 93*
Failing, George Edgar 1912- *WhoAm 92*
Failla, Frank Jerome, Jr. 1949- *St&PR 93*
Failla, Mark Edward 1962- *WhoEmL 93*
Failla, Patricia McClement 1925- *WhoAm 92*
Faillace, Michael A. *Law&B 92*
Faillace, Michael Antonio 1957- *WhoEmL 93*
Faillard, Hans 1924- *WhoScE 91-3*
Failoni, Sergio 1890-1948 *Baker 92*
Failor, William Ned 1950- *WhoEmL 93*
Fails, Donna Gail 1958- *WhoAmW 93, WhoEmL 93*
Faiman, Charles 1939- *WhoAm 92*
Faiman, Peter *MiSFD 9*
Faiman, Robert Neil 1923- *WhoAm 92*
Fain, Bill *BioIn 17*
Fain, Cheryl Ann 1953- *WhoAmW 93*
Fain, David H. 1847-1902 *BioIn 17*
Fain, Ferris Roy 1921- *BiDAMSp 1989*
Fain, Jay Lindsey 1950- *WhoEmL 93*
Fain, Jessie Bledsoe 1865-1951 *BioIn 17*
Fain, Joel Maurice 1953- *WhoEmL 93*
Fain, John Charles 1937- *St&PR 93*
Fain, John Nicholas 1934- *WhoAm 92, WhoSSW 93*
Fain, John W. 1953- *St&PR 93*
Fain, John Wood *Law&B 92*
Fain, Karen Kellogg 1940- *WhoAmW 93*
Fain, Michael 1937?- *ConAu 139*
Fain, Mickey Allen 1956- *WhoEmL 93*
Fain, Pauline *AmWomPl*
Fain, Raymond N. 1946- *St&PR 93*
Fain, Richard David 1947- *WhoAm 92, WhoWor 93*
Fain, Sammy 1902-1989 *Baker 92, BioIn 17*
Faine, Chris Wells *Law&B 92*
Faine, Solomon 1926- *WhoWor 93*
Fainman, Burt 1936- *St&PR 93*
Fainsbert, Amy 1962- *St&PR 93*
Fainstein, P.M. *Law&B 92*
Fair, Charles Maitland 1916- *WhoE 93*
Fair, Harry David 1936- *WhoAm 92*
Fair, Hudson Randolph 1953- *WhoEmL 93*
Fair, J. Milton 1934- *St&PR 93*
Fair, James Richard 1950- *WhoEmL 93*
Fair, James Rutherford, Jr. 1920- *WhoAm 92*
Fair, Jean Everhard 1917- *WhoAm 92*
Fair, Jeff 1952- *ScF&FL 92*
Fair, Jeremy George 1947- *St&PR 93*
Fair, Kathryn E. *Law&B 92*
Fair, Mary Louise 1931- *WhoAmW 93*
Fair, Morris Harley 1929- *WhoAm 92*
Fair, Norma L. 1931- *St&PR 93*
Fair, Norman Arnold 1945- *St&PR 93, WhoIns 93*
Fair, Richard Barton 1942- *WhoAm 92*
Fair, Robert James 1919- *WhoAm 92*
Fair, Russell B. 1948- *St&PR 93*
Fair, Tamera L. *Law&B 92*
Fair, Walter Russel 1936- *St&PR 93*
Fair, William R. 1922- *St&PR 93*
Fair, William Robert 1935- *WhoAm 92*
Fairbairn, Barbara Jean 1950- *WhoE 93*
Fairbairn, Ursula F. 1943- *St&PR 93*
Fairbairn, Ursula Farrell 1943- *WhoAmW 93*
Fairbairn, Walter M. *WhoScE 91-1*
Fairbairns, Zoe 1948- *ScF&FL 92*
Fairbank, Bruce Edward 1957- *St&PR 93*
Fairbank, Janet Ayer *AmWomPl*
Fairbank, John 1907-1991 *AnObit 1991*
Fairbank, John King 1907-1991 *BioIn 17*
Fairbank, William M. 1917-1989 *BioIn 17*
Fairbank, William Martin, Jr. 1946- *WhoEmL 93*
Fairbanks, Clifford Alan 1946- *WhoSSW 93*
Fairbanks, David C. 1937- *St&PR 93*
Fairbanks, Deborah M. 1954- *WhoAmW 93*
Fairbanks, Douglas 1883-1939 *BioIn 17, IntDcF 2-3 [port]*
Fairbanks, Douglas Elton, Jr. 1909- *WhoAm 92, WhoE 93, WhoWor 93*
Fairbanks, Frank B. 1930- *St&PR 93*
Fairbanks, Frank Bates 1930- *WhoAm 92*
Fairbanks, Harold Vincent 1915- *WhoAm 92*
Fairbanks, Joel Kent 1956- *WhoSSW 93*
Fairbanks, Jonathan Leo 1933- *WhoAm 92*
Fairbanks, Norman Russell, Jr. *Law&B 92*
Fairbanks, Richard Monroe 1912- *WhoAm 92*
Fairbanks, Richard Monroe, III 1941- *WhoAm 92*
Fairbanks, Robert Alvin 1944- *WhoSSW 93, WhoWor 93*
Fairbanks, Russell Norman 1919- *WhoAm 92*
Fairbanks, William J. 1931- *WhoIns 93*
Fairbanks-Graham, Bett *BioIn 17*
Fairbrook, Susan K. *Law&B 92*
Fairbrother, Jack A. 1949- *St&PR 93*
Fairbrother, Kathryn Louise 1957- *WhoAmW 93*
Fairburn, Robert G. d1992 *NewYTBS 92*
Fairburn, Robert Gordon 1911- *WhoAm 92*
Fairchild, Alexander Graham Bell 1906- *WhoSSW 93*
Fairchild, Beatrice Magdoff 1916- *WhoAm 92*
Fairchild, Blair 1877-1933 *Baker 92*
Fairchild, David Lawrence 1946- *WhoAm 92*
Fairchild, John Burr 1927- *WhoAm 92*
Fairchild, Katherine Ballenger 1923- *WhoAmW 93*
Fairchild, Kentley Robert 1961- *WhoEmL 93*
Fairchild, Melanie McDowell *Law&B 92*
Fairchild, Melody *BioIn 17*
Fairchild, Ralph G. 1935-1990 *BioIn 17*
Fairchild, Raymond Eugene 1923- *St&PR 93, WhoAm 92, WhoWor 93*
Fairchild, Raymond Francis 1946- *WhoEmL 93*
Fairchild, Robert Charles 1921- *WhoAm 92*
Fairchild, Ronald B. 1957- *St&PR 93*
Fairchild, Samuel Wilson 1954- *WhoAm 92, WhoE 93, WhoSSW 93*
Fairchild, Thomas E. 1912- *WhoAm 92*
Fairchild, Thomas Hayes 1954- *WhoEmL 93*
Faircloth, Cyril E. *ScF&FL 92*
Faircloth, Wayne Reynolds 1932- *WhoSSW 93*
Fairclough, John W. 1930- *WhoWor 93*
Faire, Virginia Brown 1904-1980 *SweetSg B [port]*
Fairey, Wendy W. *BioIn 17*
Fairfax, Charles E., III *Law&B 92*
Fairfax, Ferdinand 1944- *MiSFD 9*
Fairfax, Laura May 1943- *WhoSSW 93*
Fairfax, Marion *AmWomPl*
Fairfax, Mary Wein Symonds, Lady *BioIn 17*
Fairfax, Sally *BioIn 17*
Fairfax, Warwick *BioIn 17*
Fairfax of Cameron, Ferdinando Fairfax 1584-1648 *HarEnMi*
Fairfax of Cameron, Thomas Fairfax 1612-1671 *HarEnMi*
Fairfield, Betty Elaine Smith 1927- *WhoAm 92*
Fairfield, Frances *AmWomPl*
Fairfield, John *WhoWrEP 92*
Fairfield, Lory C. 1936- *St&PR 93*
Fairfield, Nancy A. *Law&B 92*
Fairfield-Sonn, James Willed 1948- *WhoE 93, WhoEmL 93*
Fairgrieve, Anita Belle *AmWomPl*
Fairhurst, Charles 1929- *WhoAm 92*
Fairhurst, John Arthur *WhoScE 91-1*
Fairlamb, Alan Hutchinson 1947- *WhoWor 93*
Fairlamb, James Remington 1838-1908 *Baker 92*
Fairleigh, James Parkinson 1938- *WhoSSW 93*
Fairleigh, Marlane Paxson 1939- *WhoSSW 93*
Fairley, Henry Barrie 1927- *WhoAm 92*
Fairley, Mary C. *Law&B 92*
Fairley, Michael J. 1946- *St&PR 93*
Fairley, Richard L. 1933- *WhoE 93*
Fairlie, Henry *BioIn 17*
Fairlie, Margaret C. *AmWomPl*
Fairly, Ronald Ray 1938- *BiDAMSp 1989*
Fairman, Francis E. 1957- *St&PR 93*
Fairman, Joel Martin 1929- *WhoAm 92*
Fairman, Paul W. 1909-1977 *ScF&FL 92*
Fairobent, Lynne Anne 1956- *WhoAmW 93, WhoEmL 93*
Fairstein, Linda *BioIn 17*
Fairweather, D. *WhoScE 91-1*
Fairweather, Howard Hessington 1938- *St&PR 93, WhoAm 92*
Fairweather, Robert Gordon Lee 1923- *WhoAm 92*
Fairweather, William Ross 1943- *WhoE 93*
Fairweather-Tait, Susan Jane *WhoScE 91-1*
Faisal, King of Saudi Arabia 1906-1975 *BioIn 17*
Faisal, I 1885-1933 *DcTwHis*
Faisal, II 1935-1958 *DcTwHis*
Faisal, Nabeel Jaffar 1959- *WhoWor 93*
Faisal, Sayedah Khadijah d1992 *NewYTBS 92*
Faisal ibn Abd al-Aziz 1905-1975 *DcTwHis*
Faison, Edmund Winston, Jr. 1953- *WhoEmL 93*
Faison, Ferdinand Johnson 1934- *St&PR 93*
Faison, Hawthorne 1933- *WhoSSW 93*
Faison, Holly 1953- *WhoAmW 93*
Faison, Jimmy 1947- *WhoSSW 93*
Faison, Larry Don 1949- *WhoSSW 93*
Faison, Linda Kay Gainey 1952- *WhoE 93*
Faison, Seth Shepard 1924- *WhoAm 92*
Faison, William F., II *Law&B 92*
Faissner, Helmut Carl 1928- *WhoScE 91-3*
Faisst, Immanuel 1823-1894 *Baker 92*
Faist, Andre P. 1935- *WhoScE 91-4*
Fait, George A. 1926- *St&PR 93, WhoIns 93*
Faith, Eddie Ray 1955- *WhoSSW 93*
Faith, Jane Kaelin 1952- *WhoSSW 93*
Faith, Mark David 1962- *WhoEmL 93*
Faith, Percy 1908-1976 *Baker 92*
Faithfull, Nigel Tyley 1943- *WhoWor 93*
Faivre, Gabriel 1944- *WhoScE 91-2*
Faiz, Asif 1947- *WhoE 93*
Faiz, Faiz Ahmad 1911?-1984 *BioIn 17*
Fajack, D. James 1936- *St&PR 93*
Fajans, Jack 1922- *WhoAm 92*
Fajans, Kazimierz 1887-1975 *PolBiDi*
Fajans, Maksymilian 1827-1890 *PolBiDi*
Fajans, Stefan Stanislaus 1918- *WhoAm 92*
Fajardo, Katharine Lynn 1951- *WhoAm 92, WhoAmW 93, WhoEmL 93*
Fajfar, Peter 1943- *WhoScE 91-4*
Fajgier, Susan Ellen 1958- *WhoAmW 93*
Fajon, Etienne 1906- *BioIn 17*
Fajziev, Latif 1929- *DrEEuF*
Fakazis, Melvina D. 1948- *St&PR 93*
Fakeris, Edward G. 1951- *St&PR 93*
Fakes, Mary E. A. 1962- *WhoAmW 93, WhoEmL 93*
Fakhri, Salim d1990 *BioIn 17*
Faklaris, John Richard 1949- *St&PR 93*
Fakundiny, Robert Harry 1940- *WhoE 93*
Falabella (Correa), Roberto 1926-1958 *Baker 92*
Falahee, Thomas Michael *Law&B 92*
Falana, Lola *BioIn 17*
Falat, Anna Maria 1952- *WhoAmW 93*
Falat, Julian 1853-1929 *PolBiDi*
Falb, John H. 1945- *St&PR 93*
Falb, Mark Charles 1947- *St&PR 93*
Falb, Peter Lawrence 1936- *WhoAm 92*
Falbaum, Bertram Seymour 1934- *WhoSSW 93*
Falbe, Christian Tuxen 1791-1849 *BioIn 17*
Falbe, Joachim Martin 1709-1782 *BioIn 17*
Falber, Harold Julius 1946- *WhoE 93, WhoEmL 93*
Falcam, Leo A. 1935- *WhoAsAP 91*
Falcao, Carlos 1940- *WhoWor 93*
Falchi, Stanislao 1851-1922 *Baker 92*

Falci, Nina Lansky 1958- *WhoEmL 93*
Falciani, Robert A. 1946- *St&PR 93*
Falcinelli, Rolande 1920- *Baker 92*
Falck, Alberto 1938- *WhoWor 93*
Falck, Ingeborg 1922- *WhoScE 91-3*
Falck, Maria J. 1962- *WhoAmW 93*
Falcke, Caj O. 1941- *WhoUN 92*
Falco, Charles Maurice 1948- *WhoEmL 93*
Falco, Edward 1948- *WhoWrEP 92*
Falco, JoAnn 1952- *WhoAmW 93, WhoWor 93*
Falco, Louis 1942- *WhoAm 92, WhoE 93*
Falco, Maria Josephine 1932- *WhoAm 92, WhoAmW 93*
Falco, Michele c. 1688-c. 1732 *OxDcOp*
Falcoff, E. *WhoScE 91-2*
Falcon, Cornelie 1814-1897 *OxDcOp*
Falcon, (Marie-) Cornelie 1814-1897 *Baker 92*
Falcon, Joe *BioIn 17*
Falcon, Lawrence Michael 1943- *St&PR 93*
Falcon, Louis Albert 1932- *WhoAm 92*
Falcon, Marie Cornelie 1814-1897 *IntDcOp [port]*
Falcon, Ray A. 1940- *St&PR 93*
Falcon, Raymond J., Jr. *Law&B 92*
Falcon, Raymond Jesus, Jr. 1953- *WhoE 93, WhoEmL 93*
Falcon, Walter P. 1936- *BioIn 17*
Falconar, A.E.I. *ScF&FL 92*
Falcone, Alfonso Benjamin 1923- *WhoAm 92, WhoWor 93*
Falcone, Anthony 1956- *St&PR 93*
Falcone, Charles A. 1942- *St&PR 93*
Falcone, David John 1950- *WhoE 93*
Falcone, Donna Marie 1961- *WhoEmL 93*
Falcone, Frank S. 1940- *WhoAm 92*
Falcone, Giuseppe 1926- *WhoScE 91-3*
Falcone, Louis A. 1955- *WhoEmL 93*
Falcone, Nola Maddox 1939- *WhoAm 92, WhoAmW 93*
Falcone, Patricia Kuntz 1952- *WhoAmW 93*
Falcone, Peter 1936- *WhoAm 92*
Falcone, Philip Francis 1929- *WhoWor 93*
Falcone, Sebastian Anthony 1927- *WhoE 93*
Falcone, Thomas R. 1947- *St&PR 93*
Falconer, David Duncan 1940- *WhoAm 92*
Falconer, Florence Williams *AmWomPl*
Falconer, George 1932- *St&PR 93*
Falconer, Ian Robert 1935- *WhoWor 93*
Falconer, Lee N. *ScF&FL 92*
Falconer, Ramsey Reid 1956- *WhoSSW 93*
Falconer, Robert A. *Law&B 92*
Falconer, Roger Alexander *WhoScE 91-1*
Falconer, Sovereign *ScF&FL 92*
Falconer, William B. d1990 *BioIn 17*
Falconi, R.J. *Law&B 92*
Falconieri, Andrea 1585?-1656 *Baker 92*
Falconio, Patrick E. 1941- *St&PR 93*
Falcons *SoulM*
Faldo, Nick *BioIn 17*
Faldo, Nick 1957- *CurBio 92 [port]*
Faleiro, Eduardo 1940- *WhoAsAP 91*
Falen, Melissa Ann 1956- *WhoAmW 93*
Falender-Zohn, Carol Ann 1946- *WhoAmW 93, WhoEmL 93*
Faleomavaega, Eni F.H. *CngDr 91*
Faleomavaega, Eni F. H. 1943- *WhoAm 92*
Fales, Dennis D. *Law&B 92*
Fales, Gregg Booth 1945- *WhoE 93*
Fales, Haliburton, II 1919- *WhoAm 92*
Fales, Henry Marshall 1927- *WhoE 93*
Fales, James M. 1943- *St&PR 93*
Fales, Rochelle *BioIn 17*
Faletti, Harold Everett 1952- *WhoEmL 93*
Faletti, Richard J. 1922- *St&PR 93*
Faletti, Richard Joseph 1922- *WhoAm 92*
Falge, H.-J. *WhoScE 91-3*
Falger, Vincent Stephan Eugene 1946- *WhoWor 93*
Falgoust, David M. *Law&B 92*
Falgoust, Dean Thomas 1958- *WhoEmL 93*
Falgout, Anne Frances 1967- *WhoSSW 93*
Falick, James 1936- *WhoAm 92, WhoSSW 93*
Falick, Paul 1944- *St&PR 93*
Falicki, Zdzislaw 1929- *WhoScE 91-4*
Falicov, Leopoldo Maximo 1933- *WhoAm 92*
Falieri, Marinos c. 1395-1474 *OxDcByz*
Falik, Harold N. 1949- *St&PR 93*
Falik, Joseph Laurence *Law&B 92*
Falik, Yuri 1936- *Baker 92*
Falise, Carolyn P. d1990 *BioIn 17*
Falise, Robert A. 1932- *St&PR 93*
Falisse, Andre 1947- *WhoScE 91-2*
Falk, Bernard Henry 1926- *WhoAm 92*
Falk, Bernice d1991 *BioIn 17*
Falk, Bibb August 1899-1989 *BiDAMSp 1989*
Falk, Burton Arthur 1936- *St&PR 93*
Falk, Candace 1947- *ConAu 136*
Falk, Charles David 1939- *WhoE 93*
Falk, Conrad Robert 1935- *WhoAm 92*
Falk, Dean 1944- *WhoAmW 93*
Falk, Diane M. 1947- *WhoWrEP 92*
Falk, Dick *BioIn 17*
Falk, Edgar Alan 1932- *WhoAm 92*
Falk, Elizabeth Moxley 1942- *WhoAmW 93, WhoWor 93*
Falk, Elliott George 1927- *WhoE 93*
Falk, Eugene Hannes 1913- *WhoAm 92*
Falk, Eugene L. 1943- *WhoAm 92*
Falk, Feliks 1941- *DrEEuF*
Falk, Ferdie Arnold 1928- *WhoAm 92, WhoWor 93*
Falk, Gerhard *WhoE 93*
Falk, Gerhard 1931- *ConAu 39NR, -40NR*
Falk, Glenn Edward 1965- *WhoE 93*
Falk, Harry *MiSFD 9*
Falk, Harvey L. 1934- *WhoE 93*
Falk, Heinz 1939- *WhoScE 91-4*
Falk, James Harvey, Sr. 1938- *WhoAm 92*
Falk, Joan Frances 1936- *WhoE 93*
Falk, John C. 1946- *St&PR 93*
Falk, Jonathan *ScF&FL 92*
Falk, Julia S. 1941- *WhoAm 92*
Falk, Katherine 1944- *WhoE 93*
Falk, Kathryn Colleen 1965- *WhoAmW 93*
Falk, Lawrence Claster 1942- *WhoSSW 93, WhoWor 93*
Falk, Lee Harrison *WhoAm 92, WhoWor 93*
Falk, Lloyd David 1932- *St&PR 93*
Falk, Lloyd Leopold 1919- *WhoE 93*
Falk, Margaret *ScF&FL 92*
Falk, Marshall Allen 1929- *WhoWor 93*
Falk, Myron S. d1992 *BioIn 17*
Falk, Norman 1928- *St&PR 93*
Falk, Orren Beth *Law&B 92*
Falk, Patrick George Alexander 1944- *WhoE 93*
Falk, Peter 1927- *BioIn 17, IntDcF 2-3, WhoAm 92*
Falk, Peter H(astings) 1950- *ConAu 139*
Falk, Richard S. 1941- *St&PR 93*
Falk, Richard Sands, Jr. 1941- *WhoAm 92*
Falk, Robert Barclay, Jr. 1945- *WhoE 93*
Falk, Robert Hardy 1948- *WhoEmL 93*
Falk, Sam 1903-1991 *BioIn 17*
Falk, Sigo 1934- *St&PR 93*
Falk, Stephen Thomas *Law&B 92*
Falk, Sydney Westervelt, Jr. 1947- *WhoEmL 93*
Falk, Theodore Carswell 1946- *WhoEmL 93*
Falk, Ursula Adler *WhoAmW 93*
Falk, Victor S., III *Law&B 92*
Falk, W.D. 1906-1991 *BioIn 17*
Falke, Dietrich 1927- *WhoScE 91-3*
Falkenbach, John J. *Law&B 92*
Falkenberg, Anna Woytek 1946- *WhoEmL 93*
Falkenberg, Edward 1940- *St&PR 93, WhoAm 92*
Falkenberg, John F. 1925- *St&PR 93*
Falkenberg, Mary Ann Theresa 1931- *WhoAmW 93*
Falkenberry, Joyce Knox 1955- *WhoEmL 93*
Falkenburg, Hans d1992 *NewYTBS 92*
Falkenburg, Jinx *BioIn 17*
Falkeneau, Therese *AmWomPl*
Falkenhausen, Ludwig von 1840-1936 *HarEnMi*
Falkenhayn, Erich von 1861-1922 *HarEnMi*
Falkenhorst, Nikolaus von 1885-1968 *HarEnMi*
Falkenstein, Claire 1908- *BioIn 17*
Falkenstein, Karin Edith 1950- *WhoAmW 93*
Falker, John Richard 1940- *WhoAm 92*
Falkie, Thomas Victor 1934- *St&PR 93, WhoAm 92, WhoE 93*
Falkin, Jeffrey C. *Law&B 92*
Falkingham, Donald Herbert 1918- *WhoSSW 93, WhoWor 93*
Falkmer, Sture E. 1927- *WhoScE 91-4*
Falkner, Frank Tardrew 1918- *WhoAm 92*
Falkner, J. Meade 1858-1932 *ScF&FL 92*
Falkner, Jennifer G. *Law&B 92*
Falkner, (Donald) Keith 1900- *Baker 92*
Falkner, Pandora Ilona 1958- *WhoEmL 93*
Falknor, G. Scott *Law&B 92*
Falkoff, Milton 1915- *St&PR 93*
Falkow, Stanley 1934- *WhoAm 92*
Falkowitz, Daniel 1936- *St&PR 93, WhoAm 92, WhoE 93*
Falkowitz, Ed 1946- *WhoE 93*
Falk Scott, Laura *Law&B 92*
Falkson, Susan D. *Law&B 92*
Fall, Janice Leyrer *Law&B 92*
Fall, John A. *Law&B 92*
Fall, John Alexander 1942- *St&PR 93*
Fall, Leo 1873-1925 *OxDcOp*
Fall, Leo(pold) 1873-1925 *Baker 92*
Fall, Mamadou 1948- *WhoUN 92*
Fall, Medoune 1919- *WhoWor 93*
Fall, Steven Michael 1951- *WhoEmL 93*
Fall, Thomas 1917- *DcAmChF 1960*
Falla, Enrique C. 1939- *St&PR 93*
Falla, Enrique Crabb 1939- *WhoAm 92*
Falla, Manuel de 1876-1946 *IntDcOp, OxDcOp*
Falla, Norman Alexander Richard 1943- *WhoScE 91-1*
Falla (y Matheu), Manuel (Maria) de 1876-1946 *Baker 92*
Fallaci, Oriana *BioIn 17*
Fallaci, Oriana 1930- *WhoAm 92, WhoWor 93*
Fallahi, Carolyn Ruth 1961- *WhoAmW 93*
Fallais, Charles J. 1937- *WhoScE 91-2*
Fallarino, John 1941- *St&PR 93*
Fallas, Carlos Luis 1901-1966 *SpAmA*
Fallas, Luis *DcCPCAm*
Fallas Venegas, Helio Francisco 1947- *WhoWor 93*
Fallaw, Walter Robert, Jr. 1935- *WhoE 93*
Fall Creek, Stephanie Jean 1950- *WhoEmL 93*
Fallding, Harold Joseph 1923- *WhoAm 92*
Falle, Daisy Carolyne 1940- *WhoAm 92*
Fallek, David d1992 *BioIn 17*
Faller, Brian V. *Law&B 92*
Faller, Donald E. 1927- *WhoAm 92*
Faller, Jack W. 1942- *WhoE 93*
Faller, Jeanne-Marie Elizabeth 1944- *WhoAmW 93*
Faller, Jozsef 1936- *WhoScE 91-4*
Faller, Nikola 1862-1938 *Baker 92*
Faller, Susan Grogan 1950- *WhoEmL 93*
Fallesen, Gary David 1959- *WhoE 93, WhoEmL 93*
Falletta, Jo Ann 1954- *BioIn 17, WhoAm 92, WhoAmW 93*
Falletta, John Matthew 1940- *WhoAm 92*
Fallick, Nina Shari 1961- *WhoAmW 93*
Fallick, Paul *Law&B 92*
Fallier, Charles Nicholas, Jr. 1917- *WhoWor 93*
Fallier, Jeanne Hanway 1920- *WhoWrEP 92*
Fallieres, Clement Armand 1841-1931 *BioIn 17*
Fallin, Barbara Moore 1939- *WhoAmW 93*
Fallin, Jack F., Jr. *Law&B 92*
Fallin, Mary Copeland 1954- *WhoAmW 93*
Fallingstar, Cerridwen *ScF&FL 92*
Fallis, Albert Murray 1907- *WhoAm 92*
Fallis, Alexander Graham 1940- *WhoAm 92*
Fallon, Anita *AmWomPl*
Fallon, Ann Louise 1953- *St&PR 93*
Fallon, Brett David 1961- *WhoEmL 93*
Fallon, Brian Anthony 1955- *WhoEmL 93*
Fallon, Daniel 1938- *WhoAm 92*
Fallon, Donald 1944- *St&PR 93*
Fallon, Edward George 1941- *St&PR 93*
Fallon, Harry J. 1926- *St&PR 93*
Fallon, Honore J. *Law&B 92*
Fallon, Ivan (Gregory) 1944- *ConAu 137*
Fallon, John F. *Law&B 92*
Fallon, John Golden 1946- *St&PR 93, WhoAm 92*
Fallon, Kelly *BioIn 17*
Fallon, Kristine K. 1949- *St&PR 93, WhoAmW 93, WhoEmL 93*
Fallon, Louis Fleming, Jr. 1950- *WhoWor 93*
Fallon, Malachy 1961- *St&PR 93*
Fallon, Martin 1929- *BioIn 17*
Fallon, Michael *BioIn 17*
Fallon, Moira Anne 1952- *WhoAmW 93*
Fallon, Richard Gordon 1923- *WhoAm 92*
Fallon, Stephen Francis 1956- *WhoIns 93*
Fallon, Tom 1936- *WhoWrEP 92*
Fallon, William E. 1954- *St&PR 93*
Fallon, William Hume 1956- *WhoEmL 93*
Fallon, William M. 1946- *St&PR 93*
Fallon-Walsh, Barbara *BioIn 17*
Falloon, John Howard 1942- *WhoAsAP 91*
Fallowell, Duncan (Richard) 1948- *ConAu 137*
Fallows, James Mackenzie 1949- *WhoAm 92, WhoE 93, WhoWrEP 92*
Falls, Edward Joseph 1920- *WhoAm 92*
Falls, Gerald Flynn 1949- *WhoSSW 93*
Falls, Glenn 1921- *St&PR 93*
Falls, James J. 1939- *St&PR 93*
Falls, Joseph Francis 1928- *BiDAMSp 1989, WhoAm 92*
Falls, Kathleene Joyce 1949- *WhoAmW 93, WhoWor 93*
Falls, Marilyn Lee 1949- *WhoAm 92, WhoEmL 93*
Falls, O.B., Jr. 1913- *St&PR 93*
Falls, Olive Moretz 1934- *WhoSSW 93, WhoWor 93*
Falls, Ralph Lane, Jr. 1941- *St&PR 93*
Falls, Raymond L. 1929-1991 *BioIn 17*
Falls, Robert Arthur 1954- *WhoAm 92*
Falls, Robert Glenn 1921- *St&PR 93*
Falls, William Wayne 1947- *WhoAm 92*
Fallside, Frank *WhoScE 91-1*
Fallwell, Marion A. *Law&B 92*
Falo, Giovanni Battista Antonio 1942- *WhoWor 93*
Faloon, William Wassell 1920- *WhoAm 92*
Faloona, Michael Patrick 1961- *WhoEmL 93*
Falor, Marcia Hasek 1950- *WhoAmW 93*
Falotico, Raymond 1951- *WhoE 93*
Falsetti, Christine Marie 1961- *WhoEmL 93*
Falsey, Edward F. 1910-1990 *BioIn 17*
Falsey, John Henry, Jr. 1951- *WhoAm 92*
Falsgraf, William Wendell 1933- *WhoAm 92*
Falso, Edward D. *Law&B 92*
Falso, Steven Michael 1960- *WhoE 93*
Falstad, Daniel Thomas *Law&B 92*
Falstad, David B. 1936- *St&PR 93*
Falstad, David Bergfeld *Law&B 92*
Falstad, David Bergfeld 1936- *WhoAm 92*
Faltas Youssef, Edwar Kolta *ConAu 136*
Falter, Claus 1944- *WhoScE 91-3*
Falter, John 1910-1982 *BioIn 17*
Falter, Lawrence S. *Law&B 92*
Falter, Vincent Eugene 1932- *WhoAm 92*
Falterman, Darrell John *WhoIns 93*
Falterman, Darrell John 1947- *St&PR 93*
Faltermeyer, Harold 1952- *ConTFT 10*
Falthammar, Carl-Gunne S.C. 1931- *WhoScE 91-4*
Faltin, Bruce Charles 1947- *WhoEmL 93*
Faltings, Gerd 1954- *WhoAm 92*
Faltinsen, Odd M. 1944- *WhoScE 91-4*
Faltus, Michelle 1935- *WhoAmW 93*
Faludi, Susan *BioIn 17*
Faludi, Susan 1959- *ConAu 138, News 92 [port]*
Faludi, Susan C. *WhoAmW 93, WhoE 93*
Faluyi, Akinsola Olusegun 1934- *WhoWor 93*
Falvey, Charles L. *Law&B 92*
Falvey, John W. *Law&B 92*
Falvey, Patrick Joseph 1927- *WhoAm 92*
Falvey, Paul F. *St&PR 93*
Falvo, Anthony J., Jr. *WhoAm 92*
Falvo, Donna Rose 1945- *WhoAmW 93*
Falwell, David George 1943- *St&PR 93*
Falwell, Jerry *BioIn 17*
Falwell, Jerry L. 1933- *WhoAm 92, WhoSSW 93*
Falzarano, Jeffrey Mark 1960- *WhoEmL 93*
Falzon, Anthony Alfred 1954- *WhoWor 93*
Falzon, John J. 1928- *St&PR 93*
Falzone, Joseph Sam 1917- *WhoE 93*
Fama, Donald Francis 1938- *WhoE 93*
Fama, Maria 1951- *WhoWrEP 92*
Fambrough, William Louis, Jr. 1954- *WhoEmL 93*
Famie, Keith *BioIn 17*
Famighetti, Robert Joseph 1947- *WhoE 93*
Famiglietti, Nancy Zima 1956- *WhoAmW 93, WhoE 93, WhoEmL 93, WhoWor 93*
Famintsyn, Alexander (Sergeievich) 1841-1896 *Baker 92*
Fan, Changxin 1931- *WhoWor 93*
Fan, Guoxiang 1928- *WhoUN 92*
Fan, Hai-Fu 1933- *WhoWor 93*
Fan, Hung Y. 1947- *WhoAm 92*
Fan, Jiaxiang 1924- *WhoWor 93*
Fan, John C.C. 1943- *St&PR 93*
Fan, Ky 1914- *WhoAm 92*
Fan, Linda C. 1956- *WhoAmW 93*
Fan, Peter Joseph 1907-1992 *BioIn 17, NewYTBS 92*
Fan, Rita Lai-Tai 1945- *WhoAsAP 91*
Fan, Tian-You 1939- *WhoWor 93*
Fan, Yiu-Kwan 1944- *WhoWor 93*
Fan, Yun 1946- *WhoWor 93*
Fanaka, Jamaa *MiSFD 9*
Fanaroff, Sheri V.G. *Law&B 92*
Fancelli, Giuseppe 1833-1887 *OxDcOp*
Fancher, Donald Alden 1943- *St&PR 93*
Fancher, Genevieve Louella 1927- *WhoAmW 93*
Fancher, George H., Jr. 1939- *WhoWor 93*
Fancher, Helen Irene 1931- *WhoWor 93*
Fancher, Jane S. 1952- *ScF&FL 92*
Fancher, Mary Frank 1912- *WhoAmW 93*
Fancher, Michael Reilly 1946- *WhoAm 92*
Fancher, Robert Burney 1940- *St&PR 93, WhoAm 92*
Fancher, Robert Trenor 1954- *WhoE 93*
Fancher, Ronald L. 1943- *St&PR 93*
Fanchi, Joseph B. 1936- *St&PR 93*
Fanchiotti, Huner 1936- *WhoWor 93*
Fan Chung-yen 990-1053 *HarEnMi*
Fanciulli, Francesco 1850-1915 *Baker 92*
Fanciullo, John A. *St&PR 93*
Fanconi, Sergio Mario 1949- *WhoWor 93*

Fancy, Patricia B. Law&B 92
Fandreyer, Ernest Egon 1926- WhoE 93
Fandrich, Lamont H. 1951- WhoEmL 93
Fane, Julian BioIn 17
Fane, Julian 1927- ScF&FL 92
Fane, Lawrence 1933- WhoE 93
Fane, Mildmay 1601-1666 BioIn 17
Fanella, Nicholas Robert 1936- St&PR 93
Fanella, Robert J. 1950- St&PR 93
Fanelle, Carmella 1960- WhoAmW 93
Fanelli, Emil Joseph, Jr. 1942- St&PR 93
Fanelli, Ernest 1860-1917 Baker 92
Fanelli, Irene Susan 1956- WhoEmL 93
Fanelli, Joseph James 1924- WhoE 93
Fanelli, Leslie Ellen 1957- WhoE 93
Fanelli, Michele A. 1931- WhoScE 91-3
Faneuf, Leo J. 1925- St&PR 93
Faneuil, Edward J. Law&B 92
Fanfani, Luca 1941- WhoScE 91-3
Fang, Bertrand Tien-Chueh 1932- WhoAm 92
Fang, Frank Fu 1930- WhoAm 92
Fang, Joong 1923- WhoAm 92
Fang, Li-chih BioIn 17
Fang, Pen Jeng 1931- WhoAm 92, WhoE 93
Fang, Philip Shun-Sang 1941- WhoUN 92
Fang, Russell Ju Fu 1940- WhoAm 92
Fang Chih-min d1934 HarEnMi
Fanger, Donald Lee 1929- WhoAm 92
Fanger, Mark 1943- WhoE 93
Fanger, P.O. 1934- WhoScE 91-2
Fanget, Bernard J.C. 1944- WhoWor 93
Fang La d1122 HarEnMi
Fang Lizhi BioIn 17
Fangman, Dan St&PR 93
Fangman, James Arthur 1965- WhoSSW 93
Fangman, Richard Jerome, Jr. 1935- WhoSSW 93
Fang Weizhong 1928- WhoAsAP 91
Faning, Eaton 1850-1927 Baker 92
Fankhauser, Eric 1961- St&PR 93
Fanlund, Lari Marner 1953- WhoAmW 93
Fann, Albert BioIn 17
Fannin, Leon Francis 1926- WhoE 93
Fannin, Linda R. Law&B 92
Fannin, Melanie S. Law&B 92
Fanning, Barbara Jean 1926- WhoAmW 93
Fanning, Barry Hedges 1950- WhoAm 92, WhoEmL 93
Fanning, David BioIn 17
Fanning, Delvin Seymour 1931- WhoAm 92
Fanning, Eugene Patrick 1950- WhoWor 93
Fanning, James Jeffery 1948- WhoE 93
Fanning, John F. d1990 BioIn 17
Fanning, John Harold 1916-1990 BioIn 17
Fanning, Katherine 1927- DcLB 127 [port]
Fanning, Katherine Woodruff 1927- WhoAm 92, WhoAmW 93
Fanning, Margaret Beverly 1937- WhoAm 92
Fanning, Paul Thomas 1945- WhoSSW 93
Fanning, Peter Maurice 1955- WhoEmL 93
Fanning, Robert Allen 1931- WhoAm 92
Fanning, Robin C. Law&B 92
Fanning, Ronald Heath 1935- WhoWor 93
Fanning, William James 1927- WhoAm 92
Fannon, Diane WhoAm 92
Fannon, John J. 1934- WhoAm 92
Fano, Guido 1932- WhoScE 91-3
Fano, (Aronne) Guido Alberto 1875-1961 Baker 92
Fano, Robert Mario 1917- WhoAm 92
Fano, Ugo 1912- WhoAm 92
Fanon, Frantz 1925-1961 ConLC 74 [port]
Fanseen, James Foster 1928- WhoAm 92
Fanshaw, Judith L. Law&B 92
Fanshawe, Richard 1608-1666 DcLB 126 [port]
Fanshel, David 1923- WhoAm 92
Fan Shizhong BioIn 17
Fansten, Jacques MiSFD 9
Fant, Douglas Law&B 92
Fant, Eugene Robert 1919- WhoAm 92
Fant, George C., Jr. 1926- St&PR 93
Fant, John F., Jr. Law&B 92
Fant, Joseph Lewis, III 1928- WhoAm 92
Fant, Richard E. 1961- St&PR 93
Fanta, Paul Edward 1921- WhoAm 92
Fantaci, Mary Kathryn 1962- WhoAmW 93
Fantasia, Tilia BioIn 17
Fantauzzi, David A. Law&B 92
Fantazzi, Nick 1949- St&PR 93
Fante, James Peter 1950- WhoEmL 93
Fante, John 1909-1983 BioIn 17
Fante, Ronald Louis 1936- WhoAm 92
Fantel, Jane Isaacs 1946- WhoEmL 93
Fanthorpe, Lionel 1935- ScF&FL 92
Fanthorpe, Patricia 1938- ScF&FL 92
Fantigrossi, Frank Joseph 1949- St&PR 93
Fantin, Louis Anthony Law&B 92
Fantini, Deborah Ann 1958- WhoWor 93
Fantini, Pamela Crimi WhoAmW 93
Fantini, Robert S. 1927- St&PR 93
Fantin-Latour, Ignace Henri Jean Theodore 1836-1904 BioIn 17
Fantinus the Younger OxDcByz
Fanton, Dolores Pfrengle 1952- WhoEmL 93
Fanton, Jacques 1941- WhoScE 91-2
Fanton, Jonathan Foster 1943- WhoAm 92, WhoE 93
Fanton, Roland Benjamin 1943- WhoWrEP 92
Fantozzi, Gilbert 1942- WhoScE 91-2
Fantozzi, Gilbert 1962- WhoWor 93
Fantozzi, Peggy Ryone 1948- WhoAm 92
Fantozzi, Umberto St&PR 93
Fantz, Paul Richard 1941- WhoSSW 93
Fanu, J. Sheridan Le ScF&FL 92
Fanuele, Michael Anthony 1938- WhoAm 92, WhoE 93, WhoWor 93
Fanuele, Vincent James 1950- WhoEmL 93
Fanus, Pauline Rife 1925- WhoAmW 93, WhoE 93, WhoWor 93
Fanwick, Ernest 1926- WhoAm 92
Fanwick, Kerry Law&B 92
Faour, Anna Rose 1929- WhoAmW 93
Far, Sui Sin 1865-1914 AmWomWr 92
Fara, Gaetano Maria 1934- WhoScE 91-3
Fara, Giulio 1880-1949 Baker 92
Fara, John William 1942- St&PR 93, WhoAm 92
Farabow, Ford Franklin, Jr. 1938- WhoAm 92
Farace, Gus BioIn 17
Farace, Virginia Kapes 1945- WhoAmW 93
Faraci, John Vincent, Jr. 1950- WhoAm 92
Faraday, Bruce John 1919- WhoAm 92, WhoSSW 93, WhoWor 93
Faraday, M. M. ConAu 38NR, ScF&FL 92
Faraday, Michael 1791-1867 BioIn 17
Farady, John T. 1942- St&PR 93
Farage, Donald J. WhoAm 92
Faraghan, George Telford 1926- WhoE 93
Farago, John 1917- WhoSSW 93
Farago, Vincent J. Law&B 92
Faragria, Annette Law&B 92
Farah, Ardeshir BioIn 17
Farah, Benjamin Frederick 1956- WhoEmL 93
Farah, Caesar Elie 1929- WhoAm 92
Farah, Cynthia Weber 1949- WhoAmW 93, WhoSSW 93
Farah, Elie George 1962- WhoEmL 93
Farah, Joseph Francis 1954- WhoAm 92
Farah, Nuruddin 1945- DcLB 125 [port], IntLitE, IntvWPC 92 [port]
Farahar, Robert Martin 1928- WhoWor 93
Faraldo, Claude 1936- MiSFD 9
Faran, Ellen Webster 1951- WhoAmW 93
Faranda, John Paul 1957- WhoEmL 93
Faraone, Stephen Vincent 1956- WhoE 93
Faraone, Ted 1956- WhoE 93, WhoEmL 93
Faraoni, Melvin Ray 1944- St&PR 93
Fararo, Thomas John 1933- WhoAm 92
Farashuddin, Mohammed 1942- WhoUN 92
Farat, Jean Hanri 1951- WhoWor 93
Faraut, Jean-Pierre 1944- WhoWor 93
Farawell, John M. 1956- St&PR 93
Farb, Edith H. 1928- WhoAm 92
Farb, Thomas Forest 1956- WhoE 93, WhoEmL 93
Farber, Amy B. Law&B 92
Farber, Arthur David 1947- St&PR 93
Farber, Bernard 1922- WhoAm 92
Farber, Bernard John 1948- WhoEmL 93, WhoWor 93
Farber, Charlotte R. Law&B 92
Farber, Emmanuel 1918- WhoAm 92
Farber, Evan Ira 1922- WhoAm 92
Farber, Harvey 1941- St&PR 93
Farber, Isadore E. 1917- WhoAm 92
Farber, Jackie 1927- WhoAm 92
Farber, James ScF&FL 92
Farber, Jerry S. 1932- WhoE 93
Farber, John 1925- St&PR 93
Farber, John J. 1925- WhoAm 92
Farber, Lillian 1920- WhoAmW 93
Farber, Mark Law&B 92
Farber, Milton H. d1991 BioIn 17
Farber, Norma 1909-1984 MajAI [port]
Farber, Paul Francis 1951- St&PR 93
Farber, Phillip Andrew 1934- WhoE 93
Farber, Randal Scott 1959- WhoSSW 93
Farber, Seymour Morgan 1912- WhoAm 92
Farber, Steven Glenn 1946- WhoEmL 93
Farber, Thomas A. Law&B 92
Farber, Viola Anna 1931- WhoAm 92
Farberman, Harold 1929- Baker 92
Farberman, Harold 1930- WhoAm 92
Farbiszewski, Ryszard 1928- WhoScE 91-4
Farbman, Jon 1943- St&PR 93
Farbstein, Joshua Heschel F. 1870-1948 PolBiDi
Farbstein, Marvin 1931- WhoE 93
Farcau, Bruce 1951- ConAu 138
Farcus, Joseph Jay 1944- WhoSSW 93
Fardeau, Michel WhoScE 91-2
Fardink, Michael d1991 BioIn 17
Farebrother, Robert Charles 1953- WhoWor 93
Faredin, Imre 1922- WhoScE 91-4
Fareed, Ahmed Ali 1932- WhoWor 93
Farel, Guillaume 1489-1565 BioIn 17
Farell, H. Dan 1949- St&PR 93
Farenga, Patrick Lawrence 1957- WhoEmL 93
Farenthold, Frances Tarlton 1926- PolPar, WhoAm 92, WhoAmW 93
Farentino, James 1938- WhoAm 92
Farer, Tom Joel 1935- WhoAm 92
Fares, Louis d1991 BioIn 17
Faresi, Renato 1930- WhoScE 91-3
Farey, Jan E. St&PR 93
Farge, Yves-M.P. 1939- WhoScE 91-2
Fargher, John Stanley Wakelam, Jr. 1944- WhoSSW 93
Fargis, Paul Mckenna 1939- St&PR 93, WhoAm 92
Fargnoli, John A., Jr. 1946- St&PR 93
Fargo, Alvin W. 1915-1990 BioIn 17
Fargo, James 1938- MiSFD 9
Fargo, John Jay 1950- WhoEmL 93
Fargo, Kate Mills AmWomPl
Fargo, Louis James 1938- WhoAm 92
Fargo, Wilson D. Law&B 92
Farha, Alfred S. 1933- St&PR 93
Farha, James T. Law&B 92
Farha, James Tannel 1941- St&PR 93
Farha, William Farah 1908- WhoAm 92
Farhi, Edward 1952- WhoE 93
Farhi, Leon Elie 1923- WhoAm 92
Farho, James Henry, Jr. 1924- WhoWor 93
Faria, A(nthony) J(ohn) 1944- ConAu 40NR
Faria, Jose Brandao 1952- WhoWor 93
Faria, Luciano L.O. 1921- WhoScE 91-3
Faria, Luciano L. Oliveira 1921- WhoWor 93
Faria, Thomas George 1926- St&PR 93
Farias, Fred, III 1957- WhoSSW 93
Farias de Isassi, Teresa 1878- DcMexL
Faricy, Richard Thomas 1928- WhoAm 92
Farid, Nadir Rashad 1944- WhoWor 93
Farid Ahmad Mazdak, Comrade 1958- WhoAsAP 91
Faridi, Hamed 1947- WhoE 93
Fariello, Frank Anthony 1934- St&PR 93
Faries, Charles E., Jr. 1933- St&PR 93
Farigoule, Louis ScF&FL 92
Farin BioIn 17
Farin, Lou Joseph 1943- St&PR 93
Farina, Almo 1950- WhoWor 93
Farina, Ana Beatriz 1950- WhoAmW 93, WhoEmL 93, WhoWor 93
Farina, Carlo Alessandro 1942- WhoWor 93
Farina, Carolyn BioIn 17
Farina, Francis Joseph 1951- WhoEmL 93
Farina, George Edward 1953- WhoSSW 93
Farina, John G. 1951- WhoIns 93
Farina, Julie Lynn 1950- WhoEmL 93
Farina, Mark D. 1949- St&PR 93
Farina, Nick Charles 1942- WhoAm 92
Farina, Peter R. 1946- WhoAm 92, WhoE 93, WhoEmL 93
Farina, Robert A. 1943- St&PR 93
Farina, Vincent M. 1953- St&PR 93
Farinacci, Anna 1923- WhoScE 91-3
Farina Hille, Francisco Javier 1933- WhoUN 92
Farinas, Carlos 1934- Baker 92
Farinella, Paul James 1926- WhoAm 92
Farinelli 1705-1782 Baker 92, IntDcOp [port], OxDcOp
Farinelli, Giuseppe 1769-1836 OxDcOp
Farinelli, Giuseppe (Francesco) 1769-1836 Baker 92
Farinelli, Jean L. 1946- St&PR 93, WhoAm 92
Farinelli, Ugo 1930- WhoScE 91-3
Farinholt, Larkin H. 1905-1990 BioIn 17
Farinholt, Lewis Sharp 1952- WhoSSW 93
Farino, Ernest MiSFD 9
Faris, Charlotte Lamie 1944- WhoSSW 93
Faris, Cheryl J. Law&B 92
Faris, Corinne M. 1955- St&PR 93
Faris, Eliot Tim Ransom 1942- WhoSSW 93
Faris, Frank Edgar 1919- WhoAm 92
Faris, George N. 1941- St&PR 93
Faris, Ingrid Barth 1951- WhoAmW 93, WhoEmL 93
Faris, Matthew Scott 1965- WhoEmL 93, WhoSSW 93
Faris, Mustapha 1933- WhoWor 93
Faris, Wendy Bush 1945- WhoSSW 93
Farish, Charles Morrison 1946- WhoEmL 93
Farish, Owen WhoScE 91-1
Farish, Teresa Irene 1953- WhoEmL 93
Farish, Terry 1947- ConAu 137
Farison, James Blair 1938- WhoAm 92
Fariss, Bruce Lindsay 1934- WhoAm 92
Faris-Stockem, Debbie Anne 1955- WhoEmL 93
Farjeon, Eleanor 1881-1965 ChlFicS, MajAI [port], ScF&FL 92
Farjeon, Harry 1878-1948 Baker 92
Farkas, Alan Charles 1960- WhoWor 93
Farkas, Andrew E. 1947- St&PR 93
Farkas, Charles Michael 1951- WhoE 93
Farkas, Edmund (Odon) 1851-1912 Baker 92
Farkas, Edward Barrister 1954- WhoE 93
Farkas, Endre 1948- BioIn 17, WhoCanL 92
Farkas, Ferenc 1905- Baker 92
Farkas, Israel 1948- St&PR 93
Farkas, J.H. St&PR 93
Farkas, James Paul 1947- WhoE 93
Farkas, John 1942- St&PR 93
Farkas, Jozsef 1927- WhoScE 91-4
Farkas, Jozsef 1933- WhoScE 91-4
Farkas, Laszlo 1947- WhoScE 91-4
Farkas, Laszlo Gyula 1932- WhoScE 91-4
Farkas, Laszlo Peter 1943- WhoScE 91-4
Farkas, Lisa Jean Kovacs 1962- WhoE 93
Farkas, Otto 1930- WhoScE 91-4
Farkas, Paul Stephen 1952- WhoE 93
Farkas, Philip (Francis) 1914- Baker 92
Farkas, Robin L. BioIn 17
Farkas, Robin Lewis 1933- St&PR 93, WhoAm 92
Farkas, Ruth Lewis 1906- WhoAm 92
Farkas, Scott James 1960- WhoWor 93
Farkas, Stephen Gerard 1960- WhoEmL 93
Farkas, Steven D. Law&B 92
Farkas, Tibor 1929- WhoScE 91-4
Farkes, Gary S. 1941- St&PR 93
Farland, Eugene Hector 1918- WhoWor 93
Farley, Andrew Newell 1934- WhoAm 92
Farley, Barbara Suzanne 1949- WhoEmL 93
Farley, Benjamin Wirt 1935- WhoSSW 93
Farley, Carol J. (Mcdole) 1936- DcAmChF 1960
Farley, Carole 1946- WhoAm 92
Farley, Carole Ann 1946- Baker 92
Farley, D. Stephen 1928- WhoAm 92
Farley, Daniel W. Law&B 92
Farley, Daniel W. 1955- WhoAm 92
Farley, Daniel William 1955- St&PR 93
Farley, Denise Durante 1956- WhoAmW 93
Farley, Dennis C. Law&B 92
Farley, Donal Eymard 1935- WhoE 93
Farley, Donald 1960- WhoE 93
Farley, Donald W. Law&B 92
Farley, Edward John 1934- WhoAm 92, WhoWor 93
Farley, Edward Raymond, Jr. 1918- WhoAm 92
Farley, Emma Betsey AmWomPl
Farley, Eugene Joseph 1950- WhoE 93, WhoEmL 93
Farley, Eugene Shedden, Jr. 1927- WhoAm 92
Farley, Frazier 1952- St&PR 93
Farley, Frederick A. 1952- St&PR 93
Farley, Gail Conley 1936- WhoSSW 93
Farley, Hobert Franklin 1933- St&PR 93
Farley, Hugh T. WhoE 93
Farley, J.M. WhoScE 91-1
Farley, Jacqueline Merrill 1939- WhoAmW 93
Farley, Jacquelyn Annette 1964- WhoAmW 93
Farley, James A. 1888-1976 PolPar
Farley, James Aloysius 1888-1976 BioIn 17
Farley, James B. 1930- St&PR 93
Farley, James Bernard 1930- WhoAm 92
Farley, James Duncan 1926- St&PR 93, WhoAm 92, WhoE 93
Farley, James Newton 1928- St&PR 93, WhoAm 92
Farley, James Parker 1924- WhoAm 92, WhoWor 93
Farley, James Patrick 1949- WhoEmL 93
Farley, James Thomas 1925- WhoAm 92
Farley, Jan Edwin Law&B 92
Farley, Jennie Tiffany Towle 1932- WhoAmW 93
Farley, Joan R. Law&B 92
Farley, John Joseph 1920- WhoAm 92
Farley, John Michael 1930- WhoAm 92
Farley, Joseph 1961- WhoWrEP 92
Farley, Joseph J. 1923- St&PR 93
Farley, Joseph M. 1927- St&PR 93

Farley, Joseph McConnell 1927- WhoAm 92, WhoSSW 93
Farley, Kathleen M. 1936- WhoAmW 93
Farley, Leon Alex 1935- WhoAm 92
Farley, Lyle O. 1944- St&PR 93
Farley, Margaret Mary 1926- WhoAm 92
Farley, Max F. 1944- St&PR 93
Farley, Myron Foster 1921- WhoWrEP 92
Farley, Norvil Lee 1922- St&PR 93
Farley, Paul Emerson 1930- St&PR 93, WhoAm 92
Farley, Paul John, Jr. 1951- WhoEmL 93
Farley, Peggy Ann 1947- WhoAm 92, WhoAmW 93, WhoE 93, WhoEmL 93, WhoWor 93
Farley, Philip Judson 1916- WhoAm 92
Farley, R. Frazier Law&B 92
Farley, Robert D. 1941- St&PR 93
Farley, Robert Donald 1941- WhoAm 92
Farley, Robert James 1932- WhoE 93
Farley, Robert John 1952- WhoEmL 93
Farley, Robert Joseph 1960- WhoEmL 93
Farley, Ronald E. 1962- St&PR 93
Farley, Rosemary Carroll 1952- WhoE 93
Farley, Russell Clifford 1957- WhoEmL 93
Farley, Stacey Jeanne WhoWrEP 92
Farley, Stephen A. 1944- St&PR 93
Farley, Steve d1991 BioIn 17
Farley, Terrence Michael 1930- WhoAm 92
Farley, Thomas T. 1934- WhoWor 93
Farley, Walter 1915-1989 BioIn 17, ScF&FL 92
Farley, Walter (Lorimer) 1915-1989 MajAI [port]
Farley, William 1942- St&PR 93
Farley, William Downs 1835-1863 BioIn 17
Farley, William F. 1942- WhoAm 92, WhoSSW 93
Farley, William Patrick Law&B 92
Farlie, Dennis John Gerald WhoScE 91-1
Farling, David James 1960- WhoEmL 93
Farling, Robert J. 1936- St&PR 93
Farlow, Lynne Ann 1960- WhoEmL 93
Farlow, Michael William 1957- WhoEmL 93
Farlow, Stanley Jerry 1937- WhoE 93
Farlow, Tal 1921- BioIn 17
Farmaian, Sattareh Farman- BioIn 17
Farmakides, John Basil WhoAm 92
Farman, Allan George 1949- WhoEmL 93
Farman, Richard D. 1935- St&PR 93
Farman, Richard Donald 1935- WhoAm 92
Farmanfarmaian, A. Verdi 1929- WhoE 93
Farman-Farmaian, Ghaffar 1930- WhoWor 93
Farman-Farmaian, Sattareh BioIn 17
Farmar, George Edwin 1923- St&PR 93
Farmar, Robert 1717-1778 BioIn 17
Farmen, William Newton 1939- WhoAm 92
Farmer, A.R. WhoScE 91-1
Farmer, Adella BioIn 17
Farmer, Bruce J. 1927- St&PR 93
Farmer, Bryce E. 1951- WhoIns 93
Farmer, Catherine Armbruster 1948- WhoEmL 93
Farmer, Charles Albert 1930- St&PR 93
Farmer, Clarence Eugene, Jr. Law&B 92
Farmer, Crofton Bernard 1931- WhoAm 92
Farmer, Dalen L.P. Law&B 92
Farmer, David Lowell 1945- St&PR 93
Farmer, Deborah Lyn 1954- WhoEmL 93
Farmer, Derek ScF&FL 92
Farmer, Donald Arthur, Jr. 1944- WhoAm 92
Farmer, Donald Frederick 1944- St&PR 93
Farmer, E. Peter Law&B 92
Farmer, Elaine F. 1937- WhoAmW 93
Farmer, Fannie 1857-1915 WomChHR [port]
Farmer, Fannie Merritt 1857-1915 BioIn 17, GayN
Farmer, Forest J. BioIn 17
Farmer, Frances 1913?-1970 IntDcF 2-3 [port]
Farmer, Gary P. 1943- St&PR 93
Farmer, Guy Otto, II 1941- WhoAm 92
Farmer, H. Randolph 1939- St&PR 93
Farmer, Hallie BioIn 17
Farmer, Henry George 1882-1965 Baker 92
Farmer, J.B. WhoScE 91-1
Farmer, James BioIn 17
Farmer, James 1920- EncAACR, WhoAm 92
Farmer, James A., II 1956- WhoE 93
Farmer, James B. Law&B 92
Farmer, James Prentice, Jr. 1951- WhoEmL 93
Farmer, Janene Elizabeth 1946- WhoAmW 93
Farmer, Joe Sam 1931- WhoAm 92, WhoSSW 93
Farmer, John Baker 92
Farmer, John 1836-1901 Baker 92
Farmer, John David 1939- WhoAm 92
Farmer, John Martin 1934- WhoE 93
Farmer, Kathryn Loren 1961- WhoAmW 93
Farmer, Kenneth Wayne 1938- St&PR 93
Farmer, Larry Gene 1949- WhoSSW 93
Farmer, Malcolm, III 1939- WhoAm 92
Farmer, Martha Knight 1938- WhoAmW 93, WhoSSW 93
Farmer, Martin T. 1941- St&PR 93
Farmer, Mary Bauder 1953- WhoAmW 93, WhoEmL 93
Farmer, Nellanna 1947- WhoAmW 93
Farmer, Norman Kittrell, Jr. 1934- WhoSSW 93
Farmer, Penelope 1939- BioIn 17, ScF&FL 92
Farmer, Penelope (Jane) 1939- ConAu 37NR, MajAI [port]
Farmer, Peter Brownlee WhoScE 91-1
Farmer, Philip Jose BioIn 17
Farmer, Philip Jose 1918- ScF&FL 92, WhoWrEP 92
Farmer, Phillip W. 1938- St&PR 93
Farmer, Richard Edwin 1949- WhoAm 92, WhoSSW 93
Farmer, Richard Gilbert 1931- WhoAm 92
Farmer, Richard N. 1928- ScF&FL 92
Farmer, Richard Neal Law&B 92
Farmer, Richard T. 1934- WhoAm 92
Farmer, Richard Thirl 1934- St&PR 93
Farmer, Robert E. 1929- St&PR 93
Farmer, Robert Lindsay 1922- WhoAm 92
Farmer, Roy F. 1916- St&PR 93
Farmer, Susan Baker 1953- WhoEmL 93
Farmer, Susan Lawson 1942- WhoAm 92, WhoE 93
Farmer, Thomas Laurence 1923- WhoAm 92
Farmer, Thomas Wohlsen 1914- WhoAm 92
Farmer, Timothy David 1954- WhoEmL 93
Farmer, Virginia AmWomPl
Farmer, William A. 1953- St&PR 93
Farmer, William Michael 1956- WhoEmL 93
Farmer, William Silas, Jr. 1922- WhoE 93
Farmerie, Samuel Albert 1931- WhoE 93
Farmer-Patrick, Sandra WhoAmW 93
Farmery, Peter William 1950- WhoWor 93
Farmiloe, Dorothy 1920- WhoCanL 92
Farnaby, Giles c. 1563-1640 Baker 92
Farnadi, Edith 1921-1973 Baker 92
Farnagle, Alphaed E. WhoWrEP 92
Farnam, W(alter) Lynnwood 1885-1930 Baker 92
Farnam, Walter Edward 1941- St&PR 93, WhoAm 92, WhoIns 93
Farnan, Joseph James, Jr. 1945- WhoAm 92, WhoE 93
Farncombe, Charles (Frederick) 1919- Baker 92
Farndon, John Richard WhoScE 91-1
Farndon, Peter 1953-1983 See Pretenders, The ConMus 8
Farnel, Frank Jacques 1962- WhoWor 93
Farnell, Gerald William 1925- WhoAm 92
Farnell, Kathleen Patricia 1943- WhoAmW 93
Farnell, Patricia 1949- WhoAmW 93
Farner, Eleanor G. St&PR 93
Farner, Peter Worden 1954- WhoWor 93
Farnetti, Giorgio 1923- WhoWor 93
Farney, Joseph Dale 1964- WhoSSW 93
Farney, Thomas Patrick 1948- WhoEmL 93
Farnham, Andrew Warner WhoScE 91-1
Farnham, Anthony Edward 1930- WhoAm 92
Farnham, David A. Law&B 92
Farnham, David Alexander 1946- WhoEmL 93
Farnham, George Paulding BioIn 17
Farnham, George Railton 1914- WhoAm 92
Farnham, Paulding BioIn 17
Farnham, Richard B. d1992 NewYTBS 92
Farnham, Sherman Brett 1912- WhoAm 92
Farnham, Thomas Javery 1938- WhoE 93
Farnham, Thomas Jefferson 1804-1848 BioIn 17
Farnham, Wallace Dean 1928- WhoAm 92
Farnham, Willard Carlton 1937- St&PR 93
Farnham, William H. 1936- St&PR 93
Farningham, David Alexander Halse WhoScE 91-1
Farnkart, James Edward 1946- WhoE 93
Farnow, Arthur D. 1916- St&PR 93
Farnow, Richard A. St&PR 93
Farnsley, Charles P. 1907-1990 BioIn 17
Farnsworth, A. Randall Law&B 92
Farnsworth, Cherrill Kay 1948- WhoAmW 93, WhoEmL 93
Farnsworth, Edward Allan 1928- WhoAm 92
Farnsworth, Elizabeth Brooks 1952- WhoSSW 93
Farnsworth, Frank Albert WhoAm 92
Farnsworth, Harrison E. 1896-1989 BioIn 17
Farnsworth, Jack Lee 1946- WhoAm 92
Farnsworth, James Virgel 1951- St&PR 93
Farnsworth, Janice L. 1938- WhoAmW 93
Farnsworth, Jeffrey Earl 1959- WhoEmL 93
Farnsworth, John 1828-1863 BioIn 17
Farnsworth, Karan L. Law&B 92
Farnsworth, Philip R. 1941- St&PR 93
Farnsworth, Philip Richeson 1941- WhoAm 92
Farnsworth, Philo T. 1906-1971 BioIn 17
Farnsworth, Richard 1920- WhoAm 92
Farnsworth, Shorty WhoWrEP 92
Farnsworth, T. Brooke 1945- WhoSSW 93, WhoWor 93
Farnsworth, Ted BioIn 17
Farnum, Dustin 1874-1929 BioIn 17
Farnum, Franklyn 1883-1961 BioIn 17
Farnum, Jonathan K. 1939- St&PR 93
Farnum, Mark 1923- St&PR 93
Farnum, Sylvia Arlyce 1936- WhoAm 92
Farnum, William 1876-1953 BioIn 17
Farnworth, Frank 1933- WhoScE 91-1
Faro, Geraldine AmWomPl
Farokhi, Elizabeth 1948- WhoAmW 93, WhoEmL 93
Faron, Robert Steven 1947- WhoEmL 93
Farooq, Ghazi M. 1942- WhoUN 92
Farooqi, M. Nadeem 1960- WhoWor 93
Farooqi, Zarreen Hayat 1948- WhoWor 93
Farooquee, Jim St&PR 93
Farooq Yaqubi, Ghulam 1937- WhoAsAP 91
Farouk 1920-1965 DcTwHis
Farouk, I, King of Egypt 1920-1965 BioIn 17
Farouk, Bakhtier 1951- WhoE 93
Farouq 1920-1965 BioIn 17
Farouq, Fadlullah 1934- WhoWor 93
Farquer, Thomas Lee Law&B 92
Farquhar, Beverly Kelly 1936- WhoAmW 93
Farquhar, David (Andross) 1928- Baker 92
Farquhar, Eva Lois 1935- St&PR 93
Farquhar, George WhoScE 91-1
Farquhar, George 1677?-1707 BioIn 17
Farquhar, George 1678-1707 LitC 21 [port]
Farquhar, John William 1927- WhoAm 92
Farquhar, Karen Lee 1958- WhoAmW 93
Farquhar, Karen Sachiko 1961- WhoEmL 93
Farquhar, Marilyn Gist 1928- WhoAm 92, WhoAmW 93
Farquhar, Norman 1921- WhoAm 92
Farquhar, Paul George 1949- WhoWrEP 92
Farquhar, Peter Henry 1947- WhoEmL 93
Farquhar, Robert L. 1946- WhoScE 91-1
Farquhar, Robin Hugh 1938- WhoAm 92
Farquhar, William T.N. Law&B 92
Farquharson, Donald E. 1947- St&PR 93
Farquharson, Gordon M. 1928- St&PR 93
Farquharson, Gordon MacKay 1928- WhoAm 92, WhoE 93
Farquharson, Walter Henry 1936- WhoAm 92, WhoE 93
Farr, Barry Miller 1951- WhoAm 92
Farr, Carla Lake 1949- WhoSSW 93
Farr, Charles Sims 1920- WhoAm 92, WhoE 93, WhoWor 93
Farr, Cheryl Anne 1955- WhoAmW 93
Farr, David N. BioIn 17
Farr, David N. 1955- St&PR 93
Farr, David Robert 1937- WhoScE 91-4
Farr, Eric W. 1947- St&PR 93
Farr, Fredrick Sharon 1910- WhoAm 92
Farr, Henry Bartow, Jr. 1921- WhoAm 92
Farr, James Francis 1911- WhoAm 92, WhoE 93, WhoWor 93
Farr, James Michael 1946- WhoWrEP 92
Farr, James Woodhull 1952- WhoE 93
Farr, Jo-Ann Hunter 1936- WhoAm 92, WhoE 93
Farr, John Wesley 1920- WhoSSW 93
Farr, Judith Banzer 1937- WhoE 93
Farr, Lee Edward 1907- WhoWor 93
Farr, Lona Mae 1941- WhoAmW 93, WhoE 93
Farr, Marie Terese 1940- WhoAmW 93
Farr, Mel 1944- St&PR 93
Farr, Morrill S. 1910- St&PR 93
Farr, Norman Nelson 1928- WhoAm 92
Farr, Patricia Hudak 1945- WhoAmW 93
Farr, Rebecca Ann 1958- WhoAmW 93
Farr, Richard Claborn 1928- WhoAm 92
Farr, Richard Studley 1922- WhoAm 92
Farr, Sidney Saylor 1932- WhoAmW 93
Farr, Steven 1956- WhoSSW 93
Farr, Susan Elizabeth 1955- WhoAmW 93
Farr, Thomas C. Law&B 92
Farr, Thomas Carey 1952- WhoEmL 93, WhoIns 93
Farr, Ursula Rita WhoAmW 93
Farr, Walter Emil, Jr. 1945- WhoSSW 93, WhoWor 93
Farr, Walter Greene, Jr. 1925- WhoAm 92
Farr, William Daven 1910- St&PR 93
Farr, William Joseph 1947- WhoEmL 93
Farr, William Sharon 1903- St&PR 93
Farra, Chucri Ronald 1948- WhoE 93, WhoEmL 93, WhoWor 93
Farradane, Jason 1906-1989 BioIn 17
Farragut, David Glasgow 1801-1870 BioIn 17, HarEnMi
Farrakhan, Louis BioIn 17
Farrakhan, Louis 1933- AfrAmBi, CurBio 92 [port]
Farrall, George William 1959- WhoE 93, WhoEmL 93, WhoWor 93
Farran, William N., III Law&B 92
Farrance, Roger BioIn 17
Farrand, Donald George 1939- WhoE 93
Farrand, George Nixon, Jr. 1936- WhoE 93
Farrand, James C. BioIn 17
Farrand, Livingston 1867-1939 BioIn 17
Farrant, Elizabeth 1914- WhoWrEP 92
Farrant, John fl. 16th cent.- Baker 92
Farrant, John 1575?-1618 See Farrant, John fl. 16th cent.- Baker 92
Farrant, Paul Edward WhoScE 91-1
Farrant, Richard c. 1525-1580 Baker 92
Farranto, Peter Charles Law&B 92
Farrar, Beverly Jayne 1928- WhoAm 92, WhoAmW 93
Farrar, Clarence Raymond 1934- St&PR 93
Farrar, Davis Sutcliffe 1952- WhoEmL 93
Farrar, Donald Eugene 1931- WhoAm 92
Farrar, Edward A. Law&B 92
Farrar, Elaine Willardson WhoAmW 93
Farrar, Elaine Willardson 1929- WhoAm 92, WhoWor 93
Farrar, Eleanor BioIn 17
Farrar, Elizabeth Grace Turrell 1957- WhoAmW 93, WhoEmL 93
Farrar, Ernest (Bristow) 1885-1918 Baker 92
Farrar, Fletcher F. 1921- St&PR 93
Farrar, Frank Leroy 1929- WhoAm 92
Farrar, Geraldine 1882-1967 Baker 92, IntDcOp [port], OxDcOp
Farrar, Henry Cheairs 1926- WhoSSW 93
Farrar, James Jackson 1939- St&PR 93
Farrar, James Martin 1948- WhoE 93
Farrar, Joe Edmund 1947- St&PR 93
Farrar, John Edson, II 1938- WhoWor 93
Farrar, Lynn Anne 1956- WhoSSW 93
Farrar, Marjorie S. 1922- St&PR 93
Farrar, Mark Eldon 1950- WhoEmL 93
Farrar, Pauline Elizabeth 1928- WhoAmW 93, WhoSSW 93
Farrar, Ronald 1947- St&PR 93
Farrar, Roy Alfred WhoScE 91-1
Farrar, Scott WhoAm 92
Farrar, Stephen Prescott 1944- WhoAm 92
Farrar, Stewart 1916- ScF&FL 92
Farrar, William Wesley 1940- WhoSSW 93
Farre, Thomas R. 1946- WhoWrEP 92
Farrehi, Cyrus 1935- WhoAm 92
Farrell, Anne Van Ness 1935- WhoAmW 93
Farrell, Barbara B. Law&B 92
Farrell, Bill BioIn 17
Farrell, Carmen Chidester Law&B 92
Farrell, Catherine L. Law&B 92
Farrell, Charles 1901-1990 BioIn 17
Farrell, Charles F. 1930- St&PR 93
Farrell, David C. 1933- St&PR 93
Farrell, David Coakley 1933- WhoAm 92
Farrell, David J. 1950- St&PR 93
Farrell, Dennis Joseph 1962- WhoEmL 93
Farrell, Duncan Graham Stuart 1935- WhoE 93
Farrell, Edgar Henry 1924- WhoAm 92, WhoE 93, WhoWor 93
Farrell, Edmund J. 1927- ScF&FL 92
Farrell, Edmund James 1927- WhoAm 92, WhoSSW 93, WhoWrEP 92
Farrell, Edward C. Law&B 92
Farrell, Edward Joseph 1917- WhoAm 92, WhoWor 93
Farrell, Edward Joseph 1941- WhoWor 93
Farrell, Edward Patrick 1943- WhoWor 93
Farrell, Edward Vincent 1940- St&PR 93
Farrell, Eileen 1920- Baker 92, IntDcOp
Farrell, Elaine BioIn 17
Farrell, Eugene George 1905- WhoAm 92
Farrell, Frank A., Jr. 1938- St&PR 93

Farrell, Gaston Damian 1961- WhoEmL 93
Farrell, Harold Maron, Jr. 1940- WhoE 93
Farrell, Harry (Guy) 1924- ConAu 139
Farrell, Henry Moseley 1936- St&PR 93
Farrell, J.G. 1935-1979 BioIn 17
Farrell, J. Michael 1941- WhoAm 92
Farrell, Jackson T. 1904-1978 ScF&FL 92
Farrell, James B. Law&B 92
Farrell, James E. 1940- St&PR 93
Farrell, James Gordon 1935-1979 BioIn 17
Farrell, James H. 1926- St&PR 93
Farrell, James Joseph 1949- WhoWrEP 92
Farrell, James T. 1904-1979 BioIn 17, MagSAmL [port]
Farrell, Jennette Elaine 1961- WhoAmW 93
Farrell, Jeremiah Edward 1937- WhoAm 92
Farrell, Jim BioIn 17
Farrell, John J. St&PR 93
Farrell, John L., Jr. 1929- WhoAm 92
Farrell, John R. 1950- St&PR 93
Farrell, John S. 1938- St&PR 93
Farrell, John Stanislaus 1931- WhoWor 93
Farrell, John Timothy 1947- WhoAm 92
Farrell, Joseph 1935- WhoWor 93
Farrell, Joseph Anthony Law&B 92
Farrell, Joseph Christopher 1935- St&PR 93, WhoAm 92, WhoWor 93
Farrell, Joseph Michael 1922- WhoAm 92
Farrell, June Eleanor 1916- WhoAmW 93
Farrell, June Martinick 1940- WhoAm 92, WhoAmW 93
Farrell, Kathy 1946- St&PR 93
Farrell, Kenneth Hays 1942- WhoSSW 93
Farrell, Kevin John 1957- WhoEmL 93
Farrell, Louis G. 1955- St&PR 93
Farrell, M.J. BioIn 17
Farrell, Marta Layne Engle 1960- WhoWor 93
Farrell, Mary Cooney 1949- WhoAm 92
Farrell, Mary L. Law&B 92
Farrell, Mike 1937- BioIn 17
Farrell, Mike 1939- MiSFD 9, WhoAm 92
Farrell, Neal F. Law&B 92
Farrell, Neal Francis 1934- St&PR 93, WhoAm 92
Farrell, Pamela Barnard WhoWrEP 92
Farrell, Pamela Barnard 1943- WhoAmW 93
Farrell, Patric d1992 NewYTBS 92
Farrell, Patricia Ann 1945- WhoWor 93
Farrell, Patrick L. Law&B 92
Farrell, Patrick Leo Law&B 92
Farrell, Paul Edward 1926- WhoAm 92
Farrell, Paul Harry 1927- WhoAm 92
Farrell, Perry 1960- News 92 [port]
Farrell, Peter T. d1992 NewYTBS 92 [port]
Farrell, Raymond Maurice, Jr. 1940- WhoE 93
Farrell, Regis H. 1950- St&PR 93
Farrell, Richard Davern 1960- WhoSSW 93
Farrell, Richard J. 1943- St&PR 93
Farrell, Robert G., Jr. Law&B 92
Farrell, Robert Joel, II 1965- WhoSSW 93
Farrell, Robert Steven 1960- WhoEmL 93
Farrell, Robert T. 1938- ScF&FL 92
Farrell, Rodger Edward 1932- WhoAm 92
Farrell, Ronald G. St&PR 93
Farrell, Ronald William 1951- WhoE 93
Farrell, Sally SmATA 72
Farrell, Sharon 1949- WhoAm 92
Farrell, Sherri K. Law&B 92
Farrell, Simon 1960- ScF&FL 92
Farrell, Susan Florence 1952- WhoEmL 93
Farrell, Suzanne WhoAm 92, WhoAmW 93
Farrell, Suzanne 1945- BioIn 17
Farrell, Terrence J. Law&B 92
Farrell, Thomas D. 1948- St&PR 93
Farrell, Thomas Dinan 1948- WhoEmL 93
Farrell, Thomas E. Law&B 92
Farrell, Thomas Michael Law&B 92
Farrell, William Anthony Law&B 92
Farrell, William Joseph 1936- WhoAm 92
Farrell, William Patrick 1929- St&PR 93
Farrell-Donaldson, Marie Delois 1947- WhoAmW 93
Farrell-Logan, Vivian WhoE 93
Farrelly, Alexander 1923- WhoAm 92, WhoSSW 93, WhoWor 93
Farrelly, Alexander A. 1923- DcCPCAm
Farrelly, Cyril J., Jr. 1929- St&PR 93
Farrelly, Joseph William 1944- St&PR 93
Farrelly, Thomas Joseph Law&B 92
Farren, David 1934- ScF&FL 92
Farren, J. WhoScE 91-1
Farren, J. Michael BioIn 17
Farren, J. Michael 1952- WhoAm 92
Farren, Merritt David Law&B 92
Farren, Mick 1943- ScF&FL 92
Farren, Owen 1950- St&PR 93
Farren, Pat 1944- WhoWrEP 92
Farrenc, (Jacques Hippolyte) Aristide 1794-1865 Baker 92
Farrenc, Louise 1804-1875 BioIn 17
Farrenc, (Jeanne-) Louise 1804-1875 Baker 92
Farrenc, Victorine 1826-1859 See Farrenc, (Jeanne-) Louise 1804-1875 Baker 92
Farrer, Claire Anne Rafferty 1936- WhoAmW 93
Farrer, Franklin E. 1946- St&PR 93
Farrer, Rosa Maria Zaldivar 1937- WhoAmW 93
Farrer, Sanford M. 1931-1992 BioIn 17
Farrer, William Cameron 1922- WhoAm 92
Farrer-Meschan, Rachel 1915- WhoWor 93
Farries, James M. 1940- St&PR 93
Farrigan, Julia Ann 1943- WhoAmW 93
Farrin, James Smith 1936- St&PR 93
Farringdon, Michael George 1936- WhoWor 93
Farringer, John Lee, III 1947- WhoSSW 93
Farrington, David G. Law&B 92
Farrington, Geoffrey 1955- ScF&FL 92
Farrington, Helen Agnes 1945- WhoE 93
Farrington, Hugh G. 1945- WhoAm 92, WhoE 93
Farrington, James Francis 1926- St&PR 93
Farrington, Jerry S. 1934- St&PR 93, WhoAm 92, WhoSSW 93
Farrington, John Hugh WhoScE 91-1
Farrington, John P. 1933- WhoIns 93
Farrington, John Peter 1933- St&PR 93
Farrington, Mary Elizabeth Pruett 1898- BioIn 17
Farrington, Michael H. 1940- St&PR 93
Farrington, Paul J. 1933- St&PR 93
Farrington, Robert Bois 1957- WhoEmL 93
Farrington, Russell A., Jr. 1924- St&PR 93
Farrington, Sara d1992 BioIn 17
Farrington, Sara Chisholm d1992 NewYTBS 92
Farrington, William Benford 1921- WhoAm 92
Farrington, William J. Law&B 92
Farrington-Hopf, Susan Kay 1940- WhoAmW 93
Farrior, Dianne Rodgers 1950- WhoEmL 93
Farrior, Evelyn Settle 1946- WhoSSW 93
Farrior, J. Rex, Jr. 1927- WhoWor 93
Farrior, Joseph Brown 1911- WhoAm 92
Farris, Alice Ward 1959- St&PR 93, WhoAmW 93
Farris, Bain Joseph 1949- WhoAm 92
Farris, Charles Lowell 1910- WhoAm 92
Farris, David J. 1935- St&PR 93
Farris, Edward Thompson 1925- WhoWor 93
Farris, Fred J. 1939- St&PR 93
Farris, Greer 1942- WhoSSW 93
Farris, Jack M. Law&B 92
Farris, Jefferson Davis 1927- WhoAm 92
Farris, Jeffrey Ian 1969- WhoE 93
Farris, Jerome 1930- WhoAm 92
Farris, John 1936- ScF&FL 92
Farris, John Adam 1933- St&PR 93
Farris, John Leo 1947- WhoEmL 93
Farris, John M. Law&B 92
Farris, Louis Anthony, Jr. 1936- WhoAm 92
Farris, Marc 1947- WhoEmL 93
Farris, Martin Theodore 1925- WhoAm 92, WhoWor 93
Farris, Paul Leonard 1919- WhoAm 92
Farris, Robert Earl 1928- WhoAm 92
Farris, Robert Gene 1930- WhoSSW 93
Farris, Susan Elizabeth 1966- WhoE 93
Farris, Thomas Chad 1954- WhoEmL 93
Farris, Trueman Earl, Jr. 1926- WhoAm 92
Farris, Vera King 1940- WhoAm 92, WhoAmW 93
Farrish, John R. 1945- St&PR 93
Farritor, Robert Edward 1942- WhoSSW 93
Farron, Lucien G. Law&B 92
Farron, Robert 1947- WhoE 93, WhoEmL 93
Farrow, Douglas B. Law&B 92
Farrow, Jeffrey Lloyd 1951- WhoEmL 93
Farrow, John 1904-1963 MiSFD 9N
Farrow, Margaret Ann 1934- WhoAmW 93
Farrow, Mia BioIn 17
Farrow, Mia 1946- IntDcF 2-3
Farrow, Mia Villiers 1945- WhoAm 92, WhoAmW 93, WhoE 93
Farrow, Norman D. 1916-1984 Baker 92
Farrow, Robert Scott 1952- WhoE 93, WhoEmL 93
Farrow, Sallie A. Law&B 92
Farrugia, Charles Joseph 1941- WhoWor 93
Farrukh, Marwan Omar 1946- WhoEmL 93
Farry, Michael Allen 1957- WhoEmL 93
Farsang, Csaba 1943- WhoScE 91-4
Farsetta, James Joseph 1947- WhoAm 92
Farson, Daniel 1927- ScF&FL 92
Farson, Daniel (Negley) 1927- ConAu 37NR
Farson, Richard Evans 1926- WhoAm 92, WhoWor 93
Farst, Don David 1941- WhoAm 92
Farthing, Bonnie Sherrill 1935- WhoAmW 93
Farthing, Charles Frank 1953- WhoE 93
Farthing, David Douglas 1939- WhoWor 93
Farthing, T.W. WhoScE 91-1
Faruga, Andrzej 1934- WhoScE 91-4
Faruk 1920-1965 BioIn 17
Farukhi, Suraiya 1945- WhoAmW 93
Faruki, Charles Joseph 1949- WhoEmL 93
Faruki, Mahmud Taji 1919- WhoAm 92
Farver, Mary Joan 1919- WhoAm 92
Farwell, Albert Edmond 1915- WhoAm 92
Farwell, Arthur 1877-1952 BioIn 17
Farwell, Arthur (George) 1872-1952 Baker 92
Farwell, Byron Edgar 1921- WhoAm 92, WhoWor 93, WhoWrEP 92
Farwell, Elwin D. 1919- WhoAm 92
Farwell, F. Evans 1906- St&PR 93
Farwell, Nancy Larraine 1944- WhoE 93
Farwell, Peter 1943- St&PR 93
Farwell, Robert William 1927- WhoSSW 93
Farwell, Roy P. Law&B 92
Farwell, Russ 1956- WhoE 93
Fary, Debra Faye 1957- WhoEmL 93
Faryniasz, Kirk Edward 1956- WhoSSW 93
Fasan, Peter Olusola 1935- WhoUN 92
Fasanella, Ralph 1914- BioIn 17
Fasano, Anthony 1934- WhoE 93
Fasano, Anthony A. Law&B 92
Fasano, Anthony John 1947- WhoEmL 93
Fasano, Antonio 1941- WhoScE 91-3
Fasano, Carol Fielding Law&B 92
Fasano, John MiSFD 9
Fasano, Kristine M. 1951- St&PR 93
Fasano, Renato 1902-1979 Baker 92, OxDcOp
Fascell, Dante B. 1917- CngDr 91, WhoAm 92, WhoSSW 93
Fascett, Ernest Frank 1949- St&PR 93
Fascetta, Salvatore Charles 1940- WhoAm 92, WhoE 93
Fasch, Johann Friedrich 1688-1758 Baker 92
Fasch, Karl Friedrich Christian 1736-1800 Baker 92
Faschingbauer, Thomas Richard 1942- WhoSSW 93
Fascia, Remo Mario 1922- WhoAm 92
Fasciana, Elizabeth M. Law&B 92
Fasciotti, Vittorio 1930- WhoWor 93
Fasel, Ida 1909- WhoWrEP 92
Fasella, Paolo Maria 1930- WhoScE 91-2
Fash, Charles H. Law&B 92
Fash, William Leonard 1931- WhoAm 92, WhoWor 93
Fashbaugh, Howard Dilts, Jr. 1922- WhoWor 93
Fashing, Annette Louise WhoAmW 93
Fashing, Norman James 1943- WhoSSW 93
Fasi, 'Allal 1910-1974 BioIn 17
Fasi, Frank Francis 1920- WhoAm 92
Fasi, Joseph Mario, II 1954- WhoEmL 93
Fasig, Carl E. Law&B 92
Fasing, Sandra Vayo 1957- WhoAmW 93
Fasmacht, Annette Zelder 1950- WhoE 93
Fasman, Gerald David 1925- WhoAm 92, WhoE 93
Fasman, Zachary Dean 1948- WhoEmL 93
Fasnacht, Betty Beegle 1931- WhoWrEP 92
Faso, Frank d1991 BioIn 17
Fasol, Karl H. 1927- WhoScE 91-3
Fasoldt, Sara Tullar 1945- WhoAmW 93
Fasolt, Constantin 1951- ConAu 139
Fasone, Lucille Geraldine 1954- WhoEmL 93
Fass, Peter Michael 1937- WhoAm 92
Fass, Susan R. 1941- WhoWrEP 92
Fassassi, Osseni 1944- WhoUN 92
Fassassi, Yocouba 1952- WhoUN 92
Fassbaender, Brigitte 1939- IntDcOp [port], OxDcOp, WhoAm 92
Fassbander, Brigitte 1939- Baker 92
Fassbender, Charles J. Law&B 92
Fassbender, Zdenka 1879-1954 Baker 92
Fassbinder, Rainer Werner 1946-1982 MiSFD 9N
Fasser, Paul James, Jr. 1926- WhoAm 92
Fassett, John D. 1926- WhoAm 92
Fassi, Bruno WhoScE 91-3
Fassihi, Theresa Carmela 1959- WhoAmW 93
Fassina, Giuliana 1932- WhoScE 91-3
Fassinger, Vicki Lee 1958- WhoEmL 93
Fassio, Danny Lee 1947- WhoEmL 93
Fassio, James S. 1955- St&PR 93
Fassio, Virgil 1927- St&PR 93, WhoAm 92, WhoWor 93
Fasske, Erhard Moritz Georg 1927- WhoWor 93
Fassl, Horst Erwin 1932- WhoScE 91-3
Fasslabend, Werner 1944- WhoWor 93
Fassler, Albert Franz 1943- WhoWor 93
Fassler, Bernice 1930- St&PR 93
Fassler, Charles 1946- WhoEmL 93
Fassler, Crystal G. 1942- WhoAmW 93
Fassler, Joseph K. 1942- WhoAm 92
Fassler, Leon 1933- St&PR 93
Fassler, Leonard J. 1931- St&PR 93
Fassnacht, Debra Kerr 1958- WhoAmW 93
Fassoulis, Satiris Galahad 1922- WhoE 93, WhoWor 93
Fassuliotis, Helen K. 1931- WhoSSW 93
Fast, Eric Carson 1949- WhoAm 92
Fast, Howard 1914- BioIn 17, JeAmFiW, ScF&FL 92, WhoWrEP 92
Fast, Howard Melvin 1914- WhoAm 92, WhoE 93
Fast, Jonathan 1948- ScF&FL 92
Fast, Julius 1919- WhoAm 92
Fast, Margaret Law&B 92
Fasteau, Marc 1942- St&PR 93
Faster, Walter W. 1933- St&PR 93
Fastert, Herbert P. 1936- St&PR 93
Fasthuber-Grande, Traudy 1950- WhoEmL 93
Fastiggi, Thomas St&PR 93
Fastook, Mary Ann 1944- WhoE 93
Fastoso, Bernice Kmiec 1936- WhoAmW 93
Fastuca, George P. 1952- St&PR 93
Fasullo, Peter A. 1953- St&PR 93
Fatchen, Max 1920- DcChlFi
Fate, Martin E., Jr. 1933- St&PR 93
Fate, Martin Eugene, Jr. 1933- WhoAm 92, WhoSSW 93
Fate, Weldon Lee 1937- St&PR 93
Fateley, William Gene 1929- WhoAm 92, WhoWrEP 92
Fatemi, Nasrollah S. 1910-1990 BioIn 17
Fates, Joseph Gilbert 1914- WhoAm 92
Fath Ali Tipu Sultan 1753-1799 BioIn 17
Fathalla, Mahmoud Fahmy 1935- WhoUN 92
Fathauer, Theodore Frederick 1946- WhoEmL 93, WhoWor 93
Father Divine BioIn 17, EncAACR
Father Factious ConAu 39NR
Fathy, Hassan 1900-1989 BioIn 17
Fatibello-Filho, Orlando 1952- WhoWor 93
Fatic, Vuk Marko 1932- WhoE 93
Fatin, Wendy Frances 1941- WhoAsAP 91
Fatini, Ugo 1934- WhoWor 93
Fatland, James R. WhoAm 92
Fatout, Paul 1897-1982 ScF&FL 92
Fatovic, Gregory S. Law&B 92
Fatovic, John 1932- WhoE 93
Fatovich, Mirko Ivan 1937- St&PR 93
Fatse, George 1933- St&PR 93
Fatseas, John 1946- WhoScE 91-3
Fatsis, Michael Evangelos 1961- WhoWor 93
Fatt, Irving 1920- WhoAm 92
Fattahi, Farro 1948- St&PR 93
Fattell, Edward George 1934- St&PR 93
Fattig, John J. 1924- WhoIns 93
Fattinger, Christof Peter 1954- WhoWor 93
Fattorini, Gabriele 16th cent.- Baker 92
Fatyga, Janina 1929- WhoScE 91-4
Fatzinger, Walter R., Jr. 1942- WhoAm 92
Fatzinger, Walter Robert, Jr. 1942- St&PR 93
Faubel, Gerald Lee 1941- WhoWor 93
Faubel, Manfred 1944- WhoWor 93
Fauber, Roy L. 1944- St&PR 93
Faubion, Anne WhoWrEP 92
Faubion, Charles Mann Law&B 92
Faubion, Jno. J., Jr. 1915- St&PR 93
Faubus, Orval E. 1910- PolPar
Faubus, Orval Eugene 1910- WhoAm 92
Faucera, Allen Anthony 1949- WhoEmL 93
Faucett, Sam P. 1935- St&PR 93
Faucett, Thomas Richard 1920- WhoAm 92
Fauchais, Pierre 1937- WhoScE 91-2
Faucher, Albert 1915- WhoWrEP 92
Faucher, Carol Irene Law&B 92
Faucher, Carol Irene 1953- WhoEmL 93
Faucher, Elizabeth ScF&FL 92
Faucher, Louis P. 1931- St&PR 93
Fauchet, Paul Robert 1881-1937 Baker 92
Faucheux, Claude Francois 1929- WhoWor 93
Fauchey, Paul 1858-1936 Baker 92

Fauchier, Jean Paul-Clement 1938- WhoScE 91-2
Fauci, Anthony S. BioIn 17
Fauci, Anthony S. 1940- ConHero 2 [port]
Fauci, Anthony Stephen 1940- WhoAm 92
Fauci, Lawrence Anthony 1929- St&PR 93
Fauck, Roger 1925- WhoScE 91-2
Fauconberg, Thomas c. 1450-1471 HarEnMi
Faude, William D. 1933- St&PR 93
Faue, Jeffrey Lawrence 1946- WhoE 93
Fauerbach, George, Jr. 1946- St&PR 93
Faugerolas, Laurent 1957- WhoWor 93
Faughnan, James Patrick, Jr. 1933- WhoE 93
Faughnan, Vincent M. Law&B 92
Faught, Harold Franklin 1924- St&PR 93, WhoAm 92
Faught, Ken BioIn 17
Faul, George Johnson 1918- WhoAm 92
Faul, Jan Walkley 1945- WhoE 93
Faul, June Patricia WhoAmW 93
Faulcon, Robert ScF&FL 92
Faulconer, Robert Jamieson 1923- WhoAm 92, WhoWor 93
Faulconer, Thomas Pleasant 1912- WhoWor 93
Faulders, C. Thomas, III 1949- WhoAm 92
Faulders, John David Law&B 92
Faulds, Ruth E. AmWomPl
Faulhaber, L. Michael 1937- WhoIns 93
Fauli-Trillo, Claudio 1930- WhoScE 91-3
Faulk, Elizabeth Hammond 1925- WhoAm 92, WhoAmW 93
Faulk, John Henry BioIn 17
Faulk, Marshall BioIn 17
Faulk, Michael Anthony 1953- WhoEmL 93
Faulk, Richard Oran 1951- WhoEmL 93
Faulk, Suzanne Harriet 1949- WhoEmL 93
Faulk, Terry Michael 1946- St&PR 93
Faulkenberry, Charles V. 1935- St&PR 93
Faulkenberry, Richard Ernest 1962- WhoE 93
Faulkenberry, William Leonard 1958- WhoSSW 93
Faulkenbery, Monica Anne 1957- WhoAmW 93
Faulkes, Anthony 1937- ConAu 138
Faulkner, Adele Lloyd 1911- WhoAm 92
Faulkner, Arthur Brian Deane 1921-1977 DcTwHis
Faulkner, Avery Coonley 1929- WhoAm 92
Faulkner, Benton H. 1930- St&PR 93
Faulkner, Brian 1921-1977 BioIn 17
Faulkner, Brian Fitzjames Law&B 92
Faulkner, Charles Herman 1937- WhoSSW 93
Faulkner, Claude Winston 1916- WhoAm 92, WhoWor 93
Faulkner, Cornelius J., Jr. Law&B 92
Faulkner, David Chancellor Law&B 92
Faulkner, Donald Jack 1937- WhoWor 93
Faulkner, Douglas WhoScE 91-1
Faulkner, Edwin J. 1911- St&PR 93, WhoIns 93
Faulkner, Edwin Jerome 1911- WhoAm 92
Faulkner, Frank M. 1946- WhoAm 92
Faulkner, Gerald Dale 1932- WhoAm 92
Faulkner, Jack WhoAm 92
Faulkner, Jack Sherwood 1933- St&PR 93
Faulkner, James V., Jr. Law&B 92
Faulkner, Jerry A. 1936- St&PR 93, WhoIns 93
Faulkner, Jerry Allen 1936- WhoAm 92
Faulkner, John Arthur 1923- WhoAm 92
Faulkner, John Charles 1922- WhoE 93
Faulkner, John D. 1944- St&PR 93
Faulkner, John Samuel 1932- WhoSSW 93
Faulkner, Julia Ellen 1957- WhoAm 92
Faulkner, Keith 1956- WhoWor 93
Faulkner, Kent VanHorn d1991 BioIn 17
Faulkner, Larry Ray 1944- WhoAm 92
Faulkner, Lela Emiline 1931- WhoAmW 93
Faulkner, Lloyd C. 1926- WhoAm 92, WhoSSW 93
Faulkner, Marilyn Hauch 1942- WhoE 93
Faulkner, Maurice Ervin 1912- WhoWor 93
Faulkner, Mike 1949- WhoAm 92
Faulkner, Mikel D. 1949- St&PR 93
Faulkner, Nancy 1906- DcAmChF 1960
Faulkner, Patricia Ann 1961- WhoEmL 93
Faulkner, Peter 1933- ScF&FL 92
Faulkner, Phillip Gordon 1936- St&PR 93
Faulkner, Robin Law&B 92
Faulkner, Robin Lee 1959- WhoEmL 93
Faulkner, Ronnie Wayne 1952- WhoEmL 93, WhoWrEP 92
Faulkner, Roy G. WhoScE 91-1
Faulkner, Sewell Ford 1924- WhoAm 92
Faulkner, Thomas Green, III 1945- WhoSSW 93
Faulkner, Walter Thomas 1928- St&PR 93, WhoAm 92
Faulkner, William 1897-1962 BioIn 17, MagSAmL [port], WorLitC [port]
Faulkner, Winthrop Waldron 1931- WhoAm 92
Faull, Ellen 1918- Baker 92
Faulstich, Albert Joseph 1910- WhoAm 92, WhoWor 93
Faulstich, James R. 1933- WhoAm 92
Faulwell, Gerald Edward 1942- St&PR 93, WhoAm 92
Faunce, Charles J., Jr. 1933- St&PR 93
Faunce, Robert Alan 1956- WhoE 93
Faunce, Robert L. 1941- St&PR 93
Faunce, Robert Leroy 1941- WhoAm 92
Faunce, William Dale 1947- WhoSSW 93
Fauntleroy, Dort 1925- St&PR 93
Fauntroy, Walter E. AfrAmBi [port], BioIn 17
Faupl, Peter 1943- WhoScE 91-4
Fauquier, Michelle Ruth 1951- WhoE 93
Faure, David Edward Law&B 92
Faure, Edgar 1908-1988 BioIn 17
Faure, Francois Felix 1841-1899 BioIn 17
Faure, Gabriel 1845-1924 BioIn 17, IntDcOp, OxDcOp
Faure, Gabriel (-Urbain) 1845-1924 Baker 92
Faure, Gunter 1934- WhoAm 92
Faure, Jean-Baptiste 1830-1914 Baker 92, IntDcOp [port], OxDcOp
Faure, Jean-Pierre 1931- WhoScE 91-2
Faure, Maurice Henri 1922- BioIn 17
Faure, Nicolas Law&B 92
Faure, Paul 1878-1960 BioIn 17
Faure, Robert 1919- WhoWor 93
Faure, Sebastien 1858-1942 BioIn 17
Faure, William C. MiSFD 9
Faure Benito, Roberto 1928- WhoScE 91-3
Faurer, Louis 1916- WhoAm 92
Fauri, Maurizio 1959- WhoWor 93
Faurie, Rene 1960- WhoWor 93
Fauriol, Sandie 1949- WhoAmW 93, WhoEmL 93
Faurot, Don BioIn 17
Faurot, Jeannette Louise 1943- WhoSSW 93
Faurre, Pierre Lucien 1942- WhoWor 93
Fausch, David Arthur 1935- St&PR 93, WhoAm 92
Fausch, Kurt Daniel 1955- WhoEmL 93
Fausel, Charles E. 1924- St&PR 93
Fauser, Louis 1910- WhoIns 93
Fauset, Crystal Bird 1893-1965 PolPar
Fauset, Jessie 1884?-1961 BlkAuII 92
Fauset, Jessie Redmon 1884?-1961 BioIn 17
Fauset, Jessie Redmond 1882-1961 EncAACR
Fausold, Martin Luther 1921- WhoAm 92
Faussat, A. WhoScE 91-2
Fausset, R. Roy Law&B 92
Faust fl. c. 1488-1541 OxDcOp
Faust, A. Donovan 1919- WhoAm 92
Faust, F. Leo Law&B 92
Faust, Frederick ScF&FL 92
Faust, Irvin 1924- JeAmFiW, WhoWrEP 92
Faust, Joe Clifford 1957- ScF&FL 92
Faust, John Roosevelt, Jr. 1932- WhoAm 92
Faust, John William, Jr. 1922- WhoAm 92, WhoSSW 93
Faust, Katherine AmWomPl
Faust, Leland Howard 1946- WhoEmL 93
Faust, Louis, III 1954- WhoWor 93
Faust, Marcus G. 1953- WhoAm 92, WhoE 93, WhoEmL 93, WhoWor 93
Faust, Naomi Flowe WhoAmW 93, WhoE 93, WhoWrEP 92
Faust, Owen James 1950- WhoEmL 93
Faust, Ray C., Jr. 1942- St&PR 93
Faust, Ray Clifford, Jr. 1942- WhoAm 92
Faust, Richard A., Jr. Law&B 92
Faust, Richard Alan, Jr. 1946- St&PR 93
Faust, Richard Edward 1927- WhoAm 92
Faust, Robert Lee 1938- WhoSSW 93
Faust, Robert McNeer 1939- WhoAm 92
Faust, Roger Raymond 1942- St&PR 93
Faust, Stuart L. Law&B 92
Faust, Uwe R. 1929- WhoScE 91-3
Faust, William A. 1936- St&PR 93
Faustina OxDcOp
Faustini, Giovanni c. 1619-1651 OxDcOp
Faustino, Marcilio, Jr. 1970- WhoWor 93
Fausto-Sterling, Anne 1944- ConAu 137
Fautin, Monte R. 1943- St&PR 93
Fauvarque, Renaud 1952- St&PR 93
Fauve, Robert M. 1930- WhoScE 91-2
Fauver, John William 1921- WhoAm 92
Fauvet, Jacques 1914- BioIn 17, WhoWor 93
Fauvre, John C. Law&B 92
Fauwell, Gerald Edward 1942- St&PR 93
Fava, Christopher Robert 1958- WhoEmL 93
Fava, Donald Anthony 1948- WhoE 93
Favalora, John Clement 1935- WhoAm 92
Favaro, Dennis Ray 1961- WhoEmL 93
Favaro, Mary Kaye Asperheim 1934- WhoSSW 93
Favart, Antoine Pierre Charles 1780-1867 OxDcOp
Favart, Charles Nicolas Justin 1749-1806 OxDcOp
Favart, Charles-Simon 1710-1792 Baker 92, OxDcOp
Favart, Denis 1944- WhoScE 91-2
Favart, Marie 1727-1772 Baker 92, OxDcOp
Favati, Francesco 1921- WhoScE 91-3
Favatier, Philippe 1952- WhoUN 92
Favazzo, Charles Nicholas 1941- St&PR 93
Favero, Carlo Ambrogio 1962- WhoWor 93
Favero, Mafalda 1903-1981 OxDcOp
Favero, Mafalda 1905-1981 Baker 92
Favier, Alain 1945- WhoScE 91-2
Favier, James Gordon, Jr. 1951- St&PR 93
Favier, Jean 1932- WhoWor 93
Favilla, Candice Lynn 1949- ConAu 139
Faville, Barry DcChlFi, ScF&FL 92
Faville, Jeffrey James 1956- WhoEmL 93
Favin, David Leonard 1926- WhoE 93
Favis, Roberta Smith 1946- WhoAmW 93
Favish, Jacqueline Rappaport 1929- WhoAmW 93
Favor, Suzy BioIn 17
Favorite, Amos BioIn 17
Favorite, Felix 1925- WhoAm 92
Favorite, Paul Douglas 1948- St&PR 93
Favorito, O. Mario Law&B 92
Favors, Jean M. ScF&FL 92
Favors, Malachi 1937- WhoAm 92
Favors, Sarah ScF&FL 92
Favre, Alexandre Jean 1911- WhoWor 93
Favre, Jean-Pierre 1941- WhoScE 91-2
Favreau, Donald Francis 1919- WhoAm 92
Favreau, Jean-Philippe 1956- WhoEmL 93
Favreau, Susan Debra 1955- WhoAmW 93, WhoE 93, WhoEmL 93
Favro, K.D. 1936- St&PR 93
Favrot, Leo M. Law&B 92
Faw, Duane Leslie 1920- WhoAm 92
Faw, Genevieve H. 1959- St&PR 93
Faw, Larry Dean 1948- St&PR 93
Faw, Melvin Lee 1925- WhoAm 92
Fawbush, Andrew Jackson 1946- WhoEmL 93
Fawcett, Amelia Chilcott Law&B 92
Fawcett, Bill 1947- ScF&FL 92
Fawcett, Brian 1944- WhoCanL 92
Fawcett, Charles Winton 1946- WhoEmL 93
Fawcett, Charlotte Ann 1949- WhoEmL 93
Fawcett, Cheryl Lynn 1953- WhoAmW 93
Fawcett, Don Wayne 1917- WhoAm 92
Fawcett, Dwight Winter 1927- WhoAm 92
Fawcett, Edgar 1847-1904 ScF&FL 92
Fawcett, Farrah BioIn 17
Fawcett, Farrah Leni 1947- WhoAm 92
Fawcett, Frank Conger 1934- WhoAm 92, WhoWor 93
Fawcett, George 1926- St&PR 93
Fawcett, Gerald A. 1933- St&PR 93
Fawcett, Harland Kent 1935- St&PR 93
Fawcett, Harriet B. AmWomPl
Fawcett, Howard Hoy 1916- WhoE 93, WhoWor 93
Fawcett, James 1913-1991 AnObit 1991
Fawcett, John Neville WhoScE 91-1
Fawcett, Leslie Clarence, Jr. 1920- WhoSSW 93, WhoWor 93
Fawcett, Marie Ann Formanek 1914- WhoAmW 93, WhoE 93, WhoWor 93
Fawcett, Michael James 1954- WhoWrEP 92
Fawcett, Millicent Garrett 1847-1929 BioIn 17
Fawcett, Percy 1867-1925 Expl 93
Fawcett, Richard Steven 1948- WhoEmL 93
Fawcett, Robert Earl, Jr. 1931- St&PR 93, WhoAm 92
Fawcett, Sherwood Luther 1919- St&PR 93, WhoAm 92, WhoWor 93
Fawcett, William B. ScF&FL 92
Fawcus, Robert WhoScE 91-1
Fawell, Beverly Jean 1930- WhoAmW 93
Fawell, Harris W. 1929- CngDr 91, WhoAm 92
Fawer, Martin S. 1933- St&PR 93
Fawkes, Randol DcCPCAm
Fawley, Diane Russell 1947- WhoAmW 93
Fawley, John Jones 1921- WhoAm 92
Faworski, Jozef PolBiDi
Fawsett, Patricia Combs 1943- WhoAm 92, WhoAmW 93
Fax, Charles Samuel 1948- WhoEmL 93
Fax, Elton C. 1909- BlkAuII 92
Fax, Elton Clay 1909- WhoAm 92, WhoWrEP 92
Faxon, Grace B. 1877- AmWomPl
Faxon, Thomas Baker 1924- WhoAm 92
Faxton, James Fred 1932- St&PR 93
Fay, Albert Hill 1911- WhoAm 92
Fay, Amy 1844-1928 Baker 92
Fay, Anitra Sharane 1954- WhoAmW 93
Fay, Barry George 1951- WhoE 93
Fay, Carolyn Ann 1958- WhoAmW 93
Fay, Charles Wilson, III 1946- WhoEmL 93
Fay, Christopher Ernest 1945- WhoWor 93
Fay, Conner Martindale 1929- WhoAm 92
Fay, David B. 1950- WhoE 93
Fay, Dorothy SweetSg C [port]
Fay, E.N., Jr. Law&B 92
Fay, Elvir A. Law&B 92
Fay, Fred 1946- St&PR 93
Fay, Frederic Albert 1911- WhoAm 92
Fay, James Alan 1923- WhoAm 92
Fay, James R. 1924- St&PR 93
Fay, John Thomas, Jr. 1930- St&PR 93
Fay, Julie 1951- WhoWrEP 92
Fay, Julie Diane 1950- WhoEmL 93
Fay, Kevin J. Law&B 92
Fay, Margaret F. 1949- WhoEmL 93
Fay, Maude 1878-1964 Baker 92
Fay, Maureen A. WhoAm 92, WhoAmW 93
Fay, Maureen H. Law&B 92
Fay, Nancy Elizabeth 1943- WhoAmW 93
Fay, Paul Burgess, III 1949- St&PR 93
Fay, Peter Thorp 1929- WhoAm 92, WhoSSW 93
Fay, Peter Ward 1924- WhoAm 92
Fay, Robert Clinton 1936- WhoAm 92
Fay, Robert Jesse 1920- WhoAm 92
Fay, Robert W. 1946- St&PR 93
Fay, Robert Woods 1946- WhoEmL 93
Fay, Roberta Marie WhoSSW 93
Fay, Rosemary Gerard 1958- WhoAmW 93
Fay, Rowan H. 1943- WhoE 93
Fay, Ruth Ann 1947- WhoAmW 93
Fay, Temple H. 1940- WhoSSW 93
Fay, Theresa Antonie Law&B 92
Fay, Thomas A. 1927- WhoAm 92
Fay, Thomas F. 1930- St&PR 93
Fay, Thomas Frederic 1940- WhoAm 92
Fay, Thomas Holland 1926- WhoAm 92
Fay, Toni Georgette 1947- WhoAmW 93
Fay, William M. CngDr 91
Fay, William Michael WhoAm 92
Fay, William North 1943- St&PR 93
Fayache, Mohamed Larbi 1939- WhoUN 92
Faye, Alice 1912- IntDcF 2-3
Faye, Elisa Davis 1941- WhoAmW 93
Faye, Lindsay Anton, Jr. 1932- St&PR 93
Faye, Mor 1948-1985 BioIn 17
Fayed, Mohamed al- 1933- BioIn 17
Fayed, Ramzi 1938- WhoWor 93
Fayek, Jim 1944- WhoSSW 93
Fayen, Emily Gallup 1941- WhoAmW 93
Fayer, Yuri 1890-1971 Baker 92
Fayerweather, John 1922- WhoAm 92
Fayhee, Jerry 1948- St&PR 93
Fayne, Gwendolyn Davis 1951- WhoAmW 93
Fayne, Henry W. 1946- St&PR 93
Fayolle, Francois (-Joseph-Marie) 1774-1852 Baker 92
Fayolle, Marie Emile 1852-1928 HarEnMi
Fayorsey, Clarence Bawa 1922- WhoWor 93
Fayrfax, Robert 1464?-1521 Baker 92
Faz, Gloria Aurora WhoAmW 93
Fazal, Muhammad Abul WhoScE 91-1
Fazal, Muhammad Abul 1939- WhoWor 93
Fazecas, Ioan 1921- WhoScE 91-4
Fazekas, Andras 1941- WhoScE 91-4
Fazenda, Louise 1889-1962 QDrFCA 92 [port]
Fazio, Anthony J. Law&B 92
Fazio, Carolyn Raffa 1947- WhoSSW 93
Fazio, Ellen Reidy 1962- WhoEmL 93
Fazio, Evelyn M. WhoAm 92
Fazio, Frank 1932- St&PR 93
Fazio, Gary J. 1954- St&PR 93
Fazio, Joseph F., Jr. 1957- St&PR 93
Fazio, Peter Victor, Jr. 1940- WhoAm 92
Fazio, Ronald C. 1944- WhoIns 93
Fazio, Vic 1942- BioIn 17, CngDr 91, WhoAm 92
Fazio, Victor Warren 1940- WhoAm 92
Fazli, S. Ahmet 1931- WhoScE 91-4
Fazzari, Anthony J. 1929- St&PR 93
Fazzari, Frank P. 1932- St&PR 93
Fazzina, Frederick B. 1944- WhoE 93
Fazzini, John Richard 1937- St&PR 93
Fea, Leonardo 1852-1903 IntDcAn

Fead, William Alexander Law&B 92
Feagles, Elizabeth ConAu 40NR
Feagles, Robert West 1920- WhoAm 92
Feaker, Darrell L. 1936- St&PR 93
Fealy, Maude AmWomPl
Feamster, Elizabeth Susan 1958- WhoEmL 93
Fear, Geoffrey Charles 1928- St&PR 93
Fear, Mary Alice 1959- WhoSSW 93
Fearing, Sandra Dosch 1960- WhoEmL 93
Fearing, William Kelly 1918- WhoSSW 93
Fearn, Frances Hewitt AmWomPl
Fearn, John Russell 1908-1960 ScF&FL 92
Fearn, Shirley Jane 1959- WhoAmW 93
Fearn-Banks, Kathleen 1941- WhoAmW 93
Fearnley, Neill 1953- MiSFD 9
Fearnley-Whittingstall, Jane 1939- ConAu 139
Fearnley-Whittingstall, Peter Robert 1962- WhoWor 93
Fearon, Lee Charles 1938- WhoWor 93
Fearon, Robert Henry 1900- WhoAm 92
Fearon, Robert Henry, Jr. 1927- St&PR 93
Fearons, George Hadsall 1927- WhoIns 93
Fears, Douglas Edwin 1949- St&PR 93
Fears, Jesse Rufus 1945- WhoSSW 93
Fears, Louise Mathis 1935- WhoAmW 93
Fears, Tom 1923- BioIn 17
Feast, William James WhoScE 91-1
Feaster, Dorothea Vivieene 1954- WhoE 93
Feaster, Max E. 1928- St&PR 93
Feather, Leonard (Geoffrey) 1914- Baker 92, WhoWrEP 92
Feather, Mark Randolph 1955- WhoEmL 93
Feather, Roberta Brown 1942- WhoAmW 93
Feather, William, Jr. 1915- St&PR 93
Feather, William L. Law&B 92
Featherly, Walter Thomas, III 1955- WhoEmL 93
Featherman, Bernard 1929- WhoAm 92, WhoE 93
Featherman, Donald Oscar 1936- St&PR 93
Featherman, Sandra 1934- WhoAmW 93, WhoWor 93
Featherston, C. Moxley 1914- CngDr 91
Featherston, C. Ronald 1938- St&PR 93
Featherston, Charles Ronald 1938- WhoSSW 93
Featherstone, Bruce Alan 1953- WhoAm 92
Featherstone, Harry Edwin 1929- St&PR 93
Featherstone, John Douglas Bernard 1944- WhoAm 92
Featherstone-Johnson, Monica 1946- WhoWor 93
Featherstun, Charles P. Law&B 92
Feaver, Douglas David 1921- WhoAm 92
Feaver, George A. 1937- WhoAm 92
Feaver, John Clayton 1911- WhoAm 92
Feazell, Thomas L. Law&B 92
Feazell, Thomas Lee 1937- St&PR 93, WhoAm 92
Feazell, Vic Fred 1951- WhoSSW 93
Fecher, Conrad Christopher 1946- WhoEmL 93
Fecher, Constance ConAu 40NR
Fechhelm, Paul L. Law&B 92
Fechhelm, Paul Leo 1959- WhoEmL 93
Fechik, Lloyd 1955- WhoSSW 93
Fechin, Nicolai 1881-1955 BioIn 17
Fechner, Gustave Theodor 1801-1887 Baker 92
Fechner, Robert Eugene 1936- WhoAm 92
Fecho, Cecelia Hodges 1960- WhoEmL 93, WhoSSW 93
Fechter, George A. 1946- WhoEmL 93
Fechtig, C. William Law&B 92
Fechtig, Robert 1931- WhoScE 91-4
Fechtmeyer, Gary Kevin 1963- WhoE 93
Feck, Luke M. 1935- St&PR 93
Feck, Luke Matthew 1935- WhoAm 92
Feczko, William Albert 1937- WhoAm 92, WhoE 93
Fedak, Edward 1943- St&PR 93
Fedalen, Charles H., Jr. Law&B 92
Fedalen, Richard J. 1939- WhoIns 93
Fedchak, Gregg George 1956- WhoWrEP 92
Fedchun, G.B. Law&B 92
Fedde, Paul Andrew 1925- St&PR 93
Feddeck, Michael Brendan 1944- WhoE 93
Feddema, Leonard Jay 1955- St&PR 93
Fedden, Robert Law&B 92
Feddern, Barbara Jane 1937- WhoAmW 93
Fedders, John Michael 1941- WhoAm 92
Feddes, Reinder Auke 1939- WhoScE 91-3
Feddock, John Edward 1947- St&PR 93
Feddoes, Sadie Clothil 1931- WhoE 93
Feddup, I.M. ScF&FL 92
Fedele, Charles Robert 1942- WhoE 93
Fedele, Francesco G. 1942- WhoScE 91-3
Fedele, Michael Christian 1955- WhoE 93
Fedeli, Cav. G. Uff. Enzo 1928- WhoScE 91-3
Fedeli, Enzo WhoScE 91-3
Fedeli, Vito 1866-1933 Baker 92
Fedelle, Estelle WhoAmW 93
Feder, Allan Appel 1931- WhoAm 92
Feder, Arthur A. 1927- St&PR 93, WhoAm 92
Feder, Bruce Stanley 1950- WhoEmL 93
Feder, Daniel Seth 1962- WhoE 93
Feder, Edgard 1909-1990 BioIn 17
Feder, Edward M. 1940- WhoIns 93
Feder, Gary Harold 1948- WhoEmL 93
Feder, (Franz) Georg 1927- Baker 92
Feder, Harold Abram 1932- WhoAm 92
Feder, Harriet K. 1928- SmATA 73
Feder, Harry Simon 1953- WhoE 93
Feder, Joseph 1932- St&PR 93
Feder, Kenneth L. 1952- WhoE 93
Feder, Leon A. 1920- St&PR 93
Feder, Lewis Morris Montgomery 1943- WhoE 93
Feder, Michael A. 1951- St&PR 93
Feder, Robert 1930- WhoE 93, WhoWor 93
Feder, Robert Elliot 1951- WhoE 93, WhoEmL 93
Feder, Saul E. 1943- WhoAm 92
Feder, Steven J. Law&B 92
Federa, Klaus Otto 1959- WhoWor 93
Federbush, Arnold 1935- ScF&FL 92
Federer, Richard Louis 1927- St&PR 93
Federhar, David Bernard 1951- WhoEmL 93
Federhofer, Hellmut 1911- Baker 92
Federici, Dennis Carl 1950- WhoEmL 93
Federici, Vincenzo 1764-1826 Baker 92, OxDcOp
Federici, William Vito 1931- WhoAm 92
Federico, Antonio 1948- WhoScE 91-3
Federico, Gene 1918- BioIn 17, WhoAm 92
Federico, Kathleen M. 1943- St&PR 93
Federico Goldberg, Linda 1918- WhoScE 91-3
Federighi, Christine M. 1949- WhoEmL 93, WhoSSW 93
Federing, Eric K. 1960- WhoE 93
Federle, Katherine Hunt 1958- WhoEmL 93
Federman, Daniel David 1928- WhoAm 92
Federman, Harold Barrett 1922- St&PR 93
Federman, Joseph R. 1950- St&PR 93
Federman, Lynne H. Law&B 92
Federman, Miles 1946- St&PR 93
Federman, Paula Rae 1958- St&PR 93
Federman, Raymond BioIn 17
Federman, Raymond 1928- JeAmFiW, ScF&FL 92, WhoAm 92
Federmann, Franklin Howard 1939- WhoWor 93
Federow, Harold Louis 1949- WhoEmL 93
Federspiel, Jack Weber 1953- St&PR 93
Federspiel, Jurg 1931- BioIn 17
Fedesna, Kenneth Joseph 1949- St&PR 93
Fedewa, Lawrence John 1937- St&PR 93, WhoAm 92, WhoWor 93
Fedewa, Randy 1954- St&PR 93
Fedi, Francesco 1939- WhoScE 91-3
Fedkowicz, Jerzy 1891-1959 PolBiDi
Fedo, Michael BioIn 17
Fedor, George Matthew, III 1967- WhoE 93
Fedor, Katherine Wusylko 1956- WhoE 93
Fedor, Patricia Anne 1933- WhoSSW 93
Fedor, Richard Thomas 1945- St&PR 93
Fedorchak, Timothy Hill 1958- WhoEmL 93
Fedorchik, Bette Joy Winter 1953- WhoAm 92
Fedorcsak, Imre 1926- WhoScE 91-2
Fedore, Ronald J. 1948- WhoSSW 93
Fedorich, William C. Law&B 92
Fedor-Joseph, Stephanie Rae 1956- WhoEmL 93
Fedorochko, Michael 1933- St&PR 93
Fedorochko, William, Jr. 1940- WhoAm 92
Fedoroff, Nina Vsevolod 1942- WhoAm 92, WhoAmW 93
Fedoroff, Sergey 1925- WhoAm 92
Fedorov, Alexandre Vladimirovitch 1946- WhoWor 93
Fedorov, Fedor Ivanovich 1911- WhoWor 93
Fedorov, Nikolai Fedorovich 1828-1903 BioIn 17
Fedorov, Vladimir 1901-1979 Baker 92
Fedors, John, Jr. 1953- WhoEmL 93
Fedorski, Jerzy 1947- WhoWor 93
Fedoruk, Sylvia O. 1927- WhoAm 92, WhoAmW 93
Fedoseyev, Vladimir 1932- Baker 92
Fedowich, Valerie M. Law&B 92
Fedrick, James Love 1930- WhoE 93
Feducha, Bertha 1882-1968 ScF&FL 92
Fee, Catherine Ann 1965- WhoEmL 93
Fee, Charles Thomas, Jr. Law&B 92
Fee, Charlotte Ramsey 1959- WhoAmW 93
Fee, Chong-Hwey 1959- WhoEmL 93
Fee, Ellen L. 1957- St&PR 93
Fee, Florence C. Law&B 92
Fee, Frank J. 1942- St&PR 93
Fee, Gerard Wayne Cowle 1933- WhoWor 93
Fee, Jody 1947- WhoAmW 93
Fee, Joe 1964- St&PR 93
Fee, John C. 1921- St&PR 93
Fee, John F. 1922- St&PR 93
Fee, John Gregg 1816-1901 BioIn 17
Fee, Kevin T. 1949- St&PR 93
Fee, Laurel Ruth 1950- WhoSSW 93
Fee, Michael Charles 1961- WhoEmL 93
Fee, Paul Francis 1939- St&PR 93
Fee, Paul S. St&PR 93
Fee, Thomas 1928- St&PR 93, WhoAm 92
Feedore, Jeremy Randolph 1951- WhoEmL 93
Feehan, John Joseph 1953- WhoEmL 93
Feehan, Mary Edward AmWomPl
Feehan, Thomas Joseph 1924- WhoAm 92
Feeheley, John J. 1927- St&PR 93
Feeks, J. Michael 1942- St&PR 93, WhoAm 92
Feeley, Brendan Kerry 1947- WhoSSW 93
Feeley, Edmund John 1960- WhoE 93
Feeley, Francis McCollum 1946- WhoSSW 93
Feeley, Gregory 1955- ScF&FL 92
Feeley, Henry Joseph, Jr. 1940- WhoAm 92
Feeley, James Terence 1950- WhoAm 92
Feeley, John Paul 1918- WhoAm 92
Feeley, Peter P. Law&B 92
Feeley, Sharon Denise 1949- WhoAmW 93
Feeley, Terence 1950- St&PR 93
Feelings, Muriel 1938- BlkAull 92
Feelings, Muriel (Lavita Gray) 1938- MajAI [port]
Feelings, Thomas 1933- BlkAull 92, MajAI [port]
Feelings, Tom 1933- SmATA 69 [port]
Feely, F. Joseph, III Law&B 92
Feely, Herbert William 1928- WhoE 93
Feely, John 1947- WhoScE 91-3
Feely, Matthew Stephen Anthony 1960- WhoE 93
Feely, Stephen J. 1948- St&PR 93
Feemster, Herbert 1942- See Peaches & Herb SoulM
Feeney, Carla Jean Newton 1955- WhoEmL 93
Feeney, Don Joseph, Jr. 1948- WhoEmL 93, WhoWor 93
Feeney, Frank Michael 1928- St&PR 93
Feeney, James 1936- WhoScE 91-1
Feeney, James P. 1936- St&PR 93
Feeney, Joan Louise 1950- WhoAmW 93, WhoEmL 93
Feeney, John Robert 1950- St&PR 93, WhoAm 92
Feeney, Mark 1957- WhoAm 92
Feeney, Mary Rosalind 1951- WhoEmL 93
Feeney, Patricia Boulier 1949- WhoAmW 93
Feeney, Patrick Joseph 1952- WhoEmL 93
Feeney, Richard Joseph 1944- WhoE 93
Feeney, Rosemary Stella WhoAmW 93
Feeney, Sandra Benedict 1936- WhoAmW 93
Feenker, Cherie Diane 1950- WhoAmW 93, WhoEmL 93
Feeny, Charles E. Law&B 92
Fees, James Richard 1931- WhoWor 93
Feese, Kelly Dee Law&B 92
Feeser, Larry James 1937- WhoAm 92
Feeser, Patricia 1938- WhoAmW 93
Feeser, Rosaleen Diana WhoAmW 93
Feess, Sharon Kay 1958- WhoAmW 93
Feest, Ronald L. 1927- St&PR 93
Fefer, Enrique 1939- WhoUN 92
Fefer, Leo 1921- St&PR 93
Feferman, Linda MiSFD 9
Feferman, Solomon 1928- WhoAm 92
Feffer, Gerald Alan 1942- WhoAm 92
Fefferman, Hilbert 1913- WhoE 93, WhoWor 93
Fegan, Michael 1946- St&PR 93
Fegen, David A. Law&B 92
Feger, Jean 1936- WhoScE 91-2
Fegert, Ulrich Law&B 92
Feghali, Charles Antoine 1954- WhoEmL 93
Fegley, Kenneth Allen 1923- WhoAm 92
Fegley, Randall Arlin 1955- WhoEmL 93
Feher, Franziska 1942- WhoWor 93
Feher, George 1924- WhoAm 92
Feher, Gyorgy 1928- WhoScE 91-4
Feher, Imre 1926-1975 DrEEuF
Feher, Janos 1932- WhoScE 91-4
Feher, Karen M. Law&B 92
Feher, Leslie 1944- WhoAmW 93
Feher, Milton 1912- BioIn 17
Feher, Otto 1927- WhoScE 91-4
Feher, Steve Joseph Kent 1950- WhoEmL 93
Feher, Tibor 1932- WhoScE 91-4
Fehervary, Istvan BioIn 17
Fehl, Gerhard 1934- WhoScE 91-3
Fehl, Larry Delmer 1935- WhoSSW 93
Fehlberg, Robert Erick 1926- WhoAm 92
Fehlig, Paul T. 1908- St&PR 93
Fehling, Richard Erb 1952- WhoEmL 93
Fehlinger, Irvin John 1924- St&PR 93
Fehlmann, Max WhoScE 91-2
Fehlner, Thomas Patrick 1937- WhoAm 92
Fehmers, Maarten Christiaan Otto 1938- WhoWor 93
Fehnel, Edward Adam 1922- WhoAm 92
Fehr, David S. 1935- St&PR 93
Fehr, J. Will 1926- WhoAm 92
Fehr, Kenneth Manbeck 1928- St&PR 93, WhoAm 92
Fehr, Lola Mae 1936- WhoAm 92
Fehr, Max 1887-1963 Baker 92
Fehr, Walter Ronald 1939- WhoAm 92
Fehrenbach, Franz 1949- St&PR 93
Fehrenbach, William Edward 1926- St&PR 93
Fehrenbacher, Don Edward 1920- WhoAm 92
Fehribach, Ronald Steven 1949- WhoEmL 93
Fehring, Gunter Peter 1928- WhoWor 93
Fehring, Raymond H. 1910- St&PR 93
Fehrmann, Hartmut 1933- WhoScE 91-3
Fei, James Robert 1947- WhoEmL 93
Feibelman, Peter Julian 1942- WhoAm 92
Feibleman, Gilbert Bruce 1951- WhoEmL 93
Feibleman, James Kern, Mrs. 1929- WhoSSW 93
Feicht, Hieronim 1894-1967 Baker 92, PolBiDi
Feichtinger, Thomas Jacob 1963- WhoEmL 93
Feichtner, Jacob Martin 1937- St&PR 93
Feick, Carl W. 1923- St&PR 93
Feick, Fred L. 1939- St&PR 93
Feick, John Mitchell 1951- WhoEmL 93
Feick, Ralph T. 1925- St&PR 93
Feickert, Carl William 1906- WhoAm 92
Feidler, Robert Ernest 1950- WhoEmL 93
Feidner, Lawrence J. 1927- St&PR 93
Feier, Stuart S. 1928- St&PR 93
Feierabend, Jurgen B. 1938- WhoScE 91-3
Feierstein, Larry 1948- St&PR 93
Feierstein, Mark Errol 1948- WhoEmL 93
Feifarek, A.J. 1921- St&PR 93
Feifel, Herman 1915- WhoAm 92
Feiffer, Jules BioIn 17
Feiffer, Jules 1929- WhoAm 92, WhoE 93, WhoWrEP 92
Feig, Philip J. Law&B 92
Feig, Stephen Arthur 1937- WhoAm 92
Feige, Otto ScF&FL 92
Feigel, Jane Mauldin AmWomPl
Feigelman, Theodor 1951- WhoEmL 93
Feigelson, Philip 1925- WhoAm 92
Feigen, Brenda S. 1944- WhoWor 93
Feigen, Edward d1992 BioIn 17, NewYTBS 92
Feigen, Irene 1944- WhoAmW 93, WhoE 93
Feigen, Richard L. 1930- WhoAm 92
Feigenbaum, Abraham Samuel 1929- WhoE 93
Feigenbaum, Armand Vallin 1920- WhoAm 92
Feigenbaum, Edward Albert 1936- WhoAm 92
Feigenbaum, Edward D. 1958- WhoEmL 93
Feigenbaum, Frank Law&B 92
Feigenbaum, Harriet 1939- BioIn 17
Feigenbaum, Harvey 1933- WhoAm 92
Feigenbaum, Janice Cooke 1944- WhoAmW 93
Feigenbaum, Joan 1958- WhoE 93, WhoEmL 93
Feigenbaum, Juanita Law&B 92
Feigenbaum, Larry Seth Law&B 92
Feigenbaum, Robert L. 1938- St&PR 93
Feigenbaum, Ruth I. 1944- WhoE 93
Feigenberg, Mitchell H. 1951- WhoEmL 93
Feiger, Lynn Diamond 1946- WhoEmL 93
Feighan, Edward F. 1947- CngDr 91
Feighan, Edward Farrell 1947- WhoAm 92
Feighan, Michael A. d1992 NewYTBS 92
Feighan, Michael Aloysius 1905-1992 BioIn 17
Feighery, Conleth 1946- WhoScE 91-3

Feightner, Mary Magdalene 1935- *WhoAmW 93*
Feigin, Barbara S. 1937- *St&PR 93*
Feigin, Barbara Sommer 1937- *WhoAm 92*
Feigin, Joel Stanley 1951- *WhoEmL 93*
Feigin, Ralph David 1938- *WhoAm 92*
Feigl, Dorothy Marie 1938- *WhoAm 92*
Feigl, Frank J. *BioIn 17*
Feigl, Jane Mauldin *AmWomPl*
Feigon, Judith Tova 1947- *WhoAmW 93, WhoWor 93*
Feigus, Jay d1990 *BioIn 17*
Fei Hsiao-T'ung 1910- *IntDcAn*
Feikens, John 1917- *WhoAm 92*
Feil, Ernst 1932- *WhoE 93*
Feil, Hila 1942- *ScF&FL 92*
Feil, Linda Mae 1948- *WhoEmL 93*
Feil, Richard Norman 1936- *WhoE 93*
Feil, Thomas E. 1942- *St&PR 93*
Feilchenfeldt, Marianne 1909- *BioIn 17*
Feild, James Rodney 1934- *WhoSSW 93*
Feilden, Bernard M. 1919- *BioIn 17*
Feiler, Jo Alison 1951- *WhoAm 92, WhoAmW 93, WhoEmL 93*
Feillet, Pierre 1937- *WhoScE 91-2*
Feiman, Ronald Mark 1951- *WhoEmL 93*
Feiman, Thomas E. 1940- *WhoAm 92*
Feimster, Carolyn Jane 1954- *WhoEmL 93*
Fein, Adam Richard 1957- *WhoE 93, WhoEmL 93*
Fein, Bernard 1908- *St&PR 93, WhoAm 92*
Fein, Cheri 1950- *WhoWrEP 92*
Fein, Franklin *Law&B 92*
Fein, Harold Lenard 1913- *St&PR 93*
Fein, Irving Ashley 1911- *WhoAm 92*
Fein, Lawrence Seth 1951- *WhoEmL 93*
Fein, Leah Gold 1910- *WhoAm 92, WhoAmW 93*
Fein, Leonard 1934- *WhoWrEP 92*
Fein, Linda Ann 1949- *WhoAmW 93*
Fein, Marvin M. 1923-1990 *BioIn 17*
Fein, Melanie Lippincott 1949- *WhoEmL 93*
Fein, Michael B. *Law&B 92*
Fein, Mitchell Hunter 1966- *St&PR 93*
Fein, Paul Stockser *WhoE 93*
Fein, Roger Gary 1940- *WhoAm 92*
Fein, Ronald David 1938- *St&PR 93*
Fein, Ronald Lawrence 1943- *WhoAm 92*
Fein, Seymour Howard 1948- *WhoAm 92*
Fein, Sherman Edward 1928- *WhoWor 93*
Fein, Stephen Joel 1946- *WhoEmL 93*
Fein, Thomas Paul 1946- *WhoEmL 93*
Fein, William 1933- *WhoAm 92, WhoWor 93*
Fein-Barruw, Caron 1960- *WhoSSW 93*
Feinbaum, George 1945- *WhoE 93*
Feinberg, Barbara Ellen 1957- *WhoSSW 93*
Feinberg, Barbara Jane 1938- *WhoWrEP 92*
Feinberg, David Allen 1947- *WhoEmL 93*
Feinberg, David B. 1956- *ConGAN*
Feinberg, David Erwin 1922- *St&PR 93*
Feinberg, Edward Burton 1945- *WhoAm 92*
Feinberg, Edwin J. *St&PR 93*
Feinberg, Elliot *Law&B 92*
Feinberg, Eugene Alexander 1954- *WhoE 93, WhoEmL 93*
Feinberg, Gerald d1992 *NewYTBS 92*
Feinberg, Gerald 1933-1992 *BioIn 17*
Feinberg, Glenda Joyce 1948- *WhoAmW 93, WhoEmL 93*
Feinberg, Gloria Granditer 1923- *WhoAmW 93, WhoE 93*
Feinberg, Harry *St&PR 93*
Feinberg, Harvey Michael 1938- *WhoE 93*
Feinberg, Herbert 1926- *WhoAm 92*
Feinberg, Hilda 1915- *WhoWrEP 92*
Feinberg, Irwin L. 1916- *St&PR 93, WhoAm 92*
Feinberg, Joel 1926- *WhoWrEP 92*
Feinberg, John David 1947- *WhoEmL 93*
Feinberg, Lawrence Bernard 1940- *WhoAm 92*
Feinberg, Leonard 1914- *WhoAm 92*
Feinberg, Lori A. *Law&B 92*
Feinberg, Mark Ethan 1962- *WhoEmL 93*
Feinberg, Martin Robert 1942- *WhoAm 92*
Feinberg, Milton 1926- *WhoE 93*
Feinberg, Mortimer Robert 1922- *WhoAm 92*
Feinberg, Norman E. *Law&B 92*
Feinberg, Norman Maurice 1934- *WhoE 93*
Feinberg, Paul S. *Law&B 92*
Feinberg, Peter Fredric 1962- *WhoEmL 93*
Feinberg, Richard Alan 1947- *WhoWor 93*
Feinberg, Richard B. 1945- *St&PR 93*
Feinberg, Richard Burt 1945- *WhoE 93*
Feinberg, Robert Edward 1935- *WhoAm 92, WhoE 93*
Feinberg, Robert Ira 1956- *WhoAm 92, WhoE 93, WhoEmL 93, WhoWor 93*
Feinberg, Robert Mark 1951- *WhoE 93, WhoEmL 93*
Feinberg, Robert S. 1934- *WhoAm 92, WhoE 93, WhoWor 93*
Feinberg, Robert S. 1940- *WhoAm 92*
Feinberg, Robert Samuel 1940- *St&PR 93*
Feinberg, Robert Stephen 1934- *St&PR 93*
Feinberg, Rosa Castro 1939- *WhoSSW 93*
Feinberg, Samuel 1890-1962 *Baker 92*
Feinberg, Samuel 1908- *WhoE 93*
Feinberg, Thomas Davis 1932- *St&PR 93*
Feinberg, Walter 1937- *WhoAm 92*
Feinberg, Wilfred 1920- *WhoAm 92, WhoE 93*
Feinblatt, Arlene 1938- *WhoAmW 93*
Feinblatt, Ebria 1913-1990 *BioIn 17*
Feinbloom, Helen Frenkel 1948- *WhoAmW 93*
Feinblum, David Alan 1946- *WhoE 93*
Feind, Barthold 1678-1721 *OxDcOp*
Feindel, William Howard 1918- *WhoAm 92*
Feine, Paul Money 1942- *WhoWrEP 92*
Feinendegen, Ludwig E. 1927- *WhoScE 91-3*
Feiner, Alexander 1928- *WhoAm 92*
Feiner, Arlene Marie 1937- *WhoAmW 93*
Feiner, Augusta L. *AmWomPl*
Feiner, Ava Sophia 1950- *WhoE 93, WhoEmL 93*
Feiner, Joel S. 1938- *WhoAm 92*
Feiner, Ronald Ross 1938- *St&PR 93*
Feiner, Thomas M. *Law&B 92*
Feinerman, Leon Judah 1945- *WhoE 93*
Feinglas, Mitchel Alan 1948- *WhoEmL 93*
Feingold, Alan 1938- *St&PR 93*
Feingold, Daniel Leon 1958- *WhoWor 93*
Feingold, David F. d1991 *BioIn 17*
Feingold, David Sidney 1922- *WhoAm 92*
Feingold, Eugene 1931- *WhoWrEP 92*
Feingold, Josue *WhoScE 91-2*
Feingold, Mario 1958- *WhoWor 93*
Feingold, Matthew Coleman 1945- *St&PR 93*
Feingold, Russell A. 1951- *WhoEmL 93*
Feingold, S. Norman 1914- *WhoAm 92*
Feinhals, Fritz 1869-1940 *Baker 92*
Feinhandler, Edward Sanford 1948- *WhoEmL 93*
Feininger, Andreas Bernhard Lyonel 1906- *WhoAm 92*
Feininger, Lyonel 1871-1956 *BioIn 17*
Feininger, Theodore Lux 1910- *WhoAm 92*
Feinleib, Manning 1935- *WhoAm 92*
Feinman, Valerie Louise 1937- *WhoAmW 93*
Feinn, Barbara Ann 1925- *WhoSSW 93*
Feins, Daniel M. d1990 *BioIn 17*
Feinsand, Howard L. *Law&B 92*
Feinsod, Arthur Bennett 1951- *WhoE 93*
Feinsod, Paul Martin 1955- *WhoEmL 93*
Feinstein, Alan Shawn 1931- *WhoAm 92*
Feinstein, Allen Lewis 1929- *WhoAm 92*
Feinstein, Alvan Richard 1925- *WhoAm 92, WhoE 93*
Feinstein, Dianne *BioIn 17*
Feinstein, Dianne 1933- *NewYTBS 92, PolPar, WhoAm 92, WhoAmW 93*
Feinstein, Elaine 1930- *BioIn 17*
Feinstein, Elana Beth 1962- *WhoEmL 93*
Feinstein, Fred Ira 1945- *WhoAm 92*
Feinstein, Irwin Keith 1914- *WhoAm 92*
Feinstein, Jack J. 1909- *St&PR 93*
Feinstein, Jeffrey E. 1957- *WhoEmL 93*
Feinstein, Jeffrey Mitchell 1946- *WhoEmL 93*
Feinstein, Jerald Lee 1943- *WhoSSW 93*
Feinstein, Jonathan Edward 1953- *WhoE 93*
Feinstein, Joseph 1925- *WhoAm 92*
Feinstein, Maggie d1991 *BioIn 17*
Feinstein, Martin 1921- *WhoAm 92*
Feinstein, Michael H. 1935- *St&PR 93*
Feinstein, Michael (Jay) 1956- *Baker 92, WhoAm 92*
Feinstein, Moshe 1895-1986 *BioIn 17*
Feinstein, Myron Elliot 1943- *WhoE 93*
Feinstein, Neil Jeffrey 1939- *St&PR 93*
Feinstein, Paul Louis 1955- *WhoEmL 93*
Feinstein, Peter Alan 1950- *WhoE 93*
Feinstein, Richard L. 1943- *St&PR 93*
Feinstein, Robert N(orman) 1915- *WhoWrEP 92*
Feinstein, Ronald 1946- *St&PR 93*
Feinstein, Scott D. *Law&B 92*
Feinstein, Sheldon Israel 1950- *WhoE 93*
Feinstein, Steven P. 1958- *WhoE 93*
Feinstock, Toby G. 1937- *St&PR 93*
Feintuch, Richard David 1952- *WhoEmL 93*
Feir, Dorothy Jean 1929- *WhoAm 92, WhoAmW 93*
Feir, John Douglas 1930- *WhoSSW 93*
Feirstein, Bruce Jon 1953- *WhoEmL 93*
Feirstein, Frederick 1940- *WhoAm 92, WhoWrEP 92*
Feirstein, Janice 1942- *WhoAmW 93, WhoWor 93*
Feisel, Lyle Dean 1935- *WhoAm 92*
Feiss, Carl Lehman 1907- *WhoAm 92*
Feissel, Gustave 1937- *WhoUN 92*
Feist, Ella *AmWomPl*
Feist, Gene 1930- *WhoAm 92*
Feist, Leonard 1910- *WhoAm 92*
Feist, Raymond E. 1945- *ScF&FL 92*
Feist, Stanley Charles 1924- *WhoE 93*
Feist-Fite, Bernadette 1945- *WhoAmW 93*
Feit, Dudley 1906- *St&PR 93*
Feit, Glenn M. 1929- *WhoAm 92, WhoE 93, WhoWor 93*
Feit, Richard H. 1952- *WhoE 93*
Feit, Walter 1930- *WhoAm 92*
Feitelberg, David *Law&B 92*
Feitelberg, Susan Francis 1962- *WhoE 93*
Feitler, Robert 1930- *St&PR 93, WhoAm 92, WhoWor 93*
Feito, Jose 1929- *WhoAm 92, WhoSSW 93*
Feito, Patricia Maria 1959- *WhoSSW 93*
Feitosa Teles, Francisco Franco 1941- *WhoWor 93*
Feitshans, Fred Rollin 1937- *WhoAm 92*
Feitshans, Walter Van 1947- *WhoSSW 93*
Feiwel, Henry *BioIn 17*
Feiwel, Jean Leslie 1953- *WhoWrEP 92*
Feiwell, Nancy Ann 1963- *WhoAmW 93*
Feix, Marc Roy 1928- *WhoWor 93*
Fejer, Tamas 1920- *DrEEuF*
Fejes, Pal 1931- *WhoScE 91-4*
Fejzo, Muharrem 1933- *DrEEuF*
Feke, Deborah Jo 1952- *WhoAmW 93, WhoEmL 93*
Feke, Steve *MiSFD 9*
Feken, Janet L. 1952- *WhoEmL 93*
Fekete, Andras 1936- *WhoScE 91-4*
Fekete, Attila Laszlo 1943- *WhoScE 91-4*
Fekete, Gabor 1930- *WhoScE 91-4*
Fekete, Otto 1951- *WhoWor 93*
Feketie, John J. d1992 *BioIn 17*
Fekkai, Frederic *BioIn 17*
Fekula, Walter Peter 1936- *St&PR 93*
Fel, Antoine 1694-1771 *OxDcOp*
See Also Fel, Marie 1713-1794 *Baker 92*
Fel, Edit 1910-1988 *IntDcAn*
Fel, Marie 1713-1794 *Baker 92, OxDcOp*
Fela 1938- *BioIn 17*
Felago, Ernest Michael 1944- *St&PR 93*
Feland, Armstead Milner, III 1921- *WhoAm 92*
Felando, August J. 1929- *St&PR 93*
Felber, Neil W. 1952- *St&PR 93*
Felber, Rene 1933- *WhoWor 93*
Felber, Richard J. 1928- *St&PR 93*
Felber, Ronald Jeffrey 1946- *WhoEmL 93*
Felce, David John *WhoScE 91-1*
Felch, William Campbell 1920- *WhoAm 92*
Felcher, Nancy K. *Law&B 92*
Felchlin, James Alois 1919- *St&PR 93*
Felciano, Richard (James) 1930- *Baker 92*
Felcman, Judith 1941- *WhoWor 93*
Feld, Alan David 1936- *WhoAm 92*
Feld, Arthur Michael 1942- *WhoWor 93*
Feld, Carole Leslie 1955- *WhoAmW 93*
Feld, Daniel J. *St&PR 93*
Feld, Eliot 1942- *WhoAm 92, WhoE 93*
Feld, Frederick Albert, III 1947- *WhoEmL 93, WhoSSW 93*
Feld, Fritz 1900- *QDrFCA 92 [port], WhoAm 92*
Feld, Jindrich 1925- *Baker 92*
Feld, Jonathan S. 1952- *WhoAm 92*
Feld, Joseph 1919- *WhoE 93, WhoWor 93*
Feld, Joseph, Sr. 1933- *WhoE 93*
Feld, Karen Irma 1947- *WhoE 93*
Feld, Kenneth Bernard 1955- *WhoSSW 93*
Feld, Kenneth Jeffrey 1948- *St&PR 93*
Feld, Lipman Goldman 1914- *WhoAm 92*
Feld, Michael Stephen 1940- *WhoAm 92*
Feld, Myron Jacob 1948- *WhoE 93*
Feld, Stephen Lee *Law&B 92*
Feld, Stuart Paul 1935- *WhoAm 92*
Feld, Thomas Robert 1944- *WhoAm 92*
Feld, Werner Joachim 1910- *WhoAm 92*
Feldberg, Chester Ben 1939- *WhoAm 92*
Feldberg, Meyer 1942- *WhoAm 92*
Feldberg, Stephen William 1937- *WhoE 93*
Feldberg, Sumner Lee 1924- *St&PR 93, WhoAm 92, WhoE 93*
Feldberg, Warren D. *WhoAm 92*
Feldbrill, Victor 1924- *Baker 92, WhoAm 92*
Feldbusch, Eric 1922- *Baker 92*
Feldbusch, Michael F. 1951- *WhoEmL 93*
Feldenkreis, George 1935- *WhoSSW 93*
Felder, David Wellington 1945- *WhoSSW 93*
Felder, Ernst 1920- *WhoScE 91-3*
Felder, Frederick *St&PR 93*
Felder, Lawrence Jay 1958- *WhoE 93*
Felder, Louis 1960- *St&PR 93*
Felder, Pamela Theresa 1956- *WhoEmL 93, WhoSSW 93*
Felder, Raoul Lionel 1934- *WhoE 93, WhoWor 93*
Felder, Wilson 1940- *SoulM*
Felderhof, B. Ubbo 1936- *WhoScE 91-3*
Felderhof, Herman Cornelis *Law&B 92*
Felderhof, Jan (Reindert Adriaan) 1907- *Baker 92*
Feldesman, Walter 1917- *St&PR 93*
Feldhaus, Gesina *AmWomPl*
Feldhausen, Eugene J. *Law&B 92*
Feldheim, David Allen *Law&B 92*
Feldheim, Jack 1953- *St&PR 93*
Feldheim, Mark Stephen *Law&B 92*
Feldheim, Walter H.F. 1926- *WhoScE 91-3*
Feldhoff, Gerd 1931- *Baker 92*
Feldhorn, Earl I. 1938- *St&PR 93*
Feldhusen, Hazel J. 1928- *WhoAmW 93*
Feldhusen, John Frederick 1926- *WhoAm 92*
Feldkamp, Lynn Elmer 1955- *St&PR 93*
Feldman, Adrienne Arsht 1942- *WhoAm 92*
Feldman, Barbara K. 1946- *St&PR 93*
Feldman, Barry Stewart 1940- *WhoIns 93*
Feldman, Bernard Joseph 1946- *WhoEmL 93*
Feldman, Bruce Allen 1941- *WhoE 93, WhoWor 93*
Feldman, Burton Gordon 1911- *WhoAm 92*
Feldman, Carol-Ann *Law&B 92*
Feldman, Charles K. *BioIn 17*
Feldman, Clarice Rochelle 1941- *WhoAm 92*
Feldman, Corey *BioIn 17*
Feldman, David Marc *Law&B 92*
Feldman, Debra Lynn 1955- *WhoAmW 93, WhoEmL 93, WhoWor 93*
Feldman, Dennis *MiSFD 9*
Feldman, Diane Carol Wasserman 1959- *WhoAmW 93*
Feldman, Edmund Burke 1924- *WhoAm 92, WhoSSW 93*
Feldman, Edward S. 1929- *ConTFT 10*
Feldman, Edward Steven 1947- *WhoEmL 93*
Feldman, Egal 1925- *WhoAm 92*
Feldman, Elaine Bossak 1926- *WhoAm 92, WhoAmW 93*
Feldman, Ellen (Bette) 1941- *ConAu 39NR*
Feldman, Franklin 1927- *St&PR 93, WhoAm 92*
Feldman, Frederik 1937- *St&PR 93*
Feldman, Gary Jay 1942- *WhoAm 92*
Feldman, Gary Marc 1953- *WhoE 93, WhoEmL 93, WhoWor 93*
Feldman, Gennadii 1947- *WhoWor 93*
Feldman, Gerald 1946- *WhoAm 92*
Feldman, Gordon 1928- *WhoAm 92*
Feldman, H. Larry 1941- *WhoAm 92*
Feldman, Hadley E. *Law&B 92*
Feldman, Harold Raymond 1918- *St&PR 93*
Feldman, Harold Samuel 1917- *WhoE 93*
Feldman, Harriet d1991 *BioIn 17*
Feldman, Harris Joseph 1942- *WhoWor 93*
Feldman, Harry H. 1949- *WhoE 93*
Feldman, Herbert H. 1932- *St&PR 93*
Feldman, Herbert Orville 1929- *WhoSSW 93*
Feldman, Howard S. *WhoAm 92*
Feldman, Ira S. *Law&B 92*
Feldman, Ira S. 1943- *WhoAm 92*
Feldman, Irma S. 1930- *WhoAmW 93*
Feldman, Irving 1928- *BioIn 17, WhoAm 92, WhoWrEP 92*
Feldman, Irwin Miles 1939- *WhoAm 92*
Feldman, James Benjamin 1955- *WhoSSW 93*
Feldman, Janet Diane 1958- *WhoEmL 93*
Feldman, Jay N. *Law&B 92*
Feldman, Jay N. 1936- *St&PR 93, WhoAm 92*
Feldman, Jean Frances 1955- *WhoAmW 93*
Feldman, Jeffrey M. 1950- *St&PR 93*
Feldman, Jeffrey Marc 1949- *WhoE 93*
Feldman, Jenat Levison 1951- *WhoEmL 93*
Feldman, Jerome Arthur 1938- *WhoAm 92*
Feldman, Jerome I. 1928- *St&PR 93*
Feldman, Jerome Ira 1928- *WhoAm 92*
Feldman, Jerome Myron 1935- *WhoAm 92*
Feldman, Jesse 1947- *WhoEmL 93*
Feldman, Joel Shalom 1949- *WhoAm 92*
Feldman, John *MiSFD 9*
Feldman, John R. 1947- *St&PR 93*
Feldman, Joseph David 1916- *WhoWrEP 92*
Feldman, Kathryn Lynn 1959- *WhoEmL 93*
Feldman, Larry John 1931- *WhoE 93*
Feldman, Lauren 1961- *WhoEmL 93*

Feldman, Lawrence Herbert 1942- WhoWrEP 92
Feldman, Leon D. 1929- St&PR 93
Feldman, Leonard Cecil 1939- WhoE 93
Feldman, Lillian Maltz WhoAmW 93
Feldman, Ludovic 1893-1987 Baker 92
Feldman, Lynne B. 1956- ConAu 138
Feldman, Marc Alan 1952- WhoSSW 93
Feldman, Marcie BioIn 17
Feldman, Mark B. 1935- WhoAm 92
Feldman, Mark Russel 1949- WhoAm 92
Feldman, Martin J. 1932-1991 BioIn 17
Feldman, Martin L. C. 1934- WhoAm 92, WhoSSW 93
Feldman, Martin Robert 1938- WhoE 93
Feldman, Marty 1933-1982 QDrFCA 92 [port]
Feldman, Marvin 1927- WhoAm 92, WhoE 93
Feldman, Marvin Herschel 1945- WhoWor 93
Feldman, Max 1923- St&PR 93
Feldman, Max 1935- WhoE 93
Feldman, Melvin Law&B 92
Feldman, Michael BioIn 17
Feldman, Michael Sanford 1948- WhoEmL 93
Feldman, Miriam Ellin 1924- WhoAmW 93
Feldman, Mitchell Robert 1956- WhoEmL 93
Feldman, Morton 1926-1987 Baker 92
Feldman, Myer 1917- WhoAm 92
Feldman, Natalie 1921- St&PR 93
Feldman, Oscar Henry 1921- St&PR 93
Feldman, Paula R. 1948- WhoEmL 93, WhoSSW 93
Feldman, Raymond V. 1914- St&PR 93
Feldman, Richard S. Law&B 92
Feldman, Robert A. Law&B 92
Feldman, Robert A. 1940- St&PR 93
Feldman, Robert C. 1956- WhoE 93
Feldman, Robert George 1933- WhoAm 92
Feldman, Robert M. 1932- St&PR 93
Feldman, Roberta Kirsch 1952- WhoEmL 93
Feldman, Roger Bruce 1939- WhoAm 92
Feldman, Roger David 1943- WhoAm 92, WhoE 93, WhoWor 93
Feldman, Roger David 1945- WhoAm 92
Feldman, Ronald Arthur 1938- WhoAm 92
Feldman, Rubin 1926- St&PR 93
Feldman, Ruth 1911- WhoWrEP 92
Feldman, Ruth Duskin 1934- WhoWrEP 92
Feldman, Ryszard 1953- WhoWor 93
Feldman, S. Jerome 1932- St&PR 93
Feldman, Samuel 1936- WhoE 93, WhoWrEP 92
Feldman, Samuel Mitchell 1933- WhoAm 92
Feldman, Simone Yellen d1991 BioIn 17
Feldman, Stacy R. 1949- St&PR 93
Feldman, Stanley George 1933- WhoAm 92
Feldman, Stephen 1944- WhoAm 92, WhoE 93, WhoSSW 93
Feldman, Stephen Aaron 1947- St&PR 93
Feldman, Steven 1946- WhoEmL 93
Feldman, Steven Mitchell Law&B 92
Feldman, Susan Carol 1943- WhoAmW 93
Feldman, Susan Eleanor 1947- WhoE 93
Feldman, Susan Regine Aach- 1951-1990 BioIn 17
Feldman, Walter Sidney 1925- WhoAm 92
Feldmann, Edward George 1930- WhoAm 92, WhoWor 93
Feldmann, Frank Neil 1954- WhoEmL 93
Feldmann, Marc WhoScE 91-1
Feldmann, Shirley Clark 1929- WhoAm 92, WhoE 93
Feldmesser, Julius 1918- WhoSSW 93
Feldmiller, George E. 1946- WhoAm 92
Feldner, Tim 1948- St&PR 93
Feldon, Joan Sorge 1932- WhoAmW 93
Feldon, Ruth Frankenthaler d1991 BioIn 17
Feldpausch, Sherry Miller 1961- WhoEmL 93
Feldschuh, Joseph 1935- St&PR 93
Feldshuh, Tovah S. 1952- WhoAm 92
Feldstein, Albert B. 1925- WhoAm 92, WhoWrEP 92
Feldstein, Joel Robert 1942- WhoAm 92
Feldstein, Joseph Law&B 92
Feldstein, Joseph 1933- WhoAm 92
Feldstein, Kathleen Foley 1941- WhoE 93
Feldstein, Martin Stuart 1939- WhoAm 92
Feldstein, Paul Joseph 1933- WhoAm 92
Feldstein, Richard Lawrence 1942- St&PR 93
Feldt, David Allan 1957- WhoEmL 93
Feldt, John Harrell 1940- WhoAm 92
Feldt, John Joseph Law&B 92
Feldt, Robert Hewitt 1934- WhoAm 92
Feldt, Werner WhoScE 91-3
Feldtman, Henry Douglas 1928- WhoWor 93
Feldtmose, John Nielsen 1941- WhoAm 92
Feldwisch, David Lewis Law&B 92
Feles, Gust 1927- St&PR 93
Felfe, Peter Franz 1939- WhoAm 92
Felgenhauer, Klaus M.A. 1933- WhoScE 91-3
Felger, Thomas R. Law&B 92
Felgoise, Faye 1922- St&PR 93
Felgran, Steven David 1953- WhoE 93, WhoEmL 93
Felice, Charles S. Law&B 92
Felice, Cynthia 1942- ScF&FL 92
Felice, Fortune Barthelmy de 1723-1789 BioIn 17
Felicella, Frank George 1946- WhoAm 92
Felicetti, Daniel A. 1942- WhoAm 92
Felicetty, James F. 1944- St&PR 93
Felici, Angelo Cardinal 1919- WhoWor 93
Feliciano, Donald Vincent 1952- WhoEmL 93
Feliciano, Jose 1945- Baker 92, ConHero 2 [port], WhoAm 92
Feliciano, Jose Celso 1950- WhoEmL 93
Feliciano, Julia Law&B 92
Feliciano, Wanda Ivelisse 1953- WhoAmW 93
Feliciano-Welpe, Diane 1956- WhoAmW 93
Felicier, Mae 1940- WhoAmW 93
Felicio, Diane Marie 1962- WhoE 93
Feliciotti, Enio 1926- WhoAm 92
Felicjaniak, Barbara 1940- WhoScE 91-4
Felinski, William Walter 1953- WhoE 93, WhoEmL 93, WhoWor 93
Felipe, II, King of Spain 1527-1598 BioIn 17
Felipe, IV, King of Spain 1605-1665 BioIn 17
Felipe, Leon 1884-1968 BioIn 17
Felitta, Frank De ScF&FL 92
Felitto, Bryan Joseph 1943- WhoE 93
Feliu, David Noel 1957- WhoEmL 93
Feliu Albinana, Juan Emilio 1948- WhoWor 93
Feliu Matas, Sebastian 1925- WhoScE 91-3
Felix, Charles Jeffrey 1921- WhoSSW 93
Felix, Christopher ConAu 137
Felix, David 1918- WhoAm 92
Felix, David 1921- WhoE 93
Felix, Elaine Sawtelle 1958- WhoEmL 93
Felix, Hugo 1866-1934 Baker 92
Felix, Maria 1914- IntDcF 2-3 [port]
Felix, Patricia Jean 1941- WhoAmW 93
Felix, Rainer 1945- WhoWor 93
Felix, Ray 1930-1991 BioIn 17
Felix, Robert Hanna 1904-1990 BioIn 17
Felix, Ted Mark 1947- WhoE 93, WhoEmL 93, WhoWor 93
Felix, Vaclav 1928- Baker 92
Felixmuller, Conrad 1897-1977 BioIn 17
Felkai, Ferenc 1938- WhoScE 91-4
Felkenes, August Charles 1932- St&PR 93
Felker, Allyn Caroline 1962- WhoAmW 93
Felker, David Roland 1957- WhoEmL 93
Felker, Donald William WhoAm 92
Felker, G. Stephen 1951- St&PR 93, WhoAm 92, WhoSSW 93
Felker, George W., III 1915- St&PR 93
Felker, James 1939- St&PR 93
Felker, James M. 1939- WhoAm 92
Felker, Michael David 1947- WhoSSW 93
Felker, William H. 1953- WhoEmL 93
Felkin, Alfred, Mrs. ScF&FL 92
Felkner, Butch Henry 1952- WhoWor 93
Felknor, Bruce Lester 1921- WhoAm 92
Fell, Bernhard 1929- WhoScE 91-3
Fell, David Andrew WhoScE 91-1
Fell, Derek John WhoE 93
Fell, Donald G. 1945- WhoSSW 93
Fell, Fraser M. 1928- WhoAm 92
Fell, Frederick Victor 1910- WhoAm 92, WhoWrEP 92
Fell, Gilbert Allen 1941- St&PR 93
Fell, Glen St&PR 93
Fell, Laurence T. 1937- St&PR 93
Fell, Mary Elizabeth 1947- WhoWrEP 92
Fell, Morris B. 1914- St&PR 93
Fell, Robert S. 1931- St&PR 93
Fell, Roberta Gail 1956- St&PR 93
Fell, Steven Louis 1950- St&PR 93
Fella, Charlene Ellison 1935- WhoAmW 93
Felland, Garold M. Law&B 92
Fellbaum, Christiane Dorothea 1950- WhoE 93
Fellegara, Vittorio 1927- Baker 92
Fellegi, Ivan Peter 1935- WhoAm 92
Fellenberg, Gunter Klaus Arnold 1936- WhoWor 93
Fellenberg, William Yukikazu 1948- WhoEmL 93
Fellenstein, Cora Ellen Mullikin 1930- WhoAmW 93
Feller, Benjamin E. 1947- WhoE 93, WhoEmL 93
Feller, Bob 1918- BioIn 17
Feller, Christopher Adam 1952- St&PR 93
Feller, David E. 1916- WhoAm 92
Feller, David Scott 1958- St&PR 93
Feller, Elliot D. Law&B 92
Feller, Fred d1991 BioIn 17
Feller, Marcy E. Law&B 92
Feller, Robert Coleman Law&B 92
Feller, Robert Livingston 1919- WhoAm 92
Feller, Robert William Andrew 1918- WhoAm 92, WhoWor 93
Feller, Seymour B. d1991 BioIn 17
Feller, Siegfried 1926- WhoE 93
Feller, Steven A. 1954- St&PR 93
Feller, William Frank 1925- WhoE 93
Feller, Winthrop Bruce 1950- WhoWor 93
Fellerer, Karl Gustav 1902-1984 Baker 92
Fellerman, Linden Jan 1956- WhoEmL 93
Fellers, James Davison 1913- WhoAm 92, WhoSSW 93
Fellers, James Davison, Jr. 1948- WhoAm 92
Fellers, Laura Christine 1964- WhoAmW 93
Fellers, Raymond 1923- WhoAm 92
Fellers, Rhonda Gay 1955- WhoAmW 93
Fellhauer, David E. 1939- WhoAm 92, WhoSSW 93
Fellin, Octavia Antoinette 1913- WhoAmW 93
Fellinger, Karl WhoScE 91-4
Fellingham, David Andrew 1937- St&PR 93, WhoWor 93
Fellini, Federico BioIn 17
Fellini, Federico 1920- MiSFD 9, WhoAm 92, WhoWor 93
Fellner, Bernard Samuel 1947- WhoEmL 93
Fellner, Michael Josef 1936- WhoAm 92
Fellner, Michael Joseph 1949- WhoWor 93
Fellner-Feldegg, Hugo Robert 1923- WhoWor 93
Fellous, Marc 1938- WhoScE 91-2
Fellous, Roland 1935- WhoScE 91-2
Fellowes, E(dmund) H(orace) 1870-1951 Baker 92
Fellowes, Frederick Gale, Jr. 1930- WhoAm 92
Fellowes, George W. BioIn 17
Fellowes, Peter 1944- WhoWrEP 92
Fellows, Charles Clarence Law&B 92
Fellows, Charles Robert 1950- WhoEmL 93, WhoSSW 93
Fellows, Corabelle BioIn 17
Fellows, Fred H. 1918- St&PR 93
Fellows, George Wesley 1945- WhoIns 93
Fellows, Jeff WhoScE 91-1
Fellows, John Roger 1953- WhoE 93
Fellows, L.E. 1943- WhoScE 91-1
Fellows, Peter A. 1951- St&PR 93
Fellows, R. WhoScE 91-1
Fellows, Robert Ellis 1933- WhoAm 92, WhoWor 93
Fellows, Robert Shaw 1947- St&PR 93
Fellows, Russell C. 1938- St&PR 93
Fells, Ian WhoScE 91-1
Fells, Robert Marshall 1950- WhoEmL 93
Felltham, Owen 1602?-1668 DcLB 126
Felman, Marc David 1954- WhoEmL 93, WhoSSW 93
Felmy, John 1954- St&PR 93
Felner, Glenn Lawrence 1926- WhoWor 93
Felo, Matthew Francis, Jr. 1945- St&PR 93
Felperin, Howard (Michael) 1941- ConAu 136
Felps, Paula Sue 1962- WhoAmW 93
Fels, Gerald 1943- St&PR 93
Fels, Gerhard 1939- WhoWor 93
Fels, Rendigs 1917- WhoAm 92
Fels, Robert Alan 1954- WhoEmL 93, WhoSSW 93
Fels, Stephen B. BioIn 17
Felsen, Karl Edwin 1948- WhoEmL 93, WhoWrEP 92
Felsen, Leopold B. 1924- WhoAm 92
Felsenfeld, Carl 1927- WhoUN 92
Felsenfeld, Gary 1929- WhoAm 92
Felsenstein, Walter 1901-1975 Baker 92, IntDcOp, OxDcOp
Felsenthal, Charles L. Law&B 92
Felsenthal, Gerald 1941- WhoE 93
Felsenthal, Norman Allan 1934- WhoE 93
Felsenthal, Steven Altus 1949- WhoEmL 93, WhoWor 93
Felsher, Celia Ann 1955- WhoAmW 93
Felsher, Steven G. Law&B 92
Felsher, Steven G. 1949- St&PR 93
Felske, Edwin Morgan 1934- WhoAm 92
Felsted, Carla Martindell 1947- WhoAmW 93, WhoEmL 93
Felstin, Sebastian z (von) c. 1490-c. 1543 Baker 92
Felstinensis, Sebastian z (von) c. 1490-c. 1543 Baker 92
Felsztyn, Sebastian z (von) c. 1490-c. 1543 Baker 92
Felsztyna, Sebastian z (von) c. 1490-c. 1543 Baker 92
Felsztynski, Sebastian z (von) c. 1490-c. 1543 Baker 92
Felt, D.P. Law&B 92
Felt, Donald Kyle 1934- WhoAm 92
Felt, Irving Mitchell 1910- St&PR 93, WhoAm 92
Felt, James Patterson 1950- WhoWor 93
Feltch, Cynthia Anne 1955- WhoE 93
Felten, David Lawrence 1948- WhoAm 92
Felten, Edward Joseph 1938- St&PR 93
Felten, Ross Henry 1934- St&PR 93
Feltenstein, Harry David, Jr. 1920- WhoAm 92
Feltenstein, Mary Belle Law&B 92
Feltenstein, Mary Belle 1947- St&PR 93
Feltenstein, Paul Douglas 1947- St&PR 93
Feltham, Alan Eric 1949- WhoE 93
Feltham, Ivan Reid 1930- WhoAm 92
Feltham, James E. 1930- St&PR 93
Feltham, Kerry 1939- MiSFD 9
Feltkamp, T.E.W. 1930- WhoScE 91-2
Feltman, David T. 1936- St&PR 93
Feltman, Lee 1918- St&PR 93
Feltmann, James Anthony 1925- St&PR 93
Feltner, David L. Law&B 92
Felton, Frank P., III 1928- St&PR 93
Felton, Glenn P. Law&B 92
Felton, Gordon H. 1925- WhoAm 92
Felton, Jean Spencer 1911- WhoAm 92
Felton, John W. 1929- St&PR 93
Felton, John Walter 1929- WhoAm 92
Felton, Jule Wimberly, Jr. 1932- WhoAm 92
Felton, Marion Lucy AmWomPl
Felton, Nancy Ann 1935- WhoAmW 93
Felton, Norman Francis 1913- WhoAm 92
Felton, Patricia Ann 1949- WhoEmL 93
Felton, Rebecca Ann Latimer 1835-1930 BioIn 17
Felton, Rebecca Latimer 1835-1930 PolPar
Felton, Reginald McCoy 1947- WhoEmL 93
Felton, Robert Stayton 1928- WhoIns 93
Felton, Sandra Haley 1935- WhoSSW 93
Felton, Susann D. 1948- St&PR 93
Felton, Warren Locker, II 1925- WhoAm 92
Felton, William Raymond 1956- WhoEmL 93
Feltovic, Robert J. Law&B 92
Felts, Jean Carole 1933- WhoSSW 93
Felts, Jeffrey E. 1944- St&PR 93
Felts, Joan April 1940- WhoAmW 93
Felts, John Pate 1951- WhoEmL 93
Felts, Margaret Clemen 1950- WhoEmL 93
Felts, Margaret Davis 1917- WhoAmW 93
Felts, Stephen Karey 1944- WhoSSW 93
Felts, William Robert, Jr. 1923- WhoAm 92
Feltsman, Vladimir 1952- Baker 92
Felty, James David 1947- WhoEmL 93
Felty, Kriss Delbert 1954- WhoEmL 93
Felumb, Svend Christian 1898-1972 Baker 92
Felx, Jocelyne 1949- WhoCanL 92
Felzer, Jordan Wayne 1958- WhoEmL 93
Felzer, Lionel 1923- St&PR 93
Felzer, Lionel Herbert 1923- WhoAm 92
Felzer, Stanton Bernard 1928- WhoE 93
Femal, Michael John Law&B 92
Feman, Sanford N. Law&B 92
Femenias, Victor Gonzalo 1943- WhoWor 93
Femino, Jim 1952- WhoEmL 93
Femminella, Charles J., Jr. 1938- WhoE 93
Fenady, Andrew John 1928- WhoWrEP 92
Fenady, Georg J. 1930- MiSFD 9
Fenaroli, Fedele 1730-1818 Baker 92
Fenaut, Jean-Michel 1956- WhoWor 93
Fenby, Eric (William) 1906- Baker 92
Fenchel, Gerd Herman 1926- WhoE 93
Fenchel, Tom Michael 1940- WhoScE 91-2
Fendall, Percy ScF&FL 92
Fendell, Yale M. d1991 BioIn 17
Fendelman, Burton M. Law&B 92
Fendelman, Helaine 1942- WhoAm 92
Fender, Christopher 1942- St&PR 93
Fender, Clarence Leo 1909-1991 BioIn 17
Fender, Freddy See Texas Tornados, The ConMus 8
Fender, Freddy 1937- WhoAm 92
Fender, James Ernest 1959- WhoSSW 93
Fender, Leo 1909-1991 AnObit 1991, BioIn 17, News 92
Fender, Nicole Christine 1963- WhoAmW 93
Fenderson, Caroline Houston 1932- WhoWor 93

Fenderson, Maurice Linwood 1926- St&PR 93
Fendi, Anna BioIn 17
Fendler, Janos Hugo 1937- WhoAm 92
Fendler, Jeffrey S. St&PR 93
Fendler, Oscar 1909- WhoAm 92, WhoSSW 93
Fendrich, Charles Welles, Jr. 1924- WhoAm 92
Fendrich, Harry G. 1944- St&PR 93
Fendrich, Harry George 1944- WhoAm 92
Fendrich, Roger Paul 1943- WhoAm 92
Fendrick, Alan B. 1933- St&PR 93
Fendrick, Alan Burton 1933- WhoAm 92
Feneau, Claude V. 1931- WhoScE 91-2
Fenech-Adami, Edward 1934- WhoWor 93
Fenello, Michael John 1916- WhoAm 92
Fenelonov, Evgenii Alekseevich BioIn 17
Fener, Gerald 1940- St&PR 93
Fenerty, Joseph WhoScE 91-1
Fenerty, Paul Joseph 1953- WhoE 93
Feng, Chi-ts'ai BioIn 17
Feng, Chun-Bo 1928- WhoWor 93
Feng, Cyril C.H. 1937-1990 BioIn 17
Feng, Dagan 1948- WhoWor 93
Feng, De-Xing 1940- WhoWor 93
Feng, Richard T. 1949- St&PR 93
Feng, Tse-yun 1928- WhoAm 92
Feng, Xin-De 1915- WhoWor 93
Feng, Yushu 1956- WhoWor 93
Fengel, Dietrich 1931- WhoScE 91-3
Fenger, Manfred 1928- WhoAm 92, WhoE 93
Feng Jicai BioIn 17
Feng Kuo-chang 1859-1919 HarEnMi
Fengler, John Peter 1928- WhoAm 92
Feng Tzu-ts'ai 1818-1903 HarEnMi
Feng Yu-hsiang 1882-1948 HarEnMi
Fenhaus, Louann Elta 1934- WhoAmW 93
Feniak, Juan Nicolas 1939- WhoE 93
Fenichel, Carol Hansen 1935- WhoAmW 93
Fenichel, Douglas Morgan 1953- WhoE 93
Fenichel, Norman Stewart 1924- WhoAm 92
Fenichel, Richard Lee 1925- WhoAm 92
Fenichel, Saul Michael 1952- WhoEmL 93
Fenick, Barbara Jean 1951- WhoWrEP 92
Fenig, Enrique Zvi 1945- St&PR 93
Feniger, Jerome Roland, Jr. 1927- WhoAm 92
Fenimore, Edward L. 1922- St&PR 93
Fenimore, George Wiley 1921- WhoAm 92
Feninger, Claude 1926- St&PR 93, WhoAm 92
Fenkart, Rolf Paul 1931- WhoWor 93
Fenkel, William Ralph 1952- St&PR 93
Fenker, John William 1926- WhoAm 92
Fenley, Jule Tatum Law&B 92
Fenley, Molissa BioIn 17
Fenlon, Pat BioIn 17
Fenlon, Peter C. ScF&FL 92
Fenn, Deborah Horton 1951- WhoE 93
Fenn, Eugene Henry 1930- St&PR 93
Fenn, George Junior 1926- WhoWor 93
Fenn, George Karl, Jr. Law&B 92
Fenn, James A. 1942- St&PR 93
Fenn, Lionel ScF&FL 92
Fenn, Nicholas M. 1936- WhoWor 93
Fenn, Ormon William, Jr. 1927- St&PR 93, WhoAm 92
Fenn, Raymond Wolcott, Jr. 1922- WhoAm 92
Fenn, Ruth Helen WhoScE 91-1
Fenn, Sherilyn BioIn 17, ConTFT 10
Fennario, David 1947- WhoCanL 92
Fennebresque, Kim S. 1950- St&PR 93
Fennel, Victoria May 1952- WhoAmW 93
Fennell, Christopher Connor 1961- WhoWor 93
Fennell, Diane Marie 1944- WhoAmW 93, WhoWor 93
Fennell, Dominic Joseph 1943- St&PR 93
Fennell, Francis L(e Roy), Jr. 1942- ConAu 39NR
Fennell, Frederick 1914- Baker 92
Fennell, Janice Clinedinst WhoSSW 93
Fennell, John (Lister Illingworth) 1918-1992 ConAu 139
Fennell, John Romauld 1931- St&PR 93
Fennell, Michael Daniel 1968- WhoE 93
Fennell, Peter Edward 1954- WhoIns 93
Fennell, Thomas F. 1904-1991 BioIn 17
Fennell, William Hamilton 1944- WhoWor 93
Fennell Robbins, Sally 1950- WhoAmW 93
Fennelly, Brian 1937- Baker 92
Fennelly, James Joseph 1931- WhoScE 91-3
Fennelly, Richard E. 1917- St&PR 93
Fennelly, Richard Peter Law&B 92
Fennelly, Tony 1945- WhoWrEP 92
Fennema, Owen Richard 1929- WhoAm 92
Fenner, George G. 1934- St&PR 93
Fenner, Kathleen B. Law&B 92
Fenner, Linda Lee 1947- WhoAmW 93
Fenner, Marian Warner Wildman AmWomPl
Fenner, Peter D. 1936- St&PR 93
Fenner, Peter David 1936- WhoAm 92
Fenner, Phyllis R. 1899-1982 ScF&FL 92
Fenner, Richard Dean 1947- WhoEmL 93
Fenner, Suzan Ellen 1947- WhoEmL 93
Fenner, Uwe 1943- WhoWor 93
Fennerty, Karen Sue 1962- WhoAmW 93
Fennessee, William 1951- WhoSSW 93
Fennessey, John Joseph, Jr. 1941- WhoAm 92
Fennessy, John James 1933- WhoAm 92
Fennessy, Marsha Beach Stewart 1952- WhoAmW 93, WhoE 93, WhoEmL 93, WhoWor 93
Fennestad, Knud L. 1924- WhoScE 91-2
Fenney, Nicholas William 1906- WhoE 93
Fennimore, Stephen DcChlFi
Fenning, Lisa Hill 1952- WhoAm 92, WhoAmW 93
Fenninger, Leonard Davis 1917- WhoAm 92
Fenno, Cordelia Brooks AmWomPl
Fenno, John 1751-1798 JrnUS
Fenno, John Brooks 1934- WhoE 93
Fenno, Nathan R. Law&B 92
Fenno, Nathan R. 1958- St&PR 93
Fenno, Richard Francis, Jr. 1926- WhoAm 92
Fenoglio, William Ronald 1939- St&PR 93, WhoAm 92
Fenoglio-Preiser, Cecilia Mettler WhoAm 92
Fenollosa, Ernest 1853-1908 GayN
Fenollosa, Marilyn Moore Law&B 92
Fenollosa, Mary McNeil AmWomPl
Fenselau, Catherine Clarke 1939- WhoAm 92, WhoAmW 93
Fenske, Charles Robert 1953- WhoEmL 93
Fenske, Christian Clemens 1939- WhoWor 93
Fenske, Gail Gretchen 1954- WhoEmL 93
Fenske, Sandra Lee 1955- WhoEmL 93
Fenstad, Jens Erik 1935- WhoWor 93
Fenster, Albert J. 1918- St&PR 93
Fenster, Craig Michael 1964- WhoE 93
Fenster, Harold Alan 1944- WhoSSW 93
Fenster, Harvey 1941- St&PR 93, WhoAm 92
Fenster, Herbert Lawrence 1935- WhoAm 92
Fenster, Marvin 1918- St&PR 93
Fenster, Robert David 1946- WhoEmL 93
Fenster, Robert S. 1950- St&PR 93
Fenster, Saul K. 1933- WhoAm 92
Fensterheim, Herbert 1921- WhoE 93
Fenstermacher, Carol Ann 1959- WhoAmW 93, WhoEmL 93
Fenstermacher, Robert Lane 1941- WhoE 93
Fenstermaker, John L. 1935- St&PR 93
Fenstermaker, Nancy Ruth 1930- WhoAmW 93
Fenstermaker, Scott Thomas Law&B 92
Fenster-Nunez, Rita Gail 1960- WhoE 93
Fensterstock, Blair C. Law&B 92
Fensterstock, Blair Courtney 1950- St&PR 93, WhoAm 92, WhoIns 93
Fensterstock, Joyce Narins 1948- St&PR 93, WhoAm 92, WhoAmW 93
Fensterwald, Bernard 1921-1991 BioIn 17
Fentem, Peter Harold WhoScE 91-1
Fentener van Vlissingen, Rogier 1951- WhoEmL 93
Fenter, Felix West 1926- WhoAm 92
Fenti, Daniel Joseph 1945- WhoE 93
Fenton, Alan 1927- WhoAm 92, WhoWor 93
Fenton, Arnold N. 1921- WhoAm 92
Fenton, Bruce S. Law&B 92
Fenton, Bruce Stuart 1946- St&PR 93
Fenton, Charles E. WhoAm 92
Fenton, Clifton Lucien 1943- WhoAm 92
Fenton, David Edward WhoScE 91-1
Fenton, David T. Law&B 92
Fenton, Don Alan 1951- St&PR 93
Fenton, Douglas John 1956- WhoE 93
Fenton, Edward 1917- DcAmChF 1960
Fenton, Edward 1917-1988 ScF&FL 92
Fenton, George Wallace WhoScE 91-1
Fenton, Heather Susan 1948- WhoSSW 93
Fenton, James 1949- BioIn 17
Fenton, Jeffrey Stewart 1948- WhoWor 93
Fenton, Jill Rubinson 1943- WhoE 93
Fenton, John William, Jr. 1940- St&PR 93
Fenton, Joshua Woolston 1968- St&PR 93
Fenton, Kathryn Marie 1953- WhoAmW 93
Fenton, Lavinia 1708-1760 OxDcOp
Fenton, Lawrence Jules 1940- WhoAm 92
Fenton, Lela Mae 1934- WhoWrEP 92
Fenton, Lewis Lowry 1925- WhoAm 92
Fenton, Maria Gambarelli d1990 BioIn 17
Fenton, Matthew Clark, IV 1951- WhoEmL 93
Fenton, Monica 1944- WhoAmW 93
Fenton, Noel John 1938- WhoAm 92
Fenton, Paula Blanche 1947- WhoAmW 93
Fenton, Robert Earl 1933- WhoAm 92
Fenton, Robert Leonard 1929- WhoWor 93
Fenton, Thomas C. Law&B 92
Fenton, Thomas Conner 1954- WhoEmL 93
Fenton, Thomas Eugene 1933- WhoAm 92
Fenton, Thomas Trail 1930- WhoAm 92
Fenton, Timothy M. 1943- WhoAm 92
Fenton, Wendell 1939- WhoAm 92
Fenton, William Nelson 1908- WhoAm 92
Fenton, Wilmer C. 1923- St&PR 93
Fentress, Chad A. Law&B 92
Fenves, Steven Joseph 1931- WhoAm 92
Fenvessy, Stanley John 1918- WhoAm 92, WhoE 93
Fenwick, Avril Hanning 1947- WhoEmL 93
Fenwick, Gruffydd Roger WhoScE 91-1
Fenwick, James Henry 1937- WhoAm 92
Fenwick, Millicent BioIn 17
Fenwick, Millicent H. d1992 NewYTBS 92 [port]
Fenwick, Millicent H. 1910-1992 News 93-2
Fenwick, Millicent Hammond 1910- WhoAm 92
Fenwick, Millicent Hammond 1910-1992 ConAu 139, WhoAmW 93, WhoE 93
Fenwick, Millicent (Vernon Hammond) 1910-1992 CurBio 92N
Fenyes, Tibor 1929- WhoScE 91-4
Fenyves, Ervin J. 1924- WhoSSW 93
Fenza, William J., Jr. Law&B 92
Fenza, William Joseph 1929- St&PR 93
Fenza, William Joseph, Jr. 1929- WhoAm 92
Feo, Francesco 1691-1761 Baker 92, OxDcOp
Feodosij of Pecera d1074 OxDcByz
Feofan Grek OxDcByz
Feofiloff, Paulo 1946- WhoWor 93
Feoktistov, Konstantin Petrovich 1926- BioIn 17
Feola, Arleen Helen 1938- WhoSSW 93
Feola, Eugene David 1948- WhoEmL 93
Feole, Ronald A. Law&B 92
Fer, Andre R. WhoScE 91-2
Feraca, Jean Stephanie 1943- WhoWrEP 92
Ferand, Ernst (Thomas) 1887-1972 Baker 92
Ferappi, Marcello 1934- WhoWor 93
Ferares, Kenneth 1957- WhoE 93, WhoEmL 93
Ferari, Samuel R. 1939- St&PR 93
Feraud, Louis 1920- BioIn 17
Ferazzi, Karen Z. Law&B 92
Ferbel, Thomas 1937- WhoAm 92
Ferber, Arthur Henry 1922- WhoAm 92
Ferber, David d1992 NewYTBS 92
Ferber, Edna 1885-1968 AmWomPl, JeAmFiW
Ferber, Edna 1887-1968 BioIn 17
Ferber, G.J. WhoScE 91-1
Ferber, Herbert 1906-1991 AnObit 1991, BioIn 17
Ferber, Judith R. Law&B 92
Ferber, Laurie R. Law&B 92
Ferber, Linda S. 1944- WhoAm 92
Ferber, Marianne Abeles 1923- WhoAmW 93
Ferber, Norman Alan 1948- WhoAm 92
Ferber, Rachel F. Law&B 92
Ferber, Samuel 1920- WhoAm 92
Ferbert, Frederick Winzer, Jr. 1953- St&PR 93
Ferchault, Guy 1904- Baker 92
Fercher, A.F. 1939- WhoScE 91-4
Fercho, Ivan H. 1948- St&PR 93
Ferconio, Sandra Michelle 1961- WhoAmW 93
Ferden, Bruce 1949- WhoAm 92
Ferderber-Hersonski, Boris Constantin 1943- WhoE 93
Ferdinand, Prince of Spain, Cardinal-Infante HarEnMi
Ferdinand, V, King of Spain 1452-1516 BioIn 17
Ferdinand, Frank 1923- St&PR 93
Ferdinand, William V. 1941- St&PR 93
Ferdinande, Valere A. 1930- WhoScE 91-2
Ferdinands, Ian S. 1936- St&PR 93
Fere, Vladimir 1902-1971 Baker 92
Ferebee, Gideon, Jr. 1950- WhoWrEP 92
Ferebee, John Spencer, Jr. 1947- WhoAm 92
Ferebee, Kim Louise 1966- WhoEmL 93
Ferebee, Stephen Scott, Jr. 1921- WhoAm 92
Ferebee, Valarie Jean 1955- WhoSSW 93
Ferekidis, Eleftherios 1941- WhoWor 93
Ferenbach, Richard Schooley 1928- St&PR 93
Ference, Thomas William 1959- WhoEmL 93
Ferencie, Karen Jordan 1956- WhoSSW 93
Ferencik, G.M. St&PR 93
Ferencsik, Janos 1907-1984 Baker 92, OxDcOp
Ferencz, Kalman 1923- WhoScE 91-4
Ferencz, Robert Arnold 1946- WhoEmL 93
Ferenczi, George I. 1946- WhoScE 91-4
Ferenczi, Sandor 1873-1933 BioIn 17
Ferenczy, Lajos 1930- WhoScE 91-4
Ferenczy, Oto 1921- Baker 92
Ferenczy, Paul 1931- WhoScE 91-4
Ferens, Marcella WhoE 93, WhoWor 93
Ferensowicz, Michael Jay 1952- WhoEmL 93
Ferentchak, Linda Burleigh 1955- WhoEmL 93
Ferer, Harvey Dean 1926- St&PR 93, WhoAm 92
Ferer, Kenneth Michael 1937- WhoSSW 93
Ferer, Maria Dolores 1948- WhoScE 91-3
Ferer, Whitney H. 1958- St&PR 93
Fereres, Jose 1943- WhoWor 93
Feret, Adam Edward, Jr. 1942- WhoE 93
Feretic, Eileen Susan 1949- WhoAm 92
Feretic, Geraldine Ann Marie 1958- WhoAmW 93
Ferger, Fritz Alfred 1933 WhoScE 91-4
Ferger, Lawrence A. 1934- St&PR 93, WhoAm 92
Fergus, Gary Scott 1954- WhoWor 93
Fergus, Howard 1937- DcCPCAm
Fergus, Patricia Marguerita 1918- WhoAmW 93, WhoWor 93
Ferguson, A.I. WhoScE 91-1
Ferguson, Amos 1920- BlkAuII 92
Ferguson, Amy Talley 1941- WhoAmW 93
Ferguson, Andrew WhoScE 91-1
Ferguson, Andrew Robert 1954- WhoE 93
Ferguson, Anne WhoScE 91-1
Ferguson, Anne 1956- WhoAmW 93
Ferguson, Audri Dale 1954- WhoAmW 93
Ferguson, B.A. 1931- St&PR 93
Ferguson, Betty Lou 1950- WhoEmL 93
Ferguson, Blair G. 1943- St&PR 93
Ferguson, Brad 1953- ScF&FL 92
Ferguson, Bruce W. 1954- WhoEmL 93
Ferguson, C. Alan Law&B 92
Ferguson, C. Alan 1940- WhoIns 93
Ferguson, Carolyn Sue 1935- WhoAmW 93, WhoSSW 93
Ferguson, Charles Albert 1921- WhoAm 92
Ferguson, Charles Austin 1937- WhoAm 92
Ferguson, Charles B. 1929- St&PR 93
Ferguson, Charles Winston 1913- WhoAm 92
Ferguson, Christine Joslin 1948- WhoAmW 93
Ferguson, Curtis Conway 1954- WhoAm 92
Ferguson, Daniel C. 1927- WhoAm 92
Ferguson, Daniel Cuthbert 1927- St&PR 93
Ferguson, David St&PR 93
Ferguson, David Michael 1947- WhoEmL 93
Ferguson, David Norman 1925- St&PR 93
Ferguson, David Robert 1949- WhoAm 92, WhoEmL 93, WhoSSW 93
Ferguson, Deborah Manning 1959- WhoEmL 93
Ferguson, Donald Campbell 1926- WhoAm 92
Ferguson, Donald Edward 1956- WhoSSW 93
Ferguson, Donald F. 1922- St&PR 93
Ferguson, Donald Guffey 1923- WhoE 93, WhoWor 93
Ferguson, Donald Jack 1936- St&PR 93
Ferguson, Donald John 1916- WhoAm 92
Ferguson, Donald L. 1940- St&PR 93
Ferguson, Donald (Nivison) 1882-1985 Baker 92
Ferguson, Doris Lena Wagner 1925- WhoAmW 93
Ferguson, Dorothy Margueritte WhoWrEP 92
Ferguson, Douglas Edward 1940- WhoE 93, WhoWor 93
Ferguson, E. Robert 1932- WhoAm 92
Ferguson, Earl Wilson 1943- WhoE 93
Ferguson, Edward Trevor, Jr. 1933- WhoSSW 93
Ferguson, Eileen D. Law&B 92
Ferguson, Elizabeth Ann 1932- WhoAmW 93
Ferguson, Forest D. 1933- St&PR 93
Ferguson, Frances Law&B 92
Ferguson, Frances Hand 1907- WhoAm 92

Ferguson, Francis Eugene 1921- *WhoAm 92*
Ferguson, Frank E. 1926- *St&PR 93*
Ferguson, Franklin Turner 1935- *WhoAm 92*
Ferguson, G. Richard 1942- *St&PR 93*
Ferguson, Gary Jack 1943- *WhoIns 93*
Ferguson, Gary L. 1940- *St&PR 93*
Ferguson, Gary Warren 1925- *WhoAm 92*
Ferguson, George W. *WhoIns 93*
Ferguson, George Wagoner, Jr. *Law&B 92*
Ferguson, Gerald Paul 1951- *WhoEmL 93*
Ferguson, Glenn Walker 1929- *WhoAm 92*
Ferguson, Grover Woodrow 1919- *WhoSSW 93*
Ferguson, Harley R. 1936- *St&PR 93*
Ferguson, Harley Robert 1936- *WhoAm 92*
Ferguson, Harold Vincent, Jr. 1956- *WhoEmL 93*
Ferguson, Harry 1884-1960 *BioIn 17*
Ferguson, Helaman *BioIn 17*
Ferguson, Helaman Rolfe Pratt 1940- *WhoE 93*
Ferguson, Helen 1901-1977 *SweetSg B*
Ferguson, Helen Mott 1941- *WhoAmW 93, WhoSSW 93*
Ferguson, Henry 1927- *WhoAm 92*
Ferguson, Henry L., III *Law&B 92*
Ferguson, Hill, III 1942- *St&PR 93*
Ferguson, Howard 1908- *Baker 92*
Ferguson, Ian Stewart 1935- *WhoWor 93*
Ferguson, J. Barry *BioIn 17*
Ferguson, J. Bruce *Law&B 92*
Ferguson, Jackson Robert, Jr. 1942- *WhoWor 93*
Ferguson, James *Law&B 92, WhoScE 91-1*
Ferguson, James 1935- *WhoWor 93*
Ferguson, James A. 1915- *WhoAm 92*
Ferguson, James Clarke 1938- *WhoWor 93*
Ferguson, James D. *ScF&FL 92*
Ferguson, James Joseph, Jr. 1926- *WhoAm 92*
Ferguson, James Karl 1942- *St&PR 93*
Ferguson, James Paul 1937- *WhoSSW 93*
Ferguson, James Peter 1937- *WhoAm 92*
Ferguson, James W. *Law&B 92*
Ferguson, James Warner 1950- *WhoEmL 93*
Ferguson, Jean *WhoCanL 92*
Ferguson, Jimmy Lee 1950- *WhoEmL 93*
Ferguson, Jo McCown 1915- *WhoAm 92*
Ferguson, Joan M. 1930- *WhoWrEP 92*
Ferguson, John 1931- *WhoAm 92*
Ferguson, John Cotter, II 1943- *St&PR 93*
Ferguson, John Henry 1907- *WhoAm 92, WhoWor 93*
Ferguson, John Hilton 1946- *WhoEmL 93*
Ferguson, John Lewis 1926- *WhoAm 92*
Ferguson, John Marshall 1921- *WhoAm 92*
Ferguson, John Patrick 1949- *WhoAm 92, WhoWor 93*
Ferguson, John S. 1949- *St&PR 93*
Ferguson, John T., II *Law&B 92*
Ferguson, John T., II 1946- *St&PR 93*
Ferguson, Joseph Gantt 1921- *WhoAm 92*
Ferguson, Justin G. 1941- *St&PR 93*
Ferguson, Kathy E. *St&PR 93*
Ferguson, Kingsley George 1921- *WhoAm 92*
Ferguson, Larry *BioIn 17*
Ferguson, Larry J. 1949- *St&PR 93*
Ferguson, Lloyd Elbert 1942- *WhoWor 93*
Ferguson, Lloyd N. 1918- *AfrAmBi*
Ferguson, Mable *BlkAmWO*
Ferguson, Madelyn Kristina 1948- *WhoSSW 93*
Ferguson, Margaret Geneva *WhoAmW 93*
Ferguson, Marjorie Jeanne 1928- *WhoAmW 93*
Ferguson, Mark *BioIn 17*
Ferguson, Mark William James *WhoScE 91-1*
Ferguson, Martin John 1953- *WhoAsAP 91*
Ferguson, Mary Anne Heyward 1918- *WhoAm 92*
Ferguson, Mary Kay 1944- *St&PR 93*
Ferguson, Maynard 1928- *Baker 92, BioIn 17, WhoAm 92*
Ferguson, Michael 1937- *MiSFD 9*
Ferguson, Michael 1958- *BioIn 17*
Ferguson, Michael D. *Law&B 92*
Ferguson, Michael John 1941- *WhoAm 92*
Ferguson, Milton Carr, Jr. 1931- *WhoAm 92*
Ferguson, Miriam A. 1875-1961 *PolPar*
Ferguson, Nancy Catherine *Law&B 92*
Ferguson, Nancy Jean 1954- *WhoEmL 93*
Ferguson, Neil 1947- *ScF&FL 92*
Ferguson, Pamela Anderson 1943- *WhoAm 92, WhoAmW 93*
Ferguson, Patrick 1744-1780 *HarEnMi*
Ferguson, Paul J. *St&PR 93*
Ferguson, Peter D. *Law&B 92*
Ferguson, Richard R. 1951- *St&PR 93*
Ferguson, Robert 1937- *WhoAm 92, WhoE 93*
Ferguson, Robert 1939- *BiDAMSp 1989*
Ferguson, Robert Bury 1920- *WhoAm 92*
Ferguson, Robert E. *Law&B 92*
Ferguson, Robert Harry Munro 1937- *WhoAm 92*
Ferguson, Robert R., Jr. 1923- *St&PR 93, WhoAm 92*
Ferguson, Robert R., III *WhoAm 92*
Ferguson, Robert Ray 1945- *WhoAm 92*
Ferguson, Rodney A. *Law&B 92*
Ferguson, Ronald E. 1942- *WhoIns 93*
Ferguson, Ronald Eugene 1942- *St&PR 93, WhoAm 92*
Ferguson, Roy C., III 1946- *St&PR 93*
Ferguson, S.R. *WhoScE 91-1*
Ferguson, Samuel 1810-1886 *BioIn 17*
Ferguson, Sanford Barnett 1947- *WhoEmL 93*
Ferguson, Sarah 1959- *BioIn 17*
Ferguson, Sharon Hermine 1953- *WhoAmW 93*
Ferguson, Sheila Alease 1955- *WhoAmW 93*
Ferguson, Skitch 1949- *St&PR 93*
Ferguson, Stanley L. *Law&B 92*
Ferguson, Stephen 1947- *WhoAm 92*
Ferguson, Susan Katharine Stover 1944- *WhoAmW 93*
Ferguson, Suzanne Carol 1939- *WhoAm 92, WhoAmW 93*
Ferguson, Sybil 1934- *WhoAm 92*
Ferguson, Thomas C. 1933- *WhoAm 92*
Ferguson, Thomas H. *WhoAm 92, WhoE 93*
Ferguson, Thomas K. *St&PR 93*
Ferguson, Thomas Russell 1938- *St&PR 93*
Ferguson, Tom 1943- *WhoSSW 93*
Ferguson, Tracy Heiman 1910- *WhoAm 92*
Ferguson, Trevor 1947- *ConAu 40NR, WhoCanL 92*
Ferguson, Troy *BioIn 17*
Ferguson, Virginia 1940- *ScF&FL 92*
Ferguson, Wanda Renee 1954- *WhoAmW 93*
Ferguson, Warren John 1920- *WhoAm 92*
Ferguson, Warren L. 1931- *St&PR 93*
Ferguson, Whitworth, III 1954- *WhoEmL 93*
Ferguson, William C. 1930- *St&PR 93*
Ferguson, William Charles 1930- *WhoAm 92*
Ferguson, William G. *Law&B 92*
Ferguson, William McDonald 1917- *WhoAm 92*
Ferguson, William R. 1937- *St&PR 93*
Ferguson, William R. 1943- *WhoWrEP 92*
Ferguson, William Rotch 1943- *WhoE 93*
Ferguson, Wm. Dennis 1943- *St&PR 93*
Ferguson Mann, Serena DeSantos 1957- *WhoEmL 93*
Ferguson-Pell, Margaret Alice 1951- *WhoE 93, WhoEmL 93*
Ferguson-Smith, Malcolm Andrew *WhoScE 91-1*
Fergusson, Angus Lindsay 1940- *WhoWor 93*
Fergusson, Bruce *ScF&FL 92*
Fergusson, Dianne Smith 1945- *WhoAmW 93*
Fergusson, Donald Charles 1953- *St&PR 93*
Fergusson, Frances Daly 1944- *WhoAm 92, WhoAmW 93, WhoE 93*
Fergusson, Laura 1957- *WhoAmW 93*
Fergusson, Robert 1750-1774 *BioIn 17*
Fergusson, Robert George 1911- *WhoAm 92*
Fergusson, William Blake 1924- *WhoE 93*
Ferino, Christopher Kenneth 1961- *WhoWor 93*
Ferioli, William Thomas *Law&B 92*
Ferkany, Edward A. 1937- *St&PR 93*
Ferkenhoff, Robert J. 1942- *St&PR 93, WhoAm 92*
Ferkingstad, Susanne M. 1955- *WhoAmW 93, WhoEmL 93*
Ferko, Darly W. 1954- *St&PR 93*
Ferland, Albert 1879-1943 *BioIn 17*
Ferland, Darlene Frances 1954- *WhoAmW 93, WhoEmL 93*
Ferland, E. James 1942- *St&PR 93*
Ferleger, Daniel Simon *Law&B 92*
Ferley, Lester J. 1911- *St&PR 93*
Ferlie, Ewan Balfour *WhoScE 91-1*
Ferlinghetti, Lawrence *BioIn 17*
Ferlinghetti, Lawrence 1919- *WhoAm 92*
Ferlinghetti, Lawrence 1920- *WhoWrEP 92*
Ferlinz, Jack 1942- *WhoWor 93*
Ferlinz, Rudolf 1928- *WhoScE 91-3*
Ferlito, Andrew A. 1926- *St&PR 93*
Ferm, Ari Erkki *WhoScE 91-4*
Ferm, Brita Ellen 1951- *WhoAmW 93*
Ferm, David G. *WhoAm 92*
Ferm, Robert Livingston 1931- *WhoAm 92*
Ferm, Vergil Harkness 1924- *WhoAm 92*
Ferman, Allan S. *Law&B 92*
Ferman, Allan S. 1941- *St&PR 93*
Ferman, Edward L. 1937- *ScF&FL 92*
Ferman, Irving 1919- *WhoAm 92, WhoE 93*
Ferman, Nathan 1948- *St&PR 93*
Fermi, Enrico 1901-1954 *BioIn 17*
Fermoile, Douglas Keith 1956- *WhoEmL 93*
Fermor, Patrick Leigh *BioIn 17*
Fermoy, Matthias Alexis 1737- *HarEnMi*
Fern, Alan Maxwell 1930- *WhoAm 92, WhoE 93*
Fern, Carole Lynn 1958- *WhoAmW 93*
Fern, Emma E. 1927- *WhoAmW 93*
Fern, Frederick Harold 1954- *WhoEmL 93*
Fernald, Charles E., Jr. 1939- *St&PR 93*
Fernald, Charles F., Mrs. *AmWomPl*
Fernald, David G. 1923-1990 *BioIn 17*
Fernald, George Herbert, Jr. 1926- *WhoAm 92*
Fernald, Harold Allen 1932- *WhoAm 92*
Fernald, James Michael 1964- *WhoE 93*
Fernald, Judy L. *Law&B 92*
Fernald, Linda Catherine 1943- *St&PR 93*
Fernald, Russell Dawson 1941- *WhoAm 92*
Fernan, Mary Brigid 1958- *WhoEmL 93*
Fernandel 1903-1971 *IntDcF 2-3 [port], QDrFCA 92 [port]*
Fernandes, Armando Jose 1906-1983 *Baker 92*
Fernandes, Gary J. 1943- *St&PR 93*
Fernandes, Gary Joe 1943- *WhoAm 92, WhoSSW 93*
Fernandes, George 1930- *WhoAsAP 91*
Fernandes, Gil 1937- *WhoUN 92*
Fernandes, Jeanne Mary 1948- *WhoE 93, WhoEmL 93*
Fernandes, John F. 1952- *WhoAsAP 91*
Fernandes, Joseph Edward 1923- *WhoAm 92*
Fernandes, Kathleen 1946- *WhoEmL 93*
Fernandes, Oscar 1941- *WhoAsAP 91*
Fernandes, Richard Louis 1931- *St&PR 93*
Fernandes, Tito H. 1948- *WhoScE 91-3*
Fernandes Pinheiro, Luiz Leopoldo 1945- *WhoUN 92*
Fernandes Salling, Lehua 1949- *WhoAmW 93*
Fernandez, Alejo c. 1470-1543 *BioIn 17*
Fernandez, Alfredo Jose 1957- *WhoEmL 93*
Fernandez, Angel d1991 *BioIn 17*
Fernandez, Angel Jose 1953- *DcMexL*
Fernandez, Armand 1928- *BioIn 17*
Fernandez, Beatrice 1964- *WhoAmW 93*
Fernandez, Carmen 1943- *WhoWor 93*
Fernandez, Claude 1952- *St&PR 93*
Fernandez, Eduardo Buglioni 1936- *WhoSSW 93*
Fernandez, Emilio 1904-1986 *HispAmA*
Fernandez, Emilio (El Indio) 1904-1986 *MiSFD 9N*
Fernandez, F.G. 1928- *WhoScE 91-3*
Fernandez, Ferdinand Francis 1937- *HispAmA, WhoAm 92*
Fernandez, Fernando *ScF&FL 92*
Fernandez, Filemon Lebumfacil 1938- *WhoWor 93*
Fernandez, Francisco Oves d1990 *BioIn 17*
Fernandez, Frutos M. 1937- *WhoScE 91-3*
Fernandez, Gigi 1964- *NotHsAW 93*
Fernandez, Giselle 1961- *NotHsAW 93*
Fernandez, Happy Craven 1939- *WhoAmW 93*
Fernandez, Hermes 1920- *St&PR 93*
Fernandez, Horacio M.C. *Law&B 92*
Fernandez, Ines Teresa 1952- *WhoE 93, WhoEmL 93*
Fernandez, Isabel Lidia 1964- *WhoAmW 93*
Fernandez, James D. 1961- *ConAu 139*
Fernandez, Jorge A. 1944- *St&PR 93*
Fernandez, Jose Abrantes d1991 *BioIn 17*
Fernandez, Jose B. 1948- *HispAmA*
Fernandez, Jose Raul 1935- *WhoSSW 93*
Fernandez, Jose Walfredo 1955- *WhoAm 92, WhoEmL 93*
Fernandez, Joseph A. *BioIn 17*
Fernandez, Joseph A. 1935- *WhoAm 92, WhoE 93*
Fernandez, Joseph A. 1936- *HispAmA [port]*
Fernandez, Keith Damien 1958- *WhoEmL 93*
Fernandez, Laura Bove 1915- *WhoAmW 93*
Fernandez, Linda Flawn 1943- *WhoAmW 93*
Fernandez, Luis Felipe 1958- *WhoSSW 93*
Fernandez, Macedonio 1874-1952 *SpAmA*
Fernandez, Magali 1935- *WhoAmW 93*
Fernandez, Manuel *St&PR 93*
Fernandez, Manuel 1954- *WhoSSW 93*
Fernandez, Manuel Jose 1946- *HispAmA*
Fernandez, Maria Elena 1964- *WhoAmW 93*
Fernandez, Mariano Hugo 1939- *WhoAm 92*
Fernandez, Mary Joe 1971- *BioIn 17, NotHsAW 93, WhoAmW 93*
Fernandez, Moraima 1951- *WhoEmL 93*
Fernandez, Nino J. 1941- *St&PR 93*
Fernandez, Pedro fl. 1480-1521 *BioIn 17*
Fernandez, Rene 1961- *WhoEmL 93, WhoWor 93*
Fernandez, Ricardo R. 1940- *HispAmA, WhoAm 92*
Fernandez, Richard Murray 1954- *WhoEmL 93*
Fernandez, Robert E. *Law&B 92*
Fernandez, Robert Frank 1949- *WhoSSW 93*
Fernandez, Roberto 1951- *HispAmA [port]*
Fernandez, Roldan 1946- *St&PR 93*
Fernandez, Sally Garza 1958- *NotHsAW 93*
Fernandez, Santiago *Law&B 92*
Fernandez, Sergio 1926- *DcMexL*
Fernandez, Tony 1962- *HispAmA*
Fernandez Arbos, Enrique *Baker 92*
Fernandez-Arrondo, Maria del Carmen 1931- *WhoAmW 93*
Fernandez Ballesteros, Carlos Alberto 1941- *WhoUN 92*
Fernandez Bordas, Antonio 1870-1950 *Baker 92*
Fernandez Caballero, Manuel 1835-1906 *Baker 92*
Fernandez Carrillo, Angel German 1948- *WhoWor 93*
Fernandez-Cruz, Arturo 1943- *WhoScE 91-3*
Fernandez de Cordova, Ignacio 1777-1816 *DcMexL*
Fernandez de Lizardi, Jose Joaquin 1776-1827 *DcMexL*
Fernandez de Navarrete, Juan c. 1526-1579 *BioIn 17*
Fernandez de San Salvador, Agustin Pomposo 1756-1842 *DcMexL*
Fernandez Haar, Ana Maria 1951- *NotHsAW 93*
Fernandez-Iznaola, Ricardo Jaime 1949- *WhoEmL 93*
Fernandez MacGregor, Genaro 1883-1959 *DcMexL*
Fernandez-Martinez, Jose 1930- *WhoSSW 93, WhoWor 93*
Fernandez-Moran, Humberto 1924- *WhoAm 92, WhoWor 93*
Fernandez Moreno, Baldomero 1886-1950 *SpAmA*
Fernandez-Obregon, Adolfo Carlos 1951- *WhoE 93*
Fernandez-Ochoa, Josephine 1934- *WhoAmW 93*
Fernandez Olmos, Margarita 1949- *HispAmA [port]*
Fernandez-Ordonez, Francisco 1930-1992 *NewYTBS 92 [port]*
Fernandez Ordonez, Rafael 1940- *WhoScE 91-3*
Fernandez-Pita, Rafael 1950- *WhoUN 92*
Fernandez-Pol, Blanca Dora 1932- *WhoAmW 93, WhoE'93, WhoWor 93*
Fernandez-Pol, Jose Alberto 1943- *HispAmA [port]*
Fernandez Retamar, Roberto 1930- *SpAmA, WhoWor 93*
Fernandez-Rodriguez, Maria Luisa 1952- *WhoWor 93*
Fernandez-Salguero, Jose 1948- *WhoWor 93*
Fernandez-Sanjuan, Miguél Angel 1959- *WhoWor 93*
Fernandez-Serrano, Lucrecia *Law&B 92*
Fernandez-Velazquez, Juan Ramon 1936- *WhoAm 92*
Fernandez Violante, Marcela 1941- *MiSFD 9*
Fernandez-Vives, Rafael Alberto 1953- *WhoWor 93*
Fernando, Antony Earle Z. 1939- *WhoUN 92*
Fernando, Condegamage Cecil Theodore 1924- *WhoWor 93*
Fernando, D. J. Gamini *WhoWor 93*
Fernando, Kirthi Nanda 1944- *WhoWor 93*
Fernando, Neil Vernon Patrick 1928- *WhoWor 93*
Fernando, Prasenajit Nalinaj 1965- *WhoWor 93*
Fernando-Lewis, Sonia Gabriel 1954- *WhoAmW 93*
Fernas, Edward William 1944- *WhoAm 92*

Fernbach, Alfred Phillip 1915- WhoSSW 93
Fernbach, Louise Oftedal WhoAmW 93
Fernea, Robert Alan 1932- WhoAm 92
Ferneau, Philip James 1962- WhoEmL 93
Fernendes, John Henry 1924- WhoE 93
Ferner, Anthony WhoScE 91-1
Ferney, Ralph R. Law&B 92
Ferneyhough, Brian 1943- Baker 92
Ferneyhough, Charles Joseph, III 1949- WhoEmL 93
Fernhall, Bo BioIn 17
Fernholm, Bo 1941- WhoScE 91-4
Fernholz, Gustav Johannes Hans 1915- WhoWor 93
Fernholz, H.H. 1935- WhoScE 91-3
Ferni, Caroline 1839-1926 OxDcOp
Ferni, Eugenio OxDcOp
Ferni, Vincenzina 1853-1926 OxDcOp
Ferni, Virginia 1849-1934 OxDcOp
Ferniany, Isaac William 1951- WhoEmL 93
Fernie, John Donald 1933- WhoAm 92
Ferni-Giraldoni, Carolina 1839-1926 Baker 92
Ferniot, Jean 1918- WhoWor 93
Fernlund, I. WhoScE 91-4
Fernous, Louis F., Jr. 1938- St&PR 93, WhoAm 92
Fernow, Bernhard E. 1851-1923 GayN
Ferns, C.S. ScF&FL 92
Ferns, H(enry) S(tanley) 1913-1992 ConAu 137
Fernsler, John Paul 1940- WhoAm 92
Fernstrom, John (Axel) 1897-1961 Baker 92
Fernstrom, John Dickson 1947- WhoEmL 93
Fero, Lester K. 1919- WhoSSW 93
Fero, Robert William 1927- St&PR 93
Feroe, Paul James 1951- WhoWrEP 92
Feron, David Snyder 1932- WhoAm 92
Feroz, Ehsan Habib 1952- WhoEmL 93, WhoWor 93
Ferra, Joan Miro 1893-1983 BioIn 17
Ferrabosco, Alfonso 1543?-1588 Baker 92
Ferrabosco, Alfonso c. 1575-1628 Baker 92
Ferrabosco, Domenico Maria 1513-1574 Baker 92
Ferracci, Marie-Angele Vincenti 1948- WhoWor 93
Ferracuti, Franco 1927- WhoScE 91-3
Ferracuti, Stefano Eugenio 1958- WhoWor 93
Ferradini, Christiane 1924- WhoScE 91-2
Ferragamo, Michael Charles 1952- WhoE 93
Ferragamo, Salvatore 1898-1960 BioIn 17
Ferragano, Carmen 1943- WhoAm 92
Ferragano, Carmen J. 1943- St&PR 93
Ferraio, Nicholas L. 1946- WhoE 93
Ferraioli, Armando 1949- WhoEmL 93, WhoWor 93
Ferraioli, Jose E. Law&B 92
Ferraiolo, Giuseppe 1929- WhoScE 91-3
Ferrales, Savino R. 1950- St&PR 93
Ferran, Harry A. 1936- St&PR 93
Ferran Caldero, Javier 1933- WhoScE 91-3
Ferrand, Carole Thelma 1949- WhoAmW 93, WhoE 93
Ferrand, Jean C. 1930- WhoAm 92
Ferrandes, Pierre WhoScE 91-2
Ferrandini, Giovanni Battista c. 1710-1791 OxDcOp
Ferrandino, Salvatore Anthony 1958- WhoEmL 93
Ferrando, Bruno Giovanni 1937- WhoWor 93
Ferrando, de Almedina fl. 1506-1531 BioIn 17
Ferrando, Raymond 1912- WhoWor 93
Ferrang, Edward George 1950- WhoEmL 93
Ferrani, Cesira 1863-1943 Baker 92, OxDcOp
Ferrant, Nina P. Law&B 92
Ferrante, J.F. 1925- St&PR 93
Ferrante, Jeffrey Anthony 1959- WhoEmL 93
Ferrante, Joan Marguerite 1936- WhoAm 92, WhoAmW 93
Ferrante, Louis Carl 1931- St&PR 93
Ferrante, Olivia Ann 1948- WhoAmW 93, WhoEmL 93
Ferrante, Robert Louis 1937- WhoE 93
Ferrante-Rich, Joan Law&B 92
Ferranti, Vince 1941- WhoSSW 93
Ferranto, A. WhoScE 91-3
Ferranty, Robert Johnson 1928- St&PR 93
Ferrao, J. Mendes WhoScE 91-3
Ferrara, Abel BioIn 17, MiSFD 9
Ferrara, Arthur Vincent 1930- WhoAm 92
Ferrara, Beniamino 1924- WhoScE 91-3
Ferrara, Bernadette Mary 1955- WhoE 93
Ferrara, Charles John 1939- St&PR 93
Ferrara, Dino WhoScE 91-3
Ferrara, Ferdinando 1953- St&PR 93
Ferrara, Franco 1911-1985 Baker 92
Ferrara, Giorgio WhoScE 91-3
Ferrara, Giorgio 1947- MiSFD 9
Ferrara, Giuseppe 1932- MiSFD 9
Ferrara, John Joseph Law&B 92
Ferrara, Lawrence 1949- WhoE 93
Ferrara, Luigi WhoScE 91-3
Ferrara, Mary Louise 1950- WhoAmW 93
Ferrara, Peter Biagio, Jr. 1951- WhoAm 92
Ferrara, Peter Joseph 1955- WhoAm 92
Ferrara, Roger C. 1943- St&PR 93
Ferrara, Salvatore S. 1931- St&PR 93
Ferrara, Stephen A. 1940- St&PR 93
Ferrara, Stephen Arthur 1940- WhoAm 92
Ferrara, Stephen S. Law&B 92
Ferrara, Susan Elaine 1954- WhoAmW 93
Ferrara, Thomas Charles 1951- WhoE 93
Ferrara, V. Raymond 1947- St&PR 93
Ferrara, Vincent d1992 BioIn 17
Ferrara-Hazell, Catherine Lucille 1951- WhoEmL 93
Ferrara-Sherry, Donna Layne 1946- WhoEmL 93
Ferrarese, La c. 1755-c. 1799 OxDcOp
Ferrari, Adolfo 1807-1870 OxDcOp
Ferrari, Alberto Mario 1927- WhoAm 92
Ferrari, Benedetto c. 1603-1681 Baker 92, OxDcOp
Ferrari, Carlo 1903- WhoWor 93
Ferrari, Carlotta 1837-1907 Baker 92
Ferrari, Dino d1956 BioIn 17
Ferrari, Domenico c. 1722-1780 Baker 92
Ferrari, Domenico 1940- WhoAm 92
Ferrari, Donna Mae 1931- WhoAmW 93
Ferrari, Enzo 1898-1988 BioIn 17
Ferrari, Gabrielle 1851-1921 Baker 92
Ferrari, Giacomo 1763?-1842 OxDcOp
Ferrari, Giacomo (Gotifredo) 1763?-1842 Baker 92
Ferrari, Gilbert Jacques 1946- WhoUN 92
Ferrari, Gustave 1872-1948 Baker 92
Ferrari, Joseph Richard 1956- WhoE 93
Ferrari, Marco 1952- WhoWor 93
Ferrari, Mariano 1933- WhoScE 91-3
Ferrari, Mark J. 1956- ScF&FL 92
Ferrari, Michael Richard, Jr. 1940- WhoAm 92
Ferrari, Paul Francis 1930- St&PR 93
Ferrari, Pietro 1940- WhoScE 91-3
Ferrari, Richard Harold 1956- WhoE 93, WhoWor 93
Ferrari, Robert Joseph 1930- St&PR 93
Ferrari, Robert Joseph 1936- WhoAm 92
Ferrari-Fontana, Edoardo 1878-1936 Baker 92
Ferrarin, Kimberly Lee Gardner 1961- WhoEmL 93
Ferrario, Carlo 1833-1907 OxDcOp
Ferrario, Joseph A. BioIn 17
Ferrario, Joseph A. 1926- WhoAm 92
Ferrario, Roberto Law&B 92
Ferrario, Roberto 1947- WhoWor 93
Ferraris, Giovanni 1937- WhoScE 91-3
Ferraris, Maria 1950- WhoScE 91-3
Ferrari-Trecate, Luigi 1884-1964 Baker 92
Ferraro, Antonetta d1990 BioIn 17
Ferraro, Barbara BioIn 17
Ferraro, Bernadette A. 1952- WhoWrEP 92
Ferraro, Betty Ann 1925- WhoAmW 93
Ferraro, Charles A. 1953- St&PR 93
Ferraro, Charles John 1946- St&PR 93
Ferraro, Charles Michael 1955- WhoIns 93
Ferraro, Dave BioIn 17
Ferraro, Francis Stanley 1949- St&PR 93
Ferraro, Geraldine 1935- NewYTBS 92 [port]
Ferraro, Geraldine A. BioIn 17
Ferraro, Geraldine A. 1935- PolPar
Ferraro, Geraldine Anne 1935- WhoAm 92, WhoAmW 93, WhoE 93
Ferraro, John Francis 1934- WhoWor 93
Ferraro, John Ralph 1918- WhoAm 92
Ferraro, Joseph E. 1955- St&PR 93
Ferraro, Peter L. Law&B 92
Ferrary, Jeannette Reilly 1941- WhoAmW 93
Ferras, Christian 1933-1982 Baker 92
Ferrata, Giuseppe 1865-1928 Baker 92
Ferrate Pascual, G. WhoScE 91-3
Ferrater Mora, Jose 1912-1991 BioIn 17
Ferraz, Carlos Alberto Domingues 1945- WhoWor 93
Ferraz, Francisco Marconi 1951- WhoEmL 93, WhoSSW 93
Ferraz, Silamar 1943- WhoWor 93
Ferrazzano, Fred J. 1933- St&PR 93
Ferre, Antonio Luis 1934- WhoAm 92, WhoWor 93
Ferre, Frederick Pond 1933- WhoSSW 93
Ferre, Gianfranco BioIn 17
Ferre, Gianfranco 1944- WhoAm 92
Ferre, John P. 1956- ConAu 139
Ferre, Rosario BioIn 17
Ferre, Rosario 1942- SpAmA
Ferree, Bette Micucci 1947- WhoAmW 93
Ferree, Carolyn Ruth 1944- WhoAmW 93
Ferree, John Newton, Jr. 1946- WhoWor 93
Ferree, Myra Marx 1949- WhoEmL 93
Ferree, Patricia Ann 1947- WhoEmL 93, WhoSSW 93
Ferreira, Affonso Luiz 1926- WhoWor 93
Ferreira, Armando Thomas 1932- WhoAm 92
Ferreira, Eduardo De Sousa 1936- WhoWor 93
Ferreira, Eugene A. 1940- St&PR 93
Ferreira, Gail Veronica 1952- WhoEmL 93
Ferreira, Jairo A. 1938- St&PR 93
Ferreira, Jose, Jr. 1956- WhoAm 92, WhoEmL 93
Ferreira, Jose Antonio Soeiro 1952- WhoWor 93
Ferreira, Jose Costa d1991 BioIn 17
Ferreira, Judith Anne 1940- WhoAmW 93
Ferreira, Kenneth Roy 1950- WhoE 93
Ferreira, Rick ScF&FL 92
Ferreira Falcon, Magno 1936- WhoWor 93
Ferreira Penna, Domingos Soares 1818-1888 IntDcAn
Ferreira-Worth, Deirdre Charlyn 1958- WhoEmL 93, WhoWor 93
Ferreira Xavier, Cesar Eduardo Law&B 92
Ferrel, Jill S. Law&B 92
Ferrell, Alfred Cloud 1942- WhoSSW 93
Ferrell, Barbara BlkAmWO
Ferrell, Barbara Ann 1947- BiDAMSp 1989
Ferrell, Carl 1953- WhoEmL 93, WhoSSW 93
Ferrell, Catherine Klemann 1947- WhoSSW 93
Ferrell, Conchata Galen 1943- WhoAm 92
Ferrell, David Lee 1937- WhoAm 92
Ferrell, Ernest E. 1944- St&PR 93
Ferrell, Frank 1940- ConAu 136
Ferrell, Frank M. Law&B 92
Ferrell, Jack L. 1927- St&PR 93
Ferrell, James E. 1939- St&PR 93
Ferrell, James Edwin 1939- WhoAm 92
Ferrell, John Frederick 1942- WhoAm 92
Ferrell, Keith ScF&FL 92
Ferrell, Michael W. Law&B 92
Ferrell, Milton Morgan, Jr. 1951- WhoEmL 93
Ferrell, Nancy Warren 1932- ConAu 138, SmATA 70 [port], WhoWrEP 92
Ferrell, Otis C. 1920- St&PR 93
Ferrell, Patricia Anne 1956- WhoAmW 93
Ferrell, Peter Mason, III Law&B 92
Ferrell, Robert Hugh 1921- WhoAm 92, WhoWrEP 92
Ferrell, Skip WhoWrEP 92
Ferrell, Sonja Denise 1951- WhoE 93
Ferrell, Stephanie 1963- WhoAmW 93
Ferrell, Stephen W. 1951- St&PR 93
Ferrell, Timothy L. 1946- St&PR 93
Ferrelli, Cynthia Susan 1962- WhoE 93
Ferren, Ann Speidel 1939- WhoAmW 93, WhoE 93
Ferren, Bran MiSFD 9
Ferren, John Maxwell 1937- WhoAm 92
Ferrendelli, James Anthony 1936- WhoAm 92
Ferrer, E.A. St&PR 93
Ferrer, Elizabeth Virginia 1955- WhoEmL 93
Ferrer, Francis Xavier Law&B 92
Ferrer, Heidilisa Panganiban 1965- WhoAmW 93
Ferrer, Jennifer Klatsky 1956- WhoAmW 93
Ferrer, Joan Guell y 1800-1872 BioIn 17
Ferrer, Jose d1992 NewYTBS 92 [port]
Ferrer, Jose 1912- HispAmA
Ferrer, Jose 1912-1992 BioIn 17, CurBio 92N, IntDcF 2-3, MiSFD 9N, News 92, -92-3
Ferrer, Jose Figueres 1906-1990 BioIn 17
Ferrer, Linna M. AmWomPl
Ferrer, Marie Irene 1915- WhoAm 92
Ferrer, Mateo 1788-1864 Baker 92
Ferrer, Mel 1917- HispAmA, MiSFD 9
Ferrer, Miguel BioIn 17
Ferrer, Miguel Antonio 1938- WhoAm 92
Ferrer, Rafael 1911- Baker 92
Ferrer, Rafael 1933- HispAmA
Ferrer, Rafael Douglas Paul 1957- WhoEmL 93
Ferrer, Rodolfo N. 1935- WhoWor 93
Ferrera, Arthur Rodney 1916- WhoAm 92
Ferrera, James H. 1958- St&PR 93
Ferrera, Karen Ruth 1956- WhoAmW 93
Ferrera, Kenneth Grant 1945- St&PR 93, WhoAm 92
Ferrera, Robert James 1937- WhoAm 92
Ferrera-Cerrato, Ronald 1942- WhoWor 93
Ferrer Bonsoms, Jose 1920- WhoWor 93
Ferreri, Joanne M. WhoAmW 93
Ferreri, Marco 1928- MiSFD 9
Ferreri, Nicholas Raymond 1956- WhoE 93
Ferreri, Samuel James 1955- WhoEmL 93
Ferreri, Vito Richard 1949- WhoE 93
Ferrero, Aldo 1941- WhoScE 91-3
Ferrero, Charles J. 1937- St&PR 93
Ferrero, Giovanni M. 1936- WhoWor 93
Ferrero, Lorenzo 1951- Baker 92
Ferrero, Louis Peter 1942- St&PR 93
Ferrero, Willy 1906-1954 Baker 92
Ferretis, Jorge 1902-1962 DcMexL
Ferretti, Bruno Raymond 1936- St&PR 93
Ferretti, Giovanni Maria Mastai- 1792-1878 BioIn 17
Ferretti, Giuseppe WhoScE 91-3
Ferretti, Jacopo 1784-1852 OxDcOp
Ferretti, Paolo 1866-1938 Baker 92
Ferretti, Robert A. MiSFD 9
Ferrey, Azucena DcCPCAm
Ferrey-Laughton, Barbara Eloyce 1964- WhoAmW 93
Ferreyra, Mariana 1962- WhoAmW 93
Ferri, Alessandra BioIn 17
Ferri, Alessandra Maria 1963- WhoAm 92
Ferri, Baldassare 1610-1680 Baker 92, OxDcOp
Ferri, Everett Louis, Jr. 1945- WhoE 93
Ferri, Guy 1922-1991 BioIn 17
Ferri, Richard Stephen 1956- WhoWrEP 92
Ferri, Robert Law&B 92
Ferri, Roger C. 1949-1991 BioIn 17
Ferrick, William J. 1926- St&PR 93
Ferriday, Carolyn Wolsey d1990 BioIn 17
Ferrie, Richard ScF&FL 92
Ferriell, Bruce Justin Law&B 92
Ferriell, Jeffrey Thomas 1953- WhoEmL 93
Ferrier, Allison M. Law&B 92
Ferrier, Andrew A. 1959- St&PR 93
Ferrier, Kathleen 1912-1953 IntDcOp [port], OxDcOp
Ferrier, Kathleen (Mary) 1912-1953 Baker 92
Ferrier, Loretta Jean 1937- WhoAm 92
Ferrier, Pierre Emile 1927- WhoScE 91-4
Ferrier, Robert P. WhoScE 91-1
Ferrier, Robert Patton 1934- WhoWor 93
Ferrier, Susan 1782-1854 DcLB 116 [port]
Ferries, John Charles 1937- WhoAm 92
Ferrigno, Dennis 1947- St&PR 93
Ferrigno, Thomas Howard 1925- WhoE 93
Ferril, W.C. 1931- St&PR 93
Ferrill, Harve Anthony 1932- St&PR 93
Ferrin, Allan Hogate 1951- WhoEmL 93
Ferrin, Allan Wheeler 1921- WhoAm 92
Ferrin, Mark A. Law&B 92
Ferring, David ScF&FL 92
Ferrini, Vincent 1913- WhoWrEP 92
Ferrini, Vincenzo WhoScE 91-3
Ferris, Anita Brockway 1881-1923 AmWomPl
Ferris, Barton Purdy, Jr. 1940- WhoAm 92
Ferris, Benjamin Greeley, Jr. 1919- WhoAm 92
Ferris, Brian W. Law&B 92
Ferris, Charles F. Law&B 92
Ferris, Charles Jay Law&B 92
Ferris, Dan George 1958- WhoEmL 93
Ferris, Daniel P. Law&B 92
Ferris, David Louis 1934- WhoSSW 93
Ferris, Douglas W. St&PR 93
Ferris, Ernest Joseph 1932- WhoAm 92
Ferris, Frederick Joseph 1920- WhoAm 92, WhoE 93
Ferris, Gary William 1957- WhoE 93
Ferris, George 1859-1896 GayN
Ferris, George Mallette, Jr. 1927- St&PR 93, WhoAm 92
Ferris, Helen Josephine 1890- AmWomPl
Ferris, Henry D., Jr. 1949- WhoE 93
Ferris, J. David 1937- WhoIns 93
Ferris, James Cody ConAu 37NR, MajAI
Ferris, James Leonard 1944- WhoAm 92
Ferris, James Peter 1932- WhoAm 92
Ferris, Jean 1939- ConAu 38NR, DcAmChF 1985
Ferris, John Ackel, Jr. 1928- WhoSSW 93
Ferris, Joseph Anthony Law&B 92
Ferris, Kathleen Richard 1941- WhoSSW 93
Ferris, Kent Robert 1953- St&PR 93
Ferris, Kimberlee Robin 1955- WhoWrEP 92
Ferris, Mabel AmWomPl
Ferris, Norman Bernard 1931- WhoSSW 93
Ferris, Paul 1929- ScF&FL 92
Ferris, Peter Gerard 1956- WhoE 93
Ferris, Peter Simon, Jr. 1929- WhoE 93
Ferris, Richard Foth d1990 BioIn 17
Ferris, Robert A. 1942- St&PR 93
Ferris, Robert Albert 1942- WhoAm 92
Ferris, Robert Edmund 1918- WhoAm 92
Ferris, Robert Michael 1944- WhoSSW 93
Ferris, Ronald Curry 1945- WhoAm 92
Ferris, Steve Alan 1957- WhoSSW 93

Ferris, Theodore Vincent 1919- WhoE 93
Ferris, Thomas Francis 1930- WhoAm 92
Ferris, Thomas John 1950- WhoEmL 93
Ferris, Virginia Rogers WhoAm 92
Ferris, Walter V. Law&B 92
Ferris, William (Edward) 1937- Baker 92
Ferris, William H. 1874-1941 EncAACR
Ferris, William L. 1941- WhoIns 93
Ferris, William Michael 1948- WhoEmL 93
Ferris, William R. 1942- BioIn 17, ConAu 136
Ferris, William Reynolds 1942- WhoSSW 93
Ferriss, Abbott Lamoyne 1915- WhoSSW 93, WhoWrEP 92
Ferriss, David Platt 1919- WhoAm 92
Ferriss, Lucy 1954- BioIn 17
Ferris-Shotton, Colette Law&B 92
Ferriter, John P. WhoScE 91-2
Ferriter, Warren 1938- St&PR 93
Ferriter, Warren Joseph 1938- WhoAm 92
Ferritor, Daniel E. 1939- WhoAm 92, WhoSSW 93
Ferritto, Jerauld Damian 1950- WhoEmL 93
Ferro, David Newton 1946- WhoE 93
Ferro, Deborah WhoEmL 93
Ferro, Dino R. WhoScE 91-3
Ferro, Ernest D. St&PR 93
Ferro, John Joseph 1961- WhoEmL 93
Ferro, Manuel, Jr. 1946- WhoEmL 93
Ferro, Mathilde d1990 BioIn 17
Ferro, Matthew A. 1940- St&PR 93
Ferro, Maximilian Leonida 1942- WhoAm 92
Ferro, Pablo MiSFD 9
Ferro, Ramon R. 1941- St&PR 93
Ferro, Robert 1941-1988 ConGAN
Ferro, Thomas Anthony 1954- St&PR 93
Ferro, Thomas Louis 1947- WhoEmL 93
Ferro, Walter 1925- WhoAm 92
Ferron, Jacques BioIn 17
Ferron, Jacques 1921-1985 ScF&FL 92, WhoCanL 92
Ferron, Madeleine 1922- WhoCanL 92
Ferron, Michael R. 1954- St&PR 93
Ferron, Patrick Lee 1933- St&PR 93
Ferrone, Frank A. Law&B 92
Ferrone, Gene BioIn 17
Ferrone, Soldano 1940- WhoAm 92
Ferroni, Enzo 1921- WhoScE 91-3
Ferroni, Vincenzo (Emidio Carmine) 1858-1934 Baker 92
Ferro-Nyalka, Ruth Rudys 1930- WhoAmW 93
Ferrotti, Salvatore P. 1932- St&PR 93
Ferroud, Pierre-Octave 1900-1936 Baker 92
Ferrua, Bernard Gilbert 1948- WhoScE 91-2
Ferrucci, Gabriel 1936- St&PR 93
Ferrucci, Jeanne Smith 1940- WhoE 93
Ferrucci, Raymond Vincent 1926- St&PR 93, WhoAm 92
Ferruzza, Jeanne A. 1930- St&PR 93
Ferruzzi, Arturo 1940- WhoWor 93
Ferry, Abby Farwell 1851- AmWomPl
Ferry, Andrew Peter 1929- WhoAm 92
Ferry, Bryan BioIn 17
Ferry, Bryan 1945- WhoAm 92
Ferry, Charles Brian WhoScE 91-1
Ferry, Daniel John Willard 1966- BiDAMSp 1989
Ferry, David BioIn 17
Ferry, David Keane 1940- WhoAm 92
Ferry, Diane Louise 1947- WhoAmW 93
Ferry, Donald E. 1932- WhoAm 92
Ferry, James Allen 1937- St&PR 93, WhoAm 92
Ferry, Joan Evans 1941- WhoAmW 93, WhoE 93, WhoWor 93
Ferry, Johann Urwich- BioIn 17
Ferry, John Douglass 1912- WhoAm 92
Ferry, Joseph Vincent, Jr. 1947- WhoSSW 93
Ferry, Jules 1832-1893 BioIn 17
Ferry, Lucy BioIn 17
Ferry, Michael James 1957- WhoEmL 93
Ferry, Miles Yeoman 1932- WhoAm 92
Ferry, Pamela D. Law&B 92
Ferry, Richard M. 1937- St&PR 93
Ferry, Richard Michael 1937- WhoAm 92
Ferry, Richard W. Law&B 92
Ferry, Robert Dean 1937- WhoAm 92
Ferry, Wilbur Hugh 1910- WhoAm 92
Ferry, William Curran 1949- WhoIns 93
Fersen-Osten, Renee BioIn 17
Fersht, Alan Roy WhoScE 91-1
Fershtman, Julie Ilene 1961- WhoAmW 93, WhoEmL 93
Fersini, Mario 1926- WhoScE 91-3
Ferst, Albert F. 1919- St&PR 93
Ferstadt, Louis Goodman 1900-1954 BioIn 17
Ferstandig, Louis Lloyd 1924- WhoE 93
Ferstl, Roman Karl-Heinz 1945- WhoWor 93
Ferstl, Tom Michael 1939- WhoSSW 93
Ferstler, Howard William 1943- WhoWrEP 92
Fertig, Howard WhoAm 92, WhoWrEP 92
Fertig, John F. 1926- St&PR 93
Fertig-Dyks, Susan Beatrice 1944- WhoAmW 93
Fertik, Ira J. 1940- WhoAm 92
Fertitta, George BioIn 17
Fertitta, Joseph Frank 1922- St&PR 93
Fertitta, Marian Boudreaux 1948- WhoEmL 93
Fertitta, Naomi BioIn 17
Fertner, Antoni 1950- WhoWor 93
Ferwerda, Anton 1945- St&PR 93
Ferwerda, Geert Gerrit Jan 1922- WhoWor 93
Fery, John Bruce 1930- St&PR 93, WhoAm 92
Ferzacca, William 1927- WhoWor 93
Fesca, Alexander (Ernst) 1820-1849 Baker 92
Fesca, Friedrich (Ernst) 1789-1826 Baker 92
Fesen, Michael Robert 1957- WhoEmL 93
Fesenmaier, Stephen Lee 1949- WhoSSW 93
Feser, William Joseph 1925- St&PR 93
Feshbach, Herman 1917- WhoAm 92
Feshbach, Murray 1929- WhoWor 93
Feshbach, Norma Deitch 1926- WhoAm 92
Feshbach, Seymour 1925- WhoAm 92
Feskoe, Gaffney Jon 1949- WhoAm 92, WhoEmL 93
Fesler, August WhoScE 91-2
Fesler, Daniel L. St&PR 93
Fesler, David Richard 1928- WhoAm 92, WhoWor 93
Fesler, Robert L. 1937- St&PR 93
Fess, Marilynn Elaine Ewing 1944- WhoWor 93
Fess, Philip Eugene 1931- WhoAm 92
Fess, Simeon D. 1861-1936 PolPar
Fess, Simeon Davidson 1861-1936 BioIn 17
Fessas, Phaedon 1922- WhoWor 93
Fessenden, Hart 1927- St&PR 93
Fessenden, Larry MiSFD 9
Fessenden, William P. 1806-1869 PolPar
Fesserden, Thomas Green 1771-1837 JrnUS
Fessier, Michael 1907-1988 ScF&FL 92
Fessler, Ann Helene 1949- WhoE 93
Fessler, Denis Eugene 1949- WhoEmL 93
Fessler, Donald Francis 1931- St&PR 93, WhoAm 92
Fessler, Henry WhoScE 91-1
Fest, Thorrel Brooks 1910- WhoAm 92
Festa, Costanzo c. 1480-1545 Baker 92
Festa, Francesca 1778-1835 OxDcOp
Festa, James d1992 NewYTBS 92
Festa, Roger Reginald 1950- WhoEmL 93
Feste, David A. 1951- St&PR 93
Fester, Jeffrey Thompson 1961- WhoSSW 93
Festervan, Denise Campbell 1960- WhoAmW 93
Festing, Michael (Christian) c. 1680-1752 Baker 92
Festinger, Jonathan Bernard Law&B 92
Festinger, Leon 1919-1989 BioIn 17
Festo, Charles F. Law&B 92
Festus d380 OxDcByz
Festy, Bernard R. 1935- WhoScE 91-2
Fesus, George John 1942- St&PR 93
Fesus, Laszlo 1939- WhoScE 91-4
Fetch, Alan Michael 1953- WhoEmL 93
Fetchero, James V. 1920- St&PR 93
Fetchero, John Anthony, Jr. 1951- WhoEmL 93, WhoSSW 93
Fetchin, John Allan 1942- WhoAm 92
Fetchko, Peter J. 1943- WhoAm 92, WhoE 93
Feten, Douglas Leroy 1951- WhoEmL 93
Fetherolf, Joyce Wilson 1952- WhoEmL 93
Fethke, Carol Carde 1943- WhoAmW 93
Fetin, Vladimir 1925-1981 DrEEuF
Fetis, Adolphe (-Louis-Eugene) 1820-1873 Baker 92
Fetis, Edouard (-Louis-Francois) 1812-1909 Baker 92
Fetis, Francois-Joseph 1784-1871 Baker 92, OxDcOp
Fetler, Andrew 1925- WhoAm 92, WhoWrEP 92
Fetler, Dan Gregor 1952- WhoEmL 93, WhoWor 93
Fetler, Paul 1920- Baker 92, WhoAm 92
Fetner, Charles Anthony 1951- WhoAm 92
Fetner, Gerald Lawrence 1945- WhoE 93
Fetner, R. Scott 1928- WhoAm 92
Fetner, Robert Henry 1922- WhoAm 92
Fetner, Suzanne 1929- WhoAmW 93
Fetridge, Bonnie-Jean Clark 1915- WhoAm 92, WhoWor 93
Fetridge, Clark Worthington 1946- St&PR 93, WhoAm 92
Fetrow, John Edward 1939- St&PR 93
Fetscher, Paul George William 1945- WhoAm 92, WhoE 93
Fetske, Ruth Betty 1922- WhoAmW 93
Fett, Eugene Werner 1932- WhoAm 92
Fett, Robert H. 1932- St&PR 93
Fetter, Alexander Lees 1937- WhoAm 92
Fetter, Elizabeth Ann 1958- WhoEmL 93
Fetter, Frank Whitson 1899-1991 BioIn 17
Fetter, John Branch 1951- WhoEmL 93
Fetter, Ralph R. 1943- St&PR 93
Fetter, Richard Elwood 1923- WhoAm 92
Fetter, Robert Barclay 1924- WhoAm 92
Fetter, Theodore Henry 1906- WhoAm 92
Fetter, Trevor 1960- WhoAm 92
Fetter, Vojtech 1905-1971 IntDcAn
Fetterman, Harold Ralph 1941- WhoAm 92
Fetterman, James C. 1947- WhoEmL 93
Fetterman, John Henry, Jr. 1932- WhoAm 92
Fetterman, Lynn K. 1947- St&PR 93
Fetterman, William Judd c. 1833-1866 HarEnMi
Fetterolf, Charles E. 1932- St&PR 93
Fetterolf, Donald Edward 1953- WhoE 93
Fetteroll, Eugene Carl, Jr. 1935- WhoE 93, WhoWor 93
Fetters, Joan Frances 1939- WhoAmW 93
Fetters, Norman Craig, II 1942- WhoAm 92
Fetting, Fritz 1926- WhoScE 91-3
Fetting, Rainer 1949- BioIn 17
Fettinger, Laurie A. WhoAmW 93
Fettweis, Alfred L.M. 1926- WhoScE 91-3
Fettweis, Gunter B. 1924- WhoScE 91-4
Fettweis, Gunter Bernhard Leo 1924- WhoWor 93
Fettweis, Yvonne Cache 1935- WhoAmW 93, WhoE 93, WhoWor 93
Fetz, Friedrich 1927- WhoWor 93
Fetzer, Brian Charles 1950- WhoEmL 93
Fetzer, Edward Frank 1940- WhoAm 92
Fetzer, John 1901-1991 BioIn 17
Fetzer, John Charles 1953- WhoEmL 93
Fetzer, Leland 1930- ScF&FL 92
Fetzer, Mark Stephen 1950- WhoEmL 93
Fetzer, Wallace S. 1954- St&PR 93
Fetzner, Carl G. 1934- St&PR 93
Fetzner, James Frederick 1946- St&PR 93
Feucht, Donald Lee 1933- WhoAm 92
Feucht, Robert W. 1934- St&PR 93
Feuchter, Robert 1926- St&PR 93
Feuchtwang, Thomas Emanuel 1930- WhoAm 92
Feudale, Barry Francis 1946- WhoEmL 93
Feuer, Bradley Scott 1960- WhoSSW 93
Feuer, Cy 1911- WhoAm 92, WhoE 93
Feuer, Henry 1912- WhoAm 92
Feuer, Ileana Cepeda 1960- WhoSSW 93
Feuer, Kathryn Beliveau d1992 NewYTBS 92
Feuer, Kathryn Beliveau 1926-1992 BioIn 17, ConAu 137
Feuer, Morris 1933- St&PR 93
Feuer, Robert Charles 1936- WhoE 93
Feuer, S.S. 1923- St&PR 93
Feuer, Seymour S. 1923- WhoAm 92
Feuer, Stephanie 1955- WhoEmL 93
Feuerbacher, Berndt P. 1940- WhoScE 91-3
Feuerberg, Hubert 1925- WhoScE 91-3
Feuerberg, Mark Stanley 1942- WhoE 93, WhoWor 93
Feuerberg, Paul Richard 1946- WhoEmL 93
Feuerburgh, Joseph 1908- WhoE 93
Feuereisen, Charles 1918- BioIn 17
Feuerhelm, Leonard Norman, Jr. 1949- WhoSSW 93
Feuerlein, Willy John Arthur 1911- WhoAm 92
Feuerlicht, Roberta Strauss 1931-1991 BioIn 17
Feuerman, Carol Jeanne 1945- WhoE 93
Feuermann, Emanuel 1902-1942 Baker 92
Feuerstein, Alan Ricky 1950- WhoWor 93
Feuerstein, Claude 1951- WhoWor 93
Feuerstein, Donald M. 1937- St&PR 93
Feuerstein, Donald Martin 1937- WhoAm 92
Feuerstein, Gary Ray 1950- WhoEmL 93
Feuerstein, Georg 1947- WhoWrEP 92
Feuerstein, Herbert 1927- St&PR 93
Feuerstein, Howard M. 1939- WhoAm 92
Feuerwerker, Albert 1927- WhoAm 92, WhoWrEP 92
Feuerzeig, Henry Louis 1938- WhoAm 92
Feugeas, Jorge Nestor 1944- WhoWor 93
Feuillade, Jacques Bernard 1929- WhoScE 91-2
Feuille, Richard Harlan 1920- WhoAm 92
Feuillere, Edwige 1907- IntDcF 2-3 [port]
Feuless, Scott Charles 1960- WhoEmL 93, WhoSSW 93
Feulner, Edwin John, Jr. 1941- WhoAm 92, WhoE 93, WhoWor 93
Feurey, Claudia Packer 1949- WhoEmL 93
Feurig, Thomas Leo 1950- WhoAm 92
Feurstein, Guntram 1937- WhoScE 91-4
Feusner, Randy Bruce 1960- WhoEmL 93
Feuss, Fred R. d1991 BioIn 17
Feuss, Linda U. Law&B 92
Feusse, Thomas A. 1959- St&PR 93
Feustel-Buechl, Jorg 1940- WhoScE 91-2
Feutre, Alain Philippe 1945- WhoWor 93
Fevang, Leroy Conrad 1936- WhoAm 92
Fever, Buck 1876-1941 BioIn 17
Fevin, Antoine de c. 1470-1511? Baker 92
Fevin, Robert fl. 16th cent.- Baker 92
Fevre, Michel 1943- WhoScE 91-2
Fevre, Michel F. 1936- WhoUN 92
Fevrier, Henri 1875-1957 Baker 92
Fevrier, Henry 1875-1957 OxDcOp
Fevrier, R. WhoScE 91-2
Fevurly, Keith Robert 1951- WhoEmL 93
Few, Etta Shockley AmWomPl
Few, Paula Kozicki 1943- WhoAmW 93
Few, Philip Coles WhoScE 91-1
Fewell, Anthony Roy WhoScE 91-1
Fewell, Charles K., Jr. Law&B 92
Fewell, Charles Kenneth, Jr. 1943- WhoE 93
Fewell, Kenneth Robert 1948- WhoIns 93
Fewkes, Jesse Walter 1850-1930 Baker 92
Fewson, Charles Arthur WhoScE 91-1
Fey, Charles J. 1950- WhoSSW 93
Fey, Curt F. WhoE 93
Fey, David L. 1944- St&PR 93
Fey, Dorothy WhoAm 92
Fey, Golda Conwell d1990 BioIn 17
Fey, Hans BioIn 17
Fey, Harold E. BioIn 17
Fey, John Theodore 1917- WhoAm 92
Feydeau, Georges 1862-1921 BioIn 17
Feyder, Jacques 1885-1948 MiSFD 9N
Feydy, Anne ScF&FL 92
Feyen, Jan J.A. 1942- WhoScE 91-2
Feyerabend, Paul Karl 1924- WhoAm 92
Feynman, Richard NewYTBS 92 [port]
Feynman, Richard Phillips BioIn 17
Fezandie, Clement 1865-1959 ScF&FL 92
Fezer, Fritz Erwin 1924- WhoWor 93
Ffeil, Helena A. AmWomPl
Ffinch, Michael 1934- ConAu 137
Ffowcs Williams, John Eirwyn WhoScE 91-1
Ffrangcon-Davies, David (Thomas) 1855-1918 Baker 92
Ffrangcon-Davies, Gwen 1891-1992 BioIn 17, NewYTBS 92
ffrench-Beytagh, Gonville 1912-1991 AnObit 1991
Fiacco, Norene Pfautz WhoE 93
Fiacre, Albert E. 1950- St&PR 93
Fiala, Brian D. 1950- St&PR 93
Fiala, Brian Donald 1950- WhoEmL 93
Fiala, David Marcus 1946- WhoEmL 93
Fiala, Franz 1929- WhoScE 91-4
Fiala, George (Joseph) 1922- Baker 92
Fiala, Jiri 1931- WhoScE 91-4
Fiala, John L. 1924-1990 BioIn 17
Fiala, Kenneth Richard 1932- St&PR 93
Fiala, Stephen T. 1957- St&PR 93
Fialer, Philip Anthony 1938- WhoAm 92
Fialka, John J. 1938- ConAu 139
Fialkov, Herman 1922- St&PR 93, WhoAm 92
Fialkow, Philip Jack 1934- WhoAm 92
Fialkow, Steven 1943- WhoE 93
Fialkowska, Janina 1951- Baker 92
Fialkowski, Konrad R. 1939- WhoUN 92
Fialkowski, Krzysztof Tadeusz 1944- WhoWor 93
Fiamand, Anne-Marie WhoScE 91-2
Fiamengo, Marya 1926- WhoCanL 92
Fiamingo, Nancy Anne 1949- WhoAmW 93
Fiammenghi, Gioia BioIn 17
Fiaschetti, Joanne Law&B 92
Fiaush, John C. 1930- St&PR 93
Fibich, Howard Raymond 1932- WhoAm 92
Fibich, Judith Berg d1992 NewYTBS 92
Fibich, Zdenek 1850-1900 Baker 92, OxDcOp
Fibichova, Betty 1846-1901 OxDcOp
Fibiger, John Andrew 1932- St&PR 93, WhoAm 92
Fibos, Barry 1945- St&PR 93
Fica, Juan 1949- WhoE 93
Ficarra, Bernard Joseph 1914- WhoE 93
Ficarro, John R. Law&B 92
Ficarro, John Robert 1952- WhoEmL 93
Ficat, Raymond Paul 1917- WhoScE 91-2
Ficco, Dane Patrick 1961- WhoE 93
Ficco, James Vincent, III 1954- WhoAm 92
Ficeto, Michael Joseph 1951- WhoEmL 93
Fichenberg, Robert Gordon 1920- WhoAm 92, WhoE 93
Ficher, Ilda Violeta 1928- WhoAmW 93
Ficher, Jacobo 1896-1978 Baker 92
Fichera, Lewis Carmen 1949- WhoEmL 93

Fichman, Frederick *ScF&FL 92*
Fichte, Johann Gottlieb 1762-1814 *BioIn 17*
Fichtel, Carl Edwin 1933- *WhoAm 92*
Fichtel, Mark Dilworth 1946- *St&PR 93*
Fichtel, Rudolph Robert 1915- *WhoAm 92*
Fichtenbaum, George L. d1991 *BioIn 17, NewYTBS 92*
Fichtenbaum, James Howard 1944- *WhoSSW 93*
Fichtenbaum, Paul *BioIn 17*
Fichter, Joseph H. 1908- *WhoAm 92*
Fichter, Thomas d1990 *BioIn 17*
Fichthorn, Luke Eberly, III 1941- *St&PR 93, WhoAm 92, WhoSSW 93*
Fichtner, Heinz-Joachim 1927- *WhoScE 91-3*
Fichtner, Ralph Paul *Law&B 92*
Fick, Alan J. *BioIn 17*
Fick, C. Milton *Law&B 92*
Fick, E. Dean 1944- *St&PR 93*
Fick, Eugen Georg Michael 1926- *WhoWor 93*
Fick, Gary Warren 1943- *WhoAm 92*
Fick, Georgia *BioIn 17*
Fick, Robert 1941- *St&PR 93*
Fickeisen, Cheryl L. 1946- *St&PR 93*
Fickel, Kurt 1936- *WhoScE 91-3*
Fickel, Malcolm L. 1928- *St&PR 93*
Fickel, Robert Bruce 1946- *WhoEmL 93*
Ficken, Millicent Sigler 1933- *WhoAmW 93*
Fickenscher, Arthur 1871-1954 *Baker 92*
Fickenscher, Donald A. *Law&B 92*
Fickenscher, Gerald H. 1943- *St&PR 93*
Ficker, Rudolf von 1886-1954 *Baker 92*
Ficker, Sarah Jane 1929- *WhoWrEP 92*
Fickes, Marita Clark 1946- *WhoAmW 93, WhoEmL 93*
Fickett, Edward Hale 1918- *WhoAm 92*
Fickey, Richard W. 1940- *St&PR 93*
Fickies, Robert Howard 1944- *WhoE 93*
Fickinger, Wayne Joseph 1926- *WhoAm 92*
Fickinger, William Joseph 1934- *WhoAm 92*
Fickling, Amy Leigh 1957- *WhoWrEP 92*
Fickling, David *ScF&FL 92*
Fickling, Roy Hampton 1965- *WhoSSW 93*
Fickling, William A., Jr. 1932- *St&PR 93*
Fickling, William Arthur, Jr. 1932- *WhoAm 92, WhoSSW 93*
Ficks, F. Lawrence 1930- *WhoE 93*
Ficks, Lee B. 1937- *St&PR 93*
Ficks, R. Snowden *ScF&FL 92*
Ficks, Robert L., Jr. 1919- *St&PR 93*
Ficon, Amy Schroeder 1965- *WhoAmW 93*
Ficorelli, Rick Thomas 1951- *WhoEmL 93*
Ficquette, Sharon Elaine 1956- *WhoEmL 93*
Fidanza, Gianni 1939- *St&PR 93*
Fidanza, Giovanni 1939- *WhoAm 92*
Fidanzi, Mario A. 1951- *St&PR 93*
Fiddes, Richard C. *Law&B 92*
Fiddick, Paul William *BioIn 17*
Fiddick, Paul William 1949- *WhoAm 92, WhoSSW 93*
Fiddler, Barbara Dillow 1940- *WhoE 93*
Fideghelli, Carlo 1938- *WhoScE 91-3*
Fidel, Edward Allen 1943- *WhoSSW 93*
Fidelholtz, James Lawrence 1941- *WhoWor 93*
Fidelman, Stanley J. 1936- *St&PR 93*
Fidler, Alwyn Sheppard- 1909-1990 *BioIn 17*
Fidler, Jay W. 1922- *St&PR 93*
Fidler, John Kelvin *WhoScE 91-1*
Fidler, Kathleen 1899-1980 *ScF&FL 92*
Fidler, Mark W. 1952- *St&PR 93*
Fidler, Steven E. 1943- *St&PR 93*
Fidoten, Robert Earl 1927- *WhoE 93*
Fidrych, Mariellen Johanna 1958- *WhoE 93*
Fiducia, Gene 1925- *St&PR 93*
Fidzianska-Dolot, Anna Zofia 1932- *WhoScE 91-4*
Fie, Larry Eugene 1938- *St&PR 93*
Fiebach, H. Robert 1939- *WhoAm 92*
Fiebach, Ralph Paul 1917- *WhoAm 92*
Fieber, Heribert 1927- *WhoScE 91-4*
Fiebert, Murray 1922- *St&PR 93*
Fiebig, Alexandre Marc 1968- *WhoWor 93*
Fiebig, Martin 1932- *WhoScE 91-3*
Fiebiger, Daniel Joseph 1951- *WhoEmL 93*
Fiebiger, James Russell 1941- *WhoAm 92*
Fiebrink, Mark Edward 1951- *WhoIns 93*
Fiechter, A.E. 1924- *WhoScE 91-4*
Fiechter, Georges Andre 1930- *WhoWor 93*
Fiederlein, Gustav L. 1926- *St&PR 93*
Fiederlein, Thomas R. 1946- *St&PR 93*
Fiederowicz, Walter Michael 1946- *WhoEmL 93*
Fiedler, Arkady 1894-1985 *PolBiDi*
Fiedler, Arthur 1894-1979 *Baker 92*
Fiedler, Bobbi 1937- *BioIn 17*
Fiedler, Douglas W. 1946- *St&PR 93*
Fiedler, Edgar F. 1943- *St&PR 93*
Fiedler, Edward Henry, Jr. 1932- *St&PR 93*
Fiedler, Franz 1938- *WhoScE 91-3*
Fiedler, Fred Edward 1922- *WhoAm 92*
Fiedler, Hans-Joachim 1927- *WhoScE 91-3*
Fiedler, Hans Karl 1955- *WhoEmL 93, WhoSSW 93*
Fiedler, Harold Joseph 1924- *WhoAm 92*
Fiedler, Jean 1928- *ScF&FL 92*
Fiedler, John Amberg 1941- *WhoWor 93*
Fiedler, Kurt W. 1936- *WhoScE 91-3*
Fiedler, Leslie 1917- *JeAmFiW, JeAmHC*
Fiedler, Leslie A. *BioIn 17*
Fiedler, Leslie A. 1917- *ScF&FL 92*
Fiedler, Leslie Aaron 1917- *WhoAm 92, WhoWrEP 92*
Fiedler, Marc 1955- *WhoEmL 93*
Fiedler, (August) Max 1859-1939 *Baker 92*
Fiedler, Michael Allen 1956- *WhoEmL 93, WhoSSW 93*
Fiedler, Patrick James 1953- *WhoAm 92*
Fiedler, Sally A. 1939- *WhoWrEP 92*
Fiedler, Wilfried 1940- *WhoWor 93*
Fiedoral, Joseph Fletcher 1926- *St&PR 93*
Fiedorczuk, Zygmunt 1925- *WhoScE 91-4*
Fiegel, John Leland 1944- *WhoE 93*
Fiehrer, R.A. 1934- *St&PR 93*
Fiekers, Jerome Francis 1946- *WhoE 93*
Fiel, David Hy *WhoE 93*
Fiel, Maxine Lucille *WhoAm 92, WhoAmW 93, WhoWor 93*
Fiel, Robyn Ilene 1961- *St&PR 93*
Field, A. J. 1924- *WhoAm 92*
Field, Andrea Bear 1949- *WhoAm 92, WhoAmW 93*
Field, Arthur Norman 1935- *WhoAm 92*
Field, Barry Elliot 1947- *WhoWor 93*
Field, Ben 1902?-1973? *ScF&FL 92*
Field, Benjamin R. 1938- *St&PR 93*
Field, Brian Peter 1941- *WhoWor 93*
Field, Clarence Frederick *WhoScE 91-1*
Field, Corey 1956- *WhoEmL 93*
Field, Cyrus Adams 1902- *WhoAm 92*
Field, D.B. *WhoScE 91-1*
Field, David C. *Law&B 92*
Field, David Charles 1948- *St&PR 93*
Field, David Dudley 1805-1894 *BioIn 17*
Field, David Ellis 1953- *WhoEmL 93*
Field, Dawn LeAnn Van Hoy 1965- *WhoSSW 93*
Field, Douglas Scott 1955- *WhoEmL 93*
Field, Edward 1924- *BioIn 17, WhoWrEP 92*
Field, Edwin Martin 1924- *WhoE 93*
Field, Elizabeth Farnham 1926- *St&PR 93*
Field, Ephraim Joshua 1915- *WhoWor 93*
Field, Eugene 1850-1895 *GayN, JrnUS, MajAI [port]*
Field, Flo *AmWomPl*
Field, Frank Laidley 1929- *WhoWor 93*
Field, Frederick W. *BioIn 17*
Field, Garrett 1954- *WhoEmL 93*
Field, George Brooks 1929- *WhoAm 92*
Field, George Sydney 1905- *WhoAm 92*
Field, Harold David, Jr. 1927- *WhoAm 92*
Field, Harry B. *Law&B 92*
Field, Henry Augustus, Jr. 1928- *WhoAm 92*
Field, Henry Frederick 1941- *WhoAm 92*
Field, Hermann Haviland 1910- *WhoAm 92*
Field, Jack d1990 *BioIn 17*
Field, James Bernard 1926- *WhoAm 92*
Field, Jeffrey Frederic 1954- *WhoEmL 93*
Field, John 1782-1837 *Baker 92, BioIn 17*
Field, John 1921-1991 *AnObit 1991, BioIn 17*
Field, John C. 1948- *St&PR 93*
Field, John Edwin *WhoScE 91-1*
Field, John Louis 1930- *WhoAm 92*
Field, John W. 1914 *St&PR 93*
Field, Joseph Myron 1932- *WhoAm 92*
Field, Karen Ann 1936- *WhoAmW 93*
Field, Lawrence *ScF&FL 92*
Field, Lyman 1914- *WhoAm 92*
Field, M. Patricia 1958- *WhoEmL 93*
Field, Marilyn G. *Law&B 92*
Field, Marshall 1852-1906 *GayN*
Field, Marshall 1941- *WhoAm 92, WhoWor 93*
Field, Marshall, III 1893-1956 *DcLB 127 [port], JrnUS*
Field, Marshall, IV 1916-1965 *DcLB 127*
Field, Marshall, V 1941- *DcLB 127 [port]*
Field, Michael Stanley 1940- *WhoE 93*
Field, Nathaniel d1990 *BioIn 17*
Field, Noel Macdonald, Jr. 1934- *WhoAm 92*
Field, Penny Schiffman 1960- *WhoEmL 93*
Field, Peter 1926- *St&PR 93*
Field, Rachel Lyman 1894-1942 *AmWomPl, ConAu 137, MajAI [port]*
Field, Richard Clark 1940- *WhoAm 92*
Field, Richard D. 1940- *St&PR 93*
Field, Richard L. *Law&B 92*
Field, Rikki Lamartino *Law&B 92*
Field, Robert Edward 1945- *WhoAm 92*
Field, Robert Steven 1949- *WhoEmL 93*
Field, Robert Warren 1944- *WhoAm 92*
Field, Ruth Baker *ScF&FL 92*
Field, Sally *BioIn 17*
Field, Sally 1946- *ConTFT 10, HolBB [port], IntDcF 2-3, WhoAm 92, WhoAmW 93*
Field, Sampson R. 1902-1991 *BioIn 17*
Field, Sandra Gusciora 1958- *WhoEmL 93*
Field, Sara Bard 1882- *AmWomPl*
Field, Sid 1904-1950 *QDrFCA 92 [port]*
Field, Stanley *WhoWrEP 92*
Field, Stephen H. 1948- *St&PR 93*
Field, Stephen J. 1816-1899 *BioIn 17*
Field, Stephen Johnson 1816-1899 *OxCSupC [port]*
Field, Steven Philip 1951- *WhoE 93*
Field, Ted *WhoAm 92*
Field, Ted 1952?- *ConTFT 10*
Field, Ted Wayne 1948- *WhoE 93*
Field, Thomas C. 1942- *St&PR 93*
Field, Thomas Walter, Jr. 1933- *St&PR 93*
Field, Thomas Warren 1820-1881 *BioIn 17*
Field, Virginia d1992 *NewYTBS 92 [port]*
Field, Virginia 1917-1992 *BioIn 17*
Field, William D. 1923- *St&PR 93*
Field, William Douglas, Jr. *Law&B 92*
Field, William Stephenson 1929- *WhoAm 92*
Fieldbinder, A. Christine 1951- *WhoAmW 93*
Fielden, C. Franklin, III 1946- *WhoEmL 93*
Fielden, E.M. *WhoScE 91-1*
Fielder, Cecil *BioIn 17, NewYTBS 92 [port]*
Fielder, Cecil 1963- *News 93-2 [port], WhoAm 92*
Fielder, Charles Robert 1943- *St&PR 93, WhoAm 92, WhoSSW 93*
Fielder, Dorothy Scott 1943- *WhoAmW 93*
Fielder, Douglas Stratton 1940- *WhoE 93*
Fielder, Judy Parsons 1947- *WhoEmL 93*
Fielder, Kristi Karen *Law&B 92*
Fielder, Pat *BioIn 17*
Fielder, Virginia Dodge 1948- *St&PR 93*
Fieldhouse, Lord d1992 *NewYTBS 92*
Fieldhouse, Anthony 1944- *St&PR 93*
Fieldhouse, G.E. 1917- *St&PR 93*
Fieldhouse, John David Elliott 1928-1992 *BioIn 17*
Fieldhouse of Gosport, Baron 1928-1992 *BioIn 17*
Fielding, Allen Fred 1943- *WhoAm 92*
Fielding, Elizabeth May 1917- *WhoAm 92*
Fielding, Fenella *QDrFCA 92*
Fielding, Fred Fisher 1939- *WhoAm 92*
Fielding, Henry 1707-1754 *BioIn 17, MagSWL [port], WorLitC [port]*
Fielding, Ivor Rene 1942- *WhoAm 92*
Fielding, Joy 1945- *ScF&FL 92, WhoCanL 92*
Fielding, Linden 1952- *St&PR 93*
Fielding, Peggy Lou Moss *WhoWrEP 92*
Fielding, Ronald H. 1949- *St&PR 93*
Fielding, Steven P. 1960- *St&PR 93*
Fielding, Stuart 1939- *WhoE 93*
Fielding, Tom Dennis 1940- *St&PR 93*
Fielding, Xan 1918-1991 *AnObit 1991*
Fieldman, Leon 1926- *WhoAm 92*
Fields, Anita 1940- *WhoAmW 93*
Fields, Annie 1834-1915 *BioIn 17*
Fields, Annie Adams 1834-1915 *AmWomPl*
Fields, Anthony Lindsay Austin 1943- *WhoAm 92*
Fields, Barb 1964- *St&PR 93*
Fields, Bernard Nathan 1938- *WhoAm 92*
Fields, Bertram Harris 1929- *WhoAm 92, WhoWor 93*
Fields, Bill 1949- *WhoAm 92*
Fields, Brian Jay *Law&B 92*
Fields, Carl Victor 1951- *WhoEmL 93*
Fields, Charles Richmond 1962- *WhoSSW 93*
Fields, Christine S. *Law&B 92*
Fields, Curtis Grey 1933- *St&PR 93, WhoAm 92*
Fields, Daisy Bresley 1915- *WhoAmW 93*
Fields, Darcey Ames 1950- *WhoEmL 93*
Fields, David Clark 1937- *WhoAm 92*
Fields, David M. *Law&B 92*
Fields, Debbi *BioIn 17*
Fields, Debbi 1956- *ConEn*
Fields, Dennis Franklin, Sr. 1947- *WhoSSW 93*
Fields, Dorothy 1905-1974 *AmWomPl*
Fields, Douglas Philip 1942- *St&PR 93, WhoAm 92*
Fields, Edgar M. 1939- *St&PR 93*
Fields, Edward 1945- *WhoE 93*
Fields, Ellis Kirby 1917- *WhoAm 92*
Fields, Evelyn *BioIn 17*
Fields, Freddie 1923- *WhoAm 92*
Fields, Garson R. 1949- *St&PR 93*
Fields, Gow Belton 1963- *WhoEmL 93, WhoSSW 93*
Fields, Gracie 1898-1979 *IntDcF 2-3 [port], QDrFCA 92 [port]*
Fields, Hall Ratcliff 1937- *WhoSSW 93*
Fields, Harold Thomas, Jr. 1938- *WhoAm 92*
Fields, Howard M. 1956- *WhoEmL 93*
Fields, Jack M., Jr. 1952- *CngDr 91*
Fields, Jack Milton, Jr. 1952- *WhoAm 92, WhoSSW 93*
Fields, Jackson Edward, Jr. *Law&B 92*
Fields, James 1948-1984 *Baker 92*
Fields, James Edward, Jr. 1963- *WhoEmL 93, WhoSSW 93*
Fields, James Perry 1932- *WhoSSW 93*
Fields, James Thomas 1816-1881 *BioIn 17*
Fields, Jennie 1953- *WhoAmW 93*
Fields, Jill Averly 1966- *WhoAmW 93*
Fields, Jonathan A. *Law&B 92*
Fields, Joyce M. 1947- *St&PR 93*
Fields, Kathy Ann 1958- *WhoAmW 93, WhoEmL 93*
Fields, Larry S. 1954- *WhoEmL 93, WhoSSW 93*
Fields, Leo 1928- *St&PR 93, WhoAm 92*
Fields, Mary Durland 1930- *WhoSSW 93*
Fields, Mary T. 1950- *WhoSSW 93*
Fields, Michael *MiSFD 9*
Fields, Mitchell Andrew 1952- *WhoEmL 93*
Fields, Morgan *ConAu 137, ScF&FL 92*
Fields, Nancy Carlene 1952- *WhoWrEP 92*
Fields, Patricia Helen Elder 1946- *WhoAmW 93*
Fields, Paul Robert 1919- *WhoAm 92*
Fields, Ralph Raymond 1907- *WhoAm 92*
Fields, Randy *BioIn 17*
Fields, Rick D. 1942- *WhoWrEP 92*
Fields, Robert Charles 1920- *WhoAm 92*
Fields, Robert J. *Law&B 92*
Fields, Roger Alan *Law&B 92*
Fields, Ronald Olen 1948- *WhoSSW 93*
Fields, Ruth Ann 1947- *WhoAmW 93*
Fields, Scott Michael 1957- *St&PR 93*
Fields, Shelia Rhonda 1953- *WhoSSW 93*
Fields, Stuart Howard 1943- *WhoE 93, WhoWor 93*
Fields, Susan Louise 1952- *WhoWrEP 92*
Fields, Terri 1948- *ScF&FL 92*
Fields, Theodore 1922- *WhoAm 92*
Fields, W.C. 1879?-1946 *IntDcF 2-3 [port], QDrFCA 92 [port]*
Fields, Wendy Lynn 1946- *WhoAm 92, WhoAmW 93*
Fields, William *BioIn 17*
Fields, William Albert 1939- *WhoAm 92*
Fields, William C., III *Law&B 92*
Fields, William F. 1927- *St&PR 93*
Fields, William Hudson, III 1934- *WhoAm 92*
Fields, William Jay 1936- *St&PR 93, WhoAm 92*
Fields-Babineau, Miriam Starr 1959- *WhoAmW 93*
Fielek, Etta *WhoAmW 93*
Fieleke, Norman S. 1932- *St&PR 93*
Fieleke, Norman Siegfried 1932- *WhoAm 92*
Fielitz, Alexander von 1860-1930 *Baker 92*
Fielitz, Lynn Richard 1959- *WhoSSW 93*
Fielo, Muriel Bryant 1921- *WhoAmW 93, WhoE 93*
Fielstra, Helen Adams 1921- *WhoAm 92*
Fien, Richard *St&PR 93*
Fien, Robert J. 1933- *St&PR 93*
Fienberg, Richard Tresch 1956- *St&PR 93*
Fienberg, Robert Littlewood 1939- *St&PR 93*
Fienberg, Stephen Elliott 1942- *WhoAm 92*
Fiene, Frank J. 1950- *St&PR 93*
Fier, Elihu 1931- *WhoAm 92*
Fierberg, Stephen Joel 1935- *St&PR 93*
Fierberg, Steven Edward 1954- *WhoEmL 93*
Fierce, Richard A. *Law&B 92*
Fierce, Steven W. 1949- *St&PR 93*
Fierer, Joshua Allan 1937- *WhoAm 92*
Fierheller, George Alfred 1933- *WhoAm 92, WhoE 93*
Fiering, Norman Sanford 1935- *WhoAm 92*
Fierke, Thomas G. *Law&B 92*
Fierko, Edward J. 1941- *St&PR 93*
Fierla, Linda Lea 1951- *WhoAmW 93*
Fierle, Robert Joseph 1922- *St&PR 93*
Fierman, Daniel J. *St&PR 93*
Fierman, Gerald Shea 1924- *St&PR 93, WhoE 93, WhoWor 93*
Fierman, Ronald S. 1950- *WhoAm 92*
Fiero, Patrick 1954- *WhoE 93*

Fierro, Benjamin, III 1954- *WhoEmL 93*
Fierro, Robert John 1941- *WhoSSW 93*
Fierros, Ruth Victoria 1920- *WhoSSW 93*
Fierro Sanchez, Emilia Ana 1941- *WhoWor 93*
Fiers, Alan *BioIn 17*
Fiers, Alan D. 1939- *St&PR 93*
Fiers, Walter 1931- *WhoScE 91-2*
Fierst, Bruce Philip 1951- *WhoEmL 93*
Fierstein, Harvey Forbes 1954- *WhoAm 92, WhoE 93*
Fiery, Donald Ernst 1929- *St&PR 93*
Fierz, Lukas Werner 1941- *WhoWor 93*
Fies, Marie Joyce 1939- *WhoAmW 93*
Fiest, Alan D. 1952- *St&PR 93*
Fiest, David L. 1952- *WhoE 93*
Fiett, J. *WhoScE 91-4*
Fietz, Lothar 1933- *WhoWor 93*
Fieve, Ronald Robert 1930- *WhoAm 92*
Fievet, Claude 1865-1938
See Fievet, Paul 1892-1980 *Baker 92*
Fievet, Paul 1892-1980 *Baker 92*
Fieweger, William Henry 1914- *WhoAm 92*
Fife, Bernard 1915- *St&PR 93, WhoAm 92*
Fife, Bruce Fielding 1952- *WhoWrEP 92*
Fife, Edward H. 1942- *WhoAm 92*
Fife, Elaine Harner 1950- *WhoEmL 93*
Fife, Eugene V. 1940- *St&PR 93*
Fife, Eugene Vawter 1940- *WhoAm 92*
Fife, Evelyn Henderson *AmWomPl*
Fife, John Douglas, Jr. 1955- *WhoWor 93*
Fife, Jonathan Donald 1941- *WhoAm 92*
Fife, Kenneth Gordon 1945- *St&PR 93*
Fife, Loren M. *Law&B 92*
Fife, Lorin *Law&B 92*
Fife, Lorin M. 1953- *St&PR 93*
Fife, Lorin Merrill, III *Law&B 92*
Fife, Wallace Clyde 1929- *WhoAsAP 91*
Fife, William Franklin 1921- *WhoAm 92, WhoSSW 93*
Fife, William J. *BioIn 17*
Fifer, Charles Norman 1922- *WhoAm 92*
Fifer, Elizabeth 1944- *ConAu 139*
Fifer, Kenneth 1947- *WhoE 93*
Fifer Canby, Susan Melinda 1948- *WhoAmW 93*
Fifield, Barbara Jane 1947- *WhoAmW 93*
Fifield, Cheryl Schneider 1955- *WhoAmW 93, WhoEmL 93*
Fifield, Effie Woodward *AmWomPl*
Fifield, Russell Hunt 1914- *WhoAm 92*
Fifield, William 1916-1987 *ScF&FL 92*
Fiflis, Ted J. 1933- *WhoAm 92*
Figen, I. Sevki 1924- *WhoWor 93*
Figenshu, Bill 1950- *BioIn 17*
Figes, Eva *BioIn 17*
Figg, Martin 1944- *WhoScE 91-1*
Figge, Charlene Elizabeth 1948- *WhoAmW 93, WhoEmL 93*
Figge, F. J., II *WhoSSW 93*
Figge, Frederick Henry, Jr. 1934- *WhoAm 92*
Figge, I. E. Ward 1937- *WhoSSW 93*
Figge, Kenneth J. 1933- *St&PR 93*
Figgie, Harry E., Jr. 1923- *St&PR 93*
Figgins, David F. 1929- *St&PR 93*
Figgins, David Forrester 1929- *WhoAm 92*
Figgis, Darrell 1882-1925 *ScF&FL 92*
Figgis, Mike *MiSFD 9*
Figgis, N.P. 1939- *ScF&FL 92*
Figgs, Carrie Law Morgan *AmWomPl*
Figilis, Karen 1954- *St&PR 93*
Figilis, William Murray 1940- *St&PR 93*
Figir, Issac 1947- *WhoAsAP 91*
Figlar, Anita Wise 1950- *WhoAmW 93, WhoEmL 93*
Figler, Alan Anthony 1948- *WhoEmL 93*
Figler, Michael Howard 1944- *WhoE 93*
Figley, Melvin Morgan 1920- *WhoAm 92*
Figliola, Deborah Ann 1956- *WhoAmW 93*
Figliozzi, John Philip 1946- *St&PR 93, WhoEmL 93*
Figliozzi, Robert J. 1938- *St&PR 93*
Fignar, Eugene Michael 1946- *WhoEmL 93*
Figner, Medea *IntDcOp*
Figner, Medea 1858-1952 *Baker 92*
Figner, Medea 1859-1952 *OxDcOp*
Figner, Nikolai 1857-1918 *Baker 92*
Figner, Nikolay 1857-1918 *OxDcOp*
Figner, Nikolay Nikolayevich 1857-1918 *IntDcOp [port]*
Fignole, Daniel 1915-1986 *DcCPCAm*
Figoff, Michael 1943- *St&PR 93*
Figucia, Joseph Charles, Jr. 1957- *WhoEmL 93*
Figueira, Donna D. *Law&B 92*
Figueiredo, Antonio de Albuquerque 1941- *WhoWor 93*
Figueiredo, E. 1939- *WhoScE 91-3*
Figueiredo, Hubert Fernandes 1958- *WhoEmL 93*
Figueiredo, Joao Baptista de 1918- *DcTwHis*
Figueiredo Marques, Jose J. 1937- *WhoScE 91-3*
Figuera Aymerich, Angela 1902-1984 *BioIn 17*
Figueredo, Carlos 1910- *Baker 92*
Figueredo y Clarens, Carlos *ScF&FL 92*
Figueres, Jose 1906-1990 *DcTwHis*
Figueres Ferrer, Jose 1906-1990 *BioIn 17*
Figueres Ferrer, Jose Maria Hipolito 1906-1990 *DcCPCAm*
Figueroa, Antonio 1947- *WhoE 93*
Figueroa, Boris D. 1950- *St&PR 93*
Figueroa, David *BioIn 17*
Figueroa, Gabriel 1907- *HispAmA*
Figueroa, Howard G. 1930- *St&PR 93*
Figueroa, J.F. *WhoScE 91-3*
Figueroa, Jose-Angel 1946- *BioIn 17*
Figueroa, Loida 1917- *NotHsAW 93*
Figueroa, Luis 1951- *WhoEmL 93*
Figueroa, Medardo 1887-1981 *ScF&FL 92*
Figuerola, Marcelo R. 1951- *WhoUN 92*
Figulus, Wolfgang c. 1525-1589 *Baker 92*
Figura, Phillip Michael 1949- *St&PR 93*
Figurelli, Lou *BioIn 17*
Figures, Michael Anthony 1947- *AfrAmBi [port]*
Figurski, Gerald Anthony 1945- *WhoSSW 93*
Figurski, Robert John 1943- *St&PR 93*
Figus-Bystry, Viliam 1875-1937 *Baker 92*
Fihn, Jeffrey Glaser 1949- *WhoEmL 93*
Fiigen, Bruce C. *Law&B 92*
Fiil, Niels P. 1941- *WhoScE 91-2*
Fijalkowski, Bogdan Thaddeus 1932- *WhoWor 93*
Fijnaut, H.M. *WhoScE 91-3*
Fike, Amy Drake 1956- *WhoEmL 93*
Fike, Deborah Ann 1954- *WhoSSW 93*
Fike, Edward Lake 1920- *WhoAm 92*
Fike, Elizabeth Smith 1960- *WhoAmW 93, WhoEmL 93*
Fike, William T. 1947- *St&PR 93*
Fikejs, John Wayne 1939- *St&PR 93*
Fikes, Alan Lester 1938- *St&PR 93*
Fikes, Dennis Rae 1955- *WhoWor 93*
Fiksdal, John P. 1949- *WhoEmL 93*
Fila, Joseph Duncan 1950- *WhoSSW 93*
Fila, Marian 1930- *WhoUN 92*
Filak, Richard Joseph 1946- *St&PR 93*
Filali, Abdellatif 1928- *WhoWor 93*
Filandro, Anthony Salvatore 1930- *St&PR 93*
Filanowski, Mark L. *St&PR 93*
Filante, Bill d1992 *NewYTBS 92 [port]*
Filbert, Eugene Anton 1950- *WhoSSW 93*
Filbert, John Schuyler 1924- *St&PR 93*
Filbin, Charles Everett 1955- *WhoSSW 93*
Filbrun, J.S. *ScF&FL 92*
Filby, P. William 1911- *BioIn 17*
Filby, Percy William 1911- *WhoAm 92*
Filcek, Henryk 1928- *WhoScE 91-4*
Filchock, E. *WhoWrEP 92*
Filchock, Ethel *WhoAmW 93, WhoWor 93*
Filcik, J.P. *Law&B 92*
Filderman, Rene 1930- *WhoScE 91-2*
Fildes, Robert *WhoScE 91-1*
Fildes, Robert Anthony 1938- *WhoAm 92*
File, Joseph C. *Law&B 92*
File, Sandra Elizabeth *WhoScE 91-1*
Filean, Arthur S. 1938- *St&PR 93*
Filek, Allan A. 1944- *St&PR 93*
Filelfo, Francesco 1398-1481 *OxDcByz*
Filep, Gyorgy 1932- *WhoScE 91-4*
Filepp, George Edward 1949- *WhoE 93, WhoEmL 93*
Filer, Denis E. 1932- *WhoScE 91-1*
Filer, Elizabeth Ann 1923- *WhoAm 92, WhoAmW 93*
Filer, Emily Harkins 1936- *WhoSSW 93*
Filer, John H. 1924- *St&PR 93*
Filer, Lloyd Jackson, Jr. 1919- *WhoAm 92*
Filer, Maxcy *BioIn 17*
Filer, Randall Keith 1952- *WhoEmL 93*
Filerman, Gary Lewis 1936- *WhoAm 92*
Filerman, Michael Herman 1938- *WhoAm 92*
Files, John T. 1918- *St&PR 93*
Files, Jon Mylne 1935- *St&PR 93*
Files, Mark Willard 1941- *WhoSSW 93, WhoWor 93*
Files, Meg 1946- *ScF&FL 92*
Filesi, Thomas R. 1935- *St&PR 93*
Filev, Ivan 1941- *Baker 92*
Filewood, Lewis Francis, Jr. 1931- *St&PR 93*
Filgas, James Frank 1934- *WhoAm 92*
Filho, Antunes *BioIn 17*
Fili, Pat *BioIn 17*
Filiasi, Lorenzo 1878-1963 *Baker 92*
Filiatrault, Edward J. 1938- *St&PR 93*
Filiberto, Frank Stephen Charles 1954- *WhoSSW 93*
Filimon, Ioan 1928- *WhoScE 91-4*
Filing, Nicholas A. 1947- *WhoIns 93*
Filion, Jean-Paul 1927- *WhoCanL 92*
Filion, Maurice *WhoAm 92*
Filion, Pierre 1951- *WhoCanL 92*
Filios, Louis A. 1905- *St&PR 93*
Filipczynski, Leszek 1923- *WhoScE 91-4*
Filipe, Armindo R. 1931- *WhoScE 91-3*
Filipe, Jose Antonio 1964- *WhoWor 93*
Filipek, Jan 1931- *WhoScE 91-4*
Filipi, Joan Leahy 1950- *WhoAmW 93, WhoEmL 93*
Filipiak, Boleslaw 1901-1978 *PolBiDi*
Filipiak, Francis Leonard 1938- *WhoAm 92*
Filipic, Allen Joseph 1923- *St&PR 93*
Filipkowski, Andrzej 1929- *WhoScE 91-4, WhoWor 93*
Filipkowski, Jan 1929- *WhoScE 91-4*
Filipov, Filip 1946- *St&PR 93*
Filipowicz, John David *Law&B 92*
Filipp, Carolyn Francine 1950- *WhoEmL 93*
Filipp, Mark Richard 1955- *WhoEmL 93*
Filippelli, Ann Marie 1961- *WhoAmW 93*
Filippelli, Ronald Lee 1938- *WhoAm 92*
Filippello, A. Nicholas 1942- *St&PR 93*
Filippi, Filippo 1830-1887 *Baker 92*
Filippi, Frank Joseph 1907- *WhoAm 92*
Filippi, Giorgio 1935- *WhoScE 91-3*
Filippi, Roland K. *Law&B 92*
Filippides, George John 1966- *WhoE 93*
Filippini, Christine Marie 1957- *WhoE 93*
Filippone, Vincent A. 1935- *WhoAm 92*
Filippone, Vincent Anthony 1935- *St&PR 93*
Filipps, Frank Peter 1947- *St&PR 93, WhoAm 92*
Filips, Nicholas Joseph 1925- *WhoSSW 93*
Filisko, Frank Edward 1942- *WhoAm 92*
Filistri, Antonio de' Caramondani fl. 1788-1808 *OxDcOp*
Filius, Istvan 1931- *WhoScE 91-4*
Filizetti, Gary John 1945- *WhoAm 92*
Filke, Max 1855-1911 *Baker 92*
Filker, Milton d1990 *BioIn 17*
Fill, Christopher *WhoScE 91-1*
Fill, Clifford George 1950- *WhoEmL 93*
Fill, Dennis C. 1929- *WhoAm 92*
Filla, Mark Louis 1964- *WhoSSW 93*
Filler, Gary B. 1941- *St&PR 93*
Filler, Robert 1923- *WhoAm 92*
Filler, Ronald 1957- *WhoE 93*
Filler, Ronald Howard 1948- *WhoEmL 93*
Filler, Susan Melanie 1947- *WhoEmL 93*
Fillet, Mitchell Harris 1948- *WhoAm 92, WhoEmL 93*
Fillet, Toni Dee 1957- *WhoEmL 93*
Filleul, Henry 1877-1959 *Baker 92*
Filley, Bette Elaine 1933- *WhoAmW 93*
Filley, Dorothy McCracken 1915- *WhoAmW 93*
Filley, Richard David 1955- *WhoEmL 93*
Filliatre, C. 1936- *WhoScE 91-2*
Fillingham, Patricia 1924- *WhoWrEP 92*
Fillingham, Peter J. *WhoE 93*
Fillion, Diana Sikora 1951- *WhoAmW 93*
Fillion, Joseph M. 1933- *St&PR 93*
Fillion, Michelle Marie 1949- *WhoAmW 93*
Fillion, Thomas John 1953- *WhoEmL 93*
Fillios, Louis Charles 1923- *WhoAm 92, WhoWor 93*
Fillips, Bruce Harold 1944- *St&PR 93*
Fillius, Milton Franklin, Jr. 1922- *WhoAm 92*
Fillman, James 1951- *WhoE 93*
Fillman, Jesse R. 1905-1991 *BioIn 17*
Fillman, Lee *BioIn 17*
Fillmann, William Craig 1946- *St&PR 93*
Fillmore, Abigail Powers 1798-1853 *BioIn 17*
Fillmore, Henry 1881-1956 *BioIn 17*
Fillmore, (James) Henry, (Jr.) 1881-1956 *Baker 92*
Fillmore, John Comfort 1843-1898 *Baker 92*
Fillmore, Millard 1800-1874 *BioIn 17, PolPar*
Fillmore, Peter Arthur 1936- *WhoAm 92*
Fillon, Nick J. 1926- *St&PR 93*
Filloy, Beverlee Ann Howe 1926- *WhoAmW 93*
Filmon, Gary *BioIn 17*
Filmon, Gary Albert 1942- *WhoAm 92*
Filo, John Paul *BioIn 17*
Filo, William John 1946- *St&PR 93*
Filoche, Bernard Christian 1945- *WhoScE 91-2*
Filor, Anna May 1941- *WhoE 93*
Filoramo, John Robert 1951- *WhoEmL 93*
Filoromo, Michael A. 1928- *St&PR 93*
Filosa, Gary Fairmont Randolph V., II 1931- *WhoAm 92, WhoSSW 93, WhoWor 93*
Filosa, Marvin Sam 1924- *St&PR 93*
Filowitz, Mark S. 1951- *St&PR 93*
Filpus, Uno W. 1926- *St&PR 93*
Filskov, Susan B. 1950- *WhoEmL 93, WhoSSW 93*
Filson, Ronald Coulter 1946- *WhoAm 92, WhoSSW 93*
Filston, Howard Church 1935- *WhoAm 92*
Filstrup, E. Christian 1942- *WhoAm 92*
Filstrup, Scott Hogenson 1942- *WhoWor 93*
Filter, Eunice M. *St&PR 93*
Filter, Eunice M. 1940- *WhoAm 92, WhoAmW 93*
Filter, Terrance Anderson 1950- *WhoEmL 93*
Filtz, (Johann) Anton 1733-1760 *Baker 92*
Filtz, Regis F. 1937- *St&PR 93*
Filyaw, Liston Nathaniel 1949- *WhoE 93*
Filzen, Daniel V. 1949- *St&PR 93*
Fimbel, Edward, III 1948- *St&PR 93*
Fimea, Victoria Elizabeth *Law&B 92*
Fimrite, Ron *BioIn 17*
Fina, Thomas Witmer 1924- *WhoSSW 93*
Finale, Frank Louis 1942- *WhoWrEP 92*
Finamore, Roy Edward 1953- *WhoEmL 93*
Finan, Ellen Cranston 1951- *WhoEmL 93*
Finance, Chantal 1947- *WhoScE 91-2*
Finance, Jean-Pierre 1947- *WhoScE 91-2*
Finarelli, Margaret G. 1946- *WhoAmW 93*
Finati, Claudio Roberto *Law&B 92*
Finberg, Alan Robert 1927- *St&PR 93, WhoAm 92*
Finberg, Barbara Denning 1929- *WhoAm 92, WhoAmW 93, WhoE 93*
Finberg, Donald Richard 1931- *WhoAm 92*
Finberg, Laurence 1923- *WhoAm 92*
Finburgh, Bert J. 1915- *St&PR 93*
Fincannon, L.N. *St&PR 93*
Finch, Albert M.T., Jr. *Law&B 92*
Finch, Anne 1661-1720 *BioIn 17*
Finch, Annie Ridley Crane 1956- *WhoWrEP 92*
Finch, Arthur *WhoScE 91-1*
Finch, C. Herbert 1931- *WhoAm 92*
Finch, Caleb E(llicott) 1939- *ConAu 139*
Finch, Caleb Ellicott 1939- *WhoAm 92*
Finch, Carolyn-Bogart 1938- *WhoAm 92, WhoAmW 93*
Finch, Charles *MiSFD 9*
Finch, Charles Baker 1920- *WhoAm 92, WhoE 93*
Finch, Christopher 1939- *ConAu 138, ScF&FL 92*
Finch, David S. 1941- *WhoAm 92*
Finch, Diane Shields 1947- *WhoAmW 93, WhoEmL 93*
Finch, Edward Ridley, Jr. 1919- *WhoAm 92, WhoE 93*
Finch, Eleanor Harrison 1908- *WhoE 93*
Finch, Elsie Garretson *AmWomPl*
Finch, Frank P. 1943- *St&PR 93*
Finch, George Danton, III 1946- *WhoEmL 93*
Finch, George Goode 1937- *St&PR 93*
Finch, Gordon L., Jr. 1934- *St&PR 93*
Finch, Harold Bertram, Jr. 1927- *St&PR 93, WhoAm 92, WhoWor 93*
Finch, Herman Manuel 1914- *WhoAm 92, WhoWor 93*
Finch, James M., Jr. 1909- *St&PR 93*
Finch, James Nellis 1932- *WhoE 93*
Finch, Janet Mitchell 1950- *WhoEmL 93, WhoSSW 93*
Finch, Janet Valerie *WhoScE 91-1*
Finch, Jeremiah Stanton 1910- *WhoAm 92*
Finch, Jeremy Bertrand 1950- *WhoEmL 93*
Finch, John F. 1935- *St&PR 93*
Finch, Judith Malone 1944- *WhoAm 92*
Finch, Julie Lynn *Law&B 92*
Finch, Leta CeCile 1948- *WhoEmL 93*
Finch, Lucine *AmWomPl*
Finch, Matthew James *Law&B 92*
Finch, Michael David 1946- *St&PR 93*
Finch, Michael Paul 1946- *WhoAm 92*
Finch, Nigel *MiSFD 9*
Finch, Peter 1916-1977 *IntDcF 2-3*
Finch, Phillip 1948- *ScF&FL 92*
Finch, R. Jay 1941- *St&PR 93*
Finch, Randy Carl 1955- *WhoEmL 93*
Finch, Raymond Lawrence 1940- *WhoAm 92*
Finch, Richard 1954-
See KC & the Sunshine Band *SoulM*
Finch, Robert 1900- *WhoCanL 92*
Finch, Robert (Charles) 1943- *ConAu 137*
Finch, Robert Hardin, Jr. 1953- *WhoSSW 93*
Finch, Rogers Burton 1920- *WhoAm 92*
Finch, Ronald M., Jr. 1932- *WhoAm 92*
Finch, Ruth Corbige 1916- *WhoAmW 93*
Finch, Ruth L. *Law&B 92*
Finch, Ruth W. 1916- *WhoE 93*
Finch, Sheila 1935- *ScF&FL 92*
Finch, Stephen Baker, Jr. *Law&B 92*
Finch, Stuart M. 1919-1991 *BioIn 17*
Finch, Susan Sanders 1931- *WhoAmW 93*
Finch, Walter Goss Gilchrist 1918- *WhoAm 92, WhoWor 93*
Finch, William G.H. 1897-1990 *BioIn 17*
Finchen, Jim 1952- *St&PR 93*

Fincher, Cameron Lane 1926- *WhoAm 92, WhoWor 93*
Fincher, David *MiSFD 9*
Fincher, John Albert 1911- *WhoAm 92*
Finck, Arnold J. 1925- *WhoScE 91-3*
Finck, Friedrich August von 1718-1766 *HarEnMi*
Finck, Heinrich 1444?-1527 *Baker 92*
Finck, Henry T(heophilus) 1854-1926 *Baker 92*
Finck, Hermann 1527-1558 *Baker 92*
Finck, Kevin William 1954- *WhoEmL 93, WhoWor 93*
Finck, Nancy Coombs 1951- *WhoAmW 93*
Finck, William Harry 1945- *WhoE 93*
Fincke, Gary W. 1945- *WhoWrEP 92*
Fincke, Gerald B. 1937- *St&PR 93*
Fincke, Margaret Louise d1989 *BioIn 17*
Finckh, Eberhard C. 1929- *WhoScE 91-3*
Findeisen, Nikolai (Fyodorovich) 1868-1928 *Baker 92*
Findeisen, Otto 1862-1947 *Baker 92*
Finden, Per Oistein 1947- *WhoScE 91-4*
Findenegg, Gerhard H. 1938- *WhoScE 91-3*
Findenegg, Gunter R. 1942- *WhoScE 91-3*
Finder, Alan Eliot 1952- *WhoEmL 93*
Finder, Jan Howard 1939- *ScF&FL 92*
Finder, Martin *ConAu 137, MajAI*
Finder, Robert Andrew 1947- *WhoWor 93*
Finder, Theodore Roosevelt 1914- *WhoAm 92*
Findlay, Cam *BioIn 17*
Findlay, Eric Fraser 1926- *St&PR 93, WhoAm 92*
Findlay, Harald B. 1958- *St&PR 93*
Findlay, Helen d1992 *NewYTBS 92*
Findlay, Helen T. 1909- *St&PR 93*
Findlay, John Wilson 1915- *WhoAm 92, WhoSSW 93*
Findlay, Joseph William O., Jr. 1935- *WhoUN 92*
Findlay, Michael Alistair 1945- *WhoAm 92*
Findlay, Robert B. *WhoAm 92*
Findlay, Susan 1943- *St&PR 93*
Findlay, Theodore Bernard 1939- *WhoAm 92*
Findlay, Walstein C., Jr. 1903- *St&PR 93, WhoAm 92*
Findlay, William 1768-1846 *BioIn 17*
Findlay, William Robertson 1963- *St&PR 93*
Findlay-Shirras, Alasdair R. 1949- *St&PR 93*
Findler, Jean Kerch 1951- *WhoEmL 93*
Findley, Don Aaron 1926- *WhoAm 92*
Findley, James Smith 1926- *WhoAm 92*
Findley, Jerry R. 1944- *St&PR 93*
Findley, John Allen, Jr. 1951- *WhoEmL 93*
Findley, John Sidney 1942- *WhoSSW 93, WhoWor 93*
Findley, Lynette Michelle 1954- *WhoAmW 93*
Findley, Nigel *ScF&FL 92*
Findley, Paul 1921- *WhoAm 92*
Findley, Stephen Charles 1949- *WhoEmL 93*
Findley, Thomas J. 1947- *St&PR 93*
Findley, Timothy *BioIn 17*
Findley, Timothy 1930- *IntLitE, ScF&FL 92, WhoCanL 92*
Findley, Timothy Irving 1930- *WhoWrEP 92*
Findley, William Edward, Jr. 1922- *St&PR 93*
Findley, William Nichols 1914- *WhoAm 92*
Findling, George Matthew 1942- *St&PR 93*
Findling, Jane Erwin 1947- *WhoAmW 93*
Findorff, Jean L. *Law&B 92*
Findorff, Robert L. 1929- *St&PR 93*
Findorff, Robert Lewis 1929- *WhoAm 92*
Findur, Martin A. 1926- *St&PR 93*
Fine, A. Kenneth *Law&B 92*
Fine, Allan H. 1940- *St&PR 93*
Fine, Andrea Joiner 1950- *WhoWrEP 92*
Fine, Andrew Snyder 1936- *St&PR 93*
Fine, Anne 1891- *SmATA 15AS [port]*
Fine, Anne 1947- *ChlFicS, ConAu 38NR, MajAI [port], SmATA 72 [port], WhoAm 92*
Fine, Arthur I. 1937- *WhoAm 92*
Fine, Barry 1931- *St&PR 93*
Fine, Benjamin 1948- *WhoE 93, WhoEmL 93*
Fine, Bernard J. 1926- *WhoAm 92*
Fine, Bob 1949- *WhoEmL 93*
Fine, Burton *WhoAm 92*
Fine, Charles 1944- *St&PR 93*
Fine, Charles Leon 1932- *WhoAm 92*
Fine, Daniel Matthew 1959- *WhoEmL 93*
Fine, David 1912- *St&PR 93*
Fine, David Jeffrey 1950- *WhoAm 92, WhoWor 93*
Fine, Donald Irving 1922- *WhoAm 92*
Fine, Elsa Honig 1930- *WhoWrEP 92*
Fine, Gary Alan 1950- *ScF&FL 92*
Fine, Gary Martin 1950- *WhoEmL 93*
Fine, Henri M. 1945- *St&PR 93*
Fine, Herman 1952- *St&PR 93*
Fine, Holly Katherine *BioIn 17*
Fine, Howard Alan 1941- *WhoAm 92, WhoSSW 93, WhoWor 93*
Fine, Irving (Gifford) 1914-1962 *Baker 92*
Fine, James Allen 1934- *St&PR 93*
Fine, James Stephen 1946- *WhoEmL 93*
Fine, Jane Madeline 1958- *WhoE 93*
Fine, Jeffrey I. 1939- *WhoAm 92*
Fine, Jim L. 1945- *St&PR 93*
Fine, Jo Renee 1943- *WhoAmW 93, WhoE 93*
Fine, John Sydney 1893-1978 *BioIn 17*
Fine, Karen R. *Law&B 92*
Fine, Kit 1946- *WhoWor 93*
Fine, Larry 1902-1974 *See* Stooges, Three, The *QDrFCA 92*
Fine, Larry 1902-1975 *See* Three Stooges, The *IntDcF 2-3*
Fine, Leo 1914- *St&PR 93*
Fine, Marjorie Lynn *Law&B 92*
Fine, Mark H. *Law&B 92*
Fine, Marlene Gail 1949- *WhoAmW 93, WhoE 93*
Fine, Marshall 1950- *ConAu 137*
Fine, Michael *St&PR 93*
Fine, Michael Joseph 1937- *WhoAm 92, WhoE 93*
Fine, Michael Thomas 1943- *WhoSSW 93*
Fine, Milton 1926- *WhoAm 92*
Fine, Miriam Brown 1913- *WhoE 93, WhoWor 93*
Fine, Morris Eugene 1918- *WhoAm 92*
Fine, Norman David 1935- *WhoSSW 93*
Fine, Paul Ronald *BioIn 17*
Fine, Perry Scott 1962- *St&PR 93*
Fine, Phil David 1925-1990 *BioIn 17*
Fine, Rana Arnold 1944- *WhoAm 92, WhoAmW 93*
Fine, Richard Aaron 1929- *St&PR 93*
Fine, Richard Isaac 1940- *WhoAm 92*
Fine, Samuel 1925- *WhoAm 92*
Fine, Seymour Howard 1925- *WhoAm 92*
Fine, Stanley Sidney 1927- *St&PR 93, WhoAm 92, WhoE 93*
Fine, Stephen *ScF&FL 92*
Fine, Stephen Lewis 1940- *St&PR 93*
Fine, Steven E. *Law&B 92*
Fine, Sylvia d1991 *BioIn 17*
Fine, Sylvia 1913-1991 *AnObit 1991*
Fine, Terrence Leon 1939- *WhoAm 92, WhoWor 93*
Fine, Travis *BioIn 17*
Fine, Vivian *BioIn 17*
Fine, Vivian 1913- *Baker 92, WhoAm 92*
Fine, William C. 1917-1991 *BioIn 17*
Fine, William Irwin 1928- *WhoWor 93*
Finebaum, Murray L. 1942- *St&PR 93*
Finebaum, Paul Alan 1955- *WhoSSW 93*
Fineberg, Harvey Vernon 1945- *WhoAm 92*
Fineberg, Larry 1945- *WhoCanL 92*
Fineberg, Stuart E. *Law&B 92*
Finecke, Bror Blixen- 1886-1946 *BioIn 17*
Finefrock, Donald Wendell 1930- *St&PR 93*
Finefrock, Jerome C. *Law&B 92*
Finegan, Kay *BioIn 17*
Finegan, Patrick Gerard, Jr. 1951- *WhoWrEP 92*
Finegan, Patrick T'ung 1959- *WhoEmL 93*
Finegan, Thomas Aldrich 1929- *WhoAm 92*
Finegold, H.B. 1957- *St&PR 93*
Finegold, Maurice Nathan 1932- *WhoAm 92*
Finegold, Ronald 1942- *WhoAm 92*
Finegold, Sydney Martin 1921- *WhoAm 92*
Finelli, Frederick Christopher 1954- *WhoE 93*
Finelli, Gerard Peter 1947- *WhoE 93, WhoEmL 93*
Finelli, Joseph Amilio 1915- *WhoWor 93*
Finelli, Louise Stephania 1919- *WhoAmW 93*
Finelli, Pietro *BioIn 17*
Finello, Terry Lee 1947- *WhoAmW 93, WhoEmL 93*
Fineman, Abraham H. 1896-1991 *BioIn 17*
Fineman, Bayla T. 1932- *St&PR 93*
Fineman, David 1933- *St&PR 93*
Fineman, Evan Leslie 1951- *St&PR 93*
Fineman, Samuel M. 1930- *St&PR 93*
Finer, Michael Scott 1964- *WhoE 93, WhoEmL 93, WhoWor 93*
Finerty, Martin Joseph, Jr. 1936- *WhoAm 92*
Finerty, Mary Ellen 1947- *WhoAmW 93*
Fines Fournier, Rebecca Eileen 1960- *WhoEmL 93*
Finesilver, Jay Mark 1955- *WhoEmL 93, WhoWor 93*
Finesilver, Sherman Glenn 1927- *WhoAm 92*
Finestein, Russell Mark 1956- *WhoEmL 93*
Finestone, Albert Justin 1921- *WhoE 93*
Finestone, Sheila 1927- *WhoAmW 93*
Finetti, Julian Enrique 1935- *WhoWor 93*
Fine Young Cannibals *SoulM*
Finfgeld, Richard K. 1931- *St&PR 93*
Finfrock, Ivan Ray 1929- *St&PR 93*
Fingarette, Herbert 1921- *WhoAm 92*
Finger, Bernard L. 1927- *St&PR 93*
Finger, Charles S. 1940- *St&PR 93*
Finger, Diamon Lee 1927- *St&PR 93*
Finger, Eugene P. 1938- *St&PR 93*
Finger, Frank Whitney 1915- *WhoAm 92*
Finger, Gottfried c. 1660-1730 *Baker 92*
Finger, Harold B. 1924- *WhoAm 92*
Finger, Jerry 1932- *St&PR 93*
Finger, Joel David 1956- *WhoE 93*
Finger, John F. 1919- *St&PR 93*
Finger, Judy Renee 1965- *WhoAmW 93*
Finger, Karl Hermann 1921- *WhoScE 91-3*
Finger, Kenneth Franklin 1929- *WhoAm 92*
Finger, Lisa Ann *Law&B 92*
Finger, Louis Judah 1920- *WhoE 93*
Finger, Peter Christian 1962- *WhoEmL 93*
Finger, Phyllis Thomas 1947- *WhoE 93, WhoEmL 93*
Finger, Sam P. *St&PR 93*
Finger, Seymour Maxwell 1915- *WhoAm 92*
Finger, Susan Clare 1953- *WhoAmW 93*
Finger, Thomas Emanuel 1949- *WhoEmL 93*
Finger, Wilfried Bernd 1948- *WhoWor 93*
Fingerhut, Abe 1939- *WhoWor 93*
Fingerhut, Marilyn Ann 1940- *WhoAm 92*
Fingerhut, Michael Brent *Law&B 92*
Fingerle, Lawrence Jay 1960- *St&PR 93*
Fingerman, Edward *BioIn 17*
Fingerman, Milton 1928- *WhoAm 92, WhoSSW 93*
Fingerson, Leroy Malvin 1932- *St&PR 93, WhoAm 92*
Finglass, Ronald N. 1948- *WhoEmL 93*
Fingon, Joan Carroll 1951- *WhoE 93*
Fingon, Robert James 1949- *WhoEmL 93*
Finifter, Ada W(eintraub) 1938- *WhoWrEP 92*
Finisterre *DcMexL*
Finizzi, Marguerite Helene 1934- *WhoAmW 93*
Fink, Aaron 1916- *St&PR 93*
Fink, Aaron Herman 1916- *WhoAm 92*
Fink, Abel King 1927- *WhoE 93*
Fink, Alan W. *St&PR 93*
Fink, Arthur Alan 1909- *St&PR 93*
Fink, Barbara Arlene 1949- *WhoWrEP 92*
Fink, Barry *Law&B 92*
Fink, C. *WhoScE 91-3*
Fink, Cathy DeVito 1957- *WhoAmW 93*
Fink, Charles Augustin 1929- *WhoAm 92, WhoSSW 93, WhoWor 93*
Fink, Chester Walter 1928- *WhoSSW 93*
Fink, Christian 1822-1911 *Baker 92*
Fink, Conrad Charles 1932- *WhoAm 92, WhoSSW 93*
Fink, Daniel Julien 1926- *WhoAm 92*
Fink, David Harvey 1942- *WhoAm 92*
Fink, David Leonard 1936- *WhoE 93*
Fink, David Ream, Jr. 1928- *WhoAm 92*
Fink, David Warren 1944- *WhoE 93*
Fink, Diane Joanne 1936- *WhoAm 92*
Fink, Donald Glen 1911- *WhoAm 92*
Fink, Donald Martin 1928- *St&PR 93*
Fink, Eugene Richard 1944- *WhoE 93*
Fink, George *WhoScE 91-1*
Fink, George Erwin 1949- *WhoWor 93*
Fink, Gerald Ralph 1940- *WhoAm 92*
Fink, Gordon Ian 1953- *WhoWor 93*
Fink, Gottfried Wilhelm 1783-1846 *Baker 92*
Fink, H. Bernard 1909- *WhoAm 92*
Fink, Harry Browne, III 1961- *WhoSSW 93*
Fink, Howard *ScF&FL 92*
Fink, Ida 1921- *ConAu 136*
Fink, J. Theodore 1952- *WhoEmL 93*
Fink, James Brewster 1943- *WhoWor 93*
Fink, James Curtis 1944- *St&PR 93*
Fink, Janet Rose 1950- *WhoEmL 93*
Fink, Jerold Albert 1941- *WhoAm 92*
Fink, Joanna Elizabeth 1958- *WhoAm 92, WhoE 93*
Fink, John 1926- *WhoAm 92*
Fink, John Francis 1931- *St&PR 93, WhoAm 92*
Fink, John (Philip) 1926- *ConAu 139*
Fink, Jordan Norman 1934- *WhoAm 92*
Fink, Joseph d1991 *BioIn 17*
Fink, Joseph Leslie, III 1947- *WhoEmL 93*
Fink, Joseph Richardson 1940- *WhoAm 92*
Fink, Karen G. *Law&B 92*
Fink, Karl J. 1942- *ConAu 138*
Fink, Kerry Leif 1961- *WhoEmL 93*
Fink, Lester Harold 1925- *WhoAm 92*
Fink, Lois Marie 1927- *WhoAm 92*
Fink, Lyman Roger 1912- *WhoAm 92*
Fink, Mark J. 1957- *WhoEmL 93, WhoSSW 93*
Fink, Martin Ronald 1931- *WhoE 93*
Fink, Matthew P. 1941- *WhoAm 92*
Fink, Michael F. *Law&B 92*
Fink, Michael I. *Law&B 92*
Fink, Michael Jon 1954- *Baker 92*
Fink, Paul 1926- *WhoScE 91-4*
Fink, Peter R. 1933- *St&PR 93*
Fink, R. Cullen 1955- *WhoWrEP 92*
Fink, Regina M. *Law&B 92*
Fink, Richard A. *St&PR 93*
Fink, Richard David 1936- *WhoAm 92*
Fink, Richard Merrill 1930- *St&PR 93*
Fink, Robert Louis 1958- *WhoEmL 93*
Fink, Robert Morgan 1915- *WhoAm 92*
Fink, Robert Russell 1933- *WhoAm 92*
Fink, Robert Steven 1943- *WhoAm 92*
Fink, Ronald Edward 1936- *St&PR 93*
Fink, Roy Warren 1933- *St&PR 93*
Fink, Ruth Garvey 1917- *WhoAm 92*
Fink, Scott Alan 1953- *WhoEmL 93*
Fink, Sheldon Edwin 1925- *WhoE 93*
Fink, Stephen Barry 1946- *St&PR 93*
Fink, Stuart Simon 1934- *WhoAm 92*
Fink, Teri Ann 1955- *WhoEmL 93*
Fink, Thomas Edward 1940- *WhoWor 93*
Fink, Tom *WhoAm 92*
Fink, Valerie Ann 1954- *WhoAmW 93*
Finkbeiner, Herman Lawrence 1931- *WhoE 93*
Finkbeiner, James C. 1947- *St&PR 93*
Finke, A. William *Law&B 92*
Finke, Fidelio 1891-1968 *Baker 92*
Finke, Hans-Joachim 1939- *WhoE 93*
Finke, Leonda Froehlich *WhoAm 92*
Finke, Richard Charles *Law&B 92*
Finke, Robert Forge 1941- *WhoAm 92*
Finke, Susanne Gail 1962- *WhoEmL 93*
Finke, Walter W., Jr. *Law&B 92*
Finkel, Alfred d1989 *BioIn 17*
Finkel, Bonnie Bazilian *Law&B 92*
Finkel, David 1948- *WhoSSW 93*
Finkel, Debra Paris *Law&B 92*
Finkel, Donald 1929- *WhoWrEP 92*
Finkel, Fyvush *BioIn 17*
Finkel, Gary *BioIn 17*
Finkel, George (Irvine) 1909-1975 *DcChlFi*
Finkel, Gerald Michael 1941- *WhoAm 92*
Finkel, Gilbert 1935- *WhoE 93*
Finkel, Harvey 1940- *St&PR 93*
Finkel, Jane E. *Law&B 92*
Finkel, Janet Pearl 1961- *WhoE 93*
Finkel, Judd *BioIn 17*
Finkel, Judith G. *Law&B 92*
Finkel, Judith Stillman 1934- *WhoAmW 93*
Finkel, Karen Evans 1952- *WhoSSW 93*
Finkel, Ludwik Michal 1858-1930 *PolBiDi*
Finkel, Marion Judith 1929- *WhoAm 92*
Finkel, Martin Howard 1952- *WhoEmL 93*
Finkel, Sanford Norman 1946- *WhoE 93*
Finkel, Sheila Berg 1947- *WhoAmW 93, WhoEmL 93*
Finkelday, John Paul 1943- *WhoSSW 93*
Finkelday, Karen Lynn 1944- *WhoAmW 93, WhoSSW 93, WhoWor 93*
Finkell, Max *ConAu 137*
Finkelman, Eric *Law&B 92*
Finkelman, Robert Barry 1943- *WhoSSW 93*
Finkelman, Roland I. 1928- *St&PR 93*
Finkelmeier, Philip Renner 1914- *WhoAm 92*
Finkelson, Ira *Law&B 92*
Finkelstein, Allen Lewis 1943- *WhoE 93*
Finkelstein, Barbara 1937- *WhoAm 92*
Finkelstein, Barry Marc 1954- *St&PR 93*
Finkelstein, Bernard 1930- *WhoAm 92*
Finkelstein, Bob *Law&B 92*
Finkelstein, Caroline 1941- *WhoWrEP 92*
Finkelstein, Colleen Ann 1959- *WhoAmW 93*
Finkelstein, David 1929- *WhoAm 92*
Finkelstein, Edward S. 1925- *BioIn 17, St&PR 93*
Finkelstein, Edward Sydney 1925- *WhoAm 92, WhoE 93*
Finkelstein, Evelyn M. *Law&B 92*
Finkelstein, Gary Stan 1948- *WhoE 93*
Finkelstein, George *Law&B 92*
Finkelstein, Irwin *BioIn 17*
Finkelstein, Jack, Jr. 1952- *WhoEmL 93*
Finkelstein, Jacob 1910- *WhoE 93*
Finkelstein, James Arthur 1952- *WhoEmL 93, WhoWor 93*
Finkelstein, James David 1933- *WhoAm 92, WhoE 93*
Finkelstein, Jay Jon 1959- *WhoEmL 93*
Finkelstein, Jay Laurence 1938- *WhoE 93*

Finkelstein, Jesse Adam 1955- *WhoEmL 93*
Finkelstein, Joseph Simon 1952- *WhoEmL 93*
Finkelstein, Karen Beth *Law&B 92*
Finkelstein, Lisa *Law&B 92*
Finkelstein, Louis 1895- *JeAmHC*
Finkelstein, Louis 1895-1991 *BioIn 17, ConAu 136, CurBio 92N*
Finkelstein, Ludwik *WhoScE 91-1*
Finkelstein, Mark Anderson 1959- *WhoEmL 93, WhoSSW 93*
Finkelstein, Mel d1992 *NewYTBS 92 [port]*
Finkelstein, Michael *BioIn 17*
Finkelstein, Miriam 1928- *WhoWrEP 92*
Finkelstein, Norman H. 1941- *SmATA 73 [port]*
Finkelstein, Paul D. *St&PR 93*
Finkelstein, Richard Alan 1930- *WhoAm 92*
Finkelstein, Robert 1942- *WhoE 93*
Finkelstein, Seymour 1923- *WhoAm 92*
Finkelstein, Silvio 1934- *WhoUN 92*
Finkelstein, Vicki B. *Law&B 92*
Finkelstein, William 1948- *St&PR 93*
Finkelstein, William A. *Law&B 92*
Finkenaur, E.B. 1939- *St&PR 93*
Finkenbinder, David O. *Law&B 92*
Finkenbrink, Ralph T. 1961- *St&PR 93*
Finkenkeller, John R. *St&PR 93*
Finkes, John Richard 1940- *St&PR 93*
Finkl, Charles W. 1920- *St&PR 93*
Finkl, Charles William, II 1941- *WhoAm 92, WhoSSW 93*
Finklang, Kurt Walter 1955- *WhoEmL 93*
Finkle, Beverly Arthur 1915- *WhoE 93*
Finkle, Jeffrey Alan 1954- *WhoAm 92, WhoE 93*
Finkle, Judith Tavano 1951- *WhoAmW 93*
Finkle, Morton 1927- *St&PR 93*
Finkle, Robert Andrew *Law&B 92*
Finkle, William Edward 1945- *St&PR 93*
Finklea, Tula Ellice 1923- *WhoAm 92*
Finkleman, Ken *MiSFD 9*
Finko, David 1936- *Baker 92*
Finks, James Edward 1927- *BiDAMSp 1989, WhoAm 92, WhoSSW 93*
Finks, Robert Melvin 1927- *WhoAm 92, WhoWor 93*
Finland, Tom of 1920-1991 *BioIn 17*
Finlaw, Jack D., Jr. *Law&B 92*
Finlay, Alex G. *St&PR 93*
Finlay, Carlos Juan 1833-1915 *BioIn 17*
Finlay, D.G. *ScF&FL 92*
Finlay, Frank 1926- *WhoAm 92*
Finlay, Ian C. *WhoScE 91-1*
Finlay, Ian Hamilton 1925- *BioIn 17*
Finlay, James C. d1992 *NewYTBS 92 [port]*
Finlay, James Campbell 1931- *WhoAm 92*
Finlay, John 1941-1991 *BioIn 17*
Finlay, John P. 1928- *St&PR 93*
Finlay, John W. 1923- *St&PR 93*
Finlay, John Walter 1923- *WhoAm 92*
Finlay, Julie Aileen 1965- *WhoAmW 93, WhoEmL 93*
Finlay, Louis Edward 1929- *WhoSSW 93*
Finlay, Patricia 1951- *WhoUN 92*
Finlay, R. Derek 1932- *St&PR 93*
Finlay, Robert Derek 1932- *WhoAm 92*
Finlay, Terence Edward *WhoAm 92*
Finlay, Thomas Hiram 1938- *WhoAm 92*
Finlay, Virgil 1914-1971 *ScF&FL 92*
Finlay, Warren 1950- *St&PR 93*
Finlay, William H. *Law&B 92*
Finlay, Winifred 1910- *ScF&FL 92*
Finlayson, Bruce Alan 1939- *WhoAm 92*
Finlayson, Charles J. *Law&B 92*
Finlayson, Donald Allen *Law&B 92*
Finlayson, I.E. 1948- *St&PR 93*
Finlayson, James 1887-1953 *QDrFCA 92 [port]*
Finlayson, James Bruce 1937- *WhoWor 93*
Finlayson, Jock Kinghorn 1921- *St&PR 93*
Finletter, Gretchen Damrosch *AmWomPl*
Finley, Beth *Law&B 92*
Finley, Billy R. *Law&B 92*
Finley, Charles Laughlin 1925- *St&PR 93*
Finley, Charles Oscar 1918- *WhoAm 92*
Finley, Cheryl *Law&B 92*
Finley, Chuck *BioIn 17*
Finley, David Allen 1943- *WhoE 93*
Finley, Diane L. 1952- *WhoAmW 93*
Finley, Donald J. 1956- *WhoSSW 93*
Finley, Emogene 1926- *St&PR 93*
Finley, Evelyn d1989 *SweetSg C [port]*
Finley, Fred W. 1920- *St&PR 93*
Finley, George Alvin, III 1938- *WhoSSW 93*
Finley, Glenna 1925- *WhoAm 92, WhoWrEP 92*
Finley, Gordon Ellis 1939- *WhoSSW 93*
Finley, Harold Marshall 1916- *St&PR 93, WhoAm 92*
Finley, James David 1946- *WhoEmL 93*
Finley, James Edward 1922- *WhoAm 92*
Finley, John H., III 1936- *St&PR 93*
Finley, John M., II 1948- *St&PR 93*
Finley, Joseph Michael 1952- *WhoEmL 93*
Finley, Karen *BioIn 17*
Finley, Karen 1956- *News 92 [port]*
Finley, Kathleen F. *Law&B 92*
Finley, Keith A. *St&PR 93*
Finley, Lizabeth Ann 1962- *WhoAmW 93*
Finley, Michael Valton 1947- *WhoAm 92*
Finley, Mitch *BioIn 17*
Finley, Morris 1939- *AfrAmBi*
Finley, Murray Howard 1922- *WhoAm 92*
Finley, Patrick M. 1937- *St&PR 93*
Finley, Paul C. *Law&B 92*
Finley, Robert 1772-1817 *BioIn 17*
Finley, Robert J. 1940- *St&PR 93*
Finley, Robert Van Eaton 1922- *WhoWor 93*
Finley, Rose Mary 1968- *WhoAmW 93*
Finley, Sally Maude 1954- *WhoAmW 93*
Finley, Sara Crews 1930- *WhoAm 92*
Finley, Sarah Maude Merritt 1946- *WhoEmL 93, WhoSSW 93*
Finley, Skip 1948- *BioIn 17, WhoE 93*
Finley, Wayne House 1927- *WhoAm 92, WhoSSW 93*
Finlow-Bates, Terence 1946- *WhoWor 93*
Finman, Ted 1931- *WhoAm 92*
Finn, A. Michael 1929- *WhoAm 92*
Finn, Albert E. 1927- *St&PR 93*
Finn, Andrew Lockhart 1949- *St&PR 93*
Finn, Bobby *WhoWrEP 92*
Finn, Bruce Leon 1956- *WhoEmL 93*
Finn, Chester E. 1944- *BioIn 17*
Finn, Chester Evans 1918- *WhoAm 92*
Finn, Colin Arthur *WhoScE 91-1*
Finn, Daniel Francis 1922- *WhoAm 92*
Finn, David 1921- *St&PR 93, WhoAm 92, WhoE 93*
Finn, David Thurman 1952- *WhoE 93*
Finn, Don William 1944- *WhoSSW 93*
Finn, Douglas George 1951- *WhoE 93*
Finn, F.E.S. 1916- *ScF&FL 92*
Finn, Frances Mary 1937- *WhoAmW 93, WhoE 93*
Finn, Gilbert 1920- *WhoAm 92, WhoE 93*
Finn, James Francis 1924- *WhoAm 92*
Finn, James Patrick 1947- *St&PR 93*
Finn, Janet C. *Law&B 92*
Finn, Joan Lockwood *WhoAm 92, WhoWor 93*
Finn, John McMaster 1947- *WhoE 93*
Finn, John Thomas 1948- *WhoEmL 93*
Finn, Mary Paulina 1842- *AmWomPl*
Finn, Mary Ralphe 1933- *WhoAmW 93*
Finn, Michael Steven 1955- *St&PR 93*
Finn, Patricia Ann *WhoAmW 93*
Finn, Patricia Gloria 1949- *WhoAmW 93*
Finn, Patrick Matthew 1959- *WhoE 93*
Finn, Penelope Miller B. 1951- *WhoEmL 93*
Finn, Peter 1954- *WhoE 93*
Finn, Peter Michael 1936- *WhoAm 92*
Finn, Ralph L. 1912- *ScF&FL 92*
Finn, Richard G.F. 1936- *St&PR 93*
Finn, Richard Galletly Francis 1936- *WhoAm 92*
Finn, Richard Henry 1934- *St&PR 93*
Finn, Robert 1930- *WhoAm 92*
Finn, Stephen Martin 1949- *WhoWor 93*
Finn, Steven Gerald 1946- *St&PR 93*
Finn, Thomas Macy 1927- *WhoAm 92*
Finn, Thomas P. *Law&B 92*
Finn, Timothy John 1950- *WhoAm 92*
Finn, William *BioIn 17*
Finn, William Francis 1915- *WhoAm 92, WhoWor 93*
Finn, William Lawrence 1945- *St&PR 93, WhoAm 92*
Finn, William M. *Law&B 92*
Finn, William Michael 1936- *St&PR 93*
Finnane, Daniel F. *WhoAm 92*
Finnberg, Elaine Agnes 1948- *WhoAmW 93*
Finnbogadottir, Vigdis 1930- *WhoWor 93*
Finne, Jukka 1951- *WhoScE 91-4*
Finne, Jukka Gunnar 1951- *WhoWor 93*
Finneburgh, Morris Lewis 1900- *WhoAm 92*
Finnefrock, Craig Alan 1942- *WhoE 93*
Finnegan, Cyril Vincent 1922- *WhoAm 92*
Finnegan, Dorothy Ellen 1947- *WhoAmW 93*
Finnegan, George Bernard, Jr. 1903- *WhoWor 93*
Finnegan, Hugh Patrick 1958- *WhoE 93*
Finnegan, James John, Jr. 1948- *WhoEmL 93*
Finnegan, John Robert, Sr. 1924- *WhoAm 92*
Finnegan, Kevin S. *Law&B 92*
Finnegan, Laurence P., Jr. 1937- *St&PR 93*
Finnegan, Laurence Patrick, Jr. 1937- *WhoAm 92*
Finnegan, Lawrence J. 1930- *WhoIns 93*
Finnegan, Lawrence Joseph 1930- *St&PR 93*
Finnegan, Lawrence P. 1928- *St&PR 93*
Finnegan, Martha Ann *Law&B 92*
Finnegan, Martha Ann 1953- *WhoEmL 93*
Finnegan, Neal F. 1938- *St&PR 93*
Finnegan, Neal Francis 1938- *WhoAm 92*
Finnegan, Reynold Joseph *Law&B 92*
Finnegan, Richard Brendan 1942- *WhoE 93*
Finnegan, Richard Paul 1950- *St&PR 93*
Finnegan, Sara A. 1939- *St&PR 93*
Finnegan, Sara Anne 1939- *WhoAm 92, WhoAmW 93*
Finnegan, Sharyn Marie 1946- *WhoE 93*
Finnegan, Stephen H. *Law&B 92*
Finnegan, Thomas J. *Law&B 92*
Finnegan, Thomas Joseph, Jr. 1935- *St&PR 93, WhoAm 92*
Finnegan, Thomas Joseph, III 1951- *St&PR 93*
Finnegan, William F. *Law&B 92*
Finnegan, William (Patrick) 1952- *ConAu 136*
Finnell, Alfred Wayne 1936- *WhoE 93*
Finnell, Jack Stanley 1937- *St&PR 93*
Finnell, Leonard William 1928- *WhoE 93*
Finnell, Leslie Burrow, Jr. 1939- *WhoSSW 93*
Finnell, Michael Hartman 1927- *WhoAm 92*
Finnell, Robert Kirtley 1949- *WhoEmL 93*
Finnell, Ronnie Ward *WhoE 93*
Finnemore, Douglas Kirby 1934- *WhoAm 92*
Finnen, Malachy William *Law&B 92*
Finneran, Emmett John 1944- *WhoIns 93*
Finneran, Susan Rogers 1947- *WhoEmL 93*
Finneran, Thomas A. 1949- *WhoAm 92*
Finnerty, John Dudley 1949- *WhoEmL 93*
Finnerty, Louise Hoppe 1949- *WhoAm 92*
Finnerty, Madeline Frances 1949- *WhoAmW 93*
Finnerty, Peter Joseph 1942- *St&PR 93, WhoE 93*
Finnerty, Thomas Conan 1954- *WhoE 93*
Finney, Albert 1936- *BioIn 17, IntDcF 2-3 [port], MiSFD 9, WhoAm 92, WhoWor 93*
Finney, Ann J. 1936- *St&PR 93*
Finney, Charles 1905-1984 *ScF&FL 92*
Finney, Charles Grandison 1792-1875 *BioIn 17*
Finney, David John 1917- *WhoWor 93*
Finney, David Lee 1952- *WhoEmL 93*
Finney, David Ross 1951- *WhoEmL 93*
Finney, Edward E. 1927- *St&PR 93*
Finney, Ernest Adolphus, Jr. 1931- *WhoAm 92, WhoSSW 93*
Finney, Frederic N. 1937- *St&PR 93*
Finney, J.R. *WhoScE 91-1*
Finney, Jack *BioIn 17*
Finney, Jack 1911- *ScF&FL 92*
Finney, James Nathaniel 1939- *AfrAmBi [port]*
Finney, Joan Marie McInroy 1925- *WhoAm 92, WhoAmW 93, WhoWor 93*
Finney, John Leslie *WhoScE 91-1*
Finney, Pelham Gray, III *Law&B 92*
Finney, Ray Barron 1946- *St&PR 93*
Finney, Ross Lee 1906- *Baker 92, WhoAm 92*
Finney, Roy Pelham, Jr. 1924- *WhoWor 93*
Finney, Shan *BioIn 17*
Finney, Stephen T. 1949- *St&PR 93*
Finney, Theodore M(itchell) 1902-1978 *Baker 92*
Finney, Walter B. *ScF&FL 92*
Finney-Knight, Gail Alexandria 1959- *WhoEmL 93*
Finnican, Mark H. 1957- *WhoIns 93*
Finnicum, Richard 1955- *St&PR 93*
Finnie, Doris G. 1919- *WhoAmW 93*
Finnie, Iain 1928- *WhoAm 92*
Finnie, Linda 1952- *OxDcOp*
Finnie, Neysa M. *Law&B 92*
Finnie, Phillip Powell 1933- *WhoWor 93*
Finnigan, Claire Marie 1923- *WhoAmW 93*
Finnigan, Joan 1925- *WhoCanL 92*
Finnigan, Joseph Townsend 1944- *WhoAm 92*
Finnigan, Robert E. 1927- *WhoAm 92*
Finnigan, Sheila Elizabeth 1942- *WhoAm 92*
Finnila, Birgit 1931- *Baker 92*
Finnis, John M(itchell) 1940- *ConAu 136*
Finnissy, Michael (Peter) 1946- *Baker 92*
Finniston, Monty 1912- *BioIn 17*
Finniston, Monty 1912-1991 *AnObit 1991*
Fino, Giocondo 1867-1950 *Baker 92*
Fino, Raymond M. 1942- *St&PR 93*
Finocchiaro, Alfonso G. 1932- *St&PR 93, WhoAm 92, WhoE 93*
Finocchiaro, Gaetano 1952- *WhoWor 93*
Finocchiaro, Maurice Anthony 1942- *WhoAm 92*
Finocchiaro, Paolo 1942- *WhoScE 91-3*
Finocharo, John J. *Law&B 92*
Finore, Diane 1950- *WhoEmL 93*
Finotti, J.S. 1948- *St&PR 93*
Finsberg, Geoffrey 1926- *WhoWor 93*
Finscher, Ludwig 1930- *Baker 92*
Finser, Siegfried Ernest 1932- *WhoE 93*
Finsinger, Joerg Eugen 1950- *WhoWor 93*
Finskars, Leone E. 1934- *St&PR 93*
Finson, Lowell Wayne 1949- *WhoEmL 93*
Finstad, Carl Derald 1929- *WhoWor 93*
Finstad, Donald Lee 1945- *St&PR 93*
Finstad, Suzanne 1955- *BioIn 17*
Finster, E. Burke *ScF&FL 92*
Finster, Howard *BioIn 17*
Finsterwald, Maxinne *AmWomPl*
Fintel, Dan James 1953- *WhoEmL 93*
Finter, Jurgen Erich 1948- *WhoWor 93*
Finton, Timothy Christopher 1952- *WhoEmL 93*
Finucan, John Thomas 1930- *WhoAm 92*
Finucane, Alexandra Kortschmaryk 1953- *WhoEmL 93*
Finucane, Richard Daniel 1926- *WhoAm 92*
Finver, Mary 1948- *WhoEmL 93*
Finzel, Lilja Marie Tobie 1947- *WhoEmL 93*
Finzen, Bruce Arthur 1947- *WhoEmL 93*
Finzi, Aldo F. 1931- *WhoScE 91-3*
Finzi, Gerald (Raphael) 1901-1956 *Baker 92*
Finzi, Graciane 1945- *Baker 92*
Finzi, Hilda 1925- *WhoAmW 93*
Finzi, Hilda Goldenhorn 1925- *WhoE 93*
Fiocco, Giorgio 1931- *WhoScE 91-3*
Fiocco, Jean-Joseph 1686-1746 *Baker 92*
Fiocco, Joseph-Hector 1703-1741 *Baker 92*
Fiocco, Pietro Antonio c. 1650-1714 *Baker 92*
Fiock, Shari Lee 1941- *WhoAmW 93*
Fiol Mora, Miguel Angel 1949- *WhoScE 91-3*
Fiondella, June Lea Bell 1941- *WhoAmW 93*
Fiondella, Robert William 1942- *St&PR 93, WhoAm 92*
Fiorato, Hugo 1914- *WhoAm 92, WhoE 93*
Fioravante, Janice C. 1951- *WhoEmL 93*
Fioravanti, Giuseppe c. 1795- *OxDcOp*
Fioravanti, Luigi 1829-1887 *OxDcOp*
Fioravanti, Valentino 1764-1837 *Baker 92, OxDcOp*
Fioravanti, Valentino 1827-1879 *OxDcOp*
Fioravanti, Vincenzo 1799-1877 *Baker 92, OxDcOp*
Fiore, Anthony N., Jr. *Law&B 92*
Fiore, Anthony N., Jr. 1946- *St&PR 93*
Fiore, Carole Diane 1946- *WhoEmL 93*
Fiore, David G. 1947- *St&PR 93*
Fiore, Ernest Dante, Jr. 1928- *St&PR 93*
Fiore, Joan De Wolfe 1924- *WhoWor 93*
Fiore, John *BioIn 17*
Fiore, Joseph Albert 1925- *WhoAm 92*
Fiore, Michael Thomas 1954- *St&PR 93*
Fiore, Neil A. *BioIn 17*
Fiore, Nicholas Francis 1939- *WhoAm 92, WhoE 93*
Fiore, Patrick M. d1990 *BioIn 17*
Fiore, Paul David 1964- *WhoE 93*
Fiore, Robert James 1934- *WhoAm 92*
Fiore, Ronald C. *Law&B 92*
Fiore, William Joseph 1951- *WhoEmL 93*
Fiore-Donno, Giuseppe 1927- *WhoScE 91-4*
Fiorella, Beverly Jean 1930- *WhoAmW 93*
Fiorella-Russo, D. Christine 1931- *WhoAmW 93, WhoE 93*
Fiorelli, Joseph Stephen 1950- *WhoEmL 93*
Fiorelli, Marino *WhoScE 91-3*
Fiorello, Catherine A. 1959- *WhoEmL 93*
Fiorentino, Leon F. 1925- *St&PR 93*
Fiorentino, Leon Francis 1925- *WhoAm 92*
Fiorentino, Thomas Martin 1959- *WhoAm 92, WhoE 93, WhoEmL 93*
Fiorenza, Elisabeth Schuessler 1938- *ConAu 39NR*
Fiorenza, Elisabeth Schussler 1938- *BioIn 17*
Fiorenza, Francis P. 1941- *WhoAm 92*
Fiorenza, Francis S(chuessler) 1941- *ConAu 39NR*
Fiorenza, Joseph A. 1931- *WhoAm 92, WhoSSW 93*
Fiorenza, Margaret M. *Law&B 92*
Fiori, Cesare 1945- *WhoScE 91-3*
Fiori, Michael J. 1951- *WhoE 93, WhoEmL 93, WhoWor 93*
Fiori, Pamela 1944- *WhoAm 92*
Fiori, Pamela Anne 1944- *WhoWrEP 92*
Fiorillo, Albert L. d1992 *NewYTBS 92*
Fiorillo, Elisa *BioIn 17*
Fiorillo, Federigo 1755-1823 *Baker 92*

Fiorillo, Ignazio 1715-1787 *Baker 92*
Fiorina, Carleton *St&PR 93*
Fiorini, Ettore 1933- *WhoScE 91-3*
Fiorini, Frank A. 1934- *St&PR 93*
Fiorini, Michael Vibe 1948- *WhoWor 93*
Fiorino, Christina Maria *Law&B 92*
Fiorino, Piero *WhoScE 91-3*
Fiorito, Edward G. *Law&B 92*
Fiorito, Edward G. 1936- *St&PR 93*
Fiorito, Edward Gerald 1936- *WhoAm 92*
Fiorito, Frank Anthony 1927- *WhoE 93*
Fioroni, Pio 1933- *WhoScE 91-3*
Fippinger, Grace J. 1927- *St&PR 93, WhoAm 92, WhoAmW 93*
Fippinger, Ronald Alan 1942- *WhoAm 92*
Fipps, Michael W. 1942- *WhoAm 92*
Fipps, Michael Wayne 1942- *St&PR 93*
Fique, Karl 1867-1930 *Baker 92*
Fiquet, Jeanne Adams 1955- *WhoAmW 93*
Firack, David E. *St&PR 93*
Firat, A. Ertug *WhoScE 91-4*
Firbank, Ronald 1886-1926 *BritWr S2*
Firbas, Wilhelm 1939- *WhoScE 91-4*
Firchow, Claus-Gerhard 1941- *St&PR 93*
Firchow, Evelyn Scherabon *WhoAm 92*
Firchow, Peter E. 1937- *ScF&FL 92*
Firchow, Peter Edgerly 1937- *WhoAm 92, WhoWrEP 92*
Firchow, Thomas Mark 1955- *WhoE 93*
Fire, Nancy Ann 1951- *WhoAmW 93*
Firebaugh, Francille Maloch 1933- *WhoAm 92*
Firebrace, James Henry 1951- *WhoUN 92*
Firehammer, Richard Armin, Jr. 1957- *WhoEmL 93*
Fireman, Edward L. 1922-1990 *BioIn 17*
Fireman, Jack Mervin 1926- *WhoE 93*
Fireman, Paul *BioIn 17*
Fireman, Paul 1944- *CurBio 92 [port], WhoAm 92*
Fireovid, Steve 1957- *BioIn 17*
Firer, Ben Zion 1914- *BioIn 17*
Fires, Earlie Stancel 1947- *WhoAm 92*
Fireside, Bryna J. 1932- *SmATA 73 [port]*
Fireside, Harvey Francis 1929- *WhoAm 92*
Firestein, Beth Ann 1957- *WhoAmW 93*
Firestein, Chester 1930- *WhoAm 92*
Firestien, Roger Lee 1955- *WhoE 93*
Firestone, Brooks *BioIn 17*
Firestone, Bruce Michael 1946- *WhoEmL 93*
Firestone, Catherine *WhoCanL 92*
Firestone, Charles Morton 1944- *WhoAm 92, WhoE 93*
Firestone, David 1953- *St&PR 93*
Firestone, Donald L. 1934- *St&PR 93*
Firestone, Edwin Ira 1921- *St&PR 93*
Firestone, Elaine Ruth 1959- *WhoAmW 93, WhoEmL 93*
Firestone, Elizabeth Parke d1990 *BioIn 17*
Firestone, Evan Richard 1940- *WhoAm 92*
Firestone, James H. 1937- *St&PR 93*
Firestone, Jon 1944- *WhoAm 92*
Firestone, Judith Hall 1945- *WhoAmW 93*
Firestone, Kate *BioIn 17*
Firestone, Marc S. *Law&B 92*
Firestone, Morton H. 1935- *St&PR 93, WhoAm 92*
Firestone, Nancy B. 1952- *WhoEmL 93*
Firestone, Raymond Armand 1931- *WhoE 93*
Firestone, Richard B. 1934- *St&PR 93*
Firestone, Richard Francis 1926- *WhoAm 92*
Firestone, Richard Melvin *BioIn 17*
Firestone, Ruth Roberts Hartzell 1936- *WhoAmW 93*
Firetog, Theodore Warren 1950- *WhoE 93, WhoEmL 93*
Firger, Betsy H. *Law&B 92*
Firger, Robert A. *Law&B 92*
Firket, Henri 1922- *WhoScE 91-2*
Firkin, Peter Richard 1951- *WhoWor 93*
Firkusny, Rudolf *BioIn 17*
Firkusny, Rudolf 1912- *Baker 92, WhoAm 92*
Firlit, Joseph F. 1937- *St&PR 93*
Firman, Meg Jones *Law&B 92*
Firmedow, T. *WhoScE 91-1*
Firmin, Peter 1928- *ConAu 40NR*
Firminger, Harlan Irwin 1918- *WhoAm 92*
Firmino Miguel, Mario 1938-1991 *BioIn 17*
Firor, John (Wo) 1927- *ConAu 136*
Firouz-Abadi, Abbas Alex 1927- *WhoWor 93*
Firshein, Daniel Bruce 1952- *WhoEmL 93*
First, Diane Harriet Goldey 1954- *WhoSSW 93*
First, Edward 1910-1991 *BioIn 17*
First, Harry 1945- *WhoAm 92*
First, Joseph Michael 1906- *WhoAm 92*
First, Mervin H. 1928- *St&PR 93*
First, Michael Bruce 1956- *WhoEmL 93*
First, Ruth *BioIn 17*
First, Wesley 1920- *WhoAm 92, WhoE 93*
Firstenberg, Allen 1942- *St&PR 93*
Firstenberg, Jean 1936- *WhoAm 92*
Firstenberg, Paul B. 1933- *St&PR 93*
Firstenberg, Sam 1950- *MiSFD 9*
Firstenberg, Samuel 1950- *WhoEmL 93*
Firstenburg, Bruce Edward 1942- *St&PR 93*
Firstenburg, E.W. 1913- *St&PR 93*
Firstenburg, Edward William 1913- *WhoAm 92*
Firstman, Eric Jacob 1957- *WhoEmL 93*
Firth, Brian William 1926- *WhoWor 93*
Firth, Denis Barry 1940- *WhoScE 91-1*
Firth, Everett Joseph 1930- *WhoAm 92*
Firth, Gary R. 1950- *St&PR 93*
Firth, J.G. *WhoScE 91-1*
Firth, J.R. 1890-1960 *IntDcAn*
Firth, James C. *St&PR 93*
Firth, Michael *MiSFD 9*
Firth, N. Wesley 1920-1949 *ScF&FL 92*
Firth, Raymond William 1901- *IntDcAn*
Firth, Reginald John *WhoScE 91-1*
Firth, Violet Mary 1890-1946 *BioIn 17*
Firth, William James *WhoScE 91-1*
Firth-Butterfield, Kay 1957- *WhoWor 93*
Firuta, Gary Joseph 1951- *St&PR 93*
Fisackerly, Blanche *AmWomPl*
Fisango, John 1949- *WhoAsAP 91*
Fisbeck, Weldon Henry 1935- *St&PR 93*
Fiscella, Robert Anthony *Law&B 92*
Fisch, Arline Marie 1931- *WhoAmW 93*
Fisch, Charles 1921- *WhoAm 92, WhoWor 93*
Fisch, Fredrick Lee 1955- *WhoEmL 93*
Fisch, Gerd 1942- *WhoWor 93*
Fisch, Max Harold 1900- *WhoAm 92*
Fisch, Robert Otto 1925- *WhoAm 92*
Fisch, Veronica Marie *WhoWrEP 92*
Fisch, William Bales 1936- *WhoAm 92*
Fischa, Michael *MiSFD 9*
Fischbach, Donald Richard 1947- *WhoEmL 93*
Fischbach, Ephraim 1942- *WhoAm 92*
Fischbach, Ernst-Dieter 1942- *WhoScE 91-3*
Fischbach, Gerald D. 1938- *WhoAm 92*
Fischbach, John T. *Law&B 92*
Fischbach, Joseph Franklin 1950- *St&PR 93*
Fischbach, Leroy J. 1944- *St&PR 93*
Fischbach, Marc 1946- *WhoWor 93*
Fischbacher, Siegfried *BioIn 17*
Fischbarg, Jorge 1935- *HispAmA [port]*
Fischbeck, Gerhard 1925- *WhoScE 91-3*
Fischbeck, Helmut Johannes 1928- *WhoSSW 93*
Fischel, Daniel Norman 1922- *WhoAm 92*
Fischel, Daniel R. 1950- *WhoAm 92*
Fischel, David 1936- *WhoAm 92*
Fischel, Edward Elliot 1920- *WhoAm 92*
Fischel, Shelley Duckstein 1950- *WhoEmL 93*
Fischel, William Alan 1945- *WhoAm 92*
Fischell, Robert Ellentuch 1929- *WhoAm 92*
Fischer, Aaron Jack 1947- *WhoEmL 93, WhoWor 93*
Fischer, Adam 1889-1943 *IntDcAn*
Fischer, Adam 1949- *Baker 92*
Fischer, Alice Marie 1937- *WhoSSW 93*
Fischer, Andrew *ScF&FL 92*
Fischer, Annette d1992 *NewYTBS 92*
Fischer, Annie 1914- *Baker 92*
Fischer, Anton 1778-1808 *OxDcOp*
Fischer, Barbara Anne 1960- *WhoAmW 93*
Fischer, Barbara Jean 1950- *WhoEmL 93*
Fischer, Bernhard Franz 1948- *WhoWor 93*
Fischer, Bobby 1943- *BioIn 17*
Fischer, Brent S. C. 1964- *WhoEmL 93*
Fischer, Bruce Elwood, Jr. 1951- *WhoEmL 93*
Fischer, Bruce R. 1949- *WhoIns 93*
Fischer, Carl 1849-1923 *Baker 92*
Fischer, Carl 1924- *WhoAm 92*
Fischer, Carl Robert 1939- *WhoAm 92*
Fischer, Catherine Patricia 1947- *WhoEmL 93*
Fischer, Charles B., Jr. 1943- *St&PR 93*
Fischer, Charles K. 1926- *St&PR 93*
Fischer, Christa Unzner- 1948- *BioIn 17*
Fischer, Craig Leland 1937- *WhoAm 92*
Fischer, Dale Susan 1951- *WhoAmW 93, WhoEmL 93*
Fischer, Daniel Edward 1945- *WhoSSW 93, WhoWor 93*
Fischer, David Eugene 1961- *WhoE 93*
Fischer, David J. 1933- *WhoSSW 93*
Fischer, David John 1928- *WhoSSW 93*
Fischer, David Jon 1952- *WhoEmL 93, WhoWor 93*
Fischer, David Seymour 1930- *WhoWor 93*
Fischer, Deborah Jo 1966- *WhoAmW 93*
Fischer, Dennis *ScF&FL 92*
Fischer, Dieter 1933- *WhoScE 91-3*
Fischer, Douglas James 1943- *St&PR 93*
Fischer, Edmond Henri 1920- *WhoAm 92*
Fischer, Edward (Adam) 1914- *ConAu 37NR*
Fischer, Edward John, Jr. 1942- *St&PR 93*
Fischer, Edwin 1886-1960 *Baker 92*
Fischer, Emil 1838-1914 *OxDcOp*
Fischer, Emil 1852-1919 *BioIn 17*
Fischer, Emil (Friedrich August) 1838-1914 *Baker 92*
Fischer, Emil R. 1926- *St&PR 93*
Fischer, Eric R. *Law&B 92*
Fischer, Eric Robert 1945- *St&PR 93, WhoAm 92, WhoE 93, WhoWor 93*
Fischer, Erich 1887-1977 *Baker 92*
Fischer, Ernest L. 1922- *St&PR 93*
Fischer, Ernst Otto 1918- *WhoAm 92, WhoWor 93*
Fischer, Eugene H. 1932- *WhoAm 92*
Fischer, Fayne Hirsh 1965- *WhoEmL 93*
Fischer, Floyd Brand 1916- *WhoAm 92*
Fischer, Frank E. 1933- *St&PR 93*
Fischer, Frank Ernest 1933- *WhoAm 92*
Fischer, Frank M. *St&PR 93*
Fischer, Fred Hermann Oskar 1927- *WhoWor 93*
Fischer, Gaston 1929- *WhoScE 91-4*
Fischer, George W. 1912- *St&PR 93*
Fischer, Georges 1936- *WhoScE 91-2*
Fischer, Glenn M. 1950- *St&PR 93*
Fischer, Hans H. *Law&B 92*
Fischer, Harold *BioIn 17*
Fischer, Harris E. 1922- *St&PR 93*
Fischer, Harry Arnold, Jr. 1926- *St&PR 93*
Fischer, Harry William 1921- *WhoAm 92*
Fischer, Helmut 1944- *WhoScE 91-3*
Fischer, Henri Theodore 1901-1976 *IntDcAn*
Fischer, Henry George 1923- *WhoE 93*
Fischer, Henry M. 1940- *St&PR 93*
Fischer, Herbert Martin 1931- *WhoScE 91-3*
Fischer, Hermann *WhoScE 91-4*
Fischer, Howard B. 1959- *WhoIns 93*
Fischer, Irene Kaminka 1907- *WhoAmW 93*
Fischer, Irwin 1903-1977 *Baker 92*
Fischer, Ivan 1951- *Baker 92*
Fischer, James Adrian 1916- *WhoAm 92*
Fischer, Jan A. 1936- *WhoScE 91-4*
Fischer, Jan (Frank) 1921- *Baker 92*
Fischer, Janet Jordan 1923- *WhoAm 92*
Fischer, Joel 1939- *ConAu 40NR, WhoAm 92*
Fischer, Johann Caspar Ferdinand c. 1665-1746 *Baker 92*
Fischer, John 1946- *BioIn 17*
Fischer, John Allen 1952- *WhoSSW 93*
Fischer, John Arthur 1929- *WhoSSW 93*
Fischer, John Clarence 1942- *St&PR 93*
Fischer, John J. 1950- *St&PR 93*
Fischer, John L. *Law&B 92*
Fischer, Josef E. 1937- *WhoAm 92*
Fischer, Joseph 1841-1901 *Baker 92*
Fischer, Joseph A. 1931- *St&PR 93*
Fischer, Joseph M. *Law&B 92*
Fischer, Judith Hummel 1937- *WhoE 93*
Fischer, Karen Alta 1952- *WhoEmL 93*
Fischer, Karen Ann 1947- *WhoAmW 93*
Fischer, Karl Heinz 1944- *WhoWor 93*
Fischer, Karoline Auguste Fernandine 1764-1842 *BioIn 17*
Fischer, Kenneth *St&PR 93*
Fischer, Kenneth M. 1952- *St&PR 93*
Fischer, Kenneth R. 1918- *St&PR 93*
Fischer, Kurt von 1913- *Baker 92*
Fischer, Kurt Walter 1943- *WhoE 93*
Fischer, L.P. 1935- *WhoScE 91-2*
Fischer, Larry Lee 1936- *St&PR 93*
Fischer, Lawrence Joseph 1937- *WhoAm 92*
Fischer, Lee Alan 1946- *WhoEmL 93, WhoSSW 93*
Fischer, Leopold 1923-1991 *BioIn 17*
Fischer, LeRoy Henry 1917- *WhoAm 92*
Fischer, Lindsay Koehler *WhoAm 92*
Fischer, Lisa *BioIn 17*
Fischer, Louis Wayne 1952- *WhoEmL 93*
Fischer, Lucas C. 1915- *St&PR 93*
Fischer, Lucy Rose 1944- *ConAu 138*
Fischer, Ludwig 1745-1825 *OxDcOp*
Fischer, (Johann Ignaz) Ludwig 1745-1825 *Baker 92*
Fischer, Lynn Helen 1943- *WhoWrEP 92*
Fischer, Lynn Suzanne 1951- *WhoAmW 93, WhoWor 93*
Fischer, Marlene D. *Law&B 92*
Fischer, Marsha Leigh 1955- *WhoAmW 93*
Fischer, Martin A. 1937- *WhoIns 93*
Fischer, Mary Dean Dunn 1928- *WhoAmW 93*
Fischer, Max 1929- *MiSFD 9*
Fischer, Maximilian 1929- *WhoScE 91-4*
Fischer, Michael Gottard 1773-1829 *Baker 92*
Fischer, Michael Ludwig 1940- *WhoAm 92*
Fischer, Michael S. *Law&B 92*
Fischer, Michael Stanford 1949- *St&PR 93*
Fischer, Nellie L. *AmWomPl*
Fischer, Newton Duchan 1921- *WhoAm 92*
Fischer, Nora Barry 1951- *WhoEmL 93*
Fischer, Norman, Jr. 1924- *WhoSSW 93*
Fischer, Oystein 1942- *WhoScE 91-4*
Fischer, Pamela Shadel 1959- *WhoAm 92, WhoAmW 93*
Fischer, Patrick Carl 1935- *WhoAm 92*
Fischer, Paul *Law&B 92*
Fischer, Paul David *Law&B 92*
Fischer, Paul G. 1946- *St&PR 93*
Fischer, Peter *BioIn 17*
Fischer, Peter Heinz 1942- *WhoSSW 93*
Fischer, R. M. 1947- *WhoEmL 93*
Fischer, Rainer Dietrich 1936- *WhoScE 91-3*
Fischer, Raymond Henry 1950- *WhoSSW 93*
Fischer, (Maria) Res (Theresia) 1896-1974 *Baker 92*
Fischer, Richard L. 1936- *St&PR 93*
Fischer, Richard Lawrence 1936- *WhoAm 92*
Fischer, Richard Samuel 1937- *WhoAm 92, WhoWor 93*
Fischer, Robert Andrew 1937- *WhoAm 92*
Fischer, Robert Blanchard 1920- *WhoAm 92*
Fischer, Robert Earl 1939- *WhoAm 92*
Fischer, Robert I. 1946- *St&PR 93*
Fischer, Robert Lee 1947- *WhoSSW 93*
Fischer, Robert Leigh 1926- *WhoE 93*
Fischer, Robert W. 1918- *St&PR 93*
Fischer, Robert William 1918- *WhoAm 92*
Fischer, Roger Adrian 1939- *WhoAm 92*
Fischer, Ronald J. *Law&B 92*
Fischer, Ronald Lee *WhoE 93*
Fischer, Sandi Joan 1960- *WhoAmW 93*
Fischer, Sherry Elizabeth 1967- *WhoSSW 93*
Fischer, Stanley 1943- *WhoAm 92*
Fischer, Stephen E. 1937- *St&PR 93*
Fischer, Steven Arthur 1945- *St&PR 93*
Fischer, Susan Lois 1947- *WhoEmL 93*
Fischer, Terence Joseph 1959- *WhoE 93*
Fischer, Thomas B. *Law&B 92*
Fischer, Thomas B. 1947- *St&PR 93*
Fischer, Thomas Covell 1938- *WhoAm 92*
Fischer, Thomas V. 1929- *St&PR 93, WhoAm 92*
Fischer, Timothy 1946- *WhoAsAP 91*
Fischer, Walter *St&PR 93*
Fischer, Walter S. 1882-1946 *See* Fischer, Carl 1849-1923 *Baker 92*
Fischer, Werner 1930- *WhoScE 91-3*
Fischer, Wilhelm 1886-1962 *Baker 92*
Fischer, William B. *ScF&FL 92*
Fischer, William Donald 1928- *St&PR 93, WhoAm 92*
Fischer, William G(ustavus) 1835-1912 *Baker 92*
Fischer, William Karl 1947- *St&PR 93*
Fischer, Wolfgang Georg 1933- *BioIn 17*
Fischer, Zoe Ann 1939- *WhoWor 93*
Fischer-Appelt, Peter 1932- *WhoWor 93*
Fischerauer, Bernd *MiSFD 9*
Fischer-Dieskau, Dietrich 1925- *BioIn 17, IntDcOp [port], OxDcOp, WhoAm 92*
Fischer-Dieskau, (Albert) Dietrich 1925- *Baker 92*
Fischerleitner, Franz 1947- *WhoScE 91-4*
Fischetti, Robert James 1952- *WhoAm 92*
Fischhof, Joseph 1804-1857 *Baker 92*
Fischhoff, Baruch 1946- *BioIn 17, WhoAm 92*
Fischietti, Domenico 1725?-c. 1810 *OxDcOp*
Fischkin, Theodore J. *Law&B 92*
Fischl, Alan Leslie 1955- *WhoEmL 93*
Fischl, Eric *BioIn 17*
Fischler, Abraham Saul 1928- *WhoAm 92, WhoSSW 93*
Fischler, Alan 1952- *ConAu 137*
Fischler, Barbara Brand 1930- *WhoAm 92*
Fischler, Lori Faye 1956- *WhoEmL 93*
Fischler, Shirley *BioIn 17*
Fischler, Shirley Balter 1926- *WhoAmW 93*
Fischler, Shirley (Walton) *ConAu 136*
Fischler, Stan *BioIn 17*
Fischli, Albert Edward 1940- *WhoScE 91-4*
Fischman, Bernard D. 1915- *St&PR 93, WhoAm 92*
Fischman, Burton Lloyd 1930- *WhoE 93*
Fischman, Carol O. *Law&B 92*
Fischman, Gary Joseph *WhoE 93*
Fischman, Harold Bernard 1953- *St&PR 93*
Fischman, Leonard Lipman 1919- *WhoE 93*
Fischman, Myrna Leah *WhoAm 92, WhoAmW 93, WhoE 93, WhoWor 93*
Fischman, Sheila *WhoCanL 92*

Fischman, Stanley Saul 1932- *St&PR 93*
Fischman, Stuart Lee 1935- *WhoE 93*
Fischmar, Richard Mayer 1938- *WhoWor 93*
Fischmeister, Hellmut F. 1927- *WhoScE 91-3*
Fischoff, Ephraim 1904- *WhoAm 92*
Fischoff, Gary Charles 1954- *WhoE 93, WhoEmL 93*
Fischthal, Glenn Jay 1948- *WhoAm 92*
Fiscina, Elizabeth Gladys 1944- *WhoAmW 93*
Fiscus, Robert L. 1937- *St&PR 93*
Fiscus, Robert L. 1941- *WhoAm 92*
Fiser, David J. 1939- *St&PR 93*
Fiser, Lubos 1935- *Baker 92*
Fiser, Zbynek *BioIn 17*
Fiset, Kay Patricia 1947- *WhoAmW 93*
Fisette, James J. *ScF&FL 92*
Fish, A. *WhoScE 91-1*
Fish, A. Joe 1942- *WhoSSW 93*
Fish, Aaron *BioIn 17*
Fish, Aaron Max 1932- *St&PR 93*
Fish, Albert 1870-1936 *BioIn 17*
Fish, Barbara 1920- *WhoAm 92*
Fish, Belle *AmWomPl*
Fish, Chet 1925- *WhoAm 92*
Fish, Daisy Earle *AmWomPl*
Fish, David E. 1936- *St&PR 93*
Fish, David Earl 1936- *WhoAm 92, WhoE 93, WhoWor 93*
Fish, Donald W. *Law&B 92*
Fish, Donald Winston 1930- *St&PR 93*
Fish, Donna Marie 1959- *WhoAmW 93*
Fish, Edward Anthony 1933- *WhoAm 92*
Fish, Gary R. 1958- *St&PR 93*
Fish, Gordon Edward 1951- *WhoE 93*
Fish, Hamilton 1888-1991 *AnObit 1991, BioIn 17, PolPar*
Fish, Hamilton 1951- *WhoAm 92, WhoE 93*
Fish, Hamilton, Jr. 1926- *CngDr 91, WhoAm 92, WhoE 93*
Fish, Harry G., III 1950- *St&PR 93*
Fish, Helen Therese 1944- *WhoAmW 93*
Fish, James E. 1934- *St&PR 93*
Fish, James Edmond 1945- *WhoE 93*
Fish, James Henry 1947- *WhoAm 92*
Fish, James Stuart 1915- *WhoAm 92*
Fish, Janet Isobel 1938- *WhoAm 92, WhoE 93*
Fish, Jeanne Spencer 1921- *WhoAmW 93*
Fish, Jerry Richard 1949- *WhoEmL 93*
Fish, John M., Jr. *Law&B 92*
Fish, John Perry 1949- *WhoAm 92, WhoE 93, WhoEmL 93, WhoWor 93*
Fish, John Ronald 1945- *WhoSSW 93*
Fish, Jonathan S. 1944- *St&PR 93*
Fish, Jonathon Kevin 1955- *WhoEmL 93*
Fish, June K. 1951- *St&PR 93*
Fish, Kathy Griffith 1956- *WhoSSW 93*
Fish, Leonard G. *ScF&FL 92*
Fish, Leslie *ScF&FL 92*
Fish, Lilian Mann 1901- *WhoWrEP 92*
Fish, Marcus 1925- *St&PR 93*
Fish, Mary Martha 1930- *WhoAm 92*
Fish, Patricia Ann 1931- *WhoAmW 93*
Fish, Paul Waring 1933- *WhoAm 92*
Fish, R. Talmage 1938- *St&PR 93*
Fish, Robert Jay 1947- *WhoAm 92*
Fish, Robert L. 1940- *St&PR 93*
Fish, Ruby Mae Bertram 1918- *WhoAmW 93, WhoWor 93*
Fish, Seymour L. 1930- *St&PR 93*
Fish, Stanely Eugene 1938- *WhoWrEP 92*
Fish, Stanley *NewYTBS 92 [port]*
Fish, Stanley Eugene 1938- *BioIn 17, WhoAm 92*
Fish, Stanley R. *Law&B 92*
Fish, Stephen Richard 1953- *WhoE 93, WhoEmL 93*
Fish, Stewart Allison 1925- *WhoAm 92*
Fish, Thomas C. 1933- *St&PR 93*
Fish, Virginia Dart 1954- *WhoE 93*
Fishack, Charles David, Jr. 1921- *St&PR 93*
Fishack, Charles Edward 1942- *St&PR 93*
Fishbach, Kenneth James *Law&B 92*
Fishback, Price V(anmeter) 1955- *ConAu 138*
Fishbaugh, Franklin James 1943- *WhoAm 92*
Fishbein, Barbara Tcath 1929- *WhoE 93*
Fishbein, Daniel Eli 1951- *WhoEmL 93*
Fishbein, Diana Hanna 1954- *WhoE 93*
Fishbein, Evalyn Lipton *Law&B 92*
Fishbein, Michael Claude 1946- *WhoEmL 93*
Fishbein, Peter Melvin 1934- *WhoAm 92*
Fishbein, Robert 1942- *St&PR 93*
Fishberg, Arthur M. 1898-1992 *BioIn 17*
Fishberg, Bruce 1949- *St&PR 93*
Fishberg, Gerard 1946- *WhoEmL 93*
Fishburn, Katherine 1944- *ScF&FL 92*
Fishburn, Peter Clingerman 1936- *WhoAm 92*
Fishburne, John Ingram, Jr. 1937- *WhoAm 92*
Fishburne, Larry *BioIn 17*
Fishburne, Larry 1962- *ConBlB 4 [port]*
Fishburne, Mary W. 1917- *St&PR 93*
Fishcher, Gaston 1929- *WhoWor 93*
Fishco, Robert Melvin 1939- *WhoE 93*
Fishco, Vivian Vick *WhoSSW 93*
Fishel, Carol Thomas 1949- *WhoE 93*
Fishel, Herbert Andrew *BioIn 17*
Fishel, James David 1951- *WhoAm 92*
Fishel, James Dean 1953- *WhoEmL 93*
Fishel, James Joseph 1959- *WhoEmL 93*
Fishel, Peter Livingston 1935- *WhoAm 92*
Fishel, Stanley Irvyng 1914- *WhoAm 92*
Fishelson, David *MiSFD 9*
Fisher, Adelaide 1920- *WhoSSW 93*
Fisher, Aileen (Lucia) 1906- *ConAu 37NR, MajAI [port], SmATA 73 [port]*
Fisher, Alan Washburn 1939- *WhoAm 92*
Fisher, Alfred Foster 1934- *WhoAm 92*
Fisher, Allan Campbell 1943- *WhoE 93, WhoWor 93*
Fisher, Allan Herbert, Jr. 1922- *WhoAm 92*
Fisher, Amy *BioIn 17*
Fisher, Andrea 1944- *WhoAmW 93*
Fisher, Andrew 1862-1928 *DcTwHis*
Fisher, Andrew 1920- *WhoAm 92*
Fisher, Andrew S. 1948- *St&PR 93*
Fisher, Andrew Somes 1948- *WhoEmL 93*
Fisher, Angela *BioIn 17*
Fisher, Anita Jeanne 1937- *WhoAmW 93*
Fisher, Anna Lee 1949- *WhoAmW 93*
Fisher, Anne *AmWomPl*
Fisher, Anne Elizabeth 1957- *WhoSSW 93*
Fisher, Aron Baer 1936- *WhoAm 92, WhoE 93*
Fisher, Arthur 1931- *WhoAm 92, WhoWrEP 92*
Fisher, Arthur J. *Law&B 92*
Fisher, Arthur Walter *Law&B 92*
Fisher, Avery 1906- *BioIn 17*
Fisher, Avery (Robert) 1906- *Baker 92*
Fisher, Barbara Turk 1940- *WhoAmW 93*
Fisher, Barrett C., III 1953- *St&PR 93*
Fisher, Bart Steven 1943- *WhoAm 92, WhoE 93*
Fisher, Benjamin Chatburn 1923- *WhoAm 92*
Fisher, Benjamin Franklin, IV 1940- *ScF&FL 92, WhoSSW 93*
Fisher, Bennett Lawson 1942- *St&PR 93, WhoAm 92*
Fisher, Bernard 1918- *WhoAm 92*
Fisher, Bertram Dore 1928- *WhoWor 93*
Fisher, Bill 1914-1990 *BioIn 17*
Fisher, Blanche Proctor *AmWomPl*
Fisher, Bob 1935- *BioIn 17*
Fisher, Bob 1945- *WhoAm 92*
Fisher, Bonnie Lee Michaelson 1948- *WhoAmW 93, WhoEmL 93*
Fisher, Brady Alan 1952- *WhoEmL 93*
Fisher, Bruce Dwight 1943- *WhoSSW 93*
Fisher, C. *WhoScE 91-1*
Fisher, Calvin David 1926- *WhoAm 92*
Fisher, Carl A. *BioIn 17*
Fisher, Carol Edmondson 1943- *WhoSSW 93*
Fisher, Caroline MacFadyen 1947- *WhoEmL 93, WhoSSW 93*
Fisher, Carrie *BioIn 17*
Fisher, Carrie Frances 1956- *WhoAm 92*
Fisher, Catherine *ScF&FL 92*
Fisher, Catherine Ambrosiano 1946- *WhoEmL 93*
Fisher, Catherine Ann 1955- *WhoAmW 93*
Fisher, Champe Andrews 1928- *WhoAm 92*
Fisher, Charles Frederick 1936- *WhoAm 92*
Fisher, Charles Harold 1906- *WhoAm 92, WhoSSW 93*
Fisher, Charles Page, Jr. 1921- *WhoAm 92*
Fisher, Charles T., III 1929- *St&PR 93*
Fisher, Charles Thomas, III 1929- *WhoAm 92*
Fisher, Charles Worley 1917- *WhoAm 92*
Fisher, Chester Lewis, Jr. 1911- *WhoAm 92*
Fisher, Clarkson Sherman 1921- *WhoAm 92*
Fisher, Clay 1912- *BioIn 17*
Fisher, Craig Becker 1932- *WhoAm 92*
Fisher, D. Michael 1944- *WhoE 93*
Fisher, Dale Dunbar 1945- *WhoE 93, WhoWor 93*
Fisher, Dale John 1925- *WhoAm 92*
Fisher, David 1929- *ScF&FL 92*
Fisher, David 1948- *MiSFD 9*
Fisher, David Bruce 1954- *WhoE 93*
Fisher, David Clarence 1960- *WhoWor 93*
Fisher, David E. 1931- *St&PR 93*
Fisher, David E. 1932- *ScF&FL 92*
Fisher, David F. *Law&B 92*
Fisher, David Frederick 1930- *WhoWor 93*
Fisher, David I. 1939- *St&PR 93*
Fisher, David Judson 1936- *St&PR 93*
Fisher, David Lionel *WhoScE 91-1*
Fisher, David T. *Law&B 92*
Fisher, Dean L. 1940- *St&PR 93*
Fisher, Delbert Arthur 1928- *WhoAm 92, WhoWor 93*
Fisher, Denise Danches *WhoEmL 93*
Fisher, Diane *Law&B 92*
Fisher, Dierdre Denise 1945- *WhoAmW 93*
Fisher, Don *BioIn 17*
Fisher, Donald *BioIn 17*
Fisher, Donald 1949- *WhoEmL 93*
Fisher, Donald G. 1928- *WhoAm 92*
Fisher, Donald George 1928- *St&PR 93*
Fisher, Donald Roy 1927- *St&PR 93*
Fisher, Donald Wayne 1946- *WhoAm 92*
Fisher, Donald Wiener 1923- *WhoAm 92*
Fisher, Donne F. 1938- *St&PR 93*
Fisher, Donne Francis 1938- *WhoAm 92*
Fisher, Dorothea Frances Canfield 1879-1958 *AmWomPl*
Fisher, Dorothy Canfield 1879-1958 *BioIn 17*
Fisher, Dorothy (Frances) Canfield 1879-1958 *ConAu 136, MajAI [port]*
Fisher, Douglas A. *Law&B 92*
Fisher, Douglas Arthur 1942- *St&PR 93*
Fisher, Eddie 1928- *Baker 92*
Fisher, Edward F. 1939- *St&PR 93*
Fisher, Edward Francis 1939- *WhoAm 92*
Fisher, Edward Joseph 1913- *WhoAm 92*
Fisher, Edward Walter *Law&B 92*
Fisher, Ellena Allmond *WhoAmW 93*
Fisher, Eric E. 1939- *St&PR 93*
Fisher, Eric H. *Law&B 92*
Fisher, Eric O'Neill 1954- *WhoEmL 93*
Fisher, Esther d1991 *BioIn 17*
Fisher, Eugene 1927- *WhoWor 93*
Fisher, Eugene Joseph 1943- *WhoE 93*
Fisher, Everett 1920- *WhoAm 92, WhoWor 93*
Fisher, Fenimore 1926- *WhoAm 92*
Fisher, Frances *BioIn 17*
Fisher, Franklin Adams 1929- *WhoAm 92*
Fisher, Franklin C., Jr. 1940- *St&PR 93*
Fisher, Franklin Marvin 1934- *WhoAm 92*
Fisher, Frederick Hendrick 1926- *WhoAm 92*
Fisher, Gary Alan 1951- *WhoAm 92*
Fisher, Gary Alan 1955- *WhoEmL 93*
Fisher, Gary Edwin 1948- *WhoE 93*
Fisher, Gary N. 1955- *St&PR 93*
Fisher, Gene *ScF&FL 92*
Fisher, Gene Jordan 1931- *WhoAm 92*
Fisher, Gene Lawrence 1929- *WhoAm 92*
Fisher, George Andrew 1952- *WhoEmL 93*
Fisher, George M., III *Law&B 92*
Fisher, George Myles Cordell 1940- *WhoAm 92*
Fisher, George Ross, IV 1951- *WhoEmL 93, WhoWor 93*
Fisher, George Wescott 1937- *WhoAm 92*
Fisher, George William 1946- *WhoWrEP 92*
Fisher, Gerald F. 1943- *WhoIns 93*
Fisher, Gerald Saul 1931- *WhoAm 92*
Fisher, Glenn Duane 1947- *WhoEmL 93*
Fisher, Gordon McCrea 1925- *WhoSSW 93*
Fisher, H. Joseph 1933- *WhoE 93*
Fisher, Hal Dennis 1948- *WhoWrEP 92*
Fisher, Hans 1928- *WhoE 93*
Fisher, Harold Eugene 1939- *St&PR 93*
Fisher, Harold H. d1992 *NewYTBS 92*
Fisher, Harold H. 1900-1992 *BioIn 17*
Fisher, Harold Leonard 1910- *WhoAm 92*
Fisher, Harold M. d1990 *BioIn 17*
Fisher, Harold Wallace 1904- *WhoAm 92*
Fisher, Henry 1917- *St&PR 93*
Fisher, Herbert 1921- *St&PR 93*
Fisher, Herbert O. 1909-1990 *BioIn 17*
Fisher, Herbert R. 1910- *St&PR 93*
Fisher, Herman Guy 1898-1975 *BioIn 17*
Fisher, Irving Sanborn 1920- *WhoE 93*
Fisher, J. R. 1943- *WhoAm 92*
Fisher, Jack *MiSFD 9*
Fisher, Jack Carrington 1932- *WhoAm 92*
Fisher, Jack Stuart 1949- *WhoE 93*
Fisher, Jacob Alexander Shultz 1925- *WhoSSW 93*
Fisher, James Abner, Jr. 1933- *WhoWrEP 92*
Fisher, James Aiken 1920- *WhoAm 92*
Fisher, James Burke 1932- *WhoAm 92*
Fisher, James F. 1937- *St&PR 93*
Fisher, James McFarland 1932- *St&PR 93*
Fisher, James R. 1955- *St&PR 93, WhoIns 93*
Fisher, James Richard 1955- *WhoAm 92*
Fisher, James T. 1956- *WhoEmL 93*
Fisher, James William 1925- *WhoAm 92, WhoSSW 93*
Fisher, Jan Braddock 1951- *WhoEmL 93*
Fisher, Jasper William 1914-1990 *BioIn 17*
Fisher, Jay McKean 1949- *WhoE 93*
Fisher, Jeffrey Barry 1949- *WhoEmL 93*
Fisher, Jerid Martin 1953- *WhoE 93, WhoEmL 93*
Fisher, Jerry Saul 1931- *WhoWrEP 92*
Fisher, Jewel T. 1918- *St&PR 93*
Fisher, Jewel Tanner 1918- *WhoAmW 93*
Fisher, Joan Margaret 1947- *WhoEmL 93*
Fisher, Joel Anthony 1947- *WhoE 93*
Fisher, Joel Hilton 1918- *WhoAm 92*
Fisher, Joel Marshall 1935- *WhoAm 92*
Fisher, Johanna Marie *WhoE 93*
Fisher, John 1922-1989 *BioIn 17*
Fisher, John Abraham 1744-1806 *OxDcOp*
Fisher, John Arbuthnot 1841-1920 *BioIn 17, DcTwHis, HarEnMi*
Fisher, John Berton 1951- *WhoSSW 93*
Fisher, John Christian 1954- *WhoE 93*
Fisher, John E. 1929- *WhoIns 93*
Fisher, John Edwin 1929- *St&PR 93, WhoAm 92*
Fisher, John Francis 1933- *WhoIns 93*
Fisher, John Hurt 1919- *WhoAm 92*
Fisher, John J. *BioIn 17*
Fisher, John James 1941- *WhoAm 92*
Fisher, John Morris 1922- *WhoAm 92, WhoWor 93*
Fisher, John Philip 1927- *WhoAm 92, WhoE 93*
Fisher, John Richard 1924- *WhoAm 92*
Fisher, John Sergio 1934- *WhoAm 92*
Fisher, John Stuchell 1867-1940 *BioIn 17*
Fisher, John W. *Law&B 92*
Fisher, John Welton, II 1942- *WhoSSW 93*
Fisher, John Wesley 1915- *St&PR 93, WhoAm 92*
Fisher, John William 1931- *WhoAm 92*
Fisher, Joseph Freiler 1955- *WhoEmL 93*
Fisher, Joseph Herbert 1936- *St&PR 93*
Fisher, Joseph Jefferson *WhoAm 92*
Fisher, Joseph L. d1992 *NewYTBS 92*
Fisher, Joseph L. 1914-1992 *BioIn 17*
Fisher, Joy Deborah 1952- *WhoEmL 93*
Fisher, Judith Dunn 1945- *St&PR 93, WhoAmW 93*
Fisher, Jules Edward 1937- *WhoAm 92, WhoE 93*
Fisher, Julian Hart 1947- *WhoE 93*
Fisher, Julian Potter, II 1960- *WhoE 93*
Fisher, Kenneth Deane 1932- *WhoE 93*
Fisher, Kenneth L. 1944- *WhoAm 92*
Fisher, Kerry Brant *Law&B 92*
Fisher, Kevin Bruce 1959- *WhoEmL 93*
Fisher, King 1854-1884 *BioIn 17*
Fisher, King 1916- *St&PR 93, WhoSSW 93*
Fisher, Larry J. 1951- *St&PR 93*
Fisher, Lawrence N. *Law&B 92, WhoAm 92*
Fisher, Lawrence N. 1944- *St&PR 93*
Fisher, Lawrence W. 1938- *WhoAm 92*
Fisher, Lee I. *WhoAm 92*
Fisher, Leon Harold 1918- *WhoAm 92*
Fisher, Leonard Everett *ChlBIID [port]*
Fisher, Leonard Everett 1924- *ConAu 37NR, MajAI [port], ScF&FL 92, SmATA 73 [port], WhoAm 92*
Fisher, Leonard M. *Law&B 92*
Fisher, Leonard M. 1944- *WhoIns 93*
Fisher, Lester Emil 1921- *WhoAm 92*
Fisher, Lewis Webster 1931- *St&PR 93*
Fisher, Linda J. 1952- *WhoAmW 93*
Fisher, Lloyd Edison, Jr. 1923- *WhoAm 92*
Fisher, Lou 1935- *ScF&FL 92*
Fisher, Louis McLane, Jr. 1938- *WhoAm 92*
Fisher, Lucille R. *St&PR 93*
Fisher, Lucy J. 1949- *WhoAm 92*
Fisher, M.F.K. 1908-1992 *BioIn 17, NewYTBS 92 [port], ScF&FL 92*
Fisher, M(ary) F(rances) K(ennedy) 1908-1992 *ConAu 138, CurBio 92N*
Fisher, M. Janice 1937- *WhoAmW 93*
Fisher, Maria *BioIn 17*
Fisher, Marshall Lee 1944- *WhoAm 92*
Fisher, Mary Ann *MiSFD 9*
Fisher, Mary Ann 1925- *WhoAm 92*
Fisher, Mary Ann 1926- *WhoWrEP 92*
Fisher, Mary Ann D. *Law&B 92*
Fisher, Mary Frances Kennedy 1908-1992 *BioIn 17*
Fisher, Mary M. *Law&B 92*
Fisher, Max Martin 1908- *WhoAm 92*
Fisher, McLane 1938- *St&PR 93*
Fisher, Michael Bruce 1945- *WhoAm 92, WhoWor 93*
Fisher, Michael Ellis 1931- *WhoAm 92*
Fisher, Michelle T. *Law&B 92*
Fisher, Miles Mark, IV 1932- *WhoAm 92*
Fisher, Milton Leonard 1922- *WhoAm 92*
Fisher, Mitchell Salem 1903-1990 *BioIn 17*
Fisher, Nancy 1941- *WhoAmW 93*
Fisher, Neal Floyd 1936- *WhoAm 92*
Fisher, Neil M. 1946- *WhoScE 91-1*
Fisher, Neil Mason *WhoScE 91-1*
Fisher, Nicholas Seth 1949- *WhoE 93*

Fisher, Norman Fenwick Warren 1879-1948 *DcTwHis*
Fisher, Orville E., Jr. *Law&B 92*
Fisher, Orville Earl, Jr. 1944- *WhoAm 92*
Fisher, Oscar H., Jr. 1916- *St&PR 93*
Fisher, Patricia Sweeney 1954- *St&PR 93, WhoAm 92*
Fisher, Paul C. 1913- *St&PR 93*
Fisher, Paul Douglas 1956- *WhoSSW 93*
Fisher, Paul G. *Law&B 92*
Fisher, Paul L. 1923- *St&PR 93*
Fisher, Paul R. 1960- *ScF&FL 92*
Fisher, Perry M. 1939- *St&PR 93*
Fisher, Peter 1930- *WhoWor 93*
Fisher, Peter Francis 1955- *WhoEmL 93*
Fisher, Peter Stanley 1936- *WhoAsAP 91*
Fisher, Pierre James, Jr. 1931- *WhoAm 92*
Fisher, Pieter A. d1992 *NewYTBS 92*
Fisher, Pieter A. 1931-1992 *BioIn 17*
Fisher, R. Douglas 1951- *St&PR 93*
Fisher, R.L. *ScF&FL 92*
Fisher, Ralph Edward *Law&B 92*
Fisher, Ralph J. *St&PR 93*
Fisher, Randall Eugene 1949- *WhoEmL 93*
Fisher, Raymond George 1911- *WhoAm 92*
Fisher, Raymond P. 1940- *St&PR 93*
Fisher, Rebecca Ann 1953- *St&PR 93*
Fisher, Rhoda Lee 1924- *WhoAmW 93, WhoE 93*
Fisher, Richard Alan 1950- *WhoEmL 93*
Fisher, Richard Allen 1930- *St&PR 93*
Fisher, Richard B. 1923- *St&PR 93*
Fisher, Richard B. 1936- *WhoAm 92*
Fisher, Richard Forrest 1941- *WhoAm 92*
Fisher, Richard Welton 1949- *WhoEmL 93, WhoSSW 93, WhoWor 93*
Fisher, Richard Yale 1933- *St&PR 93*
Fisher, Robert 1949- *WhoWor 93*
Fisher, Robert Alan 1943- *WhoAm 92*
Fisher, Robert Allen 1951- *WhoAm 92*
Fisher, Robert Charles 1930- *WhoAm 92*
Fisher, Robert Dale 1924- *WhoAm 92, WhoE 93*
Fisher, Robert Darryl 1939- *WhoSSW 93*
Fisher, Robert George 1917- *WhoAm 92*
Fisher, Robert Henry 1925- *WhoAm 92*
Fisher, Robert Henry 1954- *WhoEmL 93*
Fisher, Robert I. 1939- *WhoAm 92*
Fisher, Robert Joseph 1940- *WhoE 93*
Fisher, Robert S. 1907-1991 *BioIn 17*
Fisher, Robert Scott 1960- *WhoEmL 93*
Fisher, Robert Warren 1952- *WhoEmL 93*
Fisher, Roger 1922- *BioIn 17*
Fisher, Roger Dummer 1922- *WhoAm 92*
Fisher, Ronald Aylmer 1890-1962 *BioIn 17*
Fisher, Ronald C. 1950- *WhoAm 92, WhoEmL 93*
Fisher, Rosalind Anita 1956- *WhoAmW 93*
Fisher, Roy *BioIn 17*
Fisher, Roy Brent 1959- *St&PR 93*
Fisher, Rudolph 1897-1934 *BioIn 17*
Fisher, Russell George 1952- *WhoSSW 93*
Fisher, Russell S. 1949- *WhoIns 93*
Fisher, Sallie Ann 1923- *WhoAmW 93*
Fisher, Saul *Law&B 92*
Fisher, Saul Harrison 1913- *WhoAm 92*
Fisher, Seymour 1922- *WhoE 93*
Fisher, Seymour 1925- *WhoAm 92*
Fisher, Shirley Ida A. 1935- *WhoAmW 93*
Fisher, Stanley M. 1928- *St&PR 93*
Fisher, Stephen Charles *Law&B 92*
Fisher, Stephen G. *ScF&FL 92*
Fisher, Stephen Geoffrey *WhoScE 91-1*
Fisher, Stephen L(ynn) 1944- *ConAu 139*
Fisher, Stephen Lynn 1944- *WhoSSW 93*
Fisher, Stephen P. *Law&B 92*
Fisher, Steve 1912-1980 *ScF&FL 92*
Fisher, Susan Kay 1948- *WhoEmL 93*
Fisher, Susan Warwick 1956- *WhoAmW 93*
Fisher, Suzanne *SmATA 70*
Fisher, Sylvia 1910- *OxDcOp*
Fisher, Sylvia (Gwendoline Victoria) 1910- *Baker 92*
Fisher, Terence 1904-1980 *BioIn 17, MiSFD 9N*
Fisher, Thomas D. 1952- *St&PR 93*
Fisher, Thomas G. *Law&B 92*
Fisher, Thomas George 1931- *St&PR 93, WhoAm 92*
Fisher, Thomas H. 1922- *St&PR 93*
Fisher, Thomas J. 1938- *St&PR 93*
Fisher, Thomas Lee 1944- *St&PR 93, WhoAm 92*
Fisher, Thomas Michael 1951- *WhoWrEP 92*
Fisher, Todd Rogers 1949- *WhoEmL 93, WhoSSW 93*
Fisher, Tom Lyons 1942- *WhoE 93*
Fisher, Ulyss 1932- *St&PR 93*
Fisher, Walter Dummer 1916- *WhoAm 92*
Fisher, Walter Taylor 1892-1991 *BioIn 17*
Fisher, Wendy Astley-Bell 1944- *WhoAmW 93*
Fisher, Wesley Andrew 1944- *WhoE 93*
Fisher, Will Stratton 1922- *WhoAm 92*
Fisher, William Arms 1861-1948 *Baker 92*
Fisher, William B. *Law&B 92*
Fisher, William Courtney 1952- *WhoEmL 93*
Fisher, William David 1930- *WhoSSW 93*
Fisher, William Lawrence 1932- *WhoAm 92*
Fisher, William Thomas 1918- *WhoAm 92*
Fisher, Yale 1945- *St&PR 93*
Fisher, Zachary *BioIn 17*
Fisherman, Mark Frederic 1950- *WhoEmL 93*
Fishkin, Howard S. 1946- *WhoWrEP 92*
Fishkin, James S. *WhoAm 92*
Fishkin, Sonia *Law&B 92*
Fishkind, Lawrence 1936- *WhoE 93*
Fishler, Bennett Hill, Jr. 1918- *St&PR 93*
Fishler, Keith S. *Law&B 92*
Fishman, Aaron J. 1940- *St&PR 93*
Fishman, Alfred Paul 1918- *WhoAm 92*
Fishman, Barry Stuart 1943- *WhoSSW 93, WhoWor 93*
Fishman, Bernard 1920- *WhoAm 92*
Fishman, Bill *MiSFD 9*
Fishman, Charles 1942- *WhoWrEP 92*
Fishman, David Israel 1948- *WhoWor 93*
Fishman, David L. 1938- *St&PR 93*
Fishman, David S. *Law&B 92*
Fishman, Dorothy Janet *WhoAmW 93*
Fishman, Edward Marc 1946- *WhoAm 92, WhoEmL 93, WhoSSW 93*
Fishman, Felix A. 1904- *St&PR 93*
Fishman, Fred Norman 1925- *WhoAm 92*
Fishman, Gary L. 1947- *St&PR 93*
Fishman, Herbert B. 1928- *St&PR 93*
Fishman, Howard H. 1930- *St&PR 93*
Fishman, Howard Stephen 1947- *WhoEmL 93, WhoSSW 93*
Fishman, Jack 1930- *WhoAm 92*
Fishman, Jacob Robert 1930- *WhoE 93, WhoWor 93*
Fishman, James Bart 1954- *WhoEmL 93*
Fishman, James H. 1940- *WhoAm 92, WhoE 93*
Fishman, Joan *BioIn 17*
Fishman, Joshua Aaron 1926- *WhoAm 92*
Fishman, Kenneth Jay 1950- *WhoEmL 93*
Fishman, Kenneth L. *Law&B 92*
Fishman, Lawrence R. *Law&B 92*
Fishman, Leonard 1934- *WhoSSW 93*
Fishman, Lewis Warren 1951- *WhoEmL 93*
Fishman, Libby G. *Law&B 92*
Fishman, Libby G. 1940- *WhoAm 92*
Fishman, Louis Yarrut 1941- *WhoSSW 93*
Fishman, Louise 1939- *WhoAm 92*
Fishman, Mark Alan 1954- *St&PR 93, WhoEmL 93*
Fishman, Mark Brian 1951- *WhoEmL 93, WhoSSW 93, WhoWor 93*
Fishman, Marshall Lewis 1937- *WhoE 93*
Fishman, Marvin Allen 1937- *WhoAm 92*
Fishman, Merrill B. 1934- *St&PR 93*
Fishman, Mitchell Steven 1948- *WhoEmL 93*
Fishman, Richard Glenn 1952- *WhoEmL 93*
Fishman, Richard Leonard *Law&B 92*
Fishman, Robert Louis *Law&B 92*
Fishman, Robert Michael 1953- *WhoEmL 93*
Fishman, Sadie 1915-1991 *BioIn 17*
Fishman, Sara Stern 1959- *WhoAmW 93*
Fishman, Seymour 1915- *WhoSSW 93, WhoWor 93*
Fishman, Sidney 1919- *WhoE 93*
Fishman, Stan David 1951- *WhoEmL 93*
Fishman, Theodore David 1953- *WhoE 93, WhoEmL 93*
Fishman, William Harold 1914- *WhoAm 92*
Fishman, William Samuel 1916-1991 *BioIn 17*
Fishwick, John Palmer 1916- *WhoAm 92*
Fishwick, Nina Marie 1961- *WhoEmL 93, WhoWrEP 92*
Fisk, Arthur Daniel 1954- *WhoSSW 93*
Fisk, Carlton 1947- *BioIn 17*
Fisk, Carlton Ernest 1947- *WhoAm 92*
Fisk, Carol Fraser 1946- *WhoEmL 93*
Fisk, David John 1947- *WhoScE 91-1*
Fisk, David Paul *Law&B 92*
Fisk, Douglas Ray, Jr. 1948- *St&PR 93*
Fisk, Edward Ray 1924- *WhoAm 92*
Fisk, Eliot *BioIn 17*
Fisk, Eliot (Hamilton) 1954- *Baker 92*
Fisk, Erma J. *BioIn 17*
Fisk, Hayward Dan *Law&B 92*
Fisk, Jack 1945- *MiSFD 9*
Fisk, James 1835-1872 *BioIn 17*
Fisk, Lennard Ayres 1943- *WhoAm 92*
Fisk, Lloyd A. *Law&B 92*
Fisk, Margaret Cronin 1946- *WhoWrEP 92*
Fisk, May Isabel *AmWomPl*
Fisk, Nicholas 1923- *ChlFicS, ScF&FL 92*
Fisk, Pamela House 1952- *WhoAmW 93*
Fisk, Pauline *BioIn 17*
Fisk, Pauline 1948- *ConAu 136, ScF&FL 92*
Fisk, Richard L. 1944- *St&PR 93*
Fisk, Thomas Brian 1960- *WhoEmL 93*
Fisk, Trevor Anthony 1943- *WhoE 93*
Fiske, Andrew d1992 *NewYTBS 92*
Fiske, Dudley *BioIn 17*
Fiske, Edward Bogardus 1937- *WhoAm 92*
Fiske, Guy Wilbur 1924- *WhoAm 92*
Fiske, Irving L. d1990 *BioIn 17*
Fiske, Isabella Howe *AmWomPl*
Fiske, John 1842-1901 *GayN*
Fiske, John, Jr. 1935- *St&PR 93*
Fiske, Jordan Jay 1943- *WhoE 93*
Fiske, Minnie Maddern Davey 1865-1932 *AmWomPl*
Fiske, Richard Sewell 1932- *WhoAm 92*
Fiske, Robert Bishop 1900-1991 *BioIn 17*
Fiske, Robert Bishop, Jr. 1930- *WhoAm 92*
Fiske, Roger (Elwyn) 1910-1987 *Baker 92*
Fiske, Sandra Rappaport 1946- *WhoAmW 93, WhoE 93*
Fiske, Sharon *ConAu 37NR*
Fiske, Stephen Ryder 1840-1916 *JrnUS*
Fiske, Susan Tufts 1952- *WhoAmW 93*
Fiske, Terry Noble 1933- *WhoAm 92*
Fisken, Alexander McEwan 1922- *St&PR 93*
Fisketjon, Gary 1954- *BioIn 17*
Fisler, John Chester 1949- *WhoEmL 93*
Fison, Lorimer 1832-1907 *IntDcAn*
Fiss, Harry 1926- *WhoE 93*
Fiss, Owen M. 1938- *WhoAm 92*
Fissan, Heinz 1938- *WhoScE 91-3*
Fissell, William Henry 1931- *WhoAm 92, WhoE 93*
Fissot, Alexis-Henri 1843-1896 *Baker 92*
Fister, C.R. *Law&B 92*
Fistoulari, Anatole 1907- *Baker 92*
Fiszbin, Henri 1930- *BioIn 17*
Fiszdon, Wladyslaw 1912- *WhoScE 91-3, WhoWor 93*
Fiszel, Geoffrey Lynn 1942- *WhoE 93*
Fiszel, Roland *WhoWor 93*
Fiszer, Jacques 1924- *WhoScE 91-2*
Fiszer-Szafarz, Berta 1928- *WhoAm 92, WhoAmW 93*
Fitch, Alva R. 1907-1989 *BioIn 17*
Fitch, Charles Marden 1937- *WhoWrEP 92*
Fitch, Clara *AmWomPl*
Fitch, Clyde 1865-1909 *GayN*
Fitch, Coy Dean 1934- *WhoAm 92*
Fitch, David H. 1932- *St&PR 93*
Fitch, David Robnett 1921- *WhoAm 92*
Fitch, Ed *ScF&FL 92*
Fitch, Frank Wesley 1929- *WhoAm 92*
Fitch, George *BioIn 17*
Fitch, Howard Mercer 1909- *WhoAm 92, WhoSSW 93, WhoWor 93*
Fitch, James Alexander 1931- *WhoAm 92*
Fitch, James Marston 1909- *WhoAm 92*
Fitch, John, IV *MajAI*
Fitch, John Peter *WhoScE 91-1*
Fitch, Linda Bauman 1947- *WhoAmW 93, WhoEmL 93*
Fitch, Lyle Craig 1913- *WhoAm 92*
Fitch, Mary Killeen 1949- *WhoAmW 93, WhoEmL 93*
Fitch, Morgan Lewis, Jr. 1922- *WhoAm 92*
Fitch, Nancy Elizabeth 1947- *WhoAmW 93, WhoEmL 93, WhoSSW 93*
Fitch, Rachel Farr 1933- *WhoAmW 93*
Fitch, Richard 1946- *St&PR 93*
Fitch, Rita LaVerne Pickens 1936- *WhoAmW 93*
Fitch, Robert F. 1928- *St&PR 93*
Fitch, Robert McLellan 1928- *WhoAm 92*
Fitch, Rodney A. *BioIn 17*
Fitch, Sanford 1940- *St&PR 93*
Fitch, Steven Joseph 1930- *WhoAm 92*
Fitch, Stona James 1931- *WhoAm 92*
Fitch, Val Logsdon 1923- *WhoAm 92, WhoE 93, WhoWor 93*
Fitch, W. Chester 1916- *WhoAm 92*
Fitch, W.T.S. 1937- *St&PR 93*
Fitch, Walter Monroe 1929- *WhoAm 92*
Fitch, William *WhoScE 91-1*
Fitch, William C. 1934- *WhoAm 92*
Fitch, William Charles 1934- *BiDAMSp 1989*
Fitch, William D. 1950- *St&PR 93*
Fitch, William M. 1916- *St&PR 93*
Fitch, William Nelson 1941- *WhoWor 93*
Fitchen, Allen Nelson 1936- *WhoAm 92*
Fitchen, Douglas Beach 1936- *WhoAm 92*
Fitchen, Paul Russell d1990 *BioIn 17*
Fitchett, Kirsten Gloria 1963- *WhoE 93*
Fitchett, Vernon Harold 1927- *WhoWor 93*
Fitchett, William Calvin 1948- *WhoSSW 93*
Fitch-Hauser, Margaret E. 1953- *WhoSSW 93*
Fite, Jack P. 1921- *St&PR 93*
Fite, James Robert 1925- *St&PR 93*
Fite, Loran R. 1946- *St&PR 93*
Fitelberg, Gregor 1879-1953 *Baker 92*
Fitelberg, Grzegorz 1879-1953 *PolBiDi*
Fitelberg, Jerzy 1903-1951 *Baker 92, PolBiDi*
Fiterman, Charles 1933- *BioIn 17*
Fites, Donald Vester *BioIn 17*
Fites, Donald Vester 1934- *St&PR 93, WhoAm 92*
Fithian, Patricia Ann 1946- *WhoAmW 93*
Fithian, William R., Jr. 1931- *St&PR 93*
Fitilis, Theodore N. 1937- *WhoAm 92, WhoE 93*
Fitje, Andreas 1936- *WhoScE 91-4*
Fitko, James 1952- *WhoEmL 93*
Fitko, Remigiusz J. 1925- *WhoScE 91-4*
Fitremann, Jean Michel 1944- *WhoScE 91-2*
Fitt, Alfred Bradley 1923- *WhoAm 92*
Fitt, Benjamin Jones 1952- *WhoEmL 93*
Fitt, Michael George 1931- *St&PR 93, WhoAm 92*
Fitte, John Mark 1952- *St&PR 93*
Fitterer, Richard Clarence 1946- *WhoEmL 93*
Fitteron, John J. 1941- *St&PR 93*
Fitteron, John Joseph 1941- *WhoAm 92*
Fitti, Charles John 1929- *WhoE 93, WhoWor 93*
Fitti, Regina Mary 1925- *WhoE 93*
Fitting, Melvin Chris 1942- *WhoE 93*
Fitting, Robert C. 1935- *St&PR 93*
Fitting-Gifford, Marjorie Ann 1933- *WhoAmW 93*
Fittipaldi, Emerson *BioIn 17*
Fittipaldi, Emerson 1946- *CurBio 92 [port]*
Fittipaldi, Thomas Henry 1945- *WhoE 93*
Fitton, Akira *ScF&FL 92*
Fitton, David E. 1945- *St&PR 93*
Fitton, Harvey Nelson, Jr. *WhoSSW 93*
Fitton, Russell Patrick 1928- *St&PR 93*
Fitts, Bruce B. 1926- *St&PR 93*
Fitts, C. Austin 1950- *BioIn 17, WhoAm 92, WhoAmW 93, WhoE 93*
Fitts, Donald Dennis 1932- *WhoAm 92*
Fitts, Edward P., Jr. 1939- *St&PR 93*
Fitts, Jane Gale *Law&B 92*
Fitts, Jay T. *St&PR 93*
Fitts, John *Law&B 92*
Fitts, Jonathan Fairfield 1942- *WhoAm 92, WhoSSW 93*
Fitts, Thomas Allen 1966- *WhoEmL 93*
Fitz, Annette Elaine 1933- *WhoAm 92*
Fitz, David A. 1945- *St&PR 93*
Fitz, Elaine Fiber *Law&B 92*
Fitz, Harold Carlton, Jr. 1926- *WhoE 93*
Fitzalan, Richard 1307?-1376 *BioIn 17*
Fitzalan, Richard 1346-1397 *BioIn 17*
FitzAlan-Howard, Bennett-Thomas Henry Ro 1955- *WhoEmL 93*
FitzAlan-Howard, Bennett-Thomas Henry Robert 1955- *WhoE 93, WhoWor 93*
Fitzallan-Howard, R.F. *WhoWrEP 92*
Fitzenhagen, (Karl Friedrich) Wilhelm 1848-1890 *Baker 92*
Fitzgeorge, Harold James 1924- *WhoAm 92*
Fitzgeorge-Parker, Mark *ScF&FL 92*
Fitzgerald, Alan C. 1930- *St&PR 93*
Fitzgerald, Alane Diane 1962- *WhoSSW 93*
Fitzgerald, Alice Irene 1911- *WhoAmW 93*
Fitzgerald, Alice M. *Law&B 92*
Fitzgerald, Alton Leslie, Jr. 1954- *WhoEmL 93*
Fitzgerald, Arthur F. 1947- *St&PR 93*
Fitzgerald, Astrid Martha 1938- *WhoE 93*
Fitzgerald, Barry 1888-1961 *IntDcF 2-3*
Fitzgerald, Betty Vann 1940- *WhoAmW 93*
Fitzgerald, Bruce David *Law&B 92*
FitzGerald, C(harles) P(atrick) 1902-1992 *ConAu 137*
Fitzgerald, Captain Hugh *MajAI*
Fitzgerald, Caren F. *Law&B 92*
Fitzgerald, Carol Bondhus d1992 *NewYTBS 92*
Fitzgerald, Carol J. 1950- *WhoEmL 93*
Fitzgerald, Catherine T. 1933- *St&PR 93*
Fitz-Gerald, Clark *BioIn 17*
Fitzgerald, Claudia *AmWomPl*
Fitzgerald, Cynthia Lee 1946- *WhoE 93*
Fitzgerald, Daniel *Law&B 92*
Fitzgerald, Daniel Louis 1955- *WhoE 93*
Fitzgerald, Danny Christopher 1954- *WhoSSW 93*
Fitzgerald, David 1962- *St&PR 93*
Fitzgerald, David Alan 1953- *St&PR 93*
Fitzgerald, Denise Brou *Law&B 92*
Fitzgerald, Diane M. *Law&B 92*
Fitzgerald, Donal F. 1926- *St&PR 93*

Fitzgerald, Donald R. *Law&B 92*
Fitzgerald, Edith *AmWomPl*
Fitzgerald, Edmund Bacon 1926- *WhoAm 92*
Fitzgerald, Edward Earl 1919- *WhoAm 92*
Fitzgerald, Edward J. *Law&B 92*
Fitzgerald, Ella *BioIn 17*
Fitzgerald, Ella 1918- *Baker 92, WhoAm 92, WhoAmW 93, WhoWor 93*
Fitzgerald, Ernest Abner 1925- *WhoAm 92*
Fitzgerald, Eugene Francis 1925- *WhoAm 92*
Fitz-Gerald, F. Gregory 1941- *WhoAm 92*
Fitzgerald, F. Scott 1886-1940 *MagSAmL [port]*
Fitzgerald, F. Scott 1896- *DcLB Y92*
Fitzgerald, F. Scott 1896-1940 *BioIn 17, ScF&FL 92, WorLitC [port]*
FitzGerald, Frances 1940- *BioIn 17, WhoWrEP 92*
Fitzgerald, Francis Scott Key 1896-1940 *BioIn 17*
Fitzgerald, Frank 1929- *WhoScE 91-1*
Fitzgerald, Frank Thomas 1942- *WhoE 93*
Fitzgerald, Gail *BlkAmWO*
FitzGerald, Garret *BioIn 17*
Fitzgerald, Gerald d1513 *BioIn 17*
Fitzgerald, Gerald 1932-1990 *BioIn 17*
Fitzgerald, Gerald Dennis 1939- *WhoAm 92*
Fitzgerald, Gerald Francis 1925- *WhoAm 92*
Fitzgerald, Gerald Francis, Jr. 1950- *WhoAm 92*
Fitzgerald, Gerald Richard 1936- *St&PR 93*
Fitzgerald, Geraldine *AmWomPl*
Fitzgerald, Geraldine 1913- *WhoAm 92*
Fitz Gerald, Gregory 1923- *ScF&FL 92*
Fitzgerald, Harold Kenneth 1921- *WhoE 93*
Fitzgerald, Hollis *Law&B 92*
Fitzgerald, J. Robert *Law&B 92*
Fitzgerald, James Francis 1926- *WhoAm 92, WhoWor 93*
Fitzgerald, James Martin 1920- *WhoAm 92*
Fitzgerald, James Raymond, Jr. 1944- *WhoE 93*
Fitzgerald, James Richard 1939- *WhoAm 92*
FitzGerald, James W. Jay *WhoAm 92*
Fitzgerald, Janet Anne 1935- *WhoAm 92, WhoAmW 93*
Fitzgerald, Janet Marie 1943- *WhoAm 92*
Fitzgerald, Janice S. 1948- *WhoEmL 93*
Fitzgerald, Jeanette *St&PR 93*
Fitzgerald, Jeremiah Michael *Law&B 92*
Fitzgerald, John Bernard 1922- *St&PR 93*
Fitzgerald, John D(ennis) 1907- *DcAmChF 1960*
Fitzgerald, John D(ennis) 1907?-1988 *MajAI*
Fitzgerald, John Edmund 1923- *WhoAm 92*
Fitzgerald, John F. 1863-1950 *PolPar*
Fitzgerald, John James 1951- *WhoEmL 93*
Fitzgerald, John Joseph 1934- *St&PR 93*
Fitzgerald, John Paul 1951- *WhoE 93*
Fitzgerald, John Robert 1939- *St&PR 93*
Fitzgerald, John Thomas, Jr. 1948- *WhoEmL 93, WhoSSW 93, WhoWor 93*
Fitzgerald, John Warner 1924- *WhoAm 92*
Fitzgerald, Joseph Farley 1928- *WhoAm 92*
Fitzgerald, Joseph T. d1991 *BioIn 17*
Fitzgerald, Judith 1952- *WhoCanL 92*
Fitzgerald, Judith Klaswick 1948- *WhoAmW 93*
Fitzgerald, Julia 1943- *ScF&FL 92*
Fitzgerald, Julia Ann 1963- *WhoAmW 93*
Fitzgerald, Kevin M. 1954- *St&PR 93*
Fitzgerald, Kevin V. *BioIn 17*
Fitzgerald, Laurine Elisabeth 1930- *WhoAm 92*
Fitzgerald, Lee T. 1927- *St&PR 93*
Fitzgerald, Lutie *AmWomPl*
Fitzgerald, Mary Catherine 1954- *WhoEmL 93*
Fitzgerald, Mary P. 1960- *St&PR 93*
Fitzgerald, Maurice Patrick 1933- *St&PR 93*
Fitzgerald, Michael Anthony 1944- *WhoAm 92, WhoE 93*
Fitzgerald, Michael C. *Law&B 92*
Fitzgerald, Michael Eaton 1961- *WhoSSW 93*
Fitzgerald, Michael Francis 1946- *WhoWor 93*
Fitzgerald, Michael Gene 1952- *WhoEmL 93*
Fitzgerald, Michael Lee 1951- *WhoAm 92*
Fitzgerald, Michael Thomas 1948- *WhoEmL 93*
Fitzgerald, Michael William 1954- *WhoE 93*
Fitzgerald, Patrick T. 1945- *St&PR 93*
Fitzgerald, Patrishya Anne 1952- *WhoEmL 93*
Fitzgerald, Paul J. *St&PR 93*
Fitzgerald, Paula Marie Dean 1949- *WhoE 93*
Fitzgerald, Peter D. *St&PR 93*
Fitzgerald, Peter D. 1933- *St&PR 93*
Fitzgerald, Peter L. *Law&B 92*
Fitzgerald, Peter M. 1943- *St&PR 93*
Fitzgerald, Raymond Richard 1921- *WhoAm 92*
Fitzgerald, Richard Patrick 1950- *WhoEmL 93*
Fitzgerald, Robert *St&PR 93*
Fitzgerald, Robert Drake 1932- *St&PR 93*
Fitzgerald, Robert Hannon, Jr. 1942- *WhoAm 92, WhoWor 93*
Fitzgerald, Robert Maurice 1942- *St&PR 93, WhoAm 92*
Fitzgerald, Robert W. 1946- *St&PR 93*
Fitzgerald, Roger J. 1937- *WhoWrEP 92*
Fitz-Gerald, Roger Miller 1935- *WhoAm 92*
Fitzgerald, S.M.D. 1939- *WhoScE 91-1*
Fitzgerald, Sandra Patricia 1942- *WhoAmW 93*
Fitzgerald, Sandra Tucker 1955- *WhoEmL 93*
Fitzgerald, Sheryl Cunningham 1955- *WhoAmW 93*
Fitzgerald, Stephen Patrick 1954- *WhoEmL 93*
Fitzgerald, Thomas 1819-1891 *JrnUS*
Fitzgerald, Thomas Clifford 1939- *St&PR 93*
Fitzgerald, Thomas I. d1992 *NewYTBS 92 [port]*
Fitzgerald, Thomas Rollins 1922- *WhoAm 92*
Fitzgerald, Tikhon 1932- *WhoAm 92*
FitzGerald, Timothy Richard 1956- *WhoEmL 93*
Fitzgerald, Timothy Sean 1952- *WhoAm 92*
Fitzgerald, Timothy Wall 1963- *WhoEmL 93*
Fitzgerald, Vincent James 1950- *WhoEmL 93*
Fitzgerald, Walter George 1936- *WhoE 93*
Fitzgerald, Warren Franklin 1955- *WhoAm 93*
FitzGerald, Wendy Lynn 1949- *WhoAmW 93*
Fitzgerald, William Allingham 1937- *St&PR 93*
Fitzgerald, William F. 1908- *St&PR 93*
Fitzgerald, William H. 1943- *St&PR 93*
Fitz Gerald, William Henry G. 1909- *WhoAm 92*
Fitzgerald, Zelda 1900-1948 *BioIn 17*
Fitzgerald-Brown, Benita *BlkAmWO*
Fitz Gerald-Bush, Frank Shepard 1925- *WhoWor 93*
Fitzgerald Family *BioIn 17*
FitzGibbon, Constantine *BioIn 17*
FitzGibbon, Constantine 1919-1983 *ScF&FL 92*
Fitzgibbon, Donna Jean 1968- *WhoEmL 93*
Fitzgibbon, Eric John 1936- *WhoAsAP 91*
Fitzgibbon, Jane *WhoAm 92, WhoAmW 93*
Fitzgibbon, John Francis 1923- *WhoAm 92*
Fitz Gibbon, L.J. 1913- *St&PR 93*
Fitzgibbon, Patrick William 1937- *St&PR 93*
Fitzgibbon, Pierre 1954- *St&PR 93*
Fitzgibbon, Ralph Edgerton 1904- *ScF&FL 92*
Fitz Gibbon, Thomas Patrick 1913- *WhoAm 92*
Fitzgibbon, Walter J., Jr. 1933- *St&PR 93*
Fitzgibbons, David Lynn 1948- *St&PR 93*
Fitzgibbons, Donald R. 1951- *St&PR 93*
FitzGibbons, James Joseph 1958- *WhoEmL 93*
Fitzgibbons, James M. *WhoAm 92*
Fitzgibbons, James M. 1934- *St&PR 93, WhoSSW 93*
Fitzgibbons, John Murray 1950- *WhoEmL 93*
Fitzhardinge, Joan *ScF&FL 92*
Fitzhardinge, Joan Margaret 1912- *MajAI [port], SmATA 73 [port]*
Fitzharris, Timothy P. 1944- *WhoAm 92, WhoSSW 93*
Fitzhenry, Robert Irvine 1918- *WhoAm 92*
Fitz-Hugh, Glassell Slaughter, Jr. 1939- *WhoE 93*
Fitzhugh, H. Naylor d1992 *NewYTBS 92 [port]*
Fitzhugh, Louise 1928-1974 *DcAmChF 1960*
Fitzhugh, Louise (Perkins) 1928-1974 *MajAI [port]*
Fitzhugh, Lynne Dennison 1942- *WhoE 93*
Fitzhugh, Percy Keese 1876-1950 *BioIn 17*
Fitzhugh, William Wyvill, Jr. 1914- *WhoAm 92*
Fitzmaurice, Gabriel 1952- *ConAu 137*
Fitzmaurice, George 1895-1940 *MiSFD 9N*
Fitzmaurice, James 1898-1965 *BioIn 17*
Fitzmaurice, Laurence Dorset 1938- *WhoAm 92, WhoE 93*
Fitzmaurice, Robert John 1937- *St&PR 93*
Fitzmaurice, Shelley A. *Law&B 92*
Fitzmaurice, Victor E. *Law&B 92*
Fitzmorris, John Donellan, Jr. *Law&B 92*
Fitzner, Kathryn Ethridge 1953- *WhoEmL 93*
Fitzner, Werner 1954- *WhoWor 93*
Fitzpatrick, Benjamin 1802-1869 *PolPar*
Fitzpatrick, Carol Edna 1942- *St&PR 93*
Fitzpatrick, Carolyn Henley 1952- *WhoE 93*
Fitzpatrick, Charles R. 1938- *St&PR 93, WhoIns 93*
Fitzpatrick, Christopher G. *Law&B 92*
Fitzpatrick, Dana Gregory 1930- *St&PR 93*
Fitzpatrick, Daniel John *Law&B 92*
Fitzpatrick, Daniel W. *BioIn 17*
Fitzpatrick, Daniel William 1947- *WhoEmL 93*
Fitzpatrick, David William *Law&B 92*
Fitzpatrick, Denis J. 1944- *St&PR 93*
Fitzpatrick, Dennis John 1948- *WhoEmL 93*
Fitzpatrick, Duross 1934- *WhoSSW 93*
Fitzpatrick, Ellen 1957- *WhoAmW 93, WhoEmL 93*
Fitzpatrick, Eugene E. 1936- *St&PR 93*
Fitzpatrick, Francis G. d1992 *NewYTBS 92 [port]*
Fitzpatrick, Francis G. 1903-1992 *BioIn 17*
FitzPatrick, Francis James 1916- *WhoE 93, WhoWor 93*
Fitzpatrick, Frank P. 1934- *St&PR 93*
Fitzpatrick, Franklin Davidson 1952- *WhoEmL 93, WhoSSW 93*
Fitzpatrick, Gayle Daniel 1941- *WhoAmW 93*
Fitzpatrick, Gerard J. 1928- *St&PR 93*
Fitzpatrick, Gilbert Lawrence 1930- *St&PR 93, WhoAm 92*
Fitzpatrick, Gladys Eve *WhoAm 92*
Fitzpatrick, Gregory J. 1960- *St&PR 93*
Fitzpatrick, Harold Francis 1947- *WhoE 93, WhoEmL 93*
Fitzpatrick, James B. *BioIn 17*
Fitzpatrick, James David 1938- *WhoAm 92, WhoWor 93*
Fitzpatrick, James Franklin 1933- *WhoAm 92*
Fitzpatrick, James Ward, Jr. 1921- *WhoSSW 93*
Fitzpatrick, Jay W. 1941- *St&PR 93*
Fitzpatrick, Jim 1948- *ScF&FL 92*
Fitzpatrick, John 1958- *WhoWor 93*
Fitzpatrick, John A. 1949- *WhoScE 91-3*
Fitzpatrick, John B. *Law&B 92*
Fitzpatrick, John Henry 1956- *WhoAm 92*
Fitzpatrick, John J. 1918- *WhoAm 92, WhoSSW 93*
Fitzpatrick, John J., Jr. *Law&B 92*
Fitzpatrick, John Joseph 1933- *WhoAm 92*
Fitzpatrick, John M. 1948- *WhoScE 91-3*
Fitzpatrick, John Malcolm 1924- *St&PR 93, WhoAm 92*
Fitzpatrick, Joseph William 1941- *St&PR 93*
Fitzpatrick, Judith 1941- *WhoAm 92*
Fitzpatrick, Kevin Paul 1954- *WhoE 93*
Fitzpatrick, Kibbe N. 1935- *WhoUN 92*
Fitzpatrick, Lois Ann 1952- *WhoAmW 93*
Fitzpatrick, Mary Anne Theresa *WhoAmW 93*
Fitzpatrick, Michael Clifford 1953- *St&PR 93*
Fitzpatrick, Michael J. 1948- *St&PR 93*
Fitzpatrick, Nancy Soletti 1951- *WhoAmW 93*
Fitzpatrick, Philip A. 1946- *St&PR 93*
Fitzpatrick, Richard H. *Law&B 92*
Fitzpatrick, Robert F. 1931- *St&PR 93*
Fitzpatrick, Sean Kevin 1941- *WhoAm 92, WhoWor 93*
Fitzpatrick, Stephen T. 1947- *St&PR 93*
Fitzpatrick, Thomas Bernard 1919- *WhoAm 92, WhoWor 93*
Fitzpatrick, Thomas H. *Law&B 92*
Fitzpatrick, Thomas Mark 1951- *WhoAm 92*
Fitzpatrick, Timothy D. *Law&B 92*
Fitzpatrick, Tracy Elizabeth 1954- *WhoEmL 93*
Fitzpatrick, Whitfield Westfeldt 1942- *WhoWor 93*
Fitzpatrick, William Henry 1908- *WhoAm 92*
Fitzpatrick, William J. *Law&B 92*
Fitzpatrick, William Joseph 1941- *St&PR 93, WhoAm 92*
FitzRoy, Charles (Patrick Hugh) 1957- *ConAu 136*
Fitzroy, Forrest S. *Law&B 92*
Fitzroy, Nancy deLoye 1927- *WhoAm 92*
Fitzsimmons, Cotton 1931- *WhoAm 92*
Fitzsimmons, Edward J. 1932- *St&PR 93*
Fitzsimmons, Ellen Marie *Law&B 92*
Fitzsimmons, J. Patrick *Law&B 92*
Fitzsimmons, James R.B. 1939- *St&PR 93*
Fitzsimmons, John D. 1930- *St&PR 93*
Fitzsimmons, Joseph Heath 1942- *WhoAm 92*
Fitzsimmons, Joseph J. *St&PR 93*
Fitzsimmons, Joseph John 1934- *WhoAm 92*
Fitzsimmons, Kevin Michael 1956- *WhoEmL 93*
Fitzsimmons, Lowell Cotton 1931- *WhoAm 92*
FitzSimmons, Richard M. 1924- *WhoAm 92*
Fitzsimmons, Robert James 1940- *St&PR 93, WhoAm 92*
Fitzsimmons, Robert James 1946- *St&PR 93*
Fitzsimmons, Robert Prometheus 1862?-1917 *BioIn 17*
Fitzsimmons, Sophie Sonia 1943- *WhoAm 92, WhoAmW 93, WhoE 93, WhoWor 93*
Fitzsimmons, Thomas 1926- *WhoWrEP 92*
Fitzsimmons, Tina Louise *Law&B 92*
Fitzsimonds, Roger Leon 1938- *St&PR 93, WhoAm 92*
Fitzsimons, Brendan 1954- *WhoScE 91-3*
FitzSimons, Dennis Joseph *BioIn 17*
FitzSimons, Eleanor B. d1990 *BioIn 17*
Fitzsimons, George K. 1928- *WhoAm 92*
Fitzsimons, James Thomas *WhoScE 91-1*
Fitzsimons, John H. *Law&B 92*
Fitzsimons, John H. 1948- *St&PR 93*
Fitzsimons, John Thomas Raymond *WhoScE 91-1*
Fitzsimons, Marjorie Fraser 1932- *WhoSSW 93*
FitzSimons, Maureen *WhoAm 92*
Fitzsimons, Patrick S. 1930- *WhoAm 92*
Fitzsimons, Raymond 1945- *WhoAm 92*
Fitzsimons, Raymond Charles *Law&B 92*
FitzSimons, Sharon Russell 1945- *WhoAmW 93*
Fitzsimons, Thomas 1936- *WhoUN 92*
Fitzsteward, Farmer *WhoWrEP 92*
Fitzwater, Lynne E. *Law&B 92*
Fitzwater, Marlin *BioIn 17*
Fitzwater, Marlin 1942- *WhoAm 92, WhoE 93*
Fitzwater, Martha Amanda 1961- *WhoEmL 93*
Fitzwater, Ronald Lee 1953- *St&PR 93*
Fitzwater, Sidney Allen 1953- *WhoSSW 93*
Fitzwilliam, Richard 1745-1816 *Baker 92*
Fitzwilliam, William 1643-1719 *BioIn 17*
Fiumara, James Joseph 1949- *St&PR 93*
Fiume, Orazio 1908-1976 *Baker 92*
Fiumefreddo, Charles A. 1933- *St&PR 93, WhoAm 92*
Fiur, Henry Michael 1939- *St&PR 93*
Fiuza, Alejandro Daniel 1964- *WhoWor 93*
Fiuzat, Abbas Ali 1947- *WhoEmL 93, WhoSSW 93*
Fiveash, Don Pat 1956- *St&PR 93*
Fivecoate, Dennis Ray 1953- *WhoEmL 93*
Fivel, Steven E. *Law&B 92*
Fivelson, Scott 1954- *ScF&FL 92*
Five Martyrs of Sebasteia *OxDcByz*
Five Royales *SoulM*
Fives, Daniel Christopher d1990 *BioIn 17*
Five Satins *SoulM*
Fix, Alfred Harold 1930- *WhoAm 92*
Fix, James Douglas 1931- *WhoAm 92*
Fix, John Neilson 1937- *WhoAm 92*
Fix, John Robert 1934- *WhoE 93*
Fix, Meyer 1906- *WhoE 93*
Fix, Michael L. 1949- *St&PR 93*
Fix, Wilbur James 1927- *St&PR 93, WhoAm 92*
Fixel, Lawrence 1917- *ConAu 137*
Fixel, Norman *St&PR 93*
Fixler, Philip E. d1991 *BioIn 17*
Fixman, Ben 1925- *St&PR 93*
Fixman, Marshall 1930- *WhoAm 92*
Fix-Romlow, Jeanne Kay 1947- *WhoAmW 93*
Fixter, D.G. 1936- *St&PR 93*
Fixter, Scott Douglas *Law&B 92*
Fixx, David W. *Law&B 92*
Fizdale, Richard *WhoAm 92*
Fizdale, Robert 1920- *Baker 92*
Fizyta, Wojciech Leon 1948- *WhoEmL 93*
Fjeld, Magne 1939- *WhoWor 93*

Fjeldel, Mark B. *Law&B 92*
Fjeldly, Tor Arne 1943- *WhoWor 93*
Fjeldstad, Lucie J. *St&PR 93*
Fjeldstad, Oivin 1903-1983 *Baker 92*
Fjelstad, Paul 1954- *WhoEmL 93*
Fjelstul, D.M. 1942- *St&PR 93*
Fjerdingstad, Ejnar Jules 1937- *WhoWor 93*
Flaate, Kaare *WhoScE 91-4*
Flaaten, Ola 1947- *WhoWor 93*
Flacco, Elaine Germano 1959- *WhoE 93, WhoEmL 93*
Flaccus, Edward 1921- *WhoAm 92*
Flach, Frederic Francis 1927- *WhoE 93*
Flach, Gunter *WhoScE 91-3*
Flach, Victor H. 1929- *WhoAm 92*
Flachman, Leonard R. 1936- *St&PR 93*
Flachmann, Michael 1942- *ConAu 40NR*
Flack, Audrey *BioIn 17*
Flack, Charles R. 1896-1991 *BioIn 17*
Flack, David Bruce 1954- *St&PR 93*
Flack, Dora D(utson) 1919- *WhoWrEP 92*
Flack, Duane Elliott 1935- *St&PR 93*
Flack, George R. 1949- *St&PR 93*
Flack, Harold E., II 1958- *St&PR 93*
Flack, Joe Fenley 1921- *WhoAm 92*
Flack, Marjorie 1897-1958 *ChlLR 28 [port], ConAu 136, MajAI [port]*
Flack, Michael Alan 1946- *St&PR 93*
Flack, Roberta 1939- *Baker 92, SoulM, WhoAm 92, WhoAmW 93*
Flack, Warren Wade 1956- *WhoWor 93*
Flacke, Joan Wareham 1931- *WhoAmW 93*
Flacks, Louis Michael 1937- *WhoWor 93*
Flackton, William 1709-1798 *Baker 92*
Flad, H.-D. 1935- *WhoScE 91-3*
Flad, Harvey Keyes 1938- *WhoE 93*
Fladeland, Betty 1919- *WhoAm 92*
Flader, William W. 1948- *St&PR 93*
Fladmark, Lars 1935- *St&PR 93*
Fladung, Nanette Copple 1964- *WhoAmW 93*
Fladung, Richard Denis 1953- *WhoEmL 93*
Flaga, Kazimierz, Jozef 1939- *WhoScE 91-4*
Flagan, Janice 1953- *WhoAmW 93*
Flagan, Richard Charles 1947- *WhoAm 92, WhoEmL 93*
Flagel, Laverne Wayne 1934- *St&PR 93*
Flagello, Ezio (Domenico) 1931- *Baker 92*
Flagello, Ezio Domenico 1932- *WhoAm 92*
Flagello, Nicolas (Oreste) 1928- *Baker 92*
Flagg, Artemus 1953- *WhoSSW 93*
Flagg, Edmund 1815-1890 *ScF&FL 92*
Flagg, Ernest 1857-1947 *BioIn 17*
Flagg, Fannie 1941- *ConAu 40NR*
Flagg, Jeanne Bodin 1925- *WhoAm 92*
Flagg, Josiah 1737-1795? *Baker 92*
Flagg, Michael James 1958- *WhoAm 92*
Flagg, Norman Lee 1932- *WhoWor 93*
Flagg, Raymond Osbourn 1933- *St&PR 93, WhoSSW 93*
Flagg, Robert Farrington 1924- *WhoSSW 93*
Flagg, Ronald Simon 1953- *WhoEmL 93*
Flagg, Thomas *BioIn 17*
Flagg, Vivian Annette 1960- *WhoEmL 93, WhoSSW 93*
Flagle, Charles Denhard 1919- *WhoAm 92*
Flagstad, Kirsten 1895-1962 *IntDcOp [port], OxDcOp*
Flagstad, Kirsten (Malfrid) 1895-1962 *Baker 92*
Flaharty, Robert Richard 1948- *WhoEmL 93*
Flaherty, Bartley F. *Law&B 92*
Flaherty, Billie Schrecker *Law&B 92*
Flaherty, Catherine Jane 1958- *WhoAmW 93*
Flaherty, Charles Francis 1938- *WhoAm 92*
Flaherty, Daniel Martin 1960- *St&PR 93*
Flaherty, Doug 1939- *WhoWrEP 92*
Flaherty, Elizabeth B. *Law&B 92*
Flaherty, G.S. 1938- *St&PR 93*
Flaherty, Gerald A. *Law&B 92*
Flaherty, Gerlinde M. 1942- *WhoAmW 93*
Flaherty, Hugh E. 1931- *St&PR 93*
Flaherty, James Grant 1958- *WhoEmL 93*
Flaherty, James N. *Law&B 92*
Flaherty, James Robert 1946- *St&PR 93*
Flaherty, John J. d1992 *BioIn 17*
Flaherty, John Joseph 1932- *WhoAm 92*
Flaherty, John P., Jr. 1931- *WhoAm 92, WhoWor 93*
Flaherty, John Preston, Jr. 1942- *St&PR 93*
Flaherty, Lawrence M. 1952- *St&PR 93*
Flaherty, Lee F. *St&PR 93*
Flaherty, Marcia Kay 1951- *WhoEmL 93*
Flaherty, Maria Yepiz 1937- *WhoAmW 93*
Flaherty, Michael Paul 1945- *WhoAm 92*
Flaherty, Paul *MiSFD 9*
Flaherty, Peter F. 1925- *PolPar*
Flaherty, Ray *BioIn 17*
Flaherty, Richard Alan 1952- *WhoEmL 93*
Flaherty, Robert E. 1939- *St&PR 93*
Flaherty, Robert J. 1884-1951 *MiSFD 9N*
Flaherty, Roberta D. 1947- *WhoEmL 93*
Flaherty, Sharon Marie 1953- *WhoAmW 93, WhoE 93*
Flaherty, Sherri Lynne 1961- *WhoAmW 93*
Flaherty, Stephen *BioIn 17*
Flaherty, Tammy S. 1963- *St&PR 93*
Flaherty, Tina Santi *WhoAm 92, WhoAmW 93*
Flaherty, William E. 1933- *WhoAm 92, WhoE 93*
Flaherty, William Edward 1933- *St&PR 93*
Flaig, John D. *St&PR 93*
Flaig, Paul Edward 1949- *WhoEmL 93*
Flaisher, Lynn *Law&B 92*
Flajser, Steven H. 1943- *St&PR 93*
Flake, David J. 1955- *St&PR 93*
Flake, Floyd H. *BioIn 17*
Flake, Floyd H. 1945- *CngDr 91*
Flake, Floyd Harold 1945- *WhoAm 92, WhoE 93*
Flake, Janice Louise 1940- *WhoAmW 93*
Flake, John Joel 1948- *WhoEmL 93*
Flake, Robert A. 1929- *St&PR 93*
Flake, Wesley Lloyd 1952- *WhoSSW 93*
Flake, William 1839-1932 *BioIn 17*
Flakoll, Thomas Jerome 1944- *St&PR 93*
Flakus, Gregory Michael 1948- *WhoSSW 93*
Flam, Tamas 1930- *WhoScE 91-4*
Flamant, G. 1952- *WhoScE 91-2*
Flamberg, Morton 1920- *St&PR 93*
Flameng, Leopold 1831-1911 *BioIn 17*
Flament, Edouard 1880-1958 *Baker 92*
Flament-Durand, Jacqueline 1927- *WhoScE 91-2*
Flamingos *SoulM*
Flamini, Christian Joseph 1948- *WhoScE 91-2*
Flaminio, Vincenzo 1939- *WhoWor 93*
Flamm, Barry Russell 1933- *WhoWor 93*
Flamm, Donald 1899- *WhoE 93, WhoWor 93*
Flamm, Donald L. 1943- *St&PR 93*
Flamm, Eric Morton 1955- *WhoSSW 93*
Flamm, Heinz 1929- *WhoScE 91-4*
Flammang, Donna *Law&B 92*
Flammang, Donna M. 1951- *St&PR 93*
Flammang, Susann 1950- *WhoEmL 93*
Flammarion, Jean-Paul 1940- *WhoScE 91-2*
Flamme, Arthur C. *St&PR 93*
Flammer, Edward J. *St&PR 93*
Flammonde, Paris *WhoWrEP 92*
Flamson, Richard J., III *BioIn 17*
Flamson, Richard Joseph, III 1929- *St&PR 93*
Flamsteed, John 1646-1719 *BioIn 17*
Flanagan, Anita Marie 1940- *WhoAmW 93, WhoE 93, WhoWor 93*
Flanagan, Anita Mars 1961- *WhoAmW 93*
Flanagan, Barbara *WhoAm 92*
Flanagan, Barry 1941- *BioIn 17*
Flanagan, Bud 1896-1968 *See Crazy Gang, The IntDcF 2-3*
Flanagan, Bud 1896-1968 & Allen, Chesney 1893-1982 *QDrFCA 92 [port]*
Flanagan, Christie Stephen 1938- *WhoAm 92*
Flanagan, Christopher S. *Law&B 92*
Flanagan, Christopher Sean 1956- *St&PR 93*
Flanagan, Daniel d1991 *BioIn 17*
Flanagan, David J. 1924- *St&PR 93*
Flanagan, David T. 1947- *St&PR 93*
Flanagan, David Thomas *Law&B 92*
Flanagan, Deborah Mary 1956- *WhoAmW 93*
Flanagan, Dennis Patrick 1948- *St&PR 93*
Flanagan, Edward Charles 1927- *St&PR 93*
Flanagan, Edward William 1950- *WhoEmL 93*
Flanagan, Eugene John Thomas 1923- *WhoAm 92*
Flanagan, Fionnula Manon 1941- *WhoAm 92*
Flanagan, Francis Dennis 1912- *WhoAm 92*
Flanagan, Frederick James 1941- *WhoE 93*
Flanagan, Gail Claire 1952- *WhoAmW 93*
Flanagan, Glenda *St&PR 93*
Flanagan, Graeme *ScF&FL 92*
Flanagan, Hallie 1890-1969 *BioIn 17*
Flanagan, Hallie Ferguson 1890-1969 *AmWomPl*
Flanagan, Harold Thomas, Jr. 1953- *WhoEmL 93*
Flanagan, James Loton *WhoAm 92*
Flanagan, Joe *BioIn 17*
Flanagan, John Fortner 1944- *St&PR 93*
Flanagan, John J. 1906-1991 *BioIn 17*
Flanagan, John M., Jr. 1943- *St&PR 93*
Flanagan, John Terrence 1929- *St&PR 93*
Flanagan, John Theodore 1906- *WhoAm 92*
Flanagan, Joseph Charles 1938- *WhoAm 92*
Flanagan, Joseph P. 1932- *St&PR 93*
Flanagan, Joseph Patrick 1938- *WhoAm 92, WhoWor 93*
Flanagan, Joseph Patrick, Jr. 1924- *WhoAm 92*
Flanagan, Judith Ann 1950- *WhoAmW 93*
Flanagan, Kathleen T. 1954- *WhoSSW 93*
Flanagan, Kathy Marie 1952- *WhoAmW 93*
Flanagan, Kenneth Jack 1940- *St&PR 93*
Flanagan, Larry 1953- *WhoEmL 93*
Flanagan, Lillian Lee Ann 1933- *WhoAmW 93*
Flanagan, Madeline *Law&B 92*
Flanagan, Mark David 1952- *St&PR 93*
Flanagan, Martha Lang 1942- *St&PR 93, WhoAm 92*
Flanagan, Martine *Law&B 92*
Flanagan, Michael Charles 1954- *WhoEmL 93*
Flanagan, Natalie Smith 1913- *WhoAmW 93*
Flanagan, Paulette B. 1949- *St&PR 93*
Flanagan, Peter J. *Law&B 92*
Flanagan, Peter J. 1930- *WhoIns 93*
Flanagan, Richard Gerald *Law&B 92*
Flanagan, Robert 1941- *ConAu 17AS [port]*
Flanagan, Robert 1946- *WhoCanL 92*
Flanagan, Roger *WhoScE 91-1*
Flanagan, Rosemary 1956- *WhoAmW 93, WhoE 93*
Flanagan, Sean 1937- *WhoScE 91-3*
Flanagan, Sherman Edward, III *Law&B 92*
Flanagan, Stephen Roger 1956- *WhoEmL 93*
Flanagan, Terrence Girard 1952- *WhoSSW 93*
Flanagan, Terry *ScF&FL 92*
Flanagan, Therese Ann 1955- *WhoAmW 93, WhoEmL 93*
Flanagan, Thomas 1923- *BioIn 17*
Flanagan, Thomas J. *Law&B 92*
Flanagan, Thomas Patrick *WhoAm 92*
Flanagan, Tommy (Lee) 1930- *Baker 92, WhoAm 92*
Flanagan, Van Kent 1945- *WhoAm 92*
Flanagan, William, (Jr.) 1923-1969 *Baker 92*
Flanagan, William James 1934- *St&PR 93*
Flanagan, William K., Jr. *Law&B 92*
Flanagan, William M. *Law&B 92*
Flanagan, William Stanley, Jr. 1947- *WhoEmL 93*
Flanagan, William Watkins, III 1955- *WhoE 93*
Flanagan-Herstek, Katherine M. 1951- *WhoEmL 93*
Flanagan Zipperstein, Diane *Law&B 92*
Flanagin, Neil 1930- *WhoAm 92*
Flanary, Debra Wilbanks 1953- *WhoAmW 93*
Flanary, Kathy Venita Moore 1946- *WhoAmW 93*
Fland, Steve *BioIn 17*
Flanders, Allen F. 1945- *St&PR 93*
Flanders, Deanne Bowman 1946- *WhoAmW 93*
Flanders, Donald H. 1924- *St&PR 93*
Flanders, Dudley Kennedy 1952- *St&PR 93*
Flanders, Dwight Prescott 1909- *WhoAm 92, WhoWor 93*
Flanders, George James 1960- *WhoEmL 93*
Flanders, Harold H. *Law&B 92*
Flanders, Helen Driver 1947- *WhoAm 92, WhoAmW 93, WhoEmL 93*
Flanders, Henry Jackson, Jr. 1921- *WhoAm 92, WhoSSW 93*
Flanders, Howard Barrett, Jr. *Law&B 92*
Flanders, Howard Barrett, Jr. 1935- *St&PR 93*
Flanders, James Prescott 1942- *WhoSSW 93*
Flanders, Lowell L. 1942- *WhoUN 92*
Flanders, Rebecca *ScF&FL 92*
Flanders, Scott Nelson 1956- *WhoAm 92*
Flanders, Stephen Lawrence 1942- *WhoAm 92*
Flandin, Pierre Etienne 1889-1958 *BioIn 17*
Flandro, Paul Woods 1921- *St&PR 93*
Flanery, Karen *ScF&FL 92*
Flangas, William G. 1927- *St&PR 93*
Flanigan, James Conrad 1938- *WhoE 93*
Flanigan, Jeanne Marie 1946- *WhoAm 92, WhoEmL 93*
Flanigan, John Pershing 1919- *St&PR 93*
Flanigan, Michael Cletus 1936- *WhoSSW 93*
Flanigan, Michael Paul 1934- *WhoE 93*
Flanigan, Peter Magnus 1923- *St&PR 93, WhoAm 92*
Flanigan, Pierce John, III 1942- *St&PR 93*
Flanigan, Richard Joseph 1948- *WhoE 93*
Flanigan, Robert Daniel, Jr. 1949- *WhoEmL 93*
Flanigan, William Joseph 1930- *WhoAm 92*
Flaniken, Forrest W. 1954- *St&PR 93*
Flank, E.C. *Law&B 92*
Flank, Sandra Glassman 1935- *WhoE 93*
Flannagan, Benjamin Collins, IV 1927- *WhoE 93*
Flannagan, Margery Fouraker 1964- *WhoSSW 93*
Flannelly, Kevin J. 1949- *WhoWor 93*
Flannelly, Laura T. 1952- *WhoAmW 93, WhoWor 93*
Flannelly, William George 1931- *WhoE 93*
Flanner, Hildegarde 1899- *AmWomPl*
Flanner, Mary H. *AmWomPl*
Flannery, Anne *BioIn 17*
Flannery, Caroline Olson 1942- *WhoAmW 93*
Flannery, Constance O'Day- *ScF&FL 92*
Flannery, Ellen Joanne 1951- *WhoAm 92*
Flannery, Francis X. *Law&B 92*
Flannery, Frank Travers 1947- *WhoE 93, WhoEmL 93*
Flannery, Harry Audley *Law&B 92*
Flannery, Harry Audley 1947- *WhoEmL 93*
Flannery, Joseph Patrick 1932- *St&PR 93, WhoAm 92*
Flannery, Michael E. *Law&B 92*
Flannery, Nancy Gail *WhoIns 93*
Flannery, Robert James 1945- *St&PR 93*
Flannery, Thomas A. 1918- *CngDr 91*
Flannery, Thomas Aquinas 1918- *WhoAm 92, WhoE 93*
Flannery, Thomas Luke 1947- *WhoE 93*
Flannery, W. Gerald, Jr. *Law&B 92*
Flannery, Wilbur Eugene 1907- *WhoE 93, WhoWor 93*
Flannery, William Jackson, Jr. 1944- *WhoSSW 93*
Flannery, William O. *Law&B 92*
Flannigan, Anita Mae 1915-1991 *BioIn 17*
Flannigan, Edward J. 1938- *St&PR 93*
Flannigan, Timothy E. 1948- *St&PR 93*
Flansburg, James Sherman 1932- *WhoAm 92*
Flansburgh, Earl Robert 1931- *WhoAm 92, WhoE 93, WhoWor 93*
Flanzer, Robert Stephen 1934- *WhoE 93*
Flanzraich, Neil William *Law&B 92*
Flanzy, M.J. *WhoScE 91-2*
Flartey, Roger *Law&B 92*
Flasar, Aleksandar 1926- *WhoScE 91-4*
Flaschen, Evan Daniel 1957- *WhoE 93, WhoEmL 93, WhoWor 93*
Flaschen, Steward Samuel 1926- *St&PR 93, WhoAm 92*
Flaskamp, William Davidson 1924- *WhoAm 92*
Flassbeck, Heiner 1950- *WhoWor 93*
Flast, Florence d1992 *NewYTBS 92 [port]*
Flatau, Carl R. 1924- *WhoE 93*
Flaten, Alfred N. 1934- *St&PR 93*
Flaten, G. *WhoScE 91-2*
Flaten, Gunnar Arne 1956- *WhoWor 93*
Flatley, Guy 1934- *WhoAm 92*
Flatley, William M. 1934- *St&PR 93*
Flatness, Mary Linda 1942- *WhoAmW 93*
Flato, Franklin 1911- *St&PR 93*
Flaton, Johan-Martijn *ScF&FL 92*
Flatt, Adrian Ede 1921- *WhoAm 92*
Flatt, Andrew John 1946- *WhoUN 92*
Flatt, Carter J. 1943- *WhoIns 93*
Flatt, Dean 1949- *St&PR 93*
Flatt, Ernest Orville 1918- *WhoAm 92*
Flatt, George W. 1852?-1880 *BioIn 17*
Flatt, J. Bruce *St&PR 93*
Flatt, J. Ian *St&PR 93*
Flatt, Lester (Raymond) 1914-1979 *Baker 92*
Flatt, Peter Raymond *WhoScE 91-1*
Flatt, William Perry 1931- *WhoSSW 93*
Flatte, Stanley Martin 1940- *WhoAm 92*
Flatten, Jeffrey Allan 1951- *WhoEmL 93*
Flatters, Paul-Xavier 1832-1881 *Expl 93*
Flattery, Paul C. *Law&B 92*
Flattery, Thomas L. *Law&B 92*
Flattery, Thomas L. 1922- *St&PR 93*
Flattery, Thomas Long *Law&B 92*
Flattery, Thomas Long 1922- *WhoAm 92, WhoWor 93*
Flattmann, Alan Raymond 1946- *WhoEmL 93, WhoSSW 93*
Flatto, Adam R. 1963- *WhoE 93*
Flatz, Gebhard 1925- *WhoScE 91-3*
Flatz, Josef Franz 1929- *WhoScE 91-3*
Flaubert, Gustave 1821-1880 *BioIn 17, DcLB 119 [port], MagSWL [port], ShSCr 11 [port], WorLitC [port]*

Flaud, Jean-Marie Henri 1946- WhoWor 93
Flaum, Ellen M. Law&B 92
Flaum, Joel Martin 1936- WhoAm 92
Flaum, Marshall Allen WhoAm 92
Flaum, Morris Aaron 1947- WhoSSW 93
Flaum, Sander Allen 1937- WhoAm 92
Flaurier, Noel AmWomPl
Flaute, Richard Thomas 1935- St&PR 93
Flavell, Richard Bailey WhoScE 91-1
Flavian d449? OxDcByz
Flavianus OxDcByz
Flavin, Douglas E. Law&B 92
Flavin, Glennon P. 1916- WhoAm 92
Flavin, Jennifer BioIn 17
Flavin, John Joseph, Jr. 1956- WhoE 93, WhoEmL 93
Flavin, Patrick Brian 1947- St&PR 93
Flavius, Josephus BioIn 17
Flawn, Peter Tyrrell 1926- WhoAm 92
Flax, Alexander Henry 1921- WhoAm 92
Flax, Edward J. 1942- St&PR 93
Flax, Florence Roselin 1936- WhoSSW 93, WhoWor 93
Flax, Harold L. 1927- St&PR 93
Flax, Lawrence 1934- WhoSSW 93
Flax, Martin Howard 1928- WhoAm 92
Flax, Richard L. 1940- WhoE 93
Flax, Robert J. Law&B 92
Flax, Robert J. 1949- St&PR 93
Flax, Robert Leonard 1953- WhoEmL 93
Flax, Samuel Allan 1956- WhoEmL 93
Flax, Stanley 1933- WhoSSW 93
Flaxland, Gustave-Alexandre 1821-1895 Baker 92
Flay, Brian R. 1947- WhoEmL 93
Fleagle, John Gwynn 1948- WhoAm 92, WhoEmL 93
Flecha, Mateo 1481-1553 Baker 92
Flecha, Mateo c. 1530-1604 Baker 92
Fleche-Seban, C. WhoScE 91-2
Flechner, Neil 1940- St&PR 93
Flechner, Roberta Fay 1949- WhoAmW 93, WhoEmL 93
Flechsenhar, Ullrich Hans 1946- WhoUN 92
Flechtner, Richard O. 1945- St&PR 93
Fleck, Bela c. 1958- ConMus 8 [port]
Fleck, Carole Jean 1955- WhoEmL 93
Fleck, Charles L. 1952- St&PR 93
Fleck, David A. 1947- St&PR 93
Fleck, Elmer Earl 1926- WhoAm 92
Fleck, George Morrison 1934- WhoAm 92, WhoE 93
Fleck, Gustav Peter 1909- WhoAm 92
Fleck, Harold Ulrich 1935- St&PR 93
Fleck, Harry Martin Law&B 92
Fleck, Joanne Elizabeth Tuhkanen 1939- WhoAmW 93
Fleck, John BioIn 17
Fleck, Paul Duncan 1934- WhoAm 92
Fleck, Raymond Anthony, Jr. 1927- WhoAm 92
Fleck, Richard D. 1930- St&PR 93
Fleck, Richard Francis 1937- ConAu 40NR, WhoWrEP 92
Fleck, Robert John 1947- St&PR 93
Fleck, Stephen 1912- WhoWor 93
Fleck, Zachary Thomas 1961- WhoEmL 93
Fleckenstein, Agnes Elsie 1939- WhoAmW 93
Fleckenstein, Bernhard 1944- WhoScE 91-3
Flecker, James Elroy 1884-1915 BioIn 17, ScF&FL 92
Flecknell, Paul Andrew WhoScE 91-1
Fledderjohn, Karl Ross 1935- St&PR 93, WhoAm 92
Fleddermann, Stephen Roy 1956- WhoEmL 93
Fleegal, Steven Arthur 1954- WhoEmL 93, WhoSSW 93
Fleeger, Darrell Francis 1932- WhoSSW 93
Fleeger, Ron 1955- WhoE 93, WhoEmL 93
Fleener, A.D. 1930- St&PR 93
Fleenor, Judy Ann 1946- WhoAmW 93
Fleenor, Juliann E. ScF&FL 92
Fleenor, Michael Edward 1953- WhoEmL 93
Fleer, Marilyn June 1931- WhoWrEP 92
Fleeson, Doris 1901-1970 JrnUS
Fleeson, William 1915- WhoAm 92
Fleet, Brenda 1948- WhoCanL 92
Fleet, Charles S. 1931-1991 BioIn 17
Fleet, George Thurman, Jr. 1928- St&PR 93
Fleet, Jheri Chastain 1940- WhoAmW 93, WhoSSW 93
Fleet, Richard W. 1954- St&PR 93
Fleet, Thomas 1685-1758 JrnUS
Fleeter, Nancy Hartman 1956- WhoAmW 93
Fleetwood, James R. Law&B 92
Fleetwood, Jenni ScF&FL 92
Fleetwood, Michael John 1938- WhoScE 91-1
Fleetwood, Mick BioIn 17
Fleetwood, Mick 1942- Baker 92
Fleetwood, Mick 1947- WhoAm 92
Fleetwood, Rex Allen 1951- WhoAm 92, WhoE 93, WhoEmL 93
Fleetwood-Walker, Patricia WhoScE 91-1
Fleezanis, Jorja Kay 1952- WhoAm 92, WhoAmW 93
Flegal, George Blair, Jr. 1927- St&PR 93
Flegal, Janet 1944- WhoAmW 93
Flege, John Blain, Jr. 1929- WhoAm 92
Flegeal-Kipp, Sonia Ruth 1949- WhoAmW 93, WhoE 93
Flegier, Ange 1846-1927 Baker 92
Flegler, Joel B. 1941- WhoWrEP 92
Fleharty, Mary Sue 1962- WhoAmW 93
Fleisch, Herbert Andre 1933- WhoWor 93
Fleischaker, Elise Marie 1964- WhoAmW 93
Fleischaker, Ted 1950- WhoEmL 93
Fleischauer, Ben 1922- St&PR 93
Fleischauer, Emil A., Jr. 1927- St&PR 93
Fleischauer, John Frederick 1939- WhoAm 92
Fleischer, Albert Georg 1940- WhoE 93
Fleischer, Anton 1891-1945 Baker 92
Fleischer, Arthur, Jr. 1933- WhoAm 92
Fleischer, Barbara Jane 1948- WhoAmW 93
Fleischer, Carl August 1936- WhoWor 93
Fleischer, Cornell Hugh 1950- WhoAm 92
Fleischer, Debi 1950- WhoEmL 93
Fleischer, Denise M. 1958- WhoWrEP 92
Fleischer, Dorothy Ann 1957- WhoAmW 93
Fleischer, Ellen Lee 1945- WhoAmW 93
Fleischer, Everly Borah 1936- WhoAm 92
Fleischer, Gerald Albert 1933- WhoAm 92
Fleischer, Henry Law&B 92
Fleischer, Leonard T. 1911- St&PR 93
Fleischer, Leonore 1932- ScF&FL 92
Fleischer, Martha Hester Law&B 92
Fleischer, Mathew William 1944- St&PR 93
Fleischer, Max 1889-1972 ScF&FL 92
Fleischer, Michael 1908- WhoAm 92
Fleischer, Oskar 1856-1933 Baker 92
Fleischer, Paul E. 1933- WhoAm 92
Fleischer, Peter 1941- WhoSSW 93
Fleischer, Richard 1916- MiSFD 9
Fleischer, Richard O. WhoAm 92
Fleischer, Robert Louis 1930- WhoAm 92
Fleischer, William Richard 1919- WhoWor 93
Fleischhacker, W. Wolfgang 1953- WhoWor 93
Fleischhauer, Carl-August WhoUN 92
Fleischhauer, Gene Donald Law&B 92
Fleischhauer, Jorg 1939- WhoScE 91-3
Fleischhauer, Kurt 1929- WhoScE 91-3
Fleischman, Albert Sidney 1920- WhoAm 92, WhoWrEP 92
Fleischman, Barbara Greenberg 1924- WhoAmW 93
Fleischman, Charles Arthur 1945- WhoE 93
Fleischman, Donald 1934- St&PR 93
Fleischman, Edward Hirsh 1932- WhoAm 92
Fleischman, Gail Robin 1959- St&PR 93
Fleischman, Herman Israel 1950- WhoE 93, WhoEmL 93, WhoWor 93
Fleischman, Lawrence Arthur 1925- WhoAm 92
Fleischman, Marvin 1937- WhoSSW 93
Fleischman, Michael F. 1949- St&PR 93
Fleischman, Nancy Sue Law&B 92
Fleischman, Paul BioIn 17
Fleischman, Paul 1952- ConAu 37NR, DcAmChF 1985, MajAI [port], ScF&FL 92, SmATA 72 [port], WhoAm 92
Fleischman, Peter N. Law&B 92
Fleischman, Richard 1928- WhoAm 92
Fleischman, Robert L. Law&B 92
Fleischman, Sid 1920- DcAmChF 1960, DcAmChF 1985, ScF&FL 92
Fleischman, (Albert) Sid(ney) 1920- ConAu 37NR, MajAI [port]
Fleischman, Sol Joseph 1910- WhoSSW 93, WhoWor 93
Fleischman, Virginia Muse 1946- WhoEmL 93
Fleischmann, Ernest (Martin) 1924- Baker 92, WhoAm 92
Fleischmann, Fred L. 1933- St&PR 93
Fleischmann, Hans Hermann Paul 1933- WhoAm 92
Fleischmann, John 1946- WhoEmL 93
Fleischmann, Martin WhoScE 91-1
Fleischmann, Peter MiSFD 9
Fleischmann, Trude 1895-1990 BioIn 17
Fleischmann-Fellowes, Dagmar Law&B 92
Fleischmann-Fellowes, Dagmar 1958- WhoEmL 93
Fleischner, Alois Leonard 1913- WhoE 93
Fleishaker, Aaron J. Law&B 92
Fleishell, John Raymond 1942- St&PR 93
Fleisher, Bernard 1926- St&PR 93
Fleisher, Bruce BioIn 17
Fleisher, Bruce 1950- St&PR 93
Fleisher, Catherine Ellen Kate 1942- WhoAmW 93
Fleisher, David Lee 1934- St&PR 93
Fleisher, Edwin A(dler) 1877-1959 Baker 92
Fleisher, Eric Wilfrid 1926- WhoE 93, WhoWor 93
Fleisher, Gary Mitchell 1941- WhoE 93, WhoWor 93
Fleisher, Harold 1921- WhoAm 92
Fleisher, Jerrilyn 1952- WhoEmL 93, WhoWor 93
Fleisher, Leon 1928- Baker 92
Fleisher, Marcy Beth 1964- WhoAmW 93
Fleisher, Michael 1942- ScF&FL 92
Fleisher, Paul 1948- ConAu 137
Fleisher, Ronald 1947- St&PR 93
Fleisher, Seymour 1923- St&PR 93
Fleisher, Siegel Hall d1992 NewYTBS 92
Fleishman, Edwin Alan 1927- WhoAm 92
Fleishman, Ellen Marcy 1952- WhoEmL 93
Fleishman, Jay 1930- St&PR 93
Fleishman, Joel Lawrence 1934- WhoAm 92
Fleishman, Neill Howard Law&B 92
Fleishman, Philip Robert 1935- WhoAm 92, WhoE 93
Fleishman, Robert Stephen Law&B 92
Fleishman, Seymour 1918- BioIn 17
Fleisig, Calmen d1990 BioIn 17
Fleisig, David H. Law&B 92
Fleisig, Marjorie Hall 1923- WhoAmW 93
Fleisig, Norbert 1935- WhoE 93
Fleisig, Ross 1921- WhoAm 92
Fleiss, Joseph Leon 1937- WhoE 93
Fleisser, Marieluise 1901-1974 DcLB 124 [port]
Fleitz, Beverly Joyce Baker Beckett 1930- BiDAMSp 1989
Flejterski, Stanislaw 1948- WhoWor 93
Fleming, A.D. 1939- St&PR 93
Fleming, Albert 1936- DcCPCAm
Fleming, Alexander 1881-1955 BioIn 17, ConHero 2 [port]
Fleming, Alice 1882-1952 SweetSg C
Fleming, Alice Carew Mulcahey 1928- WhoAm 92, WhoAmW 93
Fleming, Andrew MiSFD 9
Fleming, Archibald MacDonald WhoScE 91-1
Fleming, Arthur Ray, III 1951- WhoEmL 93, WhoSSW 93
Fleming, Barbara R. Law&B 92
Fleming, Bartlett Sayles 1942- WhoE 93
Fleming, Becky Lynn 1942- WhoAmW 93
Fleming, Berry 1899-1989 ScF&FL 92
Fleming, Betty Corcoran 1947- WhoAmW 93
Fleming, Brian L. 1944- St&PR 93
Fleming, Brice Noel 1928- WhoAm 92
Fleming, Bruce E. 1949- St&PR 93
Fleming, Carolyn H. Law&B 92
Fleming, Charles Clifford, Jr. 1923- WhoAm 92
Fleming, Charles Stephen 1948- WhoWor 93
Fleming, Charles W. AfrAmBi
Fleming, D.G. 1930- St&PR 93
Fleming, Daniel Johnson 1871-1963 BioIn 17
Fleming, David Alan 1961- WhoSSW 93
Fleming, David Daniel 1948- St&PR 93
Fleming, Donald Charles 1949- St&PR 93
Fleming, Donald Harnish 1923- WhoAm 92
Fleming, Douglas Riley 1922- WhoAm 92, WhoSSW 93, WhoWor 93
Fleming, Duard Francis, Jr. 1946- WhoSSW 93
Fleming, Edward J. 1920- WhoAm 92, WhoE 93
Fleming, Elizabeth Joyce 1959- WhoEmL 93
Fleming, Ethel AmWomPl
Fleming, Everett R. 1928- St&PR 93
Fleming, Gail L. 1939- St&PR 93
Fleming, Garrett A. 1925- WhoScE 91-3
Fleming, Gary G. 1937- St&PR 93
Fleming, George AmWomPl, WhoScE 91-1
Fleming, George James 1904-1990 BioIn 17
Fleming, George Robert 1947- WhoEmL 93
Fleming, Gordon Ballenger 1936- St&PR 93
Fleming, Graham Richard 1949- WhoAm 92
Fleming, Harold Curtis 1922-1992 NewYTBS 92 [port]
Fleming, Harold Vincent 1922- St&PR 93
Fleming, Henry Pridgen 1932- WhoSSW 93
Fleming, Ian 1908-1964 BioIn 17
Fleming, Ian 1943- WhoScE 91-1
Fleming, J. Gordon WhoIns 93
Fleming, J. Michael 1934- St&PR 93
Fleming, J. Philip 1943- St&PR 93
Fleming, James Albert 1936- WhoSSW 93
Fleming, James Klein 1949- WhoWrEP 92
Fleming, James Stuart, Jr. 1936- WhoE 93
Fleming, Joan 1908-1980 ScF&FL 92
Fleming, Joel F. 1931- St&PR 93
Fleming, John Ambrose 1849-1945 BioIn 17
Fleming, John S. 1949- WhoScE 91-1
Fleming, John Smith WhoScE 91-1
Fleming, John V(incent) 1936- ConAu 139
Fleming, John Vincent 1936- WhoAm 92
Fleming, Jon Hugh 1941- WhoWor 93
Fleming, Joseph Benedict 1919- WhoAm 92
Fleming, Julian Denver, Jr. 1934- WhoAm 92
Fleming, Karen L. Law&B 92
Fleming, Kate 1946- ConAu 137
Fleming, Keith ScF&FL 92
Fleming, Larry A. 1949- St&PR 93
Fleming, Launcelot 1906-1990 BioIn 17
Fleming, Laurence P. Law&B 92
Fleming, Lawrence Patrick, Jr. Law&B 92
Fleming, Lee ScF&FL 92
Fleming, Lisa L. Law&B 92
Fleming, Lisa L. 1961- WhoEmL 93
Fleming, Mack Gerald 1932- WhoAm 92
Fleming, Margaret Lindsey 1955- WhoEmL 93
Fleming, Martha AmWomPl
Fleming, Martin 1953- WhoEmL 93
Fleming, May Agnes 1840-1880 BioIn 17
Fleming, Michael Paul 1963- WhoSSW 93, WhoWor 93
Fleming, Nigel ScF&FL 92
Fleming, Patricia Ann 1955- St&PR 93
Fleming, Patricia E. Law&B 92
Fleming, Patricia Jean 1942- WhoE 93
Fleming, Patrick Michael 1931- WhoWor 93
Fleming, Patrick T. Law&B 92
Fleming, Paula Ellen 1952- WhoEmL 93
Fleming, Peggy BioIn 17
Fleming, Peggy Gale 1948- WhoAm 92
Fleming, Peter d1956 BioIn 17
Fleming, Peter Emmet, Jr. 1929- WhoAm 92
Fleming, Peter John WhoScE 91-1
Fleming, Philip Andrew 1930- WhoAm 92
Fleming, Rex James 1940- WhoAm 92
Fleming, Rhonda BioIn 17, WhoAm 92
Fleming, Rhonda 1923- SweetSg D [port]
Fleming, Richard 1924- WhoAm 92
Fleming, Richard Allan 1943- WhoSSW 93
Fleming, Richard Carl Dunne 1945- WhoAm 92
Fleming, Richard E. 1917-1942 BioIn 17
Fleming, Richard Harrison 1947- St&PR 93
Fleming, Robert 1921-1976 Baker 92
Fleming, Robert Loren ScF&FL 92
Fleming, Robert T. 1923- St&PR 93
Fleming, Robert W. 1918- St&PR 93
Fleming, Robert William 1928- WhoAm 92
Fleming, Robert Wright 1918- WhoAm 92
Fleming, Ronald Lee 1941- WhoAm 92
Fleming, Russell 1938- St&PR 93
Fleming, Russell, Jr. 1938- WhoAm 92
Fleming, Samuel Crozier 1940- St&PR 93
Fleming, Samuel Crozier, Jr. 1940- WhoAm 92, WhoE 93
Fleming, Samuel M. 1908- WhoAm 92
Fleming, Scott 1923- WhoAm 92
Fleming, Scott T. 1955- St&PR 93
Fleming, Shirley (Moragne) 1931- Baker 92
Fleming, Steven Robert 1951- WhoE 93, WhoEmL 93
Fleming, Suzanne Marie 1927- WhoAm 92
Fleming, Theodore Harris 1942- WhoSSW 93
Fleming, Thomas A. NewYTBS 92 [port]
Fleming, Thomas Crawley 1921- WhoAm 92
Fleming, Thomas J. 1927- BioIn 17
Fleming, Thomas James 1927- WhoAm 92, WhoWrEP 92
Fleming, Thomas Jeffrey 1955- St&PR 93
Fleming, Thomas P. 1907-1992 BioIn 17
Fleming, Thomas P., Jr. d1992 NewYTBS 92
Fleming, Tom BioIn 17
Fleming, Victor 1883-1949 BioIn 17, MiSFD 9N
Fleming, Wendell Helms 1928- WhoAm 92
Fleming, William Charles Law&B 92
Fleming, William Charles, Sr. 1938- WhoAm 92
Fleming, William D. 1929- WhoAm 92
Fleming, William G.N. 1937- St&PR 93
Fleming, William Harrison 1915- WhoAm 92
Fleming, William J. 1922- St&PR 93

Fleming, William Launcelot Scott 1906-1990 *BioIn 17*
Fleming, William Paul 1943- *St&PR 93*
Fleming, William Sloan 1937- *WhoAm 92, WhoE 93, WhoWor 93*
Fleming, William Wright, Jr. 1932- *WhoAm 92*
Fleming, Williamina Paton Stevens 1857-1911 *BioIn 17*
Flemings, Merton Corson 1929- *WhoAm 92*
Flemister, Launcelot Johnson 1913- *WhoAm 92*
Flemister, Peter L. *Law&B 92*
Flemm, Eugene William 1944- *WhoSSW 93*
Flemma, Robert J. 1935-1990 *BioIn 17*
Flemming, Brian 1939- *WhoE 93*
Flemming, Charles Stephen 1948- *WhoUN 92*
Flemming, Claire D. 1934- *St&PR 93, WhoAm 92*
Flemming, Clente 1950- *St&PR 93*
Flemming, Edward John 1946- *St&PR 93*
Flemming, Gregory J. *Law&B 92*
Flemming, Paul Martin 1960- *St&PR 93*
Flemming, Timothy 1950- *AfrAmBi*
Flemming, Timothy Clarence 1945- *St&PR 93*
Flemming-Chamulak, Deborah Kay 1952- *WhoAmW 93*
Flemmons, Kenneth Alan 1956- *WhoEmL 93*
Flemyng, Gordon 1934- *MiSFD 9*
Flender, Rodman *MiSFD 9*
Flengmark, Poul *WhoScE 91-2*
Flengsrud, Ragnar 1942- *WhoScE 91-4*
Flentje, Horst 1925- *WhoScE 91-2*
Flerko, Bela 1924- *WhoScE 91-4*
Fleron, Theodore A. *Law&B 92*
Flers, Robert de 1872-1927 *BioIn 17*
Fles, Barthold 1902-1989 *ScF&FL 92*
Flesch, Carl 1873-1944 *Baker 92, BioIn 17*
Flesch, Rainer G. 1948- *WhoScE 91-4*
Flesch, Robert Donald 1946- *WhoEmL 93*
Flesch, Sally Jane 1948- *WhoEmL 93*
Flescher, Irwin 1926- *WhoE 93*
Fleschner, Charles d1991 *BioIn 17*
Fleseriu, Ionel Petru 1924- *WhoScE 91-4*
Fleshel, Marcia Fran 1946- *WhoEmL 93*
Flesher, Dale Lee 1945- *WhoWrEP 92*
Flesher, Hubert Louis 1933- *WhoAm 92, WhoWor 93*
Flesher, James Wendell 1925- *WhoSSW 93*
Fleshler, David 1957- *WhoEmL 93*
Fleshner, Mark Alvin 1956- *St&PR 93*
Flesner, Dean C. 1934- *St&PR 93*
Flesner, William G. *St&PR 93*
Flessland, Eric John 1958- *WhoEmL 93*
Fleta, Miguel 1893-1938 *Baker 92*
Fleta, Miguel 1897-1938 *IntDcOp [port], OxDcOp*
Fleta, Pierre 1925- *Baker 92*
Fletcher, Aaron 1934- *WhoWrEP 92*
Fletcher, Adrian *ScF&FL 92*
Fletcher, Adrian 1943- *St&PR 93*
Fletcher, Alfred John *WhoScE 91-1*
Fletcher, Alice Cunningham 1838-1923 *Baker 92, IntDcAn*
Fletcher, Angus John Stewart 1930- *WhoAm 92*
Fletcher, Anne Bosshard 1939- *WhoAmW 93*
Fletcher, Anthony L. 1935- *WhoAm 92*
Fletcher, Arthur 1885-1950 *BiDAMSp 1989*
Fletcher, Arthur A. *AfrAmBi [port], WhoAm 92*
Fletcher, Arthur Allen 1924- *BioIn 17, EncAACR*
Fletcher, Barbara Elizabeth 1936- *WhoE 93*
Fletcher, Barbara Rainbow 1935- *WhoWrEP 92*
Fletcher, Betty B. 1923- *WhoAm 92, WhoAmW 93*
Fletcher, Bradford York 1942- *WhoSSW 93*
Fletcher, Bruce W. *Law&B 92*
Fletcher, C.I. *St&PR 93*
Fletcher, Carlos Alfredo Torres 1959- *WhoEmL 93*
Fletcher, Cathy Ann 1949- *WhoAmW 93, WhoEmL 93*
Fletcher, Christine Marie 1949- *WhoAmW 93*
Fletcher, Christopher David Marsden *WhoScE 91-1*
Fletcher, Cliff 1935- *WhoAm 92*
Fletcher, Clive *WhoScE 91-1*
Fletcher, Colin 1922- *WhoAm 92*
Fletcher, D. Ed 1939- *St&PR 93*
Fletcher, Darrow 1951- *BioIn 17*
Fletcher, David B. 1952- *St&PR 93*
Fletcher, David J. 1954- *WhoEmL 93*
Fletcher, Denise K. 1948- *St&PR 93*
Fletcher, Denise Koen 1948- *WhoAm 92, WhoEmL 93*
Fletcher, Diane Miles 1956- *WhoE 93*
Fletcher, Douglas B. 1925- *St&PR 93*
Fletcher, Douglas Baden 1925- *WhoAm 92*
Fletcher, Edward Abraham 1924- *WhoAm 92*
Fletcher, Frank Jack 1885-1973 *HarEnMi*
Fletcher, G.A. *WhoScE 91-1*
Fletcher, Gilbert Hungerford 1911-1992 *BioIn 17*
Fletcher, Giles, the Younger 1585?-1623 *DcLB 121 [port]*
Fletcher, (Horace) Grant 1913- *Baker 92*
Fletcher, Harold J. 1950- *St&PR 93*
Fletcher, Harry George, III 1941- *WhoAm 92, WhoWrEP 92*
Fletcher, Hattie Bennett *AmWomPl*
Fletcher, Henry P. 1873-1959 *PolPar*
Fletcher, Henry Prather 1873-1959 *BioIn 17*
Fletcher, Homer Lee 1928- *WhoAm 92*
Fletcher, Hugh 1947- *WhoWor 93*
Fletcher, James 1919-1991 *AnObit 1991, CurBio 92N*
Fletcher, James Allen 1947- *WhoEmL 93*
Fletcher, James Andrew 1945- *WhoAm 92*
Fletcher, James C. *BioIn 17*
Fletcher, James C., III 1938- *St&PR 93*
Fletcher, James Holway 1947- *St&PR 93*
Fletcher, James Pearse *WhoScE 91-1*
Fletcher, Jane Ada *DcChlFi*
Fletcher, Jean Stout 1935- *WhoAmW 93*
Fletcher, Jeffrey Edward 1948- *WhoE 93*
Fletcher, Jerald J. 1949- *WhoSSW 93*
Fletcher, Jo 1958- *ScF&FL 92*
Fletcher, Joel Lafayette, III 1935- *WhoSSW 93*
Fletcher, John 1579-1625 *BioIn 17*
Fletcher, John Caldwell 1931- *WhoAm 92*
Fletcher, John Dexter 1940- *WhoSSW 93*
Fletcher, John Edward *WhoScE 91-1*
Fletcher, John Everett *Law&B 92*
Fletcher, John Gould 1886-1950 *BioIn 17*
Fletcher, John Jamison *Law&B 92*
Fletcher, Joseph Francis 1905-1991 *BioIn 17*
Fletcher, Julia Constance 1858-1938 *AmWomPl*
Fletcher, Karly Ann 1951- *WhoEmL 93*
Fletcher, Kathryn Sue 1960- *WhoAmW 93*
Fletcher, Keith Philip *WhoScE 91-1*
Fletcher, Kim 1927- *St&PR 93, WhoAm 92*
Fletcher, Kristin L. *Law&B 92*
Fletcher, L. John *Law&B 92*
Fletcher, Leland Vernon 1946- *WhoAm 92*
Fletcher, Leroy Stevenson 1936- *WhoAm 92, WhoSSW 93*
Fletcher, Louise 1936- *WhoAm 92, WhoAmW 93*
Fletcher, Marilyn P. 1940- *ScF&FL 92*
Fletcher, Marjorie Amos 1923- *WhoAmW 93*
Fletcher, Martin W. 1952- *St&PR 93*
Fletcher, Mary Beth 1949- *WhoE 93*
Fletcher, Mary Lee *WhoAmW 93*
Fletcher, Max Ellis 1921- *WhoAm 92*
Fletcher, Neville Horner 1930- *WhoWor 93*
Fletcher, Norman *WhoAm 92, WhoSSW 93*
Fletcher, Norman Collings 1917- *WhoAm 92*
Fletcher, Oscar Jasper, Jr. 1938- *WhoAm 92*
Fletcher, Pamela C. *Law&B 92*
Fletcher, Pamela W. *Law&B 92*
Fletcher, Paul D. 1959- *St&PR 93*
Fletcher, Pauline Charlotte 1938- *WhoWrEP 92*
Fletcher, Penny *BioIn 17*
Fletcher, Percy (Eastman) 1879-1932 *Baker 92*
Fletcher, Peter Caleb 1925- *St&PR 93*
Fletcher, Peyton B., III 1930- *WhoAm 92*
Fletcher, Philip B. *WhoAm 92*
Fletcher, Philip Bernier 1933- *St&PR 93*
Fletcher, Phillip Douglas 1957- *WhoEmL 93*
Fletcher, Phineas 1582-1650 *DcLB 121*
Fletcher, Raphael *DcCPCAm*
Fletcher, Ray Weldon 1929- *St&PR 93*
Fletcher, Raymond Harold 1914- *WhoSSW 93*
Fletcher, Raymond Russwald, Jr. 1929- *WhoAm 92*
Fletcher, Riley Eugene 1912- *WhoSSW 93, WhoWor 93*
Fletcher, Robert 1920- *WhoAm 92*
Fletcher, Robert A. *St&PR 93*
Fletcher, Robert Hillman 1940- *WhoAm 92*
Fletcher, Robert L. 1930- *St&PR 93*
Fletcher, Roger *WhoScE 91-1*
Fletcher, Ronald Darling 1933- *WhoAm 92*
Fletcher, Sarah *BioIn 17*
Fletcher, Steven John 1951- *St&PR 93*
Fletcher, Susan 1951- *ScF&FL 92*
Fletcher, Susan (Clemens) 1951- *ConAu 138, SmATA 70 [port]*
Fletcher, Terry B. 1934- *St&PR 93*
Fletcher, William Adrin 1948- *WhoEmL 93*
Fletcher, William Arthur 1947- *St&PR 93*
Fletcher, William Burke, Jr. 1958- *WhoSSW 93*
Fletcher, William Eric 1935- *St&PR 93*
Fletcher, William Wallace, Jr. 1947- *WhoEmL 93*
Fletcher-Smith, Claudia Ann 1948- *WhoEmL 93*
Fletemeyer, John R. *BioIn 17*
Flett, Una (Leonie) 1932- *ConAu 137*
Flettner, Marianne 1933- *WhoAm 92, WhoAmW 93*
Fleur, Mary Louise 1951- *WhoE 93*
Fleur, Paul *ConAu 37NR*
Fleurant, David Paul 1948- *WhoE 93*
Fleurant, Robert W. 1939- *WhoE 93*
Fleuridas, Colette Lucienne 1953- *WhoAmW 93*
Fleuridas, Jack Andre 1930- *St&PR 93*
Fleuriet, Joseph Bernard, Jr. 1953- *WhoEmL 93*
Fleury, Alain *WhoScE 91-2*
Fleury, Andre (Edouard Antoine Marie) 1903- *Baker 92*
Fleury, Joachim 1962- *WhoE 93*
Fleury, Louis (Francois) 1878-1926 *Baker 92*
Fleury, Theoren *BioIn 17*
Fleury, Thomas A. *St&PR 93*
Flew, Antony G(arrard) N(ewton) 1923- *ConAu 40NR*
Flexner, Anne Crawford 1874-1955 *AmWomPl*
Flexner, Hortense 1885- *AmWomPl*
Flexner, James Thomas 1908- *ConAu 37NR, WhoAm 92*
Flexner, Louis Barkhouse 1902- *WhoAm 92*
Flexner, Simon 1863-1946 *BioIn 17*
Flexner, Stuart Berg *BioIn 17*
Flexsenhar, William Edward 1951- *WhoSSW 93*
Flichel, Eugene Anthony 1943- *WhoAm 92*
Flick, Carl 1926- *WhoAm 92*
Flick, Donatella *BioIn 17*
Flick, Gert-Rudolf *BioIn 17*
Flick, J.A. 1930- *WhoScE 91-3*
Flick, James A. *WhoAm 92*
Flick, John Edmond 1922- *WhoAm 92*
Flick, Kay E. *Law&B 92*
Flick, Mary Jane 1958- *WhoAmW 93*
Flick, Michael Albert 1948- *St&PR 93*
Flick, Sol E. 1915- *St&PR 93, WhoAm 92*
Flick, Stephen Hunter 1949- *ConTFT 10*
Flick, Thomas Michael 1954- *WhoEmL 93*
Flick, Warren Edmond 1943- *WhoAm 92*
Flicker, Blair M. *Law&B 92*
Flicker, D.W. *Law&B 92*
Flicker, Eric L. 1949- *St&PR 93*
Flicker, Eric Lee 1949- *WhoEmL 93*
Flicker, Irving 1915- *St&PR 93*
Flicker, Norman *St&PR 93*
Flicker, Shanley E. 1917- *St&PR 93*
Flicker, Ted 1930- *WhoAm 92*
Flicker, Theodore J. 1930- *MiSFD 9*
Flicker, Warren Louis 1943- *St&PR 93*
Flickinger, Allan L. 1929- *St&PR 93*
Flickinger, Charles John 1938- *WhoAm 92, WhoSSW 93*
Flickinger, Harry Harner 1936- *WhoAm 92*
Flickinger, Joe Arden 1949- *WhoEmL 93, WhoWor 93*
Flickinger, Michele DeVoe 1961- *WhoAmW 93*
Flickinger, Peter B. 1928- *St&PR 93*
Flickinger, Thomas L. 1939- *WhoAm 92*
Flics, David Harold 1952- *WhoE 93*
Flider, Frank S. 1929- *St&PR 93*
Flieder, John J. 1936- *St&PR 93*
Flieder, John Joseph 1936- *WhoAm 92*
Fliederbaum, Merrill Edwin *Law&B 92*
Fliedner, Theodor M. 1929- *WhoScE 91-3*
Fliegel, Frederick Martin 1956- *WhoEmL 93*
Fliegel, Hellmuth *ScF&FL 92*
Fliegel, Lester *Law&B 92*
Fliegel, Robert Aalbu 1940- *WhoSSW 93*
Fliegelman, Amy Marlene *Law&B 92*
Fliegelman, Avra Leah *WhoAmW 93*
Flieger, Howard Wentworth 1909- *WhoAm 92*
Flieger, Verlyn 1933- *ScF&FL 92*
Flier, Michael Stephen 1941- *WhoAm 92*
Fliermans, Carl Bernard 1944- *WhoAm 92, WhoSSW 93*
Fliess, Michel 1945- *WhoScE 91-2*
Fliessbach, Torsten 1944- *WhoScE 91-3*
Flietstra, R.R. 1949- *St&PR 93*
Fliger, Daniel James 1940- *St&PR 93*
Fligg, James Edward 1936- *WhoAm 92*
Fligg, Loren L. 1940- *St&PR 93, WhoIns 93*
Fligg, W. Patrick *Law&B 92*
Flin, Sharon *Law&B 92*
Flinchbaugh, David Edward 1934- *WhoSSW 93*
Flinders, Matthew 1774-1814 *Expl 93 [port]*
Flindt, Homer *ScF&FL 92*
Fling, Jacqueline Ann 1947- *WhoAmW 93*
Flink, Alan J. *Law&B 92*
Flink, Barry E. 1951- *WhoSSW 93*
Flink, Frank Bernerd, Jr. *Law&B 92*
Flink, Jane Duncan 1929- *WhoAmW 93*
Flink, Marianne 1955- *St&PR 93*
Flink, Richard A. *Law&B 92*
Flink, Richard Allen 1935- *St&PR 93, WhoAm 92*
Flink, Stanley Edgar 1924- *WhoE 93*
Flinkstrom, Henry Allan 1933- *WhoE 93, WhoWor 93*
Flinn, Charles Gallagher 1938- *WhoSSW 93, WhoWor 93*
Flinn, John C. *BioIn 17*
Flinn, Lawrence, Jr. 1935- *St&PR 93*
Flinn, Michael Eugene 1946- *WhoEmL 93*
Flinn, Owen Ronald 1934- *St&PR 93*
Flinn, Patrick L. 1942- *St&PR 93*
Flinn, Roberta Jeanne 1947- *WhoAmW 93, WhoEmL 93, WhoWor 93*
Flinn, Roger Martin *WhoScE 91-1*
Flinn, Russell *ScF&FL 92*
Flinn, Stephanie Strubing 1939- *St&PR 93*
Flinn, Thomas A. d1990 *BioIn 17*
Flinn, Thomas D. 1956- *WhoEmL 93*
Flint, Anthony Patrick Fielding *WhoScE 91-1*
Flint, Colin David *WhoScE 91-1*
Flint, Daniel Waldo Boone 1926- *WhoAm 92*
Flint, Dennis F. 1943- *WhoAm 92*
Flint, Elizabeth Suzanne 1953- *WhoAmW 93*
Flint, Eva Kay 1902- *AmWomPl*
Flint, George Graham 1929- *St&PR 93*
Flint, George Lee, Jr. 1944- *WhoSSW 93*
Flint, George Squire 1930- *WhoAm 92*
Flint, Georgia D. *WhoIns 93*
Flint, Harry James *WhoScE 91-1*
Flint, Homer Eon 1892?-1924 *ScF&FL 92*
Flint, Jeremy 1928-1989 *BioIn 17*
Flint, John E. 1930- *WhoAm 92*
Flint, Kathleen Patricia 1956- *WhoEmL 93*
Flint, Kenneth A. 1940- *St&PR 93*
Flint, Kenneth C. *ScF&FL 92*
Flint, Linda Dilloway 1947- *WhoAmW 93*
Flint, Lucy *ConAu 37NR*
Flint, Mark Addison 1946- *St&PR 93, WhoAm 92, WhoEmL 93*
Flint, May Harbin *AmWomPl*
Flint, Myles Edward 1933- *WhoAm 92*
Flint, Putnam P. 1918- *St&PR 93*
Flint, Randell Sherman 1955- *WhoEmL 93*
Flint, Richard Newell 1935- *St&PR 93*
Flint, Robert H. 1913- *St&PR 93*
Flint, Robert N. 1921- *St&PR 93*
Flint, Susan Elizabeth *Law&B 92*
Flint, Susan Louise 1947- *WhoAmW 93, WhoEmL 93*
Flint-Gohlke, Lucy 1954- *ConAu 37NR*
Flintham, Lydia Stirling *AmWomPl*
Flippen, James Howard, III 1957- *WhoEmL 93*
Flipper, Henry O. 1856-1940 *BioIn 17, ConBlB 3 [port]*
Flipper, Henry Ossian 1856-1940 *EncAACR [port], HarEnMi*
Flippin, Gilmer Franklin 1947- *WhoEmL 93*
Flippo, Henry J. *Law&B 92*
Flippo, Rona Fleig 1945- *WhoE 93*
Flipse, Eduard 1896-1973 *Baker 92*
Flipse, John Edward 1921- *WhoAm 92, WhoSSW 93*
Flisi, Claudia Beth 1947- *WhoEmL 93*
Fliss, Barbara Marie 1957- *WhoAmW 93*
Fliss, Michael C. 1956- *St&PR 93*
Fliss, Raphael M. 1930- *WhoAm 92*
Flitcraft, Richard Kirby, II 1920- *WhoAm 92*
Fliter, Leah Marie 1963- *WhoAmW 93*
Flittie, Clifford Gilliland 1924- *WhoAm 92*
Flittie, John H. *WhoIns 93*
Flittie, John Howard 1936- *WhoAm 92*
Fl*m*ng, I*n *ScF&FL 92*
Floberg, Leif O.B. 1930- *WhoScE 91-4*
Floch, Herve Alexander 1908- *WhoWor 93*
Floch, Martin Herbert 1928- *WhoAm 92*
Floch-Baillet, Daniele Luce 1948- *WhoWor 93*
Floch-Prigent, Loik Le *St&PR 93*
Flock, Henry H. 1935- *St&PR 93*

Flock, R. William 1941- *St&PR 93*
Flocken, P. Jay *Law&B 92*
Flockinger, Gerda 1927- *BioIn 17*
Flocks, Marcia Lea Hinds 1955- *WhoAmW 93*
Floda, Alfred Joseph 1955- *WhoEmL 93*
Floden, Robert Edward 1949- *WhoEmL 93*
Flodin, Karl (Theodor) 1858-1925 *Baker 92*
Flodin, Nestor Winston 1915- *WhoSSW 93*
Flodine, James B. *Law&B 92*
Floe, Catherine A. *Law&B 92*
Floerchinger, Debra Sue 1959- *WhoSSW 93*
Floersch, William C. 1944- *St&PR 93*
Floersheim, Michael J. d1992 *NewYTBS 92*
Floersheim, Otto 1853-1917 *Baker 92*
Floeter, Howard A. 1953- *St&PR 93*
Flogaitis, Spyridon 1950- *WhoWor 93*
Flohr, Daniel G., III 1942- *St&PR 93*
Flohr, Hans Werner 1936- *WhoWor 93*
Flom, Edward Leonard 1929- *St&PR 93, WhoAm 92, WhoSSW 93*
Flom, Gerald Trossen 1930- *WhoAm 92*
Flom, Julia Mittle 1906- *WhoAmW 93*
Flomenhoft, Hubert Ivan 1925- *WhoSSW 93*
Flood, Aaron Ross 1910- *BiDAMSp 1989*
Flood, Ann Barry 1944- *WhoAmW 93*
Flood, Diane Lucy 1937- *WhoAmW 93*
Flood, Donald T. 1934- *St&PR 93*
Flood, Dorothy Garnett 1951- *WhoAmW 93, WhoEmL 93*
Flood, Douglas James 1955- *St&PR 93*
Flood, Francis Edward 1925- *St&PR 93*
Flood, Gay 1935- *WhoAmW 93, WhoE 93*
Flood, Howard L. 1934- *St&PR 93, WhoAm 92*
Flood, James Clair 1939- *WhoAm 92*
Flood, Joan Moore 1941- *WhoAmW 93, WhoE 93, WhoWor 93*
Flood, John Edward *WhoScE 91-1*
Flood, John Etchells, Jr. 1929- *St&PR 93*
Flood, John Joseph 1951- *WhoEmL 93*
Flood, John W. 1930- *St&PR 93*
Flood, Michael Edward *Law&B 92*
Flood, Patrick Gerard *BioIn 17*
Flood, Randolph Gene 1950- *WhoEmL 93, WhoSSW 93*
Flood, Sheila Theresa 1958- *WhoAmW 93*
Flood, Theodore C. 1930- *St&PR 93*
Flood, Timothy P. *Law&B 92*
Flood, Vincent P., Jr. *Law&B 92*
Flood, W(illiam) H(enry) Grattan 1859-1928 *Baker 92*
Flook, John C. 1947- *St&PR 93*
Floquet, Charles Thomas 1828-1896 *BioIn 17*
Floquet, Etienne 1748-1785 *OxDcOp*
Floquet, Etienne Joseph 1748-1785 *Baker 92*
Flor, Claus Peter 1953- *Baker 92*
Flor, Roger di c. 1267-1305 *HarEnMi*
Flora, Cornelia Butler 1943- *WhoAmW 93*
Flora, Edward Benjamin 1929- *St&PR 93, WhoAm 92*
Flora, Gary Stamler 1934- *WhoE 93*
Flora, George Claude 1923- *WhoAm 92*
Flora, Jairus Dale, Jr. 1944- *WhoAm 92*
Flora, James Royer 1914- *WhoE 93*
Flora, John Alan 1950- *St&PR 93*
Flora, Joseph M. 1934- *ScF&FL 92*
Flora, Joseph Martin 1934- *WhoAm 92, WhoSSW 93*
Flora, Kent Allen 1944- *WhoWor 93*
Flora, Paul 1922- *BioIn 17*
Flora, Philip Craig 1950- *WhoEmL 93, WhoSSW 93*
Florakis, Charilaos Ioannoy 1914- *WhoWor 93*
Florakis, George James 1958- *WhoE 93*
Florance, Colden l'Hommedieu Ruggles 1931- *WhoAm 92*
Florance, Sheila d1991 *BioIn 17*
Florance, Stanley Hunter 1939- *St&PR 93*
Florea, John *MiSFD 9*
Florea, Robert William 1947- *WhoE 93, WhoEmL 93*
Florean, Valeriu 1940- *WhoUN 92*
Florek, Anita Marie 1950- *St&PR 93*
Floren, Charles M. *Law&B 92*
Florence, Faye *Law&B 92*
Florence, Faye A. *Law&B 92*
Florence, Franklin Randolph, Jr. 1958- *WhoSSW 93*
Florence, Gerald P. 1933- *St&PR 93*
Florence, Lucy Mae 1942- *WhoAmW 93*
Florence, Mary Sargant 1857-1954 *BioIn 17*
Florence, Verena Magdalena 1946- *WhoAmW 93, WhoEmL 93*
Florencio, C. *WhoScE 91-3*
Florencio, I. *WhoScE 91-3*
Florendo, Norma D. *WhoAmW 93*
Florent, Jean Michel 1937- *WhoWor 93*
Florentine, Isaac *MiSFD 9*
Florentino, Vincent 1948- *WhoIns 93*
Flores, Angel 1900-1983? *ScF&FL 92*
Flores, Angel 1900-1992 *BioIn 17, ConAu 40NR*
Flores, Aurelio 1931- *WhoWor 93*
Flores, Bernal 1937- *Baker 92*
Flores, Daniel Sanchez d1990 *BioIn 17*
Flores, Frank F. *St&PR 93*
Flores, John R. *Law&B 92*
Flores, John Ruben 1956- *WhoEmL 93*
Flores, Jose 1936- *WhoScE 91-3*
Flores, Jose Obed 1954- *WhoWrEP 92*
Flores, Juan *HispAmA*
Flores, Kirk P. *Law&B 92*
Flores, Manuel M. 1840-1885 *DcMexL*
Flores, Margarita Frances 1959- *WhoAmW 93*
Flores, Marion Thomas 1946- *WhoAm 92, WhoEmL 93*
Flores, Marjorie Joice 1937- *WhoAmW 93*
Flores, Orlando 1946- *WhoEmL 93*
Flores, Patrick F. 1929- *HispAmA [port], WhoAm 92, WhoSSW 93*
Flores, Paul E. *Law&B 92*
Flores, Philip Joseph 1949- *WhoEmL 93*
Flores, Robin Ann 1949- *WhoAmW 93*
Flores, Thomas R. 1937- *WhoAm 92*
Flores, Thomas Raymond 1937- *HispAmA [port]*
Flores, William Hose 1954- *WhoEmL 93*
Florescu, I. Ion 1933- *WhoScE 91-4*
Florescu, Radu R.N. 1925- *ScF&FL 92*
Flores-De-Jacoby, Lavinia 1942- *WhoScE 91-3*
Flores Facusse, Carlos *DcCPCAm*
Flores Galindo, Alberto 1949-1990 *BioIn 17*
Flores Magon, Ricardo 1873-1922 *BioIn 17*
Florestano, Patricia Sherer 1936- *WhoAmW 93*
Floret, Paul Coste- 1911-1979 *BioIn 17*
Floreth, Frederick Dennis 1956- *WhoEmL 93*
Florey, Charles Du Ve *WhoScE 91-1*
Florey, Klaus Georg 1919- *WhoAm 92*
Florey, Robert 1900-1979 *MiSFD 9N*
Florez, Jesus 1936- *WhoScE 91-3*
Flori, Anna Marie DiBlasi LePoer 1940- *WhoWor 93*
Floria, Dolores Louella 1937- *WhoAmW 93*
Florian, Christine Marie 1965- *WhoAmW 93*
Florian, Daniel F. 1932- *St&PR 93*
Florian, Douglas 1950- *BioIn 17*
Florian, Frank Lee 1933- *WhoAm 92*
Florian, John S. 1947- *WhoWrEP 92*
Florian, Marianna Bolognesi *WhoAmW 93*
Florida, Richard (L.) 1957- *ConAu 139*
Florides, Petros Serghiou 1937- *WhoScE 91-3*
Floridia, Pietro 1860-1932 *Baker 92*
Floridis, Elizabeth 1954- *WhoAmW 93*
Florie, Terry Lynn 1956- *WhoEmL 93*
Florig, Robert R. 1940- *St&PR 93*
Florimo, Francesco 1800-1888 *Baker 92*
Florin, G. Irmela 1938- *WhoScE 91-3*
Florin, Maja Birgitta 1961- *WhoWor 93*
Florine, Jean 1934- *WhoScE 91-2*
Florini, James Ralph 1931- *WhoE 93*
Florio, Caryl 1843-1920 *Baker 92*
Florio, Ermanno 1954- *WhoAm 92*
Florio, James J. *BioIn 17*
Florio, Jim 1937- *WhoAm 92, WhoE 93, WhoWor 93*
Florio, Maryanne J. 1940- *WhoAm 92*
Florio, Patrick A. d1990 *BioIn 17*
Florio, Roger *Law&B 92*
Florio, Steven T. 1949- *WhoAm 92*
Florio, Steven Thomas 1949- *St&PR 93*
Florio, Thomas *WhoE 93*
Florio, William Francis d1991 *BioIn 17*
Florio-Norris, Donna *Law&B 92*
Floris, Bruno 1942- *WhoScE 91-2*
Florit, Eugenio 1903- *SpAmA*
Florjancic, Frederick J. 1947- *St&PR 93*
Florman, Jean Claire 1952- *WhoEmL 93*
Florman, Nils Kohler, Jr. 1943- *WhoSSW 93*
Floros, Constantin 1930- *Baker 92*
Florreich, Gary L. *Law&B 92*
Florsch, Alphonse 1929- *WhoScE 91-2*
Florsheim, Stewart Jay 1952- *WhoEmL 93*
Florsheim, Thomas W. 1930- *St&PR 93, WhoAm 92*
Flory, Douglas L. 1939- *St&PR 93, WhoAm 92*
Flory, Joyce V. 1947- *WhoWrEP 92*
Flory, Robert Mikesell 1912- *WhoSSW 93*
Flory, Robin Lane 1959- *WhoSSW 93*
Flory, Thomas Reherd 1946- *WhoE 93*
Flory, Walter S., Jr. 1907- *WhoAm 92, WhoWor 93*
Flosman, Oldrich 1925- *Baker 92*
Floss, Heinz G. 1934- *WhoAm 92*
Floss, Pit 1950- *WhoWor 93*
Floss, Rudolf 1935- *WhoScE 91-3*
Flothuis, Marius (Hendrikus) 1914- *Baker 92*
Floto, Edgardo Alfredo 1943- *WhoUN 92*
Floto, Heinz 1934- *WhoScE 91-2*
Floto, Ronald John 1942- *WhoAm 92*
Flotow, Friedrich von 1812-1883 *OxDcOp*
Flotow, Friedrich von 1813-1883 *IntDcOp [port]*
Flotow, Friedrich (Adolf Ferdinand) von 1813-1883 *Baker 92*
Flott, Andrew Frederick 1956- *St&PR 93*
Flottorp, Gordon 1920- *WhoWor 93*
Floud, Roderick *BioIn 17*
Floum, B. Robert 1935- *St&PR 93*
Flouquet, Jacques *WhoScE 91-2*
Flournoy, Dayl Jean 1944- *WhoSSW 93*
Flournoy, Houston Irvine 1929- *WhoAm 92*
Flournoy, Howard M. *Law&B 92*
Flournoy, Janie Davis 1950- *WhoAmW 93*
Flournoy, John Francis 1940- *St&PR 93*
Flournoy, Lucien 1919- *St&PR 93*
Flournoy, Melissa 1961- *WhoAmW 93*
Flournoy, Nancy 1947- *WhoAmW 93, WhoEmL 93*
Flournoy, Selwyn Lester, Jr. 1941- *WhoAm 92, WhoIns 93*
Flournoy, Valerie R. 1952- *BlkAuII 92*
Flouvat, Bernard 1939- *WhoScE 91-2*
Flowe, Benjamin Hugh, Jr. 1956- *WhoEmL 93*
Flowe, Carol Connor 1950- *WhoAmW 93, WhoEmL 93*
Flower, B.O. 1858-1918 *GayN*
Flower, George Edward 1919- *WhoAm 92*
Flower, John Arnold 1921- *WhoAm 92*
Flower, (Walter) Newman 1879-1964 *Baker 92*
Flower, Robert E. 1937- *St&PR 93*
Flower, Theodore E. 1926- *St&PR 93*
Flower, Tony *WhoScE 91-1*
Flower, Walter Chew, III 1939- *WhoSSW 93, WhoWor 93*
Flowerree, Robert Edmund 1921- *WhoAm 92*
Flowers, A.R. *ScF&FL 92*
Flowers, Amy Lee 1954- *WhoAmW 93*
Flowers, Betty Sue 1947- *WhoAm 92, WhoWrEP 92*
Flowers, Brian Hilton 1924- *WhoWor 93*
Flowers, Carolyn Dianne 1941- *WhoAmW 93*
Flowers, Chloe Anne 1939- *WhoAmW 93*
Flowers, Daniel Fort 1920- *St&PR 93*
Flowers, David 1954- *St&PR 93*
Flowers, David R. *St&PR 93*
Flowers, Francis Asbury, III 1955- *WhoEmL 93*
Flowers, Gayle Douglas 1934- *St&PR 93*
Flowers, Gennifer *BioIn 17*
Flowers, Henry *Law&B 92*
Flowers, Jack S. 1937- *St&PR 93*
Flowers, James R. 1941- *St&PR 93*
Flowers, John E. *St&PR 93*
Flowers, Joseph Stanley *Law&B 92*
Flowers, Judith Ann 1944- *WhoAmW 93*
Flowers, Kent Gordon, Jr. 1955- *WhoEmL 93*
Flowers, Langdon Strong 1922- *St&PR 93, WhoAm 92*
Flowers, Mary Evelyn 1951- *AfrAmBi [port]*
Flowers, Michael *Law&B 92*
Flowers, Michael Edward 1953- *WhoEmL 93*
Flowers, Paul William 1952- *WhoEmL 93*
Flowers, Priscilla *AmWomPl*
Flowers, Richard L., Jr. *Law&B 92*
Flowers, Richard W. 1950- *St&PR 93*
Flowers, Robert James 1943- *St&PR 93*
Flowers, Robert L. 1926- *St&PR 93*
Flowers, Robert L. 1927- *WhoAm 92*
Flowers, Ronald Alan 1954- *WhoEmL 93*
Flowers, Sally A. 1954- *WhoAmW 93*
Flowers, T.J. *ScF&FL 92*
Flowers, Virginia Anne 1928- *WhoAm 92, WhoAmW 93*
Flowers, W. Harold 1911-1990 *BioIn 17*
Flowers, William H. 1913- *St&PR 93*
Flowers, William Howard, Jr. 1913- *WhoAm 92*
Flowler, Robyn J. 1954- *St&PR 93*
Floy, Charles R. 1934- *St&PR 93, WhoIns 93*
Floyd, Alexander Graham 1947- *WhoEmL 93, WhoWor 93*
Floyd, Barry Douglas *Law&B 92*
Floyd, Camille Maxine 1940- *WhoWrEP 92*
Floyd, Carlisle 1926- *IntDcOp, OxDcOp*
Floyd, Carlisle (Sessions, Jr.) 1926- *Baker 92*
Floyd, Clark Alan 1940- *WhoWrEP 92*
Floyd, David Kenneth 1932- *WhoAm 92*
Floyd, Deborah Mae 1962- *WhoEmL 93*
Floyd, Donald J. 1943- *AfrAmBi*
Floyd, Eddie 1935- *SoulM*
Floyd, Gareth 1940- *BioIn 17*
Floyd, Glen D. 1936- *St&PR 93*
Floyd, Glenn Leslie 1954- *St&PR 93*
Floyd, J. Douglas *Law&B 92*
Floyd, Jack William 1934- *WhoAm 92*
Floyd, James Eston, Jr. 1957- *WhoEmL 93*
Floyd, John Alex *BioIn 17*
Floyd, John Alex, Jr. 1948- *WhoEmL 93, WhoSSW 93*
Floyd, John B., Jr. 1917- *WhoAm 92*
Floyd, John Buchanan 1806-1863 *HarEnMi*
Floyd, John Taylor 1942- *WhoAm 92, WhoE 93*
Floyd, Kay Cirksena 1943- *WhoSSW 93*
Floyd, Linda A. *Law&B 92*
Floyd, Linda Ann 1955- *WhoAmW 93*
Floyd, Lou Jean 1948- *WhoAmW 93*
Floyd, Marguerite Marie 1924- *WhoAmW 93*
Floyd, Mark A. 1955- *St&PR 93*
Floyd, Mark S. *Law&B 92*
Floyd, Michael *WhoScE 91-1*
Floyd, Michael Dennis 1953- *WhoEmL 93, WhoSSW 93*
Floyd, Michael Reece 1948- *WhoSSW 93*
Floyd, Nancy Arthur 1938- *WhoAmW 93*
Floyd, Otis L. *WhoAm 92, WhoSSW 93*
Floyd, Patricia A. *BioIn 17*
Floyd, Paul W. 1940- *St&PR 93*
Floyd, Raymond 1942- *WhoAm 92*
Floyd, Robert W. 1936- *WhoAm 92*
Floyd, Rodney Wayne 1938- *WhoWor 93*
Floyd, Samuel A(lexander), Jr. 1937- *ConAu 39NR*
Floyd, Steve William 1950- *WhoEmL 93*
Floyd, Thomas E. *St&PR 93*
Floyd, Wayne 1930- *WhoWrEP 92*
Floyd, William Anderson 1928- *WhoSSW 93*
Floyd, William Arthur 1946- *St&PR 93*
Floyd, William Clary, Jr. 1954- *WhoEmL 93*
Floyd, William S., IV 1950- *St&PR 93*
Floyd-Jones, William *Law&B 92*
Floyd-Teniya, Kathleen 1953- *WhoAmW 93, WhoEmL 93*
Fluck, Ekkehard Otto 1931- *WhoScE 91-3*
Fluck, Michele Marguerite 1940- *WhoAmW 93*
Fluck, Sandra Squire 1944- *WhoWrEP 92*
Fluckiger, G. Markell *Law&B 92*
Fludgate, Barrington J. 1946- *St&PR 93*
Fluegel, Elizabeth Leigh 1959- *WhoAmW 93, WhoEmL 93*
Fluegel, Susan Antoinette 1947- *WhoAmW 93*
Fluegge, Ronald Marvin 1948- *WhoWor 93*
Fluehr, Darrell Krelle 1958- *WhoEmL 93*
Fluehr, Kuhlman 1931- *St&PR 93*
Fluek, Toby Knobel *BioIn 17*
Flueler, Peter H. 1943- *WhoScE 91-4*
Flueler, Thomas *WhoScE 91-4*
Fluellen, Joel d1990 *BioIn 17*
Fluet, Michelle L. 1960- *WhoEmL 93*
Flugelman, Maximo Enrique 1945- *WhoWor 93*
Flugge, Gunter 1940- *WhoScE 91-3*
Flugger, Penelope A. 1942- *St&PR 93*
Flugger, Penelope Ann 1942- *WhoAmW 93*
Flugrath, James Marion 1934- *WhoSSW 93*
Flugsrud, Liv Birkeland 1929- *WhoScE 91-4*
Fluharty, James Robert 1943- *St&PR 93*
Fluhr, Frederick Robert 1922- *WhoE 93*
Fluke, Joanna 1942- *ScF&FL 92*
Fluke, John Maurice, Jr. 1942- *WhoAm 92*
Flum, Jerry 1940- *St&PR 93*
Flum, Ralph Allen 1954- *WhoIns 93*
Flumerfelt, Shannon Rae 1955- *WhoAmW 93*
Flummerfelt, Joseph 1937- *Baker 92*
Fluno, Jere D. 1941- *St&PR 93*
Fluno, Jere David 1941- *WhoAm 92*
Fluno, John Arthur 1914- *WhoSSW 93*
Fluor, John Robert, II 1945- *St&PR 93*
Fluor, Marjorie Letha Wade 1926- *WhoAmW 93, WhoWor 93*
Fluor, Peter J. 1947- *St&PR 93*
Flur, Wolfgang
See Kraftwerk *ConMus 9*
Fluri, Gene 1927- *St&PR 93*
Flury, Richard 1896-1967 *Baker 92*
Fluss, Sev Solomon 1934- *WhoUN 92*
Flusty, Ned E. *Law&B 92*
Flute, Molly *ScF&FL 92*
Flutie, Doug *BioIn 17*
Fluty, Steven Jay 1957- *WhoWrEP 92*
Fly, Camillus S. 1849-1901 *GayN*
Fly, Everett Lowell 1952- *WhoSSW 93*
Fly, Frederick George 1940- *St&PR 93*
Fly, Gale S. 1933- *St&PR 93*

Fly, James Lawrence, Jr. 1928- *WhoSSW 93*
Fly, Richard Nelson 1938- *WhoE 93*
Flycht, Lennart Knut Samuel 1918- *WhoWor 93*
Flye, Claudia Mae 1963- *WhoSSW 93*
Flye, M. Wayne 1942- *WhoAm 92*
Flygare, Gordon Robert 1938- *WhoSSW 93*
Flygare, Richard Watts 1955- *WhoEmL 93*
Flynn, A.V. 1942- *WhoScE 91-3*
Flynn, Anita *BioIn 17*
Flynn, Annette Theresa 1953- *WhoAmW 93, WhoEmL 93*
Flynn, Anthony 1952- *St&PR 93*
Flynn, Brian Charles, Jr. 1961- *WhoE 93*
Flynn, Carol 1933- *WhoAmW 93*
Flynn, Carolyn Ann 1948- *WhoAmW 93*
Flynn, Casey *ScF&FL 92*
Flynn, Charles E. 1912- *JrnUS*
Flynn, Charles Everette 1912- *St&PR 93*
Flynn, Charles William 1935- *St&PR 93*
Flynn, Christopher J. *Law&B 92*
Flynn, Claire Wallace *AmWomPl*
Flynn, Daniel Clarke 1939- *WhoSSW 93*
Flynn, Daniel Steven *Law&B 92*
Flynn, David *BioIn 17*
Flynn, David Kevin 1954- *WhoEmL 93*
Flynn, Dennis Michael 1956- *WhoE 93*
Flynn, Dennis Patrick 1944- *WhoAm 92*
Flynn, Donald Edward 1940- *St&PR 93*
Flynn, Donald Francis 1939- *St&PR 93*
Flynn, Donna Frances *Law&B 92*
Flynn, Edward J. 1891-1953 *BioIn 17, PolPar*
Flynn, Elizabeth Anne 1951- *WhoAmW 93*
Flynn, Errol 1909-1959 *BioIn 17, IntDcF 2-3 [port]*
Flynn, F. Patrick 1949- *St&PR 93*
Flynn, Faye Williams 1913- *WhoAmW 93*
Flynn, Frank A. 1949- *St&PR 93*
Flynn, George 1936- *ScF&FL 92*
Flynn, George Quitman 1937- *WhoSSW 93*
Flynn, George (William) 1937- *Baker 92*
Flynn, George William 1938- *WhoAm 92*
Flynn, Gerald E. 1951- *St&PR 93*
Flynn, Gregory Scott 1957- *St&PR 93*
Flynn, Harry Joseph 1933- *WhoAm 92, WhoSSW 93*
Flynn, J.M. *ScF&FL 92*
Flynn, Jackson Edward 1933- *St&PR 93*
Flynn, James J. *Law&B 92*
Flynn, James L. 1934- *St&PR 93*
Flynn, James Leonard 1934- *WhoAm 92*
Flynn, James Patrick *Law&B 92*
Flynn, James Peter 1961- *WhoE 93*
Flynn, James Rourke 1925- *WhoAm 92*
Flynn, James T. 1939- *WhoAm 92*
Flynn, Jeffrey Paul 1959- *WhoEmL 93*
Flynn, Jill Stewart 1945- *WhoAmW 93*
Flynn, John *MiSFD 9*
Flynn, John D. *Law&B 92*
Flynn, John Francis *St&PR 93*
Flynn, John H. *Law&B 92*
Flynn, John L. *ScF&FL 92*
Flynn, John M. *Law&B 92*
Flynn, John Thomas *Law&B 92*
Flynn, John Thomas 1948- *WhoE 93*
Flynn, John William 1939- *St&PR 93*
Flynn, Judith Anne 1937- *WhoAmW 93*
Flynn, Judith E. 1944- *WhoAmW 93*
Flynn, Kathleen M. *Law&B 92*
Flynn, Kevin J. *Law&B 92*
Flynn, L. Daniel 1942- *St&PR 93*
Flynn, Lawrence Pierce 1931- *WhoAm 92*
Flynn, Lefty 1893-1959 *BioIn 17*
Flynn, Leslie Bruce 1918- *ConAu 37NR*
Flynn, Margaret Alberi 1915- *WhoAmW 93*
Flynn, Marie Cosgrove 1945- *WhoAmW 93, WhoE 93*
Flynn, Mark *Law&B 92*
Flynn, Michael 1947- *ScF&FL 92*
Flynn, Michael D. *Law&B 92*
Flynn, Michael Harrington 1938- *St&PR 93*
Flynn, Michael James 1920- *WhoE 93, WhoWor 93*
Flynn, Molly Elizabeth 1958- *WhoSSW 93*
Flynn, Patricia Marie *WhoAmW 93, WhoE 93*
Flynn, Patrick J. *St&PR 93*
Flynn, Patrick J. 1942- *WhoAm 92*
Flynn, Paul Bartholomew 1935- *WhoAm 92*
Flynn, Paul M. 1953- *St&PR 93*
Flynn, Paul Michael 1953- *WhoEmL 93*
Flynn, Pauline T. 1942- *WhoAm 92*
Flynn, Peter E. 1959- *St&PR 93*
Flynn, Peter G. *Law&B 92*
Flynn, Priscilla 1948- *St&PR 93*
Flynn, R. Marshall 1959- *WhoEmL 93*
Flynn, Ralph Melvin, Jr. 1944- *WhoWor 93*
Flynn, Raymond *BioIn 17*
Flynn, Raymond Leo 1939- *WhoAm 92, WhoE 93*
Flynn, Rebecca Jo 1958- *WhoAmW 93*
Flynn, Richard J. 1924- *St&PR 93*
Flynn, Richard James 1928- *WhoAm 92, WhoWor 93*
Flynn, Richard Jerome 1924- *WhoAm 92*
Flynn, Richard Mc Donnell 1955- *WhoWrEP 92*
Flynn, Robert 1932- *BioIn 17*
Flynn, Robert Warren 1943- *WhoE 93*
Flynn, Roger Patrick 1962- *WhoWor 93*
Flynn, Sonjia Sue 1947- *WhoAmW 93*
Flynn, Steven H. *Law&B 92*
Flynn, Steven Howard *Law&B 92*
Flynn, T. Geoffrey 1937- *WhoAm 92*
Flynn, Thomas *MiSFD 9*
Flynn, Thomas Charles 1950- *WhoWor 93*
Flynn, Thomas J. *Law&B 92*
Flynn, Thomas Joseph 1936- *St&PR 93, WhoAm 92*
Flynn, Thomas Joseph 1950- *WhoEmL 93*
Flynn, Thomas Lee 1946- *WhoEmL 93*
Flynn, Thomas P. 1935- *St&PR 93*
Flynn, Thomas Patrick 1924- *WhoAm 92*
Flynn, Thomas William 1955- *WhoEmL 93*
Flynn, William *BioIn 17*
Flynn, William Frederick 1952- *WhoEmL 93*
Flynn, William J. 1932- *WhoIns 93*
Flynn, William J. 1953- *St&PR 93*
Flynn, William Joseph 1926- *WhoIns 93*
Flynn, William Sheridan 1936- *WhoAm 92*
Flynn, William Thomas 1947- *WhoIns 93*
Flynn-Connors, Elizabeth K. 1939- *WhoUN 92*
Flynn Martin, Jeanne *Law&B 92*
Flynt, Candace 1947- *WhoWrEP 92*
Flynt, Charles Homer, Jr. 1940- *WhoSSW 93*
Flynt, Clifton William 1953- *WhoWor 93*
Flynt, James Wayne 1940- *WhoSSW 93*
Flythe, Walter White 1930- *St&PR 93*
Flytzanis, Christos *WhoScE 91-2*
Fo, Dario *BioIn 17*
Foa, Joseph Victor 1909- *WhoAm 92*
Foa, Uriel G. 1916-1990 *BioIn 17*
Foard, Susan Lee 1938- *WhoAm 92*
Foat, Lawrence M. 1946- *St&PR 93*
Fobbe, Franz Caspar 1948- *WhoWor 93*
Fobbs, Joan Merna 1943- *WhoAm 92*
Foccart, Jacques 1913- *BioIn 17*
Foch, Dirk 1886-1973 *Baker 92*
Foch, Ferdinand 1851-1929 *BioIn 17, DcTwHis, HarEnMi*
Foch, Nina 1924- *WhoAm 92, WhoAmW 93*
Fochs, David M. 1958- *St&PR 93*
Focht, John Arnold, Jr. 1923- *St&PR 93, WhoAm 92, WhoSSW 93*
Focht, Michael Harrison 1942- *WhoAm 92*
Fock, Cornelia Willemina 1942- *WhoWor 93*
Fock, Dirk 1886-1973 *Baker 92*
Fockler, Herbert Hill 1922- *WhoAm 92, WhoE 93, WhoWor 93*
Foct, Jacques 1939- *WhoScE 91-2*
Foda, Faraq d1992 *BioIn 17*
Foda, Rabiz Nasir 1949- *WhoWor 93*
Fode, George Darius 1950- *WhoEmL 93*
Foden, Harry G. 1924- *St&PR 93*
Foderaro, Anthony Harolde 1926- *WhoAm 92*
Fodha, Hassen Mohamed 1945- *WhoUN 92*
Fodi, John 1944- *Baker 92*
Fodiman, Aaron Rosen 1937- *WhoSSW 93, WhoWor 93*
Fodor, Eugene 1905-1991 *AnObit 1991, BioIn 17*
Fodor, Eugene Nicholas 1950- *WhoAm 92*
Fodor, Eugene (Nicolas, Jr.) 1950- *Baker 92*
Fodor, Gabor Bela 1915- *WhoAm 92*
Fodor, Gyorgy 1929- *WhoScE 91-4*
Fodor, Istvan 1938- *WhoScE 91-4*
Fodor, Istvan 1943- *WhoWor 93*
Fodor, Istvanne Tuende 1944- *WhoUN 92*
Fodor, John 1929- *St&PR 93*
Fodor, M. Antal 1941- *WhoWor 93*
Fodor, R.V. 1944- *ScF&FL 92*
Fodor, Susanna S. *BioIn 17*
Fodor-Mainvielle, Josephine 1789-1870 *Baker 92, OxDcOp*
Fodrea, Carolyn Wrobel 1943- *WhoAm 92, WhoAmW 93*
Foege, Rose Ann Scudiero 1941- *WhoAmW 93, WhoE 93*
Foehl, Edward Albert 1942- *WhoAm 92*
Foehn, Paul M.B. 1940- *WhoScE 91-4*
Foehrkolb, Susan Mary 1948- *WhoEmL 93, WhoWor 93*
Foelker, George Albert, Jr. 1951- *WhoSSW 93*
Foell, Darrell William *Law&B 92*
Foell, Earl William 1929- *WhoAm 92, WhoWrEP 92*
Foell, Ronald R. 1929- *WhoAm 92*
Foell, Wesley Kay 1935- *WhoAm 92*
Foerder, Rudolf von Bennigsen- 1926-1989 *BioIn 17*
Foerster, Adolph Martin 1854-1927 *Baker 92*
Foerster, Bernd 1923- *WhoAm 92*
Foerster, David Wendel, Jr. 1953- *WhoSSW 93*
Foerster, Josef Bohuslav 1859-1951 *Baker 92, OxDcOp*
Foerster, Karl 1874-1970 *BioIn 17*
Foerster, Karl Heinrich 1959- *WhoE 93*
Foerster, Kathryn Stuever 1954- *WhoEmL 93*
Foerster, Paul F. 1929- *St&PR 93*
Foerster, Richard A. 1949- *WhoWrEP 92*
Foerster, Stephen Arthur 1941- *St&PR 93*
Foerster, Therese 1861-1927 *See* Herbert, Victor 1859-1924 *OxDcOp*
Foerster, Urban Michael, III 1952- *WhoAm 92*
Foerster, Valerie E. *ScF&FL 92*
Foerstrova-Lautererova, Berta 1869-1936 *Baker 92*
Foerstrova-Lautererova, Bertha 1869-1936 *OxDcOp*
Foertsch, James Gregory 1952- *WhoEmL 93*
Foffe, Maria Catherine 1948- *WhoAmW 93, WhoEmL 93*
Fofonoff, Nicholas Paul 1929- *WhoAm 92*
Foft, John William 1928- *WhoAm 92*
Fogaley, Richard Allen 1950- *WhoSSW 93*
Fogarty, Charles Joseph 1955- *WhoE 93*
Fogarty, David J. 1927- *St&PR 93*
Fogarty, Edward Michael 1948- *WhoE 93, WhoEmL 93*
Fogarty, Gerald Philip 1939- *WhoAm 92*
Fogarty, Harry 1945- *WhoE 93*
Fogarty, James E. 1913- *St&PR 93*
Fogarty, John *ScF&FL 92*
Fogarty, John E. *Law&B 92*
Fogarty, John F., Jr. 1921- *St&PR 93*
Fogarty, John T. *Law&B 92*
Fogarty, John Thomas 1929- *St&PR 93, WhoAm 92*
Fogarty, John Thomas 1940- *WhoAm 92, WhoWor 93*
Fogarty, Katrina Sibley Park 1920- *WhoE 93*
Fogarty, M.G. 1933- *St&PR 93*
Fogarty, Paul Christopher 1956- *WhoE 93*
Fogarty, Robert Edward *Law&B 92*
Fogarty, Robert Stephen 1938- *WhoAm 92*
Fogarty, Thomas Nilan 1936- *WhoSSW 93*
Fogarty, Thomas R. *St&PR 93*
Fogarty, Walter Anthony 1936- *St&PR 93*
Fogarty, William Martin, Jr. 1935- *WhoAm 92*
Fogel, Barry Steven 1952- *WhoEmL 93*
Fogel, Belle 1924- *St&PR 93*
Fogel, Bernard J. 1936- *WhoAm 92*
Fogel, Daniel Mark 1948- *WhoWrEP 92*
Fogel, Ephim G(regory) 1920-1992 *ConAu 139*
Fogel, Henry 1942- *WhoAm 92*
Fogel, Irving Martin 1929- *WhoAm 92, WhoE 93, WhoWor 93*
Fogel, Mark I. *Law&B 92*
Fogel, Meyer H. 1920- *St&PR 93*
Fogel, Neil 1954- *St&PR 93, WhoEmL 93*
Fogel, Norman 1924- *WhoSSW 93*
Fogel, Robert William 1926- *WhoAm 92*
Fogel, Steven Anthony 1951- *WhoWor 93*
Fogel, Walter *BioIn 17*
Fogel, Wieslawa Agnieszka 1949- *WhoScE 91-4*
Fogelberg, Daniel Grayling 1951- *WhoAm 92*
Fogelberg, Melissa R. *Law&B 92*
Fogelberg, Paul Alan 1951- *WhoEmL 93*
Fogelgrew, Stephen Walton 1947- *St&PR 93*
Fogelin, Russell J. 1919- *St&PR 93*
Fogelman, Harold Hugo 1943- *WhoE 93*
Fogelman, Martin 1928- *WhoAm 92*
Fogelman, Mitchell Keith 1951- *St&PR 93*
Fogelman, Morris Joseph 1923- *WhoAm 92*
Fogelmark, Staffan 1939- *ConAu 139*
Fogelnest, Robert 1946- *WhoEmL 93*
Fogelson, David 1903- *WhoAm 92*
Fogelson, James H. *BioIn 17*
Fogelson, Raymond David 1933- *WhoAm 92*
Fogelson, Wendi *Law&B 92*
Fogelsonger, Ned Raymond 1947- *WhoE 93, WhoEmL 93, WhoWor 93*
Fogerty, Arthur Joseph 1938- *St&PR 93, WhoAm 92*
Fogerty, Tom 1941-1990 *BioIn 17*
Fogg, (Charles William) Eric 1903-1939 *Baker 92*
Fogg, Ernest Leslie 1920- *WhoSSW 93*
Fogg, James Walter 1937- *St&PR 93*
Fogg, John Samuel Hill 1826-1896 *BioIn 17*
Fogg, Joseph G., III *BioIn 17*
Fogg, Joseph Graham, III 1946- *WhoAm 92*
Fogg, Mark E. 1933- *St&PR 93*
Fogg, Richard Lloyd 1937- *St&PR 93, WhoAm 92*
Fogg, Stephen Monroe 1952- *St&PR 93*
Foggia, Francesco 1604-1688 *Baker 92*
Foggie, Charles Herbert 1912- *WhoAm 92, WhoE 93*
Foggie, Samuel Lewis 1927- *St&PR 93*
Foggs, Edward L. *WhoAm 92*
Foghelin, Jan Gustaf 1944- *WhoScE 91-4*
Foght, James Loren 1936- *WhoAm 92*
Fogiel, Max 1929- *WhoE 93*
Fogland, Dennis Johan 1951- *WhoEmL 93*
Fogle, Donald Reed 1964- *WhoSSW 93*
Fogle, Edward Lawrence 1931- *St&PR 93*
Fogle, Ellen L. 1951- *WhoEmL 93*
Fogle, Fredric Dean 1936- *St&PR 93*
Fogle, Gail Cynthia 1953- *WhoAmW 93*
Fogle, Harold Warman 1918- *WhoE 93*
Fogle, James Lee 1950- *WhoEmL 93*
Fogle, Kenneth A. 1942- *St&PR 93*
Fogle, Rick Alan 1956- *WhoE 93*
Fogleman, James Hudson 1952- *WhoSSW 93*
Fogleman, John Albert 1911- *WhoAm 92*
Fogleman, John Nelson 1956- *WhoEmL 93*
Fogleman, Julian Barton 1920- *WhoAm 92*
Fogleman, Ralph William 1926- *WhoE 93*
Fogleman, Ross Lee, III 1955- *WhoEmL 93*
Fogler, Lloyd Stephen David 1933- *St&PR 93*
Foglesong, Marilee Ann 1936- *WhoE 93*
Foglesong, Paul David 1949- *WhoE 93, WhoWor 93*
Foglia, Rene A. *Law&B 92*
Fogliani, Giacomo 1468-1548 *Baker 92*
Fogliani, Ludovico d1538 *Baker 92*
Fogliano, Giacomo 1468-1548 *Baker 92*
Fogliano, Joseph F. *St&PR 93*
Fogliano, Ludovico d1538 *Baker 92*
Foglietta, Thomas M. 1928- *CngDr 91*
Foglietta, Thomas Michael 1928- *WhoAm 92, WhoE 93*
Foglietti, Vittorio 1957- *WhoWor 93*
Foglio, Phil 1956- *ScF&FL 92*
Fohl, Timothy 1934- *WhoAm 92*
Fohn, Gerald Anthony 1945- *WhoWor 93*
Fohrman, Monica M. *Law&B 92*
Foianini, Larry Dean 1949- *WhoEmL 93*
Foignet, Charles Gabriel 1750-1823 *OxDcOp*
Foignet, Francois 1782-1845 *OxDcOp*
Foil, Mary Beth 1954- *WhoAmW 93, WhoEmL 93*
Foisie, Philip Manning 1922- *WhoAm 92*
Foix, Gaston de 1489-1512 *HarEnMi*
Fojtik, John Patrick 1956- *WhoEmL 93, WhoSSW 93*
Fok, Agnes Kwan 1940- *WhoAmW 93*
Fok, Thomas Dso Yun 1921- *WhoAm 92, WhoWor 93*
Fokas, Anthony N. *St&PR 93*
Fokdal, Steffen 1939- *WhoWor 93*
Fokes, William B., II *WhoIns 93*
Fokes, William B., III *Law&B 92*
Fokine, Irine 1922- *WhoAmW 93*
Fo Kwong, Chan 1929- *WhoWor 93*
Fol, Monique Eliane 1933- *WhoAmW 93*
Folan, Martin Joseph 1945- *WhoWor 93*
Folberg, Harold Jay 1941- *WhoAm 92*
Folch-Ribas, Jacques 1928- *WhoCanL 92*
Folden, Virgil Alvis, III 1953- *WhoEmL 93*
Foldery, John Joseph 1940- *WhoSSW 93*
Foldes, Andor 1913- *Baker 92*
Foldes, Andor 1913-1992 *BioIn 17, NewYTBS 92 [port]*
Foldes, Istvan 1921- *WhoScE 91-4*
Foldes, Janos 1927- *WhoScE 91-4*
Foldes, Jozsef 1923- *WhoScE 91-4*
Foldes, Lawrence D. 1959- *MiSFD 9*
Foldes, Lawrence David 1959- *WhoEmL 93*
Foldes, Lucien Paul *WhoScE 91-1*
Foldes, Lucien Paul 1930- *WhoWor 93*
Foldes, Vilmos 1925- *WhoScE 91-4*
Foldi, Andrew Harry 1926- *WhoAm 92*
Foldi, Andrew Peter 1931- *WhoE 93*
Foldi, Michael 1920- *WhoScE 91-3*
Foldiak, Gabor 1929- *WhoScE 91-4*
Folds, Charles Weston 1910- *WhoAm 92*
Foldspang, Anders 1945- *WhoScE 91-2*
Foldvari, Istvan 1945- *WhoScE 91-4*
Foldvari, Tibor L. 1936- *St&PR 93*
Foldvary, Fred E. 1946- *WhoWrEP 92*
Foldvik, A. 1930- *WhoScE 91-4*
Folek, S. *WhoScE 91-4*
Foley *BioIn 17*

Foley, A.J. 1835-1899 OxDcOp
Foley, A(llan) J(ames) 1835-1899 Baker 92
Foley, Anne Therese 1953- WhoAmW 93
Foley, Arthur James 1946- WhoEmL 93
Foley, Barbara Wessels 1948- WhoAmW 93
Foley, Bernard James 1933- WhoE 93
Foley, Bertrand J. d1991 BioIn 17
Foley, Brian Francis 1937- St&PR 93
Foley, Brian T. 1959- WhoEmL 93
Foley, C. Patrick 1933- WhoSSW 93
Foley, Cecil B. 1933- St&PR 93
Foley, Cheryl M. Law&B 92
Foley, Cheryl M. 1947- St&PR 93
Foley, Cheryl Morgan 1947- WhoAm 92
Foley, Dan T. Law&B 92
Foley, Daniel Ronald 1941- WhoAm 92
Foley, Daniel Thomas 1957- WhoEmL 93
Foley, Diane Leigh 1961- WhoAmW 93
Foley, Duncan K. BioIn 17
Foley, Edward Francis 1954- WhoE 93, WhoEmL 93
Foley, Edward W. 1937- WhoIns 93
Foley, Edward W. 1939- St&PR 93
Foley, Eileen Mary 1954- WhoAmW 93, WhoEmL 93
Foley, Eugene Charles 1934- WhoWor 93
Foley, Gardner P.H. 1935- St&PR 93
Foley, Gerald J. 1932- St&PR 93
Foley, Gifford T. BioIn 17
Foley, Gloria Libertad 1938- WhoAmW 93
Foley, Harold Cox 1939- St&PR 93
Foley, Heather BioIn 17
Foley, Heather S. NewYTBS 92 [port]
Foley, Helen Claiborne 1945- WhoAmW 93
Foley, James MiSFD 9
Foley, James David 1942- WhoAm 92
Foley, James Edward 1950- WhoE 93
Foley, James F. Law&B 92
Foley, James F., Jr. 1942- WhoIns 93
Foley, James Francis 1946- St&PR 93
Foley, James Michael 1939- St&PR 93
Foley, James Thomas 1910-1990 BioIn 17
Foley, Jeffrey Harold 1937- WhoScE 91-1
Foley, Joe L., III 1939- St&PR 93
Foley, John A. 1956- St&PR 93
Foley, John Bliss 1948- WhoE 93
Foley, John Francis 1936- St&PR 93
Foley, John J. St&PR 93
Foley, Joseph Bernard 1929- WhoAm 92
Foley, Joseph Lawrence 1953- WhoAm 92
Foley, Joseph P. Law&B 92
Foley, Joseph Patrick 1949- WhoE 93
Foley, Katherine Elizabeth 1946- WhoAmW 93
Foley, Kathleen A. 1952- WhoAmW 93
Foley, Kathleen Mary 1947- WhoAmW 93
Foley, Kevin 1950- WhoIns 93
Foley, Kevin M. 1942- St&PR 93
Foley, L. Elizabeth Law&B 92
Foley, L. Michael 1938- St&PR 93
Foley, Lewis Michael 1938- WhoAm 92
Foley, Louise Munro 1933- ScF&FL 92
Foley, Marie Agnes AmWomPl
Foley, Maureen Frances 1946- WhoEmL 93
Foley, Michael A. 1946- WhoE 93
Foley, Michael C. 1944- St&PR 93
Foley, Michael Francis 1946- WhoAm 92, WhoSSW 93
Foley, Michael W. Law&B 92
Foley, Patricia Jean 1956- WhoAmW 93, WhoEmL 93
Foley, Patrick Francis 1950- WhoEmL 93
Foley, Patrick J. Law&B 92
Foley, Patrick J. 1930- St&PR 93
Foley, Patrick Joseph 1930- WhoAm 92, WhoIns 93
Foley, Patrick Martin 1930- WhoAm 92
Foley, Paul d1990 BioIn 17
Foley, Paula Jean 1959- WhoAmW 93
Foley, "Red" (Clyde Julian) 1910-1968 Baker 92
Foley, Richard K. 1941- St&PR 93
Foley, Robert Douglas 1954- WhoEmL 93
Foley, Robert Henry 1930- St&PR 93
Foley, Roger D. 1917- WhoAm 92
Foley, Ronald E. 1945- WhoIns 93
Foley, Stephen Bernard 1950- WhoEmL 93
Foley, Thomas 1942- WhoAm 92
Foley, Thomas C. 1952- WhoAm 92
Foley, Thomas Coleman 1952- St&PR 93
Foley, Thomas Louis 1961- WhoE 93
Foley, Thomas Michael 1943- WhoAm 92
Foley, Thomas S. 1929- BioIn 17, CngDr 91, PolPar
Foley, Thomas Stephen 1929- WhoAm 92, WhoWor 93
Foley, Timothy F. Law&B 92
Foley, Timothy Francis 1942- WhoAm 92
Foley, Vincent Paul 1947- St&PR 93
Foley, Virginia Sue Lashley 1942- WhoSSW 93
Foley, Walter P. 1936- WhoIns 93
Foley, William E. 1911-1990 BioIn 17
Foley, William Edward, Jr. 1952- WhoE 93
Foley, William P., II 1944- St&PR 93
Foley, William Patrick, II 1944- WhoAm 92
Foley, William T. d1992 NewYTBS 92 [port]
Foley, William Thomas 1911- WhoAm 92
Folgate, Homer Emmett, Jr. 1920- WhoAm 92
Folger, John Kenneth 1924- WhoSSW 93
Folger, Roger 1947- St&PR 93
Foli, A.J. 1835-1899 OxDcOp
Foli, A(llan) J(ames) 1835-1899 Baker 92
Folinsbee, Robert Edward 1917- WhoAm 92
Folinsbee, Ruth Baldwin d1991 BioIn 17
Folio, Carmen L. 1928- St&PR 93
Folio, Cynthia Jo 1954- WhoE 93
Folio, Glenn F. 1956- St&PR 93
Folio, Kathleen L. 1927- St&PR 93
Folio, Lorenzo 1938- WhoAm 92, WhoWor 93
Folk, April Lynn 1960- WhoEmL 93
Folk, Barbara Theresa 1947- WhoAmW 93, WhoEmL 93
Folk, Earl E. 1930- St&PR 93
Folk, James 1948- WhoAm 92, WhoEmL 93
Folk, Jane Champion 1959- WhoAmW 93
Folk, Katherine Pinkston 1925- WhoAmW 93
Folk, Mary Catherine 1947- WhoEmL 93
Folk, Norma H. St&PR 93
Folk, Robert L. 1925- BioIn 17
Folk, Robert Louis 1925- WhoAm 92
Folk, Roger Maurice 1936- WhoAm 92
Folk, Russell Harter 1947- WhoEmL 93
Folk, Thomas Robert 1950- WhoEmL 93
Folkenflik, Max 1948- WhoEmL 93
Folker, Cathleen Ann 1956- WhoAmW 93
Folkers, D. WhoScE 91-3
Folkers, Eugene E. 1932- St&PR 93
Folkers, Karl August 1906- WhoAm 92, WhoSSW 93
Folkert, David F. 1948- St&PR 93
Folkert, David Floyd 1948- WhoEmL 93
Folkerts, James D. 1943- St&PR 93
Folkertsma, John M. Law&B 92
Folkes, Michael John 1942- WhoWor 93
Folkman, David H. 1934- WhoAm 92
Folkman, Georgia WhoWrEP 92
Folkman, Moses Judah 1933- WhoAm 92
Folkman, Susan 1938- WhoAmW 93
Folkmar, Daniel 1861-1932 IntDcAn
Folkow, Bjorn U.G. 1921- WhoScE 91-4
Folks, J. Leroy 1929- WhoAm 92
Folks, Michael T. Law&B 92
Foll, Ronald E. Law&B 92
Folla, Paul Richard 1942- St&PR 93
Folland, Edward F. 1916- St&PR 93
Follansbee, Dorothy Leland 1911- WhoAm 92
Follari, Gregorio 1940-1991 BioIn 17
Follereau, Jacques 1923- WhoScE 91-2
Foller-Friedrich, Ingrid 1939- WhoScE 91-3
Follesdal, Dagfinn 1932- WhoAm 92
Follestad, Bjorn A. 1971- WhoScE 91-4
Follett, Brian Keith WhoScE 91-1
Follett, David B. Law&B 92
Follett, James 1939- ScF&FL 92
Follett, Ken 1949- BioIn 17, ScF&FL 92
Follett, Kenneth Martin 1949- WhoAm 92, WhoWor 93, WhoWrEP 92
Follett, Kent Albert 1937- St&PR 93
Follett, Mary Vierling 1917- WhoAmW 93
Follett, Robert J.R. 1928- St&PR 93
Follett, Robert John Richard 1928- WhoAm 92, WhoWrEP 92
Follett, Ronald Francis 1939- WhoAm 92
Follett, Ross Charles 1940- St&PR 93
Follett, Roy Hunter 1935- WhoAm 92
Follett, William S. St&PR 93
Follette, William Albert 1946- WhoEmL 93
Folley, Clyde Henry 1927- St&PR 93
Folley, Harold L. Law&B 92
Follezou, Jean-Yves 1948- WhoWor 93
Follick, Edwin Duane 1935- WhoWor 93
Follin, Jean-Claude 1940- WhoScE 91-2
Follin, Steven Ernest 1951- WhoSSW 93
Follini, George A. d1991 BioIn 17
Follini, Stefania BioIn 17
Follis, Craig Law&B 92
Follis, Cynthia A. 1941- St&PR 93
Follis, Harold W. 1945- St&PR 93
Follman, Dorothy Major 1932- WhoAm 92, WhoAmW 93
Follman, John Philip 1937- St&PR 93
Follman, Lazar St&PR 93
Follmer, John Scott 1951- WhoEmL 93
Follmer, Todd Willard 1959- WhoSSW 93
Follo, Carl R. 1944- WhoIns 93
Follosco, Ceferino L. 1931- WhoAsAP 91
Folmar, Jack Gordon 1931- St&PR 93
Folmsbee, Beulah AmWomPl
Folmsbee, Frank Arnold 1949- St&PR 93
Folse, Bart Thomas 1956- WhoE 93
Folse, Parker Camile, III 1954- WhoEmL 93
Folsom, Anita Marie 1943- WhoSSW 93
Folsom, Franklin Brewster 1907- WhoAm 92
Folsom, Henry Richard 1913- WhoAm 92
Folsom, James, Jr. 1949- WhoAm 92, WhoSSW 93, WhoWor 93
Folsom, John Roy 1918- WhoAm 92
Folsom, John W. 1950- St&PR 93
Folsom, Lowell Edwin 1947- WhoEmL 93
Folsom, Richard Gilman 1907- WhoAm 92
Folsom, Roger Lee 1952- WhoEmL 93, WhoSSW 93
Folsom, Willard V. 1936- St&PR 93
Folsom, Wynelle Stough 1924- WhoAmW 93
Folstar, Peter 1947- WhoScE 91-3
Foltanyi, Jozsef 1924- WhoScE 91-4
Folter, Roland 1943- WhoE 93
Foltinek, Herbert 1930- WhoWor 93
Foltmann, Bent 1925- WhoScE 91-2
Folts, David Jacob 1958- WhoEmL 93
Foltz, Claude A. 1932- St&PR 93
Foltz, Clinton Henry 1936- WhoAm 92
Foltz, David Allen 1937- WhoE 93
Foltz, Forrest Lowell 1926- St&PR 93
Foltz, Jack L. Law&B 92
Foltz, Jerrold Lee 1943- WhoSSW 93
Foltz, Joseph Wade Law&B 92
Foltz, Kim BioIn 17
Foltz, Michael Craig 1957- WhoEmL 93
Foltz, Richard Harry 1924- WhoAm 92
Foltz, Rodger Lowell 1934- WhoAm 92
Folville, Eugenie-Emilie Juliette 1870-1946 Baker 92
Folz, Carol Ann 1951- WhoEmL 93
Folz, Joseph S., II Law&B 92
Fomberstein, Barry Joseph 1951- WhoE 93
Fomby, Paula BioIn 17
Fomin, Evstignei 1761-1800 Baker 92
Fomin, Evstigney 1761-1800 OxDcOp
Fomon, Samuel Joseph 1923- WhoAm 92
Fonash, Stephen Joseph 1941- WhoAm 92
Foncello, Martin John, Jr. 1952- WhoE 93
Foncha, John Ngu 1916- WhoAfr
Fonck, Paul Rene 1894-1953 HarEnMi
Fonda, Alessandro 1961- WhoWor 93
Fonda, Bridget BioIn 17
Fonda, Bridget 1965?- ConTFT 10
Fonda, Henry 1905-1982 BioIn 17, IntDcF 2-3 [port]
Fonda, Jane 1937- BioIn 17, IntDcF 2-3 [port], WhoAm 92, WhoAmW 93, WhoWrEP 92
Fonda, Jane (Seymour) 1937- ConAu 138
Fonda, Jere Williams 1929- St&PR 93
Fonda, John Day 1956- St&PR 93
Fonda, Luciano 1931- WhoScE 91-3
Fonda, Margaret Lee 1942- WhoSSW 93
Fonda, Matthew W. St&PR 93
Fonda, Peter 1939- MiSFD 9
Fonda, Peter 1940- WhoAm 92
Fondahl, John Walker 1924- WhoAm 92
Fondas, Nanette Joan 1959- WhoAmW 93
Fonder, Ghislain A.J.G. 1939- WhoScE 91-2
Fondere, J.P. WhoScE 91-2
Fondiller, Robert 1916- WhoAm 92
Fondiller, Shirley Hope Alperin WhoE 93, WhoWor 93
Fondren, Kervin 1963- WhoWrEP 92
Fondren, Larry E. 1947- WhoIns 93
Fondren, William M., Jr. 1940- St&PR 93
Fondren, William Merle, Jr. 1940- WhoAm 92, WhoSSW 93
Fondu, Pierre 1938- WhoScE 91-2
Fondy, Joseph J. 1959- WhoEmL 93
Fondy, Victor L. 1931- St&PR 93
Fon Eisen, Anthony T. 1917- DcAmChF 1960
Foner, Eric 1943- WhoAm 92, WhoWrEP 92
Foner, Philip S. 1910- WhoAm 92
Foner, Simon 1925- WhoAm 92
Fong, Allen 1947- MiSFD 9
Fong, Bernard W. D. 1926- WhoAm 92
Fong, Elaine Chun 1936- WhoAmW 93
Fong, Elizabeth L. 1949- WhoUN 92
Fong, Gary Curtis 1963- WhoAm 92, WhoSSW 93
Fong, Harold Michael 1938- WhoAm 92
Fong, Henry 1935- St&PR 93
Fong, Hiram L. 1906- WhoAm 92
Fong, Jacqueline Diane 1966- WhoAmW 93
Fong, James Tse-Ming 1927- WhoE 93
Fong, Kenneth M. Law&B 92
Fong, Kuo Tye 1949- WhoWor 93
Fong, Mary Ann Law&B 92
Fong, Mervyn Mun Ngin 1958- WhoWor 93
Fong, Peter 1924- WhoAm 92
Fong, Peter C. K. 1955- WhoAm 92, WhoEmL 93, WhoWor 93
Fong, Quock Q. 1934- St&PR 93
Fong, Wang-Fun 1947- WhoWor 93
Fong, Yuen 1948- WhoWor 93
Fongaard, Bjorn 1919-1980 Baker 92
Fong Kutchins, Carole Mee Chun 1962- WhoSSW 93
Fong Wong, Nellie Kut-Man 1949- WhoAsAP 91
Fonk, James R. 1943- St&PR 93
Fonkalsrud, Eric Walter 1932- WhoAm 92
Fonken, Gerhard Joseph 1928- WhoAm 92
Fonnum, Frode 1937- WhoScE 91-4
Fono, Andrew 1923- WhoE 93
Fonollosa, Jose Adrian Rodriguez 1963- WhoWor 93
Fons, John J. Law&B 92
Fons-Boronat, Jose Maria 1930- WhoScE 91-3
Fonseca, Anthony Gutierre 1940- WhoE 93
Fonseca, Jorge Carlos Almeida WhoWor 93
Fonseca, Julio 1885-1950 Baker 92
Fonseca Amador, Carlos 1935-1976 DcCPCAm
Fonssagrives-Penn, Lisa BioIn 17
Fonssagrives-Penn, Lisa d1992 NewYTBS 92 [port]
Fonstad, Eric B. Law&B 92
Fonstad, Karen Wynn 1945- ScF&FL 92
Font, Jordi 1951- WhoScE 91-3
Fonta, Caroline 1957- WhoWor 93
Fontaine, Andre BioIn 17
Fontaine, Bernard Leo, Jr. 1956- WhoE 93, WhoEmL 93
Fontaine, Edward Paul 1936- St&PR 93, WhoAm 92
Fontaine, Eudore Joseph, Jr. 1929- WhoE 93
Fontaine, Harvey L. 1948- St&PR 93
Fontaine, Hubert 1936- WhoScE 91-2
Fontaine, Joan 1917- IntDcF 2-3 [port]
Fontaine, John C. Law&B 92, WhoAm 92
Fontaine, Marc WhoScE 91-2
Fontaine, Olivier 1952- WhoUN 92
Fontaine, Pierre J. 1924- WhoScE 91-2
Fontaine, R. Peter Law&B 92
Fontaine, Rene Georges 1932- WhoUN 92
Fontaine, Sue 1928- WhoE 93
Fontaine, Thierry 1944- WhoScE 91-2
Fontaine, Valerie Anne 1955- WhoEmL 93
Font-Altaba, Manuel 1922- WhoScE 91-3
Fontan, J. WhoScE 91-3
Fontana, Aldo A. 1917- St&PR 93
Fontana, Andre H.L. 1939- WhoScE 91-2
Fontana, Anna WhoScE 91-3
Fontana, D.C. 1939- ScF&FL 92
Fontana, Donato Maria WhoScE 91-3
Fontana, Ferdinando 1850-1919 OxDcOp
Fontana, Fontana 1933- WhoSSW 93
Fontana, Franco 1933- WhoWor 93
Fontana, Julian 1810-1869 PolBiDi
Fontana, M.P. 1941- WhoScE 91-3
Fontana, Marco 1947- WhoWor 93
Fontana, Mark Allan 1957- WhoEmL 93
Fontana, Mary Carmen Law&B 92
Fontana, Richard d1992 NewYTBS 92
Fontana, Robert Edward 1915- WhoAm 92
Fontana, Steven Anthony Law&B 92
Fontana, Thomas M. 1950- St&PR 93
Fontanals, Manuel Mila 1818-1884 BioIn 17
Fontanelli, Alfonso 1557-1622 Baker 92
Fontanelli, Renzo 1931- WhoScE 91-3
Fontanese, Richard A. 1952- WhoE 93
Fontanesi, Marcello WhoScE 91-3
Fontanez, Hector d1991 BioIn 17
Fontanilla Soriano, P. WhoScE 91-3
Fontazza, Giuseppe WhoScE 91-3
Fonte, Raul V. Law&B 92
Fontela, Emilio 1938- WhoWor 93
Fontenelle, Scuddy Francis, Jr. 1931- St&PR 93
Fontenot, Kathy Lyn Law&B 92
Fontenot, Leonard Glynn 1937- St&PR 93
Fontenot, Margaret Lynn 1963- WhoSSW 93
Fontes, Len d1992 BioIn 17, NewYTBS 92
Fontes, Montserrat 1940- ConAu 136
Fontes, Patricia J. 1936- WhoE 93
Fontes, Ron ScF&FL 92
Fontes, W.A. 1937- St&PR 93
Fontes, Wayne 1939- WhoAm 92
Fonteyn, Margot 1919-1991 AnObit 1991, BioIn 17, ConTFT 10
Fonteyne, Herman J. 1939- St&PR 93
Fonteyne, Jacques Emile 1937- St&PR 93
Fontheim, Claude G.B. 1955- WhoE 93, WhoEmL 93, WhoWor 93
Font-Llovet, Josep Maria 1954- WhoWor 93
Fonts, H. Anthony 1960- WhoE 93
Fontyn, Jacqueline 1930- Baker 92
Fonvielle, Lloyd MiSFD 9
Fonvielle, William Harold 1943- WhoAm 92

Fonville, Linda Jean 1949- *WhoEmL 93*
Fonyo, Attila 1927- *WhoScE 91-4*
Fonzi, Irene Teresa *Law&B 92*
Fonzo, John P. *Law&B 92*
Fonzo, Michael A. 1930- *St&PR 93*
Foo, Dani A.C. 1947- *WhoWor 93*
Foo, Hong Tatt 1940- *WhoE 93*
Foo, Norman Yeow-Khean 1943- *WhoWor 93*
Fooden, Bart Lewis 1955- *St&PR 93*
Fooden, Myra 1926- *WhoAmW 93, WhoE 93*
Foody, Jan Petkus 1935- *WhoAmW 93*
Foody, Richard Edward 1950- *WhoEmL 93*
Fools Crow 1890?-1989 *BioIn 17*
Foon, Dennis 1951- *BioIn 17, WhoCanL 92*
Foon, Warren David 1956- *St&PR 93*
Foor, John A. 1934- *St&PR 93*
Foor, Laurie Jeanine 1957- *WhoAmW 93*
Foor, W. Eugene 1936- *WhoE 93*
Foorman, James L. *Law&B 92*
Foos, Paul William 1946- *WhoSSW 93*
Foos, Raymond Anthony 1928- *St&PR 93*
Foose, Harry Edward, Jr. 1951- *WhoSSW 93*
Foos-Graber, Anya Elisabeth 1942- *WhoWrEP 92*
Foot, David 1929- *ConAu 136*
Foot, Mirjam M(ichaela) 1941- *ConAu 139*
Foot, Neal R. 1948- *St&PR 93*
Foot, S.B. 1947- *St&PR 93*
Foot, Solomon 1802-1866 *PolPar*
Foote, A. Peter 1941- *St&PR 93*
Foote, Andrea Davette 1946- *WhoEmL 93*
Foote, Andrew Hull 1806-1863 *HarEnMi*
Foote, Arthur (William) 1853-1937 *Baker 92*
Foote, Barbara Austin 1918- *WhoAm 92, WhoAmW 93*
Foote, Bobbie Leon 1940- *WhoSSW 93*
Foote, Bud 1930- *ScF&FL 92*
Foote, Christopher Spencer 1935- *WhoAm 92*
Foote, David Kent 1947- *St&PR 93*
Foote, Douglas Scott *Law&B 92*
Foote, Edward Potter 1949- *St&PR 93*
Foote, Edward Thaddeus, II 1937- *WhoAm 92, WhoSSW 93*
Foote, Emerson d1992 *NewYTBS 92 [port]*
Foote, Emerson 1906- *WhoAm 92, WhoWor 93*
Foote, Emmerline 1955- *WhoEmL 93*
Foote, Evelyn Patricia 1930- *WhoAm 92, WhoAmW 93*
Foote, Frances Catherine 1935- *WhoAmW 93*
Foote, Fred L. 1938- *WhoAm 92*
Foote, George (Luther) 1886-1956 *Baker 92*
Foote, Horton 1916- *WhoAm 92, WhoWrEP 92*
Foote, Irving F. *ScF&FL 92*
Foote, Irving Flint 1930- *WhoSSW 93*
Foote, James Maxwell 1941- *WhoAm 92*
Foote, Janel Toon 1950- *WhoAmW 93*
Foote, Kay Janell 1938- *WhoSSW 93*
Foote, Kevin Rafael 1964- *WhoE 93*
Foote, Lillian Vallish d1992 *NewYTBS 92*
Foote, Martha Louisa 1957- *WhoEmL 93*
Foote, Mary *AmWomPl*
Foote, Mary 1872-1968 *BioIn 17*
Foote, Ray P., Jr. 1933- *St&PR 93*
Foote, Robert A., Jr. 1962- *St&PR 93*
Foote, Robert Bruce 1834-1912 *IntDcAn*
Foote, Robert Hutchinson 1922- *WhoAm 92*
Foote, Robert Kenneth 1944- *St&PR 93*
Foote, Ruth Annette 1925- *WhoWor 93*
Foote, Samuel 1720-1777 *BioIn 17*
Foote, Shelby *BioIn 17*
Foote, Shelby 1916- *ConLC 75 [port], WhoAm 92, WhoSSW 93, WhoWrEP 92*
Foote, Sherrill Lynne 1940- *WhoAmW 93, WhoWor 93*
Foote, Timothy Gilson 1926- *WhoAm 92*
Foote, W. David 1940- *St&PR 93*
Foote, Warren Edgar 1935- *WhoE 93, WhoWor 93*
Foote, Wilson Howard *Law&B 92*
Footlik, Robert Barry 1946- *WhoEmL 93*
Footman, David J. 1895-1983 *ScF&FL 92*
Footman, Gordon Elliott 1927- *WhoWor 93*
Foott, Roger 1946- *St&PR 93, WhoEmL 93*
Fopeano, Stephan Mark 1963- *WhoEmL 93*
Foppa, Giuseppe 1760-1845 *OxDcOp*
Foppert, Deborah Ann 1961- *WhoEmL 93*
Foraboschi, Franco Paolo 1932- *WhoWor 93*
Foradori, Elizabeth Leary 1956- *St&PR 93*
Forage, A.J. *WhoScE 91-3*
Forage, Alan J. 1942- *WhoScE 91-1*
Foraker, Joseph B. 1846-1917 *PolPar*
Foraker, Joseph Benson 1846-1917 *BioIn 17*
Foran, Ed *BioIn 17*
Foran, Elizabeth Berry d1990 *BioIn 17*
Foran, Jeffrey S. *Law&B 92*
Foran, John Richard *WhoUN 92*
Foran, Kenneth Lawrence 1941- *WhoAm 92*
Foran, Margaret M. *Law&B 92*
Foran, Nancy *BioIn 17*
Foran, Robert A. *Law&B 92*
Foran, Terrence James *Law&B 92*
Foran, Thomas Aquinas 1924- *WhoAm 92*
Forant, Marie-Jean *Law&B 92*
Foraste, Roland 1938- *WhoE 93, WhoWor 93*
Forauer, Robert Richard 1946- *WhoE 93, WhoEmL 93*
Foray, June *BioIn 17*
Forbes, Allan Louis 1928- *WhoAm 92*
Forbes, Anne Pappenheimer d1992 *NewYTBS 92*
Forbes, Anne Pappenheimer 1911-1992 *BioIn 17*
Forbes, Anthony David Arnold W. 1938- *WhoWor 93*
Forbes, Arthur Patrick Hastings d1992 *NewYTBS 92*
Forbes, Barbara *WhoAm 92*
Forbes, Bryan 1926- *MiSFD 9, WhoAm 92*
Forbes, Calvin 1945- *ConAu 16AS [port]*
Forbes, Caroline 1952- *ScF&FL 92*
Forbes, Charles 1810-1870 *BioIn 17*
Forbes, Charles Douglas *WhoScE 91-1*
Forbes, Charley 1841- *BioIn 17*
Forbes, Christopher 1950- *WhoAm 92, WhoEmL 93*
Forbes, Cynthia Ann 1951- *WhoAmW 93*
Forbes, Daniel Merrill 1954- *WhoEmL 93*
Forbes, David Craig 1938- *WhoAm 92*
Forbes, David L. *Law&B 92*
Forbes, David Lowry 1950- *WhoE 93*
Forbes, David Richard 1944- *WhoIns 93*
Forbes, Edward Albert 1946- *WhoSSW 93*
Forbes, Edward Coyle 1915- *WhoAm 92, WhoWor 93*
Forbes, Elliot 1917- *Baker 92*
Forbes, Esther 1891-1967 *ChILR 27 [port], MajAI [port]*
Forbes, Eve-Lyn 1949- *WhoEmL 93*
Forbes, Franklin Sim 1936- *WhoAm 92*
Forbes, George W., III 1946- *St&PR 93*
Forbes, George William 1869-1947 *DcTwHis*
Forbes, Gilbert Burnett 1915- *WhoAm 92*
Forbes, Gordon Maxwell 1930- *WhoAm 92*
Forbes, Harland Clement 1898-1990 *BioIn 17*
Forbes, Henry 1804-1859 *Baker 92*
Forbes, Ian Scott 1930- *WhoE 93*
Forbes, Jack D. 1934- *WhoAm 92*
Forbes, James 1749-1819 *BioIn 17*
Forbes, James Wendell 1923- *WhoAm 92*
Forbes, John Alexander 1938- *St&PR 93*
Forbes, John Douglas 1910- *WhoAm 92, WhoWor 93*
Forbes, John Francis 1946- *WhoE 93, WhoEmL 93*
Forbes, John Frederick 1944- *WhoWor 93*
Forbes, John Kenneth 1956- *WhoEmL 93*
Forbes, John Michael *WhoScE 91-1*
Forbes, John Ripley 1913- *WhoAm 92, WhoWor 93*
Forbes, Kenneth Albert Faucher 1922- *WhoWor 93*
Forbes, Laurie Jane 1950- *WhoEmL 93*
Forbes, Lorna Miriam 1921- *WhoAm 92*
Forbes, Louis M. 1955- *St&PR 93*
Forbes, Lucienne *Law&B 92*
Forbes, Malcolm S., Jr. *BioIn 17*
Forbes, Malcolm S., Jr. 1947- *St&PR 93*
Forbes, Malcolm Stevenson *BioIn 17*
Forbes, Malcolm Stevenson, Jr. 1947- *WhoAm 92, WhoE 93*
Forbes, Mary Gladys 1929- *WhoAmW 93*
Forbes, Mary Jane *Law&B 92*
Forbes, Peter 1942- *WhoAm 92, WhoE 93, WhoWor 93*
Forbes, Peter William 1955- *WhoE 93*
Forbes, Philip Harris *Law&B 92*
Forbes, R. Bruce *Law&B 92*
Forbes, Richard E. 1915- *WhoAm 92*
Forbes, Richard Mather 1916- *WhoAm 92*
Forbes, Robert F. 1941- *St&PR 93*
Forbes, Roberta Laidlaw d1992 *NewYTBS 92*
Forbes, Roberta Laidlaw 1924-1992 *BioIn 17*
Forbes, Samuel E. 1944- *St&PR 93*
Forbes, Sarah Elizabeth 1928- *WhoSSW 93*
Forbes, Sebastian 1941- *Baker 92, WhoWor 93*
Forbes, Stephen W. 1942- *WhoIns 93*
Forbes, Theodore McCoy, Jr. 1929- *WhoAm 92*
Forbes, Timothy Carter 1953- *WhoAm 92, WhoWor 93*
Forbes, Walter A. 1942- *St&PR 93*
Forbes, Walter Alexander 1942- *WhoAm 92*
Forbes, William, II 1924- *WhoE 93*
Forbes-Richardson, Helen Hilda 1950- *WhoAmW 93, WhoEmL 93, WhoWor 93*
Forbes-Watt, David 1941- *WhoUN 92*
Forbis, Bryan Lester 1957- *WhoEmL 93*
Forbis, Jeff E. 1950- *St&PR 93*
Forbis, Judith Evelyn 1934- *WhoSSW 93*
Forbis, Richard George 1924- *WhoAm 92*
Forbush, Clifton Haskett, Jr. 1927- *St&PR 93*
Force, Carlton Gregory 1926- *WhoSSW 93*
Force, Elizabeth Elma 1930- *WhoAmW 93*
Force, Herman Edgar *WhoE 93*
Force, Jack Keith 1946- *WhoEmL 93*
Force, Robert 1934- *WhoAm 92*
Force, Roland Wynfield 1924- *WhoAm 92, WhoE 93*
Force, William M., Jr. 1939- *St&PR 93*
Forcellini, Lindbergh Charles 1928- *St&PR 93*
Forcese, Dennis Philip 1941- *WhoAm 92*
Forche, Carolyn *BioIn 17*
Forche, Jennifer Roth 1960- *WhoAmW 93*
Forcheskie, Carl S. 1927- *WhoAm 92*
Forchhammer, Jes 1934- *WhoScE 91-2*
Forchheimer, Otto L. 1926- *St&PR 93*
Forchheimer, Otto Louis 1926- *WhoAm 92*
Forcier, Louise Maheux- 1929- *BioIn 17*
Forcier, Richard Charles 1941- *WhoAm 92*
Forcinio, Hallie Eunice 1952- *WhoEmL 93*
Forcione, Alban Keith 1938- *WhoAm 92*
Ford, Adam 1940- *ScF&FL 92*
Ford, Albert Lee *MajAI*
Ford, Aleksander 1908- *PolBiDi*
Ford, Aleksander 1908-1980 *DrEEuF*
Ford, Allen H. 1928- *St&PR 93*
Ford, Alvin Bernard d1991 *BioIn 17*
Ford, Andrew Thomas 1944- *WhoAm 92*
Ford, Ann Suter 1943- *WhoAmW 93*
Ford, Anne *AmWomPl*
Ford, Ashley L. *Law&B 92*
Ford, Ashley Lloyd 1939- *St&PR 93, WhoAm 92*
Ford, Barbara Jean 1946- *WhoAmW 93, WhoEmL 93*
Ford, Basil H. 1944- *St&PR 93*
Ford, Becky Lynn 1953- *WhoEmL 93*
Ford, Bernard R. 1943- *St&PR 93*
Ford, Bernette *BioIn 17*
Ford, Bernette G. 1950- *BlkAuII 92*
Ford, Bessie Rainer *AmWomPl*
Ford, Betty *BioIn 17*
Ford, Betty Bloomer 1918- *WhoAm 92, WhoAmW 93, WhoWor 93*
Ford, Brendan A. *Law&B 92*
Ford, Byron Milton 1939- *WhoE 93*
Ford, Cathy 1952- *WhoCanL 92*
Ford, Cathy Zoe 1953- *WhoAmW 93*
Ford, Charles d1990 *BioIn 17*
Ford, Charles Virgil 1937- *WhoSSW 93*
Ford, Charles Willard 1938- *WhoAm 92*
Ford, Chris 1949- *WhoAm 92*
Ford, Christina 1962- *WhoAmW 93*
Ford, Christina Edwards 1955- *St&PR 93*
Ford, Clarence Quentin 1923- *WhoAm 92*
Ford, Clellan Stearns 1909-1972 *IntDcAn*
Ford, Clyde D. *Law&B 92*
Ford, Clyde Michael 1938- *St&PR 93*
Ford, Corey K. *Law&B 92*
Ford, Creed L. 1952- *St&PR 93*
Ford, Cynthia Ann 1957- *WhoAmW 93*
Ford, Daniel Francis 1931- *WhoE 93*
Ford, Danny Lee 1948- *BiDAMSp 1989*
Ford, David Clayton 1949- *WhoEmL 93*
Ford, David Graeme 1930- *WhoWor 93*
Ford, David Robert 1935- *WhoAsAP 91*
Ford, David Thurman 1950- *WhoEmL 93*
Ford, Deborah Louise 1958- *WhoSSW 93*
Ford, Deborah Mae 1950- *WhoAmW 93*
Ford, Debrah Sue 1958- *WhoEmL 93*
Ford, Derek Clifford 1935- *WhoAm 92*
Ford, Dexter 1917- *WhoAm 92*
Ford, Donald Hainline 1906- *WhoAm 92*
Ford, Donald Herbert 1926- *WhoAm 92, WhoE 93*
Ford, Donald James 1930- *WhoAm 92*
Ford, Donald Keith 1945- *St&PR 93*
Ford, Douglas 1928- *WhoE 93*
Ford, Edsel Bryant, II *BioIn 17*
Ford, Edward A. *St&PR 93*
Ford, Edwin Roe 1943- *WhoSSW 93*
Ford, Eileen Otte 1922- *WhoAm 92*
Ford, Elaine 1938- *WhoWrEP 92*
Ford, Elizabeth Martini *Law&B 92*
Ford, Ellen Hodson 1913- *WhoAm 92, WhoAmW 93, WhoWor 93*
Ford, Emory A. 1940- *WhoAm 92*
Ford, Ernest 1858-1919 *Baker 92*
Ford, Faith *BioIn 17, WhoAm 92*
Ford, Ford Barney 1922- *WhoAm 92*
Ford, Ford Madox 1873-1939 *BioIn 17, MagSWL [port]*
Ford, Francis 1882-1953 *BioIn 17*
Ford, Frankie 1940- *SoulM*
Ford, Franklin Lewis 1920- *WhoAm 92*
Ford, Fred 1930- *AfrAmBi*
Ford, G. Quinn 1949- *St&PR 93*
Ford, Gabriel H. 1765-1849 *BioIn 17*
Ford, Gary L. *Law&B 92*
Ford, George, Jr. 1936- *BlkAuII 92*
Ford, George Burt 1923- *WhoAm 92*
Ford, George W. 1957- *St&PR 93*
Ford, Gerald R. 1913- *BioIn 17, ColdWar 1 [port]*
Ford, Gerald R., Jr. 1913- *PolPar*
Ford, Gerald Rudolph 1913- *DcTwHis*
Ford, Gerald Rudolph, Jr. 1913- *WhoAm 92, WhoWor 93*
Ford, Gertrude *WhoWrEP 92*
Ford, Gilbert 1931- *St&PR 93, WhoAm 92*
Ford, Glenn 1916- *IntDcF 2-3 [port], WhoAm 92*
Ford, Gordon Buell, Jr. 1937- *WhoAm 92, WhoSSW 93*
Ford, Grace *AmWomPl*
Ford, Graham B. d1991 *BioIn 17*
Ford, Greg *MiSFD 9*
Ford, Gregory John 1961- *WhoWor 93*
Ford, Hamilton Gates d1991 *BioIn 17*
Ford, Harold 1945- *AfrAmBi, BioIn 17*
Ford, Harold E. 1945- *CngDr 91*
Ford, Harold Eugene 1945- *WhoAm 92, WhoSSW 93*
Ford, Harriet French 1863?-1949 *AmWomPl*
Ford, Harrison *BioIn 17*
Ford, Harrison 1942- *IntDcF 2-3 [port], WhoAm 92*
Ford, Harry McNamara 1932- *St&PR 93*
Ford, Henry *ScF&FL 92*
Ford, Henry 1863-1947 *BioIn 17, DcTwHis, GayN*
Ford, Henry 1917-1987 *BioIn 17*
Ford, Hilary *ConAu 37NR, MajAI*
Ford, Hugh 1913- *WhoWor 93*
Ford, Jacquelin Ann 1963- *WhoAmW 93*
Ford, James d1992 *NewYTBS 92*
Ford, James 1947?-1992 *BioIn 17*
Ford, James Alfred 1911-1968 *IntDcAn*
Ford, James Arthur 1934- *WhoSSW 93*
Ford, James David *CngDr 91*
Ford, James F. *Law&B 92*
Ford, James Francis 1942- *St&PR 93*
Ford, James Leigh *WhoScE 91-1*
Ford, James Stephen 1943- *WhoWor 93*
Ford, James W. 1893-1957 *EncAACR*
Ford, Jean Elizabeth 1923- *WhoAmW 93*
Ford, Jeffrey 1955- *ScF&FL 92*
Ford, Jeffrey Duane 1949- *WhoEmL 93*
Ford, Jerry Lee 1940- *WhoAm 92*
Ford, Jesse Hill 1928- *BioIn 17, WhoAm 92, WhoWrEP 92*
Ford, Jill Hunsberger 1950- *WhoAmW 93*
Ford, Jo-Ann *Law&B 92*
Ford, Joe T. *BioIn 17*
Ford, Joe T. 1937- *St&PR 93*
Ford, Joe Thomas 1937- *WhoAm 92*
Ford, John *St&PR 93*
Ford, John 1586-1640 *BioIn 17*
Ford, John 1895-1973 *BioIn 17, MiSFD 9N*
Ford, John Battice, III 1924- *WhoWor 93*
Ford, John Charles 1942- *WhoAm 92, WhoE 93*
Ford, John E. *Law&B 92*
Ford, John Gilmore *WhoAm 92*
Ford, John M. 1957- *ScF&FL 92*
Ford, John Salmon 1815-1897 *BioIn 17*
Ford, John Stephen 1957- *WhoEmL 93, WhoWor 93*
Ford, John T., Jr. 1953- *WhoEmL 93, WhoWor 93*
Ford, John Thomas 1932- *WhoE 93*
Ford, Jon Grant 1943- *St&PR 93*
Ford, Jonathan 1946- *St&PR 93*
Ford, Joseph 1914- *WhoAm 92*
Ford, Joseph Dillon 1952- *WhoEmL 93, WhoSSW 93*
Ford, Joseph J. *Law&B 92*
Ford, Joseph Raymond 1949- *St&PR 93, WhoAm 92, WhoEmL 93*
Ford, Judith Ann 1935- *WhoAm 92*
Ford, Julia Ellsworth Shaw 1859- *AmWomPl*
Ford, Julian R. 1932-1987 *BioIn 17*
Ford, Kathleen 1945- *WhoWrEP 92*
Ford, Kathleen J. *Law&B 92*
Ford, Kay Louise 1944- *WhoAmW 93*
Ford, Kenneth William 1926- *WhoAm 92*
Ford, Kristina *BioIn 17*
Ford, LaNelle Brigance 1924- *WhoSSW 93*

Ford, Larry John 1941- *WhoAm 92*
Ford, Latisha *BioIn 17*
Ford, Laura D. *Law&B 92*
Ford, Lauren 1891-1973 *BioIn 17*
Ford, Lawrence Howard 1948- *WhoE 93*
Ford, Lee Ellen 1917- *WhoAmW 93, WhoWor 93*
Ford, Lennie 1925?-1972 *BioIn 17*
Ford, Leslie Michelle 1950- *St&PR 93*
Ford, Lewis S. 1933- *ConAu 137*
Ford, Linda Barbara 1952- *WhoAmW 93*
Ford, Linda Lou 1948- *WhoAm 92*
Ford, Linda Maria 1949- *WhoEmL 93*
Ford, Lisa Ann 1956- *WhoSSW 93*
Ford, Lita c. 1959- *ConMus 9 [port]*
Ford, Loretta C. 1920- *WhoAm 92, WhoAmW 93*
Ford, Lucille Garber 1921- *WhoAm 92*
Ford, Marcyanne Rose 1941- *WhoAmW 93*
Ford, Marilyn Blair 1960- *WhoAmW 93*
Ford, Mary West 1965- *WhoAmW 93*
Ford, Maureen Morrissey 1936- *WhoAmW 93*
Ford, Michael Alton 1963- *WhoE 93*
Ford, Michael Raye 1945- *WhoAm 92, WhoSSW 93*
Ford, Molly Flickinger 1956- *WhoEmL 93*
Ford, Morgan 1911- *CngDr 91*
Ford, Nancy Leonard 1955- *WhoEmL 93*
Ford, Nancy Louise 1935- *WhoAm 92*
Ford, Patricia Ann *Law&B 92*
Ford, Patricia Marie 1955- *WhoEmL 93*
Ford, Patrick 1835-1913 *JrnUS*
Ford, Patrick Kildea 1935- *WhoAm 92*
Ford, Paul F. 1947- *ScF&FL 92*
Ford, Paul Leicester 1865-1902 *GayN*
Ford, Phil Jackson 1956- *BiDAMSp 1989*
Ford, Phyllis *WhoWrEP 92*
Ford, Phyllis M. 1928- *WhoAmW 93*
Ford, R.A.D. 1915- *WhoCanL 92*
Ford, Ralph A. *Law&B 92*
Ford, Regina Mae 1961- *WhoAmW 93*
Ford, Rex J. 1955- *WhoAm 92*
Ford, Richard 1944- *BioIn 17*
Ford, Richard 1948- *ScF&FL 92*
Ford, Richard Alan 1940- *WhoAm 92*
Ford, Richard Brice 1935- *WhoE 93*
Ford, Richard C. 1944- *WhoWrEP 92*
Ford, Richard Earl 1933- *WhoAm 92*
Ford, Richard Edmond 1927- *WhoAm 92*
Ford, Richard Irving 1941- *WhoAm 92*
Ford, Richard Michael 1955- *WhoEmL 93*
Ford, Richard Thomas 1935- *WhoE 93*
Ford, Robert 1862-1892 *BioIn 17*
Ford, Robert Barney 1944- *WhoAm 92*
Ford, Robert Curry *ScF&FL 92*
Ford, Robert David 1956- *WhoEmL 93*
Ford, Robert Eustace Paul 1916- *WhoWor 93*
Ford, Robert Grant 1933- *WhoSSW 93*
Ford, Robert M. *Law&B 92*
Ford, Robert MacDonald, III 1934- *WhoSSW 93*
Ford, Rodney Alan 1961- *WhoSSW 93*
Ford, Roger Hayes 1956- *WhoEmL 93, WhoSSW 93, WhoWor 93*
Ford, Ronald Glen 1947- *St&PR 93*
Ford, Sarah Litsey 1901- *WhoWrEP 92*
Ford, Sherri Ann 1960- *WhoEmL 93*
Ford, Silas M. 1937- *WhoAm 92*
Ford, Stefan *Law&B 92*
Ford, Stephen D. *Law&B 92*
Ford, Steve *MiSFD 9*
Ford, Steven Milton 1954- *WhoEmL 93*
Ford, Sue Grayson *BioIn 17*
Ford, "Tennessee Ernie" 1919- *Baker 92*
Ford, Tennessee Ernie 1919-1991 *AnObit 1991, BioIn 17, ConTFT 10, CurBio 92N, News 92*
Ford, Thomas c. 1580-1648 *Baker 92*
Ford, Thomas E. 1929- *St&PR 93*
Ford, Thomas E., III 1939- *St&PR 93*
Ford, Thomas Herbert 1953- *WhoE 93*
Ford, Thomas Jeffers 1930- *WhoSSW 93*
Ford, Thomas Milton, Jr. 1943- *St&PR 93*
Ford, Thomas Patrick 1918- *WhoAm 92*
Ford, Thomas Sparks 1944- *WhoSSW 93*
Ford, Timothy Alan 1951- *WhoAm 92, WhoSSW 93*
Ford, Timothy Graham 1945- *WhoWor 93*
Ford, Victor H.W. 1943- *WhoScE 91-1*
Ford, Wendell H. *BioIn 17*
Ford, Wendell H. 1924- *CngDr 91*
Ford, Wendell Hampton 1924- *WhoAm 92, WhoSSW 93*
Ford, William B. 1940- *St&PR 93*
Ford, William Clay 1925- *St&PR 93, WhoAm 92*
Ford, William Clay, Jr. *BioIn 17*
Ford, William D. 1927- *CngDr 91*
Ford, William David 1927- *WhoAm 92*
Ford, William F. 1925- *St&PR 93*
Ford, William F. 1936- *WhoAm 92*
Ford, William Francis 1925- *WhoAm 92*
Ford, William Leslie 1942- *St&PR 93*
Ford, William S., Jr. 1934- *St&PR 93*
Ford, William Webster 1922- *St&PR 93*
Ford, Williston *ScF&FL 92*
Ford, Yancey William, Jr. 1940- *St&PR 93, WhoAm 92*
Ford-Choyke, Phyllis *WhoWrEP 92*
Forde, Alvin Ralph 1933- *St&PR 93*
Forde, Brian Gordon *WhoScE 91-1*
Forde, Daryll 1902-1973 *IntDcAn*
Forde, Dorothy Evadne 1952- *WhoWor 93*
Forde, Harold McDonald 1916- *WhoWor 93*
Forde, Henry 1933- *DcCPCAm*
Forde, Joyce P. 1950- *WhoWrEP 92*
Forde, Larry d1990 *BioIn 17*
Forde, Michael J. *Law&B 92*
Forde, Peter C. 1955- *St&PR 93*
Forde, R.A. 1948- *ScF&FL 92*
Forde, Victoria 1896-1964 *SweetSg A*
Forde, Walter 1896-1984 *QDrFCA 92 [port]*
Fordell, Erik 1917-1981 *Baker 92*
Fordham, Benjamin Cleveland 1953- *WhoEmL 93*
Fordham, Christopher Columbus, III 1926- *WhoAm 92, WhoWor 93*
Fordham, Jefferson Barnes 1905- *WhoAm 92*
Fordham, Laurence Sherman 1929- *WhoAm 92*
Fordham, Mark *BioIn 17*
Fordham, Sharon Ann 1952- *WhoAmW 93, WhoEmL 93*
Fordham, Traci Ann 1963- *WhoAmW 93*
Fordice, Daniel Kirkwood, Jr. 1934- *WhoAm 92, WhoSSW 93, WhoWor 93*
Fordice, Daniel Kirkwood, III 1960- *St&PR 93*
Fordice, Kirk *BioIn 17, NewYTBS 92 [port]*
Fording, Edmund Howard, Jr. 1937- *WhoAm 92*
Fording, William G. 1939- *St&PR 93*
Fordtran, John Satterfield 1931- *WhoAm 92*
Fordyce, Alice Woodard d1992 *NewYTBS 92 [port]*
Fordyce, Barbara Ann 1955- *WhoAmW 93*
Fordyce, Edward, Jr. *Law&B 92*
Fordyce, Edward Winfield, Jr. 1941- *WhoAm 92*
Fordyce, Gary K. *Law&B 92*
Fordyce, James Clarence 1937- *WhoE 93*
Fordyce, James Forrest 1953- *WhoEmL 93*
Fordyce, Samuel Wesley 1927- *WhoE 93*
Fore, Edith *BioIn 17*
Fore, Gerri M. *Law&B 92*
Fore, Henrietta Holsman *WhoAm 92*
Fore, Lavonne Kelly 1952- *WhoSSW 93*
Fore, Scott E. 1954- *St&PR 93*
Fore, William R. 1941- *St&PR 93*
Forehand, Jennie Meador 1935- *WhoAmW 93*
Forehand, Margaret P. 1951- *WhoAm 92, WhoSSW 93*
Forehand, Steve R. *Law&B 92*
Forell, David C. 1947- *St&PR 93*
Forell, David Charles 1947- *WhoAm 92*
Forell, George Wolfgang 1919- *WhoAm 92*
Forelle, Helen *WhoWrEP 92*
Forelli, Matthew S. 1938- *St&PR 93*
Forelli, Sam C. 1934- *St&PR 93*
Foreman, Anne N. 1947- *WhoAm 92, WhoAmW 93*
Foreman, Bob *ScF&FL 92*
Foreman, Carl 1914-1984 *MiSFD 9N*
Foreman, Carol Lee Tucker 1938- *WhoAm 92, WhoAmW 93*
Foreman, Clark H. 1902-1977 *EncAACR*
Foreman, Clay Bertrand, Jr. 1933- *St&PR 93*
Foreman, Daphne Anne 1959- *WhoAmW 93*
Foreman, Dave *BioIn 17*
Foreman, Dave 1946- *ConAu 139*
Foreman, Domonic John 1933- *WhoAsAP 91*
Foreman, Edward Rawson 1939- *WhoAm 92*
Foreman, Edwin Francis 1931- *WhoSSW 93, WhoWor 93*
Foreman, Ellen S. 1957- *WhoEmL 93*
Foreman, Gene Clemons 1934- *WhoAm 92*
Foreman, George *BioIn 17, WhoAm 92*
Foreman, George 1948- *AfrAmBi*
Foreman, Jack P. *St&PR 93*
Foreman, James Louis 1927- *WhoAm 92*
Foreman, Jeff 1951- *WhoEmL 93*
Foreman, Joel H. 1948- *St&PR 93*
Foreman, John C. d1992 *NewYTBS 92*
Foreman, John Daniel 1940- *WhoE 93, WhoWor 93*
Foreman, John Richard 1952- *St&PR 93*
Foreman, Kenneth Martin 1925- *WhoE 93*
Foreman, Laura *WhoAm 92*
Foreman, Lucretia Jo 1963- *WhoAmW 93*
Foreman, M.H. *WhoScE 91-1*
Foreman, Michael 1938- *ConAu 38NR, MajAI, SmATA 73 [port]*
Foreman, Michael Marcellus 1941- *WhoSSW 93*
Foreman, Nancy Jean 1949- *WhoEmL 93*
Foreman, Nancy North 1938- *WhoAmW 93*
Foreman, Roberto *ScF&FL 92*
Foreman, Russell 1921- *ScF&FL 92*
Foreman, Spencer 1935- *WhoAm 92*
Foreman, Stephen H. *MiSFD 9*
Foreman, Thomas Alexander 1930- *WhoAm 92, WhoE 93, WhoWor 93*
Forer, Anne Ruth 1945- *WhoWrEP 92*
Forer, Arthur H. 1935- *WhoAm 92*
Forer, Bernard 1907- *WhoWrEP 92*
Forer, Morris L. 1912- *St&PR 93*
Forese, James J. 1935- *St&PR 93*
Forese, James John 1935- *WhoAm 92*
Foresman, James Buckey 1935- *WhoWor 93*
Forest, Charlene Lynn 1947- *WhoAmW 93, WhoEmL 93*
Forest, Dial *ConAu 37NR*
Forest, Doris Elizabeth 1936- *WhoAm 92*
Forest, Gilbert E. *Law&B 92*
Forest, Harvey 1937- *St&PR 93*
Forest, Herman Silva 1921- *WhoAm 92*
Forest, Ira 1920- *St&PR 93*
Forest, James H. 1941- *ConAu 136*
Forest, Jim *ConAu 136*
Forest, Michael Franklin 1955- *St&PR 93*
Forest, Philip Earle 1931- *WhoSSW 93*
Forest, Regan *ScF&FL 92*
Forest, Salambo *ScF&FL 92*
Foresta, Anthony J. 1942- *St&PR 93*
Forestal, Sean *ScF&FL 92*
Forester, Bernard I. 1928- *St&PR 93, WhoAm 92*
Forester, Bruce 1939- *ScF&FL 92*
Forester, Bruce Michael 1939- *WhoWrEP 92*
Forester, Donald W. *Law&B 92*
Forester, Erica Simms 1942- *WhoAm 92, WhoE 93*
Forester, Gayle Marie 1962- *WhoSSW 93*
Forester, Jean Martha Brouillette 1934- *WhoAmW 93, WhoSSW 93, WhoWor 93*
Forester, John E. 1913- *St&PR 93*
Forester, John Gordon, Jr. 1933- *WhoAm 92*
Forester, Karl S. 1940- *WhoAm 92, WhoSSW 93*
Forester, Russell 1920- *WhoAm 92*
Forester, Samuel J. *St&PR 93*
Foresti, Roy, Jr. 1925- *WhoAm 92*
Forestier, Carmen Iris 1942- *WhoSSW 93*
Forestier, Christian 1944- *WhoScE 91-2*
Forestier, Francois Lucien 1945- *WhoWor 93*
Forestier, Pierre 1902-1989 *BioIn 17*
Foret, Allen James 1947- *St&PR 93*
Foret, Mickey Phillip 1945- *WhoAm 92*
Foretich, Eric A. *BioIn 17*
Foretich, Hilary *BioIn 17*
Forfar, John Oldroyd 1916- *WhoWor 93*
Forgach, John Phillip *Law&B 92*
Forgacs, Gabor 1949- *WhoE 93*
Forgacs, Otto Lionel 1931- *WhoAm 92*
Forgan, David Waller 1933- *WhoAm 92*
Forge, John E. 1947- *St&PR 93*
Forger, Robert Durkin 1928- *WhoAm 92, WhoE 93*
Forget, Claude E. 1936- *St&PR 93*
Forget, Guy *BioIn 17*
Forgett, Valmore Joseph, Jr. 1930- *WhoWor 93*
Forgey, Benjamin Franklin 1938- *WhoAm 92*
Forgey, William W. 1942- *ScF&FL 92*
Forgione, Francesco 1887-1968 *BioIn 17*
Forgon, Mihaly 1919- *WhoScE 91-4*
Forgosh, Neil I. 1939- *St&PR 93*
Forgotson, Florence Frances 1908- *WhoAmW 93*
Forgue, Stanley Vincent 1916- *WhoAm 92*
Foriers, Andre J.M. 1949- *WhoScE 91-2*
Forino, A. *WhoScE 91-3*
Forkan, Patricia Ann 1944- *WhoAmW 93*
Forkel, Johann Nikolaus 1749-1818 *Baker 92*
Forker, Charles R(ush) 1927- *ConAu 136*
Forker, David 1937- *WhoIns 93*
Forker, Lee R. 1906- *St&PR 93*
Forker, Olan Dean 1928- *WhoAm 92*
Forkin, Patrick James 1931- *St&PR 93*
Forkman, Anders C.G. 1927- *WhoScE 91-4*
Forkman, Bengt 1930- *WhoScE 91-4*
Forkner, Claude E., Sr. d1992 *NewYTBS 92*
Forkner, Donald Maxwell 1936- *St&PR 93*
Forkner, James L. 1922- *St&PR 93*
Forkosch, Morris D. *BioIn 17*
Forks, Thomas Paul 1952- *WhoSSW 93*
Forland, Tormod 1920- *WhoScE 91-4*
Forlano, Anthony 1936- *St&PR 93, WhoAm 92*
Forlano, Frederick Peter 1947- *WhoEmL 93*
Forline, Betty M. 1933- *St&PR 93*
Forlines, John Arthur, Jr. 1918- *St&PR 93*
Forlini, Frank John, Jr. 1941- *WhoWor 93*
Forloine, William Joseph 1938- *WhoIns 93*
Form, Fredric Allan 1942- *WhoE 93, WhoWor 93*
Form, Peter Wolfgang 1931- *WhoWor 93*
Forma, Charles A. *Law&B 92*
Formaker, Susan L. *Law&B 92*
Forman, Anne 1925- *WhoAmW 93*
Forman, Beth Rosalyne 1949- *WhoAmW 93, WhoEmL 93*
Forman, Charles William 1916- *WhoAm 92*
Forman, Debra Jo 1958- *WhoAmW 93*
Forman, Donald T. 1932- *WhoAm 92*
Forman, Edgar Ross 1923- *WhoAm 92, WhoE 93*
Forman, Gail Iris 1941- *WhoAmW 93*
Forman, George Whiteman 1919- *WhoAm 92*
Forman, H. Buxton 1842-1917 *ScF&FL 92*
Forman, Henry Chandlee 1904-1991 *BioIn 17*
Forman, Howard Irving 1917- *WhoAm 92, WhoWor 93*
Forman, Jacqueline K. *Law&B 92*
Forman, James 1928- *EncAACR*
Forman, James D. 1932- *ScF&FL 92*
Forman, James (Douglas) 1932- *DcAmChF 1960, MajAI [port], SmATA 70 [port]*
Forman, Jeanne Leach 1916- *WhoAmW 93*
Forman, Jeffrey J. 1949- *St&PR 93*
Forman, Joseph Charles 1931- *WhoAm 92*
Forman, Kenneth Howard 1947- *WhoE 93*
Forman, L. Ronald *WhoAm 92*
Forman, Larry *BioIn 17*
Forman, Leona S. 1940- *WhoUN 92*
Forman, Linda Eileen 1946- *St&PR 93*
Forman, Mark Leonard 1949- *WhoEmL 93*
Forman, Maurice R. d1992 *NewYTBS 92*
Forman, Milos *BioIn 17*
Forman, Milos 1932- *DrEEuF, MiSFD 9, WhoAm 92, WhoWor 93*
Forman, Paula *WhoAmW 93*
Forman, Peter Gerald 1946- *WhoSSW 93*
Forman, Phyllis Wachs 1935- *WhoE 93*
Forman, Richard Loren 1943- *WhoE 93*
Forman, Richard T. T. 1935- *WhoAm 92*
Forman, Robert S. 1919-1990 *BioIn 17*
Forman, Sidney d1992 *NewYTBS 92*
Forman, Stuart Irving 1947- *WhoE 93*
Forman, Susan Greenberg 1948- *WhoSSW 93*
Forman, Tamara 1947- *WhoAmW 93*
Forman, Thomas Michael 1945- *St&PR 93*
Forman, Wade K. 1913- *St&PR 93*
Forman, William Gordon 1770-1812 *BioIn 17*
Forman, William Joel 1946- *WhoEmL 93*
Forman, Willis M. 1925- *St&PR 93*
Formanek, Arthur R. *Law&B 92*
Formanek, Peter Raemin 1943- *St&PR 93*
Formant, Christopher Mathew 1951- *St&PR 93*
Formby, Bent Clark 1940- *WhoWor 93*
Formby, Chip 1953- *WhoSSW 93*
Formby, George 1904-1961 *IntDcF 2-3 [port], QDrFCA 92 [port]*
Formea, Juanita Mary 1931- *WhoAmW 93*
Formeister, Richard Bruno 1946- *WhoEmL 93*
Formes, Karl Johann 1815-1889 *Baker 92*
Formes, Theodor 1826-1874 *Baker 92*
Formica, Gianni 1922- *WhoWor 93*
Formica, John Joseph 1948- *St&PR 93*
Formica, Joseph Victor 1929- *WhoSSW 93*
Formica, Peter Francis 1942- *WhoE 93*
Formichi, Cesare 1883-1949 *Baker 92*
Formicola, John Joseph 1941- *WhoE 93*
Formin, Vasiliy Ilyich 1954- *WhoWor 93*
Formisano, Mario 1923- *WhoScE 91-3*
Formosa, Daniel John 1953- *WhoE 93*
Formosinho, Sebastiao Jose 1943- *WhoScE 91-3*
Formoso, Antony 1933- *WhoScE 91-3*
Formoso, Beatrice Elena 1945- *St&PR 93*
Formoso, Esteban E. 1945- *St&PR 93*
Formosus c. 815-896 *OxDcByz*
Formwalt, Lee William 1949- *WhoEmL 93, WhoSSW 93*
Formwalt, William Alexander 1951- *WhoEmL 93*
Fornabai, Laurie Jill *Law&B 92*
Fornaciari, Gilbert Martin 1946- *WhoEmL 93*
Fornaciari, Roberta 1947- *WhoWor 93*
Fornalek, Wiktor *WhoScE 91-4*

Fornara, Charles William 1935- *WhoAm 92*
Fornari, Harry David 1919- *St&PR 93*
Fornari, Victor Masliah *WhoE 93*
Fornarotto, Felicia Agnes 1957- *WhoE 93*
Fornarotto, Michelle Lorraine 1966- *WhoAmW 93*
Fornasetti, Piero 1913-1988 *BioIn 17*
Fornatto, Elio Joseph 1928- *WhoAm 92*
Fornay, Alfred Richard *WhoE 93*
Fornell, Dave 1945- *BioIn 17*
Fornell, Martha Steinmetz 1920- *WhoAmW 93, WhoSSW 93, WhoWor 93*
Fornella, Norman G. 1948- *St&PR 93*
Forneris, Jeanne M. *Law&B 92*
Fornerod, Aloys 1890-1965 *Baker 92*
Fornes, Maria Irene 1930- *BioIn 17, ConTFT 10, HispAmA, NotHsAW 93 [port], WhoAm 92*
Fornes, Raymond Earl, Sr. 1943- *WhoSSW 93*
Fornes, Tim Michael 1966- *WhoE 93*
Forness, Steven Robert 1939- *WhoAm 92*
Fornet, Ambrosio 1932- *SpAmA*
Forney, George David, Jr. 1940- *WhoAm 92, WhoE 93*
Forney, Guy Sherman 1936- *WhoAm 92*
Forney, James L. 1945- *St&PR 93*
Forney, John Wien 1817-1881 *JrnUS*
Forney, Larry J. 1944- *WhoSSW 93*
Forney, Laurence Bruce 1925- *St&PR 93*
Forney, Mary Ann 1948- *WhoEmL 93*
Forney, Paul Joseph 1951- *St&PR 93*
Forney, Robert Clyde 1927- *St&PR 93, WhoAm 92*
Forney, Sandra Jo 1952- *WhoAmW 93*
Forney, Virginia Sue 1925- *WhoAmW 93*
Forni, Patricia Rose 1932- *WhoAm 92, WhoAmW 93, WhoSSW 93*
Fornia-Labey, Rita (Regina) 1878-1922 *Baker 92*
Fornoff, Frank, Jr. 1914- *WhoE 93, WhoWor 93*
Fornos-Asto, Joan-Josep 1957- *WhoWor 93*
Fornshell, Dave Lee 1937- *WhoAm 92*
Foroglou, George 1931- *WhoScE 91-3*
Foronda, Elena Isabel 1947- *WhoAmW 93*
Foroni, Jacopo 1825-1858 *Baker 92*
Forqueray, Antoine 1672-1745 *Baker 92*
Forqueray, Jean Baptiste 1699-1782 *See* Forqueray, Antoine 1672-1745 *Baker 92*
Forqueray, Michel 1681-1757 *See* Forqueray, Antoine 1672-1745 *Baker 92*
Forqueray, Nicolas-Gilles 1703-1761 *See* Forqueray, Antoine 1672-1745 *Baker 92*
Forr, Thomas Lee 1949- *WhoEmL 93*
Forrai, Jeno 1924- *WhoScE 91-4*
Forrer, M. *WhoScE 91-4*
Forrest, Allen Wright 1941- *WhoSSW 93*
Forrest, Archibald Robin 1943- *WhoWor 93*
Forrest, Bradley Albert *Law&B 92*
Forrest, David Vickers 1938- *WhoE 93*
Forrest, Diane 1946- *St&PR 93, WhoAmW 93*
Forrest, Douglas William 1945- *WhoE 93*
Forrest, Emmett 1927- *St&PR 93*
Forrest, Frederic *WhoAm 92*
Forrest, G.C. *WhoScE 91-1*
Forrest, Gail 1955- *WhoEmL 93*
Forrest, George 1915- *ConTFT 10*
Forrest, George William 1943- *St&PR 93*
Forrest, Hamilton 1901-1963 *Baker 92*
Forrest, Helen 1918- *BioIn 17*
Forrest, Henry J. 1933- *WhoAm 92, WhoWor 93*
Forrest, Herbert Emerson 1923- *WhoAm 92, WhoE 93, WhoWor 93*
Forrest, Hugh Sommerville 1924- *WhoSSW 93*
Forrest, James E. 1949- *St&PR 93*
Forrest, John 1847-1918 *Expl 93*
Forrest, Katherine V. 1939- *ScF&FL 92*
Forrest, Marion Patricia 1935- *WhoAmW 93*
Forrest, Muriel 1924- *WhoAmW 93*
Forrest, Nathan Bedford 1821-1877 *BioIn 17, HarEnMi*
Forrest, Nigel 1946- *WhoWor 93*
Forrest, Othello C., Jr. 1928- *St&PR 93*
Forrest, Patricia H. *Law&B 92*
Forrest, Peter *Law&B 92*
Forrest, Robert C. 1935- *St&PR 93*
Forrest, Sidney 1918- *WhoAm 92*
Forrest, Stephen 1958- *WhoEmL 93*
Forrest, Steven David *WhoWrEP 92*
Forrest, Suzanne Sims 1926- *WhoAm 92*
Forrest, Virginia R. d1991 *BioIn 17*
Forrestal, James V. 1892-1949 *BioIn 17, ColdWar 1 [port]*
Forrestal, Robert Patrick 1931- *St&PR 93, WhoAm 92*
Forrester, Alan McKay 1940- *WhoWor 93*
Forrester, Alexander R. *WhoScE 91-1*
Forrester, Alfred Whitfield 1953- *WhoEmL 93*
Forrester, Anne 1941- *WhoUN 92*
Forrester, Bernard 1908-1990 *BioIn 17*
Forrester, David Anthony 1954- *WhoEmL 93*
Forrester, David Mark 1946- *WhoEmL 93*
Forrester, Donald Dean 1945- *WhoE 93*
Forrester, Donald Williams 1939- *WhoSSW 93*
Forrester, Donna Myra 1949- *WhoAmW 93*
Forrester, Douglas Eugene 1945- *WhoSSW 93*
Forrester, Eleanor A. 1916- *St&PR 93*
Forrester, Harold C. 1908- *St&PR 93*
Forrester, Helen *WhoCanL 92*
Forrester, Helen 1919- *WhoCanL 92*
Forrester, Herb 1952- *St&PR 93*
Forrester, Jay Wright 1918- *WhoAm 92*
Forrester, Jerry Wayne 1953- *WhoSSW 93*
Forrester, John 1943- *ScF&FL 92*
Forrester, John A. 1939- *WhoAm 92*
Forrester, John Vincent *WhoScE 91-1*
Forrester, Larry L. 1944- *WhoIns 93*
Forrester, Maureen (Kathleen Stewart) 1930- *Baker 92*
Forrester, Michael Gerald 1956- *St&PR 93*
Forrester, Patrick James, Jr. 1949- *WhoEmL 93*
Forrester, Rosemary Wellington 1953- *WhoEmL 93*
Forrester, Stephen Cary 1954- *WhoEmL 93*
Forrester, Susan Annette 1962- *WhoWrEP 92*
Forrester, W. Glenn *Law&B 92*
Forrester, William Donald 1931- *WhoAm 92, WhoWor 93*
Forrette, John Elmer 1952- *WhoEmL 93*
Forrow, Brian Derek 1927- *WhoAm 92*
Forrow, Peter *WhoScE 91-1*
Forsbach, Jack Alan 1932- *WhoWor 93*
Forsberg, Charles Alton 1944- *WhoWor 93*
Forsberg, Dale John 1955- *St&PR 93*
Forsberg, David Carl 1930- *WhoAm 92*
Forsberg, Douglas L. 1945- *St&PR 93*
Forsberg, Franklin Sidney 1905- *WhoAm 92*
Forsberg, Hans G. *WhoScE 91-4*
Forsberg, Jim 1919-1991 *BioIn 17*
Forsberg, John Albert 1928- *St&PR 93*
Forsberg, Kevin John 1934- *WhoAm 92*
Forsberg, Roy Walter 1937- *WhoAm 92*
Forsberg, Shirley A. 1934- *St&PR 93*
Forsberg, Susan Marie 1953- *WhoEmL 93*
Forsberg-Rider, Eva Monica 1945- *St&PR 93*
Forsch, Mark J. *Law&B 92*
Forsch, Peter Dean d1991 *BioIn 17*
Forsching, Hans Wilhelm 1930- *WhoScE 91-3*
Forsdale, Louis 1922- *WhoAm 92*
Forse, Herbert E., Jr. 1932- *St&PR 93*
Forse, Robert Armour 1950- *WhoE 93*
Forsee, Joe Brown 1949- *WhoAm 92, WhoSSW 93*
Forselius, Randall A. 1924- *St&PR 93*
Forselius, Ruth V. 1927- *St&PR 93*
Forsell, Andrew C. *Law&B 92*
Forsell, Glenn *St&PR 93*
Forsell, John 1868-1941 *OxDcOp*
Forsell, (Carl) John 1868-1941 *Baker 92*
Forsell, Ronald O. 1928- *WhoWrEP 92*
Forsen, Harold Kay 1932- *WhoAm 92*
Forsen, K. Sture 1932- *WhoScE 91-4*
Forsey, Eugene Alfred 1904-1991 *BioIn 17*
Forsgate, Hugh Moss Gerald 1919- *WhoAsAP 91*
Forsgren, B. Arne G. 1942- *WhoScE 91-4*
Forsgren, John H., Jr. 1946- *WhoAm 92*
Forsh, Kenneth Allan 1949- *WhoE 93*
Forsha, Anita Louise 1950- *WhoEmL 93*
Forsha, Harry Irwin 1946- *WhoSSW 93*
Forshay-Lunsford, Cin *BioIn 17*
Forshey, William Osmond, III 1945- *WhoE 93*
Forshner, Hugh C. *Law&B 92*
Forsius, Henrik Runar 1921- *WhoScE 91-4*
Forslid, Anders 1955- *WhoScE 91-4*
Forsling, Willis R. 1942- *WhoScE 91-4*
Forslund, Jan Ake 1952- *WhoWor 93*
Forsman, Alpheus Edwin *Law&B 92*
Forsman, Craig H. *St&PR 93*
Forson, Norman Ray 1929- *St&PR 93, WhoAm 92*
Forssberg, K.S.E. 1943- *WhoScE 91-4*
Forssmann, Wolf-Georg 1939- *WhoWor 93*
Forst, Alan Jay 1958- *WhoEmL 93*
Forst, Eric B. 1947- *St&PR 93*
Forst, John Kelly 1960- *WhoWor 93*
Forst, Judith *BioIn 17*
Forst, Judith Doris 1943- *WhoAm 92*
Forst, Leland I. 1948- *St&PR 93*
Forst, Marion Francis 1910- *WhoAm 92*
Forst, Thomas M. 1946- *St&PR 93*
Forst, Wendell 1926- *WhoWor 93*
Forstadt, Joseph Lawrence 1940- *WhoAm 92*
Forstchen, William R. 1950- *ScF&FL 92*
Forstemann, Ernst Wilhelm 1822-1906 *IntDcAn*
Forsten, Jarl Gustav 1940- *WhoScE 91-4*
Forstenzer, Andrew P. *Law&B 92*
Förster, Alan M. 1940- *St&PR 93*
Forster, Alan Moir 1940- *WhoAm 92*
Forster, Alban 1849-1916 *Baker 92*
Forster, Antonia Averill 1949- *WhoAmW 93*
Forster, Arnold 1912- *WhoAm 92, WhoWrEP 92*
Forster, Arthur Daniel 1931- *St&PR 93*
Forster, Bruce Alexander 1948- *WhoWor 93*
Forster, Bruce Crosby 1942- *WhoWor 93*
Forster, Clinton Coutts 1939- *WhoAm 92*
Forster, Cornelius Philip 1919- *WhoAm 92*
Forster, Denis 1941- *WhoAm 92*
Forster, E.M. 1879-1970 *BioIn 17, DcLB DS10, MagSWL [port], WorLitC [port]*
Forster, Edward Morgan 1879-1970 *BioIn 17*
Forster, Emanuel Aloys 1748-1823 *Baker 92*
Forster, Eric Otto 1918- *WhoAm 92*
Forster, Francis Michael 1912- *WhoAm 92*
Forster, Georg c. 1510-1568 *Baker 92*
Forster, Georg 1754-1794 *BioIn 17*
Forster, Hansgeorg J. 1936- *WhoScE 91-3*
Forster, Homer W. 1944- *WhoSSW 93*
Forster, James E. *Law&B 92*
Forster, James Francis 1956- *WhoEmL 93*
Forster, Josef 1833-1907 *Baker 92*
Forster, Julian 1918- *WhoAm 92*
Forster, Kurt Walter 1935- *WhoAm 92*
Forster, Leslie Stewart 1924- *WhoAm 92*
Forster, Marc R. 1959- *ConAu 138*
Forster, Margaret 1938- *BioIn 17*
Forster, Merlin Henry 1928- *WhoAm 92*
Forster, Mitchell L. *Law&B 92*
Forster, Othmar 1926- *WhoScE 91-4*
Forster, Peter Hans 1942- *St&PR 93*
Forster, Robert 1941- *MiSFD 9*
Forster, Robert E., II 1919- *WhoAm 92*
Forster, Robert S. 1945- *St&PR 93*
Forster, Stuart d1991 *BioIn 17*
Forster, Virginia L. 1953- *WhoEmL 93*
Forster, William Daly 1946- *St&PR 93*
Forster, William Hull 1939- *WhoAm 92*
Forsthoff, William Earle 1924- *St&PR 93*
Forstman, Henry Jackson 1929- *WhoAm 92*
Forstmann, Theodore J. *BioIn 17*
Forstner, James A. *Law&B 92*
Forston, Sanna 1944- *WhoWrEP 92*
Forsvall, Murray Lawrence 1931- *WhoSSW 93*
Forsyth, Beverly *WhoWrEP 92*
Forsyth, Bill *BioIn 17*
Forsyth, Bill 1946- *MiSFD 9*
Forsyth, Cecil 1870-1941 *Baker 92*
Forsyth, David J.C. *WhoScE 91-1*
Forsyth, Donald William 1948- *WhoAm 92*
Forsyth, E. Jardine 1943- *St&PR 93*
Forsyth, Frederick 1938- *BioIn 17, ConAu 38NR, ScF&FL 92, WhoAm 92, WhoWor 93*
Forsyth, George Howard 1901-1991 *BioIn 17*
Forsyth, Ilene Haering 1928- *WhoAm 92*
Forsyth, Janice Condouris *Law&B 92*
Forsyth, Joseph 1942- *WhoAm 92*
Forsyth, Malcolm (Denis) 1936- *Baker 92*
Forsyth, Michael Thomas 1963- *WhoSSW 93*
Forsyth, Neil Robert 1944- *WhoWor 93*
Forsyth, Raymond Arthur 1928- *WhoAm 92*
Forsyth, Scott A. *Law&B 92*
Forsyth, Steven G. *Law&B 92*
Forsyth, Thelma Jeanne 1954- *WhoAmW 93*
Forsyth, Thomas L. *Law&B 92*
Forsythe, Alan Barry 1940- *St&PR 93*
Forsythe, Donald G. 1938- *St&PR 93*
Forsythe, Donald John 1955- *WhoE 93*
Forsythe, Earl Andrew 1904- *WhoAm 92*
Forsythe, Eric 1947- *WhoEmL 93*
Forsythe, Frank S. 1932- *St&PR 93*
Forsythe, Henderson 1917- *WhoAm 92*
Forsythe, Janet W. 1957- *WhoEmL 93*
Forsythe, John 1918- *WhoAm 92*
Forsythe, John G. 1947- *St&PR 93*
Forsythe, Lynn Maureen 1949- *WhoEmL 93*
Forsythe, Patricia Hays *WhoAmW 93, WhoWor 93*
Forsythe, Peter Winchell 1937- *WhoAm 92*
Forsythe, Richard *ScF&FL 92*
Forsythe, Richard Hamilton 1921- *WhoAm 92*
Forsythe, Roger *BioIn 17*
Forsythe, Thomas M. 1958- *WhoEmL 93*
Forsythe, Warren Murcotte 1934- *WhoWor 93*
Forsythe, William 1949- *News 93-2*
Forsythe-Schmalz, Elizabeth M. 1951- *WhoEmL 93*
Fort, Arthur Tomlinson, III 1931- *WhoAm 92, WhoWor 93*
Fort, Bernard Pierre 1942- *WhoScE 91-2*
Fort, Edward Bernard *WhoSSW 93*
Fort, Gary R. *WhoIns 93*
Fort, Gary Watt 1956- *WhoWrEP 92*
Fort, James B. 1936- *St&PR 93*
Fort, James Tomlinson 1928- *WhoAm 92*
Fort, John Franklin 1941- *St&PR 93*
Fort, John Franklin, III 1941- *WhoAm 92, WhoE 93*
Fort, Lee Earthmon 1950- *WhoEmL 93, WhoWor 93*
Fort, Linda Lee 1947- *WhoSSW 93*
Fort, Louis A. 1945- *St&PR 93*
Fort, Marron Curtis 1938- *WhoWor 93*
Fort, Paul *ConAu 137, MajAI*
Fort, Pavel 1945- *WhoE 93*
Fort, Randall Martin 1956- *WhoAm 92*
Fort, Raymond Cornelius, Jr. 1938- *WhoAm 92*
Fort, Teresa Carol 1964- *WhoAmW 93*
Fort, Timothy Lyman 1958- *WhoEmL 93*
Fort, Tomlinson 1932- *WhoAm 92, WhoSSW 93*
Fortado, Michael G. *Law&B 92*
Fortado, Michael G. 1943- *St&PR 93*
Fortado, Michael George 1943- *WhoAm 92*
Fortas, Abe 1910-1982 *BioIn 17, JeAmHC, OxCSupC [port]*
Fort-Brescia, Bernardo *BioIn 17*
Forte, Allen 1926- *Baker 92*
Forte, Charles 1908- *WhoWor 93*
Forte, Chet 1935- *BioIn 17*
Forte, Chris Eric 1956- *WhoEmL 93*
Forte, Donald, Jr. 1942- *St&PR 93*
Forte, Earl M., Jr. 1924- *St&PR 93*
Forte, Elisabeth Andersson 1959- *WhoAmW 93*
Forte, Joseph Michael 1954- *WhoEmL 93*
Forte, Nick Apollo *BioIn 17*
Forte, Stefano 1961- *WhoWor 93*
Forte, Stephen Forrest 1947- *WhoEmL 93, WhoSSW 93*
Forte, Wesley E. *Law&B 92*
Forte, Wesley E. 1933- *WhoIns 93*
Forte, Wesley Elbert 1933- *St&PR 93, WhoAm 92*
Forte-Dobson, Rosita Yevette 1954- *WhoE 93*
Fortelka, Bruce P. *St&PR 93*
Forten, James 1766-1842 *BioIn 17*
Fortenbach, Ray Thomas 1927- *WhoAm 92*
Fortenbacher, Olive White *AmWomPl*
Fortenbaugh, Samuel B., III 1933- *St&PR 93*
Fortenbaugh, Samuel Byrod, III 1933- *WhoAm 92, WhoE 93, WhoWor 93*
Fortenberry, Beverly Jeanne 1937- *WhoSSW 93*
Fortenberry, Carol Lomax 1959- *WhoEmL 93, WhoSSW 93*
Fortensky, Larry *BioIn 17*
Forter, Rodman K. 1948- *St&PR 93*
Fortes, Meyer 1906-1983 *BioIn 17, IntDcAn*
Fortescue, Margaret L. 1940- *WhoAmW 93*
Fortess, Fred 1913-1991 *BioIn 17*
Fortess, Karl Eugene 1907- *WhoAm 92*
Fortgang, Pinkus 1920- *St&PR 93*
Forth, Catherine Mary 1954- *WhoAmW 93*
Forth, Gerald Edward 1946- *St&PR 93*
Forth, Kevin Bernard 1949- *WhoAm 92, WhoEmL 93*
Forth, Stuart 1923- *WhoAm 92*
Forti, Anton 1790-1859 *Baker 92, OxDcOp*
Forti, Corinne Ann 1941- *WhoAmW 93*
Forti, Giorgio 1931- *WhoScE 91-3*
Forti, Henriette 1796-1818 *OxDcOp*
Forti, Lenore Steimle 1924- *WhoAmW 93*
Forti, Paolo 1945- *WhoScE 91-3*
Fortier, Andre Yves 1940- *WhoAm 92*
Fortier, D'Iberville 1926- *WhoAm 92*
Fortier, Jean-Marie 1920- *WhoAm 92*
Fortier, John A. 1933- *St&PR 93*
Fortier, John Bertram 1942- *WhoAm 92*
Fortier, L. Yves 1935- *WhoAm 92, WhoUN 92, WhoWor 93*
Fortier, Mark E. *Law&B 92*
Fortier, Quincy Ernest 1912- *WhoWor 93*
Fortier, Richard A. *Law&B 92*
Fortier, Ron *ScF&FL 92*
Fortier, Samuel John 1952- *WhoEmL 93*
Fortin, Harold Paul 1932- *St&PR 93*
Fortin, John J. 1922- *St&PR 93*

Fortin, Joseph Andre 1937- *WhoAm 92*
Fortin, Karen Ann 1936- *WhoSSW 93*
Fortin, Martin Emerson, Jr. 1952- *WhoEmL 93*
Fortin, Midence Mario Alberto 1954- *WhoUN 92*
Fortin, Raymond D. *Law&B 92*
Fortin, Susan Marie 1958- *WhoAmW 93, WhoE 93*
Fortin, Thaddeus J. 1959- *St&PR 93*
Fortina, Antonio Formia 1952- *WhoWor 93*
Fortina, Luigi 1931- *WhoScE 91-3*
Fortinberry, Glen W. 1927- *WhoAm 92*
Fortin Cabezas, Carlos 1940- *WhoUN 92*
Fortini, Franco 1917- *DcLB 128 [port]*
Fortini, Jack L. *Law&B 92*
Fortino, Ron *St&PR 93*
Fortinsky, Jerome Steven 1962- *WhoE 93*
Fortis, Paul de *ScF&FL 92*
Fortman, Donald J. *Law&B 92*
Fortman, Richard Allen 1936- *St&PR 93*
Fortmann, Dan 1916- *BioIn 17*
Fortmann, Thomas Edward *WhoAm 92*
Fortnagel, Peter 1938- *WhoScE 91-3*
Fortner, Brand Irving 1955- *WhoEmL 93*
Fortner, Hueston Gilmore 1959- *WhoEmL 93*
Fortner, Joseph Gerald 1921- *WhoAm 92*
Fortner, Marjorie Ann *Law&B 92*
Fortner, Robert Steven 1948- *WhoWor 93*
Fortner, Wolfgang 1907- *OxDcOp*
Fortner, Wolfgang 1907-1987 *Baker 92*
Fortney, Diane Eline Osborn 1958- *WhoAmW 93, WhoEmL 93*
Fortney, Donald Eugene 1947- *WhoEmL 93*
Fortney, Wayne Hollis, Jr. 1941- *WhoSSW 93*
Fortsch, Johann Philipp 1652?-1732 *OxDcOp*
Fortson, D. Eugene 1935- *St&PR 93*
Fortson, Edward Norval 1936- *WhoAm 92*
Fortson, Nicholas Keith 1957- *St&PR 93*
Fortuin, Johannes Martinus H. 1927- *WhoWor 93*
Fortuin, Thomas Mark 1946- *WhoEmL 93*
Fortuin, Tom *Law&B 92*
Fortuna, Barbara Ann 1952- *WhoAmW 93*
Fortuna, Frank Anthony, Jr. 1946- *WhoE 93*
Fortuna, J. Douglas 1958- *WhoEmL 93*
Fortuna, Theresa C. *Law&B 92*
Fortuna, Victoria Rettberg *Law&B 92*
Fortuna, William Frank 1948- *WhoEmL 93, WhoWor 93*
Fortunato, D'Anna 1945- *Baker 92*
Fortunato, Mark Anthony 1955- *WhoEmL 93*
Fortune, Dion 1890-1946 *BioIn 17*
Fortune, Frederic Andre 1952- *WhoEmL 93*
Fortune, Georges *DcCPCAm*
Fortune, James Michael 1947- *WhoEmL 93*
Fortune, Jan Isabelle 1892- *AmWomPl*
Fortune, Jimmy
See Statler Brothers, The *ConMus 8*
Fortune, John Alfred 1929- *WhoAsAP 91*
Fortune, Johnny 1954- *WhoWor 93*
Fortune, Lauren Susan Pitz 1948- *WhoAmW 93*
Fortune, Monique Joan 1961- *WhoWrEP 92*
Fortune, Nigel (Cameron) 1924- *Baker 92*
Fortune, Philip Robert 1913- *WhoAm 92*
Fortune, Robert R. 1916- *St&PR 93*
Fortune, Robert Russell 1916- *WhoAm 92*
Fortune, Stephen James 1951- *WhoE 93*
Fortune, T. Thomas 1856-1928 *JrnUS*
Fortune, Timothy Thomas 1856-1928 *BioIn 17, EncAACR*
Fortune, William John 1946- *St&PR 93*
Fortune, William Lemcke 1912- *WhoAm 92, WhoWor 93*
Fortuner, Lynne F. 1967- *WhoAmW 93*
Fortunet, Bruno *Law&B 92*
Forturato, John 1957- *St&PR 93*
Fortwangler, Robert W. 1946- *St&PR 93*
Forty Martyrs of Sebasteia *OxDcByz [port]*
Forty-two Martyrs of Amorion d845 *OxDcByz*
Forwalder, Beth A. *Law&B 92*
Forward, Dorothy Elizabeth 1919- *WhoAmW 93*
Forward, Gordon *BioIn 17*
Forward, Michelle Maureen 1968- *WhoAmW 93*
Forward, Richard Blair, Jr. 1943- *WhoSSW 93*
Forward, Robert 1958- *ScF&FL 92*
Forward, Robert L. 1932- *ScF&FL 92*
Forward, Robert Lull 1932- *WhoAm 92*
Forys, Conrad Walter *Law&B 92*
Forys, Karen Ann 1944- *WhoAmW 93*
Foryst, Carole *WhoAm 92*
Forzano, Giovacchino 1883-1970 *OxDcOp*
Forzano, Giovacchino 1884-1970 *IntDcOp*
Forzley, Harold Helmar Germyn 1952- *St&PR 93*
Forzley, Paul Edward 1953- *WhoE 93, WhoEmL 93*
Fosback, Norman George 1947- *WhoAm 92*
Fosberry, R.A.C. *WhoScE 91-1*
Fosburg, Richard Garrison 1930- *WhoAm 92*
Fosburgh, Lacey 1942- *WhoWrEP 92*
Fosburgh, Liza 1930- *ScF&FL 92*
Fosburgh, Minnie Astor *BioIn 17*
Fosbury, Dick 1947- *BioIn 17*
Foscante, Raymond Eugene 1942- *St&PR 93*
Foschi, Sergio 1923- *WhoScE 91-3*
Foschini, Charles Joseph 1965- *WhoSSW 93*
Fosco, Angelo *WhoAm 92*
Foscue, James E. *WhoAm 92*
Fosdick, Alice J. *AmWomPl*
Fosdick, Harry Emerson 1878-1969 *BioIn 17*
Fosgate Heggli, Julie Denise 1954- *WhoAmW 93, WhoEmL 93*
Fosha, Diana 1952- *WhoAmW 93*
Foshage, Joseph Charles 1920- *St&PR 93*
Foshage, William F., Jr. 1924- *St&PR 93*
Foshay, William W. d1992 *NewYTBS 92 [port]*
Foshee, Clyde H., Jr. *Law&B 92*
Foshee, Donald Preston 1931- *WhoSSW 93*
Fosher, Donald Hobart 1935- *WhoWor 93*
Fosholt, Sanford Kenneth 1915- *WhoAm 92*
Fosi, Polataivao 1934- *WhoAsAP 91*
Foskett, Charles T. 1943- *St&PR 93*
Fosmire, Fred Randall 1926- *WhoAm 92*
Fosnaught, Patricia S. 1943- *WhoAmW 93*
Fosnight, Alan D. 1961- *St&PR 93*
Fosnight, Dale Pennell 1923- *St&PR 93*
Fosnight, William D. *Law&B 92*
Foss, Alma Prudence *AmWomPl*
Foss, Brian Edwin 1953- *WhoEmL 93*
Foss, Charles Macleish *Law&B 92*
Foss, Charles R. 1945- *WhoWor 93*
Foss, Chris 1946- *ScF&FL 92*
Foss, Clive Frank Wilson 1939- *WhoAm 92*
Foss, Donald G. 1929- *St&PR 93*
Foss, Donald John 1940- *WhoAm 92*
Foss, Edward S. 1950- *St&PR 93*
Foss, Ernestine V. 1939- *St&PR 93*
Foss, George B., Jr. 1924- *WhoSSW 93, WhoWor 93*
Foss, George M. *Law&B 92*
Foss, Harlan 1941-1991 *BioIn 17*
Foss, Harlan Funston 1918- *WhoAm 92*
Foss, Hubert J(ames) 1899-1953 *Baker 92*
Foss, Joe *BioIn 17*
Foss, Joe 1915- *WhoAm 92*
Foss, John Frank 1938- *WhoAm 92*
Foss, John H. 1943- *St&PR 93*
Foss, John William 1933- *WhoAm 92*
Foss, Joseph Jacob 1915- *HarEnMi*
Foss, Lukas *BioIn 17*
Foss, Lukas 1922- *Baker 92, IntDcOp, OxDcOp, WhoAm 92, WhoWor 93*
Foss, Patricia Howland 1925- *WhoAmW 93*
Foss, Paulette D. 1952- *WhoEmL 93*
Foss, Ralph Scot 1945- *WhoSSW 93, WhoWor 93*
Foss, Richard F. 1917- *St&PR 93*
Foss, Ronald G. *St&PR 93*
Foss, Sam Walter 1858-1911 *JrnUS*
Foss, Stephen Danforth 1941- *WhoAm 92*
Foss, Theodore Nicholas 1950- *WhoEmL 93*
Foss, Thomas Carl 1951- *WhoSSW 93*
Foss, William Francis 1917- *St&PR 93, WhoAm 92*
Fossard, Adelaide Rawnsley *AmWomPl*
Fossat, Eric G. 1944- *WhoScE 91-2*
Fossati, Sarah 1866-1947 *BioIn 17*
Fossati, Thomas 1957- *WhoEmL 93*
Fosse, Bob *BioIn 17*
Fosse, Bob 1927-1987 *MiSFD 9N*
Fosse, Erwin Ray 1918- *WhoAm 92*
Fosse, Viggo M. 1951- *WhoScE 91-4*
Fosseen, Neal Randolph 1908- *WhoWor 93*
Fossel, Jon S. 1942- *St&PR 93*
Fossel, Peter VanBrunt 1945- *WhoAm 92*
Fosselman, J.F. 1926- *St&PR 93*
Fossen, William Van 1954- *St&PR 93*
Fossey, Dian *BioIn 17*
Fossier, Mike Walter 1928- *WhoAm 92*
Fossier, Ralph L., Jr. 1951- *St&PR 93*
Fossion, Eric M.J.A. 1943- *WhoScE 91-2*
Fossland, Joeann Jones 1948- *WhoAmW 93, WhoEmL 93*
Fossum, Donna L. 1949- *WhoEmL 93*
Fossum, Jerry George 1943- *WhoAm 92*
Fossum, Robert Merle 1938- *WhoAm 92*
Fost, Dennis L. 1944- *St&PR 93*
Foster, Abby Kelley 1811-1887 *BioIn 17*
Foster, Alan Dean 1946- *ScF&FL 92, SmATA 70 [port], WhoWrEP 92*
Foster, Alan Herbert 1925- *WhoAm 92*
Foster, Alec 1890-1972 *BioIn 17*
Foster, Allen Jay 1962- *WhoE 93*
Foster, Andrea Mary 1958- *WhoE 93*
Foster, Arlie O. 1918- *St&PR 93*
Foster, Arthur Eugene 1934- *St&PR 93*
Foster, Arthur L. 1947- *St&PR 93*
Foster, Arthur Rowe 1924- *WhoAm 92*
Foster, Barbara 1938- *WhoWrEP 92*
Foster, Barbara Anne 1955- *WhoEmL 93*
Foster, Barbara Melanie 1945- *WhoE 93*
Foster, Bert 1861-1940 *BioIn 17*
Foster, Blair 1917- *ScF&FL 92*
Foster, Bobbie Dore 1938- *WhoAmW 93*
Foster, Bobby Lynn 1946- *St&PR 93*
Foster, Brenda Kay 1953- *WhoAmW 93*
Foster, Brian Mark *Law&B 92*
Foster, Carey *AmWomPl*
Foster, Caroline Holcombe Wright 1864-1929 *AmWomPl*
Foster, Caswin Bernard 1953- *WhoEmL 93*
Foster, Catherine Rierson 1935- *WhoAm 92, WhoAmW 93, WhoE 93, WhoWor 93*
Foster, Charles Allen 1941- *WhoSSW 93*
Foster, Charles Crawford 1941- *WhoAm 92*
Foster, Charles E. *Law&B 92*
Foster, Charles Harman d1990 *BioIn 17*
Foster, Charles Henry Wheelwright 1927- *WhoAm 92*
Foster, Chris(topher Joseph) 1932- *ConAu 139*
Foster, Conrad E. 1953- *St&PR 93*
Foster, D.M. 1944- *ScF&FL 92*
Foster, Dale Warren 1950- *WhoEmL 93, WhoSSW 93, WhoWor 93*
Foster, Daniel Max, Jr. 1912- *WhoSSW 93*
Foster, David Charles 1952- *WhoEmL 93*
Foster, David Gilbert 1959- *WhoSSW 93*
Foster, David J. *St&PR 93*
Foster, David L. 1933- *St&PR 93*
Foster, David Lee 1933- *WhoAm 92*
Foster, David Manning 1944- *ConAu 39NR*
Foster, David Mark 1932- *WhoAm 92*
Foster, David R. 1920- *BioIn 17*
Foster, David Randall *Law&B 92*
Foster, David Scott 1938- *WhoAm 92*
Foster, David Smith 1927- *WhoAm 92*
Foster, David Volney 1946- *WhoE 93*
Foster, David William (Anthony) 1940- *WhoWrEP 92*
Foster, Deborah Jean 1952- *WhoEmL 93*
Foster, Dennis James 1952- *WhoEmL 93*
Foster, Dennis P. 1933- *WhoAm 92*
Foster, Donald Lee 1932- *WhoAm 92*
Foster, Doris Redman 1937- *WhoAmW 93*
Foster, Dorothy Choitz 1942- *WhoAmW 93*
Foster, Douglas Allen 1952- *WhoEmL 93, WhoSSW 93*
Foster, Dudley Edwards, Jr. 1935- *WhoWor 93*
Foster, Edith 1914- *BioIn 17*
Foster, Edson L. 1927- *WhoAm 92*
Foster, Edward E. 1939- *WhoAm 92*
Foster, Edward Halsey 1942- *ConAu 40NR*
Foster, Edward L. 1953- *WhoSSW 93*
Foster, Edward Mervyn 1933- *WhoAm 92*
Foster, Edward Paul 1945- *WhoE 93*
Foster, Edwin Powell, Jr. 1942- *WhoSSW 93*
Foster, Edwin Thomas 1923- *St&PR 93*
Foster, Elizabeth Currier 1832-1921 *BioIn 17*
Foster, Eric H., Jr. 1943- *WhoE 93*
Foster, Eugene Lewis 1922- *WhoAm 92, WhoSSW 93*
Foster, Fay 1886-1960 *Baker 92*
Foster, Frances 1924- *WhoAm 92*
Foster, Fred *SoulM*
Foster, Fred G. 1946- *St&PR 93*
Foster, Fred L. 1942- *St&PR 93*
Foster, Gary D. 1943- *St&PR 93*
Foster, Gary Dean 1944- *St&PR 93*
Foster, Genevieve 1893-1979 *MajAI [port]*
Foster, George C. 1893- *ScF&FL 92*
Foster, George McClelland 1913- *IntDcAn*
Foster, George McClelland, Jr. 1913- *WhoAm 92, WhoWor 93*
Foster, George Rainey 1943- *WhoAm 92*
Foster, George William, Jr. 1919- *WhoAm 92*
Foster, Gifford H. 1922- *St&PR 93*
Foster, Giles *MiSFD 9*
Foster, Glen R. 1908-1991 *BioIn 17*
Foster, Glenn *Law&B 92*
Foster, Gordon Kay 1927- *St&PR 93*
Foster, Grace Elizabeth 1928- *WhoWrEP 92*
Foster, Greg *BioIn 17*
Foster, Helen 1907- *SweetSg B [port]*
Foster, Helen Laura 1919- *WhoAmW 93*
Foster, Helen Montague 1946- *WhoAmW 93*
Foster, Henry Louis 1925- *WhoAm 92*
Foster, Henry Wendell 1933- *WhoAm 92*
Foster, Herman *Law&B 92*
Foster, Howard E. 1944- *St&PR 93*
Foster, Hugh Warren 1921- *WhoAm 92*
Foster, Irene Parks 1927- *WhoAmW 93*
Foster, J.B. 1934- *St&PR 93*
Foster, James Caldwell 1943- *WhoAm 92*
Foster, James Clifford 1950- *St&PR 93*
Foster, James H. *Law&B 92*
Foster, James H. 1955- *WhoIns 93*
Foster, James Henry 1930- *WhoAm 92*
Foster, James Henry 1933- *WhoAm 92*
Foster, James Howard 1947- *WhoSSW 93*
Foster, James M. d1990 *BioIn 17*
Foster, James Norton, Jr. 1954- *WhoEmL 93*
Foster, James Peter 1925- *St&PR 93*
Foster, James R. 1945- *St&PR 93*
Foster, James Reuben 1930- *WhoWor 93*
Foster, James Robert 1945- *WhoAm 92*
Foster, James Vance 1934- *St&PR 93*
Foster, Janne Castleberry *Law&B 92*
Foster, Jay W. 1957- *St&PR 93*
Foster, Jeremy James *WhoScE 91-1*
Foster, Jesse G. 1938- *St&PR 93*
Foster, Joanne Mary 1946- *WhoAmW 93*
Foster, Jodie *BioIn 17*
Foster, Jodie 1962- *CurBio 92 [port], IntDcF 2-3 [port], MiSFD 9, WhoAm 92, WhoAmW 93*
Foster, Joe B. 1934- *WhoAm 92*
Foster, Joe C., Jr. 1925- *WhoAm 92*
Foster, John Arthur 1900-1980 *BioIn 17*
Foster, John Burt, Jr. 1945- *WhoSSW 93*
Foster, John Horace 1927- *WhoAm 92*
Foster, John L. 1941- *ScF&FL 92*
Foster, John McNeely 1949- *St&PR 93, WhoAm 92*
Foster, John Odell *WhoScE 91-1*
Foster, John Stanton 1921- *WhoAm 92*
Foster, John Stuart, Jr. 1922- *WhoAm 92*
Foster, Joseph Wayne 1961- *WhoSSW 93*
Foster, Joy Via 1935- *WhoAmW 93*
Foster, Joyce Geraldine 1951- *WhoAmW 93, WhoEmL 93*
Foster, Judith Christine 1952- *WhoEmL 93*
Foster, Julian Francis Sherwood 1926- *WhoAm 92*
Foster, Julie Irene 1955- *WhoEmL 93*
Foster, Karin Marie 1959- *WhoAmW 93*
Foster, Kathleen Adair 1948- *WhoAm 92*
Foster, Kathryn Warner 1950- *WhoSSW 93*
Foster, Kenneth *DcCPCAm, WhoScE 91-1*
Foster, Lanny Gordon 1948- *WhoE 93, WhoEmL 93*
Foster, Laura Jean 1960- *WhoAmW 93*
Foster, Lawrence Gilmore 1925- *WhoAm 92*
Foster, Lawrence (Thomas) 1941- *Baker 92*
Foster, Leila Merrell 1929- *SmATA 73 [port]*
Foster, Lester Anderson, III 1962- *WhoSSW 93*
Foster, Linda Lee 1947- *St&PR 93*
Foster, Linda Nemec 1950- *WhoWrEP 92*
Foster, Liz *WhoWrEP 92*
Foster, Lloyd Arthur 1933- *WhoE 93*
Foster, Louis W. 1913- *St&PR 93*
Foster, Luther Hilton 1913- *WhoAm 92*
Foster, M.A. 1939- *ScF&FL 92*
Foster, Malcolm 1956-
See Pretenders, The *ConMus 8*
Foster, Marcia Williams 1950- *WhoAmW 93*
Foster, Margo Jill 1952- *WhoSSW 93*
Foster, Mark Alan 1956- *WhoSSW 93*
Foster, Mark Edward 1948- *WhoWor 93*
Foster, Mark Stephen 1948- *WhoEmL 93*
Foster, Martha Tyahla 1955- *WhoSSW 93*
Foster, Mary Beth 1953- *WhoAmW 93*
Foster, Mary Christine 1943- *WhoAm 92*
Foster, Mary LeCron 1914- *IntDcAn*
Foster, Maxie Elliott 1950- *WhoEmL 93*
Foster, Mayson H. 1946- *St&PR 93*
Foster, Melissa 1953- *WhoAmW 93*
Foster, Michael Edward 1949- *WhoEmL 93*
Foster, Michael H. *St&PR 93*
Foster, Michael Joseph 1954- *St&PR 93*
Foster, Michael Paul 1947- *WhoSSW 93*
Foster, Michael Thomas 1951- *WhoEmL 93*
Foster, Michelle Renee 1964- *WhoAmW 93*
Foster, Milo George 1957- *WhoEmL 93*

Foster, Morgan Lawrence 1924- *WhoAm 92*
Foster, Nancy Haston *WhoAmW 93, WhoWrEP 92*
Foster, Nicole Williams 1944- *St&PR 93*
Foster, Norman 1900-1976 *MiSFD 9N*
Foster, Norman 1949- *WhoCanL 92*
Foster, Norman P. 1935- *St&PR 93*
Foster, Norman Robert 1935- *WhoWor 93*
Foster, P.T. *ScF&FL 92*
Foster, P. Wesley, Jr. 1933- *St&PR 93*
Foster, Pamela Anne 1937- *WhoAmW 93*
Foster, Paul 1931- *WhoAm 92*
Foster, Paul M. *Law&B 92*
Foster, Paul Wesley, Jr. 1933- *WhoAm 92*
Foster, Pauline Adele 1950- *WhoEmL 93*
Foster, Peter *WhoScE 91-1*
Foster, Peter William *WhoScE 91-1*
Foster, Philip Carey 1947- *WhoEmL 93*
Foster, Prudence 1933- *ScF&FL 92*
Foster, R.A.L. 1950- *WhoScE 91-1*
Foster, R.J. *Law&B 92*
Foster, R(obert) J(ames) 1929- *WhoWrEP 92*
Foster, Rachel Ann 1955- *WhoAmW 93*
Foster, Ralph B. *Law&B 92*
Foster, Ralph B. 1928- *St&PR 93*
Foster, Randolph Courtney 1952- *WhoEmL 93*
Foster, Richard d1989 *BioIn 17*
Foster, Richard 1938- *WhoAm 92*
Foster, Richard 1946- *ConAu 137*
Foster, Richard Allen 1935- *St&PR 93*
Foster, Richard John Samuel 1954- *WhoWor 93*
Foster, Rita Dorn 1933- *WhoAm 92*
Foster, Robert 1949- *ScF&FL 92*
Foster, Robert Bruce 1950- *St&PR 93*
Foster, Robert Carmichael 1941- *St&PR 93, WhoAm 92*
Foster, Robert Francis 1926- *WhoAm 92*
Foster, Robert J. *St&PR 93*
Foster, Robert Lawson 1925- *WhoAm 92*
Foster, Robert Watson 1926- *WhoAm 92*
Foster, Roger S. d1990 *BioIn 17*
Foster, Roger Sherman, Jr. 1936- *WhoAm 92*
Foster, Roy Wayne 1938- *St&PR 93*
Foster, Ruth *ScF&FL 92*
Foster, Ruth Mary 1927- *WhoAmW 93*
Foster, Ruth Sullivan 1929- *WhoAmW 93*
Foster, Sally d1991 *BioIn 17*
Foster, Samuel Blair 1772?-1831 *BioIn 17*
Foster, Sara Mason 1957- *WhoAmW 93*
Foster, Sarah Jane 1839-1868 *BioIn 17*
Foster, Sharon Lee 1949- *WhoEmL 93*
Foster, Shirley M. *AfrAmBi*
Foster, Sidney 1917-1977 *Baker 92*
Foster, Stephen C(ollins) 1826-1864 *Baker 92*
Foster, Stephen Kent 1936- *WhoAm 92*
Foster, Steven Raymond 1953- *WhoEmL 93, WhoSSW 93*
Foster, Susan Gale 1957- *WhoAmW 93*
Foster, Susan Jane 1939- *WhoAmW 93*
Foster, Susan Weltha 1946- *WhoEmL 93*
Foster, Theda Ann *WhoSSW 93*
Foster, Theodore, II 1922- *St&PR 93*
Foster, Thomas A. 1938- *St&PR 93*
Foster, Thomas E. *Law&B 92*
Foster, Thomas H. 1940- *St&PR 93*
Foster, Thomas P. 1939- *WhoIns 93*
Foster, Timothy E. 1951- *St&PR 93*
Foster, Tom O., III *Law&B 92*
Foster, Trufant d1991 *BioIn 17*
Foster, Vere Henry Lewis 1819-1900 *BioIn 17*
Foster, Vickie Lynn 1952- *WhoWrEP 92*
Foster, Vincent Stephen 1943- *WhoE 93*
Foster, Virginia 1914- *WhoAmW 93*
Foster, Virginia Highleyman 1935- *WhoAmW 93*
Foster, W. Douglas 1942- *WhoAm 92, WhoSSW 93*
Foster, W.W. *WhoScE 91-1*
Foster, W. Wayne 1943- *St&PR 93*
Foster, Walter Herbert, Jr. 1919- *WhoE 93*
Foster, Walter Washington 1857-1935 *BioIn 17*
Foster, William Allen 1950- *WhoSSW 93*
Foster, William B. 1931- *WhoIns 93*
Foster, William Bell, Jr. 1923- *St&PR 93*
Foster, William C. *Law&B 92*
Foster, William E. 1944- *St&PR 93*
Foster, William Edwin 1930- *WhoAm 92*
Foster, William Frederick 1961- *St&PR 93*
Foster, William James, III 1953- *WhoEmL 93*
Foster, William Zebulon 1881-1961 *DcTwHis*
Foster, Willis Roy 1928- *WhoE 93*
Foster-Damigos, Patricia 1956- *WhoWor 93*
Fostier, A. *WhoScE 91-2*
Fota, Frank George 1921- *WhoWor 93*
Fotedar, Makhan Lal 1932- *WhoAsAP 91*
Fotek, Jan 1928- *Baker 92*
Fothergill, D.I. *WhoScE 91-1*
Fothergill, John Wesley, Jr. 1928- *WhoSSW 93, WhoWor 93*
Fothergill, Leslie Charles *WhoScE 91-1*
Fotheringham-Lenhart, Joy Ann 1960- *WhoAmW 93*
Foti, Andrew A. *Law&B 92*
Foti, Laurel Cohen 1943- *WhoAmW 93*
Foti, Margaret A. 1944- *WhoAm 92*
Foti, Richard Scott 1946- *WhoSSW 93*
Foti, Salvatore 1928- *WhoScE 91-3*
Fotiades, George L. 1953- *St&PR 93*
Fotinos, Katherine 1926- *WhoAmW 93*
Fotopoulos, Sophia Stathopoulos 1936- *WhoAmW 93*
Fotsch, Dan Robert 1947- *WhoEmL 93*
Fotsch, Melissa Ruth 1964- *WhoSSW 93*
Fotsch, William G. 1903- *St&PR 93*
Fottrell, Patrick F. 1933- *WhoScE 91-3*
Fotyma, Mariusz 1936- *WhoScE 91-4*
Fouassier, Claude 1938- *WhoScE 91-2*
Fouassier, Jean-Pierre 1947- *WhoScE 91-2, WhoWor 93*
Fouberg, Rodney W. 1938- *St&PR 93*
Foucauld, Charles-Eugene de 1858-1916 *BioIn 17*
Foucault, Jean Paul 1941- *WhoWor 93*
Foucault, Michel 1926-1984 *BioIn 17*
Fouch, George Daniel 1948- *St&PR 93*
Fouch, Stephanie Saunders 1947- *WhoAm 92*
Fouchard, Joseph James 1928- *WhoAm 92*
Fouchaux, Norbert Christian 1933- *WhoUN 92*
Fouche, Helen Strother 1939- *WhoAmW 93*
Foucher, Guy 1943- *WhoWor 93*
Foucher, Laure Claire *AmWomPl*
Foucher of Chartres *OxDcByz*
Fouchet, Christian 1911-1974 *BioIn 17*
Foudree, Charles M. 1944- *St&PR 93*
Fouet, Jean-Marc 1949- *WhoScE 91-2*
Fougere, Paul Francis 1932- *WhoE 93*
Fougere, Richard J. 1956- *St&PR 93*
Fougereau, Michel 1935- *WhoScE 91-2*
Fougeron, Pierre Jacques 1927- *St&PR 93, WhoAm 92*
Fougner, G. Selmer *BioIn 17*
Fougstedt, Nils-Eric 1910-1961 *Baker 92*
Foukal, Donald C. 1926- *St&PR 93*
Foukona, Ben Lucian 1959- *WhoAsAP 91*
Foulard, Claude 1939- *WhoScE 91-2*
Foulds, Donald Duane 1925- *WhoAm 92*
Foulds, Elfrida Vipont 1902- *ConAu 38NR, MajAI [port]*
Foulds, Jim *BioIn 17*
Foulds, John (Herbert) 1880-1939 *Baker 92*
Foulds, Roy 1947- *WhoWor 93*
Foulk, David Lynn 1952- *St&PR 93*
Foulk, Malcolm 1937- *St&PR 93*
Foulke, Edwin Gerhart, Jr. 1952- *WhoAm 92, WhoE 93, WhoEmL 93*
Foulke, Sarah B. 1955- *WhoAmW 93, WhoEmL 93*
Foulke, William Green 1912- *WhoAm 92*
Foulke, William Green, Jr. 1942- *WhoAm 92*
Foulkes, D.M. 1936- *WhoScE 91-1*
Foulkes, Fred Klee 1941- *WhoE 93*
Foulkes, Llyn 1934- *BioIn 17, WhoAm 92*
Foulois, Benjamin D. 1879-1967 *HarEnMi*
Foulois, Benjamin Delahauf 1879-1967 *BioIn 17*
Founds, Henry W. 1942- *St&PR 93, WhoAm 92*
Fountain, Albert Jennings 1838-1896 *BioIn 17*
Fountain, Anne Owen 1946- *WhoSSW 93*
Fountain, D. Ray 1938- *St&PR 93*
Fountain, Deward Green 1937- *St&PR 93*
Fountain, Eugenia Ferris 1959- *WhoE 93*
Fountain, Forrest Jay *Law&B 92*
Fountain, Henry Francis, Jr. 1924- *St&PR 93*
Fountain, John Ernest *Law&B 92*
Fountain, Karen Schueler 1947- *WhoE 93*
Fountain, Linda Kathleen 1954- *WhoAmW 93, WhoEmL 93, WhoSSW 93*
Fountain, M.W. *St&PR 93*
Fountain, "Pete" 1930- *Baker 92*
Fountain, Peter Dewey, Jr. 1930- *WhoAm 92*
Fountain, Primous, III 1949- *Baker 92*
Fountain, Robert Allen 1947- *WhoEmL 93*
Fountain, Robert Roy, Jr. 1932- *WhoAm 92*
Fountain, Ronald Glenn 1939- *WhoAm 92, WhoWor 93*
Fountain, Shirley Ann *Law&B 92*
Fountoulakis, Radamanthis 1960- *WhoWor 93*
Fouque, Friedrich Heinrich Karl La Motte- 1777-1843 *BioIn 17*
Fouque, Karoline Auguste La Motte- 1773-1831 *BioIn 17*
Fouquet, Leon Charles 1849-1936 *BioIn 17*
Fouraker, Lawrence Edward 1923- *WhoAm 92*
Fouras, Jim Demetrois 1938- *WhoAsAP 91*
Fourastie, Jean 1907-1990 *BioIn 17*
Fourcade, John *BioIn 17*
Fourcade, Marie Madeleine 1909-1989 *BioIn 17*
Fourcade, Vincent d1992 *NewYTBS 92 [port]*
Fourcans, Andre Georges 1946- *WhoWor 93*
Fourcard, Inez Garey *WhoAmW 93, WhoWor 93*
Fourcroy, Margarite 1956- *WhoSSW 93*
Fourdrain, Felix 1880-1923 *Baker 92*
Foureau, Fernand 1850-1914 *Expl 93*
Foureman, William C. *Law&B 92*
Fourest, Henry-Pierre 1911- *ConAu 136*
Fourestier, Louis (Felix Andre) 1892-1976 *Baker 92*
Fouret, Maurice 1888-1962 *Baker 92*
Fouret, Rene 1925- *WhoScE 91-2*
Fourkiller, Lea Duree *Law&B 92*
Fourmaux, George Marvin 1934- *St&PR 93*
Fournet, Claude Jacques 1942- *WhoWor 93*
Fournet, Gerard Lucien 1923- *WhoWor 93*
Fournet, Jean 1913- *Baker 92*
Fournet, Marilyn Michele 1949- *WhoAmW 93*
Fourney, Michael E. 1936- *WhoAm 92*
Fournie, Raymond Richard 1951- *WhoEmL 93*
Fournie, Robert G. 1920- *WhoAm 92*
Fournier, Albert Edouard 1938- *WhoWor 93*
Fournier, Arthur Edmond, Jr. *Law&B 92*
Fournier, Daniel S. 1947- *St&PR 93*
Fournier, Donald Frederick 1934- *WhoWor 93*
Fournier, Emile-Eugene-Alix 1864-1897 *Baker 92*
Fournier, F. *WhoUN 92*
Fournier, Harold Nelson 1928- *St&PR 93*
Fournier, Jean Pierre 1941- *WhoWor 93*
Fournier, Josette 1938- *WhoScE 91-2*
Fournier, Kenneth Leon 1947- *St&PR 93*
Fournier, Michael R. *Law&B 92*
Fournier, Paul Guy 1941- *WhoWor 93*
Fournier, Pierre 1916- *ConAu 40NR*
Fournier, Pierre (Leon Marie) 1906-1985 *Baker 92*
Fournier, Pierre-Simon 1712-1768 *Baker 92*
Fournier, Roger 1929- *WhoCanL 92*
Fournier, Ronald P. 1933- *St&PR 93*
Fournier, Serge Raymond-Jean 1931- *WhoAm 92*
Four Pennies *SoulM*
Fourquet, Bernard Jean 1948- *WhoWor 93*
Fourrier, Clay Joseph 1950- *WhoEmL 93*
Fourriere, Jean-Claude R. P. 1941- *WhoWor 93*
Fourroux, Melvin Ross 1944- *WhoE 93*
Fourt, Pierre Marie 1929- *WhoScE 91-2*
Four Tops *SoulM*
Fourtou, Jean-Rene 1939- *WhoAm 92*
Foury, Claude 1931- *WhoScE 91-2*
Fouse, Ron G. 1944- *St&PR 93*
Fouse, Ronald Grove 1944- *WhoSSW 93*
Fouss, James H. 1939- *WhoAm 92*
Fouss, James Helmer 1939- *St&PR 93*
Foust, Charles William 1952- *WhoEmL 93*
Foust, Kathy Ramona 1948- *WhoAmW 93*
Foust, Ronald 1942- *ScF&FL 92*
Foust, Roscoe T. 1928- *St&PR 93*
Foust, Russel Eugene 1947- *WhoE 93, WhoEmL 93*
Foust, Sharon Jeanette 1953- *WhoEmL 93*
Foust, William R. 1942- *St&PR 93*
Fout, George Douglas 1950- *WhoEmL 93*
Foutch, Michael James 1951- *WhoSSW 93, WhoWor 93*
Fouts, Donna Desti 1949- *WhoEmL 93*
Fouts, Elizabeth A.M. 1961- *WhoAmW 93*
Fouts, Elizabeth Browne 1927- *St&PR 93, WhoAmW 93, WhoSSW 93, WhoWor 93*
Fouts, James Fremont 1918- *St&PR 93, WhoSSW 93, WhoWor 93*
Fouts, James Ralph 1929- *WhoAm 92*
Fouts, Robert E. 1947- *St&PR 93*
Fouts, William P., III 1943- *St&PR 93*
Fou Ts'ong 1934- *Baker 92*
Foutz, Dell R. 1932- *WhoWrEP 92*
Foutz, Diana Lynn 1964- *WhoAmW 93*
Foutz, Samuel Theodore 1945- *WhoSSW 93*
Fovall, Nettie L. 1921- *St&PR 93*
Fovenesi, John C. 1951- *WhoAm 92*
Fowble, William Frankiln 1938- *St&PR 93*
Fowble, William Franklin 1938- *WhoAm 92*
Fowinkle, Eugene W. 1934- *WhoAm 92*
Fowke, Edith Margaret Fulton 1913- *WhoAm 92, WhoAmW 93, WhoWrEP 92*
Fowke, Helen Shirley 1914- *WhoCanL 92*
Fowkes, Charles *ScF&FL 92*
Fowkes, Richard Owen *Law&B 92*
Fowkes, William Ivor 1950- *WhoEmL 93*
Fowler, Alan Bicksler 1928- *WhoAm 92*
Fowler, Alastair (David Shaw) 1930- *ConAu 39NR*
Fowler, Anne Victoria 1945- *WhoAmW 93*
Fowler, Arden Stephanie 1930- *WhoAmW 93*
Fowler, Audrian Huff 1940- *WhoAmW 93*
Fowler, Barbara Hughes 1926- *WhoAm 92*
Fowler, Betty Janmae 1925- *WhoAm 92, WhoAmW 93*
Fowler, Bradley A. 1935- *St&PR 93*
Fowler, Bruce Andrew 1945- *WhoAm 92, WhoE 93, WhoWor 93*
Fowler, Carol F. *Law&B 92*
Fowler, Catharine W. *AmWomPl*
Fowler, Cecile Ann 1920- *WhoAmW 93, WhoE 93, WhoWor 93*
Fowler, Charles Albert 1920- *WhoAm 92*
Fowler, Charles Allison Eugene 1921- *WhoAm 92, WhoWor 93*
Fowler, Christopher 1953- *ConAu 137, ScF&FL 92*
Fowler, Clement 1924- *ConTFT 10*
Fowler, Conrad Murphree 1918- *WhoAm 92, WhoSSW 93*
Fowler, D.A. *ScF&FL 92*
Fowler, D.H. *WhoScE 91-1*
Fowler, David *WhoScE 91-1*
Fowler, David L. *Law&B 92*
Fowler, David S. 1945- *St&PR 93*
Fowler, David Wayne 1937- *WhoAm 92*
Fowler, Deborah Lynn 1952- *WhoEmL 93*
Fowler, Delbert Marcom 1924- *WhoSSW 93*
Fowler, Dolores Eleanor 1936- *WhoE 93*
Fowler, Don Wall 1944- *WhoAm 92*
Fowler, Dona Sylvia B. *WhoE 93*
Fowler, Donald Raymond 1926- *WhoAm 92*
Fowler, Douglas 1940- *ScF&FL 92*
Fowler, Douglas R. 1940- *WhoWrEP 92*
Fowler, Earle Cabell 1921- *WhoAm 92*
Fowler, Elaine Wootten 1914- *WhoAm 92*
Fowler, Elizabeth 1943- *WhoSSW 93*
Fowler, Elizabeth Milton 1919- *WhoAmW 93*
Fowler, Ellen Thorneycroft *ScF&FL 92*
Fowler, Emil Eugene 1923- *WhoE 93*
Fowler, F.G. 1870-1918 *BioIn 17*
Fowler, Francis George 1870-1918 *BioIn 17*
Fowler, Frank MacPherson 1935- *WhoWor 93*
Fowler, Fred J. 1946- *St&PR 93*
Fowler, Frederick Victor, Jr. 1933- *St&PR 93, WhoAm 92*
Fowler, Gene 1931- *WhoWrEP 92*
Fowler, Gene, Jr. *BioIn 17*
Fowler, George Selton, Jr. 1920- *WhoWor 93*
Fowler, Gilbert L. 1949- *WhoAm 92, WhoEmL 93, WhoSSW 93*
Fowler, Harriet Whittemore 1946- *WhoSSW 93*
Fowler, Harry Winthrop 1920- *St&PR 93*
Fowler, Henry H. 1908- *St&PR 93*
Fowler, Henry Hamill 1908- *WhoAm 92, WhoWor 93*
Fowler, Henry Watson 1858-1933 *BioIn 17*
Fowler, Horatio Seymour 1919- *WhoAm 92*
Fowler, Howard *St&PR 93*
Fowler, J. Edward *Law&B 92*
Fowler, J.W. 1944- *St&PR 93*
Fowler, Jack W. 1931- *WhoAm 92*
Fowler, Jaime Michael 1959- *WhoEmL 93*
Fowler, James Allan *WhoScE 91-1*
Fowler, James D., Jr. 1944- *WhoAm 92*
Fowler, James Daniel, Jr. 1944- *St&PR 93*
Fowler, James Edward 1931- *WhoAm 92*
Fowler, James M. 1939- *WhoWor 93*
Fowler, Jennifer 1939- *Baker 92*
Fowler, Joanna S. 1942- *WhoAm 92, WhoAmW 93*
Fowler, John A. 1943- *St&PR 93*
Fowler, John D. *Law&B 92*
Fowler, John Douglas 1931- *St&PR 93, WhoAm 92*
Fowler, John Moore 1949- *WhoAm 92*
Fowler, John Russell 1918- *St&PR 93, WhoAm 92*
Fowler, John Wellington 1935- *WhoAm 92*
Fowler, Joseph William 1950- *WhoEmL 93*

Fowler, Karen Anne 1958- *St&PR 93*
Fowler, Karen Joy 1950- *ScF&FL 92*
Fowler, Keith 1928- *St&PR 93*
Fowler, Keith Thomas 1950- *WhoE 93*
Fowler, Kellye *BioIn 17*
Fowler, Kenneth *St&PR 93*
Fowler, Laura Amsden *AmWomPl*
Fowler, Lee M. 1932- *St&PR 93*
Fowler, Linda McKeever 1948- *WhoAmW 93, WhoEmL 93*
Fowler, Mark Stapleton 1941- *WhoAm 92*
Fowler, Mary Ellen 1938- *St&PR 93*
Fowler, Molly Rulon-Miller 1935- *WhoE 93*
Fowler, Murray Elwood 1928- *WhoAm 92*
Fowler, Nancy *BioIn 17*
Fowler, Nancy Crowley 1922- *WhoAmW 93*
Fowler, Nicholas P. 1952- *St&PR 93*
Fowler, Noble Owen 1919- *WhoAm 92*
Fowler, Nola Faye 1934- *WhoAmW 93, WhoSSW 93*
Fowler, Norman *BioIn 17*
Fowler, Norman 1938- *WhoWor 93*
Fowler, Patricia D. 1937- *St&PR 93*
Fowler, Peter Niles 1951- *WhoEmL 93*
Fowler, Raymond D., Jr. 1930- *ScF&FL 92*
Fowler, Raymond David 1944- *WhoAm 92*
Fowler, Richard Calvin 1940- *St&PR 93*
Fowler, Richard Gildart 1916- *WhoAm 92, WhoWor 93*
Fowler, Robert *MiSFD 9*
Fowler, Robert Archibald 1931- *WhoE 93*
Fowler, Robert Asa 1928- *WhoAm 92*
Fowler, Robert G. 1926- *St&PR 93*
Fowler, Robert Glen 1930- *WhoAm 92, WhoSSW 93*
Fowler, Robert Howard 1926- *WhoAm 92*
Fowler, Robert K. 1944- *St&PR 93*
Fowler, Robert L. 1930- *St&PR 93*
Fowler, Robert Nicholas 1828-1891 *BioIn 17*
Fowler, Russell Marcus 1915- *WhoE 93*
Fowler, Samuel A., Jr. *Law&B 92*
Fowler, Sandra Smith 1961- *WhoSSW 93*
Fowler, Scott 1941- *WhoScE 91-4*
Fowler, Susan Michele 1952- *WhoAmW 93, WhoEmL 93*
Fowler, Terri 1949- *WhoAmW 93, WhoEmL 93*
Fowler, Thomas Benton, Jr. 1947- *WhoWor 93*
Fowler, Thomas Geoffrey 1924- *WhoWor 93*
Fowler, Thomas Kenneth 1931- *WhoAm 92*
Fowler, Thurley *DcChlFi*
Fowler, Tillie *WhoAmW 93*
Fowler, Vivian Delores 1946- *WhoAmW 93, WhoEmL 93, WhoSSW 93, WhoWor 93*
Fowler, Wiley Douglas 1938- *WhoSSW 93*
Fowler, William Alfred 1911- *WhoAm 92, WhoWor 93*
Fowler, William Dix 1940- *WhoAm 92*
Fowler, William Eugene 1953- *WhoSSW 93*
Fowler, William Morgan, Jr. 1944- *WhoWrEP 92*
Fowler, William Roy, Jr. 1950- *WhoEmL 93, WhoSSW 93*
Fowler, Wilton Bonham 1936- *WhoAm 92*
Fowler, Wyche, Jr. *BioIn 17*
Fowler, Wyche, Jr. 1940- *CngDr 91, WhoAm 92, WhoSSW 93*
Fowler, Wyman Beall 1937- *WhoAm 92*
Fowler-Scarpaci, Kathleen Anne 1962- *WhoEmL 93*
Fowles, George Richard 1928- *WhoAm 92*
Fowles, Gerald Wilfred Albert 1925- *WhoWor 93*
Fowles, John 1926- *BioIn 17, MagSWL [port], ScF&FL 92, WhoAm 92, WhoWor 93*
Fowles, William D. 1947- *St&PR 93*
Fowlie, Wallace 1908- *BioIn 17*
Fowlston, Brendan James 1945- *WhoScE 91-1*
Fox, A. Gardner d1992 *NewYTBS 92 [port]*
Fox, Alan L. *Law&B 92*
Fox, Alan M. 1947- *St&PR 93*
Fox, Alan S. *Law&B 92*
Fox, Alexander 1919- *St&PR 93*
Fox, Alexander E. 1906-1991 *BioIn 17*
Fox, Alistair 1948- *ConAu 39NR*
Fox, Alistair Graeme 1948- *WhoWor 93*
Fox, Allan 1935- *St&PR 93*
Fox, Ancella M. *AmWomPl*
Fox, Andrea Nancy 1949- *WhoEmL 93*
Fox, Andrew Jay, Jr. 1930- *WhoWor 93*
Fox, Andrew Mark 1957- *WhoE 93*
Fox, Angus C. *Law&B 92*
Fox, Annette Joy 1951- *WhoEmL 93*
Fox, Arthur Charles 1926- *WhoAm 92*
Fox, Arthur Joseph, Jr. 1923- *WhoAm 92*
Fox, Arturo Angel 1935- *WhoAm 92*
Fox, Barbara B. 1940- *WhoAmW 93*
Fox, Barbara C. *Law&B 92*
Fox, Barbara Jean d1991 *BioIn 17*
Fox, Barbara Ramey 1956- *WhoSSW 93*
Fox, Barry Jay 1956- *WhoWor 93*
Fox, Bennett Louis 1938- *WhoAm 92*
Fox, Bernard 1915- *St&PR 93*
Fox, Bernard Hayman 1917- *WhoAm 92*
Fox, Bernard Michael 1942- *WhoAm 92*
Fox, Betty 1935- *WhoAmW 93*
Fox, Betty Lou 1945- *WhoAmW 93*
Fox, Bill 1949- *St&PR 93*
Fox, C. Fred 1937- *WhoAm 92*
Fox, C. Joseph, III 1947- *St&PR 93*
Fox, C. Wayne 1938- *St&PR 93*
Fox, Carol 1926-1981 *OxDcOp*
Fox, Carroll Lawson 1925- *St&PR 93*
Fox, Cecelia Mary 1954- *WhoAmW 93, WhoE 93*
Fox, Charles Eldon, Jr. 1941- *WhoAm 92*
Fox, Charles Ira 1940- *WhoAm 92*
Fox, Charles J. 1907- *St&PR 93*
Fox, Charles James 1749-1806 *BioIn 17*
Fox, Charles Warren 1904-1983 *Baker 92*
Fox, Christopher W. *Law&B 92*
Fox, Clenzo B. *Law&B 92*
Fox, Clifford Gatley 1959- *WhoIns 93*
Fox, Connie T. 1932- *WhoWrEP 92*
Fox, Cynthia Austin 1954- *WhoAmW 93*
Fox, Cyril A., Jr. 1937- *WhoAm 92*
Fox, Daniel Michael 1938- *WhoAm 92*
Fox, David Eliot 1960- *WhoEmL 93*
Fox, David Louis 1949- *WhoE 93*
Fox, David Martin *BioIn 17*
Fox, David Martin 1948- *WhoEmL 93*
Fox, David W. 1931- *St&PR 93*
Fox, David Wayne 1931- *WhoAm 92*
Fox, David William 1959- *WhoEmL 93*
Fox, Dawne Marie 1948- *WhoE 93*
Fox, Dean Frederick 1944- *WhoAm 92*
Fox, Deborah *Law&B 92*
Fox, Derek *WhoScE 91-1*
Fox, Donald Melville 1942- *WhoIns 93*
Fox, Donald Thomas 1929- *WhoAm 92, WhoWor 93*
Fox, Donna Lee *BioIn 17*
Fox, Douglas Allan 1927- *WhoAm 92*
Fox, Douglas Brian 1947- *St&PR 93*
Fox, Douglas Lee 1951- *WhoEmL 93*
Fox, Duke Melvin 1919- *WhoSSW 93*
Fox, Edward A. 1936- *WhoAm 92*
Fox, Edward Alan 1950- *WhoEmL 93*
Fox, Edward Inman 1933- *WhoAm 92, WhoWrEP 92*
Fox, Eileen *Law&B 92*
Fox, Eleanor Mae Cohen 1936- *WhoAm 92, WhoWrEP 92*
Fox, Elizabeth Regina *WhoAmW 93*
Fox, Emile 1953- *WhoWor 93*
Fox, Erica *MiSFD 9*
Fox, Erwin Joseph 1930- *St&PR 93*
Fox, Eugene, III 1958- *WhoEmL 93*
Fox, Felix 1876-1947 *Baker 92*
Fox, Florence C. *AmWomPl*
Fox, Francis Haney 1933- *WhoAm 92*
Fox, Francis Henry 1923- *WhoAm 92*
Fox, Fred(erick Alfred) 1931- *Baker 92*
Fox, Frederick 1910-1991 *BioIn 17*
Fox, Frederick Gerald 1932- *St&PR 93*
Fox, Frederick I. *Law&B 92*
Fox, Gail 1942- *WhoCanL 92*
Fox, Gardner F. 1911-1986 *ScF&FL 92*
Fox, Gary 1939- *St&PR 93*
Fox, Gary Devenow 1951- *WhoEmL 93*
Fox, Geoffrey 1941- *SmATA 73 [port]*
Fox, Geoffrey Charles 1944- *WhoAm 92*
Fox, George 1624-1691 *BioIn 17*
Fox, Gerald Lynn 1942- *WhoAm 92, WhoSSW 93*
Fox, Gerson I. 1927- *St&PR 93*
Fox, Graydon C. 1933- *St&PR 93*
Fox, Gretchen Hovemeyer 1940- *WhoAmW 93*
Fox, Harold Edward 1945- *WhoE 93*
Fox, Harold J. 1958- *St&PR 93*
Fox, Harvey Michael 1942- *WhoE 93*
Fox, Hazel Metz 1921-1989 *BioIn 17*
Fox, Henry H. Bucky 1942- *WhoAm 92*
Fox, Herbert 1939- *WhoE 93*
Fox, Herbert Charles 1927- *St&PR 93*
Fox, Hugh Bernard 1932- *WhoWrEP 92*
Fox, Ira Martin 1953- *WhoE 93*
Fox, Irving H. 1943- *St&PR 93*
Fox, Jack Jay 1916- *WhoAm 92*
Fox, Jacob L. 1921- *St&PR 93*
Fox, Jacob Logan 1921- *WhoAm 92*
Fox, James *Law&B 92*
Fox, James A. *Law&B 92*
Fox, James Carroll 1928- *WhoAm 92, WhoSSW 93*
Fox, James Erwin *Law&B 92*
Fox, James Francis 1943- *St&PR 93*
Fox, James Frederick *Law&B 92*
Fox, James Frederick 1917- *WhoAm 92, WhoE 93*
Fox, James Gahan 1943- *WhoAm 92*
Fox, James H. *Law&B 92*
Fox, James Hoppes 1948- *WhoEmL 93*
Fox, James Michael 1953- *WhoEmL 93*
Fox, James W. 1947- *St&PR 93*
Fox, Janice Annette 1953- *WhoSSW 93*
Fox, Janis P. *Law&B 92*
Fox, Jean 1941- *WhoE 93*
Fox, Jean DeWitt 1918- *WhoAm 92*
Fox, Jeanne Marie 1952- *WhoEmL 93*
Fox, Jeffery Edward 1949- *WhoEmL 93*
Fox, Jeffrey 1951- *WhoEmL 93, WhoWor 93*
Fox, Jimi 1946- *WhoWor 93*
Fox, Joan Marie 1948- *WhoE 93, WhoEmL 93*
Fox, Joan Phyllis 1945- *WhoWor 93*
Fox, Joann Lewis 1931- *St&PR 93, WhoAmW 93*
Fox, Joanna Hornig 1947- *WhoSSW 93*
Fox, John 1952-1990 *BioIn 17, ConGAN*
Fox, John Bayley, Jr. 1936- *WhoAm 92*
Fox, John Charles 1933- *St&PR 93*
Fox, John David 1929- *WhoAm 92*
Fox, John Duffell 1940- *WhoAm 92*
Fox, John Edward *WhoScE 91-1*
Fox, John Joseph, Jr. 1931- *WhoE 93*
Fox, John L. 1949- *St&PR 93*
Fox, John Nicholas 1937- *WhoE 93*
Fox, Jonathan Edward 1945- *WhoWor 93*
Fox, Jonathan R. *St&PR 93*
Fox, Jonathan Randall 1958- *WhoWor 93*
Fox, Joseph Carter 1939- *St&PR 93, WhoAm 92, WhoSSW 93*
Fox, Joseph J. 1925- *St&PR 93*
Fox, Joseph Leland 1938- *WhoAm 92*
Fox, Joseph William *WhoIns 93*
Fox, Judith Hoos 1949- *WhoEmL 93*
Fox, Judy Kay 1952- *WhoEmL 93*
Fox, June T. 1924- *WhoE 93*
Fox, K.R. *St&PR 93*
Fox, Karen 1949- *WhoAm 92*
Fox, Karen Jean 1955- *WhoWrEP 92*
Fox, Karen Northridge 1956- *WhoEmL 93*
Fox, Karl August 1917- *WhoAm 92, WhoWor 93, WhoWrEP 92*
Fox, Kathryn Lynette 1966- *WhoSSW 93*
Fox, Keith Alexander Arthur *WhoScE 91-1*
Fox, Kelly Diane 1959- *WhoAmW 93, WhoE 93*
Fox, Kenneth 1929- *WhoAm 92*
Fox, Kenneth 1935- *WhoSSW 93*
Fox, Kenneth A. 1957- *St&PR 93*
Fox, Kenneth L. 1917- *WhoAm 92*
Fox, Kevin G. *Law&B 92*
Fox, Kevin Lee 1959- *WhoSSW 93*
Fox, Lafe Palmer 1915- *St&PR 93*
Fox, Laura Livingston *Law&B 92*
Fox, Lawrence 1932- *WhoAm 92*
Fox, Lawrence, III 1947- *WhoAm 92*
Fox, Lawrence Aaron 1923- *WhoAm 92*
Fox, Lawrence Alan *Law&B 92*
Fox, Lawrence Alan 1948- *WhoAm 92, WhoEmL 93*
Fox, Lawrence W. 1950- *St&PR 93*
Fox, Lee Barry 1952- *WhoEmL 93*
Fox, Leonard Dean 1950- *WhoSSW 93*
Fox, Leslie Burke 1958- *St&PR 93*
Fox, Lisa Marie 1961- *WhoAmW 93*
Fox, Lloyd Allan 1945- *WhoSSW 93*
Fox, Lorraine Susan 1956- *WhoAmW 93*
Fox, Louis 1917- *St&PR 93*
Fox, Luke 1586-1635 *Expl 93*
Fox, Lynn Marie 1967- *St&PR 93*
Fox, M. Bradford 1961- *WhoEmL 93*
Fox, Marcia Rose 1942- *WhoE 93*
Fox, Margaret Blair 1951- *WhoE 93*
Fox, Margaret L. *AmWomPl*
Fox, Marian 1950- *WhoE 93*
Fox, Marla Ann 1963- *St&PR 93*
Fox, Martin 1935- *St&PR 93*
Fox, Marvin 1922- *WhoE 93*
Fox, Mary Ann Williams 1939- *WhoE 93*
Fox, Mary Ellen 1956- *WhoEmL 93*
Fox, Marye Anne 1947- *WhoAm 92, WhoAmW 93, WhoEmL 93*
Fox, Matthew 1940- *BioIn 17, News 92 [port]*
Fox, Matthew Ignatius 1934- *WhoAm 92*
Fox, Maurice Sanford 1924- *WhoAm 92*
Fox, Maxine Randall 1924- *WhoAmW 93*
Fox, Mem 1946- *MajAI [port]*
Fox, Merrion Frances *MajAI*
Fox, Michael A. 1938- *St&PR 93*
Fox, Michael Charles *Law&B 92*
Fox, Michael Francis 1948- *WhoEmL 93*
Fox, Michael J. *BioIn 17*
Fox, Michael J. 1961- *IntDcF 2-3, WhoAm 92*
Fox, Michael Vass 1940- *WhoAm 92*
Fox, Michael Wilson 1937- *WhoAm 92, WhoWrEP 92*
Fox, Miriam Annette 1959- *WhoAmW 93, WhoE 93*
Fox, Muriel 1928- *WhoAm 92, WhoAmW 93*
Fox, Nancy Ellen 1956- *WhoAmW 93*
Fox, P.F. 1937- *WhoScE 91-3*
Fox, Patricia Ann 1942- *WhoAmW 93*
Fox, Patricia Tucker 1951- *WhoEmL 93*
Fox, Patrick Bernard 1948- *WhoEmL 93*
Fox, Paul G. 1949- *WhoE 93*
Fox, Paul J., Jr. 1952- *St&PR 93*
Fox, Paula *BioIn 17*
Fox, Paula 1923- *ChlFicS, DcAmChF 1960, DcAmChF 1985, MajAI [port], WhoAm 92*
Fox, Peter 1946- *ScF&FL 92*
Fox, Philip J. 1944- *St&PR 93*
Fox, R. Murdo *WhoWrEP 92*
Fox, Ralph W., II 1958- *WhoEmL 93*
Fox, Randolph A. *St&PR 93*
Fox, Raymond C. 1930- *St&PR 93*
Fox, Raymond F. 1942- *St&PR 93*
Fox, Raymond Graham 1923- *WhoSSW 93*
Fox, Reeder Rodman 1934- *WhoAm 92*
Fox, Renee Claire 1928- *WhoAm 92, WhoAmW 93*
Fox, Richard Allen 1954- *St&PR 93*
Fox, Richard Gabriel 1939- *WhoSSW 93*
Fox, Richard Keith 1938- *WhoE 93*
Fox, Richard Kenneth 1925- *WhoE 93*
Fox, Richard Kyle 1846-1922 *GayN*
Fox, Richard Paul 1962- *WhoWor 93*
Fox, Rick *BioIn 17*
Fox, Robert *WhoScE 91-1*
Fox, Robert 1945- *BioIn 17*
Fox, Robert A. 1937- *St&PR 93*
Fox, Robert Alan 1938- *WhoAm 92*
Fox, Robert August 1937- *WhoAm 92*
Fox, Robert Elliot 1944- *ScF&FL 92*
Fox, Robert J. 1927- *ConAu 40NR*
Fox, Robert J. 1928- *St&PR 93*
Fox, Robert Kriegbaum 1907- *WhoAm 92*
Fox, Robert R. 1943- *WhoWrEP 92*
Fox, Robert Trench 1937- *WhoWor 93*
Fox, Robert William 1934- *WhoAm 92*
Fox, Ronald Ernest 1936- *WhoAm 92*
Fox, Ronald Forrest 1943- *WhoAm 92*
Fox, Ronald Lee 1952- *WhoEmL 93, WhoWor 93*
Fox, Ronnie Ilaine 1943- *WhoSSW 93*
Fox, Roy W. 1920- *St&PR 93*
Fox, Ruth Ellen 1947- *WhoAmW 93*
Fox, Samuel 1905- *WhoAm 92*
Fox, Samuel Mickle, III 1923- *WhoAm 92*
Fox, Sharon S. *Law&B 92*
Fox, Sheila 1947- *WhoAm 92*
Fox, Sidney Walter 1912- *WhoAm 92*
Fox, Simone Martha 1961- *WhoEmL 93*
Fox, Stacy L. *Law&B 92*
Fox, Stanley Forrest 1946- *WhoSSW 93*
Fox, Stephen P. *Law&B 92*
Fox, Steven Alan 1953- *WhoWor 93*
Fox, Steven Phillip 1939- *St&PR 93*
Fox, Steven Thomas 1949- *WhoSSW 93*
Fox, Susan Christine 1943- *WhoWrEP 92*
Fox, Susan Rogan 1946- *WhoEmL 93*
Fox, Sylvan 1928- *WhoAm 92*
Fox, Talbert James *Law&B 92*
Fox, Terence J. 1938- *St&PR 93*
Fox, Terry Roy *Law&B 92*
Fox, Thomas Charles 1944- *WhoAm 92*
Fox, Thomas George 1942- *WhoAm 92*
Fox, Thomas John 1960- *WhoEmL 93*
Fox, Thomas Robert 1934- *WhoAm 92*
Fox, Thomas Walton 1923- *WhoAm 92*
Fox, Vernon Brittain 1916- *WhoAm 92, WhoWrEP 92*
Fox, Virgil (Keel) 1912-1980 *Baker 92*
Fox, W.N. *WhoScE 91-1*
Fox, W. Randolph *ScF&FL 92*
Fox, Wayne 1920- *St&PR 93*
Fox, Willard, III 1946- *WhoSSW 93*
Fox, William Joseph 1940- *St&PR 93*
Fox, William McNair 1924- *WhoSSW 93*
Fox, William Templeton 1932- *WhoAm 92*
Fox, William Waring 1968- *WhoEmL 93*
Fox-Biswell, Eileen Marie 1954- *WhoEmL 93*
Foxcroft, Kenneth B. 1944- *St&PR 93*
Foxen, Gene Louis 1936- *WhoAm 92, WhoWor 93*
Foxen, Lynne Anne 1950- *WhoEmL 93*
Foxen, Richard William 1927- *WhoAm 92*
Fox-Freund, Barbara Susan 1949- *WhoAmW 93*
Fox-Genovese, Elizabeth Ann 1941- *WhoAm 92, WhoSSW 93*
Foxhall, Irene Nene 1951- *WhoAmW 93*
Foxhall, Kathryn 1950- *WhoWrEP 92*
Fox-Hill, Emily Jean 1950- *WhoSSW 93*
Foxhoven, Michael John 1949- *WhoEmL 93*
Foxley, Alejandro 1939- *WhoAm 92*
Foxley, Griffith W. *Law&B 92*
Foxman, Abraham H. *WhoE 93*
Foxman, Bruce Mayer 1942- *WhoAm 92*
Foxman, Stephen Mark 1946- *WhoEmL 93*
Fox Strangways, A(rthur) H(enry) 1859-1948 *Baker 92*
Foxwell, Elizabeth Marie 1963- *WhoE 93*
Foxworth, Jo *WhoAm 92*
Foxworth, John Edwin, Jr. 1932- *WhoAm 92*
Foxworth, Robert Heath 1941- *WhoAm 92*

Foxx, Charlie 1939- & Foxx, Inez 1944- *SoulM*
Foxx, Inez 1944- See Foxx, Charlie 1939- & Foxx, Inez 1944- *SoulM*
Foxx, Jimmie 1907-1967 *BioIn 17*
Foxx, Redd *BioIn 17*
Foxx, Redd 1922-1991 *AnObit 1991, ConTFT 10, CurBio 92N, News 92*
Foy, Benny Earl 1948- *WhoWor 93*
Foy, Catherine Anthony 1957- *WhoWrEP 92*
Foy, Charles Daley 1923- *WhoAm 92, WhoE 93*
Foy, Denise Colleen 1960- *St&PR 93*
Foy, Edward A. 1917- *St&PR 93*
Foy, Gregory Alan 1954- *St&PR 93*
Foy, Herbert Miles, III 1945- *WhoSSW 93*
Foy, James Edward 1944- *St&PR 93*
Foy, Joe Hardeman 1926- *WhoAm 92*
Foy, John B. 1942- *St&PR 93*
Foy, Joseph C. 1937- *St&PR 93*
Foy, Louis Andre 1912- *WhoE 93*
Foy, Marguerite Elisabeth 1952- *WhoAmW 93*
Foy, Richard Daniel 1929- *St&PR 93*
Foy, Ricky Harold 1957- *WhoSSW 93*
Foye, Laurance Vincent, Jr. 1925- *WhoAm 92*
Foye, Patrick Joseph 1957- *WhoE 93*
Foye, Raymond 1957- *ScF&FL 92*
Foye, Thomas Harold 1930- *WhoAm 92*
Foyes, Betty J. 1926- *WhoE 93*
Foyt, A.J. *BioIn 17*
Foyt, Anthony Joseph, Jr. 1935- *WhoAm 92*
Foyt, Arthur George 1937- *WhoAm 92*
Fozard, John R. 1940- *WhoScE 91-2*
Fozard, John William 1928- *WhoAm 92*
Fozzati, Aldo 1950- *WhoEmL 93*
Fraad, Lewis M. 1907-1990 *BioIn 17*
Fraas, Arthur Paul 1915- *WhoSSW 93*
Fraas, Richard J. 1932- *St&PR 93*
Fraber, John W., III 1947- *St&PR 93*
Frabutt, Peter J. 1932- *St&PR 93*
Fracassi, Allen *St&PR 93*
Fracassi, Americo 1880-1936 *Baker 92*
Fracassi, Elmerico 1874-1930 *Baker 92*
Fracassi, Michael A. 1957- *WhoEmL 93*
Fraccaro, Marco 1926- *WhoScE 91-3*
Fracci, Carla 1936- *WhoWor 93*
Frachon, Benoit 1893-1975 *BioIn 17*
Frack, Joseph E. 1948- *WhoIns 93*
Frackenpohl, Arthur (Roland) 1924- *Baker 92*
Fracker, Robert Granger 1928- *WhoSSW 93, WhoWor 93*
Frackiewicz, Henryk 1929- *WhoScE 91-4*
Frackman, Noel 1930- *WhoAmW 93, WhoE 93*
Frackman, Richard Benoit 1923- *WhoAm 92*
Frackowiak, Milosz 1930- *WhoScE 91-4*
Frackowiak, Richard S.J. *WhoScE 91-1*
Frackt, Marvin Lee 1947- *WhoWor 93*
Frade, Peter Daniel 1946- *WhoAm 92*
Frade, Raymond *WhoScE 91-2*
Fradella, Frank John 1955- *WhoSSW 93*
Fradenburg, Ruth Olsen 1950- *WhoAmW 93*
Fradkin, David Milton 1931- *WhoAm 92*
Fradkin, Fredric 1892-1963 *Baker 92*
Fradkin, Howard Ross 1952- *WhoEmL 93*
Fradley, Frederick Macdonell 1924- *WhoAm 92*
Frady, Marshall Bolton 1940- *WhoWrEP 92*
Fraedrich, Klaus 1945- *WhoScE 91-3*
Fraedrich, Royal Louis 1931- *WhoAm 92*
Fraenkel, Dan Gabriel 1937- *WhoAm 92*
Fraenkel, Fred S. 1949- *St&PR 93*
Fraenkel, Fred Steven 1949- *WhoAm 92*
Fraenkel, George Kessler 1921- *WhoAm 92*
Fraenkel, Stephen Joseph 1917- *WhoAm 92*
Fraenkel, Wolfgang 1897-1983 *Baker 92*
Fraga, Jose Antonio Arbesu 1940- *BioIn 17*
Fragapane, Stephen A. 1949- *St&PR 93*
Frager, Albert S. 1922- *WhoAm 92*
Frager, Malcolm 1935-1991 *AnObit 1991, BioIn 17*
Frager, Malcolm (Monroe) 1935-1991 *Baker 92*
Frager, Marc Stephen 1949- *WhoEmL 93, WhoSSW 93*
Frager, Norman 1936- *WhoAm 92*
Fragiacomo, Giorgio 1938- *WhoWor 93*
Fragola, Anthony Nicholas 1943- *WhoWrEP 92*
Fragomen, Austin Thomas 1919- *WhoAm 92*
Fragu, P. 1941- *WhoScE 91-2*
Fragu, Philippe Michel 1941- *WhoWor 93*
Fraher, Jill Marie 1960- *WhoAmW 93*
Fraher, John P. 1942- *WhoScE 91-3*
Frahm, Donald R. 1932- *WhoIns 93*
Frahm, Donald Robert 1932- *WhoAm 92*
Frahm, Sheila 1945- *WhoAmW 93*
Fraiberg, Lawrence Phillip 1921- *St&PR 93, WhoAm 92, WhoE 93, WhoWor 93*
Fraiche, Donna DiMartino 1951- *WhoEmL 93*
Fraidin, Stephen 1939- *WhoAm 92, WhoWor 93*
Frail, Edward J. *ScF&FL 92*
Fraim, William L. 1951- *St&PR 93*
Fraiman, Genevieve Lam 1928- *WhoAm 92*
Frain, James Lee 1953- *WhoEmL 93*
Fraioli, Pamela Frances 1965- *WhoEmL 93*
Fraipont, Charles-Marie-Julien-Joseph de 1883-1946 *IntDcAn*
Fraipont, Julien 1857-1910 *IntDcAn*
Fraipont, Lucien 1933- *WhoScE 91-2*
Frair, Elizabeth Evans 1927- *WhoE 93*
Frair, Wayne Franklin 1926- *WhoWor 93*
Fraiser, Gerald P. 1943- *St&PR 93*
Frake, Charles Oliver 1930- *WhoAm 92*
Fraker, Beverley Jo 1938- *WhoSSW 93*
Fraker, William A. 1923- *BioIn 17, MiSFD 9, WhoAm 92*
Fraker, William Wootton 1949- *WhoSSW 93*
Frakes, Lawrence Austin 1930- *WhoWor 93*
Frakes, Lawrence Wright 1951- *WhoAm 92, WhoEmL 93, WhoSSW 93, WhoWor 93*
Frakes, Phillip E. 1929- *WhoIns 93*
Frakes, Randall *ScF&FL 92*
Frakes, Rod Vance 1930- *WhoAm 92*
Fraknoi, Andrew 1948- *WhoAm 92, WhoEmL 93*
Fraleigh, Donna Ellen 1956- *WhoAmW 93*
Fraleigh, John E. 1938- *St&PR 93*
Fraley, David Kennard 1952- *WhoSSW 93*
Fraley, Elwin Eugene 1934- *WhoAm 92*
Fraley, Frederick W., III *Law&B 92*
Fraley, Frederick William, III 1932- *St&PR 93*
Fraley, John L. 1920- *WhoSSW 93*
Fraley, Jonathan David, Jr. 1941- *WhoSSW 93*
Fraley, Lawrence R. *Law&B 92*
Fraley, Leonie Jeanne 1941- *WhoAmW 93*
Fraley, Mark Thomas 1952- *WhoEmL 93*
Fraley, Penny Kelly 1946- *WhoAmW 93*
Fraley, Russell Scott 1957- *WhoEmL 93*
Fralic, Bill *BioIn 17*
Fram, Frederick Gordon 1962- *WhoEmL 93, WhoSSW 93*
Fram, Sydney S. *Law&B 92*
Framberg, Norman Stokes 1934- *St&PR 93*
Frame, Anne Parsons 1904- *WhoAmW 93*
Frame, Clarence George 1918- *St&PR 93, WhoAm 92*
Frame, Donald Murdoch 1911-1991 *BioIn 17*
Frame, E. Bartram, Jr. 1944- *St&PR 93*
Frame, George D. 1936- *St&PR 93*
Frame, Helen Dunn 1939- *WhoSSW 93, WhoWrEP 92*
Frame, Janet *BioIn 17*
Frame, Janet 1924- *IntLitE, ScF&FL 92*
Frame, John *WhoScE 91-1*
Frame, John Timothy 1930- *WhoAm 92*
Frame, John Wands *WhoScE 91-1*
Frame, Paul 1913- *BioIn 17*
Frame, Raymond C. 1946- *WhoE 93*
Frame, Roger Everett *WhoSSW 93*
Frame, Russell William 1929- *WhoAm 92*
Frame, Virginia Woodson *AmWomPl*
Frame, William Douglas 1942- *St&PR 93*
Frame, William V. 1938- *St&PR 93*
Frame, William Verner 1938- *WhoAm 92*
Framery, Nicolas Etienne 1745-1810 *Baker 92*
Framme, Cynthia Clark 1955- *WhoAmW 93*
Framme, Lawrence Henry, III 1949- *WhoSSW 93*
Frampton, George Thomas 1917- *St&PR 93, WhoAm 92*
Frampton, George Thomas, Jr. 1944- *WhoAm 92, WhoE 93*
Frampton, Larry G. 1939- *St&PR 93*
Frampton, Paul Howard 1943- *WhoAm 92, WhoWor 93*
Frampton, Peter 1950- *WhoAm 92*
Frampton, Peter (Kenneth) 1950- *Baker 92*
Frampton, Walter Cobia 1948- *WhoEmL 93*
Framson, Joel 1947- *WhoEmL 93*
Fran, Paul E. d1991 *BioIn 17*
Franano, Susan Margaret Ketteman 1946- *WhoAm 92, WhoAmW 93*
Franca, Celia 1921- *WhoAm 92, WhoAmW 93*
Franca, Jose-Augusto 1922- *WhoWor 93*
Franca, Leopoldo Penna 1959- *WhoWor 93*
Francais, Ariel Patrice 1945- *WhoUN 92*
Francais, Jacques *BioIn 17*
Francaix, Jean 1912- *Baker 92, OxDcOp*
Francaviglia, Mauro 1953- *WhoWor 93*
Francaviglia, Vincenzo *WhoScE 91-3*
France, Anatole 1844-1924 *BioIn 17, DcLB 123 [port]*
France, Bill, Sr. *BioIn 17*
France, Bruce Eric, Sr. 1954- *WhoEmL 93*
France, Edward Augustine, Jr. 1937- *WhoAm 92*
France, Helen Way 1953- *St&PR 93*
France, Jacqueline Linda 1952- *WhoEmL 93*
France, James T. 1956- *St&PR 93*
France, John Naylor 1947- *WhoSSW 93*
France, Joseph David 1953- *WhoAm 92, WhoE 93*
France, Kenneth 1949- *WhoEmL 93*
France, Newell Edwin 1927- *WhoAm 92, WhoSSW 93*
France, Pierre Mendes- 1907-1982 *BioIn 17*
France, Richard E. 1926- *St&PR 93*
France, Richard William 1947- *WhoEmL 93, WhoSSW 93*
France, Richard Xavier 1938- *WhoAm 92*
France, William d1992 *NewYTBS 92*
France, William C. 1933- *St&PR 93*
Frances, Andrew Robert 1950- *WhoEmL 93*
Frances, Eddy 1940- *WhoSSW 93*
Frances, Helen *DcChlFi*
Frances, Stephen 1917-1989 *ScF&FL 92*
Francesa, Doris Tina 1927- *St&PR 93*
Francescatti, Zino 1902-1991 *BioIn 17*
Francescatti, Zino (Rene) 1902- *Baker 92*
Francesch, Homero 1947- *Baker 92*
Franceschelli, Christopher 1955- *St&PR 93*
Franceschi, Ernest Joseph, Jr. 1957- *WhoEmL 93*
Franceschina, John Charles 1947- *WhoEmL 93, WhoSSW 93*
Franceschini, Jose Inacio Gonzaga 1949- *WhoWor 93*
Franceschini, Marco Antonio 1648-1729 *BioIn 17*
Francesco, Anne Marie Carol-Theresa 1952- *WhoE 93*
Francesco, Susan G. 1954- *St&PR 93*
Francesconi, Gino *BioIn 17*
Franch, Richard Thomas 1942- *WhoAm 92*
Franchet d'Esperey, Louis Felix 1858-1942 *DcTwHis*
Franchet D'Esperey, Louis Felix Francois 1856-1942 *HarEnMi*
Franchet d'Esperey, Louis Felix Marie Francois 1856-1942 *BioIn 17*
Franchetti, Alberto 1860-1942 *Baker 92, OxDcOp*
Franchetti, Giorgio *BioIn 17*
Franchi, Giuseppe 1924- *WhoScE 91-3*
Franchi, Sergio d1990 *BioIn 17*
Franchimont, Paul 1934- *WhoScE 91-2*
Franchini, Gene Edward 1935- *WhoAm 92*
Franchini, Roxanne 1951- *WhoAmW 93, WhoEmL 93*
Franchi-Verney, Giuseppe Ippolito 1848-1911 *Baker 92*
Franchomme, Auguste (-Joseph) 1808-1884 *Baker 92*
Franchot, Yves *WhoScE 91-2*
Franci, Benvenuto 1891-1985 *Baker 92*
Franci, Carlo 1927- *Baker 92*
Franciosa, Anthony 1928- *WhoAm 92*
Francis, Albert John, II 1954- *WhoEmL 93*
Francis, Alexandria Stephanie 1952- *WhoAm 92, WhoEmL 93*
Francis, Arlene Jo-Ann *Law&B 92*
Francis, Arthur *WhoScE 91-1*
Francis, Arthur Stratton 1944- *WhoWor 93*
Francis, Arthur William *Law&B 92*
Francis, Betty Joe 1930- *WhoWrEP 92*
Francis, Bill Dean 1929- *WhoAm 92*
Francis, Bobby Marion d1991 *BioIn 17*
Francis, Brian Joseph *WhoScE 91-1*
Francis, Carolyn Rae 1940- *WhoAmW 93*
Francis, Celia *AmWomPl*
Francis, Charles Wesley, Jr. 1951- *WhoEmL 93*
Francis, Christopher Michael George *WhoScE 91-1*
Francis, Clyde Milton, Jr. 1925- *WhoSSW 93*
Francis, Cynthia Bentle 1956- *WhoAmW 93*
Francis, Cyril Lloyd 1920- *WhoAm 92*
Francis, Daniel Jerome 1955- *WhoSSW 93*
Francis, Darryl Robert 1912- *WhoAm 92*
Francis, David Anthony 1955- *WhoSSW 93*
Francis, David M. *Law&B 92*
Francis, David R. *Law&B 92*
Francis, David W. *Law&B 92*
Francis, Dennis P. 1943- *WhoIns 93*
Francis, Diana R. *Law&B 92*
Francis, Diane Marie 1946- *WhoAmW 93*
Francis, Dick *BioIn 17*
Francis, Dick 1920- *WhoAm 92*
Francis, Dorothy Brenner 1926- *ScF&FL 92*
Francis, Edward *WhoWrEP 92*
Francis, Elizabeth Adams 1923- *WhoAmW 93*
Francis, Elliot *BioIn 17*
Francis, Emile Percy 1926- *WhoAm 92*
Francis, Eulalie Marie *WhoAmW 93, WhoE 93, WhoWor 93*
Francis, Fitzgerald Andrew 1933- *WhoUN 92*
Francis, Frank J. 1948- *St&PR 93*
Francis, Freddie 1917- *BioIn 17, MiSFD 9, WhoAm 92*
Francis, Frederick John 1921- *WhoE 93*
Francis, Gail K. *ScF&FL 92*
Francis, Gerald Peter 1936- *WhoE 93*
Francis, Harry McDonald, Jr. 1933- *St&PR 93, WhoAm 92*
Francis, James Delbert 1947- *St&PR 93, WhoAm 92*
Francis, Jane Marshall 1961- *WhoE 93*
Francis, John Darrell 1904- *St&PR 93*
Francis, John Leslie *WhoScE 91-1*
Francis, Jon *BioIn 17*
Francis, Joseph A. *BioIn 17*
Francis, Karl *MiSFD 9*
Francis, Kathleen Crowley 1946- *WhoAmW 93*
Francis, Kay 1899?-1968 *IntDcF 2-3*
Francis, Lee, Mrs. 1926- *WhoE 93*
Francis, Marc Douglas *Law&B 92*
Francis, Marion David 1923- *WhoAm 92*
Francis, Merrill Richard 1932- *WhoAm 92*
Francis, Nadine Eraine *Law&B 92*
Francis, Nathaniel *DcCPCAm*
Francis, Norman Charles 1922- *WhoE 93*
Francis, Patricia Anne Shaud 1961- *WhoEmL 93*
Francis, Patricia Lynn 1952- *WhoE 93, WhoEmL 93*
Francis, Patricia Shaud *Law&B 92*
Francis, Paul Raymond 1959- *St&PR 93*
Francis, Paul Wilbur, Jr. 1929- *WhoE 93*
Francis, Philip H. 1938- *St&PR 93*
Francis, Philip Hamilton 1938- *WhoAm 92*
Francis, Philip S., Jr. 1941- *St&PR 93*
Francis, Richard *Law&B 92*
Francis, Richard 1945- *ScF&FL 92*
Francis, Richard Haudiomont 1925- *WhoAm 92*
Francis, Richard Herman 1932- *WhoAm 92*
Francis, Rodney J. *St&PR 93*
Francis, Sam 1923- *BioIn 17, WhoAm 92*
Francis, Samuel Todd 1947- *WhoAm 92*
Francis, Sheryl Ann 1957- *WhoAmW 93*
Francis, Spencer Lee 1943- *St&PR 93*
Francis, Steven Cabot 1954- *WhoEmL 93*
Francis, Sylvia Ann 1944- *WhoWor 93*
Francis, Theodore Ovil 1943- *WhoWrEP 92*
Francis, Timothy Duane 1956- *WhoEmL 93, WhoWor 93*
Francis, Virgil Walter, III 1938- *St&PR 93*
Francis, Walter Moser 1947- *WhoEmL 93*
Francis, William W. 1940- *St&PR 93*
Francis, Willie Brenard *WhoSSW 93*
Francisco, Don *BioIn 17*
Francisco, Edgar Wiggin, III 1930- *WhoSSW 93*
Francisco, James L. 1937- *WhoAm 92*
Francisco, Lawrence R. 1931- *St&PR 93*
Francisco, Louis J. 1930- *St&PR 93*
Francisco, Margaret Holmes *AmWomPl*
Francisco, Ronald Alan 1948- *WhoEmL 93*
Francisco, Sanchis Marco *WhoWor 93*
Franciscovich, George 1954- *WhoEmL 93*
Franciscus, James 1934-1991 *AnObit 1991, BioIn 17, ConTFT 10, News 92*
Francis Joseph 1830-1916 *DcTwHis*
Francis, of Assisi, Saint 1182-1226 *BioIn 17*
Francis-Vogelsang, Charee *Law&B 92*
Francis-Vogelsang, Charee 1946- *St&PR 93*
Franck, Aloyse J. P. 1953- *WhoWor 93*
Franck, Cesar 1822-1890 *BioIn 17, OxDcOp*
Franck, Cesar (-Auguste-Jean-Guillaume-Hubert) 1822-1890 *Baker 92*
Franck, Donald G. 1935- *St&PR 93*
Franck, Edouard *WhoWor 93*
Franck, Eduard 1817-1893 *Baker 92*
Franck, Frederick Sigfred 1909- *WhoAm 92*
Franck, Howard P. *Law&B 92*

Franck, Jean-Michel 1893?-1941 *BioIn 17*
Franck, Johann Wolfgang 1644?-c. 1710 *Baker 92, OxDcOp*
Franck, John M. 1953- *WhoAm 92*
Franck, Joseph 1825-1891 *Baker 92*
Franck, Melchior c. 1579-1639 *Baker 92*
Franck, Michael 1932- *WhoAm 92*
Franck, Richard 1858-1938 *Baker 92*
Franck, Stephen A. 1933- *WhoE 93*
Franck, Thomas Martin 1931- *WhoAm 92*
Franck, William Francis 1917- *St&PR 93, WhoAm 92*
Francke, Caroline *AmWomPl*
Francke, Gloria Niemeyer 1922- *WhoAm 92, WhoAmW 93*
Francke, Linda Bird *BioIn 17*
Francke, Linda Bird 1939- *WhoAm 92*
Francke, Michael *BioIn 17*
Francke, Uta 1942- *WhoAm 92*
Francke, William Bradford *Law&B 92*
Francken, Marc Emmanuel 1946- *WhoWor 93*
Franckenstein, Clemens von 1875-1942 *Baker 92*
Franckenstein, Clemens von und zu 1875-1942 *OxDcOp*
Francki, R. I. B. 1930-1990 *BioIn 17*
Franckle, Charles T. 1945- *St&PR 93*
Francklyn, Doris *AmWomPl*
Franck-Neumann, Michel 1939- *WhoScE 91-2*
Franco 1938-1989 *Baker 92*
Franco, Alain Andre 1944- *WhoScE 91-2*
Franco, Annemarie Woletz 1933- *WhoAmW 93*
Franco, Anthony M. 1933- *WhoAm 92*
Franco, Armando 1935- *St&PR 93*
Franco, Barbara Ann 1960- *St&PR 93*
Franco, Carole Ann 1948- *WhoE 93, WhoEmL 93*
Franco, Douglas Eugene 1948- *WhoEmL 93*
Franco, Ed d1992 *NewYTBS 92*
Franco, Edmund 1918- *BiDAMSp 1989*
Franco, Eloise 1910- *BioIn 17*
Franco, Francisco 1892-1975 *BioIn 17, DcTwHis*
Franco, Giuseppe *BioIn 17*
Franco, Harry 1932- *St&PR 93*
Franco, Howard 1952- *St&PR 93*
Franco, Itamar 1931- *WhoWor 93*
Franco, Itamar Augusto Cautiero 1930- *NewYTBS 92 [port]*
Franco, Johan 1908-1988 *BioIn 17*
Franco, Johan (Henri Gustav) 1908-1988 *Baker 92*
Franco, John 1960- *BioIn 17*
Franco, John Albert 1942- *St&PR 93*
Franco, John J. 1944- *St&PR 93*
Franco, Juan Roberto 1937- *WhoSSW 93*
Franco, Julio Cesar 1961- *WhoAm 92*
Franco, Kenneth Lawrence 1951- *WhoEmL 93*
Franco, Madeleine 1949- *WhoAmW 93*
Franco, Morris 1939- *St&PR 93*
Franco, Noel Bondoc 1950- *WhoWor 93*
Franco, Otto Edgar 1951- *WhoWor 93*
Franco, Raymond M. 1937- *St&PR 93*
Franco, Robert 1941- *WhoE 93, WhoUN 92*
Franco, Thomas S. *WhoIns 93*
Franco, Victor 1937- *WhoAm 92*
Franco, Walter David 1950- *WhoUN 92*
Franco-Bahamonde, Francisco Paulino Hermenegildo Teodulo 1892-1975 *HarEnMi*
Franco-Beato, Carlos Augusto 1949- *WhoSSW 93*
Franco-Bourland, Rebecca Elizabeth 1947- *WhoWor 93*
Franco de Coronado, Lila Isabel 1958- *WhoAmW 93*
Francoeur, Francois 1698-1787 *Baker 92*
Francoeur, Jacques G. 1925- *St&PR 93*
Francoeur, Louis-Joseph 1738-1804 *Baker 92*
Francoeur, Lucien 1948- *WhoCanL 92*
Francois, Christian Alexandre 1935- *WhoUN 92*
Francois, Dominique 1932- *WhoScE 91-2*
Francois, Etienne J.N.G. 1934- *WhoScE 91-2*
Francois, Francis Bernard 1934- *WhoAm 92, WhoE 93, WhoWor 93*
Francois, G.E. 1936- *WhoScE 91-2*
Francois, Gabriel Maxine 1926- *WhoWor 93*
Francois, Gregory 1946- *St&PR 93*
Francois, Jean Pierre 1943- *WhoScE 91-2*
Francois, Joseph Francis 1961- *WhoEmL 93*
Francois, Michael Brian 1950- *WhoEmL 93*
Francois, Samson 1924-1970 *Baker 92*
Francois, Theodore Noel 1932- *WhoUN 92*
Francois, William A. *Law&B 92*
Francois, William Armand 1942- *St&PR 93, WhoAm 92*
Francois, Yves Regis 1943- *ScF&FL 92*
Francoise 1863-1910 *BioIn 17*
Francoise, Anthony R. *Law&B 92*
Francois-Marsal, Frederic 1874-1958 *BioIn 17*
Francois-Poncet, Jean 1928- *BioIn 17*
Francois-Poncet, Jean Andre 1928- *WhoWor 93*
Francois-Smith, Susan Lynn 1965- *WhoAmW 93*
Francolini, Geno F. 1931- *St&PR 93*
Francomano, George 1933- *St&PR 93, WhoIns 93*
Francone, Carol A. *Law&B 92*
Franconi, C. 1929- *WhoScE 91-3*
Franco of Cologne *Baker 92*
Francos, Alexis 1949- *WhoEmL 93*
Franco Soler, J.M. *WhoScE 91-3*
Francotte, Pierre Louis 1956- *WhoUN 92*
Francovich, Carlo d1990 *BioIn 17*
Francula, Nedjeljko 1937- *WhoScE 91-4*
Franczek, Deborah C. *Law&B 92*
Franczek, James Clement, Jr. 1946- *WhoAm 92*
Frand, Jasper F. d1991 *BioIn 17*
Frandsen, John 1918- *Baker 92*
Frane, Jeff *ScF&FL 92*
Franek, Frantisek 1929- *WhoScE 91-4*
Franek, Jiri 1929- *WhoScE 91-4*
Franetovic, Vjekoslav 1946- *WhoWor 93*
Franey, Billie Nolan 1930- *WhoAmW 93*
Franey, John Thomas 1949- *St&PR 93*
Frang, Dezso 1932- *WhoScE 91-4*
Frangakis, Gerassimos P. 1940- *WhoWor 93*
Frangella, Luis *BioIn 17*
Franger, Robert Rich 1954- *WhoE 93*
Frangialli, Francisco 1947- *WhoUN 92*
Frangio, Juan Manuel *BioIn 17*
Frangipane, Joseph R. 1936- *St&PR 93*
Frangiskos, Antonis 1928- *WhoScE 91-3*
Frangopoulos, Victor Spiros 1935- *St&PR 93*
Frangopoulos, Zissimos A. 1944- *St&PR 93*
Frangos, Apostolos 1918- *WhoScE 91-3*
Frangos, Irene J. *Law&B 92*
Frangos, James George 1934- *WhoAm 92*
Frangos, James Mason 1947- *WhoE 93*
Franjieh, Suleiman 1910-1992 *NewYTBS 92 [port]*
Franjou, Marie-Helene 1946- *WhoWor 93*
Franju, Georges 1912-1987 *MiSFD 9N*
Frank, A. Peter *Law&B 92*
Frank, Adolf E. 1938- *WhoScE 91-4*
Frank, Agnes T. *WhoAmW 93*
Frank, Alan 1937- *ScF&FL 92*
Frank, Alan (Clifford) 1910- *Baker 92*
Frank, Alan I. W. 1932- *WhoWor 93*
Frank, Alfred *St&PR 93*
Frank, Allan Daniel 1930- *WhoE 93*
Frank, Alyce *BioIn 17*
Frank, Amalie Julianna 1933- *WhoAm 92*
Frank, Andre Gunder 1929- *BioIn 17*
Frank, Ann-Marie 1957- *WhoAmW 93*
Frank, Anne 1929-1945 *BioIn 17, WorLitC [port]*
Frank, Anthony M. *BioIn 17, CngDr 91*
Frank, Anthony M. c. 1931- *News 92 [port]*
Frank, Anthony Melchior 1931- *WhoAm 92*
Frank, Arthur 1934- *WhoE 93*
Frank, Arthur W. *BioIn 17*
Frank, Barbara *BioIn 17*
Frank, Barbara Ann 1939- *WhoAmW 93*
Frank, Barbara Hoffman *Law&B 92*
Frank, Barney *BioIn 17*
Frank, Barney 1940- *CngDr 91, WhoAm 92, WhoE 93*
Frank, Bena 1898-1991 *BioIn 17*
Frank, Bernard 1913- *WhoAm 92*
Frank, Bernard A. 1931- *St&PR 93*
Frank, Billy, Jr. *NewYTBS 92 [port]*
Frank, Bruce O. 1947- *WhoUN 92*
Frank, Bruno 1887-1945 *DcLB 118 [port]*
Frank, Carl John *Law&B 92*
Frank, Carol *MiSFD 9*
Frank, Celeste Mary 1949- *WhoE 93*
Frank, Charles Alexander 1948- *WhoEmL 93*
Frank, Charles Raphael, Jr. 1937- *WhoAm 92, WhoE 93*
Frank, Claude 1925- *Baker 92, BioIn 17*
Frank, Clint d1992 *NewYTBS 92*
Frank, Clinton Edward 1915- *WhoAm 92*
Frank, Courtenay *WhoWrEP 92*
Frank, Curtiss E. 1904-1990 *BioIn 17*
Frank, Cynthia Sue 1957- *WhoEmL 93*
Frank, Darlene 1946- *WhoWrEP 92*
Frank, David A. 1947- *St&PR 93*
Frank, David Thomas 1954- *WhoWor 93*
Frank, Dieter 1930- *WhoAm 92*
Frank, Edgar Gerald 1931- *WhoAm 92*
Frank, Ellen Joyce 1948- *WhoAmW 93*
Frank, Eric 1920- *St&PR 93*
Frank, Ernst 1847-1889 *Baker 92, OxDcOp*
Frank, Eugene Maxwell 1907- *WhoAm 92*
Frank, Evelyn Berman *BioIn 17*
Frank, F. Alexander 1916- *WhoAm 92*
Frank, Felicia Miller 1952- *WhoAmW 93*
Frank, Florence Kiper 1886?- *AmWomPl*
Frank, Frederick 1932- *St&PR 93, WhoAm 92, WhoE 93*
Frank, Frederick S. 1935- *ConAu 138, ScF&FL 92*
Frank, Geoffrey Edward 1955- *WhoEmL 93*
Frank, George A. *Law&B 92*
Frank, George C., Jr. 1936- *St&PR 93*
Frank, George Willard 1923- *WhoAm 92*
Frank, Gerald W. 1923- *St&PR 93*
Frank, Gerold 1907- *WhoAm 92, WhoWrEP 92*
Frank, H. Alan 1930- *St&PR 93*
Frank, Halbert 1922- *St&PR 93*
Frank, Hans 1900-1946 *BioIn 17*
Frank, Harold Roy 1924- *St&PR 93, WhoAm 92*
Frank, Harriet, Jr. *BioIn 17*
Frank, Hartmut Gottlieb 1943- *WhoWor 93*
Frank, Harvey 1944- *St&PR 93, WhoSSW 93*
Frank, Helmar Gunter 1933- *WhoScE 91-3, WhoWor 93*
Frank, Herbert Lawrence 1932- *WhoE 93*
Frank, Hilbourne 1932- *DcCPCAm*
Frank, Hilda Rhea Kaplan 1939- *WhoAm 92*
Frank, Howard *ScF&FL 92*
Frank, Howard 1941- *WhoAm 92*
Frank, Ilya 1908-1990 *BioIn 17*
Frank, Irwin Norman 1927- *WhoAm 92*
Frank, Isaiah 1917- *WhoAm 92*
Frank, J. Louis 1936- *WhoAm 92*
Frank, J. William, III *Law&B 92*
Frank, Jacob *Law&B 92*
Frank, Jacob 1936- *St&PR 93*
Frank, Jacqueline Denise 1951- *WhoAmW 93*
Frank, James A. *BioIn 17*
Frank, James Albert 1952- *WhoEmL 93*
Frank, James Henry 1940- *St&PR 93*
Frank, James Stuart 1945- *WhoAm 92*
Frank, Jean Brown *WhoAmW 93*
Frank, Jean-Michel 1893?-1941 *BioIn 17*
Frank, Jerome David 1909- *WhoAm 92, WhoE 93*
Frank, Jerome Jacques 1954- *WhoWor 93*
Frank, Jerome P. *BioIn 17*
Frank, Joan *BioIn 17*
Frank, Joe Lee, III 1947- *WhoE 93*
Frank, Joel I. 1956- *St&PR 93*
Frank, Joel Lawrence 1961- *WhoEmL 93*
Frank, John Nicholas 1953- *WhoEmL 93*
Frank, John Paul 1917- *WhoAm 92, WhoWrEP 92*
Frank, John R. 1955- *St&PR 93*
Frank, John Vincent d1991 *BioIn 17*
Frank, Joseph Nathaniel 1918- *WhoAm 92, WhoWrEP 92*
Frank, Josette 1893-1989 *BioIn 17*
Frank, Jozsef 1945- *WhoScE 91-4*
Frank, Julie Ann 1953- *WhoEmL 93*
Frank, Karen Denise 1956- *WhoEmL 93*
Frank, Katherine Marie 1952- *WhoEmL 93*
Frank, Kenneth L. 1917- *St&PR 93*
Frank, Laura Jean 1945- *WhoE 93*
Frank, Laurie 1954- *WhoEmL 93*
Frank, Leo *BioIn 17*
Frank, Leonard *ConAu 139*
Frank, Leonhard 1882-1961 *DcLB 118 [port]*
Frank, Lloyd *Law&B 92*
Frank, Lloyd 1925- *St&PR 93, WhoAm 92, WhoE 93*
Frank, Lynda Arlene 1951- *WhoAmW 93*
Frank, M. Kennith, III *Law&B 92*
Frank, Margaret Lois 1960- *WhoAmW 93*
Frank, Margaret M. *Law&B 92*
Frank, Marshall E. 1939- *WhoAm 92*
Frank, Martin 1947- *WhoAm 92*
Frank, Martin Harold 1941- *St&PR 93*
Frank, Marvin Ronald *Law&B 92*
Frank, Mary 1933- *BioIn 17, WhoAm 92*
Frank, Mary Lou 1915- *WhoAmW 93*
Frank, Mary Lou 1952- *WhoAmW 93*
Frank, Maude Morrison 1870- *AmWomPl*
Frank, Melvin 1913-1988 *MiSFD 9N*
Frank, Melvin S. 1925- *St&PR 93*
Frank, Michael B. *Law&B 92*
Frank, Michael Ian 1960- *WhoEmL 93*
Frank, Michael John 1943- *WhoWor 93*
Frank, Michael M. 1937- *WhoAm 92*
Frank, Michael S. *St&PR 93*
Frank, Michael Victor 1947- *WhoEmL 93*
Frank, Michael William 1947- *WhoEmL 93*
Frank, Milton 1919- *WhoAm 92*
Frank, Miriam J. *Law&B 92*
Frank, Mitchell A. *Law&B 92*
Frank, Nancy Gillen 1943- *WhoAmW 93*
Frank, Natalie Susan 1963- *WhoAmW 93*
Frank, Niklas 1939- *BioIn 17*
Frank, Norman 1928- *BioIn 17*
Frank, Ove A. 1937- *WhoScE 91-4*
Frank, Pamela 1967- *BioIn 17*
Frank, Pat 1907-1964 *BioIn 17*
Frank, Patricia *BioIn 17*
Frank, Paul D. 1949- *St&PR 93*
Frank, Paul M. *Law&B 92*
Frank, Paul Martin 1934- *WhoScE 91-3*
Frank, Paul Michael 1941- *St&PR 93*
Frank, Paula Feldman *WhoAmW 93*
Frank, Peter Solomon 1950- *WhoAm 92, WhoWrEP 92*
Frank, Renee Sisson 1949- *WhoSSW 93*
Frank, Reuven 1920- *WhoWrEP 92*
Frank, Richard Allan 1943- *WhoE 93*
Frank, Richard Calhoun 1930- *WhoAm 92*
Frank, Richard H. *St&PR 93*
Frank, Richard Horton, Jr. 1928- *WhoSSW 93*
Frank, Richard Lynn 1945- *St&PR 93*
Frank, Richard M. 1948- *WhoAm 92*
Frank, Richard Sanford 1931- *WhoAm 92*
Frank, Robert 1924- *MiSFD 9*
Frank, Robert Allen 1932- *WhoAm 92, WhoE 93, WhoWor 93*
Frank, Robert Allen 1950- *WhoEmL 93*
Frank, Robert E. 1949- *St&PR 93*
Frank, Robert George 1952- *WhoEmL 93*
Frank, Robert Joseph 1939- *WhoWrEP 92*
Frank, Robert Louis 1958- *WhoEmL 93*
Frank, Robert Steven 1954- *WhoE 93*
Frank, Robert Worth, Jr. 1914- *WhoAm 92*
Frank, Ronald Edward 1933- *WhoAm 92, WhoSSW 93*
Frank, Ronald W. 1947- *WhoEmL 93, WhoWor 93*
Frank, Ruby Merinda 1920- *WhoAmW 93*
Frank, Ruth Crawford 1918- *WhoAmW 93*
Frank, Sam Hager 1932- *WhoAm 92, WhoE 93*
Frank, Sanders Thalheimer 1938- *WhoAm 92, WhoWor 93*
Frank, Sandra Kaye 1941- *WhoAmW 93*
Frank, Sarah *BioIn 17*
Frank, Stacy C. *Law&B 92*
Frank, Stanley Donald 1932- *WhoAm 92*
Frank, Steven Neil 1947- *WhoWor 93*
Frank, Stuart 1934- *WhoAm 92*
Frank, Susan Marie 1949- *WhoAmW 93*
Frank, T. C. *ConAu 138*
Frank, Terri J. *Law&B 92*
Frank, Terri Joy 1957- *WhoEmL 93*
Frank, Thaisa 1943- *WhoWrEP 92*
Frank, Thomas Paul 1956- *St&PR 93*
Frank, Thomas W. d1992 *NewYTBS 92*
Frank, Tracy Steven Scott 1965- *WhoWrEP 92*
Frank, Victor H., Jr. 1927- *St&PR 93, WhoWor 93*
Frank, Waldo 1889-1967 *JeAmFiW*
Frank, Wally 1910- *St&PR 93*
Frank, Walter M. *Law&B 92*
Frank, Werner Karl Otto 1926- *WhoScE 91-3*
Frank, Werner L. 1929- *St&PR 93*
Frank, William Charles 1940- *WhoAm 92*
Frank, William Edward, Jr. 1943- *WhoSSW 93*
Frank, William Fielding 1944- *WhoAm 92, WhoE 93, WhoWor 93*
Frank, William H. 1943- *St&PR 93*
Frank, William Pendleton 1941- *WhoSSW 93*
Franke, Ann Harriet 1952- *WhoE 93*
Franke, Brent Douglas 1949- *WhoEmL 93*
Franke, Cecelia Marie 1936- *WhoSSW 93*
Franke, Charles Henry 1933- *WhoAm 92, WhoSSW 93*
Franke, D. *WhoScE 91-3*
Franke, Eileen Diane 1956- *WhoEmL 93*
Franke, Frederick Rahde 1918- *WhoAm 92*
Franke, Gunther 1930- *WhoWor 93*
Franke, Kenneth A., Jr. 1958- *St&PR 93*
Franke, Linda Frederick 1947- *WhoEmL 93*
Franke, Maripat Kemps 1960- *WhoAmW 93*
Franke, Michael Wolfgang 1948- *St&PR 93, WhoEmL 93*
Franke, Paul-Gerhard 1918- *WhoScE 91-3*
Franke, Paul W. 1929- *St&PR 93*
Franke, R.J. 1930- *St&PR 93*
Franke, Richard J. 1931- *St&PR 93*
Franke, Richard James 1931- *WhoAm 92*
Franke, S. Wolfgang 1921- *WhoScE 91-3*
Franke, Tammi K. *Law&B 92*
Franke, Thomas E., Sr. 1961- *St&PR 93*
Franke, Wayne Thomas 1950- *WhoEmL 93*
Franke, Werner Wilhelm 1940- *WhoScE 91-3*

Franke, William Augustus 1937- St&PR 93, WhoAm 92
Frankel, Alona BioIn 17
Frankel, Andrew J. 1932- St&PR 93
Frankel, Andrew Vance 1957- WhoE 93, WhoEmL 93
Frankel, Arnold J. 1922- WhoAm 92
Frankel, Arthur 1928- WhoAm 92
Frankel, Benjamin 1906-1973 Baker 92
Frankel, Benjamin Harrison 1930- WhoAm 92
Frankel, Bernard 1929- St&PR 93
Frankel, Candie 1953- WhoWrEP 92
Frankel, David 1922- WhoScE 91-4
Frankel, Dean A. Law&B 92
Frankel, Dean Alan 1957- WhoEmL 93
Frankel, Donald Leon 1931- WhoAm 92
Frankel, Edward M. 1954- St&PR 93
Frankel, Edward Michael Law&B 92
Frankel, Eliot d1990 BioIn 17
Frankel, Ellen 1938- ScF&FL 92, WhoAm 92, WhoWrEP 92
Frankel, Ephraim J. d1991 BioIn 17
Frankel, Eric Howard 1948- WhoSSW 93
Frankel, Ernest David 1924- St&PR 93
Frankel, Ernst Gabriel 1923- WhoAm 92
Frankel, Evan M. d1991 BioIn 17
Frankel, Francine Ruth 1935- WhoAm 92
Frankel, Gene 1923- WhoAm 92
Frankel, Glenn 1949- WhoAm 92, WhoE 93
Frankel, Helen Bruce 1925- WhoAmW 93
Frankel, Herbert A. 1925- St&PR 93
Frankel, J. Joseph Law&B 92
Frankel, Jeffrey A.H. Law&B 92
Frankel, Jeffrey Alexander 1952- WhoAm 92
Frankel, Jeffrey Scott 1962- WhoSSW 93
Frankel, Judith Jennifer Mariasha 1947- WhoAmW 93, WhoEmL 93
Frankel, Judith Leibholz 1961- WhoE 93
Frankel, Kenneth Mark 1940- WhoE 93, WhoWor 93
Frankel, Lawrence Stephen 1941- WhoE 93
Frankel, Martin Richard 1943- WhoAm 92, WhoE 93
Frankel, Marvin 1924- WhoAm 92
Frankel, Marvin E. 1920- WhoAm 92
Frankel, Max 1930- JrnUS, WhoAm 92, WhoE 93, WhoWrEP 92
Frankel, Michael Henry 1939- WhoAm 92
Frankel, Michael S. 1946- WhoAm 92
Frankel, Morton Sedley 1924- St&PR 93
Frankel, Nancy Jean 1953- St&PR 93
Frankel, Otto Herzberg 1900- WhoWor 93
Frankel, Richard BioIn 17
Frankel, Russell E. 1943- St&PR 93
Frankel, Ruth Leah 1957- WhoAmW 93
Frankel, S. Lee, Jr. 1948- WhoE 93
Frankel, Sandor 1943- WhoAm 92
Frankel, Saul Jacob 1917- WhoAm 92
Frankel, Sherman 1922- WhoAm 92
Frankel, Stanley Arthur 1918- WhoAm 92
Frankel, Stephen W. St&PR 93
Frankel, Steven Richard Law&B 92
Frankel, Valerie 1965- ConAu 138
Frankel, Victor Hirsch 1925- WhoAm 92
Frankel, William Harry 1955- WhoEmL 93
Franke-Mateer, June M. 1962- St&PR 93
Franken, A.A.J.M. 1959- WhoScE 91-3
Franken, Darrell 1930- WhoWrEP 92
Franken, Edmund Anthony, Jr. 1936- WhoAm 92
Franken, Thomas Joseph 1955- WhoSSW 93
Frankena, Frederick 1948- WhoEmL 93
Frankenberg, Robert Edward 1944- WhoE 93
Frankenberg, Robert Johann 1947- St&PR 93
Frankenberger, Bertram, Jr. 1933- WhoAm 92
Frankenhaeuser, Marianne 1925- WhoWor 93
Frankenheim, Samuel 1932- WhoAm 92
Frankenheimer, John 1930- MiSFD 9
Frankenheimer, John Michael 1930- WhoAm 92
Frankenhoff, William P. 1925- St&PR 93
Frankenstein, Alfred (Victor) 1906-1981 Baker 92
Frankenstein, George, IV 1935- St&PR 93
Frankenthaler, Helen 1928- WhoAm 92, WhoAmW 93
Franker, Stephen Grant 1949- WhoEmL 93
Frankfort, Howard Mark 1952- WhoE 93
Frankforter, Albertus Daniel 1939- WhoE 93
Frankforter, Weldon DeLoss 1920- WhoAm 92
Frankfurter, Felix 1882-1965 BioIn 17, JeAmHC, OxCSupC [port]
Frankfurter, Jack 1929- WhoWor 93
Frankhouser, David E. Law&B 92
Frankhouser, Homer Sheldon, Jr. 1927- WhoSSW 93, WhoWor 93
Frankhouser, Nancy L. 1935- St&PR 93
Frankiewicz, Marcia Jean 1947- WhoAmW 93, WhoEmL 93
Frankl, Daniel Richard 1922- WhoAm 92, WhoE 93
Frankl, Karl H. 1933- St&PR 93
Frankl, Kenneth Richard 1924- WhoAm 92
Frankl, Peter 1935- Baker 92
Frankl, Razelle WhoE 93
Frankl, Spencer Nelson 1933- WhoAm 92
Frankl, Steven Kenneth 1944- WhoAm 92
Frankl, Viktor E. 1905- WhoAm 92
Frankl, William Stewart 1928- WhoAm 92, WhoE 93, WhoWor 93
Frankland, Juliet Camilla WhoScE 91-1
Frankle, Edward Alan 1946- WhoEmL 93
Frankle, Jerome H., Jr. 1928- St&PR 93
Frankle, Judith ScF&FL 92
Franklin, Alan Douglas 1922- WhoE 93
Franklin, Allan Ray 1945- WhoSSW 93
Franklin, Aretha BioIn 17
Franklin, Aretha 1942- AfrAmBi, Baker 92, CurBio 92 [port], SoulM, WhoAm 92, WhoAmW 93
Franklin, Barbara Hackman BioIn 17
Franklin, Barbara Hackman 1940- WhoAm 92, WhoAmW 93, WhoE 93
Franklin, Ben T., Jr. 1944- St&PR 93
Franklin, Benjamin 1706-1790 Baker 92, BioIn 17, JrnUS, MagSAmL [port]
Franklin, Benjamin, V 1939- ConAu 39NR, WhoSSW 93
Franklin, Benjamin Barnum 1944- WhoWor 93
Franklin, Billy Joe 1940- WhoAm 92, WhoSSW 93
Franklin, Bonnie Gail 1944- WhoAm 92
Franklin, Carl MiSFD 9
Franklin, Carleen Lois Hollenbeck 1933- WhoAmW 93
Franklin, Carol Bertha 1947- WhoEmL 93
Franklin, Carolyn 1945-1988 SoulM
Franklin, Cassandra Small 1956- WhoEmL 93
Franklin, Cecil BioIn 17
Franklin, Charles E. 1938- WhoAm 92
Franklin, Charles Scothern 1937- WhoAm 92
Franklin, Cheryl J. 1955- ConAu 138, ScF&FL 92, SmATA 70 [port]
Franklin, Christine C. Law&B 92
Franklin, Christine Ladd- 1847-1930 BioIn 17
Franklin, Churchill Gibson 1948- WhoE 93, WhoEmL 93
Franklin, Cornell Law&B 92
Franklin, Dale Helaine 1940- WhoAmW 93
Franklin, Daniel 1951- WhoAm 92
Franklin, David 1908-1973 OxDcOp
Franklin, David Jansen 1951- WhoEmL 93
Franklin, Dawson Cleveland, Jr. 1922- St&PR 93
Franklin, Donald Evan 1962- St&PR 93, WhoE 93
Franklin, E. Thomas, Jr. 1944- St&PR 93
Franklin, Earl R. Law&B 92
Franklin, Earl Robert 1943- St&PR 93
Franklin, Edward Ward 1926- WhoAm 92
Franklin, Eileen BioIn 17
Franklin, Elaine M. Law&B 92
Franklin, Erma SoulM
Franklin, Frederick Russell 1929- WhoAm 92, WhoWor 93
Franklin, G. Charles 1935- WhoAm 92
Franklin, Gene Farthing 1927- WhoAm 92
Franklin, George BioIn 17
Franklin, George Charles 1935- WhoSSW 93
Franklin, George S. 1913- WhoWor 93
Franklin, Gloria Friedman d1992 BioIn 17, NewYTBS 92 [port]
Franklin, H. Allen 1945- WhoAm 92
Franklin, H. Bruce 1934- ScF&FL 92
Franklin, Hardy R. 1929- WhoAm 92, WhoE 93
Franklin, Harriet Lewis 1938- WhoAmW 93
Franklin, Herbert Mendell 1933- WhoE 93
Franklin, Howard MiSFD 9
Franklin, Howard B. 1920- St&PR 93
Franklin, J. Manning WhoWrEP 92
Franklin, Jack Lee 1931- WhoSSW 93
Franklin, James 1697-1735 JrnUS
Franklin, James E. 1943- St&PR 93
Franklin, James M. 1943- St&PR 93
Franklin, James Nathan 1949- St&PR 93
Franklin, James Robert 1951- WhoAm 92
Franklin, Jeffrey Alan 1964- WhoE 93
Franklin, Jesse 1760-1823 PolPar
Franklin, Joel Nicholas 1930- WhoAm 92
Franklin, John 1786-1847 BioIn 17, Expl 93 [port]
Franklin, John Hope 1915- BioIn 17, EncAACR, WhoAm 92, WhoWrEP 92
Franklin, Jon Daniel 1942- WhoAm 92
Franklin, Joseph Earl 1953- WhoEmL 93, WhoSSW 93
Franklin, Jude Eric 1943- WhoAm 92
Franklin, Julian Harold 1925- WhoAm 92
Franklin, K.D. ScF&FL 92
Franklin, Karen Spiegel 1954- WhoE 93
Franklin, Kathleen Anna 1957- WhoAmW 93
Franklin, Kenneth Linn 1923- WhoAm 92
Franklin, Kenneth William 1952- WhoE 93
Franklin, Kerry ConAu 136, WhoWrEP 92
Franklin, Larry Brock 1951- WhoSSW 93
Franklin, Larry Daniel 1942- St&PR 93, WhoAm 92
Franklin, Laura Huey 1926- WhoAmW 93
Franklin, Leeann T. 1958- St&PR 93
Franklin, Lewis G. 1950- St&PR 93
Franklin, Linda Lawrence 1950- WhoE 93, WhoEmL 93
Franklin, Madeleine ScF&FL 92
Franklin, Malcolm G. Law&B 92
Franklin, Marc Adam 1932- WhoAm 92
Franklin, Margaret Lavona Barnum 1905- WhoAmW 93, WhoWor 93
Franklin, Margery Bodansky 1933- WhoAm 92
Franklin, Martha Carolyn 1931- WhoAmW 93
Franklin, Max 1915-1983 ScF&FL 92
Franklin, Michael ScF&FL 92
Franklin, Michael Harold 1923- WhoAm 92
Franklin, Miriam Anna 1894- WhoWrEP 92
Franklin, Murray Joseph 1922- WhoAm 92
Franklin, Pat ScF&FL 92
Franklin, Pearl c. 1888- AmWomPl
Franklin, Phyllis 1932- WhoAm 92
Franklin, Ralph Earl, Jr. 1934- WhoSSW 93
Franklin, Ralph William 1937- WhoAm 92
Franklin, Raymond Jay 1924- WhoSSW 93
Franklin, Richard 1948- ConTFT 10, MiSFD 9
Franklin, Richard A. 1945- WhoScE 91-1
Franklin, Richard C. 1948- St&PR 93
Franklin, Richard M. 1930- WhoScE 91-4
Franklin, Richard Mark 1947- WhoEmL 93
Franklin, Richard Walter, Jr. 1955- WhoEmL 93
Franklin, Robert Brewer 1937- WhoAm 92
Franklin, Robert Charles 1936- St&PR 93
Franklin, Robert Drury 1935- St&PR 93, WhoSSW 93, WhoWor 93
Franklin, Robert J. 1928- St&PR 93
Franklin, Robert McFarland 1943- WhoSSW 93, WhoWrEP 92
Franklin, Roger Edwin, Jr. 1949- WhoEmL 93
Franklin, Rogers WhoWrEP 92
Franklin, Ronald Dewane 1953- WhoEmL 93
Franklin, Samuel Gregg 1946- WhoEmL 93
Franklin, Sheryl Renee Law&B 92
Franklin, Shirley Clarke 1945- AfrAmBi [port]
Franklin, Sidney 1893-1972 MiSFD 9N
Franklin, Stanley Phillip 1931- WhoAm 92
Franklin, Stephen 1922- ScF&FL 92
Franklin, Sylvan L. 1934- St&PR 93
Franklin, Thomas Chester 1923- WhoSSW 93
Franklin, Victor A. Law&B 92
Franklin, Victoria Thompson 1951- St&PR 93
Franklin, Wallace G. 1926- St&PR 93
Franklin, Walt 1950- WhoWrEP 92
Franklin, Warren WhoAm 92
Franklin, William 1731-1813 BioIn 17
Franklin, William Emery 1933- WhoAm 92
Franklin, William P. 1933- St&PR 93
Franklin, William P. 1953- WhoEmL 93
Franklin Family BioIn 17
Franko, Bernard Vincent 1922- WhoAm 92
Franko, Nahan 1861-1930 Baker 92
Franko, Sam 1857-1937 Baker 92
Frankovich, George Law&B 92
Frankovich, George Richard 1920- WhoAm 92
Frankovich, Mike d1992 NewYTBS 92
Frankovich, Mike 1910-1992 BioIn 17
Frankovich, Thomas Bernard 1951- WhoEmL 93
Frankowiak, James Raymond 1946- WhoAm 92, WhoSSW 93
Frankowski, Eugeniusz 1884-1962 IntDcAn
Frankowski, Leo 1943- ScF&FL 92
Franks, Charles Leslie 1934- WhoAm 92
Franks, Christopher R. 1937- WhoScE 91-2
Franks, Christopher Ralph 1937- WhoScE 91-3
Franks, Cyril Maurice 1923- WhoE 93
Franks, David A. 1929- WhoE 93
Franks, Donald J. 1950- St&PR 93
Franks, Gary BioIn 17
Franks, Gary A. 1953- CngDr 91
Franks, Gary Alvin 1953- WhoAm 92, WhoE 93
Franks, George Vincent 1963- WhoE 93
Franks, Harry Edward 1906- WhoSSW 93
Franks, Hollis Berry 1916- WhoSSW 93
Franks, J. Robert 1937- WhoAm 92
Franks, James WhoScE 91-1
Franks, James Byron 1949- WhoEmL 93
Franks, Lawrence Albert 1933- St&PR 93
Franks, Lennis Earl 1961- WhoSSW 93
Franks, Leonard M. 1921- WhoScE 91-1
Franks, Lewis E. 1931- WhoAm 92
Franks, Lucinda BioIn 17
Franks, Lucinda Laura 1946- WhoAm 92
Franks, Martin Davis 1950- BioIn 17, WhoE 93
Franks, Michael BioIn 17
Franks, Oliver Shewell 1905- DcTwHis
Franks, Oliver Shewell 1905-1992 NewYTBS 92 [port]
Franks, Philip J. Law&B 92
Franks, Richard M. 1945- St&PR 93
Franks, Robert A. Law&B 92
Franks, Ronald Dwyer 1946- WhoAm 92
Franks, Stephen WhoScE 91-1
Franks, Stephen G. 1950- WhoIns 93
Franks, Thomas Matthew 1954- WhoEmL 93
Franks, Violet 1926- WhoAmW 93
Frankson, Harry Lawrence 1942- St&PR 93
Frankson-Kendrick, Sarah Jane 1949- WhoAmW 93
Frankstone, Edward R. 1922- St&PR 93
Frankum, James Edward 1921- WhoAm 92
Frankum, Julie Margaret 1960- WhoWor 93
Frano, Andrew Joseph 1953- WhoEmL 93, WhoWor 93
Frans, W. Douglas 1950- St&PR 93
Fransen, Christine Irene 1947- WhoEmL 93
Fransen, Jan 1933- WhoUN 92
Fransman, Martin Jacques WhoScE 91-1
Franson, Carole Marie 1961- WhoAmW 93
Franson, Donald 1916- ScF&FL 92
Franson, Donald R., Jr. 1952- St&PR 93
Franson, Fredrik 1852-1908 BioIn 17
Franson, Marc Paul 1955- WhoEmL 93
Franson, Paul Oscar, III 1941- WhoAm 92
Franson, Robert Wilfred 1946- ScF&FL 92
Franta, Rosalyn 1951- St&PR 93
Franta, William Roy 1942- WhoAm 92
Frantum, Albert W., Jr. 1947- St&PR 93
Frantz, Andrew Gibson 1930- WhoAm 92
Frantz, Cecilia Aranda 1941- WhoSSW 93
Frantz, Charles 1925- WhoAm 92
Frantz, Edward J. Law&B 92
Frantz, Ferdinand 1906-1959 Baker 92, OxDcOp
Frantz, Francis X. 1953- St&PR 93
Frantz, Gerald J. 1938- St&PR 93
Frantz, Gilda Gloria 1926- WhoAmW 93
Frantz, Jack T. 1939- St&PR 93
Frantz, Jack Thomas 1939- WhoAm 92
Frantz, James J. Law&B 92
Frantz, John C. 1953- St&PR 93
Frantz, John Corydon 1926- WhoAm 92
Frantz, Justus 1944- Baker 92
Frantz, Leroy, Jr. 1927- St&PR 93
Frantz, Paul Lewis 1955- WhoEmL 93
Frantz, Ray William, Jr. 1923- WhoAm 92
Frantz, Robert Lewis 1925- WhoAm 92
Frantz, Robert W. Law&B 92
Frantz, Robert Wesley 1950- WhoEmL 93
Frantz, Roger C. 1937- St&PR 93
Frantz, Rosebud Yellow Robe d1992 NewYTBS 92
Frantz, Welby Marion 1912- WhoAm 92
Frantze, David W. 1955- WhoEmL 93
Frantzen, Henry Arthur 1942- St&PR 93, WhoAm 92
Frantzis, Charalampos 1928- WhoScE 91-3
Frantzve, Jerri Lyn 1942- WhoAmW 93, WhoSSW 93
Franz, Angela BioIn 17
Franz, Arthur 1920- BioIn 17
Franz, Daniel Thomas 1949- WhoEmL 93
Franz, Donald Eugene, Jr. 1944- WhoAm 92, WhoE 93
Franz, Frank Andrew 1937- WhoAm 92, WhoSSW 93

Franz, Frederick W. d1992 *NewYTBS 92 [port]*
Franz, Frederick William 1893- *WhoAm 92, WhoE 93*
Franz, Gerhard 1937- *WhoScE 91-3*
Franz, Jeffrey Brian 1947- *WhoWrEP 92*
Franz, Jennifer Danton 1949- *WhoEmL 93*
Franz, John E. 1929- *BioIn 17, WhoAm 92*
Franz, John H. 1928- *St&PR 93*
Franz, Judy R. *BioIn 17*
Franz, Kyleen D. *Law&B 92*
Franz, Lydia Millicent Truc 1924- *WhoAmW 93*
Franz, Marie-Luise von 1915- *ScF&FL 92*
Franz, Mike *BioIn 17*
Franz, Paul 1876-1950 *Baker 92*
Franz, Paul Allen *Law&B 92*
Franz, Richard B. 1950- *St&PR 93*
Franz, Robert 1815-1892 *Baker 92*
Franz, Robert W. 1924- *St&PR 93*
Franz, Robert Warren 1924- *WhoAm 92*
Franz, Roger Lee 1949- *WhoEmL 93*
Franz, Wendy Leigh *WhoAmW 93*
Franzblau, Carl 1934- *WhoAm 92*
Franzblau, Deborah Sharon 1957- *WhoEmL 93*
Franze, Anthony J. *Law&B 92*
Franzen, Ake Sigurd 1925- *WhoScE 91-4*
Franzen, Charles Rice 1957- *WhoWor 93*
Franzen, Ferdinand Ludwig 1929- *WhoUN 92*
Franzen, Janice Marguerite Gosnell 1921- *WhoAm 92*
Franzen, Jonathan *BioIn 17*
Franzen, Richard B. 1946- *WhoWrEP 92*
Franzen, Stephen Edwards 1953- *WhoEmL 93*
Franzen, Therese Glisson *Law&B 92*
Franzen, Ulrich J. 1921- *WhoAm 92*
Franzese, Bruce J. *Law&B 92*
Franzese, Bruce Joseph 1947- *St&PR 93*
Franzetti, Carlos Alberto 1948- *WhoE 93*
Franzetti, Joseph 1955- *St&PR 93*
Franzetti, Tony Raymond 1950- *WhoEmL 93*
Franzitta, Guglielmo *WhoScE 91-3*
Franz Josef, II, Prince of Liechtenstein 1906-1989 *BioIn 17*
Franzke, Allan 1930- *WhoAm 92*
Franzke, Hans-Hermann 1927- *WhoWor 93*
Franzke, Richard Albert 1935- *WhoAm 92*
Franzkowski, Rainer 1935- *WhoWor 93*
Franzl, Ferdinand (Ignaz Joseph) 1767-1833 *Baker 92*
Franzl, Ignaz (Franz Joseph) 1736-1811 *Baker 92*
Franzman, A. Daniel 1934- *St&PR 93*
Franzman, Thomas R. *BioIn 17*
Franzmann, Albert Wilhelm 1930- *WhoAm 92*
Franzmeier, Donald Paul 1935- *WhoAm 92*
Franzone, Andrew L. 1937- *St&PR 93*
Franzos, Karl Emil 1848-1904 *BioIn 17*
Franzosi, Mario Enrico 1934- *WhoWor 93*
Frappaolo, Carl Joseph 1956- *WhoE 93*
Frappia, Linda Ann 1946- *WhoAmW 93, WhoEmL 93*
Frappier, Gilles 1931- *WhoAm 92*
Frappier, Thomas F. 1933- *St&PR 93*
Frary, Richard Spencer 1924- *WhoAm 92*
Frary, Richard Spencer, Sr. 1924- *St&PR 93*
Frasca, Armond C. d1991 *BioIn 17*
Frasca, Robert 1933- *St&PR 93*
Frascarelli, Sergio 1939- *WhoWor 93*
Frascati, J. Michael *Law&B 92*
Frasch, Brian Bernard 1956- *WhoEmL 93*
Frasch, David E. *Law&B 92*
Frasch, David E. 1947- *St&PR 93*
Frasch, David Edward 1947- *WhoAm 92*
Fraschilla, Ceaser 1936- *St&PR 93*
Fraschini, Gaetano 1816-1887 *Baker 92, OxDcOp*
Frascino, Edward *ConAu 37NR, MajAI [port]*
Frasco, Robert Anthony *Law&B 92*
Frasconi, Antonio 1919- *MajAI [port], WhoE 93*
Frascotti, John Anthony *Law&B 92*
Fraser, Alexa Stirling 1897-1977 *BiDAMSp 1989*
Fraser, Alexander J. *Law&B 92*
Fraser, Angus S.J. *BioIn 17*
Fraser, Anne W. *Law&B 92*
Fraser, Anserd George 1952- *WhoSSW 93*
Fraser, Anthea 1930- *ScF&FL 92*
Fraser, Antonia 1932- *BioIn 17, WhoAm 92*
Fraser, Antony P. *WhoScE 91-1*
Fraser, Bertha Cooper *AmWomPl*
Fraser, Bruce Douglas 1927- *St&PR 93*
Fraser, Bruce Wickersham 1941- *WhoWrEP 92*
Fraser, C.B. Gladwin d1991 *BioIn 17*
Fraser, Campbell 1923- *WhoAm 92, WhoWor 93*
Fraser, Campbell, Sir 1923- *St&PR 93*
Fraser, Charles fl. 1813-1819 *BioIn 17*
Fraser, Charles Annand 1928- *WhoWor 93*
Fraser, Charles E. *BioIn 17*
Fraser, Charles Elbert 1929- *WhoAm 92, WhoWor 93*
Fraser, Christine Marion *ScF&FL 92*
Fraser, Craig Wilson 1948- *St&PR 93*
Fraser, D. Ian 1931- *St&PR 93, WhoIns 93*
Fraser, David 1920- *ScF&FL 92*
Fraser, David Allen 1943- *WhoE 93*
Fraser, David Charles 1942- *WhoWor 93*
Fraser, David Lawrence *Law&B 92*
Fraser, David S. 1938- *St&PR 93*
Fraser, David William 1944- *WhoAm 92*
Fraser, Dawn 1937- *BioIn 17*
Fraser, Diane Lynch *WhoE 93*
Fraser, Donald 1924- *PolPar*
Fraser, Donald Alexander Stuart 1925- *WhoAm 92*
Fraser, Donald C. 1941- *WhoAm 92, WhoE 93, WhoSSW 93*
Fraser, Donald MacKay 1924- *WhoAm 92*
Fraser, Donald Murray 1946-1985 *WhoCanL 92*
Fraser, Dorothy *ScF&FL 92*
Fraser, Douglas Andrew 1916- *BioIn 17*
Fraser, Duncan Alexander, III *Law&B 92*
Fraser, Edith L. *AmWomPl*
Fraser, Eliza W. *Law&B 92*
Fraser, Everett Mackay 1921- *St&PR 93*
Fraser, Fawnette Locktee 1952- *WhoSSW 93*
Fraser, G.A. *Law&B 92*
Fraser, Geo. B. 1930- *St&PR 93*
Fraser, Georg Richard 1946- *WhoWor 93*
Fraser, George Broadrup 1914- *WhoAm 92*
Fraser, Harry 1889-1974 *BioIn 17*
Fraser, Helen Jean Sutherland 1949- *WhoWor 93*
Fraser, Henry S. 1900- *WhoAm 92*
Fraser, Howard Michael 1943- *WhoSSW 93*
Fraser, Ian Maclean 1935- *St&PR 93*
Fraser, J.F. 1930- *St&PR 93*
Fraser, James Cavender 1941- *WhoAm 92*
Fraser, James S. *Law&B 92*
Fraser, Janet 1911-
See Fraser, Norman 1904- *Baker 92*
Fraser, Jaye *Law&B 92*
Fraser, Jeannette Lynn 1951- *WhoE 93*
Fraser, John *BioIn 17*
Fraser, John Allen 1931- *WhoAm 92*
Fraser, John Denis 1934- *WhoWor 93*
Fraser, John Foster 1930- *WhoAm 92*
Fraser, John J. 1951- *St&PR 93*
Fraser, John Keith 1922- *WhoAm 92*
Fraser, John Malcolm 1930- *DcTwHis*
Fraser, John Wayne 1944- *WhoSSW 93, WhoWor 93*
Fraser, Jon 1955- *WhoEmL 93*
Fraser, Julia Ann 1957- *WhoE 93, WhoEmL 93*
Fraser, Kathleen Joy 1937- *WhoAm 92*
Fraser, Keath 1944- *WhoCanL 92*
Fraser, Kenneth William, Jr. 1937- *St&PR 93, WhoAm 92*
Fraser, Margot *BioIn 17*
Fraser, Mary Karen 1946- *WhoAm 92*
Fraser, Neale *BioIn 17*
Fraser, Norman 1904- *Baker 92*
Fraser, Peter 1884-1950 *DcTwHis*
Fraser, R.S.S. *WhoScE 91-1*
Fraser, Randall O. 1949- *St&PR 93*
Fraser, Raymond 1941- *WhoCanL 92*
Fraser, Raymond Francis 1965- *WhoE 93*
Fraser, Robert Carson 1925- *WhoE 93*
Fraser, Robert Gordon 1921- *WhoAm 92*
Fraser, Robert Murray 1930- *WhoAm 92*
Fraser, Ron *BioIn 17*
Fraser, Ronald 1888-1974 *ScF&FL 92*
Fraser, Ronald George 1936- *BiDAMSp 1989*
Fraser, Russell Alfred 1927- *WhoAm 92, WhoWrEP 92*
Fraser, Russell Gordon 1934- *WhoAm 92*
Fraser, Scott 1958- *BioIn 17*
Fraser, Scott Alexander 1955- *WhoEmL 93*
Fraser, Simon 1726-1782 *HarEnMi*
Fraser, Simon 1729-1777 *HarEnMi*
Fraser, Simon 1776-1862 *Expl 93*
Fraser, Stanley Drew 1925- *St&PR 93*
Fraser, Sylvia 1935- *WhoCanL 92*
Fraser, Thomas Edwards *Law&B 92*
Fraser, Thomas G. *St&PR 93*
Fraser, Thomas H. 1948- *St&PR 93*
Fraser, Thomas William *WhoScE 91-1*
Fraser, W.A. 1859-1933 *ScF&FL 92*
Fraser, Warren Kenneth 1927- *WhoSSW 93*
Fraser, William Irvine *WhoScE 91-1*
Fraser, William Lawrence 1929- *WhoAm 92*
Fraser, William Neil 1932- *WhoAm 92*
Fraser, William Walker 1929- *WhoWor 93*
Fraser-Howze, Debra Yolanda 1952- *WhoE 93*
Fraser-Reid, Bertram Oliver 1934- *WhoAm 92*
Fraser-Smith, Charles d1992 *NewYTBS 92*
Fraser-Smith, Elizabeth Birdsey 1938- *WhoAm 92*
Frasher, Glenn Edward 1934- *WhoSSW 93*
Frasher, Thomas P. 1956- *St&PR 93*
Frashier, Gary E. 1936- *St&PR 93*
Frashure, Deborah Jo Carvelli 1951- *WhoAmW 93*
Frasi, Giulia fl. 1742-1772 *OxDcOp*
Frasier, Debra 1953- *BioIn 17, ConAu 137, SmATA 69 [port]*
Frasier, Delaine Rae 1956- *WhoEmL 93*
Frasier, Gary W. 1937- *WhoAm 92*
Frasier, Ralph K. *Law&B 92*
Frasier, Ralph Kennedy 1938- *St&PR 93, WhoAm 92*
Frasier, Thomas Daniel 1938- *WhoWrEP 92*
Frasier, William Marshall 1946- *St&PR 93, WhoEmL 93*
Frassinelli, Guido Joseph 1927- *WhoWor 93*
Frasure, William R. 1954- *St&PR 93*
Fratcher, William Franklin 1913- *WhoAm 92*
Fratello, Clifford *St&PR 93*
Fratello, Michael Robert 1947- *WhoAm 92*
Frater, Hal 1909- *WhoE 93*
Frater, Robert William Mayo 1928- *WhoAm 92*
Frati, Luigi 1943- *WhoWor 93*
Frati, William 1931- *WhoE 93*
Fratianni, Joseph James 1932- *St&PR 93*
Fraticelli, Marco 1942- *WhoCanL 92*
Fratt, Gerald E. 1941- *St&PR 93*
Frattali, Rose E. 1931- *WhoIns 93*
Frattali, Rose Esther 1931- *St&PR 93*
Frattaroli, Carmen Aniello 1948- *WhoEmL 93*
Frattini, Alberto 1922- *DcLB 128 [port]*
Fratz, Donald Douglas 1952- *WhoE 93, WhoWrEP 92*
Fratzke, Charles Edward 1927- *WhoIns 93*
Frauenfelder, Hans 1922- *WhoAm 92*
Frauenglas, Robert Alan 1950- *WhoWrEP 92*
Frauenhoffer, Gail Lynne 1958- *St&PR 93*
Frauenknecht, Alfred d1991 *BioIn 17*
Frauens, Marie 1902- *WhoWor 93*
Fraulo, Amadeo Andy 1920- *St&PR 93*
Fraum, Jeffrey Scott *Law&B 92*
Fraunfelder, Frederick Theodore 1934- *WhoAm 92*
Fraunholz, Wolfgang 1931- *WhoWor 93*
Fraustino, Daniel Victor 1945- *WhoWrEP 92*
Frausto, Maria 1952- *WhoAmW 93, WhoEmL 93*
Frautschi, Dorothy Jones 1903- *St&PR 93*
Frautschi, John Jones 1929- *St&PR 93*
Frautschi, Steven Clark 1933- *WhoAm 92*
Frautschi, Timothy Clark 1937- *WhoAm 92*
Frautschi, Walter Albert 1901- *St&PR 93, WhoAm 92*
Fravala, George Michael 1951- *WhoEmL 93*
Fravel, Elizabeth Whitmore 1951- *WhoAmW 93, WhoEmL 93*
Fravert, Colleen Mohnike 1951- *WhoEmL 93*
Frawley, Bernard d1992 *NewYTBS 92*
Frawley, Claire 1929- *WhoAmW 93*
Frawley, Daniel Seymour 1943- *WhoAm 92, WhoE 93*
Frawley, Elizabeth Kirk 1959- *WhoAmW 93*
Frawley, Frederic L. *Law&B 92*
Frawley, Frederic L. 1941- *St&PR 93*
Frawley, James *MiSFD 9*
Frawley, Patrick J. 1923- *St&PR 93*
Frawley, Patrick Joseph, Jr. 1923- *WhoAm 92*
Frawley, Robert Donald 1947- *WhoEmL 93*
Frawley, Sean Paul 1940- *WhoAm 92, WhoE 93*
Frawley, Thomas Francis 1919- *WhoAm 92*
Fraxedas, Ricardo 1953- *St&PR 93*
Fray, Derek John *WhoScE 91-1*
Fray, Earl Napoleon 1934- *St&PR 93*
Fray, Sharon Swenson 1951- *WhoAmW 93*
Frayling, Christopher 1946- *ScF&FL 92*
Frayn, Michael *BioIn 17*
Frayne, John G. 1894- *BioIn 17*
Fraysse, Jean-Francois 1946- *NewYTBS 92 [port]*
Fraze, Denny Turner 1940- *WhoSSW 93*
Frazee, Elizabeth Lynn 1957- *WhoEmL 93*
Frazee, Gerald Clifford 1958- *St&PR 93*
Frazee, Harry H. 1930- *St&PR 93*
Frazee, Jane 1918-1985 *SweetSg C [port]*
Frazee, John Powell, Jr. 1944- *St&PR 93, WhoAm 92*
Frazee, Ronald Leroy 1946- *WhoEmL 93*
Frazee, Rowland Cardwell 1921- *St&PR 93*
Frazee-Baldassarre, Marie Marcia 1921- *WhoAmW 93*
Frazelle, Michael Jerome 1953- *WhoEmL 93*
Frazer, Bud 1864-1896 *BioIn 17*
Frazer, Buddy 1946- *WhoSSW 93*
Frazer, Frank Reese, III 1958- *WhoSSW 93*
Frazer, Fred *ConAu 39NR*
Frazer, Gregory James 1952- *WhoEmL 93*
Frazer, Ira 1954- *WhoEmL 93*
Frazer, J. Howard 1924- *St&PR 93*
Frazer, Jack Winfield 1924- *WhoAm 92*
Frazer, James George 1854-1941 *BioIn 17, IntDcAn*
Frazer, John Howard 1924- *WhoAm 92*
Frazer, John Paul 1914- *WhoAm 92*
Frazer, Maud *AmWomPl*
Frazer, Miriam K. *St&PR 93*
Frazer, Nathaniel Blevins 1949- *WhoEmL 93*
Frazer, Nimrod Thompson 1929- *WhoAm 92, WhoSSW 93*
Frazer, Oliver 1808-1864 *BioIn 17*
Frazer, Robbin Walsh 1920- *WhoAmW 93*
Frazer, Robert 1891-1944 *BioIn 17*
Frazer, Robert H. *Law&B 92*
Frazer, Shamus 1912- *ScF&FL 92*
Frazer, Stuart Harrison, III 1948- *WhoSSW 93*
Frazer, Wendy 1943- *WhoAmW 93*
Frazetta, Frank 1928- *ScF&FL 92, WhoAm 92*
Frazeur, Joyce 1931- *WhoWrEP 92*
Frazier, A. D., Jr. 1944- *WhoAm 92*
Frazier, Alan D. 1951- *WhoEmL 93*
Frazier, Allie Robert 1933- *WhoSSW 93*
Frazier, Amy *BioIn 17*
Frazier, Amy 1971- *WhoAmW 93*
Frazier, April *WhoWrEP 92*
Frazier, Arthur *Law&B 92*
Frazier, C. Elisia *Law&B 92*
Frazier, Chet June 1924- *WhoAm 92*
Frazier, Donald 1924- *St&PR 93*
Frazier, Donald Keith 1962- *WhoSSW 93*
Frazier, Donald Tha, Sr. 1935- *WhoAm 92*
Frazier, Douglas Byron 1957- *WhoEmL 93*
Frazier, Edward Clarence *BioIn 17*
Frazier, Edward Franklin 1894-1962 *BioIn 17, EncAACR*
Frazier, Eric Dowling 1948- *WhoEmL 93*
Frazier, Gregg Gerard 1964- *WhoEmL 93*
Frazier, Henry Bowen, III 1934- *WhoAm 92*
Frazier, Howard Stanley 1926- *WhoAm 92*
Frazier, Howard Thomas 1911- *WhoE 93*
Frazier, J. Phillip 1939- *St&PR 93*
Frazier, Janice Dianne 1956- *WhoEmL 93*
Frazier, Joe 1944- *WhoAm 92*
Frazier, John E., II 1940- *St&PR 93*
Frazier, John Lionel Devin 1932- *St&PR 93, WhoAm 92*
Frazier, John Phillip 1939- *WhoAm 92*
Frazier, John Warren 1913- *WhoAm 92*
Frazier, Kendrick (Crosby) 1942- *ConAu 39NR, WhoWrEP 92*
Frazier, Kimberlee Gonterman 1953- *WhoAmW 93, WhoWor 93*
Frazier, Larry G. 1952- *St&PR 93*
Frazier, Lawrence Alan *Law&B 92*
Frazier, Lawrence Alan 1936- *St&PR 93, WhoIns 93*
Frazier, LeRoy 1946- *WhoAm 92*
Frazier, Loy William, Jr. 1938- *WhoSSW 93*
Frazier, Marjorie Derene *WhoE 93*
Frazier, Nancy Jo 1935- *WhoAmW 93*
Frazier, Neta Lohnes 1890-1990 *BioIn 17*
Frazier, Owsley B. 1935- *St&PR 93, WhoAm 92, WhoSSW 93*
Frazier, Patricia Bailey 1935- *St&PR 93*
Frazier, Peter W. 1942- *St&PR 93*
Frazier, Richard R. 1946- *St&PR 93*
Frazier, Ricks P. *Law&B 92*
Frazier, Robert 1951- *ScF&FL 92*
Frazier, Ruth Mae 1944- *WhoAmW 93*
Frazier, Terry Francis 1953- *WhoEmL 93, WhoSSW 93*
Frazier, Thomas Brooks 1947- *WhoSSW 93*
Frazier, Thomas G. 1943- *St&PR 93*
Frazier, W. Edwin, III *Law&B 92*

Frazier, Walt 1945- *WhoAm 92*
Frazier, Walter Ronald 1939- *WhoSSW 93, WhoWor 93*
Frazier, Warner C. 1932- *St&PR 93*
Frazier, William A. 1908- *WhoAm 92*
Frazier, William Francis, Jr. 1957- *WhoEmL 93*
Frazier, William Henry 1943- *WhoSSW 93*
Frazier, William J. 1925- *St&PR 93*
Frazier, Winston Earle 1930- *WhoSSW 93*
Frazier-Tsai, Karen Lynne 1952- *WhoAm 92*
Frazza, George S. *Law&B 92*
Frazza, George S. 1934- *St&PR 93, WhoAm 92*
Frazzetta, Frank *ScF&FL 92*
Frazzetta, Thomas H. 1934- *WhoAm 92*
Frazzi, Vito 1888-1975 *Baker 92, OxDcOp*
Frazzitta, Bartholomew J. 1942- *St&PR 93*
Fread, Sidney 1916-1990 *BioIn 17*
Freal, James Brendan 1962- *WhoEmL 93, WhoSSW 93*
Fream, Anita Sue 1948- *WhoAmW 93, WhoEmL 93*
Freaney, Vincent 1945- *WhoIns 93*
Frears, Stephen 1941- *BioIn 17, MiSFD 9*
Freas, Donald Hayes 1933- *St&PR 93*
Freas, Frank Kelly 1922- *ScF&FL 92, WhoAm 92*
Freas, George Craig 1947- *WhoEmL 93*
Freas, Guy James 1962- *WhoEmL 93*
Frease, Belden *Law&B 92*
Frease, John Michael 1950- *WhoWor 93*
Freathy, Paul 1958- *WhoScE 91-1*
Freberg, Stanley 1926- *WhoAm 92*
Freccia, Massimo 1906- *Baker 92*
Frech, Harry Edward, III 1946- *WhoEmL 93*
Frechet, Jean Marie Joseph 1944- *WhoE 93*
Frechette, Alfred L. 1909-1991 *BioIn 17*
Frechette, Ernest Albert 1918- *WhoSSW 93*
Frechette, Louis-Honore 1839-1908 *BioIn 17*
Frechette, Louise 1946- *WhoUN 92*
Frechette, Peter L. 1937- *St&PR 93*
Frechette, Peter Loren 1937- *WhoAm 92*
Frechette, Van Derck 1916- *WhoAm 92*
Freckelton, Sondra 1936- *WhoE 93*
Frecon, L. *WhoScE 91-2*
Fred, B. Alan 1927- *St&PR 93*
Freda, Barbara Anne 1958- *WhoEmL 93*
Fredborg, Erik Lars Arvid 1915- *WhoWor 93*
Freddi, Cris 1955- *ScF&FL 92*
Frede, Jonathan H. 1950- *WhoE 93*
Fredenslund, Aage 1941- *WhoScE 91-2*
Fredenthal, Ruth Ann 1938- *WhoE 93*
Frederic, Francis J., Jr. 1926- *St&PR 93*
Frederic, Harold 1856-1898 *GayN, JrnUS*
Frederic-Dupont, Edouard 1902- *BioIn 17*
Frederich, Kathy W. 1953- *WhoAmW 93, WhoEmL 93*
Frederick, I c. 1123-1190 *HarEnMi*
Frederick, I 1657-1713 *HarEnMi*
Frederick, II 1194-1250 *HarEnMi*
Frederick, II 1712-1786 *Baker 92, OxDcOp*
Frederick, II, King of Prussia 1712-1786 *BioIn 17*
Frederick, III 1657-1713 *HarEnMi*
Frederick, Bill *WhoAm 92*
Frederick, Charlene J. 1951- *WhoAm 92*
Frederick, Charles Osmond 1936- *WhoScE 91-1*
Frederick, Claire Cobb 1932- *WhoAmW 93*
Frederick, David Charles 1951- *WhoWor 93*
Frederick, David M. 1942- *St&PR 93*
Frederick, Dawn Hildred Ruth 1956- *WhoWrEP 92*
Frederick, Dolliver H. 1944- *WhoAm 92*
Frederick, Doyle Grimes 1935- *WhoAm 92*
Frederick, Earl James 1927- *WhoAm 92*
Frederick, Edward Charles 1930- *WhoAm 92*
Frederick, Elizabeth A. *Law&B 92*
Frederick, Gary Donnell 1947- *WhoEmL 93*
Frederick, Gary Michael 1957- *WhoSSW 93*
Frederick, Ghislaine Renee 1933- *St&PR 93*
Frederick, Herbert Stanley 1930- *St&PR 93*
Frederick, Joanne Michele 1968- *WhoAmW 93*
Frederick, Joseph Francis, Jr. 1933- *WhoAm 92*
Frederick, Karen S. 1942- *WhoAmW 93*
Frederick, Karyn Lynne 1947- *WhoAmW 93*
Frederick, Kathleen Anne 1950- *WhoAmW 93, WhoSSW 93*
Frederick, Lafayette 1923- *WhoAm 92*
Frederick, Linda Lenore 1949- *WhoWrEP 92*
Frederick, Lowell L. 1939- *St&PR 93*
Frederick, Marsha A. *Law&B 92*
Frederick, Martin Barnett 1941- *St&PR 93*
Frederick, Michael Francis 1945- *St&PR 93*
Frederick, Nancy 1932- *WhoWor 93*
Frederick, Pamela Renner 1951- *WhoAmW 93*
Frederick, Pauline d1990 *BioIn 17*
Frederick, R.L. *Law&B 92*
Frederick, Richard Andrew 1948- *WhoEmL 93*
Frederick, Richmond S. *Law&B 92*
Frederick, Robert L. 1939- *St&PR 93*
Frederick, Samuel Walter 1943- *WhoUN 92*
Frederick, Thomas James 1956- *WhoEmL 93*
Frederick, Thomas S. 1945- *St&PR 93*
Frederick, Virginia Fiester 1916- *WhoAmW 93*
Frederick, Willard Drawn, Jr. 1934- *WhoSSW 93*
Frederick, William George DeMott 1936- *WhoE 93*
Frederick, William S. 1938- *St&PR 93*
Frederick, William Sherrad 1938- *WhoAm 92*
Frederick Barbarossa, I c. 1125-1190 *OxDcByz*
Frederick Charles, Prince 1828-1885 *HarEnMi*
Frederick-Collins, Jana 1955- *WhoEmL 93*
Frederick Hohenstaufen, II 1194-1250 *OxDcByz*
Frederick Louis, Prince of Wales 1707-1751 *BioIn 17*
Frederick-Mairs, Thyra Julie 1941- *WhoAmW 93*
Fredericks, Barry Irwin 1936- *WhoE 93*
Fredericks, Casey 1943- *ScF&FL 92*
Fredericks, Dale E. *WhoAm 92*
Fredericks, Daniel Carl 1950- *WhoEmL 93*
Fredericks, David Michael 1950- *St&PR 93, WhoEmL 93*
Fredericks, James 1942- *St&PR 93*
Fredericks, James W. *Law&B 92*
Fredericks, Joan DeLanoy 1928- *WhoAmW 93*
Fredericks, Kay Louise 1943- *WhoAmW 93*
Fredericks, Marshall Maynard 1908- *WhoAm 92, WhoWor 93*
Fredericks, Norman J. 1914- *St&PR 93*
Fredericks, Norman J., Jr. 1940- *St&PR 93*
Fredericks, Norman John 1914- *WhoAm 92*
Fredericks, Robert Joseph 1934- *WhoE 93*
Fredericks, Sharon Kay 1942- *WhoAmW 93*
Fredericks, Thomas R. *Law&B 92*
Fredericks, Vic *WhoWrEP 92*
Fredericks, Walter Otto 1939- *WhoE 93*
Fredericks, Ward Arthur 1939- *WhoWor 93*
Fredericks, Wayne 1917- *WhoAm 92*
Fredericks, Wendell K. *Law&B 92*
Fredericks, Wesley C., Jr. 1948- *St&PR 93*
Fredericks, Wesley Charles, Jr. 1948- *WhoAm 92, WhoE 93, WhoEmL 93, WhoWor 93*
Fredericks, William Charles 1943- *St&PR 93*
Fredericks, William John 1924- *WhoSSW 93*
Fredericksen, Paul H. 1945- *St&PR 93*
Frederickson, Anthony *ScF&FL 92*
Frederickson, Arman Frederick 1918- *WhoAm 92*
Frederickson, Charles Richard 1938- *St&PR 93*
Frederickson, Horace George 1937- *WhoAm 92*
Frederickson, Keith Alvin 1925- *WhoAm 92*
Frederick the Great 1712-1786 *Baker 92, BioIn 17*
Frederick the Great, II 1712-1786 *HarEnMi*
Frederick William 1620-1688 *HarEnMi*
Frederick William, Crown Prince 1882-1951 *HarEnMi*
Frederick William, I 1688-1740 *HarEnMi*
Frederics, Richard 1949- *St&PR 93*
Frederiksen, Henning 1924- *St&PR 93*
Frederiksen, Marilynn Elizabeth Conners 1949- *WhoAm 92, WhoAmW 93, WhoEmL 93*
Frederiksen, Paul Asger 1946- *WhoEmL 93*
Frederiksen, Per O. 1928- *WhoScE 91-2*
Frederiksen, Robert G. 1925- *St&PR 93*
Frederiksen, Rosemary Ann 1956- *WhoE 93*
Frederiksen, William A. 1947- *St&PR 93*
Fredette, Barbara Wagner 1933- *WhoAmW 93*
Fredette, Diane Kaufman 1956- *WhoEmL 93*
Fredette, Jean Marie 1940- *WhoWrEP 92*
Fredette, Michael *Law&B 92*
Fredette, Richard Chester 1934- *WhoAm 92*
Fredette, Robert Francis 1952- *WhoEmL 93*
Fredga, Karl 1934- *WhoScE 91-4*
Fredga, Kerstin 1935- *WhoScE 91-4*
Fredholm, B. Bertil 1943- *WhoScE 91-4*
Frediani, Diane Marie 1963- *WhoAmW 93*
Frediani, Donald Joseph 1929- *St&PR 93*
Fredin, Leif Goran Reinhold 1945- *WhoSSW 93*
Fredj, Gaston H.A. 1938- *WhoScE 91-2*
Fredland, Kurt Roger 1948- *St&PR 93*
Fredman, Daniel Joseph 1949- *WhoEmL 93*
Fredmann, Martin 1943- *WhoAm 92*
Fredner, Rolf 1913- *St&PR 93*
Fredrich, Steven R. *St&PR 93*
Fredrichsen, Richard Fredrick 1934- *St&PR 93*
Fredrick, Beth M. 1959- *WhoE 93*
Fredrick, Donald Arthur 1941- *St&PR 93*
Fredrick, Laurence William 1927- *WhoAm 92*
Fredrick, Robert Frank 1948- *WhoEmL 93*
Fredrick, Susan Walker 1948- *WhoAmW 93, WhoEmL 93*
Fredrick, Thomas W. *Law&B 92*
Fredrick, Victoria M. 1950- *WhoEmL 93*
Fredricks, Jessica 1887-1979 *BioIn 17*
Fredricks, Richard 1933- *WhoAm 92*
Fredricks, Terry L. 1957- *WhoEmL 93*
Fredricksen, Cleve John 1917- *WhoAm 92*
Fredricksen, Cleve Laurance 1941- *WhoAm 92*
Fredrickson, Albert 1932- *St&PR 93*
Fredrickson, Arthur Allan 1923- *WhoAm 92*
Fredrickson, Bruce Donald 1940- *WhoE 93*
Fredrickson, Bruce R., II 1943- *St&PR 93*
Fredrickson, Bryan Timothy 1956- *WhoEmL 93*
Fredrickson, Donald Sharp 1924- *WhoAm 92*
Fredrickson, George Marsh 1934- *WhoAm 92*
Fredrickson, John Wesley 1941- *St&PR 93*
Fredrickson, Kenneth L. *Law&B 92*
Fredrickson, Lawrence Thomas 1928- *WhoAm 92*
Fredrickson, Roxanna Lynn 1952- *WhoEmL 93*
Fredrickson, Sharon Wong 1956- *WhoEmL 93*
Fredrickson, Vance O. 1928- *WhoIns 93*
Fredrik, Burry 1925- *WhoAm 92*
Fredriksen, Peter A. 1931- *St&PR 93*
Fredriksen, Wilhelm *WhoScE 91-2*
Fredrikson, Dennis Roy 1944- *St&PR 93*
Fredrikson, Gunnar F.W. 1944- *WhoScE 91-4*
Fredrikson, Per Lennart 1947- *WhoWor 93*
Fredriksson, Sverker 1946- *WhoScE 91-4*
Fredro, Aleksander 1793-1876 *PolBiDi*
Fredston, Arthur Howard 1929- *WhoAm 92*
Fredyma, James Paul 1950- *WhoE 93*
Free, Ann Cottrell *WhoAm 92, WhoE 93, WhoWor 93*
Free, Charles Alfred 1936- *WhoE 93*
Free, Dexter S. 1937- *St&PR 93*
Free, Dwayne Loy 1954- *WhoSSW 93*
Free, Helen M. 1923- *WhoAmW 93*
Free, John D. 1929- *BioIn 17*
Free, M. Virginia 1945- *St&PR 93*
Free, Mike 1952- *St&PR 93*
Free, Ross Vincent 1943- *WhoAsAP 91*
Free, Ruth Morgan 1946- *WhoAmW 93*
Free, Stephen J. 1948- *WhoE 93*
Free, William John 1943- *WhoAm 92*
Freeark, Robert James 1927- *WhoAm 92*
Freebairn-Smith, Laura 1959- *WhoAmW 93*
Freeberg, Lawrence B. 1931- *St&PR 93*
Freeburg, Jeffrey C. *Law&B 92*
Freeburg, Robert M. 1929- *St&PR 93*
Freeburger, Thomas Oliver 1948- *WhoEmL 93*
Freece, Robert A. 1941- *St&PR 93*
Freece, Todd Michael 1965- *WhoSSW 93*
Freed, Aaron David 1922- *WhoAm 92*
Freed, Alan 1922-1965 *Baker 92, BioIn 17*
Freed, Alan David 1954- *WhoEmL 93*
Freed, Barbara Faye 1941- *WhoE 93*
Freed, Bert 1919- *WhoAm 92*
Freed, Charles 1926- *WhoAm 92*
Freed, Clarence Landis 1945- *WhoE 93*
Freed, David Clark 1936- *WhoAm 92*
Freed, Dean M. *Law&B 92*
Freed, Dean Winslow 1923- *St&PR 93*
Freed, DeBow 1925- *WhoAm 92*
Freed, Edmond Lee 1935- *WhoE 93*
Freed, Herb *MiSFD 9*
Freed, Isadore 1900-1960 *Baker 92*
Freed, Jack Herschel 1938- *WhoAm 92*
Freed, James Ingo 1930- *WhoAm 92*
Freed, Jonathan Michael 1954- *WhoEmL 93*
Freed, Joshua 1925- *St&PR 93*
Freed, Karl Frederick 1942- *WhoAm 92*
Freed, Kenneth Alan 1957- *WhoEmL 93*
Freed, L.A. *ScF&FL 92*
Freed, Leonard 1929- *BioIn 17*
Freed, Lynn Ruth *WhoWrEP 92*
Freed, Marilyn J. *Law&B 92*
Freed, Murray Monroe 1924- *WhoAm 92*
Freed, Ray 1939- *ConAu 40NR*
Freed, Ray Forrest 1939- *WhoWrEP 92*
Freed, Richard D(onald) 1928- *Baker 92*
Freed, Richard Howard *Law&B 92*
Freed, Rita Evelyn 1952- *WhoAm 92*
Freed, Robert Leslie 1946- *WhoEmL 93*
Freed, Russell William 1955- *St&PR 93*
Freed, Stanley Arthur 1927- *WhoAm 92*
Freed, Stephen N. *Law&B 92*
Freedberg, A. Stone 1908- *WhoAm 92*
Freedberg, Irwin Mark 1931- *WhoAm 92*
Freedberg, Sydney Joseph 1914- *WhoAm 92*
Freedgood, Anne Goodman 1917- *WhoAm 92*
Freedland, Barbara Sharon 1955- *WhoSSW 93*
Freedland, Jacob Berke 1913- *WhoSSW 93, WhoWor 93*
Freedland, Richard Allan 1931- *WhoAm 92*
Freedland, Sidney 1926- *St&PR 93*
Freedman, Aaron David 1922- *WhoE 93*
Freedman, Alan Reinald 1935- *WhoE 93*
Freedman, Albert Z. *WhoAm 92*
Freedman, Alfred Mordecai 1917- *WhoE 93*
Freedman, Allen Royal 1940- *St&PR 93, WhoAm 92*
Freedman, Anne Beller 1949- *WhoAmW 93*
Freedman, Anne Maureen 1943- *WhoAmW 93*
Freedman, Anthony Stephen 1945- *WhoAm 92*
Freedman, Arnold Michael 1918- *WhoSSW 93*
Freedman, Arthur 1916- *St&PR 93*
Freedman, Barbara S. 1952- *WhoAmW 93*
Freedman, Barry H. *Law&B 92*
Freedman, Bart Joseph 1955- *WhoWor 93*
Freedman, Barton H. *Law&B 92*
Freedman, Ben 1924- *St&PR 93*
Freedman, Betty *WhoAm 92*
Freedman, Betty Helene 1918- *WhoAmW 93*
Freedman, Cheryl Chase *Law&B 92*
Freedman, Daniel X. 1921- *WhoAm 92*
Freedman, David 1921- *St&PR 93*
Freedman, David Amiel 1938- *WhoAm 92*
Freedman, David H. 1942- *WhoUN 92*
Freedman, David Noel 1922- *WhoAm 92, WhoWor 93*
Freedman, Dennis Buch 1951- *WhoEmL 93*
Freedman, Donald P. 1939- *St&PR 93*
Freedman, Elizabeth Anne 1961- *WhoAmW 93*
Freedman, Eric 1949- *WhoWrEP 92*
Freedman, Eugene M. 1932- *WhoAm 92*
Freedman, Frank Harlan 1924- *WhoE 93*
Freedman, Gary K. 1952- *St&PR 93*
Freedman, George 1921- *WhoE 93*
Freedman, Harry 1922- *Baker 92, WhoAm 92*
Freedman, Helen Rosengren 1952- *WhoE 93, WhoWrEP 92*
Freedman, Howard A. *Law&B 92*
Freedman, Howard Martin 1953- *WhoE 93*
Freedman, Irving H. 1935- *WhoE 93*
Freedman, James D. *Law&B 92*
Freedman, James Oliver 1935- *WhoAm 92, WhoE 93*
Freedman, Jay *Law&B 92*
Freedman, Jeffrey J. *Law&B 92*
Freedman, Jerome 1916- *WhoAm 92*
Freedman, Jerrold *MiSFD 9*
Freedman, Joel 1948- *WhoIns 93*
Freedman, Jon Bruce 1959- *WhoEmL 93*
Freedman, Jonathan Borwick 1950- *WhoAm 92*
Freedman, Joseph Joel 1926- *St&PR 93*
Freedman, Judith Greenberg 1939- *WhoAmW 93, WhoE 93*

Freedman, Kenneth David 1947- *WhoAm 92*
Freedman, Larry A. 1943- *St&PR 93*
Freedman, Lawrence Zelic 1919- *WhoAm 92*
Freedman, Lewis d1992 *NewYTBS 92 [port]*
Freedman, Lewis Alexander *Law&B 92*
Freedman, Lewis S. 1936- *WhoE 93*
Freedman, Louis Martin 1947- *WhoSSW 93*
Freedman, Marc David *Law&B 92*
Freedman, Marcia 1938- *BioIn 17*
Freedman, Martin H. 1937- *St&PR 93*
Freedman, Marvin Irving 1939- *WhoE 93*
Freedman, Mary Anne 1941- *WhoAmW 93*
Freedman, Matt *BioIn 17*
Freedman, Mervin Burton 1920- *WhoAm 92*
Freedman, Michael Alan 1960- *WhoE 93*
Freedman, Michael H. 1951- *BioIn 17*
Freedman, Michael Hartley 1951- *WhoAm 92, WhoEmL 93*
Freedman, Monroe Henry 1928- *WhoAm 92, WhoWor 93*
Freedman, Penny Millicent 1941- *WhoAm 92*
Freedman, Philip 1926- *WhoAm 92*
Freedman, Richard 1932-1991 *BioIn 17*
Freedman, Robert *MiSFD 9*
Freedman, Robert Louis 1940- *WhoAm 92*
Freedman, Roger Mitchell 1945- *WhoAm 92*
Freedman, Ronald 1917- *WhoAm 92*
Freedman, Ronald D. 1949- *St&PR 93*
Freedman, Russell 1929- *SmATA 71 [port]*
Freedman, Russell (Bruce) 1929- *MajAI [port], WhoAm 92*
Freedman, Samuel Orkin 1928- *WhoAm 92*
Freedman, Sandra Warshaw 1943- *WhoAmW 93, WhoSSW 93*
Freedman, Sandra Warshaw 1944- *WhoAm 92*
Freedman, Stanford William 1939- *St&PR 93*
Freedman, Stanley A. *Law&B 92*
Freedman, Stanley Arnold 1922- *WhoAm 92*
Freedman, Stanley Marvin 1923- *WhoAm 92*
Freedman, Steve F. *Law&B 92*
Freedman, Theodore Murray 1930- *St&PR 93*
Freedman, Walter 1914- *WhoAm 92*
Freedom, Nancy 1932- *WhoAmW 93*
Freedson, Grace Elizabeth 1951- *WhoEmL 93*
Freedy, Amos 1938- *St&PR 93*
Freeh, Cheri Hutchinson 1961- *WhoE 93*
Freeh, Edward James 1925- *WhoAm 92*
Freeh, Louis *BioIn 17*
Freehan, Philip F. 1950- *St&PR 93*
Freehan, William Ashley 1941- *BiDAMSp 1989*
Freehill, Maurice F. 1915- *WhoAm 92*
Freehill, Michael H. 1943- *St&PR 93*
Freehling, Daniel Joseph 1950- *WhoAm 92*
Freehling, Deborah June 1955- *WhoAmW 93, WhoEmL 93*
Freehling, Harold George, Jr. 1947- *WhoEmL 93, WhoWor 93*
Freehling, Norman 1905- *WhoAm 92*
Freehling, Paul Edward 1938- *WhoAm 92*
Freehling, Stanley Maxwell 1924- *WhoAm 92*
Freehling, Willard Maxwell 1913- *WhoAm 92*
Freehling, William Wilhartz 1935- *WhoAm 92, WhoWrEP 92*
Freehof, Fanny Evelyn *AmWomPl*
Freehof, Solomon B. 1892-1990 *BioIn 17*
Freel, Charles William 1945- *St&PR 93*
Freel, James E. 1949- *St&PR 93*
Freeland, Alan Edward 1939- *WhoSSW 93*
Freeland, Arthur Glenn 1956- *WhoEmL 93*
Freeland, Claire Ann Bennett 1955- *WhoEmL 93*
Freeland, James M. Jackson 1927- *WhoAm 92*
Freeland, Jerry M. 1936- *St&PR 93*
Freeland, Jesse Rae 1924- *WhoWrEP 92*
Freeland, John A. 1933- *St&PR 93*
Freeland, Kathleen S. 1938- *BioIn 17*
Freeland, Manning Corey 1925- *St&PR 93*
Freeland, William Lee 1929- *WhoE 93*
Freeland, William Thomas 1944- *St&PR 93*
Freeland-Graves, Jeanne Himich 1948- *WhoSSW 93*
Freeling, Paul *WhoScE 91-1*
Freeman, A.J. 1928- *St&PR 93*
Freeman, Albert E. 1931- *WhoAm 92*
Freeman, Anne Hobson 1934- *WhoAmW 93, WhoWrEP 92*
Freeman, Arthur 1925- *WhoAm 92*
Freeman, Arthur J. 1930- *WhoAm 92*
Freeman, Barbara C. 1906- *ScF&FL 92*
Freeman, Barbara Joyce 1953- *WhoAmW 93*
Freeman, Benjamin Harrison, II 1936- *St&PR 93*
Freeman, Betty 1921- *Baker 92*
Freeman, Betty Lou 1946- *WhoAmW 93, WhoSSW 93*
Freeman, Bill 1938- *DcChlFi, WhoCanL 92*
Freeman, Bob A. 1926- *WhoAm 92*
Freeman, Bobby 1940- *SoulM*
Freeman, Bruce 1942- *St&PR 93*
Freeman, Bruce George 1929- *WhoE 93*
Freeman, Bruce L., Jr. 1949- *WhoEmL 93*
Freeman, Bud *BioIn 17*
Freeman, Bud 1906-1991 *AnObit 1991*
Freeman, "Bud" (Lawrence) 1906-1991 *Baker 92*
Freeman, Burton M. *Law&B 92*
Freeman, Carl M. *St&PR 93*
Freeman, Carol Anne 1940- *WhoAmW 93*
Freeman, Carolyn R. *AmWomPl*
Freeman, Carolyn Ruth 1950- *WhoAm 92*
Freeman, Chas. W., Jr. 1943- *WhoAm 92, WhoWor 93*
Freeman, Clarence Calvin 1923- *WhoAm 92*
Freeman, Clifford Lee 1941- *WhoAm 92*
Freeman, Corinne 1926- *WhoAm 92*
Freeman, David *OxDcOp*
Freeman, David 1951- *IntDcOp*
Freeman, David E. 1945- *WhoCanL 92*
Freeman, David Forgan 1918- *WhoAm 92*
Freeman, David Franklin, Jr. 1959- *WhoEmL 93*
Freeman, David Haines 1931- *WhoE 93*
Freeman, David L. *Law&B 92, St&PR 93*
Freeman, David Lynn 1924- *WhoAm 92*
Freeman, Deborah Lynn 1955- *WhoEmL 93*
Freeman, Dennis Earl 1942- *St&PR 93*
Freeman, Dianne Mendoza 1947- *WhoWor 93*
Freeman, Dick *WhoAm 92*
Freeman, Dirk Blair 1935- *St&PR 93*
Freeman, Don 1908-1978 *MajAI [port]*
Freeman, Don L. *ScF&FL 92*
Freeman, Donald Chester, Jr. 1930- *WhoAm 92*
Freeman, Donald Wayne 1947- *St&PR 93*
Freeman, Donald Wilford 1929- *WhoSSW 93*
Freeman, Doris Branch 1925- *WhoSSW 93*
Freeman, Dorothy Perkins d1990 *BioIn 17*
Freeman, Douglas Southall 1886-1953 *JrnUS*
Freeman, E.M. *WhoScE 91-1*
Freeman, E.M. 1949- *ScF&FL 92*
Freeman, Edward Augustus 1823-1892 *BioIn 17*
Freeman, Elaine Lavalle 1929- *WhoAm 92, WhoAmW 93*
Freeman, Elizabeth *BioIn 17*
Freeman, Elizabeth Anne 1958- *WhoAm 92*
Freeman, Emery W., II 1961- *WhoEmL 93*
Freeman, Eric Lewis 1947- *St&PR 93*
Freeman, Ernest Lucier, III 1953- *WhoEmL 93*
Freeman, Ernest Robert 1933- *WhoAm 92*
Freeman, Ethel Hale *AmWomPl*
Freeman, Everett 1911-1991 *BioIn 17*
Freeman, Fred W. 1925- *St&PR 93*
Freeman, Gaail *ScF&FL 92*
Freeman, Gary W. 1948- *St&PR 93*
Freeman, Gaylord A. 1910-1991 *BioIn 17*
Freeman, Geoffrey E. 1949- *WhoEmL 93*
Freeman, George 1930- *St&PR 93*
Freeman, George Clemon, Jr. 1929- *WhoAm 92*
Freeman, George Henry *Law&B 92*
Freeman, Gerald M. 1937- *St&PR 93*
Freeman, Glenda Fay Allen 1950- *WhoAmW 93*
Freeman, Graham P.M. *St&PR 93*
Freeman, Graham P. M. 1946- *WhoAm 92*
Freeman, Graydon LaVerne 1904- *WhoAm 92*
Freeman, Harold Paul 1933- *WhoAm 92*
Freeman, Harrop Arthur 1907- *WhoAm 92*
Freeman, Harry B. 1926-1990 *BioIn 17*
Freeman, Harry Cole 1920- *St&PR 93*
Freeman, Harry Lawrence 1869-1954 *Baker 92*
Freeman, Harry Louis 1932- *WhoAm 92*
Freeman, Harry Lynwood 1920- *WhoAm 92*
Freeman, Helen *AmWomPl*
Freeman, Herbert 1925- *WhoAm 92*
Freeman, Horace L. 1922- *St&PR 93*
Freeman, Houghton 1921- *St&PR 93, WhoIns 93*
Freeman, Howard d1992 *NewYTBS 92*
Freeman, Howard E(dgar) 1929-1992 *ConAu 139*
Freeman, Howard Edgar 1929- *WhoAm 92*
Freeman, Howard L., Jr. 1935- *St&PR 93*
Freeman, Howard Lee, Jr. 1935- *WhoAm 92*
Freeman, Hugh James 1947- *WhoAm 92*
Freeman, Ira Henry 1906- *WhoAm 92*
Freeman, J. Derek 1916- *IntDcAn*
Freeman, Jack *St&PR 93*
Freeman, James A. 1945- *WhoIns 93*
Freeman, James Atticus, III 1947- *WhoEmL 93*
Freeman, James William 1928- *St&PR 93*
Freeman, Janet Elizabeth 1956- *WhoEmL 93*
Freeman, Janet Helfrich 1928- *WhoAmW 93*
Freeman, Jere Evans 1936- *WhoAm 92*
Freeman, Joan *MiSFD 9*
Freeman, Joan Maie 1918- *WhoWor 93*
Freeman, Joe Bailey 1937- *WhoAm 92*
Freeman, John Edward *Law&B 92*
Freeman, John Mark 1933- *WhoAm 92*
Freeman, John Paul 1937- *WhoE 93*
Freeman, John Yelverton 1950- *WhoEmL 93*
Freeman, Joseph Morris 1925- *St&PR 93*
Freeman, Josh 1949- *WhoEmL 93*
Freeman, Joshua B. 1949- *ConAu 139*
Freeman, Kathleen 1920- *QDrFCA 92 [port]*
Freeman, Kathryn 1956- *BioIn 17, WhoWor 93*
Freeman, Kenneth M. 1949- *WhoEmL 93*
Freeman, Kenneth W. 1950- *St&PR 93*
Freeman, Kester St. Clair, Jr. 1944- *WhoAm 92*
Freeman, Larramour Earl 1931- *WhoE 93*
Freeman, Laura Brewer *Law&B 92*
Freeman, Lee Allen, Jr. 1940- *WhoAm 92*
Freeman, Legh Richmond 1843-1915 *JrnUS*
Freeman, Leonard Murray 1937- *WhoAm 92*
Freeman, Leslie Gordon 1935- *WhoAm 92*
Freeman, Linton Clarke 1927- *WhoAm 92*
Freeman, Louis Barton 1935- *WhoE 93*
Freeman, Louis McDaniel 1940- *WhoAm 92, WhoSSW 93*
Freeman, Louis McDaniel, Jr. 1964- *WhoWor 93*
Freeman, Louis S. 1940- *WhoAm 92*
Freeman, Maggie *ScF&FL 92*
Freeman, Mansfield d1992 *NewYTBS 92*
Freeman, Marcus A., Jr. 1934- *WhoWrEP 92*
Freeman, Marilyn Ruth 1953- *WhoAmW 93*
Freeman, Marjorie Kler 1929- *WhoE 93*
Freeman, Mark *WhoWrEP 92*
Freeman, Mark 1908- *WhoAm 92*
Freeman, Mark William 1949- *WhoEmL 93*
Freeman, Marlou *BioIn 17*
Freeman, Mary Agnes 1943- *WhoAmW 93*
Freeman, Mary Alice *Law&B 92*
Freeman, Mary Anna 1943- *WhoSSW 93*
Freeman, Mary E. Wilkins 1852-1930 *GayN*
Freeman, Mary Eleanor Wilkins 1852-1930 *AmWomPl, BioIn 17*
Freeman, Mary Wilkins 1852-1930 *AmWomWr 92*
Freeman, Maurice Tracy 1904- *WhoAm 92*
Freeman, Meredith Norwin 1920- *WhoAm 92*
Freeman, Michael G. 1938- *St&PR 93*
Freeman, Michael Leonard 1952- *WhoSSW 93*
Freeman, Milton Malcolm Roland 1934- *WhoAm 92*
Freeman, Milton Victor 1911- *WhoAm 92, WhoE 93, WhoWor 93*
Freeman, Montine McDaniel 1915- *WhoAm 92, WhoWor 93*
Freeman, Morgan *BioIn 17*
Freeman, Morgan 1937- *WhoAm 92*
Freeman, Morton S. 1912- *WhoAm 92*
Freeman, Myrna Faye 1939- *WhoAmW 93*
Freeman, Nancy *BioIn 17*
Freeman, Natasha Matrina Leonidow 1958- *WhoAmW 93*
Freeman, Neal Blackwell 1940- *WhoAm 92*
Freeman, Neil 1948- *WhoEmL 93*
Freeman, Norman William 1933- *St&PR 93*
Freeman, Otis S. d1992 *NewYTBS 92*
Freeman, Palmer 1944- *WhoSSW 93*
Freeman, Pat S. 1943- *WhoWrEP 92*
Freeman, Patricia Elizabeth 1924- *WhoAmW 93*
Freeman, Paul (Douglas) 1936- *Baker 92*
Freeman, Paul Randolph 1957- *WhoAm 92, WhoEmL 93*
Freeman, Peter Craig 1956- *WhoAm 92*
Freeman, Peter J. *MajAI, SmATA 69, WhoWrEP 92*
Freeman, Peter Ronald *WhoScE 91-1*
Freeman, Peter Ronald 1939- *WhoWor 93*
Freeman, Philip Conrad, Jr. 1937- *WhoAm 92*
Freeman, Philip Dayne *Law&B 92*
Freeman, Phyllis Rise 1948- *WhoAmW 93*
Freeman, Ralph Douglas 1936- *St&PR 93*
Freeman, Ralph McKenzie 1902-1990 *BioIn 17*
Freeman, Raymond *WhoScE 91-1*
Freeman, Raymond L. 1920- *St&PR 93*
Freeman, Raymond Lee 1919- *WhoAm 92*
Freeman, Reino S. 1919-1990 *BioIn 17*
Freeman, Richard Benton 1931- *WhoAm 92*
Freeman, Richard Boyd 1947- *WhoEmL 93*
Freeman, Richard Francis 1934- *WhoAm 92*
Freeman, Richard Mark 1958- *WhoE 93*
Freeman, Richard Merrell 1921- *WhoAm 92*
Freeman, Robert Alan 1947- *WhoEmL 93*
Freeman, Robert Arnold 1927- *WhoWor 93*
Freeman, Robert John 1947- *WhoEmL 93*
Freeman, Robert Mallory 1941- *St&PR 93, WhoAm 92, WhoSSW 93*
Freeman, Robert Parke 1945- *St&PR 93*
Freeman, Robert (Schofield) 1935- *Baker 92, WhoAm 92*
Freeman, Robert Turner, Jr. 1918- *WhoAm 92*
Freeman, Roger A. 1904-1991 *BioIn 17*
Freeman, Roger A(dolph) 1904-1991 *ConAu 136*
Freeman, Ronald Larry 1947- *WhoEmL 93, WhoSSW 93*
Freeman, Rowland Godfrey, III 1922- *WhoSSW 93*
Freeman, Russell A. *Law&B 92*
Freeman, Russell Adams 1932- *WhoAm 92*
Freeman, Sally 1960- *WhoWor 93*
Freeman, Samuel Ralph 1929- *WhoAm 92*
Freeman, Sarah 1940- *BioIn 17*
Freeman, Scot Lewis 1958- *WhoEmL 93*
Freeman, Sheila Helene 1947- *WhoAmW 93*
Freeman, Shelley 1958- *WhoEmL 93*
Freeman, Simon 1952- *ScF&FL 92*
Freeman, Susan H. *Law&B 92*
Freeman, Susan Swartzman 1957- *WhoEmL 93*
Freeman, Susan Tax 1938- *WhoAm 92*
Freeman, Thomas E. 1930- *St&PR 93*
Freeman, Thomas French 1956- *WhoE 93*
Freeman, Thomas Lee 1951- *St&PR 93*
Freeman, Tiki d1992 *NewYTBS 92*
Freeman, Timothy James *WhoScE 91-1*
Freeman, Todd Ira 1953- *WhoEmL 93*
Freeman, Toni Lea 1956- *WhoAmW 93*
Freeman, Walter Coombs, Jr. 1941- *WhoSSW 93*
Freeman, Wanda Vest 1934- *WhoAmW 93*
Freeman, William *WhoCanL 92*
Freeman, William 1946- *St&PR 93*
Freeman, William A. 1943- *St&PR 93, WhoE 93*
Freeman, William David 1951- *WhoEmL 93*
Freeman, William Emmett 1957- *WhoSSW 93*
Freeman, William Ernest, Jr. 1913- *WhoAm 92*
Freeman-Baraka, Rhonda Nichelle 1962- *WhoAmW 93*
Freeman-Longo, Robert Earl 1951- *WhoEmL 93*
Freemann, Richard Z., Jr. *Law&B 92*
Freemyer, Reginald W. 1960- *WhoEmL 93*
Freeny, Patrick Clinton 1942- *WhoAm 92*
Freer, Coburn 1939- *WhoAm 92*
Freer, Eleanor 1864-1942 *Baker 92*
Freer, John Henry *WhoScE 91-1*
Freer, John Herschel 1938- *WhoAm 92*
Freer, John J. *Law&B 92*
Freer, Robert Elliott, Jr. 1941- *WhoAm 92, WhoWor 93*
Freericks, Mary Avakian 1935- *WhoWrEP 92*
Freerksen, Deborah Lynne 1956- *WhoEmL 93*
Freers, Theodore Frederick 1937- *St&PR 93*
Freer-Smith, Peter Hamilton *WhoScE 91-1*
Freese, Alan J. 1931- *St&PR 93*

Freese, Courtland F.H. 1928- *St&PR 93*
Freese, Frank E. 1940- *WhoIns 93*
Freese, Frank Edward 1940- *St&PR 93*
Freese, George E. 1942- *St&PR 93*
Freese, Hans-Hermann 1931- *WhoScE 91-3*
Freese, John Philip 1947- *WhoEmL 93*
Freese, Katherine 1957- *WhoAmW 93*
Freese, Margaret Poindexter 1948- *WhoAmW 93*
Freese, Melanie Louise 1945- *WhoAmW 93*
Freese, Robert Gerard 1929- *St&PR 93*
Freese, Uwe Ernest 1925- *WhoAm 92*
Freeson, Lee 1901- *BioIn 17*
Freeston, Ian Leslie *WhoScE 91-1*
Freestone, David Stanley 1933- *WhoWor 93*
Freestone, Mitchell C. *Law&B 92*
Freeth, Douglas D. 1935- *St&PR 93*
Freeth, Douglas Duncan 1935- *WhoAm 92*
Freeze, James Donald 1932- *WhoAm 92*
Freeze, Nancy Sue 1939- *St&PR 93*
Freeze, Roy Allan 1939- *WhoAm 92*
Freeze, Thomas W. 1951- *St&PR 93*
Fregetto, Eugene Fletcher 1947- *WhoEmL 93*
Fregonese, Hugo 1908-1987 *MiSFD 9N*
Fregoni, Mario 1934- *WhoScE 91-3*
Fregosi, James Louis 1942- *BiDAMSp 1989, WhoAm 92, WhoE 93*
Fre-Hiwet, Assefa 1937- *WhoUN 92*
Frei, Alphonse Emil 1938- *St&PR 93*
Frei, Eduardo 1911-1982 *DcTwHis*
Frei, Emil, III 1924- *WhoAm 92*
Frei, John Karen 1936- *WhoAmW 93, WhoSSW 93, WhoWor 93*
Frei, Michael Clark *Law&B 92*
Freiberg, Karen Louise 1944- *WhoE 93*
Freiberg, Lowell Carl 1939- *St&PR 93, WhoAm 92*
Freiberg, Margaret B.G. *Law&B 92*
Freiberg, Mira A.K. *Law&B 92*
Freiberg, Reinhard Yoav 1937- *WhoUN 92*
Freiberg, Stanley K. 1923- *ScF&FL 92, WhoCanL 92*
Freiberger, Steven Z. 1950- *ConAu 138*
Freiberger, Walter Frederick 1924- *WhoAm 92, WhoWor 93*
Freibergs, Imants 1934- *WhoWor 93*
Freibert, Lucy M. 1922- *WhoWrEP 92*
Freibrun, Eric Scott *Law&B 92*
Freiburger, Betsey *WhoWrEP 92*
Freid, Jacob *WhoAm 92*
Freidberg, Sidney 1914- *WhoAm 92, WhoWor 93*
Freidberg, Stephen P. 1939- *St&PR 93*
Freidberg, Stephen Roy 1934- *WhoE 93*
Freidel, Frank Burt, Jr. 1916- *WhoAm 92*
Freidenbergs, Ingrid 1944- *WhoE 93*
Freidenreich, Harriet Pass 1947- *WhoAmW 93*
Freidheim, Cyrus F., Jr. 1935- *St&PR 93, WhoWor 93*
Freidin, Seymour 1917-1991 *BioIn 17*
Freidinger, Roger Merlin 1947- *WhoAm 92, WhoE 93, WhoEmL 93*
Freidkin, George Jacob 1946- *WhoEmL 93, WhoSSW 93*
Freidman, Orrie M. 1915- *St&PR 93*
Freidson, Eliot Lazarus 1923- *WhoAm 92*
Freier, Susan Marcie 1953- *WhoEmL 93*
Freiert, Donald Vincent, Jr. 1947- *WhoAm 92*
Freifeld, Shlomo d1990 *BioIn 17*
Freifeld, Stanley 1954- *WhoE 93*
Freigang, Dietrich 1940- *St&PR 93*
Freiheit, Clayton Fredric 1938- *WhoAm 92*
Freiherr von Handel, Norbert Erasmus 1942- *WhoWor 93*
Freiherr von Kleydorff, Ludwig Otto Alexander 1926- *WhoAm 92*
Freiherr Von Lersner, Heinrich Ludwig 1930- *WhoScE 91-3*
Freihofer, Charles Christian 1941- *St&PR 93*
Freihofer, Hans Peter M. 1937- *WhoScE 91-3*
Freihofer, Hans Peter Michael 1937- *WhoWor 93*
Freihofer, Robert W. 1919-1991 *BioIn 17*
Freiler, Frank Joseph 1955- *WhoEmL 93*
Freiley, Dennis John 1944- *WhoSSW 93*
Freilich, David *Law&B 92*
Freilich, Jeff 1948- *WhoAm 92*
Freilich, Joan Sherman 1941- *WhoAmW 93*
Freilich, William B. *Law&B 92*
Freilicher, Jane *BioIn 17*
Freilicher, Jane 1924- *WhoAm 92*
Freilicher, Melvyn S. 1946- *WhoWrEP 92*
Freilinger, Ida M.W. 1943- *WhoWrEP 92*
Freiman, David Burl 1947- *WhoAm 92*
Freiman, David Galland 1911- *WhoAm 92*
Freiman, Hal Jeffrey 1954- *WhoE 93*
Freiman, Lela Kay 1939- *WhoAmW 93*
Freiman, Paul 1934- *St&PR 93*
Freiman, Paul E. 1932- *WhoAm 92*
Freiman, Sharon K. *Law&B 92*
Freimarck, George Stephen Alfred 1917- *WhoE 93*
Freimark, Jeffrey Philip 1955- *St&PR 93, WhoAm 92*
Freimark, Robert 1922- *WhoAm 92*
Frei Montalva, Eduardo 1911-1982 *ColdWar 2 [port]*
Freimuth, Marc W. *Law&B 92*
Freimuth, Marilyn Joan 1951- *WhoAmW 93*
Freinkel, Ruth Kimmelstiel 1926- *WhoAm 92*
Freire, Alexis Tadeu de Aguiar 1956- *WhoWor 93*
Freire, Antonio M. *Law&B 92*
Freire, Nelson (Jose) 1944- *Baker 92*
Freire, Paulo 1921- *BioIn 17*
Freire Falcao, Jose Cardinal 1925- *WhoAm 92, WhoWor 93*
Freireich, Emil J. 1927- *WhoAm 92, WhoSSW 93*
Freirich, Jeff Robert 1946- *St&PR 93*
Freirich, Jerry *St&PR 93*
Freis, Edward David 1912- *WhoAm 92*
Freischlag, Paul H., Jr. 1954- *St&PR 93*
Freise, Bruce Harry 1935- *St&PR 93*
Freise, Kathryn Maria 1962- *WhoEmL 93*
Freismuth, Thomas Patrick 1948- *WhoEmL 93*
Freitag, David Franklin, II 1945- *WhoWor 93*
Freitag, Edward G. *Law&B 92*
Freitag, Edward G. 1946- *St&PR 93*
Freitag, Frederick Gerald 1952- *WhoEmL 93*
Freitag, Harlow 1936- *WhoAm 92*
Freitag, Helmut Erich 1932- *WhoScE 91-3*
Freitag, Henry George 1932- *St&PR 93*
Freitag, Herta Therese 1908- *WhoSSW 93*
Freitag, James Milton 1953- *WhoEmL 93*
Freitag, Nicholas H. 1954- *St&PR 93*
Freitag, Robert Frederick 1920- *WhoAm 92, WhoSSW 93*
Freitag, Wolfgang Martin 1924- *WhoAm 92*
Freitag-Pace, Barbara Jo 1948- *WhoEmL 93*
Freitas, Antonio, Jr. 1908- *BiDAMSp 1989*
Freitas (Branco), Frederico (Guedes) de 1902-1980 *Baker 92*
Freitas, David M. *Law&B 92*
Freitas, Jeffrey Anthony 1946- *WhoE 93*
Freitas, Joe A. 1926- *St&PR 93*
Freitas, Louis A. *St&PR 93*
Freitas, Maria Isabel B. Sande 1949- *WhoWor 93*
Freitas, Randall William 1951- *WhoEmL 93*
Freitas Branco, Luis de 1890-1955 *Baker 92*
Freivalds, John 1944- *WhoWrEP 92*
Freiwald, David Allen 1941- *WhoWor 93*
Freizer, Louis A. 1931- *WhoAm 92, WhoE 93, WhoWor 93*
Frejacques, C. 1924- *WhoScE 91-2*
Frejacques, Claude *WhoScE 91-2*
Frelich, Phyllis 1944- *WhoAm 92*
Frelick, Linden Frederick 1938- *WhoAm 92*
Freling, Richard Alan 1932- *WhoAm 92*
Frelinger, Jeffrey Allen 1948- *WhoAm 92, WhoEmL 93*
Frelinghuysen, Joseph Sherman 1941- *St&PR 93*
Frelinghuysen, Joseph Sherman, Jr. 1941- *WhoAm 92*
Frelix, Ronald H. 1956- *WhoSSW 93*
Frell, Ellen Frances 1950- *WhoWrEP 92*
Fremaux, Bernard 1936- *WhoScE 91-2*
Fremaux, Louis 1921- *Baker 92*
Frembgen, Theodore Edward 1936- *St&PR 93*
Fremder, Marcel 1931- *St&PR 93*
Fremgen, Thomas E. *Law&B 92*
Freminet, Alain 1942- *WhoScE 91-2*
Fremlin, David Heaver 1942- *WhoWor 93*
Fremon, Richard C. 1918- *WhoE 93*
Fremont, Alicia Ann 1959- *WhoAmW 93*
Fremont, Eleanor *ScF&FL 92*
Fremont, Ernest Hoar, Jr. 1925- *WhoWor 93*
Fremont, Jessie Benton 1824-1902 *BioIn 17*
Fremont, John C. 1813-1890 *PolPar*
Fremont, John Charles 1813-1890 *BioIn 17, Expl 93 [port], HarEnMi*
Fremont-Smith, Marion R. 1926- *WhoAm 92*
Fremont-Smith, Richard 1935- *WhoE 93*
Fremont-Smith, Thayer 1931- *WhoAm 92*
Fremouw, Edward Joseph 1934- *WhoAm 92*
Fremstad, Olive 1871-1951 *Baker 92, IntDcOp, OxDcOp*
Fremund, Zdenek Anthony 1946- *WhoAm 92, WhoE 93*
French, Albert E. d1991 *BioIn 17*
French, Alden, Jr. 1934- *WhoAm 92*
French, Anne Richmond Warner 1869-1913 *AmWomPl*
French, Anthony Philip 1920- *WhoAm 92*
French, Antonia *ConAu 139, ConTFT 10*
French, Arthur Leeman, Jr. 1940- *WhoAm 92*
French, Barbara 1957- *WhoEmL 93*
French, Becky Russell 1953- *WhoEmL 93*
French, Benjamin B. 1800-1870 *BioIn 17*
French, Bertram F. 1927- *St&PR 93*
French, Bevan M. 1937- *BioIn 17*
French, Bevan Meredith 1937- *WhoAm 92, WhoE 93*
French, Bruce Hartung 1915- *WhoAm 92*
French, Carl Stuart 1947- *WhoWor 93*
French, Carolyn J. 1946- *St&PR 93*
French, Catherine 1946- *WhoAm 92*
French, Charles Ezra 1923- *WhoAm 92*
French, Charles Ferris, Jr. 1918- *St&PR 93, WhoAm 92*
French, Charles Stacy 1907- *WhoAm 92*
French, Clarence Levi, Jr. 1925- *WhoAm 92*
French, Colin Val 1957- *WhoEmL 93*
French, Daniel Chester 1850-1931 *GayN*
French, David 1939- *WhoCanL 92*
French, David H. 1942- *St&PR 93*
French, David Heath 1918- *WhoAm 92*
French, David Nichols 1936- *WhoE 93*
French, Dennis E. *Law&B 92*
French, Donald Anthony 1955- *St&PR 93*
French, E(mma) Yulee 1926- *WhoWrEP 92*
French, Edward Alexander *WhoScE 91-1*
French, Edward F. 1959- *St&PR 93*
French, Edward Ronald 1937- *WhoWor 93*
French, Eleanor Clark 1908-1990 *BioIn 17*
French, Elizabeth Irene 1938- *WhoSSW 93*
French, Eunice Pelafigue 1938- *WhoAm 92*
French, Fiona 1944- *ConAu 40NR, MajAI*
French, Georgine Louise 1934- *WhoAmW 93*
French, Glendon Everett, Jr. 1934- *WhoAm 92*
French, Gordon 1949- *WhoSSW 93*
French, H. Louis 1940- *St&PR 93*
French, Harold Stanley 1921- *WhoAm 92, WhoE 93*
French, Harold Wendell 1930- *WhoSSW 93*
French, Henry Pierson, Jr. 1934- *WhoE 93, WhoWor 93*
French, Hollis, II 1927- *St&PR 93*
French, Jacob 1754-1817 *Baker 92*
French, James Edward 1937- *WhoE 93*
French, James Kevin *Law&B 92*
French, James T. 1931- *St&PR 93*
French, James William 1935- *St&PR 93, WhoAm 92*
French, Jeffrey Stuart 1954- *WhoE 93, WhoEmL 93*
French, Jim *BioIn 17*
French, John, III 1932- *WhoAm 92, WhoWor 93*
French, John Denton Pinkstone 1852-1925 *BioIn 17, HarEnMi*
French, John Dwyer 1933- *WhoAm 92, WhoWor 93*
French, John Henry, Jr. 1911- *WhoAm 92*
French, John M. 1942- *St&PR 93*
French, Joseph Anthony *Law&B 92*
French (Judd), Laurel Kathleen *Law&B 92*
French, Judson Cull 1922- *WhoAm 92*
French, Kenneth Ronald 1954- *WhoAm 92*
French, Larry B. 1958- *St&PR 93*
French, Larry J. 1940- *St&PR 93*
French, Larry L. 1948- *WhoSSW 93*
French, Laura 1949- *ScF&FL 92*
French, Lew Daniel, III 1960- *WhoEmL 93*
French, Lexie Anne 1949- *WhoAmW 93*
French, Linda J. *Law&B 92*
French, Linda J. 1947- *St&PR 93*
French, Linda Jean 1947- *WhoAm 92*
French, Lisa 1953- *St&PR 93, WhoIns 93*
French, Lyle Albert 1915- *WhoAm 92*
French, Marcus Emmett 1929- *WhoAm 92*
French, Marilyn 1929- *BioIn 17, CurBio 92 [port], WhoAm 92, WhoAmW 93, WhoWrEP 92*
French, Maurice Lindsey *BioIn 17*
French, Melvin Perry 1962- *WhoEmL 93*
French, Michael 1944- *ScF&FL 92*
French, Michael Bruce 1954- *WhoEmL 93, WhoSSW 93*
French, Michael Harvey 1949- *WhoWrEP 92*
French, Michael Joseph *WhoScE 91-1*
French, Nelson 1925- *St&PR 93*
French, Paul *ConAu 137, MajAI*
French, Percy 1854-1920 *BioIn 17*
French, Peter A(ndrew) 1942- *ConAu 38NR*
French, Philip 1933- *BioIn 17*
French, Philip F. 1932- *St&PR 93*
French, Philip Franks 1932- *WhoAm 92*
French, Raymond 1920- *St&PR 93, WhoAm 92*
French, Richard *BioIn 17*
French, Richard Frederic 1915- *WhoAm 92*
French, Richard Harry 1947- *WhoEmL 93*
French, Richard W. *Law&B 92*
French, Robert *ScF&FL 92*
French, Robert Warren 1911- *WhoAm 92*
French, Roderick Stuart 1931- *WhoWor 93*
French, Sharon Marie 1952- *WhoSSW 93*
French, Simon *WhoScE 91-1*
French, Simon 1957- *DcChlFi*
French, Stanley George 1933- *WhoAm 92*
French, Stephanie *BioIn 17*
French, Susan *Law&B 92*
French, Thomas C. 1949- *St&PR 93*
French, Valerie 1932-1990 *BioIn 17*
French, Valerie 1965- *WhoAmW 93*
French, Virginia Lee 1939- *WhoAmW 93*
French, William 1926- *WhoCanL 92*
French, William Decker 1946- *WhoE 93*
French, William Harold 1926- *WhoAm 92*
Frenchak, Harry Nicholas 1939- *St&PR 93*
French-Davis, Ricardo 1936- *WhoWor 93*
Frendahl, Dennis Michael 1959- *WhoSSW 93*
Frendo, Michael 1955- *WhoWor 93*
Frendt, Richard J. 1942- *St&PR 93*
Frene, Jean B.M. 1941- *WhoScE 91-2*
Freneau, Philip 1752-1832 *JrnUS, MagSAmL [port]*
Freneau, Philip M. 1752-1832 *PolPar*
Frenger, Paul Fred 1946- *WhoEmL 93*
Freni, D. Richard 1914- *WhoE 93*
Freni, Melo 1934- *DcLB 128 [port]*
Freni, Mirella *BioIn 17*
Freni, Mirella 1935- *Baker 92, IntDcOp [port], OxDcOp, WhoAm 92*
Frenier, James Francis 1934- *St&PR 93*
Frenier, Thomas J. 1948- *St&PR 93*
Freni Vegeto, Maria 1928- *WhoScE 91-3*
Frenkel, Eugene Phillip 1929- *WhoAm 92*
Frenkel, Jacob A. *BioIn 17*
Frenkel, James 1948- *ScF&FL 92*
Frenkel, Joan D. *ScF&FL 92*
Frenkel, Karen A. 1955- *WhoWrEP 92*
Frenkel, Michael *Law&B 92*
Frenkel, Michael 1936- *St&PR 93, WhoAm 92*
Frenkel, Nama Rachel 1951- *WhoE 93*
Frenkel, Robert I. *Law&B 92*
Frenkel, Robert Irwin 1954- *WhoEmL 93*
Frenkel-Brunswik, Else 1908-1958 *BioIn 17*
Frenkiel, Nora *BioIn 17, NewYTBS 92 [port]*
Frenkiel, Norman N. d1992 *NewYTBS 92*
Frenkiel, Paul 1952- *St&PR 93*
Frenkiel, Richard Henry 1943- *WhoAm 92*
Frenklach, Michael Yehoshua 1947- *WhoEmL 93*
Frenn, Thomas Louis 1947- *WhoEmL 93*
Frenock, Larry 1956- *WhoEmL 93*
Frensilli, Frederick John 1936- *WhoE 93*
Frentsos, Jeanne Marie 1958- *WhoEmL 93*
Frentz, Harold George 1919- *WhoAm 92*
Frentz, William C. 1934- *St&PR 93*
Frentzen, Jeffrey 1956- *ScF&FL 92*
Frenyea, Melissa Mary 1968- *WhoEmL 93*
Frenz, Dorothy Ann 1954- *WhoE 93*
Frenzel, Bill *BioIn 17*
Frenzel, Otto Nicholas, III 1930- *St&PR 93*
Frenzer, Peter F. 1934- *WhoIns 93*
Frenzer, Peter Frederick 1934- *St&PR 93, WhoAm 92*
Frere, Jean-Marie 1943- *WhoScE 91-2*
Frere, John Edward 1947- *St&PR 93, WhoAm 92*
Frere, Maurice Herbert 1932- *WhoAm 92, WhoSSW 93*
Freres, Ronald P. 1943- *St&PR 93*
Frerichs, Ernest Sunley 1925- *WhoAm 92*
Freriks, Donald James 1944- *St&PR 93*
Freris, Leonard Leo 1934- *WhoWor 93*
Fresch, Marie Beth 1957- *WhoAmW 93, WhoWor 93*
Freschi, Bruno Basilio 1937- *WhoE 93*
Freschi, (Giovanni) Domenico c. 1625-1710 *Baker 92*
Fresco, Jacques Robert 1928- *WhoAm 92*
Fresco, Michael *MiSFD 9*
Frescobaldi, Girolamo 1583-1643 *Baker 92*
Frese, Glenn *Law&B 92*
Frese, Millie Kay 1963- *WhoWrEP 92*
Frese, Walter Wenzel 1909- *WhoAm 92*
Fresher, Brian *Law&B 92*

Freshman, Bruce *ScF&FL 92*
Fresh Prince *BioIn 17*
Freshwater, Mark Edwards 1948- *ScF&FL 92*
Freshwater, Michael Felix 1948- *WhoAm 92, WhoEmL 93, WhoSSW 93, WhoWor 93*
Fresia, Jerry *BioIn 17*
Fresiello, Carol Ann *Law&B 92*
Freske, Richard Clarence 1940- *St&PR 93*
Fresnay, Pierre 1897-1975 *IntDcF 2-3 [port]*
Fresnel, J.M. 1937- *WhoScE 91-4*
Fresno Larrain, Juan Francisco 1914- *WhoWor 93*
Freso, Tibor 1918- *Baker 92*
Fresquez, Carolina A. *St&PR 93*
Freston, Thomas E. 1945- *WhoAm 92*
Fretageot, Nora C. *AmWomPl*
Freter, Lisa 1951- *WhoAmW 93, WhoEmL 93*
Freter, Mark Allen 1947- *WhoEmL 93, WhoWor 93*
Frett, Richard W. *Law&B 92*
Frette, Donald Eugene 1947- *WhoEmL 93*
Fretter, T.W. *WhoWrEP 92*
Fretter, William Bache 1916-1991 *BioIn 17*
Fretthold, Timothy J. *Law&B 92*
Fretthold, Timothy J. 1949- *St&PR 93*
Fretthold, Timothy Jon 1949- *WhoAm 92*
Fretts, Bruce *ScF&FL 92*
Fretts, Debra Rene 1955- *St&PR 93*
Fretwell, Dorrie Shearer 1927- *WhoSSW 93*
Fretwell, Elbert Kirtley, Jr. 1923- *WhoAm 92*
Fretwell, Elizabeth 1920- *OxDcOp*
Fretwell, Lyman Jefferson, Jr. 1934- *WhoE 93*
Freuchen-Gale, Dagmar d1991 *BioIn 17*
Freud, Anna 1895-1982 *BioIn 17*
Freud, Gloria Gaca *Law&B 92*
Freud, John Sigmund 1956- *WhoEmL 93*
Freud, Lucian *BioIn 17*
Freud, Sigmund 1856-1939 *BioIn 17, DcTwHis*
Freudberg, Seth D. 1959- *WhoIns 93*
Freudenberg, Wilhelm 1838-1928 *Baker 92*
Freudenberger, Herbert Justin 1926- *WhoAm 92*
Freudenberger, Herman 1922- *WhoAm 92*
Freudenberger, Richard A. *Law&B 92*
Freudenheim, Milton B. 1927- *WhoAm 92*
Freudenheim, Tom Lippmann 1937- *WhoAm 92*
Freudenschuss, Helmut 1956- *WhoUN 92*
Freudenstein, Ferdinand 1926- *WhoAm 92*
Freudenthal, Ernest G. 1920- *St&PR 93*
Freudenthal, Hans 1905-1990 *BioIn 17*
Freudenthal, Roslyn Roth 1909- *WhoE 93*
Freudenthal, Steven Franklin 1949- *WhoAm 92*
Freudmann, Axel I. 1946- *WhoIns 93*
Freudmann, Axel Ivan 1946- *St&PR 93*
Freund, Allan G. *Law&B 92*
Freund, Carol Marguerite 1957- *WhoSSW 93*
Freund, Charles Gibson 1923- *WhoAm 92*
Freund, Douglas 1947- *St&PR 93*
Freund, Eckhard 1940- *WhoWor 93*
Freund, Edouard 1947- *WhoScE 91-2*
Freund, Edouard Franklin 1947- *WhoWor 93*
Freund, Elisabeth 1898-1982 *BioIn 17*
Freund, Elsie Marie 1912- *BioIn 17*
Freund, Emma Frances 1922- *WhoAm 92, WhoAmW 93, WhoSSW 93*
Freund, Ernst 1864-1932 *OxCSupC*
Freund, Fred A. 1928- *WhoAm 92*
Freund, Gerald 1930- *WhoAm 92, WhoWor 93*
Freund, Gisele 1912- *BioIn 17*
Freund, Hans-Joachim 1951- *WhoScE 91-3, WhoWor 93*
Freund, Hugh 1937- *St&PR 93*
Freund, Hugo Allen 1954- *WhoEmL 93*
Freund, James Coleman 1934- *WhoAm 92*
Freund, John Christian 1848-1924 *Baker 92*
Freund, Karl 1890-1969 *MiSFD 9N*
Freund, Lambert Ben 1942- *WhoAm 92*
Freund, Leopold 1808- *BioIn 17*
Freund, Lisa 1951- *WhoAmW 93*
Freund, Marya 1876-1966 *Baker 92*
Freund, Maxine B. 1946- *WhoEmL 93*
Freund, Mitchell David 1953- *WhoAm 92, WhoE 93, WhoEmL 93*
Freund, Paul A. 1908-1992 *NewYTBS 92 [port]*
Freund, Paul A(braham) 1908-1992 *ConAu 136*
Freund, Paul Abraham 1908-1992 *BioIn 17*
Freund, Richard L. 1921- *WhoAm 92*
Freund, Richard W. d1991 *BioIn 17*
Freund, Robert Michael 1953- *WhoEmL 93*
Freund, Roland Paul 1939- *WhoE 93*
Freund, Ronald S. 1934- *WhoAm 92*
Freund, Samuel J. 1949- *WhoE 93, WhoEmL 93*
Freund, William Curt 1926- *WhoAm 92*
Freundlich, August Ludwig 1924- *WhoAm 92*
Freundlich, Gloria Winifred 1936- *WhoSSW 93*
Freundt, Cornelius c. 1535-1591 *Baker 92*
Freundt, Eyvind A. 1919- *WhoScE 91-2*
Freundt, Pilar Perera 1946- *WhoAmW 93*
Frevert, Douglas James 1952- *WhoEmL 93*
Frevert, James Wilmot 1922- *WhoSSW 93*
Frevert, Richard Anton 1956- *WhoEmL 93*
Frew, Robert Simpson 1940- *WhoE 93*
Frewein, J. *WhoScE 91-4*
Frey, Albert 1903- *WhoAm 92*
Frey, Alexander M. 1881-1957 *ScF&FL 92*
Frey, Andrew Lewis 1938- *WhoAm 92*
Frey, Audrey Maxwell 1957- *WhoAmW 93*
Frey, Bob Henry 1953- *WhoSSW 93*
Frey, Charles Frederick 1929- *WhoAm 92, WhoWor 93*
Frey, Christian Miller 1923- *WhoAm 92*
Frey, Cynthia Fuller 1958- *WhoAmW 93*
Frey, Dale Franklin 1932- *St&PR 93, WhoAm 92*
Frey, David Gardner 1942- *St&PR 93, WhoAm 92*
Frey, Donald N. 1923- *St&PR 93*
Frey, Donald Nelson 1923- *WhoAm 92*
Frey, Edward R. 1944- *St&PR 93*
Frey, Emil 1889-1946 *Baker 92*
Frey, Frank William 1947- *WhoEmL 93*
Frey, Frederick August 1938- *WhoAm 92, WhoE 93*
Frey, Frederick James 1950- *WhoIns 93*
Frey, Gerard Louis 1914- *WhoAm 92*
Frey, Glenn *BioIn 17*
Frey, Glenn 1948- *WhoAm 92*
Frey, Hans-Hasso 1927- *WhoScE 91-3*
Frey, Harry J. 1941- *WhoScE 91-4*
Frey, Harry Juhana 1941- *WhoWor 93*
Frey, Henry Charles 1948- *WhoEmL 93*
Frey, Henry Montague *WhoScE 91-1*
Frey, Herman S. 1920- *WhoAm 92, WhoWor 93*
Frey, Hildebrand Wolfgang *WhoScE 91-1*
Frey, Jacques 1934- *WhoScE 91-2*
Frey, James E. 1946- *St&PR 93*
Frey, James G. 1931- *St&PR 93*
Frey, James Gottfried 1931- *WhoAm 92*
Frey, James McKnight 1932- *WhoAm 92*
Frey, James N. 1948- *ScF&FL 92*
Frey, Jan Paul 1942- *St&PR 93*
Frey, Jay J. 1932- *St&PR 93*
Frey, Jean-Jacques *Law&B 92*
Frey, Jeffery Bryan 1943- *WhoSSW 93*
Frey, Jerry McBride 1953- *St&PR 93*
Frey, John A. 1920- *St&PR 93*
Frey, John M. 1928- *St&PR 93*
Frey, Joseph Charles 1941- *St&PR 93*
Frey, Kelly Leibert 1951- *WhoEmL 93*
Frey, Kenneth John 1923- *WhoAm 92*
Frey, Lawrence D. 1950- *St&PR 93*
Frey, Leon Harry 1933- *St&PR 93*
Frey, Linda Susan 1951- *WhoEmL 93*
Frey, Lori Ann 1963- *WhoE 93*
Frey, Louis, Jr. 1934- *WhoAm 92*
Frey, Mark A. *St&PR 93*
Frey, Martin 1940- *WhoScE 91-4*
Frey, Martin Alan 1939- *WhoAm 92, WhoSSW 93*
Frey, Marvin V. d1992 *NewYTBS 92*
Frey, Mary Elizabeth *Law&B 92*
Frey, Nancy 1946- *WhoE 93*
Frey, Nicholas M. 1948- *WhoAm 92*
Frey, Oliver *ScF&FL 92*
Frey, Pearl Payne *AmWomPl*
Frey, Philip, Jr. 1927- *St&PR 93*
Frey, Rene L. 1939- *WhoWor 93*
Frey, Richard K. 1928- *St&PR 93*
Frey, Robert Imbrie 1943- *WhoAm 92*
Frey, Roger 1913- *BioIn 17*
Frey, Stuart Macklin 1925- *WhoAm 92*
Frey, Suzan Ann 1952- *WhoE 93*
Frey, Thomas Joseph 1962- *WhoE 93*
Frey, Thomas Joseph, Jr. *WhoE 93*
Frey, Timothy John 1955- *WhoEmL 93*
Frey, Walter 1898-1985 *Baker 92*
Frey, William Carl 1930- *WhoAm 92*
Frey, William Francis 1933- *WhoSSW 93*
Freyberg, Bernard Cyril 1889-1963 *DcTwHis, HarEnMi*
Freyberg, Derek Peter *Law&B 92*
Freychet, Pierre 1935- *WhoScE 91-2*
Freychet, Pierre F. 1935- *WhoScE 91-2*
Freycinet, Charles Louis de Saulces de 1828-1923 *BioIn 17*
Freyd, Jennifer Joy 1957- *WhoAmW 93, WhoEmL 93*
Freyd, Peter John 1936- *WhoAm 92, WhoE 93*
Freyd, William Pattinson 1933- *WhoE 93, WhoWor 93*
Freydank, Harri Hans-Joachim 1945- *WhoWor 93*
Freydberg, Eli A. d1990 *BioIn 17*
Freyer, Jorg 1952- *St&PR 93*
Freyer, Victoria C. *WhoAmW 93, WhoSSW 93*
Freyhardt, Herbert C. 1941- *WhoScE 91-3*
Freyland, Werner Franz 1942- *WhoWor 93*
Freymann, John Gordon 1922- *WhoE 93*
Freymuth, G. Russell 1928- *St&PR 93, WhoAm 92*
Freyre, Gilberto 1900-1987 *BioIn 17*
Freyss, David 1933- *WhoAm 92*
Freytag, David M. *Law&B 92*
Freytag, Donald Ashe 1937- *WhoAm 92*
Freytag, Rene *WhoScE 91-2*
Freytag, Sharon Nelson 1943- *WhoAmW 93*
Frey-Wettstein, Manuel 1932- *WhoWor 93*
Frez, Il'ja 1909- *DrEEuF*
Frezza, Christine Anne 1942- *WhoE 93*
Frezza, Robert 1956- *ScF&FL 92*
Frezzolini, Erminia 1818-1884 *OxDcOp*
Fri, Robert Wheeler 1935- *WhoAm 92*
Friant, Ray J. 1931- *St&PR 93*
Friar, George Edward 1916- *WhoSSW 93*
Friar, Martha Jane *Law&B 92*
Friar, Martha Jane 1952- *WhoAmW 93*
Friary, Donald Richard 1940- *WhoE 93*
Frias, Antonio 1939- *St&PR 93*
Frias, Jaime Luis 1933- *WhoAm 92, WhoWor 93*
Frias, Joseph 1940- *St&PR 93*
Frias, Marlene Citron de *NotHsAW 93*
Frias y Soto, Hilarion 1831-1905 *DcMexL*
Friauf, Katherine Elizabeth 1956- *WhoAmW 93*
Fribance, Caroline E. 1945- *St&PR 93*
Fribec, Kresimir 1908- *Baker 92*
Friberg, Emil Edwards 1935- *WhoSSW 93*
Friberg, Lars 1920- *WhoScE 91-4*
Fribourg, Michel *WhoAm 92*
Fribourgh, James Henry 1926- *WhoAm 92, WhoWor 93*
Fric, Martin 1902-1968 *DrEEuF*
Fricano, John Charles 1930- *WhoAm 92, WhoE 93, WhoWor 93*
Fricano, Wayne R. 1944- *St&PR 93, WhoAm 92*
Fricci, Antonietta 1840-1912 *Baker 92*
Frick, Dennis Duane *Law&B 92*
Frick, Flora M. *AmWomPl*
Frick, Gary John 1940- *St&PR 93*
Frick, Gottlob 1906- *Baker 92, IntDcOp, OxDcOp*
Frick, Henry Clay 1849-1919 *GayN*
Frick, Ivan Eugene 1928- *WhoAm 92*
Frick, John Paul 1955- *WhoSSW 93*
Frick, John William 1951- *WhoEmL 93, WhoWor 93*
Frick, Joseph Francis 1930- *WhoAm 92*
Frick, Mr. 1915- *WhoAm 92*
Frick, Oscar Lionel 1923- *WhoAm 92*
Frick, Robert William 1937- *WhoAm 92*
Frick, Ronald Alan 1961- *WhoEmL 93*
Frick, Sandra Groome 1935- *WhoAmW 93*
Frick, Sidney Wanning 1915- *WhoAm 92*
Frick, Werner Wilhelm 1946- *WhoWor 93*
Fricke, Burkhard 1941- *WhoScE 91-3*
Fricke, Carolyn Marie 1951- *WhoEmL 93*
Fricke, Gerhard 1921- *WhoScE 91-3*
Fricke, Herbert H. 1939- *St&PR 93*
Fricke, Hilmar L. *Law&B 92*
Fricke, Howard R. 1936- *WhoIns 93*
Fricke, Janie 1947- *WhoAm 92*
Fricke, Jochen S. 1938- *WhoWor 93*
Fricke, John *ScF&FL 92*
Fricke, John W. 1945- *St&PR 93*
Fricke, Martin P. 1937- *St&PR 93*
Fricke, Richard I. 1922- *St&PR 93*
Fricke, Richard John 1945- *WhoE 93, WhoWor 93*
Fricke, Roger Alan 1942- *WhoE 93*
Fricke, Ron *MiSFD 9*
Fricke, Thomas F. *Law&B 92*
Frickel, Donald J. *Law&B 92*
Fricker, Brenda *BioIn 17, WhoAmW 93*
Fricker, Evan N. 1938- *St&PR 93*
Fricker, Herbert (Austin) 1868-1943 *Baker 92*
Fricker, John Arthur 1931- *WhoAm 92*
Fricker, Peter Racine 1920-1990 *Baker 92*
Frickert, E.M. *WhoWrEP 92*
Frickey, Darryl Paul *Law&B 92*
Fricks, Carla Diane 1953- *WhoSSW 93*
Fricks, Ernest Eugene 1948- *WhoEmL 93*
Fricks, William Peavy 1944- *WhoAm 92*
Fricsay, Ferenc 1914-1963 *Baker 92, OxDcOp*
Frid, Geza 1904-1989 *Baker 92*
Friday, Donald Conrad 1947- *WhoE 93*
Friday, Elbert Walter, Jr. 1939- *WhoAm 92, WhoE 93*
Friday, Gilbert Anthony, Jr. 1930- *WhoE 93*
Friday, Herschel Hugar 1922- *WhoAm 92, WhoWor 93*
Friday, John Ernest, Jr. 1929- *WhoAm 92*
Friday, Karl Frederick 1957- *WhoSSW 93*
Friday, Mary H. *Law&B 92*
Friday, Nancy *BioIn 17*
Friday, Nancy 1937- *WhoWrEP 92*
Friday, Richard Harvey 1942- *St&PR 93*
Friday, William Clyde 1920- *WhoAm 92, WhoSSW 93*
Friderici, Daniel 1584-1638 *Baker 92*
Fridhandler, Michael A. *Law&B 92*
Fridkin, Alan R. *Law&B 92*
Fridley, Cheryl Lynn 1959- *WhoAmW 93*
Fridley, James Owen 1941- *WhoSSW 93*
Fridley, Robert Bruce 1934- *WhoAm 92*
Fridley, Saundra Lynn 1948- *WhoAmW 93, WhoEmL 93, WhoWor 93*
Fridling, David 1950- *St&PR 93*
Fridlington, John W. 1944- *St&PR 93*
Fridman, Josef Josel *Law&B 92*
Fridman, Josef Josel 1945- *WhoAm 92*
Fridman, W.H. *WhoScE 91-2*
Fridovich, Irwin 1929- *WhoAm 92*
Fridrik, Laszlo 1939- *WhoScE 91-4*
Fridriksson, Sturla 1922- *WhoScE 91-4*
Fridson, Martin Steven 1952- *WhoE 93*
Fridstein, Stanley M. *St&PR 93*
Frieber, Laury M. *Law&B 92*
Frieberg, John *St&PR 93*
Fried, Albert, Jr. 1930- *St&PR 93, WhoAm 92*
Fried, Alexej 1922- *Baker 92*
Fried, Barbara Brachman 1942- *WhoAmW 93*
Fried, Bernard 1928- *St&PR 93*
Fried, Brenda Lynne 1956- *WhoEmL 93*
Fried, Burton David 1925- *WhoAm 92*
Fried, Burton T. *Law&B 92*
Fried, Burton Theodore 1940- *St&PR 93, WhoAm 92*
Fried, Charles 1935- *WhoAm 92*
Fried, Charles A. 1945- *WhoAm 92*
Fried, Donald 1936- *St&PR 93*
Fried, Donald David 1936- *WhoAm 92*
Fried, Edward R. 1918- *WhoAm 92*
Fried, Elliot 1944- *WhoWrEP 92*
Fried, Harvey D. *Law&B 92*
Fried, Herbert Daniel 1928- *St&PR 93, WhoAm 92*
Fried, Ilana 1936- *WhoWor 93*
Fried, Jean J. 1940- *WhoScE 91-2*
Fried, Jeffrey Michael 1953- *WhoE 93, WhoEmL 93*
Fried, Joanne Bette 1955- *WhoAmW 93, WhoEmL 93*
Fried, Joel R. 1946- *WhoWor 93*
Fried, John 1929- *St&PR 93*
Fried, John H.E. 1905-1990 *BioIn 17*
Fried, Josef 1914- *WhoAm 92*
Fried, Karen Joan 1962- *WhoAmW 93*
Fried, Lawrence Kenneth 1952- *WhoE 93*
Fried, Lawrence Philip 1938- *WhoSSW 93*
Fried, Louis Lester 1930- *WhoWor 93*
Fried, Martin L. 1934- *WhoE 93*
Fried, Max 1932- *St&PR 93*
Fried, Miriam 1946- *Baker 92*
Fried, Nancy Elizabeth 1948- *WhoEmL 93*
Fried, Oskar 1871-1941 *Baker 92*
Fried, P.M. 1943- *WhoScE 91-4*
Fried, Peter A. 1931- *St&PR 93*
Fried, Philip Henry 1945- *WhoWrEP 92*
Fried, Rachel Shifra 1968- *WhoE 93*
Fried, Randall *MiSFD 9*
Fried, Richard 1946- *St&PR 93*
Fried, Robert Nathan 1959- *St&PR 93*
Fried, Robyn L. *Law&B 92*
Fried, Ronnee 1947- *WhoAmW 93*
Fried, Ross Stuart 1952- *WhoSSW 93*
Fried, Samuel 1951- *WhoAm 92*
Fried, Walter Jay 1904- *WhoAm 92*
Fried, Walter Rudolf 1923- *WhoAm 92*
Fried, Wendy R. *Law&B 92*
Frieda, John *BioIn 17*
Friedan, Betty *BioIn 17*
Friedan, Betty 1921- *ConLC 74 [port], PolPar, WhoAm 92, WhoAmW 93, WhoWrEP 92, WomChHR [port]*
Friedberg, Barry Sewell 1941- *WhoAm 92*
Friedberg, Burton Steven 1942- *St&PR 93*
Friedberg, Carl 1872-1955 *Baker 92*
Friedberg, Gertrude 1908-1989 *ScF&FL 92*
Friedberg, Harold David 1927- *WhoAm 92*
Friedberg, Martha A. 1916- *WhoWrEP 92*
Friedberg, Marvin Paul 1931- *WhoAm 92*
Friedberg, Maurice 1929- *BioIn 17, WhoAm 92*
Friedberg, Rick *MiSFD 9*
Friedberg, Simeon Adlow 1925- *WhoE 93*
Friedberg, Stephen M. 1935- *St&PR 93*

Friedberg, Thomas Franklin 1958- *WhoEmL 93*
Friedberg, Thomas H. 1939- *St&PR 93*
Friedberg, Thomas Harold 1939- *WhoAm 92, WhoIns 93, WhoSSW 93*
Friede, Arnold I. *Law&B 92*
Friede, Charlotte 1935- *St&PR 93*
Friede, Eleanor Kask 1920- *WhoAm 92*
Friede, Juan 1902-1990 *BioIn 17*
Friede, Reinhard L. 1926- *WhoAm 92*
Friede, William N. 1926- *St&PR 93*
Friedeberg, Pedro 1937- *WhoAm 92*
Friedeberg-Seeley, Frank (J. B.) 1912- *ConAu 138*
Friedeburg, Hans Georg von *HarEnMi*
Friedel, Jacques 1921- *WhoScE 91-2*
Friedel, Janice Nahra 1950- *WhoAmW 93*
Friedel, Lynn K. 1949- *St&PR 93*
Friedel, Michael Gerald 1948- *WhoEmL 93*
Friedel, Robert Oliver 1936- *St&PR 93, WhoAm 92*
Friedel, Wolfgang F. 1946- *WhoIns 93*
Friedell, Ellen S. *Law&B 92*
Friedell, Gilbert Hugo 1927- *WhoAm 92*
Frieden, Bernard Joel 1930- *WhoAm 92*
Frieden, Carl 1928- *WhoAm 92*
Frieden, Charles Leroy 1941- *WhoAm 92*
Frieden, Jane Heller 1926- *WhoSSW 93*
Frieden, Ken 1955- *WhoSSW 93*
Frieden, Robert M. 1955- *WhoEmL 93*
Friedenberg, Daniel Meyer 1923- *WhoAm 92, WhoE 93*
Friedenberg, Karen Rosen 1949- *WhoAmW 93*
Friedenberg, Richard *MiSFD 9*
Friedenberg, Richard Myron 1926- *WhoAm 92*
Friedensohn, Elias 1924-1991 *BioIn 17*
Friedenson, Jay Philip *Law&B 92*
Frieder, Abraham-Aba 1911-1946 *BioIn 17*
Frieder, Bill *BioIn 17*
Frieder, Gideon 1937- *WhoAm 92*
Friederich, Jan 1944- *WhoAm 92*
Friederichs, Norman Paul 1936- *WhoWor 93*
Friederici, Hartmann H. R. 1927- *WhoAm 92*
Friedes, Peter Elliot 1941- *WhoAm 92*
Friedewald, William Thomas 1939- *WhoAm 92*
Friedgen, Christina J. 1943- *St&PR 93*
Friedheim, Arthur 1859-1932 *Baker 92*
Friedheim, Eric Arthur 1910- *WhoAm 92*
Friedheim, Jerry Warden 1934- *WhoAm 92, WhoSSW 93*
Friedheim, Michael 1943- *WhoAm 92*
Friedheim, Stephen Bailey 1934- *WhoSSW 93*
Friedhofer, Hugo (William) 1901-1981 *Baker 92*
Friedhoff, Arnold J. 1923- *WhoAm 92*
Friedhoff, Karl 1932- *WhoScE 91-3*
Friedkin, Don S. 1921- *St&PR 93*
Friedkin, Joseph Frank 1909- *WhoAm 92*
Friedkin, Kenneth G. 1915-1962 *EncABHB 8 [port]*
Friedkin, William *BioIn 17*
Friedkin, William 1935- *MiSFD 9*
Friedkin, William 1939- *WhoAm 92*
Friedl, Donald George 1932- *St&PR 93*
Friedl, Francis Peter 1917- *WhoAm 92*
Friedl, Rick 1947- *WhoEmL 93*
Friedlaender, Ann Fetter 1938- *WhoAm 92*
Friedlaender, Fritz Josef 1925- *WhoAm 92*
Friedlaender, Gary Elliott 1945- *WhoAm 92*
Friedlaender, Israel 1876-1920 *JeAmHC*
Friedlaender, Jonathan Scott 1940- *WhoE 93*
Friedlaender, Max 1852-1934 *Baker 92*
Friedland, Allan S. *Law&B 92*
Friedland, Avraham Hayim d1939? *BioIn 17*
Friedland, Bernard 1930- *WhoAm 92*
Friedland, Bruce *BioIn 17*
Friedland, Claire Bertha 1915- *WhoE 93*
Friedland, Edward A. *Law&B 92*
Friedland, Edward Charles 1937- *WhoE 93*
Friedland, Ellen Beth 1958- *WhoEmL 93*
Friedland, Harvey Karron 1933- *WhoE 93*
Friedland, Jerold Arthur 1945- *WhoAm 92*
Friedland, Joanne Benazzi 1953- *WhoAmW 93*
Friedland, Lilli 1947- *WhoEmL 93*
Friedland, Louis N. 1913- *WhoAm 92*
Friedland, Norman *Law&B 92*
Friedland, Paul Jay 1961- *WhoE 93*
Friedland, Richard S. 1950- *St&PR 93*
Friedland, Richard Stewart 1950- *WhoAm 92, WhoE 93*
Friedland, Robert M. 1950- *St&PR 93*
Friedland, Sharon L. *Law&B 92*
Friedland, Susan Helen 1947- *WhoWrEP 92*
Friedlander, Benjamin 1947- *WhoAm 92*
Friedlander, Betsy A. *Law&B 92*
Friedlander, Carl I. d1991 *BioIn 17*
Friedlander, D. Gilbert *Law&B 92*
Friedlander, Daniel A. *Law&B 92*
Friedlander, David Max 1941- *St&PR 93*
Friedlander, Donald 1940- *WhoE 93*
Friedlander, Edward Jay 1945- *WhoSSW 93*
Friedlander, Gerald A. *St&PR 93*
Friedlander, Gerhart 1916- *WhoAm 92*
Friedlander, Henry Z. 1925- *WhoE 93*
Friedlander, Herbert D. 1928- *St&PR 93*
Friedlander, Jack *St&PR 93*
Friedlander, John Benjamin 1941- *WhoAm 92*
Friedlander, John Eastburn 1947- *WhoAm 92*
Friedlander, Judith Naomi 1944- *WhoE 93*
Friedlander, Leonard d1990 *BioIn 17*
Friedlander, Michael Wulf 1928- *WhoAm 92*
Friedlander, Miles Herbert 1935- *WhoAm 92*
Friedlander, Myrna Lois 1947- *WhoEmL 93*
Friedlander, Patricia Ann 1944- *WhoAmW 93*
Friedlander, Paul Josef Crost 1910-1990 *BioIn 17*
Friedlander, Paul S. *Law&B 92*
Friedlander, Paul S. 1940- *St&PR 93*
Friedlander, Ralph 1913- *WhoWor 93*
Friedlander, Raymond N. *Law&B 92*
Friedlander, Robert Lynn 1933- *WhoAm 92*
Friedlander, Saul 1932- *BioIn 17*
Friedlander, Sheldon Kay 1927- *WhoAm 92*
Friedlander, Vladimir Rostislavovich 1925- *WhoWor 93*
Friedlander, William A. 1932- *St&PR 93*
Friedland-Wechsler, Naomi *Law&B 92*
Friedlein, Matilda Mary 1936- *WhoAmW 93*
Friedlein, Mattie Mary 1936- *WhoSSW 93*
Friedley, David P. *BioIn 17*
Friedley, H. Herald 1927- *St&PR 93*
Friedli, Emilie *ScF&FL 92*
Friedlob, James Wesley 1946- *WhoEmL 93, WhoSSW 93*
Friedly, John C. 1938- *WhoAm 92*
Friedman, Abigail Sarah 1956- *WhoE 93*
Friedman, Abraham Solomon 1921- *WhoE 93*
Friedman, Adam Issac 1945- *WhoAm 92*
Friedman, Alan *WhoWrEP 92*
Friedman, Alan H. 1946- *St&PR 93*
Friedman, Alan Herbert 1937- *WhoAm 92, WhoE 93, WhoWor 93*
Friedman, Alan Jacob 1942- *WhoAm 92, WhoE 93*
Friedman, Alan Warren 1939- *WhoAm 92*
Friedman, Allan David 1950- *WhoEmL 93*
Friedman, Allen d1992 *NewYTBS 92 [port]*
Friedman, Alvin 1931- *WhoAm 92*
Friedman, Alvin E. 1919- *St&PR 93*
Friedman, Alvin Edward 1919- *WhoAm 92*
Friedman, Alvin F. 1926- *St&PR 93*
Friedman, Amy Robin 1965- *WhoAmW 93*
Friedman, Anita 1943- *WhoAmW 93*
Friedman, Arnold c. 1874-1946 *BioIn 17*
Friedman, Arnold Carl 1951- *WhoE 93*
Friedman, Arnold M. *Law&B 92, WhoAm 92*
Friedman, Arnold P. 1909-1990 *BioIn 17*
Friedman, Arnold S. 1929- *WhoAm 92, WhoE 93*
Friedman, Arthur Daniel 1940- *WhoAm 92*
Friedman, Arthur Leonard 1929- *St&PR 93*
Friedman, Arthur Meeker 1948- *WhoAm 92*
Friedman, Aryeh Shimon *Law&B 92*
Friedman, B(ernard) H(arper) 1926- *WhoWrEP 92*
Friedman, Barbara *BioIn 17*
Friedman, Barbara Bernstein 1946- *WhoEmL 93*
Friedman, Barbara Glatt 1937- *WhoAmW 93*
Friedman, Barbara Marie 1949- *WhoE 93*
Friedman, Barry 1954- *WhoEmL 93*
Friedman, Barry David 1953- *WhoSSW 93*
Friedman, Barry S. 1956- *WhoEmL 93*
Friedman, Barton Robert 1935- *WhoAm 92*
Friedman, Benjamin M. 1944- *ConAu 139*
Friedman, Benjamin Morton 1944- *WhoAm 92*
Friedman, Bernard Alvin 1943- *WhoAm 92*
Friedman, Bernard Harper 1926- *WhoAm 92*
Friedman, Bernard Leonard 1922- *St&PR 93*
Friedman, Bradley Alan 1959- *WhoEmL 93*
Friedman, Brian P. 1955- *St&PR 93*
Friedman, Brian Paul 1955- *WhoAm 92, WhoEmL 93*
Friedman, Bruce Jay 1930- *JeAmFiW*
Friedman, Bruce Stuart *Law&B 92*
Friedman, C.S. 1955?- *ScF&FL 92*
Friedman, Charles J. 1941- *St&PR 93*
Friedman, Charles Stuart 1943- *WhoWor 93*
Friedman, D.A. *St&PR 93*
Friedman, Dan 1945- *BioIn 17*
Friedman, Dana Elise 1951- *WhoEmL 93*
Friedman, Dana M. *Law&B 92*
Friedman, Daniel M. 1916- *CngDr 91*
Friedman, Daniel Mark 1958- *WhoE 93*
Friedman, Daniel Mortimer 1916- *WhoAm 92*
Friedman, David Alan 1952- *WhoEmL 93*
Friedman, David F. *BioIn 17*
Friedman, David G. *Law&B 92, ScF&FL 92*
Friedman, David Seth *Law&B 92*
Friedman, Deborah J. *Law&B 92*
Friedman, Deborah Leslie White 1950- *WhoEmL 93, WhoSSW 93*
Friedman, Denise 1952- *WhoAmW 93*
Friedman, Dennis Carl 1948- *WhoEmL 93*
Friedman, Dian Debra 1943- *WhoE 93*
Friedman, Donald Joseph 1929- *WhoAm 92*
Friedman, Dorothy *WhoWrEP 92*
Friedman, Dorothy Foster 1940- *WhoE 93*
Friedman, Douglas E. *Law&B 92*
Friedman, Edgar 1964- *WhoE 93*
Friedman, Edward Andrew 1949- *WhoEmL 93*
Friedman, Edward David *WhoAm 92*
Friedman, Eli A. 1933- *WhoAm 92*
Friedman, Ellen S. 1954- *WhoEmL 93*
Friedman, Ellis Harold Ian 1954- *WhoWor 93*
Friedman, Emanuel 1919- *WhoAm 92*
Friedman, Emanuel A. 1926- *WhoAm 92*
Friedman, Eric D. 1959- *St&PR 93*
Friedman, Erick 1939- *Baker 92*
Friedman, Ernest J. *St&PR 93*
Friedman, Estelle Rapport 1926- *WhoE 93*
Friedman, Eugene A. *Law&B 92*
Friedman, Eugene Warren 1919- *WhoAm 92*
Friedman, Frances 1928- *WhoAm 92, WhoAmW 93*
Friedman, Frank Bennett 1940- *St&PR 93, WhoAm 92*
Friedman, Frank G. 1950- *St&PR 93*
Friedman, Frederick M. 1940- *St&PR 93*
Friedman, Fredrica Schwab 1939- *WhoAm 92, WhoAmW 93*
Friedman, Gary E. 1947- *St&PR 93*
Friedman, Gene 1958- *WhoE 93*
Friedman, George H. 1954- *St&PR 93*
Friedman, George Henry 1954- *WhoEmL 93*
Friedman, George Jerry 1928- *WhoAm 92*
Friedman, Gerald Douglas *Law&B 92*
Friedman, Gerald Manfred 1921- *WhoAm 92, WhoE 93, WhoWor 93*
Friedman, Gloria d1992 *BioIn 17*
Friedman, H. Harold 1917- *WhoAm 92*
Friedman, Hans Adolf 1921- *WhoAm 92*
Friedman, Harold *Law&B 92*
Friedman, Harold d1992 *NewYTBS 92 [port]*
Friedman, Harold 1911-1992 *BioIn 17*
Friedman, Harold 1930- *St&PR 93*
Friedman, Harold B. 1904- *St&PR 93*
Friedman, Harold Edward 1934- *WhoAm 92*
Friedman, Harold Lee *ScF&FL 92*
Friedman, Harold S. 1937- *WhoAm 92*
Friedman, Harry Fred 1928- *St&PR 93*
Friedman, Harvey 1936- *St&PR 93*
Friedman, Harvey Martin 1948- *WhoAm 92*
Friedman, Helen Ruth 1951- *WhoEmL 93*
Friedman, Herbert 1916- *WhoAm 92, WhoWor 93*
Friedman, Herman 1931- *WhoSSW 93*
Friedman, Howard Martin 1948- *WhoAm 92*
Friedman, Howard Samuel 1940- *WhoE 93*
Friedman, Howard Scott 1952- *WhoEmL 93*
Friedman, Howard W. 1925- *WhoAm 92*
Friedman, Ignaz 1882-1948 *Baker 92, PolBiDi*
Friedman, Ira Hugh 1933- *WhoAm 92*
Friedman, Irving Sigmund 1915-1989 *BioIn 17*
Friedman, J. Roger 1933- *St&PR 93*
Friedman, Jack B. 1921- *St&PR 93*
Friedman, Jack R. *Law&B 92*
Friedman, Jack Raphael 1950- *WhoEmL 93*
Friedman, James Winstein 1936- *WhoAm 92*
Friedman, Janet M. 1949- *WhoAmW 93*
Friedman, Janet Teri 1957- *WhoWrEP 92*
Friedman, Jay 1963- *WhoE 93*
Friedman, Jeffrey *MiSFD 9*
Friedman, Jeffrey H. 1950- *WhoWrEP 92*
Friedman, Jeffrey L. *Law&B 92*
Friedman, Jennifer *BioIn 17*
Friedman, Jerome Isaac 1930- *BioIn 17, WhoAm 92, WhoE 93, WhoWor 93*
Friedman, Jesse I. 1918- *St&PR 93*
Friedman, Jim 1955- *WhoEmL 93*
Friedman, Joan M. 1949- *WhoAm 92*
Friedman, Joel 1939- *St&PR 93*
Friedman, Joel Matthew 1942- *WhoAm 92, WhoE 93*
Friedman, Joel Stephen 1937- *St&PR 93, WhoAm 92*
Friedman, Joel William 1951- *WhoAm 92*
Friedman, John Arthur 1952- *WhoEmL 93*
Friedman, Jon George 1951- *WhoE 93, WhoEmL 93*
Friedman, Jonathan M. 1955- *St&PR 93*
Friedman, Jonathan Mark 1958- *WhoEmL 93*
Friedman, Joseph 1947- *WhoEmL 93*
Friedman, Joseph N. *Law&B 92*
Friedman, Joshua M. 1941- *WhoAm 92*
Friedman, Judith E. *Law&B 92*
Friedman, Judy Fran 1942- *St&PR 93*
Friedman, Julie *BioIn 17*
Friedman, K. Bruce 1929- *WhoAm 92*
Friedman, Kathryn M. *Law&B 92*
Friedman, Kathy V(allone) 1943- *ConAu 38NR*
Friedman, Ken *MiSFD 9*
Friedman, Ken 1939- *Baker 92*
Friedman, Kent Bruce *Law&B 92*
Friedman, Kim *MiSFD 9*
Friedman, L. Jeanne 1951- *WhoEmL 93*
Friedman, Laurence Mark *Law&B 92*
Friedman, Lawrence A. 1951- *WhoEmL 93*
Friedman, Lawrence Carl 1956- *WhoEmL 93*
Friedman, Lawrence J. *Law&B 92*
Friedman, Lawrence M. 1930- *WhoAm 92*
Friedman, Lawrence Milton 1945- *WhoIns 93*
Friedman, Lawrence Samuel 1953- *WhoE 93*
Friedman, Lenard R. 1942- *St&PR 93*
Friedman, Lenemaja 1924- *ScF&FL 92*
Friedman, Leonard 1929- *WhoE 93*
Friedman, Leonard Howard 1953- *WhoEmL 93*
Friedman, Lester James 1951- *WhoEmL 93*
Friedman, Lewis 1922- *WhoE 93*
Friedman, Lewis Michael d1992 *BioIn 17, NewYTBS 92*
Friedman, Linda Weiser 1953- *WhoAmW 93*
Friedman, Lionel Robert *WhoE 93*
Friedman, Louis Frank 1941- *WhoAm 92*
Friedman, Lynn Joseph 1949- *WhoSSW 93*
Friedman, Malcolm 1928- *WhoE 93*
Friedman, Margaret Sue 1952- *WhoAmW 93*
Friedman, Maria Andre 1950- *WhoAmW 93, WhoE 93*
Friedman, Marion 1918- *WhoWor 93*
Friedman, Mark 1932- *WhoE 93*
Friedman, Mark Joel 1946- *WhoSSW 93*
Friedman, Mark Steven 1949- *WhoEmL 93*
Friedman, Marla G. 1953- *St&PR 93*
Friedman, Marna Wendy 1959- *WhoAmW 93, WhoEmL 93*
Friedman, Martin 1925- *WhoAm 92*
Friedman, Martin Burton 1927- *WhoAm 92*
Friedman, Martin L. 1925- *BioIn 17*
Friedman, Marty See Megadeth *ConMus 9*
Friedman, Marvin Harold 1923- *WhoE 93*
Friedman, Mary Brooks 1947- *WhoEmL 93*
Friedman, Matthew *BioIn 17, Law&B 92*
Friedman, Matthew Emanuel 1923- *St&PR 93*
Friedman, Maurice Harold 1903-1991 *BioIn 17*
Friedman, Maurice Stanley 1921- *WhoAm 92*
Friedman, Melinda Ann *Law&B 92*
Friedman, Melvin 1930- *WhoAm 92*
Friedman, Melvin Jack 1928- *WhoAm 92*
Friedman, Meyer 1910- *WhoAm 92*
Friedman, Michael Belais 1943- *WhoE 93*
Friedman, Michael Elliot 1951- *WhoEmL 93*

Friedman, Michael Jan 1955- ScF&FL 92
Friedman, Michael Phillip 1951- WhoEmL 93
Friedman, Michael Steven 1953- WhoEmL 93
Friedman, Mickey 1944- WhoAm 92
Friedman, Mildred S. BioIn 17
Friedman, Miles 1950- WhoAm 92, WhoE 93, WhoEmL 93, WhoWor 93
Friedman, Milton 1912- BioIn 17, JeAmHC, WhoAm 92, WhoWor 93
Friedman, Milton I. 1925- St&PR 93
Friedman, Monroe BioIn 17
Friedman, Morton Law&B 92
Friedman, Morton Lee 1932- WhoAm 92
Friedman, Murray 1926- WhoAm 92
Friedman, Myles Ivan 1924- WhoAm 92
Friedman, Naomi B. 1949- WhoEmL 93
Friedman, Neal Joel 1940- WhoE 93
Friedman, Neil B. 1947- St&PR 93
Friedman, Nelson 1912- St&PR 93
Friedman, Norman 1925- St&PR 93, WhoE 93, WhoWrEP 92
Friedman, Orrie M. 1915- St&PR 93
Friedman, Pamela Ruth Lessing 1950- WhoAmW 93
Friedman, Paul 1931- WhoAm 92
Friedman, Paul Alan 1937- WhoWrEP 92
Friedman, Paul Jay 1937- WhoAm 92
Friedman, Paul Lawrence 1944- WhoAm 92
Friedman, Paul Robert 1952- WhoAm 92
Friedman, Penny 1951- WhoEmL 93
Friedman, Peter Charles 1958- WhoEmL 93
Friedman, Philip Scott 1954- WhoEmL 93
Friedman, Phillip L. 1947- St&PR 93
Friedman, Philmore H. 1925- St&PR 93
Friedman, Ralph d1991 BioIn 17
Friedman, Ralph d1992 NewYTBS 92 [port]
Friedman, Ralph 1904- WhoAm 92
Friedman, Ralph 1922- WhoAm 92
Friedman, Raymond 1922- WhoAm 92
Friedman, Richard MiSFD 9
Friedman, Richard 1944- Baker 92
Friedman, Richard Everett 1942- WhoAm 92
Friedman, Richard I. Law&B 92
Friedman, Richard N. 1941- St&PR 93
Friedman, Robert 1947- WhoAm 92, WhoEmL 93
Friedman, Robert B. 1939- St&PR 93
Friedman, Robert Lee 1930- WhoAm 92
Friedman, Robert Michael 1950- WhoAm 92, WhoEmL 93, WhoSSW 93, WhoWor 93
Friedman, Robert Sidney 1927- WhoAm 92
Friedman, Rodger 1951- WhoE 93
Friedman, Ronald Benjamin Law&B 92
Friedman, Ronald Jules 1946- St&PR 93
Friedman, Ronald M. Law&B 92
Friedman, Ronald Marvin 1930- WhoAm 92, WhoWor 93
Friedman, Rose D(irector) WhoWrEP 92
Friedman, Roy Bennis 1934- WhoWrEP 92
Friedman, Samuel Arthur 1927- WhoSSW 93
Friedman, Samuel H. d1990 BioIn 17
Friedman, Samuel Selig 1935- WhoAm 92, WhoE 93, WhoWor 93
Friedman, Sanford 1926- St&PR 93
Friedman, Sanford 1928- ConGAN
Friedman, Sarah Landau 1943- WhoE 93
Friedman, Selwyn Marvin 1929- WhoE 93
Friedman, Semyon BioIn 17
Friedman, Shelly Arnold 1949- WhoAm 92, WhoWor 93
Friedman, Sholem Law&B 92
Friedman, Sidney A. 1935- WhoAm 92
Friedman, Sigmund 1938- St&PR 93
Friedman, Stanford J. 1927- St&PR 93
Friedman, Stanley 1925- WhoAm 92
Friedman, Stanley P. 1925- WhoWrEP 92
Friedman, Stephen BioIn 17
Friedman, Stephen James Law&B 92
Friedman, Stephen James 1938- WhoAm 92, WhoWor 93
Friedman, Steve BioIn 17
Friedman, Steve 1946- BioIn 17
Friedman, Steven 1945- WhoAm 92, WhoE 93
Friedman, Steven A. 1950- St&PR 93
Friedman, Steven J. 1947- WhoE 93
Friedman, Steven Lewis 1946- WhoAm 92
Friedman, Stuart ScF&FL 92
Friedman, Sue Tyler 1925- WhoAmW 93, WhoE 93, WhoWor 93
Friedman, Susan Lynn Bell 1953- WhoAmW 93
Friedman, Sydney M. 1916- WhoAm 92
Friedman, Theodore d1992 NewYTBS 92
Friedman, Thomas L. BioIn 17
Friedman, Thomas L(oren) 1953- ConAu 38NR
Friedman, Thomas Loren 1953- WhoE 93
Friedman, Townsend B., Jr. 1940- WhoAm 92, WhoWor 93
Friedman, Tully Michael 1942- WhoWor 93
Friedman, Victor Stanley 1933- WhoAm 92
Friedman, Wilbur H. 1907- St&PR 93
Friedman, Wilbur Harvey 1907- WhoAm 92, WhoE 93
Friedman, William Foster 1936- WhoAm 92
Friedman, William Hersh 1938- WhoAm 92
Friedman, William J. 1903- St&PR 93
Friedman-Blum, Janet Teri 1957- WhoEmL 93
Friedmann, Emerich Imre 1921- WhoAm 92
Friedmann, Erika 1952- WhoE 93
Friedmann, Norman E. 1929- St&PR 93
Friedmann, Paul 1933- WhoE 93, WhoWor 93
Friedmann, Peretz Peter 1938- WhoAm 92
Friedmann, Roseli Ocampo 1937- WhoAmW 93, WhoSSW 93
Friedmann, Rosemary Anne 1948- WhoEmL 93, WhoSSW 93
Friedmutter, Martin 1947- WhoE 93
Friedner, Jerry Franklin 1937- St&PR 93
Friedrich, Alexander Gunther 1923- WhoWor 93
Friedrich, Allen John 1948- WhoE 93
Friedrich, Benjamin Charles 1929- WhoE 93
Friedrich, Caspar David 1774-1840 BioIn 17
Friedrich, Charles William 1943- WhoWor 93
Friedrich, Craig William 1946- WhoE 93
Friedrich (der Grosse), II Baker 92
Friedrich, Gotz 1930- Baker 92, IntDcOp, OxDcOp
Friedrich, Gunther 1929- WhoScE 91-3
Friedrich, Gustav William 1941- WhoSSW 93
Friedrich, James F. 1951- St&PR 93
Friedrich, Joan Ann 1952- WhoAmW 93
Friedrich, Jurgen Helmut 1956- WhoWor 93
Friedrich, Karl 1905-1981 Baker 92
Friedrich, Margret Cohen 1947- WhoAmW 93, WhoE 93
Friedrich, Mariola-Elzbieta 1948- WhoWor 93
Friedrich, Otto Alva 1929- WhoWrEP 92
Friedrich, Paul 1927- WhoAm 92
Friedrich, Paul William 1927- WhoWrEP 92
Friedrich, Paula Jean 1965- WhoE 93
Friedrich, Peter 1951- WhoWor 93
Friedrich, Philip Joseph 1947- WhoE 93, WhoWor 93
Friedrich, Robert Edmund 1918- WhoAm 92
Friedrich, Robert James 1946- WhoE 93
Friedrich, Roland W. 1942- WhoScE 91-3
Friedrich, Roman, III St&PR 93
Friedrich, Rose Marie 1941- WhoAmW 93, WhoWor 93
Friedrich, Ruth Andreas- 1901-1977 BioIn 17
Friedrich, Stephen Miro 1932- WhoAm 92
Friedrich, Wayne Hurff 1928- WhoE 93
Friedrich-Patterson, Evelyn Beth 1953- WhoAmW 93
Friedrichs, Arthur Martin 1911- WhoSSW 93
Friedrichs, Wayne Lawrence 1940- St&PR 93
Friedrichsen, Rodney D. 1955- St&PR 93
Friedrichson, Sabine 1948- BioIn 17
Friedrick, Lynn Dee Law&B 92
Friedricks, Burton Lee 1928- St&PR 93
Friedricks, Larry 1937- St&PR 93
Friedsam, Ronald J. 1943- St&PR 93
Friedt, Wolfgang 1946- WhoScE 91-3
Friehe, Carl Alan 1939- WhoAm 92
Friel, Bernard Preston 1930- WhoAm 92
Friel, Brian BioIn 17
Friel, Brian 1929- ConTFT 10, WhoAm 92
Friel, Carol S. Law&B 92
Friel, Daniel Denwood, Sr. 1920- WhoAm 92, WhoE 93
Friel, James 1958- ConAu 139
Friel, Karen Eileen 1957- WhoEmL 93
Friel, Peter J. 1959- WhoEmL 93
Friel, Thomas Patrick 1936- WhoAm 92
Frieling, Barbara Johnston 1950- WhoEmL 93, WhoSSW 93
Frieling, Gerald H., Jr. 1930- St&PR 93
Frieling, Gerald Harvey, Jr. 1930- WhoAm 92
Frieling, T. WhoScE 91-3
Frieling, Thomas Jerome 1953- WhoSSW 93
Friell, James 1912- BioIn 17
Frieman, Edward Allan 1926- WhoAm 92
Frieman, Hildegarde 1948- WhoEmL 93
Frieman, Joel ScF&FL 92
Friemann, Robert Frederich 1947- WhoEmL 93
Friemann, Witold 1889-1977 Baker 92
Friend, Alexander Alan 1961- St&PR 93
Friend, Cynthia M. 1955- WhoAm 92, WhoAmW 93, WhoEmL 93
Friend, David Lee 1951- WhoEmL 93
Friend, David Robert 1956- WhoEmL 93
Friend, David Wesley 1946- St&PR 93
Friend, Dorie ConAu 138
Friend, Edward Malcolm, Jr. WhoAm 92
Friend, Edward Malcolm, III 1946- WhoAm 92, WhoSSW 93
Friend, Elaine Byrd 1930- WhoAmW 93
Friend, Frederick Law&B 92
Friend, Harold Charles 1946- WhoEmL 93, WhoSSW 93
Friend, James R. Law&B 92
Friend, John G. d1992 NewYTBS 92
Friend, Jonathan Joseph 1955- WhoAm 92
Friend, Lisa Beth 1959- WhoAmW 93
Friend, Lonn ScF&FL 92
Friend, Mark Allen 1949- WhoEmL 93
Friend, Miriam Ruth 1925- WhoAmW 93
Friend, Olen Kent 1962- WhoEmL 93
Friend, Oscar J. 1897-1963 ScF&FL 92
Friend, Robert Bartmess 1930- BiDAMSp 1989
Friend, Ross D. Law&B 92
Friend, Sandra Ann Covert 1937- WhoAmW 93
Friend, Shirley C., Jr. Law&B 92
Friend, Theodore Wood, III 1931- WhoAm 92
Friend, Theodore (Wood, III) 1931- ConAu 138
Friend, William Benedict 1931- WhoAm 92, WhoSSW 93
Friend, William K. Law&B 92
Friend, William Kagay 1946- St&PR 93, WhoAm 92
Friendly, Fred W. 1915- JrnUS, WhoAm 92
Friendly, Lynda E. WhoAm 92
Friends, Jalynn WhoWrEP 92
Friends of Darkover ScF&FL 92
Frierdich, Bruce E. Law&B 92
Frierson, Cheryl Ann 1960- WhoAmW 93
Frierson, Daniel K. 1942- WhoSSW 93
Frierson, Eleanor Grace 1949- WhoUN 92
Frierson, Paul Kruesi 1937- St&PR 93
Friery, Donna Elizabeth 1957- WhoEmL 93
Friery, John J., Jr. Law&B 92
Friery, John Joseph 1946- WhoEmL 93
Fries, Amy Rose 1958- WhoWrEP 92
Fries, Blanche Baillargeon 1914- WhoAmW 93
Fries, Cecil Edward, Jr. 1935- WhoSSW 93
Fries, Daniel 1930- WhoScE 91-2
Fries, Deborah Fay 1958- WhoE 93
Fries, Donald E. 1943- St&PR 93, WhoIns 93
Fries, Donald Eugene 1943- WhoAm 92
Fries, Donald Owen 1939- WhoE 93
Fries, Erik F.B. 1899-1990 BioIn 17
Fries, Helen Sergeant Haynes WhoAmW 93
Fries, Herluf Beck 1915- WhoWor 93
Fries, Jack 1942- St&PR 93
Fries, James Franklin 1938- WhoAm 92
Fries, James Lawrence 1932- WhoAm 92
Fries, Jay Robert 1954- WhoEmL 93
Fries, Jochen Wu 1954- WhoE 93
Fries, John Robert 1922- St&PR 93
Fries, Maureen Holmberg 1931- WhoAm 92
Fries, Maureen L. Law&B 92
Fries, Michael Thomas 1959- WhoEmL 93
Fries, Monica L. Law&B 92
Fries, Patricia Angeline 1946- WhoAmW 93
Fries, Philip J., Jr. Law&B 92
Fries, Raymond Sebastian 1919- WhoWor 93
Fries, Reinhard 1950- WhoScE 91-3
Fries, Robert Francis 1911- WhoAm 92
Fries, Robert John Law&B 92
Fries, Roger J. 1945- St&PR 93
Fries, Wulf (Christian Julius) 1825-1902 Baker 92
Friesch, Jurgen 1950- WhoScE 91-3
Friesch, Paulette M. Law&B 92
Friese, George R. 1936- St&PR 93
Friese, George Ralph 1936- WhoAm 92
Friese, Helen Marie 1925- WhoWrEP 92
Friese, Robert Charles 1943- WhoAm 92
Friese, Wilhelm 1924- WhoWor 93
Friesecke, Raymond Francis 1937- WhoAm 92
Frieseke, Frances 1914- WhoWrEP 92
Friesem, Gustave Daniel 1916- St&PR 93
Friesen, David R. 1943- St&PR 93
Friesen, Eugene Keith 1931- St&PR 93
Friesen, Gilbert Dean 1942- St&PR 93
Friesen, Henry George 1934- WhoAm 92
Friesen, Patrick 1946- WhoCanL 92
Friesen, Richard B. 1941- St&PR 93
Friesen, Wolfgang Otto 1942- WhoAm 92
Frieser, Rudolf Gruenspan 1920- WhoAm 92, WhoSSW 93
Fries Gardner, Lisa 1956- WhoEmL 93
Friesner, Esther M. 1951- Au&Arts 10 [port], ScF&FL 92, SmATA 71 [port]
Friesner-Stutzman, Esther ScF&FL 92
Friessner, Johannes 1892-1971 HarEnMi
Friestad, Arild Law&B 92
Friesz, Donald Stuart 1929- St&PR 93
Friesz, Gerald Daniel 1941- St&PR 93
Friesz, Lynda M. 1960- WhoEmL 93
Friesz, Othon 1879-1949 BioIn 17
Frietsch, Rudyard 1927- WhoScE 91-4
Frieze, P.A. WhoScE 91-1
Frieze, Stanley B. St&PR 93
Frigard, Wayne R. Law&B 92
Frigerio, Alejandro 1955- WhoEmL 93
Frigessi, Arnoldo 1959- WhoWor 93
Friggens, Arthur 1920- ScF&FL 92
Friggens, Thomas George 1949- WhoAm 92
Frigieri, Paolo 1944- WhoScE 91-3
Frigo, George G. 1940- St&PR 93
Frigoletto, Fredric David, Jr. 1933- WhoAm 92
Frigon, Chris Darwin 1949- WhoEmL 93
Frigon, Guy R. 1954- St&PR 93
Frigon, Henry Frederick 1934- St&PR 93, WhoAm 92, WhoSSW 93
Frigyes, Andor 1922- WhoScE 91-4
Friis, Erik 1931- WhoUN 92
Friis, Erik Johan 1913- WhoAm 92, WhoWor 93
Friis-Hansen, Bent Julius 1920- WhoScE 91-2
Frijsh, Povla 1881-1960 Baker 92
Frijs-Madsen, Bent 1933- WhoScE 91-2
Frikel, Protasio 1912-1974 IntDcAn
Frikert, Brian W. Law&B 92
Friligos, Nikolaos 1941- WhoScE 91-3
Frilot, Bert Clark 1939- WhoWor 93
Friman, Alice 1933- WhoWrEP 92
Frimel, (Charles) Rudolf 1879-1972 Baker 92
Frimerman, Leslie 1943- WhoAm 92, WhoWor 93
Friml, Rudolf 1879-1972 OxDcOp
Friml, (Charles) Rudolf 1879-1972 Baker 92
Frimmel, Theodor von 1853-1928 Baker 92
Frimmer, Max 1921- WhoScE 91-3
Frimmer, Paul Norman 1945- WhoAm 92
Frimmer, Rick Leslie 1951- WhoAm 92
Frindel, Emilia 1925- WhoScE 91-2
Frindt, Andrzej Jan 1928- WhoScE 91-4
Frings, Ketti 1915-1981 ScF&FL 92
Frink, George Raymond 1918- St&PR 93
Frink, Jno. Spencer 1930- WhoIns 93
Frink, Peter Hill 1939- WhoE 93
Frink, Phillip F., Jr. 1938- St&PR 93
Frink, Tommie Shelby 1937- St&PR 93
Frinking, John J. 1935- St&PR 93
Friou, George Jacob 1919- WhoAm 92
Friou, Phillip J. 1949- WhoAm 92
Friou, Roger Patteson 1934- St&PR 93
Fripp, Chandra Vanessa Law&B 92
Fripp, Robert BioIn 17
Fripp, Robert 1946- ConMus 9 [port]
Fris, Eric A., Jr. 1941- St&PR 93
Frisbee, Don C. 1923- St&PR 93
Frisbee, Don Calvin 1923- WhoAm 92
Frisbey, Bradley Alan 1964- WhoSSW 93
Frisbie, Carol ScF&FL 92
Frisbie, F. Richard 1942- St&PR 93
Frisbie, Marlene Ann 1955- WhoAmW 93
Frisbie, Richard P(atrick) 1926- ConAu 38NR
Frisbie, Ronald Edgar 1922- St&PR 93
Frisbie, Steven James 1941- St&PR 93
Frisby, Gregory S. 1959- St&PR 93
Frisby, James Curtis 1930- WhoAm 92
Frisby, Jerry B. 1937- St&PR 93
Frisby, John Peter WhoScE 91-1
Frisch, August W. Law&B 92
Frisch, August Wilbert 1940- St&PR 93
Frisch, Bertram 1931- WhoScE 91-3
Frisch, David H. 1918-1991 BioIn 17
Frisch, Frank 1898-1973 BioIn 17
Frisch, Fred I. 1935- WhoWor 93
Frisch, Harry D. Law&B 92
Frisch, Harry David 1954- WhoE 93, WhoEmL 93
Frisch, Harry Lloyd 1928- WhoAm 92, WhoE 93
Frisch, Henry Jonathan 1944- WhoAm 92
Frisch, Ivan Thomas 1937- WhoAm 92
Frisch, Joseph 1921- WhoAm 92
Frisch, Max 1911-1991 AnObit 1991, BioIn 17, DcLB 124 [port]
Frisch, Michael H. BioIn 17
Frisch, Otto Robert 1904-1979 BioIn 17
Frisch, Paula Baker 92
Frisch, Robert A. 1930- WhoAm 92

Frisch, Robert Emile 1925- WhoAm 92
Frisch, Robert Myron, Jr. 1956- WhoE 93
Frisch, Rose Epstein 1918- WhoAm 92, WhoAmW 93, WhoE 93
Frisch, Wendi J. 1960- WhoEmL 93
Frischauf, Anna-Maria 1947- WhoScE 91-1
Frischenmeyer, Michael Leo 1951- WhoEmL 93
Frischenschlager, Friedhelm 1943- WhoWor 93
Frischenschlager, Friedrich 1885-1970 Baker 92
Frischer, Murray B. 1942- St&PR 93
Frischhertz, Kristine BioIn 17
Frischhertz, Lloyd Nicholas 1948- WhoEmL 93
Frischknecht, Lee Conrad 1928- WhoAm 92
Frischknecht, Ruedi 1938- St&PR 93
Frischkorn, David Ephraim Keasbey, Jr. 1951- WhoEmL 93, WhoSSW 93
Frischling, Carl 1937- St&PR 93
Frischmann, Donald W. 1921- WhoIns 93
Frisco, Louis Joseph 1923- WhoAm 92
Frisell, Wilhelm Richard 1920- WhoAm 92
Frisell-Schroder, Sonja Bettie 1937- WhoAm 92
Frishberg, Aaron David WhoE 93
Frisina, D. Frank Law&B 92
Frisina, Robert Dana 1955- WhoAm 92, WhoE 93, WhoEmL 93, WhoWor 93
Frisk, Ruth Davis 1916- WhoAmW 93
Friskin, James 1886-1967 Baker 92
Frisman, Roger Lawrence 1952- WhoEmL 93
Frismark, Anders Olof 1943- WhoUN 92
Frisoli, John E. St&PR 93
Frison, Giuseppe 1935- WhoScE 91-3
Frison, Lisa Marie 1958- WhoSSW 93
Frison, Paul Maurice 1937- WhoAm 92
Frisone, Franco 1946- WhoWor 93
Frisque, Alvin Joseph 1923- WhoAm 92
Frist, Ramsey Hudson 1936- WhoSSW 93
Frist, Thomas Fearn 1910- WhoAm 92
Frist, Thomas Fearn, Jr. 1938- WhoSSW 93
Frist, Thomas Ferran 1945- WhoAm 92, WhoSSW 93
Frist, William H. 1952- ConAu 136
Fristacky, Norbert 1931- WhoWor 93
Fristad, Kenneth Arthur 1941- St&PR 93
Fristad, Mark Robert 1953- WhoEmL 93
Fristad, Mary Antonette 1959- WhoAmW 93
Frister, Robert Allen 1936- ScF&FL 92
Friswell, Hain 1825-1878 ScF&FL 92
Friswold, Fred Ravndahl 1937- WhoAm 92
Frit, Bernard 1939- WhoScE 91-2
Fritch, Charles E. 1927- ScF&FL 92
Fritchie, Hazel M. 1926- WhoWrEP 92
Fritchman, John Allen 1962- WhoSSW 93
Frith, David (Edward John) 1937- ConAu 138
Frith, Eugene Richard 1941- WhoSSW 93
Frith, Francis 1822-1898 BioIn 17
Frith, Margaret WhoAmW 93
Frith, Michael K. ScF&FL 92
Frith, Nigel 1941- ScF&FL 92
Fritkin, George 1938- St&PR 93
Fritsch, Allen Joseph 1930- St&PR 93
Fritsch, Billy Dale, Jr. 1956- WhoSSW 93, WhoWor 93
Fritsch, Colin Michael 1948- WhoEmL 93
Fritsch, Fritz Rudolf 1939- WhoWor 93
Fritsch, Gerhard Heinrich 1940- WhoWor 93
Fritsch, Peter 1940- WhoScE 91-4
Fritsch, Robert Bruce 1931- WhoAm 92
Fritsch, Rudolf 1928- WhoScE 91-3
Fritsch, Werner, Freiherr von 1880-1939 BioIn 17
Fritsch, Werner von 1880-1939 HarEnMi
Fritsch, Willi 1922- WhoScE 91-3
Fritsche, Claudia WhoWor 93
Fritsche, Claudia 1952- WhoUN 92
Fritsche, Joellen Marie 1951- WhoEmL 93
Fritsche, Richard Henry 1945- St&PR 93
Fritsche, Wolfgang 1928- WhoWor 93
Fritschen, Robert David 1935- WhoAm 92
Fritschi, Max Theodor 1933- WhoWor 93
Fritschler, A. Lee 1937- WhoAm 92
Fritschler, Alvin Henry Law&B 92
Frittitta, Peter Anthony 1956- WhoEmL 93, WhoWor 93
Fritton, Karl Andrew 1955- WhoEmL 93
Fritts, Donnie SoulM
Fritts, Harold Clark 1928- WhoAm 92
Fritts, Harry Washington, Jr. 1921- WhoAm 92, WhoWrEP 92
Fritts, Lillian Elizabeth 1923- WhoAmW 93
Fritts, Mary Bahr ConAu 136
Fritts, Stewart Brooks 1932- St&PR 93
Fritts, William ScF&FL 92
Fritz, Anton BioIn 17
Fritz, Arthur A. Law&B 92
Fritz, Bruce Morrell 1947- WhoAm 92
Fritz, Carol Schweinforth 1944- WhoSSW 93
Fritz, Cecil M. 1921- St&PR 93
Fritz, Cecil Morgan 1921- WhoAm 92
Fritz, Charles 1955- BioIn 17
Fritz, Daniel R. 1955- St&PR 93
Fritz, Donald Wayne 1929- St&PR 93
Fritz, Douglas Partridge 1940- WhoE 93
Fritz, Duane Clayton 1932- WhoSSW 93
Fritz, Ernest F. 1930- St&PR 93
Fritz, Ethel L. AmWomPl
Fritz, Ethel Mae Hendrickson 1925- WhoAmW 93
Fritz, Gerhard 1919- WhoScE 91-3
Fritz, Gregory Robert 1948- WhoEmL 93
Fritz, Hans 1935- WhoWor 93
Fritz, Heinz Peter William 1930- WhoScE 91-3
Fritz, Jack 1950- WhoAsAP 91
Fritz, Jack Wayne 1927- WhoAm 92
Fritz, James Edward 1938- WhoE 93
Fritz, James Sherwood 1924- WhoAm 92
Fritz, Jean 1915- ScF&FL 92
Fritz, Jean (Guttery) 1915- ConAu 37NR, DcAmChF 1960, MajAI [port], SmATA 72 [port], WhoAm 92, WhoAmW 93
Fritz, Jeanne Lynne Francis 1965- WhoEmL 93
Fritz, Joanne Lee 1936- WhoSSW 93
Fritz, Joseph W., Jr. Law&B 92
Fritz, Lance Hine 1947- WhoE 93
Fritz, Mark J. Law&B 92
Fritz, Maynard Eugene 1931- St&PR 93
Fritz, Michael A. St&PR 93
Fritz, Michael Charles 1964- WhoE 93
Fritz, Michael Joseph 1942- St&PR 93
Fritz, Rene Eugene, Jr. 1943- WhoAm 92
Fritz, Robert John Law&B 92
Fritz, Robert Lawrence 1949- WhoSSW 93
Fritz, Roger Jay 1928- WhoAm 92
Fritz, Ruby M. 1928- St&PR 93
Fritz, Ruby Morten 1928- WhoAmW 93
Fritz, Sigmund 1914- WhoE 93
Fritz, Susan Kay 1956- WhoAmW 93
Fritz, Suzanne 1961- WhoE 93
Fritz, Tage 1933- WhoScE 91-4
Fritz, Thomas Anthony 1949- St&PR 93
Fritz, Thomas Vincent 1934- WhoAm 92
Fritz, Volkmar Otto 1938- WhoWor 93
Fritz, Wayne M. 1956- St&PR 93
Fritz, Wayne Richard 1934- WhoE 93
Fritz, William Warren 1943- WhoAm 92
Fritz Cohn, Loreli Law&B 92
Fritze, James Napier 1925- St&PR 93, WhoSSW 93
Fritze, Julius Arnold 1918- WhoSSW 93
Fritze, Roger Laurence 1946- WhoEmL 93, WhoSSW 93
Fritzhand, James 1946- ScF&FL 92
Fritzhand, Marek 1913- WhoWor 93
Fritzke, Audrey Elmere 1933- WhoAm 92
Fritzke, Paul Henry 1936- St&PR 93
Fritzler, Gerald J. 1953- BioIn 17
Fritzsch, Harald 1943- WhoScE 91-3
Fritzsche, Gary Ralph Law&B 92
Fritzsche, Hellmut 1927- WhoAm 92
Fritzsche, Paul 1925- St&PR 93
Fritzsche, Peter 1959- ConAu 139
Fritzsche, R. Wayne 1949- WhoEmL 93, WhoWor 93
Fritzsche, Staffan Richard Mortimer 1954- WhoWor 93
Fritzson, Per 1922- WhoScE 91-4
Frivold, Lars Helge 1946- WhoScE 91-4
Frizzel, Terry WhoAm 92
Frizzell, Carol E. Law&B 92
Frizzell, "Lefty" (William Orville) 1928-1975 Baker 92
Frizzell, Lucille Bridgers 1925- WhoAmW 93
Frizzell, William Kenneth 1928- WhoAm 92
Frnka, Paula Kay 1953- WhoSSW 93
Frobel, Anne S. 1816-1907 BioIn 17
Frobel, Francis A. BioIn 17
Frobenius, Leo 1873-1938 IntDcAn
Froberger, Johann Jakob 1616-1667 Baker 92
Frobisher, Martin 1539-1594 Expl 93
Frock, J. Daniel 1940- WhoAm 92, WhoE 93
Froebe, Hans A. 1931- WhoScE 91-3
Froebel, Carlton Alfred, Jr. 1938- WhoE 93
Froehle, Deena Law&B 92
Froehlich, Anna Ingrid 1956- WhoEmL 93
Froehlich, Clifford Wayne 1956- WhoEmL 93
Froehlich, Dean Kenneth 1931- WhoE 93
Froehlich, Fritz Edgar 1925- WhoAm 92, WhoE 93
Froehlich, Harold Vernon 1932- WhoAm 92
Froehlich, Joachim William 1944- WhoAm 92
Froehlich, Klaus Franz Otto 1937- WhoUN 92
Froehlich, Kristi Lynn 1964- WhoEmL 93
Froehlich, Laurence Alan 1951- WhoEmL 93
Froehlich, Leonhard H. 1929- St&PR 93
Froehlich, Lynne Peterson 1958- WhoAmW 93
Froehlich, Wojciech 1943- WhoScE 91-4
Froehlke, Robert Frederick 1922- St&PR 93, WhoAm 92
Froehner, Michael Herbert 1942- WhoWor 93
Froelich, Bernard John 1936- St&PR 93
Froelich, Beverly Lorraine 1948- WhoAmW 93
Froelich, Bill MiSFD 9
Froelich, Daniel A. 1948- St&PR 93
Froelich, Wolfgang Andreas 1927- WhoAm 92
Froelicher, Franz 1936- WhoSSW 93
Froeming, Rebecca Lynn 1954- WhoAmW 93
Froemming, Herbert Dean 1936- WhoAm 92
Froemsdorf, Donald Hope 1934- WhoAm 92
Froeschle, Robert Edward 1918- WhoAm 92
Froese, Robert 1945- ScF&FL 92
Froese, Victor 1940- WhoAm 92
Froesel, David Wm. 1930- St&PR 93
Froessl, Horst Waldemar 1929- WhoWor 93
Froewiss, Kenneth Clark 1945- WhoAm 92
Froger, Claude E. 1935- WhoScE 91-2
Froglia, Carlo 1946- WhoScE 91-3
Frogner, Stein 1931- WhoScE 91-4
Frohawk, F.W. 1861-1946 BioIn 17
Frohawk, Frederick William 1861-1946 BioIn 17
Frohberg, Martin George 1929- WhoScE 91-3
Frohlich, Cheryl Jean 1951- WhoSSW 93
Frohlich, Dietmar H. 1936- WhoWor 93
Frohlich, Edward David 1931- WhoAm 92
Frohlich, Emil L. 1931- St&PR 93
Frohlich, Gustav 1902-1987 IntDcF 2-3 [port]
Frohlich, Jack T. 1950- WhoE 93, WhoEmL 93
Frohlich, Kenneth 1945- WhoIns 93
Frohlich, Kenneth R. 1945- St&PR 93, WhoAm 92
Frohlich, Marie A. 1905- St&PR 93
Frohlichstein, Alan 1953- WhoWor 93
Frohling, Edward Sebastian 1924- St&PR 93
Frohlinger, Barry Michael 1954- WhoEmL 93
Frohlinger, Joel Larry 1949- WhoE 93
Frohman, Howard Loeb 1916- WhoWrEP 92
Frohman, Lawrence Asher 1935- WhoAm 92
Frohmann, Jules 1933- St&PR 93
Frohnen, Bruce (P.) 1962- ConAu 139
Frohnmayer, David Braden 1940- WhoAm 92
Frohnmayer, John E. 1942- BioIn 17
Frohnmayer, John Edward 1942- WhoAm 92
Frohnmayer, William G. 1938- St&PR 93
Frohock, Fred Manuel 1937- WhoAm 92
Frohock, Joan 1939- WhoAm 92
Frohring, Paul Robert WhoAm 92
Froidebise, Pierre (Jean Marie) 1914-1962 Baker 92
Froideval, Francois Marcela- ScF&FL 92
Froidevaux, Claude 1930- WhoScE 91-2
Froikin, Murray Arthur 1952- WhoEmL 93
Frois, Jeanne 1953- SmATA 73 [port]
Frois, Theodore M. Law&B 92
Frolander, Ulf 1939- WhoWor 93
Frolich, B.D. 1940- St&PR 93
Frolich, (Friedrich) Theodor 1803-1836 Baker 92
Frolick, Patricia Mary 1923- WhoAmW 93
Frolio, David G. Law&B 92
Frolov, Konstantin Vasilievitch 1932- WhoWor 93
Frolund, Hakon 1916- WhoWor 93
From, Harry WhoWor 93
Fromageot, Henri Pierre-Marcel 1937- WhoE 93
Froman, Ann WhoAm 92, WhoAmW 93
Froman, Charles A., Jr. 1929- St&PR 93
Froman, Michael Braverman 1962- WhoEmL 93
Froman, Nanny Ingeborg 1922- WhoScE 91-4, WhoWor 93
Froman, Per Olof 1926- WhoScE 91-4, WhoWor 93
Froman, Rebecca Ann Law&B 92
Fromberg, Doris Pronin 1937- WhoAmW 93
Fromberg, Kurt Christian 1934- WhoWor 93
Fromboluti, Sideo 1920- WhoE 93
Frome, David Herman 1945- WhoE 93
Frome, Nils Helmer 1918-1962 ScF&FL 92
Frome, R.L. St&PR 93
Froment, Eric 1944- WhoWor 93
Froment, Gilbert F.A. 1930- WhoScE 91-2
Froment, Louis (Georges Francois) de 1921- Baker 92
Froment, Michel 1931- WhoScE 91-2
Fromentin, Eugene 1820-1876 DcLB 123 [port]
Fromer, Harvey S. 1941- St&PR 93
Fromhagen, Carl, Jr. 1926- WhoAm 92, WhoWor 93
Fromkes, Saul 1907-1991 BioIn 17
Fromkin, Victoria Alexandria 1923- WhoAm 92
Fromknecht, Thomas Gerard 1961- WhoE 93
Fromlet, K. Hubert 1947- WhoWor 93
Fromm, Alfred 1905- WhoAm 92
Fromm, Andreas 1621-1683 Baker 92
Fromm, Bernard 1935- St&PR 93
Fromm, David 1939- WhoAm 92
Fromm, Eli 1939- WhoAm 92, WhoE 93
Fromm, Erich 1900-1980 BioIn 17
Fromm, Erika 1910- WhoAm 92
Fromm, Erwin Frederick 1933- WhoSSW 93, WhoWor 93
Fromm, Frederick A., Jr. Law&B 92
Fromm, Friedrich 1888-1945 HarEnMi
Fromm, Hans 1939- WhoE 93
Fromm, Henry Gordon 1911- WhoAm 92
Fromm, Herbert 1905- Baker 92
Fromm, Jeffery B. Law&B 92
Fromm, Jeffery Bernard 1947- WhoEmL 93
Fromm, Joseph 1920- WhoAm 92
Fromm, Paul 1906-1987 Baker 92
Fromm, Paul Oliver 1923- WhoAm 92
Fromm, Pete 1958- ConAu 139
Fromm, Roger William 1933- WhoE 93
Fromm, Winfield Eric 1918- WhoAm 92
Frommell, James L. 1948- St&PR 93
Frommelt, Peter 1946- WhoWor 93
Frommer, Arthur BioIn 17
Frommer, Henry 1943- WhoAm 92, WhoE 93
Frommer, Peter Leslie 1932- WhoAm 92
Frommer, Sara Hoskinson 1938- WhoWrEP 92
Frommhold, Walter 1921- WhoWor 93
Fromming, Karl-Heinz 1925- WhoScE 91-3
Fromont, Michel Jean 1940- St&PR 93
Fromowitz, Allen 1948- WhoE 93, WhoEmL 93
Fromson, Antoinette Duval 1925- WhoAmW 93, WhoE 93, WhoWor 93
Fromson, Jeffrey 1944- St&PR 93
Fromstein, Mitchell S. BioIn 17
Fromstein, Mitchell S. 1928- WhoAm 92
Froncek, Frank X. Law&B 92
Fronckiewicz, Robert Lawrence 1936- St&PR 93
Fronczak, Thomas Allan 1946- WhoE 93
Fronduti, A. Rex 1926- St&PR 93
Froneberg, Brigitte 1945- WhoWor 93
Fronheiser, James Joseph 1930- St&PR 93
Fronk, John D. 1954- St&PR 93
Fronk, Rhonda Beth 1956- WhoEmL 93
Fronk, Robert Steven 1959- St&PR 93
Fronk, William Joseph 1925- WhoAm 92
Fronski, Andrzej 1938- WhoScE 91-4
Front, Marshall Bernard 1937- St&PR 93
Frontczak, Nancy Thal 1947- WhoAmW 93
Frontenay, Jean de Rohan d1571? BioIn 17
Frontier, Serge 1934- WhoScE 91-2
Frontiere, Georgia WhoAm 92, WhoAmW 93
Frontini, Francesco Paolo 1860-1939 Baker 92
Fronville, Claire Louise 1956- WhoEmL 93
Froom, Sharon June 1958- WhoE 93
Froom, William Watkins 1915- WhoAm 92
Frosch, James Peter 1949- WhoE 93, WhoEmL 93
Frosch, Robert Alan 1928- St&PR 93, WhoAm 92
Froschauer, Johann fl. 15th cent.- Baker 92
Froseth, Gerald O. 1931- St&PR 93
Frosner, Gert G. 1942- WhoWor 93
Fross, Lavern K. St&PR 93
Fross, Stuart E. Law&B 92
Frossard, Louis-Oscar 1889-1946 BioIn 17
Frossi, Paolo 1921- WhoWor 93

Frost, A(rthur) B(urdett) 1851-1928 ConAu 136, MajAI [port]
Frost, A. Corwin 1934- WhoE 93
Frost, Alexander ScF&FL 92
Frost, Allison K. 1956- WhoEmL 93
Frost, Andrew Richard WhoScE 91-1
Frost, Anna Eastman AmWomPl
Frost, Annamarie 1955- WhoSSW 93
Frost, Anne 1932- WhoSSW 93
Frost, Barry Warren 1947- WhoEmL 93
Frost, Bobby Jean 1932- WhoWor 93
Frost, Brian J. ScF&FL 92
Frost, Brian Standish 1958- WhoEmL 93
Frost, Charles Estes, Jr. 1950- WhoEmL 93
Frost, Charles Harper 1920- WhoSSW 93
Frost, Chester R. 1939- WhoAm 92
Frost, Chester Robert 1939- St&PR 93
Frost, David 1925- WhoE 93
Frost, David B. Law&B 92
Frost, David Paradine 1939- WhoAm 92, WhoWor 93
Frost, David Paul 1954- WhoSSW 93
Frost, Denis 1925- ScF&FL 92
Frost, Diana Law&B 92
Frost, Earle Wesley 1899- WhoAm 92
Frost, Earline Shields 1941- WhoAmW 93
Frost, Elizabeth Ann McArthur 1938- WhoE 93
Frost, Ellen Louise 1945- WhoAm 92
Frost, Faye Juanita 1927- WhoWrEP 92
Frost, Felicia Dodee 1956- WhoAmW 93
Frost, Frederick G. 1907-1991 BioIn 17
Frost, Gregory 1951- ScF&FL 92
Frost, Harlie D. Law&B 92
Frost, Herbert G., Jr. 1931- St&PR 93
Frost, J. Ormond 1927- WhoAm 92
Frost, Jacqueline Ford 1963- WhoE 93
Frost, James Arthur 1918- WhoAm 92, WhoWor 93
Frost, James Frank 1902-1991 BioIn 17
Frost, Janet Owens 1944- WhoAmW 93
Frost, Jason ScF&FL 92, WhoWrEP 92
Frost, Jerry William 1940- WhoAm 92
Frost, Joe Lindell 1933- WhoAm 92
Frost, John 1922-1990 BioIn 17
Frost, John C. 1950- WhoSSW 93
Frost, John E. d1992 NewYTBS 92
Frost, John Eldridge 1917- WhoWor 93
Frost, John Elliott 1924- WhoSSW 93, WhoWor 93
Frost, John Jared, Jr. 1954- St&PR 93
Frost, John Sidney 1949- St&PR 93
Frost, Jonas Martin 1942- WhoAm 92, WhoSSW 93
Frost, Juanita Corbitt 1926- WhoAmW 93, WhoSSW 93
Frost, Julianne Louise 1958- WhoAmW 93
Frost, Lawrence A. 1907-1990 BioIn 17
Frost, Lawrence B. 1942- St&PR 93
Frost, Lena-Carin Elizabeth 1962- St&PR 93
Frost, Lucille Joan 1940- WhoAmW 93
Frost, Margaret Anne 1935- WhoAmW 93
Frost, Mark BioIn 17, MiSFD 9, WhoAm 92
Frost, Martin 1942- CngDr 91
Frost, Michael Glynn WhoScE 91-1
Frost, Michele M. Law&B 92
Frost, Monica McAsey 1959- WhoAmW 93, WhoEmL 93
Frost, Norman Cooper 1923- WhoAm 92
Frost, O(rcutt) W(illiam) 1926- ConAu 136
Frost, Phillip 1936- St&PR 93
Frost, Raymond David 1960- WhoSSW 93
Frost, Richard George 1929- WhoWrEP 92
Frost, Robert 1874-1963 BioIn 17, MagSAmL [port], WorLitC [port]
Frost, Robert 1939- WhoAm 92
Frost, Robert Edwin 1932- WhoAm 92
Frost, Rose 1950- WhoAmW 93
Frost, Russell, III 1921- St&PR 93
Frost, S. David 1930- WhoAm 92
Frost, Stuart 1947- St&PR 93
Frost, Susan Henson 1948- WhoAmW 93
Frost, T.C., Jr. 1927- St&PR 93
Frost, Thomas ScF&FL 92
Frost, Thomas Clayborne 1927- WhoAm 92
Frost, William Lee 1926- WhoAm 92
Frost, Winston Lyle 1958- WhoEmL 93
Frostad, John P. 1958- St&PR 93
Frostell, Carl Goran G. 1920- WhoScE 91-4
Frostic, Gwen 1906- WhoAmW 93
Frostick, Frederick Charles 1922- WhoSSW 93
Frost-Tucker, Vontell Delores 1951- WhoE 93
Frot, Pierre Roland 1963- WhoWor 93
Frothingham, Eugenia Brooks 1874- AmWomPl
Frothingham, Thomas Eliot 1926- WhoAm 92
Frotscher, Gotthold 1897-1967 Baker 92
Frotzler, Carl 1873-1960 Baker 92
Froud, Brian 1948- ScF&FL 92
Froud, Ethel E. 1880?-1941 BioIn 17
Froud, Jane ScF&FL 92
Froude, James Anthony 1818-1894 BioIn 17
Froula, James 1945- WhoWrEP 92
Froula, James DeWayne 1945- WhoAm 92
Frova, Andrea 1936- WhoScE 91-3
Frowen, Stephen Francis 1923- WhoWor 93
Frowick, Robert Holmes 1929- WhoAm 92
Frowick, Roy Halston BioIn 17
Froy, Herald ConAu 137
Fruchart, Daniel 1944- WhoScE 91-2
Fruchart, Jean-Charles WhoScE 91-2
Fruchtenbaum, Edward 1948- St&PR 93
Fruchter, Scott Joseph 1951- WhoEmL 93
Fruchterman, James Robert, Jr. 1959- WhoEmL 93
Fruchthendler, Fred Barry 1951- WhoEmL 93
Fruchting, Henning C. 1940- WhoScE 91-3
Fruchtman, Arthur Law&B 92
Fruchtman, Joel ScF&FL 92
Fruchtman, Milton Allen WhoAm 92
Fruchtman, Steven Martin 1951- WhoE 93
Fructus, Jean WhoScE 91-2
Frudakis, Evangelos William 1921- WhoAm 92
Frudakis, Rosalie 1952- WhoAmW 93
Frudakis, Zenos Antonios 1951- WhoAm 92, WhoWor 93
Frueauf, Wendy Holly 1953- WhoEmL 93
Frueckert, Rolf Herbert 1945- WhoWor 93
Frueh, A.J. 1880-1968 ScF&FL 92
Frueh, Lloyd W., II 1936- St&PR 93
Fruehan, Richard J. 1942- WhoAm 92
Fruehauf, Harvey C., Jr. 1929- St&PR 93
Fruehling, Carl R. 1935- St&PR 93
Fruehling, Rosemary Therese 1933- WhoAmW 93
Fruend, Robert Allen 1940- WhoAm 92
Fruet, William 1933- MiSFD 9
Frug, Gerald E. 1939- WhoAm 92
Frug, Mary Joe 1941-1991 BioIn 17
Frugatta, Giuseppe 1860-1933 Baker 92
Fruggiero, Gerard St&PR 93
Frugoni, Orazio 1921- Baker 92
Fruhbeck, Rafael 1933- Baker 92
Fruhbeck de Burgos, Rafael 1933- Baker 92, WhoAm 92, WhoWor 93
Fruhbeck Olmedo, Federico 1955- WhoWor 93
Fruhman, Harry 1956- WhoE 93
Fruhmann, Karen Anne WhoAmW 93
Fruhwald, Arno 1944- WhoScE 91-3
Fruin, Betty Jo 1961- WhoAmW 93
Fruin, Robert Cornelius 1925- WhoAm 92
Fruit, Karen Brezina 1959- WhoAmW 93
Fruit, Melvyn Herschel 1937- WhoAm 92
Fruit, Richard E. 1941- St&PR 93
Fruitman, Frederick Howard 1950- WhoEmL 93
Fruitman, Harvey M. 1938- St&PR 93
Fruitt, Paul N. 1931- WhoAm 92, WhoE 93
Fruitt, Paul Nelson 1931- St&PR 93
Frum, Barbara BioIn 17
Frum, Barbara 1937-1992 ConAu 137, NewYTBS 92
Frum, Elsie BioIn 17
Frumerie, (Per) Gunnar (Fredrik) de 1908-1987 Baker 92
Frumerman, Marcia 1933- WhoE 93
Frumerman, Robert 1924- WhoE 93
Frumkes, Lewis Burke 1939- WhoWrEP 92
Frumkes, Roy 1944- MiSFD 9
Frumkin, Allan 1926- WhoAm 92
Frumkin, Brian E. Law&B 92
Frumkin, Neva Leslie 1954- WhoAmW 93
Frumkin, Robert Martin 1928- WhoSSW 93
Frumkin, Victor Robert 1929- St&PR 93
Frump, Robert Roy 1947- St&PR 93
Frundsberg, Georg von 1473-1528 HarEnMi
Frungillo, Nicholas Anthony, Jr. 1960- WhoEmL 93
Frunze, Mikhail Vasilyevich 1885-1925 HarEnMi
Frunzi, George Louis 1944- WhoE 93
Fruschelli, Corradino 1938- WhoScE 91-3
Frusciante, John BioIn 17
Frusciante, John c. 1970- See Red Hot Chili Peppers, The News 93-1
Frush, James Carroll, Jr. 1930- WhoWor 93
Frushour, Susan Tydings 1947- WhoSSW 93
Frutchey, Daniel Lloyd Law&B 92
Frutchey, Daphne Faye 1934- WhoAmW 93
Fruth, Beryl Rose 1952- WhoAmW 93, WhoEmL 93
Fruth, Diana Lynn 1958- WhoSSW 93
Frutkoff, Peter Harold 1953- WhoE 93
Frutos Vaesken, Alexis 1934- WhoWor 93
Frux, Gregory William 1958- WhoEmL 93
Fruzzetti, Oreste Giorgio 1938- WhoWor 93
Fry, Albert Joseph 1937- WhoAm 92
Fry, Anne Evans 1939- WhoAmW 93
Fry, Bernard Mitchell 1915- WhoWor 93
Fry, Charles E., Jr. 1952- St&PR 93
Fry, Charles George 1936- WhoWor 93
Fry, Charles L. 1934- St&PR 93
Fry, Charles Rahn BioIn 17
Fry, Christopher BioIn 17
Fry, Clarence Herbert 1926- WhoAm 92
Fry, Cynthia Anne 1953- WhoEmL 93
Fry, Darrel K. 1948- St&PR 93
Fry, Darryl Diamond 1939- WhoAm 92
Fry, David John 1929- St&PR 93
Fry, David Stow 1949- WhoAm 92
Fry, Donald Lewis 1924- WhoAm 92
Fry, Donald Owen 1921- WhoAm 92
Fry, Donna Marie 1947- WhoAmW 93, WhoEmL 93
Fry, Doris Hendricks 1918- WhoAm 92
Fry, Dorothy Whipple 1897- AmWomPl
Fry, Edward F. 1935-1992 BioIn 17, NewYTBS 92
Fry, Edwin Merritt, Jr. 1951- WhoSSW 93
Fry, Elizabeth Gurney 1780-1845 BioIn 17
Fry, Emma Viola Sheridan AmWomPl
Fry, Frederick Ernest Joseph 1908-1989 BioIn 17
Fry, Harry Wellman 1932- WhoAm 92
Fry, Hayden 1929- WhoAm 92
Fry, J. Lee 1949- St&PR 93
Fry, James Edward 1928- WhoSSW 93
Fry, James Wilson 1939- WhoAm 92
Fry, James Wilson, Jr. Law&B 92
Fry, Jennifer Goering Law&B 92
Fry, John 1930- St&PR 93, WhoAm 92, WhoWrEP 92
Fry, John C. 1949- WhoScE 91-3
Fry, John Hayden, Jr. 1929- BiDAMSp 1989
Fry, Keith A. 1955- St&PR 93
Fry, Keith E. Law&B 92
Fry, Lincoln Jacob 1937- WhoSSW 93
Fry, Linda Sue 1961- WhoAm 92, WhoAmW 93
Fry, Louis Edwin, Jr. 1928- WhoAm 92
Fry, Malcolm Craig 1928- WhoAm 92
Fry, Margery 1874-1958 BioIn 17
Fry, Marion Golda 1932- WhoAmW 93
Fry, Mark Kendrick 1967- WhoSSW 93
Fry, Mary Beth 1961- WhoE 93
Fry, Mary L. Law&B 92
Fry, Maxwell John 1944- WhoAm 92, WhoWor 93
Fry, Michael Graham 1934- WhoAm 92
Fry, Mildred Helen 1940- WhoAmW 93
Fry, Nicholas 1942- ScF&FL 92
Fry, Patricia Louise 1940- WhoAmW 93
Fry, Robert Dean 1955- St&PR 93
Fry, Roger 1866-1934 DcLB DS10
Fry, Ron W. Law&B 92
Fry, Ronald William 1949- WhoEmL 93
Fry, Russell Jackson 1928- WhoSSW 93
Fry, Samuel 1909-1991 BioIn 17
Fry, Samuel Edwin, Jr. 1934- WhoE 93
Fry, Sara Bancroft AmWomPl
Fry, Sarah BioIn 17
Fry, Shanti Addison 1951- WhoE 93
Fry, Slaton Eugene 1958- WhoSSW 93
Fry, Steve J. 1946- St&PR 93
Fry, Steven Edward 1945- St&PR 93
Fry, Ted Charles 1950- WhoEmL 93
Fry, Thomas Richard 1948- WhoEmL 93
Fry, William Frederick 1921- WhoAm 92
Fry, William Henry 1813-1864 Baker 92, BioIn 17
Fry, William Henry 1815-1864 JrnUS
Fryar, William Ronald 1951- WhoSSW 93
Fryatt, John E. WhoAm 92
Fryback, Ronald D. 1936- St&PR 93
Fryberger, H.B., Jr. 1906- St&PR 93
Fryburger, Vernon Ray, Jr. 1918- WhoAm 92
Fryczkowski, Andrzej Witold 1939- WhoWor 93
Frycz-Modrzewski, Andrzej 1503-1572 PolBiDi
Frydenberg, Cliff 1950- St&PR 93
Frydryk, Karl A. 1954- St&PR 93
Frye, Billy Eugene 1933- WhoAm 92
Frye, David Scott 1955- WhoIns 93
Frye, Della Mae 1926- WhoWrEP 92
Frye, Dexter M. 1958- St&PR 93
Frye, Don W. 1934- St&PR 93
Frye, Dwight 1899-1943 BioIn 17
Frye, George M. Law&B 92
Frye, Gilbert Bernard 1938- St&PR 93
Frye, Helen Jackson 1930- WhoAmW 93
Frye, Henry E. 1932- WhoAm 92, WhoSSW 93
Frye, Herbert David 1950- WhoEmL 93
Frye, Jack 1904-1959 EncABHB 8 [port]
Frye, Jeff 1957- St&PR 93
Frye, John H., Jr. 1908- WhoAm 92
Frye, John William, III 1929- WhoAm 92
Frye, Joseph T. 1918- St&PR 93
Frye, Judith Eleen Minor WhoAmW 93, WhoWor 93
Frye, Karen Ernst 1951- WhoWor 93
Frye, Keith Nale 1941- WhoAm 92
Frye, Mauna 1947- St&PR 93
Frye, Newton Phillips, Jr. 1918- WhoAm 92
Frye, Northrop BioIn 17
Frye, Northrop 1912-1991 AnObit 1991, ConLC 70 [port], WhoCanL 92
Frye, (Herman) Northrop 1912-1991 ConAu 37NR
Frye, Richard Nelson 1920- WhoAm 92
Frye, Robert Dean 1948- WhoE 93
Frye, Roland Mushat 1921- WhoAm 92, WhoE 93
Frye, Roland Mushat, Jr. 1950- WhoEmL 93
Frye, Victor Morse Law&B 92
Frye, Walter fl. 15th cent.- Baker 92
Frye, William P. 1830-1911 PolPar
Frye Hoffman, Lois 1955- WhoWrEP 92
Fryer, Arlene Barbara 1931- St&PR 93
Fryer, Deborah Tyler 1932- WhoE 93
Fryer, Donald Sidney ScF&FL 92
Fryer, E. Reeseman d1991 BioIn 17
Fryer, George Herbert 1877-1957 Baker 92
Fryer, Joan Cook 1952- WhoEmL 93, WhoSSW 93
Fryer, John Stanley 1937- WhoAm 92
Fryer, Patricia Ruth WhoScE 91-1
Fryer, Regina Kenny 1943- WhoAmW 93
Fryer, Robert Sherwood 1920- WhoAm 92
Fryer, Thomas Waitt, Jr. 1936- WhoAm 92
Fryer, Wendell F., Jr. 1934- St&PR 93
Fryk, Jan 1950- WhoScE 91-4
Frykberg, W. Randolph 1947- WhoEmL 93
Frykenberg, Robert Eric 1930- WhoAm 92
Fryklof, Harald (Leonard) 1882-1919 Baker 92
Fryklof, Lars-Einar 1929- WhoScE 91-4
Fryklund, (Lars Axel) Daniel 1879-1965 Baker 92
Fryklund, Linda M. 1945- WhoScE 91-4
Fryland, Sonnich Jacob 1941- WhoAm 92
Fryling, Charles, Jr. BioIn 17
Fryling, Dawn BioIn 17
Frym, Gloria Lynn 1947- WhoWrEP 92
Frym, Janet Carolyn 1946- WhoAmW 93
Fryman, Cherie Marie 1955- WhoAmW 93
Frymer, Berl 1912-1991 BioIn 17
Frymer, Murry 1934- WhoAm 92
Frymier, Jack Rimmel 1925- BioIn 17
Frymier, Phyllis Godwin 1951- WhoEmL 93
Fryml, Martin Josef 1961- St&PR 93, WhoSSW 93
Fryns, Jean-Pierre 1946- WhoScE 91-2
Fryshman, Bernard 1938- WhoE 93
Fryson, Christopher Dwayne 1963- WhoSSW 93
Fryt, Michael David 1955- WhoEmL 93
Fryt, Monte Stanislaus 1949- WhoWor 93
Fry-Wendt, Sherri Diane 1958- WhoAmW 93
Fryxell, David Allen 1956- WhoAm 92
Fryxell, Greta Albrecht 1926- WhoAmW 93
Fryxell, Paul Arnold 1927- WhoSSW 93
Fryzuk, Michael Daniel 1952- WhoAm 92
Fsadni, Ivan 1961- WhoUN 92
Fthenakis, Emanuel John 1928- WhoAm 92, WhoSSW 93
Fthenakis, Vasilis 1951- WhoE 93
Fu, Chu Li 1945- WhoWor 93
Fu, Hung-Lin 1950- WhoWor 93
Fu, Karen King-Wah 1940- WhoAm 92
Fu, Monty Mong Chen 1946- St&PR 93
Fu, Shen C. Y. 1937- WhoAm 92
Fu, Shou-Cheng Joseph 1924- WhoWor 93
Fu, Tong 1936- WhoWor 93
Fu, Xiao Feng 1956- WhoWor 93
Fu, Yu Li 1959- WhoWor 93
Fu, Yuan Chin 1930- WhoWor 93
Fua, Giorgio 1919- WhoWor 93
Fua, Orlando B. 1933- WhoAsAP 91
Fuad, I 1868-1936 DcTwHis
Fuad, Peter H. Law&B 92
Fubini, Eugene Ghiron 1913- WhoAm 92
Fuccella, Carl J. 1927- WhoAm 92
Fucci, Joseph Leonard 1950- WhoEmL 93
Fucci, Linda D. 1947- St&PR 93
Fuccillo, Arthur Nicholas 1953- WhoE 93
Fuchida, Mitsuo 1902-1976 HarEnMi

Fuchida, Mitsuo 1902- *BioIn 17*
Fu Chien 337-384 *HarEnMi*
Fuchigami, Sadao 1937- *WhoAsAP 91*
Fuchs, (Leonard Johann Heinrich) Albert 1858-1910 *Baker 92*
Fuchs, Alfred d1990 *BioIn 17*
Fuchs, Alfred Herman 1932- *WhoAm 92, WhoE 93*
Fuchs, Anna-Riitta 1926- *WhoAm 92*
Fuchs, Anne Sutherland 1947- *WhoAmW 93*
Fuchs, Arnold Carl *St&PR 93*
Fuchs, Bernard A. 1912- *St&PR 93*
Fuchs, Beth Ann 1963- *WhoAmW 93*
Fuchs, Boris 1933- *WhoScE 91-3*
Fuchs, Carl (Dorius Johannes) 1838-1922 *Baker 92*
Fuchs, Curtis Ray 1943- *WhoWor 93*
Fuchs, Daniel 1909- *ConAu 40NR, JeAmFiW*
Fuchs, Daniel Jude *Law&B 92*
Fuchs, Dieter R. 1952- *WhoScE 91-3*
Fuchs, Elaine V. 1950- *WhoAm 92, WhoAmW 93, WhoEmL 93*
Fuchs, Ewald Franz 1939- *WhoAm 92*
Fuchs, Flavio Danni 1950- *WhoWor 93*
Fuchs, Frank Joseph 1954- *WhoEmL 93*
Fuchs, Fredica Ann 1949- *WhoEmL 93*
Fuchs, Fritz 1918- *WhoAm 92*
Fuchs, Gerhard H. *Law&B 92*
Fuchs, Hanno 1928- *WhoAm 92*
Fuchs, Helmuth Hans 1931- *WhoE 93*
Fuchs, Jaime J. 1920- *WhoWor 93*
Fuchs, Jay R. 1955- *WhoIns 93*
Fuchs, Johann Nepomuk 1842-1899 *Baker 92*
Fuchs, John Michael 1945- *WhoE 93*
Fuchs, Joseph Louis 1931- *WhoAm 92*
Fuchs, Joseph (Philip) 1900- *Baker 92*
Fuchs, Jurgen Hans 1957- *WhoWor 93*
Fuchs, K. *WhoScE 91-3*
Fuchs, Kathleen Fitzgerald 1946- *WhoEmL 93*
Fuchs, Klaus 1911- *DcTwHis*
Fuchs, Klaus 1911-1988 *ColdWar 1 [port]*
Fuchs, Konrad Rudolf 1928- *WhoWor 93*
Fuchs, L. 1937- *St&PR 93*
Fuchs, Laszlo Jehoshua 1949- *WhoWor 93*
Fuchs, Laurel Bernice 1935- *WhoWrEP 92*
Fuchs, Lawrence Howard 1927- *WhoAm 92*
Fuchs, Leo L. 1929- *WhoWor 93*
Fuchs, Lillian 1903- *Baker 92*
Fuchs, Lucy Ann 1935- *WhoSSW 93*
Fuchs, Lukas *Baker 92*
Fuchs, Marc *St&PR 93*
Fuchs, Marcia Gail 1950- *WhoE 93*
Fuchs, Marta 1898-1974 *Baker 92, OxDcOp*
Fuchs, Michael 1949- *WhoE 93, WhoEmL 93*
Fuchs, Michael J. 1946- *WhoAm 92, WhoE 93*
Fuchs, Michael Joseph *BioIn 17*
Fuchs, Morton S. 1932- *WhoAm 92*
Fuchs, Nancy Kathleen 1961- *WhoAmW 93*
Fuchs, Olivia Anne Morris 1949- *WhoEmL 93*
Fuchs, Owen George 1951- *WhoWor 93*
Fuchs, Patrick Eugene 1930- *WhoWor 93*
Fuchs, Peter 1928- *WhoWor 93*
Fuchs, Renato 1942- *St&PR 93*
Fuchs, Robert 1847-1927 *Baker 92*
Fuchs, Roland John 1933- *WhoUN 92*
Fuchs, Stephen 1908- *IntDcAn*
Fuchs, Victor Robert 1924- *BioIn 17, WhoAm 92*
Fuchs, Vivian 1908- *Expl 93, WhoWor 93*
Fuchsberg, Jacob David 1913- *WhoAm 92*
Fuchs-Gioia, Joyce K. 1947- *WhoE 93*
Fuchsluger, Donna Jean 1952- *WhoEmL 93*
Fuchssteiner, Benno 1941- *WhoWor 93*
Fuchsteiner, Judith Agnes 1947- *WhoEmL 93*
Fucik, Donald Edward 1955- *WhoEmL 93*
Fucik, Frank M. 1917- *St&PR 93*
Fucik, Julius 1903-1943 *BioIn 17*
Fucik, Julius (Arnost Vilem) 1872-1916 *Baker 92*
Fucile, Frank, Jr. *Law&B 92*
Fucillo, Mike 1956- *St&PR 93*
Fuck, Reinhardt Adolfo 1940- *WhoWor 93*
Fudacz, Paul M. *Law&B 92*
Fudalla, Marvin J. 1954- *St&PR 93*
Fudenberg, Herman Hugh 1928- *WhoAm 92, WhoSSW 93*
Fudge, Ann Marie 1951- *WhoAm 92, WhoAmW 93*
Fudge, Anne M. *BioIn 17*
Fudger, Joanne Wright 1943- *WhoSSW 93*
Fudold, Wallace A. 1944- *St&PR 93*
Fuduli, Robin Ann 1947- *WhoAmW 93*
Fudurich, Edward Charles 1944- *St&PR 93*
Fuegi, John 1936- *WhoAm 92*
Fuehrer, Walter 1941- *St&PR 93*
Fuelberg, Bennie R. 1944- *St&PR 93*
Fuellgraf, Charles Louis, Jr. 1931- *St&PR 93*
Fuelling, Thomas Norton 1933- *WhoAm 92*
Fuenllana, Miguel de 16th cent.- *Baker 92*
Fuenning, Esther Renate *WhoAmW 93*
Fueno, Takayuki 1931- *WhoWor 93*
Fuente, Carmen de la 1923- *DcMexL*
Fuente, D. I. 1946- *WhoSSW 93*
Fuente, Jose E. 1946- *St&PR 93*
Fuentealba, Victor William 1922- *WhoAm 92*
Fuentes, Carlos *BioIn 17, DcCPCAm*
Fuentes, Carlos 1928- *DcMexL, MagSWL [port], ScF&FL 92, SpAmA, WhoAm 92, WhoWor 93, WorLitC [port]*
Fuentes, Juan Bautista 1869-1955 *Baker 92*
Fuentes, Martha Ayers 1923- *WhoAm 92, WhoWrEP 92*
Fuentes, Rene Ramon 1946- *St&PR 93*
Fuentes, Roberto 1934- *ScF&FL 92*
Fuentes, Rodolfo 1954- *BioIn 17*
Fuentes Mohr, Alberto *DcCPCAm*
Fuentes Mota, Jose 1944- *WhoScE 91-3*
Fuentes-Perez, Manuel 1936- *WhoScE 91-3*
Fuentes Pieruccini, Mario *DcCPCAm*
Fuentevilla, Manuel Edward 1923- *WhoE 93*
Fuenzalida, Victor Manuel 1957- *WhoWor 93*
Fuerbringer, Alfred Ottomar 1903- *WhoAm 92*
Fuerle, Richard D. *Law&B 92*
Fueroghne, Dean Keith 1952- *WhoWor 93*
Fuerst, Adolph 1925- *WhoE 93*
Fuerst, Harold T. 1909-1990 *BioIn 17*
Fuerst, Wolfgang 1938- *WhoUN 92*
Fuerste, Frederick 1921- *WhoWor 93*
Fuerstenau, Douglas Winston 1928- *WhoAm 92*
Fuerstenberg, Friedrich Karl Richard 1930- *WhoWor 93*
Fuerstenberg, Gary J. 1943- *St&PR 93*
Fuerstenburg, Anna 1948- *WhoCanL 92*
Fuerstner, Carl 1912- *Baker 92*
Fuertes, Gloria *BioIn 17*
Fuertes, Rafael Arellano 1946- *WhoWor 93*
Fuess, Billings Sibley, Jr. 1928- *WhoE 93, WhoWor 93*
Fuess, Harold George 1910- *WhoAm 92*
Fuess, Hartmut 1941- *WhoScE 91-3, WhoWor 93*
Fuessel, Diana F. *St&PR 93*
Fuessel, Frederick Dennis *St&PR 93*
Fuessel, John Frederick *St&PR 93*
Fuest, Robert 1927- *MiSFD 9*
Fufuka, Karama 1951- *BlkAuII 92*
Fufuka, Natika Njeri Yaa 1952- *WhoAmW 93*
Fuga, Sandro 1906- *Baker 92*
Fugami, Keigo 1961- *WhoWor 93*
Fugard, Athol *BioIn 17*
Fugard, Athol 1932- *DramC 3 [port], IntLitE, MiSFD 9, News 92 [port], -92-3 [port]*
Fugard, Athol Harold 1932- *WhoWor 93*
Fugate, Edward 1956- *WhoEmL 93*
Fugate, Glenn David *Law&B 92*
Fugate, Ivan Dee 1928- *WhoAm 92, WhoWor 93*
Fugate, Judith *BioIn 17, WhoAm 92*
Fugate, Kendall Morgan 1937- *St&PR 93*
Fugate, Norman G. 1925- *St&PR 93*
Fugate, Thomas Warren 1959- *WhoEmL 93*
Fugate, Wilbur Lindsay 1913- *WhoAm 92, WhoWor 93*
Fugate-Wilcox, Terry 1944- *WhoAm 92*
Fugawa, Michelle *Law&B 92*
Fugazy, William Denis *WhoWor 93*
Fugazzi, Paul Anthony 1959- *WhoEmL 93, WhoSSW 93*
Fuge, Marlena Jean 1963- *WhoAmW 93*
Fugelberg, Nancy Jean 1947- *WhoAmW 93*
Fuger, Jean *WhoScE 91-3*
Fuger, Simon J. 1952- *St&PR 93*
Fugere, Lucien 1848-1935 *Baker 92, OxDcOp*
Fuggi, Gretchen Miller 1938- *WhoAmW 93, WhoE 93*
Fugh, John Liu 1934- *WhoAm 92*
Fugiel, Frank Paul 1950- *WhoEmL 93*
Fugitt, William Joseph 1965- *WhoSSW 93*
Fuglestad, Judy Ellen 1948- *St&PR 93*
Fugl-Meyer, Axel R. 1934- *WhoScE 91-4*
Fuglsang, Annette Margarethe 1960- *WhoAmW 93*
Fugmann, Robert 1927- *WhoScE 91-3*
Fugoso, Leonardo B. 1922- *WhoAsAP 91*
Fuhlrodt, Norman Theodore 1910- *WhoWor 93*
Fuhr, Fritz 1934- *WhoScE 91-3*
Fuhr, Grant *BioIn 17*
Fuhr, Jay A. *St&PR 93*
Fuhr, Xaver 1898-1973 *BioIn 17*
Fuhrboter, Alfred 1931- *WhoScE 91-3*
Fuhrer, Arthur K. 1926- *WhoAm 92, WhoE 93*
Fuhrer, Erwin 1936- *WhoScE 91-4*
Fuhrer, Robert (Johann Nepomuk) 1807-1861 *Baker 92*
Fuhriman, David H. 1947- *St&PR 93*
Fuhrman, Charles Andrew 1933- *WhoAm 92*
Fuhrman, David A. 1951- *St&PR 93*
Fuhrman, Edward J. 1935- *St&PR 93*
Fuhrman, Frederick Alexander 1915- *WhoAm 92*
Fuhrman, Ralph Edward 1909- *WhoAm 92*
Fuhrman, Robert Alexander 1925- *St&PR 93, WhoAm 92*
Fuhrman, Roberta Jean 1946- *WhoAmW 93*
Fuhrman, Sandra Lee *Law&B 92*
Fuhrman, Sylvia Howard 1919- *WhoUN 92*
Fuhrmann, Amos Eno 1944- *WhoE 93*
Fuhrmann, Charles J., II 1945- *WhoAm 92, WhoE 93*
Fuhrmann, Debora Josephine 1957- *WhoAmW 93, WhoEmL 93*
Fuhrmann, Robert A. 1927- *WhoScE 91-2*
Fuhrmann, Stewart M. *Law&B 92*
Fuhrmann, Walter J.G. 1924- *WhoScE 91-3*
Fuhrmann, Wilfried Arthur 1945- *WhoWor 93*
Fuhs, Allen Eugene 1927- *WhoAm 92*
Fuhs, Georg Wolfgang 1932- *WhoWor 93*
Fujii, Akio 1937- *WhoWor 93*
Fujii, Akira 1942- *WhoWor 93*
Fujii, Hideo 1927- *WhoWor 93*
Fujii, Hirohisa 1918- *WhoAsAP 91*
Fujii, Hiroyuki 1928- *WhoWor 93*
Fujii, Iwane 1936- *WhoWor 93*
Fujii, Naoko *Law&B 92*
Fujii, Takao 1943- *WhoAsAP 91*
Fujii, Takeo 1930- *WhoWor 93*
Fujii Koichi 1858-1926 *HarEnMi*
Fujii-Kuriyama, Yoshiaki 1938- *WhoWor 93*
Fujikawa, Eva Eiko 1958- *WhoAmW 93, WhoEmL 93, WhoWor 93*
Fujikawa, Gyo 1908- *MajAI [port], SmATA 16AS [port]*
Fujikawa, Mayumi 1946- *Baker 92*
Fujime, Yukihiro 1945- *WhoWor 93*
Fujimori, Alberto *BioIn 17*
Fujimori, Alberto 1938- *News 92 [port], WhoWor 93*
Fujimoto, Agustin Yoshio 1928- *WhoWor 93*
Fujimoto, Fumihide 1925- *WhoWor 93*
Fujimoto, Ichiro 1951- *WhoSSW 93*
Fujimoto, James G. 1957- *WhoAm 92*
Fujimoto, Tetsuo 1930- *WhoWor 93*
Fujimura, Michio 1929- *WhoWor 93*
Fujimura, Robert Kanji 1933- *WhoSSW 93*
Fujinami, Takao 1932- *WhoAsAP 91*
Fujio, Masayuki 1917- *WhoAsAP 91*
Fujioka, Goro 1921- *WhoWor 93*
Fujisawa, Hitoshi 1936- *WhoWor 93*
Fujisawa, Norio 1925- *WhoWor 93*
Fujishima, Seitaro 1957- *WhoWor 93*
Fujishiro, Katakazu Kenneth 1932- *WhoE 93*
Fujita, Akio 1934- *WhoWor 93*
Fujita, Atsushi 1959- *WhoWor 93*
Fujita, Den *BioIn 17, NewYTBS 92 [port]*
Fujita, Hiroshi 1955- *WhoWor 93*
Fujita, Jun 1950- *WhoWor 93*
Fujita, Keiki 1935- *WhoUN 92*
Fujita, Kenji 1934- *WhoWor 93*
Fujita, Shigeji 1929- *WhoAm 92*
Fujita, Sumi 1933- *WhoAsAP 91*
Fujita, Takatoshi 1923- *WhoAsAP 91*
Fujita, Tetsuya Theodore 1920- *WhoAm 92*
Fujita, Tsuneo 1933- *WhoWor 93*
Fujita, Wayne Y. 1954- *St&PR 93*
Fujita, Yuzan 1949- *WhoAsAP 91*
Fujitani, Martin Tomio 1968- *WhoWor 93*
Fujiwara, Fusao 1929- *WhoAsAP 91*
Fujiwara, Isao 1921- *WhoWor 93*
Fujiwara, Iwaichi 1908- *HarEnMi*
Fujiwara, Murasaki 978?- *BioIn 17*
Fujiwara, Yuzo 1938- *WhoWor 93*
Fukada, Robert Mikio 1933- *WhoWor 93*
Fukae, Kensuke 1926- *WhoAm 92*
Fukai, Robert D. 1949- *St&PR 93*
Fukai, Shiro 1907-1959 *Baker 92*
Fukai, Yuh 1934- *WhoWor 93*
Fukasaku, Kinji *MiSFD 9*
Fukatsu, Tanefusa 1923- *WhoWor 93*
Fukaya, Takashi 1935- *WhoAsAP 91*
Fukida, Akira 1927- *WhoAsAP 91*
Fukofuka, Viliami 1948- *WhoWor 93*
Fuks, Zvi Y. 1936- *WhoE 93*
Fuks, Zvi Yehiel 1936- *WhoAm 92*
Fukuchi, Takao 1932- *WhoUN 92*
Fukuda, Hideomi 1928- *WhoWor 93*
Fukuda, Hikosuke 1875-1959 *HarEnMi*
Fukuda, Hiroichi 1914- *WhoAsAP 91*
Fukuda, Ichiro 1940- *WhoWor 93*
Fukuda, Margaret Mary *Law&B 92*
Fukuda, Masataro 1866-1932 *HarEnMi*
Fukuda, Michael Kiyoshi 1949- *WhoEmL 93*
Fukuda, Morimichi 1929- *WhoWor 93*
Fukuda, Shigeru 1933- *WhoWor 93*
Fukuda, Yasuo 1936- *WhoAsAP 91*
Fukuda-Parr, Sakiko 1950- *WhoUN 92*
Fukudome, Shigeru 1891-1971 *HarEnMi*
Fukuhara, Mark T. 1949- *St&PR 93*
Fukui, Hatsuaki 1927- *WhoAm 92*
Fukui, Kenichi 1918- *WhoAm 92, WhoWor 93*
Fukui, Naotaka 1935- *WhoWor 93*
Fukui, Shozo 1928- *WhoWor 93*
Fukui, Yasuyuki 1934- *WhoWor 93*
Fukuma, Tomoyuki 1927- *WhoAsAP 91*
Fukumoto, Leslie Satsuki 1955- *WhoEmL 93*
Fukumoto, Shiegeo 1934- *WhoWor 93*
Fukumoto, Yasunobu 1926- *WhoWor 93*
Fukunaga, George Joji 1924- *St&PR 93, WhoAm 92*
Fukunaga, Keinosuke 1930- *WhoAm 92*
Fukunaga, Nobuhiko 1944- *WhoAsAP 91*
Fukushima, Akira 1936- *WhoWor 93*
Fukushima, Barbara Naomi 1948- *WhoAmW 93*
Fukushima, Joji 1927- *WhoAsAP 91*
Fukushima, Kazuaki 1931- *WhoWor 93*
Fukushima, Kazuo 1930- *Baker 92*
Fukushima, Keishiro 1946- *WhoWor 93*
Fukushima, Masanori 1948- *WhoWor 93*
Fukushima, Takashi 1949- *WhoWor 93*
Fukuwatari, Shichiro 1906- *WhoWor 93*
Fukuyama, Betty M. 1922- *WhoWrEP 92*
Fukuyama, Yukio 1928- *WhoWor 93*
Fukuzawa, Yukichi 1834-1901 *BioIn 17*
Fukuzumi, Naoyoshi 1924- *WhoWor 93*
Fulbright, Harriet Mayor 1933- *WhoAmW 93, WhoE 93*
Fulbright, J. William 1905- *ColdWar 1 [port], PolPar*
Fulbright, James William 1905- *DcTwHis, WhoAm 92*
Fulbright, M. J. 1955- *WhoEmL 93*
Fulbright, Paul Edward *Law&B 92*
Fulcher, Carolyn A. *Law&B 92*
Fulcher, Claire Eleanor 1925- *WhoAmW 93*
Fulcher, James 1942- *ConAu 139*
Fulcher of Chartres c. 1058-1127? *OxDcByz*
Fulci, Lucio 1927- *MiSFD 9*
Fulco, Armand John 1932- *WhoAm 92*
Fulco, Jose Roque 1927- *WhoAm 92*
Fulcomer, Virginia Ann 1916- *WhoAmW 93*
Fuld, James Jeffrey 1916- *WhoAm 92*
Fuld, Richard Severin, Jr. 1946- *WhoAm 92*
Fuld, Stanley H. 1903- *WhoAm 92*
Fulda, Michael 1939- *WhoSSW 93*
Fulda, Myron Oscar 1930- *WhoSSW 93*
Fulde, Peter S.O. 1936- *WhoScE 91-3*
Fulde, Stefan J. 1920- *WhoScE 91-4*
Fuldheim, Dorothy Snell *BioIn 17*
Fuldner, Christopher Terry 1951- *St&PR 93*
Fuldner, William Terry 1927- *St&PR 93*
Fule, Vilma Garcia 1950- *WhoAm 92*
Fuleihan, Anis 1900-1970 *Baker 92*
Fulford, Dennis L. *BioIn 17*
Fulford, James A. 1937- *St&PR 93*
Fulgencio, Saura Calixto 1946- *WhoWor 93*
Fulgham, John Rawles, Jr. 1927- *St&PR 93*
Fulgham, Steven Ray *ScF&FL 92*
Fulghum, Brice Elwin 1919- *WhoWor 93*
Fulghum, Robert *BioIn 17*
Fulghum, Robert (L.) 1937- *ConAu 139, WhoAm 92*
Fulghum, Robert Schmidt 1929- *WhoSSW 93*
Fulgieri, Maria A. *Law&B 92*
Fulginiti, Vincent 1931- *WhoAm 92*
Fulgoney, John F. 1946- *St&PR 93*
Fulgoni, Gian Marc 1948- *WhoAm 92*
Fulgoni, Gian Mark 1948- *St&PR 93*
Fulgoni, Patricia Fecenko 1947- *WhoAmW 93*
Fulgoni, Peter A. *St&PR 93*
Fulham, Gerard A. 1920-1990 *BioIn 17*
Fuligni, F. *WhoScE 91-3*
Fulinski, Andrzej Boguslaw 1934- *WhoScE 91-4*
Fulk, Roscoe Neal 1916- *WhoAm 92*
Fulkerson, Conward Guard 1933- *WhoE 93*

Fulkerson, Frederick 1922-1991 BioIn 17
Fulkerson, Gregory (Locke) 1950- Baker 92
Fulkerson, James (Orville) 1945- Baker 92
Fulkerson, Raymond Gerald 1941- WhoSSW 93, WhoWor 93
Fulkerson, William Measey, Jr. 1940- WhoAm 92
Fulkes, Jean Aston WhoWor 93
Fulks, David Joseph 1943- WhoSSW 93
Fulks, Paula J. Law&B 92
Fulks, Robert Grady 1936- WhoAm 92, WhoE 93
Fulks, William B. 1932- St&PR 93
Full, Jerome Kendrick 1926- St&PR 93
Fullagar, Paul David 1938- WhoAm 92
Fullagar, Scott David 1960- St&PR 93
Fullagar, William Watts 1914- WhoAm 92
Fullan, Richard Kenneth 1946- WhoE 93
Fullbright, Wilbur D. 1926- WhoWor 93
Fullen, Michael Augustine 1956- WhoWor 93
Fuller, Alan Gerald 1931- WhoScE 91-1
Fuller, Albert 1926- Baker 92
Fuller, Alfred Worcester 1923- WhoAm 92
Fuller, Alice Cook AmWomPl
Fuller, Andrea B. Law&B 92
Fuller, Andrew 1754-1815 BioIn 17
Fuller, Ann L. Law&B 92
Fuller, Anne Elizabeth Havens 1932- WhoAm 92
Fuller, Anthony Thomas 1924- WhoWor 93
Fuller, Arthur D. 1944- St&PR 93
Fuller, Avard E. d1992 NewYTBS 92
Fuller, Benjamin Franklin 1922- WhoAm 92
Fuller, Betty McCall 1948- WhoAmW 93
Fuller, Blair Fairchild 1927- WhoWrEP 92
Fuller, Buckminster 1895-1983 BioIn 17
Fuller, Caroline Case 1956- WhoEmL 93
Fuller, Caroline Macomber AmWomPl
Fuller, Cassandra Miller 1965- WhoAmW 93
Fuller, Charles BioIn 17
Fuller, Charles 1939- WhoAm 92
Fuller, Charles E. BioIn 17
Fuller, Charles Lee 1957- WhoSSW 93
Fuller, Christopher Robert 1953- WhoEmL 93
Fuller, Craig Lawrence 1951- WhoAm 92
Fuller, D.E. WhoScE 91-1
Fuller, D. Ward 1945- WhoAm 92
Fuller, Daniel Gunn 1958- WhoSSW 93
Fuller, DieQie 1942- WhoAmW 93
Fuller, Donald Scott 1938- St&PR 93
Fuller, Dorothy 1930- St&PR 93
Fuller, Dwight Crowe 1919- WhoSSW 93
Fuller, Edward WhoScE 91-1
Fuller, Edwin Daniel 1945- WhoAm 92, WhoWor 93
Fuller, Ethel K. AmWomPl
Fuller, Eunice AmWomPl
Fuller, Fleming B. MiSFD 9
Fuller, Fred D. 1946- St&PR 93
Fuller, Fred H. d1991 BioIn 17
Fuller, Gilbert Amos 1941- St&PR 93, WhoAm 92
Fuller, Glenn Arthur 1940- St&PR 93
Fuller, Gloria Dawn 1953- WhoWrEP 92
Fuller, Grover Francis, Jr. Law&B 92
Fuller, Harry Laurance 1938- WhoAm 92, WhoWor 93
Fuller, Henry Blake 1857-1929 GayN
Fuller, Herbert Harold 1946- WhoEmL 93
Fuller, Ida May AmWomPl
Fuller, Jack Glendon, Jr. 1923- WhoAm 92
Fuller, Jack William 1946- WhoAm 92
Fuller, Jackson Franklin 1920- WhoAm 92
Fuller, James Law&B 92
Fuller, James Chester Eedy 1927- WhoAm 92
Fuller, James Stanley 1947- St&PR 93
Fuller, Jeanne M. 1939- WhoAmW 93
Fuller, Jeffrey P. 1950- WhoE 93
Fuller, Jeffrey R. 1953- St&PR 93
Fuller, John 1937- ScF&FL 92
Fuller, John Chisholm 1932- St&PR 93
Fuller, John Frederick Charles 1878-1964 HarEnMi
Fuller, John Frederick Charles 1878-1966 BioIn 17
Fuller, John G. 1913-1990 ScF&FL 92
Fuller, John Garsed Campbell 1930- WhoAm 92
Fuller, John Grant 1913-1990 BioIn 17
Fuller, John J. d1990 BioIn 17
Fuller, John Langworthy 1910- WhoAm 92
Fuller, Joseph 1926- St&PR 93
Fuller, Joseph, Jr. 1947- WhoAm 92
Fuller, Joseph D., III 1947- WhoEmL 93, WhoSSW 93
Fuller, Julia Pazdral 1945- WhoAmW 93
Fuller, Julia Ruth 1958- WhoEmL 93
Fuller, Justin 1926- WhoSSW 93
Fuller, K.L. WhoScE 91-1
Fuller, Karen Ann 1947- WhoEmL 93
Fuller, Karon Kathleen 1941- WhoAmW 93
Fuller, Kathryn BioIn 17
Fuller, Kathryn M. Law&B 92
Fuller, Keith 1923- WhoAm 92
Fuller, Kenneth Roller 1913- WhoAm 92
Fuller, Larry 1938- WhoAm 92
Fuller, Lawrence Benedict 1936- WhoE 93
Fuller, Lawrence Joseph 1914- WhoAm 92
Fuller, Lawrence Robert 1941- WhoAm 92
Fuller, Leslie 1889-1948 QDrFCA 92 [port]
Fuller, Mabel B. AmWomPl
Fuller, Margaret 1810-1850 AmWomWr 92, BioIn 17, JrnUS
Fuller, Margaret Cathcart 1935- WhoAmW 93, WhoWrEP 92
Fuller, Margaret Virginia 1948- WhoAmW 93
Fuller, Mark Adin, Jr. 1933- St&PR 93, WhoAm 92, WhoE 93
Fuller, Mary Falvey 1941- WhoWor 93
Fuller, Mary Margaret Stiehm 1914- WhoWrEP 92
Fuller, Maxine Compton 1921- WhoSSW 93, WhoWor 93
Fuller, Melville Weston 1833-1910 OxCSupC [port]
Fuller, Meta Vaux Warrick 1877-1968 BioIn 17, EncAACR
Fuller, Michael David 1934- WhoAm 92
Fuller, Mike Andrew 1964- WhoWrEP 92
Fuller, Millard BioIn 17
Fuller, Millard Dean 1935- WhoAm 92
Fuller, Mozelle James 1909- WhoAmW 93, WhoE 93, WhoWor 93
Fuller, Myron F. St&PR 93
Fuller, Nancy J. 1949- St&PR 93
Fuller, Orville 1925- St&PR 93
Fuller, Paul 1948- WhoSSW 93
Fuller, Paula G. 1949- WhoAmW 93, WhoEmL 93
Fuller, Perry Lucian 1922- WhoAm 92
Fuller, Peter 1923- St&PR 93
Fuller, Peter 1947-1990 BioIn 17
Fuller, R. Buckminster 1895-1983 BioIn 17
Fuller, Reginald H(orace) 1915- ConAu 39NR
Fuller, Reginald Horace 1915- WhoAm 92
Fuller, Richard Allen 1941- WhoE 93
Fuller, Richard Kenneth 1935- WhoE 93
Fuller, Robert A. Law&B 92
Fuller, Robert A. 1938- St&PR 93
Fuller, Robert A. 1951- St&PR 93
Fuller, Robert C(harles) 1952- ConAu 38NR
Fuller, Robert E. Law&B 92
Fuller, Robert Fellows BioIn 17
Fuller, Robert Ferrey 1929- WhoAm 92
Fuller, Robert Walker, III 1959- WhoEmL 93
Fuller, Robin Michael WhoScE 91-1
Fuller, Roy 1912-1991 AnObit 1991
Fuller, Roy Broadbent 1912- BioIn 17
Fuller, Roy Broadbent 1912-1991 ConLC 70
Fuller, Russell Lee 1943- WhoSSW 93
Fuller, S. Bacon 1905-1988 EncAACR
Fuller, Samuel 1911- MiSFD 9
Fuller, Samuel 1912- CurBio 92 [port], WhoAm 92
Fuller, Samuel Ashby 1924- WhoAm 92
Fuller, Samuel Henry 1946- St&PR 93
Fuller, Samuel Henry, III 1946- WhoAm 92
Fuller, Stephen Herbert 1920- St&PR 93, WhoAm 92
Fuller, Stephen Spencer 1959- WhoSSW 93
Fuller, Steve William 1959- ConAu 137
Fuller, Steven Edward 1950- WhoEmL 93, WhoSSW 93
Fuller, Steven Michael 1953- WhoEmL 93, WhoSSW 93
Fuller, Sue WhoAm 92, WhoAmW 93
Fuller, Teresa Malloy 1956- WhoAmW 93
Fuller, Thelma AmWomPl
Fuller, Theodore 1918- WhoAm 92
Fuller, Theodore, Jr. 1937- WhoSSW 93
Fuller, Thomas Ashmead 1952- WhoEmL 93
Fuller, Thomas R. 1927- St&PR 93
Fuller, Thomas Ralph 1927- WhoSSW 93
Fuller, Thomas W. St&PR 93
Fuller, Timothy Richard 1957- WhoE 93
Fuller, Tracy Annette 1962- WhoAmW 93, WhoEmL 93
Fuller, Vicki BioIn 17
Fuller, Wallace Hamilton 1915- WhoAm 92
Fuller, Warren O. 1951- St&PR 93
Fuller, Wayne Arthur 1931- WhoAm 92
Fuller, Wayne Maurice 1946- WhoEmL 93
Fuller, William Edward 1950- WhoSSW 93
Fuller, William Miles 1938- St&PR 93
Fuller, William Samuel 1926- WhoAm 92
Fuller, William Sidney 1931- WhoAm 92
Fuller Maitland, J(ohn) A(lexander) 1856-1936 Baker 92
Fullerton, Albert Louis, Jr. 1921- WhoE 93
Fullerton, Alexander 1924- ScF&FL 92
Fullerton, Arthur C. Law&B 92
Fullerton, Charles William 1917- WhoAm 92
Fullerton, Dale A. 1930- St&PR 93
Fullerton, Dorothy Mallan 1938- WhoAmW 93, WhoWor 93
Fullerton, Gail Jackson 1927- WhoAm 92, WhoAmW 93
Fullerton, Gary Dodson 1939- WhoAm 92
Fullerton, George 1903-1989 BioIn 17
Fullerton, Hugh Stuart 1873-1945 BiDAMSp 1989
Fullerton, Jane Wyatt 1932- WhoAmW 93
Fullerton, Jymie Luie 1943- WhoSSW 93
Fullerton, Lawrence Rae 1952- WhoEmL 93
Fullerton, Maryellen 1946- WhoEmL 93
Fullerton, Mollie Hays WhoAmW 93, WhoE 93
Fullerton, Philip Charles 1931- WhoWor 93
Fullerton, Philippa Stevenson 1949- WhoAm 92
Fullerton, R. Donald BioIn 17
Fullerton, R. Donald 1931- WhoAm 92, WhoWor 93
Fullerton, Robert C. 1938- St&PR 93
Fullerton, Robert Victor 1918- WhoAm 92
Fullerton, Sally Ann 1934- WhoAmW 93
Fullerton, Terrence David 1949- WhoE 93
Fullerton, William Hugh 1939- WhoWor 93
Fulleylove, Brian 1944- WhoSSW 93
Fulling, Katharine Painter WhoAmW 93, WhoWor 93
Fulling, Mark S. 1959- St&PR 93
Fullingim, John Powers 1951- WhoSSW 93
Fulljames, Sydney T. 1932- St&PR 93
Fullman, Lynn Grisard 1949- WhoEmL 93
Fullmer, Daniel Warren 1922- WhoAm 92
Fullmer, Harold Milton 1918- WhoAm 92
Fullmer, Joseph A. 1943- St&PR 93
Fullmer, Paul 1934- St&PR 93, WhoAm 92
Fullmer, Robert J. Law&B 92
Fullmer, Steven Mark 1956- WhoEmL 93
Fullmer, William Arthur Law&B 92
Fullwood, Ralph Roy 1928- WhoE 93
Fullwood, Stanley G. Law&B 92
Fulmer, Donald Book, Jr. 1928- St&PR 93
Fulmer, Gary C. 1933- St&PR 93
Fulmer, Gary Creighton 1933- WhoAm 92
Fulmer, Hugh Scott 1928- WhoAm 92, WhoWor 93
Fulmer, Jerry Brian Law&B 92
Fulmer, Joe Jeff 1936- St&PR 93
Fulmer, Michael Clifford 1954- WhoEmL 93, WhoWor 93
Fulmer, Pruitt 1942- St&PR 93
Fulmer, Richard Warren 1930- WhoAm 92
Fulmer, Robert 1920- St&PR 93
Fulmer, Sandra Lee 1953- WhoWrEP 92
Fulmer, Thomas Stephen 1934- St&PR 93
Fulmer, Vincent Anthony 1927- WhoAm 92
Fulmer, Wanda 1939- WhoSSW 93
Fulmer, Willa Lybrand 1884-1968 BioIn 17
Fulmer, William B. 1948- St&PR 93
Fulner, Tom BioIn 17
Fulop, Gabor 1928- WhoScE 91-4
Fulop, George 1954- WhoEmL 93
Fulop, Milford 1927- WhoAm 92
Fulp, James Alan 1951- WhoEmL 93
Fulpius, Bernard 1939- WhoScE 91-4
Fulrath, Irene 1945- WhoAmW 93, WhoE 93
Fulscher, Gary Vincent 1943- St&PR 93
Fulton, Alice 1952- WhoAmW 93, WhoWrEP 92
Fulton, Andy St&PR 93
Fulton, Arthur Hawling 1929- St&PR 93
Fulton, Barbara Jane 1952- WhoAmW 93
Fulton, Chandler Montgomery 1934- WhoAm 92
Fulton, Darrell Nelson 1946- WhoEmL 93
Fulton, David C. 1929- St&PR 93
Fulton, Donald William, Jr. 1946- St&PR 93, WhoEmL 93
Fulton, Duncan Thomas, III 1955- WhoSSW 93
Fulton, Eleanor Marie 1939- WhoE 93
Fulton, Elizabeth G. ScF&FL 92
Fulton, Glen Steven 1956- WhoEmL 93
Fulton, James Franklin 1930- WhoAm 92
Fulton, Janice G. 1920?-1992? NewYTBS 92
Fulton, Jay David 1960- WhoEmL 93
Fulton, Joe Kirk, Jr. 1957- WhoEmL 93, WhoSSW 93
Fulton, John J. 1928- St&PR 93
Fulton, Karen S. 1952- St&PR 93
Fulton, Katherine Nelson 1955- WhoSSW 93
Fulton, Len 1934- WhoAm 92, WhoWrEP 92
Fulton, Liz ScF&FL 92
Fulton, Marianne 1948- WhoAm 92
Fulton, Maud(e) AmWomPl
Fulton, Norman 1909-1980 Baker 92
Fulton, Richard 1921- WhoAm 92
Fulton, Richard Alsina 1926- WhoAm 92
Fulton, Richard F., Jr. 1954- St&PR 93
Fulton, Richard Harmon 1927- WhoAm 92
Fulton, Robert 1765-1815 BioIn 17
Fulton, Robert Andrew 1944- WhoUN 92
Fulton, Robert K. 1949- St&PR 93
Fulton, Robert Kevin Law&B 92
Fulton, Robert Lester 1926- WhoAm 92
Fulton, Robin BioIn 17
Fulton, Robin 1937- ConAu 38NR
Fulton, Roger ScF&FL 92
Fulton, Sandy M. 1943- St&PR 93
Fulton, Sandy Michael 1943- WhoAm 92
Fulton, Thomas Benjamin 1918- WhoAm 92
Fulton, William A. St&PR 93
Fultz, Clair Ervin 1911- WhoAm 92
Fultz, Dave 1921- WhoAm 92
Fultz, Katharine Ruth 1960- WhoE 93
Fultz, Kenneth R. 1935- St&PR 93
Fultz, Mary Catherine 1916- WhoSSW 93
Fultz, Regina Oehler ScF&FL 92
Fultz, William Joseph 1931- St&PR 93
Fulvi, Philip A. 1932-1990 BioIn 17
Fulweiler, Howard Wells 1932- WhoAm 92
Fulweiler, Marie-Louise Law&B 92
Fulweiler, Patricia Platt 1923- WhoAmW 93, WhoE 93
Fulweiler, Spencer Biddle 1913- WhoE 93
Fulwiler, Robert Neal 1937- WhoAm 92, WhoWor 93
Fulwiler, Toby Edward 1942- WhoE 93
Fulwood, S. Leigh Law&B 92
Fumagalli Baker 92
Fumagalli, Adolfo 1828-1856 Baker 92
Fumagalli, Barbara Merrill 1926- WhoAm 92
Fumagalli, Disma 1826-1893 Baker 92
Fumagalli, Luca 1837-1908 Baker 92
Fumagalli, Polibio 1830-1900 Baker 92
Fumagalli, Remo 1933- WhoScE 91-3
Fumento, Michael (Aaron) 1960- ConAu 139
Fumet, Dynam-Victor 1867-1949 Baker 92
Fumi, Fausto Gherardo 1924- WhoWor 93
Fumi, Vinceslao 1823-1880 Baker 92
Fumihito, Prince of Japan 1965- BioIn 17
Fumo, Vincent Joseph 1943- WhoE 93
Funabashi, Yoichi 1944- WhoWor 93
Funabiki, Ryuhei 1931- WhoWor 93
Funada, Hajime 1953- WhoAsAP 91
Funahashi, Akira 1928- WhoWor 93
Funari, John H. 1929- WhoAm 92
Funaro, Sergio 1922-1986 ScF&FL 92
Funasaki, Noriaki 1941- WhoWor 93
Funatsu, Isaac Hideki 1957- WhoWor 93
Funchess, Manley Lindsey 1942- St&PR 93
Funchess, Noel, Jr. 1940- WhoSSW 93
Fundaro, Frank Salvatore 1943- St&PR 93
Funderburg, I. Owen 1924- AfrAmBi [port], St&PR 93
Funderburg, Lisa A. Law&B 92
Funderburk, David B. 1944- WhoAm 92
Funderburk, Henry Hanly, Jr. 1931- WhoAm 92, WhoSSW 93
Funderburk, Jeanette Campos 1959- WhoAmW 93
Funderburke, Eugene Bryant 1938- WhoSSW 93
Funderburk-Galvan, Janet Rebecca 1951- WhoE 93
Fundingsland, O.M. 1943- St&PR 93
Funer, Rolf Edward 1940- WhoE 93
Funesti, Julie Colette 1962- WhoEmL 93
Fung, Adrian Kin-Chiu 1936- WhoAm 92
Fung, Amy Shu-Fong 1949- WhoAmW 93
Fung, Frederick Ho 1951- WhoEmL 93
Fung, Ho-Leung 1943- WhoAm 92
Fung, Kee-Ying 1948- WhoEmL 93
Fung, Mina Hsu 1947- WhoAm 92
Fung, Roland S. Law&B 92
Fung, Thomas BioIn 17
Fung, Yu-lan 1895-1990 BioIn 17
Fung, Yuan-Cheng Bertram 1919- WhoAm 92
Funge, Robert 1931- WhoWrEP 92

Fung Ket Wing *WhoAsAP 91*
Fungsang, Michael Wing 1951- *WhoEmL 93*
Funi, Achille 1890-1972 *BioIn 17*
Funicelli, Betty Lynn 1963- *WhoAmW 93*
Funk, Albert Peter 1919- *St&PR 93*
Funk, Arthur Layton 1914- *WhoSSW 93*
Funk, Arthur W. 1930- *St&PR 93*
Funk, Carole Ann 1942- *WhoSSW 93*
Funk, Cyril Reed, Jr. 1928- *WhoAm 92, WhoE 93*
Funk, David Albert 1927- *WhoAm 92, WhoWor 93*
Funk, Donald Alan 1933- *St&PR 93*
Funk, Ella Frances 1921- *WhoAmW 93, WhoWor 93*
Funk, Frank E. 1923- *WhoAm 92*
Funk, Gary Lloyd 1945- *WhoSSW 93*
Funk, George *Law&B 92*
Funk, Gernot 1924- *WhoScE 91-3*
Funk, Joel David 1946- *WhoE 93*
Funk, John A. *Law&B 92*
Funk, John W. *Law&B 92*
Funk, John William 1937- *WhoAm 92*
Funk, Joseph E., Jr. 1939- *St&PR 93*
Funk, Kazimierz 1884-1967 *PolBiDi*
Funk, L. Edward *Law&B 92*
Funk, Larry L. 1942- *St&PR 93, WhoAm 92*
Funk, Leonard A. 1916- *BioIn 17*
Funk, Lisa Averill 1957- *WhoAmW 93*
Funk, Margaret J. 1930- *St&PR 93*
Funk, Pamela Ann 1962- *WhoAmW 93*
Funk, Patricia Ann 1934- *WhoE 93*
Funk, Paul Edward 1940- *WhoAm 92*
Funk, Sherman Maxwell 1925- *WhoAm 92, WhoWor 93*
Funk, Smith Adam 1925- *WhoSSW 93*
Funk, Terry W. 1951- *St&PR 93*
Funk, Vicki Jane 1951- *WhoAmW 93, WhoEmL 93, WhoSSW 93*
Funk, Virginia B. 1923- *WhoWrEP 92*
Funk, Walter, Jr. 1916- *St&PR 93*
Funk, William Henry 1933- *WhoAm 92*
Funke, Ginny *WhoWrEP 92*
Funke, Klemens A. 1934- *St&PR 93*
Funke, Lewis B. d1992 *NewYTBS 92 [port]*
Funke, Phyllis Ellen 1941- *WhoE 93*
Funkenstein, H. Harris d1990 *BioIn 17*
Funkhouser, Eileen 1957- *WhoWrEP 92*
Funkhouser, Elmer Newton, Jr. 1916- *St&PR 93, WhoAm 92*
Funkhouser, Lawrence William 1921- *WhoAm 92*
Funkhouser, Lenore Marie 1947- *WhoSSW 93*
Funkhouser, Paul W. 1952- *St&PR 93*
Funkhouser, Paul William 1952- *WhoAm 92*
Funkhouser, Richard Daniel Brunk 1935- *St&PR 93*
Funkhouser, Robert C. *Law&B 92*
Funknouser, John W. 1944- *St&PR 93*
Funnell, Augustine 1952- *ScF&FL 92*
Funnell, Brian Michael *WhoScE 91-1*
Funnell, Donald Kevin 1955- *WhoEmL 93*
Funsch, Henry Robert 1947- *St&PR 93*
Funsch, Richard Henry 1931- *St&PR 93*
Funseth, Robert Lloyd Eric Martin 1926- *WhoAm 92*
Funston, Frederick 1865-1917 *HarEnMi*
Funston, G(eorge) Keith 1910-1992 *CurBio 92N*
Funston, Keith 1910-1992 *BioIn 17*
Funston, Mark David 1959- *St&PR 93*
Funt, Allen 1914- *MiSFD 9*
Funtash, Paul A., Jr. 1943- *St&PR 93*
Funtowitz, Joel Michael *Law&B 92*
Fuoco, Frank John 1953- *WhoWor 93*
Fuoco, Philip Stephen 1946- *WhoEmL 93*
Fuqua, Christopher Steven 1956- *WhoSSW 93*
Fuqua, Harvey 1928- *SoulM*
Fuqua, J.B. *BioIn 17*
Fuqua, John Brooks *BioIn 17*
Fuqua, John Brooks 1918- *WhoAm 92, WhoSSW 93*
Fuqua, Mary M. 1937- *WhoE 93*
Fuqua, Robert E. 1943- *St&PR 93*
Fuqua, Robert Edward 1943- *WhoAm 92*
Fuqua, Samuel G. 1899-1987 *BioIn 17*
Fu Quanyou 1930- *WhoAsAP 91*
Fur, Lajos 1930- *WhoWor 93*
Furay, Catherine J. 1952- *WhoAmW 93, WhoEmL 93*
Furay, Joseph Francis *Law&B 92*
Furbank, P(hilip) N(icholas) 1920- *ConAu 40NR*
Furbank, Philip Nicholas *BioIn 17*
Furbay, John Harvey 1903- *WhoAm 92*
Furbeck, Patricia Ann *WhoE 93*
Furbee, Carol Ann 1942- *WhoAmW 93*
Furber, Edward Bixby 1929- *St&PR 93*
Furbush, John 1937- *St&PR 93*
Furbush, Michael Rollins *Law&B 92*
Furbush, Steven Dean 1958- *WhoE 93, WhoEmL 93*
Furby, James R. 1936- *St&PR 93*
Furchtgott-Roth, Diana Elizabeth 1958- *WhoEmL 93*
Furchtgott-Roth, Harold Wilkes 1956- *WhoEmL 93*
Furci, Joan Gelormino 1939- *WhoAmW 93*
Furcon, John Edward 1942- *WhoWor 93*
Furedy, Clifton George 1945- *WhoSSW 93*
Furek, Robert M. 1942- *St&PR 93*
Furer, Martin Pius 1947- *WhoE 93*
Furer-Haimendorf, Christoph von 1909- *BioIn 17, IntDcAn*
Furet, Francois 1927- *BioIn 17*
Furey, Agnes 1937- *WhoAmW 93*
Furey, Barbara H. *Law&B 92*
Furey, John J. *Law&B 92*
Furey, Joseph Endicott 1906-1990 *BioIn 17*
Furey, Laurence Thomas 1930- *WhoSSW 93*
Furey, Robert Joseph 1956- *WhoWrEP 92*
Furey, Thomas J. 1935- *St&PR 93*
Furey, Vincent E., Jr. 1939- *St&PR 93*
Furey, Vincent Edward, Jr. 1939- *WhoAm 92*
Furfaro, Ricardo *Law&B 92*
Furgalus, Keith 1944- *St&PR 93*
Furgason, Maiya Kathryn 1944- *WhoAm 92*
Furgason, Robert Roy 1935- *WhoAm 92*
Furgison, Clifford Fredric 1948- *WhoEmL 93*
Furgiuele, Guy 1926- *St&PR 93*
Furgiuele, Margery Wood 1919- *WhoAmW 93*
Furgol, Edward Mackie 1955- *WhoAm 92, WhoE 93*
Furgurson, Ernest Baker, Jr. 1929- *WhoAm 92*
Furht, Borivoje 1946- *WhoEmL 93*
Furia, Jose Carlos Belfort 1939- *WhoWor 93*
Furia, Philip (G.) 1943- *ConAu 136*
Furiasse, Jorge Gabriel 1960- *WhoWor 93*
Furie, Bruce 1944- *WhoE 93*
Furie, Sidney J. 1933- *MiSFD 9*
Furiga, Richard Daniel 1935- *WhoAm 92*
Furigay, Rodolfo Lazo 1938- *WhoE 93*
Furihata, Takehiko 1922- *WhoWor 93*
Furillo, Carl Anthony 1922-1989 *BiDAMSp 1989*
Furimsky, Stephen, Jr. 1924- *WhoWor 93*
Furino, Antonio *WhoAm 92*
Furlan, Giuseppe 1935- *WhoScE 91-3*
Furlani Donda, Anita 1928- *WhoScE 91-3*
Furlaud, Richard M. 1923- *St&PR 93*
Furlaud, Richard Mortimer 1923- *WhoAm 92*
Furlong, Brenda J. 1948- *St&PR 93*
Furlong, Charles Richard 1950- *WhoAm 92*
Furlong, Edward *BioIn 17*
Furlong, Edward V., Jr. 1937- *St&PR 93, WhoAm 92*
Furlong, George Morgan, Jr. 1931- *WhoAm 92*
Furlong, Gregory William 1947- *WhoEmL 93*
Furlong, John M. *Law&B 92*
Furlong, John William 1932- *WhoE 93*
Furlong, Maurice B. 1909- *WhoWrEP 92*
Furlong, Monica 1930- *ChlFicS, ScF&FL 92*
Furlong, Patrick David 1948- *WhoEmL 93, WhoWor 93*
Furlong, Raymond Bernard 1926- *WhoSSW 93*
Furlong, Stewart Sadler 1939- *St&PR 93*
Furlong, Suzanne T. 1964- *WhoE 93*
Furlotte, Nicolas 1952- *WhoWrEP 92*
Furlow, Mack V., Jr. 1931- *St&PR 93*
Furlow, Mack Vernon, Jr. 1931- *WhoAm 92*
Furman, A.L. 1902-1972 *ScF&FL 92*
Furman, Anthony Michael 1934- *WhoAm 92*
Furman, Deane Philip 1915- *WhoAm 92*
Furman, Diane E. *Law&B 92*
Furman, Donald M. 1918- *St&PR 93*
Furman, Elise Catherine 1956- *WhoAmW 93*
Furman, Eric Bertram 1934- *WhoSSW 93*
Furman, Hezekiah Wyndol Carroll 1922- *WhoAm 92*
Furman, Howard 1938- *WhoSSW 93*
Furman, James Merle 1932- *WhoAm 92*
Furman, John R. 1917- *St&PR 93*
Furman, John Rockwell 1917- *WhoAm 92*
Furman, Laura *BioIn 17*
Furman, Laura 1945- *WhoWrEP 92*
Furman, Mark Steven 1951- *WhoEmL 93*
Furman, Martin Julian 1949- *WhoEmL 93*
Furman, Mignon *BioIn 17*
Furman, Norton M. *Law&B 92*
Furman, Robert Howard 1918- *WhoAm 92*
Furman, Roy L. 1939- *St&PR 93*
Furman, Roy Lance 1939- *WhoAm 92*
Furman, Samuel Elliott 1932- *WhoAm 92, WhoE 93, WhoWor 93*
Furman, Theodore Robert, Jr. *Law&B 92*
Furman, Thomas D., Jr. 1943- *St&PR 93*
Furman, Walter Laurie 1913- *WhoSSW 93*
Furman, William Stuart 1929- *WhoAm 92*
Furmanczyk, Kazimierz 1943- *WhoScE 91-4*
Furmanski, Philip 1946- *WhoAm 92, WhoE 93, WhoEmL 93*
Furnas, David William 1931- *WhoAm 92, WhoWor 93*
Furnas, Howard Earl 1919- *WhoAm 92*
Furnas, Joseph Chamberlain 1905- *WhoAm 92, WhoWrEP 92*
Furnas, Robert J. *St&PR 93*
Furness, Betty 1916- *WhoAm 92*
Furness, Edith Ellis *AmWomPl*
Furness, Peter John 1956- *WhoEmL 93*
Furness, Peter Norman 1955- *WhoWor 93*
Furness, William Henry, 3rd 1866-1920 *IntDcAn*
Furney, Linda Jeanne 1947- *WhoAmW 93*
Furniss, Grace Livingston *AmWomPl*
Furniss, Tilman H. 1948- *WhoScE 91-3*
Furniss, Todd Anthony *Law&B 92*
Furnival, George Mitchell 1908- *WhoAm 92*
Furno, Daryl Davis d1990 *BioIn 17*
Furno, Giovanni 1748-1837 *Baker 92*
Furnweger, Karen 1951- *WhoEmL 93*
Furois, Michael Carl 1960- *WhoWor 93*
Furowicz, Antoni Julian 1936- *WhoScE 91-4, WhoWor 93*
Furr, Aaron Keith 1932- *WhoSSW 93*
Furr, Anthony Lloyd 1944- *St&PR 93*
Furr, Cynthia Morgan 1954- *WhoAmW 93*
Furr, Quint Eugene 1921- *WhoAm 92*
Furr, Richard Michael 1942- *WhoSSW 93*
Furr, Robert B., Jr. *Law&B 92*
Furr, Warwick Rex, II 1940- *WhoAm 92*
Furrer, James Douglas 1952- *WhoEmL 93*
Furrer, John Rudolf 1927- *WhoAm 92, WhoSSW 93, WhoWor 93*
Furrer, Markus Julius 1955- *WhoWor 93*
Furrer, Ronald Walter 1934- *St&PR 93*
Furrey, Anne-Marie Mason 1948- *WhoWor 93*
Furry, Beth Anne 1961- *WhoAmW 93*
Furry, Donald Edward 1934- *WhoSSW 93*
Furry, Kenneth B. *Law&B 92*
Furry, Mark D. 1947- *St&PR 93*
Furry, Richard L. 1938- *St&PR 93*
Fursch-Madi(er), Emma 1847-1894 *Baker 92*
Furse, Elizabeth 1936- *WhoAmW 93*
Furse, James Robert 1939- *St&PR 93, WhoAm 92*
Furse, Katharine Symonds 1875-1952 *BioIn 17*
Fursenko, Leonid Ivanovich *BioIn 17*
Fursikov, Andrei Vladimirovich 1945- *WhoWor 93*
Furst, Alex Julian 1938- *WhoSSW 93, WhoWor 93*
Furst, Ansgar Hermann 1930- *WhoWor 93*
Furst, Anton d1991 *BioIn 17, NewYTBS 92 [port]*
Furst, Anton 1944-1991 *AnObit 1991, ConTFT 10*
Furst, Arthur 1914- *WhoAm 92, WhoWor 93*
Furst, Austin O., Jr. 1943- *ConEn*
Furst, Barry W. *Law&B 92*
Furst, Bob *BioIn 17*
Furst, Errol Kenneth 1946- *WhoAm 92, WhoEmL 93*
Furst, Gary Stuart 1951- *St&PR 93*
Furst, Henry Fairchild 1951- *WhoEmL 93*
Furst, John Douglas 1959- *WhoSSW 93*
Furst, John Frederick 1946- *WhoE 93*
Furst, Kenneth Errol 1946- *St&PR 93*
Furst, Lilian Renee 1931- *ConAu 40NR, WhoAm 92*
Furst, Norma Fields 1931- *WhoAmW 93, WhoE 93*
Furst, Patricia Ann *WhoIns 93*
Furst, Patricia Ann 1949- *St&PR 93*
Furst, Peter 1936- *WhoScE 91-3*
Furst, Rafael 1928- *St&PR 93*
Furst, Renee d1990 *BioIn 17*
Furst, Sidney Carl 1925- *WhoE 93*
Furst, Warren Arthur 1924- *St&PR 93*
Furste, Wesley Leonard, II 1915- *WhoAm 92, WhoWor 93*
Furstenau, Moritz 1824-1889 *Baker 92*
Furstenberg, Mark *BioIn 17*
Furstman, Shirley Elsie Daddow 1930- *WhoAmW 93*
Furstner, Adolph 1833-1908 *Baker 92*
Furtado, Joseph Edward, Jr. 1962- *WhoSSW 93*
Furtado, Stephen Eugene 1942- *WhoE 93*
Furter, William Frederick 1931- *WhoAm 92*
Furth, B. 1931- *WhoScE 91-3*
Furth, Frederick Paul 1934- *WhoAm 92*
Furth, George 1932- *WhoAm 92*
Furth, Harold Paul 1930- *WhoAm 92*
Furth, John Jacob 1929- *WhoAm 92, WhoE 93*
Furth, Peter David 1954- *WhoE 93, WhoEmL 93*
Furtwangler, Wilhelm 1886-1954 *BioIn 17, IntDcOp [port], OxDcOp*
Furtwangler, (Gustav Heinrich Ernst Martin) Wilhelm 1886-1954 *Baker 92*
Furubotn, Eirik G. 1923- *ConAu 137*
Furubotn, Eirik Grundtvig 1923- *WhoAm 92, WhoSSW 93*
Furugen, Saneyoshi 1929- *WhoAsAP 91*
Furuhata, Taketo 1930- *WhoAm 92*
Furuhjelm, Erik Gustaf 1883-1964 *Baker 92*
Furuichi, Susumu 1931- *WhoWor 93*
Furukawa, Junji 1912- *WhoWor 93*
Furukawa, Tasaburo 1933- *WhoAsAP 91*
Furukawa, Yusuke 1957- *WhoWor 93*
Furumoto, Horace 1931- *St&PR 93*
Furumoto, Horace Wataru 1931- *WhoAm 92*
Furuta, Naoki 1950- *WhoWor 93*
Furuya, Keiji 1952- *WhoAsAP 91*
Furuya, Masaki 1926- *WhoWor 93*
Furuya, Tsutomu 1928- *WhoWor 93*
Furuya, Yasuo 1926- *WhoWor 93*
Furvik, Nils-Bertil 1928- *WhoScE 91-4*
Fury, Mark Aaron *Law&B 92*
Fury, Mary Elizabeth 1943- *WhoAmW 93*
Furze, Edward William 1938- *WhoE 93*
Fusaro, Angelo 1950- *St&PR 93*
Fusaro, Joseph A. 1940- *WhoE 93*
Fusaro, Ramon Michael 1927- *WhoAm 92*
Fusaro, Robert Francis Xavier *Law&B 92*
Fuscaldo, Antonio Frank 1919- *WhoWor 93*
Fuscaldo, James Joseph *Law&B 92*
Fuschetti, Edward A. 1935- *St&PR 93*
Fuschillo, Charles J. d1991 *BioIn 17*
Fusco, Andrew G. 1948- *WhoEmL 93, WhoSSW 93*
Fusco, Anthony Salvatore 1954- *WhoEmL 93*
Fusco, David Michael 1959- *WhoEmL 93*
Fusco, Edmund J. 1924- *St&PR 93*
Fusco, Edmund John 1923- *WhoAm 92*
Fusco, Jacqueline Tecce 1956- *WhoAmW 93, WhoEmL 93*
Fusco, Linda Esrich 1949- *WhoAmW 93*
Fusco, Lucille Mary 1932- *WhoAmW 93*
Fusco, Mario Louis 1946- *St&PR 93*
Fusco, Raymond Arthur 1959- *WhoE 93*
Fusco, Victor 1949- *WhoE 93*
Fusco, Virginia Kathleen *Law&B 92*
Fuse, Tadashi 1927- *WhoWor 93*
Fuselier, Louis Alfred 1932- *WhoAm 92*
Fuseya, Shuji 1930- *WhoAsAP 91*
Fusfeld, Daniel Roland 1922- *WhoAm 92*
Fusfeld, Ira 1948- *St&PR 93*
Fushiki, Kazuo 1928- *WhoAsAP 91*
Fushimi, Satoshi 1946- *WhoWor 93*
Fusi, John C. 1955- *St&PR 93*
Fusilli, Donald P., Jr. *Law&B 92*
Fusillo, Thomas Victor 1953- *WhoE 93*
Fusina, Alessandro Eugenio 1937- *WhoAm 92*
Fuson, Harold W., Jr. *Law&B 92*
Fuson, Harold W., Jr. 1945- *St&PR 93*
Fuson, Laurel *Law&B 92*
Fuson, Robert Henderson 1927- *WhoWrEP 92*
Fuss, John M. 1930- *WhoE 93*
Fuss, John M., Jr. 1930- *St&PR 93*
Fuss, Peter S. 1933- *St&PR 93*
Fussan, Werner 1912-1986 *Baker 92*
Fussell, Catharine Pugh 1919- *WhoAm 92*
Fussell, Charles C(lement) 1938- *Baker 92*
Fussell, Fred Wayne 1950- *WhoSSW 93*
Fussell, Norman Coldham 1937- *WhoWor 93*
Fussell, Paul 1924- *BioIn 17, ConLC 74 [port], WhoAm 92, WhoWrEP 92*
Fussell, Ronald Moi 1956- *WhoEmL 93*
Fussell, Samuel Wilson *BioIn 17*
Fusselman, Timothy J. *Law&B 92*
Fussenegger, Gary 1949- *St&PR 93*
Fussey, David Eric *WhoScE 91-1*
Fussichen, Kenneth 1950- *WhoWor 93*
Fussl, Karl Heinz 1924- *Baker 92*
Fussler, Irene *AmWomPl*
Fussner, Liselotte Berthe 1941- *WhoWor 93*
Fuste, Jose Antonio 1943- *HispAmA, WhoAm 92*
Fuster, Jaime B. 1941- *CngDr 91, HispAmA*
Fuster, Mark 1947- *St&PR 93*
Fuster, Peter *Law&B 92*
Fuster, Valentin 1943- *WhoAm 92*
Futada, Koji 1938- *WhoAsAP 91*
Futai, Masamitsu 1940- *WhoWor 93*
Futaki, Kiyoshi 1929- *WhoWor 93*
Futami, Nobuaki 1935- *WhoAsAP 91*

Futas, Elizabeth Dorothy 1944- *WhoAm 92, WhoAmW 93*
Futas, George P. 1934- *St&PR 93*
Futatsugi, Hideo 1930- *WhoAsAP 91*
Futch, Eddie *BioIn 17*
Futch, L. Wayne 1943- *St&PR 93*
Futch, Stephen Hubbard 1953- *WhoSSW 93*
Futch, Tom R. 1951- *St&PR 93*
Futcher, Palmer Howard 1910- *WhoAm 92*
Futerman, Eli N. 1958- *St&PR 93*
Futerman, Mike 1927- *St&PR 93*
Futey, Bohdan A. 1939- *CngDr 91, WhoE 93*
Futia, Leo R. 1919- *St&PR 93, WhoIns 93*
Futia, Leo Richard 1919- *WhoAm 92*
Futoran, Herbert S. 1942- *WhoIns 93*
Futorny, Vjatcheslav Michaylovich 1961- *WhoWor 93*
Futral, Ronald Steven 1962- *WhoEmL 93*
Futrell, Anna R. 1952- *WhoAmW 93*
Futrell, Basil Lee 1937- *WhoAm 92, WhoE 93, WhoWor 93*
Futrell, J. Richard, Jr. 1931- *St&PR 93*
Futrell, John William 1935- *WhoAm 92*
Futrell, Jonas Richard, Jr. 1931- *WhoAm 92*
Futrell, Mary Alice Hatwood 1940- *WhoAm 92*
Futrell, Mary Hatwood *BioIn 17*
Futrell, Mary Hatwood 1940- *AfrAmBi*
Futrell, Robert Frank 1917- *WhoSSW 93, WhoWor 93*
Futter, Ellen Victoria 1949- *WhoAm 92, WhoAmW 93*
Futter, Jeffrey L. *Law&B 92*
Futter, Joan Babette 1921- *WhoE 93*
Futter, Victor 1919- *WhoAm 92*
Futterer, Carl 1873-1927 *Baker 92*
Futterer, Dieter Karl 1938- *WhoScE 91-3*
Futterer, Edward P. *Law&B 92*
Futterer, Edward Philip 1953- *WhoEmL 93*
Futterer, Karen Lehner 1953- *WhoSSW 93*
Futterknecht, James O. 1947- *St&PR 93*
Futterman, Jack 1933- *St&PR 93, WhoE 93*
Futura 2000 1956- *BioIn 17*
Fuwa, Keiichiro 1925- *WhoWor 93*
Fuwa, Tasuku 1915- *WhoWor 93*
Fuwa, Tetsuzo 1930- *WhoAsAP 91*
Fuwen, Yang Fuwen 1963- *WhoWor 93*
Fux, Johann Joseph 1660-1741 *Baker 92, OxDcOp*
Fux, Maria Anna 1771-1858 *See* Gassmann, Florian Leopold 1729-1774 *OxDcOp*
Fuxa, James Roderick 1949- *WhoSSW 93*
Fuxe, Kjell Gunnar 1938- *WhoScE 91-4*
Fu Xishou 1930- *WhoAsAP 91*
Fuyushiba, Tetsuzo 1936- *WhoAsAP 91*
Fuzak, Arthur Walter 1923- *St&PR 93*
Fuzak, Victor T. 1926- *WhoAm 92*
Fuzeau-Braesch, Suzel 1928- *WhoScE 91-2*
Fuzek, Bettye Lynn 1924- *WhoAmW 93*
Fuzek, John Frank 1921- *WhoSSW 93*
Fuzesi, Stephen, Jr. 1948- *WhoAm 92, WhoEmL 93*
Fuzhong, Li 1928- *WhoWor 93*
Fuzo, Frank John 1951- *WhoE 93*
Fyan, Loleta Dawson 1894-1990 *BioIn 17*
Fyda, Marianne 1946- *WhoAmW 93*
Fye, Robert Floyd 1948- *St&PR 93*
Fye, W. Bruce, III 1946- *WhoAm 92*
Fyfe, David James *WhoScE 91-1*
Fyfe, M.B. 1936- *St&PR 93*
Fyfe, Malcolm Hewer Durke Findlay *WhoScE 91-1*
Fyfe, William Sefton 1927- *WhoAm 92*
Fyffe, Elizabeth *AmWomPl*
Fyffe, Will 1884-1947 *QDrFCA 92 [port]*
Fyhn, Hans Jorgen 1940- *WhoScE 91-4*
Fyke, Tim R. *Law&B 92*
Fyleman, Rose 1877-1957 *AmWomPl*
Fyles, John Gladstone 1923- *WhoAm 92*
Fyock, Hilda Joyce 1964- *WhoAmW 93*
Fysh *ScF&FL 92*
Fytizas, Evangelos 1931- *WhoScE 91-3*
Fyvolent, Robert J. *Law&B 92*

G

G., John Scott 1948- *WhoEmL 93*
G., Mama *ConAu 39NR*
Gaab, Michael Robert 1947- *WhoWor 93*
Gaafar, Sayed Mohammed 1924- *WhoAm 92*
Gaal, Gabriel Edmund 1938- *WhoScE 91-4*
Gaal, Istvan 1933- *DrEEuF*
Gaalova, Barbara Kanzler 1953- *WhoEmL 93*
Gaan, Margaret *BioIn 17*
Gaar, Marilyn Audrey Wiegraffe 1946- *WhoAmW 93, WhoEmL 93*
Gaar, Norman Edward 1929- *WhoWor 93*
Gaar, William Charles 1941- *St&PR 93*
Gaard, David Reed 1949- *St&PR 93*
Gaard, Thomas J. 1939- *WhoIns 93*
Gaardemo, Peter Michael 1956- *WhoWor 93*
Gaarder, Marie 1935- *WhoAm 92*
Gaarder, Per Ivar 1941- *WhoScE 91-4*
Gaarslev, Knud *WhoScE 91-2*
Gaasenbeek, Matthew 1930- *St&PR 93, WhoAm 92*
Gaba, Barbara Blassingame 1947- *WhoE 93*
Gabala, James Anthony *Law&B 92*
Gabalas *OxDcByz*
Gabalas, Manuel c. 1271-c. 1359 *OxDcByz*
Gabaldon, Diana 1952- *ScF&FL 92*
Gabaldon, Ester Hao Tanco 1951- *WhoWor 93*
Gabancho, Luis Maria 1945- *WhoWor 93*
Gabarro, John Joseph 1939- *WhoAm 92*
Gabathuler, Erwin *WhoScE 91-1*
Gabay, Donald D. 1935- *WhoIns 93*
Gabbai, Alberto Alain 1953- *WhoWor 93*
Gabbai, Moni E. 1943- *WhoIns 93*
Gabbana, Stefano *BioIn 17*
Gabbard, G.N. 1941- *ScF&FL 92*
Gabbard, Glen Owens 1949- *WhoAm 92, WhoEmL 93*
Gabbard, Glenn Patrick 1954- *WhoE 93*
Gabbard, Gregory Alan 1949- *WhoEmL 93*
Gabbard, Gregory N. 1941- *WhoWrEP 92*
Gabbard, O. Gene 1940- *ConEn*
Gabbay, Dov M. *WhoScE 91-1*
Gabbay, Marcel 1923- *WhoWor 93*
Gabbe, Peter J. 1950- *St&PR 93*
Gabbe, Steven Glenn 1944- *WhoAm 92*
Gabbert, Harriet Zais 1944- *WhoUN 92*
Gabbert, James Donald 1952- *St&PR 93*
Gabbiani, Giulio 1937- *WhoScE 91-4, WhoWor 93*
Gabbour, Iskandar 1929- *WhoAm 92*
Gabe, Caryl Jacobs 1949- *WhoEmL 93*
Gabel, Allen Meredith 1943- *St&PR 93*
Gabel, Creighton 1931- *WhoAm 92*
Gabel, Edward Alexander 1947- *WhoIns 93*
Gabel, Eli 1939- *WhoE 93*
Gabel, Frederick Daniel, Jr. 1938- *WhoIns 93*
Gabel, Gary J. 1949- *St&PR 93*
Gabel, Gary Joseph 1949- *WhoEmL 93*
Gabel, George DeSaussure, Jr. 1940- *WhoAm 92, WhoSSW 93, WhoWor 93*
Gabel, Hortense W. 1912-1990 *BioIn 17*
Gabel, Jon Robert 1944- *WhoE 93*
Gabel, Katherine 1938- *WhoAmW 93*
Gabel, Kathryn Vinson 1961- *WhoSSW 93*
Gabel, Krystal Leigh 1964- *WhoAmW 93, WhoEmL 93*
Gabel, Michael V. *Law&B 92*
Gabel, Ronald Glen 1937- *WhoE 93*
Gabel, Sharon Ann 1956- *WhoAmW 93*
Gabellieri, F. Ralph 1929- *St&PR 93*
Gabelman, Irving Jacob 1918- *WhoAm 92, WhoE 93*
Gabelman, James S. 1929- *St&PR 93*
Gaber, Elsie Jean Kins 1952- *WhoAmW 93*
Gaber, Robert 1923- *WhoE 93*
Gaberino, John Anthony, Jr. 1941- *WhoWor 93*
Gaberman, Harry 1913- *WhoSSW 93*
Gaberman, Judie *ScF&FL 92*
Gabert, Lenard Morris 1925- *WhoSSW 93*
Gabert, Nori L. *Law&B 92*
Gabert, Nori Lauren 1953- *St&PR 93, WhoAmW 93*
Gabert, Shelley Lynn 1961- *WhoEmL 93*
Gabhart, Ann *ScF&FL 92*
Gabichvadze, Revaz 1913- *Baker 92*
Gabig, Robert Louis, Jr. 1953- *WhoE 93*
Gabil, Diane Rapson 1947- *WhoEmL 93*
Gabilando Soler, Francisco d1990 *BioIn 17*
Gabin, Jane Susan *WhoSSW 93*
Gabin, Jean 1904-1976 *IntDcF 2-3 [port]*
Gabis, Mark A. *Law&B 92*
Gable, Carl Irwin 1939- *WhoAm 92*
Gable, Carol Brignoli 1945- *WhoAm 92*
Gable, Clark 1901-1960 *BioIn 17, IntDcF 2-3 [port]*
Gable, Edward Brennan, Jr. 1929- *WhoWor 93*
Gable, Fred Burnard 1929- *WhoAm 92*
Gable, G. Ellis 1905- *WhoAm 92*
Gable, Joanie Carole 1954- *WhoEmL 93*
Gable, John Allen 1943- *WhoE 93*
Gable, John Oglesby, III 1944- *WhoE 93*
Gable, June 1945- *ConTFT 10*
Gable, Karen Elaine 1939- *WhoAmW 93*
Gable, L. John *St&PR 93*
Gable, Michael 1945- *WhoE 93*
Gable, Philip E. 1955- *WhoSSW 93*
Gable, Robert E. 1934- *St&PR 93*
Gable, Robert Elledy 1934- *WhoAm 92, WhoSSW 93*
Gable, Roxanna Spurgis 1952- *WhoAmW 93*
Gablehouse, Timothy Reuben 1951- *WhoEmL 93*
Gablenz, Jerzy 1888-1937 *PolBiDi*
Gabler, Marilyn Ann 1954- *WhoEmL 93*
Gabold, Ingolf 1942- *Baker 92*
Gabor, Andre 1910- *St&PR 93*
Gabor, Elisabeth 1929- *WhoScE 91-4*
Gabor, Eva 1921- *BioIn 17*
Gabor, Frank 1918- *WhoIns 93, WhoWor 93*
Gabor, Georgia Marjam 1930- *WhoAmW 93*
Gabor, Georgia Miriam 1930- *WhoWrEP 92*
Gabor, Jeffrey Alan 1942- *WhoSSW 93*
Gabor, Michael J. 1934- *St&PR 93*
Gabor, Pal 1932-1987 *DrEEuF, MiSFD 9N*
Gaborcik, Norbert 1951- *WhoScE 91-4*
Gabour, Jim 1947- *WhoEmL 93*
Gabourie, Mitchell *MiSFD 9*
Gabovitch, Steven Alan 1953- *WhoEmL 93*
Gabras *OxDcByz*
Gabras, Michael c. 1290-c. 1350 *OxDcByz*
Gabremariam, Fassil 1944- *St&PR 93, WhoAm 92*
Gabreski, Francis *BioIn 17*
Gabria, Joanne Bakaitis 1945- *WhoAmW 93, WhoWor 93*
Gabridge, Michael Gregory 1943- *WhoAm 92*
Gabriel 1912- *BioIn 17*
Gabriel, Alan H. 1933- *WhoScE 91-2*
Gabriel, Anthony Patrick 1944- *WhoE 93*
Gabriel, Arthur John 1951- *WhoEmL 93*
Gabriel, Astrik Ladislas 1907- *WhoAm 92*
Gabriel, Charles Alvin 1928- *WhoAm 92*
Gabriel, Charles H(utchinson) 1856-1932 *Baker 92*
Gabriel, Eberhard John *Law&B 92*
Gabriel, Eberhard John 1942- *St&PR 93*
Gabriel, Edward Michael 1950- *WhoAm 92*
Gabriel, Edward Paul 1945- *WhoE 93*
Gabriel, Edwin Zenith 1913- *WhoE 93*
Gabriel, Eileen M. 1951- *WhoIns 93*
Gabriel, Ethel Mary 1921- *WhoWor 93*
Gabriel, Gail Virginia 1946- *WhoEmL 93*
Gabriel, Gary A. 1942- *WhoUN 92*
Gabriel, George Peter 1923- *St&PR 93*
Gabriel, Harold John *Law&B 92*
Gabriel, Jeffrey Nikolas 1940- *St&PR 93*
Gabriel, Jill A. 1958- *St&PR 93*
Gabriel, Joseph Martin 1927- *St&PR 93*
Gabriel, Mary Ann Virginia 1825-1877 *Baker 92*
Gabriel, Michael *MiSFD 9*
Gabriel, Michael 1940- *WhoAm 92*
Gabriel, Mordecai Lionel 1918- *WhoAm 92*
Gabriel, Othmar 1925- *WhoE 93*
Gabriel, Peter *BioIn 17*
Gabriel, Peter 1950- *WhoAm 92, WhoWor 93*
Gabriel, Roger Eugene 1929- *WhoSSW 93*
Gabriele, Rosaria Vienna 1946- *WhoAmW 93*
Gabriele, Vincenzo 1948- *WhoSSW 93*
Gabriel Hieromonachos fl. 15th cent.- *OxDcByz*
Gabrieli, Andrea c. 1510-1586 *Baker 92*
Gabrieli, Giovanni 1554?-1612 *Baker 92*
Gabrielle, Anthony F. 1927- *St&PR 93*
Gabrielli, Adriana *OxDcOp*
Gabrielli, Caterina 1730-1796 *Baker 92, OxDcOp*
Gabrielli, Domenico 1651-1690 *Baker 92*
Gabrielli, Nicolo 1814-1891 *Baker 92*
Gabrielli, Thomas Robert 1947- *WhoEmL 93*
Gabrielopoulos *OxDcByz*
Gabriel-Reyes, Asteria Masangkay 1933- *WhoAmW 93*
Gabriels, Donald Maurice 1946- *WhoWor 93*
Gabriels, R. 1938- *WhoScE 91-2*
Gabrielse, Hubert 1926- *WhoAm 92*
Gabrielsen-Cabush, Diane Lynn 1957- *WhoAmW 93*
Gabrielson, Elaine Beth 1956- *WhoAmW 93*
Gabrielson, Guy G. 1891-1976 *PolPar*
Gabrielson, Guy George 1891-1976 *BioIn 17*
Gabrielson, Ira Wilson 1922- *WhoAm 92*
Gabrielsson, Juha Erkki 1931- *WhoScE 91-4*
Gabriles, George Antonio 1926- *St&PR 93*
Gabrillides, Savas Th. *WhoScE 91-3*
Gabrilove, Jacques Lester 1917- *WhoAm 92, WhoWor 93*
Gabrilowitsch, Ossip (Salomonovich) 1878-1936 *Baker 92*
Gabrini, Philippe Jean 1940- *WhoWor 93*
Gabron, Frank 1930- *St&PR 93*
Gabroy, Jane R. 1949- *St&PR 93*
Gabryelewicz, Antoni 1928- *WhoScE 91-4*
Gabrynowicz, Joanne Irene 1949- *WhoEmL 93*
Gabrys, Gerard T. 1948- *St&PR 93*
Gabryszewski Zdzislaw 1930- *WhoScE 91-4*
Gaburo, Kenneth (Louis) 1926- *Baker 92*
Gabus, Jean 1908- *IntDcAn*
Gabussi, Giulio Cesare 1555-1611 *Baker 92*
Gabussi, Rita c. 1815-1891 *See* De Bassini, Achille 1819-1881 *OxDcOp*
Gabutti, Alberto 1960- *WhoWor 93*
Gaby, Daniel M. 1933- *St&PR 93*
Gac, Andre 1924- *WhoScE 91-2*
Gaccione, Joseph Alfred 1932- *WhoSSW 93*
Gach, Gary Gregory 1947- *WhoWrEP 92*
Gach, John Paul 1946- *WhoEmL 93*
Gachet, Christian 1937- *WhoScE 91-2*
Gachet, Fred Smith, Jr. 1932- *WhoSSW 93*
Gachet, Thomas McInnis *Law&B 92*
Gachman, Leon H. 1916- *St&PR 93*
Gachon, Louis 1926- *WhoScE 91-2*
Gachot, Charles A.J., Jr. 1931- *St&PR 93*
Gachot, Charles Artur Jacques 1931- *WhoE 93*
Gack, Bruce M. *Law&B 92*
Gack, Normandy Mary 1940- *WhoAmW 93*
Gackenbach, Dick 1927- *ConAu 38NR, MajAI [port]*
Gackle, George D. 1925- *St&PR 93*
Gackowski, Dennis Edward 1948- *WhoEmL 93*
Gacto, Mariano Jose 1948- *WhoWor 93*
Gadal, Pierre 1938- *WhoScE 91-2*
Gadallah, Leslie 1939- *ScF&FL 92*
Gadamer, Hans Georg 1900- *BioIn 17*
Gadarowski, James Joseph *Law&B 92*
Gadbaw, R. Michael *Law&B 92*
Gadbois, Richard A., Jr. 1932- *WhoAm 92*
Gadbois, Sherri Lynn 1958- *WhoAmW 93*
Gadd, Maxine 1940- *WhoCanL 92*
Gadd, William H. 1930- *St&PR 93*
Gadda, David G. *Law&B 92*
Gaddafi, Muammar 1942- *BioIn 17*
Gaddas, Rachid Ridha 1935- *WhoUN 92*
Gaddes, Richard 1942- *WhoAm 92*
Gaddess, Mary L. *AmWomPl*
Gaddie, David Michael 1947- *St&PR 93*
Gaddis, John Lewis 1941- *WhoAm 92*
Gaddis, Paul Otto 1924- *WhoAm 92*
Gaddis, Robert Smith 1931- *St&PR 93*

Gaddis, William 1922- *BioIn 17, MagSAmL [port], WhoAm 92, WhoWrEP 92*
Gaddis Rose, Marilyn 1930- *WhoAm 92*
Gaddy, C. Welton *BioIn 17*
Gaddy, Gordon M. 1936- *St&PR 93*
Gaddy, James Leoma 1932- *WhoAm 92*
Gaddy, M. Gordon 1936- *WhoIns 93*
Gaddy, Margaret Elaine 1954- *WhoAmW 93*
Gaddy, Mercer Gordon 1936- *WhoAm 92*
Gaddy, Oscar Lee 1932- *WhoAm 92*
Gaddy, Robert Joseph 1924- *WhoAm 92*
Gaddy, Rodney Edwin 1955- *WhoEmL 93*
Gade, Alfred Eric *Law&B 92*
Gade, Axel Willy 1860-1921 *Baker 92*
Gade, Daniel Wayne 1936- *WhoE 93*
Gade, Jacob 1879-1963 *Baker 92*
Gade, Karl 1939- *WhoWor 93*
Gade, Marvin Francis 1924- *WhoAm 92*
Gade, Niels 1958- *WhoScE 91-2*
Gade, Niels (Wilhelm) 1817-1890 *Baker 92*
Gadefelt, Goran Robert 1921- *WhoScE 91-4*
Gaden, Elmer L. 1923- *BioIn 17*
Gaden, Elmer Lewis, Jr. 1923- *WhoAm 92, WhoSSW 93*
Gadev, Hristo 1922- *WhoScE 91-4*
Gadgil, Vithal Narhar 1928- *WhoAsAP 91*
Gadhafi, Muammar Muhammed 1942- *WhoWor 93*
Gadian, David Geoffrey *WhoScE 91-1*
Gadicke, Ansbert Schneider 1958- *WhoE 93*
Gadient, Janet Young *Law&B 92*
Gadient, Walter G. 1923- *St&PR 93*
Gadiesh, Orit *BioIn 17*
Gadigian, Paul 1933- *St&PR 93*
Gadish, Daniel Brian 1951- *WhoEmL 93*
Gadkowski, Walter I. d1991 *BioIn 17*
Gadney, Alan 1941- *MiSFD 9*
Gadol, Peter 1964- *ScF&FL 92*
Gadomski, Nina Marie 1960- *WhoEmL 93*
Gadomski, Robert Eugene 1947- *St&PR 93, WhoAm 92*
Gadon, Harold 1928- *St&PR 93*
Gadon, Steven Franklin 1931- *St&PR 93*
Gador, Witold 1929- *WhoScE 91-4*
Gadoury, Lee Joseph 1954- *St&PR 93*
Gadow, B. Curtis 1963- *St&PR 93*
Gadra, Gerald John 1939- *St&PR 93*
Gadsby, Edward Northup, Jr. 1935- *WhoAm 92*
Gadsby, Henry (Robert) 1842-1907 *Baker 92*
Gadsby, Robin Edward 1939- *WhoAm 92*
Gadsden, Christopher Henry 1946- *WhoEmL 93*
Gadsden, James 1949- *WhoEmL 93*
Gadsden, M. *WhoScE 91-1*
Gadsden, Richard Hamilton 1925- *WhoAm 92, WhoSSW 93*
Gadski, Johanna 1872-1932 *IntDcOp, OxDcOp*
Gadski, Johanna (Emilia Agnes) 1872-1932 *Baker 92*
Gadson, Gregory Pierce *Law&B 92*
Gady, Richard Lynn 1943- *St&PR 93*
Gadzhibekov, Sultan 1919-1974 *Baker 92*
Gadzhibekov, Uzeir 1885-1948 *Baker 92*
Gadzhiev, (Akhmed) Jevdet 1917- *Baker 92*
Gadzinski, Barbara Ann 1955- *WhoAmW 93*
Gadzinski, Chester 1928- *St&PR 93*
Gaebler, Richard H. 1930- *WhoIns 93*
Gaecke, Robert L. 1946- *St&PR 93*
Gaefgen, Gerard Franz Marcel 1925- *WhoWor 93*
Gaeke, Harry Francis 1923- *St&PR 93*
Gael, J.S. *WhoWrEP 92*
Gaelen, Norbert 1926- *St&PR 93*
Gaemperli, R. *WhoScE 91-4*
Gaemperli, Robert 1954- *WhoScE 91-4*
Gaeng, Paul Ami 1924- *WhoAm 92*
Gaer, Joseph 1897-1969 *ScF&FL 92*
Gaertner, Christopher Wolfgang 1962- *WhoAm 92, WhoWor 93*
Gaertner, Donell J. 1932- *WhoAm 92*
Gaertner, Kenneth Clark 1933- *WhoWrEP 92*
Gaertner, Klaus-Juergen 1939- *WhoUN 92*
Gaertner, Richard Francis 1933- *WhoAm 92*
Gaeta, Cinzia *Law&B 92*
Gaeta, Francesco Saverio 1926- *WhoScE 91-3*
Gaeta, Giuseppe 1928- *WhoWor 93*
Gaeta, Rosemarie 1947- *WhoE 93*
Gaetano dc. 1793 *OxDcOp*
Gaetano, Joyce Ann 1956- *WhoEmL 93*
Gaethe, George 1919- *WhoSSW 93*
Gaeto, Paul Joseph *Law&B 92*
Gaetz, Roy P. *Law&B 92*
Gaff, Brian Michael 1962- *WhoWor 93*
Gaff, Frank W. 1941- *St&PR 93*
Gaff, Jerry Gene 1936- *WhoAm 92*
Gaff, William A. 1957- *St&PR 93*
Gaffey, Thomas Michael, Jr. 1934- *WhoAm 92*
Gaffga, Diane 1947- *WhoEmL 93*
Gaffigan, Catherine *WhoE 93*
Gaffigan, Jacques Gardiner 1927- *St&PR 93*
Gaffin, C. Harold 1939- *St&PR 93*
Gaffin, Gerald Eliot 1932- *WhoE 93*
Gaffner, David Lewis 1954- *WhoEmL 93*
Gaffney, Beryl *WhoAmW 93*
Gaffney, Donna Mary 1946- *WhoE 93*
Gaffney, Edward S. 1945- *St&PR 93*
Gaffney, Grace *St&PR 93*
Gaffney, Grace Lee *AmWomPl*
Gaffney, J. Patrick *Law&B 92*
Gaffney, James L. *Law&B 92*
Gaffney, Jane Ellen 1949- *WhoAmW 93*
Gaffney, John *BioIn 17*
Gaffney, John Francis 1934- *WhoE 93*
Gaffney, Joseph M. 1946- *St&PR 93*
Gaffney, Lauren *BioIn 17*
Gaffney, Mark William 1951- *WhoEmL 93*
Gaffney, Martin d1991 *BioIn 17*
Gaffney, Michael David 1939- *WhoAm 92*
Gaffney, Michael Scully 1928- *St&PR 93*
Gaffney, Michele Elizabeth 1961- *WhoAmW 93*
Gaffney, Myrick William 1947- *WhoEmL 93*
Gaffney, Orville E. *St&PR 93*
Gaffney, Owen James 1935- *St&PR 93*
Gaffney, Paul Cotter 1917- *WhoAm 92*
Gaffney, Paul Golden, II 1946- *WhoAm 92, WhoSSW 93*
Gaffney, Richard C. *Law&B 92*
Gaffney, Richard C., Jr. *Law&B 92*
Gaffney, Robert D. *St&PR 93*
Gaffney, Robert Joseph 1946- *St&PR 93*
Gaffney, Stiles 1954- *St&PR 93*
Gaffney, Terrence John 1949- *WhoEmL 93*
Gaffney, Thomas 1915- *WhoAm 92*
Gaffney, Thomas Edward 1930- *WhoAm 92*
Gaffney, Thomas Francis 1945- *St&PR 93, WhoAm 92*
Gaffney, Timothy R. 1951- *ConAu 137, SmATA 69*
Gaffney, William C. 1928- *St&PR 93*
Gafford, Charlotte Kelly *WhoWrEP 92*
Gafford, Nora N. 1924- *St&PR 93*
Gafford, W. Wade 1955- *St&PR 93*
Gaffurio, Franchino 1451-1522 *Baker 92*
Gaffurius, Franchino 1451-1522 *Baker 92*
Gafner, Peter *WhoScE 91-4*
Gafney, Harry D. 1943- *WhoAm 92*
Gafurius, Franchino 1451-1522 *Baker 92*
Gafvert, Karl Olof Uno 1946- *WhoWor 93*
Gag, Wanda (Hazel) 1893-1946 *ConAu 137, MajAI [port]*
Gagain, Edward Francis, Jr. 1947- *WhoEmL 93*
Gagan, Richard D. 1936- *St&PR 93*
Gagarin, Yuri 1934-1968 *BioIn 17, Expl 93 [port]*
Gage, Calvin William 1929- *WhoAm 92*
Gage, Clarke Lyman 1921- *WhoE 93*
Gage, David Floyd 1945- *WhoSSW 93*
Gage, E. Dean 1942- *WhoAm 92*
Gage, Edwin C., III 1940- *WhoAm 92*
Gage, Fred Kelton 1925- *WhoAm 92*
Gage, Gaston Hemphill 1930- *WhoSSW 93, WhoWor 93*
Gage, George *MiSFD 9*
Gage, Irwin 1939- *Baker 92*
Gage, John 1937- *WhoAm 92*
Gage, John D. 1939- *WhoScE 91-1*
Gage, Kevin E. *BioIn 17*
Gage, Kevin E. 1959- *St&PR 93*
Gage, Lois Waite 1922- *WhoAmW 93*
Gage, N.L. 1917- *BioIn 17*
Gage, Nancy Elizabeth 1947- *WhoEmL 93*
Gage, Nathaniel Lees 1917- *BioIn 17, WhoAm 92*
Gage, Nicholas *BioIn 17*
Gage, Nicholas 1939- *WhoAm 92*
Gage, Patrick 1942- *WhoAm 92*
Gage, Steven K. 1959- *WhoEmL 93*
Gage, Thomas c. 1720-1787 *HarEnMi*
Gage, Thomas E. *ScF&FL 92*
Gage, Thomas M. *Law&B 92*
Gage, Tommy Wilton 1935- *WhoAm 92*
Gage, William James 1932- *WhoE 93*
Gage, Wilson *ConAu 139, DcAmChF 1960, MajAI, SmATA 72*
Gageby, Stephen L. 1940- *St&PR 93*
Gagen, David William 1943- *WhoSSW 93*
Gagge, Adolf Pharo 1908- *WhoAm 92*
Gaggero, James Peter 1959- *WhoWor 93*
Gaggioli, Nestor Gustavo 1940- *WhoWor 93*
Gaggioli, Richard Arnold 1934- *WhoAm 92*
Gaghan, Gloria *ScF&FL 92*
Gagher, John E. *ScF&FL 92*
Gagik, I *OxDcByz*
Gagik, II dc. 1079 *OxDcByz*
Gagliani, William Dennis 1959- *WhoWrEP 92*
Gagliano *Baker 92*
Gagliano, Alessandro *Baker 92*
Gagliano, Ferdinando c. 1724-1781 *Baker 92*
Gagliano, Frank Joseph 1931- *WhoAm 92*
Gagliano, Gennaro 1700-1788 *Baker 92*
Gagliano, Guido 1947- *St&PR 93*
Gagliano, Joseph W. 1924- *St&PR 93*
Gagliano, Marco da 1582-1643 *Baker 92, IntDcOp, OxDcOp*
Gagliano, Nicholas Joseph 1926- *St&PR 93*
Gagliano, Nicola 1695-1758 *Baker 92*
Gagliano, Thomas Dominick *Law&B 92*
Gagliardi, Annette Jane 1950- *WhoWrEP 92*
Gagliardi, Elaine Hightower 1960- *WhoEmL 93*
Gagliardi, Joseph F. 1911-1992 *BioIn 17, NewYTBS 92 [port]*
Gagliardi, Joseph J. 1939- *St&PR 93*
Gagliardi, Lee Parsons 1918- *WhoAm 92*
Gagliardi, Michael J. 1940- *St&PR 93*
Gagliardi, R.G. 1946- *St&PR 93*
Gagliardi, Raul Pedro 1944- *WhoWor 93*
Gagliardi, Raymond Alfred 1922- *WhoAm 92, WhoWor 93*
Gagliardi, Ugo Oscar 1931- *WhoAm 92, WhoE 93*
Gagliardino, Juan Jose 1938- *WhoWor 93*
Gagliardo, Joseph Michael 1952- *WhoEmL 93*
Gagliardo, Reginald Saverio 1948- *WhoEmL 93*
Gagliardo, Ruth 1895-1980 *BioIn 17*
Gaglione, Gregory *Law&B 92*
Gaglione, Robert J. 1958- *WhoEmL 93*
Gagne, Armand Joseph, Jr. 1936- *WhoWor 93*
Gagne, Faith Elizabeth 1934- *WhoE 93*
Gagne, Francois 1960- *St&PR 93*
Gagne, George Francis 1952- *WhoEmL 93*
Gagne, H. Lamontage *Law&B 92*
Gagne, Kimberly Ann 1964- *WhoE 93*
Gagne, Laura Lee 1959- *WhoE 93*
Gagne, Paul E. 1946- *St&PR 93*
Gagne, Paul Ernest 1946- *WhoAm 92*
Gagne, Paul R. 1956- *ScF&FL 92*
Gagne, Roger Owen 1931- *WhoE 93*
Gagne, Russell C. 1960- *St&PR 93*
Gagne, William Roderick 1955- *WhoE 93, WhoEmL 93, WhoWor 93*
Gagnebin, Albert Paul 1909- *WhoAm 92*
Gagnebin, Henri 1886-1977 *Baker 92*
Gagnepain, Jean-Jacques 1942- *WhoScE 91-2*
Gagner, Thomas Albert 1946- *WhoE 93, WhoEmL 93*
Gagner, Thomas F. 1928- *St&PR 93*
Gagner, Wayne P. 1938- *WhoE 93*
Gagni, Arsenio O. 1935- *WhoUN 92*
Gagnon, Alain 1943- *WhoCanL 92*
Gagnon, Alfred Joseph 1914- *WhoAm 92*
Gagnon, Cecile 1936- *WhoCanL 92*
Gagnon, Claude 1949- *MiSFD 9*
Gagnon, Daniel 1946- *WhoCanL 92*
Gagnon, Daniel Fred 1953- *St&PR 93*
Gagnon, Denis C. 1948- *St&PR 93*
Gagnon, Edith Morrison 1909- *WhoAm 92, WhoAmW 93*
Gagnon, Edouard Cardinal 1918- *WhoWor 93*
Gagnon, John Harvey 1946- *WhoE 93*
Gagnon, Joseph *BioIn 17*
Gagnon, Lee A. 1937- *St&PR 93*
Gagnon, Madeleine 1938- *WhoCanL 92*
Gagnon, Mariano *BioIn 17*
Gagnon, Maurice 1912- *WhoCanL 92*
Gagnon, Michael J. 1939- *St&PR 93*
Gagnon, Peter R. 1943- *St&PR 93*
Gagnon, Rejean 1938- *St&PR 93*
Gagnon, Roger Joseph 1946- *WhoEmL 93*
Gagnon, Ronald J. 1939- *St&PR 93*
Gagnon, Stewart Walter 1949- *WhoAm 92*
Gagnon, Yvonne 1946- *WhoEmL 93, WhoWor 93*
Gagny, Claude 1932- *WhoScE 91-2*
Gago, Jenny *BioIn 17*
Gagon, G. Scott 1946- *St&PR 93*
Gagosian, Earl d1990 *BioIn 17*
Gagosian, Larry *BioIn 17, WhoE 93*
Gagosian, Robert B. 1944- *WhoAm 92*
Gaguine, Benito 1912- *WhoAm 92*
Gahagan, James Edward 1900-1991 *BioIn 17*
Gahagan, James Edward, Jr. 1927- *WhoAm 92*
Gahagan, Marilyn Ann 1949- *WhoAmW 93*
Gahagan, Thomas Gail 1938- *WhoSSW 93*
Gahagen, Dennis L. 1945- *St&PR 93*
Gaham, Hamid 1941- *WhoUN 92*
Gahan, Gary Michael 1941- *St&PR 93*
Gahan, Kathleen Mason 1940- *WhoAmW 93*
Gahan, Peter Brian *WhoScE 91-1*
Gahan, Peter Brian 1933- *WhoWor 93*
Gahan, William Patrick, III 1954- *WhoEmL 93*
Gahm, Gosta F. 1942- *WhoScE 91-4*
Gahmberg, Carl G. 1942- *WhoScE 91-4*
Gahrton, Gosta C.A. 1932- *WhoScE 91-4*
Gahtan, Alan M. *Law&B 92*
Gai, Eliezer 1944- *WhoAm 92*
Gaia, Jeffrey P. 1953- *St&PR 93*
Gaiber, Lawrence Jay 1960- *WhoEmL 93*
Gaich, Sharon Denise 1961- *WhoAmW 93, WhoWrEP 92*
Gaida, Davida *ScF&FL 92*
Gaida, Roman 1928- *WhoWor 93*
Gaidano, Don Joseph 1948- *St&PR 93*
Gaidar, Yegor *NewYTBS 92 [port]*
Gaidemak, Joel 1931- *WhoE 93*
Gaieb, M'Hamed 1943- *WhoUN 92*
Gaige, Dorothy Dove 1945- *WhoWrEP 92*
Gaige, Peter 1942- *WhoAsAP 91*
Gaigerova, Varvara 1903-1944 *Baker 92*
Gail, Maxwell Trowbridge, Jr. 1943- *WhoAm 92*
Gail, Otto 1896-1956 *ScF&FL 92*
Gailey, Edward David 1948- *WhoEmL 93*
Gailey, Frances Harriett 1932- *WhoE 93*
Gailey, Joan Dale 1940- *WhoAmW 93*
Gailey, Susan Coia 1954- *WhoEmL 93*
Gailhard, Andre 1885-1966 *Baker 92*
Gailhard, Pierre 1848-1918 *Baker 92, OxDcOp*
Gailing, Walter 1930- *St&PR 93*
Gailius, Gilbert Keistutis 1931- *St&PR 93, WhoAm 92*
Gaillard, Anthony W.K. 1944- *WhoScE 91-3*
Gaillard, Edwin Samuel 1827-1885 *JrnUS*
Gaillard, Felix 1919-1970 *BioIn 17*
Gaillard, Franklin Delino 1946- *WhoSSW 93*
Gaillard, J.P. 1941- *WhoScE 91-2*
Gaillard, John 1765-1826 *PolPar*
Gaillard, John Palmer, Jr. 1920- *WhoAm 92*
Gaillard, Marius-Francois 1900-1973 *Baker 92*
Gaillard, Mary Katharine 1939- *WhoAm 92, WhoAmW 93*
Gaillard, Michel *WhoScE 91-2*
Gaillard, P. *WhoScE 91-2*
Gaillard, Slim *BioIn 17*
Gaillard, Slim 1916-1991 *AnObit 1991*
Gaillard, Thomas Ray 1947- *WhoEmL 93, WhoSSW 93*
Gaillard, Trudy 1962- *WhoAmW 93*
Gaillard, Yvon Andre 1923- *WhoWor 93*
Gaillardet, Theodore Frederic 1808-1882 *JrnUS*
Gailly, Pierre-Joseph 1955- *WhoWor 93*
Gailys, John M. 1941- *WhoAm 92*
Gaiman, Neil 1960- *ScF&FL 92*
Gainas dc. 401 *OxDcByz*
Gaine, Hugh 1726-1807 *JrnUS*
Gainen, Susan Rose 1950- *WhoEmL 93*
Gainer, Leila Josephine 1948- *WhoAmW 93, WhoEmL 93*
Gainer, Paul *BioIn 17*
Gainer, Rhonda Hope 1956- *WhoEmL 93*
Gainer, Sandra Gertrude 1951- *WhoEmL 93*
Gaines, Alan McCulloch 1938- *WhoAm 92*
Gaines, Anne Preston 1950- *WhoAmW 93, WhoE 93, WhoEmL 93, WhoWor 93*
Gaines, Beverly Joyce 1931- *WhoWrEP 92*
Gaines, Bobby Dean 1930- *WhoSSW 93*
Gaines, C. Ronald *Law&B 92*
Gaines, Charles Stephen 1947- *WhoEmL 93*
Gaines, Clarence *BioIn 17*
Gaines, Dennis *BioIn 17*
Gaines, Diana Torruella 1963- *WhoAmW 93*
Gaines, Donna 1951- *ConAu 136*
Gaines, Edmund Pendleton 1777-1849 *HarEnMi*
Gaines, Ernest J. *WhoWrEP 92*
Gaines, Ernest J. 1933- *BioIn 17*
Gaines, Ervin J. 1916-1986 *BioIn 17*
Gaines, Frank, Jr. 1918- *WhoE 93*
Gaines, George Bernard 1921- *St&PR 93*
Gaines, Gerald William 1956- *St&PR 93*
Gaines, H. Michael 1945- *St&PR 93, WhoIns 93*
Gaines, Howard Clarke 1909- *WhoAm 92*
Gaines, J. Donald 1936- *St&PR 93*
Gaines, James Donald 1936- *WhoAm 92*
Gaines, James Edwin, Jr. 1938- *WhoAm 92, WhoSSW 93*
Gaines, James Preston 1924- *WhoSSW 93*
Gaines, James Russell 1947- *WhoAm 92, WhoE 93*
Gaines, John Strother 1933- *WhoSSW 93*
Gaines, Jonathan E. *Law&B 92*
Gaines, Joseph Allen 1924- *St&PR 93*
Gaines, Kendra Holly 1946- *WhoEmL 93*

Gaines, Leonard M. 1956- WhoEmL 93
Gaines, Peter Mathew 1951- WhoEmL 93
Gaines, Richard Law&B 92
Gaines, Robert M. Law&B 92
Gaines, Robert Walker 1933- St&PR 93
Gaines, Rosie BioIn 17
Gaines, Sarah Fore 1920- WhoSSW 93
Gaines, Sidney d1992 NewYTBS 92
Gaines, Steve c. 1950- See Lynyrd Skynyrd ConMus 9
Gaines, Thomas, Jr. 1948- WhoSSW 93
Gaines, Thomas A. 1923- ConAu 139
Gaines, Thomas E. 1926- St&PR 93
Gaines, Tinsley Powell 1939- WhoSSW 93
Gaines, Weaver H. Law&B 92
Gaines, Weaver Henderson 1943- St&PR 93
Gaines, William Chester 1933- WhoAm 92
Gaines, William M. d1992 NewYTBS 92
Gaines, William M. 1922-1992 BioIn 17, News 93-1
Gaines, William Maxwell 1922-1992 WhoWor 93
Gaines-Shelton, Ruth AmWomPl
Gainey, Hugh Gerrard 1938- St&PR 93
Gainey, Robert Michael 1953- WhoAm 92
Gainor, James Joseph 1931- St&PR 93
Gainor, Thomas Edward 1933- St&PR 93, WhoAm 92
Gainotti, Guido 1939- WhoWor 93
Gainsborough, Thomas 1727-1788 BioIn 17
Gainsbourg, Serge 1928-1991 AnObit 1991, BioIn 17
Gainsburg, Roy Ellis 1932- WhoAm 92
Gainsford, Ian Derek 1930- WhoWor 93
Gainville, Rene MiSFD 9
Gair, Alan BioIn 17
Gair, Frederick 1926- WhoAsAP 91
Gairard, Alexis 1941- WhoScE 91-2
Gairdner, John Smith 1925- WhoAm 92
Gairy, Eric 1922- DcCPCAm
Gais, Hans-Joachim 1942- WhoWor 93
Gaisch, Helmut Werner 1933- WhoScE 91-4
Gaiser, Gary Vincent 1937- St&PR 93
Gaiser, William R. 1926- St&PR 93
Gaiseric 389-477 OxDcByz
Gaisser, Hope Owren 1946- St&PR 93
Gaisser, James H. 1943- St&PR 93
Gaisser, Julia Haig 1941- WhoAm 92
Gaiswinkler, Robert Sigfried 1932- WhoAm 92
Gait, Gary BioIn 17
Gait, Paul BioIn 17
Gaita, Marie Elaine 1938- WhoAmW 93
Gaitan, Jose BioIn 17
Gaitanos, Mario Law&B 92
Gaite, Carmen Martin BioIn 17
Gaites, Robert J. 1941- St&PR 93
Gaither, Ann Heafner 1932- WhoSSW 93
Gaither, Bill 1936- BioIn 17
Gaither, Frances Ormond Jones 1889- AmWomPl
Gaither, Gary A. 1949- St&PR 93
Gaither, Gerald Henderson 1940- WhoSSW 93
Gaither, Gloria 1942- BioIn 17
Gaither, James Law&B 92
Gaither, James C. St&PR 93
Gaither, James C. 1937- WhoAm 92
Gaither, John F. 1949- WhoAm 92
Gaither, John F., Jr. Law&B 92, WhoAm 92
Gaither, John F., Jr. 1949- St&PR 93
Gaither, John Francis 1918- WhoAm 92, WhoWor 93
Gaither, John Stokes 1944- St&PR 93, WhoAm 92
Gaither, O.D. 1927- St&PR 93
Gaither, Randy Martin 1951- WhoSSW 93
Gaither, Richard A. Law&B 92
Gaither, William Samuel 1932- WhoAm 92
Gaito, Constantino 1878-1945 Baker 92
Gaitskell, Hugh 1906-1963 ColdWar 1 [port]
Gaitskell, Hugh Todd Naylor 1906-1963 DcTwHis
Gaitz, Charles Milton 1922- WhoSSW 93
Gaius Caesar 12-41 BioIn 17
Gaj, Miron Mateusz 1927- WhoScE 91-4
Gajaria, Babu 1949- St&PR 93
Gajcy, Tadeusz Stefan 1922-1944 PolBiDi
Gajda, Anthony James 1943- WhoE 93
Gajda, James E. 1947- St&PR 93
Gajda, James Edward 1947- WhoEmL 93
Gajda, Patricia Ann 1941- WhoAmW 93
Gajda, Zbigniew 1958- WhoWor 93
Gajdaj, Leonid 1923- DrEEuF
Gajderowicz, Idzi 1942- WhoScE 91-4
Gajdusek, Daniel Carleton 1923- WhoAm 92, WhoWor 93
Gajdzik, David T. 1946- St&PR 93
Gajer, Vaclav 1923- DrEEuF
Gajewski, Antoni 1938- WhoScE 91-4
Gajewski, Christine 1946- WhoEmL 93
Gajewski, Patricia Louise 1959- WhoE 93, WhoEmL 93
Gajewski, Wieslaw Peter 1946- WhoEmL 93
Gajkowski, John Joseph 1954- WhoEmL 93
Gajowniczek, Franciszek 1900- PolBiDi
Gakov, Vladimir 1951- ScF&FL 92
Gal, Dezso 1926- WhoScE 91-4
Gal, Hans 1890-1987 Baker 92, OxDcOp
Gal, Kenneth Maurice 1954- WhoAm 92
Gal, Laszlo 1933- WhoAm 92
Gal, Richard John 1957- WhoWor 93
Gal, Sandor 1933- WhoScE 91-4
Gal, Susannah 1958- WhoWor 93
Gal, Tomas 1926- WhoWor 93
Gala, Andrew Roman 1959- WhoEmL 93
Galaba, Glenda Ann 1946- WhoAmW 93
Galaburda, Albert Mark 1948- WhoAm 92
Galajikian, Florence Grandland 1900-1970 Baker 92
Galaktionov, Victor Alexandrovich 1955- WhoWor 93
Galal Gorchev, Hend 1932- WhoUN 92
Galaly, Enan 1947- WhoWor 93
Galambos, John Thomas 1921- WhoAm 92
Galambos, Theodore Victor 1929- WhoAm 92
Galambosi, Bertalan 1946- WhoWor 93
Galamian, Ivan (Alexander) 1903-1981 Baker 92
Galamison, Milton A. 1923-1988 EncAACR
Galan, August John 1912- BiDAMSp 1989
Galan, Julio 1958- BioIn 17
Galan, Nely 1964- NotHsAW 93
Galanaud, Pierre 1944- WhoScE 91-2
Galand, Paul A. 1935- WhoScE 91-2
Galane, Morton Robert 1926- WhoAm 92, WhoWor 93
Galanis, Marian Monica 1918- St&PR 93
Galanis, Terry S., Sr. 1918- St&PR 93
Galanis, Terry S., Jr. 1947- St&PR 93
Galanko, William Andrew Law&B 92
Galanopoulou, Stella 1937- WhoScE 91-3
Galanos, James 1924- WhoAm 92
Galant, Daniel G. Law&B 92
Galant, Herbert Lewis 1928- WhoAm 92
Galant, Lisa Marie 1965- WhoAmW 93
Galant, Mark BioIn 17
Galantai, Aurel 1951- WhoScE 91-4
Galante, Anna-Marie Law&B 92
Galante, Eugene J. 1925- St&PR 93
Galante, Francine Ann Marie 1960- WhoSSW 93
Galante, Joe WhoE 93
Galante, Jorge Osvaldo 1934- WhoAm 92
Galante, Joyce M. Law&B 92
Galante, Nicholas Thomas, III 1955- WhoE 93
Galanter, Eugene 1924- WhoAm 92, WhoE 93, WhoWor 93
Galanter, Marc 1941- WhoAm 92
Galanthay, Theodore E. Law&B 92
Galantine, Kathleen Patricia 1953- WhoWrEP 92
Galantuomini, Carol Brigida 1959- WhoEmL 93
Galanty, M. 1941- St&PR 93
Galardi, John N. 1938- St&PR 93
Galardi, Joseph C. Law&B 92
Galarneau, Gerald George 1947- St&PR 93
Galarza, Ernesto 1905- HispAmA [port]
Galarza, Ernesto 1905-1984 DcLB 122 [port]
Galas, Diamanda (Dimitria Angeliki Elena) 1955- Baker 92
Galas, Edward 1928- WhoScE 91-4
Galas, Thomas A. 1947- St&PR 93
Galasiewicz, Zygmunt M. 1926- WhoScE 91-4
Galasinski, Wladyslaw 1922- WhoScE 91-4
Galask, Rudolph Peter 1935- WhoAm 92, WhoWor 93
Galaskiewicz, Joseph James 1949- WhoEmL 93
Galasko, Charles Samuel Bernard WhoScE 91-1
Galassi, Jonathan 1949- WhoWrEP 92
Galassi, Jonathan White 1949- WhoAm 92
Galassi, Peter 1951- WhoAm 92
Galasso, Attilio WhoScE 91-3
Galasso, Francis Salvatore 1931- WhoAm 92
Galatas, Pearle Edith 1927- WhoAmW 93
Galati, Frank Joseph 1943- WhoAm 92
Galati, Michael A. 1930- St&PR 93
Galati, Michael Anthony 1930- WhoIns 93
Galatianos, Gus A. 1947- WhoEmL 93, WhoWor 93
Galat-Luong, Gerard 1942- WhoScE 91-2
Galatro, Vincent T. 1929- St&PR 93
Galatte-Howard, Gail Ann 1959- WhoAmW 93, WhoEmL 93
Galaty, Carol Popper 1943- WhoAmW 93
Galatz, Henry F. Law&B 92
Galay, Ted 1941- WhoCanL 92
Galazen, Kevin Paul 1962- WhoEmL 93
Galazka, Artur 1933- WhoUN 92
Galazka, Jacek Michal 1924- WhoAm 92
Galbenu, Paul 1933- WhoScE 91-4
Galberaith, Richard O. 1939- St&PR 93
Galbershtad, Semyon 1915- WhoWor 93
Galbis, Vicente 1942- WhoUN 92
Galbo-Mangone, Roslyn 1954- WhoEmL 93
Galbraith, Bruce S. St&PR 93
Galbraith, Esther E. AmWomPl
Galbraith, Evan Griffith 1928- WhoAm 92
Galbraith, Harry Wilson 1918- St&PR 93
Galbraith, Henry Thomas 1944- WhoAm 92
Galbraith, James Kenneth 1952- WhoAm 92
Galbraith, James Marshall 1942- WhoAm 92
Galbraith, James Ronald 1936- WhoAm 92
Galbraith, John Kenneth 1908- BioIn 17, WhoAm 92, WhoWor 93, WhoWrEP 92
Galbraith, John Semple 1916- WhoAm 92
Galbraith, John William 1921- WhoAm 92
Galbraith, Kirk 1942- St&PR 93
Galbraith, Mary J. AmWomPl
Galbraith, Matthew White 1927- St&PR 93, WhoAm 92
Galbraith, Nanette G. 1928- WhoAmW 93
Galbraith, Paul E. 1951- St&PR 93
Galbraith, Roderick Allister McDonald WhoScE 91-1
Galbraith, Ruth Legg 1923- WhoAm 92
Galbreath, J. Joseph 1935- St&PR 93
Galbreath, James H. St&PR 93
Galbreath, Terry Stephen 1950- WhoEmL 93
Galbreath, Theodore Ralph 1953- WhoEmL 93
Galdan 1644-1697 HarEnMi
Galdes, Alphonse 1952- WhoE 93
Galdi, Albert Peter, Jr. 1950- WhoEmL 93
Galdieri, Anthony August 1943- WhoE 93
Galdikas, Birute BioIn 17, NewYTBS 92 [port], WhoAmW 93
Galdone, Paul 1907?-1986 MajAI [port]
Galdone, Paul 1914-1986 BioIn 17, ChlBIID [port]
Gale, Alastair George WhoScE 91-1
Gale, Anthony WhoScE 91-1
Gale, Brent E. Law&B 92
Gale, Connie 1946- St&PR 93
Gale, Connie R. Law&B 92
Gale, Connie Ruth 1946- WhoEmL 93
Gale, Dagmar Freuchen- d1991 BioIn 17
Gale, Elizabeth AmWomPl
Gale, G. Donald 1933- St&PR 93
Gale, George Alexander 1906- WhoAm 92
Gale, John MiSFD 9
Gale, John Albert 1956- WhoEmL 93
Gale, June Winsor AmWomPl
Gale, Liz BioIn 17
Gale, Mary D. St&PR 93
Gale, Michael Denis WhoScE 91-1
Gale, Nancy Ann 1947- St&PR 93
Gale, Neil Jan 1960- St&PR 93, WhoEmL 93
Gale, Paula Jane 1946- WhoAm 92
Gale, Rachel E. Baker AmWomPl
Gale, Randall Glenn 1952- WhoEmL 93
Gale, Rhonda Law&B 92
Gale, Robert Frederick Law&B 92
Gale, Robert James 1955- WhoSSW 93
Gale, Robert L(ee) 1919- ConAu 40NR
Gale, Robert Lee 1919- WhoAm 92
Gale, Robert Peter 1945- WhoAm 92
Gale, Stanley William 1947- WhoEmL 93
Gale, Steven Hershel 1940- WhoAm 92, WhoSSW 93
Gale, Thomas Charles 1943- WhoAm 92
Gale, Thomas Martin 1926- WhoAm 92
Gale, William A. 1939- WhoWrEP 92
Gale, William C. ConAu 39NR
Gale, William Henry 1905- WhoAm 92
Gale, Zona 1874-1938 AmWomPl
Galea, John Henry 1924- WhoAm 92
Galea, Rennie Renato 1966- WhoWor 93
Galeano, Eduardo 1940- ConLC 72 [port], SpAmA
Galeano, Israel d1992 BioIn 17, NewYTBS 92
Galeazzi, Lucio 1942- WhoScE 91-3
Gale-Batten, Stephen J. Law&B 92
Galecke, Robert M. 1942- St&PR 93
Galecke, Robert Michael 1942- WhoAm 92
Galecki, Marek Alfred 1965- WhoSSW 93
Galeener, Frank Lee 1936- WhoAm 92
Galeev, Albert Abubakir 1940- WhoWor 93
Galef, Andrew Geoffrey 1932- St&PR 93, WhoAm 92
Galef, David Adam 1959- WhoSSW 93
Galef, Richard G. 1923- St&PR 93
Galeffi, Carlo 1882-1961 Baker 92, OxDcOp
Galehouse, Lawrence David 1946- WhoEmL 93
Galella, Joseph Peter 1956- WhoEmL 93
Galella, Ron BioIn 17
Galella, Ronald Edward 1931- WhoAm 92
Galen 129-c. 210 OxDcByz
Galen, James 1918-1987 ScF&FL 92
Galen, Richard E. Law&B 92
Galenkamp, Jennifer Sue 1963- WhoAmW 93
Galeotti, Cesare 1872-1929 Baker 92
Galeotti, Steven 1952- WhoE 93, WhoEmL 93
Galer, Donna Lynn 1949- St&PR 93
Galer, Donna Lynn 1950- WhoIns 93
Galer, Ian A.R. 1949- WhoScE 91-1
Galer, Margaret Dawn WhoScE 91-1
Galerius c. 260-311 OxDcByz
Galerne, Andre 1926- St&PR 93
Gales, Joseph 1761-1841 BioIn 17
Gales, Joseph 1786-1860 BioIn 17, JrnUS
Gales, Weston 1877-1939 Baker 92
Galesi, Francesco BioIn 17
Galesiotes, George 1278?-c. 1346 OxDcByz
Galet, Pierre 1921- WhoScE 91-2
Galey, David Jonathan 1952- St&PR 93
Galey, George Gregory 1948- WhoE 93
Galey, John Taylor 1907- WhoAm 92
Galey, Leon 1925- St&PR 93
Galey, Thomas S. 1955- St&PR 93
Galfas, Timothy 1934- MiSFD 9
Galfas, Timothy, II 1943- WhoSSW 93
Galfo, Armand James 1924- WhoAm 92
Galford, Ellen 1947- ScF&FL 92
Galgano, Victor Joseph 1943- St&PR 93
Galgut, Peter Neil WhoScE 91-1
Galian, Laurence Joseph Anthony Michael 1954- WhoEmL 93
Galiani, Ferdinando 1728-1787 BioIn 17
Galiano, Dionisio Alcala- 1760-1805 BioIn 17
Galiardo, John W. Law&B 92
Galiardo, John W. 1933- St&PR 93
Galiardo, John William 1933- WhoAm 92
Galiber, Joseph L. 1924- AfrAmBi
Galiber, Joseph Lionel 1924- WhoE 93
Galiber, Rochelle B. Law&B 92
Galido, Alejandro 1936-1990 BioIn 17
Galie, Louis Michael 1945- WhoAm 92, WhoE 93
Galien, Kristine J. Law&B 92
Galik, Albert R. Law&B 92
Galil, Uzia 1925- St&PR 93, WhoAm 92
Galilei, Galileo 1564-1642 BioIn 17
Galilei, Vincenzo c. 1520-1591 Baker 92, OxDcOp
Galileo 1564-1642 BioIn 17
Galimer, Felix 1910- Baker 92
Galimi, Dominick Joseph 1945- WhoE 93
Galimi, Phyllis Joy 1949- WhoAmW 93
Galin, Douglas M. Law&B 92
Galin, Julius L. 1924- St&PR 93
Galin, Miles A. 1932- WhoAm 92
Galin, Mitchell ScF&FL 92
Galin, Pierre 1786-1821 Baker 92
Galina, Henryk 1946- WhoScE 91-4
Galindo, Alberto Flores 1949-1990 BioIn 17
Galindo (Dimas), Blas 1910- Baker 92
Galindo, Fernando 1951- WhoWor 93
Galindo, Gary Anthony 1947- St&PR 93
Galindo, Hermila 1896-1975? BioIn 17
Galindo, Miguel Angel 1960- WhoWor 93
Galindo, Sergio 1926- DcMexL, SpAmA
Galindo Salais, Bernardo 1946- WhoWor 93
Galindo Tixaire, Alberto 1934- WhoScE 91-3
Galinski, Heinz 1912-1992 NewYTBS 92 [port]
Galinsky, Andrew M. 1947- St&PR 93
Galinsky, Gotthard Karl 1942- WhoAm 92
Galinsky, Marsha Dee 1958- WhoEmL 93
Galinsky, Raymond Ethan 1948- WhoEmL 93
Galione, Jack BioIn 17
Galioto, Frank Martin, Jr. 1942- WhoAm 92
Galipo, Russell E. 1932- St&PR 93
Galish, Suellen M. Law&B 92
Galitz, Keith G. Law&B 92
Galivan, John Henry 1939- WhoE 93
Galkin, Elliott W. BioIn 17
Galkin, Elliott W(ashington) 1921-1990 Baker 92
Galkin, Florence 1925- WhoAmW 93
Galkin, Robert Theodore 1926- St&PR 93

Galkin, Samuel Bernard 1933- *WhoE 93, WhoWor 93*
Galkowski, Andrzej Edmund 1926- *WhoScE 91-4*
Galkowski, Raymond 1961- *St&PR 93*
Gall c. 1840-1894 *HarEnMi*
Gall, Christian F. 1927- *WhoScE 91-3*
Gall, Clarence Arthur 1945- *WhoWor 93*
Gall, David Anthony 1941- *St&PR 93*
Gall, Edward R. Home- *ScF&FL 92*
Gall, Elizabeth Benson 1944- *WhoAmW 93*
Gall, Ellen M. *AmWomPl*
Gall, Eric Papineau 1940- *WhoAm 92, WhoWor 93*
Gall, Graham Alexander Edward 1936- *WhoAm 92*
Gall, Helen Louise 1930- *WhoAmW 93*
Gall, Jan Karol 1856-1912 *PolBiDi*
Gall, John C. *Law&B 92*
Gall, Joseph Grafton 1928- *WhoAm 92*
Gall, Lenore Rosalie 1943- *WhoE 93*
Gall, Martin 1944- *WhoAm 92*
Gall, Meredith Damien 1942- *WhoAm 92, WhoWrEP 92*
Gall, Patience Beth 1936- *WhoAmW 93*
Gall, Robert Edward 1945- *St&PR 93*
Gall, Sally Moore 1941- *WhoE 93, WhoWrEP 92*
Gall, Yvonne 1885-1972 *Baker 92*
Gallacher, Gerard 1955- *WhoWor 93*
Gallager, Robert Gray 1931- *WhoAm 92*
Gallagher, Alfred Kenneth 1936- *WhoWor 93*
Gallagher, Anne Porter 1950- *WhoAmW 93, WhoEmL 93*
Gallagher, Bob *ScF&FL 92*
Gallagher, Brad K. 1944- *WhoIns 93*
Gallagher, Carole L. 1950- *WhoE 93*
Gallagher, Charlene A. *Law&B 92*
Gallagher, Charles Patrick 1938- *St&PR 93*
Gallagher, Colin Crompton *WhoScE 91-1*
Gallagher, Daniel Joseph 1951- *St&PR 93*
Gallagher, David *St&PR 93*
Gallagher, David C. *Law&B 92*
Gallagher, Deborah Rigling 1957- *WhoAmW 93*
Gallagher, Dennis *Law&B 92*
Gallagher, Dennis Vincent 1952- *WhoEmL 93*
Gallagher, Diana G. 1946- *ScF&FL 92*
Gallagher, Don *BioIn 17*
Gallagher, Ed *BioIn 17, NewYTBS 92 [port]*
Gallagher, Edward Clark 1887-1940 *BiDAMSp 1989*
Gallagher, Edward J. 1929- *St&PR 93*
Gallagher, Edward J. 1940- *ScF&FL 92*
Gallagher, Edward Peter 1951- *WhoAm 92, WhoE 93*
Gallagher, Eleanor 1939- *WhoE 93*
Gallagher, Eloise 1942- *St&PR 93*
Gallagher, F. Michael 1934- *WhoAm 92*
Gallagher, Frank W. 1925- *St&PR 93*
Gallagher, Gary W(illiam) 1950- *ConAu 136*
Gallagher, Gerald Raphael 1941- *WhoAm 92*
Gallagher, Gerhardt J. 1936- *WhoScE 91-3*
Gallagher, Gregory Allen 1953- *St&PR 93*
Gallagher, Helen 1948- *WhoAmW 93*
Gallagher, Henry Edmond, Jr. 1949- *WhoEmL 93*
Gallagher, Hubert R. 1907- *WhoAm 92*
Gallagher, Hugh *BioIn 17*
Gallagher, Hugh Gregory 1932- *WhoAm 92*
Gallagher, J. Patrick 1952- *St&PR 93*
Gallagher, J. Richard *Law&B 92*
Gallagher, Jack Burt 1947- *WhoEmL 93*
Gallagher, Jack M. 1936- *St&PR 93*
Gallagher, James D. *Law&B 92*
Gallagher, James E. 1920- *St&PR 93*
Gallagher, James G. *Law&B 92*
Gallagher, James Michael 1941- *WhoSSW 93*
Gallagher, James Paul 1948- *St&PR 93*
Gallagher, James Wes 1911- *WhoAm 92*
Gallagher, Joan Frances 1939- *WhoAmW 93*
Gallagher, Joel Peter 1942- *WhoSSW 93*
Gallagher, John A. 1955- *MiSFD 9*
Gallagher, John Austin 1935- *St&PR 93*
Gallagher, John Francis *WhoAm 92*
Gallagher, John J. d1991 *BioIn 17*
Gallagher, John Joseph 1943- *WhoAm 92*
Gallagher, John Joseph, Jr. 1940- *WhoSSW 93*
Gallagher, John P. 1927- *St&PR 93*
Gallagher, John Paul 1947- *WhoEmL 93*
Gallagher, John Pirie 1916- *WhoAm 92*
Gallagher, John Robert, Jr. 1941- *WhoWor 93*
Gallagher, John Sill, III 1947- *WhoAm 92*
Gallagher, John Thomas 1935- *St&PR 93*
Gallagher, John William 1948- *St&PR 93*
Gallagher, Joseph *BioIn 17*
Gallagher, Joseph Francis 1926- *WhoAm 92*
Gallagher, Karen 1948- *WhoWrEP 92*
Gallagher, Kathleen E. 1949- *WhoE 93*
Gallagher, Kathleen J. *Law&B 92*
Gallagher, Kevin C. *Law&B 92*
Gallagher, Kevin M. 1932- *WhoIns 93*
Gallagher, Kim *BlkAmWO*
Gallagher, Kimberly J. *Law&B 92*
Gallagher, Lacey Wingham 1962- *St&PR 93*
Gallagher, Leslieann *Law&B 92*
Gallagher, Lindy Allyn 1954- *WhoAmW 93, WhoE 93, WhoEmL 93*
Gallagher, Lorie Miller 1962- *WhoEmL 93*
Gallagher, Mark J. 1954- *St&PR 93*
Gallagher, Mary Beth 1946- *WhoWrEP 92*
Gallagher, Matthew Philip, Jr. 1944- *WhoSSW 93*
Gallagher, Michael Gerald *Law&B 92*
Gallagher, Michael Patrick 1958- *WhoEmL 93*
Gallagher, Michael Paul *BioIn 17*
Gallagher, Michael R. *St&PR 93*
Gallagher, Michael Robert 1946- *WhoAm 92*
Gallagher, Nancy Anne 1952- *WhoAmW 93*
Gallagher, Patricia C. 1957- *ConAu 138*
Gallagher, Patricia Cecilia *WhoWrEP 92*
Gallagher, Patrick 1873-1964 *BioIn 17*
Gallagher, Paul F. *Law&B 92*
Gallagher, Paul Francis *Law&B 92*
Gallagher, Paul Thomas 1928- *St&PR 93*
Gallagher, Paula Marie 1959- *WhoAmW 93*
Gallagher, Paula Marie 1964- *WhoAmW 93*
Gallagher, Phil C. 1926- *WhoIns 93*
Gallagher, R.R. 1940- *St&PR 93*
Gallagher, Rachel Mary *WhoAmW 93*
Gallagher, Raymond J. 1912-1991 *BioIn 17*
Gallagher, Richard Edward 1929- *St&PR 93*
Gallagher, Richard Hugo 1927- *WhoAm 92*
Gallagher, Rita Munley *WhoAmW 93*
Gallagher, Robert C. 1938- *St&PR 93*
Gallagher, Robert Edmond 1923- *St&PR 93*
Gallagher, Robert Francis 1934- *St&PR 93, WhoAm 92*
Gallagher, Sean 1955- *WhoE 93*
Gallagher, Stephen 1954- *ConAu 138, ScF&FL 92*
Gallagher, Steve *ScF&FL 92*
Gallagher, Susan VanZanten 1955- *ConAu 137*
Gallagher, Terence Joseph *Law&B 92*
Gallagher, Terence Joseph 1934- *St&PR 93, WhoAm 92*
Gallagher, Terrence Vincent 1946- *WhoAm 92*
Gallagher, Tess *BioIn 17*
Gallagher, Tess 1943- *DcLB 120 [port], WhoWrEP 92*
Gallagher, Theorode Joseph *Law&B 92*
Gallagher, Thomas 1918-1992 *NewYTBS 92*
Gallagher, Thomas C. 1948- *WhoSSW 93*
Gallagher, Thomas French 1939- *WhoE 93*
Gallagher, Thomas J. 1949- *St&PR 93, WhoIns 93*
Gallagher, Thomas Joseph 1949- *WhoAm 92, WhoE 93*
Gallagher, Thomas R. *Law&B 92*
Gallagher, Thomas W. *Law&B 92*
Gallagher, Tom 1944- *WhoAm 92, WhoSSW 93*
Gallagher, Vera 1917- *ConAu 38NR*
Gallagher, Vicki Morin 1948- *WhoAmW 93*
Gallagher, Vicki Smith 1950- *WhoSSW 93*
Gallagher, Vincent Patrick 1945- *St&PR 93*
Gallagher, Walter B. 1912- *St&PR 93*
Gallagher, Walter Edward 1910- *WhoAm 92*
Gallagher, Wes 1911- *DcLB 127 [port]*
Gallagher, William P. 1940- *St&PR 93*
Gallahan, John Martin 1956- *St&PR 93*
Gallahan, Ronald Nelson 1950- *WhoSSW 93*
Gallaher, Cynthia 1953- *WhoWrEP 92*
Gallaher, Frank F. 1946- *St&PR 93*
Gallaher, James A. 1947- *St&PR 93*
Gallaher, (William) Rhea, Jr. 1945- *ConAu 136*
Gallaire, Herve 1944- *WhoScE 91-3*
Gallais, Andre 1940- *WhoScE 91-2*
Gallais, Fernand Georges 1908- *WhoWor 93*
Gallamore-Capes, Betty Lou 1951- *WhoEmL 93*
Galland, Adolf 1912- *BioIn 17, HarEnMi*
Galland, China *BioIn 17*
Galland, Jacques 1935- *WhoScE 91-2*
Galland, Leo 1943- *WhoE 93*
Galland, R.I. 1916- *St&PR 93*
Gallander, Cathleen Sparks 1931- *WhoAmW 93*
Gallant, Brian J. 1955- *WhoE 93*
Gallant, Edgar 1924- *WhoAm 92*
Gallant, Esther May 1943- *WhoAmW 93*
Gallant, Francis X. 1928- *St&PR 93*
Gallant, George William 1931- *WhoE 93*
Gallant, Herbert 1922- *St&PR 93*
Gallant, James Jerome 1950- *WhoE 93*
Gallant, James T. 1937- *WhoWrEP 92*
Gallant, Mavis *BioIn 17*
Gallant, Mavis 1922- *WhoAm 92, WhoAmW 93, WhoCanL 92*
Gallant, Pamela L. 1942- *WhoWrEP 92*
Gallant, Roy A. *BioIn 17*
Gallant, Roy A(rthur) 1924- *MajAI [port]*
Gallant, Sylvie *Law&B 92*
Gallant, Thomas Grady, III 1948- *WhoEmL 93*
Galla Placidia 388?-450 *OxDcByz*
Gallardo, Gervasio 1934- *ScF&FL 92*
Gallardo, Juan 1947- *St&PR 93*
Gallardo, Sara 1931-1988 *BioIn 17, SpAmA*
Gallardo-Lancho, Juan F. 1945- *WhoScE 91-3*
Galla-Rini, Anthony 1904- *Baker 92*
Gallarini, Luciano 1932- *WhoWor 93*
Gallas, Daniel Otis 1931- *St&PR 93*
Gallas, George S. *Law&B 92*
Gallas, Matthias 1584-1647 *HarEnMi*
Gallas, Nesta Mabyn 1917- *WhoAmW 93*
Gallas, Pio Cabanillas 1923-1991 *BioIn 17*
Gallas, William Edward *Law&B 92*
Gallassero, Hilda Kilmer 1928- *WhoWrEP 92*
Gallatin, Albert 1761-1849 *IntDcAn, PolPar*
Gallatin, Albert E. 1939- *St&PR 93*
Gallatin, Ronald L. 1945- *St&PR 93*
Gallatin, Sue Ann 1955- *St&PR 93*
Gallaudet, Denison 1944- *St&PR 93*
Gallaugher, Barbara Alice 1950- *WhoAmW 93*
Gallavan, Kendra M. *Law&B 92*
Gallavotti, Giovanni 1941- *WhoScE 91-3*
Galle, Emile 1846-1904 *BioIn 17*
Galle, Fred Charles 1919- *WhoAm 92*
Galle, Per 1950- *WhoWor 93*
Galle, Richard Lynn 1947- *WhoAm 92*
Galle, Yvonne 1885-1972 *Baker 92*
Gallegly, Elton 1944- *CngDr 91*
Gallegly, Elton William 1944- *WhoAm 92*
Gallego, Donato Sitao 1944- *WhoWor 93*
Gallego, Gerald *BioIn 17*
Gallego, Ignacio *BioIn 17*
Gallego-Juarez, Juan Antonio 1941- *WhoWor 93*
Gallegos, Andres Moises 1929- *WhoWor 93*
Gallegos, Jose Manuel 1815-1875 *HispAmA*
Gallegos, Jose Ramon *St&PR 93*
Gallegos, R. Thomas *Law&B 92*
Gallegos, Romulo 1884-1969 *BioIn 17, SpAmA*
Gallegos, Russell J. 1932- *St&PR 93*
Gallegos, Tony Eismail 1924- *WhoAm 92*
Gallegos Lara, Joaquin 1909-1947 *SpAmA*
Galleher, Helen *AmWomPl*
Gallemore, Sandra Lucile 1942- *WhoSSW 93*
Gallen, Joel A. 1957- *WhoAm 92*
Gallen, Sue S. 1931- *WhoAm 92*
Gallenberg, Wenzel Robert, Graf von 1783-1839 *Baker 92*
Gallenberger, Clara 1929- *St&PR 93*
Galleno, Anthony M. 1942- *St&PR 93*
Galleno, Anthony Massimo 1942- *WhoAm 92, WhoE 93, WhoWor 93*
Galleno, Humberto 1943- *WhoWor 93*
Gallenti, Vincent James 1948- *WhoE 93*
Gallerano, A.J. *Law&B 92*
Gallerano, Andrew John 1941- *St&PR 93, WhoAm 92*
Gallery, Daniel V. 1901-1977 *ScF&FL 92*
Gallery, Sharon Mendelson 1953- *WhoWrEP 92*
Galles, Jose 1761-1836 *Baker 92*
Gallet, J.P. 1943- *WhoScE 91-2*
Gallet, Louis 1835-1898 *IntDcOp, OxDcOp*
Galletly, Donald *St&PR 93*
Galletly, Gerard Duncan *WhoScE 91-1*
Galletta, Nunzio 1927- *WhoE 93*
Galletti, Giovanni 1926- *WhoScE 91-3*
Galletti, Pierre Marie 1927- *WhoAm 92, WhoE 93*
Galletto, Dionigi 1932- *WhoScE 91-3*
Galley, Tom C. 1955- *St&PR 93*
Galley, Violet Ursula *WhoE 93*
Galli, Amintore 1845-1919 *Baker 92*
Galli, Caterina c. 1723-1804 *OxDcOp*
Galli, Claudio *WhoScE 91-3*
Galli, Enrica 1938- *WhoScE 91-3*
Galli, Ermanno 1937- *WhoScE 91-3*
Galli, Filippo 1783-1853 *Baker 92, OxDcOp*
Galli, Giovanni 1625-1665 *OxDcOp*
Galli, Robert E. *Law&B 92*
Galli, Robert G. 1933- *St&PR 93*
Galli, Vicenzo 1798-1858 *OxDcOp*
Gallia, Jay L. *Law&B 92*
Gallian, Russell Joseph 1948- *WhoWor 93*
Gallian, Virginia Anne 1933- *WhoAmW 93*
Galliard, Johann Ernst c. 1680-1749 *Baker 92*
Galliard, John Ernest c. 1687-1749 *OxDcOp*
Galliard, Terence 1939- *WhoScE 91-1*
Galliari, Bernardino 1707-1794 *OxDcOp*
Galliari, Fabrizio 1709-1790 *OxDcOp*
Galliari, Giovanni Antonio 1714-1783 *OxDcOp*
Galliari, Giovannino 1746-1818 *OxDcOp*
Galliari, Giuseppino 1742-1817 *OxDcOp*
Galli-Bibiena, Alessandro 1686-1748 *OxDcOp*
Galli-Bibiena, Antonio 1697?-1774 *OxDcOp*
Galli-Bibiena, Carlo 1721?-1787 *OxDcOp*
Galli-Bibiena, Ferdinando 1656-1743 *OxDcOp*
Galli-Bibiena, Francesco 1659-1737 *OxDcOp*
Galli-Bibiena, Giovanni Carlo c. 1720-1760 *OxDcOp*
Galli-Bibiena, Giovanni Maria 1694-1777 *OxDcOp*
Galli-Bibiena, Giuseppe 1695-1757 *OxDcOp*
Gallicchio, David Michael 1943- *WhoE 93*
Gallichio, Kathleen Anne 1955- *WhoAm 92, WhoAmW 93*
Gallico, Leo 1919- *WhoScE 91-3*
Gallico, Paolo 1868-1955 *Baker 92*
Gallico, Paul 1897-1976 *ScF&FL 92*
Gallico, Paul (William) 1897-1976 *MajAI [port]*
Galli-Curci, Amelita 1882-1963 *Baker 92, IntDcOp, OxDcOp*
Gallieni, Joseph Simon 1849-1916 *HarEnMi*
Galliera, Alceo 1910- *Baker 92*
Galliffet, Gaston Alexandre Auguste, marquis de 1830-1909 *BioIn 17*
Galligan, Edward L. 1926- *WhoWrEP 92*
Galligan, Mary Margaret 1945- *WhoAmW 93*
Galligan, Thomas Joseph, III 1944- *St&PR 93, WhoAm 92*
Gallignani, Giuseppe 1851-1923 *Baker 92*
Galligo, Jose 1951- *WhoScE 91-3*
Galliher, Charles E., IV 1958- *St&PR 93*
Galliher, Michael B. 1959- *St&PR 93*
Galliker, Franz 1926- *WhoWor 93*
Gallimard, Claude 1914-1991 *AnObit 1991, BioIn 17*
Galli-Marie, Celestine 1840-1905 *Baker 92, OxDcOp*
Galli-Marie, Celestine Laurence 1840-1905 *IntDcOp*
Gallimore, David Alfred 1939- *St&PR 93*
Gallimore, Robert Stephenson 1920- *WhoAm 92*
Gallin, Christopher H. *St&PR 93*
Gallin, John C. 1941- *St&PR 93*
Gallina, Charles Onofrio 1943- *WhoWor 93*
Gallinaro, Nicholas Francis 1930- *St&PR 93, WhoWor 93*
Galliner, Peter 1920- *WhoWor 93*
Galling, Gottfried 1937- *WhoScE 91-3*
Gallinger, Kurt D. *Law&B 92*
Gallinger, Lois Mae 1922- *WhoAm 92, WhoAmW 93*
Gallinot, Ruth Maxine 1925- *WhoAmW 93, WhoWor 93*
Gallipo, James Joseph 1946- *St&PR 93*
Gallisa, Carlos *DcCPCAm*
Gallis-Quednau, Marion Elisabeth 1934- *WhoUN 92*
Gallitto, Robyn R. 1962- *WhoAmW 93*
Gallivan, Karen Park *Law&B 92*
Gallivan, Sarah M. *Law&B 92*
Gallman, Clarence Hunter 1922- *WhoAm 92*
Gallman, David Eugene 1939- *St&PR 93*
Gallman, John Gerry 1938- *WhoAm 92*
Gallman, Robert Emil 1926- *WhoAm 92*
Gallmann, Peter Urs 1952- *WhoScE 91-4*
Gallmeyer, Charles C. 1948- *St&PR 93*
Gallo, Adam Andrew *Law&B 92*
Gallo, Amy Lynn 1966- *WhoAmW 93*
Gallo, David R. *Law&B 92*
Gallo, Dean A. 1935- *CngDr 91*
Gallo, Dean Anderson 1935- *WhoAm 92, WhoE 93*
Gallo, Dennis 1951- *St&PR 93*
Gallo, Diane 1949- *WhoWrEP 92*
Gallo, Donald Robert 1938- *WhoWrEP 92*
Gallo, Elissa E. *Law&B 92*

Gallo, Ernest BioIn 17
Gallo, Ernest 1909- WhoAm 92
Gallo, Faith Philippbar 1937- WhoAm 92
Gallo, Fortune 1878-1970 Baker 92
Gallo, Francis Carl 1943- WhoE 93
Gallo, Fred MiSFD 9
Gallo, Frederick S. 1944- St&PR 93
Gallo, George MiSFD 9
Gallo, Gerald Peter 1952- St&PR 93
Gallo, James Andrew 1950- WhoEmL 93
Gallo, Joseph, Jr. 1944- WhoE 93
Gallo, Joseph Charles 1950- WhoEmL 93
Gallo, Joseph J. Law&B 92
Gallo, Joseph John 1959- WhoSSW 93
Gallo, Julio BioIn 17
Gallo, Julio 1910- WhoAm 92
Gallo, Louis Jacob 1945- WhoWrEP 92
Gallo, Luiz Antonio 1952- WhoWor 93
Gallo, Matthew Joseph Law&B 92
Gallo, Max 1932- BioIn 17
Gallo, Nicholas A., III 1940- St&PR 93
Gallo, Patrick J. 1937- ConAu 139
Gallo, Robert C. BioIn 17
Gallo, Robert Charles 1937- WhoAm 92, WhoWor 93
Gallo, Samuel J. Law&B 92
Gallo, Sebastian John 1932- WhoE 93
Gallo, Teresa L. WhoAm 92, WhoAmW 93
Gallo, Vincent John 1943- WhoSSW 93
Gallo, William Victor 1922- WhoAm 92
Gallof, Steven 1946- St&PR 93
Gallogly, Aimee 1955- St&PR 93
Gallogly, Barry Andrew 1952- WhoEmL 93
Gallogly, Vincent Law&B 92
Gallogly, William W. Law&B 92
Gallois, A. Paul WhoScE 91-1
Gallois-Montbrun, Raymond 1918- Baker 92
Gallon, Jean 1878-1959 Baker 92
Gallon, Noel 1891-1966 Baker 92
Galloney, Frank H., III 1935- St&PR 93
Gallop, Jane Anne 1952- WhoAm 92
Gallop, John C. 1943- WhoScE 91-1
Gallop, John R. St&PR 93
Gallop, Richard C. 1938-1989 BioIn 17
Galloping Gourmet BioIn 17
Gallot, Philippe Eric 1961- WhoWor 93
Gallot, Yves Georges Charles 1936- WhoScE 91-2
Gallou-Dumiel, Elisabeth Sylvie 1948- WhoWor 93
Galloway, Alene Marsha 1949- WhoEmL 93
Galloway, Beth Anne 1953- WhoAmW 93
Galloway, Bruce 1952- ScF&FL 92
Galloway, Carl H. 1955- St&PR 93
Galloway, David Alexander 1943- WhoAm 92
Galloway, David D(arryl) 1937- ConAu 37NR
Galloway, David Darryl 1937- WhoWor 93
Galloway, Edward L. Law&B 92
Galloway, Eilene Marie 1906- WhoE 93
Galloway, Ethan Charles 1930- St&PR 93, WhoAm 92
Galloway, Gale Lee 1930- WhoSSW 93
Galloway, Gerald E., Jr. 1935- WhoAm 92
Galloway, Harvey S., Jr. 1934- WhoIns 93
Galloway, Harvey Scott, Jr. 1934- St&PR 93, WhoAm 92
Galloway, Helen A. 1925- WhoAmW 93
Galloway, Jackie BioIn 17
Galloway, Janice 1956- ConAu 137
Galloway, Kenneth Franklin 1941- WhoAm 92
Galloway, Lillian Carroll 1934- WhoAmW 93
Galloway, Norval B. Law&B 92
Galloway, Patricia Denese 1957- WhoEmL 93
Galloway, Patricia Kay 1945- WhoAm 92
Galloway, Paul Newton 1959- WhoSSW 93
Galloway, Paul V. 1904-1990 BioIn 17
Galloway, Peter S. Law&B 92
Galloway, Priscilla 1930- BioIn 17, WhoCanL 92
Galloway, Richard H. 1940- WhoWor 93
Galloway, Robert Michael 1946- WhoEmL 93
Galloway, Robert Morton 1927- St&PR 93
Galloway, Stanley Auburn 1959- WhoWrEP 92
Galloway, Thomas F. 1939- St&PR 93
Galloway, William Jefferson 1922- WhoAm 92
Galloway, William Joyce 1924- WhoAm 92
Gallu, Samuel G. d1991 BioIn 17
Gallucci, Kathryn McClanahan 1963- WhoE 93
Gallucci, Sheila S. Law&B 92
Gallun, Raymond Z. 1911- BioIn 17, ScF&FL 92
Gallup, Alan Francis 1953- St&PR 93
Gallup, Charles E. Law&B 92
Gallup, Dick 1941- WhoWrEP 92
Gallup, Donald Clifford 1913- WhoAm 92
Gallup, Frank James 1936- St&PR 93
Gallup, George 1901-1984 PolPar
Gallup, George Horace 1901- JrnUS
Gallup, Grant Morris 1932- WhoWrEP 92
Gallup, Howard Frederick 1927- WhoE 93
Gallup, Jane Harrington 1949- WhoEmL 93
Gallup, Janet Louise 1951- WhoAmW 93
Gallup, John G. 1927- St&PR 93
Gallup, John Gardiner 1927- WhoAm 92
Gallup, John Young, II 1955- WhoE 93
Gallup, Stephen Edmonds 1950- WhoWrEP 92
Gallups, Vivian Lylay Bess 1954- WhoAmW 93, WhoSSW 93
Gallus 325?-354 OxDcByz
Gallus, Aelius fl. c. 25BC- Expl 93
Gallus, Johannes dc. 1543 Baker 92
Gallus (Petelin), Jacobus 1550-1591 Baker 92
Gallusser, Werner Arnold 1929- WhoWor 93
Galluzzo, Camilla 1951- St&PR 93
Gallwitz, Dieter WhoScE 91-3
Gallwitz, Max von 1852-1932 HarEnMi
Gally, Julius 1928- WhoScE 91-4
Gally C., Hector 1942- DcMexL
Galmarini, Claudio Romulo 1962- WhoWor 93
Galnick, Mitchell Neil 1953- WhoEmL 93
Galoozis, George T. 1931- St&PR 93
Galoppini, Carlo 1924- WhoScE 91-3
Gal-Or, Esther 1951- WhoEmL 93
Galore, Mamie 1940- BioIn 17
Galotti, Donna BioIn 17
Galotti, Donna 1955- WhoAm 92, WhoAmW 93, WhoE 93
Galotti, Ronald WhoAm 92
Galovic, Thomas A. St&PR 93
Galowich, Ronald H. 1936- St&PR 93
Galowitch-Janus, Susan St&PR 93
Galper, Hal BioIn 17
Galperin, Boris 1952- WhoSSW 93
Galphin, Bruce Maxwell 1932- WhoWrEP 92
Galpin, Francis W(illiam) 1858-1945 Baker 92
Galpine, Maurice David 1936- St&PR 93
Galskoy, Constantin BioIn 17
Galsky, Desidir d1990 BioIn 17
Galston, Arthur William 1920- WhoAm 92
Galston, Clarence E. 1909- WhoIns 93
Galston, Clarence Elkus 1909- WhoAm 92
Galston, Gottfried 1879-1950 Baker 92
Galston, Nancy Lee 1954- WhoEmL 93
Galsworthy, John 1867-1933 BioIn 17, TwCLC 45 [port], WorLitC [port]
Galt, Anthony H(oward) 1944- ConAu 137
Galt, Barry J. 1933- St&PR 93, WhoAm 92
Galt, John 1779-1839 BioIn 17, DcLB 116 [port]
Galt, John Kirtland 1920- WhoAm 92
Galt, John William 1940- WhoAm 92
Galt, Thomas F., Jr. 1908- WhoWrEP 92
Galt, Thomas M. 1921- St&PR 93
Galterio, Joseph Albert 1923- St&PR 93
Galterio, Louis 1951- WhoE 93
Galterio, Robert John 1957- WhoE 93
Galtieri, Leopold Fortunato 1926- DcTwHis
Galton, David Jeremy WhoScE 91-1
Galton, Glenn Law&B 92
Galton, Peter Malcolm 1942- WhoE 93
Galton, Valerie Anne 1934- WhoAm 92, WhoE 93
Galuppi, Baldassare 1706-1785 Baker 92, IntDcOp, OxDcOp
Galvan, Elias Gabriel 1938- WhoAm 92
Galvan, Robert A. 1923- WhoWrEP 92
Galvani, Christiane Mesch 1954- WhoSSW 93
Galvani, Giacomo 1825-1889 Baker 92
Galvanin, Robert BioIn 17
Galvan Llopis, Vicente 1949- WhoScE 91-3
Galvao, Julio Pistacchini WhoScE 91-3
Galve-Basilio, Enrique 1954- WhoWor 93
Galvez, Bernardo de 1746-1786 BioIn 17
Galvez, Juan F. 1937- WhoScE 91-3
Galvez, Juan Manuel DcCPCAm
Galvez, Manuel 1887-1962 SpAmA
Galvez, Matthew S. St&PR 93
Galvin, Aaron Abraham 1932- WhoE 93
Galvin, Brendan James 1938- WhoWrEP 92
Galvin, Brian Christopher 1950- WhoE 93
Galvin, Charles O'Neill 1919- WhoAm 92
Galvin, Donald A. 1958- St&PR 93
Galvin, Edward Patrick 1933- WhoWor 93
Galvin, James Norman 1947- St&PR 93, WhoAm 92
Galvin, Jane Foulkrod 1946- WhoAmW 93
Galvin, John BioIn 17
Galvin, John Rogers 1929- WhoAm 92
Galvin, Joseph Mannion 1907- St&PR 93
Galvin, Judith Ann 1963- WhoAmW 93
Galvin, Kerry Anne Law&B 92
Galvin, Louise Leonard 1947- WhoE 93
Galvin, Maryanne 1954- WhoE 93, WhoWrEP 92
Galvin, Michael John, Jr. 1930- WhoAm 92
Galvin, Paul 1895-1959 BioIn 17
Galvin, Robert W. BioIn 17
Galvin, Robert W. 1922- St&PR 93
Galvin, Thomas F. Law&B 92
Galvin, Thomas John 1932- WhoAm 92
Galvin, Thomas Joseph 1938- St&PR 93
Galvis, Julio C. Law&B 92
Galway, James 1939- Baker 92, WhoAm 92, WhoWor 93
Galwey, Andrew Knox WhoScE 91-1
Galy, Jean 1938- WhoScE 91-2
Galya, Thomas Andrew 1947- WhoSSW 93
Galyean, George Ellsworth 1940- St&PR 93
Galyean, Howard J. 1930- St&PR 93
Galyean, Roy Allen 1942- St&PR 93
Galyon, Betty Joyce 1935- St&PR 93
Galyon, James Raymond 1929- WhoWor 93
Galzy, Pierre 1929- WhoScE 91-2
Gama, Cristovao da 1516-1542 HarEnMi
Gamache, Kathleen Anne 1956- WhoEmL 93
Gamache, R. Donald 1935- St&PR 93
Gamache, Richard A. 1944- St&PR 93
Gamar, Reginald William 1936- WhoE 93, WhoWor 93
Gamarnik, Moisey Yankelevich 1936- WhoWor 93
Gamba, Piero 1936- Baker 92
Gambacorta, Agata 1946- WhoScE 91-3
Gambal, David 1931- WhoAm 92
Gambale, Anthony J. 1927- St&PR 93
Gambale, Frank BioIn 17
Gambardella, Rosemary WhoAmW 93
Gambari, Ibrahim Agboola 1944- WhoAfr, WhoUN 92
Gambarini, Grazia Lavinia 1942- WhoWor 93
Gambaro, Griselda BioIn 17
Gambaro, Thomas M. 1932- St&PR 93
Gambarova, Pietro G. 1941- WhoScE 91-3
Gambatese, John Francis 1937- St&PR 93
Gambee, Bonnie Ford 1932- WhoAmW 93
Gambee, Eleanor Brown 1904- WhoAmW 93
Gambee, Robert Rankin 1942- WhoAm 92
Gambell, Ray 1935- WhoScE 91-1
Gamberale, Francesco 1933- WhoScE 91-4
Gambero, Darrell J. WhoIns 93
Gambet, Daniel George 1929- WhoAm 92
Gambetta, Leon 1838-1882 BioIn 17
Gambill, Barbara F. Law&B 92
Gambill, Ben S., Jr. 1945- St&PR 93
Gambill, Malcolm W. WhoAm 92, WhoE 93
Gambill, Malcolm W. 1930- St&PR 93
Gambill, R. Brent Law&B 92
Gambill, Ted R. 1948- St&PR 93
Gambill, Terry A. 1942- St&PR 93
Gambino, Diane R. WhoWrEP 92
Gambino, Robert William 1926- WhoAm 92
Gambino, Salvatore Raymond 1926- WhoAm 92
Gamble, Alvan 1916- WhoE 93
Gamble, Carol A. Law&B 92
Gamble, Charles W.K. Law&B 92
Gamble, Charles W.K. 1932- St&PR 93
Gamble, David BioIn 17
Gamble, David John 1949- St&PR 93
Gamble, Donald G.B. Law&B 92
Gamble, Edward James 1929- WhoAm 92
Gamble, Frances Nell Earle 1910- WhoAmW 93
Gamble, George Clinton 1910- WhoAm 92
Gamble, Hazel V. AmWomPl
Gamble, James 1803?- BioIn 17
Gamble, John Marshall 1863-1957 BioIn 17
Gamble, Kamy Rayburn 1960- WhoAmW 93
Gamble, Kenneth Gregory 1940- WhoAm 92
Gamble, Malcolm Robert 1937- WhoScE 91-1
Gamble, Mary Grace 1950- WhoEmL 93, WhoSSW 93
Gamble, Mary Rolofson AmWomPl
Gamble, Michael I. 1935- St&PR 93
Gamble, Norman Law&B 92
Gamble, Paul 1911- WhoE 93
Gamble, Paul Robert WhoScE 91-1
Gamble, Ranelle A. Law&B 92
Gamble, Ross A. 1938- St&PR 93
Gamble, Theodore Robert, Jr. 1953- WhoE 93, WhoEmL 93, WhoWor 93
Gamble, Thomas Ranshaw 1942- St&PR 93
Gamble, William Belser, Jr. 1925- WhoSSW 93
Gamble & Huff SoulM
Gamblin, James E. 1954- WhoSSW 93
Gamblin, Julie Ann Law&B 92
Gambling, W. Alec WhoScE 91-1
Gambling, William Alexander 1926- WhoWor 93
Gamboa, Federico 1864-1939 DcMexL
Gamboa, George Charles 1923- WhoAm 92
Gamboa, Jose Joaquin 1878-1931 DcMexL
Gamboa, Joseph C. 1951- WhoAmW 93
Gamboa, Reymundo 1948- DcLB 122 [port], WhoWrEP 92
Gambolati, Giuseppe 1944- WhoWor 93
Gambon, Michael BioIn 17
Gambone, Joseph Robert, Jr. 1953- St&PR 93
Gambrel, John, Mrs. AmWomPl
Gambrell, David Henry 1929- WhoAm 92
Gambrell, James Bruton, III 1926- WhoAm 92
Gambrell, James Bruton, IV 1959- WhoSSW 93
Gambrell, Jamey BioIn 17
Gambrell, Luck Flanders 1930- WhoAmW 93
Gambrell, Richard Donald, Jr. 1931- WhoAm 92, WhoSSW 93, WhoWor 93
Gambrell, Sarah Belk 1918- WhoAmW 93
Gambro, Michael S. 1954- WhoAm 92
Gambs, Carl M. 1943- St&PR 93
Gambulos, James C., III 1954- WhoSSW 93
Gambuti, Gary 1937- WhoAm 92
Gambuto, Elizabeth Anne 1966- WhoE 93
Game, Ramona Griffin 1940- WhoAmW 93
Gamel, Thomas W. 1940- St&PR 93
Gamel, Wendell W. 1929- St&PR 93
Gamel, Wendell Wesley 1929- WhoAm 92
Gamel, William Glenn 1936- WhoSSW 93
Gamelin, Maurice Gustave 1872-1958 DcTwHis, HarEnMi
Gamerith, Horst WhoScE 91-4
Games, David Edgar WhoScE 91-1
Games, Donald W. 1924- St&PR 93
Games, Robert F. 1930- WhoSSW 93
Games, Sonia BioIn 17
Gamet, Donald Max 1916- WhoAm 92, WhoWor 93
Gamewell, William T. 1949- St&PR 93
Gamez, Robert BioIn 17
Gaminitilake, Semage Donald Edmund 1950- WhoWor 93
Gamino, John Law&B 92
Gamio, Manuel 1883-1960 IntDcAn
Gamm, Marilyn Sue 1961- WhoAmW 93
Gammage, Andre AfrAmBi
Gammage, Robert Alton 1938- WhoAm 92, WhoSSW 93
Gammelgaard, Jorgen 1938-1991 BioIn 17
Gammell, Frances Howland 1949- St&PR 93
Gammell, Gloria Ruffner 1948- WhoAmW 93, WhoEmL 93
Gammell, Leon 1936- ScF&FL 92
Gammell, Stephen 1943- BioIn 17, MajAI [port]
Gammie, Anthony 1934- St&PR 93
Gammie, Anthony Petrie 1934- WhoE 93
Gammill, Darryl Curtis 1950- WhoEmL 93
Gammill, John Stewart 1923- WhoIns 93
Gammill, Lee M., Jr. 1934- WhoIns 93
Gammill, Lee Morgan 1934- St&PR 93
Gammill, Lee Morgan, Jr. 1934- WhoAm 92
Gammill, Martha Ann Law&B 92
Gammill, Noreen Ellers AmWomPl
Gammill, William 1949- WhoWrEP 92
Gammon, Elizabeth Ann 1946- WhoAmW 93
Gammon, Garry Brent Law&B 92
Gammon, Jack Albert 1950- WhoSSW 93
Gammon, James Alan 1934- WhoAm 92
Gammon, Joy ScF&FL 92
Gammon, Malcolm Ernest, Sr. 1947- WhoSSW 93, WhoWor 93
Gammon, Samuel Rhea, III 1924- WhoAm 92
Gammons, Kevin Trafton Law&B 92
Gammons, Peter 1945- BiDAMSp 1989
Gammons, Peter T., Jr. 1936- WhoIns 93
Gammons, Robert C. 1945- St&PR 93
Gamoneda, Francisco 1873-1953 DcMexL
Gamota, George 1939- WhoAm 92
Gamow, George 1904-1968 BioIn 17
Gampel, Elaine Susan 1950- WhoAmW 93
Gamrasni, M.A. 1938- WhoScE 91-2
Gamron, W. Anthony 1948- St&PR 93, WhoAm 92

Gams, Andrija 1911- *WhoWor 93*
Gamsakhurdia, Zviad *BioIn 17*
Gamsin, Sharon L. 1949- *WhoAmW 93*
Gamson, Anita Gordon 1917- *WhoE 93*
Gamson, Bernard William 1917- *WhoAm 92*
Gamson, Zelda Finkelstein 1936- *WhoAm 92*
Gamwell, C.C. 1924- *St&PR 93*
Gamwell, Lynn 1943- *WhoE 93*
Gamzon, Robert 1926- *St&PR 93*
Gamzu, Elkan R. *St&PR 93*
Gan, Kong Chin 1956- *St&PR 93*
Ganas, Jane Andrew 1942- *WhoWrEP 92*
Ganas, Perry Spiros 1937- *WhoAm 92*
Gance, Abel 1889-1981 *MiSFD 9N*
Gancedo, Carlos 1940- *WhoScE 91-3*
Gancer, Donald Charles 1933- *WhoAm 92*
Ganche, Edouard 1880-1945 *Baker 92*
Gancher, David Arthur 1943- *WhoAm 92*
Ganchev, Kostadin 1941- *WhoScE 91-4*
Ganchrow, Mandell I. 1937- *WhoE 93*
Ganci, James J. 1943- *St&PR 93*
Ganci, Paul J. 1938- *St&PR 93*
Ganczarczyk, Jerzy Jozef 1928- *WhoAm 92*
Gandal, Robert *Law&B 92*
Gandal, Robert 1928- *St&PR 93*
Gandarias, Patrick Alexander 1961- *WhoWor 93*
Gandelman, Robert James 1954- *WhoWor 93*
Gander, Forrest 1956- *WhoWrEP 92*
Gander, John Edward 1925- *WhoAm 92*
Ganderton, David *WhoScE 91-1*
Gandevia, Bryan Harle 1925- *WhoWor 93*
Gandhi, Bharat 1942- *St&PR 93*
Gandhi, Bharat R. 1942- *WhoAm 92*
Gandhi, Indira 1917-1984 *BioIn 17, ColdWar 2 [port], DcTwHis*
Gandhi, Joyatindra Poonam 1956- *WhoWor 93*
Gandhi, Kishore 1939- *ScF&FL 92*
Gandhi, Mahatma 1869-1948 *BioIn 17*
Gandhi, Malini Ravi 1954- *WhoWor 93*
Gandhi, Mohandas Karamchand 1869-1948 *BioIn 17, DcTwHis*
Gandhi, Om Parkash 1934- *WhoAm 92*
Gandhi, Priyanka *BioIn 17*
Gandhi, Rahul *BioIn 17*
Gandhi, Rajiv 1944- *WhoAsAP 91*
Gandhi, Rajiv 1944-1991 *AnObit 1991, BioIn 17, DcTwHis*
Gandhi, Sonia 1947- *BioIn 17*
Gandin, Andrew Mackay *Law&B 92*
Gandini, Gerardo 1932- *Baker 92*
Gandini, Marcello *BioIn 17*
Gandois, Jean Guy 1930- *WhoAm 92*
Gandolf, Raymond L. 1930- *WhoAm 92*
Gandolfi, Fred 1904-1990 *BioIn 17*
Gandolfi, Riccardo (Cristoforo Daniele Diomede) 1839-1920 *Baker 92*
Gandolfo, Giancarlo 1937- *WhoWor 93*
Gandrud, D.E. *St&PR 93*
Gandsey, Louis John 1921- *WhoWor 93*
Gandy, Bobby A. 1926- *St&PR 93*
Gandy, Charles David 1949- *WhoAm 92*
Gandy, Dean Murray 1927- *WhoAm 92*
Gandy, James Thomas 1952- *WhoSSW 93*
Gandy, Richard N. 1939- *St&PR 93*
Gandy-Diamond, Joyce Ann 1937- *WhoWor 93*
Gane, Margaret *WhoCanL 92*
Ganek, Marc E. *Law&B 92*
Ganeles, Jeffrey 1957- *WhoEmL 93*
Ganelin, Viacheslav 1944- *Baker 92*
Ganelius, Tord *WhoScE 91-4*
Ganelius, Tord Hjalmar 1925- *WhoWor 93*
Ganellin, Charon Robin *WhoScE 91-1*
Ganellin, Charon Robin 1934- *WhoWor 93*
Ganesan, Ann Katharine 1933- *WhoAm 92*
Ganeshwar Kusum 1934- *WhoAsAP 91*
Ganev, Stoyan 1955- *WhoWor 93*
Gang, Arthur *Law&B 92*
Gang, Lawrence N. *Law&B 92*
Gang, Mark Jay 1947- *WhoE 93*
Gang, Stephen 1951- *St&PR 93*
Gang, Stephen R. 1951- *WhoAm 92, WhoE 93*
Gangas, Nicholas-Hercule 1937- *WhoScE 91-3*
Gange, Charles A. 1948- *St&PR 93*
Gange, Fraser 1886-1962 *Baker 92*
Gangel, Carl A. *Law&B 92*
Gangel, Kenneth O(tto) 1935- *ConAu 39NR*
Gangemi, Kenneth 1937- *WhoWrEP 92*
Gangemi, Mary Anne 1954- *St&PR 93*
Ganger, Ira Jay 1952- *St&PR 93*
Ganger, J. Harold 1934- *St&PR 93*
Ganger, Robert M. d1992 *NewYTBS 92 [port]*
Ganger, Robert M. 1913-1992 *BioIn 17*
Gangi, Frank Joseph 1941- *St&PR 93*
Gangitano, Ernesto Sebastian 1948- *WhoEmL 93*
Gangl, Kenneth Richard 1945- *St&PR 93*
Gangloff, John Joseph 1942- *WhoAm 92*
Gangloff, Linda Lee 1942- *WhoAmW 93, WhoE 93*
Gang Lu d1991 *BioIn 17*
Gangnes, A.V. 1920- *St&PR 93*
Gang of Four *ConMus 8 [port], DcTwHis*
Gangolf, Andrew Lawrence, III *Law&B 92*
Gangolli, S.D. *WhoScE 91-1*
Gangone, Lynn M. 1957- *WhoE 93*
Gangopadhyay, Nirmal Kanti 1943- *WhoSSW 93*
Ganguly, Ashit Kumar 1934- *WhoE 93*
Ganguzza, Philip 1920- *St&PR 93*
Gangwal, Rakesh 1953- *St&PR 93, WhoAm 92*
Gani, Joseph Mark 1924- *WhoAm 92*
Gani, Marcel 1952- *St&PR 93*
Ganiere, Paul William 1922- *St&PR 93*
Ganiere, Robert C. 1936- *St&PR 93*
Ganilau, Penaia 1918- *WhoAsAP 91*
Ganilau, Penaia Kanatabatu 1918- *WhoWor 93*
Ganim, Joseph P. 1959- *WhoAm 92, WhoE 93*
Ganim, Ronald J. *Law&B 92*
Ganin, Saul 1921- *St&PR 93*
Ganin, Steven L. 1952- *St&PR 93*
Ganino, Anne Margaret 1964- *WhoAmW 93*
Ganja, Robert E. *Law&B 92*
Ganley, Glandys Dickens 1929- *WhoWrEP 92*
Ganley, James Francis 1935- *St&PR 93, WhoAm 92*
Ganley, James Powell 1937- *WhoAm 92, WhoSSW 93*
Ganley, Oswald Harold 1929- *WhoAm 92*
Ganley, Susan Anastasia 1957- *WhoE 93*
Ganley, W. Paul 1934- *ScF&FL 92*
Gann, Barbara Marie 1962- *WhoSSW 93*
Gann, Benard Wayne 1939- *WhoAm 92*
Gann, Edwin Doyle 1950- *WhoEmL 93*
Gann, Ernest K. 1910-1991 *ScF&FL 92*
Gann, Ernest Kellogg 1910- *WhoWrEP 92*
Gann, Ernest Kellogg 1910-1991 *BioIn 17, ConAu 136*
Gann, Jean Pope 1917- *WhoAmW 93*
Gann, Kenneth W. 1938- *St&PR 93*
Gann, Kyle (Eugene) 1955- *Baker 92*
Gann, Mark Stephen 1957- *WhoEmL 93, WhoSSW 93*
Gann, Richard George 1944- *WhoE 93*
Gann, Theresa Verlyn 1943- *WhoAmW 93*
Gannaway, Joann Pickering 1930- *WhoAmW 93*
Ganne, Louis Gaston 1862-1923 *Baker 92*
Gannello, Alfreda Mavis 1926- *WhoWrEP 92*
Gannett, Frank E. 1876-1957 *JrnUS*
Ganning, Bjorn 1938- *WhoScE 91-4*
Gannon, A.O. *WhoScE 91-3*
Gannon, Alice H. 1954- *WhoIns 93*
Gannon, Ann Ida 1915- *WhoAm 92, WhoAmW 93*
Gannon, Barbara Charlotte 1934- *WhoWrEP 92*
Gannon, Christian H. *Law&B 92*
Gannon, Christopher Richard *Law&B 92*
Gannon, David P. 1929- *St&PR 93*
Gannon, Dee 1953- *WhoWrEP 92*
Gannon, Francis L. *Law&B 92*
Gannon, Gerald J. *Law&B 92*
Gannon, Harold Joseph 1957- *WhoE 93*
Gannon, J. Michael *Law&B 92*
Gannon, J. Timothy *St&PR 93*
Gannon, J. Truett 1930- *WhoSSW 93*
Gannon, Jerome Aylward 1935- *WhoAm 92*
Gannon, Joseph Winfield, Jr. *Law&B 92*
Gannon, Lucinda J. *Law&B 92*
Gannon, Lucinda J. 1947- *St&PR 93*
Gannon, Lynette Marie 1948- *WhoAm 92, WhoSSW 93*
Gannon, Mary Carol 1944- *WhoAm 92*
Gannon, Michael J. 1943- *St&PR 93*
Gannon, Michael R. 1947- *St&PR 93*
Gannon, Robert Haines 1931- *WhoWrEP 92*
Gannon, Robert P. *WhoAm 92*
Gannon, Sarah Ruddiman *Law&B 92*
Gann-Wick, Lisa Marie 1966- *WhoAmW 93*
Gano, Clifton Wayne, Jr. 1941- *WhoAm 92*
Gano, John 1924- *WhoAm 92, WhoSSW 93*
Ganoe, Charles Stratford 1929- *WhoAm 92*
Ganoff, Gregory Daniel 1945- *WhoSSW 93*
Ganong, William Francis 1924- *WhoAm 92*
Ganong, William Francis, III 1951- *WhoAm 92*
Ganon-Garayalde, Victor F. 1945- *WhoWor 93*
Ganoulis, Jacques 1945- *WhoScE 91-3*
Ganoza, M. Clelia 1937- *WhoAm 92*
Ganoza-Becker, M. Clelia 1937- *WhoAmW 93*
Ganpat 1886-1951 *ScF&FL 92*
Ganry, Jacky 1946- *WhoScE 91-2*
Gans, Bruce Michael 1951- *WhoWrEP 92*
Gans, Carl 1923- *WhoAm 92*
Gans, Carol Butchko 1954- *WhoAmW 93*
Gans, Erna Irene 1925- *St&PR 93*
Gans, Eugene Howard 1929- *WhoE 93*
Gans, Herbert J. 1927- *WhoAm 92*
Gans, Leo 1926- *St&PR 93*
Gans, Robert J. 1918- *St&PR 93*
Gans, Roger *BioIn 17*
Gans, Roger Frederick 1941- *WhoAm 92*
Gans, Roma 1894- *BioIn 17*
Gans, Samuel Myer 1925- *WhoE 93, WhoWor 93*
Gans, Terry Alexander 1946- *St&PR 93*
Gans, Walter G. *Law&B 92*
Gans, Walter Gideon 1936- *WhoAm 92*
Gansbacher, Johann (Baptist) 1778-1844 *Baker 92*
Ganschow, Clifford Laurence 1935- *WhoWor 93*
Ganse, Jean Marie 1949- *WhoEmL 93*
Gansen, Ronald E. 1950- *St&PR 93*
Gansevoort, Peter 1749-1812 *HarEnMi*
Ganshert, Stephen Carl 1942- *WhoSSW 93*
Ganskopp, William Fredrick 1915- *WhoSSW 93*
Gansler, Bob *BioIn 17*
Gansovsky, Sever 1918- *BioIn 17*
Gansovsky, Sever 1918-1990 *ScF&FL 92*
Ganssauge, Eberhard 1931- *WhoScE 91-3*
Ganssle, Margaret Plank *AmWomPl*
Gant, Catherine Adamski 1936- *WhoAmW 93*
Gant, Cynthia Eleanor 1948- *WhoAmW 93*
Gant, Donald R. 1928- *St&PR 93*
Gant, Donald Ross 1928- *WhoAm 92*
Gant, Duplain Rhodes 1924- *WhoE 93*
Gant, George Arlington Lee 1941- *WhoAm 92*
Gant, Harry T. 1942- *St&PR 93*
Gant, Horace Zed 1914- *WhoWor 93*
Gant, Kevin *BioIn 17*
Gant, Norman Ferrell, Jr. 1939- *WhoAm 92*
Gant, Ronald Edwin Ron 1965- *WhoAm 92*
Gantar, Claudio 1930- *WhoScE 91-3*
Ganten, Detlev 1941- *WhoScE 91-3*
Ganten, Reinhard Hinrich 1939- *WhoWor 93*
Gantenbein, Herbert B. 1912- *St&PR 93*
Gantenbein, Larry A. *Law&B 92*
Ganter, Bernard J. 1928- *WhoAm 92, WhoSSW 93*
Ganter, Gladys Marie 1908- *WhoAmW 93*
Ganther, Howard Edward 1937- *WhoAm 92*
Gantin, Bernardin Cardinal 1922- *WhoWor 93*
Gantman, David J. 1941- *WhoAm 92*
Gantner, Bruce Alan 1950- *WhoSSW 93*
Gantner, Susan *BioIn 17*
Gantos, L. Douglas 1931- *St&PR 93*
Gantsoudes, James G. 1942- *St&PR 93*
Gantt, Cora Dick *AmWomPl*
Gantt, Harvey *BioIn 17*
Gantt, Harvey B. 1943- *WhoAm 92*
Gantt, Harvey Bernard 1943- *AfrAmBi*
Gantt, Michael Eugene 1944- *St&PR 93*
Gantt, N. Lee *St&PR 93*
Gantt, William Robert, III 1948- *St&PR 93*
Gantz, Bruce Jay 1946- *WhoAm 92*
Gantz, Carroll Melvin 1931- *WhoAm 92*
Gantz, Charles V., Jr. 1932- *St&PR 93*
Gantz, David Alfred 1942- *WhoAm 92*
Gantz, Everett Ellis 1925- *WhoSSW 93*
Gantz, John G., Jr. 1948- *St&PR 93, WhoAm 92, WhoIns 93*
Gantz, Joseph 1947- *St&PR 93*
Gantz, Nancy Rollins 1949- *WhoEmL 93*
Gantz, Robert Forrest 1925- *St&PR 93*
Gantz, Suzi Grahn 1954- *WhoAmW 93, WhoEmL 93*
Gantz, Wilbur H. 1937- *St&PR 93*
Ganulin, Neil *Law&B 92*
Ganus, Charles A. *Law&B 92*
Ganus, Clifton Loyd, III 1945- *WhoSSW 93*
Ganyard, Ivan Stanley 1929- *St&PR 93*
Ganz, Adolf 1796-1870 *See* Ganz, Wilhelm 1833-1914 *Baker 92*
Ganz, Alice 1943- *WhoWrEP 92*
Ganz, Aura 1957- *WhoE 93*
Ganz, Bruno 1941- *IntDcF 2-3 [port]*
Ganz, Cary H. 1946- *WhoE 93*
Ganz, David L. 1951- *WhoE 93*
Ganz, Erwin M. 1929- *St&PR 93, WhoAm 92*
Ganz, Kate *BioIn 17*
Ganz, Michael H. *Law&B 92*
Ganz, Rudolph 1877-1972 *Baker 92*
Ganz, Samuel 1911- *WhoAm 92*
Ganz, Susan Joyce 1959- *St&PR 93*
Ganz, Sylvia Tykie 1932- *WhoAmW 93*
Ganz, Wilhelm 1833-1914 *Baker 92*
Ganz, William I. 1951- *WhoSSW 93*
Ganz, Yaffa 1938- *BioIn 17*
Ganzarain, Ramon Cajiao 1923- *WhoSSW 93*
Ganzarolli, Wladimiro 1936- *Baker 92*
Ganzenmuller, Lisa Ann 1963- *WhoAmW 93*
Ganzi, Victor F. *Law&B 92*
Ganzoni, John Julian 1932- *WhoWor 93*
Gao, Guo Zhu 1946- *WhoWor 93*
Gao, Hong-Bo 1961- *WhoWor 93*
Gao, Ji 1941- *WhoWor 93*
Gao, Shi-an 1938- *WhoWor 93*
Gao, Wenjie 1956- *WhoWor 93*
Gao Dezhan 1932- *WhoAsAP 91*
Gao Di 1927- *WhoAsAP 91*
Gao Huanchang 1924- *WhoAsAP 91*
Gao Liang *BioIn 17*
Gaonkar, Gopal Hosabu 1937- *WhoSSW 93*
Gao Zhenning 1929- *WhoAsAP 91*
Gap Band *SoulM*
Gape, Serafina Vetrano 1945- *WhoAmW 93*
Gapen, D. Kaye *BioIn 17*
Gapen, Delores Kaye 1943- *WhoAm 92, WhoAmW 93*
Gaples, Harry S. 1935- *St&PR 93*
Gaples, Harry Seraphim 1935- *WhoAm 92*
Gapo, Branko 1931- *DrEEuF*
Gapon, Georgi Apollonovich 1870?-1906 *BioIn 17*
Gaponenko, Yuri Lukitch 1942- *WhoWor 93*
Gapp, Paul 1928-1992 *NewYTBS 92 [port]*
Gapp, Paul John 1928- *WhoAm 92*
Gapper, Patience 1928- *ConAu 139*
Gappmayer, Richard B. 1936- *St&PR 93*
Gapsis, G.J. *Law&B 92*
Gara, Michael Anthony 1953- *WhoE 93*
Garabedian, Mitchell 1937- *St&PR 93*
Garabedian, Paul Roesel 1927- *WhoAm 92*
Garafalo, Anthony Joseph 1954- *WhoE 93*
Garagiola, Joe 1926- *BioIn 17, WhoAm 92*
Garaguly, Carl von 1900-1984 *Baker 92*
Garahan, Peter Thomas 1946- *WhoAm 92*
Garam, Peter P. *Law&B 92*
Garamendi, John R. *BioIn 17*
Garance, Dominick 1912- *WhoAm 92, WhoWor 93*
Garand, Christopher Pierre 1947- *St&PR 93, WhoIns 93*
Garand, Pierre Arthur 1954- *WhoWrEP 92*
Garand, Richard A. *St&PR 93*
Garang de Mabior, John 1945- *WhoAfr*
Garant, (Albert Antonio) Serge 1929-1986 *Baker 92*
Garasky, Steven Brian 1958- *WhoE 93*
Garat, (Dominique) Pierre (Jean) 1762-1823 *Baker 92*
Garattini, Silvio 1928- *WhoScE 91-3*
Garau, Pietro A. 1942- *WhoUN 92*
Garaud, Marie-France 1934- *BioIn 17*
Garaude, Alexis (Adelaide-Gabriel) de 1779-1852 *Baker 92*
Garaudy, Roger 1913- *BioIn 17*
Garavani, Valentino *BioIn 17*
Garavani, Valentino 1932- *WhoWor 93*
Garavelli, John Stephen 1947- *WhoAm 92*
Garavito, Stephen C. *Law&B 92*
Garay, Charles James 1939- *St&PR 93*
Garay, Joseph P. *Law&B 92*
Garay, Joseph P. 1949- *St&PR 93*
Garay Narciso 1876-1953 *Baker 92*
Garazi, Ida Shwartz 1936- *WhoAm 92*
Garb, Allan E. 1929- *St&PR 93*
Garb, Ernest L. 1932- *St&PR 93*
Garb, Forrest Allan 1929- *WhoSSW 93*
Garba, Edward Aloysius 1921- *WhoAm 92*
Garba, Joseph Nanven 1943- *WhoAfr*
Garbacz, Gerald George 1936- *St&PR 93, WhoAm 92*
Garbacz, Jerzy K. 1948- *WhoScE 91-4*
Garbacz, Patricia Frances 1941- *WhoAmW 93*
Garbade, Nancy Caroline 1947- *St&PR 93*
Garbalewski, Czeslaw 1920- *WhoScE 91-4*
Garban, Douglas S. 1964- *WhoE 93*
Garbarek, Jan 1947- *Baker 92*
Garbarino, James *BioIn 17*
Garbarino, James 1947- *WhoAm 92*
Garbarino, Jean 1926- *WhoScE 91-2*
Garbarino, Joseph William 1919- *WhoAm 92*
Garbarino, Robert Paul 1929- *WhoWor 93*
Garbaty, Marie Louise 1910- *WhoAm 92, WhoAmW 93*
Garbell, Maurice 1914-1991 *BioIn 17*

Garber, Alan Joel 1943- *WhoAm 92*
Garber, Anne (Theresa) 1946- *ConAu 138*
Garber, Betty Kahn 1950- *WhoAmW 93*
Garber, Charles Allen 1941- *WhoAm 92, WhoE 93*
Garber, Charles N. 1947- *St&PR 93*
Garber, Charles Stedman, Jr. 1943- *WhoAm 92*
Garber, Daniel Elliot 1949- *WhoAm 92*
Garber, Earl S. 1932- *St&PR 93*
Garber, Eric *ScF&FL 92*
Garber, Floyd Wayne 1941- *WhoSSW 93*
Garber, Fred *BioIn 17*
Garber, Harry Douglas 1928- *St&PR 93, WhoAm 92*
Garber, Henry Eugene 1947- *BiDAMSp 1989*
Garber, Janet *WhoE 93*
Garber, John Reed *Law&B 92*
Garber, Judith Ann 1949- *WhoEmL 93*
Garber, Margaret E. *Law&B 92*
Garber, Paul E. d1992 *NewYTBS 92 [port]*
Garber, Robert E. *Law&B 92*
Garber, Robert Edward 1949- *St&PR 93, WhoAm 92*
Garber, Rosann 1955- *WhoAmW 93*
Garber, Samuel B. *Law&B 92*
Garber, Samuel B. 1934- *St&PR 93*
Garber, Samuel Baugh 1934- *WhoAm 92*
Garber, Sidney *WhoScE 91-1*
Garber, Stanley N. *Law&B 92*
Garber, Stephen L. *Law&B 92*
Garber, Stephen Meyer 1940- *St&PR 93*
Garber, Valerie L. *Law&B 92*
Garber, Walter, Jr. 1935- *WhoSSW 93*
Garberding, Larry G. 1938- *St&PR 93*
Garberding, Larry Gilbert 1938- *WhoAm 92*
Garbers, Christoph Friedrich 1929- *WhoWor 93*
Garbin, Albeno Patrick 1932- *WhoAm 92*
Garbin, Edoardo 1865-1943 *Baker 92*
Garbis, Marvin Joseph 1936- *WhoAm 92, WhoE 93*
Garbis, Michelle R. 1947- *St&PR 93*
Garbo, Greta 1905-1990 *BioIn 17, IntDcF 2-3 [port]*
Garbo, Greta Maria 1957- *WhoAmW 93*
Garbo, Paul W. 1911- *St&PR 93*
Garbose, Doris Rhoda 1924- *WhoAmW 93*
Garbose, S. Bernard 1929- *St&PR 93*
Garbousova, Raya 1905- *Baker 92*
Garbrecht, Susan Slavich 1953- *St&PR 93*
Garbus, Martin Solomon 1934- *WhoAm 92*
Garbutt, Eugene James 1925- *WhoAm 92*
Garbutt, Jeremy *BioIn 17*
Garbutt, Jeremy 1950- *WhoAm 92*
Garbutt, P. *WhoScE 91-1*
Garby, Lars E. 1924- *WhoScE 91-2*
Garces, Gerardo Orbe 1957- *WhoWor 93*
Garchik, Leah Lieberman 1945- *WhoAm 92*
Garci, Jose Luis 1944- *MiSFD 9*
Garcia, Abel 1949- *St&PR 93*
Garcia, Adalberto 1954- *WhoEmL 93*
Garcia, Adolfo Ramon 1948- *WhoAm 92*
Garcia, Albert Daniel 1943- *WhoE 93*
Garcia, Alberto *St&PR 93*
Garcia, Alberto 1875-1946 *OxDcOp*
Garcia, Alberto A. 1945- *St&PR 93*
Garcia, Alexander 1919- *WhoAm 92*
Garcia, Alfredo Mariano 1927- *HispAmA*
Garcia, Andy *BioIn 17*
Garcia, Andy 1956- *HispAmA, WhoAm 92*
Garcia, Ann Marie 1963- *WhoAmW 93*
Garcia, Antonio 1901- *HispAmA*
Garcia, Antonio Lopez *BioIn 17*
Garcia, Benjamin d1991 *BioIn 17*
Garcia, Carlos Ernesto 1936- *HispAmA*
Garcia, Catalina Esperanza 1944- *NotHsAW 93*
Garcia, Celso Ramon 1921- *HispAmA [port], WhoAm 92*
Garcia, Cristina 1958- *NotHsAW 93*
Garcia, Daniel P. 1947- *HispAmA*
Garcia, Danny Gayton 1951- *WhoSSW 93*
Garcia, David Joseph 1946- *WhoSSW 93*
Garcia, Diane 1947- *WhoEmL 93*
Garcia, Domingo 1958- *WhoWor 93*
Garcia, Domingo, Jr. *Law&B 92*
Garcia, Eddie 1970- *BioIn 17*
Garcia, Edward Harold 1942- *WhoSSW 93*
Garcia, Edward J. 1928- *HispAmA*
Garcia, Edward Miguel 1923-1986 *BiDAMSp 1989*
Garcia, Elisa D. *Law&B 92*
Garcia, Eliud 1951- *St&PR 93*
Garcia, Enrique T., Jr. 1940- *WhoAsAP 91*
Garcia, Ephrahim 1963- *WhoSSW 93*
Garcia, Ernest Carlos *Law&B 92*
Garcia, Eugenie 1815-1880 *OxDcOp*
Garcia, Eugenie 1818-1880 *Baker 92*
Garcia, Eva Cristina 1943- *WhoWor 93*
Garcia, F. Chris 1940- *WhoAm 92*
Garcia, Felix, Jr. 1941- *WhoSSW 93*
Garcia, Florina Aurora 1950- *WhoWor 93*
Garcia, Frances 1938- *NotHsAW 93 [port]*
Garcia, George Edward 1930- *WhoE 93*
Garcia, George F. 1942- *WhoAm 92*
Garcia, Gustave 1837-1925 *OxDcOp*
Garcia, Hector Perez 1914- *HispAmA*
Garcia, Henry Frank 1943- *WhoSSW 93*
Garcia, Hernando *Law&B 92*
Garcia, Hipolito Frank 1925- *HispAmA, WhoSSW 93*
Garcia, Ignacio Molina 1950- *WhoWrEP 92*
Garcia, Ignacio Razon 1953- *WhoEmL 93, WhoWor 93*
Garcia, Jerry *BioIn 17*
Garcia, Jerry 1942- *Baker 92, WhoAm 92*
Garcia, Joaquina 1780-1854 *OxDcOp*
Garcia, Jose Antonio 1954- *WhoSSW 93*
Garcia, Jose D. 1936- *HispAmA [port]*
Garcia, Jose Luix 1949- *WhoEmL 93*
Garcia, Josefina Margarita 1906- *WhoAmW 93*
Garcia, Joseph 1947- *WhoE 93*
Garcia, Joseph Charles 1931- *WhoE 93*
Garcia, Joy Paronda 1965- *WhoE 93*
Garcia, Juan Ramon *Law&B 92*
Garcia, Julian S. 1950- *WhoWrEP 92*
Garcia, Juliana Rose 1961- *WhoAmW 93*
Garcia, Juliet Villarreal 1949- *NotHsAW 93 [port]*
Garcia, Katherine Lee 1950- *WhoAmW 93, WhoEmL 93*
Garcia, Kathleen J. 1949- *WhoWrEP 92*
Garcia, Lawrence D. *Law&B 92*
Garcia, Len *WhoIns 93*
Garcia, Lionel G. 1935- *HispAmA [port]*
Garcia, Louis R. 1931- *WhoIns 93*
Garcia, Louis Richard 1931- *St&PR 93*
Garcia, Luis G. *Law&B 92*
Garcia, Manuel 1775-1832 *IntDcOp [port], OxDcOp*
Garcia, Manuel 1805-1906 *OxDcOp*
Garcia, Manuel (del Popolo Vicente Rodriguez) 1775-1832 *Baker 92*
Garcia, Manuel Domingo 1952- *WhoWor 93*
Garcia, Manuel Patricio Rodriguez 1805-1906 *Baker 92*
Garcia, Maria E. *Law&B 92*
Garcia, Maria Emilia Martin *NotHsAW 93*
Garcia, Maria Felicia 1808-1836 *OxDcOp*
Garcia, Maribel *Law&B 92*
Garcia, Mario David *DcCPCAm*
Garcia, Marissa Praxedes 1944- *WhoSSW 93*
Garcia, Marito Hernandez 1951- *WhoUN 92*
Garcia, Mary Jane Madrid 1936- *WhoAmW 93*
Garcia, Mike *ScF&FL 92*
Garcia, Nancy Yeatts 1947- *WhoAmW 93*
Garcia, Nicole *BioIn 17*
Garcia, Norma 1950- *NotHsAW 93 [port]*
Garcia, O. *WhoScE 91-3*
Garcia, Ofelia 1941- *WhoAmW 93*
Garcia, Oscar Nicolas 1936- *WhoAm 92, WhoE 93*
Garcia, Pablo P. 1925- *WhoAsAP 91*
Garcia, Patricia Ann 1959- *WhoEmL 93*
Garcia, Pauline 1821-1910 *OxDcOp*
Garcia, Pauline Viardot- *Baker 92*
Garcia, Peter Charles 1951- *WhoAm 92*
Garcia, Phyllis Josephine 1934- *WhoAmW 93*
Garcia, Raymond Lloyd 1942- *WhoSSW 93*
Garcia, Reynaldo 1939- *St&PR 93*
Garcia, Robert T. 1958- *ScF&FL 92*
Garcia, Roberto Sioson 1933- *WhoE 93*
Garcia, Roland Hidalgo 1952- *WhoWor 93*
Garcia, Rupert 1941- *HispAmA*
Garcia, Sandra Joanne Anderson 1939- *WhoAmW 93*
Garcia, Serge Michel 1945- *WhoScE 91-3, WhoUN 92*
Garcia, Sharon Kay 1956- *WhoSSW 93*
Garcia, Simeon E., Jr. 1949- *WhoAsAP 91*
Garcia, Telesforo 1844-1918 *DcMexL*
Garcia-Aracil, Vicente 1927- *WhoWor 93*
Garcia Ascot, Jomi 1929- *DcMexL*
Garcia-Barbero, Mila 1948- *WhoUN 92*
Garcia Barragan, German Alfonso 1941- *WhoWor 93*
Garcia Bish, Juan Ramon 1956- *WhoWor 93*
Garcia C., Elisa D. *Law&B 92*
Garcia C., Elisa Dolores 1957- *WhoEmL 93*
Garcia Cantu, Gaston 1917- *DcMexL*
Garcia-Castaner, Felix 1936- *WhoScE 91-3*
Garcia-Colin, Leopoldo Scherer 1930- *WhoWor 93*
Garcia-Conde, J.R. 1920- *WhoScE 91-3*
Garcia Criado, Balbino 1943- *WhoScE 91-3*
Garcia De Andres, Carlos 1948- *WhoScE 91-3*
Garcia De Castro, Jose 1927- *WhoScE 91-3*
Garcia De Diego, Jesus *WhoScE 91-3*
Garcia De Figuerola, Luis C. 1922- *WhoScE 91-3*
Garcia De Jalon, Javier 1949- *WhoScE 91-3*
Garcia-del-Solar, Lucio 1922- *WhoWor 93*
Garcia De Miguel, J.M. 1944- *WhoScE 91-3*
Garcia De Viedma, Luis 1932- *WhoScE 91-2*
Garcia Diaz-De-Villegas, Jose-Manuel 1942- *WhoScE 91-3*
Garciadiego, Alejandro Ricardo 1953- *WhoWor 93*
Garcia Fajer, Francisco Javier 1730-1809 *Baker 92*
Garcia Fernandez, Norberto Emilio 1939- *WhoUN 92*
Garcia Gancedo, Angel 1925- *WhoScE 91-3*
Garcia-Godoy, Cristian 1924- *WhoSSW 93*
Garcia Godoy, Hector *DcCPCAm*
Garcia-Granados, Sergio Eduardo 1942- *WhoAm 92, WhoE 93*
Garcia-Heras, Jaime L. 1945- *WhoScE 91-3*
Garcia Herreros, Rafael d1992 *NewYTBS 92*
Garcia-Huidobro, Guillermo 1947- *WhoUN 92*
Garcia Icazbalceta, Joaquin 1825-1894 *DcMexL*
Garcia Iglesias, Sara 1917- *DcMexL*
Garcia Lopes, Miguel 1953- *WhoWor 93*
Garcia-Lopez, Jose Gabriel 1930- *WhoUN 92*
Garcia Lorca, Federico 1898-1936 *BioIn 17, MagSWL [port], WorLitC [port]*
Garcia Luis, Julio Omar 1942- *WhoWor 93*
Garcia Mansilla, Eduardo 1870-1930 *Baker 92*
Garcia-Marcos, Luis 1957- *WhoScE 91-3*
Garcia Marquez, Gabriel 1927- *SpAmA*
Garcia Marquez, Gabriel 1928- *BioIn 17, MagSWL [port], ScF&FL 92, WorLitC [port]*
Garcia Marquez, Gabriel Jose 1928- *WhoWor 93*
Garcia Martinez, Hernando 1942- *WhoWor 93*
Garcia-Maurino, Carlos *Law&B 92*
Garcia-Merayo, Felix 1936- *WhoWor 93*
Garcia Monge, Joaquin 1881-1958 *SpAmA*
Garcia Morales, Adelaida *BioIn 17*
Garcia-Moran, Manuel 1935- *WhoWor 93*
Garcia Moreno, Antonio 1942- *WhoScE 91-3*
Garcia-Moritan, Roberto 1948- *WhoUN 92*
Garcia-Munoz, Marianela 1949- *WhoAmW 93*
Garcia Naranjo, Nemesio 1883-1962 *DcMexL*
Garcia Navarro, (Luis Antonio) *Baker 92*
Garcia Novo, Francisco 1943- *WhoScE 91-3*
Garcia Oller, Jose Luis 1923- *WhoAm 92*
Garcia-Palmieri, Mario Ruben 1927- *WhoAm 92*
Garcia-Paris, Carolina 1962- *WhoEmL 93*
Garcia Pascual, Jacinto 1949- *WhoWor 93*
Garcia Perez, Alan *DcCPCAm*
Garcia Ponce, Juan 1932- *DcMexL*
Garcia Pueyo, Felix Raul 1938- *WhoWor 93*
Garcia Ramis, Magali 1946- *SpAmA*
Garcia-Regueiro, J.A. 1954- *WhoScE 91-3*
Garcia-Rill, Edgar Enrique 1948- *WhoSSW 93*
Garcia Robles, Alfonso 1911-1991 *BioIn 17*
Garcia Rosa, Ricardo 1944- *WhoScE 91-3*
Garcia-S., Jesus Nicasio 1955- *WhoWor 93*
Garcia Samajoa, Jose Domingo *WhoWor 93*
Garcia Sanchez, Javier 1955- *ConAu 136*
Garcia Tejada, Hector *WhoWor 93*
Garcia Terres, Jaime 1924- *DcMexL*
Garcia Tomas, Jesus 1937- *WhoScE 91-3*
Garcia Vargas, Julian 1946- *WhoWor 93*
Garcia y Robertson, R. 1949- *ScF&FL 92*
Garcilaso de la Vega 1539-1616 *IntDcAn*
Garcilaso de la Vega, El Inca 1539-1616 *BioIn 17*
Garczynski, John Stephen 1937- *St&PR 93*
Garczynski, Wlodzimierz 1936- *WhoScE 91-4*
Gard, Albert Wilson, III 1941- *St&PR 93*
Gard, Beverly J. 1940- *WhoAmW 93*
Gard, Curtis Eldon 1921- *St&PR 93, WhoAm 92*
Gard, Janice *AmWomPl, MajAI*
Gard, Randy *Law&B 92*
Gard, Richard Abbott 1914- *WhoWor 93*
Garda, Patrick Florent 1957- *WhoWor 93*
Garda, Robert Allen 1939- *WhoAm 92*
Gardam, Jane *BioIn 17*
Gardam, Jane 1928- *ChlFicS, MajAI [port], ScF&FL 92*
Gardano, Antonio 1509-1569 *Baker 92*
Gardaphe, Fred L(ouis) 1952- *ConAu 136*
Gardarsson, Arnthor 1938- *WhoScE 91-4*
Garde, Abraham 1926- *St&PR 93*
Garde, Daniel Frederick 1940- *WhoE 93*
Garde, John Charles 1961- *WhoWor 93*
Garde, Michael James 1937- *WhoE 93*
Garde, Susan Reutershan 1953- *WhoAmW 93, WhoEmL 93*
Gardea, Jesus 1939- *DcMexL, SpAmA*
Gardebring, Sandra S. *WhoAmW 93*
Gardel, Andre 1922- *WhoScE 91-4*
Gardel, Carlos 1887-1935 *Baker 92*
Gardella, Libero Anthony 1935- *WhoAm 92*
Gardella, Robert R. 1934- *St&PR 93*
Gardella, William Paul *Law&B 92*
Gardelli, Lamberto 1915- *Baker 92, OxDcOp*
Gardellini, Gabriella fl. 1698- *BioIn 17*
Garden, Domnern 1928- *WhoWor 93*
Garden, Donald J. *ScF&FL 92*
Garden, Mary 1874-1967 *Baker 92, IntDcOp [port], OxDcOp*
Garden, Mary 1877-1967 *GayN*
Garden, Nancy 1938- *ScF&FL 92*
Gardener, Edward Patrick Montgomery *WhoScE 91-1*
Gardenfors, Peter Bjorn 1949- *WhoWor 93*
Gardenhour, Eugene Charles 1932- *St&PR 93*
Gardenia, Vincent d1992 *NewYTBS 92 [port]*
Gardenia, Vincent 1921- *WhoAm 92*
Gardenia, Vincent 1922-1992 *News 93-2*
Gardenier, Edna Frances 1935- *WhoAmW 93*
Gardenier, John Stark, II 1937- *WhoE 93*
Gardenier, Turkan Kumbaraci 1941- *WhoAm 92*
Gardes, Roger 1922- *Baker 92*
Gardette, Charles D. 1830-1884 *ScF&FL 92*
Gardine, Michael *ScF&FL 92*
Gardiner, A. Theodore, III *Law&B 92*
Gardiner, Arthur Zimmermann, Jr. 1935- *WhoAm 92*
Gardiner, Becky *AmWomPl*
Gardiner, Brian 1957- *St&PR 93*
Gardiner, Brian George *WhoScE 91-1*
Gardiner, Craig Alexander *Law&B 92*
Gardiner, Cyril Frederick 1930- *WhoWor 93*
Gardiner, Daryl Thomas 1949- *WhoWor 93*
Gardiner, David 1772-1815 *BioIn 17*
Gardiner, Donald Andrew 1922- *WhoAm 92*
Gardiner, Donald K. 1939- *WhoIns 93*
Gardiner, Duncan *WhoScE 91-1*
Gardiner, E. Nicholas P. 1939- *WhoAm 92*
Gardiner, Eileen 1947- *WhoEmL 93*
Gardiner, Frances R. 1926- *St&PR 93*
Gardiner, Gerald Austin 1900-1990 *BioIn 17*
Gardiner, Ginnie *BioIn 17*
Gardiner, H(enry) Balfour 1877-1950 *Baker 92*
Gardiner, Harry Walter 1938- *WhoWrEP 92*
Gardiner, Henry Gilbert 1927- *WhoSSW 93*
Gardiner, John Eliot *BioIn 17*
Gardiner, John Eliot 1943- *Baker 92, OxDcOp*
Gardiner, John Graham *WhoScE 91-1*
Gardiner, John Lyon 1770-1816 *BioIn 17*
Gardiner, John Macdonald *WhoScE 91-1*
Gardiner, John Reynolds 1944- *BioIn 17, DcAmChF 1985*
Gardiner, John W. 1931- *St&PR 93*
Gardiner, John William 1931- *WhoAm 92*
Gardiner, Joseph William Fawsitt 1920- *WhoAm 92*
Gardiner, Judith Kegan 1941- *ConAu 138*
Gardiner, Judy 1922- *ScF&FL 92*
Gardiner, Keith Mattinson 1933- *WhoAm 92*
Gardiner, Linda 1947- *WhoWrEP 92*
Gardiner, Linda Jane *WhoE 93*
Gardiner, Margaret Doane *AmWomPl*

Gardiner, Michael J. 1933- WhoScE 91-3
Gardiner, Michael James 1945- St&PR 93
Gardiner, Muriel ConAu 39NR
Gardiner, Nathan F. Law&B 92
Gardiner, Peter Alexander Jack 1935- St&PR 93
Gardiner, Piers R.R. 1940- WhoScE 91-3
Gardiner, Piers Richard Rochfort 1940- WhoWor 93
Gardiner, Robert M. 1922- St&PR 93
Gardiner, Stuart K. Law&B 92
Gardiner, Susan Niven 1956- WhoAmW 93
Gardiner, Thomas Joseph 1947- St&PR 93
Gardiner, Walter A. 1950- St&PR 93
Gardiner, Wayne Jay 1943- WhoWrEP 92
Gardiner, William 1770-1853 Baker 92
Gardiner, William Cecil, Jr. 1933- WhoAm 92
Gardiner, William Douglas Haig 1917- St&PR 93, WhoAm 92
Gardiner of Kittisford, Baron 1900-1990 BioIn 17
Gardiner-Scott, Tanya J. 1958- ScF&FL 92
Gardiner-Scott, Tanya Jane 1958- WhoE 93
Gardino, Vincent Anthony 1953- WhoE 93, WhoWor 93
Gardiol, Freddy 1935- WhoScE 91-4
Gardiol, Rita Mazzetti WhoAmW 93
Gardissat, Jean-Louis 1949- WhoWor 93
Gardner, Adrienne Albertha 1953- WhoSSW 93
Gardner, Albert Henderson 1932- WhoE 93
Gardner, Alexander 1821-1882 BioIn 17
Gardner, Allan Buchanan WhoUN 92
Gardner, Alvin Frederick 1920- WhoAm 92
Gardner, Andrew J. St&PR 93
Gardner, Ann L. 1961- WhoAmW 93
Gardner, Arnold Burton 1930- WhoAm 92
Gardner, Arthur BioIn 17
Gardner, Ava 1922-1990 BioIn 17, IntDcF 2-3 [port]
Gardner, Ava (Lavinia) 1922-1990 ConAu 139
Gardner, Averil 1937- ScF&FL 92
Gardner, Bernard 1931- WhoAm 92
Gardner, Bert Erwin 1928- WhoAm 92
Gardner, Bettiann 1930- WhoAm 92, WhoAmW 93
Gardner, Blair M. Law&B 92
Gardner, Booth 1936- WhoAm 92, WhoWor 93
Gardner, Brenda Sue 1952- WhoAmW 93
Gardner, Bruce A. Law&B 92
Gardner, Bruce D. 1951- WhoIns 93
Gardner, Bruce David Law&B 92
Gardner, Bruce L. BioIn 17
Gardner, Bruce William 1938- St&PR 93
Gardner, Burleigh B. 1902- IntDcAn
Gardner, Carol A. 1948- WhoAmW 93
Gardner, Carolanne Law&B 92
Gardner, Carole Jean 1942- St&PR 93
Gardner, Caryn Sue 1960- WhoEmL 93
Gardner, Charles Olda 1919- WhoAm 92
Gardner, Charles Sperry 1949- WhoEmL 93
Gardner, Chester Stone 1947- WhoAm 92
Gardner, Clifford Speer 1924- WhoAm 92
Gardner, Clyde Edward 1931- WhoWor 93
Gardner, Connie Louise 1947- St&PR 93, WhoAmW 93
Gardner, Conrad Oliver Law&B 92
Gardner, Craig Shaw 1949- ScF&FL 92
Gardner, David Chambers 1934- WhoE 93
Gardner, David Edward 1923- St&PR 93, WhoAm 92
Gardner, David Lance 1950- WhoE 93
Gardner, David P. 1933- St&PR 93
Gardner, David Paton 1956- WhoAm 92
Gardner, David Pierpont 1933- WhoAm 92, WhoWor 93
Gardner, David Walton 1950- WhoEmL 93, WhoSSW 93
Gardner, Dean L. Law&B 92
Gardner, Delbert R. 1923- ScF&FL 92
Gardner, Donald LaVere 1930- WhoAm 92
Gardner, Donald Ray 1937- WhoAm 92
Gardner, Dorothy AmWomPl
Gardner, Dorsey Robertson 1942- WhoAm 92
Gardner, Edward G. 1925- BioIn 17
Gardner, Edward P. 1947- WhoWor 93
Gardner, Edward Tytus, III 1949- WhoSSW 93
Gardner, Eldora A. Law&B 92
Gardner, Elizabeth Ann Hunt 1916- WhoAmW 93
Gardner, Eric 1949- WhoEmL 93
Gardner, Erle Stanley 1889-1970 BioIn 17, ScF&FL 92
Gardner, Everette Shaw, Jr. 1944- WhoSSW 93
Gardner, Flora Clark AmWomPl
Gardner, Florence Cecelia 1913- WhoWrEP 92
Gardner, Gary Alan 1945- WhoE 93
Gardner, Gaylord E., Jr. 1951- St&PR 93
Gardner, Gene Pritchard 1929- St&PR 93
Gardner, Geoffrey 1943- WhoWrEP 92
Gardner, George Peabody 1917- WhoAm 92
Gardner, Gerald 1929- ScF&FL 92
Gardner, Gerald B. ScF&FL 92
Gardner, Gerald Faye 1950- WhoWrEP 92
Gardner, Grace Daniel 1911- WhoAmW 93
Gardner, Grant Walter 1954- WhoEmL 93, WhoSSW 93
Gardner, Gwendolyn Smith 1948- WhoSSW 93
Gardner, H. Daniel Law&B 92
Gardner, Henry L. BioIn 17
Gardner, Henry Louis 1944- WhoAm 92
Gardner, Herb MiSFD 9
Gardner, Howard BioIn 17
Gardner, Howard Alan 1920- WhoAm 92
Gardner, Howard Earl 1943- WhoAm 92, WhoE 93
Gardner, Howard Garry 1943- WhoWor 93
Gardner, Howard Lane, Jr. 1919- St&PR 93
Gardner, Isabella Stewart 1840-1924 GayN
Gardner, Jack H. Law&B 92
Gardner, Jacqueline Debra Law&B 92
Gardner, James Albert 1943- WhoAm 92
Gardner, James Bailey 1950- WhoEmL 93
Gardner, James Barrington 1934- St&PR 93
Gardner, James Carson 1933- WhoAm 92, WhoSSW 93, WhoWor 93
Gardner, James Harkins 1943- WhoAm 92
Gardner, James M. 1931- St&PR 93
Gardner, James Richard 1944- WhoAm 92, WhoE 93, WhoWor 93
Gardner, Jerome ScF&FL 92
Gardner, Jerry Dean 1939- WhoAm 92
Gardner, Jess Lewis 1957- WhoEmL 93
Gardner, Jill Christopher 1948- WhoAm 92
Gardner, Joan Andrews 1933- WhoAmW 93
Gardner, Joan M. 1954- St&PR 93
Gardner, Joann Lynn 1950- WhoSSW 93
Gardner, Joel Robert 1942- WhoE 93
Gardner, John 1926- ScF&FL 92
Gardner, John 1933-1982 BioIn 17, MagSAmL [port], ScF&FL 92
Gardner, John B., III 1949- St&PR 93
Gardner, John Champlin 1933-1982 BioIn 17
Gardner, John E. 1926- BioIn 17
Gardner, John Fentress 1912- WhoE 93
Gardner, John (Linton) 1917- Baker 92
Gardner, John R. 1937- St&PR 93, WhoIns 93
Gardner, John Reed, II 1925- WhoIns 93
Gardner, John Underhill 1924- WhoE 93
Gardner, John W. 1912- PolPar
Gardner, John William 1912- WhoAm 92
Gardner, Joseph C. 1942- St&PR 93
Gardner, Joseph Lawrence 1933- WhoAm 92, WhoWrEP 92
Gardner, Joyce D. 1915- WhoWrEP 92
Gardner, Kathleen D. Law&B 92
Gardner, Kathleen D. 1947- WhoAm 92
Gardner, Keith Hadrian 1930- WhoAm 92, WhoWor 93
Gardner, Keith Howard 1950- WhoEmL 93, WhoSSW 93
Gardner, Kenneth Leroy 1941- St&PR 93
Gardner, Larry McClain 1947- St&PR 93
Gardner, Leonard 1934- St&PR 93
Gardner, Leonard Burton, II 1927- WhoAm 92
Gardner, Lisa Fries Law&B 92
Gardner, Liz 1932- WhoE 93
Gardner, Lloyd Calvin, Jr. 1934- WhoAm 92
Gardner, Lynn Sullivan 1957- WhoAmW 93
Gardner, M. Brent Law&B 92
Gardner, M. Dozier 1933- St&PR 93
Gardner, Margaret Ann 1946- WhoSSW 93
Gardner, Margaret Frances AmWomPl
Gardner, Marshall Allen 1940- WhoAm 92
Gardner, Marshall Closson 1918- WhoE 93
Gardner, Martin 1914- BioIn 17, ScF&FL 92, WhoSSW 93
Gardner, Marvin Allen, Jr. 1943- WhoE 93
Gardner, Mary AmWomPl
Gardner, Mary Ann St&PR 93
Gardner, Mary Bertha Hoeft Chadwick 1914- WhoAmW 93
Gardner, Michael Jospeh 1954- WhoE 93
Gardner, Michael Leopold George 1946- WhoWor 93
Gardner, Moe BioIn 17
Gardner, Murray Briggs 1929- WhoAm 92
Gardner, N.A. 1942- St&PR 93
Gardner, Nancy Bruff 1909- WhoWrEP 92
Gardner, Nancy K. Law&B 92
Gardner, Nord Arling 1923- WhoWor 93
Gardner, Paul Allen 1950- WhoWrEP 92
Gardner, Paul Jay 1929- WhoAm 92
Gardner, Peggy Ann 1937- WhoAmW 93
Gardner, Peter Jaglom 1958- WhoE 93
Gardner, Philip WhoAm 92
Gardner, Philip 1936- ScF&FL 92
Gardner, R.H. 1918- BioIn 17, WhoAm 92
Gardner, R. Hartwell 1934- St&PR 93
Gardner, Ralph David 1923- WhoAm 92
Gardner, Randy Clyburn 1952- WhoEmL 93
Gardner, Ray D. Law&B 92
Gardner, Richard 1931- ScF&FL 92
Gardner, Richard Alan 1931- WhoAm 92, WhoWrEP 92
Gardner, Richard Barnum 1943- St&PR 93
Gardner, Richard Ernest 1942- St&PR 93
Gardner, Richard Hartwell 1934- WhoAm 92, WhoSSW 93
Gardner, Richard Kent 1928- WhoAm 92
Gardner, Richard M. 1942- WhoWrEP 92
Gardner, Richard Newton 1927- WhoAm 92
Gardner, Richard W. 1913- St&PR 93
Gardner, Rita Kathryn 1933- WhoAmW 93
Gardner, Robert 1929- WhoE 93
Gardner, Robert Allen 1934- St&PR 93
Gardner, Robert B. 1956- St&PR 93
Gardner, Robert Charles 1961- WhoEmL 93, WhoSSW 93
Gardner, Robert H. 1913- St&PR 93
Gardner, Robert Michael 1948- WhoEmL 93
Gardner, Robert R. St&PR 93
Gardner, Robin Pierce 1934- WhoAm 92
Gardner, Rodney Earl 1953- WhoSSW 93
Gardner, Romaine L. Law&B 92
Gardner, Russell Menese 1920- WhoAm 92, WhoSSW 93
Gardner, Samuel 1891-1984 Baker 92
Gardner, Sandra 1940- ConAu 138, SmATA 70, WhoE 93
Gardner, Sharon Lee 1957- WhoSSW 93
Gardner, Sharon Marcum 1947- WhoSSW 93
Gardner, Stanley Dwain 1956- WhoSSW 93
Gardner, Stephen Henry 1951- WhoSSW 93
Gardner, Stephen Leroy 1948- WhoWrEP 92
Gardner, Stephen Symmes 1921-1978 BioIn 17
Gardner, Susan M. Law&B 92
Gardner, Terry A. 1952- St&PR 93
Gardner, Thomas E. WhoSSW 93
Gardner, Thomas Earle 1938- WhoAm 92
Gardner, Thomas Edward 1948- WhoAm 92
Gardner, Tonita S. ScF&FL 92
Gardner, Virginia 1904-1992 ConAu 136
Gardner, Walter E. 1954- WhoE 93
Gardner, Warren Joseph, Jr. 1951- WhoEmL 93, WhoWor 93
Gardner, Wendell J. 1933- St&PR 93
Gardner, William Albert, Jr. 1939- WhoAm 92
Gardner, William Alden 1902-1991 BioIn 17
Gardner, William E. BioIn 17
Gardner, William Earl 1928- WhoAm 92
Gardner, William George 1945- St&PR 93, WhoAm 92
Gardner, William Michael 1932- WhoAm 92
Gardner, William Michael 1948- WhoAm 92
Gardner, William T. d1992 BioIn 17, NewYTBS 92
Gardner, William Wayne 1946- WhoSSW 93
Gardner Dunn, Archibald DcCPCAm
Gardner-Wienick, Carol Robin 1956- WhoEmL 93
Gardom, Garde Basil 1924- WhoAm 92
Gardos, G. 1927- WhoScE 91-4
Garduce, Venancio T. 1930- WhoAsAP 91
Gardyne, Mary Elkins AmWomPl
Gareau, Joseph H. 1947- WhoIns 93
Gareeboo, Hassam 1941- WhoWor 93
Garegg, Per J. 1933- WhoScE 91-4
Garegnani, Cynthia Laine Law&B 92
Garegnani, Pierangelo 1930- BioIn 17
Gareiss, Herbert, Jr. 1945- St&PR 93
Garel, John 1958- St&PR 93
Garelick, E. Lee 1934- St&PR 93
Garelick, Martin 1924- WhoAm 92
Garelick, May 1910-1989 BioIn 17
Garesche, Julius Peter 1821-1862 BioIn 17
Garet, C. WhoScE 91-2
Garetti, Marco 1946- WhoScE 91-3
Garey, Donald Lee 1931- WhoAm 92, WhoWor 93
Garey, Jack 1930- St&PR 93
Garey, James Robert 1932- WhoE 93
Garey, Patricia Martin 1932- WhoAmW 93, WhoWor 93
Garey, Roger W. 1921- St&PR 93
Garey, Terry A. 1948- WhoWrEP 92
Garfein, Jack 1930- MiSFD 9
Garfias, Luis Francisco 1968- WhoWor 93
Garfias, Pedro 1901-1967 DcMexL
Garfield, Allen 1939- ConTFT 10, WhoAm 92
Garfield, Bernard Howard 1924- WhoAm 92
Garfield, Brian Wynne 1939- WhoAm 92, WhoWrEP 92
Garfield, Carolyn Joan 1942- WhoAmW 93
Garfield, Cathleen Beall 1961- WhoAmW 93
Garfield, David Crosby 1927- St&PR 93, WhoAm 92
Garfield, Eugene 1925- WhoAm 92
Garfield, Evelyn Picon 1940- WhoAmW 93
Garfield, Gary A. Law&B 92
Garfield, Horace Fuller 1953- WhoSSW 93
Garfield, Howard Robert 1933- St&PR 93
Garfield, Howard S., 2nd 1947- St&PR 93
Garfield, J. Brent Law&B 92
Garfield, James A. 1831-1881 BioIn 17, PolPar
Garfield, Joan Barbara 1950- WhoAmW 93
Garfield, John 1913-1952 BioIn 17, IntDcF 2-3 [port]
Garfield, Leon 1921- ChlFicS, ConAu 38NR, MajAI [port], ScF&FL 92
Garfield, Leslie Jerome 1932- WhoE 93
Garfield, Lucretia Rudolph 1832-1918 BioIn 17
Garfield, Michael R. Law&B 92
Garfield, Nancy Jane 1947- WhoAmW 93
Garfield, Randy Alan 1952- WhoSSW 93
Garfield, Robert Edward 1955- WhoAm 92
Garfield, Timothy K. 1946- St&PR 93
Garfin, Louis 1917- WhoAm 92
Garfinkel, Alan 1941- WhoWrEP 92
Garfinkel, Barry Herbert 1928- WhoAm 92
Garfinkel, Eric I. 1954- WhoAm 92
Garfinkel, Harmon M. 1933- St&PR 93
Garfinkel, Harmon Mark 1933- WhoAm 92
Garfinkel, Herbert 1920- WhoAm 92
Garfinkel, Renee Efra 1950- WhoEmL 93
Garfinkel, Steven R. 1943- St&PR 93
Garfinkle, Barry David 1946- WhoEmL 93
Garfinkle, Louis Alan 1928- WhoWor 93
Garfinkle, Mark Allen Law&B 92
Garforth-Bles, Peter D. Law&B 92
Garfunkel, Art 1941- Baker 92, WhoAm 92
Garfunkel, Florence Rubin d1990 BioIn 17
Garfunkel, Joseph M. 1926- WhoWrEP 92
Garfunkel, Steven B. Law&B 92
Garfunkle, Ellen 1948- St&PR 93
Garg, Devendra 1948- WhoAm 92
Garg, Devendra Prakash 1934- WhoAm 92, WhoSSW 93
Garg, Reva 1945- WhoWor 93
Garg, Vijayendra Kumar 1942- WhoWor 93
Gargalli, Claire W. 1942- St&PR 93
Gargallo, Pablo 1881-1934 BioIn 17
Gargan, Anthony 1942- WhoScE 91-3
Gargan, James V. Law&B 92
Gargan, John Joseph 1930- WhoSSW 93
Gargan, Thomas Joseph 1952- WhoEmL 93
Gargan, William Michael 1950- WhoWrEP 92
Gargana, John J., Jr. 1931- St&PR 93
Gargana, John Joseph, Jr. 1931- WhoAm 92
Gargano, Amil BioIn 17, WhoAm 92
Gargano, Charles Angelo 1934- WhoWor 93
Gargano, Francine Ann 1957- WhoEmL 93
Gargano, Michael Louis 1947- WhoE 93
Gargaro, J.T. 1954- St&PR 93
Gargas, Eivind 1942- WhoScE 91-2
Garges, Susan 1953- WhoAm 92, WhoAmW 93
Gargill, Robert Myron 1934- WhoAm 92

Gargione, Frank 1938- WhoE 93
Gargiul, Donna Marie 1965- WhoE 93
Gargiulo, Generio Thomas 1948- St&PR 93
Gargiulo, Gerald John 1934- WhoE 93
Gargula, Nancy Jane Law&B 92
Gari, Lutfallah T. 1953- WhoWor 93
Gari, Manfred F.H. 1938- WhoScE 91-3
Gari, Roman ScF&FL 92
Garibaldi, Giuseppe 1807-1882 BioIn 17, HarEnMi
Garibaldi, John L. 1953- St&PR 93
Garibaldi, Marie Louise 1934- WhoAmW 93
Garibay, Ricardo 1923- DcMexL
Garibay-Gutierrez, Luis 1916- WhoAm 92, WhoSSW 93, WhoWor 93
Garibay K., Angel Maria 1892- DcMexL
Garic, Harold N. 1946- St&PR 93
Garielli, Francesca c. 1735- OxDcOp
Gariepy, Henry 1930- WhoWrEP 92
Gariepy, Mark Steven 1960- WhoSSW 93
Garifo, Luciano 1949- WhoScE 91-3
Garin, Geoffrey Douglas 1953- WhoAm 92
Garin, Mary S. Painter d1991 BioIn 17
Garin, Oscar G. 1941- WhoAsAP 91
Garing, John Seymour 1930- WhoAm 92
Garinger, Louis Daniel WhoAm 92
Garis, Howard R. 1873-1962 ScF&FL 92
Garison, Lynn Lassiter 1954- WhoAmW 93, WhoEmL 93
Garita, Edgar A. 1938- WhoUN 92
Garizurieta, Cesar 1904-1961 DcMexL
Garl, Tim C. 1956- WhoEmL 93
Garland, Bennett WhoWrEP 92
Garland, Beverly 1930- SweetSg D [port]
Garland, Bruce S. 1946- St&PR 93
Garland, Carl Wesley 1929- WhoAm 92, WhoE 93
Garland, Charles S. 1927-1990 BioIn 17
Garland, Floyd Richard 1938- WhoE 93
Garland, Garfield Garrett 1945- WhoWor 93
Garland, George Arthur 1941- WhoUN 92
Garland, Hamlin 1860-1940 GayN
Garland, Howard 1946- WhoE 93
Garland, James Wilson, Jr. 1933- WhoAm 92
Garland, Joan Bruder 1931- WhoE 93
Garland, Joanne Marie 1947- WhoWrEP 92
Garland, Judy BioIn 17
Garland, Judy 1922-1969 Baker 92, IntDcF 2-3 [port]
Garland, LaRetta Matthews WhoAmW 93, WhoSSW 93
Garland, Madge d1990 BioIn 17
Garland, Michael BioIn 17
Garland, P.B. WhoScE 91-1
Garland, Patrick 1936- MiSFD 9
Garland, Patrick James 1931- St&PR 93
Garland, Peter 1952- Baker 92
Garland, Phillip E. 1932- St&PR 93
Garland, Rebecca Lynn 1953- WhoSSW 93
Garland, Richard Roger 1958- WhoEmL 93
Garland, Robert Field 1934- WhoAm 92
Garland, Sarah BioIn 17
Garland, Sherry 1948- SmATA 73 [port]
Garland, Stephen B. 1946- St&PR 93
Garland, Suzanne Marie WhoWor 93
Garland, Sylvia Dillof 1919- WhoAm 92
Garland, Wayne BioIn 17
Garland, William James 1948- WhoAm 92
Garlandia, Johannes de c. 1195- Baker 92
Garlets, Donovon G. 1938- St&PR 93
Garlette, William Henry Lee 1951- WhoEmL 93, WhoSSW 93
Garlick, Andrew Mark 1951- St&PR 93
Garlick, Jonathan Curtis 1959- St&PR 93
Garlick, Nicholas ScF&FL 92
Garlick, Peter James WhoScE 91-1
Garlick, Ralph W. 1937- WhoAm 92
Garlick, Thomas Bruce 1949- WhoE 93
Garlick, Tom Michael 1951- St&PR 93
Garlid, Kermit Leroy 1929- WhoAm 92
Garling, Carol Elizabeth 1939- WhoSSW 93
Garlinghouse, Bradley Kent 1941- St&PR 93
Garlington, Jack O'Brien 1917- WhoWrEP 92
Garlington, Robert J. 1939- St&PR 93
Garlinski, Jozef BioIn 17
Garlipp, Waldir 1924- WhoWor 93
Garlits, Don BioIn 17
Garlock, Betty Blanche 1935- St&PR 93
Garlock, Edward S. Law&B 92
Garloff, Jurgen 1950- WhoWor 93
Garloff, Samuel John 1947- WhoE 93, WhoWor 93
Garlough, William Glenn 1924- St&PR 93, WhoAm 92
Garman, Eric Thomas 1942- WhoSSW 93
Garman, Karen Ann 1960- WhoAmW 93
Garman, Kim M. Law&B 92
Garman, M. Lawrence 1943- St&PR 93
Garman, Teresa Agnes 1937- WhoAmW 93
Garman, Willard Hershel 1912- WhoAm 92
Garmatis, Iakovos WhoAm 92
Garmel, Jeffery Ira 1952- WhoEmL 93
Garmendia, Julio 1898-1977 SpAmA
Garmezy, Norman BioIn 17
Garmezy, Norman 1918- WhoAm 92
Garmire, Elsa Meints 1939- WhoAm 92, WhoAmW 93
Garmize, Sharon Marie 1950- WhoEmL 93
Garmon, Henry B. 1943- St&PR 93
Garmon, Philip B. 1944- St&PR 93
Garms, David John 1942- WhoE 93
Garms, Walter I. BioIn 17
Garn, Edwin J. ScF&FL 92
Garn, Edwin Jacob 1932- WhoAm 92
Garn, Jake 1932- CngDr 91, ScF&FL 92, WhoAm 92
Garn, Stanley Marion 1922- WhoAm 92
Garneau, Francois-Xavier 1809-1866 BioIn 17
Garneau, Hector de Saint-Denys 1912-1943 BioIn 17
Garneau, Jacques 1939- WhoCanL 92
Garneau, Lucien Joseph 1931- St&PR 93
Garneau, Michel 1939- WhoCanL 92
Garneau, Saint-Denys 1912-1943 BioIn 17
Garner, Alan 1934- BioIn 17, ChlFicS, MajAI [port], SmATA 69 [port]
Garner, Albert Headden 1955- WhoAm 92
Garner, Alto Luther 1916- WhoAm 92
Garner, Carlene Ann 1945- WhoAmW 93
Garner, Celeste Dixon 1934- WhoWor 93
Garner, Charles Kent 1946- St&PR 93, WhoAm 92
Garner, Charles William 1939- WhoAm 92, WhoE 93
Garner, Cindy Anne 1957- WhoSSW 93
Garner, Craig Andrew 1950- WhoE 93
Garner, Debra Williams 1957- WhoWrEP 92
Garner, Donald Glenn 1929- St&PR 93
Garner, Edward L. 1932- St&PR 93
Garner, Edward Markley, II 1949- WhoAm 92, WhoEmL 93
Garner, Elsie Bell 1947- WhoSSW 93
Garner, Erroll (Louis) 1921-1977 Baker 92
Garner, Frederick L. 1940- St&PR 93
Garner, Geraldine 1946- WhoAmW 93
Garner, Graham ScF&FL 92
Garner, Harvey Louis 1926- WhoAm 92
Garner, J. Michael Law&B 92
Garner, James 1928- BioIn 17, IntDcF 2-3, WhoAm 92
Garner, James Parent 1923- WhoAm 92
Garner, Jay Alan 1956- WhoSSW 93
Garner, Jo Ann Starkey 1934- WhoAmW 93
Garner, Jodi Law&B 92
Garner, John C., Jr. 1947- WhoEmL 93
Garner, John Kenneth 1953- WhoSSW 93
Garner, John Michael 1935- St&PR 93, WhoAm 92
Garner, John Nance 1868-1967 PolPar
Garner, John Patrick 1942- St&PR 93
Garner, Kim 1967- BioIn 17
Garner, LaForrest Dean 1933- WhoWor 93
Garner, Lloyd St&PR 93
Garner, Louis M. 1919- St&PR 93
Garner, Margaret BioIn 17
Garner, Mildred Maxine 1919- WhoAm 92
Garner, Paul Trantham 1951- WhoSSW 93
Garner, Peter Ward 1949- WhoE 93
Garner, Phil 1949- WhoAm 92
Garner, R. Colin 1944- WhoScE 91-1
Garner, Richard Warren 1948- St&PR 93, WhoIns 93
Garner, Robert Dale 1933- WhoAm 92
Garner, Robert Edward Lee 1946- WhoSSW 93
Garner, Samuel Paul 1910- WhoAm 92
Garner, Sharon Kay 1947- WhoWrEP 92
Garner, Stanton Berry 1925- WhoWrEP 92
Garner, Theresa Rae 1964- WhoSSW 93
Garner, Thomas Ward 1947- WhoSSW 93
Garner, Timothy David 1959- WhoEmL 93
Garner, Tony David 1945- WhoWor 93
Garner, Wendell Richard 1921- WhoAm 92
Garner, William Darrell 1933- WhoE 93
Garner, William S. 1949- St&PR 93
Garner, William S., Jr. Law&B 92
Garner-Lipman, Karen Lee 1947- WhoWrEP 92
Garnes, Delbert Franklin 1943- WhoSSW 93
Garnes, Eugene Ellsworth 1955- WhoEmL 93
Garnes, Ronald Vincent 1947- WhoSSW 93
Garnes, Wayne 1958- St&PR 93
Garnet, A.H. MajAI, SmATA 72
Garnet, Henry Highland 1815-1882 BioIn 17
Garnett, Alice 1903-1989 BioIn 17
Garnett, Angelica 1918- ConAu 136
Garnett, Bill 1941- ScF&FL 92
Garnett, David 1892-1981 ScF&FL 92
Garnett, David S. 1947- ScF&FL 92
Garnett, Dianne Kay 1948- WhoE 93
Garnett, Eve C. R. 1900-1991 SmATA 70
Garnett, Gerald 1944- St&PR 93
Garnett, Keith Jay 1938- WhoAm 92
Garnett, Louise Ayres d1937 AmWomPl
Garnett, Lynne 1942- ConAu 138
Garnett, Marion Winston 1919- WhoAm 92
Garnett, Marjorie AmWomPl
Garnett, Pryor A. Law&B 92
Garnett, Rhys 1935- ScF&FL 92
Garnett, Robert Selden 1819-1861 HarEnMi
Garnett, Stanley I., II 1943- St&PR 93
Garnett, Stanley Iredale, II 1943- WhoAm 92
Garnett, Stephen Hunter 1928- St&PR 93
Garnett, Susan Bradfield 1947- WhoSSW 93
Garnett, Tay 1894-1977 MiSFD 9N
Garnett, Timothy A. Law&B 92
Garnett, Tony MiSFD 9
Garnett, Wendall d1991 BioIn 17
Garnett, William 1916- WhoAm 92
Garnett, William J. ScF&FL 92
Garney, Charles Arthur 1931- St&PR 93
Garnham, S.P. WhoScE 91-1
Garni, Joseph C. Law&B 92
Garnier, Anton C. 1940- St&PR 93
Garnier, Francis 1839-1873 Expl 93 [port]
Garnier, Francis Gustave 1939- WhoWor 93
Garnier, Jean 1929- WhoScE 91-2
Garnier, Patrick 1944- WhoScE 91-2
Garnier, Robert Charles 1916- WhoAm 92
Garniez, Nancy Caballero 1937- WhoAmW 93
Garns, John David Martin 1933- St&PR 93
Garoeb, Moses Makue 1941- WhoAfr
Garofalo, Joseph Anthony 1953- WhoEmL 93
Garofalo, Robert Conrad 1949- WhoE 93
Garofalo, Robert Joseph 1939- WhoE 93
Garofalo, Roy Lawrence 1932- St&PR 93
Garoff, Thomas Mikael 1946- WhoWor 93
Garofola, Anthony Charles 1954- WhoEmL 93
Garoian, Charles Richard 1943- WhoE 93
Garon, Gerald Stephen 1942- St&PR 93
Garong, Peter Langir WhoAsAP 91
Garonna, Paolo 1948- WhoWor 93
Garonzik, Arnon E. Law&B 92
Garonzik, Elan David 1950- WhoWor 93
Garonzik, Sara E. 1951- WhoAmW 93
Garoogian, Rhoda WhoAm 92
Garouste, Elizabeth BioIn 17
Garouste, Gerard BioIn 17
Garoutte, Bill Charles 1921- WhoAm 92, WhoWor 93
Garpman, Sten Ivar Axel 1944- WhoWor 93
Garpow, James E. 1944- St&PR 93
Garpow, James Edward 1944- WhoAm 92
Garr, Carl R. 1927- St&PR 93
Garr, Carl Robert 1927- WhoAm 92
Garr, Donna L. Law&B 92
Garr, Louis J., Jr. 1939- WhoAm 92
Garr, Louis Joseph, Jr. Law&B 92
Garr, Louis Joseph, Jr. 1939- St&PR 93
Garr, Teri BioIn 17
Garr, Teri 1949?- ConTFT 10
Garr, Teri 1952- WhoAm 92, WhoAmW 93
Garrambone, Leonard J. BioIn 17
Garramone, Daniel Joseph, Jr. Law&B 92
Garramone, Joan Debra 1956- St&PR 93
Garrard, Christopher WhoWrEP 92
Garrard, Don Edward Burdett WhoAm 92
Garrard, Gardiner Wingfield, Jr. 1941- St&PR 93
Garrard, Mary DuBose 1937- WhoAmW 93
Garratt, G.L. 1950- St&PR 93
Garratt, Peter Joseph 1934- WhoWor 93
Garratt, Reg G. 1929- St&PR 93
Garraty, John Arthur 1920- WhoAm 92
Garre, John Michael 1949- St&PR 93, WhoAm 92
Garreans, Leonard Lansford 1942- WhoSSW 93
Garreau, Bruce John 1950- St&PR 93
Garreau, Joel Roland 1948- WhoE 93
Garrec, Jean-Pierre 1944- WhoScE 91-2
Garrelick, Joel Marc 1941- WhoE 93
Garrels, Helen Ann 1940- WhoAm 92
Garrels, John C., III 1940- St&PR 93
Garren, Bruce P. Law&B 92
Garren, Rebecca Smith 1952- WhoEmL 93, WhoSSW 93
Garret, Merril D. 1935- St&PR 93
Garret, Paula Lyn 1951- WhoAm 92, WhoAmW 93
Garreta, Julio 1875-1925 Baker 92
Garreth, Ralph H. 1943- St&PR 93
Garreton Merino, Roberto BioIn 17
Garretson, Donald Everett 1921- WhoAm 92
Garretson, Henry David 1929- WhoAm 92, WhoWor 93
Garretson, Steven Michael 1950- WhoEmL 93
Garrett, Andrea LeNaye 1962- WhoEmL 93
Garrett, Ann 1942- St&PR 93
Garrett, Barbara Jane 1950- WhoEmL 93
Garrett, Beatrice 1929- WhoWrEP 92
Garrett, Betty BioIn 17
Garrett, Brian K. 1947- St&PR 93
Garrett, Carl W. 1944- St&PR 93
Garrett, Caroline Kay 1952- WhoSSW 93
Garrett, Carolyn Joanne 1948- WhoAmW 93
Garrett, Charlene Elizabeth 1960- WhoSSW 93
Garrett, Charles Geoffrey Blythe 1925- WhoAm 92, WhoWor 93
Garrett, Charles Hope 1953- WhoEmL 93, WhoSSW 93
Garrett, Charles Ray 1955- WhoEmL 93
Garrett, Dana BioIn 17
Garrett, Dave ScF&FL 92
Garrett, David C., Jr. 1922- St&PR 93
Garrett, David Clyde, III 1948- WhoEmL 93, WhoSSW 93
Garrett, Donald William, Jr. 1949- WhoSSW 93
Garrett, Dora Melissa 1934- WhoAm 92
Garrett, Douglas Law&B 92
Garrett, Duejean Law&B 92
Garrett, Duejean C. 1942- St&PR 93
Garrett, Duejean Clements 1942- WhoAm 92
Garrett, Edward Cortez 1948- WhoWrEP 92
Garrett, Foster Dale 1935- St&PR 93
Garrett, Franklin Miller 1906- WhoSSW 93
Garrett, George (Mursell) 1834-1897 Baker 92
Garrett, George Palmer, Jr. 1929- WhoAm 92, WhoWrEP 92
Garrett, Gloria Susan 1951- WhoAmW 93
Garrett, Gregory Todd 1961- WhoSSW 93
Garrett, Henry Lawrence, III 1939- NewYTBS 92, WhoAm 92
Garrett, J. Richard 1945- WhoIns 93
Garrett, James F. d1991 BioIn 17
Garrett, James Hanen 1934- WhoSSW 93
Garrett, James Leo, Jr. 1925- WhoWor 93
Garrett, James Lowell 1946- WhoSSW 93
Garrett, James William 1946- WhoE 93
Garrett, Jeanne BioIn 17
Garrett, Jeannette Law&B 92
Garrett, Jerry Dale 1940- WhoAm 92, WhoSSW 93
Garrett, Jill Hope 1954- WhoAmW 93
Garrett, Jo Ann 1949- BioIn 17
Garrett, John 1943- WhoWor 93
Garrett, John B., Jr. St&PR 93
Garrett, John Brian 1937- WhoWor 93
Garrett, John Raymond WhoScE 91-1
Garrett, John W., III 1930- St&PR 93
Garrett, Joseph Edward 1943- WhoSSW 93
Garrett, Joyce Lynn 1946- WhoE 93, WhoEmL 93
Garrett, Kenneth W. 1946- WhoScE 91-1
Garrett, Kenny BioIn 17
Garrett, Larry Carlton 1950- WhoEmL 93, WhoSSW 93
Garrett, Laurel A. 1960- WhoEmL 93
Garrett, Laurie 1954- St&PR 93
Garrett, Lee 1925- WhoSSW 93
Garrett, Leslie 1932- WhoWrEP 92
Garrett, Lila 1925- MiSFD 9
Garrett, Luther Weaver, Jr. 1925- WhoAm 92
Garrett, M. Kerry 1943- WhoScE 91-1
Garrett, Margaret Lucretia 1931- WhoE 93
Garrett, Maurice 1925- St&PR 93
Garrett, Melissa Jo 1956- WhoAmW 93, WhoEmL 93
Garrett, Michael Law&B 92, ScF&FL 92
Garrett, Michael Lewis 1949- WhoSSW 93
Garrett, Nelson Lee 1927- WhoSSW 93
Garrett, P.C. 1936- St&PR 93
Garrett, Panchita 1946- WhoSSW 93
Garrett, Pat 1946- BioIn 17
Garrett, Pat F. 1850-1908 BioIn 17
Garrett, Peter BioIn 17
Garrett, Randall 1927-1987 BioIn 17, ScF&FL 92

Garrett, Reginald Hooker 1939- *WhoAm 92*
Garrett, Richard 1920- *ConAu 37NR*
Garrett, Richard W. 1944- *St&PR 93*
Garrett, Robert 1937- *WhoAm 92*
Garrett, Robert D. 1933- *St&PR 93*
Garrett, Roberta Kampschulte 1947- *WhoSSW 93*
Garrett, Ronald Doyle 1955- *WhoEmL 93, WhoSSW 93*
Garrett, S.D. 1906-1989 *BioIn 17*
Garrett, Sandy *WhoAm 92*
Garrett, Shirley Gene 1944- *WhoAm 92, WhoAmW 93*
Garrett, Siedah 1963- *SoulM*
Garrett, Stephen Denis 1906-1989 *BioIn 17*
Garrett, Stephen P. *Law&B 92*
Garrett, Susan Mary 1961- *WhoWrEP 92*
Garrett, Sylvester 1911- *WhoAm 92*
Garrett, Terese Lowney *Law&B 92*
Garrett, Theodore Louis 1943- *WhoAm 92*
Garrett, Todd Adams 1941- *WhoAm 92*
Garrett, Wilbur Eugene 1930- *WhoAm 92*
Garrett, Wilbur Eugene (Bill Garrett) 1930- *WhoWrEP 92*
Garrett, William Floyd, Jr. 1947- *WhoEmL 93*
Garrett-Goodyear, Joan d1992 *BioIn 17*
Garrett-Goodyear, Joan Hickcox d1992 *NewYTBS 92*
Garretto, Paolo 1903-1989 *BioIn 17*
Garrett Swierc, Glenda Darlene 1963- *WhoAmW 93*
Garrick, David 1717-1779 *BioIn 17*
Garrick, Frederick Evans *Law&B 92*
Garrick, Jacqueline 1963- *WhoAmW 93, WhoWrEP 92*
Garrick, James Joseph, Jr. 1964- *WhoSSW 93*
Garrick, Joseph Daniel 1949- *St&PR 93*
Garrick, Laura Morris 1945- *WhoAmW 93*
Garrido, Clara Zambra 1949- *WhoSSW 93*
Garrido, Mar *ScF&FL 92*
Garrido, Pablo 1905-1982 *Baker 92*
Garrido Atenas, Jorge 1940- *WhoWor 93*
Garrido-Lecca, Celso 1926- *Baker 92*
Garrier, Jo Ann Ross 1960- *WhoAmW 93*
Garriga, Erisbelia 1947- *WhoEmL 93*
Garrigan, Richard Thomas 1938- *WhoAm 92*
Garrigan, Sean *WhoWrEP 92*
Garriga Turon, Margarita 1957- *WhoScE 91-3*
Garrigle, William Aloysius 1941- *WhoE 93*
Garrigo, Jose R. 1936- *St&PR 93*
Garrigues, George Louis 1932- *WhoE 93*
Garrigues, Malvina 1825-1904 *See* Schnorr von Carolsfeld, Ludwig 1836-1865 *OxDcOp*
Garrigus, Charles B(yford) 1914- *ConAu 136*
Garrigus, Upson Stanley 1917- *WhoAm 92*
Garringer, Arthur W. 1926- *St&PR 93*
Garriott, Owen Kay 1930- *WhoAm 92*
Garris, Emilie Ross 1947- *WhoEmL 93*
Garris, Mick *MiSFD 9*
Garrish, Theodore John 1943- *WhoAm 92*
Garrison, Althea 1940- *WhoAmW 93*
Garrison, Betty Bernhardt 1932- *WhoAmW 93*
Garrison, Brenda Gail 1957- *St&PR 93*
Garrison, Clayton 1921- *WhoAm 92*
Garrison, Clifford Talmadge 1932- *St&PR 93*
Garrison, Constance Martin 1946- *WhoSSW 93*
Garrison, Dan 1949- *St&PR 93*
Garrison, Daniel H. 1937- *ConAu 136*
Garrison, David *St&PR 93*
Garrison, David Alan *Law&B 92*
Garrison, David C. 1939- *St&PR 93*
Garrison, Earl Grant *Law&B 92*
Garrison, Edwin H., Jr. *Law&B 92*
Garrison, Elizabeth Jane 1952- *WhoE 93*
Garrison, Ellen Barrier 1944- *WhoSSW 93*
Garrison, Gary 1934- *WhoWor 93*
Garrison, George Hartranft Haley 1938- *WhoSSW 93*
Garrison, George Walker, Jr. 1939- *WhoSSW 93*
Garrison, Guy Grady 1927- *WhoAm 92*
Garrison, Harry W. 1941- *St&PR 93*
Garrison, J.B. *Law&B 92*
Garrison, J. Ritchie 1951- *ConAu 137*
Garrison, Jake Patrick 1956- *St&PR 93*
Garrison, James Samuel 1922- *WhoSSW 93*
Garrison, Jane Gayle 1951- *WhoAm 92*
Garrison, Jim d1992 *NewYTBS 92*
Garrison, Jim 1922-1992 *News 93-2*
Garrison, Jim (C.) 1921-1992 *ConAu 139*
Garrison, Joanne Kathleen *Law&B 92*
Garrison, John Raymond 1938- *WhoAm 92*
Garrison, Keith Ellsworth, Jr. 1946- *WhoSSW 93*
Garrison, Lester Boyd 1948- *WhoEmL 93*
Garrison, Lloyd Kirkham 1897-1991 *BioIn 17*
Garrison, Lucy McKim 1842-1877 *Baker 92*
Garrison, Mabel 1886-1963 *Baker 92*
Garrison, Mahala *WhoWrEP 92*
Garrison, Marion Ames 1907- *WhoAm 92*
Garrison, Mark Joseph 1930- *WhoAm 92*
Garrison, Michael W. *Law&B 92*
Garrison, Michael William 1945- *St&PR 93*
Garrison, Milton 1933- *St&PR 93*
Garrison, Paul F. 1929- *WhoAm 92*
Garrison, Paul Franklin 1929- *St&PR 93*
Garrison, Phil *ConAu 38NR*
Garrison, Philip R. *Law&B 92*
Garrison, Preston Jones 1942- *WhoAm 92, WhoSSW 93*
Garrison, Ray Harlan 1922- *WhoAm 92, WhoWor 93*
Garrison, Richard Christopher 1948- *WhoAm 92*
Garrison, Robert A. 1941- *St&PR 93*
Garrison, Robert E. 1942- *St&PR 93*
Garrison, Robert Frederick 1936- *WhoAm 92*
Garrison, Roger L. 1943- *St&PR 93*
Garrison, Sara K. 1951- *St&PR 93*
Garrison, Stephen Allan 1940- *St&PR 93*
Garrison, Theodosia Pickering 1874-1944 *AmWomPl*
Garrison, Thomas S. 1952- *WhoWrEP 92*
Garrison, Tom 1960- *St&PR 93*
Garrison, Truitt B. 1936- *WhoAm 92*
Garrison, U. Edwin 1928- *WhoAm 92*
Garrison, Walter R. 1926- *St&PR 93, WhoAm 92*
Garrison, Wanda Brown 1936- *WhoAmW 93*
Garrison, William Lloyd 1805-1879 *JrnUS, PolPar*
Garrison, William Louis 1924- *WhoAm 92*
Garrison, Zina *BioIn 17*
Garrison, Zina 1963- *WhoAm 92, WhoAmW 93*
Garrison-Kilbourne, Clara Anne *WhoWrEP 92*
Garriss, James A. *Law&B 92*
Garrity, Dennis Gerard 1953- *WhoEmL 93*
Garrity, Donald Lee 1927- *WhoAm 92*
Garrity, Durwood James 1937- *St&PR 93*
Garrity, Edward Richard, Jr. 1960- *WhoE 93*
Garrity, James Dart 1929- *WhoWor 93*
Garrity, Keith Raymond 1931- *St&PR 93*
Garrity, Leo F. 1919- *St&PR 93*
Garrity, Leona Mary 1908- *WhoAmW 93*
Garrity, Mary E. *Law&B 92*
Garrity, Norman E. 1941- *St&PR 93*
Garrity, Rodman Fox 1922- *WhoAm 92*
Garrity, Sharyn Marie 1947- *WhoAmW 93*
Garrity, Vincent Francis, Jr. 1937- *WhoAm 92*
Garrity, Wendell Arthur, Jr. 1920- *WhoAm 92, WhoE 93*
Garro, Elena *BioIn 17*
Garro, Elena 1920- *DcMexL, SpAmA*
Garrod, D.J. *WhoScE 91-1*
Garrone, Gabriel Marie Cardinal 1901- *WhoWor 93*
Garrone, Gaston-Edouard 1924- *WhoScE 91-4*
Garrone, Robert 1943- *WhoScE 91-2*
Garrott, Frances Carolyn 1932- *WhoAmW 93*
Garrott, Idamae T. 1916- *WhoAmW 93, WhoE 93*
Garrott, Thomas M. 1937- *St&PR 93*
Garrott, Thomas M. 1938- *WhoAm 92*
Garrou, Donna Gaye 1960- *WhoAmW 93*
Garrow, David Jeffries 1953- *WhoAm 92, WhoE 93*
Garrow, Jack A. 1932- *St&PR 93*
Garrow, John Patrick 1928- *St&PR 93*
Garrow, John Stuart *WhoScE 91-1*
Garrow, William 1760-1840 *BioIn 17*
Garrow, William Casselman 1946- *WhoE 93*
Garruto, Michelle Bartok 1961- *WhoWor 93*
Garruto, Ralph Michael 1943- *WhoE 93*
Garry, Ben 1955- *WhoAsAP 91*
Garry, Charlene 1932-1989 *BioIn 17*
Garry, Charles 1909-1991 *AnObit 1991*
Garry, Charles R. 1909-1991 *BioIn 17*
Garry, Chee Yit Meng 1956- *WhoWor 93*
Garry, Frederick Wilton 1921- *WhoAm 92*
Garry, Jean Calvert 1922- *WhoAmW 93*
Garry, Peggy A. *Law&B 92*
Garry, Richard Leonard 1928- *St&PR 93*
Garry, William James 1944- *WhoAm 92*
Garsh, Thomas Burton 1931- *WhoAm 92*
Garshnek, Victoria 1957- *WhoEmL 93*
Garside, John *WhoScE 91-1*
Garside, John Rushforth, II 1935- *WhoAm 92*
Garside, Marlene Elizabeth 1933- *WhoAmW 93*
Garske, Kathleen Agnes Gauthier 1946- *WhoAmW 93, WhoEmL 93, WhoSSW 93*
Garson, Arthur 1914- *St&PR 93*
Garson, Barbara *BioIn 17*
Garson, Brian Keith 1944- *WhoAm 92*
Garson, Dan 1920- *St&PR 93*
Garson, Gary W. *Law&B 92*
Garson, Gary W. 1946- *St&PR 93*
Garson, Greer 1908- *IntDcF 2-3 [port], WhoAm 92*
Garst, David Blackburn 1943- *WhoIns 93*
Garst, Roswell 1898?-1977 *BioIn 17*
Garstang, Roy Henry 1925- *WhoAm 92*
Garsten, Joel Jay 1948- *WhoWor 93*
Garstka, Kenneth E. *Law&B 92*
Garston, Gerald Drexler 1925- *WhoAm 92*
Gart, Murray Joseph 1924- *WhoAm 92*
Gartel, Laurence Maury 1956- *WhoE 93*
Garten, Alan F. M. 1955- *WhoEmL 93*
Garten, David B. *Law&B 92*
Garten, David B. 1952- *WhoAm 92*
Garten, David Burton 1952- *St&PR 93*
Gartenberg, Barry Felix 1956- *St&PR 93*
Gartenberg, Leo 1906-1990 *BioIn 17*
Gartenberg, Seymour Lee 1931- *WhoAm 92, WhoE 93, WhoWor 93*
Gartenhaus, Solomon 1929- *WhoAm 92*
Garth, Bryant Geoffrey 1949- *WhoAm 92*
Garth, David 1930- *PolPar*
Garth, John Campbell 1934- *WhoE 93*
Garth, Leonard I. 1921- *WhoAm 92*
Garth, Mathew *WhoWrEP 92*
Garth, Samuel 1661-1719 *BioIn 17*
Garth, Will 1904-1956 *ScF&FL 92*
Garthoff, Raymond Leonard 1929- *WhoE 93*
Garthwaite, Nicholas 1952- *WhoWor 93*
Gartin, John P. *Law&B 92*
Gartland, James J. 1954- *St&PR 93*
Gartland, James M. 1952- *St&PR 93*
Gartland, John Joseph 1918- *WhoAm 92*
Gartland, William Joseph 1944- *St&PR 93*
Gartland, William Joseph, Jr. 1941- *WhoAm 92*
Gartler, Stanley Michael 1923- *WhoAm 92*
Gartley, Cheryle Blumberg 1947- *WhoEmL 93*
Gartley, Eleanor F. *AmWomPl*
Gartner, Alan P. 1935- *WhoAm 92*
Gartner, Bruce S. 1957- *WhoSSW 93*
Gartner, E.J. 1930- *WhoScE 91-3*
Gartner, George, III 1954- *St&PR 93*
Gartner, Harold Henry, III 1948- *WhoEmL 93, WhoWor 93*
Gartner, Helmut 1932- *WhoScE 91-3*
Gartner, Kerrin Lee- *BioIn 17*
Gartner, Lawrence Mitchel 1933- *WhoAm 92*
Gartner, Lillian Melanie *AmWomPl*
Gartner, Michael G. *BioIn 17*
Gartner, Michael Gay 1938- *WhoAm 92*
Gartner, Murray 1922- *WhoAm 92*
Gartner, Samuel 1901-1991 *BioIn 17*
Garton, Gary K. 1941- *St&PR 93*
Garton, Ray *ScF&FL 92*
Garton, Vernon Keith 1931- *St&PR 93*
Garton, William Reginald Stephen *WhoScE 91-1*
Garts, James Rufus, Jr. 1949- *WhoEmL 93*
Gartz, Linda Louise 1949- *WhoAmW 93*
Gartz, Paul Ebner 1946- *WhoWor 93*
Gartz, William Frederick 1953- *WhoEmL 93*
Gartzke, David G. 1943- *St&PR 93*
Garui, Benson 1956- *WhoAsAP 91*
Garuti, John, Jr. 1952- *St&PR 93*
Garvan, Anthony N.B. d1992 *BioIn 17, NewYTBS 92*
Garvens, James Arvine 1936- *St&PR 93*
Garver, Christian J. *St&PR 93*
Garver, Elayne Teller 1944- *WhoAmW 93*
Garver, James Amos 1937- *WhoSSW 93*
Garver, Oliver Bailey, Jr. 1925- *WhoAm 92*
Garver, Richard Lloyd 1941- *St&PR 93*
Garver, Robert S. 1942- *WhoAm 92*
Garver, Robert Vernon 1932- *WhoAm 92*
Garver, Theodore Meyer 1929- *St&PR 93, WhoAm 92*
Garver, Thomas Haskell 1934- *WhoAm 92*
Garvey, Amy Ashwood *AmWomPl*
Garvey, Amy Jacques *BioIn 17*
Garvey, Cyndy *BioIn 17*
Garvey, Doris Burmester 1936- *WhoAmW 93*
Garvey, Edmond P. d1991 *BioIn 17*
Garvey, Gerald Thomas 1935- *WhoAm 92*
Garvey, James Anthony 1923- *WhoAm 92*
Garvey, James Sutherland 1922- *St&PR 93*
Garvey, Joanne Marie 1935- *WhoAm 92*
Garvey, John Charles 1921- *WhoAm 92*
Garvey, John Leo 1927- *WhoAm 92*
Garvey, Kenneth W. 1946- *St&PR 93*
Garvey, Marcus 1887-1940 *BioIn 17, DcCPCAm, PolPar*
Garvey, Marcus Mosiah 1887-1940 *EncAACR [port]*
Garvey, Marcus Moziah 1887-1940 *DcTwHis*
Garvey, Michael Steven 1950- *WhoE 93*
Garvey, Michelle K. 1958- *St&PR 93*
Garvey, Olive White *AmWomPl*
Garvey, Patrick R. 1942- *St&PR 93*
Garvey, R. Michael 1947- *St&PR 93*
Garvey, Renee J. 1964- *WhoE 93*
Garvey, Richard Anthony 1950- *WhoAm 92, WhoE 93*
Garvey, Robert Robey, Jr. 1921- *WhoAm 92*
Garvey, Steve *BioIn 17*
Garvey, Steven Patrick 1948- *WhoAm 92*
Garvey, Susan Catherine 1958- *WhoAmW 93*
Garvey, William John 1952- *St&PR 93*
Garvin, Andrew Paul 1945- *WhoAm 92*
Garvin, Bruce M. 1933- *St&PR 93*
Garvin, Clarence Alexander, Jr. 1921- *WhoE 93*
Garvin, Clifton C., Jr. 1921- *St&PR 93*
Garvin, Clifton Canter, Jr. 1921- *WhoAm 92*
Garvin, Florence Ward 1928- *WhoE 93*
Garvin, Glenn 1954- *ConAu 136*
Garvin, Noel Jack 1948- *St&PR 93*
Garvin, Richard M. 1934-1980 *ScF&FL 92*
Garvin, Richard W. 1940- *St&PR 93*
Garvin, Richard Wade 1940- *WhoAm 92*
Garvin, Robert P. 1921- *St&PR 93*
Garvin, Thomas Michael 1935- *St&PR 93*
Garvin, Vernon Burgette, III 1950- *WhoSSW 93*
Garwin, Richard Lawrence 1928- *WhoAm 92*
Garwood, Alice *AmWomPl*
Garwood, John Delvert 1915- *WhoAm 92*
Garwood, Julie 1946- *ConAu 138*
Garwood, Victor Paul 1917- *WhoAm 92*
Garwood, William Everett 1919- *WhoE 93*
Garwood, William Lockhart 1931- *WhoAm 92*
Gary, Benjamin Walter, Jr. 1934- *WhoAm 92*
Gary, Charles Lester 1917- *WhoAm 92*
Gary, Dolores A. *Law&B 92*
Gary, Edwin d1990 *BioIn 17*
Gary, James Frederick 1920- *St&PR 93, WhoAm 92*
Gary, Jerdy *BioIn 17*
Gary, Jerome *MiSFD 9*
Gary, John 1932- *WhoAm 92*
Gary, Judson Emmet, III 1954- *WhoEmL 93*
Gary, Julia Thomas 1929- *WhoAmW 93*
Gary, Kenneth J. *Law&B 92*
Gary, Madeleine Sophie 1923- *WhoWrEP 92*
Gary, Martin Neil 1948- *WhoEmL 93, WhoSSW 93*
Gary, Nancy Elizabeth 1937- *WhoAm 92, WhoAmW 93, WhoE 93*
Gary, Robert M. 1922- *St&PR 93*
Gary, Robert W. 1938- *WhoIns 93*
Gary, Roger Vanstrom 1946- *WhoEmL 93, WhoSSW 93, WhoWor 93*
Gary, Romain *BioIn 17*
Gary, Romain 1914-1980 *ScF&FL 92*
Gary, Timothy 1952- *WhoWrEP 92*
Gary, Willie *BioIn 17*
Gary, Willie E. *NewYTBS 92 [port]*
Garyfalos, Ioannis 1922- *WhoScE 91-3*
Garza, Adolph Aranda 1959- *WhoEmL 93*
Garza, Carmen Lomas 1948- *NotHsAW 93*
Garza, Emilio M. 1947- *HispAmA, WhoSSW 93*
Garza, Emilio Miller 1947- *WhoAm 92*
Garza, J.E. *Law&B 92*
Garza, Jacqueline McFarlane 1965- *WhoAmW 93*
Garza, Lila 1953- *NotHsAW 93*
Garza, Mario Martin *Law&B 92*
Garza, Reynaldo G. 1915- *HispAmA, WhoSSW 93*
Garza, Roberto Jesus 1934- *WhoSSW 93*
Garza, Sally Fernandez *NotHsAW 93*
Garza, Ygnacio D. 1953- *HispAmA [port]*
Garzarelli, Elaine *BioIn 17*
Garzarelli, Elaine M. 1951- *News 92 [port], -92-3 [port], St&PR 93*
Garzarelli, Elaine Marie 1951- *WhoAm 92, WhoAmW 93*

Garza-Zavaleta, Peter Albert 1953- *WhoIns 93*
Garzia, Samuel Angelo 1920- *WhoAm 92*
Garzilli, Jane *Law&B 92*
Garzillo, Marcello Joseph 1932- *WhoE 93*
Garzon, Paula *Law&B 92*
Gasanov, Gasan Aziz ogly 1940- *WhoWor 93*
Gasaway, Laura Nell 1945- *WhoAm 92*
Gasaway, Rankin L. *Law&B 92*
Gasbarre, George P. 1925- *St&PR 93*
Gasbarro, Pasco, Jr. 1944- *WhoAm 92*
Gasbarro, William Edward 1947- *WhoEmL 93*
Gasca, Alfonso Flores 1955- *WhoWor 93*
Gascar, Pierre *ConAu 40NR*
Gasch, Oliver 1906- *CngDr 91*
Gasche, Louis M. 1913- *St&PR 93*
Gascho, Joseph Alvin 1947- *WhoE 93*
Gasco, Alberto 1938- *WhoScE 91-3*
Gascoigne, Bamber *BioIn 17*
Gascoigne, J.A. *WhoScE 91-1*
Gascoigne, Marc *ScF&FL 92*
Gascoigne, Toss *ScF&FL 92*
Gascon, F.M. 1956- *WhoScE 91-3*
Gascoyne, David 1916- *BioIn 17*
Gascoyne-Cecil, Robert Arthur Talbot 1830-1903 *BioIn 17*
Gash, Ira Arnold 1930- *WhoE 93*
Gash, Jeff David 1952- *St&PR 93*
Gash, Shirley Ann 1935- *WhoAmW 93*
Gasich, Welko Elton 1922- *WhoAm 92*
Gasink, Warren Alfred 1927- *WhoE 93*
Gasinski, Lech 1936- *WhoScE 91-4*
Gasior, Eugeniusz 1929- *WhoScE 91-4*
Gasior, Michael 1960- *WhoE 93*
Gasiorkiewicz, Eugene Anthony 1950- *WhoWor 93*
Gasiorowicz, Stephen George 1928- *WhoAm 92*
Gasiorowska, Xenia d1989 *BioIn 17*
Gasiorowski, Andrzej *BioIn 17*
Gaska, Christine 1965- *WhoEmL 93*
Gaskell, Mrs. 1810-1865 *ScF&FL 92*
Gaskell, Carolyn Suzanne 1954- *WhoAmW 93*
Gaskell, Colin S. *WhoScE 91-1*
Gaskell, Elizabeth C. *ScF&FL 92*
Gaskell, Jane 1941- *ScF&FL 92*
Gaskell, Robert Eugene 1912- *WhoAm 92*
Gaskell, Vernon Guy 1926- *St&PR 93*
Gaskill, Helen Gertrude *AmWomPl*
Gaskill, Jack Richard 1936- *St&PR 93*
Gaskill, Robert Clarence 1931- *AfrAmBi*
Gaskill, William 1930- *BioIn 17*
Gaskin, Carol *ScF&FL 92*
Gaskin, Felicia 1943- *WhoAm 92*
Gaskin, George Christopher *Law&B 92*
Gaskin, Jerry William 1940- *St&PR 93*
Gaskin, Mary 1925- *WhoE 93*
Gaskin, Richard L. 1954- *St&PR 93*
Gaskins, Junior Parrott Donald Henry *BioIn 17*
Gaskins, Larry Corbitt 1945- *WhoWor 93*
Gaskins, Lee O. 1937- *St&PR 93*
Gaskins, Pee Wee *BioIn 17*
Gaskins, Samuel Paul 1946- *WhoSSW 93*
Gaskins-Clark, Patricia Renae 1959- *WhoSSW 93*
Gaskoin, Catherine Bellaire *AmWomPl*
Gasn, Harvey Victor 1947- *WhoEmL 93*
Gasner, Anne 1927- *WhoWrEP 92*
Gasowski, Wlodzimierz 1933- *WhoScE 91-4*
Gaspar, Andrew 1948- *WhoAm 92*
Gaspar, Anna Louise 1935- *WhoAmW 93*
Gaspar, Charles F.M.S. 1938- *WhoScE 91-2*
Gaspar, Gary J. 1949- *WhoIns 93*
Gaspar, George Jacob 1936- *St&PR 93*
Gaspar, Helder Calado Goncalves 1941- *WhoWor 93*
Gaspar, Peter Paul 1935- *WhoAm 92*
Gaspar, Rezso 1921- *WhoScE 91-4*
Gaspar, Sandor 1929- *WhoScE 91-4*
Gaspar, Thomas E.C. 1938- *WhoScE 91-2*
Gasparac, Hanzi Predanic *WhoScE 91-4*
Gasparec, Vladimir S. *St&PR 93*
Gasparetto, Ettore 1939- *WhoScE 91-3*
Gaspari, Gaetano 1807-1881 *Baker 92*
Gaspari, James A. 1956- *St&PR 93*
Gaspari, Russell Arthur 1941- *WhoAm 92*
Gasparian, Susan A. *Law&B 92*
Gasparic, Jiri 1926- *WhoScE 91-4*
Gasparik, Frank 1938- *St&PR 93*
Gasparik, Jan *WhoScE 91-4*
Gasparik, Valerie Jean *Law&B 92*
Gasparini, Francesco 1668-1727 *Baker 92, OxDcOp*
Gasparini, Len 1941- *WhoCanL 92*
Gasparini, Thomas Arthur *Law&B 92*
Gasparo da Salo 1540-1609 *Baker 92*
Gasparrini, Claudia 1941- *WhoAmW 93*
Gasparro, Frank 1909- *WhoAm 92*
Gasparro, Madeline 1928- *WhoAmW 93*
Gaspe, Philippe-Ignace-Francois Aubert de 1814-1841 *BioIn 17*
Gaspe, Philippe-Joseph Aubert de 1786-1871 *BioIn 17*
Gasper, David A. 1956- *St&PR 93*
Gasper, Jo Ann 1946- *WhoAm 92*
Gasper, Joseph J. 1942- *WhoWor 93*
Gasper, Richard Joseph 1943- *St&PR 93*
Gasper, Ruth Eileen 1934- *WhoWor 93*
Gasper-Galvin, Lee DeLong 1956- *WhoSSW 93*
Gasperini, Elizabeth Carmela 1961- *WhoAmW 93, WhoEmL 93*
Gasperini, Gerard F. *Law&B 92*
Gasperini, Guido 1865-1942 *Baker 92*
Gasperini, Jim 1952- *ScF&FL 92*
Gasperoni, Ellen Jean Lias *WhoAmW 93, WhoSSW 93, WhoWor 93*
Gasperoni, Emil, Sr. 1926- *WhoSSW 93, WhoWor 93*
Gaspey, Thomas 1788-1871 *DcLB 116 [port]*
Gasque, Elizabeth Hawley 1896-1989 *BioIn 17*
Gasque, Harrison 1958- *WhoEmL 93, WhoSSW 93, WhoWor 93*
Gasque, Woodrow Ward 1939- *WhoE 93*
Gass, Clinton Burke 1920- *WhoAm 92*
Gass, Craig E. *Law&B 92*
Gass, Gertrude Zemon *WhoAmW 93*
Gass, Ian Graham *WhoScE 91-1*
Gass, James *St&PR 93*
Gass, James Andrew *Law&B 92*
Gass, Jerry H. 1934- *St&PR 93*
Gass, Kurt E. 1957- *St&PR 93*
Gass, Manus M. 1928- *WhoAm 92*
Gass, Raymond William *Law&B 92*
Gass, Raymond William 1937- *St&PR 93*
Gass, William H. 1924- *BioIn 17, WhoWrEP 92*
Gasse, Francois Louis 1947- *WhoUN 92*
Gassen, Joseph Albert 1926- *WhoAm 92*
Gassenheimer, Linda 1942- *ConAu 137*
Gasser, Gary Lee 1950- *St&PR 93*
Gasser, Georg *WhoScE 91-4*
Gasser, John Richard 1941- *WhoE 93*
Gasser, Richard Charles 1935- *WhoSSW 93*
Gasser, Robert Charles 1936- *St&PR 93*
Gasser, Susan Margaret 1955- *WhoWor 93*
Gasser, Thomas Peter 1933- *St&PR 93*
Gasser, Wilbert Warner, Jr. 1923- *WhoAm 92*
Gassere, Eugene Arthur *Law&B 92*
Gassere, Eugene Arthur 1930- *St&PR 93, WhoAm 92*
Gasset, Jose Ortega y 1883-1955 *BioIn 17*
Gassien, R.G. 1937- *St&PR 93*
Gassiot Matas, Miguel 1937- *WhoScE 91-3*
Gassler, David 1954- *St&PR 93*
Gassman, Catherine A. *Law&B 92*
Gassman, Jayne Dana 1957- *WhoWrEP 92*
Gassman, Paul George 1935- *WhoAm 92*
Gassman, Victor Alan 1935- *WhoWor 93*
Gassman, Vittorio 1922- *BioIn 17, IntDcF 2-3 [port], WhoWor 93*
Gassman, William G. 1926- *St&PR 93*
Gassmann, Florian Leopold 1729-1774 *Baker 92, OxDcOp*
Gassmann, Guenter E. J. 1939- *WhoWor 93*
Gassner, Dennis *BioIn 17*
Gassner, Ferdinand Simon 1798-1851 *Baker 92*
Gassner, Stuart F. *Law&B 92*
Gasso, Carlos Sprekelsen 1942- *WhoScE 91-3*
Gasson, Michael John *WhoScE 91-1*
Gast, Dwight V. 1951- *WhoE 93, WhoEmL 93*
Gast, Peter *Baker 92*
Gast, Robert Gale 1931- *WhoAm 92*
Gastaldon, Stanislas 1861-1939 *Baker 92*
Gastambide, Bernard R.A. 1922- *WhoScE 91-2*
Gastaut, Therese Genevieve 1944- *WhoUN 92*
Gasteazoro, Carlos Manuel 1922-1989 *BioIn 17*
Gasteiger, Johann 1941- *WhoWor 93*
Gastel, Barbara Jean 1952- *WhoSSW 93*
Gaster, Adele Diane 1930- *WhoAmW 93*
Gaster, David Robert 1946- *WhoE 93*
Gaster, M. *WhoScE 91-1*
Gaster, Orville Raymond, Jr. 1942- *WhoSSW 93*
Gaster, T(heodor) Herzl 1906-1992 *ConAu 136*
Gaster, Theodor Herzl 1906-1992 *BioIn 17, NewYTBS 92*
Gasteyer, Carlin Evans 1917- *WhoAmW 93*
Gasteyger, Curt Walter 1929- *WhoWor 93*
Gastfriend, David Robert 1954- *WhoEmL 93*
Gastil, Russell Gordon 1928- *WhoAm 92*
Gastineau, Clifford Felix 1920- *WhoAm 92*
Gastineau, Mark *BioIn 17*
Gastineau, Michael Keith 1957- *WhoIns 93*
Gastinel, Leon-Gustave-Cyprien 1823-1906 *Baker 92*
Gastl, Guenther Alois 1952- *WhoWor 93*
Gastman, Theodore R. 1929- *St&PR 93*
Gastoldi, Giovanni Giacomo c. 1622- *Baker 92*
Gaston, Arthur G. 1892- *ConBlB 4 [port]*
Gaston, Arthur G., Sr. 1892- *AfrAmBi [port]*
Gaston, Bill 1953- *WhoCanL 92*
Gaston, Cito 1944- *WhoAm 92*
Gaston, David Mark 1938- *WhoE 93*
Gaston, Don F. *WhoAm 92*
Gaston, E(verett) Thayer 1901-1970 *Baker 92*
Gaston, Edwin Willmer, Jr. 1925- *WhoSSW 93, WhoWrEP 92*
Gaston, Gerald N. *WhoIns 93*
Gaston, Hartley Russell 1938- *St&PR 93*
Gaston, Hugh Philip 1910- *WhoWor 93*
Gaston, Judith Ann 1950- *WhoEmL 93*
Gaston, Larry Dean 1952- *WhoSSW 93*
Gaston, Mack Charles 1940- *AfrAmBi [port], WhoAm 92*
Gaston, Paul Lee 1943- *WhoSSW 93*
Gaston, W.W. 1926- *St&PR 93*
Gaston, William P. 1950- *St&PR 93*
Gastoue, Amedee (-Henri-Gustave-Noel) 1873-1943 *Baker 92*
Gastwirth, Bart Wayne 1953- *WhoEmL 93*
Gastwirth, Donald Edward 1944- *WhoAm 92*
Gastwirth, Glenn Barry 1946- *WhoE 93*
Gastwirth, Joseph Lewis *WhoAm 92*
Gasztowtt, Guillaume Pierre 1949- *WhoWor 93*
Gatacre, William Forbes 1843-1905 *HarEnMi*
Gatch, Milton McCormick, Jr. 1932- *WhoAm 92*
Gatchel, R. *St&PR 93*
Gateff, Elisabeth 1932- *WhoScE 91-3, WhoWor 93*
Gatell, Jose Maria 1951- *WhoWor 93*
Gately, Arthur Thomas, Jr. 1927- *St&PR 93*
Gately, George 1928- *WhoAm 92*
Gately, John C. 1923- *St&PR 93*
Gately, John J. 1947- *St&PR 93*
Gately, Maurice Kent 1946- *WhoE 93*
Gately, Robert Francis 1947- *WhoE 93*
Gatenbeck, Sten V. 1926- *WhoScE 91-4*
Gatenby, Arthur Whitley 1933- *St&PR 93*
Gatenby, Greg 1950- *WhoCanL 92*
Gater, Mary Theresa 1962- *WhoWor 93*
Gates, Anthony C. 1948- *St&PR 93*
Gates, Arthur Roland, II 1941- *St&PR 93*
Gates, Barbara Lynn 1954- *WhoAmW 93*
Gates, Carmen Jean Wegener 1940- *WhoAmW 93*
Gates, Carolyn Helm 1935- *WhoSSW 93*
Gates, Charles Bradford 1921- *St&PR 93*
Gates, Charles Cassius 1921- *St&PR 93, WhoAm 92*
Gates, Charles R. 1948- *St&PR 93*
Gates, Charles W., Sr. 1943- *WhoAm 92*
Gates, Chester Robert 1925- *St&PR 93*
Gates, Connie Belinda 1965- *St&PR 93*
Gates, Crawford Marion 1921- *WhoAm 92*
Gates, Daryl F. *BioIn 17*
Gates, Daryl Francis 1926- *WhoAm 92*
Gates, Deborah W. *Law&B 92*
Gates, Donald Dean 1930- *St&PR 93*
Gates, Doris 1901- *DcAmChF 1960*
Gates, Doris 1901-1987 *MajAI [port]*
Gates, Dorothy Louise 1926- *WhoAmW 93*
Gates, Earl Dwight 1945- *WhoE 93*
Gates, Earl J. 1918- *St&PR 93*
Gates, (Mary) Eleanor 1875-1951 *AmWomPl*
Gates, Elmer D. 1929- *WhoAm 92*
Gates, Harry Irving 1934- *WhoAm 92*
Gates, Henry Louis *BioIn 17*
Gates, Henry Louis, Jr. 1950- *ConBlB 3 [port], CurBio 92 [port], WhoAm 92*
Gates, Horatio 1728-1806 *BioIn 17, HarEnMi*
Gates, J.C. 1943- *St&PR 93*
Gates, Jacquelyn *AfrAmBi*
Gates, James David 1927- *WhoAm 92*
Gates, James K., II 1944- *St&PR 93*
Gates, Jerrol A. 1941- *St&PR 93*
Gates, Jodie *WhoAm 92*
Gates, John d1992 *NewYTBS 92 [port]*
Gates, John 1913-1992 *BioIn 17*
Gates, John W., III 1939- *WhoIns 93*
Gates, John William Charles *WhoScE 91-1*
Gates, Jonathan Leland 1938- *St&PR 93*
Gates, Larry 1915- *WhoAm 92*
Gates, Leslie Clifford 1918- *WhoAm 92*
Gates, Lewis E. 1860-1924 *GayN*
Gates, M. Mike *WhoIns 93*
Gates, Madi 1938- *WhoAm 92*
Gates, Mahlon Eugene 1919- *WhoAm 92*
Gates, Marshall DeMotte, Jr. 1915- *WhoAm 92*
Gates, Marshall M. 1952- *St&PR 93*
Gates, Martina Marie 1957- *WhoAmW 93, WhoEmL 93*
Gates, Michael D. *Law&B 92*
Gates, Milo S. 1923- *St&PR 93*
Gates, Milo Sedgwick 1923- *WhoAm 92*
Gates, Nancy *SweetSg D [port]*
Gates, Nancy Gotter 1931- *WhoWrEP 92*
Gates, Philip Don 1937- *WhoAm 92*
Gates, R. Patrick 1954- *ScF&FL 92*
Gates, Reginald D. 1942- *WhoWrEP 92*
Gates, Richard Daniel 1942- *St&PR 93, WhoAm 92*
Gates, Richard Wade 1934- *WhoE 93*
Gates, Robert M. *BioIn 17*
Gates, Robert M. 1943- *CurBio 92 [port], News 92 [port], WhoAm 92*
Gates, Robert Michael 1947- *WhoEmL 93*
Gates, Sheree Hunt 1958- *WhoEmL 93, WhoSSW 93*
Gates, Signe S. *Law&B 92*
Gates, Stephen F. *St&PR 93*
Gates, Stephen Frye *Law&B 92*
Gates, Stephen Frye 1946- *WhoAm 92, WhoEmL 93*
Gates, Steven Leon 1954- *WhoEmL 93, WhoSSW 93*
Gates, Susa 1856-1933 *BioIn 17*
Gates, Theodore Ross 1918- *WhoAm 92*
Gates, Theresa Ann 1959- *WhoAmW 93*
Gates, Thomas Edward 1953- *WhoWor 93*
Gates, Timothy Joseph 1951- *St&PR 93*
Gates, Walter B. 1931- *St&PR 93*
Gates, Walter Edward 1946- *St&PR 93, WhoAm 92*
Gates, William 1917- *BiDAMSp 1989*
Gates, William Carl 1940- *St&PR 93*
Gates, William F. 1922- *St&PR 93*
Gates, William H. *BioIn 17*
Gates, William H. 1925- *WhoAm 92*
Gates, William H. 1955- *St&PR 93*
Gates, William Henry 1955- *WhoAm 92*
Gates, William S. 1944- *St&PR 93, WhoIns 93*
Gates-Cohen, Lisa 1955- *WhoAmW 93*
Gatesoupe, F.J. 1950- *WhoScE 91-2*
Gatesy, Carolyne Ilona 1950- *St&PR 93*
Gatewood, D.M. 1948- *St&PR 93*
Gatewood, Lawrence E. 1945- *St&PR 93*
Gatewood, Leonard B. 1947- *St&PR 93, WhoAm 92*
Gatewood, Robert Charles, III *Law&B 92*
Gatewood, Robert Payne 1923- *WhoWor 93*
Gatewood, Willard Badgett, Jr. 1931- *WhoAm 92*
Gath, Eugene G. 1961- *WhoWor 93*
Gath, Norman Clayton 1938- *St&PR 93*
Gath, Philip C. 1947- *St&PR 93, WhoAm 92*
Gather, Ursula 1953- *WhoWor 93*
Gathercole, Patricia May 1920- *WhoSSW 93*
Gatheridge, R. Edward *WhoWrEP 92*
Gathers, Hank *BioIn 17*
Gathers, Patricia Kathleen 1964- *WhoAmW 93*
Gathers, Thomas W. 1956- *St&PR 93*
Gathorne-Hardy, Jonathan G. 1933- *ConAu 39NR*
Gathright, John Byron, Jr. 1933- *WhoAm 92*
Gati, Gyula 1938- *WhoScE 91-4*
Gati, Norman Nandor 1924- *St&PR 93*
Gati, William Eugene 1959- *WhoE 93, WhoWor 93*
Gatineau, Lucien 1927- *WhoScE 91-2*
Gatipon, Betty Becker 1931- *WhoAmW 93*
Gatison, Sheryl Lynn 1957- *WhoAmW 93*
Gatje, Robert Frederick 1927- *WhoAm 92*
Gatliff, Roxann R. 1954- *St&PR 93*
Gatlin, Eugene S., Jr. 1935- *WhoSSW 93, WhoWor 93*
Gatlin, James Paul *Law&B 92*
Gatlin, Larry 1948- *Baker 92*
Gatlin, Larry Wayne 1948- *WhoAm 92*
Gatlin, Michael Gerard 1956- *WhoE 93, WhoEmL 93, WhoWor 93*
Gatling, Irene Banning 1956- *WhoWor 93*
Gatos, Harry Constantine 1921- *WhoAm 92*
Gatrell, Joselle Bernstein 1942- *WhoAmW 93*
Gatski, Frank *BioIn 17*
Gatsos, Dimitrios 1948- *WhoWor 93*
Gatsos, John D. *Law&B 92*
Gatsos, John G. *Law&B 92*
Gatt, Raymond 1959- *WhoWor 93*
Gatta, John Joseph, Jr. 1946- *WhoE 93*
Gattas, Fred Patrick 1914- *St&PR 93*
Gattas, James Wood 1950- *St&PR 93*
Gatter, Jeffery E. 1957- *St&PR 93*
Gatterman, William L. 1954- *St&PR 93*
Gatti, Frank R. 1947- *St&PR 93*

Gatti, Gabriele WhoWor 93
Gatti, Guido M(aggiorino) 1892-1973 Baker 92
Gatti, Juan BioIn 17
Gatti, Marco 1927- WhoScE 91-3
Gatti, Rosa Marie 1950- WhoAmW 93
Gatti-Casazza, Giulio 1868-1940 Baker 92
Gatti-Casazza, Giulio 1869-1940 OxDcOp
Gattie, Erma Charlotte 1961- WhoAm 92
Gattilusio OxDcByz
Gattinella, Wayne T. 1952- St&PR 93
Gatting, Carlene J. 1955- WhoEmL 93
Gattinger, Traugott E. WhoScE 91-4
Gattis, James Ralph 1944- WhoAm 92
Gattis, Jerry D. 1948- St&PR 93
Gatto, Dominick J. 1947- St&PR 93
Gatto, John Taylor ScF&FL 92
Gatto, Joseph Daniel 1956- WhoWor 93
Gatto, Louis Constantine 1927- WhoAm 92
Gatto, Michele S. Law&B 92
Gatto, Ottorino WhoScE 91-3
Gatton, Carol Martin 1932- WhoAm 92
Gatton, Danny BioIn 17
Gatty, Margaret 1809-1873 BioIn 17
Gatty, Nicholas Comyn 1874-1946 Baker 92
Gatty, Trevor Thomas 1930- WhoSSW 93
Gatza, James 1933- WhoIns 93
Gatza, Robert G. 1942- St&PR 93
Gatzek, Deborah R. 1948- St&PR 93
Gatzinsky, Pantalei Hristov 1932- WhoWor 93
Gaubatz, Dieter Siegfried 1952- St&PR 93
Gaube, Erhard 1936- WhoScE 91-3
Gaubert, Alain M. 1944- WhoScE 91-2
Gaubert, Jacques 1926- WhoScE 91-2
Gaubert, Kevin Joseph 1928- WhoSSW 93
Gaubert, Lloyd Francis 1921- WhoSSW 93
Gaubert, Patrice Francois 1944- WhoWor 93
Gaubert, Philippe 1879-1941 Baker 92
Gaubert, Thomas Merrill 1939- St&PR 93
Gauch, Eugene William, Jr. 1922- WhoAm 92
Gauch, Patricia Lee 1934- WhoWrEP 92
Gaucher, Richard Allen Law&B 92
Gauci, Louis 1948- WhoEmL 93
Gauck, Charlie H. Law&B 92
Gaudaire, Maurice 1935- WhoScE 91-2
Gaudemer, Yves 1935- WhoScE 91-2
Gaudens, Augustus Saint- 1848-1907 BioIn 17
Gauderon-Alec, Martine Elisabeth Law&B 92
Gaudet, Belinda 1951- St&PR 93
Gaudet, Charles Philip 1827-1917 IntDcAn
Gaudet, Denise A. Law&B 92
Gaudet, Douglas A. 1954- WhoIns 93
Gaudet, E. Hugh Law&B 92
Gaudette, Donald L., Jr. 1958- St&PR 93
Gaudette, Henri Eugene 1932- WhoAm 92
Gaudi, Antoni 1852-1926 BioIn 17
Gaudiani, Claire Lynn 1944- WhoAm 92, WhoAmW 93
Gaudie, H. Alan 1940- St&PR 93
Gaudier-Brzeska, Henri 1891-1915 BioIn 17
Gaudieri, Alexander V. J. 1940- WhoAm 92
Gaudieri, Millicent Hall 1941- WhoAm 92
Gaudimel, Claude Baker 92
Gaudin, Dean R. 1933- St&PR 93
Gaudino, Edward J. Law&B 92
Gaudino, James Lawrence 1949- WhoSSW 93
Gaudino, Mario 1918- WhoWor 93
Gaudio, Bob BioIn 17
Gaudio, Maxine Diane 1939- WhoAm 92
Gaudion, Donald Alfred 1913- WhoAm 92
Gaudlitz, William Arthur 1932- St&PR 93
Gaudreau, Bernard 1931- WhoScE 91-2
Gaudreault-Labrecque, Madeleine 1931- WhoCanL 92
Gaudry, Roger 1913- WhoAm 92
Gauen, Patrick Emil 1950- WhoAm 92
Gauer, Donald L. 1932- WhoIns 93
Gauer, Edward H. d1991 BioIn 17
Gauert, Mildred Newby 1905- WhoAmW 93
Gauf, Cynthia Green 1962- WhoAmW 93
Gaufredus Malaterra dc. 1101 OxDcByz
Gauger, Charles H. 1944- St&PR 93
Gauger, David Kenyon 1958- WhoWor 93
Gauger, Jurgen F. 1939- WhoScE 91-4
Gauger, Michele Roberta 1949- WhoAmW 93
Gauger, Richard C. ScF&FL 92
Gauger, Rick ScF&FL 92
Gaugh, Harry F. 1938-1992 NewYTBS 92
Gaughan, Eugene Francis 1945- WhoAm 92
Gaughan, Geri-Lynn M. Law&B 92
Gaughan, Gregory Michael Law&B 92
Gaughan, James D. Law&B 92
Gaughan, Norbert F. 1921- WhoAm 92
Gaughan, Thomas M. BioIn 17
Gaughan, Thomas R. 1936- St&PR 93
Gaughan Atlas, Joan M. 1952- WhoEmL 93
Gaugler, Richard L. 1925- St&PR 93
Gauguin, Paul 1848-1903 BioIn 17
Gauk, Alexander 1893-1963 Baker 92
Gaul, Alfred (Robert) 1837-1913 Baker 92
Gaul, Alice LeVeille 1940- WhoSSW 93
Gaul, Kathleen Theresa 1960- WhoEmL 93
Gaul, Lothar 1946- WhoScE 91-3
Gaul, Randy 1959- BioIn 17
Gaul, Timothy James Law&B 92
Gauldin, Michael Glen 1954- WhoSSW 93
Gaule, Beatrice AmWomPl
Gaule, Wendy Anne 1959- WhoAmW 93
Gaulin, J. Guy 1927- St&PR 93
Gaull, Gerald Edward 1930- WhoAm 92, WhoWor 93
Gaull, Natalie L. Law&B 92
Gaulle, Charles de 1890-1970 BioIn 17
Gault, Barbara Jeanne 1935- WhoAmW 93
Gault, Charlayne Hunter- BioIn 17
Gault, James L. 1928- WhoAm 92
Gault, Jean 1953- WhoScE 91-2
Gault, John Franklin 1936- St&PR 93
Gault, Julia Marie 1908- WhoAmW 93
Gault, N. L., Jr. 1920- WhoAm 92
Gault, Peter 1958- ConAu 138
Gault, Robert Allen 1959- WhoEmL 93
Gault, Robert Kruger, Jr. 1944- WhoAm 92
Gault, Seth R. 1935- WhoWrEP 92
Gault, Stanley C. 1926- St&PR 93
Gault, Stanley Carleton 1926- WhoAm 92
Gault, William Campbell 1910- ConAu 37NR
Gaulthier, Denis 1603-1672 Baker 92
Gaulthier, Ennemond 1575-1651 Baker 92
Gaultier, Denis 1603-1672 Baker 92
Gaultier, Ennemond 1575-1651 Baker 92
Gaultier, Jean-Paul BioIn 17
Gaultney, John Orton 1915- WhoAm 92
Gaum, Carl Henry 1922- WhoE 93
Gaumann, Tino 1925- WhoScE 91-4
Gaumer, Gary L. 1946- St&PR 93
Gaumond, George Raymond 1946- WhoSSW 93
Gauna, Monica Collins 1963- WhoE 93
Gaunaurd, Guillermo C. 1940- WhoAm 92
Gaunlett, Thomas R. 1945- St&PR 93
Gaunt, David Stafford WhoScE 91-1
Gaunt, Eleanor ScF&FL 92
Gaunt, Keith Hunton 1944- WhoWor 93
Gaunt, William L. Law&B 92
Gauntlett, Donald Wayne 1940- WhoE 93
Gauntner, Anthony Joseph 1954- WhoSSW 93
Gauntt, William Amor 1926- St&PR 93
Gaup, Nils MiSFD 9
Gaupp, Andrew Christopher 1954- WhoSSW 93
Gauron, Eugene F. 1935- WhoAm 92
Gaus, Bertha AmWomPl
Gaus, William Thomas 1928- St&PR 93
Gausch, Kurt 1932- WhoScE 91-4
Gause, Jeannette L. 1956- WhoSSW 93
Gauss, Louise Fallenstein AmWomPl
Gaussens, Jacques 1920- WhoScE 91-2
Gaussot, Olivier 1949- WhoWor 93
Gaustad, Edwin Scott 1923- WhoAm 92, WhoWrEP 92
Gaustad, John Eldon 1938- WhoAm 92
Gaut, C. Christopher 1956- St&PR 93
Gaut, Marvin Joseph 1911- St&PR 93, WhoAm 92
Gaut, Norman Eugene 1937- St&PR 93, WhoAm 92
Gautam, Anand Prakash 1941- WhoAsAP 91
Gautam, Kul Chandra 1949- WhoE 93, WhoUN 92
Gautam, Sunil Rashmikant 1954- WhoWor 93
Gautama Buddha BioIn 17
Gautheron, Daniele C. 1927- WhoScE 91-2
Gauthier, Alan E. 1947- St&PR 93
Gauthier, Andre Pierre 1933- WhoWor 93
Gauthier, Ann Wilmot BioIn 17
Gauthier, Clarence Joseph 1922- WhoAm 92
Gauthier, (Ida Josephine Phoebe) Eva 1885-1958 Baker 92
Gauthier, Gerald Law&B 92
Gauthier, Gerard 1923- WhoScE 91-4
Gauthier, Henry E. 1940- St&PR 93
Gauthier, Joseph Stephen 1950- WhoEmL 93, WhoSSW 93
Gauthier, Louis 1944- WhoCanL 92
Gauthier, Michel J. 1939- WhoScE 91-2
Gauthier, Paule 1943- WhoAmW 93
Gauthier, Russell John 1942- St&PR 93
Gautier, Achilles 1937- WhoScE 91-2
Gautier, Agnes M. 1939- St&PR 93
Gautier, Denis 1603-1672 Baker 92
Gautier, Dick 1937- WhoAm 92
Gautier, Ennemond 1575-1651 Baker 92
Gautier, (Jean-Francois-) Eugene 1822-1878 Baker 92
Gautier, Jean-Claude 1926- WhoScE 91-2
Gautier, Judith 1845-1917 BioIn 17
Gautier, Norman Edward 1939- St&PR 93
Gautier, Samuel Peter 1932- WhoSSW 93
Gautier, Theophile 1811-1872 DcLB 119 [port], ScF&FL 92
Gautieri, Ronald Francis 1933- WhoE 93
Gautney, George Ernest 1935- St&PR 93
Gautray, Jean Pierre 1924- WhoScE 91-2
Gautreau, Lynda Law&B 92
Gautreaux, Marcelian Francis, Jr. 1930- WhoAm 92
Gautreaux, Tim Martin 1947- WhoWrEP 92
Gautron, Rene Lucien Theophile 1932- WhoScE 91-2
Gautschi, Walter 1927- WhoAm 92
Gautschy, Gudrun Dorothea 1944- WhoE 93
Gauvain, Mary Theresa 1952- WhoAmW 93
Gauvey, Ralph Edward, Jr. 1947- WhoWrEP 92
Gauvin, Alvin L. 1947- St&PR 93
Gauvin, Alvin Lawrence 1947- WhoAm 92
Gauvin, Lise 1940- WhoCanL 92
Gauvreau, Claude 1925-1971 BioIn 17
Gauvreau, Norman Paul 1948- WhoE 93
Gauvreau, Paul Richard 1939- St&PR 93
Gavac, Donna Broderick 1926- WhoWor 93, WhoWrEP 92
Gavalas, Alexander Beary 1945- WhoE 93
Gavalas, George R. 1936- WhoAm 92
Gavalas, Nikos A. 1934- WhoScE 91-3
Gavaldon, Darcy Jo 1956- St&PR 93
Gavaldon, Roberto 1909-1990? MiSFD 9N
Gavan, James Anderson 1916- WhoAm 92
Gavan, Patricia Jane Law&B 92
Gavarni, Paul 1804-1866 BioIn 17
Gavaudan, Emilie 1775-1837 See Gaveaux, Pierre 1760-1825 OxDcOp
Gavaudan, Pierre 1772-1840 See Gaveaux, Pierre 1760-1825 OxDcOp
Gavazzeni, Gianandrea 1909- Baker 92, OxDcOp
Gavazzi, Aladino A. 1922- WhoAm 92
Gavazzi, Gino 1938- WhoWor 93
Gavazzi, Giuseppe 1936- WhoScE 91-3
Gave, Charles Jean 1943- WhoWor 93
Gaveaux, Pierre 1760-1825 OxDcOp
Gaveaux, Simon 1759- OxDcOp
Gavel-Adams, Ann-Charlotte Maria 1944- WhoAmW 93
Gavelis, Jonas Rimvydas 1950- WhoWor 93
Gavello, Donald Louis 1935- St&PR 93
Gavenda, John David 1933- WhoAm 92
Gavenus, Edward Richard 1932- St&PR 93, WhoAm 92
Gaver, Eleanor MiSFD 9
Gaver, Mary Virginia d1991 NewYTBS 92 [port]
Gaver, Mary Virginia 1906-1991 BioIn 17, ConAu 136, CurBio 92N
Gavert, Paul d1992 BioIn 17, NewYTBS 92
Gavey, James Edward 1942- St&PR 93, WhoSSW 93
Gavey, Joan Moran 1943- St&PR 93
Gavigan, Mary Teresa Andrea Law&B 92
Gavigan, Michael T. 1958- St&PR 93
Gavilan, J. Maria 1927- WhoScE 91-3
Gavin, Austin 1909- WhoAm 92
Gavin, Carol Coghlan Law&B 92
Gavin, Caroline Anne 1945- WhoAmW 93
Gavin, Herbert James 1921- WhoAm 92
Gavin, James John, Jr. 1922- WhoAm 92
Gavin, James Martin 1956- WhoE 93
Gavin, James Maurice 1907-1990 BioIn 17
Gavin, James Thomas 1934- WhoAm 92
Gavin, Jamila ChlFicS
Gavin, Jamila 1941- ScF&FL 92
Gavin, John Anthony 1932- WhoAm 92
Gavin, John T. 1951- St&PR 93
Gavin, Joseph G. Law&B 92
Gavin, Julie C. Law&B 92
Gavin, Mary AmWomPl
Gavin, Robert Michael, Jr. 1940- WhoAm 92
Gavin, Thomas Michael 1941- WhoWrEP 92
Gavin, Wendy Joan 1953- WhoAmW 93
Gavin, William Gerard 1951- St&PR 93
Gavinies, Pierre 1728-1800 Baker 92
Gaviola, Enrique d1989 BioIn 17
Gaviria, Cesar BioIn 17
Gaviria, Victor 1955- MiSFD 9
Gaviria Trujillo, Cesar 1947- WhoWor 93
Gavoty, Bernard 1908-1981 Baker 92
Gavranovic, Thomas Joseph Law&B 92
Gavras, Constantin 1933- WhoAm 92, WhoWor 93
Gavras, Costa- MiSFD 9
Gavriil of Lesnovo fl. 11th cent.-12th cent. OxDcByz
Gavrilenko, Vladimir Ivanovich 1949- WhoWor 93
Gavrilin, Valery 1939- Baker 92
Gavrilov, Andrei 1955- Baker 92
Gavrilov, Trajco Slavko 1948- WhoUN 92
Gavrin, Vladimir Nicolayevich 1941- WhoWor 93
Gavrity, John D. 1940- WhoIns 93
Gavrity, John Decker 1940- St&PR 93, WhoAm 92
Gaw, Allison AmWomPl
Gaw, Diane Leighton 1949- WhoAmW 93
Gaw, Doyle S. 1931- St&PR 93
Gaw, Edward R. 1936- St&PR 93
Gaw, Ethelean Tyson AmWomPl
Gaw, James Richard 1943- WhoE 93
Gaw, Robert Bruce 1957- WhoEmL 93
Gawalt, Gerard Wilfred 1943- WhoAm 92
Gawarecki, Carolyn Grosse 1931- WhoAmW 93
Gawchik, Sandra Mary WhoAmW 93
Gawecki, Kazimierz 1915- WhoScE 91-4
Gawehn-Frisby, Dorothy Jeanne 1931- WhoAmW 93
Gawf, John Lee 1922- WhoAm 92
Gawlak, Albert A. 1962- WhoE 93
Gawley, Robert Edgar 1948- WhoSSW 93
Gawlinski, Wladyslaw 1881-1973 PolBiDi
Gawron, Jean Mark 1953- ScF&FL 92
Gawron, Valerie J. 1954- WhoE 93
Gawronik, Aleksander BioIn 17
Gawronski, Adalbert (Wojciech) 1868-1910 Baker 92
Gawronski, Mieczyslaw 1933- WhoWor 93
Gawronski, Wojciech 1868-1910 PolBiDi
Gawryn, Marvin 1951- WhoWrEP 92
Gawthrop, Peter John WhoScE 91-1
Gawthrop, Robert S., III 1942- WhoAm 92, WhoE 93
Gay, Albert Loyal, Jr. 1940- WhoAm 92
Gay, Andrew M. 1931- St&PR 93
Gay, Anne 1952- ScF&FL 92
Gay, August Francois 1890-1949 BioIn 17
Gay, Bernd 1941- WhoScE 91-3
Gay, Brian WhoScE 91-1
Gay, Charles Edward 1940- St&PR 93
Gay, David Holden 1954- WhoE 93
Gay, Delphine 1804-1855 BioIn 17
Gay, Donald R. St&PR 93
Gay, E. Laurence 1923- St&PR 93
Gay, Ebenezer 1696-1787 BioIn 17
Gay, Emil Laurence 1923- WhoAm 92
Gay, Frances Marion Welborn 1956- WhoSSW 93
Gay, Francisque 1885-1963 BioIn 17
Gay, Ginger 1947- WhoSSW 93
Gay, Helen 1918- WhoAm 92
Gay, Jean-Bernard 1942- WhoScE 91-4
Gay, John 1685-1732 Baker 92, BioIn 17, IntDcOp, OxDcOp
Gay, John Marion 1936- WhoSSW 93, WhoWor 93
Gay, Lee Anderson 1952- WhoAm 92
Gay, Leonard Omar 1919- St&PR 93
Gay, Maria 1879-1943 Baker 92, OxDcOp
Gay, Marie-Louise 1952- BioIn 17, ChlLR 27 [port], WhoCanL 92
Gay, Matthew Thomas Law&B 92
Gay, Michael H. Law&B 92
Gay, Michel 1949- WhoCanL 92
Gay, Nancy Bingham 1923- WhoE 93
Gay, Nyra P. 1936- St&PR 93
Gay, Olin Robert, Jr. 1940- St&PR 93
Gay, Peter 1923- WhoAm 92, WhoWrEP 92
Gay, Philip T. 1949- St&PR 93
Gay, Priscilla Hale 1948- WhoAmW 93, WhoEmL 93
Gay, Robert Derril 1939- WhoAm 92
Gay, Ruth 1922- ConAu 139
Gay, Ruth Nunn 1927- WhoAmW 93
Gay, Spencer Bradley 1948- WhoEmL 93, WhoSSW 93
Gay, Sydney Howard 1814-1888 JrnUS
Gay, Tom David 1947- WhoAm 92
Gay, Volney P(atrick) 1948- ConAu 40NR
Gay, Walter 1856-1937 BioIn 17
Gay, William Arthur, Jr. 1936- WhoAm 92
Gay, William Ingalls 1926- WhoAm 92
Gayane OxDcByz
Gayarre, Julian 1844-1890 Baker 92, OxDcOp
Gay-Bryant, Claudine Moss 1915- WhoAmW 93
Gay-Crosier, Raymond 1937- WhoSSW 93
Gayda, Michael D. Law&B 92
Gaydar, Yegor Timurovich 1956- WhoWor 93
Gaydos, John Vincent 1950- St&PR 93
Gaydos, Joseph M. 1926- CngDr 91

Gaydos, Joseph Matthew 1926- *WhoAm 92, WhoE 93*
Gaydos, Michael Edward, IV 1956- *WhoE 93, WhoWor 93*
Gaydos, Michael Ross 1942- *St&PR 93*
Gaye, Marvin *BioIn 17*
Gaye, Marvin 1939-1984 *SoulM*
Gaye, Marvin (Pentz) 1939-1984 *Baker 92*
Gayer (Ashkenasi), Catherine 1937- *Baker 92*
Gayer, Catherine 1937- *OxDcOp*
Gayer, John Harrison 1919- *WhoAm 92*
Gayer, Katherine L. *Law&B 92*
Gayer, Petr 1944- *WhoScE 91-4*
Gayhart, Keith Alan 1954- *WhoEmL 93*
Gayhart, Roy L. 1950- *St&PR 93*
Gayle, Addison 1932-1991 *BioIn 17, BlkAull 92*
Gayle, Crystal *WhoAm 92*
Gayle, Crystal 1951- *Baker 92*
Gayle, Gibson, Jr. 1926- *WhoAm 92*
Gayle, Helene D. *BioIn 17*
Gayle, Helene D. 1955- *ConBlB 3 [port]*
Gayle, Joseph Central, Jr. 1942- *WhoE 93*
Gayle, Karalene Joyce *Law&B 92*
Gayle, Katherine Jean 1965- *WhoAmW 93*
Gayler, John 1943- *WhoAsAP 91*
Gayles, Joseph Nathan, Jr. *WhoAm 92*
Gaylin, Ned L. 1935- *WhoAm 92, WhoE 93*
Gaylin, Willard 1925- *WhoAm 92, WhoE 93*
Gaylis, Norman Brian 1950- *WhoSSW 93*
Gaylo, Paul Joseph *Law&B 92*
Gaylor, Bettie May 1959- *WhoEmL 93*
Gaylor, Diane Marie 1938- *WhoAmW 93*
Gaylor, Donald Hughes 1926- *WhoAm 92, WhoWor 93*
Gaylor, James Leroy 1934- *WhoE 93*
Gaylor, Madeleine 1901- *WhoAmW 93*
Gaylor, Walter Ralph 1924- *WhoSSW 93*
Gaylord, Bruce Michael *Law&B 92*
Gaylord, Edward King 1873-1974 *DcLB 127 [port]*
Gaylord, Edward Lewis 1919- *DcLB 127 [port], St&PR 93, WhoAm 92*
Gaylord, Helen *AmWomPl*
Gaylord, Kathleen A. *Law&B 92*
Gaylord, Norman Grant 1923- *WhoAm 92*
Gaylord, Robert S. *St&PR 93*
Gaylord, S. Murray 1942- *WhoAm 92*
Gaylord, Sanford Fred 1923- *WhoAm 92*
Gaylord, William O. *Law&B 92*
Gaylord-Ross, Robert 1945-1990 *BioIn 17*
Gayman, Benjamin Franklin 1947- *WhoE 93*
Gaynard, Thomas Joseph 1950- *WhoWor 93*
Gayner, Esther K. d1992 *NewYTBS 92*
Gayner, Esther K. 1914- *WhoAm 92*
Gaynes, Albert H. d1991 *BioIn 17*
Gaynier, Michael *St&PR 93*
Gaynor, Christine K. *Law&B 92*
Gaynor, David Bennett *Law&B 92*
Gaynor, Edward Barry 1941- *WhoE 93*
Gaynor, Gloria 1949- *SoulM*
Gaynor, Herbert Fred 1923- *St&PR 93*
Gaynor, Janet 1906-1984 *BioIn 17, IntDcF 2-3*
Gaynor, Joseph 1925- *WhoAm 92*
Gaynor, Joseph Patrick, III 1948- *St&PR 93*
Gaynor, Leah 1931- *WhoAmW 93, WhoSSW 93*
Gaynor, Lee 1927- *St&PR 93*
Gaynor, Martin Scott 1955- *WhoEmL 93*
Gaynor, Pamela Ariana 1939- *WhoAmW 93*
Gaynor, Paul B. *Law&B 92*
Gaynor, Ronald K. 1952- *St&PR 93*
Gayoom, Maumoon Abdul 1939- *WhoWor 93*
Gayot, Francois *DcCPCAm*
Gayral, Louis Francois 1916- *WhoScE 91-2*
Gayral, Philippe 1941- *WhoScE 91-2*
Gayssot, Jean-Claude 1946?- *BioIn 17*
Gaytan, Carol Wesselman 1958- *WhoAmW 93*
Gayton, Bradley Michael *Law&B 92*
Gayton, Joe *MiSFD 9*
Gazaix, Maurice 1928- *WhoScE 91-2*
Gazale, Midhat Joseph 1929- *WhoWor 93*
Gazarian, Armand *MiSFD 9*
Gazda, Emil 1931- *WhoScE 91-4*
Gazda, Walter Edward 1955- *WhoEmL 93*
Gazdag, Gyula *BioIn 17*
Gazdag, Gyula 1947- *MiSFD 9*
Gazdanov, Gaito 1903-1971 *ScF&FL 92*
Gazdanov, Georgii *ScF&FL 92*
Gazdar, Gerald James Michael *WhoScE 91-1*
Gazdar, Gerald James Michael 1950- *WhoWor 93*
Gazdzicki, Jerzy 1931- *WhoScE 91-4*
Gaze, Nigel Raymond 1943- *WhoWor 93*
Gaze, Raymond Michael *WhoScE 91-1*
Gazecki, William J. 1925- *St&PR 93*
Gazeley, Harold James 1923- *St&PR 93*
Gazes, Theodore c. 1400-1475? *OxDcByz*
Gazeta, Mario Joao 1959- *WhoWor 93*
Gazinski, Benon 1953- *WhoWor 93*
Gazley, John Gerow 1895-1991 *BioIn 17*
Gaztambide, Joaquin 1822-1870 *OxDcOp*
Gaztambide (y Garbayo), Joaquin (Romualdo) 1822-1870 *Baker 92*
Gazzam, A. Cheney 1965- *WhoSSW 93*
Gazzaniga, Giovanna 1946- *WhoScE 91-3*
Gazzaniga, Giuseppe 1743-1818 *Baker 92, OxDcOp*
Gazzaniga, Marietta 1824-1884 *OxDcOp*
Gazzara, Ben 1930- *BioIn 17, MiSFD 9, WhoAm 92*
Gazzelloni, Severino d1992 *NewYTBS 92*
Gazzelloni, Severino 1919- *Baker 92*
Gazzola, Kenneth Everett 1940- *St&PR 93*
Gazzoli, Joseph J. *Law&B 92*
Gazzoli, Joseph John 1952- *St&PR 93*
Gbewonyo, Sylvestre Kwadzo 1942- *WhoWor 93*
Gbezera-Bria, Michel 1946- *WhoAfr*
Gburzynski, John Joseph 1943- *WhoE 93*
G. de Zubiaurre, Leopoldo 1924- *WhoWor 93*
Gdoutos, Emmanuel E. 1948- *WhoScE 91-3*
Gdowski, Clarence John 1933- *St&PR 93, WhoAm 92*
Gdowski, Walter J. 1946- *WhoIns 93*
Gdowski, Walter John 1946- *St&PR 93*
Ge, Guang Ping 1934- *WhoWor 93*
Ge, Yubo 1942- *WhoWor 93*
Geach, John J. *St&PR 93*
Geach, Richard L. 1941- *WhoAm 92*
Geadelmann, Patricia Lou *WhoAmW 93*
Geaghan, John M. *Law&B 92*
Geair, Harry F. *Law&B 92*
Gealt, Adelheid Maria 1946- *WhoAm 92*
Geanakoplos, Deno John 1916- *WhoAm 92*
Geaney, Dennis J. *BioIn 17*
Geannopulos, Nicholas George 1930- *WhoAm 92*
Geanuracos, Elsie Da Silva 1922- *WhoAmW 93*
Gear, A. *WhoScE 91-1*
Gear, Alan 1949- *WhoScE 91-1*
Gear, Charles William 1935- *WhoAm 92*
Gear, George 1947- *WhoAsAP 91*
Gear, Kathleen O'Neal 1954- *ScF&FL 92, SmATA 71*
Gear, Marty *ScF&FL 92*
Gear, Sara Moreau 1941- *WhoAmW 93*
Gear, W. Michael 1955- *ScF&FL 92, SmATA 71*
Gearan, Mark Daniel 1956- *NewYTBS 92 [port]*
Gearde, Lisa F. 1961- *St&PR 93*
Geare, Michael 1919- *ScF&FL 92*
Gearhart, Frank Xavier 1959- *WhoSSW 93*
Gearhart, John Wesley, III 1950- *WhoEmL 93, WhoSSW 93*
Gearhart, Marilyn Kaye 1950- *WhoAmW 93*
Gearhart, Martha Susan 1953- *WhoEmL 93*
Gearhart, Marvin 1927- *WhoAm 92*
Gearhart, Pearl H. 1943- *St&PR 93*
Gearhart, Sally Miller 1931- *ScF&FL 92*
Gearhart, Thomas Lee 1942- *WhoAm 92*
Gearheart, James W. *Law&B 92*
Gearheart, Linda Beach 1949- *WhoSSW 93*
Gearon, Jamie H. *Law&B 92*
Gearon, John Michael 1934- *WhoAm 92, WhoSSW 93*
Gearty, Edward Joseph 1923- *WhoAm 92*
Geary, Anthony *BioIn 17*
Geary, David Leslie 1947- *WhoAm 92, WhoEmL 93, WhoSSW 93, WhoWor 93*
Geary, John White 1819-1873 *BioIn 17*
Geary, Joseph E., Jr. 1939- *St&PR 93*
Geary, Marie Josephine 1933- *WhoAmW 93*
Geary, Michael *BioIn 17*
Geary, Patricia 1951- *ScF&FL 92*
Geary, Patrick Joseph 1948- *WhoSSW 93*
Geary, Thomas F. 1932- *St&PR 93*
Geary, Vanessa 1953- *WhoAmW 93*
Geary, William James *WhoScE 91-1*
Geasland, Jack 1944- *ScF&FL 92*
Geasland, John B. *ScF&FL 92*
Geballe, Ronald 1918- *WhoAm 92*
Geballe, Theodore Henry 1920- *WhoAm 92*
Gebben, Charles W. 1940- *St&PR 93*
Gebbers, Jan-Olaf 1942- *WhoWor 93*
Gebbia, Karen Marie 1958- *WhoAmW 93*
Gebbia, Robert James 1947- *WhoE 93*
Gebbia, Stephen Louis 1930- *St&PR 93*
Gebbie, Kristine Moore 1943- *WhoAm 92*
Gebczynski, Marek 1938- *WhoScE 91-4*
Gebel, Georg 1709-1753 *Baker 92*
Gebelein, Richard Stephen 1946- *WhoAm 92*
Gebelein, Robert Seaver 1934- *WhoWrEP 92*
Gebel-Williams, Gunther *BioIn 17*
Gebel-Williams, Gunther 1934- *WhoAm 92*
Geber, Anthony 1919- *WhoAm 92*
Gebert, Helga 1935- *BioIn 17*
Gebert, Horst *WhoScE 91-4*
Gebert, Sandra Margot 1961- *WhoEmL 93*
Gebhard, David 1927- *WhoAm 92*
Gebhard, Heinrich 1878-1963 *Baker 92*
Gebhard, James J. 1945- *St&PR 93*
Gebhardt, Franz 1930- *WhoScE 91-3*
Gebhardt, Karl-Heinz 1924- *WhoScE 91-3*
Gebhardt, Robert A. *Law&B 92*
Gebhardt, Wolfgang 1930- *WhoScE 91-3*
Gebhart, Carl Grant 1926- *WhoAm 92*
Gebhart, Christopher W. 1951- *St&PR 93*
Gebhart, E. Roger 1957- *WhoSSW 93*
Gebhart, John E., III *St&PR 93*
Gebhart, Joseph Gilbert 1953- *WhoEmL 93*
Gebler, D.B. 1949- *St&PR 93*
Gebman, Eva Urlish 1948- *WhoWrEP 92*
Gebo, Susan Claire 1954- *WhoAmW 93*
Gebreel, Ashour Omar 1935- *WhoUN 92*
Gebre-Kidhan, Tesfaye *WhoAfr*
Gecel, Claudine 1957- *WhoAmW 93*
Gecht, Martin Louis 1920- *St&PR 93, WhoAm 92*
Gecht, Robert D. 1951- *St&PR 93*
Gechtoff, Sonia 1926- *WhoAm 92, WhoE 93*
Geckle, George Leo, III 1939- *WhoAm 92, WhoWrEP 92*
Geckle, Jerome William 1929- *St&PR 93*
Geckle, Robert A. 1944- *St&PR 93*
Geckle, Robert Alan 1944- *WhoAm 92*
Geckle, Timothy James *Law&B 92*
Geckle, William Jude 1955- *WhoE 93*
Geckler, Ralph William 1923- *St&PR 93*
Geckler, Richard Delph 1918- *WhoAm 92*
Gecowets, Jerry L. 1936- *St&PR 93*
Geczy, Paul C. 1951- *St&PR 93*
Ged, Caer *ScF&FL 92*
Gedale, William Joseph 1942- *St&PR 93*
Gedalge, Andre 1856-1926 *Baker 92*
Gedda, Giulio Cesare 1899-1970 *Baker 92*
Gedda, Nicolai 1925- *Baker 92, IntDcOp, OxDcOp*
Geddes, Adrienne *ScF&FL 92*
Geddes, Barbara Sheryl 1944- *WhoWor 93*
Geddes, Eric Campbell 1875-1937 *BioIn 17*
Geddes, F. Michael 1939- *St&PR 93*
Geddes, Gary 1940- *WhoCanL 92*
Geddes, Jane 1960- *WhoAmW 93*
Geddes, Joan K. *Law&B 92*
Geddes, LaNelle Evelyn 1935- *WhoAm 92*
Geddes, Leslie Alexander 1921- *WhoAm 92*
Geddes, Patrick 1854-1932 *BioIn 17*
Geddes, Paul 1922- *ConAu 136*
Geddes, Ray A. 1932- *St&PR 93*
Geddes, Robert 1923- *WhoAm 92*
Geddes, Robert D. *Law&B 92*
Geddes, Robert D. 1938- *St&PR 93*
Geddes, Robert Dale 1938- *WhoAm 92*
Geddes, Roger A. *Law&B 92*
Geddes, William Robert 1916-1989 *IntDcAn*
Geddis, David Christopher 1947- *WhoWor 93*
Geddy, Vernon Meredith, Jr. 1926- *WhoAm 92*
Gedeon, Alfredo 1927- *St&PR 93*
Gedeon, Lucinda Heyel 1947- *WhoE 93*
Geder, Laszlo 1932- *WhoE 93*
Gedgaudas, Eugene 1924- *WhoAm 92*
Gedge, Patrick 1949- *St&PR 93*
Gedge, Pauline 1945- *ScF&FL 92, WhoCanL 92*
Gedike, Alexander *Baker 92*
Gedin, Per 1928- *WhoWor 93*
Gedney, Richard 1948- *St&PR 93*
Gedraitis, John A. 1961- *St&PR 93*
Gedrick, Jason *BioIn 17*
Geduld, Carolyn *ScF&FL 92*
Geduld, Emanuel E. 1943- *St&PR 93*
Geduld, Harry M. 1931- *ScF&FL 92*
Geduld, Irwin 1935- *St&PR 93*
Geduldig, Dwight *Law&B 92*
Gedvila, Gabriel E. *Law&B 92*
Gedzhadze, Irakly 1925- *Baker 92*
Gee, Alvin Wong 1954- *WhoSSW 93*
Gee, Elwood Gordon 1944- *WhoAm 92*
Gee, F. Denise 1965- *WhoWrEP 92*
Gee, Gregory Williams *Law&B 92*
Gee, Gregory Williams 1948- *WhoAm 92*
Gee, Irene 1950- *WhoAmW 93*
Gee, Jean Marie d1990 *BioIn 17*
Gee, Juliet Leslie 1954- *WhoEmL 93*
Gee, Karen Kathryn 1952- *WhoAmW 93*
Gee, Kenneth Allen 1933- *St&PR 93*
Gee, Kenneth P. *WhoScE 91-1*
Gee, Louis Stark 1922- *St&PR 93*
Gee, Maggie 1948- *ScF&FL 92*
Gee, Maurice 1931- *ScF&FL 92*
Gee, Maurice (Gough) 1931- *ChlFicS, DcChlFi*
Gee, Maurine *AmWomPl*
Gee, Myrtle Garrison *AmWomPl*
Gee, Nancy Lynn 1959- *WhoAmW 93*
Gee, Norman D. 1930- *St&PR 93*
Gee, Peter *BioIn 17*
Gee, Robert LeRoy 1926- *WhoAm 92*
Gee, Robert Stark 1951- *St&PR 93*
Gee, Ronald Keith *Law&B 92*
Gee, Sherman 1937- *WhoSSW 93*
Gee, Thomas Gibbs 1925- *WhoAm 92*
Gee, Vanyoska 1948- *MiSFD 9*
Gee, William R. 1940- *St&PR 93*
Geehl, Henry Ernest 1881-1961 *Baker 92*
Geehr, Patricia Bray 1938- *WhoAmW 93*
Geehr, Richard S. 1938- *ConAu 136*
Geeker, Nicholas Peter 1944- *WhoAm 92*
Geekie, Thomas Anthony 1938- *St&PR 93*
Geelan, Peter d1992 *NewYTBS 92*
Geelan, Peter Brian Kenneth 1929- *WhoWor 93*
Geels, F. Patrick 1948- *WhoScE 91-3*
Geen, Jeffery Scott *Law&B 92*
Geen, Tim Dow 1944- *WhoSSW 93*
Geene, Patricia G. 1959- *WhoAmW 93*
Geer, Frances Pearl 1907- *WhoAmW 93*
Geer, Galen Lee 1949- *WhoWrEP 92*
Geer, Henry Daniel 1922- *WhoWor 93*
Geer, Jack Charles 1927- *WhoAm 92*
Geer, James Hamilton 1924- *WhoAm 92*
Geer, James Henderson 1932- *WhoSSW 93*
Geer, John Farr 1930- *WhoAm 92*
Geer, Johnny Glen 1938- *St&PR 93*
Geer, Roderick Leland 1928- *WhoAm 92*
Geer, Ronald Lamar 1926- *WhoAm 92, WhoSSW 93*
Geer, Stephen DuBois 1930- *WhoAm 92*
Geerdes, Cynthia E. *Law&B 92*
Geerdes, James 1924- *WhoAm 92*
Geering, Alfred Heinrich 1936- *WhoScE 91-4*
Geering, Hans Peter 1942- *WhoScE 91-4, WhoWor 93*
Geerlings, Gerald Kenneth 1897- *WhoAm 92*
Geerlings, Maurits W. 1931- *WhoScE 91-3*
Geers, Mark A. *Law&B 92*
Geers, Robert E. 1928- *St&PR 93*
Geers, Thomas Lange 1939- *WhoAm 92*
Geerts, J.P. 1946- *WhoScE 91-3*
Geerts, Stanny 1949- *WhoScE 91-2*
Geertsma, Robert Henry 1929- *WhoAm 92*
Geertz, Clifford *BioIn 17*
Geertz, Clifford James 1926- *WhoAm 92*
Geertz, Hildred Storey 1927- *WhoAmW 93*
Geeseman, Robert George 1944- *WhoE 93, WhoWor 93*
Geeslin, Bailey M. 1938- *WhoAm 92*
Geeslin, Gene Smith 1927- *WhoSSW 93*
Geeslin, Sara Chambers 1948- *WhoAmW 93*
Geest, Berber van der 1938- *BioIn 17*
Geevarghese, Puthenpeedikayil Koshy 1933- *WhoAm 92, WhoSSW 93*
Gefert, Jerome T. 1954- *St&PR 93*
Geffe, Philip Reinhold 1920- *WhoAm 92*
Geffen, Abraham 1916- *WhoE 93*
Geffen, Betty Ada 1911- *WhoAmW 93*
Geffen, David *BioIn 17*
Geffen, David 1943- *ConEn, ConMus 8 [port], CurBio 92 [port], WhoAm 92*
Geffen, Frances Pearl 1919- *WhoAmW 93, WhoE 93, WhoWor 93*
Geffen, Steven B. *Law&B 92*
Geffert, Michael Andrew 1955- *St&PR 93*
Geffken, Detlef 1943- *WhoWor 93*
Geffner, Donna Sue 1946- *WhoAm 92, WhoAmW 93, WhoE 93, WhoEmL 93*
Geffner, Linda Marie 1949- *WhoAmW 93*
Geffroy, Marc A. 1961- *WhoE 93*
Gefke, Henry Jerome 1930- *WhoAm 92*
Gefors, Hans 1952- *Baker 92*
Gefter, Malcolm L. 1942- *St&PR 93*
Gefter, William Irvin 1915- *WhoAm 92*
Gefvert, Jill Marie Hagenbuch 1949- *WhoE 93*
Gegenheimer, Harold W. 1910- *St&PR 93*
Geggie, Thomas H. *Law&B 92*
Geggus, David Patrick 1949- *ConAu 37NR*
Geghman, Yahya Hamoud 1934- *WhoUN 92*
Geh, Hans-Peter 1934- *WhoWor 93*
Geha, Alexander Salim 1936- *WhoAm 92*
Gehan, Edmund Alpheus 1929- *WhoSSW 93*
Geher, Karoly 1929- *WhoScE 91-4*
Geherin, David J(ohn) 1943- *ConAu 39NR*
Gehin, Marie Therese d1991 *BioIn 17*

Gehl, Alice Elvira 1936- *WhoAmW 93, WhoE 93*
Gehl, Eugene Othmar 1923- *WhoAm 92*
Gehl, John William 1941- *St&PR 93*
Gehl, Robert Ernest 1933- *St&PR 93*
Gehl, William D. *Law&B 92*
Gehl, William D. 1946- *St&PR 93*
Gehlbach, Kurt F. *Law&B 92*
Gehlert, Sarah Jane 1948- *WhoAmW 93*
Gehlhaar, Rolf (Rainer) 1943- *Baker 92*
Gehling, John Adam 1920- *St&PR 93*
Gehling, Michael Paul 1962- *St&PR 93*
Gehm, Charlene *WhoAm 92*
Gehm, Denise Charlene 1951- *WhoAm 92*
Gehman, Christian 1948- *WhoWrEP 92*
Geho, Walter Blair 1939- *WhoAm 92*
Ge Hongsheng 1931- *WhoAsAP 91*
Gehorsam, Leon Albert 1924- *St&PR 93*
Gehot, Jean 1756-c. 1820 *Baker 92*
Gehr, David Edward 1948- *WhoEmL 93*
Gehr, James Benjamin 1930- *St&PR 93*
Gehr, Mary *WhoAm 92*
Gehres, Ruth 1933- *WhoAmW 93, WhoSSW 93*
Gehres, Tony L. *Law&B 92*
Gehret, Jeanne Barton 1953- *WhoWrEP 92*
Gehret, Joseph B. 1919- *St&PR 93*
Gehret, Thomas M. 1955- *St&PR 93*
Gehrig, Edward Harry 1925- *WhoAm 92*
Gehrig, Henry Louis 1903-1941 *BioIn 17*
Gehrig, John Allen 1937- *WhoSSW 93*
Gehrig, Jule Lou 1935- *St&PR 93*
Gehrig, Klaus 1946- *ConAu 137*
Gehrig, Leo Joseph 1918- *WhoAm 92*
Gehrig, Lou 1903-1941 *BioIn 17, ConHero 2 [port]*
Gehring, Charles William 1956- *St&PR 93*
Gehring, David Austin 1930- *WhoAm 92, WhoE 93, WhoWor 93*
Gehring, Frederick William 1925- *WhoAm 92*
Gehring, George Joseph, Jr. 1931- *WhoWor 93*
Gehring, Gillian Anne *WhoScE 91-1*
Gehring, Pamela Lauless 1950- *St&PR 93*
Gehring, Perry James 1936- *WhoAm 92*
Gehring, Walter J. 1939- *WhoScE 91-4*
Gehring, Wes D(avid) 1950- *ConAu 137*
Gehringer, Charlie 1903- *BioIn 17*
Gehringer, Edward Francis 1950- *WhoSSW 93*
Gehringer, Martha Jean 1961- *WhoAmW 93*
Gehringer, Richard George 1949- *St&PR 93, WhoAm 92, WhoE 93*
Gehringer, William Allison 1938- *St&PR 93*
Gehrke, Allen Charles 1934- *WhoAm 92*
Gehrke, Charles William 1917- *WhoAm 92*
Gehrke, Fred C. 1935- *St&PR 93*
Gehrke, Jeanette Frances 1946- *WhoAmW 93*
Gehrke, Karen Marie 1940- *WhoAmW 93*
Gehrkens, Karl (Wilson) 1882-1975 *Baker 92*
Gehrts, Meg *BioIn 17*
Gehry, Frank *BioIn 17*
Gehry, Frank Owen 1929- *WhoAm 92*
Gehrz, Robert Gustave 1915- *WhoAm 92*
Gehu, Jean Marie 1930- *WhoScE 91-2*
Geib, Philip Oldham 1921- *WhoAm 92*
Geib, Richard G. *Law&B 92*
Geib, Richard John *Law&B 92*
Geibel, Grace Ann 1937- *WhoAmW 93*
Geidel, Wolfdietrich W. *Law&B 92*
Geiduschek, Ernest Peter 1928- *WhoAm 92*
Geier, Arnold 1926- *WhoSSW 93*
Geier, August F. 1929- *St&PR 93*
Geier, George 1918- *WhoAm 92*
Geier, James A.D. 1925- *St&PR 93*
Geier, James Aylward Develin 1925- *WhoAm 92*
Geier, Joan Austin 1934- *WhoE 93*
Geier, Leonard J. 1945- *St&PR 93*
Geier, Mark Robin 1948- *WhoAm 92*
Geier, Pattie Ann 1947- *WhoAmW 93*
Geier, Philip Henry, Jr. *BioIn 17*
Geier, Philip Henry, Jr. 1935- *St&PR 93, WhoAm 92, WhoE 93*
Geier, Richard J. 1941- *St&PR 93*
Geier, Robert M. 1927- *St&PR 93*
Geiersbach, Rachel E. *Law&B 92*
Geiger, Alfons Michael 1944- *WhoWor 93*
Geiger, David K. *WhoE 93*
Geiger, Edward R. 1942- *St&PR 93*
Geiger, Eugene Gregory 1949- *St&PR 93*
Geiger, Franz 1941- *WhoWor 93*
Geiger, Gene Edward 1928- *WhoAm 92*
Geiger, Hansjurg 1951- *WhoWor 93*
Geiger, Helene R. 1950- *WhoWrEP 92*
Geiger, Howard W. d1991 *BioIn 17*
Geiger, James Norman 1932- *WhoSSW 93*
Geiger, Joseph E. 1949- *St&PR 93*
Geiger, K.C. 1954- *St&PR 93*
Geiger, Kathleen W. *Law&B 92*
Geiger, Klaus K. 1940- *WhoScE 91-3*
Geiger, Louis George 1913- *WhoAm 92*
Geiger, Mark Watson 1949- *WhoAm 92, WhoEmL 93, WhoWor 93*
Geiger, Mary Ann 1935- *WhoE 93*
Geiger, Michele *Law&B 92*
Geiger, Peter Edward 1951- *St&PR 93*
Geiger, Philip Earl 1947- *WhoE 93*
Geiger, Randall L. 1949- *WhoAm 92*
Geiger, Raymond A. 1910- *St&PR 93*
Geiger, Raymond Aloysius 1910- *WhoAm 92*
Geiger, Raymond James 1928- *St&PR 93*
Geiger, Richard Lawrence 1917- *WhoAm 92*
Geiger, Robert 1945- *St&PR 93*
Geiger, Robert Jacob *Law&B 92*
Geiger, Robert Keith 1923- *WhoAm 92*
Geiger, Ronald R. 1942- *St&PR 93*
Geiger, Roy Stanley 1885-1947 *HarEnMi*
Geiger, Sharon Kay 1945- *WhoAmW 93*
Geiger, Victor Alan 1948- *St&PR 93, WhoAm 92*
Geiger, William H. *Law&B 92*
Geigert, Daniel P. 1937- *St&PR 93*
Geiges, Robert H. 1946- *St&PR 93*
Geiken, Alan Richard 1923- *WhoWor 93*
Geiken, John G. 1936- *St&PR 93*
Geil, Norman H. *Law&B 92*
Geilfuss, John Crittenden 1914- *St&PR 93*
Geilich, Robert A. *Law&B 92*
Geiman, J. Robert 1931- *WhoAm 92*
Geingob, Hage Gottfried 1941- *WhoAfr, WhoWor 93*
Geinitz, Hand Wolfgang 1917- *WhoWor 93*
Geiogamah, Hanay 1945- *BioIn 17*
Geipel, Ute Maja 1950- *WhoWor 93*
Geiringer, Karl (Johannes) 1899-1989 *Baker 92*
Geirlandt, Karel J. 1910-1989 *BioIn 17*
Geis, Bernard 1909- *WhoAm 92*
Geis, David M. 1950- *St&PR 93*
Geis, Duane Virgil 1923- *WhoAm 92*
Geis, Florence Lindauer 1933- *WhoAmW 93, WhoE 93*
Geis, Gilbert Lawrence 1925- *WhoAm 92*
Geis, Norman Winer 1925- *WhoAm 92*
Geis, Richard E. 1927- *ScF&FL 92*
Geisberg, Samuel P. 1936- *St&PR 93*
Geise, Herman J.V.H. 1937- *WhoScE 91-2*
Geise, Norman A. 1918- *St&PR 93*
Geisel, C. Meade, Jr. 1937- *St&PR 93*
Geisel, Cameron Meade, Jr. 1937- *WhoAm 92*
Geisel, Ernesto 1907- *DcTwHis*
Geisel, Harold Walter 1947- *WhoAm 92*
Geisel, Martin Simon 1941- *WhoAm 92, WhoSSW 93*
Geisel, Samuel George 1944- *WhoSSW 93*
Geisel, Theodor 1904-1991 *News 92*
Geisel, Theodor Seuss *BioIn 17*
Geisel, Theodor Seuss 1904- *JrnUS*
Geisel, Theodor Seuss 1904-1991 *ConLC 70, MajAI [port]*
Geiseler, J. *WhoScE 91-3*
Geiselhart, Lorene Annetta 1929- *WhoAmW 93*
Geiselman, April Lorraine 1957- *WhoAmW 93*
Geiselman, Debra Ann 1955- *WhoAmW 93*
Geiselman, LucyAnn *WhoAmW 93*
Geiselman, Paula Jeanne 1944- *WhoAm 92, WhoAmW 93*
Geisendorfer, Esther Lillian 1927- *WhoAmW 93*
Geisendorfer, James Vernon 1929- *WhoWor 93*
Geisenheimer, Emile J. 1947- *WhoAm 92, WhoE 93, WhoEmL 93*
Geiser, David F. 1952- *St&PR 93*
Geiser, Elizabeth Able 1925- *WhoAm 92*
Geiser, James 1949- *WhoEmL 93*
Geiser, Robert Neil 1961- *WhoEmL 93*
Geiser, Walther 1897- *Baker 92*
Geisert, Arthur *ChlBIID [port]*
Geisert, Gene Alvin 1927- *WhoE 93*
Geisert, Jean 1939- *WhoScE 91-2*
Geisert, Wayne Frederick 1921- *WhoAm 92, WhoSSW 93*
Geishecker, John Andrew, Jr. 1938- *St&PR 93*
Geisinger, Janice Allain 1927- *WhoAmW 93*
Geisinger, Kurt Francis 1951- *WhoE 93, WhoEmL 93*
Geisler, Brigitte J. *Law&B 92*
Geisler, Carol Joy 1948- *WhoE 93, WhoEmL 93*
Geisler, David Herbruck 1937- *WhoSSW 93*
Geisler, Ernest Keith, Jr. 1931- *WhoAm 92*
Geisler, Gerhard 1927- *WhoScE 91-3*
Geisler, Hans Emanuel 1935- *WhoAm 92, WhoWor 93*
Geisler, Harlynne 1950- *WhoEmL 93*
Geisler, John 1962- *WhoEmL 93*
Geisler, Jonathan David 1949- *WhoAm 92, WhoEmL 93*
Geisler, Karen Lee 1955- *WhoAmW 93*
Geisler, Linus Sebastian 1934- *WhoWor 93*
Geisler, Paul 1856-1919 *Baker 92*
Geisler, Rosemary P. 1947- *St&PR 93, WhoAm 92*
Geisler, Udo Kurt 1944- *WhoWor 93*
Geismar, Richard L. 1927- *St&PR 93*
Geismar, Richard Lee 1927- *WhoAm 92*
Geismar, Robert 1946- *WhoE 93*
Geismar, Sylvan d1990 *BioIn 17*
Geismar, Thomas H. 1931- *WhoAm 92*
Geisow, Michael John 1948- *WhoScE 91-1*
Geiss, David Richard 1953- *WhoEmL 93, WhoWor 93*
Geiss, Imanuel 1931- *WhoWor 93*
Geiss, Johannes 1926- *WhoScE 91-4*
Geiss, Suzanne *Law&B 92*
Geissbuhler, Stephan 1942- *WhoAm 92*
Geisse, John F. d1992 *NewYTBS 92 [port]*
Geisse, John F. 1920- *ConEn*
Geisse, John F. 1920-1992 *BioIn 17*
Geissele, Lynn Marie 1959- *WhoSSW 93*
Geisser, Peter Otto 1945- *WhoWor 93*
Geissert, Katy 1926- *WhoAm 92, WhoAmW 93*
Geissinger, Frederick W. 1945- *St&PR 93*
Geissinger, Frederick Wallace 1945- *WhoAm 92*
Geissinger, Ladnor Dale 1938- *WhoSSW 93*
Geissler, Claus Dieter 1952- *BioIn 17*
Geissler, Elmer E. 1929- *St&PR 93*
Geissler, Erhard 1930- *WhoWor 93*
Geissler, Fritz 1921-1984 *Baker 92*
Geissler, Heiner 1930- *WhoWor 93*
Geissler, Suzanne Burr 1950- *WhoE 93*
Geissler, Ursula 1931- *WhoScE 91-3*
Geissmar, Clara 1844-1911 *BioIn 17*
Geissner, Helmut Karl 1926- *WhoWor 93*
Geist, Carl William, Jr. 1938- *St&PR 93*
Geist, Frederick Stewart 1923- *WhoSSW 93*
Geist, Harold 1916- *WhoWrEP 92*
Geist, Jacob Myer 1921-1991 *BioIn 17*
Geist, James E. 1929- *St&PR 93, WhoAm 92*
Geist, Jerry Douglas 1934- *St&PR 93*
Geist, Jill Marie 1959- *WhoAmW 93*
Geist, John K. 1948- *St&PR 93*
Geist, Karin Ruth Tammeus McPhail 1938- *WhoAmW 93, WhoWor 93*
Geist, Lester 1920- *St&PR 93*
Geist, Maggie Ann 1939- *WhoWrEP 92*
Geister, Edna *AmWomPl*
Geistfeld, Ronald Elwood 1933- *WhoAm 92*
Geisweidt, Lorilee Barrick 1960- *WhoAmW 93, WhoEmL 93*
Geitgey, Doris Arlene 1920- *WhoAm 92*
Geith, Karl-Ernst 1933- *WhoWor 93*
Geithner, Paul H., Jr. 1930- *St&PR 93*
Geithner, Paul Herman, Jr. 1930- *WhoAm 92, WhoSSW 93*
Gejdenson, Sam 1948- *CngDr 91, WhoAm 92, WhoE 93*
Gekas, George 1930- *CngDr 91*
Gekas, George William 1930- *WhoAm 92, WhoE 93*
Gekeler, Ernst-Ulrich 1951- *WhoWor 93*
Gelard, Jean-Pierre 1942- *WhoScE 91-2*
Gelardin, Jacques P. *WhoAm 92*
Gelasios of Caesarea d395 *OxDcByz*
Gelasios of Kyzikos dc. 475 *OxDcByz*
Gelasius, I d496 *OxDcByz*
Gelato, Marie Catherine 1947- *WhoE 93*
Gelatt, Charles Daniel 1918- *WhoAm 92, WhoWor 93*
Gelatt, Philip Madison 1950- *St&PR 93*
Gelatt, Roland 1920-1986 *Baker 92*
Gelb, Alan Michael 1938- *WhoAm 92*
Gelb, Arthur 1924- *BioIn 17, WhoAm 92, WhoWrEP 92*
Gelb, Arthur 1937- *WhoAm 92*
Gelb, Barbara *BioIn 17*
Gelb, Bruce *BioIn 17*
Gelb, Bruce S. 1927- *WhoAm 92, WhoWor 93*
Gelb, Fannie d1990 *BioIn 17*
Gelb, Harold Seymour 1920- *WhoAm 92*
Gelb, Jeff *ScF&FL 92*
Gelb, Joseph Donald 1923- *WhoE 93, WhoWor 93*
Gelb, Judith Anne 1935- *WhoAm 92, WhoAmW 93, WhoE 93, WhoWor 93*
Gelb, Judith C. 1937- *WhoAmW 93*
Gelb, Leslie 1937- *ColdWar 1 [port]*
Gelb, Leslie Howard 1937- *WhoAm 92*
Gelb, Mike *St&PR 93*
Gelb, Richard L. 1924- *St&PR 93*
Gelb, Richard Lee 1924- *WhoAm 92, WhoE 93*
Gelb, Ronda Shainmark 1933- *WhoAmW 93*
Gelb, Victor 1926- *WhoAm 92*
Gelbach, Martha Harvey 1913- *WhoAm 92*
Gelbach, Myron S., Jr. 1921- *St&PR 93*
Gelbach, W.H., Jr. 1921- *St&PR 93*
Gelband, Henry 1936- *WhoAm 92*
Gelbart, Abe 1911- *WhoAm 92, WhoWor 93*
Gelbart, Larry *BioIn 17*
Gelbart, Larry 1925- *WhoAm 92*
Gelbart, Larry 1928- *ConTFT 10*
Gelbein, Jay Joel 1949- *WhoE 93*
Gelber, Arthur 1915- *WhoAm 92*
Gelber, Bruno-Leonardo 1941- *Baker 92*
Gelber, Don Jeffrey 1940- *WhoAm 92*
Gelber, Gabriel 1921- *St&PR 93*
Gelber, Gail 1952- *St&PR 93*
Gelber, Herbert Donald 1932- *WhoAm 92, WhoWor 93*
Gelber, Jack 1932- *WhoAm 92, WhoWrEP 92*
Gelber, Jill Barbara *WhoAmW 93*
Gelber, Robert Cary 1951- *WhoEmL 93*
Gelbier, Stanley 1935- *WhoWor 93*
Gelbke, Heinz-Peter 1943- *WhoWor 93*
Gelbrun, Artur 1913-1985 *Baker 92*
Gelburd, Diane Elizabeth 1952- *WhoEmL 93*
Gelburd, Gail Enid 1954- *WhoEmL 93*
Gelci, Gianna Maria 1957- *WhoEmL 93*
Geldart, Derek *WhoScE 91-1*
Geldart, Donald James Wallace 1938- *WhoAm 92*
Geldenhuys, Deon 1950- *ConAu 139*
Gelder, James R. *WhoIns 93*
Gelder, John William 1933- *WhoAm 92*
Gelder, Michael Graham *WhoScE 91-1*
Gelder, Nick Van 1914- *St&PR 93*
Gelders, Ludo F.L. 1943- *WhoScE 91-2*
Geldhof, Alex R. 1920- *St&PR 93*
Geldmacher, Jurgen 1929- *WhoScE 91-3*
Geldmacher, Robert Carl 1917- *WhoAm 92*
Geldof, Bob *BioIn 17*
Geldof, Bob 1954- *ConMus 9 [port]*
Geldon, Fred Wolman *Law&B 92*
Geldon, Fred Wolman 1946- *WhoSSW 93*
Geldon, Gilbert E. *Law&B 92*
Geleen, Gottfried Hunn, Count von c. 1590-1657 *HarEnMi*
Gelehrter, Ann Gorris 1949- *WhoEmL 93*
Gelehrter, Thomas David 1936- *WhoAm 92*
Gelencser, Eva 1950- *WhoScE 91-4*
Gelernt, Irwin M. 1935- *WhoE 93*
Gelernter, David *NewYTBS 92 [port]*
Gelernter, David Hillel *BioIn 17*
Gelfan, Gregory *Law&B 92*
Gelfand, David *MiSFD 9*
Gelfand, Hyman d1991 *BioIn 17*
Gelfand, Ivan 1927- *WhoAm 92*
Gelfand, Jeffrey Alan 1946- *WhoE 93*
Gelfand, Jennifer *BioIn 17*
Gelfand, M. David 1949- *WhoAm 92*
Gelfand, Mikhail Sergeevich 1963- *WhoWor 93*
Gelfand, Morris Arthur 1908- *WhoAm 92*
Gelfand, Neal 1944- *St&PR 93, WhoAm 92*
Gelfand, Steven B. 1948- *WhoE 93*
Gelfland, M. Howard *ScF&FL 92*
Gelfman, Richard David 1947- *WhoEmL 93*
Gelfman, Robert William 1932- *WhoAm 92*
Gelfond, Marjorie Pam 1948-1992 *WhoAmW 93*
Gelgoot, Arthur *BioIn 17*
Geliebter, Allan 1947- *WhoE 93*
Gelimer fl. 530-534 *OxDcByz*
Gelin, Daniel 1921- *IntDcF 2-3 [port]*
Gelinas, Charles J. 1903- *St&PR 93*
Gelinas, Gratien *BioIn 17*
Gelinas, Gratien 1909- *WhoAm 92, WhoCanL 92, WhoWrEP 92*
Gelinas, John Gerald 1929- *WhoAm 92*
Gelinas, Joseph A. 1945- *St&PR 93*
Gelinas, Marc Adrien 1947- *WhoEmL 93, WhoSSW 93*
Gelinas, Michelle Kay 1963- *WhoAmW 93*
Gelinas, Paul Joseph 1914- *WhoSSW 93*
Gelinas, Roger G. 1948- *St&PR 93*
Gelineau, Joseph 1920- *Baker 92*
Gelineau, Louis Edward 1928- *WhoAm 92*
Gelinek, Joseph 1758-1825 *Baker 92*
Geliot, Michael 1933- *OxDcOp*
Gelke, Kurt David 1957- *WhoE 93, WhoEmL 93*
Gell, Gunther 1941- *WhoWor 93*
Gellar, Glenda Aman 1941- *WhoAmW 93*
Gellenbeck, Lynne *Law&B 92*
Geller, A. Neal 1943- *WhoAm 92*
Geller, Abraham *BioIn 17*
Geller, Andrew Michael 1924- *WhoE 93*
Geller, Avrum D. 1943- *St&PR 93*
Geller, Barbara Johnson 1958- *WhoEmL 93*
Geller, Dave *BioIn 17*
Geller, Diane Joyce 1953- *WhoEmL 93*

Geller, Edward *Law&B 92*
Geller, Eric Mitchell 1949- *St&PR 93*
Geller, Eric P. *Law&B 92*
Geller, Estelle Hecht 1927- *WhoAmW 93*
Geller, Esther 1921- *WhoAm 92*
Geller, Eugene N. 1932- *St&PR 93*
Geller, Gerry *BioIn 17*
Geller, Harold Arthur 1954- *WhoE 93, WhoEmL 93, WhoWor 93*
Geller, Janice Grace 1938- *WhoAmW 93, WhoE 93, WhoWor 93*
Geller, Jeffrey Lawrence 1953- *WhoE 93*
Geller, Margaret Joan 1947- *WhoAm 92, WhoAmW 93*
Geller, Mark J. 1948- *St&PR 93*
Geller, Matthew Bruce *WhoE 93*
Geller, Robert 1931- *WhoE 93*
Geller, Robert James 1937- *WhoAm 92, WhoE 93*
Geller, Ronald Gene 1943- *WhoAm 92*
Geller, Seymour 1921- *WhoAm 92*
Geller, Stephen *ScF&FL 92*
Geller, Uri 1946- *ScF&FL 92*
Gellerman, Bruce Edward 1950- *WhoE 93*
Gellerman, Jay Michael 1938- *St&PR 93*
Gellermann, Henry 1912- *WhoAm 92*
Gellermann, William Prescott 1929- *WhoE 93*
Gellerstedt, Lawrence Love, Jr. 1925- *St&PR 93*
Gellerstedt, Marie Ada 1926- *WhoAmW 93, WhoWor 93*
Gellert, Christian Furchtegott 1715-1769 *BioIn 17*
Gellert, George Geza 1938- *WhoAm 92*
Gellert, Michael E. 1931- *St&PR 93*
Gellert, Michael Erwin 1931- *WhoAm 92*
Gelles, Harry 1934- *WhoAm 92*
Gelles, Pamela Eve 1961- *St&PR 93*
Gelles, Richard J. 1946- *WhoWrEP 92*
Gelles, Richard James 1946- *WhoAm 92*
Gellhorn, Alfred 1913- *WhoAm 92, WhoE 93*
Gellhorn, Ernest Albert Eugene 1935- *WhoAm 92*
Gellhorn, Martha *BioIn 17*
Gellhorn, Walter 1906- *WhoAm 92*
Gelling, Ralph D. *Law&B 92*
Gellis, Barrie Fabian 1950- *WhoWrEP 92*
Gellis, Roberta *ScF&FL 92*
Gellis, Roberta L(eah Jacobs) 1927- *WhoWrEP 92*
Gellis, Roberta Leah 1927- *WhoAmW 93*
Gellis, Sandy L. 1946- *WhoEmL 93*
Gellis, Sydney Saul 1914- *WhoAm 92*
Gellise, Mary Yvonne 1934- *WhoAm 92*
Gellius, Statius fl. 305BC- *HarEnMi*
Gellman, Gloria Gae Seeburger Schick 1947- *WhoAmW 93, WhoEmL 93, WhoWor 93*
Gellman, James Franklin *Law&B 92*
Gellman, Jerome I. 1927- *St&PR 93*
Gellman, Nancy Joan 1945- *WhoAmW 93*
Gellman, Steven 1947- *Baker 92*
Gellman, William d1992 *BioIn 17, NewYTBS 92*
Gellman, Yale H. 1934- *WhoAm 92*
Gell-Mann, Murray 1929- *WhoAm 92, WhoWor 93*
Gellner, Ernest *BioIn 17*
Gelman, Alex *MiSFD 9*
Gelman, Amy 1961- *SmATA 72 [port]*
Gelman, Bernard 1933- *WhoE 93, WhoWor 93*
Gelman, Bernard 1940- *WhoAm 92*
Gelman, Charles 1931- *St&PR 93*
Gelman, Daniel Harris 1961- *St&PR 93*
Gelman, David Graham 1926- *WhoAm 92*
Gelman, Dian D. 1938- *St&PR 93*
Gelman, Donald 1938- *WhoE 93*
Gelman, Elaine Edith 1927- *WhoAmW 93*
Gelman, I. Lawrence *Law&B 92*
Gelman, Jack Kenneth 1945- *St&PR 93*
Gelman, Juan 1930- *SpAmA*
Gelman, Larry 1930- *WhoAm 92*
Gelman, Norman Ira 1929- *WhoE 93*
Gelman, Rita Golden *ScF&FL 92*
Gelmetti, Gianluigi 1945- *Baker 92, WhoWor 93*
Gelmis, Joseph Stephan 1935- *WhoAm 92*
Gelo, Daniel Joseph 1957- *WhoEmL 93, WhoSSW 93*
Gelo, Helena 1929- *WhoScE 91-4*
Geloso-Barone, Rosalia Ann 1962- *WhoE 93, WhoEmL 93*
Gelpi, Albert Joseph 1931- *WhoAm 92*
Gelpi, Barbara Charlesworth 1933- *WhoAm 92*
Gelpi, Emilio 1942- *WhoScE 91-3*
Gelpi, Ettore 1933- *WhoUN 92*
Gelsand, Eugene M. *Law&B 92*
Gelsinger, James Roger *Law&B 92*
Gelsinger, Linda Mae 1950- *WhoAmW 93*
Gelson, John Francis 1931- *St&PR 93*
Gelsthorpe, Joseph Dean 1943- *WhoSSW 93*
Gelston, Stephanie M. 1960- *WhoE 93*
Geltzer, Robert Lawrence 1945- *WhoAm 92*
Geltzer, Sheila Simon 1940- *WhoAm 92*
Gelus, Maurice M. 1940- *WhoScE 91-2*
Gelvin, L. Millard 1928- *St&PR 93*
Gelvin, Lyle Millard 1928- *WhoSSW 93*
Gelwick, Richard Lee 1931- *WhoE 93*
Gelz, Desmond *BioIn 17*
Gelzer, Helen 1950- *St&PR 93*
Gelzer, Justus 1929- *WhoScE 91-4, WhoWor 93*
Gemayel, Bashir 1947-1982 *ColdWar 2 [port]*
Gemayel, Pierre 1905-1984 *BioIn 17*
Gembicki, Maciej 1928- *WhoScE 91-4*
Gemello, John Michael 1946- *WhoAm 92*
Gemery, Henry Albert 1930- *WhoAm 92*
Gemignani, Gino John, Jr. 1942- *St&PR 93*
Gemignani, Michael Caesar 1938- *WhoAm 92*
Geminiani, Francesco (Xaverio) 1687-1762 *Baker 92*
Geminus, Gnaeus Servilius d216BC *HarEnMi*
Gemke, Pieter N.M. 1926- *St&PR 93*
Gemma, John P. 1939- *WhoIns 93*
Gemma, Peter Benedict, Jr. 1950- *WhoEmL 93, WhoSSW 93*
Gemmel, Terry 1932- *WhoAmW 93*
Gemmell, David A. 1948- *ScF&FL 92*
Gemmell, Edgar Mills d1990 *BioIn 17*
Gemmell, Gavin John Norman 1941- *WhoWor 93*
Gemmell, Joseph Paul 1935- *St&PR 93, WhoAm 92*
Gemmer, H. Robert 1923- *WhoSSW 93, WhoWor 93*
Gemmett, Robert James 1936- *WhoAm 92*
Gemmill, Elizabeth H. *Law&B 92*
Gemmill, Elizabeth H. 1945- *St&PR 93*
Gemmill, Kenneth W. 1910- *St&PR 93*
Gemperle, Marcel 1930- *WhoScE 91-4*
Gemsa, Diethard 1937- *WhoWor 93*
Gemtos, Petros Anastassios 1939- *WhoWor 93*
Gemunder, August (Martin Ludwig) 1814-1895 *Baker 92*
Gemunder, Georg 1816-1899 *See* Gemunder, August (Martin Ludwig) 1814-1895 *Baker 92*
Gemunder, Joel F. 1939- *St&PR 93*
Gen, Martin 1926- *WhoE 93, WhoWor 93*
Genabith, Richard Carl 1946- *WhoE 93, WhoEmL 93*
Genack, Ahuva *Law&B 92*
Genader, Ann Marie 1932- *WhoWrEP 92*
Genain, Marc P. *WhoWor 93*
Genard, Gerald H. *Law&B 92*
Genaro, Donald Michael 1932- *WhoWor 93*
Genaro, Lorayne Edylyne 1949- *WhoEmL 93*
Genatossio, Francis Joseph 1956- *WhoE 93*
Genauer, Emanuel 1939- *St&PR 93*
Genc, Ertekin 1935- *WhoScE 91-4*
Genc, Ibrahim 1939- *WhoScE 91-4*
Gencer, Leyla 1924- *Baker 92, OxDcOp*
Genco, Robert Joseph 1938- *WhoAm 92*
Genda, Minoru 1904-1989 *HarEnMi*
Gendall, Stuart *ScF&FL 92*
Genday, Richard E. 1957- *St&PR 93*
Gendell, Gerald Stanleigh 1929- *WhoAm 92*
Gendelman, Sheldon 1930- *St&PR 93*
Gendreau, Francois Xavier 1931- *WhoWor 93*
Gendreau, Ingrid *Law&B 92*
Gendreau, Michael C. 1949- *St&PR 93*
Gendrin, Roger Emile 1932- *WhoScE 91-2*
Gendron, Jay W. *Law&B 92*
Gendron, Maurice 1920-1990 *Baker 92, BioIn 17*
Gendron, Serge 1951- *St&PR 93*
Gendron, Yvon *St&PR 93*
Gene, Jones P. 1951- *St&PR 93*
Genee, Richard 1823-1895 *OxDcOp*
Genee, (Franz Friedrich) Richard 1823-1895 *Baker 92*
Genel, Myron 1936- *WhoAm 92*
Geneletti, Ezio *BioIn 17*
Genensky, Samuel M. 1927- *BioIn 17*
General, Darrell *BioIn 17*
Generale, Robert 1952- *St&PR 93*
Generali, Pietro 1773-1832 *Baker 92, OxDcOp*
Generelli, Joseph F. *Law&B 92*
Generes, Edwin Gerard 1949- *St&PR 93*
Genereux, Robert James 1930- *WhoAm 92*
Genermont, Jean 1936- *WhoScE 91-2*
Generous, Eric Yves Jacques 1960- *WhoE 93*
Genes, James *St&PR 93*
Genes, Janice *St&PR 93*
Genesen, Judith Levin 1932- *WhoAm 92*
Genesen, Louis 1926- *St&PR 93, WhoAm 92*
Geneser, Joseph Daniel 1937- *St&PR 93*
Genesi, Robert C. *St&PR 93*
Genesios *OxDcByz*
Genest, Francois J. 1950- *St&PR 93*
Genest, Jacques 1919- *St&PR 93, WhoAm 92*
Genest, Suzanne Dreyer 1952- *WhoAmW 93*
Genet, Citizen 1763-1834 *PolPar*
Genet, Jean 1910-1986 *BioIn 17*
Genet, Taras *BioIn 17*
Genetet, Bernard 1931- *WhoWor 93*
Genetski, Robert James 1942- *St&PR 93, WhoAm 92*
Genette, Gerard Raymond 1930- *WhoWor 93*
Genetz, Emil 1852-1930 *Baker 92*
Geng, Edward Joseph 1931- *WhoAm 92*
Geng, Edward Joseph 1931-1991 *BioIn 17*
Geng, Karl H. 1941- *St&PR 93*
Genge, William Harrison 1923- *St&PR 93, WhoAm 92*
Gengenbach, Marianne S. 1956- *WhoEmL 93*
Genghis Khan 1162-1227 *BioIn 17*
Genghis Khan, Temujin 1162-1227 *HarEnMi*
Gengler, M. Jeanne 1912- *WhoAm 92*
Gengler, Norman John 1924- *WhoSSW 93*
Gengor, Virginia Anderson 1927- *WhoAmW 93, WhoWor 93*
Genheimer, J. Edward 1929- *St&PR 93*
Genia, Jack T. 1948- *WhoAsAP 91*
Genier, Robert Arthur 1941- *St&PR 93*
Geniesse, Robert John 1929- *WhoAm 92*
Genillard, Robert Louis 1929- *WhoWor 93*
Genin, Augusto 1862-1931 *DcMexL*
Genin, Paul Charles 1927- *WhoWor 93*
Genin, Roland 1927- *St&PR 93*
Genius, Garnet Lebeau 1919- *St&PR 93*
Genkin, Larry Allen 1965- *WhoE 93*
Genkin, Melanie B. *Law&B 92*
Genkins, Amy Ellen *Law&B 92*
Genkins, Gabriel 1928- *WhoAm 92*
Genlis, Stephanie Felicite, comtesse de 1746-1830 *BioIn 17*
Genn, Nancy *WhoAm 92*
Gennadios, I c. 400- *OxDcByz*
Gennadios Scholarios, II 1400?-c. 1472 *OxDcByz*
Gennadius of Marseilles d492? *OxDcByz*
Gennari, Frank John 1937- *WhoE 93*
Gennaro, Antonio 1963- *WhoWor 93*
Gennaro, Jane E. *Law&B 92*
Gennaro, John S. *Law&B 92*
Gennaro, Peter *BioIn 17*
Gennell, Mina *AmWomPl*
Gennep, Arnold van 1873-1957 *IntDcAn*
Gennet, Peter Robert 1947- *St&PR 93*
Gennett, Phillip *St&PR 93*
Gennrich, Friedrich 1883-1967 *Baker 92*
Gennrich, Robert Paul, II 1950- *WhoAm 92*
Genoni, Kenneth Allen *Law&B 92*
Genova, Anthony Charles 1929- *WhoAm 92*
Genova, Diane *Law&B 92*
Genova, John M. *Law&B 92*
Genovese, Alfred *WhoAm 92*
Genovese, Eugene Dominick 1930- *WhoAm 92*
Genovese, Francis Charles 1921- *WhoAm 92*
Genovese, Frank A. 1951- *St&PR 93*
Genovese, Michael J. *Law&B 92*
Genovese, Philip William 1917- *WhoE 93*
Genovese, Richard 1947- *WhoE 93*
Genovese, Thomas L. *Law&B 92*
Genovese, Thomas Leonardo 1936- *St&PR 93, WhoAm 92*
Genovese, Thomas M. *Law&B 92*
Genovesi, Robert P. 1928- *St&PR 93*
Genovich-Richards, Joann 1954- *WhoAmW 93*
Genoways, Hugh Howard 1940- *WhoAm 92*
Genrich, Willard Adolph 1915- *WhoWor 93*
Gens, Antonio 1950- *WhoScE 91-3*
Gens, Helen Diane 1934- *WhoAmW 93*
Gens, IUlii Borisovich 1887-1957 *BioIn 17*
Gens, Ralph Samuel 1924- *WhoAm 92*
Genscher, Hans Dietrich *BioIn 17*
Genscher, Hans-Dietrich 1927- *WhoWor 93*
Gensert, Richard Michael 1922- *WhoAm 92*
Genshaft, Judy Lynn 1948- *WhoEmL 93*
Gensheimer, Cynthia Francis 1953- *WhoE 93*
Gensheimer, Elizabeth Lucille 1955- *WhoSSW 93*
Gensheimer, Joseph M. *Law&B 92*
Gensinger, Raymond Albert 1941- *St&PR 93*
Gensler, James Thomas 1947- *St&PR 93*
Gensler, John Calvin 1936- *St&PR 93*
Genster, Helge G. 1932- *WhoScE 91-2*
Genster, Jane E. *Law&B 92*
Gent, Alan Neville 1927- *WhoAm 92*
Gent, G.P. *WhoScE 91-1*
Gent, Pamela Joyce 1957- *WhoE 93*
Gentele, Goeran 1917-1972 *Baker 92*
Gentele, Goran 1917-1972 *IntDcOp, OxDcOp*
Genter, David L. 1934- *St&PR 93*
Genter, Frances A. *BioIn 17*
Genter, John Robert 1957- *WhoEmL 93*
Genter-Knudtson, Frances d1992 *NewYTBS 92*
Genthe, William Klug 1931- *St&PR 93*
Gentile, Ann *St&PR 93*
Gentile, Anthony *ScF&FL 92*
Gentile, Antoinette M. 1936- *WhoE 93*
Gentile, Arthur Christopher 1926- *WhoAm 92*
Gentile, Dominick Edward 1932- *WhoAm 92*
Gentile, Don F. 1954- *St&PR 93*
Gentile, Doug Charles 1950- *WhoE 93*
Gentile, Fred J. 1929- *St&PR 93*
Gentile, Gary 1946- *ScF&FL 92*
Gentile, George Michael 1936- *St&PR 93*
Gentile, Giovanni 1875-1944 *DcTwHis*
Gentile, J. Ronald 1941- *WhoE 93*
Gentile, Joan McCarthy *Law&B 92*
Gentile, Joseph F. 1934- *WhoAm 92*
Gentile, Joseph J. 1958- *WhoE 93*
Gentile, Patrick J. 1917- *St&PR 93*
Gentile, Paul Louis 1940- *WhoE 93*
Gentile, Peter A. 1952- *WhoIns 93*
Gentile, Robert N. *Law&B 92*
Gentile, Salvatore *BioIn 17*
Gentile, Salvatore 1934- *WhoScE 91-3*
Gentile, Sharon Ann 1953- *WhoAmW 93, WhoEmL 93*
Gentile, Tom G. 1954- *St&PR 93*
Gentile, Tony 1920- *St&PR 93*
Gentile, Valerie Ann *Law&B 92*
Gentilello, Larry *BioIn 17*
Gentile-Rose, Gina Marie 1965- *WhoAmW 93*
Gentileschi, Artemisia 1597-1651 *BioIn 17*
Gentili, Serafino c. 1775-1835 *OxDcOp*
Gentilini, Marc *WhoScE 91-2*
Gentilizza, Mirjana 1934- *WhoScE 91-4*
Gentiloni Silveri, Fabrizio 1951- *WhoUN 92*
Gentine, Lawrence John 1946- *WhoAm 92*
Gentine, Lee M. 1952- *St&PR 93*
Gentine, Lee Michael 1952- *WhoAm 92*
Gentine, Louis P. 1947- *St&PR 93*
Gentis, Karen Ann 1959- *St&PR 93*
Gentle, Alfred Fernandez, Jr. 1953- *WhoSSW 93*
Gentle, Kenneth William 1940- *WhoAm 92*
Gentle, Mary 1956- *ScF&FL 92*
Gentleman, David 1930- *BioIn 17*
Gentleman, John F. *St&PR 93*
Gentleman, John F. 1937- *WhoIns 93*
Gentner, Brian H. *Law&B 92*
Gentner, Claudia Alene 1953- *WhoE 93*
Gentner, Russell Douglas 1954- *St&PR 93*
Gentry, Bern Leon, Sr. 1941- *WhoAm 92*
Gentry, Bobbie 1944- *Baker 92*
Gentry, Carolyn Adele 1952- *WhoAmW 93, WhoEmL 93*
Gentry, Carolyn Smith 1938- *WhoSSW 93*
Gentry, Christine 1954- *ScF&FL 92*
Gentry, Cynthia Sue 1930- *WhoAmW 93*
Gentry, David Raymond 1933- *WhoSSW 93*
Gentry, David Truett 1927- *St&PR 93*
Gentry, Deborah Brown *Law&B 92*
Gentry, Debra Sanford 1958- *WhoAmW 93*
Gentry, Don Kenneth 1939- *WhoAm 92*
Gentry, Donald Gunn 1940- *WhoE 93*
Gentry, Gregg Thornton 1957- *WhoEmL 93*
Gentry, Harold Wayne 1951- *WhoEmL 93, WhoSSW 93*
Gentry, Helen *AmWomPl*
Gentry, Hubert, Jr. *Law&B 92*
Gentry, Hubert, Jr. 1931- *St&PR 93, WhoAm 92*
Gentry, Hugh E. 1929- *St&PR 93*
Gentry, James O'Connor *Law&B 92*
Gentry, James O'Conor 1926- *St&PR 93, WhoIns 93*
Gentry, Jeanne Louise 1946- *WhoAmW 93*
Gentry, Joanne Hester 1934- *WhoAmW 93*
Gentry, Judith Anne Fenner 1942- *WhoSSW 93*
Gentry, Layne Oral 1940- *WhoSSW 93*
Gentry, Marla Jaclyn 1947- *St&PR 93*
Gentry, Michael Ray 1958- *WhoSSW 93*
Gentry, Robert Cecil 1916- *WhoAm 92, WhoSSW 93*
Gentry, Stephen John 1947- *WhoScE 91-1*

Gentry, Teddy *WhoAm 92*
Gentry, William Norton 1908- *WhoWor 93*
Gentsch, Henry W. 1904- *St&PR 93*
Genty, Richard Daniel 1926- *St&PR 93*
Gentz, William Howard 1918- *WhoWrEP 92*
Gentzkow, Gary D. 1947- *St&PR 93*
Gentzler, Doreen *BioIn 17*
Genuit, David Walter 1949- *WhoEmL 93*
Genung, Norman Bernard 1951- *WhoEmL 93*
Genung, Sharon Rose 1951- *WhoAmW 93*
Genutis, Otto M. 1943- *WhoAm 92*
Genyk, Ruth Bel 1955- *WhoAm 92*
Genz, Henning 1938- *WhoWor 93*
Genzabella, John Carmelo 1938- *St&PR 93*
Genzale, John 1954-1991 *BioIn 17*
Genzer, Marvin D. *Law&B 92*
Genzmer, Harald 1909- *Baker 92*
Geoffrey, Michel 1944- *WhoScE 91-4*
Geoffrey De Villehardouin *OxDcByz*
Geoffrey Villehardouin, I 1170?-1225? *OxDcByz*
Geoffrey Villehardouin, II c. 1195-1246 *OxDcByz*
Geoffrion, Sondra Jane 1939- *WhoAmW 93*
Geoffroy, Charles Henry 1926- *WhoAm 92*
Geoffroy, Kevin Edward 1932- *WhoAm 92*
Geoffroy, Michel Marc 1944- *WhoWor 93*
Geoffroy, Thomas A. 1961- *St&PR 93*
Geoga, Douglas G. *Law&B 92*
Geoghan, Joseph Edward *Law&B 92*
Geoghan, Joseph Edward 1937- *St&PR 93, WhoAm 92*
Geoghegan, John Joseph 1917- *WhoAm 92*
Geoghegan, John W. 1945- *St&PR 93*
Geoghegan, Joseph Edward 1932- *WhoE 93*
Geoghegan, Linda L. *Law&B 92*
Geoghegan, Michel H. 1937- *WhoUN 92*
Geoghegan, Michel Henry 1937- *WhoE 93, WhoWor 93*
Geoghegan, Thomas Edward 1948- *WhoSSW 93*
Geoghegan, William J. 1921- *St&PR 93*
Geoghegar, Andrew P. *Law&B 92*
Geo-Karis, Adeline Jay 1918- *WhoAmW 93*
Geoppinger, William Anthony 1939- *WhoAm 92*
Georgakas, Dan 1938- *WhoWrEP 92*
Georgakis, Christos 1947- *WhoAm 92*
Georgakis, Spryos 1932- *WhoScE 91-3*
Georgala, D.L. *WhoScE 91-1*
Georganas, Nicolas D. 1943- *WhoAm 92*
Georgantas, Aristides William 1943- *WhoAm 92*
Georgantas, Aristides William 1944- *St&PR 93*
George *OxDcByz*
George, IV, King of Great Britain 1762-1830 *BioIn 17*
George, V 1865-1936 *DcTwHis*
George, V, King of Great Britain 1865-1936 *BioIn 17*
George, VI 1895-1952 *DcTwHis*
George, VI, King of Great Britain 1895-1952 *BioIn 17*
George, Albert Richard 1938- *WhoAm 92, WhoE 93*
George, Alex D., Jr. 1946- *St&PR 93*
George, Alexander Andrew 1938- *WhoWor 93*
George, Alice *BioIn 17*
George, Alva *AmWomPl*
George, Anderson *BioIn 17*
George, Andrea Zoe 1946- *WhoAmW 93*
George, Anna Pritchard *AmWomPl*
George, Anne Gibbons *Law&B 92*
George, Anthony 1935- *WhoWor 93*
George, Barbara *ConAu 37NR, SoulM*
George, Barbara 1942- *WhoWrEP 92*
George, Beauford James, Jr. 1925- *WhoAm 92*
George, Beth 1946- *WhoWrEP 92*
George, Bill 1930-1982 *BioIn 17*
George, Bill 1951- *ScF&FL 92*
George, Brian James *WhoScE 91-1*
George, Carole Schroeder 1943- *WhoAmW 93*
George, Charles Frederick *WhoScE 91-1*
George, Charles William 1914- *WhoAm 92*
George, Chris Alexander *Law&B 92*
George, Claudia K. 1949- *WhoAmW 93*
George, D.J. *WhoScE 91-1*
George, D. Keith *Law&B 92*
George, David A. 1942- *St&PR 93*
George, David Alan 1942- *WhoAm 92, WhoWor 93*
George, David C. 1921- *St&PR 93*
George, David E. 1934- *St&PR 93*
George, David Lloyd George Lloyd 1863-1945 *BioIn 17*
George, David Webster 1922- *WhoAm 92*
George, Delia *BioIn 17*
George, Dennis A. 1947- *St&PR 93*
George, Deveral D. 1939- *WhoAm 92*
George, Diane Elizabeth 1952- *WhoAmW 93, WhoEmL 93*
George, Donna Flach 1947- *WhoAmW 93*
George, Dorothy Thomas *AmWomPl*
George, Doug 1949- *WhoEmL 93*
George, Earl 1924- *Baker 92, WhoAm 92*
George, Edward *ScF&FL 92*
George, Edward H. 1955- *St&PR 93*
George, Edward Metcalf 1936- *St&PR 93*
George, Elisa Suzanne 1956- *St&PR 93*
George, Elizabeth 1949- *ConAu 137*
George, Elizabeth Ann 1948- *WhoEmL 93*
George, Elizabeth Pratt 1964- *WhoAmW 93*
George, Emery Edward 1933- *WhoAm 92*
George, Emily *ConAu 37NR*
George, Francis *WhoAm 92*
George, Francisco 1947- *WhoUN 92*
George, Fredric J. *Law&B 92*
George, Gail *ConAu 37NR*
George, Gerald William 1938- *WhoAm 92*
George, Grace 1895- *AmWomPl*
George, Harry D., Jr. *Law&B 92*
George, Henry 1839-1897 *BioIn 17, GayN, JrnUS, PolPar*
George, Henry Hamilton 1934- *WhoE 93*
George, Herbert J. 1941- *St&PR 93*
George, James *BioIn 17*
George, James A. 1932- *St&PR 93*
George, James Edward 1943- *WhoSSW 93*
George, James Henry Bryn 1929- *St&PR 93*
George, Jawad F. d1990 *BioIn 17*
George, Jean *MajAI*
George, Jean Craighead 1919- *BioIn 17, DcAmChF 1960, MajAI [port], WhoAm 92, WhoWrEP 92*
George, Jeff *BioIn 17*
George, Jennifer Jill *WhoScE 91-1*
George, Jennifer Mari 1956- *WhoAmW 93, WhoSSW 93*
George, Jim *MiSFD 9*
George, Joan Marie 1932- *WhoAmW 93*
George, Joey Russell 1963- *WhoE 93, WhoEmL 93*
George, John 1961- *WhoEmL 93*
George, John Anthony 1948- *WhoEmL 93*
George, John C. 1954- *St&PR 93*
George, John Martin, Jr. 1947- *WhoAm 92*
George, Joyce Jackson 1936- *WhoAm 92, WhoAmW 93*
George, Judith Wordsworth 1940- *WhoWor 93*
George, Kenneth John *WhoScE 91-1*
George, Kenneth L. *Law&B 92*
George, Lawrence M. 1935- *St&PR 93*
George, Leonard F. 1952- *St&PR 93*
George, Lisa 1964- *WhoEmL 93*
George, Louis D. 1922- *St&PR 93*
George, Lynda Day 1946- *WhoAm 92*
George, Mary Carolyn Hollers 1930- *WhoSSW 93*
George, Mary Shannon 1916- *WhoAmW 93*
George, Melvin Douglas 1936- *WhoAm 92*
George, Merton Baron Tisdale 1920- *WhoAm 92*
George, Michael J. 1947- *St&PR 93*
George, Nicholas *WhoAm 92*
George, Pamela Carlson 1960- *WhoE 93*
George, Patrick Joseph 1951- *WhoEmL 93*
George, Paula Louise 1952- *WhoEmL 93*
George, Peter James 1941- *WhoAm 92*
George, Peter T. 1929- *WhoAm 92*
George, Phyllis *BioIn 17*
George, Raymond Eugene, Jr. 1930- *WhoAm 92*
George, Regina Jo 1949- *WhoEmL 93*
George, Richard Ervin, Jr. 1939- *WhoAm 92*
George, Richard Lee 1950- *St&PR 93*
George, Richard Neill 1933- *WhoAm 92*
George, Robert D. 1942- *St&PR 93*
George, Ron 1944- *BioIn 17*
George, Ronald Baylis 1932- *WhoAm 92*
George, Ross 1932- *St&PR 93*
George, Sara 1947- *ScF&FL 92*
George, Sarah G. 1954- *St&PR 93*
George, Screaming Mad *MiSFD 9*
George, Shirley H. 1938- *WhoAmW 93*
George, Stephan Anthony 1946- *WhoWor 93*
George, Stephen (Alan) 1949- *ConAu 139*
George, Stephen R. *ScF&FL 92*
George, Sue Ann 1948- *WhoAmW 93, WhoEmL 93, WhoSSW 93*
George, Susan G. *Law&B 92*
George, Sushil 1959- *WhoWor 93*
George, Thomas 1918- *WhoAm 92*
George, Thomas Frederick 1947- *WhoAm 92*
George, Thomas Wynne 1935- *WhoSSW 93*
George, W. Peyton 1936- *WhoAm 92*
George, Walter Eugene, Jr. 1922- *WhoAm 92*
George, Walter F. 1878-1957 *PolPar*
George, William D. 1932- *St&PR 93*
George, William David *WhoScE 91-1*
George, William Douglas, Jr. 1932- *WhoAm 92*
George, William F. *ScF&FL 92*
George, William Francis 1927- *St&PR 93*
George, William Ickes 1931- *WhoSSW 93*
George, William J. *Law&B 92*
George, William Leo, Jr. 1938- *WhoAm 92*
George, William O. *WhoScE 91-1*
George, William Wallace 1942- *St&PR 93, WhoAm 92*
George Brankovic c. 1375-1456 *OxDcByz*
Georgeff, Michael Peter 1946- *WhoWor 93*
George Hamartolos *OxDcByz*
Georgehead, Christopher William 1942- *St&PR 93*
George Komnenos c. 1254-c. 1284 *OxDcByz*
Georgelas, Anthony John 1953- *St&PR 93*
Georgelos, Peter J. 1935- *St&PR 93*
George Mt'ac'mindeli 1009-1065 *OxDcByz*
George of Amastris d802? *OxDcByz*
George of Antioch c. 1100-1150 *HarEnMi*
George of Cyprus fl. 7th cent.- *OxDcByz*
George of Mytilene *OxDcByz*
George Of Mytilene 763-844 *See* David of Mytilene 716-783? *OxDcByz*
George of Nikomedeia *OxDcByz*
George of Pisidia dc. 631 *OxDcByz*
George of Trebizond *OxDcByz*
Georges, Alexandre 1850-1938 *Baker 92*
Georges, Jean Marie 1939- *WhoScE 91-2*
Georges, John A. 1931- *St&PR 93, WhoAm 92, WhoE 93*
Georges, Maurice Ostrow 1921- *WhoAm 92*
Georges, Paul Gordon 1923- *WhoAm 92*
Georges, Peter John 1940- *WhoWor 93*
Georgescu, Dan Corneliu 1938- *Baker 92*
Georgescu, Georges 1887-1964 *Baker 92*
Georgescu, Leonida *WhoScE 91-4*
Georgescu, Peter A. 1939- *St&PR 93*
Georgescu, Peter Andrew 1939- *WhoAm 92, WhoE 93*
Georgescu, Petre Paul *WhoScE 91-4*
Georgescu-Roegen, Nicholas 1906- *BioIn 17*
Georgeson, Peter I. 1925- *St&PR 93*
George the Monk *OxDcByz*
George the Philosopher fl. 14th cent.- *OxDcByz*
George the Synkellos dc. 810 *OxDcByz*
George Trapezountios 1395-c. 1472 *OxDcByz*
George William 1595-1640 *HarEnMi*
Georghiades, Mary Elizabeth 1961- *WhoSSW 93*
Georghiou, Luke *WhoScE 91-1*
Georghiou, Luke Gregory 1955- *WhoWor 93*
Georgi, Rudolf 1943- *WhoWor 93*
Georgiade, Nicholas George 1918- *WhoAm 92*
Georgiades, George I. 1942- *WhoWor 93*
Georgiades, Thrasybulos 1907-1977 *Baker 92*
Georgiades, William Den Hartog 1925- *WhoAm 92, WhoSSW 93, WhoWor 93*
Georgiadis, Georges 1912-1986 *Baker 92*
Georgiev, Georgi Angelov 1928- *WhoScE 91-4*
Georgiev, N. Ivanov 1934- *WhoScE 91-4*
Georgiev, Vassil Stefanov 1929- *WhoWor 93*
Georgiev, Viden 1925- *WhoScE 91-4*
Georgieva-Tancheva, Kitchka 1930- *WhoScE 91-4*
Georgii, Alexander 1927- *WhoScE 91-3*
Georgii, Hans-Otto 1944- *WhoWor 93*
Georgii, Walter 1887-1967 *Baker 92*
Georgine, Robert A. *WhoIns 93*
Georgino, Damian C. *Law&B 92*
Georgino, Susan Martha 1950- *WhoAmW 93*
Georgiou, Dimitrios 1946- *WhoScE 91-3*
Georgiou, Georgios Leonidas 1947- *WhoScE 91-4*
Georgitis, John 1950- *WhoEmL 93, WhoSSW 93*
Georgitsis, Nicolas M. 1934- *St&PR 93*
Georgius, John R. 1944- *WhoAm 92*
Georgopapadakou, Nafsika Helen 1950- *WhoEmL 93*
Georgopoulos, Chris J. 1932- *WhoScE 91-3*
Georgopoulos, Maria 1949- *WhoAm 92, WhoAmW 93, WhoE 93*
Georgoulis, Stratton J. 1932- *St&PR 93*
Geosling, Gary M. *Law&B 92*
Gepfert, Alan Harry 1930- *WhoE 93*
Gepford, Daniel W. *Law&B 92*
Gephardt, Donald Louis 1937- *WhoE 93*
Gephardt, Richard A. *BioIn 17*
Gephardt, Richard A. 1941- *CngDr 91, PolPar*
Gephardt, Richard Andrew 1941- *WhoAm 92*
Gephardt, Thomas Steuber 1927- *WhoAm 92*
Gephardt, William Ellery, Jr. 1929- *St&PR 93*
Gephart, William 1913- *WhoE 93*
Gepner, Marsha Kay 1947- *WhoEmL 93*
Geppert, Kathryn Ann 1953- *WhoEmL 93*
Geppert, Marlene 1941- *WhoAmW 93*
Geppert, Richard P. 1937- *St&PR 93*
Geppert, William A., Jr. 1923- *St&PR 93*
Gera, Bernice d1992 *NewYTBS 92*
Gerace, Gregory J. 1955- *St&PR 93*
Gerace, Susan Terese 1950- *WhoEmL 93*
Geraci, Diane 1952- *WhoAmW 93*
Geraci, Giuseppe 1933- *WhoScE 91-3*
Geraci, Michael Raleigh 1937- *WhoE 93*
Geraci, Philip Charles, Jr. 1929- *WhoE 93*
Geraci, Raymond J. 1928- *St&PR 93*
Geraci, Vincent J. 1914-1991 *BioIn 17*
Gerad, R. Peter 1937- *St&PR 93*
Geradin, Michel M. 1945- *WhoScE 91-2*
Geraghty, Barbara Anne 1949- *WhoAmW 93*
Geraghty, Carmelita 1901-1966 *SweetSg B [port]*
Geraghty, Kenneth George 1950- *WhoAm 92*
Geraghty, Margaret Karl 1947- *WhoAmW 93, WhoEmL 93*
Geraghty, Roberta T. *AmWomPl*
Gerakis, Pantazis-Alexandros 1934- *WhoScE 91-3*
Gerald, Barry 1934- *WhoAm 92*
Gerald, Carolyn 1943- *WhoWrEP 92*
Gerald, Florence *AmWomPl*
Gerald, Gregory Fitz *ScF&FL 92*
Gerald, John Bart 1940- *WhoWrEP 92*
Gerald, Louis G. 1919- *St&PR 93*
Gerald, Michael Charles 1939- *WhoAm 92*
Gerald, Missy *BlkAmWO*
Gerald, Veronica Davis 1950- *WhoSSW 93*
Geraldi, Camille *BioIn 17*
Geraldi, Michael *BioIn 17*
Geraldson, Raymond I., Jr. 1940- *WhoWor 93*
Geramb, Viktor 1884-1958 *IntDcAn*
Gerani, Gary *ScF&FL 92*
Gerard, Andre 1932- *WhoScE 91-2*
Gerard, Bryan Elie *Law&B 92*
Gerard, Claude 1918- *WhoE 93*
Gerard, Emanuel 1932- *St&PR 93, WhoAm 92*
Gerard, Gale E. 1946- *St&PR 93*
Gerard, Gaston 1912-1990 *BioIn 17*
Gerard, Gil *BioIn 17*
Gerard, James Wilson 1935- *WhoAm 92*
Gerard, Jean Broward Shevlin 1938- *WhoAm 92, WhoAmW 93*
Gerard, Jim 1937- *WhoAsAP 91*
Gerard, Jules Bernard 1929- *WhoAm 92*
Gerard, Michel Marie 1934- *WhoWor 93*
Gerard, Norbert 1936- *WhoScE 91-2*
Gerard, Richard A. *Law&B 92*
Gerard, Robert A. 1944- *St&PR 93*
Gerard, Roy Dupuy 1931- *St&PR 93, WhoAm 92*
Gerard, Roy Joseph 1924- *WhoAm 92*
Gerard, Stephen S. *Law&B 92*
Gerard, Stephen Stanley 1936- *WhoWor 93*
Gerard, Thomas H. 1928- *St&PR 93*
Gerard, Whitney Ian 1934- *WhoAm 92*
Gerard, William W. *St&PR 93*
Gerard, Yves 1927- *WhoScE 91-2*
Gerardi, Maryrose Acerra 1959- *WhoEmL 93*
Gerardi, Michael T. 1952- *St&PR 93*
Gerardino, William Ernest 1933- *WhoWrEP 92*
Gerardo *BioIn 17*
Gerardo, Nunez Vargas 1949- *WhoWor 93*
Gerardy, Jean 1877-1929 *Baker 92*
Geras, Adele (Daphne) 1944- *ChlFicS*
Gerasimov, Gennadi 1930- *WhoWor 93*
Gerasimov, Sergej 1906-1985 *DrEEuF*
Gerasimow, Alexander M. *Law&B 92*
Gerathy, E. Carroll 1915- *WhoAm 92*
Gerault-Richard 1860-1911 *BioIn 17*
Geraut, Christian 1946- *WhoScE 91-2*
Gerba, Charles Peter 1945- *WhoWor 93*
Gerbaldi, Michele 1944- *WhoScE 91-2*
Gerber, Adrian Maree 1938- *St&PR 93*
Gerber, Barbara Ann Witter 1934- *WhoAm 92, WhoAmW 93*
Gerber, Barry Eldon 1942- *WhoWor 93*
Gerber, C. Richard 1959- *WhoSSW 93*
Gerber, Charles A. 1942- *St&PR 93*

Gerber, Charles J., Jr. 1935- St&PR 93
Gerber, Charles Waas 1961- WhoEmL 93
Gerber, Daniel Frank 1940- WhoWrEP 92
Gerber, David A. BioIn 17
Gerber, David J. Law&B 92
Gerber, Donald Albert 1932- WhoE 93
Gerber, Douglas Earl 1933- WhoAm 92, WhoWrEP 92
Gerber, Edward Michael Law&B 92
Gerber, Ernst Ludwig 1746-1819 Baker 92
Gerber, Eugene J. 1931- WhoAm 92
Gerber, Fritz WhoScE 91-4
Gerber, Gwendolyn Loretta WhoE 93
Gerber, Harold Bruce 1925- St&PR 93
Gerber, Harvey Franklin, Jr. 1948- WhoEmL 93
Gerber, Hazel Marie WhoAmW 93
Gerber, Heinz Joseph BioIn 17
Gerber, Heinz Joseph 1924- St&PR 93, WhoAm 92
Gerber, Heinz Peter 1934- WhoScE 91-4
Gerber, Israel Joshua 1918- WhoSSW 93
Gerber, James L. 1928- St&PR 93
Gerber, Joel 1940- CngDr 91, WhoAm 92
Gerber, John Christian 1908- WhoAm 92, WhoWrEP 92
Gerber, John R. Law&B 92
Gerber, Linda Maxine 1953- WhoEmL 93
Gerber, Louis Emil 1930- WhoAm 92
Gerber, Lucille D. 1952- WhoAmW 93, WhoEmL 93
Gerber, Marlene 1937- WhoAmW 93
Gerber, Merrill Joan BioIn 17
Gerber, Michael H. 1944- St&PR 93
Gerber, Miriam 1922- BioIn 17
Gerber, Murray A. WhoAm 92
Gerber, Murray A. 1935- St&PR 93
Gerber, Neva SweetSg B [port]
Gerber, Rene 1908- Baker 92
Gerber, Robert Alue 1927- St&PR 93
Gerber, Robert Evan 1947- WhoAm 92, WhoEmL 93
Gerber, Robert Russell 1951- WhoAm 92
Gerber, Roger A. Law&B 92
Gerber, Roger A. 1939- St&PR 93
Gerber, Roger Alan 1939- WhoAm 92
Gerber, Roman J. 1932- St&PR 93
Gerber, Ronald N. 1943- St&PR 93
Gerber, Rudolf 1899-1957 Baker 92
Gerber, Sanford Edwin 1933- WhoAm 92
Gerber, Seymour St&PR 93
Gerber, Seymour 1920- WhoAm 92
Gerber, Stanley 1941- WhoAm 92
Gerber, Thomas W. 1921-1991 BioIn 17
Gerber, William Kenton 1954- St&PR 93, WhoAm 92
Gerberding, Bette Jean 1933- WhoAmW 93
Gerberding, Elizabeth Sears AmWomPl
Gerberding, Miles Law&B 92
Gerberding, Miles Carston 1930- WhoAm 92
Gerberding, William Passavant 1929- WhoAm 92, WhoWor 93
Gerberg, Eugene Jordan 1919- WhoAm 92
Gerberg, Judith Levine 1940- WhoAmW 93
Gerberg, Mort BioIn 17
Gerberg, Mort 1931- ScF&FL 92
Gerberich, William Warren 1935- WhoAm 92
Gerbert, Goran 1938- WhoScE 91-4
Gerbert, Martin 1720-1793 Baker 92
Gerbi, Claudio 1907-1990 BioIn 17
Gerbi, Susan Alexandra 1944- WhoAm 92
Gerbie, Albert Bernard 1927- WhoAm 92
Gerbino, John 1941- WhoAm 92
Gerbitz, Lois Lynn 1954- WhoAmW 93
Gerbner, George 1919- WhoAm 92
Gerbode, Willi Franz 1955- WhoWor 93
Gerbracht, Terry Lynne 1955- WhoAmW 93
Gerchenson, Emile H. 1922- St&PR 93
Gerchenson, Jeffrey St&PR 93
Gerchunoff, Alberto 1883-1950 SpAmA
Gerdeaux, Daniel 1948- WhoScE 91-2
Gerdemann, James Wessel 1921- WhoAm 92
Gerdes, Anthony Martin 1952- WhoSSW 93
Gerdes, Gerold 1947- BioIn 17
Gerdes, John Leon 1955- WhoSSW 93
Gerdes, Michelle Ann 1961- WhoE 93
Gerdes, Neil Wayne 1943- WhoAm 92, WhoWor 93
Gerdes, Ralph Donald 1951- WhoEmL 93
Gerdes, Roberto Mauricio 1948- WhoE 93
Gerdes, Susan Taylor 1951- WhoWrEP 92
Gerdes, Thomas Robert 1948- St&PR 93
Gerdie, Raymond 1929- WhoScE 91-4
Gerdine, Leigh 1917- WhoAm 92
Gerding, Edward Y. 1926- St&PR 93
Gerding, Paul A. 1921- St&PR 93
Gerdis-Karp, Joyce Ellen 1961- WhoEmL 93
Gerdjikov, Vladimir Stefanov 1947- WhoWor 93
Gerdts, Abigail Booth 1937- WhoE 93
Gerdts, William H. BioIn 17
Gerdts, William Henry 1929- WhoAm 92
Gere, James Monroe 1925- WhoAm 92
Gere, Richard BioIn 17
Gere, Richard 1949- HolBB [port], IntDcF 2-3 [port], WhoAm 92
Gere, Terrence D. 1941- St&PR 93
Gere, Tibor 1937- WhoScE 91-4
Gereau, Mary Condon 1916- WhoAmW 93
Gereaue, Michael R. 1946- St&PR 93
Gereb, Daniel L. 1929- St&PR 93
Gerecke, William 1924- St&PR 93
Gerei, Laszlo 1929- WhoScE 91-4
Gerek, Terrence L. 1957- St&PR 93
Gerelli, Ennio 1907-1970 Baker 92
Gerely, Peter 1934- WhoScE 91-4
Geremski, Terrence Eugene 1947- WhoEmL 93
Geren, Brenda L. 1950- WhoAmW 93, WhoEmL 93
Geren, Gerald S. 1939- WhoWor 93
Geren, Pete 1952- CngDr 91, WhoAm 92
Geren, Peter 1952- WhoSSW 93
Geren, Preston Murdoch, Jr. 1923- WhoAm 92
Gerena, Ana Rodriguez 1961- WhoSSW 93
Gerencser, Miklos 1931- WhoScE 91-4
Gerendas, Thomas G. 1932- St&PR 93
Gerentz, Sven Thure 1921- WhoWor 93
Gerety, Doris W. St&PR 93
Gerety, Peter L. Law&B 92
Gerety, Peter Leo 1912- WhoAm 92
Gerety, Robert John 1939- WhoAm 92
Gerety, Tom 1946- WhoAm 92
Gerevas, Ronald E. St&PR 93
Gerfen, Henry James 1940- WhoAm 92
Gergacz, John William 1950- WhoEmL 93
Gergatz, Stephen Joseph 1946- WhoSSW 93
Gergely, Arpad Jozsef 1938- WhoWrEP 92
Gergely, Istvan 1937- WhoScE 91-4
Gergely, Janos 1925- WhoScE 91-4
Gergely, Peter 1942- WhoScE 91-4
Gergely, Stephen WhoScE 91-1
Gergen, David Richmond 1942- WhoAm 92
Gergen, Mark Joseph Law&B 92
Gerger, Haluk Bahri 1948- WhoUN 92
Gerges, Makram Amin 1942- WhoUN 92
Gergiannakis, Anthony Emmanuel 1935- WhoAm 92
Gergiev, Valery 1953- WhoWor 93
Gergis, Samir Danial 1933- WhoAm 92
Gergowicz, Zdzislaw Bernard 1920- WhoScE 91-4
Gerhard, Harry E., Jr. 1925- WhoE 93, WhoWor 93
Gerhard, Herbert Fritz 1930- St&PR 93
Gerhard, Lang Hallett 1945- WhoAm 92
Gerhard, Lee Clarence 1937- WhoAm 92
Gerhard, Roberto 1896-1970 Baker 92, OxDcOp
Gerhardie, William Alexander 1895-1977 BioIn 17
Gerhard-Multhaupt, Georg Reimund 1952- WhoWor 93
Gerhardstein, E. Michael 1923- St&PR 93
Gerhardt, Don John 1939- WhoSSW 93
Gerhardt, Elena 1883-1961 Baker 92
Gerhardt, Glenn Rodney 1923- WhoSSW 93
Gerhardt, Jon Stuart 1943- WhoAm 92
Gerhardt, Lillian Noreen 1932- WhoAm 92, WhoAmW 93, WhoWrEP 92
Gerhardt, Marion Law&B 92
Gerhardt, Philipp 1921- St&PR 93, WhoAm 92
Gerhardt, Rosario Alejandrina 1953- WhoAmW 93, WhoEmL 93
Gerhardt, Uta Emma Therese 1938- WhoScE 91-3
Gerhardy, Louis P. 1934- St&PR 93
Gerhart, Ann 1955- St&PR 93
Gerhart, Charles J. BioIn 17
Gerhart, Eugene Clifton 1912- St&PR 93, WhoAm 92
Gerhart, Glenna Lee 1954- WhoAmW 93, WhoSSW 93
Gerhart, James Basil 1928- WhoAm 92
Gerhart, Mary J. 1935- WhoAmW 93
Gerhart, Peter Milton 1945- WhoAm 92
Gerhart, Richard A. 1947- St&PR 93
Gerhart, Richard Stephen 1941- St&PR 93
Gerhart, Steven George 1948- WhoAm 92
Gerhart, William Earle 1932- St&PR 93
Gerhold, Timothy A.G. Law&B 92
Gerholm, Tor Ragnar 1925- WhoScE 91-4, WhoWor 93
Geria, Dennis WhoWor 93
Gerich, Obren B. St&PR 93
Gericke, Paul William 1924- WhoAm 92
Gericke, Wilhelm 1845-1925 Baker 92
Gerigk, K. WhoScE 91-3
Gerik, Rodney Ernest Law&B 92
Gerike, Ann Elizabeth 1933- WhoAm 92
Gering, Donald Vern 1947- WhoEmL 93
Gering, George S. 1932- St&PR 93
Gering, John P. 1953- St&PR 93
Gering, Ronald Carl 1945- WhoE 93
Gering, William J. 1945- St&PR 93
Gerin-Lajoie, Antoine 1824-1882 BioIn 17
Gerisch, Gunther WhoScE 91-3
Gerjuoy, Edward 1918- WhoAm 92, WhoE 93
Gerke, Patricia Ann 1961- WhoE 93
Gerken, Henry J. Law&B 92
Gerken, Henry J. 1940- St&PR 93
Gerken, Richard R. Law&B 92
Gerken, Richard R. 1945- St&PR 93
Gerken, Walter Bland 1922- St&PR 93, WhoAm 92
Gerkens, Robert F. Law&B 92
Gerking, Shelby Delos, Jr. 1918- WhoAm 92
Gerl, Franz Xaver 1764-1827 Baker 92, OxDcOp
Gerl, Maurice 1939- WhoScE 91-2
Gerl, Peter 1940- WhoScE 91-4
Gerlach, Carol Danese 1955- WhoEmL 93, WhoSSW 93
Gerlach, Clinton G. 1926- St&PR 93
Gerlach, Dieter L.W. 1935- WhoScE 91-3
Gerlach, Ernest John 1939- WhoSSW 93
Gerlach, Frederick Herman 1938- WhoWor 93
Gerlach, G. Donald 1933- WhoAm 92
Gerlach, Gary G. 1945- WhoAm 92, WhoSSW 93
Gerlach, Jeanne Elaine 1946- WhoAmW 93
Gerlach, John B. 1927- WhoAm 92
Gerlach, John Thomas 1932- St&PR 93, WhoE 93
Gerlach, Luther Paul 1930- WhoAm 92
Gerlach, O.H. WhoScE 91-3
Gerlach, Otto B., III 1939- St&PR 93
Gerlach, Rebecca Anne 1956- WhoAmW 93
Gerlach, Richard G. 1934- St&PR 93
Gerlach, Robert Law&B 92
Gerlach, Robert A. 1927- St&PR 93
Gerlach, Robert Louis 1940- WhoAm 92
Gerlach, Roger Harold 1945- St&PR 93
Gerlach, Scott B. 1948- WhoIns 93
Gerlach, Scott Borden 1948- St&PR 93
Gerlach, Sebastian A. 1929- WhoScE 91-3
Gerlach, Talitha BioIn 17
Gerlach, Theodor 1861-1940 Baker 92
Gerlach, Ulrich 1925- WhoScE 91-3
Gerlach, William C. 1956- WhoE 93
Gerle, Hans c. 1500-1570 Baker 92
Gerle, Robert 1924- Baker 92
Gerler, Edwin Roland, Jr. 1945- WhoSSW 93
Gerli, Karen Ann 1959- St&PR 93
Gerlich, Michael Anthony 1954- St&PR 93
Gerlicher, Andrew John Law&B 92
Gerlin, Robert A. St&PR 93
Gerling, Paul J. 1947- St&PR 93
Gerlinger, Charles D. Law&B 92
Gerlits, Francis Joseph 1931- WhoAm 92
Gerlitz, Dennis Eugene 1937- WhoIns 93
Gerlitzki, Guenther Johannes 1924- WhoE 93
Gerlough, Robert Tillman 1930- St&PR 93
Gerlt, Joseph Luther 1934- St&PR 93
Germain, Albert E. Law&B 92
Germain, Albert E. 1934- St&PR 93
Germain, Albert H.N. 1944- WhoScE 91-2
Germain, Francis Marie Auguste 1949- WhoWor 93
Germain, Gary Roger 1944- WhoAm 92
Germain, Gerald 1942- St&PR 93, WhoAm 92
Germain, Jean Claude 1939- WhoCanL 92
Germain, Jean Eugene 1922- WhoScE 91-2
Germain, Jeanette Eloise 1950- WhoWrEP 92
Germain, Paul Marie 1920- WhoScE 91-2
Germain, Sophie 1776-1831 BioIn 17
German, Aleksej 1938- DrEEuF
German, Anton L. 1939- WhoScE 91-3
German, Diane Judith 1944- WhoAmW 93
German, Dwight Charles 1944- WhoSSW 93
German, Edward 1862-1936 Baker 92, OxDcOp
German, Edward Cecil 1921- WhoE 93
German, Jeffrey Neal 1957- WhoEmL 93
German, Joan W(olfe) 1933- WhoWrEP 92
German, John George 1921- WhoAm 92
German, Karyn Marie 1962- WhoAmW 93
German, Katherine L. 1947- WhoEmL 93
German, Norman 1955- WhoWrEP 92
German, Randall Michael 1946- WhoAm 92
German, Ronald Stephen 1946- WhoAm 92, WhoEmL 93, WhoSSW 93
German, Tony 1924- WhoCanL 92
German, William 1919- WhoAm 92
Germane, Gayton Elwood 1920- WhoAm 92
Germani, Elia Law&B 92
Germani, Fernando 1906- Baker 92
Germann, Albert George 1926- St&PR 93
Germann, Klaus 1938- WhoScE 91-3
Germann, Richard Paul 1918- WhoAm 92, WhoWor 93
Germano, Fernao Stella 1932- WhoWor 93
Germano, Peter B. 1913-1983 ScF&FL 92
Germano, William Paul 1950- WhoAm 92
Germanos c. 505-550 OxDcByz
Germanos, I c. 630-c. 730 OxDcByz
Germanos, II 12th cent.- OxDcByz
Germany, Daniel Monroe 1937- WhoAm 92
Germany, John Fredrick 1923- WhoAm 92
Germer, Erich 1924- WhoWor 93
Germeshausen, Kenneth J. 1907-1990 BioIn 17
Germi, Pietro 1914-1974 MiSFD 9N
Germing, Georgus H. 1929- WhoScE 91-3
Germon, Jean-Claude 1948- WhoScE 91-2
Germond, John Louis 1929- St&PR 93
Germuska, Michael Joseph 1950- WhoSSW 93
Gernand, Bradley Elton 1964- WhoAm 92
Gernant, Karen 1938- WhoAmW 93
Gerner, Daniel F. St&PR 93
Gerner, Raymond Edwin 1926- St&PR 93
Gernert, Dieter WhoWor 93
Gernes, Sonia Grace 1942- WhoWrEP 92
Gernez WhoScE 91-2
Gernon, George Owen, Jr. 1950- WhoEmL 93, WhoSSW 93, WhoWor 93
Gernreich, Rudi 1922-1985 BioIn 17
Gernsbacher, Morton Ann 1955- WhoAmW 93
Gernsback, Hugo BioIn 17
Gernsheim, Friedrich 1839-1916 Baker 92
Gero, Anne L. Law&B 92
Gero, Anthony George 1936- WhoE 93
Gero, Erno 1898-1980 ColdWar 2 [port]
Gero, James Farrington 1945- St&PR 93, WhoAm 92
Gero, Jhan fl. 16th cent.- Baker 92
Gerogiannis, Nicholas Constantine 1945- WhoSSW 93
Gerolami, Andre WhoScE 91-2
Gerold, John Henry 1947- St&PR 93
Gerold, (Jean) Theodore 1866-1956 Baker 92
Gerome, Nick Jerry 1944- St&PR 93
Geron, Ellen Hansman 1949- St&PR 93
Geronemus, Diann Fox 1947- WhoAmW 93
Geronimo 1829-1909 BioIn 17, GayN, HarEnMi
Gerony, Francois Andre 1948- WhoWor 93
Geronzi, Cesare BioIn 17
Geroski, Paul Andrew WhoScE 91-1
Gerow, Edwin Mahaffey 1931- WhoAm 92
Gerow, Leonard Townsend 1888-1972 HarEnMi
Gerra, Martin Jerome, Jr. 1927- WhoE 93
Gerrand, Rob ScF&FL 92
Gerrard, Gene 1890-1971 QDrFCA 92 [port]
Gerrard, Robert J., Jr. Law&B 92
Gerrard, Robert W. 1927- St&PR 93
Gerrard, Robert Wilkin 1927- WhoAm 92
Gerrard, Roy 1935- BioIn 17, ChlBIID [port]
Gerrare, Wirt 1862- ScF&FL 92
Gerraughty, Richard Gerard 1940- St&PR 93
Gerrietts, John 1912-1992 ConAu 136
Gerring, Cathy BioIn 17
Gerring, Donna Maria Isabella 1957- WhoAmW 93
Gerring, Edward Lawrence WhoScE 91-1
Gerringer, Robert 1926-1989 BioIn 17
Gerringer-Busenbark, Elizabeth Jacquelin 1934- WhoAmW 93
Gerrish, Brian Albert 1931- WhoAm 92
Gerrish, Catherine R. 1911- St&PR 93
Gerrish, Catherine Ruggles 1911- WhoAmW 93, WhoE 93
Gerrish, Eileen Devine 1950- WhoE 93
Gerrish, Hollis G. 1907- St&PR 93, WhoE 93, WhoWor 93
Gerrits, J.P.G. 1938- WhoScE 91-3
Gerritsen, Frans Andreas 1953- WhoWor 93
Gerritsen, Hendrik Jurjen 1927- WhoAm 92
Gerritsen, Johannes Teengs d1990 BioIn 17
Gerritsen, Mary Ellen 1953- WhoAm 92, WhoAmW 93, WhoEmL 93

Gerritsen, Paul S. 1945- St&PR 93
Gerrity, Daniel Wallace 1948- WhoE 93
Gerrity, Frank, II 1918- WhoAm 92, WhoWor 93
Gerrity, J. Frank 1918- St&PR 93
Gerrity, James Robert 1941- WhoAm 92
Gerrity, Richard Warren 1942- St&PR 93
Gerrity, Robert M. WhoAm 92
Gerritzen, Lothar Georg 1941- WhoWor 93
Gerrold, David 1944- BioIn 17, ScF&FL 92
Gerry, Albert Cleve 1943- St&PR 93
Gerry, Dale Francis 1950- WhoE 93
Gerry, Darlene E. Law&B 92
Gerry, Elbridge 1744-1814 PolPar
Gerry, Elbridge T. 1908- St&PR 93
Gerry, Elbridge Thomas 1908- WhoAm 92
Gerry, Elbridge Thomas, Jr. 1933- WhoAm 92
Gerry, John Francis 1925- WhoAm 92, WhoE 93
Gerry, Joseph John 1928- WhoAm 92, WhoE 93
Gerry, Margarita Spalding 1870-1939 AmWomPl
Gerry, Martin Hughes, IV 1943- WhoAm 92
Gerry, Roger Goodman 1916- WhoE 93, WhoWor 93
Gers, Seymour 1931- WhoAm 92
Gersbach, Francis Collins 1939- St&PR 93
Gersch, Harold Arthur 1922- WhoAm 92
Gersch, Seth J. 1947- St&PR 93
Gerschbacher, Corine Marie 1961- WhoAmW 93
Gerschefski, Edwin 1909- Baker 92
Gerschke, Elroy Louis 1919- St&PR 93
Gersdorf, Antoinette Graham 1952- WhoWrEP 92
Gerse, Steven Law&B 92
Gersen, Michelle S. Law&B 92
Gersh, Beatrice BioIn 17
Gersh, Philip BioIn 17
Gersh, Richard L. 1952- St&PR 93
Gersh, Richard Leon 1952- WhoE 93
Gersh, Wayne David 1949- WhoE 93
Gershator, David 1937- WhoWrEP 92
Gershbein, Leon Lee 1917- WhoAm 92
Gershel, George F., Jr. 1930- St&PR 93
Gershen, Barnett Leonard 1947- St&PR 93
Gershenfeld, Matti Kibrick WhoAmW 93, WhoE 93
Gershengorn, Marvin Carl WhoAm 92, WhoE 93
Gershenson, Harry 1902- WhoAm 92
Gershfeld, David 1911- Baker 92
Gershgorn, Allan S. Law&B 92
Gershman, Elizabeth Gibson 1927- WhoE 93, WhoWrEP 92
Gershman, Karen Frances 1956- WhoSSW 93
Gershom ben Judah 960-1040 BioIn 17
Gershon, Deborah S. Law&B 92
Gershon, Julian Robert, Jr. 1953- WhoSSW 93
Gershon, Michael David 1938- WhoAm 92
Gershon, Neil D. Law&B 92
Gershon, Nina 1940- WhoAmW 93
Gershon, Samuel 1927- WhoAm 92
Gershony, Yariv St&PR 93
Gershowitz, Harold 1938- St&PR 93
Gersht, M.J. Law&B 92
Gershuny, Dianne Lynette 1952- WhoEmL 93
Gershuny, Donald N. Law&B 92
Gershuny, Edward S. Law&B 92
Gershuny, Seymour P. 1917- St&PR 93
Gershuny, Theodore MiSFD 9
Gershvin, Jacob 1898-1937 Baker 92
Gershwin, George 1898-1937 Baker 92, BioIn 17, IntDcOp [port], JeAmHC, OxDcOp
Gershwin, Ira 1896-1983 Baker 92
Gershwin, Leonore Strunsky d1991 BioIn 17
Gersie, Michael H. 1948- WhoIns 93
Gersing, James Edward 1947- WhoEmL 93
Gerske, Janet Fay 1950- WhoAmW 93, WhoEmL 93
Gersky, Robert H. 1935- St&PR 93
Gersler, I. WhoScE 91-4
Gerson, Alan H. 1946- St&PR 93
Gerson, Corinne (Schreibstein) 1927- DcAmChF 1960
Gerson, Eleanor BioIn 17
Gerson, Elliot F. 1952- WhoIns 93
Gerson, Elliot Francis 1952- WhoAm 92, WhoEmL 93
Gerson, Emily Goldsmith AmWomPl
Gerson, Fabian 1928- WhoScE 91-4
Gerson, Gordon Martin, Sr. 1936- WhoSSW 93
Gerson, Irwin Conrad 1930- WhoAm 92
Gerson, Jack ScF&FL 92
Gerson, Jacki Ellen 1949- WhoEmL 93
Gerson, Jerome Howard 1928- WhoAm 92
Gerson, Mark David 1954- WhoWrEP 92
Gerson, Maxine L. Law&B 92
Gerson, Noel B. 1914-1988 BioIn 17, ScF&FL 92
Gerson, Paulette Greer 1960- WhoAmW 93
Gerson, Ralph J. 1949- St&PR 93
Gerson, Ralph Joseph 1949- WhoAm 92, WhoEmL 93
Gerson, Robert Walthall 1935- WhoAm 92
Gerson, Steve 1947- St&PR 93
Gerson, Stuart Michael 1944- WhoAm 92
Gerson, Theodore Frederick 1920- WhoSSW 93
Gerson, Theodore S. 1915- St&PR 93
Gerson, Wojciech 1831-1901 PolBiDi
Gersoni-Edelman, Diane Claire 1947- WhoAmW 93
Gerson-Kiwi, (Esther) Edith 1908- Baker 92
Gersony, Welton Mark 1931- WhoAm 92
Gerst, Elizabeth Carlsen 1929- WhoAmW 93, WhoE 93, WhoWor 93
Gerst, John BioIn 17
Gerst, Paul Howard 1927- WhoAm 92, WhoE 93
Gerst, Steven Richard 1958- WhoSSW 93, WhoWor 93
Gerstberger, Karl 1892-1955 Baker 92
Gerstein, David B. 1936- St&PR 93
Gerstein, David Brown 1936- WhoAm 92
Gerstein, David Morris 1917- St&PR 93
Gerstein, Doryne Shari 1960- WhoE 93, WhoEmL 93
Gerstein, Esther 1924- WhoAm 92, WhoAmW 93, WhoE 93, WhoWor 93
Gerstein, Harvey S. 1935- St&PR 93
Gerstein, Hilda Kirschbaum 1911- WhoAm 92
Gerstein, Irving R. 1942- WhoAm 92
Gerstein, Kenneth Stephen 1951- WhoEmL 93
Gerstein, Mark Bender 1966- WhoWor 93
Gerstein, Mel 1936- St&PR 93
Gerstein, Mordicai 1935- MajAI [port]
Gerstein, Richard E. d1992 NewYTBS 92 [port]
Gerstein, Richard E. 1923-1992 BioIn 17
Gerstein, Richard L. Law&B 92
Gerstein, Richard L. 1942- St&PR 93
Gerstel, Leopold 1925- WhoScE 91-4
Gerstel, Martin Stephen 1941- St&PR 93
Gerstell, A. Frederick 1938- St&PR 93, WhoAm 92
Gersten, Jerome William 1917- WhoAm 92
Gersten, Mark David 1950- St&PR 93
Gersten, S. William 1943- St&PR 93
Gerstenberg, Alice (Erya) 1885-1972 AmWomPl
Gerstenberg, Heinrich Wilhelm von 1737-1823 BioIn 17
Gerstenberger, Donna Lorine 1929- WhoAm 92
Gerstenberger, Heide 1940- WhoWor 93
Gerstenecker, A. Frank BioIn 17
Gerstenecker, Carl-Erhard 1943- WhoScE 91-3
Gerstenmaier, John M. 1916-1991 BioIn 17
Gerstenzang, James Rose 1947- WhoE 93
Gerster, Alec 1948- St&PR 93
Gerster, Etelka 1855-1920 Baker 92, OxDcOp
Gerster, Ottmar 1897-1969 Baker 92, OxDcOp
Gerster, Robert Gibson 1945- WhoAm 92
Gerstgrasser, Walter BioIn 17
Gerstgrasser, Walter d1992 NewYTBS 92
Gersting, Judith Lee 1940- WhoAmW 93
Gerstl, Joel 1932- WhoE 93
Gerstle, Mark R. Law&B 92
Gerstler, Amy 1956- ConLC 70 [port]
Gerstman, Blanche 1910-1973 Baker 92
Gerstman, Henry 1938- St&PR 93
Gerstman, Louis J. d1992 NewYTBS 92
Gerstman, Louis J. 1930-1992 BioIn 17
Gerstner, John J. 1946- WhoWrEP 92
Gerstner, Lillian Polus 1951- WhoWrEP 92
Gerstner, Louis V., Jr. BioIn 17
Gerstner, Louis Vincent, Jr. 1942- WhoAm 92, WhoE 93
Gerstner, Nickolae ScF&FL 92
Gerstner, Richard Thomas 1939- St&PR 93, WhoAm 92
Gerstner, Robert William 1934- WhoAm 92
Gerstner, William L. 1939- St&PR 93
Gert, Bernard 1934- WhoAm 92
Gertenbach, Robert Frederick 1923- WhoAm 92
Gerth, Donald Rogers 1928- WhoAm 92
Gerth, Edwin Charles 1938- St&PR 93
Gertis, Karl WhoScE 91-3
Gertler, Alan William 1952- WhoEmL 93
Gertler, Alfred Martin 1922- WhoAm 92
Gertler, Andre 1907- Baker 92
Gertler, Kenneth L. Law&B 92
Gertler, Menard M. 1919- WhoAm 92, WhoWor 93
Gertler, Viktor 1901-1969 DrEEuF
Gertler, Willie 1907-1991 AnObit 1991
Gertrude, Katy 1928- WhoAmW 93
Gertsch, William Darrell 1940- WhoSSW 93
Gertsen, Celeste Regina 1957- WhoAmW 93
Gertsikova, Maya BioIn 17
Gertz, Alison BioIn 17
Gertz, Alison L. d1992 NewYTBS 92 [port]
Gertz, Alison L. c. 1966-1992 News 93-2
Gertz, Elmer 1906- BioIn 17, ScF&FL 92, WhoAm 92, WhoWrEP 92
Gertz, Junius 1928- St&PR 93
Gertz, Steven Michael 1943- WhoE 93
Gertzog, Irwin Norman 1933- WhoE 93
Gerulaitis, Vitas d1991 BioIn 17
Gerull, Douglas B. 1955- St&PR 93
Gerut, Rosalie Warszawska 1951- WhoAmW 93
Gervais, Barbara Elizabeth 1951- WhoE 93, WhoEmL 93
Gervais, C.H. 1946- WhoCanL 92
Gervais, Charles-Hubert 1671-1744 OxDcOp
Gervais, Cherie Nadine WhoAmW 93
Gervais, Donald G. 1942- St&PR 93
Gervais, Generose 1919- WhoAm 92
Gervais, Guy 1937- WhoCanL 92
Gervais, Henry Joseph 1928- St&PR 93
Gervais, Marcel Andre 1931- WhoAm 92
Gervais, Michel 1944- WhoAm 92, WhoWor 93
Gervais, Paul BioIn 17
Gervais, Paul Nelson 1947- WhoE 93, WhoEmL 93, WhoWor 93
Gervaise, Claude fl. 16th cent.- Baker 92
Gervasi, Frank Henry 1908-1990 BioIn 17
Gervasi, Joseph A. Law&B 92
Gervat, Andre Louis 1929- WhoWor 93
Gerver, Kenneth W. Law&B 92
Gerville-Reache, Jeanne 1882-1915 Baker 92, OxDcOp
Gervino, Eugene Frank Law&B 92
Gervitz, Gloria 1943- DcMexL
Gervois-Nickols, Annie Genevieve Olga 1951- WhoAmW 93
Gerwatowski, Ronald T. Law&B 92
Gerwatowski, Ronald T. 1956- St&PR 93
Gerwick, Ben Clifford, Jr. 1919- WhoAm 92
Gerwig, Edgar C. 1941- St&PR 93
Gerwin, Brenda Isen 1939- WhoAm 92, WhoAmW 93
Gerwin, Leslie Ellen 1950- WhoEmL 93
Gerwing, Maria I. 1947- St&PR 93
Gery, John Roy Octavius 1953- WhoWrEP 92
Gery, Michel 1937- WhoScE 91-2
Geryol, Andrew J. 1942- St&PR 93
Gerzel, Andrew d1990 BioIn 17
Gerzeli, Giuseppe 1931- WhoScE 91-3
Gerzina, John A. 1918- St&PR 93
Gerzon, Mark BioIn 17
Gesang Doje WhoAsAP 91
Geschwind, Russell McRae 1921- WhoAm 92
Geschwint, Ira 1931- St&PR 93
Gesell, Frederick John 1939- St&PR 93
Gesell, Geraldine Cornelia 1932- WhoSSW 93
Gesell, Gerhard A. 1910- CngDr 91
Gesell, Gerhard Alden 1910- WhoAm 92, WhoE 93
Gesensway, Louis 1906-1976 Baker 92
Gesinski, Robert George 1951- St&PR 93
Geske, Donald Charles 1947- St&PR 93
Geske, Larry D. 1939- St&PR 93
Geskey, Ronald Dale 1942- St&PR 93
Geskin, Ernest Samuel 1935- WhoE 93
Gesler, Wilbert M. 1941- ConAu 138
Geslin, Catherine WhoScE 91-2
Geslot, R. WhoScE 91-2
Gesmer, Henry 1912- WhoE 93
Gesner, Elsie Miller WhoWrEP 92
Gesner, Salomon 1730-1788 BioIn 17
Gess, Nicholas Michael 1955- WhoE 93
Gessel, Barbara F. Law&B 92
Gessel, Ira Martin 1951- WhoEmL 93
Gessel, Stanley Paul 1916- WhoAm 92
Gessing, Ryszard Stanislaw 1935- WhoWor 93
Gessner, Charles Herman 1938- WhoAm 92
Gessner, Nicolas 1931- MiSFD 9
Gessner, Salomon 1730-1788 BioIn 17
Gessow, Alfred 1922- WhoAm 92
Gest, Bernard 1924- St&PR 93
Gest, Howard 1921- WhoAm 92
Gest, Jean 1921- WhoScE 91-2
Gest, Kathryn Waters 1947- WhoAm 92
Gestal-Garcia, Jose Rogelio 1951- WhoEmL 93
Gesteland, Robert Charles 1930- WhoAm 92
Geston, Mark S. 1946- ScF&FL 92
Geston, Mark Symington 1946- WhoWrEP 92
Gestrin, B.V. 1935- St&PR 93
Gesualdo, Carlo c. 1560-1613 Baker 92
Geszty, Sylvia 1934- Baker 92
Getachew-Smith, David K. Law&B 92
Getchell, Charles Richard 1933- St&PR 93
Getchell, Charles Willard, Jr. 1929- WhoE 93
Getchell, Franklin St&PR 93
Getchell, Margaret Colby AmWomPl
Gethers, Peter BioIn 17
Gethers, Peter 1953- WhoAm 92
Gethers, Steven 1922-1989 MiSFD 9N
Gethmann, Jack B. 1937- St&PR 93
Gethmann, Kenneth W. 1913- St&PR 93
Getis, Arthur 1934- WhoAm 92
Getler, Michael 1935- WhoAm 92
Getman, Dennis Jon Law&B 92
Getman, Dennis Jon 1944- St&PR 93, WhoAm 92
Getman, Frank Newton 1910- WhoAm 92
Getman, Sheryl Marie 1947- WhoAmW 93, WhoE 93, WhoEmL 93, WhoWor 93
Getoff, Nikola 1922- WhoScE 91-4
Getske, Kathrine 1937- WhoAmW 93
Gettelfinger, Gerald Andrew 1935- WhoAm 92
Gettelfinger, Nancy WhoAmW 93
Gettelman, Kenneth Milton 1925- WhoAm 92
Gettelman, Robin Claire 1952- WhoAmW 93, WhoWor 93
Gettier, Edmund Lee, III 1927- WhoE 93
Gettier, Glenn Howard, Jr. 1942- St&PR 93
Gettig, Carl William 1928- WhoWor 93
Gettig, Martin Winthrop 1939- WhoE 93, WhoWor 93
Gettig, Philip D. Law&B 92
Getting, Ivan Alexander 1912- BioIn 17, WhoAm 92
Gettinger, Lillian 1925- St&PR 93
Gettinger, Matthew Law&B 92
Gettinger, Walter 1915- St&PR 93
Gettings, Maureen P. 1956- St&PR 93
Gettleman, Chad H. 1951- WhoEmL 93
Gettleman, Lawrence Marvin 1940- WhoSSW 93
Gettler, Benjamin 1925- WhoAm 92, WhoWor 93
Gettler, Benjamin 1927- St&PR 93
Getty, Ann BioIn 17
Getty, Balthazar BioIn 17
Getty, Benjamin H. St&PR 93
Getty, Carol Pavilack 1938- WhoAm 92, WhoAmW 93
Getty, Cheryl 1951- WhoE 93
Getty, Donald Ross 1933- WhoAm 92
Getty, Estelle BioIn 17
Getty, Estelle 1923- WhoAm 92
Getty, Ethel Salter 1921- St&PR 93
Getty, Gordon 1933- Baker 92
Getty, Gordon P. BioIn 17
Getty, Gordon Peter 1933- WhoAm 92
Getty, J. Paul 1892-1976 BioIn 17
Getty, Jill E. 1959- St&PR 93
Getty, Paul Balthazar BioIn 17
Getty, Paul Merle 1951- WhoEmL 93, WhoSSW 93
Getty, Susan 1946- WhoAmW 93
Gettys, George Anderson 1948- WhoAm 92
Getu, Seyoum 1941- WhoE 93
Getz, Bert A. 1937- St&PR 93
Getz, Bettina 1954- WhoAmW 93
Getz, Edward Randolph Law&B 92
Getz, Edwin Lee 1945- St&PR 93
Getz, Ernest John 1918- WhoAm 92
Getz, George F., Jr. 1908- St&PR 93
Getz, George Fulmer, Jr. 1908- WhoAm 92
Getz, Herbert A. Law&B 92
Getz, Herbert A. 1955- St&PR 93
Getz, Ilse d1992 NewYTBS 92
Getz, James Edward 1950- WhoEmL 93
Getz, Lowell Vernon 1932- WhoSSW 93
Getz, Mike 1938- WhoWrEP 92
Getz, Morton Ernest 1930- WhoSSW 93
Getz, Solomon 1936- WhoAm 92
Getz, Stan 1927-1991 AnObit 1991, BioIn 17
Getz, Stan(ley) 1927- Baker 92
Getz, Thomas Bethel Law&B 92
Getzel, Jeffrey Alan 1953- WhoE 93
Getzels, Jacob Warren 1912- WhoAm 92
Getzendanner, Susan 1939- WhoAm 92, WhoAmW 93
Geudeke, Peter W. 1939- WhoScE 91-3
Geupel, John C. 1927- St&PR 93
Geupel, John S. 1952- St&PR 93
Geurin, J.H. WhoScE 91-1

Geuskens, Georges 1934- *WhoScE 91-2*
Geuss, Gary George 1958- *WhoWor 93*
Geuther, Carl F. 1945- *St&PR 93*
Geuther, Carl Frederick 1945- *WhoAm 92*
Gevaert, Francois Auguste 1828-1908 *Baker 92*
Gevantman, Judith 1949- *WhoAm 92, WhoE 93*
Gevas, Philip C. *St&PR 93*
Gevers, Jan Karel Maria 1944- *WhoWor 93*
Gevers, Marcia Bonita 1946- *WhoEmL 93*
Gevirtz, Don Lee 1928- *St&PR 93*
Gewanter, Harry Lewis 1950- *WhoAm 92*
Gewartowski, James Walter 1930- *WhoAm 92*
Gewe, Raddory *MajAI, SmATA 70*
Gewecke, Michael 1938- *WhoScE 91-3*
Geweke, John Frederick 1948- *WhoAm 92*
Geweniger, Robert Arthur 1943- *St&PR 93*
Gewertz, Bruce Labe 1949- *WhoAm 92*
Gewin, Joe Crawford 1942- *St&PR 93*
Gewirtz, Gerry 1920- *WhoAm 92, WhoAmW 93*
Gewirtz, Harold 1950- *WhoEmL 93*
Gewirtz, Paul D. 1947- *WhoAm 92*
Gewirtz, Paul P. d1992 *BioIn 17, NewYTBS 92*
Gewirtzman, Garry Bruce 1947- *WhoSSW 93, WhoWor 93*
Gex, Walter Joseph, III 1939- *WhoAm 92, WhoSSW 93*
Gey, Wolfgang 1932- *WhoScE 91-3*
Geyari, Chaim 1920- *WhoWor 93*
Geyelin, Anthony A. *Law&B 92*
Geyelin, Anthony Allen 1945- *St&PR 93*
Geyer, Bodo Herbert Friedhelm 1937- *WhoWor 93*
Geyer, Carolyn Kay 1936- *WhoAmW 93*
Geyer, Donald H., Jr. 1951- *St&PR 93*
Geyer, Georg 1922- *WhoScE 91-4*
Geyer, Georgia Anne 1935- *JrnUS*
Geyer, Georgie Anne 1935- *WhoAm 92, WhoAmW 93, WhoWrEP 92*
Geyer, Harold Carl 1905- *WhoAm 92*
Geyer, Lynsey *BioIn 17*
Geyer, Stefi 1888-1956 *Baker 92*
Geylin, Michael Sola 1954- *WhoEmL 93*
Geyman, John Payne 1931- *WhoAm 92*
Geysen, Willy J.D. 1939- *WhoScE 91-2*
Geysen, Willy Josef 1939- *WhoWor 93*
Gezairy, Hussein Abdul-Razzak 1934- *WhoUN 92*
Gezelius, Goeran *WhoScE 91-4*
Gezella, Barbara Dantinne 1944- *St&PR 93*
Gfeller, Donna Kvinge 1959- *WhoAmW 93*
Gfroehrer, Martin Timithy 1960- *St&PR 93*
Ghafar Baba, Abdul 1925- *WhoWor 93*
Ghaffari, Matt *BioIn 17*
Ghaffar-Zadeh, Mansour 1952- *WhoWor 93*
Ghafoor-Ghaznawi, Abdul 1935- *WhoUN 92*
Ghai, Dharam Pal 1936- *WhoUN 92*
Ghai, Rajendra Durgaprasad 1943- *WhoE 93*
Ghalayini, Issam Muhamad Salim 1955- *WhoWor 93*
Ghali, Anwar Youssef 1944- *WhoE 93, WhoWor 93*
Ghali, Boutros 1922- *WhoAm 92*
Ghali, Boutros Boutros- *BioIn 17*
Ghali, Boutros Boutros 1922- *News 92 [port], -92-3 [port], WhoWor 93*
Ghalib 1797-1869 *NinCLC 39 [port]*
Ghalib, Mirza Asadullah Khan 1797-1869 *BioIn 17*
Ghalib, Omar Arteh *WhoWor 93*
Ghalib, Omar Arteh 1930- *WhoAfr*
Ghandour, Ali 1931- *WhoWor 93*
Ghandour, Ibrahim Ismail 1934- *WhoUN 92*
Ghani, Ashraf Muhammad 1931- *WhoWor 93*
Ghani, Mohammed Abdul 1963- *St&PR 93*
Gharbi, El Mostafa 1935- *WhoUN 92*
Ghareeb, Sami Mitri 1944- *WhoSSW 93*
Gharekhan, Chinmaya Rajaninath 1934- *WhoUN 92*
Ghasemi, Seifollah 1944- *St&PR 93*
Ghatak, Ritwik 1926-1976 *BioIn 17*
Ghattas, Ignatius 1920- *WhoE 93*
Ghauri, Yasmeen *BioIn 17*
Ghausi, Mohammed Shuaib 1930- *WhoAm 92*
Ghazi d1134 *OxDcByz*
Ghaznavi, John J. 1935- *St&PR 93*
Ghaznavi, John Jahangir 1935- *WhoAm 92*
Ghebrehiwet, Berhane 1946- *WhoEmL 93*
Ghederim, Veturia 1930- *WhoScE 91-4*
Ghedini, Giorgio 1892-1965 *OxDcOp*
Ghedini, Giorgio Federico 1892-1965 *Baker 92*
Ghee, Peter Henry *Law&B 92*
Ghee, Peter Henry 1930- *WhoSSW 93*
Ghegan, William S. 1948- *St&PR 93*
Ghelderode, Michel de 1898-1962 *ConAu 40NR*
Ghelfenstein, Michel Henri 1939- *WhoScE 91-2*
Ghelfi, Alfred R. 1939- *St&PR 93*
Ghelmansarai, Farhad Abbasi 1961- *WhoWor 93*
Gheluwe, Leon van 1837-1914 *Baker 92*
Ghendon, Yuri 1929- *WhoUN 92*
Ghenov, Paul Boiko 1942- *St&PR 93*
Ghent, Emmanuel 1925- *Baker 92*
Gheorghe, Aglaia *BioIn 17*
Gheorghiu, C. Virgil d1992 *NewYTBS 92*
Gheorghiu, Valentin 1928- *Baker 92*
Gheorghiu, (Constantin) Virgil 1916-1992 *ConAu 138*
Gheorghiu-Dej, Gheorghe 1901-1965 *ColdWar 2 [port], DcTwHis*
Gherardi, Diane 1941- *WhoAmW 93*
Gherghi, Andrei 1926- *WhoScE 91-4*
Gherlein, Gerald L. *Law&B 92*
Gherlein, Gerald L. 1938- *St&PR 93*
Gherlein, John Harlan 1926- *WhoAm 92*
Gherman, Beverly *BioIn 17*
Gherman, Beverly 1934- *ConAu 136*
Gherty, John E. 1944- *St&PR 93, WhoAm 92*
Ghess, Benjamin *Law&B 92*
Ghetti, Bernardino Francesco 1941- *WhoAm 92*
Gheyn, Matthias van den 1721-1785 *Baker 92*
Ghezzi, Victor 1910-1976 *BiDAMSp 1989*
Ghezzo, Dinu 1941- *Baker 92*
Ghezzo, Mario 1937- *WhoE 93*
Ghiara, Paolo 1958- *WhoWor 93*
Ghiardi, James Domenic 1918- *WhoAm 92*
Ghiaurov, Nicolai 1929- *Baker 92, IntDcOp, OxDcOp, WhoAm 92*
Ghidaglia, Jean-Michel 1958- *WhoWor 93*
Ghidalia, Vic 1926- *ScF&FL 92*
Ghiglia, Oscar 1938- *Baker 92*
Ghiglia, Oscar Alberto 1938- *WhoAm 92*
Ghiglieri, Dominick James 1940- *WhoE 93*
Ghigna, Charles 1946- *WhoWrEP 92*
Ghignone, Giovanni Pietro *Baker 92*
Ghilardi, Giuliana 1922- *WhoScE 91-2*
Ghilardi, Louis J. *Law&B 92*
Ghileri, Sirleen Jean 1943- *WhoAmW 93*
Ghilezan, Nicolae 1938- *WhoScE 91-4*
Ghimiray, Tulshi *MiSFD 9*
Ghimire, Bishwa 1943- *St&PR 93*
Ghimire, Laxman Prasad 1943- *WhoWor 93*
Ghini, Massimo Iosa *BioIn 17*
Ghiolman, Michael 1937- *WhoWor 93*
Ghiotto, Robert A. 1933- *St&PR 93*
Ghirardi, Gian Carlo 1935- *WhoScE 91-3*
Ghiretti, Francesco *WhoScE 91-3*
Ghiringhelli, Antonio 1903-1979 *OxDcOp*
Ghiron, Giorgio 1933- *WhoWor 93*
Ghis, Henri 1839-1908 *Baker 92*
Ghiselin, Brewster 1903- *BioIn 17, WhoAm 92, WhoWrEP 92*
Ghiselin, Johannes fl. 15th cent.-16th cent. *Baker 92*
Ghiselin, Michael Tenant 1939- *WhoAm 92*
Ghisi, Federico 1901-1975 *Baker 92*
Ghisla, Sandro 1942- *WhoScE 91-3*
Ghislanzoni, Antonio 1824-1893 *Baker 92, IntDcOp, OxDcOp*
Ghisler, Martin 1940- *WhoScE 91-2*
Ghisletta, Kristan Marie *Law&B 92*
Ghita, Ion 1924- *WhoScE 91-4*
Ghitalla, Armando 1925- *Baker 92*
Ghiz, Joseph A. 1945- *WhoAm 92, WhoE 93*
Ghobashy, Omar Zaki 1924- *WhoE 93, WhoWor 93*
Ghodse, Abdol-Hamid *WhoScE 91-1*
Gholoston, J.N. *ScF&FL 92*
Gholson, Beverly V. *Law&B 92*
Gholston, Homer N. *ScF&FL 92*
Ghomeshi, M. Mehdi 1956- *St&PR 93*
Ghoneim, Hussein Atta 1944- *WhoWor 93*
Ghooprasert, Wanchai 1952- *WhoWor 93*
Ghoos, Yvo F.C. 1938- *WhoScE 91-2*
Ghorayeb, Bechara Youssef 1945- *WhoSSW 93*
Ghormley, Ralph McDougall 1927- *WhoAm 92*
Ghormley, Robert Lee 1883-1958 *BioIn 17, HarEnMi*
Ghose, Arup Kumar 1951- *WhoE 93*
Ghose, Aurobindo 1872-1950 *BioIn 17*
Ghose, Rabindra N. 1925- *St&PR 93*
Ghose, Rabindra Nath 1925- *WhoAm 92, WhoWor 93*
Ghose, Sisirkumar 1919- *ScF&FL 92*
Ghose, Zulfikar 1935- *BioIn 17, IntvWPC 92 [port], ScF&FL 92*
Ghosez, Leon A.J. 1934- *WhoScE 91-2*
Ghosh, Arun Kumar 1930- *WhoWor 93*
Ghosh, Dipen 1932- *WhoAsAP 91*
Ghosh, Sakti Pada 1935- *WhoAm 92*
Ghosh, Swadhin Kumar *WhoScE 91-1*
Ghoshal, Nani Gopal 1934- *WhoAm 92*
Ghoshal, Subrata 1945- *WhoScE 91-4*
Ghosh Dastidar, Shib Narayan 1932- *WhoWor 93*
Ghostlaw, Donald K. *Law&B 92*
Ghozali, Djamal Eddine 1943- *WhoUN 92*
Ghozali, Sid Ahmed 1937- *WhoWor 93*
Ghrist, Bruce Charles *Law&B 92*
Ghuman, Joti 1946- *WhoAmW 93*
Ghurye, Govind Sadashiv 1893-1983 *IntDcAn*
Ghys, Joseph 1801-1848 *Baker 92*
Giacalone, Joseph Anthony 1938- *WhoE 93*
Giacalone, Rick 1932- *St&PR 93*
Giacalone, Robert Augustine 1957- *WhoEmL 93, WhoSSW 93*
Giacalone, Robert P. *Law&B 92*
Giaccio, Evelyn D. *Law&B 92*
Giacco, Alexander Fortunatus 1919- *WhoAm 92, WhoWor 93*
Giacconi, Anna Lee 1957- *WhoAmW 93*
Giacconi, Riccardo 1931- *WhoAm 92, WhoWor 93*
Giachardi, D.J. *WhoScE 91-1*
Giachardi, David J. 1948- *WhoScE 91-1*
Giachetti, Edward John 1939- *St&PR 93*
Giachetti, Ismene 1945- *WhoScE 91-2*
Giacobbe, George Antonino 1943- *WhoSSW 93*
Giacobbe, Patrick James 1953- *WhoE 93*
Giacobbi, Girolamo 1567?-1629 *OxDcOp*
Giacoletto, Lawrence Joseph 1916- *WhoAm 92*
Giacolini, Earl L. *WhoAm 92*
Giacomazzi, Frank P. 1931- *St&PR 93*
Giacomazzi, Frank Paul 1931- *WhoAm 92*
Giacomelli, Geminiano c. 1692-1740 *Baker 92*
Giacomelli, Giorgio *WhoUN 92*
Giacomelli, Giorgio 1931- *WhoScE 91-3*
Giacomelli, Giorgio Maria 1931- *WhoWor 93*
Giacomello, Pierluigi 1947- *WhoWor 93*
Giacometti, Alberto 1901-1966 *BioIn 17*
Giacometti, Giovanni 1929- *WhoScE 91-3*
Giacomin, Angelo Robert 1935- *St&PR 93*
Giacomini, Giuseppe 1940- *WhoAm 92*
Giacomini, Lynwood Laurin d1991 *BioIn 17*
Giacomini, Peter Donald 1955- *St&PR 93*
Giacomino, Robert Richard 1946- *WhoAm 92*
Giacosa, Giuseppe 1847-1906 *IntDcOp [port], OxDcOp*
Giacottino, Jean-Claude 1937- *WhoScE 91-2*
Giaever, Ivar 1929- *WhoAm 92, WhoE 93, WhoWor 93*
Giaimo, Frank J. 1943- *St&PR 93*
Giakoumakis, Lefteris 1937- *WhoScE 91-3*
Gialanella, Donald George 1956- *WhoE 93*
Gialanella, Philip Thomas 1930- *St&PR 93, WhoAm 92*
Gialdini, Gialdino 1843-1919 *Baker 92*
Giallanza, Charles Philip 1950- *WhoSSW 93*
Gialleonardo, Victor 1928- *St&PR 93, WhoAm 92*
Giallonardo, Thomas Michael 1947- *St&PR 93*
Giallorenzi, Thomas *Law&B 92*
Giallorenzi, Thomas Gaetano 1943- *WhoAm 92*
Giallorenzo, Peter *St&PR 93*
Giam, Choo-Seng 1931- *WhoAm 92*
Giamartino, Gary Attilio 1952- *WhoE 93*
Giamatti, A. Bartlett 1938-1989 *BioIn 17*
Giamatti, Angelo Barlett 1938-1989 *BiDAMSp 1989*
Giambalvo, Anthony 1946- *St&PR 93*
Giambalvo, Vincent 1942- *WhoE 93*
Giambrone, Steve 1949- *WhoSSW 93*
Giambusso, Ann M. *Law&B 92*
Giammanco, Brenda Sue 1939- *WhoAmW 93*
Giammarco, James A. *St&PR 93*
Giampalmi, Joseph John 1943- *WhoWrEP 92*
Gian, Bill *BioIn 17*
Giana, James Joseph 1946- *WhoEmL 93*
Gianakos, Irene 1954- *WhoAmW 93*
Gianakos, John N. 1954- *St&PR 93*
Gianaras, Alex A. 1954- *St&PR 93*
Gianatasio, David John 1966- *WhoE 93*
Giancana, Sam 1908-1975 *BioIn 17*
Giancano, Sam *DcCPCAm*
Giancarlo, Frank V. 1929- *St&PR 93*
Giancola, Holly Harrington 1961- *WhoAmW 93, WhoEmL 93*
Giancola, Mary Rose 1952- *WhoAmW 93*
Gianelli, Leslie Joan *Law&B 92*
Gianelli, William Reynolds 1919- *WhoAm 92*
Gianettini, Antonio 1648-1721 *Baker 92*
Giangola, Gary 1955- *WhoE 93*
Gianinno, Susan McManama 1948- *WhoAm 92*
Gianino, Frank John 1927- *St&PR 93*
Gianino, John Joseph 1935- *St&PR 93, WhoAm 92*
Giannakaris, Agiris 1933- *WhoScE 91-3*
Giannakoulas, Dimitrios 1932- *WhoScE 91-3*
Giannantonio, Rick C. *Law&B 92*
Giannaros, Demetrios Spiros 1949- *WhoE 93, WhoEmL 93, WhoWor 93*
Giannattasio, Brian Eliot *Law&B 92*
Giannella, Daniel Neto 1951- *WhoWor 93*
Giannella, Mario 1941- *WhoScE 91-3*
Giannelli, B. Francesco *WhoScE 91-1*
Gianneo, Luis 1897-1968 *Baker 92*
Giannesini, J.F. 1942- *WhoScE 91-2*
Giannetti, Donald 1955- *St&PR 93*
Giannetti, Enzo 1950- *WhoScE 91-3*
Giannetti, Giovanni 1869-1934 *Baker 92*
Giannetti, Louis Daniel 1937- *WhoAm 92*
Giannetti, Stephen J. 1949- *St&PR 93*
Giannettino, John Mark 1959- *WhoEmL 93*
Gianni, Alice *Law&B 92*
Giannini, A. James 1947- *WhoWor 93*
Giannini, Cynthia *WhoAm 92*
Giannini, David 1948- *WhoWrEP 92*
Giannini, Dusolina 1900-1986 *Baker 92, IntDcOp*
Giannini, Dusolina 1902-1986 *OxDcOp*
Giannini, Enzo 1946- *BioIn 17*
Giannini, Euphemia 1895-1979 *OxDcOp*
Giannini, Ferruccio 1868-1948 *Baker 92, OxDcOp*
Giannini, Giancarlo 1942- *IntDcF 2-3*
Giannini, Jill Marie 1966- *WhoAmW 93*
Giannini, Valerio Louis 1938- *WhoAm 92*
Giannini, Vittorio 1903-1966 *Baker 92, OxDcOp*
Gianniny, Omer Allan, Jr. 1925- *WhoAm 92*
Giannis, Athanassios 1954- *WhoWor 93*
Giannone, Joe *MiSFD 9*
Giannone, Michael 1942- *WhoE 93*
Giannone, Pietro *WhoScE 91-3*
Giannone, Richard 1934- *ScF&FL 92*
Giannopolitis, C.N. 1946- *WhoScE 91-3*
Giannopoulos, George A. 1946- *WhoScE 91-3*
Giannotti, Louis John 1945- *WhoE 93*
Giannuzzi, Alfonso *BioIn 17*
Giannuzzi, Ellen T. *Law&B 92*
Giannuzzi, Lorenzo 1950- *WhoWor 93*
Gianola, Umberto 1927- *WhoSSW 93*
Gianoli, Paul Louis 1943- *WhoWrEP 92*
Giantonio, Brian A. *Law&B 92*
Gianturco, Delio E. 1940- *WhoAm 92*
Gianturco, Francesco A. 1938- *WhoScE 91-3*
Gianturco, Maurizio Antonio 1928- *St&PR 93, WhoAm 92*
Gianutsos, Rosamond Rockwell 1945- *WhoAmW 93*
Giap, Nguyen Vo 1912- *DcTwHis*
Giap, Vo Nguyen 1912- *BioIn 17, ColdWar 2 [port], HarEnMi*
Giaquinto, Donna Marie 1951- *WhoAmW 93*
Giarchi, George Giacinto *WhoScE 91-1*
Giard, A., Q.C. *Law&B 92*
Giard, George Peter, Jr. 1938- *St&PR 93*
Giarda, Luigi Stefano 1868-1953 *Baker 92*
Giarda, Robert Lee 1960- *WhoSSW 93*
Giardina, Elsa Grace V. 1941- *WhoE 93*
Giardina, Paul Anthony 1949- *WhoAm 92*
Giardinelli, Mempo 1947- *SpAmA*
Giardini, Allegro *WhoScE 91-3*
Giardini, Angelo J.M. 1910- *St&PR 93*
Giardini, Carl P. 1935- *St&PR 93*
Giardini, Felice de' 1716-1796 *Baker 92*
Giardini, Janet *Law&B 92*
Giardini, Thomas M. 1947- *St&PR 93*
Giardino, Lorraine Fornesse 1942- *WhoSSW 93*
Giarla, William F. *Law&B 92*
Giarrano, Thomas 1953- *WhoEmL 93, WhoSSW 93*
Giarratano, Joe *BioIn 17*
Giarrusso, Alena Louisa 1951- *WhoE 93*
Giarrusso, Giovanni 1939- *WhoAm 92*
Giasemedis, Frank Steve 1940- *St&PR 93*
Giasi, Ralph William 1940- *St&PR 93*
Giauffret, A. *WhoScE 91-2*
Giauffret, Andre Jean Louis 1931- *WhoScE 91-2*
Giauque, William Francis 1895-1982 *BioIn 17*
Giazotto, Remo 1910- *Baker 92*
Gibala, Ronald 1938- *WhoAm 92*
Gibaldi, Milo 1938- *WhoAm 92*
Gibans, James David 1930- *WhoAm 92*
Gibart, Pierre J.L. 1940- *WhoScE 91-2*
Gibas, Tadeusz 1922- *WhoScE 91-4*
Gibb, Barry 1946- *WhoAm 92*

Gibb, David Fox 1934- *St&PR 93*
Gibb, Elmo *BioIn 17*
Gibb, Fergus George Ferguson 1941- *WhoWor 93*
Gibb, Forbes 1953- *WhoWor 93*
Gibb, Jeffrey B. *Law&B 92*
Gibb, Jocelyn 1907- *ScF&FL 92*
Gibb, Lee *ConAu 38NR*
Gibb, Lisa Jo Christenson 1961- *WhoAmW 93*
Gibb, Maurice 1949- *WhoAm 92*
Gibb, Richard Dean 1928- *WhoAm 92*
Gibb, Richard Fraser 1945- *WhoSSW 93*
Gibb, Robert 1946- *WhoWrEP 92*
Gibb, Roberta *BioIn 17*
Gibb, Robin 1949- *WhoAm 92*
Gibb, Ronald L. 1948- *St&PR 93*
Gibbard, Allan (Fletcher) 1942- *ConAu 136*
Gibbard, Judith R. 1945- *WhoAmW 93*
Gibbard, T.S.J. *ScF&FL 92*
Gibbens, Alfred Morton 1935- *WhoAm 92*
Gibbens, Margaret Louise 1933- *WhoAmW 93*
Gibberman, Susan R. 1958- *ScF&FL 92*
Gibbes, Frances Guignard *AmWomPl*
Gibbes, John 1765-1815 *BioIn 17*
Gibbes, Lewis Ladson 1771-1828 *BioIn 17*
Gibbes, Thomas Stanyarne 1770-1798 *BioIn 17*
Gibbes, William Holman 1930- *WhoWor 93*
Gibbings, Brian R. 1946- *St&PR 93, WhoAm 92*
Gibbings, Terence Harold Robsjohn- 1905-1976 *BioIn 17*
Gibbins, Duncan *MiSFD 9*
Gibbins, Gordon A. 1948- *WhoIns 93*
Gibbins, Malcolm George 1943- *St&PR 93*
Gibbon, C. Gilpin 1924- *St&PR 93*
Gibbon, Duke P. 1937- *St&PR 93*
Gibbon, Edward 1737-1794 *BioIn 17*
Gibbon, John 1827-1896 *HarEnMi*
Gibbon, John Murray 1875-1952 *BioIn 17*
Gibbons, Barach d1814 *BioIn 17*
Gibbons, Barry J. 1946- *St&PR 93*
Gibbons, Bob *ConAu 39NR*
Gibbons, Cedric *BioIn 17*
Gibbons, Charles T., Jr. *Law&B 92*
Gibbons, Christopher 1615-1676 *Baker 92*
Gibbons, David *DcCPCAm*
Gibbons, Dawn 1954- *WhoAmW 93*
Gibbons, Dennis *Law&B 92*
Gibbons, Edward 1568-c. 1650 *Baker 92*
Gibbons, Elizabeth Gill 1949- *WhoE 93*
Gibbons, Ellis 1573-1603 *Baker 92*
Gibbons, Faye 1938- *BioIn 17*
Gibbons, Floyd 1887-1939 *JrnUS*
Gibbons, Gail 1944- *MajAI [port]*
Gibbons, Gail (Gretchen) 1944- *SmATA 72 [port]*
Gibbons, Gregg Michael *Law&B 92*
Gibbons, Gregg Michael 1952- *St&PR 93*
Gibbons, J. Whitfield 1939- *WhoSSW 93*
Gibbons, James Franklin 1931- *WhoAm 92*
Gibbons, James Mortimer, Jr. 1930- *WhoE 93*
Gibbons, John A., Jr. 1942- *St&PR 93*
Gibbons, John Howard 1929- *WhoAm 92*
Gibbons, John Sheridan 1961- *WhoE 93*
Gibbons, Joseph John 1906- *WhoAm 92*
Gibbons, Joseph Martin 1947- *St&PR 93*
Gibbons, Julia Smith 1950- *WhoAm 92, WhoAmW 93, WhoSSW 93*
Gibbons, Mariko Uryu 1932- *St&PR 93*
Gibbons, Mary Peyser 1936- *WhoAmW 93, WhoE 93, WhoWor 93*
Gibbons, Michael *WhoScE 91-1*
Gibbons, Orlando 1583-1625 *Baker 92*
Gibbons, P. Michael 1942- *St&PR 93*
Gibbons, Patrick Chandler 1943- *WhoAm 92*
Gibbons, Paul F. 1951- *St&PR 93*
Gibbons, Reginald 1947- *DcLB 120 [port]*
Gibbons, (William) Reginald, Jr. 1947- *WhoWrEP 92*
Gibbons, Robert 1949- *ConAu 39NR*
Gibbons, Robert Ebbert 1940- *WhoAm 92*
Gibbons, Robert Edmund 1929- *St&PR 93*
Gibbons, Robert J. 1945- *WhoIns 93*
Gibbons, Robert John 1943- *St&PR 93, WhoAm 92*
Gibbons, Ronald John 1932- *WhoAm 92*
Gibbons, Ruth Elizabeth 1956- *WhoAmW 93*
Gibbons, Sam 1920- *CngDr 91*
Gibbons, Sam Melville 1920- *WhoAm 92*
Gibbons, Samuel Melville 1920- *WhoSSW 93*
Gibbons, Sheila Marie 1931- *St&PR 93, WhoAm 92, WhoAmW 93*
Gibbons, Stella 1902-1989 *BioIn 17*
Gibbons, Susan Marlene 1956- *WhoAmW 93*
Gibbons, Thomas Michael 1925- *WhoAm 92*
Gibbons, William H., Jr. 1945- *St&PR 93*
Gibbons, William Reginald, Jr. 1947- *WhoAm 92*
Gibbons Gallagher, Kerri Ann 1964- *WhoAmW 93*
Gibbs, A. Roger 1925- *St&PR 93*
Gibbs, Alace Zara *AmWomPl*
Gibbs, Ann 1941- *WhoSSW 93*
Gibbs, Anne B. 1949- *St&PR 93*
Gibbs, Anthony 1902-1975 *ScF&FL 92*
Gibbs, Barbara Francesca 1912- *WhoWrEP 92*
Gibbs, Barbara Kennedy 1950- *WhoAm 92, WhoAmW 93*
Gibbs, Carl *St&PR 93*
Gibbs, Cecil Armstrong 1889-1960 *Baker 92*
Gibbs, Charles Frederick 1917- *St&PR 93*
Gibbs, Cora Lee 1924- *WhoE 93*
Gibbs, David George 1925- *WhoAm 92*
Gibbs, David N. 1958- *ConAu 139*
Gibbs, Delbridge Lindley 1917- *WhoAm 92*
Gibbs, Dennis C. 1952- *WhoIns 93*
Gibbs, Elizabeth Villa 1935- *WhoAmW 93, WhoE 93*
Gibbs, Elsie Frances 1919- *WhoAm 92*
Gibbs, Federic A. 1903- *WhoAm 92*
Gibbs, Florence Reville 1890-1964 *BioIn 17*
Gibbs, Frederic A. 1903-1992 *NewYTBS 92 [port]*
Gibbs, Frederick Winfield 1932- *WhoAm 92*
Gibbs, Gerald D., Jr. 1959- *WhoEmL 93*
Gibbs, Henry 1913- *ScF&FL 92*
Gibbs, Humphrey Vicary 1902-1990 *BioIn 17*
Gibbs, J. David *Law&B 92*
Gibbs, J. Willard 1839-1903 *BioIn 17*
Gibbs, Jake 1938- *BioIn 17*
Gibbs, James A. 1935- *St&PR 93*
Gibbs, James Alanson 1935- *WhoAm 92, WhoSSW 93*
Gibbs, James Calvin 1924- *WhoSSW 93*
Gibbs, James Howard 1929- *WhoSSW 93*
Gibbs, James Lowell, Jr. 1931- *WhoAm 92*
Gibbs, James R. 1944- *St&PR 93*
Gibbs, Jamie 1955- *WhoWrEP 92*
Gibbs, Jason A. 1933- *St&PR 93*
Gibbs, Joe *BioIn 17*
Gibbs, Joe 1940- *CurBio 92 [port]*
Gibbs, Joe Jackson 1940- *WhoAm 92*
Gibbs, John W. 1927- *St&PR 93*
Gibbs, Josiah Willard 1839-1903 *BioIn 17*
Gibbs, June Nesbitt 1922- *WhoAm 92, WhoAmW 93, WhoE 93*
Gibbs, Lawrence B. 1938- *WhoAm 92*
Gibbs, Lawrence Charles 1948- *WhoEmL 93*
Gibbs, Lawrence Lindsay 1942- *WhoSSW 93*
Gibbs, Lippman Martin 1938- *WhoAm 92*
Gibbs, Lynn Ferguson 1949- *WhoSSW 93*
Gibbs, Marcus C. 1939- *St&PR 93*
Gibbs, Margaret Catherine 1914- *WhoAmW 93, WhoWor 93*
Gibbs, Marilyn Shisler 1948- *WhoAm 92*
Gibbs, Marla 1931- *WhoAm 92*
Gibbs, Martin 1922- *WhoAm 92*
Gibbs, Mary Bramlett 1953- *WhoAmW 93*
Gibbs, Michael Errol 1941- *WhoE 93*
Gibbs, Michael John 1962- *WhoE 93*
Gibbs, Murray 1944- *WhoUN 92*
Gibbs, Patricia Lynn 1952- *WhoAmW 93*
Gibbs, Raymond Weldon 1920- *WhoE 93*
Gibbs, Richard L. 1947- *St&PR 93*
Gibbs, Richard Leslie 1927- *WhoAm 92*
Gibbs, Robert 1930- *WhoCanL 92*
Gibbs, Robert Coleman 1930- *WhoSSW 93*
Gibbs, Rose L. 1940- *WhoAmW 93*
Gibbs, Sarah Preble 1930- *WhoAm 92, WhoAmW 93*
Gibbs, Simon John 1955- *WhoWor 93*
Gibbs, Terry 1924- *Baker 92*
Gibbs, Timothy Henry 1954- *WhoWor 93*
Gibbs, W.H. Holden 1932- *St&PR 93*
Gibbs, William Eugene 1930- *WhoAm 92*
Gibbs, William Harold 1950- *WhoAm 92*
Gibbs, William L. 1945- *St&PR 93*
Gibbs, William Lee 1945- *WhoAm 92*
Gibbs, William Nigel 1935- *WhoUN 92*
Gibbs, William Paul 1952- *WhoE 93*
Gibbs-Fisher, Carole Ann 1937- *St&PR 93*
Gibby, Mabel Enid Kunce 1926- *WhoAm 92, WhoAmW 93, WhoWor 93*
Gibby-Drake, Emma Joann 1961- *WhoAmW 93*
Gibeau, Marie 1950- *WhoAmW 93*
Gibeau, Martin G. 1954- *St&PR 93*
Gibeaut, Arthur A. 1946- *St&PR 93*
Giber, David J. 1954- *WhoE 93*
Giber, Janos 1929- *WhoScE 91-4*
Giberga, Ulises 1932- *St&PR 93*
Giberstone, Leah H. *Law&B 92*
Gibert, E.J., III *Law&B 92*
Gibert, Henri 1942- *WhoScE 91-2*
Gibert, Paul-Cesar 1717-1787 *OxDcOp*
Gibeson, Jacqueline *ScF&FL 92*
Gibian, George 1924- *WhoAm 92*
Gibian, Gerald Zachary 1938- *St&PR 93*
Gibian, Marvin Paul 1927- *St&PR 93*
Gibian, Thomas George 1922- *WhoAm 92*
Gibinski, Kornel 1915- *WhoScE 91-4*
Giblett, Eloise Rosalie 1921- *WhoAm 92*
Giblin, James A. *Law&B 92*
Giblin, James Cross 1933- *ChlLR 29 [port], MajAI [port], WhoAm 92*
Giblin, John J. 1943- *St&PR 93*
Giblin, Joseph J. *Law&B 92*
Giblin, Michael J. 1937- *St&PR 93*
Giblin, Patrick David 1932- *St&PR 93, WhoAm 92*
Giblin, Thomas Patrick 1947- *WhoE 93*
Giblon, Frank G. *Law&B 92*
Gibney, Frank Bray 1924- *WhoAm 92*
Gibney, Kristen Elaine 1948- *WhoAmW 93, WhoEmL 93*
Gibney, Lawrence John 1932- *WhoIns 93*
Gibney, Therese A. 1949- *St&PR 93*
Gibofsky, Allan 1949- *WhoE 93*
Gibofsky, Karen Beth 1955- *WhoAmW 93*
Giboney, Susan Kay 1940- *WhoAmW 93*
Gibowicz, Slawomir Jerzy 1933- *WhoScE 91-4*
Gibran, Kahlil 1922- *WhoAm 92*
Gibs, Gabriel Joseph 1936- *WhoE 93*
Gibson, Alan 1938-1987 *MiSFD 9N*
Gibson, Alexander 1926- *OxDcOp*
Gibson, Alexander (Drummond) 1926- *Baker 92, WhoWor 93*
Gibson, Alice Whitney 1939- *WhoAmW 93*
Gibson, Althea 1927- *AfrAmBi, BioIn 17, WhoAm 92, WhoAmW 93*
Gibson, Andrew (William) 1949- *SmATA 72 [port]*
Gibson, Anthea *BioIn 17*
Gibson, Arthur Geoffrey *WhoScE 91-1*
Gibson, Barry Joseph 1951- *WhoAm 92*
Gibson, Benjamin F. 1931- *WhoAm 92*
Gibson, Betty Sue 1937- *WhoAmW 93*
Gibson, Bob 1935- *BioIn 17*
Gibson, Brian *BioIn 17*
Gibson, Brian 1944- *MiSFD 9*
Gibson, Bryan 1940- *St&PR 93*
Gibson, C. Scott *BioIn 17*
Gibson, Carl Royce 1941- *St&PR 93*
Gibson, Carol Sue Anderson 1950- *WhoEmL 93*
Gibson, Carolyn Opal 1942- *WhoSSW 93*
Gibson, Charles Colmery 1914- *WhoAm 92*
Gibson, Charles Dana 1867-1944 *GayN*
Gibson, Charles DeWolf 1943- *WhoAm 92*
Gibson, Charles Ernest 1947- *WhoEmL 93*
Gibson, Charles Robert 1940- *St&PR 93*
Gibson, Clive Patrick 1948- *WhoWor 93*
Gibson, Colin *ScF&FL 92*
Gibson, Count Dillon, Jr. 1921- *WhoAm 92*
Gibson, Cynthia Marcotte 1962- *WhoAmW 93*
Gibson, D.G. *WhoScE 91-1*
Gibson, Darren *BioIn 17, NewYTBS 92*
Gibson, David Bryan 1951- *St&PR 93*
Gibson, David Eugene 1940- *St&PR 93*
Gibson, David F. 1944- *WhoAm 92, WhoE 93*
Gibson, David Mark 1923- *WhoAm 92*
Gibson, David W. 1948- *St&PR 93*
Gibson, Dirk Cameron 1953- *WhoEmL 93, WhoSSW 93*
Gibson, Don *Law&B 92*
Gibson, Donald Bernard 1933- *WhoE 93*
Gibson, Donald J., Jr. *Law&B 92*
Gibson, Douglas 1943- *WhoCanL 92*
Gibson, Douglas B. 1951- *WhoAm 92*
Gibson, E. Martin 1938- *St&PR 93*
Gibson, Edgar Thomas 1915- *WhoE 93*
Gibson, Edward 1936- *ScF&FL 92*
Gibson, Edward Fergus 1937- *WhoAm 92*
Gibson, Edwin Martin 1938- *WhoAm 92*
Gibson, Eleanor Jack 1910- *BioIn 17, WhoAm 92, WhoAmW 93*
Gibson, Elisabeth Jane 1937- *WhoAmW 93, WhoWor 93*
Gibson, Emily M. *AmWomPl*
Gibson, Ernest L., III 1945- *WhoSSW 93*
Gibson, Ernest Willard, III 1927- *WhoE 93*
Gibson, Evan K. 1909-1986 *ScF&FL 92*
Gibson, Everett Kay, Jr. 1940- *WhoAm 92*
Gibson, Florence Anderson 1924- *WhoAmW 93*
Gibson, Floyd *ScF&FL 92*
Gibson, Floyd Robert 1910- *WhoAm 92*
Gibson, Frank Alexande 1924- *WhoScE 91-3*
Gibson, Frank Andrew 1944- *St&PR 93*
Gibson, Fred D., Jr. 1927- *St&PR 93*
Gibson, Fred Daniel, III *Law&B 92*
Gibson, Gail McMurray 1948- *WhoSSW 93*
Gibson, Garland Frank 1943- *St&PR 93*
Gibson, Gary Maxwell 1945- *WhoWor 93*
Gibson, Gayle June 1960- *WhoAmW 93*
Gibson, Geoffrey Eric 1942- *WhoWor 93*
Gibson, George R. 1905- *St&PR 93*
Gibson, George W. T. 1925- *WhoSSW 93*
Gibson, Graeme 1934- *WhoCanL 92*
Gibson, Gregory G. *Law&B 92*
Gibson, Harry *Law&B 92*
Gibson, Harry William 1941- *WhoSSW 93*
Gibson, Helen 1892-1977 *SweetSg A [port]*
Gibson, Henry, Jr. *BioIn 17*
Gibson, Hoot *BioIn 17*
Gibson, Hugh 1918- *WhoAm 92*
Gibson, Ian Bennett 1936- *WhoWor 93*
Gibson, James d1992 *NewYTBS 92 [port]*
Gibson, James 1769-1856 *BioIn 17*
Gibson, James 1902-1992 *BioIn 17*
Gibson, James 1919- *ScF&FL 92*
Gibson, James B. *Law&B 92*
Gibson, James Edwin 1941- *WhoAm 92*
Gibson, James Isaac 1925- *St&PR 93*
Gibson, James John 1923- *WhoAm 92*
Gibson, James Riley, Jr. 1944- *WhoWrEP 92*
Gibson, James Thomas, Jr. 1921- *WhoAm 92*
Gibson, James Vernon 1912- *WhoSSW 93*
Gibson, Janet Marie 1959- *WhoAmW 93*
Gibson, Janet Mayo 1939- *WhoSSW 93*
Gibson, Janice Thorne 1934- *WhoAm 92*
Gibson, Jay F. *Law&B 92*
Gibson, Jerry Leigh 1930- *WhoAm 92*
Gibson, John Edward *WhoScE 91-1*
Gibson, John Egan 1926- *WhoAm 92*
Gibson, John Holden, II 1959- *St&PR 93*
Gibson, John L. 1933- *St&PR 93*
Gibson, John Robert 1925- *WhoAm 92*
Gibson, John Willis 1944- *WhoWor 93*
Gibson, Jon *Law&B 92*
Gibson, Joseph Whitton, Jr. 1922- *WhoAm 92, WhoE 93*
Gibson, Josh 1911-1947 *BioIn 17*
Gibson, Karon White 1946- *WhoAmW 93, WhoEmL 93*
Gibson, Karyn Ann 1955- *WhoAmW 93*
Gibson, Kathleen M. *Law&B 92*
Gibson, Kathleen R. *Law&B 92*
Gibson, Kathleen Rita 1942- *WhoAmW 93, WhoSSW 93, WhoWor 93*
Gibson, Keiko Matsui 1953- *WhoWrEP 92*
Gibson, Keith A. 1957- *St&PR 93*
Gibson, Kenneth A. 1931- *PolPar*
Gibson, Kenneth Allen 1932- *AfrAmBi*
Gibson, Kenneth Trigg 1947- *St&PR 93*
Gibson, Laurine Catalano 1935- *WhoE 93*
Gibson, Lisa M. *Law&B 92*
Gibson, Lois *BioIn 17*
Gibson, Lynn Allen 1955- *WhoSSW 93*
Gibson, Margaret 1944- *DcLB 120 [port]*
Gibson, Margaret 1948- *WhoCanL 92*
Gibson, Margaret Ferguson 1944- *WhoWrEP 92*
Gibson, Mary Elizabeth G. 1924- *WhoWrEP 92*
Gibson, McGuire 1938- *WhoAm 92*
Gibson, Mel *BioIn 17*
Gibson, Mel 1956- *HolBB [port], IntDcF 2-3, WhoAm 92*
Gibson, Melvin Roy 1920- *WhoAm 92*
Gibson, Michael Addison 1943- *WhoAm 92, WhoSSW 93, WhoWor 93*
Gibson, Michael Clay 1945- *St&PR 93*
Gibson, Michael Fielding 1948- *WhoEmL 93*
Gibson, Michael Vern 1950- *WhoEmL 93*
Gibson, Miles 1947- *ScF&FL 92*
Gibson, Morgan 1929- *WhoWrEP 92*
Gibson, Nancy Jones 1955- *WhoWor 93*
Gibson, Nicholas Steven *Law&B 92*
Gibson, Norman James 1931- *WhoWor 93*
Gibson, Patricia Ann 1942- *WhoAmW 93*
Gibson, Philip G. 1945- *St&PR 93*
Gibson, Quentin Howieson 1918- *WhoAm 92*
Gibson, Ralph *BioIn 17*
Gibson, Ralph Holmes 1939- *WhoAm 92*
Gibson, Rankin MacDougal 1916- *WhoAm 92*
Gibson, Ray 1946- *WhoScE 91-1*
Gibson, Raymond *WhoScE 91-1*
Gibson, Raymond E. 1939- *St&PR 93*
Gibson, Raymond Eugene 1924- *WhoAm 92*
Gibson, Reginald W. 1927- *CngDr 91*
Gibson, Reginald Walker 1927- *WhoE 93*
Gibson, Rex H. *Law&B 92*
Gibson, Richard John 1945- *WhoSSW 93*
Gibson, Richard William *WhoScE 91-1*
Gibson, Rob *BioIn 17*
Gibson, Robert 1935- *WhoAm 92*
Gibson, Robert Fisher d1990 *BioIn 17*

Gibson, Robert Lee 1946- WhoAm 92
Gibson, Robert Valentine 1921- WhoAm 92
Gibson, Robert W. 1945- St&PR 93
Gibson, Roy BioIn 17
Gibson, Roy N. 1941- St&PR 93
Gibson, Russell G. 1952- St&PR 93
Gibson, Sam Thompson 1916- WhoAm 92, WhoE 93, WhoWor 93
Gibson, Samantha Livingston 1941- WhoSSW 93
Gibson, Scott Law&B 92
Gibson, Scott Carter 1959- WhoE 93, WhoEmL 93
Gibson, Sheila Ann Law&B 92
Gibson, Stephen E. 1953- St&PR 93
Gibson, Stephen Lowell 1963- WhoE 93
Gibson, Steven H. Law&B 92
Gibson, Susan 1940- WhoAmW 93
Gibson, Thelma Hardy AmWomPl
Gibson, Thomas c. 1680-1751 BioIn 17
Gibson, Thomas Fenner, III 1955- WhoAm 92
Gibson, Thomas Joseph Law&B 92
Gibson, Thomas Joseph 1935- St&PR 93, WhoAm 92
Gibson, Thomas R. 1944- St&PR 93
Gibson, Valerie 1957- WhoEmL 93
Gibson, Virginia Lee 1946- WhoAmW 93
Gibson, Walter B. 1897-1985 ScF&FL 92
Gibson, Walter Samuel 1932- WhoAm 92
Gibson, Warren A. Law&B 92
Gibson, Weldon Bailey 1917- WhoAm 92
Gibson, Wendy Joan 1953- WhoAmW 93
Gibson, William 1914- BioIn 17, MagSAmL [port], WhoAm 92
Gibson, William 1948- BioIn 17, ScF&FL 92, WhoCanL 92
Gibson, William B. 1938- WhoAm 92
Gibson, William Edward 1944- WhoAm 92
Gibson, William Francis 1952- WhoAm 92, WhoEmL 93
Gibson, William Lee 1949- WhoEmL 93
Gibson, William M. 1945- St&PR 93
Gibson, William Michael Law&B 92
Gibson, William S. Law&B 92
Gibson, William S. 1933- WhoIns 93
Gibson, William Shepard 1933- St&PR 93, WhoAm 92
Gibson, William Willard, Jr. 1932- WhoAm 92
Gibson-Downs, Sally 1954- ScF&FL 92
Gibson-Harris, Sheree Lee 1956- WhoEmL 93, WhoSSW 93
Gibson-Jarvie, Clodagh ScF&FL 92
Gibson-Moore, David John 1943- St&PR 93
Gichev, Todor Rachev 1943- WhoWor 93
Gicking, Robert K. 1931- St&PR 93
Gidai, Laszlo 1932- WhoScE 91-4
Gidal, Nachum Tim 1909- WhoWor 93
Gidda, Jaswinder Singh 1964- WhoWor 93
Giddens, Clearance 1954- BioIn 17
Giddens, Don Peyton 1940- WhoAm 92
Giddens, Zelma Kirk WhoAmW 93
Giddings, Clifford Frederick 1936- WhoE 93
Giddings, Daniel S. 1917-1991 BioIn 17
Giddings, Debra Lynn 1956- WhoAmW 93
Giddings, Elizabeth BioIn 17
Giddings, Franklin Henry 1855-1931 GayN
Giddings, Helen 1943- WhoWor 93
Giddings, Joshua 1795-1864 PolPar
Giddings, Lauren WhoWrEP 92
Giddings, Lucille Cassell 1947- WhoWor 93
Giddings, Paula BioIn 17
Giddings, Robert 1935- ScF&FL 92
Giddings, Robert Killen 1928- St&PR 93
Giddings, S. Arthur 1929- WhoAm 92
Giddings, Wooster Philip 1913- WhoE 93
Giddins, Gary Mitchell 1948- WhoAm 92
Giddon, Donald Bernard 1930- WhoAm 92, WhoWor 93
Gide, Andre 1869-1951 BioIn 17, MagSWL [port], WorLitC [port]
Gidefeldt, Lars 1938- WhoWor 93
Gidel, John D. Law&B 92
Gidel, Robert Hugh 1951- WhoWor 93
Gideon, Clarence James WhoSSW 93
Gideon, John ScF&FL 92
Gideon, Kenneth Wayne 1946- WhoAm 92
Gideon, Miriam 1906- Baker 92, BioIn 17, WhoAm 92
Gideon, Nancy Ann 1955- WhoWrEP 92
Gideon, Sharon Lee 1955- WhoEmL 93
Gideon, William Patrick 1943- WhoSSW 93
Gideon-Hawke, Pamela Lawrence 1945- WhoAmW 93
Gidley, John Lynn 1924- WhoAm 92
Gidley, Thomas Dunne 1934- WhoE 93
Gidley, William J. 1926- St&PR 93
Gidos OxDcByz
Gidwani, Bhagwan N. 1937- St&PR 93
Gidwitz, Gerald 1906- WhoAm 92
Gidwitz, Gerald S. 1906- St&PR 93
Gidwitz, James Gerald 1946- St&PR 93
Gidwitz, Joseph L. 1905- St&PR 93
Gidwitz, Joseph Leon 1905- WhoAm 92
Gidwitz, Nancy 1948- WhoEmL 93
Gidwitz, Ronald J. 1945- St&PR 93, WhoAm 92
Giebel, Joseph L. 1930- St&PR 93
Giebel (Kanders), Agnes 1921- Baker 92
Giebisch, Gerhard Hans 1927- WhoAm 92
Gieburowski, Waclaw 1876-1943 Baker 92
Giec, Leszek 1928- WhoScE 91-4
Giedion, Sigfried 1888-1968 BioIn 17
Giedt, Bruce Alan 1937- WhoAm 92
Giedt, Warren Harding 1920- WhoAm 92
Giegerich, Paul Raymond 1953- WhoE 93
Giegling, Franz 1921- Baker 92
Giel, Paul Robert 1932- BiDAMSp 1989
Giel, Robert Laurence 1947- WhoEmL 93
Gielarowska-Sznajder, Danuta Maria 1936- WhoScE 91-4
Gieldanowski, Jerzy Zbigniew 1925- WhoScE 91-4
Gielen, Jacques Eugene 1940- WhoScE 91-2
Gielen, Marcel 1938- WhoScE 91-2
Gielen, Michael 1927- OxDcOp
Gielen, Michael (Andreas) 1927- Baker 92, WhoWor 93
Gielen, Uwe Peter 1940- WhoE 93
Gielgud, John 1904- BioIn 17, IntDcF 2-3 [port], WhoAm 92, WhoWor 93
Gielgud, Maina 1945- WhoWor 93
Gielow, Ronald W. 1952- St&PR 93
Gier, Audra May Calhoon 1940- WhoAmW 93
Gier, Deborah Lee 1953- WhoSSW 93
Gier, Karan Hancock 1947- WhoAmW 93
Gierasch, Stefan 1926- ConTFT 10
Gierbolini, Gilberto 1926- HispAmA
Gierbolini-Ortiz, Gilberto 1926- WhoSSW 93
Gierczyk, James P. 1951- St&PR 93
Giere, Horst-Henning 1942- WhoScE 91-3
Giere, Olav 1939- WhoScE 91-3
Gierek, Edward 1913- ColdWar 2 [port], DcTwHis, PolBiDi
Gierenstein, Thomas 1954- WhoWor 93
Gierer, Alfred 1929- WhoScE 91-3
Gierer, Vincent A., Jr. 1947- WhoAm 92, WhoE 93
Gierer, Vincent Andrew, Jr. 1947- St&PR 93
Gieri, Raymond 1938- WhoUN 92
Giering, John L. 1944- St&PR 93
Gierke, Sandra Jean 1937- WhoAmW 93
Gierlasinski, Kathy Lynn 1951- WhoAmW 93
Gierlinski, Jacek T. 1946- WhoScE 91-1
Giermak, Chester F. 1927- St&PR 93
Giermann, Edward Charles Law&B 92
Giermann, Gunter K.F. 1932- WhoScE 91-3
Gieroba, Jan 1927- WhoScE 91-4
Gierow, Catherine Marie 1954- WhoUN 92
Giersch, Herbert Hermann 1921- WhoWor 93
Giersing, Morten 1945- WhoUN 92
Giertych, Maciej M. 1936- WhoScE 91-4
Giertz, J. Fred 1943- WhoAm 92
Gierymski, Aleksander 1850-1901 PolBiDi
Gierymski, Maksymilian 1846-1874 PolBiDi
Gies, Jane Marie 1963- WhoAmW 93
Gies, Thomas Anthony 1930- WhoAm 92, WhoWor 93
Gies, W. Glenn 1936- St&PR 93
Giese, Richard Heinrich 1931- WhoScE 91-3
Giese, Robert 1941- St&PR 93
Giese, Roger Kent 1942- St&PR 93
Giese, Theodore Lynn 1945- WhoE 93
Giese, Werner 1936- WhoScE 91-3
Giese, William Herbert 1944- WhoAm 92, WhoE 93
Giesecke, Gustav Ernst 1908- WhoAm 92
Giesecke, Jurgen Karl 1932- WhoScE 91-3
Giesecke, Karl Ludwig 1761-1833 OxDcOp
Giesecke, Leonard Frederick 1937- WhoSSW 93
Gieseke, Corinne Joyce 1954- WhoEmL 93
Gieseking, Walter 1895-1956 BioIn 17
Gieseking, Walter (Wilhelm) 1895-1956 Baker 92
Giesekus, Hans Walter 1922- WhoWor 93
Giesel, Robert L. 1916- St&PR 93
Gieseler, Daniel J., Jr. 1938- WhoIns 93
Giesen, Dieter Joseph Heinrich Konrad 1936- WhoWor 93
Giesen, John William 1928- WhoAm 92
Giesen, Richard A. 1929- St&PR 93
Giesen, Richard Allyn 1929- WhoAm 92
Giesenhaus, William Frederick 1933- St&PR 93
Giesey, Harry George 1933- WhoIns 93
Giesler, Gareth L. 1937- St&PR 93
Giessel, Linda D. Law&B 92
Giesselmann, Michael Guenter 1956- WhoSSW 93
Giesser, Joanne M. Law&B 92
Giessmann, Ernst-Gunter 1950- WhoWor 93
Giesswein, Michael 1944- WhoWor 93
Gietzelt, Arthur Thomas 1920- WhoAsAP 91
Gifaldi, David ScF&FL 92
Giff, Patricia Reilly 1935- MajAI [port], SmATA 70 [port]
Giffard, Ingaret BioIn 17
Giffel, Terry Clyde 1945- WhoE 93
Giffels, Donald James 1935- St&PR 93
Giffen, Daniel Harris 1938- WhoAm 92
Giffen, John A. 1938- St&PR 93, WhoAm 92
Giffen, Robert Carlisle 1886-1962 HarEnMi
Giffen, Robert Henry 1922- WhoE 93
Giffen, Shavan Mary Law&B 92
Giffin, Kenneth N. 1944- St&PR 93
Giffin, Margaret Ethel 1949- WhoAmW 93
Giffin, Mary Elizabeth 1919- WhoWrEP 92
Giffin, Walter Charles 1936- WhoAm 92
Giffiths, Gregory 1951- St&PR 93
Gifford, Anita S. Law&B 92
Gifford, Barry 1946- BioIn 17
Gifford, Barry (Colby) 1946- ConAu 40NR
Gifford, Bernard R. BioIn 17
Gifford, Bernard R. 1943- WhoAm 92
Gifford, Brooks, Jr. Law&B 92
Gifford, Charles H., III Law&B 92
Gifford, Charles K. St&PR 93
Gifford, Cornelia Rogers 1923- WhoAmW 93
Gifford, Denis 1927- ScF&FL 92
Gifford, Don R. 1928- St&PR 93
Gifford, Edward Winslow 1887-1959 IntDcAn
Gifford, Ernest Milton 1920- WhoAm 92
Gifford, Frank BioIn 17
Gifford, Frank Newton 1930- WhoAm 92
Gifford, Gary L. 1947- St&PR 93
Gifford, George E. 1924- WhoAm 92, WhoSSW 93
Gifford, Harry Cortland Frey 1919- WhoAm 92
Gifford, Jeffrey Scott 1955- St&PR 93
Gifford, Kathie Lee BioIn 17
Gifford, Kathie Lee 1953- News 92 [port]
Gifford, Meredith Hayes Law&B 92
Gifford, Michael F. 1948- St&PR 93
Gifford, Myron D. 1941- St&PR 93
Gifford, Nelson Sage 1930- St&PR 93, WhoAm 92
Gifford, Page E. Law&B 92
Gifford, Porter William 1918- WhoAm 92
Gifford, Prosser 1929- ConAu 39NR, WhoAm 92
Gifford, Ray Wallace, Jr. 1923- WhoAm 92, WhoWor 93
Gifford, Russell M. 1954- St&PR 93
Gifford, Samuel Lee, II 1935- St&PR 93
Gifford, Thomas 1937- ScF&FL 92
Gifford, Timothy D. Law&B 92
Gifford, Timothy J. Law&B 92
Gifford, Timothy Penny 1947- WhoEmL 93
Gifford, Virginia Snodgrass 1936- WhoAm 92, WhoAmW 93
Gifford, William Wallace 1928- WhoAm 92
Giffuni, Cathe 1949- WhoAmW 93, WhoEmL 93, WhoWrEP 92
Gift, James Joseph 1942- St&PR 93
Gift, Roland
See Fine Young Cannibals SoulM
Giftos, Dean A. 1942- St&PR 93
Giftos, P. Michael Law&B 92
Giftos, P. Michael 1947- St&PR 93
Giftos, Peter Charles 1927- St&PR 93
Giga, Yoshikazu 1955- WhoWor 93
Gigandet, Carl Francis 1940- WhoAm 92
Gigante, Dino Vincent 1934- WhoE 93
Gigante, Nancy Eileen 1964- St&PR 93
Gigante, Sharon Anne 1962- St&PR 93
Gigante, Vincent BioIn 17
Gigas, George BioIn 17
Gigase, Paul L.J. 1930- WhoScE 91-2
Giger, H.R. 1940- ScF&FL 92
Giger, Hansruedi ScF&FL 92
Giger, Peter 1945- WhoWor 93
Giget, Marc WhoScE 91-2
Gigg, Roy Henry WhoScE 91-1
Giggey, James Walker 1931- WhoAm 92
Gigli, Beniamino 1890-1957 Baker 92, BioIn 17, IntDcOp [port], OxDcOp
Gigli, Irma 1931- NotHsAW 93, WhoAm 92
Gigli Berzolari, Alberto 1921- WhoScE 91-3, WhoWor 93
Giglietti, Patrice Ann 1964- WhoEmL 93
Giglio, Francis A. 1928- WhoSSW 93
Giglio, Frank Alan 1943- WhoSSW 93
Giglio, Frank F. 1951- St&PR 93
Giglio, James N. 1939- ConAu 138
Giglio, Jose Roberto 1934- WhoWor 93
Giglio, Kelli Ann 1966- WhoAmW 93
Giglio, Mary Ann 1946- WhoE 93
Giglio, Richard John Law&B 92
Giglio, Ronald Joseph 1933- St&PR 93
Giglioli, Enrico Hillyer 1845-1909 IntDcAn
Gigliotti, Aldo G. 1930- WhoScE 91-3
Gigliotti, Joanne Marie 1945- WhoE 93
Gigliotti, Peter Michael 1952- WhoE 93
Gigliotti, Richard Joseph 1945- WhoE 93
Gignac, Kenneth E. 1933- St&PR 93
Gignilliat, Arthur M., Jr. 1932- St&PR 93
Gignoux, Claude Joseph 1890-1966 BioIn 17
Gignoux, Dominique 1929- St&PR 93
Gigout, Eugene 1844-1925 Baker 92
Giguere, Brenda Sue 1959- WhoAmW 93
Giguere, Roland 1929- WhoCanL 92
Giheno, John 1950- WhoAsAP 91
Gijbels, Renaat H.H. 1939- WhoScE 91-2
Gijsman, H.M. 1927- WhoScE 91-3
Gikas, Paul William 1928- WhoAm 92
Gikow, Jacqueline Paula 1947- WhoEmL 93
Gikow, Louise ScF&FL 92
Gil, Andres Valerio 1954- WhoEmL 93
Gil, Avishai 1945- WhoWor 93
Gil, Federico Guillermo 1915- WhoAm 92
Gil, Joan 1940- WhoE 93
Gil, Manuel WhoScE 91-3
Gil, Maria de Fatima Santos 1962- WhoScE 91-3
Gil, Regina Keller 1948- WhoE 93
Gil-Albert Velarde, Fernando 1937- WhoScE 91-3
Gilardi, Gilardo 1889-1963 Baker 92
Gilardi, Richard D. 1936- WhoE 93
Gilb, Corinne Lathrop 1925- WhoAmW 93
Gilbane, Frank 1951- WhoEmL 93
Gilbane, Jean A. 1923- St&PR 93
Gilbane, Jean Ann 1923- WhoAm 92, WhoE 93
Gilberg, Arnold L. 1936- WhoAm 92
Gilberg, Ira Michael 1967- WhoE 93
Gilberg, Kenneth Roy 1951- WhoE 93
Gilberg, Milton Joseph 1921- St&PR 93
Gilbert, A. Kirven, III Law&B 92
Gilbert, Alan Graham WhoScE 91-1
Gilbert, Allan Arthur 1925- WhoAm 92
Gilbert, Alvin Everett 1925- WhoE 93
Gilbert, Anne Wieland 1927- WhoAm 92
Gilbert, Anthony Chapin 1937- WhoAm 92
Gilbert, Anthony (John) 1934- Baker 92
Gilbert, Arch Burton 1933- St&PR 93
Gilbert, Arthur Charles 1926- WhoSSW 93, WhoWor 93
Gilbert, Arthur Charles Francis 1929- WhoAm 92
Gilbert, Arthur Dale 1953- St&PR 93
Gilbert, Arthur Lewis 1924- St&PR 93
Gilbert, Barbara WhoWrEP 92
Gilbert, Barry Law&B 92
Gilbert, Barton 1936- St&PR 93
Gilbert, Benjamin 1929- WhoWor 93
Gilbert, Benjamin Davis d1992 BioIn 17
Gilbert, Benjamin Franklin 1918- WhoAm 92
Gilbert, Billy 1893-1971 QDrFCA 92 [port]
Gilbert, Bonnie AmWomPl
Gilbert, Brian MiSFD 9
Gilbert, Bruce C. 1938- St&PR 93
Gilbert, Bruce Charles WhoScE 91-1
Gilbert, Bruce Rits Law&B 92
Gilbert, C.M. ScF&FL 92
Gilbert, Carl Arthur 1942- St&PR 93
Gilbert, Cass 1859?-1934 BioIn 17, OxCSupC
Gilbert, Celia 1932- WhoWrEP 92
Gilbert, Charles Richard Alsop 1916- WhoAm 92
Gilbert, Christina Ida 1950- WhoWrEP 92
Gilbert, Christopher 1949- WhoWrEP 92
Gilbert, Clark William WhoIns 93
Gilbert, Creighton Eddy 1924- WhoAm 92, WhoE 93, WhoWor 93
Gilbert, Daniel Lee 1925- WhoAm 92, WhoE 93
Gilbert, David 1913- ConAu 137
Gilbert, David 1945- WhoAm 92
Gilbert, David Erwin 1939- WhoAm 92
Gilbert, David Heggie 1932- WhoAm 92
Gilbert, Denise Marie 1957- WhoAmW 93
Gilbert, Dennis Clare 1952- WhoE 93
Gilbert, Diane Victoria 1957- WhoAmW 93
Gilbert, Dorothy E. Law&B 92
Gilbert, Douglas 1942- ScF&FL 92
Gilbert, E. Penny Law&B 92

Gilbert, Edward Peter 1956- *WhoEmL 93*
Gilbert, Edward William 1938- *WhoE 93*
Gilbert, Elliot L. 1930-1991 *BioIn 17*
Gilbert, Eugenia *SweetSg B [port]*
Gilbert, Fabiola Cabeza de Baca 1898- *NotHsAW 93*
Gilbert, Felix 1905-1991 *BioIn 17*
Gilbert, Fred Ivan, Jr. 1920- *WhoAm 92*
Gilbert, Frederick S. 1939-1991 *BioIn 17*
Gilbert, Glenn Gordon 1936- *WhoAm 92, WhoWor 93*
Gilbert, Gregory Eastham 1965- *WhoSSW 93*
Gilbert, Gwen B. 1938- *St&PR 93*
Gilbert, Gwen Beryl 1938- *WhoSSW 93*
Gilbert, Harold Frederick 1916- *WhoWor 93*
Gilbert, Harold Stanley 1924- *WhoAm 92*
Gilbert, Harold Wendell 1939- *WhoAm 92*
Gilbert, Harry Ephraim, Jr. 1931- *WhoAm 92*
Gilbert, Helen *AmWomPl*
Gilbert, Henry F(ranklin Belknap) 1868-1928 *Baker 92*
Gilbert, Herman Cromwell 1923- *WhoWrEP 92*
Gilbert, Humphrey 1539-1583 *Expl 93 [port]*
Gilbert, Ilsa 1933- *WhoWrEP 92*
Gilbert, Jack *WhoWrEP 92*
Gilbert, Jackson B. 1932- *WhoAm 92*
Gilbert, Jacqueline D. *Law&B 92*
Gilbert, James Cayce 1925- *WhoAm 92*
Gilbert, James Eastham 1929- *WhoAm 92, WhoE 93*
Gilbert, James F. 1932- *St&PR 93*
Gilbert, James Freeman 1931- *WhoAm 92*
Gilbert, Jerrold *Law&B 92*
Gilbert, Jerrold 1936- *St&PR 93*
Gilbert, Jerry Lon 1947- *WhoSSW 93*
Gilbert, Jimmie D. 1934- *WhoSSW 93*
Gilbert, Jo 1949- *WhoAmW 93*
Gilbert, Joan Stulman 1934- *WhoAmW 93*
Gilbert, Joann Doris 1946- *WhoAmW 93*
Gilbert, John *ScF&FL 92*
Gilbert, John 1897?-1936 *IntDcF 2-3 [port]*
Gilbert, John Andrew 1948- *WhoSSW 93*
Gilbert, John B. 1921- *St&PR 93*
Gilbert, John Humphrey Victor 1941- *WhoAm 92*
Gilbert, John Jordan 1907- *St&PR 93*
Gilbert, John Jouett 1937- *WhoAm 92*
Gilbert, John Kenward *WhoScE 91-1*
Gilbert, John Laurence 1950- *WhoEmL 93*
Gilbert, John Neely, Jr. 1936- *St&PR 93*
Gilbert, John Nunneley, Jr. *WhoIns 93*
Gilbert, John O. 1942- *WhoIns 93*
Gilbert, John Oren 1942- *St&PR 93*
Gilbert, Judith Arlene 1946- *WhoAm 92*
Gilbert, Katherine Anne 1950- *WhoAmW 93*
Gilbert, Kathie Simon 1943- *WhoAm 92*
Gilbert, Keith Duncan 1941- *St&PR 93, WhoAm 92*
Gilbert, Keith W. 1946- *St&PR 93*
Gilbert, Kenneth 1931- *Baker 92*
Gilbert, Kenneth Albert 1931- *WhoAm 92*
Gilbert, Kenneth J. 1935- *St&PR 93*
Gilbert, L. Wolfe 1886-1970 *Baker 92*
Gilbert, Laura B. *Law&B 92*
Gilbert, Laura Jean 1938- *WhoAmW 93*
Gilbert, Laurel J. *Law&B 92*
Gilbert, Lawrence Irwin 1929- *WhoAm 92*
Gilbert, Leonard Harold 1936- *WhoAm 92*
Gilbert, Lewis 1920- *MiSFD 9, WhoWor 93*
Gilbert, Liane Marie 1949- *WhoAmW 93*
Gilbert, Linda Cheryl 1956- *WhoAmW 93*
Gilbert, Marie Rogers 1924- *WhoWrEP 92*
Gilbert, Marlene F. *Law&B 92*
Gilbert, Marlin L. *Law&B 92*
Gilbert, Martin 1936- *BioIn 17*
Gilbert, Martin B. *Law&B 92*
Gilbert, Melissa 1964- *WhoAm 92*
Gilbert, Michael *BioIn 17*
Gilbert, Michael 1912- *ScF&FL 92*
Gilbert, Michael C. *Law&B 92*
Gilbert, Michel 1938- *WhoUN 92*
Gilbert, Mildred M. d1992 *NewYTBS 92*
Gilbert, Milton Montague 1927- *St&PR 93*
Gilbert, Neil Robin 1940- *WhoAm 92*
Gilbert, Norman Sutcliffe 1919- *WhoWor 93*
Gilbert, Patrick Nigel Geoffrey 1934- *WhoWor 93*
Gilbert, Paula Ruth 1945- *WhoAmW 93*
Gilbert, Perry Webster 1912- *WhoAm 92*
Gilbert, Phil Edward, Jr. 1915- *WhoAm 92, WhoWor 93*
Gilbert, Pia 1921- *Baker 92*
Gilbert, Pia S. 1921- *WhoAm 92*
Gilbert, R.A. 1942- *ScF&FL 92*
Gilbert, Ray Wilson, Jr. 1951- *St&PR 93*
Gilbert, Real Paul 1938- *WhoE 93*
Gilbert, Rebecca 1952- *St&PR 93*
Gilbert, Richard G. 1920- *St&PR 93*
Gilbert, Richard Joel 1948- *WhoEmL 93*
Gilbert, Richard John *WhoScE 91-1*
Gilbert, Richard P. 1950- *St&PR 93*
Gilbert, Robert Edward 1941- *WhoAm 92*
Gilbert, Robert James 1923- *WhoSSW 93*
Gilbert, Robert Pettibone 1917- *WhoE 93*
Gilbert, Robert Wolfe 1920- *WhoWor 93*
Gilbert, Rodney Carson 1939- *St&PR 93*
Gilbert, Roger Whitney 1932- *WhoIns 93*
Gilbert, Ronald Rhea 1942- *WhoAm 92*
Gilbert, Ronnie *BioIn 17*
Gilbert, Ronnie c. 1927- *See* Weavers, The *ConMus 8*
Gilbert, Roy H.R. 1936- *St&PR 93*
Gilbert, Roy W., Jr. 1937- *WhoSSW 93*
Gilbert, Russell T. 1930- *St&PR 93*
Gilbert, Ruth *ScF&FL 92*
Gilbert, Ruth Gallard Ainsworth *MajAI*
Gilbert, Sandra M. *BioIn 17*
Gilbert, Sandra M(ortola) 1936- *DcLB 120 [port]*
Gilbert, Sarah 1959?- *ConAu 139*
Gilbert, Selma L. 1936- *St&PR 93*
Gilbert, Sharon 1944- *WhoE 93*
Gilbert, Shirl Edward 1945- *WhoAm 92*
Gilbert, Sky *WhoCanL 92*
Gilbert, Stephen Alan 1939- *St&PR 93, WhoIns 93*
Gilbert, Stephen L. 1943- *WhoWor 93*
Gilbert, Steven Jeffrey 1947- *WhoEmL 93*
Gilbert, Suzanne Harris 1943- *WhoAmW 93*
Gilbert, Suzanne Harris 1948- *St&PR 93*
Gilbert, Sylvio R. d1992 *NewYTBS 92*
Gilbert, Terence James 1943- *WhoSSW 93*
Gilbert, Teresan Wasie *Law&B 92*
Gilbert, Terry D. 1936- *St&PR 93*
Gilbert, Thomas Tibbals 1947- *WhoEmL 93*
Gilbert, Virginia Lee 1946- *WhoWrEP 92*
Gilbert, W.S. 1836-1911 *BioIn 17, OxDcOp*
Gilbert, W(illiam) S(chwenck) 1836-1911 *Baker 92*
Gilbert, Walter 1932- *CurBio 92 [port], WhoAm 92, WhoE 93, WhoWor 93*
Gilbert, Walter F. 1926- *St&PR 93*
Gilbert, Walter Randolph, Jr. 1936- *WhoSSW 93*
Gilbert, William Schwenck 1836-1911 *BioIn 17*
Gilbert, Willie 1916-1980 *ConAu 37NR*
Gilbert and George *BioIn 17*
Gilbert-Barness, Enid F. 1927- *WhoAm 92*
Gilberte, Hallett 1872-1946 *Baker 92*
Gilberti, Anthony F. *BioIn 17*
Gilbert-Miguet, Pascale 1952- *WhoUN 92*
Gilbertson, B(ernice) Charlotte *WhoWrEP 92*
Gilbertson, Eric Raymond 1945- *WhoAm 92*
Gilbertson, Gene Roy 1949- *St&PR 93*
Gilbertson, John Raymond 1923- *St&PR 93*
Gilbertson, John S. 1943- *St&PR 93*
Gilbertson, Larry R. *Law&B 92*
Gilbertson, Mark *BioIn 17*
Gilbertson, Moyna P. *WhoScE 91-1*
Gilbertson, Peggy Ann 1964- *WhoAmW 93*
Gilbertson, Peter Allan 1953- *WhoWor 93*
Gilbertson, Robert G. 1941- *WhoAm 92*
Gilbertson, Robert Gene 1941- *St&PR 93*
Gilbey, John W.G. *St&PR 93*
Gilbey, John Walter Guy 1941- *WhoAm 92*
Gilbo, Anna-Carolyn 1940- *WhoWrEP 92*
Gilboa, Jacob 1920- *Baker 92*
Gilboa, Nisan 1945- *WhoE 93*
Gilboa, Tsach I. *Law&B 92*
Gilbody, Henry Brian *WhoScE 91-1*
Gilboe, David Dougherty 1929- *WhoAm 92*
Gilboord, Margaret *WhoCanL 92*
Gilborn, Craig Alfred 1934- *WhoE 93*
Gilborne, Jean Elizabeth 1910- *WhoAmW 93*
Gilboy, Michael Russell 1950- *WhoEmL 93*
Gilbreath, Freida Carol 1949- *WhoAmW 93*
Gilbreath, Rex L. 1933-1991 *BioIn 17*
Gilbreth, Frank Bunker 1868-1924 *BioIn 17*
Gilbreth, Frank Bunker, Jr. 1911- *WhoAm 92*
Gilbreth, Lillian Moller 1878-1972 *BioIn 17*
Gilbride, John Thomas, Jr. 1945- *WhoAm 92*
Gilbride, William Donald 1924- *WhoAm 92*
Gilchrest, Thornton Charles 1931- *WhoAm 92*
Gilchrest, Wayne T. 1946- *CngDr 91*
Gilchrest, Wayne Thomas 1946- *WhoAm 92, WhoE 93*
Gilchrist, A.O. *WhoScE 91-1*
Gilchrist, Anne Burrows 1828-1885 *BioIn 17*
Gilchrist, Barry D. 1947- *St&PR 93*
Gilchrist, Barry Dean *Law&B 92*
Gilchrist, David M. 1949- *St&PR 93*
Gilchrist, David Walter 1931- *St&PR 93*
Gilchrist, Doris Irene 1960- *WhoEmL 93*
Gilchrist, Ellen 1935- *BioIn 17*
Gilchrist, Ellen Louise 1935- *WhoAm 92, WhoAmW 93*
Gilchrist, Frank R. d1991 *BioIn 17*
Gilchrist, Gerald Seymour 1935- *WhoAm 92*
Gilchrist, James Austin 1953- *WhoEmL 93*
Gilchrist, James B. 1939- *St&PR 93*
Gilchrist, James Beardslee 1939- *WhoAm 92*
Gilchrist, Jan Spivey 1949- *BlkAuII 92, SmATA 72 [port]*
Gilchrist, John 1932- *ScF&FL 92*
Gilchrist, Jonathan C. *Law&B 92*
Gilchrist, Kenneth 1927- *St&PR 93*
Gilchrist, Marilyn *BioIn 17*
Gilchrist, Ralph Edward 1926- *WhoSSW 93*
Gilchrist, Richard Irwin 1946- *WhoWor 93*
Gilchrist, William McKenzie 1909- *St&PR 93*
Gilchrist, William Risque, Jr. 1944- *WhoSSW 93*
Gilchrist, William Wallace 1846-1916 *Baker 92*
Gilcrease, Joy Victoria 1940- *St&PR 93*
Gilcrease, Richard 1937- *St&PR 93*
Gilcrease, Thomas 1890-1962 *BioIn 17*
Gilcrest, Linda Rae 1946- *WhoEmL 93*
Gilcrest, Roger W. 1937- *St&PR 93*
Gild, Mary Alice 1955- *WhoAmW 93*
Gilde, Thomas F. *Law&B 92*
Gildea, Brian M. 1939- *St&PR 93*
Gildea, Brian Michael 1939- *WhoE 93, WhoWor 93*
Gildea, Edward J. *Law&B 92*
Gildea, John R. 1939- *St&PR 93*
Gildea, Steven Joseph 1967- *WhoE 93*
Gil de Biedma, Jaime 1929- *BioIn 17*
Gildehaus, Thomas Arthur 1940- *St&PR 93, WhoAm 92*
Gildemeister, Jerry 1934- *WhoWrEP 92*
Gilden, David 1947- *St&PR 93*
Gilden, Joyce *Law&B 92*
Gilden, K.B. 1914-1991 *BioIn 17*
Gilden, Katya B. 1914-1991 *BioIn 17*
Gilden, Mel 1947- *ScF&FL 92*
Gildenberg, Philip Leon 1935- *WhoAm 92*
Gildenberg, Sanford R. 1942- *St&PR 93*
Gildenblatt, Stuart Alan 1950- *St&PR 93*
Gildenhorn, Joseph Bernard 1929- *WhoAm 92, WhoWor 93*
Gilder, Charles Joseph 1934- *St&PR 93*
Gilder, George F. 1939- *BioIn 17*
Gilder, Jeanette Leonard 1849-1916 *AmWomPl*
Gilder, Richard Watson 1844-1909 *GayN*
Gilderhus, Mark Theodore 1941- *WhoAm 92*
Gildersleeve, Robert F. 1942- *St&PR 93*
Gildin, Herbert *St&PR 93*
Gilding, David Brian *WhoScE 91-1*
Gildner, Gary 1938- *WhoWrEP 92*
Gildo d398 *OxDcByz*
Gildred, Theodore Edmonds 1935- *WhoAm 92*
Gildrie, Richard Peter 1945- *WhoSSW 93*
Gilds, Siegfried *WhoWor 93*
Gile, Mary Stuart 1936- *WhoAmW 93*
Gile, Selden Connor 1877-1947 *BioIn 17*
Gilejko, Leszek Kazimierz *WhoWor 93*
Gilels, Elizabeta 1919- *Baker 92*
Gilels, Emil (Grigorievich) 1916-1985 *Baker 92*
Giler, David *MiSFD 9*
Giles, Alan Edwin *WhoScE 91-1*
Giles, Allen 1924- *WhoWor 93*
Giles, Anne Diener 1948- *WhoAm 92*
Giles, Anthony Kent *WhoScE 91-1*
Giles, Barbara Joan 1945- *WhoAmW 93*
Giles, Carl H(oward) 1935- *ConAu 39NR*
Giles, Clarence Alfred 1946- *WhoEmL 93, WhoWor 93*
Giles, David K. 1945- *St&PR 93*
Giles, David Lake *Law&B 92*
Giles, Donald Earl 1931- *St&PR 93*
Giles, Ernest 1835-1897 *Expl 93 [port]*
Giles, Eugene 1933- *WhoAm 92*
Giles, Florine Bonnie 1950- *WhoAmW 93*
Giles, Harold Frazee, Jr. 1945- *WhoSSW 93*
Giles, Homer Wayne 1919- *WhoAm 92*
Giles, James T. 1943- *WhoAm 92, WhoE 93*
Giles, Jean Hall 1908- *WhoAmW 93, WhoWor 93*
Giles, Jeff *BioIn 17*
Giles, Jeff 1965- *ConAu 137*
Giles, Jeffrey Alan 1964- *WhoSSW 93*
Giles, Josephine *AmWomPl*
Giles, Judith Margaret 1939- *WhoAmW 93*
Giles, Karen Denise 1961- *WhoAmW 93*
Giles, Lynda Fern 1943- *WhoAmW 93*
Giles, Mamye Ruth 1910- *WhoSSW 93*
Giles, Marvin McCrary 1943- *WhoSSW 93*
Giles, Merle *BioIn 17*
Giles, Molly 1942- *WhoWrEP 92*
Giles, Nathaniel c. 1558-1634 *Baker 92*
Giles, Norman Henry 1915- *WhoAm 92*
Giles, Patricia Jessie 1928- *WhoAsAP 91*
Giles, Peter 1938- *St&PR 93, WhoAm 92*
Giles, Phyllis Lenore Williams 1912- *WhoAmW 93*
Giles, Richard W. 1930- *St&PR 93*
Giles, Robert Hartmann 1933- *WhoAm 92*
Giles, Thomas Wilbur 1939- *WhoE 93*
Giles, William Branch 1762-1830 *PolPar*
Giles, William Edward *Law&B 92*
Giles, William Elmer 1927- *WhoAm 92*
Giles, William Yale 1934- *WhoAm 92*
Giles, of Rome c. 1243-1316 *BioIn 17*
Gilet, M. *WhoScE 91-2*
Gilfillan, George William 1938- *WhoAm 92*
Gilfillan, Mari Margaret 1955- *WhoAmW 93*
Gilfillan, Merrill (C.) 1945- *ConAu 138*
Gilford, Jack 1907-1990 *BioIn 17*
Gilford, Leon 1917- *WhoAm 92, WhoE 93*
Gilford, Steven Ross 1952- *WhoAm 92*
Gilfrich, John Valentine 1927- *WhoE 93*
Gilgar, Arthur Emery 1944- *St&PR 93, WhoAm 92*
Gil-Gayarre, Miguel 1932- *WhoScE 91-3*
Gilger, Paul Douglass 1954- *WhoEmL 93, WhoWor 93*
Gilges, August Stephan 1936- *St&PR 93*
Gilges, Walter F. *Law&B 92*
Gil Gilbert, Enrique 1912-1973 *SpAmA*
Gilgoff, Alice 1946- *WhoAmW 93*
Gilgore, Sheldon Gerald 1932- *WhoAm 92*
Gilgun, John 1935- *ConGAN*
Gilgun, John Francis 1935- *WhoWrEP 92*
Gilham, Charles Sayel *Law&B 92*
Gilhousen, Brent J. *Law&B 92*
Gilhuley, Stephen E. *Law&B 92*
Gilhuley, Stephen E. 1944- *St&PR 93*
Gilhuly, Robert Thomas 1930- *WhoAm 92*
Gilhuly, Shannon Jones 1955- *WhoAmW 93*
Gilhuus-Moe, Ole Theodor 1929- *WhoWor 93*
Gilhuys, Charles 1934- *St&PR 93*
Gili, Phillida 1944- *SmATA 70*
Gilibert, Charles 1866-1910 *Baker 92*
Giliberti, Barbara C. *Law&B 92*
Gililland, Patrick Mark 1958- *WhoSSW 93*
Gilinsky, Stanley Ellis 1918- *WhoAm 92*
Gilinsky, Victor 1934- *WhoAm 92*
Gilinson, Philip Julius, Jr. 1914- *WhoE 93*
Gilissen, Herman Petrus 1937- *St&PR 93*
Gilje, Stephen Arne 1949- *WhoE 93*
Gilkerson, Yancey Sherard 1919- *WhoAm 92*
Gilkes, Arthur G. 1915- *St&PR 93*
Gilkes, Arthur Gwyer 1915- *WhoWor 93*
Gilkeson, Robert Fairbairn 1917- *WhoAm 92*
Gilkey, Bertha *BioIn 17, NewYTBS 92 [port]*
Gilkey, Clinton Howard 1938- *WhoE 93*
Gilkey, Gordon Waverly 1912- *WhoAm 92, WhoWor 93*
Gilkey, Herbert Talbot 1924- *WhoSSW 93*
Gilkey, Langdon Brown 1919- *BioIn 17*
Gill, Abigail Stanton 1945- *St&PR 93*
Gill, Andrew D. *Law&B 92*
Gill, Andy *See* Gang of Four *ConMus 8*
Gill, Anne Whalen 1948- *WhoEmL 93*
Gill, Ardian 1929- *WhoIns 93*
Gill, Ardian C. 1929- *WhoAm 92*
Gill, Austin 1906-1990 *BioIn 17*
Gill, Bartholomew *ConAu 37NR*
Gill, Benjamin Franklin 1917- *WhoAm 92*
Gill, Benjamin P. *Law&B 92*
Gill, Brendan 1914- *BioIn 17, ConAu 37NR, WhoAm 92, WhoWrEP 92*
Gill, C. *WhoScE 91-1*
Gill, Carole O'Brien 1946- *WhoAm 92, WhoAmW 93*
Gill, Charles B. 1938- *St&PR 93*
Gill, Charles Burroughs 1921- *WhoE 93*
Gill, Clark Cyrus 1915- *WhoAm 92*
Gill, D. Steve *Law&B 92*
Gill, Daniel E. 1936- *St&PR 93, WhoAm 92*
Gill, Darla R. 1951- *St&PR 93*

Gill, David *BioIn 17*
Gill, David Brian 1957- *WhoEmL 93, WhoSSW 93*
Gill, Diane L. 1948- *WhoAmW 93, WhoEmL 93, WhoSSW 93*
Gill, Donald Artley 1938- *WhoSSW 93*
Gill, Donald George 1927- *WhoAm 92*
Gill, Elliot M. *Law&B 92*
Gill, Eric 1882-1940 *BioIn 17*
Gill, Evalyn Pierpoint *WhoAmW 93*
Gill, George Edward *Law&B 92*
Gill, George K. 1939- *St&PR 93*
Gill, George N. *Law&B 92*
Gill, George Norman 1934- *St&PR 93, WhoAm 92*
Gill, Gerald Lawson 1947- *WhoEmL 93, WhoSSW 93, WhoWor 93*
Gill, H.R. 1936- *St&PR 93*
Gill, Harlan 1922- *St&PR 93*
Gill, Harold Edward 1957- *WhoEmL 93*
Gill, Harry S. *Law&B 92*
Gill, Harry S. 1945- *St&PR 93*
Gill, Henry Clement 1927- *St&PR 93*
Gill, Henry Herr 1930- *WhoAm 92*
Gill, Janis *BioIn 17*
Gill, John 1732-1785 *JrnUS*
Gill, John Allen 1938- *St&PR 93*
Gill, John E. 1941- *St&PR 93*
Gill, John M. 1947- *WhoScE 91-1*
Gill, John M. 1950- *St&PR 93*
Gill, John Ray 1953- *WhoE 93*
Gill, Johnny *BioIn 17, SoulM*
Gill, Joseph Peter, Jr. 1928- *St&PR 93*
Gill, Joseph S. *Law&B 92*
Gill, Kathleen Mary 1948- *WhoAmW 93*
Gill, Kenneth Paul 1926- *St&PR 93*
Gill, Lakshmi *WhoCanL 92*
Gill, Laurance Leslie 1936- *WhoWor 93*
Gill, Lawrence E. *Law&B 92*
Gill, Lucy Elizabeth 1928- *WhoAmW 93*
Gill, Lunda Lucinda 1959- *WhoAmW 93, WhoEmL 93*
Gill, Margaret S. 1941- *WhoAmW 93*
Gill, Mark James 1956- *St&PR 93*
Gill, Merwyn C. 1910- *St&PR 93*
Gill, Michael Henry 1794-1879 *BioIn 17*
Gill, Michael L. *Law&B 92*
Gill, Patricia Jane 1950- *WhoAmW 93*
Gill, Peter L. 1942- *St&PR 93*
Gill, Raymond *Law&B 92*
Gill, Raymond Joseph 1930- *St&PR 93, WhoAm 92*
Gill, Richard 1948- *ScF&FL 92*
Gill, Richard J. 1955- *St&PR 93*
Gill, Richard Lawrence 1946- *WhoEmL 93*
Gill, Richard Thomas 1927- *WhoAm 92*
Gill, Robert B. *St&PR 93*
Gill, Robert Monroe 1949- *WhoSSW 93*
Gill, Rockne 1931- *WhoAm 92*
Gill, Roger *ScF&FL 92*
Gill, Ronnie Joy 1949- *WhoAmW 93*
Gill, Ruland J., Jr. *Law&B 92*
Gill, Sabra Hall 1941- *WhoSSW 93*
Gill, Safdar Ali 1931- *St&PR 93*
Gill, Stanley Jensen 1929- *WhoAm 92*
Gill, Stephen *WhoCanL 92*
Gill, Stephen 1932- *BioIn 17, ScF&FL 92*
Gill, Stephen Paschall 1938- *WhoAm 92*
Gill, Suzanne L(utz) 1941- *ConAu 136*
Gill, Thomas *Law&B 92*
Gill, Thomas J. *St&PR 93*
Gill, Thomas James, III 1932- *WhoAm 92, WhoE 93*
Gill, Thomas M. 1941- *WhoIns 93*
Gill, Thomas Michael 1941- *St&PR 93*
Gill, Vince *BioIn 17*
Gill, Wanda Eileen 1945- *WhoE 93*
Gill, William Nelson 1928- *WhoAm 92*
Gill, William Robert 1920- *WhoAm 92*
Gill, Winifred Marie 1958- *WhoAmW 93, WhoEmL 93*
Gillaland, George S. 1939- *St&PR 93*
Gillam, Gary E. 1954- *WhoEmL 93*
Gillam, Harry Lee, Jr. 1954- *WhoEmL 93*
Gillam, James Kennedy 1922- *WhoAm 92*
Gillam, Jean Clare 1959- *WhoEmL 93*
Gillam, Max Lee 1926- *WhoAm 92*
Gillam, Patrick John 1933- *WhoAm 92*
Gillam, Robert S. *Law&B 92*
Gillam, Thomas D. 1944- *St&PR 93*
Gillan, Allan Wayne 1946- *WhoEmL 93, WhoSSW 93*
Gillan, John Terry 1937- *WhoSSW 93*
Gillan, Joseph Anthony 1940- *WhoE 93*
Gillan, Maria Mazziotti 1940- *WhoAmW 93, WhoE 93, WhoWrEP 92*
Gillanders, John David 1939- *WhoSSW 93*
Gillani, Noor Velshi 1944- *WhoWor 93*
Gillard, Robert David *WhoScE 91-1*
Gillard, Stuart 1946- *MiSFD 9*
Gillard, Stuart Thomas 1946- *WhoAm 92*
Gillaspie, Athey Graves, Jr. 1938- *WhoSSW 93*
Gillaugh, Raymond Dale 1930- *St&PR 93*
Gillberg, K. Gunnar 1942- *St&PR 93*
Gillcrist, Paul T. *BioIn 17*
Gille, Jacob Edvard 1814-1880 *Baker 92*
Gille, Lori-Jean 1952- *St&PR 93*
Gille, Marianne Birgitta 1944- *WhoWor 93*
Gille, Paul 1927- *WhoScE 91-2*
Gillece, James Patrick, Jr. 1944- *WhoAm 92*
Gillece, William F. 1939- *St&PR 93*
Gillego, Bonifacio H. 1921- *WhoAsAP 91*
Gilleland, LaRue Wesley 1930- *WhoE 93*
Gillem, Elise Marie 1958- *WhoAmW 93*
Gillen, James R. *Law&B 92*
Gillen, James Robert 1937- *St&PR 93, WhoAm 92*
Gillen, Mary Ann 1956- *St&PR 93*
Gillen, Stephen E. 1953- *St&PR 93*
Gillen, William Albert 1914- *WhoAm 92*
Gillenson, Lewis W. d1992 *NewYTBS 92*
Gillenson, Lewis William 1918-1992 *ConAu 139*
Gillenson, Mark Lee 1948- *WhoEmL 93*
Gillentine, Betty Diane 1944- *WhoAmW 93*
Gillenwater, Jay Young 1933- *WhoAm 92*
Giller, Benita 1933- *WhoAmW 93*
Giller, Edward Bonfoy 1918- *WhoAm 92*
Giller, Howard M. 1956- *St&PR 93*
Giller, Norman M. 1918- *St&PR 93*
Giller, Norman Myer 1918- *WhoAm 92*
Giller, Robert Maynard 1942- *WhoE 93*
Gillert, Stanislaw Victor 1857-1907 *PolBiDi*
Gillery, Beth-Ann 1947- *WhoAmW 93*
Gilles 1953- *BioIn 17*
Gilles, Dennis Cyril *WhoScE 91-1*
Gilles, Gemna Louis 1926- *WhoScE 91-2*
Gilles, Herbert Michael *WhoScE 91-1*
Gilles, Jean 1668-1705 *Baker 92*
Gilles, Jean-Marie 1931- *WhoScE 91-2*
Gilles, Jean-Marie Ferdinand G. 1931- *WhoWor 93*
Gilles, Raymond J.J. 1940- *WhoScE 91-2*
Gilles, Serge 1936- *DcCPCAm*
Gillespie, A.J., Jr. 1923- *St&PR 93*
Gillespie, Alastair William 1922- *WhoAm 92*
Gillespie, Alexander Joseph, Jr. 1923- *WhoAm 92*
Gillespie, Anita Wright 1953- *WhoEmL 93*
Gillespie, Arlene F. 1936- *NotHsAW 93*
Gillespie, Bertha *AmWomPl*
Gillespie, Bruce 1947- *ScF&FL 92*
Gillespie, Bruce A. 1948- *St&PR 93*
Gillespie, Carol J. *Law&B 92*
Gillespie, Carol J. 1945- *St&PR 93*
Gillespie, Carol Suzanne 1964- *WhoEmL 93*
Gillespie, Charles Anthony, Jr. 1935- *WhoAm 92, WhoWor 93*
Gillespie, Claire Seybold 1947- *St&PR 93*
Gillespie, Cliff, Jr. 1948- *WhoSSW 93*
Gillespie, Colleen P. *Law&B 92*
Gillespie, Daniel Curtis, Sr. 1922- *WhoAm 92*
Gillespie, Daniel Joseph 1928- *St&PR 93*
Gillespie, Daniel P. *St&PR 93*
Gillespie, "Dizzy" 1917- *Baker 92, BioIn 17, WhoAm 92*
Gillespie, Dizzy 1917-1993 *News 93-2*
Gillespie, Edward Malcolm 1935- *WhoAm 92, WhoSSW 93*
Gillespie, Fannie B. *AmWomPl*
Gillespie, Floyd Harold 1924- *St&PR 93*
Gillespie, Frederick S. 1916- *St&PR 93*
Gillespie, George 1613-1648 *BioIn 17*
Gillespie, George Joseph, III 1930- *WhoAm 92*
Gillespie, Gerald Ernest Paul 1933- *WhoAm 92*
Gillespie, Gwain H. 1931- *St&PR 93*
Gillespie, Gwain Homer 1931- *WhoAm 92*
Gillespie, Harry A. 1924- *St&PR 93*
Gillespie, Helen Davys 1954- *WhoAmW 93, WhoEmL 93*
Gillespie, Iain Erskine *WhoScE 91-1*
Gillespie, J. Martin 1949- *WhoEmL 93*
Gillespie, Jacquelyn Randall 1927- *WhoAmW 93*
Gillespie, James Davis 1955- *WhoSSW 93*
Gillespie, James Howard 1917- *WhoAm 92*
Gillespie, Jane *Law&B 92*
Gillespie, John Birks 1917- *BioIn 17*
Gillespie, John Spence *WhoScE 91-1*
Gillespie, John Thomas 1928- *WhoAm 92*
Gillespie, Joseph G. 1939- *St&PR 93*
Gillespie, Leonard Blackburn 1953- *WhoSSW 93*
Gillespie, Malcolm J.S. 1951- *WhoScE 91-1*
Gillespie, Mary Krempa 1941- *WhoAm 92, WhoAmW 93*
Gillespie, Nan *WhoWrEP 92*
Gillespie, Nicholas John 1963- *WhoE 93*
Gillespie, Patrick 1617-1675 *BioIn 17*
Gillespie, Ramon Edward 1928- *St&PR 93*
Gillespie, Richard *BioIn 17*
Gillespie, Richard Joseph 1944- *WhoAm 92*
Gillespie, Richard Roubaud 1930- *St&PR 93*
Gillespie, Robert Charles 1942- *WhoAm 92*
Gillespie, Robert J. 1942- *St&PR 93*
Gillespie, Robert James 1942- *WhoAm 92*
Gillespie, Robert W. 1944- *St&PR 93*
Gillespie, Ronald James 1924- *WhoAm 92*
Gillespie, Rory Andrew 1956- *WhoAm 92*
Gillespie, Samuel H., III *Law&B 92*
Gillespie, Sarah Ashman 1953- *WhoAm 92*
Gillespie, Susan M. *Law&B 92*
Gillespie, Suzanne Audrey 1938- *St&PR 93*
Gillespie, Ted C. *Law&B 92*
Gillespie, Teresa Williams *Law&B 92*
Gillespie, Thomas Francis, Jr. 1957- *WhoE 93*
Gillespie, Thomas James, III 1924- *St&PR 93*
Gillespie, Thomas Stuart 1938- *St&PR 93, WhoAm 92*
Gillespie, Thomas William 1928- *WhoAm 92, WhoE 93, WhoWor 93*
Gillespie, William A. 1924- *St&PR 93*
Gillespie, William Anthony 1950- *WhoWor 93*
Gillespie, Wilma Joan 1928- *WhoAmW 93*
Gillet, Claude Camille 1931- *WhoWor 93*
Gillet, Claude M.R.G. 1933- *WhoScE 91-2*
Gillet, Denis 1953- *WhoScE 91-2*
Gillet, Ernest 1856-1940 *Baker 92*
Gillet, J.Y. 1938- *WhoScE 91-2*
Gillet, Marcel 1935- *WhoScE 91-2*
Gillet, Roland 1962- *WhoWor 93*
Gillet, Ronald A. 1941- *St&PR 93*
Gillet, Ronald Allen 1941- *WhoSSW 93*
Gillet-Huser, Eveline 1937- *WhoScE 91-2*
Gillett, Charles 1915- *WhoAm 92*
Gillett, Franklin L. 1935- *St&PR 93*
Gillett, Frederick H. 1851-1935 *PolPar*
Gillett, George *BioIn 17*
Gillett, James Buchanan 1856-1937 *BioIn 17*
Gillett, John Robert *WhoScE 91-1*
Gillett, Jonathan Newell 1941- *WhoAm 92*
Gillett, Margaret 1930- *ConAu 39NR*
Gillett, Mary Caperton 1929- *WhoAmW 93*
Gillett, Nancy Mary 1928- *WhoAmW 93*
Gillett, Raphael 1945- *WhoWor 93*
Gillett, Richard M. 1923- *WhoAm 92*
Gillett, Roger Charles 1952- *WhoWor 9*
Gillett, Stephen L. 1953- *ScF&FL 92*
Gillett, W.B. *WhoScE 91-1*
Gillette, Anita 1938- *WhoAm 92*
Gillette, Arthur L. 1938- *WhoUN 92*
Gillette, Bob *WhoWrEP 92*
Gillette, Charlyne Clara 1950- *St&PR 93*
Gillette, Dean 1925- *WhoAm 92*
Gillette, Dennis 1939- *St&PR 93*
Gillette, Edward LeRoy 1932- *WhoAm 92*
Gillette, Ethel Morrow 1921- *WhoAmW 93*
Gillette, Ethel Perry *WhoWrEP 92*
Gillette, Halbert George 1926- *WhoSSW 93*
Gillette, Hyde 1906- *WhoAm 92*
Gillette, James R. 1943- *St&PR 93*
Gillette, John Albert 1958- *WhoEmL 93*
Gillette, Joseph Morton, Jr. 1951- *WhoSSW 93*
Gillette, King Camp 1855-1932 *BioIn 17, GayN*
Gillette, Norman John 1911- *WhoE 93*
Gillette, Paul 1938- *WhoWrEP 92*
Gillette, Paul Crawford 1942- *WhoAm 92*
Gillette, Robert S. 1913- *St&PR 93*
Gillette, Sheila Hennessey 1944- *WhoAmW 93*
Gillette, Stanley C. *WhoAm 92*
Gillette, Susan Downs 1950- *WhoAm 92, WhoAmW 93*
Gillette, W. Michael 1941- *WhoAm 92*
Gillette, William 1853-1937 *GayN*
Gillette, William 1933- *WhoAm 92*
Gillette-Baumann, Muriel Delphine 1945- *WhoAmW 93*
Gilley, Burnie Eugene 1942- *St&PR 93*
Gilley, J. Wade *WhoSSW 93*
Gilley, Mickey Leroy 1936- *WhoAm 92*
Gilley, Riley C. *Law&B 92*
Gilleylen, Bruce C. 1946- *St&PR 93*
Gillham, Brenda Keenan 1944- *BioIn 17*
Gillham, John Kinsey 1930- *WhoAm 92*
Gillham, Nicholas Wright 1932- *WhoAm 92*
Gillham, Robert 1938- *WhoAm 92*
Gillheeney, Gary S. 1955- *St&PR 93*
Gillhooly, Thomas J. d1990 *BioIn 17*
Gilli, Angelo Christopher, Sr. 1925- *WhoE 93*
Gilli, Lynne Marie 1954- *WhoE 93*
Gilli, Manfred 1942- *WhoWor 93*
Gilliam, Anita W. *Law&B 92*
Gilliam, Annette *Law&B 92*
Gilliam, Carroll Lewis 1929- *WhoAm 92*
Gilliam, Charles Phillips *Law&B 92*
Gilliam, Dorothea Cooke 1953- *WhoAmW 93*
Gilliam, Earl Ben 1931- *WhoAm 92*
Gilliam, Elizabeth M. 1930- *WhoWrEP 92*
Gilliam, Jackson Earle 1920- *WhoAm 92*
Gilliam, James H. *BioIn 17*
Gilliam, James H., Jr. *Law&B 92*
Gilliam, James Howard, Jr. 1945- *St&PR 93*
Gilliam, James N. 1942- *St&PR 93*
Gilliam, John A. 1935- *WhoAm 92*
Gilliam, John Charles 1927- *WhoAm 92*
Gilliam, Latha A. *Law&B 92*
Gilliam, Lynda Faye 1949- *WhoEmL 93*
Gilliam, Margaret Carol *Law&B 92*
Gilliam, Marion G.H. *BioIn 17*
Gilliam, Mary 1928- *WhoAmW 93*
Gilliam, Marymargaret Earle 1947- *WhoAmW 93, WhoSSW 93*
Gilliam, Melvin Randolph 1921- *WhoAm 92, WhoWor 93*
Gilliam, Michael C. 1948- *WhoIns 93*
Gilliam, Paula Hutter *WhoAmW 93*
Gilliam, Sam 1933- *BioIn 17, WhoAm 92*
Gilliam, Terry 1940- *MiSFD 9, ScF&FL 92*
Gilliam, Terry Keith 1945- *St&PR 93*
Gilliam, Terry Vance 1940- *WhoAm 92*
Gilliand, Harold 1932- *St&PR 93*
Gilliand, Merle E. 1921- *St&PR 93*
Gilliatt, Neal 1917- *St&PR 93, WhoAm 92*
Gillibrand, Michael Gray 1948- *WhoWor 93*
Gillice, Sondra Jupin *WhoAmW 93*
Gillice, Sondra Jupin 1936- *St&PR 93*
Gillick, Betsy Brinkley 1959- *WhoAmW 93*
Gillick, Patrick 1937- *WhoAm 92*
Gillick, Susan Lee 1946- *WhoAmW 93*
Gillie, Michelle Francoise 1956- *WhoAmW 93*
Gillie, Percy H. d1991 *BioIn 17*
Gillier, Jean-Claude 1667-1737 *OxDcOp*
Gillies, Donald Richard 1939- *WhoAm 92*
Gillies, John S. *Law&B 92*
Gillies, Malcolm 1954- *ConAu 137*
Gillies, Peter C. 1931- *WhoUN 92*
Gillies, Thomas Daniel 1920- *WhoAm 92*
Gillig, Stephen R. 1947- *St&PR 93*
Gilligan, Alison *ScF&FL 92*
Gilligan, Colin Thomas *WhoScE 91-1*
Gilligan, Edward John 1938- *WhoAm 92*
Gilligan, Harry E. 1931- *St&PR 93*
Gilligan, Jane *Law&B 92*
Gilligan, John R. 1927- *St&PR 93*
Gilligan, Martin Edward, Jr. 1938- *St&PR 93*
Gilligan, Mary Ann 1956- *WhoEmL 93*
Gilligan, Michael Joseph 1948- *WhoEmL 93*
Gilligan, Patrick J. 1927-1991 *BioIn 17*
Gilligan, Roy 1923- *WhoWrEP 92*
Gilligan, Shannon *ScF&FL 92*
Gillikin, Richard Charles 1952- *WhoEmL 93*
Gillikin, Virginia 1952- *WhoAmW 93*
Gillilan, William J., III 1946- *WhoAm 92, WhoSSW 93*
Gilliland, Alexis A. 1931- *ScF&FL 92*
Gilliland, Alexis A(rnaldus) 1931- *SmATA 72 [port]*
Gilliland, Charles Donald 1945- *WhoSSW 93*
Gilliland, George Samuel 1939- *St&PR 93*
Gilliland, Gerald *St&PR 93*
Gilliland, Hap 1918- *WhoWrEP 92*
Gilliland, Larry Daniel 1938- *St&PR 93*
Gilliland, Lisa Jeffrey 1958- *St&PR 93*
Gilliland, Marion Charlotte S. 1918- *WhoAmW 93, WhoSSW 93*
Gilliland, Norman Lee, Jr. 1958- *St&PR 93*
Gilliland, Theo T. 1924- *St&PR 93*
Gilliland, William Elton 1919- *WhoAm 92*
Gillilland, Thomas 1932- *WhoE 93*
Gillin, James 1925- *WhoAm 92*
Gillin, Malvin James, Jr. 1946- *WhoEmL 93*
Gillinder, Scott W. 1955- *St&PR 93*
Gillingham, Bryan Reginald 1944- *WhoAm 92*
Gillingham, John Francis 1916- *WhoWor 93*
Gillingham, Robert Fenton 1944- *WhoAm 92*
Gillingham, Stephen Thomas *Law&B 92*
Gillingham, Stephen Thomas 1944- *WhoE 93*
Gillings, Daniel Andrew 1940- *St&PR 93*
Gillings, Gary Dean 1955- *WhoEmL 93*
Gillings, Joseph J. 1941- *St&PR 93*

Gillinson, Andrew Stuart 1948- *WhoE 93, WhoEmL 93*
Gillio, Carolyn Irene 1931- *WhoAm 92*
Gilliom, Judith Carr 1943- *WhoAm 92*
Gillio-Tos, M. *WhoScE 91-3*
Gillis, Bernard Thomas 1931- *WhoAm 92*
Gillis, Chester 1951- *ConAu 136*
Gillis, Christine Diest-Lorgion *WhoAmW 93*
Gillis, Christopher *BioIn 17*
Gillis, Don 1912-1978 *Baker 92*
Gillis, Donald Paul 1941- *WhoE 93*
Gillis, Elie 1937- *WhoScE 91-2*
Gillis, Frank L. 1951- *St&PR 93*
Gillis, Frank Lauren 1951- *WhoAm 92*
Gillis, James T. 1947- *St&PR 93*
Gillis, James W. 1930- *St&PR 93*
Gillis, John Simon 1937- *WhoAm 92, WhoWor 93*
Gillis, Margaret Rose 1953- *WhoAm 92*
Gillis, Margie *BioIn 17*
Gillis, N. Scott 1953- *St&PR 93*
Gillis, Nelson Scott 1953- *WhoEmL 93*
Gillis, Paul Leonard 1953- *WhoAm 92*
Gillis, Richard Austin 1953- *WhoE 93*
Gillis, Richard Fred 1936- *WhoAm 92*
Gillis, Richard Paul 1953- *WhoSSW 93*
Gillis, Steven 1953- *WhoAm 92*
Gillis, Tamara Louise 1961- *WhoAmW 93*
Gillis, Thomas G. 1955- *St&PR 93*
Gillis, Wayne Anthony 1943- *WhoE 93*
Gillis, William Freeman 1948- *WhoAm 92*
Gillison, David E. 1952- *St&PR 93*
Gillison, Jeanette Scott 1931- *WhoAmW 93*
Gillispie, Charles Coulston 1918- *WhoE 93*
Gilliss, Barbara Ellen 1938- *WhoAmW 93*
Gillissen, Gunther Josef 1917- *WhoScE 91-3*
Gillman, Anthony Philip *Law&B 92*
Gillman, Arthur Emanuel 1927- *WhoAm 92*
Gillman, Donald O. 1930- *St&PR 93*
Gillman, Florence Morgan 1947- *WhoEmL 93*
Gillman, Leonard 1917- *WhoAm 92, WhoSSW 93, WhoWor 93*
Gillman, Nina Dorothy *Law&B 92*
Gillman, Richard 1931- *WhoAm 92, WhoE 93*
Gillman, Robert N. 1930- *St&PR 93*
Gillman, Sid 1911- *BioIn 17*
Gillmann, Harold E. *Law&B 92*
Gillmar, Stanley Frank 1935- *WhoAm 92*
Gillmaur, David W. *St&PR 93*
Gillmer, Thomas Charles 1911- *WhoWor 93*
Gillmor, Charles Stewart 1938- *WhoAm 92*
Gillmor, John Edward 1937- *WhoAm 92*
Gillmor, Karen Lako 1948- *WhoAmW 93, WhoEmL 93*
Gillmor, Paul E. 1939- *CngDr 91, WhoAm 92*
Gillmore, Kathleen C. *Law&B 92*
Gillmore, Quincy Adams 1825-1888 *HarEnMi*
Gillmore, Robert 1946- *WhoAm 92*
Gillmore, Susan Marie *Law&B 92*
Gillogly, Fred Dale 1918- *St&PR 93*
Gillogly, Terry Blake 1950- *St&PR 93*
Gillois, Michel Jean 1933- *WhoScE 91-2*
Gillon, Arie 1946- *WhoWor 93*
Gillon, David Gerard 1951- *WhoSSW 93*
Gillon, John William 1900- *WhoAm 92*
Gillon, Yves 1938- *WhoScE 91-2*
Gillooly, Ann F. *Law&B 92*
Gillooly, Greg J. 1948- *St&PR 93*
Gillooly, Susan E. *Law&B 92*
Gillow, Paul L. *Law&B 92*
Gil-Loyzaga, Pablo Enrique 1954- *WhoWor 93*
Gilloz, Andre-Pierre 1926- *WhoWor 93*
Gill Thompson, Norma N. 1920- *WhoAmW 93*
Gilluly, Sheila *ScF&FL 92*
Gillum, Keith Michael 1954- *St&PR 93*
Gillum, Roderick D. *Law&B 92*
Gillum, Ronald Lee 1938- *WhoSSW 93*
Gillum, Vern *MiSFD 9*
Gilly, Dinh 1877-1940 *Baker 92, OxDcOp*
Gilly, Philip Alain 1956- *WhoE 93*
Gilly, Richard P. *Law&B 92*
Gilman, Alan B. 1930- *WhoAm 92*
Gilman, Albert Franklin, III 1931- *WhoSSW 93*
Gilman, Alfred Goodman 1941- *WhoAm 92*
Gilman, Andrew D. 1951- *ConAu 137*
Gilman, Benjamin A. 1922- *CngDr 91*
Gilman, Benjamin Arthur 1922- *WhoAm 92, WhoE 93*
Gilman, Benjamin Ives 1852-1933 *Baker 92*
Gilman, Bill 1945- *St&PR 93*
Gilman, Charles Alan 1949- *WhoAm 92*
Gilman, Charlotte Perkins 1860-1935 *AmWomWr 92, BioIn 17, GayN, ScF&FL 92*
Gilman, Charlotte Perkins Stetson 1860-1935 *AmWomPl*
Gilman, David Alan 1933- *WhoAm 92*
Gilman, Dorothy 1923- *ScF&FL 92, WhoAm 92*
Gilman, Ernest Bernard 1946- *WhoEmL 93*
Gilman, Ethan Henry 1937- *St&PR 93*
Gilman, Greer Ilene 1951- *ScF&FL 92*
Gilman, Herbert 1924-1990 *BioIn 17*
Gilman, J. Bruce, Jr. *Law&B 92*
Gilman, John Joseph 1925- *WhoAm 92*
Gilman, Jonathan Charles 1953- *WhoE 93*
Gilman, Julia M. 1942- *WhoWrEP 92*
Gilman, Karyn Lynn 1950- *WhoSSW 93*
Gilman, Kenneth Bruce 1946- *St&PR 93*
Gilman, Lawrence 1878-1939 *Baker 92*
Gilman, Marvin Stanley 1922- *WhoAm 92*
Gilman, Michelle *BioIn 17*
Gilman, Neil Frederic 1954- *St&PR 93*
Gilman, Norman Washburn 1938- *WhoE 93*
Gilman, Peter A. *WhoAm 92*
Gilman, Richard 1925- *WhoAm 92, WhoWrEP 92*
Gilman, Richard Carleton 1923- *WhoAm 92*
Gilman, Robert Cham *ScF&FL 92*
Gilman, Robert S. 1953- *St&PR 93*
Gilman, Roger H. d1992 *NewYTBS 92 [port]*
Gilman, Roger H. 1914-1992 *BioIn 17*
Gilman, Ronald Lee 1942- *WhoAm 92*
Gilman, S.I. 1938- *St&PR 93*
Gilman, Sander Lawrence 1944- *WhoAm 92*
Gilman, Shirley J. *St&PR 93*
Gilman, Sid 1932- *WhoAm 92*
Gilman, Steven Christopher 1952- *WhoAm 92, WhoEmL 93*
Gilman, Susan Chernow 1948- *WhoEmL 93*
Gil-Marchex, Henri 1894-1970 *Baker 92*
Gilmartin, John A. 1942- *St&PR 93, WhoAm 92, WhoE 93*
Gilmartin, Karen Baust 1961- *WhoEmL 93*
Gilmartin, Patricia Purcell 1941- *WhoSSW 93*
Gilmartin, Ralph Brian *Law&B 92*
Gilmartin, Raymond V. 1941- *St&PR 93, WhoAm 92*
Gilmartin, Roger *St&PR 93*
Gilmer, B. von Haller 1909- *WhoAm 92, WhoWor 93*
Gilmer, Deborah Ann 1951- *WhoEmL 93*
Gilmer, Elizabeth Meriwether 1861-1951 *JrnUS*
Gilmer, James Christopher 1960- *WhoSSW 93*
Gilmer, La Jeanne Thompson 1934- *WhoWrEP 92*
Gilmer, Mary Elizabeth 1911- *WhoWrEP 92*
Gilmer, Robert 1938- *WhoSSW 93*
Gilmer, Thomas Edward, Jr. 1925- *WhoAm 92*
Gilmer, Wendell Jerome 1950- *WhoEmL 93*
Gilmond, James Edward 1949- *WhoE 93, WhoEmL 93*
Gilmont, Ernest Rich 1929- *WhoAm 92*
Gilmor, Robert d1989 *BioIn 17*
Gilmore, Alice F. *AmWomPl*
Gilmore, Ann Louise 1939- *WhoSSW 93*
Gilmore, Annella Slaughter *AmWomPl*
Gilmore, Anthony 1900-1981 *ScF&FL 92*
Gilmore, Art 1912- *WhoAm 92*
Gilmore, Barbara Eleanor Sale 1932- *WhoE 93*
Gilmore, Benjamin 1906- *St&PR 93*
Gilmore, Betty J. *St&PR 93*
Gilmore, Bruce *BioIn 17*
Gilmore, Charlotte Ann 1948- *WhoSSW 93*
Gilmore, Clarence Fielding 1922- *St&PR 93*
Gilmore, Clarence Percy 1926- *WhoAm 92, WhoWrEP 92*
Gilmore, David James *Law&B 92*
Gilmore, David W. 1950- *St&PR 93*
Gilmore, Donald Albert 1930- *WhoSSW 93*
Gilmore, Gordon Ray 1935- *WhoSSW 93, WhoWor 93*
Gilmore, H. William *WhoAm 92*
Gilmore, Horace Weldon 1918- *WhoAm 92*
Gilmore, Howard N., Jr. 1933- *St&PR 93*
Gilmore, Howard W. *BioIn 17*
Gilmore, Hugh Redland 1916- *WhoSSW 93*
Gilmore, James D. *St&PR 93*
Gilmore, James Stanley, Jr. 1926- *WhoAm 92*
Gilmore, Jerry Carl 1933- *WhoAm 92*
Gilmore, Jesse Lee 1920- *WhoAm 92*
Gilmore, Joan Elizabeth 1927- *WhoAmW 93*
Gilmore, Joan Marie 1959- *WhoEmL 93*
Gilmore, John F. 1940- *St&PR 93*
Gilmore, John Vaughn, Jr. 1948- *WhoE 93*
Gilmore, June Ellen 1927- *WhoAm 92, WhoAmW 93, WhoWor 93*
Gilmore, Kate *ScF&FL 92*
Gilmore, Kathryn Alice 1967- *WhoAmW 93*
Gilmore, Kenneth *BioIn 17*
Gilmore, Kenneth O. 1930- *St&PR 93*
Gilmore, Kenneth Otto 1930- *WhoAm 92*
Gilmore, Lillian *SweetSg B [port]*
Gilmore, Lloyd M. 1925- *St&PR 93*
Gilmore, Louisa Ruth 1930- *WhoAmW 93*
Gilmore, M. Reed *Law&B 92*
Gilmore, Maeve d1983 *ScF&FL 92*
Gilmore, Marjorie Havens 1918- *WhoAmW 93*
Gilmore, Mary Eugene 1938- *WhoAmW 93*
Gilmore, Michael 1952- *WhoWrEP 92*
Gilmore, Michael D. *Law&B 92*
Gilmore, Patrick S(arsfield) 1829-1892 *Baker 92*
Gilmore, Patrick Timothy 1928- *St&PR 93*
Gilmore, Richard G. 1927- *WhoAm 92*
Gilmore, Robert Ames 1930- *WhoE 93*
Gilmore, Robert Eugene 1920- *St&PR 93, WhoAm 92*
Gilmore, Robert Gordon *WhoAm 92*
Gilmore, Robert N. 1948- *WhoAm 92*
Gilmore, Robert Noel 1948- *St&PR 93*
Gilmore, Roger 1932- *WhoAm 92*
Gilmore, Russell Stanley 1936- *WhoE 93*
Gilmore, Susan Astrid Lytle 1942- *WhoAm 92*
Gilmore, Thomas Joseph *Law&B 92*
Gilmore, Thomas Meyer 1942- *WhoE 93*
Gilmore, Timothy Jonathan 1949- *WhoEmL 93*
Gilmore, Voit 1918- *WhoAm 92*
Gilmore, William Gerard 1930- *St&PR 93*
Gilmore, William Harold 1932- *St&PR 93*
Gilmour, Allan Dana 1934- *St&PR 93, WhoAm 92*
Gilmour, Cathryn A. 1945- *St&PR 93*
Gilmour, David 1949- *ConAu 138*
Gilmour, Edward Ellis 1930- *WhoAm 92*
Gilmour, Everett A. 1921- *St&PR 93*
Gilmour, H.B. 1939- *ScF&FL 92*
Gilmour, J. Lowell 1928- *St&PR 93*
Gilmour, James H. 1942- *St&PR 93*
Gilmour, John C. 1939- *ConAu 136*
Gilmour, Joseph Elliott, Jr. 1944- *WhoSSW 93*
Gilmour, Mark R. *Law&B 92*
Gilmour, Robert Arthur 1944- *WhoE 93*
Gilmour, Roger *WhoScE 91-1*
Gilmour, William *ScF&FL 92*
Gilmour-Stallsworth, Lisa Kathereyne 1959- *WhoAmW 93*
Gilner, Samuel 1952- *St&PR 93*
Giloi, Wolfgang K. 1930- *WhoScE 91-3*
Gilomen, Brian R. *Law&B 92*
Gilot, Francoise 1921- *BioIn 17*
Gilpatric, Carolyn Draper *AmWomPl*
Gilpatric, Lawrence 1948- *WhoE 93*
Gilpatric, Roswell 1904- *ColdWar 1 [port]*
Gilpatric, Roswell Leavitt 1906- *WhoAm 92*
Gilpatrick, Eleanor 1930- *WhoE 93*
Gilpatrick, Rose Adele *AmWomPl*
Gilpin, Larry Vincent 1943- *WhoAm 92*
Gilpin, Mark Edmund Michael 1949- *WhoUN 92*
Gilrain, Gerard James 1929- *St&PR 93*
Gilrain, Ronald F. 1927- *St&PR 93*
Gilrane, James Joseph 1938- *St&PR 93*
Gilreath, Jerry Hollandsworth 1934- *WhoE 93*
Gilreath, Warren Dean 1920- *WhoAm 92*
Gil-Recasens, Alejandro 1950- *WhoWor 93*
Gilrein, Sean Michael 1960- *WhoE 93*
Gil Robles, Jose Maria 1898-1980 *DcTwHis*
Gilronan, Sean-Patrick Michael 1945- *St&PR 93*
Gilroy, Edwin Bernard 1923- *St&PR 93*
Gilroy, Frank D. 1925- *MiSFD 9*
Gilroy, Frank Daniel 1925- *WhoAm 92*
Gilroy, Hollie A. 1963- *WhoEmL 93*
Gilroy, John M. 1948- *St&PR 93*
Gilroy, Michael James *Law&B 92*
Gilroy, Patricia Anne 1944- *WhoAmW 93*
Gilroy, William Francis 1936- *St&PR 93*
Gilroy, William Gerard 1954- *WhoWrEP 92*
Gilruth, Robert Rowe 1913- *WhoAm 92*
Gilsdorf, John B. *St&PR 93*
Gilsdorf, Mary Jo B. 1957- *WhoE 93*
Gilse, Jan van 1881-1944 *Baker 92*
Gil-Sevillano, Javier 1947- *WhoScE 91-3*
Gilsig, Toby 1940- *St&PR 93*
Gilsig, William 1938- *St&PR 93*
Gilsinan, James Francis, III 1945- *WhoAm 92*
Gilson, Elizabeth Anne 1945- *WhoAmW 93*
Gilson, Giles Pickering 1942- *WhoE 93*
Gilson, Goodwin W. 1918-1991 *BioIn 17*
Gilson, Greta Melissa 1957- *WhoAmW 93*
Gilson, James R. 1917- *St&PR 93*
Gilson, Paul 1865-1942 *Baker 92*
Gilson, W.E., Jr. 1936- *WhoIns 93*
Gilstad, June Russell 1928- *WhoWrEP 92*
Gilstein, Jacob Burrill 1923- *WhoAm 92*
Gilstrap, Dennis Leon 1930- *St&PR 93*
Gilstrap, Richard D., Jr. *Law&B 92*
Gilstrap, Suzanne T. 1950- *St&PR 93*
Giltay, Berend 1910-1975 *Baker 92*
Giltinan, Gerry Joseph 1955- *WhoWor 93*
Giltinan, John A. 1956- *St&PR 93*
Giltner, Alyce Sharlene 1960- *WhoEmL 93*
Giluk Dompok, Bernard *WhoAsAP 91*
Gilvary, James Joseph 1929- *WhoAm 92*
Gilvey, Edward Eugene 1926- *St&PR 93*
Gilway, Barry J. 1945- *St&PR 93*
Gilway, Barry John 1945- *WhoIns 93*
Gilzow, Homer Floyd, Jr. 1950- *WhoEmL 93*
Gimaro, Christopher Andrew 1964- *WhoE 93*
Gimbel, Louis S., III 1929- *St&PR 93*
Gimbel, Madeleine Esther 1944- *WhoSSW 93*
Gimbel, Michael Marc 1951- *WhoE 93*
Gimbel, Norman *WhoAm 92*
Gimbel, Roger 1925- *ConTFT 10*
Gimbel, William Thomas 1918- *St&PR 93*
Gimbrone, Michael Anthony, Jr. 1943- *WhoAm 92*
Gimbutas, Marija 1921- *WhoAm 92, WhoAmW 93*
Gimenez, Jeronimo 1854-1923 *Baker 92, OxDcOp*
Gimenez, Jose German 1950- *WhoScE 91-3*
Gimenez, Luis Fernando 1952- *WhoEmL 93*
Gimenez y Bellido, Jeronimo 1854-1923 *Baker 92*
Gimeno, Jose 1947- *WhoWor 93*
Gimeno Heredia, Jose 1947- *WhoScE 91-3*
Gimigliano, Alessandro 1955- *WhoWor 93*
Gimingham, Charles Henry *WhoScE 91-1*
Gimino, Frederick Anthony 1948- *WhoE 93*
Gimma, Joseph 1907- *St&PR 93*
Gimma, Joseph A. 1907-1990 *BioIn 17*
Gimmi, Kenneth James 1948- *WhoE 93*
Gimmy, Daniel P. 1946- *St&PR 93*
Gimmy, Daniel Patrick *Law&B 92*
Gimpel, Bronislaw 1911-1979 *Baker 92*
Gimpel, Jack F. 1940- *St&PR 93*
Gimpel, Jakob 1906-1989 *Baker 92*
Gimsing, Niels J. 1935- *WhoScE 91-2*
Gimson, Curtis S. *Law&B 92*
Gimson, Curtis S. 1955- *St&PR 93*
Ginader, John B. 1941- *St&PR 93*
Ginalski, Janusz 1927- *WhoScE 91-4*
Ginastera, Alberto 1916- *OxDcOp*
Ginastera, Alberto 1916-1983 *IntDcOp*
Ginastera, Alberto (Evaristo) 1916-1983 *Baker 92*
Ginchev, Ivan 1950- *WhoWor 93*
Ginden, Kathryn *WhoAm 92*
Ginder, Peter Craig 1946- *WhoEmL 93*
Gindes, Marion E. 1939- *WhoE 93*
Gindi, Joseph M. 1925- *St&PR 93*
Gindi, Roger Alan 1952- *WhoE 93*
Gindin, Irina 1938- *WhoE 93*
Gindin, Peter J. *Law&B 92*
Gindin, William Howard 1931- *WhoAm 92*
Gindlesberger, Pamela Ann 1958- *WhoAmW 93*
Gindlin, Herbert M. *Law&B 92*
Gindville, John J. 1948- *St&PR 93*
Gindy, Benjamin Lee 1929- *WhoSSW 93*
Ginell, Robert 1912-1990 *BioIn 17*
Giner, Valeriy Borisovich 1954- *WhoWor 93*
Giner de los Rios, Francisco 1917- *DcMexL*
Gineris, Thomas L. 1952- *WhoEmL 93*
Ginet, Rene-Gabriel 1927- *WhoScE 91-2*
Ginetto, Anthony Charles *Law&B 92*
Gingell, Richard 1941- *St&PR 93*
Ginger, Leonard George 1918- *St&PR 93*
Gingerich, Charles 1914- *BioIn 17*
Gingerich, Florine Rose 1951- *WhoAmW 93*
Gingerich, John Charles 1936- *St&PR 93, WhoAm 92*
Gingerich, Mark Alan 1961- *St&PR 93*
Gingerich, Owen Jay 1930- *WhoAm 92*
Gingerich, Philip Derstine 1946- *WhoAm 92*
Gingery, Donald Edward, Jr. 1951- *St&PR 93*

Gingery, Gregory William 1946- *St&PR 93*
Gingery, James Montgomery 1958- *St&PR 93*
Gingher, Marianne 1947- *ConAu 138*
Gingiss, Benjamin Jack 1911- *WhoAm 92*
Gingl, Manfred *St&PR 93*
Gingl, Manfred 1948- *WhoAm 92, WhoE 93*
Gingold, Dennis Marc 1949- *WhoAm 92, WhoE 93, WhoEmL 93, WhoWor 93*
Gingold, Elliot Bailin *WhoScE 91-1*
Gingold, George Norman *Law&B 92*
Gingold, George Norman 1939- *St&PR 93, WhoAm 92*
Gingold, Helene d1926 *AmWomPl*
Gingold, Helene E.A. *ScF&FL 92*
Gingold, Hermoine 1897-1987 *QDrFCA 92 [port]*
Gingold, Jeffrey Lee *Law&B 92*
Gingold, Josef 1909- *Baker 92, BioIn 17*
Gingras, David Alan 1946- *WhoE 93*
Gingras, Gustave 1918- *WhoAm 92, WhoWor 93*
Gingras, John R. *Law&B 92*
Gingras, Rene 1952- *WhoCanL 92*
Gingras, Yvan 1957- *St&PR 93*
Gingrich, Arnold *BioIn 17*
Gingrich, Deborah Sue 1963- *WhoAmW 93*
Gingrich, Gregg A. *Law&B 92*
Gingrich, Newell Shiffer 1906- *WhoAm 92*
Gingrich, Newt *BioIn 17, NewYTBS 92 [port]*
Gingrich, Newt 1943- *CngDr 91*
Gingrich, Newton Leroy 1943- *WhoAm 92*
Gingrich, Newton Leroy Newt 1943- *WhoSSW 93*
Gingrich, Robert P. *Law&B 92*
Gingrich, Steven Bryan 1951- *St&PR 93*
Gingrich-Petersen, Carolyn Ashcraft *WhoAm 92, WhoAmW 93*
Gingu, Vergil 1939- *WhoScE 91-4*
Ginguene, Pierre Louis 1748-1816 *Baker 92*
Giniecki, Kathleen Anne 1966- *WhoAmW 93*
Giniger, Kenneth Seeman 1919- *WhoAm 92*
Gininsky, Gail Ann 1956- *WhoAmW 93*
Ginivan, William J. *Law&B 92*
Ginkel, Godert van Reede de 1644-1703 *HarEnMi*
Ginley, Eugene D. *Law&B 92*
Ginley, Thomas J. 1938- *WhoAm 92*
Ginman, Peter John 1937- *WhoUN 92*
Ginn, Alexis *Law&B 92*
Ginn, Anna M. 1950- *St&PR 93*
Ginn, Connie Mardean 1951- *WhoEmL 93, WhoSSW 93, WhoWor 93*
Ginn, David K. 1946- *St&PR 93*
Ginn, David Kendall *Law&B 92*
Ginn, John Arthur 1918- *WhoSSW 93*
Ginn, John Charles 1937- *WhoAm 92, WhoWor 93*
Ginn, Robert Jay, Jr. 1946- *WhoE 93*
Ginn, Robert M. 1924- *St&PR 93*
Ginn, Robert Martin 1924- *WhoAm 92*
Ginn, Ronn 1933- *WhoAm 92*
Ginn, Sam 1937- *St&PR 93*
Ginn, Sam L. 1937- *WhoAm 92*
Ginn, Susan B. 1950- *WhoAmW 93*
Ginn, Walter Pope 1948- *WhoAm 92*
Ginn, William Denton 1923- *St&PR 93*
Ginna, William L., Jr. 1952- *St&PR 93*
Ginnard, Charles Raymond 1947- *WhoE 93*
Ginnetti, John P. 1945- *WhoIns 93*
Ginniff, M.E. *WhoScE 91-1*
Ginocchio, R. *WhoScE 91-2*
Ginorio, Angela Beatriz 1947- *WhoAmW 93*
Ginorio, Beatriz Angela 1947- *HispAmA*
Ginoux, Jean 1925- *WhoScE 91-2*
Ginsberg, Allen 1926- *BioIn 17, MagSAmL [port], ScF&FL 92, WhoAm 92, WhoE 93, WhoWor 93, WhoWrEP 92, WorLitC [port]*
Ginsberg, Barbara W. 1941- *WhoAmW 93*
Ginsberg, Barry Howard 1945- *WhoAm 92*
Ginsberg, Benjamin 1923- *St&PR 93*
Ginsberg, Benjamin 1947- *WhoE 93, WhoEmL 93*
Ginsberg, Daniel R. d1991 *BioIn 17*
Ginsberg, David Lawrence 1932- *WhoAm 92*
Ginsberg, David Mark 1946- *St&PR 93*
Ginsberg, Edward 1917- *WhoAm 92, WhoWor 93*
Ginsberg, Ernest 1931- *St&PR 93, WhoAm 92*
Ginsberg, Errol 1956- *St&PR 93*
Ginsberg, Frank Charles 1944- *WhoAm 92*
Ginsberg, George L. 1935-1991 *BioIn 17*
Ginsberg, Harold Louis 1903-1990 *BioIn 17*
Ginsberg, Harold Samuel 1917- *WhoAm 92, WhoE 93*
Ginsberg, Harry 1888-1991 *BioIn 17*
Ginsberg, Harvey 1930- *St&PR 93*
Ginsberg, Harvey Slom 1930- *WhoAm 92*
Ginsberg, Hersh Meier 1928- *WhoAm 92*
Ginsberg, Ira M. 1952- *St&PR 93*
Ginsberg, Jeffrey Scott 1962- *WhoEmL 93*
Ginsberg, Lawrence N. *Law&B 92*
Ginsberg, Leon Herman 1936- *WhoAm 92, WhoSSW 93*
Ginsberg, Lewis Robbins 1932- *WhoAm 92*
Ginsberg, Marilyn Kaplan 1952- *WhoAm 92*
Ginsberg, Mark Alan 1944- *WhoE 93*
Ginsberg, Milton Moses *MiSFD 9*
Ginsberg, Morris d1990 *BioIn 17*
Ginsberg, Morton A. 1919- *St&PR 93*
Ginsberg, Myron 1943- *WhoWor 93*
Ginsberg, Myron David 1939- *WhoAm 92*
Ginsberg, Phillip Carl 1954- *WhoE 93*
Ginsberg, Richard Frank 1958- *WhoAm 92*
Ginsberg, Riva Jill *St&PR 93*
Ginsberg, Robert *Law&B 92*
Ginsberg, Robert I. 1933- *St&PR 93*
Ginsberg, Ronald Lawrence 1947- *WhoEmL 93*
Ginsberg, Seymour 1931- *St&PR 93*
Ginsberg, Steven *St&PR 93*
Ginsberg, Susan Karelitz 1931-1991 *BioIn 17*
Ginsberg, Will Bruce 1944- *St&PR 93*
Ginsberg-Fellner, Fredda 1937- *WhoAm 92, WhoAmW 93*
Ginsburg, Amy Judith *Law&B 92*
Ginsburg, Ann 1932- *WhoAm 92*
Ginsburg, Barry *St&PR 93*
Ginsburg, Carl S. 1936- *WhoWrEP 92*
Ginsburg, Carol Linda 1943- *WhoAmW 93*
Ginsburg, Charles David 1912- *WhoAm 92*
Ginsburg, Charles P. d1992 *NewYTBS 92 [port]*
Ginsburg, Charles Pauson 1920-1992 *BioIn 17*
Ginsburg, Christian D. 1831-1914 *PolBiDi*
Ginsburg, Dana J. *Law&B 92*
Ginsburg, Daniel Evan 1956- *WhoAm 92*
Ginsburg, David 1952- *WhoAm 92*
Ginsburg, David Monroe 1930- *St&PR 93*
Ginsburg, Douglas Howard 1946- *CngDr 91, OxCSupC, WhoAm 92, WhoE 93*
Ginsburg, Ellin Louis *WhoAm 92*
Ginsburg, Gerald J. 1930- *WhoAm 92*
Ginsburg, Harold Heilbron 1951- *WhoSSW 93*
Ginsburg, Iona Horowitz 1931- *WhoAm 92*
Ginsburg, Lee Robert 1942- *WhoE 93*
Ginsburg, Leonard 1927- *WhoScE 91-2*
Ginsburg, Lev 1907-1981 *Baker 92*
Ginsburg, Marcus 1915- *WhoAm 92*
Ginsburg, Martin David 1932- *WhoAm 92*
Ginsburg, Mirra 1919- *ScF&FL 92*
Ginsburg, Moe d1992 *NewYTBS 92*
Ginsburg, Norton Sydney 1921- *WhoAm 92*
Ginsburg, Paul Howard *Law&B 92*
Ginsburg, Roy Allen d1992 *NewYTBS 92*
Ginsburg, Roy S. *Law&B 92*
Ginsburg, Ruth Bader 1933- *CngDr 91, WhoAm 92, WhoE 93*
Ginsburg, Semion 1901- *Baker 92*
Ginsburg, Seymour 1927- *WhoAm 92*
Ginsburg, Sigmund G. 1937- *WhoAm 92, WhoE 93*
Ginsburg, William S. *Law&B 92*
Ginsburgh, Alice R. L. *Law&B 92*
Ginsburgh, Brook 1942- *WhoE 93*
Ginsburgh, Robert N. d1992 *NewYTBS 92*
Ginsburgh, Robert N. 1923-1992 *BioIn 17*
Ginsky, Marvin H. *Law&B 92*
Ginsky, Marvin H. 1930- *St&PR 93, WhoAm 92*
Ginsztler, Janos 1943- *WhoScE 91-4*
Gintautas, Jonas 1938- *WhoE 93*
Gintel, Oliver d1991 *BioIn 17*
Gintel, Robert M. 1928- *St&PR 93*
Ginter, Catherine O'Connor 1960- *WhoAmW 93*
Ginter, Evelyn 1932- *WhoAmW 93*
Ginter, James Lee 1945- *WhoAm 92*
Ginter, Melba Arlene 1933- *WhoAmW 93*
Ginter, Valerian Alexius 1939- *WhoE 93, WhoWor 93*
Ginther, Larua Jeanne 1958- *WhoE 93*
Ginther, Richie *BioIn 17*
Gintis, Daniel 1923- *WhoSSW 93*
Gintis, Herbert *BioIn 17*
Gintoft, Ethel Margaret *WhoAmW 93*
Ginty, Robert *MiSFD 9*
Gintz, Lynda Kathryn 1949- *WhoEmL 93*
Ginwala, Kymus 1931- *St&PR 93, WhoAm 92*
Ginzberg, Asher 1856-1927 *BioIn 17*
Ginzberg, Eli 1911- *WhoAm 92*
Ginzberg, Louis 1873-1953 *JeAmHC*
Ginzburg, Carlo 1939- *BioIn 17*
Ginzburg, Lidiia 1902-1990 *BioIn 17*
Ginzburg, Natalia *BioIn 17*
Ginzburg, Natalia 1916-1991 *AnObit 1991, ConLC 70 [port]*
Ginzburg, Ralph 1929- *WhoAm 92, WhoWrEP 92*
Ginzburg, Yankel 1945- *WhoAm 92*
Ginzel, Roland 1921- *WhoE 93*
Ginzinger, Wolfgang *WhoScE 91-4*
Ginzton, Edward L. 1915- *St&PR 93*
Ginzton, Edward Leonard 1915- *WhoAm 92*
Gioannini, Theresa Lee 1949- *WhoEmL 93*
Giobbi, Chambliss Martino 1963- *WhoE 93*
Giobbi, Edward Giacchino 1926- *WhoAm 92*
Giocondi, Gino J. 1931- *WhoAm 92*
Gioello, Debbie Ann 1935- *WhoE 93*
Gioffre, Joseph D. 1943- *St&PR 93, WhoE 93*
Gioffre, Michael J. *Law&B 92*
Gioia, Anthony 1948- *St&PR 93*
Gioia, Dana *BioIn 17*
Gioia, (Michael) Dana 1950- *DcLB 120 [port], WhoWrEP 92*
Gioia, Lisa Ann 1959- *WhoAmW 93*
Gioia, Vito 1947- *WhoWor 93*
Gioiella, Russell Michael 1954- *WhoE 93*
Gioiosa, Tommy *BioIn 17*
Gioioso, Joseph 1942- *St&PR 93*
Gioioso, Joseph Vincent 1939- *WhoWor 93*
Gioka, Tina P. 1936- *WhoWor 93*
Giolito, Julie D. *St&PR 93*
Giolitti, Giovanni 1842-1928 *DcTwHis*
Giometti, Paul Francis 1936- *St&PR 93*
Gionfriddo, Paul 1953- *WhoE 93*
Giono, Jean 1895-1970 *BioIn 17*
Gionta, Tom *St&PR 93*
Gior, Fino 1936- *WhoE 93*
Giorcelli, Achille 1956- *WhoScE 91-3*
Giordan, Andre Jean Pierre Henri 1946- *WhoWor 93*
Giordani, Giuseppe 1743-1798 *Baker 92*
Giordani, John E. 1942- *St&PR 93*
Giordani, Tommaso c. 1730-1806 *Baker 92*
Giordano, Andrew 1932- *St&PR 93*
Giordano, Andrew Anthony 1932- *WhoAm 92*
Giordano, Anthony Bruno 1915- *WhoAm 92*
Giordano, Anthony Daniel 1948- *WhoEmL 93*
Giordano, Antoinette R. 1948- *WhoEmL 93*
Giordano, Arthur Anthony 1941- *WhoE 93*
Giordano, August Thomas 1923- *WhoAm 92*
Giordano, David Alfred 1930- *WhoSSW 93*
Giordano, Donald A. 1932- *St&PR 93*
Giordano, E. Lynn *WhoAm 92*
Giordano, Gene Vincent 1953- *St&PR 93*
Giordano, Gerard Ralph 1950- *St&PR 93*
Giordano, Giulio 1927- *WhoScE 91-3*
Giordano, Giuseppe Giulio 1922- *WhoScE 91-3*
Giordano, Italo *WhoScE 91-3*
Giordano, John Read 1937- *WhoAm 92*
Giordano, John Vincent 1951- *St&PR 93*
Giordano, Joseph 1932- *St&PR 93*
Giordano, Joseph Anthony 1948- *WhoWor 93*
Giordano, Joseph Francis 1932-1990 *BioIn 17*
Giordano, Kevin Henry *Law&B 92*
Giordano, Luca 1632-1705 *BioIn 17*
Giordano, Mario 1923- *WhoScE 91-3*
Giordano, Michael Francis 1943- *St&PR 93*
Giordano, Michele Cardinal 1930- *WhoWor 93*
Giordano, Nicholas Anthony 1943- *St&PR 93, WhoAm 92*
Giordano, Nicola *WhoScE 91-3*
Giordano, Patricia Schoppe 1947- *WhoAmW 93, WhoE 93, WhoEmL 93*
Giordano, Paul John 1931- *St&PR 93*
Giordano, Philip John 1947- *St&PR 93*
Giordano, Ralph J. *St&PR 93*
Giordano, Ray *Law&B 92*
Giordano, Richard V. 1934- *St&PR 93*
Giordano, Richard Vincent 1934- *WhoAm 92, WhoE 93, WhoWor 93*
Giordano, Robert J. 1956- *St&PR 93*
Giordano, Robert R. 1938- *St&PR 93*
Giordano, Rose Ann 1938- *WhoAm 92, WhoAmW 93*
Giordano, Salvatore 1910- *St&PR 93*
Giordano, Salvatore, Sr. 1910- *WhoAm 92*
Giordano, Salvatore, Jr. 1938- *St&PR 93, WhoAm 92*
Giordano, Saverio P. *WhoAm 92*
Giordano, Serafino 1936- *WhoE 93*
Giordano, Teresa Ann 1962- *WhoAmW 93*
Giordano, Tommaso c. 1733-1806 *OxDcOp*
Giordano, Tony 1939- *WhoAm 92*
Giordano, Umberto 1867-1948 *Baker 92, BioIn 17, IntDcOp, OxDcOp*
Giordano, Vincent *Law&B 92*
Giordano, Vincent S., Jr. 1946- *St&PR 93*
Giordano-Echegoyen, Diego O. *Law&B 92*
Giordano-McCanless, Angela Maria 1965- *WhoAmW 93*
Giorgi, Elsie Agnes 1911- *WhoAm 92, WhoAmW 93*
Giorgi, Teresa *OxDcOp*
Giorgianni, Albert J. 1945- *St&PR 93*
Giorgi-Banti, Brigida c. 1756-1806 *OxDcOp*
Giorgio, Robert J. 1949- *St&PR 93*
Giorgi-Righetti, Geltrude 1793-1862 *OxDcOp*
Giorloff, Ruth *AmWomPl*
Giorni, Aurelio 1895-1938 *Baker 92*
Giornovichi, Giovanni Mane c. 1735-1804 *Baker 92*
Giorza, Paolo 1832-1914 *Baker 92*
Gioseffi, Daniela 1941- *WhoAmW 93, WhoWrEP 92*
Gioseffi, Linda M. 1950- *St&PR 93*
Giovacchini, Peter Louis 1922- *WhoAm 92*
Giovacchini, Robert Peter 1928- *St&PR 93, WhoAm 92*
Giovagnotti, Celso 1925- *WhoScE 91-3*
Giovanelli, Riccardo 1946- *WhoAm 92*
Giovanisci, Stephen J. 1936- *St&PR 93*
Giovannelli, Ruggiero c. 1560-1625 *Baker 92*
Giovannetti, Sergio Giovanni 1924- *WhoScE 91-3*
Giovanni, Nikki *BioIn 17*
Giovanni, Nikki 1943- *BlkAuII 92, EncAACR, MagSAmL [port], MajAI [port], WhoAm 92, WhoAmW 93, WhoWrEP 92*
Giovanni, Paul d1990 *BioIn 17*
Giovanni Agostino, da Lodi fl. c. 1500- *BioIn 17*
Giovanni da Cascia fl. 14th cent.- *Baker 92*
Giovanni de Florentia fl. 14th cent.- *Baker 92*
Giovannini, Giovanni *WhoWrEP 92*
Giovannitti, Len d1992 *BioIn 17, NewYTBS 92*
Giovannitti, Len 1920-1992 *ConAu 137*
Giovannucci, Daniel L. 1919- *St&PR 93*
Giovannucci, Livia A. 1922- *St&PR 93*
Giove, Barbara Ann Jean 1954- *WhoEmL 93*
Giove, Robert John 1923- *St&PR 93*
Giovenco, John V. 1936- *St&PR 93*
Giovi, Lawrence A. 1923- *St&PR 93*
Giovinazzo, Paul Thomas 1957- *WhoEmL 93*
Gipe, George 1933-1986 *ScF&FL 92*
Gipps, Ruth (Dorothy Louisa) 1921- *Baker 92*
Gips, Edward U. 1922- *WhoAm 92*
Gips, Walter Fuld, Jr. 1920- *WhoAm 92, WhoE 93*
Gipson, Angela Christina 1954- *WhoWrEP 92*
Gipson, David G. 1946- *St&PR 93*
Gipson, Fred(erick Benjamin) 1908-1973 *MajAI [port]*
Gipson, Gordon 1914- *St&PR 93, WhoAm 92, WhoWrEP 92*
Gipson, Hayward R., Jr. 1945- *St&PR 93*
Gipson, Ilene Kay 1944- *WhoAmW 93*
Gipson, Jeffery 1922- *WhoSSW 93*
Gipson, Ray A. *Law&B 92*
Gipson, Robert M. 1939- *St&PR 93*
Gipson, Robert Malone 1939- *WhoAm 92*
Gipson, Steve 1950- *WhoSSW 93*
Gipson, Victor L. *BioIn 17*
Gipstein, Milton Fivenson 1951- *WhoEmL 93*
Gipsy Kings, The *ConMus 8 [port]*
Gira, Catherine Russell 1932- *WhoAm 92, WhoAmW 93*
Giradelli, Marc *BioIn 17*
Giraldi, Bob *MiSFD 9*
Giraldi, Robert Nicholas 1939- *WhoAm 92*
Giraldi, Tullio 1944- *WhoScE 91-3*
Giraldoni, Eugenio 1871-1924 *Baker 92, OxDcOp*
Giraldoni, Leone 1824-1897 *Baker 92, OxDcOp*
Girard, Andrea Eaton 1946- *WhoAmW 93, WhoEmL 93*

Girard, Ann Olson Law&B 92
Girard, Annabel Sisk 1940- WhoSSW 93
Girard, Bernard 1930- MiSFD 9
Girard, Donald M. 1958- St&PR 93
Girard, Dorothy Rosenthal 1920- St&PR 93
Girard, Edward William 1930- WhoSSW 93
Girard, Fernand St&PR 93
Girard, Francis E. 1939- St&PR 93
Girard, Helene-Marie Law&B 92
Girard, James Emery 1945- WhoAm 92
Girard, James Preston 1944- WhoWrEP 92
Girard, James R. St&PR 93
Girard, Jean Raymond 1942- WhoScE 91-2
Girard, Jeffrey Charles 1947- St&PR 93
Girard, Jurg R. 1935- WhoScE 91-4
Girard, Kenneth ScF&FL 92
Girard, Leonard A. Law&B 92
Girard, Leonard A. 1942- St&PR 93
Girard, Leonard Arthur 1942- WhoAm 92
Girard, Louis Joseph 1919- WhoAm 92
Girard, Luke N. 1951- St&PR 93
Girard, Marc 1936- WhoScE 91-2
Girard, Marc Paul 1955- WhoWor 93
Girard, Margaret F. Law&B 92
Girard, Michel 1939- WhoScE 91-2
Girard, Nettabell 1938- WhoAm 92, WhoAmW 93
Girard, Rene Noel 1923- WhoAm 92
Girard, Rodolphe 1879-1956 BioIn 17
Girard, Salli WhoWrEP 92
Girardeau, Marvin Denham 1930- WhoAm 92
Girardi, Laurence Leonard 1953- WhoEmL 93
Girardi, Lisa Florio 1963- WhoE 93
Girardi, Vicente Antonio Vitorio 1938- WhoWor 93
Girardier, Lucien 1929- WhoScE 91-4
Girardin, Carol Erickson 1957- St&PR 93
Girardin, Delphine de 1804-1855 BioIn 17
Girardot, Annie 1931- IntDcF 2-3 [port]
Giraud, Fiorello 1870-1928 Baker 92, OxDcOp
Giraud, Francis Edmond Paul M. 1932- WhoScE 91-2
Giraud, Henri 1879-1949 BioIn 17
Giraud, Ludovico 1846-1882 OxDcOp
Giraud, Raymond Dorner 1920- WhoAm 92
Giraudet, Alfred-Auguste 1845-1911 Baker 92
Giraudet, Michele 1945- WhoWor 93
Giraudier, Antonio 1926- WhoE 93
Giraudoux, Jean 1882-1944 ScF&FL 92
Girault, Suzanne 1882-1973 BioIn 17
Giraux, Jean-Jacques Edmond 1951- WhoWor 93
Giray, Safa 1931- WhoWor 93
Girden, Eugene Lawrence 1930- WhoAm 92, WhoWor 93
Girdler, Ronald William 1930- WhoWor 93
Girdlestone, Brian A. 1933- St&PR 93
Girdlestone, Cuthbert (Morton) 1895-1975 Baker 92
Girdley, James D. 1931- WhoSSW 93
Girdwood, William John 1936- St&PR 93
Gire, Sharon Lee 1944- WhoAmW 93
Giresi, Mark A. Law&B 92
Girga, Barbara Ann 1937- WhoAmW 93
Girgulis, J.D. Law&B 92
Girgus, Joan Stern 1942- WhoAm 92, WhoAmW 93
Giri, Rudra Shanker 1932- WhoUN 92
Giridhar, Garimella 1945- WhoWor 93
Giridharadas, Shyam 1951- WhoWor 93
Girimaji, Sharath Subbarao 1960- WhoSSW 93
Girkins, David R. 1951- St&PR 93
Girko, Vyacheslav Leonidovich 1946- WhoWor 93
Girle, Roderic Allen 1938- WhoWor 93
Girling, Peter Michael 1937- WhoE 93
Girling, Robert George William, III 1929- WhoWor 93
Giro, Gabriele 1941- WhoScE 91-3
Giro, Manuel 1848-1916 Baker 92
Girod, Bernard A. 1942- St&PR 93
Girod, Christian 1930- WhoScE 91-2
Girod, Frank Paul 1908- WhoWor 93
Girod, Roger 1921- WhoWor 93
Girodias, Maurice d1990 BioIn 17
Girolami, Antonio 1931- WhoScE 91-3
Girolami, James Paul 1953- WhoE 93
Girolami, Lisa S. 1960- WhoAmW 93
Girolamo, Maryanne M. 1945- WhoAm 92
Giron, Andres DcCPCAm
Girona y Agrafel, Manuel 1818-1905 BioIn 17
Girondo, Oliverio 1891-1967 SpAmA
Girone, Joan Christine Cruse 1927- WhoAmW 93
Girone, Maria Elena 1939- HispAmA
Girone, Vito Anthony 1910- WhoAm 92
Gironta, Michael 1941- St&PR 93
Girotti, Stefano 1950- WhoWor 93
Girouard, Ken BioIn 17
Girouard, Mark 1931- BioIn 17
Girouard, Peggy Jo Fulcher 1933- WhoSSW 93
Girouard, Pierre 1953- WhoWor 93
Girouard, Shirley Ann 1947- WhoEmL 93
Giroud, Francoise 1916- BioIn 17, ConAu 39NR
Giroud, Jean-Paul 1936- WhoScE 91-2
Giroult, Eric J.R. 1936- WhoUN 92
Giroux, Jacques J. 1934- WhoScE 91-2
Giroux, Leo, Jr. ScF&FL 92
Giroux, Michel R. 1946- WhoUN 92
Giroux, Richard Leonard 1945- St&PR 93
Giroux, Robert 1914- WhoAm 92
Giroux, Robert-Jean-Yvon 1939- WhoAm 92
Giroux, Stanley C. 1921- St&PR 93
Giroux, Stephen M. Law&B 92
Girsh, Faye Joan 1933- WhoAmW 93
Girsky, Joel H. 1939- St&PR 93
Girth, Marjorie Louisa 1939- WhoAm 92
Girton, Jack C. 1935- St&PR 93
Girton, Richard A., Jr. 1941- St&PR 93
Girty, Simon 1741-1818 HarEnMi
Girvan, Brian J. 1955- St&PR 93
Girvigian, Raymond 1926- WhoAm 92
Girvin, Eb Carl 1917- WhoAm 92
Girvin, Gerald Thomas 1929- WhoE 93
Girvin, John Warren, Jr. Law&B 92
Girvin, Tim BioIn 17
Girzone, Joseph F. 1930- ScF&FL 92
Gisbert-Calabuig, Juan Antonio 1922- WhoScE 91-3
Giscard d'Estaing, Valery 1926- BioIn 17, ColdWar 1 [port], DcTwHis
Gisch, Gary Raymond 1954- WhoSSW 93
Gish, Alan 1941- St&PR 93
Gish, Annabeth BioIn 17
Gish, Edward Rutledge 1908- WhoWor 93
Gish, Glenwood Littleton 1931- St&PR 93
Gish, Lillian WhoAm 92, WhoAmW 93
Gish, Lillian 1896?- BioIn 17, IntDcF 2-3 [port]
Gish, Norman Richard 1935- WhoAm 92
Gisi, David 1950- WhoE 93
Gisi, John Joseph 1945- WhoAm 92
Gislason, Eric Arni 1940- WhoAm 92
Gislason, Scott Hewitt Law&B 92
Gislason, Thorsteinn 1947- St&PR 93, WhoScE 91-4
Gisler, Richard F. Law&B 92
Gismondi, Paul Arthur 1955- WhoWor 93
Gisoldi, Antoinette Mary 1944- WhoAmW 93
Gisolf, Aart Cornelis 1937- WhoWor 93
Gisolfi, Anthony Maria 1909- WhoE 93
Gisolfi, Peter Anthony 1944- WhoAm 92
Gisolfi Pechukas, Diana 1940- WhoE 93
Gispanski, Joseph Anthony, Jr. 1965- WhoE 93
Giss, Vernon J. 1909- St&PR 93
Gisser, Rivka 1939- St&PR 93
Gissing, Bruce 1931- WhoAm 92
Gissing, George 1857-1903 TwCLC 47 [port]
Gissing, George Robert 1857-1903 BioIn 17
Gissing, Scott Richard 1963- WhoEmL 93
Gissler, Sigvard G. 1935- St&PR 93
Gissler, Sigvard Gunnar, Jr. 1935- WhoAm 92
Gist, Carole BioIn 17
Gist, Howard Battle, Jr. 1919- WhoAm 92
Gist, Michael A. Law&B 92
Gistelinck, Elias 1935- Baker 92
Gistenson, Donald E. 1932- St&PR 93
Gisvold, Sven Erik 1944- WhoScE 91-4
Gitai, Amos MiSFD 9
Giteck, Janice 1946- Baker 92
Gitelle, Elisabeth Ann 1962- WhoAmW 93
Gitelson, Susan Aurelia WhoWor 93
Gitera, Kya Kaysire 1939- WhoUN 92
Gitin, Herbert M. 1931- St&PR 93
Gitin, Teresa Angel 1957- WhoAmW 93
Gitler, Bernard 1950- WhoEmL 93
Gitler, Samuel 1933- WhoAm 92
Gitlin, Lewis D. Law&B 92
Gitlin, Michael 1943- WhoE 93
Gitlin, Todd 1943- WhoWrEP 92
Gitlis, Ivry 1922- Baker 92
Gitlitz, David Martin 1942- WhoAm 92
Gitlow, Abraham Leo 1918- WhoAm 92
Gitlow, Herman S. 1918- St&PR 93
Gitner, Deanne 1944- WhoAm 92, WhoAmW 93
Gitner, Fred Jay 1951- WhoEmL 93
Gitner, Gerald L. 1945- WhoAm 92
Gits, John Robert 1933- St&PR 93
Gitsch, Eduard 1920- WhoScE 91-4
Gitt, Werner 1937- WhoScE 91-3
Gittell, Ross Jacobs 1957- WhoE 93
Gittelman, Donald Henry 1929- WhoSSW 93
Gittelman, Marc Jeffrey 1947- St&PR 93, WhoAm 92
Gittelman, Martin 1930- WhoE 93
Gittelsohn, John Edelsohn 1955- WhoSSW 93
Gittelson, Abraham Jacob 1928- WhoSSW 93
Gittelson, Bernard 1918- WhoAm 92
Gittelson, Natalie Leavy 1929- WhoWrEP 92
Gittens, Gerald James 1935- WhoScE 91-1
Gitter, Max 1943- WhoAm 92
Gitterman, Alex WhoAm 92, WhoE 93
Gitterman, Joseph L., III 1936- St&PR 93
Gittes, Ruben Foster 1934- WhoAm 92, WhoWor 93
Gittess, Ronald Marvin 1937- WhoSSW 93
Gittinger, Paul Allen 1959- St&PR 93
Gittings, J.B. 1927- St&PR 93
Gittings, Robert (William Victor) 1911-1992 ConAu 136, SmATA 70
Gittins, Dafydd BioIn 17
Gittins, Deanna Christine 1957- WhoEmL 93
Gittleman, Sol 1934- WhoAm 92
Gittler, Joseph Bertram 1912- WhoAm 92
Gittler, Steven 1926- WhoE 93
Gittler, Sydney d1991 BioIn 17
Gittlin, Arthur Sam 1914- WhoAm 92, WhoE 93
Gittlin, B. Morton 1922- St&PR 93
Gittman, Betty 1945- WhoAmW 93
Giua, John Richard 1952- St&PR 93
Giua, P.E. WhoScE 91-3
Giudice, Giovanni 1933- WhoScE 91-3
Giudice, Giovanni Giuseppe 1933- WhoWor 93
Giudici, Giovanni 1924- DcLB 128 [port]
Giuffre, Jimmy 1921- Baker 92
Giuffre, Victor M. 1955- St&PR 93
Giuffrida, Tom A. 1946- WhoAm 92
Giuggio, John P. Law&B 92
Giuggio, John Peter 1930- St&PR 93, WhoAm 92
Giugiaro, Giorgetto BioIn 17
Giugliano, Margaret Law&B 92
Giuglini, Antonio 1827-1865 Baker 92
Giuli, Dino 1946- WhoScE 91-3
Giuliani, Alan V. 1946- St&PR 93
Giuliani, Albert H. 1922- St&PR 93
Giuliani, Alfredo 1924- DcLB 128
Giuliani, Jean-Francois 1938- WhoUN 92
Giuliani, Joseph Carl 1931- WhoAm 92
Giuliani, Luciano 1928- WhoWor 93
Giuliani, Mauro 1781-1829 Baker 92
Giuliani, Peter 1907- WhoE 93
Giuliani, Rudolph W. BioIn 17
Giuliani, Rudolph W. 1944- WhoAm 92, WhoE 93
Giuliano, Sebastian R. 1931- St&PR 93
Giulianti, Mara Selena 1944- WhoAm 92, WhoAmW 93
Giulii, Joseph N. 1930- St&PR 93
Giulini, Carlo Maria 1914- Baker 92, OxDcOp, WhoWor 93
Giulini, Carol Maria 1914- IntDcOp [port]
Giulini, Giorgio 1716-1780 Baker 92
Giulio, Ludovico 1926- WhoScE 91-3
Giumarra, John George, Jr. 1940- St&PR 93
Giumond, Lucy Law&B 92
Giunta, Mary 1962- WhoAmW 93
Giunta-Mange, Anita Diane 1960- WhoAmW 93, WhoE 93
Giuntini, Peter A. Law&B 92
Giurca, Voicu 1931- WhoScE 91-4
Giuriceo, Anthony Joseph Law&B 92
Giurickovic Simili, Pietro Silvestro 1952- WhoWor 93
Gius, Julius 1911- WhoAm 92
Giuseppetti, Gabriella 1945- WhoScE 91-3
Giuseppetti, Giuseppe 1923- WhoScE 91-3
Giusfredi, Giovanni 1950- WhoScE 91-3
Giusiana, Michele A. Law&B 92
Giussani, Pablo d1991 BioIn 17
Giusti, Gino Paul 1927- St&PR 93, WhoAm 92
Giusti, Girolamo Aloise d1766? OxDcOp
Giusti, Giuseppe 1929- WhoScE 91-3
Giusti, Giusto 1941- WhoScE 91-3
Giusti, Joseph Paul 1935- WhoAm 92
Giusti, Robert George 1937- WhoAm 92
Giusti, Susan Marie 1970- WhoAmW 93
Giustina, Daniel Della- BioIn 17
Giustini, Lodovico 1685-1743 Baker 92
Giustiniani Longo, Giovanni d1453 OxDcByz
Giusto, Joel 1954- St&PR 93
Giusto, Thomas Michael 1953- WhoEmL 93
Giustozzi, Corrado 1959- WhoWor 93
Giuttari, Theodore R. Law&B 92
Givan, Boyd Eugene WhoAm 92
Givan, Richard Martin 1921- WhoAm 92
Givant, Philip Joachim 1935- WhoWor 93
Givaudan, Ben Trested, III 1936- WhoAm 92
Givelber, Daniel James 1940- WhoAm 92
Given, Cecil A. 1946- St&PR 93
Given, H.F. 1943- WhoScE 91-3
Given, Kenna Sidney 1938- WhoAm 92, WhoSSW 93
Given, S. Perry, Jr. Law&B 92
Givenchy 1927- WhoAm 92, WhoWor 93
Givenchy, Hubert de BioIn 17
Givens, Charles J. BioIn 17
Givens, Craig Lee 1949- St&PR 93, WhoEmL 93
Givens, D.I. WhoScE 91-1
Givens, David Ian 1948- WhoScE 91-1
Givens, David W. 1932- St&PR 93, WhoAm 92
Givens, Donna Neal 1947- WhoAm 92
Givens, Helen M. AmWomPl
Givens, Hurtis Lynn 1953- WhoSSW 93
Givens, Jack Rodman 1928- WhoSSW 93, WhoWor 93
Givens, Janet E. 1921-1990 BioIn 17
Givens, Janet Eaton 1932- WhoAmW 93, WhoE 93
Givens, John Kenneth 1940- WhoAm 92
Givens, Paul Edward 1934- WhoAm 92, WhoSSW 93
Givens, Paul Ronald 1923- WhoAm 92
Givens, Randy BlkAmWO
Givens, Robin BioIn 17, WhoAm 92
Givens, Robin 1964?- ConTFT 10
Givens, Robin 1965- ConBlB 4 [port]
Givens, Stephen Bruce 1941- St&PR 93
Givens, Walter Phillip 1941- St&PR 93
Givens, William Phillip 1914- St&PR 93
Giverink, Jack E. 1931- St&PR 93
Givins, Genevieve AmWomPl
Givler, Michael E. 1955- St&PR 93
Givner, Joan 1936- WhoCanL 92
Givon, Bernd Shlomo 1932- WhoWor 93
Giwa, Lateef Olakunle 1943- WhoE 93
Giza, David A. Law&B 92
Gizinski, Gerard Howard 1944- WhoWor 93
Gizis, Evangelos John 1934- WhoE 93
Gizziello 1714-1761 OxDcOp
Gjaevenes, Kjell Martin 1937- WhoWor 93
Gjeitnes, Aasmund WhoScE 91-4
Gjelde, Earl E. 1944- St&PR 93
Gjersdal, Henry W., Jr. Law&B 92
Gjertsen, O. Gerard 1932- WhoAm 92
Gjika, Viktor 1937- DrEEuF
Gjorv, Odd E. 1935- WhoScE 91-4
Gjorv, Odd Even 1935- WhoWor 93
Glab, John D. 1917- St&PR 93
Glabas OxDcByz
Glabas, Isidore 1341?-1396 OxDcByz
Glabas, Michael Tarchaneiotes c. 1235-c. 1304 OxDcByz
Glaberson, Cory ScF&FL 92
Glabisz, Urszula Bronislawa 1922- WhoScE 91-4
Glabman, Richard J. 1945- St&PR 93
Glabrio, Manius Acilius fl. 201BC-189BC HarEnMi
Glace, Beth Winifred 1960- WhoEmL 93
Glacel, Barbara Pate 1948- WhoAmW 93, WhoEmL 93, WhoSSW 93
Glacken, Clarence 1909-1989 BioIn 17
Glackens, Ira 1907-1990 BioIn 17
Glacking, Marjorie Joyce Straub 1936- WhoAmW 93
Glad, Edward Newman 1919- WhoAm 92
Glad, John P. 1941- ScF&FL 92
Glad, Lois Gayle 1931- WhoWrEP 92
Glad, Paul Wilbur 1926- WhoAm 92, WhoSSW 93
Glad, Suzanne Lockley 1929- WhoAmW 93, WhoWor 93
Gladchun, Lawrence Law&B 92
Gladchun, Lawrence L. 1950- WhoAm 92
Gladden, Carolan 1935- WhoWrEP 92
Gladden, Joseph R., Jr. 1942- St&PR 93
Gladden, Joseph Rhea, Jr. Law&B 92
Gladden, Joseph Rhea, Jr. 1942- WhoAm 92, WhoSSW 93
Gladden, Roger Dennes 1945- WhoAm 92
Gladden, Washington 1836-1918 BioIn 17
Gladding, Everett Bushnell 1917- WhoSSW 93
Gladding, Samuel Templeman 1945- WhoSSW 93
Gladding, Walter St. G. 1936- St&PR 93
Glade, John Frederick 1943- St&PR 93
Glade, William Patton, Jr. 1929- WhoAm 92
Gladem, Martin D. 1923- St&PR 93
Glader, Mats Lennart 1945- WhoWor 93
Gladfelter, Phillip E. Law&B 92
Gladfelter, Suzanne Elaine 1950- WhoAmW 93
Gladhill, T. Sue 1952- WhoAmW 93
Gladieux, Bernard Louis 1907- WhoAm 92
Gladieux, Persis Emma d1991 BioIn 17
Gladish, Donald P. 1926- St&PR 93
Gladkin, Peter 1947- WhoE 93
Gladkowska, Konstancja 1810-1889 PolBiDi
Gladman, Jack Craig 1952- WhoSSW 93
Gladney, Heather 1957- ScF&FL 92

Gladstein, Mimi Reisel 1936- ScF&FL 92
Gladstein, Robert d1992 NewYTBS 92
Gladstein, Robert 1943-1992 BioIn 17
Gladstein, Susan P. Law&B 92
Gladstone, David John St&PR 93
Gladstone, Francis Edward 1845-1928 Baker 92
Gladstone, Herbert Jack 1924- WhoAm 92
Gladstone, Karen J. 1940- WhoAmW 93
Gladstone, Kim Diane 1957- WhoAmW 93
Gladstone, Lois A. Law&B 92
Gladstone, Louis I. 1927- St&PR 93
Gladstone, Michael D. Law&B 92
Gladstone, Milton H. d1992 NewYTBS 92
Gladstone, Milton H. 1914-1992 BioIn 17
Gladstone, Milton S. d1991 BioIn 17
Gladstone, Richard Bennett 1924- WhoAm 92
Gladstone, W.E. 1809-1898 BioIn 17
Gladstone, William 1949- WhoEmL 93
Gladstone, William Ewart 1809-1898 BioIn 17
Gladstone, William Louis 1931- WhoAm 92
Gladstone, William Sheldon, Jr. 1923- WhoAm 92
Gladue, Brian Anthony 1950- WhoEmL 93
Gladue, Philip J., Jr. 1930- St&PR 93
Gladue, Rosemary A. Law&B 92
Gladwell, David 1935- MiSFD 9
Gladwell, Graham Maurice Leslie 1934- WhoAm 92
Gladwell, John Stuart 1932- WhoUN 92
Gladwin, Harold Sterling 1883-1983 IntDcAn
Gladysz, Andrzej Wladyslaw 1940- WhoScE 91-4
Gladysz, Martin W. 1952- St&PR 93
Gladysz, Mieczyslaw 1903-1984 IntDcAn
Glaefke, Deborah S. 1956- WhoWrEP 92
Glaeser, Phyllis Sloane 1937- WhoScE 91-2
Glaeser, W. WhoScE 91-2
Glaeser, William St&PR 93
Glaeske, Hans Jurgen 1932- WhoWor 93
Glaessmann, Doris Ann 1940- WhoAmW 93, WhoE 93, WhoWor 93
Glaisner, Kurt F. 1946- St&PR 93
Glakas, Nicholas John Law&B 92
Glamann, Kristof 1923- WhoScE 91-2
Glancy, Alfred R., III 1938- St&PR 93
Glancy, Alfred Robinson, III 1938- WhoAm 92
Glancy, Diane 1941- ConAu 136, WhoWrEP 92
Glancy, Dorothy Jean 1944- WhoAmW 93
Glancy, Michael Lin WhoSSW 93
Glancy, Walter John 1942- WhoAm 92
Glancz, Gary Lewis Law&B 92
Glander, Nancy Lynn 1955- WhoAmW 93
Glander, William J. 1928- St&PR 93
Glang, Gabriele 1959- WhoWrEP 92
Glann, Elizabeth Jane 1934- WhoWrEP 92
Glann, James D. Law&B 92
Glanton, Richard H. 1946- WhoAm 92
Glantz, Gina 1943- WhoAmW 93
Glantz, Margo 1930- DcMexL
Glantz, Miles M. Law&B 92
Glantz, Miles Maurice 1934- St&PR 93
Glantz, Per-Olof J. 1936- WhoScE 91-4
Glantz, Richard G. 1931- St&PR 93
Glantz, Ronald A. 1941- St&PR 93
Glanville, James W. d1992 NewYTBS 92 [port]
Glanville, James William 1923- WhoAm 92
Glanville, Jerry BioIn 17
Glanville, Jerry 1941- WhoAm 92, WhoSSW 93
Glanville-Hicks, Peggy 1912-1990 Baker 92, BioIn 17
Glanz, Barbara Anne 1943- WhoAmW 93
Glanz, Karen 1953- WhoAmW 93
Glanz, Niki Louise 1944- WhoAmW 93
Glanz, Ruth 1928- WhoE 93
Glanzel, Richard Kurt 1944- WhoWor 93
Glapa, Kathlene Macechak 1947- St&PR 93
Glarean, Heinrich 1488-1563 Baker 92
Glareanus, Henricus 1488-1563 Baker 92
Glas, Michel 1950- WhoWor 93
Glasauer, Franz Ernst 1930- WhoAm 92
Glasberg, Herbert Mark 1939- WhoE 93, WhoWor 93
Glasberg, Laurence Brian 1943- WhoAm 92
Glasberg, Meyer Samuel 1916- WhoE 93
Glasberg, Paula Drillman 1939- WhoAm 92, WhoAmW 93, WhoWor 93
Glasby, Ian 1931- WhoWor 93
Glasby, John 1928- ScF&FL 92
Glasco, Joseph Milton 1925- WhoAm 92
Glasco, Kimberly WhoAm 92
Glascock, Anthony Philip, Jr. 1947- WhoEmL 93
Glascock, John Hays 1928- St&PR 93
Glascoe, Rosalyn B. 1944- St&PR 93
Glasenapp, Carl Friedrich 1847-1915 Baker 92
Glaser, Alvin 1932- WhoE 93, WhoWor 93
Glaser, Arthur Henry 1947- WhoEmL 93
Glaser, Bobby Gene 1954- WhoEmL 93
Glaser, Claude Edward, Jr. 1919- WhoAm 92
Glaser, Daniel 1918- WhoAm 92
Glaser, Donald Arthur 1926- WhoAm 92, WhoWor 93
Glaser, Douglas Edward 1951- WhoEmL 93
Glaser, Elizabeth BioIn 17
Glaser, Elizabeth 1947- ConAu 138
Glaser, Elizabeth 1948?- ConHero 2 [port]
Glaser, Felix Herbert 1936- WhoScE 91-3
Glaser, Franz 1798-1861 OxDcOp
Glaser, Franz (Joseph) 1798-1861 Baker 92
Glaser, Gary A. 1944- St&PR 93
Glaser, Gilbert Herbert 1920- WhoAm 92
Glaser, Harold 1924- WhoAm 92
Glaser, Henry J. 1945- St&PR 93
Glaser, Herbert O. 1927- St&PR 93
Glaser, Horst Albert 1935- WhoWor 93
Glaser, Horst Stephan Robert WhoScE 91-3
Glaser, Isabel Joshlin 1929- WhoWrEP 92
Glaser, Jeffrey G. Law&B 92
Glaser, Joseph Bernard 1925- WhoAm 92
Glaser, Joy Harriet 1941- WhoAmW 93
Glaser, Judith Entine 1946- WhoAmW 93, WhoE 93
Glaser, Louis Frederick 1933- WhoAm 92
Glaser, Luis 1932- WhoAm 92
Glaser, Margaret L. St&PR 93
Glaser, Michael Lance 1939- WhoAm 92
Glaser, Michael S. 1943- WhoWrEP 92
Glaser, Michael Schmidt 1943- WhoE 93
Glaser, Milton BioIn 17
Glaser, Milton 1929- WhoAm 92
Glaser, Paul Michael MiSFD 9
Glaser, Paul Russel 1945- WhoE 93
Glaser, Peter Edward 1923- BioIn 17, St&PR 93, WhoAm 92
Glaser, Robert Edward 1935- WhoAm 92
Glaser, Robert Edward 1954- WhoE 93
Glaser, Robert Joy 1918- St&PR 93, WhoAm 92
Glaser, Robert Leonard 1929- WhoAm 92
Glaser, Robert Leonard, Jr. 1960- WhoE 93
Glaser, Robert Vincent 1951- WhoE 93
Glaser, Ronald 1939- WhoAm 92
Glaser, Steven Jay Law&B 92
Glaser, Steven Jay 1957- WhoEmL 93
Glaser, Vera Romans WhoAm 92
Glaser, Werner Wolf 1910- Baker 92
Glaser, William A(rnold) 1925- WhoWrEP 92
Glaser, William Peter 1933- St&PR 93
Glasford, Allan John 1929- WhoAm 92
Glasgall, Franklin 1932- St&PR 93
Glasgold, Alvin I. 1936- WhoE 93
Glasgow, Agnes Jackie 1941- WhoSSW 93
Glasgow, Andrew St&PR 93
Glasgow, Ellen 1873-1945 AmWomWr 92, GayN, MagSAmL [port]
Glasgow, Ellen Anderson Gholson 1873-1945 BioIn 17
Glasgow, Jesse Edward 1923- WhoAm 92
Glasgow, John Michael 1934- WhoAm 92
Glasgow, Robert J. 1942- WhoSSW 93
Glasgow, Thomas William, Jr. 1947- St&PR 93, WhoAm 92
Glasgow, Vaughn Leslie 1944- WhoAm 92
Glasgow, Willene Graythen 1939- WhoAmW 93
Glasgow, William J. 1946- St&PR 93
Glasgow, William Jacob 1946- WhoAm 92
Glasheen, Kevin P. Law&B 92
Glashow, Sheldon Lee 1932- WhoAm 92, WhoE 93, WhoWor 93
Glasier, Alice Geneva 1903- WhoAm 92, WhoWor 93
Glasier, Charles H. 1912- St&PR 93
Glasier, George E. 1944- St&PR 93
Glasier, Katharine St. John Conway Bruce 1867-1950 BioIn 17
Glasier, Robert Allen 1946- WhoSSW 93
Glasier, Susan H. Law&B 92
Glaske, Paule E. 1933- St&PR 93
Glaskey, Susan M. 1960- WhoEmL 93
Glas-Larsson, Margareta 1911- BioIn 17
Glasner, Daniel Mayer 1940- St&PR 93, WhoE 93
Glasner, David 1948- WhoEmL 93
Glasner, Peter E. WhoScE 91-1
Glasner, Sol Y. Law&B 92
Glasow, E. Thomas 1947- WhoE 93
Glaspell, Susan 1876-1948 AmWrS3
Glaspell, Susan 1882-1948 AmWomWr 92, BioIn 17
Glaspell, Susan Keating 1876?-1948 AmWomPl
Glaspie, April BioIn 17
Glass, Alastair Malcolm 1940- WhoAm 92
Glass, Alexander Jacob 1933- WhoAm 92
Glass, Alice 1912?- BioIn 17
Glass, Amanda ConAu 139, ScF&FL 92, WhoWrEP 92
Glass, Andrew James 1935- WhoAm 92
Glass, Barbara B. 1944- St&PR 93
Glass, Benjamin 1911-1991 BioIn 17
Glass, Brent D. 1947- WhoAm 92
Glass, Burton Joel 1945- WhoE 93
Glass, Carson McElyea 1915- WhoAm 92
Glass, Carter 1858-1946 PolPar
Glass, Charles BioIn 17
Glass, Charles 1951- ConAu 139
Glass, Charles Warren 1945- WhoSSW 93
Glass, David Carter 1930- WhoAm 92
Glass, David D. 1935- St&PR 93, WhoAm 92, WhoSSW 93
Glass, David Vaughn 1955- WhoEmL 93
Glass, Deborah E. Law&B 92
Glass, Dennis R. 1949- WhoIns 93
Glass, Diane Law&B 92
Glass, Donald F. Law&B 92
Glass, Elliott Michael 1934- WhoAm 92
Glass, Ernest J., Jr. 1937- St&PR 93
Glass, Ernest Wilson, Jr. 1949- WhoEmL 93
Glass, Frederick Marion 1913- WhoWor 93
Glass, Glen A. Law&B 92
Glass, Harold A. 1919- St&PR 93
Glass, Henry Peter 1911- WhoAm 92
Glass, Herbert 1934- WhoAm 92
Glass, Irvine Israel 1918- WhoAm 92
Glass, J.E. Law&B 92
Glass, James R. 1933- St&PR 93
Glass, James William 1945- WhoSSW 93
Glass, Joanna McClelland 1936- WhoCanL 92
Glass, John Derek 1941- WhoAm 92
Glass, John Sheldon 1936- WhoE 93
Glass, John Thomas 1935- St&PR 93
Glass, Kenneth Edward 1940- WhoWor 93
Glass, Laurel 1923- WhoAm 92
Glass, Louis (Christian August) 1864-1936 Baker 92
Glass, M. Milton 1906- WhoAm 92
Glass, Margaret S. 1946- St&PR 93
Glass, Margaret Smyllie 1946- WhoAm 92, WhoAmW 93
Glass, Mary M. 1952- WhoSSW 93
Glass, Michael 1945- WhoAm 92
Glass, Michael Gwinn 1938- St&PR 93
Glass, Milton Louis 1929- St&PR 93, WhoAm 92
Glass, Molly 1925- WhoWrEP 92
Glass, Paul Jason 1953- WhoSSW 93
Glass, Philip BioIn 17
Glass, Philip 1937- Baker 92, IntDcOp, NewYTBS 92 [port], OxDcOp, WhoAm 92, WhoE 93
Glass, Phyllis Law&B 92
Glass, Robert Davis 1922- WhoAm 92
Glass, Ronald Lee 1946- St&PR 93, WhoAm 92
Glass, Susan J. Law&B 92
Glass, Theodore ScF&FL 92
Glass, Timothy J. 1951- St&PR 93
Glass, Torrey Allen 1952- WhoSSW 93
Glass, Walter 1909- St&PR 93
Glass, Werner Botho 1927- WhoE 93
Glassberg, David St&PR 93
Glassco, John 1909-1981 ScF&FL 92
Glassco, Robert B. 1917- St&PR 93
Glasscock, Larry C. 1948- St&PR 93
Glasscock, Michael Emmanuel, III 1933- WhoAm 92
Glasse, John Howell 1922- WhoAm 92
Glasse, Paul BioIn 17
Glassell, Alfred Curry, Jr. 1913- WhoWor 93
Glassenberg, Albert Bryant 1927- St&PR 93
Glasser, Alan ScF&FL 92
Glasser, Albert 1916- BioIn 17
Glasser, Allen 1918- ScF&FL 92
Glasser, Bernard 1924- BioIn 17
Glasser, Claudina Rose 1947- WhoAmW 93
Glasser, Fredrik Paul WhoScE 91-1
Glasser, Harold A. Law&B 92
Glasser, Herman 1924- St&PR 93
Glasser, Ira 1938- ConAu 137
Glasser, Ira Saul 1938- WhoAm 92
Glasser, Israel Leo 1924- WhoAm 92, WhoE 93
Glasser, James J. 1934- St&PR 93, WhoAm 92
Glasser, John L. St&PR 93
Glasser, Joseph 1925- WhoAm 92
Glasser, Marc Seth 1952- WhoE 93
Glasser, Marvin 1923- St&PR 93
Glasser, Otto John 1918- WhoAm 92
Glasser, Paul Harold 1929- WhoAm 92
Glasser, Perry 1948- WhoWrEP 92
Glasser, Stephen Andrew 1943- WhoE 93
Glasser, Stephen Paul 1940- WhoAm 92
Glasser, Wolfgang Gerhard 1941- WhoSSW 93
Glassett, Tim S. Law&B 92
Glassett, Tim S. 1956- St&PR 93
Glassford, Wilfred ScF&FL 92
Glassgold, Alfred Emanuel 1929- WhoAm 92
Glassgold, I. Leon 1923- WhoAm 92
Glasshagel, Glenn E. 1945- St&PR 93
Glassick, Charles Etzweiler 1931- WhoAm 92
Glassman, Alexander Howard 1934- WhoAm 92
Glassman, Armand Barry 1938- WhoAm 92, WhoSSW 93
Glassman, Bernie BioIn 17
Glassman, Caroline Duby 1922- WhoAm 92, WhoAmW 93
Glassman, Daniel St&PR 93
Glassman, Edward 1929- WhoAm 92
Glassman, Edwina 1939- St&PR 93
Glassman, George Morton 1935- WhoWor 93
Glassman, Gerald Seymour 1932- St&PR 93, WhoAm 92
Glassman, Herbert Haskel 1919- WhoAm 92
Glassman, Howard Theodore 1934- WhoAm 92
Glassman, Iris St&PR 93
Glassman, Irvin 1923- WhoAm 92
Glassman, James Kenneth 1947- WhoAm 92
Glassman, Jerome Martin 1919- WhoAm 92
Glassman, Jon David 1944- WhoAm 92, WhoWor 93
Glassman, Lawrence S. 1953- WhoE 93
Glassman, Marvin 1935- St&PR 93
Glassman, Meryl Linda Corsover 1954- WhoEmL 93
Glassman, Shirley Gloger 1926- WhoAmW 93
Glassmeyer, Edward 1915- WhoAm 92
Glassmeyer, James Milton 1928- WhoWor 93
Glassmoyer, Thomas Parvin 1915- WhoAm 92, WhoE 93
Glassner, Barry 1952- WhoAm 92
Glassock, Richard James 1934- WhoAm 92
Glasson, Jacques J. 1935- St&PR 93
Glasson, John WhoScE 91-1
Glasson, Lloyd 1931- WhoAm 92
Glasspole, Florizel DcCPCAm
Glast, Ben 1912- St&PR 93
Glast, Celia Gellman 1945- St&PR 93
Glast, Robert Joel 1944- St&PR 93
Glastetter, Lori Jean 1958- St&PR 93
Glastonbury, Bryan WhoScE 91-1
Glastris, Carolyn Moses 1960- WhoAmW 93
Glasunov, Igor Sergeevitch 1933- WhoUN 92
Glatfelter, Philip H., III 1916- St&PR 93
Glatfelter, Philip Henry, III 1916- WhoAm 92
Glatis, George W. 1933- WhoE 93
Glatman-Stein, Marcia 1944- WhoAmW 93
Glatt, David Allen 1960- St&PR 93
Glatt, Mitchell Steven 1957- WhoE 93, WhoEmL 93
Glatter, Lesli Linka MiSFD 9
Glattstein, Judy 1942- ConAu 137
Glatz, Herta 1908- Baker 92
Glatzer, Nahum Norbert 1903-1990 BioIn 17
Glatzer, Richard ScF&FL 92
Glatzer, Wolfgang P. W. 1944- WhoWor 93
Glaub, Kathleen Sereda 1953- St&PR 93
Glaubemsklee, Marilyn Law&B 92
Glauber, Michael A. 1943- St&PR 93, WhoAm 92
Glauber, Roy Jay 1925- WhoAm 92
Glauberman, Lionel 1930- St&PR 93
Glauberman, Stuart Craig 1953- St&PR 93
Glaubig, Judith Carol Law&B 92
Glaubinger, Alan 1940- WhoSSW 93
Glaubinger, Lawrence D. 1925- St&PR 93
Glaubinger, Lawrence David 1925- WhoE 93, WhoWor 93
Glauert, Michael Barker WhoScE 91-1
Glauner, Alfred William Law&B 92
Glauner, Alfred William 1936- WhoAm 92
Glausi, Elizabeth d1991 BioIn 17
Glauthier, T. James 1944- WhoAm 92
Glavas, Peggy BioIn 17
Glavickas, Joseph Albert 1939- St&PR 93, WhoAm 92
Glavin, James Edward 1923- WhoAm 92
Glavin, William Francis 1932- WhoAm 92
Glavine, Tom 1966- WhoAm 92

Glavopoulos, Christos Dimitrios 1958- WhoWor 93
Glaz, Edit 1926- WhoScE 91-4
Glaz, Herta 1908- Baker 92
Glaza-Herrington, Linda Law&B 92
Glaze, Eleanor 1930- ScF&FL 92
Glaze, Lynn Ferguson 1933- WhoAmW 93
Glaze, Michael James 1935- WhoWor 93
Glaze, Robert A. 1942- St&PR 93
Glaze, Robert Howe 1952- WhoEmL 93
Glaze, Robert Pinckney 1933- WhoAm 92
Glaze, Thomas A. 1947- St&PR 93
Glaze, Tom 1938- WhoAm 92, WhoSSW 93
Glazebrook, Benjamin Kirkland 1931- WhoWor 93
Glazebrook, Ted James 1956- St&PR 93
Glazek, Stanislaw Dobieslaw 1957- WhoWor 93
Glazer, Anthony Michael WhoScE 91-1
Glazer, Anthony Michael 1943- WhoWor 93
Glazer, Charles Thomas 1951- WhoE 93
Glazer, David 1913- Baker 92
Glazer, David Andrew 1953- WhoE 93
Glazer, Donald Jack 1942- WhoAm 92
Glazer, Donald Wayne 1944- WhoAm 92
Glazer, Esther WhoAm 92
Glazer, Frederic Jay 1937- WhoAm 92, WhoSSW 93
Glazer, H. 1928- St&PR 93
Glazer, Hilda Ruth 1947- WhoSSW 93
Glazer, Ira S. 1937- St&PR 93
Glazer, Jack Henry 1928- WhoWor 93
Glazer, Jennifer A. Law&B 92
Glazer, Jerome Sanford d1991 BioIn 17
Glazer, Jerome Sanford 1929- St&PR 93
Glazer, Laurence Charles 1945- St&PR 93, WhoAm 92
Glazer, Marlene L. Law&B 92
Glazer, Mary Kay 1959- WhoAmW 93
Glazer, Michael Law&B 92
Glazer, Mindy ScF&FL 92
Glazer, Nathan 1923- WhoAm 92
Glazer, Penina Migdal 1939- WhoAmW 93, WhoE 93
Glazer, Scott F. Law&B 92
Glazer, Scott F. 1962- St&PR 93
Glazer, Steven Donald 1948- WhoEmL 93
Glazier, Betty Jean 1937- WhoAmW 93
Glazier, Kenneth Charles 1949- St&PR 93
Glazier, Louis Law&B 92
Glazier, Louis 1949- St&PR 93
Glazier, Mark David 1953- St&PR 93
Glazier, Patricia Neel Law&B 92
Glazier, Raymond Earl, Jr. 1941- WhoE 93, WhoWor 93
Glazier, Robert Carl 1927- WhoAm 92
Glazunov, Alexander (Konstantinovich) 1865-1936 Baker 92
Glazunov, Ilya Sergeevich 1930- BioIn 17
Glazzard, Charles F. Law&B 92
Gleasner, Diana Cottle 1936- WhoWrEP 92
Gleason, Abbott 1938- WhoAm 92, WhoWrEP 92
Gleason, Alfred M. 1930- St&PR 93, WhoAm 92
Gleason, Alice Bryant 1940- WhoAmW 93, WhoSSW 93
Gleason, Andrew Mattei 1921- WhoAm 92
Gleason, Ann Drucker 1948- WhoAmW 93
Gleason, Anne & Gleason, Elizabeth AmWomPl
Gleason, Bradley J. 1954- St&PR 93
Gleason, Brian T. 1960- St&PR 93
Gleason, Charlotte AmWomPl
Gleason, Douglas 1916- WhoAm 92
Gleason, Edward M. 1940- St&PR 93
Gleason, Elizabeth
See Gleason, Anne & Gleason, Elizabeth AmWomPl
Gleason, Frank J., Jr. 1930- St&PR 93
Gleason, Frederick Grant 1848-1903 Baker 92
Gleason, George Donald 1920- WhoWrEP 92
Gleason, Gregory Lynn 1950- WhoEmL 93
Gleason, Gregory W. 1952- St&PR 93
Gleason, Gregory Williams 1951- WhoEmL 93
Gleason, Harold 1892-1980 Baker 92
Gleason, Harold Anthony 1945- St&PR 93
Gleason, J. Marne Law&B 92
Gleason, J. Marne 1935- St&PR 93
Gleason, Jackie 1916-1987 QDrFCA 92 [port]
Gleason, James 1886-1959 QDrFCA 92 [port]
Gleason, James Arthur 1905- WhoAm 92
Gleason, James M. Law&B 92
Gleason, James Marne 1935- WhoAm 92
Gleason, James S. 1934- WhoAm 92
Gleason, Janice Heather 1950- WhoSSW 93
Gleason, Jean Berko 1931- WhoAm 92
Gleason, Jean Wilbur 1943- WhoAm 92
Gleason, Joanna 1950- WhoAmW 93
Gleason, John F. 1928- St&PR 93
Gleason, John F. 1950- WhoEmL 93
Gleason, John Francis 1928- WhoAm 92
Gleason, John James 1941- WhoAm 92
Gleason, John Martin 1907- WhoAm 92
Gleason, John P., Jr. 1941- St&PR 93
Gleason, John Patrick, Jr. 1941- WhoAm 92
Gleason, John Scovil 1941- WhoAm 92
Gleason, Kathy A. Law&B 92
Gleason, Linda K. 1956- WhoAmW 93
Gleason, Michie MiSFD 9
Gleason, Nora L. Law&B 92
Gleason, Norman Dale 1943- WhoAm 92, WhoSSW 93
Gleason, Orissa W. AmWomPl
Gleason, Owen P. Law&B 92
Gleason, Philip James 1954- WhoEmL 93
Gleason, Ralph Newton 1922- WhoAm 92
Gleason, Robert Michael 1929- St&PR 93
Gleason, Robert Willard 1932- WhoAm 92
Gleason, Scott Douglas 1964- WhoSSW 93
Gleason, Stephen Anson 1949- WhoAm 92
Gleason, Stephen Charles 1946- WhoEmL 93
Gleason, Thomas D. 1936- St&PR 93
Gleason, Thomas Daues 1936- WhoAm 92
Gleason, Thomas W. d1992 NewYTBS 92 [port]
Gleason, Walter R. Law&B 92
Gleason, William F., Jr. Law&B 92, WhoAm 92
Gleason, William J. 1866-1933 BiDAMSp 1989
Gleason, William Newman 1951- WhoAm 92
Gleaton, Harriet E. 1937- WhoSSW 93
Gleaton, Martha McCalman 1943- WhoSSW 93
Gleaton, Tony BioIn 17
Gleaves, Edwin Sheffield 1936- WhoAm 92, WhoSSW 93
Gleaves, James L. 1952- St&PR 93
Gleaves, James Leslie 1952- WhoEmL 93
Gleaves, Leon Rogers 1939- St&PR 93
Gleazer, Edmund John, Jr. 1916- WhoAm 92
Gleb OxDcByz
Gleb d1015
See Boris and Gleb OxDcByz
Gleberman, Jules Harvey 1922- St&PR 93
Glebov, Evgeny 1929- Baker 92
Glebov, Igor Baker 92
Gleckner, Robert Francis 1925- WhoAm 92
Gledhill, Russell William 1946- St&PR 93
Glee, Glenna WhoWrEP 92
Gleed, George Clifford 1929- St&PR 93
Gleed, William H. 1933- WhoIns 93
Gleekel, Sherman Sherry 1930- St&PR 93
Gleeson, Austin Michael 1938- WhoAm 92
Gleeson, John W. d1991 BioIn 17
Gleeson, Judith Amanda Sang Coomber 1955- WhoWor 93
Gleeson, Libby 1950- DcChlFi
Gleeson, Noel Martin 1934- WhoAsAP 91, WhoWor 93
Gleeson, Pat WhoScE 91-3
Gleeson, Paul Francis 1941- WhoAm 92
Gleghorn, George Jay 1927- WhoAm 92
Glegle d1889 BioIn 17
Gleich, Carol S. 1935- WhoAmW 93
Gleich, Gerald Joseph 1931- WhoAm 92
Gleichauf, John George 1933- WhoSSW 93
Gleichenhaus, Oliver d1991 BioIn 17
Gleichenhaus, Robert D. 1929- St&PR 93
Gleichert, Gregg Charles 1948- St&PR 93
Gleichman, John Alan 1944- WhoWor 93
Gleick, James (W.) 1954- ConAu 137
Gleijeses, Mario 1955- WhoEmL 93
Gleim, James Mac 1934- WhoAm 92
Gleim, Johann Wilhelm Ludwig 1719-1803 BioIn 17
Gleim, Michael Lee 1943- St&PR 93
Gleim, Robert Alan 1968- WhoE 93
Gleis, Linda Hood 1952- WhoAm 92
Gleispach, Helmut 1937- WhoWor 93
Gleisser, Marcus David 1923- WhoAm 92
Gleiter, Herbert 1938- WhoScE 91-3
Gleitman, George 1928- St&PR 93
Gleitzer, Charles 1932- WhoScE 91-2
Glekel, Jeffrey Ives 1947- WhoAm 92
Gleklen, Donald Morse 1936- St&PR 93, WhoAm 92
Glele, King of Dahomey d1889 BioIn 17
Glemann, Richard Paul 1949- WhoSSW 93
Glemarec, Michel 1938- WhoScE 91-2
Glemp, Jozef 1928- PolBiDi
Glemp, Jozef Cardinal 1929- WhoWor 93
Glemser, Bernard ScF&FL 92
Glemser, Bernard 1908-1990 BioIn 17
Glen, Alida Mixson 1930- WhoAm 92
Glen, David McKellar WhoScE 91-1
Glen, Emilie 1937- WhoWrEP 92
Glen, Eva M. AmWomPl
Glen, John 1833-1904 Baker 92
Glen, John 1932- MiSFD 9
Glen, John Wallington 1927- WhoWor 93
Glen, Robert 1905- WhoAm 92
Glen, Thomas 1804-1873
See Glen, John 1833-1904 Baker 92
Glencer, Suzanne Thomson 1942- WhoE 93
Glencross, William Donald 1936- St&PR 93
Glendening, Bruce Bradford Law&B 92
Glendening, Everett Austin 1929- WhoAm 92
Glendening, Parris Nelson 1942- WhoE 93
Glendening, R. Bradley Law&B 92
Glendinning, Victoria BioIn 17
Glendon, John B. Law&B 92
Glenn, Albert H. 1922- WhoSSW 93
Glenn, Andrea Poutasse 1951- WhoAmW 93
Glenn, Barbara Peterson 1954- WhoAmW 93
Glenn, Belinda 1963- WhoAmW 93, WhoEmL 93
Glenn, Charles E.B. Law&B 92
Glenn, Clyde Albert, Jr. 1933- St&PR 93
Glenn, Constance White 1933- WhoAmW 93
Glenn, David Allen Law&B 92
Glenn, David Wright 1943- WhoAm 92, WhoSSW 93
Glenn, Deborah Elaine 1949- WhoAmW 93
Glenn, Dennis Wayne 1952- WhoEmL 93, WhoSSW 93
Glenn, Donald Taylor, Jr. 1948- WhoEmL 93, WhoSSW 93
Glenn, Gabriella G. Law&B 92
Glenn, George Rembert 1923- WhoSSW 93
Glenn, Gerald M. 1942- St&PR 93
Glenn, Gerald Marvin 1942- WhoAm 92
Glenn, Gordon H. Law&B 92
Glenn, Gordon S. 1948- St&PR 93
Glenn, James 1937- WhoAm 92
Glenn, James Francis 1928- WhoAm 92
Glenn, Jerry Hosmer, Jr. 1938- WhoAm 92
Glenn, Joe Davis, Jr. 1921- WhoSSW 93
Glenn, John 1921- BioIn 17, CngDr 91, Expl 93 [port]
Glenn, John Herschel, Jr. 1921- WhoAm 92
Glenn, John M. 1931- St&PR 93
Glenn, John William, Jr. 1944- WhoE 93
Glenn, Kathleen Mary 1936- WhoSSW 93
Glenn, Lawrence Randolph 1938- WhoAm 92
Glenn, Lois 1941- ScF&FL 92
Glenn, Louise A. Law&B 92
Glenn, Michael Douglas 1940- WhoAm 92
Glenn, Nancy Noyes 1953- WhoWrEP 92
Glenn, Nancy Tyler 1938- ScF&FL 92
Glenn, Norval Dwight 1933- WhoAm 92
Glenn, Patrick L. 1938- St&PR 93
Glenn, Peggy 1944- WhoWrEP 92
Glenn, Pierre William MiSFD 9
Glenn, Rhonda Faye 1946- WhoSSW 93
Glenn, Richard Wray 1936- St&PR 93
Glenn, Robert Aubrey 1930- WhoAm 92
Glenn, Robert Edward 1944- WhoAm 92
Glenn, Robin Day 1947- WhoEmL 93
Glenn, Rogers 1930- WhoSSW 93
Glenn, Roland Douglas WhoAm 92
Glenn, Scott BioIn 17
Glenn, Scott 1942- WhoAm 92
Glenn, Steven Claude 1947- WhoEmL 93
Glenn, Thomas Michael 1940- WhoAm 92
Glenn, Walter Lewis, Jr. 1940- WhoAm 92
Glenn, William Allen 1925- WhoAm 92
Glenn, William Grant 1916- WhoSSW 93
Glenn, William Wallace Lumpkin 1914- WhoAm 92, WhoWor 93
Glennen, Robert Eugene, Jr. 1933- WhoAm 92
Glenner, Richard Allen 1934- WhoWor 93
Glennerster, Howard WhoScE 91-1
Glennon, Barbara Ruth Ward 1937- WhoAmW 93
Glennon, Charles Edward 1942- WhoWor 93
Glennon, Harrison R., Jr. 1914- St&PR 93
Glennon, Harrison Randolph, Jr. 1914- WhoAm 92
Glennon, Jeremy D. 1954- WhoScE 91-3
Glennon, Robert Eugene, Jr. 1948- WhoEmL 93
Glenny, Lyman Albert 1918- WhoAm 92
Glenny, Michael BioIn 17
Glenville, Peter 1913- MiSFD 9
Gleser, Goldine Cohnberg 1915- WhoAmW 93
Gleser, Leon Jay 1939- WhoE 93
Gless, Ruth M. BioIn 17
Gless, Sharon BioIn 17, WhoAm 92, WhoAmW 93
Gleszer, Kenneth M. 1921- St&PR 93
Gleva, Karen J. 1952- WhoEmL 93
Glew, George WhoScE 91-1
Glew, Louis Wm. Law&B 92
Glewwe, Paul William 1958- WhoEmL 93
Glezen, William Paul 1931- WhoSSW 93
Glezerman, Lois P. St&PR 93
Glezerov, Valery 1939- WhoE 93
Glezos, Matthews 1927- St&PR 93, WhoAm 92
Gliatta, Ronald 1950- WhoE 93, WhoWor 93
Glicenstein, Enrico 1870-1942 PolBiDi
Glichouse, Eric Scott 1960- WhoSSW 93
Glicini, Jean Marie 1961- WhoAmW 93
Glick, Alan Harvey 1934- WhoE 93
Glick, Allan H. 1938- WhoAm 92
Glick, Alvin Louis 1926- St&PR 93
Glick, Arthur W. 1905-1991 BioIn 17
Glick, Barry 1949- St&PR 93
Glick, Carl 1921- St&PR 93
Glick, Cynthia Susan 1950- WhoAmW 93
Glick, Edward Maurice 1920- WhoSSW 93
Glick, Evelyn Harter d1990 BioIn 17
Glick, Garland Wayne 1921- WhoAm 92
Glick, George Washington 1827-1911 BioIn 17
Glick, Irvin David 1935- WhoE 93
Glick, J. Leslie 1940- WhoAm 92
Glick, Jane Mills 1943- WhoAmW 93
Glick, John 1938- BioIn 17
Glick, John H. 1943- WhoAm 92
Glick, Joseph 1935- WhoE 93
Glick, Kenneth Joel 1951- WhoE 93, WhoEmL 93
Glick, Kenneth R. Law&B 92
Glick, Leslie Alan 1946- WhoEmL 93
Glick, Mark Alan 1955- WhoE 93
Glick, Marty Gerald 1949- St&PR 93
Glick, Myrna Joan 1936- WhoE 93
Glick, Peter Allen 1947- St&PR 93
Glick, Philip J. Law&B 92
Glick, Philip Milton 1905- WhoAm 92
Glick, Robert A. 1916- St&PR 93
Glick, Robert Dunn 1936- St&PR 93
Glick, Robert Ralph 1919- St&PR 93
Glick, Ruth 1942- ScF&FL 92
Glick, Ruth Burtnick 1942- WhoAm 92
Glick, Srul Irving 1934- Baker 92
Glick, Steven Marc 1947- WhoWor 93
Glick, Todd W. 1962- WhoEmL 93
Glick, William Lee 1920- St&PR 93
Glick-Colquitt, Karen Lynne 1945- WhoAmW 93
Glickenhaus, James 1950- MiSFD 9
Glickenhaus, Sarah Brody 1919- WhoAm 92, WhoAmW 93
Glickman, A.B. 1937- St&PR 93
Glickman, Albert Seymour 1923- WhoAm 92
Glickman, Carl D. 1926- St&PR 93
Glickman, Carl Davis 1926- WhoAm 92
Glickman, Dan 1944- CngDr 91
Glickman, Daniel Robert 1944- WhoAm 92
Glickman, Edward A. 1957- St&PR 93
Glickman, Edward Alan 1957- WhoE 93
Glickman, Ernest Irwin 1940- St&PR 93
Glickman, Franklin Sheldon 1929- WhoAm 92
Glickman, Gary 1959- ConGAN
Glickman, Gerald Neal 1950- WhoEmL 93
Glickman, Gladys Law&B 92
Glickman, Gladys 1920- St&PR 93
Glickman, Harry 1924- WhoAm 92
Glickman, James A. 1948- WhoE 93
Glickman, Louis 1933- St&PR 93, WhoAm 92
Glickman, Mark Warren 1953- WhoEmL 93
Glickman, Marlene 1936- WhoAmW 93, WhoE 93
Glickman, Marshall L. 1934- St&PR 93
Glickman, Norman J. 1942- WhoE 93
Glickman, Paula Rivlin WhoE 93
Glickman, Robert Jeffrey 1947- St&PR 93
Glickman, Robert Morris 1939- WhoAm 92
Glickman, Rosalind Helen 1937- WhoE 93
Glickman, Susan 1953- ConAu 38NR, WhoCanL 92
Glicksman, Arvin Sigmund 1924- WhoAm 92
Glicksman, Frank ScF&FL 92
Glicksman, Martin Eden 1937- WhoAm 92
Glicksman, Maurice 1928- WhoAm 92
Glicksman, Michael Lewis 1941- WhoE 93

Glicksman, Russell Allen 1939- *WhoAm 92, WhoWor 93*
Glicksohn, Susan *ScF&FL 92*
Glickstein, Arthur F. 1927- *WhoE 93*
Glickstein, Neil Evans 1946- *St&PR 93*
Glidden, Allan H. 1920- *St&PR 93*
Glidden, Allan Hartwell 1920- *WhoAm 92*
Glidden, Germain G. 1913- *St&PR 93*
Glidden, John Redmond 1936- *WhoAm 92*
Glidden, Lloyd Sumner, Jr. 1922- *WhoAm 92*
Glidden, Richard M. 1924- *St&PR 93*
Glidden, Robert Burr 1936- *WhoAm 92*
Glidden, Robert Sterling 1944- *St&PR 93*
Glidden, Ronald C. 1939- *St&PR 93, WhoAm 92*
Glidewell, John Calvin 1919- *WhoSSW 93*
Glieberman, Herbert Allen 1930- *WhoAm 92*
Gliedman, Marvin L. 1929- *WhoAm 92*
Gliege, John Gerhardt 1948- *WhoEmL 93*
Gliemann, Gunter 1931- *WhoScE 91-3*
Gliemann, J. 1937- *WhoScE 91-2*
Glier, Ingeborg Johanna 1934- *WhoAm 92*
Gliere, Reinhold 1875-1956 *OxDcOp*
Gliere, Reinhold (Moritsovich) 1875-1956 *Baker 92*
Gliha, John Lee 1953- *WhoEmL 93*
Gliha, Slavko 1940- *WhoScE 91-4*
Glijansky, Alex 1948- *WhoE 93, WhoEmL 93*
Glik, Jeffrey Warren 1956- *St&PR 93*
Glik, Joseph 1926- *St&PR 93*
Glikes, Erwin Arno 1937- *WhoAm 92*
Gliklich, Jerry 1948- *WhoE 93*
Gliklikh, Yuri Evgenievich 1949- *WhoWor 93*
Glimcher, Arne *BioIn 17, MiSFD 9*
Glimcher, Arnold B. 1938- *WhoAm 92, WhoE 93*
Glimcher, Melvin Jacob 1925- *WhoAm 92*
Glimm, Adele 1937- *WhoWrEP 92*
Glimm, James Gilbert 1934- *WhoAm 92*
Glimp, H. Earl 1943- *St&PR 93*
Glincher, Andrew I. *St&PR 93*
Glindeman, Henry Peter, Jr. 1924- *WhoAm 92*
Gliner, Erast Boris 1923- *WhoWor 93*
Glines, Carroll Vane, Jr. 1920- *WhoAm 92*
Glines, John 1933- *WhoE 93*
Glines, Paul *BioIn 17*
Glines, Stephen Ramey 1952- *WhoEmL 93, WhoWor 93*
Glinka, Mikhail 1804-1857 *OxDcOp*
Glinka, Mikhail (Ivanovich) 1804-1857 *Baker 92, IntDcOp [port]*
Glinka, Ryszard Brunon 1946- *WhoScE 91-4*
Glinski, Jan Marian 1933- *WhoScE 91-4*
Glinski, Mateusz 1892-1976 *Baker 92*
Glinski, Robert C. *Law&B 92*
Gliori, Debi 1959- *SmATA 72 [port]*
Glisan, Eileen Wydo 1956- *WhoE 93*
Glissant, Edouard 1928- *BioIn 17*
Glissant, Edouard Mathieu 1928- *WhoAm 92*
Glisson, Floyd Wright 1947- *St&PR 93*
Glitman, Erik Wayne 1959- *WhoE 93*
Glitsch, Helfried Gunther 1937- *WhoScE 91-3*
Glitsch, Val *BioIn 17*
Glittenberg, Udo 1943- *WhoWor 93*
Glitz, Dohn George 1936- *WhoAm 92*
Glitz, Donald Robert 1944- *WhoE 93*
Gliwicz, Z.M. 1939- *WhoScE 91-4*
Glixon, David M(orris) 1908- *WhoWrEP 92*
Glixon, David Morris 1908- *WhoAm 92*
Gloag, John 1896-1981 *ScF&FL 92*
Glob, Peter Vilhelm 1911-1985 *IntDcAn*
Glober, George Edward, Jr. *Law&B 92*
Globerman, Linda Marilyn 1951- *WhoEmL 93*
Globerson, Peter 1927- *St&PR 93*
Globman, Richard Allen 1942- *St&PR 93*
Globokar, Vinko 1934- *Baker 92*
Glock, Albert d1992 *BioIn 17*
Glock, Charles Young 1919- *WhoAm 92*
Glock, Erich 1929- *WhoWor 93*
Glock, Marvin David 1912- *WhoAm 92, WhoE 93*
Glock, William 1908- *BioIn 17*
Glock, William (Frederick) 1908- *Baker 92*
Glocker, Theodore Wesley, Jr. 1925- *WhoAm 92*
Glocker, Theodore William 1953- *WhoEmL 93, WhoSSW 93*
Glockner, Maurice 1906- *St&PR 93*
Glockner, Peter G. 1929- *WhoAm 92*
Glod, Stanley Joseph 1936- *WhoAm 92*
Glodeanu, Liviu 1938-1978 *Baker 92*
Glodek, Peter K.F. 1934- *WhoScE 91-3*
Glodowski, Shelley Jean 1950- *WhoEmL 93*
Gloe, Christopher F. *Law&B 92*
Gloeckner, Frederick Carl d1990 *BioIn 17*
Gloetzner, Frank Ludwig 1938- *WhoWor 93*
Gloger, Zygmunt 1845-1910 *IntDcAn*
Glogower, Melanie Smith 1956- *WhoAmW 93*
Glomb, Diana *WhoAmW 93*
Glombitza, Karl-Werner 1933- *WhoScE 91-3*
Glomset, Daniel Anders 1913- *WhoAm 92*
Glonti, Omar Aleksandres 1939- *WhoWor 93*
Gloor, Kurt 1942- *MiSFD 9*
Gloor, Richard Bruce 1946- *WhoEmL 93*
Gloria, John Joseph 1930- *St&PR 93*
Glorie, Francis *St&PR 93*
Glorieux, Francois 1932- *Baker 92*
Glorioso, Pamela Mae 1960- *WhoAmW 93*
Glos, Margaret Beach 1936- *WhoAm 92*
Glosband, Daniel Martin 1944- *WhoAm 92, WhoE 93*
Gloss, Molly 1944- *ScF&FL 92*
Glosser, Caryle Rosen 1946- *WhoAm 92*
Glosser, Jeffrey Mark 1936- *WhoAm 92, WhoE 93*
Glosser, Jill Paige *Law&B 92*
Glosser, Ronald Dean 1933- *St&PR 93*
Glosser, William Louis 1929- *WhoAm 92, WhoE 93*
Glossop, Peter 1928- *Baker 92, IntDcOp [port], OxDcOp*
Glosup, Lorene 1911- *WhoAm 92, WhoAmW 93*
Glotzbecker, Paul Gerald 1953- *St&PR 93*
Gloudeman, Joseph Floyd 1935- *St&PR 93*
Glovach, David H. 1930- *St&PR 93*
Glover, Arthur W. 1929- *St&PR 93*
Glover, Charles Wayne 1953- *WhoSSW 93*
Glover, Cliff C. 1913- *St&PR 93*
Glover, Clifford Banks, Jr. 1919- *WhoSSW 93*
Glover, Clifford Clarke 1913- *WhoAm 92, WhoSSW 93*
Glover, Crispin *BioIn 17*
Glover, Crispin Hellion 1964- *WhoAm 92*
Glover, Danny *BioIn 17*
Glover, Danny 1947- *CurBio 92 [port], HolBB [port], WhoAm 92*
Glover, David Moore *WhoScE 91-1*
Glover, David Moore 1948- *WhoWor 93*
Glover, Donald E. 1933- *ScF&FL 92*
Glover, Donald Ellsworth 1933- *WhoSSW 93*
Glover, Donald Robert *WhoAm 92*
Glover, Douglas *WhoCanL 92*
Glover, Douglas 1948- *ConAu 137*
Glover, Edward Ernest *WhoScE 91-1*
Glover, Elsa Margaret 1939- *WhoAmW 93, WhoSSW 93*
Glover, Everett William, Jr. 1948- *WhoSSW 93*
Glover, Fred William 1937- *WhoAm 92, WhoWor 93*
Glover, Frederick James 1920- *WhoWor 93*
Glover, Harry Allen, Jr. 1949- *WhoEmL 93*
Glover, Henry d1991 *BioIn 17*
Glover, Henry 1922- *SoulM*
Glover, Hilda Weaver 1933- *WhoAm 92*
Glover, James T. 1939- *St&PR 93*
Glover, Jane 1949- *OxDcOp*
Glover, Jane (Alison) 1949- *Baker 92*
Glover, Joe Charles 1944- *WhoSSW 93*
Glover, John A. 1949-1989 *BioIn 17*
Glover, John William 1815-1899 *Baker 92*
Glover, K. *WhoScE 91-1*
Glover, Keith T. *St&PR 93*
Glover, Kenneth W. 1927- *St&PR 93*
Glover, Kenneth Wadd 1927- *WhoSSW 93*
Glover, Laurice White 1930- *WhoE 93*
Glover, Lisa Marie 1963- *WhoAmW 93*
Glover, Lydia M. *AmWomPl*
Glover, Maggie Wallace 1948- *WhoAmW 93*
Glover, Marion Bellinger 1942- *St&PR 93*
Glover, Marty Anne 1958- *WhoEmL 93*
Glover, Michael F. *Law&B 92*
Glover, Nan G. *AmWomPl*
Glover, Norman James 1929- *WhoAm 92, WhoE 93*
Glover, Oscar Harrison 1937- *WhoSSW 93*
Glover, Paul W. 1947- *WhoIns 93*
Glover, Paul W., III 1947- *St&PR 93*
Glover, Paul Williams, III 1947- *WhoAm 92*
Glover, Penny Neathery 1962- *WhoSSW 93*
Glover, Ralph J. 1943- *St&PR 93*
Glover, Richard 1712-1785 *BioIn 17*
Glover, Richard Edward 1950- *BiDAMSp 1989*
Glover, Richard M. *WhoAm 92*
Glover, Ron K. 1940- *WhoE 93*
Glover, Sarah Anna 1786-1867 *Baker 92*
Glover, Savion *BioIn 17*
Glover, Steven Allen *Law&B 92*
Glover, Stuart William *WhoScE 91-1*
Glover, Vern L. 1935- *St&PR 93*
Glover, Victor Joseph Patrick 1932- *WhoWor 93*
Glover, William Dwight 1954- *WhoWor 93*
Glover, William Harper 1911- *WhoAm 92*
Glover, William Howard 1819-1875 *Baker 92*
Glover, William J., Jr. 1940- *St&PR 93*
Glover-Wright, Geoffrey *ScF&FL 92*
Glovka, Richard Paul 1937- *WhoAm 92*
Glowac, Laurie A. 1947- *WhoEmL 93*
Glowacka, Barbara 1938- *WhoScE 91-4*
Glowacki, Jan Nepomucen 1802-1846 *PolBiDi*
Glowacki, Janusz *BioIn 17*
Glowacki, Richard Chester 1932- *WhoAm 92*
Glowen, Kathryn Anne 1941- *WhoAmW 93*
Glower, Donald Duane 1926- *WhoAm 92*
Glowik-Johnson, Linda Ann 1951- *WhoEmL 93*
Glowinski, J. *WhoScE 91-2*
Glowinski, Jerome James 1931- *St&PR 93*
Glowinski, Roland 1937- *WhoAm 92*
Glowka, Marek Leszek 1948- *WhoWor 93*
Glowna, Vadim *MiSFD 9*
Glowniak, Jerry Vincent 1948- *WhoEmL 93*
Glowski, Daniel T. *Law&B 92*
Gloyd, Helen P. *AmWomPl*
Gloyd, Lawrence Eugene 1932- *WhoAm 92*
Gloyd, Susan Vitali 1950- *WhoAmW 93*
Gloyna, Earnest Frederick 1921- *WhoAm 92*
Glozshteyn, Yakov 1936- *St&PR 93*
Glubb, John Bagot 1897-1986 *DcTwHis, HarEnMi*
Glube, Constance Rachelle 1931- *WhoAm 92*
Glubo, Les Jay 1951- *WhoE 93*
Glubok, Shirley 1933- *BioIn 17*
Glubok, Shirley (Astor) 1933- *MajAI [port]*
Glubrecht, Hellmut 1917- *WhoScE 91-3*
Gluck, Alma 1884-1938 *Baker 92, IntDcOp [port]*
Gluck, Barry S. 1952- *St&PR 93*
Gluck, Carol 1941- *WhoE 93*
Gluck, Christoph Willibald 1714-1787 *OxDcOp*
Gluck, Christoph Willibald, Ritter von 1714-1787 *Baker 92*
Gluck, Christoph Willibald Ritter von 1714-1787 *IntDcOp [port]*
Gluck, Dion Peter 1956- *WhoSSW 93*
Gluck, Henry 1928- *St&PR 93, WhoAm 92*
Gluck, Louise (Elisabeth) 1943- *ConAu 40NR, WhoAm 92, WhoAmW 93, WhoWrEP 92*
Gluck, Michael J. *BioIn 17*
Gluck, Michelle H. *Law&B 92*
Gluck, Michelle H. 1959- *St&PR 93*
Gluck, Nancy DeProspo 1959- *WhoE 93*
Gluck, Robert 1947- *ConGAN*
Gluck, Rudolf W. *WhoScE 91-3*
Gluck, Ruth Rubin *Law&B 92*
Gluckman, Harold L. 1938- *St&PR 93*
Gluckman, Janet 1939- *ScF&FL 92*
Gluckman, Jean-Claude 1940- *WhoScE 91-2, WhoWor 93*
Gluckman, Kenneth I. *Law&B 92*
Gluckman, Thomas S. 1943- *St&PR 93*
Glucksberg, Sam 1933- *WhoE 93*
Glucksman, David N. 1923- *St&PR 93*
Glucksman, Larry Morris 1947- *WhoEmL 93*
Gluckson, James Andrew 1956- *WhoWrEP 92*
Gluckstal, Leonard 1947- *WhoE 93*
Gluckstein, Fritz Paul 1927- *WhoAm 92*
Gluckstein, Martin Edwin 1928- *WhoSSW 93*
Gluckstern, Robert Leonard 1924- *WhoAm 92*
Glucroft, Douglas *Law&B 92*
Glueck, Louise *ConAu 40NR*
Glueck, Nelson 1900-1971 *IntDcAn*
Glueck, Peter 1942- *WhoScE 91-4*
Glueck, Sylvia Blumenfeld 1925- *WhoAmW 93, WhoSSW 93*
Glueck, Theodore P. 1934- *St&PR 93*
Glueckauf, Robert Lewis 1949- *WhoEmL 93*
Glumac, Ann Marie 1959- *WhoAmW 93*
Gluntz, Karen McHenry 1951- *WhoAmW 93*
Gluscevic, Obrad 1913-1980 *DrEEuF*
Glushenkov, Vladimir Dmitrievich 1945- *WhoWor 93*
Glushien, Morris P. 1909- *WhoAm 92, WhoWor 93*
Glushko, Robert G. 1947- *St&PR 93*
Glusker, Donald Leonard 1930- *WhoE 93*
Glusker, Jenny Pickworth 1931- *WhoAmW 93*
Gluskoter, Charles *BioIn 17*
Glusman, Paul C. *Law&B 92*
Glussman, Betty Berman 1930- *WhoAmW 93*
Glut, Donald F. 1944- *ScF&FL 92*
Glutting, Robert V. 1934- *St&PR 93*
Gluyas, Constance 1920- *ConAu 136*
Gluyas, Constance 1920-1983 *ScF&FL 92*
Glyde, L.D. *WhoScE 91-1*
Glykas, Michael 12th cent.- *OxDcByz*
Glymph, William E. 1950- *St&PR 93*
Glyn, Margaret H(enrietta) 1865-1946 *Baker 92*
Glynis, Gregory Allan *Law&B 92*
Glynn, Arthur Lawrence 1916- *WhoAm 92*
Glynn, Carlin 1940- *WhoAm 92*
Glynn, David Gerald 1952- *WhoWor 93*
Glynn, Edward 1935- *WhoAm 92*
Glynn, Edward Lewis 1944- *WhoWor 93*
Glynn, Gary Allen 1946- *WhoAm 92, WhoEmL 93*
Glynn, James Vincent 1938- *St&PR 93, WhoIns 93*
Glynn, Jeffrey Thomas 1958- *St&PR 93*
Glynn, John Joseph 1933- *St&PR 93*
Glynn, Kathy Ann 1958- *St&PR 93*
Glynn, Mary Ann Theresa 1951- *WhoAmW 93*
Glynn, Neil Held 1928- *WhoAm 92*
Glynn, Robert D., Jr. 1942- *St&PR 93*
Glynn, Sandra Lenore 1935- *WhoAmW 93*
Glynn, Timothy Kevin 1964- *WhoE 93*
Glynn, William C. 1944- *St&PR 93*
Glynn, William Thomas, Jr. 1921- *WhoE 93*
Gmach, Richard Eugene 1941- *St&PR 93*
Gmelig-Meyling, Frederik Hendrik Johan 1947- *WhoScE 91-3*
Gmernicka-Haftek, Cecylia 1928- *WhoScE 91-4*
Gmora, Barbara S. *Law&B 92*
Gmora, Joan E. *Law&B 92*
Gmora, Kenneth N. 1930- *St&PR 93*
Gmuer, Cecilia Ann 1953- *WhoEmL 93*
Gmytrasiewicz, Maria Marta 1940- *WhoWor 93*
Gnadt, Bill *BioIn 17*
Gnaedinger, John Phillip 1926- *St&PR 93*
Gnali, Mambou Aimee 1935- *WhoUN 92*
Gnall, Gregory P. *Law&B 92*
Gnanasekaran, Kottai S. 1936- *WhoUN 92*
Gnann, Alan J. 1949- *St&PR 93*
Gnann, John Wyatt, Jr. 1953- *WhoEmL 93*
Gnarowski, Michael 1934- *WhoCanL 92*
Gnat, Raymond Earl 1932- *WhoAm 92*
Gnattali, Radames 1906- *Baker 92*
Gnazzo, Anthony J(oseph) 1936- *Baker 92*
Gnazzo, Edison 1929- *WhoWor 93*
Gnecchi, Vittorio 1876-1954 *Baker 92*
Gnehm, Edward W., Jr. *BioIn 17*
Gnehm, Edward W., Jr. 1944- *WhoAm 92, WhoWor 93*
Gneisenau, August Wilhelm Anton, Count Neithardt von 1760-1831 *HarEnMi*
Gnesda, Thomas A. 1944- *St&PR 93*
Gnessin, Mikhail (Fabianovich) 1882-1957 *Baker 92*
Gniadek, Cheryl Lynn 1947- *WhoAmW 93, WhoEmL 93*
Gniazdowski, Marek 1935- *WhoScE 91-4*
Gniazdowski, Marek Andrzej 1935- *WhoWor 93*
Gniewek, Raymond 1931- *WhoAm 92*
Gniewek, Raymond Louis 1947- *WhoAm 92*
Gnoleba, Maurice Seri 1935- *WhoAfr*
Gnuse, Jeanne Pflaum 1937- *WhoAmW 93*
Gnutti, Alan N. 1950- *St&PR 93*
Gnyawali, Devi Ram 1958- *WhoWor 93*
Go, Josiah Lim 1962- *WhoWor 93*
Goad, Barry Stephens 1930- *St&PR 93*
Goad, Curtis Carl 1952- *St&PR 93*
Goad, Linda May 1948- *WhoAm 92, WhoAmW 93, WhoEmL 93*
Goad, Rachell LaGuardia 1951- *WhoEmL 93*
Goade, William Richard 1922- *WhoAm 92*
Goaley, Donald Joseph 1935- *St&PR 93, WhoIns 93*
Goas, Jean-Yves 1938- *WhoScE 91-2*
Goavec, Pierre-Yves *BioIn 17*
Gobar, Alfred Julian 1932- *St&PR 93, WhoAm 92, WhoWor 93*
Gobar, Gail Tamara 1940- *WhoAmW 93*
Gobatti, Stefano 1852-1913 *OxDcOp*
Gobbaerts, Jean-Louis 1835-1886 *Baker 92*
Gobbel, L. Russell *Law&B 92*
Gobbell, Ronald Vance 1948- *WhoEmL 93, WhoSSW 93*

Gobbi, Tito 1913-1984 *Baker 92, IntDcOp [port], OxDcOp*
Gobeil, Paul 1942- *St&PR 93*
Gobeil, Pierre *St&PR 93*
Gobel, George 1919-1991 *BioIn 17*
Gobel, George 1920-1991 *AnObit 1991*
Gobel, Jerry Walter 1943- *St&PR 93*
Gobel, John Henry 1926- *WhoAm 92*
Gobel, Rudiger Gotthard 1940- *WhoWor 93*
Goben, Michael K. *St&PR 93*
Goberna, Raimundo 1943- *WhoScE 91-3*
Gobert, Thomas c. 1640-1708 *BioIn 17*
Gobesz, Ferdinand 1929- *WhoScE 91-4*
Gobie, Henry Macaulay 1911- *WhoAm 92*
Gobind Singh, Guru 1666-1708 *BioIn 17*
Gobineau, Joseph-Arthur de 1816-1882 *DcLB 123 [port]*
Goble, Alfred Theodore 1909- *WhoE 93*
Goble, Danney 1946- *ConAu 136*
Goble, Frank G. 1917- *St&PR 93*
Goble, George G. 1929- *WhoAm 92*
Goble, Kimberly L. 1963- *St&PR 93*
Goble, Lou *ScF&FL 92*
Goble, Paul 1933- *MajAI [port], SmATA 69 [port], WhoAm 92, WhoWrEP 92*
Goble, Robert Thomas 1947- *WhoSSW 93*
Goblet, Rene 1828-1905 *BioIn 17*
Goblowsky, Michael 1962- *WhoSSW 93*
Gobrecht, Chris *BioIn 17*
Gobrecht, Heinrich Friedrich 1909- *WhoWor 93*
Gobris, Joseph J. 1936- *St&PR 93*
Gobrogge, Roger Edwin *Law&B 92*
Goc, Kazimierz 1933- *WhoScE 91-4*
Gocek, Matilda Arkenbout 1923- *WhoE 93*
Gocek, Matilda Arkensout 1923- *WhoWrEP 92*
Gochberg, Thomas J. 1939- *St&PR 93*
Gochberg, Thomas Joel 1939- *WhoAm 92*
Gochenaur, Jack A. 1948- *St&PR 93*
Gochfeld, Michael 1940- *ConAu 137*
Gochman, Eva Ruth *WhoE 93*
Gochnauer, Richard Wallis 1949- *St&PR 93, WhoAm 92*
Gocke, David Joseph 1933- *WhoAm 92*
Gockel, John Raymond 1947- *WhoEmL 93*
Gockley, Barbara Jean 1951- *WhoAmW 93, WhoEmL 93*
Gockley, David 1943- *WhoAm 92*
Gockley, David Woodrow 1918- *WhoAm 92*
Gockley, James M. *Law&B 92*
Gockley, John C., Jr. *Law&B 92*
Gockowski, Adam Stefan 1953- *St&PR 93*
Goco, Raul Ilustre 1930- *WhoWor 93*
Goda, Ellen Marie Killelea 1952- *WhoAmW 93*
Goda, J. Joe 1943- *St&PR 93*
Goda, John Michael 1964- *WhoE 93*
Godar, John F. *Law&B 92*
Godara, Lal Chand 1952- *WhoWor 93*
Godard, Alain 1929- *WhoScE 91-2*
Godard, Barbara 1941- *WhoCanL 92*
Godard, Benjamin 1849-1895 *OxDcOp*
Godard, Benjamin (Louis Paul) 1849-1895 *Baker 92*
Godard, H. *WhoScE 91-2*
Godard, James McFate 1907- *WhoAm 92*
Godard, Jean Luc 1930- *BioIn 17, MiSFD 9, WhoAm 92, WhoWor 93*
Godard, Randy E. *Law&B 92*
Godart, Bruno 1956- *WhoScE 91-2*
Godbey, Helen Kay 1946- *WhoAmW 93, WhoEmL 93*
Godbey, Robert Carson 1953- *WhoEmL 93*
Godbold, Edward Stanly, Jr. 1942- *WhoSSW 93*
Godbold, F.S. 1943- *St&PR 93*
Godbold, Francis Stanley 1943- *WhoAm 92, WhoSSW 93*
Godbold, John Cooper 1920- *WhoAm 92, WhoSSW 93*
Godbold, Mollie Moore 1877- *AmWomPl*
Godbold, N. Terry 1948- *WhoIns 93*
Godbold, Wilford, Jr. 1938- *St&PR 93*
Godbold, Wilford Darrington, Jr. 1938- *WhoAm 92*
Godbout, Gregory J. 1946- *St&PR 93*
Godbout, Jacques 1933- *BioIn 17, ScF&FL 92, WhoCanL 92*
Godbout, Pamela Sue 1948- *WhoWrEP 92*
Godchaux, Charles R. 1930- *St&PR 93*
Godchaux, Frank A., III 1927- *St&PR 93*
Godchaux, Frank Area, III 1927- *WhoAm 92*
Goddard, A.B. 1943- *St&PR 93*
Goddard, A.J.H. *WhoScE 91-1*
Goddard, Arabella 1836-1922 *Baker 92*
Goddard, Carol Ann 1941- *WhoAmW 93*
Goddard, Daniel C. 1950- *WhoIns 93*
Goddard, David Benjamin 1947- *WhoEmL 93*
Goddard, Felicia *AmWomPl*
Goddard, Gary *MiSFD 9*
Goddard, Hazel Idella 1911- *WhoWrEP 92*
Goddard, James *ScF&FL 92*
Goddard, Jim 1936- *MiSFD 9*
Goddard, Joan *WhoCanL 92*
Goddard, Joe Dean 1936- *WhoAm 92*
Goddard, John Wesley 1941- *WhoAm 92*
Goddard, Morrill 1865-1937 *JrnUS*
Goddard, Paul Robert *WhoScE 91-1*
Goddard, Paulette 1911-1990 *BioIn 17, IntDcF 2-3 [port]*
Goddard, Peter John *WhoScE 91-1*
Goddard, Pliny Earle 1869-1928 *IntDcAn*
Goddard, Robert *BioIn 17*
Goddard, Robert Clyde 1951- *WhoE 93*
Goddard, Robert E. *Law&B 92*
Goddard, Robert Hale Ives 1909- *WhoAm 92*
Goddard, Robert Hutchings 1882-1945 *BioIn 17*
Goddard, Sandra Kay 1947- *WhoAmW 93*
Goddard, Terry *WhoAm 92*
Goddard, Thomas Glen 1955- *WhoE 93*
Goddard, Thomas H. 1940- *St&PR 93*
Goddard, William 1740-1817 *JrnUS*
Goddard, William Andrew, III 1937- *WhoAm 92*
Godddaed, Sandra B. 1949- *St&PR 93*
Godden, Rumer 1907- *BioIn 17, WhoAm 92*
Godden, (Margaret) Rumer 1907- *MajAI [port]*
Godderz, James S. *Law&B 92*
Goddess, Lynn Barbara 1942- *WhoAmW 93, WhoE 93, WhoWor 93*
Goddin, Clifton Sylvanus 1914- *WhoSSW 93*
Goddin, Jean 1946- *ScF&FL 92*
Goddin, Jeffrey 1950- *ScF&FL 92*
Godding, George Arthur 1920- *WhoAm 92*
Goddu, Roland Jean-Berchmans 1936- *WhoAm 92, WhoSSW 93*
Gode, Jeanne *Law&B 92*
Godea, Ioan 1943- *WhoWor 93*
Godebski, Cyprian 1835-1909 *PolBiDi*
Godec, Maksimilijan 1937- *WhoAm 92*
Godechot, Jacques Leon 1907-1989 *BioIn 17*
Godefroid, Patrice 1966- *WhoWor 93*
Godel, Kurt *BioIn 17*
Godell, Ralph W. *Law&B 92*
Godenne, Ghislaine Dudley *WhoAm 92*
Godet, Maurice R. 1930- *WhoScE 91-2*
Godett, Wilson *DcCPCAm*
Godey, Laurence R. *Law&B 92*
Godey, Louis Antoine *BioIn 17*
Godey, Louis Antoine 1804-1878 *JrnUS*
Godez, Susan Lynn 1953- *WhoEmL 93*
Godfraind, Theophile 1931- *WhoScE 91-2*
Godfraind, Theophile Joseph 1931- *WhoWor 93*
Godfree, Kitty d1992 *NewYTBS 92 [port]*
Godfrey, Arlene R. *Law&B 92*
Godfrey, Biff *Law&B 92*
Godfrey, Cullen M. 1945- *St&PR 93*
Godfrey, Cullen Michael *Law&B 92*
Godfrey, Cullen Michael 1945- *WhoAm 92*
Godfrey, Dan(iel) 1831-1903 *Baker 92*
Godfrey, Dan(iel Eyers) 1868-1939 *Baker 92*
Godfrey, David 1938- *WhoCanL 92*
Godfrey, Donald W. 1934- *St&PR 93*
Godfrey, Edward Farley 1949- *St&PR 93*
Godfrey, Ellen 1942- *WhoCanL 92*
Godfrey, George *Baker 92*
Godfrey, George Cheeseman, II 1926- *WhoE 93*
Godfrey, H.W. 1937- *St&PR 93*
Godfrey, Henry Philip 1941- *WhoE 93*
Godfrey, Isidore 1900-1977 *Baker 92*
Godfrey, James B. 1909- *St&PR 93*
Godfrey, James Brown 1909- *WhoAm 92*
Godfrey, James William, Jr. 1951- *WhoSSW 93*
Godfrey, John Morrow 1912- *St&PR 93, WhoAm 92*
Godfrey, John Munro 1941- *WhoAm 92, WhoSSW 93*
Godfrey, John S. 1937- *St&PR 93*
Godfrey, Joline Dudley 1950- *WhoEmL 93*
Godfrey, Keith Richard *WhoScE 91-1*
Godfrey, Kirk D. 1957- *St&PR 93*
Godfrey, Leslie George *WhoScE 91-1*
Godfrey, Loren 1939- *St&PR 93*
Godfrey, Marjorie Ann *WhoWrEP 92*
Godfrey, Martyn 1949- *WhoCanL 92*
Godfrey, Martyn N. 1949- *ScF&FL 92*
Godfrey, Nancy 1948- *WhoAmW 93*
Godfrey, Paul Victor 1939- *St&PR 93, WhoAm 92*
Godfrey, Robert Gordon 1927- *WhoAm 92*
Godfrey, Robert R. 1947- *WhoAm 92, WhoEmL 93, WhoWor 93*
Godfrey, Samuel Addison 1922- *WhoAm 92*
Godfrey, Walter P., Jr. 1944- *WhoSSW 93*
Godfrey, William *ConAu 37NR, MajAI*
Godfrey, William K. 1933- *St&PR 93*
Godfrey of Bouillon c. 1060-1100 *OxDcByz*
Godicke, Horst 1940- *WhoUN 92*
Godie, Lee *BioIn 17*
Godimel, Claude *Baker 92*
Godin, Arnold L. 1943- *St&PR 93*
Godin, Gilles C. 1959- *St&PR 93*
Godin, H. Richard 1931- *WhoWrEP 92*
Godin, Marcel 1932- *WhoCanL 92*
Godin, Philip Gerald *Law&B 92*
Godin, Raymond Hervey 1949- *WhoUN 92*
Godin, William N. 1936- *St&PR 93*
Godin des Odonais, Isabel 1728-1792 *Expl 93*
Godine, David Richard 1944- *WhoAm 92*
Godiner, Donald L. *Law&B 92*
Godiner, Donald Leonard 1933- *St&PR 93, WhoAm 92*
Godinez Flores, Ramon 1936- *WhoAm 92*
Goding, Jeffrey L. 1944- *St&PR 93*
Goding, Judith Germaine 1947- *WhoAmW 93*
Godino, Rino Lodovico 1925- *WhoAm 92, WhoE 93*
Godio, Julio Felix 1939- *WhoUN 92*
Godkin, Celia 1948- *BioIn 17*
Godkin, Edwin Lawrence 1831-1902 *JrnUS*
Godkin, Lynda *Law&B 92*
Godleski, John Joseph 1943- *WhoE 93*
Godlewska-Lipowa, Waclawa-Alicja 1929- *WhoScE 91-4*
Godlewski, James Bernard 1952- *WhoE 93, WhoEmL 93*
Godlewski, Julian 1903-1983 *PolBiDi*
Godlewski, Julian 1922- *WhoScE 91-4*
Godley, Georgina *BioIn 17*
Godley, Michael H.R. *WhoScE 91-1*
Godley, Nigel 1942- *St&PR 93*
Godley, William C. 1931- *St&PR 93*
Godley, Wynne *BioIn 17*
Godman, Fred D. *St&PR 93*
Godman, Gabriel Charles 1921- *WhoAm 92*
Godmanis, Ivars 1951- *WhoWor 93*
Godmilow, Jill *MiSFD 9*
Godoff, Ann 1949- *WhoAm 92*
Godofsky, Lawrence 1938- *WhoAm 92*
Godofsky, Stanley 1928- *WhoAm 92*
Godolphin, Sidney 1610-1643 *DcLB 126 [port]*
Godon, Bernard 1932- *WhoScE 91-2*
Godonis, Thomas Gerald 1949- *WhoAm 92*
Godown, Robert Lee 1946- *St&PR 93*
Godowski, Leopold 1870-1938 *PolBiDi*
Godowsky, Barry M. 1950- *St&PR 93*
Godowsky, Leopold 1870-1938 *Baker 92, BioIn 17*
Godoy, Emma 1918- *DcMexL*
Godoy, Virgilio *DcCPCAm*
Godoy Alcayaga, Lucila 1889-1957 *BioIn 17*
Godre, John Keith *Law&B 92*
Godreche, Judith *BioIn 17*
Godridge, Joseph Edward, Jr. 1926- *St&PR 93*
Godron, Hugo 1900-1971 *Baker 92*
Godschalk, David Robinson 1931- *WhoAm 92*
Godsey, Dwayne Erwin 1931- *St&PR 93*
Godsey, John Drew 1922- *WhoAm 92*
Godsey, Linda Carol 1946- *WhoAmW 93*
Godsey, William Cole 1933- *WhoSSW 93, WhoWor 93*
Godshalk, David R. 1935- *St&PR 93*
Godshalk, Henry W. 1921- *St&PR 93*
Godshalk, James Bond 1914- *St&PR 93*
Godshall, Jonathan H. 1948- *St&PR 93*
Godsman, James Gillinder 1940- *St&PR 93*
Godsoe, P.C. 1938- *St&PR 93*
Godsoe, Peter C. *BioIn 17*
Godsoe, Peter Cowperthwaite 1938- *WhoAm 92*
Godson, Godfrey Nigel 1936- *WhoAm 92*
Godson, Warren Lehman 1920- *WhoAm 92*
Godt, Stanley 1934- *St&PR 93*
Godun, Boris Vasiljevich 1949- *WhoWor 93*
Godunov, Alexander Boris 1949- *WhoAm 92*
Godwin, Audrey Louise 1963- *WhoAmW 93*
Godwin, Edward *ScF&FL 92*
Godwin, Gail 1937- *BioIn 17*
Godwin, Gail Kathleen 1937- *WhoAm 92, WhoWrEP 92*
Godwin, Harold Norman 1941- *WhoAm 92*
Godwin, Herbert James 1922- *WhoWor 93*
Godwin, James Beckham 1918- *WhoAm 92*
Godwin, James Edward 1931- *St&PR 93*
Godwin, Johnnie C. 1937- *St&PR 93*
Godwin, Joscelyn 1945- *Baker 92*
Godwin, Joseph Lawrence 1947- *WhoE 93*
Godwin, Linda M. 1952- *WhoAmW 93*
Godwin, Mary Jo 1949- *BioIn 17, WhoAmW 93, WhoSSW 93*
Godwin, Nancy Elizabeth 1951- *WhoAmW 93*
Godwin, Nora 1947- *WhoUN 92*
Godwin, Pamela June 1949- *WhoAm 92, WhoEmL 93*
Godwin, Parke 1929- *ScF&FL 92*
Godwin, Paul Kenneth, Jr. *Law&B 92*
Godwin, Paul Milton 1942- *WhoSSW 93*
Godwin, Phillip *BioIn 17*
Godwin, R. Wayne 1941- *St&PR 93, WhoAm 92, WhoE 93*
Godwin, Ralph Lee, Jr. 1954- *WhoE 93, WhoEmL 93*
Godwin, Rebecca T. 1950- *ConAu 139*
Godwin, Richard Jeffrey *Law&B 92*
Godwin, Sara 1944- *WhoAm 92, WhoAmW 93, WhoWor 93*
Godwin, Sara Moak 1924- *WhoSSW 93*
Godwin, Stephani *ScF&FL 92*
Godwin, Thomas *ScF&FL 92*
Godwin, Tom 1915-1980 *ScF&FL 92*
Godwin, William 1756-1836 *BioIn 17*
Godwin-Austen, Pamela 1952- *WhoEmL 93*
Godwin-Jones, Robert 1949- *ConAu 137*
Godycki-Cwirko, Tadeusz 1926- *WhoScE 91-4*
Godzik, Janusz Edwin 1927- *WhoWor 93*
Godzik, Stefan 1933- *WhoScE 91-4*
Goe, Eric A. 1948- *WhoE 93*
Goeb, Roger (John) 1914- *Baker 92*
Goebbels, Joseph 1897-1945 *BioIn 17*
Goebbels, Joseph Paul 1897-1945 *DcTwHis*
Goebbels, Klaus 1942- *WhoScE 91-3*
Goebbels, Paul Joseph 1897-1945 *BioIn 17*
Goebel, Bernard 1944- *St&PR 93*
Goebel, Daniel Donnelly 1964- *WhoSSW 93*
Goebel, Earle Stanwood 1930- *St&PR 93*
Goebel, Ellis C. *St&PR 93*
Goebel, Fred J., Jr. 1942- *St&PR 93*
Goebel, Jil Therese 1958- *WhoEmL 93*
Goebel, John J. 1930- *WhoAm 92*
Goebel, Peter H. 1939- *St&PR 93*
Goebel, Reinhard 1952- *Baker 92*
Goebel, Richard Alan 1944- *WhoAm 92*
Goebel, Richard McNeil 1955- *WhoEmL 93*
Goebel, Robert J. 1923- *BioIn 17*
Goebel, Walther Frederick 1899- *WhoAm 92*
Goebel, Werner 1939- *WhoScE 91-3*
Goebel, William Douglas 1950- *WhoEmL 93, WhoSSW 93*
Goebel, William Mathers 1922- *WhoAm 92*
Goebelbecker, William John *Law&B 92*
Goebeler, George Francis 1941- *WhoAm 92*
Goebert, Donald F.U. 1936- *St&PR 93*
Goebert, Robert J. 1941- *WhoAm 92*
Goebert, Robert Jeremy 1941- *St&PR 93*
Goebes, Diane Diaz 1948- *WhoAmW 93*
Goecke, Floyd C. 1931- *St&PR 93*
Goedde, Alan George 1948- *WhoEmL 93, WhoWor 93*
Goedde, H. Werner 1927- *WhoScE 91-3*
Goedde, Josef 1953- *WhoWor 93*
Goedde, William Richard 1930- *St&PR 93, WhoIns 93*
Goedderz, Thomas Jay *Law&B 92*
Goedecke, Colin Edward 1958- *WhoEmL 93*
Goedecke, David Stewart 1929- *WhoAm 92*
Goedegebuure, Ben G. *WhoScE 91-3*
Goedeke, Nancy Lynn 1955- *WhoEmL 93*
Goedeker, Raymond Bernard 1923- *St&PR 93*
Goedert, John P. 1913- *St&PR 93*
Goedicke, Hans 1926- *WhoAm 92*
Goedicke, Patricia 1931- *WhoWrEP 92*
Goedike, Alexander 1877-1957 *Baker 92*
Goedken, Ann Mary 1949- *WhoAmW 93*
Goedken, Florian H. 1929- *St&PR 93*
Goeggel, Richard Arthur 1951- *St&PR 93*
Goeglein, John B. 1922- *St&PR 93*
Goeglein, Richard John 1934- *WhoAm 92*
Goehner, Donna Marie 1941- *WhoAmW 93*
Goehr, Alexander 1932- *IntDcOp, OxDcOp*
Goehr, (Peter) Alexander 1932- *Baker 92*
Goehr, Walter 1903-1960 *Baker 92, OxDcOp*
Goehring, John Brown 1935- *WhoAm 92, WhoWor 93*
Goehring, Kenneth 1919- *WhoAm 92*
Goehring, Maude Cope 1915- *WhoAmW 93*
Goehring, Robert E. 1944- *St&PR 93*

Goehring, Stanley E. 1944- *St&PR 93*
Goekmen, Ariel Sergio 1967- *WhoWor 93*
Goel, Amrit Lal 1938- *WhoAm 92*
Goeldi, Emilio Augusto 1859-1917 *IntDcAn*
Goeldner, Charles Raymond 1932- *WhoAm 92*
Goelet, Robert G. 1923- *WhoAm 92, WhoE 93*
Goelitz, Milly June *AmWomPl*
Goelkel, Gary Morgan 1953- *WhoEmL 93*
Goell, James Emanuel 1939- *WhoAm 92*
Goeller, Christine Jane 1951- *WhoE 93, WhoWor 93*
Goeller, Leo F. 1925- *WhoE 93*
Goeller, Roger F. 1941- *St&PR 93*
Goellner, Jack Gordon 1930- *WhoAm 92*
Goellnitz, Gerhard-Carl 1920- *WhoWor 93*
Goeltz, Richard Karl 1942- *WhoAm 92*
Goelz, John Matthew 1957- *WhoWor 93*
Goelz, Paul Cornelius 1914- *WhoAm 92*
Goelzer, Berenice Isabel Ferrari 1940- *WhoUN 92*
Goelzer, Daniel Lee 1947- *WhoAm 92, WhoE 93*
Goelzer, David Murray *Law&B 92*
Goelzer, Linda *BioIn 17*
Goelzer, Lucio 1938- *WhoUN 92*
Goemaat, John F. *Law&B 92*
Goeminne, Patrick 1945- *WhoScE 91-2*
Goen, C.C. *BioIn 17*
Goencueoglu, M. Cemal 1948- *WhoScE 91-4*
Goenner, Judith Mary 1948- *WhoWrEP 92*
Goens, Donald V. 1957- *St&PR 93*
Goepfart, Christian Heinrich 1835-1890 *See* Goepfart, Karl Eduard 1859-1942 *Baker 92*
Goepfart, Karl Eduard 1859-1942 *Baker 92*
Goepfert, Eric Richard 1946- *WhoEmL 93*
Goepfert, Robert Harold 1935- *WhoE 93*
Goepp, Philip H(enry) 1864-1936 *Baker 92*
Goepp, Robert August 1930- *WhoAm 92*
Goeppert-Mayer, Maria 1906-1972 *BioIn 17*
Goer, Alan Barry 1949- *St&PR 93*
Goerdt, Marcia Fae 1950- *WhoEmL 93*
Goergen, Jan Roger 1935- *WhoWor 93*
Goergen, John Peter 1948- *WhoEmL 93*
Goergen, Robert B. 1938- *St&PR 93*
Goergen, Ronald M. 1942- *St&PR 93*
Goering, Albert H. 1926- *St&PR 93*
Goering, Carroll E. 1934- *WhoAm 92*
Goering, George L. 1935- *St&PR 93*
Goering, Hermann 1893-1946 *BioIn 17*
Goering, Hermann Wilhelm 1893-1946 *DcTwHis*
Goering, Kenneth Justin 1913- *WhoAm 92*
Goering, Reinhard 1887-1936 *DcLB 118 [port]*
Goering, Robert Albert 1960- *WhoEmL 93*
Goerke, Glenn Allen 1931- *WhoSSW 93*
Goerler, Ronald B. 1925- *St&PR 93*
Goerner, Edward Alfred 1929- *WhoAm 92*
Goers, Melvin Armand 1918- *WhoAm 92*
Goerss, Richard G. *Law&B 92*
Goerttler, Klaus 1925- *WhoScE 91-3*
Goertz, Augustus Frederick, III 1948- *WhoAm 92*
Goertz, Christoph K. 1944-1991 *BioIn 17*
Goertz, Erik 1940- *WhoWor 93*
Goertz, Gary Wayne 1952- *St&PR 93*
Goerz, Mary Elizabeth 1935- *WhoAmW 93*
Goes, Bertha *AmWomPl*
Goes, Charles B. 1917- *St&PR 93*
Goes, Charles Berthold, IV 1947- *St&PR 93*
Goes, Gunther Walter 1921- *WhoWor 93*
Goessel, William Warren 1927- *St&PR 93*
Goessling, John Gerald 1928- *St&PR 93*
Goessling, Werner 1946- *WhoWor 93*
Goetcheus, John Stewart 1938- *WhoE 93*
Goetel, Ferdynand 1890-1960 *PolBiDi*
Goeth, Joe A. 1921- *St&PR 93*
Goethals, Angela *BioIn 17*
Goethals, Eric E.J. 1936- *WhoScE 91-2*
Goethals, George R. 1944- *WhoAm 92*
Goethals, George Washington 1856-1928 *HarEnMi*
Goethals, J.-M. *WhoScE 91-2*
Goethals, Lucien (Gustave Georges) 1931- *Baker 92*
Goethals, Patricia 1963- *WhoWor 93*
Goethe, Johann Wolfgang von 1749-1832 *Baker 92, BioIn 17, MagSWL [port], MajAI [port], OxDcOp, PoeCrit 5 [port]*
Goetsch, Alma 1901-1968 *BioIn 17*
Goetsch, Gary Gordon 1938- *WhoAm 92*
Goetsch, John Hubert 1933- *St&PR 93, WhoAm 92*
Goetsch, Richard J. *Law&B 92*
Goetsch, Virginia Louise 1955- *WhoAmW 93*
Goetschalckx, Marc 1954- *WhoEmL 93*
Goetschius, Herbert T. 1950- *St&PR 93*
Goetschius, Percy 1853-1943 *Baker 92*
Goette, Klaus H. W. 1932- *WhoWor 93*
Goettler, Herbert Rudolf Jakob 1946- *WhoWor 93*
Goettling-Krause, Gisela Erika Waltraud 1926- *WhoAm 92*
Goetz, Barbara *Law&B 92*
Goetz, Betty Barrett 1943- *WhoAmW 93*
Goetz, Cecelia Helen *WhoAmW 93*
Goetz, Curt 1888-1960 *DcLB 124 [port]*
Goetz, Donald Lee 1936- *St&PR 93*
Goetz, Hermann 1840-1876 *OxDcOp*
Goetz, Hermann (Gustav) 1840-1876 *Baker 92*
Goetz, John Bullock 1920- *WhoAm 92, WhoWrEP 92*
Goetz, Karl Georg 1930- *WhoScE 91-3*
Goetz, Kenneth D. *Law&B 92*
Goetz, Lionel John 1943- *St&PR 93*
Goetz, Lothar 1925- *WhoWor 93*
Goetz, Maurice Harold 1924- *WhoAm 92*
Goetz, Maxwell *WhoWrEP 92*
Goetz, Paul A. 1931- *St&PR 93*
Goetz, Peter Benedict 1934- *St&PR 93, WhoAm 92*
Goetz, Philip W. 1927- *WhoAm 92*
Goetz, Richard George *Law&B 92*
Goetz, Robert Clifford 1941- *WhoAm 92*
Goetz, Theodore 1947- *St&PR 93*
Goetz, Thomas Henry Paul 1936- *WhoWor 93*
Goetz, William K. 1940- *St&PR 93*
Goetzberger, Adolf 1928- *WhoScE 91-3*
Goetze, David Wesley 1954- *WhoSSW 93*
Goetze, Robert C. 1924- *St&PR 93*
Goetze, Walter W. 1883-1961 *Baker 92*
Goetzen, Bogdan Bronislaw 1925- *WhoScE 91-4*
Goetzke, Gloria Louise *WhoAmW 93, WhoWor 93*
Goetzke, Ronald Richard 1933- *St&PR 93, WhoIns 93*
Goetzl, Judith Chuckrow *WhoSSW 93*
Goetzman, John Robert 1949- *WhoEmL 93, WhoSSW 93*
Goewey, Gordon Ira 1924- *WhoAm 92*
Goewey, James Arthur 1929- *St&PR 93*
Goeyvaerts, Karel (August) 1923- *Baker 92*
Goez, Carlos R. d1990 *BioIn 17*
Goff, Christopher L. *Law&B 92*
Goff, Christopher Wallick 1948- *WhoEmL 93*
Goff, Daniel 1961- *St&PR 93*
Goff, Harry Russell 1915- *WhoAm 92*
Goff, J. Edward *Law&B 92*
Goff, J. Edward 1933- *St&PR 93*
Goff, Jerry K. 1952- *St&PR 93*
Goff, Joyce Sullivan *Law&B 92*
Goff, Kathleen Ann Murray 1960- *WhoEmL 93*
Goff, Kathleen Elaine 1954- *WhoSSW 93*
Goff, Kenneth W. 1928- *St&PR 93*
Goff, Kenneth Wade 1928- *WhoAm 92*
Goff, Laura Mae Blume 1932- *WhoAmW 93*
Goff, Lila Johnson 1944- *WhoAm 92, WhoAmW 93*
Goff, Michael Harper 1927- *WhoAm 92, WhoWor 93*
Goff, R. Garey 1943- *WhoSSW 93*
Goff, Raymond Ellis 1945- *WhoAm 92*
Goff, Robert Burnside 1924- *WhoAm 92*
Goff, Robert Edward 1952- *WhoE 93*
Goff, Robert M. *Law&B 92*
Goff, Stanley Norman 1923- *St&PR 93*
Goff, Steven Lee 1958- *WhoEmL 93*
Goff, Wayne B. 1938- *St&PR 93*
Goffart, Walter (Andre) 1934- *ConAu 38NR, WhoAm 92, WhoWrEP 92*
Goffaux, Pierre Eugene 1938- *St&PR 93*
Goffe, George Stanley 1926- *St&PR 93*
Goffe, Toni *BioIn 17*
Goffe, William A. 1929- *CngDr 91*
Goffe, William Gregory 1949- *WhoAm 92, WhoEmL 93*
Goffen, Rona 1944- *WhoAm 92*
Goffin, Dallas Clive *ScF&FL 92*
Goffin, Gerry *BioIn 17*
Goffin, Gerry 1939- *See* Goffin & King *SoulM*
Goffin, Josse 1938- *BioIn 17*
Goffin, Leon Marie 1914- *WhoWor 93*
Goffin & King *SoulM*
Goffinet, Edward Peter, Jr. 1930- *WhoE 93*
Goffinet, Francois *BioIn 17*
Goffinet, Ray Frank 1929- *St&PR 93*
Goffinet, Serge 1959- *WhoWor 93*
Goffman, Martin 1940- *WhoE 93*
Goffman, William 1924- *WhoAm 92*
Goffredo, Daniel Louis 1923- *St&PR 93*
Goffredo, R. Michael 1927- *St&PR 93*
Goffstein, Brooke *MajAI, SmATA 70*
Goffstein, M.B. *BioIn 17*
Goffstein, M. B. 1940- *SmATA 70 [port]*
Goffstein, M(arilyn) B(rooke) 1940- *MajAI [port]*
Goforth, Carolyn Mae 1931- *WhoAm 92*
Goforth, Charles D. 1921- *St&PR 93*
Goforth, Joy 1921- *WhoSSW 93*
Goforth, Mary Elaine 1922- *WhoAmW 93*
Goforth, William Clements 1937- *WhoSSW 93*
Gofrank, Frank L. 1918- *St&PR 93*
Gofrank, Frank Louis 1918- *WhoAm 92*
Goga, Fakhruddin 1948- *WhoWor 93*
Gogan, Catherine Mary 1959- *WhoAmW 93*
Gogan, James Wilson 1938- *WhoAm 92, WhoE 93*
Gogarty, William Barney 1930- *WhoAm 92*
Gogel, Timothy J. *St&PR 93*
Goggan, Celeste Roxanne 1950- *St&PR 93*
Goggans, Cathy Diane 1957- *WhoEmL 93, WhoSSW 93*
Goggans, Roberta Daily 1926- *WhoAmW 93*
Goggi, V.G. 1943- *WhoScE 91-4*
Goggi, Virginio Giorgio 1943- *WhoWor 93*
Goggin, Dan *BioIn 17*
Goggin, Daniel Brendon 1935- *St&PR 93*
Goggin, Joan Marie 1956- *WhoAmW 93*
Goggin, Joseph Robert 1926- *WhoAm 92*
Goggin, Margaret Knox 1919- *WhoAm 92*
Goggin, William E. 1945- *St&PR 93*
Goggins, Bari E. *Law&B 92*
Goggins, Glenn J. *Law&B 92*
Goggins, John Francis 1933- *WhoAm 92*
Gogh, Vincent van 1853-1890 *BioIn 17*
Goghan, Robert *St&PR 93*
Gogick, Kathleen Christine 1945- *WhoAm 92*
Gogisgi *WhoWrEP 92*
Gogliettino, John Carmine 1952- *WhoE 93, WhoEmL 93*
Gogoberidze, Lana 1928- *DrEEuF*
Gogol, John Michael 1938- *WhoWrEP 92*
Gogol, Nikolai 1809-1852 *MagSWL [port], WorLitC [port]*
Gogol, Nikolay 1809-1852 *OxDcOp*
Gogolin, Marilyn Tompkins 1946- *WhoAmW 93*
Gogorza, Emilio (Edoardo) de 1874-1949 *Baker 92*
Goguel, Claude Arnaud 1936- *WhoWor 93*
Goguen, Joseph Amadee 1941- *WhoWor 93*
Goguen, Paul Arthur 1929- *St&PR 93*
Goh, Chuen-Jin 1956- *WhoWor 93*
Goh, David Shuh-jen 1941- *WhoE 93*
Goh, Kiam Seng 1937- *WhoUN 92*
Goh, Kuang Huah 1946- *WhoWor 93*
Goh, Taijiro 1907-1970 *Baker 92*
Goh, Thong-Ngee 1947- *WhoWor 93*
Goh Cheng Teik, Dr. 1943- *WhoAsAP 91*
Goh Chok Tong 1941- *WhoAsAP 91, WhoWor 93*
Gohdes, Clarence Louis Frank 1901- *WhoSSW 93*
Goheen, Jean Holdridge 1937- *WhoAmW 93*
Goheen, Richard C. 1936- *St&PR 93*
Goheen, Robert Francis 1919- *WhoAm 92*
Goheen, Steven Charles 1951- *WhoEmL 93*
Gohil, Pratapsinh 1950- *WhoEmL 93*
Gohler, (Karl) Georg 1874-1954 *Baker 92*
Gohlke, Frank William 1942- *WhoAm 92*
Gohmann, J. Michael 1945- *St&PR 93*
Gohmann, Timothy 1947- *WhoEmL 93*
Gohn, David *BioIn 17*
Goiburn, Gordon Henry 1938- *St&PR 93*
Goichman, Jane C.L. *Law&B 92*
Goicoechea, Ana M. *ScF&FL 92*
Goidell, Sheldon W. 1927- *St&PR 93*
Goin, Dale *BioIn 17*
Goin, Gerard 1938- *WhoScE 91-2*
Going, William Thornbury 1915- *WhoAm 92*
Goings, Everett V. 1945- *St&PR 93*
Goings, Everett Vernon 1945- *WhoAm 92*
Goings, James Arden 1941- *St&PR 93*
Goings, Susan Simmons 1958- *WhoAmW 93*
Goins, Donald L. *St&PR 93*
Goins, Kenneth M., Jr. 1958- *St&PR 93*
Goins, Mary Jeanne 1921- *WhoAmW 93*
Goins, Michael Edgar 1954- *WhoEmL 93, WhoSSW 93*
Goins, Richard Anthony 1950- *WhoSSW 93*
Goiria, Mercedes *Law&B 92*
Goisman, Robert Michael 1947- *WhoEmL 93*
Goizueta, Roberto C. *BioIn 17*
Goizueta, Roberto C. 1931- *HispAmA [port], St&PR 93*
Goizueta, Roberto Crispulo 1931- *WhoAm 92, WhoSSW 93, WhoWor 93*
Gojmerac-Leiner, Georgia 1949- *WhoWrEP 92*
Gokay, Michael Alan 1951- *WhoE 93, WhoEmL 93*
Gokee, Donald LeRoy 1933- *WhoWor 93*
Gokey, Franklin Charles 1916- *WhoIns 93*
Gokhale, Maya Balkrishna 1952- *WhoAmW 93*
Gokongwei, John *BioIn 17*
Goksel, Faut A. 1926- *WhoScE 91-4*
Goksel, Selahattin A. 1925- *WhoScE 91-4*
Gol, Jean 1942- *WhoWor 93*
Gola, Sandra Valentina 1955- *WhoAmW 93, WhoEmL 93*
Golab, Boguslaw Kazimierz 1929- *WhoScE 91-4*
Golabek, Jakub 1739-1789 *PolBiDi*
Golahny, Amy 1951- *WhoAmW 93*
Golan, Amnon J. 1939- *WhoUN 92*
Golan, Menahem 1929- *MiSFD 9, WhoAm 92*
Golan, Stephen Leonard 1951- *WhoEmL 93*
Goland, Martin 1919- *St&PR 93, WhoAm 92*
Golander, Carl-Gustaf 1953- *WhoScE 91-4*
Golann, Dwight 1947- *WhoEmL 93*
Golany, Gideon Salomon 1928- *WhoAm 92*
Golar, Martha L. *Law&B 92*
Golar, Martha L. 1953- *WhoE 93*
Golashesky, Chrysa Zofia 1957- *WhoAmW 93, WhoEmL 93*
Golaski, Walter Michael 1913- *WhoAm 92, WhoWor 93*
Golaszewski, Richard Stanley 1947- *WhoE 93*
Golay, Alain *WhoScE 91-4*
Golay, Marcel 1927- *WhoScE 91-4*
Golba, Theodore T. 1958- *St&PR 93*
Golboro, Alan S. 1930- *St&PR 93*
Gold, Aaron A. 1919- *St&PR 93*
Gold, Aaron Alan 1919- *WhoAm 92*
Gold, Alan 1944- *WhoAm 92*
Gold, Alan B. 1917- *WhoAm 92*
Gold, Alan H. 1951- *St&PR 93*
Gold, Alan Stephen 1944- *WhoAm 92, WhoSSW 93*
Gold, Albert 1916- *WhoAm 92*
Gold, Alison Leslie 1945- *ConAu 136*
Gold, Allen Morton 1930- *WhoE 93*
Gold, Andrew Paul 1961- *WhoEmL 93*
Gold, Arnold Henry 1932- *WhoAm 92*
Gold, Arthur 1917-1990 *Baker 92*
Gold, Artie 1947- *WhoCanL 92*
Gold, Bela 1915- *WhoAm 92*
Gold, Bernard 1923- *WhoAm 92*
Gold, Bruce 1943- *St&PR 93*
Gold, Carol Sapin *WhoAm 92*
Gold, Clifford Charles *Law&B 92*
Gold, Daniel Howard 1942- *WhoSSW 93*
Gold, Deborah T. 1951- *WhoAmW 93*
Gold, Dennis Charles 1952- *WhoE 93*
Gold, Doris Bauman 1919- *WhoWrEP 92*
Gold, E.J. 1941- *ScF&FL 92*
Gold, Edgar 1934- *WhoAm 92*
Gold, Edwin 1931- *WhoWor 93*
Gold, Erica Louise 1959- *WhoEmL 93*
Gold, Ernest 1921- *Baker 92*
Gold, Errol Samuel 1949- *St&PR 93*
Gold, Eugene 1928- *St&PR 93*
Gold, Fay Helfano 1907- *WhoE 93*
Gold, Gerald Seymour 1931- *WhoAm 92*
Gold, Gregg *MiSFD 9*
Gold, Harold Arthur 1929- *WhoAm 92*
Gold, Harry *Law&B 92*
Gold, Heidi J. 1963- *WhoAmW 93*
Gold, Helen M. *Law&B 92*
Gold, Herbert 1924- *BioIn 17, JeAmFiW, WhoWrEP 92*
Gold, Herbert Frank 1939- *St&PR 93, WhoAm 92*
Gold, Hilary Alexander 1931- *WhoE 93*
Gold, Horace L. 1914- *ScF&FL 92*
Gold, I. Randall 1951- *WhoEmL 93, WhoSSW 93, WhoWor 93*
Gold, Ivan 1932- *WhoWrEP 92*
Gold, Jack 1930- *ConTFT 10, MiSFD 9*
Gold, Jay D. 1942- *WhoAm 92*
Gold, Jeffrey M. 1945- *St&PR 93*
Gold, Jeffrey Mark 1945- *WhoAm 92*
Gold, Jerome *ScF&FL 92*
Gold, Jimmy 1886-1967 *See* Crazy Gang, The *IntDcF 2-3*
Gold, Joe 1950- *WhoWrEP 92*
Gold, Jon H. 1947- *St&PR 93*
Gold, Joseph 1912- *BioIn 17*
Gold, Joseph 1930- *WhoAm 92, WhoWor 93*
Gold, Judith Hammerling 1941- *WhoAm 92*
Gold, Julie *BioIn 17*
Gold, Laurence Stephen 1936- *WhoAm 92*
Gold, Lawrence L. 1950- *WhoAm 92*
Gold, Leonard C. 1926- *St&PR 93*
Gold, Leonard Singer 1934- *WhoAm 92*
Gold, Leonard Steven 1954- *St&PR 93*
Gold, Lois E. *Law&B 92*

Gold, Lois Meyer 1945- *WhoAmW 93*
Gold, Lonny 1951- *St&PR 93*
Gold, Lorne W. 1928- *WhoAm 92*
Gold, Lou *BioIn 17*
Gold, Manny 1920- *St&PR 93*
Gold, Mari S. 1940- *WhoAm 92*
Gold, Mark Samuel *Law&B 92*
Gold, Mark Stephen 1949- *WhoEmL 93*
Gold, Martin Elliot 1946- *WhoAm 92*
Gold, Melissa d1991 *BioIn 17*
Gold, Michael 1893-1967 *JeAmFiW*
Gold, Michael 1950- *ConAu 139*
Gold, Michael Evan 1943- *ConAu 138*
Gold, Miriam V. *Law&B 92*
Gold, Mortimer H. d1990 *BioIn 17*
Gold, Norma Bernice 1941- *WhoAmW 93*
Gold, Norman Myron 1930- *WhoAm 92*
Gold, Patricia Mc Manus 1934- *WhoWrEP 92*
Gold, Paul Ernest 1945- *WhoSSW 93*
Gold, Paul Nicholas 1953- *WhoEmL 93*
Gold, Peter S. *Law&B 92*
Gold, Peter Stephen 1941- *St&PR 93*
Gold, Phil 1936- *WhoAm 92*
Gold, Philip William 1944- *WhoAm 92*
Gold, Phradie Kling 1933- *WhoAmW 93, WhoE 93*
Gold, R. Ilise 1954- *WhoE 93*
Gold, Richard Horace 1935- *WhoAm 92, WhoWor 93*
Gold, Richard L. *Law&B 92*
Gold, Richard L. 1925- *St&PR 93*
Gold, Rick A. 1949- *St&PR 93*
Gold, Robert F. 1953- *St&PR 93*
Gold, Robert James 1932- *St&PR 93*
Gold, Robert S. 1924- *BioIn 17*
Gold, Ronald D. 1954- *WhoSSW 93*
Gold, Sally Cohn 1948- *WhoAmW 93*
Gold, Sandra Orenberg 1937- *WhoAm 92, WhoAmW 93*
Gold, Seymour (Murray) 1933- *WhoWrEP 92*
Gold, Shirley Jeanne 1925- *WhoAmW 93*
Gold, Stanley *BioIn 17*
Gold, Stanley P. 1942- *WhoAm 92*
Gold, Steven Neal 1953- *WhoSSW 93*
Gold, Stuart 1935- *St&PR 93*
Gold, Sylviane 1948- *WhoAm 92, WhoEmL 93*
Gold, Thomas 1920- *WhoAm 92*
Gold, Thomas Robert *Law&B 92*
Gold, Todd 1958- *ConAu 136*
Gold, Tracey *BioIn 17*
Gold, Vera Johnson 1951- *WhoAm 92*
Gold, William 1937- *St&PR 93*
Gold, William Elliott 1948- *WhoE 93*
Goldammer, Kurt Moritz Artur 1916- *WhoWor 93*
Goldanskii, Vitalii Iosifovich 1923- *WhoWor 93*
Goldbach, Michael H. 1953- *WhoScE 91-3*
Goldbach, Richard Albert 1936- *St&PR 93*
Goldbach, Scott Paxton 1960- *WhoEmL 93*
Goldbarg, Jeffrey Robbins 1948- *WhoEmL 93*
Goldbarth, Albert *BioIn 17*
Goldbarth, Albert 1948- *ConAu 40NR, DcLB 120 [port]*
Goldbaum, Roberto 1951- *WhoWor 93*
Goldbeck, Carl W. 1923- *St&PR 93*
Goldbeck, George 1925- *St&PR 93*
Goldbeck, George P. 1925- *WhoIns 93*
Goldbeck, Robert 1839-1908 *Baker 92*
Goldberg, Alan Eliot 1931- *WhoAm 92*
Goldberg, Alan (Howard) 1942- *WhoWrEP 92*
Goldberg, Alan Jeffrey 1949- *WhoE 93*
Goldberg, Alan Joel 1943- *WhoWor 93*
Goldberg, Alan M. 1930- *St&PR 93*
Goldberg, Alan Marvin 1939- *WhoAm 92, WhoE 93*
Goldberg, Albert 1898-1990 *Baker 92*
Goldberg, Allan Seth 1955- *WhoE 93*
Goldberg, Anatolii Asirovich 1930- *WhoWor 93*
Goldberg, Anne Carol 1951- *WhoEmL 93*
Goldberg, Arnold Irving 1929- *WhoAm 92*
Goldberg, Arthur Abba 1940- *WhoAm 92*
Goldberg, Arthur H. 1942- *WhoAm 92*
Goldberg, Arthur Henry 1905-1990 *BioIn 17*
Goldberg, Arthur Howard 1942- *St&PR 93*
Goldberg, Arthur J. *BioIn 17*
Goldberg, Arthur J. 1908-1990 *JeAmHC*
Goldberg, Arthur Joseph 1908-1990 *OxCSupC [port]*
Goldberg, Arthur Lewis 1939- *WhoAm 92*
Goldberg, Arthur M. *WhoAm 92*
Goldberg, Arthur M. 1924-1991 *BioIn 17*
Goldberg, Avram Jacob 1930- *WhoAm 92*
Goldberg, Barbara June 1943- *WhoWrEP 92*
Goldberg, Barnet H. 1908- *St&PR 93*
Goldberg, Barton Sheldon 1933- *St&PR 93*
Goldberg, Bernard Arthur 1944- *WhoE 93*
Goldberg, Bertram J. 1942- *WhoAm 92*
Goldberg, Bertrand 1913- *WhoAm 92*
Goldberg, Beverly Rappaport 1931- *WhoE 93*
Goldberg, Bruce R. *Law&B 92*
Goldberg, Burton S. d1990 *BioIn 17*
Goldberg, Carl 1938- *WhoE 93*
Goldberg, Carol Rabb 1931- *WhoAm 92*
Goldberg, Caryn 1953- *WhoAmW 93*
Goldberg, Charles *Law&B 92*
Goldberg, Conrad Stewart 1943- *WhoE 93*
Goldberg, Dan *MiSFD 9*
Goldberg, Daniel Lewis 1939- *St&PR 93*
Goldberg, Danny *BioIn 17*
Goldberg, David Alan 1933- *WhoAm 92*
Goldberg, David Charles 1940- *WhoAm 92*
Goldberg, David Edward 1953- *WhoEmL 93*
Goldberg, David Elliott 1932- *WhoE 93*
Goldberg, David H. 1958- *St&PR 93*
Goldberg, David Meyer 1933- *WhoAm 92*
Goldberg, Deborah Baron 1942- *WhoAmW 93*
Goldberg, Dennis 1942- *St&PR 93*
Goldberg, E. Susan 1937- *St&PR 93*
Goldberg, Edward 1929- *WhoAm 92, WhoE 93*
Goldberg, Edward 1940- *WhoAm 92*
Goldberg, Edward D. *BioIn 17*
Goldberg, Edward Davidow 1921- *WhoAm 92*
Goldberg, Edward Jay 1950- *WhoSSW 93*
Goldberg, Elliott Marshall 1930- *WhoAm 92*
Goldberg, Erwin B. 1945- *WhoE 93*
Goldberg, Fred Sellmann 1941- *WhoAm 92*
Goldberg, Fred T. *BioIn 17*
Goldberg, Fred T., Jr. *WhoAm 92*
Goldberg, Gary David *BioIn 17, MiSFD 9*
Goldberg, Gary David 1944- *ConTFT 10, WhoAm 92*
Goldberg, Geraldine Elizabeth 1939- *WhoAm 92, WhoAmW 93, WhoE 93, WhoWor 93*
Goldberg, Gerry *ScF&FL 92*
Goldberg, Glenn Steven 1958- *St&PR 93*
Goldberg, Hannah Friedman 1933- *WhoAm 92*
Goldberg, Harold Howard 1924- *WhoE 93*
Goldberg, Harold Seymour 1925- *WhoAm 92, WhoE 93*
Goldberg, Harriet L. *Law&B 92*
Goldberg, Harry Finck 1936- *WhoAm 92*
Goldberg, Harry L. d1991 *BioIn 17*
Goldberg, Herman Raphael 1915- *WhoAm 92*
Goldberg, Hilary Tham 1946- *WhoWrEP 92*
Goldberg, Homer Beryl 1924- *WhoAm 92*
Goldberg, Honey L. *Law&B 92*
Goldberg, Howard E. 1946- *St&PR 93*
Goldberg, Icchok Ignacy 1916- *WhoAm 92*
Goldberg, Idelle *Law&B 92*
Goldberg, Idelle Anne *Law&B 92*
Goldberg, Ira 1948- *WhoE 93*
Goldberg, Irving Hyman 1926- *WhoAm 92*
Goldberg, Ivan D. 1934- *WhoAm 92*
Goldberg, Jacob 1926- *WhoAm 92*
Goldberg, Jane *BioIn 17*
Goldberg, Jane G. 1946- *ConAu 138*
Goldberg, Jean 1922- *St&PR 93*
Goldberg, Jerold Martin 1938- *WhoAm 92*
Goldberg, Jocelyn Hope Schnier 1953- *WhoAmW 93, WhoEmL 93*
Goldberg, Jodi Lynn 1961- *WhoEmL 93*
Goldberg, Joel Henry 1945- *WhoWor 93*
Goldberg, Johann Gottlieb 1727-1756 *Baker 92*
Goldberg, Jonathan R. 1930-1991 *BioIn 17*
Goldberg, Joseph Jim 1953- *WhoE 93, WhoEmL 93*
Goldberg, Joseph Philip 1918- *WhoE 93*
Goldberg, Kenneth Philip 1945- *WhoE 93*
Goldberg, Lawrence Irwin 1940- *WhoAm 92*
Goldberg, Lee H. *Law&B 92*
Goldberg, Lee Winicki 1932- *WhoAmW 93, WhoWor 93*
Goldberg, Leo 1913-1987 *BioIn 17*
Goldberg, Leonard 1934- *WhoAm 92*
Goldberg, Lorri Schwartz 1954- *WhoAmW 93*
Goldberg, Luella Gross 1937- *WhoAm 92*
Goldberg, Lyssa S. *Law&B 92*
Goldberg, M. A. *WhoAm 92*
Goldberg, Malcolm 1936- *WhoE 93*
Goldberg, Marc David 1944- *WhoSSW 93*
Goldberg, Marc Evan 1957- *WhoE 93, WhoEmL 93, WhoWor 93*
Goldberg, Marcel *WhoScE 91-2*
Goldberg, Mark *Law&B 92*
Goldberg, Mark Steven 1952- *St&PR 93*
Goldberg, Marlene S. *Law&B 92*
Goldberg, Marshall 1930- *ScF&FL 92*
Goldberg, Martin 1930- *WhoAm 92, WhoE 93*
Goldberg, Marvin 1928- *St&PR 93*
Goldberg, Maxwell Henry 1907- *WhoSSW 93*
Goldberg, Mel J. 1944- *St&PR 93*
Goldberg, Melvin A. *WhoE 93*
Goldberg, Melvin Arthur 1923- *WhoAm 92*
Goldberg, Michael Arthur 1941- *WhoAm 92*
Goldberg, Michael E. *Law&B 92*
Goldberg, Michael H. 1949- *WhoE 93*
Goldberg, Michael M. 1959- *St&PR 93*
Goldberg, Michel E. 1938- *WhoScE 91-2*
Goldberg, Mitchell 1957- *St&PR 93*
Goldberg, Morris M. d1991 *BioIn 17*
Goldberg, Morton Edward 1932- *WhoAm 92*
Goldberg, Morton Falk 1937- *WhoAm 92*
Goldberg, Morton Harold 1933- *WhoE 93*
Goldberg, Moses Haym 1940- *WhoSSW 93*
Goldberg, Murray M. 1929- *St&PR 93*
Goldberg, Myron Allen 1942- *WhoE 93*
Goldberg, Neil A. 1947- *WhoAm 92*
Goldberg, Norman Albert 1918- *WhoAm 92*
Goldberg, Pamela Winer 1955- *WhoAmW 93, WhoEmL 93*
Goldberg, Paul M. 1928- *St&PR 93*
Goldberg, Philip J. 1948- *St&PR 93*
Goldberg, Rachelle 1900-1991 *BioIn 17*
Goldberg, Ray Allan 1926- *WhoAm 92, WhoWor 93*
Goldberg, Reiner 1939- *Baker 92, OxDcOp*
Goldberg, Richard 1934- *St&PR 93*
Goldberg, Richard Jerome 1949- *WhoEmL 93*
Goldberg, Richard R. *Law&B 92*
Goldberg, Richard R. 1941- *St&PR 93*
Goldberg, Richard Robert 1941- *WhoAm 92*
Goldberg, Rita Maria 1933- *WhoAm 92*
Goldberg, Robert E. *Law&B 92*
Goldberg, Robert M. 1941- *WhoWor 93*
Goldberg, Robert R. *Law&B 92*
Goldberg, Robert S. 1955- *St&PR 93*
Goldberg, Roselee *WhoE 93*
Goldberg, Samuel 1925- *WhoAm 92*
Goldberg, Samuel 1928- *St&PR 93, WhoAm 92*
Goldberg, Samuel Irving 1923- *WhoAm 92*
Goldberg, Sarah A.S. 1951- *St&PR 93*
Goldberg, Sheldon Aaron 1938- *WhoE 93*
Goldberg, Sherman I. *Law&B 92, WhoAm 92*
Goldberg, Sherman I. 1941- *St&PR 93*
Goldberg, Sidney 1931- *St&PR 93, WhoAm 92, WhoWor 93*
Goldberg, Stanley Ira 1950- *St&PR 93*
Goldberg, Stanley Irwin 1934- *WhoSSW 93*
Goldberg, Stephanie Benson 1951- *WhoAm 92*
Goldberg, Stephen Z. 1947- *WhoE 93*
Goldberg, Steven C. *Law&B 92*
Goldberg, Steven Charles 1949- *WhoEmL 93*
Goldberg, Steven F. 1950- *WhoIns 93*
Goldberg, Steven Selig 1950- *WhoE 93*
Goldberg, Susan 1948- *SmATA 71 [port]*
Goldberg, Susan Solomon 1944- *WhoAm 92, WhoAmW 93*
Goldberg, Szymon 1909- *Baker 92*
Goldberg, Theo 1921- *Baker 92*
Goldberg, Victor Joel 1933- *WhoAm 92*
Goldberg, Victor Paul 1941- *WhoE 93*
Gol'dberg, Viktor Naumovich 1934- *WhoWor 93*
Goldberg, Whoopi *BioIn 17*
Goldberg, Whoopi 1949- *HolBB [port], IntDcF 2-3, QDrFCA 92 [port]*
Goldberg, Whoopi 1955- *ConBlB 4 [port], WhoAm 92, WhoAmW 93*
Goldberger, Alan Steven 1949- *WhoEmL 93*
Goldberger, Alfred L. 1932- *St&PR 93*
Goldberger, Arthur Stanley 1930- *WhoAm 92*
Goldberger, Blanche Rubin 1914- *WhoAm 92, WhoAmW 93*
Goldberger, George Stefan 1947- *WhoE 93, WhoEmL 93, WhoWor 93*
Goldberger, Marvin Leonard 1922- *WhoAm 92, WhoWor 93*
Goldberger, Neal Michael 1957- *WhoE 93*
Goldberger, Paul Jesse 1950- *WhoAm 92*
Goldberger, Stephen A. *WhoAm 92*
Goldberger, William M. 1928- *St&PR 93*
Goldberg-Mobry, Leslie Rebecca 1959- *WhoAmW 93*
Goldblatt, Barry Lance 1945- *WhoE 93, WhoWor 93*
Goldblatt, Eileen Witzman 1946- *WhoEmL 93*
Goldblatt, Hal Michael 1952- *WhoEmL 93, WhoWor 93*
Goldblatt, Irwin Leonard 1940- *WhoE 93*
Goldblatt, Mark *MiSFD 9*
Goldblatt, Michael L. *Law&B 92*
Goldblatt, Stanford Jay 1939- *WhoAm 92*
Goldblatt-Bond, Kathleen Boyle 1941- *WhoAm 92*
Goldblith, Samuel Abraham 1919- *St&PR 93, WhoAm 92*
Goldbloom, Richard Ballon 1924- *WhoAm 92*
Goldbloom, Victor *BioIn 17*
Goldbloom, Victor Charles 1923- *WhoAm 92*
Goldblum, Jeff *BioIn 17*
Goldblum, Jeff 1952- *HolBB [port], WhoAm 92*
Goldblum, Sigmund H. 1938- *St&PR 93*
Goldbrenner, Ronald S. *Law&B 92*
Goldby, Derek *BioIn 17*
Golde, David William 1940- *WhoAm 92*
Golde, Marcy *BioIn 17*
Golde, Walter 1887-1963 *Baker 92*
Goldemberg, Isaac 1945- *SpAmA, WhoWrEP 92*
Goldemberg, Robert Lewis 1925- *WhoE 93*
Golden, Alison Hope 1964- *St&PR 93*
Golden, Balfour Henry 1922- *WhoE 93*
Golden, Ben Roy 1937- *WhoSSW 93*
Golden, Beth Robinson 1959- *WhoEmL 93*
Golden, Brendan 1926- *WhoScE 91-3*
Golden, Bruce Paul 1943- *WhoAm 92*
Golden, Carol Sue 1947- *WhoAmW 93*
Golden, Carole Ann 1942- *WhoSSW 93*
Golden, Casey *BioIn 17*
Golden, Charles Josh 1949- *WhoE 93*
Golden, Christie *ScF&FL 92*
Golden, Christopher Anthony 1937- *WhoAm 92*
Golden, Dale Thomas 1952- *St&PR 93*
Golden, Dan *MiSFD 9*
Golden, David Aaron 1920- *WhoAm 92*
Golden, David Edward 1932- *WhoAm 92*
Golden, Diana *BioIn 17*
Golden, Donald L. *St&PR 93*
Golden, Eddie Lee 1955- *WhoSSW 93*
Golden, Edwin Harold 1931- *WhoSSW 93, WhoWor 93*
Golden, Eleanor *AmWomPl*
Golden, Eve 1957- *ConAu 136*
Golden, Fred Stephan 1945- *WhoE 93, WhoWor 93*
Golden, Garrett K. *Law&B 92*
Golden, Gary M. *Law&B 92*
Golden, Gordon Ray 1952- *WhoEmL 93*
Golden, Harry Lewis 1903-1981 *JeAmHC*
Golden, Jacquelyn D. *WhoE 93*
Golden, James John 1948- *St&PR 93*
Golden, James S. *Law&B 92*
Golden, John *MiSFD 9*
Golden, John F. 1949- *WhoAm 92*
Golden, John Joseph, Jr. 1943- *WhoE 93, WhoWor 93*
Golden, John Murrough 1945- *WhoWor 93*
Golden, Jonathan *St&PR 93*
Golden, Joseph A. 1949- *St&PR 93*
Golden, Kenneth Lacoy 1951- *WhoSSW 93*
Golden, L. Warren *Law&B 92*
Golden, Larry Ira *Law&B 92*
Golden, Lee M. *Law&B 92*
Golden, Leon 1930- *WhoAm 92, WhoWor 93*
Golden, Leslie Black 1955- *WhoAmW 93*
Golden, Louis M., Jr. 1919- *St&PR 93*
Golden, Marc *Law&B 92*
Golden, Marcia B. *Law&B 92*
Golden, Marita *BioIn 17*
Golden, Michael *BioIn 17*
Golden, Michael 1942- *WhoAm 92*
Golden, Michael Frank 1947- *St&PR 93*
Golden, Milton M. 1915- *WhoAm 92*
Golden, Nancy Felice 1950- *WhoAmW 93, WhoWor 93*
Golden, Pat d1991 *BioIn 17*
Golden, Patrick G. *Law&B 92*
Golden, R. Keith *BioIn 17*
Golden, Rebecca Lynne 1964- *WhoWor 93*
Golden, Reynold Stephen 1937- *WhoE 93*
Golden, Richard M(artin) 1947- *ConAu 138*
Golden, Robert Bennett 1948- *St&PR 93*
Golden, Robert Charles 1946- *WhoAm 92, WhoE 93*
Golden, Robert Edward 1945- *WhoE 93*
Golden, Ronald Aaron 1943- *WhoE 93*
Golden, Roy Eugene 1941- *WhoSSW 93*
Golden, Samuel G. A. 1939- *WhoWor 93*
Golden, Seymour W. 1921- *St&PR 93*
Golden, Sheri Dianne 1960- *WhoAmW 93*
Golden, Stephen Edward, II 1949- *WhoE 93*
Golden, Terence C. 1944- *WhoAm 92*
Golden, William C. 1936- *WhoAm 92*

Golden, William Edward 1953- *WhoSSW 93*
Golden, William T. 1909- *St&PR 93*
Golden, William Theodore 1909- *WhoAm 92*
Goldenberg, Andrew Avi 1945- *WhoAm 92*
Goldenberg, Barton Joshua 1955- *WhoEmL 93*
Goldenberg, Carl A. 1927- *St&PR 93*
Goldenberg, David Milton 1938- *WhoAm 92, WhoE 93*
Goldenberg, Debra Ann 1959- *WhoAmW 93*
Goldenberg, Elizabeth Leigh 1963- *WhoAmW 93*
Goldenberg, Eve A. 1926- *St&PR 93*
Goldenberg, George 1929- *WhoAm 92, WhoSSW 93, WhoWor 93*
Goldenberg, Gerald Joseph 1933- *WhoAm 92*
Goldenberg, Herbert J. 1939- *St&PR 93*
Goldenberg, Irene Toby 1934- *WhoAmW 93*
Goldenberg, Marvin Manus 1935- *WhoE 93*
Goldenberg, Melvyn Joel 1942- *St&PR 93*
Goldenberg, Myrna Gallant 1937- *WhoAmW 93, WhoE 93*
Goldenberg, Perry B. 1935- *St&PR 93*
Goldenberg, Ronald Edwin 1931- *WhoAm 92*
Goldenberg, Sherri Roberta 1964- *WhoE 93*
Goldenberg, Terri S. *Law&B 92*
Goldenburg, Grace Delaney *AmWomPl*
Goldenhersh, Louise *Law&B 92*
Goldenhorn, Hilda 1925- *WhoAmW 93*
Goldensohn, Barry Nathan 1937- *WhoE 93, WhoWrEP 92*
Goldenson, Leonard H. *BioIn 17*
Goldenthal, Jolene Bleich *WhoAmW 93*
Goldenweiser, Alexander A. 1880-1940 *IntDcAn*
Goldenweiser, Alexander (Borisovich) 1875-1961 *Baker 92*
Golder, Carol Warner 1959- *WhoAmW 93*
Golder, Morton I. *Law&B 92*
Golder, Stanley C. *St&PR 93*
Goldet, Cecile 1914- *WhoUN 92*
Goldetsky, Steven M. *Law&B 92*
Goldey, James Mearns 1926- *WhoAm 92*
Goldey, Michael J. *Law&B 92*
Goldfaden, Abraham 1840-1908 *JeAmHC*
Goldfader, Stanley J. 1943- *St&PR 93*
Goldfarb, Aron 1923- *BioIn 17*
Goldfarb, Bernard Sanford 1917- *WhoAm 92*
Goldfarb, David *BioIn 17*
Goldfarb, Donald 1941- *WhoAm 92*
Goldfarb, Herman d1990 *BioIn 17*
Goldfarb, Howard E. *Law&B 92*
Goldfarb, Igor Isaakovich 1962- *WhoWor 93*
Goldfarb, Irene Dale 1929- *WhoWor 93*
Goldfarb, Lewis H. *Law&B 92*
Goldfarb, Mark 1934- *St&PR 93*
Goldfarb, Marsha Geier 1942- *WhoAmW 93*
Goldfarb, Martin 1938- *WhoAm 92*
Goldfarb, Mitchell 1953- *WhoEmL 93*
Goldfarb, Muriel Gordon 1934- *WhoE 93*
Goldfarb, Richard Marc 1953- *WhoE 93*
Goldfarb, Robert Lawrence 1951- *WhoEmL 93*
Goldfarb, Robert Stanley 1943- *WhoAm 92*
Goldfarb, Ronald L. 1933- *ConAu 40NR*
Goldfarb, Ronald Lawrence 1933- *WhoAm 92*
Goldfarb, Sheldon I. *Law&B 92*
Goldfarb, Stanley 1943- *WhoE 93*
Goldfarb, Steven *Law&B 92*
Goldfarb, Warren David 1949- *WhoAm 92*
Goldfeder, Howard 1926- *St&PR 93*
Goldfeld, Dorian 1947- *WhoAm 92, WhoE 93*
Goldfeld, Stephen Michael 1940- *WhoAm 92*
Goldfleld, Alfred Sherman 1939- *WhoAm 92*
Goldfield, Edwin David 1918- *WhoAm 92*
Goldfine, Bernard 1891-1967 *PolPar*
Goldfine, Howard 1932- *WhoAm 92*
Goldfine, Mel A. 1948- *St&PR 93*
Goldfine, Miriam 1933- *WhoAm 92*
Goldfinger, Clarence S. 1923- *St&PR 93*
Goldfinger, Solomon 1950- *St&PR 93*
Goldfinger, Stephen Mark 1951- *WhoEmL 93*
Goldfischer, Sidney Leo 1926- *WhoE 93*
Goldfrank, Esther Schiff 1896- *IntDcAn*
Goldfrank, Herbert J., Mrs. 1912- *WhoE 93, WhoWor 93*
Goldfrank, Lewis Robert 1941- *WhoE 93*
Gold Franke, Paula Christine 1952- *WhoWrEP 92*
Goldfus, Donald Wayne 1934- *St&PR 93, WhoAm 92*
Goldfus, Mark B. *Law&B 92*
Goldgar, Bertrand Alvin 1927- *WhoAm 92*
Goldgar, Corinne Hartman 1928- *WhoAmW 93*
Goldhaber, F.I. *WhoWrEP 92*
Goldhaber, Gerald Martin 1944- *WhoAm 92*
Goldhaber, Gerson 1924- *WhoAm 92*
Goldhaber, Gertrude Scharff 1911- *WhoAm 92, WhoAmW 93*
Goldhaber, Jacob Kopel 1924- *WhoAm 92*
Goldhaber, Maurice 1911- *WhoAm 92*
Goldham, Bob 1922-1991 *BioIn 17*
Goldhamer, Walter M. 1911- *St&PR 93*
Goldhammer, Arthur 1946- *ConAu 139*
Goldhammer, Earl *Law&B 92*
Goldhammer, Henry N. 1943- *St&PR 93*
Goldhammer, Robert F. 1931- *St&PR 93*
Goldhirsh, Bernard A. *BioIn 17*
Goldhirsh, Bernard A. 1940- *WhoAm 92*
Goldhirsh, Martha 1960- *WhoEmL 93*
Goldhor, Herbert 1917- *BioIn 17*
Goldhurst, William 1929- *WhoAm 92, WhoWrEP 92*
Goldiamond, Israel 1919- *WhoAm 92*
Goldich, Geoffrey S. *Law&B 92*
Goldie, Alfred William 1920- *WhoWor 93*
Goldie, C.J. *Law&B 92*
Goldie, George 1927- *St&PR 93*
Goldie, Ian 1930- *WhoScE 91-4*
Goldie, James Hunter 1955- *St&PR 93*
Goldie, Kathleen *ScF&FL 92*
Goldie, L. Frederick E. 1918-1991 *BioIn 17*
Goldie, Louis Frederick Edward 1918-1991 *BioIn 17*
Goldie, Ray Robert 1920- *WhoWor 93*
Goldie, Robert *St&PR 93*
Goldie, Ron Robert 1951- *WhoEmL 93*
Goldin, Alan Gary 1942- *WhoAm 92*
Goldin, Barbara Diamond 1946- *WhoAm 92*
Goldin, Barry *St&PR 93*
Goldin, Claudia Dale 1946- *WhoAm 92, WhoAmW 93*
Goldin, Daniel *BioIn 17*
Goldin, Daniel 1940- *WhoAm 92, WhoE 93*
Goldin, Harold L. 1928- *St&PR 93*
Goldin, Harrison Jacob 1936- *WhoE 93*
Goldin, Joshua *BioIn 17*
Goldin, Judah 1914- *WhoAm 92, WhoE 93*
Goldin, Leon 1923- *WhoE 93*
Goldin, Milton 1927- *WhoAm 92*
Goldin, Sol 1909- *WhoAm 92*
Goldin, Stephen 1947- *ScF&FL 92*
Golding, Brage 1920- *WhoAm 92*
Golding, Carolyn May 1941- *WhoAmW 93*
Golding, Charles William 1931- *WhoAm 92*
Golding, Cornelius E. 1947- *WhoIns 93*
Golding, Cornelius Eugene 1947- *St&PR 93*
Golding, Jay Harold 1945- *St&PR 93*
Golding, Louis 1895-1958 *ScF&FL 92*
Golding, Martin Philip 1930- *WhoAm 92*
Golding, Michael H.B. 1943- *St&PR 93*
Golding, Paul *MiSFD 9*
Golding, Samuel Y. *St&PR 93*
Golding, William 1911- *BioIn 17, MagSWL [port], ScF&FL 92*
Golding, William 1911-1991 *WorLitC [port]*
Golding, William Gerald 1911- *WhoAm 92, WhoWor 93*
Goldis, Sy 1928- *WhoAm 92*
Goldleaf, Steven 1953- *WhoWrEP 92*
Goldmacher, Jeffery A. 1956- *WhoE 93*
Goldman, Aaron 1913- *St&PR 93, WhoAm 92*
Goldman, Alan Ira 1937- *WhoAm 92*
Goldman, Albert 1897-1960 *BioIn 17*
Goldman, Alex J. 1917- *BioIn 17*
Goldman, Alexander 1910- *WhoSSW 93*
Goldman, Alfred Emmanuel 1925- *WhoAm 92, WhoE 93*
Goldman, Alice Carla *Law&B 92*
Goldman, Allan Bailey 1937- *WhoAm 92*
Goldman, Allan Larry 1943- *WhoSSW 93*
Goldman, Allen Marshall 1937- *WhoAm 92*
Goldman, Alvin Lee 1938- *WhoAm 92*
Goldman, Andrew 1947- *WhoE 93*
Goldman, Arlene Leslie 1956- *WhoAmW 93*
Goldman, Arnold 1931- *WhoE 93*
Goldman, Arnold David 1933- *WhoE 93*
Goldman, Arnold L. 1930- *St&PR 93*
Goldman, Barbara Deren 1949- *WhoAmW 93*
Goldman, Barbara Linda 1950- *WhoAmW 93*
Goldman, Benard M. *Law&B 92*
Goldman, Bernard 1928- *St&PR 93, WhoAm 92*
Goldman, Bert Arthur 1929- *WhoAm 92, WhoSSW 93*
Goldman, Bessie d1991 *BioIn 17*
Goldman, Betsy Schein 1932- *WhoWrEP 92*
Goldman, Bettie Ellen 1958- *WhoAmW 93*
Goldman, Brian Arthur 1946- *WhoAm 92*
Goldman, Charles N. 1932- *St&PR 93*
Goldman, Charles Norton *Law&B 92*
Goldman, Charles Norton 1932- *WhoAm 92*
Goldman, Charley 1888-1968 *BioIn 17*
Goldman, Cheryl Lisa 1962- *WhoAmW 93*
Goldman, Clifford Alan 1943- *WhoAm 92*
Goldman, Clint Paul *WhoAm 92*
Goldman, Daniel C. 1943- *St&PR 93*
Goldman, Donald Howard 1942- *WhoAm 92*
Goldman, Donald L. *Law&B 92*
Goldman, Donald L. 1937- *St&PR 93*
Goldman, Donna B. *Law&B 92*
Goldman, Douglas David 1965- *WhoSSW 93*
Goldman, Edward Joseph 1938- *St&PR 93*
Goldman, Edwin Franko 1878-1956 *Baker 92*
Goldman, Emma 1869-1940 *BioIn 17, DcTwHis, JeAmHC*
Goldman, Ernest Harold 1922- *WhoE 93*
Goldman, Gary Craig *Law&B 92*
Goldman, Gary Craig 1951- *WhoEmL 93*
Goldman, George David 1923- *WhoAm 92*
Goldman, Gerald Carl *WhoSSW 93*
Goldman, Gerald Hillis 1947- *WhoAm 92*
Goldman, Harold A. 1911- *St&PR 93*
Goldman, Harvey J. 1946- *St&PR 93*
Goldman, Henry M. 1911-1991 *BioIn 17*
Goldman, Ira Steven 1951- *WhoE 93, WhoEmL 93*
Goldman, Jacob E. 1921- *St&PR 93*
Goldman, James 1927- *WhoAm 92*
Goldman, James A. 1955- *St&PR 93*
Goldman, James M. 1936- *WhoAm 92*
Goldman, Jane H. *Law&B 92*
Goldman, Janice Goldin 1938- *WhoAmW 93, WhoE 93*
Goldman, Jay 1930- *WhoAm 92*
Goldman, Jeri Joan 1934- *WhoAmW 93*
Goldman, Jerome 1936- *St&PR 93*
Goldman, Jerry Stephen 1951- *WhoE 93*
Goldman, Jill *MiSFD 9*
Goldman, Jill Minkoff 1953- *WhoAmW 93*
Goldman, Joel J. 1940- *WhoAm 92, WhoE 93, WhoWor 93*
Goldman, Joseph Elias 1923- *WhoAm 92*
Goldman, Joseph L. 1904-1991 *BioIn 17*
Goldman, Joseph Lawrence 1904- *WhoWor 93*
Goldman, Judith *WhoE 93*
Goldman, Laura S. *Law&B 92*
Goldman, Laura Sue 1958- *WhoAmW 93*
Goldman, Laurence *Law&B 92*
Goldman, Lawrence 1936- *WhoE 93*
Goldman, Lawrence Paul 1942- *WhoE 93*
Goldman, Lawrence Saul 1942- *WhoE 93*
Goldman, Leo 1920- *WhoAm 92*
Goldman, Leonard Manuel 1925- *WhoAm 92*
Goldman, Lionel *St&PR 93*
Goldman, Marilyn Barbara 1943- *WhoE 93*
Goldman, Marilyn S. 1929- *St&PR 93*
Goldman, Martin 1945- *St&PR 93*
Goldman, Martin Raymond Rubin 1920- *WhoWrEP 92*
Goldman, Martyn Alan 1930- *WhoSSW 93*
Goldman, Marvin 1928- *WhoAm 92*
Goldman, Max 1931- *WhoScE 91-2*
Goldman, Michael Paul 1936- *WhoAm 92*
Goldman, Milton 1913-1991 *BioIn 17*
Goldman, Morton Irwin 1926- *St&PR 93*
Goldman, Murray Abraham 1937- *St&PR 93, WhoAm 92*
Goldman, Nancy Joan Kramer 1953- *WhoAm 92*
Goldman, Nathan Carliner 1950- *WhoEmL 93, WhoSSW 93, WhoWor 93*
Goldman, Neal D. *Law&B 92*
Goldman, Norman Lewis 1933- *WhoAm 92*
Goldman, Patricia Ann 1942- *WhoAmW 93*
Goldman, Paul 1946?- *BioIn 17*
Goldman, Phyllis E. *WhoE 93*
Goldman, Ralph Frederick 1928- *WhoAm 92*
Goldman, Ralph Morris 1920- *WhoAm 92*
Goldman, Richard B. 1946- *St&PR 93*
Goldman, Richard Craig *Law&B 92*
Goldman, Richard Franko 1910-1980 *Baker 92*
Goldman, Richard Mark *Law&B 92*
Goldman, Richard Paul 1935- *WhoE 93*
Goldman, Richard Stewart 1948- *WhoEmL 93*
Goldman, Robert Irving 1932- *St&PR 93, WhoAm 92*
Goldman, Robert N. 1949- *St&PR 93*
Goldman, Robert W. 1942- *St&PR 93*
Goldman, Robyn S. *Law&B 92*
Goldman, Ronald Frank 1947- *WhoE 93*
Goldman, Roslyn Bakst 1938- *WhoAmW 93*
Goldman, Sam 1932- *St&PR 93*
Goldman, Samuel 1931- *WhoE 93*
Goldman, Sheldon 1939- *WhoAm 92*
Goldman, Sheldon T. *St&PR 93*
Goldman, Sherry Robin 1958- *WhoAmW 93*
Goldman, Siegmund 1924- *St&PR 93*
Goldman, Siegmund Isadore 1924- *WhoSSW 93*
Goldman, Simon 1913- *WhoAm 92*
Goldman, Stanford 1907- *WhoAm 92*
Goldman, Stephen H. *ScF&FL 92*
Goldman, Stephen Harris 1951- *St&PR 93*
Goldman, Stephen Shepard 1941- *WhoE 93*
Goldman, Steven Jason 1947- *WhoEmL 93*
Goldman, Susan *BioIn 17*
Goldman, William 1931- *BioIn 17, JeAmFiW, ScF&FL 92, WhoAm 92*
Goldman, William Jay 1936- *St&PR 93*
Goldman, Zachary C. 1929- *St&PR 93*
Goldmann, Allen A. 1919- *St&PR 93*
Goldmann, Friedrich 1941- *Baker 92*
Goldmann, Kenneth Francis 1922- *St&PR 93*
Goldmann, Morton Aaron 1924- *WhoAm 92*
Goldmann, Stanley H. 1931- *St&PR 93*
Goldmark, Karl 1830-1915 *Baker 92, IntDcOp, OxDcOp*
Goldmark, Peter Carl 1940- *WhoAm 92*
Goldmark, Rubin 1872-1936 *Baker 92*
Goldner, David W. 1961- *St&PR 93*
Goldner, George 1918-1970 *SoulM*
Goldner, Jane Schnuer 1949- *WhoEmL 93*
Goldner, Jesse Alan 1948- *WhoEmL 93*
Goldner, Leonard H. 1947- *St&PR 93*
Goldner, Orville 1906-1985 *ScF&FL 92*
Goldner, Sheldon Herbert 1928- *WhoAm 92*
Goldon, Jerry *St&PR 93*
Goldoni, Carlo 1707-1793 *IntDcOp [port], OxDcOp*
Goldovsky, Boris 1908- *Baker 92, OxDcOp, WhoAm 92*
Goldowsky, Barbara 1936- *WhoWrEP 92*
Goldress, Jerry Edwin 1930- *St&PR 93*
Goldrich, Nathan J. 1902-1991 *BioIn 17*
Goldrich, S.N. 1950- *St&PR 93*
Goldrich, S.P. 1918- *St&PR 93*
Goldring, Elizabeth 1945- *WhoE 93*
Goldring, Harold Benjamin 1929- *St&PR 93*
Goldring, Norman Max 1937- *WhoAm 92*
Goldring, Timothy John 1930- *WhoWor 93*
Golds, Cassandra 1962- *ScF&FL 92*
Goldsack, James F. 1930- *St&PR 93*
Goldsack, Stephen James *WhoScE 91-1*
Goldsamt, Bonnie Blume 1946- *WhoEmL 93*
Goldsand, Robert 1911- *Baker 92*
Goldsand, Robert 1911-1991 *BioIn 17*
Goldsberry, Fred Lynn 1947- *WhoEmL 93*
Goldsberry, Steven *WhoWrEP 92*
Goldsberry, Steven 1949- *ScF&FL 92*
Goldsborough, Carole Cole 1928- *WhoAmW 93*
Goldsborough, Louis Malesherbes 1805-1877 *HarEnMi*
Goldsborough, Robert (Gerald) 1937- *ConAu 138, WhoAm 92*
Goldsby, Crawford 1876-1896 *BioIn 17*
Goldscheider, Robert *Law&B 92*
Goldscheider, Sidney 1920- *WhoAm 92*
Goldschein, Steven Marc 1946- *St&PR 93*
Goldschlag, William 1952- *WhoAm 92*
Goldschmid, Harvey Jerome 1940- *WhoAm 92, WhoWor 93*
Goldschmid, Mary Tait Seibert 1947- *WhoE 93*
Goldschmidt, Adalbert von 1848-1906 *Baker 92*
Goldschmidt, Arthur Eduard, Jr. 1938- *WhoAm 92*
Goldschmidt, Bernd 1950- *WhoWor 93*
Goldschmidt, Berthold 1903- *Baker 92, OxDcOp*
Goldschmidt, Bertrand *BioIn 17*
Goldschmidt, Diane S. *Law&B 92*
Goldschmidt, Eliezer d1992 *BioIn 17*
Goldschmidt, Hugo 1859-1920 *Baker 92*
Goldschmidt, Joel L. 1933- *St&PR 93*
Goldschmidt, John *MiSFD 9*
Goldschmidt, Jurgen 1939- *WhoWor 93*
Goldschmidt, Lucien 1912-1992 *NewYTBS 92*

Goldschmidt, Millicent Edna 1926- *WhoSSW 93*
Goldschmidt, Otto (Moritz David) 1829-1907 *Baker 92*
Goldschmidt, Peter Graham 1945- *WhoE 93*
Goldschmidt, Robert Alphonse 1937- *WhoAm 92*
Goldschmidt, Victor Moritz 1888-1947 *BioIn 17*
Goldschmied, Fabio Renzo 1919- *WhoAm 92*
Goldsholl, Mildred 1920- *WhoAm 92*
Goldsmith, Arnold L. 1928- *ScF&FL 92*
Goldsmith, Arthur Austin 1926- *WhoAm 92, WhoWrEP 92*
Goldsmith, Barbara 1931- *WhoAm 92, WhoWrEP 92*
Goldsmith, Billy Joe 1933- *WhoAm 92*
Goldsmith, Bram 1923- *St&PR 93, WhoAm 92*
Goldsmith, Cathy Ellen 1947- *WhoAmW 93, WhoE 93, WhoEmL 93, WhoWor 93*
Goldsmith, Claude Orville 1932- *WhoAm 92*
Goldsmith, Clifford Henry 1919- *WhoAm 92*
Goldsmith, David L. *St&PR 93*
Goldsmith, Debbie Ann 1952- *St&PR 93*
Goldsmith, Debra *Law&B 92*
Goldsmith, Debra J. *Law&B 92*
Goldsmith, Diane Bradford 1951- *WhoAmW 93*
Goldsmith, Donald *BioIn 17*
Goldsmith, Elaine 1935- *WhoSSW 93*
Goldsmith, Gary Norman 1948- *WhoEmL 93*
Goldsmith, Harold d1991 *BioIn 17*
Goldsmith, Harold Davis 1947- *WhoSSW 93*
Goldsmith, Harry L. *Law&B 92*
Goldsmith, Harry Sawyer 1929- *WhoAm 92*
Goldsmith, Howard 1943- *ConAu 40NR, ScF&FL 92*
Goldsmith, Howard 1945- *WhoAm 92, WhoWrEP 92*
Goldsmith, Isabel *BioIn 17*
Goldsmith, Jack Landman 1910- *WhoAm 92*
Goldsmith, James 1933- *BioIn 17*
Goldsmith, Jeff Charles 1948- *WhoEmL 93*
Goldsmith, Jeffrey Michael *Law&B 92*
Goldsmith, Jeffrey Robert 1957- *St&PR 93*
Goldsmith, Jerry 1929- *Baker 92, WhoAm 92*
Goldsmith, John Anton 1951- *WhoAm 92*
Goldsmith, John Arthur 1947- *St&PR 93*
Goldsmith, John Graham 1947- *WhoE 93*
Goldsmith, Joseph Patrick 1944- *WhoSSW 93*
Goldsmith, Judith *BioIn 17*
Goldsmith, Julian Royce 1918- *WhoAm 92*
Goldsmith, Kathleen Mawhinney 1957- *WhoAmW 93*
Goldsmith, Kenneth 1924- *St&PR 93*
Goldsmith, Larry Dean 1952- *WhoWrEP 92*
Goldsmith, Lee Selig 1939- *WhoAm 92*
Goldsmith, Lowell Alan 1938- *WhoAm 92, WhoE 93, WhoWor 93*
Goldsmith, Luba *AmWomPl*
Goldsmith, Mark L. 1936- *WhoAm 92*
Goldsmith, Martin *Law&B 92*
Goldsmith, Martin H. 1947- *WhoAm 92*
Goldsmith, Marvin Fred 1941- *St&PR 93*
Goldsmith, Marvin L. 1925- *WhoAm 92*
Goldsmith, Maxine Iris 1947- *WhoE 93, WhoEmL 93*
Goldsmith, Melissa 1954- *WhoWrEP 92*
Goldsmith, Merwin 1937- *WhoE 93, WhoWor 93*
Goldsmith, Michael 1921-1990 *BioIn 17*
Goldsmith, Michael James Frederick *WhoScE 91-1*
Goldsmith, Mortimer Michael 1950- *WhoE 93*
Goldsmith, Nancy Carrol 1940- *WhoAmW 93*
Goldsmith, Oliver 1728-1774 *BioIn 17, MagSWL [port], WorLitC [port]*
Goldsmith, Oliver 1794-1861 *BioIn 17*
Goldsmith, Paul F. 1948- *St&PR 93*
Goldsmith, Paul Felix 1948- *WhoAm 92*
Goldsmith, Peter Arthur 1956- *WhoSSW 93*
Goldsmith, Ph. *WhoScE 91-2*
Goldsmith, Robert H. 1930- *St&PR 93*
Goldsmith, Robert Hillis 1911- *WhoAm 92*
Goldsmith, Robert Lewis 1928- *WhoAm 92*
Goldsmith, Robert W. 1952- *St&PR 93*
Goldsmith, Ruth M. 1919- *BioIn 17*
Goldsmith, Scott 1949- *St&PR 93*
Goldsmith, Shep 1928- *St&PR 93*
Goldsmith, Sidney 1930- *WhoAm 92*
Goldsmith, Sophie L. *AmWomPl*
Goldsmith, Stanley Joseph 1937- *WhoAm 92*
Goldsmith, Stephen 1946- *WhoAm 92*
Goldsmith, Victor 1940- *WhoE 93*
Goldsmith, Werner 1924- *WhoAm 92*
Goldson, Mary Funnye d1990 *BioIn 17*
Goldspink, Geoffrey *WhoScE 91-1*
Goldstein, Abraham S. 1925- *WhoAm 92*
Goldstein, Alan 1928- *St&PR 93*
Goldstein, Alan 1953- *WhoWrEP 92*
Goldstein, Alan B. *Law&B 92*
Goldstein, Alfred George 1932- *WhoAm 92*
Goldstein, Allan 1951- *MiSFD 9*
Goldstein, Allan Leonard 1937- *WhoAm 92*
Goldstein, Alvin 1929- *WhoAm 92*
Goldstein, Arnold K. 1954- *St&PR 93*
Goldstein, Arthur L. 1935- *St&PR 93*
Goldstein, Avram 1919- *WhoAm 92*
Goldstein, B.B. 1919- *St&PR 93*
Goldstein, Barry S. *Law&B 92*
Goldstein, Bernard 1929- *St&PR 93, WhoAm 92*
Goldstein, Bernard David 1939- *WhoAm 92, WhoE 93*
Goldstein, Bernard Herbert 1907- *WhoAm 92*
Goldstein, Burton Jack 1930- *WhoAm 92*
Goldstein, Charles Arthur 1936- *WhoAm 92, WhoWor 93*
Goldstein, Charles H. 1939- *WhoAm 92*
Goldstein, Charles J. *Law&B 92*
Goldstein, Charlotte Lipson 1929- *WhoAmW 93*
Goldstein, David 1898-1992 *BioIn 17*
Goldstein, David Garson 1919- *St&PR 93*
Goldstein, David H. *Law&B 92*
Goldstein, Dennis B. *Law&B 92*
Goldstein, Donald E. 1946- *St&PR 93*
Goldstein, Donald Jay 1948- *WhoEmL 93*
Goldstein, Donald Maurice 1932- *WhoE 93, WhoWor 93*
Goldstein, Donna L. *Law&B 92*
Goldstein, Dora Benedict 1922- *WhoAm 92*
Goldstein, Doris Mueller 1942- *WhoAmW 93, WhoE 93*
Goldstein, E. Alexander 1951- *St&PR 93*
Goldstein, E. Ernest 1918- *WhoAm 92, WhoWor 93*
Goldstein, Edward 1923- *WhoAm 92*
Goldstein, Edward David 1927- *WhoAm 92*
Goldstein, Eleanor 1935- *WhoE 93, WhoWor 93*
Goldstein, Elizabeth 1955- *WhoIns 93*
Goldstein, Elliott 1915- *WhoAm 92, WhoWor 93*
Goldstein, Fern 1935- *WhoAm 92, WhoWor 93*
Goldstein, Frank Robert 1943- *WhoAm 92*
Goldstein, Fred *ScF&FL 92*
Goldstein, Fred 1924- *WhoAm 92, WhoE 93*
Goldstein, Garry Arnold 1931- *WhoE 93*
Goldstein, Gary S. 1954- *WhoAm 92*
Goldstein, George A. 1942- *WhoWor 93*
Goldstein, Gerald 1931- *WhoAm 92*
Goldstein, Gerald C. *Law&B 92*
Goldstein, Gigi 1963- *WhoAmW 93*
Goldstein, Gregory Bevan 1944- *WhoUN 92*
Goldstein, Gregory Lee 1960- *WhoEmL 93*
Goldstein, Harold W. *St&PR 93*
Goldstein, Harry Harold 1922- *WhoSSW 93*
Goldstein, Harry M. 1926- *St&PR 93*
Goldstein, Harvey A. 1939- *WhoAm 92*
Goldstein, Henry 1933- *WhoE 93*
Goldstein, Howard Bernard 1943- *WhoE 93*
Goldstein, Howard J. 1944- *St&PR 93*
Goldstein, Ira M. d1992 *NewYTBS 92 [port]*
Goldstein, Irving 1938- *St&PR 93*
Goldstein, Irving Robert 1916- *WhoE 93*
Goldstein, Irving Solomon 1921- *WhoAm 92*
Goldstein, Irwin Stuart 1947- *WhoEmL 93, WhoSSW 93*
Goldstein, Jack 1938- *St&PR 93*
Goldstein, Jacob Herman 1915- *WhoAm 92*
Goldstein, Jeffrey *Law&B 92*
Goldstein, Jeffrey Haskell 1942- *WhoE 93*
Goldstein, Jeffrey Marc 1947- *WhoE 93*
Goldstein, Jeremy S. 1962- *St&PR 93*
Goldstein, Jerome Arthur 1941- *WhoAm 92, WhoSSW 93*
Goldstein, Jerome Charles 1935- *WhoAm 92*
Goldstein, Jerome J. 1922- *St&PR 93*
Goldstein, Jerome S. 1940- *WhoAm 92*
Goldstein, Jerry S. 1940- *St&PR 93*
Goldstein, Joel Samuel 1942- *WhoE 93*
Goldstein, Joel William 1939- *WhoE 93*
Goldstein, John Arthur 1937- *WhoWor 93*
Goldstein, Jonathan Amos 1929- *WhoAm 92*
Goldstein, Joseph 1923- *WhoAm 92*
Goldstein, Joseph E. 1946- *St&PR 93*
Goldstein, Joseph I. *Law&B 92*
Goldstein, Joseph Irwin 1939- *WhoAm 92*
Goldstein, Joseph Leonard 1940- *WhoAm 92, WhoSSW 93, WhoWor 93*
Goldstein, Joshua 1953- *WhoE 93*
Goldstein, Joyce *BioIn 17*
Goldstein, Judith Shelley 1935- *WhoAmW 93*
Goldstein, Julia Sonia 1923- *WhoSSW 93*
Goldstein, Kathryn Elizabeth 1962- *WhoAmW 93*
Goldstein, Kenneth B. 1949- *WhoEmL 93*
Goldstein, Kenneth F. 1944- *WhoIns 93*
Goldstein, Kenneth K. 1926- *WhoE 93*
Goldstein, Larry Joel 1944- *ConAu 139*
Goldstein, Larry Samuel 1943- *WhoE 93*
Goldstein, Laurence Alan 1943- *WhoWrEP 92*
Goldstein, Lawrence Jerome *St&PR 93*
Goldstein, Leonard Barry 1944- *WhoE 93*
Goldstein, Leonard D. 1921- *St&PR 93*
Goldstein, Leslie Joyce *Law&B 92*
Goldstein, Lester 1924- *WhoAm 92*
Goldstein, Lewis M. 1927- *St&PR 93*
Goldstein, Lisa 1953- *ScF&FL 92*
Goldstein, Louis Lazarus 1913- *WhoAm 92*
Goldstein, Lynn A. *Law&B 92*
Goldstein, Lynn E. 1932- *St&PR 93*
Goldstein, Manfred 1927- *WhoWor 93*
Goldstein, Marc Evan 1935- *WhoAm 92*
Goldstein, Marc Steven 1945- *WhoAm 92*
Goldstein, Marcus S. 1906- *IntDcAn*
Goldstein, Marilyn J. *Law&B 92*
Goldstein, Marjorie Tunick 1940- *WhoE 93*
Goldstein, Mark *Law&B 92*
Goldstein, Mark David 1947- *WhoAm 92*
Goldstein, Mark Kane 1938- *St&PR 93*
Goldstein, Mark Kingston Levin 1941- *WhoWor 93*
Goldstein, Marsha Feder 1945- *WhoAmW 93*
Goldstein, Martin 1919- *WhoAm 92*
Goldstein, Martin Barnet 1933- *WhoE 93*
Goldstein, Marvin Emanuel 1938- *WhoAm 92*
Goldstein, Marvin Norman 1940- *WhoE 93*
Goldstein, Melvyn C. 1938- *WhoAm 92*
Goldstein, Menek 1924- *WhoAm 92*
Goldstein, Michael 1941- *St&PR 93*
Goldstein, Michael B. 1943- *WhoAm 92*
Goldstein, Michael Gerald 1946- *WhoEmL 93*
Goldstein, Mikhail 1917-1989 *Baker 92*
Goldstein, Milton 1914- *WhoE 93*
Goldstein, Milton Houseman 1937- *WhoE 93*
Goldstein, Mindy Sue 1952- *WhoE 93*
Goldstein, Morris 1945- *WhoAm 92*
Goldstein, Murray 1925- *WhoAm 92*
Goldstein, Naomi 1932- *WhoE 93*
Goldstein, Neil Howard 1952- *WhoEmL 93*
Goldstein, Neil Warren 1950- *WhoE 93, WhoEmL 93*
Goldstein, Norman R. 1944- *St&PR 93, WhoAm 92, WhoWor 93*
Goldstein, Norman Robert 1928- *WhoAm 92, WhoE 93*
Goldstein, Paul 1934- *St&PR 93*
Goldstein, Paul 1943- *WhoAm 92*
Goldstein, Paul Alan 1953- *WhoSSW 93*
Goldstein, Paul E. *Law&B 92*
Goldstein, Peggy R. 1921- *WhoAm 92, WhoWor 93*
Goldstein, Richard A. 1942- *WhoAm 92, WhoE 93*
Goldstein, Richard Alan 1942- *St&PR 93*
Goldstein, Richard D. *Law&B 92*
Goldstein, Richard David *Law&B 92*
Goldstein, Richard Jay 1928- *WhoAm 92*
Goldstein, Rita B. 1933- *WhoAmW 93*
Goldstein, Robert *Law&B 92*
Goldstein, Robert Arnold 1941- *WhoAm 92*
Goldstein, Robert H. *St&PR 93*
Goldstein, Robert Lawrence 1931- *St&PR 93*
Goldstein, Robert Lee 1951- *WhoEmL 93, WhoSSW 93*
Goldstein, Robert S. 1932- *St&PR 93*
Goldstein, Roberta Eisman 1936- *WhoSSW 93*
Goldstein, Robin Ellen 1958- *WhoAmW 93*
Goldstein, Ronald *Law&B 92*
Goldstein, Ronald Erwin 1933- *WhoSSW 93*
Goldstein, Rubin 1933- *WhoE 93*
Goldstein, S.J. *Law&B 92*
Goldstein, Samuel Jack 1952- *WhoWor 93*
Goldstein, Samuel R. 1918- *WhoAm 92*
Goldstein, Sandra *WhoAmW 93*
Goldstein, Scott *MiSFD 9*
Goldstein, Shari L. *Law&B 92*
Goldstein, Shirley Jean *Law&B 92*
Goldstein, Shirley Lila 1911- *St&PR 93*
Goldstein, Sidney 1927- *WhoAm 92, WhoE 93*
Goldstein, Simeon Hai Fischel 1915- *WhoE 93*
Goldstein, Sol L. *Law&B 92*
Goldstein, Stan *ScF&FL 92*
Goldstein, Stanley P. 1934- *St&PR 93, WhoAm 92*
Goldstein, Stanley Philip 1923- *WhoAm 92*
Goldstein, Stephen Louis 1959- *WhoEmL 93*
Goldstein, Steven R. *Law&B 92*
Goldstein, Stuart Zane 1950- *WhoWor 93*
Goldstein, Susan 1952- *WhoSSW 93*
Goldstein, Sylvia Beatrice 1919- *WhoAmW 93*
Goldstein, Sylvia W. 1919- *St&PR 93*
Goldstein, Theodore Philip 1928- *WhoE 93*
Goldstein, Thomas 1944- *WhoSSW 93*
Goldstein, Walter E. 1940- *St&PR 93*
Goldstein, Walter Elliott 1940- *WhoAm 92*
Goldstein, William L. 1928- *St&PR 93*
Goldstein, William Marks 1935- *WhoAm 92*
Goldstein, William Steven 1941- *St&PR 93*
Goldstick, Thomas Karl 1934- *WhoAm 92*
Goldsticker, Ralph Philip 1952- *St&PR 93*
Goldstine, Abner D. 1929- *St&PR 93, WhoAm 92*
Goldstine, Herman Heine 1913- *WhoAm 92*
Goldstine, Jonathan Heine 1959- *WhoEmL 93, WhoSSW 93*
Goldstine, Sandra Dawn 1940- *WhoSSW 93*
Goldstine, Stephen Joseph 1937- *WhoAm 92*
Goldston, Barbara M. Harral 1937- *WhoAmW 93, WhoWor 93*
Goldston, David B. *Law&B 92*
Goldston, Harold M. 1930- *WhoIns 93*
Goldston, Stephen Eugene 1931- *WhoAm 92*
Goldston, William Frank 1947- *St&PR 93*
Goldstone, Adrian 1897-1977 *ScF&FL 92*
Goldstone, Allen Richard 1952- *St&PR 93*
Goldstone, Bette Perilstein 1947- *WhoE 93*
Goldstone, James 1931- *MiSFD 9*
Goldstone, Jeffrey 1933- *WhoAm 92*
Goldstone, Leslie 1939- *WhoScE 91-1*
Goldstone, Mark L. *Law&B 92*
Goldstone, Robert 1952- *WhoIns 93*
Goldstone, Sanford 1926- *WhoAm 92*
Goldsweig, David N. *Law&B 92*
Goldsworthy, Andy 1956- *BioIn 17*
Goldsworthy, Earl E. 1934- *St&PR 93*
Goldsworthy, Frederick Allin *WhoScE 91-1*
Goldszmit, Henryk 1878-1942 *BioIn 17*
Goldthorpe, John Clifford 1931- *WhoAm 92, WhoSSW 93*
Goldthwait, Bob 1962- *ConTFT 10*
Goldthwait, Bobcat *ConTFT 10, MiSFD 9*
Goldthwaite, Mary Jane *Law&B 92*
Goldthwaite, Richard A(llen) 1933- *ConAu 136*
Goldthwatt, Sheldon Forrest, Jr. 1938- *St&PR 93*
Goldwasser, A. Norman 1956- *WhoSSW 93*
Goldwasser, Edwin Leo 1919- *WhoAm 92*
Goldwasser, Eugene 1922- *WhoAm 92*
Goldwasser, Jane Salmon 1945- *WhoAmW 93*
Goldwasser, Judith Wax 1944- *WhoAmW 93, WhoWrEP 92*
Goldwasser, Michael 1823-1903 *PolBiDi*
Goldwasser, Ralph A. 1947- *St&PR 93*
Goldwasser, Robert Ellis 1945- *St&PR 93*
Goldwater, Barry 1909- *ColdWar 1 [port]*
Goldwater, Barry M. 1909- *PolPar*
Goldwater, Barry Morris 1909- *WhoAm 92*
Goldwater, Deena *Law&B 92*
Goldwater, France *AmWomPl*
Goldwater, John L. 1916- *WhoAm 92*
Goldwater, Leonard John 1903- *WhoAm 92*
Goldwater, Morris 1852-1939 *BioIn 17*
Goldwater, Walter d1985 *BioIn 17*
Goldway, David d1990 *BioIn 17*
Goldweitz, Saul 1920- *WhoAm 92*
Goldwire, Michael M. *St&PR 93*
Goldwitz, Susan 1949- *WhoWrEP 92*
Goldworm, Robert d1991 *BioIn 17*
Goldwurm, Jean d1990 *BioIn 17*

Goldwyn, Craig D. 1949- *WhoWrEP 92*
Goldwyn, Judith S. 1940- *WhoE 93*
Goldwyn, Robert M. 1930- *WhoWrEP 92*
Goldwyn, Samuel, Jr. *BioIn 17, St&PR 93*
Goldwyn, Samuel John, Jr. 1926- *WhoAm 92*
Goldwyn, Sheree Diane 1955- *St&PR 93*
Goldwyn, Tony *BioIn 17*
Goldzung, Harold John 1933- *WhoE 93*
Golea, Antoine 1906-1980 *Baker 92*
Golebiewski, Alojzy Ferdynand 1927- *WhoScE 91-4*
Golebiowski, Andrzej 1940- *WhoScE 91-4*
Golebiowski, Bernardo 1947- *WhoWor 93*
Golec, Janusz Stanislaw 1959- *WhoEmL 93*
Goleizovsky, Kasyan *BioIn 17*
Golemansky, Vassil 1933- *WhoScE 91-4*
Golemba, Beverly Eve 1931- *WhoSSW 93*
Golemba, Michael Edward 1940- *WhoSSW 93*
Golembeski, Jerome John 1931- *WhoAm 92*
Golembeski, Matthew *St&PR 93*
Golembieski, Michael Edward 1946- *WhoAm 92*
Golembiewski, Robert M. *Law&B 92*
Golembiewski, Robert Thomas 1932- *WhoWrEP 92*
Goleminov, Marin 1908- *Baker 92*
Golemme, Richard E. 1955- *St&PR 93*
Golemo, Stanley Michael, Jr. 1938- *St&PR 93*
Golenia, Antoni 1923- *WhoScE 91-4*
Goler, Angel Lopez *WhoScE 91-3*
Goler, Karl Andrew 1950- *WhoEmL 93, WhoSSW 93*
Golestan, Stan 1875-1956 *Baker 92*
Goley, Frank Renfro 1933- *St&PR 93*
Goley, Mary Anne 1945- *WhoE 93*
Golfier, Michel J.F. 1935- *WhoScE 91-2*
Golfman, Margarita M. 1937- *WhoAmW 93*
Golia, Gerald E. 1945- *St&PR 93*
Golia, Mary Ann 1957- *WhoEmL 93*
Golia, Peter R. 1926- *WhoE 93*
Golia, Stephen Thomas *Law&B 92*
Golian, Andrew G. *Law&B 92*
Golich, Vicki Lynne 1950- *WhoAmW 93*
Golightly, Donald Edward 1942- *WhoAm 92*
Golightly, Lena Mills *WhoAm 92*
Golik, Donald Edward 1943- *St&PR 93*
Golik, Kreso 1922- *DrEEuF*
Golin, Milton 1921- *WhoWrEP 92*
Golin, Simon 1958- *WhoWor 93*
Golinkin, Webster Fowler 1951- *St&PR 93*
Golino, Andre Joseph 1949- *WhoSSW 93*
Golino, Carlo Luigi 1913-1991 *BioIn 17*
Golino, Valeria *BioIn 17*
Golinowski, Joseph 1930- *St&PR 93*
Golinski, Jan 1957- *ConAu 139*
Golinski, Joseph John 1955- *St&PR 93*
Golis, Paul *ScF&FL 92*
Golisek, Robert J. 1940- *St&PR 93*
Golitz, Loren Eugene 1941- *WhoAm 92*
Golitzin, Nikolai (Borisovich) 1794-1866 *Baker 92*
Goll, Gillien *WhoE 93*
Goll, Karen Marie *WhoAmW 93*
Golland, Jeffrey H. 1941- *WhoE 93*
Golleher, George 1948- *WhoAm 92*
Goller, Karlene W. *Law&B 92*
Goller, Norman James 1930- *St&PR 93, WhoAm 92*
Gollerich, August 1859-1923 *Baker 92*
Golles, Josef *WhoScE 91-4*
Gollin, Albert Edwin 1930- *WhoAm 92*
Gollin, Stuart Allen 1941- *WhoAm 92*
Gollin, Susanne Merle 1953- *WhoAm 92, WhoAmW 93, WhoEmL 93*
Gollis, Elaine Sandra 1938- *WhoAmW 93*
Golliver, Robert Russell 1935- *St&PR 93*
Gollmick, Adolf 1825-1883 *Baker 92*
Gollmick, Friedrich Karl 1774-1852 *See* Gollmick, Karl 1796-1866 *Baker 92*
Gollmick, Karl 1796-1866 *Baker 92*
Gollner, Joseph Edward Lawrence 1937- *WhoAm 92*
Gollner, Marie Louise 1932- *WhoAm 92*
Gollnick, Philip 1934-1991 *BioIn 17*
Gollob, Herman Cohen 1930- *WhoAm 92*
Gollob, Marvin E. 1931- *St&PR 93*
Gollobin, Leonard Paul 1928- *WhoAm 92*
Gollon, Barbara Ann 1944- *WhoAmW 93*
Golly, Lynette Alice 1957- *WhoAmW 93*
Golly, Richard William 1949- *WhoEmL 93*
Golman, Jeffrey A. 1955- *WhoAm 92*
Golmen, Lars G. 1954- *WhoScE 91-4*
Golner, Jerold J. 1935- *St&PR 93*
Golob, David Richard, II 1968- *WhoE 93*
Golobic, Anton 1944- *St&PR 93*
Golobic, Robert A. *St&PR 93*
Goloby, George William, Jr. 1949- *WhoEmL 93, WhoSSW 93*
Golodner, Jack 1931- *WhoAm 92*
Golodner, Linda Fowler 1940- *WhoWor 93*
Golomb, Claire 1928- *WhoAmW 93, WhoE 93*
Golomb, D.L. *St&PR 93*
Golomb, Frederick Martin 1924- *WhoAm 92, WhoWor 93*
Golomb, Harvey Morris 1943- *WhoAm 92*
Golomb, Richard Moss 1958- *WhoE 93*
Golomb, Solomon Wolf 1932- *WhoAm 92*
Golomski, William Arthur J. *WhoAm 92*
Golonka, Sheila Lorraine 1958- *WhoEmL 93*
Golovanov, Nikolai (Semyonovich) 1891-1953 *Baker 92*
Golovchan, Vladimir Terentievich 1938- *WhoWor 93*
Golovskoy, Val Semion 1938- *WhoE 93*
Gols, A. George 1928- *St&PR 93*
Golschmann, Vladimir 1893-1972 *Baker 92*
Golson, Afton Almeda 1932- *WhoAm 92, WhoSSW 93*
Golson, George Barry 1944- *WhoAm 92, WhoWrEP 92*
Golsong, Dominique *Law&B 92*
Golstein, Pierre 1939- *WhoScE 91-2*
Golter, Harry 1924- *WhoAm 92*
Golterman, Han L. 1928- *WhoScE 91-2*
Goltermann, Georg (Eduard) 1824-1898 *Baker 92*
Goltra, David Dwight, Jr. 1954- *WhoEmL 93, WhoSSW 93*
Goltz, Alan 1947- *WhoAm 92*
Goltz, Christel 1912- *Baker 92, OxDcOp*
Goltz, Kolmar von der 1843-1916 *HarEnMi*
Goltz, Robert William 1923- *WhoAm 92*
Goltz, Sonia May 1959- *WhoAmW 93*
Goltz, Susan Ackerman 1946- *WhoEmL 93*
Goltzius, Hendrick 1558-1617 *BioIn 17*
Goltzman, David 1944- *WhoAm 92*
Golub, Barry Eric 1957- *WhoIns 93*
Golub, Gary E. 1943- *St&PR 93*
Golub, Gene Howard 1932- *WhoAm 92*
Golub, Harvey 1939- *WhoAm 92*
Golub, Howard V. *Law&B 92*
Golub, Howard V. 1945- *St&PR 93*
Golub, Howard Victor 1945- *WhoAm 92*
Golub, Leon Albert 1922- *BioIn 17, WhoAm 92*
Golub, Marcia Helene 1953- *WhoWrEP 92*
Golub, Maryln Lambert *Law&B 92*
Golub, Neil 1937- *WhoAm 92*
Golub, Rachelle Elias 1952- *St&PR 93*
Golub, Robert *BioIn 17*
Golub, Samuel Joseph 1915- *WhoE 93*
Golub, Sharon Bramson 1937- *WhoAmW 93*
Golub, Stephen Bruce 1941- *WhoAm 92*
Golub, William 1904- *St&PR 93*
Golub, William Weldon 1914- *WhoAm 92*
Golubev, Evgeny 1910-1988 *Baker 92*
Golubiew, Antoni 1907-1979 *PolBiDi*
Golubock, Harvey L. 1942- *St&PR 93*
Golubock, Harvey Lewis 1942- *WhoAm 92*
Golubovic, Predrag 1935- *DrEEuF*
Golubow Pollock, Karen G. *Law&B 92*
Goluskin, Norman Lewis 1938- *St&PR 93*
Golyn, Rudi Franklin 1938- *WhoAm 92*
Golyscheff, Jefim 1897-1970 *Baker 92*
Golz, James F. 1947- *St&PR 93, WhoIns 93*
Golz, Ronald A. 1934- *St&PR 93*
Golz, William C., Jr. 1947- *St&PR 93*
Golz, William Carl, Jr. 1947- *WhoEmL 93*
Golzman, Ita Hass 1951- *WhoEmL 93*
Gom, Leona 1946- *ScF&FL 92, WhoCanL 92*
Goma, Lameck Kazembe Haza 1930- *WhoAfr*
Goma, Louis Sylvain 1941- *WhoAfr*
Gomango, Girdhar 1943- *WhoAsAP 91*
Gombach, Raymond 1937- *St&PR 93*
Gombar, Csaba 1939- *WhoWor 93*
Gombeaud, Marc 1947- *WhoUN 92*
Gomberg, Edith S. Lisansky 1920- *WhoAm 92*
Gomberg, Henry Jacob 1918- *WhoAm 92*
Gomberg, Ira A. 1943- *St&PR 93*
Gomberg, Sydelle *WhoAm 92*
Gombert, Nicolas c. 1495-c. 1560 *Baker 92*
Gombi, Rosa 1933- *WhoScE 91-4*
Gombler, Willy Hans 1941- *WhoWor 93*
Gombos, Bruce William 1950- *WhoEmL 93*
Gombos, Ervin 1941- *WhoUN 92*
Gombos, Robert Steven 1943- *St&PR 93*
Gombosi, Otto (Janos) 1902-1955 *Baker 92*
Gombosuren, Tserenpilyn 1943- *WhoAsAP 91, WhoWor 93*
Gombrich, E.H. 1909- *BioIn 17*
Gombrich, Ernst Hans 1909- *BioIn 17*
Gombrich, Ernst Hans Josef 1909- *WhoWor 93*
Gombrich, Richard Francis 1937- *ConAu 138*
Gombrowicz, Witold 1904-1969 *PolBiDi*
Gomel, Maurice 1938- *WhoScE 91-2*
Gomena, John Edward 1927- *WhoAm 92*
Gomer, Robert 1924- *WhoAm 92*
Gomer, Steve *MiSFD 9*
Gomercic, Hrvoje 1940- *WhoScE 91-4*
Gomersall, Earl Raymond 1930- *WhoAm 92*
Gomery, Douglas 1945- *WhoE 93, WhoWrEP 92*
Gomery, Percy 1881- *ScF&FL 92*
Gomes, Antonio Carlos 1836-1896 *IntDcOp*
Gomes, Aquiles Coelho 1940- *WhoWor 93*
Gomes, Brian E. 1951- *St&PR 93*
Gomes, Carlos 1836-1896 *OxDcOp*
Gomes, (Antonio) Carlos 1836-1896 *Baker 92*
Gomes, Francisco Neves *WhoScE 91-3*
Gomes, J.A.N.F. 1947- *WhoScE 91-3*
Gomes, Jim A. 1940- *St&PR 93*
Gomes, Joao Fernando Pereira 1960- *WhoWor 93*
Gomes, Pericles Ferreira 1931- *WhoUN 92*
Gomes, Peter John 1942- *BioIn 17, WhoAm 92*
Gomes, Richard David 1937- *St&PR 93*
Gomes, Wayne Reginald 1938- *WhoAm 92*
Gomes, Zachary 1955- *St&PR 93*
Gomes de Araujo, Joao 1846-1942 *Baker 92*
Gomez, Al Ralph 1957- *WhoEmL 93*
Gomez, Alain *BioIn 17*
Gomez, Alseny Rene 1936- *WhoWor 93*
Gomez, Alvar 1936- *WhoAm 92*
Gomez, Calleja *Baker 92*
Gomez, Carol Vartuli 1950- *WhoAmW 93*
Gomez, Daniel B. 1936- *St&PR 93*
Gomez, Deborah Lou 1957- *WhoSSW 93*
Gomez, Didier *BioIn 17*
Gomez, Edgardo Dizon 1938- *WhoWor 93*
Gomez, Edward Casimiro 1938- *WhoAm 92*
Gomez, Elizabeth Ann 1960- *WhoAmW 93*
Gomez, Elsa *WhoAmW 93*
Gomez, Elsa 1938- *HispAmA [port], NotHsAW 93*
Gomez, Francis Dean 1941- *WhoAm 92, WhoWor 93*
Gomez, Gilberto Florentino 1946- *WhoWor 93*
Gomez, Jewelle *BioIn 17*
Gomez, Jewelle 1948- *ScF&FL 92*
Gomez, Jill 1942- *Baker 92, OxDcOp*
Gomez, John *BioIn 17*
Gomez, Juan Gualberto *DcCPCAm*
Gomez, Juan Vicente 1864-1935 *DcTwHis*
Gomez, Julie 1946- *WhoEmL 93*
Gomez, Keith Andrew 1950- *WhoSSW 93*
Gomez, Lefty 1908-1988 *HispAmA*
Gomez, Lefty 1908?-1989 *BioIn 17*
Gomez, Lloyd Edward 1933- *St&PR 93*
Gomez, Lucas 1940- *WhoSSW 93*
Gomez, Luis Maria 1924- *WhoUN 92*
Gomez, Luis Oscar 1943- *WhoAm 92*
Gomez, M. F. da Costa *DcCPCAm*
Gomez, Madeleine Yvonne 1956- *WhoEmL 93*
Gomez, Magdalena 1954- *BioIn 17*
Gomez, Manuel Rodriguez 1928- *WhoAm 92*
Gomez, Marco *Law&B 92*
Gomez, Mary Alice 1953- *WhoSSW 93*
Gomez, Max *BioIn 17*
Gomez, Michael John 1949- *WhoWor 93*
Gomez, Oscar C. 1946- *St&PR 93*
Gomez, Rajan Gaetan 1938- *WhoWor 93*
Gomez, Ralph d1990 *BioIn 17*
Gomez, Ramon *Law&B 92*
Gomez, Ricardo G. 1955- *WhoWor 93*
Gomez, Rogelio Roberto 1950- *WhoWrEP 92*
Gomez, Tony *BioIn 17*
Gomez-Acebo, Luis 1934-1991 *BioIn 17*
Gomezanda, Antonio 1894-1961 *Baker 92*
Gomez-Bezares, Fernando 1956- *WhoWor 93*
Gomez-Campo, Cesar 1933- *WhoScE 91-3*
Gomez Canedo, Lino 1908-1990 *BioIn 17*
Gomez de Avellaneda y Arteaga, Gertrudis 1814-1873 *BioIn 17*
Gomez de la Cortina, Jose 1799-1860 *DcMexL*
Gomez De Las Heras, Federico 1947- *WhoScE 91-3*
Gomez Del Prado, Jose L. 1937- *WhoUN 92*
Gomez Duran, Carlos 1932- *WhoScE 91-3*
Gomez-Fatou, Jose Maria 1928- *WhoScE 91-3*
Gomez-Gallego, Julian 1933- *WhoScE 91-3*
Gomez Haro, Enrique 1877-1956 *DcMexL*
Gomez Larraneta, M. 1924- *WhoScE 91-3*
Gomez-Martinez, Jose Luis 1943- *WhoSSW 93*
Gomez Martinez, Miguel Angel 1949- *Baker 92*
Gomez Mayorga, Mauricio 1913- *DcMexL*
Gomez Morin, Manuel *DcCPCAm*
Gomez-Oliver, Antonio 1942- *WhoUN 92*
Gomez Palacio, Martin 1893- *DcMexL*
Gomez-Pena, Guillermo *BioIn 17*
Gomez-Preston, Cheryl *BioIn 17*
Gomez-Quinones, Juan 1940- *HispAmA*
Gomez-Quinones, Juan 1942- *DcLB 122 [port]*
Gomez-Reino, Carlos 1946- *WhoWor 93*
Gomez Robelo, Ricardo 1884-1924 *DcMexL*
Gomez-Rodriguez, Manuel 1940- *WhoAm 92*
Gomez-Rosa, Alexis 1950- *WhoE 93*
Gomez-Sanchez, Antonio 1926- *WhoScE 91-3*
Gomi, Taro *BioIn 17*
Gomide, Aloysio Mares Dias 1929- *WhoWor 93*
Gomide, Fernando de Mello 1927- *WhoWor 93*
Gomilak, Thomas A., Jr. 1932- *St&PR 93*
Gomillion, Charles G. 1900- *EncAACR*
Gomis Soler, Jose 1900- *DcMexL*
Gomis y Colomber, Jose 1741-1836 *OxDcOp*
Gomm, Peter Albert 1931- *St&PR 93*
Gomme, Alice Bertha 1852-1938 *BioIn 17*
Gomolka, Michal 1564-1609 *Baker 92*
Gomolka, Mikolaj c. 1535-c. 1591 *Baker 92, PolBiDi*
Gomoll, Allen Warren 1933- *WhoE 93*
Gomolski, Thomas Frank 1947- *St&PR 93*
Gomor, Bela 1938- *WhoScE 91-4*
Gomory, Ralph E. *BioIn 17*
Gomory, Ralph Edward 1929- *St&PR 93, WhoAm 92, WhoE 93*
Gomozov, Eugene Pavlovitch 1947- *WhoWor 93*
Gompers, Samuel 1850-1924 *BioIn 17, GayN, PolPar*
Gompers, William C. 1949- *St&PR 93*
Gompertz, Mark Alan 1954- *St&PR 93*
Gompertz, Martin *ScF&FL 92*
Gompertz, Rolf 1927- *WhoWrEP 92*
Gomperz, Paul Andreas 1937- *WhoE 93*
Gompf, Arthur Milton 1909- *St&PR 93*
Gompf, Clayton N., Jr. *Law&B 92*
Gomulka, Wladyslaw 1905-1982 *ColdWar 2 [port], DcTwHis, PolBiDi*
Gomurgen, Erol 1933- *WhoWor 93*
Goncalves, Fernando Inocencio 1949- *WhoScE 91-3*
Goncalves, Francisco 1926- *WhoScE 91-3*
Goncalves, Joao G.M. 1952- *WhoScE 91-3*
Goncalves, Marcos Pereira 1958- *WhoWor 93*
Goncalves da Silva, Cylon Eudoxio Tricot 1946- *WhoWor 93*
Goncebate, Rodolfo Sixto 1945- *WhoWor 93*
Gonchar, Rosalie James 1927- *WhoSSW 93*
Goncharov, Sergei S 1951- *WhoWor 93*
Goncher, Susan Ellen 1950- *WhoAmW 93*
Goncourt, Edmond de 1822-1896 *BioIn 17*
Goncourt, Edmond de 1822-1896 & Goncourt, Jules de 1830-1870 *DcLB 123 [port]*
Goncourt, Jules de 1830-1870 *BioIn 17*
Goncourt, Jules de 1830-1870 *See* Goncourt, Edmond de 1822-1896 & Goncourt, Jules de 1830-1870 *DcLB 123*
Goncz, Arpad *BioIn 17*
Goncz, Arpad 1922- *WhoWor 93*
Gondek, Janice Ruth 1934- *St&PR 93*
Gondek, Robert Joseph 1943- *St&PR 93*
Gondek, Therese M. 1950- *St&PR 93*
Gondek, Therese Marie 1950- *WhoEmL 93*
Gonder, David Wooddell 1942- *WhoSSW 93*
Gondimel, Claude *Baker 92*
Gondles, James A., Jr. *BioIn 17*
Gondo, Tsuneo 1930- *WhoAsAP 91*
Gondo, Yasuo 1926- *WhoWor 93*
Gondola, Istvan 1951- *WhoScE 91-4*
Gondosch, Linda 1944- *ScF&FL 92*
Gondosch, Linda Ann 1944- *WhoWrEP 92*
Gondra, Ernesto S.M. 1949- *WhoUN 92*
Gondran, Jean 1932- *WhoScE 91-2*
Gondswaard, J.M. *WhoScE 91-3*
Gonelevu, Villiame Sakaraia Jonathan 1941- *WhoAsAP 91*
Gonella, Joseph A. 1937- *WhoScE 91-2*
Gonella, Robert J. *Law&B 92*
Gonen, Shmuel d1991 *BioIn 17*
Gonet, Boleslaw 1920- *WhoScE 91-4*
Gonet, Zdzislaw 1925- *WhoScE 91-4*
Gonfiantini, Roberto 1932- *WhoUN 92*

Gong, Carolyn Lei Chu 1949- WhoAmW 93
Gong, Edmond Joseph 1930- WhoAm 92
Gong, Nancy Yee 1957- WhoE 93
Gong, Vincent 1929- St&PR 93
Gongaware, Donald Francis 1935- St&PR 93, WhoAm 92
Gongora-Trejos, Enrique 1931- WhoWor 93
Gonia, Charles 1925- St&PR 93, WhoAm 92
Gonick, Harvey Craig 1930- WhoAm 92
Gonick, Paul 1930- WhoAm 92
Gonne, Maud 1866-1953 BioIn 17
Gonnella, Eleanor Ann 1954- WhoE 93
Gonnella, Nina Celeste 1953- WhoAm 92, WhoAmW 93, WhoEmL 93
Gonnella-Sheridan, Eleanor Ann 1954- WhoAmW 93
Gonnenwein, Friedrich 1933- WhoScE 91-2
Gonnenwein, Wolfgang 1933- Baker 92
Gonnerman, Mary F. 1927- St&PR 93
Gonnoud, Urban d1990 BioIn 17
Gonon, Phyllis WhoAmW 93
Gonor, Robert F. 1949- WhoIns 93
Gonsalkorale, Mahendra 1944- WhoWor 93
Gonsalves, Donald John 1931- St&PR 93
Gonsalves, Gregory Jay 1968- WhoE 93, WhoEmL 93
Gonsalves, Ralph 1946- DcCPCAm
Gonsalves, Sandra Virginia 1960- WhoAmW 93
Gonsalves, Stephanie A. Law&B 92
Gonsalves, Victor L. 1952- St&PR 93
Gonsalves-Sabola, Joaquim Claudino 1929- WhoWor 93
Gonser, Ulrich 1922- WhoScE 91-3
Gonseth, Walter C. 1931- St&PR 93
Gonshak, Isabelle Lee 1932- WhoSSW 93
Gonson, S. Donald 1936- WhoWor 93
Gonsoulin Ghattas, Wendy Ann 1965- WhoAmW 93
Gontard, Thierry 1962- WhoWor 93
Gontarek, Paul J. Law&B 92
Gonthier, Charles Doherty 1928- WhoAm 92
Gontier, Jean Roger 1927- WhoWor 93
Gonya, Patrice Yeager 1951- WhoAmW 93
Gonye, Laszlo K. 1922- WhoIns 93
Gonyo, Marilyn E. 1943- WhoE 93
Gonzaga, Isabella d'Este 1474-1539 BioIn 17
Gonzaga, Pietro 1751-1831 OxDcOp
Gonzaga family OxDcOp
Gonzague, Maria Ludwika 1611-1667 PolBiDi
Gonzales, Adrian Sada St&PR 93
Gonzales, Alexis 1931- WhoAm 92
Gonzales, Andre Agustine 1943- WhoAm 92
Gonzales, (Elizabeth) Anne H. 1944- ConAu 138
Gonzales, Cesar I. 1934- St&PR 93
Gonzales, Diana Espana 1947- WhoSSW 93
Gonzales, Edward C. 1930- St&PR 93
Gonzales, Frank Law&B 92
Gonzales, Fred Patrick 1947- St&PR 93
Gonzales, John Edmond 1924- WhoAm 92
Gonzales, Lucille Contreras 1937- WhoAmW 93
Gonzales, Marjorie Elaine 1927- WhoAm 92
Gonzales, Michael Law&B 92
Gonzales, Myrtle 1891-1918 SweetSg A
Gonzales, Neptali A. WhoAsAP 91
Gonzales, Paul Villareal 1952- St&PR 93
Gonzales, Rebecca Eliza 1963- WhoAmW 93
Gonzales, Rodolfo 1928- DcLB 122 [port]
Gonzales, Ronald Rene Law&B 92
Gonzales, Rosa Ontiveros 1964- WhoAmW 93
Gonzales, Stephanie 1950- HispAmA [port], WhoAm 92, WhoAmW 93
Gonzales, Sylvia Alicia 1943- NotHsAW 93
Gonzales-Berry, Erlinda 1942- NotHsAW 93
Gonzales Martin, Marcelo Cardinal 1918- WhoWor 93
Gonzalez, Abel Julio 1941- WhoUN 92
Gonzalez, Adalberto Elias HispAmA
Gonzalez, Ana Maria Law&B 92
Gonzalez, Angel 1925- BioIn 17
Gonzalez, Avelino Juan 1951- WhoEmL 93, WhoSSW 93
Gonzalez, Bradford J. 1950- WhoSSW 93
Gonzalez, Carlos Manuel 1946- St&PR 93
Gonzalez, Carlos Miguel 1941- WhoSSW 93
Gonzalez, Carmen G. Law&B 92
Gonzalez, Catherine Gunsalus 1934- ConAu 136
Gonzalez, Celedonio 1923- HispAmA
Gonzalez, Cheryl Diana 1951- WhoAmW 93
Gonzalez, Deena J. 1952- HispAmA
Gonzalez, Edgardo Law&B 92
Gonzalez, Edwin Law&B 92
Gonzalez, Efren William 1929- WhoAm 92
Gonzalez, Elma 1942- HispAmA
Gonzalez, Emilio M. 1913- WhoWor 93
Gonzalez, Ervin Amado 1960- WhoEmL 93
Gonzalez, Eugene Robert WhoAm 92, WhoWor 93
Gonzalez, Felipe BioIn 17
Gonzalez, Floyd A. Law&B 92
Gonzalez, Frederick Mark Law&B 92
Gonzalez, Fredrick J. 1949- HispAmA [port]
Gonzalez, Genaro 1949- DcLB 122 [port]
Gonzalez, Georgina S. WhoAmW 93
Gonzalez, Gisela Alexandra 1949- WhoAmW 93, WhoEmL 93
Gonzalez, Gladys M. 1955- WhoEmL 93, WhoSSW 93
Gonzalez, Gloria 1940- ScF&FL 92
Gonzalez, Hector Hugo 1937- WhoAm 92
Gonzalez, Hector R. 1933- St&PR 93
Gonzalez, Henry B. BioIn 17
Gonzalez, Henry B. 1916- CngDr 91
Gonzalez, Henry Barbosa 1916- HispAmA, NewYTBS 92 [port], WhoAm 92, WhoSSW 93
Gonzalez, Herlinda Law&B 92
Gonzalez, Hernan 1949- WhoAm 92, WhoEmL 93, WhoSSW 93, WhoWor 93
Gonzalez, Ileana 1958- WhoAmW 93
Gonzalez, Jacqueline C. Lytle 1955- WhoAmW 93
Gonzalez, James Raymond 1953- WhoEmL 93
Gonzalez, Javier J. Law&B 92
Gonzalez, Jerry BioIn 17
Gonzalez, Jesse 1936- St&PR 93
Gonzalez, Joe Manuel 1950- WhoAm 92
Gonzalez, Jose 1933- HispAmA
Gonzalez, Jose Alejandro, Jr. 1931- WhoAm 92, WhoSSW 93
Gonzalez, Jose E. Law&B 92
Gonzalez, Jose Luis 1926- DcMexL, SpAmA
Gonzalez, Jose Luis, Jr. Law&B 92
Gonzalez, Jose R. 1954- St&PR 93
Gonzalez, Jose Ramon 1930- WhoAm 92
Gonzalez, Jose Ramon 1951- WhoEmL 93
Gonzalez, Jose Victoriano 1887-1927 BioIn 17
Gonzalez, Julio 1876-1942 BioIn 17
Gonzalez, Karen Eileen 1960- WhoAmW 93
Gonzalez, Kimberly Regina 1964- WhoAmW 93, WhoEmL 93, WhoWor 93
Gonzalez, Lauren Yvonne 1952- WhoAmW 93
Gonzalez, Leonel DcCPCAm
Gonzalez, Lucia Parsons 1852-1942 HispAmA
Gonzalez, Lynn Ammirato 1948- WhoAmW 93
Gonzalez, Manuel John 1963- WhoSSW 93
Gonzalez, Mario Octavio 1913- WhoSSW 93
Gonzalez, Orlando G. 1927- St&PR 93
Gonzalez, Pacita T. 1940- WhoAsAP 91
Gonzalez, Patricia 1958- BioIn 17, NotHsAW 93
Gonzalez, Paula 1932- HispAmA
Gonzalez, Philip Albert 1946- WhoEmL 93
Gonzalez, Rafael Ceferino 1942- WhoAm 92
Gonzalez, Raquel Maria 1952- WhoSSW 93
Gonzalez, Raul 1948- WhoE 93
Gonzalez, Raul A. 1940- WhoAm 92, WhoSSW 93
Gonzalez, Ray 1952- DcLB 122 [port]
Gonzalez, Raymond Emmanuel 1924- HispAmA
Gonzalez, Raymond G. Law&B 92
Gonzalez, Renee E. Law&B 92
Gonzalez, Richard Alonzo 1928- HispAmA [port]
Gonzalez, Richard Peter 1942- St&PR 93
Gonzalez, Richard Rafael 1942- HispAmA
Gonzalez, Ruben WhoAm 92
Gonzalez, Servando 1925- MiSFD 9
Gonzalez, Wenceslao Jose 1957- WhoWor 93
Gonzalez, William G. 1940- WhoAm 92
Gonzalez, Xavier d20th cent. HispAmA
Gonzalez, Zoe Mirella 1958- WhoE 93
Gonzalez-Acosta, Alejandro Jose 1953- WhoWor 93
Gonzalez-Acuna, Jose 1952- WhoE 93
Gonzalez-Alexopoulos 1945- WhoAm 92
Gonzalez Amezcua, Consuelo 1903-1975 NotHsAW 93
Gonzalez-Avila, Jorge 1925- Baker 92
Gonzalez-Ayela, Antonio 1946- WhoWor 93
Gonzalez Bernaldo De Quiros, Julio 1930- WhoScE 91-3
Gonzalez-Berry, Erlinda 1942- HispAmA [port]
Gonzalez Bocanegra, Francisco 1824-1861 DcMexL
Gonzalez Caballero, Antonio 1931- DcMexL
Gonzalez Caballero de Castillo Ledon, Amalia 1902-1974 DcMexL
Gonzalez Calzada, Manuel 1915- DcMexL
Gonzalez Casanova, Pablo 1922- WhoWor 93
Gonzalez-Cruz, Luis Francisco 1943- WhoE 93
Gonzalez de Eslava, Fernan DcMexL
Gonzalez de Mendoza, Jose Maria 1893-1967 DcMexL
Gonzalez de Mireles, Jovita 1899-1983 DcLB 122
Gonzalez de Rivera, Jose Luis 1944- WhoWor 93
Gonzalez Duran, Jorge 1918- DcMexL
Gonzalez Estrada, N. WhoScE 91-3
Gonzalez Fernandez, Jose Antonio 1937- WhoScE 91-3
Gonzalez Gago, Nestor Jose 1946- WhoWor 93
Gonzalez-Gascon, Francisco 1945- WhoScE 91-3
Gonzalez-Gerth, Miguel 1926- DcMexL
Gonzalez Gonzalez, Fernando Luis 1958- WhoWor 93
Gonzalez-Hernandez, Oscar 1930- WhoUN 92
Gonzalez-Lama, Zoilo 1949- WhoWor 93
Gonzalez-Lauck, Victor Walton 1955- WhoWor 93
Gonzalez Leon, Francisco 1862-1945 DcMexL
Gonzalez Luna, Efrain DcCPCAm
Gonzalez-Marina, Joaquina Dolores 1935- WhoWor 93
Gonzalez Martinez, Enrique 1871-1952 DcMexL
Gonzalez-Mena, Janet 1937- WhoWrEP 92
Gonzalez-Navarro, Andres 1946- WhoScE 91-3
Gonzalez Obregon, Luis 1865-1938 DcMexL
Gonzalez Pena, Carlos 1885-1955 DcMexL
Gonzalez Pineda, Francisco 1918- DcMexL
Gonzalez Pino, Barbara 1941- WhoSSW 93
Gonzalez Ponce, Ricardo 1941- WhoScE 91-3
Gonzalez Real, Osvaldo 1938- SpAmA
Gonzalez Revilla, Antonio DcCPCAm
Gonzalez Rivadeneyra, Marino Cesar 1933- WhoWor 93
Gonzalez Rojo, Enrique 1899-1939 DcMexL
Gonzalez Rojo, Enrique, Jr. 1928- DcMexL
Gonzalez Santander, Rafael 1932- WhoScE 91-3
Gonzalez Sanz, Julio 1945- WhoWor 93
Gonzalez Sfeir, Mauricio Jorge 1956- WhoWor 93
Gonzalez Urena, Angel 1947- WhoWor 93
Gonzalez Vera, Jose Santos 1897-1970 SpAmA
Gonzalo, Julio Antonio 1936- WhoWor 93
Gonzalo de Cordoba, Hernandez 1453-1515 HarEnMi
Gonzelez Merquez, Felipe 1942- WhoWor 93
Gonzo, Elio Emilio 1945- WhoWor 93
Goo, Abraham Meu Sen 1925- St&PR 93, WhoAm 92
Goo, Donald Wah Yung 1934- WhoAm 92
Gooch, Anthony Cushing 1937- WhoAm 92
Gooch, Carolyn Frances 1951- WhoAmW 93
Gooch, Frances Pusey AmWomPl
Gooch, J. Glenn 1922- St&PR 93, WhoAm 92
Gooch, James Oliver 1913- WhoAm 92
Gooch, Lawrence Boyd 1942- WhoAm 92
Gooch, Lowell Thomas St&PR 93
Gooch, Patricia Carolyn 1935- WhoAm 92, WhoAmW 93, WhoSSW 93
Gooch, Phillip W. 1943- St&PR 93
Gooch, Robert Miletus WhoWrEP 92
Gooch, Stan 1932- ScF&FL 92
Gooch, Stephen Grant Law&B 92
Gooch, Walter Lewis 1937- WhoSSW 93
Gooch, William DeWitt 1935- WhoSSW 93
Gooch, William Kevin 1954- WhoSSW 93
Goocher, R.L. 1950- St&PR 93
Good, Albert F. 1915- St&PR 93
Good, Alice 1950- SmATA 73 [port]
Good, Allen Hovey 1930- WhoE 93
Good, Anne Leeper 1923- WhoAmW 93
Good, Barbara J. 1927- WhoAmW 93
Good, Bonnie Mae 1952- WhoAmW 93
Good, Charles E. 1948- St&PR 93
Good, Cynthia Annette 1951- WhoAm 92
Good, Daniel James 1940- WhoAm 92, WhoE 93
Good, David Allen 1954- St&PR 93
Good, David H. Law&B 92
Good, Deborah Hoven 1955- WhoEmL 93
Good, Donald Wayne 1956- WhoEmL 93, WhoSSW 93
Good, Edward K. 1931- St&PR 93
Good, Edwin Stanton 1871-1957 BioIn 17
Good, Gayle Fitzpatrick 1945- WhoAmW 93
Good, Gregory Elmer, Jr. 1941- WhoAm 92
Good, Irving John 1916- WhoAm 92, WhoSSW 93, WhoWor 93
Good, Jack Duane 1936- St&PR 93
Good, James Robert 1947- St&PR 93
Good, Janis Caroline 1958- WhoEmL 93
Good, Joan Duffey 1939- WhoAmW 93, WhoWor 93
Good, Joan R. Law&B 92
Good, John BioIn 17
Good, John Dudley 1928- St&PR 93
Good, John Edward George WhoScE 91-1
Good, John Leon, III 1943- WhoE 93
Good, John Scott 1957- St&PR 93
Good, Joseph R. 1911- St&PR 93
Good, Joseph Samuel 1939- St&PR 93
Good, Judith Marie 1955- WhoAmW 93
Good, Larry J. 1952- St&PR 93
Good, Laurance Frederic 1932- WhoAm 92
Good, Leonard Phelps 1907- WhoAm 92, WhoWor 93
Good, Linda Lou 1941- WhoAmW 93
Good, Mary L. 1931- St&PR 93
Good, Mary Lowe BioIn 17
Good, Mary Lowe 1931- WhoAm 92, WhoAmW 93
Good, Michael Clay 1956- WhoSSW 93
Good, Norma Lee 1932- WhoAmW 93
Good, Paul Joseph 1929- WhoAm 92
Good, Ralph E. 1937-1991 BioIn 17
Good, Raymond F. 1928- WhoAm 92
Good, Rebecca Mae Wertman 1943- WhoE 93
Good, Robert Alan 1922- WhoAm 92, WhoWor 93
Good, Roy M. 1916- St&PR 93
Good, Sharon 1950- WhoE 93
Good, Sheldon Fred 1933- WhoWor 93
Good, Susan Pauline 1953- WhoAmW 93
Good, Thomas Lindall 1943- WhoAm 92, WhoWrEP 92
Good, Tim 1958- St&PR 93
Good, Virginia Johnson 1919- WhoAmW 93, WhoE 93
Good, Walter 1932- WhoScE 91-4
Good, Walter Raymond 1924- WhoAm 92
Good, Wendy Rae 1951- WhoEmL 93
Good, William Allen 1949- WhoAm 92
Goodacre, Glenna 1939- BioIn 17
Goodacre, Jill BioIn 17
Goodale, Eugene Clark Law&B 92
Goodale, James Campbell 1933- St&PR 93, WhoAm 92
Goodale, Jennifer Paine 1962- WhoE 93
Goodale, Robert Seldon 1933- WhoAm 92
Goodale, Toni Krissel 1941- WhoAm 92, WhoAmW 93
Goodall, Brian WhoScE 91-1
Goodall, Frances Louise 1915- WhoAmW 93, WhoWor 93
Goodall, Frederique Vincent 1959- WhoAmW 93
Goodall, Harry Alonzo 1932- WhoAm 92
Goodall, Harvey L. 1836-1900 JrnUS
Goodall, Hurley Charles 1927- AfrAmBi
Goodall, Jackson Wallace, Jr. BioIn 17
Goodall, Jackson Wallace, Jr. 1938- St&PR 93, WhoAm 92
Goodall, Jane BioIn 17
Goodall, John S. 1908- BioIn 17
Goodall, John S(trickland) 1908- MajAI [port]
Goodall, Leon S. 1925- St&PR 93
Goodall, Leon Steele 1925- WhoAm 92, WhoIns 93
Goodall, Leonard Edwin 1937- WhoAm 92
Goodall, Marcus Campbell 1914- WhoWor 93
Goodall, Reginald 1901-1990 Baker 92, IntDcOp
Goodall, Reginald 1905-1990 BioIn 17, OxDcOp
Gooday, Graham William WhoScE 91-1

Goodban, Maurice G. 1930- St&PR 93
Goodby, Donald Rhodes 1926- St&PR 93
Goodby, James Eugene 1929- WhoAm 92
Goodby, Jeffrey WhoAm 92
Goodby, Richard W. 1917- St&PR 93
Goodby, Scott R. 1955- St&PR 93, WhoAm 92
Goodchild, George 1888-1969 ScF&FL 92
Goodchild, Heather Margaret 1957- St&PR 93
Goodchild, John Charles, Jr. 1945- WhoAm 92
Goodchild, Phillip E. Law&B 92
Goodchild, Robert Marshall 1933- St&PR 93, WhoAm 92
Goode, Alexander David 1911-1943 BioIn 17
Goode, Brad BioIn 17
Goode, Bryan C. 1935- St&PR 93
Goode, Caron Banta 1951- WhoE 93
Goode, Celia Ross 1950- WhoEmL 93, WhoSSW 93
Goode, Clement Tyson 1929- WhoAm 92
Goode, Constance Loper 1950- WhoSSW 93
Goode, Cynthia Baird 1957- WhoE 93, WhoEmL 93
Goode, David R. Law&B 92
Goode, David Ronald 1941- St&PR 93, WhoSSW 93
Goode, Diane BioIn 17, ChlBIID [port]
Goode, Erica Tucker 1940- WhoAmW 93
Goode, Erich 1938- ConAu 37NR
Goode, Gwendolyn Marie 1949- WhoAmW 93
Goode, Ian R. Law&B 92
Goode, James A. d1992 NewYTBS 92
Goode, James Emory 1935- St&PR 93
Goode, James Moore 1939- WhoAm 92
Goode, John Law&B 92
Goode, John Martin 1934- St&PR 93, WhoAm 92
Goode, Martin 1928- St&PR 93
Goode, Richard Benjamin 1916- WhoAm 92
Goode, Richard Harris 1939- WhoWor 93
Goode, Richard (Stephen) 1943- Baker 92, WhoAm 92
Goode, S.M. 1943- St&PR 93
Goode, Seddon, Jr. 1932- St&PR 93
Goode, Stephen Hogue 1924- WhoAm 92
Goode, Vickie Catherine 1949- WhoAmW 93
Goode, W. Wilson 1938- AfrAmBi [port], ConBlB 4 [port], WhoAm 92, WhoE 93
Goode, William Josiah 1917- WhoAm 92
Goode-Elman, Alice Neufeld 1949- WhoE 93
Goodell, Charles E. 1926-1987 PolPar
Goodell, Christina Marie 1959- WhoAmW 93
Goodell, George Sidney 1921- WhoAm 92
Goodell, Horace Grant 1925- WhoAm 92
Goodell, John Dewitte 1909- WhoWor 93
Goodell, Joseph Edward 1937- WhoAm 92
Goodell, Larry 1935- WhoWrEP 92
Goodell, Robert P., Jr. 1928- St&PR 93
Goodell, Sol 1906- WhoAm 92
Goodell, Warren Franklin 1924- WhoAm 92
Goodell, William 1792-1878 PolPar
Goodelman, Aaron J. 1890-1978 BioIn 17
Goodelman, Alan Frank 1931- St&PR 93
Goodelman, Arthur Michael 1953- St&PR 93
Goodelman, Hilda 1931- St&PR 93
Goodelman, Ruth N. 1914- WhoE 93
Gooden, C. Michael 1946- ConEn
Gooden, Dwight BioIn 17
Gooden, Dwight Eugene 1964- WhoAm 92, WhoE 93
Gooden, Melinda Grady 1963- WhoSSW 93
Gooden, Philip ScF&FL 92
Gooden, Romone PeeWee See Digital Underground ConMus 9
Goodenough, Andrew Lewis 1955- St&PR 93
Goodenough, David John 1944- WhoE 93
Goodenough, Florence Laura 1886-1959 BioIn 17
Goodenough, John 1940- WhoWor 93
Goodenough, John Bannister 1922- WhoAm 92, WhoSSW 93
Goodenough, Judith B. 1942- WhoWrEP 92
Goodenough, Judith Elizabeth 1948- WhoEmL 93
Goodenough, Peter William WhoScE 91-1
Goodenough, Walter H. 1939- St&PR 93
Goodenough, Ward Hunt 1919- WhoAm 92
Gooder, Harry 1928- WhoSSW 93
Goodes, Melvin Russell 1935- St&PR 93, WhoAm 92, WhoE 93
Goodey, Ila Marie WhoWrEP 92
Goodey, Ila Marie 1948- WhoAm 92, WhoEmL 93
Goodfellow, E.H., Mrs. AmWomPl
Goodfellow, George 1855-1910 BioIn 17
Goodfellow, Peggy Jo 1947- WhoAmW 93
Goodfellow, Robin Irene 1945- WhoAm 92
Goodfellow, William Chester 1947- WhoEmL 93
Goodfriend, B. Dale, Jr. Law&B 92
Goodfriend, Douglas Edward 1951- WhoEmL 93
Goodfriend, Herbert Jay 1926- WhoAm 92
Goodfriend, Marvin S. 1950- St&PR 93
Goodfriend, Robert M. St&PR 93
Goodgame, Ronald Edward Law&B 92
Goodgame, Ronald Edward 1938- St&PR 93, WhoAm 92
Goodger, John Verne 1936- St&PR 93, WhoAm 92
Goodgold, Edwin 1944- ScF&FL 92
Goodhart, Diane Williams 1944- WhoAmW 93
Goodhart, Karen Stephan 1947- WhoAmW 93
Goodhartz, Gerald 1938- WhoE 93, WhoWor 93
Goodhead, Dudley Trevor WhoScE 91-1
Goodheart, Barbara Jean 1934- WhoWrEP 92
Goodheart, Eugene 1931- ConAu 39NR
Goodheer, Wil Charles 1932- WhoWor 93
Goodhew, Howard R., Jr. 1923- St&PR 93
Goodhew, J. Mark 1955- St&PR 93
Goodhew, Peter John WhoScE 91-1
Goodhew, Peter John 1943- WhoWor 93
Goodhue, Francis A. 1916-1990 BioIn 17
Goodhue, Mary Brier 1921- WhoAmW 93, WhoE 93
Goodier, Fred 1938- WhoScE 91-1
Goodier, J. Leslie 1920- WhoAm 92
Goodier, John Jefferis 1931- St&PR 93
Goodin, Cynthia Dawn 1964- WhoAmW 93
Goodin, John Walter 1946- St&PR 93
Goodin, Julia C. 1957- WhoAmW 93
Goodin, Michael Anthony 1951- WhoWrEP 92
Goodin, Robert Edward 1950- WhoWrEP 92
Goodin, William Charles 1917- WhoAm 92
Goodine, Francena White 1940- WhoWrEP 92
Goodine, Isaac Thomas 1932- WhoWor 93
Gooding, Charles Arthur 1936- WhoAm 92
Gooding, Charles Thomas 1931- WhoAm 92
Gooding, Gretchen Ann Wagner 1935- WhoAmW 93
Gooding, James Henry 1837-1864 BioIn 17
Gooding, John T., II Law&B 92
Gooding, Judson 1926- WhoAm 92, WhoWrEP 92
Gooding, Paul H. Law&B 92
Gooding, Theodore J. Law&B 92
Gooding, Timothy James 1949- St&PR 93
Goodkin, Deborah Gay 1951- WhoAmW 93
Goodkin, Michael Jon 1941- WhoAm 92
Goodkind, Conrad George 1944- WhoAm 92
Goodkind, Louis William 1914- WhoAm 92
Goodkind, Robert H. 1921- St&PR 93
Goodlad, John I. BioIn 17
Goodlad, John Inkster 1920- WhoAm 92
Goodland, Katharine 1958- WhoE 93
Goodlander, Mabel Ray AmWomPl
Goodlett, James Campbell 1937- St&PR 93
Goodley, George Richard 1932- WhoSSW 93
Goodling, William F. CngDr 91
Goodling, William F. 1927- WhoAm 92, WhoE 93
Goodloe, James Edward 1951- WhoSSW 93
Goodloe, John Duncan, IV 1935- St&PR 93, WhoAm 92
Goodloe, Mary R. 1962- St&PR 93
Goodluck, Bruce John 1933- WhoAsAP 91
Goodman, Abbie Rebecca 1961- WhoE 93
Goodman, Abraham H. 1910-1990 BioIn 17
Goodman, Alfred 1920- Baker 92, WhoAm 92
Goodman, Alfred Nelson 1945- WhoE 93
Goodman, Allen C. BioIn 17
Goodman, Allen Charles 1947- WhoAm 92
Goodman, Alvin Malcolm 1930- WhoSSW 93
Goodman, Alvin S. 1925- WhoAm 92
Goodman, Andrew 1943-1964 EncAACR
Goodman, Audrey Ruth 1949- WhoAmW 93
Goodman, Barbara Eason 1949- WhoEmL 93
Goodman, Benjamin 1904- WhoAm 92
Goodman, Benny 1909-1986 Baker 92, BioIn 17, JeAmHC
Goodman, Bernard 1923- WhoAm 92
Goodman, Bernard J. 1923- WhoAm 92
Goodman, Blanche AmWomPl
Goodman, Brian William WhoE 93
Goodman, Bruce Bailey 1928- WhoWor 93
Goodman, Bruce G. Law&B 92
Goodman, Bruce G. 1948- St&PR 93
Goodman, Bruce Gerald 1948- WhoAm 92
Goodman, Bruce K. 1926- St&PR 93
Goodman, C.H. Law&B 92
Goodman, Carolyn 1956- WhoAmW 93
Goodman, Charles Schaffner 1916- WhoAm 92
Goodman, Constance Beth 1963- WhoWrEP 92
Goodman, Corey Scott 1951- WhoAm 92
Goodman, David BioIn 17
Goodman, David 1912-1991 BioIn 17
Goodman, David Barry Poliakoff 1942- WhoAm 92, WhoE 93
Goodman, David J. 1931- BioIn 17
Goodman, David Joel 1939- WhoAm 92
Goodman, David M. 1920- St&PR 93
Goodman, David Richard, Jr. 1949- St&PR 93
Goodman, Deborah Lerme 1956- ScF&FL 92
Goodman, DeWitt S. BioIn 17
Goodman, Dody BioIn 17, WhoAm 92
Goodman, Donald C. 1927- WhoAm 92
Goodman, E. Frank Law&B 92
Goodman, Eileen H. Law&B 92
Goodman, Elaine Iris 1963- WhoE 93
Goodman, Elena Patrice 1966- WhoAmW 93
Goodman, Ellen BioIn 17
Goodman, Ellen Holtz 1941- WhoAm 92, WhoAmW 93
Goodman, Elliot Raymond 1923- WhoAm 92
Goodman, Elliott Irvin 1934- WhoAm 92
Goodman, Ellis M. 1937- St&PR 93
Goodman, Erik David 1944- WhoAm 92
Goodman, Erika WhoAm 92
Goodman, Frank H. 1947- St&PR 93
Goodman, Gail Busman 1953- WhoAmW 93
Goodman, Gary Alan 1947- WhoEmL 93
Goodman, George Jerome Waldo 1930- WhoAm 92
Goodman, Gertrude Amelia 1924- WhoAmW 93, WhoSSW 93, WhoWor 93
Goodman, Gordon T. 1926- WhoScE 91-4
Goodman, Gwendolyn Ann 1955- WhoEmL 93
Goodman, Harold S. 1937- WhoAm 92
Goodman, Harriet J. Law&B 92
Goodman, Helen G. St&PR 93
Goodman, Henry Maurice 1934- WhoAm 92
Goodman, Herbert Irwin 1923- St&PR 93, WhoAm 92, WhoWor 93
Goodman, Isidore BioIn 17
Goodman, Jacob Eli 1933- WhoE 93
Goodman, Jacquelyn Lepak 1949- WhoAmW 93
Goodman, James A. Law&B 92
Goodman, James Benjamin Law&B 92
Goodman, Jean A. 1934- St&PR 93
Goodman, Jo 1940- ScF&FL 92
Goodman, Joan Frances 1941- WhoAmW 93
Goodman, Joel Barry 1948- WhoWrEP 92
Goodman, Joel Harry, Jr. 1944- WhoAm 92
Goodman, Joel Kopel 1935- St&PR 93
Goodman, Joel Warren 1933- WhoAm 92
Goodman, John BioIn 17, WhoAm 92
Goodman, John 1952- HolBB [port]
Goodman, John B. d1990 BioIn 17
Goodman, John M. Law&B 92
Goodman, John M. 1947- St&PR 93
Goodman, John P. Law&B 92
Goodman, John P. 1945- St&PR 93
Goodman, John Sefton 1934- St&PR 93
Goodman, Jordan Elliot 1954- WhoE 93
Goodman, Joseph Champion 1937- WhoSSW 93
Goodman, Joseph Wilfred 1936- WhoAm 92
Goodman, Judith Ross 1950- WhoWor 93
Goodman, Julius ScF&FL 92
Goodman, Kenneth Edward 1947- St&PR 93
Goodman, Kenneth Wayne 1946- WhoEmL 93
Goodman, Kimberly Swain 1963- WhoEmL 93
Goodman, Laurie 1962- ScF&FL 92
Goodman, Lawrence Eugene 1920- WhoAm 92
Goodman, Leon 1920- WhoAm 92
Goodman, Leslie E. 1943- St&PR 93
Goodman, Linda WhoWor 93
Goodman, Madeleine Joyce 1945- WhoAmW 93
Goodman, Major Merlin 1938- WhoAm 92
Goodman, Martin d1992 BioIn 17, NewYTBS 92
Goodman, Martin M. 1938- St&PR 93
Goodman, Marv 1943- WhoAm 92
Goodman, Marvin David 1933- WhoWor 93
Goodman, Max A. 1924- WhoAm 92
Goodman, Melvin A. 1938- ConAu 138
Goodman, Michael Barry 1949- WhoE 93
Goodman, Morris St&PR 93
Goodman, Morris 1925- WhoAm 92
Goodman, N.N., Jr. 1925- St&PR 93
Goodman, Neal Robert 1947- WhoE 93
Goodman, Nelson BioIn 17
Goodman, Norman 1934- WhoAm 92
Goodman, Norton Victor 1936- WhoAm 92
Goodman, Pamela Beth 1964- WhoE 93
Goodman, Paul 1911-1972 BioIn 17
Goodman, Phillip Lane 1948- WhoEmL 93
Goodman, R. Gail Law&B 92
Goodman, Richard 1931- WhoE 93
Goodman, Richard 1945- ConAu 136
Goodman, Richard E. 1928-1990 BioIn 17
Goodman, Richard Henry WhoSSW 93
Goodman, Richard Merle 1932- ConAu 40NR
Goodman, Richard Shalem WhoE 93
Goodman, Robert A. Law&B 92
Goodman, Robert L. 1940- WhoAm 92
Goodman, Robert Merwin 1945- WhoAm 92
Goodman, Robert Philip 1950- WhoE 93
Goodman, Robert Stewart 1951- St&PR 93
Goodman, Roberta L. Law&B 92
Goodman, Roland Alfred 1933- WhoAm 92
Goodman, Ronald D. 1935- St&PR 93
Goodman, Roy B. 1957- St&PR 93
Goodman, Roy Matz 1930- WhoAm 92, WhoE 93
Goodman, Sam R. 1930- St&PR 93
Goodman, Sam Richard 1930- WhoAm 92
Goodman, Sara B. Law&B 92
Goodman, Seymour S. 1931- WhoAm 92
Goodman, Sherri Leigh 1962- WhoAmW 93
Goodman, Shirley SoulM
Goodman, Shirley d1991 BioIn 17
Goodman, Shiroxley Huoswald 1941- WhoWor 93
Goodman, Stanley 1931- WhoAm 92
Goodman, Stanley J. 1910- St&PR 93
Goodman, Stanley Joshua 1910- WhoAm 92
Goodman, Stanley Leonard 1920- WhoAm 92
Goodman, Stephen H. 1944- WhoAm 92
Goodman, Stephen Nathaniel 1932- St&PR 93
Goodman, Stuart Lauren 1938- WhoAm 92
Goodman, Susan C. Law&B 92
Goodman, Theodore Russell 1927- St&PR 93
Goodman, Thomas Andrew 1954- WhoAm 92
Goodman, Toby Ray 1948- WhoSSW 93
Goodman, Valerie Dawson 1948- WhoAmW 93
Goodman, Velma C. 1901- St&PR 93
Goodman, Wallace Richard 1941- WhoE 93
Goodman, Walter 1927- WhoWrEP 92
Goodman, William Beehler 1923- WhoAm 92, WhoWrEP 92
Goodman, William Dale 1926-1984 BiDAMSp 1989
Goodman, William E., IV 1932- St&PR 93
Goodman, William I. 1919- WhoAm 92
Goodman, William Richard 1930- WhoE 93
Goodman, Yetta M. 1931- WhoAmW 93
Goodman-Miller, Dorothy Victory 1945- WhoE 93
Goodnature, Susan Law&B 92
Goodner, Dwight Benjamin 1913- WhoAm 92
Goodner, Harland M. 1935- WhoSSW 93
Goodner, Homer Wade 1929- WhoSSW 93, WhoWor 93
Goodner, John Ross, Jr. 1927- WhoAm 92
Goodnick, Paul Joel 1950- WhoEmL 93, WhoSSW 93, WhoWor 93
Goodnow, Jacqueline J. 1924- BioIn 17
Goodnow, Wilma Elizabeth 1944- WhoWor 93
Goodof, Robert Steven 1950- St&PR 93
Goodpaster, Andrew Jackson 1915- WhoAm 92
Goodpaster, William Van 1925- St&PR 93
Goodpasture, Dennis Laroy 1948- WhoSSW 93
Goodpasture, Frank, Jr. 1923- St&PR 93

Goodpasture, James Dale 1942- WhoAm 92
Goodreau, Robert M. 1938- St&PR 93
Goodreds, John Stanton 1934- St&PR 93, WhoAm 92
Goodrich, Alan Owens Law&B 92
Goodrich, Alan Owens 1958- WhoSSW 93
Goodrich, Bradley 1950- St&PR 93
Goodrich, Charles S. 1957- St&PR 93
Goodrich, Chauncey Glenn 1928- WhoE 93
Goodrich, Cheryl Yund 1956- WhoAmW 93
Goodrich, Clifford ScF&FL 92
Goodrich, David WhoScE 91-1
Goodrich, David Michael 1936- WhoSSW 93
Goodrich, Donna Marie 1938- WhoWrEP 92
Goodrich, Frances 1890- AmWomPl
Goodrich, George Herbert 1925- WhoAm 92
Goodrich, H.L. Law&B 92
Goodrich, Henry Calvin 1920- WhoAm 92
Goodrich, Isaac 1939- WhoE 93
Goodrich, James N. 1943- St&PR 93
Goodrich, James Tait 1946- WhoE 93, WhoEmL 93, WhoWor 93
Goodrich, James William 1939- WhoAm 92
Goodrich, John Bernard 1928- WhoAm 92
Goodrich, John M. 1950- St&PR 93
Goodrich, Kenneth Paul 1933- WhoAm 92
Goodrich, Leland 1899-1990 BioIn 17
Goodrich, Leon Raymond 1936- WhoAm 92
Goodrich, Marcus 1897-1991 BioIn 17
Goodrich, Marcus (Aurelius) 1897-1991 CurBio 92N
Goodrich, Maurice Keith 1935- St&PR 93, WhoAm 92
Goodrich, Michael R. St&PR 93
Goodrich, Nathaniel Herman 1914- WhoAm 92
Goodrich, Nelson R. Law&B 92
Goodrich, Richard ScF&FL 92
Goodrich, Ronald K. St&PR 93
Goodrich, Ronald Leonard 1934- St&PR 93
Goodrich, Samuel Griswold 1793-1860 BioIn 17
Goodrich, Samuel Melvin 1936- WhoSSW 93
Goodrich, Stephen W. Law&B 92
Goodrich, Thomas Michael 1945- WhoAm 92
Goodrich, Wallace 1871-1952 Baker 92
Goodrich, William Bruce 1926- WhoSSW 93
Goodridge, Alan Gardner 1937- WhoAm 92
Goodridge, Allan D. 1936- WhoAm 92
Goodridge, Georgia Esther 1950- WhoWrEP 92
Goodridge, Gregory C. 1953- St&PR 93
Goodridge, Noel Herbert Alan 1930- WhoAm 92, WhoE 93
Goodridge Roberts, Theodore 1877-1953 BioIn 17
Goodrum, Daniel Shepard 1926- St&PR 93
Goodrum, Richard W. 1928- St&PR 93
Goodrum, Wayne L. Law&B 92
Goodrum, William James 1958- St&PR 93
Goodsell, Eugene H. 1953- St&PR 93
Goodsell, James Nelson 1929- WhoE 93
Goodsell, Steven A. Law&B 92
Goodson, Carol Faye 1947- WhoSSW 93
Goodson, Carole Edith McKissock 1946- WhoAmW 93
Goodson, Charles L. 1928- WhoSSW 93
Goodson, George Royden, III 1955- St&PR 93
Goodson, Katharine 1872-1958 Baker 92
Goodson, Louie Aubrey, Jr. 1922- St&PR 93, WhoAm 92
Goodson, Mark BioIn 17
Goodson, Mark d1992 NewYTBS 92 [port]
Goodson, Mark 1915- WhoAm 92, WhoE 93
Goodson, Peter BioIn 17
Goodson, R. Eugene 1935- St&PR 93
Goodson, Raymond Eugene 1935- WhoAm 92
Goodson, Richard Carle, Jr. 1945- WhoE 93
Goodson, Shannon Lorayn 1952- WhoAmW 93
Goodson, William Wilson, Jr. 1951- WhoEmL 93
Goodspeed, Barbara 1919- WhoAm 92, WhoAmW 93
Goodspeed, Elizabeth Fuller AmWomPl
Goodspeed, Scott Winans 1954- WhoE 93
Goodstein, Barnett Maurice 1921- WhoAm 92
Goodstein, Daniel Victor 1932- St&PR 93
Goodstein, David Louis 1939- WhoAm 92
Goodstein, Maurice Mac 1909- St&PR 93
Goodstein, Richard Edward 1953- WhoEmL 93
Goodstein, Sanders A. 1918- St&PR 93
Goodstone, Edward H. 1934- WhoIns 93
Goodstone, Edward Harold 1934- St&PR 93, WhoAm 92
Goodstone, Rosemary Ann 1947- WhoAmW 93, WhoEmL 93
Goodstone, Tony ScF&FL 92
Goodvich, Eugene Walter 1934- St&PR 93
Goodwick, David Lee 1954- WhoEmL 93
Goodwill, Donald Joseph 1944- WhoE 93
Goodwill, Margaret Jane 1950- WhoAm 92
Goodwin, Alfred Theodore 1923- WhoAm 92
Goodwin, Andrew Wirt, II 1932- WhoSSW 93
Goodwin, Barbara A. 1938- WhoAm 92, WhoAmW 93
Goodwin, Barbara Sue 1950- WhoEmL 93, WhoSSW 93
Goodwin, Bernard 1907- WhoAm 92
Goodwin, Bill 1942- WhoWrEP 92
Goodwin, Brian Carey WhoScE 91-1
Goodwin, Bruce Kesseli 1931- WhoAm 92
Goodwin, Carl E. 1947- St&PR 93
Goodwin, Claude Elbert 1910- WhoAm 92
Goodwin, Craufurd David 1934- WhoAm 92
Goodwin, Dean 1955- WhoSSW 93
Goodwin, Donald A. 1950- St&PR 93
Goodwin, Donald G. 1927- St&PR 93
Goodwin, Donald William 1931- WhoAm 92
Goodwin, Douglas Ira 1946- WhoAm 92
Goodwin, E.L. 1899- St&PR 93
Goodwin, Elizabeth Tanner 1957- WhoAmW 93, WhoE 93
Goodwin, Ellen Pemberton 1938- WhoAmW 93
Goodwin, Francis Maurice 1956- WhoWrEP 92
Goodwin, Frank Erik 1954- WhoSSW 93
Goodwin, Frederick King 1936- WhoAm 92
Goodwin, George Evans 1917- WhoAm 92, WhoSSW 93
Goodwin, Glenn Arthur 1946- St&PR 93
Goodwin, Graham 1946- WhoScE 91-1
Goodwin, H. Clark 1934- St&PR 93
Goodwin, Hal ScF&FL 92
Goodwin, Hal 1914-1990 BioIn 17
Goodwin, Harold Leland 1914-1990 BioIn 17
Goodwin, Harry Eugene 1922- WhoAm 92
Goodwin, James Alton, Jr. 1949- WhoE 93
Goodwin, James Michael 1938- WhoSSW 93
Goodwin, Jean McClung 1946- WhoAm 92, WhoAmW 93
Goodwin, Jeffrey 1946- St&PR 93
Goodwin, Jesse C. d1991 BioIn 17, NewYTBS 92
Goodwin, Joel Franklin, Sr. 1924- WhoSSW 93
Goodwin, John B. d1990 BioIn 17
Goodwin, John J. Law&B 92
Goodwin, John R. 1941- St&PR 93
Goodwin, Joseph J. 1926- St&PR 93
Goodwin, Kemper 1906- WhoAm 92
Goodwin, Lewis Billings 1957- St&PR 93
Goodwin, Louis 1906- St&PR 93
Goodwin, Maria Capone 1952- WhoAmW 93
Goodwin, Marie D. ScF&FL 92
Goodwin, Mark B. Law&B 92
Goodwin, Maryellen 1964- WhoAmW 93
Goodwin, Matthew Law&B 92
Goodwin, Maureen Ann Law&B 92
Goodwin, Maurice Roy 1911- WhoE 93
Goodwin, Michael 1951- ScF&FL 92
Goodwin, Michael John WhoScE 91-1
Goodwin, Mildred 1926- WhoE 93
Goodwin, Nancy Lee 1940- WhoAm 92
Goodwin, Nicholas Peter 1959- WhoWor 93
Goodwin, Paul 1919- St&PR 93, WhoAm 92
Goodwin, Paul Richard 1943- WhoAm 92
Goodwin, Peggy BioIn 17
Goodwin, Peter Wentworth Law&B 92
Goodwin, Phillip Bramley WhoScE 91-1
Goodwin, Phillip Hugh 1940- WhoAm 92, WhoSSW 93
Goodwin, Phillip Knowles 1934- WhoE 93
Goodwin, Ralph Roger 1917- WhoAm 92
Goodwin, Rhoda Sherman 1938- WhoAmW 93
Goodwin, Richard Clarke 1949- WhoWor 93
Goodwin, Richard G. 1935- St&PR 93
Goodwin, Richard M. 1913- BioIn 17
Goodwin, Richard T. 1953- St&PR 93
Goodwin, Robert Delmege 1920- WhoAm 92
Goodwin, Robert L. 1924- St&PR 93
Goodwin, Rodney Keith Grove 1944- WhoAm 92
Goodwin, Rolf Ervine 1956- WhoE 93
Goodwin, Rosanne 1954- WhoEmL 93
Goodwin, Sarah Webster 1953- WhoAmW 93
Goodwin, Sheila Diane 1958- WhoAmW 93
Goodwin, Stephen 1943- WhoWrEP 92
Goodwin, Susan Ann 1944- WhoE 93
Goodwin, Thomas J. Law&B 92
Goodwin, Todd 1931- WhoAm 92
Goodwin, Tony McDaniel 1962- WhoEmL 93, WhoSSW 93
Goodwin, Wayne Edward 1940- WhoSSW 93
Goodwin, Willard Elmer 1915- WhoAm 92
Goodwin, William Dean 1937- WhoSSW 93
Goodwin-Diaz, Celso Michael 1941- WhoUN 92
Goodwyn, Andrew 1954- ScF&FL 92
Goodwyn, James Turner, Jr. 1928- St&PR 93, WhoAm 92
Goodwyn, Kendall W. 1911-1990 BioIn 17
Goodwyn, Richard Blackwood 1939- St&PR 93
Goody, Alycia L. Law&B 92
Goody, Joan 1935- WhoAm 92
Goody, Richard Mead 1921- WhoAm 92
Goody, Sam 1904-1991 BioIn 17, News 92
Goodyear, Austin 1919- St&PR 93, WhoAm 92
Goodyear, Charles W. 1958- St&PR 93
Goodyear, Edward Stephen, Jr. 1954- WhoE 93
Goodyear, Frank Henry, Jr. 1944- WhoAm 92, WhoE 93
Goodyear, Holly Sue 1942- WhoAmW 93
Goodyear, Joan Garrett- d1992 BioIn 17
Goodyear, John L. 1936- St&PR 93
Goodyear, John Lake 1930- WhoAm 92, WhoE 93
Goodyear, John Lee 1936- WhoE 93
Goodyear, John W. 1941- St&PR 93
Goodyear, William M. 1948- St&PR 93
Goodyer, Ian Michael 1949- WhoWor 93
Goodykoontz, Bess 1894-1990 BioIn 17
Goodykoontz, Charles Alfred 1928- WhoAm 92
Gooel, Bert J. 1904- St&PR 93
Googasian, George Ara 1936- WhoAm 92
Googe, James P., Jr. Law&B 92
Googins, Dorothy Rose AmWomPl
Googins, Robert R. 1937- WhoIns 93
Googins, Robert Reville 1937- WhoAm 92
Googins, Sonya Forbes 1936- WhoAmW 93
Gooi Hock Seng WhoAsAP 91
Gookin, Thomas Allen Jaudon 1951- WhoEmL 93
Gookin, William Scudder 1914- WhoWor 93
Gool, Reshard 1931-1989 WhoCanL 92
Goolishian, Harold A. 1924-1991 BioIn 17
Goolkasian, Aram Richard 1924- WhoAm 92
Goolkasian, Paula A. 1948- WhoAmW 93, WhoEmL 93, WhoSSW 93
Goolsbee, Charles Thomas 1935- St&PR 93
Goon, Dickson Bing 1954- WhoE 93
Goon, Eric Hean-Tat 1937- WhoUN 92
Goonrey, Charles W. Law&B 92
Goor, Ronald Stephen 1940- WhoAm 92
Goorey, Nancy Jane 1922- WhoAm 92, WhoAmW 93
Goorley, John Theodore 1907- WhoSSW 93, WhoWor 93
Goos, Cees 1941- WhoUN 92
Goos, Gerhard T. 1937- WhoScE 91-3
Goos, Kathryn A. 1958- St&PR 93
Goos, Roger Delmon 1924- WhoAm 92
Gooskens, Robert Henricus Johannus 1948- WhoWor 93
Goosman, Arlys N. 1932- St&PR 93
Goosman, Eleanor McKee 1917- WhoAmW 93
Gooss, Henry E. 1941- St&PR 93
Goossen, Jacob Frederic 1927- WhoSSW 93
Goossens Baker 92
Goossens, Eugene 1845-1906 Baker 92, OxDcOp
Goossens, Eugene 1867-1958 Baker 92, OxDcOp
Goossens, Eugene 1893-1962 Baker 92, OxDcOp
Goossens, Jozef Elisa 1943- WhoAm 92
Goossens, Leon 1897-1988 Baker 92
Goossens, Marie 1894-1991 AnObit 1991
Goossens, Marie (Henriette) 1894- Baker 92
Goossens, Pierre 1961- WhoWor 93
Goossens, Sidonie 1899- Baker 92
Goostree, Robert Edward 1923- WhoAm 92
Goot, Joanne Gunvor 1953- WhoE 93
Gootman, Gerald Martin 1937- St&PR 93
Gootman, Norman 1933- WhoE 93
Gootman, Phyllis Myrna 1938- WhoAmW 93
Gootman, Phyllis Myrna Adler WhoE 93
Gootnick-Bruce, Stephanie 1954- WhoWrEP 92
Goott, Daniel 1919- WhoAm 92
Gootzeit, Jack Michael 1924- WhoAm 92, WhoWor 93
Goovaerts, Alphonse (Jean Marie Andre) 1847-1922 Baker 92
Gopal, Nanda 1965- WhoSSW 93
Gopal, Sarvepalli 1923- WhoWor 93
Gopal, Vishnu 1946- WhoWor 93
Gopalan, Coluthur 1918- WhoWor 93
Gopalan, R.T. 1943- WhoAsAP 91
Gopalsary, V. 1944- WhoAsAP 91
Gopfert, Alfred 1934- WhoWor 93
Gopinath, Anand 1936- WhoAm 92
Gopinath, Padmanabh 1939- WhoUN 92
Gopinath, Sivasankar 1946- WhoWor 93
Gopman, Glenn Henry 1955- WhoEmL 93
Gopon, Gene George 1944- WhoIns 93
Goppel, Wilma Henriette 1945- WhoUN 92
Goppelt, John Walter 1924- WhoE 93
Gopu, Vijaya K.A. 1949- WhoAm 92
Goral, Stanislaw 1930- WhoScE 91-4
Goral, Turker 1945- WhoScE 91-4
Goralcyzk, Steven Michael 1955- WhoSSW 93
Goralczyk, Jozef Andrzej 1924- WhoScE 91-4
Goralnick, L. Arnold 1930- St&PR 93
Goralski, Donald John 1957- WhoE 93
Gorans, Gerald Elmer 1922- WhoAm 92
Goranson, Harold Theodore 1947- WhoEmL 93, WhoSSW 93
Goray, Gerald Allen 1939- WhoSSW 93, WhoWor 93
Gorbachev, Maria Panteleyevna BioIn 17
Gorbachev, Mikhail BioIn 17
Gorbachev, Mikhail 1931- ColdWar 2 [port], ConHero 2 [port]
Gorbachev, Mikhail Sergeyevich 1931- DcTwHis, WhoWor 93
Gorbachev, Raisa Maksimovna BioIn 17
Gorbitz, Barbara Elizabeth 1953- WhoAmW 93
Gorbunovs, Anatolijs 1942- WhoWor 93
Gorcey, Leo 1915-1969 See Bowery Boys, The QDrFCA 92
Gorchakov, Sergei 1905-1976 Baker 92
Gorcyca, Raymond M. 1942- St&PR 93
Gorczyca, Fryderyk Emil WhoE 93
Gorczyca, Richard Marian 1949- WhoEmL 93
Gorczycki, Grzegorz Gerwazy c. 1647-1734 Baker 92
Gorczycki, Grzegorz Gerwazy 1666-1734 PolBiDi
Gorczynski, Izabelle J. Law&B 92
Gordan, Andrew Leb 1923- WhoWor 93
Gordan, Gilbert Saul 1916- WhoAm 92
Gordan, Vicki Jolene Tripp 1956- WhoEmL 93
Gordan-Feller, Carla Janine 1936- WhoAmW 93
Gordaninejad, Faramarz 1953- WhoEmL 93
Gorday, Carl Leonard Law&B 92
Gordeli, Otar 1928- Baker 92
Gorden, Fred Augustus 1940- AfrAmBi [port]
Gorden, Nancy D. 1937- WhoWrEP 92
Gordenker, Leon 1923- WhoAm 92
Gorder, Herbert W. 1935- St&PR 93
Gordesky, Morton 1929- WhoE 93, WhoWor 93
Gordett, Marea Beth 1949- WhoWrEP 92
Gordevitch, Igor 1924- WhoWor 93
Gordian, I d238 HarEnMi
Gordian, Marcus Antonius, II 192-238 HarEnMi
Gordian, Marcus Antonius, III c. 225-244 HarEnMi
Gordien, Fortune Everett 1922-1990 BiDAMSp 1989
Gordievsky, Oleg BioIn 17
Gordigiani, Luigi 1806-1860 Baker 92
Gordimer, Nadine 1923- BioIn 17, BritWr S2, ConLC 70 [port], IntLitE, MagSWL [port], WhoWor 93
Gordin, Dean Lackey 1935- WhoAm 92
Gordin, George, Jr. Law&B 92
Gordinier, Richard B. 1942- St&PR 93
Gordis, David Moses 1940- WhoAm 92
Gordis, Leon 1934- WhoAm 92
Gordis, Robert d1992 NewYTBS 92 [port]
Gordis, Robert 1908- JeAmHC
Gordis, Robert 1908-1992 BioIn 17
Gordman, A. Dan 1912- WhoAm 92
Gordon, Alan George 1929- WhoWor 93
Gordon, Alan Ira 1958- WhoEmL 93
Gordon, Alan L. 1935- St&PR 93
Gordon, Alan M. Law&B 92
Gordon, Alan R. 1943- St&PR 93

Gordon, Albert Hamilton 1901- WhoAm 92
Gordon, Albert Saul d1992 NewYTBS 92
Gordon, Alden Edgar 1933- WhoSSW 93
Gordon, Alice Jeannette Irwin 1934- WhoAmW 93
Gordon, Alison 1943- WhoCanL 92
Gordon, Andrew Mark 1945- WhoSSW 93
Gordon, Angus Neal, Jr. 1919- WhoAm 92
Gordon, Arlene Cahn 1958- WhoE 93
Gordon, Aron Samuel 1911- St&PR 93
Gordon, Arthur 1922- St&PR 93
Gordon, Audrey Kramen 1935- WhoAmW 93
Gordon, Aviva Yocheved 1968- WhoAmW 93
Gordon, Barbara Arenette 1933- WhoAmW 93
Gordon, Barry BioIn 17
Gordon, Barry 1951- WhoE 93
Gordon, Barry Joel 1945- St&PR 93, WhoAm 92
Gordon, Bart 1949- CngDr 91
Gordon, Barton Jennings 1949- WhoAm 92, WhoEmL 93, WhoSSW 93
Gordon, Basil 1932- WhoAm 92
Gordon, Beate BioIn 17
Gordon, Bernard 1922- WhoAm 92
Gordon, Bernard Marshall 1927- St&PR 93
Gordon, Bert I. 1922- MiSFD 9
Gordon, Bette MiSFD 9
Gordon, Betty Turner 1945- WhoAmW 93
Gordon, Bonnie Bilyeu 1945- WhoAmW 93, WhoSSW 93
Gordon, Bonnie Heather 1952- WhoAm 92, WhoAmW 93
Gordon, Bruce W. 1948- St&PR 93
Gordon, Bryan MiSFD 9
Gordon, Cameron Elliott 1962- WhoE 93
Gordon, Caroline 1895-1981 BioIn 17, ScF&FL 92
Gordon, Charles ConTFT 10
Gordon, Charles 1905- WhoAm 92
Gordon, Charles A. Law&B 92
Gordon, Charles A. 1928- St&PR 93
Gordon, Charles Edmund 1961- WhoSSW 93
Gordon, Charles George 1833-1885 HarEnMi
Gordon, Charles William 1860-1937 BioIn 17
Gordon, Conrad J. 1937- St&PR 93
Gordon, Conrad Jack 1937- WhoAm 92
Gordon, Craig Jeffrey 1953- WhoWor 93
Gordon, Cyrus Herzl 1908- WhoAm 92
Gordon, Dale C. Law&B 92
Gordon, Dale C. 1948- St&PR 93
Gordon, Dane Rex 1925- WhoAm 92
Gordon, David 1936- WhoAm 92
Gordon, David J. Law&B 92
Gordon, David Jamieson 1947- WhoAm 92
Gordon, David Jeremy 1946- WhoE 93
Gordon, David M. BioIn 17
Gordon, Deborah Robin 1964- WhoAmW 93
Gordon, Dena Walters 1950- WhoAmW 93
Gordon, Dexter BioIn 17
Gordon, Dexter (Keith) 1923-1990 Baker 92
Gordon, Diana Greene Law&B 92
Gordon, Diana Russell 1938- WhoAm 92
Gordon, Donald Howard 1954- WhoEmL 93
Gordon, Doris Yetta 1928- WhoE 93
Gordon, Douglas Ironside WhoScE 91-1
Gordon, Douglas N. Law&B 92
Gordon, Edward 1930- WhoAm 92
Gordon, Ellen R. 1931- St&PR 93
Gordon, Ellen Rubin WhoAm 92, WhoAmW 93
Gordon, Emmajean Elizabeth 1920- WhoAmW 93
Gordon, Ernest 1916- WhoAm 92
Gordon, Eugene Andrew 1917- WhoAm 92
Gordon, Eugene Irving 1930- WhoAm 92
Gordon, Ezra 1921- WhoAm 92
Gordon, F.J. WhoScE 91-1
Gordon, Felton Hays 1915- WhoSSW 93, WhoWor 93
Gordon, Florence Shanfield 1942- WhoAmW 93, WhoE 93
Gordon, Francine E. 1948- WhoEmL 93
Gordon, Frank N., Jr. 1924- St&PR 93
Gordon, Frank Wallace 1935- WhoAm 92
Gordon, Frank X., Jr. 1929- WhoAm 92
Gordon, Fritz WhoWrEP 92
Gordon, G. Barry 1931- St&PR 93
Gordon, G.D. Law&B 92
Gordon, G.M.W. WhoScE 91-1
Gordon, George WhoScE 91-1
Gordon, George Angier 1853-1929 BioIn 17
Gordon, George Minot 1947- WhoAm 92
Gordon, George Stanley 1931- WhoAm 92
Gordon, Gerard James 1941- St&PR 93
Gordon, Gerd Stray 1912- WhoAmW 93, WhoE 93
Gordon, Gilbert 1911- St&PR 93
Gordon, Gilbert 1933- WhoAm 92
Gordon, Giles 1940- ScF&FL 92
Gordon, Gloria Kathleen 1938- WhoAmW 93
Gordon, Guanetta Stewart WhoWrEP 92
Gordon, Hal 1914-1990 BioIn 17
Gordon, Harris A. 1907- WhoWrEP 92
Gordon, Harrison J. 1950- WhoEmL 93
Gordon, Harry ConAu 137
Gordon, Harry 1925- BioIn 17
Gordon, Harry H. 1938- WhoIns 93
Gordon, Harry William 1924- WhoE 93
Gordon, Harvey Charles Law&B 92
Gordon, Helen Tate 1948- WhoAmW 93
Gordon, Herbert David 1938- St&PR 93, WhoAm 92
Gordon, Herman Law&B 92
Gordon, Howard 1938- WhoWor 93
Gordon, Howard D. Law&B 92
Gordon, Howard F. Law&B 92
Gordon, Iain James WhoScE 91-1
Gordon, Ilene S. 1953- St&PR 93
Gordon, Irwin Glenn 1965- WhoE 93
Gordon, Ivan H. 1934- St&PR 93
Gordon, J.P. 1920- St&PR 93
Gordon, Jack 1953- WhoWor 93
Gordon, Jack David 1922- WhoAm 92
Gordon, Jack Leonard 1928- St&PR 93
Gordon, Jack Marshall 1949- WhoWrEP 92
Gordon, Jacques 1899-1948 Baker 92
Gordon, Jaimy 1944- WhoWrEP 92
Gordon, James Braund 1911- WhoAm 92
Gordon, James Carel Gerhard 1791-c. 1845 Baker 92
Gordon, James Fleming 1918-1990 BioIn 17
Gordon, James M. d1988 BioIn 17
Gordon, James Vohndrow 1929- WhoSSW 93
Gordon, Jan Baker 1941- WhoWor 93
Gordon, Janet Hill 1915-1990 BioIn 17
Gordon, Janine M. 1946- St&PR 93, WhoAm 92, WhoAmW 93
Gordon, Jaquelyn Ruth Anma 1943- WhoE 93
Gordon, Jeffie Ross ScF&FL 92, WhoWrEP 92
Gordon, Jeffrey Mark 1952- WhoE 93
Gordon, Jeffrey Neil 1942- St&PR 93
Gordon, Jeffrey Neil 1949- WhoE 93
Gordon, Jerold James 1930- St&PR 93
Gordon, Joan 1947- ScF&FL 92
Gordon, Joel C. 1929- St&PR 93
Gordon, Joel Charles 1929- WhoAm 92
Gordon, Joel Ethan 1930- WhoAm 92
Gordon, John BioIn 17
Gordon, John 1925- ScF&FL 92
Gordon, John Brown 1832-1904 HarEnMi
Gordon, John C. 1925- St&PR 93
Gordon, John Charles 1939- WhoAm 92
Gordon, John Donald Munro 1942- WhoScE 91-1
Gordon, John E. WhoAm 92
Gordon, John L. 1944- WhoScE 91-1
Gordon, John Leo 1933- WhoAm 92
Gordon, John P. Law&B 92
Gordon, John Steele BioIn 17
Gordon, John (William) 1925- ChlFicS
Gordon, Jonathan C. Law&B 92
Gordon, Jonathan David 1949- WhoAm 92
Gordon, Joseph Elwell 1921- WhoAm 92
Gordon, Joseph H. 1909- St&PR 93
Gordon, Joseph Harold 1909- WhoAm 92
Gordon, Joseph K. 1925- St&PR 93
Gordon, Joseph Lowell 1915-1978 BiDAMSp 1989
Gordon, Julian M. 1930- St&PR 93
Gordon, Julie Peyton 1940- WhoAm 92
Gordon, Julien AmWomPl
Gordon, Julien 1850?-1920 ScF&FL 92
Gordon, June 1929- WhoAmW 93
Gordon, Katherine H. 1948- WhoAsAP 91
Gordon, Kathryn Lee 1947- WhoAmW 93
Gordon, Keith 1961- MiSFD 9
Gordon, Kenneth Antony 1937- WhoAm 92
Gordon, Kenneth Robert 1935- St&PR 93
Gordon, Kim c. 1953- See Sonic Youth ConMus 9
Gordon, Kurtiss Jay 1940- WhoE 93
Gordon, Lance Bennett Law&B 92
Gordon, Larry David 1938- WhoWor 93
Gordon, Larry Jean 1926- WhoAm 92
Gordon, Lawrence 1936- ConTFT 10
Gordon, Lawrence M. Law&B 92
Gordon, Leonard 1935- WhoAm 92
Gordon, Leonard Victor 1917- WhoAm 92
Gordon, Levan AfrAmBi [port]
Gordon, Lewis 1937- St&PR 93
Gordon, Lincoln 1913- WhoAm 92
Gordon, Linda S. Law&B 92
Gordon, Lloyd Baumgardner 1952- WhoSSW 93
Gordon, Lloyd Reid 1916- St&PR 93
Gordon, Lois Goldfein 1938- WhoAm 92, WhoE 93
Gordon, Lori BioIn 17
Gordon, Lorne Bertram 1945- WhoAm 92
Gordon, Lynne Verdelle 1959- WhoEmL 93
Gordon, Mack 1915- St&PR 93
Gordon, Malcolm Stephen 1933- WhoAm 92
Gordon, Marcia Laura 1925- WhoAmW 93
Gordon, Margaret H. 1957- St&PR 93
Gordon, Margaret Shaughnessy 1910- WhoAm 92
Gordon, Maria T. 1965- WhoEmL 93
Gordon, Marian Helene 1954- WhoAmW 93
Gordon, Marjorie WhoAm 92
Gordon, Mark 1926- WhoE 93, WhoWor 93
Gordon, Mark 1942- WhoCanL 92
Gordon, Mark Alan Law&B 92
Gordon, Marshall 1937- WhoAm 92
Gordon, Martin 1939- WhoAm 92
Gordon, Martin Eli 1921- WhoE 93
Gordon, Marvin B. 1916- St&PR 93
Gordon, Mary 1949- BioIn 17, MagSAmL [port]
Gordon, Mary Catherine 1949- WhoAm 92, WhoAmW 93
Gordon, Max BioIn 17
Gordon, Maxwell 1921- WhoAm 92
Gordon, Melvin J. 1919- St&PR 93
Gordon, Melvin Jay 1919- WhoAm 92
Gordon, Merrill Kern 1919- St&PR 93
Gordon, Michael 1909- MiSFD 9, WhoAm 92
Gordon, Michael 1923- St&PR 93
Gordon, Michael 1953- WhoE 93, WhoEmL 93
Gordon, Michael Duane 1949- WhoWor 93
Gordon, Michael R. 1951- St&PR 93
Gordon, Milton A. 1908-1990 BioIn 17
Gordon, Milton Andrew 1935- WhoAm 92
Gordon, Milton G. 1922- WhoAm 92
Gordon, Milton Paul 1930- WhoAm 92
Gordon, Minita Elmira 1930- WhoWor 93
Gordon, Minnie E. AmWomPl
Gordon, Monte J. 1923- St&PR 93
Gordon, Morris Aaron 1920- WhoE 93
Gordon, Myron 1920- WhoE 93
Gordon, Myron L. 1918- WhoAm 92
Gordon, Nathan 1916- BioIn 17
Gordon, Nathan 1938- St&PR 93
Gordon, Neal Law&B 92
Gordon, Neil R. 1948- St&PR 93
Gordon, Nicholas 1928- WhoAm 92
Gordon, Nicole Ann 1954- WhoAm 92
Gordon, Nina Marlene 1951- WhoEmL 93
Gordon, Nina Robin 1959- WhoAm 92
Gordon, Norman Botnick 1921- WhoAm 92
Gordon, P.S. 1953- BioIn 17
Gordon, Patricia Ann 1957- WhoAmW 93
Gordon, Paul 1942- St&PR 93
Gordon, Paul David 1941- WhoE 93, WhoWor 93
Gordon, Paul John 1921- WhoAm 92
Gordon, Paul Perry 1927- WhoWrEP 92
Gordon, Paula Rossbacher 1953- WhoE 93
Gordon, Peggy Zeeman 1946- WhoAmW 93
Gordon, Philip Lynn 1960- St&PR 93
Gordon, R. Bruce Law&B 92
Gordon, Ralph A. 1944- St&PR 93
Gordon, Ralph D. 1940- St&PR 93
Gordon, Ralph Dearing 1940- WhoAm 92
Gordon, Randall Eugene 1949- St&PR 93
Gordon, Randall Joe 1941- WhoAm 92
Gordon, Renee Adele Law&B 92
Gordon, Rhea Juanita 1954- WhoAmW 93
Gordon, Richard Law&B 92
Gordon, Richard Edwards 1922- WhoAm 92
Gordon, Richard H. WhoE 93
Gordon, Richard Joseph 1933- WhoAm 92
Gordon, Richard Lewis 1934- WhoAm 92, WhoE 93
Gordon, Richard M. Erik 1949- WhoEmL 93
Gordon, Ricky Dean 1955- WhoEmL 93
Gordon, Rita Simon 1929- WhoAmW 93
Gordon, Robert Boyd 1929- WhoAm 92
Gordon, Robert Dana 1945- WhoE 93
Gordon, Robert Edward 1925- WhoAm 92
Gordon, Robert James 1940- WhoAm 92
Gordon, Robert Jay 1942- WhoSSW 93
Gordon, Robert Lynn 1935- WhoAm 92
Gordon, Robert M. Law&B 92
Gordon, Robert P. 1935- WhoWor 93
Gordon, Roger L. WhoAm 92
Gordon, Roy Gerald 1940- WhoAm 92
Gordon, Roy Harris 1926- WhoAm 92
Gordon, Ruth 1896-1985 IntDcF 2-3
Gordon, Ruth I. 1933- WhoAmW 93
Gordon, Sandra Claire Law&B 92
Gordon, Scott 1949- WhoE 93
Gordon, Scott Robert 1948- WhoSSW 93
Gordon, Seymour 1932- St&PR 93
Gordon, Shana WhoAm 92
Gordon, Sheila 1927- ChlLR 27 [port], DcAmChF 1985
Gordon, Sheri Spires 1967- WhoSSW 93
Gordon, Siamon WhoScE 91-1
Gordon, Sidney 1917-1975 BiDAMSp 1989
Gordon, Stephen Maurice 1942- WhoAm 92
Gordon, Steven BioIn 17
Gordon, Steven Joe 1956- WhoEmL 93
Gordon, Steven Stanley 1919- WhoAm 92
Gordon, Stewart George 1937- St&PR 93, WhoAm 92
Gordon, Storrow M. Law&B 92
Gordon, Stuart MiSFD 9
Gordon, Stuart 1947- ScF&FL 92
Gordon, Stuart Paul 1952- WhoEmL 93
Gordon, Theodore Jay 1930- WhoAm 92
Gordon, Thomas Christian, Jr. 1915- WhoAm 92
Gordon, Timothy William 1965- WhoE 93
Gordon, Tina WhoE 93
Gordon, Trina D. 1954- St&PR 93
Gordon, Walter 1907- WhoAm 92
Gordon, Walter Kelly 1930- WhoAm 92, WhoE 93
Gordon, Ward B. 1931-1991 BioIn 17
Gordon, Ward Blake 1931- St&PR 93
Gordon, Wendell Chaffee 1916- WhoAm 92
Gordon, Wendy Jane WhoAmW 93
Gordon, William E., Jr. Law&B 92
Gordon, William Edwin 1918- WhoAm 92
Gordon, William Morrison WhoScE 91-1
Gordon, William Richard 1913- WhoAm 92
Gordone, Charles 1925- BioIn 17
Gordone, Charles 1927- WhoAm 92
Gordon-Kirsch, Mary T. 1957- St&PR 93
Gordon-Mountian, Lesley Dara 1954- WhoAmW 93
Gordon of Auchleuchies, Patrick 1635-1699 HarEnMi
Gordon-Smith, Edward Colin WhoScE 91-1
Gordonsmith, John Arthur Harold 1942- St&PR 93, WhoAm 92
Gordon-Somers, Trevor 1938- WhoUN 92
Gordonson, Robert Martin 1935- St&PR 93, WhoAm 92
Gordon-Watson, Mary 1948- ConAu 37NR
Gordon-Wise, Barbara Ann 1946- ScF&FL 92
Gordy, Berry 1929- MiSFD 9, WhoAm 92
Gordy, Berry, Jr. BioIn 17
Gordy, Berry, Jr. 1929- AfrAmBi, Baker 92, SoulM
Gordy, Charlie Leon 1938- WhoSSW 93
Gordy, Denise Marie 1958- WhoAmW 93, WhoEmL 93
Gordy, Emory BioIn 17
Gordy, Fuller d1991 BioIn 17
Gordy, Michael A. 1947- St&PR 93
Gordy, Susan BioIn 17
Gordy, Vaunda St&PR 93
Gore, Albert, Jr. BioIn 17
Gore, Albert, Jr. 1948- CngDr 91, News 93-2 [port], WhoAm 92, WhoEmL 93, WhoSSW 93
Gore, Albert Arnold, Jr. 1948- NewYTBS 92 [port]
Gore, Barry Maurice 1944- WhoAm 92
Gore, Brian H. 1951- St&PR 93
Gore, Catherine 1800-1861 DcLB 116 [port]
Gore, David Eugene 1935- St&PR 93, WhoAm 92
Gore, Donald E. Law&B 92
Gore, Genevieve Walton 1913- St&PR 93, WhoAmW 93
Gore, George 1857-1933 BiDAMSp 1989
Gore, George 1939- WhoAm 92
Gore, H. Joseph Law&B 92
Gore, Jacques 1937- WhoScE 91-2
Gore, Jayavant Prabhakar 1956- WhoE 93
Gore, Jeanne Guerrero 1945- WhoWrEP 92
Gore, Lesley BioIn 17
Gore, Nanette Brittain 1954- WhoAmW 93
Gore, Peter Henry WhoScE 91-1
Gore, Philip Larner 1911- St&PR 93
Gore, Richard Michael 1953- WhoEmL 93
Gore, Robert Fisher 1932- WhoSSW 93
Gore, Stephen J. 1947- St&PR 93
Gore, Susan Belinda 1949- WhoAmW 93
Gore, Thomas Pryor 1870-1949 BioIn 17
Gore, Tipper 1948- WhoAmW 93
Gore, William Jay 1924- WhoAm 92
Goreau, Angeline W. 1951- WhoWrEP 92
Gorecki, Henryk 1920- WhoScE 91-4
Gorecki, Henryk (Mikolaj) 1933- Baker 92
Gorecki, Jan 1926- WhoAm 92
Gorecki, Jan 1934- WhoScE 91-4

Gorecki, Joseph F. 1953- St&PR 93
Gorecki, Piotr K. 1928- WhoScE 91-4
Gorecki, Stanley L. 1941- St&PR 93
Goreglad, Ramon Pedro 1954- WhoWor 93
Goreham, B. Sheldon 1915- St&PR 93
Gorelick, Joseph 1962- St&PR 93
Gorelick, Shelton 1929- St&PR 93
Gorelick, Shirley 1924- WhoAmW 93
Gorelik, Asher Raphael 1957- WhoEmL 93
Goren, Alexander Mircea 1940- WhoAm 92, WhoE 93
Goren, Arnold Louis WhoAm 92
Goren, Charles 1901-1991 AnObit 1991
Goren, Charles Henry 1901-1991 BioIn 17
Goren, Herbert d1991 BioIn 17
Goren, Howard Joseph 1941- WhoAm 92
Gorena, Guadalupe Garcia 1941- WhoSSW 93
Gorenc, William, Jr. Law&B 92
Gorenstein, Daniel d1992 NewYTBS 92 [port]
Gorenstein, Shirley Slotkin 1928- WhoAm 92, WhoE 93
Gorer, Geoffrey 1905-1985 ScF&FL 92
Gores, Alida Van ScF&FL 92
Gores, E.A. Law&B 92
Gores, Joseph Nicholas 1931- WhoAm 92, WhoWrEP 92
Gores, Landis 1919-1991 BioIn 17
Gores, Nancy L. Law&B 92
Goretchkine, Iouri Alexeevich 1936- WhoUN 92
Goretta, Claude 1929- MiSFD 9
Gorevitz, Richard D. Law&B 92
Gorewitz, Rubin Leon 1924- WhoE 93, WhoWor 93
Gorey, Edward (St. John) 1925- MajAI [port], SmATA 70 [port], WhoAm 92, WhoWrEP 92
Gorez, Raymond D.R. 1934- WhoWor 93
Gorfine, Stephen Richard 1949- WhoEmL 93
Gorges, Heinz August 1913- WhoSSW 93
Gorgi, Habib Y. 1956- St&PR 93
Gorguze, V.T. 1916- St&PR 93
Gorham, Barry James WhoScE 91-1
Gorham, David L. 1932- St&PR 93, WhoAm 92
Gorham, Edwin L. Law&B 92
Gorham, Eville 1925- WhoAm 92
Gorham, Frank D., Jr. 1921- St&PR 93
Gorham, Frank DeVore, Jr. 1921- WhoAm 92
Gorham, John Patrick 1942- WhoE 93
Gorham, Linda Joanne 1951- WhoAmW 93, WhoEmL 93
Gorham, Melvin 1910- ScF&FL 92
Gorham, William 1930- WhoAm 92
Gorham, William Hartshorne 1933- WhoAm 92
Gorham-Smith, Rosella Dorita 1948- WhoAmW 93
Gori, Esmond T. St&PR 93
Gori, Giuliano BioIn 17
Gorichan, Bonnie Sue Law&B 92
Gorigin, Eugene Boris 1919- WhoAm 92
Gorin, Evgeniy Alexeevich 1936- WhoWor 93
Gorin, George 1925- WhoAm 92
Gorin, Igor 1908-1982 Baker 92
Gorin, Jean-Pierre MiSFD 9
Gorin, Michael 1941- St&PR 93
Gorin, Natalio 1933- WhoScE 91-3
Gorin, Norman W. 1952- St&PR 93
Gorin, Robert Murray, Jr. 1948- WhoE 93, WhoEmL 93, WhoWor 93
Gorin, Robert S. 1935- St&PR 93
Gorin, Robert Seymour Law&B 92
Gorin, William 1908- WhoAm 92
Gorinevsky, Dimitry Markovitch 1960- WhoWor 93
Goring, Arthur William 1915- WhoSSW 93
Goring, David Arthur Ingham 1920- WhoAm 92
Goring, Edda 1938- BioIn 17
Goring, George 1608-1657 HarEnMi
Goring, Hermann 1893-1946 BioIn 17
Goring, Hermann William 1893-1946 HarEnMi
Goring, Peter Allan Elliott 1943- WhoAm 92
Gorini, Gino 1914-1989 Baker 92
Gorissen, Jan Law&B 92
Goritz, Otto 1873-1929 Baker 92
Gorka, Sandra J. Law&B 92
Gorke, Thomas Peter 1948- St&PR 93
Gorkin, Jess 1913- WhoWrEP 92
Gorkuscha, Mischa 1946- St&PR 93
Gorky, Arshile 1904-1948 BioIn 17
Gorky, Maksim 1868-1936 BioIn 17
Gorky, Maxim 1868-1936 BioIn 17, WorLitC [port]
Gorla, Carlo 1942- St&PR 93
Gorlach, Eugeniusz 1926- WhoScE 91-4
Gorland, Ronald K. 1944- St&PR 93
Gorland, Ronald Kent 1944- WhoAm 92
Gorlick, Alan E. 1948- St&PR 93
Gorlick, Sheldon H. d1992 NewYTBS 92
Gorlick, Sheldon H. 1928-1992 BioIn 17
Gorlicki, Michael 1957- WhoWor 93
Gorlin, Rena Ann 1957- WhoE 93
Gorlin, Richard 1926- WhoAm 92
Gorlin, Robert H. Law&B 92
Gorlin, Robert James 1923- WhoAm 92
Gormally, Laura E. Law&B 92
Gorman, Aileen Patricia 1946- St&PR 93
Gorman, Alan Thomas 1952- St&PR 93
Gorman, Alvin L. 1933- St&PR 93
Gorman, Alvin Larry 1933- WhoAm 92
Gorman, Arthur P. 1839-1906 PolPar
Gorman, Bonnie BioIn 17
Gorman, Burton William 1907- WhoAm 92
Gorman, Cheryl Lee 1962- WhoAmW 93
Gorman, Chris 1943- WhoAm 92
Gorman, Cliff WhoAm 92
Gorman, Daniel Geelan WhoScE 91-1
Gorman, David H. 1946- WhoAm 92
Gorman, David Harlan 1946- St&PR 93
Gorman, Dennis Gregory Cates 1960- WhoSSW 93
Gorman, Ed ConAu 138
Gorman, Ed 1941- ScF&FL 92
Gorman, Edward 1941- ConAu 138
Gorman, Edward H. Law&B 92
Gorman, Gary Alan Law&B 92
Gorman, Gerald Allen 1929- St&PR 93
Gorman, Gerald Warner 1933- WhoAm 92
Gorman, Harold V., Jr. Law&B 92
Gorman, Herbert 1893-1954 ScF&FL 92
Gorman, Ida Niebauer 1949- WhoE 93
Gorman, J.V. Law&B 92
Gorman, James Carvill 1924- St&PR 93, WhoAm 92
Gorman, James Lou WhoAm 92, WhoE 93
Gorman, Jeff BioIn 17, Law&B 92
Gorman, Jeffrey Scott 1952- St&PR 93
Gorman, John Andrew 1938- WhoWrEP 92
Gorman, John H. 1942- St&PR 93
Gorman, John J. d1991 BioIn 17
Gorman, John William 1950- WhoAm 92
Gorman, Joseph Gregory, Jr. 1939- WhoAm 92
Gorman, Joseph M. Law&B 92
Gorman, Joseph P., Jr. 1943- St&PR 93
Gorman, Joseph Tolle 1937- St&PR 93, WhoAm 92
Gorman, Judy 1942- WhoWrEP 92
Gorman, Karen Machmer 1955- WhoAmW 93, WhoEmL 93
Gorman, Kenneth J. 1932- WhoIns 93
Gorman, Kenneth T. 1954- St&PR 93
Gorman, Kirk Edward 1950- St&PR 93
Gorman, Leon A. 1934- WhoAm 92
Gorman, LeRoy 1949- WhoCanL 92
Gorman, Lynn R. 1942- St&PR 93
Gorman, Marcie Sothern 1949- WhoAmW 93, WhoEmL 93, WhoSSW 93, WhoWor 93
Gorman, Margaret Mary WhoAmW 93, WhoE 93
Gorman, Marilyn Grace 1966- WhoE 93
Gorman, Martin D. Law&B 92
Gorman, Marvin BioIn 17
Gorman, Marvin 1928- St&PR 93
Gorman, Maureen J. 1955- WhoAmW 93
Gorman, Michael C. Law&B 92
Gorman, Michael E. 1952- ConAu 139
Gorman, Michael Joseph 1941- WhoAm 92
Gorman, Michael P. Law&B 92
Gorman, Ned WhoAm 92
Gorman, Patricia Jane 1950- WhoAm 92
Gorman, Raymond James 1953- WhoE 93
Gorman, Robert Francis 1950- WhoSSW 93
Gorman, Robert Saul 1933- WhoE 93, WhoWor 93
Gorman, Russell Neville Joseph 1926- WhoAsAP 91
Gorman, Sarah E. Law&B 92
Gorman, Sue M. d1991 BioIn 17
Gorman, Susan Marie 1946- WhoAmW 93
Gorman, Thomas J. 1947- St&PR 93
Gorman, Tom d1992 NewYTBS 92
Gorman, William David 1925- WhoAm 92
Gorman, William Moore 1923- WhoWor 93
Gorman, William Thomas 1936- St&PR 93
Gorman, Wilma Rose 1923- WhoAmW 93
Gorme, Eydie NewYTBS 92 [port], WhoAm 92
Gorme, Eydie 1932- Baker 92
Gormezano, Keith Stephen 1955- WhoEmL 93, WhoWor 93, WhoWrEP 92
Gormezano, Rebecca Law&B 92
Gormley, Beatrice 1942- ScF&FL 92
Gormley, Charles MiSFD 9
Gormley, David Michael 1955- St&PR 93
Gormley, Dennis James 1939- St&PR 93, WhoAm 92
Gormley, Edward Joseph 1928- St&PR 93
Gormley, Franics Xavier, Jr. 1953- WhoEmL 93
Gormley, Gerard Majella 1957- WhoE 93
Gormley, James John WhoE 93
Gormley, James R. Law&B 92
Gormley, Kathleen J. Law&B 92
Gormley, Myra DeVee 1940- WhoAm 92
Gormley, Nancy Elzabeth Law&B 92
Gormley, Nancy H. Law&B 92
Gormley, Peter V. Law&B 92
Gormley, Robert James 1921- WhoAm 92
Gormley, Robert John 1939- WhoAm 92
Gormley, T.R. 1941- WhoScE 91-3
Gormley, W. Clarke Law&B 92
Gormly, Barbara Diesner 1943- WhoAmW 93
Gormly, Ilene T. Law&B 92
Gormly, John Matthew 1947- St&PR 93
Gormsen, Erdmann 1929- WhoScE 91-3
Gormus, Bobby Joe 1941- WhoSSW 93
Gorn, Janet Marie 1938- WhoAm 92
Gorn, Michael H. 1950- ConAu 139
Gornall, Glenn A. 1933- St&PR 93
Gorney, Henry S. 1942- St&PR 93
Gorney, Jay BioIn 17
Gorney, Jay 1896-1990 Baker 92, BioIn 17
Gorney, Jay Philip 1952- WhoEmL 93
Gorney, Mary Jane 1939- WhoAmW 93
Gorney, Roderic 1924- WhoAm 92
Gornichec, Roger F. 1949- St&PR 93
Gornick, Alan Lewis 1908- WhoAm 92, WhoWor 93
Gornick, Michael MiSFD 9
Gornick, Michael George 1947- St&PR 93
Gornick, Vivian BioIn 17
Gornicki, Jaroslaw 1959- WhoWor 93
Gorniewicz, Lech 1941- WhoWor 93
Gornik, Erich 1944- WhoScE 91-3
Gorniok, Alfred 1926- WhoScE 91-4
Gornish, Gerald 1937- WhoAm 92
Gornitsky, Rhonda Law&B 92
Gorno, Albino 1859-1945 Baker 92
Gorny, Peter Hanns 1935- WhoScE 91-3, WhoWor 93
Gorny, Zbigniew WhoScE 91-4
Gorny, Zbigniew 1927- WhoScE 91-4
Goro, Cynthia A. 1955- St&PR 93
Gorodetzky, Charles William 1937- WhoAm 92
Gorodnitzki, Sascha 1904-1986 Baker 92
Gorog, Judith 1938- ScF&FL 92
Gorog, Katalin 1927- WhoScE 91-4
Gorog, William Francis 1925- WhoAm 92
Goronkin, Herbert 1936- WhoAm 92
Gorosh, Alan S. Law&B 92
Gorostiza, Celestino 1904-1967 DcMexL
Gorostiza, Jose 1901-1973 DcMexL
Gorostiza, Jose 1901-1979 SpAmA
Gorostiza, Manuel Eduardo 1789-1851 DcMexL
Gorr, Ivan William WhoAm 92
Gorr, Ivan William 1929- St&PR 93
Gorr, Louis Frederick 1941- WhoAm 92, WhoSSW 93
Gorr, Rita 1926- Baker 92, IntDcOp, OxDcOp
Gorra, Marilyn Noval 1948- WhoWor 93
Gorrell, Dena Ruth 1932- WhoWrEP 92
Gorrell, Edgar S. 1891-1945 EncABHB 8 [port]
Gorres, Joseph von 1776-1848 BioIn 17
Gorretta, Laura J. Law&B 92
Gorriaran, Al Juaquin 1955- WhoE 93
Gorrin, Eugene 1956- WhoE 93, WhoEmL 93
Gorrio, Tobia OxDcOp
Gorris, Henrietta BioIn 17
Gorriti, Juana Manuela 1818-1892 BioIn 17
Gorrod, John William 1931- WhoWor 93
Gorry, F. Jack 1933- St&PR 93
Gorsche, David V. Law&B 92
Gorshkov, Sergei 1910-1988 ColdWar 2 [port]
Gorska-Brylass, Alicja 1933- WhoScE 91-4
Gorske, Robert H. Law&B 92
Gorske, Robert H. 1932- St&PR 93
Gorske, Robert Herman 1932- WhoAm 92
Gorski, Adam 1924- WhoScE 91-4
Gorski, Andrzej Zbigniew 1954- WhoWor 93
Gorski, Ben 1930- St&PR 93
Gorski, Daniel Alexander 1939- WhoAm 92
Gorski, Eugeniusz 1924- WhoScE 91-4
Gorski, Janet Weinberg Law&B 92
Gorski, Jerzy 1937- WhoScE 91-4
Gorski, Ludwik 1924- WhoScE 91-4
Gorski, Robert Alexander 1922- WhoE 93
Gorski, Roger BioIn 17
Gorski, Roger Anthony 1935- WhoAm 92
Gorski, Stanislaw 1927- WhoScE 91-4
Gorski, Tadeusz 1930- WhoScE 91-4
Gorski, Walter J. Law&B 92
Gorski, Walter J. 1943- WhoIns 93
Gorski, Walter Joseph 1943- St&PR 93
Gorski, William Edward 1950- WhoWor 93
Gorsky, Alexander 1871-1924 BioIn 17
Gorslene, Bessie M. AmWomPl
Gorsline, Russell Elvin 1943- WhoWor 93
Gorson, S. Marshall 1924- St&PR 93
Gorst, H.E. 1868-1950 ScF&FL 92
Gorst, Norma 1936- WhoWrEP 92
Gorst, Vern C. 1876-1953 EncABHB 8 [port]
Gorsuch, John Wilbert 1930- WhoAm 92
Gort, Douglas Jon 1953- St&PR 93
Gort, Michael 1923- WhoAm 92, WhoE 93
Gort, Randall J. Law&B 92
Gort, Seymour 1923- St&PR 93
Gortari, Carlos Salinas de BioIn 17
Gorter, James Polk 1929- St&PR 93, WhoAm 92
Gorth, William Phillip 1943- WhoAm 92
Gortler, Elaine Law&B 92
Gortler, Hugh Phillip Law&B 92
Gortler, Leon Bernard 1935- WhoE 93
Gortner, Susan Reichert 1932- WhoAmW 93
Gorton, Arlene Elizabeth 1931- WhoAm 92
Gorton, Azita Bagherz Law&B 92
Gorton, Gregg Emmanuel 1953- WhoEmL 93
Gorton, Kaitlyn WhoWrEP 92
Gorton, Ron ScF&FL 92
Gorton, Roy E. 1936- St&PR 93
Gorton, Slade 1928- CngDr 91, WhoAm 92
Gortsema, Janet Phillips WhoWrEP 92
Gorum, Victoria 1951- WhoAmW 93
Gorup, Gregory James 1948- WhoE 93, WhoWor 93
Gorup, Slavo 1930- WhoScE 91-4
Gorval, B.J. 1951- St&PR 93
Gorvetzian, Kenneth R. Law&B 92
Goryn, Sara 1944- WhoAmW 93
Gorzalczany, Marian Boleslaw 1955- WhoWor 93
Gorzynski, Eugene Arthur 1919- WhoE 93
Gos, Reinhard 1948- WhoScE 91-4
Gosch, Cheryl M. Law&B 92
Goschi, Nicholas Peter 1925- WhoAm 92
Gosciewski, Robert Louis 1957- WhoEmL 93
Gosciminski, Bonnie Marie Kifer 1947- WhoAmW 93
Goscinski, Osvaldo 1938- WhoScE 91-4
Gosden, Freeman F. 1928- St&PR 93
Gosdis, Sherry 1947- WhoE 93
Gose, Celeste Marlene 1959- WhoAmW 93
Gose, Elliott B. 1926- ScF&FL 92
Gose, Elliott Bickley, Jr. 1926- WhoWrEP 92
Gose, Wulf Achim 1938- WhoAm 92
Gosewehr, Carl Louis 1926- St&PR 93
Gosha, Hideo MiSFD 9
Gosha, Hideo d1992 NewYTBS 92
Goshen-Gottstein, Esther 1928- ConAu 137
Goshen-Gottstein, Moshe Henry 1925-1991 BioIn 17
Gosho, Heinosuke BioIn 17
Goshorn, Myrtle Warner AmWomPl
Gosiewski, Anatol 1928- WhoScE 91-4
Gosine, Raymond Francis 1934- St&PR 93
Goskowski, Francis Michael 1950- WhoE 93
Goslawski, Maurycy 1802-1834 PolBiDi
Goslee, James d1990 BioIn 17
Goslicki, Wawrzyniec 1530-1607 PolBiDi
Goslin, David Alexander 1936- WhoAm 92
Goslin, Goose 1900-1971 BioIn 17
Goslin, John Alan 1947- St&PR 93
Gosline, Robert Bradley 1913- WhoAm 92
Gosling, L.M. 1943- WhoScE 91-1
Gosling, Paula ScF&FL 92
Gosling, Peter G. 1954- WhoScE 91-1
Gosman, A.D. WhoScE 91-1
Gosman, Abraham D. 1928- St&PR 93
Gosman, Albert Louis 1923- WhoAm 92
Gosnell, Abigail Reardon 1956- WhoAmW 93
Gosnell, Candace Shealy 1948- WhoSSW 93
Gosnell, Harold F. 1896- PolPar
Gosnell, J. Richard 1947- St&PR 93
Gosnell, John R. 1939- St&PR 93
Gosnell, M. Ann Law&B 92
Gosney, John Roy 1955- WhoWor 93
Gosney, Nora Katherine 1927- St&PR 93
Gospe, Sidney Maloch, Jr. 1952- WhoEmL 93
Goss, Barbara Craig 1945- WhoAmW 93
Goss, Charles H. 1930- St&PR 93
Goss, Charles Henry 1930- WhoAm 92
Goss, Colleen Flynn Law&B 92
Goss, David Arthur 1948- WhoSSW 93

Goss, Edwin J. 1926- St&PR 93
Goss, Eileen Abel 1942- WhoAmW 93
Goss, Frederick Daniel 1941- WhoAm 92
Goss, Georgia Bulman 1939- WhoAmW 93, WhoWor 93
Goss, Howard S. 1933- St&PR 93
Goss, Howard Simon 1933- WhoAm 92
Goss, Irving Joseph 1943- St&PR 93
Goss, James Leslie 1930- St&PR 93
Goss, James Walter 1924- WhoAm 92
Goss, Jeffery Alan 1953- WhoWor 93
Goss, Joel Francis 1955- WhoE 93
Goss, John 1800-1880 Baker 92
Goss, John Howard 1946- WhoSSW 93
Goss, John Reed, III 1955- WhoE 93
Goss, Kenneth George 1922- WhoAm 92
Goss, L.R. 1940- WhoScE 91-3
Goss, Louise Chitwood 1918- WhoSSW 93
Goss, Mary E. Weber 1926- WhoAm 92, WhoAmW 93
Goss, Porter J. 1938- CngDr 91, WhoAm 92, WhoSSW 93
Goss, Rebecca O. Law&B 92
Goss, Richard Henry 1935- WhoAm 92
Goss, Richard Johnson 1925- WhoAm 92
Goss, Richard Oliver WhoScE 91-1
Goss, Robert Mitchell 1956- St&PR 93, WhoEmL 93
Goss, Roger Alfred Ernest 1940- WhoUN 92
Goss, Rosemary Carucci 1952- WhoSSW 93
Goss, Tina R. Law&B 92
Gossage, E. Gene 1935- St&PR 93
Gossage, John Ralph 1946- WhoAm 92
Gossage, Rich 1951- BioIn 17
Gossage, Thomas Layton 1934- St&PR 93, WhoAm 92, WhoE 93, WhoWor 93
Gossage, Wayne 1926- WhoE 93
Gossard, Arthur Charles 1935- WhoAm 92
Gossard, Earl Everett 1923- WhoAm 92
Gossard, William Herbert, Jr. 1945- WhoE 93
Goss-Custard, John Douglas WhoScE 91-1
Gossec, Francois-Joseph 1734-1829 Baker 92, OxDcOp
Gosselaar, Mark-Paul BioIn 17
Gosselin, Kenneth James 1960- WhoE 93
Gosselin, Peter Gordon 1951- WhoE 93
Gosselin, Robert Edmond 1919- WhoAm 92, WhoE 93
Gosselink, Charlotte Penfield BioIn 17
Gosselink, James Gordon 1931- WhoSSW 93
Gosselink, Jerry Dean 1943- St&PR 93
Gosselink, Sara Elizabeth 1893- AmWomPl
Gossels, Claus Peter Rolf 1930- WhoE 93
Gossen, Emmett Joseph, Jr. 1942- St&PR 93, WhoAm 92
Gossens, Salvador Allende 1908-1973 BioIn 17
Gossett, Bruce 1947- St&PR 93
Gossett, Donald Lance 1954- WhoEmL 93
Gossett, Earl Fowler, Jr. 1933- WhoSSW 93
Gossett, Harry A. 1939- St&PR 93
Gossett, Kimberly A. 1960- WhoEmL 93
Gossett, Louis, Jr. BioIn 17
Gossett, Louis, Jr. 1936- WhoAm 92
Gossett, Nellie Jane 1951- WhoAmW 93
Gossett, Oscar Milton 1925- WhoAm 92, WhoE 93
Gossett, Philip 1941- Baker 92, WhoAm 92, WhoWor 93
Gossett, Robert Francis, Jr. 1943- WhoAm 92, WhoE 93
Gossett, Robert M. 1938- WhoAm 92
Gossett, Sharron BioIn 17
Gossett, William H. 1930- St&PR 93
Gossick, Lee Van 1920- WhoAm 92
Gossling, Harry Robert 1922- WhoAm 92
Gossman, Francis Joseph 1930- WhoAm 92, WhoSSW 93
Gossman, Lionel 1929- WhoAm 92, WhoWrEP 92
Gossman, Robert G. 1931- St&PR 93
Gossmann, Hans-Joachim L. 1955- WhoE 93
Gosstola, David John 1959- St&PR 93
Gossweiler, Robert Martin 1949- WhoEmL 93
Gosswein, Claus F. 1931- WhoScE 91-3
Gostin, Judson Jacob 1935- WhoAm 92
Gostkowski, Anthony James 1944- St&PR 93
Gostling, Richard John 1944- WhoScE 91-1
Gostovich, David M. St&PR 93
Gostuski, Dragutin 1923- Baker 92
Goswami, Amit 1936- ScF&FL 92
Goswami, Dinesh d1991 BioIn 17
Goswami, Dinesh 1935- WhoAsAP 91
Goswami, Maggie 1937- ScF&FL 92
Goswami, Ramnarayan 1935- WhoAsAP 91
Goszczynski, Seweryn 1801-1876 PolBiDi
Gotard, Jan 1898-1943 PolBiDi
Gotay, Carolyn Cook 1951- WhoAmW 93, WhoE 93
Gotbaum, Betsy BioIn 17
Gotbaum, Joshua 1951- St&PR 93
Gotch, Frank BioIn 17
Gotcher, Deryl L., Jr. Law&B 92
Gotchey, Shelley Smith 1951- WhoEmL 93, WhoSSW 93
Gotfredson, James C. 1954- St&PR 93
Gotfryd, Alex 1931-1991 BioIn 17
Goth, Jorge Andres 1945- WhoWor 93
Goth, Louis A. ScF&FL 92
Goth, Robert William 1927- WhoE 93
Gothar, Peter 1947- DrEEuF, MiSFD 9
Gothard, Donald Lee 1934- WhoAm 92
Gothard, Donita 1932- WhoAmW 93
Gothberg, Loren A. 1920- St&PR 93
Gothefors, Leif 1940- WhoScE 91-4
Gothenborg, Bent 1941- WhoWor 93
Gotherman, John E. 1933- WhoAm 92
Gothers, Daniel Edward 1935- St&PR 93
Gothler, Ann Marie WhoAmW 93
Gothlin, Jan Herman 1933- WhoScE 91-4
Gotkin, Michael S. Law&B 92
Gotkin, Michael Stanley 1942- St&PR 93
Gotlib, Henryk 1892-1966 PolBiDi
Gotlib, Lorraine 1931- WhoAm 92
Gotlieb, Allan E. BioIn 17
Gotlieb, Allan E. 1928- WhoAm 92, WhoE 93
Gotlieb, Calvin Carl 1921- WhoAm 92
Gotlieb, Irwin I. 1949- WhoAm 92, WhoEmL 93
Gotlieb, Jaquelin Smith 1946- WhoEmL 93, WhoSSW 93
Gotlieb, Lawrence B. Law&B 92
Gotlieb, Lawrence Barry 1948- WhoEmL 93
Gotlieb, Phyllis 1926- ScF&FL 92, WhoCanL 92
Gotlieb, Phyllis Fay Bloom 1926- WhoAm 92
Gotlieb, Sondra 1936- WhoCanL 92
Gotlin, Josip 1922- WhoScE 91-4
Goto, Ken 1952- WhoWor 93
Goto, Kenji 1958- WhoWor 93
Goto, Kimio 1926- WhoWor 93
Goto, Masanori 1939- WhoAsAP 91
Goto, Masao 1913- WhoAsAP 91
Goto, Midori 1971- BioIn 17
Goto, Mitsuo 1935- WhoWor 93
Goto, Nobuo 1938- WhoWor 93
Goto, Nobuo 1956- WhoWor 93
Goto, Shigeru 1925- WhoAsAP 91
Gotoda, Masaharu 1914- WhoAsAP 91
Gotoh, Hideo 1927- WhoWor 93
Gotoh, Tetsuya 1952- WhoWor 93
Gotovac, Jakov 1895-1982 Baker 92, OxDcOp
Gotovac, Tomislav BioIn 17
Gotowko, John Francis 1950- WhoE 93
Gotsch, John Warren 1937- WhoE 93
Gotschalk, Felix C. 1929- ScF&FL 92
Gotschall, Buck BioIn 17
Gotschall, George D. 1920- St&PR 93
Gotschall, Jeffrey P. 1948- St&PR 93
Gotschlich, Emil Claus 1935- WhoAm 92
Gotsch-Thomson, Susan Dorothea 1942- WhoE 93
Gotsdiner, Judy Zaiman Law&B 92
Gotstein, Michael E. 1933- St&PR 93
Gott, J. Richard, III 1947- WhoAm 92
Gott, James L. 1933- St&PR 93
Gott, Marjorie 1944- WhoWor 93
Gotta, Alexander Walter 1935- WhoAm 92, WhoE 93, WhoWor 93
Gottelt, Herbert R. 1936- St&PR 93
Gotter, Friedrich Wilhelm 1746-1797 OxDcOp
Gottesfeld, Gary ScF&FL 92
Gottesman, Callman 1909- WhoAm 92
Gottesman, David Sanford 1926- WhoAm 92
Gottesman, Edward H. d1992 NewYTBS 92
Gottesman, Irving Isadore 1930- WhoAm 92, WhoSSW 93
Gottesman, Ronald 1933- ScF&FL 92
Gottesman, Roy Tully 1928- WhoAm 92
Gottesman, S. D. ConAu 37NR
Gottesman, Scott 1957- WhoIns 93
Gottesman, Stephen Thancy 1939- WhoSSW 93
Gottesman, Walter St&PR 93
Gottesmann, Claude 1936- WhoScE 91-2
Gottesmann, Susan Roberta 1945- WhoSSW 93
Gottfeld, Gunther Max 1934- WhoE 93
Gottfredson, Don Martin 1926- WhoAm 92
Gottfried, Benjamin Frank 1939- WhoE 93
Gottfried, Byron Stuart 1934- WhoAm 92
Gottfried, Chet 1947- ScF&FL 92
Gottfried, Eugene Leslie 1929- WhoAm 92, WhoWor 93
Gottfried, Gary Jay 1948- WhoEmL 93
Gottfried, Harold d1990 BioIn 17
Gottfried, Ira Sidney 1932- WhoAm 92
Gottfried, Kurt 1929- WhoAm 92
Gottfried, Leon Albert 1925- WhoAm 92, WhoWrEP 92
Gottfried, Mark Ellis 1953- WhoEmL 93
Gottfried, Martha A. St&PR 93
Gottfried von Strassburg fl. c. 1210- ClMLC 10 [port]
Gottfries, Carl-Gerhard 1928- WhoScE 91-4
Gottheimer, George M., Jr. 1933- WhoIns 93
Gotthelf, Ezra Gerson 1907-1981 ScF&FL 92
Gotti, Demos 1915- WhoScE 91-3
Gotti, John BioIn 17
Gotti, Margaret R. WhoAmW 93
Gottier, Richard Chalmers 1918- St&PR 93, WhoAm 92
Gotting, Klaus-Jurgen 1936- WhoScE 91-3, WhoWor 93
Gottlieb, A. Arthur 1937- St&PR 93
Gottlieb, Abraham Arthur 1937- WhoAm 92
Gottlieb, Adolph 1903-1974 BioIn 17
Gottlieb, Aida 1937- WhoAmW 93
Gottlieb, Alan Law&B 92
Gottlieb, Allen Sandford 1928- WhoAm 92
Gottlieb, Alma 1954- ConAu 138
Gottlieb, Anna 1774-1856 OxDcOp
Gottlieb, Arnold 1926- WhoE 93
Gottlieb, Arthur 1929- ConAu 137
Gottlieb, Bernard 1912- St&PR 93
Gottlieb, Carl 1938- MiSFD 9
Gottlieb, Edward 1910- WhoAm 92
Gottlieb, Freema (Peninah) 1946- ConAu 137
Gottlieb, Gidon Alain Guy 1932- WhoAm 92
Gottlieb, Gilbert 1929- ConAu 138
Gottlieb, Gordon Stuart 1948- WhoEmL 93
Gottlieb, H. David 1956- WhoE 93
Gottlieb, Harry d1992 NewYTBS 92
Gottlieb, Hinko 1886-1948 ScF&FL 92
Gottlieb, Jack 1930- Baker 92
Gottlieb, James Allen 1956- WhoWor 93
Gottlieb, Jane Ellen 1954- WhoAm 92
Gottlieb, Jerrold Howard 1946- WhoAm 92
Gottlieb, Julius Judah 1919- WhoE 93, WhoWor 93
Gottlieb, Krista 1955- WhoE 93
Gottlieb, Leonard Solomon 1927- WhoAm 92, WhoE 93
Gottlieb, Lester M. 1932- St&PR 93, WhoE 93
Gottlieb, Lisa MiSFD 9
Gottlieb, Louis L. 1923- St&PR 93
Gottlieb, Lucille Montrose Fox 1929- WhoAmW 93, WhoSSW 93
Gottlieb, Manuel Walter Law&B 92
Gottlieb, Marc M. 1930- WhoAm 92
Gottlieb, Marilyn Ann 1942- WhoAm 92, WhoAmW 93
Gottlieb, Marilynn Payne 1956- WhoEmL 93
Gottlieb, Marise S. 1938- St&PR 93
Gottlieb, Martin BioIn 17, Law&B 92
Gottlieb, Martin Morris 1959- WhoE 93
Gottlieb, Maurice 1856-1879 PolBiDi
Gottlieb, Meyer St&PR 93
Gottlieb, Michael MiSFD 9
Gottlieb, Morton Edgar 1921- WhoAm 92
Gottlieb, Myron I. 1943- St&PR 93
Gottlieb, Paul Law&B 92
Gottlieb, Paul 1935- WhoAm 92
Gottlieb, Paul 1936- WhoWrEP 92
Gottlieb, Paul Erwin 1935- St&PR 93
Gottlieb, Richard Douglas 1942- St&PR 93
Gottlieb, Richard Michael Law&B 92
Gottlieb, Robert Adams 1931- BioIn 17, WhoAm 92, WhoE 93
Gottlieb, Sheldon Fred 1932- WhoAm 92
Gottlieb, Sherry Gershon 1947?- ScF&FL 92
Gottlieb, Sidney Alan WhoSSW 93, WhoWor 93
Gottlieb, Stephen E. 1941- ConAu 138
Gottlieb, Theodore ScF&FL 92
Gottman, Jerome E. 1939- St&PR 93
Gottmann, Jean 1915- WhoAm 92
Gotto, Antonio Marion, Jr. 1935- WhoAm 92
Gottovi, Karen Elizabeth 1941- WhoAmW 93
Gottron, Carol Ann 1945- WhoAmW 93
Gottron, Debra S. 1957- WhoEmL 93
Gottron, Harry P., Jr. 1918- St&PR 93
Gottry, Karla Mae Styer 1951- WhoEmL 93
Gottry, Steven Roger 1946- WhoWor 93
Gottschalk, Alexander 1932- WhoAm 92
Gottschalk, Alfons 1932- WhoScE 91-3
Gottschalk, Alfred 1930- WhoAm 92
Gottschalk, Bernard 1935- WhoE 93
Gottschalk, Carl William 1922- WhoAm 92
Gottschalk, Charles Max 1928- WhoAm 92
Gottschalk, Donna M. 1964- WhoAmW 93
Gottschalk, Frank Klaus 1932- WhoAm 92
Gottschalk, Fritz 1937- BioIn 17
Gottschalk, Gerhard 1935- WhoScE 91-3
Gottschalk, Jere Leroy 1924- St&PR 93
Gottschalk, John Simison 1912- WhoAm 92
Gottschalk, Louis August 1916- WhoAm 92
Gottschalk, Louis Moreau 1829-1869 Baker 92, BioIn 17
Gottschalk, Mary Therese 1931- WhoAm 92
Gottschalk, Norman E., Jr. 1944- St&PR 93
Gottschalk, Walter Helbig 1918- WhoE 93
Gottschalk, Werner Max 1920- WhoScE 91-3, WhoWor 93
Gottschall, Edward Maurice 1915- WhoAm 92, WhoWrEP 92
Gottschall, Victor P. Law&B 92
Gottsched, Johann Christoph 1700-1766 BioIn 17
Gottschewski, Jurgen H.M. 1935- WhoScE 91-3
Gottschild, Hellmut BioIn 17
Gottsching, Lothar 1936- WhoScE 91-3
Gottsegen, Gloria 1930- WhoSSW 93
Gottsegen, Mark David 1948- WhoSSW 93
Gottshall, Kevin Lee Law&B 92
Gottsman, Earl Eugene 1946- WhoAm 92, WhoE 93
Gottsman, Jennifer Woods 1958- WhoEmL 93
Gottstein, Barnard Jacob 1925- St&PR 93
Gottstein, Esther Goshen ConAu 137
Gottstein, Karen 1946- WhoWrEP 92
Gottstein, Klaus L.F. 1924- WhoScE 91-3
Gottstein, Moshe Henry Goshen- 1925-1991 BioIn 17
Gottwald, Bruce C. 1933- St&PR 93
Gottwald, Bruce Cobb 1933- WhoSSW 93
Gottwald, Bruce Cobb, Jr. 1957- WhoAm 92
Gottwald, Clytus 1925- Baker 92
Gottwald, Floyd Dewey, Jr. 1922- St&PR 93, WhoAm 92, WhoSSW 93
Gottwald, John D. 1954- WhoSSW 93
Gottwald, Klement 1896-1953 ColdWar 2 [port], DcTwHis
Gottwald, Siegfried Johannes 1943- WhoWor 93
Gotwals, Charles Place, Jr. 1917- WhoAm 92
Gotwals, William Logan 1942- St&PR 93
Gotz, Johann Nikolaus 1721-1781 BioIn 17
Gotz, Karl Georg 1930- WhoScE 91-3
Gotz, Manfred H. 1942- WhoScE 91-4
Gotze, Johann Nikolaus Konrad 1791-1861 Baker 92
Gotze, Karl 1836-1887 Baker 92
Gotze, Wolfgang 1937- WhoScE 91-3
Gotzoyannis, Stavros Eleutherios 1933- WhoWor 93
Goubarev, Alexandre 1950- WhoUN 92
Goubert, Pierre 1915- ConAu 136
Goudaras, Argirios 1941- WhoScE 91-3
Goude, Jean-Paul BioIn 17
Goudeau, Alain M. 1950- WhoScE 91-2
Goudeles OxDcByz
Goudge, Eileen BioIn 17
Goudge, Eileen 1950- ScF&FL 92
Goudge, Elizabeth 1900-1984 ScF&FL 92
Goudge, Elizabeth (de Beauchamp) 1900-1984 MajAI [port]
Goudie, Andrew Shaw WhoScE 91-1
Goudie, Andrew Shaw 1945- ConAu 38NR, WhoWor 93
Goudie, Kenneth R. 1948- St&PR 93
Goudimel, Claude c. 1510-1572 Baker 92
Goudis, Christos 1947- WhoScE 91-3
Goudmand, Pierre W.N. 1934- WhoScE 91-2
Goudmel, Claude c. 1510-1572 Baker 92
Goudoever, Henri Daniel van 1898-1977 Baker 92
Goudreau, Roland H. 1938- St&PR 93
Goudy, Frederic W. 1865-1947 BioIn 17
Goudy, James Joseph Ralph 1952- WhoWor 93
Goudy, Josephine Gray 1925- WhoAmW 93
Goudy, Robert Schwalm Law&B 92
Gouesbet, Gerard 1947- WhoWor 93
Gouge, Susan Cornelia Jones 1924- WhoAm 92, WhoAmW 93, WhoWor 93
Gougenheim, Jacques Henri 1932- WhoWor 93
Gougeon, Len Girard 1947- WhoWrEP 92

Gouger, Dale Bartlett 1942- *WhoE 93, WhoWor 93*
Gough, Brandon *BioIn 17*
Gough, Carolyn Harley 1922- *WhoAm 92*
Gough, Cecile S. *St&PR 93*
Gough, Colin Edward *WhoScE 91-1*
Gough, Denis Ian 1922- *WhoAm 92*
Gough, Gary William 1942- *St&PR 93*
Gough, Hubert de la Poer 1870-1963 *HarEnMi*
Gough, Hugh 1779-1869 *HarEnMi*
Gough, Jessie Post 1907- *WhoAmW 93, WhoSSW 93*
Gough, John Bernard 1928- *WhoWor 93*
Gough, John Francis 1934- *WhoE 93*
Gough, Joseph M. 1927- *St&PR 93*
Gough, Michael 1917- *BioIn 17*
Gough, Michael John 1939- *WhoIns 93*
Gough, Pauline Bjerke 1935- *WhoAm 92, WhoAmW 93*
Gough, Phillip Alan 1955- *St&PR 93*
Gough, Ronald 1936- *WhoScE 91-1*
Gough, Stephen Bradford 1950- *WhoSSW 93*
Gough, Steven *MiSFD 9*
Gough, Terry A. 1939- *WhoScE 91-1*
Gough, William 1945- *WhoCanL 92*
Gougher, Ronald Lee 1939- *WhoE 93, WhoWor 93*
Goughler, Donald H. 1945- *WhoE 93*
Goughnour, Roy Robert 1928- *WhoSSW 93*
Gougov, Nikola Delchev 1914- *ConAu 37NR*
Gouguenheim, Lucienne 1935- *WhoScE 91-2*
Gouig, Steven J. *Law&B 92*
Gouilloud, Michel 1930- *WhoAm 92*
Gouin, Felix 1884-1977 *BioIn 17*
Gouin, Francis R. 1938- *WhoAm 92*
Gouin, Serge 1943- *WhoAm 92*
Goulard, Guy Yvon 1940- *WhoAm 92*
Goulart, Ron 1933- *ScF&FL 92*
Goulart, Ron(ald Joseph) 1933- *WhoWrEP 92*
Goulart, Ronald Joseph 1933- *WhoAm 92*
Goulazian, Peter *BioIn 17*
Goulazian, Peter Robert 1939- *WhoAm 92*
Goulbourne, Donald Samuel, Jr. 1950- *WhoE 93*
Goulbourne, Harry 1948- *ConAu 137*
Gould, Alan *ScF&FL 92*
Gould, Alan Brant 1938- *WhoAm 92*
Gould, Alice *AmWomPl*
Gould, Alvin R. 1922- *WhoAm 92*
Gould, Barbara Bodichon Ayrton 1886-1950 *BioIn 17*
Gould, Bernard 1912- *St&PR 93*
Gould, Bonnie Marie 1947- *WhoEmL 93*
Gould, Brian S. 1947- *St&PR 93*
Gould, Bruce Grant 1942- *WhoWrEP 92*
Gould, Bryan 1939- *ConAu 136*
Gould, Carol Cirelle 1946- *WhoAmW 93*
Gould, Charles Howard 1935- *WhoE 93*
Gould, Charles L. 1942- *St&PR 93*
Gould, Charles Perry 1909- *WhoAm 92*
Gould, Chester 1900-1985 *BioIn 17*
Gould, Courtney A. 1915- *St&PR 93*
Gould, D.M. 1939- *St&PR 93*
Gould, David I. 1930- *St&PR 93*
Gould, David J. *Law&B 92*
Gould, Dirk S. *Law&B 92*
Gould, Donald Everett 1932- *WhoE 93, WhoWor 93*
Gould, Edward P. 1931- *St&PR 93*
Gould, Edwin Sheldon 1926- *WhoAm 92*
Gould, Eileen Gordon 1948- *WhoEmL 93*
Gould, Elizabeth Lincoln *AmWomPl*
Gould, Elliott 1938- *IntDcF 2-3 [port], WhoAm 92*
Gould, F.J. 1855-1938 *ScF&FL 92*
Gould, Frank Joseph *Law&B 92*
Gould, Frank Nelson 1926- *St&PR 93*
Gould, Fredric H. 1935- *St&PR 93*
Gould, George D. 1927- *WhoAm 92*
Gould, George M. *Law&B 92*
Gould, Georgeanne Helen *Law&B 92*
Gould, Glen Miller 1961- *WhoSSW 93*
Gould, Glenn 1932-1982 *BioIn 17, ConMus 9 [port]*
Gould, Glenn (Herbert) 1932-1982 *Baker 92*
Gould, Glenn Hunting 1949- *WhoSSW 93*
Gould, Gordon 1920- *St&PR 93*
Gould, Gregory 1920- *St&PR 93*
Gould, H.J. *WhoScE 91-1*
Gould, Harold 1923- *WhoAm 92*
Gould, Harry Edward, Jr. 1938- *St&PR 93, WhoAm 92, WhoE 93, WhoWor 93*
Gould, Harry J., III 1947- *WhoSSW 93*
Gould, Harvey Allen 1938- *WhoE 93*
Gould, Heywood *MiSFD 9*
Gould, Irving 1919- *St&PR 93*
Gould, Jack Richard 1922- *WhoE 93*
Gould, James C. 1945- *St&PR 93*
Gould, James Spencer 1922- *WhoAm 92*
Gould, James Warren 1924- *WhoE 93*
Gould, Jay 1836-1892 *GayN*
Gould, Jay 1940- *St&PR 93*
Gould, Jay Martin 1915- *WhoAm 92*
Gould, Jean Rosalind 1919- *WhoWrEP 92*
Gould, Jerry 1934- *St&PR 93*
Gould, Joan 1927- *ScF&FL 92*
Gould, Joann E. *Law&B 92*
Gould, Jodie Ellen 1957- *WhoAmW 93*
Gould, John *ConTFT 10*
Gould, John Joseph 1930- *WhoAm 92*
Gould, John Philip, Jr. 1939- *WhoAm 92*
Gould, John T., Jr. *St&PR 93*
Gould, Judith *ConAu 136*
Gould, Kathleen Simpson 1914- *WhoAmW 93*
Gould, Kenneth Dean *Law&B 92*
Gould, Kenneth Lance 1938- *WhoAm 92*
Gould, Lawrence Alren 1930- *WhoE 93*
Gould, Lewis Ludlow 1939- *WhoAm 92*
Gould, Lois *BioIn 17, WhoWrEP 92*
Gould, Loyal Norman 1927- *WhoAm 92*
Gould, Marie 1962- *WhoAmW 93*
Gould, Marilyn A. 1928- *WhoAmW 93*
Gould, Martha B. 1931- *WhoAmW 93*
Gould, Maxine Lubow 1942- *WhoAmW 93*
Gould, Milton S. 1909- *St&PR 93*
Gould, Milton Samuel 1909- *WhoAm 92*
Gould, Morley David 1936- *WhoAm 92*
Gould, Morton 1913- *Baker 92, WhoAm 92*
Gould, Nathaniel Duren 1781-1864 *Baker 92*
Gould, Paul *BioIn 17, St&PR 93*
Gould, Peter John 1941- *St&PR 93*
Gould, Peter Robin 1932- *WhoAm 92*
Gould, Philip 1922- *WhoE 93*
Gould, Phillip L. 1937- *WhoAm 92*
Gould, R. Max 1939- *St&PR 93*
Gould, Ralph Albert, Jr. 1923- *St&PR 93*
Gould, Raphael L. d1991 *BioIn 17*
Gould, Richard Allan 1939- *WhoAm 92*
Gould, Robert A. 1951- *St&PR 93*
Gould, Robert Bryan 1956- *WhoE 93*
Gould, Robert L. 1938- *WhoAm 92*
Gould, Roberta 1941- *WhoWrEP 92*
Gould, Roberta Berkley 1936- *WhoAmW 93*
Gould, Ronald James 1950- *WhoSSW 93*
Gould, Roy Walter 1927- *WhoAm 92*
Gould, Sherri Hallerman *Law&B 92*
Gould, Stanley Farrell 1949- *WhoEmL 93*
Gould, Stephen Jay 1941- *BioIn 17, WhoAm 92*
Gould, Stuart S. 1906- *St&PR 93*
Gould, Syd S. 1912- *WhoSSW 93, WhoWor 93*
Gould, Wayne Curtis 1960- *WhoE 93*
Gould, Wesley Larson 1917- *WhoAm 92*
Gould, William Allen 1941- *WhoE 93*
Gould, William F. 1934- *WhoIns 93*
Gould, William Henry Mercur 1951- *WhoE 93*
Gould, William Richard 1919- *St&PR 93*
Gould, William Thomas 1946- *St&PR 93*
Goulden, Joseph Chesley 1934- *WhoAm 92, WhoWrEP 92*
Goulder, Caroljean Hempstead 1933- *WhoAm 92, WhoAmW 93, WhoE 93*
Goulder, George V. 1914- *St&PR 93*
Goulder, Gerald Polster 1953- *WhoEmL 93*
Gouldey, Bruce K. 1952- *St&PR 93*
Gouldey, Glenn Charles 1952- *WhoEmL 93*
Gouldin, Norman Hadley 1921- *St&PR 93*
Goulding, Charles Edwin 1916- *WhoSSW 93*
Goulding, Edmund 1891-1959 *MiSFD 9N*
Goulding, Marrack Irvine 1936- *WhoUN 92*
Goulding, Nora 1944- *WhoAm 92, WhoAmW 93*
Goulding, Ray 1922-1990 *BioIn 17*
Goulding, Robert 1920-1991 *BioIn 17*
Gouldner, Alvin Ward 1920-1980 *BioIn 17*
Gouldthorpe, Kenneth Alfred Percival 1928- *WhoAm 92*
Gouled Aptidon, Hassan 1916- *WhoAfr, WhoWor 93*
Goulet, Carole *Law&B 92*
Goulet, Charles Rudolfe 1933- *St&PR 93*
Goulet, Charles Ryan 1927- *WhoAm 92*
Goulet, Cynthia Wagner 1957- *WhoAmW 93, WhoEmL 93*
Goulet, Denis Andre 1931- *WhoAm 92*
Goulet, Lorrie 1925- *WhoAm 92, WhoAmW 93*
Goulet, M.L. *Law&B 92*
Goulet, Robert 1933- *BioIn 17*
Goulet, Robert (Gerard) 1933- *Baker 92, WhoAm 92*
Goulianos, Konstantin 1935- *WhoAm 92*
Goullet, Alf *BioIn 17*
Goullet, Philippe 1927- *WhoScE 91-2*
Goulletquer, Herve 1956- *WhoWor 93*
Goulon, M. 1919- *WhoScE 91-2*
Goulston, Marilyn Gwen 1949- *WhoEmL 93*
Gounard, Beverley Elaine 1942- *WhoE 93*
Gounaris, Anne Demetra 1924- *WhoAm 92, WhoE 93*
Goundji, Aziz Philippe 1956- *WhoUN 92*
Goune, Steven Etienne 1956- *WhoE 93*
Gounelle, J.-C. 1932- *WhoScE 91-2*
Gouner, Farley A. 1941- *St&PR 93*
Gounod, Charles 1818-1893 *OxDcOp*
Gounod, Charles (Francois) 1818-1893 *Baker 92, IntDcOp [port]*
Gounot, Anne-Monique 1935- *WhoScE 91-2*
Gourad Hamadou, Barkat *WhoWor 93*
Gouran, Dennis Stephen 1941- *WhoAm 92*
Gouras, Peter 1930- *WhoAm 92*
Gouraud, Jackson S. 1923- *WhoAm 92*
Gouraud, Marie-Michel 1905-1991 *BioIn 17*
Gourbin, Jean-Louis 1947- *St&PR 93*
Gourdeau, Danielle *Law&B 92*
Gourdeau, Jean-Guy 1964- *St&PR 93*
Gourdikian, Adelina Lena 1965- *WhoSSW 93*
Gourdine, Anthony 1940- *See* Little Anthony & the Imperials *SoulM*
Gourdine, Meredith Charles 1929- *WhoAm 92*
Gourdine, Simon Peter 1940- *WhoAm 92, WhoWor 93*
Gourdji, Joseph 1926- *WhoE 93*
Gourdon, Charles Maurice d1991 *BioIn 17*
Goureaux, Guy 1930- *WhoScE 91-2*
Gourevitch, Peter Alexis 1943- *WhoAm 92*
Gourevitch, Victor 1925- *WhoAm 92*
Gourgue, Gerard 1925- *DcCPCAm*
Gourias, Samonas, and Abibas *OxDcByz*
Gourio, Herve 1940- *WhoWor 93*
Gourlay, Elizabeth 1917- *WhoCanL 92*
Gourley, Dick R. 1944- *WhoAm 92*
Gourley, James Leland 1919- *WhoAm 92, WhoWor 93*
Gourley, Keith D. *Law&B 92*
Gourley, Marshall *BioIn 17*
Gourley, Paula Marie 1948- *WhoAmW 93*
Gourley, Ronald Robert 1919- *WhoAm 92*
Gourley, Theodore Joseph, Jr. 1944- *WhoE 93*
Gourlie, Jonathan William 1942- *WhoE 93*
Gourlie, Rebecca Elizabeth 1948- *WhoEmL 93*
Gournay, Marie le Jars de d1645 *BioIn 17*
Goursat, Paul 1942- *WhoScE 91-2*
Goursaud, Anne *BioIn 17*
Gouse, S. William, Jr. 1931- *WhoAm 92, WhoSSW 93*
Gousha, Richard Paul 1923- *WhoAm 92*
Goussault, Y. *WhoScE 91-2*
Gousseland, Pierre 1922- *St&PR 93*
Goussetis, Harry A. *Law&B 92*
Gouterman, Martin Paul 1931- *WhoAm 92*
Gouterman, Robert Gerald 1938- *WhoAm 92*
Goutier, Roland 1927- *WhoScE 91-2*
Goutte, R. *WhoScE 91-2*
Goutte, Rene 1935- *St&PR 93*
Gouveia, Diana Brigitta *Law&B 92*
Gouveia, Judith Kathleen Blake 1944- *WhoAmW 93*
Gouverneur, Simon 1934-1990 *BioIn 17*
Gouvy, Louis Theodore 1819-1898 *Baker 92*
Gouyon, Paul Cardinal 1910- *WhoAm 92, WhoWor 93*
Govaerts, Paul E.J. 1947- *WhoScE 91-2*
Govan, James Fauntleroy 1926- *WhoAm 92*
Gove, C. John 1926- *St&PR 93*
Gove, Christopher David 1948- *WhoWor 93*
Gove, Doris 1944- *SmATA 72 [port]*
Gove, Jeanne 1927- *St&PR 93*
Gove, John C. 1926- *St&PR 93*
Gove, Samuel Kimball 1923- *WhoAm 92*
Goved Njayick, Emmanuel Christian 1941- *WhoUN 92*
Gover, Alan Shore 1948- *WhoAm 92, WhoSSW 93*
Gover, James Edwin 1940- *WhoAm 92*
Gover, Raymond Lewis 1927- *St&PR 93, WhoAm 92*
Goverman, Barry 1945- *St&PR 93*
Govern, Frank Stanley 1951- *WhoE 93*
Governali, Paul V. 1921-1978 *BiDAMSp 1989*
Governor, Richard *MiSFD 9*
Govey, Charles W. *St&PR 93*
Govi, Mario *WhoScE 91-3*
Govier, Katherine 1948- *ConAu 40NR, WhoCanL 92*
Govier, William Charles 1936- *WhoAm 92*
Govig, Valerie Cowls 1934- *WhoWrEP 92*
Govil, Narendra Kumar 1940- *WhoSSW 93*
Govindaraju, Kuppusami 1928- *WhoScE 91-2*
Govindarajulu, Zakkala 1933- *WhoSSW 93*
Govindjee 1933- *WhoAm 92*
Govoni, Amy Louise 1953- *WhoEmL 93*
Govoni, Virginia Deliso 1934- *St&PR 93*
Govreau, Lisa Carol 1959- *WhoAmW 93*
Govreau, Mary Frances 1949- *WhoAmW 93*
Gow, Ellen B. 1950- *WhoWrEP 92*
Gow, Ian 1937-1990 *BioIn 17*
Gow, Nathaniel 1763-1831 *Baker 92*
Gow, Niel 1727-1807 *Baker 92*
Gowac, John Joseph 1957- *St&PR 93*
Gowan, Alastair C. 1935- *St&PR 93*
Gowan, Donald Elmer 1929- *WhoE 93*
Gowan, Joseph Patrick, Jr. 1939- *WhoAm 92, WhoWor 93*
Gowanny, Helen 1957- *WhoAmW 93*
Gowans, Alan 1923- *ConAu 40NR, WhoE 93*
Gowar, Michael R. *ScF&FL 92*
Gowar, Mick 1951- *ScF&FL 92*
Gowda, D.B. Chandre 1936- *WhoAsAP 91*
Gowda, K.G. Thimme 1915- *WhoAsAP 91*
Gowda, Narasimhan Ramaiah 1949- *WhoEmL 93, WhoWor 93*
Gowden, Virginia Mary 1947- *WhoAmW 93*
Gowdy, Curtis 1919- *WhoAm 92*
Gowdy, Miriam Betts 1928- *WhoAm 92, WhoAmW 93*
Gowdy, Robert C. 1943- *WhoIns 93*
Gowen, Clarence William, Jr. 1952- *WhoEmL 93, WhoSSW 93*
Gowen, Jerry Dale 1943- *St&PR 93*
Gowen, Nancy Adele 1934- *WhoAmW 93*
Gowen, Paul H. 1925- *St&PR 93*
Gowen, Richard Joseph 1935- *WhoAm 92*
Gowen, Sheryl Ann 1946- *WhoSSW 93*
Gowens, Verneeta Viola 1913- *WhoAmW 93*
Gower, Bob G. 1937- *St&PR 93, WhoSSW 93*
Gower, Charlotte Day *IntDcAn*
Gower, David Benjamin *WhoScE 91-1*
Gower, John Clifford *WhoScE 91-1*
Gower, Richard Maynard 1925- *WhoAm 92*
Gower, Robert J. *Law&B 92*
Gowing, Lawrence 1918-1991 *AnObit 1991, BioIn 17*
Gowl, Colleen Butler *WhoAmW 93*
Gowland, Karen E. *Law&B 92*
Gowland, M.S. *WhoScE 91-1*
Gowon, Yakubu 1934- *ColdWar 2 [port], DcTwHis, WhoAfr*
Gowsell, R.W. 1925- *St&PR 93*
Goy, Patrick *St&PR 93*
Goya, Francisco 1746-1828 *BioIn 17*
Goyal, Hari Chand 1924- *WhoWor 93*
Goyal, Raj Kumar 1937- *WhoAm 92*
Goyal, Saroj 1949- *WhoEmL 93*
Goyal, Vinod Kumar 1948- *St&PR 93*
Goyan, Jere Edwin 1930- *WhoAm 92*
Goyan, Michael Donovan 1938- *WhoAm 92*
Goya y Lucientes, Francisco Jose de 1746-1828 *BioIn 17*
Goydan, Paul Alexander 1947- *St&PR 93*
Goyer, Jane *BioIn 17*
Goyer, Robert Andrew 1927- *WhoAm 92*
Goyer, Robert Stanton 1923- *WhoAm 92*
Goyer, Virginia L. 1942- *WhoAmW 93*
Goyet, Jean-Marie 1945- *St&PR 93*
Goyette, Denis *St&PR 93*
Goyette, John H. 1946- *St&PR 93*
Goyette, Marc L. 1955- *St&PR 93*
Goyne, William M. 1931- *WhoSSW 93*
Goy-Severino, Paula Anne 1957- *WhoAmW 93*
Goytisolo, Juan *BioIn 17*
Goytortua, Jesus 1910- *DcMexL*
Goz, Harry G. 1932- *WhoWor 93*
Gozani, Tsahi 1934- *WhoAm 92*
Gozder, Charles 1935- *St&PR 93*
Gozleveli, Tamer Mehmet 1952- *WhoSSW 93*
Gozon, Felipe Lapus 1939- *WhoWor 93*
Gozon, Richard C. 1938- *St&PR 93*
Gozonsky, Edwin S.P. 1930- *St&PR 93*
Gozukara, Engin M. 1939- *WhoScE 91-4*
Gozzi, Carlo 1720-1806 *OxDcOp*
Graae, Flemming Gomme 1948- *WhoEmL 93*
Graaf, Peter *ConAu 37NR, MajAI*
Graaskamp, Charles Fiske 1934- *St&PR 93*
Graass, James Henry *Law&B 92*
Grab, John M. 1946- *St&PR 93*
Grabar, Andre 1896-1990 *BioIn 17*
Grabar, Oleg 1929- *WhoAm 92*
Grabarek, William C. *Law&B 92*
Grabbe, Crockett L(ane) 1951- *ConAu 138*
Grabbe, Klaus 1932- *WhoScE 91-3*
Grabda, Eugeniusz Jan 1908- *WhoWor 93*
Grabek, James R. 1945- *St&PR 93*
Grabel, Lawrence 1947- *WhoE 93*
Grabelsky, Glen H. 1953- *St&PR 93*

Grabemann, Karl W. 1929- *WhoAm 92*
Graben-Hoffmann, Gustav (Heinrich) 1820-1900 *Baker 92*
Graber, Arnold S. *Law&B 92*
Graber, Doris Appel 1923- *WhoAm 92, WhoWrEP 92*
Graber, Edith E. 1924- *WhoAmW 93*
Graber, Edward Alex 1914- *WhoAm 92*
Graber, Kathleen Sue 1945- *WhoSSW 93*
Graber, Lee A. 1947- *St&PR 93*
Graber, Richard Allan 1933- *St&PR 93*
Graber, Robert 1946- *St&PR 93*
Graber, Robert Philip 1918- *WhoWor 93*
Graber, Sarah J. *Law&B 92*
Graber, Steve L. 1960- *St&PR 93*
Graber, Steven Wayne 1950- *WhoEmL 93*
Graber, Susan P. 1949- *WhoAm 92, WhoAmW 93*
Graber, Thomas M. 1917- *WhoAm 92*
Grabert, Hellmut 1920- *WhoScE 91-3*
Grabfield, Deborah Diller 1954- *WhoAmW 93*
Grabham, David A. *Law&B 92*
Grabherr, Rolf 1944- *WhoScE 91-4*
Grabiel, Floyd E. 1946- *St&PR 93*
Grabien, Deborah *ScF&FL 92*
Grabill, Gloria Elizabeth 1938- *WhoE 93*
Grabill, James Roscoe, Jr. 1949- *WhoWrEP 92*
Grabinska, Wanda G. 1902-1980 *PolBiDi*
Grabinski, Carl S. *Law&B 92*
Grabke, Hans Jurgen 1935- *WhoWor 93*
Grable, Betty 1916-1973 *IntDcF 2-3 [port]*
Grable, Edward E. 1926- *WhoAm 92*
Grabner, George John 1918- *St&PR 93, WhoAm 92*
Grabner, Hermann 1886-1969 *Baker 92*
Grabner, Peter 1935- *WhoScE 91-3*
Grabo, Anders P. 1950- *WhoIns 93*
Grabo, Norman S. 1930- *ScF&FL 92*
Grabo, Norman Stanley 1930- *WhoAm 92, WhoWrEP 92*
GraBois, Stuart *BioIn 17*
Grabon, Henry 1917- *St&PR 93*
Graboski, Thomas Walter 1947- *WhoAm 92*
Grabosky, Terri Jo 1949- *WhoEmL 93*
Grabovsky, Leonid 1935- *Baker 92*
Grabow, Barry G. 1943- *St&PR 93*
Grabow, Laura M. *Law&B 92*
Grabow, Stephen Harris 1943- *WhoAm 92*
Grabowska, Arthur Joseph 1953- *WhoEmL 93, WhoSSW 93*
Grabowska, James A. 1956- *WhoSSW 93*
Grabowska-Olszewska, Barbara 1933- *WhoScE 91-4*
Grabowski, Chester Adam 1946- *WhoAm 92*
Grabowski, Edward Joseph John 1940- *WhoE 93*
Grabowski, Elizabeth 1940- *WhoAmW 93*
Grabowski, Hans 1934- *WhoScE 91-3*
Grabowski, Janice Lynn 1948- *WhoAmW 93*
Grabowski, John Francis 1947- *WhoWrEP 92*
Grabowski, Joseph James 1956- *WhoE 93*
Grabowski, Klaus H. 1943- *WhoScE 91-3*
Grabowski, Marianne *Law&B 92*
Grabowski, Maureen Mona 1951- *WhoAmW 93*
Grabowski, Mieczyslaw Jerzy 1928- *WhoScE 91-4, WhoWor 93*
Grabowski, Piotr Ludwik 1952- *WhoWor 93*
Grabowski, Raymond 1950- *St&PR 93*
Grabowski, Roger J. 1947- *WhoAm 92*
Grabowski, Sandra Reynolds 1943- *WhoAmW 93*
Grabowski, Stanislaw 1940- *WhoWor 93*
Grabowski, William J(ohn) 1958- *WhoWrEP 92*
Grabowsky, Axel L. 1937- *St&PR 93*
Grabowsky, Nicholas *ScF&FL 92*
Graboys, George 1932- *WhoAm 92*
Grabske, William John 1943- *WhoAm 92*
Grabski, Donald E. 1927- *St&PR 93*
Grabski, Maciej W. 1934- *WhoScE 91-4*
Grabski, Maciej Wladyslaw 1934- *WhoWor 93*
Grabski, Ronald John 1946- *St&PR 93*
Grabu Louis fl. 1665-1694 *OxDcOp*
Graburn, Nelson Hayes Henry 1936- *WhoAm 92*
Gracchus, Tiberius Sempronius d212BC *HarEnMi*
Grace, Princess of Monaco 1929-1982 *BioIn 17*
Grace, Alexander M. *ConAu 138*
Grace, Bob L. 1938- *St&PR 93*
Grace, Carol *ConAu 139*
Grace, Catherine D. 1964- *WhoWrEP 92*
Grace, Charles Brown, Jr. 1934- *WhoAm 92, WhoE 93*
Grace, Charles Edward 1957- *WhoEmL 93*
Grace, Charles L. 1935- *St&PR 93*
Grace, Charles Manuel 1881-1960 *BioIn 17*
Grace, Corinne Bissette 1929- *WhoWor 93*
Grace, Daddy 1881-1960 *BioIn 17*
Grace, Deborah *ConAu 136*
Grace, Dixie Lee 1948- *WhoAmW 93*
Grace, Donna-Marie Angela 1959- *WhoSSW 93*
Grace, Edward Laurence 1931- *WhoAsAP 91*
Grace, Eugene *Law&B 92*
Grace, Eugene P. 1951- *St&PR 93*
Grace, Eugene Vernon 1927- *WhoWrEP 92*
Grace, George *Law&B 92*
Grace, H. David 1936- *WhoAm 92*
Grace, Harvey 1874-1944 *Baker 92*
Grace, J. Peter *BioIn 17*
Grace, J. Peter 1913- *St&PR 93, WhoAm 92, WhoSSW 93*
Grace, James M. 1943- *St&PR 93*
Grace, James Martin 1943- *WhoAm 92*
Grace, James W. *Law&B 92*
Grace, Jason Roy 1936- *St&PR 93, WhoAm 92*
Grace, Jerry L. 1941- *St&PR 93*
Grace, John Eugene 1931- *WhoAm 92*
Grace, John Kenneth 1945- *WhoAm 92, WhoE 93*
Grace, John Robert 1926- *St&PR 93*
Grace, John Ross 1943- *WhoAm 92*
Grace, John William 1927- *WhoAm 92*
Grace, Joseph Peter *BioIn 17*
Grace, Judy Diane 1946- *WhoAmW 93, WhoEmL 93*
Grace, Julianne Alice 1937- *St&PR 93, WhoAm 92, WhoAmW 93*
Grace, Kevin Henry 1956- *WhoWor 93*
Grace, Linda Ann 1952- *WhoE 93*
Grace, Lola Nashashibi 1958- *WhoAmW 93*
Grace, Marcia Bell 1937- *WhoAm 92*
Grace, Mark *BioIn 17*
Grace, Michael J. 1946- *St&PR 93*
Grace, Nancy O. 1936- *St&PR 93*
Grace, Oliver R. d1992 *NewYTBS 92 [port]*
Grace, Oliver R. 1909- *St&PR 93*
Grace, Oliver R. 1909-1992 *BioIn 17*
Grace, Patricia N. *Law&B 92*
Grace, Priscilla Anne 1943- *WhoAmW 93*
Grace, Richard Edward 1930- *WhoAm 92*
Grace, Robert M., Jr. *Law&B 92*
Grace, Robert Mitchell, Jr. 1947- *St&PR 93*
Grace, Roy 1936- *St&PR 93*
Grace, Stephen S. *Law&B 92*
Grace, Thomas Edward 1954- *WhoEmL 93*
Grace, Thomas Lee 1955- *WhoE 93, WhoEmL 93*
Grace, Thomas P. *Law&B 92*
Grace, Virginia 1901- *BioIn 17*
Grace, W. R. *DcCPCAm*
Grace, Wesley Gee, Jr. 1945- *WhoSSW 93*
Grace, William J(oseph), Jr. 1948- *ConAu 38NR*
Gracey, Dan J. 1948- *St&PR 93*
Gracey, Douglas Robert 1936- *WhoAm 92*
Gracey, J. Donald *Law&B 92*
Gracey, James Steele 1927- *WhoAm 92*
Grachev, Pavel *WhoWor 93*
Grachev, Victor Pavlovich 1932- *WhoUN 92*
Gracia, Charles 1944- *WhoUN 92*
Gracia, Jorge Jesus Emiliano 1942- *WhoAm 92*
Gracia, Juan Miguel 1945- *WhoWor 93*
Gracia, Pilar 1953- *WhoScE 91-3*
Gracia-Navarro, Francisco 1952- *WhoWor 93*
Gracida, Rene Henry 1923- *WhoAm 92, WhoSSW 93*
Gracie, Christopher A.J. 1945- *WhoScE 91-1*
Gracis, Ettore 1915- *Baker 92*
Gracq, Julien 1910- *BioIn 17*
Gracy, David Bergen, II 1941- *WhoAm 92*
Graczyk, Alan Edward 1953- *WhoEmL 93*
Graczyk, Ryszard 1926- *WhoScE 91-4*
Graczynska, Ewa Wanda *WhoWor 93*
Grad, David *Law&B 92*
Grad, David Allan 1952- *St&PR 93*
Grad, Frank Paul 1924- *WhoAm 92*
Grad, Gabriel 1890-1950 *Baker 92*
Grad, John J. 1938- *St&PR 93*
Grad, John Joseph 1938- *WhoAm 92*
Grad, Rae *BioIn 17*
Graddick, Charles Allen 1944- *WhoAm 92*
Graddick, Richard Adolph 1918- *WhoWrEP 92*
Grade, Chaim 1910-1982 *BioIn 17*
Grade, Jeffery T. 1943- *WhoAm 92*
Grade, Lew 1906- *BioIn 17, WhoAm 92*
Gradeen, G.D. 1954- *St&PR 93*
Gradeless, Donald Eugene 1949- *WhoEmL 93*
Graden, John Joseph 1960- *WhoEmL 93*
Gradener, Carl (Georg Peter) 1812-1883 *Baker 92*
Gradener, Hermann (Theodor Otto) 1844-1929 *Baker 92*
Gradenwitz, Peter (Werner Emanuel) 1910- *Baker 92*
Grader, Charles Raymond 1931- *WhoWor 93*
Grader, Ralph Howard 1922- *St&PR 93*
Gradin, Anita 1933- *WhoWor 93*
Gradinger, J. Gary 1943- *St&PR 93*
Gradinger, Joseph F. *St&PR 93*
Gradisar, Helen Margaret 1922- *WhoAmW 93*
Gradishar, Randy Charles 1952- *BiDAMSp 1989*
Gradison, Heather Jane 1952- *WhoAm 92*
Gradison, Willis D., Jr. 1928- *CngDr 91*
Gradison, Willis David, Jr. 1928- *WhoAm 92*
Gradmann, Ulrich 1931- *WhoScE 91-3*
Grado, Angelo John 1922- *WhoAm 92*
Grado, John 1927- *St&PR 93*
Grado, John Angelo 1953- *St&PR 93*
Gradoville, Savory M. *Law&B 92*
Gradowski, Stanley J., Jr. 1938- *St&PR 93*
Gradowski, Stanley Joseph, Jr. 1938- *WhoAm 92*
Gradstein, Alfred 1904-1954 *Baker 92*
Gradus, Ben d1990 *BioIn 17*
Grady, Christine S. *Law&B 92*
Grady, David F. 1938- *St&PR 93*
Grady, David J. 1941- *WhoIns 93*
Grady, Duane G. 1936- *St&PR 93*
Grady, Edward C. 1947- *St&PR 93*
Grady, Edward F. 1936- *St&PR 93*
Grady, Gilbert Robidoux, Jr. 1936- *St&PR 93*
Grady, Gregory 1945- *WhoE 93*
Grady, Harvell 1949- *St&PR 93*
Grady, Henry Woodfin 1850-1889 *BioIn 17, JrnUS*
Grady, James (Thomas) 1949- *WhoWrEP 92*
Grady, John *BioIn 17*
Grady, John F. 1929- *WhoAm 92*
Grady, John Joseph 1920- *WhoAm 92*
Grady, Kevin T. *Law&B 92*
Grady, Lee Timothy 1937- *WhoAm 92*
Grady, Maureen Frances 1960- *WhoWor 93*
Grady, Perry Linwood 1940- *WhoSSW 93*
Grady, Stafford Robert 1921- *St&PR 93*
Grady, Thomas J. 1914- *WhoAm 92*
Grady, Thomas Michael *Law&B 92*
Grady, Wayne 1948- *WhoCanL 92*
Grady, Wayne Desmond 1957- *WhoAm 92*
Grady, William Earl 1953- *WhoWor 93*
Grady, William G. 1932- *WhoAm 92*
Gradziel, Carol Elizabeth 1950- *WhoAmW 93*
Grae, Camarin *ScF&FL 92*
Graeb, Thelma Savard 1934- *WhoAmW 93*
Graebner, Carol F. *Law&B 92*
Graebner, Fritz 1877-1934 *IntDcAn*
Graebner, James Herbert 1940- *WhoAm 92*
Graebner, Norman Arthur 1915- *WhoAm 92*
Graedon, Joe David 1945- *WhoSSW 93*
Graef, Luther William 1931- *WhoAm 92*
Graef, Volkmar 1931- *WhoScE 91-3*
Graeff, David Wayne 1946- *WhoE 93, WhoEmL 93*
Graeffe, Gunnar Thor 1935- *WhoScE 91-4*
Graeme, Bruce 1900-1982 *ScF&FL 92*
Graener, Paul 1872-1944 *Baker 92, OxDcOp*
Graening, Paige L. *Law&B 92*
Graepel, Barbara Jean 1958- *WhoAmW 93*
Graese, Clifford Ernest 1927- *WhoAm 92*
Graeser, Wolfgang 1906-1928 *Baker 92*
Graesser, Carl 1929-1989 *BioIn 17*
Graessley, William Walter 1933- *WhoAm 92*
Graettinger, John Sells 1921- *WhoAm 92, WhoWor 93*
Graetz, Michael J. 1944- *WhoAm 92*
Graetzel, Michael 1944- *WhoScE 91-4*
Graetzer, Guillermo 1914- *Baker 92*
Graf, Alan B., Jr. 1953- *St&PR 93*
Graf, Ann B. *Law&B 92*
Graf, Donald L. 1937- *St&PR 93*
Graf, Donald Leroy 1937- *WhoAm 92*
Graf, Doran H. 1931- *St&PR 93*
Graf, Dorothy Ann 1935- *WhoAmW 93*
Graf, Edward Louis 1938- *St&PR 93*
Graf, Edward Louis, Jr. 1938- *WhoAm 92*
Graf, Engelbert F. 1922- *WhoScE 91-3*
Graf, Eric K. *Law&B 92*
Graf, Erich Louis 1948- *WhoAm 92*
Graf, Gary R. 1947- *WhoWrEP 92*
Graf, George N., Jr. 1933- *St&PR 93*
Graf, Heiner 1943- *WhoScE 91-3*
Graf, Herbert 1903-1973 *Baker 92*
Graf, Herbert 1904-1973 *IntDcOp, OxDcOp*
Graf, Horst *Law&B 92*
Graf, James E. 1947- *St&PR 93*
Graf, Jeffrey Howard 1955- *WhoE 93*
Graf, John C. 1948- *St&PR 93*
Graf, John Christian, Jr. 1948- *WhoEmL 93*
Graf, John Kenneth *St&PR 93*
Graf, Joseph Charles 1928- *WhoAm 92, WhoSSW 93*
Graf, Kermit Wilmer 1952- *WhoE 93*
Graf, L.R. 1946- *St&PR 93*
Graf, Larry W. 1938- *St&PR 93*
Graf, Max 1873-1958 *Baker 92*
Graf, Paul E. 1944- *St&PR 93*
Graf, Paul Edward 1944- *WhoAm 92*
Graf, Peter *BioIn 17*
Graf, Peter Gustav 1936- *WhoAm 92, WhoE 93*
Graf, Robert Arlan 1933- *St&PR 93, WhoAm 92*
Graf, Roland 1934- *DrEEuF*
Graf, Steffi *BioIn 17*
Graf, Steffi 1969- *WhoAm 92, WhoWor 93*
Graf, Thomas 1944- *WhoScE 91-3*
Graf, Thomas J. 1948- *WhoIns 93*
Graf, Truman Frederick 1922- *WhoAm 92*
Graf, Ulrich 1943- *WhoScE 91-4*
Graf, Walter 1903-1982 *Baker 92*
Graf, Walter 1929- *WhoScE 91-3*
Graf, Walter 1933- *WhoScE 91-4*
Graf, Walter 1941- *WhoScE 91-4*
Graf, Wayne 1943- *St&PR 93*
Graf, Zinita *AmWomPl*
Grafarend, Erik Wilhelm 1939- *WhoWor 93*
Grafe, Donna Sue 1957- *WhoAmW 93*
Grafe, Karl J. *Law&B 92*
Grafe, Vicki C. *BioIn 17*
Grafe, Warren Blair 1954- *WhoEmL 93, WhoWor 93*
Graff, Cynthia Stamper 1953- *WhoAmW 93*
Graff, David Austin 1949- *WhoE 93*
Graff, George Stephen 1917- *WhoAm 92*
Graff, Guy L.A. 1932- *WhoScE 91-2*
Graff, Harold 1932- *WhoAm 92, WhoWor 93*
Graff, Henry Franklin 1921- *WhoAm 92, WhoWor 93*
Graff, Hettie Westbrook Murphy 1928- *WhoE 93*
Graff, J. William 1930- *WhoWrEP 92*
Graff, John R. 1935- *St&PR 93*
Graff, Louise M. *AmWomPl*
Graff, M.B. *Law&B 92*
Graff, Marguerite Scifo 1919- *WhoSSW 93*
Graff, Marnette Kathleen 1951- *WhoAmW 93*
Graff, Michael H. 1943- *St&PR 93*
Graff, Milton Arthur 1929- *St&PR 93*
Graff, Morris U. 1920- *St&PR 93*
Graff, Philip 1931- *St&PR 93*
Graff, Philippe 1941- *WhoScE 91-2*
Graff, Randy 1955- *WhoAmW 93, WhoE 93*
Graff, Robert Alan 1953- *WhoWor 93*
Graff, Roger David 1955- *St&PR 93*
Graff, Stephen Ney 1934- *WhoAm 92, WhoWor 93*
Graff, Stuart Leslie 1945- *WhoAm 92*
Graff, William 1925- *WhoAm 92*
Graff, William M. 1940- *St&PR 93*
Graffeo, Anthony P. 1947- *St&PR 93*
Graffeo, Anthony Salvatore 1938- *St&PR 93*
Graffigna, Achille 1816-1896 *Baker 92*
Graffigna-Sperling, Carlotta 1955- *WhoUN 92*
Graffigny, Francoise d'Issembourg d'Happoncourt de 1695-1758 *BioIn 17*
Graffin, Guillaume *WhoAm 92*
Graffis, Kathleen McDermott 1953- *WhoEmL 93*
Graffman, Gary 1928- *Baker 92, WhoAm 92*
Grafft, B.C. 1911- *St&PR 93*
Grafft, James 1950- *St&PR 93*
Grafigny, Mme de 1695-1758 *BioIn 17*
Grafigny, Francoise d'Issembourg d'Happoncourt de 1695-1758 *BioIn 17*
Grafin von Bethusy-Huc, Viola Marie Elisabeth Sibylle 1927- *WhoWor 93*
Grafke, Alfred G. 1940- *St&PR 93*
Grafstein, Bernice *WhoAm 92*
Grafstein, Norm 1944- *St&PR 93*
Grafstrom, Jan Olof 1951- *St&PR 93*
Graft, M. Lee *Law&B 92*
Grafton, Clive Llewellyn 1930- *WhoAm 92*
Grafton, Edwin Gulledge 1916- *WhoSSW 93*
Grafton, Eugene S. 1930- *St&PR 93*
Grafton, Robert Bruce 1935- *WhoE 93*
Grafton, Sue 1940- *WhoAmW 93*
Grafton, T.J. 1949- *St&PR 93*
Graf von Schweinitz, Konstantin Nikolaus 1961- *WhoWor 93*

Graf zu Rantzau, Detlev 1930- *WhoUN 92*
Gragasin, Jose Valliente 1900- *WhoWrEP 92*
Gragert, Steven Keith 1950- *WhoEmL 93, WhoSSW 93*
Gragg, Gary S. 1959- *St&PR 93*
Gragg, Perry Earl 1929- *WhoSSW 93*
Gragg, Thomas P. 1950- *St&PR 93*
Gragnola, John B. 1929- *St&PR 93*
Grah, Karen Elizabeth 1953- *WhoAmW 93, WhoEmL 93*
Graham, Aaron Richard 1944- *WhoE 93*
Graham, Albert Bruce 1919- *WhoAm 92*
Graham, Albert Darlington, Jr. 1948- *WhoE 93, WhoEmL 93, WhoWor 93*
Graham, Alberta Newsome 1955- *WhoAmW 93*
Graham, Alex 1917-1991 *AnObit 1991*
Graham, Alexander John 1930- *WhoAm 92*
Graham, Alicia Marie 1964- *WhoAmW 93*
Graham, Allister P. 1936- *St&PR 93*
Graham, Angus Frederick 1916- *WhoAm 92*
Graham, Anna Regina 1947- *WhoEmL 93*
Graham, Arnold Harold 1917- *WhoAm 92*
Graham, B. Paige 1953- *St&PR 93*
Graham, Barbara F. 1950- *WhoE 93*
Graham, Barbara Jeannette 1936- *WhoAmW 93*
Graham, Beardsley 1914- *WhoAm 92*
Graham, Bernard Allen 1933- *WhoE 93*
Graham, Bett Fairbanks- *BioIn 17*
Graham, Betty Gay 1942- *WhoSSW 93*
Graham, Bill *BioIn 17*
Graham, Bill 1931-1991 *AnObit 1991, News 92*
Graham, Billy d1992 *NewYTBS 92*
Graham, Billy 1918- *BioIn 17, News 92 [port], WhoAm 92*
Graham, Billy 1923-1992 *BioIn 17*
Graham, Bob 1936- *CngDr 91*
Graham, Bob 1942- *BioIn 17*
Graham, Bruce Douglas 1915- *WhoAm 92*
Graham, Bruce John 1925- *WhoAm 92*
Graham, Bryan Alaster 1962- *WhoEmL 93*
Graham, Calvin L. d1992 *NewYTBS 92 [port]*
Graham, Cameron R. *Law&B 92*
Graham, Camille Frances 1960- *WhoAmW 93*
Graham, Carl Francis 1915- *WhoAm 92*
Graham, Carol Ethlyn 1941- *WhoAmW 93*
Graham, Catharine Macaulay 1731-1791 *BioIn 17*
Graham, Catherine Creighton 1947- *WhoSSW 93*
Graham, Charles, Jr. 1940- *WhoE 93*
Graham, Charles Eugene 1930- *WhoSSW 93*
Graham, Charles George 1946- *St&PR 93*
Graham, Charles John 1929- *WhoAm 92*
Graham, Charles Passmore 1927- *WhoAm 92*
Graham, Charlotte Raye 1958- *WhoAmW 93*
Graham, Christopher 1946- *WhoEmL 93*
Graham, Christopher Forbes *WhoScE 91-1*
Graham, Clark A. 1950- *St&PR 93*
Graham, Clayton James 1942- *St&PR 93*
Graham, Clayton R. 1950- *ConGAN*
Graham, Clyde Benjamin, Jr. 1931- *WhoAm 92*
Graham, Colin *WhoAm 92*
Graham, Colin 1931- *IntDcOp [port], OxDcOp*
Graham, Cora Joyce 1948- *WhoAmW 93*
Graham, Cosmo 1956- *ConAu 138*
Graham, Craig Edmund 1955- *WhoEmL 93*
Graham, Curly Bill *BioIn 17*
Graham, Cynthia Armstrong 1950- *St&PR 93, WhoAm 92, WhoAmW 93*
Graham, D.C. *WhoScE 91-1*
Graham, D. Richard 1944- *St&PR 93*
Graham, D. Robert Bob 1936- *WhoSSW 93*
Graham, David 1919- *ScF&FL 92*
Graham, David 1947- *WhoE 93*
Graham, David Ian *WhoScE 91-1*
Graham, David Tredway 1917- *WhoAm 92*
Graham, Dayton *BioIn 17*
Graham, Dean S. 1955- *St&PR 93*
Graham, Dee McDonald 1927- *WhoAm 92*
Graham, Dellas Ray 1934- *St&PR 93*
Graham, Diana *Law&B 92*
Graham, Dianne *BioIn 17*
Graham, Don B. 1940- *ConAu 39NR*
Graham, Don Ballew 1940- *WhoAm 92*
Graham, Donald B. 1940- *St&PR 93*
Graham, Donald Edward 1945- *St&PR 93, WhoAm 92, WhoE 93*
Graham, Dorothy Ruth 1944- *WhoWor 93*
Graham, Doug 1942- *WhoAsAP 91*
Graham, Douglas C. 1957- *St&PR 93*
Graham, Edward 1765?-1833 *BioIn 17*
Graham, Edward Henry *Law&B 92*
Graham, Elizabeth Ann 1965- *WhoAmW 93*
Graham, Eric Kevin 1963- *WhoSSW 93*
Graham, Evelyne Moore 1929- *WhoSSW 93*
Graham, Ford Mulford 1911- *WhoAm 92*
Graham, Frances Keesler 1918- *WhoAm 92, WhoAmW 93, WhoE 93*
Graham, Frances Kelso 1938- *BioIn 17*
Graham, Francis Ronald 1920- *WhoAm 92*
Graham, Frank Porter 1886-1972 *EncAACR*
Graham, Fred *BioIn 17*
Graham, Fred Patterson 1931- *JrnUS, WhoAm 92*
Graham, Frederick E. *St&PR 93*
Graham, Frederick Mitchell 1921- *WhoAm 92*
Graham, G.C. *Law&B 92*
Graham, G. Edwin 1924- *WhoAm 92*
Graham, Gail *DcAmChF 1960*
Graham, George *BioIn 17*
Graham, George A. 1909- *St&PR 93*
Graham, George Adams 1904- *WhoAm 92*
Graham, George Gordon 1923- *WhoAm 92*
Graham, George Malcolm Roger 1939- *WhoWor 93*
Graham, Greta J. *Law&B 92*
Graham, Greta Jouce *Law&B 92*
Graham, Hampton Davidson, Jr. 1945- *St&PR 93, WhoAm 92*
Graham, Hardy Moore 1912- *WhoSSW 93, WhoWor 93*
Graham, Harold Grove, Jr. 1929- *St&PR 93*
Graham, Heather *ScF&FL 92*
Graham, Hilary *WhoScE 91-1*
Graham, Howard Barrett 1929- *WhoAm 92*
Graham, Howard H. 1947- *St&PR 93*
Graham, Howard Holmes 1947- *WhoAm 92, WhoEmL 93*
Graham, Howard Lee 1934- *St&PR 93*
Graham, Howard Lee, Sr. 1942- *WhoSSW 93, WhoWor 93*
Graham, Hugh Davis 1936- *WhoAm 92*
Graham, Irene T. 1921- *St&PR 93*
Graham, Irwin Patton 1927- *WhoAm 92*
Graham, J.F. *WhoScE 91-1*
Graham, Jack N. 1931- *St&PR 93*
Graham, James 1907-1991 *BioIn 17*
Graham, James 1929- *BioIn 17, WhoWor 93*
Graham, James Bernard 1923- *WhoAm 92*
Graham, James Cornelius Ruddell 1950- *WhoEmL 93*
Graham, James E. 1953- *St&PR 93*
Graham, James Edmund 1933- *WhoAm 92*
Graham, James Herbert 1921- *WhoAm 92, WhoWor 93*
Graham, James Otis *BioIn 17*
Graham, James Robert, III 1943- *WhoAm 92*
Graham, Janet Ellen 1941- *WhoAmW 93*
Graham, Jarlath John 1919- *WhoAm 92*
Graham, Jay Elmer 1922- *WhoWor 93*
Graham, Jean *ScF&FL 92*
Graham, Joe Michael 1952- *WhoWrEP 92*
Graham, Joel Michael *Law&B 92*
Graham, John 1908-1991 *BioIn 17*
Graham, John Albert 1942- *WhoAm 92*
Graham, John Borden 1918- *WhoAm 92*
Graham, John Brett 1959- *WhoEmL 93*
Graham, John Collins 1952- *WhoIns 93*
Graham, John Dalby 1937- *WhoAm 92*
Graham, John E. 1938- *St&PR 93*
Graham, John Finlayson 1924-1990 *BioIn 17*
Graham, John Francis 1948- *WhoE 93*
Graham, John Gourlay 1938- *St&PR 93*
Graham, John H., IV *St&PR 93*
Graham, John Joseph 1939- *St&PR 93*
Graham, John MacAdam 1943- *WhoWor 93*
Graham, John R. 1945- *St&PR 93, WhoIns 93*
Graham, John Robert, Jr. 1930- *WhoAm 92*
Graham, John Ruskin 1909-1990 *BioIn 17*
Graham, John Webb 1912- *St&PR 93, WhoAm 92, WhoE 93*
Graham, Jon Fredrick 1952- *WhoEmL 93*
Graham, Jorie 1951- *DcLB 120 [port], WhoAmW 93*
Graham, Jul Eliot 1953- *WhoEmL 93*
Graham, Katharine *BioIn 17*
Graham, Katharine 1917- *St&PR 93, WhoAm 92, WhoAmW 93, WhoE 93, WhoWor 93*
Graham, Katharine (Meyer) 1917- *DcLB 127 [port]*
Graham, Katherine Meyer 1917- *JrnUS*
Graham, Kathleen Margaret 1913- *WhoAm 92*
Graham, Kenneth Robert 1943- *WhoE 93*
Graham, Kenneth W. 1938- *ScF&FL 92*
Graham, Kent Hill 1937- *WhoSSW 93*
Graham, Kirsten R. 1946- *WhoAmW 93, WhoEmL 93, WhoWor 93*
Graham, Lanier 1940- *WhoAm 92, WhoWor 93*
Graham, Larry 1946- *SoulM*
Graham, Larry H. 1947- *St&PR 93*
Graham, Laurie *BioIn 17*
Graham, Lawrence *BioIn 17*
Graham, Lawrence E. *Law&B 92*
Graham, Lawrence E. 1936- *WhoIns 93*
Graham, Lawrence Edward *Law&B 92*
Graham, Lawrence Edward 1936- *St&PR 93*
Graham, Lawrence Lee 1935- *WhoSSW 93*
Graham, Lawrence Sherman 1936- *WhoSSW 93*
Graham, Lois Charlotte 1917- *WhoAmW 93, WhoWor 93*
Graham, Lola Amanda 1896- *WhoAm 92, WhoAmW 93, WhoWor 93*
Graham, Lola Amanda Beall 1896- *WhoWrEP 92*
Graham, Loren Raymond 1933- *WhoAm 92*
Graham, Lorenz 1902-1989 *BlkAull 92*
Graham, Lorenz B. 1902-1989 *BioIn 17*
Graham, Lorenz (Bell) 1902- *DcAmChF 1960*
Graham, Lorenz (Bell) 1902-1989 *MajAI [port]*
Graham, Louis 1939- *AfrAmBi*
Graham, M.A. 1947- *WhoScE 91-1*
Graham, Malcolm Scott 1932- *St&PR 93*
Graham, Manta S. 1883- *AmWomPl*
Graham, Marsha *St&PR 93*
Graham, Martha *BioIn 17*
Graham, Martha 1894-1991 *AnObit 1991*
Graham, Mary *AmWomPl*
Graham, Mary Anne 1947- *WhoAmW 93*
Graham, Mary E. 1945- *WhoAmW 93*
Graham, Mary Fawcett 1959- *WhoAmW 93*
Graham, Maury 1917- *BioIn 17*
Graham, Michael D. 1956- *St&PR 93*
Graham, Nan Wood d1990 *BioIn 17*
Graham, Neil Bonnette *WhoScE 91-1*
Graham, Neil Bonnette 1933- *WhoWor 93*
Graham, Neil H. 1933- *St&PR 93*
Graham, Nicholas *BioIn 17*
Graham, Nicol G. 1952- *St&PR 93*
Graham, Norman Christopher *WhoScE 91-1*
Graham, Norman Lewis 1934- *St&PR 93*
Graham, Otis Livingston, Jr. 1935- *WhoAm 92*
Graham, Otto 1921- *BioIn 17*
Graham, Otto Everett, Jr. 1921- *WhoAm 92*
Graham, Patricia Albjerg 1935- *WhoAm 92*
Graham, Patrick Francis 1940- *WhoAm 92*
Graham, Perry Page 1956- *WhoEmL 93*
Graham, Peter William 1951- *WhoSSW 93*
Graham, Philip Leslie 1915-1963 *DcLB 127 [port]*
Graham, Precious Jewel 1925- *WhoAm 92*
Graham, R.B. Cunninghame 1852-1936 *BioIn 17*
Graham, Raymond J. *St&PR 93*
Graham, Rhea Lydia 1952- *WhoAm 92, WhoEmL 93*
Graham, Richard 1941- *WhoAm 92*
Graham, Richard A. 1947- *St&PR 93*
Graham, Richard Douglas 1947- *WhoSSW 93*
Graham, Richard Harper 1911- *WhoAm 92*
Graham, Richard Newell 1947- *WhoSSW 93, WhoWor 93*
Graham, Richard R. 1950- *St&PR 93*
Graham, Richard Zoll 1929- *St&PR 93*
Graham, Robert *ScF&FL 92*
Graham, Robert Arlington 1938- *WhoAm 92*
Graham, Robert C. 1925- *WhoAm 92*
Graham, Robert Clare, III 1955- *WhoEmL 93*
Graham, Robert Davis *Law&B 92*
Graham, Robert Davis 1948- *WhoIns 93*
Graham, Robert Grant 1931- *St&PR 93, WhoAm 92*
Graham, Robert Klark 1906- *WhoWor 93*
Graham, Robert William 1922- *WhoAm 92*
Graham, Ronald Eugene 1955- *WhoSSW 93*
Graham, Ronald F. 1951- *WhoEmL 93*
Graham, Ronald Jonathan, Jr. 1963- *WhoSSW 93*
Graham, Ronald Lewis 1935- *WhoAm 92*
Graham, Ronny 1919- *BioIn 17*
Graham, Russell D. 1930- *St&PR 93*
Graham, Sam R. 1941- *St&PR 93*
Graham, Saxon 1922- *WhoAm 92*
Graham, Seymour C. 1914- *St&PR 93*
Graham, Sharon Shanks 1946- *WhoAmW 93*
Graham, Sheilah *BioIn 17*
Graham, Sheilah 1904-1989 *JrnUS*
Graham, Sheldon Marcellus 1954- *WhoE 93*
Graham, Shirley 1906-1977 *BioIn 17*
Graham, Shirley 1907-1977 *AmWomPl*
Graham, Shirley Lola 1906-1977 *BlkAull 92*
Graham, Stephen Douglas Andrews 1955- *WhoAm 92*
Graham, Stephen Michael 1951- *WhoEmL 93*
Graham, Stuart Edward 1946- *St&PR 93, WhoAm 92*
Graham, Susan Lois 1942- *WhoAm 92*
Graham, Sylvia Swords 1935- *WhoAmW 93*
Graham, Theodora Rapp 1938- *WhoAmW 93*
Graham, Thomas, Jr. 1933- *WhoAm 92*
Graham, Thomas C. 1927- *St&PR 93*
Graham, Thomas Carlisle 1927- *WhoAm 92*
Graham, Thomas Hardy 1945- *St&PR 93*
Graham, Thomas Pegram, Jr. 1937- *WhoAm 92*
Graham, Tony d1992 *BioIn 17, NewYTBS 92 [port]*
Graham, Tony M. 1949- *WhoAm 92*
Graham, Victor Ernest 1920- *WhoAm 92, WhoWrEP 92*
Graham, Vincent Gradford 1964- *WhoEmL 93*
Graham, Violetta G. Peterson 1902-1989 *BioIn 17*
Graham, W.R. *WhoScE 91-1*
Graham, Walter E. *Law&B 92*
Graham, Wesley Thomas *Law&B 92*
Graham, William A. *MiSFD 9*
Graham, William A. 1930?- *ConTFT 10*
Graham, William Arthur 1921- *St&PR 93*
Graham, William Aubrey, Jr. 1930- *WhoSSW 93, WhoWor 93*
Graham, William B. 1911- *St&PR 93, WhoAm 92, WhoWor 93*
Graham, William Edgar, Jr. 1929- *St&PR 93, WhoAm 92*
Graham, William Franklin 1918- *WhoAm 92*
Graham, William Henry *Law&B 92*
Graham, William James 1923- *WhoAm 92*
Graham, William Patton, III 1934- *WhoAm 92*
Graham, William Robert 1937- *WhoAm 92, WhoWor 93*
Graham, William Thomas 1933- *WhoSSW 93*
Graham, William Thomas, III 1950- *WhoEmL 93*
Graham, William W. 1949- *St&PR 93*
Graham, Winifred d1950 *ScF&FL 92*
Grahame, Gloria 1925?-1981 *BioIn 17, IntDcF 2-3 [port]*
Grahame, Kenneth 1859-1932 *ConAu 136, MajAI [port], ScF&FL 92*
Graham-Elliott, Clara Anne 1943- *WhoAmW 93*
Grahame-Smith, D.G. *WhoScE 91-1*
Grahame-White, Claude 1879-1959 *ScF&FL 92*
Graham-Henry, Diane Michelle 1946- *WhoWrEP 92*
Graham-Moore, Brian Edward 1935- *WhoSSW 93*
Grahati, Jan *WhoAmW 93*
Grahl, Timothy Galen 1948- *St&PR 93*
Grahl-Madsen, Atle 1922- *WhoWor 93*
Grahm, Randall *BioIn 17*
Grahmann, Charles V. 1931- *WhoAm 92, WhoSSW 93*
Grahn, Barbara Ascher 1929- *WhoAmW 93*
Grahn, Ulf 1942- *Baker 92*
Grahn, Ulf Ake Wilhelm 1942- *WhoSSW 93*
Grain, Jean 1936- *WhoScE 91-2*
Grainger, Andrew R. *Law&B 92*
Grainger, David William 1927- *St&PR 93*
Grainger, Edmund C., Jr. 1922- *WhoAm 92*
Grainger, John Noel Rowland 1925- *WhoScE 91-3*
Grainger, Martin Allerdale 1874-1941 *BioIn 17*
Grainger, Nessa *WhoE 93*

Grainger, (George) Percy (Aldridge) 1882-1961 *Baker 92*
Grainger, Peter *WhoScE 91-1*
Grainger, Stephen Richard William *WhoScE 91-1*
Grala, Jane Marie *WhoWor 93*
Gralapp, Marcelee Gayl 1931- *WhoAmW 93*
Gralen, Donald John 1933- *WhoAm 92*
Gralish, Tom *WhoE 93*
Grall, N. *Law&B 92*
Grall, Yvon Jean-Pierre 1936- *WhoWor 93*
Gralla, Arthur R. *St&PR 93*
Gralla, Eugene 1924- *St&PR 93, WhoAm 92*
Gralla, Lawrence 1930- *WhoAm 92*
Gralla, Milton 1928- *WhoAm 92*
Grallo, Richard Martin 1947- *WhoE 93*
Gram, Anita Marie 1950- *WhoE 93*
Gram, Christian 1932- *WhoScE 91-2*
Gram, Christine Elise 1924- *WhoAmW 93*
Gram, Hans 1754-1804 *Baker 92*
Gram, Peder 1881-1956 *Baker 92*
Gram, William H. *Law&B 92*
Gram, William Harold 1937- *St&PR 93*
Gramaccioli, Carlo Maria 1935- *WhoScE 91-3*
Gramain, Jean-Claude 1937- *WhoScE 91-2*
Gramatges, Harold 1918- *Baker 92*
Gramatidis, Yanos 1952- *WhoWor 93*
Gramatky, Hardie 1907-1979 *MajAI [port]*
Grambasch, Donald (John) 1927-1983 *Baker 92*
Grambling, Lois G. 1927- *SmATA 71 [port]*
Grambow, Martin E. *Law&B 92*
Grambs, Jean Dresden 1919-1989 *BioIn 17*
Gramchev, Todor Vassilev 1956- *WhoWor 93*
Gramelspacher, Glenn H. 1925- *St&PR 93*
Gramer, George Kerr, Jr. 1952- *WhoEmL 93*
Grames, Conan P. *Law&B 92*
Gramke, Donald J. *Law&B 92*
Gramley, Lyle E. *BioIn 17*
Gramlich, Allan A. 1925- *St&PR 93*
Gramling, George F., III *Law&B 92*
Gramling, John Sheriff 1956- *WhoSSW 93*
Gramling, Mitzi Tousman *Law&B 92*
Gramling, Oliver S. d1992 *NewYTBS 92*
Gramling, Oliver S. 1904-1992 *BioIn 17*
Gramm, Barbara Fairchild 1936- *WhoWrEP 92*
Gramm, Donald (John) 1927-1983 *Baker 92*
Gramm, Frank G. *Law&B 92*
Gramm, Phil 1942- *CngDr 91*
Gramm, Wendy Lee *WhoAm 92, WhoAmW 93*
Gramm, Wendy Lee 1945- *BioIn 17*
Gramm, William Philip 1942- *PolPar, WhoAm 92, WhoSSW 93*
Gramman, E.G. 1922- *St&PR 93*
Grammann, Karl 1844-1897 *Baker 92*
Grammaticas, W. *St&PR 93*
Grammatico, Maria *BioIn 17*
Grammatikov, Vladimir 1942- *DrEEuF*
Grammeltvedt, A. *WhoScE 91-4*
Grammenopoulos, Anthony Filios 1948- *WhoE 93, WhoEmL 93*
Grammer, Frank Clifton 1943- *WhoSSW 93*
Grammer, Kelsey *BioIn 17, WhoAm 92*
Gramont, John R., Jr. *Law&B 92*
Gramont, Sanche de *ScF&FL 92*
Grams, Armin Edwin 1924- *WhoE 93*
Grams, Jack I. 1943- *St&PR 93*
Grams, Jerry J. 1930- *St&PR 93*
Grams, William E. 1943- *St&PR 93*
Grams, William Edmund 1943- *WhoIns 93*
Gramsci, Antonio 1891-1937 *BioIn 17, DcTwHis*
Gramse, Richard G. 1935- *St&PR 93*
Gramza, Felix J. 1934- *St&PR 93*
Gran, Gale I. *WhoIns 93*
Gran, James M. *Law&B 92*
Granacki, Victoria Ann 1947- *WhoEmL 93*
Granada, Jose Rolando 1950- *WhoWor 93*
Granados, Edoardo 1894-1928 *OxDcOp*
Granados, Enrique 1867-1916 *BioIn 17, IntDcOp, OxDcOp*
Granados, Onnie *ScF&FL 92*
Granados (y Campina), Eduardo 1894-1928 *Baker 92*
Granados (y Campina), Enrique 1867-1916 *Baker 92*
Granahan, Kathryn Elizabeth 1894-1979 *BioIn 17*
Granahan, Patrick John 1941- *St&PR 93*
Granai, Edwin 1931- *WhoE 93*
Granat, Laurence Ronald 1938- *St&PR 93*
Granat, Robert *WhoWrEP 92*
Granata, Robert John 1934- *St&PR 93*
Granatelli, Andy 1923- *BioIn 17*
Granath, Herbert A. 1928- *St&PR 93, WhoE 93*
Granath, Lars 1931- *WhoScE 91-4*
Granath, Marvin O. *Law&B 92*
Granath, Olof Erik Tryggve 1940- *WhoWor 93*
Granatir, William Louis 1916- *WhoE 93*
Granato, F. Mark 1952- *St&PR 93*
Granato, James R. 1943- *St&PR 93*
Granatstein, Jack Lawrence 1939- *WhoAm 92, WhoWrEP 92*
Granatstein, Victor Lawrence 1935- *WhoAm 92*
Granberg, Per-Ola 1921- *WhoScE 91-4*
Granberry, Clyde Wilfred 1928- *St&PR 93*
Granberry, Edwin Phillips, Jr. 1926- *WhoWor 93*
Granberry, W. Preston *Law&B 92*
Granbery, Edwin Carleton, Jr. 1913- *WhoAm 92*
Granchalek, Dale R. *Law&B 92*
Granchelli, Ralph S. 1955- *WhoEmL 93*
Grancini, Michel'Angelo 1605-1669 *Baker 92*
Grancino *Baker 92*
Grancino, Andrea *Baker 92*
Grancino, Francesco fl. 1715-1746 *Baker 92*
Grancino, Giovanni *Baker 92*
Grancino, Giovanni Battista fl. 1715-1746 *Baker 92*
Grancino, Michel'Angelo 1605-1669 *Baker 92*
Grancino, Paolo *Baker 92*
Grand, Bernard 1928- *St&PR 93*
Grand, Guy *BioIn 17*
Grand, Mary Ann *BioIn 17*
Grand, Paul *BioIn 17*
Grand, Rebecca *ScF&FL 92*
Grand, Richard D. 1930- *WhoAm 92*
Grand, Richard Joseph 1937- *WhoE 93*
Grand, Robert Alan 1948- *WhoSSW 93*
Grand, Sarah 1854-1943 *BioIn 17*
Grandbois, Alain 1900-1975 *BioIn 17*
Grand Central Station *SoulM*
Grandcourt, Robert 1944- *WhoUN 92*
Grand D'Esnon, Antoine 1957- *WhoScE 91-2*
Grande, Brian Craig 1956- *WhoEmL 93*
Grande, Charles W. 1940- *St&PR 93*
Grande, Frank A. 1923- *St&PR 93*
Grande, John *BioIn 17*
Grande, Joseph Anthony 1932- *WhoE 93*
Grande, Rutilio *DcCPCAm*
Grande, Thomas Robert 1952- *WhoEmL 93*
Grande, Virginia A. *Law&B 92*
Grandert, Johnny 1939- *Baker 92*
Grandgent, Charles Malcolm 1953- *WhoE 93*
Grandguillotte, Bruno *Law&B 92*
Grandi, Alessandro c. 1577-1630 *Baker 92*
Grandi, Attilio 1929- *WhoWor 93*
Grandi, Margherita 1894- *Baker 92, OxDcOp*
Grandin, Georges P. 1938- *WhoScE 91-2*
Grandin, Glenn M. 1943- *St&PR 93*
Grandin, Temple 1947- *WhoAmW 93, WhoEmL 93*
Grandinetti, Linda Terese 1947- *WhoAmW 93*
Grandinetti, Michael Lawrence 1960- *WhoEmL 93*
Grandizio, John F. 1943- *St&PR 93*
Grandjany, Marcel (Georges Lucien) 1891-1975 *Baker 92*
Grandjean, Axel Karl William 1847-1932 *Baker 92*
Grandjean, Cyrille Maurice 1959- *WhoEmL 93*
Grandjean, Fernande Julia 1947- *WhoWor 93*
Grandjean, Philippe 1950- *WhoScE 91-2*
Grandjean, Philippe Adam 1950- *WhoWor 93*
Grandle, Ralph W. 1936- *St&PR 93*
Grand-Lubell, Stephanie 1953- *WhoEmL 93*
Grandma Moses 1860-1961 *BioIn 17*
Grandmaster Flash 1958- *SoulM*
Grandolfi, Mia Nicole 1965- *WhoSSW 93*
Grandolfo, Joe Frank 1947- *St&PR 93*
Grandon, Gary Michael 1948- *WhoSSW 93*
Grandon, Pamela Jo 1953- *WhoEmL 93*
Grandon, Raymond Charles 1919- *WhoE 93, WhoWor 93*
Grandone, Eugene 1948- *St&PR 93*
Grandone, Vincenzo 1934- *WhoUN 92*
Grandval, Gilbert 1904-1981 *BioIn 17*
Grandval, Marie de 1830-1907 *BioIn 17*
Grandval, Marie Felicie Clemence de Reiset 1830-1907 *Baker 92*
Grandy, Charles C. 1928- *St&PR 93*
Grandy, Charles Creed 1928- *WhoSSW 93*
Grandy, Fred 1948- *CngDr 91, WhoAm 92*
Grandy, James Frederick 1919- *WhoAm 92*
Grandy, Jay Franklin 1939- *St&PR 93*
Grandy, Leonard A. 1916- *WhoAm 92*
Grandy, Nita Mary 1915- *WhoAm 92, WhoWor 93*
Grandy, Susan Punnen 1956- *WhoAmW 93*
Grandy, Walter Thomas, Jr. 1933- *WhoAm 92*
Granell, Francisco 1944- *WhoWor 93*
Graner, Georges 1933- *WhoScE 91-2*
Graner, Jane *BioIn 17*
Granet, Irving 1924- *WhoE 93*
Granet, Lloyd 1958- *WhoSSW 93*
Granet, Roger B. 1947- *WhoAm 92*
Graney, Marshall John 1939- *WhoSSW 93*
Grangaard, Daniel Robert 1950- *WhoSSW 93*
Grangaard, Paul D. 1958- *St&PR 93*
Grange, John Michael 1943- *WhoScE 91-1*
Grange, Red *BioIn 17*
Grange, Red 1903-1991 *AnObit 1991*
Granger, Alan N. *Law&B 92*
Granger, Beth 1962- *WhoEmL 93*
Granger, Betsy S. *Law&B 92*
Granger, Bill 1941- *WhoAm 92, WhoWor 93, WhoWrEP 92*
Granger, Charles *BioIn 17*
Granger, David 1903- *St&PR 93, WhoAm 92, WhoWor 93*
Granger, David Mason 1952- *WhoSSW 93*
Granger, David William 1951- *WhoEmL 93*
Granger, Dennis Lee 1938- *WhoWrEP 92*
Granger, Douglas Scott 1960- *WhoEmL 93*
Granger, Francis 1792-1868 *PolPar*
Granger, Geddes *DcCPCAm*
Granger, Gordon 1822-1876 *HarEnMi*
Granger, Harvey, Jr. 1928- *St&PR 93, WhoAm 92*
Granger, Helen *DcChlFi*
Granger, Karla Annette 1964- *WhoAmW 93*
Granger, Kay 1943- *WhoAmW 93, WhoSSW 93*
Granger, Lester B. 1896-1976 *EncAACR*
Granger, Lester Blackwell 1896-1976 *BioIn 17*
Granger, Luc Andre 1944- *WhoAm 92*
Granger, Percy 1945- *ConAu 136*
Granger, Philip Richard 1943- *WhoWor 93*
Granger, Pierre 1936- *WhoScE 91-2*
Granger, R.J. *WhoScE 91-1*
Granger, Raymond Earl, III 1948- *St&PR 93*
Granger, Robert Alan 1928- *WhoE 93*
Granger, Stewart 1913- *IntDcF 2-3 [port]*
Granger, Welsey Miles 1951- *WhoSSW 93*
Granholm, Lars G. 1929- *WhoScE 91-4*
Granichstaedten, Bruno 1879-1944 *Baker 92*
Granick, David *BioIn 17*
Granick, Elissa Susan 1953- *St&PR 93*
Granick, Lois Wayne 1932- *WhoAm 92, WhoE 93*
Granick, Michael 1932- *St&PR 93*
Graniczny, Marek 1947- *WhoScE 91-4*
Graniela-Rodriguez, Magda *WhoSSW 93*
Granier, Olivier L. 1959- *WhoWor 93*
Granieri, George John 1939- *WhoE 93*
Granieri, Michael Nicholas 1943- *WhoAm 92, WhoSSW 93*
Granieri, Vincent J. 1957- *St&PR 93*
Granirer, Edmond Ernest 1935- *WhoAm 92*
Granlund, Thomas Arthur 1951- *WhoWor 93*
Grann, Phyllis 1937- *WhoAm 92*
Grannan, Caroline Moira 1954- *WhoAmW 93*
Grannan, Robert J. 1952- *St&PR 93*
Granner, Daryl Kitley 1936- *WhoAm 92*
Grannon, Charles Lee 1915- *St&PR 93*
Grano, Joseph, Jr. *BioIn 17*
Grano, Olavi Johannes 1925- *WhoWor 93*
Granof, Michael H. 1942- *WhoAm 92*
Granoff, Gail P. 1951- *St&PR 93*
Granoff, Gail Patricia *Law&B 92*
Granoff, Gail Patricia 1952- *WhoAm 92*
Granoff, Gary Charles 1948- *WhoE 93, WhoEmL 93, WhoWor 93*
Granofsky, Jack d1992 *NewYTBS 92*
Granops, Marian 1938- *WhoScE 91-4*
Granovetter, Mark 1943- *WhoE 93*
Granowetter, Linda 1951- *WhoEmL 93*
Granowitz, Marian A. d1992 *NewYTBS 92*
Granquist, Victor Martin 1955- *WhoEmL 93*
Granquist, Wayne George 1935- *St&PR 93*
Granstedt, Greta 1907-1987 *SweetSg C*
Granston, David Wilfred 1939- *WhoE 93, WhoWor 93*
Granston, Larry R. 1938- *St&PR 93*
Granstrom, Marvin Leroy 1920- *WhoAm 92*
Grant, A. James 1940- *St&PR 93*
Grant, A.M. *Law&B 92*
Grant, Adrian Maxwell *WhoScE 91-1*
Grant, Adrian Maxwell 1948- *WhoWor 93*
Grant, Alan J. 1925- *WhoAm 92*
Grant, Alexander Marshall 1928- *WhoAm 92*
Grant, Aline *ScF&FL 92*
Grant, Alistair 1925- *BioIn 17*
Grant, Amy *BioIn 17*
Grant, Andrew Merritt 1943- *St&PR 93*
Grant, Anthony 1914- *ScF&FL 92*
Grant, Arnold *Law&B 92*
Grant, Barbara Lee 1946- *WhoAmW 93*
Grant, Barry Keith 1947- *ConAu 138, ScF&FL 92*
Grant, Barry Marvin 1936- *WhoAm 92*
Grant, Betty Dayvault 1940- *WhoAmW 93*
Grant, Betty Ruth 1937- *WhoAmW 93*
Grant, Bob 1954- *St&PR 93*
Grant, Bradley Cameron 1954- *WhoEmL 93*
Grant, Brian *MiSFD 9*
Grant, Bruce E. 1935- *St&PR 93*
Grant, Bruce T. 1931- *St&PR 93*
Grant, Carl N. 1939- *WhoAm 92*
Grant, Carol Sawyer 1962- *WhoE 93*
Grant, Carolyn Virginia 1949- *WhoSSW 93*
Grant, Cary 1904-1986 *BioIn 17, IntDcF 2-3 [port]*
Grant, Charles B. 1944- *St&PR 93*
Grant, Charles Brasfield, III 1951- *St&PR 93*
Grant, Charles L. 1942- *ScF&FL 92*
Grant, Charles L. 1950- *St&PR 93*
Grant, Charles Truman 1946- *WhoAm 92*
Grant, Cheryl 1944- *WhoAm 92, WhoAmW 93*
Grant, Claude De Witt 1944- *WhoWrEP 92*
Grant, Clay *ScF&FL 92*
Grant, Clifford (Scantlebury) 1930- *Baker 92*
Grant, Colin D. *WhoScE 91-1*
Grant, Conrad Joseph 1956- *WhoE 93*
Grant, Cora DeForest *AmWomPl*
Grant, Dale Bezar 1942- *St&PR 93*
Grant, Daniel Angus 1944- *St&PR 93*
Grant, Daniel Ross 1923- *WhoAm 92*
Grant, David *ConTFT 10, ScF&FL 92*
Grant, David A.W. 1949- *WhoScE 91-1*
Grant, David Aaron *Law&B 92*
Grant, David B. 1915- *St&PR 93*
Grant, David James William 1937- *WhoAm 92*
Grant, David Marshall 1955- *ConTFT 10*
Grant, David Morris 1931- *WhoAm 92*
Grant, Dennis Duane 1940- *WhoAm 92*
Grant, Donald B. *St&PR 93*
Grant, Donald M. 1927- *ScF&FL 92*
Grant, Donald W. 1924- *St&PR 93*
Grant, Donna Marie *BioIn 17*
Grant, Duncan 1885-1978 *DcLB DS10*
Grant, Duncan James Corrowr 1885-1978 *BioIn 17*
Grant, Edith Ingram *AfrAmBi*
Grant, Edward *ScF&FL 92*
Grant, Edward 1936- *WhoE 93, WhoWor 93*
Grant, Edward Hector *WhoScE 91-1*
Grant, Edwin R. 1943- *St&PR 93*
Grant, Elizabeth Jane Thurmond 1950- *WhoSSW 93*
Grant, Elmer G. 1925- *St&PR 93*
Grant, Ethel Watts Mumford 1878-1940 *AmWomPl*
Grant, Franklin Dean 1941- *WhoSSW 93*
Grant, Fred T., Jr. 1955- *St&PR 93*
Grant, Frederick Anthony 1949- *WhoAm 92, WhoE 93*
Grant, Gary L., Jr. *Law&B 92*
Grant, George Clifford 1929- *WhoSSW 93*
Grant, George Monro 1835-1902 *BioIn 17*
Grant, Gerald 1938- *WhoE 93*
Grant, Gordon William Burton *WhoScE 91-1*
Grant, Gwen 1940- *ScF&FL 92*
Grant, Gwen(doline Ellen) 1940- *ChlFicS*
Grant, Harry J. 1881-1963 *JrnUS*
Grant, Ian *WhoScE 91-1*
Grant, Ian D.R. *WhoScE 91-1*
Grant, Ian J. 1937- *St&PR 93*
Grant, Ian Stanley 1940- *WhoAm 92, WhoE 93*
Grant, Isabella Horton 1924- *WhoAmW 93*
Grant, J.B. 1940- *WhoWrEP 92*
Grant, Jacquelyn *BioIn 17*
Grant, Jacquelyn 1948- *WhoAmW 93, WhoSSW 93*
Grant, James 1720-1806 *HarEnMi*
Grant, James 1822-1887 *ScF&FL 92*
Grant, James Augustus 1827-1892 *Expl 93 [port]*
Grant, James Colin 1937- *WhoAm 92*

Grant, James Deneale 1932- *WhoAm 92*
Grant, James Francis 1940- *WhoAm 92*
Grant, James Morgan 1943- *St&PR 93*
Grant, James Pineo 1922- *WhoAm 92, WhoUN 92*
Grant, Janet *WhoScE 91-1*
Grant, Jeff 1958- *WhoAsAP 91*
Grant, Jeffery Mark 1956- *WhoSSW 93*
Grant, Jim *BioIn 17*
Grant, Jim 1940- *WhoSSW 93*
Grant, Joan Salzman *Law&B 92*
Grant, Joanne Catherine 1940- *WhoAm 92, WhoAmW 93*
Grant, Joe *Law&B 92*
Grant, John 1949- *ScF&FL 92*
Grant, John Rogers 1956- *WhoSSW 93*
Grant, John Thomas 1920- *WhoAm 92*
Grant, John Wallace 1942- *WhoSSW 93*
Grant, Joseph M. *Law&B 92*
Grant, Joseph M. 1938- *St&PR 93*
Grant, Juanita G. 1930- *WhoAmW 93*
Grant, Julia Dent 1826-1902 *BioIn 17*
Grant, Julie Ann 1958- *WhoEmL 93*
Grant, Julius *WhoScE 91-1*
Grant, Julius 1901-1991 *AnObit 1991*
Grant, Karen Gallagher 1957- *WhoAmW 93*
Grant, Kathryn *ScF&FL 92*
Grant, Kathryn Ann 1946- *WhoEmL 93*
Grant, Kathryn Hoban 1937- *WhoAmW 93*
Grant, Kay Lallier 1951- *WhoSSW 93*
Grant, Kenneth Tyrone 1955- *WhoEmL 93*
Grant, Kim Delayne 1955- *WhoAmW 93*
Grant, Larry L. *Law&B 92*
Grant, Lawrence 1938- *WhoIns 93*
Grant, Lee *BioIn 17*
Grant, Lee 1926?- *IntDcF 2-3*
Grant, Lee 1927- *MiSFD 9*
Grant, Lee 1931- *WhoAm 92*
Grant, Leonard J. 1933- *WhoWor 93*
Grant, Leonard O. *Law&B 92*
Grant, Leonard Tydings 1930- *WhoAm 92*
Grant, Linda Kathleen 1939- *WhoAmW 93*
Grant, Lois Margaret 1937- *WhoSSW 93*
Grant, Marcus 1945- *WhoUN 92*
Grant, Marion Hepburn d1986 *BioIn 17*
Grant, Mark *ScF&FL 92*
Grant, Mark Antonio 1954- *WhoEmL 93*
Grant, Mary Lynn Johnson 1937- *WhoAmW 93*
Grant, Matthew 1934- *St&PR 93*
Grant, Maxwell *ScF&FL 92*
Grant, Merrill Theodore 1932- *WhoAm 92*
Grant, Merwin Darwin 1944- *WhoWor 93*
Grant, Michael 1952- *MiSFD 9*
Grant, Michael Kevin 1961- *WhoE 93*
Grant, Michael Peter 1936- *WhoAm 92, WhoWor 93*
Grant, Miriam Rosenbloum *WhoAmW 93*
Grant, N. Gunnar 1932- *WhoScE 91-4*
Grant, Nicholas John 1915- *St&PR 93, WhoAm 92*
Grant, (William) Parks 1910- *Baker 92*
Grant, Patrick Gerard *Law&B 92*
Grant, Paul Bernard 1931- *WhoAm 92*
Grant, Paul Jared *Law&B 92*
Grant, Penelope 1942- *ScF&FL 92*
Grant, Penny 1959- *WhoAmW 93*
Grant, Peter Mitchell *WhoScE 91-1*
Grant, Phyllis Hunt 1951- *WhoEmL 93*
Grant, Raymond Thomas 1957- *WhoAm 92*
Grant, Rhoda 1902- *WhoAm 92, WhoAmW 93, WhoWor 93*
Grant, Rhondda Elaine Stout *Law&B 92*
Grant, Richard 1952- *ScF&FL 92*
Grant, Richard Evans 1927- *WhoAm 92*
Grant, Richard Lee 1955- *St&PR 93*
Grant, Richard S. 1946- *St&PR 93*
Grant, Rob *ScF&FL 92*
Grant, Robert 1852-1940 *GayN*
Grant, Robert Allen 1905- *WhoAm 92*
Grant, Robert Bruce 1933- *WhoE 93*
Grant, Robert Gobel *Law&B 92*
Grant, Robert James 1937- *WhoE 93*
Grant, Robert L. 1925- *WhoWrEP 92*
Grant, Robert McQueen 1917- *WhoAm 92*
Grant, Robert Nathan 1930- *WhoAm 92*
Grant, Robert Stephen 1942- *WhoWrEP 92*
Grant, Robert Ulysses 1929- *WhoAm 92*
Grant, Robert Yearington 1913- *WhoAm 92*
Grant, Rodney A. *BioIn 17*
Grant, Rodney A. c. 1960- *News 92 [port]*
Grant, Sandra Milliken 1958- *WhoAm 92*
Grant, Sandra Swearingen 1944- *WhoAmW 93*
Grant, Sara Catherine 1950- *WhoAmW 93*
Grant, Sheila Ann *WhoScE 91-1*
Grant, Shirley Mae 1936- *WhoAmW 93*
Grant, Stephen Allen 1938- *WhoAm 92, WhoE 93*
Grant, Stephen R. *Law&B 92*
Grant, Stephen R. 1939- *St&PR 93*
Grant, Steven 1953- *ScF&FL 92*
Grant, Steven C. 1942- *St&PR 93*
Grant, Stuart *Law&B 92*
Grant, Susan 1954- *WhoEmL 93*
Grant, Susan B. 1949- *St&PR 93*
Grant, Susan Irene 1953- *WhoE 93*
Grant, Sydney Robert 1926- *WhoAm 92*
Grant, Thomas 1763-1811 *BioIn 17*
Grant, Thomas James 1957- *WhoEmL 93*
Grant, Thomas Jeffrey *Law&B 92*
Grant, Thomas W. 1951- *St&PR 93*
Grant, Timothy J. 1959- *St&PR 93*
Grant, Tone N. *Law&B 92*
Grant, Ulysses S. 1822-1885 *BioIn 17, PolPar*
Grant, Ulysses Simpson 1822-1885 *CmdGen 1991 [port], HarEnMi*
Grant, Verne Edwin 1917- *WhoAm 92*
Grant, Vernon 1902-1990 *BioIn 17*
Grant, Vicki Cain 1954- *WhoAmW 93*
Grant, Virginia Annette 1941- *WhoAm 92*
Grant, Virginia Lee King 1918- *WhoSSW 93*
Grant, W. Thomas, II 1950- *WhoAm 92*
Grant, Walter Burton 1934- *St&PR 93*
Grant, Walter King, Sr. 1906- *St&PR 93*
Grant, Walter M. *Law&B 92*
Grant, Walter Matthews 1945- *St&PR 93, WhoAm 92*
Grant, William D. 1917- *St&PR 93*
Grant, William Downing 1917- *WhoAm 92*
Grant, William Frederick 1924- *WhoAm 92*
Grant, William John *Law&B 92*
Grant, William Packer, Jr. 1942- *WhoE 93, WhoWor 93*
Grant, William R. 1925- *St&PR 93*
Grant, William Robert 1925- *WhoAm 92*
Grant, William W., III 1932- *St&PR 93*
Grant, William West, III 1932- *WhoAm 92*
Grant-Berger, Lynn 1950- *WhoSSW 93*
Grant-Cobb, Peggy *Law&B 92*
Grant Goldman, Pamela 1961- *WhoEmL 93*
Grantham, Alexandra Etheldred 1867- *AmWomPl*
Grantham, Charles Edward 1950- *WhoSSW 93*
Grantham, Dewey Wesley 1921- *WhoAm 92*
Grantham, Donald 1947- *Baker 92*
Grantham, George Farley 1900-1954 *BiDAMSp 1989*
Grantham, George Leighton 1920- *WhoAm 92*
Grantham, Geraldine Keeney 1931- *WhoAmW 93, WhoSSW 93*
Grantham, Pamela Maas 1962- *WhoAmW 93*
Grantham, Richard Ludwell 1922- *WhoScE 91-2*
Grantham, Richard Robert 1927- *St&PR 93, WhoAm 92*
Grantham, Robert William 1931- *St&PR 93*
Grantham, Thomas Robinson 1738-1786 *BioIn 17*
Grantier, Barry Murdock 1942- *St&PR 93*
Grantley, Robert C. 1949- *St&PR 93*
Grant-Mann, Genie 1951- *WhoEmL 93*
Grants, Andris 1943- *St&PR 93*
Grantzau, Erich 1942- *WhoScE 91-3*
Granum, Robert Marion 1924- *St&PR 93*
Granville, Charles Strecker 1951- *WhoE 93*
Granville-Barker, Harley 1877-1946 *BioIn 17*
Granzer, Friedrich 1926- *WhoScE 91-3*
Granzier, Paul A. *Law&B 92*
Granzier, Paul A. 1927- *St&PR 93*
Grape, Lee d1990 *BioIn 17*
Grapes, David Gene, II 1951- *WhoEmL 93*
Grapes, Marcus Jack 1942- *WhoWrEP 92*
Graphia, Anthony V. 1938- *St&PR 93*
Graphos, Gerald G. 1937- *St&PR 93*
Grapin, Jacqueline G. 1942- *WhoE 93*
Grappe, Ronald E. 1953- *St&PR 93*
Grappelli, Stephane 1908- *Baker 92, WhoAm 92*
Grappelly, Stephane 1908- *Baker 92*
Grapski, Ladd Raymond 1942- *WhoAm 92*
Grare, Didier R. 1956- *WhoScE 91-2*
Gras, Emmanuel Michel 1937- *WhoWor 93*
Gras, Robert 1930- *WhoScE 91-2*
Grasbeck, Gottfrid (Gustaf Unosson) 1927- *Baker 92*
Grasbeck, Ralph G.A. 1930- *WhoScE 91-4*
Grasek, Peter *WhoScE 91-4*
Graser, Merle Lawrence 1929- *St&PR 93, WhoAm 92*
Graskamp, Frederick Allan 1945- *St&PR 93*
Graskemper, Joseph Peter 1951- *WhoEmL 93*
Grasley, Michael Howard 1937- *St&PR 93*
Graslund, L. Christian 1942- *WhoScE 91-4*
Grasmick, Joseph Christian 1949- *WhoEmL 93*
Grasmick, Nana *ScF&FL 92*
Grass, Alex *BioIn 17*
Grass, Alex 1927- *St&PR 93*
Grass, Alexander 1927- *WhoAm 92, WhoE 93*
Grass, Charla Elaine 1949- *WhoSSW 93*
Grass, Gunter 1927- *BioIn 17, DcLB 124 [port], MagSWL [port], ScF&FL 92, WorLitC [port]*
Grass, Gunter Wilhelm 1927- *WhoWor 93*
Grass, Joseph J. *Law&B 92*
Grass, Martin L. 1954- *St&PR 93*
Grass, Martin Lehrman 1954- *WhoAm 92, WhoE 93*
Grassa, Jose Maria 1956- *WhoScE 91-3*
Grasse, Donald Anthony 1929- *St&PR 93*
Grasse, Edwin 1884-1954 *Baker 92*
Grasse, Francois Joseph Paul de 1722-1788 *HarEnMi*
Grasse, John M., Jr. 1927- *WhoSSW 93*
Grasselli, Jeanette Gecsy 1928- *WhoAm 92, WhoAmW 93*
Grasselli, Robert Karl 1930- *WhoAm 92*
Grasser, George Robert 1939- *WhoAm 92*
Grasserbauer, Manfred 1945- *WhoScE 91-4*
Grasset, Bernard 1933- *WhoWor 93*
Grasset, Bernard Michel 1933- *WhoAsAP 91*
Grasshoff, Alex *WhoAm 92*
Grasshoff, Alex 1930- *MiSFD 9*
Grassi, Anthony Michael 1944- *St&PR 93*
Grassi, Anthony Prentice 1944- *WhoAm 92*
Grassi, Carlo 1926- *WhoScE 91-3, WhoWor 93*
Grassi, Cecila *OxDcOp*
Grassi, Dominic J. *BioIn 17*
Grassi, Ellen Elizabeth 1949- *WhoEmL 93*
Grassi, Eugene 1881-1941 *Baker 92*
Grassi, Joseph F. 1949- *WhoE 93*
Grassi, Louis C. 1955- *WhoE 93*
Grassi, Marco 1934- *BioIn 17*
Grassi, Mario 1927- *St&PR 93*
Grassi, Paolo Silvio *Law&B 92*
Grassi, Robert G. *Law&B 92*
Grassie, Norman *WhoScE 91-1*
Grassini, Giuseppina 1773-1850 *OxDcOp*
Grassini, Josephina 1773-1850 *Baker 92*
Grassle, Karen *WhoAm 92*
Grassler, Frank P. *Law&B 92*
Grassley, Charles E. 1933- *CngDr 91*
Grassley, Charles Ernest 1933- *WhoAm 92*
Grassmick, Eugene R. 1928- *St&PR 93*
Grassmuck, George Ludwig 1919- *WhoAm 92*
Grasso, Doreen Marie 1955- *WhoAmW 93, WhoEmL 93*
Grasso, Ella 1919-1980 *BioIn 17*
Grasso, Ella T. 1919-1981 *PolPar*
Grasso, Mary Ann 1952- *WhoAm 92*
Grasso, Patrick 1925- *St&PR 93*
Grasso, Paul *WhoScE 91-1*
Grasso, Randall C. *Law&B 92*
Grasso, Richard A. *WhoAm 92, WhoE 93*
Grasty, Charles H. 1863-1924 *JrnUS*
Grasty, James K. *Law&B 92*
Grasty, Phillip Elwood 1930- *WhoSSW 93*
Grastyan, Endre 1924- *WhoScE 91-4*
Graswich, Vicki *BioIn 17*
Grasz, Lynne Anne Morian 1943- *WhoAmW 93*
Gratch, Linda Vaden 1953- *WhoAmW 93*
Gratch, Serge 1921- *WhoAm 92*
Grathwohl, Joseph A. 1937- *St&PR 93*
Grathwohl, Thomas Judd 1955- *St&PR 93*
Gratian 359-383 *OxDcByz*
Gratianus, Flavius 359-383 *HarEnMi*
Graton, Milton Stanley 1908- *WhoE 93*
Gratovich, Eugene Alexis 1941- *WhoSSW 93*
Grattan, C. Hartley 1902-1980 *ScF&FL 92*
Grattan, Edward Patrick *Law&B 92*
Grattan, George H. 1923- *St&PR 93*
Grattan, Henry 1746-1820 *BioIn 17*
Grattan, John Lawrence 1830-1854 *HarEnMi*
Grattan, Kenneth Thomas Victor 1953- *WhoWor 93*
Grattan, Patricia Elizabeth 1944- *WhoAm 92*
Grattarola, Massimo Italo 1950- *WhoWor 93*
Gratto, Joseph M. 1936- *WhoSSW 93*
Grattoni, Paolo 1946- *WhoScE 91-3*
Gratwick, John 1923- *WhoAm 92*
Gratz, Hyman 1776-1857 *JeAmHC*
Gratz, L. *WhoScE 91-4*
Gratz, Pauline 1924- *WhoAm 92*
Gratz, Rebecca 1781-1869 *BioIn 17*
Gratz, Roy Fred 1942- *WhoSSW 93*
Gratz, Samuel 1920- *St&PR 93*
Gratzer, George Andrew 1936- *WhoAm 92*
Grau, Fred V. 1902-1990 *BioIn 17*
Grau, Gerard 1927- *WhoScE 91-2*
Grau, John Michael 1952- *WhoAm 92, WhoE 93*
Grau, Jorge 1962- *WhoSSW 93*
Grau, Juan Vilarrubias 1917- *WhoWor 93*
Grau, Marcy Beinish 1950- *WhoAmW 93, WhoE 93, WhoWor 93*
Grau, Maurice 1849-1907 *Baker 92, OxDcOp*
Grau, Shirley Ann 1929- *BioIn 17, WhoAm 92, WhoAmW 93, WhoSSW 93, WhoWrEP 92*
Grau, Wilfried 1943- *St&PR 93*
Graubard, Seymour 1911- *WhoAm 92*
Graubard, Stephen Richards 1924- *WhoAm 92*
Graubart, Renee *BioIn 17*
Graudan, Nicolai 1896-1964 *Baker 92*
Graue, Donna Marie 1963- *WhoAmW 93*
Grauer, Allan L. 1930- *WhoAm 92*
Grauer, Eva Marie 1925- *WhoAmW 93, WhoSSW 93, WhoWor 93*
Grauer, Frederick Miller, Jr. 1942- *St&PR 93*
Grauer, Manfred 1945- *WhoWor 93*
Grauer, William Kale, III 1958- *WhoE 93*
Graugnard, F.A., Jr. 1916- *St&PR 93*
Graul, Emil Heinz 1920- *WhoScE 91-3*
Graul, Joseph F. *Law&B 92*
Graul, Lonnie Milton 1952- *St&PR 93*
Graule, Raymond Siegfried 1932- *WhoSSW 93*
Graulich, Robert H. *St&PR 93*
Grauman, Walter 1922- *MiSFD 9*
Graumann, William Albert 1932- *St&PR 93*
Graun, August Friedrich 1698-1765 *OxDcOp*
Graun, August Friedrich 1699-1765 *Baker 92*
Graun, Carl Heinrich 1703?-1759 *OxDcOp*
Graun, Carl Heinrich 1704-1759 *Baker 92, IntDcOp*
Graun, Johann Gottlieb c. 1703-1771 *Baker 92*
Graun, Johann Gottlob 1702?-1771 *OxDcOp*
Graunke, Kurt 1915- *Baker 92*
Graupe, Daniel 1934- *WhoAm 92*
Graupmann, Thomas L. 1957- *St&PR 93*
Graupner, Christoph 1683-1760 *OxDcOp*
Graupner, (Johann) Christoph 1683-1760 *Baker 92*
Graupner, (Johann Christian) Gottlieb 1767-1836 *Baker 92*
Grau San Martin, Ramon *DcCPCAm*
Grauslund, Jorgen 1935- *WhoScE 91-2*
Grava, Donald Walter, Jr. 1955- *WhoE 93, WhoEmL 93*
Gravano, Salvatore *BioIn 17*
Gravatt, Chris-Tina Millen 1947- *WhoE 93*
Grave, Floyd Kersey 1945- *WhoE 93*
Grave, Jean 1854-1939 *BioIn 17*
Gravel, Camille Francis, Jr. 1915- *WhoWor 93*
Gravel, David Charles 1956- *St&PR 93*
Gravel, Francois *WhoCanL 92*
Gravel, Geary 1951- *ScF&FL 92*
Gravel, Helene Cecile 1960- *WhoAmW 93*
Gravel, James 1943- *St&PR 93*
Gravel, John Cook 1947- *WhoEmL 93*
Graveling, Richard Alan 1951- *WhoScE 91-1*
Gravelle, Peter W. 1938- *St&PR 93*
Gravelle, Pierre 1941- *WhoAm 92*
Gravelle, Pierre C. 1931- *WhoScE 91-2*
Gravely, Edward Martin 1945- *St&PR 93*
Gravely, Jane Candace 1952- *WhoAmW 93*
Gravely, Samuel L., Jr. *BioIn 17*
Gravely, Samuel Lee 1922- *AfrAmBi [port]*
Graven, Stanley Norman 1932- *WhoSSW 93*
Graven, Timothy M. 1951- *St&PR 93*
Gravenstein, Joachim Stefan 1925- *WhoAm 92*
Graver, Elizabeth 1965- *ConLC 70 [port]*
Graver, Fred *ScF&FL 92*
Graver, Gary *MiSFD 9*
Graver, Jack Edward 1935- *WhoAm 92*
Graver, Lawrence Stanley 1931- *WhoAm 92*
Graver, Nancy J. 1951- *WhoEmL 93*
Graver, Suzanne Levy 1936- *WhoAmW 93, WhoE 93*
Graversen, Ole 1944- *WhoScE 91-2*
Graversen, Pat 1935- *ScF&FL 92*
Gravert, Hans O. 1928- *WhoScE 91-3*
Graves, Alan Scott 1957- *WhoSSW 93*
Graves, Allen D. d1992 *BioIn 17*
Graves, Austin T. 1908-1991 *BioIn 17*

Graves, Ben E. 1925- *WhoSSW 93*
Graves, Benjamin Barnes 1920- *WhoAm 92*
Graves, Bernard J., Jr. *Law&B 92*
Graves, C. Dean 1957- *WhoSSW 93*
Graves, C. Wayne 1942- *WhoSSW 93*
Graves, Caroline McCall 1947- *WhoWor 93*
Graves, Charles Allen 1941- *St&PR 93*
Graves, Charles E. *Law&B 92*
Graves, Clotilde Inez Mary 1863-1932 *AmWomPl*
Graves, Curtis M. *AfrAmBi [port]*
Graves, Daniel B. *Law&B 92*
Graves, Dean Layton, Jr. *Law&B 92*
Graves, Denise Browne 1948- *WhoE 93*
Graves, Denyce *BioIn 17*
Graves, Denyce Antoinette 1964- *WhoAm 92*
Graves, Dixie Bibb 1882-1965 *BioIn 17*
Graves, Earl G. 1935- *AfrAmBi [port], BioIn 17, St&PR 93*
Graves, Earl Gilbert 1935- *WhoAm 92*
Graves, Ernest, Jr. 1924- *WhoAm 92*
Graves, Frank X. d1990 *BioIn 17*
Graves, Fred Hill 1914- *WhoAm 92*
Graves, G.T., III 1949- *St&PR 93*
Graves, Geoffrey Basil 1928- *WhoScE 91-1*
Graves, Gordon Harwood 1884-1973 *ScF&FL 92*
Graves, H. Brice 1912- *WhoAm 92*
Graves, Harry Hammond 1956- *WhoEmL 93, WhoWor 93*
Graves, Harry M., Jr. 1953- *St&PR 93*
Graves, Herbert C., IV *Law&B 92*
Graves, Howard Dwayne 1939- *WhoAm 92, WhoE 93*
Graves, J. Stanley 1936- *St&PR 93*
Graves, Jean Frankye 1932- *WhoAmW 93*
Graves, Jeanne Reinert 1941- *WhoAmW 93*
Graves, John Alexander 1920- *WhoWrEP 92*
Graves, John Temple 1856-1925 *JrnUS*
Graves, John William 1942- *WhoSSW 93*
Graves, Johnny B., Jr. 1960- *WhoSSW 93*
Graves, Judson 1947- *WhoEmL 93*
Graves, Kathleene J. *Law&B 92*
Graves, Kenneth Martin 1943- *WhoSSW 93*
Graves, Kenny Max 1949- *St&PR 93*
Graves, Lawrence Lester 1917- *WhoAm 92*
Graves, Lorraine Elizabeth 1957- *WhoAm 92*
Graves, Malcolm J. 1932- *St&PR 93*
Graves, Matthew C. 1956- *St&PR 93*
Graves, Maureen Ann 1946- *WhoAmW 93, WhoWor 93*
Graves, Michael 1934- *BioIn 17, WhoAm 92, WhoE 93*
Graves, Nancy 1940- *BioIn 17*
Graves, Nancy Stevenson *WhoAm 92, WhoAmW 93*
Graves, Patrick Lee 1945- *WhoWor 93*
Graves, Peter 1926- *WhoAm 92*
Graves, Pirkko Maija-Leena 1930- *WhoAm 92*
Graves, R.J. *WhoScE 91-1*
Graves, Ralph (Augustus) 1924- *ConAu 138*
Graves, Ralph Huntington 1926- *St&PR 93*
Graves, Ray 1924- *WhoAm 92*
Graves, Ray Reynolds 1946- *WhoAm 92*
Graves, Richard 1715-1804 *BioIn 17*
Graves, Richard H. *DcChlFi*
Graves, Robert 1895-1985 *BioIn 17, MagSWL [port], PoeCrit 6 [port], ScF&FL 92*
Graves, Robert Jackson 1913- *St&PR 93*
Graves, Robert Lawrence 1926- *WhoAm 92*
Graves, Robert Roy 1930- *St&PR 93*
Graves, Ronald N. *Law&B 92*
Graves, Ronald Norman 1942- *St&PR 93*
Graves, Roy Neil 1939- *WhoWrEP 92*
Graves, Roy Stanley 1951- *St&PR 93*
Graves, Ruth *BioIn 17*
Graves, Ruth Parker 1934- *WhoE 93*
Graves, Samuel 1713-1787 *HarEnMi*
Graves, Sandra L. 1943- *WhoAmW 93*
Graves, Sid Foster, Jr. 1946- *WhoSSW 93*
Graves, Thomas c. 1725-1802 *HarEnMi*
Graves, Thomas Ashley, Jr. 1924- *WhoAm 92, WhoE 93*
Graves, Wallace Billingsley 1922- *WhoAm 92*
Graves, Walter Albert 1920- *WhoAm 92*
Graves, Warren 1933- *WhoCanL 92*
Graves, Willard Lee 1940- *WhoE 93*
Graves, William H.B. 1928- *St&PR 93*
Graves, William P. E. 1926- *WhoAm 92, WhoE 93*
Graves, William Preston 1953- *WhoAm 92*
Graves, William Sidney 1865-1940 *HarEnMi*
Graves, William T. 1934- *WhoAm 92*
Graves, William Terrell 1934- *St&PR 93*
Graves-Morris, Peter Russell *WhoScE 91-1*
Gravett, Linda Sue 1950- *WhoEmL 93*
Graveure, Louis 1888-1965 *Baker 92*
Gravgaard, Miles A. 1946- *St&PR 93*
Graville-Flaten, Susan Annette 1952- *WhoAmW 93*
Gravina, Federico Carlos, Duke of 1756-1806 *HarEnMi*
Gravina, John 1930- *St&PR 93*
Gravine, Catherine Ann 1953- *WhoAmW 93*
Gravink, Philip Ton 1935- *St&PR 93*
Gravino, Nelson 1951- *WhoWor 93*
Graviros, Ruth *ConAu 139*
Gravis, Helen Meany d1991 *BioIn 17*
Gravlee, Grace Downing 1913- *WhoWrEP 92*
Gravley, Ernestine Hudlow *WhoWrEP 92*
Grawehr, Mark 1957- *St&PR 93*
Grawemeyer, Joy 1934- *WhoAmW 93*
Gray, Alan 1855-1935 *Baker 92*
Gray, Alan John *WhoScE 91-1*
Gray, Alasdair *BioIn 17*
Gray, Alasdair 1934- *ScF&FL 92*
Gray, Alfred Orren 1914- *WhoAm 92*
Gray, Alice Wirth 1934- *WhoWrEP 92*
Gray, Allen A. *Law&B 92*
Gray, Allen Gibbs 1915- *WhoAm 92*
Gray, Alvin L. 1928- *St&PR 93, WhoAm 92*
Gray, Amlin 1946- *ConAu 138*
Gray, Angela *ScF&FL 92*
Gray, Ann Maynard 1945- *St&PR 93, WhoAmW 93*
Gray, Anthony Rollin 1939- *WhoAm 92, WhoSSW 93*
Gray, Arnold Lee 1945- *WhoE 93*
Gray, Arthur, Jr. 1922- *WhoAm 92*
Gray, Audrey Nesbitt 1920- *WhoAmW 93*
Gray, Augustine Heard, Jr. 1936- *WhoAm 92*
Gray, Aurum 1935- *St&PR 93*
Gray, Barbara Bronson 1955- *WhoAmW 93*
Gray, Barry *BioIn 17*
Gray, Barry Lyndon 1942- *St&PR 93*
Gray, Barry Sherman 1916- *WhoAm 92*
Gray, Barry W. 1931- *St&PR 93*
Gray, Bartley 1952- *St&PR 93*
Gray, Basil 1904-1989 *BioIn 17*
Gray, Betsy d1798 *BioIn 17*
Gray, Beverly Wills 1952- *WhoAmW 93*
Gray, Bonnie Andrea *WhoAmW 93*
Gray, Braley 1941- *St&PR 93*
Gray, Brian Anton 1939- *WhoE 93*
Gray, Brian Mark 1939- *WhoWor 93*
Gray, Brian V. *Law&B 92*
Gray, C. Boyden *BioIn 17*
Gray, C.C. Howard 1949- *St&PR 93*
Gray, C. G. 1927- *WhoSSW 93*
Gray, C. Jackson 1947- *St&PR 93*
Gray, C. Vernon 1939- *AfrAmBi [port]*
Gray, Carl Eugene, Jr. 1950- *WhoSSW 93*
Gray, Carol Hickson 1958- *WhoEmL 93, WhoSSW 93, WhoWor 93*
Gray, Carol Joyce *WhoAm 92*
Gray, Carol Lippert 1950- *WhoWrEP 92*
Gray, Carol M. *Law&B 92*
Gray, Carrie L.P. *Law&B 92*
Gray, Catherine Darlene 1948- *WhoWrEP 92*
Gray, Cecil 1895-1951 *Baker 92*
Gray, Charles Agustus 1938- *WhoAm 92*
Gray, Charles Augustus 1928- *WhoE 93, WhoWor 93*
Gray, Charles Buffum 1934- *WhoAm 92*
Gray, Charles Elmer 1919- *WhoAm 92*
Gray, Charles Jackson 1947- *WhoAm 92*
Gray, Charlinda Davis 1962- *WhoEmL 93*
Gray, Christopher Donald 1951- *WhoEmL 93*
Gray, Clarence Jones 1908- *WhoSSW 93, WhoWor 93*
Gray, Clayland Boyden 1943- *WhoAm 92*
Gray, Clayton Howard 1912- *WhoE 93*
Gray, Cleve 1918- *WhoAm 92*
Gray, Coleen 1922- *SweetSg D*
Gray, Curme 1910-1980 *ScF&FL 92*
Gray, Dahli 1948- *WhoAmW 93, WhoEmL 93*
Gray, Daniel M. *Law&B 92*
Gray, Darlene Agnes 1957- *WhoEmL 93*
Gray, David A. *Law&B 92*
Gray, David G. *Law&B 92*
Gray, David L. *Law&B 92*
Gray, David Lawrence 1930- *WhoAm 92*
Gray, David Martin 1933- *WhoE 93*
Gray, David Ross 1940- *St&PR 93*
Gray, David William 1948- *WhoE 93*
Gray, Deborah Dolia 1952- *WhoAmW 93*
Gray, Deborah Mary 1952- *WhoAmW 93*
Gray, Denis John Pereira *WhoScE 91-1*
Gray, Diane 1941- *WhoAm 92*
Gray, Dobie 1942- *SoulM*
Gray, Don 1935- *WhoE 93*
Gray, Donald Lyman 1929- *WhoSSW 93*
Gray, Donna Mae 1933- *WhoAm 92*
Gray, Duncan Montgomery, Jr. 1926- *WhoAm 92*
Gray, D'Wayne 1931- *WhoAm 92*
Gray, Edman Lowell 1939- *WhoAm 92*
Gray, Edward Barton, Jr. 1924- *WhoE 93*
Gray, Edward John 1930- *WhoAm 92*
Gray, Edward P. *Law&B 92*
Gray, Eileen 1879-1976 *BioIn 17*
Gray, Elizabeth Janet *MajAI*
Gray, Elizabeth Keighley 1958- *WhoAmW 93*
Gray, Ellen M. *St&PR 93*
Gray, Enid Maurine 1943- *WhoAm 92*
Gray, Ernest Paul 1926- *WhoE 93*
Gray, Ethel Cooper *AmWomPl*
Gray, Eunice T. *AmWomPl*
Gray, Festus Gail 1943- *WhoWor 93*
Gray, Frances *AmWomPl*
Gray, Frances M. 1910- *WhoAm 92*
Gray, Francine du Plessix *BioIn 17, WhoAm 92*
Gray, Francine Du Plessix 1930- *WhoWrEP 92*
Gray, Francis Campbell 1940- *WhoAm 92*
Gray, Francis I. *Law&B 92*
Gray, Frank George 1942- *St&PR 93*
Gray, Frank Truan 1920- *WhoAm 92*
Gray, Fred 1942- *St&PR 93*
Gray, Fred L. 1938- *St&PR 93*
Gray, Frederick James *Law&B 92*
Gray, Frederick Thomas, Jr. 1951- *WhoAm 92*
Gray, Frederick William, III 1944- *WhoAm 92*
Gray, G.M. *WhoScE 91-1*
Gray, Gary Michael 1950- *WhoEmL 93*
Gray, George 1840-1925 *PolPar*
Gray, George 1907- *WhoAm 92, WhoWor 93*
Gray, George Francis 1956- *WhoE 93*
Gray, George W. 1940- *St&PR 93*
Gray, George William *WhoScE 91-1*
Gray, Gerald R. 1930- *WhoAm 92*
Gray, Gilda 1898-1959 *PolBiDi*
Gray, Glenn Shelton *Law&B 92*
Gray, Gloria Jean 1948- *WhoSSW 93*
Gray, Gordon Joseph Cardinal 1910- *WhoWor 93*
Gray, Gordon L. 1924- *WhoAm 92*
Gray, Grattan 1925- *St&PR 93*
Gray, Gregory Nolan *Law&B 92*
Gray, Gwen Cash 1943- *WhoAmW 93*
Gray, Hanna 1930- *News 92 [port]*
Gray, Hanna Holborn 1930- *WhoAm 92, WhoAmW 93, WhoWor 93*
Gray, Harold 1894-1968 *BioIn 17*
Gray, Harry B. *BioIn 17*
Gray, Harry Barkus 1935- *WhoAm 92*
Gray, Harry J. 1919- *St&PR 93*
Gray, Harry Jack 1919- *WhoAm 92, WhoWor 93*
Gray, Harry Joshua 1924- *WhoAm 92*
Gray, Henry David 1908- *WhoAm 92, WhoWor 93*
Gray, Hope Diffenderfer 1917- *WhoAm 92, WhoSSW 93*
Gray, Horace 1828-1902 *OxCSupC [port]*
Gray, Howard *WhoWrEP 92*
Gray, Ian Keith 1941- *WhoWor 93*
Gray, Isabel McReynolds *AmWomPl*
Gray, Jack 1927- *WhoCanL 92*
Gray, James 1923- *WhoAm 92*
Gray, James Alexander 1920- *WhoAm 92*
Gray, James Gordon 1919- *St&PR 93*
Gray, James P., II 1953- *St&PR 93*
Gray, James Patrick 1958- *St&PR 93*
Gray, James Peyton 1943- *WhoAm 92*
Gray, James William, Jr. 1928- *St&PR 93*
Gray, Jan Charles *Law&B 92*
Gray, Jan Charles 1947- *WhoEmL 93*
Gray, Jason Stephen 1943- *St&PR 93*
Gray, Jeanne 1917- *WhoAmW 93*
Gray, Jeanne Hull 1946- *WhoAmW 93*
Gray, Jeffrey Alan *WhoScE 91-1*
Gray, Jeffrey Huston *Law&B 92*
Gray, Jeffrey Huston 1950- *St&PR 93*
Gray, Jerry 1915-1976 *Baker 92*
Gray, John *BioIn 17, MiSFD 9*
Gray, John 1946- *WhoCanL 92*
Gray, John Archibald Browne 1918- *WhoWor 93*
Gray, John Augustus 1924- *WhoAm 92*
Gray, John B., Jr. 1951- *WhoIns 93*
Gray, John Bullard 1927- *St&PR 93*
Gray, John D. 1919- *St&PR 93*
Gray, John Delton 1919- *WhoAm 92*
Gray, John Douglas 1945- *St&PR 93*
Gray, John Edmund 1922- *WhoAm 92, WhoWor 93*
Gray, John H. 1939- *St&PR 93*
Gray, John Lathrop, III 1931- *WhoAm 92*
Gray, John Martin Fisher *Law&B 92*
Gray, John Oliver *WhoScE 91-1*
Gray, John P. *St&PR 93*
Gray, John Robert 1952- *WhoE 93*
Gray, John S. 1941- *WhoScE 91-4*
Gray, John Walker 1931- *WhoAm 92*
Gray, John Willard 1935- *WhoE 93*
Gray, John Wylie 1935- *WhoAm 92*
Gray, Joseph W. 1813-1862 *JrnUS*
Gray, Juanita Hamilton 1928- *WhoWor 93*
Gray, Judith Neapolitan 1945- *WhoAmW 93*
Gray, Karla Marie *WhoAm 92, WhoAmW 93*
Gray, Kenneth D. 1940- *St&PR 93*
Gray, Kenneth Eugene 1930- *WhoAm 92*
Gray, Kenneth John 1919- *WhoAm 92*
Gray, Kenneth Wayne 1944- *WhoSSW 93*
Gray, Kerwin L. *Law&B 92*
Gray, Laman A., Jr. 1940- *WhoAm 92*
Gray, Larry A. 1940- *St&PR 93*
Gray, Lawrence Clarke, Jr. 1942- *St&PR 93*
Gray, Lawrence Neal 1953- *WhoE 93*
Gray, Lawrence W. 1948- *St&PR 93*
Gray, Linda *BioIn 17, WhoAm 92*
Gray, Linda Crockett 1943- *ScF&FL 92*
Gray, Linda Diane 1953- *WhoAmW 93*
Gray, Linda Esther 1948- *Baker 92*
Gray, Liz *WhoWrEP 92*
Gray, Lois Howard 1920- *St&PR 93*
Gray, Lorna 1924- *SweetSg C [port]*
Gray, Margaret Ann 1950- *WhoAmW 93*
Gray, Marie Elise 1914- *WhoAmW 93*
Gray, Marvin Lee, Jr. 1945- *WhoAm 92*
Gray, Mary Wheat 1939- *WhoAm 92*
Gray, Maurine *WhoSSW 93*
Gray, Maurisse Taylor 1954- *St&PR 93*
Gray, Melvin 1932- *St&PR 93*
Gray, Michael *ScF&FL 92*
Gray, Michael Charles 1951- *WhoEmL 93*
Gray, Michael Phillip *Law&B 92*
Gray, Mike *MiSFD 9*
Gray, Milton H. 1910- *St&PR 93*
Gray, Milton Hefter 1910- *WhoAm 92*
Gray, Morris 1921- *St&PR 93*
Gray, Morris G. *Law&B 92*
Gray, Myles McClure 1932- *WhoAm 92*
Gray, N.F. 1952- *WhoScE 91-3*
Gray, Nancy Ann Oliver 1951- *WhoAmW 93, WhoEmL 93*
Gray, Nancy Isabel 1950- *WhoAmW 93*
Gray, Neil S. *Law&B 92*
Gray, Nicholas Stuart 1922-1981 *ScF&FL 92*
Gray, Olwen Leigh *WhoWrEP 92*
Gray, Oscar Shalom 1926- *WhoAm 92, WhoE 93, WhoWor 93*
Gray, Patricia A. *Law&B 92*
Gray, Patricia Ellen 1939- *WhoAm 92*
Gray, Patrick Worth 1937- *WhoWrEP 92*
Gray, Paul Edward 1932- *WhoAm 92, WhoE 93, WhoWor 93*
Gray, Paul Russell 1942- *WhoAm 92*
Gray, Paulette Styles 1943- *WhoE 93*
Gray, Percy 1869-1952 *BioIn 17*
Gray, Peter 1954- *St&PR 93*
Gray, Peter Michael David *WhoScE 91-1*
Gray, Philip Elza 1937- *St&PR 93*
Gray, Philip Howard 1926- *WhoAm 92*
Gray, Phyllis Anne 1926- *WhoAm 92*
Gray, Ralph 1915- *WhoAm 92*
Gray, Rhoshon *BioIn 17*
Gray, Richard 1928- *WhoAm 92*
Gray, Richard Alexander, Jr. 1927- *WhoAm 92*
Gray, Richard L. *Law&B 92*
Gray, Richard Michael 1932- *St&PR 93*
Gray, Richard Moss 1924- *WhoWor 93*
Gray, Robert Apsey 1957- *WhoEmL 93*
Gray, Robert Curtis 1946- *WhoE 93*
Gray, Robert Earl 1941- *AfrAmBi*
Gray, Robert Edmond 1938- *St&PR 93*
Gray, Robert Harley 1942- *WhoSSW 93*
Gray, Robert Hugh *WhoScE 91-1*
Gray, Robert K. 1956- *St&PR 93*
Gray, Robert Keith 1923- *St&PR 93, WhoAm 92, WhoE 93*
Gray, Robert Kevin 1953- *WhoEmL 93*
Gray, Robert Molten 1943- *WhoAm 92*
Gray, Robert Steele 1923- *WhoAm 92, WhoSSW 93, WhoWor 93*
Gray, Robin 1931- *WhoAsAP 91*
Gray, Robin Trevor 1940- *WhoAsAP 91*
Gray, Rod *ScF&FL 92*
Gray, Roland William 1947- *WhoEmL 93, WhoSSW 93*
Gray, Ronald *Law&B 92*
Gray, Ronald D. 1942- *WhoAm 92*
Gray, Ronald P. 1939- *St&PR 93*
Gray, Ross E.S. *Law&B 92*
Gray, Ross E.S. 1954- *St&PR 93*
Gray, S. Garrett *Law&B 92*
Gray, Samuel P.M. 1937- *St&PR 93*
Gray, Sarah Virginia 1934- *WhoSSW 93*
Gray, Seymour 1911- *WhoAm 92*
Gray, Sharon Ann 1953- *WhoAmW 93*
Gray, Sheila Hafter 1930- *WhoAm 92, WhoAmW 93, WhoE 93*
Gray, Sheldon 1938- *WhoAm 92*
Gray, Sheldon W. 1938- *St&PR 93*
Gray, Sidney John *WhoScE 91-1*
Gray, Simon James Holliday 1936- *BioIn 17, WhoWor 93*
Gray, Sonia Lee 1957- *WhoEmL 93*

Gray, Spalding NewYTBS 92 [port]
Gray, Spalding 1941- WhoAm 92, WhoWrEP 92
Gray, Spalding 1942?- BioIn 17
Gray, Stephen E. Law&B 92
Gray, Stephen T. 1950- St&PR 93
Gray, Sylvia Inez 1946- WhoAmW 93
Gray, Sylvia Ruth 1945- WhoAmW 93
Gray, Teresa A. Law&B 92
Gray, Thaddeus Ives 1959- WhoE 93
Gray, Thomas 1716-1771 BioIn 17, WorLitC [port]
Gray, Thomas Stephen 1950- WhoAm 92
Gray, Timothy Robert George WhoScE 91-1
Gray, Tracey L. 1932- St&PR 93
Gray, Truman Stretcher 1906- WhoAm 92
Gray, Virginia Hickman 1945- WhoAm 92
Gray, Walter Franklin 1929- St&PR 93, WhoAm 92
Gray, William Bennett 1935- WhoSSW 93
Gray, William D. 1912-1990 BioIn 17
Gray, William Frederick Law&B 92
Gray, William Guerin 1948- WhoAm 92
Gray, William H. 1941- AfrAmBi [port]
Gray, William H., III BioIn 17
Gray, William H., III 1941- CngDr 91, ConBlB 3 [port], PolPar, WhoAm 92, WhoE 93
Gray, William J., Jr. 1953- St&PR 93
Gray, William L. 1946- St&PR 93
Gray-Aldrich, Gretchen Elise 1934- WhoE 93
Graybar, Andrew T. 1944- St&PR 93
Graybeal, D. Scudder 1941- St&PR 93
Graybeal, Sidney Norman 1924- WhoAm 92
Graybill, Ben F. 1933- St&PR 93
Graybill, David Wesley 1949- WhoAm 92
Graybill, James B. 1938- St&PR 93
Graybill, V. Lynn 1944- St&PR 93
Graybow, Marvin 1925- St&PR 93
Grayck, Marcus Daniel 1927- WhoAm 92
Graydon, Frank Drake 1921- WhoSSW 93
Graydon, William Murray 1877?-1963? ScF&FL 92
Gray-Fisk, Delphine Isabel 1945- WhoWor 93
Grayhack, John Thomas 1923- WhoAm 92
Grayheck, Ronald J. 1934- WhoAm 92
Gray-Little, Bernadette 1944- WhoAm 92, WhoAmW 93, WhoSSW 93
Gray-Nix, Elizabeth Whitwell 1956- WhoAmW 93, WhoEmL 93
Graysmark, John BioIn 17
Graysmith, Robert 1942- WhoAm 92
Grayson, A.J. 1929- WhoScE 91-1
Grayson, Albert Kirk 1935- WhoAm 92
Grayson, C. Jackson St&PR 93
Grayson, Charles Jackson, Jr. 1923- WhoAm 92
Grayson, Darryl Stephen 1961- WhoE 93
Grayson, David 1870-1946 BioIn 17
Grayson, David D. 1920- St&PR 93
Grayson, David Edward 1943- St&PR 93
Grayson, David L. Law&B 92
Grayson, Edward D. Law&B 92
Grayson, Edward Davis 1938- St&PR 93, WhoAm 92
Grayson, Edward Victor 1943- WhoSSW 93
Grayson, Gene 1928- St&PR 93
Grayson, Gerald Herbert 1940- WhoAm 92
Grayson, Grace Riethmuller 1917- WhoAmW 93
Grayson, Joel 1938- St&PR 93
Grayson, John Allan 1930- WhoAm 92
Grayson, John R. 1925- St&PR 93
Grayson, Kathryn 1922- IntDcF 2-3 [port]
Grayson, Lawrence Peter 1937- WhoAm 92
Grayson, Richard 1951- WhoWrEP 92
Grayson, Richard E. 1929- St&PR 93
Grayson, Robert Allen 1927- WhoAm 92
Grayson, Sandra Lynn Law&B 92
Grayson, Susan Cubillas 1946- WhoAm 92
Grayson, Walton George, III 1928- WhoAm 92
Grayson, Warren B. Law&B 92
Grayson, William Jackson, Jr. 1930- St&PR 93, WhoAm 92
Grayson, William John 1788-1863 BioIn 17
Grayson Ford, Sue BioIn 17
Gray-Stoewsand, Lorraine Rae 1963- WhoAmW 93
Grayston, J. Thomas 1924- WhoAm 92
Grayzel, Arthur Irwin 1932- WhoSSW 93
Graze, Robert L. 1936- WhoE 93
Grazer, Brian BioIn 17
Grazer, Brian 1951- ConTFT 10
Grazi, Abraham V. St&PR 93
Grazi, Jack V. St&PR 93
Grazi, Maurice V. St&PR 93
Graziadei, William Daniel, III 1943- WhoAm 92
Graziani, Augusto 1933- BioIn 17
Graziani, Bonifazio 1604?-1664 Baker 92
Graziani, Francesco 1828-1901 Baker 92, OxDcOp
Graziani, Leonard Joseph 1929- WhoAm 92
Graziani, Lodovico 1820-1885 Baker 92, OxDcOp
Graziani, N. Jane 1958- WhoSSW 93
Graziani, Rudolfo 1882-1955 DcTwHis
Graziani, Vincenzo 1836-1906 OxDcOp
Graziano, Anthony Walter, Jr. Law&B 92
Graziano, Catherine Elizabeth 1931- WhoAmW 93
Graziano, Cynthia Kay S. 1955- WhoAmW 93
Graziano, Frank D. 1933- St&PR 93
Graziano, Joseph Harold 1947- WhoE 93
Graziano, Rocky 1921-1990 BioIn 17
Graziano, Thomas Anthony 1943- St&PR 93
Graziano, Vincent James 1933- St&PR 93
Grazin, Igor Nikolai 1952- WhoAm 92
Graziosi, Cherry Lynn 1957- WhoAmW 93
Graziunas, Daina 1953- ScF&FL 92
Grbceva, Ivanka 1946- DrEEuF
Grcevic, Barbara Helen 1951- WhoAmW 93
Greacen, Thomas Edmund, II 1907- WhoAm 92
Grealish, Helena Mary WhoScE 91-1
Grealy, Cornelius Joseph Law&B 92
Greaney, Dennis Michael 1946- WhoAm 92
Greaney, James M. 1941- St&PR 93
Greaney, John Francis 1950- WhoEmL 93
Greaney, Patrick Joseph 1939- St&PR 93, WhoAm 92
Greanias, Stanley Louis 1949- WhoAm 92
Greany, Catherine I. St&PR 93
Greaser, Constance Udean 1938- WhoAmW 93, WhoWor 93
Greaser, Marion Lewis 1942- WhoAm 92
Greashabet, Anna M. 1957- St&PR 93
Greason, Arthur LeRoy, Jr. 1922- WhoAm 92
Greason, Katherine Law&B 92
Greason, Murray Crossley, Jr. 1936- WhoWor 93
Great, Don Charles 1951- WhoWor 93
Greatbatch, Wilson 1919- WhoAm 92
Greated, Clive Alan WhoScE 91-1
Greathead, David John WhoScE 91-1
Greathouse, Cynthia Joyce 1953- WhoSSW 93
Greathouse, Patricia Dodd 1935- WhoAmW 93
Greathouse, Terrence Ray 1932- WhoAm 92
Greatorex, Henry Wellington 1813-1858 See Greatorex, Thomas 1758-1831 Baker 92
Greatorex, Thomas 1758-1831 Baker 92
Greaver, Harry 1929- WhoAm 92
Greaver, Joanne Hutchins 1939- WhoAmW 93, WhoSSW 93
Greaves, Brian L. 1943- St&PR 93
Greaves, David William Law&B 92
Greaves, Derrick 1927- BioIn 17
Greaves, George 1909-1990 BioIn 17
Greaves, George Richard 1941- WhoWor 93
Greaves, J. Randall 1955- WhoSSW 93
Greaves, James Louis 1943- WhoAm 92
Greaves, M.F. WhoScE 91-1
Greaves, Malcolm Watson WhoScE 91-1
Greaves, Margaret 1914- ChlFicS, ScF&FL 92
Greaves, Michael Prior WhoScE 91-1
Greaves, Philip 1931- DcCPCAm
Greaves, Philip Hugh 1955- WhoWor 93
Greaves, R.B. 1944- SoulM
Greaves, Richard L(ee) 1938- ConAu 39NR
Greaves, Thomas Guy, Jr. 1918- WhoAm 92
Greaves, William Garfield WhoAm 92
Greb, Gordon Barry 1921- WhoAm 92
Grebe, Henry L. 1932- St&PR 93
Grebe, Thomas William 1934- St&PR 93
Greben, Stanley Edward 1927- WhoAm 92
Grebens, G.V. 1943- ScF&FL 92
Grebenschikov, G.V. ScF&FL 92
Grebler, Leo 1900-1991 BioIn 17
Grebner, Bernice May Prill WhoWrEP 92
Grebner, Dennis William 1932- WhoAm 92
Grebow, Edward 1949- St&PR 93, WhoAm 92
Grebow, Peter Eric 1946- WhoE 93
Grebowsky, Joseph Mark 1941- WhoE 93
Grebstein, Sheldon Norman 1928- WhoAm 92
Grecco, Patrick Ronald 1949- WhoE 93
Grecenko, Alexandr 1930- WhoScE 91-4
Grechko, Andrei Antonovich 1903-1976 ColdWar 2 [port]
Grecky, Joseph M. 1939- St&PR 93
Greco, El 1541-1614 BioIn 17
Greco, Albert Nicholas 1945- WhoE 93
Greco, Charles 1949- WhoE 93
Greco, Edgar J. St&PR 93
Greco, Frank J. 1951- St&PR 93
Greco, Frank Joseph 1946- WhoSSW 93
Greco, Guy Benjamin 1951- WhoEmL 93
Greco, Ignazio J. 1961- WhoIns 93
Greco, Jean-Marie 1921- WhoScE 91-2
Greco, Joann 1960- WhoWrEP 92
Greco, Jose 1918- WhoAm 92
Greco, Juliette 1927- BioIn 17, CurBio 92 [port]
Greco, Karen A. Law&B 92
Greco, Michael S. 1942- WhoAm 92
Greco, Philip Anthony 1932- WhoAm 92
Greco, Thomas Joseph 1957- WhoEmL 93
Greco, Vito Louis 1943- St&PR 93
Grecu, Virgil 1930- WhoScE 91-4
Grecula, Pavol 1936- WhoScE 91-4
Gredal, Otto 1925- WhoWor 93
Grede, Kjell 1936- MiSFD 9
Grede, William J. 1897-1989 BioIn 17
Greden, John Francis 1942- WhoAm 92
Gredys, Keith J. 1955- St&PR 93
Greebel, Janet St&PR 93
Greeenberg, Marilyn Werstein 1937- WhoWrEP 92
Greef, Arthur de 1862-1940 Baker 92
Greeff, Kurt Rudolf 1920- WhoScE 91-3
Greehey, William Eugene 1936- St&PR 93, WhoSSW 93
Greek, Darold I. 1909- WhoAm 92
Greek, Janet MiSFD 9
Greek, William J., Sr. St&PR 93
Greeler, Gwendolyn B. 1950- St&PR 93
Greeley, Andrew M. 1928- BioIn 17, ScF&FL 92
Greeley, Andrew Moran 1928- WhoAm 92, WhoWrEP 92
Greeley, Horace 1811-1872 JrnUS, PolPar
Greeley, Joseph May 1902- WhoAm 92
Greeley, Michael H. St&PR 93
Greeley, Richard Stiles 1927- WhoE 93
Greeley, Sean McGovern 1961- WhoE 93
Greeley, Walter Franklin 1931- St&PR 93, WhoAm 92
Greelish, Thomas W. 1939-1991 BioIn 17
Greely, Adolphus Washington 1844-1935 HarEnMi
Greely, Augusta AmWomPl
Green, A.P. WhoScE 91-1
Green, Adam MajAI
Green, Adeline Mandel WhoAmW 93
Green, Adolph 1915- Baker 92, BioIn 17, ConTFT 10, WhoAm 92, WhoE 93
Green, Al 1946- Baker 92, ConMus 9 [port], SoulM, WhoAm 92
Green, Alan Ivan 1943- WhoE 93
Green, Alan Jay 1947- WhoAm 92
Green, Alan M. Law&B 92
Green, Alfred E. 1889-1960 MiSFD 9N
Green, Allan 1928- WhoE 93
Green, Allen Russell 1949- St&PR 93
Green, Allison Anne 1936- WhoAmW 93
Green, Alvar James 1946- St&PR 93
Green, Alvin Law&B 92
Green, Alvin 1931- WhoAm 92
Green, Andrew Wilson 1923- WhoAm 92
Green, Anne Canevari BioIn 17
Green, Anthony M. 1938- WhoScE 91-4
Green, Anthony Raymond 1930- St&PR 93
Green, Anthony Sidney Geoffrey 1936- WhoWor 93
Green, Arlena 1940- WhoAmW 93
Green, Arthur Christopher Haughton 1943- WhoWor 93
Green, Arthur L. d1991 BioIn 17
Green, Arthur Nelson 1941- WhoAm 92
Green, Asa Norman 1929- WhoAm 92
Green, Ashbel 1928- WhoAm 92, WhoWrEP 92
Green, Barbara Jean 1939- WhoAmW 93
Green, Barbara-Marie 1928- WhoAmW 93
Green, Barbara Strawn 1938- WhoAm 92, WhoAmW 93
Green, Barry 1948- WhoEmL 93
Green, Bartholomew 1666-1732 JrnUS
Green, Benigna Regina 1956- WhoEmL 93
Green, Benjamin F. Law&B 92
Green, Bennett Donald 1950- WhoE 93
Green, Bernard 1917- St&PR 93
Green, Bert Franklin, Jr. 1927- WhoE 93
Green, Beverly J. 1951- St&PR 93
Green, Bill 1929- CngDr 91, WhoAm 92, WhoE 93
Green, Bonnie Jean 1950- WhoAmW 93
Green, Brenda Moss Law&B 92
Green, Brent B. Law&B 92
Green, Brian Austin BioIn 17
Green, Brian Michael 1939- WhoSSW 93
Green, Bruce Seth MiSFD 9
Green, Brynmor Hugh 1941- WhoWor 93
Green, Carl R. 1932- ScF&FL 92
Green, Carol BioIn 17
Green, Carol H. 1944- WhoAm 92, WhoAmW 93
Green, Carole L. Law&B 92
Green, Catherine Gertrude 1945- WhoAmW 93
Green, Cecil Howard 1900- WhoAm 92
Green, Charles Dickinson 1771-1857 BioIn 17
Green, Charles K. 1943- St&PR 93
Green, Charles LaVerne 1932- WhoSSW 93
Green, Charles Leon 1960- WhoEmL 93
Green, Cindy Austin 1967- WhoAmW 93
Green, Claire Magidovitch 1953- WhoEmL 93
Green, Clara S. AmWomPl
Green, Clay S. 1945- St&PR 93
Green, Clifford Scott 1923- WhoAm 92
Green, Colin James WhoScE 91-1
Green, Coppie 1946- WhoWrEP 92
Green, Cora Mae AmWomPl
Green, Curtis H. 1925- St&PR 93
Green, Cyril K. 1931- St&PR 93
Green, Dale F. 1945- WhoSSW 93
Green, Dale Monte 1922- WhoAm 92
Green, Dan 1935- WhoAm 92
Green, Dana Ione Law&B 92
Green, Daniel 1907- WhoSSW 93
Green, Daniel G. 1937- WhoAm 92
Green, Daniel S. 1947- St&PR 93
Green, David MiSFD 9
Green, David 1899- WhoAm 92
Green, David 1922- WhoWor 93
Green, David Edward 1937- WhoE 93
Green, David Henry 1921- WhoAm 92
Green, David Marvin 1932- BioIn 17
Green, David O. 1923- WhoAm 92
Green, David T. 1962- WhoSSW 93
Green, David Thomas 1925- WhoAm 92
Green, Dennis BioIn 17, WhoAm 92
Green, Dennis J. Law&B 92
Green, Dennis Joseph 1941- St&PR 93, WhoAm 92
Green, Dianna AfrAmBi [port]
Green, Don Wesley 1932- WhoAm 92
Green, Donald M. 1932- St&PR 93
Green, Donald Webb 1944- WhoAm 92
Green, Dorothy BioIn 17
Green, Dottie d1992 NewYTBS 92 [port]
Green, Douglas Alvin 1925- WhoSSW 93
Green, Douglas Brant 1931- St&PR 93
Green, Douglas Carson 1945- St&PR 93
Green, Duff 1791-1875 JrnUS
Green, E.F. 1918- St&PR 93
Green, Earl Leroy 1913- WhoAm 92
Green, Edith 1910-1987 BioIn 17
Green, Edith Pinero 1929- ScF&FL 92
Green, Edith S. 1910-1987 PolPar
Green, Edward Crocker 1944- WhoE 93, WhoWor 93
Green, Edward Lewis 1946- WhoSSW 93
Green, Edwin 1948- ConAu 38NR
Green, Eliot I. 1935- St&PR 93
Green, Elizabeth A(dine) H(erkimer) 1906- Baker 92
Green, Elizabeth Adine Herkimer 1906- WhoWrEP 92
Green, Elizabeth Atkinson Lay 1897- AmWomPl
Green, Ellen Carraway 1949- WhoAmW 93
Green, Eric BioIn 17
Green, Erma AmWomPl
Green, Eva A. 1958- St&PR 93
Green, Fitzhugh 1917-1990 BioIn 17
Green, Flora Hungerford 1941- WhoAm 92, WhoAmW 93
Green, Fred Wallace 1945- WhoE 93, WhoIns 93
Green, G.W. d1991 BioIn 17
Green, Gareth Montraville 1931- WhoAm 92
Green, Garland 1942- BioIn 17
Green, Gaylon Wayne 1947- St&PR 93
Green, Geoffrey D. Law&B 92
Green, George 1793-1841 BioIn 17
Green, George Joseph 1938- WhoAm 92
Green, Gerald 1922- WhoAm 92, WhoWrEP 92
Green, Gerard Leo 1928- WhoE 93
Green, Gertrude Dorsey 1949- WhoAm 92, WhoEmL 93
Green, Goldie AmWomPl
Green, Gordon Jay 1957- WhoAm 92
Green, Grant Douglas Law&B 92
Green, Guy 1913- MiSFD 9
Green, Guy Mervin Charles WhoAm 92
Green, H. Gordon 1912-1991 WhoCanL 92
Green, Hamilton WhoWor 93
Green, Harry Joyce, Jr. 1930- WhoSSW 93
Green, Harry Western, II 1940- WhoAm 92
Green, Harry William 1932- St&PR 93
Green, Harvey 1946- ConAu 37NR, WhoE 93, WhoEmL 93
Green, Henry 1905-1973 BritWr S2

Green, Henry 1905-1974 ScF&FL 92
Green, Hetty 1834-1916 BioIn 17
Green, Hilary ScF&FL 92
Green, Holcombe Tucker, Jr. 1939- WhoAm 92
Green, Hollis L. Law&B 92
Green, Holly Ann 1962- WhoAmW 93
Green, Holly Mary 1962- WhoAmW 93
Green, Hope Stuart 1944- WhoE 93
Green, Howard 1925- WhoAm 92
Green, Howard I. 1936- WhoWor 93
Green, Howard Peyton, III 1949- WhoAm 92
Green, Hubert 1946- WhoAm 92
Green, J.H. WhoScE 91-1
Green, Jack Allen Law&B 92
Green, Jack Allen 1945- WhoAm 92
Green, Jack Peter 1925- WhoAm 92
Green, James WhoScE 91-1
Green, James 1928- WhoWor 93
Green, James Craig 1955- WhoEmL 93
Green, James David Law&B 92
Green, James Harry 1932- WhoWrEP 92
Green, James Lewis 1944- St&PR 93
Green, James Weston 1913- WhoAm 92
Green, James Wilder 1927- WhoAm 92
Green, James Wyche 1915- WhoAm 92
Green, Jane Ann 1947- WhoAmW 93
Green, Jay Martin 1947- St&PR 93
Green, Jean Susanne 1949- WhoWrEP 92
Green, Jeffrey Emanuel 1954- WhoEmL 93
Green, Jeffrey Harris 1956- WhoEmL 93
Green, Jeffrey S. Law&B 92
Green, Jen 1954- ScF&FL 92
Green, Jerome Frederic 1928- WhoAm 92
Green, Jerome George 1929- WhoAm 92
Green, Jerry Howard 1930- WhoWor 93
Green, Jerry Richard 1946- WhoAm 92
Green, Jersey Michael-Lee 1952- WhoAm 92
Green, Jesse 1958- ConAu 139
Green, Joe C. 1941- St&PR 93
Green, John Alden 1925- WhoAm 92
Green, John Cawley 1910- WhoAm 92
Green, John Clancy 1949- WhoEmL 93, WhoSSW 93
Green, John Douglas 1939- WhoWor 93
Green, John E. 1937- WhoScE 91-1
Green, John Hampson 1932- WhoE 93
Green, John Henry 1929- WhoSSW 93
Green, John Joseph 1931- St&PR 93, WhoAm 92
Green, John Lafayette, Jr. 1929- WhoWrEP 92
Green, John Lafayette, Jr. 1933- WhoAm 92
Green, John Orne 1922- WhoAm 92
Green, John Theodore 1937- St&PR 93
Green, John (Waldo) 1908-1989 Baker 92
Green, John Wickliffe 1769-1813 BioIn 17
Green, Jonathan BioIn 17
Green, Jonathan D. Law&B 92
Green, Jonathan D. 1946- St&PR 93
Green, Jonathan David 1946- WhoEmL 93
Green, Jonathan William 1939- WhoAm 92
Green, Jonathon 1948- ScF&FL 92
Green, Jordan Mark 1961- WhoWor 93
Green, Joseph 1928- WhoAm 92
Green, Joseph 1931- ScF&FL 92
Green, Joseph Barnet 1928- WhoAm 92
Green, Joshua, III 1936- St&PR 93, WhoAm 92
Green, Joyce 1928- WhoWor 93
Green, Joyce Hens 1928- CngDr 91, WhoAmW 93, WhoE 93
Green, Judith WhoE 93
Green, Judy 1943- WhoAmW 93
Green, Julia Lynne 1959- WhoE 93
Green, Julien 1900- BioIn 17
Green, Julius Curtis 1957- WhoE 93
Green, June Lazenby 1914- CngDr 91, WhoAm 92, WhoAmW 93, WhoE 93
Green, Karen Ann 1957- WhoAmW 93
Green, Karen Ina Margulies 1939- WhoAm 92, WhoAmW 93
Green, Karen Tracy Law&B 92
Green, Karin Marie 1935- WhoAmW 93
Green, Karl Walter 1940- WhoSSW 93
Green, Kate 1950- ScF&FL 92
Green, Katherine Ann 1947- WhoEmL 93
Green, Keith 1940- WhoSSW 93
Green, Kevin A. 1954- St&PR 93
Green, Larry Allen 1947- WhoWrEP 92
Green, Larry Alton 1948- WhoAm 92
Green, Larry Ray Law&B 92
Green, Lauralee Maynard 1959- WhoEmL 93
Green, Lawrence David 1952- St&PR 93
Green, Lennis Harris 1940- WhoAmW 93
Green, Leon, Jr. 1922- WhoAm 92
Green, Leon Morton 1949- WhoE 93
Green, Leon William 1925- WhoAm 92
Green, Leonard I. 1933- St&PR 93
Green, Leslie Claude 1920- WhoAm 92
Green, Lester Duane 1925- St&PR 93
Green, Lewis 1946- WhoWrEP 92
Green, Linda Lou 1946- WhoAmW 93, WhoSSW 93
Green, Lisa Michele 1957- WhoE 93, WhoEmL 93
Green, Lynne Annette 1965- WhoAmW 93
Green, M.B. Law&B 92, WhoScE 91-1
Green, M.J. 1957- WhoScE 91-1
Green, Malcolm 1942- WhoScE 91-1
Green, Malcolm Leslie Hodder WhoScE 91-1
Green, Malcolm Leslie Hodder 1936- WhoWor 93
Green, Marbley Law&B 92
Green, Margaret Lucy WhoScE 91-1
Green, Marguerite 1922- WhoAm 92
Green, Maria C. Law&B 92
Green, Marjorie 1943- WhoAmW 93
Green, Mark J. BioIn 17
Green, Mark Joseph 1945- WhoAm 92
Green, Mark V. Law&B 92
Green, Marsha Ann WhoSSW 93
Green, Marshall 1916- WhoAm 92
Green, Marti Law&B 92
Green, Martin 1927- ScF&FL 92
Green, Marvin Howe, Jr. 1935- St&PR 93, WhoAm 92, WhoWor 93
Green, Mary d1992 NewYTBS 92
Green, Mary Hester 1941- WhoAmW 93, WhoWor 93
Green, Mary Wolcott AmWomPl
Green, Maurice 1926- WhoAm 92
Green, Maurice Berkeley 1920- WhoWor 93
Green, Maurice Richard 1922- WhoAm 92, WhoE 93
Green, Maurice Warner 1927- St&PR 93
Green, Maury 1916- ScF&FL 92
Green, Melvia B. 1953- AfrAmBi
Green, Meredith W. 1922- WhoSSW 93
Green, Meyra Jeanne 1946- WhoAmW 93
Green, Michael 1943- ScF&FL 92
Green, Michael Alan WhoScE 91-1
Green, Michael B. BioIn 17
Green, Michael Ben 1943- WhoScE 91-1
Green, Michael D. 1944- St&PR 93
Green, Michael Enoch 1938- WhoE 93
Green, Michael Frederick BioIn 17
Green, Michael John 1942- WhoWor 93
Green, Michael Kent 1951- WhoE 93
Green, Mino WhoScE 91-1
Green, Miranda J(ane Aldhouse) 1947- ConAu 139
Green, Miriam Blau 1932- WhoAmW 93
Green, Mitzi Chandler 1956- WhoSSW 93
Green, Morris 1922- WhoAm 92
Green, Nancy Elizabeth 1955- WhoEmL 93
Green, Nancy H. 1944- St&PR 93
Green, Nancy L. 1947- St&PR 93
Green, Nancy Loughridge 1942- WhoAm 92, WhoAmW 93
Green, Nehemiah 1837-1890 BioIn 17
Green, Nelson F. 1929- St&PR 93
Green, Norman WhoAm 92
Green, Norman H. 1929- St&PR 93
Green, Norman Kenneth 1924- WhoAm 92
Green, Norman Marston, Jr. 1932- WhoE 93
Green, Norman Michael WhoScE 91-1
Green, Norman Whitaker 1951- WhoScE 91-4
Green, Orville Cronkhite, III 1926- WhoAm 92
Green, Patricia ConTFT 10
Green, Patrick E. 1954- St&PR 93
Green, Paul C. 1919- WhoIns 93
Green, Paul Eliot 1894-1981 EncAACR
Green, Paul Eliot, Jr. 1924- WhoAm 92
Green, Paul H. Law&B 92
Green, Paula WhoAm 92
Green, Paula Ann 1953- WhoAmW 93
Green, Peggy Meyers 1943- WhoAm 92, WhoAmW 93
Green, Peter 1946- See Fleetwood, Mick 1942- Baker 92
Green, Peter James WhoScE 91-1
Green, Peter L. 1939- St&PR 93
Green, Peter Morris 1924- WhoAm 92
Green, Philip Bevington 1933- WhoAm 92
Green, Phillip C. 1940- St&PR 93
Green, Phillip Dale 1954- WhoAm 92
Green, R. Keith 1951- St&PR 93
Green, R. P. H. 1943- ConAu 138
Green, Rachael Paulette 1953- WhoEmL 93, WhoSSW 93
Green, Raleigh E., II 1951- WhoWrEP 92
Green, Ray BioIn 17
Green, Ray (Burns) 1909- Baker 92
Green, Raymond Bert 1929- WhoAm 92, WhoWor 93
Green, Raymond Ferguson St. John 1950- WhoE 93
Green, Raymond Robert 1946- WhoE 93
Green, Raymond Silvernail 1915- WhoAm 92, WhoE 93, WhoWor 93
Green, Reuven BioIn 17
Green, Richard 1936- WhoWor 93
Green, Richard A. Law&B 92
Green, Richard Alan 1926- WhoAm 92
Green, Richard B. 1942- St&PR 93
Green, Richard Brownlow 1940- WhoSSW 93
Green, Richard C., Jr. 1954- St&PR 93
Green, Richard Calvin, Jr. 1954- WhoAm 92
Green, Richard G. 1913- St&PR 93
Green, Richard James 1928- WhoAm 92
Green, Richard John 1944- WhoAm 92
Green, Richard K. 1939- St&PR 93
Green, Richard Lancelyn Gordon 1953- WhoAm 92
Green, Richard M. Law&B 92
Green, Richard M. 1940- St&PR 93
Green, Richard Manners WhoScE 91-1
Green, Richard Michael 1944- WhoE 93
Green, Ricki Kutcher 1943- WhoAmW 93
Green, Robert A. Law&B 92
Green, Robert B. Law&B 92
Green, Robert B. 1941- WhoIns 93
Green, Robert Edward 1921- WhoE 93, WhoWor 93
Green, Robert Edward 1953- St&PR 93
Green, Robert Edward, Jr. 1932- WhoAm 92
Green, Robert Kent Law&B 92
Green, Robert Lamar 1914- WhoAm 92
Green, Robert Leonard 1931- St&PR 93, WhoAm 92
Green, Robert Lynn 1955- WhoEmL 93
Green, Robert S. 1927- WhoAm 92
Green, Robert Scott 1953- WhoAm 92
Green, Roger WhoScE 91-1
Green, Roger J. 1944- ChlFicS, ScF&FL 92
Green, Roger Lancelyn 1918-1987 ScF&FL 92
Green, Roland 1944- ScF&FL 92
Green, Ronald Michael 1942- WhoAm 92
Green, Rose Basile 1914- ConAu 39NR, WhoAm 92, WhoAmW 93, WhoE 93, WhoWor 93
Green, Russell M. 1938- St&PR 93
Green, Ruth R. WhoE 93
Green, RuthAnn 1935- WhoAmW 93, WhoWor 93
Green, Samuel Leonard 1948- WhoWrEP 92
Green, Samuel R. 1919-1991 BioIn 17
Green, Sandra Staap 1944- WhoSSW 93
Green, Sara Edmond 1954- WhoAmW 93, WhoWor 93
Green, Saul 1925- WhoAm 92
Green, Scott E. 1951- ScF&FL 92
Green, Sharon 1942- ScF&FL 92
Green, Sharon Alligood 1950- WhoAmW 93
Green, Sharon Jordan 1948- WhoEmL 93, WhoSSW 93
Green, Sheila Ellen 1934- ConAu 39NR
Green, Shia Toby Riner WhoAmW 93
Green, Shia Toby Riner 1937- WhoAm 92
Green, Shirley Moore 1933- WhoAm 92, WhoAmW 93
Green, Sihugo 1934-1980 BiDAMSp 1989
Green, Simon 1955- ScF&FL 92
Green, Stanley BioIn 17
Green, Stanley Bruce 1937- WhoSSW 93
Green, Stephanie ScF&FL 92
Green, Stephen Law&B 92
Green, Stephen Joel 1940- WhoE 93
Green, Steven J. 1952- St&PR 93
Green, Stewart E. Law&B 92
Green, Stewart E. 1944- St&PR 93
Green, Susan Blair 1945- WhoSSW 93
Green, Susan Kohn 1941- ScF&FL 92
Green, Susan P. 1947- St&PR 93
Green, Ted WhoAm 92
Green, Terence C. Law&B 92
Green, Terence M. 1947- ScF&FL 92
Green, Terence Michael 1947- WhoEmL 93
Green, Terrence C. 1944- St&PR 93
Green, Terry MiSFD 9
Green, Theo 1956- WhoWrEP 92
Green, Theodore 1946- St&PR 93
Green, Theodore, III 1938- WhoAm 92
Green, Theodore F. 1868-1966 PolPar
Green, Thomas B. Law&B 92
Green, Thomas Edward 1948- WhoEmL 93, WhoSSW 93
Green, Thomas George 1931- WhoAm 92
Green, Timothy Avery Law&B 92
Green, Tom L. Law&B 92
Green, Traci BioIn 17
Green, Traci Leigh 1966- WhoAmW 93
Green, Vera Mae 1951- WhoSSW 93
Green, Walon 1936- MiSFD 9
Green, Walter Luther 1934- WhoAm 92
Green, Warren Arthur WhoE 93
Green, Warren Harold 1915- WhoAm 92
Green, William 1942- St&PR 93
Green, William A. 1951- WhoEmL 93, WhoSSW 93
Green, William Anthony 1951- WhoE 93
Green, William Edward 1943- WhoE 93
Green, William G. Law&B 92
Green, William Hadfield Law&B 92
Green, William J., Sr. 1910-1963 PolPar
Green, William L. 1941- St&PR 93
Green, William Lohr 1945- WhoSSW 93
Green, William O., III Law&B 92
Green, William Porter 1920- WhoAm 92, WhoWor 93
Green, William W. d1992 BioIn 17, NewYTBS 92
Green, William Wells 1911- WhoSSW 93
Green, Willie Harold 1940- WhoSSW 93
Green, Woodrow, Jr. 1952- BiDAMSp 1989
Greenan, Frank Joseph 1920- St&PR 93
Greenan, Russell H. 1925- ScF&FL 92
Greenawald, Sheri (Kay) 1947- Baker 92
Greenawalt, David Franklin 1933- St&PR 93
Greenawalt, Donald Ralph 1931- WhoE 93
Greenawalt, Jane Burdette 1951- WhoAmW 93, WhoSSW 93
Greenawalt, Karen Louise 1951- WhoSSW 93
Greenawalt, Nancy Putnam 1945- WhoSSW 93
Greenawalt, Peggy Freed Tomarkin 1942- WhoAm 92, WhoAmW 93, WhoE 93
Greenawalt, Robert Kent 1936- WhoAm 92
Greenawalt, Ruth Marjorie 1942- WhoSSW 93
Greenawalt, William Sloan 1934- WhoE 93, WhoWor 93
Greenaway, David WhoScE 91-1
Greenaway, David 1952- WhoWor 93
Greenaway, Emerson 1906-1990 BioIn 17
Greenaway, Frederick Thomas WhoE 93
Greenaway, Joseph Anthony, Jr. Law&B 92
Greenaway, Kate 1846-1901 BioIn 17, ConAu 137, MajAI [port]
Greenaway, Peter BioIn 17
Greenaway, Peter 1942- ConTFT 10, MiSFD 9
Greenaway, Peter John WhoScE 91-1
Greenaway, Peter Van ScF&FL 92
Greenaway, Rosemary Maureen 1959- WhoAmW 93
Greenbacker, John Everett 1917- WhoAm 92
Greenbaum, Alvin M. d1992 BioIn 17
Greenbaum, Bruce 1964- WhoE 93
Greenbaum, Carol Ann 1947- WhoAmW 93, WhoEmL 93
Greenbaum, Daniel Wolf 1926- St&PR 93
Greenbaum, David 1946- WhoE 93
Greenbaum, Donald Reuben 1951- St&PR 93
Greenbaum, Elias 1944- WhoSSW 93
Greenbaum, Henry 1907-1992 BioIn 17
Greenbaum, James R. 1933- St&PR 93
Greenbaum, James Richard 1933- WhoAm 92
Greenbaum, Kenneth Law&B 92
Greenbaum, Kenneth 1944- WhoAm 92
Greenbaum, Lowell Marvin 1928- WhoAm 92
Greenbaum, Maurice C. 1918- WhoAm 92
Greenbaum, Melvin 1923- St&PR 93
Greenbaum, Monroe d1991 BioIn 17
Greenbaum, Richard d1990 BioIn 17
Greenbaum, Robert S. 1922- WhoAm 92
Greenbaum, Steven Marc Law&B 92
Greenbaum, Stuart I. 1936- WhoAm 92
Greenbaum, William I. Law&B 92
Greenbaum, William Ivan 1950- WhoEmL 93
Greenberg, Aaron Rosmorin 1932- WhoE 93
Greenberg, Alan C. 1927- St&PR 93
Greenberg, Alan Courtney 1927- WhoAm 92
Greenberg, Albert 1924- WhoAm 92
Greenberg, Alfred H. 1924-1990 BioIn 17
Greenberg, Alice BioIn 17
Greenberg, Allan BioIn 17
Greenberg, Allan 1917- WhoAm 92
Greenberg, Allan Carl 1940- WhoE 93
Greenberg, Allan David 1945- St&PR 93
Greenberg, Allan E. 1942- St&PR 93
Greenberg, Allan Jeffrey 1960- WhoE 93
Greenberg, Allen Leonard Law&B 92
Greenberg, Alvin David 1932- WhoWrEP 92
Greenberg, Arline Francine WhoAmW 93
Greenberg, Barbara H. Law&B 92
Greenberg, Barbara Levenson 1932- WhoWrEP 92
Greenberg, Barbara Reynolds 1947- WhoAmW 93
Greenberg, Ben S. 1925- St&PR 93
Greenberg, Bernard 1922- WhoAm 92
Greenberg, Blu 1936- BioIn 17, WhoAm 92
Greenberg, Bonnie Lynn 1955- WhoAmW 93

Greenberg, Bradley Sander 1934- WhoAm 92
Greenberg, Bruce MiSFD 9
Greenberg, Bruce C. BioIn 17
Greenberg, Byron Stanley 1919- WhoAm 92
Greenberg, Carl 1934- WhoAm 92
Greenberg, Charles Steven 1950- WhoEmL 93, WhoSSW 93
Greenberg, Clement 1909- BioIn 17
Greenberg, Dan Leonard 1954- WhoSSW 93
Greenberg, Daniel 1941- WhoAm 92
Greenberg, David A. 1936- St&PR 93
Greenberg, David Bernard 1928- WhoAm 92
Greenberg, David Gordon 1947- WhoE 93
Greenberg, Edward Alan 1941- St&PR 93
Greenberg, Edward Seymour 1942- WhoAm 92
Greenberg, Elizabeth Law&B 92
Greenberg, Esther 1923-1991 BioIn 17
Greenberg, Frank Edgar 1933- WhoE 93
Greenberg, Frank S. 1929- WhoAm 92, WhoSSW 93
Greenberg, Frank Stanford 1929- St&PR 93
Greenberg, Geoffrey Andrew 1948- WhoE 93
Greenberg, Hank 1911-1986 BioIn 17
Greenberg, Harry Bertrand 1920- WhoSSW 93
Greenberg, Harvey Roy 1935- WhoE 93
Greenberg, Henry Morton 1940- WhoE 93
Greenberg, Herbert Marvin 1929- WhoAm 92
Greenberg, Howard R. Law&B 92
Greenberg, Hoyne St&PR 93
Greenberg, Irving 1933- BioIn 17, JeAmHC
Greenberg, Irwin E. St&PR 93
Greenberg, Jack Law&B 92
Greenberg, Jack 1924- OxCSupC, WhoAm 92
Greenberg, Jack M. 1942- WhoAm 92
Greenberg, Jacob 1929- WhoAm 92
Greenberg, Jan 1942- BioIn 17
Greenberg, Jay (R.) 1942- ConAu 137
Greenberg, Jay Richard 1943- WhoE 93
Greenberg, Jeanne LeCrann 1935- WhoAm 92
Greenberg, Jeffrey W. St&PR 93, WhoIns 93
Greenberg, Jerome 1936- WhoAm 92
Greenberg, Jerrold Selig 1942- WhoAm 92
Greenberg, Joanne 1932- WhoWrEP 92
Greenberg, Joel S. 1931- WhoAm 92
Greenberg, John Leonard 1945- WhoWor 93
Greenberg, Jonathan 1950- WhoEmL 93, WhoSSW 93
Greenberg, Joseph H. 1915- WhoAm 92
Greenberg, Joseph Harold 1915- BioIn 17, IntDcAn
Greenberg, Joseph J. 1915-1991 BioIn 17
Greenberg, Joshua F. 1933- WhoAm 92
Greenberg, Joyce Irene 1952- WhoAm 92
Greenberg, Judith Horovitz 1947- WhoEmL 93
Greenberg, Larry 1937- St&PR 93
Greenberg, Lawrence MiSFD 9
Greenberg, Leon 1931- WhoE 93
Greenberg, Les Paul 1946- WhoSSW 93
Greenberg, Linda WhoE 93
Greenberg, Lon R. Law&B 92
Greenberg, Lon R. 1950- St&PR 93
Greenberg, Marc L. Law&B 92
Greenberg, Margaret H. 1935- WhoWrEP 92
Greenberg, Mark Lawrence 1948- WhoE 93
Greenberg, Marshall Gary 1935- WhoAm 92
Greenberg, Martin 1918- ScF&FL 92
Greenberg, Martin Burt 1939- WhoAm 92
Greenberg, Martin H. 1941- ScF&FL 92
Greenberg, Martin Stephen 1940- WhoAm 92
Greenberg, Maurice R. 1925- St&PR 93
Greenberg, Maurice Raymond 1925- WhoAm 92, WhoIns 93
Greenberg, Max d1992 NewYTBS 92
Greenberg, Maxwell Elfred 1922- WhoAm 92
Greenberg, Mel 1932- St&PR 93
Greenberg, Melanie Hope 1954- SmATA 72 [port], WhoE 93
Greenberg, Melvin Nathaniel 1928- WhoAm 92
Greenberg, Michael John 1931- WhoAm 92
Greenberg, Michael Richard 1943- WhoE 93
Greenberg, Milton 1918- WhoAm 92
Greenberg, Milton 1927- WhoAm 92, WhoE 93
Greenberg, Morton Ira 1933- WhoAm 92, WhoE 93
Greenberg, Morton Paul 1946- WhoEmL 93
Greenberg, Myron Silver 1945- WhoWor 93
Greenberg, Nancy Jean 1947- WhoWrEP 92
Greenberg, Nat 1918- WhoAm 92
Greenberg, Nathan 1919- WhoAm 92, WhoWor 93
Greenberg, Nathan Abraham 1928- WhoAm 92
Greenberg, Neville Geoffrey 1943- St&PR 93
Greenberg, Noah 1919-1966 Baker 92
Greenberg, Oscar Wallace 1932- WhoAm 92
Greenberg, Paul BioIn 17
Greenberg, Paul 1937- WhoAm 92, WhoSSW 93, WhoWrEP 92
Greenberg, Reuben M. 1944- BioIn 17
Greenberg, Richard 1959?- ConAu 138
Greenberg, Richard A. 1931- St&PR 93, WhoAm 92
Greenberg, Richard Alan MiSFD 9
Greenberg, Richard Alan 1946- WhoE 93, WhoEmL 93, WhoWor 93
Greenberg, Richard S. 1960- WhoEmL 93
Greenberg, Robert Law&B 92
Greenberg, Robert A. 1939- WhoAm 92
Greenberg, Robert I. 1930- WhoAm 92
Greenberg, Robert Milton 1916- WhoAm 92
Greenberg, Robert Y. 1940- ConEn
Greenberg, Ronald David 1939- WhoAm 92
Greenberg, Ronald M. Law&B 92
Greenberg, Rosalind M. 1951- ScF&FL 92
Greenberg, Ruthanne 1948- WhoAmW 93
Greenberg, Sanford David 1940- WhoAm 92
Greenberg, Saul Norman 1923- WhoE 93
Greenberg, Sheldon Burt 1948- WhoE 93, WhoEmL 93
Greenberg, Shelley St&PR 93
Greenberg, Sidney S. 1912-1991 BioIn 17
Greenberg, Sigmund Robert 1930- WhoSSW 93
Greenberg, Simon 1901- WhoAm 92
Greenberg, Stanley B. 1945- NewYTBS 92 [port]
Greenberg, Stephen Jay 1941- WhoAm 92
Greenberg, Stephen Michael 1944- WhoAm 92
Greenberg, Steven A. NewYTBS 92 [port]
Greenberg, Steven Morey 1949- WhoE 93, WhoEmL 93
Greenberg, Susan Law&B 92
Greenberg, Toni d1990 BioIn 17
Greenberg, William Michael 1946- WhoE 93, WhoEmL 93, WhoWor 93
Greenberger, Daniel Mordecai 1933- WhoE 93
Greenberger, Ellen 1935- WhoAm 92
Greenberger, Ellen L. Law&B 92
Greenberger, Ernest 1923- WhoAm 92
Greenberger, George M. 1912- St&PR 93
Greenberger, Howard Leroy 1929- WhoAm 92
Greenberger, I. Michael 1945- WhoAm 92
Greenberger, Josh 1948- WhoE 93
Greenberger, Marsha Moses 1943- WhoAmW 93
Greenberger, Martin 1931- WhoAm 92
Greenberger, Norton Jerald 1933- WhoAm 92
Greenberger, Raymond Stuart 1945- St&PR 93
Greenberger, Robert 1958- ScF&FL 92
Greenbie, Barrie Barstow 1920- WhoE 93
Greenblat, Rodney Alan 1960- BioIn 17
Greenblatt, A. Martha 1941- WhoAmW 93
Greenblatt, Arthur Edwin 1942- WhoE 93
Greenblatt, Daniel St&PR 93
Greenblatt, David J. 1945- WhoAm 92
Greenblatt, Deana Charlene 1948- WhoAmW 93
Greenblatt, Hellen Chaya 1947- WhoAmW 93
Greenblatt, Kenneth D. 1946- St&PR 93
Greenblatt, Maurice 1928- St&PR 93
Greenblatt, Maurice Theodore 1928- WhoAm 92
Greenblatt, Milton 1914- WhoAm 92
Greenblatt, Miriam WhoAmW 93
Greenblatt, Nancy St&PR 93
Greenblatt, Ray Harris 1931- WhoAm 92
Greenblatt, Rena Matison 1955- WhoE 93
Greenblatt, Robert Ira 1953- WhoE 93
Greenblatt, Sherwin BioIn 17
Greenblatt, Sherwin 1941- St&PR 93, WhoAm 92
Greenblatt, Stephen 1943- ScF&FL 92
Greenblatt, Walter Charles 1956- WhoE 93
Greenblum, J. Bradley 1958- WhoWor 93
Green-Buckner, SueCarol Law&B 92
Greenburg, Dan BioIn 17
Greenburg, Dan 1936- ScF&FL 92, WhoAm 92, WhoWrEP 92
Greenburg, David Julius 1925- WhoAm 92
Greenburg, Leonard 1892-1991 BioIn 17
Greenburg, Sharon Louise 1941- WhoAmW 93
Greenburg, Virginia Hoff d1991 BioIn 17
Greenbury, Richard 1936- WhoAm 92
Greendlinger, Michael Leonard 1938- WhoE 93
Greene, A.C. 1923- BioIn 17
Greene, A. Crawford, Jr. 1922- WhoAm 92
Greene, Adele S. WhoAmW 93
Greene, Al 1946- Baker 92
Greene, Alan I. 1929- St&PR 93
Greene, Alan S. 1930- St&PR 93
Greene, Albert Gorton 1802-1868 BioIn 17
Greene, Alexander Plunket d1990 BioIn 17
Greene, Allen Earl 1929- WhoWor 93
Greene, Allen Steven 1946- WhoE 93
Greene, Alvin 1932- WhoAm 92
Greene, Alvin Carl 1923- WhoAm 92
Greene, Arthur Edward 1945- WhoAm 92
Greene, Aubrey E. St&PR 93
Greene, Balcomb 1904-1990 BioIn 17
Greene, Bancroft Farrar 1941- WhoSSW 93
Greene, Barbara Ann Mary 1945- WhoAmW 93
Greene, Barbara Ellen Law&B 92
Greene, Barnett Alan 1907- WhoE 93
Greene, Barry S. Law&B 92
Greene, Barry Steven 1946- St&PR 93
Greene, Belle da Costa 1883-1950 BioIn 17
Greene, Benjamin 1932- St&PR 93
Greene, Benjamin Carroll 1937- WhoSSW 93
Greene, Bernard Harold 1925- WhoAm 92
Greene, Bette 1934- DcAmChF 1960, MajAI [port], SmATA 16AS [port], WhoWrEP 92
Greene, Beverly Ann 1950- WhoE 93
Greene, Bill 1931- AfrAmBi [port]
Greene, Bob 1947- WhoAm 92
Greene, Bradford Marson 1920- WhoAm 92
Greene, Bruce Howard 1958- WhoEmL 93
Greene, Bruce Wilkie 1939- St&PR 93
Greene, Carl William 1935- St&PR 93
Greene, Carla 1916- BioIn 17, WhoWrEP 92
Greene, Carol BioIn 17
Greene, Catherine Antoinette 1958- WhoEmL 93
Greene, Charles BioIn 17
Greene, Charles Cassius 1897- WhoAm 92, WhoWor 93
Greene, Charles E., III WhoWrEP 92
Greene, Charles Sumner 1868-1957 BioIn 17
Greene, Christopher 1737-1781 HarEnMi
Greene, Constance C(larke) 1924- ConAu 38NR, MajAI [port], SmATA 72 [port]
Greene, Constance (Clarke) 1924- DcAmChF 1960
Greene, Curtis Densmore 1929- WhoIns 93
Greene, Dale E. 1946- St&PR 93
Greene, Dallas Whorton, Jr. 1923- WhoAm 92
Greene, Danford B. MiSFD 9
Greene, David 1921- MiSFD 9
Greene, David E. Law&B 92
Greene, David L. 1944- ScF&FL 92
Greene, David Lee 1938- WhoAm 92
Greene, David Mason 1920- WhoAm 92
Greene, David Paul 1941- St&PR 93
Greene, Deborah 1951- WhoWrEP 92
Greene, Deborah Lyn 1955- WhoAmW 93, WhoEmL 93
Greene, Debra A.S. Law&B 92
Greene, Don Harold Law&B 92
Greene, Donald Johnson 1916- WhoAm 92, WhoWrEP 92
Greene, Donald Richard 1947- WhoEmL 93
Greene, Donna Sue 1956- WhoEmL 93
Greene, Douglas G. 1944- ScF&FL 92
Greene, Douglas George 1944- WhoSSW 93
Greene, Edith Leslie 1952- WhoAmW 93
Greene, Edward Allen 1926- WhoE 93
Greene, Edward Forbes 1922- WhoAm 92
Greene, Edward Gregory 1957- WhoSSW 93
Greene, Elizabeth Law&B 92
Greene, Ellen 1952?- ConTFT 10
Greene, Ernest Lonzo 1931- WhoSSW 93
Greene, Ernest Rinaldo, Jr. 1941- WhoSSW 93, WhoWor 93
Greene, Ettie Mae 1877-1992 BioIn 17, NewYTBS 92
Greene, Frank Sullivan, Jr. 1938- WhoAm 92
Greene, Freda 1929- WhoAmW 93
Greene, Frederick D., II 1927- WhoAm 92
Greene, Gael BioIn 17
Greene, Gayle 1943- ConAu 137
Greene, George H. 1938- St&PR 93
Greene, Graham BioIn 17
Greene, Graham 1904-1991 AnObit 1991, BioIn 17, ConLC 70 [port], -72 [port], MagSWL [port], ScF&FL 92, WorLitC [port]
Greene, Graham Carleton 1936- WhoWor 93
Greene, Harlan 1953- ConAu 137, ConGAN
Greene, Harold A. Law&B 92
Greene, Harold H. 1923- CngDr 91
Greene, Harris 1921- WhoWor 93
Greene, Henry Mather 1870-1954 BioIn 17
Greene, Herbert Bruce 1934- St&PR 93, WhoAm 92
Greene, Herman Paul, Jr. 1936- WhoE 93
Greene, Howard Paul 1931- WhoAm 92
Greene, Howard Roger 1937- WhoE 93
Greene, Ida 1938- WhoAmW 93
Greene, Jack P(hillip) 1931- ConAu 40NR
Greene, Jack Phillip 1931- WhoAm 92
Greene, James Douglas 1957- WhoEmL 93
Greene, James L. 1934- WhoIns 93
Greene, James R. 1929- St&PR 93
Greene, James R., III Law&B 92
Greene, James W. Law&B 92
Greene, Janelle L. 1940- St&PR 93
Greene, Janelle Langley 1940- WhoAmW 93
Greene, Jay E. 1914-1987 ScF&FL 92
Greene, Jerry George 1937- WhoAm 92
Greene, Jesse J., Jr. 1945- WhoE 93
Greene, Joe BioIn 17
Greene, Joe 1946- WhoAm 92
Greene, John d1991 BioIn 17
Greene, John Burkland 1939- WhoAm 92
Greene, John Clifford 1926- WhoAm 92
Greene, John Colton 1917- WhoAm 92
Greene, John Frederick 1940- WhoAm 92, WhoSSW 93
Greene, John Joseph 1946- WhoAm 92, WhoWor 93
Greene, John Robert 1955- WhoE 93
Greene, John Thomas, Jr. 1929- WhoAm 92
Greene, Jonathan Edward 1943- WhoSSW 93
Greene, Joseph Nathaniel, Jr. 1920- WhoAm 92, WhoE 93
Greene, Joshua Eli 1951- WhoEmL 93, WhoUN 92
Greene, Joyce Meller 1927- WhoAm 92
Greene, Judith C. Law&B 92
Greene, Jule Blounte 1922- WhoAm 92
Greene, Karen Sandra 1942- WhoAmW 93, WhoE 93
Greene, Kenneth A. Law&B 92
Greene, Kermit 1925- St&PR 93
Greene, Kevin Darwin BioIn 17
Greene, Larry BioIn 17
Greene, Laurence Whitridge, Jr. 1924- WhoWor 93
Greene, Lawrence M. 1911- St&PR 93
Greene, Lawrence William 1950- WhoEmL 93
Greene, Leonard Michael 1918- WhoAm 92
Greene, Liliane 1928- WhoAm 92
Greene, Liz 1946- ScF&FL 92
Greene, Lorenzo Johnston 1899-1988 BioIn 17
Greene, Lorna WhoWrEP 92
Greene, Lorraine Williams 1950- WhoSSW 93
Greene, Lynne Jeannette 1938- WhoAm 92, WhoAmW 93, WhoE 93
Greene, Margaret Lyford 1942- St&PR 93
Greene, Margaret McCaffrey WhoE 93
Greene, Mark 1942- St&PR 93
Greene, Marlin SoulM
Greene, Maureen P. Law&B 92
Greene, Maurice 1696-1755 Baker 92
Greene, Maxine BioIn 17
Greene, Melissa Fay 1952- ConAu 138
Greene, Michael A. Law&B 92
Greene, Michael Edward 1935- WhoAm 92, WhoE 93
Greene, Michael R. Law&B 92
Greene, Michele WhoAm 92
Greene, Mildred Sarah 1929- WhoAmW 93
Greene, Milton Anthony 1938- WhoAm 92
Greene, Mott Tuthill 1945- WhoAm 92
Greene, Nancy Ellen 1947- WhoAmW 93
Greene, Natalie Constance 1960- WhoAmW 93
Greene, Nathanael 1742-1786 HarEnMi
Greene, Nathanael 1935- WhoAm 92
Greene, Oscar, III 1948- St&PR 93

Greene, Pat Ryan 1930- WhoWrEP 92
Greene, Paul Irving 1933- St&PR 93
Greene, Percy 1898-1977 EncAACR
Greene, Peter A. 1946- WhoAm 92
Greene, Philip James 1961- WhoE 93
Greene, (Harry) Plunket 1865-1936 Baker 92
Greene, Raleigh Williams 1927- St&PR 93
Greene, Randall Frederick 1949- St&PR 93
Greene, Renez Law&B 92
Greene, Richard 1948- St&PR 93
Greene, Richard E. 1938- St&PR 93, WhoAm 92
Greene, Richard H. 1955- WhoE 93
Greene, Richard Myron 1953- WhoE 93
Greene, Richard Tucker 1941- St&PR 93
Greene, Robert BioIn 17
Greene, Robert Allan 1931- WhoAm 92
Greene, Robert Bernard, Jr. 1947- WhoAm 92, WhoWrEP 92
Greene, Robert Edward Lee, Jr. 1941- St&PR 93
Greene, Robert Jay 1930- WhoE 93
Greene, Robert Michael 1945- WhoAm 92
Greene, Robert Warren 1928- WhoE 93
Greene, Robert William 1929- WhoAm 92
Greene, Robin Lea 1954- WhoAmW 93
Greene, Ruth AmWomPl
Greene, Sarah Laschinger 1929- WhoSSW 93
Greene, Sarah Lee 1955- WhoSSW 93
Greene, Sarah Louise 1952- WhoAmW 93
Greene, Sharon Louise 1960- WhoAmW 93
Greene, Shecky 1926- WhoAm 92
Greene, Sonia ScF&FL 92
Greene, Sparky 1948- MiSFD 9
Greene, Stefanie Krainin 1937- WhoAmW 93
Greene, Stephanie Harrison 1950- WhoAmW 93
Greene, Theodore J. 1934- St&PR 93
Greene, Thomas Alan 1934- St&PR 93
Greene, Thomas Edward Law&B 92
Greene, Thomas McLernon 1926- WhoAm 92
Greene, Timothy G. Law&B 92
Greene, Tony 1955-1990 BioIn 17
Greene, Virginia A. d1984 BioIn 17
Greene, Virginia Carvel 1934- WhoAm 92
Greene, Walter Skinner 1951- WhoEmL 93
Greene, Warren H., Jr. Law&B 92
Greene, Warren K. 1936- St&PR 93
Greene, Warren Keeler 1936- WhoAm 92
Greene, Wendy Segal 1929- WhoAmW 93
Greene, William Henry L'Vel 1943- WhoAm 92
Greene, Willie Donald 1939- WhoSSW 93
Greenebaum, James Eugene, II 1927- St&PR 93
Greenebaum, Leonard Charles 1934- WhoAm 92, WhoE 93, WhoWor 93
Greene-Mercier, Marie Zoe 1911- WhoWor 93
Greener, Judith Robin 1953- St&PR 93
Greener, Leslie 1900-1974 DcChlFi
Greener, William I., III 1950- WhoAm 92
Greener, William O. ScF&FL 92
Greenes, Robert B. 1921- St&PR 93
Greenewalt, Crawford Hallock 1902- WhoAm 92
Greeney, Laura Anne 1961- WhoEmL 93
Greenfeld, Josh BioIn 17
Greenfeld, Liah 1954- ConAu 138
Greenfest, Robert 1960- WhoE 93
Greenfield, Adrienne I. Law&B 92
Greenfield, Amy Beth Law&B 92
Greenfield, Bruce Harold 1917- WhoAm 92
Greenfield, Carol Nathan 1942- WhoAm 92, WhoAmW 93
Greenfield, Charles d1989 BioIn 17
Greenfield, Cheryl S. 1959- WhoE 93
Greenfield, Craig Bennett 1962- WhoEmL 93
Greenfield, Daniel Paul 1945- WhoE 93
Greenfield, David W. Law&B 92
Greenfield, David W. 1940- WhoAm 92
Greenfield, Eloise 1929- BioIn 17, BlkAull 92, DcAmChF 1960, MajAI [port], SmATA 16AS [port], WhoAm 92
Greenfield, Eloise Little 1929- WhoWrEP 92
Greenfield, George B. 1928- WhoAm 92
Greenfield, Gerald 1939- WhoAm 92
Greenfield, Gordon Kraus 1915- WhoAm 92
Greenfield, Helen Meyers 1908- WhoAm 92, WhoAmW 93, WhoE 93, WhoWor 93
Greenfield, Helen Muehl 1910- WhoAmW 93
Greenfield, Irving A. 1928- ScF&FL 92
Greenfield, James Robert 1926- WhoAm 92
Greenfield, Jane BioIn 17
Greenfield, Jay 1932- WhoAm 92
Greenfield, Jerry BioIn 17
Greenfield, John Charles 1945- WhoAm 92
Greenfield, Joseph Cholmondeley, Jr. 1931- WhoAm 92
Greenfield, Julia Leah Law&B 92
Greenfield, Karyn Allison Law&B 92
Greenfield, Kenneth Darwin 1927- St&PR 93
Greenfield, Lazar John 1934- WhoAm 92
Greenfield, Mark A. Law&B 92
Greenfield, Marsha Karen Law&B 92
Greenfield, Martin K. 1924- St&PR 93
Greenfield, Maurice H. 1942- St&PR 93
Greenfield, Meg 1930- WhoAm 92, WhoAmW 93, WhoE 93
Greenfield, Nancy Reuben 1961- WhoSSW 93
Greenfield, Norman Samuel 1923- WhoAm 92
Greenfield, Robert K. 1915- St&PR 93
Greenfield, Robert Kauffman 1915- WhoAm 92
Greenfield, Robert Thomas, Jr. 1933- WhoE 93
Greenfield, Ronald Alan 1951- WhoSSW 93
Greenfield, Sanford Raymond 1926- WhoAm 92
Greenfield, Seymour Stephen 1922- St&PR 93, WhoAm 92
Greenfield, Stanley WhoScE 91-1
Greenfield, Stanley Marshall 1927- WhoAm 92
Greenfield, Stanley R. 1925- WhoUN 92
Greenfield, Steven E. 1947- WhoE 93
Greenfield, Val Shea 1932- WhoAm 92, WhoE 93, WhoWor 93
Greenfield, W. 1944- WhoAmW 93
Greenfield-Sanders, Timothy 1952- WhoEmL 93
Greengard, Paul 1925- WhoAm 92
Greengrass, Paul MiSFD 9
Greengrass, Shirley d1992 NewYTBS 92
Greengus, Samuel 1936- WhoAm 92
Greenhagen, Suzette BioIn 17
Greenhalgh, Douglas Anthony 1951- WhoWor 93
Greenhalgh, Frederick A. 1942- St&PR 93
Greenhalgh, James D. Law&B 92
Greenhalgh, James Francis Derek WhoScE 91-1
Greenhalgh, Jo Lynn 1949- St&PR 93
Greenhalgh, Lorene Mason 1943- WhoAmW 93
Greenhalgh, Richard Justin S. 1958- WhoScE 91-1
Greenhalgh, Roger Malcolm WhoScE 91-1
Greenhalgh, Terry L. 1950- WhoEmL 93, WhoSSW 93
Greenhalgh, Thomas J. 1949- St&PR 93
Greenhalgh, Zohra ScF&FL 92
Greenhall, Arthur Merwin 1911- WhoE 93
Greenhall, Ken ScF&FL 92
Greenhaw, Dale 1921- St&PR 93
Greenhaw, Thomas Benton, IV 1925- WhoWor 93
Greenhawt, Charles Eric Law&B 92
Greenhill, Basil (Jack) 1920- ConAu 38NR
Greenhill, Colin Roger 1937- WhoUN 92
Greenhill, James Giffard 1964- WhoSSW 93
Greenhill, Richard Harry 1939- St&PR 93
Greenhill, Robert Foster 1936- WhoAm 92
Greenhill, William Duke 1946- WhoSSW 93
Greenholtz, Wayne Maurice 1941- St&PR 93
Greenhough, John Hardman 1939- WhoAm 92, WhoE 93
Greenhough, Terence ScF&FL 92
Greenhough, Terry 1944- ScF&FL 92
Greenhouse, Bernard 1916- Baker 92, WhoAm 92
Greenhouse, Linda Joyce 1947- WhoAmW 93
Greenhouse, Lloyd 1923- St&PR 93
Greenhouse, N. Barry 1940- WhoIns 93
Greenhut, Arnold 1928- St&PR 93
Greenhut, Deborah Schneider 1951- WhoEmL 93
Greenhut, Melvin Leonard 1921- WhoAm 92, WhoSSW 93
Greeniaus, H. John BioIn 17
Greening, Bruce Craig 1954- St&PR 93
Greenky, Seth Richard 1948- WhoE 93
Greenland, Colin 1954- ScF&FL 92
Greenland, Gregory Lance 1945- St&PR 93
Greenland, Leo 1920- St&PR 93, WhoAm 92
Greenland, Rita d1991 BioIn 17
Greenland, Steven St&PR 93
Greenland, Thomas E. Law&B 92
Greenleaf, Daniel Edward 1951- WhoWrEP 92
Greenleaf, Katherine Maxim 1948- St&PR 93
Greenleaf, Mary K. 1927- St&PR 93
Greenleaf, Richard Edward 1930- WhoAm 92
Greenleaf, Robert K. 1904-1990 BioIn 17
Greenleaf, Robert T. 1926- St&PR 93
Greenleaf, Thomas 1755-1798 JrnUS
Greenleaf, William ScF&FL 92
Greenlee, Billy C. 1930- St&PR 93
Greenlee, Bruce Carleton 1931- St&PR 93
Greenlee, Gus 1897-1952 BioIn 17
Greenlee, Herbert Breckenridge 1927- WhoAm 92
Greenlee, John Alden 1911- WhoAm 92
Greenlee, Kenneth William 1916- WhoWor 93
Greenlee, Mark B. Law&B 92
Greenlee, Mark William 1956- WhoWor 93
Greenlee, Stewart David Law&B 92
Greenlees, John Patrick Campbell 1959- WhoWor 93
Greenlees, Thomas William 1926- WhoE 93
Greenley, Ken BioIn 17
Greenlick, Merwyn Ronald 1935- WhoAm 92
Greenly, Colin 1928- WhoAm 92, WhoE 93
Greenly, Lewis Allen WhoWor 93
Greenman, Frederic E. Law&B 92
Greenman, Frederic Edward 1936- St&PR 93, WhoAm 92
Greenman, Jeffrey Matthew Law&B 92
Greenman, Norman Lawrence 1923- St&PR 93, WhoAm 92
Greenman, Paula S. Law&B 92
Greenman, Robert 1939- ConAu 38NR
Greenman, Seymour Law&B 92
Greenman, W. Frank St&PR 93
Greenman, William G. 1948- St&PR 93
Greeno, John Ladd 1949- St&PR 93, WhoAm 92, WhoE 93, WhoEmL 93, WhoWor 93
Greenop, David C. 1932- St&PR 93
Greenough, William Bates, III 1932- WhoAm 92
Greenough, William Edward, Jr. 1942- St&PR 93
Greenough, William Tallant 1944- WhoAm 92
Greenquist, Thomas Alfred 1928- St&PR 93
Greenshields, Jack Browning 1949- WhoEmL 93
Greenshields, Raymond 1947- WhoWor 93
Greenslade, Brian 1930- St&PR 93
Greenslade, Forrest Charles 1939- WhoAm 92
Greenslade, Thomas B. 1910-1990 BioIn 17
Greenspan, Alan BioIn 17, NewYTBS 92 [port]
Greenspan, Alan 1926- News 92 [port], WhoAm 92, WhoE 93, WhoWor 93
Greenspan, Alan George 1943- WhoE 93
Greenspan, Arnold Michael 1938- St&PR 93, WhoAm 92
Greenspan, Bud BioIn 17, MiSFD 9
Greenspan, David d1991 BioIn 17
Greenspan, David Arnold 1940- WhoSSW 93
Greenspan, David Ellison 1959- WhoEmL 93
Greenspan, David J. Law&B 92
Greenspan, Deborah WhoAm 92
Greenspan, Donald 1928- WhoAm 92
Greenspan, Francis S. 1920- WhoAm 92
Greenspan, Harvey Philip 1933- WhoAm 92
Greenspan, Jay Scott 1959- WhoAm 92
Greenspan, Jodi Carpey Law&B 92
Greenspan, Joel Daniel 1952- WhoE 93
Greenspan, Joseph 1930- St&PR 93
Greenspan, Leon Joseph 1932- WhoE 93
Greenspan, Ronald I. 1947- St&PR 93
Greenspan, Sandra L. Law&B 92
Greenspan, Sara Theodora 1940- WhoE 93
Greenspan, Stanley Ira 1941- WhoE 93
Greenspan, Stanley Michael 1956- WhoEmL 93
Greenspan, Stuart d1990 BioIn 17
Greenspan-Margolis, June Rita Edelman 1934- WhoAm 92, WhoAmW 93
Greenspon, Herbert Mitchell 1917- St&PR 93
Greenspon, Jeffrey Mark 1952- WhoE 93
Greenspon, Lawrence Harris 1966- WhoSSW 93
Greenstadt, Melvin 1918- WhoAm 92
Greensted, Christopher Stanford WhoScE 91-1
Greenstein, Abraham Jacob 1949- WhoAm 92, WhoE 93, WhoEmL 93
Greenstein, Alvin 1928- St&PR 93
Greenstein, Edward Theodore 1923- WhoE 93
Greenstein, Fred Irwin 1930- WhoAm 92
Greenstein, James F. 1924- St&PR 93
Greenstein, Jesse Leonard 1909- WhoAm 92
Greenstein, Joel Robert 1937- WhoE 93
Greenstein, Julius Sidney 1927- WhoAm 92
Greenstein, Martin Richard 1944- WhoAm 92
Greenstein, Merle Edward 1937- WhoWor 93
Greenstein, Michael Kenneth 1946- St&PR 93
Greenstein, Milton BioIn 17
Greenstein, Rita Rappoport 1928- WhoAmW 93
Greenstein, Ruth Louise 1946- WhoAm 92
Greenstein, Scott Andrew Law&B 92
Greenstone, J. David 1937-1990 BioIn 17
Greenstone, James Lynn 1943- WhoAm 92
Greenstreet, John R. Law&B 92
Greenstreet, Sydney 1879-1954 IntDcF 2-3 [port]
Greenthal, Charles H. d1991 BioIn 17
Greentree, I. Richard 1948- WhoSSW 93
Greentree, Leanne Marie 1960- WhoEmL 93
Greenwade, George Dennis 1956- WhoSSW 93
Greenwald, Alan Frank 1944- WhoAm 92
Greenwald, Carol Schiro 1939- WhoAm 92
Greenwald, Caroline Meyer 1936- WhoAm 92
Greenwald, Dorothy I. 1920- WhoE 93
Greenwald, Douglas 1913- WhoWor 93
Greenwald, Floyd T. 1934- St&PR 93
Greenwald, Gerald BioIn 17
Greenwald, Gerald 1935- St&PR 93, WhoAm 92
Greenwald, Gerald Bernard 1929- WhoAm 92
Greenwald, Gilbert Saul 1927- WhoAm 92
Greenwald, Harry J. ScF&FL 92
Greenwald, Harry R. 1930- St&PR 93
Greenwald, Herbert 1910- WhoE 93
Greenwald, Howard 1918- St&PR 93
Greenwald, James L. 1927- St&PR 93
Greenwald, Jawj E. Law&B 92
Greenwald, Jean 1942- WhoAmW 93
Greenwald, Jerry 1946- St&PR 93
Greenwald, Jim 1938- WhoAm 92
Greenwald, John Edward 1942- WhoAm 92
Greenwald, Larry L. Law&B 92
Greenwald, Maggie MiSFD 9
Greenwald, Martin 1942- WhoAm 92
Greenwald, Michael Jay 1953- WhoE 93
Greenwald, Peter 1936- WhoAm 92
Greenwald, Robert 1927- WhoAm 92
Greenwald, Robert 1945- MiSFD 9
Greenwald, Robert A. 1947- St&PR 93
Greenwald, Sheila ConAu 39NR
Greenwald, Sheila Ellen 1934- WhoAm 92
Greenwald, Thomas Edward 1960- WhoE 93
Greenwald Hendler, Lynne Law&B 92
Greenwalt, Clifford Lloyd 1933- St&PR 93, WhoAm 92
Greenwalt, David MiSFD 9
Greenwalt, Lynn Adams 1931- WhoAm 92
Greenwalt, Sandra Joyce 1962- WhoEmL 93
Greenwalt, Tibor Jack 1914- WhoAm 92
Greenwalt, William Earl, Jr. 1962- WhoE 93
Greenway, Hugh Davids Scott 1935- WhoAm 92
Greenway, Isabella Selmes 1886-1953 BioIn 17
Greenway, John Selmes 1924- WhoAm 92
Greenway, Patsy Jo 1937- WhoWrEP 92
Greenway, Robert Charles Stuart 1928- WhoE 93
Greenway, Robert Stuart 1960- WhoE 93
Greenway, William Charles 1958- WhoE 93
Greenway, William Henry, Jr. 1947- WhoWrEP 92
Greenwell, Arnold 1956- WhoEmL 93
Greenwell, Donald Edward, III Law&B 92
Greenwell, James Joseph 1959- St&PR 93
Greenwell, Kathleen Mary 1947- WhoAmW 93
Greenwell, Kevin James 1958- WhoE 93
Greenwell, Michael Lewis 1963- WhoAm 92
Greenwell, Pamela M. Law&B 92
Greenwell, Roger Allen 1941- WhoWor 93
Greenwell, Ronald Everett 1938- WhoAm 92
Greenwich, Ellie 1940- SoulM
Greenwold, Douglas Jay 1942- St&PR 93

Greenwold, Warren Eldon 1923- WhoAm 92
Greenwood, Alan G. Law&B 92
Greenwood, Allan N. WhoAm 92
Greenwood, Audrey Gates 1917- WhoE 93
Greenwood, Charles F. 1947- St&PR 93
Greenwood, Charlotte 1890-1978 QDrFCA 92 [port]
Greenwood, Colin WhoScE 91-1
Greenwood, David WhoScE 91-1
Greenwood, David Kasim 1957- BiDAMSp 1989
Greenwood, Ed ScF&FL 92
Greenwood, Frank 1924- WhoWor 93
Greenwood, Fred Henry 1927- WhoE 93
Greenwood, Fred M., III Law&B 92
Greenwood, G.B. WhoScE 91-1
Greenwood, Gaynol DeWane 1935- WhoSSW 93
Greenwood, Geoffrey Wilson WhoScE 91-1
Greenwood, Gordon Edward 1935- WhoSSW 93
Greenwood, Harriet Lois 1950- WhoAmW 93
Greenwood, Helen Maxine 1916- WhoAmW 93
Greenwood, Ivan Anderson 1921- WhoWor 93
Greenwood, James ScF&FL 92
Greenwood, Janet Kae Daly 1943- WhoAm 92
Greenwood, Janet Kingham 1939- WhoAmW 93
Greenwood, Joan 1921-1987 IntDcF 2-3 [port]
Greenwood, Joen Elizabeth 1934- WhoAmW 93
Greenwood, John Edson 1927- WhoWrEP 92
Greenwood, John Edward Douglas 1923- WhoE 93, WhoWor 93
Greenwood, John Malcolm 1941- St&PR 93
Greenwood, L. C. Henderson 1946- BiDAMSp 1989
Greenwood, Lawrence George 1921- St&PR 93, WhoAm 92
Greenwood, M. R. C. 1943- WhoAm 92, WhoAmW 93
Greenwood, Marion 1909-1970 BioIn 17
Greenwood, Norman Neill WhoScE 91-1
Greenwood, P. WhoScE 91-1
Greenwood, Patrick E. Law&B 92
Greenwood, Richard Edwin 1938- St&PR 93
Greenwood, Richard M. 1947- St&PR 93
Greenwood, Robert N. 1935- St&PR 93
Greenwood, Roger K. 1943- St&PR 93
Greenwood, Scott Alson 1949- WhoE 93
Greenwood, Sharon A. Law&B 92
Greenwood, Susan Fowle 1941- WhoE 93
Greenwood, Susan Grossman 1946- WhoAm 92, WhoAmW 93
Greenwood, Ted 1930- DcChlFi
Greenwood, Thomas S. 1921- St&PR 93
Greenwood, Tim S. 1949- St&PR 93
Greenwood, Virginia Maxine McLeod 1930- WhoSSW 93
Greenwood, William Edward 1938- St&PR 93
Greenwood, William Warren 1942- WhoAm 92
Greenwood, Wilson 1923- St&PR 93
Greenwood, Winifred 1885-1961 SweetSg A
Greenwood-Harris, Janie Law&B 92
Greep, Linda Caryl 1947- WhoAmW 93, WhoWor 93
Greer, Allen Curtis, II 1951- WhoAm 92
Greer, Beverly S. Law&B 92
Greer, Billy Louis 1959- WhoE 93
Greer, Brent Wesley 1967- WhoSSW 93
Greer, Carl C. 1940- St&PR 93
Greer, Carl Crawford 1940- WhoAm 92
Greer, Darrell Ray 1950- WhoEmL 93
Greer, David S. 1925- WhoAm 92
Greer, Dennis L. 1945- St&PR 93
Greer, Dorothy Elizabeth 1946- WhoSSW 93
Greer, Dwain 1950- St&PR 93
Greer, Edward 1924- WhoAm 92
Greer, Edward Gabriel 1920- WhoE 93
Greer, Eric Reginald 1904-1983 BioIn 17
Greer, Gayle BioIn 17
Greer, George C. 1932- St&PR 93
Greer, George W., III 1939- St&PR 93
Greer, Germaine 1939- BioIn 17, WhoAm 92
Greer, Gery ScF&FL 92
Greer, Gordon Bruce 1932- WhoAm 92, WhoE 93, WhoWor 93
Greer, Herschel Lynn, Jr. 1941- WhoSSW 93
Greer, Howard Earl 1921- WhoAm 92
Greer, J. Wayne 1942- St&PR 93
Greer, Jack P. 1928- St&PR 93
Greer, James Alexander, II 1932- WhoAm 92
Greer, James Bradford 1934- WhoSSW 93
Greer, James Pete Law&B 92
Greer, Jane H. 1938- St&PR 93
Greer, Jeanette Mulder 1924- WhoAmW 93
Greer, John J. 1942- St&PR 93
Greer, Joseph Epps 1923- WhoAm 92
Greer, Joseph Terrence BioIn 17
Greer, Leonard W. 1934- St&PR 93
Greer, Melvin 1929- WhoAm 92
Greer, Monte Arnold 1922- WhoAm 92, WhoWor 93
Greer, Patric Robert 1954- St&PR 93
Greer, Paul W. 1951- St&PR 93
Greer, Randall Dewey 1951- St&PR 93, WhoAm 92, WhoEmL 93
Greer, Raymond White 1954- WhoSSW 93
Greer, Reg 1904-1983 BioIn 17
Greer, Richard MajAI
Greer, Richard R. 1952- St&PR 93
Greer, Richard Ray 1952- WhoAm 92
Greer, Rita Gilbert 1948- WhoEmL 93
Greer, Robert A. 1953- St&PR 93
Greer, Scott 1935- WhoSSW 93
Greer, Thomas H. 1942- WhoAm 92
Greer, Thomas Hoag 1914- WhoAm 92
Greer, Thomas Upton 1928- WhoAm 92
Greer, Thomas Vernon 1932- WhoAm 92
Greer, Tom 1846?-1904 ScF&FL 92
Greer, Victoria Marie Law&B 92
Greer, William J., Sr. 1947- St&PR 93
Greer, William Wayne 1942- St&PR 93
Greet, Norman Roy 1947- St&PR 93
Gref, Robert 1939- St&PR 93
Grefe, Richard 1945- WhoAm 92
Grefe, Rolland Eugene 1920- WhoAm 92
Grefenstette, Carl G. 1927- St&PR 93
Greff, John T. St&PR 93
Grefinger, Wolfgang 1470?-1515? Baker 92
Gregan, Edmund Robert 1936- WhoAm 92
Gregan, John Patrick 1947- WhoE 93, WhoEmL 93, WhoWor 93
Greganti, Mac Andrew 1947- WhoAm 92
Gregentios fl. 6th cent.- OxDcByz
Greger, Harald 1942- WhoScE 91-4
Greger, Janet Lee 1948- WhoAmW 93
Gregersen, Kenneth A. 1931- St&PR 93
Gregerson, Byron Arnold 1942- WhoIns 93
Gregerson, Rebecca Ostar 1955- WhoAmW 93
Gregerson, Robert Louis 1938- St&PR 93
Gregg, Andrew 1755-1835 PolPar
Gregg, Candace Carlene 1961- WhoEmL 93
Gregg, Charles Haynie 1939- WhoSSW 93
Gregg, Charles T. 1927- BioIn 17
Gregg, Charles T(hornton) 1927- ConAu 40NR
Gregg, Charles Thornton 1927- WhoAm 92
Gregg, Colin 1947- MiSFD 9
Gregg, David, III 1933- WhoWor 93
Gregg, David Paul 1923- WhoWor 93
Gregg, Davis Weinert 1918- WhoAm 92
Gregg, Donald Phinney 1927- WhoAm 92, WhoWor 93
Gregg, Eric 1951- BioIn 17
Gregg, Forrest BioIn 17
Gregg, Forrest 1933- WhoAm 92
Gregg, Gary R. St&PR 93
Gregg, Gloria E. 1924- St&PR 93
Gregg, Hugh 1917- WhoAm 92
Gregg, J. Robby, Jr. 1961- WhoE 93
Gregg, Jamie V. 1953- St&PR 93
Gregg, Jamie Vincent 1953- WhoEmL 93
Gregg, John Franklin 1943- WhoAm 92
Gregg, John Nathan 1934- WhoAm 92
Gregg, John William Law&B 92
Gregg, Judd 1947- WhoAm 92, WhoE 93, WhoWor 93
Gregg, Lucius Perry, Jr. 1933- WhoAm 92
Gregg, Lynne Diana Williams 1956- WhoAmW 93
Gregg, Marie Byrd 1930- WhoSSW 93
Gregg, Marjorie AmWomPl
Gregg, Martin d1992 NewYTBS 92
Gregg, Michael B. 1930- WhoAm 92
Gregg, Michael T. Law&B 92
Gregg, Michael W. 1935- St&PR 93, WhoAm 92
Gregg, Raymond Harry 1930- St&PR 93
Gregg, Stephen R. 1914- BioIn 17
Gregg, Stewart D. 1954- St&PR 93
Gregg, Susan Sampson 1947- WhoSSW 93
Gregg, Walter E., Jr. Law&B 92
Gregg, Walter Emmor, Jr. 1941- WhoAm 92
Greggains, Joanie Catherine WhoAmW 93
Greggs, Elizabeth May Bushnell 1925- WhoAmW 93, WhoWor 93
Gregh, Louis 1843-1915 Baker 92
Grego, Claudio 1947- St&PR 93
Gregoir, Edouard (Georges Jacques) 1822-1890 Baker 92
Gregoir, Jacques (Mathieu Joseph) 1817-1876 Baker 92
Gregoir, Willy-Louis 1920- WhoScE 91-2
Gregoire, Christine WhoAmW 93
Gregoire, Dennis James 1954- St&PR 93
Gregoire, Ghislain 1939- WhoScE 91-2
Gregoire, Marc 1955- WhoWor 93
Gregoire, Michel R. 1946- WhoWor 93
Gregoire, Paul Cardinal 1911- WhoAm 92, WhoWor 93
Gregoire, Sylvie Law&B 92
Gregoire, Timothy Gordon 1949- WhoSSW 93
Gregor, Andrew St&PR 93
Gregor, Andrew, Jr. 1948- WhoAm 92
Gregor, Arthur 1923- BioIn 17, WhoWrEP 92
Gregor, Bohumil 1926- Baker 92, OxDcOp
Gregor, Cestmir 1926- Baker 92
Gregor, Christian Friedrich 1723-1801 Baker 92
Gregor, Clunie Bryan 1929- WhoAm 92
Gregor, Dorothy Deborah 1939- WhoAm 92, WhoAmW 93
Gregor, Eduard 1936- WhoWor 93
Gregor, Harriet Elizabeth Wilson 1950- WhoWor 93
Gregor, Joseph 1888-1960 IntDcOp, OxDcOp
Gregor, Lee ConAu 37NR
Gregor, Mary Jeanne 1928- WhoAmW 93
Gregor, Tibor Philip 1919- WhoAm 92
Gregoras, Nikephoros c. 1290-c. 1358 OxDcByz
Gregorczyk, Florian S. Law&B 92
Gregoriadis, Gregory WhoScE 91-1
Gregorian, Joyce Ballou 1946-1991 ScF&FL 92
Gregorian, Vartan BioIn 17
Gregorian, Vartan 1934- WhoAm 92, WhoE 93, WhoWor 93
Gregorian, Victoria BioIn 17
Gregorich, Barbara BioIn 17
Gregorich, Penny Denise 1968- WhoAmW 93
Gregorio, Frank Michael 1948- St&PR 93
Gregorio, Luis J.L. 1929- St&PR 93
Gregorio, Luis Justino Lopes 1929- WhoAm 92
Gregorio, M.V.M. 1946- WhoScE 91-3
Gregorio, Peter Anthony 1916- WhoSSW 93
Gregorio, Robert Domenic 1966- WhoE 93
Gregoriou, Gregor Georg 1937- WhoWor 93
Gregorius, Beverly June 1915- WhoAm 92, WhoAmW 93
Gregorski, Peggy Wilk 1959- WhoEmL 93
Gregory d647 OxDcByz
Gregory, Lady 1852-1932 BioIn 17
Gregory, I c. 540-604 Baker 92
Gregory, I, Saint c. 540-604 BioIn 17
Gregory, II 669-731 OxDcByz
Gregory, III OxDcByz
Gregory, V OxDcByz
Gregory, VII c. 1020-1085 OxDcByz
Gregory, IX c. 1170-1241 OxDcByz
Gregory, X 1210-1276 OxDcByz
Gregory, XI 1329-1378 OxDcByz
Gregory, Alfred Thorne 1901-1991 BioIn 17
Gregory, Alfred William 1928- St&PR 93
Gregory, Ann Young 1935- WhoAmW 93, WhoSSW 93
Gregory, Arthur Stanley 1914- WhoAm 92
Gregory, Augustus 1819-1905 Expl 93
Gregory, Bettina Louise 1946- WhoAm 92, WhoAmW 93
Gregory, Bobby Lee 1938- WhoAm 92
Gregory, Bruce Craig 1937- WhoAsAP 91
Gregory, Calvin 1942- WhoWor 93
Gregory, Calvin Luther 1942- WhoIns 93
Gregory, Carolyn Holmes 1950- WhoWrEP 92
Gregory, Cynthia BioIn 17
Gregory, Cynthia Kathleen 1946- WhoAm 92, WhoAmW 93
Gregory, D.P. WhoScE 91-1
Gregory, Daniel Kevin 1958- WhoSSW 93
Gregory, David Wilson 1941- WhoSSW 93
Gregory, Dennis Edward 1949- WhoEmL 93, WhoSSW 93
Gregory, Dick BioIn 17
Gregory, Dick 1932- WhoAm 92
Gregory, Don E. St&PR 93
Gregory, Donald Munson 1897- WhoAm 92
Gregory, Edward Meeks 1922- WhoSSW 93
Gregory, Ena 1905-1965 SweetSg B
Gregory, Fern Alexandra 1951- WhoAmW 93
Gregory, Franklin 1905-1985 ScF&FL 92
Gregory, Frederick 1942- ConAu 138
Gregory, Frederick D. 1941- AfrAmBi [port]
Gregory, Frederick Drew BioIn 17
Gregory, Geoffrey WhoScE 91-1
Gregory, George G. Law&B 92
Gregory, George G. 1932- WhoAm 92
Gregory, George Martin 1934- St&PR 93
Gregory, George Tillman, Jr. 1921- WhoSSW 93
Gregory, Gus 1940- WhoSSW 93
Gregory, Guy ScF&FL 92
Gregory, Harold Anthony 1919- WhoE 93
Gregory, Harry L. 1943- St&PR 93
Gregory, Helen Emelee 1936- WhoAmW 93
Gregory, Henry C. 1935-1990 BioIn 17
Gregory, Herold La Mar 1923- WhoAm 92
Gregory, Holly Wanda Januszkiewicz 1956- WhoAmW 93
Gregory, Horace 1898-1982 BioIn 17
Gregory, Jack 1925- St&PR 93
Gregory, Jamee BioIn 17
Gregory, James 1911- WhoAm 92
Gregory, Jane Thurmond 1930- St&PR 93
Gregory, Jean MajAI
Gregory, Jean Winfrey 1947- WhoAmW 93, WhoSSW 93
Gregory, Jerrold W. BioIn 17
Gregory, Joel Edward 1939- St&PR 93
Gregory, John ScF&FL 92
Gregory, John Harry 1950- WhoEmL 93
Gregory, John Lunsford, III 1947- WhoEmL 93
Gregory, Joseph Tracy 1914- WhoAm 92
Gregory, Josephine Lane 1955- WhoWrEP 92
Gregory, Julia P. 1952- St&PR 93
Gregory, Julia Paige 1952- WhoE 93
Gregory, Kathrine Patricia 1952- WhoAmW 93
Gregory, Kenneth BioIn 17
Gregory, Kenneth John WhoScE 91-1
Gregory, Laura Rachford 1946- WhoEmL 93
Gregory, Leigh P. Law&B 92
Gregory, Linda Susan 1952- St&PR 93
Gregory, Louis P. Law&B 92
Gregory, Marian Frances 1919- WhoAmW 93
Gregory, Martha Ann 1942- WhoAmW 93
Gregory, Mary L. ScF&FL 92
Gregory, Mel Hyatt, Jr. 1936- WhoAm 92
Gregory, Mercedes d1992 BioIn 17, NewYTBS 92
Gregory, Michael 1940- WhoWrEP 92
Gregory, Michael J. 1947- WhoSSW 93
Gregory, Michael Strietmann 1929- WhoAm 92
Gregory, Mollie 1940- ScF&FL 92
Gregory, Myra May 1912- WhoAmW 93, WhoE 93
Gregory, Nelson Bruce 1933- WhoWor 93
Gregory, Neville George WhoScE 91-1
Gregory, Norman Wayne 1920- WhoAm 92
Gregory, Patricia Diane 1952- WhoWrEP 92
Gregory, Paul Eugene 1929- St&PR 93
Gregory, Philippa 1954- ScF&FL 92
Gregory, Richard Claxton BioIn 17
Gregory, Richard Claxton 1932- EncAACR [port]
Gregory, Richard Thomas 1948- WhoE 93
Gregory, Richard W. Law&B 92
Gregory, Rick Dean 1954- WhoSSW 93
Gregory, Robert D. 1929- St&PR 93
Gregory, Robert E., Jr. 1942- St&PR 93
Gregory, Robert Earle, Jr. 1942- WhoAm 92
Gregory, Robert Scott 1954- WhoSSW 93
Gregory, Ross 1933- WhoAm 92
Gregory, Sharon McWhirter 1948- WhoSSW 93
Gregory, Stephen 1952- ConAu 136, ScF&FL 92
Gregory, Theodore Law&B 92
Gregory, Thomas L. 1926- St&PR 93
Gregory, Thomas Raymond 1951- WhoSSW 93
Gregory, Tullio 1929- WhoWor 93
Gregory, Victoria Law&B 92
Gregory, Walter Martin 1956- WhoWor 93
Gregory, Walter R. 1945- St&PR 93
Gregory, Wanda Jean 1925- WhoAmW 93
Gregory, William N., Jr. 1929- WhoIns 93
Gregory, William Wallace, Jr. Law&B 92
Gregory, Wilton D. BioIn 17
Gregory Abu'l-Faraj 1225-1286 OxDcByz
Gregory Degha Pahlavuni OxDcByz
Gregory Magistros c. 990-c. 1058 OxDcByz
Gregory of Akragas fl. c. 700- OxDcByz
Gregory of Corinth OxDcByz
Gregory of Cyprus, II c. 1241-1290 OxDcByz
Gregory of Dekapolis c. 797-c. 842 OxDcByz
Gregory of Nazianzos 329?-c. 390. OxDcByz [port]
Gregory, of Nazianzus, Saint d390 BioIn 17

Gregory of Nyssa c. 335-c. 394 OxDcByz
Gregory of Tours c. 540-593? OxDcByz
Gregory Sinaites c. 1255-c. 1337 OxDcByz
Gregory, the Great c. 540-604 BioIn 17
Gregory the Great, I c. 540-604 OxDcByz
Gregory the Illuminator fl. 4th cent.- OxDcByz
Gregory Tlay 1133-1193 OxDcByz
Gregson, Dana Alan 1955- St&PR 93
Gregson, Edward 1945- Baker 92
Gregson, Maureen ScF&FL 92
Gregus, Linda Anna 1956- WhoAmW 93, WhoE 93, WhoEmL 93
Gregware, James Murray 1956- WhoE 93
Greh, Deborah Ellen 1948- WhoAmW 93
Grehan, Harold Simon, Jr. 1927- St&PR 93, WhoAm 92, WhoSSW 93
Greher, Gena R. 1951- WhoAm 92
Greher, Lawrence S. Law&B 92
Greider, Bettina Louise 1958- WhoAmW 93
Greider, John 1952- St&PR 93
Greidinger, B. Bernard 1906- WhoAm 92
Greif, Edward Louis 1909- WhoAm 92
Greif, Lloyd BioIn 17
Greif, Mortimer 1926- St&PR 93
Greif, Robert 1938- WhoAm 92
Greif, Toni Anne 1954- WhoE 93
Greifer, Aaron P. 1919- WhoE 93
Greifer, Ira 1931- WhoAm 92
Greig, Alastair 1944- WhoScE 91-1
Greig, Brian Strother 1950- WhoAm 92, WhoWor 93
Greig, Denis WhoScE 91-1
Greig, Edvard 1843-1907 OxDcOp
Greig, John Angus 1941- St&PR 93
Greig, N.A. 1927- St&PR 93
Greig, Rita AmWomPl
Greig, Russell G. 1952- WhoE 93, WhoEmL 93
Greig, Thomas Currie 1931- WhoAm 92
Greig, William James 1927- WhoWor 93
Greig, William Taber, Jr. 1924- WhoAm 92
Greil, Arthur L(awrence) 1949- ConAu 139
Greiling, James A. 1957- St&PR 93
Greiling, Paul Theodore 1939- WhoAm 92
Greilsheimer, James Gans 1937- WhoAm 92
Greim, Jon Edward 1949- St&PR 93
Greiman, April 1948- WhoAm 92, WhoAmW 93
Greimes, Christopher ScF&FL 92
Grein, Richard Frank 1932- WhoAm 92
Greindl, Josef 1912- Baker 92, OxDcOp
Greiner, David Lee 1964- WhoEmL 93, WhoSSW 93
Greiner, Dolores Mohr 1954- WhoAmW 93
Greiner, Donald J(ames) 1940- ConAu 37NR
Greiner, Donald James 1940- WhoSSW 93
Greiner, G. Roger 1942- WhoIns 93
Greiner, Gordon Gary 1934- WhoAm 92
Greiner, Harold Fredric 1922- St&PR 93
Greiner, Jeffrey H. Law&B 92
Greiner, Linda Wright 1940- WhoAmW 93
Greiner, Mary L. Law&B 92
Greiner, Morris Esty, Jr. 1920- WhoAm 92
Greiner, Nick 1947- WhoAsAP 91
Greiner, Paul Calvin 1926- St&PR 93
Greiner, Peter Charles 1938- WhoAm 92
Greiner, William Robert 1934- WhoAm 92, WhoE 93
Greinke, Everett Donald 1929- WhoAm 92
Greis, Howard Arthur 1925- St&PR 93
Greisen, Gorm 1951- WhoWor 93
Greisen, Kenneth Ingvard 1918- WhoAm 92
Greisler, Howard Parker 1950- WhoAm 92
Greisman, Harvey William 1948- WhoEmL 93
Greisman, Kenneth D. Law&B 92
Greissle, Felix 1894-1982 Baker 92
Greist, Mary Coffey 1947- WhoAm 92, WhoEmL 93
Greiter, Matthaeus c. 1490-1550 Baker 92
Greiter, W.D. 1954- St&PR 93
Greitzer, Edward Marc 1941- WhoAm 92
Greitzer, Robert Warren 1946- St&PR 93
Greive, Donald William WhoScE 91-1
Greiver, Sanford Philip 1930- WhoSSW 93
Grekoussis, Robert 1941- WhoScE 91-3
Grele, Milton Drummer 1925- St&PR 93
Grell, (August) Eduard 1800-1886 Baker 92
Grell, Harald Wolfgang 1944- WhoUN 92
Grell, Lewis Adam 1932- WhoE 93
Grella, Robert Alan 1939- WhoIns 93
Grelle, Francis Gerard 1948- St&PR 93
Grellet, Guy R. 1937- WhoScE 91-2
Grellier, Arthur Winslow 1921- St&PR 93
Grellier, Nancy C. 1929- St&PR 93
Grellier, Patrick 1941- WhoScE 91-2
Grelon, Bernard 1945- WhoWor 93
Grembowski, Eugene 1938- WhoWor 93
Gremeaux, Paul M. 1940- St&PR 93
Gremelsbacker, John Andrews 1942- WhoE 93
Gremetz, Maxime 1940- BioIn 17
Gremillion, Curtis Lionel, Jr. 1924- WhoAm 92, WhoWor 93
Gremillion, Denise 1955- WhoEmL 93
Gremillion, F. Marcel Law&B 92
Gremley, Robert C. 1929- St&PR 93
Gremmels, Luther Lloyd 1959- WhoSSW 93
Gremy, Francois 1929- WhoScE 91-2
Gren, Conrad Roger 1955- WhoWor 93
Grena, Barbara Waszak 1942- WhoE 93
Grenache, Claude Laurent 1937- WhoE 93
Grenald, Raymond 1928- WhoAm 92
Grenander, M.E. 1918- ScF&FL 92, WhoAm 92
Grenda-Lukas, John Michael 1945- WhoWrEP 92
Grende, Carol Ann 1955- WhoAmW 93
Grendell, Timothy Joseph 1953- WhoAm 92
Grendi, Ernest Walter 1946- St&PR 93
Grendler, Paul Frederick 1936- WhoAm 92
Greneker, Lillian Lidman d1990 BioIn 17
Grenell, James Henry 1924- WhoAm 92
Grenesko, Don WhoAm 92
Grenesko, Donald C. 1948- St&PR 93
Grenfell, Clarine Coffin 1910- WhoWrEP 92
Grenfell, Joyce 1910-1979 QDrFCA 92 [port]
Grenfell, Thomas Nicholas 1940- St&PR 93
Grenfell, Wilfred Thomason 1865-1940 BioIn 17
Grenga, Helen Eva 1938- WhoAm 92
Grenier, Bernard 1925- WhoScE 91-2
Grenier, Donald P. 1931- St&PR 93
Grenier, Edward Joseph, Jr. 1933- WhoAm 92
Grenier, Jacques Felix 1928- WhoScE 91-2
Grenier, Normand G. Law&B 92
Grenier, Patricia Brosnihan 1954- WhoAmW 93
Grenier, Pierre 1958- WhoScE 91-2
Greninger, Edwin Thomas 1918- WhoSSW 93
Grenley, Philip 1912- WhoWor 93
Grennan, Jim 1933- WhoSSW 93
Grennan, Margaret R. 1912- ScF&FL 92
Grennell, Robert Lovell 1910- WhoE 93
Grennfelt, Peringe 1944- WhoScE 91-4
Grenon, Timothy Louis 1963- WhoEmL 93
Grenquist, Peter Carl 1931- WhoAm 92, WhoE 93
Grenquist, Scott Anthony Francis 1959- WhoWor 93
Grensing, Linda Leigh 1959- WhoWrEP 92
Grentz, Theresa NewYTBS 92 [port]
Grenville, George 1920- WhoAm 92
Grenville, William Wyndham 1759-1834 BioIn 17
Grenville-Wood, Geoffrey G.C. 1943- WhoUN 92
Grenzke, Norman Frederick, Jr. 1946- St&PR 93
Grenzke, Richard A. 1946- St&PR 93
Greppin, Hubert Romain 1934- WhoScE 91-4
Greppin, John Aird Coutts 1937- WhoAm 92, WhoWor 93
Grepstad, Jostein Kvaal 1951- WhoWor 93
Gres, Alfred D. 1923- St&PR 93
Gresak, Jozef 1907- Baker 92
Gresham, Ann Elizabeth 1933- WhoWor 93
Gresham, Douglas H. 1945- ScF&FL 92
Gresham, Gary Stuart 1951- WhoAm 92
Gresham, Geoffrey Austin WhoScE 91-1
Gresham, Georgia Carol 1949- WhoAmW 93
Gresham, Glen Edward 1931- WhoAm 92
Gresham, Gloria 1946?- ConTFT 10
Gresham, James Arthur 1928- WhoAm 92
Gresham, James B. 1939- St&PR 93
Gresham, Perry Epler 1907- WhoAm 92, WhoWor 93
Gresham, Robert Coleman 1917- WhoAm 92
Gresham, Robert Lee 1942- St&PR 93, WhoAm 92
Gresham, Robert M. 1943- St&PR 93
Gresham, Rupert N., Jr. 1922- St&PR 93
Gresham, Stephen 1947- ScF&FL 92
Gresham, Stephen Deane 1960- WhoE 93, WhoEmL 93
Gresham, Walter Q. 1832-1895 PolPar
Gresham, Wayne E. Law&B 92
Gresko, Maureen Anne 1956- WhoAmW 93
Gresla, Jack F. 1920- St&PR 93
Gresnick, Antoine-Frederic 1755-1799 Baker 92
Gresov, Boris 1914- St&PR 93
Gresov, Boris Vladimir 1914- WhoAm 92
Gress, Gerald L. 1944- St&PR 93
Gress, Jean Elaine 1946- WhoAmW 93
Gress, Rose Marie 1930- WhoE 93
Gressak, Anthony Raymond, Jr. 1947- WhoAm 92
Gressel, Alan 1930- St&PR 93
Gressent, Alfred Georges 1878-1945 BioIn 17
Gresser, Jacklyn S. 1951- WhoAmW 93
Gresser, Mark Geoffrey 1958- WhoE 93
Gresser, Monika Jean 1964- WhoAmW 93
Gresser, Seymour Gerald 1926- WhoE 93
Gressette, Lawrence M., Jr. 1932- St&PR 93, WhoAm 92
Gressley, Gene Maurice 1931- WhoAm 92
Gressman, Eugene 1917- WhoAm 92
Gresso, Vernon Riddle 1927- WhoSSW 93
Grestoni, Angelo Frank 1957- St&PR 93
Gretchaninoff, Alexander (Tikhonovich) 1864-1956 Baker 92
Greten, Heiner 1939- WhoScE 91-3
Gretes, Frances Constance 1948- WhoE 93
Grethen-Gold, Kim L. 1963- WhoE 93
Grether, David Maclay 1938- WhoAm 92
Gretry, Andre-Ernest-Modeste 1741-1813 Baker 92, IntDcOp [port], OxDcOp
Gretry, Lucille 1772-1790 See Gretry, Andre-Ernest-Modeste 1741-1813 Baker 92
Gretsch, Judith Constance 1963- WhoEmL 93
Gretsch, Richard F. 1908- St&PR 93
Grettenberger, John O. 1937- St&PR 93
Gretton, Robert BioIn 17
Gretz, Stephen Randolph 1948- WhoAm 92, WhoE 93, WhoEmL 93
Gretzinger, Jeffrey Alan 1959- WhoEmL 93
Gretzinger, Ralph Edwin, III 1948- WhoEmL 93, WhoSSW 93, WhoWor 93
Gretzky, Walter BioIn 17
Gretzky, Wayne BioIn 17
Gretzky, Wayne 1961- WhoAm 92
Greubel, Joseph E. 1937- St&PR 93
Greuel, David Paul 1945- WhoE 93
Greulich, Richard Curtice 1928- WhoAm 92
Greulich, Richard E. 1926- St&PR 93
Greulich, Robert Charles 1958- WhoE 93
Greuter, W.F. WhoScE 91-4
Greuter, Werner R. 1938- WhoScE 91-3
Greve, Bertrand Joseph 1923- St&PR 93
Greve, Felix ScF&FL 92
Greve, Felix Paul 1879-1948 BioIn 17
Greve, Gerald V. 1948- St&PR 93
Greve, Guy Robert 1947- WhoEmL 93
Greve, J. William 1929- St&PR 93
Greve, John Henry 1934- WhoAm 92
Greve, Lucius, II 1915- WhoWor 93
Greve, Otto WhoScE 91-3
Greven, H.C. 1936- WhoScE 91-3
Grevendonk, Willy L.G. 1937- WhoScE 91-2
Grever, Frederik Law&B 92
Grever, Maria 1894-1951 NotHsAW 93
Greves, Larry Allen 1947- St&PR 93
Greville, Nicholas A. 1943- St&PR 93
Greville, Nicholas Anthony 1943- WhoAm 92
Grevillius, Nils 1893-1970 Baker 92
Greving, Robert C. 1951- St&PR 93
Grevy, Jules 1807-1891 BioIn 17
Grew, Edward Sturgis 1944- WhoE 93
Grew, Kimberly Ann 1962- WhoEmL 93
Grew, Mary 1813-1896 BioIn 17
Grew, Priscilla Croswell 1940- WhoAmW 93
Grew, Robert Ralph 1931- WhoE 93, WhoWor 93
Grewcock, William L. 1925- WhoAm 92
Grewe, Arthur H. 1926- St&PR 93
Grewe, John Mitchell 1938- WhoAm 92, WhoE 93
Grewelle, Larry Allan 1937- WhoSSW 93
Grey, A.W. ScF&FL 92
Grey, Alan Lewis 1919- WhoAm 92
Grey, Charles 1729-1807 HarEnMi
Grey, Deborah BioIn 17
Grey, Deborah Cleland 1952- WhoAmW 93
Grey, Edward 1862-1933 BioIn 17, DcTwHis
Grey, Francis Joseph 1931- WhoAm 92, WhoE 93, WhoWor 93
Grey, Gloria 1909-1947 SweetSg B [port]
Grey, Henry 1954- St&PR 93, WhoAm 92
Grey, Holly Sue 1960- WhoAmW 93
Grey, Joel 1932- WhoAm 92
Grey, Leslie WhoWrEP 92
Grey, Linda WhoAm 92
Grey, Lloyd Eric ScF&FL 92
Grey, M. Cameron ScF&FL 92
Grey, Madeleine 1896- Baker 92
Grey, Margery Lynn 1960- WhoAmW 93, WhoEmL 93
Grey, Mary AmWomPl
Grey, Michael 1937- ScF&FL 92
Grey, Richard WhoAm 92
Grey, Robert Constantine 1928- St&PR 93
Grey, Robert Dean 1939- WhoAm 92
Grey, Robert T., Jr. 1936- WhoUN 92
Grey, Roberta 1936- WhoWor 93
Grey, Shirley SweetSg C [port]
Grey, Virginia 1917- SweetSg C [port]
Grey, Zane 1872-1939 BioIn 17
Grey Morgan, Colyn WhoScE 91-1
Grey of Fallodon 1862-1933 BioIn 17
Grey Owl 1888-1938 BioIn 17
Greyson, Charles Bruce 1946- WhoEmL 93
Greyson, John BioIn 17
Greytak, David Edward 1941- WhoE 93
Greytak, Gil Guy 1941- St&PR 93
Greytak, Thomas John 1940- WhoAm 92
Greywhiskers, Fifi ScF&FL 92
Greze, Jean-Louis 1931- St&PR 93, WhoAm 92
Griaule, Marcel 1898-1956 IntDcAn
Grib, Boris F. 1924- St&PR 93
Gribanov, Gennady Alexandrovich 1940- WhoWor 93
Gribben, Alan 1941- WhoAm 92, WhoSSW 93
Gribben, Carolyn Eckhaus 1957- WhoE 93
Gribben, James Joseph 1942- St&PR 93
Gribbens, Lorraine Eloise 1920- WhoSSW 93
Gribbin, David James, III 1939- WhoAm 92
Gribbin, John 1946- ScF&FL 92
Gribbins, Richard James 1944- St&PR 93
Gribble, Charles Edward 1936- WhoWor 93
Gribbon, Daniel McNamara 1917- WhoAm 92
Gribbon, William L. ScF&FL 92
Gribbs, Roman S. 1925- WhoAm 92
Gribeauval, Jean Baptiste Vaquette de 1715-1789 HarEnMi
Gribi, John F. 1941- WhoAm 92
Gribler, Michael Alan Law&B 92
Grice, Douglas Lynn 1955- WhoSSW 93
Grice, George Daniel 1929- WhoAm 92
Grice, Ian Eric 1937- WhoWor 93
Grice, Julia 1940- ScF&FL 92
Grice, Michael W. Law&B 92
Grice, Richard Lee 1946- St&PR 93
Grice, Roger WhoScE 91-1
Grich, Bobby BioIn 17
Grich, Robert Anthony 1949- BiDAMSp 1989
Grickis, William V. Law&B 92
Gricks, Thomas C., III Law&B 92
Grider, George W. 1912-1991 BioIn 17
Grider, John Raymond 1952- WhoSSW 93
Grider, Joseph Kenneth 1921- WhoAm 92
Grider, Kathy Jill 1954- WhoAmW 93
Grider, Rufus 1817- Baker 92
Gridley, Henry Meeker 1933- St&PR 93
Gridley, Mark Charles 1947- WhoEmL 93
Gridley, Mary Theresa 1935- WhoE 93
Gridley, Michael C. Law&B 92
Grieb, R.W. 1930- St&PR 93
Grieb, Robert William 1930- WhoIns 93
Griebe, Mark Henry 1942- St&PR 93
Griebling-Long, Karen Jean 1957- Baker 92
Griech, Fred George 1944- St&PR 93
Griech, Frederick G. 1944- WhoAm 92
Grieco, John Louis 1956- St&PR 93
Grieco, Paul Anthony 1944- WhoAm 92
Grieco, Richard BioIn 17
Grieco, Richard 1965?- ConTFT 10
Grieder, Karen Suzanne 1957- WhoAmW 93
Griefen, John Adams 1942- WhoAm 92, WhoE 93
Grieg, Edvard (Hagerup) 1843-1907 Baker 92
Grieg, Nina 1845-1935 Baker 92
Grieger, Gunter 1931- WhoScE 91-3, WhoWor 93
Grieger, Ronald Dean 1945- WhoE 93
Griego, Linda 1935- NotHsAW 93
Griego, Pancho d1875 BioIn 17
Griek, Martin Richard 1943- WhoSSW 93
Griem, Hans Rudolf 1928- WhoAm 92
Griem, John Michael 1945- St&PR 93, WhoWor 93
Grieman, John Joseph 1944- St&PR 93
Grieme, Rosemary E. Law&B 92
Griend, Koss van de 1905-1950 Baker 92
Grienenberger, Warren F. Law&B 92
Griep, Clifford M. 1951- St&PR 93
Griepenkerl, Friedrich

See Griepenkerl, Wolfgang Robert 1810-1868 Baker 92
Griepenkerl, Wolfgang Robert 1810-1868 Baker 92
Griepp, Randall Bertram 1940- WhoAm 92
Grier, Barbara G. 1933- WhoAmW 93, WhoWrEP 92
Grier, Baxter 1919- St&PR 93
Grier, Charles F. 1951- St&PR 93
Grier, Charles Paul 1930- St&PR 93
Grier, Eldon 1917- WhoCanL 92
Grier, Herbert E. 1911- St&PR 93
Grier, Herbert Earl 1911- WhoAm 92
Grier, James Edward 1935- WhoAm 92
Grier, James R., III 1938- St&PR 93
Grier, Joseph Williamson, Jr. 1915- WhoAm 92
Grier, Phillip Michael 1941- WhoAm 92
Grier, Robert Cooper 1794-1870 OxCSupC [port]
Grier, Ruth 1936- WhoAmW 93
Grier, William A. 1912-1990 BioIn 17
Grier, William E. 1933- WhoAm 92
Grier, William Milton 1878-1935 BioIn 17
Grierson, Benjamin Henry 1826-1911 HarEnMi
Grierson, Donald WhoScE 91-1
Grierson, Francis D. 1888-1972 ScF&FL 92
Grierson, Letitia d1991 BioIn 17
Grierson, Ronald H. 1921- WhoScE 91-1
Grierson, William 1917- WhoAm 92
Grier-Wallen, Mary Elizabeth 1912- WhoAmW 93
Gries, Brett E. 1948- St&PR 93
Gries, Brett Evan 1948- WhoEmL 93
Gries, David Joseph 1939- WhoAm 92
Gries, James Patrick 1946- WhoEmL 93
Gries, John Paul 1911- WhoAm 92
Gries, Tom 1922-1977 MiSFD 9N
Griesa, Thomas Poole 1930- WhoAm 92, WhoE 93
Griesar, William Howard 1932- WhoE 93
Griesbach, John Henry 1798-1875 Baker 92
Griesbacher, Peter 1864-1933 Baker 92
Griese, Bob 1945- BioIn 17
Griese, John William, III 1955- WhoWor 93
Griese, R. Paul Law&B 92
Griesedieck, Ellen 1948- WhoE 93
Griesemer, John N. WhoAm 92
Griesinger, David Hadley 1944- WhoE 93
Griesse, Paul D. 1943- St&PR 93
Griesser, Michael S. Law&B 92
Griessman, Benjamin Eugene 1934- WhoWor 93
Griest, Debra Lynn 1959- WhoEmL 93
Griev, R. WhoScE 91-1
Grieve, Andrew MiSFD 9
Grieve, Catherine Macy 1926- WhoAmW 93
Grieve, Christopher Murray 1892-1978 BioIn 17
Grieve, Harold Walter 1901- WhoAm 92
Grieve, Leona Lee 1954- WhoWrEP 92
Grieve, Margaret M. Law&B 92
Grieve, Pierson M. 1927- St&PR 93
Grieve, Pierson MacDonald 1927- WhoAm 92
Grieve, Thomas Alan 1948- WhoAm 92
Grieves, Richard W. Law&B 92
Grieves, Robert Belanger 1935- WhoAm 92
Griewahn, Robert David, Jr. Law&B 92
Grifalconi, Ann BioIn 17, ChlBIID [port]
Grifalconi, Ann 1929- MajAI [port], SmATA 16AS [port]
Griff, Bernard Matthew 1935- WhoWrEP 92
Griff, Donna Lynn 1964- WhoAmW 93
Griffel, Lois BioIn 17
Griffen, Clyde Chesterman 1929- WhoAm 92
Griffen, Elizabeth L. ScF&FL 92
Griffen, Ward O., Jr. 1928- WhoAm 92
Griffenhagen, George Bernard 1924- WhoAm 92
Griffes, Charles T(omlinson) 1884-1920 Baker 92
Griffes, Elliot 1893-1967 Baker 92
Griffeth, Paul Lyman 1919- WhoAm 92
Griffey, Dick BioIn 17
Griffey, Dick 1943- AfrAmBi
Griffey, George Kenneth, Sr. 1950- BiDAMSp 1989
Griffey, Ken, Jr. BioIn 17
Griffey, Ken, Jr. 1969- WhoAm 92
Griffey, Lee 1936- St&PR 93
Griffey, Linda Boyd 1949- WhoAmW 93
Griffin, Albert Bruce 1946- WhoEmL 93
Griffin, Anna Helena AmWomPl
Griffin, Barbara Ellen 1946- WhoSSW 93
Griffin, Ben Hill, Jr. BioIn 17
Griffin, Ben L., Jr. 1946- WhoIns 93
Griffin, Billy Loyd 1930- St&PR 93
Griffin, Bob Franklin 1935- WhoAm 92, WhoE 93
Griffin, Brian 1941- ScF&FL 92
Griffin, Bryant Wade 1915- WhoAm 92
Griffin, Byron Kent 1942- St&PR 93
Griffin, Campbell Arthur, Jr. 1929- WhoAm 92
Griffin, Carleton Hadlock 1928- WhoAm 92
Griffin, Caroline Stearns 1868- AmWomPl
Griffin, Carroll W. 1949- WhoSSW 93
Griffin, Catherine Ann Law&B 92
Griffin, Charles 1825-1867 HarEnMi
Griffin, Charles R. Law&B 92
Griffin, Charles Steven 1956- WhoSSW 93
Griffin, Christopher Gordon 1952- St&PR 93
Griffin, Clayton Houstoun 1925- WhoAm 92
Griffin, Cornelius F. 1939- St&PR 93
Griffin, David ConAu 40NR
Griffin, DeWitt James 1914- WhoAm 92, WhoWor 93
Griffin, Diane Edmund 1940- WhoAmW 93
Griffin, Donald Redfield 1915- WhoAm 92
Griffin, Donald W. 1937- St&PR 93
Griffin, Donna Osborne 1956- WhoEmL 93
Griffin, Dye Ann Law&B 92
Griffin, Edward D. 1940- St&PR 93
Griffin, Edward Michael 1937- WhoAm 92
Griffin, Emilie Russell Dietrich 1936- WhoWrEP 92
Griffin, Eugene F. 1926- St&PR 93
Griffin, F. O'Neil 1926- St&PR 93, WhoAm 92
Griffin, G. Edward 1931- WhoAm 92
Griffin, Gary A. 1937- St&PR 93
Griffin, Gene R. Law&B 92
Griffin, George Edward WhoScE 91-1
Griffin, George Thomas 1921- WhoSSW 93
Griffin, Gerald F. 1934- St&PR 93
Griffin, Gerald G. 1933- ScF&FL 92
Griffin, Gerard Francis WhoScE 91-1
Griffin, Gladys Bogues 1937- WhoSSW 93
Griffin, Graham Keith WhoScE 91-1
Griffin, Gregory 1770-1827 BioIn 17
Griffin, Harriet M. 1903-1991 BioIn 17
Griffin, Harry Frederick 1951- WhoEmL 93
Griffin, Haynes Glen 1947- St&PR 93
Griffin, Haynes Glenn 1947- WhoSSW 93
Griffin, Henry E. 1943- St&PR 93
Griffin, Herman A. 1932- WhoAm 92
Griffin, Herman Talmadge 1948- WhoEmL 93, WhoSSW 93
Griffin, Herschel Emmett 1918- WhoAm 92
Griffin, J. Eric Law&B 92
Griffin, J.M. Law&B 92
Griffin, J. Philip, Jr. 1932- WhoIns 93
Griffin, J. Timothy 1951- St&PR 93
Griffin, J. William 1939- WhoWrEP 92
Griffin, Jack Kennedy 1958- WhoEmL 93
Griffin, James Alton 1956- WhoEmL 93
Griffin, James Anthony 1934- WhoAm 92
Griffin, James Bennett 1905- IntDcAn, WhoAm 92
Griffin, James C. 1940- St&PR 93
Griffin, James Donald 1929- WhoE 93
Griffin, James Edwin 1927- St&PR 93, WhoAm 92
Griffin, James M. 1934- St&PR 93
Griffin, James Philip 1932- St&PR 93
Griffin, Jane Whittington 1916-1979 ScF&FL 92
Griffin, Jasper BioIn 17
Griffin, Jean 1931- WhoAmW 93
Griffin, Jeanne A. Law&B 92
Griffin, Jeffrey Thomas 1944- St&PR 93
Griffin, Jo Ann Thomas 1933- WhoAmW 93, WhoE 93
Griffin, Joan Solomon 1958- WhoAmW 93
Griffin, John ScF&FL 92
Griffin, John C. Law&B 92
Griffin, John Howard 1920-1980 EncAACR
Griffin, John Lee 1943- WhoSSW 93
Griffin, John R. 1942- St&PR 93
Griffin, Joseph 1932- St&PR 93
Griffin, Joseph J. 1932- WhoAm 92
Griffin, Joseph Parker 1944- WhoAm 92
Griffin, Judith Ann 1948- WhoAm 92
Griffin, Judith Berry BlkAuII 92
Griffin, Karen Elaine 1957- WhoEmL 93
Griffin, Katherine Hoeh 1959- WhoE 93
Griffin, Kathleen Christina 1948- WhoE 93
Griffin, Kay Loy 1948- WhoAmW 93
Griffin, Keith B. BioIn 17
Griffin, Keith Broadwell 1938- WhoAm 92
Griffin, Kenneth Lee 1945- WhoSSW 93
Griffin, Kenneth Patrick 1930- St&PR 93
Griffin, Kim 1955- WhoWor 93
Griffin, Kirk St&PR 93
Griffin, Larry Don 1951- WhoEmL 93, WhoSSW 93
Griffin, Larry Paul 1947- WhoEmL 93, WhoSSW 93
Griffin, Laura M. 1925- WhoAmW 93
Griffin, Linda L. 1942- WhoSSW 93
Griffin, Louis Austin 1931- St&PR 93
Griffin, Lyle N. 1961- WhoSSW 93
Griffin, Margaret Elizabeth 1952- WhoE 93
Griffin, Mark Edward St&PR 93
Griffin, Martin WhoScE 91-1
Griffin, Marvin Anthony 1923- WhoAm 92
Griffin, Mary 1916- WhoAm 92
Griffin, Mary Ann 1946- WhoAmW 93
Griffin, Mary C.A. 1952- WhoScE 91-1
Griffin, Mary Frances 1925- WhoAmW 93
Griffin, Mary Winifred 1906- WhoAmW 93
Griffin, Melanie Hunt 1949- WhoAmW 93, WhoSSW 93
Griffin, Melissa Gaye 1956- WhoEmL 93
Griffin, Merv 1925- BioIn 17
Griffin, Merv Edward 1925- WhoAm 92
Griffin, Michael Charles 1950- St&PR 93
Griffin, Moira 1954- BioIn 17
Griffin, Norris Samuel 1931- WhoAm 92
Griffin, O. Daniel, Jr. 1960- WhoSSW 93
Griffin, O.W., Mrs. AmWomPl
Griffin, Oscar O'Neal, Jr. 1933- WhoAm 92
Griffin, P.G. 1946- St&PR 93
Griffin, P.M. 1947- ScF&FL 92
Griffin, Patricia 1953- St&PR 93
Griffin, Paul David 1944- WhoUN 92
Griffin, Paul M. Law&B 92
Griffin, Peni R. BioIn 17
Griffin, Peni R. 1961- ScF&FL 92
Griffin, Peni Rae 1961- WhoWrEP 92
Griffin, Peter 1942- ConAu 136
Griffin, Peter J. 1943- WhoAm 92
Griffin, Phillip Stone 1938- St&PR 93
Griffin, Phillip Stone, I 1938- WhoAm 92
Griffin, Priscilla Loring 1930- WhoAm 92, WhoE 93
Griffin, Rachel 1917- WhoWrEP 92
Griffin, Richard BioIn 17
See Also Public Enemy News 92
Griffin, Richard Brent 1966- WhoSSW 93
Griffin, Rick d1991 BioIn 17
Griffin, Robert A. 1944- WhoSSW 93
Griffin, Robert Emmett 1935- St&PR 93
Griffin, Robert G. 1951- St&PR 93
Griffin, Robert P. 1923- PolPar
Griffin, Robert Paul 1923- WhoAm 92
Griffin, Robert Thomas 1917- WhoAm 92
Griffin, Robert Wooten 1952- WhoSSW 93
Griffin, Rodney d1991 BioIn 17, NewYTBS 92
Griffin, Roger Francis WhoScE 91-1
Griffin, Roland I. Law&B 92
Griffin, Russell M. 1943-1986 ScF&FL 92
Griffin, Rutledge Avalon 1944- St&PR 93
Griffin, Samuel M. 1951- St&PR 93
Griffin, Scott 1938- St&PR 93, WhoAm 92
Griffin, Sean Young 1961- WhoWor 93
Griffin, Sharon L. 1939- WhoAm 92
Griffin, Sheila 1951- WhoEmL 93
Griffin, Suzanne Elizabeth 1963- WhoEmL 93
Griffin, Sylvia Gail 1935- WhoAmW 93, WhoWor 93
Griffin, Thomas A. 1931- St&PR 93
Griffin, Thomas Aquinas, Jr. 1927- WhoAm 92
Griffin, Thomas H. 1931- St&PR 93
Griffin, Thomas Lee, Jr. 1929- WhoWor 93
Griffin, Thomas McLean 1922- WhoAm 92
Griffin, Thomas Norfleet, Jr. 1933- WhoAm 92
Griffin, Thomas W. 1945- WhoAm 92
Griffin, Timothy G. Law&B 92
Griffin, Tom 1926- WhoAm 92
Griffin, Tommy Brewer 1936- WhoSSW 93
Griffin, Trenholme J. Law&B 92
Griffin, Villard Stuart, Jr. 1937- WhoAm 92
Griffin, W. E. B. ConAu 40NR
Griffin, W.L. Hadley 1918- St&PR 93
Griffin, Wallace Kennon, Jr. 1943- WhoSSW 93
Griffin, Walter 1937- WhoWrEP 92
Griffin, Walter Wanzel 1926- WhoSSW 93
Griffin, Wesley K. Law&B 92
Griffin, William 1935- ScF&FL 92
Griffin, William Dallas 1925- WhoE 93
Griffin, William J. 1936- St&PR 93
Griffin, William Leonard, Jr. 1948- St&PR 93
Griffin, William Lester Hadley 1918- WhoAm 92
Griffin, William M. 1926- St&PR 93
Griffin, William Thomas 1905- WhoAm 92
Griffin, William Thomas Jackson 1928- WhoWor 93
Griffin, Yvonne Marie 1952- WhoAmW 93
Griffing, Robert G. 1927- WhoIns 93
Griffin-Holst, Jean 1943- WhoAmW 93, WhoWor 93
Griffins, Herbert R. 1938- St&PR 93
Griffis, David R. 1939- St&PR 93
Griffis, Mona Crisp 1961- WhoSSW 93
Griffis, Roy A. 1936- St&PR 93
Griffith, A. Wayne 1938- St&PR 93
Griffith, Alan R. 1941- St&PR 93
Griffith, Alan Richard 1941- WhoAm 92
Griffith, Alice Mary Matlock AmWomPl
Griffith, Aline BioIn 17
Griffith, Andy 1926- BioIn 17, ConTFT 10, WhoAm 92
Griffith, Arthur 1872-1922 BioIn 17, DcTwHis
Griffith, Beverly Hutcheson Law&B 92
Griffith, Bezaleel Herold 1925- WhoAm 92
Griffith, Boulden Galbreath Law&B 92
Griffith, C. Wayne 1933- St&PR 93
Griffith, C. Wayne 1935- WhoE 93
Griffith, Charles B. MiSFD 9
Griffith, Clark Calvin, II 1941- WhoAm 92
Griffith, Clem ScF&FL 92
Griffith, D.W. 1875-1948 BioIn 17, MiSFD 9N
Griffith, Daniel Alva 1948- WhoE 93
Griffith, Daniel Boyd 1934- St&PR 93, WhoAm 92
Griffith, David J. St&PR 93
Griffith, David Jackson 1946- St&PR 93
Griffith, David M. 1943- St&PR 93
Griffith, David Wark 1875-1948 BioIn 17
Griffith, Delorez Florence BiDAMSp 1989
Griffith, Donald Kendall 1933- WhoAm 92
Griffith, Douglas 1946- WhoSSW 93
Griffith, Edward David 1944- WhoWor 93
Griffith, Eleanor Glendower AmWomPl
Griffith, Elizabeth 1727-1793 BioIn 17
Griffith, Elwin Jabez 1938- WhoAm 92
Griffith, Emlyn Irving 1923- WhoAm 92, WhoE 93, WhoWor 93
Griffith, Ernest Ralph 1928- WhoAm 92
Griffith, Evert Willem 1949- WhoWor 93
Griffith, F. Lee, III 1947- WhoE 93, WhoEmL 93
Griffith, Fred Dean, Jr. 1934- St&PR 93
Griffith, G. Larry 1937- WhoAm 92
Griffith, G. Sanders, III Law&B 92
Griffith, Garth Ellis 1928- WhoAm 92
Griffith, Gary Ernest 1948- WhoEmL 93
Griffith, George Thomas Law&B 92
Griffith, Gerald P. 1948- St&PR 93
Griffith, Geraline Moeller 1916- WhoWrEP 92
Griffith, Gloria Dodie 1932- WhoSSW 93
Griffith, Helen Sherman 1873- AmWomPl
Griffith, Helen V(irginia) 1934- WhoWrEP 92
Griffith, Howard Morgan 1958- WhoEmL 93
Griffith, Jack BioIn 17
Griffith, Jack William 1929- WhoAm 92
Griffith, James Clifford 1948- WhoWor 93
Griffith, James Joseph 1927- WhoE 93
Griffith, James William 1922- WhoAm 92
Griffith, Jefferson Davis, III Law&B 92
Griffith, Jerry Dice 1933- WhoAm 92
Griffith, John H. 1925- St&PR 93
Griffith, John Keith 1946- St&PR 93
Griffith, John Vincent WhoAm 92
Griffith, Katherine Scott 1942- WhoAmW 93, WhoWor 93
Griffith, Kathryn Meyer 1950- ScF&FL 92
Griffith, Ladd Ray 1930- WhoAm 92
Griffith, Lawrence Stacey Cameron 1937- WhoAm 92
Griffith, Leah Marie 1956- WhoEmL 93
Griffith, Lee B. 1940- St&PR 93
Griffith, Linda Claire 1951- WhoAmW 93
Griffith, Linda Gail Law&B 92
Griffith, Madlynne Veil 1951- WhoE 93, WhoEmL 93
Griffith, Martha 1945- WhoAmW 93
Griffith, Mary 1800?-1877 ScF&FL 92
Griffith, Mary Louise Kilpatrick 1926- WhoAmW 93, WhoE 93
Griffith, Melanie BioIn 17
Griffith, Melanie 1957- HolBB [port], WhoAm 92
Griffith, Melvin Eugene 1912- WhoSSW 93, WhoWor 93
Griffith, Michael John 1949- WhoEmL 93
Griffith, Nancy Snell 1946- ScF&FL 92

Griffith, Osbie Hayes 1938- WhoAm 92
Griffith, Owen Wendell 1946- WhoE 93
Griffith, Patricia Browning WhoWrEP 92
Griffith, Peter 1927- WhoAm 92
Griffith, R. Keeffe Law&B 92
Griffith, Rashard BioIn 17
Griffith, Raymond 1890-1957 QDrFCA 92 [port]
Griffith, Reese Ann 1959- WhoE 93
Griffith, Richard Robert 1947- St&PR 93
Griffith, Robert Charles 1939- WhoWor 93
Griffith, Robert W. 1930- St&PR 93
Griffith, Ronald L. 1934- St&PR 93
Griffith, Stanley N. Law&B 92
Griffith, Steve C., Jr. 1933- St&PR 93
Griffith, Steve Campbell, Jr. Law&B 92
Griffith, Steve Campbell, Jr. 1933- WhoAm 92
Griffith, Steven Franklin, Sr. 1948- WhoEmL 93, WhoSSW 93, WhoWor 93
Griffith, Steven Morgan 1961- WhoE 93
Griffith, Susan Buffington 1956- WhoAmW 93
Griffith, Thomas Jefferson 1923- WhoSSW 93
Griffith, Vanessa W. Law&B 92
Griffith, Wayland Coleman 1925- WhoAm 92
Griffith, William 1921- ScF&FL 92
Griffith, William Alexander 1922- St&PR 93, WhoAm 92
Griffith, William F.R. BioIn 17
Griffith, William Harry 1931- WhoE 93
Griffith, William Schuler 1949- WhoEmL 93, WhoSSW 93
Griffith-Joyner, Delorez Florence 1959- BiDAMSp 1989
Griffith Joyner, Florence BioIn 17
Griffith-Joyner, Florence 1959- BlkAmWO [port]
Griffith-Joyner, Florence Delores WhoAm 92
Griffiths, Alan Gordon 1952- WhoAsAP 91
Griffiths, Anthony F. 1930- WhoE 93
Griffiths, Anthony Frear 1930- St&PR 93
Griffiths, Barclay H. 1942- St&PR 93
Griffiths, Brian BioIn 17
Griffiths, Charles Robert 1941- WhoSSW 93
Griffiths, Clive Edward 1928- WhoAsAP 91
Griffiths, Daniel Edward 1917- WhoAm 92
Griffiths, David Arthur ScF&FL 92
Griffiths, David Neil 1935- St&PR 93, WhoAm 92
Griffiths, Denwood Vaughan 1953- WhoWor 93
Griffiths, Donald P., Sr. 1919- St&PR 93
Griffiths, Ellis WhoScE 91-1
Griffiths, Gail Hayes Law&B 92
Griffiths, Georgia Dorothy 1951- WhoAmW 93, WhoEmL 93
Griffiths, Georgia Gregory 1939- St&PR 93
Griffiths, Hubert Brian WhoScE 91-1
Griffiths, Ian WhoScE 91-1
Griffiths, Iorwerth David Ace WhoAm 92
Griffiths, James Watters 1927- St&PR 93
Griffiths, Jeanne ScF&FL 92
Griffiths, Jeffrey Deacon WhoScE 91-1
Griffiths, Jeremy Bransom WhoScE 91-1
Griffiths, John 1934- ScF&FL 92
Griffiths, John B. 1937- St&PR 93
Griffiths, John Brittain 1937- WhoAm 92
Griffiths, John Bryan WhoScE 91-1
Griffiths, John E. Law&B 92
Griffiths, John Richard WhoScE 91-1
Griffiths, John William Roger WhoScE 91-1
Griffiths, Ken BioIn 17
Griffiths, Kenney E. 1939- St&PR 93
Griffiths, L. Gene 1940- St&PR 93
Griffiths, Linda WhoCanL 92
Griffiths, Lloyd Joseph 1941- WhoAm 92
Griffiths, Lynn Christopher 1940- WhoAm 92
Griffiths, Mark MiSFD 9
Griffiths, Martha W. 1912- PolPar
Griffiths, Martha Wright 1912- BioIn 17
Griffiths, Norman D. Law&B 92
Griffiths, Paul 1947- ScF&FL 92
Griffiths, Paul David WhoScE 91-1
Griffiths, Paul F. Law&B 92
Griffiths, Peter Boyd 1956- WhoE 93
Griffiths, Philip John 1948- St&PR 93
Griffiths, Phillip A. WhoAm 92
Griffiths, R. WhoScE 91-3
Griffiths, R.F. WhoScE 91-1
Griffiths, Richard R. 1959- St&PR 93
Griffiths, Richard Reese 1931- WhoAm 92
Griffiths, Robert Budington 1937- WhoAm 92, WhoE 93
Griffiths, Robert P. 1949- St&PR 93
Griffiths, Roland Redmond 1946- WhoE 93
Griffiths, Susan BioIn 17
Griffiths, Sylvia Preston 1924- WhoAm 92
Griffiths, Thomas Alan 1951- BioIn 17
Griffiths, Vivien ScF&FL 92
Griffo, James Vincent, Jr. 1928- WhoAm 92
Griffo, John Thomas 1948- St&PR 93
Griffo, Lynn Jennifer 1957- WhoWrEP 92
Griffon, Joseph P. 1914- St&PR 93
Griffuelhes, Jean Victor 1874-1922 BioIn 17
Griffy, Thomas Alan 1936- WhoAm 92
Grigalonis, Mary Lou 1962- WhoE 93
Grigely, Joseph Constantine, Jr. 1956- WhoE 93
Grigereit, Hugh Reeves, Jr. 1930- WhoSSW 93
Grigg, Betty Ann Carpenter 1932- WhoAmW 93
Grigg, Charles M. d1992 NewYTBS 92
Grigg, George Cary 1946- WhoSSW 93
Grigg, Richard R. 1948- St&PR 93
Grigg, Ronald WhoScE 91-1
Grigg, Ted W. 1946- WhoAm 92
Grigg, William 1934- WhoWrEP 92
Grigg, William Humphrey 1932- St&PR 93, WhoAm 92
Griggs, Benjamin Glyde, Jr. 1928- St&PR 93
Griggs, Bobbie June 1938- WhoAmW 93, WhoSSW 93, WhoWor 93
Griggs, Carole A. 1947- St&PR 93
Griggs, John 1941-1991 BioIn 17
Griggs, John Wyeth 1947- WhoEmL 93
Griggs, K. Scott Law&B 92
Griggs, Leonard LeRoy, Jr. 1931- WhoAm 92
Griggs, Phyllis Kay 1937- WhoAmW 93
Griggs, Ralph William 1955- WhoSSW 93
Griggs, Robert Charles 1939- WhoAm 92
Griggs, Robyn BioIn 17
Griggs, Ron 1940- St&PR 93
Griggs, Shirley Ann 1931- WhoE 93
Griggs, Stephen Layng 1947- WhoE 93
Griggs, Stephen P. 1957- St&PR 93
Griggs, Terry 1951- WhoCanL 92
Griggy, Kenneth Joseph 1934- St&PR 93, WhoAm 92
Griglak, Martin Samuel 1927- WhoE 93
Griglock, William John 1948- WhoIns 93
Grignac, Pierre 1926- WhoScE 91-2
Grignon, Albina Yvonne 1949- WhoAmW 93, WhoE 93
Grignon, Claude 1942- WhoScE 91-2
Grignon, Georges 1927- WhoScE 91-2
Grignon, Richard Lamote de Baker 92
Grigny, Nicolas de 1672-1703 Baker 92
Grigor, Wallace Gladstone 1929- WhoWor 93
Grigor'ev, IU. V. 1899-1973 BioIn 17
Grigor'ev, IUrii Vladimirovich 1899-1973 BioIn 17
Grigoriadis, Mary 1942- WhoE 93
Grigorian, Sergei Vagharshak 1934- WhoWor 93
Grigorieff, Rolf Dieter 1938- WhoWor 93
Grigoriev, Dima Yu 1954- WhoWor 93
Grigoriu, Theodor 1926- Baker 92
Grigorov, Grigory I. 1935- WhoScE 91-4
Grigorov, L. WhoScE 91-4
Grigorovich, IUrii Nikolaevich 1927- BioIn 17
Grigsby, Alcanoan O. ScF&FL 92
Grigsby, Chester Poole, Jr. 1929- St&PR 93, WhoSSW 93, WhoWor 93
Grigsby, Daryl Russell 1955- WhoWrEP 92
Grigsby, E.K. 1939- St&PR 93
Grigsby, Gordon 1927- WhoWrEP 92
Grigsby, Henry Jefferson, Jr. 1930- WhoAm 92
Grigsby, Jack Webster 1923- St&PR 93
Grigsby, James A. 1942- WhoIns 93
Grigsby, James Alfred A. 1942- St&PR 93
Grigsby, Jefferson Eugene, Jr. 1918- WhoAm 92
Grigsby, John L. 1928-1988 BioIn 17
Grigsby, Lonnie O. 1939- St&PR 93
Grigsby, Lonnie Oscar 1939- WhoAm 92
Grigsby, Maggie Barrios 1950- WhoSSW 93
Grigsby, Margaret Elizabeth 1923- WhoAm 92, WhoAmW 93
Grigsby, Marshall C. 1946- WhoAm 92
Grigsby, Richard Paul 1954- St&PR 93
Grigsby-Stephens, Klaron 1952- WhoAmW 93, WhoEmL 93, WhoWor 93
Grigson, Geoffrey 1905-1985 BioIn 17
Grigson, Jane 1928-1990 BioIn 17
Grijalva, Beth N. Law&B 92
Grijalva, Douglas Cole Law&B 92
Grijpma, Peter 1932- WhoScE 91-3
Grile, Don ConAu 139
Griley, Theodore D. 1932- St&PR 93
Griliches, Zvi 1930- WhoAm 92
Grilk, Thomas S. Law&B 92
Grill, David BioIn 17
Grill, Donna P. Law&B 92
Grill, Jeffrey W. 1957- WhoEmL 93
Grill, Joseph C. 1944- St&PR 93
Grill, Laurence Kay 1949- WhoAm 92
Grill, Lawrence J. 1936- WhoAm 92
Grill, Murray M. Law&B 92
Grill, Wolfgang 1946- WhoScE 91-3
Grillenzoni, Maurizio 1937- WhoScE 91-3
Griller, David 1948- WhoAm 92
Grillet, Alain Robbe- 1922- BioIn 17
Grilli, Chloe Lenore WhoWrEP 92
Grilli, Enzo R. 1943- WhoUN 92
Grilli, Marcel F. d1990 BioIn 17
Grilli, Mario 1928- WhoScE 91-3
Grilliot, Mary I. 1954- St&PR 93
Grilliot, William Lawrence 1949- St&PR 93
Grillis, Lucas Chris 1931- St&PR 93
Grillner, Sten 1941- WhoScE 91-4
Grillo, A.G. Law&B 92
Grillo, Gary MiSFD 9
Grillo, Hermes Conrad 1923- WhoAm 92
Grillo, Janet St&PR 93
Grillo, Joann Danielle 1939- WhoAm 92, WhoAmW 93, WhoE 93, WhoWor 93
Grillo, Leo Francis 1949- WhoEmL 93
Grillo, T. Adesanya Ige 1927- WhoWor 93
Grillo, Thomas F. Law&B 92
Grillo-Bernstein, Kimberly Law&B 92
Grillos, John J. 1947- St&PR 93
Grillos, John Joseph Law&B 92
Grillos, Patricia Marshall 1954- WhoSSW 93
Grillparzer, Franz 1791-1872 OxDcOp
Grills, George B. 1940- St&PR 93
Grim, Eugene Donald 1922- WhoAm 92
Grim, Harry G. Law&B 92
Grim, J. Lawrence, Jr. 1933- St&PR 93
Grim, James Roy 1952- WhoSSW 93
Grim, Linn I. Law&B 92
Grim, Patricia Ann 1940- WhoAmW 93
Grim, Patrick 1950- ConAu 37NR
Grim, Samuel Oram 1935- WhoAm 92
Grim, Shelle K. 1955- St&PR 93
Grim, Wayne Martin 1930- WhoE 93
Grimaldi, Andrew C. 1935- St&PR 93
Grimaldi, Anthony Julio 1933- St&PR 93
Grimaldi, David A. BioIn 17
Grimaldi, Jack P. Law&B 92
Grimaldi, Jack Philip 1946- WhoEmL 93
Grimaldi, James Thomas 1928- WhoSSW 93, WhoWor 93
Grimaldi, Janette Pienkny 1938- ConAu 139
Grimaldi, Nicholas Lawrence 1950- WhoAm 92
Grimaldi, Nicolo Baker 92, OxDcOp
Grimaud, Jean-Alexis 1943- WhoScE 91-2
Grimaud, Maurice 1913- BioIn 17
Grimault, Paul 1905- BioIn 17
Grimball, Caroline Gordon 1946- WhoAmW 93, WhoSSW 93
Grimball, Edward B. 1944- St&PR 93
Grimball, Elizabeth Berkeley AmWomPl
Grimball, William Heyward 1917- WhoAm 92
Grimberg, Raimond 1944- WhoScE 91-4
Grimble, George Kenneth 1951- WhoWor 93
Grimble, Ian 1921- ConAu 39NR
Grimble, Michael John WhoScE 91-1
Grimby, Gunnar L. 1933- WhoScE 91-4
Grime, J.P. WhoScE 91-1
Grimes, Cathy Margaret 1956- WhoAmW 93
Grimes, Charles B., Jr. 1927- St&PR 93, WhoAm 92
Grimes, Connie Carr 1960- WhoEmL 93
Grimes, Dale Mills 1926- WhoAm 92
Grimes, Darrell Jay 1944- WhoE 93
Grimes, David Lynn 1947- WhoAm 92, WhoEmL 93, WhoSSW 93
Grimes, Debra Louise 1954- WhoSSW 93
Grimes, Don W. 1944- St&PR 93
Grimes, Edward L. 1958- WhoSSW 93
Grimes, Elmer Louis 1914-1990 BioIn 17
Grimes, Gary Joe 1947- WhoEmL 93
Grimes, Gary Wayne 1946- WhoE 93
Grimes, Howard Ray 1918- St&PR 93, WhoAm 92
Grimes, Howard W. 1922- St&PR 93
Grimes, Howard Warren 1922- WhoE 93
Grimes, Hubert L. AfrAmBi
Grimes, Hugh Gavin 1929- WhoAm 92
Grimes, James Alan 1948- St&PR 93
Grimes, James Joseph 1949- WhoEmL 93
Grimes, John Phillip 1961- WhoSSW 93
Grimes, John Wade Law&B 92
Grimes, Joseph Edward 1941- WhoWor 93
Grimes, Katherine Atherton AmWomPl
Grimes, Lee 1920- BioIn 17, ConAu 37NR
Grimes, Margaret Katherine 1955- WhoAmW 93, WhoEmL 93
Grimes, Martha BioIn 17, WhoAmW 93
Grimes, Mary Phyllis 1946- WhoEmL 93, WhoSSW 93
Grimes, Michael Duane 1946- WhoEmL 93, WhoSSW 93
Grimes, Nikki 1950- BlkAuII 92, WhoWrEP 92
Grimes, Richard Stuart 1939- WhoSSW 93
Grimes, Robert C. 1923- St&PR 93
Grimes, Robert O. 1920- St&PR 93
Grimes, Russell Newell 1935- WhoAm 92, WhoSSW 93
Grimes, Ruth Elaine 1949- WhoAmW 93, WhoEmL 93, WhoWor 93
Grimes, Sondra Lynn 1949- WhoAmW 93
Grimes, Stephen Henry 1927- WhoAm 92, WhoSSW 93
Grimes, Tammy 1934- WhoAm 92
Grimes, Terry Glen 1957- WhoSSW 93
Grimes, William Alvan 1911- WhoAm 92
Grimke, Angelina 1805-1879 See Grimke Sisters, The PolPar
Grimke, Angelina Emily 1805-1879 BioIn 17
Grimke, Angelina Weld 1880-1958 AmWomPl, EncAACR
Grimke, Archibald 1849-1930 EncAACR
Grimke, Francis James 1850-1937 EncAACR
Grimke, Sarah Moore 1792-1873 BioIn 17 See Also Grimke Sisters, The PolPar
Grimke Sisters, The PolPar
Grimland, John Martin, Jr. 1917- WhoSSW 93
Grimley, Jeffrey Michael 1957- WhoAm 92
Grimley, Liam Kelly 1936- WhoAm 92
Grimley, Robert G. 1940- St&PR 93
Grimley, Robert Thomas 1930- WhoAm 92
Grimley Evans, John 1936- WhoWor 93
Grimm, Ben Emmet 1924- WhoAm 92
Grimm, Carl Hugo 1890-1978 Baker 92
Grimm, Charles E. 1943- St&PR 93
Grimm, Cherry ScF&FL 92
Grimm, Eldon A. d1990 BioIn 17
Grimm, Friedrich Melchior, Baron von 1723-1807 Baker 92
Grimm, Gerhard A.H. 1926- WhoScE 91-3
Grimm, Hazel AmWomPl
Grimm, Heinrich c. 1593-1637 Baker 92
Grimm, Jack BioIn 17
Grimm, Jacob 1785-1863 BioIn 17, MagSWL [port]
Grimm, Jacob Ludwig Karl 1785-1863 MajAI [port]
Grimm, James C. 1932- WhoSSW 93
Grimm, James R. 1935- WhoAm 92
Grimm, Jay Vaughn 1926- St&PR 93, WhoE 93
Grimm, John Lloyd 1945- WhoSSW 93
Grimm, Julius Otto 1827-1903 Baker 92
Grimm, Karl 1819-1888 Baker 92
Grimm, Kathleen 1946- WhoAmW 93
Grimm, Kurt R. Law&B 92
Grimm, Lloyd Richard 1934- St&PR 93
Grimm, Louis John 1933- WhoAm 92
Grimm, (Karl Konstantin) Louis (Ludwig) 1820-1882 Baker 92
Grimm, Paul Edward 1931- St&PR 93
Grimm, Paula 1950- WhoAmW 93
Grimm, Peter Michael 1942- St&PR 93
Grimm, Phyllis E. Law&B 92
Grimm, Robert 1915- St&PR 93
Grimm, Roland D. 1926- St&PR 93
Grimm, Roland DuBois 1926- WhoAm 92
Grimm, Stefan Karol 1937- WhoScE 91-4
Grimm, Thomas L. St&PR 93
Grimm, Victor E. 1937- WhoAm 92
Grimm, W. Thomas Law&B 92
Grimm, Wilhelm 1786-1859 BioIn 17, MagSWL [port]
Grimm, Wilhelm Karl 1786-1859 MajAI [port]
Grimm, William Arthur 1939- St&PR 93
Grimm, Willis McClellan 1935- WhoSSW 93
Grimme, A. Jeannette 1921- WhoAmW 93
Grimme, Lothar Horst 1939- WhoScE 91-3
Grimme, Michael J. BioIn 17
Grimmeau, Jean-Pierre WhoScE 91-2
Grimmeiss, Hermann Georg 1930- WhoScE 91-4, WhoWor 93
Grimmel, Eckhard 1941- WhoScE 91-3
Grimmell, Karen Ethel 1937- WhoAmW 93
Grimmer, John C. St&PR 93
Grimmer, Margot 1944- WhoAm 92, WhoAmW 93
Grimmett, Geoffrey Richard WhoScE 91-1
Grimmett, Gerald Glen 1942- WhoWrEP 92
Grimmig, Eugene M. Law&B 92
Grimmig, Robert John 1928- St&PR 93
Grimm-Richardson, Anna Louise 1927- WhoWrEP 92
Grimond, Joseph 1913- DcTwHis
Grimsel 1831-1913 BioIn 17

Grimshaw, David *Law&B 92*
Grimshaw, James Albert, Jr. 1940- *WhoAm 92, WhoSSW 93*
Grimshaw, Nigel 1925- *ScF&FL 92*
Grimshaw, Paul *WhoAm 92*
Grimshaw, Thomas Drysdale 1933- *WhoWrEP 92*
Grimsley, Ann *ScF&FL 92*
Grimsley, James Alexander, Jr. 1921- *WhoAm 92, WhoSSW 93*
Grimsley, Will Henry 1914- *WhoAm 92, WhoWrEP 92*
Grimsley, William Elmer, Jr. 1943- *WhoSSW 93*
Grimson, Bettina Warburg 1900-1990 *BioIn 17*
Grimson, Malcolm John *WhoScE 91-1*
Grimvall, N. Goran 1940- *WhoScE 91-4*
Grimwade, Peter *ScF&FL 92*
Grimwade, R. Reed 1929- *St&PR 93*
Grimwood, Ken *ScF&FL 92*
Grinage, Lauren B. *Law&B 92*
Grinage, Lauren B. 1939- *St&PR 93*
Grinberg, Meyer Stewart 1944- *WhoAm 92, WhoWor 93*
Grinblat, Romuald 1930- *Baker 92*
Grinch, Robert Paul 1956- *WhoEmL 93*
Grinchuk, Mikhail Ivanovich 1964- *WhoWor 93*
Grinde, Erick R. 1949- *St&PR 93*
Grinde, Kjell 1929- *WhoWor 93*
Grinde, Ralph Wayne 1943- *St&PR 93*
Grindea, Daniel 1924- *St&PR 93, WhoAm 92*
Grindel, Patricia Diane 1957- *WhoEmL 93, WhoSSW 93*
Grindem, Carol Beth 1951- *WhoAmW 93*
Grinder, Olle 1945- *WhoScE 91-4*
Grindlay, Jonathan Ellis 1944- *WhoAm 92*
Grindlay, Robert Melville 1786-1877 *BioIn 17*
Grindle, Crosby Redman 1925- *WhoSSW 93*
Grindley, Mitchell P. 1959- *St&PR 93*
Grindley, Robert B. 1929- *St&PR 93*
Grindlinger, Benjamin 1938- *St&PR 93*
Grindon, Arthur St. Leger 1949- *WhoE 93*
Grine, Donald Reaville 1930- *WhoAm 92*
Grinell, Sheila 1945- *WhoAm 92*
Griner, George Wesley, Jr. 1895- *HarEnMi*
Griner, Jimmy Wayne 1949- *WhoEmL 93*
Griner, Kenneth Edward 1948- *WhoEmL 93*
Griner, Norman 1932- *WhoE 93*
Griner, Paul Francis 1933- *WhoAm 92*
Griner, Terry Wyn 1947- *St&PR 93*
Grinevald, Jacques Marie Leon 1946- *WhoWor 93*
Gring, David M. 1945- *WhoAm 92*
Gringer, Donald 1933- *St&PR 93*
Grinham, A.R. *WhoScE 91-1*
Grinker, Morton 1928- *WhoWrEP 92*
Grinker, Roy Richard, Sr. 1900- *WhoAm 92*
Grinker, Roy Richard, Jr. 1927- *WhoAm 92*
Grinker, Susan Ann 1948- *St&PR 93*
Grinker, William Stephen 1934- *St&PR 93, WhoAm 92*
Grinko, Sigmund John 1924- *St&PR 93*
Grinnan, Richardson 1940- *St&PR 93*
Grinnell, Alan Dale 1936- *WhoAm 92*
Grinnell, Charles W. *Law&B 92*
Grinnell, David *SmATA 69*
Grinnell, Frederick 1945- *WhoSSW 93*
Grinnell, George Bird 1849-1938 *BioIn 17*
Grinnell, Helene Dunn 1936- *WhoAmW 93*
Grinold, Richard C. *St&PR 93*
Grinshpan, Arcadii Zaharovich 1945- *WhoWor 93*
Grinshpan, Leonid Abramovich 1946- *WhoWor 93*
Grinspan, Mel G. 1917- *WhoSSW 93*
Grinstead, William Carter, Jr. 1930- *WhoAm 92*
Grinstein, Benjamin 1958- *WhoE 93*
Grinstein, Gerald 1932- *St&PR 93, WhoAm 92, WhoSSW 93*
Grinstein, Keith D. *Law&B 92*
Grinstein Richman, Louise Sonia 1929- *WhoAmW 93*
Grint, Alan *MiSFD 9*
Grinyer, John Raymond *WhoScE 91-1*
Grinyer, John Raymond 1935- *WhoWor 93*
Grip, Carl Manfred, Jr. 1921- *WhoAm 92*
Grip, Goran 1945- *WhoWor 93*
Gripaldo, Rolando Menardo 1948- *WhoWor 93*
Gripe, Maria 1923- *ScF&FL 92*
Gripe, Maria (Kristina) 1923- *ConAu 39NR, MajAI [port]*
Gripkey, Theodore F., Jr. *Law&B 92*
Grippa, Anthony John 1945- *WhoIns 93*
Grippe, Peter Joseph 1912- *WhoE 93*
Grippi, Salvatore William 1921- *WhoAm 92*
Grippin, Eugene W. 1931- *St&PR 93*
Gris, Charles Edouard Jeanneret- 1887-1965 *BioIn 17*
Gris, Juan 1887-1927 *BioIn 17*
Grisanti, Anthony F. 1949- *St&PR 93*
Grisanti, Eugene Philip 1929- *WhoAm 92, WhoE 93*
Grisar, Albert 1808-1869 *Baker 92, OxDcOp*
Grisar, Johann Martin 1929- *WhoWor 93*
Grisart, Charles Jean Baptiste 1837-1904 *Baker 92*
Griscelli, C. 1936- *WhoScE 91-2*
Grischkowsky, Daniel Richard 1940- *WhoAm 92*
Griscom, David Lawrence 1938- *WhoE 93*
Griscom, Nina *BioIn 17*
Griscom, Thomas Cecil 1949- *WhoAm 92*
Griscti, Alfred Edward 1936- *WhoWor 93*
Grise, Wilma Marie 1937- *WhoAmW 93, WhoWor 93*
Grisebach, Hans 1926- *WhoScE 91-3*
Grisebach, Hans 1926-1990 *BioIn 17*
Griselle, Thomas 1891-1955 *Baker 92*
Grisez, Germain G. 1929- *WhoWrEP 92*
Grisham, Charles Milton 1947- *WhoAm 92, WhoSSW 93*
Grisham, Joe Wheeler 1931- *WhoAm 92, WhoWor 93*
Grisham, John 1955?- *ConAu 138*
Grisham, Larry Richard 1949- *WhoE 93*
Grisham, Michael J. *Law&B 92*
Grisham, Richard Bond *Law&B 92*
Grisham, Sandra Ann 1949- *WhoEmL 93*
Grishchenko, Anatoly d1990 *BioIn 17*
Grishin, V.V. 1914-1992 *BioIn 17*
Grishin, Viktor V. d1992 *NewYTBS 92*
Grishin, Viktor Vasil'evich 1914-1992 *BioIn 17*
Grishkat, Hans (Adolf Karl Willy) 1903-1977 *Baker 92*
Grisi, Arthur John 1952- *St&PR 93*
Grisi, Carlotta *OxDcOp*
Grisi, Giuditta 1805-1840 *Baker 92, IntDcOp [port], OxDcOp*
Grisi, Giulia 1811-1869 *Baker 92, IntDcOp [port], OxDcOp*
Griskey, Richard George 1931- *WhoAm 92*
Grisolia, Santiago 1923- *WhoScE 91-3, WhoWor 93*
Grispino, Maria Genevieve 1954- *WhoEmL 93*
Grissom, Beverly McMurtry 1946- *WhoAmW 93*
Grissom, Gail Coffin 1942- *WhoE 93*
Grissom, Garth Clyde 1930- *WhoAm 92*
Grissom, J. David 1938- *St&PR 93*
Grissom, J. David 1939- *WhoAm 92*
Grissom, Joseph Carol 1931- *WhoAm 92*
Grissom, Lee Alan 1942- *WhoAm 92*
Grissom, Monte T. *St&PR 93*
Grissom, Patsy Coleen 1934- *WhoAmW 93*
Grissom, Stephen David 1952- *St&PR 93*
Grissom, Steven Edward 1949- *WhoWrEP 92*
Grist, Reri 1932- *OxDcOp*
Grist, Reri 1934- *Baker 92, IntDcOp*
Gristy, Bill *BioIn 17*
Griswell, J. Barry 1949- *WhoIns 93*
Griswold, Benjamin Howell, IV 1940- *WhoAm 92, WhoE 93*
Griswold, Bruce 1916- *WhoAm 92*
Griswold, Denny *WhoAm 92, WhoE 93, WhoWor 93*
Griswold, Edward J. *BioIn 17*
Griswold, Erwin Nathaniel 1904- *WhoAm 92*
Griswold, Frank Tracy, III 1937- *WhoAm 92*
Griswold, Gary Lee *Law&B 92*
Griswold, Gary Norris 1947- *WhoE 93*
Griswold, George 1919- *WhoSSW 93*
Griswold, Gerald W. 1938- *WhoIns 93*
Griswold, Grace d1927 *AmWomPl*
Griswold, Jean *BioIn 17*
Griswold, Norman H. 1929- *St&PR 93*
Griswold, Oscar Wolverton 1886-1959 *HarEnMi*
Griswold, Phillip Dwight 1948- *WhoSSW 93*
Griswold, Putnam 1875-1914 *Baker 92*
Griswold, Richard Bruce 1947- *St&PR 93*
Griswold, Richard Merle 1931- *St&PR 93*
Griswold, Thomas Hays *Law&B 92*
Griswold, Valerie Anne 1962- *WhoAmW 93, WhoEmL 93*
Griswold, Virginia A. *AmWomPl*
Griswold, William G. 1949- *St&PR 93*
Griswold, William Tudor, II 1921- *St&PR 93*
Griswold del Castillo, Richard A. 1942- *HispAmA*
Grittman, Ronald 1933- *St&PR 93*
Gritton, Eugene Charles 1941- *WhoAm 92*
Gritz, Louis 1925- *St&PR 93*
Grivas, Theodore 1922- *WhoAm 92, WhoWor 93*
Griver, Michael A. 1942- *WhoIns 93*
Grixti, Joseph 1950- *ScF&FL 92*
Grizi, Samir Amine 1942- *WhoWor 93*
Grizzard, George 1928- *WhoAm 92*
Grizzard, Lewis *BioIn 17*
Grizzell, Roy Ames 1918- *WhoSSW 93*
Grizzle, Charles Leslie 1948- *WhoAm 92*
Grizzle, J. David *Law&B 92*
Grizzle, J. David 1954- *St&PR 93*
Grizzle, Rhonda Mewborn 1952- *WhoAmW 93*
Grlic, Rajko 1947- *DrEEuF*
Grmek, Dorothy Antonia 1930- *WhoAmW 93*
Groah, Linda Kay 1942- *WhoAmW 93*
Groark, Eunice 1938- *WhoAm 92, WhoAmW 93, WhoE 93*
Grob, Bruce Russell 1951- *WhoEmL 93, WhoSSW 93*
Grob, Gerald N. 1931- *WhoAm 92, WhoWrEP 92*
Grob, Howard S. 1932-1990 *BioIn 17*
Grobart, David Lee *Law&B 92*
Grobbel, Mark A. *Law&B 92*
Grobe, Albert A. d1990 *BioIn 17*
Grobe, Charles Stephen 1935- *WhoAm 92*
Grobe, Kenneth A. 1927- *St&PR 93*
Grobe, William Howard 1916- *WhoWor 93*
Groberg, Dick *BioIn 17*
Groberg, James J. 1928- *St&PR 93*
Groberg, James Jay 1928- *WhoAm 92*
Groberg, Neil H. *Law&B 92*
Grobman, Alexander 1927- *WhoWor 93*
Grobman, Arnold Brams 1918- *WhoAm 92*
Grobman, Hulda Gross 1920- *WhoAm 92*
Grobois, Brian Saul 1957- *WhoEmL 93*
Grobowsky, George Erwin 1934- *St&PR 93*
Grob-Prandl, Gertrud 1917- *Baker 92, OxDcOp*
Grobstein, Clifford 1916- *WhoAm 92*
Groce, James Freelan 1948- *WhoEmL 93, WhoSSW 93*
Groce, Larry *BioIn 17*
Groce, William John 1947- *St&PR 93*
Grochala, Richard John *Law&B 92*
Grocheo, Johannes de fl. 14th cent.- *Baker 92*
Grochoski, Gregory Thomas 1946- *St&PR 93, WhoAm 92*
Grochowska, Maria J. 1926- *WhoScE 91-4*
Grochulski, Pawel 1955- *WhoWor 93*
Grocott, Ann 1938- *ScF&FL 92*
Groda, Borivoj 1945- *WhoScE 91-4*
Grodberg, Eva M. 1960- *WhoAmW 93*
Grodberg, Marcus Gordon 1923- *WhoE 93, WhoWor 93*
Grodberg, Robert S. *Law&B 92*
Grodd, Clifford 1924- *St&PR 93*
Grode, Murray T. *WhoIns 93*
Groden, Gerald 1931- *WhoE 93*
Grodhaus, Greg R. 1947- *St&PR 93*
Grodin, Charles *BioIn 17*
Grodin, Charles 1935- *WhoAm 92*
Grodins, Fred S. *BioIn 17*
Grodinsky, Jack 1923- *St&PR 93*
Grodman, Robert Frederic 1952- *WhoWor 93*
Grodnik, Daniel 1952- *St&PR 93*
Grodsky, Gerold Morton 1927- *WhoAm 92*
Grody, Donald 1927- *WhoAm 92*
Grody, Gary Lance 1949- *WhoE 93*
Grody, Mark Stephen 1938- *WhoAm 92*
Grodzicki, Antoni 1936- *WhoScE 91-4*
Grodzinsky, Zvi Hirsch 1857?-1947 *JeAmHC*
Groebel, Anna Margarete 1960- *WhoWor 93*
Groebel, Jo 1950- *WhoWor 93*
Groeber, David Paul 1935- *St&PR 93*
Groebli, Werner Fritz 1915- *WhoAm 92*
Groefsema, Bruce Kenneth 1950- *St&PR 93*
Groeger, Joseph Herman 1925- *WhoAm 92*
Groeger, Phyllis J. 1940- *St&PR 93*
Groemer, Gerald 1957- *ConAu 139*
Groen, Frances K. *BioIn 17*
Groen, Pieter Maria 1941- *WhoWor 93*
Groener, Wilhelm 1867-1939 *HarEnMi*
Groeneveld, Arie 1934- *WhoScE 91-3*
Groeneveld, Karl-Ontjes E. 1935- *WhoScE 91-3*
Groeneveld, Karl-Ontjes Ernst 1935- *WhoWor 93*
Groenewegen, Peter D. 1939- *BioIn 17*
Groening, Matt *BioIn 17*
Groening, Matt 1954- *ConAu 138, ConTFT 10*
Groening, Matthew Akbar 1954- *WhoAm 92*
Groening, William Andrew, Jr. 1912- *WhoAm 92*
Groenke, Theodore Arthur 1921- *WhoAm 92*
Groennert, Charles Willis 1937- *St&PR 93, WhoAm 92*
Groennings, Sven Ole 1934- *WhoAm 92*
Groesbeck, Elise de Branges de Bourica 1936- *WhoAmW 93, WhoSSW 93, WhoWor 93*
Groeschel, Benedict J(oseph) 1933- *ConAu 37NR*
Groesschen, Heribert Johannes 1943- *WhoWor 93*
Groetzinger, Jon, Jr. *Law&B 92*
Groetzinger, Jon, Jr. 1949- *WhoAm 92*
Grofe, Ferde 1892-1972 *Baker 92*
Groff, Alice *AmWomPl*
Groff, Harold Allen 1931- *WhoE 93*
Groff, James B. 1932- *WhoE 93*
Groff, Jim *St&PR 93*
Groff, JoAnn 1956- *WhoAmW 93*
Groff, John d1990 *BioIn 17*
Groff, John Marshall 1951- *WhoE 93*
Groff, Jon P. 1939- *St&PR 93*
Groff, Kenelm A. 1929- *St&PR 93*
Groff, Marlin *BioIn 17*
Groff, Pamela Joanne 1961- *WhoWrEP 92*
Groff, Raymond David 1933- *St&PR 93*
Groff, Regis F. 1935- *AfrAmBi*
Grogan, Alice Washington *Law&B 92*
Grogan, Alice Washington 1956- *WhoAmW 93, WhoSSW 93*
Grogan, Barbara B. 1947- *ConEn*
Grogan, Bette Lowery 1931- *WhoAmW 93*
Grogan, Donald W. 1947- *St&PR 93*
Grogan, Earlean Stanley 1922- *WhoWrEP 92*
Grogan, John J. *St&PR 93*
Grogan, Kenneth Augustine 1924- *WhoAm 92*
Grogan, Kevin 1948- *WhoAm 92*
Grogan, Michael Kevin 1951- *WhoSSW 93*
Grogan, Michael T. *Law&B 92*
Grogan, Oliver 1948- *WhoUN 92*
Grogan, Richard B. 1937- *St&PR 93, WhoAm 92*
Grogan, Robert Edward 1914- *St&PR 93*
Grogan, Robert Harris 1933- *WhoSSW 93*
Grogan, Stanley Joseph, Jr. 1925- *WhoWor 93*
Grogan, Steven James 1953- *WhoAm 92*
Grogan, Thomas F. *Law&B 92*
Grogan, Timothy James 1940- *WhoAm 92*
Grogan, William McLean, Jr. 1944- *WhoSSW 93*
Grogan, William Robert 1924- *WhoAm 92*
Grogg, Tim Allen *Law&B 92*
Grogg, Timothy A. *Law&B 92*
Groh, Clifford J., Sr. 1926- *WhoAm 92, WhoWor 93*
Groh, Gabor Gyula 1948- *WhoWor 93*
Groh, Irwin 1894-1985 *ScF&FL 92*
Groh, Lawrence Paul 1947- *WhoEmL 93*
Groh, LeAnna Wheaton 1916- *WhoE 93*
Grohl, Dave
See Nirvana *ConMus 8*
See Also Nirvana *News 92*
Grohman, Paul William, Jr. 1954- *WhoAm 92*
Grohmann, Eckhart Georg 1936- *St&PR 93*
Grohol, Robert M. 1932- *St&PR 93*
Groholski, John S. 1939- *St&PR 93*
Grohs, Saul Ernest 1937- *St&PR 93*
Grohskopf, Bernice *WhoWrEP 92*
Groiss, Fred George 1936- *WhoAm 92*
Groiss, Josef Theodor 1933- *WhoScE 91-3*
Grokoest, Albert W. 1917-1991 *BioIn 17*
Grolier, Eric de 1911- *BioIn 17*
Groll, Horst P. 1924- *WhoScE 91-3*
Groll, Horst Peter 1924- *WhoWor 93*
Groller, Richard 1955- *WhoEmL 93, WhoSSW 93*
Grollman, Sigmund Sidney 1923- *WhoE 93*
Grollmes, Eugene Edward 1931- *WhoWrEP 92*
Grollmus, Pablo W. 1952- *St&PR 93*
Grolnick, Don *BioIn 17*
Grolnick, Herbert Norman 1932- *St&PR 93, WhoAm 92*
Grolnick, Simon A. 1930-1990 *BioIn 17*
Grom, Bogdan 1918- *WhoE 93*
Grom, George W. 1931- *St&PR 93*
Gromada, John *BioIn 17*
Gro Mambo Angela Novanyon Idizol 1953- *WhoE 93*
Groman, Arthur 1914- *WhoAm 92*
Groman, David 1937- *WhoUN 92*
Groman, Linda R. *Law&B 92*
Groman, Neal Benjamin 1921- *WhoAm 92*
Gromelski, Stanley John 1942- *WhoAm 92*
Gromen, Richard John 1930- *WhoAm 92*
Gromfin, Herbert 1930- *St&PR 93*

Gromiller, James William 1931- *WhoE 93*
Gromisz, Michal 1925- *WhoScE 91-4*
Grommesh, Donald Joseph 1931- *St&PR 93*
Grommet, Allen Norman 1954- *WhoEmL 93*
Gromosiak, Paul 1942- *WhoE 93*
Gromov, Boris *BioIn 17*
Grompone, Juan 1939- *WhoWor 93*
Gromyko, Andrei 1909-1989 *ColdWar 2 [port]*
Gron, Gary M. *Law&B 92*
Gronau, Crystal Lynn 1957- *WhoAmW 93*
Gronau, Hans von fl. c. 1914- *HarEnMi*
Gronau, Magdala 1947- *WhoWor 93*
Gronau, Mary Ellen *ScF&FL 92*
Gronbach, Robert Charles 1928- *WhoE 93*
Gronbech, Michael 1946- *WhoWor 93*
Groncki, Paul John 1949- *WhoAm 92, WhoE 93*
Gronda, Richard F. 1941- *St&PR 93*
Grondahl, Agathe Backer- 1847-1907 *BioIn 17*
Grondahl, Kirsti Kolle 1943- *WhoWor 93*
Grondahl, Launy 1886-1960 *Baker 92*
Grondal, Benedikt 1924- *WhoUN 92*
Grondalen, Jorunn 1937- *WhoScE 91-4*
Grondin, Conrad A. 1926- *St&PR 93*
Grondin, Mary L. 1941- *WhoWor 93*
Grondin, Robert J. 1936- *St&PR 93*
Grondine, Robert Francis 1952- *WhoWor 93*
Grondine, Susan E. *Law&B 92*
Grondin-Francella, Barbara Jean 1962- *WhoAmW 93*
Grone, James A. 1945- *St&PR 93*
Gronemann, Sammy 1875-1952 *BioIn 17*
Gronemeyer, Lyman Schoonmaker *Law&B 92*
Gronemeyer, Suzanne Alsop 1941- *WhoAmW 93*
Gronenborn, Angela Maria 1950- *WhoE 93*
Groner, Bernd 1946- *WhoScE 91-4*
Groner, Beverly Anne *WhoAm 92*
Groner, Frank Shelby 1911- *WhoSSW 93*
Groner, Pat Neff 1920- *WhoAm 92*
Groner, Samuel Brian 1916- *WhoAm 92*
Groner, Sheldon M. 1960- *St&PR 93*
Gronhaug, Arne 1933- *WhoScE 91-4*
Gronich, Dan Neal Jonathan 1942- *WhoE 93*
Gronich, Daphne *Law&B 92*
Gronick, Patricia Ann Jacobsen 1930- *WhoAmW 93*
Groningen, Stefan van 1851-1926 *Baker 92*
Groninger, Cheryl Kay 1949- *WhoAmW 93*
Groninger, Donald L. 1941- *St&PR 93*
Gronka, Martin Steven 1952- *WhoE 93*
Gronlie, Olav 1946- *WhoUN 92*
Gronlund, J. Anders 1948- *WhoScE 91-4*
Gronmark, Scott *ScF&FL 92*
Gronowicz, Antoni c. 1912-1985 *PolBiDi*
Gronowska, Janina 1922- *WhoScE 91-4*
Gronowska-Senger, Anna 1940- *WhoScE 91-4*
Gronowski, Paul *ScF&FL 92*
Gronquist, Carl Harry 1903-1991 *BioIn 17*
Gronqvist, Anders Henrik 1954- *WhoScE 91-4*
Gronroos, Matti 1931- *WhoScE 91-4*
Gronstol, Hallstein 1939- *WhoScE 91-4*
Gronvall, John A. 1931-1990 *BioIn 17*
Grooer, Hans Herrmann Cardinal 1919- *WhoWor 93*
Groom, Dale 1912- *WhoAm 92*
Groom, Donald Joseph 1947- *WhoE 93, WhoEmL 93*
Groom, Gary L. 1946- *St&PR 93*
Groom, Gary Lee 1946- *WhoAm 92*
Groom, John *St&PR 93*
Groom, John Miller 1936- *WhoAm 92*
Groom, Sharon E. *Law&B 92*
Groome, Reginald K. 1927- *St&PR 93, WhoAm 92*
Grooms, H.H. 1900-1991 *BioIn 17*
Grooms, James Trenton 1931- *WhoWor 93*
Grooms, Red 1937- *WhoAm 92*
Grooms, Robert P. *WhoE 93*
Grooms, Suzanne Simmons 1945- *WhoAmW 93, WhoSSW 93*
Grooms, Vicki Lynn 1960- *WhoSSW 93*
Grooms, Vickie Lynn 1955- *WhoEmL 93*
Groorachurn, Fanjay *Law&B 92*
Groos, Arthur Bernhard, Jr. 1943- *WhoAm 92*
Groos, Margaret *BioIn 17*
Groos, Richard John 1958- *WhoEmL 93*
Groos, Richard T. 1929- *St&PR 93*
Groot, Cor de 1914- *Baker 92*
Groot, Gary J. *Law&B 92*
Groot, Huub Johannes Maria 1958- *WhoWor 93*
Groot, Lonnie Neil 1950- *WhoEmL 93*
Groothuis, Martin J. *Law&B 92*
Groothuis, Richard Bernard 1937- *St&PR 93*
Grootjans, J.F. 1945- *WhoScE 91-2*
Grootkerk, Paul 1946- *WhoSSW 93*
Groot-Koerkamp, Irene M. *Law&B 92*
Grootveld, John E. *St&PR 93*
Groover, Marion D. *Law&B 92*
Gropius, Walter 1883-1969 *BioIn 17*
Gropp, Louis Oliver 1935- *WhoAm 92, WhoWrEP 92*
Gropp, Walter Edward 1930- *St&PR 93*
Groppa, Carlos G. 1931- *WhoWrEP 92*
Gropper, Allan Louis 1944- *WhoAm 92*
Gropper, Edward 1920- *St&PR 93*
Gropper, William 1897-1977 *BioIn 17*
Gropsian, Zeno 1920- *WhoScE 91-4*
Gros, Claudius 1961- *WhoWor 93*
Gros, Ridley Joseph 1941- *WhoSSW 93*
Grosanu, I. 1982- *WhoScE 91-4*
Grosbard, Ulu 1929- *MiSFD 9, WhoAm 92*
Grosberg, Percy *WhoScE 91-1*
Grosby, Herbert Leon 1919- *St&PR 93*
Grosch, Barbara Ann 1945- *WhoAmW 93*
Grosch, Lucia Leokadia 1911- *WhoE 93*
Grosch, Timothy Leo *Law&B 92*
Grosclaude, Francois 1933- *WhoScE 91-2*
Grose, Ann Bawden Huntington 1926- *WhoAmW 93*
Grose, B. Donald 1943- *WhoAm 92*
Grose, B(url) Donald 1943- *WhoWrEP 92*
Grose, Becki Gail 1958- *WhoAmW 93*
Grose, David E. 1952- *St&PR 93*
Grose, Donald Gene 1935- *St&PR 93*
Grose, Geri Lynn 1958- *WhoAmW 93*
Grose, Kate *St&PR 93*
Grose, Robert Freeman 1924- *WhoAm 92*
Grose, Robert Warfield 1941- *WhoAm 92*
Grose, Thomas Lucius Trowbridge 1924- *WhoAm 92*
Grose, William Rush 1939- *WhoAm 92*
Groseclos, Gene *Law&B 92*
Groseclose, Everett Harrison 1938- *WhoAm 92*
Groseclose, William H. 1930- *St&PR 93*
Groseilliers, Medard Chouart des 1618-1696? *Expl 93*
Grosfeld, James 1938- *WhoAm 92*
Grosfeld, Jay Lazar 1935- *WhoAm 92*
Grosheim, Georg Christoph 1764-1841 *Baker 92*
Groshek, Michael Dean 1932- *WhoAm 92*
Groshner, Maria Star 1961- *WhoAmW 93, WhoEmL 93*
Groshong, Claudia Clark 1949- *WhoAm 92*
Grosjean, Ernest 1844-1936 *Baker 92*
Grosjean, Henri 1941- *WhoScE 91-2*
Grosjean, Jean Romary 1815-1888 *Baker 92*
Groskopf, John E. 1945- *WhoIns 93*
Grosland, Emery Layton 1929- *WhoAm 92*
Grosland, Knut 1946- *WhoScE 91-4*
Gros Louis, Kenneth Richard Russell 1936- *WhoAm 92, WhoWor 93*
Grosman, Alan M. 1935- *WhoE 93*
Grosman, Meta 1936- *WhoWor 93*
Grosof, Miriam Schapiro 1932- *WhoE 93*
Gross, Abraham 1928- *WhoAm 92*
Gross, Al 1918- *WhoAm 92*
Gross, Alan John 1934- *WhoSSW 93*
Gross, Alexander S. d1990 *BioIn 17*
Gross, Alfred d1992 *BioIn 17*
Gross, Beatrice Schaap 1935- *WhoE 93*
Gross, Bennett S. *Law&B 92*
Gross, Beverly *Law&B 92*
Gross, Beverly Ann 1951- *WhoAmW 93*
Gross, Carol Cott 1942- *WhoWrEP 92*
Gross, Carol Jane 1949- *WhoWrEP 92*
Gross, Caroline Lord 1940- *WhoAmW 93*
Gross, Chaim 1904-1991 *BioIn 17*
Gross, Charles Gordon 1936- *WhoAm 92*
Gross, Charles Wayne 1930- *WhoAm 92*
Gross, Cynthia Ann 1964- *WhoAmW 93*
Gross, David Danforth 1949- *St&PR 93*
Gross, David E. 1937- *St&PR 93*
Gross, David J. *Law&B 92*
Gross, David Jay 1958- *WhoEmL 93*
Gross, David John 1953- *WhoE 93*
Gross, David Lee 1943- *WhoAm 92*
Gross, Debra Marie 1953- *WhoAmW 93*
Gross, Dennis S. 1958- *St&PR 93*
Gross, Denyse Robin *Law&B 92*
Gross, Donald 1947- *WhoE 93*
Gross, Dorine Miles *BioIn 17*
Gross, Douglas Hale *Law&B 92*
Gross, Edmund S. *Law&B 92*
Gross, Edward *WhoAm 92*
Gross, Edward 1960- *ScF&FL 92*
Gross, Egon Miller 1934- *WhoSSW 93*
Gross, Ernest Arnold 1906- *WhoAm 92*
Gross, Ernie *BioIn 17*
Gross, Ernie 1913- *ConAu 136*
Gross, Esther Moneysmith 1936- *WhoWrEP 92*
Gross, Eugene P. d1991 *BioIn 17*
Gross, Feliks 1906- *WhoE 93, WhoWor 93*
Gross, Francis McKenzie 1941- *WhoSSW 93*
Gross, Franz 1923- *WhoScE 91-3*
Gross, Fredye Wright 1949- *WhoE 93*
Gross, Fritz A. 1910- *WhoAm 92*
Gross, Gad d1991 *BioIn 17*
Gross, George 1934- *WhoE 93*
Gross, George, Jr. 1941- *WhoE 93*
Gross, Gregory M. 1952- *St&PR 93*
Gross, Hal Raymond 1914- *WhoAm 92*
Gross, Hans Joachim 1936- *WhoScE 91-3*
Gross, Harriet P. Marcus 1934- *WhoAmW 93, WhoSSW 93*
Gross, Harriet Sharon 1958- *WhoE 93*
Gross, Harvey 1922- *St&PR 93*
Gross, Henry 1949- *WhoAm 92, WhoE 93*
Gross, Ian 1943- *WhoE 93*
Gross, Iris Lee 1941- *WhoAmW 93*
Gross, Irwin Lee 1943- *WhoAm 92, WhoE 93*
Gross, Jack 1910- *St&PR 93*
Gross, James Dehnert 1929- *WhoAm 92*
Gross, Jane *BioIn 17*
Gross, Jenard Morris 1929- *WhoAm 92*
Gross, Jerome 1917- *WhoAm 92*
Gross, Jerry M. *Law&B 92*
Gross, Jerry M. 1935- *St&PR 93*
Gross, Jildy H. *Law&B 92*
Gross, Jimmie Frank 1936- *WhoSSW 93*
Gross, John Birney 1924- *WhoAm 92*
Gross, John E. 1936- *St&PR 93*
Gross, John F. 1942- *St&PR 93*
Gross, John (Jacob) 1935- *ConAu 39NR, WhoWor 93*
Gross, John Richard 1931- *St&PR 93*
Gross, Jonathan Light 1941- *WhoAm 92*
Gross, Joseph Haim 1934- *WhoWor 93*
Gross, Jozef 1921-1991 *BioIn 17*
Gross, Judith E. *Law&B 92*
Gross, Julia Ann 1957- *WhoAmW 93*
Gross, Julie 1959- *WhoE 93, WhoEmL 93*
Gross, Justin A. *Law&B 92*
Gross, Karen P. 1954- *St&PR 93*
Gross, Kenneth J. 1944- *St&PR 93*
Gross, Kenneth Paul 1952- *WhoEmL 93*
Gross, Larry *MiSFD 9*
Gross, Larry Paul 1942- *WhoAm 92*
Gross, Laura Ann 1948- *WhoAmW 93, WhoEmL 93*
Gross, Laurie Carol 1953- *St&PR 93*
Gross, Lawrence Robert 1941- *St&PR 93, WhoAm 92*
Gross, Leo 1903-1990 *BioIn 17*
Gross, Leonard 1935- *St&PR 93*
Gross, Leroy 1926- *WhoAm 92*
Gross, Leslie Pamela 1952- *WhoAmW 93, WhoEmL 93*
Gross, Lisse R. *Law&B 92*
Gross, Louis 1930- *St&PR 93*
Gross, Louis S. 1954- *ScF&FL 92*
Gross, Ludwik 1904- *WhoAm 92*
Gross, Marilyn Agnes 1937- *WhoWrEP 92*
Gross, Marjorie E. *Law&B 92*
Gross, Mary Anne 1943- *WhoE 93*
Gross, Maurice 1941- *WhoScE 91-2*
Gross, Max Menachem 1951- *WhoEmL 93*
Gross, Melanie B. 1946- *St&PR 93*
Gross, Meredith R. *Law&B 92*
Gross, Merryl Jane 1963- *WhoEmL 93*
Gross, Michael 1947- *WhoAm 92*
Gross, Michael 1948- *BioIn 17*
Gross, Michael 1957- *ScF&FL 92*
Gross, Michael Lawrence 1940- *WhoAm 92*
Gross, Michael M. 1936- *St&PR 93*
Gross, Michael Raymond 1952- *WhoE 93*
Gross, Miriam 1936?- *ScF&FL 92*
Gross, Morton 1923- *St&PR 93*
Gross, Murray *Law&B 92, St&PR 93*
Gross, Nathan 1933- *WhoE 93, WhoWor 93*
Gross, Nelson Boon 1929- *St&PR 93*
Gross, Pamela Heather Boxwood 1949- *WhoAmW 93*
Gross, Pamela Robyn 1963- *WhoAmW 93*
Gross, Patricia Louise 1952- *WhoSSW 93*
Gross, Patrick Walter 1944- *St&PR 93, WhoAm 92, WhoWor 93*
Gross, Paul 1902- *WhoAm 92*
Gross, Paul A. 1937- *St&PR 93*
Gross, Paul Allan 1937- *WhoAm 92, WhoSSW 93*
Gross, Paul Dwayne 1947- *WhoSSW 93*
Gross, Paul Randolph 1928- *WhoAm 92*
Gross, Peter Alan 1938- *WhoAm 92, WhoE 93, WhoWor 93*
Gross, Priva d1990 *BioIn 17*
Gross, Priva Baidaff 1911- *WhoAmW 93, WhoE 93*
Gross, Rainer 1943- *WhoWor 93*
Gross, Richard Charles 1939- *St&PR 93*
Gross, Richard Edmund 1920- *WhoAm 92*
Gross, Richard Warren 1945- *St&PR 93*
Gross, Richard Wilson 1948- *WhoEmL 93*
Gross, Robert Alan 1945- *WhoAm 92*
Gross, Robert E. 1911- *St&PR 93*
Gross, Robert Emanuel 1920- *WhoE 93*
Gross, Robert R. d1991 *BioIn 17*
Gross, Ronald Martin *WhoAm 92*
Gross, Ronald Martin 1933- *St&PR 93*
Gross, Ruth Taubenhaus 1920- *WhoAm 92, WhoAmW 93*
Gross, Sally Lucille 1943- *WhoSSW 93*
Gross, Sanford 1921- *St&PR 93*
Gross, Sarah Kerstin 1952- *WhoAmW 93*
Gross, Selma d1991 *BioIn 17*
Gross, Seth S. *Law&B 92*
Gross, Sharon Clare 1954- *WhoAmW 93*
Gross, Sharon Ruth 1940- *WhoAmW 93*
Gross, Shelley *WhoWrEP 92*
Gross, Shelly 1921- *WhoAm 92*
Gross, Shirley Ann 1959- *WhoAmW 93*
Gross, Shirley Marie 1917- *WhoAmW 93*
Gross, Sid *BioIn 17*
Gross, Sidney W. 1904- *WhoAm 92, WhoWor 93*
Gross, Sonja Keller 1926- *WhoE 93*
Gross, Stanislaw 1924- *WhoWor 93*
Gross, Stanley Carl 1938- *WhoWor 93*
Gross, Stanley Jay 1927- *WhoE 93*
Gross, Stephen Mark 1938- *WhoAm 92*
Gross, Stephen Randolph 1947- *WhoEmL 93, WhoSSW 93, WhoWor 93*
Gross, Steven 1946- *WhoE 93*
Gross, Stuart *St&PR 93*
Gross, Susan English *Law&B 92*
Gross, Theodore Lawrence 1930- *WhoAm 92, WhoWrEP 92*
Gross, Walter Otto 1912- *WhoWor 93*
Gross, Wendy S. 1942- *WhoAmW 93*
Gross, William H. 1944- *WhoIns 93*
Gross, Willis Charles, Jr. 1924- *WhoWor 93*
Gross, Yoram *MiSFD 9*
Grossart, Gordon Smith 1923- *WhoWor 93*
Grossbach, Robert 1941- *ScF&FL 92*
Grossbard, Arthur Jerome 1938- *WhoE 93*
Grossbard, Janet 1938- *WhoAmW 93*
Grossbart, Ted Alan 1946- *WhoE 93*
Grossberg, David Burton 1956- *WhoE 93*
Grossberg, Kenneth Alan 1946- *WhoEmL 93*
Grossberg, Sidney Edward 1929- *WhoAm 92*
Grosschmid-Zsogod, Geza Benjamin 1918- *WhoAm 92*
Grosscup, Bryan D. 1950- *St&PR 93*
Grosse, Bill 1947- *St&PR 93*
Grosse, Eduard 1928- *St&PR 93*
Grosse, Edward Ralph 1940- *WhoSSW 93, WhoWor 93*
Grosse, Richard R. 1942- *St&PR 93*
Grosseau, A. *WhoScE 91-2*
Grosse-Middeldorf Viola, Birgit Elisabet 1958- *WhoE 93*
Grosser, Bernard Irving 1929- *WhoAm 92*
Grosser, George E. *Law&B 92*
Grosser, Morton 1931- *ScF&FL 92*
Grosset, Jessica Ariane 1952- *WhoAmW 93*
Grosseteste, Robert c. 1168-1253 *OxDcByz*
Grossetete, Bernard 1938- *WhoScE 91-2*
Grossetete, Ginger Lee 1936- *WhoAmW 93*
Grossett, Deborah Lou 1957- *WhoSSW 93*
Grosse-Wilde, Hans 1943- *WhoScE 91-3*
Grossfeld, Stan 1951- *ConAu 136, WhoAm 92*
Grosshans, Edouard 1937- *WhoScE 91-2*
Grossi, Giovanni *OxDcOp*
Grossi, Olindo 1909- *WhoAm 92*
Grossi, Ralph Edward 1949- *WhoAm 92, WhoE 93*
Grossi, Richard J. 1935- *WhoAm 92*
Grossi, Richard John *Law&B 92*
Grossich, Mark Chris 1950- *WhoEmL 93*
Grossinger, Tania Seifer 1937- *WhoWrEP 92*
Grossi-Tyson, Laura *Law&B 92*
Grossklaus, Dieter 1930- *WhoScE 91-3*
Grosskopf, Dean Alan 1949- *St&PR 93*
Grosskopf, Erhard 1934- *Baker 92*
Grosskopf, Rudolf E. 1935- *WhoScE 91-3*
Grosskreutz, Joseph Charles 1922- *WhoAm 92*
Grossman, Allen Neil 1946- *WhoE 93*
Grossman, Allen (R.) 1932- *ConAu 38NR*
Grossman, Allen Richard 1932- *WhoAm 92*
Grossman, Andrew Joseph 1958- *WhoWrEP 92*
Grossman, Anne Chotzinoff 1930- *WhoE 93*
Grossman, Arnold *ScF&FL 92*
Grossman, Barbara *BioIn 17*
Grossman, Barbara Susanne 1951- *WhoAmW 93*
Grossman, Barbara Therese 1943- *WhoAmW 93*
Grossman, Bernard 1942- *WhoSSW 93*
Grossman, Bernard I. *St&PR 93*
Grossman, Bill 1948- *SmATA 72 [port]*
Grossman, Burt *BioIn 17*

Grossman, Burton Alan 1940- *WhoSSW 93*
Grossman, Carl L. *Law&B 92*
Grossman, Carl Stuart 1949- *St&PR 93*
Grossman, David *BioIn 17, MiSFD 9*
Grossman, David 1954- *ConAu 138*
Grossman, David Z. 1938- *St&PR 93*
Grossman, Deborah C. *Law&B 92*
Grossman, Debra A. 1951- *WhoAm 92*
Grossman, Edgar 1919- *St&PR 93*
Grossman, Eileen Gordon 1945- *St&PR 93*
Grossman, Elizabeth Korn 1923- *WhoAm 92, WhoAmW 93*
Grossman, Elmer Roy 1929- *WhoAm 92*
Grossman, Everett Philip 1924- *WhoAm 92*
Grossman, Frances Kaplan 1929- *WhoAm 92, WhoAmW 93*
Grossman, Fred 1921- *WhoE 93*
Grossman, Gabrielle 1940- *WhoAmW 93*
Grossman, Gary H. 1948- *ScF&FL 92*
Grossman, Gordon William 1932- *St&PR 93*
Grossman, Herschel I. 1939- *WhoAm 92*
Grossman, Howard Jeffry *Law&B 92*
Grossman, Howard M. d1990 *BioIn 17*
Grossman, Hyman C. 1935- *St&PR 93*
Grossman, Ira Joseph *Law&B 92*
Grossman, Irving 1926- *WhoAm 92, WhoWor 93*
Grossman, Irving J. *St&PR 93*
Grossman, Jack 1925- *WhoAm 92*
Grossman, Jacob S. 1930- *WhoAm 92*
Grossman, Janice 1949- *WhoAm 92, WhoAmW 93*
Grossman, Jeffrey W. 1963- *St&PR 93*
Grossman, Jerome *BioIn 17*
Grossman, Jerome Barnett 1919- *St&PR 93, WhoAm 92*
Grossman, Jerome Harvey 1939- *WhoAm 92*
Grossman, Jerrold B. 1947- *WhoE 93*
Grossman, Joan Delaney 1928- *WhoAm 92*
Grossman, Joan W. *Law&B 92*
Grossman, Joel Barry 1936- *WhoAm 92*
Grossman, Joel M. *Law&B 92*
Grossman, John Henry, III 1945- *WhoAm 92*
Grossman, John Joseph 1924- *WhoAm 92*
Grossman, Josephine *ScF&FL 92*
Grossman, Karl H. 1942- *WhoAm 92*
Grossman, Lawrence 1924- *WhoAm 92*
Grossman, Lawrence Morton 1922- *WhoAm 92*
Grossman, Leonard Albert 1926- *St&PR 93*
Grossman, Leonard E. 1935- *St&PR 93*
Grossman, Louis 1914- *St&PR 93*
Grossman, Ludwik 1835-1915 *PolBiDi*
Grossman, Marshall Bruce 1939- *WhoAm 92*
Grossman, Martin Allen 1943- *WhoWrEP 92*
Grossman, Marvin 1927- *St&PR 93*
Grossman, Matthew Rodney 1948- *WhoSSW 93*
Grossman, Merilyn M. 1935- *St&PR 93*
Grossman, Michael 1942- *WhoAm 92*
Grossman, Michael Jay *Law&B 92*
Grossman, Michael Ross 1962- *WhoE 93*
Grossman, Miriam 1955- *St&PR 93*
Grossman, Mitchell 1954- *St&PR 93*
Grossman, N. Bud 1921- *St&PR 93*
Grossman, Nancy *WhoAm 92*
Grossman, Patricia 1951- *SmATA 73 [port]*
Grossman, Paul Leslie 1960- *WhoSSW 93*
Grossman, Peter J. 1956- *St&PR 93*
Grossman, Richard Leslie 1948- *WhoE 93*
Grossman, Richard Parker 1934- *St&PR 93*
Grossman, Robert Allen 1941- *St&PR 93*
Grossman, Robert George 1933- *WhoAm 92*
Grossman, Robert Mayer 1934- *WhoAm 92*
Grossman, Roberta d1992 *BioIn 17*
Grossman, Roberta Bender d1992 *NewYTBS 92*
Grossman, Ronald 1936- *St&PR 93, WhoAm 92*
Grossman, Samuel 1897- *WhoWor 93*
Grossman, Sanford 1929- *WhoAm 92*
Grossman, Sanford Jay 1953- *WhoAm 92*
Grossman, Stanley H. *St&PR 93*
Grossman, Stephen Lewin 1935- *WhoE 93*
Grossman, Steven J. 1942- *St&PR 93*
Grossman, Vasilii Semenovich 1905-1964 *BioIn 17*
Grossman, William 1940- *WhoAm 92*
Grossman, William C. *Law&B 92*
Grossmann, Deena Michele 1959- *WhoAmW 93*
Grossmann, Donald E. 1939- *St&PR 93*
Grossmann, Elihu David 1927- *WhoE 93*
Grossmann, Ferdinand 1887-1970 *Baker 92*
Grossmann, Friedrich K.W. 1927- *WhoScE 91-3*
Grossmann, Hartmut Georg 1946- *WhoEmL 93*
Grossmann, Ignacio Emilio 1949- *WhoAm 92*
Grossmann, Ralph L. *Law&B 92*
Grossmann, Ralph L. 1939- *St&PR 93*
Grossmann, Stanley M. *Law&B 92*
Grossnickle, William Foster 1930- *WhoSSW 93*
Grosso, Anthony Joseph 1926- *St&PR 93*
Grosso, George D. 1941- *St&PR 93*
Grosso, Gino 1948- *WhoE 93, WhoEmL 93*
Grosso, John 1946- *St&PR 93*
Grosso, Patrick F. 1937- *St&PR 93*
Grosso, Rubina Irene 1929- *St&PR 93*
Grosso, Vance 1959- *St&PR 93*
Grossolano, Peter d1117 *OxDcByz*
Grossvogel, David I. 1925- *WhoE 93*
Grossvogel, Jill Elyse 1945- *WhoE 93*
Gross Watkins, Rochelle 1949- *WhoAmW 93, WhoEmL 93*
Grossweiner, Leonard Irwin 1924- *WhoAm 92*
Grosveld, Frank *WhoScE 91-1*
Grosvenor, Edwin Stuart 1951- *WhoWrEP 92*
Grosvenor, Gilbert Hovey *BioIn 17*
Grosvenor, Gilbert Hovey 1875-1966 *JrnUS*
Grosvenor, Gilbert Melville 1931- *WhoAm 92, WhoE 93, WhoWrEP 92*
Grosvenor, Sarah d1742 *BioIn 17*
Grosvenor, William Mason 1835-1900 *JrnUS*
Grosz, Barbara Jean 1948- *WhoAm 92, WhoAmW 93*
Grosz, George 1893-1959 *BioIn 17*
Grosz, Karoly 1930- *ColdWar 2 [port]*
Groszek, William Alexander 1935- *St&PR 93*
Grot, Anton Franciszek 1886-1974 *PolBiDi*
Grot, John B. 1943- *St&PR 93*
Grote, Claus 1927- *WhoScE 91-3*
Grote, Richard Charles 1941- *WhoSSW 93*
Grote, Robert E., III 1943- *St&PR 93*
Grote, William Dominic 1939- *St&PR 93*
Groteluschen, David 1953- *St&PR 93*
Groten, Barnet 1933- *WhoAm 92*
Groten, Dallas 1951- *BioIn 17, ConAu 38NR*
Grotenfelt, Sten Nils Bosson 1939- *WhoWor 93*
Grotens, A.H.P. *WhoScE 91-3*
Groth, A. Nicholas 1937- *WhoSSW 93*
Groth, Alexander Jacob 1932- *WhoAm 92*
Groth, Betty *WhoWor 93*
Groth, Brian Joseph 1960- *WhoWrEP 92*
Groth, Hans Lennart 1955- *WhoWor 93*
Groth, Klaus 1923- *WhoScE 91-3*
Groth, Patricia Celley 1932- *WhoWrEP 92*
Groth, Raymond Clarence 1947- *St&PR 93*
Groth, Richard Henry 1929- *WhoE 93*
Groth, Robert William 1947- *WhoEmL 93*
Grothe, Barbara Ann 1953- *WhoEmL 93*
Grothe, Dale F. 1930- *St&PR 93*
Grothe, Robert N. 1945- *St&PR 93*
Grothe, Susan K. 1962- *WhoAmW 93*
Grotheer, Morris Paul 1928- *WhoSSW 93*
Grotmol, Frode 1949- *WhoWor 93*
Grotnes, Milford *BioIn 17*
Groton, James Purnell 1927- *WhoAm 92*
Grotowski, Jerzy 1933- *WhoAm 92, WhoWor 93*
Grott, Catherine Jane 1960- *WhoAmW 93*
Grotta, Louis William 1933- *St&PR 93*
Grotta, Sandra Brown 1934- *WhoE 93*
Grotta-Kurska, Daniel 1944- *ScF&FL 92*
Grottanelli, Vinigi Lorenzo 1912- *IntDcAn, WhoWor 93*
Grotte, Jeffrey Harlow 1947- *WhoSSW 93*
Grotterod, Knut 1922- *WhoAm 92*
Grottger, Artur 1837-1867 *PolBiDi*
Grotz, Paul 1902-1990 *BioIn 17*
Grotzinger, Laurel Ann 1935- *WhoAm 92, WhoAmW 93*
Grouchy, Emmanuel, Marquis of 1766-1847 *HarEnMi*
Groudan, Ethel Fishman 1935- *WhoAmW 93*
Groult, Benoite 1920- *BioIn 17*
Groumy, Claude *WhoScE 91-2*
Grounes, Mikael 1933- *WhoWor 93*
Groussard, Serge Hariton 1921- *WhoWor 93*
Groussman, Dean G. *WhoAm 92, WhoWor 93*
Groussman, Ray G. *Law&B 92*
Groussman, Ray G. 1935- *St&PR 93*
Grout, Bill *BioIn 17*
Grout, Coral May 1953- *WhoAmW 93*
Grout, Donald J(ay) 1902-1987 *Baker 92*
Grout, R.J. *WhoScE 91-1*
Grout, Stephen C. 1955- *WhoEmL 93*
Groux, Guy Marc 1945- *WhoWor 93*
Groux, Peter John 1960- *WhoEmL 93, WhoSSW 93*
Grovan, Cynthia Lee 1965- *WhoAmW 93*
Grove, Alfred Frank, Jr. 1939- *St&PR 93*
Grove, Andrew S. *BioIn 17*
Grove, Andrew S. 1936- *St&PR 93, WhoAm 92*
Grove, Bernard L. 1933- *St&PR 93*
Grove, Brandon Hambright, Jr. 1929- *WhoAm 92*
Grove, David Lawrence 1918- *WhoAm 92*
Grove, E.L., Jr. 1924- *St&PR 93*
Grove, Edward Ryneal 1912- *WhoAm 92*
Grove, Fred(erick) 1913- *ConAu 37NR*
Grove, Frederick Philip 1879-1948 *BioIn 17, ScF&FL 92*
Grove, Garry R. 1946- *St&PR 93*
Grove, Garth Walden 1945- *WhoSSW 93*
Grove, Gary *BioIn 17*
Grove, George 1820-1900 *Baker 92*
Grove, Helen Harriet *WhoAm 92, WhoWor 93*
Grove, Henry S. 1933- *St&PR 93*
Grove, J.R. *WhoScE 91-1*
Grove, Jack F. 1953- *St&PR 93*
Grove, James B. 1928- *St&PR 93*
Grove, James W. 1929- *St&PR 93*
Grove, Janet Elaine 1951- *St&PR 93*
Grove, John Landis 1921- *St&PR 93*
Grove, Kalvin Myron 1937- *WhoAm 92*
Grove, Lefty 1900-1975 *BioIn 17*
Grove, Lester W. 1944- *St&PR 93*
Grove, Michael E. *BioIn 17*
Grove, Michael James 1958- *WhoE 93*
Grove, Myrna Jean 1949- *WhoAmW 93*
Grove, N.M. *Law&B 92*
Grove, Patricia Ann 1952- *WhoAmW 93*
Grove, Peter J. *ScF&FL 92*
Grove, Richard Martin 1950- *WhoWor 93*
Grove, Robert W. *Law&B 92*
Grove, Russell Sinclair, Jr. 1939- *WhoAm 92*
Grove, Stefans 1922- *Baker 92*
Grove, Ted Russell 1961- *WhoEmL 93, WhoSSW 93*
Grove, William Boyd 1929- *WhoAm 92*
Grove, William Johnson 1920- *WhoAm 92*
Groven, Eivind 1901-1977 *Baker 92*
Groven, I. 1923- *WhoScE 91-2*
Grover, Brent R. 1950- *St&PR 93*
Grover, Cathy A. *BioIn 17*
Grover, Charles W. 1948- *St&PR 93*
Grover, Darlene 1951- *WhoAmW 93*
Grover, Dorys C. 1921- *ScF&FL 92*
Grover, Dorys Crow 1921- *WhoSSW 93*
Grover, Eve Ruth 1929- *WhoAm 92*
Grover, Herbert Joseph 1937- *WhoAm 92*
Grover, James P. *Law&B 92*
Grover, James Robb 1928- *WhoE 93*
Grover, John Henry 1927- *St&PR 93*
Grover, Mark Donald 1955- *WhoE 93*
Grover, Michael R. *Law&B 92*
Grover, Neal 1950- *St&PR 93*
Grover, Norman LaMotte 1928- *WhoAm 92, WhoSSW 93*
Grover, Phyllis Florence Bradman 1924- *WhoAm 92, WhoAmW 93*
Grover, Rebekah Rachel 1954- *WhoEmL 93*
Grover, Robert Arthur 1953- *WhoSSW 93*
Grover, Robert Lawrence 1910- *WhoAm 92*
Grover, Robinson Allen 1936- *WhoE 93*
Grover, Rosalind Redfern 1941- *WhoAmW 93, WhoSSW 93, WhoWor 93*
Grover, Roy *St&PR 93*
Grover, Stanley 1926- *ConTFT 10*
Grover, Terry L. *Law&B 92*
Grover, Wayne 1934- *ConAu 137, SmATA 69 [port]*
Grover, Wayne Clayton 1906-1970 *BioIn 17*
Grover, William Herbert 1938- *WhoAm 92*
Grover, William Joseph 1948- *WhoE 93*
Grover-Haskin, Kim Arleen 1960- *WhoEmL 93*
Groverman, David *St&PR 93*
Groves, Ann *ScF&FL 92*
Groves, Charles 1915- *OxDcOp*
Groves, Charles 1915-1992 *NewYTBS 92*
Groves, Charles (Barnard) 1915- *Baker 92*
Groves, Donald George *WhoSSW 93*
Groves, Dorothy Eloise 1931- *WhoAmW 93, WhoSSW 93*
Groves, Eileen Anne *Law&B 92*
Groves, Franklin Nelson 1930- *St&PR 93, WhoAm 92*
Groves, G.L. *St&PR 93*
Groves, George H. 1944- *St&PR 93, WhoAm 92*
Groves, George L., Jr. *St&PR 93*
Groves, George L., Jr. 1928- *WhoAm 92*
Groves, Gordon Capron 1930- *St&PR 93*
Groves, Hurst Kohler *Law&B 92*
Groves, Hurst Kohler 1941- *WhoAm 92, WhoE 93*
Groves, J. Randall 1939- *St&PR 93*
Groves, John R. *Law&B 92*
Groves, John Taylor, III 1943- *WhoAm 92*
Groves, John Thomas d1811 *BioIn 17*
Groves, Michael 1936- *St&PR 93, WhoAm 92*
Groves, Monica Renae 1959- *WhoAmW 93*
Groves, Naomi Jackson 1910- *ConAu 40NR*
Groves, Paul 1930- *ScF&FL 92*
Groves, Richard Melvin 1929- *St&PR 93*
Groves, Rockwell M. 1934- *St&PR 93*
Groves, Rodger Duclos 1945- *WhoAm 92*
Groves, Sharon Darlene 1951- *WhoEmL 93, WhoSSW 93*
Groves, Sheridon Hale 1947- *WhoEmL 93, WhoWor 93*
Groves, Stephen Peterson, Sr. 1956- *WhoEmL 93*
Groves, Theodore Francis, Jr. 1941- *WhoAm 92*
Groves, Thomas H. *Law&B 92*
Groves, Vaughn Ray *Law&B 92*
Groves, Wallace *DcCPCAm*
Grovlez, Gabriel (Marie) 1879-1944 *Baker 92*
Grow, Galusha A. 1822-1907 *PolPar*
Grow, Michael Abbott 1947- *WhoEmL 93*
Grow, Robert Theodore 1948- *WhoE 93*
Growe, Joan Anderson 1935- *WhoAm 92, WhoAmW 93*
Groza, Alex John 1926- *BiDAMSp 1989*
Groza, Lou 1924- *BioIn 17*
Groza, Petru 1921- *WhoScE 91-4*
Grozavescu, Trajan 1895-1927 *Baker 92*
Grozdev, Sava Ivanov 1950- *WhoWor 93*
Grozev, Georgi Rangelov 1958- *WhoWor 93*
Grua, Carlo Luigi Pietro c. 1665- *Baker 92*
Grua, Carlo Pietro c. 1700-1773 *Baker 92*
Grua, Franz Paul 1753-1833 *Baker 92*
Grua, Rudolph 1928- *St&PR 93*
Grub, Phillip Donald 1931- *WhoAm 92*
Grubaugh, Virginia Jane 1923- *WhoAmW 93*
Grubb, Albany Delmer 1942- *St&PR 93*
Grubb, Bradley Nelson 1959- *WhoSSW 93*
Grubb, Clare M. *AmWomPl*
Grubb, David H. 1936- *St&PR 93*
Grubb, Davis 1919-1980 *ScF&FL 92*
Grubb, Donald H. 1924- *St&PR 93*
Grubb, Donald Hartman 1924- *WhoAm 92*
Grubb, Edgar Harold 1939- *WhoAm 92*
Grubb, Eric A. 1936- *St&PR 93*
Grubb, Farley Ward 1954- *WhoE 93, WhoEmL 93*
Grubb, Jeff *ScF&FL 92*
Grubb, Linda Fern 1944- *WhoAm 92*
Grubb, Linda Sue 1953- *WhoEmL 93*
Grubb, Robert Lynn 1927- *WhoSSW 93*
Grubb, Rune 1920- *WhoScE 91-4*
Grubb, Stephen Bunyan 1945- *WhoSSW 93*
Grubb, William Francis X. 1944- *WhoAm 92*
Grubb, Wilson Lyon 1910- *WhoAm 92*
Grubbe, Kenneth S. 1935- *St&PR 93*
Grubbs, David Allen 1957- *WhoSSW 93*
Grubbs, Donald Ray 1947- *WhoSSW 93*
Grubbs, Donald Shaw, Jr. 1929- *St&PR 93, WhoAm 92, WhoWor 93*
Grubbs, Elven Judson 1930- *WhoAm 92*
Grubbs, Geoffrey Hilton 1951- *WhoAm 92*
Grubbs, Gerald Reid 1947- *St&PR 93, WhoAm 92, WhoEmL 93*
Grubbs, Louise Capel 1931- *WhoAmW 93*
Grubbs, Robert H. 1942- *WhoAm 92*
Grubbs, Stephen *BioIn 17*
Grubbs, Wilbur Charles 1929- *St&PR 93*
Grube, Charles A. *Law&B 92*
Grube, Eitel Friedrich 1928- *WhoScE 91-3*
Grube, Elizabeth 1917- *WhoAmW 93*
Grube, John P. 1946- *St&PR 93*
Grube, John S. *Law&B 92*
Grube, Karl Bertram 1946- *WhoAm 92*
Grube, Lewis Blaine 1917- *St&PR 93*
Grube, Rebecca Sue 1945- *WhoAmW 93*
Grube, Terrence Craig *Law&B 92*
Gruber, Alan Richard 1927- *St&PR 93, WhoAm 92*
Gruber, Arnold 1940- *WhoE 93*
Gruber, Aspasia 1948- *WhoIns 93*
Gruber, Barbara Miklos 1946- *WhoE 93*
Gruber, Christina Ellis d1990 *BioIn 17*
Gruber, Chuck *BioIn 17*
Gruber, Debra R. 1951- *St&PR 93*
Gruber, Donald F. *Law&B 92*
Gruber, Douglas Lloyd 1920- *WhoE 93*
Gruber, Franz Xaver 1787-1863 *Baker 92*
Gruber, Fred 1947- *St&PR 93*
Gruber, Fredric Francis 1931- *WhoAm 92*
Gruber, Gary John 1955- *WhoIns 93*
Gruber, Georg 1904- *Baker 92*
Gruber, H(einz) K(arl) 1943- *Baker 92*

Gruber, Harald 1961- *WhoWor 93*
Gruber, Helen Elizabeth 1946- *WhoEmL 93*
Gruber, Ira Dempsey 1934- *WhoAm 92*
Gruber, J. Richard 1948- *WhoAm 92*
Gruber, Jerome C. 1945- *St&PR 93*
Gruber, Johann 1621-1680 *Expl 93*
Gruber, John Balsbaugh 1935- *WhoAm 92*
Gruber, Kenneth J. 1951- *St&PR 93*
Gruber, L. Fritz *BioIn 17*
Gruber, Robert Stuart 1932- *St&PR 93*
Gruber, Rolf 1935- *WhoScE 91-3*
Gruber, Rosalind H. 1943- *WhoE 93*
Gruber, Rudolf Franz Josef 1937- *WhoWor 93*
Gruber, Ruth *BioIn 17*
Gruber, Samuel Harvey 1938- *WhoSSW 93*
Gruber, Sheldon 1930- *WhoAm 92*
Gruber, Sylvia E. *St&PR 93*
Gruber, Terry deRoy *BioIn 17*
Gruber, Thomas A. 1940- *WhoAm 92*
Gruber, William Paul 1932- *WhoAm 92*
Gruberg, Cy 1928- *WhoAm 92*
Gruberg, Martin 1935- *WhoAm 92*
Gruberova, Edita 1946- *Baker 92, IntDcOp, OxDcOp*
Grubiak, James Francis 1947- *WhoEmL 93*
Grubiak, James Frank 1938- *St&PR 93*
Grubic, Aleksandar 1929- *WhoScE 91-4*
Grubin, Arnold 1929- *St&PR 93*
Grubisic, Vatroslav Vicko 1933- *WhoScE 91-3*
Grubman, Allen 1942- *BioIn 17*
Grubman, Herman Joseph 1927- *St&PR 93*
Grubman, Stanley D. *Law&B 92*
Grubman, Wallace Karl 1928- *St&PR 93, WhoAm 92, WhoWor 93*
Gruchacz, Robert S. 1929- *WhoAm 92*
Gruchalla, Michael Emeric 1946- *WhoEmL 93*
Gruchman, Monika Maria 1922- *WhoWor 93*
Gruchow, Paul *BioIn 17*
Gruchy, Allan Garfield 1906-1990 *BioIn 17*
Gruchy, Lydia d1992 *BioIn 17*
Grucza, Nancy Marceca 1955- *WhoEmL 93*
Grude, Ulrich 1944- *WhoWor 93*
Grudzewski, Wieslaw Maria 1933- *WhoScE 91-4*
Grudzina, John J. *Law&B 92*
Grue, Howard W. 1927- *St&PR 93*
Grue, Howard Wood 1927- *WhoAm 92*
Grue, Lee Meitzen *WhoWrEP 92*
Grueber, Cynthia Marie 1957- *WhoEmL 93*
Gruehn, Reginald 1929- *WhoScE 91-3*
Gruen, Armin 1944- *WhoWor 93*
Gruen, Arno 1923- *WhoWor 93*
Gruen, David Henry 1929- *WhoAm 92*
Gruen, Erich Stephen 1935- *WhoAm 92*
Gruen, G. John 1945- *St&PR 93*
Gruen, Gerald Elmer 1937- *WhoAm 92*
Gruen, Michael Stephan 1942- *WhoWor 93*
Gruen, Peter H. 1939- *WhoAm 92*
Gruen, Von *ScF&FL 92*
Gruenbaum, Gerald Carlton 1944- *WhoSSW 93*
Gruenberg, Don 1942- *St&PR 93*
Gruenberg, Elliot Lewis 1918- *WhoAm 92, WhoE 93, WhoWor 93*
Gruenberg, Erich 1924- *Baker 92*
Gruenberg, Ernest M. 1915-1991 *BioIn 17*
Gruenberg, Eugene 1854-1928 *Baker 92*
Gruenberg, Gladys Walleman 1920- *WhoAmW 93*
Gruenberg, K.W. *WhoScE 91-1*
Gruenberg, Louis 1884-1964 *Baker 92, IntDcOp*
Gruenberg, Mark Jonathan 1953- *WhoE 93*
Gruenberg, Ruth 1922- *WhoAmW 93*
Gruenberger, Peter 1937- *WhoAm 92*
Gruendel, Aileen Dopp 1939- *WhoAmW 93*
Gruenewald, Carl William, II 1933- *St&PR 93*
Gruenewald, Doris 1916- *WhoAmW 93*
Gruenewald, Max d1992 *NewYTBS 92*
Gruenhut, Egon 1922- *St&PR 93*
Gruenling, Edwin H. 1939- *St&PR 93*
Gruennert, Kenneth E. d1942 *BioIn 17*
Gruenther, Alfred Maximilian 1899-1983 *HarEnMi*
Gruenwald, George Henry 1922- *WhoAm 92, WhoWrEP 92*
Gruenwald, James Howard 1949- *WhoEmL 93*
Gruer, William E. 1937- *WhoSSW 93*
Grueser, Suzanne Haile 1958- *WhoAmW 93*
Grueskin, William Steven 1956- *WhoSSW 93*
Grueter, Thomas Hans 1957- *WhoWor 93*
Gruetzmacher, Cheryl Kay *WhoAmW 93*
Grufferman, Seymour 1937- *WhoE 93*
Gruhl, Andrea Morris 1939- *WhoAmW 93, WhoE 93, WhoWor 93*
Gruhl, James 1945- *WhoWor 93*
Gruhl, Robert H. 1945- *St&PR 93, WhoIns 93*
Gruhl, Robert Herbert 1945- *WhoAm 92*
Gruhl, William Wagner 1941- *St&PR 93*
Gruhle, Wolfgang Hans-Dieter 1925- *WhoWor 93*
Gruhn, Carrie E. 1907-1990 *ScF&FL 92*
Gruhn, Joel D. 1947- *St&PR 93*
Gruhn, Nora 1905- *Baker 92, OxDcOp*
Gruidl, Thomas G. 1937- *St&PR 93*
Gruin, Sandra Keller 1949- *WhoAmW 93*
Grulkowski, Ray A. 1937- *St&PR 93*
Grum, Clifford J. 1934- *St&PR 93, WhoAm 92, WhoSSW 93*
Grum, Janez 1946- *WhoScE 91-4*
Gruman, William P. 1928- *St&PR 93*
Grumbach, Cheryl Lynn 1960- *WhoAmW 93*
Grumbach, Doris *BioIn 17*
Grumbach, Doris 1918- *WhoAm 92, WhoWrEP 92*
Grumbach, Melvin Malcolm 1925- *WhoAm 92*
Grumbacher, M. Thomas *St&PR 93*
Grumbaum, Caroline 1814-1868
See Grunbaum, Therese 1791-1876 *OxDcOp*
Grumbine, David L. *Law&B 92*
Grumbine, David Lee 1951- *WhoEmL 93*
Grumer, Eugene Lawrence 1940- *WhoE 93*
Grumet, Priscilla Hecht 1943- *WhoAmW 93*
Grumet, Robert Steven 1949- *WhoEmL 93*
Grumiaux, Arthur 1921-1986 *Baker 92*
Grumke, Clay L. *Law&B 92*
Grumm, Hans 1919- *WhoScE 91-4*
Grumman, Fredric Russell *Law&B 92*
Grumman, Robert Jeremy 1941- *WhoSSW 93*
Grummer, Elisabeth 1911-1986 *Baker 92, OxDcOp*
Grummer, Paul 1879-1965 *Baker 92*
Grumpelt, Harry C. d1990 *BioIn 17*
Grun, Jakob 1837-1916 *Baker 92*
Grun, Jean-Bernard 1935- *WhoScE 91-2*
Grunbaum, Adolf 1923- *WhoAm 92, WhoWor 93*
Grunbaum, Therese 1791-1876 *Baker 92, OxDcOp*
Grunberg, Robert Leon Willy 1940- *WhoAm 92, WhoE 93, WhoWor 93*
Grunberger, Dezider 1922- *WhoAm 92, WhoE 93*
Grunblatt, Hilda Ruth 1922- *WhoE 93*
Grund, Friedrich Wilhelm 1791-1874 *Baker 92*
Grund, Walter James, Jr. 1927- *WhoAm 92*
Grundahl, John Alvin 1946- *WhoEmL 93*
Grundbacher, Frederick John 1926- *WhoAm 92*
Grundboeck, Marian 1923- *WhoScE 91-4*
Grundboeck-Jusko, Jadwiga 1925- *WhoScE 91-4*
Grunder, Arthur Neil 1936- *WhoAm 92*
Grunder, Fred Irwin 1940- *WhoSSW 93*
Grunder, Paul Edwin 1931- *WhoAm 92*
Grunder, Robert Douglas 1953- *WhoEmL 93*
Grundey, Klaus 1948- *WhoWor 93*
Grundfest, Joseph Alexander 1951- *WhoAm 92*
Grundgens, Gustaf 1899-1963 *BioIn 17*
Grundgens, Gustav 1899-1963 *IntDcF 2-3*
Grundhaus, William E. 1942- *St&PR 93*
Grundhofer, John F. 1939- *WhoAm 92*
Grundhofer, John Francis 1939- *St&PR 93*
Grundin, Katherine G. *Law&B 92*
Grundlehner, Conrad Ernest 1942- *WhoSSW 93*
Grundman, V. Rock, Jr. *Law&B 92*
Grundmann, Ekkehard 1921- *WhoScE 91-3*
Grundmann, Volker Robert 1931- *St&PR 93*
Grundmeyer, Douglas Lanaux 1948- *WhoEmL 93, WhoSSW 93*
Grundstein, Nathan David 1913- *WhoAm 92*
Grundstrom, David N. 1952- *St&PR 93*
Grundy, Betty Lou Bottoms 1940- *WhoAm 92, WhoAmW 93*
Grundy, Dorothy A. *AmWomPl*
Grundy, Jess W. 1918- *St&PR 93*
Grundy, Kenneth William 1936- *WhoAm 92*
Grundy, Nigel Arthur 1944- *WhoWor 93*
Grundy, Rhea Joy 1955- *WhoAmW 93*
Grundy, Richard Dennis 1959- *WhoEmL 93*
Grundy, Virginia Rudder *AmWomPl*
Grune, George *BioIn 17*
Grune, George Vincent 1929- *St&PR 93, WhoAm 92*
Grunebach, Georgan S. *Law&B 92*
Grunebaum, Ernest F. *Law&B 92*
Grunebaum, Ernest Michael 1934- *WhoAm 92*
Grunebaum, Hermann 1872-1954 *OxDcOp*
Grunebaum, Nora 1905- *Baker 92*
Gruneich, Kevin Ross 1958- *St&PR 93*
Gruneklee, Dieter Alfred Hermann 1938- *WhoWor 93*
Grunenwald, Jean-Jacques 1911-1982 *Baker 92*
Gruner, Charles Ralph 1931- *WhoWrEP 92*
Gruner, Glen *MiSFD 9*
Gruner, Max-Jean 1935- *WhoScE 91-2*
Gruner-Hegge, Odd 1899-1973 *Baker 92*
Grunert, Eberhard 1930- *WhoScE 91-3*
Grunert, Gunther 1955- *WhoWor 93*
Grunert, Klaus Gunter 1953- *WhoWor 93*
Grunes, David Leon 1921- *WhoAm 92*
Grunes, Robert Lewis 1941- *WhoAm 92, WhoE 93*
Grunewald, Bjorn Mikael 1940- *WhoWor 93*
Grunewald, Donald 1934- *WhoWor 93*
Grunewald, Gary Lawrence 1937- *WhoAm 92*
Grunewald, John H. 1936- *St&PR 93*
Grunewald, Michael 1954- *WhoWor 93*
Grunfeld, Alfred 1852-1924 *Baker 92*
Grunfeld, Heinrich 1855-1931 *Baker 92*
Grunfeld, Rudy 1919- *St&PR 93*
Grunick, Rebecca J. *Law&B 92*
Grunig, James Elmer 1942- *WhoAm 92*
Grunik, Sally Ann 1955- *WhoEmL 93*
Gruninger, Gerhard 1932- *WhoScE 91-3*
Gruninger, John E. 1939- *WhoIns 93*
Grunke, Mary Ellen 1950- *WhoEmL 93*
Grunlan, Stephen Arthur 1942- *ConAu 39NR*
Grunland, Paul Allen 1924- *St&PR 93*
Grunling, Hermann W. *WhoScE 91-3*
Grunn, John Homer 1880-1944 *Baker 92*
Grunnah, S. Thomas 1936- *St&PR 93*
Grunseth, Jon *BioIn 17*
Grunsfeld, Ernest Alton, III 1929- *WhoAm 92*
Grunt, Jerome Alvin 1923- *WhoAm 92*
Grunwald, Ernest Max 1923- *WhoAm 92*
Grunwald, John J. 1929- *WhoAm 92*
Grunwald, Katharine E. *Law&B 92*
Grunwell, Pamela *WhoScE 91-1*
Grupas, Constance Kathryn 1942- *WhoAmW 93*
Grupe, Amy Elizabeth 1958- *WhoEmL 93*
Grupe, Robert Charles 1948- *WhoSSW 93*
Grupe, Warren Edward 1933- *WhoAm 92, WhoWor 93*
Grupen, Claus 1941- *WhoScE 91-3*
Grupka, Richard Allen 1952- *St&PR 93*
Grupp, Hariolf 1950- *WhoScE 91-3*
Gruppe, Charles Camille 1928- *WhoE 93*
Gruppe, Werner 1920- *WhoScE 91-3*
Gruppuso, Frank M. 1950- *St&PR 93*
Grush, Helen Butler 1921- *WhoAmW 93*
Grushkin, Philip 1921- *St&PR 93*
Grushow, Ira 1933- *WhoE 93*
Grusin, Dave 1934- *ConTFT 10, WhoAm 92*
Gruske, Karl-Dieter 1946- *WhoWor 93*
Gruskin, Alan Burton 1937- *WhoAm 92*
Gruskin, Edward *ScF&FL 92*
Gruskin, Mary J. *WhoAm 92*
Gruson, Hiroko Tsubota 1940- *WhoAm 92, WhoE 93*
Gruson, Sydney 1916- *St&PR 93*
Gruss, William Andre 1951- *WhoWor 93*
Gruszczynski, Stanislaw 1891-1959 *PolBiDi*
Gruszecki, Jan 1941- *WhoScE 91-4*
Gruszka, James Richard 1948- *WhoE 93*
Gruszka, Robert Jerome 1942- *WhoUN 92*
Grutzmacher, Friedrich (Wilhelm Ludwig) 1832-1903 *Baker 92*
Grutzmacher, Hans-Friedrich Artur 1932- *WhoWor 93*
Grutzmacher, Hansjorg Friedrich 1959- *WhoWor 93*
Grutzmacher, June Edith 1956- *WhoEmL 93*
Gruver, Suzanne Cary *AmWomPl*
Gruver, William Rolfe 1944- *WhoAm 92*
Gruverman, Irwin J. 1933- *St&PR 93*
Gruy, Henry Jones 1915- *St&PR 93, WhoAm 92*
Gruy, Robert H. 1942- *St&PR 93*
Gruys, Erik 1944- *WhoScE 91-3*
Gruzleski, Thomas Floyd 1945- *WhoE 93*
Gruzlewski, Bernard J. 1934- *St&PR 93*
Gryazin, Victor Pavlovich 1951- *WhoUN 92*
Gryce, David Conrad 1955- *WhoE 93*
Grycz, Monica Dodds 1949- *WhoAmW 93*
Gryder, Janet Arleen 1964- *WhoAmW 93*
Gryder, Rosa Meyersburg 1926- *WhoAm 92*
Grygiel, John Andrew 1926- *St&PR 93*
Grygiencza, Diana J. *Law&B 92*
Gryglas, Ronald J. 1945- *St&PR 93*
Gryglas, Stephen 1915- *St&PR 93*
Gryglas, Steven E. 1943- *St&PR 93*
Grygorenko, Wiktor 1927- *WhoScE 91-4*
Gryka, George Edwin 1932- *WhoWor 93*
Grylicki, Miroslaw 1926- *WhoScE 91-4*
Grylls, Rosalie Glynn 1905-1988 *ScF&FL 92*
Grynbaum, Bruce B. 1920- *WhoE 93*
Grynkiewicz, Grzegorz 1939- *WhoScE 91-4*
Grynszpan, Herschel 1921-1943? *BioIn 17*
Gryntakis, Angelos Nicholas 1940- *WhoWor 93*
Gryp, Firmin A. 1927- *St&PR 93*
Gryska, Ted M. 1954- *St&PR 93*
Gryski, Camilla 1948- *BioIn 17, SmATA 72 [port]*
Gryson, Joseph Anthony 1932- *WhoAm 92*
Gryzlo, Joseph William *Law&B 92*
Grzanka, Leonard 1947- *WhoWrEP 92*
Grzaslewicz, Ryszard 1953- *WhoWor 93*
Grzechowiak, Jerzy 1929- *WhoScE 91-4*
Grzedzielski, Stanislaw J. 1933- *WhoScE 91-4*
Grzegorz, Kiedrowicz 1953- *WhoScE 91-4*
Grzegorzewski, Adam 1911- *PolBiDi*
Grzelak, David W. 1949- *St&PR 93*
Grzelakowska-Sztabert, Barbara 1938- *WhoScE 91-4*
Grzesik, Mieczyslaw 1948- *WhoWor 93*
Grzesik, Tadeusz 1933- *WhoWor 93*
Grzesiuk, Stanislaw 1926- *WhoScE 91-4*
Grzeskowiak, J. *WhoScE 91-4*
Grzeszczyk, Szczepan Jan 1901-1967 *PolBiDi*
Grzezinski, Dennis Michael 1950- *WhoEmL 93*
Grzimek, Martin 1950- *ScF&FL 92*
Grzonka, Zbigniew 1938- *WhoScE 91-4*
Grzyb, Stanislaw 1919- *WhoScE 91-4*
Grzybowski, Kazimierz 1911- *WhoAm 92, WhoWor 93*
Grzybowski, Walter T. *St&PR 93*
Grzywa, Edward J. 1933- *WhoScE 91-4*
Gschneidner, Karl Albert, Jr. 1930- *WhoAm 92*
Gschwind, A. Edward 1932- *St&PR 93*
Gschwind, Donald 1933- *WhoAm 92*
Gschwind, John C. *Law&B 92*
Gschwind, John K. 1934- *St&PR 93*
Gschwind, John Karl 1934- *WhoAm 92*
Gschwindt de Gyor, Peter George 1945- *WhoE 93*
Gsell, Roland Arnold 1896-1991 *BioIn 17*
Gu, Bing-Lin 1945- *WhoWor 93*
Gu, Claire Xiang-Guang *WhoWor 93*
Guadagni, Gaetano c. 1725-1792 *Baker 92, IntDcOp, OxDcOp*
Guadagni, Lavinia-Maria 1735-c. 1790 *OxDcOp*
Guadagnini *Baker 92*
Guadagnini, Gaetano 1745-1831 *Baker 92*
Guadagnini, Giovanni Battista 1711-1786 *Baker 92*
Guadagnini, Giuseppe 1736-1805 *Baker 92*
Guadagnini, Lorenzo 1689-1748 *Baker 92*
Guadagnini, Paolo d1942 *Baker 92*
Guadagno, Anton 1925- *Baker 92*
Guadagno, Betty Ann 1955- *WhoEmL 93*
Guadagno, Mary Ann Noecker 1952- *WhoAmW 93*
Guadalajara, Jose Rafael 1863- *DcMexL*
Guadalupi, Gianni 1945- *ScF&FL 92*
Guaglianone, Denise Marie 1958- *WhoAmW 93*
Guaglianone, Victor F. *Law&B 92*
Guajardo, Maria Resendez 1959- *WhoAmW 93*
Guala, Peter J. *St&PR 93*
Gualde, Norbert 1943- *WhoScE 91-2*
Gualdo, John (Giovanni) d1771 *Baker 92*
Gualtieri, Devlin Michael 1947- *WhoE 93*
Gualtieri, John P., Jr. *Law&B 92*
Gualtieri, Joseph Peter 1916- *WhoAm 92, WhoE 93*
Guaman Poma de Ayala, Felipe 1534?-1615 *IntDcAn*
Guami, Francesco c. 1544-1602 *Baker 92*
Guami, Gioseffo c. 1540-1611 *Baker 92*
Guancione, Karen Ann 1957- *WhoEmL 93*
Guandalini, Bruno 1941- *WhoUN 92*
Guandolo, John 1919- *WhoAm 92*
Guan Guangfu 1931- *WhoAsAP 91*
Guanzon, Romeo G. 1921- *WhoAsAP 91*
Guarascio, Anthony R. 1953- *St&PR 93*
Guard, Dave 1934-1991 *AnObit 1991*
See Also Kingston Trio, The *ConMus 9*
Guard, David 1934-1991 *BioIn 17, ScF&FL 92*
Guard, Leonard A. 1942- *WhoAm 92*
Guard, Mary Beth 1955- *WhoAmW 93*
Guarda, Pedro B. 1952- *WhoUN 92*

Guarda, Roger Francois 1941- WhoUN 92
Guardalabene, John T. Law&B 92
Guardia, Enrique Jose 1938- WhoAm 92
Guardia, Gilberto F. 1930- WhoWor 93
Guardia, Gloria 1941- SpAmA
Guardia, John BioIn 17
Guardia, Miguel 1924- DcMexL
Guardino, Harry 1925- WhoAm 92
Guardino, Stephen P. d1991 BioIn 17
Guardo, Carol J. 1939- WhoAm 92, WhoAmW 93
Guarducci, Tommaso c. 1720-c. 1770 OxDcOp
Guare, John BioIn 17
Guare, John 1938- WhoAm 92, WhoE 93
Guariglia, Pierre 1927- St&PR 93
Guarini, Frank J. 1924- CngDr 91, WhoAm 92, WhoE 93
Guarino, Annette L. Law&B 92
Guarino, Carl Anthony 1957- St&PR 93
Guarino, Carmine 1893-1965 Baker 92
Guarino, Dagmar ConAu 136
Guarino, Deborah 1954- BioIn 17, ConAu 136
Guarino, John Ralph 1915- WhoAm 92
Guarino, Joseph A. d1991 BioIn 17
Guarino, Marsula Gail 1942- WhoE 93
Guarino, Michael Anthony Law&B 92
Guarino, Michael J. 1953- WhoE 93
Guarino, Patrick J. Law&B 92
Guarino, Piero 1919- Baker 92
Guarino, Roger Charles 1929- WhoAm 92, WhoSSW 93
Guarino, Salvatore Frank 1937- WhoAm 92
Guarino, Thomas V. 1953- St&PR 93
Guarino, Walter F. 1942- St&PR 93
Guarise, Christine Louise 1948- WhoAmW 93
Guarise, Gian Berto 1932- WhoScE 91-3
Guarnaccia, Steven BioIn 17
Guarneri Baker 92
Guarneri, Andrea c. 1625-1698 Baker 92
Guarneri, Giuseppe Antonio 1698-1744 Baker 92
Guarneri, Giuseppe Giovanni Battista 1666-c. 1740 Baker 92
Guarneri, Pietro 1695-1762 Baker 92
Guarneri, Pietro Giovanni 1655-1720 Baker 92
Guarnerius Baker 92
Guarneschelli, Philip George 1932- St&PR 93, WhoE 93
Guarnieri Baker 92
Guarnieri, Albina 1953- WhoAmW 93
Guarnieri, Antonio 1880-1952 Baker 92
Guarnieri, (Mozart) Camargo 1907- Baker 92
Guarnieri, Robert Joseph 1952- St&PR 93
Guarr, Michael J. Law&B 92
Guarrera, Frank 1923- Baker 92
Guastaferro, Angelo 1932- WhoAm 92
Guastalla Lucchini, Gherarda 1937- WhoWor 93
Guastamachio, Wende W. Law&B 92
Guastavino, Carlos 1912- Baker 92
Guattari, Felix 1930-1992 NewYTBS 92 [port]
Guay, Edward 1943- WhoAm 92
Guay, Georgette 1952- WhoCanL 92
Guay, Gordon Hay 1948- WhoEmL 93
Guay, Jean-Pierre 1946- WhoCanL 92
Guayacan Gutierrez, Saul 1950- WhoWor 93
Guazzi, Mario WhoScE 91-3
Guba, Ferenc 1919- WhoScE 91-4
Guba, Vladimir 1938- Baker 92
Gubaidulina, Sofia 1931- Baker 92
Gubala, Jerzy Maciej 1935- WhoScE 91-4
Gubar, Susan 1944- BioIn 17
Gubbins, David WhoScE 91-1
Gubbins, Keith Edmund 1937- WhoAm 92
Gubbins, Terry Van 1958- WhoSSW 93
Gubenko, Nikolaj 1941- DrEEuF
Guber, Peter BioIn 17
Guber, Peter 1942- WhoAm 92
Guberman, Ronald Mark 1960- WhoE 93
Gubernatis, Thomas Frank, Sr. 1947- WhoE 93
Gubin, Ronald WhoAm 92
Gubler, Duane J. 1939- WhoAm 92
Gublin, Fernand 1936- WhoScE 91-2
Gubray, Anthony Roy 1932- WhoWor 93
Gubrud, Irene (Ann) 1947- Baker 92
Gubser, Carole Ethel 1956- WhoSSW 93
Gubser, Donald Urban 1940- WhoE 93
Gubser, Lyn M. 1939- WhoE 93
Gubser, Peter Anton 1941- WhoE 93
Guccion, Brian Edward 1955- St&PR 93
Guccione, Bob 1930- BioIn 17
Guccione, Leslie Davis 1946- SmATA 72 [port]
Guccione, Robert Charles Joseph Edward Sabatini 1930- WhoAm 92
Guccione, Samuel Anthony 1941- WhoE 93
Gu Chuanxun 1935- WhoAsAP 91
Guckenheimer, Daniel P. 1943- St&PR 93
Gucker, Jane Gleason 1951- WhoAm 92, WhoEmL 93
Guckert, Harry James 1934-1991 BioIn 17
Guckes, William Ruhland, Jr. 1944- WhoAm 92
Gucluer, Sevket WhoScE 91-4
Gucovsky, Michael Moshe 1931- WhoUN 92
Guczi, Laszlo 1932- WhoScE 91-4
Gudanek, Lois Bassolino 1944- WhoAmW 93
Gudberg, Paul 1946- WhoWor 93
Gudding, Roar 1944- WhoScE 91-4
Gude, Alberto, Jr. 1939- WhoAm 92
Gude, Gilbert 1923- WhoAm 92
Gude, Nancy Carlson 1948- WhoAmW 93
Gude, William Morgan 1934- St&PR 93
Gudehus, Donald Henry WhoSSW 93
Gudehus, Heinrich 1845-1909 Baker 92, OxDcOp
Gudelis, Drasutis 1933- St&PR 93
Gudeman, Stephen Frederick 1939- WhoAm 92
Gudeman, Timothy Allan 1958- WhoEmL 93
Gudemann, Moritz 1835-1918 BioIn 17
Guden, Paul Alexander 1944- St&PR 93
Gudenberg, Harry Richard 1933- WhoAm 92
Gudeon, Arthur 1935- WhoE 93
Guderian, Heinz 1888-1953 HarEnMi
Guderian, Heinz 1888-1954 BioIn 17
Gudev, Vladimir 1940- WhoWor 93
Gudgel, Dean W. Law&B 92
Gudgel, Tom Law&B 92
Gudgeon, Donald L. 1931- WhoScE 91-1
Gudin, Charles-Etienne 1946- WhoWor 93
Gudin, Serge 1959- WhoWor 93
Gudinas, Donald Jerome 1933- WhoAm 92
Gudino Kieffer, Eduardo 1935- SpAmA
Gudis, Malcolm J. 1941- St&PR 93, WhoAm 92
Gudjonsson, Birgir 1938- WhoWor 93
Gudmel, Claude Baker 92
Gudmestad, Terje Law&B 92
Gudmundsen, Vance C. Law&B 92
Gudmundsen-Holmgreen, Pelle 1932- Baker 92
Gudmundson, Barbara Rohrke WhoWor 93
Gudmundsson, Agust 1953- WhoScE 91-4
Gudmundsson, Finnbogi 1924- WhoWor 93
Gudmundsson, Olafur 1942- WhoScE 91-4
Gudmundsson, Sigurdur Elimundur 1932- WhoWor 93
Gudmundsson, Thorir 1960- WhoWor 93
Gudorf, Kenneth Francis 1939- St&PR 93, WhoAm 92
Gudyka, Louis Carl 1930- St&PR 93
Gudykust, Thomas 1948- St&PR 93
Gudz, Michael 1951- St&PR 93
Gudzak, Shelley Overholt 1958- WhoSSW 93
Gue, Andre Robert 1933- WhoUN 92
Gue, Belle Willey AmWomPl
Gue, Benjamin F. 1828-1904 JrnUS
Guebriant, Jean Baptiste Budes, Count of 1602-1643 HarEnMi
Guebuza, Armando Emilio 1943- WhoAfr
Gueden, Hilde 1915-1988 OxDcOp
Gueden, Hilde 1917-1988 Baker 92, IntDcOp
Guedes, Amancio d'Alpoim Miranda 1925- WhoWor 93
Guedes, Carlos BioIn 17
Guedes, Maria Eduarda G. Miranda 1932- WhoScE 91-3
Guedes-Silva, Antonio Alberto Matos 1948- WhoWor 93
Guedes-Vieira, Manuel Jose 1943- WhoWor 93
Guedj, R. 1936- WhoScE 91-2
Guedon, Jacques 1927- WhoScE 91-2
Guedron, Pierre 1570?-1619? Baker 92
Guedry, James W. Law&B 92
Guedry, James Walter 1941- WhoAm 92
Guedry, Leo J. 1940- WhoAm 92
Gueft, Boris 1916- WhoE 93
Guegen, Yves WhoScE 91-2
Gueguen, M. WhoScE 91-2
Gueguen, Yves 1949- WhoScE 91-2
Guehria, Said 1939- WhoUN 92
Gueldner, Helmar 1939- St&PR 93
Gueldner, Robert F., III 1950- St&PR 93
Guelfi, Giangiacomo 1924- Baker 92
Guelich, Robert Vernon 1917- WhoAm 92
Guell y Bacigalupi, Eusebi 1847-1918 BioIn 17
Guell y Ferrer, Joan 1800-1872 BioIn 17
Guen, Moncef WhoUN 92
Guenault, Anthony Michael WhoScE 91-1
Guencheva, Guenka Petrova 1941- WhoScE 91-4
Guendel, Thomas Joseph 1927- St&PR 93
Guendelsberger, Robert Joseph 1950- WhoEmL 93
Guenet, Jean-Louis 1938- WhoScE 91-2
Guenet, Jean-Michel 1951- WhoWor 93
Guenette, Francoise 1951- WhoAm 92
Guenette, Robert 1935- MiSFD 9
Guengerich, Gary David 1945- St&PR 93, WhoAm 92
Guenin, Gerard 1945- WhoScE 91-2
Guenin, Marcel Andre 1937- WhoScE 91-4
Guenin, Marie-Alexandre 1744-1835 Baker 92
Guenin-Lelle, Dianne Paula 1957- WhoAmW 93
Guennewig, Victoria Brosokas 1950- WhoSSW 93
Guennoc, Pol 1953- WhoScE 91-2
Guenst, Rodney S. 1956- St&PR 93
Guenter, Helen Marie Giessen 1944- WhoSSW 93
Guenter, Raymond A. Law&B 92
Guenter, Raymond Albert 1932- St&PR 93, WhoAm 92
Guenther, Arthur Henry 1931- WhoAm 92
Guenther, Bob Dean 1939- WhoSSW 93
Guenther, Charles John 1920- WhoAm 92, WhoWrEP 92
Guenther, Daniel 1956- WhoSSW 93
Guenther, George C. 1931- St&PR 93
Guenther, George Carpenter 1931- WhoAm 92
Guenther, Jack Donald 1929- WhoAm 92
Guenther, Jack Egon 1934- WhoAm 92
Guenther, James R. 1945- St&PR 93
Guenther, John S. 1942- St&PR 93
Guenther, Karl Heinz 1947- WhoSSW 93
Guenther, Kenneth A. BioIn 17
Guenther, Kenneth Allen WhoAm 92, WhoE 93
Guenther, Paul B. 1940- St&PR 93
Guenther, Paul Bernard 1940- WhoAm 92
Guenther, Robert Anthony 1942- WhoWor 93
Guenther, Robert Stanley, II 1950- WhoEmL 93
Guenther, Thomas P. 1932- St&PR 93
Guenther, Wolfgang A. Law&B 92
Guentner, Gail Marie 1961- WhoAmW 93, WhoEmL 93
Guenzel, Frank Bernhard 1938- WhoAm 92
Guenzel, Paul Walter 1910- WhoAm 92
Guenzel, Rudolf Paul 1940- St&PR 93
Guenzel, Steven Eric 1953- WhoEmL 93
Guequierre, John Phillip 1946- St&PR 93
Gueranger, Prosper Louis Pascal 1805-1875 Baker 92
Guerard, Albert Joseph 1914- WhoAm 92, WhoWrEP 92
Guerard, Daniel L. 1941- WhoScE 91-2
Guerci, Agnes Paule 1956- WhoWor 93
Guerci, Christine M. Law&B 92
Guercino 1591-1666 BioIn 17
Guercio, Baldovino dc. 1201 OxDcByz
Guercio, James William MiSFD 9
Guerin, Bernard 1942- WhoScE 91-2
Guerin, Camille A. 1938- St&PR 93
Guerin, Charles Anthony Law&B 92
Guerin, Christopher David 1953- WhoAm 92
Guerin, Daniel 1904-1988 BioIn 17
Guerin, Dean P. 1922- St&PR 93
Guerin, Dean Patrick 1922- WhoAm 92
Guerin, Didier 1950- WhoAm 92
Guerin, Gerard M.P. 1948- WhoScE 91-2
Guerin, Herve Bernard 1941- WhoWor 93
Guerin, James K. Law&B 92
Guerin, Jean Louis 1935- WhoAm 92
Guerin, Joel F. 1948- St&PR 93
Guerin, John
See Byrds, The ConMus 8
Guerin, John J. 1926- St&PR 93
Guerin, Kenneth Joseph 1948- WhoEmL 93
Guerin, Michelle WhoCanL 92
Guerin, Patrick Gerard 1965- WhoWor 93
Guerin, Wilfred Louis 1929- WhoSSW 93
Guerine, Morton 1934- St&PR 93
Gueritee, Nicolas 1920- WhoWor 93
Gueritey, Harold Charles, Jr. 1939- St&PR 93
Guerithault, Vincent BioIn 17
Guermonprez, Jean-Leon 1937- WhoScE 91-2
Guernsey, Anthony H. 1936- St&PR 93
Guernsey, Louis Harold 1923- WhoAm 92
Guernsey, Nancy Patricia 1955- WhoEmL 93, WhoWrEP 92
Guernsey, Otis Love, Jr. 1918- WhoAm 92, WhoWor 93
Guernsey, Peter E. 1921- St&PR 93
Guernsey, Royal Thomas d1990 BioIn 17
Gueron, Jules 1907-1990 BioIn 17
Guerra, Armando J. 1951- WhoEmL 93, WhoSSW 93
Guerra, Carlos A. Law&B 92
Guerra, Charles Albert 1960- WhoSSW 93, WhoWor 93
Guerra, Debra Sharon 1953- WhoAmW 93
Guerra, Emma Maria 1956- WhoAmW 93
Guerra, Eutimio DcCPCAm
Guerra, Juan 1950- St&PR 93
Guerra, Juan Luis BioIn 17
Guerra, Justino WhoScE 91-3
Guerra, Michael Law&B 92
Guerra, Nancy 1951- WhoAmW 93
Guerra, Olivia Margaret Law&B 92
Guerra, Roland 1961- WhoSSW 93
Guerra, Ruy 1931- MiSFD 9
Guerra, Silvio Neto Bezerra 1956- WhoWor 93
Guerra, Stella G. NotHsAW 93
Guerra, Stella Garcia 1945- WhoAmW 93
Guerra, Tonino 1920- DcLB 128 [port]
Guerra-Melick, Judith Inez 1961- WhoAmW 93
Guerrant, David Edward 1919- WhoAm 92
Guerrant, John Lippincott 1910- WhoSSW 93
Guerra Ord, Angustias de la NotHsAW 93
Guerra-Peixe, Cesar 1914- Baker 92
Guerrerio, Richard Law&B 92
Guerrero, Anthony R., Jr. 1945- St&PR 93, WhoAm 92
Guerrero, Dolores 1941- NotHsAW 93
Guerrero, Francisco 1528-1599 Baker 92
Guerrero, Hernan Gilberto 1935- WhoWor 93
Guerrero, Jesus R. 1911- DcMexL
Guerrero, Jose d1991 NewYTBS 92
Guerrero, Jose 1914-1991 BioIn 17
Guerrero, Jose Jesus 1961- WhoWor 93
Guerrero, Jose Lino Balbin 1933- WhoUN 92
Guerrero, Lena BioIn 17
Guerrero, Lena 1957- NotHsAW 93 [port]
Guerrero, Leonardo L. 1924- WhoAsAP 91
Guerrero, Maria Elena 1954- WhoAmW 93
Guerrero, Mario, Jr. 1962- WhoE 93
Guerrero, Pedro 1956- WhoAm 92
Guerrero, Reynaldo David 1948- WhoWor 93
Guerrero, Tito, III 1947- WhoSSW 93
Guerrette, Richard Hector 1930- WhoE 93
Guerri, Sergio Cardinal 1905- WhoWor 93
Guerri, William Grant 1921- WhoAm 92
Guerrier, Edith 1870-1958 BioIn 17
Guerrieri, Kevin Scott 1962- WhoE 93
Guerrieri, Lisa R. 1960- WhoAmW 93
Guerrieri, Michael Anthony 1946- St&PR 93
Guerriero, Michael d1991 BioIn 17
Guerriero, Michael J. Law&B 92
Guerrin, J. 1934- WhoScE 91-2
Guerrin, Jacques 1934- WhoScE 91-2
Guerrini, Guido 1890-1965 Baker 92
Guerrini, Paolo (Antigono) 1880-1960 Baker 92
Guerrini, Zelma Maria Varella 1943- WhoWor 93
Guerrise, Patrick P. 1943- St&PR 93, WhoAm 92
Guerster, Rene L. 1938- St&PR 93, WhoAm 92
Guertin, Louis Law&B 92
Guertin, Robert G. 1947- St&PR 93
Guertin, Robert Powell 1939- WhoAm 92
Guertler, Walter St&PR 93
Guesde, Jules 1845-1922 BioIn 17
Guess, George 1770?-1843 BioIn 17
Guess, Harry Adelbert 1940- WhoSSW 93
Guess, John Adam, IV 1946- WhoSSW 93
Guest, Barbara WhoWrEP 92
Guest, Barbara 1920- WhoAm 92
Guest, Brian Milton 1948- WhoEmL 93
Guest, Charlotte Bertie Elizabeth 1812-1895 BioIn 17
Guest, Christopher 1948- MiSFD 9
Guest, Cynthia Jean 1963- WhoAmW 93
Guest, Diane ScF&FL 92
Guest, Donald Britnor 1929- WhoSSW 93, WhoWor 93
Guest, George (Howell) 1924- Baker 92
Guest, Gerald Bentley 1936- WhoAm 92
Guest, James Alfred 1940- WhoAm 92
Guest, Jane Mary c. 1762-1846 BioIn 17
Guest, John Franklin, Jr. 1944- WhoSSW 93
Guest, John Rodney WhoScE 91-1
Guest, Judith BioIn 17
Guest, Judith Ann 1936- WhoAm 92, WhoWrEP 92
Guest, Karl Macon 1915- WhoAm 92
Guest, L.R. Law&B 92
Guest, Lynn 1939- ScF&FL 92
Guest, Raymond 1907-1991 AnObit 1991
Guest, Raymond R. d1991? NewYTBS 92
Guest, Raymond Richard 1907-1991 BioIn 17
Guest, Robert Henry 1916- WhoAm 92
Guest, Val 1911- MiSFD 9
Guest, William F. 1931- St&PR 93
Guettel, Henry Arthur 1928- WhoAm 92
Guetterman, Janet A. 1967- WhoAmW 93

Guettinger, Thomas Wolfgang 1954- *WhoWor 93*
Guetzkow, Daniel 1949- *St&PR 93*
Guetzkow, Daniel Steere 1949- *WhoAm 92, WhoE 93, WhoEmL 93, WhoWor 93*
Guetzkow, Diana 1947- *WhoAmW 93*
Guevara, Alex, Jr. *Law&B 92*
Guevara, Anibal *DcCPCAm*
Guevara, Che 1928-1967 *BioIn 17*
Guevara, Ernesto 1928-1967 *BioIn 17, DcTwHis*
Guevara, Juan Manuel 1953- *WhoWor 93*
Guevara, Miguel de 1585-1646? *DcMexL*
Guevara de la Serna, Ernesto 1928-1967 *ColdWar 2 [port]*
Guevara de la Serna, Ernesto Che 1928-1967 *DcCPCAm*
Guevara-Lacki, Nanette Rose 1953- *WhoAmW 93*
Guevremont, Germaine 1893-1968 *BioIn 17*
Gueymard, Louis 1822-1880 *OxDcOp*
Gueymard, Pauline Lauters 1834- *OxDcOp*
Guezec, Jean-Pierre 1934-1971 *Baker 92*
Guffey, George R. 1932- *ScF&FL 92*
Guffey, James Roger 1929- *St&PR 93, WhoAm 92*
Guffey, Joe Lynn 1952- *WhoSSW 93*
Guffey, John W. 1938- *St&PR 93*
Guffey, Wendell Ray *Law&B 92*
Guffey, Wendell Ray 1951- *WhoEmL 93*
Guffin, Peter J. *Law&B 92*
Gugas, Chris 1921- *WhoWor 93*
Gugel, Craig Thomas 1954- *WhoAm 92, WhoE 93, WhoEmL 93, WhoWor 93*
Gugelot, Piet Cornelis 1918- *WhoAm 92*
Guggenheim, Alan Andre Albert Paul Edouard 1950- *WhoEmL 93*
Guggenheim, Charles 1924- *PolPar*
Guggenheim, Charles E. 1924- *WhoAm 92*
Guggenheim, Daniel 1856-1930 *EncABHB 8 [port]*
Guggenheim, Harry F. 1890-1971 *EncABHB 8 [port]*
Guggenheim, Richard E. 1913- *WhoAm 92*
Guggenheimer, Elinor 1912- *WhoAmW 93*
Guggenheimer, Heinrich Walter 1924- *WhoAm 92*
Guggenheimer, James 1936- *WhoE 93*
Guggenheimer, Joan *Law&B 92*
Guggenhime, Richard Johnson 1940- *WhoAm 92, WhoWor 93*
Gugger, Heinrich 1950- *WhoWor 93*
Gugic, Petar 1924- *WhoScE 91-4*
Gugino, Carmelo, Jr. 1915- *St&PR 93*
Gugino, Wade *BioIn 17*
Gugler, Anne Tonetti d1990 *BioIn 17*
Guglielmetti, Robert 1937- *WhoScE 91-2*
Guglielmi, Frank A. 1951- *St&PR 93*
Guglielmi, Jacopo d1731? *OxDcOp*
Guglielmi, Pietro Alessandro 1728-1804 *Baker 92, OxDcOp*
Guglielmi, Pietro Carlo c. 1763-1817 *Baker 92*
Guglielmi, Robert Vincent 1936- *St&PR 93*
Guglielmino, Paul Joseph 1942- *WhoSSW 93*
Gugliotta, Robert *St&PR 93*
Gugliuzza, Kristene Koontz 1956- *WhoAmW 93*
Guha, Anton-Andreas 1937- *ScF&FL 92*
Guha, Subhendu 1942- *St&PR 93*
Guha, Sunil 1931- *WhoUN 92*
Guhawardana, Kanti Kumudadati 1941- *WhoUN 92*
Gu Hui 1930- *WhoAsAP 91*
Gui, James Edmund 1928- *WhoAm 92, WhoE 93*
Gui, Vittorio 1885-1975 *Baker 92, OxDcOp*
Guiart, Jean 1925- *WhoScE 91-2*
Guiberson, Brenda Z. 1946- *SmATA 71 [port]*
Guibert, Herve 1955-1991 *BioIn 17*
Guibert, Jacques Antoine Hippolyte, Count of 1743-1790 *HarEnMi*
Guibert of Nogent c. 1053-c. 1124 *OxDcByz*
Guibord, Jerry E. *BioIn 17*
Guibord, Linda Bergendahl 1946- *WhoE 93*
Guibord, Scott Laurence *Law&B 92*
Guice, John Thompson 1923- *WhoAm 92*
Guice, Leslie Kieth 1954- *WhoAm 92*
Guichard, Antoine Hubert 1954- *WhoWor 93*
Guichard, Olivier 1920- *BioIn 17*
Guichen, Luc Urbain de Bouexic, Count of 1712-1790 *HarEnMi*
Guida, F.A. 1934- *St&PR 93*
Guida, Pat 1929- *WhoAmW 93*
Guida, Peter Matthew 1927- *WhoAm 92*
Guida, Ronald J. 1958- *WhoEmL 93*
Guidacci, Margherita 1921-1992 *DcLB 128 [port]*
Guidano, Vittorio Filippo 1944- *WhoWor 93*
Guide, Robert George 1933- *St&PR 93*
Guidebeck, Ronald Patrick 1936- *St&PR 93*
Guidera, Brian M. 1939- *St&PR 93*
Guidette, Christopher Lino 1946- *WhoE 93*
Guidetti, Beniamino 1918- *WhoScE 91-3*
Guidetti, Giovanni Domenico 1531?-1592 *Baker 92*
Guidi, Doris Fraser 1934- *WhoAmW 93*
Guidi, Giulio 1933- *WhoScE 91-3*
Guidi, Virgilio 1891-1984 *BioIn 17*
Guiditta, Thomas Anthony 1944- *St&PR 93*
Guido, Beatriz 1925-1988 *SpAmA*
Guido, Clemente *DcCPCAm*
Guido, Jo Ann 1952- *WhoWrEP 92*
Guido, Joseph Matthew 1934- *WhoAm 92*
Guido, Richard Lawrence *Law&B 92*
Guido, Shareon Christine 1946- *WhoAmW 93, WhoEmL 93*
Guido Aretinus c. 991-c. 1033 *Baker 92*
Guidobono Cavalchini, Luigi 1939- *WhoScE 91-3*
Guido d'Arezzo c. 991-c. 1033 *Baker 92*
Guidos-Maruskin, Marie 1937- *WhoE 93*
Guidotti, D. Bruce 1943- *WhoAm 92*
Guidotti, Richard John 1942- *WhoUN 92*
Guidry, Diane Tilton 1953- *WhoAmW 93*
Guidry, George Harrel, Jr. *Law&B 92*
Guidry, Glenn Alan 1956- *WhoSSW 93*
Guidry, John R. *Law&B 92*
Guidry, Krisandra Ann 1963- *WhoEmL 93, WhoSSW 93*
Guidry, Rodney-Lee Joseph 1935- *WhoSSW 93*
Guidry, Susan Diane Arnold 1953- *WhoEmL 93*
Guidry, William A. 1947- *WhoSSW 93*
Guidugli, Piero Angelo 1952- *St&PR 93*
Guier, William Howard 1926- *WhoAm 92*
Guiffre, Jean Ellen 1942- *WhoAmW 93*
Guifre fl. 870?-897 *BioIn 17*
Guifred, Count of the Spanish March fl. 870?-897 *BioIn 17*
Guigal, R. *WhoScE 91-2*
Guignon, Jean-Pierre 1702-1774 *Baker 92*
Guigonnat, Henri *ScF&FL 92*
Guigou, Elisabeth *BioIn 17*
Guihan, J. Lawrence 1952- *St&PR 93*
Guiheneuc, Pierre 1939- *WhoScE 91-2*
Guiher, James Morford, Jr. 1927- *WhoAm 92*
Guiho, Gerard D. 1945- *WhoScE 91-2*
Guijt, Jacob 1934- *WhoUN 92*
Guikema, Dale J. 1940- *St&PR 93*
Guilaran, Alfonso Posadas, Jr. 1930- *WhoWor 93*
Guilbault, Lawrence James 1940- *St&PR 93*
Guilbault, Pierre 1954- *St&PR 93*
Guilbeaux, Murphy Joseph, Jr. 1955- *WhoSSW 93*
Guilbert, Yvette 1865-1944 *Baker 92*
Guild, Alden 1929- *St&PR 93, WhoAm 92*
Guild, Clark Joseph, Jr. 1921- *WhoAm 92*
Guild, Curtis 1827-1911 *JrnUS*
Guild, Henry Rice, Jr. 1928- *St&PR 93*
Guild, Jeffrey Warren *Law&B 92*
Guild, Nelson Prescott 1928- *WhoAm 92*
Guild, Richard Samuel 1925- *WhoE 93, WhoWor 93*
Guilds, John Caldwell *DcLB Y92 [port]*
Guiles, Carol Ellis 1950- *WhoSSW 93*
Guiles, Paula Grace 1948- *WhoAmW 93*
Guilet, Daniel 1899-1990 *BioIn 17*
Guiley, Rosemary *ScF&FL 92*
Guilford, Colin Michael 1929- *WhoWor 93*
Guilford, Marjorie Bryan 1957- *WhoSSW 93*
Guilford, Morgan B. 1935- *St&PR 93*
Guilford, Nanette 1903-1990 *BioIn 17*
Guilfoyle, David *St&PR 93*
Guilfoyle, George H. 1913-1991 *BioIn 17*
Guilfoyle, Richard J. 1935- *WhoIns 93*
Guill, Margaret Frank 1948- *WhoAmW 93*
Guillame, Raymond Kendrick 1943- *St&PR 93*
Guillard, Joanny Pierre 1923- *WhoScE 91-2*
Guillard, Nicolas Francais 1752-1814 *OxDcOp*
Guillard, Robert Russell Louis 1921- *WhoE 93*
Guillaumat, Pierre 1909-1991 *BioIn 17*
Guillaume, Gilbert 1930- *WhoUN 92, WhoWor 93*
Guillaume, Jean-Charles 1936- *WhoWor 93*
Guillaume, Marnix L.K. 1938- *St&PR 93*
Guillaume, Marnix Leo Karl 1938- *WhoAm 92*
Guillaume, Raymond Kendrick 1943- *WhoAm 92*
Guillaume, Robert 1927- *ConBlB 3 [port]*
Guillaumont, Patrick 1939- *WhoWor 93*
Guillaumont, Robert 1933- *WhoScE 91-2*
Guillaumot, Jacques *WhoScE 91-2*
Guille, Alain 1937- *WhoScE 91-2*
Guillebeau, Julie Graves 1948- *WhoWrEP 92*
Guillem, Sylvie 1965- *ConTFT 10*
Guillemain, Bernard 1942- *WhoScE 91-2*
Guillemain, Louis-Gabriel 1705-1770 *Baker 92*
Guillemette, A. Roger 1934- *St&PR 93*
Guillemette, Gloria Vivian 1929- *WhoAm 92, WhoAmW 93*
Guillemin, Michel P. 1943- *WhoScE 91-4*
Guillemin, Roger 1924- *WhoAm 92, WhoWor 93*
Guillen, Fedro 1920- *DcMexL*
Guillen, Jorge 1893-1984 *BioIn 17*
Guillen, Jorge Eduardo 1957- *WhoE 93*
Guillen, Mauro Federico 1964- *WhoE 93*
Guillen, Michael Arthur *WhoE 93*
Guillen, Nicolas 1902-1989 *SpAmA*
Guillen, Oswaldo Jose Barrios 1964- *WhoAm 92*
Guillerman, A. Pierre *WhoSSW 93*
Guillermin, Armand Pierre 1936- *WhoSSW 93*
Guillermin, John 1925- *MiSFD 9*
Guillermo, Linda Sue 1951- *WhoAmW 93*
Guillery, R.W. *WhoScE 91-1*
Guillery, Rainer Walter 1929- *WhoAm 92*
Guillet, James Edwin 1927- *WhoAm 92*
Guillevin Wood, Jeannine *BioIn 17*
Guilliouma, Larry Jay, Jr. 1950- *WhoEmL 93, WhoSSW 93*
Guillon, Pierre 1947- *WhoScE 91-2*
Guillory, Elbert Lee 1944- *WhoSSW 93*
Guillory, Elizabeth Brown- *BioIn 17*
Guillot, Daniel Francois 1939- *WhoScE 91-2*
Guillot, G. 1947- *WhoScE 91-2*
Guillot, Rene 1900-1969 *ConAu 39NR*
Guilloton, Sheila Kahoe *Law&B 92*
Guillotte, Preston J. 1938- *St&PR 93*
Guillou, Jean 1930- *Baker 92*
Guillouzo, Andre 1946- *WhoScE 91-2*
Guilmant, (Felix) Alexandre 1837-1911 *Baker 92*
Guilmette, Joanne 1951- *WhoAmW 93*
Guilmette, Larry Gene 1948- *WhoE 93*
Guilmino, Carol Sue 1933- *WhoSSW 93*
Guimaraes, Andre 1932- *WhoWor 93*
Guimaraes, George Gomes 1944- *WhoAm 92*
Guimaraes, Ulysses d1992 *NewYTBS 92 [port]*
Guimond, A. Roger 1954- *St&PR 93*
Guimond, Gerard J., Jr. *Law&B 92*
Guimond, John Patrick 1927- *WhoAm 92*
Guimond, Richard Joseph 1947- *WhoAm 92*
Guimond, Robert Wilfrid 1938- *WhoE 93*
Guin, David Jonathan 1960- *WhoSSW 93*
Guin, Debra Mauriece 1953- *WhoEmL 93, WhoSSW 93*
Guin, Don Lester 1940- *WhoSSW 93, WhoWor 93*
Guin, James Patrick 1946- *St&PR 93*
Guin, Junius Foy, Jr. 1924- *WhoAm 92, WhoSSW 93*
Guin, Marilyn Potts- d1989 *BioIn 17*
Guin, Ursula K. Le *ScF&FL 92*
Guin, Winford Harold 1926- *WhoAm 92*
Guin, Wyman 1915-1989 *ScF&FL 92*
Guinan, James M. *St&PR 93*
Guinan, Joanne K. *Law&B 92*
Guinan, Mary Elizabeth 1939- *WhoAmW 93*
Guinan, Texas 1884?-1933 *SweetSg A [port]*
Guinard, Daniel *WhoScE 91-2*
Guindon, Yvan 1951- *WhoAm 92*
Guinea, Francisco 1953- *WhoWor 93*
Guinee, A.W. *WhoScE 91-3*
Guinee, William T. 1932- *St&PR 93*
Guingona, Teofisto Tayco, Jr. 1928- *WhoAsAP 91*
Guinier, Ewart 1910-1990 *BioIn 17*
Guinivan, Thomas W. 1922- *St&PR 93*
Guinn, David Crittenden 1926- *WhoAm 92, WhoSSW 93*
Guinn, Donald Edgell *Law&B 92*
Guinn, Dorothy C. *AmWomPl*
Guinn, Dotson R. 1939- *St&PR 93*
Guinn, Franketta *BioIn 17*
Guinn, Gary Mark 1948- *WhoWrEP 92*
Guinn, Geoffrey Kyle 1948- *St&PR 93*
Guinn, Janet Martin 1942- *WhoAmW 93, WhoWor 93*
Guinn, Jerry Hill 1929- *St&PR 93*
Guinn, John Rockne 1936- *WhoAm 92*
Guinn, Kenny C. 1936- *St&PR 93*
Guinn, Linda A. *Law&B 92*
Guinn, Stanley Willis 1953- *WhoEmL 93*
Guinness, Alec 1914- *IntDcF 2-3 [port], QDrFCA 92 [port], WhoAm 92, WhoWor 93*
Guinness, Arthur 1725-1803 *BioIn 17*
Guinness, Bryan (Walter) 1905-1992 *ConAu 139*
Guinot, Bernard 1925- *WhoScE 91-2*
Guinot, Herve Marie Camille 1955- *WhoWor 93*
Guinot, J.C. 1942- *WhoScE 91-2*
Guinsburg, Philip Fried 1946- *WhoSSW 93*
Guinter, John Robert 1922- *St&PR 93*
Guinther, Frederick E. 1932- *St&PR 93*
Guinto-Juco, Estelita 1930- *WhoAsAP 91*
Guion, David (Wendell Fentress) 1892-1981 *Baker 92*
Guion, Paul David *WhoScE 91-1*
Guionnet, Michel 1940- *WhoScE 91-2*
Guion-Shipley, Joyce 1946- *WhoWrEP 92*
Guior, Glenn L. *Law&B 92*
Guiora, Susie Nira 1932- *WhoWor 93*
Guirado, Burt 1955- *WhoSSW 93*
Guiraldenq, P.H. 1934- *WhoScE 91-2*
Guiraldes, Ricardo 1886-1927 *BioIn 17, SpAmA*
Guiraud, C.Y. 1933- *WhoScE 91-2*
Guiraud, Ernest 1837-1892 *Baker 92, OxDcOp*
Guiraud, Jean-Baptiste 1803-c. 1864 *OxDcOp*
Guirdham, Arthur 1905- *ScF&FL 92*
Guirguis, Raouf Albert 1953- *WhoWor 93*
Guirlinger, Richard B. 1953- *St&PR 93*
Guirma, Frederic *BlkAull 92*
Guisan, Olivier 1938- *WhoScE 91-4*
Guise, David Earl 1931- *WhoAm 92*
Guise, Edward J., III *Law&B 92*
Guise, Francois de Lorraine, Duke of 1519-1563 *HarEnMi*
Guise, Frank W. 1945- *St&PR 93*
Guise, Henri de Lorraine, Duke of 1550-1588 *HarEnMi*
Guise, Thomas James 1944- *St&PR 93*
Guiseley, Kenneth Balm 1933- *WhoE 93*
Guisewite, Cathy *BioIn 17*
Guisewite, Cathy Lee 1950- *WhoAm 92, WhoAmW 93*
Gui Shiyong 1934- *WhoAsAP 91*
Guist, Carl G. 1946- *St&PR 93*
Guist, Fredric Michael 1946- *WhoAm 92*
Guitar Slim 1926-1959 *BioIn 17*
Guiterman, Anthony T. 1949- *St&PR 93*
Guiton, Bonnie 1941- *AfrAmBi [port]*
Guiton, Bonnie F. 1941- *WhoAm 92, WhoAmW 93*
Guiton, Jacques *BioIn 17*
Guiton, John H. 1929- *St&PR 93*
Guiton, John P. *Law&B 92*
Guittar, Lee J. 1931- *St&PR 93*
Guittarr, Dennis C. 1947- *St&PR 93*
Guizar, Ricardo Diaz 1933- *WhoAm 92*
Guizzardi, Gustavo 1943- *WhoWor 93*
Guizzetti, Joe Dale 1951- *St&PR 93*
Guizzo, Mary Lou 1954- *WhoAmW 93*
Guja, Arthur T. *Law&B 92*
Gujer, Willi 1946- *WhoScE 91-4*
Gu Jinchi 1932- *WhoAsAP 91*
Gujral, Inder Kumar 1919- *WhoAsAP 91*
Guju, John G. 1924- *WhoAm 92*
Gulak, Morton Blum 1938- *WhoSSW 93*
Gulak-Artemovsky, Semyon Stepanovich 1813-1873 *Baker 92*
Gulas, Edward John 1932- *St&PR 93*
Gulas, Theodore Constantine 1950- *WhoEmL 93*
Gulati, Dhiraj 1949- *WhoE 93*
Gulati, Jagdish 1942- *WhoE 93*
Gulati, R.D. 1935- *WhoScE 91-3*
Gulati, Ramesh Datt 1935- *WhoWor 93*
Gulbenkian, Paul *WhoAm 92*
Gulbenkian, Paul Basil 1940- *WhoWor 93*
Gulbin, John George 1935- *St&PR 93*
Gulbinowicz, Henryk Roman Cardinal 1928- *WhoWor 93*
Gulbrandsen, Shari *Law&B 92*
Gulbransen, Capron R. 1923- *St&PR 93*
Gulbransen, Margery Elizabeth *WhoWrEP 92*
Gulbranson, Ellen 1863-1947 *Baker 92, OxDcOp*
Gulbranson, Jeanne Marie 1947- *WhoAmW 93*
Gulbranson, Rex A. 1951- *WhoEmL 93*
Gulcher, Robert Harry 1925- *WhoAm 92*
Gulczynski, Frank B. 1925- *St&PR 93*
Gulczynski, Maureen E. 1933- *St&PR 93*
Gulda, Edward J. *St&PR 93*
Gulda, Edward James 1945- *WhoAm 92, WhoWor 93*
Gulda, Friedrich 1930- *Baker 92*
Guldberg, Tatiana 1913- *WhoWor 93*
Guldborg, Soren 1943- *WhoWor 93*
Gulden, Simon *Law&B 92*
Gulden, Simon 1938- *St&PR 93, WhoAm 92*
Gulden, Vern Theodore 1948- *St&PR 93*
Guldenstern, David L. 1943- *St&PR 93*

Guldimann, Till M. 1949- *WhoAm 92, WhoEmL 93*
Guldimann, Werner 1916- *WhoWor 93*
Guldner, Mary Ellen *WhoWrEP 92*
Guler, Mengu *WhoScE 91-4*
Gulia, Joseph Paul 1934- *WhoE 93*
Gulia, Peter Joseph *Law&B 92*
Gulicher, Herbert 1930- *WhoWor 93*
Gulick, Betty 1929- *St&PR 93*
Gulick, Bill *ConAu 39NR*
Gulick, Deborah Jean 1953- *WhoAmW 93*
Gulick, Donald E. 1942- *St&PR 93*
Gulick, Donna Marie 1956- *WhoAmW 93, WhoEmL 93*
Gulick, Grover C. 1916- *ConAu 39NR*
Gulick, Henry G. *WhoIns 93*
Gulick, John 1924- *WhoAm 92*
Gulick, John Alexander, III 1955- *WhoEmL 93*
Gulick, Luther Halsey 1892- *BioIn 17, WhoAm 92*
Gulick, Robert Walter 1949- *WhoEmL 93*
Gulick, Roy M. 1934- *St&PR 93*
Gulick, Walter Lawrence 1927- *WhoAm 92*
Gulinello, Joan R. *Law&B 92*
Gulino, Daniel V. *Law&B 92*
Gulka, John Matthew 1953- *WhoE 93, WhoEmL 93*
Gulkan, H. Polat 1944- *WhoScE 91-4*
Gulker, Myron 1939- *St&PR 93*
Gulkin, Harry 1927- *WhoAm 92*
Gulko, Paul Michael 1944- *WhoAm 92*
Gulko, Ralph 1953- *WhoEmL 93*
Gull, Keith *WhoScE 91-1*
Gull, Paula Mae 1955- *WhoEmL 93*
Gull, Theodore Raymond 1944- *WhoE 93*
Gulla, Robert Joseph 1935- *WhoE 93*
Gullace, Marlene Frances 1952- *WhoAmW 93*
Gullan, Richard Wilson 1953- *WhoWor 93*
Gullander, Werner Paul 1908- *WhoAm 92*
Gullans, Charles (Bennett) 1929- *ConAu 39NR, WhoWrEP 92*
Gullapalli, S.M. 1936- *St&PR 93*
Gullatt, Jane 1932- *WhoAmW 93*
Gulledge, Karen Stone 1941- *WhoAmW 93*
Gulledge, Sidney Loy, Jr. 1921- *St&PR 93*
Gullen, Christopher R. *Law&B 92*
Gullen, Christopher Roy 1950- *WhoEmL 93*
Gullen, John Douglas *Law&B 92*
Guller, Marjorie Ann *Law&B 92*
Gullett, Donald Edward 1951- *BiDAMSp 1989*
Gullett, John Estes 1941- *St&PR 93*
Gullette, Ethel Mae Bishop 1908- *WhoAmW 93, WhoE 93*
Gullette, Robert L. *Law&B 92*
Gulley, Don R. 1940- *St&PR 93*
Gulley, Joan L. 1947- *St&PR 93*
Gulley, Joan Long 1947- *WhoAm 92*
Gulley, Leona Grace 1935- *WhoSSW 93*
Gulley, Wilbur Paul, Jr. 1923- *WhoAm 92*
Gulley, William Louis 1930- *WhoIns 93*
Gulli, Franco 1926- *Baker 92*
Gullick, William John 1954- *WhoWor 93*
Gullickson, Glenn, Jr. 1919- *WhoAm 92*
Gullickson, Grant *Law&B 92*
Gullickson, William Dean 1924- *St&PR 93*
Gulliford, Andrew *BioIn 17*
Gulliksen, Harold 1903- *BioIn 17*
Gulliver, Dorothy 1908- *SweetSg B [port]*
Gullo, Johnni Lee 1962- *WhoE 93*
Gullo, Robert J. *Law&B 92*
Gullon, German 1945- *WhoAm 92*
Gullo-Siotkas, Dorothy 1942- *WhoAmW 93*
Gullotta, Thomas P. 1948- *WhoE 93*
Gullstrand, Tore R. 1921- *WhoScE 91-4*
Gullvag, Barbro M. 1927- *WhoScE 91-4*
Gully, Chester *WhoWrEP 92*
Gulmezoglu, Ekrem 1927- *WhoScE 91-4*
Gulmi, James Singleton 1946- *St&PR 93, WhoAm 92*
Gulotta, Gerald David 1921- *WhoE 93*
Gulotta, Victor 1954- *WhoE 93*
Gulpen, J.C. 1955- *St&PR 93*
Gulsoy, H. Erden 1939- *WhoScE 91-4*
Gultekin, Ergun 1938- *WhoScE 91-4*
Gultekin, Selahattin 1950- *WhoWor 93*
Gulvin, David H. 1934- *St&PR 93*
Gulvin, David Horner 1934- *WhoAm 92*
Gulyas, Bela Janos 1938- *WhoE 93*
Gum, Dawn Alicia 1956- *WhoEmL 93*
Guma, Greg 1947- *WhoWrEP 92*
Guma, Greg William 1947- *WhoAm 92*
Gumaer, Elliott Wilder, Jr. 1933- *WhoAm 92*
Guman, William John 1929- *WhoE 93*
Gumaniuc, Nicolae 1927- *WhoScE 91-4*
Gumb, Dana Frederic 1924- *St&PR 93*
Gumbel, Bryant *NewYTBS 92 [port]*
Gumbel, Bryant 1948- *BioIn 17*
Gumbel, Bryant Charles 1948- *AfrAmBi, WhoAm 92, WhoE 93*
Gumbel, Greg *BioIn 17*
Gumber, Paul Michael James 1962- *WhoE 93*
Gumbert, Ferdinand 1818-1896 *Baker 92*
Gumbiner, Anthony Joseph 1945- *St&PR 93*
Gumbiner, Lewis Robert 1923- *St&PR 93*
Gumbiner, Robert L. 1923- *WhoAm 92*
Gumbinner, Paul S. 1942- *WhoAm 92, WhoE 93*
Gumble, Arthur Robert 1920- *WhoWor 93*
Gumbleton, Thomas J. 1930- *WhoAm 92*
Gumbs, Emile 1928- *DcCPCAm*
Gumbs, Juliet Louise 1949- *WhoAmW 93*
Gumerman, Steve Howard 1957- *WhoE 93*
Gumerson, Jean Gilderhus 1923- *WhoAm 92*
Guminski, John A. 1930- *St&PR 93*
Gummel, Hermann Karl 1923- *WhoAm 92*
Gummer, Charles L. 1946- *St&PR 93*
Gummer, Peter Selwyn 1942- *WhoWor 93*
Gummere, Jerry D. 1932- *St&PR 93*
Gummere, John 1928- *St&PR 93, WhoAm 92, WhoIns 93*
Gummere, Walter Cooper 1917- *WhoAm 92*
Gummert, Helmut 1929- *WhoScE 91-3*
Gump, Mary G. *Law&B 92*
Gump, Richard Anthony 1917- *WhoAm 92*
Gumpel, Glenn J. *WhoAm 92*
Gumpelzhaimer, Adam 1559-1625 *Baker 92*
Gumpert, Friedrich Adolf 1841-1906 *Baker 92*
Gumpert, Gunther 1919- *WhoAm 92*
Gumpertz, Werner Herbert 1917- *St&PR 93, WhoAm 92*
Gumplowicz, Ludwig 1838-1909 *PolBiDi*
Gumppert, Karella Ann 1942- *WhoAmW 93*
Gumprecht, Elizabeth Ann Nace 1941- *WhoAmW 93*
Gumpright, Herbert Lawrence, Jr. 1946- *WhoE 93*
Gumucio Dagron, Alfonso 1950- *SpAmA*
Gumusdere, Ismet 1944- *WhoScE 91-4*
Gun, Guneli *ScF&FL 92*
Gunapala, Ragalkande Arachchillage 1940- *WhoWor 93*
Gunar, Lee Roy 1938- *WhoIns 93*
Gunaratnam, Kathiresapillai 1951- *WhoWor 93*
Gunawardana, Ranaweera L. Herbert 1938- *WhoWor 93*
Gunawardena, Chandra 1940- *WhoWor 93*
Gunawardena, Munugoda Hewage 1932- *WhoUN 92*
Gunbak, Ali Riza 1948- *WhoScE 91-4*
Gunby Kelly, Carolyn 1954- *WhoWor 93*
Gunckel, Stuart S. *Law&B 92*
Gunckel, Stuart S. 1936- *St&PR 93*
Gunczler, Paul 1957- *MiSFD 9*
Gund, Agnes *BioIn 17, WhoE 93*
Gund, Agnes 1938- *News 93-2 [port]*
Gund, George, III 1937- *WhoAm 92*
Gund, Gordon *BioIn 17*
Gund, Gordon 1939- *St&PR 93, WhoAm 92*
Gund, Sharon Smallwood *BioIn 17, WhoAmW 93*
Gundel, Norman L. *Law&B 92*
Gundelfinger, Genevieve May 1956- *WhoWor 93*
Gundelfinger, John 1937-1991 *BioIn 17*
Gundelfinger, Margaret Ellen 1956- *WhoEmL 93*
Gunden, Kenneth Von *ScF&FL 92*
Gunderloy, Mike *ScF&FL 92*
Gundermann, Knut-Olaf W. 1933- *WhoScE 91-3*
Gunderode, Karoline von 1780-1806 *BioIn 17*
Gundersen, Allison Maureen 1959- *WhoAmW 93*
Gundersen, Mark J. *Law&B 92*
Gundersen, Sonja J. *Law&B 92*
Gundersen, Wayne Campbell 1936- *WhoAm 92*
Gundersen, Wenche Blix 1933- *WhoScE 91-4*
Gundersheimer, Werner Leonard 1937- *WhoAm 92, WhoE 93*
Gunderson, Clark Alan 1948- *WhoEmL 93, WhoSSW 93*
Gunderson, Elmer Millard 1929- *WhoAm 92*
Gunderson, Gerald Axel 1940- *WhoAm 92*
Gunderson, Joanna 1932- *WhoWrEP 92*
Gunderson, John Brooks 1931- *St&PR 93*
Gunderson, Judith Keefer 1939- *WhoAmW 93*
Gunderson, Julie L. 1956- *St&PR 93*
Gunderson, Louise *BioIn 17*
Gunderson, Richard L. 1933- *St&PR 93, WhoIns 93*
Gunderson, Robert Vernon, Jr. 1951- *WhoAm 92*
Gunderson, Steve 1951- *CngDr 91*
Gunderson, Steve Craig 1951- *WhoAm 92*
Gunderson, Steven Alan 1949- *WhoEmL 93*
Gundlach, Heinz L. 1937- *St&PR 93*
Gundlach, Heinz Ludwig 1937- *WhoAm 92*
Gundlach, T.F. 1924- *St&PR 93*
Gundlach, Wladyslaw Rudolf 1921- *WhoScE 91-4*
Gundrum, James Richard 1929- *WhoAm 92*
Gundrum, Lawrence Joseph 1943- *St&PR 93*
Gundrum, Russell Fred 1948- *St&PR 93*
Gundry, Inglis 1905- *Baker 92*
Gundry, Jo Ann 1945- *WhoAmW 93*
Gunduz, Turgut 1926- *WhoScE 91-4*
Guneli, Zulkuf 1946- *WhoScE 91-4*
Gunerman, Penny Ann 1953- *WhoE 93*
Guney, Yilmaz 1937-1984 *MiSFD 9N*
Gungl, Joseph 1810-1889 *Baker 92*
Gungwu, Wang 1930- *WhoWor 93*
Gunjaadorg, Sharavyn 1937- *WhoAsAP 91*
Gunji, Hiromi 1939- *St&PR 93, WhoAm 92*
Gunkel, Carroll Reese 1937- *WhoE 93*
Gunkel, Claus Wilhelm 1954- *WhoWor 93*
Gunn, A.J. 1945- *ScF&FL 92*
Gunn, Alan 1940- *WhoAm 92*
Gunn, Alan Richard 1936- *WhoWor 93*
Gunn, Albert Edward, Jr. 1933- *WhoAm 92*
Gunn, Bill d1989 *BioIn 17*
Gunn, Charles William 1939- *WhoSSW 93*
Gunn, Christy Howard 1954- *WhoAmW 93*
Gunn, David W. 1960- *St&PR 93*
Gunn, Edgar Lindsey 1950- *WhoEmL 93, WhoSSW 93*
Gunn, G. Greg 1958- *WhoE 93*
Gunn, George 1939- *WhoAm 92*
Gunn, George F., Jr. 1927- *WhoAm 92*
Gunn, George R., Jr. 1939- *WhoAm 92*
Gunn, Giles Buckingham 1938- *WhoAm 92*
Gunn, Glenn Dillard 1874-1963 *Baker 92*
Gunn, H. Michael 1946- *WhoScE 91-3*
Gunn, James 1923- *ScF&FL 92*
Gunn, James Edward 1938- *WhoAm 92*
Gunn, James Edwin 1923- *WhoWrEP 92*
Gunn, John *DcChlFi*
Gunn, John c. 1765-c. 1824 *Baker 92*
Gunn, John 1952- *WhoWor 93*
Gunn, John D. 1941- *St&PR 93*
Gunn, John Michael Ferguson 1954- *WhoWor 93*
Gunn, John Reginald 1943- *WhoAm 92, WhoWor 93*
Gunn, Karen Sue 1951- *WhoAm 92, WhoAmW 93, WhoEmL 93*
Gunn, Kenneth David 1940- *WhoSSW 93*
Gunn, Kenneth T. 1936- *St&PR 93*
Gunn, Larry J. *Law&B 92*
Gunn, Mary Elizabeth 1914- *WhoAmW 93*
Gunn, Michael William 1945- *St&PR 93, WhoAm 92*
Gunn, Morey Walker, Jr. 1939- *WhoSSW 93, WhoWor 93*
Gunn, Moses 1929- *WhoAm 92*
Gunn, Neil M. *BioIn 17*
Gunn, Neil M. 1891-1973 *ScF&FL 92*
Gunn, Robert Burns 1939- *WhoAm 92*
Gunn, Robert Dewey 1928- *WhoAm 92*
Gunn, Robert Murray 1927- *WhoAm 92*
Gunn, Roderick James 1945- *WhoAm 92*
Gunn, Thom *BioIn 17*
Gunn, Thom 1929- *WhoWrEP 92*
Gunn, Thomas Allen, Jr. 1931- *St&PR 93*
Gunn, Thomas Hilton 1940- *WhoSSW 93*
Gunn, Thomas M. *WhoAm 92*
Gunn, Thomson William 1929- *WhoAm 92*
Gunn, Walter Joseph 1935- *WhoSSW 93*
Gunn, Wendell L. 1932- *WhoIns 93*
Gunn, Wendell Lavelle 1932- *St&PR 93, WhoAm 92*
Gunn, William John 1920- *WhoE 93*
Gunn, William T. d1992 *NewYTBS 92 [port]*
Gunnars, Kristjana 1948- *WhoCanL 92*
Gunnarson, John A. 1925- *St&PR 93*
Gunnarsson, Olafur *ScF&FL 92*
Gunnarsson, Sturla 1951- *MiSFD 9*
Gunnarsson, Thorarinn 1957- *ScF&FL 92*
Gunnell, John A. 1947- *WhoWrEP 92*
Gunnell, Kenneth A. 1946- *St&PR 93*
Gunnells, Charlene Marie 1964- *WhoSSW 93*
Gunnels, Lawrence 1931- *St&PR 93*
Gunner, George William, III 1959- *WhoEmL 93*
Gunner, Mary Frances *AmWomPl*
Gunnerod, Tor B. 1940- *WhoScE 91-4*
Gunnerson, Robert M. 1949- *St&PR 93*
Gunnerson, Robert Mark 1949- *WhoAm 92*
Gunness, Robert Charles 1911- *WhoAm 92*
Gunnestedt, Leif Peder 1944- *WhoUN 92*
Gunning, Francis Patrick 1923- *WhoAm 92*
Gunning, Gerald 1932-1991 *BioIn 17*
Gunning, James R. 1933- *St&PR 93*
Gunning, John Thaddeus 1917- *WhoAm 92*
Gunning, Robert Clifford 1931- *WhoAm 92*
Gunnison, Douglas 1944- *WhoAm 92*
Gunnison, Hugh 1929- *WhoE 93*
Gunnlaugsson, Gordon Harvey 1944- *WhoAm 92*
Gunnlaugsson, Hrafn 1948- *MiSFD 9*
Gunnoe, Nancy Lavenia 1921- *WhoAmW 93, WhoSSW 93, WhoWor 93*
Gunsalus, Irwin C. 1912- *WhoAm 92*
Gunsalus Gonzalez, Catherine *ConAu 136*
Gunsbourg, Raoul 1859-1955 *Baker 92, OxDcOp*
Gunset, Joseph P. *Law&B 92*
Gunson, Allister L. *Law&B 92*
Gunsser, Walter 1927- *WhoScE 91-3*
Gunst, Morgan A., Jr. 1918- *St&PR 93*
Gunst, Robert A. 1948- *St&PR 93*
Gunst, Robert Allen 1948- *WhoAm 92*
Gunstone, Frank Denby *WhoScE 91-1*
Gunsul, Brooks R. W. 1928- *WhoAm 92*
Gunter, Bradley Hunt 1940- *WhoSSW 93, WhoWor 93*
Gunter, Cornell d1990 *BioIn 17*
Gunter, Denise Colburn 1955- *WhoAmW 93*
Gunter, Emily Diane 1948- *WhoEmL 93*
Gunter, Frank Delano 1933- *St&PR 93*
Gunter, Frank Elliott 1934- *WhoAm 92*
Gunter, Franklin Delano 1933- *WhoAm 92*
Gunter, Ivy *BioIn 17*
Gunter, Joe T. *Law&B 92*
Gunter, John B. 1919- *St&PR 93*
Gunter, John Brown, Jr. 1919- *WhoAm 92*
Gunter, John David 1947- *WhoE 93*
Gunter, John L. *St&PR 93*
Gunter, John M. *Law&B 92*
Gunter, John Ralph 1943- *WhoScE 91-4*
Gunter, John Richmond 1941- *WhoAm 92*
Gunter, Karen Johnson 1948- *WhoAmW 93, WhoEmL 93*
Gunter, Michael Donwell 1947- *WhoEmL 93, WhoSSW 93*
Gunter, Michael Martin 1943- *WhoSSW 93*
Gunter, Nancy Richey 1942- *BiDAMSp 1989*
Gunter, Pete Addison Yancey, III 1936- *WhoSSW 93*
Gunter, Rickey Van 1944- *WhoSSW 93*
Gunter, Russell Allen 1950- *WhoEmL 93, WhoSSW 93*
Gunter, Wilkin Jacob 1948- *WhoEmL 93, WhoSSW 93*
Gunter, William D., Jr. 1934- *WhoIns 93*
Gunter, William Dawson, Jr. 1934- *WhoAm 92*
Gunter, William Joseph 1942- *St&PR 93*
Guntert, B. *WhoScE 91-4*
Gunther, Conrad J., Jr. 1946- *St&PR 93*
Gunther, Curt *BioIn 17*
Gunther, Egon 1927- *DrEEuF*
Gunther, Elisabeth 1925- *WhoWor 93*
Gunther, Erna 1896-1982 *IntDcAn*
Gunther, Gary A. 1947- *St&PR 93*
Gunther, George Lackman 1919- *WhoE 93*
Gunther, Gerald 1927- *WhoAm 92*
Gunther, Harald *WhoScE 91-3*
Gunther, Herbert Chao 1951- *WhoAm 92*
Gunther, Herbert Otto 1922- *WhoWor 93*
Gunther, Jane Perry 1916- *WhoAm 92*
Gunther, John 1901-1970 *BioIn 17, JrnUS*
Gunther, John A. 1947- *St&PR 93*
Gunther, John David 1944- *WhoUN 92*
Gunther, John E. *Law&B 92*
Gunther, John M. *Law&B 92*
Gunther, Karl Michael 1952- *WhoEmL 93, WhoSSW 93*
Gunther, Klaus-Dietrich 1926- *WhoScE 91-3*
Gunther, Leon 1939- *WhoAm 92*
Gunther, Marc 1951- *WhoAm 92*
Gunther, Marian Waclaw Jan 1923- *WhoWor 93*
Gunther, Max 1927- *ScF&FL 92*
Gunther, Michael John 1949- *WhoE 93*
Gunther, Robert 1922- *WhoScE 91-4*
Gunther, Robert Alan *Law&B 92*
Gunther, Rolf W. 1943- *WhoScE 91-3*
Gunther, William David 1940- *WhoSSW 93*
Gunther of Pairis c. 1150-c. 1208 *OxDcByz*

Guntheroth, Warren Gaden 1927- *WhoAm 92*
Gunton, James Douglas 1937- *WhoE 93*
Gunton, Thomas E. *Law&B 92*
Guntow, James 1942- *St&PR 93*
Guntrum, Suzanne Simmons 1946- *WhoWrEP 92*
Guntsch, Fritz-Rudolf 1925- *WhoScE 91-3*
Gunzberg, Guy Walter 1940- *St&PR 93*
Gunzburger, Gerard J. 1931- *St&PR 93*
Gunzenhauser, Gerard Ralph, Jr. 1936- *WhoAm 92*
Gunzenhauser, Keith 1933- *St&PR 93*
Gunzenhauser, Rul 1933- *WhoScE 91-3*
Gunzenhauser, Stephen Charles 1942- *WhoAm 92*
Gunzl, Leopold 1926- *WhoScE 91-4*
Guo, Di 1911- *WhoWor 93*
Guo, Guo-Qiang 1963- *WhoWor 93*
Guo, Xin Kang 1938- *WhoWor 93*
Guo, Yu Qi 1940- *WhoWor 93*
Guo Chaoren 1934- *WhoAsAP 91*
Guohui, Zhang 1932- *WhoWor 93*
Guokas, Matt 1944- *WhoAm 92*
Guokas, Matthew George, Jr. 1944- *WhoSSW 93*
Guon, Ellen 1964- *ScF&FL 92*
Guo Zhenqian 1931- *WhoAsAP 91*
Gup, Benton Eugene 1936- *WhoAm 92, WhoSSW 93*
Gup, Nancy Jane 1961- *WhoSSW 93*
Gupit, Fortunato Icasiano 1936- *WhoWor 93*
Guppy, Stephen 1951- *WhoCanL 92*
Gupta, Anil Kumar 1949- *WhoE 93, WhoEmL 93*
Gupta, Ashwani Kumar 1948- *WhoAm 92, WhoEmL 93*
Gupta, Bhagwandas 1946- *WhoEmL 93*
Gupta, Brij Lal *WhoScE 91-1*
Gupta, Chandra 1954- *St&PR 93*
Gupta, Derek 1928- *WhoScE 91-3*
Gupta, Girish Chandra 1941- *WhoE 93*
Gupta, Gopal Krishna 1942- *WhoWor 93*
Gupta, Indra Jit 1919- *WhoAsAP 91*
Gupta, Krishna Chandra 1948- *WhoAm 92*
Gupta, Kuldip Chand 1940- *WhoAm 92, WhoWor 93*
Gupta, Linda Ayscue 1949- *WhoSSW 93*
Gupta, Madan Mohan 1936- *WhoAm 92*
Gupta, Madhu Sudan 1945- *WhoAm 92*
Gupta, Nirmal Kumar 1934- *WhoWor 93*
Gupta, Prafulla Chandra 1944- *St&PR 93*
Gupta, Rajendra 1943- *WhoSSW 93*
Gupta, Rajiv Lochan 1945- *WhoWor 93*
Gupta, Ram Swaroop 1940- *WhoE 93*
Gupta, Ramesh Kumar 1953- *WhoE 93*
Gupta, Ravi Chandra 1956- *WhoE 93*
Gupta, Satish Kumar 1943- *WhoScE 91-4*
Gupta, Shiv K(umar) 1930- *ConAu 37NR*
Gupta, Subhash Chandra 1941- *WhoE 93*
Gupta, Sunetra 1965- *ConAu 137*
Gupta, Suraj Narayan 1924- *WhoAm 92, WhoWor 93*
Gupta, Surendra Kumar 1938- *WhoAm 92*
Gupta, Venu Gopal 1934- *WhoE 93*
Gupta, Vijay Kumar 1941- *WhoAm 92*
Gupta, Vinod *St&PR 93*
Gupta, Vinod 1946- *WhoAm 92*
Gupta, Virendra Kumar 1941- *St&PR 93*
Gupta, Vishwa Bandhu 1927- *WhoAsAP 91*
Gupte, Subhash 1939- *WhoWor 93*
Guptill, Elizabeth Frances Ephraim 1870- *AmWomPl*
Guptill, Paul *ScF&FL 92*
Gupton, John Thomas, III 1946- *WhoSSW 93*
Gur, Adnan 1938- *WhoUN 92*
Gura, David Alexander 1957- *WhoSSW 93*
Gura, Eugen 1842-1906 *Baker 92, OxDcOp*
Gura, Hermann 1870-1944 *Baker 92, OxDcOp*
Gurak, Kathleen Theresa 1943- *WhoAmW 93*
Guralnick, Sidney Aaron 1929- *WhoAm 92*
Guran, Marius 1936- *WhoWor 93*
Gurash, John Thomas 1910- *St&PR 93, WhoAm 92*
Gurbuz, Ahmet 1943- *WhoScE 91-4*
Gurcay, Ali Aydemir 1928- *WhoScE 91-4*
Gurd, John Richard *WhoScE 91-1*
Gurd, Robert Preston 1949- *WhoWor 93*
Gurdal, Zafer 1956- *WhoSSW 93*
Gurdjian, Pierre Louis 1961- *WhoWor 93*
Gurdjieff, Georges Ivanovitch 1872-1949 *BioIn 17*
Gurdon, John *WhoScE 91-1*
Gurdon, Madeleine *BioIn 17*
Gureckas, Algimantas Petras 1923- *WhoUN 92*
Gurecky, Marcia *Law&B 92*
Guren, Sheldon B. 1924- *St&PR 93*
Gurevich, David *BioIn 17*
Gurevich, Linda Schiller *Law&B 92*
Gurevitch, Arnold William 1936- *WhoAm 92*
Gurevitz, Mark Stuart *Law&B 92*
Gurewich, Marinka d1990 *BioIn 17*
Gurewitz, Barton I. 1941- *St&PR 93*
Gurfein, Pamela Linda *Law&B 92*
Gurfein, Richard Alan 1946- *WhoEmL 93*
Gurfein, Stuart James 1947- *WhoAm 92, WhoE 93*
Gurfel, Benor 1932- *WhoE 93*
Gurganus, Allan *BioIn 17*
Gurganus, Allan 1947- *ConGAN, ConLC 70 [port]*
Gurgen, Baydar 1937- *WhoUN 92*
Gurgen, Emily *AmWomPl*
Gurgin, Vonnie Ann 1940- *WhoAm 92*
Gurgulino de Souza, Heitor 1928- *WhoUN 92*
Gurian, Mal 1926- *WhoAm 92, WhoE 93, WhoWor 93*
Gurian, Stanley 1930- *St&PR 93*
Guridi (Bidaola), Jesus 1886-1961 *Baker 92*
Guridi, Jesus 1886-1961 *OxDcOp*
Guridi y Alcocer, Jose Miguel 1763-1828 *DcMexL*
Gurik, Robert 1932- *WhoCanL 92*
Gurin, Arnold 1917-1991 *BioIn 17*
Gurin, Cheryl Bernstein 1957- *WhoAmW 93*
Gurin, Jane Roberta 1953- *WhoSSW 93*
Gurin, Maurice G. d1990 *BioIn 17*
Gurin, Meg *WhoAm 92*
Gurin, Richard S. 1940- *St&PR 93*
Gurin, Richard Stephen 1940- *WhoAm 92*
Gurin, Timothy Benjamin *Law&B 92*
Gurion, David Ben- 1886-1973 *BioIn 17*
Gurion, Henry 1950- *St&PR 93*
Gurion, Henry B. *Law&B 92*
Gurirab, Joan *BioIn 17*
Gurirab, Theo Ben *WhoAfr*
Gurirab, Theo-Ben 1938- *WhoWor 93*
Guritz, G. Robert *Law&B 92*
Gurka, Allen S. 1939- *St&PR 93*
Gurkan, Elcin 1939- *WhoScE 91-4*
Gurkan, Turker 1948- *WhoScE 91-4*
Gurke, Sharon McCue 1949- *WhoAmW 93, WhoSSW 93, WhoWor 93*
Gurkewitz, Rona Norma *WhoAmW 93*
Gurkin, Kathryn Bright 1934- *WhoWrEP 92*
Gurkoff, Jon Buch 1951- *St&PR 93*
Gurland, Doris Fanette 1924- *WhoE 93*
Gurland, Joseph 1923- *WhoAm 92*
Gurley, Anthony J. 1945- *St&PR 93*
Gurley, Clair E. 1907- *St&PR 93*
Gurley, Elisabeth Anne 1927- *WhoWor 93*
Gurley, Franklin Louis 1925- *WhoAm 92, WhoWor 93*
Gurley, George *BioIn 17*
Gurley, Geraldine Marie 1947- *WhoAmW 93*
Gurley, James A. 1933- *St&PR 93*
Gurley, Karen Anne 1967- *WhoAmW 93*
Gurley, Margot Carmichael Lester 1962- *WhoSSW 93*
Gurley, Steven Harrison 1957- *WhoEmL 93, WhoSSW 93*
Gurlitt, Cornelius 1820-1901 *Baker 92*
Gurlitt, Manfred 1890-1972 *Baker 92*
Gurlitt, Manfred 1890-1973 *OxDcOp*
Gurlitt, Wilibald 1889-1963 *Baker 92*
Gurman, Ernest Basil 1933- *WhoSSW 93*
Gurman, Ina Ruth 1944- *WhoE 93*
Gurmankin, Alan E. 1935- *St&PR 93*
Gurne, Patricia Dorothy 1941- *WhoAmW 93*
Gurnee, Hal 1935- *WhoAm 92*
Gurnee, Janice Fenley 1948- *WhoAmW 93*
Gurnee, Steven Hazard 1949- *WhoEmL 93*
Gurnee, W.H. *Law&B 92*
Gurnett, Donald Alfred 1940- *WhoAm 92*
Gurney, A.R. 1930- *BioIn 17*
Gurney, Albert Ramsdell 1930- *BioIn 17, WhoAm 92, WhoE 93*
Gurney, Albert Ramsdell, Jr 1930- *WhoWrEP 92*
Gurney, Brian Jeffrey 1949- *WhoEmL 93*
Gurney, Daniel Sexton 1931- *WhoAm 92*
Gurney, David *ScF&FL 92*
Gurney, Elizabeth Tucker Guice 1941- *WhoAmW 93*
Gurney, Gene *BioIn 17*
Gurney, Ivor (Bertie) 1890-1937 *Baker 92*
Gurney, James Thomas 1901- *WhoAm 92, WhoWor 93*
Gurney, John Michael 1933- *WhoUN 92*
Gurney, John Steven 1962- *WhoE 93*
Gurney, Mary Kathleen 1964- *WhoAmW 93*
Gurney, Patricia Louise 1957- *WhoAmW 93*
Gurney, Patrick Joseph 1952- *WhoSSW 93*
Gurney, Susan Lee 1958- *WhoEmL 93*
Gurnham, Robert F. 1951- *St&PR 93*
Gurnitz, Robert N. 1938- *St&PR 93*
Gurnitz, Robert Ned 1938- *WhoAm 92*
Gurnsey, Kathleen Wallace *WhoAmW 93*
Gurov, Prokopii Ivanovich 1890-1958 *BioIn 17*
Gurowski, Adam 1805-1866 *PolBiDi*
Gurpinar, Aybars 1944- *WhoUN 92*
Gurr, David 1936- *WhoCanL 92*
Gurr, Ted Robert 1936- *WhoAm 92*
Gurry, Francis Gerard 1951- *WhoUN 92*
Gurs, Karl A. 1927- *WhoScE 91-3*
Gursey, Feza 1921-1992 *BioIn 17*
Gursky, Alvin 1919- *St&PR 93*
Gursky, Deborah Ann 1966- *WhoAmW 93*
Gursky, Herbert 1930- *WhoAm 92*
Gursky, Mary Patricia 1960- *WhoE 93*
Gurstel, Norman Keith 1939- *WhoWor 93*
Gurtin, Morton Edward 1934- *WhoAm 92*
Gurtler, Oswald 1928- *WhoScE 91-3*
Gurtler, Peter *BioIn 17*
Guru, Narayana 1856-1928 *BioIn 17*
Gurule, Jimmy 20th cent.- *HispAmA*
Gurule, Jimmy 1951- *WhoAm 92*
Guru Ma *BioIn 17*
Gurung, T.S. 1923- *WhoAsAP 91*
Gurung, Vishnu Maya *BioIn 17*
Gurupadaswamy, Malangi Shivalingadevaru 1923- *WhoAsAP 91*
Gurvich, Alexander Marcovich 1925- *WhoWor 93*
Gurvich, Vladimir Alexander 1952- *WhoWor 93*
Gurvis, Sandra Jane 1951- *WhoWrEP 92*
Gurvitch, Helen W. 1924- *WhoE 93*
Gurvitz, Milton Solomon 1919- *WhoAm 92*
Gurwitch, Arnold Andrew 1925- *WhoAm 92*
Gury, David J. 1938- *St&PR 93*
Gury, Jeremy 1913- *WhoAm 92, WhoWrEP 92*
Gus, Walter R. 1945- *St&PR 93*
Gusberg, Saul Bernard 1913- *WhoAm 92*
Guschlbauer, Theodor 1939- *Baker 92*
Guschlbauer, Wilhelm Theodor 1932- *WhoWor 93*
Guscott, Kenneth Irvin 1925- *St&PR 93*
Gusdon, John Paul, Jr. 1931- *WhoSSW 93, WhoWor 93*
Guse, Carl Edward 1929- *St&PR 93*
Gusenleitner, Josef *WhoScE 91-4*
Gusewelle, C.W. 1933- *WhoWrEP 92*
Gusewelle, Charles Wesley 1933- *WhoAm 92*
Gushard, Keith Lee 1958- *WhoE 93*
Gushchin, Boris Petrovich 1874-1936? *BioIn 17*
Gushee, Allison Taylor 1962- *WhoAmW 93, WhoEmL 93*
Gushee, Charles H. 1903- *St&PR 93*
Gushman, John Louis 1912- *WhoAm 92*
Gu Shunzhang 1902?- *BioIn 17*
Gusikoff, Michel 1893-1978 *Baker 92*
Guske, Lawrence Arthur 1944- *St&PR 93*
Guskey, Thomas Robert 1950- *WhoSSW 93*
Guskin, Alan E. 1937- *WhoAm 92*
Gusman, Patrick Mark *Law&B 92*
Gusman, Rico *ScF&FL 92*
Gusman, Robert C. *Law&B 92*
Gusmao, Renato d'Affonseca 1950- *WhoUN 92*
Gusmer, John H. 1932- *St&PR 93*
Gusmer, William E. 1934- *St&PR 93*
Gusmorino, Paul 1948- *WhoEmL 93*
Gusner, Iris 1941- *DrEEuF*
Gusoff, Patricia Kearney 1951- *WhoE 93*
Gusrae, Wendy Carol 1952- *St&PR 93*
Guss, Mitchell F. *Law&B 92*
Gussack, Allan J. d1992 *NewYTBS 92*
Gussak, Elizabeth Emmons 1919- *WhoAmW 93*
Gussakovsky, Apollon 1841-1875 *Baker 92*
Gussenhoven, John W. 1946- *St&PR 93*
Gussin, Robert Zalmon 1938- *WhoAm 92*
Gussoni, Gerald O., Jr. *Law&B 92*
Gussow, Alan 1931- *WhoAm 92*
Gussow, Don *BioIn 17*
Gussow, Don d1992 *NewYTBS 92*
Gussow, Don 1907-1992 *ConAu 136*
Gussow, John Andrew 1946- *WhoE 93*
Gussow, Mel 1933- *WhoAm 92*
Gussow, Michelle Denise 1963- *WhoEmL 93*
Gussow, William Carruthers 1908- *WhoAm 92*
Gust, Alfred C. 1932- *St&PR 93*
Gust, Anne Baldwin *Law&B 92*
Gust, Gerald Norman 1946- *WhoEmL 93*
Gust, LeRoy Charles 1941- *St&PR 93*
Gust, Lysle A. 1931- *St&PR 93*
Gustaf, III, King of Sweden 1746-1792 *BioIn 17*
Gustaf Adolf, II, King of Sweden 1594-1632 *BioIn 17*
Gustafson, Albert Katsuaki 1949- *WhoEmL 93, WhoWor 93*
Gustafson, Barbara A. *Law&B 92*
Gustafson, Barbara Ann Helton 1948- *WhoAmW 93*
Gustafson, C. Donald 1930- *St&PR 93*
Gustafson, C. Gunnar 1945- *WhoScE 91-4*
Gustafson, Charles B. *Law&B 92*
Gustafson, Claes-Goran *WhoScE 91-4*
Gustafson, Clifford 1931- *WhoAm 92*
Gustafson, Clifford Lincoln 1931- *BiDAMSp 1989*
Gustafson, Deborah Lee 1948- *WhoEmL 93*
Gustafson, Frances Decker 1928- *WhoSSW 93*
Gustafson, Frances Goodwin 1917- *St&PR 93*
Gustafson, Gayle Lee 1959- *WhoE 93*
Gustafson, Glendon Davis 1938- *St&PR 93*
Gustafson, James E. 1946- *WhoIns 93*
Gustafson, James M(oody) 1925- *ConAu 37NR*
Gustafson, John Alfred 1925- *WhoAm 92*
Gustafson, Jon 1945- *ScF&FL 92*
Gustafson, Karl Erik 1950- *St&PR 93*
Gustafson, Nancy 1956- *OxDcOp*
Gustafson, Norman C. 1938- *St&PR 93*
Gustafson, Pamela Weber 1961- *WhoAmW 93*
Gustafson, Paula 1941- *WhoWrEP 92*
Gustafson, Philip Edward 1916- *St&PR 93*
Gustafson, Ralph 1909- *WhoCanL 92*
Gustafson, Ralph Barker 1909- *WhoAm 92, WhoWrEP 92*
Gustafson, Randall Lee 1947- *WhoEmL 93, WhoWor 93*
Gustafson, Rebecca Susanne 1962- *WhoAmW 93*
Gustafson, Richard Alrick 1941- *WhoAm 92*
Gustafson, Richard Charles 1942- *WhoAm 92*
Gustafson, Richard Paul 1957- *WhoEmL 93, WhoWor 93*
Gustafson, Robert L. *St&PR 93*
Gustafson, Sandra Lynne 1948- *WhoAmW 93*
Gustafson, Smith *ScF&FL 92*
Gustafson, Steven R. *Law&B 92*
Gustafson, Victoria *ScF&FL 92*
Gustafson, William Robert 1943- *St&PR 93*
Gustafson, Winthrop Adolph 1928- *WhoAm 92*
Gustafsson, Bengt Harald *WhoWor 93*
Gustafsson, Bengt S.H. 1930- *WhoScE 91-4*
Gustafsson, Bertil 1939- *WhoScE 91-4*
Gustafsson, Borje Karl 1930- *WhoAm 92*
Gustafsson, Georg 1932- *WhoScE 91-4*
Gustafsson, Gosta 1951- *WhoScE 91-4*
Gustafsson, Hakan Vilhelm 1961- *WhoWor 93*
Gustafsson, Jan-Ake 1943- *WhoScE 91-4*
Gustafsson, Kersti *WhoScE 91-4*
Gustafsson, Lars 1936- *BioIn 17*
Gustafsson, Lars B. 1927- *WhoScE 91-4*
Gustafsson, Lars Erik Einar 1936- *WhoAm 92, WhoSSW 93, WhoWor 93*
Gustav, Karl *WhoWrEP 92*
Gustavson, Carl Gustav 1915- *WhoAm 92*
Gustavson, Dean Leonard 1924- *WhoAm 92*
Gustavson, Erik *MiSFD 9*
Gustavson, Henry Bradford 1954- *WhoE 93*
Gustavson, Joan Ellen Carlson 1947- *WhoAmW 93, WhoEmL 93*
Gustavson, Mark Steven 1951- *WhoEmL 93*
Gustavus Adolphus 1594-1632 *BioIn 17, HarEnMi*
Guste, Roy Francis, Jr. 1951- *WhoWrEP 92*
Guste, William Joseph, Jr. 1922- *WhoSSW 93*
Guster, Timothy Staten *Law&B 92*
Gusterson, Barry Austin *WhoScE 91-1*
Gustin, Ann Winifred 1941- *WhoAmW 93*
Gustin, David *BioIn 17*
Gustin, James Frederick *Law&B 92*
Gustin, Lawrence Robert 1937- *ConAu 37NR*
Gustin, William Arnett 1960- *WhoE 93*
Gustina, Charles Francis 1957- *WhoE 93*
Gustine, Frank 1920-1991 *BioIn 17*
Gustlin, Philip Raymond 1934- *WhoAm 92*
Gustman, Alan Leslie 1944- *WhoAm 92*
Guston, David H. 1965- *WhoWrEP 92*
Guston, Musa McKim 1908-1992 *BioIn 17, NewYTBS 92*
Guston, Sheila E. 1936- *WhoE 93*
Gustowska, Leokadia 1940- *WhoWor 93*
Gustus, Rudolph Conway 1933- *WhoAm 92*
Gut, Rainer E. 1932- *St&PR 93*

Gutang, Rodrigo B. 1933- *WhoAsAP 91*
Gutberlet, Phyllis Joanne 1958- *WhoAmW 93*
Gutche, Gene 1907- *Baker 92, WhoAm 92, WhoWor 93*
Gutek, Gerald L(ee) 1935- *ConAu 40NR*
Gutek, Gerald Lee 1935- *WhoAm 92*
Gutekanst, William P. *St&PR 93*
Gutekunst, Richard Ralph 1926- *WhoAm 92, WhoSSW 93*
Gutelius, Edward Warner 1922- *WhoSSW 93*
Gutenbaum, Jakub 1929- *WhoScE 91-4*
Gutenberg, Johann 1397?-1468 *BioIn 17*
Gutenkunst, Richard Laacke 1933- *St&PR 93*
Gutenstein, Robert G. 1933- *St&PR 93*
Guterding, William F. 1952- *WhoIns 93*
Gutermann, Peter A. *Law&B 92*
Gutermann, Thomas 1937- *WhoScE 91-4*
Gutermuth, Paul-Georg 1935- *WhoScE 91-3*
Gutfeld, Norman E. 1911- *WhoAm 92*
Gutfreund, John *BioIn 17*
Gutfreund, John H. 1929- *WhoAm 92*
Gutfreund, Susan *BioIn 17*
Guth, Alan Harvey 1947- *WhoAm 92*
Guth, Beth Ann 1958- *WhoAmW 93*
Guth, Eugene 1905-1990 *BioIn 17*
Guth, Gary Robert 1944- *WhoAm 92*
Guth, Marshall C. 1955- *St&PR 93*
Guth, Paul C. 1922- *WhoAm 92*
Guth, Paul David 1932- *WhoAm 92*
Guth, Robert 1929- *St&PR 93*
Guth, Sherman Leon 1932- *WhoAm 92*
Guthans, Robert Anthony 1929- *St&PR 93*
Guthart, Leo 1937- *St&PR 93*
Gutheil, John Gordon 1944- *WhoAm 92*
Gutheil-Schoder, Marie 1874-1935 *Baker 92, OxDcOp*
Gutheim, Allen Herman 1945- *WhoWor 93*
Gutheim, Frederick 1908- *WhoAm 92*
Gutheim, Frederick Albert 1908- *BioIn 17*
Gutheim, Robert Julius 1911- *WhoAm 92*
Gutherie, Melvin Charles, III 1959- *St&PR 93*
Gutherie, William Thomas 1963- *St&PR 93*
Guthke, Karl S. 1933- *ScF&FL 92*
Guthke, Karl S(iegfried) 1933- *ConAu 37NR*
Guthke, Karl Siegfried 1933- *WhoAm 92, WhoWor 93*
Guthman, Jack 1938- *WhoAm 92*
Guthman, William H(arold) 1924- *ConAu 37NR*
Guthmann, Louis B., Jr. 1923- *St&PR 93*
Guthorn, Amanda May 1961- *WhoAmW 93*
Guthridge, George 1948- *ScF&FL 92*
Guthrie, A.B. 1901-1991 *BioIn 17*
Guthrie, A.B., Jr. 1901-1991 *AnObit 1991*
Guthrie, Alfred Bertram 1901-1991 *BioIn 17*
Guthrie, Alfred Bertram, Jr. 1901-1991 *ConLC 70*
Guthrie, Arlo 1947- *See* Guthrie, Woody 1912-1967 *Baker 92*
Guthrie, Bill M. 1933- *St&PR 93*
Guthrie, Bill Myers 1933- *WhoAm 92*
Guthrie, Brian T. *Law&B 92*
Guthrie, Catherine S. Nicholson *WhoAm 92*
Guthrie, Diana Fern 1934- *WhoAmW 93*
Guthrie, Donna 1946- *BioIn 17*
Guthrie, Edward A. 1944- *St&PR 93*
Guthrie, Edward Everett 1941- *WhoAm 92*
Guthrie, Eleanor Y. 1915- *St&PR 93*
Guthrie, Francis J., Jr. 1937- *St&PR 93*
Guthrie, Frank Albert 1927- *WhoAm 92*
Guthrie, George Ralph 1928- *WhoAm 92, WhoSSW 93, WhoWor 93*
Guthrie, Gerald Ray 1934- *St&PR 93*
Guthrie, Gloria Jean 1941- *WhoAmW 93*
Guthrie, Harvey Henry, Jr. 1924- *WhoAm 92*
Guthrie, Helen A. 1925- *WhoAm 92, WhoAmW 93*
Guthrie, Hugh Delmar 1919- *WhoWor 93*
Guthrie, James Russell 1940- *WhoE 93*
Guthrie, James Williams 1936- *WhoAm 92*
Guthrie, Janet 1938- *BioIn 17, WhoAm 92*
Guthrie, Jeffrey Allen *Law&B 92*
Guthrie, John Craver 1946- *WhoSSW 93*
Guthrie, John F., Jr. 1943- *St&PR 93*
Guthrie, John Francis 1957- *WhoE 93*
Guthrie, John Gilkeson 1936- *St&PR 93*
Guthrie, John Reiley 1921- *WhoAm 92*
Guthrie, John Robert 1942- *WhoSSW 93*
Guthrie, Judith K. 1948- *WhoAmW 93*
Guthrie, Mearl Raymond, Jr. 1922- *WhoAm 92*
Guthrie, Pamela *BioIn 17*
Guthrie, Patricia Sue 1958- *WhoAm 92*
Guthrie, Paul A. *Law&B 92*
Guthrie, Randolph Hobson, Jr. 1934- *WhoAm 92*
Guthrie, Ray 1934- *St&PR 93*
Guthrie, Richard Alan 1935- *WhoAm 92*
Guthrie, Richard Y. 1944- *St&PR 93*
Guthrie, Robert Val 1930- *WhoAm 92*
Guthrie, Roy A. 1953- *St&PR 93*
Guthrie, Sally Record 1929- *WhoWrEP 92*
Guthrie, Theron A., Jr. *Law&B 92*
Guthrie, Thomas Lee 1928- *St&PR 93*
Guthrie, Tyrone 1900-1971 *BioIn 17, IntDcOp, OxDcOp*
Guthrie, Wallace Nessler, Jr. 1939- *WhoAm 92*
Guthrie, Wayne E. 1919- *St&PR 93*
Guthrie, William *BioIn 17*
Guthrie, William David 1935- *WhoE 93*
Guthrie, Woody 1912-1967 *Baker 92, BioIn 17*
Gutierrez, Adolfo Osvaldo 1959- *WhoE 93*
Gutierrez, Ana Sol 20th cent.- *HispAmA*
Gutierrez, Ana Sol 1942- *NotHsAW 93*
Gutierrez, Carlos M. 1953- *St&PR 93*
Gutierrez, Claudio 1942- *WhoScE 91-3, WhoWor 93*
Gutierrez, Eduardo Francisco 1942- *WhoUN 92*
Gutierrez, Elia Garza 1932- *WhoAmW 93*
Gutierrez, Gerald Andrew 1952- *WhoEmL 93*
Gutierrez, Gonzalo c. 1540-1605 *Baker 92*
Gutierrez, Guillermo Tirona 1924- *WhoWor 93*
Gutierrez, Gustavo *DcCPCAm*
Gutierrez, Horacio 1948- *Baker 92*
Gutierrez, Horacio Tomas 1948- *WhoWor 93*
Gutierrez, Juan Francisco, Jr. 1947- *WhoEmL 93*
Gutierrez, Manuel 1923- *WhoScE 91-3*
Gutierrez, Mario Tirona 1928- *WhoWor 93*
Gutierrez, Max, Jr. 1930- *WhoAm 92, WhoWor 93*
Gutierrez, Nancy C. 1941- *NotHsAW 93*
Gutierrez, Pamela Jean Holbrook 1956- *WhoWor 93*
Gutierrez, Peter Luis 1939- *WhoE 93*
Gutierrez, Ramon 1951- *HispAmA*
Gutierrez, Ramon Arturo 1957- *WhoAm 92*
Gutierrez Alea, Tomas 1928- *MiSFD 9*
Gutierrez Aragon, Manuel 1942- *MiSFD 9*
Gutierrez de Mendoza, Juana Belen 1880-1942 *BioIn 17*
Gutierrez Freyberg, Eduardo 1940- *WhoWor 93*
Gutierrez Heras, Joaquin 1927- *Baker 92*
Gutierrez Hermosillo, Alfonso 1905-1935 *DcMexL*
Gutierrez-Jodra, Luis 1922- *WhoScE 91-3*
Gutierrez-Leyton, Hernan 1927- *WhoUN 92*
Gutierrez-Najera, Manuel 1859-1895 *DcMexL*
Gutierrez-Santos, Luis Emiliano 1945- *WhoAm 92*
Gutin, Irving *Law&B 92*
Gutin, Irving 1932- *St&PR 93*
Gutin, Myra Gail 1948- *WhoAmW 93*
Gutjahr, H.C. 1930- *St&PR 93*
Gutkiewicz, Piotr 1951- *WhoScE 91-4*
Gutknecht, James Evan 1950- *St&PR 93*
Gutknecht, Marianne Sciabica 1960- *WhoAmW 93*
Gutkowski, Witold 1928- *WhoScE 91-4*
Gutlich, Philipp 1934- *WhoScE 91-3*
Gutman, Alfred Elihu 1916- *St&PR 93*
Gutman, Amos *MiSFD 9*
Gutman, Bill *BioIn 17*
Gutman, Bobbi *BioIn 17*
Gutman, D. Milton 1933- *WhoWor 93*
Gutman, Harry Largman 1942- *WhoAm 92*
Gutman, I. Cyrus 1912- *WhoAm 92, WhoE 93, WhoWor 93*
Gutman, Ivan 1947- *WhoScE 91-4*
Gutman, John d1992 *NewYTBS 92*
Gutman, Lucy Toni 1936- *WhoSSW 93*
Gutman, Madeleine Feldman d1992 *BioIn 17, NewYTBS 92*
Gutman, Mindi S. 1958- *St&PR 93*
Gutman, Nathaniel *MiSFD 9*
Gutman, Richard E. *Law&B 92*
Gutman, Richard Edward 1944- *WhoSSW 93*
Gutman, Richard Martin 1946- *WhoWor 93*
Gutman, Robert William 1925- *WhoAm 92*
Gutman, Semion 1950- *WhoEmL 93, WhoSSW 93*
Gutman, Stanley E. *Law&B 92*
Gutman, Steven *Law&B 92*
Gutmann, Adolph 1819-1882 *Baker 92*
Gutmann, Barbara S. *Law&B 92*
Gutmann, Bessie Pease 1876-1960 *SmATA 73 [port]*
Gutmann, David Leo 1925- *WhoAm 92*
Gutmann, Joseph 1923- *ConAu 37NR, WhoAm 92*
Gutmann, Leonard M. 1930- *St&PR 93*
Gutmann, Reinhart Bruno 1916- *WhoAm 92*
Gutmann, Ronald J. 1940- *WhoAm 92*
Gutmann, Viktor 1921- *WhoScE 91-4*
Gutmann, William C. 1927- *St&PR 93*
Gutmanski, Izydor 1930- *WhoScE 91-4*
Gutowicz, Matthew Francis, Jr. 1945- *WhoWor 93*
Gutowitz, Samuel 1904-1991 *BioIn 17*
Gutowski, Armin (Ferdinand) 1930-1987 *ConAu 136*
Gutowski, Roman Wojciech 1926- *WhoScE 91-4*
Gutowsky, H. S. 1919- *WhoAm 92*
Gutrath, Gordon C. 1937- *St&PR 93*
Gutridge, Thomas Ray, Jr. 1943- *WhoSSW 93*
Guts, Alexander Konstantinovich 1947- *WhoWor 93*
Gutsch, William Anthony, Jr. 1946- *WhoAm 92, WhoE 93*
Gutsche, Carl David 1921- *WhoAm 92, WhoSSW 93*
Gutsche, Romeo Maximilian Eugene Ludwig *Baker 92*
Gutsche, Steven Lyle 1946- *WhoAm 92*
Gutshall, Arthur Robert 1948- *St&PR 93*
Gutshall, Frederick Raym 1946- *WhoEmL 93*
Gutshall, Priscilla Jean 1944- *WhoAmW 93*
Gutshall, Richard Brice, Jr. 1938- *WhoAm 92*
Gutstein, Debra Lee 1954- *WhoAmW 93*
Gutt, Daniel Z. 1948- *St&PR 93*
Guttag, E.W. *Law&B 92*
Guttay, Andrew John Robert 1924- *WhoAm 92*
Guttenberg, Albert Ziskind 1921- *WhoAm 92*
Guttenberg, Elyse 1952- *ScF&FL 92*
Guttenberg, Steve *BioIn 17*
Guttenberg, Steve 1958- *HolBB [port], QDrFCA 92 [port], WhoAm 92*
Guttenplan, Harold E. 1924- *St&PR 93*
Guttenplan, Harold Esau 1924- *WhoAm 92*
Guttentag, Gilbert 1940- *St&PR 93*
Guttentag, Joseph Harris 1929- *WhoAm 92*
Gutter, Robert Harold 1938- *WhoAm 92, WhoSSW 93*
Gutteridge, Colin Stuart 1954- *WhoScE 91-1*
Gutteridge, Don 1937- *WhoCanL 92*
Gutteridge, Lindsay 1923- *ScF&FL 92*
Gutterman, Bernard 1926- *St&PR 93*
Gutterman, Gerald S. 1929- *St&PR 93*
Gutterman, Marvin 1922- *St&PR 93*
Gutterman, Scott 1958- *St&PR 93*
Gutterman-Reinfeld, Debra Ellen 1948- *WhoAmW 93*
Gutterson, Gerald 1930- *St&PR 93*
Gutterson, Janet Miriam 1939- *WhoAmW 93*
Guttfreund, Andre *MiSFD 9*
Guttierrez Martinez, Salvador Jesus 1951- *WhoWor 93*
Gutting, Gary (Michael) 1942- *ConAu 37NR, WhoAm 92*
Guttler, Ludwig 1943- *Baker 92*
Guttman, Alan J. *Law&B 92*
Guttman, Charles Martin 1939- *WhoE 93*
Guttman, Dena Ann 1934- *WhoWrEP 92*
Guttman, Egon 1927- *WhoAm 92*
Guttman, Gilda Rae 1951- *WhoE 93, WhoWor 93*
Guttman, Helene Nathan 1930- *WhoAm 92, WhoAmW 93, WhoE 93*
Guttman, Irving Allen 1928- *WhoAm 92*
Guttman, Louis 1916-1987 *BioIn 17*
Guttman, Richard T. *Law&B 92*
Guttman, Robert S. *Law&B 92*
Guttman, Ronald E. *Law&B 92*
Guttman, Steven J. 1946- *St&PR 93*
Guttmann, Allen 1932- *ConAu 39NR*
Guttmann, H. Peter 1919- *St&PR 93*
Guttmann, Martin *BioIn 17*
Guttmann, Simon 1892-1990 *BioIn 17*
Guttormsen, Magne Sveen 1950- *WhoWor 93*
Guttosch, Thomas James 1950- *St&PR 93*
Guttowa, Alicja 1924- *WhoScE 91-4*
Guttshall, Russell Moyer, III *Law&B 92*
Gutzeit, Fred Ernst 1940- *WhoE 93*
Gutzke, Karl Norbert 1933- *WhoSSW 93*
Gutzmer, Peter E. *Law&B 92*
Gutzwiller, Felix 1948- *WhoScE 91-4*
Gutzwiller, Frank William 1926- *WhoAm 92*
Gu Xiulian 1936- *WhoAsAP 91*
Guy, Arthur William 1928- *WhoAm 92*
Guy, Barbara Buxton 1957- *WhoSSW 93*
Guy, Bernard 1952- *WhoScE 91-2*
Guy, Bruce Michael 1949- *WhoE 93*
Guy, Buddy *BioIn 17*
Guy, Buddy 1936- *WhoAm 92*
Guy, C.W. 1948- *St&PR 93*
Guy, Carol Ann 1943- *WhoWrEP 92*
Guy, Clarence Caldwell 1932- *St&PR 93*
Guy, Donald Russell 1945- *St&PR 93*
Guy, Eleanor Bryenton 1930- *WhoAmW 93*
Guy, Jasmine *BioIn 17, WhoAm 92*
Guy, John M. 1929- *St&PR 93*
Guy, Kirk Nelson *Law&B 92*
Guy, Leona Ruth 1913- *WhoAmW 93, WhoSSW 93*
Guy, Louis L., Jr. 1938- *St&PR 93*
Guy, M. Russell *Law&B 92*
Guy, Mary E. 1947- *ConAu 138*
Guy, Matthew Joel 1945- *WhoWor 93*
Guy, Michel 1927-1990 *BioIn 17*
Guy, Ralph B., Jr. 1929- *WhoAm 92*
Guy, Ray 1939- *WhoCanL 92*
Guy, Richard 1932- *WhoAm 92*
Guy, Richard S. *Law&B 92*
Guy, Robert D. *Law&B 92*
Guy, Rosa *BioIn 17*
Guy, Rosa 1928- *BlkAuII 92*
Guy, Rosa (Cuthbert) 1925- *MajAI [port]*
Guy, Sharon Kaye 1958- *WhoAmW 93*
Guy, Stuart R. 1955- *St&PR 93*
Guyader, J.L. *WhoScE 91-2*
Guyan, Cheryl Ann 1964- *WhoSSW 93*
Guyard, Marius-Francois 1921- *WhoWor 93*
Guybon, Francis *BioIn 17*
Guyer, Charles Grayson, II 1949- *WhoSSW 93*
Guyer, Joe E. 1924- *St&PR 93*
Guyer, John C.L. *Law&B 92*
Guyer, Nancy Porter 1943- *WhoSSW 93*
Guyer, Paul David 1948- *WhoAm 92*
Guyer, Raymond L. 1944- *St&PR 93*
Guyer, Steven C. *Law&B 92*
Guyer, Walter Albert 1937- *St&PR 93*
Guyet *WhoScE 91-2*
Guyett, Robert Losee 1937- *St&PR 93, WhoAm 92, WhoE 93*
Guyette, James M. 1945- *St&PR 93, WhoAm 92*
Guyker, William Charles, Jr. 1933- *WhoAm 92*
Guymon, Gary LeRoy 1935- *WhoAm 92*
Guymont, Philip J. 1950- *St&PR 93*
Guynn, Jack 1942- *St&PR 93*
Guynn, Robert William 1942- *WhoAm 92*
Guyon, Etienne Marie 1935- *WhoWor 93*
Guyon, Joe 1892-1971 *BioIn 17*
Guyon, John Carl 1931- *WhoAm 92*
Guyon, Stephen A. 1948- *St&PR 93*
Guyonnet, Jacques 1933- *Baker 92*
Guyonnet, Jean-Francois Rene Claude 1933- *WhoUN 92*
Guyot, A. *WhoScE 91-2*
Guyot, Alain 1931- *WhoScE 91-2*
Guyot, Alain 1944- *WhoScE 91-2*
Guyot, Jean 1512-1588 *Baker 92*
Guyot, Philippe Adelin 1950- *St&PR 93*
Guyre, William H. 1942- *St&PR 93*
Guy-Ropartz *Baker 92*
Guyton, Arthur Clifton 1919- *WhoAm 92*
Guyton, Kathleen Elizabeth 1943- *WhoAmW 93*
Guyton, Richard Lent 1941- *St&PR 93*
Guyton, Robert P. 1937- *St&PR 93*
Guyton, Robert Pool 1937- *WhoSSW 93*
Guyton, Samuel Percy 1937- *WhoAm 92, WhoWor 93*
Guyton, William J. 1922- *St&PR 93*
Guz Aguila *HispAmA*
Guze, Samuel Barry 1923- *WhoAm 92*
Guzek, Jan Wojciech 1924- *WhoScE 91-4, WhoWor 93*
Guzewski, Adolf 1876-1920 *PolBiDi*
Guzik, Ronald Edward 1960- *WhoEmL 93*
Guzikov, Michal Jozef 1806-1837 *Baker 92*
Guzinski, Andrzej 1939- *WhoScE 91-4*
Guzman, Antonio 1911-1982 *DcCPCAm*
Guzman, Claudio *MiSFD 9*
Guzman, Franciso de Paula 1843-1884 *DcMexL*
Guzman, Gaspar de 1587-1645 *BioIn 17*
Guzman, Juanita Elizabeth 1961- *WhoEmL 93*
Guzman, Martin Luis 1887-1976 *DcMexL, SpAmA*
Guzman, Pato 1933?-1991 *ConTFT 10*
Guzman, Ricardo Mosquera 1949- *WhoWor 93*
Guzman, Rodolfo Manuel 1966- *WhoE 93*
Guzman, Roxana *Law&B 92*
Guzman, Suzanna 1955- *HispAmA*
Guzowski, Bruce Thomas 1953- *St&PR 93*
Guzowski, Lawrence F. 1942- *St&PR 93*
Guzowski, Lawrence T. 1944- *St&PR 93*
Guzy, Marguerita Linnes 1938- *WhoWor 93*
Guzzardi, Walter Peter 1950- *WhoE 93*
Guzzetta, Joe *BioIn 17*
Guzzetta, Salvatore Joseph 1936- *WhoSSW 93*

Guzzetti, Alfred F. 1942- *ConAu 136*
Guzzetti, Louis A., Jr. 1939- *St&PR 93*
Guzzetti, William Louis 1943- *St&PR 93*
Guzzi, Patricia Ann 1936- *WhoAmW 93*
Guzzi, Paul 1942- *St&PR 93*
Guzzi, Rodolfo 1942- *WhoScE 91-3*
Guzzle, Timothy L. 1936- *St&PR 93, WhoAm 92, WhoSSW 93*
Guzzo, Sandra Elizabeth 1941- *WhoWrEP 92*
Gvosdovich, Nikolai Vasiljevich 1953- *WhoWor 93*
Gvozdenovic-Simovic, Vjera 1929- *WhoScE 91-4*
Gvozdev, Mikhail Spiridonovich *BioIn 17*
Gwaltney, Corbin 1922- *WhoAm 92, WhoWor 93*
Gwaltney, Donald Marvin 1936- *WhoAm 92*
Gwaltney, E.C. 1918- *St&PR 93*
Gwaltney, Eugene C. *BioIn 17*
Gwaltney, Eugene C., Jr. 1918- *WhoSSW 93*
Gwaltney, Jack Merrit, Jr. 1930- *WhoAm 92*
Gwaltney, John Langston 1928- *WhoAm 92*
Gwaltney, Renee Hamilton *Law&B 92*
Gwartney, Stephen W. 1949- *St&PR 93*
Gwathmey, Archibald L. 1951- *St&PR 93*
Gwathmey, Charles 1938- *WhoAm 92*
Gwathmey, Frank Winston 1942- *WhoSSW 93*
Gwathmey, Robert 1903-1988 *BioIn 17*
Gwiazda, Stanley John 1922- *WhoAm 92*
Gwillim, Russell Adams 1922- *St&PR 93, WhoAm 92*
Gwin, Billy *BioIn 17*
Gwin, Dorothy Jean Bird 1934- *WhoSSW 93*
Gwin, James Ellsworth 1947- *WhoEmL 93, WhoSSW 93*
Gwin, Robert H., Jr. 1930- *St&PR 93*
Gwin, William Rayford 1941- *WhoSSW 93*
Gwinn, Geraldine B. 1952- *WhoE 93*
Gwinn, John C. 1929- *St&PR 93*
Gwinn, Mary Ann 1951- *WhoAmW 93*
Gwinn, Nancy Elizabeth 1945- *WhoAmW 93*
Gwinn, Robert P. 1907- *St&PR 93, WhoAm 92*
Gwinn, Terri Lynne 1965- *WhoSSW 93*
Gwinn, William Dulaney 1916- *WhoAm 92*
Gwinnell, Harry J. *Law&B 92*
Gwinner, Joachim Ulrich 1950- *WhoWor 93*
Gwinner, Robert Fred, Jr. 1935- *WhoAm 92*
Gwinup, Kimberly Sue 1965- *WhoAmW 93*
Gwizdz, Richard Gary *Law&B 92*
Gwozdz, Boleslaw Michael 1928- *WhoWor 93*
Gwozdz, Ronald E. 1939- *St&PR 93*
Gwyn, Douglas Allan 1948- *WhoEmL 93*
Gwyn, Linda J. 1949- *St&PR 93*
Gwyn, Richard Jermy 1934- *WhoAm 92*
Gwyn, William B. 1927- *WhoSSW 93*
Gwynn, Anthony Keith 1960- *WhoAm 92*
Gwynn, Brian Joseph 1965- *WhoSSW 93*
Gwynn, Darrell *BioIn 17*
Gwynn, Price *BioIn 17*
Gwynn, R(obert) S(amuel) 1948- *WhoWrEP 92*
Gwynn, Tony *BioIn 17*
Gwynne, Anne 1918- *BioIn 17, SweetSg C [port]*
Gwynne, Arthur V. 1936- *St&PR 93*
Gwynne, Elizabeth W. *AmWomPl*
Gwynne, Fred 1926- *WhoAm 92*
Gwynne, Michael Douglas 1932- *WhoUN 92*
Gyarfas, Ivan George 1934- *WhoUN 92*
Gyarmathy, Livia 1932- *DrEEuF*
Gyaw, Ohn 1932- *WhoWor 93*
Gydikov, Alexander 1929- *WhoScE 91-4*
Gye, Ernest *OxDcOp*
Gye, Frederick 1809-1878 *OxDcOp*
Gyenes, George 1925- *WhoScE 91-4*
Gyenis, Janos 1939 *WhoScE 91-4*
Gyetvan, Angela Wilson 1962- *WhoEmL 93*
Gyftopoulos, Elias Panayiotis 1927- *WhoAm 92*
Gygax, Gary 1938- *ScF&FL 92*
Gygi, Richard W. 1945- *St&PR 93*
Gyles, John 1680-1775 *BioIn 17*
Gylfason, Thorvaldur 1951- *WhoWor 93*
Gylfe, Carl E. 1925- *St&PR 93*
Gylippus fl. 414BC-404BC *HarEnMi*
Gyllander, Nikki K. 1946- *WhoAmW 93*
Gyllenhaal, Stephen 1949- *MiSFD 9*
Gyllenhammar, Pehr Gustaf 1935- *WhoAm 92, WhoE 93, WhoWor 93*
Gyllensten, Lars *WhoScE 91-4*
Gyllerup, Christer 1943- *WhoScE 91-4*
Gyorffy, Balazs Laszlo *WhoScE 91-1*
Gyorffy, Bela 1928- *WhoScE 91-4*
Gyorffy, Istvan 1884-1939 *IntDcAn*
Gyori, Alberta Rose 1955- *St&PR 93*
Gyori, Daniel 1924- *WhoScE 91-4*
Gyory, Attila Nicholas 1933- *WhoWor 93*
Gypsy Mueller 1874-1930 *BioIn 17*
Gyrowetz, Adalbert 1763-1850 *OxDcOp*
Gyrowetz, Adalbert (Mathias) 1763-1850 *Baker 92*
Gysbers, Norman Charles 1932- *WhoAm 92*
Gyselen, Andries K.T. 1914- *WhoScE 91-2*
Gysen, Paul-Hubertus 1953- *WhoWor 93*
Gysi, Charles L., III 1957- *WhoWrEP 92*
Gysin, Brion 1916-1986 *ScF&FL 92*
Gyulai, Laszlo 1949- *WhoEmL 93*
Gyulai, Peter 1950- *WhoScE 91-4*
Gyurk, Istvan 1935- *WhoScE 91-4*
Gyurko, Istvan 1932- *WhoScE 91-4*
Gyzi, Fritz 1888-1967 *Baker 92*
Gzowski, Casimir Stanislaw 1813-1898 *PolBiDi*
Gzowski, Olgierd 1929- *WhoScE 91-4*
Gzowski, Peter 1934- *ConAu 40NR*

H

H. D. 1886-1961 *ConLC 73 [port], MagSAmL [port], PoeCrit 5 [port]*
H., D.E.W. *ScF&FL 92*
Ha, Chong Wan 1938- *WhoWor 93*
Ha, Tai-You 1933- *WhoWor 93*
Haab, Larry D. 1937- *St&PR 93*
Haab, Larry David 1937- *WhoAm 92*
Haab, Peter William 1931- *St&PR 93*
Haac, Gunilla N. *Law&B 92*
Haack, Alfred 1940- *WhoScE 91-3, WhoWor 93*
Haack, Richard Wilson 1935- *WhoWor 93*
Haack, Robert W(illiam) 1917-1992 *CurBio 92N*
Haack, Robert William 1917-1992 *NewYTBS 92 [port]*
Haack, Sandra Jeanne 1952- *WhoAmW 93*
Haack, Thomas Robert 1945- *WhoAm 92*
Haack, Wolfgang 1902- *WhoWor 93*
Haacke, Harry Henry 1928- *WhoE 93*
Haack-Rogers, Linda Marie 1962- *WhoAmW 93*
Haaf, Beverly T. 1936- *ScF&FL 92*
Haag, Arthur Paul 1929- *WhoSSW 93*
Haag, Barbara Larrabee 1953- *St&PR 93*
Haag, Carol Ann Gunderson *WhoAmW 93*
Haag, David E. 1946- *St&PR 93*
Haag, David Earl 1946- *WhoE 93*
Haag, Ernst 1932- *WhoWor 93*
Haag, Eugene Paul 1937- *WhoE 93*
Haag, Everett Keith 1928- *WhoAm 92*
Haag, Fred George 1931- *WhoE 93*
Haag, Gary L. *Law&B 92*
Haag, James Joseph 1941- *WhoE 93*
Haag, Joyce Pluta *Law&B 92*
Haag, Marty *BioIn 17*
Haag, Walter Monroe, Jr. 1940- *WhoAm 92*
Haag, William George 1910- *WhoAm 92*
Haaga, Candice Ann Fogel 1960- *WhoEmL 93*
Haaga, David Andrew Fogel 1961- *WhoE 93*
Haaga, Paul G., Jr. *Law&B 92*
Haagensen, C.D. 1900-1990 *BioIn 17*
Haagensen, C. Gabriel 1941- *St&PR 93*
Haagensen, Cushman Davis 1900-1990 *BioIn 17*
Haagsma, J. 1933- *WhoScE 91-3*
Haahr, Joan Gluckauf 1940- *WhoAmW 93*
Haahr, Jorn Christian 1935- *WhoE 93*
Haaijman, Joost J. 1947- *WhoScE 91-3*
Haak, Alex Johan Henri 1930- *WhoWor 93*
Haak, Daniel H. 1944- *St&PR 93*
Haak, Harold Howard 1935- *WhoAm 92*
Haake, F. Peter 1934- *St&PR 93*
Haake, Paul 1932- *WhoAm 92*
Haake, Robert A., Jr. 1946- *St&PR 93*
Haakon, VII 1872-1957 *DcTwHis*
Haakon, Paul d1992 *NewYTBS 92*
Haakon Haakonsson, IV 1204-1263 *HarEnMi*
Haakonsen, Bent 1936- *WhoUN 92*
Haakon the Good, I c. 920-961 *HarEnMi*
Haaksma, Jimke 1938- *WhoScE 91-3*
Haaland, Douglas 1952- *WhoWor 93*
Haan, Arthur G. 1941- *St&PR 93*
Haan, Charles Thomas 1941- *WhoAm 92*
Haan, Rick Allan 1953- *WhoE 93*
Haan, Tom de *ScF&FL 92*
Haanen, Clemens 1924- *WhoScE 91-3*
Haapala, Ilmari J. 1939- *WhoScE 91-4*
Haapala, Kirsti Inkeri 1937- *WhoScE 91-4*
Haapanen, Toivo (Elias) 1889-1950 *Baker 92*
Haapiainen, Kari Eino Antero 1958- *WhoScE 91-4*
Haar, Ana Maria Fernandez *NotHsAW 93*
Haar, Charles Monroe 1920- *WhoAm 92*
Haar, James 1929- *Baker 92*
Haarer, Dietrich 1938- *WhoScE 91-3*
Haarer, G. Donald *Law&B 92*
Haarklou, Johannes 1847-1925 *Baker 92*
Haarlander, John R. 1936- *St&PR 93*
Haarmann, Bruce Donald *Law&B 92*
Haarmeyer, David Alan 1958- *WhoE 93*
Haars, Neil Wayne 1939- *WhoWor 93*
Haarsma, J.N.P. *WhoScE 91-3*
Haarz, David R. *Law&B 92*
Haas, Barbara Dolores 1940- *WhoAmW 93*
Haas, Bruce Randy 1952- *St&PR 93*
Haas, Candice *BioIn 17*
Haas, Carl Christian 1947- *St&PR 93*
Haas, Carolyn Buhai 1926- *WhoAm 92, WhoAmW 93*
Haas, Carroll *St&PR 93*
Haas, Charles *Law&B 92*
Haas, Colleen Anne 1959- *WhoAmW 93, WhoSSW 93*
Haas, David Robert 1941- *St&PR 93*
Haas, Deborah Lynn 1952- *WhoAmW 93, WhoSSW 93*
Haas, Donald F. *Law&B 92*
Haas, Dorothy *ScF&FL 92*
Haas, Dorothy F(rances) *DcAmChF 1985*
Haas, Edward Lee 1935- *WhoAm 92, WhoWor 93*
Haas, Eleanor A. *WhoE 93, WhoWor 93*
Haas, Ellen Roberta 1942- *WhoAmW 93*
Haas, Ernst Bernard 1924- *WhoAm 92*
Haas, Felix 1921- *WhoAm 92*
Haas, Francis Eugene 1938- *WhoAm 92*
Haas, Francis J. 1889-1953 *EncAACR*
Haas, Frank Joseph 1911- *St&PR 93*
Haas, Frederick Carl 1936- *St&PR 93, WhoAm 92*
Haas, Frederick Peter 1911- *WhoAm 92*
Haas, Geoffrey J. *Law&B 92*
Haas, George Aaron 1919- *WhoAm 92*
Haas, George William, Jr. 1924- *St&PR 93*
Haas, Gregory George 1949- *WhoSSW 93*
Haas, Harold Murray 1925- *WhoAm 92*
Haas, Henry Richard 1940- *St&PR 93*
Haas, Hermann Josef 1929- *WhoScE 91-3*
Haas, Howard Brian 1960- *WhoEmL 93*
Haas, Howard Green 1924- *WhoAm 92*
Haas, Ingrid Elizabeth 1953- *WhoEmL 93*
Haas, Jacqueline Crawford 1935- *WhoAmW 93, WhoE 93*
Haas, Jere Douglas 1945- *WhoE 93*
Haas, Joanna Faith 1947- *WhoWor 93*
Haas, John Allen 1936- *WhoAm 92*
Haas, John C. 1934- *WhoAm 92*
Haas, John F. 1949- *St&PR 93*
Haas, John Howard 1948- *WhoEmL 93*
Haas, Joseph 1879-1960 *Baker 92*
Haas, Joseph Marshall 1927- *St&PR 93, WhoAm 92*
Haas, Karl (Wilhelm Jacob) 1900-1970 *Baker 92*
Haas, Kenneth Fred 1946- *WhoE 93*
Haas, Kenneth Gregg 1943- *WhoAm 92, WhoE 93*
Haas, Lester Carl 1913- *WhoAm 92*
Haas, Lisa E. *Law&B 92*
Haas, Marc 1908- *St&PR 93*
Haas, Marc 1908-1990 *BioIn 17*
Haas, Marvin I. 1942- *St&PR 93*
Haas, Mary R. 1910- *IntDcAn*
Haas, Melinda Annette 1964- *WhoAmW 93*
Haas, Merrill Wilber 1910- *WhoAm 92*
Haas, Mindy B. *Law&B 92*
Haas, Monique 1906-1987 *Baker 92*
Haas, Paul Arnold 1929- *WhoSSW 93*
Haas, Paul R. 1915- *St&PR 93*
Haas, Paul Raymond 1915- *WhoAm 92, WhoWor 93*
Haas, Pavel 1899-1944 *Baker 92*
Haas, Peter E. 1918- *BioIn 17, St&PR 93, WhoAm 92*
Haas, Peter Edgar, Jr. 1947- *WhoAm 92*
Haas, Rae Marie 1929- *WhoE 93*
Haas, Ralph Arthur 1916- *St&PR 93*
Haas, Richard A. *Law&B 92*
Haas, Richard Allen 1951- *WhoEmL 93*
Haas, Richard C. *BioIn 17*
Haas, Richard J. 1937- *WhoIns 93*
Haas, Richard John 1936- *WhoE 93*
Haas, Robert *BioIn 17*
Haas, Robert D. 1942- *BioIn 17, St&PR 93*
Haas, Robert Donnell 1953- *WhoSSW 93, WhoWor 93*
Haas, Robert Douglas 1942- *WhoAm 92*
Haas, Robert (Maria) 1886-1960 *Baker 92*
Haas, Robert Terry 1947- *WhoEmL 93*
Haas, Susanne Ingeburg *Law&B 92*
Haas, Suzanne Newhouse 1945- *WhoWor 93*
Haas, Thomas Craig 1943- *St&PR 93*
Haas, Tom d1991 *BioIn 17*
Haas, Tracy L. 1958- *St&PR 93*
Haas, Walter A. 1889-1979 *BioIn 17*
Haas, Walter A. 1916- *BioIn 17*
Haas, Walter A., Jr. 1916- *St&PR 93, WhoAm 92*
Haas, Walter J. *WhoAm 92*
Haas, Ward John 1921- *WhoAm 92*
Haas, Warren James 1924- *WhoAm 92*
Haas, Wayne Paul 1950- *St&PR 93*
Haas, Werner 1931-1976 *Baker 92*
Haas, William Paul 1927- *WhoAm 92*
Haas, Yvette Renee 1963- *WhoAmW 93, WhoEmL 93*
Haase, Ashley Thomson 1939- *WhoAm 92*
Haase, Craig *St&PR 93*
Haase, David Glen 1948- *WhoEmL 93*
Haase, Glenn R. *Law&B 92*
Haase, Gunter 1918- *WhoScE 91-3, WhoWor 93*
Haase, Hans 1929- *Baker 92*
Haase, Harley Dean 1946- *St&PR 93*
Haase, Marilee Ellen 1947- *WhoEmL 93*
Haase, Volkmar Helmut 1940- *WhoWor 93*
Haase, William Edward 1943- *WhoAm 92*
Haase, Wolfgang 1936- *WhoScE 91-3*
Haasemann, Frauke Petersen d1991 *BioIn 17*
Haasen, Peter 1927- *WhoScE 91-3*
Haaser, Diana L. *Law&B 92*
Haass, Cheryl Lynn 1955- *WhoAmW 93*
Haass, Erwin Herman 1904- *St&PR 93, WhoAm 92*
Haass, Richard Nathan 1951- *WhoAm 92*
Haass, Terry 1923- *BioIn 17*
Haas-Wilson, Deborah Ann 1955- *WhoE 93*
Haavelmo, Trygve 1911- *WhoWor 93*
Haaverstad, Ole Aage 1949- *WhoWor 93*
Haavikko, Paavo 1931- *BioIn 17*
Haavikko, Paavo Juhani 1931- *WhoWor 93*
Haayen, Richard Jan 1924- *WhoAm 92*
Haba, Alois 1893-1973 *Baker 92, OxDcOp*
Haba, Karel 1898-1972 *Baker 92, OxDcOp*
Habachy, Suzan S. 1933- *WhoUN 92*
Habakkuk, John Hrothgar 1915- *WhoWor 93*
Habakus, Lisa Ann 1967- *WhoAmW 93*
Habal, Mutaz Billah 1938- *WhoSSW 93*
Habash, George 1925- *BioIn 17*
Habash, George 1926- *ColdWar 2 [port]*
Habbart, Ellisa Opstbaum 1959- *WhoAmW 93, WhoWor 93*
Habbas, Kelly Atwa 1931- *St&PR 93*
Habbe, John 1948- *St&PR 93*
Habbe, Karl Albert 1928- *WhoScE 91-3*
Habbestad, Kathryn Louise 1949- *WhoAm 92, WhoAmW 93, WhoEmL 93*
Habbick, Brian Ferguson 1939- *WhoAm 92*
Habbishaw, John A. 1947- *St&PR 93*
Habeck, Dietrich A. E. 1925- *WhoWor 93*
Habeck, Frederic Harvey 1933- *WhoE 93*
Habecker, Eugene Brubaker 1946- *WhoAm 92*
Habeeb, Patricia Ann 1947- *WhoEmL 93*
Habeeb, Virginia Thabet *WhoAm 92*
Habegger, Gary L. 1944- *St&PR 93*
Habel, J. *Law&B 92*
Habel, Janette *ConAu 139*
Habelt, William W. *Law&B 92*
Haben, Mary Kay 1956- *WhoAmW 93*
Habeneck, Francois-Antoine 1781-1849 *Baker 92*
Habenicht, Wenda 1956- *WhoE 93*
Habenstreit, Abraham Isaac 1937- *WhoE 93*
Haber, Alan d1991 *BioIn 17*
Haber, Bruce J. 1952- *St&PR 93*
Haber, Bruce Michael 1957- *WhoE 93*
Haber, Edgar 1932- *WhoAm 92*
Haber, Emanuel Milton 1958- *WhoE 93*
Haber, Fred 1925- *St&PR 93*
Haber, Fred 1928- *St&PR 93*
Haber, Frederic 1958- *WhoEmL 93*
Haber, Henry 1922- *St&PR 93*
Haber, Ira Joel 1947- *WhoAm 92*
Haber, Jane Murchison d1991 *BioIn 17*
Haber, Jeffry Robert 1960- *WhoEmL 93*
Haber, Jerome 1941- *St&PR 93*
Haber, Jerzy 1930- *WhoScE 91-4*
Haber, John d1992 *BioIn 17, NewYTBS 92*
Haber, Joyce 1932- *WhoAm 92, WhoWor 93*
Haber, Judith Ellen *WhoAmW 93*
Haber, Karen 1955- *ScF&FL 92*

Haber, Lawrence G. 1941- *St&PR 93*
Haber, Leonard V. d1992 *NewYTBS 92*
Haber, Lynn C. *Law&B 92*
Haber, Marsha Hilla 1939- *WhoSSW 93*
Haber, Martin David *Law&B 92*
Haber, Martin David 1946- *St&PR 93*
Haber, Marvin S. *Law&B 92*
Haber, Meryl Harold 1934- *WhoAm 92*
Haber, Norman 1929- *St&PR 93*
Haber, Paul 1936- *WhoSSW 93*
Haber, Pierre Claude 1931- *WhoE 93*
Haber, Ralph Norman 1932- *WhoAm 92*
Haber, Theda R. *Law&B 92*
Haber, Warren H. 1941- *St&PR 93, WhoAm 92*
Haber, Wlynski Adam 1883-1921 *PolBiDi*
Haber, Wolfgang 1925- *WhoScE 91-3*
Haberaecker, Heather Jean 1949- *WhoAmW 93*
Haberberger, Mark Joseph *Law&B 92*
Haberbier, Ernst 1813-1869 *Baker 92*
Haberer, Jean-Yves 1932- *WhoWor 93*
Haberfeld, Bert John 1930- *St&PR 93*
Haberkorn, Axel W.H. 1933- *WhoScE 91-3*
Haberl, Franz Xaver 1840-1910 *Baker 92*
Haberl, Valerie Elizabeth 1947- *WhoAmW 93*
Haberland, David Lee 1960- *WhoEmL 93, WhoSSW 93*
Haberland, Paul Mallory 1935- *WhoSSW 93*
Haberle, Heinz H. 1935- *WhoScE 91-3*
Haberle, Joan Baker *WhoAm 92, WhoAmW 93*
Haberle, Siegfried *WhoScE 91-3*
Haberlin, Gail Maureen 1962- *WhoAmW 93*
Haberman, Daniel 1933- *WhoWrEP 92*
Haberman, Daniel 1933-1991 *BioIn 17*
Haberman, Irwin L. 1946- *St&PR 93*
Haberman, Louise Shelly *WhoAmW 93*
Haberman, Monte *BioIn 17*
Haberman, Roger *BioIn 17*
Haberman, Shelby Joel 1947- *WhoAm 92*
Haberman, Steven *WhoScE 91-1*
Haberman, Susan Roberta 1948- *WhoAmW 93*
Haberman, Ted R. *Law&B 92*
Habermann, Arie Nicolaas 1932- *WhoAm 92*
Habermann, Ernst R. 1926- *WhoScE 91-3*
Habermann, Helen Margaret 1927- *WhoAm 92*
Habermann, Michael R. 1950- *WhoEmL 93*
Habermann, Norman Neil 1933- *St&PR 93*
Habermann, Vlastimil 1930- *WhoScE 91-4*
Habermehl, Gerhard G.K. 1931- *WhoScE 91-3*
Habermehl, Gerhard Georg 1931- *WhoWor 93*
Habermehl, Lawrence LeRoy 1937- *WhoE 93*
Haberstock, Roy A. 1934- *St&PR 93, WhoAm 92*
Haberstroh, James Howard 1948- *St&PR 93*
Haberstroh, Jon A. 1940- *St&PR 93*
Habert, Johannes Evangelista 1833-1896 *Baker 92*
Habetha, Klaus Otto Paul 1932- *WhoWor 93*
Habgood, Anthony John 1946- *WhoAm 92*
Habib, Edmund J. 1927- *WhoE 93*
Habib, Fortuna Simcha 1963- *WhoAmW 93*
Habib, Philip *DcCPCAm*
Habib, Philip C. d1992 *NewYTBS 92 [port]*
Habib, Philip Charles *BioIn 17*
Habib, Philip (Charles) 1920-1992 *CurBio 92N*
Habib, Pierre A. 1925- *WhoScE 91-2*
Habib, R. *WhoScE 91-2*
Habib, Robert 1954- *WhoWor 93*
Habib, Sally Ann 1954- *WhoAmW 93*
Habib Abdelsayed, Habib Adly 1955- *WhoWor 93*
Habibie, Bacharuddin Jusuf *BioIn 17*
Habibie, Bachruddin Jusuf 1936- *WhoAsAP 91*
Habibullah, Ghulam Mustafa 1941- *WhoWor 93*
Habiby, Emile *BioIn 17*
Habic, Frank Joseph 1939- *St&PR 93*
Habich, Eduard 1880-1960 *Baker 92*
Habicht, Allen R. 1946- *St&PR 93*
Habicht, Christian Herbert 1926- *WhoAm 92*
Habicht, Edna Lina 1927- *WhoAmW 93*
Habicht, Frank H. 1920- *St&PR 93*
Habicht, Frank Henry 1920- *WhoAm 92*
Habicht, Frank Henry, II 1953- *WhoAm 92*
Habicht, Jean-Pierre 1934- *WhoAm 92*
Habicht, Patricia T. *Law&B 92*
Habif, David V. 1914-1992 *BioIn 17*
Habif, Robert Alan 1950- *WhoEmL 93*
Habig, Anthony P. 1925- *St&PR 93*
Habig, Arnold Frank 1907- *St&PR 93, WhoAm 92*
Habig, Douglas Arnold 1946- *St&PR 93, WhoAm 92*
Habig, John Basil 1933- *St&PR 93*
Habig, Thomas L. 1928- *St&PR 93*
Habington, William 1605-1654 *DcLB 126*
Haborak, George Edward 1936- *WhoSSW 93*
Habre, Hissene 1936- *WhoAfr*
Habsburg family *OxDcOp*
Habsburg-Lothringen, Otto von *BioIn 17*
Habschmidt, James J. 1955- *St&PR 93*
Habush, Robert Lee 1936- *WhoAm 92, WhoWor 93*
Haby, Rene 1919- *BioIn 17*
Habyarimana, Juvenal 1937- *WhoAfr, WhoWor 93*
Hacault, Antoine Joseph Leon 1926- *WhoAm 92*
Haccoun, David 1937- *WhoAm 92*
Hach, Robert William 1917- *St&PR 93*
Hacha, Anna M. *Law&B 92*
Hachar, Adrienne La Verne 1947- *WhoAmW 93*
Hachar, Edward Charles 1956- *St&PR 93*
Hachar, George L. 1931- *St&PR 93*
Hache, J. *WhoScE 91-2*
Hachen, Hans Juerg 1936- *WhoWor 93*
Hachenburg, Peter H. *Law&B 92*
Hachette, Jean-Louise 1925- *WhoWor 93*
Hachey, Thomas Eugene 1938- *WhoAm 92, WhoWrEP 92*
Hachida, Howard Mitsugi 1953- *WhoE 93*
Hachim, Said Hassan Said *WhoWor 93*
Hachiro, Yoshio 1948- *WhoAsAP 91*
Hachman, Cheryl K. *Law&B 92*
Hachtel, Gary H. 1951- *St&PR 93*
Hachten, William Andrews 1924- *WhoAm 92*
Hachuel, Herve *MiSFD 9*
Hachuel, Jacques 1930- *BioIn 17*
Hack, Carole Mae 1942- *WhoAm 92*
Hack, E.W. *Law&B 92*
Hack, Mardi 1940- *WhoAmW 93*
Hack, Martin Howard *Law&B 92*
Hack, Richard 1947- *WhoWrEP 92*
Hackam, Reuben 1936- *WhoAm 92*
Hackbirth, David William 1935- *WhoAm 92*
Hackborn, Richard *BioIn 17*
Hackborn, Richard A. *NewYTBS 92 [port]*
Hacke, Werner 1948- *WhoWor 93*
Hackel, Emanuel 1925- *WhoAm 92*
Hackel, Hans 1942- *WhoScE 91-3*
Hackel-Sims, Stella Bloomberg 1926- *WhoAm 92*
Hackenberg, Audrey Susanna 1960- *WhoAmW 93, WhoSSW 93*
Hackenberg, Barbara Jean Collar 1927- *WhoAmW 93*
Hackenbroch, Matthias Heinrich 1935- *WhoScE 91-3*
Hackenbrock, Charles R. 1929- *WhoAm 92*
Hacker, Alan (Ray) 1938- *Baker 92*
Hacker, Andrew 1929- *WhoAm 92*
Hacker, Anthony Wayne 1956- *WhoSSW 93*
Hacker, Benjamin T. 1935- *AfrAmBi [port]*
Hacker, Cyndi *BioIn 17*
Hacker, Jeffrey R. *Law&B 92*
Hacker, Jon Christopher 1950- *WhoAm 92, WhoE 93, WhoEmL 93*
Hacker, Joshua 1910- *St&PR 93*
Hacker, Larry E. 1943- *WhoSSW 93*
Hacker, Marilyn 1942- *ConLC 72 [port], DcLB 120 [port]*
Hacker, Michael A. *Law&B 92*
Hacker, Peter 1944- *WhoScE 91-4*
Hacker, Randi *BioIn 17*
Hacker, Robert William 1923- *WhoWor 93*
Hacker, Sally 1936-1988 *BioIn 17*
Hacker, Shelley Gordon 1956- *WhoSSW 93*
Hackerman, Hallie Maxine 1963- *WhoAmW 93*
Hackerman, Norman 1912- *WhoAm 92*
Hackes, Peter Sidney 1924- *WhoAm 92*
Hackett, Barbara Kloka 1928- *WhoAm 92, WhoAmW 93*
Hackett, Bobby 1915-1976 *Baker 92*
Hackett, Buddy 1924- *QDrFCA 92 [port], WhoAm 92*
Hackett, Carol Ann Hedden 1939- *WhoAm 92, WhoAmW 93*
Hackett, Charles 1889-1942 *Baker 92*
Hackett, Christopher Fitzherbert 1943- *WhoUN 92*
Hackett, David Kramer 1948- *WhoEmL 93, WhoSSW 93*
Hackett, Dianne 1937- *WhoAmW 93*
Hackett, Earl J. 1941- *St&PR 93*
Hackett, Earl Randolph 1932- *WhoAm 92*
Hackett, Edward Vincent 1946- *WhoSSW 93*
Hackett, Harry Leonard 1942- *WhoE 93*
Hackett, James Edwin, Jr. 1943- *WhoIns 93*
Hackett, Jean Marie 1956- *WhoE 93*
Hackett, John 1910- *ScF&FL 92*
Hackett, John Byron 1933- *WhoAm 92*
Hackett, John Francis 1911-1990 *BioIn 17*
Hackett, John Francis 1956- *WhoAm 92*
Hackett, John Peter 1942- *WhoAm 92*
Hackett, John Thomas 1932- *St&PR 93, WhoAm 92*
Hackett, John Winthrop 1910- *BioIn 17*
Hackett, Lance B. 1951- *WhoEmL 93*
Hackett, Lee Philip 1939- *St&PR 93*
Hackett, Louise 1933- *WhoAmW 93*
Hackett, Luther Frederick 1933- *St&PR 93, WhoAm 92*
Hackett, Martin *ScF&FL 92*
Hackett, Mary Alice *Law&B 92*
Hackett, Patricia *Law&B 92*
Hackett, Peter Andrew 1948- *WhoAm 92*
Hackett, Randall Winslow 1935- *WhoAm 92*
Hackett, Roger Fleming 1922- *WhoAm 92*
Hackett, Suzanne Frances 1961- *WhoWrEP 92*
Hackett, Wesley Palmer 1930- *WhoAm 92*
Hackett, William Earle 1921- *WhoWor 93*
Hackey, Doris Plummer 1928- *WhoE 93*
Hackford, Taylor 1944- *MiSFD 9*
Hackh, Otto (Christoph) 1852-1917 *Baker 92*
Hacking, Ian MacDougall 1936- *WhoAm 92, WhoWrEP 92*
Hackinson, Robert Ralph 1936- *St&PR 93*
Hackl, Alphons J. *WhoAm 92*
Hackl, Donald John 1934- *WhoAm 92*
Hackl, Erich 1954- *ConAu 137*
Hackler, John Byron, III 1925- *WhoAm 92*
Hackler, Michael Lewis 1960- *WhoSSW 93*
Hackler, Russell *BioIn 17*
Hackler, Ruth Ann 1924- *WhoAmW 93*
Hackler, Wallace Leroy 1926- *St&PR 93*
Hackley, Jerry R., Sr. 1929- *St&PR 93*
Hackley, Lloyd Vincent 1940- *WhoAm 92, WhoSSW 93*
Hackman, Elmer Ellsworth, III 1928- *WhoE 93*
Hackman, Gene 1930- *WhoAm 92*
Hackman, Gene 1931- *BioIn 17, IntDcF 2-3 [port]*
Hackman, John Clement 1947- *WhoEmL 93, WhoSSW 93*
Hackman, John Edward 1940- *WhoSSW 93*
Hackman, Mark Thomas *Law&B 92*
Hackman, Martin 1928- *St&PR 93*
Hackman, Martin Robert 1942- *WhoE 93*
Hackman, Roger L. 1930- *St&PR 93*
Hackman, Timothy B. *Law&B 92*
Hackman, Tracy L. *Law&B 92*
Hackman, Vicki Lou 1952- *WhoEmL 93*
Hackmann, Glen F. 1941- *St&PR 93*
Hackmann, Jan *BioIn 17*
Hackmann, Kathy A. *Law&B 92*
Hackney, Edward T. *Law&B 92*
Hackney, Elizabeth Herrington 1947- *WhoAmW 93*
Hackney, Francis Sheldon 1933- *WhoAm 92, WhoWor 93*
Hackney, Gertrude M. *Law&B 92*
Hackney, Howard Smith 1910- *WhoWor 93*
Hackney, Hoyt M. 1938- *St&PR 93*
Hackney, James Acra, Jr. 1917- *St&PR 93*
Hackney, James Acra, III 1939- *St&PR 93, WhoAm 92*
Hackney, R. 1949- *WhoScE 91-1*
Hackney, Ralph Hodges 1941- *St&PR 93*
Hackney, Ray Wesley 1934- *St&PR 93*
Hackney, Roger 1902-1991 *BioIn 17*
Hackney, Ronald Delpho 1941- *WhoSSW 93*
Hackney, Sheldon *WhoE 93*
Hackney, Virginia Howitz 1945- *WhoAmW 93*
Hackney, William P. 1924- *St&PR 93*
Hackney, William Pendleton 1924- *WhoAm 92*
Hackney-Simmons, Mary Alice 1955- *WhoAmW 93*
Hacks, Peter 1928- *DcLB 124 [port]*
Hackstein, K.G. *WhoScE 91-3*
Hackwood, Susan 1955- *WhoAm 92*
Hackworth, Arthur A. *Law&B 92*
Hackworth, Brett Alan 1958- *St&PR 93*
Hackworth, Donald E. 1937- *WhoAm 92*
Hackworth, Gary N. 1949- *St&PR 93*
Hacthoun, Augusto 1945- *WhoWrEP 92*
Hada, Shigeki 1940- *WhoWor 93*
Hadad, Henry d1990 *BioIn 17*
Hadad, Herbert 1937?- *BioIn 17*
Hadamard, Jacques Salomon 1865-1963 *BioIn 17*
Hadar, Mary 1945- *WhoAm 92*
Hadary, Jonathan 1948- *ConTFT 10*
Hadas, Elizabeth Chamberlayne 1946- *WhoAm 92, WhoAmW 93*
Hadas, Pamela White 1946- *WhoWrEP 92*
Hadas, Rachel 1948- *DcLB 120 [port], WhoWrEP 92*
Hadas-Lebel, Raphael *St&PR 93*
Hadassah d1992 *NewYTBS 92*
Haddad, Abraham Herzl 1938- *WhoAm 92*
Haddad, Edward Raouf 1926- *WhoWor 93*
Haddad, Ernest Mudarri 1938- *WhoAm 92, WhoE 93, WhoWor 93*
Haddad, Faris Mohammad 1963- *WhoWor 93*
Haddad, George Alphonse 1937- *WhoUN 92*
Haddad, George Ilyas 1935- *WhoAm 92*
Haddad, George Richard 1918- *WhoAm 92, WhoWor 93*
Haddad, Georges Joseph 1951- *WhoWor 93*
Haddad, Gladys 1930- *ConAu 138*
Haddad, Heskel Marshall 1930- *WhoAm 92, WhoWor 93*
Haddad, Inad 1953- *WhoWor 93*
Haddad, James Henry 1923- *WhoE 93*
Haddad, Jamil Raouf 1923- *WhoAm 92*
Haddad, Jerrier Abdo 1922- *WhoAm 92*
Haddad, John Michael 1935- *WhoWor 93*
Haddad, Marc 1962- *WhoWor 93*
Haddad, Thurayya Hanna 1939- *WhoE 93*
Haddan, Laverne Lincoln 1948- *St&PR 93*
Haddaway, James D. 1933- *St&PR 93*
Hadden, Barbara *BioIn 17*
Hadden, Briton 1898-1929 *BioIn 17*
Hadden, David Robert *WhoScE 91-1*
Hadden, E.M. 1955- *St&PR 93*
Hadden, J(ames) Cuthbert 1861-1914 *Baker 92*
Hadden, Laura Lee 1953- *WhoAmW 93*
Hadden, Martha J. 1951- *WhoE 93*
Hadden, Mayo Addison 1943- *WhoWor 93*
Hadden, Richard *BioIn 17*
Hadden, Scott Robert 1952- *WhoEmL 93*
Haddican, Mary Pat *Law&B 92*
Haddick, R.D. *WhoScE 91-1*
Haddick, Reid Johnson *Law&B 92*
Haddie *WhoWrEP 92*
Haddix, Carol Ann 1946- *WhoAm 92*
Haddix, Harvey 1925- *BiDAMSp 1989, BioIn 17*
Haddock, A.K. *WhoScE 91-1*
Haddock, Arthur *BioIn 17*
Haddock, Bradley E. *Law&B 92*
Haddock, Fred Theodore 1919- *WhoAm 92, WhoWor 93*
Haddock, Harold, Jr. 1932- *WhoAm 92*
Haddock, Jane W. *Law&B 92*
Haddock, John O. 1946- *St&PR 93*
Haddock, Jorge 1955- *WhoE 93*
Haddock, Randy D. *Law&B 92*
Haddock, Randy D. 1947- *St&PR 93*
Haddock, Raymond Earl 1936- *WhoAm 92*
Haddock, Richard Marshall 1951- *St&PR 93*
Haddock, Robert Lynn 1945- *WhoAm 92, WhoE 93, WhoWor 93*
Haddock, Robert M. 1945- *St&PR 93*
Haddock, Ronald Wayne 1940- *St&PR 93, WhoAm 92, WhoSSW 93*
Haddon, A.C. 1855-1940 *IntDcAn*
Haddon, Beverly Jeanne 1941- *St&PR 93, WhoAm 92*
Haddon, Dayle *BioIn 17*
Haddon, Harold Alan 1940- *WhoAm 92*
Haddon, Leigh *Law&B 92*
Haddon, Phoebe Anniese 1950- *WhoEmL 93*
Haddon, Sam Ellis 1937- *WhoAm 92*
Haddon, Timothy J. 1948- *St&PR 93*
Haddow, Margaret Maureen *WhoScE 91-1*
Haddox, Charles Edward 1951- *WhoSSW 93*
Haddox, Mark *WhoAm 92*
Haddy, Francis John 1922- *WhoAm 92, WhoE 93*
Hademenos, James George 1931- *WhoSSW 93*
Haden, Charles 1937- *WhoAm 92*
Haden, Charles H., II 1937- *WhoAm 92, WhoSSW 93*
Haden, Clovis Roland 1940- *WhoAm 92*
Haden, E.D. 1929- *St&PR 93*
Haden, Etta Weaver *AmWomPl*
Haden, Hugh H. 1924- *WhoSSW 93*
Haden, Kathrin P. *AmWomPl*
Haden, Richard Max 1939- *St&PR 93*
Haden, Walter Darrell 1931- *WhoSSW 93, WhoWor 93*
Hadenfeldt, Jerry L. *Law&B 92*

Hader, Berta 1890-1976 *ScF&FL 92*
Hader, Berta (Hoerner) 1891-1976 *MajAI [port]*
Hader, Elmer 1889-1973 *ScF&FL 92*
Hader, Elmer (Stanley) 1889-1973 *MajAI*
Haderer, Harry W., II 1962- *WhoE 93*
Hadermann, Albert Felix 1938- *WhoE 93*
Hadewijch 13th cent.- *BioIn 17*
Hadfield, A.M. 1908- *ScF&FL 92*
Hadfield, Christopher 1953- *WhoScE 91-1*
Hadfield, James Irvine Havelock 1930- *WhoWor 93*
Hadfield, Kathleen Joy Halverson 1938- *WhoSSW 93*
Hadfield, Michael James 1934- *WhoWor 93*
Hadfield, Ronald C. 1940- *St&PR 93*
Hadges, Thomas Richard 1948- *WhoEmL 93, WhoWor 93*
Hadgraft, Jonathan *WhoScE 91-1*
Hadi, Abdullah 1943- *WhoUN 92*
Hadi, Mohammed Sharif 1943- *WhoWor 93*
Hadi bin Derani, Dr. *WhoAsAP 91*
Hadida, Serge-Harry 1960- *WhoWor 93*
Hadidian, Dikran Yenovk 1920- *WhoAm 92*
Hadik, Robert Edward 1932- *St&PR 93*
Hadipriono, Fabian Christy 1947- *WhoEmL 93*
Hadithi, Mwenye *BioIn 17*
Hadji, Serge B. *Law&B 92*
Hadjibekov, Hussein Aga Sultan-ogly 1898-1972 *OxDcOp*
Hadjibekov, Sultan Ismail-ogly 1919- *OxDcOp*
Hadjibekov, Uzeir Abdul Hussein-ogly 1885-1948 *OxDcOp*
Hadjibekov, Zulfugar Abdul Hussein-ogly 1884-1950 *OxDcOp*
Hadjichristodoulou, Andreas 1938- *WhoScE 91-4*
Hadjidemetriou, Demetrios G. 1940- *WhoScE 91-4*
Hadjidemetriou, John 1937- *WhoScE 91-3*
Hadjimatheou, George 1943- *WhoWor 93*
Hadjimichael, Michael T. 1952- *WhoUN 92*
Hadjiolov, Asen A. 1930- *WhoScE 91-4*
Hadjistamov, Dimiter 1940- *WhoWor 93*
Hadjitofis, Pavlos 1937- *WhoUN 92*
Hadjoudis, Eugene 1929- *WhoScE 91-3*
Hadl, John Willard 1940- *BiDAMSp 1989*
Hadland, Kenneth W. *Law&B 92*
Hadley, Carolyn Beth 1945- *WhoAmW 93*
Hadley, Charles A. 1931- *St&PR 93*
Hadley, Donald Hale, II 1951- *St&PR 93*
Hadley, Elizabeth Harrison 1955- *WhoAmW 93, WhoE 93*
Hadley, Gregory A. *Law&B 92*
Hadley, Gregory Brown 1946- *WhoEmL 93*
Hadley, Henry 1871-1937 *OxDcOp*
Hadley, Henry (Kimball) 1871-1937 *Baker 92*
Hadley, Herbert S. 1872-1927 *PolPar*
Hadley, J.L. 1926- *St&PR 93*
Hadley, Jane Byington 1929- *WhoAmW 93, WhoE 93*
Hadley, Jerry *BioIn 17*
Hadley, Jerry 1952- *OxDcOp, WhoAm 92*
Hadley, Lee 1934- *MajAI [port]*
Hadley, Leila Eliott-Burton 1925- *WhoAmW 93, WhoWor 93*
Hadley, Leonard A. 1934- *St&PR 93*
Hadley, Leonard Anson 1934- *WhoAm 92*
Hadley, Lizzie M. *AmWomPl*
Hadley, Marlin LeRoy 1931- *WhoAm 92*
Hadley, Patrick *Law&B 92*
Hadley, Patrick (Arthur Sheldon) 1899-1973 *Baker 92*
Hadley, Paul Ervin 1914- *WhoAm 92*
Hadley, Peter Starr 1928- *St&PR 93*
Hadley, Ralph Vincent, III 1942- *WhoSSW 93*
Hadley, Robert James 1938- *WhoAm 92*
Hadley, Roger Denham *WhoScE 91-1*
Hadley, Rollin van N. 1927-1992 *BioIn 17*
Hadley, Rollin Van Nostrand 1927-1992 *NewYTBS 92*
Hadley, Stanton Thomas 1936- *St&PR 93, WhoAm 92*
Hadley, Susan Marie 1952- *WhoEmL 93*
Hadley, Theodore D., Jr. *BioIn 17*
Hadley, Thomas Mark 1940- *WhoSSW 93*
Hadlock, Charles Robert 1947- *WhoE 93*
Hadlock, Timothy J. *Law&B 92*
Hadlow, David Moore 1928- *St&PR 93*
Hadlow, Earl Bryce 1924- *WhoAm 92*
Hadlow, S. Gertrude *AmWomPl*
Hadow, W(illiam) H(enry) 1859-1937 *Baker 92*
Hadrian 76-138 *HarEnMi*
Hadrian, Emperor of Rome 76-138 *BioIn 17*
Hadrian, I *OxDcByz*
Hadrian, II 792-872 *OxDcByz*
Hadrian, IV c. 1110-1159 *OxDcByz*
Hadro, Timothy C. *St&PR 93*
Hadwiger, Don Frank 1930- *WhoAm 92*
Hadzi, Dimitri 1921- *WhoAm 92*
Hadzi, Dusan 1921- *WhoScE 91-4*
Hadzic, Fadil 1922- *DrEEuF*
Hadzidakis, Manos 1925- *Baker 92*
Hadzikadic, Mirsad 1955- *WhoSSW 93*
Hadziyiannakis, Stavros 1930- *WhoScE 91-3*
Hadzor, Thomas Baylor 1954- *WhoE 93*
Haebel, Robert Edward 1927- *WhoAm 92*
Haeberle, Warren Keith 1956- *WhoEmL 93*
Haeberlin, Herman 1891-1918 *IntDcAn*
Haeberlin, Peter 1947- *WhoWor 93*
Haebler, Ingrid 1926- *Baker 92*
Haeck, Christel 1948- *WhoAmW 93*
Haeck, James F. 1946- *St&PR 93*
Haeck, Philippe 1946- *WhoCanL 92*
Haecker, Arthur John, III *Law&B 92*
Haeder, Hans-Eckhard 1931- *WhoScE 91-3*
Haedicke, Mark E. *Law&B 92*
Haedo, Jorge Alberto 1945- *WhoE 93, WhoWor 93*
Haedrich, Thomas W. *St&PR 93*
Haefele, Edwin Theodore 1925- *WhoAm 92*
Haeffner, Johann Christian Friedrich 1759-1833 *Baker 92*
Haefliger, Ernst 1919- *Baker 92, OxDcOp*
Haefner, Bridget A. *Law&B 92*
Haefner, George R. 1932- *WhoAm 92, WhoSSW 93*
Haefner, Klaus 1936- *WhoScE 91-3*
Haefner, Klaus Dieter Jurgen 1936- *WhoWor 93*
Haege, Ivan Delius *WhoWor 93*
Haegel, Nancy M. 1959- *BioIn 17*
Haegele, John Ernest 1941- *WhoAm 92*
Haegeman, Jozef F.V. 1935- *WhoScE 91-2*
Haeger, John Denis 1942- *ConAu 137*
Haeger, M.R. 1936- *St&PR 93*
Haeger-Aronsen, Birgitta 1926- *WhoScE 91-4*
Haehl, John George 1922- *St&PR 93*
Haehl, John George, Jr. 1922- *WhoAm 92*
Haelsig, Claus-Peter 1947- *WhoScE 91-1*
Haelterman, Edward Omer 1918- *WhoAm 92*
Haemers, Achiel 1943- *WhoScE 91-2*
Haemmel, William Gordon 1924- *WhoSSW 93*
Haemmerlie, Frances Montgomery 1948- *WhoAmW 93, WhoEmL 93, WhoWor 93*
Haen, Victor Raymond 1938- *St&PR 93*
Haenchen, Hans Michael 1949- *WhoWor 93*
Haendel, Ida 1923- *Baker 92*
Haenel, Matthias Walter 1944- *WhoWor 93*
Haenicke, Diether Hans 1935- *WhoAm 92*
Haenlein, George Friedrich Wilhelm 1927- *WhoAm 92*
Haenni, Anne-Lise 1931- *WhoScE 91-2*
Haensel, Vladimir 1914- *WhoAm 92*
Haensel, William B. 1945- *St&PR 93*
Haenssler, Friedrich 1927- *WhoWor 93*
Haenszel, William Manning 1910- *WhoAm 92*
Haentjens, Richard Peter 1944- *St&PR 93*
Haentjens, W.D. 1921- *St&PR 93*
Haerer, Carol 1933- *WhoAm 92*
Haerig, Rainer 1947- *WhoScE 91-3*
Haering, Edwin Raymond 1932- *WhoAm 92*
Haering, Rudolph Roland 1934- *WhoAm 92*
Haerle, Paul Raymond 1932- *WhoAm 92*
Haerther, Daniel P. 1925- *St&PR 93*
Haertling, Peter 1933- *MajAI [port]*
Haeseler, John A. d1990 *BioIn 17*
Haeske, Horst 1925- *WhoAm 92*
Haessle, Jean-Marie Georges 1939- *WhoAm 92*
Haessler, Gregory David 1950- *St&PR 93*
Haessler, John F. 1936- *St&PR 93*
Haessly, Jacqueline 1937- *WhoAmW 93, WhoWrEP 92*
Haessner, Frank 1927- *WhoScE 91-3*
Haeuseler, Hartmut E.W. 1943- *WhoScE 91-3*
Haeussinger, Dieter Lothar 1951- *WhoWor 93*
Hafele, Wolf 1927- *WhoScE 91-3*
Hafeman, Lyle R. 1930- *St&PR 93*
Hafemann, William C. 1928- *St&PR 93*
Hafen, Brent Q(ue) 1940- *ConAu 40NR*
Hafen, Bruce Clark 1940- *WhoAm 92*
Hafen, Elizabeth Susan Scott 1946- *WhoE 93*
Hafen, Mary Ann 1854- *BioIn 17*
Hafenbreidel, Louis B. 1937- *St&PR 93*
Hafer, Duane R. 1933- *St&PR 93*
Hafer, Frederick Douglass 1941- *St&PR 93, WhoAm 92*
Hafer, Henry M. 1917- *St&PR 93*
Hafer, Thomas Franklin *Law&B 92*
Haferkamp, H.J. 1927- *St&PR 93*
Haferkamp, Otto F.Th. 1926- *WhoScE 91-3*
Hafertepe, Kenneth 1955- *ConAu 137*
Hafets, Richard Jay 1951- *WhoE 93, WhoWor 93*
Hafez (Shabana), Abdel Halim 1929-1977 *Baker 92*
Haff, Richard W. 1945- *St&PR 93*
Haffen, Katy *WhoScE 91-2*
Haffenden, Philip Evans *Law&B 92*
Haffenreffer, Rudolf F. d1991 *BioIn 17*
Haffner, Alden Norman 1928- *WhoAm 92*
Haffner, Alfred Loveland, Jr. 1925- *WhoAm 92*
Haffner, C.C., III 1928- *St&PR 93*
Haffner, Charles Christian, III 1928- *WhoAm 92*
Haffner, David S. 1952- *St&PR 93*
Haffner, Debra Wynne 1954- *WhoAmW 93, WhoE 93*
Haffner, Mark Davis 1965- *WhoSSW 93*
Haffner, Marlene Elisabeth 1941- *WhoAm 92, WhoAmW 93*
Haffner, Oscar Harvey 1926- *St&PR 93*
Hafford, Lida *AmWomPl*
Hafford, Mary Louise Gale d1992 *NewYTBS 92*
Hafford, Mary Louise Gale 1902-1992 *BioIn 17*
Hafford, Patricia Ann 1947- *WhoAmW 93*
Hafgren, Lily (Johana Maria) 1884-1965 *Baker 92*
Hafiz, Quazi M. 1934- *WhoUN 92*
Hafkenschiel, Joseph Henry, Jr. 1916- *WhoE 93*
Hafkin, Berry 1947- *St&PR 93*
Hafling, William Russell 1936- *WhoSSW 93*
Hafner, Arthur Wayne 1943- *WhoAm 92*
Hafner, Dudley H. 1935- *WhoAm 92*
Hafner, German 1911- *WhoWor 93*
Hafner, Heinz 1926- *WhoScE 91-3*
Hafner, Jodie Marie 1959- *WhoAmW 93*
Hafner, John Henry 1938- *WhoSSW 93*
Hafner, Joseph A., Jr. 1944- *WhoAm 92*
Hafner, Joseph Albert, Jr. 1944- *St&PR 93*
Hafner, Klaus 1927- *WhoScE 91-3*
Hafner, Lawrence Erhardt 1924- *WhoAm 92*
Hafner, Michael John 1963- *WhoE 93*
Hafner, Theodore d1990 *BioIn 17*
Hafner, Thomas M. *Law&B 92*
Hafner, Thomas M. 1943- *St&PR 93*
Hafner, Thomas Mark 1943- *WhoAm 92*
Hafner, Volker W. 1936- *St&PR 93*
Hafner, Warren Grimm, Jr. 1955- *WhoEmL 93*
Hafskjold, Bjorn 1947- *WhoScE 91-4*
Haft, Marilyn Geisler 1943- *WhoAm 92, WhoAmW 93, WhoE 93*
Haft, Robert Stephen 1929- *St&PR 93*
Haftek, Stanley R. 1942- *St&PR 93*
Haftel, Howard W. 1925- *St&PR 93*
Haftel, Jan 1954- *WhoE 93*
Hafter, Martin 1923- *St&PR 93*
Hafter, Robert 1951- *St&PR 93*
Haftl, Franklin Dale 1934- *WhoIns 93*
Haftorn, Svein 1925- *WhoScE 91-4*
Haga, Judith Ann 1939- *WhoAmW 93*
Haga, Takahiro 1942- *WhoWor 93*
Hagaman, Frank Leslie 1894-1966 *BioIn 17*
Hagaman, Gwendolyn Racine 1957- *WhoAmW 93*
Hagan, Adrienne Joyce 1951- *WhoEmL 93*
Hagan, Chet 1922- *ScF&FL 92*
Hagan, Donald Frank 1954- *WhoSSW 93*
Hagan, Donald Kieth 1949- *St&PR 93*
Hagan, Epsie Lewis 1927- *WhoAm 92*
Hagan, Frank Edward 1945- *WhoE 93*
Hagan, Frank M. 1918- *St&PR 93*
Hagan, George Thomas 1961- *WhoSSW 93*
Hagan, Henry Guy 1953- *St&PR 93*
Hagan, James A. 1946- *St&PR 93*
Hagan, John Aubrey 1936- *St&PR 93, WhoAm 92*
Hagan, John Charles, III 1943- *WhoAm 92*
Hagan, Joseph C. *Law&B 92*
Hagan, Joseph Henry 1935- *WhoAm 92*
Hagan, Joseph L. 1942- *St&PR 93*
Hagan, Juanice M. 1949- *St&PR 93*
Hagan, Katherine Ellen 1959- *WhoAmW 93*
Hagan, Kenneth James 1936- *WhoE 93*
Hagan, Linda Bailey 1944- *WhoSSW 93*
Hagan, Myles Christian 1920- *WhoWor 93*
Hagan, Peter A. *Law&B 92*
Hagan, Randall Lee 1945- *St&PR 93, WhoAm 92*
Hagan, Robert Leslie 1923- *WhoAm 92*
Hagan, Roger Lee 1947- *WhoSSW 93*
Hagan, Timothy P. 1942- *St&PR 93*
Hagan, Victoria *BioIn 17*
Hagan, Wallace Woodrow 1913- *WhoAm 92*
Hagan, William E. *St&PR 93*
Hagan, William John, Jr. 1956- *WhoE 93*
Hagan, William T. *BioIn 17*
Hagan, William Thomas 1918- *WhoAm 92*
Hagans, Karen Carter 1958- *WhoAmW 93*
Hagans, Robert Frank 1926- *St&PR 93, WhoAm 92*
Hagans, William Fred 1947- *WhoEmL 93*
Hagar, Al 1930- *St&PR 93*
Hagar, James Thomas 1950- *WhoSSW 93*
Hagar, Joseph Archibald 1896-1989 *BioIn 17*
Hagar, Robert Montel 1942- *WhoSSW 93*
Hagar, Sammy c. 1949- See Van Halen *ConMus 8*
Hagar, Walter F. *St&PR 93*
Hagarman, John A. 1935- *St&PR 93*
Hagat, Mrunal N.B. *St&PR 93*
Hagauer, Richard William 1928- *WhoSSW 93*
Hagberg, Bengt A. 1923- *WhoScE 91-4*
Hagberg, Carl Thomas 1942- *WhoAm 92*
Hagberg, Daniel John 1960- *WhoEmL 93*
Hagberg, David 1942- *ScF&FL 92*
Hagberg, Jeff Leigh 1951- *St&PR 93*
Hagberg, Sture H. 1924- *WhoScE 91-4*
Hagberg, Viola Wilgus 1952- *WhoAmW 93*
Hage, Candace L. *Law&B 92*
Hage, George Campbell 1944- *WhoSSW 93*
Hagebak, Beaumont Roger 1936- *WhoSSW 93*
Hagebo, Einar 1933- *WhoScE 91-4*
Hagedoorn, John 1950- *WhoWor 93*
Hagedorn, Alfred Arthur, III 1948- *WhoE 93*
Hagedorn, Donald James 1919- *WhoAm 92*
Hagedorn, Dorothy Louise 1929- *WhoAm 92*
Hagedorn, Fred B. 1928- *WhoSSW 93*
Hagedorn, George Allan 1953- *WhoSSW 93*
Hagedorn, Henry Howard 1940- *WhoAm 92*
Hagedorn, Jessica *ConAu 139*
Hagedorn, Jessica Tarahata 1949- *ConAu 139*
Hagedorn, Jurgen 1933- *WhoScE 91-3*
Hagedorn, Peter B. 1941- *WhoScE 91-3*
Hagedorn, Raymond Thomas 1947- *St&PR 93*
Hagefstration, John E., Jr. 1961- *WhoEmL 93*
Hagegard, Hakan 1945- *Baker 92, WhoAm 92, WhoWor 93*
Hagege, Raoul 1934- *WhoScE 91-2*
Hagel, Barbara *BioIn 17*
Hagel, Frank *BioIn 17*
Hagel, Gali L. *Law&B 92*
Hagel, John, III 1950- *WhoEmL 93, WhoWor 93*
Hagel, Peter *BioIn 17*
Hagel, Raymond Charles 1916- *WhoAm 92*
Hagel, William R. 1945- *St&PR 93*
Hagele, Glenn Fred, Jr. 1957- *St&PR 93*
Hagele, Mary Catherine 1942- *WhoAmW 93*
Hagelman, Charles William, Jr. 1920- *WhoAm 92*
Hagelstein, Robert P. 1942- *St&PR 93*
Hagelstein, Robert Philip 1942- *WhoAm 92*
Hageman, Andrew F. *Law&B 92*
Hageman, Douglas L. *Law&B 92*
Hageman, Gilbert Robert 1947- *WhoEmL 93, WhoSSW 93*
Hageman, Howard G. d1992 *NewYTBS 92*
Hageman, Howard Garberich 1921- *WhoAm 92*
Hageman, John A. *Law&B 92*
Hageman, Maurits (Leonard) 1829-1906 *Baker 92*
Hageman, Paul Henry Kivett 1956- *WhoEmL 93*
Hageman, Richard 1882-1966 *Baker 92*
Hageman, Richard Harry 1917- *WhoAm 92*
Hageman, Richard Philip, Jr. 1941- *WhoE 93, WhoWor 93*
Hageman, William Eugene 1939- *WhoE 93*
Hagemann, Dolores Ann 1935- *WhoAmW 93*
Hagemann, Douglas Lee 1936- *St&PR 93*
Hagemann, Frederik *WhoScE 91-4*
Hagemann, Gisela Krohne 1946- *WhoWor 93*
Hagemann, Manfred Dieter 1952- *WhoWor 93*
Hagemeister, George 1925- *St&PR 93*
Hagen, Ann Marie *Law&B 92*

Hagen, Arthur Ainsworth 1933- *WhoAm 92*
Hagen, Carsten 1942- *St&PR 93*
Hagen, Charles William, Jr. 1918- *WhoAm 92*
Hagen, Daniel Russell 1952- *WhoE 93*
Hagen, David Russell 1956- *WhoEmL 93*
Hagen, Donald Floyd 1938- *WhoAm 92*
Hagen, Everett Einar 1906- *BioIn 17*
Hagen, Francis Florentine 1815-1907 *Baker 92*
Hagen, Friedrich Heinrich von der 1780-1856 *Baker 92*
Hagen, George Leon 1924- *St&PR 93, WhoAm 92*
Hagen, Gina Elaine 1961- *WhoAmW 93*
Hagen, Harold Alfred 1926- *St&PR 93*
Hagen, James A. 1932- *St&PR 93*
Hagen, James Alfred 1932- *WhoAm 92, WhoE 93*
Hagen, John P. 1908-1990 *BioIn 17*
Hagen, John Robert 1948- *WhoEmL 93*
Hagen, John William 1940- *WhoAm 92*
Hagen, Kathryn Eileen 1952- *WhoEmL 93*
Hagen, Kevin A. 1956- *WhoAm 92, WhoSSW 93*
Hagen, Lorinda *ScF&FL 92*
Hagen, Michael E. 1947- *St&PR 93*
Hagen, Nicholas Stewart 1942- *WhoWor 93*
Hagen, Oliver H. 1932- *St&PR 93*
Hagen, Patricia Funderburke *Law&B 92*
Hagen, Paul Beo 1920- *WhoAm 92*
Hagen, R. E. 1933- *WhoAm 92*
Hagen, Ross *MiSFD 9*
Hagen, Stephen A. *Law&B 92*
Hagen, Stephen Close 1942- *St&PR 93*
Hagen, Stuart Martin 1950- *St&PR 93*
Hagen, Ted Williamson, II 1948- *WhoSSW 93*
Hagen, Thomas Bailey 1935- *St&PR 93, WhoAm 92, WhoIns 93*
Hagen, Uta 1919- *BioIn 17*
Hagen, Uta Thyra 1919- *WhoAm 92, WhoAmW 93*
Hagen, Walter 1892-1969 *BioIn 17*
Hagenau, Bernd 1958- *WhoWor 93*
Hagenau, Steven E. 1951- *St&PR 93*
Hagenbruch, Harriet Ann *WhoAmW 93, WhoE 93*
Hagenbuch, Hans 1945- *WhoWor 93*
Hagenbuch, John Jacob 1951- *WhoWor 93*
Hagenbuch, Rodney Dale *WhoWor 93*
Hagenbuch, William H. 1918- *St&PR 93*
Hagenbush, Christopher Lee *Law&B 92*
Hagendorn, William 1925- *WhoAm 92*
Hagener, Maria N. *Law&B 92*
Hagen-Groll, Walter 1927- *Baker 92*
Hagen-Lautrup, Carlos B. *BioIn 17*
Hagenmuller, Paul 1921- *WhoScE 91-2*
Hagenstein, Perry Reginald 1931- *WhoAm 92, WhoE 93*
Hagenstein, William David 1915- *WhoAm 92*
Hager, Amy Wertz 1959- *WhoAmW 93*
Hager, Bronson Q. 1959- *St&PR 93*
Hager, Charles Read 1937- *WhoAm 92*
Hager, Don *Law&B 92*
Hager, E.B. 1931- *St&PR 93*
Hager, Edward Paul 1948- *WhoE 93, WhoEmL 93*
Hager, Elizabeth Sears 1944- *WhoAmW 93*
Hager, Frederick H. 1957- *St&PR 93*
Hager, Fritz-Peter P. 1939- *WhoWor 93*
Hager, Gary *BioIn 17*
Hager, George Washington, Jr. *Law&B 92*
Hager, Hellmut Wilhelm 1926- *WhoAm 92*
Hager, Henry Brandebury 1926- *WhoWrEP 92*
Hager, Jennifer M. *Law&B 92*
Hager, Jimmy Nelson 1947- *WhoWrEP 92*
Hager, John Patrick 1936- *WhoAm 92*
Hager, Kathy Elaine 1951- *WhoAmW 93, WhoWor 93*
Hager, Larry Stanley 1942- *WhoAm 92, WhoWrEP 92*
Hager, Leopold 1935- *Baker 92*
Hager, Linda Wesseling 1941- *WhoAmW 93*
Hager, Lowell Paul 1926- *WhoAm 92*
Hager, Mary Hastings 1948- *WhoAmW 93, WhoE 93*
Hager, Orval O. 1918- *WhoAm 92*
Hager, Paul Calvin 1931- *WhoSSW 93*
Hager, Robert *WhoAm 92*
Hager, Robert L. 1947- *St&PR 93*
Hager, Robert Worth 1928- *WhoAm 92*
Hager, Stanley Lee 1946- *WhoSSW 93*
Hager, Wayne Richard 1941- *WhoE 93*
Hager, William Ward 1948- *WhoEmL 93, WhoSSW 93*
Hagerman, Allen R. 1951- *St&PR 93*
Hagerman, Allen Reid 1951- *WhoAm 92*
Hagerman, John David 1941- *WhoSSW 93*
Hagerman, Lars 1941- *WhoScE 91-2*
Hagerman, Peter Stanley 1939- *WhoAm 92*
Hagerman, Theodore Frederick 1908- *St&PR 93*
Hagerson, John David 1966- *WhoEmL 93, WhoWor 93*
Hagerty, Betty Lee *St&PR 93, WhoAmW 93, WhoWor 93*
Hagerty, Carol K. 1954- *St&PR 93*
Hagerty, George James, III 1952- *WhoE 93*
Hagerty, James J. 1941- *St&PR 93*
Hagerty, Laurence J. 1953- *St&PR 93*
Hagerty, Michael d1991 *BioIn 17*
Hagerty, Polly Martiel 1946- *WhoAmW 93*
Hagerup, Richard II. 1952- *St&PR 93*
Hagerup Bull, Edvard 1922- *Baker 92*
Hageseth, Christian, III 1941- *WhoWrEP 92*
Hagey, Walter Rex 1909- *WhoE 93, WhoWor 93*
Hagfors, Tor 1930- *WhoAm 92*
Hagg, Jakob Adolf 1850-1928 *Baker 92*
Hagg (Peterson), Gustaf Wilhelm 1867-1925 *Baker 92*
Hagg, Russell *MiSFD 9*
Haggai, Thomas Stephens 1931- *St&PR 93*
Haggar, Edmond Ralph 1916- *WhoAm 92*
Haggar, Sara Thompson 1963- *WhoEmL 93*
Haggard, Audrey *AmWomPl*
Haggard, David Eugene 1934- *St&PR 93*
Haggard, Forrest Deloss 1925- *WhoAm 92*
Haggard, H. Rider 1856-1925 *ScF&FL 92*
Haggard, Jolene M. *Law&B 92*
Haggard, Lilias Rider 1892-1968 *ScF&FL 92*
Haggard, Mark P. *WhoScE 91-1*
Haggard, Merle (Ronald) 1937- *Baker 92*
Haggard, Paul Wintzel 1933- *WhoSSW 93*
Haggard, Piers 1939- *MiSFD 9*
Haggard, Tamara C. 1949- *St&PR 93*
Haggard, William Henry 1920- *WhoSSW 93*
Haggard-Martinez, Donna Lynn 1952- *WhoAmW 93*
Haggbom, Nils-Ake 1942- *WhoWor 93*
Haggen, Donald Edmund 1931- *St&PR 93*
Haggen, Richard R. 1945- *St&PR 93*
Haggendal, C. Jan 1932- *WhoScE 91-4*
Haggerty, Allen C. 1936- *St&PR 93*
Haggerty, Allen Charles 1936- *WhoAm 92*
Haggerty, Brian John 1945- *WhoIns 93*
Haggerty, David M. 1942- *St&PR 93, WhoIns 93*
Haggerty, Frederick *St&PR 93*
Haggerty, George W. 1891-1961 *BiDAMSp 1989*
Haggerty, James Joseph 1920- *WhoE 93, WhoWor 93*
Haggerty, James Joseph 1936- *WhoAm 92*
Haggerty, John Edward 1918- *WhoAm 92*
Haggerty, John Richard 1935- *St&PR 93, WhoAm 92*
Haggerty, Joseph Kevin *Law&B 92*
Haggerty, Lawrence G. 1916- *St&PR 93*
Haggerty, Lawrence George 1916- *WhoAm 92*
Haggerty, Mary Ann 1945- *WhoAmW 93*
Haggerty, Mary Ellen 1920- *St&PR 93*
Haggerty, Richard Paul 1939- *St&PR 93*
Haggerty, Robert H., Jr. *Law&B 92*
Haggerty, Robert Henry 1919- *WhoAm 92*
Haggerty, Robert Johns 1925- *WhoAm 92*
Haggerty, Robert V.J. 1937- *St&PR 93*
Haggerty, Roger E. *St&PR 93*
Haggerty, Warren H., Jr. *WhoE 93*
Haggerty, William J. 1930- *St&PR 93*
Haggett, William *St&PR 93*
Haggin, B(ernard) H. 1900-1987 *Baker 92*
Haggis, Arthur George, Jr. 1924- *WhoSSW 93, WhoWor 93*
Hagglund, Bjorn *WhoScE 91-4*
Hagglund, Clarance Edward 1927- *WhoAm 92*
Haggren, Bert Goran 1952- *WhoWor 93*
Haggstrom, Stig Olof 1924- *WhoWor 93*
Hagin, Kenneth 1917- *BioIn 17*
Hagins, Thomas C. 1913- *St&PR 93*
Hagiochristophorites, Stephen d1185 *OxDcByz*
Hagiotheodorites *OxDcByz*
Hagiwara, Kokichi 1924- *St&PR 93, WhoAm 92*
Hagiwara, Teruhiko 1944- *WhoSSW 93*
Hagiyama, Kyogon 1945- *WhoAsAP 91*
Hagiz, Moses c. 1671-c. 1750 *BioIn 17*
Hagland, Mark Martin *WhoWrEP 92*
Hagle, George Herbert, Jr. 1936- *WhoAm 92*
Hagleitner, Diane J. 1951- *St&PR 93*
Hagler, Christine Louise 1963- *WhoEmL 93, WhoSSW 93*
Hagler, Daniel R. *Law&B 92*
Hagler, Jon Lewis 1936- *WhoAm 92*
Hagler, Lillie Mae 1916- *WhoAmW 93, WhoWor 93*
Hagler, Marion Otho 1939- *WhoAm 92*
Hagler, Marvin *BioIn 17*
Hagler, Marvin 1954- *WhoAm 92*
Hagler, Samuel Henry 1940- *St&PR 93*
Hagler, Thomas 1920- *WhoSSW 93*
Haglund, Gerhard Oscar, Sr. 1916- *WhoAm 92*
Haglund, Marlene Linda 1959- *WhoAmW 93*
Hagmajer, Marek 1945- *WhoUN 92*
Hagman, Harlan Lawrence 1911- *WhoAm 92, WhoWor 93*
Hagman, Larry *BioIn 17*
Hagman, Larry 1931- *MiSFD 9, WhoAm 92*
Hagman, Max *WhoScE 91-4*
Hagman, Sally Wingchong 1962- *WhoEmL 93*
Hagmann, Stuart 1942- *MiSFD 9*
Hagmann-Petersen, Sooren 1937- *WhoScE 91-2*
Hagn, George Hubert 1935- *WhoAm 92*
Hagnell, Erik Olof (Olle) 1924- *WhoScE 91-4*
Hagner, Arthur Feodor 1911- *WhoAm 92*
Hagner, Guy R. 1960- *St&PR 93*
Hagner, Mats 1934- *WhoScE 91-4*
Hagner, Samuel Benedict 1925- *WhoE 93*
Hagni, Richard Davis *WhoAm 92*
Hagon, Priscilla *MajAI*
Hagood, Annabel Dunham 1924- *WhoAm 92*
Hagood, Bo L. 1949- *St&PR 93*
Hagood, Louis R. 1944- *WhoE 93*
Hagood, Margaret Jarman 1907-1963 *BioIn 17*
Hagood, Susan Stewart Hahn 1953- *WhoEmL 93, WhoSSW 93*
Hagood, Thomas Richard, Jr. 1954- *WhoSSW 93*
Hagoort, Nancy Lynn 1956- *WhoWor 93*
Hagoort, Thomas Henry 1932- *WhoAm 92*
Hagopian, Berge Kipling 1941- *St&PR 93*
Hagopian, David Malcolm 1960- *WhoEmL 93*
Hagopian, Deriar N. *St&PR 93*
Hagopian, Gary *Law&B 92*
Hagopian, Larry S. 1947- *St&PR 93*
Hagopian, Louis Thomas 1925- *St&PR 93*
Hagopian, Zgon Der d1991 *BioIn 17*
Hagqvist, Risto Kalevi 1956- *WhoScE 91-4*
Hagrup, Knut 1913- *WhoWor 93*
Hagson, Carl Allan 1921- *WhoWor 93*
Hagstrom, Jon 1939- *St&PR 93*
Hagstrom, Stig Bernt 1932- *WhoAm 92*
Hagstrom, Tony Gunnar 1936- *WhoWor 93*
Hagstrum, Homer Dupre 1915- *WhoAm 92*
Hagstrum, Jean Howard 1913- *WhoAm 92*
Hagting, Albert 1939- *WhoScE 91-3*
Hague, Albert Frederick 1947- *WhoE 93, WhoEmL 93*
Hague, Donald Victor 1926- *WhoAm 92*
Hague, Douglas Ian *Law&B 92*
Hague, Elizabeth F. *AmWomPl*
Hague, Frank 1876-1956 *PolPar*
Hague, Harlan 1932- *ConAu 40NR*
Hague, John William, Jr. 1943- *WhoAm 92*
Hague, Michael R. 1948- *MajAI [port]*
Hague, Paul Richard 1940- *WhoE 93*
Hague, Raoul 1905- *WhoAm 92*
Hague, Richard 1947- *WhoWrEP 92*
Hague, Robert W. 1926- *St&PR 93*
Hague, Roger S. 1928- *St&PR 93*
Hague, William 1952- *WhoE 93, WhoEmL 93*
Hague, William Edward 1919- *WhoWrEP 92*
Hagues, Michael David 1952- *WhoSSW 93*
Hagura, Nobuya 1919- *St&PR 93*
Hagvar, Sigmund 1944- *WhoScE 91-4*
Hagwood, Henry Melvin, Jr. 1937- *WhoAm 92*
Hagy, Alyson 1960- *ConAu 137*
Hagy, David W. *Law&B 92*
Hagy, Teresa Jane 1950- *WhoAmW 93, WhoEmL 93*
Hagye, Melissa Marie 1952- *WhoEmL 93*
Hahl, Albert 1868-1945 *BioIn 17*
Hahl, Hermann Winfried 1945- *WhoWor 93*
Hahl, Neil M. 1948- *St&PR 93*
Hahlbeck, Edwin C. 1940- *St&PR 93*
Hahlbrock, Klaus *WhoScE 91-3*
Hahm, David Edgar 1938- *WhoAm 92*
Hahm, Kyung-Soo 1946- *WhoWor 93*
Hahn, Arthur W. 1944- *WhoAm 92*
Hahn, Bessie King 1939- *WhoAm 92, WhoAmW 93*
Hahn, Betty 1940- *WhoAm 92*
Hahn, Bradley D. 1942- *St&PR 93*
Hahn, Carl Horst 1926- *WhoAm 92, WhoWor 93*
Hahn, Cathy Ann Clifford 1947- *WhoEmL 93, WhoSSW 93*
Hahn, Celia Allison 1931- *WhoE 93*
Hahn, Celia Ferner 1942- *WhoE 93*
Hahn, Charles Julien 1925- *WhoScE 91-4*
Hahn, Davis Milford 1946- *WhoE 93*
Hahn, Dean LuVerne 1933- *St&PR 93*
Hahn, Edward Lorenz 1937- *St&PR 93*
Hahn, Elliot Frank 1944- *WhoSSW 93*
Hahn, Emily 1905- *WhoAmW 93*
Hahn, Ernest W. d1992 *NewYTBS 92 [port]*
Hahn, Erwin Louis 1921- *WhoAm 92*
Hahn, Eugene Richard 1938- *St&PR 93*
Hahn, Frank *BioIn 17*
Hahn, Frank George 1879-1960 *BiDAMSp 1989*
Hahn, Frank Horace 1925- *WhoWor 93*
Hahn, Fred 1906- *WhoE 93*
Hahn, Fred K., III 1954- *St&PR 93*
Hahn, Frederic Louis 1941- *WhoAm 92*
Hahn, George E. *St&PR 93*
Hahn, George LeRoy 1934- *WhoAm 92*
Hahn, George Thomas 1930- *WhoAm 92*
Hahn, Gilbert, Jr. 1921- *WhoAm 92*
Hahn, Glenda F. *Law&B 92*
Hahn, Hans Georg 1929- *WhoScE 91-3*
Hahn, Harlan Dean 1939- *WhoAm 92*
Hahn, Harriet Luisa Paine 1919- *WhoAmW 93*
Hahn, Helen L. 1920- *St&PR 93*
Hahn, Helene *BioIn 17, Law&B 92, St&PR 93*
Hahn, Helene B. *WhoAmW 93*
Hahn, Helmut 1937- *WhoScE 91-3*
Hahn, Hermann H. 1940- *WhoScE 91-3*
Hahn, Hong Thomas 1942- *WhoWor 93*
Hahn, James Maglorie 1936- *WhoAm 92*
Hahn, Jeffrey P. *Law&B 92*
Hahn, Jeffrey P. 1944- *St&PR 93*
Hahn, Jerome P. 1924- *St&PR 93*
Hahn, Jessica *BioIn 17*
Hahn, John Charles 1943- *WhoE 93*
Hahn, John W. 1940- *WhoIns 93*
Hahn, John William 1940- *WhoAm 92, WhoE 93*
Hahn, Karl Wilhelm 1829-1887 *BioIn 17*
Hahn, Kenneth H. 1922- *St&PR 93*
Hahn, Kent S. 1955- *St&PR 93*
Hahn, Kurt 1886-1974 *BioIn 17*
Hahn, Laura J. *Law&B 92*
Hahn, Laura L. 1959- *St&PR 93*
Hahn, Lewis Edwin 1908- *WhoAm 92, WhoWor 93*
Hahn, Lithia B. 1951- *WhoAmW 93, WhoEmL 93*
Hahn, Lloyd C. 1919- *St&PR 93*
Hahn, Lloyd Edward 1925- *St&PR 93*
Hahn, Lorna *WhoE 93*
Hahn, Lucille Denise 1940- *WhoAmW 93*
Hahn, Malvine, Mrs. *AmWomPl*
Hahn, Margaret H. *AmWomPl*
Hahn, Marjorie 1933- *St&PR 93*
Hahn, Mary Downing 1937- *DcAmChF 1985, MajAI [port], ScF&FL 92, WhoAm 92*
Hahn, Moira *BioIn 17*
Hahn, Natalie D. 1945- *WhoUN 92*
Hahn, Norman Jacob 1965- *WhoE 93*
Hahn, Oscar 1938- *SpAmA*
Hahn, Oswald 1928- *WhoWor 93*
Hahn, Paul Frederick 1930- *St&PR 93*
Hahn, Philip M. *Law&B 92*
Hahn, Reynaldo 1874-1947 *Baker 92*
Hahn, Reynaldo 1875-1947 *OxDcOp*
Hahn, Richard Christian 1939- *St&PR 93*
Hahn, Richard Eric *Law&B 92*
Hahn, Richard H. *Law&B 92*
Hahn, Richard Ray 1930- *WhoAm 92*
Hahn, Richard S. 1951- *St&PR 93*
Hahn, Robert A. *Law&B 92*
Hahn, Robert E. 1957- *St&PR 93*
Hahn, Robert G. 1928- *St&PR 93*
Hahn, Roger Carl 1932- *WhoE 93*
Hahn, Sandra Elaine 1964- *WhoSSW 93*
Hahn, Sharon Lee 1939- *WhoAmW 93*
Hahn, Stanley Robert, Jr. 1946- *WhoSSW 93*
Hahn, Stefan L. 1921- *WhoScE 91-4*
Hahn, Stephen 1929- *St&PR 93*
Hahn, Stephen Walter 1950- *WhoE 93*
Hahn, Steve *ScF&FL 92*
Hahn, Steven *MiSFD 9*
Hahn, Steven William 1947- *WhoAm 92*
Hahn, Theo 1928- *WhoWor 93*
Hahn, Theodor 1928- *WhoScE 91-3*
Hahn, Theodore Thomas 1942- *St&PR 93*
Hahn, Thomas Marshall, Jr. 1926- *St&PR 93, WhoAm 92, WhoSSW 93, WhoWor 93*
Hahn, Ulrich *Baker 92*

Hahn, Volker Heinz-Ulrich 1945- *WhoWor 93*
Hahn, Warren E. *St&PR 93*
Hahn, William 1829-1887 *BioIn 17*
Hahn, William Harry 1946- *St&PR 93*
Hahn, William M. 1933- *St&PR 93*
Hahn, Yubong 1942- *WhoAm 92*
Hahne, C. E. 1940- *WhoSSW 93, WhoWor 93*
Hahne, Erich W.P. 1932- *WhoScE 91-3*
Hahne, Erich Wilhelm Perikles 1932- *WhoWor 93*
Hahne, Robert Louis 1938- *WhoAm 92*
Hahner, Moritz Julius 1931- *WhoE 93*
Hahon, Nicholas 1924- *WhoSSW 93*
Hahs, Dale E. 1963- *St&PR 93*
Hai, Carol Sue 1938- *WhoAm 92, WhoAmW 93*
Hai, Zafar *MiSFD 9*
Haibel, Jakob 1762-1826 *OxDcOp*
Haibel, (Johann Petrus) Jakob 1762-1826 *Baker 92*
Haiblum, Isidore 1935- *ScF&FL 92*
Haich, Elisabeth 1897- *ScF&FL 92*
Haid, Charles M. 1943- *WhoAm 92*
Haidar, Salim Mohammad 1958- *WhoEmL 93*
Haidari, Iqbal 1929- *WhoWor 93*
Haider, Jorg 1950- *WhoWor 93*
Haider, Syed Jawad 1944- *WhoWor 93*
Haidt, Harold 1926- *WhoAm 92, WhoWor 93*
Haiduc, Ionel 1937- *WhoScE 91-4*
Haiech, Jacques 1954- *WhoScE 91-2*
Haieff, Alexei (Vasilievich) 1914- *Baker 92*
Haier, Eva Meier 1963- *WhoAmW 93*
Haifleigh, Debra Grace *Law&B 92*
Haifley, Sharon Virginia 1951- *WhoAmW 93*
Haig, Al(lan Warren) 1924-1982 *Baker 92*
Haig, Alexander M., Jr. 1924- *ColdWar 1 [port]*
Haig, Alexander M(eigs), Jr. 1924- *ConAu 138*
Haig, Alexander Meigs 1924- *BioIn 17*
Haig, Alexander Meigs, Jr. 1924- *HarEnMi, WhoAm 92, WhoWor 93*
Haig, Douglas 1861-1926 *HarEnMi*
Haig, Douglas 1861-1928 *BioIn 17, DcTwHis*
Haig, Frank Rawle 1928- *WhoAm 92*
Haig, Robert Leighton 1947- *WhoAm 92, WhoE 93, WhoEmL 93, WhoWor 93*
Haig, Robert M. 1887-1953 *BioIn 17*
Haig, Robert W. *Law&B 92*
Haig, Theodor 1913- *WhoWor 93*
Haig, Ylva Christina 1945- *WhoWor 93*
Haig-Brown, Roderick (Langmere) 1908-1976 *ConAu 38NR, DcChlFi, MajAI [port]*
Haigh, John 1953- *WhoWor 93*
Haigh, John C. 1930- *St&PR 93*
Haigh, John Richard 1953- *St&PR 93*
Haigh, Richard *ScF&FL 92*
Haigh, Robert William 1926- *WhoAm 92*
Haigh, Ronald K. 1934- *St&PR 93*
Haigh, Sheila *ScF&FL 92*
Haight, Barbara Kavanagh 1937- *WhoSSW 93*
Haight, Barrett Slocum 1937- *WhoSSW 93*
Haight, Carol Barbara 1945- *WhoAmW 93*
Haight, Charles Sherman, Jr. 1930- *WhoAm 92*
Haight, Donald Alexander 1946- *WhoE 93*
Haight, Edward Allen 1910- *WhoAm 92*
Haight, Fulton Wilbur 1923- *WhoAm 92*
Haight, Gordon 1946- *WhoAm 92*
Haight, Gordon Sherman 1901-1985 *BioIn 17*
Haight, James T. *Law&B 92*
Haight, James Theron 1924- *St&PR 93, WhoAm 92*
Haight, Katherine Witt *Law&B 92*
Haight, Kenneth Lee 1955- *WhoEmL 93*
Haight, Lee Charles 1952- *WhoSSW 93*
Haight, Marcia Kae 1939- *WhoAmW 93*
Haight, Mary Ellen Jordan *ConAu 136*
Haight, Peter V. 1937- *St&PR 93*
Haight, Warren Gazzam 1929- *WhoAm 92, WhoWor 93*
Haigler, Theodore E., Jr. 1924- *St&PR 93*
Haigood, Lyndell Wayne 1949- *St&PR 93*
Haik, Joseph 1930- *St&PR 93*
Haiken, Leatrice Brown 1934- *WhoAm 92*
Haiko, Geraldine Mae 1940- *WhoAmW 93*
Hail, John Wesley 1930- *WhoWor 93*
Haile, Eugen 1873-1933 *Baker 92*
Haile, Getatchew 1931- *WhoAm 92*
Haile, H. G. 1931- *WhoAm 92, WhoWrEP 92*
Haile, James Francis 1920- *WhoAm 92*
Haile, Jane Elizabeth 1944- *WhoUN 92*
Haile, L. John, Jr. 1945- *WhoAm 92*
Haile, Lawrence Barclay 1938- *WhoAm 92, WhoWor 93*
Haile, Raymond Alderson, Jr. 1930- *WhoAm 92*
Haile, Terence *ScF&FL 92*
Haile Giorgis, Workneh 1930- *WhoWor 93*
Hailes, Norman Stanley James *WhoScE 91-1*
Haile Selassie 1892-1975 *DcTwHis*
Haile Selassie, I 1892-1975 *ColdWar 2 [port]*
Haile Selassie, I, Emperor of Ethiopia 1891-1975 *BioIn 17*
Hailey, Anthony Eugene 1959- *WhoE 93*
Hailey, Arthur *BioIn 17*
Hailey, Arthur 1920- *WhoAm 92, WhoWor 93, WhoWrEP 92*
Hailey, Hans Ronald 1950- *WhoEmL 93*
Hailey, Jacob Joseph 1949- *WhoE 93*
Hailey, Johanna *ScF&FL 92*
Hailey, (Elizabeth) Kendall 1966- *ConAu 136*
Hailey, Richard A. 1949- *WhoEmL 93, WhoSSW 93*
Hailey, Shawn *BioIn 17*
Hailpern, Brent Tzion 1955- *WhoE 93*
Hails, Barbara *BioIn 17*
Hails, Robert Emmet 1923- *WhoAm 92, WhoWor 93*
Hailsham of St. Marylebone, Baron 1907- *BioIn 17*
Hailstork, Adolphus (Cunningham) 1941- *Baker 92*
Hailu, Solomon 1939- *WhoUN 92*
Haim, Corey *BioIn 17*
Haim, Ruth *St&PR 93*
Haiman, Franklyn Saul 1921- *WhoAm 92*
Haiman, Irwin Sanford 1916- *WhoAm 92*
Haiman, Mieczislaus 1888-1949 *PolBiDi*
Haiman, Robert James 1936- *WhoAm 92, WhoSSW 93*
Haimann, Theo 1911- *WhoAm 92*
Haimbaugh, George Dow, Jr. 1916- *WhoAm 92*
Haimendorf, Christoph von Furer- 1909- *BioIn 17*
Haimes, Rand S. *Law&B 92*
Haimes, Yacov Yosseph 1936- *WhoAm 92*
Haimo, Deborah Tepper 1921- *WhoAm 92*
Haimo, Michael Jay 1941- *WhoSSW 93*
Haimowitz, Natalie Reader 1923- *WhoAmW 93*
Haims, Anna *St&PR 93*
Haimsohn, Henry 1947- *ConEn*
Haimsohn, Michael Anthony d1990 *BioIn 17*
Hain, Charles R. 1942- *St&PR 93*
Hain, Uwe 1944- *WhoUN 92*
Hainard, Pierre 1936- *WhoScE 91-4*
Haine, John Wesley *Law&B 92*
Haine, Peter Michael *WhoScE 91-1*
Haine, Susan J. *Law&B 92*
Haines, Albert E. 1944- *WhoAm 92*
Haines, Andrew Paul *WhoScE 91-1*
Haines, Barry Gordon 1961- *WhoEmL 93*
Haines, Byron *BioIn 17*
Haines, Charlene J. *Law&B 92*
Haines, Charles Davis 1927- *WhoSSW 93*
Haines, Dennis *Law&B 92*
Haines, Elizabeth Joan 1958- *WhoE 93*
Haines, Frank S. 1921- *St&PR 93*
Haines, Genevieve Greville *AmWomPl*
Haines, George William 1941- *St&PR 93*
Haines, James S., Jr. 1946- *St&PR 93*
Haines, Janine 1945- *WhoAsAP 91*
Haines, John Alan 1938- *WhoUN 92*
Haines, John M. 1924- *WhoWrEP 92*
Haines, Lawrence Archibald 1928- *St&PR 93*
Haines, Lee Mark, Jr. 1927- *WhoAm 92*
Haines, Leslie Ian Bullin *WhoScE 91-1*
Haines, M.G. *WhoScE 91-1*
Haines, Mary June 1932- *WhoWrEP 92*
Haines, Michael *WhoScE 91-1*
Haines, Michael Robert 1944- *WhoE 93, WhoWor 93*
Haines, Milton L. 1940- *WhoAm 92*
Haines, Perry Vansant 1944- *St&PR 93, WhoAm 92*
Haines, Philip C. 1936- *St&PR 93*
Haines, Randa *BioIn 17, MiSFD 9*
Haines, Randa 1945- *ConTFT 10*
Haines, Richard Foster 1937- *WhoAm 92*
Haines, Robert Earl 1929- *WhoAm 92*
Haines, Robert William *Law&B 92*
Haines, Robin Lynn 1961- *WhoWor 93*
Haines, Ronald *St&PR 93*
Haines, Ronald H. 1934- *WhoAm 92*
Haines, Samuel L. 1944- *St&PR 93*
Haines, Shirley Lynn 1951- *WhoAmW 93*
Haines, Stephen W. 1936- *St&PR 93*
Haines, Thomas Joseph *Law&B 92*
Haines, Thomas W. W. 1941- *WhoAm 92*
Haines, Walter Wells 1918- *WhoAm 92*
Haines, William 1900-1973 *BioIn 17*
Haines, William Joseph 1919- *WhoAm 92, WhoWor 93*
Haines, William Stokes 1921- *St&PR 93*
Haines, William Wister 1908-1989 *BioIn 17*
Haing S. Ngor *BioIn 17*
Haining, James Howard 1950- *WhoWrEP 92*
Haining, Peter 1940- *ScF&FL 92*
Hainl, Francois 1807-1873 *Baker 92*
Hainley, Gary *St&PR 93*
Hainline, Forrest Arthur, Jr. 1918- *WhoAm 92, WhoSSW 93, WhoWor 93*
Hainline, Louise 1947- *WhoAmW 93, WhoE 93*
Hainline, Wallace F. 1906- *WhoE 93*
Hainsworth-Straus, Christine Louise 1962- *WhoAmW 93*
Hainy, Keith W. 1951- *St&PR 93*
Haipt, Mildred Mary 1928- *WhoE 93*
Hair, Don B. 1950- *St&PR 93*
Hair, Donald W. 1938- *St&PR 93*
Hair, James E. d1992 *BioIn 17, NewYTBS 92*
Hair, Leroy McCurry 1937- *WhoSSW 93*
Hair, Marcia Elizabeth 1948- *WhoAmW 93, WhoSSW 93*
Hair, Mattox Strickland 1938- *WhoSSW 93*
Hair, Paul E. 1928- *St&PR 93*
Hairald, Mary Payne 1936- *WhoAmW 93*
Haire, Bill Martin 1936- *WhoAm 92*
Haire, Christie K. *St&PR 93*
Haire, James 1938- *WhoAm 92*
Haire, James R. *WhoAm 92*
Haire, James R. 1947- *WhoIns 93*
Haire, John R. 1925- *St&PR 93*
Haire, John Russell 1925- *WhoAm 92*
Haire, Thomas B. d1990 *BioIn 17*
Haire, Thomas E. 1944- *ConEn*
Haire, Thomas Edwin 1944- *St&PR 93*
Hairell, Melvin L. 1938- *WhoIns 93*
Hairell, Melvin Lloyd 1938- *St&PR 93*
Haire-Sargeant, Lin 1946- *ConAu 139*
Hairs, Hugh Michael 1940- *WhoWrEP 92*
Hairston, Jay Timothy 1956- *WhoWor 93*
Hairston, Julie Janette 1963- *WhoEmL 93*
Hairston, Miriam Estelle 1959- *WhoAmW 93*
Hairston, Nelson George 1917- *WhoAm 92*
Hairston, Peyton T., Jr. *Law&B 92*
Hairston, Robert Conway 1951- *WhoE 93*
Hairston, William George 1944- *St&PR 93*
Hairston, William Michael 1947- *WhoAm 92, WhoEmL 93, WhoSSW 93*
Hairston, William Russell, Jr. 1928- *WhoAm 92, WhoSSW 93*
Haisch, Karl Heinrich 1933- *WhoScE 91-3*
Haisch, Udo Manfred Dieter 1940- *WhoWor 93*
Haise, Fred Wallace, Jr. 1933- *WhoAm 92*
Haiser, Gary Martin 1945- *WhoSSW 93, WhoWor 93*
Haislett, Nicole *WhoAmW 93*
Haislmaier, Robert Joseph 1929- *WhoAm 92*
Haist, Dennis P. *Law&B 92*
Haisten, Marilyn Majors 1946- *WhoAmW 93*
Hait, Fred Harold 1947- *WhoEmL 93*
Hait, Gershon 1927- *WhoAm 92*
Hait, Richard Scott 1926- *WhoAm 92*
Haitink, Bernard 1929- *OxDcOp*
Haitink, Bernard J. H. 1929- *WhoWor 93*
Haitink, Bernard (Johann Herman) 1929- *Baker 92*
Haitzinger, Anton 1796-1869 *Baker 92*
Haizinger, Anton 1796-1869 *Baker 92, OxDcOp*
Haizlip, Ellis B. *BioIn 17*
Haizlip, Henry H., Jr. 1913- *St&PR 93*
Haizlip, Henry Hardin, Jr. 1913- *WhoAm 92*
Haizlip, Jeannine LaMair *Law&B 92*
Haizlip, Wilson Williamson *Law&B 92*
Hajah Rahmah Osman 1939 *WhoAsAP 91*
Haj Amin al-Husseini 1897-1974 *DcTwHis*
Hajda, Nina J. *ScF&FL 92*
Hajda, Thomas A. *Law&B 92*
Hajdin, Rade 1961- *WhoWor 93*
Hajdinyak, John Steven 1953- *WhoE 93*
Hajdu, Andre 1932- *Baker 92*
Hajdu, Janos 1934- *WhoScE 91-3*
Hajdu, Joseph 1921- *WhoScE 91-4*
Hajdu, Mihaly 1909- *Baker 92*
Hajduk, Boguslaw 1948- *WhoWor 93*
Haje, Pater R. *Law&B 92*
Haje, Peter Robert 1934- *WhoAm 92*
Hajec, Richard George 1935- *St&PR 93*
Hajek, Bradley Carr 1963- *WhoE 93*
Hajek, Francis Paul 1958- *WhoEmL 93*
Hajek, Joseph C. 1942- *St&PR 93*
Hajek, Monika D. *Law&B 92*
Hajek, Otomar 1930- *WhoAm 92*
Hajek, Stanislav 1919- *WhoScE 91-4*
Hajek, Vaclav 1934- *WhoScE 91-4*
Haji, Iqbal 1940- *WhoUN 92*
Hajian, Gerald 1940- *WhoSSW 93*
Hajicek, Robert A. 1937- *St&PR 93*
Hajim, Edmund A. 1936- *WhoAm 92*
Hajime 1932- *WhoAsAP 91*
Hajinian, Nazar 1925- *St&PR 93*
Haji-Sheikh, Abdol Hossein 1933- *WhoSSW 93*
Hajivassiliou, Vassilis Argyrou 1957- *WhoEmL 93*
Hajj, Ibrahim Nasri 1942- *WhoAm 92*
Hajjan, Mohammed el- *ScF&FL 92*
Hajjar, Jean-Jacques Joseph 1961- *WhoE 93*
Hajko, V. *WhoScE 91-4*
Hajko, Vladimir 1920- *WhoWor 93*
Hajmasy, Tibor *WhoScE 91-4*
Hajmasy, Tibor 1927- *WhoScE 91-4*
Haj Muhammad Hassan Amin al-Zarb d1898 *BioIn 17*
Hajnoczi, Thomas 1955- *WhoUN 92*
Hajos, Ferenc 1936- *WhoScE 91-4*
Hakala, Judyth Ann 1955- *WhoEmL 93*
Hakala, Thomas John 1948- *WhoE 93*
Hakala, Thomas Richard 1936- *WhoAm 92*
Hakala, Veli Jaakko 1954- *WhoWor 93*
Hakalahti, Hannu *WhoScE 91-4*
Hakama, Matti 1939- *WhoScE 91-4*
Hakani, Hysen 1932- *DrEEuF*
Hakansson, Inge L. 1929- *WhoScE 91-4*
Hakansson, Kjell *WhoScE 91-4*
Hakansson, Kjell G. 1929- *WhoWor 93*
Hakansson, Knut (Algot) 1887-1929 *Baker 92*
Hake, Rodger B. 1940- *WhoScE 91-1*
Hake, Terry *BioIn 17*
Hake, William M. 1953- *St&PR 93*
Hakel, Milton Daniel, Jr. 1941- *WhoAm 92*
Hakemi, Hassan-Ali 1946- *WhoWor 93*
Haken, Hermann P.J. 1927- *WhoScE 91-3*
Hakes, Beth *WhoEmL 93*
Hakes, James Edward *Law&B 92*
Hakes, John Earl 1932- *St&PR 93*
Hakes, John M. 1940- *St&PR 93*
Hakim, Carla Susan 1961- *WhoAmW 93*
Hakim, Masud 1936- *St&PR 93, WhoAm 92*
Hakim, Maximos V. 1908- *WhoWor 93*
Hakim, Seymour 1933- *WhoWor 93*
Hakim, Talib Rasul 1940-1988 *Baker 92*
Hakim, Tawfiq al- 1898-1987 *BioIn 17*
Hakim-Elahi, Enayat 1934- *WhoE 93*
Hakimi, S. Louis 1932- *WhoAm 92*
Hakimoglu, Ayhan 1927- *St&PR 93*
Hakimoglu, Geraldine A. 1950- *St&PR 93*
Hakimoglu, Geraldine Ann 1950- *WhoAmW 93*
Hakkarainen, Jorma *WhoScE 91-4*
Hakkarainen, Tero J. 1941- *WhoScE 91-4*
Hakkila, Pentti Tapani 1935- *WhoScE 91-4*
Hakkinen, Raimo Jaakko 1926- *WhoAm 92*
Hakli, Esko Antero 1936- *WhoWor 93*
Hakola, Hannu Panu Aukusti 1932- *WhoWor 93*
Hakovirta, Harto Kalevi 1941- *WhoWor 93*
Hakozaki, Katsuya 1941- *WhoWor 93*
Hakstege, C. *WhoScE 91-3*
Hakulin, Bertel Kristian 1930- *WhoWor 93*
Halabi, Jorge Alberto 1952- *WhoWor 93*
Halabi, Walid M. K. 1957- *WhoWor 93*
Halaby, Henry Joseph 1928- *St&PR 93*
Halaby, Lisa *BioIn 17*
Halaby, Najeeb E. 1915- *EncABHB 8 [port], WhoAm 92*
Halaby, Samia Asaad 1936- *WhoAm 92*
Haladej, M. Andrew 1927- *St&PR 93*
Halal, William Enitt 1933- *WhoWor 93*
Halam, Ann *ScF&FL 92*
Halam, Ann 1952- *ChlFicS*
Halamandaris, Harry 1938- *WhoAm 92*
Halan, John Paul 1928- *WhoAm 92, WhoWor 93*
Halard, Francois *BioIn 17*
Halaris, Angelos 1942- *WhoAm 92*
Halas, Andrej 1934- *WhoScE 91-4*
Halas, Cynthia Ann 1961- *WhoAmW 93, WhoEmL 93*
Halas, Edward J. 1943- *St&PR 93*
Halas, George Stanley 1895-1983 *BioIn 17*
Halas, Paul J. *Law&B 92*
Halaseh, Khalil Tawfic 1959- *WhoWor 93*
Halasi, Rozsa 1933- *WhoScE 91-4*
Halasi-Kun, George Joseph 1916- *WhoAm 92*
Halasi-Kun, Tibor 1914-1991 *BioIn 17*
Halaska, Howard E. 1919- *St&PR 93*
Halaska, Robert H. 1940- *WhoAm 92*
Halaska, Thomas Edward 1945- *WhoSSW 93*
Halasz, Anna 1938- *WhoScE 91-4*

Halasz, Aurel 1923- *WhoScE 91-4*
Halasz, Laszlo 1905- *Baker 92*
Halasz, Nicholas Alexis 1931- *WhoAm 92*
Halasz, Otto 1927- *WhoScE 91-4*
Halata, Zdenek 1939- *WhoScE 91-3*
Halbach, Patrice H. *Law&B 92*
Halbach, Patrice Haley 1953- *WhoEmL 93*
Halbach, Susan T. *Law&B 92*
Halbe, Max 1865-1944 *DcLB 118 [port]*
Halberg, Charles John August, Jr. 1921- *WhoAm 92, WhoWor 93*
Halberg, G. Peter 1915- *WhoAm 92*
Halberstadt, Robert Bilheimer 1918- *WhoE 93, WhoWor 93*
Halberstam, David 1934- *ColdWar 1 [port], WhoAm 92, WhoWrEP 92*
Halberstam, Heini 1926- *WhoAm 92*
Halberstam, Malvina 1937- *WhoAm 92*
Halberstam, Michael 1932-1980 *ScF&FL 92*
Halberstein, Joseph L. 1915- *St&PR 93*
Halbert, Dohsis 1949- *WhoAsAP 91*
Halbert, Melvyn Leonard 1929- *WhoSSW 93*
Halbmayr, Helmut 1942- *WhoScE 91-4*
Halbouty, Manah Robert 1914- *WhoSSW 93, WhoWor 93*
Halbouty, Michel T. 1909- *St&PR 93*
Halbouty, Michel Thomas 1909- *WhoAm 92*
Halbrecht, Kenneth Ashley 1960- *WhoE 93*
Halbreich, Kathy *BioIn 17*
Halbreich, Kathy 1949- *WhoAm 92, WhoAmW 93*
Halbritter, Marc A. *Law&B 92*
Halbritter, Marc Alan *Law&B 92*
Halbritter, Marc Alan 1955- *St&PR 93*
Halbrook, Duane *ScF&FL 92*
Halbrook, Jack 1943- *St&PR 93*
Halbrooks, Carol A. *BioIn 17*
Halbstein, Bernard M. 1910-1991 *BioIn 17*
Halby, William G. *Law&B 92*
Halby, William Grandjean 1931- *St&PR 93*
Halcolm *WhoWrEP 92*
Haldane, Elizabeth Sanderson 1862-1937 *BioIn 17*
Haldane, J.B.S. 1892-1964 *ScF&FL 92*
Haldane, Richard Burdon 1856-1928 *BioIn 17, DcTwHis, HarEnMi*
Haldar, Dipak 1937- *WhoE 93*
Haldeman, Candace *ScF&FL 92*
Haldeman, Charles Waldo, III 1936- *WhoE 93*
Haldeman, Harry R. 1926- *WhoAm 92*
Haldeman, Jack C., II 1941- *ScF&FL 92*
Haldeman, Janice Hamilton 1936- *WhoAmW 93*
Haldeman, Joe 1943- *ScF&FL 92*
Haldeman, Joe W. 1943- *BioIn 17*
Haldeman, Joe William 1943- *WhoWrEP 92*
Haldeman, Laurie *ScF&FL 92*
Haldeman, Linda 1935?-1988 *ScF&FL 92*
Haldeman, Robert B. 1934- *St&PR 93*
Haldeman, Susan Ward 1951- *WhoAmW 93*
Haldeman, Vol 1946- *ScF&FL 92*
Haldeman-Julius, Anna Marcet *AmWomPl*
Haldeman-Julius, E. 1889-1951 *ScF&FL 92*
Halder, Chris *BioIn 17*
Halder, Franz 1884-1972 *BioIn 17, DcTwHis, HarEnMi*
Halderman, John W. 1907-1989 *BioIn 17*
Halderman, Ken *St&PR 93*
Halderson, Clark A. *Law&B 92*
Haldimann, Martha Marian 1940- *WhoWor 93*
Haldin, Rikard Valter 1959- *WhoWor 93*
Hale, A. Dean 1929- *WhoWrEP 92*
Hale, Adam de la *Baker 92*
Hale, Alan 1892-1950 *BioIn 17*
Hale, Alan 1918-1990 *BioIn 17*
Hale, Alan L. d1991 *BioIn 17*
Hale, Alan P. 1960- *St&PR 93*
Hale, Allean Lemmon 1914- *WhoWrEP 92*
Hale, Andrew 1939- *ScF&FL 92*
Hale, Arnold Wayne 1934- *WhoSSW 93, WhoWor 93*
Hale, Barbara 1921- *SweetSg D*
Hale, Beverly Ann 1939- *WhoWor 93*
Hale, Billy 1934- *ConTFT 10*
Hale, Cecil Harrison 1919- *St&PR 93*
Hale, Charles F. *Law&B 92*
Hale, Charles F. 1931- *St&PR 93*
Hale, Charles Martin 1936- *WhoAm 92, WhoWor 93*
Hale, Charles Russell 1916- *WhoAm 92*
Hale, Charlotte 1928- *WhoAm 92*
Hale, Clara *BioIn 17*
Hale, Clara M. d1992 *NewYTBS 92 [port]*
Hale, D. Curtis 1951- *WhoSSW 93*
Hale, Daniel R. *Law&B 92*
Hale, Danny Lyman 1944- *St&PR 93, WhoAm 92, WhoWor 93*
Hale, David Peter 1958- *WhoSSW 93*
Hale, Dean Edward 1950- *WhoEmL 93*
Hale, Donald J. *Law&B 92*
Hale, Donald J. 1937- *St&PR 93*
Hale, F.J. *ScF&FL 92*
Hale, Ford R., Jr. 1918- *WhoSSW 93*
Hale, Gina LaStelle 1959- *WhoAmW 93*
Hale, Glenn *ScF&FL 92*
Hale, Gregory A. *Law&B 92*
Hale, H. David 1944- *St&PR 93*
Hale, Hamilton Orin 1906- *WhoAm 92*
Hale, Hershel David 1944- *WhoAm 92, WhoSSW 93*
Hale, Hilton Ingram 1956- *WhoWor 93*
Hale, Hope *WhoWrEP 92*
Hale, Horatio Emmons 1817-1896 *IntDcAn*
Hale, Jack K. 1928- *WhoAm 92*
Hale, James *ScF&FL 92*
Hale, James Pierce 1928- *WhoSSW 93*
Hale, James Randolph 1951- *St&PR 93*
Hale, James Russell 1918- *WhoAm 92*
Hale, James T. *Law&B 92*
Hale, James Thomas 1940- *WhoAm 92*
Hale, Jennifer *ScF&FL 92*
Hale, Jerry Wayne 1951- *WhoSSW 93*
Hale, John 1926- *ScF&FL 92*
Hale, John Dewey 1937- *WhoAm 92*
Hale, John L. 1940- *St&PR 93*
Hale, John Mathew 1962- *WhoSSW 93*
Hale, John McKee 1935- *WhoSSW 93*
Hale, John P. 1806-1873 *PolPar*
Hale, John Rigby 1923- *WhoWor 93*
Hale, Joseph Rice 1935- *WhoAm 92*
Hale, Judson D. 1933- *St&PR 93*
Hale, Judson Drake 1933- *WhoWrEP 92*
Hale, Judson Drake, Sr. 1933- *WhoAm 92, WhoE 93*
Hale, Karyn *BioIn 17*
Hale, Katherine Lee 1951- *St&PR 93*
Hale, Kathleen 1898- *BioIn 17*
Hale, Kaycee *BioIn 17*
Hale, Kyleen K. 1953- *St&PR 93*
Hale, Laurence Swart 1925- *WhoAm 92*
Hale, Louise Closser 1872-1933 *AmWomPl*
Hale, Lucretia Peabody 1820-1900 *ConAu 136, MajAI [port]*
Hale, Margaret Smith 1945- *WhoAmW 93*
Hale, Marilyn Carlene 1951- *WhoAmW 93*
Hale, Martin De Mora 1941- *St&PR 93*
Hale, Michael *ConAu 38NR, ScF&FL 92*
Hale, Oliver Daniel *WhoScE 91-1*
Hale, Oron J. 1902-1991 *BioIn 17*
Hale, Philip 1854-1934 *Baker 92*
Hale, R. Walter, III 1943- *St&PR 93*
Hale, Ralph Webster 1935- *WhoAm 92*
Hale, Richard Lee 1930- *WhoAm 92, WhoSSW 93, WhoWrEP 92*
Hale, Richard Thomas, Jr. 1945- *WhoAm 92, WhoE 93*
Hale, Robert Beverly 1901-1985 *ScF&FL 92*
Hale, Robert Graham 1934- *WhoE 93*
Hale, Roger Loucks 1934- *St&PR 93, WhoAm 92*
Hale, Russell Thomas 1939- *St&PR 93*
Hale, Ruth Ann 1956- *WhoEmL 93*
Hale, Sandra J. *BioIn 17*
Hale, Sarah Josepha *BioIn 17*
Hale, Sarah Josepha Buell 1788-1879 *JrnUS*
Hale, Sheila B. 1944- *St&PR 93*
Hale, Sonnie 1902-1959 *QDrFCA 92 [port]*
Hale, Thomas 1937- *BioIn 17*
Hale, Truman W. 1953- *St&PR 93*
Hale, William *MiSFD 9*
Hale, William Gregson *WhoScE 91-1*
Hale, William Henry, Jr. 1940- *WhoSSW 93*
Hale, Willie *SoulM*
Hale, Willis H. 1893-1961 *HarEnMi*
Halecki, Oscar 1891-1973 *PolBiDi*
Halecky, Benedicta Martha 1958- *WhoAmW 93*
Halegua, Alfredo 1930- *WhoE 93*
Halein, Kathinka 1801-1877 *BioIn 17*
Haleman, Laura Rand 1946- *WhoEmL 93*
Hale O'Connor, Diann 1934- *WhoAm 92*
Haler, Lawrence Eugene 1951- *WhoWor 93*
Hales, Alfred Washington 1938- *WhoAm 92*
Hales, Brad Lee 1953- *WhoEmL 93*
Hales, Charles Albert 1941- *WhoE 93*
Hales, Charles Nicholas *WhoScE 91-1*
Hales, Daniel B. 1941- *WhoAm 92*
Hales, Duke C. 1941- *St&PR 93*
Hales, E.E.Y. 1908- *ScF&FL 92*
Hales, Lisa Herman 1961- *WhoSSW 93*
Hales, Myrt T. 1956- *WhoEmL 93*
Hales, Patricia Louise 1955- *WhoAmW 93*
Hales-Mabry, Celia Elaine 1946- *WhoAmW 93, WhoEmL 93*
Halevi, Yehudah 12th cent.- *BioIn 17*
Halevy, Abraham Hayim 1927- *WhoWor 93*
Halevy, Beth M. *Law&B 92*
Halevy, Fromental 1799-1862 *OxDcOp*
Halevy, (Jacques-Francois-) Fromental (-Elie) 1799-1862 *Baker 92*
Halevy, Jacques-Francois-Fromental-Elie 1799-1862 *IntDcOp*
Halevy, Simon 1929- *WhoAm 92*
Halevy, Uzi 1936- *St&PR 93*
Haley, Alex *BioIn 17*
Haley, Alex 1921-1992 *ConBlB 4 [port], ConHero 2 [port]*
Haley, Alex 1924-1992 *NewYTBS 92 [port], News 92, -92-3*
Haley, Alex(ander Murray Palmer) 1921-1992 *ConAu 136*
Haley, Alex Palmer 1921- *WhoWrEP 92*
Haley, Alex (Palmer) 1921-1992 *CurBio 92N, EncAACR*
Haley, Andrew G. *BioIn 17*
Haley, Bill 1925-1981 *Baker 92*
Haley, C. James, Jr. 1942- *St&PR 93*
Haley, Claud *ScF&FL 92*
Haley, Clifton E. 1931- *St&PR 93, WhoAm 92*
Haley, Clifton Edward 1931- *WhoAm 92*
Haley, Craig P. 1946- *St&PR 93*
Haley, Dianne Rae 1944- *St&PR 93*
Haley, Donald S. *Law&B 92*
Haley, Frederick Thomas 1912- *St&PR 93*
Haley, Gail E(inhart) 1939- *MajAI [port]*
Haley, Gail Einhart 1939- *WhoAm 92*
Haley, George 1929- *WhoAm 92*
Haley, George Brock, Jr. 1926- *WhoAm 92*
Haley, George H. d1991 *BioIn 17*
Haley, George Williford Boyce 1925- *WhoAm 92*
Haley, Harry F. 1883-1965 *ScF&FL 92*
Haley, J. Evetts 1901- *BioIn 17*
Haley, Jack 1899-1979 *QDrFCA 92 [port]*
Haley, Jack 1964- *BioIn 17*
Haley, Jack, Jr. 1933- *MiSFD 9, WhoAm 92*
Haley, James L. 1951- *ScF&FL 92*
Haley, Jean Rodger 1936- *WhoAmW 93*
Haley, John Charles 1929- *WhoAm 92*
Haley, John David 1924- *WhoWor 93*
Haley, Johnetta Randolph *WhoAmW 93, WhoWor 93*
Haley, Keith Brian *WhoScE 91-1*
Haley, Kevin Jon 1959- *WhoEmL 93*
Haley, Mark *Law&B 92*
Haley, Mark Tyler 1951- *St&PR 93*
Haley, Michael John 1948- *WhoE 93*
Haley, Michael Wayne 1948- *WhoSSW 93*
Haley, Nedom Angier 1943- *WhoSSW 93*
Haley, Neil B. 1934- *WhoUN 92*
Haley, Priscilla Jane 1926- *WhoAm 92*
Haley, Richard Charles 1942- *WhoSSW 93*
Haley, Robert Lewis 1919- *WhoSSW 93*
Haley, Roger Kendall 1938- *WhoAm 92*
Haley, Rosemary Elizabeth 1926-1992 *WhoWor 93*
Haley, Roy W. 1946- *St&PR 93, WhoAm 92, WhoIns 93*
Haley, Roy W. 1947- *WhoSSW 93*
Haley, Russell John 1931- *St&PR 93*
Haley, Shawna M. *Law&B 92*
Haley, Simon Alexander *BioIn 17*
Haley, Stephen B. 1942- *WhoAm 92*
Haley, Thomas E. 1938- *St&PR 93*
Haley, Vanessa Leigh 1954- *WhoWrEP 92*
Haley, Vincent Peter 1931- *WhoAm 92*
Haley, Wayne William 1947- *WhoIns 93*
Half, Robert 1918- *WhoAm 92, WhoWor 93*
Halfant, Gary D. 1953- *WhoEmL 93, WhoWor 93*
Halfen, Abraham 1947- *WhoE 93*
Halfen, David 1924- *WhoAm 92*
Halff, Alex Hart 1931- *St&PR 93*
Halff, Bro 1946- *WhoWrEP 92*
Halff, Henry Mayer 1942- *WhoSSW 93*
Halffter (Escriche), Ernesto 1905-1989 *Baker 92*
Halffter (Escriche), Rodolfo 1900-1987 *Baker 92*
Halffter (Jimenez), Cristobal 1930- *Baker 92*
Halfin, Bobbie *BioIn 17*
Halfman, Margaret L. *Law&B 92*
Halfon, Peter B. 1938- *St&PR 93*
Halford, Carol Ann 1960- *WhoAmW 93*
Halford, Donna LaNelle 1942- *WhoAmW 93*
Halford, William Dean 1938- *WhoWor 93*
Halfvarson, Lucille Robertson 1919- *WhoAmW 93*
Halgren, Donald Nelson *Law&B 92*
Haliassos, Michael 1959- *WhoEmL 93*
Haliburton, Thomas Chandler 1796-1865 *BioIn 17*
Halicky, John P. 1950- *St&PR 93*
Haliczer, James Solomon 1952- *WhoEmL 93, WhoSSW 93, WhoWor 93*
Halifax, Edward Frederick Lindley Wood, Viscount and Earl of 1881-1959 *DcTwHis*
Halik, Nancy Lickerman 1954- *WhoEmL 93*
Halim, Eduardus *BioIn 17*
Halimi, Gisele 1927- *BioIn 17*
Halinski, Linda Lee 1945- *WhoAmW 93*
Halinski, Richard Thomas, Jr. *Law&B 92*
Halio, Jay Leon 1928- *WhoAm 92*
Halir, Carl 1859-1909 *Baker 92*
Haliw, Andrew Jerome, III 1946- *WhoAm 92*
Halka, Kathleen Grace 1953- *WhoEmL 93*
Halkes, C.J.J. *WhoScE 91-3*
Halket, Thomas D. 1948- *WhoEmL 93*
Halkett, Alan Neilson 1931- *WhoAm 92*
Halki, John Joseph 1926- *WhoAm 92*
Halkias, Christos 1933- *WhoScE 91-3*
Halkias, Demetrios George 1932- *WhoSSW 93*
Halkin, Abraham S. 1903-1990 *BioIn 17*
Halkin, Hubert 1936- *WhoAm 92*
Halkin, John 1927- *ScF&FL 92*
Halkka, Olli J. 1928- *WhoScE 91-4*
Halkyard, Edwin Milton 1934- *St&PR 93, WhoAm 92*
Halkyard, Robert C. 1935- *St&PR 93*
Hall, Abraham 1826-1898 *JrnUS*
Hall, Adam *ScF&FL 92*
Hall, Adrian *MiSFD 9*
Hall, Adrian 1927- *WhoWrEP 92*
Hall, Adrienne Ann *WhoAmW 93*
Hall, Alan F. *Law&B 92*
Hall, Albert Leander 1926- *WhoAm 92*
Hall, Alden Barker 1927- *WhoE 93*
Hall, Alexander 1894-1968 *MiSFD 9N*
Hall, Alma L. *AmWomPl*
Hall, Almon C. 1946- *St&PR 93*
Hall, Alvin M. *Law&B 92*
Hall, Alvin Owsley, Jr. 1931- *WhoSSW 93*
Hall, Alvin Stewart, Jr. 1942- *St&PR 93*
Hall, Andrew Clifford 1944- *WhoAm 92, WhoSSW 93, WhoWor 93*
Hall, Andrew J. *WhoAm 92*
Hall, Ann Louise 1946- *WhoWrEP 92*
Hall, Anna Christene 1946- *WhoAmW 93*
Hall, Annette Howard 1941- *WhoAmW 93*
Hall, Anthony Ray 1962- *WhoSSW 93*
Hall, Anthony Robert 1938- *St&PR 93, WhoAm 92*
Hall, Aristides 1936- *WhoScE 91-3*
Hall, Arnold Alexander 1915- *WhoAm 92*
Hall, Arsenio *BioIn 17*
Hall, Arsenio 1955- *AfrAmBi, WhoAm 92*
Hall, Arsenio 1957- *HolBB [port]*
Hall, Arthur James *Law&B 92*
Hall, Arthur Raymond, Jr. 1922- *WhoAm 92*
Hall, Arthur W. 1943- *St&PR 93*
Hall, Asaph H. 1933- *St&PR 93*
Hall, Asaph Hale 1933- *WhoAm 92*
Hall, Austin 1880-1933 *ScF&FL 92*
Hall, Barbara 1960- *BioIn 17*
Hall, Bernard 1925- *WhoAm 92*
Hall, Bernard Joseph 1955- *WhoEmL 93*
Hall, Bertha Parker *AmWomPl*
Hall, Beth S. 1946- *St&PR 93*
Hall, Beth Shand 1946- *WhoAmW 93*
Hall, Betty Jane 1928- *WhoAmW 93, WhoWor 93*
Hall, Betty Kathleen 1908- *WhoWrEP 92*
Hall, Beverly Adele 1935- *WhoAm 92*
Hall, Beverly Elaine 1957- *WhoAmW 93*
Hall, Beverly Stewart 1939- *WhoAmW 93*
Hall, Bill 1948- *BioIn 17*
Hall, Blanche Barbara 1928- *WhoSSW 93*
Hall, Bradley Clarke 1941- *St&PR 93*
Hall, Brenda Yvonne 1957- *WhoAmW 93*
Hall, Brian 1935- *ScF&FL 92*
Hall, Brian Barrie *WhoScE 91-1*
Hall, Brian H. 1947- *St&PR 93*
Hall, Brian (Jonathan) 1959- *ConAu 137*
Hall, Brian Keith 1941- *WhoAm 92*
Hall, Brian Olliff *WhoScE 91-1*
Hall, Brooks 1921- *St&PR 93*
Hall, Bruce W. *St&PR 93*
Hall, Burton H. 1929-1991 *BioIn 17*
Hall, Carl William 1924- *WhoAm 92*
Hall, Carlyle Washington, Jr. 1943- *WhoAm 92*
Hall, Carole *BioIn 17*
Hall, Cathy Jayne Wright 1951- *WhoAmW 93*
Hall, Charles Allan 1941- *WhoAm 92*
Hall, Charles Allen 1933- *WhoAm 92*
Hall, Charles Douglas 1948- *WhoEmL 93*
Hall, Charles F. 1920- *BioIn 17*
Hall, Charles Francis 1821-1871 *Expl 93*
Hall, Charles Frederick 1920- *WhoAm 92*
Hall, Charles M. 1932- *St&PR 93*
Hall, Charles P. *BioIn 17*
Hall, Charles Philip 1886-1953 *HarEnMi*
Hall, Charles W. 1944- *St&PR 93*

Hall, Charles Washington 1930- WhoAm 92
Hall, Charles William 1922- WhoAm 92
Hall, Charlotte Hauch 1945- WhoAm 92
Hall, Christie Lea 1958- WhoWrEP 92
Hall, Christopher George Longden 1956- WhoE 93, WhoEmL 93, WhoWor 93
Hall, Clarence Albert, Jr. 1930- WhoAm 92
Hall, Claude Hampton 1922- WhoAm 92
Hall, Conrad 1926- WhoAm 92
Hall, Conrad Mercer 1943- St&PR 93
Hall, Craig P. Law&B 92
Hall, Crystal S. 1962- WhoSSW 93
Hall, Cynthia B. Law&B 92
Hall, Cynthia Holcomb 1929- WhoAm 92, WhoAmW 93
Hall, D. Helaine 1949- WhoWrEP 92
Hall, Daniel G. Law&B 92
Hall, Daniel G. 1938- WhoIns 93
Hall, Daniel G. 1946- St&PR 93
Hall, Daniel N. Law&B 92
Hall, Daniel Weston 1841- BioIn 17
Hall, Daryl 1949- WhoAm 92
Hall, Daryl 1949- & Oates, John 1949- SoulM
Hall, Dave BioIn 17
Hall, David 1714-1772 JrnUS
Hall, David 1916- Baker 92, WhoAm 92
Hall, David 1943- WhoE 93
Hall, David Benjamin 1951- WhoE 93
Hall, David Charles 1944- WhoAm 92
Hall, David Earl Law&B 92
Hall, David Edward 1940- WhoAm 92
Hall, David K. Law&B 92
Hall, David N. 1939- St&PR 93
Hall, David Oakley WhoScE 91-1
Hall, David Spencer 1929- St&PR 93
Hall, David W. 1947- WhoIns 93
Hall, Deanna BioIn 17
Hall, Deborah Jane 1952- WhoE 93
Hall, Dennis Gene 1948- WhoE 93
Hall, Dennis J. 1941- St&PR 93
Hall, Denver George WhoScE 91-1
Hall, Derek Harry 1945- WhoAm 92
Hall, Desmond ScF&FL 92
Hall, Desmond W. d1992 NewYTBS 92
Hall, Dewey Eugene 1932- WhoWor 93
Hall, Don Alan 1938- WhoAm 92
Hall, Donald 1928- BioIn 17, WhoAm 92, WhoWrEP 92
Hall, Donald Joyce 1928- WhoAm 92
Hall, Donald Keith 1931- St&PR 93
Hall, Donald M. 1920- St&PR 93
Hall, Donald Norman Blake 1944- WhoAm 92
Hall, Donald Perry 1927- St&PR 93
Hall, Donald S. 1940- WhoAm 92
Hall, Donna Ann 1962- St&PR 93
Hall, Donna F. 1927- St&PR 93
Hall, Dorothy Day 1929- WhoAmW 93
Hall, Dorothy Gay Nell 1941- St&PR 93, WhoAm 92
Hall, Douglas Lee 1947- WhoEmL 93, WhoSSW 93, WhoWor 93
Hall, Douglas N. 1930- WhoIns 93
Hall, Douglas Scott 1940- WhoSSW 93
Hall, Dwayne Allen 1958- WhoEmL 93, WhoSSW 93
Hall, E. Eugene 1932- WhoAm 92
Hall, Ed 1931-1991 ConTFT 10
Hall, Edd NewYTBS 92 [port]
Hall, Edith BioIn 17
Hall, Edmond 1901-1967 Baker 92
Hall, Edmund Joseph, Jr. 1930- St&PR 93
Hall, Edward H., Jr. 1935- St&PR 93
Hall, Edward T. 1914- CurBio 92 [port], IntDcAn
Hall, Edward Twitchell BioIn 17
Hall, Edward Twitchell 1914- WhoAm 92
Hall, Edwin Presley, Jr. 1941- WhoSSW 93
Hall, Elizabeth 1929- WhoAm 92
Hall, Ella Mae 1945- WhoAmW 93
Hall, Ellen SweetSg C
Hall, Ellen Wood WhoAm 92, WhoAmW 93
Hall, Elliott Sawyer 1938- St&PR 93, WhoAm 92
Hall, Ernest L. 1940- WhoAm 92
Hall, Ernst Paul 1925- WhoAm 92
Hall, Eula BioIn 17
Hall, Everett BioIn 17
Hall, F. McKamy 1942- St&PR 93
Hall, Fawn BioIn 17
Hall, Floyd 1938- WhoAm 92
Hall, Frances 1914- ScF&FL 92
Hall, Francoise Puvrez 1932- WhoAm 92, WhoAmW 93
Hall, Frank K. 1942- St&PR 93
Hall, Franklin R. d1991 BioIn 17
Hall, Frederick Douglass 1898-1982 Baker 92
Hall, Frederick Keith 1930- WhoAm 92, WhoE 93
Hall, Frederick Lee 1916-1970 BioIn 17
Hall, G. Stanley 1844-1924 GayN
Hall, Garrett W. 1946- St&PR 93
Hall, Geoffrey WhoScE 91-1
Hall, Geoffrey E. 1946- WhoScE 91-1
Hall, Geoffrey Walsh 1937- WhoSSW 93
Hall, Georganna Mae 1951- WhoEmL 93, WhoSSW 93
Hall, George Atwater 1925- WhoAm 92
Hall, George F(ridolph) 1908- WhoWrEP 92
Hall, Gloria Jean BioIn 17
Hall, Gordon R. 1926- WhoAm 92
Hall, Grace Rosalie 1921- WhoE 93
Hall, Graham Ainsley WhoScE 91-1
Hall, Gregory J. St&PR 93
Hall, Gus BioIn 17
Hall, Gus 1910- ConAu 137, PolPar, WhoAm 92
Hall, Hal W. 1941- ScF&FL 92
Hall, Harold G. 1922- St&PR 93
Hall, Harold H. 1926-1991 BioIn 17
Hall, Harry A., III 1928- St&PR 93
Hall, Harry H. 1934- WhoSSW 93
Hall, Harvey Dale 1925- WhoSSW 93
Hall, Hazel A. Law&B 92
Hall, Helen Frances 1946- WhoAmW 93
Hall, Helen Marian Law&B 92
Hall, Helen Norton 1911- WhoSSW 93
Hall, Henry B. 1933- St&PR 93
Hall, Henry Edgar WhoScE 91-1
Hall, Henry Lee 1949- WhoEmL 93
Hall, Henry Lyon, Jr. 1931- WhoAm 92
Hall, Houghton Alexander 1936- WhoSSW 93
Hall, Howard E. 1930- St&PR 93
Hall, Howard Henry 1939- St&PR 93
Hall, Howard Kingsley 1967- WhoE 93
Hall, Howard Tracy 1919- WhoAm 92
Hall, Howard Wesley 1949- WhoEmL 93
Hall, Hugh David 1931- WhoAm 92
Hall, Hugh Gaston 1931- WhoWor 93
Hall, Huntz 1920- See Bowery Boys, The QDrFCA 92
Hall, Idaline L. Law&B 92
Hall, J. Diana Law&B 92
Hall, Jack Gilbert 1927- WhoAm 92
Hall, James 1900-1940 BioIn 17
Hall, James A. 1942- St&PR 93
Hall, James Alexander 1920- WhoAm 92
Hall, James Bryan 1946- WhoEmL 93, WhoSSW 93
Hall, James Byron 1918- WhoWrEP 92
Hall, James Curtis 1926- WhoAm 92
Hall, James E. 1933- WhoAm 92
Hall, James Edward 1933- St&PR 93
Hall, James Fay, Jr. 1916- WhoAm 92
Hall, James Frederick 1921- WhoAm 92
Hall, James Granville, Jr. 1917- WhoSSW 93
Hall, James Henry 1939- WhoAm 92, WhoWor 93
Hall, James Herrick, Jr. 1933- WhoSSW 93
Hall, James Leo, Jr. 1936- WhoAm 92
Hall, James N. ScF&FL 92
Hall, James Parker 1906- WhoAm 92
Hall, James Reginald, Jr. 1936- AfrAmBi [port]
Hall, James Stanley 1930- WhoAm 92
Hall, James William 1937- WhoAm 92
Hall, James William 1953- WhoEmL 93
Hall, Jane Anna 1959- WhoAm 92, WhoAmW 93, WhoE 93, WhoWor 93
Hall, Janice 1953- WhoAm 92
Hall, Janice Lynn 1953- WhoAmW 93
Hall, Jay 1932- WhoAm 92, WhoWrEP 92
Hall, Jeannine D. 1973- WhoWrEP 92
Hall, Jeffrey Stuart 1951- WhoAm 92
Hall, Jerald Culver 1931- St&PR 93
Hall, Jerome d1992 NewYTBS 92
Hall, Jerome 1901- WhoWrEP 92
Hall, Jerome 1901-1992 BioIn 17, ConAu 137
Hall, Jerome William 1943- WhoAm 92
Hall, Jerry BioIn 17
Hall, Jesse Lee 1849-1911 BioIn 17
Hall, Jesse Seaborn 1929- WhoAm 92
Hall, Jim BioIn 17
Hall, Jim 1930- Baker 92, BioIn 17
Hall, Jimmy Dwain, Sr. 1929- St&PR 93
Hall, Joan Joffe 1936- WhoWrEP 92
Hall, Joan M. 1939- WhoAm 92, WhoAmW 93
Hall, Joe E. 1938- WhoAm 92
Hall, Joel Allen 1934- St&PR 93
Hall, Joel R. Law&B 92
Hall, John St&PR 93
Hall, John c. 1529-c. 1566 Baker 92
Hall, John 1937- WhoUN 92
Hall, John Allen 1914- WhoAm 92
Hall, John Allen 1952- WhoEmL 93
Hall, John C. 1936- St&PR 93
Hall, John Daniel, II 1947- WhoSSW 93
Hall, John Emmett 1925- WhoAm 92
Hall, John F. Law&B 92
Hall, John Frederick 1941- St&PR 93
Hall, John Fry 1919- WhoAm 92
Hall, John Glenn 1948- WhoEmL 93
Hall, John Herbert 1942- WhoAm 92
Hall, John Hopkins 1925- WhoAm 92, WhoSSW 93, WhoWor 93
Hall, John Lewis 1934- WhoAm 92
Hall, John Lloyd WhoScE 91-1
Hall, John Louis 1946- WhoSSW 93
Hall, John Marshall 1935- WhoAm 92
Hall, John R. BioIn 17
Hall, John R. 1932- St&PR 93
Hall, John Richard 1932- WhoAm 92, WhoSSW 93, WhoWor 93
Hall, John Ryder ScF&FL 92
Hall, John S. 1949- St&PR 93
Hall, John Scoville 1908-1991 BioIn 17
Hall, John Thomas 1938- WhoSSW 93
Hall, John W. 1929- WhoIns 93
Hall, John Wesley, Jr. 1948- WhoEmL 93
Hall, John Whitling 1934- WhoAm 92, WhoSSW 93
Hall, Joseph 1574-1656 DcLB 121 [port]
Hall, Joseph A. 1931- St&PR 93
Hall, Joseph E. 1914- St&PR 93
Hall, Joseph Gustave WhoScE 91-1
Hall, Joseph Lindley 1936- WhoE 93
Hall, Joyce Turner 1948- WhoAmW 93, WhoEmL 93
Hall, Juanita D. 1919- St&PR 93
Hall, Judith Kay 1943- St&PR 93
Hall, Judy Marie 1948- WhoAmW 93
Hall, June BioIn 17
Hall, Karen Marie 1953- WhoAmW 93
Hall, Kate d1991 BioIn 17
Hall, Kathleen Ann 1948- WhoEmL 93, WhoSSW 93
Hall, Kathryn Evangeline WhoAm 92, WhoAmW 93, WhoWor 93
Hall, Kathryn Sandra Kaur 1958- WhoAmW 93
Hall, Katie 1938- BioIn 17
Hall, Keith A. Law&B 92
Hall, Kenneth F. Law&B 92
Hall, Kenneth F. 1952- St&PR 93
Hall, Kenneth J. MiSFD 9
Hall, Kenneth Keller 1918- WhoAm 92, WhoSSW 93
Hall, Kenneth Octavius 1941- WhoE 93
Hall, Kenneth Richard 1939- WhoAm 92
Hall, Kenneth William 1944- St&PR 93
Hall, Kent Strange, Sr. 1928- WhoSSW 93
Hall, Kevin Peter BioIn 17
Hall, Kevin Peter 1955?-1991 ConTFT 10
Hall, Kirsten 1974- BioIn 17
Hall, Larry C. Law&B 92
Hall, Larry D. 1942- St&PR 93, WhoAm 92
Hall, Laurance David WhoScE 91-1
Hall, Lawrie Pitcher Platt 1942- WhoSSW 93
Hall, Layne BioIn 17
Hall, Lee 1934- WhoAm 92, WhoAmW 93
Hall, Lee Boaz 1928- St&PR 93, WhoAm 92, WhoWor 93
Hall, Leo E. 1917- St&PR 93
Hall, Leon W. BioIn 17
Hall, Leonard W. 1900-1979 PolPar
Hall, Leonard Wood 1900-1979 BioIn 17
Hall, Les Law&B 92
Hall, Leslie Carlton 1952- WhoEmL 93
Hall, Linda E. Law&B 92
Hall, Lois 1926- SweetSg C
Hall, Lora A. 1932- St&PR 93
Hall, Loretta J. 1932- WhoAmW 93, WhoWor 93
Hall, Luther Egbert, Jr. 1926- WhoAm 92
Hall, Lynn 1937- ConAu 37NR, DcAmChF 1960, MajAI [port], ScF&FL 92, WhoAm 92
Hall, Lynn Reeves 1953- WhoSSW 93
Hall, Madelon Carol Syverson 1937- WhoAmW 93
Hall, Mamie Barton 1928- WhoAmW 93, WhoWor 93
Hall, Manly P. 1901-1990 ScF&FL 92
Hall, Marcel Scott 1926- WhoSSW 93
Hall, Marcia Joy 1947- WhoAmW 93, WhoE 93
Hall, Marian Ella 1920- WhoAmW 93, WhoWor 93
Hall, Marie 1884-1956 Baker 92
Hall, Marion H. 1925- WhoIns 93
Hall, Marion Trufant 1920- WhoAm 92
Hall, Marjorie Frederica 1924- WhoAmW 93
Hall, Marjory 1908- WhoAm 92
Hall, Martha T. 1932- St&PR 93
Hall, Mary Fields 1934- WhoAm 92
Hall, Mary-jo 1947- WhoEmL 93
Hall, Mary Leora AmWomPl
Hall, Matthew ScF&FL 92
Hall, Maude L. AmWomPl
Hall, Maudie Catherine 1939- WhoAmW 93
Hall, Maureen Therese 1963- WhoAmW 93
Hall, Melville Wakeman d1991 BioIn 17
Hall, Michael Anthony WhoScE 91-1
Hall, Michael Garibaldi 1926- WhoSSW 93
Hall, Michael James 1944- St&PR 93
Hall, Michael Lee 1946- WhoE 93
Hall, Michelle Marie 1961- St&PR 93
Hall, Miles Lewis, Jr. 1924- WhoAm 92, WhoWor 93
Hall, Millard Frank, Jr. 1945- WhoAm 92
Hall, Milton Reese 1932- WhoAm 92
Hall, Monty 1925- WhoAm 92
Hall, N. John 1933- WhoE 93
Hall, Nancy Christensen 1946- WhoAm 92
Hall, Nancy F. 1947- WhoAmW 93
Hall, Nancy Lee BioIn 17
Hall, Nancy Schafer 1942- WhoAmW 93
Hall, Nechie Tesitor 1946- WhoEmL 93
Hall, Newman A. 1913- WhoAm 92
Hall, Nicholas 1949- WhoAm 92, WhoWor 93
Hall, Nicholas C.D. Law&B 92
Hall, Norman 1904- ScF&FL 92
Hall, O. Glen 1929- WhoAm 92
Hall, Ogden Henderson 1922- WhoAm 92
Hall, P. WhoScE 91-1
Hall, Pamela Elizabeth 1957- WhoE 93
Hall, Pamela S. 1944- WhoAm 92, WhoAmW 93
Hall, Patrick Andrew Voss WhoScE 91-1
Hall, Pauline (Margarete) 1890-1969 Baker 92
Hall, Peggy Kubicz Law&B 92
Hall, Perry E. d1992 NewYTBS 92 [port]
Hall, Peter 1930- BioIn 17, IntDcOp, MiSFD 9, OxDcOp
Hall, Peter Andrew 1950- WhoE 93
Hall, Peter Francis 1924- WhoAm 92
Hall, Peter Michael 1934- WhoAm 92, WhoSSW 93
Hall, Peter (Reginald Frederick) 1930- Baker 92, WhoAm 92, WhoWor 93
Hall, Phil 1953- WhoCanL 92
Hall, Phil 1964- WhoWrEP 92
Hall, Philip WhoScE 91-1
Hall, Philip H. Law&B 92
Hall, Philip H. 1917- St&PR 93
Hall, Philip Layton 1940- WhoSSW 93
Hall, Phoebe Poulterer 1941- WhoAmW 93
Hall, Pike, Jr. WhoSSW 93
Hall, Preston Winship 1932- St&PR 93
Hall, Prince 1748-1807 BioIn 17
Hall, R. Vance 1928- WhoAm 92
Hall, R.W.J. WhoScE 91-1
Hall, Radclyffe 1886-1943 BioIn 17
Hall, Ralph Carr 1928- WhoSSW 93
Hall, Ralph Foster Law&B 92
Hall, Ralph M. 1923- CngDr 91
Hall, Ralph Macon 1941- St&PR 93
Hall, Ralph Moody 1923- WhoAm 92, WhoSSW 93
Hall, Ray C. 1944- St&PR 93, WhoIns 93
Hall, Richard 1926- ConGAN
Hall, Richard C. W. 1942- WhoAm 92, WhoSSW 93
Hall, Richard Clayton 1931- WhoE 93
Hall, Richard John 1856-1897 BioIn 17
Hall, Richard Leland 1923- WhoAm 92
Hall, Richard S. 1944- St&PR 93
Hall, Richard W. d1992 NewYTBS 92
Hall, Rick 1932- SoulM
Hall, Rita Hudson 1961- WhoAmW 93
Hall, Robert AfrAmBi, DcCPCAm
Hall, Robert Alan 1958- WhoEmL 93
Hall, Robert Browne 1858-1907 Baker 92
Hall, Robert Chambers 1931- St&PR 93
Hall, Robert Ernest 1943- WhoAm 92
Hall, Robert Givin 1953- WhoEmL 93
Hall, Robert Gordon Law&B 92
Hall, Robert Howell 1921- WhoAm 92, WhoSSW 93
Hall, Robert J. WhoAm 92, WhoE 93
Hall, Robert Joseph 1926- WhoAm 92
Hall, Robert Lee 1941- ScF&FL 92
Hall, Robert Lee 1951- WhoSSW 93
Hall, Robert Leicester 1905-1991 BioIn 17
Hall, Robert Lynn 1945- St&PR 93
Hall, Robert M. Law&B 92
Hall, Robert McClellan 1942- WhoAm 92
Hall, Robert Pierce 1963- WhoEmL 93
Hall, Robert Preston 1954- WhoSSW 93
Hall, Robert Turnbull, III 1945- WhoWor 93
Hall, Robert William 1928- WhoAm 92
Hall, Rodney 1935- ScF&FL 92
Hall, Roger Dale 1955- St&PR 93
Hall, Ronald Arthur 1941- WhoSSW 93
Hall, Ronald E. 1933- WhoAm 92, WhoSSW 93
Hall, Rosanne M. Law&B 92
Hall, Ruth 1912- SweetSg C [port]
Hall, Ruth Ann 1950- WhoAmW 93
Hall, Ruth Arlene 1923- WhoAmW 93
Hall, Sam 1936- ConAu 137
Hall, Sam Blakeley, Jr. 1924- WhoAm 92, WhoSSW 93
Hall, Samuel M., Jr. 1937- WhoE 93
Hall, Sandi 1942- ScF&FL 92
Hall, Sandra Jean 1958- WhoWrEP 92
Hall, Sarah E. Law&B 92
Hall, Sharlot Mabridth 1870-1943 BioIn 17
Hall, Shawn Law&B 92
Hall, Sherrill Gray 1933- St&PR 93

Hall, Sibyl Eloise 1940- *WhoSSW 93*
Hall, Stanley Eckler 1934- *St&PR 93, WhoE 93, WhoWor 93*
Hall, Steele 1928- *WhoAsAP 91*
Hall, Stephen Charles 1948- *WhoSSW 93, WhoWor 93*
Hall, Stephen Gardner 1949- *WhoEmL 93*
Hall, Stephen M. 1921- *St&PR 93*
Hall, Stephen Pudney 1950- *WhoAm 92*
Hall, Steven Edward 1954- *WhoE 93*
Hall, Stewart K. *Law&B 92*
Hall, Stewart Kent 1947- *St&PR 93*
Hall, Susan *WhoAm 92*
Hall, Susan J. 1944- *St&PR 93*
Hall, Susan Jean 1951- *WhoEmL 93*
Hall, Susan Liddell 1951- *WhoAmW 93*
Hall, Suzanne Marie 1962- *WhoEmL 93*
Hall, Telka Mowery Elium 1936- *WhoAmW 93*
Hall, TennieBee M. 1940- *WhoAmW 93*
Hall, Terrance Hamilton *Law&B 92*
Hall, Theodore Dana 1943- *WhoWrEP 92*
Hall, Theodore Thomas 1940- *St&PR 93*
Hall, Therese Mary Yarborough 1946- *WhoAmW 93*
Hall, Thomas Edward 1946- *WhoSSW 93*
Hall, Thomas Forrest 1939- *WhoAm 92*
Hall, Thomas J. *Law&B 92*
Hall, Thomas J. 1923- *St&PR 93*
Hall, Thomas Jennings 1948- *WhoEmL 93*
Hall, Thor 1927- *WhoAm 92*
Hall, Timothy C. 1937- *WhoAm 92, WhoWor 93*
Hall, Tom T. 1936- *Baker 92, WhoAm 92*
Hall, Tony P. 1942- *CngDr 91, WhoAm 92*
Hall, Trevor James 1956- *WhoWor 93*
Hall, Vera P. Webb 1937- *WhoAmW 93*
Hall, W. Reginald 1936- *WhoAm 92*
Hall, Wade Henry 1934- *WhoSSW 93*
Hall, Walter 1933- *St&PR 93*
Hall, Wanda Jean 1943- *WhoE 93*
Hall, Warden Reginald 1921- *WhoWor 93*
Hall, Warren F. 1937- *St&PR 93*
Hall, Wayne Lee 1953- *WhoSSW 93*
Hall, Wilbur Dallas, Jr. 1938- *WhoAm 92*
Hall, William Austin 1945- *WhoAm 92*
Hall, William C. 1922- *WhoIns 93*
Hall, William Darlington 1914- *WhoAm 92*
Hall, William Donald 1932- *WhoSSW 93*
Hall, William E. 1942- *WhoAm 92*
Hall, William Edward 1923-1991 *BioIn 17*
Hall, William Edward 1940- *St&PR 93*
Hall, William Edward, Jr. 1951- *WhoEmL 93*
Hall, William G. 1929- *St&PR 93*
Hall, William Joel 1926- *WhoAm 92*
Hall, William Keith 1954- *WhoSSW 93*
Hall, William King 1943- *St&PR 93, WhoAm 92*
Hall, William Lloyd 1925- *WhoSSW 93*
Hall, William Robert, Jr. 1953- *WhoEmL 93, WhoSSW 93*
Hall, William Shield *WhoScE 91-1*
Hall, William Smith, Jr. 1941- *WhoE 93*
Hall, William Stone 1915- *WhoAm 92*
Hall, Willis *BioIn 17*
Hall, Willis 1929- *ChlFicS, ScF&FL 92*
Hall, Wilson Dudley 1922-1991 *BioIn 17*
Hall, Yong Ok 1950- *WhoAm 92*
Halla, Judy Webb 1941- *WhoSSW 93*
Halla, Robert Christian 1949- *WhoWrEP 92*
Hallacher, Lester L. *Law&B 92*
Hallack, John James 1938- *St&PR 93*
Halladay, Laurie Ann 1945- *WhoAm 92*
Hallahan, Carolyn Patricia 1958- *WhoAmW 93*
Hallahan, Edward V. 1932- *WhoScE 91-3*
Hallahan, William H. *ScF&FL 92*
Hallak, Ahmad 1939- *WhoUN 92*
Hallal, Jean 1942- *WhoCanL 92*
Hallam, Arthur Henry 1811-1833 *BioIn 17*
Hallam, Atlantis 1915-1987 *ScF&FL 92*
Hallam, Beverly 1923- *WhoAm 92, WhoAmW 93*
Hallam, Robert Gaston 1941- *St&PR 93*
Hallam, Robert J. 1952- *WhoAm 92*
Hallamshire, David *ScF&FL 92*
Hallanan, Elizabeth V. 1925- *WhoAm 92, WhoAmW 93, WhoSSW 93*
Hallard, Peter *ConAu 38NR, MajAI*
Hallard, Wayne Bruce 1951- *WhoE 93, WhoEmL 93, WhoWor 93*
Hallas, Henry 1924- *St&PR 93*
Hallas, Richard *ConAu 137, MajAI*
Hallas, Thorkil Erling 1943- *WhoScE 91-2*
Hallauer, Arnel Roy 1932- *WhoAm 92*
Hallawell, Philip Charles 1951- *WhoWor 93*
Hallbauer, Robert E. 1930- *St&PR 93*
Hallbauer, Robert Edward 1930- *WhoAm 92, WhoWor 93*
Hallbauer, Rosalie Carlotta 1939- *WhoAmW 93*
Hallberg, Bengt Olof *WhoWor 93*
Hallberg, Bjorn Wilho 1938- *Baker 92*
Hallberg, Budd Jaye 1942- *WhoE 93, WhoWor 93*
Hallberg, Garth Ragnar 1944- *WhoAm 92*
Halldor, Laxness 1902- *BioIn 17*
Halldorsson, Gudmundur 1952- *WhoScE 91-4*
Halle, Adam de la *Baker 92*
Halle, Charles 1819-1895 *Baker 92, OxDcOp*
Halle, James 1916- *St&PR 93*
Halle, Louis Joseph 1910- *WhoAm 92*
Halle, Merle Henry *Law&B 92*
Halle, Morris 1923- *WhoAm 92*
Halle, Peter Edward 1944- *WhoAm 92*
Halleck, Charles A. 1900-1986 *PolPar*
Halleck, Charles White 1929- *WhoAm 92*
Halleck, Donald Richard 1954- *WhoSSW 93*
Halleck, Henry Wager 1815-1872 *CmdGen 1991 [port], HarEnMi*
Hallee, Lisa A. *Law&B 92*
Hallee, Neal David 1943- *WhoE 93*
Halleen, Otis H. *Law&B 92*
Halleen, Otis H. 1934- *St&PR 93*
Halleen, Owen Paul 1934- *St&PR 93*
Halle Keyloun, Susan Anne 1952- *WhoAmW 93, WhoEmL 93*
Halleman, Norman Lee 1938- *St&PR 93*
Hallen, (Johannes) Andreas 1846-1925 *Baker 92*
Hallen, Arvid *WhoScE 91-4*
Hallen, E. Donald 1930- *St&PR 93*
Hallen, Hans A. 1951- *WhoScE 91-4*
Hallen, Kenneth Peter 1943- *WhoIns 93*
Hallen, Philip Burgh 1930- *WhoAm 92*
Hallenbeck, Alfred Madison 1930- *WhoAm 92*
Hallenbeck, Kenneth Luster 1931- *WhoAm 92*
Hallenbeck, Lane William 1955- *WhoEmL 93*
Hallenbeck, Mark D. *Law&B 92*
Hallenbeck, Pomona Juanita 1938- *WhoWor 93*
Hallenbeck, Robert M. *Law&B 92*
Hallenberg, Nancy Lee 1941- *WhoSSW 93*
Hallene, Alan Montgomery 1929- *WhoAm 92, WhoWor 93*
Hallensleben, Manfred L. 1936- *WhoScE 91-3*
Halle-Pannenko, Olga *WhoScE 91-2*
Halle-Pannenko, Olga 1934- *WhoScE 91-2*
Haller, Amelia Jane 1927- *WhoWrEP 92*
Haller, Andrew P. *Law&B 92*
Haller, Archibald Orben 1926- *WhoAm 92, WhoWor 93*
Haller, Calvin John 1925- *WhoAm 92*
Haller, Charles Edward 1924- *WhoAm 92*
Haller, Daniel 1926- *MiSFD 9*
Haller, Donald B. *Law&B 92*
Haller, Fred J. 1954- *St&PR 93*
Haller, Harlan Thomas 1924- *St&PR 93, WhoAm 92*
Haller, Heinz 1914- *WhoWor 93*
Haller, Howard Edward 1947- *WhoWor 93*
Haller, Jacob Alexander, Jr. 1927- *WhoAm 92*
Haller, Joann *Law&B 92*
Haller, John C. 1945- *WhoAm 92*
Haller, John Charles 1950- *St&PR 93*
Haller, Jordan Daniel 1932- *WhoAm 92*
Haller, Joseph E. 1929- *St&PR 93*
Haller, Jozef 1873-1960 *PolBiDi*
Haller, Karen S. *St&PR 93*
Haller, Karl *St&PR 93*
Haller, Kenneth E. 1941- *WhoIns 93*
Haller, Lee Higdon 1947- *WhoE 93*
Haller, Michael 1840-1915 *Baker 92*
Haller, Ralph A. 1948- *WhoAm 92*
Haller, Robert Terrence 1930- *WhoE 93, WhoWor 93*
Haller, Russell W. 1923- *St&PR 93*
Haller, Scot *BioIn 17*
Haller, Sonja Maria *Law&B 92*
Haller, Terry 1934- *WhoWrEP 92*
Haller, Terry Lyndon 1948- *St&PR 93*
Halleran, Arthur Joseph, Jr. 1947- *St&PR 93*
Halleran, Richard Carroll 1941- *St&PR 93*
Hallerberg, Gretchen A. 1949- *BioIn 17*
Hallermann, Gisela Elizabeth 1936- *WhoAmW 93*
Hallett, Benjamin F. 1797-1862 *PolPar*
Hallett, Benjamin Franklin 1797-1862 *BioIn 17*
Hallett, Carol *BioIn 17*
Hallett, Carol Boyd 1937- *WhoAm 92, WhoAmW 93*
Hallett, Charles Arthur, Jr. 1939- *WhoAm 92*
Hallett, Charles Lee 1958- *WhoSSW 93*
Hallett, Elizabeth M. *Law&B 92*
Hallett, Fred N. 1938- *St&PR 93*
Hallett, Fred Norton 1938- *WhoAm 92*
Hallett, Frederick Howard 1929- *St&PR 93*
Hallett, Laurence S. 1957- *WhoIns 93*
Hallett, Lewellyn 1953- *WhoWrEP 92*
Hallett, Mark 1943- *WhoAm 92*
Hallett, Phyllis May 1926-1990 *BioIn 17*
Hallett, Richard E. 1939- *St&PR 93*
Hallett, Thomas P. 1955- *WhoEmL 93*
Hallett, William Jared 1923- *WhoAm 92*
Halleux, Albert Martin Julien 1920- *WhoWor 93*
Halley, Barbara Jean 1951- *WhoAmW 93*
Halley, Edmond 1656-1742 *BioIn 17*
Halley, Fred Nicholas 1938- *WhoAm 92*
Halley, James Alfred 1948- *WhoSSW 93*
Halley, James Woods, Jr. 1938- *WhoAm 92*
Halley, John A. *Law&B 92*
Halley, Shawn Ellen 1957- *WhoEmL 93, WhoSSW 93*
Hallgren, Richard Edwin 1932- *WhoAm 92*
Hallgrimsson, Haflidi (Magnus) 1941- *Baker 92*
Hallgrimsson, Sveinn 1936- *WhoScE 91-4*
Halliburton, Alan D. 1945- *St&PR 93*
Halliburton, David 1933- *ScF&FL 92*
Halliburton, John Robert 1934- *WhoWor 93*
Halliday, A. Martin 1926- *WhoScE 91-1*
Halliday, D.B. *WhoScE 91-1*
Halliday, David *WhoScE 91-1*
Halliday, David John 1936- *WhoUN 92*
Halliday, Denis J. 1941- *WhoUN 92*
Halliday, Diana *WhoScE 91-1*
Halliday, Gordon T. 1953- *St&PR 93*
Halliday, Harriet Hudnut 1941- *WhoAmW 93*
Halliday, Ian 1928- *WhoAm 92*
Halliday, John Meech 1936- *WhoAm 92, WhoWor 93*
Halliday, Laura Alice McCarty 1928- *WhoE 93*
Halliday, Mary M. *AmWomPl*
Halliday, Michael Sebastian *WhoScE 91-1*
Halliday, R. Michael 1955- *St&PR 93*
Halliday, Rene Bruton 1955- *St&PR 93*
Halliday, Stephen M. 1927- *St&PR 93*
Halliday, Susan Marie *Law&B 92*
Halliday, Walter John 1907- *WhoAm 92*
Halliday, William R. 1952- *St&PR 93*
Halliday, William Ross 1926- *WhoAm 92, WhoWor 93*
Hallier, Gerard Edouard 1941- *WhoAm 92*
Hallier, Hans-Joachim 1930- *WhoWor 93*
Halligan, Howard Ansel 1937- *WhoAm 92*
Halligan, James Edmund 1936- *WhoAm 92*
Halligan, T.W. 1922- *St&PR 93*
Halligan, Theodore H. 1923- *St&PR 93*
Halligan, Thomas William 1921- *WhoSSW 93*
Hallila, Bruce Allan 1950- *WhoEmL 93, WhoSSW 93*
Hallin, Gayle Annette 1948- *WhoEmL 93*
Hallinan, Hazel Hunkins- 1890-1982 *BioIn 17*
Hallinan, Joseph Thomas 1960- *WhoAm 92*
Hallinan, Maureen Teresa *WhoAm 92*
Hallinan, Vincent W. d1992 *NewYTBS 92*
Hallinan, Vincent (W.) 1896-1992 *CurBio 92N*
Hallinan, William J. *St&PR 93*
Hallinan, William James *Law&B 92*
Halling, Hal P. 1937- *St&PR 93*
Halling, Leonard William 1927- *WhoAm 92*
Halling, Peter James *WhoScE 91-1*
Halling, Roderick Peter 1955- *WhoWor 93*
Halling, William Russell 1939- *WhoAm 92*
Hallingby, Paul, Jr. 1919- *St&PR 93, WhoAm 92*
Hallisey, John Francis 1906- *St&PR 93*
Hallisey, Michael Joseph 1929- *St&PR 93*
Hallisey, Paul Michael 1947- *St&PR 93*
Hallissey, Michael 1943- *WhoWor 93*
Halliwell, Barry *WhoScE 91-1*
Halliwell, Janet Elizabeth 1945- *WhoAm 92*
Halliwell, Leslie 1929-1989 *ScF&FL 92*
Halliwell, Neil Anthony *WhoScE 91-1*
Halliwell, Walter G. 1953- *St&PR 93*
Halliwell, William Henry 1939- *WhoE 93*
Hallman, Ake 1942- *WhoWor 93*
Hallman, Donald U. *WhoIns 93*
Hallman, Dwayne Duncan 1962- *WhoIns 93*
Hallman, Gary L. 1940- *WhoAm 92*
Hallman, Glen *Law&B 92*
Hallman, Grady Lamar, Jr. 1930- *WhoAm 92*
Hallman, Henry Theodore, Jr. 1933- *WhoAm 92*
Hallman, Michael R. *BioIn 17*
Hallman, Richard Douglas 1951- *WhoE 93*
Hallman, Stanley P. *St&PR 93*
Hallman, Thomas Lee 1947- *WhoSSW 93*
Hallmans, Goran 1947- *WhoScE 91-4*
Hallmark, Nelson Stephen 1942- *WhoSSW 93*
Hall-McDermott, Kimberly Ann 1962- *WhoSSW 93*
Hallmen, David R. *St&PR 93*
Hallmundsson, Hallberg 1930- *WhoWrEP 92*
Hallnas, (Johan) Hilding 1903-1984 *Baker 92*
Hallo, William Wolfgang 1928- *WhoAm 92*
Hallock, Alan David *Law&B 92*
Hallock, C. Wiles, Jr. 1918- *WhoAm 92*
Hallock, Gilbert Vinton 1925- *WhoE 93*
Hallock, Grace Tabor 1893- *AmWomPl*
Hallock, Henry A., Mrs. *AmWomPl*
Hallock, James Anthony 1942- *WhoAm 92*
Hallock, Kurt David *Law&B 92*
Hallock, Paul L. 1948- *St&PR 93*
Hallock, Robert J. *Law&B 92*
Hallock, Rusty *ScF&FL 92*
Hallock, Suzy 1942- *WhoE 93*
Hallock-Muller, Pamela 1948- *WhoAmW 93, WhoEmL 93*
Halloran, Bernard Thorpe 1931- *WhoAm 92*
Halloran, Daniel F. 1926- *WhoWrEP 92*
Halloran, David G. 1932- *St&PR 93*
Halloran, John J. 1942- *St&PR 93*
Halloran, John M. 1952- *St&PR 93*
Halloran, Kathleen L. 1952- *St&PR 93, WhoAm 92*
Halloran, Kevin J. *Law&B 92*
Halloran, Leo Augustine 1931- *WhoE 93*
Halloran, Michael J. *Law&B 92*
Halloran, Michael James 1941- *WhoAm 92*
Halloran, Mike John 1948- *St&PR 93*
Halloran, Richard Colby 1930- *WhoAm 92*
Halloran, Richard Francis 1922- *St&PR 93*
Halloran, William Frank 1934- *WhoAm 92*
Halloun, Elyssa Nadia *WhoAmW 93, WhoE 93*
Halloway, H. Stephen 1946- *WhoUN 92*
Hallowell, Alfred Irving 1892-1974 *IntDcAn*
Hallowell, Burton Crosby 1915- *St&PR 93, WhoAm 92*
Hallowell, Eleanor *AmWomPl*
Hallowell, John *BioIn 17*
Hallowell, Michael Geoffrey 1954- *WhoWor 93*
Hallowell, Nancy S. *AmWomPl*
Hallowell, Robert Edward 1918- *WhoAm 92*
Hallowell, Todd *MiSFD 9*
Hallowell, Walter H. 1943- *St&PR 93*
Hallowell, Walter Henry 1943- *WhoAm 92*
Hallows, Michael C.L. 1941- *St&PR 93*
Hallows, Michael Colin Lloyd 1941- *WhoAm 92*
Hallpike, Jeremy Frank 1936- *WhoWor 93*
Hallquist, Age *WhoScE 91-4*
Hallquist, Scott G. *Law&B 92*
Hallquist, Scott G. 1953- *St&PR 93*
Hall-Sheedy, Leslee 1955- *St&PR 93*
Hallstead, William Finn, III *ScF&FL 92*
Hallstead, William Finn, III 1924- *WhoWrEP 92*
Hallstein, Walter 1901-1982 *ColdWar 1 [port]*
Hallsten, Bertil Erik 1932- *WhoWor 93*
Hallsten Mc Garry, Susan Joan 1948- *WhoWrEP 92*
Hallstrom, Ivar 1826-1901 *OxDcOp*
Hallstrom, Ivar (Christian) 1826-1901 *Baker 92*
Hallstrom, Lasse 1946- *MiSFD 9*
Halluin, Albert P. 1939- *St&PR 93*
Hallward, M.B. 1955- *St&PR 93*
Hallworth, Grace *ChlFicS*
Hally, Michael Joseph, Jr. *Law&B 92*
Hally, Paul F. *Law&B 92*
Halm, August Otto 1869-1929 *Baker 92*
Halm, Klaus 1929- *WhoSSW 93*
Halm, Margo Anne 1961- *WhoAmW 93*
Halm, Nancye Studd 1932- *WhoAmW 93*
Halm, Willard Kim *Law&B 92*
Halman, Doris Friend 1895- *AmWomPl*
Halman, Talat Sait 1931- *WhoAm 92*
Halme, Aarne 1943- *WhoScE 91-4*
Halme, Seppo J. 1938- *WhoScE 91-4*
Halme, Timo Ilari 1951- *WhoWor 93*
Halmekoski, Jaakko Juhani 1928- *WhoScE 91-4*
Halmi, Robert 1924- *WhoAm 92*
Halmo, R.M. *Law&B 92*

Hamburger, Jean 1909-1992 *BioIn 17, NewYTBS 92*
Hamburger, Jeffrey Allen 1947- *WhoEmL 93*
Hamburger, John Andrew *Law&B 92*
Hamburger, Mary Ann 1939- *WhoAmW 93, WhoE 93, WhoWor 93*
Hamburger, Philip Paul 1914- *WhoAm 92*
Hamburger, Richard James 1937- *WhoAm 92, WhoWor 93*
Hamburger, Robert Jay 1941- *WhoE 93*
Hamburger, Stephen Charles 1946- *WhoAm 92*
Hamburger, Ursula 1907- *BioIn 17*
Hamburger, Viktor 1900- *WhoAm 92*
Hamby, A. Garth 1938- *WhoSSW 93*
Hamby, Alonzo Lee 1940- *WhoAm 92*
Hamby, George Russell 1935- *St&PR 93*
Hamby, J.W. 1925- *St&PR 93*
Hamby, James A. 1943- *WhoWrEP 92*
Hamby, Jeannette 1933- *WhoAmW 93*
Hamby, John Holden 1938- *St&PR 93*
Hamby, Michael E. 1952- *WhoIns 93*
Hamby, R.C. *WhoScE 91-1*
Hamby, Robert E., Jr. 1946- *St&PR 93*
Hamby, William H. *Law&B 92*
Hamdan, Lawrence Anise 1961- *WhoE 93*
Hamdan ibn Rashid Al-Maktum, Sheikh 1945- *WhoWor 93*
Hamdan Sheikh Tahir, Tuan Yang Terutama Tun Tan Sri Datuk Haji 1921- *WhoAsAP 91*
Hamdoon, Nizar *BioIn 17*
Hamed, Martha Ellen 1950- *WhoAmW 93*
Hameen-Anttila, Antero 1931- *WhoScE 91-4*
Hameenniemi, Eero 1951- *Baker 92*
Hameister, Lavon Louetta 1922- *WhoAmW 93, WhoWor 93*
Hameka, Hendrik Frederik 1931- *WhoAm 92, WhoWor 93*
Hamel, Aldona Mary 1946- *WhoAmW 93*
Hamel, Bruce Roger 1951- *WhoE 93*
Hamel, Dana Bertrand 1923- *WhoAm 92*
Hamel, David Charles 1953- *WhoSSW 93*
Hamel, Elizabeth Cecil 1918- *WhoAmW 93*
Hamel, Emilienne M. 1919- *St&PR 93*
Hame'l, Esther Veramae 1922- *WhoAmW 93*
Hamel, Fred 1903-1957 *Baker 92*
Hamel, Gilles 1945- *St&PR 93*
Hamel, Hannelore 1930- *WhoWor 93*
Hamel, James Victor 1944- *WhoE 93*
Hamel, Jean-Louis 1942- *St&PR 93*
Hamel, Jean-Marc 1925- *WhoAm 92*
Hamel, Marie-Pierre 1786-1879 *Baker 92*
Hamel, Peter G. 1936- *WhoScE 91-3*
Hamel, Reginald 1931- *WhoAm 92*
Hamel, Rodolphe *Law&B 92*
Hamel, Rodolphe 1929- *St&PR 93, WhoAm 92*
Hamel, Veronica 1943- *WhoAm 92*
Hamelin, Jean-Guy 1925- *WhoAm 92*
Hamelin, Marcel 1937- *WhoAm 92*
Hamelin, Raymond 1930- *WhoScE 91-2*
Hamel Peifer, Kathleen *ScF&FL 92*
Hament, Andrew Stanton *Law&B 92*
Hament, Joel I. 1950- *St&PR 93*
Hamen y Leon, Juan van der 1596-c. 1632 *BioIn 17*
Hamer, David John 1923- *WhoAsAP 91*
Hamer, Douglas Winford 1942- *St&PR 93*
Hamer, Eberhard Ernst Heinrich 1921- *WhoWor 93*
Hamer, Fannie Lou 1917-1977 *EncAACR [port], PolPar*
Hamer, Fannie Lou Townsend 1917-1977 *BioIn 17*
Hamer, James M. 1951- *St&PR 93*
Hamer, Jean Jerome Cardinal 1916- *WhoWor 93*
Hamer, Rob J. 1957- *WhoScE 91-3*
Hamer, Robert 1911-1963 *MiSFD 9N*
Hamer, Robert E. 1951- *St&PR 93*
Hamer, Walter Jay 1907- *WhoE 93*
Hamerik, Asger 1843-1923 *Baker 92*
Hamerik, Ebbe 1898-1951 *Baker 92*
Hamerman, David Jay 1925- *WhoE 93*
Hamermesh, Daniel Selim 1943- *WhoAm 92*
Hamermesh, Morton 1915- *WhoAm 92*
Hamermesh, Richard G. 1948- *WhoEmL 93*
Hamerow, Eleanor *BioIn 17*
Hamerow, Theodore Stephen 1920- *WhoAm 92*
Hamerski, Susan Thurston 1959- *WhoAmW 93*
Hamerstrom, Frances 1907- *WhoAmW 93*
Hamerstrom, Frederick *BioIn 17*
Hamerton, John Laurence 1929- *WhoAm 92*
Hames, Carl Martin 1938- *WhoSSW 93*
Hames, Clifford M. 1926- *St&PR 93*
Hames, Clifford Moffett 1926- *WhoAm 92*
Hames, Curtis Gordon 1920- *WhoAm 92*
Hames, John Foster 1928- *St&PR 93*
Hamid, Ansley 1944- *WhoE 93*
Hamid, Hael Abdel d1991 *BioIn 17*
Hamid, Michael 1934- *WhoAm 92*
Hamid, Mohammad 1936- *WhoUN 92*
Hamid, Qutayba A. 1953- *WhoWor 93*
Hamidjaja, Wiriadi Willy 1962- *WhoWor 93*
Hamil, Jack Robinson 1941- *St&PR 93*
Hamil, Peggy Penelope *WhoAmW 93*
Hamilburg, Joseph Daniel 1948- *St&PR 93*
Hamilburg, Maurice Joseph 1946- *St&PR 93*
Hamill, Dorothy 1956- *BioIn 17*
Hamill, Elizabeth Allison 1959- *WhoE 93*
Hamill, John P. 1940- *St&PR 93, WhoAm 92*
Hamill, Judith Ellen 1953- *WhoAmW 93*
Hamill, Kathleen M. *Law&B 92*
Hamill, Mark 1951- *WhoAm 92*
Hamill, Mary Kay 1956- *WhoEmL 93*
Hamill, Pete *BioIn 17*
Hamill, Pete 1935- *WhoAm 92, WhoWrEP 92*
Hamill, Richard D. 1939- *St&PR 93*
Hamilton, A. Lamar 1930- *St&PR 93*
Hamilton, Agnes *AmWomPl*
Hamilton, Alan *BioIn 17*
Hamilton, Alan Galbraith 1943- *WhoWor 93*
Hamilton, Albert Charles 1921- *WhoAm 92*
Hamilton, Albert Garland 1927- *St&PR 93*
Hamilton, Alex 1930- *ScF&FL 92*
Hamilton, Alexander 1712-1756 *BioIn 17*
Hamilton, Alexander 1755?-1804 *JrnUS*
Hamilton, Alexander 1757-1804 *BioIn 17, CmdGen 1991 [port], HarEnMi, OxCSupC, PolPar*
Hamilton, Alice *BioIn 17*
Hamilton, Allan Corning 1921- *WhoAm 92*
Hamilton, Allen Philip 1937- *WhoWor 93*
Hamilton, Alvin 1912- *BioIn 17*
Hamilton, Amy Elizabeth *Law&B 92*
Hamilton, Andrew *ScF&FL 92*
Hamilton, Angela L. 1955- *WhoAmW 93*
Hamilton, Ann E. *Law&B 92*
Hamilton, Anne Linnea 1949- *WhoEmL 93*
Hamilton, Anthony Robert 1936- *WhoE 93*
Hamilton, Arthur Francis 1934- *WhoScE 91-3*
Hamilton, Barbara 1944- *St&PR 93*
Hamilton, Barbara Yvonne 1958- *WhoAmW 93*
Hamilton, Beatrice 1947- *WhoAm 92, WhoAmW 93*
Hamilton, Beverly Lannquist 1946- *St&PR 93, WhoAm 92*
Hamilton, Bill *WhoAm 92*
Hamilton, Brooks Witham 1918- *WhoE 93*
Hamilton, Bruce E. *St&PR 93*
Hamilton, Brutus 1900-1970 *BioIn 17*
Hamilton, Brutus Kerr 1900-1970 *BiDAMSp 1989*
Hamilton, C. Michael *St&PR 93*
Hamilton, Calvin Sargent 1924- *WhoAm 92*
Hamilton, Carol Jean 1935- *WhoWrEP 92*
Hamilton, Carolyn C. *Law&B 92*
Hamilton, Chad James 1937- *St&PR 93*
Hamilton, Charles 1913- *BioIn 17*
Hamilton, Charles Henry 1903- *WhoAm 92*
Hamilton, Chico 1921- *WhoAm 92*
Hamilton, Christina Sundlof 1959- *WhoEmL 93*
Hamilton, Christopher John 1947- *WhoE 93*
Hamilton, Cicely 1872-1952 *BioIn 17*
Hamilton, Cindy Jean 1949- *WhoAmW 93*
Hamilton, Clarence Grant 1865-1935 *Baker 92*
Hamilton, Clive *MajAI*
Hamilton, Clyde Henry 1934- *WhoAm 92, WhoSSW 93*
Hamilton, D.D. 1920- *St&PR 93*
Hamilton, D.S. *Law&B 92*
Hamilton, Dagmar Strandberg 1932- *WhoAm 92, WhoAmW 93*
Hamilton, Dana F. 1948- *St&PR 93*
Hamilton, Daniel Stephen 1932- *WhoAm 92*
Hamilton, David *MiSFD 9*
Hamilton, David John 1956- *WhoE 93, WhoEmL 93*
Hamilton, David Lee 1937- *WhoAm 92*
Hamilton, David (Peter) 1935- *Baker 92*
Hamilton, David R. 1939- *St&PR 93*
Hamilton, David Wendell 1953- *WhoAm 92, WhoWor 93*
Hamilton, Diane Slaughter 1957- *WhoSSW 93*
Hamilton, Donald (Bengtsson) 1916- *ConAu 39NR, WhoAm 92, WhoWrEP 92*
Hamilton, Donald Emery 1938- *WhoAm 92*
Hamilton, Doris Jean *WhoWrEP 92*
Hamilton, Douglas G. *Law&B 92*
Hamilton, E. Haden, Jr. 1942- *St&PR 93*
Hamilton, Earle Grady, Jr. 1920- *WhoAm 92*
Hamilton, Ed 1970- *BioIn 17*
Hamilton, Edith 1867-1963 *AmWomPl*
Hamilton, Edmond 1904-1977 *BioIn 17, ScF&FL 92*
Hamilton, Edward J., Jr. *Law&B 92*
Hamilton, Edward Jackson, Jr. 1947- *St&PR 93*
Hamilton, Edward Marsh 1941- *WhoWor 93*
Hamilton, Elissa Lynn Alkoff 1958- *WhoWrEP 92*
Hamilton, Elizabeth 1758-1816 *DcLB 116 [port]*
Hamilton, Elmer, Jr. *ScF&FL 92*
Hamilton, Frank
See Weavers, The *ConMus 8*
Hamilton, Frank 1918- *ScF&FL 92*
Hamilton, Frank 1925-1991 *BioIn 17*
Hamilton, Frank Roy 1945- *St&PR 93*
Hamilton, Franklin *MajAI*
Hamilton, Frederic Crawford 1927- *St&PR 93, WhoAm 92*
Hamilton, Gail 1833-1896 *BioIn 17*
Hamilton, Gary Glen 1943- *WhoAm 92*
Hamilton, George *BioIn 17*
Hamilton, George, IV 1937- *Baker 92*
Hamilton, George E. 1895-1990 *BioIn 17*
Hamilton, George Ernest 1951- *WhoEmL 93*
Hamilton, George Ernest, III 1926- *WhoE 93*
Hamilton, George Heard 1910- *WhoAm 92*
Hamilton, George T. *ScF&FL 92*
Hamilton, Gordon Brown 1922- *St&PR 93*
Hamilton, Gordon D. 1953- *St&PR 93*
Hamilton, Grace T. d1992 *NewYTBS 92 [port]*
Hamilton, Guy 1922- *MiSFD 9*
Hamilton, Harold Philip 1924- *WhoAm 92*
Hamilton, Harry Lemuel, Jr. 1938- *WhoAm 92*
Hamilton, Helen *AmWomPl*
Hamilton, Henning 1929- *WhoScE 91-4*
Hamilton, Henry d1796 *HarEnMi*
Hamilton, Henry Ronald 1932- *WhoAm 92*
Hamilton, Horace George 1925- *WhoAm 92*
Hamilton, Howard Britton 1923- *WhoAm 92, WhoE 93*
Hamilton, Howard Henry 1935- *WhoE 93*
Hamilton, Howard Laverne 1916- *WhoAm 92*
Hamilton, Hugh Alexander 1929- *WhoAm 92*
Hamilton, Hugh B., Jr. 1946- *St&PR 93*
Hamilton, Hughbert Clayton 1903- *WhoE 93*
Hamilton, Hugo 1953- *ConAu 138*
Hamilton, Iain 1922- *OxDcOp*
Hamilton, Iain (Ellis) 1922- *Baker 92*
Hamilton, Ian Standish Monteith 1853-1947 *HarEnMi*
Hamilton, J. Marshall *Law&B 92*
Hamilton, J. Scott 1961- *WhoE 93*
Hamilton, Jack H. 1941- *WhoAm 92*
Hamilton, Jackson Douglas 1949- *WhoSSW 93*
Hamilton, Jacqueline 1942- *WhoAmW 93, WhoSSW 93*
Hamilton, James 1938- *WhoWrEP 92*
Hamilton, James, Marquess and Duke of 1606-1649 *HarEnMi*
Hamilton, James Andrew 1930- *St&PR 93*
Hamilton, James Arthur 1947- *WhoE 93*
Hamilton, James B. 1949- *St&PR 93*
Hamilton, James Bruce 1910-1991 *BioIn 17*
Hamilton, James Marvie 1950- *WhoAm 92, WhoEmL 93*
Hamilton, James P. 1946- *WhoIns 93*
Hamilton, James Theodore 1931- *WhoE 93*
Hamilton, Janet Virginia 1936- *WhoSSW 93*
Hamilton, Jay W. 1927- *St&PR 93*
Hamilton, Jeff *BioIn 17*
Hamilton, Jerald 1927- *WhoAm 92*
Hamilton, Jessica *ScF&FL 92*
Hamilton, Jimmie J. *Law&B 92*
Hamilton, Jimmy *BioIn 17*
Hamilton, Joe d1991 *BioIn 17*
Hamilton, Joe 1929-1991 *ConTFT 10*
Hamilton, John Alfred 1929- *WhoAm 92*
Hamilton, John Bruce 1943- *WhoE 93*
Hamilton, John D. M. 1892-1973 *PolPar*
Hamilton, John Daniel Miller 1892-1973 *BioIn 17*
Hamilton, John Dayton, Jr. 1934- *WhoAm 92*
Hamilton, John Kent 1945- *WhoSSW 93*
Hamilton, John L. Jack 1918- *St&PR 93*
Hamilton, John Ross 1924- *WhoAm 92*
Hamilton, John Thomas, Jr. 1951- *WhoEmL 93*
Hamilton, John W. 1939- *St&PR 93*
Hamilton, Joseph Hants, Jr. 1932- *WhoAm 92*
Hamilton, Joseph Henry Michael, Jr. 1929- *WhoAm 92*
Hamilton, Joshua Pearre 1938- *WhoE 93*
Hamilton, Judith Ann 1946- *WhoAmW 93*
Hamilton, Kimberly Darlene 1960- *WhoAmW 93, WhoEmL 93, WhoSSW 93*
Hamilton, Laura Ann 1939- *WhoAmW 93*
Hamilton, Lee H. 1931- *CngDr 91*
Hamilton, Lee Herbert 1931- *WhoAm 92*
Hamilton, Leona 1915- *WhoWrEP 92*
Hamilton, Leonard Derwent 1921- *WhoAm 92*
Hamilton, Linda Helen 1952- *WhoAmW 93*
Hamilton, Linda Kay 1945- *WhoWrEP 92*
Hamilton, Lisa 1961- *WhoE 93*
Hamilton, Lyman Critchfield, Jr. 1926- *WhoAm 92*
Hamilton, M. Raymond 1953- *WhoSSW 93*
Hamilton, Malcolm Cowan 1938- *WhoAm 92*
Hamilton, Marcella Denise 1954- *WhoWrEP 92*
Hamilton, Margaret 1941- *ScF&FL 92*
Hamilton, Margaret Letitia *St&PR 93*
Hamilton, Margaret Porch 1867- *AmWomPl*
Hamilton, Margaret Stewart 1940- *WhoAmW 93*
Hamilton, Marian Eloise 1931- *WhoSSW 93*
Hamilton, Mark B. *Law&B 92*
Hamilton, Mark Robert *St&PR 93*
Hamilton, Mary Agnes Adamson 1883-1966 *BioIn 17*
Hamilton, Mary K. 1926- *St&PR 93*
Hamilton, Mary Lucia Kerr 1926- *WhoAmW 93*
Hamilton, Mary M. *ScF&FL 92*
Hamilton, Melinda R. 1954- *WhoIns 93*
Hamilton, Melvin Charles 1950- *St&PR 93*
Hamilton, Michael H. *Law&B 92*
Hamilton, Michael Scott 1953- *WhoAm 92, WhoWor 93*
Hamilton, Michaela Ann 1948- *St&PR 93*
Hamilton, Michelle Renee 1956- *WhoAmW 93*
Hamilton, Milton Holmes, Sr. 1925- *WhoAm 92*
Hamilton, Mykol Cecilia 1952- *WhoEmL 93*
Hamilton, Nancy Beth 1948- *WhoAmW 93, WhoWor 93*
Hamilton, Nancy Corinne Miller 1929- *WhoSSW 93*
Hamilton, Nancy Elizabeth *Law&B 92*
Hamilton, Patricia Ann 1930- *WhoE 93*
Hamilton, Patricia Wardley 1930- *WhoWrEP 92*
Hamilton, Peter Bannerman 1946- *St&PR 93, WhoAm 92*
Hamilton, Peter Boris 1928- *WhoWor 93*
Hamilton, Peter Owen 1944- *WhoAm 92*
Hamilton, Peter Scott 1945- *WhoSSW 93*
Hamilton, Philip R. 1945- *St&PR 93*
Hamilton, Phillip Douglas 1954- *WhoEmL 93*
Hamilton, Phillip Larry 1960- *WhoSSW 93*
Hamilton, Pierpont Morgan 1898-1982 *BioIn 17*
Hamilton, Ralph *MajAI*
Hamilton, Ralph Lloyd 1928- *WhoSSW 93*
Hamilton, Ralph West 1933- *WhoAm 92*
Hamilton, Rhoda Lillian Rosen 1915- *WhoAmW 93*
Hamilton, Richard 1922- *BioIn 17*
Hamilton, Richard Daniel 1928- *WhoAm 92*
Hamilton, Richard Frederick 1930- *WhoWrEP 92*
Hamilton, Richard Freeman 1936- *WhoE 93*
Hamilton, Richard John *WhoScE 91-1*
Hamilton, Richard Lee 1939- *WhoAm 92*
Hamilton, Robert Brooks 1936- *WhoSSW 93*
Hamilton, Robert Morrison 1936- *WhoAm 92*
Hamilton, Robert T. *St&PR 93*
Hamilton, Robert William 1930- *WhoE 93*

Hamilton, Robert William 1939- *WhoAm 92*
Hamilton, Robert Woodruff 1931- *WhoAm 92*
Hamilton, Ronald *WhoScE 91-1*
Hamilton, Ross Aitken *WhoScE 91-1*
Hamilton, Russell *BioIn 17*
Hamilton, Russell George, Jr. 1934- *WhoAm 92*
Hamilton, Ruth Ethelmae *WhoAmW 93*
Hamilton, Sandra 1959- *WhoEmL 93*
Hamilton, Scott *BioIn 17*
Hamilton, Scott 1953- *WhoEmL 93*
Hamilton, Scott 1954- *BioIn 17*
Hamilton, Scott D'Arcy 1958- *WhoEmL 93*
Hamilton, Scott Scovell 1958- *WhoAm 92*
Hamilton, Scott W. 1954- *St&PR 93*
Hamilton, Shirley Siekmann 1928- *WhoAmW 93*
Hamilton, Stephen George *Law&B 92*
Hamilton, Stephen K. 1946- *WhoIns 93*
Hamilton, Steven G. *Law&B 92*
Hamilton, Steven G. 1939- *St&PR 93*
Hamilton, Strathford *MiSFD 9*
Hamilton, Susan Owens 1951- *WhoSSW 93*
Hamilton, Suzy *BioIn 17*
Hamilton, T. Earle 1905- *WhoAm 92*
Hamilton, Thomas A. *Law&B 92*
Hamilton, Thomas Allen 1947- *WhoSSW 93*
Hamilton, Thomas Herman 1931- *WhoAm 92*
Hamilton, Thomas James 1905- *BiDAMSp 1989*
Hamilton, Thomas Michael 1947- *WhoAm 92, WhoE 93, WhoWor 93*
Hamilton, Thomas Stewart 1911- *WhoAm 92*
Hamilton, Thomas Woolman 1948- *WhoWor 93*
Hamilton, Todd Cameron *ScF&FL 92*
Hamilton, Victor *BioIn 17*
Hamilton, Virginia 1936- *BioIn 17, ConAu 37NR, MajAI [port], ScF&FL 92, WhoAm 92, WhoAmW 93, WhoWrEP 92*
Hamilton, Virginia Esther 1933- *BlkAuII 92*
Hamilton, Virginia (Esther) 1936- *ChlFicS, DcAmChF 1960, DcAmChF 1985*
Hamilton, Virginia Van der Veer 1921- *WhoAm 92*
Hamilton, W. Allan *WhoScE 91-1*
Hamilton, W.D. *WhoScE 91-1*
Hamilton, Walter Scott 1931- *WhoSSW 93*
Hamilton, Warren Bell 1925- *WhoAm 92*
Hamilton, William 1730-1803 *BioIn 17*
Hamilton, William Berry, Jr. 1929- *WhoAm 92*
Hamilton, William Douglas, II 1948- *WhoEmL 93, WhoSSW 93*
Hamilton, William Ernest 1951- *WhoE 93*
Hamilton, William Frank 1939- *WhoAm 92*
Hamilton, William G. 1936- *St&PR 93*
Hamilton, William Howard 1918- *WhoAm 92*
Hamilton, William L. 1941- *St&PR 93*
Hamilton, William Lardner 1952- *WhoEmL 93*
Hamilton, William Leonard 1944- *WhoAm 92*
Hamilton, William Milton 1925- *St&PR 93, WhoAm 92*
Hamilton, William Rowan 1805-1865 *BioIn 17*
Hamilton, William T. 1939- *WhoAm 92*
Hamilton, Winthrop W. 1941- *St&PR 93*
Hamilton-Craig, Ian 1944- *WhoWor 93*
Hamilton-Finlay, Ian 1925- *BioIn 17*
Hamilton-Kemp, Thomas Rogers 1942- *WhoSSW 93*
Hamilton-McLeod, Rosemary *Law&B 92*
Hamilton-Miller, Jeremy Marcus Tom *WhoScE 91-1*
Hamilton-Paterson, James *BioIn 17*
Hamilton-Paterson, James 1941- *ConAu 137*
Hamington, Armand 1933- *St&PR 93*
Hamister, Donald Bruce 1920- *St&PR 93, WhoAm 92*
Hamity, Victor Hugo 1941- *WhoWor 93*
Ham Jong Han 1945- *WhoAsAP 91*
Hamlen, Robert Paul 1929- *WhoE 93*
Hamlet, Burgess Harrison 1937- *WhoSSW 93*
Hamlet, Joseph Frank 1934- *St&PR 93, WhoAm 92*
Hamlett, Donald Perry 1946- *WhoSSW 93*
Hamlett, George F. 1935- *St&PR 93*
Hamlett, James Gordon *WhoE 93, WhoWor 93*
Hamlett, Robert Barksdale 1949- *WhoEmL 93, WhoSSW 93*
Hamley, Dennis *ChlFicS*
Hamley, Dennis 1935- *ScF&FL 92, SmATA 69 [port]*
Hamley, James *Law&B 92*
Hamlin, A.H. 1934- *St&PR 93*
Hamlin, Arthur Tenney 1913- *WhoAm 92*
Hamlin, Cary Lee 1949- *WhoE 93*
Hamlin, Charles Sumner 1861-1938 *BioIn 17*
Hamlin, Dan William 1947- *WhoSSW 93*
Hamlin, Deborah Anne *Law&B 92*
Hamlin, George William 1948- *WhoSSW 93*
Hamlin, Hannibal 1809-1891 *BioIn 17, PolPar*
Hamlin, Harry *BioIn 17*
Hamlin, Harry 1951- *HolBB [port]*
Hamlin, Harry Robinson 1951- *WhoAm 92, WhoEmL 93*
Hamlin, Henry Allen 1930- *St&PR 93*
Hamlin, Isadore 1917-1991 *BioIn 17*
Hamlin, James Turner, III 1929- *WhoAm 92*
Hamlin, Janet *BioIn 17*
Hamlin, Kenneth Eldred, Jr. 1917- *WhoAm 92*
Hamlin, Mary Kay 1944- *WhoSSW 93*
Hamlin, Mary P. *AmWomPl*
Hamlin, Melissa Belote *BiDAMSp 1989*
Hamlin, Orrin Kenneth, II 1946- *WhoEmL 93*
Hamlin, Richard E. 1939- *St&PR 93*
Hamlin, Robert Henry 1923- *WhoAm 92*
Hamlin, Roger Eugene 1945- *WhoAm 92*
Hamlin, Ross J. *Law&B 92*
Hamlin, Sonya B. *WhoAmW 93*
Hamlin, Susan Lynn 1962- *WhoEmL 93*
Hamlin, Tim Allen 1960- *St&PR 93*
Hamling, James L. 1941- *St&PR 93*
Hamlisch, Marvin 1944- *WhoAm 92*
Hamlisch, Marvin (Frederick) 1944- *Baker 92*
Hamlyn, Adrian Noel 1944- *WhoWor 93*
Hamlyn, Jane *BioIn 17*
Hamlyn, Paul Bertrand 1926- *WhoWor 93*
Hamlyn, Richard L. 1950- *St&PR 93*
Hamm, Charles (Edward) 1925- *Baker 92*
Hamm, Charles J. 1937- *St&PR 93*
Hamm, Charles John 1937- *WhoAm 92*
Hamm, Diane Johnston 1949- *WhoAm 92*
Hamm, Donald George, Jr. 1954- *St&PR 93*
Hamm, Donald Ivan 1928- *WhoAm 92*
Hamm, Fred P. 1924- *WhoIns 93*
Hamm, Jerry Wid 1950- *WhoSSW 93*
Hamm, Louise Rarey 1927- *WhoAmW 93*
Hamm, Robert B. 1940- *St&PR 93*
Hamm, Stuart *BioIn 17*
Hamm, Suzanne Margaret 1943- *WhoAm 92, WhoAmW 93*
Hamm, Theodore 1825-1903 *BioIn 17*
Hamm, Thomas D. 1957- *ConAu 137*
Hamm, Wanda Sue 1944- *WhoAmW 93*
Hamm, William 1929- *ScF&FL 92*
Hamm, William Joseph 1910- *WhoAm 92*
Hamm, William R. *Law&B 92*
Hamm, William Robert 1952- *St&PR 93*
Hammacher, A.M. 1897- *ScF&FL 92*
Hammack, Charles Joseph 1923- *St&PR 93*
Hammack, Floyd Morgan 1944- *WhoE 93*
Hammack, Henry Edgar 1928- *WhoSSW 93*
Hammad, Alam E. 1943- *WhoWor 93*
Hammaker, Paul M. 1903- *WhoAm 92*
Hammalian, John Boyd *Law&B 92*
Hammalian, Stephen John 1941- *St&PR 93*
Hammam, Habib N. 1944- *WhoUN 92*
Hammam, M. Shawky 1919- *WhoAm 92*
Hamman, Robert J. 1914- *St&PR 93*
Hamman, Steven Roger 1946- *WhoEmL 93*
Hammann, Chester A. 1948- *WhoIns 93*
Hammans, Charles Erle, Jr. 1926- *St&PR 93*
Hammar, Hans B. 1936- *WhoUN 92*
Hammar, John C. *Law&B 92*
Hammar, Lester E. 1927- *St&PR 93*
Hammar, Lester Everett 1927- *WhoAm 92*
Hammargren, Sten-Peter 1923- *WhoWor 93*
Hammarskjold, Dag 1905-1961 *BioIn 17, ColdWar 1 [port]*
Hammarskjold, Dag Hjalmar Agne Carl 1905-1961 *DcTwHis*
Hammarsten, James Francis 1920- *WhoAm 92*
Hammarstrom, Lars E. 1936- *WhoScE 91-4*
Hammas, Refik 1935- *WhoWor 93*
Hammatt, Meryle Grace *Law&B 92*
Hamme, Robert K. 1942- *St&PR 93*
Hammel, Charles Louis 1925- *St&PR 93*
Hammel, Eileen Noel 1964- *WhoE 93*
Hammel, Frank Elliott 1959- *WhoE 93*
Hammel, Harold Theodore 1921- *WhoWor 93*
Hammel, Jay E. 1921-1990 *BioIn 17*
Hammel, Richard Warren 1956- *St&PR 93*
Hammel, Robert Edward 1935- *St&PR 93*
Hammel, Robert F. 1956- *St&PR 93*
Hammele, Joseph F. 1929- *St&PR 93*
Hammele, Joseph Francis 1929- *WhoAm 92*
Hammel-Geiger, Mary Celeste 1956- *WhoAm 92*
Hammell, Grandin Gaunt 1945- *WhoWor 93*
Hammell, Randall W. 1944- *St&PR 93*
Hammell, Thomas James 1944- *WhoE 93*
Hammen, Carl Schlee 1923- *WhoE 93*
Hammer *BioIn 17, WhoAm 92*
Hammer, Alfred Emil 1925- *WhoAm 92*
Hammer, Armand 1898-1990 *BioIn 17, JeAmHC*
Hammer, Carl 1914- *WhoAm 92*
Hammer, Daniel William 1932- *WhoAm 92*
Hammer, David Lindley 1929- *WhoWor 93*
Hammer, Dennis Glen 1953- *St&PR 93*
Hammer, Dietrich Hermann 1930- *WhoWor 93*
Hammer, Donald Price 1921- *WhoAm 92*
Hammer, Edward David 1957- *WhoAm 92*
Hammer, Emanuel Frederick 1926- *WhoAm 92*
Hammer, Erich 1935- *WhoScE 91-4*
Hammer, Erling A. 1934- *WhoScE 91-4*
Hammer, Harold Harlan 1920- *St&PR 93, WhoAm 92*
Hammer, Heinrich (Albert Eduard) 1862-1954 *Baker 92*
Hammer, Herman N. 1924- *St&PR 93*
Hammer, Ina *AmWomPl*
Hammer, Jacob 1950- *WhoEmL 93, WhoSSW 93*
Hammer, Jacob Myer 1927- *WhoAm 92*
Hammer, Jan 1948- *ConTFT 10*
Hammer, John William 1952- *St&PR 93*
Hammer, Karen A. *Law&B 92*
Hammer, Katherine Gonet 1946- *WhoAmW 93*
Hammer, Kenneth B. *Law&B 92*
Hammer, Klaus 1942- *WhoScE 91-3*
Hammer, Le *Law&B 92*
Hammer, Louis L. 1945- *St&PR 93*
Hammer, Louis (Zelig) 1931- *ConAu 139, WhoWrEP 92*
Hammer, M.C. *BioIn 17*
Hammer, Mark 1943- *St&PR 93*
Hammer, Mark Eugene 1944- *WhoSSW 93*
Hammer, Michael *NewYTBS 92 [port]*
Hammer, Michael Richard 1957- *WhoSSW 93*
Hammer, Mitchell A. *St&PR 93*
Hammer, N. Robert 1942- *St&PR 93*
Hammer, Nancy Johannaber *Law&B 92*
Hammer, R. Brooks 1937- *St&PR 93*
Hammer, Robert H., III *Law&B 92*
Hammer, Robert J. *Law&B 92*
Hammer, Roger A. 1934- *WhoWrEP 92*
Hammer, Roy Armand 1934- *WhoAm 92*
Hammer, Russell Jeffrey 1953- *St&PR 93*
Hammer, Sanford S. d1990 *BioIn 17*
Hammer, Sharon Elise 1958- *WhoEmL 93*
Hammer, Susan W. 1938- *WhoAm 92, WhoAmW 93*
Hammer, Theodore S. 1945- *St&PR 93*
Hammer, Thomas Allen 1947- *WhoE 93*
Hammer, Wade Burke 1932- *WhoAm 92*
Hammer, Wilfried 1927- *WhoScE 91-3*
Hammer, William Charles 1929- *St&PR 93*
Hammer, William P., Jr. *Law&B 92*
Hammer, Zevulun *BioIn 17*
Hammerich, Angul 1848-1931 *Baker 92*
Hammerle, Fredric Joseph 1944- *WhoAm 92*
Hammerling, Gunter *WhoScE 91-3*
Hammerly, David L. 1941- *St&PR 93*
Hammerly, Harry Allan 1934- *St&PR 93, WhoAm 92*
Hammerman, David Lewis 1935- *WhoE 93*
Hammerman, Irving Harold, II 1920- *WhoWor 93*
Hammerman, Joy Kaufman 1950- *WhoAmW 93*
Hammerman, Pat Jo 1954- *WhoEmL 93*
Hammerman, Stephen L. *Law&B 92*
Hammerman, Stephen Lawrence 1938- *WhoAm 92*
Hammerschick, Joseph 1937- *WhoScE 91-3*
Hammerschlag, Janos 1885-1954 *Baker 92*
Hammerschlag, Marianne 1932- *WhoAmW 93*
Hammerschmidt, Andreas 1612?-1675 *Baker 92*
Hammerschmidt, John A. *Law&B 92*
Hammerschmidt, John Paul 1922- *CngDr 91, WhoAm 92, WhoSSW 93*
Hammersen, Frithjof 1932- *WhoScE 91-3*
Hammersley, Frederick 1919- *BioIn 17*
Hammersmith, Jack Leonard 1941- *WhoSSW 93*
Hammerstein, Jurgen K.G.D. 1925- *WhoScE 91-3*
Hammerstein, Oscar 1846-1919 *Baker 92, OxDcOp*
Hammerstein, Oscar 1895-1960 *BioIn 17*
Hammerstein, Oscar, II 1895-1960 *OxDcOp*
Hammerstein, Oscar (Greeley Clendenning), II 1895-1960 *Baker 92*
Hammert, Dorothy Savage *WhoAmW 93*
Hammert, Marian Carol Dieckman 1939- *WhoAmW 93*
Hammerton, Max *WhoScE 91-1*
Hammes, Gordon G. 1934- *WhoAm 92*
Hammes, Kathryn Marie 1962- *WhoAmW 93*
Hammes, Lynn F. 1951- *St&PR 93*
Hammes, Robert Matthew, Jr. *Law&B 92*
Hammes, Terry Marie 1955- *WhoAmW 93*
Hammes, Walter P. 1939- *WhoScE 91-3*
Hammes, William James *Law&B 92*
Hammett, Dashiell 1894-1961 *BioIn 17, MagSAmL [port]*
Hammett, Dorothy T. *Law&B 92*
Hammett, Ellis Theodore 1920- *WhoWrEP 92*
Hammett, James Lincoln, Jr. 1943- *WhoE 93*
Hammett, John R. 1948- *St&PR 93*
Hammett, Michael F. 1956- *St&PR 93*
Hammett, Roy 1933- *St&PR 93*
Hammett, Samuel Dashiell 1894-1961 *BioIn 17*
Hammett, William M. H. 1944- *WhoAm 92*
Hammil, Joel 1909- *ScF&FL 92*
Hammill, Edward I. 1918- *St&PR 93*
Hammill, John Roberts 1931- *St&PR 93*
Hammill, R. Joseph 1942- *WhoSSW 93*
Hamming, Richard Wesley 1915- *WhoAm 92*
Hammis, James E. *Law&B 92*
Hammitt, Harry Andrew 1953- *WhoEmL 93, WhoSSW 93*
Hammitt, John Michael 1943- *WhoAm 92*
Hammon, Arthur Christopher 1951- *WhoWrEP 92*
Hammon, Patricia Jane 1946- *WhoAmW 93*
Hammond, Alice Fay 1949- *WhoAmW 93*
Hammond, Allen Lee 1943- *WhoAm 92*
Hammond, Betty Rae 1942- *WhoAmW 93*
Hammond, C. Dean, III 1947- *St&PR 93*
Hammond, Caleb D. 1915- *St&PR 93*
Hammond, Charles 1779-1840 *JrnUS*
Hammond, Charles Ainley 1933- *WhoAm 92*
Hammond, Charles Bessellieu 1936- *WhoAm 92*
Hammond, Christopher Fitzsimons, III 1939- *St&PR 93*
Hammond, Clarke Randolph 1945- *WhoSSW 93*
Hammond, Clement Milton *ScF&FL 92*
Hammond, Constance Elaine 1964- *WhoAmW 93*
Hammond, Dale 1947- *WhoIns 93*
Hammond, David Alan 1948- *WhoAm 92, WhoSSW 93*
Hammond, David Greene 1913- *WhoAm 92*
Hammond, Deanna Lindberg 1942- *WhoAm 92, WhoAmW 93*
Hammond, Donald L. 1927- *WhoAm 92*
Hammond, Dorothy Lee 1924- *WhoAmW 93*
Hammond, Duane Allen 1940- *WhoE 93*
Hammond, Edward H. 1944- *WhoAm 92*
Hammond, Edwin Hughes 1919- *WhoAm 92*
Hammond, Eleanor Agnes Merriam 1924- *WhoE 93*
Hammond, Eleanor Prescott 1866-1933 *AmWomPl*
Hammond, Frances L. 1957- *WhoSSW 93*
Hammond, Francis *BioIn 17*
Hammond, Frank Jefferson, III 1953- *WhoEmL 93*
Hammond, Frank Joseph 1919- *WhoAm 92*
Hammond, Frederick (Fisher) 1937- *Baker 92*
Hammond, G.A. *WhoScE 91-1*
Hammond, George Denman 1923- *WhoAm 92*
Hammond, George Simms 1921- *WhoAm 92*
Hammond, Gilbert Palmer, Jr. 1944- *St&PR 93*
Hammond, Glen R. 1937- *St&PR 93*
Hammond, Harold Francis 1908- *WhoAm 92*
Hammond, Harold Logan 1934- *WhoAm 92*

Hammond, Henry 1914-1989 *BioIn 17*
Hammond, J. D. 1933- *WhoAm 92*
Hammond, J(ames) D(illard) 1933- *WhoWrEP 92*
Hammond, J.R. 1933- *ScF&FL 92*
Hammond, Jack Arnold 1938- *St&PR 93*
Hammond, Jane Laura *WhoAm 92, WhoE 93*
Hammond, Jerome Jerald 1942- *WhoAm 92*
Hammond, Joan 1912- *IntDcOp, OxDcOp*
Hammond, Joan (Hood) 1912- *Baker 92*
Hammond, JoAnn 1957- *WhoEmL 93*
Hammond, Joanne Kugler 1951- *WhoAmW 93*
Hammond, Joe *BioIn 17*
Hammond, John Arlen 1937- *St&PR 93*
Hammond, John Hays, Jr. 1888-1965 *Baker 92*
Hammond, Joseph Charles Anthony 1934- *WhoAsAP 91*
Hammond, Joseph Kenneth *WhoScE 91-1*
Hammond, Joseph M. 1928- *St&PR 93*
Hammond, Josephine 1876- *AmWomPl*
Hammond, Judy Oliver 1946- *WhoEmL 93*
Hammond, Karen Smith 1954- *WhoAmW 93, WhoEmL 93, WhoSSW 93, WhoWor 93*
Hammond, Kathleen Doorish 1950- *St&PR 93*
Hammond, Kathryn Wire 1877- *AmWomPl*
Hammond, Kevin W. 1960- *St&PR 93*
Hammond, Lambert P. 1932- *St&PR 93*
Hammond, Lane E. *Law&B 92*
Hammond, Laurens 1895-1973 *Baker 92*
Hammond, Lou Rena Charlotte 1939- *WhoAm 92*
Hammond, M.J. *WhoScE 91-1*
Hammond, Mark B. *Law&B 92*
Hammond, Mark B. 1945- *St&PR 93*
Hammond, Mary Elizabeth Hale 1942- *WhoAm 92*
Hammond, Michael Peter 1932- *WhoAm 92*
Hammond, Michael W. 1938- *St&PR 93*
Hammond, Norman David Curle 1944- *WhoAm 92*
Hammond, Pamela 1938- *WhoAmW 93*
Hammond, Pat Wilcox 1937- *WhoSSW 93*
Hammond, Patricia Flood 1948- *WhoAmW 93, WhoEmL 93*
Hammond, Paul Young 1929- *WhoAm 92*
Hammond, Peter *MiSFD 9, WhoScE 91-1*
Hammond, R. Philip 1916- *WhoAm 92*
Hammond, Ralph Charles 1916- *WhoSSW 93*
Hammond, Red 1947- *WhoE 93*
Hammond, Richard J. *Law&B 92*
Hammond, Richard M. 1934- *St&PR 93*
Hammond, Richard W. 1946- *St&PR 93*
Hammond, Rick L. 1951- *WhoIns 93*
Hammond, Robert Alexander, III 1930- *WhoAm 92*
Hammond, Robert Lee *Law&B 92*
Hammond, Robert Lee 1926- *WhoAm 92*
Hammond, Robert Morris 1920- *WhoAm 92*
Hammond, Robert Tracy 1944- *St&PR 93*
Hammond, Roger Charles 1949- *WhoScE 91-4*
Hammond, Ronald B. *St&PR 93*
Hammond, Rose Marie 1949- *WhoAmW 93, WhoEmL 93*
Hammond, Roy Joseph 1929- *St&PR 93, WhoAm 92*
Hammond, Ruth 1896-1992 *BioIn 17, NewYTBS 92*
Hammond, Ruth Elizabeth 1954- *WhoWrEP 92*
Hammond, S. Katharine 1949- *WhoAmW 93*
Hammond, Stuart Lindsley 1922- *St&PR 93*
Hammond, Susan *BioIn 17*
Hammond, Teresa Lynn 1961- *WhoEmL 93*
Hammond, Thomas L. 1936- *St&PR 93*
Hammond, Thomas T. 1938- *St&PR 93*
Hammond, Virginia Maye *AmWomPl*
Hammond, William Alexander 1828-1900 *BioIn 17*
Hammond, Wilton N. 1927- *St&PR 93*
Hammond-Chambers, Robert Alexander 1942- *St&PR 93*
Hammond Innes, Ralph 1913- *WhoWor 93*
Hammond-Kominsky, Cynthia Cecelia 1957- *WhoAmW 93*
Hammonds, Deborah Jenkins 1950- *WhoAmW 93*
Hammonds, Elizabeth Ann 1968- *WhoAmW 93*
Hammonds, Michael 1942- *ScF&FL 92*
Hammond-Stroud, Derek 1926- *WhoWor 93*
Hammond-Stroud, Derek 1929- *Baker 92, OxDcOp*
Hammons, Brian Kent 1958- *St&PR 93*
Hammons, David *BioIn 17*
Hammons, James Hutchinson 1934- *WhoAm 92*
Hammontree, Charle F. 1960- *St&PR 93*
Hammontree, R. James 1933- *St&PR 93*
Hammurabi, King of Babylonia *BioIn 17*
Hamner, Charles Edward, Jr. 1935- *WhoAm 92*
Hamner, Earl Henry, Jr. 1923- *WhoAm 92*
Hamner, Homer Howell 1915- *WhoAm 92, WhoWor 93*
Hamner, Laura Vernon *AmWomPl*
Hamner, Patrick F. 1955- *St&PR 93*
Hamner, Sharon Boone 1939- *WhoSSW 93*
Hamner, Suzanne Leath 1940- *WhoAmW 93*
Hamner, W. Easley 1937- *St&PR 93*
Hamnett, Andrew *WhoScE 91-1*
Hamnett, Katharine *BioIn 17*
Hamod, (Hamode) Sam(uel) 1936- *WhoWrEP 92*
Hamolsky, Milton William 1921- *WhoAm 92*
Hamon, Michel *WhoScE 91-2*
Hamon, Richard Grady 1937- *WhoAm 92*
Hamor, Geza 1934- *WhoScE 91-4*
Hamori, Shigeyuki 1959- *WhoWor 93*
Hamosh, Margit 1933- *WhoE 93*
Hamot, Esse *AmWomPl*
Hamovitch, William 1922- *WhoAm 92*
Hamowy, Albert 1923- *St&PR 93*
Hamp, Eric Pratt 1920- *WhoAm 92*
Hampar, Berge 1932- *WhoE 93*
Hamparson, George Crosby 1924- *St&PR 93*
Hampe, Henry Theodore 1934- *St&PR 93*
Hampel, Alfred H. 1926- *St&PR 93*
Hampel, Alvin 1927- *WhoAm 92*
Hampel, David A. *Law&B 92*
Hampel, R.V. *Law&B 92*
Hampel, Robert Edward 1941- *St&PR 93, WhoAm 92*
Hampel, Werner A. 1942- *WhoScE 91-4*
Hamper, Ben *BioIn 17*
Hamper, Ben 1956?- *ConAu 138*
Hamper, Robert Joseph 1956- *WhoEmL 93, WhoWor 93*
Hampers, L. Joyce *WhoAmW 93*
Hampilos, Gus Theodore *Law&B 92*
Hampl, Arnost 1931- *WhoScE 91-4*
Hampl, Patricia 1946- *BioIn 17, WhoWrEP 92*
Hampshire, Damian Peter 1961- *WhoWor 93*
Hampshire, Joyce *ScF&FL 92*
Hampshire, Michael John *WhoScE 91-1*
Hampshire, Stuart 1950- *WhoScE 91-3*
Hampshire, Susan 1942- *WhoAm 92*
Hampson, C.P. *WhoScE 91-1*
Hampson, Christopher J. 1953- *WhoScE 91-1*
Hampson, Gary T. *Law&B 92*
Hampson, Mary Joan 1947- *WhoAmW 93, WhoE 93*
Hampson, Richard Kenneth 1942- *St&PR 93*
Hampson, Thomas *BioIn 17*
Hampson, Thomas 1955- *Baker 92*
Hampson, Thomas Lee 1948- *WhoE 93, WhoEmL 93*
Hampton, Benjamin Bertram 1925- *WhoAm 92*
Hampton, Bethany Russell 1952- *WhoSSW 93*
Hampton, Bill 1934- *ScF&FL 92*
Hampton, C. L. 1917- *WhoSSW 93*
Hampton, Calvin 1938-1984 *Baker 92*
Hampton, Carol McDonald 1935- *WhoAmW 93*
Hampton, Carolyn Hutchins 1936- *WhoAmW 93, WhoSSW 93*
Hampton, Christopher 1946- *BioIn 17*
Hampton, Christopher James 1946- *WhoWor 93*
Hampton, Cindy *BioIn 17*
Hampton, Clark W. 1934- *St&PR 93*
Hampton, Daniel Oliver 1957- *WhoAm 92*
Hampton, David *BioIn 17*
Hampton, Delon 1933- *WhoAm 92*
Hampton, E. Lynn 1947- *WhoAm 92*
Hampton, Edward John 1952- *WhoWor 93*
Hampton, Gena Faye 1959- *WhoEmL 93, WhoSSW 93*
Hampton, Glen Richard 1948- *WhoWor 93*
Hampton, Gordon Francis 1912- *WhoAm 92*
Hampton, Henry Eugene, Jr. 1940- *WhoAm 92*
Hampton, Henry (Eugene, Jr.) 1940- *ConAu 139*
Hampton, James Wilburn 1931- *WhoWor 93*
Hampton, Jay *ScF&FL 92*
Hampton, Jean Elizabeth 1954- *WhoAmW 93*
Hampton, John L.M. *Law&B 92*
Hampton, John Lewis 1935- *WhoAm 92*
Hampton, John N. 1944- *St&PR 93*
Hampton, John Reynolds *WhoScE 91-1*
Hampton, Leroy 1927- *WhoAm 92*
Hampton, Lionel *BioIn 17*
Hampton, Lionel 1909- *Baker 92*
Hampton, Lionel Leo 1913- *WhoAm 92*
Hampton, Louis R. 1920- *St&PR 93*
Hampton, Luann *ScF&FL 92*
Hampton, Margaret Frances 1947- *St&PR 93*
Hampton, Margaret Josephine 1935- *WhoAmW 93*
Hampton, Mark *BioIn 17*
Hampton, Mark 1940- *WhoE 93*
Hampton, Mark Garrison 1923- *WhoAm 92*
Hampton, Michael Douglas 1954- *WhoEmL 93*
Hampton, Morgan C. 1938- *St&PR 93*
Hampton, Oscar P., III 1933- *St&PR 93*
Hampton, Patty K. 1947- *St&PR 93*
Hampton, Philip McCune 1932- *St&PR 93, WhoAm 92*
Hampton, Phillip Michael 1932- *WhoAm 92*
Hampton, Ralph Clayton, Jr. 1934- *WhoAm 92*
Hampton, Raymond O. 1936- *St&PR 93*
Hampton, Rex H. 1918- *St&PR 93*
Hampton, Rex Herbert 1918- *WhoAm 92*
Hampton, Robert W. 1951- *St&PR 93*
Hampton, Robert Wesley 1951- *WhoSSW 93*
Hampton, Thomas Edward 1943- *WhoSSW 93*
Hampton, Trevor Allan *WhoSSW 93*
Hampton, Verne C., II 1934- *St&PR 93*
Hampton, Verne Churchill, II 1934- *WhoAm 92*
Hampton, Wade 1818-1902 *BioIn 17, HarEnMi, PolPar*
Hampton-Kauffman, Margaret Frances 1947- *WhoAmW 93*
Hamraev, Ali 1937- *DrEEuF*
Hamric, Frederick Leonidas 1923- *WhoAm 92*
Hamrick, C. Rush, Jr. 1921- *St&PR 93*
Hamrick, C. Wake 1941- *St&PR 93*
Hamrick, Gordon Grice 1930- *St&PR 93*
Hamrick, John M. 1913- *St&PR 93*
Hamrick, Joseph Thomas 1921- *WhoAm 92, WhoSSW 93*
Hamrick, Marie Ann 1968- *WhoSSW 93*
Hamrick, Richard Minor, III 1956- *WhoEmL 93*
Hamsaki, James S. *Law&B 92*
Ham-Seidel, Lorri Lynn 1965- *WhoAmW 93*
Hamsten, Bengt G. 1946- *WhoScE 91-4*
Hamstra, Christine Josephine 1953- *WhoSSW 93*
Hamsun, Knut 1859-1952 *MagSWL [port]*
Hamsun, Kunt 1859-1952 *BioIn 17*
Hamualainen, Martti M.J. 1939- *WhoScE 91-4*
Hamutenya, Hidipo 1939- *WhoAfr*
Hamvas, John Peter 1966- *St&PR 93*
Hamway, Edward George, Jr. 1942- *St&PR 93*
Hamway, Michael C. 1946- *St&PR 93*
Hamwee, Sally Rachel 1947- *WhoWor 93*
Hamy, Theodore 1842-1908 *IntDcAn*
Ham-Ying, Lemoy *Law&B 92*
Hamza, Janosne 1942- *WhoScE 91-4*
Hamza, Mohamed Carim Mohamed 1943- *WhoWor 93*
Hamzaee, Reza Gholi 1951- *WhoEmL 93, WhoWor 93*
Hamzah, Hamzah Sulaiman 1948- *WhoWor 93*
Hamzaoui, Abdelaziz 1935- *WhoAm 92*
Han, Cher Kwang 1965- *WhoWor 93*
Han, Chien-Pai 1936- *WhoAm 92*
Han, Chingping Jim 1957- *WhoSSW 93*
Han, Chong Kyu 1946- *WhoWor 93*
Han, Francis Tingpi d1991 *BioIn 17*
Han, Jaok 1930- *WhoAm 92*
Han, Jiawei 1949- *WhoWor 93*
Han, Kyung-Chik *BioIn 17*
Han, Lit S. 1925- *WhoAm 92*
Han, Moo-Young 1934- *WhoAm 92*
Han, Peter *BioIn 17*
Han, Sang Kil 1933- *St&PR 93*
Han, Sang Tae 1928- *WhoUN 92*
Han, Suyin 1917- *ScF&FL 92*
Han, Tian Xiong 1947- *WhoWor 93*
Han, Ulrich c. 1425-c. 1478 *Baker 92*
Han, Yanbin 1938- *WhoWor 93*
Han, Young Jo 1956- *WhoEmL 93, WhoSSW 93*
Han, Young Seok 1963- *WhoWor 93*
Hanache, Marie Adele 1932- *WhoE 93*
Hanack, Michael 1931- *WhoScE 91-3*
Hanada, Nobuhiro 1953- *WhoWor 93*
Hanafi, Waguih S. 1951- *WhoUN 92*
Hanafin, Bernard M. 1954- *St&PR 93*
Hanafusa, Hidesaburo 1929- *WhoAm 92*
Hanahan, Donald James 1919- *WhoAm 92*
Hanahan, James Lake 1932- *WhoSSW 93*
Hanak, Dusan 1938- *DrEEuF*
Hanak, Hynek *BioIn 17*
Hanamirian, Varujan 1952- *WhoEmL 93, WhoWor 93*
Hanan, Joe John 1931- *WhoAm 92*
Hanan, Patrick Dewes 1927- *WhoAm 92*
Han An-kuo fl. 135BC-129BC *HarEnMi*
Hanas, Robert J. *St&PR 93*
Hanas, Sven Ragnar 1951- *WhoWor 93*
Hanashi, Nobuyuki 1928- *WhoAsAP 91*
Hanau, Kenneth John, Jr. 1927- *WhoAm 92*
Hanau, Rudolf *St&PR 93*
Hanauer, Joe Franklin 1937- *WhoAm 92*
Hanauer, Jonathan 1961- *St&PR 93*
Hanauske, Axel Rainer 1953- *WhoWor 93*
Hanawalt, Philip Courtland 1931- *WhoAm 92*
Hanaya, Tadashi 1894-1957 *HarEnMi*
Hanback, Christopher Brecht 1950- *St&PR 93, WhoEmL 93*
Hanback, Hazel Marie Smallwood 1918- *WhoAmW 93, WhoWor 93*
Hanboys, John fl. 15th cent.- *Baker 92*
Hanburger, Christian, Jr. 1941- *BiDAMSp 1989*
Hanbury, George Lafayette, II 1943- *WhoAm 92*
Hanbury, Raymond Francis, Jr. 1945- *WhoE 93*
Hanby, Bernadine C. d1991 *BioIn 17*
Hanby, John E. 1941- *St&PR 93*
Hanby, John Estes, Jr. 1941- *WhoAm 92*
Hanby, Robert M. Butch 1940- *St&PR 93*
Hanby, Walter Dana 1944- *WhoSSW 93*
Hance, Allan *WhoScE 91-2*
Hance, Frank W. 1950- *St&PR 93*
Hance, James H., Jr. 1944- *St&PR 93*
Hance, James Henry, Jr. 1944- *WhoAm 92*
Hance, Laconla Hinson 1923- *WhoAm 92*
Hance, Margaret T. d1990 *BioIn 17*
Hance, Raymond John 1936- *WhoUN 92*
Hancell, Peter James *WhoScE 91-1*
Hancevic, Janko 1933- *WhoScE 91-4*
Hanchett, Henry Granger 1853-1918 *Baker 92*
Hanchey, Frederick L. *Law&B 92*
Hancke, Karen Lee 1967- *WhoE 93*
Hancock, Alan 1935- *WhoUN 92*
Hancock, Alexander DiGiulio 1952- *WhoWrEP 92*
Hancock, Arthur Stewart 1926- *St&PR 93*
Hancock, Barry Anthony 1960- *St&PR 93*
Hancock, Barry William *WhoScE 91-1*
Hancock, Brent H. 1942- *St&PR 93*
Hancock, Carol Brooks 1941- *St&PR 93*
Hancock, Charles Cavanaugh, Jr. 1935- *WhoAm 92, WhoE 93*
Hancock, Clenric Guy 1948- *WhoEmL 93, WhoSSW 93*
Hancock, Cynthia Chapman 1936- *WhoSSW 93*
Hancock, Dain Michael 1941- *St&PR 93*
Hancock, Don *St&PR 93*
Hancock, Don Edward 1952- *WhoEmL 93*
Hancock, Edward Lee, Jr. *Law&B 92*
Hancock, Ellen M. 1943- *St&PR 93*
Hancock, Ellen Marie 1943- *WhoAm 92, WhoAmW 93*
Hancock, Emily Stone 1945- *WhoAm 92*
Hancock, Ernest William 1927- *WhoAm 92*
Hancock, G.J. *WhoScE 91-1*
Hancock, Geoff 1946- *ScF&FL 92*
Hancock, Geoffrey 1946- *WhoCanL 92*
Hancock, Geoffrey White 1946- *WhoAm 92*
Hancock, Gerre Edward 1934- *WhoAm 92*
Hancock, Herbert Jeffrey 1940- *WhoAm 92*
Hancock, Herbie 1940- *Baker 92, BioIn 17, ConMus 8 [port]*
Hancock, Ian Francis 1942- *WhoAm 92*
Hancock, Jaci S. *Law&B 92*
Hancock, James Hughes 1931- *WhoAm 92*
Hancock, John *WhoScE 91-1*
Hancock, John d1992 *NewYTBS 92*
Hancock, John 1939- *MiSFD 9*
Hancock, John Ansel 1956- *WhoSSW 93*
Hancock, John B. *Law&B 92*
Hancock, John Coulter 1929- *St&PR 93, WhoAm 92*
Hancock, John D. 1939- *WhoAm 92*
Hancock, John M. *Law&B 92*
Hancock, John W. 1931- *WhoAm 92*
Hancock, John W. 1937- *St&PR 93*
Hancock, John Walker, III 1937- *WhoAm 92*
Hancock, Judith Louise 1951- *WhoEmL 93*
Hancock, Katherine Pohl 1960- *WhoAmW 93*

Hancock, Kathleen Elizabeth 1955- *WhoSSW 93*
Hancock, Kathy Marie 1952- *WhoAmW 93*
Hancock, Langley George 1909- *WhoWor 93*
Hancock, Loni 1940- *WhoAm 92, WhoAmW 93*
Hancock, Lyn 1938- *WhoCanL 92*
Hancock, Malcolm *BioIn 17*
Hancock, Marion Donald 1939- *WhoAm 92*
Hancock, Mel 1929- *CngDr 91, WhoAm 92*
Hancock, Monte Floyd, Jr. 1953- *WhoEmL 93, WhoSSW 93*
Hancock, Nancy L. *Law&B 92*
Hancock, Nannette Beatrice Finley 1937- *WhoAmW 93*
Hancock, Niel 1941- *ScF&FL 92*
Hancock, Paul David *Law&B 92*
Hancock, S. Lee 1955- *WhoWor 93*
Hancock, Sandra Olivia 1947- *WhoAmW 93, WhoEmL 93*
Hancock, Stewart F. 1950- *St&PR 93*
Hancock, Thomas 1913- *WhoAm 92*
Hancock, Tony 1924-1968 *QDrFCA 92 [port]*
Hancock, Vernon Ray 1926- *WhoSSW 93*
Hancock, Walker Kirtland 1901- *WhoAm 92*
Hancock, Wayne M. *Law&B 92*
Hancock, Wayne Mitchell 1931- *St&PR 93*
Hancock, William Frank, Jr. 1942- *WhoWor 93*
Hancock, William Glenn 1950- *St&PR 93, WhoAm 92*
Hancock, William John 1942- *WhoAm 92*
Hancock, Winfield S. 1824-1886 *PolPar*
Hancock, Winfield Scott 1824-1886 *HarEnMi*
Hancocks, David Morgan 1941- *WhoAm 92*
Hancox, David Robert 1951- *WhoE 93*
Hancox, Nancie 1890-1978 *BioIn 17*
Hancox, Ralph 1929- *St&PR 93, WhoAm 92*
Hancox, Robert Ernest 1943- *WhoAm 92, WhoE 93, WhoWor 93*
Hanczor, Joseph *Law&B 92*
Hand, Bethlyn Jean *St&PR 93*
Hand, Billings Learned 1872-1961 *OxCSupC*
Hand, Brian Edward 1963- *WhoE 93*
Hand, Cadet Hammond, Jr. 1920- *WhoAm 92*
Hand, Charles T. 1928- *St&PR 93*
Hand, Cora McWhiney *AmWomPl*
Hand, David John 1950- *WhoWor 93*
Hand, David John 1959- *WhoScE 91-1*
Hand, Dent N., Jr. *Law&B 92*
Hand, Elizabeth 1957- *ConAu 136, ScF&FL 92*
Hand, Gerry 1942- *WhoAsAP 91*
Hand, Gertrude 1886- *AmWomPl*
Hand, Herbert Hensley 1931- *WhoAm 92, WhoSSW 93*
Hand, James Stanley 1949- *WhoEmL 93*
Hand, John 1926- *WhoAm 92*
Hand, John Oliver 1941- *WhoAm 92*
Hand, John Thomas, Jr. *Law&B 92*
Hand, Judith Hayes 1939- *WhoAmW 93*
Hand, Kathleen Margaret 1947- *WhoAmW 93*
Hand, Kerry Wayne 1952- *St&PR 93*
Hand, Matthew H. *Law&B 92*
Hand, Olivia Browing d1990 *BioIn 17*
Hand, Paul E. 1931- *St&PR 93*
Hand, Paul Edgar 1931- *WhoE 93, WhoWor 93*
Hand, Peter James 1937- *WhoAm 92, WhoE 93*
Hand, Ralph, III *BioIn 17*
Hand, Robert E. *Law&B 92*
Hand, Robert Frank 1939- *St&PR 93*
Hand, Robert James 1938- *WhoWor 93*
Hand, Robert Stephens 1915- *WhoE 93*
Hand, Roger 1938- *WhoAm 92*
Hand, Scott M. 1942- *St&PR 93*
Hand, Scott McKee *Law&B 92*
Hand, Stephen *ScF&FL 92*
Hand, Susan *WhoWrEP 92*
Hand, William Brevard 1924- *WhoAm 92, WhoSSW 93*
Handahl, Donald H. 1924- *St&PR 93*
Handal, Schafick Jorge *DcCPCAm*
Handberg, Irene Deak *WhoAm 92*
Handberg, Ronald 1938- *St&PR 93*
Handel, Bernard 1926- *WhoE 93*
Handel, David Jonathan 1946- *WhoAm 92*
Handel, George Frideric 1685-1759 *Baker 92, BioIn 17, IntDcOp [port], OxDcOp*
Handel, Gerald Seidman 1924- *WhoE 93*
Handel, Katharine Carter 1945- *WhoSSW 93*
Handel, Maurice d1990 *BioIn 17*
Handel, Morton E. 1935- *St&PR 93*
Handel, Morton Emanuel 1935- *WhoAm 92*
Handel, Nancy H. 1951- *St&PR 93*
Handel, Peter H. 1937- *WhoAm 92*
Handelman, Alice Roberta 1943- *WhoAmW 93*
Handelman, David Y. *Law&B 92*
Handelman, David Y. 1938- *St&PR 93*
Handelman, David Yale 1938- *WhoAm 92*
Handelman, Edward I. *Law&B 92*
Handelman, Eileen Tannenbaum 1928- *WhoAmW 93*
Handelman, Lester J. 1911- *St&PR 93*
Handelman, Neil J. 1935- *St&PR 93*
Handelman, Susan A. 1949- *ConAu 137*
Handelman, William Alan 1948- *WhoEmL 93*
Handelsman, Harold S. *Law&B 92*
Handelsman, Harold S. 1946- *WhoAm 92*
Handelsman, Harold Samuel 1946- *St&PR 93*
Handelsman, M. Gene 1923- *WhoAm 92*
Handelsman, Marceli 1882-1945 *PolBiDi*
Handerek, Jan 1934- *WhoScE 91-4*
Handford, Martin *BioIn 17*
Handford, Martin (John) 1956- *ConAu 137, MajAI [port]*
Handford, Maurice 1929-1986 *Baker 92*
Handford, Nourma 1911- *DcChlFi*
Handin, John Walter 1919- *WhoAm 92*
Handke, Peter 1942- *BioIn 17, DcLB 124 [port], MagSWL [port]*
Handl, Irene 1901-1987 *QDrFCA 92 [port]*
Handl, Jacob *Baker 92*
Handleman, Claiborne P. *Law&B 92*
Handleman, David 1914- *WhoAm 92*
Handleman, David 1915- *St&PR 93*
Handleman, David Y. 1938- *WhoAm 92*
Handler, Alan B. 1931- *WhoAm 92*
Handler, Douglas Perry 1957- *WhoE 93, WhoEmL 93*
Handler, Elisabeth Helen 1944- *WhoAmW 93*
Handler, Elliot 1916- *BioIn 17*
Handler, Enid Irene 1932- *WhoAmW 93*
Handler, Evan *BioIn 17*
Handler, Evelyn Erika 1933- *WhoWor 93*
Handler, Harold Robert 1935- *WhoAm 92*
Handler, Jerome Sidney 1933- *WhoAm 92*
Handler, Julian H. 1921-1991 *BioIn 17*
Handler, Lawrence David 1945- *WhoAm 92*
Handler, Leslie 1901-1991 *BioIn 17*
Handler, Lowell *BioIn 17*
Handler, Mark S. 1933- *St&PR 93, WhoAm 92, WhoE 93*
Handler, Milton 1903- *WhoAm 92*
Handler, Milton E. 1926- *St&PR 93*
Handler, Mimi 1934- *WhoAm 92*
Handler, R. Arnold *Law&B 92*
Handler, Ruby Ann *WhoAm 92*
Handler, Ruth 1916- *BioIn 17*
Handler, Sidney 1932- *WhoAm 92*
Handlery, Paul R. 1920- *St&PR 93*
Handlery, Paul Robert 1920- *WhoAm 92*
Handley, Earl L. *Law&B 92*
Handley, Eleanor Lucristor 1950- *WhoAmW 93*
Handley, Elisabeth Anne 1957- *WhoAmW 93*
Handley, G. Kenneth *Law&B 92*
Handley, Graham 1926- *ScF&FL 92*
Handley, Kaye C. *St&PR 93*
Handley, Leon Hunter 1927- *WhoAm 92, WhoSSW 93, WhoWor 93*
Handley, Margie Lee 1939- *WhoAmW 93*
Handley, Max 1945- *ScF&FL 92*
Handley, Patricia Carol Bell 1940- *WhoSSW 93*
Handley, Ray 1944- *WhoAm 92, WhoE 93*
Handley, Richard Lowry *Law&B 92*
Handley, Roger Patrick 1945- *WhoAm 92*
Handley, Thomas P. 1963- *St&PR 93*
Handley, Tommy 1894-1949 *QDrFCA 92 [port]*
Handley, Vernon (George) 1930- *Baker 92*
Handley-Poteat, Sue Ann 1955- *WhoAmW 93*
Handlin, Oscar 1915- *JeAmHC, WhoAm 92*
Handling, Piers *ScF&FL 92*
Handlir, David Y. 1947- *St&PR 93*
Handlir, Jiri Vladimir 1946- *WhoWor 93*
Handly, Earl John 1922- *St&PR 93*
Handmaker, Stuart Allen 1930- *St&PR 93*
Han Dongfang *NewYTBS 92 [port]*
Handrich, Rita Rae 1958- *WhoAmW 93*
Handrock, Julius 1830-1894 *Baker 92*
Hands, Rachel Indra 1961- *WhoAmW 93*
Hands, Terence David 1941- *WhoWor 93*
Handschin, Edmund 1941- *WhoScE 91-3*
Handschin, Jacques (Samuel) 1886-1955 *Baker 92*
Handschuh, Dawn 1959- *WhoAmW 93*
Handschuh, G. Gregory *Law&B 92*
Handschumacher, Albert Gustave 1918- *WhoAm 92, WhoWor 93*
Handschumacher, Robert Edmund 1927- *WhoE 93*
Handshaw, Gordon Frank 1950- *WhoE 93*
Handspicker, Brian DeWitt 1957- *WhoE 93*
Handt, Herbert 1926- *Baker 92*
Handville, Robert Tompkins 1924- *WhoAm 92*
Handwerger, Sandra 1955- *WhoE 93*
Handwerker, A. M. 1928- *WhoWor 93*
Handwerker, Earl Howard 1946- *WhoEmL 93*
Handwerker, Murray 1921- *St&PR 93*
Hand Wright, Laura Bella 1950- *WhoAmW 93*
Handy, Alice Warner 1948- *WhoAm 92*
Handy, Charles Brooks 1924- *WhoAm 92*
Handy, Daniel Nash 1875?-1948 *BioIn 17*
Handy, Drucilla 1924- *WhoAmW 93*
Handy, Edward Otis, Jr. 1929- *WhoAm 92*
Handy, Edward Smith Craighill 1892-1980 *IntDcAn*
Handy, Ellen Joan 1961- *WhoE 93*
Handy, Howard P.G. 1944- *WhoUN 92*
Handy, Lyman Lee 1919- *WhoAm 92*
Handy, Mary Catherine Lipham 1947- *WhoAmW 93, WhoE 93, WhoEmL 93*
Handy, Mary Nixeon Civille 1909- *WhoWrEP 92*
Handy, Merriam Joan 1952- *WhoAmW 93*
Handy, Richard Lincoln 1929- *WhoAm 92*
Handy, Robert Maxwell 1931- *WhoAm 92*
Handy, Robert Truman 1941- *WhoSSW 93*
Handy, Rollo Leroy 1927- *WhoAm 92, WhoE 93*
Handy, W(illiam) C(hristopher) 1873-1958 *Baker 92*
Handy, Will *Baker 92*
Handy, William Talbot, Jr. 1924- *WhoAm 92*
Handy, Willowdean Chatterson 1889-1965 *IntDcAn*
Hane, Antonio C.P. 1939- *St&PR 93*
Hane, Guy Elliott 1952- *WhoEmL 93*
Hane, Mikiso 1922- *WhoAm 92*
Hanebrink, Earl Lee 1924- *WhoSSW 93*
Hanegan, Herbert Michael *Law&B 92*
Haneke, Dianne Myers 1941- *WhoWrEP 92*
Hanel, Lewis Sterling 1916- *St&PR 93*
Hanelius, Antti Juhani 1931- *WhoScE 91-4*
Hanen, Marsha *BioIn 17*
Hanes, Andrew Guy 1929- *St&PR 93*
Hanes, Darlene Marie 1956- *WhoEmL 93*
Hanes, Donald Keith 1933- *WhoE 93*
Hanes, Elson C. 1924- *St&PR 93*
Hanes, Frank Borden 1920- *WhoAm 92, WhoWrEP 92*
Hanes, Hope Yandell d1992 *NewYTBS 92*
Hanes, Hugh D. 1935- *St&PR 93*
Hanes, James Henry 1922- *WhoAm 92*
Hanes, John Grier 1936- *St&PR 93*
Hanes, John T. 1936- *WhoAm 92*
Hanes, Lee Duncan 1927- *WhoE 93*
Hanes, Ralph Philip, Jr. 1926- *St&PR 93, WhoAm 92*
Hanes, Robert G. 1936- *St&PR 93*
Hanesian, Deran 1927- *WhoAm 92, WhoE 93*
Hanesworth, Daniel J. 1944- *St&PR 93*
Hanesworth, L. Michael *Law&B 92*
Hanevik, Amund 1932- *WhoScE 91-4*
Haney, Arthur John 1942- *WhoSSW 93*
Haney, Dan *Law&B 92*
Haney, David P. 1938- *WhoWrEP 92*
Haney, Elizabeth Marie 1968- *WhoSSW 93*
Haney, Hoyt A. 1933- *St&PR 93*
Haney, J. Terrence 1933- *WhoAm 92, WhoWor 93*
Haney, James W. *St&PR 93*
Haney, Jay Bernard 1947- *WhoSSW 93*
Haney, John Benjamin 1931- *WhoE 93*
Haney, John Keith 1962- *WhoSSW 93*
Haney, Joseph Donald 1936- *St&PR 93*
Haney, Judith Louise 1946- *WhoE 93*
Haney, Julia Jamison 1942- *WhoWor 93*
Haney, Lee *BioIn 17*
Haney, Lynn 1941- *ScF&FL 92*
Haney, R. Lee 1939- *St&PR 93*
Haney, Raymond Lee 1939- *WhoAm 92*
Haney, Rebecca S. *Law&B 92*
Haney, Robert E. *BioIn 17*
Haney, Robert Locke 1928- *WhoWor 93*
Haney, Roger A. 1938- *St&PR 93*
Haney, Sharon 1950- *WhoWrEP 92*
Haney, Thomas Victor d1991 *BioIn 17*
Haney, William V. 1936- *St&PR 93*
Hanf, Charles David 1950- *WhoE 93*
Hanff, Helene 1916- *WhoWrEP 92*
Hanff, Johann Nikolaus 1665-1711? *Baker 92*
Hanff, Peter E. 1944- *ScF&FL 92*
Hanfling, Robert Irwin 1938- *WhoAm 92*
Hanford, Agnes Rutledge 1927- *WhoSSW 93*
Hanford, Aubrey L., III 1939- *St&PR 93*
Hanford, Craig Bradley 1953- *WhoE 93, WhoEmL 93*
Hanford, George Hyde 1920- *WhoAm 92*
Hanford, Grail Stevenson 1932- *WhoSSW 93*
Hanford, Mary Cathey *BioIn 17*
Hanford, Patrick Joseph 1952- *WhoSSW 93*
Hanfstangel, Marie 1846-1917 *Baker 92*
Hanft, John D. 1943- *WhoIns 93*
Hanft, Noah Jonathan 1953- *WhoEmL 93*
Hanft, Ruth S. Samuels 1929- *WhoAm 92, WhoAmW 93*
Han Fu-ch'u 1890-1938 *HarEnMi*
Hanganut, Marius 1929- *WhoScE 91-4*
Hangen, Bruce Boyer 1947- *WhoAm 92*
Hanger, Clifford *WhoWrEP 92*
Hanger, Robert Edwin 1934- *WhoSSW 93*
Hanger, Wallace Carlton, Jr. 1955- *WhoE 93*
Hangley, William Thomas 1941- *WhoE 93*
Ha-Ngoc, Tuan 1952- *St&PR 93*
Hangstefer, James B. 1927- *St&PR 93*
Hangyal, Karoly 1928- *WhoScE 91-4*
Hanhausen, Edward Henry 1926- *WhoE 93*
Hani, "Chris" Martin Thembisile 1942- *WhoAfr*
Hani, Heinz *WhoScE 91-4*
Hani, Motoko 1873-1957 *BioIn 17*
Hanifen, Richard Charles 1931- *WhoAm 92*
Hanifin, Leo Eugene 1946- *WhoAm 92*
Hanify, Edward B. 1912- *St&PR 93*
Hanig, Carl Jesse 1955- *WhoE 93*
Hanigan, Francis Lawrence 1935- *WhoSSW 93*
Hanigan, Lawrence 1925- *WhoAm 92*
Hanigan, Marvin Frank 1931- *St&PR 93, WhoAm 92*
Hanigan, Thomas E. 1922- *St&PR 93*
Hanigan, Thomas E. 1922-1991 *BioIn 17*
Hanik, Peter 1946- *WhoAm 92*
Hanin, Israel 1937- *WhoAm 92*
Haning, Charles Robert 1934- *St&PR 93*
Hanis, Gregory Richard 1950- *WhoEmL 93*
Hanisch, Joseph 1812-1892 *Baker 92*
Hanisee, Jeanette Lester 1940- *WhoAmW 93*
Hanisee, Mark Steven 1958- *WhoSSW 93*
Hank, Bernard J., Jr. 1929- *St&PR 93, WhoAm 92*
Hank, Lois *BioIn 17*
Hankamer, Michael 1944- *WhoSSW 93*
Hanke, Byron Reidt 1911- *WhoAm 92*
Hanke, Karl c. 1750-1803 *Baker 92*
Hanke, Ken 1954- *ScF&FL 92*
Hanke, Lewis Ulysses 1905- *WhoAm 92*
Hanke, Wilfried F. 1927- *WhoScE 91-3*
Hankenson, Edward Craig, Jr. 1935- *WhoAm 92*
Hanket, Mark J. *Law&B 92*
Hanket, Mark J. 1943- *St&PR 93*
Hanket, Mark John 1943- *WhoAm 92*
Hankey, David Lawrence *Law&B 92*
Hankey, James Nelson 1957- *WhoSSW 93*
Hankey, Maurice Pascal Alars 1877-1963 *DcTwHis*
Hankey, Paul V. 1931- *St&PR 93*
Hankin, Ann Dunlap *Law&B 92*
Hankin, Bernard Jacob 1913- *WhoAm 92*
Hankin, Elaine Krieger 1938- *WhoAm 92*
Hankin, Errol Patrick 1942- *WhoAm 92*
Hankin, Janet R. *BioIn 17*
Hankin, Leonard J. 1917- *WhoAm 92*
Hankin, Robert Michael 1930- *WhoAm 92*
Hankin, William Henry 1946- *WhoE 93, WhoEmL 93*
Hankins, G. William *Law&B 92*
Hankins, Hesterly G., III 1950- *WhoWor 93*
Hankins, Hugh Walter 1933- *St&PR 93*
Hankins, Marie Garner 1943- *WhoAmW 93*
Hankins, Raleigh Walter 1958- *WhoWor 93*
Hankins, Winston H. 1932- *WhoIns 93*
Hankinson, Charlene Joy 1949- *WhoAmW 93*
Hankinson, Harriette Foster 1942- *WhoSSW 93*
Hankinson, James F. 1943- *WhoAm 92*
Hankinson, James Floyd 1943- *WhoE 93, WhoWor 93*
Hankinson, Risdon William 1938- *WhoAm 92*
Hankla, Cathryn 1958- *ConAu 39NR, WhoWrEP 92*

Hankoff, Jeffrey Frank 1948- *WhoEmL 93*
Hanks, Alan R. 1939- *WhoAm 92*
Hanks, Bob D. 1939- *St&PR 93*
Hanks, Camilla 1863-1902 *BioIn 17*
Hanks, David Allen 1940- *WhoE 93*
Hanks, David Terry 1951- *WhoSSW 93*
Hanks, Deaf Charlie 1863-1902 *BioIn 17*
Hanks, Don F., II 1953- *WhoSSW 93*
Hanks, Gordon R. 1946- *WhoScE 91-1*
Hanks, Grace Mary 1954- *WhoAm 92, WhoAmW 93, WhoEmL 93*
Hanks, James Judge, Jr. 1943- *WhoAm 92*
Hanks, John Donald 1920- *St&PR 93*
Hanks, Kenneth R. 1954- *St&PR 93*
Hanks, Linda A. *Law&B 92*
Hanks, Robert J. 1943- *WhoE 93*
Hanks, Robert Jack 1923- *WhoAm 92*
Hanks, Roma Stovall 1947- *WhoSSW 93*
Hanks, Sandra May 1940- *WhoAmW 93*
Hanks, Stephen Grant *Law&B 92*
Hanks, Timothy Wayne 1960- *WhoSSW 93*
Hanks, Tom *BioIn 17*
Hanks, Tom 1956- *HolBB [port], IntDcF 2-3, QDrFCA 92 [port], WhoAm 92*
Hanks, William Bruce 1954- *St&PR 93*
Han Kwang Ok 1942- *WhoAsAP 91*
Hanle, Paul Arthur 1947- *WhoAm 92*
Hanle, William Scott 1948- *St&PR 93*
Hanlen, John Garrett 1922- *WhoAm 92, WhoE 93*
Hanley, Boniface 1924- *BioIn 17*
Hanley, Charles 1920- *WhoAm 92*
Hanley, Charles E. *St&PR 93*
Hanley, Edward Thomas 1932- *WhoAm 92*
Hanley, Elizabeth *ScF&FL 92*
Hanley, Elizabeth Hines *AmWomPl*
Hanley, Frank 1930- *WhoAm 92*
Hanley, Gerald d1992 *NewYTBS 92*
Hanley, Gerald (Anthony) 1916-1992 *ConAu 139*
Hanley, James 1901-1985 *BioIn 17, ScF&FL 92*
Hanley, James A. 1931- *WhoAm 92*
Hanley, Jane W. *St&PR 93*
Hanley, Joseph A. 1922- *St&PR 93*
Hanley, Julia Elizabeth Burns 1953- *WhoSSW 93*
Hanley, Kenneth T. *Law&B 92*
Hanley, Mary Lynn 1937- *WhoUN 92*
Hanley, Michael J. 1948- *St&PR 93*
Hanley, Michael Joseph 1940- *WhoSSW 93*
Hanley, Peter R. 1939- *St&PR 93*
Hanley, Peter Ronald 1939- *WhoAm 92*
Hanley, Philip M. 1945- *St&PR 93*
Hanley, Priscilla E. *St&PR 93*
Hanley, Raymond Joseph 1955- *WhoE 93*
Hanley, Robert 1933- *St&PR 93*
Hanley, Robert, Jr. 1933- *WhoAm 92*
Hanley, Robert F. 1924-1991 *BioIn 17*
Hanley, Robert Francis 1924-1991 *WhoAm 92*
Hanley, Thomas Aquinas, Jr. 1954- *WhoE 93*
Hanley, Thomas Patrick 1951- *WhoEmL 93*
Hanley, Thomas Richard 1945- *WhoAm 92, WhoSSW 93*
Hanley, Wayne S. 1945- *St&PR 93*
Hanley, William H. 1942- *WhoAm 92*
Hanley, William T. 1947- *St&PR 93*
Hanlin, Hugh Carey 1925- *WhoAm 92, WhoSSW 93*
Hanlin, R.L. 1932- *St&PR 93*
Hanlin, Richard Thomas 1931- *WhoSSW 93*
Hanlin, Russell L. 1932- *WhoAm 92*
Hanlon, Betty Ellen 1935- *WhoAmW 93*
Hanlon, David Patrick 1944- *WhoE 93, WhoSSW 93*
Hanlon, Emily 1945- *ScF&FL 92, WhoWrEP 92*
Hanlon, Gayle E. *Law&B 92*
Hanlon, James Allison 1937- *St&PR 93, WhoAm 92*
Hanlon, John L. 1935- *St&PR 93*
Hanlon, Patricia Mary 1956- *WhoEmL 93*
Hanlon, Thomas William 1948- *St&PR 93*
Hanlon, William John *Law&B 92*
Hanmer, Read *BioIn 17*
Hanmer, Stephen Read, Jr. 1933- *WhoAm 92*
Hann, Barbara JoAnn 1946- *WhoAmW 93*
Hann, Daniel P. *Law&B 92*
Hann, Don Robert 1946- *WhoEmL 93*
Hann, Elmer L. d1990 *BioIn 17*
Hann, Georg 1897-1950 *Baker 92, OxDcOp*
Hann, George Charles 1924- *WhoAm 92*
Hann, George R. 1891-1979 *EncABHB 8 [port]*
Hann, James David 1931- *WhoAm 92*
Hann, Kimberly Marie 1959- *WhoE 93*
Hann, Robert Kenneth 1945- *St&PR 93*
Hann, Roy William, Jr. 1934- *WhoAm 92*
Hanna, Arthur *DcCPCAm*
Hanna, Barsoum Elerian Misiha 1943- *WhoWor 93*
Hanna, Charlotte 1951- *WhoE 93*
Hanna, Cheryl Irene 1951- *BlkAull 92*
Hanna, David Colin *WhoScE 91-1*
Hanna, Edgar E. 1933- *WhoE 93*
Hanna, Eduardo Zacarias 1941- *WhoE 93, WhoWor 93*
Hanna, Elizabeth Heming *AmWomPl*
Hanna, Frank F. 1945- *St&PR 93*
Hanna, Frank Joseph 1939- *WhoSSW 93, WhoWor 93*
Hanna, Geoffrey Chalmers 1920- *WhoAm 92*
Hanna, George Verner, III 1943- *WhoSSW 93*
Hanna, Harry Adolphus 1940- *WhoAm 92*
Hanna, Jack Bushnell 1947- *WhoAm 92*
Hanna, Jan McDonald *Law&B 92*
Hanna, John A. 1942- *St&PR 93, WhoAm 92*
Hanna, John P. 1918- *WhoIns 93*
Hanna, Kathryn Lura 1947- *WhoAmW 93*
Hanna, Louis James 1967- *WhoE 93*
Hanna, Marcus A. 1837-1904 *PolPar*
Hanna, Mark 1837-1904 *BioIn 17, GayN*
Hanna, Mark E. 1937- *St&PR 93*
Hanna, Martin Shad 1940- *WhoAm 92*
Hanna, Michael George, Jr. 1936- *WhoAm 92*
Hanna, Michael James 1954- *WhoAm 92*
Hanna, Nellie *AmWomPl*
Hanna, Nessim 1938- *WhoAm 92*
Hanna, Noreen Anelda 1939- *WhoAmW 93*
Hanna, Paul Johnston 1915- *St&PR 93*
Hanna, Pricie 1948- *St&PR 93*
Hanna, Ralph, III 1942- *WhoAm 92*
Hanna, Richard W. 1930- *St&PR 93*
Hanna, Robert C. 1933- *WhoSSW 93*
Hanna, Robert Clyde 1928- *St&PR 93*
Hanna, Roberta Jones 1925- *WhoAm 92, WhoAmW 93, WhoSSW 93*
Hanna, Roland 1932- *Baker 92*
Hanna, Samir A. 1934- *WhoE 93*
Hanna, Sherman Davie 1946- *WhoEmL 93*
Hanna, Suzanne Louise 1953- *WhoEmL 93*
Hanna, Tacie May *AmWomPl*
Hanna, Terry Ross 1947- *WhoSSW 93, WhoWor 93*
Hanna, Thomas Hamilton *WhoScE 91-1*
Hanna, Thomas Louis *WhoWrEP 92*
Hanna, William 1911- *MiSFD 9*
Hanna, William Brian 1939- *St&PR 93*
Hanna, William Brooks 1936- *WhoAm 92*
Hanna, William Denby 1910- *WhoAm 92*
Hanna, William Johnson 1922- *WhoAm 92*
Hannafin, James D. 1946- *St&PR 93*
Hannaford, D.C. 1930- *St&PR 93*
Hannaford, Peter Dor 1932- *WhoAm 92*
Hannah *BioIn 17*
Hannah, Barry *BioIn 17*
Hannah, Carol 1950- *WhoAmW 93*
Hannah, Daryl *BioIn 17*
Hannah, Daryl 1961- *WhoAm 92*
Hannah, David H. 1951- *St&PR 93*
Hannah, Drew *BioIn 17*
Hannah, Duncan Rathbun 1952- *WhoE 93*
Hannah, Gloria Jean 1960- *WhoAmW 93*
Hannah, Hamner, III 1939- *WhoAm 92*
Hannah, John *BioIn 17*
Hannah, John A. 1902-1991 *BioIn 17*
Hannah, John David 1945- *WhoSSW 93*
Hannah, John H., Jr. *WhoAm 92, WhoSSW 93*
Hannah, John Robert, Sr. 1939- *WhoSSW 93*
Hannah, Larry W. *Law&B 92*
Hannah, Martin John 1926- *St&PR 93*
Hannah, Mary Elizabeth 1940- *WhoAmW 93*
Hannah, Mary-Emily 1936- *WhoAm 92*
Hannah, Mosie R. 1949- *St&PR 93*
Hannah, Norma Rathbun 1909-1990 *BioIn 17*
Hannah, Norman Britton 1919- *WhoAm 92*
Hannah, Paul F. 1905- *St&PR 93*
Hannah, Ray Eugene 1936- *St&PR 93*
Hannah, Selden J. d1991 *BioIn 17*
Hannah, Steven R. *Law&B 92*
Hannah, Wayne Robertson, Jr. 1931- *WhoAm 92*
Hannah-Ross, Dianne Lorraine 1954- *WhoE 93*
Hannallah, Raafat Samy 1944- *WhoE 93*
Hannan, Bradley 1935- *WhoAmW 93*
Hannan, Charles *ScF&FL 92*
Hannan, Edward J. 1942- *St&PR 93*
Hannan, John 1931- *WhoScE 91-3*
Hannan, Joseph Francis 1945- *WhoE 93*
Hannan, Mark C., III 1947- *WhoIns 93*
Hannan, Michael (Francis) 1949- *Baker 92*
Hannan, Michael Joseph 1963- *WhoE 93*
Hannan, Robert W. *St&PR 93*
Hannan, Robert William 1939- *WhoAm 92*
Hannant, Brian *MiSFD 9*
Hannant, Duncan 1947- *WhoScE 91-1*
Hannawalt, Willis Dale 1928- *WhoAm 92*
Hannay, David Hugh Alexander 1935- *WhoUN 92, WhoWor 93*
Hannay, David Rainsford *WhoScE 91-1*
Hannay, Margaret P. 1944- *ScF&FL 92*
Hannay, Margaret Patterson 1944- *WhoWrEP 92*
Hannay, Norman Bruce 1921- *WhoAm 92*
Hannay, Roger D(urham) 1930- *Baker 92*
Hann-Byrd, Adam *BioIn 17*
Hanneborg, Knut 1929- *WhoWor 93*
Hannegan, Robert E. 1903-1949 *PolPar*
Hannegan, Robert Emmet 1903-1949 *BioIn 17*
Hanneken, John William 1949- *WhoEmL 93, WhoSSW 93*
Hannema, Dirk Petrus 1953- *WhoWor 93*
Hanneman, Elaine Esther 1928- *WhoAmW 93*
Hanneman, Rodney E. 1936- *St&PR 93*
Hanneman, Rodney Elton 1936- *WhoAm 92*
Hannemann, Timothy William 1942- *St&PR 93*
Hannen, John Edward 1937- *WhoAm 92*
Hannenberg, Vera Losev 1923- *WhoE 93*
Hanner, Dawna Melanson 1947- *WhoEmL 93*
Hanner, Emil Joseph 1929- *St&PR 93*
Hanner, Jerome S. *Law&B 92*
Hanners, David *WhoAm 92*
Hannerz, D.G. Lennart 1922- *WhoScE 91-4*
Hannes, James A. 1943- *St&PR 93*
Hannes, James Alan 1943- *WhoIns 93*
Hannes, Peter John 1942- *St&PR 93*
Hannesson, John David *Law&B 92*
Hannesson, Ketill Arnar H. 1937- *WhoScE 91-4*
Hannesson, Paul Edward 1940- *St&PR 93*
Hannevig, Veronica Ann 1942- *WhoE 93*
Hanni, R.B. 1928- *St&PR 93*
Hannibal d406BC *HarEnMi*
Hannibal 247BC-183BC *BioIn 17*
Hannibal, Bruce J. *St&PR 93*
Hannibal Barca 247BC-183BC *HarEnMi*
Hannibaledward, L. 1936- *WhoWrEP 92*
Hannibal Gisco fl. 264BC-260BC *HarEnMi*
Hannibalsson, Jon Baldvin 1939- *WhoWor 93*
Hannig, Kurt 1920- *WhoScE 91-3*
Hannigan, Donald E. *Law&B 92*
Hannigan, Eugene Joseph 1939- *WhoE 93*
Hannigan, Frank 1931- *WhoAm 92*
Hannigan, Gregory Stewart 1950- *St&PR 93*
Hannigan, John David 1947- *WhoE 93*
Hannigan, John Joseph 1947- *St&PR 93*
Hannigan, Mark *BioIn 17*
Hannigan, Vera Simmons 1932- *WhoAm 92*
Hannikainen *Baker 92*
Hannikainen, Arvo (Sakari) 1897-1942 *Baker 92*
Hannikainen, (Toivo) Ilmari 1892-1955 *Baker 92*
Hannikainen, Pekka 1854-1924 *Baker 92*
Hannikainen, Tauno (Heikki) 1896-1968 *Baker 92*
Hannikainen, Vaino (Aatos) 1900-1960 *Baker 92*
Hanninen, Osmo O.P. 1939- *WhoScE 91-4*
Hanninen, Osmo Otto 1939- *WhoWor 93*
Hanning, Elizabeth Ann *Law&B 92*
Hanning, Gary William 1942- *WhoSSW 93, WhoWor 93*
Hannington, Robert James 1955- *WhoWor 93*
Hannity, Vincent Thomas 1944- *St&PR 93*
Hannley, Patricia Jean 1950- *St&PR 93*
Hanno fl. c. 264BC-256BC *HarEnMi*
Hanno fl. 500BC- *Expl 93*
Hanno, Marshall 1945- *St&PR 93*
Hannon, Beverly A. 1932- *WhoAmW 93*
Hannon, Brian Owens 1959- *WhoWrEP 92*
Hannon, Bruce M. 1934- *WhoAm 92*
Hannon, Byron L. 1951- *St&PR 93*
Hannon, Debra Sue 1960- *WhoAm 92*
Hannon, Donald F. 1927- *St&PR 93*
Hannon, Ezra *ConAu 38NR*
Hannon, Heather M. *Law&B 92*
Hannon, James E. 1949- *St&PR 93*
Hannon, James T. *Law&B 92*
Hannon, John Robert 1945- *WhoAm 92, WhoE 93*
Hannon, John W. 1920- *St&PR 93*
Hannon, Kathleen Mary *Law&B 92*
Hannon, Kathy Maley 1954- *St&PR 93*
Hannon, Kevin P. 1949- *WhoIns 93*
Hannon, Michael Stewart-Moore 1942- *WhoWor 93*
Hannon, Norman Leslie 1923- *WhoWor 93*
Hannon, Raymond E. 1938- *St&PR 93*
Hannon, Thomas A. d1991 *BioIn 17*
Hannon, Thomas Michael 1939- *WhoWrEP 92*
Hanno the Great fl. c. 247BC-237BC *HarEnMi*
Hannoun, Claude M.P. 1926- *WhoScE 91-2*
Hannula, Tapio K. 1953- *WhoScE 91-4*
Hannum, David Lawrence 1945- *WhoE 93*
Hannum, John Berne 1915- *WhoAm 92*
Hannum-Cox, Susan Michelle 1956- *WhoWrEP 92*
Hano, Arnold 1922- *BiDAMSp 1989*
Hano, Frank E. 1933- *St&PR 93*
Hano, George 1929- *St&PR 93*
Hanoa, Rolf Otto IIoc 1944- *WhoScE 91-4*
Hanofee, Eugene M. 1922-1990 *BioIn 17*
Hanold, Terrance 1912- *WhoAm 92*
Hanon, Charles-Louis 1819-1900 *Baker 92*
Hanooka, Izhak *MiSFD 9*
Hanotaux, Gabriel 1853-1944 *BioIn 17*
Hanotiaux, Gustave 1927- *WhoScE 91-2*
Hanoune, Jacques 1936- *WhoScE 91-2*
Hanover, Alain J. 1950- *St&PR 93*
Hanover, Irwin d1991 *BioIn 17*
Hanover, Marc J. 1950- *St&PR 93*
Hanower, L. David *Law&B 92*
Han Peixin 1923- *WhoAsAP 91*
Hanrahan, Jeffrey Russell *Law&B 92*
Hanrahan, Jeremiah Joseph *Law&B 92*
Hanrahan, John Joseph 1932- *WhoE 93*
Hanrahan, Joyce Yancey 1933- *WhoE 93*
Hanrahan, Patrick Jude 1954- *WhoEmL 93, WhoSSW 93*
Hanrahan, Robert Joseph 1932- *WhoAm 92, WhoSSW 93*
Hanrath, David Allen 1935- *St&PR 93*
Hanratty, Carin Gale 1953- *WhoAmW 93, WhoEmL 93*
Hanratty, Lawrence Charles 1935- *St&PR 93*
Hanratty, Peter *ScF&FL 92*
Hanratty, Thomas Joseph 1926- *WhoAm 92*
Hans, Allen A. *Law&B 92*
Hans, Harry L. 1933- *WhoAm 92*
Hans, Paul Charles 1946- *St&PR 93, WhoEmL 93*
Hans-Adam 1945- *WhoWor 93*
Hansan, Mary Anne 1961- *WhoAmW 93*
Hansard, James William 1936- *WhoAm 92*
Hansard, William Ney 1951- *WhoSSW 93*
Hansbarger, Larry DeFord 1921- *St&PR 93*
Hansberger, Allan P. 1924- *St&PR 93*
Hansberger, William Lyle 1921- *WhoSSW 93*
Hansberry, Lorraine 1930-1965 *BioIn 17, MagSAmL [port]*
Hansberry, Timothy Joseph 1943- *WhoAm 92*
Hansche, Heather *Law&B 92*
Hanscom, Beatrice *AmWomPl*
Hanscom, Fred Robert, III 1942- *WhoSSW 93*
Hanscom, Lisa Ellen 1964- *WhoAmW 93*
Hansel, Georges 1936- *WhoWor 93*
Hansel, Gregory Paul 1960- *WhoEmL 93*
Hansel, John Parker 1924- *WhoE 93*
Hansel, Paul George 1917- *WhoAm 92*
Hansel, Stephen Arthur 1947- *St&PR 93, WhoAm 92*
Hansell, Edgar Frank 1937- *WhoAm 92*
Hansell, Haywood Shepard, Jr. 1909- *HarEnMi*
Hansell, Heidi Nerwin 1953- *WhoEmL 93*
Hansell, John Royer 1931- *WhoAm 92*
Hansell, Richard Stanley 1950- *WhoEmL 93*
Hanselman, Orlando B. 1959- *St&PR 93*
Hanselman, Richard Wilson 1927- *St&PR 93, WhoAm 92*
Hanseman, Dennis J. 1950- *St&PR 93*
Hansen, Alan Lee 1951- *WhoSSW 93*
Hansen, Albert L. 1954- *St&PR 93*
Hansen, Alex 1955- *WhoWor 93*
Hansen, Alfred G. 1933- *WhoAm 92*
Hansen, Andrew Marius 1929- *WhoAm 92*
Hansen, Ann C. *Law&B 92*
Hansen, Ann Natalie 1927- *WhoWrEP 92*
Hansen, Anne Bagger *WhoScE 91-2*
Hansen, Arne Rae 1940- *WhoAm 92*
Hansen, Arnold *WhoScE 91-4*
Hansen, Arthur Gene 1925- *WhoAm 92*
Hansen, Arthur Magne 1946- *St&PR 93*
Hansen, Arvid R. 1920- *St&PR 93*
Hansen, Barbara Caleen 1941- *WhoAm 92, WhoAmW 93, WhoE 93*
Hansen, Barbara J. *Law&B 92*
Hansen, Barbara J. 1947- *St&PR 93*

Hansen, Bennett Roy 1945- *WhoSSW 93*
Hansen, Bobby J. 1926- *WhoSSW 93, WhoWor 93*
Hansen, Bonnie Jo 1950- *WhoEmL 93*
Hansen, Brooks 1965- *BioIn 17*
Hansen, Bryan C. 1943- *St&PR 93*
Hansen, Charles 1926- *WhoAm 92*
Hansen, Charles J. *Law&B 92*
Hansen, Charles Medom 1938- *WhoScE 91-2, WhoWor 93*
Hansen, Charles W. 1930- *St&PR 93*
Hansen, Christian Andreas, Jr. 1926- *WhoAm 92*
Hansen, Christina Flores 1951- *WhoEmL 93*
Hansen, Claire V. 1925- *St&PR 93, WhoAm 92*
Hansen, Clifford Peter 1912- *WhoAm 92*
Hansen, Colin Henry 1951- *WhoWor 93*
Hansen, Colleen Comer 1957- *WhoAmW 93*
Hansen, Dale J. 1939- *WhoAm 92*
Hansen, David E. 1940- *St&PR 93*
Hansen, David L. 1961- *St&PR 93*
Hansen, David R. *Law&B 92*
Hansen, David Rasmussen 1938- *WhoAm 92*
Hansen, David Thomas *Law&B 92*
Hansen, Deborah A. 1957- *WhoAmW 93*
Hansen, Deborah Ann 1950- *WhoAmW 93*
Hansen, Deborah Kay 1952- *WhoSSW 93*
Hansen, Dennis L. 1944- *St&PR 93*
Hansen, Donald 1909- *St&PR 93*
Hansen, Donald D. 1928- *St&PR 93, WhoIns 93*
Hansen, Donald W. 1924- *WhoAm 92*
Hansen, Donald W. 1927- *St&PR 93*
Hansen, Donna Lauree 1939- *WhoAmW 93*
Hansen, Doris Anne 1937- *WhoAmW 93*
Hansen, Douglas Brayshaw 1929- *WhoSSW 93*
Hansen, Edward Allen 1929- *WhoAm 92*
Hansen, Edward W. 1956- *St&PR 93*
Hansen, Elisa Marie 1952- *WhoAm 92, WhoAmW 93*
Hansen, Elizabeth J. 1930- *WhoWrEP 92*
Hansen, Eric *BioIn 17, MiSFD 9*
Hansen, Eric P. *Law&B 92*
Hansen, Erik Denslow 1940- *WhoSSW 93*
Hansen, Erling K. 1934- *WhoScE 91-4*
Hansen, Finn 1945- *WhoWor 93*
Hansen, Florence Marie Congiolosi 1934- *WhoAmW 93*
Hansen, Francis Eugene 1925- *WhoAm 92*
Hansen, Frank J. 1941- *St&PR 93*
Hansen, Fred Wilcox 1946- *WhoSSW 93*
Hansen, Gary B(arker) 1935- *WhoWrEP 92*
Hansen, Gary Lee 1951- *WhoEmL 93, WhoSSW 93*
Hansen, George K. *WhoAm 92*
Hansen, George K. 1935- *St&PR 93*
Hansen, Glen *BioIn 17*
Hansen, Grant Lewis 1921- *WhoAm 92*
Hansen, Gregg Allan *Law&B 92*
Hansen, Gregg Allan 1946- *St&PR 93*
Hansen, Gunnar 1947- *WhoWrEP 92*
Hansen, Gwen *ScF&FL 92*
Hansen, H.J.S. 1939- *WhoScE 91-2*
Hansen, H. Jack 1922- *WhoWor 93*
Hansen, Hans Bertil Harald 1921- *WhoWor 93*
Hansen, Hans George 1922- *WhoScE 91-3*
Hansen, Hardy 1941- *ConAu 139*
Hansen, Harry 1884-1977 *BioIn 17*
Hansen, Harry L. d1992 *NewYTBS 92*
Hansen, Heine Hoi *WhoScE 91-2*
Hansen, Henny Harald 1900- *IntDcAn*
Hansen, Herbert Edwin 1920- *WhoAm 92*
Hansen, Herbert W. 1935- *WhoAm 92*
Hansen, Howard Louis 1915- *St&PR 93*
Hansen, Hugh 1927- *St&PR 93*
Hansen, Hugh Justin 1923- *WhoAm 92*
Hansen, Jacqueline Rider 1959- *WhoAmW 93*
Hansen, James Bernard 1934- *St&PR 93*
Hansen, James E. 1941- *BioIn 17*
Hansen, James L. 1930- *St&PR 93*
Hansen, James Lee 1925- *WhoAm 92*
Hansen, James V. 1932- *CngDr 91, WhoAm 92*
Hansen, Jane 1946- *WhoAmW 93*
Hansen, Jean Marie 1937- *WhoAmW 93*
Hansen, Jeanne Bodine 1930- *WhoE 93*
Hansen, Jeffrey Peter 1954- *WhoEmL 93*
Hansen, Jo-Ida Charlotte 1947- *WhoAmW 93, WhoEmL 93*
Hansen, John *WhoScE 91-2*
Hansen, John Patrick 1949- *WhoSSW 93*
Hansen, John Paul 1928- *WhoAm 92, WhoWor 93*
Hansen, John Peter *Law&B 92*
Hansen, Jorgen Hartmann 1936- *St&PR 93*
Hansen, Jorn Dines 1940- *WhoScE 91-2*
Hansen, Joseph 1923- *ConAu 17AS [port], ConGAN*
Hansen, Joyce 1942- *DcAmChF 1985, MajAI [port], SmATA 15AS [port]*
Hansen, Joyce Viola 1942- *BlkAull 92*
Hansen, Judith Ann 1938- *WhoAmW 93*
Hansen, Julia Butler 1907-1988 *BioIn 17*
Hansen, Jurgen 1944- *WhoScE 91-2*
Hansen, Kai P.M. 1935- *WhoScE 91-3*
Hansen, Kaj Lykke Karmark 1923- *WhoWor 93*
Hansen, Karen Delegesa 1961- *WhoAmW 93*
Hansen, Karen Elizabeth 1964- *WhoAmW 93*
Hansen, Karen L. 1958- *St&PR 93*
Hansen, Karen Thornley 1945- *WhoAmW 93*
Hansen, Karen Vyonne 1955- *WhoEmL 93*
Hansen, Karl 1950- *ScF&FL 92*
Hansen, Kathleen Ann 1954- *WhoAmW 93*
Hansen, Kathryn Gertrude 1912- *WhoAmW 93*
Hansen, Kay Sorup 1922- *WhoWor 93*
Hansen, Kent E. *Law&B 92*
Hansen, Kent E. 1947- *St&PR 93*
Hansen, Kent Forrest 1931- *WhoAm 92*
Hansen, Kermit Read 1917- *WhoAm 92*
Hansen, Kevin *St&PR 93*
Hansen, Kim Loren 1953- *WhoEmL 93*
Hansen, Knud Henrik 1927- *WhoScE 91-2*
Hansen, Knud Waede 1944- *WhoWor 93*
Hansen, Kurt Paul 1938- *St&PR 93*
Hansen, Larry E. 1949- *St&PR 93*
Hansen, Larry Keith 1940- *St&PR 93*
Hansen, Lars Marcel 1966- *WhoWor 93*
Hansen, Leif 1942- *WhoUN 92*
Hansen, Leland Joe 1944- *WhoWor 93*
Hansen, Leonard Joseph 1932- *WhoWor 93*
Hansen, Leroy E. 1932- *St&PR 93*
Hansen, Linda R. *Law&B 92*
Hansen, Lisbeth M. 1955- *WhoAmW 93*
Hansen, Lisbeth Valentin *WhoScE 91-2*
Hansen, Lois M. 1931- *St&PR 93*
Hansen, Lorens *WhoScE 91-2*
Hansen, Lorraine Sundal 1929- *WhoAmW 93*
Hansen, Louis Rovs 1926- *WhoWor 93*
Hansen, Matilda 1929- *WhoAmW 93*
Hansen, Maynard Lawrence 1931- *St&PR 93*
Hansen, Michael Roy 1953- *WhoWor 93*
Hansen, Morris Howard 1910-1990 *BioIn 17, WhoAm 92*
Hansen, Nancy Siegfried 1946- *St&PR 93*
Hansen, Neil William 1932- *WhoAm 92*
Hansen, Nick Dane 1938- *St&PR 93, WhoAm 92*
Hansen, Niels 1933- *WhoScE 91-2*
Hansen, Orval 1926- *WhoAm 92*
Hansen, Per Brinch 1938- *WhoAm 92, WhoWor 93*
Hansen, Per Christian 1957- *WhoWor 93*
Hansen, Per Kristian 1932- *WhoAm 92, WhoE 93, WhoWor 93*
Hansen, Peter 1941- *WhoUN 92*
Hansen, Peter F. 1925- *St&PR 93*
Hansen, Peter Henry 1954- *WhoE 93*
Hansen, Peter T. 1943- *WhoE 93*
Hansen, Poul 1927- *WhoScE 91-2*
Hansen, Poul 1931- *WhoScE 91-2*
Hansen, Ralph Holm 1923- *WhoAm 92*
Hansen, Randall L. *Law&B 92*
Hansen, Ray Blain *Law&B 92*
Hansen, Reimer Johannes 1937- *WhoWor 93*
Hansen, Richard Arthur 1941- *WhoAm 92*
Hansen, Richard Fred 1932- *WhoAm 92*
Hansen, Richard H. 1929-1991 *BioIn 17*
Hansen, Richard W. 1919- *WhoAm 92*
Hansen, Richard W. 1937- *St&PR 93, WhoAm 92*
Hansen, Robert Clinton 1926- *WhoAm 92*
Hansen, (Emil) Robert 1860-1926 *Baker 92*
Hansen, Robert Joseph 1918- *WhoAm 92*
Hansen, Robert Suttle 1918- *WhoAm 92*
Hansen, Robert William 1924- *WhoAm 92*
Hansen, Roger B. 1943- *St&PR 93*
Hansen, Roger D. 1935-1991 *BioIn 17*
Hansen, Roger Towner 1934- *St&PR 93*
Hansen, Ronald D. 1938- *St&PR 93*
Hansen, Rosanna Lee 1947- *WhoAmW 93*
Hansen, Scott William 1953- *WhoEmL 93*
Hansen, Soeren Halling 1946- *St&PR 93*
Hansen, Svend Erik 1921- *WhoScE 91-2*
Hansen, Theodore Carl 1935- *WhoSSW 93*
Hansen, Theodore L. 1911- *St&PR 93*
Hansen, Thomas Duane 1944- *WhoE 93*
Hansen, Thomas W. *St&PR 93*
Hansen, Torben Christen 1933- *WhoScE 91-2*
Hansen, Torben Ingemann 1936- *WhoWor 93*
Hansen, Vern 1921- *ScF&FL 92*
Hansen, W.E. 1921- *St&PR 93*
Hansen, W. Lee 1928- *WhoAm 92*
Hansen, Walter Eugene 1929- *WhoWor 93*
Hansen, Wayne W. 1942- *WhoAm 92*
Hansen, Wendell Jay 1910- *WhoWor 93*
Hansen, Wilhelm *Baker 92*
Hansen, William R. *Law&B 92*
Hansen, Zenon C.R. 1909-1990 *BioIn 17*
Hansen-Flaschen, John Hyman 1950- *WhoEmL 93*
Hansenne, Michel 1940- *WhoUN 92*
Han Seoung-Soo 1938- *WhoAsAP 91*
Hanser, Mary Julia 1941- *WhoAmW 93*
Hanseth, George L. 1944- *St&PR 93*
Hansgen, Walter Edwin 1919-1966 *BioIn 17*
Hanshaw, Annette 1910-1985 *BioIn 17*
Hanshaw, James Barry 1928- *WhoAm 92*
Hanshaw, Kenneth J. *Law&B 92*
Hanshue, Harris M. 1881-1937 *EncABHB 8 [port]*
Hanska, Ewelina 1804-1882 *PolBiDi*
Hansler, Eberhard *WhoScE 91-3*
Hansler, Mark W. *Law&B 92*
Hanslick, Eduard 1825-1904 *Baker 92, OxDcOp*
Hanslin, Tony 1943- *St&PR 93*
Hansl-Kozanecka, Traudl 1940- *WhoWor 93*
Hansma, Paul K. 1946- *BioIn 17*
Hansman, Robert John, Jr. 1954- *WhoEmL 93*
Hansmann, Ralph Emil 1918- *WhoAm 92*
Hansmeier, Ralph Henry 1912- *St&PR 93*
Hansmeier, Wanda Violet 1917- *St&PR 93*
Hans-Moevi, Roger Alexandre 1934- *WhoUN 92*
Hansohm, Dirk Christian 1956- *WhoWor 93*
Hanson, Albert LeRoy 1952- *WhoEmL 93*
Hanson, Allen Dennis 1936- *WhoAm 92*
Hanson, Angus Alexander 1922- *WhoAm 92*
Hanson, Anne Coffin 1921- *WhoAm 92*
Hanson, Arnold Philip 1924- *WhoAm 92*
Hanson, Avarita Laurel 1953- *WhoSSW 93*
Hanson, Barbara L. *Law&B 92*
Hanson, Barbara L. 1957- *St&PR 93*
Hanson, Beverly Jill 1965- *WhoSSW 93*
Hanson, Carl Malmrose 1941- *WhoAm 92*
Hanson, Carol Francine Weckler 1933- *WhoAmW 93*
Hanson, Charles G. 1912- *St&PR 93*
Hanson, Charles G(oring) 1934- *ConAu 138*
Hanson, Clifford R. 1936- *WhoIns 93*
Hanson, Curtis *MiSFD 9*
Hanson, Dale S. 1938- *WhoAm 92*
Hanson, Dale Sven 1938- *St&PR 93*
Hanson, David Alan 1956- *WhoSSW 93*
Hanson, David Bigelow 1946- *WhoAm 92, WhoE 93, WhoEmL 93, WhoWor 93*
Hanson, David Justin 1941- *WhoE 93*
Hanson, David Parker 1939- *WhoE 93*
Hanson, David S. *Law&B 92*
Hanson, Diane Charske 1946- *WhoAmW 93, WhoEmL 93*
Hanson, Dick Vincent 1925- *WhoWrEP 92*
Hanson, Donald Wayne 1937- *WhoAm 92*
Hanson, Earl Dorchester 1927- *WhoAm 92*
Hanson, Earl T. 1934- *St&PR 93*
Hanson, Edward J., Jr. *Law&B 92*
Hanson, Eric Alan 1953- *WhoEmL 93, WhoWor 93*
Hanson, Eugene Nelson 1917- *WhoAm 92*
Hanson, Floyd Bliss 1939- *WhoAm 92*
Hanson, Gaylord Heber 1936- *St&PR 93*
Hanson, George 1925- *WhoWor 93*
Hanson, George Alfred 1940- *WhoSSW 93*
Hanson, George Fulford 1916- *WhoAm 92*
Hanson, George Victor 1908- *St&PR 93*
Hanson, Gilbert Nikolai 1936- *WhoAm 92*
Hanson, Grant W. *Law&B 92*
Hanson, Gregg W. 1948- *St&PR 93*
Hanson, Gregory Paul 1959- *WhoSSW 93*
Hanson, Haldore d1992 *NewYTBS 92 [port]*
Hanson, Hans J. 1955- *St&PR 93*
Hanson, Harold Palmer 1921- *WhoAm 92, WhoWor 93*
Hanson, Howard (Harold) 1896-1981 *Baker 92*
Hanson, J. David *Law&B 92*
Hanson, James Austin 1947- *WhoAm 92*
Hanson, James Eric 1946- *St&PR 93*
Hanson, Jane Marie *Law&B 92*
Hanson, Jason *BioIn 17*
Hanson, Jean Elizabeth 1949- *WhoAm 92*
Hanson, Jean M. 1958- *St&PR 93*
Hanson, Jeanne Carol 1947- *WhoAmW 93*
Hanson, Jeanne Sutley 1946- *WhoSSW 93*
Hanson, Jill Alane 1949- *WhoEmL 93*
Hanson, Jo *WhoAm 92*
Hanson, Joan Catherine 1965- *WhoAmW 93*
Hanson, John 1942- *MiSFD 9*
Hanson, John J. 1922- *WhoAm 92*
Hanson, John K. d1991 *BioIn 17*
Hanson, John K. 1913- *St&PR 93, WhoAm 92*
Hanson, John L. 1933- *St&PR 93*
Hanson, John M. 1932- *WhoAm 92*
Hanson, John Melvin 1932- *St&PR 93*
Hanson, John Nils 1942- *WhoAm 92*
Hanson, Joseph E. d1989 *BioIn 17*
Hanson, Joseph J. 1930- *WhoAm 92*
Hanson, Karl Gustaf Anders Ludvig *Law&B 92*
Hanson, Katharine Heard 1947- *WhoE 93*
Hanson, Kathryn Marie 1962- *WhoAmW 93*
Hanson, Kenneth Ralph 1930- *WhoE 93*
Hanson, Kermit Osmond 1916- *WhoAm 92*
Hanson, Kirk L. 1938- *St&PR 93*
Hanson, Kristen Kay 1965- *WhoAmW 93*
Hanson, Larry K. 1932- *St&PR 93*
Hanson, Larry Keith 1932- *WhoAm 92*
Hanson, Lars A. 1934- *WhoScE 91-4*
Hanson, Leila Fraser 1942- *WhoAm 92, WhoAmW 93*
Hanson, Lowell Knute 1935- *WhoSSW 93*
Hanson, Mamie B. *AmWomPl*
Hanson, Marlene *Law&B 92*
Hanson, Mary Jane Shirar 1953- *WhoEmL 93*
Hanson, Mary Lou 1927- *WhoAmW 93*
Hanson, Maurice Francis 1907- *WhoAm 92*
Hanson, Michael *BioIn 17*
Hanson, Michael J. *Law&B 92*
Hanson, Monte R. *Law&B 92*
Hanson, Morgan Alfred 1930- *WhoSSW 93*
Hanson, Myrna A. *Law&B 92*
Hanson, Noel K. 1940- *St&PR 93*
Hanson, Norma Saliba 1934- *WhoSSW 93*
Hanson, Norman Leonard 1909-1990 *BioIn 17*
Hanson, Owen Jerrold *WhoScE 91-1*
Hanson, Palmer Oliver, Jr. 1929- *WhoSSW 93*
Hanson, Patricia Rose 1961- *WhoAmW 93*
Hanson, Paul David 1939- *WhoAm 92*
Hanson, Paul David 1946- *WhoWor 93*
Hanson, Paul Nathan 1946- *St&PR 93*
Hanson, Peg 1946- *WhoE 93, WhoEmL 93, WhoWor 93*
Hanson, Philip Slade 1921- *WhoSSW 93*
Hanson, Raymond Lester 1912- *WhoAm 92*
Hanson, Richard Edwin 1931- *WhoSSW 93, WhoWor 93*
Hanson, Richard Eric 1952- *WhoSSW 93*
Hanson, Richard Wayne 1946- *St&PR 93*
Hanson, Richard Winfield 1935- *WhoAm 92*
Hanson, Robert A. 1924- *St&PR 93*
Hanson, Robert Arthur 1924- *WhoAm 92*
Hanson, Robert Carl 1926- *WhoAm 92*
Hanson, Robert DeLolle 1916- *WhoE 93, WhoWor 93*
Hanson, Robert Duane 1935- *WhoAm 92*
Hanson, Robert Eugene 1947- *WhoAm 92*
Hanson, Roger Gordon 1931- *WhoSSW 93*
Hanson, Roger James 1927- *WhoAm 92*
Hanson, Roger Kvamme 1932- *WhoAm 92*
Hanson, Ronald Lee 1944- *WhoE 93*
Hanson, Ronald Lee 1949- *St&PR 93*
Hanson, Ronald William 1950- *WhoAm 92, WhoEmL 93*
Hanson, Roy Carl 1938- *St&PR 93*
Hanson, Rudolph A. 1924- *St&PR 93*
Hanson, Samuel Lee 1939- *WhoAm 92*
Hanson, Sandra D. 1946- *St&PR 93*
Hanson, Sandra J. McKenzie 1949- *WhoAmW 93*
Hanson, Shirley Ann 1934- *WhoAmW 93*
Hanson, Simon Peter 1953- *WhoE 93, WhoEmL 93*
Hanson, Stephanie Lee 1958- *WhoAmW 93*
Hanson, Susan Easton 1943- *WhoAm 92*
Hanson, Susan Ruth 1953- *WhoEmL 93*
Hanson, Thomas E. *St&PR 93*
Hanson, Thomas Earl 1941- *WhoE 93*
Hanson, Thomas Edward 1963- *WhoSSW 93*
Hanson, Thomas L. 1953- *St&PR 93*
Hanson, Thomas Michael 1947- *WhoEmL 93*
Hanson, Thor 1928- *WhoAm 92*

Hanson, Toni Jo 1949- WhoAmW 93
Hanson, Victor ScF&FL 92
Hanson, Victor Henry, II 1930- St&PR 93, WhoAm 92, WhoSSW 93
Hanson, Victor Henry, III 1956- WhoSSW 93
Hanson, Victoria Mary 1950- WhoWor 93
Hanson, Walter Edmund 1916- WhoAm 92
Hanson, Wendi Kay 1964- WhoEmL 93, WhoSSW 93
Hanson, William Cook 1909- WhoAm 92
Hanson, William F. Law&B 92
Hanson, William Herbert 1936- WhoAm 92
Hanson-McDonald, Susan Margaret 1962- St&PR 93
Hanspal, Harvendra Singh 1938- WhoAsAP 91
Hans Sachs OxDcOp
Hanssen, Gary Michael 1938- St&PR 93
Hanssens, Charles-Louis 1802-1871 Baker 92
Hansson, A. Lennart 1938- WhoScE 91-4
Hansson, Bo Alfred 1937- WhoUN 92
Hansson, Gunilla 1939- BioIn 17
Hansson, Jan-Erik 1928- WhoScE 91-4
Hansson, Jan Erik 1950- WhoSSW 93
Hansson, Margaret Sutherland St&PR 93
Hansson, Oli Valur 1922- WhoScE 91-4
Hansson, Richard John 1952- WhoE 93
Hansteen, Henry B. 1904-1991 BioIn 17
Hanstein, Penelope 1948- WhoEmL 93
Hanstein, Walter G. 1934- WhoScE 91-3
Hanstein, Walter Georg 1934- WhoWor 93
Hansuld, John A. St&PR 93
Hansum, Richard V. Law&B 92
Hansum, Richard Valentine 1946- WhoEmL 93
Hantho, Charles 1931- St&PR 93
Hantho, Charles Harold 1931- WhoAm 92, WhoE 93
Hanthorn, Dennis Wayne 1951- WhoAm 92
Hanthorn, George Wilmot Law&B 92
Han Tingpi, Francis d1991 NewYTBS 92
Hantler, Steven B. Law&B 92
Hantman, Lawrence Law&B 92
Hantman, Ronald David Law&B 92
Hantman, Sarah Ann 1952- WhoAmW 93
Hanton, Emile Michael WhoE 93, WhoWor 93
Hanton, Sharon Eleanor 1939- WhoAmW 93
Hantula, Richard Michael 1945- WhoE 93
Hantze, Karen BiDAMSp 1989
Hanula, Robert Walter Law&B 92
Hanumanthappa, H. 1932- WhoAsAP 91
Hanus, Borek BioIn 17
Hanus, Frank Jay, III 1949- St&PR 93
Hanus, Jan 1915- Baker 92
Hanus, Jean G. 1936- WhoScE 91-2
Hanus, Jerome 1940- WhoAm 92
Hanus, Thomas Joel 1940- St&PR 93
Hanuschak, George Alan 1949- WhoAm 92
Hanuschak, Lee Nicholas 1947- WhoEmL 93
Hanushek, Eric Alan 1943- WhoAm 92
Hanuszewska-Schaeffer, Mieczyslawa Janina
See Schaeffer, Boguslaw (Julien) 1929- Baker 92
Hanuszewska-Schaeffer, Mieczyslawa Janina 1929- Baker 92
Hanwacker, Patricia Aileen 1951- WhoAmW 93
Hanway, Donald Grant 1918- WhoAm 92
Hanway, H. Edward 1952- WhoIns 93
Hanway, John, III 1952- WhoEmL 93
Hanwright, Joseph C. MiSFD 9
Han Xu 1924- BioIn 17, WhoAsAP 91
Hanyga, Andrzej Jerzy 1938- WhoWor 93
Hanysak, Denny Paul 1944- St&PR 93
Hanzak, Gary A. John 1957- WhoSSW 93
Hanzalek, Astrid Teicher 1928- WhoAmW 93
Hanzel, Michael Collins Law&B 92
Hanzel, Vladimir 1937- WhoScE 91-4
Hanzlicek, Charles George 1942- WhoWrEP 92
Hanzlick, Glenn P. Law&B 92
Hanzlik, Alan Edward 1947- St&PR 93, WhoAm 92
Hanzlik, Rayburn DeMara 1938- WhoAm 92
Hanzlik, Stephen John 1957- WhoEmL 93
Hao, Oliver Jing 1946- WhoE 93
Hao Jianxiu 1935- WhoAsAP 91
Haole, Janet Lani 1956- WhoAmW 93
Haozous 1914?- BioIn 17
Haozous, Robert 1943- BioIn 17
Hapala, Milan Ernest 1919- WhoAm 92
Hapeman, John William 1942- WhoE 93
Hapgood, Norman 1868-1937 BioIn 17, GayN
Hapgood, Robert Derry 1928- WhoAm 92
Hapka, Catherine M. St&PR 93
Hapka, Gerald A. Law&B 92
Hapke, Bruce William 1931- WhoE 93
Hapke, Daniel Super, Jr. Law&B 92
Hapke, Hans-Jurgen 1931- WhoScE 91-3
Hapke, Jobst 1940- WhoScE 91-3
Hapke, Laura 1946- ConAu 138
Haploucheir, Michael OxDcByz
Hapoienu, Spencer L. 1950- WhoAm 92
Happ, Harvey Heinz 1928- WhoAm 92
Happ, Helmut 1927- WhoScE 91-3
Happel, John 1908- WhoAm 92, WhoE 93
Happel, Marvin H. 1939- St&PR 93
Happel, Ruth Emilie 1958- WhoAmW 93
Happer, William, Jr. 1939- WhoAm 92
Happle, Rudolf 1938- WhoWor 93
Hapsara, Habib Rachmat 1938- WhoUN 92
Hapsburg, Elizabeth d1505 PolBiDi
Haq, Iftikhar Ul 1939- WhoWor 93
Haq, Nazmul WhoScE 91-1
Haque, Aziz 1949- WhoWor 93
Haque, Habib Quazi 1936- WhoUN 92
Haque, Malika Hakim WhoAm 92, WhoAmW 93, WhoWor 93
Haque, Mohammed Azizul 1939- WhoWor 93
Haque, Nadeem Ul 1950- WhoUN 92
Haque, Shahudul 1946- WhoWor 93
Hara, Bunbee 1913- WhoAsAP 91
Hara, Chuichi 1889-1964 HarEnMi
Hara, Ernest Hideo 1909- WhoAm 92
Hara, Hiroko 1934- WhoWor 93
Hara, Hiroshi 1946- WhoWor 93
Hara, Kenzaburo 1907- WhoAsAP 91, WhoWor 93
Hara, Setsuko 1920- IntDcF 2-3 [port]
Hara, Tameichi 1900- HarEnMi
Hara, Toshio 1935- BioIn 17
Hara, Yasuo 1934- WhoWor 93
Harab, Elliot Peter Law&B 92
Harabin, Zdzislaw 1935- WhoScE 91-4
Harad, George Jay 1944- St&PR 93, WhoAm 92
Harada, Akira 1949- WhoWor 93
Harada, Curtis Y. 1955- St&PR 93
Harada, Ken 1919- WhoAsAP 91
Harada, Shinji 1950- WhoWor 93
Harada, Shozo 1923- WhoAsAP 91
Harada, Tokuya 1918- WhoWor 93
Harada, Yoshiaki 1944- WhoAsAP 91
Harada, Yoshiya 1934- WhoWor 93
Haradhvala, Adil 1958- WhoEmL 93
Haragan, Donald Robert 1936- WhoAm 92
Harahap, Filino 1938- WhoWor 93
Harahap, Hasjrul 1931- WhoAsAP 91
Hara-Isa, Nancy Jeanne 1961- WhoAmW 93, WhoEmL 93
Harakas, Stanley Samuel 1932- WhoWrEP 92
Harakson, Susan Christine 1953- WhoAmW 93
Haralampu, George Stelios 1925- WhoAm 92
Harald, V 1937- WhoWor 93
Haraldson, Deborah Law&B 92
Haraldson, Jo-Nell Law&B 92
Haraldsted, Hans Henrik 1942- WhoWor 93
Haralick, Robert Martin 1943- WhoAm 92
Haralson, Carol Louise 1948- WhoWrEP 92
Haralson, Jeremiah 1846-1916 BioIn 17
Haralson, Linda Jane 1959- WhoAmW 93
Haramati, Aviad 1954- WhoE 93
Haran, Maeve 1950- ConAu 136
Harari, Carmi 1920- WhoE 93
Harari, Hananiah 1912- WhoAm 92
Harari, Justine BioIn 17
Harari, Raimondo 1943- WhoUN 92
Harary, Frank 1921- WhoAm 92
Harary, Joel T. Law&B 92
Harasek, Elizabeth F. Law&B 92
Harasiewicz, Adam 1932- Baker 92
Harasowski, Adam 1904- Baker 92
Harasty, Zoltan A. 1930- St&PR 93
Harasym, Willa F. Law&B 92
Harasymowicz, Jan 1921- WhoScE 91-4, WhoWor 93
Haraszti, Emile 1885-1958 Baker 92
Haraszti, Janos 1924- WhoScE 91-4
Hara Takashi 1856-1921 DcTwHis
Haratunian, Michael 1933- St&PR 93
Harawi, Al- d1215 OxDcByz
Harb, Larry E. 1953- St&PR 93
Harb, Said T. WhoUN 92
Harbach, Barbara Carol 1946- WhoEmL 93
Harbach, Chet Marvin 1955- WhoSSW 93
Harbach, Otto 1873-1963 Baker 92
Harbach, Ralph Edward 1948- WhoE 93
Harbater, David 1952- WhoEmL 93
Harbaugh, Daniel Paul 1948- WhoEmL 93
Harbaugh, George Milton 1930- WhoAm 92
Harbaugh, John Warvelle 1926- WhoAm 92
Harbaugh, Virginia Ann 1939- WhoAmW 93
Harbaugh, William Henry 1920- WhoSSW 93
Harbaugh, William L. 1940- St&PR 93
Harbeck, William James 1921- WhoAm 92
Harbeke, Gunther BioIn 17
Harber, Loretta Michele 1954- WhoAmW 93
Harberd, Nicholas Paul WhoScE 91-1
Harberger, Arnold Carl 1924- WhoAm 92
Harbers, Volkert 1945- WhoScE 91-3
Harbert, Bill Lebold 1923- St&PR 93, WhoAm 92
Harbert, Chick d1992 NewYTBS 92
Harbert, Edward Wesley, III BioIn 17
Harbert, Guy Morley, Jr. 1929- WhoAm 92
Harbert, John Murdoch, III 1921- St&PR 93
Harbert, Norman C. 1933- St&PR 93
Harbert, Pamela Annett 1963- WhoAmW 93
Harbert, Ted BioIn 17
Harbeson, Paul Cret 1919- WhoAm 92
Harbi, Djamal 1940- WhoUN 92
Harbin, John Pickens 1917- WhoAm 92, WhoSSW 93
Harbin, Lyle D. 1934- St&PR 93
Harbin, Thomas Shelor, Jr. 1945- WhoSSW 93
Harbinson, Allen ScF&FL 92
Harbinson, W.A. 1941- ScF&FL 92
Harbison, Earle Harrison, Jr. 1928- St&PR 93, WhoAm 92
Harbison, Gregory A. 1958- St&PR 93
Harbison, James Prescott 1951- WhoE 93
Harbison, John 1938- WhoAm 92
Harbison, John (Harris) 1938- Baker 92
Harbison, John R. 1953- St&PR 93
Harbison, Lawrence Roehm 1951- St&PR 93
Harbison, Robert Gene 1939- St&PR 93
Harbison, W. 1922- St&PR 93
Harbison, William James 1923- WhoAm 92, WhoSSW 93
Harbit, Douglas Alan 1949- WhoE 93
Harbolt, James G. 1933- St&PR 93
Harbord, James Guthrie 1866-1947 HarEnMi
Harbordt, Charles Michael 1942- WhoSSW 93
Harbottle, Philip 1941- ScF&FL 92
Harbottle, Scott A. Law&B 92
Harbou, Thea von 1888-1954 ScF&FL 92
Harbour, John W. Law&B 92
Harbour, John W., Jr. Law&B 92
Harbour, Mary Frances 1954- WhoAmW 93
Harbour, Nancy Caine 1949- WhoEmL 93
Harbour, Robert L. 1929- St&PR 93
Harbour, Tracy Ray 1963- WhoEmL 93
Harbrant, Robert Francis 1942- WhoAm 92
Harbrecht, Joseph William 1944- St&PR 93
Harbuck, Edwin Charles 1934- WhoSSW 93
Harbur, Nathan Clayton 1951- WhoEmL 93
Harburg, E.Y. 1898-1981 Baker 92
Harbury, Henry Alexander 1927- WhoAm 92
Harbutt, Charles 1935- WhoAm 92
Harby, Levi Myers 1793-1870 BioIn 17
Harcarik, Joseph T. Law&B 92
Harchut, Robert Francis Law&B 92
Harcleroad, Fred Farley 1918- WhoAm 92, WhoWrEP 92
Harclerode, Jack Edgar 1935- WhoAm 92
Harcourt, Edgar A. 1927-1990 BioIn 17
Harcourt, Eugene d' 1859-1918 Baker 92
Harcourt, Geoffrey Colin BioIn 17
Harcourt, Geoffrey Colin 1931- WhoWor 93
Harcourt, Glenn ScF&FL 92
Harcourt, John Kenneth 1931- WhoWor 93
Harcourt, Marguerite d' 1884-1964 Baker 92
Harcourt, Michael BioIn 17
Harcourt, Michael Franklin 1943- WhoAm 92
Harcourt, Richard Douglas 1939- St&PR 93
Hard, David BioIn 17
Hard, Edward W. ScF&FL 92
Hard, Josephine Wilhelm AmWomPl
Hard, T.W. 1939- ScF&FL 92
Hard, Torleif R. 1959- WhoWor 93
Hardage, Page Taylor 1944- WhoAmW 93, WhoSSW 93
Hardaway, Anfernee BioIn 17
Hardaway, Robert Morris, III 1916- WhoAm 92
Hardaway, Tim BioIn 17
Hardaway, Timothy Duane 1966- WhoAm 92
Hardbeck, George William 1925- WhoAm 92
Hardberger, Phillip Duane 1934- WhoAm 92
Hardcastle, Alan John 1958- WhoEmL 93
Hardcastle, Clifford WhoScE 91-1
Hardcastle, Jack Donald WhoScE 91-1
Hardcastle, Jack Donald 1933- WhoWor 93
Hardcastle, Kenneth Lloyd 1934- St&PR 93
Hardcastle, Michael 1933- ChlFicS
Hardee, Alvin J., Jr. 1942- WhoSSW 93
Hardee, Evelyn Rocker 1921- WhoAmW 93, WhoWor 93
Hardee, Lewis Jefferson, Jr. 1937- WhoE 93
Hardee, Ray McKay 1961- WhoSSW 93
Hardee, William Covington 1919- WhoAm 92
Hardee, William Joseph 1815-1873 BioIn 17, HarEnMi
Hardegg, Grad 1834-1867 Baker 92
Hardegree, Arthur Lee, III Law&B 92
Hardelot, Guy d' 1858-1936 Baker 92
Harden, Alice V. 1948- WhoAmW 93
Harden, Anita Joyce 1947- WhoEmL 93
Harden, Blaine Charles 1952- WhoAm 92
Harden, Cecil Murray 1894-1984 BioIn 17
Harden, David E. 1927- St&PR 93
Harden, Douglas W. 1948- St&PR 93
Harden, Doyle Benjamin 1935- WhoSSW 93, WhoWor 93
Harden, Joan Piper 1947- WhoEmL 93
Harden, Jon Bixby 1944- WhoAm 92
Harden, Kirk B. 1951- St&PR 93
Harden, Lydia Dixon 1959- WhoAm 92
Harden, Marcia Gay BioIn 17, NewYTBS 92 [port]
Harden, Marvin WhoAm 92
Harden, Mary Emily AmWomPl
Harden, Michael Patrick 1952- WhoWrEP 92
Harden, Michele Louise 1958- WhoWrEP 92
Harden, Oleta Elizabeth 1935- WhoAm 92
Harden, Patrick Alan 1936- WhoAm 92
Harden, Richard Lee 1946- St&PR 93
Harden, Robert Lawson 1945- St&PR 93
Harden, Ronald McGlashan WhoScE 91-1
Hardenberg, Friedrich, Freiherr von 1772-1801 BioIn 17
Hardenbrook, Kirsten BioIn 17
Hardenbrook, Yvonne Imogene 1928- WhoWrEP 92
Hardenburg, Robert Earle 1919- WhoAm 92, WhoSSW 93
Harder, Brittany BioIn 17
Harder, Charles J. Law&B 92
Harder, Gary Ray 1944- St&PR 93
Harder, Heather Anne 1948- WhoEmL 93
Harder, Hermann 1923- WhoScE 91-3
Harder, Jane Daniels 1950- St&PR 93
Harder, John E. 1930- WhoAm 92
Harder, Kelsie B(rown) 1922- ConAu 139
Harder, Kelsie Brown 1922- WhoAm 92
Harder, Kristine 1949- WhoEmL 93
Harder, Laura BioIn 17
Harder, Lewis B. 1918- St&PR 93
Harder, Lewis Bradley 1918- WhoAm 92
Harder, Marilyn Anne 1951- WhoEmL 93
Harder, Martin David 1940- St&PR 93
Harder, Michael J. 1950- St&PR 93
Harder, Paul Richard Law&B 92
Harder, Robert Clarence 1929- WhoAm 92
Harder, Rolf Peter 1929- WhoAm 92
Harder, Ronald R. 1943- St&PR 93, WhoIns 93
Harder, Sarah Snell 1937- WhoAmW 93
Harder, Virgil Eugene 1923- WhoAm 92
Harder, William E. Law&B 92
Harder, William Ewald 1932- St&PR 93
Hardester, Royce Dean 1952- WhoWrEP 92
Hardesty, C. Howard, Jr. 1922- WhoAm 92
Hardesty, Christopher Scott 1945- St&PR 93
Hardesty, Egbert Railey 1915- WhoAm 92
Hardesty, Hiram Haines 1914- WhoAm 92
Hardesty, James Dunn 1946- St&PR 93, WhoAm 92
Hardesty, Joseph L. Law&B 92
Hardesty, Larry Lynn 1947- WhoSSW 93
Hardesty, Michael BioIn 17
Hardesty, Robert Lynch 1940- WhoAm 92
Hardesty, Rodney d1991 BioIn 17
Hardesty, Steven 1946- ScF&FL 92
Hardesty, Steven Conway 1951- WhoSSW 93
Hardey, Mathew W. 1952- St&PR 93
Hardgrave, Robert Lewis, Jr. 1939- WhoSSW 93
Hardie, Dianne Law&B 92
Hardie, Eldridge BioIn 17

Hardie, George Graham 1933- *WhoAm 92*
Hardie, James Hiller 1929- *WhoAm 92*
Hardie, Michael C. 1946- *St&PR 93*
Hardie, Raymond *ScF&FL 92*
Hardiek, Bernard L. 1940- *St&PR 93*
Hardigg, James Sutton 1922- *St&PR 93*
Hardigg, Jamie M. 1958- *St&PR 93*
Hardigree, Randolph Stephen 1938- *St&PR 93*
Hardiman, Joseph Raymond 1937- *St&PR 93, WhoAm 92, WhoE 93*
Hardiman, Roy Charles *Law&B 92*
Hardiman, S.A. *WhoScE 91-1*
Hardiman, Therese Anne 1956- *WhoAmW 93, WhoE 93*
Hardin, Adlai S. 1901-1989 *BioIn 17*
Hardin, Adlai Stevenson, Jr. 1937- *WhoAm 92*
Hardin, Clifford Morris 1915- *WhoAm 92, WhoWor 93*
Hardin, Edwin Milton 1926- *St&PR 93*
Hardin, Elizabeth Ann 1959- *WhoAmW 93, WhoEmL 93*
Hardin, Eugene B., Jr. 1930- *St&PR 93*
Hardin, Eugene Brooks, Jr. 1930- *WhoAm 92*
Hardin, George Cecil, Jr. 1920- *WhoAm 92*
Hardin, Hal D. 1941- *WhoAm 92*
Hardin, Henry Townes, III *Law&B 92*
Hardin, Hilliard Frances 1917- *WhoAm 92, WhoAmW 93*
Hardin, James *DcLB Y92 [port]*
Hardin, James 1936- *WhoAm 92*
Hardin, James Michael 1956- *WhoEmL 93, WhoSSW 93*
Hardin, James Neal 1939- *WhoAm 92*
Hardin, James Neal, Jr. 1939- *WhoWrEP 92*
Hardin, Janice E. *Law&B 92*
Hardin, John 1957- *St&PR 93*
Hardin, John Alexander 1911- *WhoAm 92*
Hardin, John Wesley 1853-1895 *BioIn 17*
Hardin, Joseph S. 1945- *St&PR 93*
Hardin, Kenneth Lee 1916- *WhoWrEP 92*
Hardin, Leslie Ann 1959- *WhoSSW 93*
Hardin, Lloyd T., Jr. 1949- *St&PR 93*
Hardin, Lowell Stewart 1917- *WhoAm 92*
Hardin, Lynn Frank 1948- *St&PR 93*
Hardin, Michael J. *Law&B 92*
Hardin, Michael J. 1947- *St&PR 93*
Hardin, Paul 1931- *WhoAm 92, WhoSSW 93, WhoWor 93*
Hardin, Richard V. 1939- *St&PR 93*
Hardin, Russell 1940- *WhoAm 92*
Hardin, Sondra Higdon 1958- *WhoAmW 93*
Hardin, Tammy Jo 1963- *WhoEmL 93*
Hardin, Thomas Jefferson, II 1945- *WhoSSW 93*
Hardin, William Downer 1926- *WhoAm 92*
Hardin, William Jefferson 1830?-1890? *PolPar*
Hardin, William Samuel 1946- *St&PR 93*
Harding, A(lbert) A(ustin) 1880-1958 *Baker 92*
Harding, Barry 1952- *WhoSSW 93*
Harding, C.G.S. *WhoScE 91-1*
Harding, Constance Arlene Etzold 1936- *WhoAmW 93*
Harding, D.E. d1909 *BioIn 17*
Harding, Darlene Carol 1945- *WhoE 93*
Harding, Douglas Edison *BioIn 17*
Harding, Edward 1951- *St&PR 93*
Harding, Elizabeth Lee *Law&B 92*
Harding, Enoch, Jr. 1931- *WhoE 93*
Harding, Ethel M. 1927- *WhoAmW 93*
Harding, Eva Victoria 1913- *WhoWrEP 92*
Harding, Fann 1930- *WhoAm 92*
Harding, Florence Kling De Wolfe 1860-1924 *BioIn 17*
Harding, Frank I. 1944- *WhoAm 92*
Harding, Frank I., III 1944- *St&PR 93*
Harding, Fred R. 1943- *St&PR 93*
Harding, G. Homer *WhoAm 92*
Harding, George, IV *BioIn 17*
Harding, George Ann *Law&B 92*
Harding, Graham Frederick Anthony *WhoScE 91-1*
Harding, Harry 1946- *WhoAm 92*
Harding, Henry W. 1910- *St&PR 93*
Harding, James Warren 1918- *WhoAm 92*
Harding, John David 1944- *St&PR 93*
Harding, John Edmond *WhoScE 91-1*
Harding, John Hibbard 1936- *St&PR 93, WhoAm 92*
Harding, Karen Anne *Law&B 92*
Harding, Khit 1942- *WhoWrEP 92*
Harding, Lee 1937- *ScF&FL 92*
Harding, (John) Lee 1937- *DcChlFi*
Harding, Lila E. d1992 *BioIn 17*
Harding, Mabel Traer *AmWomPl*
Harding, Major Best 1935- *WhoAm 92, WhoSSW 93*
Harding, Maureen 1953- *WhoEmL 93*
Harding, Nancy *ScF&FL 92*
Harding, Paul J. *Law&B 92*
Harding, Richard *ScF&FL 92*
Harding, Richard S. 1923- *St&PR 93*
Harding, Robert Douglas *WhoScE 91-1*
Harding, Robert E. 1935- *St&PR 93*
Harding, Thomas Lynn 1927- *St&PR 93*
Harding, Tim *BioIn 17*
Harding, Toehl *Law&B 92*
Harding, Trewitt DeLano 1934- *WhoSSW 93, WhoWor 93*
Harding, Victor Mathews 1908- *WhoAm 92*
Harding, Walter 1917- *WhoWrEP 92*
Harding, Walter Roy 1917- *BioIn 17*
Harding, Warren G. 1865-1923 *BioIn 17, PolPar*
Harding, Wayne Edward, III 1954- *WhoEmL 93*
Harding, William Malcolm 1933- *St&PR 93*
Harding, William Proctor Gould 1864-1930 *BioIn 17*
Hardingham, Timothy E. 1942- *WhoScE 91-1*
Hardis, Stephen Roger 1935- *St&PR 93, WhoAm 92*
Hardison, Donald Leigh 1916- *WhoAm 92*
Hardison, Kadeem *BioIn 17*
Hardison, Leslie C. 1929- *St&PR 93*
Hardison, O.B. *BioIn 17*
Hardison, O(sborne) B(ennett, Jr.) 1928-1990 *ConAu 40NR*
Hardison, Richard Lee 1941- *St&PR 93*
Hardison, Ruth Inge *WhoAm 92*
Hardisson, Carlos 1939- *WhoScE 91-3*
Hardister, Darrell Edward 1934- *WhoSSW 93*
Hardisty, Huntington *WhoAm 92*
Hardisty, Roger Michael *WhoScE 91-1*
Hardisty, William Lucas c. 1822-1881 *IntDcAn*
Hardjotanojo, Witjaksono 1940- *WhoUN 92*
Hardle, Wolfgang Karl 1953- *WhoWor 93*
Hardman, Curtis Thomas 1946- *WhoSSW 93*
Hardman, D.J. *WhoScE 91-1*
Hardman, Daniel Clarke 1954- *WhoEmL 93, WhoSSW 93*
Hardman, Harold Francis 1927- *WhoAm 92*
Hardman, James Charles 1931- *WhoAm 92*
Hardman, James Felix 1941- *St&PR 93*
Hardman, Joel Griffeth 1933- *WhoAm 92*
Hardman, John Herbert 1929- *WhoE 93*
Hardman, John Maley 1933- *WhoAm 92*
Hardman, Katherine Elizabeth 1955- *WhoAmW 93*
Hardman, Kathleen Goldie Brown 1915- *WhoE 93*
Hardman, Lamartine Griffin, III 1939- *St&PR 93*
Hardman, William Victor, Jr. 1945- *WhoE 93*
Hardnett, Charlotte Jefferson 1944- *WhoAmW 93*
Hardon, J.J. *WhoScE 91-3*
Hardon, John Anthony 1914- *WhoAm 92*
Hardon, Michiel 1943- *WhoWor 93*
Hardouin, Jacques E. 1929- *WhoScE 91-2*
Hardrick, Maria Darshell 1966- *WhoAmW 93*
Hardrick, Seledith Elaine 1962- *WhoAmW 93*
Hardt, Aaron L. *Law&B 92*
Hardt, Hanno Richard Eduard 1934- *WhoAm 92*
Hardt, John Stephen 1951- *WhoSSW 93*
Hardt, Nancy Franck 1943- *WhoAmW 93*
Hardway, Wendell Gary 1927- *WhoAm 92*
Hardwick, Charles Leighton 1941- *WhoAm 92*
Hardwick, David Francis 1934- *WhoAm 92*
Hardwick, Elizabeth *BioIn 17*
Hardwick, Elizabeth 1916- *AmWrS3, WhoAmW 93, WhoWrEP 92*
Hardwick, Gary Clifford 1960- *WhoEmL 93*
Hardwick, John F. *Law&B 92*
Hardwick, Joy *BioIn 17*
Hardwick, Karen Lee 1952- *WhoSSW 93*
Hardwicke, David Haliburton *Law&B 92*
Hardy, Antoine 1929- *WhoScE 91-2*
Hardy, Arthur B. 1913-1991 *BioIn 17*
Hardy, Barbara Gladys 1924- *WhoWor 93*
Hardy, Beatriz Betancourt 1961- *WhoAmW 93*
Hardy, Benjamin A., Jr. *Law&B 92*
Hardy, Benson B. 1920- *WhoWor 93*
Hardy, Bernice *AmWomPl*
Hardy, Brandt N. *Law&B 92*
Hardy, Bruce Blondel 1930- *St&PR 93*
Hardy, C. Colbuxrn 1910- *WhoWrEP 92*
Hardy, Carol Elizabeth 1951- *WhoAmW 93*
Hardy, Catherine *BlkAmWO*
Hardy, Charles E. *Law&B 92*
Hardy, Charles Jeffrey 1956- *WhoSSW 93*
Hardy, Charles Leach 1919- *WhoAm 92*
Hardy, David 1924- *WhoAm 92*
Hardy, David A. 1936- *ScF&FL 92*
Hardy, David Walter 1942- *WhoE 93*
Hardy, Deborah Welles 1927- *WhoAm 92*
Hardy, Donna Dee 1941- *WhoE 93*
Hardy, Dorcas Ruth 1946- *WhoAm 92*
Hardy, Earl M. *St&PR 93*
Hardy, Edward Clark 1934- *St&PR 93*
Hardy, Ellen Marie 1964- *WhoEmL 93*
Hardy, Florence Emily 1881-1937 *BioIn 17*
Hardy, Gail Brewster *BioIn 17*
Hardy, Gene B. 1936- *ScF&FL 92*
Hardy, Gene M. 1937- *St&PR 93*
Hardy, George 1911-1990 *BioIn 17*
Hardy, Gordon Alfred 1918- *WhoAm 92*
Hardy, Gyme Dufault 1952- *WhoAm 92*
Hardy, Harvey Louchard 1914- *WhoSSW 93*
Hardy, Hilbert 1906- *ScF&FL 92*
Hardy, Hugh 1932- *BioIn 17*
Hardy, Hugh Gelston 1932- *WhoAm 92, WhoWor 93*
Hardy, J.C. *WhoScE 91-1*
Hardy, James Chester 1930- *WhoAm 92*
Hardy, James Daly 1948- *WhoAm 92*
Hardy, James Deane 1929- *St&PR 93*
Hardy, Jane Elizabeth 1930- *WhoAmW 93*
Hardy, Jerome S. 1918- *St&PR 93*
Hardy, John Christopher 1941- *WhoAm 92*
Hardy, John Edward 1922- *WhoAm 92, WhoWrEP 92*
Hardy, John J. 1937- *WhoIns 93*
Hardy, Joseph 1929- *MiSFD 9*
Hardy, June Dorflinger 1929- *WhoE 93*
Hardy, Lester Babbitt 1932- *WhoAm 92*
Hardy, Linda B. 1955- *WhoAmW 93*
Hardy, Linda Lea Sterlock 1947- *WhoAmW 93*
Hardy, Lois Lynn 1928- *WhoAmW 93, WhoWor 93*
Hardy, Lyndon 1941- *ScF&FL 92*
Hardy, Major Preston, Jr. 1937- *WhoWor 93*
Hardy, Mark G. *St&PR 93*
Hardy, Maurice G. 1930- *St&PR 93*
Hardy, Maurice G. 1931- *WhoE 93*
Hardy, Naomi *ScF&FL 92*
Hardy, Oliver 1892-1957 *BioIn 17*
Hardy, Oliver 1892-1957 *See* Laurel, Stan 1890-1965 & Hardy, Oliver 1892-1957 *QDrFCA 92*
Hardy, Paul Jude 1942- *WhoAm 92, WhoWor 93*
Hardy, Phil 1945- *ScF&FL 92*
Hardy, Ralph Eugene *Law&B 92*
Hardy, Ralph W. F. 1934- *WhoAm 92, WhoE 93, WhoWor 93*
Hardy, Richard B. 1932- *St&PR 93*
Hardy, Richard Earl 1938- *WhoAm 92*
Hardy, Richard L. 1924- *St&PR 93*
Hardy, Robert Gerald 1944- *WhoAm 92*
Hardy, Robin 1929- *MiSFD 9, ScF&FL 92*
Hardy, Sandra Jane *Law&B 92*
Hardy, Sherry Frances *Law&B 92*
Hardy, Thomas 1840-1928 *BioIn 17, MagSWL [port], OxDcOp, ScF&FL 92, TwCLC 48, WorLitC [port]*
Hardy, Thomas Austin 1921- *WhoAm 92*
Hardy, Thomas Cresson 1942- *St&PR 93, WhoAm 92, WhoIns 93*
Hardy, Thomas G. 1945- *St&PR 93*
Hardy, Thomas George 1945- *WhoAm 92, WhoE 93*
Hardy, Tom Charles, Jr. 1945- *WhoAm 92*
Hardy, Victoria Elizabeth 1947- *WhoAmW 93, WhoEmL 93*
Hardy, W.G. 1895-1979 *ScF&FL 92*
Hardy, Walter Newbold 1940- *WhoAm 92*
Hardy, William H., Jr. *Law&B 92*
Hardy, William Robinson 1934- *WhoAm 92, WhoWor 93*
Hardy-Beierl, Barbara *WhoE 93*
Hardy Havens, Debra Mae 1953- *WhoAmW 93*
Hardymon, James 1934- *St&PR 93*
Hardymon, James F. 1934- *WhoAm 92*
Hardymon, James Franklin 1934- *WhoWor 93*
Hare, Ann Tingle *WhoSSW 93*
Hare, Daphne Kean 1937- *WhoWor 93*
Hare, David *BioIn 17*
Hare, David 1917- *WhoAm 92*
Hare, David 1917-1992 *NewYTBS 92 [port]*
Hare, David 1947- *ConAu 39NR, MiSFD 9, WhoAm 92, WhoWor 93*
Hare, Diana S. *Law&B 92*
Hare, Donald Eustis 1929- *St&PR 93*
Hare, Eleanor O'Meara 1936- *WhoAmW 93*
Hare, Frederick Kenneth 1919- *WhoAm 92*
Hare, Glenn F. 1931- *St&PR 93*
Hare, J. Patrick 1953- *St&PR 93*
Hare, James H. 1856-1946 *GayN*
Hare, Jerry *BioIn 17*
Hare, Maud Cuney *AmWomPl*
Hare, Michael John 1938- *WhoWor 93*
Hare, Nathan 1933- *WhoAm 92*
Hare, Peter Hewitt 1935- *WhoAm 92, WhoWor 93*
Hare, Richard 1938- *St&PR 93*
Hare, Richard Williams 1924-1989 *BioIn 17*
Hare, Robert Lee, Jr. 1920- *WhoWor 93*
Hare, Robert Lewis 1923- *WhoAm 92*
Hare, Robert Yates 1921- *WhoAm 92*
Hare, Robertson 1891-1979 *QDrFCA 92 [port]*
Hare, Sandra Florence 1952- *WhoAmW 93, WhoEmL 93, WhoWor 93*
Hare, Susan Yvonne 1953- *WhoEmL 93*
Hare, William *BioIn 17*
Harel, Ezra 1950- *St&PR 93*
Harell, George S. 1937- *WhoSSW 93*
Harelson, Hugh 1930- *WhoAm 92*
Haren, Charles Wells, Jr. 1933- *St&PR 93*
Haren, Lawrence P. 1954- *St&PR 93*
Haren, Nathalie S. 1932- *St&PR 93*
Harenchar, Michael J. 1926- *St&PR 93*
Harens, Ann Therese 1961- *WhoAmW 93*
Harens, Paul Arthur 1951- *WhoEmL 93*
Harer, Kathleen Frances 1947- *WhoEmL 93*
Hares, William Joseph 1949- *WhoEmL 93*
Har-Even, Reuven 1948- *WhoAm 92*
Harewood, Earl of 1923- *OxDcOp*
Harewood, George (Henry Hubert Lascelles), Earl of 1923- *Baker 92*
Harff, Charles H. *Law&B 92*
Harff, Charles H. 1929- *St&PR 93*
Harff, Charles Henry 1929- *WhoAm 92*
Harford, James Joseph 1924- *WhoAm 92*
Harfors, Claes B. 1948- *WhoScE 91-4*
Hargadon, Bernard Joseph, Jr. 1927- *WhoAm 92*
Hargadon, Bro Kevin 1930- *WhoE 93*
Hargens, Charles William, III 1918- *WhoAm 92, WhoE 93*
Hargens, William Garman 1943- *WhoAm 92*
Harger, Robert Owens 1932- *WhoAm 92*
Hargett, Charles B. *Law&B 92*
Hargett, Donald Edward 1945- *St&PR 93*
Hargett, Paul Glenn 1954- *St&PR 93, WhoAm 92*
Hargis, Billy James 1925- *BioIn 17, WhoAm 92, WhoWor 93*
Hargis, Darel Edwin 1955- *WhoEmL 93, WhoSSW 93*
Hargis, Frances *AmWomPl*
Hargiss, James Leonard 1921- *WhoAm 92*
Hargitai, Laszlo 1930- *WhoScE 91-4*
Hargitt, Rollin Jerry 1931- *St&PR 93*
Hargrave, Alexander Davidson 1920- *WhoAm 92*
Hargrave, Cecille Terry 1917- *WhoAm 92*
Hargrave, Eustace *AmWomPl*
Hargrave, Irvin P.H. 1935- *St&PR 93*
Hargrave, Irvin P.H., Jr. 1935- *WhoIns 93*
Hargrave, John 1894-1982 *ScF&FL 92*
Hargrave, Judith Ann *Law&B 92*
Hargrave, Leonie *MajAI*
Hargrave, Mary Anne 1959- *WhoAmW 93*
Hargrave, R.W. 1920- *St&PR 93*
Hargrave, Robert Larson 1941- *St&PR 93*
Hargrave, Robert Warren 1944- *WhoSSW 93, WhoWor 93*
Hargrave, Robert Webb 1920- *WhoAm 92*
Hargrave, Rowena 1906- *ConAu 40NR*
Hargrave, Rudolph 1925- *WhoAm 92, WhoSSW 93*
Hargrave, Sarah Quesenberry 1944- *WhoAm 92*
Hargrave, Victoria Elizabeth 1913- *WhoAm 92*
Hargrave, Willie Lee 1943- *WhoSSW 93*
Hargraves, David G. 1949- *St&PR 93*
Hargraves, Gordon Sellers 1932- *WhoAm 92*
Hargraves, Melody Manor 1964- *WhoSSW 93*
Hargreaves, David William 1943- *WhoAm 92, WhoE 93, WhoWor 93*
Hargreaves, George Henry 1916- *WhoAm 92*
Hargreaves, H.A. 1928- *ScF&FL 92*
Hargreaves, Kenneth L. 1948- *St&PR 93*
Hargreaves, Mary-Wilma Massey 1914- *WhoAmW 93*
Hargroder, Charles Merlin 1926- *WhoSSW 93, WhoWor 93*
Hargrove, Dean 1938- *MiSFD 9*

Hargrove, Dudley Michael 1949- *BiDAMSp 1989*
Hargrove, G. Thomas 1939- *St&PR 93*
Hargrove, George Matthew, Jr. 1951- *St&PR 93*
Hargrove, Gerry Lyndon *Law&B 92*
Hargrove, James Ward 1922- *WhoAm 92*
Hargrove, James Ward, Jr. 1944- *WhoSSW 93*
Hargrove, John R. 1923- *WhoE 93*
Hargrove, John Russell 1947- *WhoAm 92*
Hargrove, Laurie Elizabeth 1927- *WhoSSW 93*
Hargrove, Lisa K. *Law&B 92*
Hargrove, Logan E. 1935- *WhoSSW 93*
Hargrove, Marguerite *ScF&FL 92*
Hargrove, Michael B. 1941- *WhoE 93, WhoWor 93*
Hargrove, Mike 1949- *WhoAm 92*
Hargrove, R.L., Jr. 1932- *St&PR 93*
Hargrove, Roy *BioIn 17*
Hargrove, Thomas Stephen 1954- *WhoEmL 93*
Harguem, Abdelhafidh 1954- *WhoWor 93*
Hargus, Susan Diane 1964- *WhoAmW 93*
Hari, Kenneth Stephen 1947- *WhoAm 92*
Harich-Schneider, Eta 1897-1986 *Baker 92*
Haridakis, Paul Michael *Law&B 92*
Haried, James Andrew 1956- *WhoSSW 93*
Harig, Bernhardt Peter Gold 1926- *St&PR 93*
Harig, John Joseph 1951- *WhoEmL 93*
Harig, Rainer 1947- *WhoScE 91-3*
Harigan, John D. 1934- *St&PR 93*
Harigel, Gert Gunter 1930- *WhoWor 93*
Harijan, Ram 1938- *WhoWor 93*
Harik, Issam Elias 1952- *WhoEmL 93, WhoSSW 93*
Harinasuta, Tranakchit *BioIn 17*
Haring, Douglas Gilbert 1894-1970 *IntDcAn*
Haring, Ellen Stone 1921- *WhoAm 92*
Haring, Eugene Miller 1927- *WhoAm 92*
Haring, Howard Jack 1924- *WhoAm 92*
Haring, Keith 1958-1990 *BioIn 17*
Haring, Marilyn Joan 1941- *WhoAm 92*
Haring, Olga Munk 1917- *WhoAm 92*
Haring, Robert W. 1932- *WhoSSW 93*
Haring, Scott D. *ScF&FL 92*
Haring-Smith, Tori 1953- *WhoE 93*
Harington, Charles Richard 1933- *WhoAm 92*
Harington, Donald 1935- *ScF&FL 92*
Hario, M. *WhoScE 91-4*
Haririan, Mehdi 1950- *WhoEmL 93*
Haris, Mary Papajohn d1990 *BioIn 17*
Harisdangkul, Valee 1941- *WhoAm 92*
Hari Singh 1929- *WhoAsAP 91*
Harisis, T.G. 1930- *St&PR 93*
Haritatos, George M. 1959- *WhoWor 93*
Harith, Al- *OxDcByz*
Harito, Sadamoto 1948- *WhoWor 93*
Hariton, Morris Bernard 1911- *WhoE 93*
Haritos, Dolores Jean *WhoE 93*
Hariu, Yukichi 1937- *WhoAsAP 91*
Harjo, Joy *BioIn 17*
Harjo, Joy 1951- *DcLB 120 [port], WhoWrEP 92*
Harjung, Kurt Stephen 1950- *WhoEmL 93*
Hark, Tsui 1951- *MiSFD 9*
Harkala, Walter H. *St&PR 93*
Harkarvy, Benjamin 1930- *WhoWor 93*
Harkavy, Jack Z. 1939- *St&PR 93*
Harkavy, Minna d1987 *BioIn 17*
Harkaway, Hal *MajAI*
Harkay, Robert L. d1992 *NewYTBS 92*
Harke, Douglas James 1942- *WhoE 93*
Harkema, Steven J. 1963- *St&PR 93*
Harker, David 1906-1991 *BioIn 17*
Harker, Gordon 1885-1967 *QDrFCA 92 [port]*
Harker, Howard R. 1933- *St&PR 93*
Harker, John V. 1934- *St&PR 93*
Harker, Joseph Edward 1936- *WhoAm 92*
Harker, Kenneth Reid, Jr. *Law&B 92*
Harker, Lizzie Allen 1863-1933 *AmWomPl*
Harker, Norrene 1927- *WhoAmW 93*
Harker, Robert Ian 1926- *WhoAm 92*
Harkes, John *BioIn 17*
Harkey, Amy Lord 1954- *WhoSSW 93*
Harkey, C. Dee 1952- *St&PR 93*
Harkey, Dee 1866-1948 *BioIn 17*
Harkey, Ira Brown, Jr. 1918- *WhoAm 92*
Harkey, John D., Jr. 1960- *St&PR 93*
Harkey, John Norman 1933- *WhoAm 92*
Harkey, Robert S. *Law&B 92*
Harkey, Robert Shelton 1940- *WhoAm 92*
Harkin, Daniel John 1955- *WhoSSW 93*
Harkin, James C. 1926- *WhoSSW 93*
Harkin, Thomas Richard 1939- *WhoAm 92*
Harkin, Tom *NewYTBS 92 [port]*
Harkin, Tom 1939- *BioIn 17, CngDr 91, CurBio 92 [port]*
Harkins, Ann Elizabeth 1952- *WhoAmW 93*
Harkins, C. Patrick 1950- *St&PR 93*
Harkins, Edwin L. 1940- *WhoAm 92*
Harkins, Eugene *Law&B 92*
Harkins, George F. 1913-1991 *BioIn 17*
Harkins, Herbert Perrin 1912- *WhoE 93*
Harkins, Ignatius John, III 1936- *WhoE 93*
Harkins, James Stanley, Sr. 1932- *WhoSSW 93*
Harkins, Jayne Michele Mosser 1960- *WhoAmW 93*
Harkins, John Graham, Jr. 1931- *WhoAm 92*
Harkins, Joseph Francis 1938- *WhoAm 92*
Harkins, Joseph James *St&PR 93, WhoAm 92*
Harkins, Kenneth R. 1921- *CngDr 91, WhoAm 92*
Harkins, Kenneth V. *Law&B 92*
Harkins, Laurie Neville *Law&B 92*
Harkins, Michael E. 1941- *WhoAm 92, WhoE 93*
Harkins, Richard A. *Law&B 92*
Harkins, Richard Wesley 1946- *WhoEmL 93*
Harkins, Susan E. *Law&B 92*
Harkins, William Daniel 1943- *WhoAm 92*
Harkins, William Edward 1921- *WhoAm 92*
Harkleroad, William Derryl 1938- *St&PR 93*
Harkless, David G. 1952- *St&PR 93*
Harkna, Eric 1940- *St&PR 93, WhoAm 92*
Harkness, Bruce 1923- *WhoAm 92*
Harkness, Donald Ray 1921- *WhoWrEP 92*
Harkness, Donald Richard 1932- *WhoAm 92*
Harkness, James Linwood 1931- *St&PR 93*
Harkness, James Willard 1941- *St&PR 93*
Harkness, John C. 1916- *St&PR 93*
Harkness, John Cheesman 1916- *WhoAm 92*
Harkness, Kenneth Kohlsaat 1934- *WhoE 93*
Harkness, M. Stephen 1948- *St&PR 93*
Harkness, Mabel Gleason 1913- *WhoAmW 93*
Harkness, Mary Lou 1925- *WhoAm 92*
Harkness, Maurice Stephen 1948- *WhoAm 92*
Harkness, R. Kenneth 1949- *WhoEmL 93, WhoSSW 93*
Harkness, Robert Douglas *WhoScE 91-1*
Harkness, Ruth *BioIn 17*
Harkness, Samuel Dacke, III 1940- *WhoE 93*
Harkness, Sarah Pillsbury 1914- *WhoAm 92*
Harkness, Scott J. 1955- *St&PR 93*
Harkness, Stephanie Diane 1943- *WhoAmW 93*
Harkness, William Leonard 1934- *WhoAm 92*
Harknett, John 1942- *St&PR 93*
Harknett, Richard F. 1938- *St&PR 93*
Harkon, Franz *ScF&FL 92*
Harkow, Jaye Fredrica 1959- *WhoEmL 93, WhoSSW 93*
Harkrader, Carleton Allen 1917- *WhoAm 92*
Harkrader, Charles Johnston, Jr. 1913- *WhoAm 92*
Harkrader, Milton K., Jr. 1938- *St&PR 93*
Harkrader, Milton Keene, Jr. 1939- *WhoAm 92*
Harkrader, Sue Robertson 1941- *WhoSSW 93*
Harkrider, David Garrison 1931- *WhoAm 92*
Harkrider, Harold G. 1928- *St&PR 93*
Harl, Neil Eugene 1933- *WhoAm 92*
Harlacher, Meredith I. 1942- *St&PR 93*
Harlan, David C. 1950- *St&PR 93*
Harlan, F. James 1948- *St&PR 93*
Harlan, Irma *WhoSSW 93*
Harlan, Jack Rodney 1917- *WhoAm 92*
Harlan, Jane Ann 1947- *WhoAmW 93, WhoEmL 93*
Harlan, Jean Durgin 1924- *WhoAm 92*
Harlan, John Belat 1957- *WhoEmL 93*
Harlan, John G. d1990 *BioIn 17*
Harlan, John Marshall *WhoAm 92*
Harlan, John Marshall 1833-1911 *EncAACR [port], OxCSupC [port]*
Harlan, John Marshall 1899-1971 *BioIn 17*
Harlan, John Marshall 1933- *St&PR 93*
Harlan, John Marshall, II 1899-1971 *OxCSupC [port]*
Harlan, Kathleen T. 1934- *WhoWor 93*
Harlan, Kenneth 1895-1967 *BioIn 17*
Harlan, Leonard Morton 1936- *WhoAm 92, WhoE 93, WhoWor 93*
Harlan, Louis Rudolph 1922- *WhoAm 92*
Harlan, Mark Evan 1953- *WhoE 93*
Harlan, Neil Eugene 1921- *WhoAm 92*
Harlan, Norman Ralph 1914- *WhoWor 93*
Harlan, Robert Dale 1929- *WhoAm 92*
Harlan, Robert Ernest 1936- *WhoAm 92*
Harlan, Robert Ridge 1953- *WhoEmL 93*
Harlan, Robert Warren 1921- *WhoAm 92*
Harlan, Roma Christine *WhoAm 92, WhoAmW 93*
Harlan, Ross 1919- *WhoWrEP 92*
Harlan, Ross Edgar 1919- *WhoAm 92, WhoSSW 93*
Harlan, Stephen Donald 1933- *WhoAm 92*
Harlan, William Robert, Jr. 1930- *WhoAm 92*
Harland, Brian James 1944- *WhoWor 93*
Harland, David A.K. *Law&B 92*
Harland, David Anthony Knox 1955- *WhoEmL 93*
Harlander, Leslie Albert 1923- *WhoAm 92*
Harlass, Sherry Ellen Pool 1961- *WhoAmW 93*
Harle, Franz 1937- *WhoScE 91-3*
Harlem, Susan Lynn 1950- *WhoAm 92*
Harleman, Ann *WhoAmW 93*
Harleman, Ann 1945- *WhoWrEP 92*
Harleman, Donald Robert Fergusson 1922- *WhoAm 92*
Harless, Byron Brittingham 1916- *WhoAm 92*
Harless, James Malcolm 1948- *WhoWor 93*
Harless, James Warren 1937- *WhoSSW 93*
Harless, Keith Weston 1946- *WhoEmL 93*
Harless, Lynette Leanne Satterfield 1959- *WhoAmW 93*
Harleston, Bernard Warren 1930- *WhoAm 92*
Harleston, Kathleen M. *Law&B 92*
Harley, Alan A. *Law&B 92*
Harley, Brian 1932-1991 *AnObit 1991*
Harley, Ellen A. 1946- *WhoAmW 93*
Harley, Geoffrey John 1953- *WhoWor 93*
Harley, George T. *St&PR 93*
Harley, J.B. *BioIn 17*
Harley, J. Michael *Law&B 92*
Harley, John Brian *BioIn 17*
Harley, Marjorie d1991 *BioIn 17*
Harley, Naomi Hallden 1932- *WhoAm 92, WhoE 93*
Harley, Robison Dooling 1911- *WhoAm 92*
Harley, Wayne Chapin 1947- *St&PR 93*
Harley, William Gardner 1911- *WhoAm 92*
Harlin, Andreas 1951- *BioIn 17*
Harlin, Marilyn Miler 1934- *WhoAmW 93*
Harlin, Renny *BioIn 17, MiSFD 9*
Harlin, Renny 1959?- *ConTFT 10*
Harline, Leigh 1907-1969 *Baker 92*
Harling, Carlos Gene 1946- *WhoAm 92*
Harling, Robert Allen 1930- *WhoSSW 93*
Harling, William Franke 1887-1958 *Baker 92*
Harllee, Frederick Earl, III 1945- *WhoSSW 93*
Harllee, John 1914- *WhoE 93*
Harllee, John Thomas 1935- *WhoWrEP 92*
Harloff, Robert C. 1943- *St&PR 93*
Harlow, Bryce L. 1949- *WhoAm 92*
Harlow, Gary Lee 1945- *St&PR 93*
Harlow, George Eugene 1949- *WhoAm 92*
Harlow, James Gindling, Jr. 1934- *St&PR 93, WhoAm 92, WhoSSW 93*
Harlow, Jean 1911-1937 *BioIn 17, IntDcF 2-3 [port]*
Harlow, John Gronbech 1944- *St&PR 93*
Harlow, LeRoy Francis 1913- *WhoAm 92, WhoWor 93*
Harlow, Lisa Lavoie 1951- *WhoEmL 93*
Harlow, Paul S. 1941- *St&PR 93*
Harlow, Robert 1923- *WhoCanL 92*
Harlow, Robert Dean 1938- *St&PR 93, WhoAm 92*
Harlow, Steven Michael 1963- *WhoEmL 93, WhoSSW 93*
Harm, Duane R. 1939- *St&PR 93*
Harma, Laurence E. 1944- *St&PR 93*
Harman, Avraham d1992 *NewYTBS 92 [port]*
Harman, Avraham 1914-1992 *BioIn 17*
Harman, Carter 1918- *Baker 92*
Harman, Charles A. 1942- *St&PR 93*
Harman, Charles Michael 1947- *St&PR 93, WhoAm 92*
Harman, Charles Morgan 1929- *WhoAm 92*
Harman, Daniel T. *Law&B 92*
Harman, David E. 1933- *St&PR 93*
Harman, Donald J. *Law&B 92*
Harman, Donald Lee 1948- *WhoEmL 93, WhoWor 93*
Harman, Dudley M. 1935- *St&PR 93*
Harman, Fred 1902-1982 *BioIn 17*
Harman, G. Don 1949- *St&PR 93*
Harman, George Gibson 1924- *WhoAm 92*
Harman, Gilbert Helms 1938- *WhoAm 92*
Harman, Harry E., III 1917- *ConAu 39NR*
Harman, James Richard 1952- *WhoAm 92*
Harman, Jane Lakes 1945- *WhoAmW 93*
Harman, Jeanne Perkins 1919- *ConAu 39NR*
Harman, John Robert, Jr. 1921- *WhoAm 92*
Harman, John Royden 1921- *WhoAm 92*
Harman, Julie Ann 1958- *WhoEmL 93*
Harman, Michele Lee 1959- *WhoAmW 93*
Harman, Nigel *ScF&FL 92*
Harman, Patt Claude, III 1947- *St&PR 93*
Harman, Pete *BioIn 17*
Harman, Sidney 1918- *WhoE 93*
Harman, Theodore Carter 1929- *WhoE 93*
Harman, Thomas *Law&B 92*
Harman, Willard Nelson 1937- *WhoAm 92*
Harman, William Boys, Jr. 1930- *WhoAm 92, WhoIns 93, WhoWor 93*
Harman, William E. 1906-1985 *BioIn 17*
Harmar, Josiah 1753-1813 *CmdGen 1991 [port], HarEnMi*
Harmat, Artur 1885-1962 *Baker 92*
Harmati, Istvan 1929- *WhoScE 91-4*
Harmati, Sandor 1892-1936 *Baker 92*
Harmaty, Myron Bohdand 1945- *WhoSSW 93*
Harmatz, Fred Mark 1954- *St&PR 93*
Harmatz, Morton Gerald 1939- *WhoE 93*
Harmel, Hilda Herta *WhoAmW 93*
Harmel, Merel Hilber 1917- *WhoAm 92*
Harmelin, Stephen Joseph 1939- *WhoAm 92, WhoE 93, WhoWor 93*
Harmell, Pamela Hersh 1947- *WhoAm 92*
Harmening, Denise M. 1952- *WhoAmW 93*
Harmenopoulos, Constantine fl. 14th cent.- *OxDcByz*
Harmer, David G. 1943- *St&PR 93*
Harmer, Don S. *WhoSSW 93*
Harmer, Lee DeLoache 1936- *WhoSSW 93*
Harmer, Patricia Gail 1963- *WhoAmW 93*
Harmer, Rose 1939- *WhoSSW 93*
Harmes, Johann Oswald 1643?-1708 *OxDcOp*
Harmeson, Greg 1946- *St&PR 93*
Harmet, A(rnold) Richard 1932- *WhoWrEP 92*
Harmetz, Aljean *ConAu 139*
Harmey, Matthew A. 1938- *WhoScE 91-3*
Harmeyer, Johein 1934- *WhoScE 91-3*
Harmoko 1939- *WhoAsAP 91*
Harmon, Adrian 1919- *St&PR 93*
Harmon, Alfred 1929- *St&PR 93*
Harmon, Allen D. 1951- *St&PR 93*
Harmon, Artice Ward 1940- *WhoAmW 93*
Harmon, Benjamin Franklin, IV *Law&B 92*
Harmon, Bert 1906-1991 *BioIn 17*
Harmon, Brent Lowell 1947- *WhoSSW 93*
Harmon, Bud Gene 1931- *WhoAm 92*
Harmon, Caroline Hoff 1927- *WhoE 93*
Harmon, Charles T. 1960- *BioIn 17*
Harmon, Cynthia Ann 1956- *WhoEmL 93*
Harmon, Dale Lynn 1931- *WhoSSW 93*
Harmon, Dan D. *Law&B 92*
Harmon, Daniel Patrick 1938- *WhoAm 92*
Harmon, David Eugene 1951- *WhoSSW 93*
Harmon, Douglas Alexander 1946- *St&PR 93*
Harmon, Ellen T. *Law&B 92*
Harmon, Ernest Nason 1894-1979 *HarEnMi*
Harmon, Foster 1912- *WhoAm 92, WhoSSW 93, WhoWor 93*
Harmon, Gail McGreevy 1943- *WhoAmW 93*
Harmon, Gary Lee 1935- *WhoAm 92*
Harmon, George Lamar 1931- *WhoSSW 93*
Harmon, George Marion 1934- *WhoAm 92*
Harmon, Grant Stephen *Law&B 92*
Harmon, Harry William 1918- *WhoAm 92*
Harmon, Jacqueline Baas 1934- *WhoSSW 93*
Harmon, James Allen 1935- *St&PR 93, WhoAm 92, WhoE 93*
Harmon, James J. *ScF&FL 92*
Harmon, Jerald Scott 1962- *WhoSSW 93*
Harmon, Jim 1933- *ScF&FL 92*
Harmon, Joanne Marie *Law&B 92*
Harmon, Keith Hanna 1952- *WhoSSW 93*
Harmon, Keith James 1950- *WhoEmL 93*
Harmon, Lily 1912- *WhoAm 92*
Harmon, Lynn Adrian 1944- *St&PR 93, WhoAm 92*
Harmon, Margaret K. 1923- *St&PR 93*

Harmon, Marian Sanders 1916- *WhoAmW 93*
Harmon, Mark *BioIn 17*
Harmon, Mark 1951- *HolBB [port], WhoAm 92*
Harmon, Mary Joann 1941- *WhoSSW 93*
Harmon, Megan Elizabeth *Law&B 92*
Harmon, Melinda Furche 1946- *WhoAm 92, WhoAmW 93, WhoSSW 93*
Harmon, Patrick 1916- *WhoAm 92*
Harmon, Paul A. 1957- *St&PR 93*
Harmon, Philip M. *ScF&FL 92*
Harmon, Raymond William 1925- *St&PR 93*
Harmon, Reginald C. d1992 *NewYTBS 92*
Harmon, Richard L. 1950- *WhoE 93*
Harmon, Richard Wingate 1958- *WhoE 93*
Harmon, Robert *MiSFD 9*
Harmon, Robert E. 1939- *St&PR 93*
Harmon, Robert Lee 1926- *St&PR 93, WhoAm 92*
Harmon, Robert Lon 1938- *WhoWor 93*
Harmon, Robert W. *Law&B 92*
Harmon, Robert Wayne 1929- *WhoAm 92*
Harmon, Scott McKneely 1951- *WhoEmL 93*
Harmon, Stanley A. *Law&B 92*
Harmon, Terry 1940- *WhoAm 92*
Harmon, Thomas J. 1950- *St&PR 93*
Harmon, Tina Louisa 1962- *WhoAmW 93*
Harmon, Todd A. 1958- *St&PR 93*
Harmon, Tom 1919-1990 *BioIn 17*
Harmon, Tom D. *Law&B 92*
Harmon, Victoria Tham 1956- *WhoAmW 93, WhoEmL 93*
Harmon, W. David 1943- *WhoE 93*
Harmon, William 1938- *BioIn 17*
Harmon, William J. *Law&B 92*
Harmon Brown, Valarie Jean 1948- *WhoAm 92, WhoAmW 93, WhoEmL 93*
Harmond, R.E. 1944- *St&PR 93*
Harmond, Richard Peter 1929- *WhoE 93*
Harmon Hanna, Emma 1939- *WhoAmW 93*
Harmon-Sanders, Gail Ann 1955- *WhoAmW 93*
Harmony, Marlin Dale 1936- *WhoAm 92*
Harmony, Terrence *WhoWrEP 92*
Harms, Barbara J. 1947- *St&PR 93*
Harms, Barbara Jean 1947- *WhoAmW 93*
Harms, Brian G. *Law&B 92*
Harms, Carol J. 1953- *St&PR 93*
Harms, Daniel Carl 1956- *St&PR 93*
Harms, Deborah Gayle 1950- *WhoAmW 93*
Harms, Elizabeth Louise 1924- *WhoAm 92*
Harms, Ernst H. 1939- *WhoScE 91-3*
Harms, Fred D. 1946- *St&PR 93*
Harms, Gregory Martin 1949- *WhoSSW 93*
Harms, John E. 1946- *St&PR 93*
Harms, John Kevin 1960- *WhoEmL 93*
Harms, Judy Ann 1949- *WhoAmW 93*
Harms, Jurgen 1937- *WhoScE 91-4*
Harms, Nancy Isabel Fitch 1939- *WhoAmW 93*
Harms, Robert Thomas 1932- *WhoAm 92*
Harms, Shelley E. *Law&B 92*
Harms, Steven Alan 1949- *WhoEmL 93*
Harms, U. *WhoScE 91-3*
Harms, Valerie 1940- *WhoWrEP 92*
Harmsen, Harlan F. 1927- *St&PR 93*
Harmsen, Karl 1947- *WhoScE 91-3*
Harmsen, Tyrus George 1924- *WhoAm 92*
Harn, Rebecca Claire 1950- *WhoSSW 93*
Harnack, Curtis 1927- *WhoWrEP 92*
Harnack, Don Steger 1928- *WhoAm 92*
Harnack, Robert Spencer 1918- *WhoAm 92*
Harnden, David Gilbert 1932- *WhoScE 91-1*
Harnden, Michael Raymond 1938- *WhoWor 93*
Harnden, Ruth (Peabody) *DcAmChF 1960*
Harned, David Baily 1932- *WhoAm 92*
Harned, Herbert Spencer, Jr. 1921- *WhoSSW 93*
Harned, Keith Wayne 1966- *WhoSSW 93*
Harned, Roger Kent 1934- *WhoAm 92*
Harnedy, Joan Catherine Holland 1936- *WhoAmW 93*
Harner, James Lowell 1946- *WhoSSW 93*
Harner, James Philip 1943- *WhoE 93*
Harner, Linda Jeane 1952- *WhoAmW 93*
Harner, Michael James 1929- *WhoAm 92, WhoWor 93*
Harner, Paul B. 1909- *WhoAm 92*
Harnesk, Priscilla Ann 1955- *WhoEmL 93*
Harness, Charles L. 1915- *ScF&FL 92*
Harness, Hugh Gregory 1930- *St&PR 93*
Harness, J.M. *WhoScE 91-1*
Harness, John Parker 1937- *St&PR 93*
Harness, Robert L. *St&PR 93*
Harness, William Edward 1940- *WhoAm 92*
Harness, William Walter 1945- *WhoSSW 93*
Harnett, Craig Curtiss 1952- *WhoE 93*
Harnett, Daniel Joseph 1930- *WhoAm 92*
Harnett, David S. *WhoEmL 93*
Harnett, Donald Lee 1937- *WhoAm 92*
Harnett, James Francis 1921- *WhoAm 92*
Harnett, Joseph Durham 1917- *WhoAm 92*
Harnett, Lila 1926- *WhoAmW 93*
Harnett, Thomas Aquinas 1924- *WhoAm 92, WhoIns 93*
Harnett, William Michael 1848-1892 *BioIn 17*
Harney, Charles F. 1951- *St&PR 93*
Harney, Charles Francis 1951- *WhoAm 92*
Harney, David Moran 1924- *WhoWor 93*
Harney, Kenneth Robert 1944- *WhoAm 92, WhoWrEP 92*
Harney, William John 1932- *St&PR 93*
Harney, William Selby 1800-1889 *HarEnMi*
Harnick, Sheldon Mayer 1924- *WhoAm 92*
Harnik, Hans 1918-1991 *BioIn 17*
Harning, Daniel Thomas 1935- *St&PR 93*
Harnisch, Linda Lee *Law&B 92*
Harnish, Stephen Norman 1948- *WhoEmL 93*
Harnois, J. Paul 1945- *St&PR 93*
Harnois, L. Paul 1931- *St&PR 93*
Harnoncourt, Alice 1930- See Harnoncourt, Nikolaus 1929- *Baker 92*
Harnoncourt, Karl 1934- *WhoScE 91-4*
Harnoncourt, Nikolaus 1929- *Baker 92, BioIn 17, WhoWor 93*
Harnoy, Ofra 1965- *Baker 92*
Harnsberger, Therese Coscarelli *WhoAmW 93*
Harnwell, Anna Jane Wilcox 1872- *AmWomPl*
Haro, John Calvin 1928- *St&PR 93, WhoAm 92*
Haroian, Gary E. 1951- *St&PR 93*
Harold, Edmund *ScF&FL 92*
Harold, Elliotte M., Jr. *Law&B 92*
Harold, John Gordon 1955- *WhoAm 92, WhoWor 93*
Harold, John Thomas 1950- *St&PR 93*
Harold, Michael C. *Law&B 92*
Harold, Paul Dennis 1948- *WhoE 93*
Harold, Susan *Law&B 92*
Harold, Vincent John 1941- *St&PR 93*
Harold Hardrada 1015-1066 *OxDcByz*
Haroldson, Glenn Victor 1951- *St&PR 93*
Haroldson, Steven A. 1946- *WhoIns 93*
Haroon, Abdullah Hussain 1950- *WhoWor 93*
Harowitz, Charles Lichtenberg 1926- *WhoSSW 93*
Haroz, Richard K. 1941- *WhoScE 91-3, -91-4*
Harp, Donald Leon 1928- *St&PR 93*
Harp, Emile Francis 1928- *St&PR 93*
Harp, Paul Lindsey 1948- *St&PR 93*
Harp, Rufus William 1923- *WhoAm 92, WhoWor 93*
Harp, Steven Ray 1952- *St&PR 93*
Harper, Aja C. 1919- *St&PR 93*
Harper, Alan A. d1991 *BioIn 17*
Harper, Alan G. 1945- *WhoAm 92*
Harper, Alexander Murray *WhoScE 91-1*
Harper, Alfred John, II 1942- *WhoAm 92*
Harper, Andrew *ScF&FL 92*
Harper, Ashby d1992 *NewYTBS 92*
Harper, Bland Harvey 1949- *WhoSSW 93*
Harper, Blaney *Law&B 92*
Harper, Carey Davis, III 1945- *St&PR 93*
Harper, Catherine Marie 1956- *WhoEmL 93*
Harper, Charles F. 1948- *St&PR 93*
Harper, Charles Michael *BioIn 17*
Harper, Charles Michael 1927- *St&PR 93*
Harper, Charles Michel 1927- *WhoAm 92, WhoWor 93*
Harper, Chris B. *Law&B 92*
Harper, Clyde Maurice 1931- *St&PR 93*
Harper, Conrad Kenneth 1940- *WhoAm 92*
Harper, Cynthia Anne 1936- *WhoAmW 93*
Harper, David Edwin 1939- *St&PR 93*
Harper, David Michael 1953- *WhoEmL 93, WhoSSW 93*
Harper, Dean Harrison 1929- *WhoAm 92*
Harper, Deborah Ann Flammer 1953- *WhoAmW 93*
Harper, Debra Kay 1963- *WhoAmW 93*
Harper, Delphine Bernice 1947- *WhoAmW 93, WhoE 93, WhoWor 93*
Harper, Denise Clonez 1955- *WhoEmL 93*
Harper, Derry *Law&B 92*
Harper, Don Ray 1926- *WhoSSW 93*
Harper, Donald Jack 1928- *St&PR 93*
Harper, Donald Victor 1927- *WhoAm 92*
Harper, Donna Akiba Sullivan 1954- *WhoSSW 93*
Harper, Douglas C. 1934- *WhoWrEP 92*
Harper, Doyal Alexander, Jr. 1944- *WhoAm 92*
Harper, Edward (James) 1941- *Baker 92*
Harper, Edwin Albert *Law&B 92*
Harper, Edwin Leland 1941- *WhoAm 92, WhoE 93*
Harper, Emery Walter 1936- *WhoAm 92*
Harper, Emma Jane 1935- *WhoAmW 93*
Harper, Ernest Bouldin, Jr. 1924- *St&PR 93*
Harper, Ernest Martin, Jr. *Law&B 92*
Harper, Fletcher 1806-1877 *JrnUS*
Harper, Frances 1825-1911 *GayN*
Harper, Frances Ellen Watkins 1825-1911 *AmWomWr 92, BioIn 17*
Harper, Genevieve *AmWomPl*
Harper, George Mills 1914- *ConAu 136, WhoAm 92*
Harper, George W. 1927- *ScF&FL 92*
Harper, Gerald 1945- *St&PR 93*
Harper, Gladys Coffey *WhoAm 92, WhoAmW 93*
Harper, Gwendolyn 1927- *WhoAmW 93*
Harper, Harlan, Jr. 1928- *WhoAm 92*
Harper, Harry 1880-1960 *ScF&FL 92*
Harper, Harry Clifford 1939- *St&PR 93*
Harper, Heather 1930- *OxDcOp*
Harper, Heather (Mary) 1930- *Baker 92, WhoAm 92, WhoWor 93*
Harper, Henry H. 1934- *WhoAm 92*
Harper, Howard Fyfe 1930- *WhoWor 93*
Harper, Howard M(orrall), Jr. 1930- *WhoWrEP 92*
Harper, Iva *BioIn 17*
Harper, James d1991 *BioIn 17*
Harper, James Allie, Jr. 1929- *WhoAm 92*
Harper, James Eugene 1940- *WhoAm 92*
Harper, James Roland 1918- *WhoSSW 93, WhoWor 93*
Harper, James Thomas 1949- *WhoEmL 93*
Harper, James Weldon, III 1937- *WhoE 93*
Harper, James William 1944- *St&PR 93*
Harper, Jane 1951- *WhoAmW 93*
Harper, Jane Armstrong 1942- *WhoSSW 93*
Harper, Janet Sutherlin Lane 1940- *WhoAm 92, WhoAmW 93*
Harper, Jene Paul 1910- *St&PR 93*
Harper, Jerry Warren, Jr. *Law&B 92*
Harper, Jewel Benton 1925- *WhoSSW 93*
Harper, John R. 1931- *St&PR 93*
Harper, John Ross *WhoScE 91-1*
Harper, Joseph Stafford 1959- *WhoSSW 93*
Harper, Judith C. *Law&B 92*
Harper, Judson Morse 1936- *WhoAm 92*
Harper, Kay Ann Bean Matthews 1955- *WhoEmL 93*
Harper, Lawrence Vernon 1935- *WhoAm 92*
Harper, Leonard A. 1920-1991 *BioIn 17*
Harper, Linda *WhoWrEP 92*
Harper, Lucy Lowrey *AmWomPl*
Harper, Lyndus E. 1905- *St&PR 93*
Harper, Malcolm Charles 1939- *WhoUN 92*
Harper, Margaret Earl 1924- *WhoAmW 93*
Harper, Margaret Mills 1957- *WhoSSW 93*
Harper, Marion 1916-1989 *BioIn 17*
Harper, Mary Sadler 1941- *St&PR 93, WhoAmW 93*
Harper, Michael John Kennedy 1935- *WhoAm 92, WhoSSW 93*
Harper, Michael S. *BioIn 17*
Harper, Norman Bernard 1923- *St&PR 93*
Harper, Patricia Ann 1957- *WhoAmW 93*
Harper, Peter S. *WhoScE 91-1*
Harper, Philip George *WhoScE 91-1*
Harper, Ralph Champlin 1916- *WhoAm 92*
Harper, Ralph E. *Law&B 92*
Harper, Richard *BioIn 17*
Harper, Richard Henry 1950- *WhoEmL 93, WhoWor 93*
Harper, Richard Russell 1944- *St&PR 93*
Harper, Robert *St&PR 93*
Harper, Robert Alexander 1924- *WhoAm 92*
Harper, Robert Allan 1915- *WhoAm 92*
Harper, Robert Gale 1944- *WhoSSW 93*
Harper, Robert Goodloe 1765-1825 *BioIn 17*
Harper, Robert James 1940- *WhoWor 93*
Harper, Robert Leslie 1939- *WhoAm 92*
Harper, Robert Stevens 1922- *WhoSSW 93*
Harper, Roger Alan 1955- *WhoWor 93*
Harper, Ron 1951- *WhoEmL 93*
Harper, Rory *ScF&FL 92*
Harper, Roy W. 1905- *WhoAm 92*
Harper, Ruth B. *AfrAmBi [port]*
Harper, S. Birnie 1944- *WhoAm 92*
Harper, Sandra Stecher 1952- *WhoAmW 93*
Harper, Sarah Watson 1942- *WhoSSW 93*
Harper, Shirley Fay 1943- *WhoSSW 93*
Harper, Spencer, III *Law&B 92*
Harper, Stephen Coale 1947- *WhoEmL 93, WhoSSW 93*
Harper, Stephen Lee *Law&B 92*
Harper, Sylvia K. 1949- *St&PR 93*
Harper, Tara K. *ScF&FL 92*
Harper, Ted Alan 1947- *WhoIns 93*
Harper, Thelma 1940- *WhoAmW 93*
Harper, Tim R. 1943- *WhoScE 91-1*
Harper, Valerie *BioIn 17*
Harper, Valerie 1940- *WhoAm 92*
Harper, W. Wayne *Law&B 92*
Harper, Walter Joseph 1947- *WhoAm 92*
Harper, William Charles *WhoSSW 93*
Harper, William Curtis 1942- *St&PR 93*
Harper, William H. 1934- *St&PR 93*
Harper, William Thomas, III 1956- *WhoEmL 93, WhoSSW 93, WhoWor 93*
Harper, Willie Miles 1950- *BiDAMSp 1989*
Harper, Wyatt Eugene, III 1946- *WhoEmL 93*
Harper, Zenola *Law&B 92*
Harpham, Virginia Ruth 1917- *WhoAm 92*
Harpin, Lorna Rae 1958- *WhoEmL 93*
Harpold, Lew *Law&B 92*
Harpole, B.C. 1934- *St&PR 93*
Harpole, Joseph Hunter 1924- *WhoSSW 93*
Harpole, Murray J. 1921- *St&PR 93*
Harpool, Robert Thomas, Jr. 1918- *St&PR 93*
Harps, Joseph P. *Law&B 92*
Harpster, James Erving 1923- *WhoSSW 93*
Harpster, Norman Ray 1951- *WhoE 93*
Harpum, Richard 1951- *WhoSSW 93*
Harpur, Gina *St&PR 93*
Harpur, Patrick *ScF&FL 92*
Harpur, Thomas William 1929- *ConAu 137*
Harpur, Tom *ConAu 137*
Harr, Clair H. 1939- *St&PR 93*
Harr, Karl Gottlieb, Jr. 1922- *WhoAm 92, WhoWor 93*
Harr, Lawrence F. *Law&B 92*
Harr, Lawrence F. 1938- *WhoIns 93*
Harr, Lawrence Francis 1938- *St&PR 93, WhoAm 92*
Harr, Lucy Loraine 1951- *WhoAm 92*
Harradine, Brian 1935- *WhoAsAP 91*
Harrah, Arnett A., III 1951- *WhoSSW 93*
Harrah, Colbert Dale 1948- *BiDAMSp 1989*
Harrah, Helen Faye 1953- *WhoAmW 93*
Harrah, Robert Eugene 1916- *WhoAm 92*
Harral, John Menteith 1948- *WhoAm 92*
Harralson, James G. *Law&B 92*
Harrap, Kenneth R. 1931- *WhoScE 91-1*
Harrawood, Paul 1928- *WhoAm 92*
Harre, Alan Frederick 1940- *WhoAm 92*
Harre, Wolfgang 1938- *WhoScE 91-3*
Harreis, Horst Hermann 1940- *WhoScE 91-3*
Harreld, J. Bruce 1950- *St&PR 93*
Harreld, James Bruce 1950- *WhoAm 92*
Harreld, Michael Neal 1944- *St&PR 93*
Harrell, Barbara R. *Law&B 92*
Harrell, Benjamin Carlton 1929- *WhoSSW 93*
Harrell, Brandon Hayes 1960- *St&PR 93*
Harrell, Bruce A. *Law&B 92*
Harrell, Charles Lydon, Jr. 1916- *WhoSSW 93, WhoWor 93*
Harrell, Charles M. 1928- *St&PR 93*
Harrell, Don W. 1938- *WhoIns 93*
Harrell, Earl *BioIn 17*
Harrell, Edward H. 1939- *St&PR 93*
Harrell, Edward Harding 1939- *WhoAm 92*
Harrell, Elizabeth Nunez- *BioIn 17*
Harrell, Ernest James 1936- *AfrAmBi, WhoAm 92*
Harrell, Gwen B. *Law&B 92*
Harrell, Henry Howze 1939- *St&PR 93, WhoAm 92, WhoSSW 93*
Harrell, Herman Lester 1933- *WhoSSW 93*
Harrell, Horace William 1947- *WhoEmL 93, WhoSSW 93*
Harrell, Irene Burk 1927- *WhoSSW 93, WhoWrEP 92*
Harrell, James Earl 1931- *WhoAm 92*
Harrell, James J. 1943- *St&PR 93*
Harrell, Janice 1945- *ConAu 138, SmATA 70 [port]*
Harrell, Jean Gabbert 1921- *WhoAmW 93*
Harrell, Jerry A. 1961- *WhoE 93*
Harrell, Jerry Wayne 1953- *WhoEmL 93*
Harrell, Lloyd Vernell 1944- *WhoSSW 93*
Harrell, Lyman Christian, III 1937- *St&PR 93*

Harrell, Lynn 1944- *Baker 92*
Harrell, Lynn Morris 1944- *WhoAm 92*
Harrell, Mack 1909-1960 *Baker 92*
Harrell, Melton L. 1940- *St&PR 93*
Harrell, Michele Yvonne 1955- *WhoAmW 93*
Harrell, Minnie *WhoSSW 93*
Harrell, Redin Paul 1932- *St&PR 93*
Harrell, Richard 1951- *St&PR 93*
Harrell, Roy Harrison, Jr. 1928- *WhoSSW 93, WhoWor 93*
Harrell, Royce D. 1945- *St&PR 93*
Harrell, Samuel Delargy 1958- *St&PR 93*
Harrell, Samuel M. 1931- *St&PR 93*
Harrell, Samuel Macy 1931- *WhoAm 92, WhoWor 93*
Harrell, Sara Gordon 1938- *ScF&FL 92*
Harrell, Sherri Jo 1955- *WhoAmW 93*
Harrell, Wanda Faye 1942- *WhoSSW 93*
Harrell, William Edward, Jr. 1948- *WhoEmL 93, WhoSSW 93*
Harrell, William G. 1922-1964 *BioIn 17*
Harrelson, Linda T. 1944- *WhoAmW 93*
Harrelson, Thomas William 1943- *WhoWor 93*
Harrelson, Walter Joseph 1919- *WhoAm 92, WhoSSW 93, WhoWor 93*
Harrelson, Woody *BioIn 17, WhoAm 92*
Harrelson, Woody 1962?- *ConTFT 10*
Harrer, Gustave Adolphus 1924- *WhoAm 92*
Harreus, Elizabeth Anne 1961- *WhoAmW 93*
Harreys, John Fisher 1933- *St&PR 93*
Harri, Mikko N.E. 1942- *WhoScE 91-4*
Harriau, Robert Raymond 1929- *St&PR 93*
Harrice, Nicholas Cy 1915- *WhoE 93*
Harrick, Jim *BioIn 17*
Harrie, Jeanne Ellen 1947- *WhoAmW 93*
Harries, Hugo James *WhoScE 91-1*
Harries, James 1978- *BioIn 17*
Harries, John V. *Law&B 92*
Harries, Karsten 1937- *WhoAm 92*
Harries, Michael *BioIn 17*
Harries, Paula *BioIn 17*
Harries-Jenkins, Gwyn 1931- *WhoWor 93*
Harriett, Judy Anne 1960- *WhoAmW 93*
Harriff, Suzanna Elizabeth 1953- *WhoEmL 93*
Harrigan, Anthony Hart 1925- *WhoAm 92*
Harrigan, Gail Labruzza 1951- *St&PR 93, WhoE 93*
Harrigan, John Frederick 1925- *WhoAm 92*
Harrigan, John Thomas, Jr. 1929- *WhoAm 92*
Harrigan, Kenneth W. 1927- *St&PR 93*
Harrigan, Kenneth William J. 1927- *WhoAm 92*
Harrigan, Laura G. 1953- *WhoAmW 93*
Harrigan, Susan *BioIn 17*
Harrigan, William Sweetser 1943- *St&PR 93*
Harriger, Gary C. *Law&B 92*
Harriger, Gary Carl 1940- *St&PR 93*
Harrigian, Harold 1935- *St&PR 93*
Harrill, Donald L. 1950- *St&PR 93*
Harriman, Arthur J. 1906-1991 *BioIn 17*
Harriman, Constance Bastine *WhoAm 92, WhoAmW 93*
Harriman, Edward Henry 1848-1909 *GayN*
Harriman, Gerald Eugene 1924- *WhoAm 92*
Harriman, John Howland 1920- *WhoAm 92*
Harriman, Lucy Lynn 1951- *WhoEmL 93*
Harriman, Malcolm Bruce 1950- *WhoSSW 93*
Harriman, Pamela *BioIn 17*
Harriman, Pamela Digby Churchill 1920- *WhoAm 92, WhoAmW 93*
Harriman, W. Averell 1891-1986 *ColdWar 1 [port]*
Harriman, William Averell 1891-1986 *DcTwHis*
Harring, Dean K. 1951- *WhoIns 93*
Harring, Dean Kenneth 1951- *WhoEmL 93*
Harring, Michael A. *Law&B 92*
Harringer, Olaf Carl 1919- *WhoAm 92*
Harrington, Alan 1919- *ScF&FL 92*
Harrington, Alan M. *Law&B 92*
Harrington, Barbara *ScF&FL 92*
Harrington, Barbara Sue 1957- *WhoSSW 93*
Harrington, Barry *ScF&FL 92*
Harrington, Bart, Jr. 1951- *WhoEmL 93*
Harrington, Benjamin Davis, Jr. 1952- *St&PR 93*
Harrington, Benjamin Franklin, III 1922- *WhoAm 92*
Harrington, Bob d1992 *NewYTBS 92*
Harrington, Bob 1950- *WhoE 93*
Harrington, Bruce Michael 1933- *WhoAm 92*
Harrington, Carol A. 1953- *WhoAmW 93*
Harrington, Charles T. *Law&B 92*
Harrington, Chester D., Jr. 1927- *St&PR 93*
Harrington, Cornelius Daniel, Jr. 1927- *St&PR 93*
Harrington, Craig Jerome 1957- *WhoEmL 93*
Harrington, Curtis *BioIn 17*
Harrington, Curtis 1928- *MiSFD 9*
Harrington, Daniel Leo John *Law&B 92*
Harrington, Daniel P. 1956- *St&PR 93*
Harrington, David 1949- *See* Kronos Quartet, The *News 93-1*
Harrington, Dean Butler *WhoAm 92*
Harrington, Diane Gail 1963- *WhoAmW 93, WhoWor 93*
Harrington, Donald C. 1912- *WhoAm 92*
Harrington, Donald James 1945- *WhoAm 92*
Harrington, Donald P. 1941- *WhoE 93*
Harrington, Edward F. 1933- *WhoAm 92, WhoE 93*
Harrington, Elizabeth Dallas 1965- *St&PR 93*
Harrington, Evaline *AmWomPl*
Harrington, Frances Ward d1990 *BioIn 17*
Harrington, Francis L. 1913- *St&PR 93*
Harrington, Fred Harvey 1912- *WhoAm 92*
Harrington, G. *WhoScE 91-1*
Harrington, Gary Burnes 1934- *WhoSSW 93, WhoWor 93*
Harrington, Gary Michael 1953- *WhoE 93*
Harrington, George Edward, Jr. 1948- *WhoSSW 93*
Harrington, George Fred 1923- *WhoSSW 93*
Harrington, George Walter 1914-1990 *BioIn 17*
Harrington, George William 1929- *WhoAm 92*
Harrington, Gerard, III 1956- *WhoE 93, WhoEmL 93*
Harrington, Geri *WhoWrEP 92*
Harrington, Geri Spolane *WhoE 93*
Harrington, Glenn Lewis 1942- *St&PR 93, WhoWor 93*
Harrington, Helen *AmWomPl*
Harrington, Herbert H. 1946- *WhoEmL 93, WhoWor 93*
Harrington, James P. *Law&B 92*
Harrington, James V. 1939- *St&PR 93*
Harrington, Jean Patrice *WhoAm 92*
Harrington, Jeremiah J. 1936- *St&PR 93*
Harrington, Jeremy Thomas 1932- *WhoAm 92*
Harrington, Jesse Moye, III 1940- *St&PR 93, WhoAm 92*
Harrington, John Charles 1955- *WhoEmL 93*
Harrington, John Malcolm *WhoScE 91-1*
Harrington, John Michael, Jr. 1921- *WhoAm 92*
Harrington, John Norris 1939- *WhoSSW 93*
Harrington, John P. 1952- *ConAu 138*
Harrington, John Peabody 1884-1961 *IntDcAn*
Harrington, John Timothy 1921- *WhoAm 92*
Harrington, John Vincent 1919- *WhoAm 92, WhoSSW 93*
Harrington, Joseph 1939- *St&PR 93*
Harrington, Joseph John 1937- *WhoAm 92*
Harrington, Kenneth Alan 1948- *WhoE 93*
Harrington, Kim M. *Law&B 92*
Harrington, LaMar 1917- *WhoAm 92*
Harrington, Lee K. 1946- *St&PR 93*
Harrington, Leonard 1922- *WhoIns 93*
Harrington, Margaret Helen 1945- *WhoAmW 93*
Harrington, Marguerite A. 1949- *St&PR 93*
Harrington, Marguerite Ann 1949- *WhoEmL 93*
Harrington, Marion Ray 1924- *WhoAm 92*
Harrington, Mary Evelina Paulson *WhoAmW 93*
Harrington, Matthew Jerome 1962- *WhoE 93, WhoEmL 93*
Harrington, Michael Francis 1916- *WhoAm 92*
Harrington, Michael Gerard 1930- *WhoScE 91-3*
Harrington, Michael James *Law&B 92*
Harrington, Michael P. 1936- *St&PR 93*
Harrington, Michaele Mary 1946- *WhoE 93, WhoEmL 93, WhoWor 93*
Harrington, Nancy D. *WhoAmW 93*
Harrington, Nancy Elaine 1955- *WhoEmL 93*
Harrington, Nancy Patricia 1938- *WhoAmW 93*
Harrington, Nancy T. *Law&B 92*
Harrington, Orville *BioIn 17*
Harrington, Othella *NewYTBS 92 [port]*
Harrington, Patricia Nichols 1948- *WhoAmW 93*
Harrington, Patrick, Jr. *WhoAm 92*
Harrington, Patrick Anthony *Law&B 92*
Harrington, Paul H. *Law&B 92*
Harrington, Peter Tyrus 1951- *WhoEmL 93*
Harrington, Phillip John, Jr. 1957- *WhoE 93*
Harrington, R.A. 1945- *St&PR 93*
Harrington, Rick A. *Law&B 92*
Harrington, Robert Dudley, Jr. 1932- *WhoE 93*
Harrington, Robert Sutton 1942- *WhoE 93*
Harrington, Roger Fuller 1925- *WhoAm 92*
Harrington, Ronald George 1940- *St&PR 93*
Harrington, Rory 1945- *WhoScE 91-3*
Harrington, Shaun Donald 1949- *St&PR 93*
Harrington, Susan Marie 1946- *WhoAmW 93*
Harrington, Sybil *BioIn 17*
Harrington, Theodore J. 1937- *St&PR 93*
Harrington, Thomas Daniel 1952- *WhoEmL 93, WhoSSW 93*
Harrington, Thomas Joseph 1935- *WhoAm 92*
Harrington, Thomas More 1937- *WhoWor 93*
Harrington, Thomas Neal 1953- *WhoEmL 93*
Harrington, Tim J., Jr. *Law&B 92*
Harrington, Timothy J. 1918- *WhoAm 92*
Harrington, William D. 1930- *St&PR 93*
Harrington, William Fields d1992 *NewYTBS 92*
Harrington, William Fields 1920- *WhoAm 92*
Harrington, William J. 1923-1992 *NewYTBS 92 [port]*
Harrington-Connors, Erin 1959- *WhoWrEP 92*
Harrington-Hughes, Kathryn 1955- *WhoWrEP 92*
Harrington-Lloyd, Jeanne Leigh *WhoWor 93*
Harrington-Lynn, John *WhoScE 91-1*
Harrington-Trenbeth, Joan 1935- *WhoAmW 93*
Harris, Aaron 1930- *WhoAm 92*
Harris, Abram Lincoln 1899-1963 *EncAACR*
Harris, Ada Leonora *AmWomPl*
Harris, Adrian Llewellyn 1950- *WhoWor 93*
Harris, Alan 1944- *ConAu 139, SmATA 71 [port]*
Harris, Albert Josiah 1908-1990 *BioIn 17*
Harris, Alfred 1919- *WhoAm 92*
Harris, Alfred Gene 1939- *St&PR 93*
Harris, Alfred Peter 1932- *WhoE 93*
Harris, Alison S. *Law&B 92*
Harris, Allan E. 1908- *St&PR 93*
Harris, Allen 1929- *WhoAm 92, WhoE 93, WhoWor 93*
Harris, Allen Lee *ScF&FL 92*
Harris, Allena *AmWomPl*
Harris, Andrew Van Vleet, Jr. 1953- *WhoEmL 93*
Harris, Anita Louise 1952- *WhoAmW 93*
Harris, Ann Birgitta Sutherland 1937- *WhoAm 92*
Harris, Ann Marie 1959- *WhoAmW 93, WhoEmL 93*
Harris, Ann S. *WhoAm 92*
Harris, Annie Elizabeth *AmWomPl*
Harris, Anthony Leonard *WhoScE 91-1*
Harris, Anthony Spencer 1900-1982 *BiDAMSp 1989*
Harris, April Lee 1953- *WhoSSW 93*
Harris, Arthur Travers 1892-1984 *HarEnMi*
Harris, Audrey Ellen 1916- *WhoWrEP 92*
Harris, Augustus 1852-1896 *OxDcOp*
Harris, Augustus (Henry Glossop) 1852-1896 *Baker 92*
Harris, Aurand 1915- *WhoAm 92*
Harris, Austin Francis 1928- *St&PR 93*
Harris, B. Clare 1937- *WhoAm 92*
Harris, B. Meyer 1910- *St&PR 93*
Harris, Ballard *Law&B 92*
Harris, Barbara 1930- *ConHero 2 [port]*
Harris, Barbara 1935- *WhoAm 92*
Harris, Barbara Ann 1951- *AfrAmBi [port], WhoEmL 93*
Harris, Barbara Anne 1962- *WhoAmW 93*
Harris, Barbara C. *BioIn 17*
Harris, Barbara Clementine 1930- *AfrAmBi, WhoAm 92, WhoAmW 93*
Harris, Barbara Jane 1953- *WhoAmW 93, WhoEmL 93*
Harris, Barbara S. 1927- *ScF&FL 92*
Harris, Barry Lee 1939- *St&PR 93*
Harris, Beaver 1936-1991 *BioIn 17*
Harris, Belinda Kay 1952- *WhoAmW 93*
Harris, Ben Maxwell 1923- *WhoAm 92*
Harris, Benjamin 1673-1716 *JrnUS*
Harris, Benjamin Harte, Jr. 1937- *WhoAm 92*
Harris, Benjamin Louis 1917- *WhoE 93*
Harris, Benjamin P., III 1936- *St&PR 93*
Harris, Bernard David 1956- *St&PR 93*
Harris, Bernard P. 1918- *St&PR 93*
Harris, Bernice Eisen 1927- *WhoE 93*
Harris, Bernice Ellen 1957- *WhoAmW 93*
Harris, Betty *SoulM*
Harris, Betty Wesson 1930- *WhoSSW 93*
Harris, Bill Jasper 1947- *WhoSSW 93*
Harris, Bob J. 1926- *WhoSSW 93*
Harris, Brian *ScF&FL 92*
Harris, Brian Craig 1941- *WhoE 93, WhoWor 93*
Harris, Brooks Arthur 1959- *WhoSSW 93*
Harris, Bruce Eugene 1950- *WhoEmL 93*
Harris, Bryan *WhoScE 91-1*
Harris, Burt Irving 1922- *WhoAm 92*
Harris, Burton Henry 1941- *WhoE 93*
Harris, C.F. *WhoScE 91-1*
Harris, C. Ian *WhoScE 91-1*
Harris, C. Philip 1949- *St&PR 93*
Harris, Carl R. 1951- *St&PR 93*
Harris, Carmon Coleman 1904- *WhoAm 92*
Harris, Carol Margaret 1947- *WhoAmW 93*
Harris, Carole Casey *Law&B 92*
Harris, Cassandra *BioIn 17*
Harris, Charlene Durae 1961- *WhoAmW 93*
Harris, Charles Alan 1953- *WhoSSW 93*
Harris, Charles Edgar 1915- *WhoAm 92, WhoSSW 93*
Harris, Charles Edison 1946- *WhoAm 92*
Harris, Charles Elmer 1922- *WhoAm 92*
Harris, Charles Frederick 1934- *WhoAm 92*
Harris, Charles Keith 1961- *WhoSSW 93*
Harris, Charles Randy 1954- *St&PR 93*
Harris, Charles Thomas 1943- *WhoAm 92*
Harris, Charles Upchurch 1914- *WhoWor 93*
Harris, Charles Ward 1926- *WhoAm 92*
Harris, Chauncy Dennison 1914- *WhoAm 92, WhoWor 93*
Harris, Cheryl Montgomery 1949- *WhoWor 93*
Harris, Chester 1938- *WhoSSW 93*
Harris, Christie 1907- *WhoCanL 92*
Harris, Christie (Lucy) Irwin 1907- *MajAI [port]*
Harris, Christie Lucy 1907- *WhoAm 92, WhoWrEP 92*
Harris, Christie (Lucy Irwin) 1907- *DcChlFi*
Harris, Christopher 1933- *WhoAm 92*
Harris, Clare Winger 1891-1968 *ScF&FL 92*
Harris, Claude 1940- *CngDr 91, WhoAm 92, WhoSSW 93*
Harris, Claudia Lucas *AmWomPl*
Harris, Clifford John 1948- *WhoWor 93*
Harris, Clifton Dunn, Jr. *Law&B 92*
Harris, Colin Cyril 1928- *WhoAm 92*
Harris, Conrad Michael *WhoScE 91-1*
Harris, Coralee 1954- *St&PR 93*
Harris, Craig *BioIn 17*
Harris, Curtis B., Jr. 1944- *St&PR 93*
Harris, Cynthia M. 1934- *WhoAmW 93*
Harris, Cyril Manton *WhoAm 92, WhoE 93*
Harris, D. George 1933- *WhoAm 92*
Harris, D.M. *Law&B 92*
Harris, Dale Benner 1914- *WhoAm 92*
Harris, Dale Hutter 1932- *WhoAmW 93*
Harris, Dale Ray 1937- *WhoAm 92*
Harris, Damian *MiSFD 9*
Harris, Daniel, Jr. *Law&B 92*
Harris, Daniel E. *Law&B 92*
Harris, Darryl L. 1951- *St&PR 93*
Harris, Darryl Wayne 1941- *WhoAm 92*
Harris, David Golightly 1824-1875 *BioIn 17*
Harris, David Henry 1924- *WhoAm 92*
Harris, David Joel 1950- *WhoWor 93*
Harris, David Mayer 1944- *St&PR 93*
Harris, David P. 1937- *St&PR 93*
Harris, Dawn Francine 1935- *WhoSSW 93*
Harris, Dawn Stewart *Law&B 92*
Harris, Debbie Crabtree 1950- *WhoAmW 93*
Harris, Deborah Turner 1951- *ScF&FL 92*
Harris, Debra Lynne 1956- *WhoAmW 93*
Harris, Denise Koppelman 1953- *WhoEmL 93*
Harris, Denny *MiSFD 9*
Harris, Diana Koffman 1929- *WhoAmW 93*
Harris, Diane 1947- *WhoEmL 93*
Harris, Diane Carol 1942- *St&PR 93, WhoAm 92, WhoAmW 93*
Harris, Diane Feuillan 1932- *WhoWrEP 92*

Harris, Don Victor, Jr. 1921- WhoAm 92
Harris, Donald 1931- Baker 92, WhoAm 92
Harris, Donald Dean 1943- WhoSSW 93
Harris, Donald Leonard 1966- WhoSSW 93
Harris, Donald Wayne 1948- WhoSSW 93
Harris, Donald Wilson 1927- WhoSSW 93
Harris, Donna Adams Law&B 92
Harris, Donna Lee 1949- WhoAmW 93
Harris, Donna M. Law&B 92
Harris, Dorothy Clark 1949- WhoAm 92, WhoAmW 93
Harris, Dorthy Forbes 1944- WhoSSW 93
Harris, Douglas Clay 1939- St&PR 93, WhoAm 92
Harris, Douglas E. Law&B 92
Harris, Douglas J. 1955- St&PR 93
Harris, Dunstan Alexander 1947- WhoWrEP 92
Harris, Dwayne Matthew 1967- WhoE 93
Harris, E. Burt Law&B 92
Harris, E. Ray Law&B 92
Harris, Earl Douglas 1947- WhoSSW 93
Harris, Earl Edward 1931- WhoAm 92
Harris, Earl F. 1921- St&PR 93
Harris, Earl Lynn 1941- AfrAmBi
Harris, Earle H. 1906-1990 BioIn 17
Harris, Edna Mae 1950- WhoWrEP 92
Harris, Edna May 1900- AmWomPl
Harris, Edward Allen 1950- WhoAm 92
Harris, Edward D., Jr. 1937- WhoAm 92
Harris, Edward L. AfrAmBi
Harris, Eldon Dwayne 1938- St&PR 93
Harris, Elihu Mason 1947- WhoAm 92
Harris, Elizabeth 1944- ConAu 136
Harris, Elizabeth Ann Law&B 92
Harris, Elizabeth Ann 1957- WhoEmL 93
Harris, Elizabeth Claudia 1942- WhoE 93
Harris, Elizabeth Holder 1944- WhoAm 92
Harris, Elizabeth Jane 1964- WhoAmW 93
Harris, Ella Mae 1930- WhoSSW 93
Harris, Ellen Gandy 1910- WhoAm 92, WhoWor 93
Harris, Elliott Stanley 1922- WhoAm 92
Harris, Elmer Beseler 1939- WhoAm 92
Harris, Emily Katharine WhoWrEP 92
Harris, Emma Earl 1936- WhoAmW 93
Harris, Emmylou BioIn 17
Harris, Emmylou 1947- Baker 92, WhoAm 92, WhoAmW 93
Harris, Eric I. Law&B 92
Harris, Eva Pittard 1955- WhoAmW 93
Harris, Everett 1916- St&PR 93
Harris, Frances Helen AmWomPl
Harris, Francesca Treppeda 1958- WhoAmW 93, WhoE 93
Harris, Franco 1950- BioIn 17
Harris, Frank MiSFD 9
Harris, Frank, III 1956- WhoWrEP 92
Harris, Frank C. WhoScE 91-1
Harris, Frank J.T. 1927- WhoScE 91-1
Harris, Fred R. 1930- PolPar, WhoAm 92
Harris, Frederick George 1922- WhoAm 92
Harris, Frederick Holladay 1949- WhoSSW 93
Harris, Frederick John 1943- WhoE 93
Harris, Gail Pilley 1941- WhoAmW 93
Harris, Gary Brooks 1955- WhoEmL 93, WhoSSW 93
Harris, Gary W. Law&B 92
Harris, Gayle Marie 1954- WhoAmW 93
Harris, Geneva Duke 1946- WhoAmW 93
Harris, George Clinton 1925- WhoAm 92
Harris, Geraldine 1951- ScF&FL 92
Harris, Glen WhoAm 92
Harris, Glenda Stange 1954- WhoSSW 93
Harris, Glynda J. 1937- St&PR 93
Harris, Gordon ScF&FL 92
Harris, Gregory Scott 1955- WhoAm 92
Harris, Guy D. 1943- St&PR 93
Harris, Harold Daniel 1942- St&PR 93
Harris, Harriett Smitherman 1932- WhoAmW 93
Harris, Harry 1922- MiSFD 9
Harris, Harwell Hamilton 1903-1990 BioIn 17
Harris, Hazel Harper AmWomPl
Harris, Henry WhoScE 91-1
Harris, Henry Hiter, Jr. 1922- WhoAm 92
Harris, Henry U., Jr. 1926- St&PR 93
Harris, Henry Upham, Jr. 1926- WhoAm 92
Harris, Henry William 1919- WhoAm 92
Harris, Henry Wood 1938- WhoAm 92
Harris, Hollis Loyd 1931- St&PR 93, WhoAm 92
Harris, Holton E. 1923- St&PR 93
Harris, Howard E. BioIn 17
Harris, Howard E. 1929- St&PR 93
Harris, Howard Elliott 1943- WhoAm 92
Harris, Howard Hunter 1924- WhoAm 92
Harris, Howard S. Law&B 92
Harris, Hoyt Clark 1920- WhoSSW 93
Harris, Hugh BioIn 17
Harris, Hyde ConTFT 10
Harris, Irving 1927- WhoAm 92, WhoWor 93
Harris, Irving Brooks 1910- BioIn 17, St&PR 93, WhoAm 92
Harris, Isaac Henson 1912- WhoAm 92
Harris, Israel 1770-1816 BioIn 17
Harris, J. Robin 1926- WhoAm 92
Harris, J. Roy 1901- St&PR 93
Harris, Jack Howard, II 1945- WhoWor 93
Harris, Jacob George 1938- WhoAm 92
Harris, Jacqueline L. 1929- BioIn 17
Harris, James 1709-1780 BioIn 17
Harris, James B. 1928- MiSFD 9
Harris, James Carroll, II 1951- WhoEmL 93, WhoSSW 93
Harris, James Dexter 1919- WhoAm 92
Harris, James Edward 1947- WhoSSW 93
Harris, James Franklin 1941- WhoAm 92
Harris, James Fulbright 1929- WhoE 93
Harris, James H. Law&B 92
Harris, James H. 1942- St&PR 93
Harris, James Herman 1942- WhoWor 93
Harris, James Jeffrey Law&B 92
Harris, James Martin 1928- WhoAm 92
Harris, James Stewart, Jr. 1942- WhoAm 92
Harris, Jana N. 1947- WhoWrEP 92
Harris, Jane Yancey AmWomPl
Harris, Janel Kay 1949- WhoAmW 93
Harris, Janet 1932-1979 ScF&FL 92
Harris, Janine Law&B 92
Harris, Jared BioIn 17
Harris, Jay Howard 1936- WhoAm 92
Harris, Jean BioIn 17
Harris, Jean Louise 1931- WhoAm 92, WhoAmW 93
Harris, Jean O'Brien 1951- WhoAmW 93
Harris, Jean (S.) 1923- ConAu 137
Harris, Jed Gilbert, Jr. 1954- WhoSSW 93
Harris, Jeffrey 1944- WhoAm 92
Harris, Jeffrey Earl 1948- WhoE 93
Harris, Jeffrey Sherman 1944- WhoAm 92
Harris, Jenny Lou 1948- WhoSSW 93
Harris, Jerilyn Rolinson 1942- WhoAmW 93
Harris, Jerome Sylvan 1909- WhoAm 92
Harris, Jerrold B. 1942- WhoAm 92
Harris, Jessie G. 1909- WhoAmW 93
Harris, Joan Patricia 1930- St&PR 93
Harris, Joan White 1931- WhoAmW 93
Harris, Joe Frank 1936- WhoAm 92, WhoSSW 93, WhoWor 93
Harris, Joel Bruce 1941- WhoAm 92
Harris, Joel Chandler 1848-1908 BioIn 17, ConAu 137, GayN, JrnUS, MajAI [port]
Harris, Johana 1913- See Harris, Roy (Leroy Ellsworth) 1898-1979 Baker 92
Harris, Johanna Law&B 92
Harris, Johanna 1879-1964 BioIn 17
Harris, John 1916-1991 AnObit 1991, ScF&FL 92
Harris, John A. 1932- St&PR 93
Harris, John Allen 1962- WhoEmL 93
Harris, John B. 1940- WhoScE 91-1
Harris, John Beynon ScF&FL 92
Harris, John Bunyan, III 1952- WhoEmL 93
Harris, John Charles 1943- WhoAm 92
Harris, John Clinton, Jr. 1946- WhoEmL 93
Harris, John Corydon 1947- St&PR 93
Harris, John Edward 1936- WhoAm 92
Harris, John Fitzgerald Law&B 92
Harris, John Kenneth 1948- WhoE 93
Harris, John N. 1939- St&PR 93
Harris, John Patrick 1942- WhoE 93, WhoWor 93
Harris, John William 1920- WhoAm 92
Harris, John Woods 1893- WhoSSW 93, WhoWor 93
Harris, John Wyndham Parkes Lucas Beynon 1903-1969 BioIn 17
Harris, Jonathan David Law&B 92
Harris, Jonathan M. 1947- St&PR 93
Harris, Jonathan Mark 1948- WhoEmL 93
Harris, Jordan WhoAm 92
Harris, Joseph 1918- WhoWrEP 92
Harris, Joseph Lamar 1951- WhoEmL 93, WhoSSW 93
Harris, Joseph P. 1935- St&PR 93
Harris, Judith Ann White 1939- WhoWor 93
Harris, Judith Hill 1949- WhoAmW 93
Harris, Judith Lynn Law&B 92
Harris, Jules Eli 1934- WhoAm 92
Harris, Julie BioIn 17
Harris, Julie 1925- WhoAm 92
Harris, June Starkey 1932- St&PR 93
Harris, K. David 1927- WhoAm 92
Harris, K.M. WhoScE 91-1
Harris, Karen H(arriman) 1934- WhoWrEP 92
Harris, Karen Kostock 1942- St&PR 93, WhoAmW 93
Harris, Katherine Leidel 1954- WhoAmW 93, WhoEmL 93
Harris, Kathleen Law&B 92
Harris, Kathryn R. AmWomPl
Harris, Kathy Wilson 1958- WhoAmW 93
Harris, Keith Dwain 1938- St&PR 93
Harris, Keith Edward Law&B 92
Harris, Kenneth David d1992 BioIn 17
Harris, Kenneth Henry 1956- WhoSSW 93
Harris, Kerry Francis Patrick 1941- WhoSSW 93
Harris, Kevin J. 1953- WhoWrEP 92
Harris, Kim Sutherland 1952- St&PR 93
Harris, Kimberly Anne 1965- WhoEmL 93
Harris, King W. 1943- St&PR 93
Harris, Lara BioIn 17
Harris, Lawrence Kenneth 1935- WhoWor 93
Harris, Lenore Zobel 1944- WhoAmW 93
Harris, Leon A., Jr. 1926- WhoAm 92
Harris, Leonard 1927- St&PR 93
Harris, Leonard 1929- ScF&FL 92
Harris, Leonard R. 1922-1991 BioIn 17
Harris, Lillian AmWomPl
Harris, Linda Gaye 1964- WhoAmW 93
Harris, Linda Kay 1947- WhoAmW 93, WhoEmL 93
Harris, Linda M. Law&B 92
Harris, Lloyd G. Law&B 92
Harris, Lorraine 1955- WhoAmW 93
Harris, Louis 1902-1970 BioIn 17
Harris, Louis 1921- WhoAm 92
Harris, Louis A. 1932- St&PR 93
Harris, Louis Selig 1927- WhoWor 93
Harris, Louise 1903- WhoE 93
Harris, Loyd Ervin 1900- WhoSSW 93
Harris, Lucy AmWomPl
Harris, Lucy Brown 1924- WhoAmW 93
Harris, Lula Marie Irene 1962- WhoAmW 93
Harris, Lynn Farmer 1948- WhoSSW 93
Harris, Lyttleton Tazwell, IV 1940- WhoSSW 93
Harris, M.M. 1916- St&PR 93
Harris, Mac Donald 1921- WhoWrEP 92
Harris, MacDonald 1921- ScF&FL 92
Harris, Madalene Ruth 1925- WhoWrEP 92
Harris, Major SoulM
Harris, Malcolm WhoScE 91-1
Harris, Marc Matthew 1965- WhoWor 93
Harris, Marcelite Jordan 1943- WhoAm 92, WhoAmW 93
Harris, Margaret 1943- WhoAm 92, WhoAmW 93, WhoWor 93
Harris, Marie 1943- WhoWrEP 92
Harris, Marie-Therese 1939- WhoWrEP 92
Harris, Marilyn WhoAmW 93
Harris, Marilyn 1931- DcAmChF 1960, ScF&FL 92
Harris, Marilyn Irene 1938- WhoAmW 93
Harris, Marion Hopkins 1938- WhoAmW 93
Harris, Mark 1922- JeAmFiW, WhoAm 92, WhoWrEP 92
Harris, Mark 1960- ScF&FL 92
Harris, Mark Jonathan 1941- DcAmChF 1960, WhoWrEP 92
Harris, Martha G. 1943- WhoWrEP 92
Harris, Martin Harvey 1932- WhoAm 92
Harris, Martin Seymour 1935- WhoE 93
Harris, Martyn Rutherford WhoScE 91-1
Harris, Marvin 1927- WhoWrEP 92
Harris, Mary B. 1933- WhoAmW 93
Harris, Mary Bierman 1943- WhoAmW 93
Harris, Matthew Jeffrey 1959- St&PR 93
Harris, Maury Norton 1947- WhoAm 92
Harris, May AmWomPl
Harris, May Pashley AmWomPl
Harris, Mel BioIn 17, ConTFT 10, WhoAm 92
Harris, Melanie Gause 1949- WhoWrEP 92
Harris, Melba Iris 1945- WhoSSW 93
Harris, Melissa Jane 1959- WhoSSW 93
Harris, Melva J. 1944- WhoE 93
Harris, Merry WhoWrEP 92
Harris, Micalyn Shafer 1941- WhoAmW 93, WhoE 93, WhoWor 93
Harris, Michael BioIn 17
Harris, Michael 1944- WhoCanL 92
Harris, Michael James 1954- WhoEmL 93
Harris, Michael Philip WhoScE 91-1
Harris, Michael S. Law&B 92
Harris, Michael William Greville WhoScE 91-1
Harris, Mildred 1903- WhoWrEP 92
Harris, Mildred Willis AmWomPl
Harris, Miles Fitzgerald 1913- WhoE 93
Harris, Milton 1906-1991 BioIn 17
Harris, Milton M. 1916- WhoAm 92
Harris, N. Stuart 1967- WhoWor 93
Harris, Nancy 1950- St&PR 93
Harris, Natholyn Dalton 1939- WhoAmW 93
Harris, Neil 1938- WhoAm 92
Harris, Neil Patrick BioIn 17
Harris, Neison 1915- St&PR 93, WhoAm 92
Harris, Nell H. WhoAm 92
Harris, Nelson G. 1926- St&PR 93
Harris, Nelson George 1926- WhoAm 92
Harris, Neville Robert 1938- WhoScE 91-3
Harris, Nicholas George 1939- WhoAm 92
Harris, Norman Duncan Campany WhoScE 91-1
Harris, Ola Winifred Moulton 1917- WhoAmW 93
Harris, Orville Jeff, Jr. 1937- WhoSSW 93
Harris, P. Stephen Law&B 92
Harris, Pamela Marcia 1964- WhoAmW 93
Harris, Patricia 1924-1985 BioIn 17
Harris, Patricia Ann 1959- WhoScE 91-1
Harris, Patricia Roberts 1924- AfrAmBi
Harris, Patricia Roberts 1924-1985 EncAACR [port]
Harris, Patricia Steele 1958- WhoAmW 93
Harris, Patricia Stewart 1950- WhoSSW 93
Harris, Patrick Donald 1940- WhoAm 92
Harris, Paul 1925- WhoAm 92
Harris, Paul Lynwood, Jr. 1945- WhoAm 92
Harris, Paul N. Law&B 92
Harris, Paul S. 1945- St&PR 93
Harris, Paul Smith 1935- WhoE 93
Harris, Paul Stewart 1906- WhoAm 92
Harris, Peggy Aline 1948- WhoAmW 93
Harris, Penelope Claire 1952- WhoAmW 93
Harris, Penny Smith 1941- WhoE 93
Harris, Peter J. BioIn 17
Harris, Peter James WhoScE 91-1
Harris, Peter Quincy 1947- WhoEmL 93
Harris, Philip Edwin 1947- WhoE 93
Harris, Philip John 1926- WhoAm 92
Harris, Philip Robert 1926- WhoAm 92
Harris, Priscilla A. Law&B 92
Harris, R. Eleanor M. WhoAmW 93
Harris, R. Jeffrey Law&B 92
Harris, R. Robert Law&B 92
Harris, R. Robert 1933- WhoAm 92
Harris, Ralph F. 1951- St&PR 93
Harris, Randy A. WhoAm 92
Harris, Randy Hayes 1956- WhoE 93
Harris, Randy Jay 1946- WhoWor 93
Harris, Raymond 1953- ScF&FL 92
Harris, Raymond Jesse 1916- WhoE 93, WhoWor 93
Harris, Raymond Richard WhoScE 91-1
Harris, Reese H., Jr. 1911- St&PR 93
Harris, Rhonda Kidd 1957- St&PR 93
Harris, Rhonda L. 1966- WhoAmW 93
Harris, Richard 1932- MiSFD 9
Harris, Richard 1933- IntDcF 2-3 [port], WhoAm 92
Harris, Richard Foster, Jr. 1918- WhoAm 92, WhoSSW 93
Harris, Richard Foster, III 1942- WhoSSW 93
Harris, Richard Franklin 1940- St&PR 93, WhoIns 93
Harris, Richard Guy Law&B 92
Harris, Richard Hayden 1928- St&PR 93
Harris, Richard J. Law&B 92
Harris, Richard John 1936- St&PR 93, WhoAm 92
Harris, Richard Lee 1928- WhoAm 92
Harris, Richard Max 1935- WhoAm 92
Harris, Richard Steven 1949- WhoEmL 93
Harris, Robert Law&B 92
Harris, Robert 1952- WhoAm 92
Harris, Robert Allen 1938- WhoAm 92
Harris, Robert Allison 1939- WhoAm 92
Harris, Robert Alton BioIn 17
Harris, Robert Charles 1952- WhoE 93
Harris, Robert D. Law&B 92
Harris, Robert Edward 1940- WhoSSW 93
Harris, Robert Glen 1933- St&PR 93
Harris, Robert Laird 1911- WhoAm 92
Harris, Robert Lewis Law&B 92
Harris, Robert Norman 1920- WhoAm 92
Harris, Roberta Lucas 1916- WhoAmW 93
Harris, Robin SmATA 71
Harris, Robin 1953-1990 BioIn 17
Harris, Robin Kingsley WhoScE 91-1
Harris, Robin Kingsley 1936- WhoWor 93
Harris, Robin Rose 1963- WhoE 93
Harris, Rodney WhoScE 91-1
Harris, Roger Clark 1938- WhoE 93
Harris, Roger Noel 1933- WhoUN 92
Harris, Roger S. 1930- WhoAm 92
Harris, Ronald David 1938- WhoAm 92
Harris, Ronald Harvey 1947- St&PR 93
Harris, Ronell F. 1934- St&PR 93
Harris, Rosa S. AmWomPl

Harris, Rosalie 1937- *WhoAmW 93*
Harris, Rosalind Dale *ScF&FL 92*
Harris, Rosemary 1923- *ScF&FL 92*
Harris, Rosemary Ann 1930- *WhoAm 92*
Harris, Roy 1898- *BioIn 17*
Harris, Roy Hartley 1928- *WhoAm 92*
Harris, Roy (Leroy Ellsworth) 1898-1979 *Baker 92*
Harris, Ruby Lee 1939- *WhoAmW 93*
Harris, Rue M. 1931- *St&PR 93*
Harris, Ruth Berman 1916- *WhoAm 92, WhoAmW 93*
Harris, Ruth Ellen Beall 1947- *WhoE 93*
Harris, Ruth Josell 1947- *St&PR 93*
Harris, Ruth Ruhr 1927- *WhoAmW 93*
Harris, Samuel d1789 *BioIn 17*
Harris, Sandra Ann 1944- *WhoE 93*
Harris, Sandra Lee 1942- *WhoE 93*
Harris, Sharon Mae 1957- *WhoAm 92*
Harris, Sharon Marie 1949- *WhoAmW 93*
Harris, Shelley Follansbee 1949- *WhoAmW 93*
Harris, Shirley *Law&B 92*
Harris, Stacy *WhoAm 92, WhoAmW 93, WhoWrEP 92*
Harris, Stanley S. 1927- *CngDr 91, WhoAm 92*
Harris, Stephen 1945- *WhoScE 91-3*
Harris, Stephen E. 1943- *St&PR 93*
Harris, Stephen Ernest 1936- *WhoAm 92*
Harris, Steve 1954- *ScF&FL 92*
Harris, Steven Michael 1952- *WhoEmL 93*
Harris, Stuart d1991 *BioIn 17*
Harris, Susan *BioIn 17, WhoAm 92, WhoAmW 93*
Harris, Susan Fox 1955- *WhoAmW 93*
Harris, Susan Hunt 1959- *WhoAmW 93*
Harris, Susan L. *Law&B 92*
Harris, Susan Louise *WhoAm 92*
Harris, Susanna 1919- *WhoE 93*
Harris, Suzanne Straight 1944- *WhoAm 92*
Harris, Sydney Malcolm 1917- *WhoAm 92*
Harris, T. George 1924- *WhoAm 92, WhoWrEP 92*
Harris, Temple W. 1948- *St&PR 93*
Harris, Teresa Yvonne 1953- *WhoAmW 93*
Harris, Terry G. 1947- *WhoSSW 93*
Harris, Theodore Edward 1919- *WhoAm 92*
Harris, Theodore Wilson 1921- *BioIn 17*
Harris, Thomas 1940- *BioIn 17*
Harris, Thomas Everett 1912- *WhoAm 92*
Harris, Thomas L. 1931- *St&PR 93, WhoAm 92*
Harris, Thomas Laxson 1943- *WhoSSW 93*
Harris, Thomas R., Jr. 1931- *St&PR 93*
Harris, Thomas Raymond 1937- *WhoAm 92*
Harris, Thomas Sarafen 1947- *WhoEmL 93, WhoWor 93*
Harris, Tim *ConTFT 10*
Harris, Timothy 1946- *ConTFT 10*
Harris, Timothy Francis 1948- *St&PR 93*
Harris, Timothy John Roy 1950- *WhoWor 93*
Harris, Timothy Patrick *Law&B 92*
Harris, Tom P. 1951- *St&PR 93*
Harris, Tracey E. 1967- *WhoSSW 93*
Harris, Tracy B. *Law&B 92*
Harris, Trent *MiSFD 9*
Harris, Trudier 1948- *ConAu 40NR*
Harris, Vera Evelyn 1932- *WhoAmW 93*
Harris, (William) Victor 1869-1943 *Baker 92*
Harris, Vincent Crockett 1913- *WhoAm 92*
Harris, W. Alden 1932- *St&PR 93*
Harris, W. David *Law&B 92*
Harris, W. Wayne 1946- *WhoSSW 93*
Harris, Walte Davis 1936- *WhoE 93*
Harris, Walter 1925- *ScF&FL 92*
Harris, Walter E. d1990 *BioIn 17*
Harris, Walter Edgar 1915- *WhoAm 92*
Harris, Warren Wayne 1962- *WhoSSW 93, WhoWor 93*
Harris, Wayne Manley 1925- *WhoAm 92*
Harris, Wayne W. *Law&B 92*
Harris, Wendell B., Jr. *MiSFD 9*
Harris, Wendell V. 1932- *WhoE 93*
Harris, Wesley L. 1941- *WhoSSW 93*
Harris, Whitney Robson 1912- *WhoAm 92*
Harris, Wiley Lee 1949- *WhoE 93*
Harris, Wilhelmina d1991 *BioIn 17*
Harris, William Cecil 1913- *WhoAm 92*
Harris, William E. d1991 *BioIn 17*
Harris, William Edward 1961- *WhoEmL 93*
Harris, William Enoch, Jr. 1955- *WhoSSW 93*
Harris, William G. d1991 *NewYTBS 92*
Harris, William Gibson, II 1944- *WhoAm 92*
Harris, William Hamilton 1927- *WhoAm 92*
Harris, William Hamilton 1944- *WhoSSW 93*
Harris, William J. 1944- *WhoScE 91-1*
Harris, William James, Jr. 1918- *WhoAm 92*
Harris, William John 1928- *WhoAm 92*
Harris, William McKinley 1941- *WhoWor 93*
Harris, William Norman 1952- *WhoE 93, WhoEmL 93*
Harris, William North 1938- *WhoE 93, WhoSSW 93, WhoWor 93*
Harris, William S. 1938- *St&PR 93*
Harris, William Thomas d1989 *BioIn 17*
Harris, William Vernon 1938- *WhoAm 92*
Harris, Wilson 1921- *BioIn 17, ConAu 16AS [port], IntLitE*
Harris, (Theodore) Wilson 1921- *DcLB 117 [port]*
Harris, Y. L. *ConAu 138*
Harris, Yvonne L. *ConAu 138*
Harris-Ching, Raymond 1939- *BioIn 17*
Harrises, Antonio Efthemios 1926- *WhoE 93*
Harris-Hobbs, Bernice Lee 1946- *WhoSSW 93*
Harris-Holloway, Geraldine 1958- *WhoEmL 93*
Harrison, Alan *WhoScE 91-1*
Harrison, Alan V. 1952- *St&PR 93*
Harrison, Allen 1940- *St&PR 93*
Harrison, Anna Jane 1912- *WhoAm 92, WhoAmW 93*
Harrison, Anna Symmes 1775-1864 *BioIn 17*
Harrison, Barbara Grizzuti *BioIn 17*
Harrison, Barbara Grizzuti 1934- *WhoAm 92*
Harrison, Barry 1951- *WhoWor 93*
Harrison, Beatrice 1892-1965 *Baker 92*
Harrison, Beatrice Marie 1958- *WhoWor 93*
Harrison, Benjamin 1833-1901 *BioIn 17, GayN, PolPar*
Harrison, Benjamin Leslie 1928- *WhoAm 92*
Harrison, Betty Carolyn Cook 1939- *WhoAmW 93*
Harrison, Brenda Carole Vogelsang 1942- *WhoSSW 93*
Harrison, Bryan Desmond 1931- *WhoWor 93*
Harrison, Byron Patton 1881-1941 *PolPar*
Harrison, Carl W. 1936- *St&PR 93*
Harrison, Carol Lynn 1946- *WhoAmW 93*
Harrison, Caroline Scott 1832-1892 *BioIn 17*
Harrison, Carter Henry 1935- *WhoAm 92*
Harrison, Charles Edgar 1926- *St&PR 93*
Harrison, Charles Edward 1923- *WhoWrEP 92*
Harrison, Charles J. *Law&B 92*
Harrison, Charles Maurice 1927- *WhoAm 92*
Harrison, Charles Robert, Jr. 1957- *WhoE 93*
Harrison, Charles Wagner, Jr. 1913- *WhoAm 92, WhoWor 93*
Harrison, Charles William 1940- *St&PR 93*
Harrison, Christine Delane 1947- *WhoAmW 93*
Harrison, Christopher George Alick 1936- *WhoSSW 93*
Harrison, Clifford Joy, Jr. 1925- *WhoAm 92*
Harrison, Colin 1945- *WhoWor 93*
Harrison, Colin 1960- *ConAu 138*
Harrison, Colin Young 1960- *WhoE 93*
Harrison, Constance Cary 1843-1920 *AmWomPl*
Harrison, Craig 1942- *ScF&FL 92*
Harrison, Craig Donald 1956- *WhoEmL 93, WhoWor 93*
Harrison, David James 1959- *WhoWor 93*
Harrison, David Keith *WhoScE 91-1*
Harrison, David Lee 1937- *St&PR 93*
Harrison, David Lombard 1953- *WhoEmL 93*
Harrison, David Wesley 1954- *WhoEmL 93*
Harrison, Deborah Ann 1957- *WhoAmW 93*
Harrison, Denise Lee 1960- *WhoAmW 93*
Harrison, Don E. 1927-1988 *BioIn 17*
Harrison, Donald *BioIn 17*
Harrison, Donald 1928- *WhoE 93*
Harrison, Donald Carey 1934- *WhoAm 92*
Harrison, Donald Frederick Norris, Sir *WhoScE 91-1*
Harrison, Donald Gilmour 1920- *St&PR 93*
Harrison, Dorothy Wood 1935- *WhoSSW 93*
Harrison, Douglas Edwin 1937- *St&PR 93*
Harrison, Douglas Patrick 1937- *WhoSSW 93*
Harrison, Earl David 1932- *WhoAm 92, WhoE 93, WhoWor 93*
Harrison, Earle 1903- *WhoAm 92*
Harrison, Edna (Lucella) Brigham 1902- *WhoWrEP 92*
Harrison, Edward Hardy 1926- *ConAu 39NR*
Harrison, Edward Robert 1919- *WhoAm 92*
Harrison, Edward Thomas, Jr. 1929- *WhoE 93*
Harrison, Elliott, Jr. *Law&B 92*
Harrison, Emmett Bruce, Jr. 1932- *WhoAm 92*
Harrison, Eric E. 1955- *WhoSSW 93*
Harrison, Ernest *BioIn 17*
Harrison, Ernest Franklin 1929- *WhoAm 92*
Harrison, Francis Patrick 1950- *WhoE 93*
Harrison, Frank 1913- *WhoAm 92*
Harrison, Frank Joseph 1919- *WhoWor 93*
Harrison, Frank Ll(ewellyn) 1905-1987 *Baker 92*
Harrison, Frank Russell, III 1935- *WhoSSW 93*
Harrison, Frederick Joseph 1951- *WhoEmL 93*
Harrison, G.B. 1894-1991 *AnObit 1991*
Harrison, G(eorge) B(agshawe) 1894-1991 *ConAu 136*
Harrison, Geoffrey Ainsworth *WhoScE 91-1*
Harrison, George *BioIn 17*
Harrison, George 1943- *Baker 92, WhoAm 92, WhoWor 93*
Harrison, George Brooks 1940- *WhoAm 92*
Harrison, Gerald 1929- *St&PR 93, WhoAm 92*
Harrison, Geraldine Lenore 1922- *WhoAmW 93*
Harrison, Gilbert Warner 1940- *WhoAm 92*
Harrison, Gordon Ray 1931- *WhoAm 92*
Harrison, Graham *WhoScE 91-1*
Harrison, Gregory 1952- *WhoAm 92*
Harrison, Gregory, q 1950- *HolBB [port]*
Harrison, Gregory Arnold 1944- *WhoE 93*
Harrison, Guy Fraser 1894-1986 *Baker 92*
Harrison, Harold 1948- *WhoE 93*
Harrison, Harry 1925- *BioIn 17, ScF&FL 92*
Harrison, Harry (Max) 1925- *WhoWrEP 92*
Harrison, Helen Coplan 1911- *WhoAmW 93*
Harrison, Helen Mayer 1929- *BioIn 17*
Harrison, Henry Starin 1930- *WhoAm 92*
Harrison, Henry T. 1903-1991 *BioIn 17*
Harrison, Henry Walter *WhoScE 91-1*
Harrison, Herman A. 1932- *St&PR 93*
Harrison, Howard R. *Law&B 92*
Harrison, Ira Enell 1933- *WhoSSW 93*
Harrison, Jaime *BioIn 17*
Harrison, James 1925-1990 *BioIn 17*
Harrison, James Anthony 1945- *WhoSSW 93*
Harrison, James C., IV 1947- *St&PR 93*
Harrison, James Joshua, Jr. 1936- *WhoAm 92*
Harrison, James L., Sr. 1948- *St&PR 93*
Harrison, James Martin 1951- *St&PR 93*
Harrison, James Ostelle 1920- *WhoSSW 93*
Harrison, James S. 1929- *WhoScE 91-1*
Harrison, James Thomas 1937- *WhoAm 92, WhoWrEP 92*
Harrison, James Wilburn 1918- *WhoSSW 93*
Harrison, James William *Law&B 92*
Harrison, Jane Friendly *Law&B 92*
Harrison, Jeffrey Woods 1957- *WhoWrEP 92*
Harrison, Jeremy Thomas 1935- *WhoAm 92*
Harrison, Jerome P. *Law&B 92*
Harrison, Jerry Calvin 1941- *WhoAm 92*
Harrison, Jim 1937- *BioIn 17, CurBio 92 [port], WhoAm 92*
Harrison, Jimmy 1900-1931 *Baker 92*
Harrison, Joel S. *Law&B 92*
Harrison, John *BioIn 17, MiSFD 9*
Harrison, John Alexander 1944- *WhoAm 92*
Harrison, John Armstrong 1915- *WhoAm 92*
Harrison, John Arthur 1936- *WhoAm 92*
Harrison, John C. *Law&B 92*
Harrison, John Clement 1913-1989 *BioIn 17*
Harrison, John Conway 1913- *WhoAm 92*
Harrison, John Devereux, Jr. 1955- *WhoWrEP 92*
Harrison, John H. 1928- *St&PR 93*
Harrison, John Ray 1930- *WhoAm 92, WhoSSW 93*
Harrison, John Raymond 1933- *WhoAm 92, WhoWor 93*
Harrison, Joseph 1962- *WhoSSW 93*
Harrison, Joseph Heavrin 1929- *WhoWor 93*
Harrison, Joy *BioIn 17*
Harrison, Judy Aline 1949- *WhoSSW 93*
Harrison, Julius 1885-1963 *Baker 92*
Harrison, Kathryn 1961- *ConLC 70 [port]*
Harrison, Ken 1942- *MiSFD 9*
Harrison, Ken L. 1942- *St&PR 93, WhoAm 92*
Harrison, Lois Smith 1924- *WhoAmW 93, WhoE 93*
Harrison, Lou 1917- *Baker 92*
Harrison, Lowell Hayes 1922- *WhoSSW 93*
Harrison, Lynn Henry, Jr. 1944- *WhoSSW 93*
Harrison, M. John 1945- *ScF&FL 92*
Harrison, Mannie Pascal, Jr. 1931- *WhoSSW 93*
Harrison, Margaret L. *Law&B 92*
Harrison, Marion Edwyn 1931- *WhoAm 92*
Harrison, Marjorie Jeanne 1923- *WhoAm 92*
Harrison, Mark 1951- *ScF&FL 92*
Harrison, Mark Alan 1931- *St&PR 93*
Harrison, Mark I. 1934- *WhoAm 92*
Harrison, Mark M. *Law&B 92*
Harrison, Mark S. 1945- *St&PR 93*
Harrison, Marshall 1933- *ConAu 138*
Harrison, Martin Edward 1937- *WhoWor 93*
Harrison, Mary *ConAu 37NR*
Harrison, Mary Anne *Law&B 92*
Harrison, Mary Frances Nall 1918- *WhoAmW 93*
Harrison, Matthew Clarence, Jr. 1944- *WhoE 93*
Harrison, May 1891-1959 *Baker 92*
Harrison, Michael 1907-1991 *ScF&FL 92*
Harrison, Michael 1940- *WhoAm 92*
Harrison, Michael Allen 1960- *WhoE 93*
Harrison, Michael Douglas *WhoScE 91-1*
Harrison, Michael Jay 1932- *WhoAm 92*
Harrison, Michael R. 1944- *BioIn 17*
Harrison, Michael Roger *WhoScE 91-1*
Harrison, Monika Edwards 1949- *WhoAm 92*
Harrison, Nancy J. *Law&B 92*
Harrison, Nelsine Frances 1941- *WhoAmW 93*
Harrison, Newton 1932- *BioIn 17*
Harrison, Otis Gene 1929- *St&PR 93*
Harrison, Pamela Marie 1953- *WhoAmW 93*
Harrison, Patricia de Stacy *WhoAm 92*
Harrison, Patricia Greenwood 1937- *WhoAmW 93*
Harrison, Patti Lynne 1955- *WhoSSW 93*
Harrison, Paula R. 1941- *St&PR 93*
Harrison, Pauline May *WhoScE 91-1*
Harrison, Payne *BioIn 17, ScF&FL 92*
Harrison, Payne 1949?- *ConAu 139*
Harrison, Peter 1946- *BioIn 17*
Harrison, Peter Jeffrey *WhoScE 91-1*
Harrison, Philip Lewis 1945- *WhoWrEP 92*
Harrison, R.D. 1923- *St&PR 93*
Harrison, R.G. *WhoScE 91-1*
Harrison, R.S. 1931- *St&PR 93*
Harrison, Ralph Kent *Law&B 92*
Harrison, Rex *BioIn 17*
Harrison, Rex 1908-1990 *IntDcF 2-3*
Harrison, Richard 1920- *WhoWor 93*
Harrison, Richard A. 1948- *St&PR 93*
Harrison, Richard Donald 1923- *WhoAm 92*
Harrison, Richard Edward 1948- *WhoEmL 93*
Harrison, Richard Norris 1949- *WhoEmL 93*
Harrison, Robert Carter *Law&B 92*
Harrison, Robert Charles 1933- *St&PR 93*
Harrison, Robert Drew 1923- *WhoAm 92*
Harrison, Robert F. 1940- *WhoScE 91-3*
Harrison, Robert H. 1745-1790 *OxCSupC*
Harrison, Robert J. 1928- *WhoSSW 93*
Harrison, Robert John 1961- *WhoWor 93*
Harrison, Robert Lee 1930- *St&PR 93*
Harrison, Robert Mark 1958- *WhoWor 93*
Harrison, Robert Pogue 1954- *ConAu 138*
Harrison, Robert Vernon McElroy 1935- *WhoAm 92*
Harrison, Robert W. 1927- *St&PR 93*
Harrison, Robert William 1915- *WhoE 93, WhoWor 93*
Harrison, Roger Gran 1943- *WhoAm 92*
Harrison, Roger Michael *WhoScE 91-1*
Harrison, Rosalie Thornton 1917- *WhoAmW 93*
Harrison, S. David 1930- *WhoAm 92*
Harrison, Samuel Hughel 1956- *WhoEmL 93, WhoSSW 93*
Harrison, Sarah 1946- *BioIn 17*
Harrison, Selig Seidenman 1927- *WhoAm 92*

Harrison, Sherry *BioIn 17*
Harrison, Shirley Wanda 1923- *WhoAmW 93*
Harrison, Stanley Earl 1930- *WhoAm 92*
Harrison, Stephen Brian 1964- *WhoSSW 93*
Harrison, Stephen Coplan 1943- *WhoAm 92*
Harrison, Stephen Earle 1941- *St&PR 93*
Harrison, Steve 1958- *WhoEmL 93, WhoSSW 93, WhoWor 93*
Harrison, Steven R. 1951- *St&PR 93*
Harrison, Sue 1950- *ScF&FL 92*
Harrison, Susan Frances 1859-1935 *BioIn 17*
Harrison, Suzanne Marie 1961- *WhoAmW 93*
Harrison, Ted *ConAu 39NR*
Harrison, Ted 1926- *BioIn 17*
Harrison, Thomas Emil, Jr. *Law&B 92*
Harrison, Thomas James 1935- *WhoAm 92*
Harrison, Tillson Lever 1888-1946 *BioIn 17*
Harrison, Timothy George *WhoScE 91-1*
Harrison, Timothy Phillips 1961- *WhoEmL 93*
Harrison, Timothy Stone 1927- *WhoAm 92*
Harrison, Tony 1937- *BioIn 17*
Harrison, Utta Karin 1936- *St&PR 93*
Harrison, Vicky Ann 1963- *WhoAmW 93*
Harrison, Virginia Budd 1927- *WhoSSW 93*
Harrison, W. Allen 1932- *St&PR 93*
Harrison, Wallace Kirkman 1895-1981 *BioIn 17*
Harrison, Wendell *BioIn 17*
Harrison, Wilbert 1929- *SoulM*
Harrison, William 1813-1868 *Baker 92, OxDcOp*
Harrison, William 1933- *ScF&FL 92*
Harrison, William B. 1943- *St&PR 93*
Harrison, William Burwell, Jr. 1943- *WhoAm 92*
Harrison, William Hardin 1933- *WhoAm 92*
Harrison, William Henry 1773-1841 *BioIn 17, HarEnMi, PolPar*
Harrison, William Henry 1896-1990 *BioIn 17*
Harrison, William K. *Law&B 92*
Harrison, William L. 1936- *WhoIns 93*
Harrison, William Loring 1936- *St&PR 93*
Harrison, William Neal 1933- *WhoAm 92, WhoWrEP 92*
Harrison, William Oliver, Jr. 1945- *WhoSSW 93*
Harrison, William R. *Law&B 92*
Harrison, William Shaw 1922- *WhoE 93*
Harrison, William Wright 1915- *WhoAm 92*
Harrison, William Wright, Jr. 1953- *WhoEmL 93*
Harrison, Yola G. 1947- *WhoEmL 93, WhoSSW 93*
Harrison-Johnson, Yvonne Elois 1939- *WhoAm 92*
Harriss, Charles (Albert Edwin) 1862-1929 *Baker 92*
Harriss, Cynthia Therese 1952- *WhoAm 92*
Harriss, Herbert Lynch 1943- *St&PR 93*
Harriss, Lucas Edward 1934- *St&PR 93*
Harrisson, Tom 1911-1976 *IntDcAn*
Harris-Warrick, Ronald Morgan 1949- *WhoE 93*
Harritt, Norman L. 1941- *St&PR 93, WhoAm 92*
Harrity, William F. 1850-1912 *PolPar*
Harro, Barbara Leigh 1928- *WhoAmW 93*
Harrod, Billy Joe 1933- *WhoAm 92, WhoE 93, WhoWor 93*
Harrod, Brian *BioIn 17*
Harrod, Donald Joseph 1944- *St&PR 93*
Harrod, Lawrence Wayne 1950- *WhoEmL 93*
Harrod, Pamala A. *Law&B 92*
Harrod, Roger 1945- *St&PR 93*
Harrod, Scott 1910- *WhoAm 92*
Harroff, Jerry Marlin 1932- *St&PR 93*
Harrold, Bernard 1925- *WhoAm 92*
Harrold, Dennis Edward 1947- *WhoEmL 93*
Harrold, Gordon Coleson 1906- *WhoSSW 93, WhoWor 93*
Harrold, Orville Robert 1932- *St&PR 93*
Harrold, Rebecca Susan 1963- *WhoAmW 93*
Harrold, Ronald Thomas 1933- *WhoAm 92*
Harrold, William Eugene 1936- *WhoWrEP 92*
Harron, Donald 1924- *WhoCanL 92*
Harron, Gerald A. 1943- *St&PR 93*
Harrop, Daniel Smith, III 1954- *WhoEmL 93*
Harrop, William Caldwell 1929- *WhoAm 92, WhoWor 93*
Harrover, Roy Perkins 1928- *WhoAm 92*
Harrow, Barry Richard 1949- *WhoEmL 93*
Harrow, Gustave 1930-1990 *BioIn 17*
Harrow, Nancy *WhoAm 92*
Harrower, George Alexander 1924- *WhoAm 92*
Harrs, Leland Allen 1936- *WhoIns 93*
Harry, Bill *ScF&FL 92*
Harry, Deborah *BioIn 17*
Harry, Deborah Ann 1945- *WhoAm 92*
Harry, Jackee *BioIn 17, ConTFT 10*
Harry, Jacqueline *ConTFT 10*
Harry, John David 1937- *WhoScE 91-1*
Harry, Marina Matlin *Law&B 92*
Harry, Richard *BioIn 17*
Harry, Robert Hayden 1918- *WhoAm 92*
Harry, William, III 1955- *WhoAm 92*
Harryhausen, Ray 1920- *ScF&FL 92*
Harryhausen, Ray Frederick 1920- *WhoAm 92*
Harry the Kid d1881 *BioIn 17*
Harsanyi, Fruzsina M. 1942- *St&PR 93*
Harsanyi, Janice 1929- *WhoAm 92*
Harsanyi, John Charles 1920- *WhoAm 92*
Harsanyi, Tibor 1898-1954 *Baker 92*
Harsch, Joseph C. 1905- *WhoAm 92*
Harsdorff, Manfred 1932- *WhoScE 91-3*
Harsdorffer, Georg Philipp 1607-1658 *OxDcOp*
Harsen, Edward Charles 1958- *WhoWrEP 92*
Harsev, Emil Manolov 1961- *WhoWor 93*
Harsh, Donald Ramon, Jr. 1946- *St&PR 93*
Harsh, Fred (T.) 1925- *SmATA 72 [port]*
Harsha, Edward Houston 1916- *WhoAm 92*
Harsha, Mary Ruth *Law&B 92*
Harshavardhana 590-648 *HarEnMi*
Harshaw, David Hare 1904-1991 *BioIn 17*
Harshaw, Margaret 1909- *Baker 92*
Harshaw, Margaret 1912- *OxDcOp*
Harshaw, Nannie M. 1932- *St&PR 93*
Harshaway, Bobby Lee 1954- *St&PR 93*
Harshbarger, Dwight 1938- *WhoAm 92*
Harshbarger, Richard B. 1934- *WhoAm 92*
Harshbarger, Scott 1941- *WhoAm 92, WhoE 93*
Harshfield, Edward G. 1937- *St&PR 93*
Harshfield, Edward Gordon 1937- *WhoAm 92*
Harshman, Daniel James 1951- *WhoSSW 93*
Harshman, Marc 1950- *SmATA 71 [port]*
Harshman, Morton Leonard 1932- *WhoAm 92*
Harshman, R. Brent *Law&B 92*
Harshman, Tonya Lynn 1959- *WhoWor 93*
Harshman-Green, Amy *WhoSSW 93*
Harsin, Diane Kay 1963- *WhoAmW 93*
Harsing, Laszlo 1920- *WhoScE 91-4*
Harsney, Johanna Marie Offner 1914- *WhoAmW 93*
Harstad, Clifford Allen 1947- *St&PR 93*
Harstela, Pertti Juhani 1946- *WhoScE 91-4*
Hart, Alan Robert 1947- *WhoE 93*
Hart, Alden Sherburne, Jr. 1956- *WhoEmL 93*
Hart, Alex *BioIn 17*
Hart, Alex Way 1940- *St&PR 93*
Hart, Alison Ann 1963- *WhoEmL 93*
Hart, (Jill) Alison 1948- *WhoWrEP 92*
Hart, Alvin Leroy 1925- *WhoAm 92*
Hart, Amy S. 1962- *WhoE 93*
Hart, Antonio *BioIn 17*
Hart, Arthur Alvin 1921- *WhoAm 92*
Hart, Augustin Snow, Jr. 1915- *WhoAm 92*
Hart, Barbara Lane 1941- *WhoSSW 93*
Hart, Basil Henry Liddell 1895-1970 *BioIn 17*
Hart, Bobby Sidna 1954- *WhoWrEP 92*
Hart, Brenda Ayres *Law&B 92*
Hart, Brenda Ayres 1956- *WhoEmL 93*
Hart, Bruce 1938- *MiSFD 9*
Hart, C. Allan 1909- *WhoAm 92*
Hart, Catherine 1948- *ConAu 139*
Hart, Cecil William Joseph 1931- *WhoAm 92*
Hart, Charles Anthony *WhoScE 91-1*
Hart, Charles Anthony 1945- *WhoWor 93*
Hart, Charles Franklin 1925- *St&PR 93*
Hart, Charles H. 1944- *St&PR 93*
Hart, Charles Willard, Jr. 1928- *WhoAm 92, WhoE 93*
Hart, Chris *ScF&FL 92*
Hart, Christopher *BioIn 17, MiSFD 9*
Hart, Craig Michael 1958- *WhoWor 93*
Hart, Cynthia Louise 1948- *WhoEmL 93*
Hart, Dabney Adams 1926- *ScF&FL 92*
Hart, Dabney Gardner 1940- *WhoAmW 93*
Hart, Daniel Anthony 1927- *WhoAm 92*
Hart, David A. 1947- *St&PR 93*
Hart, David C. *Law&B 92*
Hart, David Churchill 1940- *WhoAm 92*
Hart, David M(ontgomery) 1927- *ConAu 136*
Hart, Dean Evan 1957- *WhoE 93*
Hart, Derek *MiSFD 9*
Hart, Dick *Law&B 92*
Hart, Dominick Joseph 1942- *WhoSSW 93*
Hart, Don Allen *Law&B 92*
Hart, Donald J. 1933- *St&PR 93*
Hart, Donald L. 1933- *St&PR 93*
Hart, Donald Milton 1914- *WhoAm 92*
Hart, Donald Purple 1937- *WhoAm 92*
Hart, Donn Vorhis 1918-1983 *IntDcAn*
Hart, Dorothy *WhoAm 92*
Hart, Dorothy Lea Cramer 1940- *St&PR 93*
Hart, Douglas C. 1950- *ScF&FL 92*
Hart, Edith Wade *AmWomPl*
Hart, Edward LeRoy 1916- *WhoAm 92, WhoWrEP 92*
Hart, Edwin James 1910- *WhoAm 92*
Hart, Edwin Robert, Jr. 1953- *WhoEmL 93, WhoSSW 93*
Hart, Eileen Kelly 1947- *WhoAmW 93*
Hart, Elizabeth Harriet *AmWomPl*
Hart, Elizabeth Street *AmWomPl*
Hart, Elsie Faye 1920- *WhoAmW 93*
Hart, Eric Mullins 1925- *WhoAm 92*
Hart, Evelyn 1956- *WhoAm 92*
Hart, Fay Maria Mitchell 1935- *WhoSSW 93*
Hart, Francis Russell *ScF&FL 92*
Hart, Frank E. *WhoScE 91-1*
Hart, Frank Lee *Law&B 92*
Hart, Fred Clinton 1940- *WhoAm 92*
Hart, Frederic Patton 1894- *Baker 92*
Hart, Frederick Donald 1915- *WhoAm 92*
Hart, Frederick E. *BioIn 17*
Hart, Frederick Michael 1929- *WhoAm 92*
Hart, Fritz 1874-1949 *OxDcOp*
Hart, Fritz (Bennicke) 1874-1949 *Baker 92*
Hart, G. Allen 1948- *St&PR 93*
Hart, G.F.J. *WhoScE 91-1*
Hart, Gary 1936- *BioIn 17*
Hart, Gary W. 1936- *WhoAm 92*
Hart, George 1839-1891 *Baker 92*
Hart, George E. *Law&B 92*
Hart, George E. 1951- *St&PR 93*
Hart, George H. 1883-1959 *BioIn 17*
Hart, George Vaughan 1947- *WhoSSW 93*
Hart, Gerald E. 1931- *St&PR 93*
Hart, Gurnee Fellows 1929- *WhoAm 92, WhoE 93*
Hart, Harry 1907-1964 *BioIn 17*
Hart, Harry James 1918- *WhoWor 93*
Hart, Harvey 1928-1989 *MiSFD 9N*
Hart, Helen P. 1927- *WhoAmW 93*
Hart, Henry 1903-1990 *BioIn 17*
Hart, Henry Walker 1954- *WhoWrEP 92*
Hart, Herbert Michael 1928- *WhoAm 92, WhoE 93, WhoSSW 93*
Hart, Horace 1910-1991 *BioIn 17*
Hart, Howard F. *Law&B 92*
Hart, Howard Roscoe, Jr. 1929- *WhoAm 92*
Hart, J. Philip *Law&B 92*
Hart, James 1647-1718 *Baker 92*
Hart, James David 1911-1990 *BioIn 17*
Hart, James Francis 1948- *St&PR 93*
Hart, James G. 1959- *St&PR 93*
Hart, James V. d1991 *BioIn 17*
Hart, James W., Jr. 1953- *St&PR 93, WhoAm 92*
Hart, James Warren 1944- *WhoAm 92*
Hart, James Whitfield, Jr. 1935- *WhoAm 92*
Hart, Jean Hardy 1942- *WhoAmW 93*
Hart, Jeanne 1906- *WhoWrEP 92*
Hart, Jeff Roderick 1944- *WhoAm 92*
Hart, Jenifer 1914- *ConAu 138*
Hart, Jerome Anthony 1933- *St&PR 93*
Hart, John *BioIn 17*
Hart, John 1948- *WhoWrEP 92*
Hart, John C. *Law&B 92*
Hart, John Edward 1937- *St&PR 93*
Hart, John Lewis 1931- *WhoAm 92*
Hart, John Mason 1935- *WhoSSW 93*
Hart, John Richard 1932- *WhoAm 92*
Hart, John Thomas 1805-1874 *Baker 92*
Hart, Joseph H. 1931- *WhoAm 92*
Hart, Josephine *BioIn 17*
Hart, Josephine 1942?- *ConAu 138, ConLC 70 [port]*
Hart, Judith Constance Mary 1924-1991 *BioIn 17*
Hart, Julia Catherine 1796-1867 *BioIn 17*
Hart, Karen Kay 1947- *St&PR 93*
Hart, Kathryn Mary 1947- *WhoSSW 93*
Hart, Kenneth Einar *WhoE 93*
Hart, Kenneth Nelson 1930- *WhoAm 92*
Hart, Kenneth Wayne 1939- *WhoSSW 93*
Hart, Kevin John 1954- *WhoWor 93*
Hart, Kimberly Ann 1966- *WhoSSW 93*
Hart, Kitty Carlisle *BioIn 17*
Hart, Kitty Carlisle 1917- *WhoAm 92, WhoAmW 93*
Hart, Larry A. 1912- *St&PR 93*
Hart, Larry Edward 1945- *WhoAm 92*
Hart, Larry M. 1940- *St&PR 93*
Hart, Leslie James *Law&B 92*
Hart, Lewis Justice, Jr. 1945- *WhoAm 92*
Hart, Linda Dixon 1948- *WhoSSW 93*
Hart, Lois Borland 1941- *WhoAmW 93, WhoWrEP 92*
Hart, Lorenz (Milton) 1895-1943 *Baker 92*
Hart, Loring Edward 1924- *WhoAm 92*
Hart, M.R. 1891-1990 *BioIn 17*
Hart, Marian Griffith 1929- *WhoAmW 93*
Hart, Marie D. 1932- *St&PR 93*
Hart, Marion Rice 1891-1990 *BioIn 17*
Hart, Mark Carlisle 1921- *St&PR 93*
Hart, Martin B. 1950- *St&PR 93*
Hart, Martin J. 1924- *St&PR 93*
Hart, Marvin C. 1938- *St&PR 93*
Hart, Marvin Eugene 1959- *WhoEmL 93*
Hart, Mary *BioIn 17*
Hart, Mary T. *AmWomPl*
Hart, Matthew J. 1952- *St&PR 93*
Hart, Maxine Barton 1934- *WhoAm 92*
Hart, Mel 1938- *St&PR 93*
Hart, Melissa Joan *BioIn 17*
Hart, Michael A. 1953- *St&PR 93*
Hart, Mickey *BioIn 17*
Hart, Milledge A., III 1934- *St&PR 93*
Hart, Moss 1904-1961 *BioIn 17*
Hart, Nathaniel Irwin 1930- *WhoAm 92*
Hart, Neal 1879-1949 *BioIn 17*
Hart, Nelson S. 1926- *St&PR 93*
Hart, Oliver D'Arcy 1948- *WhoAm 92, WhoEmL 93*
Hart, Pamela Heim 1946- *WhoAmW 93*
Hart, Patricia A. *Law&B 92*
Hart, Patricia Ann 1957- *WhoEmL 93*
Hart, Patrick Joseph 1925- *WhoAm 92, WhoWrEP 92*
Hart, Paul 1955- *WhoE 93*
Hart, Paul Robert 1956- *WhoSSW 93*
Hart, Pearl fl. 1898-1901 *BioIn 17*
Hart, Peter David 1942- *WhoAm 92*
Hart, Philip c. 1674-1749 *Baker 92*
Hart, Ralph A. 1904- *St&PR 93*
Hart, Raymond Kenneth 1928- *WhoSSW 93*
Hart, Richard B. *Law&B 92*
Hart, Richard Banner 1932- *WhoAm 92*
Hart, Richard Nevel, Jr. 1940- *WhoAm 92*
Hart, Richard Oliver 1949- *WhoE 93, WhoEmL 93, WhoWor 93*
Hart, Richard Thomas *Law&B 92*
Hart, Richard Trapnell 1953- *WhoSSW 93*
Hart, Richard Wesley 1933- *WhoSSW 93, WhoWor 93*
Hart, Robert 1835-1911 *BioIn 17*
Hart, Robert C. *Law&B 92*
Hart, Robert Camillus 1934- *WhoAm 92, WhoWor 93*
Hart, Robert Gordon 1921- *WhoAm 92*
Hart, Robert John Kirkland 1916- *St&PR 93*
Hart, Robert Joseph 1937- *WhoAm 92*
Hart, Robert Leonard 1927- *WhoAm 92*
Hart, Robert M. 1944- *WhoAm 92*
Hart, Roderick P. 1945- *WhoAm 92*
Hart, Roger C. *Law&B 92*
Hart, Ronald Wilson 1942- *WhoAm 92*
Hart, Rosana L. 1942- *WhoWrEP 92*
Hart, Sally Millner 1953- *WhoEmL 93*
Hart, Sandra Hile 1947- *WhoSSW 93*
Hart, Sean Timothy 1953- *WhoE 93*
Hart, Stanley Robert 1935- *WhoAm 92*
Hart, Stephen R. *Law&B 92*
Hart, Stephen Strong 1952- *WhoEmL 93*
Hart, Steven Weber 1956- *St&PR 93, WhoAm 92*
Hart, Terry Jonathan 1946- *WhoAm 92*
Hart, Thomas Charles 1877-1971 *HarEnMi*
Hart, Thomas E. 1943- *St&PR 93*
Hart, Thomas F. 1929- *St&PR 93*
Hart, Thomas Judson 1958- *WhoWor 93*
Hart, Thomas Paul 1951- *WhoAm 92*
Hart, Weldon 1911-1957 *Baker 92*
Hart, Wilbert 1947- *See* Delfonics *SoulM*
Hart, William 1945- *WhoWrEP 92* *See Also* Delfonics *SoulM*
Hart, William C. 1933- *WhoIns 93*
Hart, William D., Jr. 1950- *WhoAm 92*
Hart, William Douglas *Law&B 92*
Hart, William L. 1917- *St&PR 93*
Hart, William Milton 1913- *WhoAm 92*
Hart, William O. *Law&B 92*
Hart, William S. 1865?-1946 *IntDcF 2-3 [port]*
Hart, William S. c. 1870-1946 *BioIn 17*
Hart, William Thomas 1929- *WhoAm 92*
Hartal-Dreissinger, Michelle 1961- *BioIn 17*
Hart & Sons *Baker 92*
Hartarto 1932- *WhoAsAP 91*
Hartdegen, Carl 1918-1991 *BioIn 17*
Hartdegen, Stephen J. 1907-1989 *BioIn 17*

Harte, Andrew Dennis 1946- *WhoE 93, WhoEmL 93*
Harte, Betty d1965 *SweetSg A*
Harte, Bret 1836-1902 *MagSAmL [port], WorLitC [port]*
Harte, Christopher M. 1947- *St&PR 93*
Harte, Christopher McCutcheon 1947- *WhoAm 92*
Harte, Edward Holmead 1922- *DcLB 127 [port], WhoSSW 93*
Harte, Houston Harriman 1927- *DcLB 127 [port], St&PR 93, WhoAm 92*
Harte, John Joseph Meakins 1914- *WhoAm 92*
Harte, Joseph Michael 1940- *St&PR 93*
Harte, Lisa R. 1966- *St&PR 93*
Harte, Marjorie *ConAu 40NR*
Harte, Rebecca Elizabeth 1967- *WhoSSW 93, WhoWor 93*
Hartel, Gottfried Christoph 1763-1827 See Breitkopf & Hartel *Baker 92*
Hartel, Hermann 1803-1875 See Breitkopf & Hartel *Baker 92*
Hartell, John 1902- *WhoE 93*
Hartenberger, Robert *Law&B 92*
Hartenstein, Geoffrey Robert *Law&B 92*
Hartenstine, Warren Richard 1945- *WhoAm 92*
Harter, Alvin Adam 1927- *St&PR 93*
Harter, Carol Clancey *WhoAm 92, WhoAmW 93*
Harter, David John 1942- *WhoWor 93*
Harter, Diana J. *Law&B 92*
Harter, Donald Harry 1933- *WhoAm 92, WhoE 93, WhoWor 93*
Harter, Duane L. 1932- *St&PR 93*
Harter, Franklin C. *Law&B 92*
Harter, Hugh Anthony 1922- *WhoAm 92*
Harter, Jean Ann 1959- *WhoAmW 93*
Harter, Lafayette George, Jr. 1918- *WhoAm 92, WhoWor 93*
Harter, Lisa Reidy 1966- *WhoAmW 93*
Harter, Michael Thomas 1942- *WhoAm 92*
Harter, Paul Robert 1957- *WhoEmL 93*
Harter, Penny 1940- *WhoWrEP 92*
Harter, Richard *ScF&FL 92*
Harter, Robert Duane 1936- *WhoAm 92*
Harter, Robert J., Jr. *Law&B 92*
Harter, Robert Jackson, Jr. 1944- *WhoAm 92*
Hartfeld, Hermann 1942- *ConAu 136*
Hartfiel, Darald Joe 1939- *WhoSSW 93*
Hartfield, Elizabeth Ann 1950- *WhoSSW 93*
Hartfield, Richard A. *Law&B 92*
Hartfield, Roy James, Jr. 1963- *WhoSSW 93*
Hartford, Brian Arnold 1943- *WhoE 93*
Hartford, Huntington 1911- *BioIn 17, WhoAm 92*
Hartford, John Cowan 1937- *WhoAm 92*
Hartford, Phyllis K. *Law&B 92*
Hartford, Robert Lionel *WhoE 93*
Hartford, Sallie Rogers 1947- *WhoSSW 93*
Hartford, Thomas James, III *Law&B 92*
Hartford, William H. 1938- *WhoAm 92*
Hartgen, Vincent Andrew 1914- *WhoAm 92*
Hartgraves, Joni Kaye 1960- *WhoAmW 93*
Hartgrove, Richard C. *Law&B 92*
Harth, Erica *WhoAm 92*
Harth, Robert James 1956- *WhoAm 92*
Harth, Sidney 1929- *Baker 92, WhoAm 92*
Harth, Wolfgang 1932- *WhoScE 91-3*
Harthan, Hans 1855-1936 *Baker 92*
Harthan, Stephen Carrol 1948- *WhoSSW 93*
Harthern, Anthony Barrie 1936- *WhoWor 93*
Harthoorn, Rudolf 1946- *WhoWor 93*
Harthun, Luther A. *Law&B 92*
Harthun, Luther A. 1935- *St&PR 93*
Harthun, Luther Arthur 1935- *WhoAm 92*
Hartig, Dale Joseph 1950- *St&PR 93*
Hartig, Heinz (Friedrich) 1907-1969 *Baker 92*
Hartigan, Grace 1922- *WhoAm 92*
Hartigan, MaryEllen 1957- *WhoEmL 93*
Hartigan, Michael J., Jr. *Law&B 92*
Hartigan, Neil F. 1938- *WhoAm 92*
Hartigan, Patrick J. 1931- *WhoScE 91-3*
Hartikainen, Olli-Pekka 1937- *WhoScE 91-4, WhoWor 93*
Hartin, Robert Marvin 1949- *WhoSSW 93*
Harting, Emilie Clothier 1942- *WhoWrEP 92*
Harting, G. Robert 1927- *St&PR 93*
Hartje, Keith Douglas 1950- *St&PR 93*
Hartje, Robert Wayne, Sr. 1938- *WhoAm 92*
Hartje, Tod D(ale) 1968- *ConAu 139*
Hartl, Albert Victor 1911- *WhoAm 92*
Hartl, Charles *St&PR 93*
Hartl, Daniel Lee 1943- *WhoAm 92*
Hartl, Richard James 1937- *St&PR 93*
Hartl, Wilbur Michael 1916- *St&PR 93*
Hartl, William Parker 1935- *WhoE 93, WhoWor 93*
Hartlage, James A. 1938- *St&PR 93*
Hartlage, Lawrence Clifton 1934- *WhoAm 92*
Hartland, Anthony 1937- *WhoScE 91-1*
Hartland, Clive *WhoScE 91-1*
Hartle, Anthony E. 1942- *ConAu 137*
Hartle, Kent Lewis 1952- *WhoEmL 93*
Hartle, Robert Wyman 1921- *WhoAm 92, WhoSSW 93*
Hartle, William George 1948- *St&PR 93*
Hartleb, David Frederick 1944- *WhoAm 92*
Hartleb, Emil A. 1938- *St&PR 93*
Hartleben, Faye Pearl 1940- *WhoWrEP 92*
Hartleben, Otto Erich 1864-1905 *DcLB 118 [port]*
Hartlen, J. *WhoScE 91-4*
Hartlen, Jan E.B. 1944- *WhoScE 91-4*
Hartlep, Ralph Q. 1946- *St&PR 93*
Hartler, Nils 1926- *WhoScE 91-4*
Hartley, Baron Manning 1924- *WhoE 93*
Hartley, Bonalyn J. 1944- *St&PR 93*
Hartley, Brian *WhoScE 91-1*
Hartley, Brian Selby *WhoScE 91-1*
Hartley, Brian Selby 1926- *WhoWor 93*
Hartley, Bruce Maxwell 1940- *WhoWor 93*
Hartley, Craig Hilliard 1953- *WhoSSW 93*
Hartley, Craig Sheridan 1937- *WhoSSW 93*
Hartley, David Fielding *WhoScE 91-1*
Hartley, Domenic G. 1947- *St&PR 93*
Hartley, Donald 1941- *WhoSSW 93*
Hartley, Donald V. *Law&B 92*
Hartley, Duncan 1941- *WhoE 93*
Hartley, Edon V. *Law&B 92*
Hartley, Fred *BioIn 17*
Hartley, George R. *Law&B 92*
Hartley, George S. 1946- *St&PR 93*
Hartley, Hal *MiSFD 9*
Hartley, James *WhoScE 91-1*
Hartley, James Harrison 1946- *WhoEmL 93*
Hartley, Jean Ayres 1914- *WhoWrEP 92*
Hartley, John T., Jr. 1930- *St&PR 93, WhoAm 92, WhoSSW 93*
Hartley, Joseph Wayman, Jr. 1933- *St&PR 93, WhoAm 92*
Hartley, Karen Jeanette 1950- *WhoAmW 93, WhoEmL 93, WhoWor 93*
Hartley, Keith *WhoScE 91-1*
Hartley, Keith 1940- *ConAu 37NR*
Hartley, Kevin F. *Law&B 92*
Hartley, L.P. 1895-1972 *BioIn 17, ScF&FL 92*
Hartley, Leslie Poles 1895-1972 *BioIn 17*
Hartley, Linda Maie 1943- *WhoAmW 93*
Hartley, Livingston 1900-1981 *ScF&FL 92*
Hartley, Mariette *BioIn 17*
Hartley, Mariette 1940- *WhoAm 92, WhoAmW 93*
Hartley, Marsden 1877-1943 *BioIn 17*
Hartley, Paul *BioIn 17*
Hartley, Polly *BioIn 17*
Hartley, Richard Glendale 1926- *WhoAm 92*
Hartley, Robert Frank 1927- *WhoAm 92*
Hartley, Roger *WhoScE 91-1*
Hartley, Shiela L. 1953- *WhoIns 93*
Hartley, Stephen Louis *Law&B 92*
Hartley, Steven W. 1956- *ConAu 139*
Hartley, Stuart Leslie 1938- *WhoAm 92*
Hartley, Trevor C. *WhoScE 91-1*
Hartley, Walter S(inclair) 1927- *Baker 92*
Hartley, William H. 1926- *St&PR 93*
Hartley-Leonard, Darryl *WhoAm 92*
Hartley-Linse, Bonnie Jean 1923- *WhoAmW 93, WhoWor 93*
Hartline, Lamar G. 1934- *St&PR 93*
Hartling, Peter 1933- *BioIn 17, ChILR 29 [port], WhoWor 93*
Hartling, Poul 1914- *WhoWor 93*
Hartloff, Stephen Alexander 1947- *WhoEmL 93*
Hartlove, Michele Denise 1959- *WhoEmL 93*
Hartly, Michelle Jeannette 1959- *WhoEmL 93*
Hartlyn, Jonathan *WhoSSW 93*
Hartman, Alan James *Law&B 92*
Hartman, Ann 1948- *St&PR 93*
Hartman, Arthur A. 1926- *WhoAm 92*
Hartman, Ashley Powell 1922- *WhoAm 92*
Hartman, Burton Arthur 1924- *WhoAm 92*
Hartman, Carl 1917- *WhoAm 92*
Hartman, Charles Henry 1933- *WhoAm 92, WhoE 93*
Hartman, Cherry 1947- *WhoEmL 93*
Hartman, Darlene *ScF&FL 92*
Hartman, David 1955- *St&PR 93*
Hartman, David Downs 1935- *WhoAm 92*
Hartman, David G. 1942- *St&PR 93, WhoIns 93*
Hartman, David Gardiner 1942- *WhoAm 92*
Hartman, David Gene 1951- *St&PR 93*
Hartman, David James 1948- *WhoEmL 93*
Hartman, Dennis A. 1951- *St&PR 93*
Hartman, Diane B. 1942- *WhoAmW 93*
Hartman, Douglas Arthur 1938- *St&PR 93*
Hartman, Elizabeth Ann 1959- *WhoWrEP 92*
Hartman, Elliott Morgan, Jr. 1938- *WhoE 93*
Hartman, Emily Lou 1932- *WhoAm 92, WhoAmW 93*
Hartman, Ernest Ortiz 1954- *WhoSSW 93*
Hartman, Estelle Stein d1990 *BioIn 17*
Hartman, Frank L. *Law&B 92*
Hartman, Gary T. *Law&B 92*
Hartman, Geoffrey H. 1929- *WhoAm 92*
Hartman, George Eitel 1936- *WhoAm 92, WhoE 93*
Hartman, Gerald Charles 1936- *St&PR 93*
Hartman, Hedy Ann 1954- *WhoAm 92, WhoE 93*
Hartman, Henry A. 1929- *St&PR 93*
Hartman, Henry Bob 1951- *WhoE 93*
Hartman, Hope Janine 1947- *WhoAmW 93, WhoE 93*
Hartman, James Austin 1928- *WhoSSW 93*
Hartman, James D. *St&PR 93*
Hartman, James Le-Roy 1940- *WhoWor 93*
Hartman, James Theodore 1925- *WhoAm 92*
Hartman, Jane E(vangeline) 1928- *WhoWrEP 92*
Hartman, Janet Digges 1946- *WhoAmW 93*
Hartman, Janine Cey 1952- *WhoAmW 93*
Hartman, Jeannette Marie 1952- *WhoAmW 93, WhoEmL 93*
Hartman, Jennifer Weaver 1947- *WhoE 93*
Hartman, Joan Edna 1930- *WhoAmW 93*
Hartman, John E. *Law&B 92*
Hartman, John R. 1950- *WhoIns 93*
Hartman, John Wheeler 1922- *WhoAm 92, WhoSSW 93*
Hartman, Joy C. 1948- *St&PR 93*
Hartman, Kathi L. *Law&B 92*
Hartman, Kenneth Shane 1955- *WhoE 93*
Hartman, Kevin John 1960- *WhoE 93*
Hartman, Lars Olov 1930- *WhoWor 93*
Hartman, Lawrence M. 1943- *St&PR 93*
Hartman, Lee Ann Walraff 1945- *WhoAmW 93, WhoE 93, WhoWor 93*
Hartman, Leonard S. 1935- *WhoUN 92*
Hartman, Lisa *BioIn 17*
Hartman, Margaret J. 1943- *WhoAm 92*
Hartman, Mark William 1937- *St&PR 93*
Hartman, Mary Louise 1942- *WhoE 93*
Hartman, Mary S. 1941- *WhoAm 92*
Hartman, Morris J. 1956- *St&PR 93*
Hartman, Nancy Lee 1951- *WhoAmW 93*
Hartman, Paul Arthur 1926- *WhoAm 92*
Hartman, Paul J. d1992 *NewYTBS 92*
Hartman, Peter M. *Law&B 92*
Hartman, Phil *BioIn 17*
Hartman, Philip *MiSFD 9*
Hartman, Phillip Anthony 1950- *WhoAm 92*
Hartman, Richard E. 1940- *St&PR 93*
Hartman, Richard Leon 1937- *WhoAm 92*
Hartman, Richard Russell 1926- *WhoAm 92*
Hartman, Robert F. 1947- *St&PR 93*
Hartman, Robert James 1937- *St&PR 93, WhoIns 93*
Hartman, Robert L. 1930- *St&PR 93*
Hartman, Robert Leroy 1926- *WhoAm 92*
Hartman, Robert S. 1914- *WhoAm 92*
Hartman, Robert William 1938- *WhoE 93*
Hartman, Ruth Ann 1938- *WhoAmW 93*
Hartman, Ruth Gayle 1948- *WhoAmW 93*
Hartman, Ruth Looper 1937- *WhoAmW 93*
Hartman, Sheldon Roy *Law&B 92*
Hartman, Stephen Jennings, Jr. 1945- *WhoAm 92*
Hartman, Steven H. *Law&B 92*
Hartman, Stewart Eugene, Jr. 1931- *WhoAm 92*
Hartman, Terry Lee 1948- *St&PR 93*
Hartman, Thomas Jeffery 1966- *WhoE 93*
Hartman, Timothy P. 1939- *St&PR 93*
Hartman, Timothy Patwill 1939- *WhoAm 92*
Hartman, Wallace R. 1940- *St&PR 93*
Hartman, William Arthur 1955- *WhoAm 92*
Hartman, William Ellis 1919- *WhoWor 93*
Hartman, William R., Jr. *Law&B 92*
Hartman, Zoe *AmWomPl*
Hartman-Abramson, Ilene 1950- *WhoAmW 93, WhoEmL 93, WhoWor 93*
Hartman-Goldsmith, Joan 1933- *WhoAm 92, WhoAmW 93*
Hartman-Irwin, Mary Frances 1925- *WhoAmW 93*
Hartmanis, Juris 1928- *WhoAm 92*
Hartmann *Baker 92*
Hartmann, A. *WhoScE 91-4*
Hartmann, Arthur (Martinus) 1881-1956 *Baker 92*
Hartmann, August Wilhelm 1775-1850 *Baker 92*
Hartmann, Carl 1895-1969 *Baker 92*
Hartmann, E. Jan 1929- *St&PR 93*
Hartmann, Edward George 1912- *WhoAm 92*
Hartmann, Edward H. 1940- *St&PR 93*
Hartmann, Elmar 1941- *WhoScE 91-3*
Hartmann, Emil (Wilhelm Emilius Zinn) 1836-1898 *Baker 92*
Hartmann, Ervin 1935- *WhoScE 91-4*
Hartmann, Erwin 1924- *WhoScE 91-3*
Hartmann, Frederick Howard 1922- *ConAu 38NR, WhoAm 92*
Hartmann, Frederick William 1928- *WhoAm 92*
Hartmann, George Herman 1927- *WhoAm 92*
Hartmann, Hans Dieter 1925- *WhoScE 91-3*
Hartmann, Hans Gregory 1961- *WhoSSW 93*
Hartmann, Heidrun E.K. 1942- *WhoScE 91-3*
Hartmann, Hermann 1914- *WhoScE 91-3*
Hartmann, Horst Alfred 1927- *WhoWor 93*
Hartmann, Hudson Thomas 1914- *WhoAm 92*
Hartmann, Johann Ernst (Joseph) 1726-1793 *Baker 92*
Hartmann, Johann Peter Emilius 1805-1900 *Baker 92*
Hartmann, Jurgen Heinrich 1945- *WhoWor 93*
Hartmann, Karl Amadeus 1905-1963 *Baker 92, OxDcOp*
Hartmann, Karl Max 1935- *WhoWor 93*
Hartmann, Ludwig 1929- *WhoScE 91-3*
Hartmann, Martin R. 1948- *St&PR 93*
Hartmann, Pater 1863-1914 *Baker 92*
Hartmann, Peggy Lynn 1964- *WhoAmW 93*
Hartmann, Richard J. 1933- *St&PR 93*
Hartmann, Robert Carl 1919- *WhoAm 92*
Hartmann, Robert E. 1926- *St&PR 93*
Hartmann, Robert Elliott 1926- *WhoAm 92*
Hartmann, Robert Sankey 1948- *WhoE 93*
Hartmann, Robert Trowbridge 1917- *WhoAm 92*
Hartmann, Ronald T. *Law&B 92*
Hartmann, Rudolf 1900-1988 *Baker 92, IntDcOp, OxDcOp*
Hartmann, Rudolf 1929- *WhoSSW 93*
Hartmann, Ruth Annemarie 1936- *WhoAmW 93*
Hartmann, Sadakichi 1867-1944 *BioIn 17*
Hartmann, Svend E. 1931- *St&PR 93*
Hartmann, Thomas (Alexandrovich de) 1885-1956 *Baker 92*
Hartmann, Uwe 1942- *WhoWor 93*
Hartmann, Werner 1927- *WhoScE 91-3*
Hartmann, Werner 1955- *WhoWor 93*
Hartmann, William Edward 1916- *WhoAm 92*
Hartmann, William K. 1939- *ScF&FL 92*
Hartmann, William Kenneth 1939- *WhoAm 92*
Hartmann, Zoe *AmWomPl*
Hartmann-Downing, Nancy L. *St&PR 93*
Hartmann-Johnsen, Olaf Johan 1924- *WhoWor 93*
Hartnagel, Hans L. 1934- *WhoScE 91-3*
Hartnall, Michael James 1942- *WhoWor 93*
Hartnedy, Peter Gerard 1949- *St&PR 93*
Hartness, John Douglas, Jr. 1949- *WhoSSW 93*
Hartness, Sandra Jean 1944- *WhoAmW 93*
Hartness, Thomas Signor 1918- *St&PR 93*
Hartnett, Edmond A. 1945- *St&PR 93*
Hartnett, Elizabeth A. 1952- *WhoAmW 93*
Hartnett, Gabby 1900-1972 *BioIn 17*
Hartnett, J. Michael *Law&B 92*
Hartnett, James Patrick 1924- *WhoAm 92, WhoWor 93*
Hartnett, John A. 1936- *St&PR 93*
Hartnett, John F. 1937- *WhoE 93, WhoWor 93*
Hartnett, Katherine 1951- *WhoAm 92*
Hartnett, Kathleen Mary 1960- *WhoWor 93*
Hartnett, Koula C. 1938- *WhoSSW 93*

Hartnett, Patricia L. *Law&B 92*
Hartnett, Richard E. 1947- *St&PR 93*
Hartnett, Robert Lee 1932- *WhoSSW 93*
Hartnett, Thomas J., Jr. 1942- *St&PR 93*
Hartnett, Thomas Patrick 1942- *St&PR 93, WhoAm 92*
Hartnett, Thomas Robert, III 1920- *WhoSSW 93, WhoWor 93*
Hartnett, W.J. Bill *Law&B 92*
Hartnett, Will Ford 1956- *WhoEmL 93, WhoSSW 93*
Hartnett-Henderson, Jennifer Lynne 1964- *WhoEmL 93*
Hartney, Joseph C. d1991 *BioIn 17*
Hartoch, Kenneth 1927- *St&PR 93*
Hartocollis, Peter 1922- *WhoScE 91-3*
Hart of South Lanark, Baroness 1924-1991 *AnObit 1991, BioIn 17*
Hartog, Diana 1942- *WhoCanL 92*
Hartog, Eduard de 1829-1909 *Baker 92*
Hartog, Jack Byron 1927- *St&PR 93*
Hartog, Jacob Pieter Den 1901-1989 *BioIn 17*
Hartog, Jan de *ScF&FL 92*
Hartogensis, Stephen 1931- *St&PR 93*
Harton, Ernest H. 1936- *St&PR 93, WhoIns 93*
Harton, John James 1941- *St&PR 93, WhoAm 92*
Harton, Thomas Dean 1945- *St&PR 93*
Harton, Thomas Gordon 1909- *WhoSSW 93*
Hartpence, Patricia Ann 1956- *WhoAmW 93*
Hartrack, Richard C. 1945- *St&PR 93*
Hartranft, John Frederick 1830-1889 *BioIn 17*
Hartrick, A.S. 1864-1950 *BioIn 17*
Hartrick, Archibald Standish 1864-1950 *BioIn 17*
Hartrick, Janice K. *Law&B 92*
Hartridge, David Charles 1939- *WhoUN 92*
Hartridge, Jon 1934- *ScF&FL 92*
Hartsaw, William O. 1921- *WhoAm 92*
Hartse, Denise Yvonne 1951- *WhoAmW 93*
Hartsel, Donald Ralph, Jr. 1947- *WhoEmL 93*
Hartsfield, Donald Wayne 1949- *WhoSSW 93*
Hartsfield, Henry Warren, Jr. 1933- *WhoAm 92*
Hartsfield, James Kennedy, Jr. 1955- *WhoSSW 93*
Hartsfield-Thomas, Stephanie Laverne 1962- *WhoAmW 93*
Hartshorn, Elizabeth 1908- *WhoSSW 93*
Hartshorn, Harry Sherwin 1943- *WhoSSW 93*
Hartshorn, W.T. 1944- *St&PR 93*
Hartshorne, Charles 1897- *BioIn 17, WhoAm 92*
Hartshorne, Henry 1823-1897 *ScF&FL 92*
Hartshorne, Richard d1992 *NewYTBS 92*
Hartsock, Linda Sue 1940- *WhoAm 92*
Hartsock, Robert L. 1939- *St&PR 93*
Hartsoe, Joseph R. *Law&B 92*
Hartson, Maurice J., III 1936- *WhoIns 93*
Hartson, Susan Belt 1958- *WhoEmL 93*
Hartsook, David L. 1948- *WhoIns 93*
Hartsook, Larry D. 1943- *St&PR 93, WhoAm 92*
Hartsough, Cheryl Marie 1959- *WhoSSW 93*
Hartsough, Gayla A. Kraetsch 1949- *WhoEmL 93*
Hartsough, Walter Douglas 1924- *WhoAm 92*
Hartstein, Jacob I. 1912-1991 *BioIn 17*
Hartsuck, Jean Ann 1939- *WhoAm 92*
Hartt, Andrew Douglas 1947- *St&PR 93*
Hartt, Frederick 1914-1991 *BioIn 17*
Hartt, Julian Norris 1911- *WhoAm 92*
Hartt, Stanley Herbert 1937- *WhoE 93*
Hartt, Susan Kay *Law&B 92*
Hartt, Susan Kay 1948- *WhoAmW 93*
Hartung, Dale E. *Law&B 92*
Hartung, Debbie Jean 1951- *WhoAmW 93*
Hartung, Glenn J. 1935- *St&PR 93*
Hartung, Hans 1904-1989 *BioIn 17*
Hartung, Klaus 1938- *WhoScE 91-3*
Hartung, Mary *WhoAmW 93*
Hartung, Paul William, Jr. 1927- *St&PR 93*
Hartung, Roderick Lee 1935- *WhoAm 92*
Hartung, Ronald Frederick 1952- *WhoEmL 93*
Hartung, Steven Joseph 1960- *WhoEmL 93*
Hartung, Steven Lee 1946- *St&PR 93*
Hartung, Susan Enid 1954- *WhoAmW 93*
Hartung, Walter Magnus 1907- *WhoAm 92*
Hartung, Wolfgang 1926- *WhoScE 91-3*
Hartung, Wolfgang 1937- *St&PR 93*
Hartvig, Tor 1933- *WhoScE 91-4*
Hartweg, Dale S. 1933- *St&PR 93*
Hartwell, David G. 1941- *ScF&FL 92*
Hartwell, David Geddes 1941- *WhoE 93*
Hartwell, Frederic Peck 1947- *WhoE 93*
Hartwell, George *BioIn 17*
Hartwell, Irene V. *AmWomPl*
Hartwell, Janice K. *Law&B 92*
Hartwell, John M. 1916- *St&PR 93*
Hartwell, Margaret Carroll 1937- *St&PR 93*
Hartwell, Ronald G. *Law&B 92*
Hartwell, Samuel A. 1930- *St&PR 93*
Hartwell, Stephen 1915- *St&PR 93*
Hartwell, Stephen 1916- *WhoAm 92*
Hartwich, Dieter 1927- *WhoWor 93*
Hartwich, Peter Michael 1955- *WhoSSW 93*
Hartwig, Charles Walter 1941- *WhoSSW 93*
Hartwig, Dieter 1934- *Baker 92*
Hartwig, Eugene L. *Law&B 92*
Hartwig, Eugene L. 1933- *St&PR 93*
Hartwig, Eugene Lawrence 1933- *WhoAm 92*
Hartwig, Gordon E. *Law&B 92*
Hartwig, Hans-Georg 1944- *WhoScE 91-3*
Hartwig, Harvey L. 1943- *WhoIns 93*
Hartwig, Irene Anita 1967- *WhoAmW 93*
Hartwig, Karl Theodore, Jr. 1946- *WhoEmL 93, WhoSSW 93*
Hartwig, Larry D. 1940- *St&PR 93*
Hartwig, Larry Dean 1940- *WhoAm 92*
Hartwig, Thomas Leo 1952- *WhoAm 92, WhoE 93*
Hartwig, Thomas Roger 1936- *St&PR 93*
Harty, Emmett Joseph 1946- *WhoE 93*
Harty, Hamilton 1879-1941 *BioIn 17*
Harty, (Herbert) Hamilton 1879-1941 *Baker 92*
Harty, James D. 1929- *St&PR 93, WhoAm 92*
Harty, James Quinn 1925- *WhoAm 92*
Harty, Roger Philip 1916- *St&PR 93*
Harty, Sheila Therese 1948- *WhoAm 92*
Hartz, Charles A. 1938- *St&PR 93*
Hartz, Charles A., Jr. *Law&B 92*
Hartz, Deborah Dillingham 1953- *WhoEmL 93*
Hartz, Fred Robert 1933- *WhoAm 92, WhoSSW 93*
Hartz, John Ernest, Jr. 1935- *St&PR 93*
Hartz, Luetta Bertha 1947- *WhoAmW 93*
Hartz, Renee Semo 1946- *WhoAm 92, WhoAmW 93*
Hartzel, David M. 1948- *St&PR 93*
Hartzel, Gerald 1927- *St&PR 93*
Hartzel, Randall L. 1957- *St&PR 93*
Hartzel, Terry J. *Law&B 92*
Hartzell, Andrew Cornelius, Jr. 1927- *WhoAm 92*
Hartzell, Charles R. 1941- *WhoAm 92*
Hartzell, David Edward 1946- *St&PR 93, WhoSSW 93*
Hartzell, Eugene 1932- *Baker 92*
Hartzell, Frank Carlisle 1925- *St&PR 93*
Hartzell, George Turner 1920- *WhoAm 92, WhoE 93*
Hartzell, Irene Janofsky 1938- *WhoAmW 93*
Hartzell, James R. 1934- *St&PR 93*
Hartzell, Robert L. 1934- *St&PR 93*
Hartzell, Susan *ScF&FL 92*
Hartzell, Suzy 1959- *ScF&FL 92*
Hartzler, Cheryl Elaine 1945- *WhoAmW 93*
Hartzler, Stanley James 1947- *WhoWor 93*
Haruki, Warren H. 1952- *St&PR 93*
Haruki Murakami 1949- *ConAu 136*
Harun, Joseph Stanley 1925- *St&PR 93*
Harun, Tun Datu Haji Mustapha Bin Datu 1918- *WhoAsAP 91*
Haruna, Mikio 1946- *WhoWor 93*
Harun Al-Rashid 766-809 *OxDcByz*
Harun Ibn Yahya fl. 9th cent.-10th cent. *OxDcByz*
Haruta, Shigeaki 1940- *WhoAsAP 91*
Harva, Uno 1882-1949 *IntDcAn*
Harvald, Bent J. 1924- *WhoScE 91-2*
Harvald, Sv. Aa. 1921- *WhoScE 91-2*
Harvanek, Robert Francis 1916- *WhoAm 92*
Harvard, Andrew Carson *Law&B 92*
Harvard, Beverly Joyce Bailey 1950- *WhoEmL 93*
Harvard, Julia Ross 1934- *WhoAmW 93*
Harvatin, Anthony Christopher 1951- *WhoE 93, WhoEmL 93*
Harvell, Cecil C. 1927- *St&PR 93*
Harvell, Grady E. 1949- *St&PR 93*
Harvell, Grady Edwin 1949- *WhoSSW 93*
Harvengt, C. 1935- *WhoScE 91-2*
Harvengt, Carl 1934- *WhoWor 93*
Harvester, James Vernon 1921- *WhoSSW 93*
Harvey, A. Mosby, Jr. *Law&B 92*
Harvey, Abner McGehee 1911- *WhoAm 92*
Harvey, Alan Lang *WhoScE 91-1*
Harvey, Alexander, II 1923- *WhoAm 92, WhoE 93*
Harvey, Alva L. d1992 *NewYTBS 92*
Harvey, Andrew Charles *WhoScE 91-1*
Harvey, Ann Gray 1956- *WhoSSW 93*
Harvey, Anthony 1931- *MiSFD 9*
Harvey, Anthony Kesteven 1931- *WhoWor 93*
Harvey, Audrey *WhoScE 91-1*
Harvey, Augustus William 1772-1856 *BioIn 17*
Harvey, Bernard S. 1941- *St&PR 93*
Harvey, Billie Faye 1926- *WhoSSW 93*
Harvey, Brett *BioIn 17*
Harvey, Brian 1926- *St&PR 93*
Harvey, Bruce Dewolfe 1928- *St&PR 93*
Harvey, Bryan Laurence 1937- *WhoAm 92*
Harvey, Calvin Rea 1943- *WhoAm 92, WhoE 93*
Harvey, Cannon Y. *Law&B 92*
Harvey, Charles A. *St&PR 93*
Harvey, Charles Ernest 1963- *WhoE 93, WhoEmL 93*
Harvey, Charles Richard Musgrave 1937- *WhoWor 93*
Harvey, Colin Edwin 1944- *WhoAm 92*
Harvey, Colleen Curran *Law&B 92*
Harvey, Curran W. 1928- *St&PR 93*
Harvey, Curran Whitthorne, Jr. 1928- *WhoAm 92*
Harvey, Cynthia *WhoAm 92*
Harvey, Daniel A. *Law&B 92*
Harvey, Darryl Lee *Law&B 92*
Harvey, David *WhoScE 91-1*
Harvey, David 1946- *ScF&FL 92*
Harvey, David Alan *BioIn 17*
Harvey, David Christopher 1959- *St&PR 93*
Harvey, David R. *WhoScE 91-1*
Harvey, David W. 1942- *WhoScE 91-1*
Harvey, Della Shaw *AmWomPl*
Harvey, Donald 1930- *WhoAm 92*
Harvey, Donald Joseph 1922- *WhoAm 92*
Harvey, Donald Phillips 1924- *WhoAm 92*
Harvey, Doris Cannon 1930- *WhoAmW 93*
Harvey, Doug 1924-1989 *BioIn 17*
Harvey, Douglas Stewart 1952- *WhoEmL 93*
Harvey, Douglass Coate 1917- *WhoAm 92*
Harvey, Edith Mary *AmWomPl*
Harvey, Edmund Huxley, Jr. 1934- *WhoAm 92, WhoWrEP 92*
Harvey, Edward Douglas *WhoScE 91-1*
Harvey, Edward J. 1936- *St&PR 93*
Harvey, Edward James 1936- *WhoAm 92*
Harvey, Edward Thomas 1948- *St&PR 93, WhoAm 92*
Harvey, Edwin Malcolm 1928- *WhoAm 92*
Harvey, Elizabeth Robyn 1946- *WhoAsAP 91*
Harvey, F. Barton, Jr. 1921- *WhoAm 92*
Harvey, F. Reese 1941- *WhoAm 92*
Harvey, Frank 1913-1982 *ScF&FL 92*
Harvey, Frank W. 1931- *St&PR 93*
Harvey, Fred *BioIn 17*
Harvey, Fred 1932- *St&PR 93*
Harvey, Frederick Parker 1920- *WhoAm 92*
Harvey, George Brinton McClellan 1864-1928 *JrnUS*
Harvey, George Burton 1931- *St&PR 93, WhoAm 92*
Harvey, George E. 1945- *St&PR 93*
Harvey, George Edwin 1938- *WhoAm 92*
Harvey, Gerald Joseph 1925- *St&PR 93*
Harvey, Gregory Alan 1949- *WhoEmL 93, WhoWor 93*
Harvey, Harold Douglas 1930- *BiDAMSp 1989*
Harvey, Herk *BioIn 17*
Harvey, Herschel A., Jr. 1929- *St&PR 93*
Harvey, Herschel Ambrose, Jr. 1929- *WhoSSW 93, WhoWor 93*
Harvey, Irwin M. 1931- *WhoAm 92*
Harvey, J. Bailey 1905-1991 *BioIn 17*
Harvey, Jacqueline Verlena 1933- *WhoAmW 93*
Harvey, James *ScF&FL 92*
Harvey, James Douglas 1929- *WhoAm 92*
Harvey, James Madison 1833-1894 *BioIn 17*
Harvey, James Mathews, Jr. 1964- *WhoSSW 93, WhoWor 93*
Harvey, James Neal 1925- *WhoAm 92*
Harvey, James R. d1992 *BioIn 17, NewYTBS 92*
Harvey, James R. 1934- *St&PR 93*
Harvey, James Ross 1934- *WhoAm 92*
Harvey, Jane R. 1945- *WhoAmW 93*
Harvey, Jean Gilmour *ScF&FL 92*
Harvey, Joan Carol 1943- *WhoAmW 93*
Harvey, Joanne H. 1932- *WhoAm 92, WhoAmW 93*
Harvey, John Adriance 1930- *WhoAm 92*
Harvey, John Collins 1923- *WhoAm 92*
Harvey, John Douglas 1960- *WhoEmL 93*
Harvey, John Grover 1934- *WhoAm 92*
Harvey, John Kenneth *WhoScE 91-1*
Harvey, Jon M. *ScF&FL 92*
Harvey, Jonathan (Dean) 1939- *Baker 92*
Harvey, Joseph Paul, Jr. 1922- *WhoAm 92*
Harvey, Joseph Seep 1920- *St&PR 93*
Harvey, Judith Gootkin 1944- *WhoAmW 93*
Harvey, Judith Weller 1932- *WhoSSW 93*
Harvey, Julia *WhoWrEP 92*
Harvey, Kate *AmWomPl*
Harvey, Katherine Abler 1946- *WhoAmW 93*
Harvey, Kenneth Ricardo 1956- *WhoWrEP 92*
Harvey, Laura S. *St&PR 93*
Harvey, Laurence 1928-1973 *IntDcF 2-3*
Harvey, Lenis Arlee 1935- *WhoSSW 93*
Harvey, Leslie Leo 1926- *WhoE 93*
Harvey, Linda Anne *Law&B 92*
Harvey, Lorena Kay 1943- *WhoAmW 93*
Harvey, Lynne Cooper *WhoAmW 93*
Harvey, M. Elayn 1945- *ScF&FL 92*
Harvey, Malcolm 1936- *WhoAm 92*
Harvey, Marc Sean 1960- *WhoEmL 93, WhoWor 93*
Harvey, Maria Luisa Alvarez *WhoSSW 93*
Harvey, Marion *AmWomPl*
Harvey, Martha Elizabeth 1949- *WhoEmL 93*
Harvey, Mary Bird 1929- *WhoE 93*
Harvey, Maurine Nelson 1943- *WhoAmW 93*
Harvey, Melinda Ann 1958- *WhoAmW 93*
Harvey, Michael *BioIn 17*
Harvey, Michael L. *Law&B 92*
Harvey, Michael Lee 1944- *WhoAm 92*
Harvey, Michelle Mauthe 1954- *WhoAmW 93, WhoEmL 93, WhoSSW 93*
Harvey, Mona R. *Law&B 92*
Harvey, Morris Lane 1950- *WhoEmL 93*
Harvey, Neil 1921- *WhoE 93*
Harvey, Norman 1931- *ScF&FL 92*
Harvey, Norman Ronald 1933- *WhoAm 92*
Harvey, Patricia Jean 1931- *WhoWor 93*
Harvey, Paul 1918- *JrnUS, WhoAm 92*
Harvey, Peter James 1941- *WhoAm 92*
Harvey, R. Carol *Law&B 92*
Harvey, Ralph 1901-1991 *BioIn 17*
Harvey, Raymond Norman 1932- *WhoE 93*
Harvey, Richard Cleveland 1936- *St&PR 93*
Harvey, Robert D.H. 1920- *St&PR 93*
Harvey, Robert Dixon Hopkins 1920- *WhoAm 92*
Harvey, Rodney *BioIn 17*
Harvey, Roger C. d1990 *BioIn 17*
Harvey, Roland 1945- *SmATA 71 [port]*
Harvey, Ronald Gilbert 1927- *WhoAm 92*
Harvey, Rose Marie 1924- *WhoE 93*
Harvey, Roy Sears 1920- *WhoSSW 93*
Harvey, Rupert *MiSFD 9*
Harvey, Sanford William, Jr. *Law&B 92*
Harvey, Stanley Joseph *WhoScE 91-1*
Harvey, Stuart C., Jr. *Law&B 92*
Harvey, Stuart Charles, Jr. 1961- *WhoEmL 93*
Harvey, Susan d1990 *BioIn 17*
Harvey, Terry Dale *Law&B 92*
Harvey, Thomas F. *Law&B 92*
Harvey, Thomas J. 1939- *WhoAm 92*
Harvey, Thomas W. 1946- *St&PR 93*
Harvey, Timothy R. 1951- *St&PR 93*
Harvey, Van Austin 1926- *WhoAm 92*
Harvey, Virginia Smith 1950- *WhoAmW 93*
Harvey, William *Law&B 92*
Harvey, William Andre 1941- *WhoE 93*
Harvey, William Bernard 1948- *WhoSSW 93*
Harvey, William Brantley, Jr. 1930- *WhoAm 92*
Harvey, William Burnett 1922- *WhoAm 92*
Harvey, William D. *Law&B 92*
Harvey, William Fryer 1885-1937 *ScF&FL 92*
Harvey, William Morris 1942- *WhoE 93*
Harvey, William R. *AfrAmBi*
Harvey, William Robert 1941- *WhoSSW 93*
Harvey & the Moonglows *SoulM*
Harvey-Brown, Cynthia Ann 1968- *WhoAmW 93*
Harvey-Jones, John *BioIn 17*
Harvie, Crawford Thomas *Law&B 92*
Harvie, Donald Southam 1924- *St&PR 93*
Harvie, James 1933- *St&PR 93*
Harvie, Peggy Ann 1936- *WhoAmW 93*
Harvieux, Anne Marie 1945- *WhoAm 92*
Harville, James M. 1940- *WhoSSW 93*
Harville, Lisa D. *Law&B 92*
Harvin, David Tarleton 1945- *WhoAm 92*

Harvin, Lucius H., III 1938- *WhoSSW 93*
Harvin, William Charles 1919- *WhoAm 92*
Harvitt, Adrianne Stanley 1954- *WhoEmL 93*
Harvot, Ronald A., Jr. *Law&B 92*
Harvout, Clifford 1912-1990 *BioIn 17*
Harward, Donald *WhoAm 92*
Harward, Gary John 1941- *St&PR 93*
Harward, Valerie Pierce 1928- *WhoAmW 93*
Harwayne, Frank 1920- *WhoIns 93*
Harwell, Aubrey Biggs 1942- *WhoAm 92*
Harwell, Charles Horace 1939- *WhoSSW 93*
Harwell, David Walker 1932- *WhoAm 92, WhoSSW 93*
Harwell, Eddy G. 1952- *St&PR 93*
Harwell, Edwin Whitley 1929- *WhoAm 92*
Harwell, Ernie *BioIn 17*
Harwell, Frances Olivia 1960- *WhoAmW 93*
Harwell, Paul Lafayette 1930- *WhoSSW 93*
Harwell, Robert E., Jr. 1935- *St&PR 93*
Harwell, Thomas Meade 1913- *ScF&FL 92*
Harwell, William Earnest 1916- *BiDAMSp 1989*
Harwell, William Earnest 1918- *WhoAm 92*
Harwell, William J. 1932- *St&PR 93*
Harwerth, E. Noel *Law&B 92*
Harwick, B.L. *ConAu 38NR*
Harwick, Cheryl Lee *Law&B 92*
Harwitt, Carla Schiller *Law&B 92*
Harwood, Basil 1859-1949 *Baker 92*
Harwood, Bernice Baumel 1923- *WhoE 93*
Harwood, Brian Dennis 1932- *WhoAm 92*
Harwood, Colin Frederick 1937- *WhoE 93*
Harwood, Daniel H. 1953- *St&PR 93*
Harwood, Deborah Johnson *Law&B 92*
Harwood, Eleanor Cash 1921- *WhoAmW 93, WhoWor 93*
Harwood, Elizabeth 1938-1990 *BioIn 17, OxDcOp*
Harwood, Elizabeth (Jean) 1938-1990 *Baker 92*
Harwood, Francis fl. 1748-1783 *BioIn 17*
Harwood, Gwen 1920- *IntLitE*
Harwood, Ivan Richmond 1939- *WhoAm 92*
Harwood, Jerry 1926- *WhoAm 92*
Harwood, Jim 1939- *St&PR 93*
Harwood, John *ScF&FL 92*
Harwood, John 1949- *WhoScE 91-1*
Harwood, John A. *Law&B 92*
Harwood, John L. *WhoScE 91-1*
Harwood, Lowell Richard 1929- *St&PR 93*
Harwood, Michael *BioIn 17*
Harwood, Peter Keith 1939- *WhoWor 93*
Harwood, Richard Lee 1925- *WhoAm 92*
Harwood, Richard Roberts, Jr. 1921- *WhoAm 92*
Harwood, Sanford E. 1924- *St&PR 93*
Harwood, Vanessa Clare 1947- *WhoAm 92*
Harwood, Virginia Ann 1925- *WhoAmW 93, WhoWor 93*
Harwood, William Bradford 1925- *WhoE 93*
Harz, Christopher R. 1944- *St&PR 93*
Has, Alanur 1953- *WhoScE 91-4*
Has, Wojciech Jerzy 1925- *DrEEuF*
Has, Zdzislaw J. 1930- *WhoScE 91-4*
Hasak, Janet E. *Law&B 92*
Hasan, Harris 1956- *WhoWor 93*
Hasan, Ibnul 1925- *WhoWor 93*
Hasan, Jeddi 1931- *WhoScE 91-4*
Hasan, Mahmudul 1936- *WhoAsAP 91*
Hasan, Malik M. *St&PR 93*
Hasan, Maria Rosaria 1947- *WhoIns 93*
Hasan, Muhammad Abdille Sayyid 1864-1920 *DcTwHis*
Hasan, Nurul 1921- *WhoAsAP 91*
Hasan, Razia Qureshi 1944- *WhoWor 93*
Hasan al-Banna 1906-1949 *DcTwHis*
Hasanen, Erkki Kalevi 1931- *WhoScE 91-4*
Hasbrook, Denise M. *Law&B 92*
Hasbrouck, Elizabeth (Louise) Seymour 1883- *AmWomPl*
Hasbrouck, Kenneth Edward 1916- *WhoE 93*
Hasbrouck, Olive 1905- *SweetSg B [port]*
Hasbrouck, Robert Wilson 1896-1985 *HarEnMi*
Hasbrouck, Stephen J. 1940- *St&PR 93*
Hasbrouck, Wilbert Roland 1931- *WhoAm 92*
Hascall, James George 1938- *St&PR 93*
Hasche, Bruce A. 1953- *St&PR 93*
Haschek, Horst *WhoScE 91-4*
Hasdrubal fl. 150BC-146BC *HarEnMi*
Hasdrubal Barca d207BC *HarEnMi*
Hasdrubal Gisgo 202BC- *HarEnMi*
Hase, Anneli 1937- *WhoScE 91-4*
Hase, David John 1940- *WhoAm 92*
Hase, Donald A. 1928- *St&PR 93*
Hase, Hellmuth von 1891-1979 *See* Breitkopf & Hartel *Baker 92*
Hase, Hermann von 1880-1945 *See* Breitkopf & Hartel *Baker 92*
Hase, Oskar von 1846-1921 *See* Breitkopf & Hartel *Baker 92*
Hase, Richard Arthur 1945- *WhoE 93*
Hase, Tapio A. 1937- *WhoScE 91-4*
Hase, Yuriko 1947- *WhoAsAP 91*
Hasebe, Kotondo 1882-1969 *IntDcAn*
Hasegawa, Akinori 1941- *WhoWor 93*
Hasegawa, Akira 1934- *WhoAm 92*
Hasegawa, Hideki 1941- *WhoWor 93*
Hasegawa, Hiroshi 1928- *WhoWor 93*
Hasegawa, Kazuo 1908-1984 *IntDcF 2-3 [port]*
Hasegawa, Mitsuo 1913- *WhoWor 93*
Hasegawa, Morihiko d1990 *BioIn 17*
Hasegawa, Norishige 1907- *St&PR 93*
Hasegawa, Shin 1918-1990 *BioIn 17*
Hasegawa, Sukehiro 1942- *WhoUN 92*
Hasegawa, Takashi 1911- *WhoAsAP 91*
Hasegawa, Takemitsu 1944- *WhoWor 93*
Hasegawa, Tatsuo 1916- *WhoWor 93*
Hasegawa, Tomohiro 1962- *WhoE 93, WhoEmL 93*
Hasegawa, Tony Seisuke 1941- *WhoWor 93*
Hasegawa, Yoshimichi 1850-1924 *HarEnMi*
Hasegawa Kiyoshi 1883-1970 *HarEnMi*
Hasek, Jaroslav 1883-1923 *BioIn 17*
Hasek, John Allan 1936- *WhoE 93*
Hasel, Norman L. 1932- *St&PR 93*
Haselbach, Edwin J. 1940- *WhoScE 91-4*
Haselden, Catherine Anderson 1957- *WhoEmL 93*
Haselden, Clyde LeRoy 1914- *WhoAm 92*
Haselden, Geoffrey G. *WhoScE 91-1*
Haseley, Susan L. 1959- *St&PR 93, WhoIns 93*
Haselkorn, David 1944- *St&PR 93*
Haselkorn, Robert 1934- *WhoAm 92*
Haselmann, John Philip 1940- *WhoAm 92, WhoWor 93*
Haselmayer, Louis August 1911- *WhoAm 92*
Haselrig, Carlton Lee 1966- *BiDAMSp 1989*
Haseltine, Florence Pat 1942- *WhoAm 92, WhoAmW 93*
Haselton, Forrest Ronald 1938- *WhoAm 92*
Haselton, Rick Thomas 1953- *WhoEmL 93*
Haseman, Paul B. *Law&B 92*
Hasemann, Klaus 1944- *WhoWor 93*
Hasen, Burton Stanly 1921- *WhoAm 92*
Hasenclever, Wolfgang *WhoScE 91-3*
Hasenfratz, Sally A. 1960- *WhoEmL 93*
Hasenmiller, Stephen J. 1949- *WhoIns 93*
Hasenoehrl, Roland 1945- *WhoAm 92*
Hasenour, Lee 1936- *WhoSSW 93*
Hasenpflug, Jerome Francis 1955- *WhoEmL 93*
Haser, August Ferdinand 1779-1844 *Baker 92, OxDcOp*
Haser, Charlotte 1784-1871 *Baker 92, OxDcOp*
Haser, Johann Georg 1729-1809 *OxDcOp*
Haser, Richard Michel 1942- *WhoScE 91-2*
Haserick, John Roger 1915- *WhoAm 92*
Hasford, Gustav 1947- *ScF&FL 92*
Hash, John Frank 1944- *WhoAm 92*
Hashagen, John D. 1941- *St&PR 93*
Hashem, Abul 1938- *WhoUN 92*
Hashemi, Reza Attar 1947- *WhoE 93*
Hashemi-Rafsanjani, Ali Akbar 1935- *WhoWor 93*
Hasher, Lynn Ann 1944- *WhoAmW 93*
Hashim, Elinor Marie 1933- *WhoAm 92*
Hashim Bin Safin, Hashim Bin 1949- *WhoAsAP 91*
Hashimoto, Akira 1936- *St&PR 93*
Hashimoto, Atsushi 1928- *WhoAsAP 91*
Hashimoto, Frances Kazuko 1943- *WhoWor 93*
Hashimoto, Kingoro 1890-1957 *HarEnMi*
Hashimoto, Kiyoshi 1933- *St&PR 93*
Hashimoto, Koichi 1921- *WhoWor 93*
Hashimoto, Koichiro 1926- *WhoAsAP 91*
Hashimoto, Mochitsura 1909- *HarEnMi*
Hashimoto, Namio 1922- *WhoWor 93*
Hashimoto, Paulo Hitonari 1930- *WhoWor 93*
Hashimoto, Ronald G. 1938- *St&PR 93*
Hashimoto, Ryutaro 1937- *WhoAsAP 91*
Hashimoto, Shigeo 1934- *WhoWor 93*
Hashimoto, Takeji 1942- *WhoWor 93*
Hashimoto, Tatsuichiro 1924- *WhoWor 93*
Hashimoto, Tooru 1925- *WhoWor 93*
Hashimoto, Toru *BioIn 17*
Hashimoto, Toru 1934- *WhoWor 93*
Hashimoto, Tsuneyuki 1950- *WhoWor 93*
Hashimoto, Yoshikazu 1927- *WhoWor 93*
Hashimoto Gun 1886-1963 *HarEnMi*
Hashimoto-Sinclair, Yoko 1939- *WhoE 93*
Hashmi, Safdar 1954-1989 *BioIn 17*
Hashmi, Sajjad Ahmad 1933- *WhoAm 92, WhoIns 93*
Hashmi, Shamim 1940- *WhoAsAP 91*
Hashmi, Syed Haseen 1935- *WhoWor 93*
Hashmi, Syed Muhammad Wajid 1933- *WhoWor 93*
Hasholt, Bent 1941- *WhoScE 91-2*
Hasiak, Raymond J. *Law&B 92*
Hasija, Om P. 1943- *St&PR 93*
Hasina Wajed, Sheikh *WhoAsAP 91*
Hasiuk, Cynthia Lee 1950- *WhoE 93*
Haskayne, Richard Francis 1934- *WhoAm 92*
Haskell, Arthur Jacob 1926- *WhoAm 92*
Haskell, Barbara 1946- *WhoAm 92, WhoE 93*
Haskell, Barry Geoffry 1941- *WhoAm 92*
Haskell, Blanton Winship 1920- *WhoAm 92*
Haskell, Dan L. *Law&B 92*
Haskell, Donald McMillan 1932- *WhoAm 92*
Haskell, Helen Lacey d1991 *BioIn 17*
Haskell, John Henry Farrell, Jr. 1932- *St&PR 93, WhoAm 92*
Haskell, Keith 1939- *WhoWor 93*
Haskell, Molly *BioIn 17*
Haskell, Molly 1939- *WhoAmW 93*
Haskell, Paul Gershon 1927- *WhoAm 92*
Haskell, Paul S. 1938- *St&PR 93*
Haskell, Peter Abraham 1934- *WhoAm 92*
Haskell, Peter Thomas *WhoScE 91-1*
Haskell, Preston Hampton 1938- *St&PR 93*
Haskell, Preston Hampton, III 1938- *WhoAm 92*
Haskell, Rachel 19th cent.- *BioIn 17*
Haskell, Raymond H. 1930- *WhoIns 93*
Haskell, Raymond Hilbert 1930- *St&PR 93*
Haskell, Robert G. 1952- *St&PR 93*
Haskell, Sandra Jo 1963- *WhoAmW 93*
Haskell, Thomas Langdon 1939- *WhoAm 92*
Haskell, Valerie Kropotkin 1950- *WhoAmW 93*
Haskell-Robinson, Patricia Corbin 1931- *WhoSSW 93*
Haskew, George M. 1927- *St&PR 93*
Haskew, George M., Jr. 1927- *WhoAm 92*
Haskil, Clara 1895-1960 *Baker 92*
Haskin, Byron 1899-1984 *MiSFD 9N*
Haskin, David Warren 1933- *St&PR 93*
Haskin, Dayton William 1946- *WhoE 93*
Haskin, Donald Lee 1945- *WhoAm 92*
Haskin, Lynn Martin 1947- *WhoAmW 93*
Haskin, Marvin Edward 1930- *WhoAm 92*
Haskins, Arthur Lyman, III 1944- *St&PR 93*
Haskins, Caryl Parker 1908- *WhoAm 92, WhoWor 93*
Haskins, George Lee 1915-1991 *BioIn 17*
Haskins, Jack Lionel 1935- *St&PR 93*
Haskins, James 1941- *SmATA 69 [port], WhoAm 92*
Haskins, James S. 1941- *BlkAuII 92, MajAI [port]*
Haskins, Jim *MajAI, SmATA 69*
Haskins, Kristen Elizabeth 1944- *WhoAmW 93*
Haskins, Linda M. 1954- *St&PR 93*
Haskins, Luther Granville, III 1951- *WhoEmL 93*
Haskins, Mary Sumerlin *Law&B 92*
Haskins, Michael A. d1991 *BioIn 17*
Haskins, Michael Anthony 1957- *WhoSSW 93*
Haskins, Sandra L. 1944- *St&PR 93*
Haskins, Thomas Alexander 1950- *WhoEmL 93*
Haskins, Victoria Jean 1953- *WhoAmW 93*
Haskit, Roberta Tefft 1944- *St&PR 93*
Hasko, Ferenc 1929- *WhoScE 91-4*
Haskova, Vera 1927- *WhoScE 91-4*
Haskowitz, Howard 1947- *WhoIns 93*
Haskvitz, Alan *BioIn 17*
Hasl, Hannelore V.M. *Law&B 92*
Haslam, David *WhoScE 91-4*
Haslam, Douglas Frank 1941- *St&PR 93*
Haslam, Gerald W. 1937- *BioIn 17*
Haslam, Gerald William 1937- *WhoWrEP 92*
Haslam, Robert *BioIn 17, WhoScE 91-1*
Haslam, Robert Frank *WhoScE 91-1*
Haslego, Kathlyn Joy 1957- *WhoAmW 93*
Haslem, Edwin *WhoScE 91-1*
Haslem, John Arthur 1934- *WhoE 93*
Hasle Nielsen, Arne 1937- *WhoScE 91-2*
Hasler, Bonnie Sether 1944- *WhoAmW 93*
Hasler, E.A. 1949- *St&PR 93*
Hasler, Joachim 1929- *DrEEuF*
Hasler, Joseph William 1934- *St&PR 93*
Hasler, Rudolf 1942- *WhoScE 91-4*
Hasler, Stephan *WhoScE 91-4*
Haslerud, Bruce Daniel *Law&B 92*
Haslerud, George M. 1906-1990 *BioIn 17*
Haslett, Betty Jeanne 1945- *WhoAmW 93*
Haslett, Caroline 1895-1957 *BioIn 17*
Haslett, Harriet Holmes *AmWomPl*
Hasley, Michael A. 1941- *WhoIns 93*
Hasley, Michael James 1946- *St&PR 93*
Hasling, Jill Freeman 1952- *WhoAm 92, WhoEmL 93*
Hasling, Robert J. *Law&B 92*
Hasling, Robert John 1929- *St&PR 93*
Haslinger, Carl 1816-1868 *See* Haslinger, Tobias 1787-1842 *Baker 92*
Haslinger, Kenneth Robert 1940- *St&PR 93*
Haslinger, Tobias 1787-1842 *Baker 92*
Haslip, Katrina d1992 *NewYTBS 92*
Hasluck, Nicholas 1942- *ConAu 137*
Haslund-Christensen, Henning 1896-1948 *IntDcAn*
Haslup, Allen Lee 1926- *WhoWor 93*
Hasman, Gary Francis 1946- *WhoE 93*
Haspel, Arthur Carl 1945- *WhoAm 92*
Haspel, David K. 1949- *WhoWor 93*
Haspel, Martin Victor 1945- *WhoE 93*
Haspeslagh, Mary-Cyriel 1955- *WhoWor 93*
Hass, Anthony 1923- *WhoAm 92*
Hass, Charles John William 1934- *WhoWor 93*
Hass, Georg Hartwig 1913- *WhoSSW 93*
Hass, Heidi Elyse 1959- *WhoAmW 93*
Hass, Hyman 1934- *St&PR 93*
Hass, Robert *BioIn 17*
Hass, William H. 1934- *St&PR 93*
Hassabis, K. *WhoScE 91-4*
Hassam, Childe 1859-1935 *GayN*
Hassan, II 1929- *DcTwHis, WhoWor 93*
Hassan, II, King of Morocco 1929- *BioIn 17*
Hassan, Abdelmeguid Bayoumi 1938- *WhoUN 92*
Hassan, Aftab Syed 1952- *WhoE 93, WhoEmL 93, WhoWor 93*
Hassan, Fuad 1929- *WhoAsAP 91*
Hassan, Haidar 1951- *WhoUN 92*
Hassan, Hosni Moustafa 1937- *WhoWor 93*
Hassan, Ihab Habib 1925- *WhoAm 92, WhoWrEP 92*
Hassan, Khan Mamnoon 1941- *WhoSSW 93*
Hassan, M. Zia 1933- *WhoAm 92*
Hassan, Sandro 1954- *WhoWor 93*
Hassan, Sayed Mohammed 1944- *WhoSSW 93*
Hassan, William Ephriam, Jr. 1923- *WhoAm 92*
Hassan, Yassin Abdel 1945- *WhoAm 92*
Hassan Alban Haji Sandukong 1948- *WhoAsAP 91*
Hassanal Bolkiah, Sultan of Brunei 1946- *BioIn 17*
Hassanal Bolkiah, Mui'zzaddin Waddaulah 1946- *WhoWor 93*
Hassanal Bolkiah Mu'izzaddin Waddaulah, Paduka Seri Baginda Sultan Haji 1946- *WhoAsAP 91*
Hassan bin T al al 1947- *WhoWor 93*
Hassanein, Khatab M. 1926- *WhoAm 92*
Hassan Rida El-Senussi, Prince of Libya 1928-1992 *BioIn 17*
Hassard, Howard 1910- *St&PR 93, WhoAm 92*
Hassard, John Rose Greene 1836-1888 *JrnUS*
Hassberger, Richard L. *WhoIns 93*
Hassberger, Richard Lord 1949- *St&PR 93*
Hasse, Arthur A. 1940- *St&PR 93*
Hasse, D.E. *Law&B 92*
Hasse, Faustina c. 1700-1781 *Baker 92*
Hasse, Faustina Bordoni 1693-1783 *BioIn 17*
Hasse, Glenn Warren, Jr. 1941- *St&PR 93*
Hasse, Henry L. 1913-1977 *ScF&FL 92*
Hasse, Johann Adolf 1699-1783 *Baker 92, OxDcOp*
Hasse, Johann Adolph 1699?-1783 *IntDcOp*
Hasse, Karl 1883-1960 *Baker 92*
Hasse, Lutz K.R. 1930- *WhoScE 91-3*
Hasse, Stephan 1950- *WhoScE 91-4*
Hassebrock, Steve Allen 1945- *St&PR 93*
Hassel, James Craig 1960- *WhoE 93*
Hassel, Rudolph Christopher 1939- *WhoSSW 93*
Hasselbach, Wilhelm *WhoScE 91-3*
Hasselbalch, Marilyn Jean 1930- *WhoAmW 93*
Hasselbalch, Ole Jacob 1945- *WhoWor 93*
Hasselbarth, Ulrich Hans 1928- *WhoScE 91-3*
Hasselbring, Bruce A. 1955- *St&PR 93*
Hasselbring, Jane R. 1931- *St&PR 93*

Hasselgren, Robert William 1949- *St&PR 93, WhoIns 93*
Hasselhoff, David *BioIn 17*
Hassell, Aarno A. 1939- *St&PR 93*
Hassell, Frances Massey 1925- *WhoIns 93*
Hassell, Gerald L. 1951- *WhoAm 92*
Hassell, Jon 1937- *Baker 92*
Hassell, Leroy Rountree 1955- *WhoSSW 93*
Hassell, Martin 1927- *St&PR 93*
Hassell, Michael Patrick *WhoScE 91-1*
Hassell, Morris William 1916- *WhoSSW 93, WhoWor 93*
Hassell, Stephen P. 1949- *St&PR 93*
Hassell, Ulrich von 1881-1944 *BioIn 17*
Hasselman, Peter Morton 1937- *WhoAm 92*
Hasselman, Richard B. 1926- *WhoAm 92*
Hasselmann, Gert 1933- *WhoScE 91-2*
Hasselmann, Klaus F. 1931- *WhoScE 91-3*
Hasselmann, Klaus Ferdinand 1931- *WhoWor 93*
Hasselmans *Baker 92*
Hasselmans, Alphonse (Jean) 1845-1912 *Baker 92*
Hasselmans, Josef H. 1814-1902 *Baker 92*
Hasselmans, Louis 1878-1957 *Baker 92*
Hasselmeier, A. Gale 1944- *St&PR 93*
Hasselmeyer, Eileen Grace 1924- *WhoAm 92*
Hasselmo, Nils 1931- *WhoAm 92, WhoWor 93*
Hasselquist, M.B. 1919- *St&PR 93*
Hasselquist, Maynard Burton 1919- *WhoAm 92, WhoWor 93*
Hasselstromlinda, M. 1943- *WhoWrEP 92*
Hasselwander, Carl A. *Law&B 92*
Hasseman, Dean M. *Law&B 92*
Hasseman, Dean Michael 1946- *WhoEmL 93*
Hassen, Joel *Law&B 92*
Hassen, Philip C. 1943- *WhoAm 92*
Hassen, Russell *Law&B 92*
Hassenfeld, Alan Geoffrey 1948- *St&PR 93, WhoAm 92*
Hassenfeld, Harold 1916- *St&PR 93*
Hassenfeld, John Eliot 1957- *St&PR 93*
Hassenfeld, Stephen David *BioIn 17*
Hassenstein, Bernhard 1922- *WhoScE 91-3*
Hasser, Michael D. 1946- *St&PR 93*
Hassert, Elizabeth Anne 1956- *WhoAmW 93*
Hasset, Neil A. *Law&B 92*
Hassett, Carol Alice 1947- *WhoAm 92, WhoAmW 93, WhoE 93, WhoWor 93*
Hassett, James Manning 1947- *WhoE 93*
Hassett, Joseph Malk 1943- *WhoWrEP 92*
Hassett, Joseph Mark 1943- *WhoAm 92, WhoWor 93*
Hassett, Michael James *Law&B 92*
Hassett, Robert Emmett 1932- *St&PR 93*
Hassi, Juhani 1943- *WhoScE 91-4*
Hassi, Osmo Samuel 1921- *WhoScE 91-4*
Hassid, Sami 1912- *WhoAm 92*
Hassiepen, John Paul *Law&B 92*
Hassine, Samuel F. 1953- *St&PR 93*
Hassinger, Herman A. 1929- *WhoAm 92*
Hassinger, Maren *BioIn 17*
Hassinger, Robert Conery 1941- *WhoSSW 93*
Hassiotis, Anthony Constantine 1954- *WhoWor 93*
Hassiotis, Nicholas Daniel 1926- *St&PR 93*
Hasslein, George Johann 1917- *WhoAm 92*
Hassler *Baker 92*
Hassler, Alfred d1991 *BioIn 17*
Hassler, Caspar 1562-1618 *Baker 92*
Hassler, Donald M. 1937- *ScF&FL 92*
Hassler, Donald Mackey, II 1937- *WhoAm 92, WhoWrEP 92*
Hassler, Hans Leo 1564-1612 *Baker 92*
Hassler, Isaak c. 1530-1591 *Baker 92*
Hassler, Jakob 1569-1622 *Baker 92*
Hassler, Johann Wilhelm 1747-1822 *Baker 92*
Hassler, Jon *BioIn 17*
Hassler, Jon (Francis) 1933- *WhoWrEP 92*
Hassler, Ove 1932- *WhoScE 91-4*
Hassler, Paul Mark, Sr. 1927- *St&PR 93*
Hasso, Signe Eleonora Cecilia 1915- *WhoAm 92*
Hasson, James K. 1916- *St&PR 93*
Hasson, Moises *ScF&FL 92*
Hasson, Nathan 1945- *St&PR 93*
Hasson, Raymond I. 1950- *St&PR 93*
Hasson-Voloch, Aida 1922- *WhoWor 93*
Hassoun, Jacques 1941- *WhoScE 91-2*
Hassoun, Jacques A. 1941- *WhoScE 91-2*
Hassrick, Peter Heyl 1941- *WhoAm 92*
Hast, Adele 1931- *WhoAm 92*
Hast, Herbert H., Jr. 1938- *St&PR 93*
Hast, Joan Eileen 1955- *WhoAmW 93, WhoEmL 93*
Hast, Malcolm Howard 1931- *WhoAm 92*
Hast, Robert 1945- *WhoWor 93*
Hastein, Tore 1937- *WhoScE 91-4*
Hasten, Bradley A. *Law&B 92*
Hastert, Dennis 1942- *WhoAm 92*
Hastert, J. Dennis 1942- *CngDr 91*
Hastie, William Henry 1904-1976 *EncAACR*
Hasting, Glen Richard, II 1945- *WhoAm 92*
Hastings, Adrian Christopher 1929- *WhoWor 93*
Hastings, Alcee L. *BioIn 17*
Hastings, Andre *BioIn 17*
Hastings, Arthur L. *Law&B 92*
Hastings, Bee *AmWomPl*
Hastings, Beverly *ScF&FL 92*
Hastings, Catherine Manson 1959- *WhoWrEP 92*
Hastings, Charles W. 1936- *St&PR 93*
Hastings, Constance Moore 1941- *WhoAmW 93*
Hastings, Dana Gay 1961- *WhoEmL 93*
Hastings, Daniel Hartman 1849-1903 *BioIn 17*
Hastings, Deborah 1959- *WhoAmW 93*
Hastings, Donald Francis 1934- *WhoAm 92*
Hastings, Donald J. 1934- *St&PR 93*
Hastings, Edward Walton 1931- *WhoAm 92*
Hastings, Elizabeth Margaret 1950- *WhoAmW 93*
Hastings, Evelyn Grace 1938- *WhoAmW 93, WhoSSW 93*
Hastings, Frances *AmWomPl*
Hastings, Francis Rawdon 1754-1826 *HarEnMi*
Hastings, Gerard Bernard *WhoScE 91-1*
Hastings, Harold Keith *Law&B 92*
Hastings, Ian 1912- *BioIn 17*
Hastings, Joel Prescott 1948- *WhoWrEP 92*
Hastings, John d1991 *BioIn 17*
Hastings, John Woodland 1927- *WhoAm 92*
Hastings, Joseph H. 1949- *St&PR 93*
Hastings, June *St&PR 93*
Hastings, Kevin Lee 1937- *St&PR 93*
Hastings, Lawrence Vaeth 1919- *WhoAm 92, WhoWor 93*
Hastings, Lois Jane 1928- *WhoAm 92, WhoAmW 93*
Hastings, Maryann Shayegan 1945- *WhoAmW 93*
Hastings, Matthew Tate 1952- *WhoEmL 93, WhoSSW 93*
Hastings, Michael D. 1951- *St&PR 93*
Hastings, Michael E. 1943- *St&PR 93*
Hastings, Molly K. *Law&B 92*
Hastings, Nancy Peters 1952- *WhoAmW 93*
Hastings, Nellie Mae 1953- *WhoAmW 93*
Hastings, Otis H. *St&PR 93*
Hastings, Philip Kay 1922- *WhoAm 92*
Hastings, Richard G., III 1941- *St&PR 93*
Hastings, Robert D. 1940- *St&PR 93*
Hastings, Robert Eugene 1932- *WhoWor 93*
Hastings, Robert Pusey 1910- *WhoAm 92*
Hastings, Scott Alan 1966- *WhoSSW 93*
Hastings, Steven C. 1954- *St&PR 93*
Hastings, Susan Ann 1955- *WhoEmL 93*
Hastings, Thomas 1784-1872 *Baker 92*
Hastings, W. Bradford T. d1992 *NewYTBS 92*
Hastings, William *ScF&FL 92*
Hastings, William 1430-1483 *HarEnMi*
Hastings, William Charles 1921- *WhoAm 92*
Hastings, Wilmot Reed 1935- *WhoAm 92*
Haston, C. Cleo *Law&B 92*
Haston, Jack Steve 1946- *WhoEmL 93, WhoSSW 93*
Haston, Richard Thomas 1946- *WhoSSW 93*
Haston, Ronni Meritt 1958- *WhoAmW 93*
Hastreiter, Marge Thielman 1934- *WhoWrEP 92*
Hastreiter, Roberta *Law&B 92*
Hastrich, Jerome Joseph 1914- *WhoAm 92*
Hasty, Charles Ransom, Jr. 1960- *WhoSSW 93*
Hasty, Doyle Edwin 1945- *WhoSSW 93*
Hasty, Jack *St&PR 93*
Hasty, William Grady, Jr. 1947- *WhoSSW 93*
Hasumi, Hiroaki 1933- *WhoWor 93*
Haswell, Carleton Radley 1939- *WhoAm 92*
Haswell, Karen Lois 1954- *WhoSSW 93*
Haswin, Frances Rosina *AmWomPl*
Haszpra, Otto 1928- *WhoScE 91-4*
Hata, Eijiro 1928- *WhoAsAP 91*
Hata, Ikuhiko 1932- *WhoWor 93*
Hata, Kazuhiko R. 1943- *WhoUN 92*
Hata, Masami *MiSFD 9*
Hata, Masanori *MiSFD 9*
Hata, Masayoshi 1954- *WhoWor 93*
Hata, Shunroku 1879-1962 *HarEnMi*
Hata, Takamasa 1935- *WhoWor 93*
Hata, Tsukomu 1935- *WhoAsAP 91*
Hata, Yoshiteru 1930- *WhoWor 93*
Hatada, Kazuyuki 1951- *WhoWor 93*
Hatada, Koichi 1934- *WhoWor 93*
Hatakeyama, Shiro 1951- *WhoWor 93*
Hatanaka, Atsushi 1961- *WhoWor 93*
Hatanaka, Hiroshi 1932- *WhoWor 93*
Hatanaka, Masakazu Shoichi 1933- *WhoWor 93*
Hatanaka, Thomas Toby 1926- *St&PR 93*
Hatano, Masami 1940- *WhoWor 93*
Hatano, Sadashi 1929- *WhoWor 93*
Hatano, Tetsuro 1936- *WhoWor 93*
Hatano, Yoshio 1932- *WhoWor 93*
Hatasu *BioIn 17*
Hatch, Adelaide Westcott *AmWomPl*
Hatch, Arthur A. 1930- *St&PR 93*
Hatch, Barry Marcal *Law&B 92*
Hatch, Carl A. 1889-1963 *BioIn 17*
Hatch, David Charles *Law&B 92*
Hatch, David Lincoln 1910- *WhoAm 92*
Hatch, Dorothy L. 1920- *WhoWrEP 92*
Hatch, Edwin I. 1913- *St&PR 93*
Hatch, Frederick Tasker 1924- *WhoE 93*
Hatch, George *ScF&FL 92*
Hatch, George Clinton 1919- *St&PR 93, WhoAm 92*
Hatch, Gordon Lee 1933- *St&PR 93*
Hatch, H. Clifford 1916- *St&PR 93*
Hatch, Harold Arthur 1924- *WhoAm 92*
Hatch, Harold Eugene 1935- *St&PR 93*
Hatch, Henry Albert 1927- *St&PR 93*
Hatch, Henry J. *BioIn 17, WhoAm 92*
Hatch, Jack 1950- *WhoEmL 93*
Hatch, James Alfred 1939- *WhoAm 92*
Hatch, James Stokes 1943- *St&PR 93*
Hatch, John Davis 1907- *WhoAm 92, WhoWor 93*
Hatch, John Phillip 1946- *WhoSSW 93*
Hatch, Katharine *AmWomPl*
Hatch, Lynda Sylvia 1950- *WhoEmL 93*
Hatch, Mary Gies 1913- *WhoAm 92, WhoSSW 93*
Hatch, Mary R. Platt 1848-1935 *AmWomPl*
Hatch, Mary Wendell Vander Poel 1919- *WhoAmW 93, WhoE 93, WhoWor 93*
Hatch, Michael Francis 1947- *St&PR 93*
Hatch, Michael Ward 1949- *WhoEmL 93*
Hatch, Monroe W., Jr. 1933- *WhoAm 92*
Hatch, Nathan Orr 1946- *WhoAm 92*
Hatch, Norman S. 1950- *St&PR 93*
Hatch, Orrin G. *BioIn 17*
Hatch, Orrin G. 1934- *CngDr 91*
Hatch, Orrin Grant 1934- *WhoAm 92*
Hatch, Patricia Ann 1950- *WhoE 93*
Hatch, Patricia M. 1953- *WhoWrEP 92*
Hatch, Randall Clinton 1951- *WhoAm 92*
Hatch, Ric *BioIn 17*
Hatch, Richard 1948- *WhoSSW 93*
Hatch, Richard W. 1898-1985? *ScF&FL 92*
Hatch, Robert Allen 1947- *St&PR 93*
Hatch, Robert Norris 1914- *WhoAm 92*
Hatch, Robert Norris, Jr. 1952- *St&PR 93*
Hatch, Robert Winslow 1938- *St&PR 93, WhoAm 92, WhoSSW 93*
Hatch, Sandra Lee 1948- *WhoEmL 93*
Hatch, T. Brad 1924- *St&PR 93*
Hatch, Tracy Soper 1960- *WhoEmL 93*
Hatch, Wilda Gene 1917- *St&PR 93*
Hatchell, Steven James 1947- *WhoSSW 93*
Hatchepset *BioIn 17*
Hatcher, Aileen Ponder 1949- *WhoAmW 93*
Hatcher, Allen Edward 1944- *WhoAm 92*
Hatcher, Barbara A. *Law&B 92*
Hatcher, Bruce Alderman 1960- *WhoSSW 93*
Hatcher, Charles 1939- *CngDr 91, WhoAm 92, WhoSSW 93*
Hatcher, Charles Ross, Jr. 1930- *WhoAm 92*
Hatcher, David E. 1923- *St&PR 93*
Hatcher, Donald Buford 1938- *WhoSSW 93*
Hatcher, Everett d1989 *BioIn 17*
Hatcher, James A. *Law&B 92*
Hatcher, James A. 1952- *St&PR 93*
Hatcher, James Mitchell 1950- *WhoEmL 93, WhoSSW 93*
Hatcher, Joe Branch 1936- *WhoAm 92*
Hatcher, Kenneth Wayne 1943- *St&PR 93*
Hatcher, Larry Lee 1956- *WhoSSW 93*
Hatcher, Lib *BioIn 17*
Hatcher, Melvin N. *Law&B 92*
Hatcher, Mickey *BioIn 17*
Hatcher, Ray F. 1939- *St&PR 93*
Hatcher, Richard G. 1933- *PolPar*
Hatcher, Richard Gordon 1933- *AfrAmBi, EncAACR*
Hatcher, Robert Douglas 1924- *WhoAm 92*
Hatcher, Robin Lee 1951- *WhoWrEP 92*
Hatcher, Samuel F. *Law&B 92*
Hatcher, Samuel Fox *Law&B 92*
Hatcher, Sharna D. *Law&B 92*
Hatcher, Stanley Ronald 1932- *WhoAm 92, WhoWor 93*
Hatcher, Stephen Randolph 1942- *St&PR 93*
Hatcher, William Claude 1922- *St&PR 93*
Hatcher, William Julian, Jr. 1935- *WhoAm 92*
Hatcher, William Spottswood 1935- *WhoAm 92*
Hatchett, Edward Earl 1923- *WhoAm 92*
Hatchett, John Garner 1939- *WhoSSW 93*
Hatchett, Joseph Woodrow 1932- *WhoAm 92, WhoSSW 93*
Hatchett, R. Bryan *Law&B 92*
Hatchett, Sharon Denise *Law&B 92*
Hatchigan, Jessica *ScF&FL 92*
Hately, Maurice C. 1928- *WhoScE 91-1*
Hatfield, Bessie *AmWomPl*
Hatfield, Charles Donald 1935- *WhoAm 92*
Hatfield, Charles H. 1937- *St&PR 93*
Hatfield, David Underhill 1940- *WhoAm 92*
Hatfield, Elaine (Catherine) 1937- *ConAu 38NR, WhoAm 92, WhoAmW 93*
Hatfield, Eloise Janette 1947- *WhoWrEP 92*
Hatfield, Gretchen R. *Law&B 92*
Hatfield, Gus D., Jr. *Law&B 92*
Hatfield, Hurd 1920?- *ConTFT 10*
Hatfield, Jack Kenton 1922- *WhoWor 93*
Hatfield, James Allen 1953- *WhoSSW 93, WhoWor 93*
Hatfield, James Walker 1942- *St&PR 93*
Hatfield, Jerry Lee 1949- *WhoAm 92*
Hatfield, Jim *BioIn 17*
Hatfield, Jim G. 1941- *WhoSSW 93*
Hatfield, Joe Sweatt, Jr. 1924- *WhoAm 92*
Hatfield, Julie Stockwell 1940- *WhoAm 92*
Hatfield, Leonard Fraser 1919- *WhoAm 92*
Hatfield, Lynda Sue 1950- *WhoAmW 93*
Hatfield, Mark O. 1922- *BioIn 17, CngDr 91, PolPar, WhoAm 92*
Hatfield, Paul H. 1936- *WhoAm 92*
Hatfield, Phillip L. 1945- *St&PR 93*
Hatfield, Richard B. *BioIn 17*
Hatfield, Robert Sherman 1916- *WhoAm 92*
Hatfield, Thomas Barlow 1933- *WhoE 93*
Hatfield, Thomas E. 1949- *St&PR 93*
Hatfield, W.C. 1926- *St&PR 93, WhoAm 92*
Hatfield, William Emerson 1937- *WhoAm 92*
Hatfield, William (Ernest Chapman) 1892?- *DcChlFi*
Hatfield, William F. 1956- *St&PR 93*
Hatfield Sallee, Tiffany Clellan 1964- *WhoAmW 93*
Hathaway, Amos Townsend 1913- *WhoSSW 93*
Hathaway, Bert 1943- *BioIn 17*
Hathaway, Brian John 1929- *WhoScE 91-3*
Hathaway, Carl Emil 1933- *WhoAm 92*
Hathaway, Carmrid Glaston 1922- *WhoE 93*
Hathaway, Charles G. 1929- *St&PR 93*
Hathaway, Charles Michael 1945- *WhoAm 92*
Hathaway, David Henry 1951- *WhoSSW 93*
Hathaway, Donny 1945- *SoulM*
Hathaway, Donny 1945-1979 *Baker 92*
Hathaway, Esse Virginia 1871- *AmWomPl*
Hathaway, George *Law&B 92*
Hathaway, Harold Grant 1927- *St&PR 93*
Hathaway, Henry 1898-1985 *MiSFD 9N*
Hathaway, John David 1934- *St&PR 93*
Hathaway, John Michael 1952- *WhoEmL 93*
Hathaway, John Scott *Law&B 92*
Hathaway, Kathy R. Moore 1953- *WhoWrEP 92*
Hathaway, Kent Stuart *Law&B 92*
Hathaway, Lalah *BioIn 17, SoulM*
Hathaway, Leah 1938- *WhoAmW 93*
Hathaway, Michael Jerry 1961- *WhoWrEP 92*
Hathaway, Paul L., Jr. 1934- *WhoAm 92*
Hathaway, Paul Lawrence 1934- *St&PR 93*
Hathaway, Raeburn B., Jr. 1934- *St&PR 93*
Hathaway, Raeburn Burton, Jr. 1934- *WhoAm 92*
Hathaway, Richard Dean 1927- *WhoAm 92*
Hathaway, Robert E., II *Law&B 92*
Hathaway, Robert Lawton 1932- *WhoAm 92*
Hathaway, Roger 1933- *St&PR 93*

Hathaway, William 1944- *DcLB 120 [port]*
Hathaway, William Dodd 1924- *WhoAm 92*
Hathaway, William Kitchen 1944- *WhoWrEP 92*
Hathcoat, Ronald Andrew 1949- *WhoSSW 93*
Hathcock, Bob *MiSFD 9*
Hatherill, William A. 1951- *St&PR 93*
Hatherley, Frank *ScF&FL 92*
Hatheway, John Harris 1926- *WhoAm 92*
Hatheway, John L. 1930- *St&PR 93*
Hatheway, Robert James 1946- *WhoE 93*
Hathorne, Trese Evans 1956- *WhoSSW 93*
Hathway, Alan 1906-1977 *ScF&FL 92*
Hatie, George Daniel 1910- *WhoAm 92*
Hatjoullis, Michael Christos *WhoScE 91-1*
Hatkoff, Craig Mitchell 1954- *WhoE 93*
Hatle, Liv K. 1936- *WhoScE 91-4*
Hatle, Zdenek 1935- *WhoScE 91-4*
Hatleberg, Karen Lynn 1953- *WhoAmW 93*
Hatlen, Burton Norval 1936- *WhoAm 92*
Hatler, Patricia Ruth *Law&B 92*
Hatley, Bobby Gene 1937- *St&PR 93*
Hatley-Brickey, Lael Ann 1956- *WhoEmL 93*
Hatoff, Howard Ira 1931- *WhoAm 92*
Haton, Jean-Paul 1943- *WhoScE 91-2*
Hatoyama, Kunio 1948- *WhoAsAP 91*
Hatoyama, Lichiro 1918- *WhoAsAP 91*
Hatoyama, Yukio 1947- *WhoAsAP 91*
Hatridge, Stephen A. *Law&B 92*
Hatrik, Juraj 1941- *Baker 92*
Hatschek, Rudolf Alexander 1918- *WhoWor 93*
Hatshepsut, Queen of Egypt *BioIn 17*
Hatsopoulos, G.N. *BioIn 17*
Hatsopoulos, George N. *BioIn 17*
Hatsopoulos, George N. 1927- *St&PR 93*
Hatsopoulos, George Nicholas 1927- *WhoAm 92, WhoE 93*
Hatsopoulos, John Nicholas 1934- *St&PR 93*
Hatsukade, Shigeo 1932- *WhoWor 93*
Hatsumura, Takiichiro 1913- *WhoAsAP 91*
Hatt, Brice V. *Law&B 92*
Hatt, George E. 1947- *WhoSSW 93*
Hatt, Peter McLeod 1942- *WhoAm 92*
Hatta, Mohammad 1902-1980 *BioIn 17*
Hattabaugh, Aaron Eugene 1964- *WhoSSW 93*
Hattaway, Michael 1941- *ConAu 39NR, WhoWor 93*
Hatteberg, Larry Merle 1944- *WhoAm 92*
Hattem, Albert Worth 1951- *WhoSSW 93*
Hattem, Robert Paul 1952- *St&PR 93*
Hattemer, Hans H. 1935- *WhoScE 91-3*
Hatten, Donald G. 1930- *St&PR 93*
Hatten, Mark William 1957- *WhoE 93*
Hatten, Robert Randolph 1948- *WhoEmL 93*
Hatten, William Seward 1917- *WhoAm 92, WhoSSW 93*
Hattendorf, J. Mark 1950- *WhoEmL 93*
Hatterer, Andre 1928- *WhoScE 91-2*
Hattersley, Robert Sherwood 1931- *WhoSSW 93*
Hattersley, Roy *BioIn 17*
Hattersley, William Martin *WhoScE 91-1*
Hattersley-Smith, Geoffrey Francis 1923- *WhoAm 92*
Hattery, Robert R. 1939- *WhoAm 92*
Hattin, Donald Edward 1928- *WhoAm 92*
Hattingh, Johan Christiaan 1953- *WhoWor 93*
Hattis, Philip David 1952- *WhoE 93*
Hatton, Aiden Emmet, Jr. 1933- *St&PR 93*
Hatton, Bessie *AmWomPl*
Hatton, Candace Lee 1948- *St&PR 93*
Hatton, Catherine *Law&B 92*
Hatton, Donald H. 1938- *WhoE 93*
Hatton, Fanny Cottinet Locke 1869-1930 *AmWomPl*
Hatton, Francoise *WhoScE 91-2*
Hatton, Frank 1846-1894 *JrnUS*
Hatton, Frederick L. 1943- *St&PR 93*
Hatton, Henry Robert 1940- *WhoUN 92*
Hatton, John Liptrot 1808-1886 *Baker 92*
Hatton, Maurice *MiSFD 9*
Hatton, Raymond 1887-1971 *BioIn 17*
Hatton, Richard L. 1950- *St&PR 93*
Hatton, Robert Wayland 1934- *WhoWrEP 92*
Hatton, Rondo 1894-1946 *BioIn 17*
Hatton, Steve 1948- *WhoAsAP 91*
Hatton, Vincent P. *Law&B 92*
Hattori, Akira 1949- *WhoWor 93*
Hattori, Iwakazu 1951- *WhoWor 93*
Hattori, Kenjiro 1942- *WhoWor 93*
Hattori, Noriyasu 1943- *St&PR 93*
Hattori, Seisaku 1913- *WhoWor 93*
Hattori, Shoji 1937- *St&PR 93*
Hattori, Takushiro 1901-1960 *HarEnMi*
Hattori, Yasushi 1915- *WhoAsAP 91*
Hattox, Brock Alan 1948- *St&PR 93, WhoAm 92*
Hattox, Patsy Leeth 1949- *St&PR 93*
Hattula, Jorma S. 1940- *WhoScE 91-4*
Hatvary, George Egon 1921- *WhoWrEP 92*
Hatz, Stephen J. 1951- *St&PR 93*
Hatz, Volker 1965- *WhoWor 93*
Hatzakis, Michael 1928- *WhoAm 92*
Hatze, Josip 1879-1959 *Baker 92*
Hatzes, Robert Louis, Jr. 1953- *WhoE 93*
Hatzfeld, Jacques Alexandre 1940- *WhoWor 93*
Hatzicharissis, John Ioannis 1943- *WhoScE 91-3*
Hatzikonstantinou, Paul 1949- *WhoWor 93*
Hatzios, Kriton Kelanthis 1949- *WhoSSW 93*
Hatziotls, J.Ch. *WhoScE 91-3*
Hatzistergiou, Thomas Constantine 1957- *WhoWor 93*
Hau, Emmanuel 1939- *WhoWor 93*
Hau, Steen 1947- *WhoWor 93*
Hau, Thomas C. 1935- *St&PR 93*
Hau, Toni 1941- *WhoWor 93*
Hauben, Ronald Bruce *Law&B 92*
Haubenreich, George R., Jr. 1948- *St&PR 93*
Haubenreich, George Raymond, Jr. *Law&B 92*
Haubenstoch, Alfred B. 1916- *St&PR 93*
Haubenstock-Ramati, Roman 1919- *Baker 92*
Hauber, Patricia Anne 1953- *WhoE 93, WhoEmL 93, WhoWor 93*
Hauber, William M. 1929- *St&PR 93*
Hauberg, Allen Bernard 1937- *St&PR 93*
Hauberg, John H. 1916- *St&PR 93*
Haubert, Juanita 1916- *WhoAmW 93*
Haubiel, Charles Trowbridge 1892-1978 *Baker 92*
Haubold, Fred G. 1934- *St&PR 93*
Haubold, Wolfgang 1937- *WhoScE 91-3*
Haubold, Wolfgang Johannes 1937- *WhoWor 93*
Haubs, Helmut 1926- *WhoScE 91-3*
Hauch, Emma Bell *AmWomPl*
Hauck, C. Peter 1930- *St&PR 93*
Hauck, Charles Francis 1912- *WhoAm 92*
Hauck, Elaine Marie 1950- *WhoEmL 93*
Hauck, Frederick A. 1894- *St&PR 93*
Hauck, Frederick Hamilton 1941- *WhoAm 92*
Hauck, Gilda Tan 1949- *WhoWor 93*
Hauck, John M. 1926- *St&PR 93*
Hauck, L. Christian 1941- *St&PR 93*
Hauck, Leonore Crary *BioIn 17*
Hauck, Luella Ruth 1922- *WhoAmW 93*
Hauck, Marguerite Hall 1948- *WhoAm 92, WhoAmW 93*
Hauck, Molly Perkins 1943- *WhoAmW 93*
Hauck, Neil Tod 1954- *WhoE 93*
Hauck, Richard Henry 1930- *WhoE 93*
Hauck, Robert John 1954- *WhoSSW 93*
Hauck, Roger Paul 1936- *St&PR 93*
Hauck, Steven Barry 1951- *St&PR 93*
Hauck, Terry C. 1941- *WhoAm 92*
Hauck, Thomas R. d1992 *NewYTBS 92*
Hauck, William Edward 1932- *WhoE 93*
Hauck-Fugitt, Christine Claire Kraus 1951- *WhoAmW 93*
Haudebert, Lucien 1877-1963 *Baker 92*
Haudenschild, Christian Charles 1939- *WhoAm 92*
Haudin, Jean-Marc 1946- *WhoScE 91-2*
Haueisen, William David 1943- *WhoSSW 93*
Hauenstein, Henry William 1924- *WhoAm 92*
Hauenstein, Nancy Dean 1961- *WhoAmW 93, WhoEmL 93*
Hauenstein, Thomas G. 1933- *St&PR 93*
Hauer, Daniel 1937- *St&PR 93*
Hauer, Hansjorg 1948- *WhoScE 91-4*
Hauer, Jeanne T. 1951- *WhoAmW 93*
Hauer, Josef 1883-1959 *OxDcOp*
Hauer, Josef Matthias 1883-1959 *Baker 92*
Hauet, J.P. *WhoScE 91-2*
Hauet, Jean-Pierre 1945- *WhoScE 91-2*
Haueter, Eric D. 1925- *St&PR 93*
Haufe, Bonnie Campbell 1961- *WhoAmW 93*
Hauff, Anne Katherine 1965- *WhoAmW 93*
Hauff, Wilhelm 1802-1827 *BioIn 17*
Haufler, Christopher Hardin 1950- *WhoAm 92*
Haufler, George J. 1932- *St&PR 93*
Hauft, Amy Gilbert 1957- *WhoAmW 93, WhoE 93*
Haug, Arthur John 1919- *WhoSSW 93*
Haug, C(harles) James 1946- *ConAu 38NR*
Haug, Charles James 1946- *WhoEmL 93, WhoSSW 93*
Haug, Edward Joseph, Jr. 1940- *WhoAm 92*
Haug, Gustav 1871-1956 *Baker 92*
Haug, Hans 1900-1967 *Baker 92*
Haug, Hartmut A. 1936- *WhoScE 91-3*
Haug, Peter K. 1941- *WhoScE 91-3*
Haug, Richard Leo 1939- *St&PR 93*
Haug, Roar Brandt 1928- *WhoWor 93*
Haugaard, Erik Christian 1923- *BioIn 17, ConAu 38NR, DcAmChF 1960, DcAmChF 1985, MajAI [port]*
Haugaard, Niels 1920- *WhoAm 92*
Haugan, Richard D. 1944- *St&PR 93*
Hauge, Jens G. 1927- *WhoScE 91-4*
Hauge, Jens Gabriel 1927- *WhoWor 93*
Hauge, Keith A. 1938- *St&PR 93*
Hauge, Marilyn I. 1948- *St&PR 93*
Hauge, Richard Andrew 1956- *WhoE 93*
Hauge, Ron O. *St&PR 93*
Hauge, Sharon Kaye 1943- *WhoE 93*
Haugedal, Arnar 1938- *WhoWor 93*
Haugen, Aage 1946- *WhoScE 91-4*
Haugen, David William 1942- *St&PR 93*
Haugen, Einar Ingvald 1906- *WhoAm 92*
Haugen, Gerald Alan 1940- *St&PR 93, WhoAm 92*
Haugen, Harald 1939- *WhoWor 93*
Haugen, Heidi Lee 1966- *WhoAmW 93*
Haugen, J. *WhoScE 91-4*
Haugen, Juanita Harriet 1937- *WhoAmW 93*
Haugen, Karen A. *Law&B 92*
Haugen, Marilyn Anne 1932- *WhoAmW 93*
Haugen, Rolf Eugene 1936- *WhoAm 92*
Haugen, Tiffany Suzanne 1951- *WhoAmW 93*
Haugen, Tormod 1945- *BioIn 17*
Hauger, Leslie Starr 1904- *WhoSSW 93, WhoWrEP 92*
Haugh, Barbara Ann 1950- *WhoWrEP 92*
Haugh, Clarence Gene 1936- *WhoAm 92*
Haugh, Robert C. 1920- *St&PR 93*
Haugh, Robert J. 1926- *St&PR 93*
Haugh, Robert James 1926- *WhoAm 92*
Haugh, Stephen J. *Law&B 92*
Haughey, Charles *BioIn 17*
Haughey, Charles James 1925- *DcTwHis*
Haughey, James McCrea 1914- *WhoAm 92*
Haughland, Aage 1944- *Baker 92*
Haughney, Michael 1963- *ScF&FL 92*
Haught, James Albert, Jr. 1932- *WhoAm 92, WhoSSW 93*
Haught, Sharon K. *Law&B 92*
Haught, William Dixon 1939- *WhoAm 92*
Haughton, Dominique Marie Annick 1955- *WhoE 93*
Haughton, James Gray 1925- *WhoAm 92*
Haugland, Brynhild 1905- *WhoAmW 93*
Haugland, Loren Andrew 1941- *St&PR 93*
Haugland, Richard C. 1935- *St&PR 93*
Haugo, Cheryl Marie 1960- *WhoAmW 93*
Haugstad, Bjarne S. 1945- *WhoScE 91-4*
Hauk, A. Andrew 1912- *WhoAm 92*
Hauk, Carol *BioIn 17*
Hauk, Donald B. 1944- *St&PR 93*
Hauk, Donald Benjamin 1944- *WhoAm 92*
Hauk, Minnie 1851-1929 *Baker 92, OxDcOp*
Hauke, Mary Elizabeth 1911- *WhoAmW 93*
Hauke, Paul Richard 1951- *WhoE 93*
Haukenes, Gunnar Carl 1927- *WhoWor 93*
Haukeness, Helen Liza 1938- *WhoWrEP 92*
Haukioja, Erkki A.J. 1941- *WhoScE 91-4*
Haukland, Joanne Marie 1944- *WhoAmW 93*
Haulman, Harry Lindsay 1917- *St&PR 93*
Haumer, Hans 1940- *WhoWor 93*
Haumschild, Mark James 1951- *WhoEmL 93, WhoSSW 93*
Haun, Blair A. 1891-1968 *ScF&FL 92*
Haun, James Michael 1945- *St&PR 93*
Haun, James William 1924- *WhoAm 92*
Haun, John Daniel 1921- *WhoAm 92*
Haunschild, Hellmut 1928- *WhoScE 91-3*
Haunschild, Willard Marion 1922- *St&PR 93*
Hau Pei-Tsun, His Excellency Gen. 1919- *WhoAsAP 91*
Haupenthal, Laura Ann 1951- *WhoAmW 93*
Haupt, Adrienne Lynn 1948- *WhoAmW 93, WhoEmL 93*
Haupt, Charles V. 1939- *WhoAm 92*
Haupt, H. James 1940- *WhoWor 93*
Haupt, Hans-Jurgen 1936- *WhoScE 91-3*
Haupt, Hellmut Lehmann- 1903-1992 *BioIn 17*
Haupt, Herbert 1938- *WhoScE 91-3*
Haupt, Hermann F. 1926- *WhoScE 91-4*
Haupt, Karl August 1810-1891 *Baker 92*
Haupt, Wolfgang 1921- *WhoScE 91-3*
Hauptfuhrer, George Jost, Jr. 1926- *WhoAm 92*
Hauptfuhrer, Robert P. 1931- *St&PR 93*
Hauptfuhrer, Robert Paul 1931- *WhoAm 92*
Hauptli, Barbara Beatrice 1953- *WhoAmW 93, WhoEmL 93*
Hauptli, Thomas 1956- *St&PR 93, WhoIns 93*
Hauptman, Don 1947- *ConAu 138*
Hauptman, Edie 1946- *WhoAmW 93*
Hauptman, Herbert Aaron 1917- *WhoAm 92, WhoE 93, WhoWor 93*
Hauptman, Laurence Marc 1945- *ConAu 139, WhoE 93*
Hauptman, Madeline Mishel *BioIn 17*
Hauptman, Marjorie Anne Leahy 1938- *WhoAmW 93*
Hauptman, Michael 1933- *WhoAm 92*
Hauptman, Theodore 1952- *WhoE 93, WhoEmL 93*
Hauptmann, Carl 1858-1921 *DcLB 118 [port]*
Hauptmann, Gerhart (Johann Robert) 1862-1946 *DcLB 118 [port]*
Hauptmann, Moritz 1792-1868 *Baker 92*
Hauptschein, Martin 1953- *WhoEmL 93*
Haury, Alain 1944- *WhoScE 91-2*
Haury, Emil W. d1992 *NewYTBS 92 [port]*
Haury, Emil Walter 1904- *IntDcAn, WhoAm 92*
Haus, Hermann Anton 1925- *WhoAm 92*
Hauschild, Douglas Carey 1955- *WhoSSW 93, WhoWor 93*
Hauschild, Natalie J. *Law&B 92*
Hauschka, Stephen Denison 1940- *WhoAm 92*
Hauschka, Theodore Spaeth 1908- *WhoAm 92, WhoWor 93*
Hauschka, Vincenz 1766-1840 *Baker 92*
Hause, Edith Collins 1933- *WhoAmW 93*
Hause, Jesse Gilbert 1929- *WhoAm 92*
Hause, John W. 1943- *St&PR 93*
Hausegger, Friedrich von 1837-1899 *Baker 92*
Hausegger, Siegmund von 1872-1948 *Baker 92*
Hauselt, Denise Ann *Law&B 92*
Hauseman, Cass *WhoWrEP 92*
Hausen, Jeffrey J. 1964- *St&PR 93*
Hausen, Jutta 1943- *WhoSSW 93*
Hausen, Klaus 1944- *WhoScE 91-3*
Hausen, Laura I. 1955- *St&PR 93*
Hausen, Max Klemens von 1846-1922 *HarEnMi*
Hausen, Peter *WhoScE 91-3*
Hauser, Bruce H. 1943- *St&PR 93*
Hauser, Carl 1949- *WhoE 93*
Hauser, Charles Newland McCorkle 1929- *WhoAm 92*
Hauser, Christopher George 1954- *WhoE 93, WhoEmL 93*
Hauser, Fred Paul 1937- *St&PR 93*
Hauser, Fritz *BioIn 17*
Hauser, Gerd 1948- *WhoScE 91-3*
Hauser, Gustave M. 1929- *WhoAm 92*
Hauser, Gwen 1944- *WhoCanL 92*
Hauser, Hansjorg 1949- *WhoScE 91-3*
Hauser, Harry Raymond 1931- *WhoAm 92*
Hauser, John Reid 1938- *WhoAm 92*
Hauser, Joseph John 1899- *BiDAMSp 1989*
Hauser, Martin 1934- *St&PR 93*
Hauser, Matthew J. 1955- *St&PR 93*
Hauser, Michael George 1939- *WhoAm 92*
Hauser, Miska 1822-1887 *Baker 92*
Hauser, Norbert A. 1935- *St&PR 93*
Hauser, Paul J. 1942- *St&PR 93*
Hauser, Peter Paul 1955- *WhoEmL 93*
Hauser, Richard Alan 1943- *WhoAm 92*
Hauser, Rita Eleanore Abrams 1934- *WhoAm 92, WhoAmW 93*
Hauser, Robert Eugene 1948- *WhoEmL 93*
Hauser, Robert Mason 1942- *WhoAm 92*
Hauser, Steven F. *Law&B 92*
Hauser, Stewart Barry 1942- *WhoE 93*
Hauser, Susan Elisabeth 1936- *WhoAmW 93*
Hauser, Sylvia *BioIn 17*
Hauser, Tim c. 1942- *See* Manhattan Transfer, The *ConMus 8*
Hauser, Ulrich A.L. 1926- *WhoScE 91-3*
Hauser, Warren J. *St&PR 93*
Hauser, Willard Allen 1937- *WhoE 93*
Hauser, William Barry 1939- *WhoAm 92*
Hauser, Wings *MiSFD 9*
Hauser, Wolfhart 1949- *WhoScE 91-3*
Hauser, Wolfhart Gunnar 1949- *WhoWor 93*
Hauserman, W.F. 1919- *St&PR 93*
Hauserman, William Foley 1919- *WhoAm 92*
Hauserman, William Franklin, III 1949- *WhoSSW 93*
Hausgen, Mattie Lee *AmWomPl*
Haushofer, Marie *ScF&FL 92*
Haushofer, Marlen 1920-1970 *ScF&FL 92*
Hauske, Thomas John 1936- *St&PR 93*

Hauskens, Allan 1949- *St&PR 93*
Hausladen, Robert Henry, Jr. 1950- *WhoSSW 93*
Hauslein, R.E. 1929- *St&PR 93*
Hausler, Eberhard 1926- *WhoScE 91-3*
Hausler, William John, Jr. 1926- *WhoAm 92*
Hausman, Arthur H. 1923- *St&PR 93*
Hausman, Arthur Herbert 1923- *WhoAm 92*
Hausman, B. Mark *Law&B 92*
Hausman, Bogumil 1956- *WhoWor 93*
Hausman, Bruce *Law&B 92*
Hausman, Bruce 1930- *St&PR 93, WhoAm 92*
Hausman, Dion F. *Law&B 92*
Hausman, Faryl *Law&B 92*
Hausman, Gerald 1945- *ConAu 38NR, ScF&FL 92*
Hausman, Gerald Andrews 1945- *WhoWrEP 92*
Hausman, Gerry *ConAu 38NR*
Hausman, Helen M. 1924- *WhoAmW 93*
Hausman, Howard 1945- *WhoAm 92, WhoE 93, WhoWor 93*
Hausman, Jerry Allen 1946- *WhoAm 92*
Hausman, Leo 1909- *St&PR 93*
Hausman, Robert J. 1923- *St&PR 93*
Hausman, Samuel 1897- *St&PR 93*
Hausman, Samuel A. d1992 *NewYTBS 92 [port]*
Hausman, Suzanne Iris 1938- *WhoE 93*
Hausman, William Ray 1941- *WhoAm 92*
Hausmann, Albert Charles 1932- *WhoSSW 93*
Hausmann, Klaus Wilhelm 1947- *WhoWor 93*
Hausmann, Paul J. 1938- *St&PR 93*
Hausmann, Raoul 1886-1971 *BioIn 17*
Hausmann, Robert 1852-1909 *Baker 92*
Hausmann, Ronald Lee 1949- *St&PR 93*
Hausmann, Werner Karl 1921- *WhoAm 92*
Hausmanowa-Petrusewicz, Irena 1917- *WhoScE 91-4*
Hausner, Gideon 1915-1990 *BioIn 17*
Hausner, Stowe Whitman d1992 *BioIn 17, NewYTBS 92*
Hauspurg, Arthur 1925- *St&PR 93, WhoAm 92*
Hausrath, David Lewis *Law&B 92*
Hausrath, Ralph Allan 1918- *WhoWrEP 92*
Hauss, Deborah 1955- *WhoWrEP 92*
Haussamen, Carol Weil d1992 *NewYTBS 92 [port]*
Hausser, Gerald Arthur 1931- *WhoAm 92*
Hausser, Paul 1880-1972 *HarEnMi*
Hausser, Robert Louis 1914- *WhoAm 92*
Haussermann, John William, Jr. 1909-1986 *Baker 92*
Haussermann, Oscar William, Jr. 1921- *WhoAm 92*
Haussermann, Wolfgang 1932- *WhoScE 91-2*
Hausslein, Robert William 1937- *WhoE 93*
Haussler, Jerrilynn Reher 1946- *WhoAmW 93*
Haussmann, Valentin c. 1565-c. 1614 *Baker 92*
Hausswald, Gunter 1908-1974 *Baker 92*
Haust, Wilhelm Marian *Law&B 92*
Hausvater, Alexander 1948- *WhoCanL 92*
Hauswald, Jeananne Kay 1944- *St&PR 93, WhoAm 92, WhoAmW 93*
Hauswirth, Otto K. 1932- *WhoScE 91-3*
Hauswirth, Robert J. 1923- *St&PR 93*
Hautala, Judith Ann 1945- *St&PR 93*
Hautala, Richard A. *ScF&FL 92*
Hautala, Rick 1949- *ScF&FL 92*
Hautanen, Sandra L. *Law&B 92*
Hauth, Willard Ellsworth, III 1948- *WhoE 93*
Hautojarvi, Pekka Juhani 1944- *WhoScE 91-4*
Hautvast, Joseph G.A.J. 1938- *WhoScE 91-3*
Hautzig, Esther 1930- *SmATA 15AS [port]*
Hautzig, Esther Rudomin 1930- *BioIn 17, MajAI [port]*
Hautzig, Walter 1921- *Baker 92*
Hautzinger, Richard J. *Law&B 92*
Hauver, Constance Longshore 1938- *WhoAm 92*
Hauver, Larry King 1945- *WhoE 93*
Hauvonen, Jouko J. 1933- *WhoUN 92*
Havas, Paavo Johannes 1929- *WhoScE 91-4*
Havas, Peter 1916- *WhoAm 92*
Havas, Vera *WhoScE 91-4*
Havasy, Edward Stephen 1925- *St&PR 93*
Havasy, Judith Esther 1942- *WhoAmW 93*
Havdala, Ellen 1966- *WhoAmW 93*
Havdala, Henri Salomon 1931- *WhoAm 92*
Havekost, Daniel John 1936- *WhoAm 92*
Havel, Ivan *BioIn 17*
Havel, Jan 1934- *WhoScE 91-4*
Havel, Jean Eugene Martial 1928- *WhoAm 92, WhoWrEP 92*
Havel, Olga *BioIn 17*
Havel, Stanislav 1930- *WhoScE 91-4, WhoWor 93*
Havel, Vaclav *BioIn 17*
Havel, Vaclav 1936- *ColdWar 2 [port], ConHero 2 [port], DcTwHis, MagSWL [port], WhoWor 93*
Havelka, Svatopluk 1925- *Baker 92*
Havelka, Thomas Edward 1947- *WhoEmL 93*
Havelock, Christine Mitchell 1924- *WhoAm 92*
Havelock, Henry 1795-1857 *HarEnMi*
Havelock-Allan, Anthony 1904- *BioIn 17*
Haveman, Jacqueline Ruth 1948- *WhoAmW 93*
Havemann, Carol A. *Law&B 92*
Havemann, Ernst 1918- *WhoCanL 92*
Havemann, Gustav 1882-1960 *Baker 92*
Havemeyer, Horace 1914-1990 *BioIn 17*
Havemeyer, Robert G. 1927- *St&PR 93*
Haven, Granville James 1927- *St&PR 93*
Haven, Larry Allan 1953- *WhoSSW 93*
Haven, Miles Jonathan 1945- *St&PR 93*
Haven, Thomas Edward 1920- *WhoAm 92*
Haven, Thomas Kenneth 1906- *WhoAm 92*
Haven, Tom de *ScF&FL 92*
Havener, Marlin R. 1942- *St&PR 93*
Havener, Norma Jean 1936- *WhoAmW 93*
Havener, Robert Dale 1930- *WhoAm 92*
Havenick, Fred Stanley 1943- *St&PR 93*
Havens, Candace Jean 1952- *WhoAmW 93*
Havens, Carolyn Clarice 1953- *WhoAmW 93, WhoSSW 93*
Havens, Charles W., III 1936- *WhoAm 92, WhoIns 93*
Havens, David Atwater 1964- *St&PR 93*
Havens, John F. 1927- *St&PR 93*
Havens, John Franklin 1927- *WhoAm 92*
Havens, Kevin Louis 1957- *WhoEmL 93*
Havens, Leston Laycock 1924- *WhoAm 92*
Havens, Murray Clark 1932- *WhoAm 92*
Havens, Oliver Hershman 1917- *WhoAm 92*
Havens, Pamela Ann 1956- *WhoAmW 93, WhoEmL 93*
Havens, Rex A. *Law&B 92*
Havens, Timothy Markle 1945- *WhoAm 92, WhoE 93, WhoWor 93*
Havens, W. Paul 1911-1992 *BioIn 17*
Havens, W. Paul, Jr. d1992 *NewYTBS 92*
Havens, William W. 1920- *BioIn 17*
Haver, Jack Richard 1931- *St&PR 93*
Haveraaen, Oddvar 1931- *WhoScE 91-4*
Haverhals, J. 1944- *WhoScE 91-3*
Haverkamp, Ona (Winants) *AmWomPl*
Haverkampf, Kathleen Lea 1959- *WhoEmL 93*
Haverkamp Hildebrand, Vicky Ruth *Law&B 92*
Haverkate, Frits 1931- *WhoScE 91-3*
Haverkort, Anton J. 1951- *WhoScE 91-3*
Haverland, Edgar Marion 1925- *WhoSSW 93*
Haverland, Richard Michael 1941- *WhoIns 93*
Haverly, Douglas Lindsay 1925- *WhoE 93*
Haverly, Paul F. 1934- *St&PR 93*
Haveron, Patrick J. 1961- *St&PR 93*
Havers, Michael d1992 *NewYTBS 92*
Havers, Michael 1923-1992 *BioIn 17*
Havers, Robert Michael Oldfield 1923-1992 *BioIn 17*
Haverstock, James Edward 1925- *St&PR 93*
Haverty, Harold V. *BioIn 17*
Haverty, Harold V. 1930- *St&PR 93*
Haverty, John Rhodes 1926- *WhoAm 92*
Haverty, Patrick Joseph 1931- *St&PR 93*
Haverty, Rawson 1920- *St&PR 93, WhoAm 92, WhoSSW 93*
Haveson, Alan Michael 1937- *WhoAm 92*
Havet, Jose (L.) 1937- *ConAu 137*
Havewala, Noshir Behram 1938- *WhoWor 93*
Havey, Elizabeth A. 1947- *WhoWrEP 92*
Havey, Lois Arlene 1935- *WhoAmW 93*
Havey, Peter Sunil 1960- *WhoWor 93*
Havez, Jean C. *AmWomPl*
Haviaras, Stratis 1935- *WhoWrEP 92*
Havice, James F. 1938- *St&PR 93*
Havighurst, Alfred F. 1904-1991 *BioIn 17*
Havighurst, Clark Canfield 1933- *WhoAm 92*
Havighurst, Robert James 1900-1991 *BioIn 17*
Haviland, Bancroft Dawley 1925- *WhoAm 92*
Haviland, Camilla Klein 1926- *WhoAmW 93*
Haviland, David Sands 1942- *WhoAm 92*
Haviland, James West 1911- *WhoAmW 93*
Haviland, Leona 1916- *WhoAmW 93*
Haviland, Robert Paul 1913- *WhoAm 92*
Haviland, William 1718-1784 *HarEnMi*
Havilland, Ben 1924- *WhoE 93*
Havinga, Egbert 1909-1988 *BioIn 17*
Havinga, Nick *MiSFD 9*
Havingha, Gerhardus 1696-1753 *Baker 92*
Havir, Bryan Thomas 1963- *WhoE 93*
Havir, Darrell David 1929- *St&PR 93*
Havira, R. Mark 1944- *St&PR 93*
Havist, Marjorie Victoria 1931- *WhoAmW 93*
Haviv, Elana *BioIn 17*
Havlicek, Franklin J. 1947- *WhoAm 92, WhoE 93*
Havlicek, Jaroslav 1931- *WhoScE 91-4*
Havlicek, John 1940- *WhoAm 92*
Havlicek, Joseph 1934- *BioIn 17*
Havlicek, Karel 1821-1856 *BioIn 17*
Havlicek, Vladimir 1930- *WhoScE 91-4*
Havlik, Jiri 1928- *WhoScE 91-4*
Havlovick, James J. 1947- *St&PR 93*
Havner, Galen Clifford 1949- *WhoSSW 93*
Havner, Ronald L., Jr. 1957- *St&PR 93*
Havoc, June 1916- *WhoAm 92*
Havory de Soucy, Roberto Michel 1953- *WhoUN 92*
Havran, Martin Joseph 1929- *WhoAm 92, WhoSSW 93*
Havranek, Peter Harry 1933- *WhoScE 91-4*
Havranek, Wilhelm 1941- *WhoScE 91-4*
Havrda, Miroslav 1938- *WhoScE 91-4*
Havrilko, Jo-Ann P. 1942- *WhoE 93*
Havsteen, Bent Heine 1933- *WhoScE 91-3, WhoWor 93*
Haw, Cecile Elaine 1953- *St&PR 93*
Haw, George Gordon 1939- *St&PR 93*
Hawdon, Robin *ScF&FL 92*
Hawe, David Lee 1938- *WhoWor 93*
Hawel, Jan Wincenty 1936- *Baker 92*
Hawerchuk, Dale *WhoAm 92*
Hawes, Alexander Boyd, Jr. 1947- *WhoAm 92*
Hawes, Christine Debouvry 1943- *WhoUN 92*
Hawes, Douglas Wesson 1932- *St&PR 93, WhoAm 92*
Hawes, Elizabeth 1903-1971 *BioIn 17*
Hawes, Gene R(obert) 1922- *ConAu 39NR*
Hawes, Gregg W. 1959- *WhoEmL 93*
Hawes, John Kennedy 1930- *WhoE 93*
Hawes, Kenneth Monroe 1937- *St&PR 93*
Hawes, Kinne F. *Law&B 92*
Hawes, Kinne F. 1947- *St&PR 93*
Hawes, Louise 1943- *BioIn 17, ScF&FL 92*
Hawes, Lynne Gusikoff Salop 1931- *WhoWrEP 92*
Hawes, Nancye Elizabeth 1932- *WhoAmW 93*
Hawes, Richard Manning 1931- *WhoSSW 93*
Hawes, Velpeau Elwyn, Jr. 1936- *WhoAm 92*
Hawes, William 1785-1846 *Baker 92, OxDcOp*
Hawes, William Francis 1940- *WhoE 93*
Hawk, Charles R. *St&PR 93*
Hawk, Chester *ScF&FL 92*
Hawk, Dale V. 1938- *St&PR 93*
Hawk, Donald Lee 1947- *St&PR 93, WhoAm 92*
Hawk, Douglas D. 1948- *ScF&FL 92*
Hawk, George Wayne 1928- *St&PR 93, WhoAm 92*
Hawk, Janet Corey 1960- *WhoEmL 93*
Hawk, M.D. *Law&B 92*
Hawk, Phillip Michael 1939- *WhoAm 92*
Hawk, Rick Lynn 1952- *WhoSSW 93*
Hawk, Robert Dooley 1940- *WhoAm 92*
Hawk, Robert Steven 1949- *WhoAm 92*
Hawkanson, David R. 1946- *WhoAm 92*
Hawke, Bernard Ray 1946- *WhoAm 92*
Hawke, Edward 1705-1781 *BioIn 17, HarEnMi*
Hawke, Ethan *BioIn 17*
Hawke, John Daniel, Jr. 1933- *WhoAm 92*
Hawke, Robert J.L. 1929- *BioIn 17*
Hawke, Robert James Lee 1929- *DcTwHis, WhoAsAP 91, WhoWor 93*
Hawke, Roger Jewett 1935- *WhoAm 92*
Hawke, Rose Lagman 1931- *WhoWrEP 92*
Hawke, Simon 1951- *ScF&FL 92*
Hawken, Patty Lynn 1932- *WhoAmW 93*
Hawker, David Peter Maxwell 1949- *WhoAsAP 91*
Hawker, George Wiley 1943- *St&PR 93*
Hawker, H.G. 1889-1921 *BioIn 17*
Hawker, Harry George 1889-1921 *BioIn 17*
Hawker, Robert A. 1915- *St&PR 93*
Hawkes, Alan Geoffrey *WhoScE 91-1*
Hawkes, Alan Geoffrey 1938- *WhoWor 93*
Hawkes, Carol Ann *WhoAm 92, WhoAmW 93, WhoE 93*
Hawkes, David R. 1947- *WhoEmL 93*
Hawkes, Dennis Leslie *WhoScE 91-1*
Hawkes, Elizabeth H. 1943- *WhoE 93*
Hawkes, Elizabeth Lawrence 1944- *WhoAmW 93*
Hawkes, G(ary) W(arren) 1953- *ConAu 138*
Hawkes, Glenn Rogers 1919- *WhoAm 92*
Hawkes, Jacquetta 1910- *ScF&FL 92*
Hawkes, John 1925- *BioIn 17, WhoAm 92, WhoWrEP 92*
Hawkes, Judith 1949- *ScF&FL 92*
Hawkes, Kevin *BioIn 17*
Hawkes, Peter William 1937- *WhoScE 91-2, WhoWor 93*
Hawkes, Robert E. 1930- *WhoCanL 92*
Hawkes, Robert Howie 1930- *St&PR 93*
Hawkes, Sidney Gerard 1933- *St&PR 93*
Hawkes, Trevor Ongley 1936- *WhoWor 93*
Hawkes, William Henry *See* Boosey & Hawkes *Baker 92*
Hawkeswood, William Gordon 1951- *WhoE 93*
Hawkey, G. Michael 1941- *WhoAm 92*
Hawkey, Penelope J. 1942- *WhoAm 92, WhoAmW 93*
Hawkey, Philip A. 1946- *WhoAm 92*
Hawkey, Raymond *ScF&FL 92*
Hawking, S.W. *BioIn 17*
Hawking, Stephen W. *BioIn 17*
Hawking, Stephen W. 1942- *ConHero 2 [port], WhoWor 93*
Hawking, Stephen William *WhoScE 91-1*
Hawkins, Albert Douglas, Jr. 1947- *St&PR 93*
Hawkins, Andre *AfrAmBi*
Hawkins, Armis Eugene 1920- *WhoSSW 93*
Hawkins, Ashton 1937- *WhoAm 92*
Hawkins, Augustus F. *BioIn 17*
Hawkins, Augustus F. 1907- *AfrAmBi [port]*
Hawkins, Benjamin Sanford 1909- *WhoSSW 93*
Hawkins, Brett William 1937- *WhoAm 92*
Hawkins, Brian Lee 1948- *WhoE 93*
Hawkins, Bruce 1930- *WhoE 93*
Hawkins, Charles Earl, III 1943- *WhoE 93*
Hawkins, Charles Edward 1941- *WhoSSW 93*
Hawkins, Cheri J. *BioIn 17*
Hawkins, Christine Marguerite 1952- *WhoAmW 93*
Hawkins, Coleman (Randolph) 1904-1969 *Baker 92*
Hawkins, Cornelius L. 1942- *BiDAMSp 1989*
Hawkins, Corrine M. *Law&B 92*
Hawkins, Dale Louis 1945- *St&PR 93*
Hawkins, Dallas E. 1923- *St&PR 93*
Hawkins, David Arnold 1952- *WhoWor 93*
Hawkins, David Cartwright 1913- *WhoAm 92*
Hawkins, David Frederick 1933- *WhoAm 92*
Hawkins, David H. 1940- *St&PR 93*
Hawkins, David Rollo 1923- *WhoAm 92*
Hawkins, Diane *BioIn 17*
Hawkins, Donald Lee 1941- *St&PR 93*
Hawkins, Donald Merton 1921- *WhoAm 92*
Hawkins, Donna Faye 1943- *WhoAmW 93*
Hawkins, Donna Jean 1944- *WhoAmW 93*
Hawkins, Dorisula Wooten 1941- *WhoSSW 93*
Hawkins, Edward Jackson 1927- *WhoAm 92*
Hawkins, Elinor Dixon 1927- *WhoAmW 93, WhoSSW 93*
Hawkins, Eliot Dexter 1932- *WhoAm 92*
Hawkins, Ellen Marguerite 1960- *WhoAmW 93*
Hawkins, Erick *BioIn 17, WhoAm 92*
Hawkins, Falcon Black, Jr. 1927- *WhoAm 92, WhoSSW 93*
Hawkins, Francis Glenn 1917- *WhoAm 92*
Hawkins, Frank Nelson 1940- *St&PR 93*
Hawkins, Franklin D. *St&PR 93*
Hawkins, Fred Hopka, Jr. 1949- *St&PR 93*
Hawkins, Gail Nathena 1952- *WhoAmW 93*
Hawkins, Gene Russell 1928- *St&PR 93*
Hawkins, Geoffrey John *WhoScE 91-1*
Hawkins, Howard John 1918- *St&PR 93*
Hawkins, Hunt 1943- *WhoWrEP 92*
Hawkins, Ida Faye 1928- *WhoAmW 93*
Hawkins, Jack 1910-1973 *IntDcF 2-3 [port]*
Hawkins, Jacquelinn 1938- *WhoAmW 93*

Hawkins, Jacquelyn 1943- *WhoAmW 93*
Hawkins, James *BioIn 17*
Hawkins, James Alexander, II 1929- *WhoAm 92*
Hawkins, James Barrett 1956- *WhoEmL 93*
Hawkins, James Dale 1944- *St&PR 93*
Hawkins, James Gregory 1951- *St&PR 93*
Hawkins, James M. 1924- *St&PR 93*
Hawkins, James Victor 1936- *WhoAm 92*
Hawkins, Jasper Stillwell, Jr. 1932- *WhoAm 92*
Hawkins, Jim 1944- *ScF&FL 92*
Hawkins, Joellen Margaret Beck 1941- *WhoAmW 93*
Hawkins, John 1719-1789 *Baker 92, BioIn 17*
Hawkins, John 1944- *Baker 92*
Hawkins, John B. 1946- *St&PR 93*
Hawkins, John Lee, II 1916- *WhoSSW 93*
Hawkins, John S. 1956- *St&PR 93*
Hawkins, Joseph Elmer 1914- *WhoAm 92*
Hawkins, Karen Frances 1947- *WhoEmL 93*
Hawkins, Katherine Ann 1947- *WhoAm 92, WhoEmL 93*
Hawkins, Katherine Warfel 1958- *WhoAmW 93*
Hawkins, Kenneth D. 1950- *St&PR 93*
Hawkins, Kim Michael 1954- *St&PR 93*
Hawkins, Leslie *WhoScE 91-1*
Hawkins, Linda Parrott 1947- *WhoAmW 93, WhoSSW 93*
Hawkins, Margaret Albright 1951- *WhoAmW 93*
Hawkins, Mark F. d1992 *NewYTBS 92*
Hawkins, Mary Bess 1951- *WhoAmW 93*
Hawkins, Mary Ellen 1923- *WhoAmW 93*
Hawkins, Mary Helen 1932- *WhoSSW 93*
Hawkins, Mary Ruth Reynolds 1944- *WhoAmW 93*
Hawkins, Melvin L. *Law&B 92*
Hawkins, Merrill Morris 1914- *WhoAm 92*
Hawkins, Micah 1777-1825 *Baker 92*
Hawkins, Michael Daly 1945- *WhoAm 92*
Hawkins, Michael William 1952- *St&PR 93*
Hawkins, Naomi Ruth 1947- *WhoAmW 93*
Hawkins, Neil Middleton 1935- *WhoAm 92*
Hawkins, Osie Penman, Jr. 1913- *WhoAm 92*
Hawkins, Pamela Leigh Huffman 1950- *WhoSSW 93*
Hawkins, Paula *BioIn 17, WhoAm 92, WhoAmW 93*
Hawkins, Peter 1924- *ScF&FL 92*
Hawkins, Phillip Lee 1926- *WhoWor 93*
Hawkins, Phyllis Ann 1945- *WhoAmW 93*
Hawkins, Ralph W. 1938- *St&PR 93*
Hawkins, Rebecca Rusack *Law&B 92*
Hawkins, Reginald C. *Law&B 92*
Hawkins, Richard C. 1940- *St&PR 93*
Hawkins, Richard Michael 1949- *WhoWor 93*
Hawkins, Richard Spencer Daddow 1943- *WhoWor 93*
Hawkins, Robert 1930- *St&PR 93*
Hawkins, Robert Garvin 1936- *WhoAm 92*
Hawkins, Robert L. 1922- *St&PR 93*
Hawkins, Robert Pearson 1931- *WhoSSW 93*
Hawkins, Roger *SoulM*
Hawkins, Roger Keith *WhoScE 91-1*
Hawkins, Ronald Harris 1932- *St&PR 93*
Hawkins, Scott Alexis 1954- *WhoEmL 93*
Hawkins, Screamin' Jay 1929- *ConMus 8 [port], SoulM*
Hawkins, Shirley Maynard 1939- *St&PR 93*
Hawkins, Terence Ronald Wilfred *WhoScE 91-1*
Hawkins, Thomas Cleve 1949- *St&PR 93*
Hawkins, Thomas H. *Law&B 92*
Hawkins, Timothy d1992 *NewYTBS 92*
Hawkins, Travis Montgomery 1959- *WhoSSW 93*
Hawkins, Vinton J. *Law&B 92*
Hawkins, W. Lincoln d1992 *NewYTBS 92*
Hawkins, Walter Lincoln 1911- *WhoAm 92*
Hawkins, Ward 1912-1990 *ScF&FL 92*
Hawkins, William 1895-1990 *BioIn 17*
Hawkins, William A. 1954- *St&PR 93*
Hawkins, William D. 1914-1942 *BioIn 17*
Hawkins, William F. *BioIn 17*
Hawkins, William F. 1931- *St&PR 93, WhoAm 92*
Hawkins, William R. *Law&B 92, WhoIns 93*
Hawkins, Willis E., Jr. 1928- *St&PR 93*
Hawkins, Willis M. 1913- *St&PR 93*
Hawkins, Willis Moore 1913- *WhoAm 92*
Hawkins, Wilton A. 1922- *St&PR 93*
Hawkins, Yusuf *BioIn 17*
Hawkinson, Gary M. 1948- *St&PR 93*
Hawkinson, Gary Michael 1948- *WhoAm 92*
Hawkinson, John 1912- *St&PR 93*
Hawkinson, Leona A. 1944- *St&PR 93*
Hawkinson, Robert W. 1920- *St&PR 93*
Hawkinson, Thomas Edwin 1952- *WhoWor 93*
Hawkridge, Winifred *AmWomPl*
Hawkrigg, Melvin Michael 1930- *WhoAm 92*
Hawks, Brenda Kay 1955- *WhoAmW 93*
Hawks, Carol Pitts 1958- *WhoEmL 93*
Hawks, Howard 1896-1977 *BioIn 17, MiSFD 9N*
Hawks, Irene Kaminsky 1945- *WhoE 93*
Hawks, Kitty *BioIn 17*
Hawks, Lee *ScF&FL 92*
Hawks, Robert *BioIn 17*
Hawksford, Malcolm Omar 1947- *WhoWor 93*
Hawksworth, David Leslie *WhoScE 91-1*
Hawksworth, Paul D. 1934- *WhoIns 93*
Hawksworth, Paul David 1934- *St&PR 93*
Hawkwood, John c. 1321-1394 *HarEnMi*
Hawlett, Frank K. 1937- *St&PR 93*
Hawlett, Mark K. *St&PR 93*
Hawley, Anne 1943- *WhoAm 92, WhoAmW 93*
Hawley, Bonnie Lois 1945- *WhoAmW 93*
Hawley, Charles Beach 1858-1915 *Baker 92*
Hawley, Donald Springer 1928- *WhoWrEP 92*
Hawley, Ellis Wayne 1929- *WhoAm 92*
Hawley, Frank Jordan, Jr. 1927- *WhoAm 92, WhoE 93*
Hawley, Frederick William, III 1931- *WhoAm 92*
Hawley, J. Jeffrey *Law&B 92*
Hawley, James C. 1954- *St&PR 93*
Hawley, Jean Gannett 1924- *WhoAm 92, WhoAmW 93, WhoE 93*
Hawley, Jeffrey Lance 1948- *St&PR 93, WhoEmL 93*
Hawley, John L., Jr. 1953- *WhoSSW 93*
Hawley, Michael Christopher 1938- *St&PR 93*
Hawley, Nanci Elizabeth 1942- *WhoAmW 93*
Hawley, Philip Metschan 1925- *St&PR 93, WhoAm 92, WhoWor 93*
Hawley, Renee Elizabeth 1956- *WhoAmW 93*
Hawley, Richard S. *Law&B 92*
Hawley, Robert B. 1955- *St&PR 93*
Hawley, Robert C(oit) 1933- *WhoWrEP 92*
Hawley, Robert J. *Law&B 92*
Hawley, Robert P. 1933- *St&PR 93*
Hawley, Robert William, Jr. 1948- *WhoWor 93*
Hawley, Ronald I. 1941- *St&PR 93*
Hawley, Sandra Sue 1948- *WhoAmW 93*
Hawley, Wanda 1895-1963 *SweetSg B [port]*
Hawley, Wayne Curtis 1946- *WhoEmL 93*
Hawley, Wendell Charles 1930- *St&PR 93*
Hawn, Eric Dana 1950- *St&PR 93*
Hawn, Gates Helms 1948- *WhoAm 92*
Hawn, Goldie *BioIn 17*
Hawn, Goldie 1945- *IntDcF 2-3, QDrFCA 92 [port], WhoAm 92, WhoAmW 93*
Hawn, James F. 1927- *St&PR 93*
Hawn, Van Zandt 1945- *St&PR 93*
Hawn, Virginia Shuford 1928- *WhoSSW 93*
Haworth, Charles Dale 1932- *WhoAm 92*
Haworth, Charles Ray 1943- *WhoAm 92, WhoSSW 93*
Haworth, Charles Taylor 1937- *WhoSSW 93*
Haworth, Dale Keith 1924- *WhoAm 92*
Haworth, Daniel Thomas 1928- *WhoAm 92*
Haworth, Don *BioIn 17*
Haworth, Gerrard W. 1911- *St&PR 93*
Haworth, Gerrard Wendell 1911- *WhoAm 92*
Haworth, James Chilton 1923- *WhoAm 92*
Haworth, Joan Gustafson 1938- *WhoAmW 93*
Haworth, Lawrence Lindley 1926- *WhoAm 92, WhoWrEP 92*
Haworth, Leslie W. 1943- *St&PR 93*
Haworth, Michael Elliott, Jr. 1928- *WhoAm 92*
Haworth, Richard G. *BioIn 17*
Haworth, Richard G. 1942- *St&PR 93*
Haworth, Steven Clay 1950- *St&PR 93*
Haworth, Thomas Howard 1940- *St&PR 93*
Haworth, Trevor 1947- *St&PR 93*
Hawpe, David Vaughn 1943- *WhoAm 92*
Hawran, Paul William 1952- *St&PR 93, WhoAm 92*
Hawranko, George E. *Law&B 92*
Hawrylak, Henryk 1924- *WhoScE 91-4*
Hawrylko, Eugenia Anna 1942- *WhoE 93*
Hawryluk, Allan A. *Law&B 92*
Hawrylyshyn, Bohdan Wolodymyr 1926- *WhoWor 93*
Hawrys, Zbigniew Stanislaw 1940- *WhoScE 91-4*
Haws, Edmund John *WhoScE 91-1*
Haws, Janet Agnes 1939- *WhoAmW 93*
Hawthorn, Scott R. *Law&B 92*
Hawthorne, Betty E. d1990 *BioIn 17*
Hawthorne, Dent, Jr. 1922- *St&PR 93*
Hawthorne, Douglas Lawson 1942- *St&PR 93, WhoAm 92*
Hawthorne, Frank Christopher 1946- *WhoAm 92*
Hawthorne, Frank Howard 1923- *WhoAm 92*
Hawthorne, H. Bagley 1949- *St&PR 93*
Hawthorne, Henry Wilson 1937- *St&PR 93*
Hawthorne, Hildegarde *ScF&FL 92*
Hawthorne, J.N. *WhoScE 91-1*
Hawthorne, Jewell Ann 1952- *WhoAmW 93*
Hawthorne, Julian 1846-1934 *BioIn 17*
Hawthorne, Karen M. 1956- *St&PR 93*
Hawthorne, Marion Frederick 1928- *WhoAm 92*
Hawthorne, Nathaniel *Law&B 92*
Hawthorne, Nathaniel 1804-1864 *BioIn 17, MagSAmL [port], NinCLC 39 [port], WorLitC [port]*
Hawthorne, Nigel *BioIn 17*
Hawthorne, Nigel 1929- *ConTFT 10*
Hawthorne, Rose 1851-1926 *BioIn 17*
Hawthorne, Ruby *AmWomPl*
Hawthorne, Ruth Warren *AmWomPl*
Hawthorne, Timothy Robert 1950- *WhoEmL 93*
Hawthorne, Victor Morrison 1921- *WhoAm 92*
Hawthorne, Violet *ScF&FL 92*
Hawthorne, William L., III *Law&B 92*
Hawthorne, William Rede 1913- *WhoWor 93*
Hawtin, Geoffrey 1949- *WhoScE 91-3*
Hawtin, Geoffrey Charles 1949- *WhoUN 92*
Hawtin, P. *WhoScE 91-1*
Hawtrey, Charles 1914-1988 *QDrFCA 92 [port]*
Hawxhurst, William E. *Law&B 92*
Hax, Arnoldo Cubillos 1936- *WhoAm 92*
Haxo, Francis Theodore 1921- *WhoAm 92*
Haxton, David 1943- *WhoAm 92*
Haxton, David Page 1928- *WhoSSW 93*
Haxton, Josephine *BioIn 17*
Haxton, Wick Christopher 1949- *WhoAm 92*
Hay, Alan Malcolm *WhoScE 91-1*
Hay, Alexandre 1919-1991 *AnObit 1991, BioIn 17*
Hay, Allan Stuart 1929- *WhoAm 92*
Hay, (George) Austin 1915- *WhoWrEP 92*
Hay, Betty Jo 1931- *WhoAmW 93*
Hay, Clara *BioIn 17*
Hay, Daisy Baker *AmWomPl*
Hay, Diana 1962- *WhoAmW 93*
Hay, Edward James 1937- *St&PR 93*
Hay, Edward Norman 1889-1943 *Baker 92*
Hay, Elizabeth Claire 1967- *WhoSSW 93*
Hay, Elizabeth Dexter 1927- *WhoAm 92*
Hay, Eloise Knapp 1926- *WhoAm 92*
Hay, Frank Charles *WhoScE 91-1*
Hay, Frederick Charles 1888-1945 *Baker 92*
Hay, Frederick Dale 1944- *WhoAm 92*
Hay, George 1922- *ScF&FL 92*
Hay, George Austin 1915- *WhoAm 92, WhoE 93, WhoWor 93*
Hay, Jack Lee 1925- *WhoWrEP 92*
Hay, Jacob 1920-1976 *ScF&FL 92*
Hay, James D. *Law&B 92*
Hay, James D. 1940- *St&PR 93*
Hay, James F. 1952- *St&PR 93*
Hay, James Miller 1929- *WhoAm 92*
Hay, Jess Thomas 1931- *St&PR 93*
Hay, John 1838-1905 *GayN*
Hay, John 1915- *WhoAm 92*
Hay, John A. 1931- *St&PR 93*
Hay, John Milton 1838-1905 *BioIn 17*
Hay, John Thomas 1921- *WhoAm 92*
Hay, Louis d1991 *BioIn 17*
Hay, Mark H. 1944- *St&PR 93*
Hay, Nelson Edward 1945- *WhoWrEP 92*
Hay, Oswyn *ScF&FL 92*
Hay, Peter M. 1921- *St&PR 93*
Hay, Ralph E. 1891-1944 *BiDAMSp 1989*
Hay, Raymond Alexander 1928- *St&PR 93*
Hay, Richard Carman 1921- *WhoWor 93*
Hay, Richard Laurence 1929- *WhoAm 92*
Hay, Richard Le Roy 1926- *WhoAm 92*
Hay, Robert Dean 1921- *WhoAm 92*
Hay, Robert John 1926- *St&PR 93*
Hay, Robert K.M. 1946- *WhoScE 91-1*
Hay, Roderick James *WhoScE 91-1*
Hay, Timothy *ConAu 136, MajAI*
Hay, Timothy 1910-1952 *BioIn 17*
Hay, Will 1888-1949 *IntDcF 2-3 [port], QDrFCA 92 [port]*
Hay, William John *Law&B 92*
Hay, William Winn 1934- *WhoAm 92*
Haya, Kenichi 1929- *WhoWor 93*
Haya de la Torre, Victor Raul *DcCPCAm*
Haya de la Torre, Victor Raul 1895-1979 *DcTwHis*
Hayaishi, Osamu 1920- *WhoWor 93*
Hayakawa, Kan-Ichi 1931- *WhoAm 92, WhoWor 93*
Hayakawa, Katumitu 1943- *WhoWor 93*
Hayakawa, Margedant Peters *BioIn 17*
Hayakawa, Masaru 1940- *WhoAsAP 91*
Hayakawa, Milton 1928- *St&PR 93*
Hayakawa, S.I. *BioIn 17*
Hayakawa, S. I. 1906-1992 *NewYTBS 92 [port]*
Hayakawa, S(amuel) I(chiye) 1906-1992 *ConAu 137, CurBio 92N*
Hayakawa, Samuel Ichiye 1906-1992 *News 92, -92-3*
Hayakawa, Sessue 1890-1973 *IntDcF 2-3 [port]*
Hayami, Isao 1928- *WhoAsAP 91*
Hayami, Yujiro 1932- *WhoWor 93*
Hayano, David M. *BioIn 17*
Hayano, Shigeo 1925- *WhoWor 93*
Hayasaka, Fumio 1914-1955 *Baker 92*
Hayasaka, Taijiro 1923- *WhoWor 93*
Hayase, Fumitaka 1946- *WhoWor 93*
Hayase, Linda Michi 1963- *WhoAmW 93*
Hayase, Paul H. *Law&B 92*
Hayashi, Chikio 1918- *WhoWor 93*
Hayashi, Eizi *BioIn 17*
Hayashi, Elmer Kinji 1938- *WhoSSW 93*
Hayashi, George Yoichi 1920- *WhoWor 93*
Hayashi, Hikaru 1931- *Baker 92*
Hayashi, Hiroko 1943- *WhoWor 93*
Hayashi, Hisashi 1928- *WhoWor 93*
Hayashi, Kaizo 1957- *MiSFD 9*
Hayashi, Kenjiro 1925- *WhoWor 93*
Hayashi, Kichiro 1936- *WhoWor 93*
Hayashi, Kozaburo 1942- *WhoWor 93*
Hayashi, Masahisa 1942- *WhoWor 93*
Hayashi, Michael K. *Law&B 92*
Hayashi, Mitsuhiko 1930- *WhoWor 93*
Hayashi, Moritaka 1938- *WhoUN 92*
Hayashi (Nagaya), Kenzo 1899-1976 *Baker 92*
Hayashi, Nancy *ScF&FL 92*
Hayashi, Senjuro 1876-1942 *HarEnMi*
Hayashi, Shizuo 1922- *WhoWor 93*
Hayashi, Tadao *WhoWor 93*
Hayashi, Tadashi 1959- *WhoWor 93*
Hayashi, Taikan 1922- *WhoAsAP 91*
Hayashi, Taizo 1920- *WhoWor 93*
Hayashi, Takao 1949- *WhoWor 93*
Hayashi, Takemi 1938- *WhoWor 93*
Hayashi, Tetsumaro 1929- *WhoWrEP 92*
Hayashi, Toshiko 1940- *WhoAsAP 91*
Hayashi, Yoshihiro 1940- *WhoWor 93*
Hayashi, Yoshio 1922- *WhoWor 93*
Hayashi, Yoshiro 1927- *WhoAsAP 91*
Hayashi, Yutaro 1935- *St&PR 93*
Hayashida, Joel J. *Law&B 92*
Hayashida, Motoi 1932- *WhoE 93*
Hayashida, Yukio 1915- *WhoAsAP 91*
Hayasi, Nisiki 1929- *WhoE 93, WhoWor 93*
Hayat, Marcel 1932- *WhoScE 91-2*
Hayatou, Sadou *WhoWor 93*
Hayatou, Sadou 1942- *WhoAfr*
Hayatsu, Hikoya 1934- *WhoWor 93*
Haycock, Kathryn Proffitt 1951- *WhoWor 93*
Haycock, Kenneth Roy 1948- *WhoAm 92*
Haycox, Sue Ellen *Law&B 92*
Haycraft, Howard 1905-1991 *BioIn 17, ConAu 136, CurBio 92N, SmATA 70*
Haydanek, Ronald Edward 1932- *WhoAm 92*
Hayde, Daniel Francis 1942- *St&PR 93*
Haydee, Marcia 1937- *WhoWor 93*
Hayden, Alvin Lee 1943- *St&PR 93*
Hayden, Bertha Marie Brechet *AmWomPl*
Hayden, Bill H. *BioIn 17*
Hayden, Bruce P. 1915- *WhoE 93*
Hayden, Carl T. 1877-1972 *PolPar*
Hayden, Carl Trumbull 1877-1972 *BioIn 17*
Hayden, David Lee 1954- *St&PR 93*
Hayden, Dolores 1945- *WhoWrEP 92*
Hayden, Donna-Ann Patricia 1955- *St&PR 93*
Hayden, Edgar Clay 1922- *WhoSSW 93*
Hayden, Gary Lynn *Law&B 92*
Hayden, George Allen 1928- *WhoE 93*
Hayden, Gerald F. 1924- *St&PR 93*
Hayden, Harold Stephen 1955- *WhoSSW 93*
Hayden, Hugh M. *Law&B 92*
Hayden, J.P. *WhoScE 91-3*
Hayden, J. Page, Jr. 1929- *St&PR 93*

Hayden, Jeffrey MiSFD 9
Hayden, Jerry L. 1933- St&PR 93
Hayden, Joanne Schreyer 1942- WhoAmW 93
Hayden, John Carleton 1933- WhoSSW 93
Hayden, John Joseph Law&B 92
Hayden, John Michael 1944- BioIn 17
Hayden, John Olin 1932- WhoAm 92
Hayden, Jon E. Law&B 92
Hayden, Joseph A., Jr. 1944- WhoE 93
Hayden, Joseph P., Jr. 1929- WhoIns 93
Hayden, Joseph Page, Jr. 1929- WhoAm 92
Hayden, Karen ScF&FL 92
Hayden, Kathleen Bernadette 1948- WhoAmW 93
Hayden, Leroy Robert, Jr. 1935- WhoIns 93
Hayden, Linda D. 1951- WhoAmW 93
Hayden, Marna 1938- St&PR 93, WhoAmW 93
Hayden, Mary Law&B 92
Hayden, Michael Joseph 1964- WhoE 93
Hayden, Mildred S. 1944- St&PR 93
Hayden, Neil Steven 1937- WhoAm 92, WhoE 93
Hayden, Patricia Rogers 1945- WhoAmW 93
Hayden, Ralph Frederick 1922- WhoAm 92
Hayden, Raymond Paul 1939- WhoAm 92
Hayden, Richard M. 1945- St&PR 93
Hayden, Richard Michael 1945- WhoAm 92
Hayden, Robert 1913-1980 PoeCrit 6 [port]
Hayden, Robert E. 1913-1980 EncAACR
Hayden, Robert Earl 1913-1980 BioIn 17
Hayden, Robert Russell 1934- WhoE 93
Hayden, Sterling 1916-1986 IntDcF 2-3 [port]
Hayden, Steven Charles 1946- St&PR 93
Hayden, Tom BioIn 17
Hayden, Tom 1939- WhoWrEP 92
Hayden, Torey L. BioIn 17
Hayden, Virgil O. 1921- WhoAm 92
Hayden, William George 1933- WhoAsAP 91, WhoWor 93
Hayden, William Hughes 1940- St&PR 93
Hayden, William Joseph 1929- St&PR 93, WhoAm 92
Hayden, William Taylor 1954- WhoEmL 93
Hayden-Wing, Larry Dean 1935- WhoWor 93
Haydn, Franz Joseph 1732?-1809 IntDcOp [port]
Haydn, Joseph 1732-1809 BioIn 17, OxDcOp
Haydn, (Franz) Joseph 1732-1809 Baker 92
Haydn, Michael 1737?-1806 OxDcOp
Haydn, (Johann) Michael 1737-1806 Baker 92
Haydock, Michael Damean 1940- WhoE 93
Haydock, Michael Patrick 1951- WhoEmL 93
Haydock, Tim ScF&FL 92
Haydocks, Roger S. 1945- St&PR 93
Haydon, Benjamin Robert 1786-1846 BioIn 17
Haydon, Edward Eliot 1940- St&PR 93
Haydon, Glen 1896-1966 Baker 92
Haydu, Juan B. 1930- St&PR 93
Haydu, Richard A. Law&B 92
Haye, Mary Teressa 1953- WhoEmL 93
Hayek, Carolyn Jean 1948- WhoAm 92, WhoAmW 93
Hayek, F(riedrich) A(ugust von) 1899-1992 ConAu 137
Hayek, Friedrich A(ugust Von) 1899-1992 CurBio 92N
Hayek, Friedrich A. von 1899-1992 BioIn 17
Hayek, Friedrich August von 1899- DcTwHis
Hayek, Friedrich von 1899-1992 NewYTBS 92 [port]
Hayek, Lee-Ann Collins 1943- WhoAm 92
Hayek, Mary Annie WhoSSW 93
Hayek, William Edward 1947- WhoAm 92, WhoE 93
Hayen, William Joseph 1948- St&PR 93
Hayers, Sidney MiSFD 9
Hayes, Alberta Phyllis Wildrick 1918- WhoAmW 93
Hayes, Alexandria Lynn 1957- WhoEmL 93
Hayes, Alfred 1910-1989 BioIn 17
Hayes, Alfred Jackson 1944- St&PR 93
Hayes, Alice Bourke 1937- WhoAm 92, WhoAmW 93
Hayes, Allene Valerie Farmer 1958- WhoAmW 93
Hayes, Allison 1930-1977 BioIn 17
Hayes, Alton Odis 1936- WhoSSW 93
Hayes, Andrew Patrick 1958- WhoE 93
Hayes, Andrew Wallace, II 1939- WhoAm 92, WhoSSW 93
Hayes, Ann Carson 1941- WhoSSW 93, WhoWor 93
Hayes, Ann Louise 1924- WhoAm 92, WhoWrEP 92
Hayes, Arthur Chester 1918- WhoWor 93
Hayes, Arthur Hull, Jr. 1933- WhoAm 92
Hayes, Arthur Michael 1915- WhoAm 92
Hayes, Benjamin Holt 1934- St&PR 93
Hayes, Bernadette Marie WhoAmW 93
Hayes, Bernardine Frances 1939- WhoAmW 93
Hayes, Bob 1942- BioIn 17
Hayes, Bobby K. 1930- St&PR 93
Hayes, Bree Audrey 1945- WhoSSW 93
Hayes, Brenda Sue 1941- WhoAmW 93, WhoWor 93
Hayes, Brian F. BioIn 17
Hayes, Brian F. d1992 NewYTBS 92
Hayes, Bridget T. AmWomPl
Hayes, Carl Richard 1945- St&PR 93
Hayes, Carol Crofoot Law&B 92
Hayes, Carol J. 1940- WhoE 93
Hayes, Cathy Sumner 1953- WhoAmW 93
Hayes, Charles 1950- WhoWor 93
Hayes, Charles A. AfrAmBi [port], BioIn 17
Hayes, Charles A. 1918- CngDr 91, WhoAm 92
Hayes, Charles A. 1935- WhoSSW 93
Hayes, Charles Albert 1934- St&PR 93
Hayes, Charles Austin 1946- WhoSSW 93
Hayes, Charles Curtis, III 1959- WhoSSW 93
Hayes, Charles Lawton 1927- WhoAm 92
Hayes, Charles Leonard 1940- WhoWrEP 92
Hayes, Daniel 1952- SmATA 73 [port]
Hayes, Darlene BioIn 17
Hayes, David John Arthur, Jr. 1929- WhoAm 92, WhoWor 93
Hayes, David M. Law&B 92
Hayes, David M. 1943- St&PR 93
Hayes, David Matthew 1959- WhoSSW 93
Hayes, David Michael 1943- WhoAm 92
Hayes, David Vaughn 1954- WhoSSW 93
Hayes, David Vincent 1931- WhoAm 92
Hayes, David W. Law&B 92
Hayes, David W. 1942- WhoAm 92
Hayes, David Warren 1946- WhoEmL 93
Hayes, Denis BioIn 17
Hayes, Denis Allen 1944- WhoAm 92
Hayes, Dennis Edward 1938- WhoAm 92
Hayes, Dennis Joseph 1934- WhoAm 92
Hayes, Derek C. Law&B 92
Hayes, Derek Cumberland 1936- WhoAm 92
Hayes, Diahann Fowler 1959- WhoE 93
Hayes, Donald E., Jr. Law&B 92
Hayes, Donald Horace 1931- St&PR 93
Hayes, Donald J. 1933- St&PR 93
Hayes, Donald Powell 1948- St&PR 93
Hayes, Donald R. Law&B 92
Hayes, Dor-Tensia BioIn 17
Hayes, Dorothy Damon 1950- St&PR 93
Hayes, Dorsha d1990 BioIn 17
Hayes, Douglas A. WhoAm 92
Hayes, Douglas Martin 1943- WhoWor 93
Hayes, Edward J. 1924- St&PR 93
Hayes, Edwin Junius, Jr. 1932- WhoAm 92
Hayes, Edwin Keith 1956- WhoWrEP 92
Hayes, Everett Allison 1921- WhoSSW 93
Hayes, Everett Russell 1917- WhoE 93
Hayes, Francis Mahon 1930- WhoUN 92
Hayes, Frank N. 1938- St&PR 93
Hayes, Gayle Arline 1936- WhoSSW 93
Hayes, Gaynelle Hasselmeier 1943- WhoSSW 93
Hayes, George Stephen 1947- WhoE 93
Hayes, Gerald Joseph 1950- WhoAm 92, WhoEmL 93, WhoWor 93
Hayes, Gladys Lucille Allen 1913- WhoAmW 93
Hayes, Gordon Glenn 1936- WhoWor 93
Hayes, Harold BioIn 17
Hayes, Helen 1900- BioIn 17, ConAu 138, WhoAm 92, WhoAmW 93
Hayes, Howard Randolph 1935- St&PR 93
Hayes, Isaac 1938- Baker 92
Hayes, Isaac 1942- SoulM, WhoAm 92
Hayes, Jack Dee 1940- St&PR 93
Hayes, Jack Irby 1944- WhoSSW 93
Hayes, Jacqueline Crement 1941- WhoAmW 93
Hayes, James A. 1930- St&PR 93
Hayes, James A. 1946- CngDr 91
Hayes, James Alison 1946- WhoAm 92, WhoSSW 93
Hayes, James B. Law&B 92, WhoAm 92, WhoE 93
Hayes, James Edward 1928- WhoAm 92
Hayes, James Joseph, IV Law&B 92
Hayes, James Mark 1958- WhoEmL 93
Hayes, James Robert 1946- St&PR 93
Hayes, James W., III Law&B 92
Hayes, James W., III 1948- St&PR 93
Hayes, Janet Gray 1926- WhoAm 92
Hayes, Janice BioIn 17
Hayes, Janice Cecile Osgard 1941- WhoSSW 93
Hayes, Jere Glen Law&B 92
Hayes, Jeremiah Francis 1934- WhoAm 92
Hayes, John Bruton, Jr. 1942- WhoAm 92, WhoE 93
Hayes, John Desmond WhoScE 91-1
Hayes, John E., Jr. 1937- St&PR 93
Hayes, John Edward 1941- WhoE 93, WhoSSW 93
Hayes, John Edward, Jr. 1937- WhoAm 92
Hayes, John F(rancis) 1904-1980 DcChlFi
Hayes, John Francis 1919- WhoAm 92
Hayes, John Freeman 1926- WhoAm 92
Hayes, John J. 1930- St&PR 93
Hayes, John O. Law&B 92
Hayes, John Patrick 1921- WhoAm 92
Hayes, John Patrick 1944- WhoAm 92
Hayes, John Patrick, Jr. 1949- WhoAm 92
Hayes, John R. 1939- St&PR 93
Hayes, John Thompson 1940- WhoSSW 93
Hayes, John Trevor 1929- WhoWor 93
Hayes, John W. BioIn 17
Hayes, Joseph 1918- WhoWrEP 92
Hayes, Joseph A. Law&B 92
Hayes, Joseph M. Law&B 92
Hayes, Joyce Koria Law&B 92
Hayes, K. William 1943- WhoSSW 93, WhoWor 93
Hayes, Karen Lee Carter 1963- WhoAmW 93
Hayes, Katherine M. AmWomPl
Hayes, Kirk M. 1936- WhoIns 93
Hayes, Kirk Monroe 1936- St&PR 93
Hayes, Larry D. 1938- St&PR 93
Hayes, Linda Holmes 1947- WhoAmW 93
Hayes, Lor-Tensia BioIn 17
Hayes, Lucy Webb 1831-1889 BioIn 17
Hayes, Maria Mitchell WhoWrEP 92
Hayes, Marian Mercer 1963- WhoAmW 93, WhoEmL 93
Hayes, Mark P. 1953- WhoScE 91-1
Hayes, Mark S. Law&B 92
Hayes, Mark S. 1946- St&PR 93
Hayes, Mark Stephen 1946- WhoAm 92
Hayes, Marshall Anderson 1914- St&PR 93
Hayes, Martha Bell 1943- WhoSSW 93
Hayes, Mary Eshbaugh 1928- WhoAmW 93
Hayes, Mary Phyllis 1921- WhoAmW 93
Hayes, Michael A. 1936- WhoScE 91-3
Hayes, Michael Bernard 1958- WhoSSW 93
Hayes, Michael Patrick John 1941- WhoWor 93
Hayes, Mike WhoScE 91-1
Hayes, Mildred A. AmWomPl
Hayes, Myra Nell 1943- WhoAmW 93
Hayes, Nancy Jean 1963- WhoAmW 93
Hayes, Neville A. 1936- St&PR 93
Hayes, Nicholas 1947- WhoE 93
Hayes, Nicholas L. 1941- St&PR 93
Hayes, Norman Robert, Jr. 1948- WhoE 93
Hayes, Patricia Ann 1944- WhoAm 92, WhoAmW 93
Hayes, Paul Gordon 1934- WhoAm 92, WhoWrEP 92
Hayes, Peter 1938- WhoScE 91-1
Hayes, Peter J. 1942- St&PR 93
Hayes, Peter John 1942- WhoAm 92, WhoSSW 93
Hayes, Peter Lind 1915- WhoAm 92
Hayes, Philip 1738-1797 Baker 92
Hayes, R. Chetwynd- ScF&FL 92
Hayes, R.W. Law&B 92
Hayes, Ralph 1927- ScF&FL 92
Hayes, Rebecca Anne 1950- WhoWor 93
Hayes, Richard Alan 1957- WhoWrEP 92
Hayes, Richard J. 1932-1989 BioIn 17
Hayes, Richard Johnson 1933- WhoAm 92, WhoWor 93
Hayes, Richard L. 1941- St&PR 93
Hayes, Richard L. 1946- WhoEmL 93, WhoSSW 93
Hayes, Robert A. Law&B 92
Hayes, Robert B. 1942- St&PR 93
Hayes, Robert Bruce 1925- WhoAm 92
Hayes, Robert Emmet 1920- WhoAm 92
Hayes, Robert Herrick 1936- WhoAm 92
Hayes, Robert Mac 1945- WhoSSW 93
Hayes, Robert Mayo 1926- WhoAm 92
Hayes, Roland 1887-1976 EncAACR
Hayes, Roland 1887-1977 Baker 92, ConBlB 4 [port]
Hayes, Ron 1956- St&PR 93
Hayes, Ronald J. 1931- WhoWor 93
Hayes, Rutherford B. 1822-1893 BioIn 17, PolPar
Hayes, Samuel Banks, III 1936- St&PR 93
Hayes, Samuel Linton, III 1935- WhoAm 92, WhoWor 93
Hayes, Samuel Perkins 1910- WhoAm 92
Hayes, Sarah Hall 1934- WhoAm 92, WhoWrEP 92
Hayes, Scott Birchard 1926- WhoAm 92
Hayes, Scott M. 1947- St&PR 93
Hayes, Sheila 1937- WhoWrEP 92
Hayes, Stephen Kurtz 1949- WhoWor 93
Hayes, Steven Douglas 1949- St&PR 93
Hayes, Suzanne Downey 1953- WhoAmW 93
Hayes, Thomas A. Law&B 92
Hayes, Thomas A. 1943- WhoIns 93
Hayes, Thomas Anthony 1943- St&PR 93
Hayes, Thomas Jay, III 1914- WhoAm 92
Hayes, Thomas Parker Law&B 92
Hayes, Thomas Patrick 1940- St&PR 93
Hayes, Tom WhoIns 93
Hayes, Vertis Clemon 1911- WhoAm 92
Hayes, Waldron Stanley, Jr. 1938- WhoAm 92
Hayes, Wayland Jackson, Jr. 1917- WhoAm 92
Hayes, Webb Cook, III 1920- WhoAm 92
Hayes, Wendy Jennings 1942- WhoAmW 93
Hayes, Wilbur Frank 1936- WhoE 93
Hayes, William 1707-1777 Baker 92
Hayes, William Aloysius 1920- WhoAm 92
Hayes, William Ellie, Jr. 1930- St&PR 93
Hayes, William G. Law&B 92
Hayes, William V. 1935- St&PR 93
Hayes, Woody BioIn 17
Hayes, Zachary (Jerome) 1932- ConAu 39NR
Hayez, Jean-Yves 1946- WhoScE 91-2
Hayflick, Leonard 1928- WhoAm 92
Hayford, Charles W. 1941- ConAu 136
Hayford, John Sargent 1940- St&PR 93, WhoAm 92
Haygood, John Thomas Law&B 92
Hayhurst, David Robert WhoScE 91-1
Hayhurst, James Frederick Palmer 1941- WhoAm 92
Hayhurst, Richard Allen 1948- WhoEmL 93
Hayhurst, Susan Ann 1960- WhoAmW 93
Hayko, Dianne 1949- WhoEmL 93
Hayko, Leonard J. 1942- St&PR 93
Hayler, Jorge M. 1944- WhoWor 93
Hayles, Brian 1931-1976 ScF&FL 92
Hayles, N. Katherine 1943- ScF&FL 92
Haylett, Margaret Wendy 1953- WhoAmW 93
Hayley, William 1745-1820 BioIn 17
Haym, Nicola Francesco 1678-1729 Baker 92, IntDcOp, OxDcOp
Haym, Rudolf 1821-1901 BioIn 17
Haymaker, Douglas James 1957- WhoEmL 93
Haymaker, Gideon Timberlake 1958- St&PR 93
Hayman, Carol Bessent 1927- WhoAm 92
Hayman, David MiSFD 9
Hayman, Diane W. 1961- St&PR 93
Hayman, Fred BioIn 17
Hayman, Harry 1917- WhoAm 92
Hayman, Helen Feeley 1918- WhoAmW 93
Hayman, James Alexander 1920- St&PR 93
Hayman, Jeffrey L. Law&B 92
Hayman, Jeffrey Lloyd 1955- WhoAm 92
Hayman, Muriel Jane 1948- WhoAmW 93
Hayman, Richard 1951- Baker 92
Hayman, Richard (Warren Joseph) 1920- Baker 92, WhoAm 92
Hayman, Robert 1575-1629 BioIn 17
Hayman, Robyne Marie 1961- WhoEmL 93
Hayman, Seymour 1914- WhoAm 92
Hayman, Walter Kurt WhoScE 91-1
Haymann, Mary Dunn 1945- WhoE 93
Haymer, Matthew A. Law&B 92
Haymes, Dick 1918-1980 Baker 92, BioIn 17
Haymes, Harmon Hayden 1927- WhoAm 92
Haymes, Malcolm Douglas 1955- WhoEmL 93, WhoSSW 93
Haymes, Robert C. 1931- WhoAm 92, WhoSSW 93
Haymon, Monte Roy 1937- WhoAm 92
Haymond, Edward Owen, Jr. 1936- St&PR 93
Haymond, Paula J. 1949- WhoAm 92, WhoEmL 93
Haynal, Adre 1930- WhoScE 91-4
Hayne, C. Peck 1934- St&PR 93
Hayne, David Mackness 1921- WhoAm 92
Hayne, Paul Hamilton 1830-1886 BioIn 17
Hayne, Thomas A. 1937- St&PR 93
Hayner, George Oliver 1945- WhoSSW 93

Hayner, Herman Henry 1916- *WhoWor 93*
Hayner, Jeannette Clare 1919- *WhoAmW 93*
Hayner, Kimerick F. 1941- *St&PR 93*
Hayner, Linda Kay 1946- *WhoEmL 93, WhoSSW 93*
Haynes, Arden R. *WhoAm 92*
Haynes, Betsy 1937- *ScF&FL 92*
Haynes, Boyd Withers, Jr. 1917- *WhoAm 92*
Haynes, Buren Thomas 1937- *St&PR 93*
Haynes, Caleb Vance, Jr. 1928- *WhoAm 92*
Haynes, Caroline Hopper 1959- *WhoAm 92, WhoAmW 93*
Haynes, Charlene Lee 1963- *WhoSSW 93*
Haynes, Charles C. 1949- *WhoSSW 93*
Haynes, Cheryl Ettora 1948- *WhoAmW 93*
Haynes, Christy Ray 1939- *St&PR 93*
Haynes, Clyde Ethelbert *Law&B 92*
Haynes, Deborah Gene 1954- *WhoAmW 93*
Haynes, Donna Groves 1963- *WhoAmW 93*
Haynes, Douglas Martin 1922- *WhoAm 92*
Haynes, Elizabeth Gillespie 1918- *WhoAmW 93*
Haynes, Frank L. 1944-1990 *BioIn 17*
Haynes, Frederick Leslie 1934- *WhoWor 93*
Haynes, Garry Locklyn 1953- *WhoE 93*
Haynes, Gary Allen 1936- *WhoAm 92*
Haynes, George Edmund 1880-1960 *BioIn 17, EncAACR*
Haynes, Gerald D. *Law&B 92*
Haynes, Gwendolyn Mary Duhon 1963- *WhoAmW 93*
Haynes, James 1932- *ScF&FL 92*
Haynes, James Earl, Jr. 1943- *WhoAm 92*
Haynes, Jean Reed 1949- *WhoAm 92, WhoAmW 93, WhoEmL 93*
Haynes, Jimmy Lee 1936- *WhoWor 93*
Haynes, John Earl 1944- *WhoE 93*
Haynes, John Lenneis 1934- *WhoSSW 93*
Haynes, John Mabin 1928- *WhoAm 92*
Haynes, John Roland *WhoScE 91-1*
Haynes, Karen Sue 1946- *WhoAm 92*
Haynes, Kenneth W. 1942- *St&PR 93*
Haynes, Leonard L., Jr. 1923- *WhoAm 92*
Haynes, Leonard L., III 1947- *WhoAm 92*
Haynes, Lincoln Murray 1924- *WhoWrEP 92*
Haynes, Lloyd R., Sr. 1916- *AfrAmBi [port]*
Haynes, Martha Patricia 1951- *WhoAm 92, WhoAmW 93*
Haynes, Mary *BioIn 17*
Haynes, Mary 1938- *ScF&FL 92*
Haynes, Max 1956- *SmATA 72 [port]*
Haynes, Moses Alfred 1921- *WhoAm 92*
Haynes, Norris Michael 1950- *WhoE 93*
Haynes, Phil *BioIn 17*
Haynes, R. Michael 1940- *WhoAm 92*
Haynes, Renee (Oriana Tickell) 1906-1992 *ConAu 139*
Haynes, Richard Anthony 1948- *WhoSSW 93*
Haynes, Richie 1936- *DcCPCAm*
Haynes, Robert Hall 1931- *WhoAm 92, WhoWor 93*
Haynes, Robert Vaughn 1929- *WhoAm 92*
Haynes, Roslynn D. *ScF&FL 92*
Haynes, Roy 1926- *BioIn 17*
Haynes, Roy (Owen) 1926- *Baker 92*
Haynes, Sean Aaron Russel 1968- *WhoE 93*
Haynes, Sherwood K. 1910-1990 *BioIn 17*
Haynes, Suzanne G. 1947- *WhoAmW 93*
Haynes, Teresa Wathenia 1953- *WhoAmW 93*
Haynes, Thomas Beranek 1956- *WhoE 93*
Haynes, Thomas Morris 1918- *WhoAm 92, WhoE 93*
Haynes, Todd *MiSFD 9*
Haynes, Ulric St. Clair, Jr. 1931- *WhoAm 92*
Haynes, W. Thomas *Law&B 92*
Haynes, Walter Battison 1859-1900 *Baker 92*
Haynes, Walter M. 1921- *WhoSSW 93*
Haynes, William Eli 1943- *WhoAm 92*
Haynes, William James, II 1958- *WhoAm 92*
Haynes Family *BioIn 17*
Haynes-Palmquist, Karen *Law&B 92*
Haynie, Anna Mae Dowdell 1944- *WhoSSW 93*
Haynie, B. Don 1947- *St&PR 93*
Haynie, Betty Jo Gillmore 1937- *WhoSSW 93*
Haynie, Fred Hollis 1932- *WhoSSW 93*
Haynie, Howard Edward 1928- *WhoAm 92*
Haynie, Louis M. *Law&B 92*
Haynie, Sandra 1943- *BiDAMSp 1989*
Haynie, Thomas Powell, III 1932- *WhoAm 92*
Haynor, Patricia Manzi *WhoAmW 93*
Haynos, Robert Alex 1932- *St&PR 93*
Haynsworth, Clement F., Jr. *BioIn 17*
Haynsworth, Clement Furman, Jr. 1912-1989 *OxCSupC*
Haynsworth, Harry Jay, IV 1938- *WhoAm 92*
Hayon, Elie M. 1932- *WhoAm 92*
Hayos, Meridith L. *Law&B 92*
Hayoun, Albert 1949- *St&PR 93*
Hay-Roe, Hugh 1928- *WhoSSW 93*
Hayry, Pekka J. 1939- *WhoScE 91-4*
Hayry, Pekka Juha 1939- *WhoWor 93*
Hays, Bob *BioIn 17*
Hays, Bob d1896 *BioIn 17*
Hays, Bonnie Linn 1950- *WhoAmW 93, WhoEmL 93*
Hays, Brooks 1898-1981 *BioIn 17*
Hays, Charles Francis 1946- *St&PR 93*
Hays, Dan Andrew 1939- *WhoE 93*
Hays, David Arthur 1930- *WhoAm 92*
Hays, Dennis L. *Law&B 92*
Hays, Diana Joyce Watkins 1945- *WhoAmW 93, WhoE 93*
Hays, Donald *BioIn 17*
Hays, Donald Osborne 1907- *WhoAm 92, WhoWor 93*
Hays, Elizabeth Loretta 1937- *WhoAmW 93*
Hays, Ernest Frederick, II *Law&B 92*
Hays, Frances *AmWomPl*
Hays, Fred H. 1953- *WhoSSW 93*
Hays, Gary Palmer 1945- *St&PR 93*
Hays, Harry Sanders 1935- *St&PR 93*
Hays, Herschel Martin 1920- *WhoWor 93*
Hays, Holly Mary 1952- *WhoAmW 93*
Hays, Howard H. 1917- *WhoAm 92*
Hays, Howard H., Jr. 1917- *St&PR 93*
Hays, James A. 1936- *St&PR 93*
Hays, James Fred 1933- *WhoAm 92, WhoE 93*
Hays, John Edward 1948- *St&PR 93*
Hays, Kathryn *WhoAm 92*
Hays, Larry Weldon 1936- *WhoSSW 93*
Hays, Lee 1914-1981 *Baker 92*
See Also Weavers, The *ConMus 8*
Hays, Lewis W. 1914- *WhoAm 92*
Hays, Louis Anthony, Jr. 1954- *WhoWor 93*
Hays, Marguerite Johnston 1931- *WhoAmW 93, WhoSSW 93*
Hays, Marguerite Thompson 1930- *WhoAm 92*
Hays, Marjorie Jean 1933- *WhoAmW 93*
Hays, Mary Katherine Jackson *WhoAmW 93, WhoWor 93*
Hays, Patricia *BioIn 17*
Hays, Patricia L. *Law&B 92*
Hays, Patrick Gregory 1942- *WhoAm 92*
Hays, Peggy Ann 1948- *WhoAmW 93*
Hays, Peter L. 1938- *WhoAm 92*
Hays, Randy Kert 1953- *St&PR 93*
Hays, Richard M. *Law&B 92*
Hays, Richard M. 1927- *St&PR 93*
Hays, Richard Martin 1927- *WhoAm 92*
Hays, Rick F. 1952- *WhoEmL 93*
Hays, Robert 1947- *WhoAm 92*
Hays, Robert Alexander 1944- *WhoE 93*
Hays, Robert L. 1942- *St&PR 93*
Hays, Robert William 1925- *WhoSSW 93, WhoWor 93*
Hays, Ron d1991 *BioIn 17*
Hays, Ronald Jackson 1928- *WhoAm 92*
Hays, Ronnie Dale 1946- *St&PR 93*
Hays, S. Robert *St&PR 93*
Hays, Sidney Brooks 1931- *WhoAm 92*
Hays, Sorrel 1941- *Baker 92*
Hays, Spencer B. *Law&B 92*
Hays, Steele 1925- *WhoSSW 93*
Hays, Thomas A. 1932- *St&PR 93, WhoAm 92*
Hays, Thomas Anthony 1957- *WhoWrEP 92*
Hays, Thomas Chandler 1935- *WhoAm 92, WhoE 93, WhoWor 93*
Hays, Thomas R. *Law&B 92*
Hays, Thomas R. 1915- *WhoAm 92, WhoE 93, WhoWor 93*
Hays, W(illiam) S(hakespeare) 1837-1907 *Baker 92*
Hays, Wayne Levere 1911-1989 *BioIn 17*
Hays, Will H. 1879-1954 *BioIn 17*
Hays, William Grady, Jr. 1927- *WhoWor 93*
Hays, William H. 1879-1954 *PolPar*
Hays, William Orchard- *BioIn 17*
Hays, William Paul 1929- *WhoE 93*
Hays, Wilma Pitchford 1909- *MajAI [port]*
Haysbert, Raymond V., Sr. 1920- *St&PR 93*
Haysbert, Reginald 1948- *St&PR 93*
Hays Butler, Holly Lynn 1962- *WhoAmW 93*
Hayslett, John Paul 1935- *WhoAm 92*
Hayslett, Richard R. *Law&B 92*
Hayslett, Roderick James 1945- *St&PR 93, WhoAm 92*
Haysom, Ian Richard 1949- *WhoAm 92*
Haystead, Wesley 1942- *WhoWrEP 92*
Hayt, John T. 1938- *St&PR 93*
Haytayan, Harry M. *St&PR 93*
Hayter, Robert P. *Law&B 92*
Haythe, Winston McDonald 1940- *WhoE 93, WhoWor 93*
Haythornthwaite, Robert Morphet 1922- *WhoAm 92*
Haytin, Harold A. 1918- *St&PR 93*
Haytin, Harold Alexander 1918- *WhoAm 92*
Hayton, Jacob William 1926- *WhoAm 92*
Hayton, Lennie 1908-1971 *Baker 92*
Hayton, Richard Neil 1916- *WhoWrEP 92*
Hayutin, David Lionel 1930- *WhoAm 92*
Hayward, Austin L. 1924- *St&PR 93*
Hayward, Charles E. 1951- *WhoAm 92*
Hayward, Charles W. 1927- *St&PR 93*
Hayward, Charles William 1937- *WhoAm 92, WhoE 93*
Hayward, Charles Winthrop 1927- *WhoAm 92*
Hayward, Diane *BioIn 17*
Hayward, George J. *Law&B 92*
Hayward, George J. 1944- *WhoE 93*
Hayward, Grace *AmWomPl*
Hayward, Graham George 1938- *WhoWor 93*
Hayward, H. Gerrett 1947- *St&PR 93*
Hayward, Harold 1920- *WhoE 93*
Hayward, Jane 1918- *WhoAm 92, WhoE 93*
Hayward, John Tucker 1910- *WhoAm 92*
Hayward, Lance d1991 *BioIn 17*
Hayward, Merle A. 1924- *St&PR 93*
Hayward, Richard William 1932- *WhoE 93*
Hayward, Ronald Hamilton 1927- *WhoAm 92*
Hayward, Sally Jane 1960- *WhoEmL 93*
Hayward, Susan 1918-1975 *SweetSg D [port]*
Hayward, Susan 1919-1975 *IntDcF 2-3*
Hayward, Teresa Calcagno 1907- *WhoAmW 93, WhoE 93*
Hayward, Thomas Zander, Jr. 1940- *St&PR 93, WhoAm 92*
Hayward, Troy E. 1939- *St&PR 93*
Hayward, William Robert *St&PR 93*
Hayward-Surry, Jeremy 1942- *WhoAm 92*
Hayward-Surry, Jeremy Keith 1942- *St&PR 93*
Haywood, Anne Mowbray 1935- *WhoE 93*
Haywood, Barbara Smith 1951- *WhoEmL 93*
Haywood, Betty Jean 1942- *WhoAm 92, WhoAmW 93*
Haywood, Bruce 1925- *WhoAm 92*
Haywood, C. Robert 1921- *ConAu 137*
Haywood, Carolyn 1898-1990 *BioIn 17, MajAI [port]*
Haywood, Charles Richard 1940- *St&PR 93*
Haywood, Eliza Fowler 1693?-1756 *BioIn 17*
Haywood, Herbert Carlton 1931- *WhoAm 92*
Haywood, L. Julian 1927- *WhoAm 92*
Haywood, Laura W. *ScF&FL 92*
Haywood, Mary Carolyn 1898-1990 *BioIn 17*
Haywood, Oliver Garfield 1911- *WhoAm 92*
Haywood, Stephen Patrick 1949- *ConAu 138*
Haywood, Steve *ConAu 138*
Haywood, Theodore Joseph 1929- *WhoAm 92*
Hayworth, Curtis Benjamin 1920- *WhoE 93*
Hayworth, Nan Alison Sutter 1959- *WhoAmW 93*
Hayworth, Rita 1918-1987 *BioIn 17, HispAmA, IntDcF 2-3 [port], NotHsAW 93*
Hayworth, Rita (Cansino) 1918-1988 *SweetSg D [port]*
Hayworth, Robert Wilson, III 1963- *WhoEmL 93, WhoSSW 93*
Hayworth, Scott David 1956- *WhoE 93*
Hazaimeh, Rifai Awad 1937- *WhoWor 93*
Hazama, Hidebumi 1928- *WhoWor 93*
Hazan, Jack *MiSFD 9*
Hazan, Marcella Maddalena 1924- *WhoAm 92*
Hazan, Martin 1928- *St&PR 93*
Hazan, Yaakov 1899-1992 *NewYTBS 92*
Hazard, Christopher Wedvik 1943- *WhoSSW 93*
Hazard, Gary M. 1951- *St&PR 93*
Hazard, Geoffrey Cornell, Jr. 1929- *WhoAm 92, WhoE 93*
Hazard, James Arthur 1935- *WhoWrEP 92*
Hazard, Joe *BioIn 17*
Hazard, John Newbold 1909- *WhoAm 92, WhoWor 93*
Hazard, John Wharton 1912- *WhoAm 92*
Hazard, Nancy 1944- *WhoE 93*
Hazard, Neil Livingstone 1952- *WhoAm 92*
Hazard, Phyllis *BioIn 17*
Hazard, Roberta Louise 1934- *WhoAm 92*
Hazarian, Tina Lola Rebecca *WhoAm 92, WhoAmW 93, WhoWor 93*
Hazebroucq, Georges F. 1935- *WhoScE 91-2*
Hazel, Carolyn S. *Law&B 92*
Hazel, Diane Hunter 1949- *WhoEmL 93*
Hazel, George McLean *WhoScE 91-1*
Hazel, Gerald Vernon 1931- *St&PR 93*
Hazel, Joanie Beverly 1946- *WhoAmW 93, WhoWor 93*
Hazel, John Tilghman, Jr. 1930- *WhoAm 92*
Hazel, Joseph Ernest 1933- *WhoAm 92*
Hazel, Paul 1944- *ScF&FL 92*
Hazelett, Leonard Walsine 1954- *WhoEmL 93*
Hazelgrove, William E(lliot, III) 1959- *ConAu 138*
Hazelgrove, William Elliot, III 1959- *WhoWrEP 92*
Hazelip, Herbert Harold 1930- *WhoAm 92*
Hazell, Peter Brian Reginald 1944- *WhoE 93*
Hazelman, Donald Frederick 1930- *St&PR 93*
Hazelman, Herbert R. *BioIn 17*
Hazelrig, Paul Edward, Sr. 1916- *St&PR 93*
Hazelrigg, Mark D. 1958- *WhoSSW 93*
Hazeltine, Barrett 1931- *WhoAm 92*
Hazeltine, Herbert S., Jr. 1908- *St&PR 93*
Hazeltine, Herbert Samuel, Jr. 1908- *WhoAm 92, WhoWor 93*
Hazeltine, Joyce *WhoAm 92, WhoAmW 93*
Hazelton, Harold d1991 *BioIn 17*
Hazelton, John Richard 1946- *WhoE 93*
Hazelton, Jon G. 1938- *St&PR 93*
Hazelton, Nika *BioIn 17*
Hazelton, Nika d1992 *NewYTBS 92 [port]*
Hazelton, Vina Jane 1931- *WhoAmW 93*
Hazelwood, Carroll T. 1941- *St&PR 93*
Hazelwood, John A. 1938- *WhoAm 92*
Hazelwood, Joseph J. *BioIn 17*
Hazen, Barbara Shook 1930- *ScF&FL 92, WhoWrEP 92*
Hazen, Lee 1905-1991 *BioIn 17*
Hazen, Paul 1941- *St&PR 93*
Hazen, Paul Mandeville 1941- *WhoAm 92*
Hazen, Richard 1911-1990 *BioIn 17*
Hazen, Robert Blyth 1932- *St&PR 93*
Hazen, Robert Miller 1948- *WhoAm 92*
Hazen, Thomas N. 1935- *St&PR 93*
Hazen, Wallace Richard 1934- *St&PR 93*
Hazen, William H. 1931- *St&PR 93*
Hazen, William Harris *Law&B 92*
Hazen, William Harris 1931- *WhoAm 92*
Hazi, Endre 1926- *WhoScE 91-4*
Hazle, Bob 1930- *BioIn 17*
Hazlehurst, John Livingston 1931- *WhoSSW 93*
Hazlehurst, Robert, Jr. *Law&B 92*
Hazlehurst, Robert Purviance, Jr. 1919- *WhoAm 92*
Hazleton, Lloyd Walter d1990 *BioIn 17*
Hazlett, David Charles 1962- *WhoE 93*
Hazlett, James Arthur 1917- *WhoAm 92*
Hazlett, James Stephen 1940- *WhoAm 92*
Hazlett, Suzanne Oteriea 1950- *WhoAmW 93*
Hazlett, Timothy James 1960- *WhoEmL 93*
Hazlewood, Barbara Ann 1931- *WhoSSW 93*
Hazlewood, Mark Philip 1953- *St&PR 93*
Hazlitt, Henry 1894- *WhoAm 92*
Hazlitt, William 1778-1830 *BioIn 17*
Haznadar, Zijad 1935- *WhoScE 91-4*
Hazners, Vit 1939- *St&PR 93*
Hazou, Peter J. 1916-1991 *BioIn 17*
Hazou, Tuma J. 1938- *WhoUN 92*
Hazouri, Louis Abraham, Jr. 1948- *St&PR 93, WhoAm 92*
Hazra, B.K. 1946- *St&PR 93*
Hazucha, Joy Fisher 1960- *WhoAmW 93*
Hazy, James Kent 1955- *WhoE 93, WhoEmL 93*
Hazzard, Alvira *AmWomPl*
Hazzard, Frances Jane Osborn 1925- *WhoSSW 93*
Hazzard, Marguerite *AmWomPl*
Hazzard, Mary Dwight 1928- *WhoWrEP 92*
Hazzard, Shirley 1931- *BioIn 17, IntLitE, WhoAm 92, WhoAmW 93, WhoWrEP 92*
Hazzard, Walter R., Jr. *BiDAMSp 1989*

Hazzard, William Russell 1936- *WhoAm 92*
H.D. 1886-1961 *BioIn 17, WorLitC [port]*
H'Doubler, Francis Todd, Jr. 1925- *WhoAm 92*
He, Da-Ren 1941- *WhoWor 93*
He, Duo-Min 1941- *WhoWor 93*
He, En-dian 1920- *WhoWor 93*
He, Guozhu 1922- *WhoWor 93*
He, Jianxun 1928- *WhoWor 93*
He, Lian-fa 1942- *WhoWor 93*
He, Qi 1956- *WhoWor 93*
He, Xing-Fei 1958- *WhoWor 93*
He, Xu-Chang 1941- *WhoWor 93*
Heaberlin, David A. 1949- *St&PR 93*
Heaberlin, David Allen 1949- *WhoAm 92*
Heacker, Terrill Dyanne 1957- *WhoEmL 93, WhoSSW 93*
Heacock, Donald Dee 1934- *WhoSSW 93*
Heacock, Laurel E. *Law&B 92*
Heacock, Timothy P. 1954- *St&PR 93*
Heacox, Annette Elisabeth 1963- *WhoAmW 93*
Heacox, Kim 1951- *ConAu 137*
Head, Asbury J. 1914- *St&PR 93*
Head, Barbara Jean 1945- *WhoAmW 93*
Head, Bessie 1937-1986 *BioIn 17, DcLB 117 [port], IntLitE*
Head, Christopher A. 1951- *St&PR 93*
Head, Dale Anthony *Law&B 92*
Head, Edward Dennis 1919- *WhoAm 92*
Head, Elizabeth Spoor 1928- *WhoSSW 93*
Head, Evelyn Harris-Shields 1944- *WhoWrEP 92*
Head, George Lewis 1941- *WhoE 93, WhoIns 93*
Head, Glenn O. 1925- *WhoIns 93*
Head, Gregory A. 1955- *WhoSSW 93*
Head, Harry d1881 *BioIn 17*
Head, Hayden Wilson, Jr. 1944- *WhoAm 92, WhoSSW 93*
Head, Howard *BioIn 17*
Head, Ivan Leigh 1930- *WhoAm 92, WhoWor 93*
Head, Jacqueline M. 1921- *St&PR 93*
Head, James Crawford 1943- *WhoSSW 93*
Head, John Douglas 1927- *WhoAm 92*
Head, John Francis, Jr. 1920- *St&PR 93, WhoAm 92*
Head, John Tarpley, Jr. 1954- *WhoSSW 93*
Head, Jonathan Frederick 1949- *WhoEmL 93, WhoSSW 93, WhoWor 93*
Head, Keith Louis *Law&B 92*
Head, Marsha Marie 1951- *WhoEmL 93*
Head, Michael B. 1946- *St&PR 93*
Head, Michael (Dewar) 1900-1976 *Baker 92*
Head, Mitchell Ernest 1955- *WhoEmL 93, WhoSSW 93*
Head, Patrick J. *Law&B 92*
Head, Patrick J. 1932- *St&PR 93*
Head, Patrick James 1932- *WhoAm 92*
Head, Raymond (Victor) 1948- *ConAu 136*
Head, Richard Louis 1931- *St&PR 93*
Head, Robert 1942- *WhoWrEP 92*
Head, Robert Vincent 1929- *WhoSSW 93*
Head, Roy *SoulM*
Head, Thomas F., III 1929- *St&PR 93*
Head, Thomas Floyd 1937- *WhoIns 93*
Head, Tony *BioIn 17*
Head, Violet Beryl 1922- *WhoAm 92*
Head, William Iverson, Sr. 1925- *WhoSSW 93, WhoWor 93*
Head, Yvonne 1948- *WhoWrEP 92*
Headd, Kevin 1966- *BioIn 17*
Headding, Lillian Susan 1944- *WhoAm 92, WhoAmW 93*
Headington, Christopher (John Magenis) 1930- *Baker 92*
Headlam, Catherine 1960- *ConAu 139*
Headland, J.P. *St&PR 93*
Headlee, Raymond 1917- *WhoAm 92*
Headlee, Richard Harold 1930- *St&PR 93, WhoAm 92, WhoIns 93*
Headlee, Rolland Dockeray 1916- *WhoAm 92*
Headley, Anne Renouf 1937- *WhoAm 92*
Headley, Elizabeth *MajAI*
Headley, Oliver St. Clair 1942- *WhoWor 93*
Headly, Glenne Aimee 1958- *WhoAm 92, WhoAmW 93*
Headrick, John Anderson 1931- *WhoWor 93*
Headrick, Jon C. 1943- *St&PR 93, WhoIns 93*
Headrick, Linda Ann 1955- *WhoAmW 93*
Headrick, Roger L. 1936- *St&PR 93*
Headrick, Roger Lewis 1936- *WhoAm 92*
Headrick, Thomas Edward 1933- *WhoAm 92, WhoE 93*
Heady, Ferrel 1916- *WhoAm 92*
Heady, James *BioIn 17*
Heady, Judith Emily 1939- *WhoAmW 93*
Heady, Susan L. *Law&B 92*
Heafey, Edwin Austin, Jr. 1930- *WhoAm 92*
Heafey, Michael J. 1951- *St&PR 93*
Heagy, Lorraine Mary 1935- *WhoAmW 93*
Heagy, Thomas Charles 1945- *WhoAm 92*
Heal, Edith 1903- *AmWomPl*
Heal, Geoffrey Martin 1944- *WhoE 93*
Heal, Kenneth Lee 1942- *St&PR 93*
Heal, Richard Albert 1945- *St&PR 93*
Healan, Arthur Lee 1949- *St&PR 93*
Heald, Alberta Powell *AmWomPl*
Heald, Bruce Day 1935- *WhoE 93*
Heald, Darrel Verner 1919- *WhoAm 92, WhoE 93*
Heald, David L. 1943- *St&PR 93*
Heald, Emily Eastham 1917- *WhoAmW 93*
Heald, Jane Dewey 1931- *WhoWrEP 92*
Heald, Lucy 1872- *AmWomPl*
Heald, Melinda Merle 1962- *WhoAmW 93, WhoEmL 93*
Heald, Morrell 1922- *WhoAm 92*
Heald, Phillip P. 1939- *St&PR 93*
Heald, Randell M. *Law&B 92*
Heald, Tim 1944- *ScF&FL 92*
Healey, Ann Ruston 1939- *WhoAmW 93*
Healey, Arthur H. 1920- *WhoAm 92*
Healey, Brooks *WhoWrEP 92*
Healey, David Clayton 1946- *St&PR 93*
Healey, David Lee 1950- *WhoSSW 93*
Healey, Deirdre 1963- *WhoAmW 93*
Healey, Denis *BioIn 17*
Healey, Derek 1936- *Baker 92*
Healey, Derek Edward 1936- *WhoAm 92*
Healey, Dorothy *BioIn 17*
Healey, Dorothy (Ray) 1914- *ConAu 138*
Healey, E. Claire 1924- *WhoSSW 93*
Healey, Ed 1894-1978 *BioIn 17*
Healey, Edward Hopkins 1925- *WhoAm 92*
Healey, Frances *AmWomPl*
Healey, Frank Henry 1924- *WhoAm 92*
Healey, Jack *BioIn 17*
Healey, James E. 1941- *St&PR 93*
Healey, James Francis 1920- *St&PR 93*
Healey, James Stewart 1931- *WhoAm 92*
Healey, Jeff *BioIn 17*
Healey, Joe d1992 *BioIn 17*
Healey, John Andrew 1939- *WhoE 93*
Healey, John G. *BioIn 17*
Healey, John G. 1938- *WhoAm 92*
Healey, Joseph G(raham) 1938- *ConAu 40NR*
Healey, Laurette Ann 1954- *WhoAmW 93*
Healey, Louis P. 1950- *St&PR 93*
Healey, Lynne Kover *WhoAmW 93*
Healey, Michael John *WhoScE 91-1*
Healey, Myron 1922- *BioIn 17*
Healey, Patsy *WhoScE 91-1*
Healey, Robert Joseph 1925- *WhoAm 92*
Healey, Timothy Craig 1950- *WhoE 93*
Healey, William J. 1927- *St&PR 93*
Healey, William Vincent *Law&B 92*
Healey, William Vincent 1931- *WhoSSW 93*
Healing, Dewey d1992 *BioIn 17*
Healing, Robert E. *Law&B 92*
Healslip, John Gerald 1929- *St&PR 93*
Healton, Donald Carney 1930- *WhoAm 92*
Healy, Alice Fenvessy 1946- *WhoAm 92*
Healy, Barbara Anne 1951- *WhoAmW 93, WhoEmL 93, WhoWor 93*
Healy, Bernadine 1944- *CurBio 92 [port], News 93-1 [port]*
Healy, Bernadine P. *BioIn 17*
Healy, Bernadine P. 1944- *WhoAm 92, WhoAmW 93*
Healy, Carol Lynn 1951- *WhoAmW 93*
Healy, Charles B. 1937- *St&PR 93*
Healy, David George 1949- *WhoE 93*
Healy, Donald J., Jr. *Law&B 92*
Healy, Edward John, Jr. 1935- *St&PR 93*
Healy, Elizabeth B. *Law&B 92*
Healy, Francis Patrick 1932- *St&PR 93*
Healy, George William, III 1930- *WhoAm 92*
Healy, Gerald Burke 1942- *WhoE 93*
Healy, Grace M. *Law&B 92*
Healy, Harold Harris, Jr. 1921- *WhoAm 92*
Healy, J.C. 1942- *WhoScE 91-2*
Healy, James A. d1991 *BioIn 17*
Healy, James B. 1930- *WhoE 93, WhoWor 93*
Healy, James Casey 1956- *WhoE 93, WhoEmL 93, WhoWor 93*
Healy, James Gerard 1957- *WhoEmL 93*
Healy, James Joseph 1948- *St&PR 93, WhoAm 92*
Healy, Jane Elizabeth 1949- *WhoAm 92, WhoAmW 93*
Healy, Jane MacDonald *WhoAmW 93*
Healy, Janet *WhoAm 92*
Healy, Jeremiah (F.), III 1948- *ConAu 137*
Healy, John J. 1936- *St&PR 93*
Healy, John Joseph 1943- *WhoSSW 93*
Healy, John M. *Law&B 92*
Healy, John M. 1932- *St&PR 93*
Healy, John McLean 1954- *WhoEmL 93*
Healy, John Thomas *BioIn 17*
Healy, Joseph Francis, Jr. 1930- *WhoAm 92, WhoSSW 93*
Healy, Joyce A. *BioIn 17*
Healy, Julia Schmitt 1947- *WhoE 93*
Healy, Justin D. 1949- *St&PR 93*
Healy, Kenneth C. 1905- *St&PR 93*
Healy, Kevin George 1920- *WhoScE 91-3*
Healy, Kevin J. *Law&B 92*
Healy, Kieran John Patrick 1957- *WhoWor 93*
Healy, Margaret Anna O'Toole 1946- *WhoSSW 93*
Healy, Martin John 1939- *WhoE 93*
Healy, Mary 1918- *WhoAm 92*
Healy, Nicholas Joseph 1910- *WhoAm 92, WhoWor 93*
Healy, Patricia A. 1932- *St&PR 93*
Healy, Patrick Francis 1834-1910 *BioIn 17*
Healy, Patrick Joseph 1840-1905 *See Lyon & Healy Baker 92*
Healy, Paul Michael 1914- *St&PR 93*
Healy, Robert Danforth 1939- *WhoE 93, WhoWor 93*
Healy, Robert Edward 1904- *WhoAm 92*
Healy, Sean d1990 *BioIn 17*
Healy, Sophia (Warner) 1938- *ConAu 136*
Healy, Theresa Ann 1932- *WhoAm 92*
Healy, Thomas B., Jr. 1928- *St&PR 93*
Healy, Thomas Edward John *WhoScE 91-1*
Healy, Thomas Martin 1921- *WhoAm 92*
Healy, Timothy Stafford 1923- *BioIn 17, WhoWor 93*
Healy, Walter F. X. 1941- *WhoWor 93*
Healy, William Kent 1930- *St&PR 93, WhoAm 92*
Heaner, William E., Jr. *Law&B 92*
Heaney, Anne B. 1928- *WhoAmW 93*
Heaney, Gerald William 1918- *WhoAm 92*
Heaney, Harry *WhoScE 91-1*
Heaney, Howell J. 1917-1991 *BioIn 17*
Heaney, Joe 1947- *St&PR 93*
Heaney, Michael Francis, Jr. 1938- *WhoE 93*
Heaney, Patrick G. 1938- *St&PR 93*
Heaney, Robert Proulx 1927- *WhoAm 92*
Heaney, Robert S. d1991 *BioIn 17*
Heaney, Samuel W. 1916- *St&PR 93*
Heaney, Seamus *BioIn 17*
Heaney, Seamus 1939- *BritWr S2, ConLC 74 [port]*
Heaney, Seamus Justin 1939- *WhoAm 92, WhoWor 93*
Heaney, Tim J. 1952- *WhoEmL 93*
Heanue, Anne Allen 1940- *WhoE 93*
Heap, Charles Swinnerton 1847-1900 *Baker 92*
Heap, Frank K. 1941- *WhoAm 92*
Heap, Ian R. *St&PR 93*
Heap, R.B. *WhoScE 91-1*
Heap, Robert D. 1942- *WhoScE 91-1*
Heap, S. Allan *WhoScE 91-1*
Heap, Sylvia Stuber 1929- *WhoAmW 93*
Heaphy, Edward T. 1938- *St&PR 93*
Heaphy, Eileen Michele 1945- *WhoAmW 93*
Heaphy, James Cullen, III 1952- *WhoWrEP 92*
Heaphy, John Merrill 1927- *WhoAm 92*
Heaphy, Karen A. *Law&B 92*
Heaphy, Thomas M. 1931- *St&PR 93*
Heaps, Harry D. 1922- *St&PR 93*
Heaps, Marvin Dale 1932- *WhoAm 92*
Heard, A.L. *WhoScE 91-1*
Heard, Alexander 1917- *PolPar, WhoAm 92*
Heard, Barbara Muse 1958- *WhoAmW 93*
Heard, Carrie L. 1958- *WhoAmW 93*
Heard, Chauncy Lee 1950- *WhoEmL 93*
Heard, Craig P. 1945- *St&PR 93*
Heard, D. Dennis 1940- *St&PR 93*
Heard, David Dennis 1940- *WhoAm 92*
Heard, Dow H. 1945- *St&PR 93*
Heard, Drayton 1941- *St&PR 93*
Heard, Edwin Anthony 1926- *St&PR 93, WhoAm 92*
Heard, Elliott G. 1932-1991 *BioIn 17*
Heard, Gerald 1889-1971 *BioIn 17*
Heard, H.F. 1889-1971 *ScF&FL 92*
Heard, Henry Fitzgerald 1889-1971 *BioIn 17*
Heard, James Loyd 1954- *WhoAm 92*
Heard, John 1947- *WhoAm 92*
Heard, John Beaton 1929- *WhoAm 92*
Heard, John McDonald 1939- *St&PR 93*
Heard, Lawrence M. 1950- *St&PR 93*
Heard, Mary Anne 1946- *WhoSSW 93*
Heard, Patricia Loader 1930- *WhoAmW 93*
Heard, Ronald Roy 1947- *WhoEmL 93*
Heard, William R. 1925- *St&PR 93*
Heard, William Robert 1925- *WhoAm 92, WhoIns 93*
Hearden, Patrick J. 1942- *ConAu 138*
Hearin, Joe 1912- *St&PR 93*
Hearin, Robert M. *BioIn 17*
Hearin, William J. 1909- *St&PR 93*
Hearin, William Jefferson 1909- *WhoAm 92, WhoSSW 93*
Hearity, Thomas James *Law&B 92*
Hearle, Douglas Geoffrey 1933- *WhoAm 92*
Hearn, A.G. *WhoScE 91-3*
Hearn, Christine Agnes 1950- *WhoE 93*
Hearn, David W., Jr. 1930- *St&PR 93*
Hearn, Edell Midgett 1929- *WhoAm 92*
Hearn, Edward Joseph 1949- *WhoSSW 93*
Hearn, George Henry 1927- *WhoAm 92*
Hearn, George W. *Law&B 92*
Hearn, Grant Ernest *WhoScE 91-1*
Hearn, James Woodrow 1931- *WhoAm 92*
Hearn, Joyce Camp *WhoAmW 93*
Hearn, Kathleen K. 1947- *WhoAmW 93*
Hearn, Lafcadio 1850-1904 *BioIn 17, GayN, ScF&FL 92*
Hearn, Michael D. *Law&B 92*
Hearn, Michael Patrick 1950- *ScF&FL 92*
Hearn, Paula Clarice 1955- *WhoEmL 93*
Hearn, Richard E. 1936- *St&PR 93*
Hearn, Rosamond Ernst 1924- *WhoE 93*
Hearn, Rosemary 1929- *WhoAmW 93*
Hearn, Ruby Puryear 1940- *WhoAm 92, WhoAmW 93*
Hearn, Sharon Sklamba 1956- *WhoAmW 93*
Hearn, Susan 1955- *WhoAmW 93*
Hearn, Thomas K., Jr. *BioIn 17*
Hearn, Thomas K., Jr. 1937- *WhoSSW 93*
Hearn, Wendy Lee 1958- *WhoEmL 93*
Hearnburg, William *Law&B 92*
Hearne, Betsy Gould 1942- *ScF&FL 92*
Hearne, Edmund Joseph 1952- *WhoWor 93*
Hearne, Elizabeth G. *ScF&FL 92*
Hearne, George Archer 1934- *WhoAm 92*
Hearne, John 1926- *BioIn 17*
Hearne, John (Edgar Caulwell) 1926- *DcLB 117 [port]*
Hearne, John William 1942- *WhoSSW 93*
Hearne, Richard 1908-1979 *QDrFCA 92 [port]*
Hearne, Samuel 1745-1792 *BioIn 17, Expl 93, IntDcAn*
Hearne, Stephen Zachary 1952- *WhoSSW 93*
Hearne, Thomas 1744-1817 *BioIn 17*
Hearne, Thomas M. 1943- *St&PR 93*
Hearne, Timothy C., Jr. 1956- *St&PR 93*
Hearne, Vicki 1946- *ConAu 139*
Hearne, William Blaisdell 1932- *WhoSSW 93*
Hearn-Haynes, Theresa 1954- *WhoSSW 93, WhoWor 93*
Hearns, Thomas 1958- *AfrAmBi, BiDAMSp 1989, WhoAm 92*
Hearnsberger, Carla Wilson *Law&B 92*
Hearnshaw, Leslie 1907-1991 *AnObit 1991*
Hearon, James Hamilton, III 1934- *WhoAm 92*
Hearon, Shelby 1931- *WhoAmW 93, WhoWrEP 92*
Hearse, David J. *WhoScE 91-1*
Hearshman, Timothy W. *Law&B 92*
Hearst, Austine McDonnell 1920-1991 *BioIn 17*
Hearst, George Randolph, Jr. 1927- *WhoAm 92*
Hearst, Gladys Whitley Henderson *WhoAm 92*
Hearst, John Eugene 1935- *WhoAm 92*
Hearst, Patricia Campbell 1954- *ConAu 136*
Hearst, Patty *ConAu 136*
Hearst, Randolph A. 1915- *St&PR 93*
Hearst, Randolph Apperson 1915- *BioIn 17, WhoAm 92*
Hearst, Veronica *BioIn 17*
Hearst, William Randolph 1863-1951 *BioIn 17, GayN, JrnUS, PolPar*
Hearst, William Randolph, Jr. 1908- *ConAu 139, DcLB 127 [port], St&PR 93, WhoAm 92, WhoWor 93*
Hearst, William Randolph, III 1949- *WhoAm 92*
Heartfield, Jewele Lynn 1946- *WhoAmW 93*
Hearth, Blair Anthony 1950- *WhoE 93*
Heartman, Charles F. 1883-1953 *ScF&FL 92*
Heartman, Charles Fred 1883-1953 *BioIn 17*
Heartt, Charlotte Beebe 1933- *WhoE 93*
Heartz, Daniel (Leonard) 1928- *Baker 92*
Heasley, Roderick *St&PR 93*
Heasley, Ross E. *Law&B 92*
Heasley, Ross Edward 1939- *St&PR 93*
Heaslip, Joy Gail 1953- *St&PR 93*
Heaslip, William R. 1944- *St&PR 93*
Heaster, Arlene Louise 1958- *WhoAm 92*
Heaston, William P. *Law&B 92*

Heat, Moon *BioIn 17*
Heath, Alan F. *Law&B 92*
Heath, Alan Frank 1943- *St&PR 93*
Heath, Anna Lenington *AmWomPl*
Heath, Arthur J. *Law&B 92*
Heath, Benjamin W. 1914- *St&PR 93*
Heath, Bernard Oliver *WhoScE 91-1*
Heath, Bradley Webster 1947- *WhoEmL 93*
Heath, Catherine 1924-1991 *ConAu 136, ConLC 70*
Heath, Charisse L. *Law&B 92*
Heath, Charles Chastain 1921- *WhoSSW 93*
Heath, Charles D. *Law&B 92*
Heath, Claude Robert 1947- *WhoSSW 93*
Heath, Comer, III 1935- *AfrAmBi*
Heath, Cynthia G. *Law&B 92*
Heath, Cynthia Marie 1947- *WhoEmL 93*
Heath, D. *WhoScE 91-1*
Heath, David G. *BioIn 17*
Heath, David J. *Law&B 92*
Heath, Derek N. *Law&B 92*
Heath, Donald Albert *WhoScE 91-1*
Heath, Donald Malone 1940- *WhoSSW 93*
Heath, Douglas Hamilton 1925- *WhoAm 92*
Heath, Dwight Braley 1930- *WhoAm 92*
Heath, Edward 1916- *ColdWar 1 [port]*
Heath, Edward Richard George 1916- *DcTwHis, WhoWor 93*
Heath, Florence E. *AmWomPl*
Heath, Frank Bradford 1938- *WhoSSW 93, WhoWor 93*
Heath, George Ross 1939- *WhoAm 92*
Heath, Gilbert A. 1936- *St&PR 93*
Heath, Gloria Whitton 1922- *WhoAm 92*
Heath, Gordon 1918-1991 *BioIn 17*
Heath, H. Ellis 1912- *St&PR 93*
Heath, Harriet Elizabeth 1928- *WhoE 93*
Heath, Ivor *DcCPCAm*
Heath, James Albert 1912- *St&PR 93*
Heath, James Lee 1939- *WhoAm 92*
Heath, James Milton 1948- *WhoIns 93*
Heath, Jeffrey A. 1950- *WhoEmL 93*
Heath, Jennifer Rokus *Law&B 92*
Heath, Jim N. 1942- *St&PR 93*
Heath, Joel 1941- *St&PR 93*
Heath, John d1884 *BioIn 17*
Heath, John L. 1935- *St&PR 93*
Heath, Larry Gene d1992 *BioIn 17*
Heath, Lyn Barrett 1934- *WhoWrEP 92*
Heath, Mariwyn Dwyer 1935- *WhoAmW 93, WhoWor 93*
Heath, Milton Weeks, Jr. 1929- *St&PR 93*
Heath, Percy 1923- *WhoAm 92*
Heath, Peter 1938- *ScF&FL 92*
Heath, Peter J. 1959- *St&PR 93*
Heath, Richard Eddy 1930- *WhoAm 92*
Heath, Richard Murray 1927- *WhoAm 92*
Heath, Richard Raymond 1929- *WhoAm 92*
Heath, Robert Everett 1941- *St&PR 93, WhoE 93*
Heath, Robert F. *Law&B 92*
Heath, Roger Charles 1943- *WhoE 93*
Heath, Roy 1928- *IntvWPC 92 [port]*
Heath, Roy A.K. *BioIn 17*
Heath, Roy A(ubrey) K(elvin) 1926- *DcLB 117 [port]*
Heath, Shirley Brice *BioIn 17*
Heath, Simon *MiSFD 9*
Heath, Terrence 1936- *WhoCanL 92*
Heath, Verna *BioIn 17*
Heath, Vernon H. 1929- *WhoAm 92*
Heath, William Henry 1944- *St&PR 93*
Heath, William P., Jr. *Law&B 92*
Heathcoat-Amory, Lady 1901- *BioIn 17*
Heathcock, Clayton Howell 1936- *WhoAm 92*
Heathcock, Geoffrey Herbert 1944- *St&PR 93*
Heathcock, John Herman 1943- *WhoWor 93*
Heather, Jim *Law&B 92*
Heather, Michael *WhoWor 93*
Heather, William Paul Francis 1939- *WhoWor 93*
Heatherington, J. Scott 1919- *WhoAm 92*
Heatherley, Gail *BioIn 17*
Heatherly, David A. 1950- *WhoIns 93*
Heatherly, David Alan 1950- *St&PR 93*
Heatherly, Henry Edward 1936- *WhoAm 92*
Heatherly, Terrie Lynn 1955- *WhoAmW 93*
Heatherton, Todd Frederick 1961- *WhoE 93*
Heathfield, George Augustus Eliott 1717-1790 *HarEnMi*
Heath-Stubbs, John 1918- *ScF&FL 92*
Heathwood, Cecilia *ScF&FL 92*
Heatley, Connie Frances 1942- *WhoAmW 93, WhoE 93*
Heatley, Norman George *BioIn 17*
Heatley, Sidney M. 1928- *St&PR 93*
Heatly, Danny J. 1955- *St&PR 93*
Heat-Moon, William Least 1939- *Au&Arts 9 [port], WhoAm 92*
Heaton, Andrew Patrick 1946- *St&PR 93*
Heaton, Augustus George 1844-1930 *GayN*
Heaton, Brian Thomas *WhoScE 91-1*
Heaton, Christine Joy 1951- *WhoEmL 93*
Heaton, Clifford O. 1939- *St&PR 93*
Heaton, Culver 1912- *WhoAm 92*
Heaton, Deborah McGann 1957- *WhoE 93*
Heaton, Donald Slade 1946- *St&PR 93, WhoE 93*
Heaton, Eric F. 1941- *St&PR 93*
Heaton, Kathleen Hoge 1948- *WhoSSW 93*
Heaton, Larry Cadwalder, II 1956- *WhoE 93*
Heaton, Linda Medlen 1942- *WhoAmW 93*
Heaton, Mary Margaret J. *Law&B 92*
Heaton, Maurice *BioIn 17*
Heaton, Melinda Ann 1960- *WhoEmL 93*
Heaton, R. Kirk *Law&B 92*
Heaton, Richard L. 1936- *St&PR 93*
Heaton, Robert C. 1933- *St&PR 93*
Heaton, Timothy John Barclay 1951- *WhoWor 93*
Heaton, William Sutcliffe, Jr. 1925- *St&PR 93*
Heatter, Gabriel 1890-1972 *JrnUS*
Heatwave *SoulM*
Heatwole, Davis G. *Law&B 92*
Heatwole, Davis G. 1941- *St&PR 93*
Heatwole, Milton 1936- *St&PR 93*
Heaven, Constance 1911- *ConAu 40NR*
Heavener, David *MiSFD 9*
Heavener, David E. 1947- *St&PR 93*
Heavenrich, Robert Maurice 1913- *WhoAm 92*
Heavens, Oliver Samuel *WhoScE 91-1*
Heavens, Oliver Samuel 1922- *WhoWor 93*
Heavenston, Debra Belzer 1953- *WhoAmW 93*
Heaviside, W. Timothy *Law&B 92*
Heavner, Ann Denise 1956- *WhoE 93, WhoEmL 93*
Heavner, Martin Luther 1955- *WhoE 93*
Heavy D. *BioIn 17*
Heavysege, Charles 1816-1876 *BioIn 17*
Heazel, Francis James, Jr. 1920- *St&PR 93*
Hebald, Carol 1934- *WhoE 93, WhoWrEP 92*
Hebald, Milton Elting 1917- *WhoAm 92*
Hebard, Emory A. 1917- *WhoAm 92*
Hebard, Robert R. 1953- *St&PR 93*
Hebart, Siegfried Paul 1909-1990 *BioIn 17*
Hebb, Bobby 1941- *SoulM*
Hebb, Christopher Edmund 1951- *WhoSSW 93*
Hebb, George Sanford, Jr. 1921- *St&PR 93*
Hebb, Joseph Stephen 1948- *St&PR 93*
Hebb, Malcolm Hayden 1910- *WhoAm 92*
Hebb, Peter Harvey 1938- *St&PR 93*
Hebbard, Neysa Stanley *WhoWrEP 92*
Hebbeler, Regis J. *Law&B 92*
Hebbelinck, Marcel 1931- *WhoScE 91-2*
Hebborn, Eric *BioIn 17*
Hebborn, Nigel Peter 1958- *WhoIns 93*
Hebda, Robert Edward *Law&B 92*
Hebda-Grabowska, Halina 1951- *WhoWor 93*
Hebden, Julian 1935- *WhoAm 92*
Hebe, James L. *St&PR 93*
Hebeka, Elias Khalil 1936- *St&PR 93*
Hebel, Doris A. 1935- *WhoWor 93*
Hebel, Gail Suzette 1949- *WhoAmW 93*
Hebel, George J., Jr. 1948- *WhoIns 93*
Hebel, Johann Peter 1760-1826 *BioIn 17*
Hebeler, Henry Koester 1933- *WhoAm 92*
Hebenstreit, Jacques 1926- *WhoScE 91-2*
Hebenstreit, Jean Estill Stark *WhoAmW 93*
Hebenstreit, Johann Ernst 1702?-1757 *BioIn 17*
Hebenstreit, Pantaleon 1667-1750 *Baker 92*
Hebenstreit, Richard Henry 1925- *St&PR 93*
Hebenstreit, Stephen Louis *Law&B 92*
Heber, Albert H. *Law&B 92*
Heber, Albert James 1956- *WhoEmL 93*
Heber, Fritz Gerhard 1927- *WhoScE 91-3*
Heber, Gordon Eric 1952- *WhoEmL 93*
Heber, Ruth R. 1935- *WhoE 93*
Heber, Ulrich Wolfgang 1930- *WhoScE 91-3*
Heberer, James H. 1955- *St&PR 93*
Heberger, John Michael 1944- *WhoSSW 93*
Heberlein, Thomas Addison 1945- *WhoAm 92*
Heberlig, Harold Dean, Jr. 1944- *WhoAm 92*
Hebert, Anne *BioIn 17*
Hebert, Anne 1916- *ScF&FL 92, WhoCanL 92*
Hebert, Bliss Edmund 1930- *WhoAm 92*
Hebert, Charles Alexandre 1906- *WhoE 93*
Hebert, Donna Marie 1951- *WhoE 93*
Hebert, Edward M. 1950- *St&PR 93*
Hebert, Francois *Law&B 92*
Hebert, Francois 1946- *WhoCanL 92*
Hebert, Gene Paul 1941- *WhoSSW 93*
Hebert, Guy 1949- *St&PR 93*
Hebert, Harold R. 1940- *St&PR 93*
Hebert, Howard Neil 1928- *St&PR 93*
Hebert, J. Diane *Law&B 92*
Hebert, John L. 1920- *St&PR 93*
Hebert, John R. 1929- *St&PR 93*
Hebert, Leon P. 1931- *St&PR 93*
Hebert, Leonard Bernard, Jr. 1924- *St&PR 93*
Hebert, Linda Lempicki 1950- *WhoSSW 93*
Hebert, Maria Darene 1956- *WhoEmL 93*
Hebert, Mary Olivia 1921- *WhoAmW 93*
Hebert, Melvin Roy 1935- *WhoWor 93*
Hebert, Nick P. 1947- *St&PR 93*
Hebert, Paul *Law&B 92*
Hebert, Richard K. 1951- *St&PR 93*
Hebert, Robert D. 1938- *WhoAm 92, WhoSSW 93*
Hebert, Stanley P. *Law&B 92*
Hebert, Theresa R. *Law&B 92*
Hebert, Victor A. 1937- *St&PR 93*
Hebert, William Harvey 1929- *WhoE 93*
Hebertson, Val M. 1935- *WhoAm 92*
Hebestreit, Randall 1946- *St&PR 93*
Hebig-Naff, Kathleen Joyce 1938- *WhoAmW 93*
Hebin, Ole Martin 1937- *WhoUN 92*
Hebner, Paul C. 1919- *St&PR 93*
Hebner, Paul Chester 1919- *WhoAm 92*
Hebold, Walter C. 1949- *St&PR 93*
Hebra, Alexius Johannes 1919- *WhoSSW 93*
Hebrank, Roger Adolph 1932- *St&PR 93*
Hebron, Robert J. *Law&B 92*
Heceta, Estherbelle Aguilar 1935- *WhoAm 92*
Hechelmann, Friedrich 1948- *BioIn 17*
Hechenberger, Dieter Anton 1936- *WhoScE 91-3*
Hechenberger, Nan Bell 1932- *WhoAmW 93*
Hechinger, Brian Michael *Law&B 92*
Hechinger, Fred Michael 1920- *WhoAm 92, WhoE 93*
Hechinger, John W., Jr. 1950- *St&PR 93, WhoAm 92, WhoE 93*
Hechinger, John Walter 1920- *WhoAm 92*
Hechler, Ken 1914- *WhoAm 92, WhoSSW 93*
Hechler, Robert Lee 1936- *St&PR 93, WhoAm 92*
Hechmer, Teresa Marie *Law&B 92*
Hecht, Alan Dannenberg 1918- *WhoAm 92*
Hecht, Alice 1949- *WhoUN 92*
Hecht, Amy Blatchford 1930- *WhoAmW 93*
Hecht, Anthony Evan 1923- *WhoAm 92, WhoWrEP 92*
Hecht, Ben 1893?-1964 *JeAmFiW, MiSFD 9N*
Hecht, Ben 1894-1964 *BioIn 17, JeAmHC, JrnUS*
Hecht, Bill *BioIn 17*
Hecht, Carl E. 1925- *St&PR 93*
Hecht, Chic 1928- *WhoAm 92, WhoWor 93*
Hecht, Dennis J. *Law&B 92*
Hecht, Emil 1924- *WhoAm 92*
Hecht, Ethel Morell *WhoAmW 93*
Hecht, Eugene 1938- *WhoE 93*
Hecht, F. *WhoScE 91-4*
Hecht, Frederick 1930- *WhoAm 92*
Hecht, Harold Michael 1939- *WhoAm 92*
Hecht, Harvey E. 1939- *WhoWrEP 92*
Hecht, Howard A. 1928- *St&PR 93*
Hecht, Irene 1949- *WhoEmL 93*
Hecht, Irene Winchester D. 1932- *WhoAm 92*
Hecht, Jacob J. 1923-1990 *BioIn 17*
Hecht, James B. *Law&B 92*
Hecht, James Lee 1926- *WhoE 93*
Hecht, Joseph 1891-1951 *BioIn 17*
Hecht, Larry M. 1951- *St&PR 93*
Hecht, Lawrence W. d1991 *BioIn 17*
Hecht, Lee 1942- *St&PR 93*
Hecht, Lee Martin 1942- *WhoAm 92*
Hecht, Louis A. *Law&B 92*
Hecht, Louis A. 1944- *St&PR 93*
Hecht, Louis Alan 1944- *WhoAm 92*
Hecht, Marie Armstrong *AmWomPl*
Hecht, Marie Bergenfeld 1918- *WhoAmW 93*
Hecht, Marjorie Mazel 1942- *WhoAm 92*
Hecht, Michael Allen 1945- *St&PR 93*
Hecht, Nathan Lincoln 1949- *WhoAm 92, WhoSSW 93*
Hecht, Norman Bernard 1940- *WhoAm 92*
Hecht, Norman F. *St&PR 93*
Hecht, Norman Karl 1960- *WhoSSW 93*
Hecht, Patricia Layton 1935- *WhoE 93*
Hecht, Paul N. *Law&B 92*
Hecht, Robert Earl, Sr. 1925- *WhoAm 92*
Hecht, Robert William 1945- *WhoE 93*
Hecht, Roger D. 1945- *St&PR 93*
Heck, Albert, Jr. 1927- *WhoE 93*
Heck, Alfons 1928- *BioIn 17*
Heck, Andre *WhoScE 91-2*
Heck, Harold D., Jr. *Law&B 92*
Heck, James Baker 1930- *WhoAm 92, WhoSSW 93*
Heck, Jeffrey M. 1948- *St&PR 93*
Heck, L. Douglas 1918- *WhoAm 92*
Heck, Nancy J. *Law&B 92*
Heck, R.J. 1933- *St&PR 93*
Heck, Ronald Marshall 1943- *WhoE 93*
Heck, Walter Webb 1926- *WhoSSW 93*
Heckadon, Robert Gordon 1933- *WhoWor 93*
Heckaman, Curtis R. *St&PR 93*
Heckaman, David F. *St&PR 93*
Heckaman, Patricia A. *St&PR 93*
Heckart, Eileen 1919- *WhoAm 92, WhoAmW 93*
Heckathon, Glen J. 1946- *WhoIns 93*
Heckathorn, Glen James 1946- *St&PR 93*
Heckel, Charles Gordon 1946- *WhoEmL 93*
Heckel, Edgar 1936- *WhoScE 91-3*
Heckel, Edgar Ernst 1936- *WhoWor 93*
Heckel, Emil 1831-1908 *Baker 92*
Heckel, Erich 1883-1970 *BioIn 17*
Heckel, Johann Adam 1856-1909 *Baker 92*
Heckel, John Louis 1931- *St&PR 93, WhoAm 92*
Heckel, Richard Wayne 1934- *WhoAm 92*
Heckel, Wilhelm 1812-1877 *See* Heckel, Johann Adam 1856-1909 *Baker 92*
Heckelmann, Charles Newman 1913- *WhoAm 92, WhoWrEP 92*
Heckendorf, Glenn 1942- *WhoAm 92*
Hecker, Bruce Albert 1919- *WhoAm 92*
Hecker, Burton Glenn 1932- *St&PR 93*
Hecker, David *BioIn 17, Law&B 92*
Hecker, Debra Lynn 1953- *WhoAmW 93*
Hecker, Erich 1926- *WhoScE 91-3*
Hecker, George Sprake 1922- *WhoAm 92*
Hecker, Guy Jackson 1856-1939 *BiDAMSp 1989*
Hecker, Guy Leonard, Jr. 1932- *WhoAm 92*
Hecker, Hans-Dietrich 1941- *WhoWor 93*
Hecker, Helen Jean *WhoWrEP 92*
Hecker, Jack E. 1921- *St&PR 93*
Hecker, Jo Anne Kathryn *WhoSSW 93*
Hecker, Richard Bernard 1951- *WhoSSW 93*
Hecker, Richard Jacob 1928- *WhoAm 92*
Hecker, Siegfried Stephen 1943- *WhoAm 92*
Hecker, William Fulham 1936- *WhoSSW 93*
Hecker, Zvi 1931- *WhoWor 93*
Heckerling, Amy *BioIn 17*
Heckerling, Amy 1954- *ConAu 139, ConTFT 10, MiSFD 9, WhoAmW 93*
Heckerman, Jerry D. 1938- *St&PR 93*
Heckert, Josiah Brooks 1893-1990? *BioIn 17*
Heckert, Paul Andrew 1953- *WhoSSW 93*
Heckert, Paul Charles 1929- *WhoAm 92, WhoE 93*
Heckert, Rebecca Jean 1943- *WhoAmW 93*
Heckert, Richard Edwin 1924- *St&PR 93, WhoAm 92*
Heckhausen, Heinz *BioIn 17*
Hecking, Erwin Hans 1943- *WhoWor 93*
Heckler, Edward Eugene 1946- *WhoSSW 93*
Heckler, Gerard Vincent 1941- *WhoWor 93*
Heckler, John Maguire 1927- *WhoAm 92, WhoE 93, WhoWor 93*
Heckler, Jonellen Beth 1943- *WhoWrEP 92*
Heckler, Margaret *BioIn 17*
Heckler, Margaret Mary 1931- *WhoAmW 93*
Heckler, Maureen Kelly 1961- *WhoAmW 93*
Heckler, Paul Scott 1954- *St&PR 93*
Heckler, Sheryl Bills 1945- *WhoAm 92*
Heckler, Walter Tim 1942- *WhoSSW 93*
Heckman, Carey E. 1954- *St&PR 93*
Heckman, Carol A. 1944- *WhoAmW 93*
Heckman, D. Christopher *Law&B 92*
Heckman, H. Edward 1950- *St&PR 93*
Heckman, Henry Trevennen Shick 1918- *WhoWor 93*
Heckman, James Joseph 1944- *WhoAm 92*
Heckman, James R. 1931- *St&PR 93*

Heckman, JoAnn 1950- WhoAmW 93, WhoE 93, WhoEmL 93
Heckman, Richard Ainsworth 1929- WhoWor 93
Heckman, Stephen Paul 1939- St&PR 93
Heckman, William Guy 1925- St&PR 93
Heckmann, Irvin Lee 1925- WhoAm 92
Heckmann, Klaus H. 1934- WhoScE 91-3
Heckscher, August 1913- WhoAm 92
Heckscher, Celeste de Longpre 1860-1928 Baker 92
Heckscher, Morrison Harris 1940- WhoAm 92
Heckscher, William S. BioIn 17
Hecksher, Henry D. d1990 BioIn 17
Hecktman, Jerold Allen 1937- St&PR 93
Hecquet, Bernard 1947- WhoScE 91-2
Hector, Bruce J. Law&B 92
Hector, Louis Julius 1915- WhoAm 92
Hector, Tim 1942- DcCPCAm
Hedahl, Richard Neil 1950- St&PR 93
Hedal, Joseph A. Law&B 92
Hedaya, Dan ConTFT 10
Hedaya, Robert Joseph 1952- WhoE 93, WhoEmL 93
Hedback, Brenda Lee 1940- WhoAmW 93
Hedberg, Franklin Augustin 1946- WhoE 93
Hedberg, K. Olov 1923- WhoScE 91-4
Hedberg, Paul Clifford 1939- WhoAm 92
Hedberg, Richard J. 1935- WhoAm 92
Hedblom, Lawrence James 1955- St&PR 93
Hedborg, Jarrett BioIn 17
Heddaeus, David R. 1944- St&PR 93
Hedden, David L. Law&B 92
Hedden, Gregory Dexter 1919- WhoAm 92
Hedden, Kurt 1927- WhoScE 91-3
Hedden, Monty Scott St&PR 93
Hedden, Peter WhoScE 91-1
Hedden, Rob MiSFD 9
Hedden, William Russell, Jr. Law&B 92
Heddens, Robert D. 1938- St&PR 93
Hedderwick, Mairi 1939- ConAu 137, MajAI [port]
Heddesheimer, Walter Jacob 1910- WhoAm 92
Heddle, Douglas William Orr WhoScE 91-1
Hedelin, Per H. 1948- WhoScE 91-4
Hedeman, Richard NewYTBS 92 [port]
Hedeman, Robert J. 1954- St&PR 93
Hedeman, Robert M. 1919- St&PR 93
Hedeman, Tuff BioIn 17
Hedemann, G. Christian Law&B 92
Hedemark, N. Charles 1942- St&PR 93
Heden, Eileen May 1941- WhoAmW 93
Hedenstierna, Goran 1941- WhoScE 91-4
Hederman, H. Henry 1920- St&PR 93, WhoSSW 93
Hederman, Rea S. WhoAmW 93, WhoE 93
Hedge, Arthur Joseph, Jr. 1936- WhoAm 92
Hedge, George Albert 1939- WhoAm 92
Hedge, Jeanne Colleen 1960- WhoAmW 93, WhoE 93, WhoEmL 93, WhoWor 93
Hedgecock, Dixie Lee 1962- WhoEmL 93
Hedgepeth, Chester Melvin, Jr. 1937- WhoE 93
Hedgepeth, Richard L. 1928- St&PR 93
Hedges, Anthony (John) 1931- Baker 92
Hedges, Bertha AmWomPl
Hedges, Carl Devon 1924- WhoWor 93
Hedges, Carl Edward 1920- St&PR 93
Hedges, Charles F., Jr. Law&B 92
Hedges, Charles F., Jr. 1951- St&PR 93
Hedges, Dan 1951- WhoWrEP 92
Hedges, Donald Walton 1921- WhoAm 92
Hedges, Harry George 1923- WhoAm 92
Hedges, James 1938- WhoWrEP 92
Hedges, Jean Kyle 1930- WhoAmW 93
Hedges, John Wesley Law&B 92
Hedges, Lorrette Jean WhoAmW 93
Hedges, Marion Hawthorne AmWomPl
Hedges, Mollie Ellen 1952- WhoEmL 93
Hedges, Richard H. 1952- WhoWor 93
Hedges, Robert E.M. WhoScE 91-1
Hedges, Robert J. 1948- WhoIns 93
Hedges, Robert W. 1945- St&PR 93
Hedges, Thomas D. 1949- St&PR 93
Hedges, William A. 1941- St&PR 93
Hedien, Wayne Evans 1934- St&PR 93, WhoAm 92, WhoIns 93
Hediger, Gary Roddey 1944- St&PR 93
Hediger, Gary Roddy 1944- WhoAm 92
Hediger, Robert Thomas 1963- WhoWor 93
Hedin, Anne Miller 1944- WhoAmW 93
Hedin, Lars 1930- WhoScE 91-4
Hedin, Sven 1865-1952 Expl 93 [port], IntDcAn
Hedinger, Christoph Ernst 1917- WhoWor 93
Hedinsson, Bolli 1954- WhoWor 93
Hedley, Arthur 1905-1969 Baker 92
Hedley, Clifford Leonard WhoScE 91-1
Hedley, David Van Houten 1945- WhoAm 92
Hedley, Gerald d1990 BioIn 17
Hedley, Leslie Woolf 1921- WhoWrEP 92
Hedley, Robert Peveril 1937- St&PR 93
Hedley-Whyte, Elizabeth Tessa 1937- WhoAm 92
Hedley-Whyte, John 1933- WhoAm 92
Hedlund, Dennis 1946- WhoEmL 93
Hedlund, James BioIn 17
Hedlund, James Lane 1928- WhoAm 92
Hedlund, Lowell A. Law&B 92
Hedlund, Richard Thomas 1948- St&PR 93
Hedlund, Richard Warren 1935- WhoSSW 93
Hedlund, Robert L. WhoE 93
Hedlund, Ronald 1934- WhoAm 92
Hedlund, Ronald David 1941- WhoE 93
Hedman, Dale Eugene 1935- WhoAm 92
Hedman, Frederick Alvin 1937- WhoE 93
Hedman, Janice Lee 1938- WhoAmW 93
Hedman, Jonathan W. 1943- St&PR 93
Hedman, Martha AmWomPl
Hedner-Flodmark, Ulla K.E. 1939- WhoScE 91-2
Hedon, Bernard 1951- WhoWor 93
He Dongchang 1923- WhoAsAP 91
Hedouin, Pierre 1789-1868 Baker 92
Hedqvist, Per O. 1936- WhoScE 91-4
Hedren, Paul L(eslie) 1949- ConAu 37NR
Hedren, Tippi BioIn 17
Hedrick, Basil Calvin 1932- WhoAm 92, WhoWrEP 92
Hedrick, Charles Larry 1941- St&PR 93
Hedrick, Charles Lynnwood 1934- St&PR 93, WhoAm 92
Hedrick, David Warrington 1917- WhoAm 92, WhoSSW 93
Hedrick, Floyd Dudley 1927- WhoAm 92
Hedrick, Frederic Cleveland, Jr. 1911- WhoAm 92
Hedrick, Gary R. 1954- St&PR 93
Hedrick, Hal C., Jr. 1945- St&PR 93
Hedrick, Hal Clemmons, Jr. Law&B 92
Hedrick, Hal Clemmons, Jr. 1945- WhoAm 92
Hedrick, Jerry Leo 1936- WhoAm 92
Hedrick, John R. Law&B 92
Hedrick, Marilyn Couey 1946- WhoSSW 93
Hedrick, Max A. Law&B 92
Hedrick, Robert Kenny, Jr. 1949- WhoAm 92
Hedrick, Steve Brian 1958- WhoSSW 93
Hedrick, Thelma Ruth 1944- WhoSSW 93
Hedrick, Wally 1928- BioIn 17
Hedstrom, Ana Lisa BioIn 17
Hedstrom, Clas Ake WhoScE 91-4
Hedstrom, Eric Leonard, Jr. 1922- WhoE 93
Hedstrom, Joseph Charles 1952- WhoSSW 93
Hedstrom, Mitchell Warren 1951- WhoAm 92, WhoE 93, WhoEmL 93, WhoWor 93
Hedstrom, Scottye Law&B 92
Hedtkamp, Gunter 1928- WhoWor 93
Hedtke, Barbara Ann 1956- WhoEmL 93
Hedwall, Lennart 1932- Baker 92
Hee, Leona Lai Hung 1938- WhoAmW 93
Heeb, Donald B. Law&B 92
Heeb, Louis F. Law&B 92, WhoAm 92
Heeb, Louis F. 1930- St&PR 93
Heebe, Frederick Jacob Regan 1922- WhoSSW 93
Heebner, Albert Gilbert 1927- WhoAm 92
Heebner, David Richard 1927- St&PR 93, WhoAm 92
Heed, Hans H. 1945- WhoUN 92
Heed, James Robert Law&B 92
Heeding, Michelle Anne 1953- WhoAmW 93
Heefner, William Frederick 1922- WhoAm 92
Heeg, Peggy A. Law&B 92
Heeger, Alan Jay 1936- WhoAm 92
Heekin, James Robson, III 1949- WhoAm 92
Heekin, Judith Ann Miller 1939- WhoAmW 93
Heeks, Robert Eugene 1928- WhoE 93
Heelan, Patrick Aidan 1926- WhoAm 92
Heeling, Hendrik Aaltinus 1955- WhoWor 93
Heemskerck van Beest, Jacoba van 1876-1923 BioIn 17
Heemskerk, Johan W.M. 1953- WhoScE 91-3
Heenan, David A. 1940- WhoAm 92
Heenan, Edward J. 1947- St&PR 93
Heenan, Greg Stephen 1950- WhoEmL 93, WhoSSW 93
Heenan, Patrick Michael 1946- WhoEmL 93
Heenan, William Patrick 1954- WhoWrEP 92
Heene, Rainer J. 1930- WhoScE 91-3
Heer, David Macalpine 1930- WhoAm 92
Heer, Edwin Le Roy 1938- St&PR 93
Heer, Edwin LeRoy 1938- WhoE 93
Heer, Ernst 1928- WhoScE 91-4
Heer, Ewald 1930- WhoWor 93
Heer, Nicholas Lawson 1928- WhoAm 92
Heer, Paul Edward 1936- St&PR 93
Heer, William 1921- St&PR 93
Heerdt, Alfred A. 1881-1958 BiDAMSp 1989
Heere, Karen R. 1944- WhoAm 92, WhoAmW 93
Heeremans, Carl R. 1940- WhoWor 93
Heereman von Zuydtwyck, Valentin, Freiherr 1942- WhoWor 93
Heeren, Henk Jan 1922- WhoWor 93
Heeren, Reid L. St&PR 93
Heerens, Robert Edward 1915- WhoAm 92
Heeringa, George D. 1914- St&PR 93
Heeringa, Jaap E. Law&B 92
Heerman, William R. 1933- WhoIns 93
Heermann, Hugo 1844-1935 Baker 92
Heers, Arthur Frank 1944- WhoWor 93
Heerwagen, Herbert Alfred 1910- WhoE 93, WhoWor 93
Heerwagen, Louie M. 1935- St&PR 93
Heerwagen, Peter H. 1945- WhoE 93
Heery, Myrtle Wise 1946- WhoAmW 93
Hees, Gebhard 1926- WhoScE 91-3
Hees, George Harris 1910- WhoAm 92
Heesacker, Martin 1956- WhoSSW 93
Heeschen, David Sutphin 1926- WhoAm 92
Heeschen, George M., Jr. 1941- St&PR 93
Heeschen, W. WhoScE 91-3
Heeseler, Richard Carlton 1946- WhoAm 92
Heeseman, Rex 1942- WhoAm 92
Heesing, Albert 1926- WhoScE 91-3
Heeter, Gregory DeWayne 1955- WhoSSW 93
Heeter, Joseph Laken Law&B 92
Heetland, David Lee 1948- WhoEmL 93
Heetman, Alphonsus 1924- WhoScE 91-3
Heezen, Bruce C. BioIn 17
Heffelbower, Dwight Earl 1925- St&PR 93, WhoAm 92
Heffelfinger, Royce St&PR 93
Heffer, Eric 1922-1991 AnObit 1991
Heffer, Janet Cassandra 1947- WhoWor 93
Hefferan, Colien Joan 1949- WhoEmL 93
Hefferan, Ellen Monica Law&B 92
Hefferan, Richard P. Law&B 92
Hefferin, Douglas J. Law&B 92
Hefferlin, Ray Alden 1929- WhoSSW 93
Heffern, Debbi Marie 1956- WhoAmW 93
Heffern, Gordon E. 1924- St&PR 93
Heffern, Gordon Emory 1924- WhoAm 92
Heffern, Richard Charles 1944- WhoAm 92
Heffernan, Bart T. 1925-1990 BioIn 17
Heffernan, Carol Falvo 1944- WhoE 93
Heffernan, Catherine Mary 1965- WhoAmW 93
Heffernan, Daniel Michael 1951- WhoWor 93
Heffernan, Gerard E. 1937- St&PR 93
Heffernan, James Vincent 1926- WhoAm 92
Heffernan, John BioIn 17
Heffernan, John Joseph 1958- St&PR 93
Heffernan, Kathleen Marie Law&B 92
Heffernan, Michael 1942- ConAu 40NR
Heffernan, Michael Joseph 1942- WhoWrEP 92
Heffernan, Nathan Stewart 1920- WhoAm 92
Heffernan, Patricia Conner 1946- WhoAmW 93
Heffernan, Phillip Thomas, Jr. 1922- WhoAm 92
Heffernan, Ray W. d1990 BioIn 17
Heffernan, Richard Joseph 1951- WhoAm 92
Heffernan, Robert Russell 1952- WhoSSW 93
Heffernan, Robert Vincent 1955- WhoE 93
Heffernan, Roger Leonard 1940- St&PR 93
Heffernan, Ruth Marie 1963- WhoEmL 93
Heffernan, Terry 1951- BioIn 17
Heffernan, Thomas (Carroll), Jr. 1939- WhoWrEP 92
Heffernan, Wilbert Joseph 1932- WhoAm 92
Heffernan, William Joseph, II 1935- St&PR 93
Heffes, Harry 1939- WhoAm 92
Heffington, Joseph A., III Law&B 92
Heffner, Daniel Jason 1956- WhoEmL 93, WhoWor 93
Heffner, Grover Chester 1919- WhoAm 92
Heffner, Ralph H. 1938- WhoAm 92, WhoE 93
Heffner, Richard Douglas 1925- WhoAm 92
Heffner, Timothy Douglas 1949- St&PR 93
Heffner, William Joseph 1928- St&PR 93
Heffron, Dorris 1944- BioIn 17, WhoCanL 92
Heffron, Howard A. 1927- WhoAm 92
Heffron, James J.A. 1943- WhoScE 91-3
Heffron, Michael Edward 1949- WhoEmL 93
Heffron, Richard T. 1930- MiSFD 9
Hefler, Peter Richard 1940- WhoE 93
Hefler, Roger H. 1912- St&PR 93
Hefley, Joel 1935- CngDr 91
Hefley, Joel M. 1935- WhoAm 92
Hefley, Margie Rudene 1929- WhoSSW 93
Hefley, Robert M. ScF&FL 92
Heflin, Howell BioIn 17
Heflin, Howell T. 1921- CngDr 91
Heflin, Howell Thomas 1921- WhoAm 92, WhoSSW 93
Heflin, Martin Ganier 1932- WhoAm 92
Heflin-Wells, E. Neil 1951- WhoEmL 93, WhoSSW 93
Hefner, Calvin Eugene 1938- WhoSSW 93
Hefner, Christie BioIn 17
Hefner, Christie 1952- St&PR 93
Hefner, Christie Ann 1952- WhoAm 92, WhoAmW 93
Hefner, Hugh BioIn 17, NewYTBS 92 [port]
Hefner, Hugh M. 1926- St&PR 93
Hefner, Hugh Marston 1926- WhoAm 92
Hefner, James A. WhoAm 92, WhoSSW 93
Hefner, James Homer 1932- WhoSSW 93
Hefner, Jerrie Lou 1957- WhoAmW 93
Hefner, Kimberly Sue 1963- WhoSSW 93
Hefner, Philip James 1932- WhoAm 92
Hefner, Raymond H., Jr. 1927- St&PR 93
Hefner, Robert Alan 1929- WhoAm 92
Hefner, Robert Eugene 1927- WhoAm 92, WhoSSW 93
Hefner, Terry Thomas 1949- WhoSSW 93
Hefner, W. G. 1930- CngDr 91, WhoSSW 93
Hefner, W. G. Bill 1930- WhoAm 92
Heft, James Lewis 1943- WhoAm 92
Hefte, Carrie A. Law&B 92
Hefter, Benjamin Richard 1916- St&PR 93
Hefter, Laurence Roy 1935- WhoAm 92
Hefter, Wilfred Roy 1937- St&PR 93
Heftman, Kurt 1928- WhoScE 91-3
Hefty, Thomas R. Law&B 92
Hegan, James Edward 1920-1984 BiDAMSp 1989
Hegan, Robert S. 1928- St&PR 93
Hegar, Friedrich 1841-1927 Baker 92
Hegarty, Anthony Francis 1942- WhoScE 91-3
Hegarty, George John 1948- WhoEmL 93, WhoWor 93
Hegarty, James P. 1935- St&PR 93
Hegarty, Jo Ann M. 1945- St&PR 93
Hegarty, John J.P. 1958- WhoWor 93
Hegarty, Kathleen B. St&PR 93
Hegarty, Martin J. BioIn 17
Hegarty, Mary Frances 1950- WhoEmL 93
Hegarty, Michael J. 1939- St&PR 93
Hegarty, Thomas Joseph 1935- WhoAm 92
Hegarty, Timothy F., Jr. 1948- St&PR 93
Hegarty, William E. d1992 NewYTBS 92
Hegarty, William Edward 1926- WhoAm 92
Hegarty, William Kevin 1926- WhoAm 92
Hegebarth, Kevin Glenn 1960- WhoSSW 93
Hegedus, Chris MiSFD 9
Hegedus, Ferenc 1881-1944 Baker 92
Hegedus, L. Louis 1941- WhoAm 92
Hegedus, Lajos 1934- WhoScE 91-4
Hegedus, Peter 1951- WhoUN 92
Hegedus, Sharon Hayner Law&B 92
Hegel, Carolyn Marie 1940- WhoAm 92, WhoAmW 93
Hegel, Garrett R. 1950- St&PR 93
Hegel, Georg Wilhelm Friedrich 1770-1831 BioIn 17
Hegel, Pamela Rene 1958- WhoAmW 93
Hegel, Paul Thomas 1947- St&PR 93
Hegel, Ulrich 1930- WhoScE 91-3
Hegelmann, Julius 1921- WhoAm 92
Hegeman, James Alan 1943- WhoAm 92, WhoE 93, WhoWor 93
Hegenderfer, Jonita Susan 1944- WhoAm 92, WhoAmW 93
Heger, Frank J. 1927- St&PR 93
Heger, Frank Joseph 1927- WhoE 93
Heger, Gernot W. 1943- WhoScE 91-2
Heger, Herbert Krueger 1937- WhoAm 92

Heger, Robert 1886-1978 *Baker 92, OxDcOp*
Hegerfeldt, Gerhard Christian 1939- *WhoWor 93*
Hegerhorst, Pat *WhoWor 93*
Hegerich, Robert Lawrence 1936- *WhoSSW 93*
Hegering, Heinz-Gerd 1943- *WhoScE 91-3, WhoWor 93*
Hegerle, Henry Aloysius 1937- *WhoE 93*
Hegg, George Lennart 1930- *St&PR 93, WhoAm 92*
Hegg, Tom *BioIn 17*
Heggeland, Robert A. *St&PR 93*
Heggen, Arthur W. 1945- *WhoIns 93*
Heggen, Arthur William 1945- *St&PR 93*
Heggen, Ivar Nelson 1954- *WhoEmL 93*
Heggers, John Paul 1933- *WhoSSW 93*
Heggestad, Howard Edwin 1915- *WhoE 93*
Heggestad, Robert E. 1939- *St&PR 93*
Heggie, Robah Gray, Jr. 1929- *St&PR 93, WhoIns 93*
Heggie, Robert James 1913- *WhoAm 92*
Heggs, P.J. *WhoScE 91-1*
Heghinian, Elizabeth Alban Trumbower 1917- *WhoAmW 93, WhoE 93, WhoWor 93*
Heghmann, Robert A. *Law&B 92*
Hegi, Ursula Johanna 1946- *WhoWrEP 92*
Heginbotham, Erland Howard 1931- *WhoAm 92*
Heginbotham, Jan Sturza 1954- *WhoAm 92, WhoEmL 93*
Hegji, Charles Edward 1945- *WhoSSW 93*
Heglin, Richard Theodore 1936- *St&PR 93*
Hegner, Anna 1881-1963 *Baker 92*
Hegner, Frank D. *Law&B 92*
Hegner, Otto 1876-1907 *Baker 92*
Hegrenes, Jack Richard 1929- *WhoWor 93*
Hegstad, Roland Rex 1926- *WhoAm 92*
Hegstrom, Robert Arthur 1942- *St&PR 93*
Hegstrom, William Jean 1923- *WhoSSW 93, WhoWor 93*
He Guangyuan 1930- *WhoAsAP 91*
He Guoqiang 1944- *WhoAsAP 91*
Hegyeli, Ruth Ingeborg Elisabeth Johnsson 1931- *WhoWor 93, WhoWrEP 92*
Hegyesi, Louis 1853-1894 *Baker 92*
Hegyi, Albert Paul 1944- *WhoAm 92*
Hegyi, Julius 1923- *WhoAm 92*
Hehenkamp, Theodor H.G. 1930- *WhoScE 91-3*
Hehir, J. Bryan *BioIn 17*
Hehir, Michael K. 1947- *St&PR 93*
Hehl, Friedrich W. 1937- *WhoScE 91-3*
Hehlmann, Hanns Rudiger *WhoWor 93*
Hehmeyer, Alexander 1910- *WhoAm 92*
Hehmeyer, Alexander M. *Law&B 92*
Hehn, Barry 1949- *St&PR 93*
Heibel, Patricia Marie 1956- *WhoE 93*
Heiberg, Elisabeth 1945- *WhoAmW 93*
Heiberg, Harold Willard 1922- *WhoSSW 93*
Heiberg, Robert Alan 1943- *WhoAm 92*
Heiberger, Michael H. 1940- *WhoE 93*
Heichel, Corey 1978- *BioIn 17*
Heichel, Gary Harold 1940- *WhoAm 92*
Heid, Markham Alexander 1949- *St&PR 93*
Heidbreder, Edna 1890-1985 *BioIn 17*
Heidbreder, Warren W. 1946- *St&PR 93*
Heidbrink, Virgil Eugene 1925- *WhoSSW 93*
Heide, Christopher 1951- *WhoCanL 92*
Heide, Florence Parry 1919- *MajAI [port], SmATA 69 [port], WhoWrEP 92*
Heide, Ola M. 1931- *WhoScE 91-4*
Heide, Stanley J. 1949- *St&PR 93*
Heidebrecht, John Stanley 1938- *St&PR 93*
Heidebrecht, Norman 1938- *St&PR 93*
Heidegger, Johann Jakob 1666-1749 *OxDcOp*
Heidegger, Martin 1889-1976 *BioIn 17*
Heidelbach, Nikolaus 1955- *BioIn 17*
Heidelberg, Helen Susan Hatvani 1957- *WhoAmW 93*
Heidelberger, Kathleen Patricia 1939- *WhoAm 92*
Heidelberger, Michael 1888-1991 *BioIn 17*
Heideman, Richard Dennis 1947- *WhoAm 92*
Heideman, Richard Oliver 1948- *St&PR 93*
Heidemann, Anton 1940- *WhoScE 91-2*
Heidemann, Claus 1933- *WhoScE 91-3*
Heidemann, Robert Albert 1936- *WhoAm 92*
Heiden, Bernhard 1910- *Baker 92*
Heiden, Charles Kenneth 1925- *WhoAm 92*
Heiden, Christoph 1935- *WhoScE 91-3*
Heiden, David 1946- *ConAu 139*
Heiden, Eric *BioIn 17*
Heiden, William Mark 1952- *WhoEmL 93*
Heidenberger, Kurt Harald 1951- *WhoWor 93*
Heidenheim, Roger Stewart 1909- *WhoAm 92*
Heidenreich, Arturo 1928- *WhoWor 93*
Heidenreich, Douglas Robert 1932- *WhoAm 92*
Heidenreich, James R. *St&PR 93*
Heider, David Arthur 1941- *St&PR 93*
Heider, Jon V. 1934- *St&PR 93*
Heider, Jon Vinton *Law&B 92*
Heider, Jon Vinton 1934- *WhoAm 92*
Heider, Karl Gustav 1935- *WhoAm 92*
Heider, Patrick F. *Law&B 92*
Heider, Richard Alan 1946- *WhoEmL 93*
Heidinger, James Vandaveer, II 1941- *WhoSSW 93*
Heidinger, Marjorie Christine 1967- *WhoAmW 93*
Heidinger, Sonia Lynn 1963- *WhoAmW 93*
Heidingsfeld, Ludwig 1854-1920 *Baker 92*
Heidkamp, Walter Gerald 1936- *St&PR 93*
Heidke, Ronald L. *St&PR 93*
Heidke, Ronald Lawrence 1937- *WhoAm 92*
Heidlage, Katharine Sanderson 1951- *WhoAmW 93, WhoEmL 93*
Heidlage, Katherine S. *Law&B 92*
Heidlauf, Howard A. 1934- *St&PR 93*
Heidler, Wilfried-Gerd 1937- *WhoScE 91-3*
Heidorn, Fred Robert 1941- *St&PR 93*
Heidrich, James K., Jr. 1944- *St&PR 93*
Heidrich, William Albert, III *Law&B 92*
Heidrick, Gardner W. 1911- *St&PR 93*
Heidrick, Gardner Wilson 1911- *WhoAm 92*
Heidrick, Robert Lindsay 1941- *WhoAm 92*
Heidrick, Virginia Louise 1951- *WhoWrEP 92*
Heidt, Bill *BioIn 17*
Heidt, Carl Elmer 1928- *WhoAm 92*
Heidtman, Martin Carl 1924- *St&PR 93*
Heie, Ole E. 1926- *WhoScE 91-2*
Heiens, Richard Allen 1940- *WhoSSW 93*
Heier, Ed 1947- *St&PR 93*
Heier, Hans Erik 1944- *WhoScE 91-4*
Heier, Knut S. 1929- *WhoScE 91-4*
Heier, Knut Sigurdson 1929- *WhoWor 93*
Heier, Ronald Omer *Law&B 92*
Heier, Thomas Eugene 1948- *St&PR 93*
Heierli, Werner *WhoScE 91-4*
Heifetz, Alan William 1943- *WhoAm 92*
Heifetz, Daniel (Alan) 1948- *Baker 92*
Heifetz, Jascha 1899-1987 *Baker 92*
Heifetz, Louis James 1947- *WhoE 93*
Heifetz, Paul 1927- *St&PR 93*
Heifetz, Sonia 1929- *WhoAmW 93*
Heigel, James Edward 1940- *WhoSSW 93*
Heiges, Donald R. 1910-1990 *BioIn 17*
Heiges, Jesse G. 1914-1991 *BioIn 17*
Heigham, James Crichton 1930- *WhoAm 92*
Height, Dorothy Ephrates 1950- *WhoAmW 93*
Height, Dorothy I. 1912- *BioIn 17*
Height, Dorothy Irene 1912- *AfrAmBi*
Heighton, William 1800- *BioIn 17*
Heighway, James Edward 1946- *St&PR 93*
Heigl, James John, Jr. 1940- *St&PR 93*
Heij, Christiaan 1957- *WhoWor 93*
Heijboer, Roel Johan 1925- *WhoWor 93*
Heijbroek, Willem 1940- *WhoScE 91-3*
Heijnen, Willem Jan 1925- *WhoScE 91-3*
Heikal, Morgan *WhoScE 91-1*
Heiker, Vincent Edward 1942- *WhoSSW 93*
Heikkenen, Herman John 1930- *WhoSSW 93*
Heikkila, Esco Henrikki 1930- *WhoScE 91-4*
Heikkila, Heikki 1946- *WhoScE 91-4*
Heikkinen, Dale Wayne 1944- *St&PR 93*
Heikkinen, Raimo Allan 1955- *WhoWor 93*
Heikkonen, P. *WhoScE 91-4*
Heil, Balint 1935- *WhoScE 91-4*
Heil, Jeffrey E. 1953- *St&PR 93*
Heil, Louis John 1942- *St&PR 93*
Heil, Mark S. 1961- *St&PR 93*
Heil, Mary Ruth 1921- *WhoSSW 93*
Heil, Roland Lee 1933- *St&PR 93*
Heil, Russell Howard 1942- *St&PR 93, WhoAm 92*
Heil, Terry W. *WhoAm 92*
Heil, William H. 1949- *WhoSSW 93*
Heilberg, Robert *WhoE 93*
Heilborn, George H. 1935- *St&PR 93*
Heilbron, David Michael 1936- *WhoAm 92*
Heilbron, John L. 1934- *WhoAm 92*
Heilbron, Louis Henry 1907- *WhoAm 92*
Heilbron, Marie 1851-1886 *OxDcOp*
Heilbron, Patricia Barnett *Law&B 92*
Heilbron, Richard H. *Law&B 92*
Heilbron, Susan Mae 1945- *WhoAm 92*
Heilbroner, David *BioIn 17*
Heilbroner, Joan 1922- *BioIn 17*
Heilbroner, Robert L. *BioIn 17*
Heilbroner, Robert L. 1919- *WhoAm 92*
Heilbronn, W. Michael 1946- *St&PR 93*
Heilbronner, Edgar 1921- *WhoScE 91-4*
Heilbrun, Carolyn Gold 1926- *NewYTBS 92 [port], WhoAm 92, WhoAmW 93, WhoWrEP 92*
Heilbrun, James 1924- *WhoAm 92*
Heilbrunn, Jeffrey 1950- *WhoAm 92, WhoEmL 93, WhoWor 93*
Heilbrunn, Lorraine Judith *WhoAmW 93*
Heile, Leo James 1941- *WhoAm 92*
Heiler, Alfred G. 1938- *St&PR 93*
Heiles, Carl Eugene 1939- *WhoAm 92*
Heilferty, Henry W. 1930- *St&PR 93*
Heilig, Terry Len 1947- *WhoSSW 93*
Heilig, William Wright 1940- *WhoAm 92*
Heiliger, Wilbur David 1946- *St&PR 93*
Heiligman, Deborah *BioIn 17*
Heiller, Anton 1923-1979 *Baker 92*
Heilman, Carl Edwin 1911- *WhoAm 92, WhoE 93, WhoWor 93*
Heilman, E. Bruce 1926- *WhoAm 92*
Heilman, Harlan David *Law&B 92*
Heilman, Joan Rattner *WhoWrEP 92*
Heilman, Linda *Law&B 92*
Heilman, M. Grant 1919- *WhoWrEP 92*
Heilman, Mary Lou *BioIn 17*
Heilman, Richard Dean 1937- *WhoAm 92*
Heilman, Robert Leo 1952- *WhoWrEP 92*
Heilman, Samuel C. *BioIn 17*
Heilman, William Clifford 1877-1946 *Baker 92*
Heilmann, Christian Flemming 1936- *St&PR 93, WhoAm 92, WhoE 93*
Heilmann, Hans Dietrich 1940- *WhoWor 93*
Heilmann, Leroy W. 1932- *St&PR 93*
Heilmeier, George Harry 1936- *St&PR 93, WhoAm 92*
Heiloms, May *WhoAm 92, WhoE 93*
Heilprin, Laurence Bedford 1906- *WhoAm 92*
Heilweil, Murray d1991 *BioIn 17*
Heim, Bruce Kennedy 1941- *WhoE 93*
Heim, Bruno Bernard 1911- *WhoWor 93*
Heim, Carol Elizabeth 1955- *WhoEmL 93*
Heim, Donald John 1927- *St&PR 93, WhoAm 92*
Heim, Edgar 1930- *WhoScE 91-4*
Heim, Frederic A. 1926- *St&PR 93*
Heim, Joni Joy 1962- *WhoAmW 93*
Heim, Kathryn Marie 1952- *WhoAmW 93, WhoEmL 93*
Heim, Marcy Lynn Schultz 1957- *WhoAmW 93, WhoEmL 93*
Heim, Paul J. *Law&B 92*
Heim, Ray Vincent 1920- *WhoSSW 93*
Heim, Robert Charles 1942- *WhoAm 92*
Heim, Stephanie G. *Law&B 92*
Heim, Tonya Sue 1948- *WhoAmW 93, WhoEmL 93*
Heiman, David Gilbert 1945- *WhoAm 92*
Heiman, Diane Sanchez *BioIn 17*
Heiman, Frederic Paul 1939- *WhoAm 92*
Heiman, Gary L. 1951- *St&PR 93*
Heiman, Grover George, Jr. 1920- *WhoAm 92*
Heiman, John Charles 1947- *WhoSSW 93*
Heiman, Mark J. 1954- *St&PR 93*
Heiman, Maxwell 1932- *WhoAm 92*
Heiman, Michael Kenneth 1949- *WhoE 93*
Heiman, Paul L. 1926- *St&PR 93*
Heimann, Brenda Sue Caudill 1957- *WhoAmW 93*
Heimann, Edward A. 1937- *St&PR 93*
Heimann, Fritz F. *Law&B 92*
Heimann, Janet Barbara 1931- *WhoAmW 93*
Heimann, John Gaines 1929- *WhoAm 92*
Heimann, Joshua Gaines 1959- *WhoE 93*
Heimann, Robert Alvin 1942- *St&PR 93*
Heimann, Robert Karl 1918-1990 *BioIn 17*
Heimann, Sandra Anne 1943- *St&PR 93*
Heimann, Sandra Woeste 1943- *WhoIns 93*
Heimann, Stephen B. *Law&B 92*
Heimann, William Emil 1928- *WhoAm 92*
Heimann-Hast, Sybil Dorothea 1924- *WhoAmW 93*
Heimbaugh, James Ross 1918- *WhoAm 92, WhoE 93*
Heimberg, Eugene B. 1933- *St&PR 93*
Heimberg, Murray 1925- *WhoAm 92, WhoSSW 93*
Heimbinder, Isaac 1943- *St&PR 93, WhoAm 92, WhoSSW 93*
Heimbold, Charles Andreas, Jr. 1933- *WhoAm 92*
Heimbold, Margaret Byrne 1946- *WhoAmW 93, WhoWor 93*
Heimburger, Donald James 1947- *WhoWrEP 92*
Heimdal, Scott *BioIn 17*
Heime, Klaus 1935- *WhoScE 91-3*
Heimerl, Gerhard 1933- *WhoScE 91-3*
Heimerl, John Jules 1950- *WhoEmL 93*
Heimerl, Richard Charles 1943- *St&PR 93*
Heimerl, Richard E. *Law&B 92*
Heimerl, Richard R. *Law&B 92*
Heimert, Alan Edward 1928- *WhoAm 92*
Heimes, Joseph C. 1928- *St&PR 93*
Heimlich, Barry N. 1941- *St&PR 93*
Heimlich, Henry Jay 1920- *WhoAm 92*
Heimlich, Philip F. 1942- *St&PR 93*
Heimlich, Richard Allen 1932- *WhoAm 92*
Heimo, Maija 1953- *WhoScE 91-4*
Heimowitz, Daniel N. 1953- *St&PR 93*
Heimrath, Tadeusz Edward 1927- *WhoWor 93*
Heimsch, Charles 1914- *WhoAm 92*
Hein, Angeline McCormick *Law&B 92*
Hein, Arturo 1933- *WhoUN 92*
Hein, August Henry 1931- *WhoE 93*
Hein, Carl C. 1939- *St&PR 93*
Hein, Cheryl 1945- *WhoSSW 93*
Hein, Christoph 1944- *DcLB 124 [port]*
Hein, David Leon 1939- *St&PR 93*
Hein, Eckhard W. 1943- *WhoUN 92*
Hein, Fritz Eugen 1926- *WhoWor 93*
Hein, Glen Orville 1945- *St&PR 93*
Hein, Jerry M. *BioIn 17*
Hein, John William 1920- *WhoAm 92*
Hein, Leonard William 1916- *WhoAm 92*
Hein, Mel d1992 *NewYTBS 92 [port]*
Hein, Mel 1909-1992 *BioIn 17*
Hein, Robert E. 1929- *St&PR 93*
Hein, Rolland 1932- *ScF&FL 92*
Hein, Ulrich F. 1949- *WhoScE 91-3*
Hein, Walter C. 1930- *St&PR 93*
Hein, William J. *Law&B 92*
Heindel, Ned Duane 1937- *WhoAm 92*
Heindl, Clifford Joseph 1926- *WhoAm 92*
Heindl, Dennis Duane 1942- *WhoE 93*
Heindl, Walter E. *Law&B 92*
Heindl, Warren Anton 1922- *WhoAm 92*
Heine, Andrew N. 1928- *St&PR 93*
Heine, Andrew Noah 1928- *WhoAm 92*
Heine, Arthur J. 1940- *ConAu 138*
Heine, Edward Joseph, Jr. 1925- *WhoAm 92*
Heine, Frederick Ernest 1944- *St&PR 93*
Heine, Harold Warren 1922- *WhoE 93*
Heine, Heinrich 1797-1856 *BioIn 17, MagSWL [port], OxDcOp*
Heine, Helme *BioIn 17*
Heine, Helme 1941- *ChlBIID [port], MajAI [port]*
Heine, Horst *WhoScE 91-3*
Heine, Leonard M., Jr. 1924- *WhoE 93, WhoWor 93*
Heine, Mary Elizabeth 1961- *WhoEmL 93*
Heine, Peter Johannes 1955- *WhoWor 93*
Heine, Richard Atherton 1946- *WhoEmL 93*
Heine, Richard Walter 1918- *WhoAm 92*
Heine, Spencer H. 1942- *WhoAm 92*
Heine, Timothy J. *Law&B 92*
Heine, Ursula Ingrid 1926- *WhoAm 92*
Heine, Volker *WhoScE 91-1*
Heine, Volker 1930- *WhoWor 93*
Heine, Wilhelm 1827-1885 *BioIn 17*
Heine, Willi O.P. 1930- *WhoScE 91-3*
Heine, William C. 1919- *ScF&FL 92, WhoCanL 92*
Heinecken, Robert Friedli 1931- *WhoAm 92*
Heinefetter *Baker 92*
Heinefetter, Clara 1813-1857 *Baker 92*
Heinefetter, Kathinka 1819-1858 *Baker 92*
Heinefetter, Sabine 1809-1872 *Baker 92*
Heine-Geldern, Robert von 1885-1968 *IntDcAn*
Heineken, Alfred Henry 1923- *WhoWor 93*
Heine-Koehn, Lala *WhoCanL 92*
Heineman, Andrew David 1928- *WhoAm 92*
Heineman, Ben W., Jr. *Law&B 92*
Heineman, Ben Walter 1914- *WhoAm 92*
Heineman, Benjamin W., Jr. 1944- *St&PR 93*
Heineman, Benjamin Walter, Jr. 1944- *WhoAm 92*
Heineman, Harry Francis 1920- *St&PR 93*
Heineman, Heinz 1913- *WhoAm 92*
Heineman, Herbert A., Jr. 1932- *St&PR 93*
Heineman, Jacklyn Kay 1939- *WhoWor 93*
Heineman, Melvin L. *Law&B 92*
Heineman, Natalie *WhoAm 92*
Heineman, Paul Lowe 1924- *WhoAm 92*
Heineman, Ronald E. 1957- *St&PR 93*
Heineman, Steven *Law&B 92*
Heinemann, Alfred 1908- *Baker 92*
Heinemann, Edward H. *BioIn 17*
Heinemann, Katherine 1918- *WhoAmW 93*
Heinemann, Kirsten S. 1959- *St&PR 93*
Heinemann, Larry *BioIn 17*

Heinemann, Peter 1931- *WhoE 93*
Heinemann, Robert Klaus 1926- *WhoWor 93*
Heinemann, William 1863-1910 *GayN*
Heinemeyer, Ernst Wilhelm 1827-1869 *Baker 92*
Heinen, Gloria Jean 1942- *WhoAmW 93*
Heinen, James Albin 1943- *WhoAm 92*
Heinen, Paul A. *Law&B 92*
Heinen, Paul A. 1930- *St&PR 93*
Heinen, Peter H. 1944- *St&PR 93*
Heiner, Clyde Mont 1938- *St&PR 93, WhoAm 92*
Heiner, Dennis Grant 1943- *St&PR 93, WhoE 93*
Heiner, Earl W. 1935- *St&PR 93*
Heiner, Lawrence E. 1938- *St&PR 93*
Heines, Molly K. *Law&B 92*
Heines, Molly K. 1953- *St&PR 93*
Heinesen, William 1900-1991 *BioIn 17*
Heiney, Donald W. *ScF&FL 92*
Heiney, J.W. 1913- *St&PR 93*
Heiney, John Weitzel 1913- *WhoAm 92*
Heinichen, Jeffrey Kirk 1952- *WhoEmL 93*
Heinichen, Johann David 1683-1729 *Baker 92*
Heinicke, Ralph Martin 1914- *WhoSSW 93*
Heiniger, Ursula 1944- *WhoScE 91-4*
Heininen, Paavo (Johannes) 1938- *Baker 92*
Heininger, David Francis 1942- *St&PR 93*
Heininger, Erwin Carl 1921- *WhoAm 92*
Heininger, Kenneth Lloyd *Law&B 92*
Heininger, S. Allen 1925- *St&PR 93*
Heininger, Samuel Allen 1925- *WhoAm 92*
Heinio, Mikko 1948- *Baker 92*
Heinis, Julius Lee 1926- *WhoSSW 93*
Heinitz, Wilhelm 1883-1963 *Baker 92*
Heinke, John D. *St&PR 93*
Heinkel, Fred V. d1990 *BioIn 17*
Heinle, Robert Alan 1933- *WhoE 93, WhoWor 93*
Heinle, Robert G. 1946- *St&PR 93*
Heinlein, Robert A. 1907-1988 *BioIn 17, MagSAmL [port], ScF&FL 92, SmATA 69 [port]*
Heinlein, Robert A(nson) 1907-1988 *MajAI [port]*
Heinlein, Robert Anthony 1953- *WhoSSW 93*
Heinlein, Walter E. 1930- *WhoScE 91-3*
Heinlen, Ronald Eugene 1937- *WhoAm 92*
Heinol, Dennis *St&PR 93*
Heinold, S. Lynn 1951- *WhoEmL 93*
Heinonen, Olavi Ensio 1938- *WhoWor 93*
Heinonen, Olli P. 1934- *WhoScE 91-4*
Heinonen, Pekka J. 1955- *WhoScE 91-4*
Heinonen, Reijo 1923- *WhoScE 91-4*
Heinonen, Reijo Jorma 1939- *WhoWor 93*
Heinonen, Unto Kalervo 1942- *WhoWor 93*
Heinrich, Anthony Philip 1781-1861 *Baker 92*
Heinrich, Bonnie *WhoAmW 93*
Heinrich, Brett David *Law&B 92*
Heinrich, Daniel J. 1956- *St&PR 93*
Heinrich, Don d1992 *BioIn 17, NewYTBS 92 [port]*
Heinrich, Donna Trauscht 1960- *WhoAmW 93, WhoEmL 93*
Heinrich, Dorothea Josephine 1917- *WhoAmW 93*
Heinrich, Edwin C. 1925- *St&PR 93*
Heinrich, Gerald 1950- *St&PR 93*
Heinrich, Hans-Jurgen 1927- *WhoScE 91-3*
Heinrich, Helmut 1938- *WhoScE 91-4*
Heinrich, John E. 1944- *St&PR 93*
Heinrich, Peggy 1929- *WhoWrEP 92*
Heinrich, Randall Wayne 1958- *WhoSSW 93*
Heinrich, Raymond Lawrence 1911- *WhoSSW 93*
Heinrich, Ross Raymond 1915- *WhoAm 92*
Heinrich, Rudolf 1941- *WhoScE 91-3*
Heinrich, Thomas Paul 1946- *St&PR 93*
Heinrichs, Jean Joseph 1938- *WhoWor 93*
Heinrichs, Mary Ann 1930- *WhoAmW 93*
Heinrichs, William LeRoy 1932- *WhoAm 92*
Heinricht, D.J. *WhoScE 91-3*
Heinroth, Johann August Gunther 1780-1846 *Baker 92*
Heins, Albert Edward 1912- *WhoAm 92*
Heins, Bronwen Ann *Law&B 92*
Heins, Donald Ernest 1932- *WhoSSW 93*
Heins, Ethel L. 1918- *WhoAm 92*
Heins, Gordon Lawrence 1929- *St&PR 93*
Heins, James Edward 1930- *St&PR 93*
Heins, Marilyn 1930- *WhoAm 92*
Heins, Maurice Haskell 1915- *WhoE 93*
Heins, Robert William 1933- *WhoE 93*
Heins, Roger G. 1939- *St&PR 93*
Heinse, Wilhelm 1746-1803 *BioIn 17*
Heinsheimer, Hans (Walter) 1900- *Baker 92*
Heinsohn, Robert Jennings 1932- *WhoE 93*
Heintz, Carolinea Cabaniss 1920- *WhoAmW 93, WhoWor 93*
Heintz, Jack 1907- *WhoAm 92*
Heintz, Natascha 1930- *WhoScE 91-4*
Heintz, Roger Lewis 1937- *WhoAm 92*
Heintz, William Walter 1928- *WhoAm 92*
Heintze, Gustaf (Hjalmar) 1879-1946 *Baker 92*
Heintze, Juliette C. 1947- *St&PR 93*
Heintze, Juliette Chiodo 1947- *WhoAmW 93*
Heintzelman, Carol Ann 1942- *WhoE 93*
Heintzelman, Samuel Peter 1805-1880 *HarEnMi*
Heintzen, Markus Rudolf 1960- *WhoWor 93*
Heintzenberg, Jost 1943- *WhoScE 91-4*
Heintzleman, Mary Strickler 1921- *WhoAmW 93*
Heiny, Lisa Marie Aplikowski 1963- *WhoAmW 93*
Heinz, Bradley Donald *Law&B 92*
Heinz, Brian James 1946- *WhoWrEP 92*
Heinz, Drue *BioIn 17, WhoAm 92, WhoAmW 93*
Heinz, Elise Brookfield 1935- *WhoAm 92*
Heinz, Gerald J. *Law&B 92*
Heinz, H. John *BioIn 17*
Heinz, Henry John 1844-1919 *GayN*
Heinz, James Joseph 1941- *St&PR 93*
Heinz, Joan M. *Law&B 92*
Heinz, John 1938-1991 *AnObit 1991*
Heinz, John, III *BioIn 17*
Heinz, John Peter 1936- *WhoAm 92*
Heinz, Klaus 1937- *WhoScE 91-3*
Heinz, Leonard R. *Law&B 92*
Heinz, Maureen Carol-Robb 1965- *WhoEmL 93*
Heinz, Ulrich Walter 1955- *WhoWor 93*
Heinz, Walter Ernst Edward 1920- *WhoAm 92*
Heinze, Bernard (Thomas) 1894-1982 *Baker 92*
Heinze, F. Augustus 1869-1914 *BioIn 17, GayN*
Heinze, Gustav Adolf 1820-1904 *Baker 92*
Heinze, Joachim 1948- *WhoWor 93*
Heinze, Karl Godfried 1929- *St&PR 93*
Heinze, Linda Holli 1939- *WhoAmW 93*
Heinze, Peter R. 1942- *St&PR 93*
Heinzelman, Carl 1919- *St&PR 93*
Heinzelman, Fred 1914- *St&PR 93*
Heinzelmann de Rubio, Ute 1940- *WhoWor 93*
Heinzen, Bernard George 1930- *WhoE 93, WhoWor 93*
Heinzen, Karl Peter 1809-1880 *JrnUS*
Heinzerling, Larry Edward 1945- *WhoAm 92*
Heinzl, Joachim Lothar 1940- *WhoScE 91-3*
Heinzl, Susanne Beate 1950- *WhoWor 93*
Heinzman, Gail E.D. 1955- *St&PR 93*
Heinzman, Patricia Ann 1957- *WhoAmW 93, WhoEmL 93, WhoWor 93*
Heinzman, Richard Ruel 1942- *WhoSSW 93*
Heip, Carlo 1945- *WhoScE 91-3*
Heiple, James Dee 1933- *WhoAm 92*
Heiple, Robert Jay 1947- *St&PR 93*
Heir, Douglas 1960- *WhoWor 93*
Heir, Kal M. 1919- *WhoE 93*
Heirman, Donald N. 1940- *WhoAm 92, WhoWor 93*
Heironimus, Robert A. 1922- *St&PR 93*
Heisbourg, Francois *WhoScE 91-1*
Heisch, James A. 1943- *St&PR 93*
Heise, George Armstrong 1924- *WhoAm 92*
Heise, John Frederick 1926- *St&PR 93*
Heise, Kathleen Rocco 1952- *WhoSSW 93*
Heise, Keith A. 1955- *St&PR 93*
Heise, Knut C. *Law&B 92*
Heise, Peter 1830-1879 *OxDcOp*
Heise, Peter (Arnold) 1830-1879 *Baker 92*
Heise, Ulrich 1944- *WhoScE 91-3*
Heise, Wendy Sue Pinnow 1956- *WhoAmW 93*
Heisel, Ralph Arthur 1935- *WhoAm 92, WhoE 93, WhoWor 93*
Heisenberg, Martin 1940- *WhoScE 91-3*
Heisenberg, Werner 1901-1976 *BioIn 17*
Heiser, Arnold Melvin 1933- *WhoAm 92*
Heiser, Charles Bixler, Jr. 1920- *WhoAm 92*
Heiser, David E. *Law&B 92*
Heiser, James S. *Law&B 92*
Heiser, James S. 1956- *St&PR 93*
Heiser, John Edward 1931- *St&PR 93*
Heiser, Joseph Miller, Jr. 1914- *WhoAm 92, WhoSSW 93*
Heiser, Loretta Jane 1966- *WhoSSW 93*
Heiser, Rolland Valentine 1925- *WhoSSW 93, WhoWor 93*
Heiser, Wayne 1952- *WhoE 93*
Heiser, William E. 1950- *St&PR 93*
Heiser, William Ellwood 1950- *WhoE 93*
Heiserer, Albert, Jr. 1937- *WhoE 93, WhoWor 93*
Heiserman, Robert Gifford 1946- *WhoEmL 93*
Heisey, Lowell Vernon 1919- *WhoSSW 93*
Heisey, Sandra Lee Siegrist 1963- *WhoAmW 93*
Heisey, Walter F. 1919- *St&PR 93*
Heisey, William Lawrence 1930- *WhoAm 92*
Heishman, Charles M. *St&PR 93*
Heishman, Stephen Jay 1953- *WhoE 93*
Heiskanen, Eero Sakari 1922- *WhoScE 91-4*
Heiskanen, Kari Gustav Henrik 1946- *WhoScE 91-4*
Heiskell, John Netherland 1872-1972 *DcLB 127 [port]*
Heisler, Albert 1924- *St&PR 93*
Heisler, Brian Jan *Law&B 92*
Heisler, David M. *Law&B 92*
Heisler, Elwood Douglas 1935- *WhoE 93, WhoWor 93*
Heisler, James T. 1946- *St&PR 93*
Heisler, John Columbus 1926- *WhoAm 92*
Heisler, Quentin George, Jr. 1943- *WhoAm 92*
Heisler, Robert B., Jr. 1948- *St&PR 93*
Heisler, Stanley Dean 1946- *WhoAm 92, WhoE 93, WhoEmL 93*
Heisler, Stuart 1894-1979 *MiSFD 9N*
Heisler, William John 1942- *WhoSSW 93*
Heisman, Norman M. *Law&B 92*
Heismeyer, Fred Charles, III 1955- *WhoEmL 93, WhoSSW 93*
Heiss, Alanna *BioIn 17*
Heiss, Carol 1940- *BioIn 17*
Heiss, Harry Glen 1953- *WhoAm 92*
Heiss, Hermann 1897-1966 *Baker 92*
Heiss, John 1938- *Baker 92*
Heiss, Paul Kenneth 1948- *St&PR 93*
Heiss, Richard Walter 1930- *St&PR 93, WhoAm 92*
Heiss, Wolf-Dieter 1939- *WhoScE 91-3*
Heissenbuttel, Walter John 1947- *St&PR 93*
Heist, Charles Henry 1950- *St&PR 93*
Heist, L.C. 1931- *St&PR 93*
Heist, Lewis Clark 1931- *WhoAm 92*
Heistand, Coleen Renee 1948- *WhoE 93, WhoEmL 93*
Heistand, Donald Lee 1935- *St&PR 93*
Heistand, Joseph Thomas 1924- *WhoAm 92*
Heistand, Paul Kenneth 1949- *WhoEmL 93, WhoSSW 93*
Heistein, Robert Kenneth 1940- *WhoWor 93*
Heister, Robert John, Jr. 1953- *WhoE 93*
Heisterberg, Robert G. 1937- *St&PR 93*
Heistracher, Peter Georg 1931- *WhoScE 91-4*
Heit, Ivan 1946- *WhoEmL 93*
Heithoff, Ronald Elmer 1936- *St&PR 93*
Heitkamp, Dennis Michael 1934- *WhoSSW 93*
Heitland, Jon *ScF&FL 92*
Heitler, George 1915- *WhoAm 92*
Heitler, Susan McCrensky 1945- *WhoAmW 93*
Heitman, Frederick C. 1936- *St&PR 93*
Heitman, Gregory Erwin 1947- *WhoEmL 93*
Heitman, Richard Edgar 1930- *St&PR 93*
Heitmann, Fred W., Jr. 1918- *St&PR 93*
Heitmann, Frederick William 1922- *WhoAm 92*
Heitmann, George Joseph 1933- *WhoAm 92*
Heitmann, Richard J. *Law&B 92*
Heitmeyer, Roderick 1933- *WhoUN 92*
Heitner, John A. 1931- *WhoE 93*
Heitner, Robert Richard 1920- *WhoAm 92*
Heitz, Edward Fred 1930- *WhoSSW 93*
Heitz, Ewald 1931- *WhoScE 91-3*
Heitz, John Gregory 1943- *St&PR 93*
Heitz, Mark V. 1952- *WhoAm 92*
Heitz, Raymond J. 1932- *St&PR 93*
Heitzer, Donald Alfred 1925- *St&PR 93*
Heitzman, Frank Edward 1946- *WhoEmL 93*
Heitzman, Robert Edward 1927- *WhoAm 92*
Heitzman, William Ray 1948- *WhoWrEP 92*
Heitzmann, William Ray 1948- *SmATA 73 [port]*
Heivilin, Fred G. 1941- *St&PR 93*
Heiwig, Eugene A. 1939- *St&PR 93*
Heizer, Edgar Francis, Jr. 1929- *WhoAm 92, WhoWor 93*
Heizer, Ida Ann 1919- *WhoAmW 93*
Heizer, Michael *BioIn 17*
Heizer, Ruth Bradfute 1933- *WhoAmW 93, WhoSSW 93*
Heizman, Leslie Anne Doubleday 1957- *WhoSSW 93*
Heizmann, Philippe Henri 1942- *WhoScE 91-2*
Hejduk, John 1929- *BioIn 17*
Hejduk, John Quentin 1929- *WhoAm 92*
Hejfic, Iosif 1905- *DrEEuF*
Heji, Tibor *BioIn 17*
He Jingzhi 1924- *WhoAsAP 91*
Hejl, James George 1939- *WhoSSW 93*
Hejnowicz, Zygmunt 1929- *WhoScE 91-4*
Hejny, Slavomil 1924- *WhoScE 91-4*
Hejtmancik, Milton Rudolph 1919- *WhoSSW 93*
Hejtmanek, Danton Charles 1951- *WhoEmL 93*
He Kang 1923- *WhoAsAP 91*
Hekking, Andre 1866-1925 *Baker 92*
Hekking, Anton 1856-1935 *Baker 92*
Hekking, Gerard 1879-1942 *Baker 92*
Hekster, Walter 1937- *Baker 92*
Helander, Bruce Paul 1947- *WhoEmL 93*
Helander, Elisabeth 1942- *WhoScE 91-4*
Helander, Herbert F. 1935- *WhoScE 91-4*
Helander, Robert Charles 1932- *WhoAm 92*
Helander, Robert E. 1930- *St&PR 93*
Helbach, Conrad D. 1946- *St&PR 93*
Helber, Larry Charles 1947- *St&PR 93*
Helberg, Barbara Anne 1946- *WhoWrEP 92*
Helberg, Shirley Adelaide Holden *WhoAm 92, WhoAmW 93, WhoE 93*
Helberger, Christof 1942- *WhoWor 93*
Helbert, Clifford L. 1920- *WhoAm 92*
Helbig, Alethea K. 1928- *ConAu 37NR*
Helbig, Doris Ann 1957- *WhoSSW 93*
Helbig, Gerhard 1929- *WhoWor 93*
Helbig, Wolfgang 1839-1915 *BioIn 17*
Helbling, Paul Arthur 1953- *St&PR 93*
Helburn, Isadore B. 1938- *WhoAm 92*
Helburn, Nicholas 1918- *WhoAm 92*
Helburn, Stephen 1946- *St&PR 93*
Helburn, Theresa 1887-1959 *AmWomPl*
Held, Al 1928- *WhoAm 92*
Held, Bryan H. 1948- *St&PR 93*
Held, Charles W. *St&PR 93*
Held, Claude C., II 1943- *St&PR 93*
Held, Gary S. *St&PR 93*
Held, Gerald N. *Law&B 92*
Held, Gerrit Jan 1906-1955 *IntDcAn*
Held, Heinz Joachim 1928- *WhoWor 93*
Held, James Robert 1961- *WhoE 93*
Held, Joe Roger 1931- *WhoAm 92*
Held, John *Law&B 92*
Held, K. Lars 1946- *St&PR 93*
Held, Katy Lynn 1960- *WhoAmW 93*
Held, Lila M. 1925- *WhoAm 92, WhoAmW 93*
Held, Matthew 1929- *St&PR 93*
Held, Peter *BioIn 17*
Held, Peter Allen 1949- *WhoEmL 93*
Held, Philip 1920- *WhoAm 92*
Held, Richard Marx 1922- *WhoAm 92*
Held, Virginia 1929- *WhoAm 92*
Held, Walter George 1920- *WhoAm 92*
Heldenbrand, Keith 1950- *WhoE 93*
Heldenbrand, Marilyn Louise 1939- *WhoAmW 93*
Heldenfels, Frederick William, Jr. 1911- *WhoAm 92*
Helder, Bartholomaus 1585-1635 *Baker 92*
Helderman, Bernard D. 1920- *St&PR 93*
Heldin, Carl-Henrik 1952- *WhoWor 93*
Heldman, Alan Wohl 1936- *WhoAm 92*
Heldman, Daniel Paul 1941- *WhoAm 92*
Heldman, Dennis R. 1938- *WhoAm 92*
Heldman, Gladys M. 1922- *ScF&FL 92*
Heldman, Gladys Vivian Medalie 1922- *BiDAMSp 1989*
Heldman, Louis Marc 1949- *WhoEmL 93, WhoSSW 93*
Heldman, Paul W. *Law&B 92, WhoAm 92*
Heldman, Thomas S. 1923- *St&PR 93*
Heldreth, Joseph B. 1955- *St&PR 93*
Heldreth, Leonard Guy 1939- *WhoWrEP 92*
Heldrich, Eleanor Maar 1929- *WhoAmW 93*
Heldstab, John Christian 1940- *WhoAm 92*
Heldt, Randall J. *Law&B 92*
Heldt, W.D. 1936- *St&PR 93*
Heldy, Fanny 1888-1973 *IntDcOp, OxDcOp*
Helemish, Mohamed Abdelwahab 1936- *WhoWor 93*
Helemskii, Alexander Yakovlevich 1943- *WhoWor 93*
Helen, Claude M. 1938- *WhoScE 91-2*
Helena c. 250-c. 330 *OxDcByz*
Helena, Saint *BioIn 17*
Helene, Claude M. 1938- *WhoScE 91-2*
Heleskivi, Jouni Martti 1938- *WhoScE 91-4*
Helf, Gary L. 1946- *St&PR 93*

Helf, Marvin M. 1919- *St&PR 93*
Helf, Steven *St&PR 93*
Helfand, Arthur E. 1935- *WhoAm 92, WhoE 93*
Helfand, Elizabeth 1931- *St&PR 93*
Helfand, Eugene 1934- *WhoAm 92*
Helfand, Leon 1920- *St&PR 93*
Helfand, Margaret 1947- *WhoAmW 93*
Helfand, Robert Yisrael 1955- *WhoE 93*
Helfant, Martin Barry *Law&B 92*
Helfend, Steven *Law&B 92*
Helfer, Andrew 1958- *ScF&FL 92*
Helfer, Erica Tina 1956- *WhoEmL 93*
Helfer, Jeffrey Joseph 1943- *St&PR 93*
Helfer, Michael Stevens 1945- *WhoAm 92*
Helfer, Ray E. *BioIn 17*
Helfer, Ray E. d1992 *NewYTBS 92 [port]*
Helfer, Walter 1896-1959 *Baker 92*
Helfer, Wayne C. 1941- *St&PR 93*
Helferich, Gerard Marion 1954- *WhoE 93*
Helfert, Erich Anton 1931- *WhoAm 92*
Helfert, Thomas Louis 1947- *St&PR 93*
Helfert, Vladimir 1886-1945 *Baker 92*
Helfferich, Friedrich G. 1922- *WhoAm 92*
Helfgott, Daniel 1952- *ScF&FL 92*
Helfgott, Daniel (Andrew) 1952- *WhoWrEP 92*
Helfgott, Roy B. 1925- *WhoAm 92*
Helfinstine, Kelly Ann 1957- *WhoAmW 93*
Helfman, Dennis J. *Law&B 92*
Helfman, Max 1901-1963 *Baker 92*
Helford, Irwin 1934- *St&PR 93*
Helfrecht, Gary Frederick 1947- *WhoAm 92*
Helfrich, James C. *Law&B 92*
Helfrich, Leonard J. *Law&B 92*
Helfrich, Thomas E. 1950- *WhoIns 93*
Helfrick, John James 1961- *WhoSSW 93*
Helfritz, Hans 1902- *Baker 92*
Helft, Jorge *BioIn 17*
Helft, Marion *BioIn 17*
Helft, Michael R. 1941- *St&PR 93*
Helgason, Dean Eugene 1940- *WhoWor 93*
Helgason, Haukur 1936- *WhoWor 93*
Helgason, Orn 1938- *WhoScE 91-4*
Helgason, Sigurdur 1921- *WhoWor 93*
Helgason, Sigurdur 1927- *WhoAm 92*
Helgason, Tomas 1927- *WhoScE 91-4*
Helgeland, Walter 1935- *St&PR 93*
Helgenberger, Marg *BioIn 17, ConTFT 10, WhoAmW 93*
Helgerson, John Walter 1938- *WhoAm 92*
Helgesson, Lars-Ake 1941- *WhoAm 92*
Helguera, Ignacio 1899- *DcMexL*
He liang, Tan 1942- *WhoWor 93*
Helie, Claude 1943- *St&PR 93*
Heligman, Larry 1946- *WhoUN 92*
Heliker, John 1909- *WhoAm 92*
Helin, Eleanor *BioIn 17*
Helin, James Dennis 1942- *WhoAm 92*
Helinger, Michael Green 1947- *WhoE 93, WhoEmL 93, WhoWor 93*
Helinski, Donald Raymond 1933- *WhoAm 92*
Helio, Lima 1945- *St&PR 93*
Heliodoros fl. 2nd cent.-4th cent. *OxDcByz*
Helioff, Anne Graile *WhoAm 92, WhoAmW 93, WhoWor 93*
Heliovaara, Kari T. 1954- *WhoScE 91-4*
Helke, Cinda Jane 1951- *WhoAmW 93, WhoEmL 93*
Helke, Michael 1943- *WhoUN 92*
Helland, Diane Marie *Law&B 92*
Helland, Douglas Rolf 1945- *WhoUN 92, WhoWor 93*
Helland, George Archibald, Jr. 1937- *WhoAm 92, WhoE 93*
Helland, Richard Erling 1931- *St&PR 93*
Hellauer, James Carroll 1939- *St&PR 93*
Hellawell, Robert 1928- *WhoAm 92*
Hellberg, Clifford William 1925- *St&PR 93*
Hellbusch, Jay Jay 1939- *WhoWrEP 92*
Hellebuyck, Jean-Pierre 1947- *WhoWor 93*
Helleiner, Gerald Karl 1936- *WhoAm 92*
Hellemans, Jacques Lucien 1962- *WhoWor 93*
Hellen, Betty Dianne 1944- *WhoAmW 93*
Hellen, Paul W. 1937- *St&PR 93*
Hellenbrand, Samuel Henry 1916- *St&PR 93, WhoAm 92*
Hellenbrand, Vernon John 1933- *St&PR 93*
Hellendaal, Pieter 1721-1799 *Baker 92*
Hellendale, Robert 1917- *WhoAm 92*
Hellenschmidt, Barbara J. *Law&B 92*
Hellenthal, Wolfgang 1926- *WhoScE 91-3*
Helleny, Edward Joseph 1955- *WhoEmL 93*
Heller, Adam 1933- *WhoAm 92*
Heller, Amy Anne 1957- *WhoEmL 93*
Heller, Andrew T. *Law&B 92*
Heller, Aniko Nagy *St&PR 93*
Heller, Arthur 1930- *WhoAm 92*
Heller, Blossom 1927-1990 *BioIn 17*
Heller, Bruce David 1955- *WhoEmL 93*
Heller, Cheryl *BioIn 17*
Heller, Cheryl Christine 1950- *WhoAm 92*
Heller, Clarence E. 1926- *St&PR 93*
Heller, David J. *Law&B 92*
Heller, David R. 1953- *WhoE 93*
Heller, Devorah d1991 *BioIn 17*
Heller, Donald *St&PR 93*
Heller, Douglas Max 1918- *WhoAm 92*
Heller, E. Michael 1958- *St&PR 93*
Heller, Edgar Elwood 1922- *WhoSSW 93*
Heller, Edward M. 1926- *St&PR 93*
Heller, Erich 1911-1990 *BioIn 17*
Heller, Francis Howard 1917- *WhoAm 92*
Heller, Fred 1924- *WhoAm 92*
Heller, Frederick 1932- *WhoAm 92*
Heller, George 1922- *St&PR 93*
Heller, Gerald Mark 1964- *WhoE 93*
Heller, H. Robert 1940- *BioIn 17*
Heller, Hanes A. *Law&B 92*
Heller, Hans Ewald 1894-1966 *Baker 92*
Heller, Harry George *WhoScE 91-1*
Heller, Heinz Robert 1940- *WhoAm 92, WhoWor 93*
Heller, Herbert A. 1930- *St&PR 93*
Heller, Honey Harlene 1946- *WhoAmW 93*
Heller, Ira I. 1954- *St&PR 93*
Heller, J. Roderick, III 1937- *St&PR 93*
Heller, Jack Isaac 1932- *WhoAm 92*
Heller, James G. 1892-1971 *Baker 92*
Heller, Janet Ruth 1949- *WhoWrEP 92*
Heller, Jeffrey S. *Law&B 92*
Heller, Jessy *Law&B 92*
Heller, John 1949- *St&PR 93*
Heller, John Herbert 1921- *WhoAm 92*
Heller, John L., II 1953- *WhoEmL 93*
Heller, John Roderick, III 1937- *WhoAm 92*
Heller, Jonathan L. *Law&B 92*
Heller, Joseph *BioIn 17*
Heller, Joseph 1923- *MagSAmL [port], ScF&FL 92, WhoAm 92, WhoWrEP 92, WorLitC [port]*
Heller, Jules 1919- *WhoAm 92*
Heller, Julia Marcia *Law&B 92*
Heller, Leon *Law&B 92*
Heller, Lois Jane 1942- *WhoAmW 93*
Heller, Marc *WhoWrEP 92*
Heller, Mark 1955- *WhoEmL 93, WhoWor 93*
Heller, Marlene Ann 1953- *WhoWrEP 92*
Heller, Michael David 1937- *WhoE 93*
Heller, Mitchell Thomas 1948- *WhoAm 92*
Heller, Norman 1927- *St&PR 93*
Heller, Pamela 1954- *WhoE 93*
Heller, Paul *Law&B 92*
Heller, Paul 1914- *WhoAm 92*
Heller, Paul Michael 1927- *WhoAm 92*
Heller, Peter 1920- *WhoE 93*
Heller, Peter S. 1946- *WhoUN 92*
Heller, Philip 1952- *WhoEmL 93*
Heller, Preston B., Jr. 1929- *St&PR 93*
Heller, Preston Benjamin, Jr. 1929- *WhoAm 92*
Heller, Rachael F. *BioIn 17*
Heller, Reinhold August 1940- *WhoAm 92*
Heller, Richard F. *BioIn 17*
Heller, Robert Andrew 1928- *WhoSSW 93*
Heller, Robert H. 1940- *St&PR 93*
Heller, Robert James 1934- *WhoSSW 93*
Heller, Robert Leo 1919- *WhoAm 92*
Heller, Robert Martin 1942- *WhoAm 92*
Heller, Ronald G. *Law&B 92*
Heller, Ronald G. 1946- *St&PR 93*
Heller, Ronald Gary 1946- *WhoAm 92*
Heller, Ronald Ian 1956- *WhoAm 92, WhoEmL 93*
Heller, Ruth *BioIn 17*
Heller, Stephen (Istvan) 1813-1888 *Baker 92*
Heller, Stephen Richard 1943- *WhoE 93*
Heller, Steve 1949- *WhoE 93*
Heller, Stuart S. *Law&B 92*
Heller, Terry 1947- *ScF&FL 92*
Heller, Theodore F. 1942- *St&PR 93, WhoIns 93*
Heller, Walter W. *BioIn 17*
Heller, William Benjamin d1991 *BioIn 17*
Heller, William Russell 1920- *WhoAm 92*
Heller, Zachary I. *WhoAm 92*
Hellerman, Fred 1927- *WhoAm 92*
See Also Weavers, The *ConMus 8*
Hellerman, Marvin Lawrence 1927- *WhoAm 92, WhoE 93*
Hellers, Bo Goran 1939- *WhoScE 91-4*
Hellerson, Robert Keith 1944- *St&PR 93*
Hellerstein, Alvin Kenneth 1933- *WhoAm 92*
Hellerstein, David Joel 1953- *WhoEmL 93*
Hellerstein, Jerome Robert 1907- *WhoAm 92*
Hellerstein, Nina Salant 1946- *WhoSSW 93*
Hellerstein, Walter 1946- *WhoEmL 93*
Hellerstrom, Claes 1932- *WhoScE 91-4*
Helles, Finn 1938- *WhoScE 91-2*
Hellew, Joyce Virginia 1949- *WhoWrEP 92*
Hellgren, Lars G.I. 1930- *WhoScE 91-4*
Hellickson, Dean Robert 1962- *WhoEmL 93, WhoSSW 93*
Hellickson, Kazuko Sato 1947- *WhoEmL 93*
Hellie, Richard 1937- *WhoAm 92, WhoWrEP 92*
Helliker, Carol R. *Law&B 92*
Helliker, Steven A. 1948- *WhoE 93*
Hellinck, Lupus (Wulfaert) c. 1496-1541 *Baker 92*
Helling, Charles Siver 1940- *WhoE 93*
Helling, Dennis Keith 1948- *WhoAm 92*
Helling, Jurgen 1928- *WhoScE 91-3*
Hellinger, Douglas A(lan) 1948- *WhoWrEP 92*
Hellinger, Gary Lloyd 1940- *St&PR 93*
Hellinger, Marilyn 1941- *St&PR 93*
Hellinger, Stephen H(enry) 1948- *WhoWrEP 92*
Hellinx, Willy Bernard 1945- *WhoE 93*
Helliwell, David Leedom 1935- *WhoAm 92*
Helliwell, John Richard *WhoScE 91-1*
Helliwell, John Richard 1953- *WhoWor 93*
Helliwell, Thomas McCaffree 1936- *WhoAm 92*
Hellman, Arthur David 1942- *WhoAm 92*
Hellman, Bo O.A. 1930- *WhoScE 91-4*
Hellman, Bo Olof Alexander 1930- *WhoWor 93*
Hellman, F. Warren 1934- *St&PR 93*
Hellman, Frances 1956- *WhoAmW 93*
Hellman, Frederick Warren 1934- *WhoAm 92, WhoWor 93*
Hellman, Glenn M. 1952- *St&PR 93*
Hellman, Hal 1927- *WhoWrEP 92*
Hellman, Herbert M. *Law&B 92*
Hellman, Herbert M. 1943- *St&PR 93*
Hellman, Herbert Martin 1943- *WhoAm 92*
Hellman, Jack M. 1931- *St&PR 93*
Hellman, Jane Elizabeth 1934- *WhoAmW 93*
Hellman, Jay M. 1941- *St&PR 93*
Hellman, Jerome 1928- *MiSFD 9*
Hellman, Lillian 1905-1984 *MagSAmL [port]*
Hellman, Lillian 1906-1984 *BioIn 17*
Hellman, Louis M. 1908-1990 *BioIn 17*
Hellman, Madie G. *Law&B 92*
Hellman, Monte 1932- *MiSFD 9*
Hellman, Murray 1934- *St&PR 93*
Hellman, Patrick D. 1941- *St&PR 93*
Hellman, Per *BioIn 17*
Hellman, Peter S. 1949- *St&PR 93*
Hellman, Peter Stuart 1949- *WhoAm 92, WhoEmL 93*
Hellman, Samuel 1934- *WhoAm 92*
Hellman, Sheila Almer 1928- *WhoWrEP 92*
Hellman, Thomas A. 1944- *St&PR 93*
Hellman, William 1920- *St&PR 93*
Hellmandonna, Lee 1958- *WhoWrEP 92*
Hellmann, Donald Charles 1933- *WhoAm 92*
Hellmann, Norma Janelle 1949- *WhoAm 92*
Hellmann, Selden Stuart, Jr. 1930- *St&PR 93*
Hellmann, Sylvia 1911- *BioIn 17*
Hellmesberger *Baker 92*
Hellmesberger, Ferdinand 1863-1940 *Baker 92*
Hellmesberger, George, Sr. 1800-1873 *Baker 92*
Hellmesberger, George, Jr. 1830-1852 *Baker 92*
Hellmesberger, Joseph, Sr. 1828-1893 *Baker 92*
Hellmesberger, Joseph, Jr. 1855-1907 *Baker 92*
Hellmold, Ralph O. 1940- *WhoAm 92*
Hellmuth, C.T. 1926- *WhoIns 93*
Hellmuth, George Francis 1907- *WhoAm 92, WhoWor 93*
Hellmuth, James G. 1923- *St&PR 93*
Hellmuth, Theodore Henning 1949- *WhoEmL 93*
Hellmuth, William Frederick, Jr. 1920- *WhoAm 92*
Hellriegel, Martin B. 1890-1981 *BioIn 17*
Hellring, Bernard 1916-1991 *BioIn 17*
Hellrung, Stephen A. *Law&B 92*
Hellrung, Stephen Andrew 1947- *WhoAm 92*
Hellstern, Gerd-Michael 1947- *WhoWor 93*
Hellstrom, Gunnar *MiSFD 9*
Hellstrom, John G. 1929- *St&PR 93*
Hellstrom, Kjell H.S. 1930- *WhoScE 91-4*
Hellstrom, Ward 1930- *WhoSSW 93*
Hellums, Jesse David 1929- *WhoAm 92*
Hellwarth, Robert Willis 1930- *WhoAm 92*
Hellwege, Donald J. *Law&B 92*
Hellwig, Frank Z. *Law&B 92*
Hellwig, Helmut Wilhelm 1938- *WhoAm 92*
Hellwig, Karl (Friedrich) Ludwig 1773-1838 *Baker 92*
Helly, Walter Sigmund 1930- *WhoAm 92*
Hellyer, Clement David 1914- *WhoAm 92*
Hellyer, Constance Anne 1937- *WhoAmW 93*
Hellyer, Timothy Michael 1954- *WhoWor 93*
Helm, Anny 1903- *Baker 92*
Helm, Buck *BioIn 17*
Helm, Deborah Kathryn 1950- *WhoAmW 93*
Helm, DeWitt Frederick, Jr. 1933- *WhoAm 92*
Helm, Donald Cairney 1937- *WhoAm 92*
Helm, E(rnest) Eugene 1928- *Baker 92*
Helm, Everett (Burton) 1913- *Baker 92*
Helm, Frederick 1926- *WhoAm 92*
Helm, George Neville, III 1954- *WhoEmL 93*
Helm, Hugh Barnett 1914- *WhoSSW 93, WhoWor 93*
Helm, Jack d1873 *BioIn 17*
Helm, James M. 1947- *St&PR 93*
Helm, Joan Mary 1934- *WhoAmW 93*
Helm, Jolene DeAnn 1950- *WhoSSW 93*
Helm, Joseph Burge 1931- *WhoAm 92*
Helm, June 1924- *WhoAm 92*
Helm, Levon 1942-
See Band, The *ConMus 9*
Helm, Lewis Marshall 1931- *WhoAm 92*
Helm, Lorraine Lipski 1947- *WhoAmW 93*
Helm, Mike 1942- *WhoWrEP 92*
Helm, Murray M., Jr. *Law&B 92*
Helm, P. Ralph 1926- *St&PR 93*
Helm, Percy Ralph 1926- *WhoAm 92, WhoWor 93*
Helm, Robert Meredith 1917- *WhoAm 92*
Helm, Roger M. 1941- *St&PR 93*
Helm, Shelli Lynn 1956- *WhoSSW 93*
Helm, Sherrell 1935- *St&PR 93*
Helm, Theodor (Otto) 1843-1920 *Baker 92*
Helman, Alfred Blair 1920- *WhoAm 92*
Helman, Andrea Jean 1946- *WhoWrEP 92*
Helman, Barry Saul 1939- *St&PR 93*
Helman, Gerald Bernard 1932- *WhoAm 92*
Helman, Henri *MiSFD 9*
Helman, Joseph Arthur 1937- *WhoAm 92*
Helman, Mark A. *Law&B 92*
Helman, Richard K. *Law&B 92*
Helman, Robert Alan 1934- *WhoAm 92*
Helman, William Wilson 1928- *St&PR 93*
Helmbold, Nancy Pearce 1918- *WhoAm 92*
Helmbold, William Ross 1947- *WhoWor 93*
Helmchen, Hanfried 1933- *WhoScE 91-3, WhoWor 93*
Helme, Edward Alfred 1947- *WhoAm 92*
Helmeczi, Balazs 1928- *WhoScE 91-4*
Helmer, David Alan 1946- *WhoEmL 93, WhoWor 93*
Helmer, Hamilton Wright 1947- *WhoEmL 93*
Helmer, Paul John 1926- *St&PR 93*
Helmer, Star 1950- *WhoWrEP 92*
Helmerich, Hans Christian 1958- *St&PR 93, WhoAm 92*
Helmerich, W.H., III 1923- *St&PR 93*
Helmericks, Harmon 1917- *WhoAm 92*
Helmers, Carl 1948- *St&PR 93*
Helmers, Eric V. *Law&B 92*
Helmes, L. Scott 1945- *WhoWrEP 92*
Helmetag, Carl 1948- *WhoAm 92, WhoE 93, WhoEmL 93*
Helmetag, Carl, III 1947- *St&PR 93*
Helmetag, Charles Hugh 1935- *WhoAm 92*
Helmholtz, Hermann (Ludwig Ferdinand) von 1821-1894 *Baker 92*
Helmholz, August Carl 1915- *WhoAm 92*
Helmholz, Richard Henry 1940- *WhoAm 92*
Helmick, Aileen Barnett 1930- *WhoWor 93*
Helmick, Charles Gardiner, III 1950- *WhoEmL 93*
Helmick, L.G., Jr. 1920- *St&PR 93*
Helmick, Robert *BioIn 17*
Helmick, Susan Taylor 1945- *St&PR 93*
Helminen, H.J. 1943- *WhoScE 91-4*
Helming, Larry 1942- *St&PR 93*
Helming, Scott Bryon 1953- *WhoEmL 93*
Helminger, Paul Andrew 1941- *WhoSSW 93*
Helminiak, Daniel Albert 1942- *WhoSSW 93*
Helminski, Camille Adams 1951- *WhoEmL 93*

Henderson, Ann 1951- *WhoAmW 93, WhoSSW 93*
Henderson, Archibald 1877-1963 *BioIn 17*
Henderson, Archibald 1916- *WhoWrEP 92*
Henderson, Arnold Glenn 1934- *WhoAm 92*
Henderson, Arthur P., Jr. 1943- *St&PR 93*
Henderson, Arvis Burl 1943- *WhoSSW 93, WhoWor 93*
Henderson, Bernard Levie, Jr. 1950- *WhoAm 92*
Henderson, Betty W. 1933- *St&PR 93*
Henderson, Brian *WhoScE 91-1*
Henderson, Brian Edmond 1937- *WhoAm 92*
Henderson, Bruce B. 1946- *ConAu 139*
Henderson, Bruce D. 1915-1992 *NewYTBS 92 [port]*
Henderson, Bruce Doolin 1915- *WhoAm 92*
Henderson, Bruce E. *Law&B 92*
Henderson, Bruce Raymond 1948- *WhoWrEP 92*
Henderson, Butler *BioIn 17*
Henderson, C.J. 1951- *ScF&FL 92*
Henderson, C.R. 1911-1989 *BioIn 17*
Henderson, Carol Lee 1957- *WhoEmL 93*
Henderson, Charles Brooke 1929- *WhoAm 92, WhoSSW 93*
Henderson, Charles L. *Law&B 92*
Henderson, Charles R. 1911-1989 *BioIn 17*
Henderson, Clark *MiSFD 9*
Henderson, Claude Brooks 1925- *WhoSSW 93*
Henderson, Clay 1955- *WhoSSW 93*
Henderson, Clyde H. 1946- *St&PR 93*
Henderson, Cole 1960- *WhoE 93*
Henderson, Conway Wilson 1942- *WhoSSW 93*
Henderson, Cynthia Rena 1967- *WhoAmW 93*
Henderson, Dan 1953?-1991 *ScF&FL 92*
Henderson, Dan Fenno 1921- *WhoAm 92, WhoWor 93*
Henderson, Daniel *Law&B 92*
Henderson, Daniel Gardner 1941- *WhoE 93*
Henderson, Dave *BioIn 17*
Henderson, David B. 1840-1906 *PolPar*
Henderson, David Lesley 1942- *WhoSSW 93*
Henderson, David Steven 1965- *WhoSSW 93*
Henderson, Debra Lynn 1964- *WhoAmW 93*
Henderson, Deirdre Healy 1942- *WhoAmW 93*
Henderson, Denise Laureen 1952- *WhoEmL 93*
Henderson, Denys 1932- *St&PR 93*
Henderson, Denys H. *BioIn 17*
Henderson, Diana Elizabeth 1957- *WhoAmW 93, WhoEmL 93*
Henderson, Donald *ConAu 138*
Henderson, Donald 1938- *WhoAm 92*
Henderson, Donald Ainslie 1928- *WhoAm 92*
Henderson, Donald Blanton 1949- *WhoEmL 93, WhoSSW 93*
Henderson, Donald Eugene 1955- *WhoSSW 93*
Henderson, Donald Grey 1957- *WhoSSW 93*
Henderson, Dorland John 1898- *WhoAm 92*
Henderson, Douglas Boyd 1935- *WhoAm 92, WhoE 93, WhoWor 93*
Henderson, Dwight Franklin 1937- *WhoAm 92, WhoSSW 93*
Henderson, Edward Hugh 1939- *WhoSSW 93*
Henderson, Edward P. d1992 *NewYTBS 92*
Henderson, Edward Richards *Law&B 92*
Henderson, Edward Shelton 1932- *WhoAm 92*
Henderson, Edwin Harold 1927- *WhoAm 92*
Henderson, Edyth May 1945- *WhoAmW 93*
Henderson, Eli Camden 1890-1956 *BiDAMSp 1989*
Henderson, Erma 1917- *AfrAmBi*
Henderson, Ernest, III 1924- *St&PR 93, WhoAm 92*
Henderson, Erskine D. 1949- *WhoWrEP 92*
Henderson, Euan Scott *WhoScE 91-1*
Henderson, Eugene Leroy 1925- *WhoAm 92*
Henderson, Fergus *Law&B 92*
Henderson, (James) Fletcher 1897-1952 *Baker 92*
Henderson, Florence 1934- *BioIn 17, WhoAm 92*
Henderson, Frank Ellis 1928- *WhoAm 92*
Henderson, Frederick B. 1941- *St&PR 93*
Henderson, Garry Couch 1935- *WhoE 93*
Henderson, Gary D. *Law&B 92*
Henderson, George *WhoScE 91-1*
Henderson, George 1932- *WhoAm 92*
Henderson, George Miller 1915- *WhoAm 92*
Henderson, Gerald Gordon Lewis 1926- *WhoAm 92*
Henderson, Geraldine Thomas 1924- *WhoAmW 93*
Henderson, Gertrude Mevis 1888- *AmWomPl*
Henderson, Gladys Sigler *AmWomPl*
Henderson, Gloria Mason 1936- *WhoSSW 93*
Henderson, Gordon *BioIn 17*
Henderson, Gordon J. *Law&B 92*
Henderson, Grace Van Schoen Der Woert Hogeboom *AmWomPl*
Henderson, Greer F. 1932- *WhoIns 93*
Henderson, Greer Francis 1932- *St&PR 93*
Henderson, H.F. *WhoScE 91-3*
Henderson, H. Harry 1926- *St&PR 93*
Henderson, Harold R. 1942- *St&PR 93*
Henderson, Harold Richard, Jr. 1942- *WhoAm 92*
Henderson, Harriet *BioIn 17*
Henderson, Harriet 1949- *WhoAm 92, WhoAmW 93, WhoSSW 93*
Henderson, Harry Brinton, Jr. 1914- *WhoAm 92, WhoWrEP 92*
Henderson, Hazel 1933- *WhoSSW 93*
Henderson, Henry F., Jr. *AfrAmBi [port]*
Henderson, Herbert 1951- *St&PR 93*
Henderson, Herbert Wayne 1953- *WhoE 93*
Henderson, Horace Edward *WhoAm 92*
Henderson, Howard Bart 1957- *WhoSSW 93*
Henderson, Howard DeWeese 1907- *WhoAm 92*
Henderson, Hubert Platt 1918- *WhoAm 92*
Henderson, James A. 1934- *St&PR 93*
Henderson, James Alan 1934- *WhoAm 92*
Henderson, James Alexander 1921- *WhoAm 92*
Henderson, James David 1942- *WhoSSW 93*
Henderson, James Gary 1954- *WhoEmL 93*
Henderson, James Harold 1948- *WhoEmL 93, WhoWor 93*
Henderson, James L. 1921- *St&PR 93*
Henderson, James Marvin 1921- *St&PR 93, WhoAm 92*
Henderson, James Taylor 1931- *WhoSSW 93*
Henderson, Jana L. 1944- *WhoAmW 93*
Henderson, Jane Whalen 1913- *WhoAmW 93*
Henderson, Jeanne Lynne 1961- *WhoAmW 93*
Henderson, Jerry Y. 1938- *St&PR 93*
Henderson, Jessie E. *AmWomPl*
Henderson, Joe *BioIn 17*
Henderson, John Atkins *Law&B 92*
Henderson, John Brown 1918- *WhoAm 92*
Henderson, John Drews 1933- *WhoAm 92*
Henderson, John Thomson *WhoScE 91-1*
Henderson, John W. *Law&B 92*
Henderson, John Woodworth 1916- *WhoAm 92*
Henderson, Jon Loren 1951- *St&PR 93*
Henderson, Joseph Welles 1920- *WhoAm 92*
Henderson, Joshua 1965- *WhoSSW 93*
Henderson, Julian Crowder 1938- *WhoSSW 93*
Henderson, Julie K. 1950- *WhoWrEP 92*
Henderson, Julie L. *Law&B 92*
Henderson, Karen 1954- *WhoE 93, WhoEmL 93*
Henderson, Karen Jane 1955- *WhoEmL 93*
Henderson, Karen LeCraft 1944- *WhoAm 92, WhoAmW 93, WhoE 93*
Henderson, Kathleen Hayden 1919- *WhoWrEP 92*
Henderson, Kathleen Susan 1952- *WhoWrEP 92*
Henderson, Kathryn Luther *WhoAmW 93*
Henderson, Kaye Neil 1933- *WhoAm 92, WhoSSW 93*
Henderson, Kenneth Atwood 1905- *WhoE 93, WhoWor 93*
Henderson, Kenneth Douglas 1951- *WhoEmL 93*
Henderson, Kevin A. 1950- *WhoAm 92*
Henderson, Kevin James *Law&B 92*
Henderson, Kyle W. *Law&B 92*
Henderson, Larry Alvin 1937- *St&PR 93*
Henderson, Larry Ray 1950- *WhoEmL 93, WhoSSW 93*
Henderson, Lenneal Joseph, Jr. 1946- *WhoAm 92*
Henderson, Lother Salome 1952- *WhoE 93*
Henderson, Louis Clifton, Jr. 1937- *WhoAm 92*
Henderson, Loy Wesley 1892-1986 *BioIn 17*
Henderson, Lucile d1990 *BioIn 17*
Henderson, Luther A. 1920- *St&PR 93*
Henderson, Lynn Allyson *Law&B 92*
Henderson, Madeline Mary 1922- *WhoAm 92*
Henderson, Marc C. 1959- *St&PR 93*
Henderson, Maria Eleanor 1949- *WhoSSW 93*
Henderson, Marilyn Ann 1949- *WhoEmL 93*
Henderson, Marilyn Ruth 1927- *WhoAmW 93*
Henderson, Marion K. *Law&B 92*
Henderson, Marsha Roslyn Thaw 1946- *WhoAmW 93*
Henderson, Marvin L. 1943- *WhoSSW 93*
Henderson, Mary Blanton 1964- *WhoAmW 93*
Henderson, Mary C. 1928- *WhoAmW 93*
Henderson, Mary Louise 1928- *WhoAmW 93*
Henderson, Maureen McGrath 1926- *WhoAm 92, WhoAmW 93*
Henderson, Maurice Brian 1961- *WhoWrEP 92*
Henderson, Maxine Olive Book 1924- *WhoAmW 93*
Henderson, Melford J. 1950- *WhoEmL 93*
Henderson, Melody Massee 1963- *WhoAmW 93*
Henderson, Michael Douglas 1932- *WhoWrEP 92*
Henderson, Michael K. 1954- *St&PR 93*
Henderson, Mildred K. 1931- *WhoWrEP 92*
Henderson, Milton Arnold 1922- *WhoAm 92*
Henderson, Mina Louise *AmWomPl*
Henderson, Nancy Grace 1947- *WhoAmW 93*
Henderson, Neil M. 1942- *St&PR 93*
Henderson, Nolan B. *Law&B 92*
Henderson, Patricia Letourneau 1962- *WhoAmW 93*
Henderson, Patrick David 1927- *WhoWor 93*
Henderson, Paul 1884-1951 *EncABHB 8 [port]*
Henderson, Paul Audine 1925- *WhoAm 92*
Henderson, Paul Bargas, Jr. 1928- *WhoAm 92*
Henderson, Peter *WhoScE 91-1*
Henderson, Peter Ben 1936- *St&PR 93*
Henderson, Philip 1906-1977 *ScF&FL 92*
Henderson, Phillip Theodore 1945- *St&PR 93*
Henderson, Ralph Hale 1937- *WhoAm 92, WhoUN 92, WhoWor 93*
Henderson, Randy 1952- *WhoSSW 93*
Henderson, Ray(mond) 1896-1970 *Baker 92*
Henderson, Richard *WhoScE 91-1*
Henderson, Richard 1916- *WhoE 93*
Henderson, Richard 1928- *St&PR 93*
Henderson, Richard Albert, III 1943- *WhoAm 92*
Henderson, Richard Anthony *WhoScE 91-1*
Henderson, Richard C. *Law&B 92*
Henderson, Richard Cleveland, III 1948- *St&PR 93*
Henderson, Richard Colin *Law&B 92*
Henderson, Rickey *BioIn 17*
Henderson, Rickey 1958- *AfrAmBi*
Henderson, Rickey Henley 1958- *WhoAm 92*
Henderson, Robbye Robinson 1937- *WhoAm 92*
Henderson, Robert Alan *Law&B 92*
Henderson, Robert C. 1940- *St&PR 93*
Henderson, Robert Cameron 1940- *WhoAm 92*
Henderson, Robert Earl 1935- *WhoAm 92*
Henderson, Robert Franklin, Jr. 1944- *WhoAm 92*
Henderson, Robert Gordon 1903-1989 *BioIn 17*
Henderson, Robert Jules 1943- *WhoAm 92*
Henderson, Robert Morton 1931- *WhoSSW 93*
Henderson, Robert W. 1925- *St&PR 93*
Henderson, Robert Waugh 1920- *WhoAm 92*
Henderson, Roberta Marie 1929- *WhoAmW 93*
Henderson, Rodney James 1946- *St&PR 93*
Henderson, Roger C. 1938- *WhoAm 92*
Henderson, Roger D. 1953- *St&PR 93*
Henderson, Ronald A. 1946- *St&PR 93*
Henderson, Ronald Holstein 1931- *WhoSSW 93*
Henderson, Ronald Wilbur 1933- *WhoAm 92*
Henderson, Roy 1899- *OxDcOp*
Henderson, Roy (Galbraith) 1899- *Baker 92*
Henderson, Ruth Evelyn *AmWomPl*
Henderson, S.M. *Law&B 92*
Henderson, Safiya (Sharon) 1950- *WhoWrEP 92*
Henderson, Samuel Judson, III *Law&B 92*
Henderson, Sandra Lee 1943- *WhoAmW 93*
Henderson, Sara *AmWomPl*
Henderson, Shirley Johnson 1946- *WhoSSW 93*
Henderson, "Skitch" 1918- *Baker 92, WhoAm 92*
Henderson, Sonya Lee 1960- *WhoSSW 93*
Henderson, Stanley Dale 1935- *WhoAm 92*
Henderson, Stephen P. *Law&B 92*
Henderson, Susan Ayleen 1945- *WhoAmW 93*
Henderson, T.J. *St&PR 93*
Henderson, Tamara Lynn 1966- *WhoAmW 93*
Henderson, Terrill Leland *Law&B 92*
Henderson, Thomas K. *Law&B 92*
Henderson, Thomas K. 1940- *St&PR 93*
Henderson, Thomas Shields 1932- *St&PR 93*
Henderson, Victor Maurice 1924- *WhoWrEP 92*
Henderson, W(illiam) J(ames) 1855-1937 *Baker 92*
Henderson, W.T.K. *WhoScE 91-1*
Henderson, W.W. 1927- *St&PR 93*
Henderson, Walter G. 1930- *St&PR 93, WhoAm 92*
Henderson, Wellington *BioIn 17*
Henderson, William Boyd 1928- *WhoAm 92*
Henderson, William Boyd 1936- *WhoAm 92*
Henderson, William Charles 1941- *WhoAm 92, WhoE 93, WhoWrEP 92*
Henderson, William Lee 1929- *St&PR 93*
Henderson, William Wilmot 1926- *St&PR 93*
Henderson, Willie 1941- *BioIn 17*
Henderson, Zenna 1917-1983 *ScF&FL 92*
Henderson, Zenna 1917-1989 *BioIn 17*
Henderson-Dixon, Karen Sue 1946- *WhoAm 92*
Hendig, Klaus G. 1939- *St&PR 93*
Hendin, David 1945- *St&PR 93*
Hendin, David Bruce 1945- *WhoAm 92*
Hendin, Roy Allen *Law&B 92*
Hendl, Walter 1917- *Baker 92, WhoAm 92*
Hendler, Edwin 1922- *WhoE 93*
Hendler, Mark Stephen 1948- *WhoEmL 93*
Hendler, Samuel I. 1922- *St&PR 93, WhoAm 92*
Hendler, Yehudi Leon 1944- *St&PR 93*
Hendley, Dan Lunsford 1938- *WhoAm 92, WhoSSW 93*
Hendley, Edith Di Pasquale 1927- *WhoAmW 93, WhoE 93*
Hendley, James C. 1908- *St&PR 93*
Hendon, Betty Joyce 1935- *WhoSSW 93*
Hendon, Marvin Keith 1960- *WhoSSW 93*
Hendon, Robert Caraway 1912- *WhoAm 92*
Hendra, Barbara Jane 1938- *WhoAmW 93*
Hendrawan, Frans 1936- *WhoWor 93*
Hendren, Gary E. 1943- *WhoAm 92*
Hendren, Jo Ann 1935- *WhoSSW 93*
Hendren, Merlyn Churchill 1926- *WhoAmW 93*
Hendren, Robert Lee, Jr. 1925- *WhoAm 92*
Hendrich, Paula 1928- *ScF&FL 92*
Hendrichs, Wolfgang 1926- *WhoScE 91-3*
Hendrick, Eugene 1952- *WhoScE 91-3*
Hendrick, George 1929- *WhoAm 92*
Hendrick, George Andrew, Jr. 1949- *BiDAMSp 1989*
Hendrick, Gerald P. 1949- *St&PR 93*
Hendrick, Howard H. 1954- *WhoAm 92, WhoSSW 93*
Hendrick, Irving Guilford 1936- *WhoAm 92*
Hendrick, J.R., III *BioIn 17*
Hendrick, James Pomeroy 1901-1990 *BioIn 17*
Hendrick, Jean Patrick 1942- *WhoAmW 93*
Hendrick, Keith Coleman 1926- *WhoAm 92*
Hendrick, Ronald L. 1946- *St&PR 93*
Hendrick, Veronica Connors 1932- *WhoAmW 93*
Hendricks, Adeline *AmWomPl*
Hendricks, Barbara *BioIn 17*

Hendricks, Barbara 1948- Baker 92, ConBlB 3 [port], OxDcOp, WhoAm 92, WhoAmW 93
Hendricks, Brian James 1948- WhoWor 93
Hendricks, Bruce J. Law&B 92
Hendricks, Charles Francis 1943- St&PR 93
Hendricks, Charles Henning 1917- WhoAm 92
Hendricks, Curtis B., Jr. Law&B 92
Hendricks, Donald Duane 1931- WhoAm 92
Hendricks, Duane C. Law&B 92
Hendricks, Ed Jerald 1935- WhoAm 92
Hendricks, Edward David 1946- WhoAm 92
Hendricks, Geoffrey 1931- WhoAm 92
Hendricks, Jack E. 1948- WhoEmL 93
Hendricks, James Edwin 1935- WhoAm 92
Hendricks, James Powell 1938- WhoAm 92
Hendricks, John Aloysius 1940- St&PR 93
Hendricks, John K. Law&B 92
Hendricks, Joseph Avery 1942- St&PR 93
Hendricks, Katherine 1949- WhoEmL 93
Hendricks, Kathleen 1939- WhoWrEP 92
Hendricks, Kenneth A. 1941- ConEn
Hendricks, Marla Karen 1954- WhoAmW 93
Hendricks, Maureen BioIn 17
Hendricks, Nancy Ann 1960- St&PR 93
Hendricks, Paige Kelly 1949- WhoEmL 93, WhoSSW 93
Hendricks, Rayman Michael 1937- WhoAm 92
Hendricks, Richard Larry 1960- WhoSSW 93
Hendricks, Robert Bruce 1934- St&PR 93
Hendricks, Robert Michael 1943- WhoIns 93, WhoWor 93
Hendricks, Robert Wayne 1937- WhoSSW 93
Hendricks, S. Kenneth 1941- St&PR 93
Hendricks, Suzanne Haskins 1940- WhoAmW 93
Hendricks, Ted BioIn 17
Hendricks, Terence Rapier Law&B 92
Hendricks, Thomas A. 1819-1885 PolPar
Hendricks, Thomas L. 1940- St&PR 93
Hendricks, Thomas M. 1935- St&PR 93
Hendricks, Thomas Manley 1949- WhoWrEP 92
Hendricks, William H. 1932- St&PR 93
Hendricks, William Hulin 1932- WhoAm 92
Hendricks, William L. d1992 BioIn 17, NewYTBS 92
Hendricks, William Lawrence 1929- WhoSSW 93
Hendrickse, Ralph George WhoScE 91-1
Hendrickson, Alan Bryce 1945- WhoE 93
Hendrickson, Boyde W. 1945- WhoSSW 93
Hendrickson, Bruce C. 1930- WhoIns 93
Hendrickson, Bruce Carl 1930- WhoAm 92
Hendrickson, Candace Sue 1959- WhoEmL 93
Hendrickson, Carl H. Law&B 92
Hendrickson, Carol Follmuth 1920- WhoWrEP 92
Hendrickson, Charles John 1950- St&PR 93, WhoAm 92
Hendrickson, Chris Thompson 1950- WhoE 93
Hendrickson, Constance Marie McRight 1949- WhoAm 92, WhoEmL 93, WhoSSW 93
Hendrickson, Darlene 1941- St&PR 93
Hendrickson, Donald S. St&PR 93
Hendrickson, J. Wilbur, Jr. 1919- St&PR 93
Hendrickson, Jeffrey Thomas 1944- WhoAm 92
Hendrickson, Jerome Orland 1918- WhoAm 92
Hendrickson, Jo Ann Elizabeth 1944- WhoWrEP 92
Hendrickson, John S. Law&B 92
Hendrickson, Kevin Hugh 1953- WhoEmL 93
Hendrickson, Lisa A. 1958- WhoAmW 93
Hendrickson, Marshall D. 1935- St&PR 93
Hendrickson, Marshall David 1935- WhoAm 92
Hendrickson, Mary Angela 1953- WhoE 93
Hendrickson, Mona Lynn 1951- WhoEmL 93
Hendrickson, Olaf Knute 1961- WhoWor 93
Hendrickson, R. David Law&B 92
Hendrickson, Robert Augustus 1923- WhoAm 92
Hendrickson, Robert Frederick 1933- WhoAm 92
Hendrickson, Robert M. 1929- St&PR 93
Hendrickson, Roland M. 1923- St&PR 93
Hendrickson, Susan 1958- WhoAmW 93
Hendrickson, Susan Emery 1966- WhoAmW 93
Hendrickson, Thomas N. 1942- St&PR 93
Hendrickson, Tom Allen 1935- St&PR 93
Hendrickson, Vanessa M. 1959- WhoEmL 93
Hendrickson, Walter B., Jr. 1936- ScF&FL 92
Hendrickson, William George 1918- WhoWor 93
Hendrickx, J.M.H. 1948- WhoScE 91-3
Hendrie, Elaine WhoAmW 93
Hendrie, Joseph Mallam 1925- WhoAm 92
Hendriks, J.A.H. 1925- WhoScE 91-3
Hendriks, Ludger 1947- WhoScE 91-3
Hendrikson, Lisa A. 1960- St&PR 93
Hendriksz, Anton Rene 1948- St&PR 93
Hendrix, Claude Raymond 1889-1944 BiDAMSp 1989
Hendrix, David Woodrow 1951- WhoSSW 93
Hendrix, Dennis Ralph 1940- St&PR 93, WhoAm 92, WhoSSW 93
Hendrix, Floyd Fuller, Jr. 1933- WhoSSW 93
Hendrix, Grady Hinson 1933- WhoSSW 93
Hendrix, Howard V. 1959- ScF&FL 92
Hendrix, James Easton 1941- WhoAm 92
Hendrix, James Walter 1930- WhoAm 92
Hendrix, Jimi BioIn 17
Hendrix, Jimi 1942-1970 Baker 92, SoulM
Hendrix, Jon Richard 1938- WhoAm 92
Hendrix, Loren Ervin 1942- WhoE 93
Hendrix, Louise Butts 1911- WhoWor 93
Hendrix, Marvin L. 1942- St&PR 93
Hendrix, Michael 1937- St&PR 93
Hendrix, Randy Lee 1956- WhoEmL 93
Hendrix, Rebecca Louise Johns 1942- WhoAmW 93
Hendrix, Robert E. 1946- St&PR 93
Hendrix, Rufus Sam, Jr. 1949- WhoAm 92
Hendrix, Sarah Elizabeth 1948- WhoSSW 93
Hendrix, Stephen C. 1941- WhoAm 92
Hendrix, Susan Clelia Derrick 1920- WhoAmW 93
Hendrix-Ward, Nancy Katherine 1944- WhoAmW 93
Hendry, Aaron W. 1936- St&PR 93
Hendry, Alan WhoScE 91-1
Hendry, Andrew D. Law&B 92
Hendry, Andrew Dalency WhoAm 92
Hendry, Camilla Jean 1963- WhoSSW 93
Hendry, Diana 1941- BioIn 17, ConAu 136
Hendry, Frances Mary ScF&FL 92
Hendry, George Orr 1937- St&PR 93, WhoAm 92
Hendry, James E. 1912- WhoSSW 93
Hendry, Jean Sharon 1947- WhoAm 92, WhoAmW 93, WhoE 93
Hendry, Joe B., Jr. BioIn 17
Hendry, John WhoScE 91-1
Hendry, John (Lovat) 1952- ConAu 136
Hendry, Leo Brough WhoScE 91-1
Hendry, Lloyd G. 1922- St&PR 93
Hendry, Robert Ryon 1936- WhoSSW 93
Hendry, Scott Law&B 92
Hendry, Thomas 1929- WhoCanL 92
Hendrych, Radovan 1971- WhoScE 91-4
Hendryx, Nona 1945- SoulM
Hendy, M(ichael) F(rank) 1942- ConAu 137
Heneage, Simon ScF&FL 92
Heneberry, David Arthur 1931- WhoAm 92
Henecke, Brian S. 1960- St&PR 93
Henegan, James K. Law&B 92
Henegan, John Clark 1950- WhoEmL 93, WhoSSW 93
Henegar-Prather, Lisa Marie 1966- WhoSSW 93
Heneghan, Francis Michael 1932- St&PR 93
Heneghan, John J. d1989 BioIn 17
Heneghan, John James 1940- St&PR 93
Henel, Rolf Heinrich 1937- WhoAm 92
Henely, Bernard Dwight Law&B 92
Henely, Joann Housh 1928- WhoAmW 93
Henenlotter, Frank MiSFD 9
Henes, Donna 1945- WhoWrEP 92
Henes, James Robert Law&B 92
Henes, Samuel Ernst 1937- WhoAm 92
Henestrosa, Andres 1906- DcMexL
Heney, Joseph Edward 1927- St&PR 93, WhoAm 92
Henfling, Jan W.D.M. 1946- WhoScE 91-3
Heng, Arthur Edward 1937- WhoSSW 93
Heng, Donald James, Jr. 1944- WhoAm 92
Heng, Siang Gek 1960- WhoAmW 93
Heng, Stanley Mark 1937- WhoAm 92
Heng, William E. 1945- St&PR 93
Hengels, Charles F. St&PR 93
Hengen, William Lincoln 1914- WhoAm 92
Hengesbaugh, Bernard L. 1946- WhoIns 93
Hengeveld, Gerard 1910- Baker 92
Hengge, Edwin F. 1930- WhoScE 91-4
Henglein, Arnim WhoScE 91-3
Heng Samrin 1934- WhoAsAP 91, WhoWor 93
Hengsbach, Franz 1910-1991 BioIn 17
Hengstler, Gary Ardell 1947- WhoAm 92
Henguinet, Wayne K. 1944- St&PR 93
Henham, Alexander William Edward WhoScE 91-1
Henham, Ernest G. 1870- ScF&FL 92
Henican, Caswell Ellis 1905- WhoAm 92, WhoSSW 93
Henican, Joseph P., III St&PR 93
Henick, Steven T. 1942- St&PR 93
Henick, Steven Titman 1942- WhoE 93
Henie, Sonja BioIn 17
Henie, Sonja 1912-1969 IntDcF 2-3 [port]
Henig, Robin Marantz BioIn 17
Henig, Sammy S. Law&B 92
Henige, David 1938- ConAu 39NR
Henighan, Tom ScF&FL 92
Henigson, David 1957- St&PR 93
Henikoff, Leo M., Jr. 1939- WhoAm 92
Heninger, Simeon Kahn, Jr. 1922- WhoAm 92, WhoSSW 93
Henington, David Mead 1929- WhoAm 92, WhoSSW 93
Henion, David L. 1944- St&PR 93
Henisch, Heinz K. 1922- BioIn 17
Henisch, Heinz Kurt 1922- WhoE 93
Henisch, Peter 1943- BioIn 17
Henke, Ana Mari 1954- WhoAmW 93
Henke, C.J., Jr. Law&B 92
Henke, Emerson Overbeck 1916- WhoAm 92
Henke, Janice Carine 1938- WhoAmW 93, WhoWor 93
Henke, Michael John 1940- WhoAm 92
Henke, Steven J. 1946- St&PR 93
Henke, Sue Ellen 1951- WhoEmL 93
Henke, Theodore R. 1952- St&PR 93
Henke, Theodore Robert 1952- WhoIns 93
Henke, Werner d1991 BioIn 17
Henkel, Arthur John, Jr. 1945- WhoAm 92, WhoE 93
Henkel, David R. 1946- St&PR 93
Henkel, David Richard 1951- WhoEmL 93
Henkel, Eloise Elizabeth 1923- WhoAmW 93
Henkel, Gerhard 1943- WhoWor 93
Henkel, Heinrich 1822-1899 Baker 92
Henkel, Konrad Karl 1954- St&PR 93
Henkel, (Johann) Michael 1780-1851 Baker 92
Henkel, William 1941- WhoAm 92
Henkels, Paul M. 1924- St&PR 93
Henkels, Paul MacAllister 1924- WhoAm 92
Henkemans, Hans 1913- Baker 92
Henken, Bernard Samuel 1919- WhoE 93
Henken, Willard John 1927- WhoAm 92
Henkes, Kevin 1960- ChlBIID [port], ConAu 38NR, MajAI [port]
Henkin, Louis 1917- WhoAm 92
Henkin, Patricia 1947- WhoAmW 93
Henkin, Robert Irwin 1930- WhoAm 92
Henkin, Roxanne Lee 1951- WhoEmL 93
Henkin-Bookman, Jean Patricia 1948- WhoWrEP 92
Henkle, Roger B. d1991 BioIn 17
Henkle, Roger Black 1935- WhoWrEP 92
Henkus, Ira 1949- St&PR 93
Henkus, Irving St&PR 93
Henle, Fritz 1909- BioIn 17
Henle, Guy d1992 NewYTBS 92
Henle, Guy 1920-1992 BioIn 17
Henle, Mary 1913- BioIn 17, WhoE 93
Henle, Peter 1919- WhoAm 92
Henle, Robert Athanasius 1924- WhoAm 92
Henle, Robert John 1909- WhoAm 92
Henley, Anne AmWomPl
Henley, Arthur 1921- WhoAm 92, WhoWrEP 92
Henley, Arthur Boyden, Jr. 1933- St&PR 93
Henley, Beth BioIn 17
Henley, Beth 1952- WhoAm 92, WhoAmW 93
Henley, Cheryl Chris 1948- WhoEmL 93
Henley, Darl Heathcott 1944- WhoSSW 93
Henley, Don BioIn 17
Henley, Don 1948- WhoAm 92
Henley, Ernest Mark 1924- WhoAm 92
Henley, Gail 1950- WhoWrEP 92
Henley, Henry Howard, Jr. 1921- St&PR 93, WhoAm 92
Henley, Joseph Oliver 1949- WhoE 93, WhoEmL 93, WhoWor 93
Henley, Joseph P. 1926- St&PR 93
Henley, Lila Mary 1926- WhoAmW 93
Henley, Malcolm Wendel 1951- WhoSSW 93
Henley, Nixon Carr 1936- St&PR 93
Henley, Regina Ann Cato 1937- WhoAmW 93
Henley, Richard Merle 1952- WhoEmL 93
Henley, Terry Lew 1940- WhoWor 93
Henley, Thomas W. 1932- St&PR 93
Henley, Vernard William 1929- St&PR 93, WhoAm 92
Henley-Berg, Judy Kay 1944- WhoAmW 93
Henn, Catherine E.C. Law&B 92
Henn, Catherine Emily Campbell 1942- St&PR 93
Henn, Eugene Law&B 92
Henn, Eugene E. Law&B 92
Henn, Fritz Albert 1941- WhoAm 92, WhoE 93
Henn, John Howard 1942- WhoAm 92
Henn, Mary Ann 1930- WhoWrEP 92
Henn, Robert B. Law&B 92
Henn, Shirley Emily 1919- WhoSSW 93
Henn, Volker 1943- WhoWor 93
Hennage, Joseph Howard 1921- WhoWor 93
Hennard, George J. 1956-1991 BioIn 17
Hennart, Jean Pierre 1942- WhoWor 93
Henne, Frances E. 1906-1985 BioIn 17
Henne, James Earl 1947- WhoE 93
Henne, Nancy Diane 1955- WhoWrEP 92
Henneberg, (Carl) Albert (Theodor) 1901- Baker 92
Henneberg, Charles 1899-1959 ScF&FL 92
Henneberg, Johann Baptist 1768-1822 Baker 92
Henneberg, Nathalie 1917-1977 ScF&FL 92
Henneberg, Richard 1853-1925 Baker 92
Henneberger, John A. Law&B 92
Henneberger, Lawrence Francis 1938- WhoAm 92
Hennebert, Gregoire Laurent 1929- WhoScE 91-2
Hennebert, Paul 1923- WhoScE 91-2
Hennecke, Dietmar K. 1939- WhoScE 91-3
Hennecy, Bobbie Bobo 1922- WhoAmW 93, WhoSSW 93
Hennefer, David A. 1948- St&PR 93
Hennel, Jacek Witold 1925- WhoScE 91-4
Hennell, Michael Anthony WhoScE 91-1
Hennelly, Edmund Paul 1923- WhoAm 92, WhoE 93, WhoWor 93
Henneman, John Bell, Jr. 1935- WhoAm 92
Henneman, Stephen Charles 1949- WhoEmL 93
Hennemann, Georg 1932- WhoScE 91-3
Hennemeyer, Robert Thomas 1925- WhoAm 92
Hennen, Georges Paul 1936- WhoScE 91-2
Hennen, Thomas Robert Law&B 92
Hennen, Thomas Waldo Law&B 92
Hennenhoefer, Earl 1943- St&PR 93
Hennenhoefer, Gerald J. 1947- St&PR 93
Hennenhofer, G. WhoScE 91-3
Hennepin, Louis 1626-1705? Expl 93
Hennequin, Jean-Francois 1937- WhoScE 91-2
Henner, Marilu 1952- WhoAm 92
Hennerberg, Carl Fredrik 1871-1932 Baker 92
Hennes, Aloys 1827-1889 Baker 92
Hennes, Harvey 1947- St&PR 93
Hennes, Robert Taft 1930- WhoAm 92
Hennessee, Keith C. Law&B 92
Hennessee, Manassa Nixon 1930- St&PR 93, WhoSSW 93
Hennessey, Alice Elizabeth 1936- WhoAm 92, WhoAmW 93
Hennessey, Audrey Kathleen 1936- WhoAmW 93
Hennessey, Daniel F. 1941- St&PR 93
Hennessey, Frank Martin 1938- WhoAm 92
Hennessey, Jevera Kaye 1960- WhoEmL 93
Hennessey, John Philip WhoAm 92
Hennessey, John Philip 1937- St&PR 93
Hennessey, John William, Jr. 1925- WhoAm 92
Hennessey, Joseph Mark Law&B 92
Hennessey, Lisa Ivy 1959- WhoE 93
Hennessey, Marianne Minutola 1940- WhoAmW 93
Hennessey, Neil William 1943- St&PR 93
Hennessey, Patrick Lee 1950- St&PR 93
Hennessey, Patrick Leo 1934- St&PR 93
Hennessey, Peter J., Jr. 1920- WhoIns 93
Hennessey, Peter John, III 1943- WhoSSW 93

Hennessey, Ralph Edward 1916- *St&PR 93*
Hennessey, Raymond Frank 1925- *WhoE 93*
Hennessey, Robert J. 1941- *St&PR 93*
Hennessey, Robert John 1941- *WhoAm 92*
Hennessey, Robert Joseph 1952- *St&PR 93*
Hennessey, Thomas V., Jr. *St&PR 93*
Hennessey, William John 1948- *WhoAm 92*
Hennessey, William Joseph 1947- *WhoWor 93*
Hennessy, Betty Frances *BioIn 17*
Hennessy, Charlene C. 1928- *WhoE 93*
Hennessy, Daniel Kraft 1941- *WhoAm 92*
Hennessy, Dean McDonald 1923- *WhoAm 92, WhoWor 93*
Hennessy, Debra 1959- *St&PR 93*
Hennessy, Edward L., Jr. *BioIn 17*
Hennessy, Edward Lawrence, Jr. 1928- *WhoE 93*
Hennessy, Eileen Bernadette 1937- *WhoWrEP 92*
Hennessy, Hugh J. 1917- *St&PR 93*
Hennessy, James Ernest 1933- *WhoAm 92*
Hennessy, John *BioIn 17*
Hennessy, John Francis, III 1955- *St&PR 93, WhoE 93, WhoEmL 93*
Hennessy, John M. 1936- *St&PR 93, WhoAm 92, WhoE 93*
Hennessy, John Pope- *BioIn 17*
Hennessy, Joseph John 1953- *St&PR 93*
Hennessy, Madeleine Joyce 1948- *WhoWrEP 92*
Hennessy, Margaret Barrett 1952- *WhoAmW 93, WhoEmL 93*
Hennessy, Patrick J. 1948- *St&PR 93*
Hennessy, Paul Raymond 1925- *St&PR 93*
Hennessy, Richard *BioIn 17*
Hennessy, Robert Bruce 1934- *St&PR 93*
Hennessy, Shay 1947- *WhoWor 93*
Hennessy, Susan Margaret 1961- *WhoAmW 93*
Hennessy, Swan 1866-1929 *Baker 92*
Hennessy, Thomas Christopher 1916- *WhoAm 92*
Hennessy, Thomas F. 1911-1991 *BioIn 17*
Hennessy, Thomas P.J. 1933- *WhoScE 91-3*
Hennessy, Wesley J. 1914-1991 *BioIn 17*
Hennesy, Gerald Craft 1921- *WhoAm 92*
Hennewinkel, Michael *Law&B 92*
Henney, Christopher S. *St&PR 93*
Hennie, Dale P. 1940- *St&PR 93*
Hennig, Carl 1819-1873 *Baker 92*
Hennig, Carl Rafael 1845-1914 *Baker 92*
Hennig, Charles William 1949- *WhoSSW 93*
Hennig, Frederick E. *WhoE 93*
Hennig, Frederick E. 1932- *St&PR 93*
Hennig, Janet Lynn *Law&B 92*
Hennig, Jeffrey Carlton 1944- *St&PR 93*
Hennig, Richard Paul *Law&B 92*
Hennig, Robert Ernest 1941- *WhoSSW 93*
Hennig, Wolfgang 1941- *WhoScE 91-3*
Hennigan, John J. *Law&B 92*
Hennigan, Patrick John 1945- *WhoAm 92, WhoE 93*
Hennigan, Robert Dwyer 1925- *WhoE 93*
Hennigar, Dana E. 1933- *St&PR 93*
Hennigar, David J. 1939- *WhoAm 92*
Hennigar, Gordon Ross, Jr. 1919- *WhoSSW 93*
Hennigar, Harold Frank, Jr. 1953- *WhoEmL 93*
Hennigar, William Grant, Jr. 1947- *WhoEmL 93*
Hennike, Toni *Law&B 92*
Henniker, Florence d1923 *BioIn 17*
Henniker-Heaton, J. Lindsey 1946- *WhoScE 91-1*
Henning, Barbara J. 1948- *WhoWrEP 92*
Henning, Charles E. 1937-1991 *BioIn 17*
Henning, Charles Nathaniel 1915- *WhoAm 92*
Henning, David Richard 1943- *St&PR 93*
Henning, Doug 1947- *WhoAm 92*
Henning, Ervin Arthur 1910-1982 *Baker 92*
Henning, Gary 1951- *St&PR 93*
Henning, George A. 1947- *St&PR 93*
Henning, George Thomas, Jr. 1941- *WhoAm 92*
Henning, Harold O. 1924- *St&PR 93*
Henning, Joel Frank 1939- *WhoAm 92*
Henning, John F., Jr. 1923- *St&PR 93*
Henning, John Frederick, Jr. 1923- *WhoAm 92*
Henning, John J. 1941- *St&PR 93*
Henning, John R. 1934- *St&PR 93*
Henning, Kathleen Ann 1963- *WhoAmW 93*
Henning, Mark L. 1948- *WhoSSW 93*
Henning, Michael D. 1944- *St&PR 93*
Henning, Michael Fredrick 1963- *WhoEmL 93*
Henning, Otto 1927- *WhoScE 91-3*
Henning, Paul Francis, Jr. 1932- *St&PR 93*
Henning, Robert D. *Law&B 92*
Henning, Robert V. 1916- *St&PR 93*
Henning, Ronda Regina 1957- *WhoAmW 93*
Henning, Rudolf Ernst 1923- *WhoAm 92, WhoSSW 93*
Henning, Susan June 1946- *WhoAm 92, WhoAmW 93, WhoEmL 93*
Henning, Thomas E. 1953- *St&PR 93*
Henning, Thomas Edward 1953- *WhoAm 92*
Henning, Ulf 1929- *WhoScE 91-3*
Henning, Walter F. 1939- *WhoScE 91-3*
Henning, William Clifford 1918- *WhoWor 93*
Henning, William Wilson 1946- *St&PR 93*
Henninge, Richard Allen 1950- *WhoWor 93*
Henninge, Rose Priscilla 1922- *WhoAmW 93*
Henninger, Ann Louise 1946- *WhoEmL 93*
Henninger, Daniel Paul 1946- *WhoAm 92*
Henninger, John G. 1916- *St&PR 93*
Henninger, Kenneth Alan 1938- *St&PR 93*
Henninger, Peter Richard 1960- *WhoEmL 93*
Henninger, Polly 1946- *WhoAmW 93*
Hennings, Deirdre Ellen 1951- *WhoAmW 93*
Hennings, Dorothy Grant 1935- *WhoE 93*
Hennings, Laury H. *Law&B 92*
Hennings, William M. 1950- *St&PR 93*
Henningsen, Dierk 1935- *WhoScE 91-3*
Henningsen, Knud W. 1933- *WhoScE 91-2*
Henningsen, Linda Joyce 1954- *WhoAmW 93*
Henningsen, Peter, Jr. 1926- *St&PR 93, WhoAm 92*
Henningsen, Peter James *Law&B 92*
Henningsen, Robert C. 1939- *St&PR 93*
Henningsen, Victor William, Jr. 1924- *St&PR 93, WhoAm 92, WhoE 93*
Henningson, Carol B. *Law&B 92*
Henningsson, Bjorn 1934- *WhoScE 91-4*
Hennion, Carolyn Laird 1943- *WhoAmW 93*
Hennion, Reeve Lawrence 1941- *WhoAm 92*
Heno, Harold Joseph 1942- *WhoSSW 93*
Henquinet, Wayne K. 1944- *St&PR 93*
Henrard, Fredy L. 1940- *WhoUN 92*
Henrard, Jacques R.V.M. 1940- *WhoScE 91-2*
Henrard, Jean-Claude 1938- *WhoScE 91-2*
Henreid, Paul 1908- *IntDcF 2-3*
Henreid, Paul 1908-1992 *BioIn 17, CurBio 92N, NewYTBS 92 [port]*
Henri, Adrian 1932- *BioIn 17*
Henri, David C. *Law&B 92*
Henri, David C. 1943- *St&PR 93*
Henri, Janine Jacqueline 1955- *WhoSSW 93*
Henri, Jean Pierre *Law&B 92*
Henri, Robert 1865-1929 *BioIn 17, GayN*
Henrich, Jean MacKay 1909- *WhoE 93*
Henrich, Thomas David 1916- *BiDAMSp 1989*
Henrich, Victor Eugene 1939- *WhoE 93*
Henrichs, Albert Maximinus 1942- *WhoAm 92*
Henrichs, Paul Mark 1943- *WhoSSW 93*
Henrichsen, Jorgen *WhoScE 91-2*
Henrick, Richard P. *ScF&FL 92*
Henrick, William R. *Law&B 92*
Henricks, Jerry Arnold 1934- *St&PR 93*
Henricks, Jon M. 1935- *St&PR 93*
Henricksen, Bruce Conley 1941- *WhoWrEP 92*
Henrickson, Charles Henry 1938- *WhoSSW 93*
Henrickson, Eiler Leonard 1920- *WhoAm 92*
Henricson, Bengt Viking 1953- *WhoWor 93*
Henricson, Jan 1943- *WhoScE 91-4*
Henri de Valenciennes *OxDcByz*
Henrie, David Eugene 1940- *WhoE 93*
Henrie, Sally Anne 1953- *WhoSSW 93*
Henrie-Strup, Sue 1960- *WhoAmW 93*
Henriette, Jean M.E. 1940- *WhoScE 91-2*
Henriksen, Aage 1920- *WhoScE 91-2*
Henriksen, Anders Finn 1947- *WhoE 93*
Henriksen, David K. *Law&B 92*
Henriksen, David L. 1954- *St&PR 93*
Henriksen, Jan Fr. 1938- *WhoScE 91-4*
Henriksen, Jerry Lee 1935- *St&PR 93*
Henriksen, Kaj *WhoScE 91-2*
Henriksen, Mary Jo 1954- *WhoWrEP 92*
Henriksen, Thomas Hollinger 1939- *WhoAm 92*
Henriksen, Thormod 1928- *WhoScE 91-4*
Henriksen, Ulf Sigurd 1942- *WhoWor 93*
Henrikson, Lois Elizabeth 1921- *WhoAm 92, WhoAmW 93, WhoWor 93*
Henrikson, Pamela Smith 1940- *WhoE 93*
Henrikson, Ray Charles 1937- *WhoE 93*
Henriksson, Jan E. 1947- *WhoScE 91-4*
Henriksson, Jan Hugo Lennart 1933- *WhoWor 93*
Henriksson, Rolf 1928- *WhoScE 91-4*
Henrion, F.H.K. 1914-1990 *BioIn 17*
Henrion, Paul B. *Law&B 92*
Henriot, Nicole 1925- *Baker 92*
Henriot, Philippe 1889-1944 *BioIn 17*
Henrique, Jorge Bolivar 1944- *WhoWor 93*
Henriques, Diana Blackmon 1948- *WhoAm 92*
Henriques, Fini (Valdemar) 1867-1940 *Baker 92*
Henriques, Laurence B. d1990 *BioIn 17*
Henriques, Michael Erik 1953- *WhoUN 92*
Henriques, Robert 1858-1914 *Baker 92*
Henriquez, Salome Urena de 1850-1897 *BioIn 17*
Henriquez-Freeman, Hilda Josefina 1938- *WhoAmW 93*
Henriquez Gaztanondo, Antonio Santos 1936- *WhoWor 93*
Henriquez-Herrera, Teodulo Antonio 1956- *WhoEmL 93*
Henriquez Urena, Pedro 1884-1946 *DcMexL*
Henritze, Bette *ConTFT 10*
Henritze, Thomas King 1932- *St&PR 93*
Henrot, Antoine 1957- *WhoWor 93*
Henrot, Jacques Franklin 1952- *WhoWor 93*
Henry, Infante of Portugal 1394-1460 *BioIn 17*
Henry, Prince of Great Britain 1984- *BioIn 17*
Henry, Prince of Hesse *BioIn 17*
Henry, II 1133-1189 *HarEnMi*
Henry, III, King of England 1207-1272 *BioIn 17*
Henry, IV 1366-1413 *HarEnMi*
Henry, IV 1553-1610 *HarEnMi*
Henry, V 1387-1422 *Baker 92, HarEnMi*
Henry, V, King of England 1387-1422 *BioIn 17*
Henry, VI 1165-1197 *OxDcByz*
Henry, VI 1421-1471 *Baker 92*
Henry, VII 1457-1509 *HarEnMi*
Henry, VIII 1491-1547 *Baker 92, HarEnMi*
Henry, VIII, King of England 1491-1547 *BioIn 17*
Henry, Aaron 1922- *EncAACR, PolPar*
Henry, Alan Pemberton 1949- *WhoAm 92*
Henry, Alan Ray 1941- *WhoAm 92*
Henry, Alexander 1739-1824 *BioIn 17*
Henry, Alice 1857-1943 *BioIn 17*
Henry, Ann Rainwater 1939- *WhoSSW 93*
Henry, Anne P. *Law&B 92*
Henry, Ardith Martin 1959- *WhoAmW 93*
Henry, Arthur W. 1896-1988 *BioIn 17*
Henry, Barbara A. 1952- *WhoAm 92, WhoAmW 93*
Henry, Barbara Jayne 1956- *WhoAmW 93*
Henry, Bill E. *Law&B 92*
Henry, Bill W. 1934- *St&PR 93*
Henry, Bruce Edward 1952- *WhoEmL 93*
Henry, Buck 1930- *MiSFD 9, WhoAm 92*
Henry, Carl Ferdinand Howard 1913- *WhoAm 92*
Henry, Carolyn Mary 1964- *WhoAmW 93*
Henry, Catherine 1949- *WhoAmW 93*
Henry, Catherine Theresa 1934- *WhoE 93*
Henry, Charles E. 1930- *St&PR 93*
Henry, Charles Joseph 1936- *WhoAm 92*
Henry, Charles Robert 1937- *WhoAm 92*
Henry, Charles Wolcott 1926- *St&PR 93*
Henry, Claudette 1947- *WhoAm 92, WhoAmW 93, WhoSSW 93*
Henry, Clifford Hugh, Jr. 1928- *WhoSSW 93*
Henry, Cyrus A., Jr. 1931- *WhoIns 93*
Henry, Daniel J. *Law&B 92*
Henry, David Howe, II 1918- *WhoAm 92, WhoSSW 93, WhoWor 93*
Henry, De Witt P. 1941- *WhoWrEP 92*
Henry, Deborah J. *Law&B 92*
Henry, Deborah Jane 1952- *WhoEmL 93*
Henry, DeLysle Leon 1935- *WhoWor 93*
Henry, Denis E. *Law&B 92*
Henry, DeWitt Pawling, II 1941- *WhoAm 92*
Henry, Donald Owen 1945- *WhoSSW 93*
Henry, Donna Edwards 1949- *WhoAmW 93, WhoEmL 93*
Henry, Douglass, Jr. *St&PR 93*
Henry, Duane G. *Law&B 92*
Henry, Edward A. 1910- *St&PR 93*
Henry, Edward Frank 1923- *WhoWor 93*
Henry, Edward LeRoy 1921- *WhoAm 92*
Henry, Ellen Kay 1947- *WhoSSW 93*
Henry, Frances Ann 1939- *WhoAmW 93, WhoWor 93*
Henry, Francis B. *Law&B 92*
Henry, Francis Bradford *St&PR 93*
Henry, Frederick Edward 1947- *WhoAm 92*
Henry, Garth W. *St&PR 93*
Henry, Geoffrey Arama 1940- *WhoWor 93*
Henry, Grace R. *AmWomPl*
Henry, J.C. 1932- *WhoScE 91-2*
Henry, J.D. *St&PR 93*
Henry, James C., Jr. 1926- *St&PR 93*
Henry, Jane Stinnett 1952- *WhoAm 92, WhoEmL 93*
Henry, Jay Edward 1950- *WhoEmL 93*
Henry, Joe E. 1933- *St&PR 93*
Henry, John B. 1948- *ConEn, St&PR 93*
Henry, John P., Jr. 1935- *St&PR 93*
Henry, John Porter, Jr. 1911- *WhoAm 92*
Henry, John T. 1933- *St&PR 93*
Henry, John Vernor 1767-1829 *BioIn 17*
Henry, Jonathan Flake 1951- *WhoSSW 93*
Henry, Joseph C. 1952- *St&PR 93*
Henry, Joseph Louis 1924- *WhoAm 92*
Henry, Karen Schwab 1954- *WhoE 93*
Henry, Katherine Savage 1944- *WhoSSW 93*
Henry, Kathleen Marie 1950- *WhoAmW 93, WhoEmL 93*
Henry, Kathrine L. *Law&B 92*
Henry, Kenneth Alan 1951- *WhoEmL 93*
Henry, Kimberly Taylor *Law&B 92*
Henry, Laurin Luther 1921- *WhoAm 92*
Henry, Leigh Vaughan 1889-1958 *Baker 92*
Henry, Lenny *BioIn 17*
Henry, Maeve *ScF&FL 92*
Henry, Margaret 1914- *WhoAm 92*
Henry, Marguerite *WhoAm 92, WhoWrEP 92*
Henry, Marguerite 1902- *MajAI [port], SmATA 69 [port]*
Henry, Marguerite (Breithaupt) 1902- *DcAmChF 1960*
Henry, Marie H. *BioIn 17*
Henry, Mark *BioIn 17*
Henry, Marshall Webster, Jr. 1946- *St&PR 93*
Henry, Martha L. *St&PR 93*
Henry, Martha Venning 1950- *WhoE 93*
Henry, Mary 1913- *BioIn 17*
Henry, Michael Joseph *Law&B 92*
Henry, Michel 1555- *Baker 92*
Henry, Nicholas Llewellyn 1943- *WhoAm 92, WhoSSW 93*
Henry, O. 1862-1910 *BioIn 17, GayN, WorLitC [port]*
Henry, Palmira d1990 *BioIn 17*
Henry, Patrick 1736-1799 *BioIn 17, PolPar*
Henry, Patrick G. 1939- *WhoAm 92*
Henry, Patrick L. *Law&B 92*
Henry, Paul 1876-1958 *BioIn 17*
Henry, Paul B. 1942- *CngDr 91*
Henry, Paul Brentwood 1942- *WhoAm 92*
Henry, Paul James 1927- *WhoAm 92*
Henry, Paul Raleigh 1928- *St&PR 93*
Henry, Paul Shala 1944- *WhoAm 92*
Henry, Paula Louise 1947- *WhoAmW 93*
Henry, Paula Waldrop 1956- *WhoSSW 93*
Henry, Pete 1897-1952 *BioIn 17*
Henry, Peter York 1951- *WhoEmL 93, WhoSSW 93*
Henry, Philip Clark 1932- *St&PR 93*
Henry, Philippe Francois-Xavier 1942- *WhoWor 93*
Henry, Pierre 1927- *Baker 92*
Henry, Pierre Yves 1932- *WhoE 93*
Henry, Ragan *BioIn 17*
Henry, Ragan A. 1934- *WhoAm 92*
Henry, Ralph S. 1921- *St&PR 93*
Henry, Randolph Marshall 1946- *WhoEmL 93, WhoSSW 93*
Henry, Raquel Maria del Carmen 1956- *WhoSSW 93*
Henry, Rene Arthur, Jr. 1933- *WhoAm 92, WhoSSW 93*
Henry, Rene Paul 1917- *WhoSSW 93*
Henry, Richard Conn 1940- *WhoAm 92*
Henry, Robert Arrel 1954- *WhoSSW 93*
Henry, Robert Fillmore 1934- *St&PR 93*
Henry, Robert J. *Law&B 92*
Henry, Robert J. 1950- *St&PR 93*
Henry, Robert John 1950- *WhoAm 92*
Henry, Robert Joseph 1946- *St&PR 93*
Henry, Robert W., Jr. *Law&B 92*
Henry, Ronald James Whyte 1940- *WhoAm 92*
Henry, Roy Monroe 1939- *WhoWor 93*
Henry, Sally McDonald 1948- *WhoAmW 93*
Henry, Sharon 1963- *WhoAmW 93*
Henry, Shirley Ann 1937- *WhoWor 93*
Henry, Steven Carl 1948- *WhoAm 92*
Henry, Susan Armstrong 1946- *WhoAm 92, WhoAmW 93*
Henry, Taylor Hill, Jr. 1935- *WhoAm 92*
Henry, Thomas J., Jr. 1943- *St&PR 93*
Henry, Thomas Joseph 1934- *St&PR 93*
Henry, Vickie Lea 1945- *WhoAmW 93*

Henry, Walter L. 1941- WhoAm 92
Henry, Walter Lester, Jr. 1915- WhoAm 92
Henry, Warner W. 1938- St&PR 93
Henry, Wayne Edward 1932- St&PR 93
Henry, Will 1912- BioIn 17
Henry, William Abbott 1939- St&PR 93
Henry, William Alfred, III 1950- WhoAm 92
Henry, William Aloysius 1956- WhoE 93
Henry, William Arthur, II Law&B 92
Henry, William Lockwood 1948- WhoAm 92
Henry, William Oscar Eugene 1927- WhoAm 92
Henry, William Ray 1925- WhoAm 92
Henry, Yves-M. 1930- WhoScE 91-2
Henry, Zachary Adolphus 1930- WhoAm 92
Henry of Babenberg c. 1114-1177 OxDcByz
Henry of Hainault c. 1174-1216 OxDcByz
Henry of Navarre, II 1503-1555 HarEnMi
Henry-Parton, Kathleen 1952- WhoAmW 93
Henryson, Robert 1430?-1506? LitC 20
Henry, the Navigator 1394-1460 BioIn 17
Henry the Navigator, Prince 1394-1460 Expl 93 [port]
Henry-Thiel, Lois Hollender 1941- WhoAmW 93
Hens, Hugo S.J.C. 1943- WhoScE 91-2
Hensch, Shirley Anne 1955- WhoAmW 93
Henschel, David F. Law&B 92
Henschel, (Isidor) George (Georg) 1850-1934 Baker 92
Henschel, Herbert J. Law&B 92
Henschel, Lillian June 1860-1901 Baker 92
Hensel, Cornelius Leroy 1936- St&PR 93
Hensel, Fanny (Cacilie) 1805-1847 Baker 92
Hensel, Fanny Cecile Mendelssohn 1805-1847 BioIn 17
Hensel, Friedrich 1933- WhoScE 91-3
Hensel, H. Stuve 1901-1991 BioIn 17
Hensel, Heinrich 1874-1935 Baker 92
Hensel, Howard Milton 1946- WhoSSW 93
Hensel, John Charles 1930- WhoE 93
Hensel, Karen A. Law&B 92
Hensel, Kimberly J. Law&B 92
Hensel, Luise 1798-1876 BioIn 17
Hensel, Richard John 1952- St&PR 93
Hensel, Robin Ann Morgan 1960- WhoEmL 93
Hensel, Steven James 1956- WhoEmL 93, WhoSSW 93
Hensel, Steven Mark 1955- WhoEmL 93
Hensel, Walther 1887-1956 Baker 92
Hensel, Witold 1917- WhoWor 93
Henseler, Gerald A. 1940- St&PR 93
Henseler, Gerald Anthony 1940- WhoAm 92
Henseler, Suzanne Marie 1942- WhoAmW 93
Henselmann, Hermann 1905- BioIn 17
Henselmeier, Sandra Nadine 1937- WhoAmW 93
Henselt, Adolf 1814-1889 Baker 92
Hensen, Karl 1935- WhoScE 91-3
Hensgen, Herbert Thomas 1947- WhoWor 93
Henshall, David ScF&FL 92
Henshall, J.D. 1938- WhoScE 91-1
Henshall, Ronald S. Law&B 92
Henshaw, Edgar Cummings 1929- WhoAm 92
Henshaw, Henry Wetherbee 1850-1930 IntDcAn
Henshaw, Jonathan Cook 1922- WhoAm 92
Henshaw, Marion Updike 1945- WhoSSW 93
Henshaw, William Raleigh 1932- WhoSSW 93, WhoWor 93
Henshel, Harry B. 1919- St&PR 93
Henshel, Harry Bulova 1919- WhoAm 92
Henshell, Mort 1926- St&PR 93
Hensinger, Margaret Elizabeth 1950- WhoAm 92, WhoEmL 93, WhoSSW 93, WhoWor 93
Henske, John M. BioIn 17
Henslee, Lee W., III Law&B 92
Hensler, Guenter Manfred 1939- WhoAm 92
Hensley, Allan Lance 1944- WhoSSW 93
Hensley, Chad L. 1924- WhoIns 93
Hensley, Dennis C. Law&B 92
Hensley, Dwayne Scott 1961- WhoEmL 93
Hensley, Edward Randolph 1933- St&PR 93
Hensley, Elizabeth Catherine 1921- WhoAm 92
Hensley, Eugene Benjamin 1918- WhoAm 92
Hensley, J.L. 1926- ScF&FL 92
Hensley, Joe L. 1926- WhoWrEP 92
Hensley, Joseph Paul 1958- WhoE 93
Hensley, Lana Jane 1947- WhoSSW 93
Hensley, Max D. Law&B 92
Hensley, Robert T., Jr. 1932- St&PR 93
Hensley, Sharon Quan 1947- WhoEmL 93
Hensley, Sophie Almon 1866-1946 BioIn 17
Hensley, Stephen Allan 1950- WhoSSW 93
Hensley, Stephen Lloyd Law&B 92
Hensley, Stephen Ray WhoSSW 93
Hensley, Verna Wilkins 1957- WhoAmW 93
Hensley, William Andrew 1946- WhoAm 92
Henson, Ahnahkaq BioIn 17
Henson, Anna Miriam Morgan 1935- WhoAmW 93
Henson, Arnold 1931- St&PR 93, WhoAm 92
Henson, Bernice Ellean 1932- WhoSSW 93
Henson, Brian BioIn 17
Henson, Brian 1964?- News 92 [port]
Henson, C. Ward 1940- WhoAm 92
Henson, Carolyn Regina 1953- WhoAmW 93
Henson, Cheryl BioIn 17
Henson, Colleen A. Law&B 92
Henson, Daniel P., III 1943- St&PR 93
Henson, E. Eddie 1936- St&PR 93
Henson, Frank Herman 1938- St&PR 93
Henson, Gail Ritchie 1951- WhoAmW 93
Henson, Gene Ethridge 1924- WhoAmW 93
Henson, Glenda Maria 1960- WhoAm 92, WhoAmW 93
Henson, H. Kirk Law&B 92
Henson, Henry Paul 1931- WhoSSW 93
Henson, Jackson W. Law&B 92
Henson, James Bond 1933- WhoAm 92
Henson, Jeffery Weldon 1958- WhoEmL 93, WhoSSW 93
Henson, Jim BioIn 17
Henson, Jim 1936-1990 ConHero 2 [port], MiSFD 9N
Henson, John Clark, Sr. 1945- St&PR 93
Henson, John Ely 1947- WhoEmL 93, WhoSSW 93
Henson, Josiah 1789-1883 BioIn 17
Henson, Keith BioIn 17
Henson, L. Luton 1906- St&PR 93
Henson, Lance 1944- BioIn 17
Henson, Larry William Law&B 92
Henson, Leslie 1891-1957 QDrFCA 92 [port]
Henson, Lisa BioIn 17
Henson, Llewellyn Lafayette, III WhoSSW 93
Henson, Lou BioIn 17
Henson, Louis Ray 1932- BiDAMSp 1989
Henson, Margaret Swett 1924- WhoSSW 93
Henson, Matthew 1866-1955 ConHero 2 [port]
Henson, Matthew A. 1866-1955 Expl 93 [port]
Henson, Matthew Alexander 1866-1955 BioIn 17
Henson, O'Dell Williams, Jr. 1934- WhoSSW 93
Henson, Paul Harry 1925- St&PR 93, WhoAm 92
Henson, Ray David 1924- WhoAm 92
Henson, Richard Lay 1946- St&PR 93
Henson, Robert Frank 1925- WhoAm 92
Henson, William L. 1934- WhoE 93
Henss, Phillip S. 1933- St&PR 93
Henstell, Diana 1936- ScF&FL 92
Henstock, Barry A. 1939- St&PR 93
Henstock, Ralph WhoScE 91-1
Henstock, Ralph 1923- WhoWor 93
Henstra, Friso 1928- SmATA 73 [port]
Hentges, Alison Jane 1952- WhoSSW 93
Hentges, David John 1928- WhoSSW 93
Hentges, Edward Joel 1931- St&PR 93
Hentges, Richard Joseph 1938- St&PR 93
Hentinen, Viljo WhoScE 91-4
Hentinen, Viljo Olavi 1934- WhoWor 93
Hentkowski, Larry Peter 1953- St&PR 93
Hentoff, Margot 1930- WhoAm 92, WhoWrEP 92
Hentoff, Nat BioIn 17
Hentoff, Nat 1925- SmATA 69 [port]
Hentoff, Nat(han Irving) 1925- DcAmChF 1960, MajAI [port]
Hentoff, Nathan Irving 1925- WhoAm 92, WhoWrEP 92
Henton, Willis Ryan 1925- WhoAm 92, WhoSSW 93
Hentschel, David A. 1934- St&PR 93, WhoSSW 93
Hentschel, Franz 1814-1889 Baker 92
Hentschel, Theodor 1830-1892 Baker 92
Hentschel, Uwe 1940- WhoWor 93
Henttonen, Heikki A. 1950- WhoScE 91-4
Henty, G.A. 1832-1902 BioIn 17
Henty, George Alfred 1832-1902 BioIn 17
Hentz, Marie Eva 1920- WhoAmW 93
Hentzen, Herbert D., Jr. 1927- St&PR 93
Hentzen, William R., Sr. 1932- St&PR 93
Henwood, David John WhoScE 91-1
Henwood, Derek Edwin WhoAm 92
Henwood, Douglas Francis 1952- WhoEmL 93
Henz, Donald John 1937- St&PR 93
Henz, Hubert Joseph 1926- WhoWor 93
Henze, Hans Werner 1926- Baker 92, BioIn 17, IntDcOp [port], OxDcOp, WhoWor 93
Henze, Howard Martin 1947- WhoE 93
Henze, Paul Bernard 1924- WhoAm 92, WhoWrEP 92
Henzell-Lopez, Holly 1957- St&PR 93
Henzler, Martin 1935- WhoScE 91-3
Hepburn, Audrey 1929- BioIn 17, IntDcF 2-3 [port], WhoAm 92
Hepburn, Audrey 1929-1993 News 93-2
Hepburn, Christine Renee 1956- WhoAmW 93
Hepburn, George C., III Law&B 92
Hepburn, Katharine 1907- BioIn 17, IntDcF 2-3 [port]
Hepburn, Katharine Houghton d1951 BioIn 17
Hepburn, Katharine Houghton 1907- WhoAm 92, WhoAmW 93, WhoWor 93
Hepburn, Katharine (Houghton) 1909- ConAu 139
Hepfer, John William, Jr. 1924- WhoAm 92
Hepguler, Yasar Metin 1931- WhoWor 93
Hephaistion of Thebes 380- OxDcByz
Hepler, Ernest M. 1930- St&PR 93
Hepler, Kenneth Russel 1926- WhoWor 93
Hepler, Robert Sidney 1934- WhoAm 92
Hepler, Thomas E. 1932- St&PR 93
Hepner, Betty Shore 1927- WhoAmW 93
Hepner, Janet Smith Law&B 92
Hepp, Peter S. 1929- St&PR 93
Heppe, Ralph Richard 1923- WhoAm 92
Heppel, Alan Bruce Law&B 92
Heppel, Leon Alma 1912- WhoAm 92
Heppener, Robert 1925- Baker 92
Heppenstall, Barry 1946- St&PR 93
Heppenstall, Rayner 1911-1981 ScF&FL 92
Hepper, Carol 1953- WhoEmL 93
Heppermann, Donald C. 1943- St&PR 93
Heppermann, Jo Ann Law&B 92
Heppler, Robin Lee 1953- WhoAmW 93
Heppner, Ben BioIn 17
Heppner, Gloria Hill 1940- WhoAmW 93
Heppner, John Bernhard 1947- WhoSSW 93
Hepting, George Henry 1907-1988 BioIn 17
Heptinstall, Debra Lou 1952- WhoEmL 93
Heptinstall, Robert Hodgson 1920- WhoAm 92
Heptulla, Najma 1940- WhoAsAP 91
Hepworth, Barbara 1903-1975 BioIn 17
Hepworth, H. Jed Law&B 92
Hepworth, John David WhoScE 91-1
Hepworth, Joseph M. Law&B 92
Hepworth, Kenneth 1931- St&PR 93
Hepworth, Nigel Jeffrey 1957- WhoWor 93
Hepworth, Robert Jennings 1934- WhoWor 93
He Qizong 1936- WhoAsAP 91
Hera, Christian Ioan 1933- WhoScE 91-4
Hera, Christian-Ioan Dumitru 1933- WhoUN 92
Heraclius c. 575-641 HarEnMi
Heragu, Sunderesh Sesharanga 1959- WhoE 93
Herak, Charles Law&B 92
Herak, Janko N. 1937- WhoScE 91-4
Herak, Marko J. 1922- WhoScE 91-4
Herakleios c. 575-641 OxDcByz
Herakleios Constantine 612-641 OxDcByz
Heraklonas 626- OxDcByz
Herakovich, Carl Thomas 1937- WhoAm 92
Herald, Alice A. Law&B 92
Herald, Beverly Taylor 1946- WhoEmL 93, WhoSSW 93
Herald, Cherry Lou 1940- WhoAmW 93
Herald, Christopher E. St&PR 93
Herald, Diana Tixier ScF&FL 92
Herald, George William 1911- WhoWor 93
Herald, Kathleen MajAI
Herald, Kathleen 1929- BioIn 17
Heran, Herbert 1920- WhoScE 91-4
Heras Cobo, Luis 1927- WhoScE 91-3
Herasimchuk, David Alexander 1942- St&PR 93
Herath, Harold WhoAsAP 91, WhoWor 93
Herath, Pushpa Rukmani 1939- WhoUN 92
Herb, Jerome Bruce 1940- St&PR 93
Herb, Raymond G. 1908- WhoAm 92
Herb, Raymond George 1908- St&PR 93
Herbage, Julian (Livingston) 1904-1976 Baker 92
Herbeck, Johann (Franz), Ritter von 1831-1877 Baker 92
Herbein, John Giles 1938- St&PR 93
Herbel, LeRoy Alec, Jr. 1954- WhoSSW 93
Herber, Arnie 1910-1969 BioIn 17
Herber, Pamela Lynn 1957- WhoAmW 93
Herber, Robert Franciscus Martin 1940- WhoScE 91-3
Herber, Rolfe H. 1927- WhoE 93
Herber, Steven Carlton 1960- WhoE 93
Herberg, Will 1901-1977 JeAmHC
Herberger, A. David Law&B 92
Herberhold, Max 1936- WhoScE 91-3
Herberich, Frederick D. 1925- St&PR 93
Herberich, Frederick David 1925- WhoAm 92
Herberich, Gerhard E. 1936- WhoScE 91-3
Herberigs, Robert 1886-1974 Baker 92
Herbers, Tod Arthur 1948- WhoAm 92
Herbert, A.P. 1890-1971 ScF&FL 92
Herbert, Adam William, Jr. 1943- WhoSSW 93
Herbert, Albert Edward, Jr. 1928- WhoAm 92
Herbert, Andrew James 1954- WhoWor 93
Herbert, Anne Timbrook 1934- WhoE 93
Herbert, April Hodges 1934- WhoE 93
Herbert, Bart 1955- St&PR 93
Herbert, Billie DcCPCAm
Herbert, Brian 1947- ScF&FL 92
Herbert, Charles Emmet 1925- WhoAm 92
Herbert, Damon Charles 1945- WhoSSW 93
Herbert, David T(homas) 1935- ConAu 40NR
Herbert, David Thomas WhoScE 91-1
Herbert, Don BioIn 17
Herbert, Edward 1583-1648 BioIn 17
Herbert, Edwin L., III Law&B 92
Herbert, Frank BioIn 17
Herbert, Frank 1920-1986 MagSAmL [port], ScF&FL 92
Herbert, Frank Leonard 1926- WhoSSW 93
Herbert, Gavin S. 1932- St&PR 93
Herbert, Gavin Shearer, Jr. 1932- WhoAm 92
Herbert, George 1593-1633 DcLB 126 [port]
Herbert, George Edward Law&B 92
Herbert, George L. Law&B 92
Herbert, George R. 1922- St&PR 93
Herbert, George Richard 1922- WhoAm 92
Herbert, Gorden Law&B 92
Herbert, Henry W. Law&B 92
Herbert, Hugh 1887-1952 QDrFCA 92 [port]
Herbert, Ira C. 1927- St&PR 93, WhoSSW 93
Herbert, James 1943- ScF&FL 92
Herbert, James Arthur 1938- WhoAm 92
Herbert, James Dalton 1962- WhoE 93
Herbert, James Keller 1938- WhoAm 92
Herbert, James Paul 1941- WhoAm 92
Herbert, Jan BioIn 17
Herbert, Janine Marie 1958- WhoAmW 93, WhoEmL 93, WhoWor 93
Herbert, Jennette Campbell 1942- WhoAmW 93
Herbert, Johann Friedrich 1776-1841 Baker 92
Herbert, John 1926- WhoCanL 92
Herbert, John Campbell 1950- WhoAm 92
Herbert, John David Law&B 92
Herbert, John Warren 1924- St&PR 93, WhoAm 92
Herbert, Joseph F. 1936- St&PR 93
Herbert, Karen Elizabeth Law&B 92
Herbert, Kathleen ScF&FL 92
Herbert, Kathy Lynne Law&B 92
Herbert, Kevin Barry John 1921- WhoAm 92
Herbert, LeRoy James 1923- WhoAm 92
Herbert, Marilynne 1944- WhoAmW 93
Herbert, Mary H. ScF&FL 92
Herbert, Mary Katherine Atwell 1945- WhoAmW 93
Herbert, Michael Kinzly 1942- WhoAm 92, WhoWrEP 92
Herbert, Peter Noel 1941- WhoAm 92
Herbert, Raymond L. Law&B 92
Herbert, Richard D. 1935- St&PR 93
Herbert, Robert L. 1929- WhoAm 92
Herbert, Robert Michael 1954- WhoEmL 93
Herbert, Robert V. Law&B 92
Herbert, Robt. K. 1942- St&PR 93
Herbert, Sally Mary 1948- WhoEmL 93

Herbert, Seth E. *Law&B 92*
Herbert, Stephen W. 1941- *WhoAm 92*
Herbert, Steve Lloyd 1947- *St&PR 93*
Herbert, Teri Lynn 1948- *WhoAmW 93*
Herbert, Theodore Terence 1942- *WhoSSW 93*
Herbert, Victor *WhoAm 92*
Herbert, Victor 1859-1924 *GayN, OxDcOp*
Herbert, Victor (August) 1859-1924 *Baker 92*
Herbert, Victor James 1917- *WhoAm 92*
Herbert, Wally 1934- *Expl 93*
Herbert, Xavier 1901-1984 *BioIn 17*
Herbert, Zbigniew *BioIn 17*
Herbert, Zbigniew 1924- *PolBiDi*
Herbert of Cherbury, Edward 1583-1648 *BioIn 17*
Herbert of Cherbury, Edward, Lord 1583-1648 *DcLB 121 [port]*
Herbertz, Joachim 1940- *WhoScE 91-3*
Herbes, Frans *St&PR 93*
Herbich, John Bronislaw 1922- *WhoAm 92*
Herbig, George Howard 1920- *WhoAm 92*
Herbig, Gunther 1931- *Baker 92, WhoAm 92, WhoE 93*
Herbillon, Adrien J. 1934- *WhoScE 91-2*
Herbin, Reece A. 1946- *WhoAmW 93*
Herbison, John Stephen 1939- *St&PR 93*
Herbison, Robin J. 1961- *WhoEmL 93*
Herbison-Evans, Don 1937- *WhoWor 93*
Herbits, Stephen E. 1942- *St&PR 93*
Herbits, Stephen Edward 1942- *WhoAm 92*
Herblock 1909- *BioIn 17, WhoAm 92, WhoE 93*
Herborg-Nielsen, Thorkild 1921- *WhoWor 93*
Herbosch, Alain 1942- *WhoScE 91-2*
Herbruck, W. Gibbs 1923- *St&PR 93*
Herbst, Arthur Lee 1931- *WhoAm 92*
Herbst, Douglas James 1955- *St&PR 93*
Herbst, Edward I. 1945- *St&PR 93*
Herbst, Edward Ian 1945- *WhoAm 92*
Herbst, Eva *AmWomPl*
Herbst, Hartwig Martin 1945- *WhoWor 93*
Herbst, Jan Francis 1947- *WhoAm 92*
Herbst, Joachim 1928- *St&PR 93*
Herbst, Johannes 1735-1812 *Baker 92*
Herbst, Josephine 1892-1969 *BioIn 17*
Herbst, Jurgen 1928- *WhoAm 92*
Herbst, Lawrence Robert 1946- *WhoAm 92*
Herbst, Ludwig Josef *WhoScE 91-1*
Herbst, Marie A. 1930- *St&PR 93*
Herbst, Marie Antoinette *WhoAmW 93, WhoE 93*
Herbst, Melinda Socol *Law&B 92*
Herbst, Paul M. *Law&B 92*
Herbst, Robert 1925- *St&PR 93*
Herbst, Robert LeRoy 1935- *WhoAm 92, WhoE 93*
Herbst, Stanislaw 1906-1973 *PolBiDi*
Herbst, Todd Leslie 1952- *WhoWor 93*
Herbst, Walter Joseph 1942- *WhoE 93*
Herbster, David Parke 1941- *St&PR 93, WhoAm 92*
Herbster, James Richard 1941- *St&PR 93, WhoAm 92*
Herbster, William Gibson 1933- *WhoAm 92*
Herbstreith, Yvonne Mae 1942- *WhoAmW 93*
Herburger, Gunter 1932- *DcLB 124 [port]*
Herch, Frank Alan 1949- *WhoAm 92, WhoEmL 93*
Herchel, Dennis S. *Law&B 92*
Herchler, Duane Leonard 1944- *St&PR 93*
Hercigonja, Nikola 1911- *Baker 92*
Hercules, David Michael 1932- *WhoAm 92*
Hercus, J.W. *Law&B 92*
Herczeg, Janos 1941- *WhoScE 91-4*
Herd, Charmian June 1930- *WhoAmW 93*
Herd, Shirley *WhoWrEP 92*
Herd, Thomas Carroll *Law&B 92*
Herda, Ralph Edward 1953- *St&PR 93*
Herda, Thilo H. 1949- *WhoIns 93*
Herdan, Bernard *WhoScE 91-1*
Herde, Eugene W. *Law&B 92*
Herdeg, Howard Brian 1929- *WhoWor 93*
Herdemian, Gregory John 1954- *St&PR 93*
Herder, Gary Alan 1947- *St&PR 93*
Herder, Johann Gottfried 1744-1803 *BioIn 17, IntDcAn*
Herder, Stephen Rendell 1928- *WhoAm 92*
Herder, Thomas J. *Law&B 92*
Herdewijn, Piet Andre Maurits Maria 1954- *WhoWor 93*
Herdina, Eileen C. 1927- *St&PR 93*
Herdle, William Bruce 1947- *WhoEmL 93*
Herdman, Christine L. *Law&B 92*
Herdman, David Allan *Law&B 92*
Herdman, John Mark Ambrose 1932- *WhoWor 93*
Herdrich, Norman Wesley 1942- *WhoAm 92*
Heredia, Claudio 1931- *WhoScE 91-3*
Heredia, Manuel Agustin 1786-1846 *BioIn 17*
Heredia, Raymundo 1944- *WhoWor 93*
Heredia-Schulenburg, Jose Raul *Law&B 92*
Heredia y Heredia, Jose Maria 1803-1839 *DcMexL*
Hereford, Frank Loucks, Jr. 1923- *WhoAm 92*
Herek, Stephen 1958- *MiSFD 9*
Herendeen, Carol Denise 1955- *WhoSSW 93*
Herendeen, David Warren 1956- *WhoE 93*
Herendeen, Warren Richard 1934- *WhoE 93*
Herenton, Willie W. 1943- *WhoAm 92, WhoSSW 93*
Heresniak, Edward 1945- *St&PR 93*
Herfindahl, Lloyd Manford 1922- *WhoWor 93*
Herford, Beatrice *AmWomPl*
Herford, Julius *BioIn 17*
Herford, Julius 1901-1981 *Baker 92*
Herford, Robert David 1938- *WhoSSW 93*
Herfort, Robert A. 1919-1991 *BioIn 17*
Herforth, Pamela 1954- *WhoAmW 93*
Herforth, Sandra Lee 1951- *WhoEmL 93*
Herfurth, Egbert 1944- *BioIn 17*
Herfurth, Renate 1943- *BioIn 17*
Herge, Henry Curtis, Sr. 1905- *WhoAm 92, WhoSSW 93*
Herge, Henry Curtis, Jr. 1950- *WhoAm 92*
Herge, J. Curtis 1938- *WhoAm 92*
Hergenhan, Joyce 1941- *St&PR 93, WhoAmW 93*
Hergenhan, Kenneth William 1931- *WhoAm 92*
Hergenrather, Edmund Richard 1917- *St&PR 93, WhoAm 92*
Hergenrather, K.M. 1918- *St&PR 93*
Hergenrather, Richard Ames 1949- *St&PR 93*
Herger, Wally 1945- *CngDr 91*
Herger, Wally W., Jr. 1945- *WhoAm 92*
Hergert, David Evan 1955- *St&PR 93*
Hergert, Louis George, Jr. 1927- *St&PR 93*
Hergesheimer, Joseph 1880-1954 *BioIn 17*
Herguner, Umit 1957- *WhoWor 93*
Herguth, Robert John 1926- *WhoAm 92*
Herin, Susan Marie 1967- *WhoAmW 93*
Herincx, Raimund 1927- *OxDcOp*
Herincx, Raimund (Frederick) 1927- *Baker 92*
Hering, Doris Minnie 1920- *WhoAm 92*
Hering, Grant Barnitz 1936- *WhoAm 92*
Hering, Janet Gordon 1958- *WhoWor 93*
Hering, Karl Gottlieb 1765-1853 *Baker 92*
Hering, Louis *Law&B 92*
Hering, Meczyslaw 1937- *WhoScE 91-4*
Hering, Robert Gustave 1934- *WhoAm 92*
Hering, Wilhelm Tim 1928- *WhoWor 93*
Herington, Cecil John 1924- *WhoAm 92*
Herink, Richie 1932- *WhoE 93*
Heriot, John Ouldfield 1768-1833 *BioIn 17*
Heris, Toni 1932- *WhoAm 92, WhoAmW 93*
Heriteau, Jacqueline 1925- *ConAu 37NR*
Heritier, Charles Andre 1931- *WhoWor 93*
Heritte-Viardot, Louise-Pauline-Marie 1841-1918 *Baker 92*
Herkamp, Nathan D. *Law&B 92*
Herke, Robert, Sr. 1932- *WhoSSW 93*
Herkenham, Lorraine Ann 1958- *WhoAmW 93*
Herker, Larry V. 1938- *St&PR 93*
Herkimer, Nicholas 1728-1777 *HarEnMi*
Herklots, Carl Alexander 1759-1830 *OxDcOp*
Herkness, Lindsay Coates, III 1943- *WhoAm 92*
Herko, Carl Henry 1955- *WhoE 93*
Herkomer, Hubert von 1849-1914 *BioIn 17*
Herlache, Thomas L. 1942- *St&PR 93*
Herley, Richard 1950- *ScF&FL 92*
Herlihy, David *BioIn 17*
Herlihy, Dirlie Anne 1935- *SmATA 73 [port]*
Herlihy, James E. 1942- *St&PR 93*
Herlihy, James Edward 1942- *WhoAm 92*
Herlihy, James Leo 1927- *WhoAm 92*
Herlihy, Maura Ann 1953- *WhoAmW 93*
Herlihy, Robert Edward 1931- *WhoAm 92*
Herlihy, Walter C. 1951- *St&PR 93*
Herlihy, William F. *Law&B 92*
Herlin, Robert M. 1934- *St&PR 93*
Herling, John 1905- *WhoAm 92*
Herling, Marc Jay *Law&B 92*
Herling, Marc Jay 1959- *WhoEmL 93*
Herling, Michael *WhoAm 92*
Herlitzka, Ina Lynn 1955- *WhoAmW 93*
Herlong, D. C. *WhoAm 92, WhoSSW 93*
Herlong, Daniel Webster, III 1945- *WhoWrEP 92*
Herlt, Jasmine M. *Law&B 92*
Hermach, Francis Lewis 1917- *WhoAm 92*
Herman, A.G. 1942- *WhoScE 91-2*
Herman, Alan *ScF&FL 92*
Herman, Alan John 1943- *St&PR 93*
Herman, Allen Ian 1950- *WhoE 93*
Herman, Andrea Bettina 1960- *WhoEmL 93*
Herman, Andrea Maxine 1938- *WhoAm 92, WhoAmW 93*
Herman, Barbara F. 1941- *WhoAm 92*
Herman, Barry M. 1943- *WhoUN 92*
Herman, Bernard 1927- *St&PR 93*
Herman, Bernard Albert 1910- *St&PR 93, WhoE 93, WhoWor 93*
Herman, Beth Warshofsky 1963- *WhoE 93*
Herman, Bill Bradley 1952- *WhoE 93*
Herman, Billy 1909-1992 *NewYTBS 92 [port]*
Herman, Bruce *Law&B 92*
Herman, Bruce Whitney 1953- *WhoE 93*
Herman, Carl A. 1930- *St&PR 93*
Herman, Charles Jacob 1937- *WhoAm 92*
Herman, Charles Robert 1925-1991 *BioIn 17*
Herman, Chester Joseph 1941- *WhoAm 92*
Herman, Chloe Anna 1937- *WhoAmW 93*
Herman, David 1917- *St&PR 93*
Herman, David Jay 1954- *WhoSSW 93*
Herman, Dennis Andrew 1946- *WhoIns 93*
Herman, Diana Mary 1957- *WhoAmW 93*
Herman, Dorothy 1953- *WhoE 93*
Herman, Edith Carol 1944- *WhoAm 92*
Herman, Edward Jayson *Law&B 92*
Herman, Edward Roy 1928- *St&PR 93*
Herman, Ellen Dora 1950- *WhoE 93*
Herman, Felicia Gail 1955- *WhoAmW 93*
Herman, Frances 1951- *WhoAmW 93*
Herman, Friedl 1944- *WhoScE 91-4*
Herman, George Edward 1920- *WhoAm 92*
Herman, Grace G. 1926- *WhoWrEP 92*
Herman, Hank 1949- *WhoAm 92*
Herman, Herbert 1934- *WhoAm 92*
Herman, Irving Leonard 1920- *WhoAm 92*
Herman, Irving Philip 1951- *WhoE 93*
Herman, J.B. *ScF&FL 92*
Herman, Jeffrey Alan 1959- *WhoE 93*
Herman, Jerry *WhoAm 92*
Herman, Jerry 1933- *Baker 92*
Herman, Joan E. 1953- *St&PR 93, WhoIns 93*
Herman, Joan Elizabeth 1953- *WhoAm 92, WhoAmW 93*
Herman, John Joseph 1944- *WhoAm 92*
Herman, Josef 1934- *WhoScE 91-4*
Herman, Judith Lewis 1942- *WhoAmW 93*
Herman, Judith Mudge 1956- *WhoAmW 93*
Herman, Kenneth 1927- *WhoAm 92, WhoWor 93*
Herman, Kenneth Neil 1954- *WhoAm 92*
Herman, Larry Marvin 1951- *WhoSSW 93*
Herman, M. Jean d1992 *BioIn 17, NewYTBS 92*
Herman, Maja B. *WhoE 93*
Herman, Malcolm Jay 1930- *St&PR 93*
Herman, Mario Luis 1958- *WhoE 93, WhoEmL 93*
Herman, Mark *MiSFD 9*
Herman, Mary Ann d1992 *BioIn 17, NewYTBS 92*
Herman, Mary Elizabeth 1943- *WhoAmW 93*
Herman, Mary Margaret 1935- *WhoAmW 93*
Herman, Melvin Duaine 1925- *St&PR 93*
Herman, Michael Edward 1941- *St&PR 93*
Herman, Michael Lee 1947- *WhoEmL 93, WhoSSW 93*
Herman, Michael R. *Law&B 92*
Herman, Michaela Rossner- *ScF&FL 92*
Herman, Michelle 1955- *ConAu 136, WhoWrEP 92*
Herman, Mindy L. *Law&B 92*
Herman, Nancy Jo *Law&B 92*
Herman, Nathaniel 1930- *St&PR 93*
Herman, Paul *BioIn 17*
Herman, Pee-Wee *BioIn 17, QDrFCA 92*
Herman, Peter Simon 1938- *WhoSSW 93*
Herman, R. Dixon 1911-1990 *BioIn 17*
Herman, Reuben A. 1931- *St&PR 93*
Herman, Richard, Jr. 1939- *ConAu 137*
Herman, Robert 1914- *WhoAm 92*
Herman, Robert Lewis 1927- *St&PR 93, WhoAm 92, WhoE 93*
Herman, Robert S. 1919- *WhoAm 92*
Herman, Robin A. *Law&B 92*
Herman, Samuel 1928- *St&PR 93*
Herman, Sharon L. *Law&B 92*
Herman, Shelli Ann 1966- *WhoSSW 93*
Herman, Shirley Yvonne 1941- *WhoAmW 93*
Herman, Stephen 1942- *St&PR 93*
Herman, Stephen Allen 1943- *WhoAm 92*
Herman, Stephen Edward 1949- *WhoEmL 93*
Herman, Stephen Gerald 1939- *WhoSSW 93*
Herman, Steven 1943- *BioIn 17*
Herman, Susan Jane *WhoE 93*
Herman, Theodore L. 1936- *St&PR 93, WhoIns 93*
Herman, Thomas *BioIn 17*
Herman, Vasile 1929- *Baker 92*
Herman, William *ConAu 139*
Herman, William, III 1938- *St&PR 93*
Herman, William Hickey 1948- *St&PR 93*
Herman, William John 1942- *WhoE 93*
Herman, William Sparkes 1931- *WhoAm 92*
Herman, Woody *BioIn 17*
Herman, Woody 1913-1987 *Baker 92*
Herman, Zbigniew Stanistaw 1935- *WhoWor 93*
Herman, Zdzislaw 1945- *WhoScE 91-4*
Hermance, Frank S. 1948- *St&PR 93*
Hermance, Richard Thomas 1928- *St&PR 93*
Hermanek, Don 1948- *St&PR 93*
Hermanek, Paul 1924- *WhoScE 91-3*
Hermanies, John Hans 1922- *WhoAm 92*
Hermaniuk, Maxim 1911- *WhoAm 92*
Hermann, Allen Max 1938- *WhoAm 92*
Hermann, Anton 1945- *WhoScE 91-4*
Hermann, Arthur W. 1944- *St&PR 93*
Hermann, Edward Robert 1920- *WhoAm 92, WhoWor 93*
Hermann, Frederick A., Jr. 1924- *St&PR 93*
Hermann, Gerald W. 1934- *St&PR 93*
Hermann, Gerd M. 1941- *WhoScE 91-3*
Hermann, Hans 1870-1931 *Baker 92*
Hermann, Horst 1930- *WhoWor 93*
Hermann, Howard William *Law&B 92*
Hermann, Jane Pomerance 1935- *WhoAm 92, WhoE 93*
Hermann, John Arthur 1943- *WhoWor 93*
Hermann, Lawrence Shepley 1952- *St&PR 93*
Hermann, Linda C. *Law&B 92*
Hermann, Margaret Gladden 1938- *WhoAmW 93*
Hermann, Martin 1949- *WhoWor 93*
Hermann, Naomi Basel 1918- *WhoAmW 93*
Hermann, Paul David 1925- *WhoAm 92*
Hermann, Philip J. 1916- *WhoAm 92*
Hermann, Robert 1869-1912 *Baker 92*
Hermann, Robert J. 1933- *St&PR 93*
Hermann, Robert J. 1944- *St&PR 93*
Hermann, Robert Jay 1933- *WhoAm 92*
Hermann, Robert John 1944- *WhoAm 92*
Hermann, Robert R. 1923- *St&PR 93*
Hermann, Robert Ringen 1923- *WhoAm 92*
Hermann, Steven Istvan 1934- *WhoAm 92, WhoE 93*
Hermann, Wilfred Leroy 1933- *St&PR 93*
Hermann, William Henry 1924- *WhoAm 92*
Hermannsson, Steingrimur 1928- *WhoWor 93*
Hermannus 1013-1054 *Baker 92*
Hermanova, Hana 1934- *WhoUN 92*
Hermanovski, Egils P. *WhoAm 92*
Hermanowicz, Henry Joseph 1928- *WhoAm 92*
Hermans, Franciscus Maria Henricus 1926- *WhoWor 93*
Hermans, Hubert John 1937- *WhoWor 93*
Hermans, Reginald Boydell, Jr. 1937- *St&PR 93*
Herman-Sekulich, Maya B. *WhoE 93*
Hermansen, Martin *Law&B 92*
Hermanson, Ake (Oscar Werner) 1923- *Baker 92*
Hermanson, Harvey Philip *WhoSSW 93*
Hermanson Ogilvie, Judith 1945- *WhoAm 92*
Hermansson, Anne-Marie *WhoScE 91-4*
Hermansson, Bjorn Robert 1953- *WhoWor 93*
Hermele, Jules Joseph 1951- *St&PR 93*
Hermelin, Victor M. 1914- *St&PR 93*
Hermenet, Eugene W. 1936- *St&PR 93*
Hermes, Ethelle Manning *AmWomPl*
Hermes, Frank J. 1943- *St&PR 93*
Hermes, Jean-Louis Dumas- *BioIn 17*
Hermes, Johann Timotheus 1738-1821 *BioIn 17*
Hermes, Juanita H. 1943- *St&PR 93*
Hermesch, Alan L. 1946- *WhoE 93*

Hermesdorf, James E. 1943- *St&PR 93*
Hermesdorff, Michael 1833-1885 *Baker 92*
Hermia, Jacques 1938- *WhoScE 91-2*
Herminghouse, Patricia Anne 1940- *WhoAm 92*
Hermogenes c. 160-c. 230 *OxDcByz*
Hermoniakos, Constantine fl. 14th cent.- *OxDcByz*
Hermosillo, Jaime Humberto 1942- *MiSFD 9*
Hermsen, Gail Marie 1951- *WhoEmL 93*
Hermstedt, (Johann) Simon 1778-1846 *Baker 92*
Hermus, Rudolf J.J. 1941- *WhoScE 91-3*
Hern, John Robert 1953- *St&PR 93*
Hern, Joseph George *Law&B 92*
Hern, Kenneth Truman 1937- *WhoWor 93*
Hernacki, Mike *BioIn 17*
Hernadi, Ferenc Jozsef 1929- *WhoScE 91-4*
Hernadi, Paul 1936- *WhoAm 92, WhoWrEP 92*
Hernadi, Tibor *MiSFD 9*
Hernady, Bertalan Fred 1927- *WhoWor 93*
Hernandez, A. *Law&B 92*
Hernandez, Abisail 1949- *WhoE 93*
Hernandez, Aileen Clarke 1926- *WhoAmW 93*
Hernandez, Alfonso C. 1938- *DcLB 122 [port]*
Hernandez, Angel 1947- *WhoScE 91-3*
Hernandez, Anna Maria 1960- *St&PR 93*
Hernandez, Antonia *HispAmA [port]*
Hernandez, Antonia 1948- *NotHsAW 93 [port], WhoAmW 93*
Hernandez, Benigno Cardenas 1862-1954 *HispAmA*
Hernandez, Carlos M. *Law&B 92*
Hernandez, Carlos Manuel 1954- *WhoEmL 93*
Hernandez, Christine 1951- *NotHsAW 93, WhoAmW 93*
Hernandez, Daniel Arthur 1945- *WhoSSW 93*
Hernandez, Diego Edyl 1934- *HispAmA, WhoAm 92*
Hernandez, Efren 1904-1958 *DcMexL*
Hernandez, Enrique 1951- *HispAmA, WhoE 93*
Hernandez, Ester 1944- *HispAmA*
Hernandez, Felipe d1992 *NewYTBS 92*
Hernandez, Felisberto 1902-1964 *SpAmA*
Hernandez, Florante Dela Cruz 1963- *WhoWor 93*
Hernandez, Frances 1926- *WhoAmW 93*
Hernandez, Francisco 1946- *DcMexL*
Hernandez, Frank Bernard 1939- *WhoE 93*
Hernandez, Gonzalo J. *HispAmA*
Hernandez, Hermilio 1931- *Baker 92*
Hernandez, Humberto d1991 *BioIn 17*
Hernandez, Ines 1947- *DcLB 122 [port]*
Hernandez, Irene R. *St&PR 93*
Hernandez, Jacqueline Charmaine 1960- *WhoE 93, WhoEmL 93, WhoWor 93*
Hernandez, Jesus Horacio 1943- *WhoWor 93*
Hernandez, Jo Farb 1952- *WhoAmW 93*
Hernandez, Jose Manuel 1925- *HispAmA*
Hernandez, Julio R. 1931- *WhoIns 93*
Hernandez, Kara *BioIn 17*
Hernandez, Keith 1953- *HispAmA [port]*
Hernandez, Linda Louise 1952- *WhoEmL 93, WhoSSW 93*
Hernandez, Linda Luree Welch 1952- *WhoSSW 93*
Hernandez, Louis Robert 1947- *St&PR 93*
Hernandez, Lourdes T. *Law&B 92*
Hernandez, Luis Islas 1946- *WhoWor 93*
Hernandez, Luisa Josefina 1928- *BioIn 17, DcMexL*
Hernandez, Lupe G. 1944- *WhoAmW 93*
Hernandez, Maria Latigo 1893?-1986 *NotHsAW 93*
Hernandez, Marjorie Ray 1927- *WhoAmW 93*
Hernandez, Marvin Donald 1958- *WhoSSW 93*
Hernandez, Raul 1957- *WhoWor 93*
Hernandez, Robert M. 1944- *St&PR 93*
Hernandez, Roberto *BioIn 17*
Hernandez, Roberto Reyes 1950- *WhoEmL 93, WhoSSW 93, WhoWor 93*
Hernandez, Tomas Capatan 1946- *WhoE 93*
Hernandez, Wanda Grace 1942- *WhoAmW 93*
Hernandez, Wilbert Eduardo 1916- *WhoWor 93*
Hernandez, William H. 1948- *WhoAm 92*
Hernandez, William Hector, Jr. 1930- *WhoAm 92*
Hernandez-Agosto, Miguel Angel 1927- *WhoSSW 93*
Hernandez Alvarez, Jose 1948- *WhoWor 93*
Hernandez-Avila, Manuel Luis 1935- *WhoAm 92*
Hernandez Campos, Jorge 1921- *DcMexL*
Hernandez-Cata, Ernesto 1942- *WhoUN 92*
Hernandez Cifuentes, J. Alfredo 1952- *WhoWor 93*
Hernandez Colon, Rafael 1936- *DcCPCAm, WhoAm 92, WhoSSW 93, WhoWor 93*
Hernandez Cruz, Victor 1949- *BioIn 17*
Hernandez de Alba, Guillermo 1906-1988 *BioIn 17*
Hernandez De Arteaga, Esther Elena 1955- *WhoWor 93*
Hernandez-Denton, Federico 1954- *WhoAm 92, WhoSSW 93*
Hernandez Galicia, Joaquin *DcCPCAm*
Hernandez Gamboa, Patricio 1943- *WhoWor 93*
Hernandez-Lopez, Rhazes 1918- *Baker 92*
Hernandez-Machado, Aurora 1959- *WhoWor 93*
Hernandez Moncada, Eduardo 1899- *Baker 92*
Hernandez-Pinero, Sally B. 1952- *NotHsAW 93*
Hernandez-Ramos, Florence 1950- *NotHsAW 93*
Hernandez Sales, Pablo 1834-1910 *Baker 92*
Hernandez Sanchez, Homero Luis 1941- *WhoUN 92*
Hernandez-Sanchez, Juan Longino 1928- *WhoWor 93*
Hernandez-Vela Salgado, Edmundo 1940- *WhoWor 93*
Hernandez Xolocotzi, Efraim *BioIn 17*
Hernandez-Yago, Jose 1942- *WhoScE 91-3*
Hernandez y Aguirre, Mario 1928-1984 *SpAmA*
Hernando (y Palomar), Rafael (Jose Maria) 1822-1888 *Baker 92*
Hernandorena, Eduardo Andres 1944- *WhoWor 93*
Hernberg, Sven *WhoScE 91-4*
Herndon, Alice *AmWomPl*
Herndon, Alice Patterson Latham 1916- *WhoAmW 93, WhoSSW 93, WhoWor 93*
Herndon, Angelo. 1913- *EncAACR*
Herndon, Betty LaRue 1936- *WhoAmW 93*
Herndon, Boyd K. *Law&B 92*
Herndon, Charles Harbison 1915- *WhoAm 92*
Herndon, Claude Nash 1916- *WhoAm 92*
Herndon, Crystal Gerise 1963- *WhoSSW 93*
Herndon, D.A., Jr. 1908- *St&PR 93*
Herndon, Donna Ruth Grogan 1942- *WhoAmW 93*
Herndon, Gayle W. *Law&B 92*
Herndon, James Francis 1929- *WhoAm 92*
Herndon, James H., Jr. 1939- *WhoSSW 93*
Herndon, James Henry 1938- *WhoAm 92, WhoE 93*
Herndon, Jerry W. *Law&B 92*
Herndon, John Joyce Carter 1931- *WhoAm 92*
Herndon, John V. 1941- *St&PR 93*
Herndon, Mark *WhoAm 92*
Herndon, Michael N. 1939- *St&PR 93*
Herndon, Noah Twist 1932- *St&PR 93*
Herndon, Rhonda Dianne 1960- *WhoSSW 93*
Herndon, Robert G. 1934- *St&PR 93*
Herndon, Robert McCulloch 1935- *WhoAm 92*
Herndon, Rosemary Van Vleet 1931- *WhoAmW 93*
Herndon, Sandra Lee Fish 1941- *WhoAmW 93*
Herndon, Steven L. *Law&B 92*
Herndon, Terry Eugene 1939- *WhoAm 92*
Herndon, Thomas Glenn 1920- *WhoSSW 93*
Herndon, Ursule *ScF&FL 92*
Herndon, William d1990 *BioIn 17*
Herndon, William Henry 1818-1891 *BioIn 17*
Herne, James A. 1839-1901 *GayN*
Herne, Julie Adrienne *AmWomPl*
Hernes, Seymour Irwin 1927- *St&PR 93*
Herney, Susan Ann 1942- *WhoAmW 93*
Hernke, Richard R. 1954- *St&PR 93*
Hernon, Joseph Martin, Jr. 1936- *WhoAm 92, WhoWor 93*
Hernon, Richard Francis 1940- *WhoE 93*
Hernried, Robert (Franz Richard) 1883-1951 *Baker 92*
Hernstadt, Judith Filenbaum 1942- *WhoAm 92, WhoWor 93*
Hernstadt, William H. 1935- *WhoWor 93*
Hernton, Calvin C. 1934- *WhoWrEP 92*
Hernu, Charles 1923-1990 *BioIn 17*
Hero, Andrew W. *Law&B 92*
Hero, Barbara Ferrell 1925- *WhoE 93*
Hero, Byron A. 1950- *WhoAm 92*
Herod, Beatrice Ann 1937- *WhoAmW 93*
Herodian fl. 2nd cent.- *OxDcByz*
Herodotus *BioIn 17, OxDcByz*
Herodotus 485?BC-425?BC *Expl 93 [port]*
Herod the Great, I, King of Judea 73BC-4BC *BioIn 17*
Herold, Ann Bixby 1937- *SmATA 72 [port]*
Herold, Bernardo Jerosch 1933- *WhoScE 91-3*
Herold, Charles W., Jr. 1929- *St&PR 93*
Herold, David d1865 *BioIn 17*
Herold, Edward William 1907- *WhoAm 92, WhoE 93*
Herold, Ferdinand 1791-1833 *IntDcOp [port], OxDcOp*
Herold, (Louis-Joseph) Ferdinand 1791-1833 *Baker 92*
Herold, Francois-Joseph 1755-1802 *See* Herold, (Louis-Joseph) Ferdinand 1791-1833 *Baker 92*
Herold, Istvan 1930- *WhoScE 91-4*
Herold, John W., Jr. *BioIn 17*
Herold, Karl Guenter 1947- *WhoAm 92, WhoWor 93*
Herold, Lucia Pozzi-Escot 1921- *WhoWor 93*
Herold, Manfred *WhoScE 91-4*
Herold, Richard Carl 1927- *WhoE 93*
Herold, Ronald Joseph 1939- *St&PR 93*
Herold, Vilhelm (Kristoffer) 1865-1937 *Baker 92*
Heroman, Donald T. 1951- *St&PR 93*
Heron, Antoinette Tomai 1947- *St&PR 93*
Heron, David Winston 1920- *WhoAm 92*
Heron, Henrietta *AmWomPl*
Heron, Iver *WhoScE 91-2*
Heron, J.F. 1946- *WhoScE 91-2*
Heron, Jacqueline Brenda 1949- *WhoWrEP 92*
Heron, Joanne Elizabeth 1944- *WhoAmW 93*
Heron, Nye Brian 1952- *WhoE 93*
Heron, Patrick 1920- *WhoWor 93*
Heron, Timothy Edward 1948- *WhoWor 93*
Heron, William J., Jr. 1941- *St&PR 93*
Heron, Wm. B. 1940- *St&PR 93*
Heroux, Denis 1940- *MiSFD 9*
Heroy, William Bayard, Jr. 1915- *WhoAm 92*
Herpe, David A. 1953- *WhoEmL 93*
Herpel, George Lloyd 1921- *WhoAm 92*
Herpetz, E. *WhoScE 91-3*
Herpich, William Arthur 1922- *WhoAm 92*
Herpin, Eric J. *Law&B 92*
Herpst, Robert Dix 1947- *WhoE 93*
Herr, Charlotte *AmWomPl*
Herr, Cynthia Greco *Law&B 92*
Herr, Dan *BioIn 17*
Herr, Dan 1917-1990 *ScF&FL 92*
Herr, Earl Binkley, Jr. 1928- *WhoAm 92*
Herr, Henry D. *St&PR 93*
Herr, Hugh *BioIn 17*
Herr, John Mervin, Jr. 1930- *WhoSSW 93*
Herr, Judy Ann 1941- *WhoAmW 93*
Herr, Kenneth Julian 1927- *WhoAm 92*
Herr, Lucien 1864-1926 *BioIn 17*
Herr, Michael *BioIn 17*
Herr, Ober Samuel, Jr. 1927- *St&PR 93*
Herr, Philip Michael 1955- *WhoE 93*
Herr, Richard 1922- *WhoAm 92*
Herr, Richard C. *Law&B 92*
Herr, Robert C. 1939- *St&PR 93*
Herr, Terry Edward 1959- *WhoEmL 93*
Herra, Rafael Angel 1943- *SpAmA*
Herrbold, William Philip 1945- *St&PR 93*
Herre, Michael F. 1948- *St&PR 93*
Herregat, Guy-Georges Jacques 1939- *WhoAm 92, WhoE 93, WhoWor 93*
Herrell, Dennis James 1942- *WhoSSW 93*
Herrell, James Milton 1943- *WhoE 93*
Herrell, Wallace Edgar 1909- *WhoAm 92*
Herrema, Donald J. 1952- *St&PR 93*
Herrema, Donald James 1952- *WhoAm 92*
Herren, Daniel E. *Law&B 92*
Herren, Mary Catherine 1948- *WhoAmW 93*
Herren, Nanon Lee *AmWomPl*
Herren, Patricia Eads 1931- *WhoAmW 93*
Herren, Stanley A. 1947- *St&PR 93*
Herren, William Richard 1946- *St&PR 93*
Herrera, Anthony *MiSFD 9*
Herrera, Bill 1953- *WhoAm 92*
Herrera, Carolina *BioIn 17*
Herrera, Carolina 20th cent.- *HispAmA [port]*
Herrera, Carolina 1939- *NotHsAW 93 [port]*
Herrera, Cristina 1955- *WhoWrEP 92*
Herrera, Ernesto Falar 1942- *WhoAsAP 91*
Herrera, Eusebio Stenio 1945- *WhoWor 93*
Herrera, Flavio 1895-1968 *SpAmA*
Herrera, Francisco de c. 1576-1656 *BioIn 17*
Herrera, Francisco de 1622-1685 *BioIn 17*
Herrera, Georgina 1936- *SpAmA*
Herrera, Jaime L. 1940- *WhoUN 92*
Herrera, John *WhoAm 92*
Herrera, Juan Felipe 1948- *DcLB 122 [port]*
Herrera, Mary Cardenas 1938- *WhoAmW 93, WhoSSW 93, WhoWor 93*
Herrera, Miguel 1835-1905 *HispAmA*
Herrera, Moises Torrijos d1990 *BioIn 17*
Herrera, Omar Torrijos 1929-1981 *BioIn 17*
Herrera, Paul Fredrick 1948- *WhoAm 92, WhoE 93, WhoEmL 93*
Herrera, Robert N. *Law&B 92*
Herrera, Sandra Johnson 1944- *WhoAmW 93*
Herrera, Shirley Mae 1942- *WhoAmW 93, WhoWor 93*
Herrera de la Fuente, Luis 1916- *Baker 92*
Herrera de Noble, Ernestina Laura 1925- *WhoWor 93*
Herrera-Esparza, Rafael 1949- *WhoWor 93*
Herrera-Estrella, Luis Rafael 1956- *WhoWor 93*
Herrera Mesa, Luis 1949- *WhoScE 91-3*
Herrera-Sobek, Maria *HispAmA*
Herrera-Vegas, Jorge Hugo 1941- *WhoWor 93*
Herrerias, Catalina 1948- *WhoEmL 93*
Herres, Phillip Benjamin 1941- *WhoAm 92*
Herres, Robert T. 1932- *WhoIns 93*
Herres, Robert Tralles 1932- *WhoAm 92*
Herreshoff, Halsey Chase 1933- *St&PR 93, WhoE 93*
Herreweghe, Philippe 1947- *Baker 92*
Herrhausen, Alfred *BioIn 17*
Herrick, Bruce Hale 1936- *WhoAm 92*
Herrick, Bruce W. 1944- *WhoIns 93*
Herrick, Christine Comeaux 1954- *WhoAmW 93*
Herrick, Clarence J. 1907- *St&PR 93*
Herrick, Daniel P. *Law&B 92*
Herrick, Donald T. 1943- *St&PR 93*
Herrick, Elbert Charles 1919- *WhoE 93*
Herrick, Gerald D. 1934- *WhoAm 92*
Herrick, Gertrude *AmWomPl*
Herrick, John D. 1932- *St&PR 93*
Herrick, John Dennis 1932- *WhoAm 92, WhoWor 93*
Herrick, Kathleen Magara 1943- *WhoAmW 93*
Herrick, Kenneth Gilbert 1921- *WhoAm 92*
Herrick, Kristine Ford 1947- *WhoE 93, WhoEmL 93*
Herrick, Paul 1938- *WhoSSW 93*
Herrick, Paul 1949- *St&PR 93*
Herrick, Peter 1926- *St&PR 93, WhoAm 92, WhoE 93*
Herrick, Robert 1591-1674 *DcLB 126*
Herrick, Robert 1868-1938 *GayN*
Herrick, Robert Ford 1912- *WhoAm 92*
Herrick, Sonja Jane 1949- *WhoEmL 93*
Herrick, Stephen G. 1909- *St&PR 93*
Herrick, Todd W. 1942- *WhoAm 92*
Herrick, Todd Wesley 1942- *St&PR 93*
Herrick, Virginia *SweetSg C*
Herrick, William 1915- *WhoWrEP 92*
Herrick, William Duncan *Law&B 92*
Herridge, Charles *ScF&FL 92*
Herridge, Julie Anne 1958- *WhoEmL 93*
Herridge, Peter Lamont 1951- *WhoE 93*
Herrier, Mark *MiSFD 9*
Herriford, Robert Levi, Sr. 1931- *WhoAm 92*
Herrigel, Howard Ralph 1924- *St&PR 93*
Herriman, George 1880-1944 *BioIn 17*
Herrin, Gene Ann *Law&B 92*
Herrin, Joseph Richard 1923- *WhoSSW 93*
Herrin, M. Gwen *Law&B 92*
Herrin, Mary Lu 1944- *WhoAmW 93*
Herrin, Moreland 1922- *WhoAm 92*
Herrin, Phyllis Marshall 1947- *WhoAmW 93*
Herrin, Tammy Sue *Law&B 92*
Herring, Allen Victor 1944- *St&PR 93*
Herring, Alvan A., Jr. 1943- *St&PR 93*
Herring, Art 1907- *BioIn 17*
Herring, Charlanne Fields 1947- *WhoWrEP 92*
Herring, David Lawrence 1946- *WhoE 93*
Herring, Doris Anna 1937- *WhoAmW 93*
Herring, Edward Pendleton 1903- *BioIn 17*
Herring, Gregory 1950- *St&PR 93*
Herring, Jack William 1925- *WhoAm 92*
Herring, Jerone Carson *Law&B 92*
Herring, Jerone Carson 1938- *St&PR 93, WhoAm 92*
Herring, John R. 1931- *St&PR 93*
Herring, Lawrence Shepard 1946- *WhoEmL 93*

Herring, Leonard G. 1927- St&PR 93
Herring, Leonard Gray 1927- WhoAm 92, WhoSSW 93
Herring, Lucy BioIn 17
Herring, Michelle Denise 1965- WhoAmW 93
Herring, Nancy L. 1956- WhoEmL 93
Herring, Paul Francis 1956- WhoWor 93
Herring, Paul W. Law&B 92
Herring, Pendleton 1903- BioIn 17
Herring, Reuben 1922- WhoAm 92
Herring, Robert H(erschel) 1938- WhoWrEP 92
Herring, Shirley Macklin 1954- St&PR 93
Herring, Susan Weller 1947- WhoAm 92, WhoAmW 93, WhoEmL 93
Herring, Vincent BioIn 17
Herring, William Conyers 1914- WhoAm 92
Herringer, Frank C. 1942- St&PR 93
Herringer, Frank Casper 1942- WhoAm 92
Herringshaw, Pamela Margaret 1946- WhoAmW 93
Herrington, E. Paul Law&B 92
Herrington, Hardy R. 1943- St&PR 93
Herrington, James Benjamin, Jr. 1953- WhoEmL 93
Herrington, John David, III 1934- WhoAm 92
Herrington, John Stewart 1939- WhoSSW 93
Herrington, Marion Law&B 92
Herrington, Mark Bruce 1959- WhoSSW 93
Herrington, Raymond F. St&PR 93
Herrington, Roger D. Law&B 92
Herrington, Rowdy MiSFD 9
Herrington, Terri 1957- WhoWrEP 92
Herrington, William C. 1930-1989 BioIn 17
Herrington-Borre, Frances June 1935- WhoAmW 93
Herrinton, John Peter 1943- WhoAm 92
Herriot, Edouard 1872-1957 BioIn 17
Herriot, James 1916- ConAu 40NR, WhoWor 93
Herriott, Donald Richard 1928- WhoAm 92
Herriott, Roger M. d1992 NewYTBS 92
Herriott, Roger M. 1908-1992 BioIn 17
Herriott, Scott H. 1945- St&PR 93
Herritt, David Michael 1957- St&PR 93
Herrlich, Frank Dieter 1952- WhoWor 93
Herrlich, Peter A. 1940- WhoScE 91-3
Herrlich, Peter Albert 1940- WhoWor 93
Herrman, Barbara A. Law&B 92
Herrman, James R. 1950- St&PR 93
Herrmann, Andrea Watson 1942- WhoSSW 93
Herrmann, Andrew B. Law&B 92
Herrmann, Barbara H. 1946- St&PR 93
Herrmann, Benjamin Edward 1919- WhoAm 92
Herrmann, Bernard 1911-1975 Baker 92, BioIn 17
Herrmann, Bryan Louis 1935- St&PR 93
Herrmann, Carol 1944- WhoAmW 93
Herrmann, Cynthia Cecilia Wieber 1951- WhoE 93
Herrmann, Douglas J. 1941- WhoAm 92
Herrmann, Duane Lawrence 1951- WhoWrEP 92
Herrmann, Eberhard Bruno 1947- WhoWor 93
Herrmann, Eduard 1850-1937 Baker 92
Herrmann, Edward Kirk 1943- WhoAm 92
Herrmann, Eric P. Law&B 92
Herrmann, George 1921- WhoAm 92
Herrmann, Gerold H. 1941- WhoUN 92
Herrmann, Gunter 1925- WhoScE 91-3
Herrmann, Gunter Friedrich 1925- WhoWor 93
Herrmann, Hajo 1913- BioIn 17
Herrmann, Helen d1991 BioIn 17
Herrmann, Hugo 1896-1967 Baker 92
Herrmann, John 1931- WhoSSW 93, WhoWrEP 92
Herrmann, John A., Jr. 1935- St&PR 93
Herrmann, John B. 1932- WhoE 93
Herrmann, John Robert 1928- St&PR 93
Herrmann, Keith R. 1960- St&PR 93
Herrmann, Kenneth John, Jr. 1943- WhoE 93, WhoWor 93
Herrmann, Klaus Peter 1937- WhoScE 91-3
Herrmann, Lacy Bunnell 1929- WhoAm 92, WhoE 93, WhoWor 93
Herrmann, Lisa C. Law&B 92
Herrmann, Manfred 1941- WhoScE 91-3
Herrmann, Mary Margaret 1950- WhoAm 92
Herrmann, Norbert 1943- WhoWor 93
Herrmann, Raymond R. 1920- St&PR 93
Herrmann, Robert William 1941- WhoSSW 93
Herrmann, Thomas Francis 1951- WhoEmL 93
Herrmann, William J. 1919- St&PR 93
Herrnstadt, Richard Lawrence 1926- WhoAm 92
Herrnstein, Richard Julius 1930- WhoAm 92
Herrnstein, William Henry 1936- St&PR 93
Herro, John Joseph 1945- WhoSSW 93
Herrod, David J. Law&B 92
Herroelen, Pascal G. Law&B 92
Herrold, Edmund McMahan 1949- WhoE 93
Herrold, Kenneth Frederick 1913- WhoAm 92
Herrold, Paul R. St&PR 93
Herrold, Russell Phillips, Jr. 1924- WhoAm 92
Herron, Andrew 1909- BioIn 17
Herron, Anita Marie 1940- WhoAmW 93
Herron, Carol Christine 1944- WhoAmW 93
Herron, Carolivia 1947- WhoAmW 93, WhoEmL 93
Herron, David William 1940- St&PR 93
Herron, Don 1952- ScF&FL 92
Herron, Ellen Patricia 1927- WhoAmW 93
Herron, Francis Jay 1837-1902 HarEnMi
Herron, Georgia Johnson 1924- WhoE 93
Herron, Gregory Light 1956- St&PR 93
Herron, Hal F. 1953- St&PR 93
Herron, James Dudley 1936- WhoAm 92
Herron, James M. 1934- WhoAm 92
Herron, James Michael Law&B 92
Herron, James Michael 1934- St&PR 93
Herron, John Lewis 1944- St&PR 93
Herron, Julie Anne 1957- WhoSSW 93
Herron, Lee Scott 1956- WhoEmL 93
Herron, Linda J. Law&B 92
Herron, Orley R. 1933- WhoAm 92
Herron, Patsy Ludgood 1953- WhoEmL 93
Herron, Philip Meredith 1940- WhoSSW 93
Herron, R. Lane WhoWrEP 92
Herron, Stephen House 1925- WhoAm 92
Herron, Thomas J. 1947- WhoE 93
Herron, Wendy Watts 1952- WhoAmW 93, WhoSSW 93, WhoWor 93
Hersant, Robert BioIn 17
Hersant, Robert Joseph Emile 1920- WhoWor 93
Hersberger, Jill Ann Gosma 1954- WhoEmL 93
Hersch, Henry H. 1925- St&PR 93
Hersch, Joseph 1925- WhoWor 93
Herschbach, Diana Lee 1944- WhoAmW 93
Herschbach, Dudley Robert 1932- WhoAm 92, WhoE 93, WhoWor 93
Herschel, Abraham Joshua 1907-1972 JeAmHC
Herschel, William 1738-1822 BioIn 17
Herschel, (Frederick) William 1738-1822 Baker 92
Herschelman, Dianne Albert 1936- WhoAmW 93
Herschensohn, Bruce 1932- WhoAm 92
Herschitz, Roman 1954- WhoE 93
Herschkowitz, Janis 1959- St&PR 93
Herschler, Dale C. 1911- WhoWrEP 92
Herschler, Ed 1918-1990 BioIn 17
Herschler, Robert John 1923- WhoAm 92
Herschman, Arthur 1929-1991 BioIn 17
Herschorn, Michael Julius 1933- WhoAm 92
Herscovici, Alan 1948- ConAu 138
Herscovici, Michael 1964- WhoWor 93
Herseth, Adolph 1921- Baker 92
Hersey, David Floyd 1928- WhoAm 92
Hersey, David Kenneth 1939- WhoAm 92
Hersey, Donald E. 1944- St&PR 93
Hersey, Frederic T. 1933- St&PR 93
Hersey, Garry L. 1929- St&PR 93
Hersey, George Leonard 1927- WhoAm 92
Hersey, George Willis, Jr. 1944- St&PR 93
Hersey, John 1914- BioIn 17, JrnUS, WhoAm 92, WhoWrEP 92
Hersey, Jude Sullivan 1941- WhoE 93
Hersey, Marilyn Elaine 1943- WhoAmW 93
Hersey, Stephen P. Law&B 92
Hersh, Barry Fred 1947- WhoE 93
Hersh, Bernard 1922- WhoE 93
Hersh, Ira Paul 1948- WhoE 93, WhoWor 93
Hersh, Leroy 1920- WhoAm 92
Hersh, Raymond T. 1937- St&PR 93
Hersh, Robert 1946- St&PR 93
Hersh, Robert Lawrence 1954- WhoSSW 93
Hersh, Seymour 1937- JrnUS
Hersh, Seymour M. BioIn 17
Hersh, Seymour M. 1937- WhoAm 92
Hersh, Sheldon Paul 1947- WhoE 93
Hersh, Stanley Blair 1943- WhoE 93
Hersh, Stephen Peter 1940- WhoAm 92
Hersha, Linda Law&B 92
Hershaft, Arthur N. 1937- St&PR 93
Hershaft, Leon d1991 BioIn 17
Hershberg, David S. 1941- St&PR 93
Hershberg, Philip Isaac 1935- WhoE 93
Hershberger, John Wayne, II 1946- WhoIns 93
Hershberger, Larry D. 1944- WhoIns 93
Hershberger, Willard BioIn 17
Hershcopf, Berta Ruth 1924- WhoE 93
Hershenov, Bernard Zion 1927- WhoAm 92
Hershenson, Arthur Law&B 92
Hershenson, Herbert Malcolm 1929- WhoE 93
Hersher, Kurt B. 1928- St&PR 93
Hershey, Alan Davis 1957- WhoWor 93
Hershey, Alfred Day 1908- WhoAm 92, WhoE 93, WhoWor 93
Hershey, Barbara 1948- ConTFT 10, WhoAm 92, WhoAmW 93
Hershey, Colin Harry 1935- WhoAm 92, WhoE 93
Hershey, Dale 1941- WhoAm 92
Hershey, Daniel 1931- WhoWrEP 92
Hershey, Falls Bacon 1918- WhoAm 92
Hershey, Gerald Lee 1931- WhoAm 92
Hershey, H. Garland, Jr. 1940- WhoAm 92
Hershey, Henry E. 1930- St&PR 93
Hershey, John 1925- St&PR 93
Hershey, Jonathan Richard 1956- WhoWrEP 92
Hershey, Lisa L. Law&B 92
Hershey, Lori O'Mel Harrell 1964- WhoWrEP 92
Hershey, Lowell Jay 1947- WhoEmL 93
Hershey, Mark A. 1952- St&PR 93
Hershey, Milton Snavely 1857-1945 BioIn 17
Hershey, Nathan 1930- WhoAm 92
Hershey, Philip 1913- WhoSSW 93
Hershey, Robert Lewis 1941- WhoE 93
Hershfield, Lotte Cassel 1931- WhoE 93
Hershiser, Orel BioIn 17
Hershiser, Orel Leonard, IV 1958- WhoAm 92
Hershkowitz, Noah 1941- WhoAm 92
Hershkowitz, Ronald M. Law&B 92
Hershman, Christopher Noel 1955- WhoE 93
Hershman, Daniel A. Law&B 92
Hershman, Ethan J. 1963- St&PR 93
Hershman, Jack I. 1955- WhoE 93
Hershman, Jerome 1924- St&PR 93
Hershman, Joel MiSFD 9
Hershman, Judith 1949- WhoE 93
Hershman, Lynn Lester WhoAm 92
Hershman, Mendes d1992 NewYTBS 92 [port]
Hershman, Mendes 1911-1992 BioIn 17
Hershman, Morris 1926- ScF&FL 92
Hershman, Robert Scott 1951- St&PR 93
Hershner, Robert Franklin, Jr. 1944- WhoSSW 93
Hershock, Howard Lester 1919- WhoE 93
Hersholt, Jean 1886-1956 BioIn 17
Hershon, Judith G. Law&B 92
Hershon, Robert Myles 1936- WhoE 93, WhoWrEP 92
Hershorn, Michael 1956- WhoSSW 93
Hersi, Abdalla Farah 1931- WhoUN 92
Herskind, Carl C., Jr. 1937- St&PR 93
Hersko, Bart S. Law&B 92
Hersko, Janos 1926- DrEEuF
Herskovits, Lily Eva 1933- WhoAmW 93
Herskovits, Melville J. 1895-1963 IntDcAn
Herskovits, Melville Jean 1895-1963 EncAACR
Herskovitz, Janis St&PR 93
Herskovitz, Marshall BioIn 17, MiSFD 9
Herskovitz, Sam Marc 1949- WhoEmL 93
Herskovitz, Stuart St&PR 93
Herskowitz, Ira 1946- WhoAm 92
Herskowitz, Jeffrey Mark 1954- St&PR 93
Herskowitz, Morton Stanley 1918- WhoE 93
Herslow, Ernst Carl Fredrik 1961- WhoWor 93
Hersly, Isaac BioIn 17
Hersman, Marion Frank 1932- WhoAm 92
Hersom, Kathleen ScF&FL 92
Hersom, Kathleen 1911- SmATA 73 [port]
Herson, Arlene Rita WhoE 93
Herson, Eugene M. 1942- St&PR 93
Herst, Douglas Julian 1943- St&PR 93
Herst, Herman, Jr. 1909- WhoAm 92
Herst, Michael Alan 1955- WhoEmL 93
Herst, Perry Stern, Jr. 1929- St&PR 93
Herst, Robert L. Law&B 92
Herstad, John WhoScE 91-4
Herstad, Knut 1943- WhoScE 91-4
Herstand, Arnold 1925-1989 BioIn 17
Herstand, Theodore 1930- WhoAm 92
Herszdorfer, Pierre Jacques 1939- WhoSSW 93
Hersztajn Moldau, Juan 1945- WhoWor 93
Hert, Bernhard 1934- WhoScE 91-4
Herte, Mary Charlotte 1951- WhoAm 92, WhoAmW 93
Hertefeld, Philipp Eulenburg-, Furst zu 1847-1921 BioIn 17
Hertel, Dennis M. 1948- CngDr 91
Hertel, Dennis Mark 1948- WhoAm 92
Hertel, Eike 1940- WhoWor 93
Hertel, Francois 1905- WhoCanL 92
Hertel, Gary William 1947- St&PR 93
Hertel, Johann Christian 1699-1754 See Hertel, Johann Wilhelm 1727-1789 Baker 92
Hertel, Johann Wilhelm 1727-1789 Baker 92
Hertel, Paul R. 1928- St&PR 93
Hertel, Paul R., Jr. 1928- WhoIns 93
Hertel, Suzanne Marie 1937- WhoAmW 93, WhoE 93
Hertenberg, Rachel 1954- WhoWor 93
Hertenstein, Myrna Lynn 1937- WhoAmW 93
Herter, Christian A. 1895-1967 ColdWar 1 [port]
Herter, Loretta M. ScF&FL 92
Herter, Lori ScF&FL 92
Herter, Walter Charles 1940- St&PR 93
Hertfelder, Eric Karl 1947- WhoE 93
Hertha, Frederick E. 1927- St&PR 93
Hertig, Arthur Tremain 1904-1990 BioIn 17
Herting, David N. 1939- St&PR 93
Herting, Robert Leslie 1929- WhoAm 92
Hertl, William 1932- WhoE 93
Hertlein, Rudolph L. 1940- St&PR 93
Hertler, Walter Raymond 1933- WhoE 93
Hertog, Johannes den 1904- Baker 92
Hertog, Mary Kay 1956- WhoAmW 93
Hertsch, Bodo 1943- WhoScE 91-3
Hertweck, Alma Louise 1937- WhoAmW 93
Hertweck, E. Romayne 1928- WhoWor 93
Hertweck, Friedrich R. 1930- WhoScE 91-3
Hertz, Alfred 1872-1942 Baker 92, OxDcOp
Hertz, Arthur H. 1933- St&PR 93
Hertz, Arthur Herman 1933- WhoAm 92, WhoWor 93
Hertz, Benedykt 1872-1952 PolBiDi
Hertz, Bruce L. Law&B 92
Hertz, C. Hellmuth 1920- WhoScE 91-4
Hertz, Daniel Leroy, Jr. 1930- St&PR 93
Hertz, David Bendel 1919- WhoAm 92
Hertz, David N. Law&B 92
Hertz, Harry Steven 1947- WhoAm 92
Hertz, James G. Law&B 92
Hertz, Jean 1934- WhoScE 91-2
Hertz, John A. 1945- WhoScE 91-2
Hertz, Kenneth Theodore 1951- WhoAm 92, WhoEmL 93
Hertz, Leon 1938- WhoAm 92
Hertz, Marilyn Judith 1927- WhoAmW 93
Hertz, Marylyn Judith 1927- St&PR 93
Hertz, Richard Cornell 1916- WhoAm 92
Hertz, Robert 1881-1915 IntDcAn
Hertz, Roy 1909- WhoAm 92
Hertz, Rudolf H. 1917- St&PR 93
Hertz, Rudolf Heinrich 1917- WhoAm 92
Hertz, Uri L. 1949- WhoWrEP 92
Hertz, Vivienne Lucas 1928- WhoAmW 93
Hertzberg, Abraham 1922- WhoAm 92
Hertzberg, Arthur 1921- BioIn 17, WhoAm 92
Hertzberg, Daniel WhoE 93
Hertzberg, Hans T.E. 1905- IntDcAn
Hertzberg, Hendrik 1943- WhoAm 92
Hertzberg, Michael Law&B 92
Hertzberg, Paul Stuart 1949- WhoAm 92
Hertzberg, Richard Warren 1937- WhoAm 92
Hertzberg, Robert Steven 1954- WhoEmL 93
Hertzberger, Herman 1932- WhoWor 93
Hertzfeld, Kurt Maximilian 1918- St&PR 93
Hertzig, David 1932- WhoAm 92
Hertzka, Emil 1869-1932 Baker 92
Hertzman, Len Law&B 92
Hertzman, Staffan N. 1948- WhoScE 91-4
Hertzmann, Erich 1902-1963 Baker 92
Hertzog, Ardith Elyse 1964- WhoAmW 93
Hertzog, David Ray 1952- WhoE 93
Hertzog, James Barry Munuik 1866-1942 DcTwHis
Hertzson, Leon 1929- St&PR 93
Heru, Alison Margaret 1953- WhoEmL 93
Herve 1825-1892 Baker 92, OxDcOp
Herve, Claude BioIn 17
Herve, Gustave 1871-1944 BioIn 17
Herve, Guy WhoScE 91-2
Herve, Jacques Marie 1930- WhoWor 93
Herve, Jacques Marie 1944- WhoScE 91-2
Herve, Jean Francois 1950- WhoWor 93
Herve, Pierre 1913- BioIn 17

Herve-Bazin, Jean-Pierre Marie 1911- *WhoWor 93*
Herve Frankopoulos fl. 11th cent.- *OxDcByz*
Hervey, Albert Eugene 1939- *WhoE 93*
Hervey, Arthur 1855-1922 *Baker 92*
Hervey, Evelyn 1926- *BioIn 17*
Hervey, Frederick Augustus 1730-1803 *BioIn 17*
Hervey, Homer Vaughan 1936- *WhoE 93*
Hervey, Jason *BioIn 17*
Hervey, Maurice H. *ScF&FL 92*
Hervey of Ickworth, Baron 1696-1743 *BioIn 17*
Hervig, Richard (Bilderback) 1917- *Baker 92*
Hervonen, Antti L.J. 1944- *WhoScE 91-4*
Herwald, Kurt A. 1954- *St&PR 93*
Herwarth von Bittenfeld, Karl Eberhard 1796-1884 *HarEnMi*
Herway, Michael Jacob 1943- *WhoAm 92*
Herwitz, Carla B. 1932- *WhoAm 92*
Herwood, Mary Carol 1931- *WhoE 93*
Herwood, Michael G. 1939- *St&PR 93*
Herz, Albert X. 1921- *WhoScE 91-3*
Herz, Bill *BioIn 17*
Herz, Carl Samuel 1930- *WhoAm 92*
Herz, Cornelius 1845?-1898 *BioIn 17*
Herz, Fritz 1930- *WhoE 93*
Herz, George Peter 1928- *WhoWor 93*
Herz, Henri 1803-1888 *Baker 92*
Herz, Jack L. *St&PR 93*
Herz, Jean E. 1928- *WhoScE 91-2*
Herz, Joachim 1924- *Baker 92, IntDcOp, OxDcOp*
Herz, John 1930- *St&PR 93*
Herz, Juraj 1934- *DrEEuF*
Herz, Leonard 1931- *St&PR 93, WhoAm 92*
Herz, Martin Florian 1917-1983 *BioIn 17*
Herz, Marvin Ira 1927- *WhoAm 92*
Herz, Michael *BioIn 17*
Herz, Michael 1949- *MiSFD 9*
Herz, Michael Joseph 1936- *WhoAm 92*
Herz, Norman 1923- *WhoSSW 93*
Herz, Peter William 1945- *WhoE 93*
Herz, Werner 1921- *WhoSSW 93*
Herzar-Petri, Gizella 1927- *WhoScE 91-4*
Herzberg, Frederick 1923- *WhoAm 92*
Herzberg, Gerhard 1904- *WhoAm 92, WhoWor 93*
Herzberg, Sydelle Shulman 1933- *WhoE 93*
Herzberg, Waldron d1990 *BioIn 17*
Herzberger, Eugene E. 1920- *WhoAm 92*
Herzberger, Juergen Paul 1940- *WhoWor 93*
Herzberger, Jurgen 1940- *WhoScE 91-3*
Herzbrun, David Joseph 1927- *WhoAm 92*
Herzeca, Lois Friedman 1954- *WhoAmW 93, WhoEmL 93, WhoWor 93*
Herzel, Hans Peter 1957- *WhoWor 93*
Herzenberg, Arvid 1925- *WhoAm 92*
Herzenberg, Caroline Littlejohn 1932- *WhoAm 92, WhoAmW 93*
Herzenberg, John Eric 1955- *WhoE 93*
Herzer, Richard Kimball 1931- *St&PR 93, WhoAm 92, WhoWor 93*
Herzfeld, Alex R. *Law&B 92*
Herzfeld, Charles Maria 1925- *WhoAm 92, WhoWor 93*
Herzfeld, Donald 1937- *St&PR 93*
Herzfeld, Georg M. 1926- *St&PR 93*
Herzfeld, John *MiSFD 9*
Herzfeld, Judith 1948- *WhoE 93*
Herzfeld, Ronald *Law&B 92*
Herzfeld, Russell Loren 1927- *St&PR 93*
Herzig, Bruce David 1944- *WhoE 93*
Herzig, Buell Shields 1948- *WhoSSW 93*
Herzig, Charles E. 1929- *WhoAm 92*
Herzig, Julie Esther 1951- *WhoE 93*
Herzig, Stefan Walter 1957- *WhoWor 93*
Herziger, Gerd 1932- *WhoScE 91-3*
Herzing, Henry George 1936- *St&PR 93*
Herzka, A. *WhoScE 91-1*
Herzl, Theodor 1860-1904 *BioIn 17*
Herzlich, Claudine *WhoScE 91-2*
Herzman, Adele Sharpe d1990 *BioIn 17*
Herzog, Alan B. *St&PR 93*
Herzog, Arthur 1927- *ScF&FL 92*
Herzog, Arthur, III 1927- *WhoAm 92, WhoWrEP 92*
Herzog, Beverly Leah 1954- *WhoAm 92, WhoEmL 93*
Herzog, Bruno 1932- *WhoScE 91-4*
Herzog, Chaim 1918- *WhoWor 93*
Herzog, Cindy Ellen 1961- *WhoAmW 93*
Herzog, David Brandeis 1946- *WhoEmL 93*
Herzog, David Paul 1949- *WhoE 93*
Herzog, Dorrell Norman Elvert 1931- *BiDAMSp 1989*
Herzog, Elsie Gross d1992 *BioIn 17*
Herzog, Emile *ScF&FL 92*
Herzog, Emilie 1859-1923 *Baker 92*
Herzog, Ernest 1934- *St&PR 93*
Herzog, Forrest Edward 1951- *St&PR 93*
Herzog, Fred F. 1907- *WhoAm 92*
Herzog, George 1901-1983 *Baker 92*
Herzog, Gerhard W. 1938- *WhoScE 91-4*
Herzog, Harold Kenneth 1924- *St&PR 93*
Herzog, Hermann 1832-1932 *BioIn 17*
Herzog, Jacob Hawley 1911- *St&PR 93, WhoWor 93*
Herzog, Jesus Silva *BioIn 17*
Herzog, Joan Dorothy 1938- *WhoAmW 93*
Herzog, Johann Georg 1822-1909 *Baker 92*
Herzog, John E. 1936- *WhoAm 92*
Herzog, Kathryn Rose 1955- *WhoAmW 93, WhoEmL 93*
Herzog, Klaus Dieter 1933- *WhoWor 93*
Herzog, Mitchell Langr *Law&B 92*
Herzog, Norbert Karl 1955- *WhoEmL 93, WhoSSW 93*
Herzog, Peter Emilius 1925- *WhoAm 92*
Herzog, Philippe 1940- *BioIn 17*
Herzog, Renee Barbara 1947- *WhoAmW 93, WhoEmL 93*
Herzog, Richard Barnard 1939- *WhoAm 92*
Herzog, Richard Dennis 1950- *WhoEmL 93*
Herzog, Robert I. d1990 *BioIn 17*
Herzog, Stanley 1937- *WhoAm 92*
Herzog, Stephen B. *Law&B 92*
Herzog, Susan *BioIn 17*
Herzog, Thomas Nelson 1946- *WhoE 93*
Herzog, Todd A. 1944- *St&PR 93*
Herzog, Werner 1942- *MiSFD 9, WhoWor 93*
Herzog, Whitey 1931- *WhoAm 92*
Herzogenberg, (Leopold) Heinrich (Picot de Peccaduc), Freiherr von 1843-1900 *Baker 92*
Herzstein, Robert Erwin 1931- *WhoAm 92*
Hes, Vilem 1860-1908 *Baker 92*
Hesburgh, Theodore M. 1917- *EncAACR*
Hesburgh, Theodore Martin *BioIn 17*
Hesburgh, Theodore Martin 1917- *WhoAm 92*
Hesch, Wilhelm 1860-1908 *Baker 92*
Heschel, Abraham Joshua 1907-1972 *BioIn 17*
Heschuk, Craig Stephen *Law&B 92*
Heseltine, Michael *BioIn 17*
Heseltine, Michael Ray Dibdin 1933- *WhoWor 93*
Heseltine, Nigel Covernton de Rougemont 1926- *WhoWor 93*
Heseltine, Philip (Arnold) 1894-1930 *Baker 92*
Heselton, Frank R. 1941- *St&PR 93*
Heselton, Patricia Ann 1946- *WhoAm 92*
Hesen, Jan Christiaan 1930- *WhoScE 91-3*
Heshusius, Monda J.M. 1942- *WhoScE 91-3*
Hesingut, Henu M. 1950- *WhoAsAP 91*
Hesiod c. 750BC- *OxDcByz*
Hesjedal, Kare *WhoScE 91-4*
Hesketh, Baron 1950- *BioIn 17*
Hesketh, Christopher Edwin Dale 1951- *WhoWor 93*
Hesketh, Howard Edward 1931- *WhoAm 92*
Hesketh, John Edward *WhoScE 91-1*
Heskija, Zako 1922- *DrEEuF*
Hesky, Olga L. 1912-1974 *ScF&FL 92*
Hesley, John Maurice 1948- *WhoSSW 93*
Heslin, Cathleen Jane 1929- *WhoWor 93*
Heslin, James J. 1916- *WhoAm 92*
Heslin, James William, Jr. 1944- *WhoIns 93*
Heslin, Jo-Ann 1946- *WhoE 93*
Heslin, John Thomas 1927- *WhoE 93*
Heslin, Martin Francis *Law&B 92*
Heslop, Terence Murray 1942- *WhoAm 92*
Heslot, Henri 1921- *WhoScE 91-2*
Hespanhol, Ivanildo 1934- *WhoUN 92*
Hespos, Richard Franklin 1934- *WhoAm 92*
Hess, Alan Marshall 1942- *WhoAm 92*
Hess, Amy Morris 1947- *WhoAmW 93*
Hess, Ann Marie 1944- *WhoAmW 93*
Hess, Armand Melvin 1935- *St&PR 93*
Hess, Arthur 1927- *WhoAm 92*
Hess, Bartlett Leonard 1910- *WhoWor 93*
Hess, Benno *WhoScE 91-3*
Hess, Bernard Andes, Jr. 1940- *WhoAm 92*
Hess, Catherine Ann *Law&B 92*
Hess, Charles Edward 1931- *WhoAm 92, WhoE 93*
Hess, Charles James 1950- *WhoE 93*
Hess, Charles W. *Law&B 92*
Hess, Charles W. 1917- *St&PR 93*
Hess, Cheryl D. 1947- *St&PR 93*
Hess, Daniel J. 1939- *St&PR 93*
Hess, David Graham 1957- *WhoEmL 93*
Hess, David H.A. 1930- *St&PR 93*
Hess, David Willard 1933- *WhoAm 92*
Hess, Dennis John 1940- *St&PR 93, WhoAm 92*
Hess, Dianne Martin 1943- *WhoSSW 93*
Hess, Dieter F. 1933- *WhoScE 91-3*
Hess, Donald *BioIn 17*
Hess, Donald K. 1930- *WhoAm 92, WhoE 93*
Hess, Donald Marc 1936- *WhoWor 93*
Hess, Earl Hollinger 1928- *WhoAm 92*
Hess, Edward John 1936- *St&PR 93*
Hess, Edwin John 1933- *WhoAm 92*
Hess, Eileen Sweeten 1949- *WhoEmL 93*
Hess, Elizabeth B. *Law&B 92*
Hess, Elizabeth Guion *AmWomPl*
Hess, Emil Carl 1918- *WhoAm 92*
Hess, Eugene Lyle 1914- *WhoAm 92*
Hess, Evelyn Victorine 1926- *WhoAm 92*
Hess, Frances Leedom *AmWomPl*
Hess, Frederick J. 1941- *WhoAm 92*
Hess, Gary Steven *Law&B 92*
Hess, Geoffrey LaVerne 1949- *WhoE 93*
Hess, George Kellogg, Jr. 1922- *WhoAm 92*
Hess, George Paul 1926- *WhoAm 92*
Hess, George Robert 1941- *WhoAm 92*
Hess, Geraldo 1942- *WhoWor 93*
Hess, Glen E. *St&PR 93*
Hess, Hans Ober 1912- *WhoAm 92*
Hess, Heinz-Juergen 1941- *WhoWor 93*
Hess, Henry Richard 1936- *St&PR 93*
Hess, Irma 1939- *WhoAmW 93, WhoWor 93*
Hess, James T. 1945- *St&PR 93*
Hess, Jean-Claude 1926- *WhoScE 91-2*
Hess, Joan 1949- *ScF&FL 92*
Hess, John J. *Law&B 92*
Hess, John Warren 1947- *WhoAm 92*
Hess, Jon *MiSFD 9*
Hess, Josef 1878-1932 *BioIn 17*
Hess, Judith Anne 1949- *WhoAmW 93*
Hess, Karen Jo Matison 1939- *WhoWrEP 92*
Hess, Karl 1945- *WhoAm 92*
Hess, Karsten 1930- *St&PR 93, WhoAm 92*
Hess, Lawrence Eugene, Jr. 1923- *WhoE 93, WhoWor 93*
Hess, Lee Howard 1947- *St&PR 93, WhoAm 92, WhoEmL 93*
Hess, Leon *BioIn 17*
Hess, Leon 1914- *St&PR 93, WhoAm 92*
Hess, Leonard Wayne 1949- *WhoEmL 93, WhoWor 93*
Hess, Lester Victor 1955- *WhoEmL 93*
Hess, Loretta Rooney *WhoWrEP 92*
Hess, Lucille Jane 1945- *WhoAmW 93*
Hess, Lucy *St&PR 93*
Hess, Ludwig 1877-1944 *Baker 92*
Hess, Lynn Howard *Law&B 92*
Hess, Marcia Wanda 1934- *WhoAmW 93, WhoWor 93*
Hess, Margaret Johnston 1915- *WhoAmW 93, WhoWor 93*
Hess, Mark G. *Law&B 92*
Hess, Marshall 1927- *St&PR 93*
Hess, Mary Barbara 1953- *WhoWrEP 92*
Hess, Merrill R. 1923- *St&PR 93*
Hess, Michael *St&PR 93*
Hess, Milton S. 1941- *St&PR 93*
Hess, Milton Siegmund 1941- *WhoAm 92*
Hess, Myra 1890-1965 *Baker 92*
Hess, Orvan W. *WhoAm 92*
Hess, Oswald 1930- *WhoScE 91-3*
Hess, P. Gregory 1946- *WhoE 93, WhoEmL 93*
Hess, Patrick Henry 1931- *WhoAm 92*
Hess, Peter L. *Law&B 92*
Hess, Philip K. 1960- *WhoEmL 93*
Hess, Richard 1934-1991 *BioIn 17*
Hess, Robert C. 1947- *St&PR 93*
Hess, Robert Daniel 1920- *WhoAm 92*
Hess, Robert John 1937- *St&PR 93*
Hess, Robert L. d1992 *NewYTBS 92*
Hess, Robert L(ee) 1932-1992 *ConAu 136*
Hess, Robert Lee 1932-1992 *BioIn 17*
Hess, Robert Pratt 1942- *WhoWor 93*
Hess, Roger 1937- *WhoScE 91-4*
Hess, Ronald L. 1942- *St&PR 93*
Hess, Roy E. 1945- *St&PR 93*
Hess, Rudolf 1894-1987 *BioIn 17*
Hess, Sidney J., Jr. 1910- *WhoAm 92*
Hess, Sidney Wayne 1932- *WhoAm 92*
Hess, Stanford Donald 1943- *WhoAm 92*
Hess, Stephen 1933- *WhoAm 92, WhoWrEP 92*
Hess, Steven 1938- *St&PR 93*
Hess, Steven Charles *Law&B 92*
Hess, Terry W. 1958- *St&PR 93*
Hess, W.J. 1937- *St&PR 93*
Hess, Walter Otto 1918- *WhoWor 93*
Hess, Walter Richard Rudolf 1894-1987 *DcTwHis*
Hess, Wanda Jean 1949- *WhoEmL 93*
Hess, William d1991 *BioIn 17*
Hess, William E. 1936- *St&PR 93*
Hess, William J. *Law&B 92*
Hess, Willy 1859-1939 *Baker 92*
Hess, Willy 1906- *Baker 92*
Hess, Wilmot Norton 1926- *WhoAm 92*
Hess, Wolf 1937- *BioIn 17*
Hess, Wolfgang Josef 1940- *WhoWor 93*
Hess-Cole, Serena Dianne *WhoAmW 93, WhoSSW 93*
Hesse, Adolph (Friedrich) 1808-1863 *Baker 92*
Hesse, Albert 1938- *WhoScE 91-2*
Hesse, Carolyn Sue 1949- *WhoAmW 93*
Hesse, Christian August 1925- *St&PR 93*
Hesse, Egbert 1932- *WhoScE 91-3*
Hesse, Ernst Christian 1676-1762 *Baker 92*
Hesse, Eva 1936-1970 *BioIn 17*
Hesse, Grete Anna Erna 1933- *WhoAm 92*
Hesse, Hartmut Guenther 1949- *WhoUN 92*
Hesse, Hermann 1877-1962 *BioIn 17, MagSWL [port], ScF&FL 92, WorLitC [port]*
Hesse, James D. 1938- *St&PR 93*
Hesse, Karl O. *Law&B 92*
Hesse, Manfred 1935- *WhoScE 91-4*
Hesse, Martha O. 1942- *WhoAm 92, WhoAmW 93*
Hesse, Max 1858-1907 *Baker 92*
Hesse, Michael F. 1943- *WhoScE 91-4*
Hesse, Nancy Jane 1948- *WhoEmL 93*
Hesse, Paul A. 1941- *St&PR 93*
Hesse, Philip *BioIn 17*
Hesse, Reiner 1942- *WhoWor 93*
Hesse, Stephen Mox 1948- *WhoAm 92*
Hesse, Steve Max 1948- *St&PR 93*
Hesse, William Blass 1948- *WhoE 93*
Hesse, William R. 1914- *WhoAm 92, WhoE 93, WhoWor 93*
Hesse-Bukowska, Barbara 1930- *Baker 92*
Hessel, Dorothy Elizabeth 1963- *WhoSSW 93*
Hessel, Helena 1949- *St&PR 93*
Hessel, Louwrens W. 1931- *WhoScE 91-3, WhoWor 93*
Hessel, Susan Lee 1961- *WhoEmL 93*
Hesselbach, Bruce William 1950- *WhoWrEP 92*
Hesselbein, Frances Richards *WhoAm 92, WhoAmW 93, WhoWor 93*
Hesselberg, Edouard Gregory 1870-1935 *Baker 92*
Hesselbrock, John Joseph 1950- *St&PR 93*
Hesselgreaves, John Edward *WhoScE 91-1*
Hesselink, Ann Patrice 1954- *WhoAm 92*
Hesselroth, Warren 1926- *St&PR 93*
Hessels, Jan-Michiel 1942- *WhoAm 92*
Hesseman, Howard 1940- *WhoAm 92*
Hessen, Alexander Friedrich, Landgraf von 1863-1945 *Baker 92*
Hessenberg, Kurt 1908- *Baker 92*
Hesser, Danielle Elan 1949- *WhoAmW 93*
Hesser, E. Grant 1919- *St&PR 93*
Hesser, Grant V. 1947- *St&PR 93*
Hesser, James E. 1941- *WhoAm 92*
Hesse-Wartegg, Ernst 1854-1918 *BioIn 17*
Hessinger, Carl John William 1915- *WhoE 93*
Hession, Eileen Melia *WhoWrEP 92*
Hession, Jeanne M. *Law&B 92*
Hession, Jeanne M. 1930- *St&PR 93*
Hession, Joseph Michael 1955- *WhoWrEP 92*
Hesske, Daniel J. 1943- *St&PR 93*
Hessler, Catherine Fox 1950- *WhoAmW 93*
Hessler, Curtis Alan 1943- *WhoAm 92*
Hessler, David William 1932- *WhoAm 92*
Hessler, Gordon 1930- *BioIn 17, MiSFD 9*
Hessler, Robert John *Law&B 92*
Hessler, Robert Roamie 1918- *WhoAm 92*
Hesslund, Bradley Harry 1958- *WhoEmL 93*
Hess-Luttich, Ernest Walter Bernhard 1949- *WhoWor 93*
Hessol, Gail I. 1953- *St&PR 93*
Hesson, Paul Anthony 1923- *WhoAm 92*
Hest, Lionel G. 1946- *St&PR 93*
Hestand, Cynthia Ann 1955- *WhoEmL 93*
Hestehave, Borge Tage 1923- *St&PR 93*
Hestehave, Marianne 1924- *St&PR 93*
Hestenes, Roberta Rae 1939- *WhoAmW 93, WhoE 93*
Hester, Albert Lee 1932- *WhoSSW 93*
Hester, Bob Drerve 1928- *St&PR 93*
Hester, Donnie Phil 1950- *St&PR 93*
Hester, Douglas Benjamin 1927- *WhoAm 92*
Hester, Elizabeth James 1963- *WhoAmW 93, WhoEmL 93*
Hester, Eugene Alfred 1932- *WhoSSW 93*
Hester, Hal d1992 *NewYTBS 92*
Hester, Harris Ryland 1942- *WhoAm 92*
Hester, James McNaughton 1924- *WhoAm 92*
Hester, John Hutchison 1886-1976 *HarEnMi*
Hester, John Milton, Jr. 1960- *WhoSSW 93*
Hester, John W. *Law&B 92*
Hester, John W. 1947- *St&PR 93*

Hester, Jon Lee 1948- *WhoEmL 93*
Hester, Joseph H. *Law&B 92*
Hester, Judy G. *Law&B 92*
Hester, Karlton Edward 1949- *WhoE 93, WhoEmL 93*
Hester, Larry B. 1938- *St&PR 93*
Hester, Linda Hunt 1938- *WhoSSW 93*
Hester, Marcus Baxter 1937- *WhoSSW 93*
Hester, Mark Alan *Law&B 92*
Hester, Martin Luther 1947- *WhoWrEP 92*
Hester, Molly *BioIn 17*
Hester, Nancy Elizabeth 1950- *WhoAmW 93*
Hester, Norman Eric 1946- *WhoAm 92*
Hester, Patrick J. *Law&B 92*
Hester, Randolph Thompson, Jr. 1944- *WhoAm 92*
Hester, Ronald Ernest *WhoScE 91-1*
Hester, Ross Wyatt 1924- *WhoSSW 93*
Hester, Stephen Michael *Law&B 92*
Hester, Terry L. 1954- *St&PR 93*
Hester, Thomas P. *Law&B 92*
Hester, Thomas P. 1937- *St&PR 93*
Hester, Thomas Patrick 1937- *WhoAm 92*
Hester, Thomas Roy 1946- *WhoAm 92*
Hester, Wayne 1948- *WhoSSW 93*
Hester-Mitich, Louis John 1929- *WhoWrEP 92*
Hestler, Ralph 1930- *St&PR 93*
Heston, Charlton *BioIn 17*
Heston, Charlton 1924?- *IntDcF 2-3 [port], MiSFD 9, WhoAm 92, WhoWor 93*
Heston, Fraser C. *MiSFD 9*
Heston, James R. *Law&B 92*
Heston, W. Craig 1935- *St&PR 93*
Heston, William May 1922- *WhoE 93*
Hesychios dc. 582 *OxDcByz*
Hesychios of Alexandria fl. 5th cent.-6th cent. *OxDcByz*
Hesychios of Jerusalem dc. 451 *OxDcByz*
Heszky, Laszlo Emil 1945- *WhoScE 91-4*
Hetenyi, R. *WhoScE 91-4*
Hetfield, Walter L. 1906-1991 *BioIn 17*
Heth, Diana Sue 1948- *WhoEmL 93*
Heth, Gene A. *Law&B 92*
Heth, Henry 1825-1899 *HarEnMi*
Heth, Meir 1932- *St&PR 93*
Heth, Rhonda J. *Law&B 92*
Hetherington, Charles R. 1919- *St&PR 93*
Hetherington, Colin Mitchell *WhoScE 91-1*
Hetherington, David L. 1943- *St&PR 93*
Hetherington, Edwin S. *Law&B 92*
Hetherington, Edwin S. 1949- *St&PR 93*
Hetherington, Gordon Scott 1960- *WhoSSW 93*
Hetherington, James Richard 1931- *St&PR 93*
Hetherington, James S. 1939- *WhoScE 91-1*
Hetherington, John Warner *Law&B 92*
Hetherington, John Warner 1938- *St&PR 93, WhoAm 92*
Hetherington, Keith 1929- *ScF&FL 92*
Hetherly, Katheryn Johnson 1928- *WhoSSW 93*
Hetland, James Lyman, Jr. 1925- *WhoAm 92, WhoWor 93*
Hetland, Jerry E. 1947- *St&PR 93*
Hetland, John Robert 1930- *WhoAm 92, WhoWor 93*
Hetman, Nicholas Wayne *Law&B 92*
Hetrick, Charles Brady 1932- *WhoSSW 93*
Hetrick, Christopher Jon 1958- *St&PR 93*
Hetrick, James Edward 1960- *WhoWor 93*
Hetrick, Lenore Hazel *AmWomPl*
Hetrick, Michelle 1958- *WhoAmW 93*
Hetsch, (Karl) Ludwig Friedrich 1806-1872 *Baker 92*
Hetsko, Cyril Francis 1911- *WhoAm 92, WhoE 93, WhoWor 93*
Hettche, L. Raymond 1930- *WhoAm 92*
Hetterick, John F. 1945- *St&PR 93*
Hettiaratchi, Shennan Channa 1961- *WhoWor 93*
Hettich, Arthur Matthias 1925- *WhoAm 92, WhoE 93*
Hettich, Michael 1953- *WhoWrEP 92*
Hettich, Michael Fitz Randolph 1953- *WhoSSW 93*
Hettiger-Jacobs, Lorin J. 1956- *WhoEmL 93*
Hettinger, Sheila Kay 1960- *WhoAmW 93*
Hettinger, Steve *WhoSSW 93*
Hettleman, Michael Kalman 1936- *St&PR 93*
Hettler, Madeline Therese 1949- *WhoAmW 93*
Hettler, Paul *WhoAm 92*
Hettrick, James Parkinson 1958- *St&PR 93*
Hettrick, John L. 1934- *St&PR 93*
Hettrick, John Lord 1934- *WhoAm 92*
Hettrick, William Eugene 1939- *WhoE 93*
Hetu, Jacques (Joseph Robert) 1938- *Baker 92*
Hetu, Lise *Law&B 92*
Het'umids *OxDcByz*
Hetzel, C. Charles 1941- *St&PR 93*
Hetzel, Carl Paul 1929- *St&PR 93*
Hetzel, Dennis Richard 1952- *St&PR 93, WhoAm 92*
Hetzel, Donald Stanford 1941- *St&PR 93*
Hetzel, Frederick Armstrong 1930- *WhoAm 92*
Hetzel, Ralph Dorn, Jr. 1912- *WhoAm 92*
Hetzel, William Gelal 1933- *WhoAm 92*
Hetzer, Richard Michael 1941- *St&PR 93*
Hetzer, William J., Jr. 1942- *WhoUN 92*
Hetzler, Dale C. *Law&B 92*
Hetzron, Robert 1937- *WhoAm 92*
Heuberger, Anton 1942- *WhoScE 91-3*
Heuberger, Richard 1850-1914 *OxDcOp*
Heuberger, Richard (Franz Joseph) 1850-1914 *Baker 92*
Heubner, Konrad 1860-1905 *Baker 92*
Heubner, Ulrich Leonhard 1932- *WhoWor 93*
Heuchling, Theodore Paul 1925- *St&PR 93*
Heuck, Claus Christian 1943- *WhoUN 92*
Heuck, Roger William 1939- *St&PR 93*
Heudier, Jean-Louis 1944- *WhoScE 91-2*
Heuer, Arthur Harold 1936- *WhoAm 92*
Heuer, Gerald Arthur 1930- *WhoAm 92*
Heuer, Helmut Herbert 1932- *WhoWor 93*
Heuer, Kenneth John 1927- *WhoAm 92*
Heuer, Margaret B. 1935- *WhoAmW 93*
Heuer, Martin 1934- *WhoSSW 93*
Heuer, Marvin Arthur 1947- *WhoE 93, WhoEmL 93*
Heuer, Michael Alexander 1932- *WhoAm 92*
Heuer, Robert Maynard, II 1944- *WhoAm 92*
Heuer, Walter J. *Law&B 92*
Heuerman, Richard Arnold 1930- *St&PR 93*
Heuertz, John Anthony 1949- *WhoEmL 93*
Heuertz, Sarah Jane 1950- *WhoAm 92, WhoEmL 93*
Heugel, Henry 1789-1841 *Baker 92*
Heugel, Jacques-Leopold 1811-1883 *Baker 92*
Heughan, D.M. *WhoScE 91-1*
Heuman, D.H. 1951- *St&PR 93*
Heuman, Warner J. 1924- *St&PR 93*
Heumann, Klemens R. 1931- *WhoScE 91-3*
Heumann, Peter L. 1945- *WhoE 93*
Heumann, Roger Jay 1954- *St&PR 93*
Heumann, Scott Fredric 1951- *WhoAm 92*
Heumann, Stephen Michael 1941- *St&PR 93*
Heuman-Perl, Joan Alice 1950- *WhoE 93*
Heupel, Donald Dean 1947- *St&PR 93*
Heurich, Charles Richard 1925- *St&PR 93*
Heursel, Joseph M.R.L. 1935- *WhoScE 91-2*
Heurtematte, Roberto 1908- *St&PR 93*
Heusch, Clemens August 1932- *WhoAm 92*
Heusch, Robert W. *St&PR 93*
Heuschele, Sharon Jo 1936- *WhoAmW 93*
Heuschele, Werner Paul 1929- *WhoAm 92*
Heu-Scrivani, Allison Margaret 1953- *WhoAmW 93*
Heusel, Gary Lee 1947- *WhoEmL 93*
Heuser, Beatrice 1961- *ConAu 138*
Heuser, H.H. *WhoScE 91-3*
Heuser, Henry Vogt 1914- *St&PR 93, WhoAm 92*
Heuser, Lothar Jost Gregor 1947- *WhoWor 93*
Heuser, Thomas Stephen 1952- *WhoWor 93*
Heusinkveld, G.W.H. *WhoScE 91-3*
Heusler, Konrad E. 1931- *WhoScE 91-3*
Heusmann, Richard Warren 1948- *WhoEmL 93*
Heuss, Alfred (Valentin) 1877-1934 *Baker 92*
Heusser, Calvin John 1924- *WhoAm 92*
Heussner, G. James 1935- *St&PR 93*
Heuving, Jeanne 1951- *ConAu 138*
Hevener, Fillmer, Jr. 1933- *WhoSSW 93*
Heveran, Ronald D. 1932- *St&PR 93*
Heverin, Edward John 1946- *WhoEmL 93, WhoSSW 93*
Heverly, Richard Charles 1928- *St&PR 93*
Hevia, David Rene 1943- *St&PR 93*
Hevle, Eric Jonathan 1965- *WhoSSW 93*
Hevner, Alan Raymond 1950- *WhoEmL 93*
Hevor, Tobias 1949- *WhoScE 91-2*
Hevrdejs, Richard Jerome 1933- *St&PR 93*
Hew, Robert C. 1957- *St&PR 93*
Heward, Leslie (Hays) 1897-1943 *Baker 92*
Hewat, William Brian 1936- *WhoAm 92, WhoE 93*
Heweliusz, Jan 1611-1687 *PolBiDi*
Hewell, James R., Jr. 1930- *St&PR 93*
Hewes, Amy 1877-1970 *BioIn 17*
Hewes, George B., III *Law&B 92*
Hewes, Hayden Cooper 1943- *WhoSSW 93*
Hewes, Henry 1917- *WhoAm 92*
Hewes, Laurence Ilsley, III 1933- *WhoAm 92*
Hewes, Philip A. *Law&B 92*
Hewes, Phillip A. 1929- *St&PR 93*
Hewes, Robert Charles 1953- *WhoEmL 93*
Hewetson, Christopher Raynor 1929- *WhoWor 93*
Hewett, Arthur Edward 1935- *WhoAm 92*
Hewett, Christopher Benjamin 1958- *WhoAm 92*
Hewett, Dwight Cecil 1959- *WhoEmL 93*
Hewett, Ed Albert 1942- *WhoAm 92*
Hewett, Howard *SoulM*
Hewett, Howard, Jr. *BioIn 17*
Hewett, James Veith 1921- *WhoSSW 93*
Hewett, JoAnne Lea 1960- *WhoEmL 93*
Hewett, Peter John 1936- *St&PR 93*
Hewish, Antony *WhoScE 91-1*
Hewish, Antony 1924- *WhoWor 93*
Hewit, James Robert *WhoScE 91-1*
Hewitt, Abram S. 1822-1903 *PolPar*
Hewitt, Abram Stevens 1822-1903 *BioIn 17*
Hewitt, Adrian *WhoScE 91-1*
Hewitt, Ann Elizabeth 1934- *WhoAmW 93*
Hewitt, Benjamin Attmore 1921- *WhoE 93*
Hewitt, Bill 1909-1947 *BioIn 17*
Hewitt, Carl Herbert 1952- *WhoAm 92, WhoEmL 93*
Hewitt, Charles M. *BioIn 17*
Hewitt, Dennis Edwin 1944- *WhoAm 92*
Hewitt, Don 1922- *BioIn 17*
Hewitt, Don S. 1922- *WhoAm 92, WhoE 93*
Hewitt, Donald O. 1943- *WhoAm 92*
Hewitt, Edwin 1920- *BioIn 17, WhoAm 92*
Hewitt, Elinor Amram 1937- *WhoE 93*
Hewitt, Eliza E. *AmWomPl*
Hewitt, Frank Seaver 1941- *St&PR 93*
Hewitt, Frankie Lea 1931- *WhoAm 92, WhoAmW 93*
Hewitt, Geary Lee 1942- *St&PR 93*
Hewitt, Geoffrey Frederick *WhoScE 91-1*
Hewitt, Godfrey Matthew *WhoScE 91-1*
Hewitt, Graves Desha 1928- *WhoIns 93*
Hewitt, Harry Donald 1921- *Baker 92*
Hewitt, Harvey John 1934- *WhoE 93*
Hewitt, Helen (Margaret) 1900-1977 *Baker 92*
Hewitt, Henry Kent 1887-1972 *HarEnMi*
Hewitt, Hugh 1956- *WhoAm 92*
Hewitt, James 1770-1827 *Baker 92*
Hewitt, James J. 1933- *WhoAm 92*
Hewitt, James Lang 1803-1853 *See* Hewitt, James 1770-1827 *Baker 92*
Hewitt, James W. *Law&B 92*
Hewitt, James Watt 1932- *WhoAm 92*
Hewitt, Jerene Cline 1917- *WhoWrEP 92*
Hewitt, John Harold 1907-1987 *BioIn 17*
Hewitt, John Hill 1801-1890 *See* Hewitt, James 1770-1827 *Baker 92*
Hewitt, John R. *Law&B 92*
Hewitt, Karen Renee 1950- *WhoAmW 93, WhoWor 93*
Hewitt, Marilyn Jean 1937- *WhoAmW 93*
Hewitt, Marilyn Patricia 1947- *WhoAm 92*
Hewitt, Mark *BioIn 17*
Hewitt, Marsha 1948- *DcChlFi*
Hewitt, Marsha A. 1945- *St&PR 93*
Hewitt, Maurice 1884-1971 *Baker 92*
Hewitt, Norma Jean 1949- *WhoAmW 93*
Hewitt, Peter *MiSFD 9*
Hewitt, Peter E. *Law&B 92*
Hewitt, Peter John *WhoScE 91-1*
Hewitt, Robert C. 1945- *St&PR 93*
Hewitt, Robert E. 1947- *St&PR 93*
Hewitt, Robert Lee 1934- *WhoAm 92*
Hewitt, Rod *MiSFD 9*
Hewitt, Thomas Edward 1939- *WhoAm 92*
Hewitt, Thomas Francis 1943- *WhoAm 92*
Hewitt, Vivian Ann Davidson *WhoAm 92*
Hewitt, W(arren) E(dward) 1954- *ConAu 139*
Hewitt, William Harley 1954- *WhoWor 93*
Hewitt, William M. 1946- *St&PR 93*
Hewitt-Couturier, Naomi *BioIn 17*
Hewlett, Cecil James 1923- *WhoAm 92*
Hewlett, Horace Wilson 1915- *WhoAm 92*
Hewlett, Jimmy Lane 1942- *WhoSSW 93*
Hewlett, Richard Greening 1923- *WhoAm 92*
Hewlett, Sylvia Ann 1946- *BioIn 17*
Hewlett, William R. *BioIn 17*
Hewlett, William Redington 1913- *WhoAm 92*
Hewlett-Kierstead, Nancy Carrick 1927- *WhoWor 93*
Hewson, Donna Walters 1947- *WhoAmW 93, WhoEmL 93, WhoSSW 93, WhoWor 93*
Hewson, Estelle Simms *AmWomPl*
Hewson, Irene Dale *AmWomPl*
Hewson, Jeffrey K. 1943- *St&PR 93*
Hewson, John Robert 1910- *WhoAsAP 91*
Hewson, Martin Gerard 1929- *WhoE 93*
Hewson, Peter James *WhoScE 91-1*
Hexapterygos, Theodore c. 1180-c. 1236 *OxDcByz*
Hext, Kathleen Florence 1941- *WhoAm 92, WhoAmW 93*
Hextall, Ron 1964- *WhoAm 92*
Hexter, Jack H. 1910- *WhoAm 92*
Hexter, Maurice B. 1891-1990 *BioIn 17*
Hexter, Michael 1942- *St&PR 93*
Hey, A.J.G. *WhoScE 91-1*
Hey, David Anthony *Law&B 92*
Hey, James Conrad 1959- *WhoE 93*
Hey, John Charles 1935- *WhoAm 92*
Hey, John Denis *WhoScE 91-1*
Hey, Julius 1832-1909 *Baker 92*
Hey, Robert Pierpont 1935- *WhoAm 92*
Hey, Thomas H. 1947- *St&PR 93*
Heyamoto, Craig R. *Law&B 92*
Heybach, John Peter 1950- *WhoEmL 93, WhoWor 93*
Heyborne, Robert Linford 1923- *WhoAm 92*
Heyck, Gertrude Paine Daly 1910- *WhoAmW 93, WhoSSW 93, WhoWor 93*
Heyck, Theodore Daly 1941- *WhoWor 93*
Heyde, James Wallace 1933- *St&PR 93*
Heyde, Lalla J. 1933- *St&PR 93*
Heyde, Martha Bennett 1920- *WhoAm 92, WhoAmW 93, WhoE 93*
Heyde, Norma Lee 1927- *WhoAmW 93*
Heydebrand, Wolf Von 1930- *WhoAm 92, WhoE 93*
Heydemann, Lillian P. *AmWomPl*
Heyden, Francis J. *BioIn 17*
Heyden, Hans 1536-1613 *Baker 92*
Heyden, Sebald 1499-1561 *Baker 92*
Heyderhoff, Peter Gerhardt 1935- *WhoWor 93*
Heyderman, Arthur Jerome 1946- *WhoWor 93*
Heydlauff, Dale E. 1957- *St&PR 93*
Heydorn, Kaj 1931- *WhoScE 91-2, WhoWor 93*
Heydrich, Reinhard 1904-1942 *DcTwHis*
Heydron, Vicki Ann 1945- *ScF&FL 92*
Heydtmann, Horst Max 1931- *WhoScE 91-3*
Heyel, Carl 1908- *WhoWrEP 92*
Heyen, Beatrice J. 1925- *WhoAmW 93*
Heyen, William H. 1940- *WhoWrEP 92*
Heyer, Anna Harriet 1909- *WhoAmW 93, WhoSSW 93*
Heyer, Georgette 1902-1974 *BioIn 17*
Heyer, Grace *AmWomPl*
Heyer, John Hajdu 1945- *WhoE 93*
Heyer, John Henry, II 1946- *WhoEmL 93*
Heyer, Marilee 1942- *BioIn 17*
Heyer, Miriam Harriet 1942- *WhoAmW 93, WhoSSW 93*
Heyer, Paul Otto 1936- *WhoAm 92*
Heyer, Peter *Law&B 92*
Heyer, Terrence E. 1945- *St&PR 93*
Heyer, Wilhelm (Ferdinand) 1849-1913 *Baker 92*
Heyerdahl, Thor *BioIn 17*
Heyerdahl, Thor 1914- *ConHero 2 [port], DcTwHis, IntDcAn, WhoWor 93*
Heyert, Martin David 1934- *WhoAm 92*
Heyes, Douglas *MiSFD 9*
Heyes, Fred L. d1990 *BioIn 17*
Heyes, J. *WhoScE 91-1*
Heykants, Joseph J.P. 1941- *WhoScE 91-2*
Heykes, Nancy Nelson 1952- *St&PR 93*
Heyl, Allen Van, Jr. 1918- *WhoWor 93*
Heyl, Donald C. 1921- *St&PR 93*
Heyl, Larry Gerald 1947- *WhoEmL 93*
Heyland, Geoffrey Peter *Law&B 92*
Heyler, Grover Ross 1926- *WhoAm 92*
Heylin, Michael 1930- *WhoAm 92*
Heylman, Warren Cummings 1923- *WhoAm 92*
Heym, Christine 1932- *WhoScE 91-3*
Heym, George 1887-1912 *BioIn 17*
Heym, Stefan 1913- *ScF&FL 92*
Heyman, Annette Helen 1926- *WhoE 93*
Heyman, Art *BioIn 17*
Heyman, Arthur Bruce 1941- *BiDAMSp 1989*
Heyman, Charles Stuart 1950- *WhoSSW 93*
Heyman, David 1935- *St&PR 93*
Heyman, George Harrison, Jr. 1916- *WhoAm 92*
Heyman, Harriet *BioIn 17*
Heyman, Ira Michael 1930- *WhoAm 92, WhoWor 93*
Heyman, Jacques *WhoScE 91-1*
Heyman, James Harold 1931- *St&PR 93*

Heyman, Katherine Ruth Willoughby 1877-1944 Baker 92
Heyman, Lawrence Murray 1932- WhoAm 92
Heyman, Leonard J. 1925- St&PR 93
Heyman, Matthew David 1961- WhoEmL 93
Heyman, Ralph Edmond 1931- WhoAm 92
Heyman, Samuel J. BioIn 17, St&PR 93
Heyman, Samuel J. 1939- WhoAm 92
Heyman, Stephen J. 1939- St&PR 93
Heyman, William Herbert 1948- WhoAm 92
Heymann, C. David WhoWrEP 92
Heymann, C. David 1945- BioIn 17
Heymann, Clemens Claude 1945- WhoWrEP 92
Heymann, Clemens David 1945- BioIn 17, WhoAm 92
Heymann, Monica Golda 1959- WhoAmW 93
Heymann, Paul F. 1926- St&PR 93
Heymann, Philip B. 1932- WhoAm 92
Heymann, Stephen Timothy 1940- WhoAm 92
Heymont, George 1947- WhoWrEP 92
Heymoss, Jennifer Marie 1958- WhoAmW 93
Heymsfeld, Carla Raskin 1941- WhoAmW 93
Heyn, Arno Harry Albert 1918- WhoAm 92
Heyn, Ernest V. 1904- WhoAm 92
Heyn, William Carveth WhoE 93
Heyndrickx, Aubin Marie Achille Cesar 1927- WhoScE 91-2
Heyndrickx, Bruno Pierre Paul Philippe 1960- WhoWor 93
Heyne, Herbert Barthel 1940- St&PR 93
Heyne, William P. 1910-1985 ScF&FL 92
Heyneker, Herbert Louis 1944- WhoAm 92
Heyneman, Donald 1925- WhoAm 92
Heyneman, Ellen Katherine 1958- WhoEmL 93
Heyns, Roger William 1918- WhoAm 92
Heyns, Walter 1938- WhoScE 91-2
Heyrman, Heidi A. Law&B 92
Heys, Edward Scarborough 1935- St&PR 93
Heys, John Richard 1947- WhoE 93
Heys, Sue Ellen 1948- WhoAmW 93
Heyser, Wolfgang R.A. 1942- WhoScE 91-3
Heyssel, Robert Morris 1928- WhoAm 92, WhoWor 93
Heystek, Kristen Margaret 1949- WhoSSW 93
Heyszenau, Heinrich 1942- WhoScE 91-3
Heyward, Andrew John 1950- WhoAm 92, WhoE 93
Heyward, Andy BioIn 17
Heyward, Andy 1949- WhoEmL 93
Heyward, Charles Edward 1933- St&PR 93
Heyward, Dorothy Hartzell Kuhns 1890-1961 AmWomPl
Heyward, George Harry 1947- St&PR 93
Heyward, Louis M. 1920- BioIn 17
Heywood, Delia A. AmWomPl
Heywood, Eddie 1915-1989 Baker 92
Heywood, George H., Jr. 1920- St&PR 93
Heywood, John Benjamin 1938- WhoAm 92
Heywood, Kenneth S. Law&B 92
Heywood, Kenneth Stephen Law&B 92
Heywood, Peter 1943- WhoWrEP 92
Heywood, Robert Wales 1933- WhoAm 92
Heywood, Thomas Richard 1938- WhoScE 91-1
Heywood, Victor D. ScF&FL 92
Heyworth, Anthony A. 1944- St&PR 93
Heyworth, James O. 1942- WhoAm 92
Heyworth, Lawrence, III 1948- WhoE 93
Heyworth, Peter 1921-1991 AnObit 1991, BioIn 17
He Zhiqiang 1935- WhoAsAP 91
He Zhukang 1932- WhoAsAP 91
Hezlet, May 1882-1978 BioIn 17
Hezzelwood, William L. 1947- WhoIns 93
H.G. Wells Society ScF&FL 92
Hiaasen, Carl BioIn 17
Hiaasen, Carl 1953- WhoWrEP 92
Hiaring, Robert Dale 1941- WhoAm 92
Hiatt, Arnold 1927- WhoAm 92
Hiatt, Duane Evan 1937- WhoWrEP 92
Hiatt, Gustaves Paige 1949- WhoWor 93
Hiatt, Howard H. 1925- WhoAm 92
Hiatt, Jane Crater 1944- WhoSSW 93
Hiatt, John BioIn 17
Hiatt, John c. 1952- ConMus 8 [port]
Hiatt, John D. 1940- St&PR 93
Hiatt, Mabel Strader 1921- WhoSSW 93
Hiatt, Marjorie McCullough 1923- WhoAm 92, WhoWor 93
Hiatt, Paul F. 1927- St&PR 93
Hiatt, Peter 1930- WhoAm 92
Hiatt, Robert Nelson 1936- WhoAm 92
Hiatt, Robert Worth 1913- WhoAm 92
Hiatt, Susan K. 1959- WhoAmW 93
Hibbard, Allen Eugene 1956- WhoSSW 93
Hibbard, Dwight H. 1923- St&PR 93, WhoAm 92
Hibbard, Irving E. 1939- St&PR 93
Hibbard, J.W. Kearny 1937- St&PR 93
Hibbard, John Eugene 1936- WhoE 93
Hibbard, Richard Arthur Law&B 92
Hibbard, Robert A. 1937- St&PR 93
Hibbard, Robert L. Law&B 92
Hibbard, Walter Rollo, Jr. 1918- WhoAm 92
Hibberd, Adrian Donald 1946- WhoWor 93
Hibberd, Roy Wayne Law&B 92
Hibberd, William James 1952- WhoIns 93
Hibbert, Alun 1949- WhoCanL 92
Hibbert, Eleanor 1906- WhoWor 93
Hibbert, Gary Francis 1948- St&PR 93
Hibbert, Geoffrey WhoScE 91-1
Hibbert, Jocelyn Clare 1963- WhoE 93
Hibbert, Sherry Ann Law&B 92
Hibbert, William Andrew, Jr. 1932- WhoSSW 93, WhoWor 93
Hibbett, Howard Scott 1920- WhoAm 92
Hibbett, Robert Neland 1960- WhoEmL 93
Hibbin, Sally ScF&FL 92
Hibbitts, Bernard John 1959- WhoE 93
Hibbitts, Charles Logan Law&B 92
Hibbitts, James R. 1935- WhoIns 93
Hibbs, Cathryn Ann 1952- WhoAmW 93
Hibbs, Euthymia D. 1937- WhoAmW 93
Hibbs, Glen H. 1940- St&PR 93
Hibbs, Gwenn L. Law&B 92
Hibbs, John David 1948- WhoEmL 93, WhoWor 93
Hibbs, John J. 1936- St&PR 93
Hibbs, John Stanley 1934- WhoAm 92
Hibbs, Loyal Robert 1925- WhoAm 92
Hibbs, Robert Andrews 1923- WhoAm 92
Hibdon, James Edward 1924- WhoAm 92
Hibel, Bernard 1916- WhoAm 92
Hibino, Masaaki 1936- WhoWor 93
Hibler, Christopher MiSFD 9
Hibler, Douglas Harry 1935- WhoAm 92
Hibner, Geoffrey 1949- St&PR 93
Hibner, Geoffrey John 1949- WhoAm 92
Hibner, Rae A. 1956- WhoAmW 93, WhoEmL 93
Hibnick, Gerald R. Law&B 92
Hibschweiler, Barbara Mary 1945- WhoAmW 93
Hibshman, Norbert K. 1915- St&PR 93
Hibst, Hartmut 1950- WhoWor 93
Hibt, David Law&B 92
Hichar, Barbara June 1916- WhoAmW 93
Hichar, Joseph Kenneth 1928- WhoAm 92
Hichar, Mark N.G. Law&B 92
Hick, Jochen MiSFD 9
Hick, John Harwood 1922- WhoAm 92, WhoWrEP 92
Hick, Kenneth William 1946- WhoWor 93
Hick, Wallace Leonard, Jr. 1935- WhoAm 92
Hickcox, Curtiss Bronson 1913- WhoAm 92
Hickel, Maggie BioIn 17
Hickel, Walter Joseph 1919- BioIn 17, WhoAm 92, WhoWor 93
Hickenlooper, George MiSFD 9
Hickerson, Glenn Lindsey 1937- WhoAm 92
Hickerson, Melinda Kay 1949- WhoAmW 93
Hickerson, Patricia Parsons 1942- WhoAmW 93
Hickerson, Robert Gene 1936- BiDAMSp 1989
Hickey, Bonnie Anne 1945- WhoAmW 93
Hickey, Brian Edward 1945- St&PR 93
Hickey, Bruce MiSFD 9
Hickey, Daniel C. Law&B 92
Hickey, Delina Rose 1941- WhoWor 93
Hickey, Edward Joseph, Jr. 1912- WhoAm 92
Hickey, Francis Roger 1942- WhoWor 93
Hickey, Frank G. St&PR 93
Hickey, Howard Wesley 1930- WhoAm 92
Hickey, James Aloysius 1920- WhoE 93
Hickey, James Aloysius Cardinal 1920- WhoAm 92, WhoWor 93
Hickey, John E. Law&B 92
Hickey, John E. 1943- St&PR 93
Hickey, John Edmund 1943- WhoAm 92
Hickey, John M. 1944- WhoIns 93
Hickey, John Michael 1944- WhoSSW 93
Hickey, John T. 1934- St&PR 93
Hickey, John Thomas 1925- St&PR 93, WhoAm 92
Hickey, John W. 1916- St&PR 93
Hickey, Joseph A. St&PR 93
Hickey, Joseph James 1907- WhoAm 92
Hickey, Joseph Michael, Jr. 1940- WhoAm 92
Hickey, Kate Donnelly 1943- WhoE 93
Hickey, Kevin Francis 1951- WhoAm 92
Hickey, Laurence L. Law&B 92
Hickey, Leo Joseph 1940- WhoAm 92
Hickey, Leonard Edward 1929- St&PR 93
Hickey, Margaret A. 1902- WhoAm 92
Hickey, Michael Harold Law&B 92
Hickey, Patricia Alice 1935- WhoE 93
Hickey, Patrick Joseph 1938- St&PR 93
Hickey, Raymond 1936- ConAu 37NR
Hickey, Robert Nelson 1941- WhoAm 92
Hickey, Robert Philip, Jr. 1942- WhoAm 92
Hickey, Robert W. Law&B 92
Hickey, Thomas J. Law&B 92
Hickey, Thomas Joseph 1934- WhoAm 92
Hickey, Timothy Daniel 1949- WhoAm 92
Hickey, W. Douglas Law&B 92
Hickey, Walter B.D., Jr. 1937- St&PR 93
Hickey, William Vincent, Jr. 1944- St&PR 93
Hickinbotham, Donald Eugene 1933- St&PR 93
Hickingbotham, Frank D. 1936- ConEn, St&PR 93, WhoSSW 93
Hickingbotham, Herren C. 1959- WhoSSW 93
Hickl, Barbara C. Law&B 92
Hickland, Edward Lee 1948- WhoEmL 93
Hicklin, James F. 1946- St&PR 93
Hicklin, John 1953- WhoUN 92
Hickman, Alan Douglas Vernon 1932-1990 BioIn 17
Hickman, Bertram Raymond 1946- St&PR 93
Hickman, Bryan D. 1945- St&PR 93
Hickman, Cleveland Pendleton, Jr. 1928- WhoAm 92
Hickman, David Gordon 1953- WhoEmL 93
Hickman, David Scott 1940- St&PR 93
Hickman, Frederic W. 1927- WhoAm 92
Hickman, Gertrude A. AmWomPl
Hickman, Grace Marguerite 1921- WhoAm 92, WhoAmW 93
Hickman, Halbert I. 1939- St&PR 93
Hickman, Hans (Robert Hermann) 1908-1968 Baker 92
Hickman, Harold E. 1920- St&PR 93
Hickman, Herman Michael, Jr. 1911-1958 BiDAMSp 1989
Hickman, Irene WhoWrEP 92
Hickman, J. Kenneth 1928- WhoAm 92
Hickman, James Charles 1927- WhoAm 92
Hickman, James Donald 1951- WhoSSW 93
Hickman, Janet Susan 1948- WhoE 93
Hickman, Jeannine Frances 1944- WhoWrEP 92
Hickman, John C. 1927- St&PR 93
Hickman, John Hampton, III 1937- St&PR 93, WhoAm 92, WhoWor 93
Hickman, Jolene Kay 1954- WhoAmW 93
Hickman, Leon Edward 1900- WhoAm 92
Hickman, Lucille 1949- WhoAm 92, WhoEmL 93
Hickman, Marjorie Anderson 1918- WhoAmW 93
Hickman, Martha Whitmore 1925- WhoWrEP 92
Hickman, Mary Frey 1927- WhoAmW 93
Hickman, Maude Hicks AmWomPl
Hickman, Peter A. Law&B 92
Hickman, Peter James 1931- WhoE 93
Hickman, Richard H. 1942- St&PR 93
Hickman, Richard Lonnie 1950- WhoEmL 93, WhoWor 93
Hickman, Robert Alan 1944- St&PR 93
Hickman, Robert Harrison 1953- WhoAm 92
Hickman, Robert Norman 1935- St&PR 93, WhoAm 92
Hickman, Stephen F. 1949- ScF&FL 92
Hickman, Stephen Lee 1942- St&PR 93
Hickman, Tracy 1955- ScF&FL 92
Hickman, Traphene Parramore 1933- WhoAm 92
Hickman, Waymon Logan 1934- St&PR 93
Hickman, William Albert 1877-1957 BioIn 17
Hickner, Gail Marie 1953- WhoAmW 93
Hickok, David Keith 1936- WhoWor 93
Hickok, Floyd A. 1907- WhoWrEP 92
Hickok, Gloria Vando 1934- WhoWrEP 92
Hickok, Lorena A. 1893-1968 BioIn 17
Hickok, Lucretia Ann 1932- WhoAmW 93
Hickok, Raymond P. d1992 NewYTBS 92 [port]
Hickok, Richard Sanford 1925- WhoAm 92
Hickok, Robert Lyman, Jr. 1929- WhoAm 92
Hickok, Wild Bill 1837-1876 BioIn 17
Hickox, Anthony MiSFD 9
Hickox, Douglas d1988 MiSFD 9N
Hickox, Gary Randolph 1952- WhoSSW 93
Hickox, Richard (Sidney) 1948- Baker 92
Hickrod, George Alan Karnes Wallis 1930- WhoWor 93
Hicks, Alice Blackmore 1946- WhoEmL 93
Hicks, Arthur Meredith 1917- WhoSSW 93
Hicks, Arthur Wesley, Jr. 1958- St&PR 93
Hicks, Audrey Marion Grabfield 1957- WhoEmL 93
Hicks, Bethany Gribben 1951- WhoAmW 93, WhoEmL 93
Hicks, Chas. E. 1919- St&PR 93
Hicks, Claude Alvis 1932- WhoSSW 93
Hicks, Clifford Byron 1920- WhoWrEP 92
Hicks, David Earl 1931- WhoWor 93
Hicks, David John 1945- WhoSSW 93
Hicks, David L. Law&B 92
Hicks, David L. 1939- BioIn 17
Hicks, Donald 1927- WhoScE 91-1
Hicks, Donald W. 1943- St&PR 93
Hicks, E.M. 1915- St&PR 93
Hicks, Edna Earle 1930- WhoAmW 93
Hicks, Edwin Hugh 1932- WhoAm 92
Hicks, Ele Wyatte 1926- WhoAm 92
Hicks, Eleanor B. MajAI
Hicks, Frances Ross 1900- WhoAmW 93
Hicks, Fred L., Jr. 1926- St&PR 93
Hicks, Gary Ellis 1953- WhoEmL 93
Hicks, George R. Law&B 92
Hicks, Gilbert, IV 1945- St&PR 93
Hicks, Granville 1901-1982 ScF&FL 92
Hicks, Guy M., III Law&B 92
Hicks, Harold J. 1940- WhoSSW 93
Hicks, Harvey MajAI
Hicks, Helen Clarice 1914- WhoAmW 93
Hicks, Irle Raymond 1928- WhoAm 92
Hicks, Irvin 1938- WhoAm 92
Hicks, Jack Morgan 1930- WhoWrEP 92
Hicks, James Robert 1929- St&PR 93
Hicks, James Thomas WhoWor 93
Hicks, Janet Kelty 1949- WhoEmL 93, WhoSSW 93
Hicks, Janice Marie 1958- WhoE 93
Hicks, Jennifer Lee 1964- WhoSSW 93
Hicks, John Bradford 1944- WhoSSW 93
Hicks, John Charles, Jr. 1951- BiDAMSp 1989
Hicks, John Douglas 1952- WhoEmL 93
Hicks, John Mark 1957- WhoEmL 93, WhoSSW 93
Hicks, John Trimmer 1946- WhoWor 93
Hicks, John V. WhoCanL 92
Hicks, John Victor 1907- WhoWrEP 92
Hicks, Joseph Bryan 1936- WhoE 93
Hicks, Juanita AfrAmBi [port]
Hicks, June Tucker 1932- WhoSSW 93
Hicks, Ken Carlyle 1953- WhoAm 92
Hicks, Kima Rene 1960- WhoEmL 93
Hicks, L. Westcott 1920- St&PR 93
Hicks, Lawrence E. Law&B 92
Hicks, Lawrence Robert 1944- St&PR 93, WhoAm 92
Hicks, Lawrence Wayne 1940- WhoAm 92
Hicks, Leslie Hubert 1927- WhoAm 92
Hicks, Linda Carlen 1948- WhoAmW 93
Hicks, Linda Joyce 1946- WhoEmL 93
Hicks, Louise Day 1923- BioIn 17
Hicks, Lucile P. 1938- WhoAmW 93
Hicks, M. Elizabeth 1944- WhoAm 92
Hicks, Mark Stuart Law&B 92
Hicks, Maryellen Whitlock 1949- AfrAmBi, WhoAmW 93
Hicks, Mercer, III 1940- St&PR 93
Hicks, Mildred Walker WhoAmW 93
Hicks, Noel Jeffrey 1940- WhoAsAP 91
Hicks, Orton Havergal 1900- WhoAm 92
Hicks, Paul B., Jr. 1925- WhoAm 92, WhoE 93
Hicks, Paul Burton, Jr. 1925- St&PR 93
Hicks, Paul Burton, III 1956- WhoEmL 93
Hicks, Paul William 1937- St&PR 93
Hicks, Peggy Glanville- 1912-1990 BioIn 17
Hicks, Robert B. Law&B 92
Hicks, Robin Edgcumbe 1942- WhoWor 93
Hicks, Sandra Lois 1950- WhoAmW 93
Hicks, Sandy Lee 1959- WhoEmL 93
Hicks, Sarah 1967- WhoAmW 93
Hicks, Susan Lynn Bowman 1952- WhoAmW 93
Hicks, Thomas H. 1946- St&PR 93
Hicks, Thomas Howard 1946- WhoAm 92
Hicks, Tyler Gregory 1921- WhoAm 92
Hicks, Walter Joseph 1935- WhoE 93
Hicks, Wayland R. 1942- St&PR 93
Hicks, William Albert, III 1942- WhoAm 92
Hicks, William Hampton 1956- WhoWor 93
Hicks, Winston Oliver 1942- WhoWor 93

Hicks-Caskey, William Edward 1925- WhoSSW 93
Hickson, David John WhoScE 91-1
Hickson, Eileen Hassett 1916- WhoAmW 93
Hickson, Larry W. 1953- St&PR 93
Hickson, Marcus Lafayette, III 1945- WhoSSW 93
Hickson, Shirley Ann 1944- WhoSSW 93
Hickton, Dawne S. Law&B 92
Hida, Kinzo 1922- WhoWor 93
Hida, Miyoko 1941- WhoAsAP 91
Hida, Takeyuki 1927- WhoWor 93
Hidaka, Hisao 1942- WhoWor 93
Hidaka, Sonojo 1848-1932 HarEnMi
Hidalgo, Alberto F. 1935- WhoAm 92
Hidalgo, Carlos Fernando 1933- WhoWor 93
Hidalgo, Edward 1912- HispAmA, WhoAm 92
Hidalgo, Elvira de 1892-1980 IntDcOp [port], OxDcOp
Hidalgo, Hilda 1928- NotHsAW 93
Hidalgo, Jose Luis 1919-1947 BioIn 17
Hidalgo, Joy Faye 1950- WhoWrEP 92
Hidalgo, Juan c. 1612-1685 Baker 92, OxDcOp
Hidalgo, Liverson WhoWrEP 92
Hidalgo, Manuel T. WhoIns 93
Hidalgo, Maria Luisa 1918- DcMexL
Hidalgo, Miguel 1958- WhoEmL 93
Hidalgo, Monica 1965- WhoAmW 93
Hidalgo Maynar, Fernando 1932- WhoScE 91-3
Hidalgo y Costilla, Miguel 1753-1811 BioIn 17
Hidas, Frigyes 1928- Baker 92
Hiddema, J. 1946- WhoScE 91-3
Hide, Geoffrey Alan WhoScE 91-1
Hideaki, Okada 1935- WhoWor 93
Hiden, Charles Edward 1926- St&PR 93
Hiden, John William WhoScE 91-1
Hiden, Robert Battaile, Jr. 1933- WhoAm 92, WhoE 93, WhoWor 93
Hidenari Ito 1941- WhoAsAP 91
Hidenori, Kimura 1941- WhoWor 93
Hider, Robert Charles WhoScE 91-1
Hidore, John Junior 1932- WhoAm 92
Hidvegi, Egon J. 1931- WhoScE 91-4
Hidy, George Martel 1935- WhoAm 92
Hieatt, Allen Kent 1921- WhoAm 92, WhoWrEP 92
Hieatt, Constance Bartlett 1928- WhoAm 92, WhoAmW 93, WhoWrEP 92
Hieber, Lutz Albrecht 1944- WhoWor 93
Hiebert, Paul 1892-1987 WhoCanL 92
Hiebert, Ray Eldon 1932- WhoAm 92
Hieblinger, Leo B. 1938- WhoWor 93
Hiedemann, Annette Regine 1936- WhoSSW 93
Hiegel, Jerry M. 1927- St&PR 93
Hieggelke, Brian Jay 1962- WhoEmL 93
Hielkema, Hindrik Wiebren 1948- WhoWor 93
Hielscher, Robert A. 1948- St&PR 93
Hielscher, Robert Allen 1948- WhoAm 92
Hielscher, Udo Artur 1939- WhoWor 93
Hiemeyer, Volker 1932- WhoScE 91-3
Hiemstra, John E. 1928- WhoE 93
Hiemstra, R.J.J. 1941- St&PR 93
Hiemstra, Roger 1938- WhoAm 92
Hienke, John D. St&PR 93
Hienton, Diane DeBrosse 1948- WhoAmW 93
Hiepko, Paul 1932- WhoScE 91-3
Hier, Ethel Glenn 1889-1971 Baker 92
Hierholzer, Klaus Hermann 1929- WhoScE 91-3
Hiernaux, Jean Robert 1921- WhoScE 91-2
Hiero, I c. 535BC-467BC HarEnMi
Hiero, II c. 306BC-215BC HarEnMi
Hierokles OxDcByz
Hierokles fl. 5th cent.- OxDcByz
Hieronymus OxDcByz
Hieronymus, Clara Booth Wiggins 1913- WhoAm 92
Hieronymus, Edward Whittlesey 1943- WhoAm 92
Hieronymus, Eusebius d419? BioIn 17
Hierro, Jose 1922- BioIn 17
Hiers, James Alton 1944- WhoSSW 93
Hiers, Richard Hyde 1932- WhoSSW 93
Hiers, Thomas S. Law&B 92
Hiester, Joseph 1752-1832 BioIn 17
Hietala, Sven-Ola 1936- WhoScE 91-4
Hiett, Chanley Joseph 1947- WhoSSW 93
Hiett, David Scott 1954- WhoSSW 93
Hiett, Edward Emerson 1922- WhoAm 92
Hieu, Nguyen Van 1918- DcTwHis
Hiew Min Kong WhoAsAP 91
Higa, Tatsuo 1939- WhoWor 93
Higashi, Chikara 1941- WhoAsAP 91
Higashi, Junji 1946- WhoAsAP 91
Higashi, Ken 1934- WhoWor 93
Higashiguchi, Minoru 1930- WhoWor 93
Higashikuni, Naruhiko 1887- HarEnMi
Higashinaka, Mitsuo 1924- WhoAsAP 91
Higatsberger, Michael J. 1924- WhoScE 91-4
Higbee, David M. Law&B 92
Higbee, David M. 1944- St&PR 93
Higbee, Florence Salick WhoAmW 93
Higbee, Lawrence E. 1949- St&PR 93
Higbee, Ronald Wayne 1947- St&PR 93
Higbie, Leslie Wilson 1914- WhoE 93
Higbie, Ruth Griggs 1909- WhoWrEP 92
Higby, Edward Julian 1939- WhoSSW 93
Higby, Gregory James 1953- WhoAm 92
Higby, James Harland 1946- WhoAm 92
Higby, John H. St&PR 93
Higby, Kathleen Rose 1950- WhoE 93
Higdon, Barbara J. 1930- WhoAm 92, WhoAmW 93
Higdon, Bernice Cowan 1918- WhoAmW 93, WhoWor 93
Higdon, Charles E. 1941- St&PR 93
Higdon, David Leon 1939- WhoAm 92, WhoWrEP 92
Higdon, Jerry L. 1930- St&PR 93
Higdon, Joe M. 1940- St&PR 93
Higdon, Leo I. WhoAm 92
Higdon, Margaret B. Law&B 92
Higdon, Norris Bruce 1950- WhoSSW 93
Higdon, Polly Susanne 1942- WhoAmW 93
Higelmire, Melissa 1951- WhoEmL 93
Higenbotham, Evelyn AmWomPl
Higerd, Thomas Braden 1942- WhoSSW 93
Higginbotham, A. C. 1927- WhoSSW 93
Higginbotham, A. Leon, Jr. 1928- AfrAmBi, WhoAm 92, WhoE 93
Higginbotham, Charles Edwin 1941- WhoSSW 93
Higginbotham, David Ballard 1929- St&PR 93
Higginbotham, Glenn Bruce Law&B 92
Higginbotham, J.C. 1906-1973 Baker 92
Higginbotham, (Prieur) Jay 1937- ConAu 37NR
Higginbotham, John Taylor 1947- WhoE 93
Higginbotham, Marcus H. 1940- St&PR 93
Higginbotham, Patricia Law&B 92
Higginbotham, Patrick Errol 1938- WhoAm 92, WhoSSW 93
Higginbotham, Richard Alan 1947- St&PR 93
Higginbotham, William Allen 1957- WhoSSW 93
Higginbottom, David ScF&FL 92
Higginbottom, Samuel Logan 1921- WhoAm 92
Higgins, A. Lawrence 1922- WhoAm 92
Higgins, Adam Doby 1965- WhoSSW 93
Higgins, Aileen Cleveland 1882- AmWomPl
Higgins, Andrew Jackson 1921- WhoAm 92
Higgins, Angie Castleberry 1952- WhoAmW 93
Higgins, Anthony Paul 1940- St&PR 93
Higgins, Barbara Lorene 1947- WhoAmW 93
Higgins, Barbara S. 1955- WhoE 93
Higgins, Carlisle Wallace, Jr. 1918- St&PR 93
Higgins, Christina Johnson 1962- WhoAmW 93
Higgins, Christopher F. WhoScE 91-1
Higgins, Christopher Ian d1990 BioIn 17
Higgins, Clark Worthen 1944- St&PR 93
Higgins, Colin 1941-1988 MiSFD 9N
Higgins, Craig Stockton 1943- WhoE 93
Higgins, D. S. 1938- ScF&FL 92
Higgins, David C. 1948- St&PR 93
Higgins, David L. 1945- St&PR 93
Higgins, Dennis Roy 1937- WhoWor 93
Higgins, Dick 1938- Baker 92, WhoAm 92, WhoE 93
Higgins, Donald E. BioIn 17
Higgins, Dorothy Marie 1930- WhoAmW 93
Higgins, Doug BioIn 17
Higgins, Edward Aloysius 1931- WhoAm 92
Higgins, Fred R. BioIn 17
Higgins, Frederick Benjamin, Jr. 1936- WhoAm 92
Higgins, Geoffrey Trevor 1932- WhoAm 92
Higgins, George Edward 1930- WhoAm 92
Higgins, George Herman, Jr. 1954- WhoSSW 93
Higgins, George V. 1939- BioIn 17
Higgins, George Vincent 1939- WhoAm 92, WhoWrEP 92
Higgins, Graham McLean 1928- WhoScE 91-3
Higgins, Harold Bailey 1922- WhoAm 92
Higgins, Irving John WhoScE 91-1
Higgins, Irwin Raymond 1919- WhoSSW 93
Higgins, Isabelle Jeanette 1919- WhoAmW 93
Higgins, J. Thomas R. BioIn 17
Higgins, Jack 1929- BioIn 17, WhoAm 92
Higgins, Jack 1954- WhoAm 92
Higgins, Jack Kirby 1928- St&PR 93
Higgins, James Bruce 1947- WhoE 93
Higgins, James C. 1940- St&PR 93
Higgins, James C., Jr. Law&B 92
Higgins, James Charles, III 1947- WhoEmL 93
Higgins, James Clifford, Jr. Law&B 92
Higgins, James Henry 1916- WhoAm 92
Higgins, James Henry, III 1940- WhoE 93
Higgins, James K. Law&B 92
Higgins, Jane Margaret 1954- WhoAmW 93, WhoE 93
Higgins, Jay F. 1945- St&PR 93
Higgins, Jay Francis 1945- WhoAm 92
Higgins, Jenny L. Law&B 92
Higgins, Jerry M. 1934- St&PR 93
Higgins, Joan Marie WhoAmW 93
Higgins, John 1934- ConAu 138
Higgins, John J. Law&B 92
Higgins, John J. 1943- St&PR 93
Higgins, John Joseph 1934- WhoAm 92
Higgins, John R. d1990 BioIn 17
Higgins, John T. Law&B 92
Higgins, Joseph WhoScE 91-1
Higgins, Joseph Wayne 1949- WhoSSW 93
Higgins, Joy AmWomPl
Higgins, Julia Stretton WhoScE 91-1
Higgins, Julia Stretton 1942- WhoWor 93
Higgins, Julianne McKenna Law&B 92
Higgins, Katharine Elizabeth Chapin 1847-1925 AmWomPl
Higgins, Kathleen M(arie) 1954- ConAu 138
Higgins, Kenneth Raymond 1915- WhoAm 92
Higgins, L. Boyd 1927- St&PR 93
Higgins, Leo Michael, III 1950- WhoAm 92
Higgins, Linda Westapal 1960- WhoE 93
Higgins, Maggie Rose 1957- WhoAmW 93
Higgins, Marguerite 1920-1966 JrnUS
Higgins, Marion West 1915-1991 BioIn 17
Higgins, Matthew Joseph 1938- WhoAm 92
Higgins, Michael Joseph 1951- WhoEmL 93
Higgins, Nancy Carol 1951- WhoAmW 93
Higgins, Nancy McCready Law&B 92
Higgins, Norma Louise Jobe 1939- WhoAmW 93
Higgins, Patricia Ann 1951- WhoAmW 93, WhoWor 93
Higgins, Paula Elizabeth 1954- WhoWrEP 92
Higgins, Pauline Edwards Law&B 92
Higgins, Peter T. 1946- St&PR 93
Higgins, Peter Thomas 1943- WhoE 93
Higgins, Philip John WhoScE 91-1
Higgins, Pink 1848-1914 BioIn 17
Higgins, Prentiss C. 1939- St&PR 93
Higgins, R. Scott 1956- St&PR 93
Higgins, Richard B. 1937- St&PR 93
Higgins, Richard Carter 1938- WhoWrEP 92
Higgins, Robert Arthur 1924- WhoAm 92
Higgins, Robert E. Law&B 92
Higgins, Robert Emmett 1932- St&PR 93
Higgins, Robert J. 1945- St&PR 93
Higgins, Robert Joseph 1945- WhoAm 92
Higgins, Robert Louis 1919- WhoAm 92
Higgins, Robert Price 1932- WhoE 93
Higgins, Robert Walter 1934- WhoAm 92
Higgins, Robin BioIn 17
Higgins, Shaun Law&B 92
Higgins, Shaun Brian 1950- St&PR 93, WhoEmL 93
Higgins, Therese 1925- WhoAm 92, WhoAmW 93
Higgins, Thomas A. 1932- WhoAm 92, WhoSSW 93
Higgins, Trumbull BioIn 17
Higgins, Victor 1884-1949 BioIn 17
Higgins, Wilhemina AmWomPl
Higgins, William Henry Clay, III 1908- WhoAm 92
Higgins, William R. BioIn 17
Higgins, William Waugh 1935- St&PR 93, WhoAm 92
Higginson, Anthony Michael WhoScE 91-1
Higginson, Bernard E. 1932- St&PR 93
Higginson, Don Lee Law&B 92
Higginson, Francis 1586?-1630 BioIn 17
Higginson, Henry Lee 1834-1919 Baker 92
Higginson, James Jackson 1921- WhoAm 92
Higginson, Nathaniel Cabot 1768-1794 BioIn 17
Higginson, Sheila Elizabeth 1940- WhoWor 93
Higginson, Thomas Wentworth 1823-1911 BioIn 17, ScF&FL 92
Higginson, William J. 1938- WhoWrEP 92
Higgins-Stahulak, Elizabeth Jean 1950- WhoEmL 93
Higgo, Jennifer Joan Wynne WhoScE 91-1
Higgs, DeWitt A. 1907- WhoAm 92
Higgs, Elizabeth Jo 1960- WhoAmW 93
Higgs, Eric C. ScF&FL 92
Higgs, Jeffrey B. 1948- St&PR 93
Higgs, John H. 1934- WhoAm 92
Higgs, Lloyd Albert 1937- WhoAm 92
Higgs, W. Victor Law&B 92
High, Dallas Milton 1931- WhoSSW 93
High, Danette Colleen 1964- WhoE 93
High, Danny William 1955- WhoSSW 93
High, David Scherer 1940- St&PR 93
High, Dorothy BioIn 17
High, Edward Garfield 1919-1986 BioIn 17
High, George Borman 1931- WhoAm 92
High, Joshua 1950- St&PR 93
High, Lee E. 1951- St&PR 93
High, Mari Helen 1940- WhoAmW 93
High, Michael B. 1948- St&PR 93
High, Monique Raphel 1949- WhoAm 92, WhoEmL 93, WhoWrEP 92
High, Philip E. 1914- ScF&FL 92
High, S. Dale 1942- St&PR 93, WhoAm 92
High, Steven Samuel 1956- WhoEmL 93
High, Thomas W. 1947- WhoAm 92
High, William A. 1948- St&PR 93
Higham, Charles 1931- ScF&FL 92
Higham, John 1920- WhoAm 92
Higham, Robin 1925- WhoAm 92, WhoWrEP 92
Highberger, Craig Bender 1953- WhoWrEP 92
Highberger, William Foster 1950- WhoAm 92, WhoWor 93
Highbloom, Lloyd Henry 1939- WhoAm 92
Highet, Gilbert Keith MacInnes 1933- WhoAm 92
Highet, Helen MacInnes 1907-1985 BioIn 17
Highfield, Gary Allen 1952- WhoSSW 93
Highfield, Laurene AmWomPl
Highfield, Robert Edward 1930- WhoAm 92
Highfill, Philip Henry, Jr. 1918- WhoAm 92
Highhouse, Kent E. 1942- St&PR 93
Highland, Cecil Blaine, Jr. 1918- WhoAm 92
Highland, Dora ConAu 39NR
Highland, Harold Joseph 1917- WhoE 93
Highland, Selby Arnett, Jr. 1945- WhoAm 92
Highlands, Donald Bruce 1939- St&PR 93
Highlen, Pamela S. 1946- WhoAmW 93
Highleyman, Samuel Locke, III 1928- WhoAm 92
Highman, Barbara WhoAmW 93
Highmore, Joseph 1692-1780 BioIn 17
Highsmith, Anna Bizzell 1947- WhoSSW 93
Highsmith, Cynthia Simms 1956- WhoSSW 93
Highsmith, Duncan 1948- St&PR 93
Highsmith, Hugh Purcell 1914- St&PR 93
Highsmith, Jasper Habersham 1940- WhoSSW 93
Highsmith, Jimmy D. 1933- St&PR 93
Highsmith, Linda Yvonne 1949- WhoEmL 93
Highsmith, Patricia 1921- BioIn 17, ScF&FL 92
Highsmith, Shelby 1929- WhoAm 92
Highsmith, Wanda Law 1928- WhoAmW 93
Hight, B. Boyd 1939- St&PR 93
Hight, Joe Irvin 1958- WhoSSW 93
Hight, Mary AmWomPl
Hight, Roy Van 1955- WhoSSW 93
Hightower, Anthony 1961- WhoEmL 93
Hightower, Arlene Janice 1949- WhoEmL 93
Hightower, Christopher BioIn 17
Hightower, David Earl Law&B 92
Hightower, David Lee 1953- WhoSSW 93
Hightower, Dennis Fowler 1941- WhoWor 93
Hightower, Florence (Cole) 1916-1981 DcAmChF 1960
Hightower, Geraldine Heres 1930- WhoAmW 93
Hightower, Glenda Phillips 1944- WhoAmW 93
Hightower, Jack English 1926- WhoAm 92, WhoSSW 93
Hightower, Jim BioIn 17
Hightower, Joe Walter 1936- WhoAm 92
Hightower, John Brantley 1933- WhoAm 92
Hightower, Lloyd Arthur 1934- St&PR 93
Hightower, Michael AfrAmBi [port]

Hightower, Michael 1957- WhoEmL 93
Hightower, Neil Hamilton 1940- St&PR 93, WhoAm 92, WhoSSW 93
Hightower, Wanda Morris Law&B 92
Hightower, William Allen 1943- St&PR 93
Hightower, William Harrison, III 1936- St&PR 93
Highwater, Jamake BioIn 17, WhoAm 92
Highwater, Jamake 1942- DcAmChF 1985, SmATA 69 [port], WhoWrEP 92
Highwater, Jamake (Mamake) 1942?- MajAI [port]
Highway, Tomson 1952- WhoCanL 92
Higi, William L. 1933- WhoAm 92
Higie, William F. 1926- St&PR 93
Higinbotham, Betty Louise Wilson 1910- WhoAm 92, WhoAmW 93
Higinbotham, William Alfred 1910- WhoAm 92
Higler, L.W.G. Bert 1939- WhoScE 91-3
Higley, Albert M., Jr. 1928- St&PR 93
Higley, Bruce Wadsworth 1928- WhoAm 92
Higley, David L. 1952- St&PR 93, WhoIns 93
Higley, Kathleen Ann 1948- WhoAm 92
Higley, L. William Law&B 92
Higley, Thomas Carlton 1938- WhoSSW 93
Higley, Thomas D. 1952- St&PR 93
Higman, Dennis J. 1940- ScF&FL 92
Higman, Sally Lee 1945- WhoAmW 93
Hignard, (Jean-Louis) Aristide 1822-1898 Baker 92
Higonnet, Anne 1959- ConAu 139
Higson, Gregory Joseph Law&B 92
Higton, Gary 1960- WhoWor 93
Higuchi, C. Glen Law&B 92
Higuchi, Hiroshi 1953- WhoWor 93
Higuchi, Kichiro 1888-1970 HarEnMi
Higuchi, Masaaki 1928- WhoWor 93
Higuchi, Takayoshi 1927- WhoWor 93
Hiirsalmi, Heimo Martti 1932- WhoScE 91-4
Hiismaki, Pekka 1939- WhoScE 91-4
Hijazi, Mohammed Saeed 1950- WhoWor 93
Hijazi, Oussama 1954- WhoWor 93
Hijikata, Takeshi 1915- St&PR 93
Hijman, Julius 1901-1969 Baker 92
Hijuelos, Oscar 1951- HispAmA
Hijuelos, Oscar 1952- WhoAm 92
Hikasa, Katsuyuki 1945- WhoAsAP 91
Hikawa, Christine 1951- St&PR 93
Hiken Lapins, Cynthia E. Law&B 92
Hiland, Alinda M. AmWomPl
Hilary, Saint, Bishop of Poitiers d367? BioIn 17
Hilb, Robert H. 1927- St&PR 93
Hilberg, Wolfgang 1932- WhoScE 91-3
Hilberry, Conrad (Arthur) 1928- DcLB 120 [port], WhoWrEP 92
Hilbers, Charlotte Marie 1962- WhoAmW 93
Hilbert, Angelia Hulda 1949- WhoAmW 93
Hilbert, Bernard Charles 1921- WhoAm 92
Hilbert, Rita L. 1942- WhoAmW 93
Hilbert, Robert Backus 1929- WhoAm 92
Hilbert, Robert Saul 1941- WhoAm 92
Hilbert, Virginia Lois 1935- WhoAmW 93
Hilbert, William M. 1936- St&PR 93
Hilboldt, James S., Jr. Law&B 92
Hilborn, Michael G. Law&B 92
Hilborn, Michael G. 1943- WhoAm 92
Hilborn, Robert Clarence 1943- WhoE 93
Hilborne, Rebecca Higgins Law&B 92
Hilbrecht, Norman Ty 1933- WhoAm 92, WhoWor 93
Hilbrink, William John 1928- WhoSSW 93
Hilburg, Alan Jay 1948- WhoWor 93
Hilburn, Carol Sabel Law&B 92
Hilburn, Katherine B. Law&B 92
Hilburn, O. Nathaniel, Jr. Law&B 92
Hilburn, William Robert 1946- St&PR 93, WhoEmL 93
Hilbush, Edward O. 1918- St&PR 93
Hilby, Bruce Titus 1944- WhoWor 93
Hild, Larence C. 1928- St&PR 93
Hild, Nancy 1942- WhoWrEP 92
Hildach, Eugen 1849-1924 Baker 92
Hildebolt, William Morton 1943- St&PR 93, WhoAm 92
Hildebrand, Charles F. Law&B 92
Hildebrand, Clive Perry 1937- WhoWor 93
Hildebrand, Connie Marie 1944- WhoAmW 93
Hildebrand, David Floyd 1955- WhoEmL 93
Hildebrand, David Kent 1940- WhoAm 92
Hildebrand, Don Cecil 1943- WhoWor 93
Hildebrand, Donald Allen 1937- WhoE 93
Hildebrand, Francis Begnaud 1915- WhoAm 92, WhoE 93
Hildebrand, James A. Law&B 92
Hildebrand, Janet Elizabeth 1949- WhoAmW 93, WhoSSW 93
Hildebrand, Jerzy Georges 1936- WhoScE 91-2, WhoWor 93
Hildebrand, Joanna Lynn 1960- WhoAmW 93
Hildebrand, John Frederick 1940- WhoAm 92
Hildebrand, John Grant 1942- WhoAm 92
Hildebrand, John W. 1953- St&PR 93
Hildebrand, Karl-Gustaf 1911- WhoWor 93
Hildebrand, Krista Willett 1957- WhoE 93
Hildebrand, Mark Lane 1945- WhoUN 92
Hildebrand, Reinhard Friedrich Hans 1943- WhoWor 93
Hildebrand, Roger Henry 1922- WhoAm 92
Hildebrand, Thomas Brian 1952- WhoEmL 93
Hildebrand, Verna Lee 1924- WhoAm 92
Hildebrand, Willard Ray 1939- WhoAm 92
Hildebrandt, Alfred Georg 1937- WhoScE 91-3
Hildebrandt, Bradford Walter 1940- WhoAm 92
Hildebrandt, Brothers ScF&FL 92
Hildebrandt, Claudia Joan 1942- WhoAmW 93
Hildebrandt, Frederick Dean, Jr. 1933- WhoAm 92, WhoE 93
Hildebrandt, Gerd 1923- WhoScE 91-3
Hildebrandt, Goetz 1941- WhoScE 91-3
Hildebrandt, Greg 1939- ScF&FL 92
Hildebrandt, Rita 1948- ScF&FL 92
Hildebrandt, Stephanie Chisholm Law&B 92
Hildebrandt, Stephen Austin Law&B 92
Hildebrandt, Theodore Ware 1922- WhoAm 92
Hildebrandt, Thomas 1950- WhoIns 93
Hildebrandt, Thomas James Law&B 92
Hildebrandt, Tim 1939- ScF&FL 92
Hildebrandt, Uwe W. 1941- WhoScE 91-3
Hildebrant, Andy McClellan 1929- WhoWor 93
Hildegard, Von Bingen, Saint 1098-1179 BioIn 17
Hildegard of Bingen 1098-1179 OxDcOp
Hildegard von Bingen 1098-1179 Baker 92
Hilden, Joseph P. Law&B 92
Hilden, Patricia Jane 1944- WhoSSW 93
Hilder, Rowland 1905- BioIn 17
Hilderbrandt, Donald Franklin, II 1939- WhoAm 92
Hilderson, Herwig J.J. 1938- WhoScE 91-2
Hildesheimer, Azriel 1820-1899 BioIn 17
Hildesheimer, Wolfgang 1916- ScF&FL 92
Hildesheimer, Wolfgang 1916-1991 AnObit 1991, BioIn 17, ConLC 70, DcLB 124 [port]
Hildesley, Michael Edmund 1948- WhoWor 93
Hildestad, Terry Dean 1949- St&PR 93
Hildick, E. W. MajAI
Hildick, E.W. 1925- BioIn 17, ScF&FL 92
Hildick, Edmund Wallace 1925- BioIn 17
Hildick, (Edmund) Wallace 1925- MajAI [port]
Hilding, Jerel Lee 1949- WhoAm 92
Hildner, Ernest Gotthold, III 1940- WhoAm 92
Hildner, Phillips Brooks, II 1944- WhoWor 93
Hildon, Michael A. 1942- St&PR 93
Hildreth, Carol Temple 1943- WhoAmW 93
Hildreth, Carolyn June 1940- WhoAmW 93
Hildreth, Clifford 1917- WhoAm 92
Hildreth, Eugene A. 1924- WhoAm 92
Hildreth, Gary R. Law&B 92
Hildreth, James Robert 1927- WhoAm 92
Hildreth, Joseph Alan 1947- WhoEmL 93
Hildreth, Richard 1807-1865 JrnUS
Hildreth, Richard Mansfield 1948- WhoEmL 93, WhoSSW 93
Hildreth, Roland James 1926- WhoAm 92
Hildreth, Samuel Clay 1866-1929 BiDAMSp 1989
Hildreth, William Bartley 1949- WhoSSW 93
Hildrum, Kjell Ivar 1940- WhoScE 91-4
Hile, Jeanette Theresa 1949- WhoAmW 93
Hileman, Dorothy BioIn 17
Hileman, Michael James 1952- St&PR 93
Hiler, Dale Courtlan 1937- St&PR 93
Hiler, Edward Allan 1939- WhoAm 92
Hiler, John BioIn 17
Hiler, John Patrick 1953- WhoAm 92
Hiles, Henry 1826-1904 Baker 92
Hiles, Nancy Jane 1951- WhoSSW 93
Hiles, William Gayle, Jr. 1945- WhoSSW 93
Hiley, Paul Culverwell 1939- WhoE 93
Hilf, Eberhard R. 1935- WhoScE 91-3
Hilf, Russell 1931- WhoAm 92
Hilfer, Anthony Channell 1936- WhoAm 92
Hilferding, Rudolf 1877-1941 BioIn 17
Hilferty, Robert D. 1952- St&PR 93
Hilferty, Susan BioIn 17
Hilfinger, Dean Farrar 1912- WhoAm 92
Hilford, Lawrence B. d1992 NewYTBS 92
Hilford, Lawrence B. 1934-1992 BioIn 17
Hilfstein, Erna WhoAmW 93, WhoE 93, WhoWor 93
Hilgard, Ernest Ropiequet 1904- WhoAm 92, WhoWor 93
Hilgard, Heinrich 1835-1900 BioIn 17
Hilgard, Josephine Rohrs 1906-1989 BioIn 17
Hilgart, Donna BioIn 17
Hilgart, John Matthew 1961- WhoWor 93
Hilgart, Travis BioIn 17
Hilgartner, Beth 1957- ScF&FL 92
Hilgartner, Margaret Wehr 1924- WhoAm 92
Hilgeman, Charles E. 1934- St&PR 93
Hilgenberg, Eve Brantly Handy 1942- WhoAm 92, WhoAmW 93
Hilgenberg, Jay 1960- WhoAm 92
Hilgenberg, John Christian 1941- WhoAm 92
Hilgendorf, Jill Rae 1952- WhoAmW 93
Hilgendorf, Robert Lee 1936- St&PR 93
Hilgenfeld, Rolf 1954- WhoWor 93
Hilger, Daniel 1940- St&PR 93
Hilger, Erwin 1941- WhoScE 91-3
Hilger, Frederick Lee, Jr. 1946- WhoWor 93
Hilger, Inez 1891-1977 IntDcAn
Hilgermann, Reinhard 1933- WhoScE 91-3
Hilgers, J.H.M. 1940- WhoScE 91-3
Hilgert, Raymond Lewis 1930- WhoAm 92
Hilinski, Chester C. 1917- WhoAm 92
Hilinski, John C. Law&B 92
Hilke, John Coryell 1950- WhoEmL 93
Hilker, Walter Robert, Jr. 1921- WhoAm 92
Hilkert, David Law&B 92
Hilkert, James Michael 1945- WhoSSW 93
Hill, A. Karen Law&B 92
Hill, Aaron 1685-1750 BioIn 17
Hill, Adrian D.G. Law&B 92
Hill, Alan Jackson 1944- St&PR 93
Hill, Alan M. 1939- St&PR 93
Hill, Alan R. 1942- St&PR 93
Hill, Alan William WhoScE 91-1
Hill, Albert Alan 1938- WhoAm 92
Hill, Albert Fay 1925- ScF&FL 92
Hill, Albert Gordon 1910- WhoAm 92
Hill, Alden Eugene 1926- St&PR 93
Hill, Alfred 1870-1960 OxDcOp
Hill, Alfred 1917- WhoAm 92
Hill, Alfred 1959-1988 BioIn 17
Hill, Alfred Daniel 1952- WhoEmL 93
Hill, Alfred Ebsworth 1862-1940 See Hill, W.E. & Sons Baker 92
Hill, Alfred (Francis) 1870-1960 Baker 92
Hill, Allen Edward Law&B 92
Hill, Allen Frank 1952- WhoAm 92
Hill, Allen M. 1945- St&PR 93
Hill, Alton David, Jr. 1933- WhoAm 92
Hill, Ambrose Powell 1825-1865 HarEnMi
Hill, Andrew 1942- See Hill, W.E. & Sons Baker 92
Hill, Andrew William 1937- WhoAm 92
Hill, Anita BioIn 17
Hill, Anita Carraway 1928- WhoAmW 93
Hill, Anita F. WhoAmW 93
Hill, Ann Marie 1951- WhoEmL 93
Hill, Anna Marie 1938- WhoAmW 93
Hill, Anne Lynn 1944- WhoE 93
Hill, Anne Pendergrass Law&B 92
Hill, April Lee 1953- WhoSSW 93
Hill, Archibald Govan, IV 1950- WhoEmL 93, WhoSSW 93
Hill, Arthur 1922- ConTFT 10, WhoAm 92
Hill, Arthur Frederick 1860-1939 See Hill, W.E. & Sons Baker 92
Hill, Arthur Henry 1932- WhoE 93
Hill, Arthur J. BioIn 17
Hill, Arthur James 1948- WhoAm 92
Hill, Austin Bradford 1897-1991 AnObit 1991, BioIn 17
Hill, Barbara Ann 1944- WhoAm 92, WhoAmW 93
Hill, Barbara June 1948- WhoAmW 93
Hill, Barry Morton 1946- WhoEmL 93
Hill, Benjamin Harvey, III 1941- WhoAm 92
Hill, Bennett David 1934- WhoAm 92
Hill, Benny 1925-1992 BioIn 17, CurBio 92N, NewYTBS 92 [port], News 92, -92-3, QDrFCA 92 [port]
Hill, Berhard 1938- WhoScE 91-3
Hill, Bertha 1905-1950 Baker 92
Hill, Betty Jean 1937- WhoAmW 93
Hill, Bill WhoWrEP 92
Hill, Bob WhoAm 92
Hill, Boyd H., Jr. 1931- WhoAm 92
Hill, Brian Ernest 1937- WhoWor 93
Hill, Brice Edward 1951- WhoE 93
Hill, Bridget T. 1942- WhoScE 91-1
Hill, Bruce Marvin 1935- WhoAm 92, WhoWor 93
Hill, Bryan W. Law&B 92
Hill, Carlene Bay 1957- WhoWrEP 92
Hill, Carlos O'Brien BioIn 17
Hill, Carol 1942- ScF&FL 92
Hill, Catherine WhoWrEP 92
Hill, Catherine E. Law&B 92
Hill, Cathy 1944- ScF&FL 92
Hill, Cathy Lynn D'Amico 1958- WhoAmW 93
Hill, Charles Graham, Jr. 1937- WhoAm 92
Hill, Charles K. 1928- St&PR 93
Hill, Charles Strunk 1919- St&PR 93, WhoSSW 93
Hill, Charlie BioIn 17
Hill, Cherry Lynn 1947- WhoWrEP 92
Hill, Christina Donna Law&B 92
Hill, Christopher 1912- WhoWor 93
Hill, Christopher D. 1962- WhoSSW 93
Hill, Christopher Rowland WhoScE 91-1
Hill, Christy BioIn 17
Hill, Clara Edith 1948- WhoAmW 93, WhoE 93, WhoEmL 93
Hill, Claude BioIn 17
Hill, Claude 1911-1991 ConAu 136
Hill, Claudia Adams 1949- WhoAmW 93
Hill, Clinton 1922- WhoAm 92
Hill, Crag A. 1957- WhoWrEP 92
Hill, Curtis V. 1947- St&PR 93
Hill, Daina H. Law&B 92
Hill, Dan J. 1940- St&PR 93
Hill, Daniel George 1956- WhoIns 93
Hill, Daniel Harvey 1821-1889 BioIn 17, HarEnMi
Hill, David 1952- See Hill, W.E. & Sons Baker 92
Hill, David Allan 1942- WhoAm 92
Hill, David B. 1843-1910 PolPar
Hill, David Campbell ScF&FL 92
Hill, David Francis 1955- St&PR 93
Hill, David Jerome 1948- St&PR 93
Hill, David L. Law&B 92
Hill, David Lawrence 1919- WhoE 93, WhoWor 93
Hill, David Octavius 1802-1870 BioIn 17
Hill, David Simmons 1955- WhoSSW 93
Hill, David Stewart 1947- WhoE 93
Hill, David Thomas 1947- WhoSSW 93
Hill, David Warren 1946- WhoEmL 93
Hill, Dean Allen 1934- WhoWor 93
Hill, Deborah Brooks 1942- WhoAmW 93
Hill, Debra Elene 1957- St&PR 93
Hill, Deirdre DcChlFi
Hill, Dennis Joseph 1954- WhoSSW 93
Hill, Dennis Patrick 1960- WhoEmL 93, WhoWor 93
Hill, Denson 1939- WhoWor 93
Hill, Diane Seldon 1943- WhoAm 92
Hill, Dolores Jean 1937- St&PR 93
Hill, Donald T. 1934- St&PR 93
Hill, Donna BioIn 17
Hill, Donna Marie 1957- WhoAmW 93, WhoEmL 93
Hill, Doris SweetSg C [port]
Hill, Dorothy J. 1922- WhoWrEP 92
Hill, Dorothy S. 1925- St&PR 93
Hill, Douglas 1935- ScF&FL 92
Hill, Douglas (Arthur) 1935- ChlFicS, WhoCanL 92
Hill, Douglas K. 1935- St&PR 93
Hill, Douglass Orville 1922- WhoSSW 93
Hill, Drake D. Law&B 92
Hill, Draper 1935- WhoAm 92
Hill, Dumond Peck 1923-1991 BioIn 17
Hill, E. Franklin Law&B 92
Hill, Earl McColl 1926- WhoAm 92
Hill, Edward Burlingame 1872-1960 Baker 92
Hill, Edward D. Law&B 92
Hill, Edward F. 1936- WhoSSW 93
Hill, Elizabeth Trezise 1936- WhoE 93
Hill, Emily Katharine 1921- WhoWrEP 92
Hill, Emita Brady 1936- WhoAmW 93
Hill, Emma Lee 1949- WhoSSW 93
Hill, Eric BioIn 17
Hill, Eric 1927- MajAI [port]
Hill, Ernest 1914- ScF&FL 92
Hill, Errol Gaston 1921- WhoAm 92
Hill, Eugene Law&B 92
Hill, Eugene Bruce 1935- WhoSSW 93
Hill, Eula Vertner 1928- WhoAmW 93
Hill, Evelyn K. d1990 BioIn 17
Hill, F. Trent, Jr. 1952- St&PR 93
Hill, Fitzmaurice 1898- DcChlFi
Hill, Frances P. AmWomPl
Hill, Francis Frederick 1908- WhoAm 92
Hill, Frank B. Law&B 92

Hill, Frank Whitney, Jr. 1914- WhoAm 92
Hill, Fred Gene 1933- WhoSSW 93
Hill, Fred James 1945- WhoSSW 93
Hill, Frederick Wells Law&B 92
Hill, G. Eugene 1933- WhoE 93
Hill, G.F. Law&B 92
Hill, Gary C. 1948- St&PR 93
Hill, Geoffrey BioIn 17
Hill, George C. 1938- WhoIns 93
Hill, George H. 1936- St&PR 93
Hill, George Jackson, III 1932- WhoAm 92
Hill, George James 1932- WhoAm 92
Hill, George Leonard WhoScE 91-1
Hill, George Morey 1908- St&PR 93
Hill, George Richard 1921- WhoAm 92
Hill, George Ronald 1946- WhoWrEP 92
Hill, George Roy WhoAm 92
Hill, George Roy 1922- MiSFD 9
Hill, George S. 1926- St&PR 93
Hill, George William 1838-1914 BioIn 17
Hill, Gerald Wayne 1947- WhoSSW 93
Hill, Gladwin 1914-1992 NewYTBS 92 [port]
Hill, Glenda Cassell 1953- WhoAmW 93
Hill, Gordon Charles, III 1948- WhoE 93, WhoEmL 93
Hill, Grace Lucile Garrison 1930- WhoAm 92, WhoAmW 93, WhoSSW 93
Hill, Graham Lancelot 1939- WhoWor 93
Hill, Graham Roderick 1946- WhoAm 92
Hill, Gregory S. Law&B 92
Hill, H. Jay 1939- St&PR 93
Hill, H.W. WhoScE 91-1
Hill, Harlon Junious 1942- BiDAMSp 1989
Hill, Harold Eugene 1918- WhoAm 92
Hill, Harold Nelson, Jr. 1930- WhoAm 92
Hill, Harry E. 1948- St&PR 93
Hill, Harry Edward, III 1948- WhoE 93
Hill, Heather WhoCanL 92
Hill, Helen M. 1915- ScF&FL 92
Hill, Henry BioIn 17
Hill, Henry Allen 1933- WhoAm 92
Hill, Henry Forrest 1917- WhoSSW 93
Hill, Henry Parker 1918- WhoAm 92
Hill, Howard W. 1926- St&PR 93
Hill, Hugh Allen Oliver 1937- WhoWor 93
Hill, Hugh Kenneth 1937- WhoAm 92, WhoWor 93
Hill, Hulene Dian 1948- WhoSSW 93
Hill, Hyacinthe 1920- WhoWrEP 92
Hill, I. Kathryn 1950- WhoAmW 93, WhoEmL 93
Hill, Ian Roland 1942- WhoWor 93
Hill, Irving 1915- WhoAm 92
Hill, Isaac William 1908- WhoAm 92, WhoWrEP 92
Hill, Ivan d1990 BioIn 17
Hill, J. WhoScE 91-1
Hill, J. Stanley 1914- St&PR 93
Hill, Jack 1933- MiSFD 9
Hill, James 1919- MiSFD 9
Hill, James Bayer 1911- St&PR 93
Hill, James Benjamin, Jr. 1948- WhoWor 93
Hill, James Berry BioIn 17
Hill, James C. d1991 BioIn 17
Hill, James Clinkscales 1924- WhoAm 92, WhoSSW 93
Hill, James Jerome 1838-1916 BioIn 17
Hill, James Lee 1941- WhoSSW 93
Hill, James R. BioIn 17
Hill, James Scott 1924- WhoAm 92
Hill, James Stanley 1914- WhoAm 92
Hill, James Tomilson 1948- WhoAm 92, WhoEmL 93
Hill, James Warren 1941- St&PR 93
Hill, Jane Bowers 1950- WhoSSW 93
Hill, Jane Edna BioIn 17
Hill, Jeff BioIn 17
Hill, Jefferson Borden 1941- WhoE 93
Hill, Jeri Linda 1949- WhoWor 93
Hill, Jesse SoulM
Hill, Jessie, Jr. AfrAmBi
Hill, Jimmie Dale 1933- WhoAm 92
Hill, Joan Ann 1934- WhoSSW 93
Hill, Joe 1879-1915 BioIn 17
Hill, John ScF&FL 92
Hill, John 1937- WhoWor 93
Hill, John Alexander 1907- WhoAm 92
Hill, John Campbell 1938- WhoAm 92
Hill, John David 1920- St&PR 93
Hill, John deKoven 1920- WhoAm 92
Hill, John Edward, Jr. 1927- WhoWor 93
Hill, John F. 1855-1912 PolPar
Hill, John Howard 1940- WhoAm 92
Hill, John Luke, Jr. 1923- WhoAm 92
Hill, John McGregor 1921- WhoWor 93
Hill, John Richard 1943- WhoUN 92
Hill, John Rutledge, Jr. 1922- WhoAm 92
Hill, John S. 1957- WhoIns 93
Hill, Johnson D., Jr. 1916- St&PR 93
Hill, Jonel C. 1925- St&PR 93
Hill, Joseph Gray 1950- St&PR 93
Hill, Joseph Havord Law&B 92
Hill, Joseph Martin 1946- WhoEmL 93
Hill, Josephine 1902- SweetSg B [port]
Hill, Josephine Carmela 1932- WhoSSW 93
Hill, Josiah F. ScF&FL 92
Hill, Joyce P. Law&B 92
Hill, Judith 1945- WhoWrEP 92
Hill, Judith Deegan 1940- WhoAmW 93
Hill, Judith Swigost 1942- WhoAmW 93
Hill, Kathleen St&PR 93
Hill, Kathy Louise 1951- WhoEmL 93
Hill, Kay (Kathleen Louise) 1917- DcChlFi
Hill, Keith Maurice 1954- WhoEmL 93
Hill, Kenneth Clyde 1953- WhoSSW 93
Hill, Kenneth Douglas 1934- WhoAm 92
Hill, Kirkpatrick 1938- SmATA 72 [port]
Hill, La Joyce Carmichael 1952- WhoAmW 93
Hill, Larkin Payne 1954- WhoAmW 93, WhoSSW 93
Hill, Larry Michael 1948- St&PR 93
Hill, Laura Carnes 1936- WhoAmW 93
Hill, Laura Jo 1959- WhoEmL 93
Hill, Lawrence Michael Law&B 92
Hill, Lawrence W. d1991 BioIn 17
Hill, Lee H., Jr. 1924- St&PR 93
Hill, Lee H., III St&PR 93
Hill, Lee Halsey, Jr. 1924- WhoSSW 93
Hill, Lee Wayne 1944- WhoAm 92
Hill, Lenora Mae 1937- WhoAm 92
Hill, Lenwood Rembert, Jr. 1941- WhoSSW 93
Hill, Leslie Rowland WhoScE 91-1
Hill, Levi Walter 1928- St&PR 93
Hill, Lorie Elizabeth 1946- WhoAmW 93
Hill, Lorraine Hulpieu Loy 1915- WhoAmW 93
Hill, Louis Allen, Jr. 1927- WhoAm 92
Hill, Lowell Dean 1930- WhoAm 92
Hill, Lowell James 1945- WhoE 93
Hill, Lura Pearl 1919- WhoAmW 93
Hill, Luther Lyons, Jr. 1922- St&PR 93, WhoAm 92
Hill, Lynix S. 1940- St&PR 93
Hill, Lynn BioIn 17
Hill, Marcus Edward 1947- WhoIns 93
Hill, Margaret F. AmWomPl, St&PR 93
Hill, Marilyn J. 1929- WhoAmW 93
Hill, Marjorie Jean 1956- WhoE 93
Hill, Mark C. 1951- WhoEmL 93
Hill, Mary Christina 1949- WhoEmL 93
Hill, Mary Lou 1936- WhoAmW 93
Hill, Max Lloyd, Jr. 1927- WhoSSW 93
Hill, Melvin James 1919- WhoAm 92
Hill, Merton 1895-1989 ScF&FL 92
Hill, Millicent Elizabeth WhoWrEP 92
Hill, Milton Monroe 1919- St&PR 93
Hill, Monte Scott 1950- St&PR 93
Hill, Murray BioIn 17
Hill, Murray William 1945- WhoWor 93
Hill, Nancy 1949- WhoAmW 93
Hill, Nancy Davis 1933- WhoSSW 93
Hill, Norma Louise WhoWor 93
Hill, Norman Ellison 1939- St&PR 93
Hill, Norman Julius 1925- WhoWrEP 92
Hill, Oliver W. 1907- EncAACR
Hill, Orion Alvah, Jr. 1920- WhoAm 92
Hill, Othmar Emanuel 1948- WhoWor 93
Hill, Owen Leslie, Jr. 1938- St&PR 93
Hill, Pamela 1920- ConAu 37NR
Hill, Pamela 1938- BioIn 17
Hill, Patricia 1932- WhoWrEP 92
Hill, Patricia Arnold 1936- WhoAmW 93
Hill, Patricia Evridge 1958- WhoAmW 93
Hill, Patricia Francine 1955- WhoAmW 93, WhoEmL 93
Hill, Patricia Lispenard 1937- WhoAmW 93
Hill, Paul C. Law&B 92
Hill, Paul Drennen 1941- St&PR 93, WhoAm 92
Hill, Peter Charles John WhoScE 91-1
Hill, Peter Grey Law&B 92
Hill, Peter Waverly 1953- WhoE 93, WhoEmL 93
Hill, Phil BioIn 17
Hill, Philip Graham 1932- WhoAm 92
Hill, Prescott F. 1934- St&PR 93, WhoIns 93
Hill, Ralph 1900-1950 Baker 92
Hill, Ralph G. Law&B 92
Hill, Ralph Kelly 1952- WhoEmL 93, WhoSSW 93
Hill, Ralph Nading 1917-1987 BioIn 17
Hill, Ralph Stroud, III 1948- WhoSSW 93
Hill, Randall William 1933- St&PR 93
Hill, Ray Thomas, Jr. 1926- WhoWor 93
Hill, Raymond A. d1991 BioIn 17
Hill, Raymond J. 1935- St&PR 93
Hill, Raymond Joseph 1935- WhoAm 92
Hill, Reba Dickerson 1918- WhoE 93
Hill, Rebecca Irene 1963- WhoAmW 93
Hill, Regina Eileen 1962- WhoAmW 93, WhoEmL 93
Hill, Reginald 1936- ScF&FL 92
Hill, Richard BioIn 17
Hill, Richard D. 1919- St&PR 93
Hill, Richard Devereux 1919- WhoAm 92
Hill, Richard Earl 1929- WhoAm 92
Hill, Richard Lee 1931- WhoWor 93
Hill, Richard Lee 1951- WhoEmL 93
Hill, Richard S(ynyer) 1901-1961 Baker 92
Hill, Richard T. 1945- St&PR 93
Hill, Robb B. 1957- WhoIns 93
Hill, Robert WhoScE 91-1
Hill, Robert 1946- WhoAsAP 91
Hill, Robert A. Law&B 92
Hill, Robert Arthur 1961- WhoAm 92
Hill, Robert B. 1933- St&PR 93
Hill, Robert Charles 1952- WhoE 93
Hill, Robert F. 1936- St&PR 93
Hill, Robert Folwell, Jr. 1946- WhoEmL 93, WhoSSW 93
Hill, Robert Gilbert 1934- WhoSSW 93
Hill, Robert L. AfrAmBi [port]
Hill, Robert L. 1930- St&PR 93
Hill, Robert Lee 1928- WhoAm 92
Hill, Robert Martin 1949- WhoEmL 93
Hill, Robert Mount WhoScE 91-1
Hill, Robert Raymond, II 1922- WhoAm 92
Hill, Robert Thomas 1940- WhoWor 93
Hill, Robert W. 1927- St&PR 93
Hill, Robyn Lesley 1942- WhoAm 92, WhoAmW 93
Hill, Roderick Jeffrey 1949- WhoWor 93
Hill, Roger ScF&FL 92, WhoScE 91-1
Hill, Roger Wendell 1939- WhoAm 92
Hill, Rolla B. 1929- WhoAm 92
Hill, Ron BioIn 17
Hill, Ronald Charles 1948- WhoEmL 93, WhoSSW 93
Hill, Ronald Paul 1954- WhoE 93
Hill, Rowland 1772-1842 HarEnMi
Hill, Rubye Robinson 1926- WhoAmW 93
Hill, Russell ScF&FL 92
Hill, Ruth AmWomPl
Hill, Ruth Foell 1931- WhoAmW 93
Hill, Ruth Mary d1991 BioIn 17
Hill, Ruthie C. Randle 1951- WhoAmW 93
Hill, S.J. Law&B 92
Hill, Samuel Richardson, Jr. 1923- WhoAm 92, WhoSSW 93
Hill, Samuel Smythe, Jr. 1927- WhoSSW 93
Hill, Sharon Lee 1947- WhoAmW 93
Hill, Sheila Karen 1948- WhoWrEP 92
Hill, Shirley A. BioIn 17
Hill, Shirley Ann 1927- WhoAm 92
Hill, Stacie Leianne 1964- WhoAmW 93
Hill, Stella Richmond AmWomPl
Hill, Stephen David 1962- WhoWor 93
Hill, Stephen M. 1930- St&PR 93, WhoAm 92
Hill, Steve BioIn 17
Hill, Steven Devereux 1949- St&PR 93
Hill, Steven Richard 1947- WhoAm 92
Hill, Sue Annette 1964- WhoEmL 93
Hill, Susan WhoScE 91-1
Hill, Susan 1942- BioIn 17, ScF&FL 92
Hill, Susan Sloan 1952- WhoAmW 93, WhoSSW 93
Hill, Suzanne Marie 1958- WhoAmW 93
Hill, Sylvia Sandra 1949- WhoAmW 93
Hill, Terrel Morgan 1943- WhoUN 92
Hill, Terrell Leslie 1917- WhoAm 92
Hill, Thomas 1829-1908 BioIn 17
Hill, Thomas Allen 1958- WhoEmL 93, WhoWor 93
Hill, Thomas Bowen, III 1929- WhoAm 92, WhoSSW 93
Hill, Thomas E(nglish), Jr. 1937- ConAu 137
Hill, Thomas Glenn, III 1942- WhoAm 92
Hill, Thomas Harry 1925- WhoSSW 93
Hill, Thomas S. 1936- St&PR 93
Hill, Thomas Stewart 1936- WhoAm 92
Hill, Thomas W. 1956- St&PR 93
Hill, Thomas William, Jr. 1924- WhoE 93, WhoWor 93
Hill, Timotej 1920- WhoScE 91-4
Hill, Tom Law&B 92
Hill, Tom d1878 BioIn 17
Hill, Ureli Corelli c. 1802-1875 Baker 92
Hill, Valerie Charlotte 1932- WhoE 93, WhoWor 93
Hill, Vernon C., Jr. 1958- WhoSSW 93
Hill, Victor Ernst, IV 1939- WhoAm 92
Hill, Virgil B. Law&B 92
Hill, Virginia Watson 1959- WhoAmW 93
Hill, W.E. & Sons Baker 92
Hill, Walter 1942- MiSFD 9, WhoAm 92
Hill, Weldon ConAu 136
Hill, Weldon Kim 1948- WhoEmL 93
Hill, Wesley S. 1930- WhoAm 92
Hill, Wilhelm 1838-1902 Baker 92
Hill, William ScF&FL 92
Hill, William David 1928- WhoE 93
Hill, William Ebsworth 1817-1895 See Hill, W.E. & Sons Baker 92
Hill, William George WhoScE 91-1
Hill, William H. 1925- St&PR 93
Hill, William Henry 1857-1927 See Hill, W.E. & Sons Baker 92
Hill, William M. 1933- St&PR 93
Hill, William Plummer 1908- WhoE 93, WhoWor 93
Hill, William Thomas 1925- WhoAm 92
Hill, William Victor, II 1936- WhoSSW 93
Hill, Williard I., Jr. Law&B 92
Hill, Wilmer Bailey 1928- WhoAm 92
Hill, Winslow Smith 1925- WhoE 93
Hill, Z.Z. 1935-1984 SoulM
Hillaire-Marcel, Claude WhoScE 91-2
Hillan, Dennis Carl 1947- St&PR 93
Hillard, Lloyd C., Jr. 1946- St&PR 93
Hillard, Robert Ellsworth 1917- WhoAm 92
Hillary, Edmund BioIn 17
Hillary, Edmund 1919- Expl 93 [port]
Hillary, Edmund Percival 1919- WhoWor 93
Hillary, Richard 1919-1943 BioIn 17
Hillas, Roger S. 1927- WhoAm 92
Hillberg, Loren E. Law&B 92
Hillberry, Benny Max 1937- WhoAm 92
Hill-Beuf, Ann Harper 1938- WhoWrEP 92
Hillcourt, William d1992 NewYTBS 92 [port]
Hillcourt, William 1900-1992 ConAu 139
Hilldrup, Mary Eileen 1946- WhoAmW 93
Hille, Bertil 1940- WhoAm 92
Hille, Robert John 1953- WhoEmL 93
Hille, Stanley James 1937- WhoAm 92
Hillebrand, Lawrence John 1939- WhoE 93
Hillebrecht, Hildegard 1927- Baker 92
Hillegas, Mark R. 1926- ScF&FL 92
Hillegass, Christine Ann 1952- WhoAm 92, WhoAmW 93
Hillegass, Cliff BioIn 17
Hillegass, Clifton K. 1918- ScF&FL 92
Hillegass, Clifton Keith 1918- WhoAm 92
Hillegeist, Douglas R. Law&B 92
Hillegeist, Willard McConkey 1940- St&PR 93
Hillel 1st cent.BC-01st cent.AD BioIn 17
Hillel, Daniel 1930- WhoAm 92
Hillemacher Baker 92
Hillemacher, August 1942- WhoScE 91-3
Hillemacher, Lucien Joseph Edouard 1860-1909 Baker 92
Hillemacher, Paul Joseph Guillaume 1852-1933 Baker 92
Hilleman, Jeryl Lynn 1957- WhoAmW 93
Hilleman, Maurice Ralph 1919- WhoAm 92
Hillenbrand, David M. 1947- St&PR 93
Hillenbrand, Fredric C. 1937- St&PR 93
Hillenbrand, Martin Joseph 1915- WhoAm 92
Hillenbrand, Susan Diane 1963- WhoAmW 93
Hillenbrand, W. August 1940- St&PR 93, WhoAm 92
Hillenbrand, Will BioIn 17
Hillenmeyer, Ernest Bernard, Jr. 1922- St&PR 93
Hillenmeyer, Henry Reiling 1943- St&PR 93
Hiller, Arthur 1923- MiSFD 9, WhoAm 92
Hiller, B.B. ScF&FL 92
Hiller, Dale Murray 1924- WhoE 93
Hiller, David D. 1953- WhoAm 92
Hiller, David Dean Law&B 92
Hiller, Ferdinand 1811-1885 Baker 92
Hiller, Friedrich Adam c. 1767-1812 Baker 92
Hiller, Johann Adam 1728-1804 Baker 92, OxDcOp
Hiller, Lee 1941- St&PR 93
Hiller, Lejaren 1924- Baker 92
Hiller, Melvin Jackson 1941- St&PR 93
Hiller, Neil W. ScF&FL 92
Hiller, Stanley, Jr. 1924- St&PR 93
Hiller, Susan 1940- BioIn 17
Hiller, Wendy WhoAm 92
Hiller, William Arlington 1928- St&PR 93, WhoAm 92
Hillerbrand, Carl Michael 1961- WhoSSW 93
Hillerbrand, Hans Joachim 1931- WhoAm 92
Hiller-Laramie, Dagmar C. 1962- WhoEmL 93
Hillerman, Tony BioIn 17
Hillerman, Tony 1925- CurBio 92 [port], WhoAm 92, WhoWrEP 92
Hillers, Delbert Roy 1932- WhoAm 92
Hillers, Ellen Marsh 1961- WhoAmW 93
Hillert, Gloria Bonnin 1930- WhoAmW 93
Hillert, Margaret 1920- ConAu 40NR, WhoWrEP 92
Hillert, Mats H. 1924- WhoScE 91-4
Hillerton, John Eric WhoScE 91-1
Hillerud, Kai-Inge 1937- WhoWor 93
Hillery, Mary Jane Larato 1931- WhoAm 92, WhoAmW 93, WhoE 93, WhoWor 93

Hillery, Patrick John 1923- *WhoWor 93*
Hillery, Thomas J. d1991 *BioIn 17*
Hilles, Charles D. 1867-1949 *PolPar*
Hilles, Charles Dewey 1867-1949 *BioIn 17*
Hillestad, Donna Dawn 1938- *WhoAmW 93*
Hillesum, Etty 1914-1943 *BioIn 17, ConAu 137*
Hilley, Joseph Henry 1956- *WhoSSW 93*
Hillgren, Sonja Dorothy 1948- *WhoAm 92, WhoAmW 93*
Hillhouse, James 1754-1832 *PolPar*
Hillhouse, Thomas R. *Law&B 92*
Hilliard, Asa G. 1933- *BioIn 17*
Hilliard, Curtis R. *Law&B 92*
Hilliard, D. Mark *Law&B 92*
Hilliard, David Craig 1937- *WhoWor 93*
Hilliard, Earl F. 1942- *AfrAmBi [port]*
Hilliard, Earl Frederick 1942- *WhoSSW 93*
Hilliard, Frederick 1935- *St&PR 93*
Hilliard, Garrison Lee 1960- *WhoWrEP 92*
Hilliard, Jack Briggs 1931- *WhoAm 92*
Hilliard, James M. 1921- *St&PR 93*
Hilliard, L.E. 1945- *St&PR 93*
Hilliard, Landon 1939- *St&PR 93, WhoAm 92*
Hilliard, Mark D. *Law&B 92*
Hilliard, R. Glenn 1943- *WhoIns 93*
Hilliard, Robert Glenn 1943- *St&PR 93, WhoAm 92*
Hilliard, Sam Bowers 1930- *WhoAm 92*
Hilliard, Sharen Anne 1942- *WhoAmW 93*
Hillie, Verna 1914- *SweetSg C [port]*
Hillier, Donald Edward 1947- *WhoIns 93*
Hillier, Ian Harvey *WhoScE 91-1*
Hillier, James 1915- *WhoAm 92, WhoE 93*
Hillier, James Robert 1937- *WhoAm 92*
Hillier, Jay D. 1949- *St&PR 93*
Hillier, Paul 1949- *Baker 92*
Hillier, Stanley Kenneth 1918- *WhoSSW 93*
Hillier, Stephen Gilbert *WhoScE 91-1*
Hilligoss, Candace *BioIn 17*
Hilliker, John Arthur Charles 1928- *St&PR 93*
Hillila, Bernhard Hugo Paul 1919- *WhoAm 92*
Hillin, Henderson, Jr. 1930- *WhoWrEP 92*
Hillin, Wayne K. 1942- *St&PR 93*
Hillin, Wayne Kirby *Law&B 92*
Hillings, E. Joseph 1937- *St&PR 93, WhoAm 92*
Hillion, Pierre Theodore Marie 1926- *WhoWor 93*
Hillips, Gordon 1929- *St&PR 93*
Hillis, Durrell *BioIn 17*
Hillis, Madalyn Louise 1951- *WhoE 93*
Hillis, Margaret 1921- *Baker 92, WhoAm 92, WhoAmW 93*
Hillis, Marjorie *AmWomPl*
Hillis, Mark 1942- *St&PR 93*
Hillis, Neva Ruth 1937- *WhoAmW 93*
Hillis, Rick 1956- *WhoCanL 92*
Hillis, Shelby Ross 1940- *WhoWor 93*
Hillis, William Daniel 1933- *WhoAm 92, WhoSSW 93*
Hillman, Aaron Waddell 1926- *WhoWrEP 92*
Hillman, Arthur B., III *Law&B 92*
Hillman, Arthur L., Jr. *Law&B 92*
Hillman, Arye Laib 1947- *WhoWor 93*
Hillman, Brenda Lynn 1951- *WhoWrEP 92*
Hillman, Carol Barbara 1940- *WhoAmW 93, WhoE 93*
Hillman, Carolyn Phillips 1944- *WhoSSW 93*
Hillman, Charles W. 1929- *St&PR 93*
Hillman, Chris 1942- See Byrds, The *ConMus 8*
Hillman, Cindy Kay 1956- *WhoAmW 93*
Hillman, David *St&PR 93*
Hillman, Douglas Woodruff 1922- *WhoAm 92*
Hillman, Gary 1938- *St&PR 93*
Hillman, Harold Hyran 1930- *WhoWor 93*
Hillman, Henry L. 1918- *St&PR 93, WhoAm 92*
Hillman, Howard Budrow 1934- *WhoWrEP 92*
Hillman, James Calvin 1944- *St&PR 93*
Hillman, Janice Louise 1951- *WhoE 93*
Hillman, Jennifer Anne 1957- *WhoAmW 93*
Hillman, Joel, III 1922- *St&PR 93*
Hillman, John Richard *WhoScE 91-1*
Hillman, Joyce 1936- *WhoAmW 93*
Hillman, Katharine Ann 1952- *WhoAmW 93*
Hillman, Lee S. 1955- *St&PR 93*
Hillman, Leon 1921- *WhoE 93*
Hillman, Lin 1948- *WhoAmW 93*
Hillman, Martin *WhoCanL 92*
Hillman, Melville Ernest Douglas 1926- *WhoAm 92*
Hillman, Richard B. 1944- *St&PR 93*
Hillman, Richard Ephraim 1940- *WhoAm 92*
Hillman, Rita 1912- *WhoAmW 93, WhoE 93*
Hillman, Robert Sandor 1939- *WhoAm 92*
Hillman, S.A. *ScF&FL 92*
Hillman, S.E.G. 1911- *St&PR 93*
Hillman, Sidney 1887-1946 *BioIn 17, PolPar*
Hillman, Stanley Eric Gordon 1911- *WhoAm 92*
Hillman, Tommy 1936- *WhoAm 92, WhoSSW 93*
Hillman, William Byron *MiSFD 9*
Hillman, William T. 1953- *St&PR 93*
Hillman-Jones, Gladys Cornelia 1938- *WhoAmW 93*
Hillman-Kinelski, Julie Renae 1962- *WhoAmW 93, WhoEmL 93*
Hillmer, Duane H. 1916- *St&PR 93*
Hill-Miller, Katherine C(ecelia) 1949- *ConAu 139*
Hillquit, Morris 1869-1933 *PolPar*
Hills, Argentina Schifano 1921- *ConAu 136*
Hills, Austin Edward 1934- *St&PR 93, WhoAm 92*
Hills, Carla A. 1934- *NewYTBS 92 [port], St&PR 93*
Hills, Carla Anderson 1934- *AfrAmBi, BioIn 17, WhoAm 92, WhoAmW 93, WhoE 93*
Hills, David Warren *Law&B 92*
Hills, Frederic Wheeler 1934- *WhoAm 92*
Hills, G.J. *St&PR 93*
Hills, Howard Loomis *Law&B 92*
Hills, John Merrill 1944- *WhoAm 92*
Hills, Lee 1906- *DcLB 127 [port], St&PR 93*
Hills, Linda Launey 1947- *WhoWor 93*
Hills, Patricia Annette 1949- *WhoAmW 93*
Hills, Patricia Gorton Schulze 1936- *WhoAm 92*
Hills, Patti Lynn 1953- *WhoAmW 93, WhoEmL 93*
Hills, Peter John *WhoScE 91-1*
Hills, Philip K. 1932-1991 *BioIn 17*
Hills, Regina J. 1953- *WhoAm 92*
Hills, Richard A., Jr. 1940- *St&PR 93*
Hills, Richard Edwin *WhoScE 91-1*
Hills, Roderick M. 1931- *WhoAm 92*
Hills, Ruth Elliott *AmWomPl*
Hills, Steven 1956- *St&PR 93*
Hills, Tina *ConAu 136*
Hillsdon-Hutton, Valerie 1943- *WhoWrEP 92*
Hillsman, Regina Onie 1955- *WhoAmW 93*
Hillsman, William Gerard 1953- *WhoEmL 93*
Hillson, Jan Leslie 1952- *WhoEmL 93*
Hillsten, Kenneth Leroy 1937- *WhoSSW 93*
Hillstrom, Paul John 1930- *St&PR 93*
Hill-Tout, Charles 1858-1944 *IntDcAn*
Hillway, Tyrus 1912- *WhoAm 92*
Hilly, John C. d1991 *BioIn 17*
Hillyard, Ira William 1924- *WhoAm 92*
Hillyer, Carter Sinclair 1948- *WhoWrEP 92*
Hillyer, Mary W. *AmWomPl*
Hillyer, William Hudson 1928- *St&PR 93*
Hilmes, Michele 1953- *ConAu 136*
Hilmi, Haluk Ahmed 1930- *WhoScE 91-3*
Hilne, Alastair David 1942- *WhoScE 91-1*
Hilpert, Edward Theodore, Jr. 1928- *WhoWor 93*
Hilpert, Heinz 1890-1967 *BioIn 17*
Hilpinen, Risto Juhani 1943- *WhoWor 93*
Hilsabeck, Frank H. 1944- *St&PR 93*
Hilsberg, Aleksander 1900-1961 *PolBiDi*
Hilsberg, Alexander 1897-1961 *Baker 92*
Hilseberg, Richard T. 1952- *St&PR 93*
Hilsen, John C. 1931- *St&PR 93*
Hilsenrath, Lee Betty 1934- *WhoE 93*
Hilsinger, Arthur R., Jr. 1927- *St&PR 93*
Hilson, Barry Oliver *WhoScE 91-1*
Hilson, George Richard Forsyth 1919- *WhoScE 91-1*
Hilson, John S. d1991 *BioIn 17*
Hilstad, Paul A. *Law&B 92*
Hilstad, Paul Arnold *Law&B 92*
Hilstad, Paul Arnold 1942- *St&PR 93*
Hilt, Diane Elaine 1944- *WhoSSW 93*
Hiltbrunner, Otto Ernst 1913- *WhoWor 93*
Hilton, Alice Mary 1929- *WhoAm 92*
Hilton, Andrew C. 1928- *St&PR 93*
Hilton, Andrew Carson 1928- *WhoAm 92*
Hilton, Anthony John William 1941- *WhoWor 93*
Hilton, Barron 1927- *WhoAm 92*
Hilton, Christina Elizabeth 1966- *WhoAmW 93*
Hilton, Claude Meredith 1940- *WhoSSW 93*
Hilton, Clifford Thomas 1934- *WhoSSW 93*
Hilton, Donald Dean 1930- *St&PR 93*
Hilton, Eva Mae 1950- *WhoAmW 93*
Hilton, Gary Michael 1941- *St&PR 93*
Hilton, Glenn C., Jr. 1936- *St&PR 93*
Hilton, Hart Dale 1913- *WhoWor 93*
Hilton, James Gorton 1923- *WhoAm 92*
Hilton, James L. 1930- *WhoAm 92*
Hilton, James R. *Law&B 92*
Hilton, Jeff *BioIn 17*
Hilton, John David 1958- *WhoE 93, WhoEmL 93*
Hilton, John (the Elder) d1608 *Baker 92*
Hilton, John (the Younger) 1599-1657 *Baker 92*
Hilton, Kenneth M. 1926- *WhoIns 93*
Hilton, Leo 1918- *WhoE 93*
Hilton, Linda Ann 1948- *WhoWrEP 92*
Hilton, Margaret Lynette 1946- *ConAu 136*
Hilton, Michael E. *Law&B 92*
Hilton, Michael R. 1951- *St&PR 93*
Hilton, Nette *ConAu 136*
Hilton, Nette 1946- *BioIn 17*
Hilton, Ordway 1913- *WhoAm 92*
Hilton, Peter John 1923- *WhoAm 92*
Hilton, R. Donn *Law&B 92*
Hilton, Robert E. *Law&B 92*
Hilton, Robert L. *WhoIns 93*
Hilton, Robert Parker, Sr. 1927- *WhoAm 92, WhoWor 93*
Hilton, Robin Harvey 1934- *WhoWor 93*
Hilton, Ronald G. 1948- *St&PR 93*
Hilton, Ronald James 1932- *WhoWrEP 92*
Hilton, Theodore Craig 1949- *WhoSSW 93*
Hilton, Thomas Scott 1952- *WhoAm 92*
Hilton, W. Eugene 1945- *WhoE 93*
Hilton, William Barron 1927- *St&PR 93*
Hilton, William D. 1929- *St&PR 93*
Hilton-Regan, Judith Ann 1938- *WhoWrEP 92*
Hiltunen, Risto Aulis 1948- *WhoWor 93*
Hiltunen, Vaino Juhani 1944- *WhoWor 93*
Hiltz, Arnold Aubrey 1924- *WhoE 93*
Hiltz, Dawn Papp 1959- *WhoE 93, WhoEmL 93, WhoWor 93*
Hiltz, Robert Murray 1946- *WhoEmL 93*
Hiltz, William Otis 1951- *St&PR 93, WhoAm 92*
Hilvert, W.T. 1936- *St&PR 93*
Hilz, Helmuth 1924- *WhoScE 91-3*
Hilzendeger, Connie Colleen 1950- *WhoAmW 93*
Himathongkam, Thep 1942- *WhoWor 93*
Himel, Edmond E., Jr. 1921- *St&PR 93*
Himel, Elizabeth Grace 1960- *WhoEmL 93, WhoSSW 93*
Himel, Shelley Jeanne *Law&B 92*
Himeles, Martin Stanley, Sr. 1923- *St&PR 93*
Himelfarb, Richard Jay 1942- *St&PR 93, WhoAm 92, WhoE 93*
Himelick, Alan E. 1929-1991 *BioIn 17*
Himelstein, Monroe 1924- *WhoE 93*
Himelstein, Morgan Yale 1926- *WhoE 93*
Himelstein, Peggy Donn 1932- *WhoAm 92, WhoSSW 93*
Himelstein, Philip Nathan 1923- *WhoSSW 93*
Himelstein, Susan 1951- *WhoAmW 93*
Himeno, Masako 1939- *WhoWor 93*
Himerios d912? *OxDcByz*
Himerios c. 30-?-c. 380 *OxDcByz*
Himes, Chester 1909-1984 *BioIn 17*
Himes, Chester Bomar 1909-1984 *EncAACR*
Himes, Geoffrey 1952- *WhoWrEP 92*
Himes, George Elliott 1922- *WhoWor 93*
Himes, Laurence Austin 1940- *WhoAm 92*
Himes, Norman S. 1943- *St&PR 93*
Himilco dc. 389BC *HarEnMi*
Himler, James B. 1944- *St&PR 93*
Himler, Jeffrey Eugene 1959- *WhoEmL 93*
Himler, Ronald *ChlBIID [port]*
Himmel, Friedrich Heinrich 1765-1814 *Baker 92, OxDcOp*
Himmel, Harold S. 1922- *St&PR 93*
Himmel, Larry William 1953- *St&PR 93*
Himmel, Martin d1991 *BioIn 17*
Himmel, Mitchell A. 1942- *St&PR 93*
Himmel, Patricia A. 1947- *St&PR 93*
Himmel, Richard C. 1920- *WhoAm 92*
Himmelbauer, Linda Dianne 1965- *WhoAmW 93*
Himmelberg, Barbara Taylor 1951- *WhoAmW 93*
Himmelberg, Charles John, III 1931- *WhoAm 92*
Himmelberg, Robert Franklin 1934- *WhoAm 92*
Himmelblau, David Mautner 1923- *WhoAm 92, WhoSSW 93*
Himmelfarb, Gertrude *BioIn 17*
Himmelfarb, Gertrude 1922- *WhoWrEP 92*
Himmelfarb, Milton 1918- *WhoAm 92*
Himmelhaver, Kevin J. 1956- *St&PR 93*
Himmelman, Gerald Leon 1934- *St&PR 93*
Himmelreich, Bruce Edwin *Law&B 92*
Himmelreich, David Baker 1954- *WhoEmL 93*
Himmelreich, Faith 1921- *St&PR 93*
Himmelright, Robert John, Jr. 1926- *WhoAm 92*
Himmelspach, Mark L. *Law&B 92*
Himmelstein, Carole Shapiro *WhoAmW 93*
Himmer, Jill M. *Law&B 92*
Himmer, Richard Edward 1945- *St&PR 93*
Himmler, Heinrich 1900-1945 *BioIn 17, DcTwHis*
Himms-Hagen, Jean Margaret 1933- *WhoAm 92, WhoAmW 93*
Himoto, Teruo 1923- *St&PR 93*
Himrod, Brenda *ScF&FL 92*
Himsworth, Harold Percival 1905- *WhoWor 93*
Himsworth, Richard Lawrence *WhoScE 91-1*
Himsworth, Winston E. 1940- *St&PR 93*
Hincal, A. Atilla 1940- *WhoScE 91-4*
Hinch, William Harry 1919- *WhoWor 93*
Hinchcliff, John Clarence 1939- *WhoWor 93*
Hinchcliff, Richard Henry, Jr. 1948- *WhoIns 93*
Hinchcliffe, Philip *ScF&FL 92*
Hinchey, Keith 1933- *St&PR 93*
Hinchey, Patricia Ann 1952- *WhoAmW 93*
Hinchliff, James Thomas 1939- *WhoAm 92*
Hinchliffe, E. *WhoScE 91-1*
Hinchliffe, John Richard *WhoScE 91-1*
Hinchliffe, Stephen F., Jr. 1933- *St&PR 93*
Hinchman, John Sanger 1931- *St&PR 93*
Hinck, Lawrence Wilson 1940- *WhoSSW 93*
Hinck, Walter Johann 1922- *WhoWor 93*
Hinckle, Warren James, III 1938- *WhoAm 92*
Hinckley, Benjamin Barrett, Jr. 1913- *St&PR 93*
Hinckley, Betty Burnham d1990 *BioIn 17*
Hinckley, Christa Meyer *Law&B 92*
Hinckley, Gordon B. 1910- *WhoAm 92*
Hinckley, Gregory K. 1946- *St&PR 93*
Hinckley, Gregory Keith 1946- *WhoAm 92*
Hinckley, Kenneth R. 1946- *St&PR 93*
Hinckley, Lynn Schellig 1944- *WhoE 93*
Hinckley, Richard L. *Law&B 92*
Hinckley, Robert Craig 1947- *St&PR 93, WhoAm 92*
Hinckley, Ted C(harles) 1925- *ConAu 40NR*
Hincks, John Winslow 1931- *WhoAm 92*
Hincks, Marcia L. *Law&B 92*
Hincmar *OxDcByz*
Hind, Harry William 1915- *WhoAm 92*
Hind, Robert James 1931- *WhoWor 93*
Hinde, Brian John 1939- *WhoScE 91-1*
Hinde, John Gordon 1939- *WhoWor 93*
Hinde, Robert Aubrey *WhoScE 91-1*
Hindemith, Paul 1895-1963 *Baker 92, IntDcOp, OxDcOp*
Hinden, Milton 1922- *St&PR 93*
Hinden, Stanley Jay 1927- *WhoAm 92*
Hindenburg, Paul Ludwig Hans von Beneckendorff und von 1847-1934 *HarEnMi*
Hindenburg, Paul von 1847-1934 *BioIn 17, DcTwHis*
Hinder, David 1950- *St&PR 93*
Hinderaker, Ivan 1916- *WhoAm 92*
Hinderas, Natalie 1927-1987 *Baker 92*
Hinderberger, Philip R. *Law&B 92*
Hinderberger, Stephen J. 1954- *St&PR 93*
Hinderberger, Stephen John 1954- *WhoAm 92*
Hinderer, Amy Rehm *Law&B 92*
Hinderhofer, Kathryn M. 1951- *St&PR 93*
Hinderliter, Marie A. 1952- *St&PR 93*
Hindermann, Mark John 1935- *St&PR 93*
Hindermann, Richard L. *WhoIns 93*
Hindermann, Richard Lane 1923- *St&PR 93*
Hinders, Rodney J. *Law&B 92*
Hindersinn, Raymond Richard 1918- *WhoE 93*
Hindes, Van G. *Law&B 92*
Hindle, David D. 1939- *St&PR 93*
Hindle, Lee J. 1965- *ScF&FL 92*
Hindle, Paula Alice 1952- *WhoAmW 93, WhoEmL 93*
Hindle, Walter H. d1992 *NewYTBS 92*

Hindle, Winston Russell, Jr. 1930- *St&PR 93, WhoAm 92*
Hindley, Edward Dal 1938- *St&PR 93*
Hindley, James Roger 1939- *WhoWor 93*
Hindman, Dean R. *Law&B 92*
Hindman, Don J. 1926- *WhoAm 92*
Hindman, Edward Evans 1942- *WhoE 93*
Hindman, George W. d1878 *BioIn 17*
Hindman, Harold 1917- *St&PR 93*
Hindman, Joanne O'Rourke 1954- *St&PR 93*
Hindman, John William, III 1951- *WhoEmL 93*
Hindman, Leslie *BioIn 17*
Hindman, Leslie Susan 1954- *WhoAmW 93*
Hindman, Margaret Horton 1947- *WhoAmW 93, WhoE 93*
Hindman, Randall Kevin 1952- *WhoEmL 93, WhoSSW 93*
Hindman, Robert A. 1939- *St&PR 93*
Hindman, Roger *ScF&FL 92*
Hindman, Thomas Carmichael 1828-1868 *BioIn 17, HarEnMi*
Hindmarch, Gladys 1940- *WhoCanL 92*
Hindmarch, Ian *WhoScE 91-1*
Hindmarch, Thomas M. *Law&B 92*
Hindo, Walid Afram 1940- *WhoAm 92, WhoWor 93*
Hinds, Alfred 1917-1991 *AnObit 1991*
Hinds, Alfred George d1991 *BioIn 17*
Hinds, Artis Ann 1939- *WhoSSW 93*
Hinds, Barbara Marie 1949- *WhoAmW 93*
Hinds, Caroline Wells 1953- *WhoEmL 93*
Hinds, Cathy *BioIn 17*
Hinds, Edward Allen 1949- *WhoE 93*
Hinds, Eldon L. *Law&B 92*
Hinds, Elizabeth *WhoAmW 93*
Hinds, Glester Samuel 1951- *WhoE 93*
Hinds, Jackson C. 1921- *St&PR 93*
Hinds, Jacqueline Rene 1960- *WhoAmW 93*
Hinds, Jean Phillips 1931- *WhoSSW 93*
Hinds, Joe M., Jr. 1937- *St&PR 93*
Hinds, John G. 1941- *St&PR 93*
Hinds, Richard Clayton 1948- *St&PR 93*
Hinds, Richard Ely 1936- *WhoIns 93*
Hinds, Sallie Ann 1930- *WhoWrEP 92*
Hinds, Thomas Sheldon 1943- *WhoAm 92, WhoUN 92*
Hindus, Michael S. *Law&B 92*
Hindus, Milton 1916- *WhoAm 92, WhoWrEP 92*
Hine, Al 1915-1974 *ScF&FL 92*
Hine, Daryl *BioIn 17*
Hine, Daryl 1936- *WhoCanL 92*
Hine, John P. 1924- *St&PR 93*
Hine, Muriel *ScF&FL 92*
Hine, Robert Van Norden, Jr. 1921- *WhoAm 92*
Hine, William 1687-1730 *Baker 92*
Hineline, Philip Neil 1940- *WhoE 93*
Hineman, Nancy Lee 1951- *WhoAmW 93, WhoWor 93*
Hiner, David L. 1948- *St&PR 93*
Hiner, Doug *BioIn 17*
Hiner, Gladys Webber 1907- *WhoAmW 93*
Hiner, Leslie Davis 1957- *WhoAmW 93, WhoEmL 93*
Hiner, Myriel *BioIn 17*
Hinerfeld, Norman M. 1929- *St&PR 93*
Hinerfeld, Norman Martin 1929- *WhoAm 92*
Hinerfeld, Robert Elliot 1934- *WhoAm 92*
Hinerfeld, Ruth J. 1930- *WhoAm 92, WhoAmW 93*
Hines, Andrew Hampton, Jr. 1923- *WhoAm 92*
Hines, Angus I., Jr. 1923- *St&PR 93*
Hines, Angus Irving, Jr. 1923- *WhoAm 92*
Hines, Anna Grossnickle 1946- *ScF&FL 92, SmATA 16AS [port], WhoAm 92*
Hines, Anthony Loring 1941- *WhoAm 92*
Hines, Arline Van Ness *AmWomPl*
Hines, Bede 1918- *ScF&FL 92*
Hines, Bernard L., Jr. *BioIn 17*
Hines, Charles Alfonso 1935- *WhoAm 92*
Hines, Daisy Marie 1913- *WhoAmW 93*
Hines, Danny Ray 1947- *WhoAm 92, WhoSSW 93*
Hines, Dean Howard 1935- *WhoAm 92*
Hines, Donald Eugene 1947- *WhoSSW 93*
Hines, Donald M. 1931- *ConAu 136*
Hines, Donald Merrill 1931- *WhoWrEP 92*
Hines, Donald William 1935- *St&PR 93*
Hines, Earl (Kenneth) 1905-1983 *Baker 92*
Hines, Edward Francis, Jr. 1945- *WhoAm 92*
Hines, Edward Joseph 1951- *WhoE 93*
Hines, George Lawrence 1946- *WhoE 93*
Hines, Glenn Morris 1950- *WhoEmL 93*
Hines, Gregory *BioIn 17*
Hines, Gregory 1946- *HolBB [port], News 92 [port]*
Hines, Gregory Oliver 1946- *AfrAmBi, WhoAm 92*
Hines, Hubert Orville 1942- *WhoE 93*
Hines, Hugh Francis 1932- *WhoAm 92*
Hines, James Rodger 1923- *WhoAm 92*
Hines, Jerome 1921- *BioIn 17, OxDcOp*
Hines, Jerome (Albert Link) 1921- *Baker 92, IntDcOp*
Hines, Jerry E. *Law&B 92*
Hines, John C. 1958- *St&PR 93*
Hines, John Leonard 1868-1968 *CmdGen 1991 [port], HarEnMi*
Hines, Johnny 1898-1970 *BioIn 17*
Hines, Kingsley *Law&B 92*
Hines, Lawrence Gregory 1915-1990 *BioIn 17*
Hines, Marion Ernest 1918- *WhoAm 92*
Hines, Marshall 1923- *St&PR 93, WhoAm 92*
Hines, Mary Elizabeth 1937- *WhoE 93*
Hines, Merrill Odom 1909- *WhoAm 92, WhoWor 93*
Hines, N. William 1936- *WhoAm 92*
Hines, Norris Lee 1929- *St&PR 93*
Hines, Patricia 1947- *WhoAmW 93*
Hines, Roger *BioIn 17*
Hines, Ruth Ann 1958- *WhoEmL 93*
Hines, Sharon L. *Law&B 92*
Hines, Sherman Edwards, Jr. 1940- *St&PR 93*
Hines, Thomas S. *BioIn 17*
Hines, Voncile 1945- *WhoAmW 93*
Hines, Walter J. 1947- *St&PR 93*
Hines, Wilbur Eugene 1948- *WhoAm 92*
Hines, William Eugene 1914- *WhoAm 92*
Hines, William Everett 1923- *WhoWor 93*
Hines, Yvonne Maria 1953- *WhoEmL 93*
Hines, Zoe Ann 1949- *St&PR 93*
Hinesley, William Fred, III 1959- *WhoEmL 93*
Hingeston, John c. 1610-1683 *Baker 92*
Hinghofer-Szalkay, Helmut G. 1948- *WhoWor 93*
Hingle, Pat 1924- *WhoAm 92*
Hingle, Patricia *BioIn 17*
Hingorani, Narain G. 1931- *BioIn 17, WhoAm 92*
Hingson, Ralph W. 1948- *WhoAm 92, WhoWor 93*
Hingson, Robert Andrew 1913- *WhoAm 92, WhoE 93, WhoWor 93*
Hingst, Lawrence W. 1940- *St&PR 93, WhoIns 93*
Hingst, Robert A. 1959- *St&PR 93*
Hingston, John c. 1610-1683 *Baker 92*
Hingtgen, Joseph Nicholas 1936- *WhoAm 92*
Hiniker, Kevin James *Law&B 92*
Hinitz, Blythe Simone Farb 1944- *WhoE 93*
Hinkal, Sanford Wayne 1944- *WhoE 93*
Hinkaty, Charles J. 1950- *St&PR 93*
Hinke, C.J. *ScF&FL 92*
Hinke, Karl H. d1990 *BioIn 17*
Hinkebein, Nancy Elaine 1962- *WhoAmW 93*
Hinkel, Frederick Bruce 1927- *WhoE 93*
Hinkel, Richard Robert 1935- *St&PR 93*
Hinkeldey, Nancy Sue 1955- *WhoAmW 93*
Hinkel-Lipsker, Denise Elizabeth 1957- *WhoAmW 93*
Hinkelman, Loren G. 1931- *WhoAm 92*
Hinkelman, Ruth A. 1949- *St&PR 93, WhoIns 93*
Hinkelman, Ruth Amidon 1949- *WhoAmW 93, WhoEmL 93*
Hinkemeyer, Michael T. 1940- *ScF&FL 92*
Hinken, Elisa Bachrow 1958- *WhoAmW 93*
Hinkes, Dave 1958- *WhoSSW 93*
Hinkle, Anita Louise 1943- *WhoAmW 93*
Hinkle, B. J. 1922- *WhoAm 92*
Hinkle, Barton Leslie 1925- *WhoAm 92*
Hinkle, Buckner 1914- *St&PR 93*
Hinkle, Catherine D. *Law&B 92*
Hinkle, Charles Nelson 1930- *WhoAm 92*
Hinkle, Clarke d1988 *BioIn 17*
Hinkle, Donald Earl 1952- *St&PR 93*
Hinkle, Douglas Paddock 1923- *BioIn 17*
Hinkle, Harriett Walker 1943- *WhoAmW 93*
Hinkle, Jane Katherine 1937- *St&PR 93*
Hinkle, Jim 1924-1990 *BioIn 17*
Hinkle, John M. 1948- *St&PR 93*
Hinkle, Kelli Cyrese 1962- *WhoAmW 93*
Hinkle, Kenneth Albert, II 1946- *St&PR 93*
Hinkle, Larry W. 1946- *St&PR 93*
Hinkle, Michael Glenn 1947- *St&PR 93*
Hinkle, Muriel Ruth Nelson 1929- *WhoAm 92, WhoAmW 93*
Hinkle, Norman Wayne 1943- *WhoSSW 93*
Hinkle, Patricia Mills 1943- *WhoE 93*
Hinkle, Richard Paul 1946- *WhoWrEP 92*
Hinkle, Robert Alan 1944- *St&PR 93*
Hinkle, Steven D. *Law&B 92*
Hinkle, Talmadge Gray 1924- *St&PR 93*
Hinkle, Tony d1992 *NewYTBS 92*
Hinkle, Tony 1898- *BioIn 17*
Hinkle, Walter C. 1936- *St&PR 93*
Hinkle, Walter C., Jr. 1936- *WhoAm 92*
Hinkley, Carol Edward 1929- *St&PR 93*
Hinkley, Eleanor Holmes *AmWomPl*
Hinkley, Everett David, Jr. 1936- *WhoAm 92*
Hinkley, Laura *AmWomPl*
Hinkley, Mark W. 1945- *WhoIns 93*
Hinkley, Robert Edwin, Jr. 1943- *WhoSSW 93*
Hinkovski, Tzeno Stojanov 1927- *WhoScE 91-4*
Hinkson, John c. 1610-1683 *Baker 92*
Hinkstone, John c. 1610-1683 *Baker 92*
Hinman, Brian L. 1961- *St&PR 93*
Hinman, Charles B. 1932- *WhoAm 92*
Hinman, David N. 1950- *St&PR 93*
Hinman, Eve Elizabeth 1959- *WhoAmW 93*
Hinman, Frank, Jr. 1915- *WhoAm 92*
Hinman, George Lyon 1905- *WhoAm 92*
Hinman, Mark Hancock 1953- *WhoSSW 93*
Hinman, Martha L. *AmWomPl*
Hinman, Myra Mahlow 1926- *WhoWor 93*
Hinman, Richard Leslie 1927- *WhoAm 92*
Hinman, Rosalind Virginia 1938- *WhoAmW 93*
Hinman, Suki 1948- *WhoAmW 93*
Hinman-Sweeney, Elaine Marie 1960- *WhoAmW 93, WhoWor 93*
Hinn, Benny *BioIn 17*
Hinnant, Charles Asbell 1950- *WhoAm 92*
Hinnant, Clarence Henry, III 1938- *WhoSSW 93*
Hinnant, Debra Ridout 1963- *WhoAmW 93*
Hinnant, Donald Wayne 1950- *WhoSSW 93*
Hinnant, Hilari Anne 1953- *WhoAmW 93*
Hinnau, Irving N. d1990 *BioIn 17*
Hinneburg, Patricia Ann 1937- *WhoAmW 93*
Hinnebusch, Raymond A. 1946- *ConAu 136*
Hinnenkamp, Lawrence F. 1952- *WhoE 93*
Hinnenthal, Anne M. *Law&B 92*
Hino, Ichiro 1934- *WhoAsAP 91*
Hino, Shojun 1948- *WhoWor 93*
Hino, Shun'ya 1933- *WhoWor 93*
Hino, Terumasa *BioIn 17*
Hinojosa, Conrado A., Jr. *Law&B 92*
Hinojosa, Maria 1961- *NotHsAW 93*
Hinojosa, Noe, Jr. 1961- *St&PR 93*
Hinojosa, Raul 1928- *WhoAm 92, WhoWor 93*
Hinojosa, Ricardo H. 1950- *HispAmA, WhoAm 92, WhoSSW 93*
Hinojosa, Rolando 1929- *BioIn 17, HispAmA [port], IntvWPC 92 [port]*
Hinojosa, Santiago Noel 1943- *WhoAm 92*
Hinojosa-Smith, Roland 1929- *WhoAm 92*
Hinojosa-Smith, Rolando 1929- *ConAu 16AS [port]*
Hinote, Bill *BioIn 17*
Hinote, Samuel I. 1942- *ConEn*
Hinrichs, Gina Burns 1954- *WhoEmL 93*
Hinrichs, Gustav 1850-1942 *Baker 92*
Hinrichs, Horst 1933- *St&PR 93*
Hinrichsen, Evelyn Elizabeth Merrell 1910- *WhoWor 93*
Hinrichsen, Klaus Volquardt 1927- *WhoScE 91-3*
Hinsahw, J. Raymond 1923- *WhoE 93*
Hinsch, Gertrude Wilma 1932- *WhoAmW 93*
Hinsch, Klaus D. 1941- *WhoScE 91-3*
Hinsdale, Maryann 1947- *WhoAmW 93*
Hinsdill, Ronald Dwight 1933- *WhoAm 92*
Hinshaw, Anita Louise 1950- *WhoAmW 93*
Hinshaw, Carroll Elton 1936- *WhoAm 92*
Hinshaw, David B., Jr. 1945- *WhoAm 92*
Hinshaw, David L. *Law&B 92*
Hinshaw, Donald Gray 1934- *WhoSSW 93*
Hinshaw, Edward Banks 1940- *WhoAm 92*
Hinshaw, Ernest T., Jr. 1928- *St&PR 93*
Hinshaw, Ernest Theodore, Jr. 1928- *WhoAm 92*
Hinshaw, Gaylord Carlyle 1933- *St&PR 93*
Hinshaw, Horton Corwin 1902- *WhoAm 92*
Hinshaw, Juanita H. 1945- *St&PR 93*
Hinshaw, Lerner Brady 1921- *WhoAm 92*
Hinshaw, Randall Weston 1915- *WhoAm 92*
Hinshaw, Seth B. *BioIn 17*
Hinshaw, Virgil Goodman, Jr. 1919- *WhoAm 92*
Hinshaw, W. Eric 1949- *St&PR 93*
Hinshaw, William Wade 1867-1947 *Baker 92*
Hinske, Gerd 1932- *St&PR 93*
Hinske, Gerd Friedrich Heinrich 1932- *WhoWor 93*
Hinsley, George Raymond, III 1960- *WhoSSW 93*
Hinsley, R.S. *WhoScE 91-1*
Hinsley-Loeber, Charles Ernest 1962- *WhoWrEP 92*
Hinson, David R. 1933- *St&PR 93*
Hinson, Derl Jason 1933- *WhoAm 92*
Hinson, Everette C. 1929- *St&PR 93*
Hinson, Howard Houston 1913- *WhoAm 92*
Hinson, Jack Allsbrook 1944- *WhoSSW 93*
Hinson, Jerry Lee 1951- *WhoWrEP 92*
Hinson, John Morgan 1945- *St&PR 93*
Hinson, Laura K. 1961- *St&PR 93*
Hinson, (Grady) Maurice 1930- *ConAu 38NR*
Hinson, Phillip Wade 1957- *WhoSSW 93*
Hinson, Robert Wayne 1949- *WhoEmL 93, WhoSSW 93*
Hinson, Robert William 1944- *WhoAm 92, WhoE 93*
Hinson, Robin Ledbetter 1931- *St&PR 93*
Hinson, Trish Marie 1957- *WhoAmW 93*
Hinson, Waymon Ray 1949- *WhoSSW 93*
Hinson, Wayne E. *Law&B 92*
Hinson, William H. 1915- *St&PR 93*
Hintenlang, David Eric 1958- *WhoSSW 93*
Hinterbuchner, Catherine N. 1926- *WhoE 93*
Hinteregger, Gerald 1928- *WhoUN 92*
Hinterhaeuser, Hermann 1941- *St&PR 93, WhoAm 92*
Hintermann, Hans Erich 1929- *WhoWor 93*
Hintikka, Jaakko 1929- *WhoAm 92*
Hintlian, James T. 1924- *St&PR 93*
Hinton, Arthur 1869-1941 *Baker 92*
Hinton, Barbara Venice 1952- *WhoAmW 93*
Hinton, Brian *ScF&FL 92*
Hinton, Bruce *WhoScE 91-1*
Hinton, C. Bruce *St&PR 93*
Hinton, C. Bruce 1936- *WhoAm 92*
Hinton, C.H. 1853-1907 *ScF&FL 92*
Hinton, Carol D. *Law&B 92*
Hinton, Christine L. *Law&B 92*
Hinton, Christopher Jerrod 1961- *WhoAm 92*
Hinton, David *MiSFD 9*
Hinton, Deane Roesch 1923- *WhoAm 92, WhoWor 93*
Hinton, Eddie *SoulM*
Hinton, Estelle *AmWomPl*
Hinton, Howard W. 1946- *St&PR 93*
Hinton, John E. 1937- *St&PR 93*
Hinton, John Wallace *WhoScE 91-1*
Hinton, Julian Jay 1934- *St&PR 93*
Hinton, Kenneth M. *St&PR 93*
Hinton, Leslie Frank 1944- *WhoAm 92, WhoE 93*
Hinton, LuAnn Burkhart 1958- *WhoAmW 93*
Hinton, Michael R. 1954- *St&PR 93*
Hinton, Milt 1910- *BioIn 17*
Hinton, Norman Wayne 1944- *WhoSSW 93*
Hinton, Paula Weems 1954- *WhoAmW 93*
Hinton, Perry *ScF&FL 92*
Hinton, Quincey T., Jr. *Law&B 92*
Hinton, Robert Charles, Jr. 1948- *WhoSSW 93*
Hinton, S.E. *BioIn 17*
Hinton, S. E. 1948- *MagSAmL [port]*
Hinton, S(usan) E(loise) 1950- *DcAmChF 1960, MajAI [port]*
Hinton, Susan Eloise 1948- *WhoAm 92, WhoAmW 93*
Hinton, Terry *WhoScE 91-1*
Hinton, William H. 1919- *ConAu 40NR*
Hinton-Kedo, Jane C. *Law&B 92*
Hintsa, Mark LeRoy 1955- *WhoEmL 93*
Hintz, Bernd Jurgen 1942- *WhoAm 92*
Hintz, Charles Bradley 1949- *WhoE 93, WhoEmL 93, WhoWor 93*
Hintz, Eduard A.K. 1929- *WhoScE 91-3*
Hintz, Greg *WhoIns 93*
Hintz, Robert L. 1930- *St&PR 93*
Hintz, Robert Louis 1930- *WhoAm 92, WhoSSW 93*
Hintz, Russell Berg 1944- *St&PR 93*
Hintz, Thomas F. 1945- *St&PR 93*
Hintz, Victoria Jean 1963- *WhoAmW 93*
Hintz, Walter Gene 1945- *St&PR 93*
Hintz, Walter Richard 1937- *St&PR 93*
Hintze, Barry John 1956- *St&PR 93*
Hintze, Courtland T. 1945- *St&PR 93*
Hintze, Frank D. 1919- *St&PR 93*
Hintze, Herbert Owen, Jr. *Law&B 92*
Hintze, John D. *Law&B 92*
Hintze, Naomi A. 1909- *ScF&FL 92*

Hintze-Podufal, Christel 1938- *WhoWor 93*
Hinueber, Mark A. *Law&B 92*
Hinz, Carl Frederick, Jr. 1927- *WhoAm 92*
Hinz, Christopher 1951- *ScF&FL 92*
Hinz, Dorothy Elizabeth *WhoAm 92*
Hinz, Erhard H.A.G. 1931- *WhoScE 91-3*
Hinz, James Thomas 1926- *St&PR 93*
Hinz, Karl-Heinz 1936- *WhoScE 91-3*
Hinz, Mittie Dean 1941- *WhoAmW 93*
Hinz, Pamela Sheila 1949- *WhoSSW 93*
Hinz, Walter Fred 1946- *St&PR 93*
Hinze, Juergen Andreas Michael 1937- *WhoWor 93*
Hinze, Reinhild *St&PR 93*
Hinze, Willie Lee 1949- *WhoSSW 93*
Hiotis, Christ George 1939- *St&PR 93*
Hiott, David L. 1942- *St&PR 93*
Hipfner, L.A. *Law&B 92*
Hipkins, Alfred (James) 1826-1903 *Baker 92*
Hipkins, Brenda Leigh 1944- *WhoAmW 93*
Hipkins, Thomas Corwin 1956- *WhoEmL 93*
Hipolit, James E. *Law&B 92*
Hipolito, Jane 1942- *ScF&FL 92*
Hipp, Augustus J. *Law&B 92*
Hipp, Billy Wayne 1933- *WhoSSW 93*
Hipp, Clare Armitage 1940- *WhoE 93*
Hipp, Francis Moffett 1911- *St&PR 93, WhoAm 92, WhoSSW 93*
Hipp, Frederick L. 1908-1991 *BioIn 17*
Hipp, Frederick R. 1950- *St&PR 93*
Hipp, H. Neel 1951- *St&PR 93*
Hipp, Paul *BioIn 17, ConTFT 10*
Hipp, Urban 1913- *St&PR 93*
Hipp, W. Hayne 1940- *St&PR 93*
Hipp, William Hayne 1940- *WhoAm 92*
Hippe, Norman Douglas 1939- *St&PR 93*
Hippe, Zdzislaw S. 1930- *WhoScE 91-4*
Hippel, Theodor Gottlieb von 1741-1796 *BioIn 17*
Hippen, Gordon W. 1939- *St&PR 93*
Hipper, Franz von 1863-1932 *HarEnMi*
Hippias dc. 490BC *HarEnMi*
Hipple, James Blackman 1934- *St&PR 93, WhoAm 92*
Hipple, Theodore W. 1935- *ScF&FL 92*
Hipple, Walter John 1921- *WhoAm 92*
Hippner, Richard 1938- *St&PR 93*
Hippocrates fl. 215BC-212BC *HarEnMi*
Hippolyte, Alexander Gregory *MiSFD 9*
Hippopotamus, Eugene H. *MajAI*
Hipps, J. Robert 1939- *St&PR 93*
Hipps, Kevin D. 1958- *St&PR 93*
Hipsley, Jane Frances 1926- *WhoAmW 93*
Hipwell, Arthur P. *Law&B 92*
Hiraga, Sota 1936- *WhoWor 93*
Hirahara, Patti 1955- *WhoWor 93*
Hirai, Craig Kazuo 1949- *WhoEmL 93*
Hirai, Denitsu 1943- *WhoWor 93*
Hirai, Hidefumi 1926- *WhoWor 93*
Hirai, Kazumasa 1931- *ScF&FL 92*
Hirai, Kentaro 1931- *WhoWor 93*
Hirai, Kihei 1930- *St&PR 93*
Hirai, Kozaburo 1910- *Baker 92*
Hirai, Mikihisa 1955- *St&PR 93*
Hirai, Naofusa 1922- *WhoWor 93*
Hirai, Noriyuki 1942- *WhoWor 93*
Hirai, Takushi 1931- *WhoAsAP 91*
Hiraishi, Nagahisa 1925- *WhoWor 93*
Hiraishi, Takahiko 1944- *WhoUN 92*
Hiraizumi, Wataru 1929- *WhoAsAP 91*
Hirakawa, Kenji 1936- *WhoWor 93*
Hirama, Minoru 1946- *WhoWor 93*
Hiramatsu, Toshisuke 1947- *WhoWor 93*
Hiramoto, Koichiro 1934- *St&PR 93*
Hiranandani, Hiro R. 1938- *St&PR 93*
Hirano, Akio Pierre 1941- *WhoUN 92*
Hirano, Asao 1926- *WhoAm 92*
Hirano, Cathy 1957- *BioIn 17*
Hirano, June Yamada 1943- *WhoAmW 93*
Hirano, Ken-ichi 1927- *WhoWor 93*
Hirano, Kiyoshi 1929- *WhoAsAP 91*
Hirano, Masami 1936- *WhoWor 93*
Hirano, Michio 1960- *WhoE 93*
Hirano, Steven S. 1946- *St&PR 93*
Hirano-Nakanishi, Marsha Joyce 1949- *WhoAmW 93*
Hiranuma, Takeo 1939- *WhoAsAP 91*
Hirao, Kishio 1907-1953 *Baker 92*
Hirao, Toshikazu 1949- *WhoWor 93*
Hiraoka, Chiyuki 1930- *WhoWor 93*
Hiraoka, Leslie Satoshi 1941- *WhoE 93*
Hirasaki, George Jiro 1939- *WhoAm 92*
Hirasuna, Thomas Jyun 1955- *WhoE 93*
Hirata, Hirotaka 1932- *WhoWor 93*
Hirata, Shinichiro 1940- *WhoAsAP 91*
Hirata, Thomas *BioIn 17*
Hirata, Toshifumi 1944- *WhoWor 93*
Hirata, Yasushi 1930- *WhoWor 93*
Hirata, Yoneo 1948- *WhoAsAP 91*
Hirayama, Chisato 1923- *WhoWor 93*
Hirayama, Makoto 1961- *WhoWor 93*
Hirayoshi, Takekuni 1936- *Baker 92*
Hire, Richard C. 1928- *St&PR 93*
Hires, William Leland 1918- *WhoAm 92, WhoE 93*
Hirko, Joseph M. 1956- *St&PR 93*
Hirl, J. Roger 1931- *St&PR 93, WhoAm 92*
Hirman, Arland E. 1941- *St&PR 93*
Hirmez, Waad *BioIn 17*
Hirn, Doris Dreyer 1933- *WhoAmW 93*
Hirn, George 1941- *St&PR 93*
Hirn, Jorma Antero 1945- *WhoScE 91-4*
Hirner, Johann Josef 1956- *WhoWor 93*
Hirohara, Hideo 1941- *WhoWor 93*
Hirohito 1901-1989 *DcTwHis*
Hirohito, Emperor of Japan *BioIn 17*
Hirokawa, Shoji 1942- *WhoWor 93*
Hiromi, Kawakami 1938- *St&PR 93*
Hiromoto, Toshiro 1952- *WhoWor 93*
Hiron, Robert W.P. 1946- *WhoScE 91-1*
Hironaka, Colleen Chieko 1953- *WhoAmW 93*
Hironaka, Wakako 1934- *WhoAsAP 91*
Hirono, Mazie Keiko 1947- *WhoAmW 93*
Hirono, Yosuke 1941- *WhoWor 93*
Hironomiya Naruhito, Prince 1960- *BioIn 17*
Hirooka, Masaaki 1931- *WhoWor 93*
Hirooka, Sueyuki 1937- *WhoE 93*
Hirose, Akira 1941- *WhoAm 92*
Hirose, Takao 1959- *St&PR 93*
Hirose, Takeo 1868-1904 *HarEnMi*
Hirose, Teruo Terry 1926- *WhoAm 92*
Hiroshima, Koji Edmund 1924- *WhoAm 92*
Hiroshima, Toshifumi 1928- *WhoWor 93*
Hirota, Jitsuya 1924- *WhoWor 93*
Hirota, Minoru 1933- *WhoWor 93*
Hirrel, Michael John 1951- *WhoE 93*
Hirsch, Alex 1924- *St&PR 93*
Hirsch, Allen Vernon 1953- *St&PR 93, WhoAm 92*
Hirsch, Andy *BioIn 17*
Hirsch, Arlene Sharon 1951- *WhoAmW 93*
Hirsch, Arthur Abraham 1921- *WhoE 93*
Hirsch, B. *WhoScE 91-2*
Hirsch, Barry *Law&B 92*
Hirsch, Barry 1933- *St&PR 93, WhoAm 92*
Hirsch, Bette Gross 1942- *WhoAmW 93*
Hirsch, Bettina *MiSFD 9*
Hirsch, Carl E. 1946- *WhoAm 92*
Hirsch, Carl Herbert 1934- *St&PR 93, WhoAm 92*
Hirsch, Charles Bronislaw 1919- *WhoAm 92*
Hirsch, Charlotte Teller 1876- *AmWomPl*
Hirsch, Daniel 1940- *St&PR 93, WhoE 93*
Hirsch, David *ScF&FL 92*
Hirsch, David Jeffrey *Law&B 92*
Hirsch, David L. *WhoAm 92*
Hirsch, David M. 1944- *St&PR 93*
Hirsch, Donald Earl 1924- *WhoSSW 93*
Hirsch, Dorothy T. 1919- *St&PR 93*
Hirsch, E.D. 1928- *BioIn 17*
Hirsch, E. Franklin 1931- *St&PR 93*
Hirsch, Edward 1950- *DcLB 120 [port], WhoWrEP 92*
Hirsch, Edward Mark 1950- *WhoAm 92, WhoEmL 93, WhoSSW 93*
Hirsch, Edwin Waixel 1904- *St&PR 93*
Hirsch, Elisabeth Schiff 1918- *WhoE 93*
Hirsch, Elroy *BioIn 17*
Hirsch, Eric Donald 1928- *BioIn 17*
Hirsch, Eric Donald, Jr. 1928- *WhoAm 92*
Hirsch, Foster (Lance) 1943- *ConAu 39NR*
Hirsch, George Aaron 1934- *WhoAm 92, WhoWrEP 92*
Hirsch, Glenn Stuart 1954- *WhoEmL 93*
Hirsch, Gordon 1943- *ScF&FL 92*
Hirsch, Gregg P. *Law&B 92*
Hirsch, H.E. 1933- *St&PR 93*
Hirsch, Hans A. 1930- *WhoScE 91-3*
Hirsch, Harold S. 1907-1990 *BioIn 17*
Hirsch, Harvey Stuart 1950- *WhoE 93, WhoEmL 93*
Hirsch, Henriette 1884-1970 *BioIn 17*
Hirsch, Henry David 1943- *WhoSSW 93*
Hirsch, Horst Eberhard 1933- *WhoAm 92*
Hirsch, Hortense 1887-1990 *BioIn 17*
Hirsch, Irma Lou Kolterman 1934- *WhoAmW 93*
Hirsch, James L. 1952- *St&PR 93*
Hirsch, Jay G. 1930- *WhoAm 92*
Hirsch, Jeffrey Mark 1950- *WhoSSW 93*
Hirsch, Joel 1942- *St&PR 93*
Hirsch, Jon H. 1955- *St&PR 93*
Hirsch, Joseph Allen 1950- *WhoE 93, WhoWor 93*
Hirsch, Joseph I. *Law&B 92*
Hirsch, Judd 1935- *BioIn 17, WhoAm 92, WhoE 93*
Hirsch, Karen 1941- *BioIn 17*
Hirsch, Kennard N. *Law&B 92*
Hirsch, Klaus 1941- *WhoWor 93*
Hirsch, Larry Joseph 1938- *WhoE 93*
Hirsch, Laurence E. 1945- *St&PR 93, WhoAm 92*
Hirsch, Laurence Eliot 1945- *WhoSSW 93, WhoWor 93*
Hirsch, Lawrence Leonard 1922- *WhoAm 92*
Hirsch, Leon C. 1927- *St&PR 93*
Hirsch, Leon Charles 1927- *WhoAm 92*
Hirsch, Mark F. *St&PR 93*
Hirsch, Marla Durben *Law&B 92*
Hirsch, Martin Stanley 1939- *WhoE 93*
Hirsch, Mary Tone 1944- *WhoWrEP 92*
Hirsch, Maximilian Justice 1880-1969 *BiDAMSp 1989*
Hirsch, Melvin L. 1923- *St&PR 93, WhoAm 92*
Hirsch, Michael D. 1945- *St&PR 93*
Hirsch, Morris W. *Law&B 92*
Hirsch, Morris William 1933- *WhoAm 92*
Hirsch, Moshe *NewYTBS 92 [port]*
Hirsch, Myrtle G. d1990 *BioIn 17*
Hirsch, Neil S. 1947- *St&PR 93*
Hirsch, Paul (Adolf) 1881-1951 *Baker 92*
Hirsch, Paul J. 1937- *WhoE 93*
Hirsch, Peter 1928- *WhoScE 91-3, WhoWor 93*
Hirsch, Peter Bernhard *WhoScE 91-1*
Hirsch, Peter Bernhard 1925- *WhoAm 92*
Hirsch, Philip Francis 1925- *WhoAm 92, WhoSSW 93*
Hirsch, Raymond R. *Law&B 92*
Hirsch, Raymond Robert 1936- *WhoAm 92*
Hirsch, Richard Arthur 1925- *WhoAm 92, WhoE 93*
Hirsch, Richard B. 1921- *St&PR 93*
Hirsch, Robert Bruce 1926- *WhoAm 92*
Hirsch, Robert F. 1933- *St&PR 93*
Hirsch, Robert George 1946- *WhoE 93*
Hirsch, Robert Louis 1935- *WhoAm 92*
Hirsch, Robert W. 1939- *St&PR 93, WhoAm 92*
Hirsch, Robert W., Jr. 1947- *St&PR 93*
Hirsch, Robert William 1925- *WhoAm 92*
Hirsch, Roseann Conte 1941- *WhoAm 92*
Hirsch, Samson Raphael 1808-1888 *BioIn 17*
Hirsch, Stefan 1899-1964 *BioIn 17*
Hirsch, Stephen *Law&B 92*
Hirsch, Stephen Charles 1941- *WhoIns 93*
Hirsch, Susan *Law&B 92*
Hirsch, Walter 1917- *WhoWor 93*
Hirsch, Werner Zvi 1920- *WhoAm 92*
Hirschberg, Arthur A. 1927- *St&PR 93*
Hirschberg, D. Jeffrey *Law&B 92*
Hirschberg, Gerald A. 1945- *St&PR 93*
Hirschberg, Mark Gerald 1958- *St&PR 93*
Hirschberg, Sheldon M. 1947- *St&PR 93*
Hirschberg, Vera Hilda 1929- *WhoAm 92*
Hirschberg, Walter 1904- *IntDcAn*
Hirschberg, William S. d1992 *NewYTBS 92*
Hirschberg, William S. 1889-1992 *BioIn 17*
Hirschboeck, John Karl 1946- *WhoAm 92*
Hirschburg, Peter Lofton 1922- *St&PR 93*
Hirschel, Lieselotte Anne 1926- *WhoWrEP 92*
Hirschey, David B. *Law&B 92*
Hirschfeld, Abraham Jacob 1919- *WhoE 93*
Hirschfeld, Al 1903- *BioIn 17, News 92 [port], -92-3 [port]*
Hirschfeld, Albert 1903- *WhoAm 92, WhoE 93*
Hirschfeld, Arlene F. 1944- *WhoAmW 93*
Hirschfeld, Gerald Joseph 1921- *WhoAm 92*
Hirschfeld, I. Alan *St&PR 93*
Hirschfeld, Isidor 1868-1937 *BioIn 17*
Hirschfeld, Linda E. 1947- *St&PR 93*
Hirschfeld, Linda Evelyn 1947- *WhoEmL 93*
Hirschfeld, Michael 1950- *WhoAm 92*
Hirschfeld, Ronald Colman 1930- *WhoAm 92*
Hirschfeld, Sue Ellen 1941- *WhoAmW 93*
Hirschfelder, Arlene Phyllis 1943- *WhoAmW 93*
Hirschfelder, Joseph Oakland 1911-1990 *BioIn 17*
Hirschfield, John A. *WhoScE 91-1*
Hirschfield, Miriam Judith 1942- *WhoUN 92*
Hirschfield, Robert S. 1928- *WhoAm 92*
Hirschhorn, Austin 1936- *WhoAm 92*
Hirschhorn, Fred, Jr. 1919- *St&PR 93*
Hirschhorn, Kurt 1926- *WhoAm 92, WhoE 93*
Hirschhorn, Laurence H. 1936- *St&PR 93*
Hirschhorn, Richard S. 1935- *St&PR 93*
Hirschler, Edward S. 1914- *St&PR 93*
Hirschler, Emery Lewis 1941- *St&PR 93*
Hirschler, Philip 1955- *WhoE 93*
Hirschman, A. O. *ConAu 37NR*
Hirschman, Albert 1921- *WhoE 93*
Hirschman, Albert O. *BioIn 17*
Hirschman, Albert O. 1915- *ConAu 37NR*
Hirschman, Albert Otto 1915- *WhoAm 92, WhoE 93*
Hirschman, Edward 1950- *ScF&FL 92*
Hirschman, Frank Frederick 1936- *St&PR 93*
Hirschman, Rose Korn d1992 *BioIn 17*
Hirschman, Shalom Zarach 1936- *WhoAm 92, WhoE 93*
Hirschman, Sharon Ann 1951- *WhoAmW 93*
Hirschmann, Ralph Franz 1922- *WhoAm 92*
Hirschorn, Martin 1921- *St&PR 93*
Hirschowitz, Basil Isaac 1925- *WhoAm 92*
Hirschson, Albert Martin 1936- *St&PR 93*
Hirschson, Niel 1934- *WhoWor 93*
Hirsekorn, Robert Dean 1949- *St&PR 93*
Hirsh, Allan T., III 1949- *WhoAm 92*
Hirsh, Allan Thurman, Jr. 1920- *WhoAm 92*
Hirsh, Deborah Draughon 1949- *WhoAmW 93*
Hirsh, Ira Jean 1922- *WhoAm 92*
Hirsh, James Baker 1949- *WhoE 93*
Hirsh, James Eric 1946- *WhoSSW 93*
Hirsh, James G. *Law&B 92*
Hirsh, Norman Barry 1935- *WhoAm 92, WhoWor 93*
Hirsh, Richard M. *Law&B 92*
Hirsh, Stephanie Abraham 1954- *WhoEmL 93*
Hirsh, Sylvia *St&PR 93*
Hirsh, Thomas G. *Law&B 92*
Hirshberg, Gerald P. *NewYTBS 92 [port]*
Hirshen, Sanford 1935- *WhoAm 92*
Hirshenson, Janet *BioIn 17*
Hirshfield, Carol Roslyn 1950- *WhoEmL 93*
Hirshfield, Jane 1953- *WhoWrEP 92*
Hirshfield, Stuart 1941- *WhoAm 92, WhoE 93*
Hirshler, Eric Ernest 1924- *WhoE 93*
Hirshman, Carol Ann 1944- *WhoE 93*
Hirshman, Harold Carl 1945- *WhoAm 92*
Hirshman, Karl Jonathan 1936- *St&PR 93*
Hirshon, Maynard Jerome 1930- *WhoSSW 93*
Hirshon, Robert Edward 1948- *WhoAm 92*
Hirshon, Walter d1991 *BioIn 17*
Hirshson, Stanley Philip 1928- *WhoAm 92*
Hirshson, William Roscoe 1928- *WhoAm 92*
Hirsig, Alan R. 1939- *St&PR 93*
Hirson, David *WhoE 93*
Hirson, Estelle *WhoAmW 93*
Hirst, Grayson 1939- *Baker 92*
Hirst, Heston Stillings 1915- *WhoAm 92*
Hirst, Lawrence Martin 1949- *St&PR 93*
Hirst, Richard B. *Law&B 92*
Hirst, Wilma Elizabeth *WhoAm 92, WhoAmW 93, WhoWor 93*
Hirszfeld, Ludwik 1884-1954 *PolBiDi*
Hirt, Al(ois Maxwell) 1922- *Baker 92*
Hirt, David M. *Law&B 92*
Hirt, Franz Josef 1899-1985 *Baker 92*
Hirt, Fritz 1888-1970 *Baker 92*
Hirt, Robert W. 1943- *St&PR 93*
Hirth, John Price 1930- *WhoAm 92*
Hirtzler, Raoul 1923- *WhoScE 91-4*
Hiruki, Chuji 1931- *WhoAm 92*
Hirvela, Harold J. 1932- *St&PR 93*
Hirvonen, Ahti Ilmari 1931- *WhoWor 93*
Hirvonen, J.I. 1938- *WhoScE 91-4*
Hirvonen, Leo Leopold 1924- *WhoScE 91-4, WhoWor 93*
Hirvonen, Martti Tauno Sakari 1946- *WhoScE 91-4*
Hiryok, Kathryn Ann 1942- *WhoAmW 93*
Hisada, Mituhiko 1929- *WhoWor 93*
Hisashige, Tadao 1936- *WhoWor 93*
Hiscock, Keith 1947- *WhoScE 91-1*
Hiscock, Merrill Charles 1944- *WhoSSW 93*
Hiscoe, Helen B. 1919- *ConAu 137*
Hise, Della Van *ScF&FL 92*
Hise, James V. Van *ScF&FL 92*
Hise, William P. *Law&B 92*
Hiser, Constance 1950- *SmATA 71 [port]*
Hiser, Harold R., Jr. 1931- *St&PR 93*
Hiser, Harold Russell, Jr. 1931- *WhoAm 92*
Hiser, Max *St&PR 93*
Hisey, Richard M. 1958- *St&PR 93*
Hishida, Tomi-O 1927- *WhoWor 93*
Hishinuma, Kathleen K. 1954- *WhoEmL 93*
Hishmeh, Bassem L. 1941- *St&PR 93*
Hisle, Dewitt T. 1934- *St&PR 93*
Hisley, Martha Shelton 1951- *WhoSSW 93*
Hislop, Eric Charles *WhoScE 91-1*
Hislop, Ian *BioIn 17*
Hislop, J.S. *WhoScE 91-1*
Hislop, John T. 1941- *St&PR 93*
Hislop, Joseph 1884-1977 *OxDcOp*
Hislop, Mervyn Warren 1937- *WhoAm 92*
Hiss, Alger *BioIn 17*
Hiss, Alger 1904- *ColdWar 1 [port], DcTwHis, PolPar*
Hiss, Roland Graham 1932- *WhoAm 92*

Hiss, Tony 1941- WhoAm 92
Hissa, Raimo K. 1936- WhoScE 91-4
Histed, William Mark 1953- WhoSSW 93
Hitam, Mohamad Yusof 1936- WhoUN 92
Hitch, Charles Johnston 1910- WhoAm 92
Hitch, Horace 1921- WhoAm 92, WhoWor 93
Hitch, Robert Landis 1947- WhoWor 93
Hitchborn, James Brian 1938- WhoSSW 93
Hitchcock, A. WhoScE 91-1
Hitchcock, Alfred 1899-1980 BioIn 17, MiSFD 9N, ScF&FL 92
Hitchcock, Bion Earl Law&B 92
Hitchcock, Christopher Brian 1947- WhoE 93, WhoEmL 93, WhoWor 93
Hitchcock, D. Phil 1943- St&PR 93
Hitchcock, David Gridley 1956- St&PR 93
Hitchcock, David Ingersoll, Jr. 1928- WhoAm 92
Hitchcock, Donald BioIn 17
Hitchcock, Donald Simon 1929- St&PR 93
Hitchcock, Edward 1793-1864 BioIn 17
Hitchcock, Edward Keith 1941- WhoIns 93
Hitchcock, Ethan Allen 1798-1870 HarEnMi
Hitchcock, Ethan Allen 1909- WhoAm 92
Hitchcock, Frank H. 1867-1935 PolPar
Hitchcock, Frank Harris 1869-1935 BioIn 17
Hitchcock, Frederick L. Law&B 92
Hitchcock, George Parks 1914- WhoWrEP 92
Hitchcock, Georgia Magdalene 1903- WhoAmW 93
Hitchcock, Gregory Todd 1947- St&PR 93
Hitchcock, H(ugh) Wiley 1923- Baker 92
Hitchcock, Harold Bradford 1903- WhoAm 92
Hitchcock, Henry Russell 1903-1987 BioIn 17
Hitchcock, J. Gareth 1914- WhoAm 92
Hitchcock, Karen Ruth 1943- WhoAm 92, WhoAmW 93
Hitchcock, Laura Stern 1951- WhoAmW 93
Hitchcock, Lillian Dorothy Staw 1922- WhoAmW 93
Hitchcock, Mary S. AmWomPl
Hitchcock, Paul R. Law&B 92
Hitchcock, Peter Law&B 92
Hitchcock, Robyn BioIn 17
Hitchcock, Robyn 1953- ConMus 9 [port]
Hitchcock, Thomas S. 1939- St&PR 93
Hitchcock, Timothy Randall 1941- St&PR 93
Hitchcock, Vernon Thomas 1919- WhoWor 93
Hitchcock, Walter Anson 1918- WhoAm 92
Hitchcock, Walter Bertram, Jr. 1941- WhoSSW 93
Hitchen, Ann Jones WhoE 93
Hitchen, Harold, Jr. 1934- WhoIns 93
Hitchens, Ivon 1893-1979 BioIn 17
Hitchery, Mary McCrary Law&B 92
Hitchin, Nigel James WhoScE 91-1
Hitching, Harry James 1909- WhoAm 92
Hitchings, David Allyn 1964- WhoEmL 93
Hitchings, George Herbert 1905- WhoAm 92, WhoSSW 93, WhoWor 93
Hitchings, Herbert William 1930- St&PR 93
Hitchings, Owen Lyman 1937- WhoSSW 93
Hitchins, Ronald Joseph 1940- St&PR 93
Hitchman, J.M. 1946- St&PR 93
Hitchman, Richard Alan 1944- WhoWor 93
Hitchner, Dell Gillette 1914- WhoAm 92, WhoWor 93
Hitchner, Stephen B. d1991 BioIn 17
Hite, Arthur Joseph 1942- St&PR 93
Hite, Betsy Mallory 1944- WhoAmW 93
Hite, Catharine Leavey 1924- WhoAmW 93
Hite, Chris A. 1965- St&PR 93
Hite, David Nelson 1938- St&PR 93
Hite, Gary Paul 1935- WhoAm 92, WhoWor 93
Hite, James Tillman, III 1938- WhoAm 92
Hite, John Eric Law&B 92
Hite, Joseph Patrick 1948- St&PR 93
Hite, Mark Richard 1949- WhoEmL 93
Hite, Molly 1947- ScF&FL 92
Hite, R. Lee 1944- St&PR 93
Hite, Rhonda Ann 1965- WhoAmW 93
Hite, Robert Edelen 1937- St&PR 93
Hite, Robert Woodson d1882 BioIn 17
Hite, Shere BioIn 17
Hite, Shere D. WhoWrEP 92
Hite, Shere D. 1942- WhoAmW 93
Hite, William Knowles, III 1963- WhoE 93
Hites, Ronald Atlee 1942- WhoAm 92
Hiti, Pamela Sue 1953- WhoSSW 93
Hiti, Usamah 'Abd al-Razzaq Hummadi al- WhoWor 93
Hitler, Adolf 1889-1945 BioIn 17, DcTwHis, HarEnMi
Hitlin, David George 1942- WhoAm 92
Hitomi, Georgia Kay 1952- WhoAmW 93
Hitpas, Robert E. 1938- St&PR 93
Hitt, David Hamilton 1925- WhoAm 92
Hitt, Iola Haley 1919- WhoAmW 93
Hitt, James Alfred 1927- WhoSSW 93
Hitt, John Charles, Jr. 1940- WhoE 93, WhoSSW 93
Hitt, Leo N. 1955- WhoAm 92
Hitt, Mary E. Law&B 92
Hitt, Mary Elizabeth 1949- WhoEmL 93
Hitt, Michael A. 1946- WhoAm 92
Hitt, Robert M., III 1949- WhoEmL 93, WhoSSW 93
Hitt, Steven M. 1950- St&PR 93
Hitte, Ernie Lawrence 1941- WhoSSW 93
Hitti, Said H. WhoUN 92
Hittinger, William Charles 1922- St&PR 93, WhoAm 92
Hittle, James D. 1915- WhoAm 92, WhoSSW 93
Hittle, Richard Howard 1923- WhoAm 92
Hittleman, Ben 1920- St&PR 93
Hittmair, Otto 1924- WhoScE 91-4
Hittmair, Otto Heinrich 1924- WhoWor 93
Hittner, Carol Brenner 1942- WhoAm 92
Hittner, David 1939- WhoAm 92, WhoSSW 93, WhoWor 93
Hittner, Steven Bryan 1942- WhoAm 92
Hitz, Demi 1942- BioIn 17, MajAI [port]
Hitz, Frederick Porter 1939- WhoAm 92
Hitz, Kingman L. 1948- St&PR 93
Hitz, Warren Harding, Jr. 1947- WhoE 93
Hitzig, Bernard Michael 1935- WhoWor 93
Hitzig, Rupert MiSFD 9
Hitzman, Donald Oliver 1926- WhoSSW 93
Hively, Charles 1946- BioIn 17
Hively, Charles Edward 1947- WhoSSW 93
Hively, Jack B. MiSFD 9
Hively, Jane Stewart Wilcox 1952- WhoE 93
Hivry, Arnold Herbert 1945- St&PR 93
Hiwatashi, Koichi 1921- WhoWor 93
Hix, Charles Richard 1952- WhoSSW 93
Hix, James William 1947- WhoE 93
Hixenbaugh, Lyle H. 1931- St&PR 93
Hixon, James A. Law&B 92
Hixon, Robert Charles 1922- WhoAm 92
Hixon, Susan Dorr 1958- WhoAmW 93
Hixson, Nathan Hanks 1913- WhoSSW 93
Hiyama, Tetsuo 1939- WhoWor 93
Hiyoshi, Junichi 1923- WhoWor 93
Hizal, Ali Yilmaz 1943- WhoScE 91-4
Hizal, N. Aydin 1943- WhoScE 91-4
Hizawa, Kazuo 1930- WhoWor 93
Hizer, Marlene Brown 1940- WhoAmW 93
Hjelde, Hans Jorgen 1936- St&PR 93
Hjellum, John 1910- WhoAm 92
Hjelm, Peter Robert 1942- St&PR 93
Hjelme, Jorgen 1928- WhoScE 91-2
Hjelt, Sven-Erik O. 1939- WhoScE 91-4
Hjeltnes, Stein Harald WhoScE 91-4
Hjerner, Lars A.E. 1922- WhoWor 93
Hjerpe, Edward Alfred, III 1959- WhoAm 92
Hjerten, Stellan Vilhelm Einar 1928- WhoScE 91-4
Hjerto, Kjell Brynjulf 1947- WhoWor 93
Hjort, Barry L. Law&B 92
Hjort, Howard Warren 1931- WhoAm 92, WhoUN 92
Hjort, James William ScF&FL 92
Hjort, Peter F. Holst 1924- WhoScE 91-4
Hjort Albertsen, Per Baker 92
Hjortenberg, Erik 1930- WhoScE 91-2
Hjorth, Niels 1919- WhoScE 91-2
Hjorth, Poul Georg 1955- WhoWor 93
Hjorth, William Thomas 1937- St&PR 93
Hjortkjaer, Jes 1937- WhoWor 93
Hjortsberg, William 1941- ScF&FL 92
Hjortsberg, William Reinhold 1941- WhoAm 92, WhoWrEP 92
Hla, Nay-Myo 1946- WhoUN 92
Hlad, Gregory Michael 1947- WhoEmL 93, WhoSSW 93
Hladik, Jean 1935- WhoScE 91-2
Hladky, Joseph F., Jr. 1910- WhoAm 92
Hladkyj, Yaropolk Roland Law&B 92
Hladnik, Bostjan 1929- DrEEuF
Hlasko, Marek 1934-1969 PolBiDi
Hlasta, Dennis John 1953- WhoE 93
Hlasz, Anna 1938- WhoScE 91-4
Hlathein, Dennis 1935- St&PR 93
Hlavac, Phyllis Joan Idle 1949- WhoEmL 93
Hlavacek, James J. 1946- St&PR 93
Hlavacek, Jan WhoScE 91-4
Hlavacek, Joseph J. Law&B 92
Hlavacek, Roy George 1937- St&PR 93, WhoAm 92
Hlavaty, Marie L. 1936- St&PR 93
Hlavaty, Michael Carl Law&B 92
Hlavaty, Ted J. 1949- St&PR 93
Hlavay, Jay Alan 1956- WhoEmL 93, WhoSSW 93
Hlavinka, Paul Thomas 1950- WhoEmL 93
Hlavka, Edwin J. 1937- St&PR 93
Hlavka, Edwin John 1937- WhoAm 92
Hlawatsch, George Oliver 1945- WhoWor 93
Hliniak, Andrzej 1926- WhoScE 91-4
Hliniak, Irena 1921- WhoScE 91-4
Hlobil, Emil 1901-1987 Baker 92
Hlond, August 1881-1948 PolBiDi
Hlousek, George J. 1931- St&PR 93
Hlousek, Timothy J. 1947- St&PR 93
Hlozanek, Ivo 1936- WhoScE 91-4
Hlozek, Carole Diane Quast 1959- WhoAmW 93, WhoEmL 93
Hnatyshyn, Ramon John 1934- WhoAm 92, WhoE 93, WhoWor 93
Hnilica, Klaus D. 1941- WhoScE 91-3
Ho, Betty Yu-Lin 1930- WhoWrEP 92
Ho, Chi Minh 1890-1969 BioIn 17
Ho, Chien 1934- WhoAm 92
Ho, Chih-Chang 659-744 BioIn 17
Ho, Choon-Lin 1956- WhoWor 93
Ho, Dam d1991 BioIn 17
Ho, Dean T.W. St&PR 93
Ho, Donald Tai Loy 1930- WhoAm 92
Ho, Edward Sing-Tin 1938- WhoAsAP 91
Ho, Eric Peter 1927- WhoAsAP 91
Ho, Frank F. 1950- St&PR 93
Ho, Geoffrey T.C. Law&B 92
Ho, Irwine W. 1913- WhoAsAP 91
Ho, James K. 1952- St&PR 93
Ho, Kenneth Kin-Leung 1954- St&PR 93
Ho, Kuochu 1922- WhoWor 93
Ho, Kwon Ping BioIn 17
Ho, Mary Hao Tze 1958- WhoEmL 93
Ho, Minfong 1951- ChILR 28 [port]
Ho, Paul Siu-Chung 1936- WhoAm 92
Ho, Quang 1963- BioIn 17
Ho, Samuel Pao-San 1936- WhoAm 92
Ho, Simon Shun Man 1956- WhoWor 93
Ho, Stuart Tse Kong 1935- WhoAm 92
Ho, Tao 1936- WhoWor 93
Ho, Thomas Inn Min 1948- WhoAm 92
Ho, Thomas Tong-Yun 1931- WhoSSW 93
Ho, Tommy BioIn 17
Ho, Wei 1933- WhoWor 93
Ho, Weifan Lee 1951- WhoAmW 93, WhoEmL 93
Ho, Yan-Ki Richard 1952- WhoWor 93
Ho, Yhi-Min 1934- WhoAm 92
Ho, Yim 1952- MiSFD 9
Ho, Yu-Chi 1934- WhoAm 92
Hoad, Gordon Victor WhoScE 91-1
Hoad, William Robert 1932- St&PR 93
Hoadley, Alfred Warner 1934- WhoUN 92
Hoadley, David N. 1933- St&PR 93
Hoadley, Diana L. 1958- St&PR 93
Hoadley, Irene Braden 1938- WhoAm 92, WhoAmW 93
Hoadley, Peter George 1934- WhoAm 92
Hoadley, Robert Law&B 92
Hoadley, Robert Bruce 1933- WhoE 93
Hoadley, Walter E. 1916- St&PR 93
Hoadley, Walter Evans 1916- WhoAm 92, WhoWor 93
Hoag, Arthur Howard, Jr. 1923- WhoAm 92
Hoag, David Garratt 1925- WhoAm 92
Hoag, David H. St&PR 93
Hoag, David H. 1939- WhoAm 92, WhoSSW 93
Hoag, Emily Florence Alger 1890- AmWomPl
Hoag, John Arthur 1932- St&PR 93, WhoAm 92
Hoag, Judith BioIn 17
Hoag, Paul Sterling 1913- WhoAm 92
Hoag, Roland B., Jr. 1945- St&PR 93
Hoag, Sharon Kay 1963- WhoEmL 93
Hoag, Tami 1959- ConAu 138
Hoag, Terry S. 1942- WhoIns 93
Hoag, Thomas Robert 1947- St&PR 93
Hoag, William James 1939- St&PR 93
Hoag, Winifred A. AmWomPl
Hoagland, Albert Joseph, Jr. 1939- WhoWor 93
Hoagland, Albert Smiley 1926- WhoAm 92
Hoagland, Alexander Campbell, Jr. 1927- WhoAm 92
Hoagland, Donald Romeyne 1928- St&PR 93
Hoagland, Donald Wright 1921- WhoAm 92
Hoagland, Edward BioIn 17
Hoagland, Edward 1932- WhoAm 92, WhoWrEP 92
Hoagland, Glenn Daniel 1959- WhoE 93
Hoagland, Guy Whitney 1920- WhoWrEP 92
Hoagland, James Lee 1922- WhoAm 92
Hoagland, Jimmie Lee 1940- WhoAm 92, WhoE 93
Hoagland, John H., Jr. St&PR 93
Hoagland, Karl King, Jr. Law&B 92
Hoagland, Karl King, Jr. 1933- St&PR 93, WhoAm 92
Hoagland, Laurance Redington, Jr. 1936- WhoAm 92
Hoagland, Mahlon Bush 1921- WhoAm 92
Hoagland, Peter 1941- BioIn 17, CngDr 91
Hoagland, Peter Jackson 1941- WhoAm 92
Hoagland, Robert Earl 1951- WhoE 93, WhoEmL 93
Hoagland, Robert L. Law&B 92
Hoagland, Steven William 1948- WhoAm 92
Hoagland, William H. Law&B 92
Hoaglund, Glenn Carl 1937- WhoAm 92
Hoaglund, Susan M. Law&B 92
Hoak, James McClain 1918- WhoAm 92
Hoak, James McClain, Jr. 1944- WhoAm 92
Hoak, Jonathan S. Law&B 92
Hoak, W. McDowell 1958- St&PR 93
Hoal, Alan Law&B 92
Hoan, Hoang Van 1905?-1991 BioIn 17
Hoang, Anh Chau 1979?- BioIn 17
Hoang, Duc Van 1926- WhoAm 92
Hoang, Tuy 1927- BioIn 17
Hoang-Trong, Pho 1940- WhoScE 91-2
Hoang Van Hoan 1905?-1991 BioIn 17
Hoar, Ebenezer Rockwood 1816-1895 OxCSupC
Hoar, George F. 1826-1904 PolPar
Hoar, J. William 1938- St&PR 93
Hoar, James Clark Law&B 92
Hoar, John F. 1931- St&PR 93
Hoar, Joseph P. 1934- WhoAm 92
Hoar, Richard Morgan 1927- WhoE 93
Hoar, Samuel 1927- WhoAm 92
Hoar, Wayne Nichols 1950- St&PR 93
Hoar, William Patrick 1945- WhoE 93, WhoWor 93
Hoar, William Stewart 1913- WhoAm 92
Hoarau, Elie 1938- WhoAsAP 91
Hoard, Linda Jane Law&B 92
Hoard, Philip H. St&PR 93
Hoare, Agnes D. ScF&FL 92
Hoare, Carol Hren 1940- WhoE 93
Hoare, Charles Antony Richard WhoScE 91-1
Hoare, Dorothy M. 1901- ScF&FL 92
Hoare, Malcolm Vincent 1912-1991 BioIn 17
Hoare, Samuel John Gurney 1880-1959 DcTwHis
Hoarty, John Joseph 1950- WhoAm 92
Hoback, Florence Kunst 1922- WhoAmW 93
Hoban, George Savre 1914- WhoAm 92
Hoban, Lillian MajAI [port], SmATA 69, WhoAmW 93
Hoban, Russell BioIn 17
Hoban, Russell 1925- DcAmChF 1960, ScF&FL 92
Hoban, Russell (Conwell) 1925- ChlFicS, ConAu 37NR, MajAI [port], WhoAm 92
Hoban, Tana MajAI [port], SmATA 70 [port]
Hobart, Billie 1935- WhoAmW 93
Hobart, Doty AmWomPl
Hobart, James L. 1933- St&PR 93
Hobart, Lawrence Scott 1931- WhoAm 92
Hobart, Margaret Jefferys AmWomPl
Hobart, Marie Elizabeth 1860-1928 AmWomPl
Hobart, Peter Cahill 1934- St&PR 93
Hobart, Richard B. 1944- St&PR 93
Hobart, Robert Hobart Bull Wingfield Smith, Jr. 1932- WhoSSW 93
Hobart, William Harrison, Jr. 1924- St&PR 93, WhoAm 92
Hobaugh, Regina Margaret 1945- WhoE 93
Hobbes, Laurence Parsons Law&B 92
Hobbie, A. Clark, Jr. 1941- St&PR 93
Hobbie, Holly BioIn 17
Hobbie, Russell Klyver 1934- WhoAm 92
Hobbie, Susan Janet 1943- WhoAm 92, WhoAmW 93
Hobbs, Arthur Marmaduke 1940- WhoSSW 93
Hobbs, C. D. 1943- WhoAm 92
Hobbs, Carl Fredric 1931- WhoAm 92, WhoWor 93
Hobbs, Caswell O., III 1941- WhoAm 92
Hobbs, Douglas 1934- St&PR 93
Hobbs, Franklin Warren, IV 1947- WhoAm 92

Hobbs, G. *WhoScE 91-1*
Hobbs, G. Warfield 1905-1991 *BioIn 17*
Hobbs, Gayle Bodner 1963- *WhoAmW 93*
Hobbs, George Dever, II *Law&B 92*
Hobbs, Guy Stephen 1955- *WhoWor 93*
Hobbs, Isabelle Lucille 1944- *WhoSSW 93*
Hobbs, J. Edwin 1916- *WhoAm 92*
Hobbs, J. Timothy, Sr. 1941- *WhoE 93*
Hobbs, James Allen 1930- *St&PR 93, WhoAm 92*
Hobbs, James Baxter 1926- *WhoSSW 93*
Hobbs, James Beverly 1930- *WhoAm 92*
Hobbs, James D. 1943- *St&PR 93*
Hobbs, Jerry Chilton 1939- *St&PR 93*
Hobbs, Joan Pizzo 1957- *WhoAmW 93*
Hobbs, John Michael *WhoScE 91-1*
Hobbs, Kenneth Edward Frederick *WhoScE 91-1*
Hobbs, Lewis Mankin 1937- *WhoAm 92*
Hobbs, Linder Charlie 1925- *WhoAm 92*
Hobbs, Lottie Beth 1921- *WhoSSW 93*
Hobbs, Lucy Edith *AmWomPl*
Hobbs, Lyndall *MiSFD 9*
Hobbs, Mabel Foote *AmWomPl*
Hobbs, Marcus Edwin 1909- *WhoAm 92*
Hobbs, Matthew Hallock 1946- *WhoAm 92*
Hobbs, Michael 1954- *WhoSSW 93*
Hobbs, Michael Edwin 1940- *WhoAm 92*
Hobbs, Nila Alene 1949- *WhoEmL 93*
Hobbs, Peter D. 1945- *St&PR 93*
Hobbs, R.H. 1955- *St&PR 93*
Hobbs, Ranald Purcell 1907- *WhoAm 92*
Hobbs, Richard F. 1947- *St&PR 93*
Hobbs, Robert E. 1930- *St&PR 93*
Hobbs, Robert G. *Law&B 92*
Hobbs, Robert Henry *Law&B 92*
Hobbs, Robert Wesley 1938- *WhoAm 92*
Hobbs, Roland L. 1932- *St&PR 93*
Hobbs, Sharon Stanley 1953- *WhoEmL 93, WhoSSW 93*
Hobbs, Thomas D. 1946- *St&PR 93*
Hobbs, Thomas William 1953- *WhoSSW 93*
Hobbs, Truman McGill 1921- *WhoAm 92, WhoSSW 93*
Hobbs, Valine *AmWomPl*
Hobbs, Wilbur Eugene 1921- *WhoE 93*
Hobbs, Will *BioIn 17*
Hobbs, Will 1947- *SmATA 72 [port]*
Hobbs, William Barton Rogers 1949- *WhoAm 92, WhoEmL 93*
Hobbs, William Beers 1960- *WhoSSW 93*
Hobbs, William P. 1924- *St&PR 93*
Hobbs-Tsikos, Heidi Lou 1959- *WhoSSW 93*
Hobby, John B. *Law&B 92*
Hobby, Kenneth L. 1932- *St&PR 93*
Hobby, Kenneth Lester 1947- *WhoSSW 93*
Hobby, Oveta Culp 1905- *DcLB 127 [port], St&PR 93, WhoAm 92*
Hobby, William 1878-1964 *DcLB 127 [port]*
Hobby, William Matthews, III 1935- *WhoSSW 93*
Hobby, William Pettus 1932- *St&PR 93, WhoAm 92, WhoSSW 93*
Hobday, John Charles 1935- *WhoAm 92*
Hobdell, A.C. *WhoScE 91-1*
Hobdell, Martin Howard 1938- *WhoScE 91-3*
Hobe, Robert Donald 1958- *St&PR 93*
Hobelman, Carl Donald 1931- *WhoAm 92, WhoWor 93*
Hoben, Edmond H. *BioIn 17*
Hoberecht, Earnest 1918- *WhoAm 92, WhoWor 93*
Hoberg, Heinz 1932- *WhoScE 91-3*
Hoberg, Timothy Emil 1944- *WhoAm 92*
Hoberman, Chuck *BioIn 17*
Hoberman, Chuck 1956- *WhoE 93*
Hoberman, David *WhoAm 92*
Hoberman, Henry Don 1914- *WhoAm 92*
Hoberman, Mary Ann 1930- *MajAI [port], SmATA 72 [port], WhoE 93*
Hoberman, Solomon 1914- *WhoE 93*
Hobey, Jack 1947- *St&PR 93*
Hobhouse, Caroline d1991 *BioIn 17*
Hobhouse, Janet 1948-1991 *BioIn 17*
Hobin, Gary Russell 1946- *WhoEmL 93, WhoSSW 93*
Hobin, Patrick S. *Law&B 92*
Hoblin, Philip J., Jr. 1929- *WhoAm 92*
Hoblit, Gregory *MiSFD 9*
Hoblitzell, Alan Penniman, Jr. 1931- *WhoAm 92*
Hoblitzelle, George Knapp 1921- *WhoAm 92*
Hoboken, Anthony van 1887-1983 *Baker 92*
Hobratschk, Martin Glenn 1944- *St&PR 93*
Hobsbaum, Philip Dennis *WhoScE 91-1*
Hobscheid, Fred John *St&PR 93*
Hobson, Anthony *BioIn 17*
Hobson, Bulmer 1883-1969 *BioIn 17*
Hobson, Burton H. 1933- *St&PR 93*
Hobson, Butch 1951- *WhoAm 92, WhoE 93*
Hobson, Carroll Dean 1928- *St&PR 93*
Hobson, Clifford Allan *WhoScE 91-1*
Hobson, David L. 1936- *CngDr 91*
Hobson, David Lee 1936- *WhoAm 92*
Hobson, Derrick Anthony *Law&B 92*
Hobson, Donald *WhoScE 91-1*
Hobson, Ervin A. 1956- *St&PR 93*
Hobson, Ervin J. *St&PR 93*
Hobson, George *BioIn 17*
Hobson, George Donald 1923- *WhoAm 92*
Hobson, Harold 1904-1992 *ConAu 137*
Hobson, Harry E., Jr. 1948- *WhoWor 93*
Hobson, Harry Edward 1934- *St&PR 93*
Hobson, Harry Lee, Jr. 1929- *WhoAm 92*
Hobson, Howard 1903-1991 *BioIn 17*
Hobson, Ian 1952- *Baker 92*
Hobson, Irene *AmWomPl*
Hobson, James Lynn, Jr. 1942- *WhoAm 92*
Hobson, James Richmond 1937- *WhoAm 92, WhoE 93*
Hobson, John Allan 1933- *WhoAm 92*
Hobson, John Atkinson 1858-1940 *BioIn 17*
Hobson, Laura Z. 1900-1986 *JeAmFiW*
Hobson, Leslie *WhoScE 91-1*
Hobson, Mary S. *Law&B 92*
Hobson, Michael Lee 1950- *WhoEmL 93*
Hobson, Robert Wayne, II 1939- *WhoAm 92*
Hobson, Victor L. 1943- *St&PR 93*
Hobson, W. Edmund 1949- *St&PR 93*
Hobson, William Frederick 1951- *WhoE 93*
Hoburg, James Frederick 1946- *WhoAm 92*
Hoby, William fl. 1453- *BioIn 17*
Hocart, A.M. 1883-1939 *IntDcAn*
Hocevar, Burgess Lee 1947- *St&PR 93*
Hocevar, Janez 1943- *WhoScE 91-4*
Hoch, Carol W. *Law&B 92*
Hoch, Edward D. 1930- *ScF&FL 92, WhoWrEP 92*
Hoch, Edward Dentinger 1930- *WhoAm 92*
Hoch, Edward Wallis 1849-1925 *BioIn 17*
Hoch, Frank W. 1921- *St&PR 93*
Hoch, Frederic Louis 1920- *WhoAm 92*
Hoch, James R. 1951- *St&PR 93*
Hoch, Jeanne Marie 1949- *WhoAmW 93*
Hoch, John Joseph 1927- *St&PR 93*
Hoch, Joseph (Paul Johannes) 1815-1874 *Baker 92*
Hoch, Karl J., Jr. *Law&B 92*
Hoch, Laurence A. *Law&B 92*
Hoch, Linda Lou 1952- *WhoEmL 93*
Hoch, Orion L. 1928- *St&PR 93*
Hoch, Orion Lindel 1928- *WhoAm 92, WhoWor 93*
Hoch, Paul Kenneth *WhoScE 91-1*
Hoch, Peggy Marie 1959- *WhoE 93*
Hoch, Robert Charles 1948- *St&PR 93*
Hoch, Roland Franklin 1940- *WhoAm 92*
Hoch, Sallie O'Neil 1941- *WhoAmW 93*
Hochadel, Jack Birch *St&PR 93*
Hochbaum, Godfrey Martin 1916- *WhoAm 92*
Hochberg, Andrew S. *Law&B 92*
Hochberg, Ann P. *Law&B 92*
Hochberg, Bayard Zabdial 1932- *WhoAm 92*
Hochberg, David C. 1956- *St&PR 93*
Hochberg, Fred P. 1952- *St&PR 93*
Hochberg, Gertrude Meth 1911- *WhoAmW 93*
Hochberg, Hans Heinrich, XIV, Bolko Graf von 1843-1926 *Baker 92*
Hochberg, Jerome A. 1933- *WhoAm 92*
Hochberg, Joel Morton 1939- *WhoAm 92*
Hochberg, Julian 1923- *WhoAm 92*
Hochberg, Kathi Linn 1951- *WhoAmW 93*
Hochberg, Marcia Gail 1957- *WhoE 93*
Hochberg, Marilyn B. 1926- *St&PR 93*
Hochberg, Mark S. 1947- *WhoE 93, WhoEmL 93*
Hochberg, Martin I. 1931- *St&PR 93*
Hochberg, Martin N. 1937- *WhoE 93*
Hochberg, Richard Barry 1938- *WhoE 93*
Hochberg, Ronald Mark 1955- *WhoE 93*
Hochberg, Victoria *MiSFD 9*
Hochberger, Simon 1912- *WhoAm 92*
Hochbrueckner, George J. 1938- *CngDr 91, WhoAm 92, WhoE 93*
Hoche, Louis Lazare 1768-1797 *HarEnMi*
Hoche, Philip A. 1906- *WhoIns 93*
Hoche, Philip Anthony 1906- *WhoAm 92*
Hocheid, B.J. 1928- *WhoScE 91-2*
Hochenegg, Leonhard 1942- *WhoWor 93*
Hocherman, Henry W. *ScF&FL 92*
Hochgesang, Gerald Ray 1953- *St&PR 93*
Hochhalter, Gordon Ray 1946- *WhoEmL 93, WhoWor 93*
Hochhauser, Richard Michael 1944- *St&PR 93*
Hochhuth, Rolf *BioIn 17*
Hochhuth, Rolf 1931- *DcLB 124 [port]*
Ho Chi Minh 1890-1969 *ColdWar 2 [port], DcTwHis, HarEnMi*
Hochman, Benjamin 1925- *WhoSSW 93*
Hochman, James Alan 1949- *WhoEmL 93*
Hochman, Michele 1939- *WhoE 93*
Hochman, Neal Stuart 1934- *St&PR 93*
Hochman, Richard H. 1945- *St&PR 93*
Hochman, Ronald Norman 1951- *WhoE 93*
Hochman, Steven H. 1946- *St&PR 93*
Hochman, Todd Scott *Law&B 92*
Hochmeister, Angela Beth 1958- *WhoAmW 93*
Hochmuth, Robert Milo 1939- *WhoAm 92*
Hochrainer, Dieter 1940- *WhoScE 91-3*
Hochreiter, Edward John 1941- *St&PR 93*
Hochreiter, Joseph Christian, Jr. 1955- *WhoE 93*
Hochscheid, Robert E. 1924-1991 *BioIn 17*
Hochschild, Adam 1942- *WhoAm 92*
Hochschild, Carroll Shepherd 1935- *WhoAmW 93*
Hochschwender, Herman Karl 1920- *WhoWor 93*
Hochstadt, Harry 1925- *WhoAm 92*
Hochstadt, Joy 1939- *WhoAm 92, WhoAmW 93, WhoE 93*
Hochstein, Anatoly Boris 1932- *WhoAm 92*
Hochstein, Anita Claire *Law&B 92*
Hochstein, Eric Cameron 1956- *WhoEmL 93*
Hochster, Melvin 1943- *WhoAm 92*
Hochstetler, Alan Ray 1939- *WhoE 93*
Hochstetler, David R. 1944- *St&PR 93*
Hochstrasser, Donald Lee 1927- *WhoAm 92, WhoSSW 93*
Hochstrasser, John Michael 1938- *WhoE 93*
Hochstrasser, Marie *BioIn 17*
Hochstrasser, U. *WhoScE 91-4*
Hochwalder, Fritz 1911-1986 *BioIn 17*
Hochwarth, Robert Frederick *Law&B 92*
Hociota, Dorin *WhoScE 91-4*
Hock, Bertold 1939- *WhoScE 91-3*
Hock, Dee Ward *BioIn 17*
Hock, Delwin D. 1935- *St&PR 93, WhoAm 92*
Hock, Fromund M.L. 1927- *WhoScE 91-3*
Hock, Gregory Howard *Law&B 92*
Hock, Harlan H. *St&PR 93*
Hock, Morton 1929- *WhoAm 92, WhoWor 93*
Hock, Roy E. 1929- *St&PR 93*
Hock, Vincent M. *Law&B 92*
Hock, Vincent Michael 1942- *St&PR 93*
Hock, W. Fletcher, Jr. 1931- *St&PR 93*
Hockaday, Donald E., III *Law&B 92*
Hockaday, Irvine O., Jr. 1936- *St&PR 93, WhoAm 92*
Hockaday, Margaret d1992 *NewYTBS 92 [port]*
Hocke, Martin *ScF&FL 92*
Hockeimer, Henry Eric 1920- *WhoWor 93*
Hocken, Peter Dudley 1932- *WhoE 93*
Hocken, Robert John 1944- *WhoSSW 93*
Hockenberg, Harlan David 1927- *WhoAm 92*
Hockenberger, Susan Jane 1948- *WhoAmW 93*
Hockenberry, Debra Pearl 1961- *WhoWrEP 92*
Hockenberry, John F. *Law&B 92*
Hockenbrocht, David William 1935- *St&PR 93, WhoAm 92*
Hocker, F.H. Hartwig 1937- *WhoScE 91-3*
Hocker, John Kells 1949- *WhoEmL 93*
Hocker, John Robert 1935- *WhoE 93*
Hocker, Karla 1946- *ScF&FL 92, WhoWrEP 92*
Hockersmith, Harold M. 1927- *St&PR 93*
Hockett, Charles Francis 1916- *WhoAm 92*
Hockey, John Albert 1936- *St&PR 93*
Hockh, Carl 1707-1773 *Baker 92*
Hockin, Alan Bond 1923- *St&PR 93*
Hockin, Thomas Alexander 1938- *WhoAm 92*
Hocking, John Edwin 1926- *St&PR 93*
Hocking, John Gilbert 1920- *WhoAm 92*
Hocking, Leslie Morison *WhoScE 91-1*
Hocking, Mary (Eunice) 1921- *ConAu 40NR*
Hocking, Trevor John *WhoScE 91-1*
Hocking-Fetter, Julie 1965- *St&PR 93*
Hockley, Chris 1950- *ScF&FL 92*
Hockman, Bruce Richard 1948- *St&PR 93*
Hockman, Richard Elton 1945- *WhoAm 92*
Hockney, David *BioIn 17*
Hockney, David 1937- *ConTFT 10, IntDcOp, OxDcOp, WhoAm 92, WhoWor 93*
Hockney, Richard L. 1949- *St&PR 93*
Hockridge, Robert George 1920- *St&PR 93*
Hocks, Paula Jeanne *WhoWrEP 92*
Hocott, Claude Richard 1909- *WhoAm 92*
Hocott, Joe Bill 1921- *WhoSSW 93, WhoWor 93*
Hocutt, Max Oliver 1936- *WhoAm 92*
Hocutt, Thomas R. *EncAACR*
Hodapp, Don Joseph 1937- *St&PR 93, WhoAm 92*
Hodapp, James Dean *Law&B 92*
Hodapp, Leroy Charles 1923- *WhoAm 92*
Hodara, Henri 1926- *St&PR 93*
Hodder, Michael John 1946- *WhoE 93*
Hodder, R. Frederick 1941- *St&PR 93*
Hodder, William Alan 1931- *St&PR 93, WhoAm 92*
Hodder, William Reginald *ScF&FL 92*
Hodder-Williams, Christopher 1926- *ScF&FL 92*
Hoddinott, Alfred H., Jr. *Law&B 92*
Hoddinott, Alun 1929- *Baker 92, OxDcOp*
Hoddy, George Warren 1905- *WhoAm 92*
Hoddy, Raymond Arthur 1921- *WhoAm 92*
Hode, Lars Gunnar 1942- *WhoWor 93*
Hodeir, Andre 1921- *Baker 92*
Hodel, Christian M. 1936- *WhoWor 93*
Hodemont, Leonard (Collet) de c. 1575-1636 *Baker 92*
Hodenfield, Mabel *AmWomPl*
Hodes, Alan 1943- *St&PR 93*
Hodes, Barbara 1941- *WhoAmW 93*
Hodes, Barton L. 1940- *WhoAm 92*
Hodes, Linda *WhoAm 92*
Hodes, Marion Edward 1925- *WhoAm 92*
Hodes, Robert B. 1925- *St&PR 93*
Hodes, Robert Bernard 1925- *WhoAm 92*
Hodes, Scott 1937- *St&PR 93, WhoAm 92*
Hodes, William Dierks 1934- *St&PR 93*
Hodess, Arthur Bart 1950- *WhoE 93*
Hodgdon, Harry Edward 1946- *WhoAm 92, WhoEmL 93*
Hodgdon, Herbert James 1924- *WhoAm 92*
Hodge, Alan M. *St&PR 93*
Hodge, Anne Harkness 1951- *WhoAmW 93, WhoEmL 93*
Hodge, Bartow Michael *Law&B 92*
Hodge, Benjamin Keith 1959- *WhoSSW 93*
Hodge, Bernice Keith 1943- *WhoSSW 93*
Hodge, Bobby Lynn 1956- *WhoEmL 93, WhoSSW 93, WhoWor 93*
Hodge, Brian 1960- *ScF&FL 92*
Hodge, Carleton Taylor 1917- *WhoAm 92*
Hodge, Charles Joseph, Jr. 1941- *WhoAm 92*
Hodge, Conrad Vere- *ScF&FL 92*
Hodge, David Vaugn 1934- *WhoE 93*
Hodge, Deborah Lou 1956- *WhoEmL 93, WhoSSW 93*
Hodge, Decca Renee Carter 1956- *WhoSSW 93*
Hodge, Frederick Webb 1864-1956 *IntDcAn*
Hodge, G. Lowrance 1934- *St&PR 93*
Hodge, Garrick J. *Law&B 92*
Hodge, George Lowrance 1934- *WhoAm 92*
Hodge, Gerald Britton 1934- *St&PR 93*
Hodge, Glenn Roy 1947- *WhoEmL 93*
Hodge, Hester Wayne 1931- *St&PR 93*
Hodge, James Dwight 1933- *WhoSSW 93*
Hodge, James Lee 1935- *WhoAm 92*
Hodge, James Robert 1927- *WhoAm 92*
Hodge, Jeffrey *Law&B 92*
Hodge, John Reed 1893-1963 *HarEnMi*
Hodge, Kathleen O'Connell 1948- *WhoAmW 93*
Hodge, Kerwyn Christopher 1964- *WhoEmL 93*
Hodge, Linda Joyce *Law&B 92*
Hodge, Malcolm H. 1942- *St&PR 93*
Hodge, Martha Elizabeth 1950- *WhoAmW 93*
Hodge, Mary Gretchen Farnam 1943- *WhoAmW 93*
Hodge, Mary Jo 1935- *WhoAmW 93*
Hodge, Omar *DcCPCAm*
Hodge, Paul William 1934- *WhoAm 92*
Hodge, Pearl McDonald 1950- *WhoAmW 93*
Hodge, Philip *WhoScE 91-1*
Hodge, Philip Gibson, Jr. 1920- *WhoAm 92*
Hodge, Raymond D. d1990 *BioIn 17*
Hodge, Verne Antonio 1933- *WhoAm 92*
Hodgell, Murlin Ray 1924- *WhoAm 92*
Hodgell, P.C. 1951- *ScF&FL 92*
Hodgell, Patricia Christine 1951- *WhoWrEP 92*
Hodgell, Robert Overman 1922- *WhoAm 92*
Hodgen, Maurice Denzil 1929- *WhoAm 92*
Hodgens, Randall Wayne 1966- *WhoSSW 93*
Hodges, A. Earl *Law&B 92*
Hodges, Allen M. 1947- *St&PR 93*
Hodges, Andrew Fullarton *Law&B 92*

Hodges, Ann *WhoAmW 93, WhoSSW 93*
Hodges, Ann 1928- *WhoAm 92, WhoAmW 93*
Hodges, Ann E. 1931- *WhoAmW 93*
Hodges, Bessie Bell 1923- *St&PR 93*
Hodges, Carl G. 1902-1964 *DcAmChF 1960*
Hodges, Charles H. 1949- *St&PR 93*
Hodges, Charles Thomas 1951- *WhoAm 92*
Hodges, Cheryl D. 1952- *St&PR 93*
Hodges, Clarence Eugene 1939- *WhoAm 92*
Hodges, Courtney Hicks 1887-1966 *HarEnMi*
Hodges, Daniel M. 1949- *St&PR 93*
Hodges, David Albert 1937- *WhoAm 92*
Hodges, David Leslie 1938- *WhoScE 91-1*
Hodges, Dewey Harper 1948- *WhoAm 92, WhoSSW 93*
Hodges, Donald Wayne 1934- *St&PR 93*
Hodges, Doris *ScF&FL 92*
Hodges, Douglas John *WhoScE 91-1*
Hodges, Earl A. 1933- *St&PR 93*
Hodges, Eddie Valson 1932- *WhoSSW 93*
Hodges, Edward 1796-1867 *Baker 92*
Hodges, Everett L. 1932- *St&PR 93*
Hodges, Faustina Hasse 1823-1895 *See* Hodges, Edward 1796-1867 *Baker 92*
Hodges, Frederick James 1939- *St&PR 93*
Hodges, Gayla Dianne 1950- *WhoAmW 93*
Hodges, George Hartshorn 1866-1947 *BioIn 17*
Hodges, Gil 1924-1972 *BioIn 17*
Hodges, Gil Denny *WhoSSW 93*
Hodges, H. Gaylord, Jr. 1941- *WhoAm 92, WhoIns 93*
Hodges, H. Raiford, Jr. 1932- *St&PR 93*
Hodges, Harland Edward 1950- *St&PR 93*
Hodges, Harry Ellis, Jr. 1942- *WhoSSW 93*
Hodges, Heidi Ann 1953- *WhoAmW 93*
Hodges, J. Drew *BioIn 17*
Hodges, J(ohn) Sebastian B(ach) 1830-1915 *See* Hodges, Edward 1796-1867 *Baker 92*
Hodges, Jack Douglas 1953- *WhoEmL 93*
Hodges, James Ronald 1952- *St&PR 93*
Hodges, Jeanette Kay 1950- *WhoSSW 93*
Hodges, Jill *BioIn 17*
Hodges, John B. 1936- *St&PR 93*
Hodges, John Hendricks 1914- *WhoAm 92*
Hodges, Johnny 1906-1970 *Baker 92*
Hodges, Kenneth Stuart 1955- *WhoE 93*
Hodges, Lammie Blackwell *AmWomPl*
Hodges, Leigh Mitchell 1876-1954 *AmWomPl*
Hodges, Luther Hartwell, Jr. 1936- *St&PR 93*
Hodges, M. Ray 1931- *WhoAm 92*
Hodges, Margaret Moore 1911- *MajAI [port], WhoAm 92*
Hodges, Mary Frances 1936- *WhoAmW 93*
Hodges, Melvin S. *Law&B 92*
Hodges, Michael P. 1941- *ConAu 136*
Hodges, Mike 1932- *MiSFD 9*
Hodges, Mitchell 1959- *WhoEmL 93, WhoSSW 93*
Hodges, Paul Joseph 1959- *WhoAm 92*
Hodges, Ralph B. 1930- *WhoSSW 93*
Hodges, Richard E. 1928- *St&PR 93*
Hodges, Robert H., Jr. 1944- *WhoE 93*
Hodges, Robert Hayne, Jr. 1944- *CngDr 91*
Hodges, Ronald William 1934- *WhoE 93*
Hodges, Rose *BioIn 17*
Hodges, Russell Patrick 1910-1971 *BiDAMSp 1989*
Hodges, Sheryl L. *Law&B 92*
Hodges, Stephen *BioIn 17*
Hodges, Thomas d1856 *BioIn 17*
Hodges, Thomas Kent 1936- *WhoAm 92*
Hodges, Thompson Gene 1913- *WhoAm 92, WhoWor 93*
Hodges, Wilfrid Augustine *WhoScE 91-1*
Hodges, William Terrell 1934- *WhoSSW 93*
Hodges, Zachary Ross 1947- *WhoEmL 93, WhoSSW 93*
Hodges-McLain, Vivan Pauline 1929- *WhoSSW 93*
Hodge-Spencer, Cheryl Ann 1952- *WhoAmW 93*
Hodgin, Katharine Wyatt 1926- *WhoSSW 93*
Hodgins, Daniel Stephen 1939- *WhoSSW 93*
Hodgins, Eric 1899-1971 *BioIn 17*
Hodgins, Jack 1938- *WhoCanL 92*
Hodgins, Jack Stanley 1938- *WhoAm 92, WhoWrEP 92*
Hodgins, William *BioIn 17*
Hodgkin, Alan Lloyd 1914- *WhoAm 92, WhoWor 93*
Hodgkin, Dorothy Crowfoot 1910- *WhoAm 92, WhoWor 93*
Hodgkin, Howard 1932- *BioIn 17*
Hodgkin, Thomas 1798-1866 *BioIn 17, IntDcAn*
Hodgkins, H.F., Jr. 1928- *St&PR 93*
Hodgkins, Margaret H. 1939- *St&PR 93*
Hodgkins, Paul 1917- *WhoScE 91-1*
Hodgkinson, Charles Paul 1907- *WhoAm 92*
Hodgkinson, Elizabeth *AmWomPl*
Hodgkinson, Robert Donald *WhoScE 91-1*
Hodgkinson, Virginia Ann 1941- *WhoE 93*
Hodgkinson, William James 1939- *WhoAm 92, WhoE 93*
Hodgman, Ann *ScF&FL 92*
Hodgman, George *BioIn 17*
Hodgman, Joan Elizabeth 1923- *WhoAm 92*
Hodgman, Richard Morey 1949- *WhoE 93*
Hodgson, Adelaide *AmWomPl*
Hodgson, Agnes *BioIn 17*
Hodgson, Allan Archibald 1937- *St&PR 93, WhoAm 92*
Hodgson, Allan Ferguson 1945- *WhoWor 93*
Hodgson, Amanda *ScF&FL 92*
Hodgson, Arthur Clay 1907- *WhoWor 93*
Hodgson, Clarence H. N. *BioIn 17*
Hodgson, Edward William, Jr. 1946- *WhoEmL 93*
Hodgson, Ernest 1932- *WhoAm 92*
Hodgson, Frederick Matthew 1930- *St&PR 93*
Hodgson, Gertrude Simms *AmWomPl*
Hodgson, Ian 1945- *WhoWor 93*
Hodgson, James Stanley 1942- *WhoAm 92*
Hodgson, Jane *BioIn 17*
Hodgson, John Michael *WhoScE 91-1*
Hodgson, Matthew Marshall Neil 1926- *WhoAm 92*
Hodgson, Morgan Day 1947- *WhoEmL 93*
Hodgson, Paul Edmund 1921- *WhoAm 92*
Hodgson, Peter Crafts 1934- *WhoSSW 93*
Hodgson, Peter John 1929- *WhoAm 92*
Hodgson, Ralph E. 1906-1991 *BioIn 17*
Hodgson, Reginald Hutchins, Jr. 1939- *WhoSSW 93, WhoWor 93*
Hodgson, Richard 1917- *St&PR 93, WhoAm 92*
Hodgson, Robert Arnold 1924- *WhoE 93*
Hodgson, Robert James 1938- *St&PR 93*
Hodgson, Thomas Richard 1941- *St&PR 93, WhoAm 92, WhoWor 93*
Hodgson, Walter John Barry 1939- *WhoE 93*
Hodgson, William Hope 1877-1918 *ScF&FL 92*
Hodgson Steele, Hilda Berneice 1911- *WhoAmW 93*
Hodik, Frantisek 1955- *WhoScE 91-4*
Hodin, Joseph S. 1922- *St&PR 93*
Hodin, William 1920- *St&PR 93*
Hodinko, Robert G. 1934- *St&PR 93*
Hodkinson, Henry Malcolm *WhoScE 91-1*
Hodkinson, Sydney P(hillip) 1934- *Baker 92*
Hodkinson, Sydney Phillip 1934- *WhoAm 92*
Hodne, Thomas Harold, Jr. 1927- *WhoAm 92*
Hodnett, Byron E. 1945- *St&PR 93*
Hodnett, Charles Nicholas 1942- *WhoE 93*
Hodnett, John Phillip 1962- *WhoE 93*
Hodnett, P.F. 1939- *WhoScE 91-3*
Hodnett, Wanda Welch 1946- *WhoAmW 93*
Hodnik, David Francis 1947- *St&PR 93*
Hodo, Edward Douglas *WhoAm 92*
Hodorowicz, Stanislaw Andrzej 1941- *WhoWor 93*
Hodos, James Joseph 1946- *WhoEmL 93*
Hodous, Robert Power 1945- *WhoAm 92*
Hodowal, John Raymond 1945- *St&PR 93*
Hodsdon, Anne C. 1953- *St&PR 93*
Hodsoll, Francis Samuel Monaise 1938- *WhoAm 92*
Hodson, Charles Andrew 1947- *WhoSSW 93*
Hodson, Dale M. *St&PR 93*
Hodson, Ellenor L. *BioIn 17*
Hodson, Frank *WhoScE 91-1*
Hodson, Frank Roy *WhoScE 91-1*
Hodson, Janet Dawn 1947- *WhoEmL 93*
Hodson, Kathleen Karen 1963- *WhoAmW 93*
Hodson, Kenneth Joe 1913- *WhoAm 92*
Hodson, Susan McLoon *Law&B 92*
Hodson, Thomas Francis Xavier *Law&B 92*
Hodson, Thomas William 1946- *St&PR 93, WhoAm 92*
Hodson, William Alan 1935- *WhoAm 92*
Hodus, Herbert J. 1930- *St&PR 93*
Hodzar, Slavko 1923- *WhoScE 91-4*
Hoe, Boon Long 1943- *St&PR 93*
Hoe, Rebecca J. *Law&B 92*
Hoe, Richard March 1939- *WhoSSW 93*
Hoebel, Bartley Gore 1935- *WhoAm 92*
Hoebel, E. Adamson 1906- *IntDcAn*
Hoebel, Edward Adamson 1906- *WhoAm 92*
Hoeber, Francis Walter 1942- *WhoE 93*
Hoeber, Paul B. 1914-1991 *BioIn 17*
Hoeberg, Georg 1872-1950 *Baker 92*
Hoeberichts, Joan B. 1942- *St&PR 93*
Hoechstetter, Harvey 1941- *St&PR 93*
Hoeck, Darlene B. 1956- *WhoEmL 93*
Hoecke, David A. 1938- *St&PR 93*
Hoeckele, Stephan John 1947- *St&PR 93, WhoAm 92*
Hoeckele, Walter J. 1921- *St&PR 93*
Hoecker, Burdet Wesley 1942- *St&PR 93*
Hoecker, David 1948- *WhoAm 92*
Hoecker, F.H. Hartwig 1937- *WhoWor 93*
Hoecker, Wayne *Law&B 92*
Hoedemaker, David C. 1933- *St&PR 93*
Hoefel, H.T. 1927- *St&PR 93*
Hoefer, Margaret J. 1909- *WhoSSW 93*
Hoeffding, Wassily 1914-1991 *BioIn 17*
Hoeffe, Dietmar 1942- *WhoWor 93*
Hoeffner, Warren 1932- *St&PR 93*
Hoefler, Heinz Karl 1949- *WhoWor 93*
Hoefler, William R. 1946- *St&PR 93*
Hoeflich, Charles Hitschler 1914- *WhoAm 92*
Hoeflin, Ronald Kent 1944- *WhoE 93*
Hoefling, John Alan 1925- *WhoAm 92*
Hoefling, John Erwin 1927- *WhoWrEP 92*
Hoefling, Judy Elaine 1946- *WhoEmL 93*
Hoefling, Rudolf Joachim 1942- *WhoAm 92*
Hoeft, Elizabeth Bayless 1942- *WhoAm 92*
Hoeft, Jerald R. 1942- *St&PR 93*
Hoeft, Julius Albert 1946- *WhoAm 92*
Hoeft, Marjorie Claire 1938- *WhoAmW 93*
Hoeft, Richard James 1946- *WhoEmL 93*
Hoeft, Robert Gene 1944- *WhoAm 92*
Hoeg, Donald Francis 1931- *WhoAm 92*
Hoeg, Kaare 1938- *WhoScE 91-4*
Hoeg, Thomas E. 1953- *St&PR 93, WhoIns 93*
Hoegberg, Lars G. 1936- *WhoScE 91-4*
Hoegh, Birthe 1930- *WhoScE 91-2*
Hoegh, Hans 1926- *WhoUN 92*
Hoeh, Theodore J. 1946- *WhoIns 93*
Hoehling, A. A. *BioIn 17*
Hoehling, Adolph A. *BioIn 17*
Hoehn, Elmer L. 1915- *WhoAm 92*
Hoehn, Larry Paul 1942- *WhoSSW 93*
Hoehn, Robert A. 1941- *St&PR 93*
Hoehn, William Edwin 1937- *WhoAm 92*
Hoehnke, Hans-urgen Karl Otto 1925- *WhoWor 93*
Hoehn-Saric, Rudolf 1929- *WhoE 93*
Hoekema, David Andrew 1950- *WhoAm 92*
Hoeksema, Timothy E. *WhoAm 92*
Hoekstra, Djoerd 1934- *St&PR 93*
Hoekstra, Karl E. 1935- *St&PR 93*
Hoekwater, James Warren 1946- *WhoAm 92*
Hoel, David Gerhard 1939- *WhoAm 92*
Hoel, John E. *Law&B 92*
Hoel, Lester A. 1935- *WhoAm 92*
Hoel, Robert Fredrick, Jr. 1949- *WhoEmL 93, WhoSSW 93*
Hoellering, Michael F. 1929- *St&PR 93*
Hoelmer, Karl Heinz 1941- *St&PR 93*
Hoelscher, Crispin *BioIn 17*
Hoelscher, John Henry 1932- *WhoAm 92*
Hoelscher, Ludwig 1907- *Baker 92*
Hoelscher, Margie *BioIn 17*
Hoelscher, Ulf 1942- *Baker 92*
Hoelter, Timothy K. *Law&B 92*
Hoelter, Timothy K. 1946- *St&PR 93, WhoAm 92*
Hoelterhoff, Manuela Vali 1949- *WhoAmW 93*
Hoeltzel, David Albert 1954- *WhoEmL 93*
Hoelzeman, Ronald George 1940- *WhoE 93*
Hoen, Hudson Philip, III 1945- *St&PR 93*
Hoenack, August Frederick 1908- *WhoAm 92*
Hoene, Mary Joan *Law&B 92*
Hoene, Mary Joan 1949- *St&PR 93*
Hoeneisen, Bruce 1944- *WhoWor 93*
Hoene-Wronski, Jozef Maria 1776-1853 *PolBiDi*
Hoengen, Elisabeth 1906- *OxDcOp*
Hoenig, Carol Irene 1955- *WhoAmW 93*
Hoenig, Gerald J. *Law&B 92*
Hoenig, Moses H. 1898-1990 *BioIn 17*
Hoenig, Ronald H. *St&PR 93*
Hoenig, Thomas Michael 1946- *St&PR 93*
Hoenig, William C. 1931- *St&PR 93*
Hoenigswald, Henry M(ax) 1915- *ConAu 39NR*
Hoenigswald, Henry Max 1915- *WhoAm 92, WhoE 93, WhoWor 93*
Hoenmans, Paul John 1932- *St&PR 93, WhoAm 92*
Hoeper, Bonnie Mae 1940- *WhoE 93*
Hoeper, Jeffrey David 1948- *WhoEmL 93, WhoSSW 93*
Hoepker, Wilhelm-Wolfgang 1942- *WhoWor 93*
Hoepner, Carol Ann 1947- *WhoSSW 93*
Hoepner, Erich 1886-1944 *HarEnMi*
Hoepner, Theodore John 1941- *WhoAm 92*
Hoepper, Charles Thomas 1949- *WhoE 93*
Hoeppner, Iona Ruth 1939- *WhoWrEP 92*
Hoeppner, Thomas Joseph 1941- *St&PR 93*
Hoerber, Mary Elizabeth 1960- *WhoEmL 93*
Hoerburger, Felix 1916- *Baker 92*
Hoeree, Arthur (Charles Ernest) 1897-1986 *Baker 92*
Hoerig, Gerald Lee 1943- *WhoAm 92*
Hoerle, James R. 1934- *St&PR 93*
Hoermander, Olof 1923- *WhoScE 91-4*
Hoermann, Helmut Heinz 1941- *St&PR 93*
Hoermann, Klaus Albrecht 1956- *WhoWor 93*
Hoerner, Dennis Russell, Jr. *Law&B 92*
Hoerner, George Milton, Jr. 1929- *WhoE 93*
Hoerner, John Finch 1939- *WhoWor 93*
Hoerner, Robert Jack 1931- *WhoAm 92*
Hoerni, Jean Amedee 1924- *WhoAm 92*
Hoernle, Agnes Winifred 1885-1960 *IntDcAn*
Hoerr, Kenneth Edward 1937- *St&PR 93*
Hoersch, Alice L. 1950- *WhoE 93*
Hoes, Larry M. 1946- *St&PR 93*
Hoes, Tom L. 1953- *St&PR 93*
Hoeschen, B.W. *Law&B 92*
Hoeschen, Dietmar 1938- *WhoScE 91-3, WhoWor 93*
Hoesel, J.D. 1941- *St&PR 93*
Hoesick, Ferdinand 1867-1941 *Baker 92*
Hoessle, Charles Herman 1931- *WhoAm 92*
Hoesslin, Franz von 1885-1946 *Baker 92*
Hoest, Bill 1926-1988 *BioIn 17*
Hoest, Bunny *BioIn 17*
Hoesterey, Richard Kenneth 1942- *St&PR 93*
Hoetker, William James 1932- *WhoAm 92*
Hoeveler, William M. 1922- *BioIn 17, WhoAm 92*
Hoevenaars, J.P.M. 1948- *WhoScE 91-3*
Hoewing, Karen L. *Law&B 92*
Hoexter, Rolf 1927- *WhoE 93*
Hoey, Allen S. 1952- *WhoWrEP 92*
Hoey, Christopher J. *Law&B 92*
Hoey, Clyde Roark, II 1939- *St&PR 93*
Hoey, Edwin Anderson 1930- *WhoAm 92*
Hoey, Elizabeth W. 1941- *St&PR 93*
Hoey, James Joseph 1936- *St&PR 93, WhoAm 92*
Hoey, Marjorie Mary *Law&B 92*
Hoey, Mark Christopher *Law&B 92*
Hoey, Richard Benedict 1943- *WhoAm 92*
Hoey, Rita Marie 1950- *WhoAm 92, WhoEmL 93*
Hof, Henry 1937- *WhoUN 92*
Hof, Liselotte Bertha 1937- *WhoAm 92, WhoE 93*
Hofacker, G. Ludwig 1930- *WhoScE 91-3*
Hofacker, Jane 1957- *WhoAmW 93*
Hofbauer, Rita Anne 1936- *WhoAmW 93*
Hofeldt, John W. 1920- *WhoAm 92*
Hofener, Steven David 1954- *WhoSSW 93*
Hofer, Erwin Helmuth 1949- *WhoWor 93*
Hofer, Hans Werner 1941- *WhoScE 91-3*
Hofer, Hermann Theodor 1938- *WhoWor 93*
Hofer, Josepha *OxDcOp*
Hofer, Judith K. *WhoAm 92, WhoAmW 93*
Hofer, Karl 1878-1955 *BioIn 17*
Hofer, Kathy J. *Law&B 92*
Hofer, Kurt Gabriel 1939- *WhoSSW 93*
Hofer, Mari Ruef 1866- *AmWomPl*
Hofer, Myron Arms 1931- *WhoAm 92*
Hofer, Rudolf *WhoScE 91-4*
Hofert, Jack 1930- *WhoWor 93*
Hoff, B.J. 1940- *WhoWrEP 92*
Hoff, Charles Worthington, III 1934- *St&PR 93, WhoAm 92*
Hoff, David Jordan 1924- *St&PR 93*
Hoff, Donnafred Mary 1903- *WhoWrEP 92*
Hoff, Edwin Frank, Jr. 1938- *WhoWor 93*
Hoff, G.H. *Law&B 92*
Hoff, George L. *Law&B 92*
Hoff, Gerhardt Michael 1930- *St&PR 93, WhoAm 92, WhoIns 93*
Hoff, Henry Bainbridge 1946- *WhoE 93*
Hoff, James Edwin 1932- *WhoAm 92*
Hoff, Jonathan Morind 1955- *WhoAm 92*
Hoff, Julian Theodore 1936- *WhoAm 92*
Hoff, Lawrence C. 1929- *St&PR 93*
Hoff, Lynnette Ann 1951- *WhoAmW 93*
Hoff, Marcian Edward, Jr. 1937- *WhoAm 92*
Hoff, Margo 1912- *BioIn 17, WhoAm 92*

Hoff, Mary Kathryn 1953- *WhoEmL 93*
Hoff, Nancy Kay 1953- *WhoEmL 93*
Hoff, Nanette Hillman *Law&B 92*
Hoff, Nicholas John 1906- *WhoAm 92*
Hoff, Peter Leroy 1940- *WhoE 93*
Hoff, Randal Mark 1952- *St&PR 93*
Hoff, Randy A. 1949- *St&PR 93*
Hoff, Samuel Boyer 1957- *WhoE 93*
Hoff, Samuel R. 1930- *St&PR 93*
Hoff, Syd(ney) 1912- *ConAu 38NR, MajAI [port], SmATA 72 [port]*
Hoff, Sydney 1912- *WhoAm 92*
Hoff, Timothy 1941- *WhoAm 92, WhoSSW 93*
Hoffa, Harlan 1925- *BioIn 17*
Hoffa, Harlan Edward 1925- *WhoAm 92*
Hoffa, James Riddle *BioIn 17*
Hoffa, Jimmy *BioIn 17*
Hoffa, Portland d1990 *BioIn 17*
Hoffait, Alfred 1937- *WhoScE 91-2*
Hoffart, Louis Frank 1939- *St&PR 93*
Hoffbauer, Diane Kaye 1955- *WhoEmL 93*
Hoffberg, Judith A. 1934- *WhoWrEP 92*
Hoffberg, Norman Charles 1947- *St&PR 93*
Hoffberg, Theodore J. 1932- *St&PR 93*
Hoffberg, William E. 1923- *St&PR 93*
Hoffberger, Bruce Silver 1948- *WhoIns 93*
Hoffberger, Charles H. 1912- *St&PR 93*
Hoffberger, Jerold C. 1919- *St&PR 93*
Hoffberger, Jerold Charles 1919- *WhoAm 92*
Hoffberger, LeRoy E. 1925- *St&PR 93*
Hoffberger, LeRoy Edward 1925- *WhoAm 92*
Hoffberger, Stanley A. 1929- *St&PR 93*
Hoffbrand, Allan Victor *WhoScE 91-1*
Hoffding, (Niels) Finn 1899- *Baker 92*
Hoffecker, Pamela Hobbs 1942- *WhoWrEP 92*
Hoffee, Patricia Anne 1937- *WhoAmW 93*
Hoffen, John F., Jr. *Law&B 92*
Hoffenberg, Martin 1945- *St&PR 93, WhoAm 92*
Hoffenberg, Marvin 1914- *WhoAm 92*
Hoffend, Donald A., Jr. 1949- *St&PR 93*
Hoffer, Alma Jeanne 1932- *WhoAmW 93*
Hoffer, Charles R(ussell) 1929- *WhoWrEP 92*
Hoffer, Charles Russell 1929- *WhoAm 92*
Hoffer, John Louis 1931- *St&PR 93, WhoAm 92*
Hoffer, Mary Jane 1947- *WhoAmW 93*
Hoffer, Michael G. 1939- *St&PR 93*
Hoffer, Paul 1895-1949 *Baker 92*
Hoffer, Paul B. 1939- *WhoAm 92*
Hoffer, Robert M. 1921- *St&PR 93*
Hoffer, Robert Morrison 1921- *WhoAm 92*
Hoffer, Stuart H. 1937- *St&PR 93*
Hoffer, Thomas William 1938- *WhoSSW 93*
Hoffer, William A. 1949- *St&PR 93*
Hoffer, William Albert 1949- *WhoEmL 93*
Hoffert, J. Stan 1947- *St&PR 93*
Hoffert, J. Stanley *Law&B 92*
Hoffert, J. Stanley 1947- *WhoIns 93*
Hoffert, Martin Irving 1938- *WhoAm 92*
Hoffert, Paul Washington 1923- *WhoE 93*
Hoffgen, Marga 1921- *Baker 92*
Hoffheimer, Craig 1950- *St&PR 93*
Hoffheimer, Daniel Joseph 1950- *WhoEmL 93, WhoWor 93*
Hoffheimer, James M. 1955- *St&PR 93*
Hoffinger, Roy E., Sr. *Law&B 92*
Hoffius, Stephen Glenn 1950- *WhoSSW 93*
Hoffleit, Ellen Dorrit 1907- *WhoAm 92*
Hofflund, Paul 1928- *WhoWor 93*
Hoffman, Abbie *BioIn 17*
Hoffman, Adonis Edward 1954- *WhoWor 93*
Hoffman, Alan B. 1938- *St&PR 93*
Hoffman, Alan Jay 1948- *WhoE 93, WhoEmL 93*
Hoffman, Alan Jerome 1924- *WhoAm 92*
Hoffman, Alfred John 1917- *WhoAm 92*
Hoffman, Alice *BioIn 17*
Hoffman, Alice 1952- *CurBio 92 [port], ScF&FL 92*
Hoffman, Allan Augustus 1934- *WhoSSW 93*
Hoffman, Allan Sachs 1932- *WhoAm 92*
Hoffman, Allan Stuart 1945- *WhoE 93*
Hoffman, Andrew Jay 1956- *ConAu 138*
Hoffman, Andy *ConAu 138*
Hoffman, Ann Fleisher 1942- *WhoAmW 93*
Hoffman, Anna Rosenberg 1902-1983 *BioIn 17*
Hoffman, Annette Kathleen 1963- *WhoE 93*
Hoffman, Arlene Faun 1941- *WhoAmW 93*
Hoffman, Arthur Wolf 1921- *WhoAm 92*
Hoffman, Audrey Iris 1938- *WhoE 93*
Hoffman, B. Carole *Law&B 92*
Hoffman, Barbara A. 1940- *WhoAmW 93*
Hoffman, Barbara Kriete 1963- *WhoAmW 93*
Hoffman, Barry H. *Law&B 92*
Hoffman, Barry P. *Law&B 92*
Hoffman, Beth Lynn 1943- *WhoAmW 93*
Hoffman, Bradley J. 1961- *St&PR 93*
Hoffman, C.N., Jr. 1918- *St&PR 93*
Hoffman, C. Roger *Law&B 92*
Hoffman, Carl *ScF&FL 92*
Hoffman, Carol Knight 1943- *WhoAmW 93*
Hoffman, Carolyn 1951- *WhoAmW 93*
Hoffman, Charles *Law&B 92*
Hoffman, Charles E. 1954- *ScF&FL 92*
Hoffman, Charles J. 1929- *St&PR 93*
Hoffman, Charles Steven 1949- *WhoAm 92*
Hoffman, Christian Matthew 1944- *WhoAm 92*
Hoffman, Claudia Ann 1952- *WhoAmW 93*
Hoffman, Curtis P. *St&PR 93*
Hoffman, D. 1932- *St&PR 93*
Hoffman, Dale Marland 1940- *WhoSSW 93*
Hoffman, Dan Lawrence 1946- *WhoE 93*
Hoffman, Daniel 1923- *ScF&FL 92, WhoWrEP 92*
Hoffman, Daniel Gerard 1923- *WhoAm 92*
Hoffman, Daniel Paul 1912- *WhoWrEP 92*
Hoffman, Daniel Steven 1931- *WhoAm 92*
Hoffman, Daniel W. 1952- *St&PR 93*
Hoffman, Darleane Christian 1926- *WhoAm 92, WhoAmW 93*
Hoffman, David Allen 1962- *WhoE 93*
Hoffman, David John 1944- *WhoE 93*
Hoffman, David N. 1910- *St&PR 93*
Hoffman, David Robert 1934- *WhoE 93*
Hoffman, Dean Allen 1949- *WhoWrEP 92*
Hoffman, Diane J. 1943- *St&PR 93*
Hoffman, Donald B. 1911- *BioIn 17*
Hoffman, Donald Bertrand 1939- *WhoE 93*
Hoffman, Donald D. *BioIn 17*
Hoffman, Donald David 1955- *WhoWor 93*
Hoffman, Donald Howard 1933- *St&PR 93*
Hoffman, Donald M. 1935- *WhoAm 92*
Hoffman, Donald Richard 1943- *WhoSSW 93*
Hoffman, Dorothy Shaw 1944- *WhoAmW 93*
Hoffman, Dustin 1937- *BioIn 17, IntDcF 2-3*
Hoffman, Dustin Lee 1937- *WhoAm 92, WhoWor 93*
Hoffman, Earl Kenneth 1944- *WhoE 93*
Hoffman, Edward Fenno 1916-1991 *BioIn 17*
Hoffman, Edward Francis 1948- *WhoEmL 93*
Hoffman, Edward Michael 1945- *WhoE 93*
Hoffman, Edward Richard, III 1928- *WhoSSW 93*
Hoffman, Edward Robert 1923- *St&PR 93*
Hoffman, Edwin K. 1922- *St&PR 93*
Hoffman, Edwin Lippincott *Law&B 92*
Hoffman, Edwin P. *BioIn 17*
Hoffman, Edwin Philip 1942- *WhoAm 92*
Hoffman, Elin M. *St&PR 93*
Hoffman, Elizabeth Hanson 1946- *WhoAmW 93*
Hoffman, Ercell H. 1941- *WhoWrEP 92*
Hoffman, Erica A. *Law&B 92*
Hoffman, Ethan *BioIn 17*
Hoffman, Eva *BioIn 17*
Hoffman, Floyd G. *Law&B 92*
Hoffman, Floyd Gerry 1943- *St&PR 93*
Hoffman, Francois-Benoit 1760-1828 *OxDcOp*
Hoffman, Frank P. *Law&B 92*
Hoffman, Franklin David, Jr. 1945- *WhoAm 92*
Hoffman, Frederick 1903- *St&PR 93*
Hoffman, Frederick 1937- *WhoSSW 93*
Hoffman, G.L. *St&PR 93*
Hoffman, Gary *MiSFD 9*
Hoffman, Gary Keith *Law&B 92*
Hoffman, Gary Wayne *Law&B 92*
Hoffman, Gene 1927- *WhoAm 92*
Hoffman, Gene D. 1927- *St&PR 93*
Hoffman, Gloria L. 1933- *WhoWrEP 92*
Hoffman, Gloria Levy 1933- *WhoWor 93*
Hoffman, Grace (Goldie) 1925- *Baker 92*
Hoffman, Harold Wayne 1930- *WhoAm 92*
Hoffman, Harry Theodore 1927- *BioIn 17*
Hoffman, Harvey Bradford *Law&B 92*
Hoffman, Hazel R. *Law&B 92*
Hoffman, Hebert W. *Law&B 92*
Hoffman, Helga 1938- *WhoUN 92*
Hoffman, Henry William 1925- *WhoWrEP 92*
Hoffman, Herbert E. *Law&B 92*
Hoffman, Herbert H(einz) 1928- *ConAu 40NR*
Hoffman, Herbert W. 1939- *St&PR 93*
Hoffman, Howard S. 1925- *BioIn 17*
Hoffman, Howard Stanley 1925- *WhoAm 92*
Hoffman, Ira Eliot 1952- *WhoEmL 93*
Hoffman, Irwin 1924- *WhoAm 92*
Hoffman, Jack Leroy 1922- *WhoAm 92*
Hoffman, Jacqueline 1947- *WhoAmW 93*
Hoffman, James E. *Law&B 92*
Hoffman, James L., Jr. *WhoAm 92, WhoWor 93*
Hoffman, James Paul 1943- *WhoWor 93*
Hoffman, James R. 1932- *WhoAm 92*
Hoffman, Jane E. 1953- *St&PR 93*
Hoffman, Janet N. 1936- *WhoAmW 93*
Hoffman, Jeffrey Marc 1954- *WhoE 93*
Hoffman, Jeffrey William 1952- *St&PR 93*
Hoffman, Jennifer Isobel 1948- *WhoAmW 93*
Hoffman, Jerry Carl 1943- *St&PR 93*
Hoffman, Jerzy 1932- *DrEEuF*
Hoffman, Joel Elihu 1937- *WhoAm 92*
Hoffman, Joel Jeffrey 1944- *St&PR 93*
Hoffman, John Ernest, Jr. 1934- *WhoAm 92*
Hoffman, John Fletcher 1946- *WhoEmL 93*
Hoffman, John R. *Law&B 92*
Hoffman, John Raleigh 1926- *WhoAm 92*
Hoffman, John Raymond 1945- *St&PR 93, WhoAm 92*
Hoffman, Joseph Anthony 1933- *WhoAm 92*
Hoffman, Joseph Frederick 1925- *WhoAm 92*
Hoffman, Joyce N. 1952- *WhoIns 93*
Hoffman, Judy Greenblatt 1932- *WhoAmW 93, WhoWor 93*
Hoffman, Julien Ivor Ellis 1925- *WhoAm 92*
Hoffman, Karen Sue 1953- *WhoAmW 93*
Hoffman, Karla Ann 1953- *WhoE 93, WhoEmL 93*
Hoffman, Karla Leigh 1948- *WhoSSW 93*
Hoffman, Kenneth D. *Law&B 92*
Hoffman, Kenneth D. 1928- *St&PR 93*
Hoffman, Kenneth Myron 1930- *WhoAm 92*
Hoffman, Kenneth O. *St&PR 93*
Hoffman, Kevin *Law&B 92*
Hoffman, Larry J. 1930- *WhoAm 92*
Hoffman, Lawrence J. *St&PR 93*
Hoffman, Lee 1932- *ScF&FL 92*
Hoffman, Linda A. *Law&B 92*
Hoffman, Linda June 1944- *WhoAmW 93*
Hoffman, Linda R. 1940- *WhoAmW 93*
Hoffman, Lloyd O. 1927- *St&PR 93*
Hoffman, Lois Wladis 1929- *WhoAmW 93*
Hoffman, Lou Duane 1946- *WhoEmL 93*
Hoffman, Lowell William 1954- *WhoE 93*
Hoffman, M. *WhoScE 91-4*
Hoffman, Mandy Lippman 1956- *WhoE 93*
Hoffman, Margaret W. 1954- *St&PR 93*
Hoffman, Marie Therese 1953- *WhoAmW 93*
Hoffman, Marilyn Friedman *WhoAm 92, WhoE 93*
Hoffman, Mark B. *St&PR 93*
Hoffman, Mark Leslie 1952- *WhoEmL 93*
Hoffman, Marshall 1942- *WhoWrEP 92*
Hoffman, Martin 1933- *St&PR 93*
Hoffman, Martin Leon 1924- *WhoAm 92*
Hoffman, Marvin Kenneth 1945- *WhoSSW 93*
Hoffman, Mary Catherine 1923- *WhoAmW 93*
Hoffman, Mary Juanita 1933- *WhoAmW 93*
Hoffman, Maryhelen H. Paulick 1943- *WhoAm 92*
Hoffman, Max 1869-1927 *HarEnMi*
Hoffman, Melchior d1543? *BioIn 17*
Hoffman, Melvin B. 1919- *St&PR 93*
Hoffman, Merle Holly 1946- *WhoAm 92, WhoAmW 93, WhoE 93, WhoEmL 93*
Hoffman, Michael *MiSFD 9*
Hoffman, Michael Duncan 1945- *WhoAm 92*
Hoffman, Michael Eugene 1942- *WhoAm 92*
Hoffman, Michael George 1947- *St&PR 93*
Hoffman, Michael Jerome 1939- *WhoAm 92*
Hoffman, Michael W. 1948- *St&PR 93*
Hoffman, Michel *BioIn 17*
Hoffman, Mitchell Wade 1954- *WhoEmL 93*
Hoffman, Nanci L. 1948- *WhoIns 93*
Hoffman, Neil James 1938- *WhoAm 92*
Hoffman, Nina Kiriki 1955- *ScF&FL 92*
Hoffman, Oscar Allen 1920- *WhoAm 92*
Hoffman, Patricia Ann *Law&B 92*
Hoffman, Patricia Ann 1962- *WhoAmW 93*
Hoffman, Paul *ScF&FL 92*
Hoffman, Paul Felix 1941- *WhoAm 92*
Hoffman, Paul Roger 1934- *WhoAm 92, WhoE 93*
Hoffman, Paul W. 1925- *St&PR 93*
Hoffman, Peter *MiSFD 9*
Hoffman, Peter Conrad Werner 1930- *WhoWrEP 92*
Hoffman, Peter Ivan 1954- *WhoE 93*
Hoffman, Peter M. *BioIn 17*
Hoffman, Peter Toll 1946- *WhoAm 92*
Hoffman, Philip Andrew 1931- *WhoAm 92, WhoWor 93*
Hoffman, Philip Eisinger 1908- *WhoAm 92*
Hoffman, Philip Guthrie 1915- *WhoAm 92*
Hoffman, Phoebe 1894- *AmWomPl*
Hoffman, Ralph G. *St&PR 93*
Hoffman, Randy Michael 1965- *WhoEmL 93, WhoWor 93*
Hoffman, Richard 1831-1909 *Baker 92*
Hoffman, Richard Bruce 1947- *WhoAm 92*
Hoffman, Richard E. 1932- *St&PR 93*
Hoffman, Richard K. 1928- *St&PR 93*
Hoffman, Richard M. 1942- *WhoAm 92*
Hoffman, Richard William 1918- *WhoAm 92*
Hoffman, Roald 1937- *PolBiDi*
Hoffman, Robert B. 1947- *WhoIns 93*
Hoffman, Robert Philip 1945- *WhoE 93*
Hoffman, Roger P. 1944- *St&PR 93*
Hoffman, Ronald 1945- *WhoAm 92*
Hoffman, Ronald Bruce 1939- *WhoAm 92, WhoSSW 93*
Hoffman, Ronald H. 1947- *St&PR 93*
Hoffman, Ronald Robert 1934- *St&PR 93, WhoAm 92*
Hoffman, Ronne *Law&B 92*
Hoffman, Rosemary Ann 1948- *WhoAmW 93*
Hoffman, Roy A., Jr. 1940- *WhoSSW 93*
Hoffman, S. David 1922- *WhoAm 92*
Hoffman, S. Joseph 1920- *WhoAm 92*
Hoffman, Saul 1931- *WhoE 93*
Hoffman, Sharon L. *WhoAmW 93*
Hoffman, Shirley B. *ScF&FL 92*
Hoffman, Stephen M. 1945- *St&PR 93*
Hoffman, Stephen Max, Jr. 1949- *WhoE 93*
Hoffman, Steven Craig *Law&B 92*
Hoffman, Sue Ellen 1945- *WhoAmW 93*
Hoffman, Teresa Esther 1957- *WhoAm 92*
Hoffman, Thomas 1945- *WhoWor 93*
Hoffman, Thomas D. *Law&B 92*
Hoffman, Thomas E. *Law&B 92*
Hoffman, Timothy Herman 1953- *WhoE 93*
Hoffman, Valerie 1953- *ScF&FL 92*
Hoffman, Valerie Jane 1953- *WhoAmW 93, WhoEmL 93*
Hoffman, Walter Edward 1907- *WhoAm 92, WhoSSW 93*
Hoffman, Wayne Edwin 1929- *WhoSSW 93*
Hoffman, Wayne Leslie, Jr. 1960- *WhoE 93*
Hoffman, Wayne Melvin 1923- *WhoAm 92*
Hoffman, William 1925- *WhoAm 92*
Hoffman, William Albert 1928- *WhoE 93*
Hoffman, William Earl, Jr. 1955- *WhoSSW 93*
Hoffman, William G. 1937- *WhoIns 93*
Hoffman, William K. *Law&B 92*
Hoffman, William M. 1939- *WhoAm 92*
Hoffman, William O. 1943- *St&PR 93*
Hoffmann, Alex *St&PR 93*
Hoffmann, Antonia 1842-1897 *PolBiDi*
Hoffmann, Arnold 1915-1991 *BioIn 17*
Hoffmann, Barry L. 1946- *St&PR 93*
Hoffmann, Bernhard 1932- *St&PR 93*
Hoffmann, Berud 1940- *WhoScE 91-3*
Hoffmann, Betty L. *Law&B 92*
Hoffmann, Bruno 1913-1991 *Baker 92*
Hoffmann, Camille Oliver- *BioIn 17*
Hoffmann, Carol Tomb 1952- *WhoAmW 93*
Hoffmann, Cecil *BioIn 17*
Hoffmann, Charles Wesley 1929- *WhoAm 92*
Hoffmann, Christoph *Law&B 92*
Hoffmann, Christoph L. 1944- *St&PR 93*
Hoffmann, Christoph Ludwig 1944- *WhoAm 92*
Hoffmann, Cindy Jane 1946- *WhoWrEP 92*
Hoffmann, Curtis H. 1958- *ScF&FL 92*
Hoffmann, D. 1947- *WhoScE 91-3*
Hoffmann, David 1909-1990 *BioIn 17*
Hoffmann, Dennis Erwin 1942- *St&PR 93*
Hoffmann, Dietrich Karl 1924- *WhoE 93*
Hoffmann, Donald 1933- *WhoAm 92*
Hoffmann, E.T.A. 1776-1822 *BioIn 17, MagSWL [port], OxDcOp*

Hoffmann, E(rnst) T(heodor) A(madeus) 1776-1822 *Baker 92 IntDcOp [port]*
Hoffmann, Eivind 1943- *WhoUN 92*
Hoffmann, Ernst Theodor Amadeus 1776-1822 *BioIn 17*
Hoffmann, Friedrich Gottlob 1741-c. 1806 *BioIn 17*
Hoffmann, Grace 1925- *OxDcOp*
Hoffmann, Gunter Georg 1954- *WhoWor 93*
Hoffmann, Gunter Martin 1923- *WhoScE 91-3*
Hoffmann, Hans 1902-1949 *Baker 92*
Hoffmann, Hans E.W. 1934- *WhoScE 91-3*
Hoffmann, Hans Martin Rudolf 1934- *WhoScE 91-3*
Hoffmann, Heinrich August 1798-1874 *Baker 92*
Hoffmann, Heinz Katl 1918- *WhoE 93*
Hoffmann, Ilse 1934- *WhoE 93*
Hoffmann, Janice Elaine 1948- *WhoAmW 93*
Hoffmann, Joan Carol 1934- *WhoAmW 93*
Hoffmann, John Baldwin 1940- *St&PR 93*
Hoffmann, Leanne Renee 1964- *WhoAmW 93*
Hoffmann, Leon Roger 1949- *St&PR 93*
Hoffmann, Louis Gerhard 1932- *WhoAm 92*
Hoffmann, Luc 1923- *WhoScE 91-2*
Hoffmann, Lutz 1934- *WhoWor 93*
Hoffmann, Malcolm Arthur 1912- *WhoAm 92*
Hoffmann, Manfred Walter 1938- *WhoSSW 93*
Hoffmann, Mark Stephen *Law&B 92*
Hoffmann, Martin R. *Law&B 92*
Hoffmann, Martin R. 1932- *WhoAm 92*
Hoffmann, Mary Linn 1940- *WhoAmW 93*
Hoffmann, Michael Richard 1947- *WhoEmL 93*
Hoffmann, Nancy Larraine *WhoAmW 93*
Hoffmann, Oswald Carl Julius 1913- *WhoAm 92*
Hoffmann, Paul Oliver- *BioIn 17*
Hoffmann, Peter Toll 1946- *WhoEmL 93*
Hoffmann, Przemyslaw-Marian 1922- *WhoScE 91-4*
Hoffmann, Randall Walrath d1990 *BioIn 17*
Hoffmann, Reinhard W. 1933- *WhoScE 91-3*
Hoffmann, Reinhard Walther 1933- *WhoWor 93*
Hoffmann, Richard 1925- *Baker 92*
Hoffmann, Richard Arthur 1941- *WhoSSW 93*
Hoffmann, Richard W. *Law&B 92*
Hoffmann, Roald 1937- *BioIn 17, WhoAm 92, WhoE 93, WhoWor 93*
Hoffmann, Robert *Law&B 92*
Hoffmann, Robert George *Law&B 92*
Hoffmann, Robert Shaw 1929- *WhoAm 92*
Hoffmann, Rudolf W. 1941- *WhoScE 91-3*
Hoffmann, Thomas Russell 1933- *WhoAm 92*
Hoffmann, Ulrich 1938- *WhoScE 91-3*
Hoffmann, Werner 1955- *WhoScE 91-3*
Hoffmann, William Frederick 1933- *WhoAm 92*
Hoffmann, William Frederick, III 1940- *WhoE 93*
Hoffmann, Wolfgang 1935- *WhoScE 91-3*
Hoffmann-Krayer, Eduard 1864-1936 *IntDcAn*
Hoffmann-Ostenhof, Otto 1914- *WhoWor 93*
Hoffmaster, Jon D. *St&PR 93*
Hoffmaster, Nancy Jo Clement 1940- *WhoAmW 93*
Hoffmaster, Stephanie Joan 1953- *WhoEmL 93*
Hoffmeier, Kathy Ann 1956- *WhoEmL 93*
Hoffmeister, David Michael *Law&B 92*
Hoffmeister, Donald Frederick 1916- *WhoAm 92*
Hoffmeister, Franz Anton 1754-1812 *Baker 92*
Hoffmeister, Hans 1932- *WhoScE 91-3*
Hoffmeister, James F. 1944- *St&PR 93*
Hoffmeister, Jana Marie *WhoAmW 93, WhoE 93*
Hoffmeyer, Charles Kenneth 1914- *WhoSSW 93*
Hoffmeyer, Erik 1924- *WhoWor 93*
Hoffner, Brian Kent 1961- *WhoE 93*
Hoffner, Larry *BioIn 17*
Hoffner, Marilyn 1929- *WhoAmW 93, WhoE 93*
Hoffner, Robert A. 1942- *St&PR 93*
Hoffner, Steve *BioIn 17*
Hoffnung, Audrey Sonia 1928- *WhoAmW 93*
Hofford, Meredith 1952- *WhoEmL 93*
Hoffs, Susanna *BioIn 17*
Hoffs, Tamar Simon *MiSFD 9*
Hoffstetter, Roman 1742-1815 *Baker 92*
Hoffstot, Henry Phipps, Jr. 1917- *WhoAm 92*
Hofgren, Daniel W. d1990 *BioIn 17*
Hofhaimer, Paul 1459-1537 *Baker 92*
Hofhaymer, Paul 1459-1537 *Baker 92*
Hofheimer, Gilbert 1943- *St&PR 93*
Hofheimer, Hannah Falk d1991 *BioIn 17*
Hofherr, Halfred Martin *Law&B 92*
Hofland, John Pieter Wilhelmus 1940- *WhoE 93*
Hofle, Gerhard 1940- *WhoScE 91-3*
Hofler, Peter Karl 1905-1952 *BioIn 17*
Hofler, Thomas J. 1955- *BioIn 17*
Hofley, Carole S. *St&PR 93*
Hofley, Norman H. 1932- *St&PR 93*
Hofling, A. Alden 1929- *St&PR 93*
Hofman, Albert 1951- *WhoScE 91-3*
Hofman, Georges 1942- *WhoScE 91-2*
Hofman, Hans 1923- *WhoWrEP 92*
Hofman, Leonard John 1928- *WhoAm 92*
Hofman, Marcel J.A. 1934- *WhoScE 91-2*
Hofman, Peter David 1946- *St&PR 93*
Hofman, Shlomo 1909- *Baker 92*
Hofman, Steven Ira 1953- *WhoEmL 93*
Hofmann, Adele Dellenbaugh 1926- *WhoAm 92, WhoAmW 93*
Hofmann, Alan Frederick 1931- *WhoAm 92*
Hofmann, Albert Josef 1933- *WhoWor 93*
Hofmann, Albrecht *WhoScE 91-3*
Hofmann, Arthur G. *Law&B 92*
Hofmann, Bernard M. 1934- *St&PR 93*
Hofmann, Bernd 1953- *WhoWor 93*
Hofmann, Casimir 1842-1911 *Baker 92, PolBiDi*
Hofmann, Daniel 1930- *St&PR 93*
Hofmann, Dieter *WhoScE 91-1*
Hofmann, Eberhard 1930- *WhoScE 91-3*
Hofmann, Edward Hamilton 1946- *WhoSSW 93*
Hofmann, Evita Sixta Maria 1954- *WhoAmW 93*
Hofmann, Franz 1942- *WhoScE 91-3*
Hofmann, Frieder Karl 1949- *WhoWor 93*
Hofmann, Gert *BioIn 17*
Hofmann, Gustav 1921- *WhoScE 91-3*
Hofmann, Hanns P.K. 1923- *WhoScE 91-3*
Hofmann, Hans 1880-1966 *BioIn 17*
Hofmann, Harald 1932- *WhoWor 93*
Hofmann, Heinrich (Karl Johann) 1842-1902 *Baker 92*
Hofmann, Hellmut Robert Hugo 1921- *WhoScE 91-4*
Hofmann, Herbert Charles 1942- *St&PR 93*
Hofmann, J. Michael 1943- *St&PR 93*
Hofmann, John Richard, Jr. 1922- *WhoAm 92*
Hofmann, Josef 1876-1957 *Baker 92*
Hofmann, Jozef Casimir 1876-1957 *PolBiDi*
Hofmann, Klaus 1911- *WhoAm 92*
Hofmann, Klaus D. 1936- *WhoWor 93*
Hofmann, Leopold 1738-1793 *Baker 92*
Hofmann, Marcia Lynn *WhoAmW 93*
Hofmann, Paul *WhoScE 91-3*
Hofmann, Paul Bernard 1941- *WhoAm 92*
Hofmann, Peter 1944- *Baker 92, OxDcOp*
Hofmann, Robert D. 1960- *St&PR 93*
Hofmann, Siegfried 1938- *WhoWor 93*
Hofmann, Theo 1924- *WhoAm 92*
Hofmann, Thomas J. 1942- *St&PR 93*
Hofmann, Ulrich 1931- *WhoScE 91-3*
Hofmann, Wilfred A.O. 1931- *WhoWor 93*
Hofmann, William F., III 1943- *WhoE 93*
Hofmannsthal, Hugo von 1874-1929 *DcLB 118 [port], IntDcOp [port]*
Hofmannsthal, Hugo von 1874-1929 *OxDcOp*
Hofmans, Cornelis M. 1929- *St&PR 93*
Hofmeister, Adolf c. 1802-1870 *See* Hofmeister, Friedrich 1782-1864 *Baker 92*
Hofmeister, Adolf K. 1936- *St&PR 93*
Hofmeister, Friedrich 1782-1864 *Baker 92*
Hofmeister, Rachel Ann 1965- *WhoAmW 93*
Hofmeyer, Johan 1952- *WhoUN 92*
Hofmeyr, Gray *MiSFD 9*
Hofmokl, Tomasz 1936- *WhoScE 91-4*
Hofnung, Maurice J. 1942- *WhoScE 91-2*
Hofnung, Maurice Jacky 1942- *WhoWor 93*
Hofrichter, David Alan 1948- *WhoEmL 93, WhoWor 93*
Hofrichter, Lawrence S. *Law&B 92*
Hofrichter, Paul *ScF&FL 92*
Hofschneider, Peter Hans 1929- *WhoScE 91-3*
Hofsinde, Robert 1902-1973 *BioIn 17*
Hofsiss, Jack 1950- *MiSFD 9*
Hofstad, Alice May 1948- *WhoAmW 93*
Hofstad, Ole 1949- *WhoScE 91-4*
Hofstadter, Douglas R. 1945- *BioIn 17*
Hofstadter, Douglas Richard 1945- *WhoAm 92*
Hofstadter, Robert 1915-1990 *BioIn 17*
Hofstaedter, Charles Andreas 1961- *WhoSSW 93*
Hofstatter, Leopold 1902- *WhoAm 92*
Hofstatter, Stephen Lewis 1958- *WhoEmL 93*
Hofstede, David *ScF&FL 92*
Hofstedt, Klaus Oskar 1937- *WhoWor 93*
Hofstein, Riquette *BioIn 17*
Hofstetter, Edward Max 1932- *WhoE 93*
Hofstetter, Eleanore Ottilia 1939- *WhoE 93*
Hofstetter, Hans 1947- *WhoScE 91-4*
Hofstetter, Kenneth John 1940- *WhoAm 92, WhoSSW 93*
Hofstrand, Judith Lynn 1941- *WhoAmW 93*
Hoft, Lynne Ann 1945- *WhoAmW 93*
Hoft, Thomas W. *Law&B 92*
Hofton, Andrew Nigel 1944- *WhoWor 93*
Hog, Erik 1932- *WhoScE 91-2*
Hogan, Ben 1912- *BioIn 17, WhoAm 92*
Hogan, Brian Joseph 1943- *WhoE 93*
Hogan, Charles Carlton 1921- *WhoE 93, WhoWor 93*
Hogan, Clarence Lester 1920- *WhoAm 92, WhoWor 93*
Hogan, Claude Hollis 1920- *WhoAm 92*
Hogan, Curtis Jule 1926- *WhoAm 92*
Hogan, D.M. 1947- *St&PR 93*
Hogan, Daniel Bolten 1943- *WhoE 93*
Hogan, Daniel E., Jr. *BioIn 17*
Hogan, Daniel E., Jr. 1917- *St&PR 93*
Hogan, Daniel Michael 1950- *WhoAm 92, WhoEmL 93*
Hogan, David 1953- *ScF&FL 92*
Hogan, Deborah Sue 1957- *WhoAmW 93*
Hogan, Diarmuid M. 1944- *St&PR 93*
Hogan, Donald Jack 1945- *St&PR 93*
Hogan, Douglas J. *Law&B 92*
Hogan, Edward Joseph 1950- *WhoEmL 93*
Hogan, Edward Leo 1932- *WhoAm 92*
Hogan, Edward Robert 1939- *WhoE 93*
Hogan, Ellen Joan 1945- *St&PR 93*
Hogan, Ernest *ScF&FL 92*
Hogan, Francis d1990 *BioIn 17*
Hogan, Francis P. 1941- *St&PR 93*
Hogan, Francis Xavier 1927- *WhoUN 92*
Hogan, Gerald P. 1946- *WhoIns 93*
Hogan, Gerald W. *Law&B 92*
Hogan, Guy Theodore 1933- *WhoE 93*
Hogan, Henry Leon, III 1920- *WhoAm 92*
Hogan, Henry M., Jr. 1932- *St&PR 93*
Hogan, Hulk *BioIn 17*
Hogan, Ilona Modly 1947- *WhoAm 92*
Hogan, James Charles 1936- *WhoAm 92*
Hogan, James Edward 1944- *WhoE 93*
Hogan, James L. 1930- *St&PR 93*
Hogan, James P. *BioIn 17*
Hogan, James P. 1941- *ScF&FL 92*
Hogan, James W. 1948- *St&PR 93*
Hogan, Jerry Harold 1937- *St&PR 93*
Hogan, John *BioIn 17*
Hogan, John Charles 1953- *WhoSSW 93*
Hogan, John D. 1927- *WhoIns 93*
Hogan, John Donald 1927- *WhoAm 92*
Hogan, John Francis 1940- *WhoWor 93*
Hogan, John H. 1946- *St&PR 93*
Hogan, John Joseph 1951- *WhoSSW 93*
Hogan, John Paul 1919- *WhoAm 92*
Hogan, John Thomas 1943- *WhoE 93*
Hogan, John W., Jr. *Law&B 92*
Hogan, Joseph Thomas 1943- *WhoWor 93*
Hogan, Judith R. *Law&B 92*
Hogan, Judy 1937- *ConAu 39NR*
Hogan, Judy Fordham 1937- *WhoWrEP 92*
Hogan, Karen Cooper 1956- *WhoSSW 93*
Hogan, Katherine *Law&B 92*
Hogan, Kenneth William 1944- *St&PR 93*
Hogan, Linda 1947- *ConLC 73 [port]*
Hogan, Linda K. 1947- *WhoWrEP 92*
Hogan, Linda Marie 1955- *WhoE 93*
Hogan, Lisa Edwards 1964- *WhoAmW 93, WhoSSW 93*
Hogan, Lois Sekerak 1948- *WhoE 93*
Hogan, Marie F. *Law&B 92*
Hogan, Mark 1931- *WhoAm 92*
Hogan, Mark D. 1957- *St&PR 93*
Hogan, Mark James 1956- *WhoEmL 93*
Hogan, Mary Ellyn R. *Law&B 92*
Hogan, Mervin Booth 1906- *WhoAm 92, WhoWor 93*
Hogan, Michael J. *Law&B 92*
Hogan, Michael Ray 1953- *St&PR 93*
Hogan, Patricia Susan 1944- *St&PR 93*
Hogan, Patrick Michael *Law&B 92*
Hogan, Paul *WhoWor 93*
Hogan, Paul 1940- *QDrFCA 92 [port]*
Hogan, Paul 1941?- *BioIn 17*
Hogan, Robert Ball 1947- *St&PR 93*
Hogan, Robert Francis, Jr. 1956- *WhoEmL 93*
Hogan, Robert Henry 1926- *WhoAm 92*
Hogan, Robert J. 1897-1963 *ScF&FL 92*
Hogan, Robert N.D. 1938- *St&PR 93*
Hogan, Roberta *BioIn 17*
Hogan, Ronald P. 1940- *WhoSSW 93*
Hogan, Terrence Patrick 1937- *WhoAm 92*
Hogan, Thomas David *Law&B 92*
Hogan, Thomas F. 1938- *CngDr 91*
Hogan, Thomas Francis 1938- *WhoAm 92, WhoE 93*
Hogan, Thomas Harlan 1944- *WhoAm 92*
Hogan, Thomas John 1946- *WhoAm 92*
Hogan, Thomas Joseph 1955- *St&PR 93*
Hogan, Thomas Joseph 1957- *WhoE 93*
Hogan, Thomas Michael 1941- *St&PR 93*
Hogan, Timothy J. *Law&B 92*
Hogan, Timothy J. 1951- *St&PR 93*
Hogan, William C. *Law&B 92*
Hogan, William Robert 1927- *St&PR 93*
Hogan, William T. 1933- *WhoE 93*
Hogan-Murphy, Moira Anita *Law&B 92*
Hogans, Mack L. 1949- *St&PR 93*
Hogarth, Burne 1911- *BioIn 17, WhoAm 92, WhoWor 93*
Hogarth, Cyril Alfred *WhoScE 91-1*
Hogarth, Emmett *ConTFT 10*
Hogarth, George 1783-1870 *Baker 92*
Hogarth, Peter 1945- *ScF&FL 92*
Hogarth, Robert James 1948- *WhoEmL 93*
Hogarth, William 1697-1764 *BioIn 17*
Hogarty, Richard Anthony 1933- *WhoE 93*
Hogate, Julian D., Mrs. *AmWomPl*
Hogberg, Carl Gustav 1913- *WhoE 93*
Hogberg, Lars *WhoScE 91-4*
Hogbin, Herbert Ian 1904-1989 *BioIn 17*
Hogbin, Myrtle 1943- *WhoSSW 93*
Hoge, Douglas L. 1921- *St&PR 93*
Hoge, Franz Joseph 1944- *WhoAm 92*
Hoge, Geraldine Rajacich 1937- *WhoAmW 93*
Hoge, James F., Jr. 1935- *St&PR 93*
Hoge, James Fulton, Jr. 1935- *WhoAm 92, WhoE 93*
Hoge, John Herman 1932- *St&PR 93*
Hoge, Marlin Boyd 1914- *WhoSSW 93*
Hoge, Robert Clyde 1947- *St&PR 93*
Hoge, Warren M. 1941- *WhoAm 92*
Hoge, William Hamilton d1990 *BioIn 17*
Hogeboom, Jan C. 1944- *St&PR 93*
Hogeboom, Patricia Ann Schrack 1937- *WhoAmW 93*
Hogeman, Hubert H., III *Law&B 92*
Hogen, Glenn A. 1928- *St&PR 93*
Hogenauer, Gregor 1933- *WhoScE 91-4*
Hogenboom, N.G. 1937- *WhoScE 91-3*
Hogenkamp, Henricus Petrus Cornelis 1925- *WhoAm 92*
Hogensen, Margaret Hiner 1920- *WhoAmW 93, WhoE 93, WhoWor 93*
Hogg, Brian William *WhoScE 91-1*
Hogg, Christopher Anthony 1936- *St&PR 93*
Hogg, David Clarence 1921- *WhoAm 92*
Hogg, David Edward 1936- *WhoSSW 93*
Hogg, James 1770-1835 *BioIn 17, DcLB 116 [port]*
Hogg, James (Dalby) 1937- *ConAu 137*
Hogg, James Henry, Jr. 1926- *WhoE 93*
Hogg, James R. 1934- *WhoAm 92*
Hogg, James S. *Law&B 92*
Hogg, James Stephen 1851-1906 *BioIn 17*
Hogg, James Stuart 1952- *WhoEmL 93*
Hogg, Joseph Paul *BioIn 17*
Hogg, Michael John 1945- *St&PR 93*
Hogg, Michael Lindsay- *BioIn 17*
Hogg, Randall Gregory 1949- *WhoSSW 93*
Hogg, Robert Lawrence 1942- *WhoCanL 92*
Hogg, Robert Vincent, Jr. 1924- *WhoAm 92*
Hogg, Rozalia Cruise 1931- *WhoAm 92, WhoAmW 93, WhoSSW 93, WhoWor 93*
Hogg, Sara Marie 1949- *WhoWrEP 92*
Hogg, Thomas F. *St&PR 93*
Hoggard, James Martin 1941- *WhoWrEP 92*
Hoggard, Jay *BioIn 17*
Hoggard, Lara Guldmar 1915- *WhoAm 92, WhoWor 93*
Hoggard, Michael 1953- *St&PR 93*
Hoggard, V. Kim 1956- *WhoAm 92*
Hoggard, William Zack, Jr. 1951- *WhoSSW 93*
Hoggatt, Clela Allphin 1932- *WhoAmW 93*
Hogge, John William 1939- *St&PR 93*
Hogland, Alfred T. 1934- *St&PR 93*
Hogle, Cheryl Mae 1945- *WhoAmW 93*
Hoglund, Forrest E. 1933- *St&PR 93*
Hoglund, Ingemar 1927- *WhoScE 91-4*
Hoglund, John Andrew 1945- *WhoWor 93*
Hoglund, John B. 1930- *St&PR 93*
Hoglund, Raymond C. *St&PR 93*
Hoglund, Richard Frank 1933- *WhoAm 92*
Hoglund, Rudolph *BioIn 17*

Hoglund, William David 1956- WhoSSW 93
Hoglund, William Elis 1934- WhoAm 92
Hogness, John Rusten 1922- WhoAm 92
Hognestad, Eivind 1921- WhoAm 92
Hognestad, Per T. 1925- WhoScE 91-4
Hogoboom, Belford E. 1926- WhoIns 93
Hogrefe, Pearl AmWomPl
Hogrogian, Nonny 1932- MajAI [port]
Hogseth, John M. 1939- St&PR 93
Hogsett, Chief 1903- BioIn 17
Hogsett, Elon Chester 1903- BioIn 17
Hogsett, Joseph WhoAm 92
Hogsett, William F. Law&B 92
Hogsette, Sarah M. Law&B 92
Hogue, Alexandre 1898- WhoAm 92, WhoWor 93
Hogue, Carol Jane Rowland 1945- WhoAm 92, WhoAmW 93
Hogue, James BioIn 17
Hogue, James Claude 1932- St&PR 93
Hogue, John G. 1948- St&PR 93
Hogue, Michael E. 1942- St&PR 93
Hogue, Terry Glynn 1944- WhoAm 92
Hogue, William C. 1941- St&PR 93
Hoguet, Geoffrey Robert 1950- WhoE 93, WhoWor 93
Hoguet, Robert Louis 1908- WhoAm 92
Hogwood, Christopher (Jarvis Haley) 1941- Baker 92, WhoAm 92
Hoh, Diane 1937- ScF&FL 92
Hohage, Frederick William 1938- WhoAm 92
Hohauser, William Law&B 92
Hoheisel, Robert Arthur 1925- St&PR 93
Hohenadel, John Herman 1950- WhoE 93
Hohenberg, Charles Morris 1940- WhoAm 92
Hohenberg, John 1906- WhoAm 92
Hohenberg, Julien BioIn 17
Hohenberg, Pierre Claude 1934- WhoAm 92
Hohendahl, Peter Uwe 1936- ConAu 40NR, WhoAm 92, WhoE 93
Hohenemser, Christoph 1937- WhoAm 92
Hohener, Conrad F., III 1952- St&PR 93
Hohenfellner, Peter 1939- WhoUN 92
Hohenlohe-Ingelfingen, Friedrich Ludwig 1746-1818 HarEnMi
Hohenlohe-Ingelfingen, Kraft Karl August Eduard Friedrich 1827-1892 HarEnMi
Hohenlohe-Schillingsfurst, Chlodwig Karl Viktor, Furst zu 1819-1901 BioIn 17
Hohenrath, William Edward 1922- WhoAm 92
Hohenschuh, Paul F. 1943- St&PR 93
Hohenshell, Jeffrey John Law&B 92
Hohl, Dawn Marie 1967- WhoSSW 93
Hohl, Hans Rudolf 1933- WhoScE 91-4, WhoWor 93
Hohl, Joan ScF&FL 92
Hohler, G. Robert WhoAm 92
Hohler, Gerhard 1921- WhoScE 91-3
Hohler, Peter 1941- WhoWor 93
Hohlneicher, Georg 1937- WhoScE 91-3
Hohlov, Yuri E. 1954- WhoWor 93
Hohm, Dale Jonathan 1958- St&PR 93
Hohman, Clifford C. 1909- St&PR 93
Hohman, Russell J. Law&B 92
Hohmann, Jere W. St&PR 93
Hohmeier, Friedrich W. 1935- WhoWor 93
Hohmeyer, Olav Hans 1953- WhoWor 93
Hohm-Nielsen, G. 1934- WhoScE 91-2
Hohmuth, Karl 1929- WhoScE 91-3
Hohn, Harry G. 1932- WhoIns 93
Hohn, Harry George 1932- WhoAm 92
Hohn, Harry George, Jr. 1932- St&PR 93
Hohn, James Samonte 1946- WhoE 93
Hohn, Jayne Marie 1957- WhoAmW 93, WhoEmL 93
Hohn, Linda C. Law&B 92
Hohn, Richard G. 1936- St&PR 93, WhoIns 93
Hohn, Richard Gregory Law&B 92
Hohn, Siegfried Robert 1933- WhoWor 93
Hohn, Thomas 1938- WhoWor 93
Hohnbaum, Carl 1936- St&PR 93
Hohne, Carolyn Kay 1963- WhoAmW 93
Hohne, Karl Heinz 1937- WhoScE 91-3
Hohner, Bill Bela 1948- St&PR 93
Hohner, Frank d1990 BioIn 17
Hohner, Kenneth Dwayne 1934- WhoWor 93
Hohner, Vicki Kathleen 1955- WhoAmW 93
Hohns, William Allin 1952- St&PR 93
Hohnstein, Robert P. 1930- St&PR 93
Hoi, Abu al- d1991 BioIn 17
Hoiby, Lee 1926- Baker 92, WhoAm 92
Hoien, Robert Donald 1940- St&PR 93
Hoigaard, Conrad J. 1936- St&PR 93
Hoigne, J. 1930- WhoScE 91-4
Hoijer, Harry 1904-1976 IntDcAn
Hoiland, Andrew Calvin 1926- WhoAm 92
Hoin, Stacy Law&B 92
Hoins, Thorsten 1965- WhoWor 93
Hois, Laura L. Law&B 92
Hoisington, Harland Steven Law&B 92
Hoit, Kenneth R. 1937- St&PR 93
Hoitt, Kenneth 1947- St&PR 93
Hoit-Thetford, Elizabeth 1948- WhoEmL 93
Hojer, Svante Erik 1961- WhoWor 93
Hojerslev, Niels Kristian 1943- WhoScE 91-2
Hojo, Masaki 1957- WhoWor 93
Hojo, Masashi 1952- WhoWor 93
Hojo, Soun 1432-1519 HarEnMi
Hojo, Tokimasa 1138-1215 HarEnMi
Hojo, Ujitsuna 1487-1541 HarEnMi
Hojo, Ujiyasu 1515-1570 HarEnMi
Hojo, Yasutoki 1183-1242 HarEnMi
Hojo, Yoshitoki 1163-1224 HarEnMi
Hojo Masako 1157-1225 BioIn 17
Hok, Peter WhoScE 91-4
Ho Kah Leong 1937- WhoAsAP 91
Hokanson Hawks, Jane Esther 1955- WhoAmW 93
Hoke, Anna D. AmWomPl
Hoke, Charles Pawling 1942- St&PR 93
Hoke, Donald Edwin 1919- WhoSSW 93
Hoke, Donald Edwin, Jr. 1948- St&PR 93
Hoke, Franklin ScF&FL 92
Hoke, Helen 1903-1990 BioIn 17, ScF&FL 92
Hoke, Robert Frederick 1837-1912 HarEnMi
Hoke, Robert W., II Law&B 92
Hokenson, Frank E. 1931- St&PR 93
Hokenson, Frank Eugene 1931- WhoAm 92
Hokenson, H. John Law&B 92
Hokenson, Jan 1942- ScF&FL 92
Hokenstad, Merl Clifford, Jr. 1936- WhoAm 92, WhoWor 93
Hokin, Edwin E. 1915-1990 BioIn 17
Hokin, Lowell Edward 1924- WhoAm 92
Hoklin, Lonn ScF&FL 92
Ho Kung-sun fl. 129BC-103BC HarEnMi
Hokusai 1760-1849 BioIn 17
Hol, Richard 1825-1904 Baker 92
Holabird, Jean 1946- WhoE 93
Holabird, John Augur, Jr. 1920- WhoAm 92
Holabird, Katharine BioIn 17
Holaday, Allan Gibson 1916- WhoAm 92
Holaday, James Clifton 1935- WhoWrEP 92
Holaday, Susan Mirles 1938- WhoWrEP 92
Holahan, John W. d1991 BioIn 17
Holahan, Marie Elisha 1959- WhoE 93
Holahan, Richard Vincent 1909- WhoAm 92
Holan, Jerri-Ann 1959- WhoAmW 93, WhoEmL 93
Holand, Ivar 1924- WhoScE 91-4
Holand, Steinar 1934- WhoUN 92
Holappa, Lauri Elias Kalevi 1941- WhoScE 91-4
Holbaek-Hanssen, Erik 1943- WhoScE 91-4
Holben, Ralph Erdman 1916- WhoE 93
Holberg, Ralph Gans, Jr. 1908- WhoAm 92
Holberg, Sven Ludvig 1927- WhoSSW 93, WhoWor 93
Holbert, Sue Elisabeth 1935- WhoAm 92, WhoAmW 93
Holbert, Theodore F. 1921- St&PR 93
Holbert, Theodore Frank 1921- WhoAm 92
Holberton, Philip Vaughan 1942- WhoAm 92
Holbik, Karel 1920- WhoAm 92
Holbik, Thomas 1960- WhoEmL 93
Holborne, Antony d1602 Baker 92
Holbrook, Alfred Samson, III 1957- WhoEmL 93, WhoSSW 93
Holbrook, Amelia Weed AmWomPl
Holbrook, Barbara Carr San WhoAmW 93, WhoE 93
Holbrook, Charles Darrell 1939- WhoSSW 93
Holbrook, Charles W. 1940- St&PR 93
Holbrook, Coit Conger 1936- St&PR 93
Holbrook, Connie Cannon Law&B 92
Holbrook, David D. WhoIns 93
Holbrook, David D. 1935- St&PR 93
Holbrook, Donald B. Law&B 92
Holbrook, Donald Benson 1925- WhoAm 92, WhoWor 93
Holbrook, Douglas Cowan 1934- WhoAm 92
Holbrook, Florence 1860-1932 AmWomPl
Holbrook, Hal 1925- WhoAm 92
Holbrook, James J. WhoWrEP 92
Holbrook, James Robert 1956- WhoWor 93
Holbrook, Jane Elaine 1936- WhoAmW 93
Holbrook, Joan 1934- WhoAm 92
Holbrook, Joseph John WhoScE 91-1
Holbrook, Lee Bruce 1950- WhoWor 93
Holbrook, Margaret Louise AmWomPl
Holbrook, Marion AmWomPl
Holbrook, Marla Davis WhoSSW 93
Holbrook, Norma Jeannette 1939- WhoAmW 93
Holbrook, Richard E. St&PR 93
Holbrook, Rita Karen Thomas 1953- WhoAmW 93
Holbrook, Robert Berryman 1941- St&PR 93
Holbrook, Robert Sumner 1932- WhoAm 92
Holbrook, S. Dennis Law&B 92
Holbrook, Stephen Fuller 1934- WhoE 93
Holbrook, Vincent Avery 1960- WhoSSW 93
Holbrook, William Harold 1924- St&PR 93
Holbrooke, Joseph 1878-1958 Baker 92, OxDcOp
Holbrooke, Richard Charles 1941- St&PR 93
Holbrow, Charles Howard 1935- WhoAm 92
Holcenberg, John Stanley 1935- WhoAm 92
Holch, Eric Sanford 1948- WhoE 93
Holch, Klaus 1941- WhoScE 91-2
Holck, Frederick H. George 1927- WhoAm 92
Holck, Philip Carl 1960- WhoSSW 93
Holcom, Thomas Howard, Jr. 1946- WhoEmL 93
Holcomb, Andrew C. Law&B 92
Holcomb, Barbara Ann 1928- WhoAmW 93
Holcomb, Bruce D. 1947- St&PR 93
Holcomb, Caramine Kellam 1941- WhoAmW 93
Holcomb, Charles Crawford 1956- WhoSSW 93
Holcomb, Constance L. 1942- WhoAmW 93
Holcomb, Daryl K. 1951- St&PR 93
Holcomb, David Wallace, Jr. 1937- WhoSSW 93
Holcomb, Donald Frank 1925- WhoAm 92
Holcomb, Dorothy Turner 1924- WhoAmW 93
Holcomb, Edward Orr, Jr. 1941- WhoSSW 93
Holcomb, George 1936- St&PR 93
Holcomb, George Ruhle 1927- WhoAm 92
Holcomb, Grant, III 1944- WhoAm 92, WhoE 93
Holcomb, Homer Simmons 1925- WhoSSW 93
Holcomb, Horace Hale, III 1930- St&PR 93
Holcomb, Hubert D. 1930- St&PR 93
Holcomb, James Robert 1937- WhoSSW 93
Holcomb, Jerry Kimble WhoWrEP 92
Holcomb, M. Staser 1932- WhoAm 92, WhoIns 93
Holcomb, Mary Lou Law&B 92
Holcomb, Norman C. 1944- St&PR 93
Holcomb, Philip H. 1938- WhoUN 92
Holcomb, Rod MiSFD 9
Holcomb, Thomas 1879-1965 HarEnMi
Holcomb, William A. 1926- WhoAm 92
Holcombe, Anna Calluori 1952- WhoE 93
Holcombe, Arthur N. 1940- WhoUN 92
Holcombe, Dorothy Freeman 1926- WhoE 93
Holcombe, Homer Wayne 1949- WhoWor 93
Holcombe, James C. 1945- St&PR 93
Holcombe, John Howard Law&B 92
Holcombe, Juanita Holden 1952- WhoAmW 93
Holcombe, Milton Winford 1932- St&PR 93
Holcombe, Patricia Fukai 1957- WhoAmW 93
Holcombe, Paul Amos, Jr. Law&B 92
Holcombe, Randall Gregory 1950- WhoAm 92
Holcombe, Robert S. Law&B 92
Holcombe, Robert Swaine 1942- WhoAm 92
Holcombe, Stephen L. 1956- St&PR 93
Holcombe, Stephen Patrick 1953- WhoSSW 93
Holcombe, Thomas Charles 1948- WhoE 93
Holcombe, Wesley Glenn 1924- St&PR 93
Holcombe, William J. 1925- WhoAm 92, WhoE 93
Holcombe, William Jones 1925- St&PR 93
Holcombe, William Michael Lloyd WhoScE 91-1
Holcombe, William Michael Lloyd 1944- WhoWor 93
Holcroft, Thomas 1745-1809 BioIn 17
Holczer, Geoffrey M. 1949- St&PR 93
Holdar, Robert Martin 1949- WhoSSW 93
Holdas, Sandor 1931- WhoScE 91-4
Holdaway, Jeffrey Alan Law&B 92
Holdcroft, James P. 1954- St&PR 93
Holde, Artur 1885-1962 Baker 92
Holdeman, Ralph M. 1906-1990 BioIn 17
Holden, Al 1931- St&PR 93
Holden, Andrea Rose 1958- WhoWor 93
Holden, Ann Marie 1954- St&PR 93
Holden, Arthur BioIn 17
Holden, Audrey P. d1992 NewYTBS 92
Holden, Budd BioIn 17
Holden, David Johnston 1930- St&PR 93
Holden, David Morgan 1938- WhoAm 92
Holden, Donald 1931- WhoAm 92
Holden, Edward F. 1930- WhoIns 93
Holden, Elizabeth R. ScF&FL 92
Holden, Gary 1951- WhoE 93
Holden, George Fredric 1937- WhoWor 93
Holden, Glen A. 1927- WhoAm 92, WhoWor 93
Holden, Gloria d1991 BioIn 17
Holden, Harold Benjamin WhoScE 91-1
Holden, Helene P. WhoCanL 92
Holden, James Phillip 1932- WhoAm 92
Holden, James Stuart 1914- WhoAm 92, WhoE 93
Holden, John Bernard 1910- WhoAm 92
Holden, John C. Law&B 92
Holden, Jonathan BioIn 17
Holden, Jonathan 1941- ConAu 37NR, WhoWrEP 92
Holden, Melvin Lee AfrAmBi [port]
Holden, Michael James 1951- St&PR 93
Holden, Myretta WhoSSW 93
Holden, Norman Edward 1936- WhoWor 93
Holden, Oliver 1765-1844 Baker 92
Holden, Patrick John 1949- St&PR 93
Holden, Peter Drew 1940- WhoE 93
Holden, Raymond Henry 1924- WhoE 93, WhoWor 93
Holden, Raymond Thomas 1904- WhoAm 92
Holden, Reuben Andrus 1918- WhoAm 92
Holden, Rick Marshall 1952- WhoE 93, WhoEmL 93
Holden, Robert Stuart 1929- St&PR 93
Holden, Ross J. Law&B 92
Holden, Sandra Sue 1938- WhoAmW 93
Holden, Scott L. Law&B 92
Holden, Steven Howie 1944- St&PR 93
Holden, Thomas B. 1948- St&PR 93
Holden, Ursula 1921- ScF&FL 92
Holden, Virginia Hamilton Law&B 92
Holden, William 1918-1981 BioIn 17
Holden, William 1918-1982 IntDcF 2-3 [port]
Holden, William Hoyt, Jr. WhoE 93
Holden, William P. 1933- WhoAm 92
Holden, William Roger 1946- WhoEmL 93
Holden, William V. 1949- St&PR 93
Holder, Angela Roddey 1938- WhoAm 92, WhoAmW 93
Holder, Annamaria Jude McGarvey 1964- WhoAmW 93, WhoE 93
Holder, Anthony Arthur WhoScE 91-1
Holder, Barry Keith 1933- WhoWor 93
Holder, Donald BioIn 17
Holder, Fabian Grafton 1931- WhoUN 92
Holder, Gail Jillian 1953- WhoAm 92
Holder, Geoffrey BioIn 17
Holder, Geoffrey 1930?- ConTFT 10, WhoAm 92
Holder, George H. 1936- St&PR 93
Holder, Harold Douglas, Sr. 1931- WhoAm 92
Holder, Holly Irene 1952- WhoAmW 93, WhoEmL 93
Holder, Howard Randolph, Sr. 1916- WhoSSW 93, WhoWor 93
Holder, Janice Marie 1949- WhoEmL 93
Holder, John E. Law&B 92
Holder, Lee 1932- WhoAm 92
Holder, Nancy 1953- ScF&FL 92
Holder, P. WhoScE 91-3
Holder, Patricia Wenzel 1925- WhoAmW 93
Holder, Richard G. WhoAm 92, WhoWor 93
Holder, Sallie Lou 1939- WhoAm 92
Holder, Sandra Sue 1938- WhoAmW 93
Holder, Susan McCaskill 1956- WhoAmW 93
Holder, Thomas Martin 1926- WhoAm 92
Holder, Timothy Scott 1955- WhoE 93
Holder, Virginia Mary 1942- WhoAmW 93
Holder, William Eilif 1939- WhoUN 92
Holderlin, Friedrich 1770-1843 BioIn 17
Holderman, Melanie 1954- WhoAmW 93
Holderman, Sandra Ann 1966- WhoAmW 93
Holderness, Algernon Sidney, Jr. 1938- WhoAm 92
Holderness, Susan Rutherford 1941- WhoAmW 93, WhoWor 93
Holderried, Siegbert 1941- WhoScE 91-3
Holder-Thomas, Jean D. Law&B 92

Holdgate, M.W. *WhoScE 91-1*
Holdgraf, Michael 1946- *St&PR 93*
Holdgrafer, Michael E. *Law&B 92*
Holdheim, William Wolfgang 1926- *WhoSSW 93*
Holding, Allan Clyde 1931- *WhoAsAP 91*
Holding, Dennis Harry 1925- *WhoSSW 93*
Holding, Frank B. 1929- *WhoAm 92*
Holding, Harvey R. 1934- *St&PR 93*
Holding, Lewis R. 1927- *WhoAm 92*
Holding, William Burton 1933- *WhoAm 92*
Holditch, W. Kenneth 1933- *WhoWrEP 92*
Holditch, William Kenneth 1933- *WhoSSW 93*
Holdman, Holly 1948- *WhoAmW 93*
Holdom, Lynne *ScF&FL 92*
Holdorf, Paul S. *Law&B 92*
Holdowsky, Michael Martin 1953- *WhoEmL 93*
Holdredge, Ransom Gillet 1836-1899 *BioIn 17*
Holdren, Cynthia Wills 1948- *WhoEmL 93, WhoSSW 93*
Holdren, John Paul 1944- *WhoAm 92*
Holdridge, Barbara 1929- *WhoAm 92, WhoWrEP 92*
Holdridge, Herbert C. 1892-1974 *ScF&FL 92*
Holdridge, Thomas D. 1941- *St&PR 93*
Holdstock, Pauline J. *WhoCanL 92*
Holdstock, Robert 1948- *ScF&FL 92*
Holdsworth, Charles Derek *WhoScE 91-1*
Holdsworth, David *WhoScE 91-1*
Holdsworth, Janet Nott 1941- *WhoAmW 93, WhoWor 93*
Holdsworth, P.J. *WhoScE 91-1*
Holdsworth, Robert Leo, Jr. 1959- *WhoWor 93*
Holdt, Leland 1930- *St&PR 93*
Holdt, Leland LaMar Stark 1930- *WhoAm 92*
Holdway, Douglas Alan 1954- *WhoWor 93*
Holdway, Michael Leon 1952- *WhoEmL 93*
Hole, Donald E. 1951- *St&PR 93*
Hole, Frank 1931- *WhoAm 92*
Ho-Le, Ken Khoa 1955- *WhoWor 93*
Holec, Anita Kathryn Van Tassel 1947- *WhoAmW 93*
Holec, James Michael, Jr. 1949- *WhoAm 92*
Hole-in-the-Day d1868 *BioIn 17*
Holeman, George Robert 1937- *WhoE 93*
Holeman, Marilyn Batey 1938- *WhoWrEP 92*
Holeman, Steven Clark 1962- *WhoSSW 93*
Holen, Eugene Dwayne 1928- *St&PR 93*
Holenbaugh, Robert Allan 1942- *St&PR 93*
Holender, Barbara D. 1927- *WhoWrEP 92*
Holenia, Alexander Lernet- *ScF&FL 92*
Holenweger, Oscar 1944- *WhoWor 93*
Holes, Andrew 15th cent.- *BioIn 17*
Holevas, C.D. *WhoScE 91-3*
Holewa, Hans 1905- *Baker 92*
Holewinski, Andrzej 1938- *WhoScE 91-4*
Holeyfield, Richard Wayne 1946- *WhoSSW 93*
Holfinger, Robert R. 1930- *St&PR 93*
Holford, Neal Scott *Law&B 92*
Holgaard, Conrad J. *WhoAm 92*
Holgate, George Jackson 1933- *WhoAm 92*
Holgate, Michael John *WhoScE 91-1*
Holgate, Stephen Townley *WhoScE 91-1*
Holguin, Alfonso Hudson 1931- *WhoAm 92*
Holguin, Guillermo *Baker 92*
Holian, Gail Conca 1948- *WhoE 93*
Holian, Katherine Stover 1947- *WhoEmL 93*
Holiday, Billie 1915-1959 *BioIn 17*
Holiday, Billie (Eleanora) 1915-1959 *Baker 92*
Holiday, Edith Elizabeth 1952- *WhoAm 92, WhoAmW 93*
Holiday, Jane *ChlFicS*
Holiday, Martha 1926- *WhoAmW 93, WhoE 93*
Holiday, Michael *Law&B 92*
Holiday, Patrick James 1947- *WhoEmL 93*
Holien, Kim Bernard 1948- *WhoE 93, WhoEmL 93, WhoSSW 93, WhoWor 93*
Holifield, John 1956- *St&PR 93*
Holifield, Marianne K. *Law&B 92*
Holifield, Patricia DiMiceli 1945- *WhoSSW 93*
Holiga, Ludomil Andrew 1920- *WhoAm 92*
Holik, Bobby *BioIn 17*
Holinger, Richard 1949- *WhoWrEP 92*
Holinger, William 1944- *WhoWrEP 92*
Holinka, John G. *Law&B 92*
Holkar, Mo 1967- *ScF&FL 92*
Holkeri, Harri Hermanni 1937- *WhoWor 93*
Holl, Donald Richard 1947- *WhoEmL 93*
Holl, Jane Ellen 1956- *WhoE 93*
Holl, John William 1928- *WhoAm 92*
Holl, Philip Kenneth *Law&B 92*
Holl, Richard Henry 1929- *St&PR 93*
Holl, Rose E. 1920- *St&PR 93*
Holl, Steven Myron 1947- *WhoAm 92*
Hollabaugh, Mark 1949- *WhoWrEP 92*
Holladay, Charles O. 1931- *WhoAm 92*
Holladay, Charles Otis 1931- *St&PR 93*
Holladay, Harlan 1925- *WhoE 93*
Holladay, James Frank 1922- *WhoAm 92*
Holladay, Janice W. 1932-1989 *BioIn 17*
Holladay, Wendell Gene 1925- *WhoAm 92*
Holladay, Wilhelmina Cole 1922- *WhoAm 92, WhoAmW 93*
Hollaender, Alexis 1840-1924 *Baker 92*
Hollaender, Fredrick 1896-1976 *See* Hollaender, Viktor 1866-1940 *Baker 92*
Hollaender, Gustav 1855-1915 *Baker 92*
Hollaender, Viktor 1866-1940 *Baker 92*
Hollaman, Keith *ScF&FL 92*
Hollan, Laszlo 1936- *WhoScE 91-2*
Hollan, Susan 1920- *WhoScE 91-4*
Hollan, Susan R. 1920- *WhoWor 93*
Holland, Agnieszka 1948- *DrEEuF, MiSFD 9*
Holland, Andrew McDonald 1933- *St&PR 93*
Holland, Arthur J. 1918-1989 *BioIn 17*
Holland, Bart Keith 1956- *WhoE 93*
Holland, Bernard George 1948- *WhoWor 93*
Holland, Beth *WhoAm 92, WhoAmW 93*
Holland, Bradford Wayne 1943- *WhoAm 92*
Holland, Brenda Jo *WhoAmW 93*
Holland, Brian 1941- *BioIn 17* *See Also* Holland, Dozier & Holland *SoulM*
Holland, Catherine Pauline 1951- *St&PR 93*
Holland, Cecelia 1943- *ScF&FL 92*
Holland, Charles 1909-1987 *Baker 92*
Holland, Charles Donald 1921- *WhoAm 92*
Holland, Charles Edward 1940- *WhoSSW 93*
Holland, Charles Hepworth 1923- *WhoScE 91-3*
Holland, Charles K. 1951- *St&PR 93*
Holland, Charles Malcolm, Jr. 1932- *WhoAm 92*
Holland, Christie Anna 1950- *WhoAm 92, WhoEmL 93*
Holland, Daniel M. 1920-1991 *BioIn 17*
Holland, Darryl Boyd 1953- *WhoE 93*
Holland, David Michael 1946- *St&PR 93, WhoIns 93*
Holland, David Thurston 1923- *WhoAm 92*
Holland, Debbie Jan 1957- *WhoAmW 93*
Holland, Dennis J. 1949- *WhoE 93*
Holland, Dennis K. *Law&B 92*
Holland, Diane G. *Law&B 92*
Holland, Dianna Gwin 1948- *WhoAm 92*
Holland, Don R. 1930- *St&PR 93*
Holland, Donald Ray 1943- *WhoSSW 93*
Holland, Donald Reginald 1940- *WhoAm 92*
Holland, Dulcie 1913- *Baker 92*
Holland, Eddie 1939- *BioIn 17* *See Also* Holland, Dozier & Holland *SoulM*
Holland, Elizabeth 1928- *ScF&FL 92*
Holland, Endesha Ida Mae *BioIn 17*
Holland, Endesha Ida Mae 1944- *ConBlB 3 [port]*
Holland, Eugene, Jr. 1922- *WhoAm 92*
Holland, Evan Marc 1955- *St&PR 93*
Holland, Garvin E. *Law&B 92*
Holland, Gary Alexander 1933- *WhoAm 92*
Holland, Gary Richard 1942- *St&PR 93*
Holland, Gene Grigsby 1928- *WhoAm 92, WhoAmW 93*
Holland, George H. *St&PR 93*
Holland, Gerald J. 1951- *St&PR 93*
Holland, Gerald M. 1935- *St&PR 93*
Holland, H. Russel 1936- *WhoAm 92*
Holland, Harold Herbert 1932- *WhoAm 92*
Holland, Heinrich Dieter 1927- *WhoAm 92*
Holland, Henry Preston 1948- *St&PR 93*
Holland, Hubert Brian 1904- *WhoAm 92*
Holland, Hudson, Jr. 1939- *WhoE 93*
Holland, Isabelle 1920- *DcAmChF 1960, MajAI [port], SmATA 70 [port]*
Holland, Isabelle Christian 1920- *WhoAm 92, WhoWor 93*
Holland, J.P. *St&PR 93*
Holland, James, Sr. *Law&B 92*
Holland, James Michael 1945- *St&PR 93*
Holland, James Paul 1948- *WhoAm 92*
Holland, James R. 1944- *WhoE 93, WhoWor 93*
Holland, James Richard, Jr. 1943- *WhoAm 92*
Holland, James Ricks 1929- *WhoAm 92*
Holland, James T. 1940- *St&PR 93*
Holland, James Tulley 1940- *WhoAm 92*
Holland, Janet M. *Law&B 92*
Holland, Janice Arlene 1951- *WhoEmL 93*
Holland, Jeffrey R. 1940- *WhoAm 92*
Holland, Jeffrey Stuart 1951- *WhoSSW 93*
Holland, Jerome Heartwell 1916-1985 *BiDAMSp 1989*
Holland, Jimmy *Law&B 92*
Holland, John B. 1932- *WhoAm 92, WhoSSW 93*
Holland, John Ben 1932- *WhoAm 92, WhoSSW 93, WhoWor 93*
Holland, John Madison 1927- *WhoAm 92*
Holland, John Philip 1841?-1914 *BioIn 17*
Holland, John Ray 1933- *WhoAm 92*
Holland, Joseph R. 1936- *WhoE 93*
Holland, Joy 1946- *WhoAmW 93*
Holland, Joyce *WhoWrEP 92*
Holland, Julie *BioIn 17*
Holland, Kathie Kunkel 1949- *WhoAmW 93*
Holland, Kenneth John 1918- *WhoAm 92*
Holland, Kenneth M. 1923- *St&PR 93*
Holland, Larry O. 1949- *St&PR 93*
Holland, Leland 1927-1990 *BioIn 17*
Holland, Leo Laverne 1941- *WhoE 93*
Holland, Leslie Arthur 1921- *WhoWor 93*
Holland, Lindsay Bradford 1947- *St&PR 93*
Holland, Lori *St&PR 93*
Holland, Louisa Emma *AmWomPl*
Holland, Lyman Faith, Jr. 1931- *WhoAm 92*
Holland, Malvern Carlyle 1926- *WhoSSW 93*
Holland, Marilyn Basye 1947- *WhoEmL 93*
Holland, Marion 1908-1989 *BioIn 17*
Holland, Marjorie Miriam 1947- *WhoEmL 93*
Holland, Merle Susan 1945- *WhoAm 92, WhoAmW 93*
Holland, Michael Francis 1944- *WhoAm 92*
Holland, Michael M. 1948- *WhoAm 92*
Holland, Nancy E. *Law&B 92*
Holland, Nancy Hinkle 1921- *WhoAm 92*
Holland, Norman Norwood 1927- *WhoSSW 93*
Holland, Pamela B. *Law&B 92*
Holland, Patricia Marcus 1952- *WhoEmL 93*
Holland, Paul Deleval 1910- *WhoAm 92*
Holland, Peter 1934- *WhoScE 91-1*
Holland, Peter Marc 1944- *WhoSSW 93*
Holland, Randy James 1947- *WhoAm 92, WhoEmL 93*
Holland, Rebecca Lou 1949- *St&PR 93*
Holland, Richard Edward 1935- *WhoWor 93*
Holland, Richard L. 1926- *St&PR 93*
Holland, Robert Campbell 1923- *WhoAm 92, WhoSSW 93*
Holland, Robert Carl 1925- *BioIn 17, WhoAm 92*
Holland, Robert L. 1939- *St&PR 93*
Holland, Robert Stevens 1945- *WhoE 93, WhoWor 93*
Holland, Robert T. 1948- *St&PR 93*
Holland, Samuel 1803-1892 *BioIn 17*
Holland, Savage Steve *MiSFD 9*
Holland, Sheila 1937- *ScF&FL 92*
Holland, Sidney George 1893-1961 *DcTwHis*
Holland, Stephen Thomas 1952- *WhoWrEP 92*
Holland, Steven A. *Law&B 92*
Holland, Susan Palmieri 1956- *WhoWrEP 92*
Holland, Theodore (Samuel) 1878-1947 *Baker 92*
Holland, Thomas Powell 1942- *WhoAm 92*
Holland, Thomas R. *ScF&FL 92*
Holland, Todd *MiSFD 9*
Holland, Tom *MiSFD 9*
Holland, Tom 1936- *WhoAm 92*
Holland, Walter W. *WhoScE 91-1*
Holland, Willard R. 1936- *St&PR 93*
Holland, William R. *Law&B 92*
Holland, William Ray 1938- *St&PR 93, WhoAm 92, WhoSSW 93*
Holland, Dozier & Holland *SoulM*
Hollande, Etienne 1937- *WhoScE 91-2*
Hollander, Betty Ruth 1930- *WhoAm 92*
Hollander, Brian W. *Law&B 92*
Hollander, Charles Simche 1934- *WhoAm 92*
Hollander, Daniel 1939- *WhoAm 92*
Hollander, David 1952- *WhoE 93*
Hollander, Edwin Paul 1927- *WhoAm 92*
Hollander, Ella H. 1908- *WhoWrEP 92*
Hollander, Ellen Collins 1946- *WhoEmL 93*
Hollander, Eric 1957- *WhoEmL 93*
Hollander, Gerhard Ludwig 1922- *WhoAm 92*
Hollander, Herbert I. 1924- *WhoAm 92*
Hollander, Howard Robert 1952- *WhoE 93, WhoEmL 93*
Hollander, Jean *WhoWrEP 92*
Hollander, Jeffrey Michael 1961- *St&PR 93*
Hollander, John *BioIn 17*
Hollander, John 1929- *WhoAm 92, WhoWrEP 92*
Hollander, Lawrence Jay 1940- *WhoE 93*
Hollander, Leo L. 1937- *St&PR 93*
Hollander, Lorin 1944- *Baker 92, BioIn 17, WhoAm 92*
Hollander, Luella Jean 1935- *WhoAmW 93*
Hollander, Marshall J. 1919- *St&PR 93*
Hollander, Milton Bernard 1928- *WhoAm 92, WhoE 93*
Hollander, Morton Joseph 1913- *WhoAm 92*
Hollander, Patricia Ann 1928- *WhoAmW 93*
Hollander, Paul *MajAI*
Hollander, Richard C. 1946- *St&PR 93*
Hollander, Richard Edward 1947- *WhoAm 92*
Hollander, Robert B., Jr. 1933- *WhoAm 92*
Hollander, Samuel 1937- *WhoAm 92*
Hollander, Samuel Steven 1938- *St&PR 93*
Hollander, Toby Edward 1931- *WhoAm 92*
Hollander, Zander *BioIn 17*
Holland-Jones, Paula Elaine 1955- *WhoAmW 93*
Hollands, John Henry 1929- *WhoAm 92*
Hollands, Roy (Derrick) 1924- *ConAu 37NR*
Hollans, Irby Noah, Jr. 1930- *WhoAm 92*
Hollar, Dale E. *Law&B 92*
Hollar, Jan H. 1955- *St&PR 93*
Hollar, Richard A. 1947- *St&PR 93*
Hollas, Donna Marie 1962- *WhoEmL 93, WhoSSW 93*
Hollatz, Horst 1941- *WhoWor 93*
Hollaway, Leonard Charles *WhoScE 91-1*
Hollaway, Peter *BioIn 17*
Holldobler, Berthold K. 1936- *WhoScE 91-3*
Holldobler, Berthold Karl 1936- *WhoE 93*
Holldorf, August W. 1932- *WhoScE 91-3*
Holle, Hugo 1890-1942 *Baker 92*
Holleb, Allen *MiSFD 9*
Holleb, Arthur Irving 1921- *WhoAm 92*
Holleb, Doris B. 1922- *WhoWor 93*
Hollebone, Christopher John 1951- *WhoWor 93*
Hollein, Helen Conway 1943- *WhoAmW 93*
Holleman, Boyce 1924- *WhoAm 92*
Holleman, John Albert 1939- *St&PR 93*
Holleman, Matthew Louis 1951- *St&PR 93*
Holleman, Pamela Smith 1953- *WhoE 93*
Holleman, Sandy Lee 1940- *WhoAmW 93*
Hollenbach, Edwin A. 1918- *St&PR 93*
Hollenbach, Eleanor P. 1922- *St&PR 93*
Hollenbach, Mark A. 1954- *St&PR 93*
Hollenbach, Ruth *WhoAm 92, WhoAmW 93*
Hollenback, William Marshall 1886-1968 *BiDAMSp 1989*
Hollenbaugh, Dave *BioIn 17*
Hollenbeck, Albert Russell 1948- *WhoE 93*
Hollenbeck, Burton G. 1927- *St&PR 93*
Hollenbeck, Donald Craig 1953- *St&PR 93*
Hollenbeck, Jot Niclas 1954- *St&PR 93*
Hollenbeck, Karen Fern 1943- *WhoAmW 93*
Hollenbeck, Marynell 1939- *WhoAmW 93, WhoWor 93*
Hollenbeck, Ralph Anthony 1925- *WhoAm 92*
Hollenberg, Charles Herbert 1930- *WhoAm 92*
Hollenberg, Cornelis P. 1940- *WhoScE 91-3*
Hollenberg, Norman Kenneth 1936- *WhoE 93*
Hollender, Alfred L. 1912-1990 *BioIn 17*
Hollender, Jeffrey *BioIn 17*
Hollender, John Edward 1941- *WhoWor 93*
Hollender, Lars G. 1933- *WhoScE 91-4*
Hollender, Sheridan H. *Law&B 92*
Hollensbe, Ronda Lee 1953- *WhoAmW 93*
Hollensworth, Mayme Stevens 1910- *WhoWrEP 92*

Holler, Adlai Cornwell, Jr. 1925- *WhoSSW 93, WhoWor 93*
Holler, Cindy Margaret 1961- *WhoAmW 93*
Holler, Dennis Keith 1951- *WhoEmL 93*
Holler, Eggehard 1940- *WhoScE 91-3*
Holler, Grover M., Jr. 1921- *St&PR 93*
Holler, John H. 1946- *St&PR 93*
Holler, Karl 1907-1987 *Baker 92*
Holler, Kenny G. 1945- *St&PR 93*
Holler, P. *WhoScE 91-3*
Holler, York (Georg) 1944- *Baker 92*
Holleran, Andrew 1943?- *ConGAN*
Holleran, John W. *Law&B 92*
Holleran, John W. 1954- *St&PR 93*
Holleran, Lawrence P. 1931- *St&PR 93*
Holleran, Paula Rizzo *WhoAmW 93*
Hollerbach, Alfred 1942- *WhoScE 91-3*
Hollerbach, Louis V. 1930- *St&PR 93*
Hollerith, Herman *BioIn 17*
Hollerith, Richard, Jr. 1926- *WhoAm 92*
Hollerman, Charles Edward 1929- *WhoAm 92*
Hollermann, Peter W. 1931- *WhoScE 91-3*
Hollern, Thomas R. 1943- *St&PR 93*
Hollesen, Hollie Marie 1959- *WhoEmL 93*
Hollett, Grant Thomas, Jr. 1942- *St&PR 93, WhoAm 92*
Holleweg dit Wegman, Willy 1934- *WhoWor 93*
Holley, Audrey Rodgers 1939- *WhoAmW 93*
Holley, Bryan R. 1961- *St&PR 93*
Holley, C. Roy 1936- *St&PR 93*
Holley, Carol Ann 1942- *WhoAmW 93*
Holley, Charlotte Marie 1950- *WhoWrEP 92*
Holley, Cyrus Helmer 1936- *WhoAm 92*
Holley, Deborah Jon 1953- *St&PR 93*
Holley, Edgar *BioIn 17*
Holley, Edward Gailon 1927- *WhoAm 92*
Holley, Gerald Neal 1938- *St&PR 93*
Holley, Howard George 1943- *St&PR 93*
Holley, Irving Brinton, Jr. 1919- *WhoAm 92, WhoSSW 93*
Holley, James W., III *WhoAm 92*
Holley, Joseph Cohron 1928- *St&PR 93*
Holley, Joseph Thomas 1946- *St&PR 93*
Holley, Kay Moffitt 1943- *WhoSSW 93*
Holley, Larry Jay 1936- *St&PR 93*
Holley, Lauren Allana 1948- *WhoAm 92, WhoAmW 93*
Holley, Lawrence Alvin 1924- *WhoAm 92*
Holley, Major Quincy 1924-1990 *BioIn 17*
Holley, Marietta 1836-1926 *AmWomPl*
Holley, Mary Anne *BioIn 17*
Holley, Monelle Boyett 1935- *WhoWrEP 92*
Holley, Mule 1924-1990 *BioIn 17*
Holley, Robert William 1922- *WhoAm 92, WhoWor 93*
Holley, Russell G. 1919- *St&PR 93*
Holley, William Arthur, III *Law&B 92*
Holleyman, Robert Walker, II 1955- *WhoE 93*
Holli, Betsy Biggar 1933- *WhoAmW 93*
Holli, Jerzy 1951- *WhoWor 93*
Hollich, Stephen Eugene 1932- *WhoSSW 93*
Holliday, Doc 1852?-1887 *BioIn 17*
Holliday, Anne Elaine 1962- *WhoAmW 93, WhoEmL 93*
Holliday, Bruce Nichols *Law&B 92*
Holliday, C.I. 1952- *WhoScE 91-1*
Holliday, Don *ScF&FL 92*
Holliday, Frederick William MacKey 1828-1898 *BioIn 17*
Holliday, George *BioIn 17*
Holliday, George Washington *Law&B 92*
Holliday, James 1936- *BioIn 17*
Holliday, Jennifer *BioIn 17*
Holliday, Jennifer 1960- *SoulM*
Holliday, Jennifer Yvette 1960- *WhoAm 92, WhoAmW 93*
Holliday, Joan Elizabeth 1959- *WhoAmW 93*
Holliday, John Henry 1852?-1887 *BioIn 17*
Holliday, John M. 1939- *St&PR 93*
Holliday, John Moffitt 1935- *WhoAm 92*
Holliday, Judy 1921-1965 *IntDcF 2-3*
Holliday, Judy 1922?-1965 *BioIn 17, QDrFCA 92 [port]*
Holliday, Karen Kahler 1959- *WhoEmL 93*
Holliday, Linda L. 1951- *WhoAmW 93*
Holliday, Michael *Law&B 92*
Holliday, Polly Dean 1937- *WhoAm 92*
Holliday, Randall H. *Law&B 92*
Holliday, Richard Carter 1938- *St&PR 93, WhoE 93*
Holliday, Robert Kelvin 1933- *WhoSSW 93*
Holliday, Susan J. *Law&B 92*
Holliday, Susan Riedman *WhoAmW 93*
Holliday, Terry Lynn 1955- *WhoEmL 93, WhoSSW 93*
Holliday, Tom E. 1929- *St&PR 93*
Hollidge, Kenneth Blake, Jr. 1945- *St&PR 93*
Hollie, Thad, Jr. *Law&B 92*
Hollien, Harry Francis 1926- *WhoAm 92, WhoSSW 93*
Hollien, Patricia Ann 1938- *WhoAmW 93, WhoSSW 93*
Hollier, Robert Henry *WhoScE 91-1*
Hollies, Linda Hall 1943- *WhoAmW 93*
Hollifield, James F. 1954- *ConAu 139*
Hollifield, Kay Mobley 1949- *WhoAmW 93*
Holliger, Heinz 1939- *Baker 92*
Holliman, Dan Clark 1932- *WhoSSW 93*
Holliman, Joe M. 1921- *St&PR 93*
Holliman, Joe Milton 1921- *WhoAm 92*
Holliman, John *BioIn 17*
Hollimon, Dianne Witt 1958- *WhoAmW 93*
Hollin, Betty A. 1956- *WhoAmW 93*
Hollin, Mitchell Louis 1962- *WhoE 93*
Hollin, Shelby W. 1925- *WhoSSW 93, WhoWor 93*
Hollinbeck, Bob *BioIn 17*
Hollinden, Christine Melanie 1960- *WhoAmW 93*
Holling, Crawford Stanley 1930- *WhoAm 92*
Holling, Holling C(lancy) 1900-1973 *MajAI [port]*
Hollinger, Arlene Utz 1916- *St&PR 93*
Hollinger, Charlotte Elizabeth 1951- *WhoSSW 93*
Hollinger, Gilbert Russell, III 1953- *WhoSSW 93*
Hollinger, Paula Colodny 1940- *WhoAmW 93, WhoE 93*
Hollinger, Peggy Louise 1956- *WhoSSW 93*
Hollinger, Peter Bracken 1948- *WhoEmL 93, WhoSSW 93*
Hollinger, Rosemary 1953- *WhoEmL 93*
Hollinger, Susan Barbara 1962- *WhoAmW 93*
Hollings, Ernest F. 1922- *CngDr 91*
Hollings, Ernest Frederick 1922- *WhoAm 92, WhoSSW 93*
Hollingshead, Barbara J. *Law&B 92*
Hollingshead, Barbara Jane *Law&B 92*
Hollingshead, Greg 1947- *WhoCanL 92*
Hollingsworth, Abner Thomas 1939- *WhoSSW 93*
Hollingsworth, Anthony 1943- *WhoScE 91-1*
Hollingsworth, Bobby J. 1927- *WhoSSW 93*
Hollingsworth, Carey Ferguson, Jr. 1929- *St&PR 93*
Hollingsworth, Carolyn Kennedy *St&PR 93*
Hollingsworth, Clyde Dixon, Jr. 1920- *WhoSSW 93*
Hollingsworth, David S. *BioIn 17*
Hollingsworth, David S. 1928- *St&PR 93*
Hollingsworth, Dennis L. 1934- *St&PR 93*
Hollingsworth, Diane Lucile 1952- *WhoSSW 93*
Hollingsworth, Fred, III 1930- *St&PR 93*
Hollingsworth, Gary Mayes 1944- *WhoWor 93*
Hollingsworth, Grace *AmWomPl*
Hollingsworth, Helen 1930- *WhoSSW 93*
Hollingsworth, Helen Partello- *BioIn 17*
Hollingsworth, Jack Waring 1924- *WhoAm 92*
Hollingsworth, James D. *Law&B 92*
Hollingsworth, John Mark *Law&B 92*
Hollingsworth, Jordan Marcus, Jr. 1941- *WhoSSW 93*
Hollingsworth, Joseph Rogers 1932- *WhoAm 92, WhoWrEP 92*
Hollingsworth, Kent 1929- *WhoWrEP 92*
Hollingsworth, Margaret *WhoCanL 92*
Hollingsworth, Margaret Camille 1929- *WhoAmW 93*
Hollingsworth, Margie Ellen 1951- *WhoAmW 93*
Hollingsworth, Martha Lynette 1951- *WhoAmW 93*
Hollingsworth, Mary Carolyn 1947- *WhoWrEP 92*
Hollingsworth, Meredith Beaton 1941- *WhoAmW 93, WhoWor 93*
Hollingsworth, Michael 1950- *WhoCanL 92*
Hollingsworth, Randolph 1957- *WhoSSW 93*
Hollingsworth, Robert Edgar 1918- *WhoAm 92*
Hollingsworth, Samuel Hawkins, Jr. 1922- *WhoAm 92*
Hollingsworth, Stanley 1924- *Baker 92*
Hollingsworth, Susan M. *Law&B 92*
Hollingworth, Beverly A. 1935- *WhoAmW 93*
Hollingworth, Charles Edward 1950- *WhoWor 93*
Hollingworth, John *WhoScE 91-1*
Hollingworth, Leta Stetter 1886-1939 *BioIn 17*
Hollingworth, Pamela d1992 *NewYTBS 92*
Hollingworth, R. *WhoScE 91-1*
Hollingworth, Sheila *WhoScE 91-1*
Hollins, Alfred 1865-1942 *Baker 92*
Hollins, Arthur, III 1930- *St&PR 93*
Hollins, Elizabeth Jay d1991 *BioIn 17*
Hollins, Harry B. d1991 *BioIn 17*
Hollins, Mitchell Leslie 1947- *WhoEmL 93*
Hollins, Sheila Clare *WhoScE 91-1*
Hollinshead, Ariel Cahill 1929- *WhoAm 92*
Hollinshead, Byron Sharpe, Jr. 1929- *WhoAm 92*
Hollinshead, Earl Darnell, Jr. 1927- *WhoE 93, WhoWor 93*
Hollinshead, May Block 1913- *WhoAmW 93*
Hollis, Bruce Warren 1951- *WhoSSW 93*
Hollis, Charles Carroll 1911- *WhoSSW 93*
Hollis, Charles Eugene, Jr. 1948- *WhoAm 92*
Hollis, Christopher 1902-1977 *ScF&FL 92*
Hollis, Colin 1938- *WhoAsAP 91*
Hollis, David Bernard 1946- *WhoWor 93*
Hollis, Donald Roger 1936- *St&PR 93, WhoAm 92*
Hollis, Douglas *BioIn 17*
Hollis, Eleanor Hannah 1931- *WhoAmW 93*
Hollis, Guy Houston 1926- *WhoSSW 93*
Hollis, Howell 1919- *WhoAm 92*
Hollis, Jocelyn 1927- *WhoWrEP 92*
Hollis, John E. 1931- *WhoIns 93*
Hollis, Kathleen Sue 1955- *WhoAmW 93*
Hollis, Lee J. *Law&B 92*
Hollis, Linda Eardley 1948- *WhoE 93*
Hollis, Loucille 1949- *WhoAmW 93*
Hollis, Mark C. 1934- *WhoSSW 93*
Hollis, Mark D. 1908- *WhoAm 92*
Hollis, Mary Dean 1928- *WhoAmW 93*
Hollis, Mary Lynn *Law&B 92*
Hollis, Peter B. 1943- *WhoE 93*
Hollis, Reginald 1932- *WhoAm 92*
Hollis, Roger 1905-1973 *BioIn 17*
Hollis, Roy Estes 1946- *WhoE 93*
Hollis, Samuel Brinson 1929- *St&PR 93*
Hollis, Sheila Slocum 1948- *WhoAm 92*
Hollis, Thomas 1720-1774 *BioIn 17*
Hollis, Timothy Martin 1962- *WhoSSW 93*
Hollis, Tony *St&PR 93*
Hollis, Virginia Weare 1948- *WhoE 93*
Hollis, William S. 1930- *WhoAm 92, WhoWor 93*
Hollis-Allbritton, Cheryl Dawn 1959- *WhoAmW 93*
Hollis-Coburn, Deborah Marie 1964- *WhoAmW 93*
Hollister, A.D. *St&PR 93*
Hollister, Bernard C. 1938- *ScF&FL 92*
Hollister, Cash 1845-1884 *BioIn 17*
Hollister, Charles Davis 1936- *WhoAm 92*
Hollister, Charles Warren 1930- *WhoAm 92*
Hollister, Jeffrey Lynn 1949- *St&PR 93*
Hollister, John C. *Law&B 92*
Hollister, Leo Edward 1920- *WhoAm 92*
Hollister, Lynda Jeanne 1960- *WhoAmW 93, WhoEmL 93*
Hollister, Raymond Lawrence *Law&B 92*
Hollister, William Gray 1915- *WhoAm 92*
Hollitt, Raye *BioIn 17*
Hollman, Richard Martin 1932- *St&PR 93*
Hollmann, Joseph 1852-1927 *Baker 92*
Hollmann, Rudolf Werner 1931- *WhoWor 93*
Hollmen, Arno Ilmari 1930- *WhoScE 91-4*
Hollo, Erkki J. 1940- *WhoScE 91-4*
Hollo, Istvan 1926- *WhoScE 91-4*
Hollo, Janos 1919- *WhoScE 91-4*
Hollo, Sandor 1958- *WhoScE 91-4*
Holloman, Deborah Ann *Law&B 92*
Holloman, Haskell Andrew 1907- *WhoSSW 93*
Holloman, Hugh Jerry 1947- *WhoWrEP 92*
Holloman, Otis Jack 1926- *St&PR 93*
Holloman, Robert C. 1928- *WhoIns 93*
Hollon, William Eugene 1913- *WhoAm 92, WhoWrEP 92*
Hollonquest, Barbara J. *Law&B 92*
Holloran, Margaret Rose 1965- *WhoAmW 93*
Holloran, Thomas Edward 1929- *St&PR 93, WhoAm 92*
Hollos, Marida 1940- *ConAu 139*
Hollosi, Gabor 1935- *WhoScE 91-4*
Hollosi, Szilard 1952- *WhoScE 91-4*
Hollow, John 1939- *ScF&FL 92*
Holloway, Benjamin Duke 1925- *St&PR 93, WhoAm 92*
Holloway, Brenda 1946- *SoulM*
Holloway, Brian *ScF&FL 92*
Holloway, Bruce Keener 1912- *WhoAm 92*
Holloway, Carol *SweetSg A [port]*
Holloway, Carol Lee 1948- *St&PR 93*
Holloway, Charles Arthur 1936- *WhoAm 92*
Holloway, Clayton Glenn 1945- *WhoSSW 93*
Holloway, Clyde C. 1943- *CngDr 91*
Holloway, Clyde Cecil 1943- *WhoAm 92, WhoSSW 93*
Holloway, David 1942- *WhoAm 92*
Holloway, Donald Phillip 1928- *WhoWor 93*
Holloway, Dorothy *AmWomPl*
Holloway, Douglas P. 1938- *St&PR 93*
Holloway, Douglas Patrick 1938- *WhoAm 92*
Holloway, Edgar Austin 1925- *WhoAm 92*
Holloway, Edna LaRue 1942- *WhoAmW 93*
Holloway, Edward Olin 1944- *WhoSSW 93*
Holloway, Elton Dewitt 1945- *WhoSSW 93*
Holloway, Emory 1885-1977 *BioIn 17*
Holloway, Eric A. 1965- *St&PR 93*
Holloway, Ernest L. *AfrAmBi [port]*
Holloway, Esther W. 1945- *St&PR 93*
Holloway, Eugene C. *Law&B 92*
Holloway, Frank Albert, Jr. 1940- *WhoSSW 93*
Holloway, Frank Burnley 1931- *St&PR 93*
Holloway, Frederic Ancrum Lord 1914-1990 *BioIn 17*
Holloway, Giselle P. 1962- *WhoAmW 93*
Holloway, Glenna Preston 1938- *WhoWrEP 92*
Holloway, Herman M., Sr. 1922- *AfrAmBi [port]*
Holloway, Hiliary Hamilton 1928- *St&PR 93, WhoAm 92*
Holloway, James Brian 1957- *WhoEmL 93*
Holloway, James Curtis 1951- *WhoE 93*
Holloway, James J. 1936- *St&PR 93*
Holloway, James Lemuel, III 1922- *WhoAm 92, WhoE 93, WhoWor 93*
Holloway, Jeanette 1949- *WhoSSW 93*
Holloway, Jeffrey John 1948- *WhoE 93*
Holloway, Jerome Knight 1923- *WhoAm 92*
Holloway, John Christopher *WhoScE 91-1*
Holloway, John Henry *WhoScE 91-1*
Holloway, John Laws, III 1937- *St&PR 93*
Holloway, John Thomas 1922- *WhoAm 92*
Holloway, Julia Bolton 1937- *WhoAmW 93, WhoWor 93*
Holloway, Kenneth A. 1934- *St&PR 93*
Holloway, Lawrence Milton, Sr. 1913- *WhoWor 93*
Holloway, Leonard Leveine 1923- *WhoAm 92*
Holloway, Lisabeth Marie 1926- *WhoAmW 93*
Holloway, Loverta Ruth *WhoE 93*
Holloway, Marcella Marie 1913- *WhoWrEP 92*
Holloway, Marvin Lawrence 1911- *WhoAm 92*
Holloway, Michael Bernice 1957- *WhoWor 93*
Holloway, Paul Fayette 1938- *WhoAm 92*
Holloway, Paul Howard 1943- *WhoSSW 93*
Holloway, Pearl 1888- *AmWomPl*
Holloway, Peter *BioIn 17*
Holloway, Peter John *WhoScE 91-1*
Holloway, Philip John *WhoScE 91-1*
Holloway, Ralph Leslie 1935- *WhoE 93*
Holloway, Reid Loren 1953- *WhoE 93*
Holloway, Richard A. 1941- *St&PR 93*
Holloway, Robert A. 1930- *St&PR 93*
Holloway, Robert Anthony 1946- *WhoWor 93*
Holloway, Robert Ross 1934- *WhoAm 92*
Holloway, Robin 1934- *OxDcOp*
Holloway, Robin (Greville) 1943- *Baker 92*
Holloway, Stanley 1890-1982 *QDrFCA 92 [port]*
Holloway, Sterling 1905-1992 *NewYTBS 92 [port]*
Holloway, Sterling Price *WhoAm 92*
Holloway, Thomas F. 1947- *St&PR 93*
Holloway, Wanda Webb *BioIn 17*
Holloway, William J., Jr. 1923- *WhoAm 92, WhoSSW 93*
Holloway, William Jimmerson 1917- *WhoAm 92*
Holloway, William Weller, Jr. *Law&B 92*
Hollowell, David *BioIn 17*
Hollowell, William George 1931- *St&PR 93*
Hollowood, James Richard 1943- *WhoE 93*
Hollox, Graham Edward 1940- *WhoScE 91-3*
Hollreiser, Heinrich 1913- *Baker 92*
Holls, William M., Jr. 1923- *St&PR 93*
Hollums, W.H. 1912- *St&PR 93*

Hollweg, Ilse 1922-1990 Baker 92
Hollweg, Robert W. Law&B 92
Hollweg, Theobald von Bethmann- 1856-1921 BioIn 17
Hollweg, Werner (Friedrich) 1936- Baker 92
Holly, Buddy 1936-1959 Baker 92, BioIn 17
Holly, Donald E. Law&B 92
Holly, Ellen 1931- ConTFT 10
Holly, Ellistine Perkins 1934- WhoSSW 93
Holly, Frank Joseph 1934- WhoSSW 93
Holly, Joan Hunter 1932-1982 ScF&FL 92
Holly, John Durward, III 1950- WhoSSW 93
Holly, Martin 1931- DrEEuF
Holly, Mary Lynne Andrews 1957- WhoSSW 93
Holly, Norman Dale Law&B 92
Hollyday, Christopher BioIn 17
Hollyday, Guy T.O. 1892-1991 BioIn 17
Hollyer, Lauraine 1947- WhoAmW 93
Hollywood, Edwin L. 1923- St&PR 93
Hollywood, John Matthew 1910- WhoAm 92
Hollywood Flames SoulM
Holm, Anne 1922- ScF&FL 92
Holm, (Else) Anne (Lise) 1922- MajAI [port]
Holm, Carl-Eric Ove 1946- WhoWor 93
Holm, Carol Elizabeth Sachs 1932- WhoAm 92
Holm, Celeste 1919- WhoAm 92
Holm, Dennis James 1931- WhoSSW 93
Holm, Eleanor 1914- BioIn 17
Holm, Gerald Lange 1938- St&PR 93
Holm, Gunnar Vilhelm 1916- WhoWor 93
Holm, Hanya WhoAm 92
Holm, Hanya d1992 NewYTBS 92 [port]
Holm, Ian 1931- WhoAm 92
Holm, Ingrid Margareta 1961- WhoE 93
Holm, Jeanne Marjorie 1921- WhoAm 92
Holm, Jens Hintze 1955- WhoWor 93
Holm, John Cecil 1904-1981 ScF&FL 92
Holm, Kim R. 1956- St&PR 93
Holm, Kurt Harri 1943- WhoScE 91-4
Holm, Melvin C. 1916-1991 BioIn 17
Holm, Mogens Winkel 1936- Baker 92
Holm, Peder 1926- Baker 92
Holm, Peter Christian Achilles 1936- WhoWor 93
Holm, Phillip Howard 1931- WhoAm 92
Holm, Renate 1931- Baker 92
Holm, Richard 1912- OxDcOp
Holm, Richard 1912-1988 Baker 92
Holm, Robert Arthur 1935- WhoAm 92
Holm, Stig E. 1933- WhoScE 91-4
Holm, Sture Axel 1936- WhoWor 93
Holman, Alan B. 1944- St&PR 93
Holman, Arthur Stearns 1926- WhoAm 92
Holman, Bob 1948- WhoWrEP 92
Holman, Bud George 1929- WhoAm 92
Holman, Carl Reyburn 1942- St&PR 93
Holman, Charles Richardson 1915- WhoAm 92
Holman, Clyde Joe 1930- WhoSSW 93
Holman, Cranston William 1907- WhoAm 92
Holman, Currier J. 1911-1977 BioIn 17
Holman, Daniel G. 1945- St&PR 93
Holman, David ScF&FL 92
Holman, Diane R. Law&B 92
Holman, Donald Reid 1930- St&PR 93, WhoAm 92
Holman, Felice 1919- ConAu 40NR, DcAmChF 1960
Holman, Francis Wade, Jr. 1939- WhoAm 92
Holman, Frederick John 1947- WhoE 93
Holman, Halsted Reid 1925- WhoAm 92
Holman, Harland Eugene 1914- WhoAm 92
Holman, James Bradley 1935- St&PR 93
Holman, Jay MiSFD 9
Holman, John Foster 1946- WhoEmL 93, WhoWor 93
Holman, John Leonard 1929- WhoAm 92, WhoWor 93
Holman, Karen Marie 1962- WhoEmL 93
Holman, Kenneth Inge 1938- WhoSSW 93
Holman, Kermit Layton 1935- WhoAm 92
Holman, Margaret Mezoff 1951- WhoAm 92, WhoE 93, WhoEmL 93
Holman, Miriam d1991 BioIn 17
Holman, Ralph Theodore 1918- WhoAm 92
Holman, Russell ScF&FL 92
Holman, Russell A. Law&B 92
Holman, Russell A. 1955- St&PR 93
Holman, Tomlinson 1946- WhoAm 92
Holman, W. H., Jr. WhoAm 92
Holman, William Henry, Jr. 1930- WhoAm 92
Holman-Hunt, William 1827-1910 BioIn 17
Holmberg, A. William 1923- St&PR 93
Holmberg, Albert William, Jr. 1923- WhoAm 92, WhoSSW 93
Holmberg, Allan R. 1909-1966 IntDcAn
Holmberg, Bo E.G. 1930- WhoScE 91-4
Holmberg, Branton Kieth 1936- WhoWor 93
Holmberg, Georgia McKee 1946- WhoAmW 93
Holmberg, James J. 1928- St&PR 93
Holmberg, Joan Joanna 1939- WhoAmW 93
Holmberg, Joyce 1930- WhoAmW 93
Holmberg, Kaj 1934- WhoScE 91-4
Holmberg, Olof W. 1931- WhoScE 91-4
Holmberg, Ronald K. 1932- WhoAm 92
Holmberg, Ronald Keith 1932- St&PR 93
Holmberg, Roy Hopkins 1939- WhoE 93
Holmberg, Ruth S. 1921- St&PR 93
Holmberg, Ruth Sulzberger 1921- WhoAm 92, WhoSSW 93
Holmberg, Uno IntDcAn
Holmblad, John B. 1950- St&PR 93
Holmbo, Dwight N. Law&B 92
Holmboe, Vagn 1909- Baker 92
Holmbom, Bjarne R. 1943- WhoScE 91-4
Holme, Bryan 1913-1990 BioIn 17
Holme, Constance ScF&FL 92
Holme, Richard Phillips 1941- WhoAm 92
Holme, Thomas Timings 1913- WhoAm 92
Holme, Tord E.B. 1927- WhoScE 91-4
Holmegaard, Poul 1927- WhoScE 91-2
Holmen, George Robert 1933- St&PR 93
Holmen, Orrie Jeffrey 1953- WhoSSW 93
Holmer, Edwin Carl 1921- WhoAm 92
Holmer, Nils-Gunnar 1943- WhoScE 91-4
Holmes, A.W. WhoScE 91-1
Holmes, Abraham S. 1821?-1908 BioIn 17
Holmes, Albert William, Jr. 1932- WhoAm 92
Holmes, Alfred 1837-1876 Baker 92
Holmes, Allen C. 1920-1990 BioIn 17
Holmes, Andrew James Timothy 1946- WhoWor 93
Holmes, Ann Hitchcock 1922- WhoAm 92
Holmes, Anna WhoWrEP 92
Holmes, Archie E., Jr. 1935- St&PR 93
Holmes, Arthur, Jr. 1931- AfrAmBi
Holmes, Augusta 1847-1903 Baker 92, BioIn 17
Holmes, Barbara Ann Krajkoski 1946- WhoAmW 93
Holmes, Barbara Jean 1948- WhoE 93, WhoEmL 93
Holmes, Barbara W. Law&B 92
Holmes, Barbara Ware BioIn 17
Holmes, Barbara Ware 1945- WhoWrEP 92
Holmes, Barry WhoScE 91-1
Holmes, Bert Otis E., Jr. 1921- WhoAm 92
Holmes, Bonnie Tansill 1946- WhoEmL 93
Holmes, Bradley Paul 1953- WhoAm 92
Holmes, Bradly J. Law&B 92
Holmes, Broox Garrett 1932- WhoAm 92
Holmes, Bruce John 1948- WhoAm 92
Holmes, Bruce T. 1946- ScF&FL 92
Holmes, Catherine Rains 1960- WhoAmW 93
Holmes, Charles E. Law&B 92
Holmes, Charles M. 1923- ScF&FL 92
Holmes, Christopher Francis 1959- WhoE 93, WhoEmL 93
Holmes, Colgate Frederick 1935- WhoAm 92
Holmes, Curtis Frank 1943- St&PR 93
Holmes, Cynthia Misao Bell 1949- WhoAmW 93
Holmes, D. Brainerd 1921- St&PR 93
Holmes, Daniel P. Law&B 92
Holmes, Daniel W., Jr. 1938- St&PR 93
Holmes, Darrell 1921- WhoAm 92
Holmes, David Bryan 1936- WhoE 93
Holmes, David Gordon 1943- WhoAm 92
Holmes, David Iain 1944- WhoWor 93
Holmes, David Richard 1940- St&PR 93, WhoAm 92
Holmes, David S. BioIn 17
Holmes, David S., Jr. 1914- AfrAmBi
Holmes, Debbie BioIn 17
Holmes, Donald Dean 1930- WhoE 93
Holmes, Dwight Ellis 1938- WhoAm 92
Holmes, Dyer Brainerd 1921- WhoAm 92
Holmes, Edward 1797-1859 Baker 92
Holmes, Elaine Louise 1958- WhoAmW 93
Holmes, Elizabeth Holbert Harris 1941- WhoSSW 93
Holmes, Francis Oliver 1899-1990 BioIn 17
Holmes, Francis William 1929- WhoAm 92
Holmes, Frank E. 1955- St&PR 93
Holmes, Frankie Ann 1950- WhoEmL 93
Holmes, Fred MiSFD 9
Holmes, Fred Gillespie 1913- WhoAm 92
Holmes, Frederic Lawrence 1932- WhoAm 92
Holmes, G.W. WhoScE 91-1
Holmes, Gary Paul 1955- WhoSSW 93
Holmes, Genta Hawkins 1940- WhoAmW 93
Holmes, Gerald E. 1940- St&PR 93
Holmes, Grace Narua 1961- WhoAmW 93
Holmes, Harry L. 1945- St&PR 93
Holmes, Helen 1892-1950 SweetSg A [port]
Holmes, Helen Bequaert 1929- WhoAm 92
Holmes, Helen Juanita WhoWrEP 92
Holmes, Henry 1839-1905 See Holmes, Alfred 1837-1876 Baker 92
Holmes, Henry Allen 1933- WhoAm 92
Holmes, Houston Eccleston, Jr. Law&B 92
Holmes, Houston Eccleston, Jr. 1938- St&PR 93
Holmes, Howard S. 1913- St&PR 93
Holmes, Ivar Hugh 1953- WhoWor 93
Holmes, J.N. Law&B 92
Holmes, Jack Edward 1934- St&PR 93
Holmes, Jack Edward 1941- WhoWor 93
Holmes, Jacquelin Ann 1947- WhoAmW 93
Holmes, Jacqueline Suzanne 1955- WhoEmL 93
Holmes, James 1919- WhoAm 92
Holmes, James Richard 1955- WhoEmL 93
Holmes, Jay Thorpe 1942- St&PR 93, WhoAm 92
Holmes, Jeffrey 1934- ScF&FL 92, WhoCanL 92
Holmes, Jeffrey E. Law&B 92
Holmes, Jeni Rose 1961- WhoAmW 93
Holmes, Jerry Dell 1935- WhoAm 92
Holmes, John BioIn 17, WhoCanL 92
Holmes, John Eric 1930- ScF&FL 92
Holmes, John Leonard 1931- WhoAm 92
Holmes, John Michael 1946- St&PR 93
Holmes, John Richard 1917- WhoAm 92
Holmes, Julia Faye 1950- WhoAmW 93
Holmes, Karen M. Law&B 92
Holmes, Kenneth Law&B 92
Holmes, Kenneth C. 1934- WhoScE 91-3
Holmes, Kenneth E. 1942- WhoIns 93
Holmes, Larry 1949- AfrAmBi, WhoAm 92
Holmes, Leonard George 1954- WhoSSW 93
Holmes, Malcolm Herbert 1934- St&PR 93
Holmes, Margaret R. 1942- St&PR 93
Holmes, Marilyn Adams 1930- WhoWrEP 92
Holmes, Marilyn Janet 1934- WhoE 93
Holmes, Marion 1940- St&PR 93
Holmes, Marjorie Law&B 92
Holmes, Marjorie Rose WhoAm 92, WhoWor 93, WhoWrEP 92
Holmes, Marjory Ann 1931- St&PR 93
Holmes, Martha 1961- SmATA 72 [port]
Holmes, Martin M. 1939- St&PR 93
Holmes, Melvin Almont 1919- WhoAm 92
Holmes, Michael A. Law&B 92
Holmes, Michael Dale 1962- WhoSSW 93
Holmes, Michael Denison 1935- St&PR 93
Holmes, Miller P., Jr. 1943- St&PR 93
Holmes, Monica Bychowski 1937- WhoAmW 93
Holmes, Neil E. 1944- St&PR 93
Holmes, Neil Edward 1944- WhoAm 92
Holmes, Nicholas Hanson, Jr. 1924- WhoAm 92
Holmes, Norman Leonard 1928- WhoAm 92
Holmes, Oliver Wendell 1841-1932 OxCSupC [port]
Holmes, Oliver Wendell 1841-1935 BioIn 17, GayN
Holmes, P.H. 1943- St&PR 93
Holmes, Patricia Anne 1927- WhoAmW 93
Holmes, Patrick WhoScE 91-1
Holmes, Paul Kinloch, Jr. 1915- WhoSSW 93
Holmes, Peggy 1897- BioIn 17
Holmes, Peter Geoffery WhoScE 91-1
Holmes, Peter Henry WhoScE 91-1
Holmes, R.L. WhoScE 91-1
Holmes, Ralph 1937-1984 Baker 92
Holmes, Randall Kent 1940- WhoAm 92
Holmes, Raymond WhoCanL 92
Holmes, Raymond V. 1937- St&PR 93
Holmes, Reed K. 1952- Baker 92
Holmes, Reed M. 1917- WhoAm 92
Holmes, Richard Brooks 1959- WhoWor 93
Holmes, Richard Hugh Morris 1925- WhoAm 92
Holmes, Richard V. 1929- St&PR 93
Holmes, Richard Winn 1923- WhoAm 92
Holmes, Robert 1926- ScF&FL 92
Holmes, Robert A. 1943- AfrAmBi [port]
Holmes, Robert Allen 1947- WhoAm 92, WhoWor 93
Holmes, Robert Lawrence 1935- WhoAm 92
Holmes, Robert Raymond 1937- WhoSSW 93
Holmes, Robert Richard 1928- WhoE 93
Holmes, Robert William 1929- WhoAm 92
Holmes, Ronald ScF&FL 92
Holmes, Roy WhoScE 91-1
Holmes, Russell Porter 1939- St&PR 93
Holmes, Sharon Ann 1959- WhoAmW 93
Holmes, Sheila Louise 1956- WhoSSW 93
Holmes, Sherie Bell Shortridge 1956- WhoSSW 93
Holmes, Steven R. Law&B 92
Holmes, Susan Annette 1957- WhoAmW 93
Holmes, Susan G. 1955- WhoAmW 93, WhoEmL 93
Holmes, Susan K. 1951- St&PR 93
Holmes, Theophilus Hunter 1804-1880 BioIn 17
Holmes, Thomas James, Jr. 1948- WhoEmL 93, WhoSSW 93
Holmes, Thomas Joseph 1953- WhoWor 93
Holmes, Thomas T. Law&B 92
Holmes, Vernon Harrison 1920- WhoAm 92
Holmes, Walter John 1906- WhoE 93
Holmes, Walter Stephen, Jr. 1919- WhoAm 92
Holmes, Willard WhoAm 92
Holmes, William Charles, Jr. 1917- WhoAm 92
Holmes, William D. 1929- St&PR 93
Holmes, William Dee 1929- WhoAm 92
Holmes, William Ernest 1947- WhoIns 93
Holmes, William Henry 1846-1933 IntDcAn
Holmes, William James WhoE 93
Holmes, William M. WhoIns 93
Holmes a Court, Janet BioIn 17
Holmes a Court, Robert BioIn 17
Holmes-Lupi, Margaret 1958- WhoEmL 93
Holmgrain, Floyd Harold, Jr. 1928- WhoE 93
Holmgren, Adriana Mcdona 1943- WhoE 93
Holmgren, Alf G.M. 1924- WhoScE 91-4
Holmgren, Arne 1940- WhoScE 91-4
Holmgren, Edwin Surl 1934- WhoAm 92
Holmgren, Jan R. 1944- WhoScE 91-4
Holmgren, Laton Earle 1915- WhoAm 92
Holmgren, Mike 1948- WhoAm 92
Holmgren, Paul WhoAm 92
Holmgren, Robert Bruce 1920- WhoAm 92
Holmgren, Theodore J. 1927-1990 BioIn 17
Holm-Nielsen, Lauritz B. 1946- WhoScE 91-2
Holmquest, Donald Lee 1939- WhoAm 92
Holmquist, Barton 1943- WhoE 93
Holmquist, Paul R. 1943- WhoIns 93
Holmquist, Paul Raymond Law&B 92
Holmquist, Walter Richard 1934- WhoAm 92
Holmquist, William Randall 1925- St&PR 93
Holms, John 1830-1891 BioIn 17
Holmsgaard, Erik WhoScE 91-2
Holmstead, Jeffrey R. 1960- WhoAm 92
Holmstedt, Bo R. 1918- WhoScE 91-4
Holmsten, Victoria Lynn 1953- WhoWrEP 92
Holmstrom, Frank Ross 1936- WhoE 93
Holmstrom, Gustaf Werner 1923- WhoWor 93
Holmstrom, Hans 1939- WhoScE 91-4
Holmstrom, Michael Edward 1942- St&PR 93
Holmstrup, Palle 1945- WhoScE 91-2
Holmwood, James Morley 1937- WhoE 93
Holness, Gordon V.R. 1939- St&PR 93
Holnick, Catherine Sigmund 1959- WhoWrEP 92
Holo, Selma Reuben 1943- WhoAm 92
Holo, Theodore 1948- WhoWor 93
Holobolos, Manuel c. 1245-c. 1310 OxDcByz
Holograf, Michael R. 1946- St&PR 93
Holoman, D(allas) Kern 1947- Baker 92
Holoman, Dallas Kern 1947- WhoAm 92
Ho Long 1896-1967 HarEnMi
Holonyak, Nick, Jr. 1928- WhoAm 92
Holoubek, Ladislav 1913- Baker 92
Holovak, Michael Joseph 1919- BiDAMSp 1989
Holovak, Mike WhoAm 92, WhoSSW 93
Holoviak, Stephen Julian 1948- WhoEmL 93
Holowesko, Mark G. 1960- St&PR 93
Holowiak, Robert W. 1947- St&PR 93
Holp, Carolyn Elaine 1947- WhoWrEP 92
Holp, Karen Patricia 1950- WhoAmW 93

Holquist, James Michael 1935- WhoAm 92
Holran, Bruce Grenville 1934- WhoE 93
Holroyd, Gregory E. 1955- St&PR 93
Holroyd, Joseph Armitage 1939- WhoAm 92
Holroyd, Michael BioIn 17
Holroyd, Michael 1935- WhoAm 92
Holroyd, Richard Allan 1930- WhoE 93
Holroyd, Sam ScF&FL 92
Holsaert, Faith S. 1943- WhoWrEP 92
Holscher, Richard Harry 1928- St&PR 93, WhoAm 92
Holschuh, John David 1926- WhoAm 92
Holschuh, John David, Jr. 1955- WhoEmL 93
Holschuh, L.J. WhoScE 91-2
Holschuh, Laurel A. Law&B 92
Holsclaw, Robert Graydon 1934- St&PR 93, WhoAm 92
Holsen, James Noble, Jr. 1924- WhoAm 92
Holsen, Robert Charles 1913- WhoAm 92
Holsenbeck, G. Penn Law&B 92
Holshey, Michael L. 1941- St&PR 93
Holshouser, Thomas Edward 1958- WhoEmL 93
Holsinger, James Wilson, Jr. 1939- WhoAm 92, WhoSSW 93
Holsinger, John Paul Law&B 92
Holsinger, Mary Frances 1938- WhoAmW 93
Holsinger, Steven J. Law&B 92
Holsinger, Virginia Harris WhoE 93
Holsinger, W. Preston 1942- St&PR 93, WhoAm 92
Holsinger, Wayne Townsend 1931- WhoAm 92
Holslag, John F. 1946- WhoSSW 93
Holst, Edvard 1843-1899 Baker 92
Holst, Erik 1929- WhoScE 91-2
Holst, Gustav 1874-1934 BioIn 17, IntDcOp [port], OxDcOp
Holst, Gustav(us Theodore von) 1874-1934 Baker 92
Holst, Henry 1899- Baker 92
Holst, Imogen (Clare) 1907-1984 Baker 92
Holst, Johan Jorgen 1937- WhoWor 93
Holst, Norman Dolcy 1943- St&PR 93
Holst, Valerie Fisher 1964- WhoAmW 93
Holst, Willem 1911- WhoAm 92, WhoE 93
Holstead, John Burnham 1938- WhoAm 92
Holstead, Marjorie ScF&FL 92
Holstein, Anne Louise Germaine Stael- 1766-1817 BioIn 17
Holstein, Bruce Jay 1947- WhoEmL 93
Holstein, Elaine BioIn 17
Holstein, Franz (Friedrich) von 1826-1878 Baker 92
Holstein, Friedrich von 1837-1909 BioIn 17
Holstein, Jay Allen 1938- WhoAm 92
Holstein, John Charles 1945- WhoAm 92
Holstein, Marilyn Anne 1958- WhoAm 92
Holstein, Mark E. Law&B 92
Holstein, William Kurt 1936- WhoAm 92
Holsten, Fred 1944- WhoScE 91-4
Holstener-Jorgensen, Helge 1924- WhoScE 91-2
Holster, Robert Marc 1946- WhoAm 92
Holsti, Kalevi Jacque 1935- WhoAm 92
Holsti, Ole Rudolf 1933- WhoAm 92
Holstius, Elvin Albert 1921- WhoSSW 93
Holston, James Benjamin, III BioIn 17
Holston, James Eugene 1951- WhoWrEP 92
Holstrom, Carleton Arthur 1935- WhoAm 92
Holsworth, Doris Campbell AmWomPl
Holsworth, Mark E. Law&B 92
Holsworth, William C. 1949- St&PR 93
Holt, Alan Craig 1945- WhoSSW 93
Holt, Alan George James WhoScE 91-1
Holt, Amos E. 1940- St&PR 93
Holt, Andrew ConTFT 10
Holt, Arthur H., Jr. 1931- WhoAm 92
Holt, Barbara Bertany 1940- WhoAmW 93
Holt, Ben d1990 BioIn 17
Holt, Betty Carolyn 1951- WhoEmL 93
Holt, Beverly Elaine 1945- WhoAmW 93
Holt, Brent Marion 1953- WhoE 93
Holt, Calvin d1991 BioIn 17
Holt, Charles Asbury 1948- WhoAm 92
Holt, Charles Carter 1921- WhoAm 92
Holt, Christopher Martin 1954- WhoWor 93
Holt, David Earl 1928- WhoSSW 93
Holt, David Tim 1943- WhoWor 93
Holt, Dennis Franklin BioIn 17
Holt, Donald A. 1932- WhoAm 92
Holt, Donald Dale 1936- WhoAm 92, WhoWrEP 92
Holt, Donald Edward, Jr. 1945- WhoAm 92
Holt, Douglas Eugene 1924- WhoAm 92
Holt, Edwin Joseph WhoSSW 93
Holt, Ellen Marie 1945- WhoAmW 93
Holt, Erick Robert Law&B 92
Holt, Florence Taber AmWomPl
Holt, G. WhoScE 91-1
Holt, G. Woodrow Law&B 92
Holt, Georgina L. 1934- WhoAm 92
Holt, Gerald F. 1923- St&PR 93
Holt, (Wilma) Geraldene ConAu 137
Holt, Guy 1892-1934 ScF&FL 92
Holt, Harold 1908-1967 DcTwHis
Holt, Helen Keil 1937- WhoAm 92
Holt, Henry 1934- Baker 92
Holt, Herbert 1912- WhoE 93
Holt, Herbert 1912-1991 BioIn 17
Holt, J.M. 1939- WhoScE 91-1
Holt, Jack W. 1936- WhoIns 93
Holt, Jack Wilson, Jr. 1929- WhoAm 92, WhoSSW 93
Holt, James 1955- WhoSSW 93
Holt, James Richard, Jr. 1958- WhoIns 93
Holt, Jason MiSFD 9
Holt, Jennifer 1920- SweetSg C [port]
Holt, Jennifer Dean Law&B 92
Holt, John d1504 BioIn 17
Holt, John 1721-1784 JrnUS
Holt, John B. 1915- WhoAm 92
Holt, John Briggs WhoScE 91-1
Holt, John C. St&PR 93
Holt, John C. 1940- WhoAm 92
Holt, John Caldwell 1923-1985 BioIn 17
Holt, John E. Law&B 92
Holt, John R. ScF&FL 92
Holt, Jonathan Turner 1949- WhoAm 92
Holt, Kenneth Sunderland WhoScE 91-1
Holt, Larry D. 1940- St&PR 93
Holt, Laura Davies AmWomPl
Holt, Laurence WhoScE 91-1
Holt, Leon Conrad, Jr. 1925- WhoAm 92
Holt, Linda Lee 1947- WhoE 93
Holt, Marjorie S. BioIn 17
Holt, Marjorie Sewell 1920- WhoAm 92, WhoAmW 93
Holt, Mary Louise 1945- WhoAmW 93
Holt, Michael ScF&FL 92
Holt, Nancy Louise 1938- WhoAm 92
Holt, Olav 1935- WhoScE 91-4
Holt, P.O. WhoScE 91-1
Holt, Patricia Lester 1944- WhoAm 92
Holt, Peter Rolf 1930- WhoAm 92
Holt, Philetus H. d1991 BioIn 17
Holt, Philetus Havens, III 1928- WhoAm 92
Holt, Ralph Manning, Jr. 1931- St&PR 93
Holt, Robert Lawrence 1939- ScF&FL 92
Holt, Robert LeRoi 1920- WhoAm 92
Holt, Robert Theodore 1928- WhoAm 92
Holt, Robert W. 1949- St&PR 93
Holt, Rochelle Lynn 1946- WhoWrEP 92
Holt, Seth 1923-1971 MiSFD 9N
Holt, Shirley Wayne Law&B 92
Holt, Sidney Clark 1955- WhoAm 92
Holt, Simeon ten 1923- Baker 92
Holt, Stephen S. 1940- WhoAm 92
Holt, T.J. 1952- St&PR 93
Holt, Terry ScF&FL 92
Holt, Terry W. 1954- WhoAm 92
Holt, Thomas C.L. ScF&FL 92
Holt, Timothy A. 1953- WhoIns 93
Holt, Timothy Arthur 1953- St&PR 93, WhoAm 92, WhoE 93
Holt, Tom 1961- ScF&FL 92
Holt, Victoria WhoAm 92, WhoWrEP 92
Holt, Walter L., Jr. 1928- St&PR 93
Holt, Wayne Gary Law&B 92
Holt, Wayne Gary 1937- St&PR 93
Holt, William H. 1929- St&PR 93
Holt, William Henry 1939- WhoSSW 93, WhoWor 93
Holt, Wilma Jean 1941- WhoAmW 93
Holtaling, Michael E. Law&B 92
Holtan, Boyd DeVere 1928- WhoAm 92, WhoSSW 93
Holtan, Daniel A. 1945- St&PR 93
Holtby, Douglas M. 1947- St&PR 93
Holtby, Douglas Martin 1947- WhoAm 92
Holtby, Kenneth Fraser 1922- WhoAm 92
Holtby, Maurice Law&B 92
Holtby, Winifred 1898-1935 BioIn 17
Holte, Debra Leah 1952- WhoAm 92, WhoAmW 93, WhoEmL 93, WhoWor 93
Holtel, Michael Ray 1958- WhoEmL 93, WhoSSW 93
Holten, Henning 1945- WhoWor 93
Holten, Virginia Lois Zewe 1938- WhoAmW 93
Holter, Arlen Rolf 1946- WhoEmL 93
Holter, Don Wendell 1905- WhoAm 92
Holter, Gail L. 1937- St&PR 93
Holter, Iver (Paul Fredrik) 1850-1941 Baker 92
Holter, Marvin Rosenkrantz 1922- WhoAm 92
Holter, Wesley Keith 1937- St&PR 93
Holtfreter, Johannes F. C. d1992 NewYTBS 92
Holtfreter, Johannes Friedrich Karl 1901- WhoAm 92
Holthaus, Dennis B. 1949- St&PR 93
Holthaus, Gerard Gustav 1962- St&PR 93
Holthaus, Hollis Lee 1936- WhoWor 93
Holthausen, Martha Anne 1934- WhoAmW 93
Holthuysen, A.M. WhoScE 91-3
Holtkamp, Dorsey Emil 1919- WhoAm 92
Holtkamp, James Arnold 1949- WhoEmL 93
Holtkamp, Richard G. Law&B 92
Holtkamp, Ronald W. 1952- WhoIns 93
Holtkamp, Wilhelm Bernhard 1953- WhoWor 93
Holtman, Robert Barney 1914- WhoSSW 93
Holtman, William J. 1921- WhoAm 92
Holtmann, John A. Law&B 92
Holton, A. Linwood, Jr. 1923- WhoAm 92
Holton, Earl D. 1934- WhoAm 92
Holton, Elwood Francis, III 1957- WhoSSW 93
Holton, Gerald 1922- WhoAm 92, WhoE 93
Holton, James Jerome 1963- WhoEmL 93
Holton, John J. 1933- St&PR 93
Holton, Mary Pearce 1939- WhoAmW 93, WhoSSW 93
Holton, Raymond William 1929- WhoAm 92
Holton, Richard Henry 1926- WhoAm 92
Holton, Robert Page 1938- WhoAm 92
Holton, Samuel Melanchthon 1922- WhoSSW 93
Holton, Scot 1939?-1991 ScF&FL 92
Holton, Susan A 1948- WhoE 93, WhoEmL 93
Holton, William Coffeen 1930- WhoAm 92, WhoSSW 93
Holton, William Milne 1931- WhoAm 92
Holton, William Roy, Jr. Law&B 92
Holtrust, Gezina Law&B 92
Holtsford, Alex LaFayette, Jr. 1959- WhoEmL 93
Holtsinger, Christine L. 1899- St&PR 93
Holtsmark, Erling B. 1936- ScF&FL 92
Holtum, Alfred Gerard 1918- WhoSSW 93
Holty, Ludwig Christoph Heinrich 1748-1776 BioIn 17
Holtz, Abel 1935- St&PR 93
Holtz, Aliza 1952- WhoE 93
Holtz, Caludia Patrizia 1964- WhoAmW 93
Holtz, Charles H. 1940- St&PR 93
Holtz, Claire J. 1958- WhoEmL 93
Holtz, Daniel M. 1959- St&PR 93
Holtz, Donald J. 1949- St&PR 93
Holtz, Edgar Wolfe 1922- WhoAm 92
Holtz, Gilbert Joseph 1924- WhoWor 93
Holtz, Glenn Edward 1938- WhoAm 92
Holtz, H. Edward Law&B 92
Holtz, Harry Lawrence 1918- St&PR 93
Holtz, Herman 1919- WhoWrEP 92
Holtz, Itshak 1925- WhoE 93
Holtz, Lou BioIn 17
Holtz, Louis Leo 1937- BiDAMSp 1989, WhoAm 92
Holtz, Mary Heston 1926- WhoSSW 93
Holtz, Michael P. 1956- St&PR 93
Holtz, Noel 1943- WhoSSW 93, WhoWor 93
Holtz, Richard L. St&PR 93
Holtz, Sara Law&B 92
Holtz, Sidney 1925- WhoAm 92
Holtz, Steven M. Law&B 92
Holtz, W. Bradley 1955- WhoEmL 93
Holtz, William V. BioIn 17
Holtz, Wolfgang H. 1941- WhoScE 91-3
Holtzapfel, Patricia Kelly 1948- WhoAmW 93, WhoEmL 93, WhoWor 93
Holtzberg, Frederic 1922- WhoAm 92
Holtzclaw, Cynthia Bennett 1953- WhoSSW 93
Holtzclaw, Diane Smith 1936- WhoAmW 93
Holtze, Sally Holmes BioIn 17
Holtzendorff, Richard Lee 1926- St&PR 93
Holtzer, Alfred Melvin 1929- WhoAm 92
Holtzman, Alexander 1924- WhoAm 92
Holtzman, Arnold Harold 1932- WhoE 93
Holtzman, Eleanor Fenster 1931- WhoAm 92
Holtzman, Elizabeth BioIn 17
Holtzman, Elizabeth 1941- WhoAm 92, WhoAmW 93
Holtzman, Ellen A. 1952- WhoAm 92
Holtzman, Gary Yale 1936- WhoAm 92
Holtzman, Jerome 1926- WhoAm 92
Holtzman, Kenneth Dale 1945- BiDAMSp 1989
Holtzman, Marcia ScF&FL 92
Holtzman, Norman 1944- St&PR 93
Holtzman, Roberta Lee 1938- WhoAmW 93
Holtzman, Scott Russell Law&B 92
Holtzman, Wayne Harold 1923- WhoAm 92
Holtzmann, Howard Marshall 1921- WhoAm 92, WhoWor 93
Holtzner, Anton d1635 Baker 92
Holtzschue, Karl Bressem 1938- WhoAm 92, WhoE 93, WhoWor 93
Holub, Charles Michael 1948- WhoE 93
Holub, Edward BioIn 17
Holub, Edward Joseph, II 1952- WhoE 93
Holub, Martin 1938- WhoAm 92
Holub, Miroslav 1923- BioIn 17, WhoWor 93
Holubowicz, Tadeusz 1929- WhoScE 91-4
Holum, Laura Lynn 1956- WhoEmL 93
Holveck, Eleanore 1942- WhoAmW 93
Holverson, Harmon E. 1924- WhoAm 92
Holverson, John 1946- WhoE 93
Holvoet, Marc A.J. 1939- WhoScE 91-2
Holway, Florence BioIn 17
Holway, James Colin 1927- WhoWor 93
Holway, Michael Paul 1955- WhoE 93
Holway, Richard A. 1937- St&PR 93
Holweger, L.M. 1948- St&PR 93
Holwell, Peter 1936- WhoWor 93
Holy, Alfred 1866-1948 Baker 92
Holy, Antonin 1936- WhoScE 91-4
Holy, Milos 1924- WhoScE 91-4
Holy, Ondrej Frantisek c. 1747-1783 OxDcOp
Holy, Sherrie Lynne 1952- WhoSSW 93
Holyer, Erna Maria 1925- WhoWrEP 92
Holyfield, Evander BioIn 17, WhoAm 92
Holyfield, Evander 1962- AfrAmBi
Holyfield, James Robert 1940- WhoSSW 93
Holyoak, William Harding 1937- WhoSSW 93
Holyoake, Keith Jacka 1904-1983 DcTwHis
Holyoke, Samuel (Adams) 1762-1820 Baker 92
Holz, Arno 1863-1929 DcLB 118 [port]
Holz, George Gilbert 1922-1989 BioIn 17
Holz, George H. 1922- St&PR 93
Holz, Hans Heinz 1927- WhoWor 93
Holz, Harold A. 1925- WhoAm 92
Holz, Harry George 1934- WhoAm 92
Holz, Jacques 1931- WhoScE 91-4
Holz, Kenneth 1959- St&PR 93
Holz, Richard Lee Law&B 92
Holz, Robert Kenneth 1930- WhoAm 92, WhoSSW 93
Holzapfel, Christina Marie 1942- WhoAm 92
Holzapfel, Wilfried B. 1938- WhoScE 91-3
Holzapfel, Wilhelm H. 1942- WhoScE 91-3
Holzapfl, Robert WhoScE 91-3
Holzbach, Raymond Thomas 1929- WhoAm 92
Holzbauer, Ignaz 1711-1783 OxDcOp
Holzbauer, Ignaz (Jakob) 1711-1783 Baker 92
Holzberg, Roger MiSFD 9
Holzberger, Sheila Marie 1960- WhoEmL 93
Holzberger, William George 1932- WhoWrEP 92
Holzel, David Benjamin 1958- WhoAm 92
Holzemer, David Charles 1966- WhoE 93
Holzendorf, Betty Smith 1939- WhoAmW 93
Holzer, Adela BioIn 17
Holzer, Edwin 1933- WhoAm 92
Holzer, Edwin H. 1933- St&PR 93
Holzer, Hans WhoAm 92
Holzer, Hans 1920- ScF&FL 92
Holzer, Harold 1949- ConAu 39NR, WhoE 93
Holzer, Hellfried Peter 1926- WhoAm 92
Holzer, Helmut 1921- WhoScE 91-3
Holzer, Jenny BioIn 17
Holzer, Joseph Alfred 1914- WhoWor 93
Holzer, Thomas Lequear 1944- WhoAm 92
Holzgreve, Alfred 1953- WhoScE 91-3
Holzhauser, Ronald C. 1944- St&PR 93
Holzheimer, Jorge 1945- St&PR 93
Holzinger, James Jay 1935- St&PR 93, WhoAm 92
Holzinger, Richard L. St&PR 93
Holzman, Allan MiSFD 9
Holzman, D. Keith 1936- WhoAm 92
Holzman, Esther Rose WhoAmW 93
Holzman, Franklyn Dunn 1918- WhoAm 92, WhoE 93
Holzman, Herbert S. 1934- St&PR 93
Holzman, Howard Eugene 1934- WhoAm 92
Holzman, Jacquelin WhoE 93
Holzman, Malcolm 1940- WhoAm 92
Holzman, Philip Seidman 1922- WhoAm 92, WhoWor 93
Holzman, Robert Stuart 1907- WhoAm 92, WhoWor 93
Holzman, Ronald R. 1931- St&PR 93
Holzman, Seymour 1936- WhoE 93
Holzmann, Hans 1929- WhoScE 91-3
Holzner, Burkart 1931- WhoAm 92
Holzner, J. Heinrich 1924- WhoScE 91-4

Holzner, Marilee Theresa 1932- *WhoAmW 93*
Holzschuher, Louisa *Law&B 92*
Holzwasser, Harry A. 1924- *St&PR 93*
Holzwasser, Robert A. 1954- *St&PR 93*
Holzworth, Richard Carl 1929- *St&PR 93*
Hom, Cynthia L. *Law&B 92*
Hom, David 1952- *St&PR 93*
Hom, David A. *Law&B 92*
Hom, Richard Yee 1950- *WhoEmL 93*
Homan, Arthur W. *Law&B 92*
Homan, Charles I. 1943- *St&PR 93*
Homan, Gerlof 1930- *WhoWor 93*
Homan, Helen Walker *AmWomPl*
Homan, John F. 1943- *St&PR 93*
Homan, Mary Carolyn 1958- *WhoEmL 93*
Homan, Paul M. 1940- *St&PR 93*
Homan, Ralph William 1951- *WhoEmL 93, WhoWor 93*
Homan, William E. 1919-1991 *BioIn 17*
Homans, Peter 1930- *WhoAm 92*
Homayssi, Ruby Lee 1945- *WhoAmW 93*
Homberger, E. *WhoScE 91-4*
Homburg, Stefan 1961- *WhoWor 93*
Homburger, Eve Alice 1955- *WhoEmL 93, WhoSSW 93*
Homburger, Freddy 1916- *WhoAm 92, WhoWrEP 92*
Homburger, Thomas Charles 1941- *WhoAm 92*
Home, Daniel Dunglas 1833-1886 *BioIn 17*
Home, Elizabeth Alington Douglas d1990 *BioIn 17*
Home, Henry *BioIn 17*
Home, Ina *AmWomPl*
Home, John 1722-1808 *BioIn 17*
Home, William Douglas 1912-1992 *ConAu 139*
Home, William Scott 1940- *ScF&FL 92*
Home-Gall, Edward R. 1899- *ScF&FL 92*
Homeier, Lon Williams 1927- *St&PR 93*
Homel, David 1952- *WhoCanL 92*
Homelson, Rochelle 1954- *WhoAmW 93*
Homeniuk, Richard R. *St&PR 93*
Homer *OxDcByz*
Homer c. 8th cent.BC- *MagSWL*
Homer, Ben R. 1936- *St&PR 93*
Homer, Bruce A. 1931- *St&PR 93*
Homer, Charles T. 1938- *St&PR 93*
Homer, F.G. *Law&B 92*
Homer, F.G. 1937- *St&PR 93*
Homer, Frances *AmWomPl*
Homer, Frieda Moffshow 1948- *WhoAmW 93*
Homer, Irvin 1924- *WhoE 93*
Homer, John Thomas 1945- *St&PR 93*
Homer, Louis David 1935- *WhoE 93*
Homer, Louise 1871-1947 *IntDcOp, OxDcOp*
Homer, Louise (Dilworth) 1871-1947 *Baker 92*
Homer, Marion 1948- *St&PR 93*
Homer, Peter Kemp 1961- *WhoE 93*
Homer, Ronald *AfrAmBi [port]*
Homer, Sidney 1864-1953 *Baker 92*
Homer, Stephen Mark 1958- *WhoSSW 93*
Homer, William Innes 1929- *WhoAm 92*
Homer, Winslow 1836-1910 *BioIn 17, GayN*
Homes, A. M. *WhoE 93*
Homes, A(my) M. *ConAu 136*
Homes, Geoffrey d1978 *BioIn 17*
Homes, Jacques 1930- *WhoScE 91-2*
Homesley, Horace Edward 1928- *WhoSSW 93, WhoWrEP 92*
Homestead, Susan 1937- *WhoAm 92, WhoAmW 93, WhoWor 93*
Homeyer, Howard C. 1933- *WhoAm 92*
Homeyer, Karen Queen *Law&B 92*
Homeyer, Michael Lee *Law&B 92*
Homiak, Albert S. 1949- *WhoIns 93*
Homick, Daniel John 1947- *WhoSSW 93*
Homilius, Gottfried August 1714-1785 *Baker 92*
Homma, Hiroomi 1944- *WhoWor 93*
Homma, Masaharu 1887-1946 *HarEnMi*
Homma, Morio 1930- *WhoWor 93*
Hommel, Thomas E. *Law&B 92*
Hommel, William Sam, Jr. 1960- *WhoEmL 93*
Hommen, Jan H.M. 1943- *St&PR 93*
Hommes, Frits Aukustinus 1934- *WhoAm 92*
Hommes, Robert Lee 1934- *St&PR 93*
Hommeyer, Pamela Crisafulli 1966- *WhoAmW 93*
Homolka, Oscar 1898?-1978 *IntDcF 2-3 [port]*
Homonnay, Gabriella 1935- *WhoScE 91-4*
Homonoff, Howard *Law&B 92*
Homs (Oller), Joaquin 1906- *Baker 92*
Homsey, Samuel Eldon 1904- *WhoAm 92*
Homsky, Marie D. *St&PR 93*
Homulos, Peter Stephen 1948- *WhoAm 92*
Homuth, Horst 1940- *WhoScE 91-3*
Homuth, Ruth Elizabeth 1947- *WhoAmW 93*
Hon, David Nyok-Sai 1947- *WhoEmL 93*
Hon, Ralph Clifford 1903- *WhoSSW 93, WhoWor 93*
Honaker, Janice Marie 1957- *WhoEmL 93*
Honaker, Richard Henderson 1951- *WhoEmL 93*
Honaman, David Gerald 1951- *St&PR 93*
Honaman, J. Craig 1943- *WhoSSW 93*
Honan, Elliot F. 1937- *St&PR 93*
Honan, James Patrick 1956- *WhoE 93*
Honan, James Terry 1946- *WhoSSW 93*
Honan, Park *BioIn 17*
Honan, William H. 1930- *ScF&FL 92*
Honan, William Holmes 1930- *WhoAm 92*
Honchell, Charlene 1943- *WhoAmW 93*
Honda, Hiroshi 1950- *WhoWor 93*
Honda, Inoshiro *MiSFD 9*
Honda, Katsuji 1950- *WhoWor 93*
Honda, Kazuo 1949- *WhoWor 93*
Honda, Masaki 1889-1964 *HarEnMi*
Honda, Masanobu 1538-1616 *HarEnMi*
Honda, Minoru *BioIn 17*
Honda, Natsuo 1930- *WhoWor 93*
Honda, Soichiro 1906-1991 *AnObit 1991, BioIn 17, News 92*
Honda, Tadakatsu 1548-1610 *HarEnMi*
Honda, Toshio 1956- *WhoWor 93*
Honderich, John Allen 1946- *WhoAm 92*
Hondre, Anthony Rodney 1939- *St&PR 93*
Hondros, E.D. *WhoScE 91-3*
Hone, James A. 1944- *St&PR 93*
Hone, Joseph 1937- *ScF&FL 92*
Hone, L. Michael 1949- *St&PR 93*
Hone, Michael Curran 1937- *St&PR 93*
Hone, Robert E. 1942- *St&PR 93*
Hone, William d1522 *BioIn 17*
Hone, William 1780-1842 *BioIn 17*
Honecker, Erich *BioIn 17*
Honecker, Erich 1912- *DcTwHis*
Honecker, Martin 1934- *WhoWor 93*
Honegger, Arthur 1892-1955 *IntDcOp, OxDcOp*
Honegger, Arthur (Oscar) 1892-1955 *Baker 92*
Honegger, Gottfried 1917- *BioIn 17*
Honegger, Henri (Charles) 1904- *Baker 92*
Honegger, Jean Ann 1942- *WhoAmW 93*
Honegger, Marc 1926- *Baker 92*
Honek, Andrew P. 1960- *St&PR 93*
Honek, J. Frank 1958- *St&PR 93*
Honemann, Daniel Henry 1929- *WhoAm 92*
Honer, Robert B. 1926- *St&PR 93*
Honerkamp, Nicholas 1950- *ConAu 138*
Honesty, Edward Franklin, Jr. *Law&B 92*
Honet, Joseph C. 1933- *WhoAm 92*
Honey, Richard Churchill 1924- *WhoAm 92*
Honeycheck, Linda J. *Law&B 92*
Honeycheck, Linda Jean 1949- *WhoAmW 93*
Honeycomb, Maurine E. *AmWomPl*
Honey Cone *SoulM*
Honeycutt, George Leonard 1936- *WhoAm 92*
Honeycutt, J. David *Law&B 92*
Honeycutt, John B. *Law&B 92*
Honeyman, Nan Wood 1881-1970 *BioIn 17*
Honeyman-Scott, James 1957-1982 *See* Pretenders, The *ConMus 8*
Honeystein, Karl 1932- *WhoAm 92*
Honeywell, Larry G. 1935- *St&PR 93*
Honeywell, Larry Gene 1935- *WhoAm 92*
Hong, Elliott *MiSFD 9*
Hong, Howard Vincent 1912- *WhoAm 92*
Hong, James *MiSFD 9*
Hong, James Ming 1940- *WhoAm 92, WhoSSW 93*
Hong, Jane Cooper 1954- *ScF&FL 92*
Hong, Peter L. 1956- *St&PR 93*
Hong, Richard 1929- *WhoAm 92*
Hong, Rose Lee 1946- *WhoAmW 93*
Hong, Se June 1944- *WhoAm 92*
Hong, Stanley W. 1936- *St&PR 93*
Hong, Sung-Rye *BioIn 17*
Hong, Yi 1943- *WhoWor 93*
Hong, Yong Shik 1932- *WhoWor 93*
Hongen, Elisabeth *OxDcOp*
Hongen, Elisabeth 1906- *Baker 92*
Hong Hee Pyo 1939- *WhoAsAP 91*
Hongler, Max-Olivier 1951- *WhoWor 93*
Hongo, Garrett Kaoru 1951- *DcLB 120 [port], WhoWrEP 92*
Hongo, Kohei 1939- *WhoWor 93*
Hong Se Kie 1930- *WhoAsAP 91*
Hong Young Kee 1920- *WhoAsAP 91*
Honhart, Barbara Ann Baker 1942- *WhoAmW 93*
Honig, Alice Sterling 1929- *WhoE 93*
Honig, Arnold 1928- *WhoAm 92*
Honig, Barry Hirsh 1941- *WhoAm 92*
Honig, Burton A. 1937- *St&PR 93*
Honig, Edwin 1919- *WhoAm 92*
Honig, Edwin B. 1919- *WhoWrEP 92*
Honig, George Raymond 1936- *WhoAm 92*
Honig, John 1924- *St&PR 93*
Honig, Lawrence Edward 1948- *St&PR 93*
Honig, Leslie *Law&B 92*
Honig, Nancy E. *Law&B 92*
Honig, Steven 1931- *St&PR 93*
Honig, Uwe 1962- *WhoWor 93*
Honig, William Martin 1933- *WhoWor 93*
Honigberg, Bronislaw Mark 1920- *WhoAm 92*
Honigberg, Irving 1916- *St&PR 93*
Honigman, Daniel M. 1933- *St&PR 93*
Honigman, Howard Aron 1946- *WhoE 93*
Honigmann, John Joseph 1914-1977 *IntDcAn*
Honikel, Karl-Otto 1942- *WhoScE 91-3*
Honikman, Larry Howard 1936- *WhoWor 93*
Honiss, Robin 1937- *St&PR 93, WhoAm 92*
Honjo, Shigeru 1876-1945 *HarEnMi*
Honkisz, James Edward *Law&B 92*
Honko, Jaakko *WhoScE 91-4*
Honner, B. Joan 1952- *WhoAmW 93*
Honneus, Geoffrey 1940- *St&PR 93*
Honnold, John Otis, Jr. 1915- *WhoAm 92*
Honnold, W. Dean 1940- *St&PR 93*
Honold, Kristen B. *Law&B 92*
Honor, Edward 1933- *AfrAmBi*
Honor, Robert S. *Law&B 92*
Honore, Anthony *St&PR 93*
Honore, Bent 1958- *WhoWor 93*
Honore, Jean-Gabriel d1990 *BioIn 17*
Honorius 384-423 *OxDcByz*
Honorius, Flavius 384-423 *HarEnMi*
Honorof, Ida 1914- *WhoAmW 93*
Honors, Mildred Olive *AmWomPl*
Honroth, Kenneth Arthur 1914- *St&PR 93*
Hons, Craig E. 1951- *St&PR 93*
Honse, Robert W. 1943- *WhoAm 92*
Honsowitz, Herbert 1944- *WhoUN 92*
Honts, George Edward, III 1940- *WhoSSW 93*
Hontz, Robert Milton, Jr. 1943- *WhoE 93*
Hontzas, Thomas Milton 1944- *St&PR 93*
Honzel, Andrew J. 1931- *St&PR 93*
Honzl, John Joseph 1942- *St&PR 93*
Hoobler, Sibley Worth 1911- *WhoAm 92*
Hoobler, Thomas 1942?- *ScF&FL 92*
Hood, A. Thomas 1946- *St&PR 93*
Hood, Alan Condit 1940- *WhoE 93*
Hood, Alexander 1726-1814 *HarEnMi*
Hood, Ann 1956- *ConAu 136*
Hood, Charles H. *St&PR 93*
Hood, Charles Harvey 1929- *WhoAm 92*
Hood, Charles Hurlburt 1938- *WhoAm 92*
Hood, Charles R. 1948- *St&PR 93*
Hood, D.E. 1936- *WhoScE 91-3*
Hood, Dale A. d1991 *BioIn 17*
Hood, Dan *BioIn 17*
Hood, David *SoulM*
Hood, David Davies 1942- *St&PR 93*
Hood, David Murl 1950- *St&PR 93*
Hood, Douglas Crary 1932- *WhoWor 93*
Hood, Earl James 1947- *WhoEmL 93*
Hood, Edward Exum, Jr. 1930- *St&PR 93, WhoAm 92, WhoE 93*
Hood, Geoffrey d1990 *BioIn 17*
Hood, George 1807-1882 *Baker 92*
Hood, George W., Jr. *St&PR 93*
Hood, Gwenyth 1955- *ScF&FL 92*
Hood, Gwenyth Elise 1955- *WhoWrEP 92*
Hood, Helen 1863-1949 *Baker 92*
Hood, Henry Lyman 1921- *WhoAm 92*
Hood, Hugh *BioIn 17*
Hood, Hugh 1928- *ConAu 17AS [port], WhoCanL 92*
Hood, James B. 1937- *WhoIns 93*
Hood, James Byron 1951- *WhoWrEP 92*
Hood, John Bell 1831-1879 *BioIn 17, HarEnMi*
Hood, John David 1955- *WhoSSW 93*
Hood, Joseph M. 1942- *WhoAm 92, WhoSSW 93*
Hood, Kevin *BioIn 17*
Hood, Lamartine Frain 1937- *WhoAm 92*
Hood, Leroy Edward 1938- *WhoAm 92*
Hood, Louie Franklin 1954- *WhoSSW 93*
Hood, Malcolm Ralph 1932- *WhoUN 92*
Hood, Mantle 1918- *Baker 92*
Hood, Mary Bryan 1938- *WhoAm 92, WhoSSW 93*
Hood, Mary Dullea 1947- *WhoEmL 93*
Hood, Ollie Ruth 1947- *WhoAmW 93*
Hood, Paul Bernard 1927- *St&PR 93*
Hood, Philip Boyce 1951- *WhoWrEP 92*
Hood, Robert 1951- *ScF&FL 92*
Hood, Robert Eric 1926- *WhoWrEP 92*
Hood, Robert K. *Law&B 92*
Hood, Robert R. 1949- *St&PR 93*
Hood, Roger William 1948- *WhoEmL 93*
Hood, Ronald Chalmers, III 1947- *WhoSSW 93*
Hood, Ronald S. *St&PR 93*
Hood, Ronnie Lee 1934- *St&PR 93*
Hood, Samuel 1724-1816 *HarEnMi*
Hood, Stuart *BioIn 17*
Hood, Thomas 1799-1845 *BioIn 17*
Hood, Thomas Charles 1938- *WhoSSW 93*
Hood, Timothy Michael 1968- *WhoEmL 93*
Hood, Walter Kelly 1928- *WhoSSW 93*
Hood, William Boyd, Jr. 1932- *WhoAm 92, WhoE 93*
Hood, William Clarence 1921- *WhoAm 92*
Hood, William E. 1909- *St&PR 93*
Hood, William Stanley, Jr. *Law&B 92*
Hoodwin, Lou W. 1915- *St&PR 93*
Hoof, David *ScF&FL 92*
Hoof, David Lorne 1945- *WhoWrEP 92*
Hoof, Jef van 1886-1959 *Baker 92*
Hoofnagle, Gail Susan 1956- *WhoEmL 93*
Hoofnagle, Joseph Bruce, Jr. *Law&B 92*
Hoog, Michel 1932- *WhoWor 93*
Hoogenboom, Ari Arthur 1927- *WhoAm 92*
Hoogendoorn, J. 1955- *WhoScE 91-3*
Hoogerkamp, D. 1937- *WhoScE 91-3*
Hoogerwerf, Judy Fay 1943- *WhoAmW 93*
Hoogewind, William H. 1948- *St&PR 93*
Hooghwinkel, Gerrit Josephus M. 1926- *WhoWor 93*
Hoogland, J. 1934- *WhoScE 91-3*
Hooglandt, J.D. *WhoScE 91-3*
Hoogmartens, Michael 1937- *WhoScE 91-2*
Hoogmoed, Neil 1934- *St&PR 93*
Hoogmoed, Walter Leonard 1938- *St&PR 93*
Hoogsteden, Aloysius Franciscus 1936- *WhoWor 93*
Hoogstraten, Willem van 1884-1965 *Baker 92*
Hook, Cornelius Henry 1929- *WhoSSW 93*
Hook, Edward Watson, Jr. 1924- *WhoAm 92*
Hook, Fred E. *Law&B 92*
Hook, Gary S. *Law&B 92*
Hook, George Matthew Verity 1917- *WhoWor 93*
Hook, Harold S. *BioIn 17*
Hook, Harold S. 1931- *St&PR 93*
Hook, Harold Swanson 1931- *WhoAm 92, WhoIns 93, WhoSSW 93*
Hook, Harry *MiSFD 9*
Hook, Henry B. 1909- *St&PR 93*
Hook, J(ulius) N(icholas) 1913- *ConAu 38NR*
Hook, James 1746-1827 *Baker 92, OxDcOp*
Hook, James H. *St&PR 93*
Hook, Jeffrey Robbins 1954- *St&PR 93*
Hook, Jerry Bruce 1937- *WhoAm 92*
Hook, John Burney 1928- *WhoAm 92*
Hook, Lewis William 1924- *St&PR 93*
Hook, Martha Ann 1936- *WhoWrEP 92*
Hook, Olle 1918- *WhoScE 91-4*
Hook, R.C. *WhoScE 91-1*
Hook, Ralph Clifford, Jr. 1923- *WhoAm 92*
Hook, Rodney N. 1946- *St&PR 93*
Hook, Sanders H.B. 1939- *St&PR 93*
Hook, Sidney 1902-1989 *BioIn 17, ColdWar 1 [port]*
Hook, Theodore 1788-1841 *DcLB 116 [port]*
Hook, Virginia May 1932- *WhoAmW 93*
Hook, William C. 1956- *BioIn 17*
Hooke, Christopher 1949- *St&PR 93*
Hooke, John Anthony Lionel 1933- *WhoWor 93*
Hooke, Roger LeBaron 1939- *WhoAm 92*
Hooker, Alan C. *Law&B 92*
Hooker, Alice Louise Ingram *WhoAmW 93*
Hooker, David Andrew 1954- *WhoE 93, WhoEmL 93*
Hooker, J. Clyde, Jr. 1920- *St&PR 93*
Hooker, James A. 1936- *St&PR 93*
Hooker, John Lee *BioIn 17*
Hooker, John Lee 1917- *WhoAm 92*
Hooker, John Lee 1920?- *CurBio 92 [port]*
Hooker, Joseph *BioIn 17*
Hooker, Joseph 1814-1879 *HarEnMi*
Hooker, Michael Kenneth 1945- *WhoAm 92, WhoE 93*
Hooker, Robert Wright 1947- *WhoSSW 93*
Hooker, Rodman Lent, Jr. 1940- *WhoAm 92*
Hooker, Ruth 1920- *ScF&FL 92*
Hooker, Steven L. 1954- *St&PR 93*
Hooker, Thomas 1586-1647 *BioIn 17*
Hooker, Van Dorn 1921- *WhoAm 92*
Hooker-Haring, Christopher Alan 1950- *WhoEmL 93*
Hooks, Bell *BioIn 17*
Hooks, Benjamin L. 1924- *BioIn 17*
Hooks, Benjamin Lawson 1925- *AfrAmBi, EncAACR, NewYTBS 92 [port], WhoAm 92*
Hooks, David *ScF&FL 92*
Hooks, George Bardin 1945- *WhoSSW 93*
Hooks, James E. 1937- *St&PR 93*
Hooks, Jan *BioIn 17*

Hooks, Kevin 1958- MiSFD 9
Hooks, Lonna R. Law&B 92
Hooks, Perry W. Law&B 92
Hooks, Vandalyn Lawrence 1935- WhoAmW 93
Hooks, Vendie Hudson, III 1948- WhoEmL 93
Hooks, William Gary 1927- WhoAm 92
Hookway, Warren Arthur 1936- St&PR 93
Hool, Lance 1948- MiSFD 9
Hoolboom, Henri 1929- WhoScE 91-3
Hoole, Alan Norman 1942- WhoWor 93
Hoole, James Edward 1947- St&PR 93
Hoole, W. Stanley 1903-1990 BioIn 17
Hooley, James Robert 1932- WhoAm 92
Hooley, John Hadrath 1951- WhoEmL 93
Hooley, Robert C. 1927- St&PR 93
Hooley, Robert Childs 1927- WhoAm 92
Hoolihan, Thomas Joseph Law&B 92
Hoon Choi 1932- WhoAsAP 91
Hoop, Rita Caporicci 1963- WhoE 93
Hooper, Arthur G. 1942- St&PR 93
Hooper, Arthur William 1919- WhoAm 92
Hooper, Barbara Bush 1909- St&PR 93
Hooper, Billy Ernest 1931- WhoAm 92
Hooper, Blake Howard 1922- WhoAm 92
Hooper, Carl Glenn 1936- WhoSSW 93
Hooper, Catherine Evelyn 1939- WhoAmW 93, WhoWor 93
Hooper, David John WhoScE 91-1
Hooper, Dean R. 1943- St&PR 93
Hooper, Donald Robert 1935- WhoE 93
Hooper, Edith Ferry 1909- WhoAm 92
Hooper, Hedda 1890-1966 BioIn 17
Hooper, Henry Olcott 1935- WhoAm 92
Hooper, Ian 1941- WhoAm 92
Hooper, Ian Derek 1941- St&PR 93
Hooper, Irene Upshaw 1935- WhoSSW 93
Hooper, J.N. WhoScE 91-1
Hooper, James Bryan 1941- WhoE 93
Hooper, James William 1937- WhoAm 92, WhoSSW 93
Hooper, Jere Mann 1933- St&PR 93, WhoAm 92
Hooper, John Allen 1922- WhoAm 92
Hooper, John Edward 1926- WhoWor 93
Hooper, John P. Law&B 92
Hooper, Johnston Jones 1815-1862 JrnUS
Hooper, Josh 1952- WhoEmL 93
Hooper, Judith 1949- ConAu 136
Hooper, Kay 1957- ScF&FL 92
Hooper, Lucy Hamilton 1835-1893 JrnUS
Hooper, M.D. WhoScE 91-1
Hooper, Malcolm WhoScE 91-1
Hooper, Marcia Jacobs 1954- WhoAmW 93
Hooper, Matthew R. Law&B 92
Hooper, Michele St&PR 93
Hooper, Michele J. BioIn 17
Hooper, Nancy Lou 1936- WhoAmW 93
Hooper, Patricia 1941- WhoWrEP 92
Hooper, R.A.E. WhoScE 91-1
Hooper, Rebecca L. AmWomPl
Hooper, Robert Alexander 1947- WhoEmL 93
Hooper, Robert Earle 1954- WhoSSW 93
Hooper, Roy B. 1947- WhoSSW 93
Hooper, Sidney Francis 1941- St&PR 93
Hooper, Stephen Ray 1954- WhoSSW 93
Hooper, Tobe 1943- MiSFD 9
Hooper, Van B. WhoSSW 93
Hooper, Virginia Fite 1917- WhoAmW 93
Hooper, Walter 1931- ScF&FL 92
Hooper, William Douglas 1949- WhoEmL 93
Hoopes, Janet Louise 1923- WhoAm 92
Hoopes, John Michael 1947- St&PR 93
Hoopes, Joseph Coudon, Jr. 1943- St&PR 93
Hoopes, Katherine Turben 1965- WhoAmW 93
Hoopes, Kathleen Ann 1957- WhoAmW 93
Hoopes, Lorenzo Neville 1913- WhoAm 92
Hoopes, Spencer Wendell 1947- St&PR 93
Hoopes, Townsend Walter 1922- WhoAm 92
Hoopes, Walter Ronald 1933- WhoAm 92, WhoE 93
Hoopis, Harry Peter 1947- WhoEmL 93
Hoople, Sally Crosby 1930- WhoWrEP 92
Hoops, Alan 1947- WhoAm 92
Hoops, Diane Kinuko 1961- WhoEmL 93
Hoops, Jeffrey Robert 1953- WhoAm 92
Hoops, Timothy G. Law&B 92
Hoornaert, Georges J. 1938- WhoScE 91-2
Hoornstra, E.H. 1921- St&PR 93
Hoornstra, Edward H. 1921- WhoAm 92
Hoose Quincey, Shelley 1955- WhoWrEP 92
Hoosin, Janice 1942- WhoAmW 93
Hoot, Joyce Jeannie Law&B 92
Hoot, Patricia Lynch 1921- WhoWrEP 92
Hoot, William John 1916- St&PR 93, WhoAm 92
Hooten, Leon E., III 1952- WhoSSW 93
Hootkin, Pamela N. 1947- St&PR 93
Hootkin, Pamela Nan 1947- WhoAm 92, WhoAmW 93
Hootman, Harry Edward 1933- WhoSSW 93, WhoWor 93
Hootnick, Laurence R. 1942- WhoAm 92
Hooton, Bruce Duff 1928- WhoE 93
Hooton, E.A. 1887-1954 IntDcAn
Hooton, Michael E. Law&B 92
Hoots, Helen Hardin WhoWrEP 92
Hoover, Albert K. Law&B 92
Hoover, Betty-Bruce Howard 1939- WhoAmW 93
Hoover, Carol Faith 1921- WhoWrEP 92
Hoover, Claude W. 1953- St&PR 93
Hoover, Cove d1990 BioIn 17
Hoover, Cynthia Jane 1953- WhoAmW 93
Hoover, Dale ScF&FL 92
Hoover, Dale L. 1934- St&PR 93
Hoover, David Carlson 1950- WhoE 93, WhoEmL 93
Hoover, Dean Robert 1935- St&PR 93
Hoover, Donald Barry 1950- WhoSSW 93
Hoover, Dorothy R. 1907- St&PR 93
Hoover, Duane BioIn 17
Hoover, Dwight Wesley 1926- WhoAm 92
Hoover, Eddie Lee 1944- WhoE 93
Hoover, Francis Louis 1913- WhoAm 92
Hoover, George Schweke 1935- WhoAm 92
Hoover, George W. BioIn 17
Hoover, H.M. 1935- ScF&FL 92
Hoover, H(elen) M(ary) 1935- MajAI [port], WhoWrEP 92
Hoover, Hap 1951- St&PR 93
Hoover, Harold Lee 1953- WhoEmL 93
Hoover, Helen Mary 1935- ChlFicS
Hoover, Herbert DcCPCAm
Hoover, Herbert 1874-1964 BioIn 17
Hoover, Herbert, III 1927- St&PR 93
Hoover, Herbert Arnold 1930- St&PR 93, WhoAm 92
Hoover, Herbert C. 1874-1964 PolPar
Hoover, Howard S., Jr. WhoAm 92
Hoover, J. Edgar 1895-1972 BioIn 17
Hoover, Jacqueline Sue 1966- WhoE 93
Hoover, James Bentley 1955- St&PR 93, WhoE 93
Hoover, Jesse Wilbert 1908- WhoWrEP 92
Hoover, Jessica Mary 1957- WhoAmW 93
Hoover, Jimmie Hartman 1930- WhoSSW 93
Hoover, John Edgar BioIn 17
Hoover, John Edgar 1895-1972 DcTwHis
Hoover, John Edward 1929- WhoE 93
Hoover, John Elwood 1924- WhoAm 92
Hoover, Julie T. St&PR 93
Hoover, Kelly Lynn 1965- WhoSSW 93
Hoover, Ken 1938- St&PR 93
Hoover, Larry Allan 1940- WhoSSW 93
Hoover, Lawrence Richard 1935- St&PR 93
Hoover, Lloyd G. 1940- St&PR 93
Hoover, Lola Mae 1947- WhoAmW 93, WhoEmL 93
Hoover, Lou Henry d1944 BioIn 17
Hoover, Mae Morgan 1940- WhoWrEP 92
Hoover, Mary N. St&PR 93
Hoover, Melinda Mader Law&B 92
Hoover, Mike J. Law&B 92
Hoover, Molly Ann 1948- WhoAmW 93
Hoover, Paul Russell 1941- St&PR 93
Hoover, Paul Williams, Jr. 1942- WhoSSW 93
Hoover, Pearl Rollings 1924- WhoWor 93
Hoover, Ralph ScF&FL 92
Hoover, Rayallen 1932- St&PR 93
Hoover, Richard WhoAm 92
Hoover, Robert Cleary 1928- WhoWor 93
Hoover, Roderick P., Jr. 1954- WhoIns 93
Hoover, Rodger S. 1927- St&PR 93
Hoover, Roger K. Law&B 92
Hoover, Roger K. 1939- St&PR 93
Hoover, Roland Armitage 1929- WhoAm 92
Hoover, Saranne ScF&FL 92
Hoover, Stephanie Ann 1960- WhoE 93
Hoover, Susan Frantz 1939- WhoWrEP 92
Hoover, Theresa L. Law&B 92
Hoover, Thomas 1941- ScF&FL 92
Hoover, Tuck d1894 BioIn 17
Hoover, William Howard 1951- WhoEmL 93
Hoover, William Leichliter 1944- WhoAm 92
Hoover, William M. St&PR 93
Hoover, William Ray 1930- St&PR 93
Hoovler, Paul Vincent 1927- St&PR 93
Hopcke, Klaus 1933- WhoWor 93
Hopcroft, John Edward 1939- WhoAm 92
Hopcus, Ernest Anthony 1946- WhoSSW 93
Hope, A. D. 1907- IntLitE
Hope, A.D. (Alec Derwent) 1907- BioIn 17
Hope, Akua Lezli 1957- WhoWrEP 92
Hope, Alec Derwent BioIn 17
Hope, Ammie Deloris 1946- WhoAmW 93, WhoEmL 93
Hope, Bob 1903- BioIn 17, IntDcF 2-3 [port], QDrFCA 92 [port], WhoAm 92, WhoWor 93
Hope, Christopher BioIn 17
Hope, Clarence Caldwell, Jr. 1920- WhoAm 92
Hope, Cliff BioIn 17
Hope, Florence Isbell AmWomPl
Hope, Frank Lewis, Jr. 1930- WhoAm 92
Hope, Garland Howard 1911- WhoAm 92
Hope, George Marion 1938- WhoSSW 93
Hope, Gerri Danette 1956- WhoAmW 93, WhoEmL 93
Hope, James WhoScE 91-1
Hope, Jemmy 1764-1853 BioIn 17
Hope, John 1868-1936 EncAACR
Hope, John Charles, Jr. 1948- WhoEmL 93
Hope, Judith Richards 1940- WhoAm 92, WhoAmW 93
Hope, Laura Lee ScF&FL 92
Hope, Lawrence Latimer 1939- WhoAm 92
Hope, Margaret Lautem WhoAmW 93, WhoSSW 93
Hope, Marjorie AmWomPl
Hope, Mark Alan 1960- WhoEmL 93, WhoSSW 93
Hope, Maury M. 1949- St&PR 93
Hope, Michael S. 1942- St&PR 93, WhoAm 92
Hope, Richard F. Law&B 92
Hope, Ronald Anthony WhoScE 91-1
Hope, Samuel Howard 1946- WhoAm 92
Hope, Theodore Sherwood, Jr. 1903- WhoWor 93
Hope, Thomas Walker 1920- WhoAm 92
Hope, Warren T. 1944- WhoIns 93
Hope, William Duane 1935- WhoAm 92
Hope, Winifred Ayres AmWomPl
Hope Cawdery, Michael J.H. 1933- WhoScE 91-3
Hope-Jones, Robert 1859-1914 Baker 92
Hopekirk, Helen 1856-1945 Baker 92, BioIn 17
Hopen, Herbert John 1934- WhoAm 92
Hope-Ross, W.J. Law&B 92
Hopes, David Brendan 1953- WhoWrEP 92
Hopewell, Barbara Ann Law&B 92
Hopewell, Craig S. Law&B 92
Hopf, Adolf Richard 1923- WhoScE 91-3
Hopf, Alice ScF&FL 92
Hopf, Frank Rudolph 1920- WhoE 93, WhoWor 93
Hopf, Hans 1916- Baker 92, OxDcOp
Hopfenbeck, George Martin, Jr. 1929- WhoAm 92
Hopfer, Andrzej Jerzy Tadeusz 1933- WhoScE 91-4
Hopfield, John Joseph 1933- WhoAm 92
Hopgood, Debra Jo 1958- WhoWor 93
Hopgood, James F. 1943- WhoAm 92, WhoSSW 93, WhoWor 93
Hopkin, Alfred W. St&PR 93
Hopkin, Lois Ann 1947- WhoEmL 93
Hopkins, Anthony BioIn 17
Hopkins, Anthony 1937- IntDcF 2-3 [port], News 92 [port]
Hopkins, Anthony Philip WhoScE 91-1
Hopkins, Anthony Philip 1937- WhoAm 92, WhoWor 93
Hopkins, Antony 1921- Baker 92
Hopkins, Arlene 1949- WhoAmW 93
Hopkins, Bruce Bond 1949- WhoEmL 93
Hopkins, Bruce Paul d1992 BioIn 17, NewYTBS 92
Hopkins, Budd 1931- WhoAm 92
Hopkins, Carl Edward 1912- WhoAm 92
Hopkins, Cecilia Ann 1922- WhoAmW 93
Hopkins, Charles I., Jr. 1927- St&PR 93
Hopkins, Charles Jerome 1836-1898 Baker 92
Hopkins, Charles Peter, II 1953- WhoE 93, WhoEmL 93, WhoWor 93
Hopkins, Chester Arthur 1928- St&PR 93
Hopkins, Claude (Driskett) 1903-1984 Baker 92
Hopkins, David L., Jr. 1928- WhoAm 92
Hopkins, Denise S. 1965- WhoAmW 93
Hopkins, Donald Roswell 1941- WhoAm 92
Hopkins, Donald W. St&PR 93
Hopkins, Drusilla K. 1956- St&PR 93
Hopkins, Edward Donald 1937- St&PR 93, WhoAm 92
Hopkins, Edward John 1818-1901 Baker 92
Hopkins, Edwina Weiskittel 1947- WhoWor 93
Hopkins, Emma B. AmWomPl
Hopkins, Esek 1718-1802 HarEnMi
Hopkins, Esther Arvilla Harrison 1926- WhoE 93
Hopkins, Everett Harold 1912- WhoAm 92
Hopkins, Frank H. 1927- St&PR 93
Hopkins, Gail Ethel 1941- WhoE 93
Hopkins, Gary B. 1949- St&PR 93
Hopkins, Gary L. Law&B 92
Hopkins, Gary L. 1955- St&PR 93
Hopkins, George Mathews Marks 1923- WhoAm 92, WhoSSW 93
Hopkins, Gerard Manley 1844-1889 BioIn 17, MagSWL [port], WorLitC [port]
Hopkins, Grover Prevatte 1933- WhoWor 93
Hopkins, Harrison WhoWrEP 92
Hopkins, Harry A. 1951- ScF&FL 92
Hopkins, Harry L. 1890-1946 ColdWar 1 [port], PolPar
Hopkins, Harry Lloyd 1890-1946 BioIn 17, DcTwHis
Hopkins, Hector K. ScF&FL 92
Hopkins, Hester A. AmWomPl
Hopkins, J. Wallace WhoScE 91-2
Hopkins, Jack Walker 1930- WhoAm 92
Hopkins, Jacques Vaughn 1930- WhoAm 92
Hopkins, James ScF&FL 92
Hopkins, James 1762-1834 BioIn 17
Hopkins, James D. 1961- WhoWrEP 92
Hopkins, James Farris 1932- WhoSSW 93
Hopkins, James Ray 1936- St&PR 93
Hopkins, James Roy 1944- WhoE 93
Hopkins, James Vinton 1949- WhoSSW 93
Hopkins, James William 1946- WhoWrEP 92
Hopkins, Jeanne Sulick 1952- WhoE 93
Hopkins, Jeannette E. 1922- WhoAm 92
Hopkins, Jerome Kirklin 1934- St&PR 93
Hopkins, Jerry Berl 1945- WhoSSW 93
Hopkins, Jerry Wayne 1947- St&PR 93
Hopkins, Jim D. 1935- St&PR 93
Hopkins, John MiSFD 9
Hopkins, John David 1938- WhoAm 92, WhoSSW 93
Hopkins, John Henry 1820-1891 Baker 92
Hopkins, John J. Law&B 92
Hopkins, John P. Law&B 92
Hopkins, John Robert 1930- St&PR 93
Hopkins, John T. 1956- St&PR 93
Hopkins, Joseph W. 1949- WhoEmL 93
Hopkins, Judith Owen 1952- WhoAm 92, WhoEmL 93
Hopkins, Karen Martin 1945- WhoSSW 93
Hopkins, Kenneth ScF&FL 92
Hopkins, Kenneth 1914-1988 BioIn 17
Hopkins, L. Wallace Law&B 92
Hopkins, L. Wallace 1925- St&PR 93
Hopkins, Larry J. 1933- CngDr 91, WhoAm 92, WhoSSW 93
Hopkins, Lee Bennett 1938- BioIn 17, MajAI [port], ScF&FL 92, WhoAm 92
Hopkins, Linda Ann 1937- WhoAmW 93
Hopkins, Malcolm John 1948- St&PR 93
Hopkins, Margaret Sutton Briscoe AmWomPl
Hopkins, Mariane S. 1951- ScF&FL 92
Hopkins, Mark 1802-1887 BioIn 17
Hopkins, Mark 1813-1878 GayN
Hopkins, Mary Ellen 1951- WhoAmW 93
Hopkins, Mary Evelyn 1919- WhoAmW 93
Hopkins, Miriam d1972 IntDcF 2-3 [port]
Hopkins, Paul Allen 1931- St&PR 93
Hopkins, Paul Jeffrey 1940- WhoAm 92
Hopkins, Peter Gerald WhoScE 91-1
Hopkins, Philip Joseph 1954- WhoEmL 93
Hopkins, R. Howard 1939- WhoIns 93
Hopkins, Raymond Edmund Law&B 92
Hopkins, Raymond Frederick 1939- WhoAm 92
Hopkins, Robert 1947- WhoScE 91-1
Hopkins, Robert Arthur 1920- WhoWor 93
Hopkins, Robert Elliott 1931- WhoWor 93
Hopkins, Robert Howard Law&B 92
Hopkins, Robert S(ydney) ConAu 38NR
Hopkins, Roy M. St&PR 93
Hopkins, Sam 1912-1982 Baker 92
Hopkins, Samuel 1721-1803 BioIn 17
Hopkins, Samuel 1913- WhoAm 92
Hopkins, Sarah Winnemucca GayN
Hopkins, Sarah Winnemucca 1844?-1891 AmWomWr 92, BioIn 17
Hopkins, Speed Elliott 1948- WhoEmL 93
Hopkins, Stephen MiSFD 9
Hopkins, Stephen A. Law&B 92
Hopkins, Telma BioIn 17
Hopkins, Thomas Arscott 1931- WhoAm 92
Hopkins, Thomas D., Jr. 1934- St&PR 93
Hopkins, Thomas Duvall 1942- WhoE 93, WhoWor 93
Hopkins, Thomas Gene 1932- WhoAm 92
Hopkins, Thomas Matthews 1927- WhoAm 92
Hopkins, Timothy 1859-1936 BioIn 17
Hopkins, Virginia Lee 1938- WhoSSW 93
Hopkins, W. Dean 1909- St&PR 93
Hopkins, Wanda Sue 1935- St&PR 93
Hopkins, Wayne W. 1947- St&PR 93

Hopkins, William Hugh 1941- BioIn 17
Hopkins, William Leatherbury 1938- St&PR 93
Hopkinson, Alan Rodney 1942- St&PR 93
Hopkinson, Arthur, Mrs. AmWomPl
Hopkinson, B. Todd 1946- St&PR 93
Hopkinson, D.A. WhoScE 91-1
Hopkinson, Francis 1737-1791 Baker 92
Hopkinson, Henry Thomas ScF&FL 92
Hopkinson, M. 1947- St&PR 93
Hopkinson, Shirley Lois 1924- WhoAmW 93
Hopkinson, T.D. St&PR 93
Hopkinson, Tom 1905-1990 BioIn 17, ScF&FL 92
Hopkins-Turkett, Bridget Ann 1960- WhoAmW 93
Hopley, David Philip 1932- WhoAm 92
Hopman, Ellen Evert 1952- WhoE 93
Hopmann, Philip Terrence 1942- WhoAm 92
Hopmeier, Arthur P. 1928- St&PR 93
Hopner, Thomas 1936- WhoScE 91-3
Hopp, Anthony J. 1945- St&PR 93
Hopp, Daniel F. Law&B 92
Hopp, Daniel Frederick 1947- St&PR 93, WhoAm 92
Hopp, James Lee 1949- WhoWrEP 92
Hopp, Manfred Ernst 1936- St&PR 93, WhoAm 92, WhoE 93
Hopp, William A. 1942- St&PR 93
Hoppa, Mary Ann 1959- WhoEmL 93
Hoppe, A.D. Law&B 92
Hoppe, Arthur Watterson 1925- WhoAm 92
Hoppe, Charles W. BioIn 17
Hoppe, Charles W. 1935- WhoAm 92
Hoppe, Charles William 1935- St&PR 93
Hoppe, Edward Henry, III 1927- St&PR 93
Hoppe, Edward P. St&PR 93
Hoppe, Eleanor Sellers 1933- WhoAmW 93
Hoppe, Hal F. 1938- St&PR 93
Hoppe, Judeth P. 1940- St&PR 93
Hoppe, Manley Robert 1910- St&PR 93
Hoppe, Michael Law&B 92
Hoppe, Murl Vern 1941- St&PR 93
Hoppe, Peter Christian 1942- WhoAm 92
Hoppe, Rudolf R.O. 1922- WhoScE 91-3
Hoppe, Stephanie T. 1947- ScF&FL 92
Hoppe, Wolfgang 1933- WhoAm 92
Hoppenstand, Gary ScF&FL 92
Hoppensteadt, Frank Charles 1938- WhoAm 92
Hoppensteadt, Thomas R. 1955- St&PR 93
Hoppenstedt, Robert M. 1951- St&PR 93
Hoppenstein, Abraham Solomon 1931- WhoWor 93
Hoppenstein, Jay Marshall 1938- WhoSSW 93
Hopper, A.G. WhoScE 91-1
Hopper, Alan T. 1947- WhoAm 92
Hopper, Andy WhoScE 91-1
Hopper, Anita Klein 1945- WhoAmW 93
Hopper, Arthur Frederick 1917- WhoSSW 93
Hopper, Carl Jefferson 1944- St&PR 93
Hopper, Dave M. 1932- St&PR 93
Hopper, David A. 1941- St&PR 93
Hopper, David Henry 1927- WhoAm 92
Hopper, Dennis BioIn 17
Hopper, Dennis 1936- IntDcF 2-3 [port], MiSFD 9, WhoAm 92
Hopper, Edward 1882-1967 BioIn 17
Hopper, Frank Ambrose, III 1944- St&PR 93
Hopper, Grace BioIn 17
Hopper, Grace Murray 1906-1992 NewYTBS 92 [port]
Hopper, Hedda 1885-1966 JrnUS
Hopper, Jack Pollard Law&B 92
Hopper, Jeannette M. 1959- WhoWrEP 92
Hopper, Jerry 1907-1988 MiSFD 9N
Hopper, Lloyd Wade 1956- WhoSSW 93
Hopper, Lyn Watson 1953- WhoSSW 93
Hopper, Margaret Sue 1937- WhoSSW 93
Hopper, Mary A. 1942- St&PR 93
Hopper, Nancy J. 1937- ConAu 38NR
Hopper, Nancy Jane 1937- WhoAmW 93
Hopper, Rea 1906-1991 BioIn 17
Hopper, Robert William 1945- WhoAm 92
Hopper, Sally WhoAmW 93
Hopper, Trevor Martin WhoScE 91-1
Hopper, Victor D. 1918- St&PR 93
Hopper, Virginia Shearer 1940- WhoWrEP 92
Hopper, Walter Everett 1915- WhoAm 92, WhoWor 93
Hopper, Wilbert H. St&PR 93
Hopper, Wilbert Hill 1933- WhoAm 92, WhoWor 93
Hopper, William Bertrand 1939- WhoAm 92
Hopper, William David 1927- WhoAm 92
Hoppert, Earl William 1939- WhoWor 93
Hoppert, Gloria Jean 1949- WhoAmW 93
Hoppin, Richard H(allowell) 1913- Baker 92
Hoppin, Thomas E. 1941- St&PR 93
Hoppin, Thomas Edward 1941- WhoAm 92
Hopping, Daniel M.C. 1905-1990 BioIn 17
Hopping, Edwin N. Law&B 92
Hopping, Jamie Evelyn 1953- WhoSSW 93
Hopping, Richard Lee 1928- WhoAm 92
Hopple, Richard Van Tromp, Jr. 1947- WhoAm 92
Hopps, Raymond, Jr. 1949- WhoWor 93
Hopps, Sidney Bryce 1934- WhoAm 92
Hopps, Walter BioIn 17
Hoppstein, Lois Dent 1958- WhoSSW 93
Hopson, Howel H. 1924- St&PR 93
Hopson, James Warren 1946- St&PR 93
Hopson, Sharilyn Jane 1960- WhoEmL 93
Hopson Lamar, Rochelle Lenae 1965- WhoAmW 93
Hopsu-Havu, Vaino K. 1933- WhoScE 91-4
Hopt, Klaus Juergen 1940- WhoWor 93
Hopta, Anna Marie 1961- WhoEmL 93
Hopta, Steven M. Law&B 92
Hopton, Ralph 1598-1652 HarEnMi
Hopton, Susanna 1627-1709 BioIn 17
Hopwood, Anthony George WhoScE 91-1
Hopwood, David Alan WhoScE 91-1
Hopwood, Howard H. 1945- WhoAm 92
Hopwood, Howard H., III Law&B 92
Hopwood, Susan Kaplan d1992 BioIn 17, NewYTBS 92
Hora, Heinrich 1931- WhoWor 93
Hora, Michael E. 1943- St&PR 93
Horace BioIn 17
Horace 65BC-8BC MagSWL [port]
Horace, Charles C. 1924- St&PR 93
Horace, Stephen J. Law&B 92
Horacek, Frank J. 1945- St&PR 93
Horack, Thomas Borland 1946- WhoAm 92
Horai, Joann WhoAmW 93, WhoE 93
Horak, Adolph 1850-1921 Baker 92
Horak, Antonin 1875-1910 Baker 92
Horak, Donna Christine 1947- WhoE 93
Horak, Eduard 1838-1892 Baker 92
Horak, Jan-Christopher 1951- WhoAm 92
Horak, Josef 1931- Baker 92
Horak, Wenzel (Vaclav) Emanuel 1800-1871 Baker 92
Horakova, Zdenka Zahutova 1925- WhoAm 92
Horan, Anthony J. Law&B 92
Horan, Clark J., III 1950- WhoWor 93
Horan, Dennis 1937- St&PR 93
Horan, Don ScF&FL 92
Horan, Donald Burke 1934- St&PR 93
Horan, Douglas S. Law&B 92
Horan, Edward J. 1921- St&PR 93
Horan, Eugene L., III 1947- St&PR 93
Horan, Harold Eugene 1927- WhoAm 92
Horan, Hume Alexander 1934- WhoAm 92
Horan, James Craig 1960- WhoSSW 93
Horan, James Daniel 1925- St&PR 93
Horan, James Joseph 1936- St&PR 93
Horan, John J. 1920- WhoAm 92
Horan, Justin Thomas 1927- WhoAm 92
Horan, Leo Gallaspy 1925- WhoAm 92
Horan, Paul K. St&PR 93
Horan, Raymond Edward, Jr. 1917- St&PR 93
Horan, Roy Allison 1953- WhoEmL 93, WhoSSW 93
Horatius Cocles fl. c. 494BC- HarEnMi
Horatius Flaccus BioIn 17
Horbach, Lothar 1927- WhoScE 91-3
Horbach, Michael 1924-1986 ScF&FL 92
Horbach, Stephen 1917- St&PR 93
Horbaczewski, Henry Z. Law&B 92
Horbal, John St&PR 93
Horberg, Samuel Bernard 1926- St&PR 93
Horbert, Janet L.H. WhoWrEP 92
Horca, Manuel L., Jr. 1948- WhoAsAP 91
Horch, Nettie S. 1896-1991 BioIn 17
Horchow, S. Roger 1928- St&PR 93
Horchow, Samuel Roger 1928- WhoAm 92, WhoSSW 93
Hord, Bruce Taylor 1937- St&PR 93
Hord, Kathy Blalock 1942- WhoAmW 93
Hord, Michael Foster Law&B 92
Horde, G. Wilson Law&B 92
Horder, Mogens 1940- WhoScE 91-2
Hordon, Robert Marshall 1936- WhoE 93
Hore, John Edward 1929- WhoAm 92, WhoE 93
Hore, Marlene BioIn 17
Hore, Marlene Carole 1944- WhoAm 92
Hore, Terry 1932- WhoWor 93
Horecker, Bernard Leonard 1914- WhoAm 92
Horein, James R. 1937- St&PR 93
Horejs, Josef 1922- WhoScE 91-4
Horekens, John F.L. 1947- WhoUN 92
Horel, Lisa Stander 1955- WhoEmL 93
Horel, Tom 1947- St&PR 93
Horen, I. Richard 1946- St&PR 93
Horenstein, Cynthia Ann 1961- WhoEmL 93
Horenstein, Jascha 1898-1973 Baker 92
Horey, Edward C. 1937- St&PR 93
Horgan, Cornelius Oliver 1944- WhoAm 92, WhoSSW 93
Horgan, Dennis William 1963- WhoE 93
Horgan, Dianne Daugherty 1948- WhoEmL 93
Horgan, Edward Daniel, III 1942- WhoWor 93
Horgan, John J. 1942- St&PR 93
Horgan, John P. 1924- St&PR 93
Horgan, Maryellyn 1945- WhoSSW 93
Horgan, Paul 1903- BioIn 17, WhoAm 92
Horgan, Susan Bedsow 1947- WhoEmL 93
Horgan-Aguado, Joseph Patrick 1955- WhoE 93
Horger, Edgar Olin, III 1937- WhoAm 92
Horger, Robert V. 1911- St&PR 93
Hori, Keiko 1954- WhoWor 93
Hori, Kosuke 1934- WhoAsAP 91
Hori, Masao 1916- WhoAsAP 91
Hori, Ryohei 1929- WhoWor 93
Hori, Toshikazu 1950- WhoAsAP 91
Hori, Yukio 1927- WhoWor 93
Horianopoulos, Gus 1938- St&PR 93
Horie, Kazuyuki 1941- WhoWor 93
Horigome, Ikuo 1942- WhoAsAP 91
Horiguchi, Atsuko 1962- WhoE 93
Horiguchi, Shun'ichi 1927- WhoWor 93
Horiguchi, Takao 1929- WhoWor 93
Horii, Howard Nobuo 1923- WhoAm 92
Horii, Reiichi 1925- WhoWor 93
Horii, Tomitaro 1890-1942 HarEnMi
Horiike, Hideto 1949- WhoWor 93
Horik, Tom Manahayu 1952- WhoAsAP 91
Horikoshi, Neil H. Law&B 92
Horine, Nelson Charles, II 1947- WhoE 93, WhoEmL 93
Horing, Sheldon 1936- St&PR 93
Horisberger, Don Hans 1951- WhoEmL 93
Horisberger, Marc 1939- WhoScE 91-4
Horisk, Anthony Bane 1947- St&PR 93
Horiszny, Laurene H. Law&B 92
Horiuchi, Atsushi 1929- WhoWor 93
Horiuchi, Gen 1964- WhoAm 92
Horiuchi, Toshihiro 1949- WhoWor 93
Horiuchi, Toshikazu 1939- WhoWor 93
Horka, Alfred Edward 1921- WhoE 93
Horkey, William R. 1925- St&PR 93
Horkey, William Richard 1925- WhoAm 92
Horkowitz, John Paul 1957- WhoSSW 93
Horkowitz, Sylvester Peter 1921- WhoWor 93
Horky, Karel 1909-1988 Baker 92
Horl, M. 1929- WhoScE 91-4
Horlak, E. E. ConAu 137, ScF&FL 92
Horler, Sydney 1888-1954 ScF&FL 92
Horlick, Allan WhoE 93
Horlick, Gary Norman 1947- WhoAm 92, WhoEmL 93
Horlick, Robert Allan 1956- WhoEmL 93
Horman, Charles H. 1939- St&PR 93
Horman, Hermine Briggs BioIn 17
Horman, Ian 1939- WhoScE 91-4
Hormander, Hans Olof 1923- WhoScE 91-4
Hormander, Lars V. 1931- WhoScE 91-4
Hormats, Robert David 1943- WhoAm 92
Hormisdas d523 OxDcByz
Hormozi, Farrokh Zad 1937- WhoE 93
Horn, Alan Law&B 92
Horn, Albrecht A. 1940- WhoUN 92
Horn, Alec H. Law&B 92
Horn, Andrew Warren 1946- WhoEmL 93
Horn, Audrey Jean 1951- WhoAmW 93
Horn, August 1825-1893 Baker 92
Horn, Barbara Ruth 1945- WhoE 93
Horn, Camillo 1860-1941 Baker 92
Horn, Carl, Jr. 1921- St&PR 93
Horn, Carol Lynn 1948- WhoAmW 93
Horn, Charles Edward 1786-1849 Baker 92, OxDcOp
Horn, Charles G. 1939- WhoAm 92, WhoSSW 93
Horn, Christian F. 1927- St&PR 93
Horn, Christian Friedrich 1927- WhoAm 92
Horn, Claire Helen 1934- WhoWor 93
Horn, Daniel d1992 NewYTBS 92
Horn, Daniel 1934-1991 BioIn 17
Horn, David D. St&PR 93
Horn, David D. 1941- WhoIns 93
Horn, David Dinsmore 1941- WhoAm 92
Horn, Dawson, III Law&B 92
Horn, Deborah Sue 1954- WhoAm 92
Horn, Donald Noel 1928- St&PR 93
Horn, Donna Kay 1951- WhoAmW 93
Horn, Dwain R. 1930- St&PR 93
Horn, Edward Newman 1903-1976 ScF&FL 92
Horn, Everett B., Jr. Law&B 92
Horn, Everett Byron, Jr. 1927- St&PR 93, WhoIns 93
Horn, Francis Henry 1908- WhoAm 92
Horn, Frederick E. d1992 BioIn 17
Horn, Gabriel WhoScE 91-1
Horn, Gerald Anthony 1941- WhoAm 92
Horn, Guenther 1943- St&PR 93
Horn, Gwendolyn 1952- WhoAmW 93
Horn, Helmut BioIn 17
Horn, Henry Stainken 1941- WhoE 93
Horn, James H. 1919- WhoIns 93
Horn, Janet 1950- WhoE 93
Horn, Jerry Dean 1937- St&PR 93, WhoAm 92
Horn, Jim Nathan 1941- WhoSSW 93
Horn, Joan Kelly 1936- CngDr 91, WhoAm 92, WhoAmW 93
Horn, John BioIn 17
Horn, John C. 1915- St&PR 93
Horn, John Chisolm 1915- WhoAm 92, WhoE 93, WhoWor 93
Horn, John J. Law&B 92
Horn, John R. Law&B 92
Horn, Jonathan F. 1955- WhoEmL 93
Horn, Karen BioIn 17
Horn, Karen Elaine Laukka 1958- WhoAmW 93
Horn, Karen Nicholson 1943- WhoAm 92, WhoAmW 93
Horn, Karl Friedrich 1762-1830 Baker 92
Horn, Kim Marie 1964- WhoEmL 93
Horn, Klaus Friedrich 1928- WhoScE 91-3
Horn, L. B., III 1953- WhoSSW 93
Horn, Lawrence S. 1944- WhoAm 92
Horn, Linda BioIn 17
Horn, Ludwig Paul 1930- St&PR 93
Horn, Lyle William 1943- WhoE 93
Horn, Marcia Davidson 1944- WhoAmW 93, WhoSSW 93
Horn, Margaret A. Law&B 92
Horn, Marian Blank 1943- CngDr 91, WhoAmW 93, WhoE 93
Horn, Marie E. Law&B 92
Horn, Martin Robert 1928- WhoAm 92
Horn, Maude Hulbert 1875-1935 BioIn 17
Horn, Michiel Steven Daniel 1939- WhoE 93
Horn, Milton 1906- WhoAm 92
Horn, Myron Kay 1930- WhoAm 92
Horn, Paul 1930- BioIn 17
Horn, Paul Joseph 1930- WhoAm 92
Horn, Paula Lois 1947- WhoAmW 93
Horn, Phyllis 1938- ScF&FL 92
Horn, Ralph E. 1937- St&PR 93
Horn, Randall C. 1952- St&PR 93
Horn, Rebecca BioIn 17, MiSFD 9
Horn, Richard 1930- St&PR 93
Horn, Richard E. WhoAm 92
Horn, Robert A. 1943- St&PR 93
Horn, Robert Ernest 1926- St&PR 93
Horn, Roger Alan 1942- WhoAm 92
Horn, Ronald C. 1936- WhoIns 93
Horn, Rose Mary 1921- WhoAmW 93
Horn, Rosemarie 1939- WhoScE 91-3
Horn, Roy BioIn 17
Horn, Russell Eugene 1912- St&PR 93
Horn, Russell Eugene, Jr. 1934- WhoAm 92, WhoE 93
Horn, Sharon McCole 1958- WhoAmW 93
Horn, Sheila Turner 1951- St&PR 93
Horn, Shirley BioIn 17, WhoAm 92
Horn, Stephen 1931- WhoAm 92, WhoWor 93
Horn, Susan Andrews 1946- WhoAmW 93, WhoEmL 93
Horn, Susan Dadakis 1943- WhoAmW 93
Horn, Thomas Carl 1916- WhoAm 92
Horn, Thomas Darrough 1918- WhoAm 92
Horn, Thomas J. Law&B 92
Horn, Thomas Lefler, Jr. 1922- St&PR 93
Horn, Tom 1860-1903 BioIn 17
Horn, Trevor
See Yes ConMus 8
Horn, Wade Frederick 1954- WhoAm 92
Horn, Walter William 1908- BioIn 17
Horn, William Fred AfrAmBi [port]
Horn, Wolfgang 1925- WhoScE 91-3
Horna, Alan Roger 1949- St&PR 93
Hornacek, Jeff BioIn 17
Hornacek, Thomas K. Law&B 92
Hornaday, David Samuel 1959- St&PR 93
Hornaday, F.D. 1950- St&PR 93
Hornaday, Jeffrey MiSFD 9
Hornaday, Jon Russell 1935- WhoSSW 93
Hornady, John R., III 1929- St&PR 93
Hornady, Marval 1913- St&PR 93
Hornak, Anna Frances 1922- WhoAm 92
Hornak, Thomas 1924- WhoAm 92
Hornback, Joseph Hope 1910- WhoAm 92
Hornback, Michelle 1958- WhoAmW 93
Hornbaker, Alice Joy 1927- WhoAm 92, WhoAmW 93
Hornbaker, Renee Jean 1952- WhoAm 92
Hornbeck, Daniel L. Law&B 92
Hornbeck, Ellen P. AmWomPl
Hornbeck, Helen P. AmWomPl

Hornbein, Thomas Frederic 1930- *WhoAm 92*
Hornbein, Victor 1913- *WhoAm 92*
Hornberger, George Milton 1942- *WhoAm 92*
Hornberger, H.D. 1927- *St&PR 93*
Hornberger, Lee 1946- *WhoEmL 93*
Hornberger, Robert Howard 1933- *WhoSSW 93*
Hornberger, Ronald 1943- *WhoAm 92*
Hornblass, Albert 1939- *WhoE 93*
Hornblass, Bernice Miriam 1951- *WhoE 93*
Hornblow, Arthur 1893-1976 *BioIn 17*
Hornblower, G.M. *Law&B 92*
Hornblower, William Butler 1851-1914 *OxCSupC*
Hornbostel, Erich Moritz von 1877-1935 *Baker 92*
Hornbostel, John F., Jr. *Law&B 92*
Hornbostel, John F., Jr. 1940- *St&PR 93, WhoAm 92*
Hornbostel, Linda 1953- *WhoAmW 93*
Hornbuckle, Franklin L. 1941- *WhoAm 92*
Hornbuckle, James Kenneth 1945- *St&PR 93*
Hornburg, Tanya Verena 1960- *WhoEmL 93*
Hornby, David Brock 1944- *WhoAm 92, WhoE 93*
Hornby, Derek 1930- *BioIn 17*
Hornby, George A. d1990 *BioIn 17*
Hornby, Lesley 1949- *WhoAm 92*
Hornby, Thomas Richard 1936- *WhoAm 92*
Hornby-Anderson, Sara Ann 1952- *WhoAmW 93*
Horne, Aaron 1940- *ConAu 138*
Horne, Alice Merrill *AmWomPl*
Horne, Carl A. 1929- *St&PR 93*
Horne, Charles E., III 1932- *St&PR 93, WhoIns 93*
Horne, Charles Hugh Wilson *WhoScE 91-1*
Horne, Colin James 1912- *WhoWor 93*
Horne, Donald Richmond 1921- *WhoWor 93*
Horne, Douglas Allan 1966- *St&PR 93*
Horne, Douglas Stuart 1934- *WhoE 93*
Horne, Eugene Barron, Jr. 1942- *St&PR 93, WhoAm 92*
Horne, Frederick Herbert 1934- *WhoAm 92*
Horne, George d1990 *BioIn 17*
Horne, George R. 1936- *St&PR 93*
Horne, Grant N. 1931- *St&PR 93*
Horne, Grant Nelson 1931- *WhoAm 92*
Horne, Herbert Percy 1864-1916 *BioIn 17*
Horne, Janis Mayo 1955- *WhoEmL 93*
Horne, John C. 1948- *St&PR 93*
Horne, John R. 1938- *St&PR 93, WhoAm 92*
Horne, Joy Luana 1948- *WhoAmW 93*
Horne, L. Donald 1933- *St&PR 93, WhoAm 92*
Horne, Lena 1917?- *IntDcF 2-3 [port], WhoAm 92, WhoAmW 93*
Horne, Lena (Calhoun) 1917- *Baker 92*
Horne, Malaika Beverly 1946- *WhoEmL 93*
Horne, Marilyn *BioIn 17*
Horne, Marilyn 1929- *OxDcOp*
Horne, Marilyn 1934- *ConMus 9 [port], IntDcOp [port], WhoAm 92, WhoWor 93*
Horne, Marilyn (Bernice) 1934- *Baker 92*
Horne, Mary Barnard 1845- *AmWomPl*
Horne, Michael Stewart 1938- *WhoAm 92*
Horne, Michael Thomas *WhoScE 91-1*
Horne, Nettie A. *Law&B 92*
Horne, Scott J. *Law&B 92*
Horne, Scott Jeffrey 1955- *WhoE 93*
Horne, Susie 1929- *WhoAmW 93*
Horne, Thomas Lee, III 1950- *WhoEmL 93, WhoSSW 93*
Horne, Timothy P. 1938- *St&PR 93*
Horne, Vernon Alvin 1947- *St&PR 93*
Horne, William E. 1946- *St&PR 93*
Horne, William Parrish 1924- *St&PR 93*
Hornecker, Wendell E. 1941- *WhoAm 92*
Horneman, Christian Frederik Emil 1840-1906 *Baker 92*
Horneman, Johan Ole Emil 1809-1870 *Baker 92*
Hornemann, Friedrich 1772-1801 *Expl 93*
Horner, Althea Jane 1926- *WhoAm 92, WhoWor 93*
Horner, Carl Matthew 1930- *WhoE 93*
Horner, Charles A. *BioIn 17*
Horner, Charles Albert 1936- *WhoAm 92*
Horner, Constance *BioIn 17*
Horner, Constance J. 1942- *WhoAmW 93*
Horner, David Edward *Law&B 92*
Horner, Donald G. 1950- *St&PR 93*
Horner, Donald William 1874- *ScF&FL 92*
Horner, Elizabeth West *AmWomPl*
Horner, Harry 1910- *WhoAm 92*
Horner, Henry H. 1878-1940 *PolPar*
Horner, Jack *BioIn 17*
Horner, Jack B. *Law&B 92*
Horner, Jack B. 1927- *St&PR 93*
Horner, James *ConTFT 10*
Horner, Joe 1849-1927 *BioIn 17*
Horner, John D. 1949- *St&PR 93*
Horner, John R. *BioIn 17*
Horner, John R. 1946- *CurBio 92 [port]*
Horner, John Robert 1946- *WhoAm 92*
Horner, Kenneth D. 1935- *St&PR 93*
Horner, Larry Dean 1934- *WhoAm 92*
Horner, Leonard M. 1927- *St&PR 93*
Horner, Mary Kay 1940- *St&PR 93*
Horner, Matina S. 1939- *WhoIns 93*
Horner, Matina Souretis 1939- *WhoAm 92, WhoAmW 93, WhoWor 93*
Horner, Maxine Edwyna Cissel 1933- *WhoAmW 93*
Horner, Ralph Joseph 1848-1926 *Baker 92*
Horner, Richard Elmer 1917- *WhoAm 92*
Horner, Robert James 1957- *BiDAMSp 1989*
Horner, Robert Malcolm Wigglesworth *WhoScE 91-1*
Horner, Russell G., Jr. *WhoAm 92*
Horner, Russell Grant, Jr. *Law&B 92*
Horner, Russell W. 1925- *St&PR 93*
Horner, Sally McKay Melvin 1935- *WhoSSW 93*
Horner, Stephen R. *St&PR 93*
Horner, Steven Mark 1951- *WhoE 93*
Horner, Thomas Harvey 1928- *WhoAm 92*
Horner, William Edwin, III 1963- *St&PR 93*
Horner, William Harry 1923- *WhoAm 92*
Horner, Winifred Bryan 1922- *WhoAmW 93*
Horney, Karen 1885-1952 *BioIn 17*
Horngren, Charles Thomas 1926- *WhoAm 92*
Hornibrook, Walter J. 1916-1991 *BioIn 17*
Hornick, Betty Stanley 1948- *WhoSSW 93*
Hornick, Gerald Charles 1932- *St&PR 93*
Hornick, Joshua 1959- *WhoEmL 93*
Hornick, Katherine Joyce Kay 1940- *WhoAm 92, WhoAmW 93*
Hornick, Lita R. 1927- *BioIn 17*
Hornick, Richard Bernard 1929- *WhoAm 92*
Hornicke, Heiko 1927- *WhoScE 91-3*
Hornickel, John H. *Law&B 92*
Hornickel, Laura *AmWomPl*
Hornig, Dana Theodore 1929- *St&PR 93*
Hornig, Donald F. 1920- *St&PR 93*
Hornig, Donald Frederick 1920- *WhoAm 92*
Hornig, Doug 1943- *ConAu 40NR*
Hornig, Douglas 1943- *WhoWrEP 92*
Hornik, Joseph William 1929- *WhoAm 92, WhoWor 93*
Hornik, Richard *BioIn 17*
Horning, Alice S. 1950- *ConAu 137, WhoAmW 93*
Horning, Arthur Alan *Law&B 92*
Horning, Dixie Dianna 1949- *WhoAmW 93*
Horning, Jerome Kay 1935- *WhoAm 92*
Horning, Martin Stuart 1942- *St&PR 93*
Horning, Michael F. 1957- *St&PR 93*
Horning, Minnie B. *AmWomPl*
Horning, Robert Alan 1954- *WhoWor 93*
Horning, Ross Charles, Jr. 1920- *WhoAm 92*
Horning, Thomas L. 1931- *St&PR 93*
Horning, Timothy John 1950- *WhoSSW 93*
Hornocker, Maurice *BioIn 17*
Hornok, Laszlo 1941- *WhoScE 91-4*
Hornok, Laszlo 1947- *WhoScE 91-4*
Hornor, Frank Berkshire 1923- *WhoAm 92*
Horns, Howard Lowell 1912- *WhoAm 92*
Hornsby, Alton, Jr. 1940- *WhoSSW 93*
Hornsby, Andrew Preston, Jr. 1943- *WhoSSW 93*
Hornsby, Bruce *BioIn 17*
Hornsby, Bruce Randall 1954- *WhoSSW 93*
Hornsby, Gerald 1934- *St&PR 93*
Hornsby, Joan Rigney 1940- *WhoAmW 93, WhoE 93*
Hornsby, John Slindon *WhoScE 91-1*
Hornsby, Richard L. 1936- *St&PR 93*
Hornsby, Roger Allen 1926- *WhoAm 92*
Hornsby, Rogers 1896-1963 *BioIn 17*
Hornsby, Sonny *WhoAm 92, WhoSSW 93*
Hornsey, Evelyn Grant *AmWomPl*
Hornsey, Pat *ScF&FL 92*
Hornsleth, Henrik Oscar 1960- *WhoWor 93*
Hornstein, Alvin Sidney 1926- *WhoE 93*
Hornstein, Barry Martin *Law&B 92*
Hornstein, Eugene 1940- *St&PR 93*
Hornstein, Harold 1920- *WhoWrEP 92*
Hornstein, Mark 1947- *St&PR 93*
Hornstein, Norbert Richard 1951- *WhoEmL 93*
Hornstein, Otto Paul 1926- *WhoWor 93*
Hornstein, Reuben Aaron 1912- *BioIn 17*
Hornstein, Robert von 1833-1890 *Baker 92*
Hornsten, Lawrence A. *WhoAm 92*
Hornung, Hans Georg 1934- *WhoAm 92*
Hornung, Klaus 1939- *WhoScE 91-3*
Hornung, Leonard Matthew 1934- *St&PR 93*
Hornung, Paul 1935- *BioIn 17*
Hornung, Robert Paul 1923- *St&PR 93*
Hornung, Ulrich 1941- *WhoWor 93*
Hornyak, Annamaria 1965- *WhoAmW 93*
Hornyak, Ronald F. 1947- *St&PR 93*
Horonzy, Joseph G. 1947- *WhoAm 92*
Horoschak, Donna *Law&B 92*
Horosko, Marian 1927- *WhoE 93*
Horoszewicz, Juliusz Stanislaw 1931- *WhoE 93, WhoWor 93*
Horovitz, Adam c. 1967- *See* Beastie Boys, The *ConMus 8*
Horovitz, Israel Arthur 1939- *WhoAm 92*
Horovitz, Joseph 1926- *Baker 92*
Horovitz, Richard d1991 *BioIn 17*
Horovitz, Stanley 1933- *St&PR 93*
Horovitz, Zola Philip 1934- *St&PR 93, WhoAm 92*
Horowitz, Alan David 1948- *St&PR 93*
Horowitz, Anthony 1955- *ChlFicS, ScF&FL 92*
Horowitz, Barney Louis 1938- *WhoWor 93*
Horowitz, Barry M. 1943- *St&PR 93*
Horowitz, Beverly Phyllis 1949- *WhoAm 92*
Horowitz, Carl 1923- *St&PR 93, WhoAm 92*
Horowitz, Daniel 1938- *WhoE 93*
Horowitz, David Charles 1937- *WhoAm 92*
Horowitz, David H. 1928- *WhoAm 92*
Horowitz, David Joel 1939- *WhoAm 92, WhoWrEP 92*
Horowitz, David K. 1928- *St&PR 93*
Horowitz, Dennis *WhoAm 92*
Horowitz, Don Roy 1930- *WhoAm 92*
Horowitz, Donald Leonard 1939- *WhoAm 92*
Horowitz, Edwin 1931- *St&PR 93*
Horowitz, Eugene B. d1992 *NewYTBS 92*
Horowitz, Eve 1963- *ConAu 139*
Horowitz, Flavio 1953- *WhoWor 93*
Horowitz, Frances Degen 1932- *WhoAm 92*
Horowitz, Fred L. 1954- *WhoWor 93*
Horowitz, Gedale B. 1932- *St&PR 93*
Horowitz, Gene 1930-1992 *BioIn 17*
Horowitz, Harold 1927- *WhoAm 92*
Horowitz, Harry I. 1915- *WhoSSW 93*
Horowitz, Herbert Eugene 1930- *WhoAm 92*
Horowitz, Hugh H. 1928- *WhoE 93*
Horowitz, Irene 1923- *St&PR 93, WhoAmW 93*
Horowitz, Irving Louis *BioIn 17*
Horowitz, Irving Louis 1929- *WhoAm 92, WhoWrEP 92*
Horowitz, Jack 1931- *WhoAm 92*
Horowitz, Jefferey R. *Law&B 92*
Horowitz, John David 1948- *WhoWor 93*
Horowitz, Julie K. *Law&B 92*
Horowitz, Kenneth Lee 1941- *WhoE 93*
Horowitz, Kenneth Paul 1956- *WhoE 93*
Horowitz, Larry *BioIn 17*
Horowitz, Lenore Wisney 1946- *WhoWrEP 92*
Horowitz, Leon 1925- *WhoSSW 93*
Horowitz, Leonard I. *Law&B 92*
Horowitz, Leonard N. *BioIn 17*
Horowitz, Leonard N. d1992 *NewYTBS 92*
Horowitz, Lewis J. 1935- *St&PR 93*
Horowitz, Lewis Jay 1935- *WhoAm 92*
Horowitz, Lois 1940- *ScF&FL 92*
Horowitz, Mary Curtis 1946- *WhoAm 92, WhoAmW 93*
Horowitz, Morris A. 1919- *WhoAm 92*
Horowitz, Paul 1942- *BioIn 17*
Horowitz, Raymond J. 1916- *St&PR 93, WhoAm 92*
Horowitz, Richard 1949- *Baker 92*
Horowitz, Richard Andrew 1950- *St&PR 93*
Horowitz, Rosalind 1946- *WhoAmW 93, WhoSSW 93*
Horowitz, Samuel d1990 *BioIn 17*
Horowitz, Samuel Boris 1927- *WhoAm 92*
Horowitz, Shel Alan 1956- *WhoWrEP 92*
Horowitz, Sheldon N. 1946- *St&PR 93*
Horowitz, Sidney 1920- *St&PR 93, WhoAm 92*
Horowitz, Stephen Paul 1943- *WhoWor 93*
Horowitz, Susan J. *Law&B 92*
Horowitz, Vladimir 1903-1989 *Baker 92*
Horowitz, Vladimir 1904-1989 *BioIn 17*
Horowitz, Winona Laura 1971- *WhoAm 92*
Horowitz, Zachary I. 1953- *WhoAm 92, WhoWor 93*
Horozko, Beverly A. 1948- *WhoAmW 93*
Horr, David A. 1938- *St&PR 93*
Horr, William Henry 1914- *WhoAm 92*
Horrall, Curtis L. 1930- *St&PR 93*
Horrell, Ben d1873 *BioIn 17*
Horrell, Jeffrey Lanier 1952- *WhoE 93*
Horrell, Karen Holley *Law&B 92*
Horrell, Karen Holley 1952- *St&PR 93, WhoEmL 93, WhoIns 93*
Horrell, Mark B. 1962- *St&PR 93*
Horrell, Martin d1878 *BioIn 17*
Horrell, Merritt d1877 *BioIn 17*
Horrell, Sam *BioIn 17*
Horrell, Tom d1878 *BioIn 17*
Horrey, C. Douglas 1937- *St&PR 93*
Horrigan, Brian *ScF&FL 92*
Horrigan, Brian Richard 1951- *WhoEmL 93*
Horrigan, D. Greg 1943- *WhoAm 92*
Horrigan, D. Gregory 1943- *St&PR 93*
Horrigan, Edward A., Jr. 1929- *WhoAm 92*
Horrigan, Patricia Ann 1934- *WhoWrEP 92*
Horrigan, Thomas H. 1926- *WhoE 93*
Horrigmoe, Geir 1946- *WhoScE 91-4*
Horrocks, Arthur Richard *WhoScE 91-1*
Horrocks, Geoffrey *WhoScE 91-1*
Horrocks, Jay B. 1930- *St&PR 93*
Horrocks, Norman 1927- *St&PR 93, WhoAm 92*
Horrocks, William DeWitt, Jr. 1934- *WhoE 93*
Horrox, Alberta W. 1938- *St&PR 93*
Horsbrugh, Patrick 1920- *WhoAm 92*
Horsch, Kathleen Joanne 1936- *WhoAm 92*
Horsch, Lawrence Leonard 1934- *WhoAm 92*
Horsell, Mary Kay 1917- *WhoAm 92, WhoWor 93*
Horseman, Roy Mertzell 1935- *WhoE 93*
Horsey, Geraldine Elizabeth 1946- *WhoAmW 93*
Horsey, James J. 1949- *St&PR 93*
Horsey, William Grant 1915- *WhoAm 92*
Horsfall, Bruce D. 1933- *St&PR 93*
Horsfield, J.M.F. *WhoScE 91-1*
Horsfield, John A. *Law&B 92*
Horsford, Anna Maria *BioIn 17*
Horsford, Anna Maria 1947- *ConTFT 10*
Horsford, Howard C(larke) 1921- *ConAu 136*
Horsford, Howard Clarke 1921- *WhoAm 92*
Horsky, Charles Antone 1910- *WhoAm 92*
Horsley, Charles Edward 1822-1876 *Baker 92*
Horsley, Jack Everett 1915- *WhoAm 92*
Horsley, Lee *BioIn 17*
Horsley, Paula Rosalie 1924- *WhoAmW 93*
Horsley, R.M. *WhoScE 91-1*
Horsley, Richard David 1942- *St&PR 93*
Horsley, Stuart E. 1945- *WhoScE 91-1*
Horsley, Teri Lynne 1961- *WhoAmW 93*
Horsley, Waller Holladay 1931- *WhoAm 92*
Horsley, William 1774-1858 *Baker 92*
Horsman, Anthony *WhoScE 91-1*
Horsman, David A. Elliott 1932- *WhoAm 92, WhoE 93*
Horsman, Greg *BioIn 17*
Horsman, James Deverell 1935- *WhoAm 92*
Horsman, John G., Jr. 1938- *St&PR 93*
Horsman, John Gordon, Jr. 1938- *WhoAm 92*
Horsman, Reginald 1931- *WhoAm 92*
Horsnell, Christopher Owen 1955- *WhoSSW 93*
Horsnell, Margaret Eileen 1928- *WhoAmW 93, WhoE 93*
Horsnell, Walter Cecil 1911- *WhoWor 93*
Horst 1906- *BioIn 17, CurBio 92 [port]*
Horst, Anthon van der 1899-1965 *Baker 92*
Horst, Bruce Everett 1921- *WhoAm 92*
Horst, Donald John 1932- *St&PR 93*
Horst, J. Robert *Law&B 92*
Horst, Katie ter d1992 *BioIn 17*
Horst, Louis 1884-1964 *Baker 92*
Horst, Nancy Carroll 1933- *WhoAmW 93*
Horst, Neal A. 1941- *St&PR 93*
Horst, Pamela Jane 1957- *WhoEmL 93*
Horst, R.G. 1919- *St&PR 93*
Horst, Tom Emil 1951- *WhoEmL 93*
Horst, Walter J. 1946- *WhoScE 91-3*
Horsted, Sv. Aa. *WhoScE 91-2*
Horsting, Jessie 1950- *ScF&FL 92*
Horstman, Randall L. 1944- *St&PR 93*
Horstman, Richard Leopold *Law&B 92*
Horstman, Suzanne Rucker 1945- *WhoAmW 93*

Horstman, Thomas ScF&FL 92
Horstmann, Dorothy Millicent 1911- WhoAm 92, WhoAmW 93
Horstmann, James Douglas 1933- WhoAm 92
Horstmann, Manfred 1928- WhoScE 91-3
Horstmeyer, John A. WhoAm 92
Horszowski, Mieczyslaw BioIn 17
Horszowski, Mieczyslaw 1892- Baker 92, PolBiDi
Hort, Michael David 1941- St&PR 93
Hort, Waldemar 1925- WhoScE 91-3
Horta, Toninho BioIn 17
Horta, Victor 1861-1947 BioIn 17
Horte, R.V. Law&B 92
Horten, Carl Frank 1914- WhoAm 92
Horter, Patricia B. Law&B 92
Horthy de Nagybanya, Nikolaus Miklos 1868-1957 DcTwHis
Horton, Andrew Marcus 1949- WhoEmL 93
Horton, Ann Mitchell 1949- WhoAmW 93
Horton, Arthur MacNeill, Jr. 1947- WhoE 93
Horton, Austin Asadata Dafora 1890-1965 Baker 92, BioIn 17
Horton, Barbara Elizabeth 1953- WhoEmL 93
Horton, Barbara Marion Deady 1930- WhoAmW 93
Horton, Bernard Francis 1916- WhoAm 92
Horton, Bobby BioIn 17
Horton, Bruce M. 1934- WhoIns 93
Horton, Byron W. 1909- St&PR 93
Horton, Claude Wendell 1915- WhoAm 92
Horton, Donna Alberg 1935- WhoSSW 93
Horton, Edward Everett 1886-1970 IntDcF 2-3, QDrFCA 92 [port]
Horton, Elliott Argue, Jr. 1926- WhoAm 92
Horton, Forest W., Jr. 1930- ScF&FL 92
Horton, Frank 1919- CngDr 91, WhoAm 92, WhoE 93
Horton, Frank Elba 1939- WhoAm 92
Horton, Frank L. 1918- BioIn 17
Horton, Gary Bruce 1943- WhoAm 92
Horton, George R. Law&B 92
Horton, Gerald Talmadge 1934- WhoAm 92
Horton, Gerald W. 1943- St&PR 93
Horton, Gordon T. 1924- ScF&FL 92
Horton, Granville Eugene 1927- WhoSSW 93
Horton, Gwendolyn 1914- WhoAmW 93
Horton, Hamilton Cowles, Jr. 1931- St&PR 93
Horton, Harland B., Jr. Law&B 92
Horton, Herbert 1945- St&PR 93
Horton, Honey ScF&FL 92
Horton, Horace Robert 1935- WhoAm 92
Horton, J.T. 1928- St&PR 93
Horton, J(ames) Wright, (Jr.) 1950- ConAu 138
Horton, James Bawden 1930- WhoAm 92
Horton, James Wallace 1951- WhoSSW 93
Horton, James William, Jr. 1959- WhoE 93
Horton, James Wright 1919- WhoAm 92
Horton, James Wright, Jr. 1950- WhoSSW 93
Horton, Jared C. 1924- WhoAm 92
Horton, Jeanne M. Law&B 92
Horton, Jeffrey Michael 1956- WhoSSW 93
Horton, John Alden 1920- WhoAm 92
Horton, John Edward 1930- WhoAm 92
Horton, John Tod 1928- WhoAm 92
Horton, Joseph Julian, Jr. 1936- WhoE 93
Horton, June Carol Law&B 92
Horton, K.C. 1956- St&PR 93
Horton, Kate AmWomPl
Horton, Larry Alan 1958- WhoSSW 93
Horton, Larry Bruce 1942- WhoSSW 93, WhoWor 93
Horton, Leonard W., III Law&B 92
Horton, Louise (Walthall) 1916- ConAu 40NR
Horton, Madeline Mary 1939- WhoAmW 93
Horton, Marcia L. 1947- St&PR 93
Horton, Martha Louise 1934- WhoE 93
Horton, Michael 1918- WhoE 93
Horton, Michael Patrick 1942- St&PR 93
Horton, Myles BioIn 17
Horton, Odell 1929- WhoAm 92, WhoSSW 93
Horton, Patrick John 1954- WhoEmL 93
Horton, Paul Bradfield 1920- WhoAm 92, WhoSSW 93, WhoWor 93
Horton, Paul Chester 1942- WhoE 93
Horton, Peter BioIn 17, MiSFD 9
Horton, Philip Giles 1930- St&PR 93
Horton, Richard L. 1943- St&PR 93
Horton, Robert Baynes 1939- St&PR 93, WhoAm 92, WhoWor 93
Horton, Robert Carlton 1926- WhoAm 92
Horton, Roger 1944- St&PR 93
Horton, Ruth AmWomPl
Horton, Sharon Rene 1958- WhoEmL 93
Horton, Sherman D. WhoAm 92
Horton, Stephen L. Law&B 92
Horton, Thelma White 1949- WhoEmL 93
Horton, Thomas Edward, Jr. 1935- WhoAm 92
Horton, Thomas Mark 1952- WhoSSW 93
Horton, Thomas R. 1926- WhoAm 92
Horton, William Alan 1955- WhoSSW 93
Horton, William R. 1931- St&PR 93
Horton, William Russell 1931- WhoAm 92
Horton-Hill, Elizabeth Carlton 1960- WhoSSW 93
Hortop, Kenneth C. Law&B 92
Horty, J.F. 1928- St&PR 93
Horvat, Dilwyn ScF&FL 92
Horvat, Edwina Marie 1953- WhoEmL 93
Horvat, Laura Jean 1947- WhoAmW 93
Horvat, Martin Michael 1946- WhoWrEP 92
Horvat, Milan 1919- Baker 92
Horvat, Peter Daniel 1937- St&PR 93
Horvat, Stanko 1930- Baker 92
Horvat, Stephen P., Jr. Law&B 92
Horvath, Arpad BioIn 17
Horvath, Attila 1939- WhoScE 91-4
Horvath, Csaba 1930- WhoAm 92
Horvath, Daniel C. 1954- WhoE 93
Horvath, Deszo 1946- WhoScE 91-4
Horvath, Elemer (George) 1933- WhoWrEP 92
Horvath, Elizabeth Iren 1966- WhoAmW 93
Horvath, Gary 1946- St&PR 93
Horvath, Gyorgy 1928- WhoScE 91-4
Horvath, Ian BioIn 17
Horvath, Imre 1935- WhoScE 91-4
Horvath, James Julius 1945- St&PR 93, WhoAm 92
Horvath, John 1948- WhoWrEP 92
Horvath, John 1949- St&PR 93
Horvath, Josef Maria 1931- Baker 92
Horvath, Joseph J. Law&B 92
Horvath, Joseph John 1936- St&PR 93, WhoAm 92
Horvath, Kathleen 1965?- BioIn 17
Horvath, Louis 1923- St&PR 93
Horvath, Lynda WhoAm 92
Horvath, Michael R. 1951- St&PR 93
Horvath, Odon von 1901-1938 DcLB 124 [port], TwCLC 45 [port]
Horvath, Richard George 1933- WhoE 93
Horvath, Steven M. 1932- St&PR 93
Horvath, Tibor 1928- WhoScE 91-4
Horvath, Vincent V. 1942- St&PR 93
Horvath, William F. d1991 BioIn 17
Horvath, Zoltan 1921- WhoScE 91-4
Horve, Leslie A. 1938- St&PR 93
Horvick, Neil M. 1954- St&PR 93
Horvitz, Abraham 1911- WhoE 93
Horvitz, Harry R. d1992 BioIn 17, NewYTBS 92
Horvitz, Howard Robert 1947- WhoAm 92
Horvitz, Leslie ScF&FL 92
Horvitz, Martha E. Law&B 92
Horvitz, Paul Michael 1935- WhoAm 92
Horwath, Mary BioIn 17
Horwedel, Lowell Charles 1932- St&PR 93
Horwege, Ronald Eugene 1944- WhoSSW 93
Horwell, David Christopher 1945- WhoScE 91-1
Horwich, Alan WhoScE 91-1
Horwich, Allan 1944- WhoAm 92
Horwich, George 1924- WhoAm 92
Horwick, Stephen Henry 1953- WhoSSW 93
Horwitch, Elaine d1991 BioIn 17
Horwitch, Marilyn Dolores 1927- WhoAmW 93
Horwith, Susan Kardos WhoE 93
Horwitt, Max Kenneth 1908- WhoAm 92
Horwitt, Nathan George 1897-1990 BioIn 17
Horwitz, Alan Fredrick 1944- WhoAm 92
Horwitz, Alan Steven 1955- St&PR 93
Horwitz, Albert Abram 1935- St&PR 93
Horwitz, Anthony Lander 1958- WhoAm 92
Horwitz, Barbara Ann 1940- WhoAm 92, WhoAmW 93
Horwitz, David Michael 1953- St&PR 93
Horwitz, Don L. Law&B 92
Horwitz, Donald Paul 1936- WhoAm 92
Horwitz, Eleanor Catherine 1941- WhoE 93
Horwitz, Ellis A. Law&B 92
Horwitz, Gary Bruce Law&B 92
Horwitz, Harry 1927- WhoAm 92
Horwitz, Irwin Daniel 1920- WhoAm 92
Horwitz, Jack BioIn 17
Horwitz, Jacob H. d1992 NewYTBS 92
Horwitz, John R. Law&B 92
Horwitz, Karl 1884-1925 Baker 92
Horwitz, Kathryn Bloch 1941- WhoAmW 93
Horwitz, Larry BioIn 17
Horwitz, Lawrence David 1939- WhoAm 92
Horwitz, Louis B. 1927- St&PR 93
Horwitz, Martha Kay 1958- WhoAmW 93
Horwitz, Michael M. 1948- St&PR 93
Horwitz, Murray 1949- WhoEmL 93
Horwitz, Orville 1909- WhoAm 92
Horwitz, Paul 1938- WhoAm 92
Horwitz, Ralph Irving 1947- WhoAm 92
Horwitz, Robert P. 1932- St&PR 93
Horwitz, Ronald M. 1938- WhoAm 92
Horwitz, Saul 1925- St&PR 93
Horwood, Ellis George 1911- WhoWor 93
Horwood, Harold 1923- WhoCanL 92
Horwood, John Michael Kerry WhoScE 91-1
Horwood, William 1944- ScF&FL 92
Horz, Friedrich 1940- WhoSSW 93
Horzinek, Marian C. 1936- WhoScE 91-3
Horzyca, Wilam 1889-1959 PolBiDi
Hosack, David 1769-1835 BioIn 17
Hosage, Daniel A. 1932- St&PR 93
Ho Sai-Chu 1937- WhoAsAP 91
Hosaka, Sakae 1930- St&PR 93
Hosaki, Shari N. Law&B 92
Hosang, Leon W. 1938- WhoUN 92
Hosbach, Howard D. 1931-1990 BioIn 17
Hosbach, Marguerette N. Law&B 92
Hosch, Burton B., Jr. 1947- St&PR 93
Hoschka, Peter 1936- WhoScE 91-3
Hoschke, Agoston 1938- WhoScE 91-4
Hoschl, Cyril 1949- WhoScE 91-4
Hoschna, Karl 1876-1911 Baker 92
Hoschner, Karl 1876-1911 Baker 92
Hoscoe, Julie B. Law&B 92
Hose, Charles 1863-1929 IntDcAn
Hose, John Robert 1940- WhoE 93
Hose, Sam d1899 EncAACR
Hosea, Julia Hiller 1952- WhoEmL 93
Hosek, Eric Allan 1956- WhoSSW 93
Hosek, Laverne R. Law&B 92
Hosek, Laverne R. 1933- St&PR 93
Hosek, Louis Otto, III 1952- WhoEmL 93, WhoSSW 93
Hoselton, Scott Allan 1964- WhoEmL 93
Hosemann, Gerhard W. 1922- WhoScE 91-3
Hosemann, Rolf 1912- WhoScE 91-3
Hosenball, S. Neil WhoAm 92
Hosey, R. Fred Law&B 92
Hosford, Jessie 1892- DcAmChF 1960
Hosford, Stephen E. Law&B 92
Hosford, William R. 1935- St&PR 93
Hoshi, Shin'ichi 1926- ScF&FL 92
Hoshikawa, Yasumatsu 1930- WhoAsAP 91
Hoshino, Eiichi 1953- WhoWor 93
Hoshino, Robert S., Jr. Law&B 92
Hoshino, Tomoichi 1918- WhoAsAP 91
Hoshino, Yoshiro 1922- WhoWor 93
Hoshino, Yukio 1932- WhoAsAP 91
Hosick, Howard Lawrence 1943- WhoAm 92
Hosie, John James 1940- WhoE 93
Hosken, Franziska Porges 1919- WhoAmW 93
Hosken, John ScF&FL 92
Hosken, Richard Bruce 1942- WhoSSW 93
Hosker, Rayford Peter, Jr. 1943- WhoAm 92
Hoskin, C.H. ScF&FL 92
Hoskin, Sandra Ruble 1935- WhoAmW 93
Hoskin, William Dickel 1920- WhoE 93
Hosking, Eric 1909-1991 AnObit 1991
Hosking, Eric John 1909-1991 BioIn 17
Hosking, John D. Law&B 92
Hosking, Richard Frank 1933- WhoWor 93
Hoskins, B. Wayne 1949- St&PR 93, WhoSSW 93
Hoskins, Bob 1942- BioIn 17, ConTFT 10, IntDcF 2-3 [port], MiSFD 9, WhoAm 92
Hoskins, Curtis Lynn 1937- St&PR 93, WhoAm 92
Hoskins, Dan MiSFD 9
Hoskins, Deborah Lebo 1960- WhoAmW 93, WhoEmL 93
Hoskins, Edwin Campbell 1928- St&PR 93
Hoskins, George Wilson 1944- WhoSSW 93
Hoskins, Geraldine 1940- WhoAmW 93
Hoskins, Harry G. Law&B 92
Hoskins, Howard Paul 1946- WhoSSW 93
Hoskins, John H. 1934- WhoAm 92
Hoskins, Lowell 1927-1990 BioIn 17
Hoskins, Richard Jerold 1945- WhoAm 92
Hoskins, Robert 1933- ScF&FL 92
Hoskins, Roland Frank WhoScE 91-1
Hoskins, Tammy Gwyn 1965- WhoSSW 93
Hoskins, W. Lee 1941- BioIn 17, WhoAm 92
Hoskins, William George 1908-1992 ConAu 136
Hoskins, William John 1940- WhoAm 92, WhoWor 93
Hoskins, William K. Law&B 92
Hoskins, William Keller 1935- St&PR 93, WhoAm 92
Hoskinson, Anne Tolson Law&B 92
Hoskinson, Carol Rowe 1947- WhoAmW 93
Hoskinson, David Wilber 1935- St&PR 93
Hoskinson, William R. 1948- St&PR 93
Hoskyns, John 1566-1638 DcLB 121 [port]
Hosler, Charles Luther, Jr. 1924- WhoAm 92, WhoE 93
Hosler, Darrell M. 1936- St&PR 93
Hosler, David Eugene 1950- St&PR 93
Hosler, Michael J. Law&B 92
Hosler, Russell John 1906- WhoAm 92
Hoslet, Gary E. Law&B 92
Hosley, Richmond B. 1947- St&PR 93
Hosli, Leo 1934- WhoScE 91-4
Hosmane, Narayan Sadashiv 1948- WhoWor 93
Hosmer, Bradley Clark 1937- WhoAm 92
Hosmer, Bradley Edwin 1940- WhoAm 92
Hosmer, C.F. Law&B 92
Hosmer, Harriet 1830-1908 BioIn 17
Hosmer, John W., Jr. 1943- St&PR 93
Hosmer, Lucius 1870-1935 Baker 92
Hosmon, Robert Stahr 1943- WhoSSW 93
Hosner, James Robert 1944- WhoWor 93
Hosni, Mahmoud Naguib 1928- WhoWor 93
Hosoda, Hiroyuki 1935- WhoAsAP 91
Hosoe, Eikoh 1933- WhoWor 93
Hosogaya, Boshiro 1888-1964 HarEnMi
Hosoi, Shigeru 1949- WhoWor 93
Hosoi, Tameyuki 1943- WhoWor 93
Hosoi, Tsutomu 1937- WhoWor 93
Hosokawa, Katsumoto 1430-1473 HarEnMi
Hosokawa, Mikio 1934- WhoWor 93
Hosokawa, Peter E. 1948- St&PR 93
Hosokawa, Ritsuo 1943- WhoAsAP 91
Hosokawa, William K. 1915- WhoAm 92
Hosokawa, Yoriyuki 1329-1392 HarEnMi
Hosono, Toshio 1922- WhoWor 93
Hosoya, Akio 1927- WhoAsAP 91
Hosoya, Harumichi 1939- WhoAsAP 91
Hosoya, Yoshi 1932- WhoWor 93
Hospers, Jan 1925- WhoScE 91-4
Hospers, John 1918- WhoAm 92
Hospes, Otto 1963- WhoWor 93
Hospital, Janette Turner 1942- WhoCanL 92
Hospodar, R.S. 1929- St&PR 93
Hospodor, Andrew Thomas 1937- WhoAm 92
Hoss, Donald Adron 1940- WhoWor 93
Hoss, Marwan BioIn 17
Hossack, Catherine Hazlett 1951- WhoAmW 93
Hossack, Charles Henry 1935- St&PR 93
Hossain, Belal 1960- WhoWor 93
Hossain, M. Kamal 1948- WhoScE 91-1
Hossain, Moazzam 1939- WhoAsAP 91
Hossain, Rokeya ScF&FL 92
Hossellman, Vernon Christopher, Jr. 1921- St&PR 93
Hossenlopp, Joseph E. 1940- WhoScE 91-2
Hossfeld, John A. 1928- St&PR 93
Hossmann, Konstantin-Alexander 1937- WhoScE 91-3
Host, Stig 1926- WhoAm 92
Hoste, Serge Charles Felix 1949- WhoWor 93
Hoster, David William 1915- WhoSSW 93
Hoster, Fred William 1939- WhoSSW 93
Hoster, George S., Jr. 1931- St&PR 93
Hoster, Jeffrey M. Law&B 92
Hoster, Richard Henry 1921- St&PR 93
Hoster, William Henry, Jr. 1912- WhoSSW 93
Hostetler, Bonnie J. Law&B 92
Hostetler, Brian J. Law&B 92
Hostetler, James M., Jr. Law&B 92
Hostetler, Jeff BioIn 17
Hostetler, Jeff W. 1961- WhoE 93
Hostetler, Sheri Ann 1962- WhoWrEP 92
Hostetler, Stan St&PR 93
Hostetter, Carl Franklin 1965- WhoE 93
Hostetter, Charles Heiges 1950- WhoAm 92
Hostetter, Hendey 1950- WhoSSW 93
Hostetter, Madonna M. 1941- St&PR 93
Hostetter, Mary Elizabeth Nieha 1961- WhoEmL 93
Hostettler, Stephen John 1931- WhoAm 92
Hosticka, Bedrich Jaroslav 1944- WhoWor 93
Hostinsky, Otakar 1847-1910 Baker 92

Hostler, Charles Warren 1919- *WhoAm 92, WhoWor 93*
Hostler, D. David *Law&B 92*
Hostrop, Bernard Warren 1933- *WhoSSW 93*
Hostrop, Richard Winfred 1925- *WhoWrEP 92*
Hotaling, Daniel L. 1914- *St&PR 93*
Hotaling, Diane Elizabeth Hickey 1961- *WhoAmW 93*
Hotaling, Larry W. 1949- *St&PR 93*
Hotard, Julie Harriet 1950- *WhoAmW 93*
Hotard, Keith C., Jr. *Law&B 92*
Hotchin, John Elton 1921- *WhoE 93*
Hotchkies, Barry 1945- *WhoAm 92*
Hotchkiss, Bill 1936- *WhoWrEP 92*
Hotchkiss, Charles Albert 1927- *St&PR 93*
Hotchkiss, Clarence Francis, Jr. 1928- *St&PR 93*
Hotchkiss, David Robert 1936- *St&PR 93*
Hotchkiss, Eugene, III 1928- *WhoAm 92*
Hotchkiss, Henry Washington 1937- *WhoE 93*
Hotchkiss, Jessie Sheehan 1906- *WhoAmW 93*
Hotchkiss, Ralf David 1947- *WhoAm 92*
Hotchkiss, Rollin Douglas 1911- *WhoAm 92*
Hotchkiss, Sally McMurdo 1929- *WhoAmW 93*
Hotchkiss, Winchester Fitch 1928- *WhoAm 92*
Hotchner, Aaron Edward 1920- *WhoAm 92*
Hotchner, Beverly June 1928- *WhoAmW 93*
Hotchner, John Mc Clure 1943- *WhoWrEP 92*
Hoth, Agustin Carlos 1937- *St&PR 93*
Hothby, John c. 1415-1487 *Baker 92*
Hotokka, Matti 1950- *WhoScE 91-4*
Hotopp, Thomas Bruce 1941- *St&PR 93*
Hotovy, Steven *BioIn 17*
Hotson, Cornelia Hinkley 1890-1977 *ScF&FL 92*
Hotson, John Leslie d1992 *NewYTBS 92 [port]*
Hott, Donald John Zink *Law&B 92*
Hotta, Yasushi 1931- *WhoAm 92*
Hotte, A. Paul L. 1920- *St&PR 93*
Hottel, Hoyt Clarke 1903- *WhoAm 92*
Hottel, Patricia Anne 1955- *WhoAmW 93*
Hotten, John Camden 1832-1873 *BioIn 17*
Hotter, Hans 1909- *Baker 92, IntDcOp [port], OxDcOp*
Hottes, Ronald W. 1944- *St&PR 93*
Hotteterre *Baker 92*
Hotteterre, Jacques 1674-1762 *Baker 92*
Hotteterre, Martin d1712 *Baker 92*
Hotteterre, Nicolas d1727 *Baker 92*
Hotteterre, Nicolas 1637-1694 *Baker 92*
Hottinger, Paul *St&PR 93*
Hottois, Lawrence Daniel 1933- *St&PR 93, WhoAm 92*
Hottovy, Ronald J. *St&PR 93*
Hoty, Dee 1952- *ConTFT 10*
Hotz, Gunter 1931- *WhoScE 91-3*
Hotz, Henry Palmer 1925- *WhoAm 92, WhoWor 93*
Hotz, John A. 1943- *St&PR 93*
Hotz, Peter R. 1942- *WhoScE 91-4*
Hotz, Robert Bergmann 1914- *WhoE 93*
Hotz, Robert H. 1944- *St&PR 93*
Hotze, Charles Wayne 1919- *WhoAm 92*
Hou, Dingyong 1956- *WhoWor 93*
Hou, Fong Joe *Law&B 92*
Hou, Guang Kun 1941- *WhoWor 93*
Hou, Hsaio-Hsien *BioIn 17*
Hou, Hsiao-Hsien *MiSFD 9*
Hou, Jin Chuan 1954- *WhoWor 93*
Hou, Kenneth Chaing 1929- *WhoAm 92*
Hou, Sui-Hoi Edwin 1960- *WhoE 93*
Hou, Zi-Xin 1941- *WhoWor 93*
Houarner, Gerard Daniel 1955- *ScF&FL 92*
Houblot, John C. 1919- *BioIn 17*
Houbolt, John Cornelius 1919- *WhoAm 92*
Houchard, Michael Harlow 1935- *WhoSSW 93*
Houchin, Jerry D. 1935- *WhoSSW 93*
Houchin, John Frederick, Sr. 1945- *WhoE 93, WhoWor 93*
Houchtaling, Harry E., Jr. *St&PR 93*
Houck, Arthur Dean 1938- *St&PR 93*
Houck, Charles S. 1947- *St&PR 93*
Houck, Charles Weston 1933- *WhoSSW 93*
Houck, David Connell *Law&B 92*
Houck, Derek R. *St&PR 93*
Houck, Donald 1932- *St&PR 93*
Houck, Donna June 1942- *St&PR 93*
Houck, Edward Bernard, II 1948- *WhoEmL 93, WhoSSW 93*
Houck, James I. 1941- *WhoAm 92*
Houck, John Burton 1928- *WhoAm 92*
Houck, John Candee 1931- *WhoAm 92*
Houck, John M. 1946- *St&PR 93*
Houck, John Roland 1923- *WhoAm 92*
Houck, Lewis Daniel, Jr. 1932- *WhoE 93, WhoWor 93*
Houck, Sharon Lu Thomas 1952- *WhoAmW 93*
Houck, William Russell 1926- *WhoAm 92, WhoSSW 93*
Houck, William Whitman 1936- *WhoE 93*
Houdard, Georges 1860-1913 *Baker 92*
Houdas, Yvon Jules 1932- *WhoWor 93*
Houde, Edward Donald 1941- *WhoE 93*
Houde, John Michael 1959- *WhoEmL 93*
Houdek, Robert G. 1940- *WhoAm 92*
Houdeshel, William R. 1928- *St&PR 93*
Houdeshell, Monty Alan 1948- *St&PR 93*
Houdin, Jean-Eugene Robert- 1805-1871 *BioIn 17*
Houdini, Harry 1874-1926 *BioIn 17*
Houel, Patrick 1942- *WhoAm 92*
Hougan, Carolyn 1943?- *ConAu 139*
Hougan, Tom McKay 1935- *St&PR 93*
Hougen, H. Montgomery 1935- *St&PR 93*
Hougen, Howard Montgomery *Law&B 92*
Hougen, Jon Torger 1936- *WhoAm 92*
Hough, Aubrey Johnston, Jr. 1944- *WhoAm 92*
Hough, Bruce Robert 1954- *WhoEmL 93*
Hough, Cass Sheffield d1990 *BioIn 17*
Hough, Charles N., Jr. 1934- *St&PR 93*
Hough, Charles Oliver 1948- *BiDAMSp 1989*
Hough, Charles Royce, III 1937- *St&PR 93*
Hough, David Allen 1946- *WhoWor 93*
Hough, Ellen Evans *AmWomPl*
Hough, George Anthony, III 1920- *WhoAm 92*
Hough, Gina A. *Law&B 92*
Hough, Gordon M. 1963- *St&PR 93*
Hough, Grant H. 1941- *St&PR 93*
Hough, Harry E. 1933- *WhoSSW 93*
Hough, Jack Van Doren 1920- *WhoSSW 93*
Hough, James *WhoScE 91-1*
Hough, James Harley *WhoScE 91-1*
Hough, James N. 1939- *St&PR 93*
Hough, James Richard *WhoScE 91-1*
Hough, Janet Gerda Campbell 1948- *WhoAmW 93, WhoEmL 93*
Hough, Jerry F(incher) 1935- *ConAu 137*
Hough, John 1941- *MiSFD 9*
Hough, John Gordon 1936- *St&PR 93*
Hough, Lawrence A. *WhoAm 92*
Hough, Lawrence Alan 1944- *St&PR 93*
Hough, Lawrence Edwin 1935- *WhoSSW 93*
Hough, Leslie *WhoScE 91-1*
Hough, Leslie Seldon 1946- *WhoSSW 93*
Hough, Mark Taylor 1949- *WhoE 93, WhoEmL 93*
Hough, Richard *ScF&FL 92*
Hough, Richard R. d1992 *NewYTBS 92 [port]*
Hough, Richard Ralston 1917- *WhoAm 92*
Hough, Richard T. 1923- *WhoAm 92*
Hough, Stephen (Andrew Gill) 1961- *Baker 92*
Hough, Steven Hedges 1938- *WhoWor 93*
Hough, Thomas Henry Michael 1933- *WhoAm 92*
Hough, Walter 1859-1935 *IntDcAn*
Hough-Dunnette, Leaetta Marie 1947- *WhoEmL 93*
Hough-Ross, Richard Thomas 1951- *WhoE 93*
Houghtaling, Pamela Ann 1949- *WhoEmL 93*
Houghtaling Colleen Joy 1957- *WhoWrEP 92*
Houghtby, Carol Mary 1960- *WhoEmL 93*
Houghtlen, Frances Elizabeth 1945- *WhoAmW 93*
Houghton, A.E. 1931- *St&PR 93*
Houghton, Alan Nourse 1924- *WhoAm 92*
Houghton, Amo 1926- *CngDr 91*
Houghton, Amory, Jr. 1926- *WhoAm 92, WhoE 93*
Houghton, Arthur Amory 1906-1990 *BioIn 17*
Houghton, Carol *AmWomPl*
Houghton, Charles Norris 1909- *WhoAm 92*
Houghton, Daniel 1740-1791 *Expl 93*
Houghton, David Drew 1938- *WhoAm 92*
Houghton, David L. 1953- *St&PR 93*
Houghton, Donald Cary 1946- *WhoAm 92*
Houghton, Donald Charles 1934- *St&PR 93*
Houghton, Eric 1930- *ScF&FL 92*
Houghton, F.J. *WhoScE 91-1*
Houghton, Francis X. d1990 *BioIn 17*
Houghton, Frederick C. *Law&B 92*
Houghton, George Knight 1929- *St&PR 93*
Houghton, James Anthony 1944- *WhoScE 91-3*
Houghton, James R. 1936- *St&PR 93*
Houghton, James Richardson 1936- *WhoAm 92, WhoE 93, WhoWor 93*
Houghton, Judith Dean 1939- *WhoAmW 93*
Houghton, Katharine 1945- *WhoAm 92, WhoE 93*
Houghton, Kenneth Sinclair, Sr. 1940- *WhoAm 92*
Houghton, Norris 1909- *BioIn 17*
Houghton, Priscilla Dewey 1924- *WhoAmW 93*
Houghton, Proctor Willis 1916- *St&PR 93*
Houghton, Sidney Paul 1938- *St&PR 93*
Houghton, Timothy Dane 1955- *WhoWrEP 92*
Houghton, W.H. 1950- *St&PR 93*
Hougland, Charles A. *Law&B 92*
Hougland, Whayne Miller *Law&B 92*
Hougland, William G. *Law&B 92*
Houin, Georges 1948- *WhoScE 91-2*
Houin, Rene 1936- *WhoScE 91-2*
Hou Jie 1930- *WhoAsAP 91*
Houk, Arlene Helen 1962- *WhoAmW 93*
Houk, Kendall Newcomb 1943- *WhoAm 92*
Houk, Marion D. 1933- *St&PR 93*
Houk, Nancy Mia 1940- *WhoAm 92, WhoAmW 93*
Houk, Paul John *Law&B 92*
Houk, Robert W. *BioIn 17*
Houk, Robert William 1927- *WhoAm 92*
Houk, Stephen Donald 1956- *St&PR 93*
Houk, Vernon Neal 1929- *WhoAm 92*
Houland, E. Keith *St&PR 93*
Houlares, Pamela Bassil 1947- *WhoAmW 93*
Houlden, Brian Thomas *WhoScE 91-1*
Houldsworth, Harry Kenneth *WhoScE 91-1*
Houle, Diane Elizabeth 1930- *WhoAmW 93*
Houle, Eugene S. 1936- *St&PR 93*
Houle, Frances Anne 1952- *WhoAm 92, WhoEmL 93*
Houle, Gerard 1953- *St&PR 93*
Houle, Guy 1935- *St&PR 93*
Houle, J. Barker 1920- *St&PR 93*
Houle, Joseph E. 1930- *WhoAm 92*
Houle, Rita C. 1947- *WhoEmL 93*
Houley, Helen M. *Law&B 92*
Houlihan, Brian T. 1944- *WhoWrEP 92*
Houlihan, Christina Erin 1962- *WhoWrEP 92*
Houlihan, Gerald John 1943- *WhoAm 92*
Houlihan, Hilda Imelio 1937- *WhoAm 92*
Houlihan, Jane Kopp 1961- *WhoAmW 93*
Houlihan, Robert A. 1938- *St&PR 93*
Houlihan, Robert Alan 1938- *WhoIns 93*
Houlihan, William Joseph 1930- *WhoE 93*
Houllier, Francois 1959- *WhoScE 91-2*
Houlne, Lois Lamoreaux 1910- *WhoAmW 93*
Houlne, Paul Joseph 1931- *St&PR 93*
Hoult, David Parks 1935- *WhoE 93*
Houlton, Loyce J. 1926- *WhoAm 92*
Houminer, Ehud *St&PR 93*
Houn, Cho Choong 1920- *WhoWor 93*
Houndjahoue, Michel 1949- *WhoWor 93*
Hounsfield, Godfrey Newbold 1919- *WhoWor 93*
Hounshell, Charles David 1920- *WhoAm 92*
Hountras, Peter Timothy 1927- *WhoAm 92*
Houot, Robert 1933- *WhoScE 91-2*
Houphouet-Boigny, Felix *BioIn 17*
Houphouet-Boigny, Felix 1905- *ConBlB 4 [port], DcTwHis, WhoAfr, WhoWor 93*
Houphouet-Boigny, Marie-Therese *BioIn 17*
Houpis, Constantine Harry 1922- *WhoAm 92*
Houpt, Grover K. 1932- *St&PR 93*
Houpt, Grover Krewson 1932- *WhoE 93*
Houpt, Jeffrey Lyle 1941- *WhoAm 92*
Houpt, Richard V. *Law&B 92*
Hourican, Thomas P. 1954- *St&PR 93*
Hourigan, Timothy Alan 1957- *WhoSSW 93*
Hourigan, William Patrick 1944- *WhoE 93*
Hourihan, Paul F. *Law&B 92*
Hourihan, Thomas J. 1934- *St&PR 93*
Hours, Bernard 1943- *WhoScE 91-2*
Housch, Kay B. *Law&B 92*
House, Antoinette Aiello 1943- *WhoE 93*
House, Arthur H. 1942- *St&PR 93*
House, Arthur Kinnear 1932- *St&PR 93*
House, Arthur S. 1921- *BioIn 17*
House, Brant *ScF&FL 92*
House, Charles Randall *WhoScE 91-1*
House, Charles Robert 1930- *St&PR 93*
House, Charles Staver 1908- *WhoAm 92*
House, Christy M. *Law&B 92*
House, David L. 1943- *WhoAm 92*
House, Diane Jean 1948- *WhoAmW 93*
House, Donald Lee, Sr. 1941- *WhoAm 92, WhoSSW 93*
House, Douglas Wayne 1955- *WhoE 93*
House, Edward M. 1858-1938 *PolPar*
House, Edward Mandell 1858-1938 *BioIn 17*
House, Edwin Wesley 1939- *WhoAm 92*
House, Emmitt C. *Law&B 92*
House, Gary W. *Law&B 92*
House, Harry *WhoScE 91-1*
House, Howard P. 1908- *BioIn 17*
House, Joseph W. 1931- *WhoIns 93*
House, Karen Elliott *St&PR 93*
House, Karen Elliott 1947- *WhoAm 92, WhoAmW 93*
House, Michael Robert *WhoScE 91-1*
House, Nicole Lomangino 1947- *WhoAmW 93*
House, Patricia Goodyear 1952- *WhoAmW 93*
House, Richard A. *St&PR 93*
House, Richard Calvin 1927- *WhoWrEP 92*
House, Robert James 1932- *WhoAm 92*
House, Robert N. *Law&B 92*
House, Robert William 1920- *WhoAm 92*
House, Robert William 1927- *WhoAm 92*
House, Roy C. 1917- *WhoAm 92*
House, Sherwood G. 1935- *St&PR 93*
House, Susan Jean 1951- *WhoAmW 93, WhoEmL 93*
House, W. *WhoScE 91-1*
Houseal, John Irving, Jr. 1945- *WhoAm 92*
Household, Geoffrey 1900-1988 *ScF&FL 92*
Householder, Joseph A. *Law&B 92*
Householder, Joseph A. 1955- *St&PR 93*
Householder, Steven L. *Law&B 92*
Housel, Jerry Winters 1912- *WhoAm 92*
Houseley, Henry 1852-1925 *Baker 92*
Houseman, Ann Elizabeth Lord 1936- *WhoAmW 93*
Houseman, David E. 1941- *St&PR 93*
Houseman, Terence H. 1943- *WhoScE 91-1*
Housen, Sevrin 1948- *WhoWrEP 92*
House of Windsor *BioIn 17*
Housepian, Edgar Minas 1928- *WhoE 93*
Houser, Allan 1914?- *BioIn 17*
Houser, Carrol D. 1929- *St&PR 93*
Houser, Cheryl Lynn *Law&B 92*
Houser, Christopher I.M. 1936- *St&PR 93*
Houser, Douglas Guy 1935- *WhoAm 92*
Houser, Dwane R. 1935- *St&PR 93*
Houser, Gregory John 1948- *St&PR 93*
Houser, H. Neil *Law&B 92*
Houser, Harold Byron 1921- *WhoAm 92*
Houser, James Cowing, Jr. 1928- *WhoSSW 93, WhoWor 93*
Houser, John Edward 1928- *WhoSSW 93*
Houser, Michael Lawrence 1952- *WhoEmL 93*
Houser, Michael Robert 1951- *St&PR 93*
Houser, Robert Lee 1943- *BioIn 17*
Houser, Ruth Gertrude 1953- *WhoAmW 93*
Houser, William Douglas 1921- *WhoAm 92*
Houseworth, Richard Court 1928- *St&PR 93, WhoAm 92*
Housewright, Artemis Skevakis 1927- *WhoE 93*
Housewright, Riley Dee 1913- *WhoAm 92*
Housewright, Wiley Lee 1913- *WhoAm 92*
Housey, John James, Jr. 1942- *St&PR 93*
Housh, Barbara 1937- *ScF&FL 92*
Houshmand, Enayat 1933- *WhoUN 92*
Houska, Catherine Mary 1960- *WhoAmW 93*
Houslay, Miles Douglas *WhoScE 91-1*
Housley, Phil 1964- *BiDAMSp 1989*
Housley-Anthony, Mary Pat 1944- *WhoAmW 93*
Housman, A.E. 1859-1936 *BioIn 17, MagSWL [port]*
Housman, Alfred Edward 1859-1936 *BioIn 17*
Housman, Arthur 1888-1942 *QDrFCA 92 [port]*
Housman, Charles J. 1927- *St&PR 93*
Housman, Clemence 1861-1955 *BioIn 17*
Housman, Harry J. 1942- *St&PR 93*
Housman, Kenneth A. 1955- *St&PR 93*
Housman, Laurence 1865-1959 *BioIn 17*
Housman, Rosalie 1888-1949 *Baker 92*
Housner, George William 1910- *WhoAm 92*
Houssier, Claude 1938- *WhoScE 91-2*
Houston, Alfred Dearborn 1940- *St&PR 93, WhoAm 92*
Houston, Bobbie Wyatt 1943- *WhoSSW 93*
Houston, Caroline Margaret 1964- *WhoAmW 93, WhoEmL 93*
Houston, Chandra Gay *Law&B 92*
Houston, Charles H. 1895-1950 *EncAACR*
Houston, Charles Hamilton 1895-1950 *BioIn 17, ConBlB 4 [port], OxCSupC*
Houston, Cissy 1932- *SoulM*
Houston, David 1938- *ScF&FL 92*

Houston, Donald 1923-1991 AnObit 1991
Houston, Dorine Syme 1951- WhoEmL 93
Houston, Eliza Allen 1809-1861 BioIn 17
Houston, Elizabeth Reece Manasco 1935- WhoAmW 93
Houston, Gary William 1948- St&PR 93
Houston, Gloria 1940- WhoSSW 93
Houston, Heather Ann 1955- WhoEmL 93
Houston, Howard Edwin 1910- WhoAm 92, WhoWor 93
Houston, Ivan J. 1925- St&PR 93, WhoIns 93
Houston, Ivan James 1925- WhoAm 92
Houston, James 1921- DcChlFi, ScF&FL 92, WhoCanL 92
Houston, James A(rchibald) 1921- ConAu 38NR, MajAI [port]
Houston, James Archibald 1921- WhoAm 92
Houston, James D. 1933- ConAu 16AS [port], WhoWrEP 92
Houston, James Gorman, Jr. 1933- WhoAm 92, WhoSSW 93
Houston, Jamie Giles, III 1952- WhoEmL 93
Houston, Jeanne Wakatsuki 1934- ConAu 16AS [port]
Houston, John Albert 1914- WhoAm 92
Houston, John Albert 1940- WhoSSW 93
Houston, John B. 1952- St&PR 93
Houston, John Coates, Jr. 1909- WhoAm 92
Houston, John R. BioIn 17
Houston, Johnny Lee 1941- WhoAm 92
Houston, Ken BioIn 17
Houston, Lisa Shelton 1957- WhoAmW 93
Houston, Neal Bryan 1928- WhoSSW 93
Houston, Pam NewYTBS 92 [port]
Houston, Patrick BioIn 17
Houston, Paul David 1944- WhoAm 92
Houston, Penelope BioIn 17
Houston, Peyton Hoge 1910- WhoAm 92, WhoWor 93
Houston, Robert MiSFD 9
Houston, Robert Alan 1946- St&PR 93
Houston, Robert Ewing, Jr. 1943- WhoSSW 93
Houston, S.J. Law&B 92
Houston, Sam 1932- St&PR 93
Houston, Samuel 1793-1863 BioIn 17, HarEnMi, PolPar
Houston, Samuel Lee 1951- WhoAm 92
Houston, Seawadon L. 1942- St&PR 93
Houston, Shirley Mae 1938- WhoWor 93
Houston, Stanley Dunsmore 1930- WhoAm 92
Houston, Temple Lea 1860-1905 BioIn 17
Houston, Thelma SoulM
Houston, Tom d1893 BioIn 17
Houston, W(illiam) Robert, Jr. 1928- ConAu 40NR
Houston, Whitney BioIn 17
Houston, Whitney 1963- AfrAmBi, Baker 92, ConMus 8 [port], SoulM, WhoAm 92, WhoAmW 93
Houston, William Edward 1956- WhoAm 92
Houston, William John Ballantyne WhoScE 91-1
Houston, William Robert Montgomery 1922- WhoWor 93
Houston, William Tennent 1950- St&PR 93
Houstoun, Lawrence Orson, Jr. 1929- WhoAm 92
Houtchens, Barnard 1911- WhoAm 92
Houtchens, Robert Austin, Jr. 1953- WhoAm 92
Houtepen, Anton Willem Joseph 1940- WhoWor 93
Houtman, Cornelius 1540-1599 Expl 93
Houtman, Richard D. Law&B 92
Houtmann, Jacques 1935- Baker 92
Houton, Kathleen ScF&FL 92
Houts, Marshall Wilson 1919- WhoAm 92, WhoWor 93
Houts, Peter Stevens 1933- WhoE 93
Houts, Ronald Carl 1937- WhoSSW 93
Houtsma, Adrianus Johannes Maria 1938- WhoWor 93
Houtz, Duane Talbott 1933- WhoAm 92
Houtz, Heywood Barron 1936- St&PR 93
Houtz, Jim H. 1936- St&PR 93
Houtz, K.H. 1927- St&PR 93
Houvenaghel, Guy T. 1943- WhoScE 91-2
Houwald, Ernst von 1778-1845 BioIn 17
Houweling, Bert St&PR 93
Houwelingen, Adriana C.v. 1950- WhoScE 91-3
Houwer, Joel Law&B 92
Houwing, Helperi 1929- WhoScE 91-3
Houwink, Eric H. 1929- WhoScE 91-3
Houx, Shirley Ann 1931- WhoAmW 93
Houzeau, Jean-Charles 1820-1888 BioIn 17
Houziaux, Leo N.O.G.G. 1932- WhoScE 91-2
Hou Zongbin 1929- WhoAsAP 91
Hovanec, Robert Michael 1954- St&PR 93
Hovanesian, Joseph Der 1930- WhoAm 92
Hovanessian, Shahen Alexander 1931- WhoAm 92
Hovannesian, Albert S. 1924- St&PR 93
Hovannesian, Rose A. 1920- St&PR 93
Hovannisian, Raffi K. WhoWor 93
Hovannisian, Richard G. 1932- WhoAm 92
Hovart, Pierre J.F. 1931- WhoScE 91-2
Hovda, Robert W. d1992 NewYTBS 92
Hovda, Robert W. 1920-1992 BioIn 17
Hovda, Robert W(alker) 1920-1992 ConAu 136
Hovde, Carl Frederick 1926- WhoAm 92
Hovde, Ellen MiSFD 9
Hovdesven, Arne 1928- WhoAm 92
Hove, Andrew Christian 1934- WhoE 93
Hove, Julian Phillops 1937- St&PR 93
Hove, Leon van d1990 BioIn 17
Hove, Randall A. Law&B 92
Hove, Richard Chemist 1935- WhoWor 93
Hovekamp, George D. St&PR 93
Hoveke, William John 1950- St&PR 93
Hovell, C. Ronald 1938- WhoAm 92
Hovell, Walter Lee 1928- St&PR 93
Hovenga, Trent LaVern 1958- WhoE 93
Hover, John Calvin, II 1943- St&PR 93, WhoAm 92
Hover, Leila Messing WhoE 93
Hovermale, Ronald L. 1939- St&PR 93
Hoversland, Arthur Stanley 1922- WhoE 93
Hovestreydt, Eric Robert 1957- WhoWor 93
Hovey, Alan Edwin, Jr. 1933- WhoE 93
Hovey, Charles F. 1909- St&PR 93
Hovey, George Melvin 1929- St&PR 93
Hovey, Justus Allan, Jr. 1922- WhoAm 92, WhoWor 93
Hovey, Kenneth Alan 1945- WhoSSW 93
Hovey, Louis Mealus 1930- St&PR 93
Hovey, Richard 1864-1900 GayN
Hovhaness, Alan 1911- OxDcOp, WhoAm 92
Hovhaness (Chakmakjian), Alan (Vaness Scott) 1911- Baker 92
Hovi, Tapani 1942- WhoScE 91-4
Hovick, Kevin J. 1954- St&PR 93
Hovig, Torstein 1928- WhoScE 91-4
Hovin, Arne William 1922- WhoAm 92
Hovind, David J. 1940- WhoAm 92
Hovind, Havard 1944- WhoScE 91-4
Hoving, Jane Pickens d1992 BioIn 17, NewYTBS 92 [port]
Hoving, John Hannes Forester 1923- WhoAm 92, WhoWor 93
Hoving, Thomas 1931- WhoAm 92, WhoWrEP 92
Hoving, Walter 1897-1989 BioIn 17
Hovis, Cherie Lynn 1952- WhoAmW 93, WhoEmL 93
Hovis, Gene BioIn 17
Hovis, Janet Fowler 1931- WhoSSW 93
Hovland, Egil 1924- Baker 92
Hovmand, Beverly Ann 1941- WhoAmW 93
Hovnanian, Ara K. 1957- WhoAm 92
Hovnanian, Armen 1930- St&PR 93
Hovnanian, H. Philip 1920- WhoAm 92
Hovnanian, Kevork S. BioIn 17
Hovnanian, Kevork S. 1923- WhoAm 92
Hovorka, Robert L., Jr. 1955- ScF&FL 92
Hovsepian, Abraham 1926- St&PR 93
How, Peter Cecil 1931- WhoWor 93
Howalt, F. Harvey, Jr. 1926- St&PR 93
Howalt, Frederick Harvey, Jr. 1926- WhoAm 92
Howaniec, Susan BioIn 17
Howard, Alan Dighton 1939- WhoAm 92
Howard, Alan Graham WhoScE 91-1
Howard, Alan Mackenzie 1937- WhoWor 93
Howard, Albert Jesse 1929- St&PR 93
Howard, Alex T., Jr. 1924- WhoAm 92
Howard, Alex Wayne 1946- WhoSSW 93
Howard, Allan ScF&FL 92
Howard, Allen Richmond, Jr. 1920- WhoWor 93
Howard, Alton Johnathan 1951- WhoEmL 93
Howard, Andree 1910-1968 BioIn 17
Howard, Ann 1936- Baker 92
Howard, Ann 1939- WhoAmW 93
Howard, Ann Hubbard 1938- WhoE 93
Howard, Annie S. AmWomPl
Howard, Arthur Ellsworth Dick 1933- WhoAm 92
Howard, Aughtum Luciel Smith 1906- WhoAmW 93, WhoSSW 93
Howard, Barbara Ann 1932- WhoAmW 93
Howard, Barbara June 1957- WhoSSW 93
Howard, Barbara Sue Mesner 1944- WhoAm 92
Howard, Barbara Viventi 1941- WhoE 93
Howard, Benjamin Chew 1791-1872 OxCSupC
Howard, Benjamin W. 1944- WhoWrEP 92
Howard, Bernadette Bunny 1956- WhoAmW 93
Howard, Bernard Eufinger 1920- WhoAm 92, WhoWor 93
Howard, Bernard L. Law&B 92
Howard, Betty Ruth 1946- WhoWrEP 92
Howard, Bion Dickerson 1950- WhoEmL 93
Howard, Blanche 1923- WhoCanL 92
Howard, Bradford Reuel 1957- WhoEmL 93
Howard, Brenda Jane WhoScE 91-1
Howard, Bruce L. St&PR 93
Howard, Bryan Robert WhoScE 91-1
Howard, Burton D. 1938- St&PR 93
Howard, C.C. Law&B 92
Howard, Carl Michael 1920- WhoAm 92
Howard, Carl V. Law&B 92
Howard, Carole Margaret 1945- St&PR 93
Howard, Carolyn Law&B 92
Howard, Cary ScF&FL 92
Howard, Cecil Gerald 1929- WhoE 93
Howard, Charles 1536-1624 HarEnMi
Howard, Charles 1919- WhoAm 92
Howard, Cheryl Lynn 1947- WhoEmL 93
Howard, Christina Schneider 1945- St&PR 93
Howard, Christopher John WhoScE 91-1
Howard, Clark 1934- ScF&FL 92
Howard, Clifford Norman 1926- St&PR 93
Howard, Clifton Merton 1922- WhoE 93
Howard, Clinton H. 1928- St&PR 93
Howard, Curly 1903-1952
See Three Stooges, The IntDcF 2-3
See Also Stooges, Three, The QDrFCA 92
Howard, Cy 1915- MiSFD 9
Howard, Daggett Horton 1917- WhoAm 92
Howard, Darcie Sheila 1946- WhoAmW 93
Howard, Darryl W. Law&B 92
Howard, Daryl 1948- BioIn 17
Howard, David 1929- WhoE 93, WhoWor 93, WhoWrEP 92
Howard, David 1937- WhoAm 92
Howard, David E. 1952- WhoAm 92
Howard, David G. BioIn 17
Howard, David H. 1944- WhoWrEP 92
Howard, David P. 1950- St&PR 93
Howard, Davis Jonathan 1954- WhoEmL 93
Howard, Dean Denton 1927- WhoAm 92
Howard, Deborah Susanne 1956- WhoAmW 93, WhoEmL 93
Howard, Denean & Howard, Sherri & Howard, Tina BlkAmWO
Howard, Dennis Martin 1930- WhoE 93
Howard, Derek 1934- St&PR 93
Howard, Desmond BioIn 17
Howard, Don (Marcel) 1940- WhoWrEP 92
Howard, Donald F. 1928- St&PR 93
Howard, Donald John Law&B 92
Howard, Donald Lee 1938- St&PR 93
Howard, Donald Roy 1927-1987 BioIn 17
Howard, Donald Searcy 1928- St&PR 93, WhoAm 92
Howard, Douglas B. Law&B 92
Howard, Earl Loren 1950- WhoEmL 93
Howard, Edward Neal 1920-1990 BioIn 17
Howard, Elena Robaina 1941- WhoUN 92
Howard, Elizabeth 1907- ScF&FL 92
Howard, Elizabeth 1950- WhoAmW 93
Howard, Elizabeth Crawford 1939- WhoWrEP 92
Howard, Elizabeth Fitzgerald 1927- BlkAuII 92
Howard, Elizabeth Jane 1923- ScF&FL 92
Howard, Ellen BioIn 17
Howard, Ellen 1943- DcAmChF 1985
Howard, Elston Gene 1929-1980 BiDAMSp 1989
Howard, Ernest E., III 1943- St&PR 93, WhoAm 92
Howard, Etchell 1942- St&PR 93
Howard, Eugene C. 1921- St&PR 93
Howard, Florence AmWomPl
Howard, Forrest William 1936- WhoSSW 93
Howard, Frances Estella Humphrey 1914- WhoAmW 93
Howard, Frank James 1909- BiDAMSp 1989
Howard, Frederic K. Law&B 92
Howard, Fredric Timothy 1939- WhoSSW 93
Howard, Gary Scott 1951- WhoAm 92
Howard, Gene Claude 1926- WhoAm 92
Howard, Gene Lebron 1940- WhoSSW 93
Howard, George 1944- WhoSSW 93
Howard, George, Jr. 1924- WhoAm 92
Howard, George Pratt 1930- WhoE 93
Howard, George Sallade 1903- WhoAm 92
Howard, George Stephen 1948- WhoEmL 93
Howard, Gerald Thomas 1938- St&PR 93
Howard, Graeme Keith, Jr. 1932- St&PR 93
Howard, Gregory Charles 1947- WhoE 93
Howard, Harold Charles 1926- WhoE 93
Howard, Harry Clay 1929- WhoAm 92
Howard, Helen Arlene 1927- WhoAm 92
Howard, Helen Cunningham 1954- WhoAmW 93
Howard, Henrietta 1681-1767 BioIn 17
Howard, Henry 1517?-1547 BioIn 17
Howard, Herbert Hoover 1928- WhoSSW 93
Howard, Hildegarde 1901- WhoAm 92
Howard, Howell H. 1927- St&PR 93
Howard, Hubert Wendell 1927- WhoAm 92
Howard, Hugh C. 1929- St&PR 93
Howard, J. Daniel 1943- WhoAm 92
Howard, J. Woodford, Jr. 1931- WhoAm 92
Howard, Jack 1924- WhoAm 92
Howard, Jack Monroe 1931- WhoWor 93
Howard, Jack Rohe 1910- WhoAm 92
Howard, Jack Wayne 1942- WhoSSW 93
Howard, Jacqueline Sue 1954- WhoEmL 93
Howard, James Law&B 92
Howard, James, III 1935- St&PR 93
Howard, James H. 1913- BioIn 17
Howard, James Joseph 1950- WhoE 93
Howard, James Joseph, III 1935- WhoAm 92
Howard, James L. d1990 BioIn 17
Howard, James Lawrence 1941- WhoSSW 93
Howard, James Merriam, Jr. 1922- WhoAm 92
Howard, James Webb 1925- WhoAm 92
Howard, Jane Temple 1935- WhoWrEP 92
Howard, Janet Anne 1946- WhoAmW 93
Howard, Janet R. Law&B 92
Howard, Janet Schlenker 1950- WhoEmL 93
Howard, Jay Lloyd 1951- St&PR 93
Howard, Jean BioIn 17
Howard, Jeffrey Hjalmar 1944- WhoAm 92
Howard, Jeffrey R. WhoAm 92
Howard, Jennifer Leigh 1963- WhoSSW 93
Howard, Jerry A. 1942- St&PR 93
Howard, Jerry Wayne 1944- St&PR 93
Howard, Jimmie BioIn 17
Howard, Joan Alice 1929- WhoAm 92, WhoAmW 93, WhoE 93, WhoWor 93
Howard, Joanne Maria 1956- WhoAmW 93
Howard, Joe L. 1941- St&PR 93
Howard, Joel L. 1941- WhoAm 92
Howard, John 1913- BioIn 17
Howard, John A. 1925- WhoScE 91-3
Howard, John A. 1950- WhoAm 92
Howard, John Addison 1921- WhoAm 92
Howard, John Arnold 1915- WhoAm 92
Howard, John B. 1932- St&PR 93
Howard, John Brigham 1912- WhoAm 92
Howard, John E. 1752-1827 PolPar
Howard, John Fitzallen 1930- St&PR 93
Howard, John Lindsay 1931- WhoAm 92
Howard, John Lindsay, Q.C. Law&B 92
Howard, John Michael 1949- St&PR 93
Howard, John Robert 1940- St&PR 93
Howard, John Tasker 1890-1964 Baker 92
Howard, John Tasker 1911- WhoAm 92
Howard, John Vincent 1933- St&PR 93
Howard, John Wilfred 1924- WhoSSW 93
Howard, John Winston 1939- WhoAsAP 91
Howard, Josefina WhoE 93
Howard, Joseph ConAu 139, ScF&FL 92
Howard, Joseph Clemens 1922- WhoE 93
Howard, Joseph Harvey 1931- WhoAm 92
Howard, Judith Ann 1942- WhoAmW 93
Howard, Judith Anne 1944- WhoAmW 93
Howard, Julie Day 1949- WhoE 93
Howard, Julie E. Law&B 92
Howard, Karin MiSFD 9
Howard, Katharine 1858- AmWomPl
Howard, Kathleen 1884-1956 Baker 92
Howard, Kathleen 1947- WhoAmW 93, WhoEmL 93
Howard, Keith WhoScE 91-1
Howard, Kenneth Joseph, Jr. 1944- WhoAm 92
Howard, Kenneth Lee 1945- WhoE 93
Howard, Kevin WhoScE 91-1
Howard, Kingston Lee 1929- St&PR 93, WhoAm 92
Howard, Kipland 1954- WhoEmL 93
Howard, Kirk E. 1952- St&PR 93
Howard, Laurence Webb, III Law&B 92
Howard, Lawrence Cabot 1925- WhoAm 92
Howard, Lee Milton 1922- WhoAm 92

Howard, Leonard Ambers 1952- *WhoSSW 93*
Howard, Leopoldine Blaine Damrosch *AmWomPl*
Howard, Leslie 1893-1943 *IntDcF 2-3 [port], MiSFD 9N*
Howard, Leslie James 1960- *WhoEmL 93, WhoSSW 93*
Howard, Linda Ann 1953- *WhoAmW 93*
Howard, Linda Darlene 1967- *WhoAmW 93*
Howard, Linda Kay *WhoSSW 93*
Howard, Linda M. *Law&B 92*
Howard, Lynn David *Law&B 92*
Howard, M. Francine 1939- *WhoAm 92, WhoAmW 93*
Howard, Malcolm Jones 1939- *WhoAm 92, WhoSSW 93*
Howard, Margaret *AmWomPl*
Howard, Margaret Mary 1957- *WhoE 93*
Howard, Marguerite Evangeline Barker 1921- *WhoAmW 93*
Howard, Mark Gorman *Law&B 92*
Howard, Marla Elaine 1955- *WhoAmW 93*
Howard, Marvin 1918- *BioIn 17*
Howard, Mary Cynthia 1950- *WhoWrEP 92*
Howard, Mary Pease 1945- *WhoAmW 93*
Howard, Matthew Aloysius 1940- *WhoAm 92*
Howard, Maureen 1930- *BioIn 17*
Howard, Mel 1935- *WhoE 93*
Howard, Melvin 1935- *St&PR 93, WhoAm 92*
Howard, Merrill J. 1930- *St&PR 93*
Howard, Michael *BioIn 17*
Howard, Michael D. 1954- *St&PR 93*
Howard, Michael R. 1945- *WhoIns 93*
Howard, Milford W. 1862- *ScF&FL 92*
Howard, Moe 1895-1975
  See Stooges, Three, The *QDrFCA 92*
Howard, Moe 1897-1975
  See Three Stooges, The *IntDcF 2-3*
Howard, Moses Leon 1928- *BlkAuII 92*
Howard, Moses William, Jr. 1946- *WhoAm 92*
Howard, Nathan Southard 1941- *WhoAm 92*
Howard, Nic *ScF&FL 92*
Howard, Noel 1920-1987 *MiSFD 9N*
Howard, Nora Oakes 1954- *WhoEmL 93*
Howard, Norman E. 1947- *St&PR 93*
Howard, O.M. Zack 1961- *WhoE 93*
Howard, Oliver Otis 1830-1909 *EncAACR [port], HarEnMi*
Howard, Patrick Edward 1947- *St&PR 93*
Howard, Paul B. 1955- *St&PR 93*
Howard, Paul Leroy 1925- *St&PR 93*
Howard, Paul Lindsay 1909- *WhoE 93*
Howard, Paul Noble, Jr. 1922- *WhoAm 92*
Howard, Paul Samuel 1954- *WhoEmL 93*
Howard, Paula Walton Ollick 1944- *WhoAmW 93*
Howard, Peggy Ann *Law&B 92*
Howard, Percy *BioIn 17*
Howard, Peter M. *Law&B 92*
Howard, Pierre *WhoAm 92, WhoSSW 93*
Howard, Randy DeWayne 1934- *WhoWor 93*
Howard, Richard 1929- *WhoAm 92, WhoWrEP 92*
Howard, Richard Charles 1929- *WhoE 93*
Howard, Richard James 1952- *WhoEmL 93*
Howard, Richard R. *St&PR 93*
Howard, Richard Ralston, II 1948- *WhoEmL 93, WhoSSW 93, WhoWor 93*
Howard, Richard Turner 1935- *WhoAm 92*
Howard, Rick *BioIn 17*
Howard, Robert C. 1931- *St&PR 93*
Howard, Robert Clark 1931- *WhoAm 92*
Howard, Robert D. 1927- *St&PR 93*
Howard, Robert E. 1906-1936 *ScF&FL 92*
Howard, Robert Elliott 1933- *WhoAm 92*
Howard, Robert Ernest 1947- *WhoSSW 93*
Howard, Robert Ervin 1906-1936 *BioIn 17*
Howard, Robert Franklin 1932- *WhoAm 92*
Howard, Robert Lowell 1936- *St&PR 93*
Howard, Robert Miller 1919- *WhoAm 92*
Howard, Robert P. 1922- *St&PR 93*
Howard, Robert Staples 1924- *WhoAm 92*
Howard, Robert W. 1954- *St&PR 93*
Howard, Roger 1938- *ConAu 39NR*
Howard, Ron *BioIn 17*
Howard, Ron 1954- *MiSFD 9, WhoAm 92*
Howard, Rosalind 1845-1921 *BioIn 17*
Howard, Roy B. 1929- *St&PR 93*
Howard, Roy W. 1883-1964 *JrnUS*
Howard, Rufus Oliver 1929- *WhoE 93*
Howard, Rustin Ray 1956- *WhoE 93*
Howard, Ruth Colette 1958- *WhoAmW 93*
Howard, Sandy 1927- *WhoAm 92*
Howard, Sarah Jean 1924- *WhoAmW 93*
Howard, Sarah L. *Law&B 92*
Howard, Sharon Vines 1959- *WhoAmW 93*
Howard, Shemp 1891-1955
  See Stooges, Three, The *QDrFCA 92*
Howard, Shemp 1895-1955
  See Three Stooges, The *IntDcF 2-3*
Howard, Sherri
  See Howard, Denean & Howard, Sherri & Howard, Tina *BlkAmWO*
Howard, Shirley Ann 1935- *WhoSSW 93*
Howard, Stanley Louis 1948- *WhoAm 92, WhoE 93*
Howard, Stephen P. *Law&B 92*
Howard, Stephen Wrigley 1940- *WhoE 93*
Howard, Steven H. 1951- *St&PR 93*
Howard, Susanne C. 1951- *WhoAmW 93*
Howard, Suzanne M. 1941- *St&PR 93*
Howard, Sydney 1884-1946 *QDrFCA 92 [port]*
Howard, Theodore Walter 1942- *St&PR 93, WhoAm 92*
Howard, Thomas 1935- *ScF&FL 92*
Howard, Thomas Bailey, Jr. 1928- *WhoAm 92*
Howard, Thomas Jackson 1942- *St&PR 93*
Howard, Timothy George 1946- *St&PR 93*
Howard, Timothy J. *Law&B 92*
Howard, Tina
  See Howard, Denean & Howard, Sherri & Howard, Tina *BlkAmWO*
Howard, Tom 1886-1955 *QDrFCA 92 [port]*
Howard, Trevor 1916-1988 *BioIn 17, IntDcF 2-3 [port]*
Howard, Troy *ScF&FL 92*
Howard, Vance F. 1937- *St&PR 93, WhoIns 93*
Howard, Vernon Alfred 1937- *WhoE 93*
Howard, Vernon (Linwood) 1918-1992 *ConAu 139, SmATA 73*
Howard, Virginia Fall 1951- *WhoAmW 93*
Howard, W. Wayne 1949- *St&PR 93*
Howard, Walter Burke 1916- *WhoAm 92*
Howard, Warren F. *ConAu 37NR*
Howard, William C. 1933- *St&PR 93*
Howard, William F. 1916- *St&PR 93*
Howard, William Gates, Jr. 1941- *WhoAm 92*
Howard, William Jack 1922- *WhoAm 92*
Howard, William Jay *Law&B 92*
Howard, William Matthew 1934- *WhoAm 92, WhoWor 93*
Howard-Carter, Theresa 1929- *WhoAm 92*
Howard-Hill, Trevor Howard 1933- *WhoAm 92, WhoSSW 93*
Howard-Howard, Margo Chanler 1935- *WhoWrEP 92*
Howards, Stuart S. 1937- *WhoSSW 93*
Howard-Smith, Richard Hugh 1959- *WhoEmL 93*
Howarth, Andrew Trevor *WhoScE 91-1*
Howarth, Charles Ian *WhoScE 91-1*
Howarth, David *BioIn 17*
Howarth, David H. 1936- *WhoAm 92*
Howarth, David John *WhoScE 91-1*
Howarth, Elgar 1935- *Baker 92, OxDcOp*
Howarth, John N. *Law&B 92*
Howarth, Robert 1931- *St&PR 93*
Howarth, Steven P. *Law&B 92*
Howarth, Thomas 1921- *WhoAm 92*
Howarth, William L. 1940- *ScF&FL 92*
Howarth, William Louis 1940- *WhoE 93*
Howat, Bruce B. *Law&B 92*
Howat, Bruce B. 1945- *WhoAm 92*
Howat, Bruce Bradshaw, Jr. 1945- *St&PR 93*
Howat, John Keith 1937- *WhoAm 92*
Howatch, Susan *BioIn 17*
Howatch, Susan 1940- *ScF&FL 92*
Howatt, Helen Clare 1927- *WhoAmW 93, WhoWor 93*
Howbert, Edgar Charles 1937- *WhoAm 92*
How-Downing, Lindsey *Law&B 92*
Howdyshell, Roger d1991 *BioIn 17*
Howe, Adrian Martin 1945- *WhoUN 92*
Howe, Ann Clark *WhoE 93*
Howe, Art 1946- *WhoAm 92*
Howe, Arthur *WhoE 93*
Howe, Arthur Henry, Jr. 1946- *WhoSSW 93*
Howe, Bette *ConTFT 10*
Howe, Brian Leslie 1936- *WhoAsAP 91, WhoWor 93*
Howe, Bruce Anthony 1955- *WhoWor 93*
Howe, Bruce Iver 1936- *WhoAm 92*
Howe, Carroll V. 1923- *St&PR 93*
Howe, Carroll Victor 1923- *WhoAm 92*
Howe, Christopher D. 1960- *St&PR 93*
Howe, Clare M. *Law&B 92*
Howe, Daniel Walker 1937- *WhoAm 92*
Howe, Danlias Francis *Law&B 92*
Howe, David *WhoScE 91-1*
Howe, David E. *Law&B 92*
Howe, Dean R. 1946- *St&PR 93*
Howe, Deborah 1946-1978 *ScF&FL 92*
Howe, Denis *WhoScE 91-1*
Howe, E. W. 1853-1937 *JrnUS*
Howe, Evelyn Freeman 1929- *WhoAmW 93*
Howe, Everett R. 1942- *St&PR 93*
Howe, Fanny 1940- *WhoAm 92*
Howe, Fisher 1914- *WhoAm 92*
Howe, Florence *BioIn 17*
Howe, Florence 1929- *WhoAm 92*
Howe, Gary Woodson 1936- *WhoAm 92*
Howe, Geoffrey 1926- *WhoWor 93*
Howe, George M. 1944- *St&PR 93*
Howe, Gordie *BioIn 17*
Howe, Gordon 1928- *WhoAm 92, WhoE 93*
Howe, Graham Lloyd 1950- *WhoAm 92*
Howe, H. W., Mrs. *AmWomPl*
Howe, Harold, II *BioIn 17*
Howe, Herbert Marshall 1912- *WhoAm 92*
Howe, Hugh Philip 1932- *WhoAm 92*
Howe, Imogen *ScF&FL 92*
Howe, Irving *BioIn 17*
Howe, Irving 1920- *JeAmHC, ScF&FL 92, WhoAm 92, WhoWrEP 92*
Howe, James 1946- *ChlFicS, MajAI [port], ScF&FL 92, SmATA 71 [port]*
Howe, James Alexander Macgregor *WhoScE 91-1*
Howe, James Everett 1930- *WhoAm 92, WhoE 93*
Howe, James Lewis 1897-1990 *BioIn 17*
Howe, James Lewis, III *Law&B 92*
Howe, James Michael *WhoScE 91-1*
Howe, James Murray 1924- *WhoAm 92*
Howe, James Tarsicius 1924- *WhoAm 92*
Howe, Jas. Murray 1924- *St&PR 93*
Howe, John P. *Law&B 92*
Howe, John Perry 1910- *WhoAm 92*
Howe, John Prentice, III 1943- *WhoAm 92, WhoSSW 93, WhoWor 93*
Howe, Jonathan Thomas 1940- *WhoAm 92*
Howe, Jonathan Trumbull 1935- *WhoAm 92*
Howe, Joseph 1804-1873 *BioIn 17*
Howe, Julia Ward 1819-1910 *BioIn 17*
Howe, Kevin P. *Law&B 92*
Howe, Kevin Paul 1934- *St&PR 93*
Howe, Larry M. *Law&B 92*
Howe, Lawrence 1921- *WhoAm 92*
Howe, Lenore Ann 1948- *WhoEmL 93*
Howe, Lyman H. 1856-1923 *BioIn 17*
Howe, Lyman Harold, III 1938- *WhoSSW 93*
Howe, Manthei *AmWomPl*
Howe, Margaret Rose 1937- *WhoAmW 93*
Howe, Margherita *BioIn 17*
Howe, Marie Jenney *AmWomPl*
Howe, Marolyn Louise 1957- *WhoSSW 93*
Howe, Martha Morgan 1945- *WhoAm 92, WhoSSW 93*
Howe, Mary *BioIn 17*
Howe, Mary 1882-1964 *BioIn 17*
Howe, Mary (Carlisle) 1882-1964 *Baker 92*
Howe, Michael William 1948- *WhoEmL 93*
Howe, Murray Joseph 1931- *St&PR 93*
Howe, Murrill Norton, Jr. 1937- *St&PR 93*
Howe, Nancy Litterman *BioIn 17*
Howe, Nathaniel 1764-1837 *BioIn 17*
Howe, Neil *BioIn 17*
Howe, Nicholas *BioIn 17*
Howe, Patricia M. *Law&B 92*
Howe, Richard 1726-1799 *HarEnMi*
Howe, Richard Cuddy 1924- *WhoAm 92*
Howe, Richard Davis 1939- *WhoSSW 93*
Howe, Richard J. 1928- *WhoAm 92*
Howe, Richard Karl 1943- *WhoAm 92*
Howe, Richard M. *Law&B 92*
Howe, Richard Marshall 1952- *WhoEmL 93*
Howe, Richard Rives 1942- *WhoAm 92*
Howe, Robert 1732-1786 *BioIn 17, HarEnMi*
Howe, Robert M. 1939- *St&PR 93*
Howe, Robert Melvin 1939- *WhoAm 92*
Howe, Robert Wilson 1932- *WhoAm 92*
Howe, Roger Evans 1945- *WhoAm 92*
Howe, Rosemarie Russi 1947- *WhoSSW 93*
Howe, Russ 1962- *BioIn 17*
Howe, Russell Warren 1925- *WhoE 93*
Howe, Stanley M. 1924- *St&PR 93*
Howe, Stanley Merrill 1924- *WhoAm 92*
Howe, Steve *BioIn 17*
Howe, Steve 1947-
  See Yes *ConMus 8*
Howe, Susan 1937- *ConLC 72 [port], DcLB 120 [port]*
Howe, Susan Patricia 1945- *WhoAmW 93*
Howe, Tina *BioIn 17*
Howe, Victor H. 1928- *St&PR 93*
Howe, Walter Charles, Jr. 1934- *WhoAm 92*
Howe, Wesley Jackson 1921- *St&PR 93, WhoAm 92, WhoE 93*
Howe, William 1729-1814 *HarEnMi*
Howe, William Hugh 1928- *WhoWor 93*
Howell, Alfred Hunt 1912- *WhoAm 92, WhoWor 93*
Howell, Allen Windsor 1949- *WhoEmL 93*
Howell, Allie Rhea 1927- *WhoAmW 93*
Howell, Alvin Harold 1908- *WhoAm 92*
Howell, Arthur 1918- *WhoAm 92*
Howell, Barbara Fennema 1924- *WhoAm 92, WhoE 93*
Howell, Barbara Miles 1937- *WhoWrEP 92*
Howell, Benjamin Franklin, Jr. 1917- *WhoAm 92, WhoE 93*
Howell, Bill 1946- *WhoCanL 92*
Howell, Bonnie Howard 1947- *WhoAmW 93*
Howell, Brad *BioIn 17*
Howell, Brian Graham 1954- *WhoEmL 93*
Howell, Brian L. 1929- *St&PR 93*
Howell, Bruce Inman 1942- *WhoSSW 93*
Howell, C. Thomas *BioIn 17*
Howell, Catherine Jeanine 1935- *WhoAmW 93*
Howell, Charles Maitland 1914- *WhoAm 92, WhoWor 93*
Howell, Christopher *ScF&FL 92*
Howell, Clark 1863-1936 *JrnUS*
Howell, Copperthite Charlotte *Law&B 92*
Howell, Corrie Crandall *AmWomPl*
Howell, David S. 1944- *St&PR 93*
Howell, Dean Myral 1932- *WhoWrEP 92*
Howell, Denis 1923- *BioIn 17*
Howell, Donald Herbert 1942- *St&PR 93*
Howell, Donald Lee 1935- *WhoAm 92, WhoSSW 93, WhoWor 93*
Howell, Dorothy 1898-1982 *Baker 92*
Howell, Dyke 1940- *St&PR 93*
Howell, E.B. 1929- *St&PR 93*
Howell, Embry Martin 1945- *WhoAmW 93*
Howell, Eric B. *Law&B 92*
Howell, Evan P. 1839-1905 *JrnUS*
Howell, Everette Irl 1914- *WhoAm 92*
Howell, Florence *AmWomPl*
Howell, Francis Clark 1925- *WhoAm 92*
Howell, Gary Allen 1943- *St&PR 93*
Howell, George Bedell 1919- *WhoAm 92, WhoWor 93*
Howell, George Washington 1927- *WhoAm 92*
Howell, Gloria Lellen 1948- *WhoE 93*
Howell, Gwynne 1938- *OxDcOp*
Howell, Gwynne (Richard) 1938- *Baker 92*
Howell, H. Scott 1929- *St&PR 93, WhoAm 92*
Howell, Harley Thomas 1937- *WhoAm 92, WhoE 93*
Howell, James 1594?-1666 *BioIn 17*
Howell, James D. *Law&B 92*
Howell, James Edwin 1928- *WhoAm 92*
Howell, James Morgan 1961- *WhoSSW 93*
Howell, James Theodore 1919- *WhoAm 92*
Howell, Janet D. 1944- *WhoAmW 93*
Howell, Jay R. 1955- *St&PR 93*
Howell, Jennifer Chandler 1956- *WhoSSW 93*
Howell, Joel DuBose 1953- *WhoAm 92*
Howell, Joel Walter, III 1949- *WhoEmL 93*
Howell, John *WhoScE 91-1*
Howell, John Alfred 1929- *WhoAm 92*
Howell, John Anthony *WhoScE 91-1*
Howell, John B. *Law&B 92*
Howell, John F. 1932- *St&PR 93*
Howell, John Floyd 1932- *WhoAm 92, WhoSSW 93*
Howell, John M. *Law&B 92*
Howell, John McDade 1922- *WhoAm 92*
Howell, John R. 1933- *WhoAm 92*
Howell, John Reid 1936- *WhoAm 92, WhoSSW 93*
Howell, John Williams 1941 *St&PR 93*
Howell, Joseph Edwin *Law&B 92*
Howell, Joyce Ann 1955- *WhoAmW 93*
Howell, Laura Sue 1937- *WhoAmW 93*
Howell, Leo A. 1921- *WhoSSW 93*
Howell, Leonard Lee 1956- *WhoSSW 93*
Howell, Lynda Edwina 1959- *WhoEmL 93*
Howell, Margie *BioIn 17*
Howell, Mark W. 1951- *St&PR 93*
Howell, Mary Elizabeth 1942- *WhoAmW 93*
Howell, Mary Jo Owens 1936- *WhoAmW 93*
Howell, Mary L. 1952- *St&PR 93, WhoAm 92*
Howell, Millard Fillmore 1913-1971 *BiDAMSp 1989*
Howell, Nancy Ward 1946- *WhoSSW 93*
Howell, Nathaniel *BioIn 17*
Howell, Nathaniel Woodhull 1770-1852 *BioIn 17*
Howell, P.P. 1917- *IntDcAn*

Howell, Paul Neilson 1918- *St&PR 93, WhoAm 92*
Howell, Peter 1947- *WhoWor 93*
Howell, Peter Jonathan 1959- *WhoScE 91-1*
Howell, R. Thomas, Jr. *Law&B 92*
Howell, Ralph Rodney 1931- *WhoAm 92, WhoSSW 93, WhoWor 93*
Howell, Richard Louis 1933- *St&PR 93*
Howell, Richard Paul, Sr. 1927- *WhoAm 92, WhoE 93*
Howell, Robert Edward 1949- *WhoAm 92*
Howell, Robert Leslie 1931- *St&PR 93*
Howell, Robert Thomas, Jr. 1942- *St&PR 93, WhoAm 92*
Howell, Robert Wayne 1916- *WhoAm 92*
Howell, Ronnie Allen *Law&B 92*
Howell, Roy Allen, Jr. 1925- *WhoSSW 93*
Howell, Russel D. *Law&B 92*
Howell, Sarah Smith 1929- *WhoSSW 93*
Howell, Scott *ScF&FL 92*
Howell, Sharon Kay 1953- *WhoAmW 93*
Howell, Simon L. *WhoScE 91-1*
Howell, Steven Kendrick 1949- *WhoAm 92*
Howell, Stewart Leslie 1942- *St&PR 93*
Howell, Thomas 1944- *WhoAm 92*
Howell, Thomas Edwin 1918- *WhoAm 92*
Howell, Thomas Jefferson 1842-1912 *BioIn 17*
Howell, Walter B. *St&PR 93*
Howell, Wilbur Samuel 1904-1992 *BioIn 17, ConAu 137*
Howell, William Ashley, III 1949- *WhoEmL 93, WhoSSW 93*
Howell, William J. 1946- *WhoIns 93*
Howell, William James 1929- *WhoAm 92*
Howell, William Leonard 1952- *WhoSSW 93*
Howell, William Page 1952- *WhoE 93*
Howell, William Robert 1936- *St&PR 93, WhoAm 92, WhoSSW 93*
Howell-Carter, Josephine *AmWomPl*
Howell-Jones, David 1923- *WhoE 93*
Howells, Anne (Elizabeth) 1941- *Baker 92*
Howells, Coral Ann 1939- *ScF&FL 92*
Howells, E.R. *WhoScE 91-1*
Howells, Edgar H. 1946- *St&PR 93*
Howells, Edward Macfarlane *WhoScE 91-1*
Howells, Herbert (Norman) 1892-1983 *Baker 92*
Howells, Kenneth Frank *WhoScE 91-1*
Howells, Michael *BioIn 17*
Howells, Muriel Gurdon Seabury 1910- *WhoWor 93*
Howells, R. Tim *WhoAm 92*
Howells, W.W. 1908- *IntDcAn*
Howells, William Dean 1837-1920 *BioIn 17, GayN, JrnUS, MagSAmL [port]*
Howells, William Dean 1932- *WhoE 93*
Howells, William White 1908- *WhoAm 92, WhoWor 93*
Howell-Sickles, Donna 1949- *BioIn 17*
Howell-Tayloe, Margaret Affarene 1926- *WhoSSW 93*
Hower, Debra Kay 1954- *WhoAmW 93, WhoEmL 93, WhoSSW 93*
Hower, Edward 1941- *WhoWrEP 92*
Hower, Frank Beard, Jr. 1928- *St&PR 93, WhoAm 92*
Hower, Matt 1957- *St&PR 93*
Howerd, Frankie 1917-1992 *QDrFCA 92 [port]*
Howerton, George 1905- *WhoAm 92*
Howerton, Helen V. 1933- *WhoAm 92*
Howerton, Herman H. *Law&B 92*
Howerton, John Benjamin 1928- *WhoAm 92*
Howerton, Tina Marie 1961- *WhoAmW 93*
Howery, Donald E. 1941- *St&PR 93*
Howery, Sharon C. 1962- *WhoEmL 93*
Howes, Alfred S. 1917- *WhoE 93, WhoIns 93, WhoWor 93*
Howes, Barbara 1914- *WhoWrEP 92*
Howes, Benjamin Durward, III 1922- *WhoAm 92*
Howes, Bobby 1895-1972 *QDrFCA 92 [port]*
Howes, Carol Susan 1960- *WhoEmL 93*
Howes, Dwight A. *Law&B 92*
Howes, Frank (Stewart) 1891-1974 *Baker 92*
Howes, Gloria *WhoAmW 93*
Howes, Jean Marie 1944- *WhoAmW 93*
Howes, Lorraine de Wet 1933- *WhoAm 92*
Howes, Melinda Sue 1947- *WhoAmW 93*
Howes, Michael Frank 1951- *WhoE 93, WhoEmL 93*
Howes, Michael John *WhoScE 91-1*
Howes, Paddy Rudd 1909- *WhoWor 93*
Howes, Robert Alan 1928- *WhoAm 92*
Howes, Theodore Clark 1929- *WhoE 93*
Howes, Thomas P. 1934- *St&PR 93*
Howes, William Browning 1937- *St&PR 93*
Howes, William Carter 1936- *St&PR 93*
Howeth, Lynda Carol 1949- *WhoAmW 93*
Howeth, Robert W. 1948- *St&PR 93, WhoAm 92*
Howett, Dicky *ScF&FL 92*
Howett, John 1926- *WhoSSW 93*
Howey, John Richard 1933- *WhoAm 92*
Howey, Margaret Eileen 1919- *WhoAmW 93*
Howgate, Ann 1945- *WhoWor 93*
Howie, Archibald *WhoScE 91-1*
Howie, David Ian Dickson 1928- *WhoScE 91-3*
Howie, Hellen Morrison *AmWomPl*
Howie, John G.R. *WhoScE 91-1*
Howie, John Mackintosh *WhoScE 91-1*
Howie, John Robert 1946- *WhoAm 92, WhoSSW 93*
Howie, John Sharp 1939- *St&PR 93*
Howie, Peter W. *WhoScE 91-1*
Howie, Robin M. *WhoScE 91-1*
Howison, George Everett 1944- *WhoAm 92*
Howitt, Arnold Martin 1947- *WhoE 93*
Howitt, Mary Botham 1799-1888 *BioIn 17*
Howitt, Pamela Tesler 1955- *WhoE 93*
Howitt, William 1792-1879 *BioIn 17*
Howker, Janni 1957- *Au&Arts 9 [port], ConAu 137, MajAI [port], SmATA 72 [port]*
Howkins, John Blair 1932- *WhoAm 92*
Howl, Joanne Healey 1957- *WhoAmW 93, WhoEmL 93*
Howl, Marcia Yvonne 1947- *ScF&FL 92*
Howland, Allen H. 1921- *St&PR 93*
Howland, Amy D. *Law&B 92*
Howland, Beth *WhoAm 92*
Howland, Bette 1937- *WhoAm 92*
Howland, Grafton Dulany 1943- *WhoSSW 93, WhoWor 93*
Howland, James Chase 1916- *St&PR 93*
Howland, Jim *BioIn 17*
Howland, John Hathaway 1946- *St&PR 93*
Howland, Murray Shipley, Jr. 1911- *WhoAm 92*
Howland, Richard Hubbard 1910- *WhoE 93*
Howland, Richard Moulton 1940- *WhoE 93*
Howland, Robert A. 1923- *St&PR 93*
Howland, Robert G. 1928- *St&PR 93*
Howland, Robert Herbert 1960- *WhoE 93*
Howland, Walter Warren 1933- *St&PR 93*
Howland, Willard J. 1927- *WhoAm 92*
Howland, William Goldwin Carrington 1915- *WhoAm 92*
Howland, William Legrand 1873-1915 *Baker 92*
Howland, William Stapleton 1919- *WhoAm 92*
Howle, C. Tycho 1949- *WhoEmL 93*
Howlett, C.T. 1945- *St&PR 93*
Howlett, C.T., Jr. *Law&B 92*
Howlett, Carolyn Svrluga 1914- *WhoAm 92*
Howlett, Donald Roger 1945- *WhoE 93*
Howlett, Joan Gail 1943- *WhoWrEP 92*
Howlett, Joe Richard 1928- *St&PR 93*
Howlett, John d1991 *BioIn 17*
Howlett, Lisa Jo 1957- *St&PR 93*
Howlett, Phyllis Lou 1932- *WhoAmW 93, WhoWor 93*
Howlett, Stephanie Ann 1957- *WhoAmW 93*
Howlett, Winston A. *ScF&FL 92*
Howley, David A. *Law&B 92*
Howley, John *MiSFD 9*
Howley, Patrick J. *Law&B 92*
Howlin' Wolf 1910-1976 *BioIn 17*
How-Martyn, Edith 1875-1953 *BioIn 17*
Howorth, Charles L., Jr. *Law&B 92*
Howorth, Lucy Somerville *WhoAmW 93*
Howorth, Lucy Somerville 1895- *WhoAm 92, WhoSSW 93, WhoWor 93*
Howrey, Edward F. 1903- *WhoAm 92*
Howrey, Eugene Philip 1937- *WhoAm 92*
Howrey, Linda McKay 1953- *WhoAmW 93*
Howse, Ben T. 1952- *St&PR 93*
Howse, Ernest Marshall 1902- *WhoAm 92*
Howse, George A. *Law&B 92*
Howse, Gregory Lawson 1955- *WhoSSW 93*
Howse, Harold D. 1928- *WhoWrEP 92*
Howse, Harold Darrow 1928- *WhoAm 92*
Howse, Robert Davis 1908- *WhoAm 92*
Howse, Robert G. 1938- *St&PR 93*
Howse, W. Frances 1947- *WhoE 93*
Howser, Nancy Paris 1933- *WhoAmW 93*
Howsmon, Roger L. 1944- *St&PR 93*
Howson, A.G. *WhoScE 91-1*
Howson, Bruce K. 1942- *WhoIns 93*
Howson, Bruce Kenneth 1942- *St&PR 93*
Howson, David Philip *WhoScE 91-1*
Howson, Frank *MiSFD 9*
Howson, Robert E. 1932- *WhoAm 92, WhoSSW 93*
Howson, Robert Edward 1931- *St&PR 93*
Howze, Harry Whitfield d1991 *BioIn 17*
Howze, Joseph Lawson Edward 1923- *WhoAm 92*
Howze, Karen Aileen 1950- *WhoAm 92*
Howze, Patricia Jeanne *Law&B 92*
Howze, Wendell Morgan 1947- *WhoEmL 93, WhoSSW 93*
Hoxha, Enver 1908-1985 *BioIn 17, ColdWar 2 [port], DcTwHis*
Hoxie, Evelyn *AmWomPl*
Hoxie, Henry Wayne 1947- *St&PR 93*
Hoxie, Jack 1885-1965 *BioIn 17*
Hoxie, Louise L. d1992 *NewYTBS 92*
Hoxie, Ralph Gordon 1919- *WhoAm 92, WhoE 93, WhoWor 93*
Hoxter, Allegra Branson 1934- *WhoE 93, WhoWor 93*
Hoxter, Curtis Joseph 1922- *WhoAm 92, WhoE 93, WhoWor 93*
Hoy, Annegret 1958- *WhoWor 93*
Hoy, Cyrus Henry 1926- *WhoAm 92*
Hoy, Eric Stuart 1948- *WhoWor 93*
Hoy, Harold Joseph 1934- *WhoE 93*
Hoy, Linda 1946- *BioIn 17*
Hoy, Marjorie Ann 1941- *WhoAm 92*
Hoy, Mary Priscilla *WhoAmW 93*
Hoy, Robert Chin 1933- *WhoSSW 93*
Hoy, Robert Joseph 1929- *WhoAm 92, WhoWor 93*
Hoy, Ronald Raymond 1939- *WhoAm 92*
Hoy, Thomas Lester 1948- *St&PR 93*
Hoy, William Ivan 1915- *WhoAm 92*
Hoye, Anita 1938- *WhoAmW 93*
Hoye, John Stephen 1949- *WhoSSW 93*
Hoye, Robert Earl 1931- *WhoSSW 93*
Hoye, Vincent Joseph 1933- *WhoE 93*
Hoyem, Andrew Lewison 1935- *WhoAm 92*
Hoyem, David S. 1944- *St&PR 93*
Hoyem, Tore *WhoScE 91-4*
Hoyer, Carl Ivan 1930- *WhoIns 93*
Hoyer, David Ralph 1931- *WhoAm 92*
Hoyer, Edward Joseph, Jr. 1952- *WhoE 93*
Hoyer, Harvey Conrad 1907- *WhoAm 92*
Hoyer, John Richard 1938- *WhoE 93*
Hoyer, Karl 1891-1936 *Baker 92*
Hoyer, Lars 1957- *WhoScE 91-2*
Hoyer, Leon William 1936- *WhoE 93*
Hoyer, Paul Jean 1943- *WhoE 93*
Hoyer, Phyllis Scarborough 1938- *WhoAmW 93, WhoE 93*
Hoyer, Steny H. *BioIn 17*
Hoyer, Steny H. 1939- *CngDr 91*
Hoyer, Steny Hamilton 1939- *WhoAm 92, WhoE 93*
Hoyer, Vincent Edgar 1924- *St&PR 93, WhoAm 92*
Hoyeraal, Hans Martin 1936- *WhoScE 91-4*
Hoyes, Donald James 1932- *WhoE 93*
Hoying, John C. 1948- *St&PR 93*
Ho Ying-ch'in 1890- *HarEnMi*
Hoyland, Arnljot 1924- *WhoScE 91-4*
Hoyland, Vic(tor) 1945- *Baker 92*
Hoyle, Edith L. *AmWomPl*
Hoyle, Fred *BioIn 17*
Hoyle, Fred 1915- *ScF&FL 92*
Hoyle, Geoffrey 1942- *ScF&FL 92*
Hoyle, Kenneth Samuel 1953- *WhoEmL 93*
Hoyle, Randy Lowell 1953- *WhoE 93*
Hoyle, Rick Harold 1956- *WhoSSW 93*
Hoyle, Sally Georgette 1957- *WhoAmW 93*
Hoyle, Trevor 1940- *ScF&FL 92*
Hoyme, Chad E. 1933- *St&PR 93*
Hoyme, Chad Earl 1933- *WhoAm 92*
Hoynacki, Jan J. *Law&B 92*
Hoynes, Louis L. *Law&B 92*
Hoynes, Louis L., Jr. 1935- *St&PR 93*
Hoynes, Louis LeNoir, Jr. 1935- *WhoAm 92*
Hoyos, Angela de *NotHsAW 93*
Hoyos, Arturo 1948- *WhoWor 93*
Hoyos, Debora de *NotHsAW 93*
Hoyos Gomez, Manuel 1944- *WhoScE 91-3*
Hoyos Sainz, Luis de 1868-1951 *IntDcAn*
Hoysgaard, Robert William 1941- *WhoSSW 93*
Hoysradt, Jean E. 1950- *St&PR 93*
Hoyt, Bradley James 1949- *WhoEmL 93*
Hoyt, Brooks Pettingill 1929- *WhoAm 92*
Hoyt, C. Douglas 1916-1990 *BioIn 17*
Hoyt, Charlee Van Cleve 1936- *WhoAmW 93*
Hoyt, Charles E. *Law&B 92*
Hoyt, Charles Lindsay 1925- *St&PR 93*
Hoyt, Charles Orcutt 1929- *WhoAm 92*
Hoyt, Clark Freeland 1942- *WhoAm 92*
Hoyt, Craig Robert 1949- *St&PR 93*
Hoyt, Darlene Prandine 1942- *WhoAmW 93*
Hoyt, David Lemire 1951- *WhoAm 92*
Hoyt, David P. 1959- *St&PR 93*
Hoyt, David Richard 1950- *WhoAm 92*
Hoyt, Diek A. *St&PR 93*
Hoyt, Earl Edward, Jr. 1936- *WhoAm 92, WhoE 93, WhoWor 93*
Hoyt, Edmund *St&PR 93*
Hoyt, Eleanor *AmWomPl*
Hoyt, Elizabeth E. *Law&B 92*
Hoyt, Ella M. *AmWomPl*
Hoyt, Ellen 1933- *WhoE 93*
Hoyt, Erich 1950- *BioIn 17*
Hoyt, F. Timothy *Law&B 92*
Hoyt, Frank Russell 1916- *WhoAm 92*
Hoyt, H. Gunther *St&PR 93*
Hoyt, Harry E. *Law&B 92, WhoIns 93*
Hoyt, Harry Edward 1931- *St&PR 93*
Hoyt, Henry H. 1895-1990 *BioIn 17*
Hoyt, Henry Hamilton, Jr. 1927- *WhoE 93*
Hoyt, Henry Martyn 1830-1892 *BioIn 17*
Hoyt, Herbert Austin Aikins 1937- *WhoAm 92*
Hoyt, James Lawrence 1943- *WhoAm 92*
Hoyt, James W. 1947- *St&PR 93*
Hoyt, John 1905-1991 *BioIn 17*
Hoyt, John Arthur 1932- *WhoAm 92, WhoWor 93*
Hoyt, John Taylor, Jr. 1942- *St&PR 93*
Hoyt, John William 1945- *WhoE 93*
Hoyt, Keith A. *Law&B 92*
Hoyt, Kenneth Boyd 1924- *WhoAm 92*
Hoyt, Kenneth M. 1948- *WhoAm 92, WhoSSW 93*
Hoyt, Leon G., Jr. 1925- *St&PR 93*
Hoyt, Lynner R. 1947- *St&PR 93*
Hoyt, Mary Finch *WhoAm 92*
Hoyt, Matthew Buckingham 1957- *WhoEmL 93, WhoSSW 93*
Hoyt, Mont Powell 1940- *WhoAm 92, WhoSSW 93*
Hoyt, Monty 1944- *WhoAm 92*
Hoyt, Nelly Schargo 1920- *WhoAm 92*
Hoyt, Olga Gruhzit 1922- *ScF&FL 92*
Hoyt, Palmer 1897-1979 *DcLB 127 [port]*
Hoyt, Priscilla Kay 1950- *WhoAmW 93*
Hoyt, Richard 1941- *ScF&FL 92*
Hoyt, Robert Dan 1941- *WhoSSW 93*
Hoyt, Roger Wilson 1937- *St&PR 93*
Hoyt, Scott C. *Law&B 92*
Hoyt, Seth *WhoAm 92*
Hoyt, Wade Arthur 1943- *WhoAm 92*
Hoyt, William B. d1992 *NewYTBS 92*
Hoyt, William B. 1937-1992 *BioIn 17*
Hoyt, William C. 1946- *St&PR 93, WhoAm 92*
Hoyt, William V. 1937- *St&PR 93*
Hoyt, William Vernor 1937- *WhoAm 92*
Hoyte, David S. 1947- *St&PR 93*
Hoyte, Hugh Desmond 1929- *WhoWor 93*
Hoyte, Robert Mikell 1943- *WhoE 93*
Hoza, Frank George 1943- *St&PR 93*
Hozack, William James 1956- *WhoE 93*
Hozer, Jozef 1948- *WhoScE 91-4*
Hozjusz, Stanislaw 1504-1579 *PolBiDi*
Hozumi, Yoshiyuki 1935- *WhoAsAP 91*
Hrabik, George John 1947- *St&PR 93*
Hrabovsky, Joseph Emil 1942- *St&PR 93*
Hrabowski, Freeman Alphonsa, III 1950- *WhoE 93*
Hrachovina, Frederick Vincent 1926- *WhoAm 92*
Hracs, Frank John 1951- *St&PR 93*
Hradilek, Zdenek 1940- *WhoScE 91-4*
Hrascinski, Jo Anne Victoria 1967- *WhoWrEP 92*
Hraska, Stefan 1933- *WhoScE 91-4*
Hrasko, Juraj 1931- *WhoScE 91-4*
Hrawi, Elias 1926- *BioIn 17, CurBio 92 [port]*
Hrayssi, Walid 1934- *WhoWor 93*
Hrazanek, Richard J. 1937- *WhoIns 93*
Hrbacek, Jaroslav 1921- *WhoScE 91-4*
Hrbek, Friedrich 1935- *WhoScE 91-4*
Hrbek, Vladimir *WhoScE 91-4*
Hrdlicka, Ales 1869-1943 *IntDcAn*
Hrdlicka, Charles R. 1938- *St&PR 93*
Hrdlicka, Richard F. 1932- *St&PR 93*
Hrdlicka, Richard Franklin 1932- *WhoAm 92*
Hrdy, Ivan 1928- *WhoScE 91-4*
Hrdy, Sarah Blaffer 1946- *WhoAm 92*
Hrebicek, Jiri 1947- *WhoScE 91-4*
Hreha, Donald William 1934- *St&PR 93*
Hreidarsson-Downey, Robert Arni 1946- *WhoWor 93*
Hresan, Sally L. 1946- *WhoEmL 93, WhoSSW 93*
Hretzay, Eugene 1948- *St&PR 93*
Hribek, Mary Ann 1941- *WhoAmW 93*
Hrimaly, Adalbert (Vojtech) 1842-1908 *Baker 92*
Hrimaly, Johann (Jan) 1844-1915 *Baker 92*
Hrimaly, Otakar 1883-1945 *Baker 92*
Hrinda, John Joseph 1951- *WhoE 93*
Hrinko, Daniel Dean 1955- *WhoEmL 93*
Hrip'sime *OxDcByz*
Hrisak, Daniel Michael 1945- *WhoWor 93*
Hrisanide, Alexandre 1936- *Baker 92*
Hrisanidis, Alexandre 1936- *Baker 92*
Hriskevich, Michael Edward 1926- *WhoAm 92*
Hristic, Stevan 1885-1958 *Baker 92*

Hristov, Hristo *WhoScE 91-4*
Hristov, Hristo 1926- *DrEEuF*
Hristov, Valentin Zdravkov 1950- *WhoWor 93*
Hrivnak, Ivan 1931- *WhoScE 91-4*
Hrna, Daniel Joseph 1940- *WhoSSW 93*
Hromadko, George 1920- *WhoAm 92*
Hromy, John G. *Law&B 92*
Hron, Ihor Walter 1943- *St&PR 93*
Hron, Jan 1941- *WhoScE 91-4*
Hron, Jaroslav 1943- *WhoScE 91-4*
Hron, Richard W. 1940- *St&PR 93*
Hronas, Michael J. 1961- *St&PR 93*
Hroncich, Edward F. 1934- *St&PR 93*
Hrones, John Anthony 1912- *WhoAm 92*
Hrouz, Jiri *WhoScE 91-4*
Hrtanek, Bohdan 1933- *WhoScE 91-4*
Hrubes, Donna Bleich 1940- *WhoAmW 93*
Hruby, Blahoslav S. d1990 *BioIn 17*
Hruby, Francis J. *Law&B 92*
Hruby, Frank M. 1918- *WhoAm 92*
Hruby, Patricia Lucille 1934- *WhoAmW 93*
Hruby, Roger Francis 1935- *St&PR 93*
Hruska, Alan 1933- *ScF&FL 92*
Hruska, Alan J. 1933- *WhoAm 92*
Hruska, Boris 1926- *WhoScE 91-4*
Hruska, Elias Nicolas 1943- *WhoWrEP 92*
Hruska, Francis John 1935- *WhoWor 93*
Hruska, Karel 1935- *WhoScE 91-4*
Hruska, Roman Lee 1904- *WhoAm 92*
Hruska-Claeys, Lucinda *Law&B 92*
Hrusovsky, Ivan 1927- *Baker 92*
Hruzek, S. Leonard 1954- *St&PR 93*
Hrycak, Peter 1923- *WhoAm 92, WhoE 93, WhoWor 93*
Hryniewicz, Olgierd 1948- *WhoScE 91-4*
Hryniewicz, Tadeusz 1945- *WhoWor 93*
Hrynkiewicz, Andrzej 1925- *WhoScE 91-4*
Hrynkiewicz, Andrzej Zygmunt 1925- *WhoWor 93*
Hrynkiewicz-Sudnik, Jerzy 1926- *WhoScE 91-4*
Hrynyk, John Paul 1949- *St&PR 93*
Hryshko, Paul Anthony 1957- *WhoEmL 93*
Hryszko, Walter J. *Law&B 92*
Hsi, David Ching Heng 1928- *WhoAm 92*
Hsi, Edward Yang 1957- *WhoEmL 93, WhoWor 93*
Hsia, James Ching 1946- *St&PR 93*
Hsia, Pei-Jan 1939- *WhoUN 92*
Hsia, Richard C. 1948- *WhoIns 93*
Hsia Erh-Kang 1908- *WhoAsAP 91*
Hsia Han-Min 1932- *WhoAsAP 91*
Hsiang T'ing-pi d1620 *HarEnMi*
Hsiang Yu d202BC *HarEnMi*
Hsiao, George Chia-Chu 1934- *WhoE 93*
Hsiao, Mu-Yue 1933- *WhoAm 92*
Hsiao, Roger Chenfang 1955- *WhoEmL 93, WhoSSW 93, WhoWor 93*
Hsiao-Hsien, Hou 1947- *MiSFD 9*
Hsieh, Dennis P. H. 1937- *WhoAm 92*
Hsieh, Din-Yu 1933- *WhoWor 93*
Hsieh, Henry Lien 1930- *WhoSSW 93*
Hsieh, Jui Sheng 1921- *WhoAm 92, WhoWor 93*
Hsieh, Lai-Fa *BioIn 17*
Hsieh, Lamont 1946- *St&PR 93*
Hsieh, Ling-Ling 1955- *WhoWor 93*
Hsieh, Richard Kin Tchang 1950- *WhoScE 91-4, WhoUN 92, WhoWor 93*
Hsieh, Rudy Ru-Pin 1950- *WhoWor 93*
Hsieh, T'iao 464-499 *BioIn 17*
Hsieh Xie, Shu-Sen 1919- *WhoWor 93*
Hsin, Victor Jun-Kuan 1945- *WhoE 93, WhoWor 93*
Hsiung, Robert Yuan Chun 1935- *WhoAm 92*
Hsu, Albert Yu Tien 1922- *WhoWor 93*
Hsu, Charles Jui-cheng 1930- *WhoE 93, WhoWor 93*
Hsu, Chen Chao 1940- *WhoAm 92*
Hsu, Chen-Chia 1929- *WhoWor 93*
Hsu, Cheng 1951- *WhoE 93, WhoWor 93*
Hsu, Chieh Su 1922- *WhoAm 92*
Hsu, Ching-Hsin 1956- *WhoAmW 93, WhoEmL 93*
Hsu, Ching-yu 1898- *WhoAm 92*
Hsu, Cho-yun 1930- *WhoAm 92*
Hsu, Chung Shih 1944- *WhoWor 93*
Hsu, Chung Yi 1944- *WhoSSW 93*
Hsu, Donald Kung-Hsing 1947- *WhoE 93*
Hsu, Hsi Fan 1906-1990 *BioIn 17*
Hsu, Hsiung 1920- *WhoAm 92*
Hsu, Immanuel Chung Yueh 1923- *WhoAm 92*
Hsu, John J. 1919- *WhoAm 92*
Hsu, John (Tseng-Hsin) 1931- *Baker 92, WhoAm 92*
Hsu, Jong-Pyng 1951- *WhoEmL 93*
Hsu, Katharine Han Kuang 1914- *WhoAmW 93*
Hsu, Ken Yuh 1951- *WhoWor 93*
Hsu, Kenneth J. 1929- *WhoScE 91-4*
Hsu, Ming Chen 1924- *WhoAm 92*
Hsu, Ming-Yu 1925- *WhoSSW 93, WhoWor 93*
Hsu, Paul Sho-Po 1939- *WhoWor 93*
Hsu, Roger Y.K. 1927- *St&PR 93, WhoAm 92*
Hsu, Samuel 1947- *WhoE 93*
Hsu, Thomas Tseng-Chuang 1933- *WhoAm 92*
Hsu, Tsang-houei 1929- *Baker 92*
Hsu, V. V. *MiSFD 9*
Hsu, Yu-Chih *WhoAm 92*
Hsu, Yu Kao 1922- *WhoWor 93*
Hsuan, Hulbert Chien-Shuan 1939- *WhoE 93*
Hsuan-Chuang 602-649 *Expl 93 [port]*
Hsueh, Chun-tu 1922- *WhoAm 92*
Hsu Lin-Nung 1921- *WhoAsAP 91*
Hsu Shu-cheng 1902-1925 *HarEnMi*
Hsu Shui-Teh 1931- *WhoAsAP 91*
Hsu Yih-Yun 1930- *WhoAsAP 91*
Hu, Baosheng 1930- *WhoWor 93*
Hu, Chenming 1947- *WhoAm 92*
Hu, Chi Yu 1933- *WhoAm 92, WhoWor 93*
Hu, Ching-Li 1932- *WhoUN 92*
Hu, Hong 1959- *WhoSSW 93*
Hu, Jimmy 1936- *WhoE 93*
Hu, Joseph Chi-Ping 1946- *WhoAm 92, WhoE 93, WhoEmL 93*
Hu, King 1931- *MiSFD 9*
Hu, Ping 1947- *WhoE 93*
Hu, Serena Shaw 1959- *WhoAmW 93*
Hu, Sheng-Cheng 1940- *WhoAm 92*
Hu, Sheng-Zhi 1932- *WhoWor 93*
Hu, Shouwei 1929- *WhoWor 93*
Hu, Steve Seng-Chiu 1922- *WhoAm 92*
Hu, Sze-Tsen 1914- *WhoAm 92*
Hu, Tsay-Hsin Gilbert 1956- *WhoSSW 93*
Hu, Yao-Su 1946- *WhoWor 93*
Hu, Zhengjia 1930- *WhoWor 93*
Hu, Zhu-Xin 1956- *WhoWor 93*
Hua, Sheng 1953- *WhoWor 93*
Hua, Timothy 1959- *WhoEmL 93*
Hua Guofeng *WhoWor 93*
Hua Guofeng 1920- *DcTwHis*
Hua Guofeng 1921- *ColdWar 2 [port], WhoAsAP 91*
Huaman, Dennis Ernest 1941- *WhoE 93*
Huan, Ignatius H. *Law&B 92*
Huang, Aixiang 1935- *WhoWor 93*
Huang, Alice Shih-hou 1939- *WhoAmW 93, WhoE 93*
Huang, Barney Kuoyen 1931- *WhoSSW 93*
Huang, Cham-Ber 1925- *Baker 92*
Huang, Christopher Li-Hur 1951- *WhoWor 93*
Huang, David Tishih 1941- *WhoUN 92*
Huang, Deng Hang 1935- *WhoWor 93*
Huang, Denis K. 1925- *WhoSSW 93*
Huang, Eugene Yuching 1917- *WhoAm 92, WhoWor 93*
Huang, Fan-Zhang 1931- *WhoWor 93*
Huang, Francis Chang Hsun 1949- *WhoWor 93*
Huang, Francis Fu-Tse 1922- *WhoAm 92*
Huang, Hong Ci 1936- *WhoWor 93*
Huang, Hsing Hua 1932- *WhoWor 93*
Huang, Hua-Feng 1935- *WhoAm 92*
Huang, Huey Wen 1940- *WhoSSW 93*
Huang, Jacob Chen-ya 1937- *WhoE 93*
Huang, Jen-Kuang 1953- *WhoSSW 93*
Huang, Jianxin *MiSFD 9*
Huang, Jin-ding 1955- *WhoWor 93*
Huang, John Hsu-Li 1959- *WhoSSW 93*
Huang, Joseph Chen-Huan 1933- *WhoE 93, WhoWor 93*
Huang, Kee Chang 1917- *WhoAm 92*
Huang, Keh-Ning 1947- *WhoWor 93*
Huang, Kerson 1928- *WhoAm 92*
Huang, Langhui 1947- *WhoWor 93*
Huang, Lin 1935- *WhoWor 93*
Huang, Minsiu *St&PR 93*
Huang, Molly Vivian 1951- *WhoAmW 93*
Huang, Pan Ming 1934- *WhoAm 92, WhoWor 93*
Huang, Pien Chien 1931- *WhoAm 92*
Huang, Po-Wen 1939- *WhoWor 93*
Huang, Raymond Hsing Yun 1939- *WhoUN 92*
Huang, Ru Chih Chow 1932- *WhoE 93*
Huang, Shiling 1928- *WhoWor 93*
Huang, Suei-rong 1932- *WhoE 93*
Huang, Theresa C. *WhoAmW 93, WhoWor 93*
Huang, Thomas Shi-Tao 1936- *WhoAm 92*
Huang, Thomas Tao-shing 1939- *WhoAm 92, WhoSSW 93*
Huang, Tien-Shang 1949- *WhoWor 93*
Huang, Ting-Chia 1932- *WhoWor 93*
Huang, Victor Tsangmin 1951- *WhoWor 93*
Huang, Wen Qi 1938- *WhoWor 93*
Huang, Yang-Tung 1955- *WhoWor 93*
Huang, Yao-wen 1947- *WhoEmL 93, WhoSSW 93*
Huang, Yin Zhu 1932- *WhoWor 93*
Huang, Yuxiang 1940- *WhoWor 93*
Huang, Zhenbang 1916- *WhoWor 93*
Huang, Zheng-Shu 1931- *WhoWor 93*
Huang, Zhenqi 1931- *WhoWor 93*
Huang, Zhirui 1937- *WhoWor 93*
Huang, Zhiyuan 1934- *WhoWor 93*
Huang Chao d884 *HarEnMi*
Huang He 1963- *BioIn 17*
Huang Hsing 1874-1916 *HarEnMi*
Huang Hua 1913- *ColdWar 2 [port]*
Huang Ju *BioIn 17*
Huang Ju 1939- *WhoAsAP 91*
Huang Kun-Hui 1936- *WhoAsAP 91*
Huang Shih-Cheng 1935- *WhoAsAP 91*
Huang Yicheng 1926- *WhoAsAP 91*
Huanzhulouzhu 1902-1961 *ScF&FL 92*
Huarachi Revollo, Gualberto 1949- *WhoWor 93*
Huard, David L. *Law&B 92*
Huard, Pierre-Alphonse 1901-1983 *IntDcAn*
Huart, Michel L. *Law&B 92*
Huas, Herve Rene 1953- *WhoAm 92*
Hubachek, Elise M. *AmWomPl*
Huband, A. Rolph 1929- *St&PR 93*
Huband, Frank Louis 1938- *WhoAm 92, WhoE 93*
Huband, P.A. *Law&B 92*
Hubatka, Milton Anthony *WhoWor 93*
Hubay, Jeno 1858-1937 *Baker 92*
Hubbard, Albert *BioIn 17*
Hubbard, Allan B. *BioIn 17*
Hubbard, Amy Nix 1949- *WhoE 93*
Hubbard, Ann Louise Cox 1943- *WhoAm 92*
Hubbard, Arthur Thornton 1941- *WhoAm 92*
Hubbard, Bruce d1991 *BioIn 17*
Hubbard, Cal 1900-1977 *BioIn 17*
Hubbard, Carroll, Jr. 1937- *CngDr 91, WhoAm 92, WhoSSW 93*
Hubbard, Charles W. 1943- *WhoIns 93*
Hubbard, Charlotte Amelia 1879- *AmWomPl*
Hubbard, Colin David 1939- *WhoWor 93*
Hubbard, David Allan 1928- *ConAu 40NR, WhoAm 92*
Hubbard, Dean Leon 1939- *WhoAm 92*
Hubbard, Dolan 1949- *WhoSSW 93*
Hubbard, Eddie 1889-1928 *EncABHB 8 [port]*
Hubbard, Elaine Marjorie 1950- *WhoSSW 93*
Hubbard, Elbert 1856-1915 *BioIn 17, GayN*
Hubbard, Eleanor(e) *AmWomPl*
Hubbard, Elizabeth *WhoAm 92*
Hubbard, Elizabeth Louise 1949- *WhoAmW 93*
Hubbard, Emma *BioIn 17*
Hubbard, Eugene P. *Law&B 92*
Hubbard, Frances Virginia Thomas *AmWomPl*
Hubbard, Frank G. 1937- *St&PR 93*
Hubbard, "Freddie" 1938- *Baker 92, BioIn 17*
Hubbard, Frederick Dewayne 1938- *WhoAm 92*
Hubbard, Gregory Lynn 1958- *WhoSSW 93*
Hubbard, Gregory Scott 1948- *WhoWor 93*
Hubbard, Harold M. 1924- *St&PR 93*
Hubbard, Harold Mead 1924- *WhoAm 92*
Hubbard, Harvey Hart 1921- *WhoAm 92*
Hubbard, Herbert Hendrix 1922- *WhoAm 92*
Hubbard, Howard James 1938- *WhoAm 92*
Hubbard, Howard L. 1927- *St&PR 93*
Hubbard, Howard Leland 1931- *WhoAm 92*
Hubbard, Jeanne Delaney 1948- *WhoEmL 93, WhoSSW 93*
Hubbard, Jesse Donald 1920- *WhoAm 92*
Hubbard, John 1931- *BioIn 17*
Hubbard, John Dana *Law&B 92*
Hubbard, John H. 1935-1991 *BioIn 17*
Hubbard, John Hamal 1945- *WhoE 93*
Hubbard, John Henry 1934- *St&PR 93*
Hubbard, John Ingram 1930- *WhoWor 93*
Hubbard, John L. 1935- *St&PR 93*
Hubbard, John Lewis 1947- *WhoAm 92, WhoEmL 93, WhoSSW 93*
Hubbard, John O'Connor 1933- *St&PR 93*
Hubbard, John Perry 1903-1990 *BioIn 17*
Hubbard, John Randolph 1918- *WhoAm 92*
Hubbard, Judy *WhoScE 91-1*
Hubbard, Julia Faye 1948- *WhoAm 92, WhoAmW 93*
Hubbard, Kenneth Earl 1942- *WhoSSW 93*
Hubbard, L. Ron 1911-1986 *BioIn 17, ScF&FL 92*
Hubbard, L. Ron, Jr. 1934- *ScF&FL 92*
Hubbard, La Fayette Ron 1911-1986 *BioIn 17*
Hubbard, Louise *AmWomPl*
Hubbard, Margaret Anna 1947- *WhoAmW 93*
Hubbard, Mark *St&PR 93*
Hubbard, Mark O. 1949- *St&PR 93*
Hubbard, Michelle Jeanine 1964- *WhoAmW 93*
Hubbard, Nancy Jane 1961- *WhoAmW 93*
Hubbard, Nerman Dobynes *Law&B 92*
Hubbard, Paul Stancyl, Jr. 1931- *WhoAm 92*
Hubbard, Peter Claire 1951- *WhoSSW 93*
Hubbard, Peter E. 1942- *WhoAm 92*
Hubbard, Peter Lawrence 1946- *WhoEmL 93*
Hubbard, Preston John 1918- *BioIn 17*
Hubbard, Randall D. 1935- *St&PR 93*
Hubbard, Reginald Hampton 1948- *St&PR 93*
Hubbard, Richmond Chase 1916- *WhoE 93*
Hubbard, Robert Gregg 1958- *WhoSSW 93*
Hubbard, Robert Hamilton 1916- *WhoAm 92*
Hubbard, Robert Hamilton 1916-1989 *BioIn 17*
Hubbard, Robert Lynwood 1934- *St&PR 93*
Hubbard, Robert R. *Law&B 92*
Hubbard, Roger D. 1957- *St&PR 93*
Hubbard, Rubye Mae Annen 1935- *WhoSSW 93*
Hubbard, Ruth 1924- *WhoAm 92, WhoAmW 93, WhoE 93*
Hubbard, Ruth 1942- *WhoAm 92*
Hubbard, Samuel T., Jr. 1950- *WhoAm 92*
Hubbard, Sandra Sue 1959- *WhoEmL 93*
Hubbard, Sonja Y. 1961- *St&PR 93*
Hubbard, Stanley Eugene 1897- *WhoAm 92*
Hubbard, Stanley S. 1933- *St&PR 93*
Hubbard, Stanley Stub 1933- *WhoAm 92, WhoWor 93*
Hubbard, Susan (S.) 1951- *ConAu 138*
Hubbard, Ted *St&PR 93*
Hubbard, Thomas Edwin 1944- *WhoSSW 93*
Hubbard, Thomas K. 1955- *St&PR 93*
Hubbard, Thomas K. 1956- *ConAu 136*
Hubbard, Van Saxton 1945- *WhoE 93*
Hubbard, Vance Matthew 1940- *St&PR 93*
Hubbard, Veronica Lynne 1960- *WhoEmL 93*
Hubbard, William Bogel 1940- *WhoAm 92*
Hubbard, William Neill, Jr. 1919- *WhoAm 92*
Hubbartt-Browne, Peggy Sue 1958- *WhoEmL 93*
Hubbe, Nikolaj *WhoAm 92*
Hubbel, Michael Robert 1954- *WhoWor 93*
Hubbeling, Edwin L. 1933- *St&PR 93*
Hubbell, Carl 1903-1988 *BioIn 17*
Hubbell, Ernest 1914- *WhoAm 92*
Hubbell, Frank Allen 1907-1971 *Baker 92*
Hubbell, Fred Shelton 1951- *WhoAm 92*
Hubbell, Frederick S. 1951- *St&PR 93*
Hubbell, George L. 1894-1990 *BioIn 17*
Hubbell, James Windsor, Jr. 1922- *St&PR 93, WhoAm 92*
Hubbell, John Howard 1925- *WhoAm 92*
Hubbell, Jonathan Allan *Law&B 92*
Hubbell, Joseph G. 1933- *St&PR 93*
Hubbell, Patricia Ann 1928- *WhoWrEP 92*
Hubbell, Richard A. 1944- *WhoSSW 93*
Hubbell, Thomas C. 1936- *St&PR 93*
Hubbell, William L. 1943- *St&PR 93*
Hubbert, James F. 1939- *St&PR 93*
Hubble, Beverly *WhoWrEP 92*
Hubble, Don Wayne 1939- *WhoSSW 93*
Hubble, Edwin Powell 1889-1953 *BioIn 17*
Hubble, Harry Moran *Law&B 92*
Hubble, Steven G. 1948- *St&PR 93*
Hubbs, Alyce Leah 1934- *WhoWrEP 92*
Hubbs, Clark 1921- *WhoAm 92*
Hubbs, Donald Harvey 1918- *WhoAm 92*
Hubbs, Galen Jay 1941- *WhoWrEP 92*
Hubbs, John Brewster 1941- *WhoE 93*
Hubbs, Ronald M. 1908- *WhoWor 93*
Hubbs, Terry D. *Law&B 92*
Hubbuck, John Reginald *WhoScE 91-1*
Hubbuck, John Reginald 1941- *WhoWor 93*
Hubeau, Jean 1917- *Baker 92*
Hubel, David Hunter 1926- *WhoAm 92, WhoE 93, WhoWor 93*
Huber, Albert Frank 1953- *St&PR 93*
Huber, Alberta 1917- *WhoAm 92*
Huber, Allan J. 1929- *St&PR 93*
Huber, Arthur Francis, II 1960- *WhoSSW 93*
Huber, Bettina Julia 1943- *WhoAmW 93, WhoE 93*
Huber, Bruce C. 1947- *St&PR 93*
Huber, Charles G., Jr. *Law&B 92*

Huber, Clayton Lloyd 1955- WhoEmL 93, WhoSSW 93, WhoWor 93
Huber, Colleen Adlene 1927- WhoAmW 93
Huber, Daniel Jurg 1963- WhoWor 93
Huber, Don Lawrence 1928- WhoAm 92
Huber, Douglas Crawford 1939- WhoSSW 93
Huber, Elizabeth Ann Law&B 92
Huber, Eugene Robert 1947- WhoE 93
Huber, Franz 1925- WhoScE 91-3, WhoWor 93
Huber, Fred W. 1931- St&PR 93
Huber, Friedo 1929- WhoWor 93
Huber, G. Ben 1934- St&PR 93
Huber, Gary Louis 1939- WhoSSW 93
Huber, Gerd G. 1921- WhoWor 93
Huber, Gordon Floyd 1921- St&PR 93
Huber, Gunter 1947- WhoScE 91-3
Huber, Hans 1852-1921 Baker 92
Huber, Helmuth Paul 1937- WhoScE 91-4
Huber, Ivan 1931- WhoE 93
Huber, J.F.K. WhoScE 91-4
Huber, J. Kendall Law&B 92
Huber, Jack Travis WhoE 93
Huber, James A. 1951- St&PR 93
Huber, Joan 1925- BioIn 17
Huber, Joan Althaus 1925- WhoAm 92
Huber, Joan Joyce 1941- WhoE 93
Huber, Johannes C. 1946- WhoScE 91-4
Huber, John David 1946- WhoAm 92
Huber, John Lawrence 1944- St&PR 93
Huber, Joseph Fowler 1946- St&PR 93
Huber, Kathleen Dorothy 1946- WhoAmW 93
Huber, Klaus 1924- Baker 92
Huber, Klaus Roland 1956- WhoWor 93
Huber, Kurt 1893-1943 Baker 92
Huber, Larry Gene 1953- WhoEmL 93
Huber, Laurence Edward 1961- WhoEmL 93
Huber, Lee M. Law&B 92
Huber, Maksymilian Tytus 1872-1950 PolBiDi
Huber, Marie Oh Law&B 92
Huber, Martin C.E. 1936- WhoScE 91-3
Huber, Michael S. 1943- St&PR 93
Huber, Michael W. 1926- WhoAm 92
Huber, Michael William Law&B 92
Huber, Mortimer G. 1932- St&PR 93
Huber, Paul Edward 1939- WhoAm 92
Huber, Rafael M. 1942- WhoScE 91-3
Huber, Richard Glen 1937- WhoWor 93
Huber, Richard Gregory 1919- WhoAm 92
Huber, Richard L. 1942- St&PR 93
Huber, Richard Leslie 1936- St&PR 93, WhoAm 92
Huber, Richard Miller 1922- WhoE 93
Huber, Rita Norma 1931- WhoAmW 93
Huber, Robert 1937- WhoScE 91-3, WhoWor 93
Huber, Robert Edger 1931- WhoWrEP 92
Huber, Ronald Frank 1923- St&PR 93
Huber, Therese 1764-1829 BioIn 17
Huber, Thomas Martin 1919- WhoAm 92
Huber, Thomas Wayne 1942- WhoSSW 93
Huber, Walter Dean, Jr. 1944- WhoSSW 93
Huber, Warren V. d1992 NewYTBS 92
Huberfeld, Harold Law&B 92
Huberman, Benjamin 1938- WhoE 93
Huberman, Bronislaw 1882-1947 Baker 92
Hubermann, Bronislaw 1882-1947 PolBiDi
Hubers, David R. 1943- St&PR 93
Huber-Stemich, Felix 1956- WhoWor 93
Hubert, A.J. 1933- WhoScE 91-2
Hubert, Bernard 1947- WhoScE 91-2
Hubert, Cam ConAu 136, WhoCanL 92
Hubert, Cam 1938- ScF&FL 92
Hubert, Christian Jean-Michel 1941- WhoUN 92
Hubert, Frank William Rene 1915- WhoAm 92
Hubert, Helen Betty 1950- WhoAm 92
Hubert, James B. Law&B 92
Hubert, Janet BioIn 17
Hubert, Jean-Loup 1949- MiSFD 9
Hubert, Jean-Luc 1960- WhoEmL 93
Hubert, Kimberly Jo 1962- WhoAm 92
Hubert, Nikolai 1840-1888 Baker 92
Hubert, Pierre 1943- WhoScE 91-2
Hubert, Virginia Elizabeth 1954- WhoAmW 93
Hubert, Walter 1956- WhoWor 93
Hubert, William J. Law&B 92
Huberti, Gustave (-Leon) 1843-1910 Baker 92
Huberty, Carl J. 1934- WhoSSW 93
Huberty, Daniel John 1943- St&PR 93
Hubicki, Donald Edward 1961- WhoE 93
Hubisz, John L., Jr. BioIn 17
Hubka, Vladimir 1924- WhoScE 91-4
Hubl, Lothar 1941- WhoWor 93
Hubler, Bruce A. 1944- St&PR 93
Hubler, Bruce Albert 1944- WhoAm 92
Hubler, David E. 1941- ScF&FL 92
Hubler, David Elliot 1941- WhoWrEP 92
Hubler, H. Clark 1910- WhoWor 93, WhoWrEP 92
Hubler, James T. Law&B 92
Hubler, James T. 1943- St&PR 93
Hubler, James Terrence 1943- WhoAm 92
Hubler, Julius 1919- WhoAm 92, WhoE 93
Hubler, Klaus K(arl) 1956- Baker 92
Hubler, William Forest 1963- WhoWor 93
Hubley, Faith Elliott 1924- WhoAm 92
Hubley, Ralph I., III Law&B 92
Hubley, Reginald Allen 1928- WhoAm 92
Hublitz, Sue 1940- WhoAmW 93
Hubner, Donald Anthony 1926- St&PR 93
Hubner, John A. 1932- St&PR 93
Hubner, Maren BioIn 17
Hubner, Robert Wilmore 1918- WhoAm 92
Hubrich, Walter 1938- WhoUN 92
Hubscher, William Donald 1956- WhoWrEP 92
Hubschman, David Neil 1946- St&PR 93
Hubschman, Henry Allan 1947- WhoAm 92
Hubschman, Thomas ScF&FL 92
Hubshman, Emanuel Edward 1916- St&PR 93
Hubsmith, Robert James 1930- WhoE 93
Huc, Evariste Regis 1813-1860 Expl 93 [port]
Hucbald c. 840-930 Baker 92
Huch, Mary Halley 1938- WhoAmW 93
Huchet-Bishop, Claire MajAI [port]
Huchok, James Paul 1952- St&PR 93
Huchtmeier, Walter Karl-Heinz 1941- WhoWor 93
Huchzermeyer, Bernhard 1950- WhoWor 93
Huciev, Marlen 1925- DrEEuF
Huck, Antie E. Law&B 92
Huck, Janet M. Law&B 92
Huck, John Lloyd 1922- St&PR 93, WhoAm 92
Huck, Leonard William 1922- WhoAm 92
Huck, Lewis Francis 1912- WhoWor 93
Huck, Paul George Law&B 92
Huck, Richard Felix, III 1957- WhoWor 93
Huck, Winnifred Sprague Mason 1882-1936 BioIn 17
Huckabee, Brian Edward 1963- WhoSSW 93
Huckabee, Carol Brooks 1945- WhoAm 92, WhoE 93
Huckabee, Phyllis 1963- WhoAmW 93
Huckabee, Tom 1955- MiSFD 9
Huckaby, Gary Carlton 1938- WhoAm 92
Huckaby, Jerry 1941- CngDr 91
Huckaby, Thomas Jerald 1941- WhoAm 92
Huckaby, Thomas Jerald Jerry 1941- WhoSSW 93
Huckeba, Judy Dianne 1944- WhoAmW 93
Huckel, Hubert E. WhoAm 92
Huckell, Sharon Anne Law&B 92
Hucker, Charles Oscar 1919- WhoAm 92
Hucker, Charles William 1947- St&PR 93
Huckert, John W. 1954- MiSFD 9
Huckins, Cora-Mae 1925- WhoSSW 93
Huckins, Harold Aaron 1924- WhoE 93, WhoWor 93
Huckins, William Judd Law&B 92
Huckins, William Judd 1927- WhoAm 92
Huckman, Michael Saul 1936- WhoAm 92
Hucknall, Nanette Veda 1933- WhoAmW 93
Huckstead, Charlotte Van Horn 1920- WhoAmW 93
Huckstep, April Yvette 1961- WhoAmW 93
Huckstep, Lee Law&B 92
Huckvale, John Frederick 1937- St&PR 93, WhoAm 92
Huda, Syed Monirul 1917- WhoWor 93
Hudachek, Carol Ann 1952- WhoSSW 93
Hudak, Christine Angela 1950- WhoEmL 93
Hudak, Kristen M. WhoAm 92, WhoAmW 93
Hudak, Linda Elise 1960- WhoE 93
Hudak, Thomas F. 1942- St&PR 93
Hudak, Thomas Francis 1942- WhoAm 92
Hudak, Thomas Michael 1937- WhoAm 92
Hudak, Timothy Qualey Law&B 92
Hudd, Nicholas Payne 1945- WhoWor 93
Huddart, David WhoScE 91-1
Huddart, Joseph 1741-1816 BioIn 17
Huddilston, Robert P. 1934- St&PR 93
Huddle, David 1942- WhoWrEP 92
Huddle, David Ross 1942- WhoE 93
Huddle, Robert H., Jr. 1947- WhoE 93
Huddleson, Edwin Emmet, Jr. 1914- WhoAm 92
Huddleston, Barbara 1939- WhoUN 92
Huddleston, David 1938- WhoAm 92
Huddleston, David William 1930- WhoAm 92
Huddleston, Donna Ruth 1958- WhoEmL 93
Huddleston, Elizabeth Sabo 1960- WhoWor 93
Huddleston, Emma Jean 1931- WhoAmW 93
Huddleston, Eugene Lee 1931- WhoAm 92
Huddleston, Joe B. 1949- WhoSSW 93
Huddleston, John D. 1934- WhoUN 92
Huddleston, Judy BioIn 17
Huddleston, Kathleen Gregory 1954- WhoAmW 93
Huddleston, Kathy Nash 1949- WhoEmL 93
Huddleston, Lee W. 1919- St&PR 93
Huddleston, Marilyn Anne 1953- WhoAmW 93
Huddleston, Megan Ann Law&B 92
Huddleston, Patrick Robinson WhoScE 91-1
Huddleston, Samuel 1953- BioIn 17
Huddleston, Sheila Law&B 92
Huddlestone, Roy Victor 1930- WhoWor 93
Huddy, Delia 1934- ScF&FL 92
Hudec, Robert Emil 1934- WhoAm 92
Hudecheck, Rosemary Anne 1949- WhoE 93
Hudecki, Gregory Edward 1946- WhoE 93
Hudell Hoffman, Nancie S. Law&B 92
Hudgens, Abigail Sadler 1946- WhoAmW 93
Hudgens, Janet Walden 1964- WhoSSW 93
Hudgens, Michael Thomas, Sr. 1938- WhoWor 93
Hudgens, Robert Pierce 1915- St&PR 93
Hudgens, Ronald C. Law&B 92
Hudgens, William Thomas 1954- St&PR 93
Hudgeons, Thomas E., III ScF&FL 92
Hudgin, Donald Edward 1917- WhoAm 92, WhoWor 93
Hudgins, Andrew 1951- WhoWrEP 92
Hudgins, Andrew (Leon, Jr.) 1951- DcLB 120 [port]
Hudgins, Barbara 1932- WhoWrEP 92
Hudgins, Catherine Harding 1913- WhoAmW 93, WhoSSW 93, WhoWor 93
Hudgins, David Drake 1955- WhoEmL 93
Hudgins, Gary A. 1953- WhoEmL 93
Hudgins, Jack Sanders, Jr. 1959- St&PR 93
Hudgins, Kenneth Wayne 1936- WhoSSW 93
Hudgins, Mary Dengler 1901- BioIn 17
Hudgins, Mary K. 1938- St&PR 93
Hudgins, Patricia Jo 1943- WhoAmW 93
Hudgins, William Freeman, Jr. 1953- WhoWrEP 92
Hudgins, William S., Jr. Law&B 92
Hudgins, William Sheppard, Jr. 1944- St&PR 93
Hudgson, Peter 1936- WhoScE 91-1
Hudiak, David Michael 1953- WhoE 93, WhoEmL 93, WhoWor 93
Hudiburg, John Justus, Jr. 1928- WhoAm 92
Hudick, Andrew Michael, II 1958- WhoEmL 93, WhoSSW 93
Hudik, Martin Francis 1949- WhoEmL 93
Hudkins, Daniel F. 1951- St&PR 93
Hudkins, John W. Law&B 92
Hudley, Donald Lee 1946- WhoE 93
Hudlin, Reginald BioIn 17, MiSFD 9
Hudlin, Warrington BioIn 17
Hudnall, David Harrison 1948- St&PR 93, WhoAm 92
Hudnall, Jarrett, Jr. 1931- WhoAm 92
Hudner, Philip 1931- WhoAm 92
Hudnut, David Beecher 1935- WhoAm 92
Hudnut, Robert K(ilborne) 1934- ConAu 38NR
Hudnut, Robert Kilborne 1934- WhoAm 92
Hudnut, Stewart 1939- WhoAm 92
Hudnut, William Herbert, III 1932- WhoAm 92
Hudobenko, Diane 1957- WhoAmW 93
Hudock, Anne Emerson 1934- WhoAmW 93
Hudock, John Paul Law&B 92
Hudolin, Vladimir 1922- WhoScE 91-4
Hudrlik, Paul Frederick 1941- WhoE 93
Hudson, A.P. WhoScE 91-1
Hudson, Alice M. 1930- St&PR 93
Hudson, Alice Peterson 1942- WhoAm 92
Hudson, Anthony P. 1939- WhoScE 91-1
Hudson, Anthony Webster 1937- WhoAm 92
Hudson, B. WhoScE 91-1
Hudson, Bannus B. 1945- St&PR 93
Hudson, Bannus B. 1946- WhoAm 92
Hudson, Barbara T. 1952- WhoIns 93
Hudson, Barton 1936- WhoSSW 93
Hudson, Benjamin, Jr. Law&B 92
Hudson, Betty 1949- St&PR 93
Hudson, C.B. WhoIns 93
Hudson, Calvin L. 1946- St&PR 93
Hudson, Carolyn E. 1944- St&PR 93
Hudson, Charles Daugherty 1927- WhoSSW 93, WhoWor 93
Hudson, Charles L. 1904-1992 NewYTBS 92 [port]
Hudson, Charles L(owell) 1904-1992 CurBio 92N
Hudson, Cheryl Willis 1948- BlkAull 92
Hudson, Christopher John 1948- WhoWor 93
Hudson, Claude Earl 1946- WhoAm 92
Hudson, Clifford 1954- St&PR 93
Hudson, Courtney Morley 1955- WhoAmW 93, WhoEmL 93, WhoSSW 93
Hudson, Dale Monroe 1934- St&PR 93
Hudson, Dean Allen 1935- WhoSSW 93
Hudson, Dennis L. Law&B 92
Hudson, Dennis Lee 1936- WhoWor 93
Hudson, Dennis S., III 1955- St&PR 93
Hudson, Desmond F. WhoAm 92
Hudson, Donald Ellis 1916- WhoAm 92
Hudson, Donald J. 1930- WhoAm 92
Hudson, Douglas Fillmore, Jr. 1945- St&PR 93
Hudson, Dyan Grayless 1965- WhoAmW 93
Hudson, Edward Allan 1946- WhoWor 93
Hudson, Edward S. ScF&FL 92
Hudson, Elizabeth Hamilton 1945- WhoAmW 93
Hudson, Ellen Matilda 1915- WhoWrEP 92
Hudson, Ethel d1992 NewYTBS 92
Hudson, Frank N. 1949- WhoAm 92
Hudson, Frank Parker 1918- WhoSSW 93
Hudson, Franklin Donald 1933- WhoAm 92
Hudson, Frederick 1913- Baker 92
Hudson, G. Donald 1897-1989 BioIn 17
Hudson, G. Kirk 1941- St&PR 93
Hudson, Garth c. 1943- See Band, The ConMus 9
Hudson, Gary MiSFD 9
Hudson, Gary Michael 1946- WhoEmL 93
Hudson, George Elbert 1916- WhoAm 92
Hudson, Gladys W. 1926- St&PR 93
Hudson, Grace Debrovner 1932- WhoSSW 93
Hudson, Gregory E. 1946- St&PR 93
Hudson, Hal D. 1931- St&PR 93
Hudson, Harold Jordon, Jr. 1924- WhoAm 92
Hudson, Harry Robinson WhoScE 91-1
Hudson, Helen BioIn 17
Hudson, Henry d1611 Expl 93 [port]
Hudson, Henry 1575?-1611 BioIn 17
Hudson, Howard V. 1945- St&PR 93
Hudson, Howard V., Jr. Law&B 92
Hudson, Hubert R. 1928- WhoWor 93
Hudson, Hugh ConTFT 10
Hudson, Hugh 1936- MiSFD 9
Hudson, Ian BioIn 17
Hudson, J. Clifford Law&B 92
Hudson, J. Clifford 1954- St&PR 93
Hudson, J.W. 1939- St&PR 93
Hudson, Jacqueline WhoAm 92, WhoAmW 93
Hudson, James Rogers 1950- WhoSSW 93
Hudson, James T. 1924- WhoSSW 93
Hudson, Jan 1954- ConAu 136, DcChlFi, ScF&FL 92
Hudson, Jan 1954-1990 BioIn 17
Hudson, Janet R. 1956- St&PR 93
Hudson, Jeffrey ConAu 40NR
Hudson, Jerry E. 1938- WhoAm 92
Hudson, Jesse Tucker, Jr. 1920- WhoAm 92
Hudson, John WhoScE 91-1
Hudson, John Balch 1934- WhoE 93
Hudson, John Irvin 1932- WhoAm 92
Hudson, John Lester 1937- WhoAm 92
Hudson, Joseph D. 1946- St&PR 93
Hudson, Joseph Douglas Law&B 92
Hudson, Judith L. Law&B 92
Hudson, Karl Grier, Jr. 1919- St&PR 93
Hudson, Katherine M. St&PR 93
Hudson, Katherine Mary 1947- WhoAm 92, WhoAmW 93
Hudson, Lee 1936- WhoAmW 93
Hudson, Leonard Harlow 1915- WhoAm 92
Hudson, Lester A., Jr. 1939- St&PR 93
Hudson, Linda 1950- WhoAmW 93
Hudson, Lizann R. AfrAmBi
Hudson, Louis Mark 1952- WhoEmL 93
Hudson, Manley O., Jr. 1932- WhoAm 92
Hudson, Marcus Allan 1947- WhoWrEP 92
Hudson, Margaret Stover 1947- WhoAmW 93
Hudson, Mark Woodbridge 1940- WhoAm 92
Hudson, Martha 1939- BioIn 17

Hudson, Martha B. BlkAmWO [port]
Hudson, Michael ScF&FL 92
Hudson, Michael Craig 1938- WhoAm 92
Hudson, Michael T. 1947- WhoSSW 93
Hudson, Molly Ann 1941- St&PR 93, WhoAm 92, WhoAmW 93
Hudson, Myra Linden Frank 1950- WhoAmW 93, WhoSSW 93
Hudson, Peter John 1953- WhoScE 91-1
Hudson, Phillip Frank 1936- WhoAm 92
Hudson, Ralph P. 1924- WhoAm 92
Hudson, Ray WhoScE 91-1
Hudson, Ray Truman 1929- WhoSSW 93
Hudson, Rebecca Dobbins 1939- WhoAmW 93
Hudson, Richard BioIn 17
Hudson, Richard Anthony WhoScE 91-1
Hudson, Richard Cloyd 1948- WhoSSW 93
Hudson, Robert Franklin, Jr. 1946- WhoAm 92, WhoEmL 93, WhoSSW 93, WhoWor 93
Hudson, Robert Paul 1926- WhoAm 92
Hudson, Robin Lyth WhoScE 91-1
Hudson, Rock 1925-1985 BioIn 17, IntDcF 2-3 [port]
Hudson, Rolando MiSFD 9
Hudson, Sally Lynn 1949- WhoSSW 93
Hudson, Samuel T. 1927- St&PR 93
Hudson, Samuel W., III 1940- AfrAmBi
Hudson, Stanton Harold, Jr. 1951- WhoE 93
Hudson, Stephen Arthur WhoScE 91-1
Hudson, Steven C. 1953- St&PR 93
Hudson, Suncerray Ann 1960- WhoAmW 93, WhoEmL 93
Hudson, Tajquah Jaye 1959- WhoEmL 93
Hudson, Terri Powell 1958- WhoAmW 93
Hudson, Thomas 1954- WhoEmL 93, WhoSSW 93, WhoWor 93
Hudson, W. Francis 1923- WhoSSW 93
Hudson, W. Gail 1953- WhoSSW 93
Hudson, W.H. 1841-1922 BioIn 17, ScF&FL 92
Hudson, Wade 1945- BlkAuII 92
Hudson, Walter BioIn 17
Hudson, Wendy Joy 1955- WhoAmW 93
Hudson, William Henry 1841-1922 BioIn 17
Hudson, William J. 1934- St&PR 93
Hudson, William L. WhoAm 92
Hudson, William Mark 1932- WhoSSW 93
Hudson, William Parke Custis 1954- St&PR 93
Hudson, William Ronald 1933- WhoAm 92
Hudson, William Thomas 1929- WhoAm 92
Hudson, Winthrop Still 1911- WhoAm 92
Hudson, Woodruff Lylle 1958- St&PR 93
Hudson, Yeager 1931- WhoAm 92
Hudson-Bauman, Sharon 1961- St&PR 93
Hudson-McQueen, Josephine 1945- WhoAmW 93
Hudson-Phillips, Karl 1933- DcCPCAm
Hudson-Young, Jane Smither 1937- WhoAmW 93
Hudspeth, Albert James 1945- WhoAm 92
Hudspeth, Chalmers Mac 1919- WhoAm 92
Hudspeth, Emmett LeRoy 1916- WhoAm 92
Hudspeth, Harry Lee 1935- WhoAm 92, WhoSSW 93
Hudspeth, Juanita Lois 1923- BioIn 17
Hudspeth, Nora Jo 1936- WhoSSW 93
Hudspeth, Robert Scott 1936- St&PR 93
Hudspeth, William Junia, Jr. 1939- St&PR 93
Hudspeth, William R. 1944- St&PR 93
Hudzik, Henryk Teodor 1945- WhoWor 93
Hue, Georges (-Adolphe) 1858-1948 Baker 92
Hue, Joseph Alphonse 1932- WhoWor 93
Huebbers, Carl George, Jr. 1952- WhoEmL 93
Huebener, Rudolf P. 1931- WhoScE 91-3
Huebener, Rudolf Peter 1931- WhoWor 93
Huebner, Allen G. Law&B 92
Huebner, Donald Frank 1925- St&PR 93
Huebner, Harlan Pierce 1927- WhoAm 92
Huebner, Jay Stanley 1939- WhoAm 92, WhoSSW 93
Huebner, John Stephen 1940- WhoAm 92
Huebner, Kurt Walter 1960- WhoSSW 93
Huebner, Lauren Jeanne 1959- WhoE 93
Huebner, Ronald Gene 1943- St&PR 93
Huebner, S.S. 1882-1964 BioIn 17
Huebner, Solomon Stephen 1882-1964 BioIn 17
Huebsch, Michael Christie 1958- WhoE 93
Huebsch, William L. Law&B 92
Huebschman, Martin John 1947- St&PR 93
Hueck, George DcCPCAm
Hueffer, Francis 1843-1889 Baker 92
Huegel, Peter A.V. Law&B 92
Hueglin, Steven BioIn 17
Huehn, Julius 1904-1971 Baker 92
Hueholt, Richard L. 1929- St&PR 93
Huelke, Donald Fred 1930- WhoAm 92
Huelskamp, Raymond L. 1927- St&PR 93
Huelsman, Albert John, Jr. 1936- St&PR 93
Huelsman, Joanne B. 1938- WhoAmW 93
Huelsmann, Thomas Cyril 1940- St&PR 93
Huemer, Dick 1898-1979 ScF&FL 92
Huemer, Joseph Wilson 1913- WhoWrEP 92
Huenefeld, Robert C. 1936- St&PR 93
Huenefeld, Thomas Ernst 1937- St&PR 93
Huenemann, Ruben Henry 1909- WhoAm 92
Huening, Walter Carl, Jr. 1923- WhoAm 92, WhoWor 93
Huenink, Dirk William 1935- St&PR 93
Huerlimann, Bettina 1909-1983 MajAI [port]
Huerta, David 1949- DcMexL
Huerta, Dolores 1930- NotHsAW 93 [port]
Huerta, Dolores Fernandez 1930- HispAmA [port]
Huerta, Efrain 1914-1982 DcMexL, SpAmA
Huerta, M. Regina Law&B 92
Huerta, Victoriano DcCPCAm
Huerta, Victoriano 1854-1916 DcTwHis
Huerta-Pavia, Eva Yolanda 1962- WhoAmW 93
Hueseman, John Alexander 1956- St&PR 93
Huesing, Elizabeth T. 1908- St&PR 93
Huesman, Cynthia Ann 1949- WhoAmW 93
Huesped, Estimado Huevos 1923- WhoAm 92
Huestis, Charles Benjamin 1920- WhoAm 92
Hueston, Robert Edward 1929- St&PR 93
Huet, Christian 1936- WhoScE 91-2
Huet, David R. Law&B 92
Huet, Jean 1930- WhoScE 91-2
Huet, Jean 1934- WhoScE 91-2
Huet, Marie-Helene Jaqueline 1944- WhoAm 92
Huet, Raymond 1926- WhoScE 91-2
Hueter, Ernest B. 1920- St&PR 93
Huether, Barbara Lee 1954- WhoAm 92
Huetsch, Larry C. 1947- St&PR 93
Huette, Robert Barrett, III 1946- St&PR 93
Huetteman, Raymond Theodore, Jr. 1929- WhoAm 92
Huetteman, Susan Ann Bice 1934- WhoWrEP 92
Huettner, Richard Alfred 1927- WhoAm 92
Huey, Elizabeth A. 1953- St&PR 93
Huey, H. Gregg 1953- St&PR 93
Huey, John H. 1934- St&PR 93
Huey, John W. Law&B 92
Huey, Joseph Wistar, III 1938- WhoE 93
Huey, Karen Annette 1944- WhoAmW 93
Huey, Ken BioIn 17
Huey, Robert Davis 1958- WhoE 93
Huey, Ward L. BioIn 17
Huey, Ward Ligon, Jr. 1938- WhoAm 92
Huf, Carol Elinor 1940- WhoAmW 93
Huf, Ernst Gustav Rudolf 1907- WhoWor 93
Hufbauer, Gary Clyde 1939- WhoAm 92, WhoWor 93
Huff, Al R. 1938- St&PR 93
Huff, Barbara A. BioIn 17
Huff, Bruce N. 1950- St&PR 93
Huff, Bruce O. 1946- WhoEmL 93
Huff, Charles F. Law&B 92
Huff, Clarence Ronald 1945- WhoAm 92, WhoWor 93
Huff, David L. Law&B 92, WhoAm 92
Huff, Edgar J. St&PR 93
Huff, Gayle C. 1956- St&PR 93
Huff, Gayle Compton 1956- WhoAmW 93, WhoEmL 93, WhoWor 93
Huff, Helmut W. 1934- WhoScE 91-3
Huff, Henry Blair 1924- WhoSSW 93
Huff, James Francis 1939- WhoE 93
Huff, Jay Scott Law&B 92
Huff, Jerome Joseph, Jr. 1943- WhoSSW 93
Huff, Jimmy Laurence 1950- WhoSSW 93
Huff, Joe Elmer 1953- WhoSSW 93
Huff, John Craig, Jr. 1920- St&PR 93
Huff, John David 1952- WhoEmL 93
Huff, John Rossman 1946- St&PR 93, WhoWor 93
Huff, John Wesley 1927- WhoSSW 93
Huff, Jonathan O. 1941- St&PR 93
Huff, Leon SoulM
Huff, Luella M. AmWomPl
Huff, Lula Eleanor Lunsford 1949- WhoAmW 93
Huff, Margaret Joan Farris 1925- WhoSSW 93
Huff, Margaret M. Law&B 92
Huff, Marilyn L. 1951- WhoAmW 93
Huff, Norman Nelson 1933- WhoWor 93
Huff, Pamela Jean 1946- WhoEmL 93
Huff, Paul Emlyn 1916- WhoAm 92
Huff, Penny 1944- St&PR 93
Huff, Richard (M.) 1962- ConAu 139
Huff, Ronald E. 1955- St&PR 93
Huff, Russell Joseph 1936- WhoSSW 93, WhoWor 93
Huff, Sam 1934- BioIn 17
Huff, Stanley Eugene 1918- WhoAm 92
Huff, Talbot S., Jr. 1940- St&PR 93
Huff, Tanya 1957- ScF&FL 92
Huff, Thomas A. 1939- St&PR 93
Huff, Thomas Allen 1935- WhoSSW 93
Huff, Thomas D. St&PR 93
Huff, Welcome Rex Anthony 1967- WhoWor 93
Huff, William Braid 1950- WhoAm 92
Huff, William Henry, III Law&B 92
Huff, William Henry, III 1937- St&PR 93, WhoIns 93
Huff, William Jennings 1919- WhoSSW 93, WhoWor 93
Huffaker, Carla Sue 1951- WhoEmL 93
Huffaker, Craig Jackson 1945- WhoAm 92
Huffaker, John Boston 1925- WhoAm 92
Huffard, Elvis Henry 1918- WhoSSW 93
Huffard, Jay C. 1941- St&PR 93
Huffenus, Alan Michael 1947- St&PR 93
Huffer, Franz 1843-1889 Baker 92
Huffine, Coy Lee 1924- WhoAm 92
Huffine, Gary Wayne 1948- St&PR 93
Huffington, Roy M. 1917- St&PR 93
Huffington, Roy Michael 1917- WhoAm 92, WhoWor 93
Huffman, A. Richard 1939- St&PR 93
Huffman, Barry Law&B 92
Huffman, Barry L. Law&B 92
Huffman, Cady BioIn 17
Huffman, Celia Ann 1953- WhoEmL 93
Huffman, Claudia Sue 1954- WhoEmL 93
Huffman, Cyrus Martin 1960- WhoSSW 93
Huffman, Dale E. Law&B 92
Huffman, Darlene A. Law&B 92
Huffman, David A. 1925- BioIn 17
Huffman, David Lloyd 1965- WhoSSW 93
Huffman, Delton Cleon, Jr. 1943- WhoAm 92
Huffman, Dennis A. 1951- St&PR 93
Huffman, Diane Rausch 1952- WhoEmL 93
Huffman, Edgar Joseph 1939- St&PR 93, WhoAm 92
Huffman, Gary Claud 1944- St&PR 93
Huffman, Gregory A. Law&B 92
Huffman, Harry V. Law&B 92
Huffman, James Thomas 1947- St&PR 93
Huffman, James Thomas William 1947- WhoAm 92
Huffman, Jan 1943- WhoE 93
Huffman, Joan Brewer 1937- WhoSSW 93
Huffman, John Curtis 1941- WhoAm 92
Huffman, John William 1932- WhoSSW 93
Huffman, Kenneth Jay 1953- St&PR 93
Huffman, Leslie, Jr. 1929- WhoAm 92
Huffman, Mark R. Law&B 92
Huffman, Marlys ScF&FL 92
Huffman, Mary Frances 1911- WhoAmW 93
Huffman, Mona Lou 1956- WhoEmL 93
Huffman, Nona Gay 1942- WhoAmW 93
Huffman, Patricia Ann 1936- WhoAmW 93
Huffman, Robert Allen, Jr. 1950- WhoEmL 93, WhoSSW 93, WhoWor 93
Huffman, Robert Earl 1928- St&PR 93
Huffman, Rodney Lee 1953- WhoSSW 93
Huffman, Ruth Webb AmWomPl
Huffman-Hine, Ruth Carson 1925- WhoAmW 93
Huffman-Klinkowitz, Julie 1956- ScF&FL 92
Huffmann, Gert 1930- WhoScE 91-3
Hufford, David Clinton 1945- WhoSSW 93
Huffstetler, Edward Wright 1958- WhoSSW 93
Huffstetler, Palmer Eugene 1937- St&PR 93, WhoAm 92, WhoSSW 93
Huffstetler, Palmer Eugene, Sr. Law&B 92
Huffstodt, Karen WhoAm 92
Huffstutler, John H. Law&B 92
Hufft, John Carlton 1925- St&PR 93
Hufham, Barbara Law&B 92
Hufham, Barbara Frances 1939- St&PR 93, WhoAmW 93
Hufnagel, Ellen M. 1948- WhoEmL 93
Hufnagel, Katherine L. Law&B 92
Hufnagel, Leon Clement, Jr. 1947- St&PR 93
Hufnagel, Linda Ann 1939- WhoAmW 93
Hufnagel, Robert Joseph 1953- St&PR 93
Hufnagle, Richard Angell 1950- St&PR 93
Hufner, Jorg 1937- WhoScE 91-3
Hufner, Michael 1940- WhoWor 93
Hufner, Stefan 1935- WhoScE 91-3
Hufschmidt, Maynard Michael 1912- WhoAm 92
Hufstedler, Seth Martin 1922- WhoAm 92
Hufstedler, Shirley Mount 1925- WhoAm 92, WhoAmW 93
Huftalen, Lisa Freeman 1953- WhoE 93, WhoEmL 93, WhoWor 93
Hug, James Edward 1941- WhoE 93
Hug, K. WhoScE 91-4
Hug, Procter Ralph, Jr. 1931- WhoAm 92
Hug, Richard E. 1935- St&PR 93
Hug, Richard Ernest 1935- WhoAm 92
Hug, Robert Charles, Jr. 1940- St&PR 93
Hug, Stephen Louis 1956- WhoEmL 93
Huge, Arthur W. 1945- St&PR 93
Huge, Thomas Arnold 1944- WhoWor 93
Hugeburg fl. 8th cent.- OxDcByz
Hugel, Charles E. 1928- St&PR 93
Hugel, Rene P. 1937- WhoScE 91-2
Hugener, Franz 1956- WhoWor 93
Huger, Benjamin 1805-1877 HarEnMi
Huger, Daniel Lionel 1768-1798 BioIn 17
Huget, Eugene Floyd 1931- WhoSSW 93
Huget, Larry R. 1945- St&PR 93
Hugg, Sondra Kay 1943- WhoAmW 93
Huggan, Isabel 1943- WhoCanL 92
Huggard, Eileen Elisabeth 1957- WhoAmW 93
Huggard, Ernest Douglas 1933- St&PR 93
Huggel, Hansjorg 1926- WhoScE 91-4
Hugghins, Beverly Kennon 1927- St&PR 93
Hugghins, Ernest Jay 1920- WhoAm 92
Hugghins, Joseph Harris 1925- St&PR 93
Huggins, Alonzo Lee, Jr. 1944- St&PR 93
Huggins, Charles Brenton 1901- WhoAm 92, WhoWor 93
Huggins, Charles Edward 1929-1990 BioIn 17
Huggins, Charlotte Susan Harrison 1933- WhoAmW 93
Huggins, Dorothy AmWomPl
Huggins, Elaine Jacqueline 1954- WhoAmW 93, WhoEmL 93
Huggins, Godfrey 1883-1971 DcTwHis
Huggins, Mary Dean 1934- WhoAmW 93
Huggins, Mary Helen 1952- WhoSSW 93
Huggins, Nancy J. 1952- St&PR 93
Huggins, Nathan Irvin 1927-1989 BioIn 17
Huggins, R. Troy 1936- St&PR 93
Huggins, Rollin Charles, Jr. 1931- WhoAm 92
Huggins, Roy 1914- MiSFD 9
Huggins, Ruth M. ScF&FL 92
Huggins, Susan Jane 1938- WhoSSW 93
Huggins, Tryon K., Jr. 1931- St&PR 93
Huggins, William 1824-1910 BioIn 17
Huggins, William 1935- WhoAm 92
Huggins, William Herbert 1919- WhoAm 92
Huggler, John 1928- Baker 92
Huggler, Lyndall J. Law&B 92
Hugh, Dafydd ab ScF&FL 92
Hugh, George M. WhoAm 92
Hughart, Barry 1934- ConAu 137, ScF&FL 92
Hughen, Lowell Harry 1937- WhoAm 92
Hughes, A.A. 1941- WhoScE 91-1
Hughes, A.J. Law&B 92
Hughes, Abbie Angharad 1940- WhoWor 93
Hughes, Ada Marean 1848-1929 BioIn 17
Hughes, Aidan 1952- St&PR 93
Hughes, Alan 1939- WhoCanL 92
Hughes, Alan 1952- St&PR 93
Hughes, Alan Richard 1936- WhoAm 92
Hughes, Albert R., Jr. 1927- St&PR 93
Hughes, Alfred Clifton 1932- WhoAm 92
Hughes, Alice Cecile 1929- WhoAmW 93
Hughes, Allan Bebout 1924- WhoAm 92
Hughes, Allen 1921- WhoAm 92
Hughes, Ann Hightower 1938- WhoAm 92, WhoAmW 93
Hughes, Ann Nolen WhoAmW 93, WhoSSW 93
Hughes, Anselm 1889-1974 Baker 92
Hughes, Arthur Hyde 1952- WhoSSW 93
Hughes, Arwel 1909- OxDcOp
Hughes, Arwel 1909-1988 Baker 92
Hughes, Author E. 1929- WhoAm 92
Hughes, B. Wayne St&PR 93
Hughes, Babette Plechner 1906- AmWomPl
Hughes, Barbara Ann 1938- WhoAmW 93
Hughes, Barbara Bradford 1941- WhoAmW 93, WhoWor 93
Hughes, Barbara Sue 1932- WhoAmW 93
Hughes, Barnard 1915- WhoAm 92
Hughes, Barry Peter WhoScE 91-1
Hughes, Bernard A. 1930- St&PR 93

Hughes, Betty 1922- St&PR 93
Hughes, Blake 1914- WhoAm 92
Hughes, Bradley Richard 1954- WhoEmL 93
Hughes, Brett G. Law&B 92
Hughes, Caleb BioIn 17
Hughes, Carl Andrew 1948- WhoWor 93
Hughes, Carl Douglas 1946- WhoEmL 93
Hughes, Carl Wilson 1914- WhoAm 92
Hughes, Carol MiSFD 9
Hughes, Carol 1915- SweetSg C [port]
Hughes, Carroll Thornton, Jr. 1931- St&PR 93
Hughes, Catherine Liggins 1947- AfrAmBi [port]
Hughes, Charles E. 1931- WhoIns 93
Hughes, Charles Evans 1862-1948 DcTwHis, OxCSupC [port], PolPar
Hughes, Charles Evans 1938- St&PR 93
Hughes, Charles Jackson 1954- WhoEmL 93
Hughes, Charles Joseph WhoScE 91-1
Hughes, Christine G. Law&B 92
Hughes, Christine Georgette 1946- WhoAm 92
Hughes, Cledwyn 1920-1978 ScF&FL 92
Hughes, Daniel Richard WhoScE 91-1
Hughes, Dave W. ScF&FL 92
Hughes, David BioIn 17, MiSFD 9
Hughes, David 1930- BioIn 17
Hughes, David Emery 1947- St&PR 93, WhoAm 92
Hughes, David Henry 1942- WhoSSW 93
Hughes, David Henry 1943- WhoAm 92
Hughes, David John 1942- St&PR 93
Hughes, David Lewis WhoScE 91-1
Hughes, David Michael 1939- WhoAm 92, WhoSSW 93
Hughes, David R. Law&B 92
Hughes, David W. ScF&FL 92
Hughes, David William 1953- WhoSSW 93
Hughes, Dean 1943- WhoWrEP 92
Hughes, Deborah Pifer 1963- WhoEmL 93
Hughes, Delia Ann 1947- WhoEmL 93
Hughes, Delos Dyson 1934- WhoAm 92
Hughes, Dennis Talbot ScF&FL 92
Hughes, Derek 1934- WhoIns 93
Hughes, Dianne Hunter 1946- WhoAmW 93
Hughes, Donald J. 1941- St&PR 93
Hughes, Dorothea M. AmWomPl
Hughes, Dwain H. 1947- St&PR 93
Hughes, Eden ConAu 40NR
Hughes, Edward c. 1718-1794 HarEnMi
Hughes, Edward Cyril 1935- WhoAm 92
Hughes, Edward D. 1942- St&PR 93
Hughes, Edward Hunter 1921- WhoAm 92
Hughes, Edward J. ScF&FL 92
Hughes, Edward James 1930- BioIn 17
Hughes, Edward John 1913- WhoAm 92
Hughes, Edward P. ScF&FL 92
Hughes, Edward T. 1920- WhoAm 92, WhoE 93
Hughes, Edwin 1884-1965 Baker 92
Hughes, Edwin Ross 1928- WhoAm 92
Hughes, Eleanor Pollock d1991 BioIn 17
Hughes, Elinor Lambert 1906- WhoAm 92
Hughes, Elizabeth AmWomPl
Hughes, Emmet John 1920-1982 PolPar
Hughes, Eril Barnett 1953- WhoSSW 93
Hughes, Eugene Morgan 1934- WhoAm 92
Hughes, Everett Clark 1904- WhoAm 92
Hughes, F. Patrick 1948- St&PR 93
Hughes, Fred BioIn 17
Hughes, Fred George 1915- WhoAm 92
Hughes, G. Michael W. Law&B 92
Hughes, G. Philip 1953- WhoAm 92, WhoWor 93
Hughes, Gareth R. 1945- WhoAm 92
Hughes, George Law&B 92
Hughes, George Allen 1940- St&PR 93
Hughes, George David 1930- WhoAm 92
Hughes, George Edward 1950- WhoSSW 93
Hughes, George Nelson 1957- WhoSSW 93
Hughes, George R. d1992 NewYTBS 92
Hughes, George Vincent 1930- St&PR 93
Hughes, George Wendell 1929- WhoAm 92
Hughes, Georgia Becker Law&B 92
Hughes, Gerald T. Law&B 92
Hughes, Glenn D. 1949- WhoE 93
Hughes, Gordon Langford 1949- WhoWor 93
Hughes, Grace-Flores 1946- WhoAm 92
Hughes, Graham Alexander 1949- WhoWor 93
Hughes, Graham Robert Vivian WhoScE 91-1
Hughes, Gwilym 1937- WhoWor 93
Hughes, H. Stuart 1916- BioIn 17
Hughes, Hal Law&B 92
Hughes, Hallie Cavett 1950- WhoSSW 93
Hughes, Harold E. 1922- PolPar
Hughes, Harold Hasbrouck, Jr. 1930- WhoAm 92
Hughes, Harold J. 1947- St&PR 93
Hughes, Helen MacGill 1903- BioIn 17
Hughes, Helen Ruth 1914- WhoWrEP 92
Hughes, Henry Stuart 1916- BioIn 17
Hughes, Herbert 1882-1937 Baker 92
Hughes, Hollis E., Jr. 1943- AfrAmBi [port]
Hughes, Holly BioIn 17
Hughes, Howard 1905-1976 BioIn 17, EncABHB 8 [port], MiSFD 9N
Hughes, I.C.H. WhoScE 91-1
Hughes, Ian Edward WhoScE 91-1
Hughes, Ian Frank 1940- St&PR 93, WhoAm 92
Hughes, Ian Simpson WhoScE 91-1
Hughes, Ian Simpson 1930- WhoWor 93
Hughes, Ida Hudson 1965- WhoSSW 93
Hughes, Idwal Wyn 1932- WhoWor 93
Hughes, Ieuan Arwel WhoScE 91-1
Hughes, James A. 1912- St&PR 93
Hughes, James Arthur 1939- WhoWor 93
Hughes, James Baker, Jr. 1938- WhoSSW 93
Hughes, James Donald 1951- WhoEmL 93
Hughes, James Edward 1938- St&PR 93
Hughes, James G. 1910- WhoSSW 93
Hughes, James Gordon 1957- WhoWor 93
Hughes, James Joseph 1956- St&PR 93
Hughes, James M. 1950- St&PR 93
Hughes, James Paul 1920- WhoAm 92
Hughes, James Sinclair 1934- WhoE 93, WhoWor 93
Hughes, Janice Deborah 1948- WhoAmW 93
Hughes, Janice Ruth 1939- WhoAmW 93
Hughes, Jay W., Jr. Law&B 92
Hughes, Jerome Michael 1929- WhoAm 92
Hughes, Jimmy SoulM
Hughes, Jimmy H. 1921- St&PR 93
Hughes, Jo Blair d1990 BioIn 17
Hughes, Joe Don 1933- WhoSSW 93
Hughes, Joe Kenneth 1927- WhoAm 92
Hughes, John BioIn 17, WhoScE 91-1
Hughes, John 1677-1720 BioIn 17
Hughes, John 1797-1864 BioIn 17
Hughes, John 1943- WhoAm 92
Hughes, John 1950- MiSFD 9
Hughes, John D. 1935- St&PR 93
Hughes, John Edwin 1927- St&PR 93
Hughes, John Farrell WhoScE 91-1
Hughes, John Farrell 1946- St&PR 93, WhoAm 92
Hughes, John Francis Law&B 92
Hughes, John G. 1930- WhoIns 93
Hughes, John L. 1937- St&PR 93
Hughes, John Lawrence 1925- St&PR 93, WhoAm 92
Hughes, John Llewellyn Mostyn 1951- WhoWor 93
Hughes, John M. 1934- St&PR 93
Hughes, John R. 1855-1947 BioIn 17
Hughes, John Russell 1928- WhoAm 92
Hughes, John Russell 1949- WhoEmL 93
Hughes, John T. d1992 NewYTBS 92
Hughes, John Vance 1946- WhoAm 92
Hughes, John W. WhoAm 92
Hughes, Jon Christopher 1945- WhoWrEP 92
Hughes, Jonathan R(oberts) T(yson) 1928-1992 ConAu 137
Hughes, Jonathan Roberts Tyson 1928- WhoAm 92
Hughes, Joseph D. 1910- WhoAm 92
Hughes, Juanita Q. 1940- St&PR 93
Hughes, Judy Lynne 1939- WhoAmW 93
Hughes, Judy Sanders 1957- WhoEmL 93
Hughes, Juliana Genine 1962- WhoEmL 93
Hughes, Karen S. 1954- St&PR 93
Hughes, Karen Smith 1954- WhoAmW 93
Hughes, Karen Woodbury 1940- WhoAm 92, WhoAmW 93
Hughes, Katherine Elaine 1950- WhoWrEP 92
Hughes, Kay SweetSg C [port]
Hughes, Keith W. 1946- St&PR 93
Hughes, Ken(neth) 1922- ConAu 39NR
Hughes, Kenneth 1922- MiSFD 9
Hughes, Kenneth Russell 1925- WhoAm 92
Hughes, Kevin Arthur 1950- WhoUN 92
Hughes, Kevin Bernard 1947- WhoEmL 93
Hughes, Kevin T. Law&B 92
Hughes, Kim Knox 1953- WhoWrEP 92
Hughes, Kimberly Arden 1960- WhoWor 93
Hughes, Kristine Fugal 1938- St&PR 93
Hughes, Langston 1902-1967 BioIn 17, BlkAuII 92, ConBlB 4 [port], ConHero 2 [port], DramC 3 [port], EncAACR [port], MagSAmL [port], WorLitC [port]
Hughes, (James Mercer) Langston 1902-1967 MajAI [port]
Hughes, Laurel Ellen 1952- WhoAmW 93
Hughes, Laurie Law&B 92
Hughes, Lawrence Edwin, III 1951- WhoSSW 93
Hughes, Lenore Harris 1914- WhoWrEP 92
Hughes, Leslie Ernest WhoScE 91-1
Hughes, Libby SmATA 71 [port]
Hughes, Libby 1932- WhoAmW 93
Hughes, Linda J. 1950- WhoAmW 93
Hughes, Linda Kay 1948- WhoSSW 93
Hughes, Linda Renate 1947- WhoEmL 93
Hughes, Louis B. 1938- St&PR 93
Hughes, Lynn Feeney 1939- St&PR 93
Hughes, Lynn Nettleton 1941- WhoAm 92, WhoSSW 93
Hughes, Malcolm Kenneth 1943- WhoAm 92
Hughes, Marcia Marie 1949- WhoAmW 93
Hughes, Margaret Eileen 1943- WhoAm 92
Hughes, Marie Sharon 1955- WhoAmW 93, WhoEmL 93
Hughes, Marija Matich WhoAm 92, WhoAmW 93
Hughes, Mark E. 1957- WhoAm 92
Hughes, Mark Reynolds 1956- St&PR 93
Hughes, Martin Neville WhoScE 91-1
Hughes, Mary Beth 1919- SweetSg C [port]
Hughes, Mary Elizabeth 1940- WhoAm 92
Hughes, Mary Elizabeth 1946- WhoEmL 93
Hughes, Matilda ConAu 40NR
Hughes, Michael Charles 1949- St&PR 93
Hughes, Michael E. Law&B 92
Hughes, Michael H. 1954- WhoIns 93
Hughes, Michael Joseph Law&B 92
Hughes, Michael Joseph 1951- WhoEmL 93
Hughes, Michaela Kelly WhoAm 92
Hughes, Monica BioIn 17
Hughes, Monica 1925- DcChlFi, ScF&FL 92, WhoCanL 92
Hughes, Monica (Ince) 1925- MajAI [port], SmATA 70 [port]
Hughes, N.H. WhoScE 91-1
Hughes, Neville Anthony 1939- St&PR 93
Hughes, Nicholas David 1945- St&PR 93
Hughes, Norah Ann O'Brien 1948- WhoAm 92, WhoAmW 93
Hughes, Owain Arwel 1942- Baker 92
Hughes, Patricia Saddler 1931- WhoWrEP 92
Hughes, Patrick H. 1942- St&PR 93
Hughes, Patrick Henry 1942- WhoIns 93
Hughes, Paul Cecil 1946- WhoEmL 93, WhoSSW 93
Hughes, Paul Craig 1921- St&PR 93
Hughes, Paula Guilfoyle 1955- WhoEmL 93
Hughes, Peter James 1933- WhoAm 92
Hughes, Peter M. 1952- WhoE 93
Hughes, Peter Tuesday ScF&FL 92
Hughes, Peter William 1947- WhoE 93
Hughes, Philip WhoScE 91-1
Hughes, Philip C. 1940- St&PR 93
Hughes, Phillip Samuel 1917- WhoAm 92
Hughes, Ralph Lyle 1924- St&PR 93
Hughes, Ray Harrison 1924- WhoAm 92
Hughes, Raymond Hargett 1927- WhoSSW 93
Hughes, Raymond John 1956- St&PR 93
Hughes, Reuben Paul d1990 BioIn 17
Hughes, Richard 1937- St&PR 93
Hughes, Richard Anthony Cranmer WhoScE 91-1
Hughes, Richard Arthur Warren 1900-1976 BioIn 17
Hughes, Richard Glynne 1955- WhoWrEP 92
Hughes, Richard J. 1909-1992 NewYTBS 92 [port]
Hughes, Richard T. Law&B 92
Hughes, Richard William 1933- St&PR 93
Hughes, Riley 1914-1981 ScF&FL 92
Hughes, Robert BioIn 17, ScF&FL 92
Hughes, Robert 1767-1829 BioIn 17
Hughes, Robert A. Law&B 92
Hughes, Robert C. MiSFD 9
Hughes, Robert Davis, III 1943- WhoSSW 93
Hughes, Robert Don 1949- ScF&FL 92
Hughes, Robert Edward 1924- WhoAm 92
Hughes, Robert Edwin 1931- WhoAm 92
Hughes, Robert Harrison 1917- WhoAm 92
Hughes, Robert John 1946- WhoAm 92
Hughes, Robert N. 1938- WhoIns 93
Hughes, Robert Powell 1940- WhoIns 93
Hughes, Robert Studley Forrest 1938- WhoAm 92
Hughes, Robert Watson 1912- Baker 92
Hughes, Robert Wayne 1942- WhoSSW 93
Hughes, Robert William 1935- St&PR 93
Hughes, Roger K. WhoAm 92
Hughes, Roger Neville WhoScE 91-1
Hughes, Rupert 1872-1956 Baker 92
Hughes, Ryan James 1979- BioIn 17
Hughes, Sally Page WhoE 93
Hughes, Sara ScF&FL 92
Hughes, Sarah Gillette 1947- WhoEmL 93
Hughes, Sarah Shaver 1933- WhoE 93
Hughes, Sean Patrick Francis WhoScE 91-1
Hughes, Sean Patrick Francis 1941- WhoWor 93
Hughes, Sharon Ann 1958- WhoAmW 93
Hughes, Sharon Mary 1952- WhoE 93
Hughes, Shelia Elizabeth Ann 1965- WhoSSW 93
Hughes, Shirley BioIn 17
Hughes, Shirley 1927- MajAI [port], SmATA 70 [port]
Hughes, Shirley 1929- ChlFicS
Hughes, Stanley John 1918- WhoAm 92
Hughes, Steve WhoScE 91-1
Hughes, Steven Jay 1948- WhoEmL 93, WhoSSW 93
Hughes, Steven William 1952- St&PR 93
Hughes, Sue Margaret WhoAm 92, WhoAmW 93, WhoSSW 93, WhoWor 93
Hughes, Susan Kay Tauscher 1962- WhoWor 93
Hughes, Susan Kutscher 1946- WhoSSW 93, WhoWrEP 92
Hughes, Ted 1930- BioIn 17, ChlFicS, MagSWL [port], MajAI [port], ScF&FL 92, WhoAm 92, WhoWor 93
Hughes, Ted Warrington 1934- St&PR 93
Hughes, Teresa P. AfrAmBi [port]
Hughes, Terry MiSFD 9
Hughes, Theodore E(rmond) 1942- ConAu 40NR
Hughes, Thomas A. Law&B 92
Hughes, Thomas Allen 1955- WhoE 93
Hughes, Thomas H. 1929- St&PR 93, WhoAm 92
Hughes, Thomas J. 1911-1991 BioIn 17
Hughes, Thomas Joseph 1926- WhoAm 92
Hughes, Thomas Joseph 1943- WhoAm 92
Hughes, Thomas Leland 1924- WhoWor 93
Hughes, Thomas Lowe 1925- WhoAm 92
Hughes, Thomas Parke 1923- WhoAm 92
Hughes, Thomas R. 1944- St&PR 93
Hughes, Tracy WhoWrEP 92
Hughes, Travis Hubert 1937- WhoSSW 93
Hughes, Vester Thomas, Jr. 1928- WhoAm 92, WhoWor 93
Hughes, Vincent George 1958- St&PR 93
Hughes, Virginia Marie 1954- WhoAmW 93
Hughes, Walter Jay, Sr. 1942- WhoWrEP 92
Hughes, Walter Jones 1941- WhoAm 92
Hughes, Walter L. ScF&FL 92
Hughes, Walter Thompson 1930- WhoAm 92
Hughes, Waunell McDonald 1928- WhoAmW 93
Hughes, Wiley R. 1940- St&PR 93
Hughes, William Law&B 92, ScF&FL 92
Hughes, William Alan 1952- St&PR 93
Hughes, William Anthony 1921- WhoAm 92, WhoSSW 93
Hughes, William Cofer 1936- St&PR 93
Hughes, William Drennan 1928- St&PR 93
Hughes, William Frank 1930- WhoAm 92
Hughes, William Franklin, Jr. 1913- WhoAm 92
Hughes, William J. 1932- CngDr 91
Hughes, William J. 1951- St&PR 93
Hughes, William John 1932- WhoAm 92, WhoE 93
Hughes, William Joseph 1953- WhoSSW 93
Hughes, William Lesley 1924- St&PR 93
Hughes, William Lewis 1926- WhoAm 92
Hughes, William Morris 1864-1952 DcTwHis
Hughes, William Silent d1990 BioIn 17
Hughes, William Taylor 1936- WhoAm 92
Hughes, William Thomas 1940- WhoE 93
Hughes, Winifred Shirley 1927- WhoAm 92
Hughes, Woody 1956- BioIn 17
Hughes, Zach 1928- ScF&FL 92
Hughes-Calero, Heather 1938- WhoWrEP 92
Hughes-Fulford, Millie 1945- WhoAmW 93
Hughes Hallett, Andrew WhoScE 91-1
Hughes-Hallett, Lucy 1951- ConAu 138

Hughes-Stanton, Blair 1902-1981 *BioIn 17*
Hughett, John Paul 1946- *WhoEmL 93, WhoSSW 93*
Hughey, Bill G. 1935- *St&PR 93*
Hughey, Don W. 1941- *St&PR 93*
Hughey, Eric Joseph 1950- *WhoEmL 93*
Hughey, Jane Bond 1935- *WhoSSW 93*
Hughey, Jo A. 1966- *WhoWrEP 92*
Hughey, Michele Annette 1956- *WhoAmW 93*
Hughey, Roberta 1942- *BioIn 17*
Hughey, Susan Sparks *Law&B 92*
Hughitt, Jeremiah Keefe 1930- *WhoAm 92*
Hugh of Vermandois d1101 *OxDcByz*
Hughs, Mary Geraldine 1929- *WhoAmW 93*
Hughs, Richard Earl 1936- *WhoAm 92, WhoE 93*
Hughs, Robert Nathaniel 1917- *WhoAm 92*
Hughston, Boots Rolf 1948- *WhoEmL 93*
Hughston, Jess 1923- *WhoAm 92*
Hugi, Maurice Gaspard 1904-1947 *ScF&FL 92*
Hugin, Adolph Charles Eugene 1907- *WhoAm 92, WhoSSW 93, WhoWor 93*
Hugo, Frank Trimble 1927- *WhoE 93*
Hugo, John Adam 1873-1945 *Baker 92*
Hugo, Norman Eliot 1933- *WhoAm 92*
Hugo, Victor 1802-1885 *BioIn 17, MagSWL [port], OxDcOp, WorLitC [port]*
Hugo, Victor (Marie) 1802-1885 *DcLB 119 [port]*
Hugo & Luigi *SoulM*
Hugon, Georges 1904-1980 *Baker 92*
Hugon, Marilyn Maurer 1955- *WhoAmW 93*
Hugoson, Goran H. 1933- *WhoScE 91-4*
Hugot-Le Goff, Anne J. 1939- *WhoScE 91-2*
Hugo-Vidal, Ross Alexander *Law&B 92*
Hugstad, Paul Steven 1943- *WhoAm 92*
Hugue, Manuel Martinez 1876-1945 *BioIn 17*
Huguenin, G. Richard 1937- *St&PR 93*
Huguenin, George Richard 1937- *WhoE 93*
Hugues, Francois-Claude 1936- *WhoScE 91-2*
Huguet, Jean Gerard 1939- *WhoScE 91-2*
Huguet, Louis 1920- *WhoScE 91-2*
Huguier, Michel Alphonse 1937- *WhoWor 93*
Huguley, Arthur Whitfield, III 1933- *St&PR 93*
Hugus, Z. Zimmerman, Jr. 1923- *WhoAm 92, WhoSSW 93*
Huh, Oscar Karl 1935- *WhoSSW 93*
Huh Kyung Man 1939- *WhoAsAP 91*
Huh Man Ki 1931- *WhoAsAP 91*
Huhmann, Paula M. 1934- *St&PR 93*
Huhmann, William Joseph 1938- *St&PR 93*
Huhn, Al H. 1938- *St&PR 93*
Huhn, Bruno 1871-1950 *Baker 92*
Huhn, Gary R. 1949- *St&PR 93*
Huhn, Stephen T. *Law&B 92*
Huhn, William D. *Law&B 92*
Huhnermann, Harry 1938- *WhoScE 91-3*
Huhta, James Kenneth 1937- *WhoAm 92, WhoSSW 93, WhoWor 93*
Huhta, Richard S. 1931- *WhoWrEP 92*
Huhtanen, Wayne H. 1954- *St&PR 93*
Huhtaniemi, Jukka Ilmari 1955- *WhoWor 93*
Huhtikangas, Aarre Erkki 1938- *WhoScE 91-4*
Hui, Ann 1947- *MiSFD 9*
Hui, Jacques A. 1933- *WhoWor 93*
Hui, Koon-Sea 1948- *WhoE 93*
Hui, Louis 1953- *WhoWor 93*
Hui, Steve L.W. 1949- *St&PR 93*
Huidekoper, Catherine Kruchen *Law&B 92*
Huidobro, Vicente 1893-1948 *SpAmA*
Huie, Robert Edwin 1929- *St&PR 93*
Huie, William Orr 1911- *WhoAm 92*
Huige, John D. *Law&B 92*
Huignard, Jacques 1938- *WhoScE 91-2*
Huijer Abu-Saad, Huda 1949- *WhoScE 91-3*
Huillet, Daniele *MiSFD 9*
Huins, John Michael Mantle 1937- *WhoUN 92*
Huisinga, Alan D. 1945- *WhoIns 93*
Huis In 'T Veld, Jos H.J. 1943- *WhoScE 91-3*
Huiskes, Adrianus H.L. 1947- *WhoScE 91-3*
Huiskes, Hendrik W.J. Rik 1944- *WhoWor 93*
Huisman, Elbertus Abraham 1943- *WhoScE 91-3*
Huisman, J.G. *WhoScE 91-3*
Huisman, Titus Hendrik Jan 1923- *WhoAm 92*
Huismans, Jan Willem 1934- *WhoUN 92*
Huitt, Jimmie L. 1923- *WhoAm 92*
Hui Yin-Fat, Hon 1936- *WhoAsAP 91*
Huizar (Garcia de la Cadena), Candelario 1883-1970 *Baker 92*
Huizenga, H. Wayne *BioIn 17*
Huizenga, H. Wayne 1937- *ConEn, St&PR 93*
Huizenga, Harry Wayne 1937- *WhoAm 92*
Huizenga, Harry Wayne 1939- *WhoSSW 93*
Huizenga, John Robert 1921- *WhoAm 92*
Huizenga, Karen *Law&B 92*
Huizenga, Robert *BioIn 17*
Huizenga, Wayne c. 1938- *News 92 [port]*
Huizing, Egbert Hendrik 1932- *WhoScE 91-3*
Huizingh, William 1919- *WhoAm 92*
Hujar, Randal Joseph 1959- *WhoE 93*
Hu Jintao 1943- *WhoAsAP 91*
Hujsak, Ruth Joy 1924- *WhoAmW 93*
Hujubregts, A.W.M. 1952- *WhoScE 91-3*
Huk, William J. 1943- *St&PR 93*
Hukill, Beth Ann 1962- *WhoEmL 93*
Hukill, Peter Biggs 1927- *WhoE 93*
Hukovic, Seid 1925- *WhoScE 91-4*
Hulanicka, Maria Danuta 1929- *WhoScE 91-4*
Hulanicki, Adam A. 1929- *WhoScE 91-4*
Hulanicki, Slawomir 1938- *WhoScE 91-4*
Hulatt, J. *WhoScE 91-1*
Hulbert, Ann 1956- *ConAu 138*
Hulbert, Bruce Walker 1937- *WhoAm 92*
Hulbert, Claude 1900-1964 *QDrFCA 92 [port]*
Hulbert, Deborah Ann *Law&B 92*
Hulbert, Jack 1892-1978 *QDrFCA 92 [port]*
Hulbert, Mary Frances 1942- *WhoAmW 93*
Hulbert, Phillip Phillip 1962- *WhoE 93*
Hulbert, Richard Woodward 1929- *WhoAm 92*
Hulbert, Samuel Foster 1936- *WhoAm 92*
Hulbert, William Ambrose 1832-1882 *BioIn 17*
Hulce, Tom 1953- *WhoAm 92*
Hulcher, Deanne Marie 1961- *WhoAmW 93*
Huldt, S. Lennart 1918- *WhoScE 91-4*
Hulegu 1217?-1265 *BioIn 17*
Hulen, James R. *Law&B 92*
Hulen, James Rozier 1933- *St&PR 93*
Hulet, Ervin Kenneth 1926- *WhoAm 92*
Hulett, Barbara June 1933- *WhoAmW 93*
Hulett, Nora Jane 1952- *WhoAmW 93*
Hulett, William *BioIn 17*
Hulette, Donald 1937- *MiSFD 9*
Hulick, Charles Henry 1943- *WhoSSW 93*
Hulick, Marjorie *AmWomPl*
Hulick, Timothy P. 1942- *St&PR 93*
Hulin, Colin Joseph 1958- *St&PR 93*
Huling, Kendell Faye 1965- *WhoAmW 93*
Hulings, A. D. 1913- *WhoAm 92*
Hulings, Henry B. 1937- *St&PR 93*
Hulings, Norman McDermott, Jr. 1923- *WhoAm 92*
Hu Lin-i 1812-1861 *HarEnMi*
Hulitar, Philip d1992 *NewYTBS 92*
Hulka, Barbara Sorenson 1931- *WhoAm 92, WhoAmW 93, WhoSSW 93*
Hulka, Jaroslav Fabian 1930- *WhoAm 92*
Hulke, Malcolm 1924-1979 *ScF&FL 92*
Hulkko, Jouko Antero 1937- *WhoWor 93*
Hulkower, Neal David 1949- *WhoEmL 93*
Hull, Amy Gayle 1967- *St&PR 93*
Hull, Anne 1888-1984 *Baker 92*
Hull, Arthur Eaglefield 1876-1928 *Baker 92*
Hull, Bobby 1939- *WhoAm 92*
Hull, Brett *BioIn 17*
Hull, Brett 1964- *CurBio 92 [port], WhoAm 92*
Hull, Cathy 1946- *WhoAm 92*
Hull, Charles Eugene 1944- *St&PR 93*
Hull, Charles William 1936- *WhoAm 92, WhoWor 93*
Hull, Christopher James *WhoScE 91-1*
Hull, Cordell *DcCPCAm*
Hull, Cordell 1871-1955 *BioIn 17, DcTwHis, PolPar*
Hull, Cordell William 1933- *WhoAm 92, WhoWor 93*
Hull, Dallas Carl 1949- *WhoE 93*
Hull, David George 1937- *WhoAm 92*
Hull, David P. 1935- *St&PR 93*
Hull, David Stewart 1938- *WhoE 93*
Hull, Derek *WhoScE 91-1*
Hull, Diana Helen *Law&B 92*
Hull, Don *Law&B 92*
Hull, Donald R. *St&PR 93*
Hull, Earl J. 1933- *St&PR 93*
Hull, Edward Whaley Seabrook 1923- *WhoSSW 93*
Hull, Elaine Mangelsdorf 1940- *WhoAmW 93*
Hull, Elizabeth Anne 1937- *ScF&FL 92*
Hull, Eugene R. 1933- *St&PR 93*
Hull, Fred T. 1937- *St&PR 93*
Hull, Harold Eugene 1932- *WhoSSW 93*
Hull, Harry Herschel 1911- *WhoSSW 93*
Hull, Helen Rose 1888-1971 *AmWomPl*
Hull, Henrietta Goodnough 1889-1967 *BioIn 17*
Hull, Herbert Mitchell 1919- *WhoAm 92*
Hull, Ida Mary Butler 1948- *WhoAmW 93*
Hull, Isaac 1773-1843 *HarEnMi*
Hull, J. Richard *Law&B 92*
Hull, J. Richard 1933- *St&PR 93*
Hull, J. Webster 1943- *St&PR 93*
Hull, James C. 1937- *St&PR 93*
Hull, James Charles 1937- *WhoAm 92*
Hull, James Clark 1945- *WhoE 93*
Hull, James K. 1928- *St&PR 93*
Hull, James Richard 1933- *WhoAm 92*
Hull, Jane Laurel Leek 1923- *WhoAmW 93*
Hull, John Daniel, IV 1953- *WhoEmL 93*
Hull, John Doster 1924- *WhoSSW 93*
Hull, John E. 1946- *St&PR 93*
Hull, John Laurence 1924- *St&PR 93*
Hull, John M. *BioIn 17*
Hull, John M. 1935- *ConAu 137*
Hull, John T., Jr. 1944- *St&PR 93*
Hull, John Thomas, Jr. 1944- *WhoAm 92*
Hull, Joseph Daniel 1948- *WhoSSW 93*
Hull, Karen Palma *Law&B 92*
Hull, Ken *BioIn 17*
Hull, Kenneth J. 1936- *St&PR 93*
Hull, Kenneth James 1936- *WhoAm 92*
Hull, Kent 1961- *WhoAm 92*
Hull, Lewis Woodruff 1916- *St&PR 93, WhoAm 92, WhoWor 93*
Hull, Linda Lee Schick 1946- *WhoAmW 93*
Hull, Louise Knox 1912- *WhoAmW 93*
Hull, M. Elizabeth C. *WhoScE 91-1*
Hull, Margaret Ruth 1921- *WhoAmW 93, WhoSSW 93*
Hull, McAllister Hobart, Jr. 1923- *WhoAm 92*
Hull, Michael B. *Law&B 92*
Hull, Norman J., Jr. 1918- *St&PR 93*
Hull, Paul G. 1940- *St&PR 93*
Hull, Peggy 1889-1967 *BioIn 17*
Hull, Peggy Fiess 1950- *WhoAmW 93*
Hull, Philip Glasgow 1925- *WhoAm 92, WhoE 93, WhoWor 93*
Hull, Piatt Harold 1914- *St&PR 93*
Hull, Raymond Whitford 1946- *WhoE 93*
Hull, Richard F. 1931- *WhoIns 93*
Hull, Rita Prizler 1936- *WhoAmW 93*
Hull, Robert Fulton 1943- *WhoSSW 93*
Hull, Robert Glenn 1929- *WhoAm 92*
Hull, Robert Kingsley 1951- *WhoEmL 93*
Hull, Roger *WhoScE 91-1*
Hull, Roger Harold 1942- *WhoAm 92, WhoE 93*
Hull, Sally Diane 1960- *WhoWor 93*
Hull, Suzanne White 1921- *WhoAm 92, WhoAmW 93*
Hull, Thomas Gray 1926- *WhoSSW 93*
Hull, Treat Clark 1921- *WhoAm 92*
Hull, W. Edward *Law&B 92*
Hull, Warren K. 1943- *St&PR 93*
Hull, Wesley Vannoy 1937- *WhoAm 92*
Hull, William Edward 1930- *WhoAm 92, WhoSSW 93*
Hull, William Floyd, Jr. 1920- *WhoAm 92*
Hull, William Henry 1918- *WhoAm 92*
Hull, William Martin, Jr. 1937- *WhoSSW 93*
Hullaby, Brenda Elizabeth 1955- *WhoAmW 93*
Hullah, John 1812-1884 *OxDcOp*
Hullah, John (Pyke) 1812-1884 *Baker 92*
Hullar, Leonard E. *ScF&FL 92*
Hullar, Link 1954- *ScF&FL 92*
Hullar, Theodore Lee 1935- *WhoAm 92, WhoWor 93*
Hullay, Joseph 1921- *WhoScE 91-4*
Hullemann, Klaus-Diethart 1938- *WhoWor 93*
Huller, Mark J. *Law&B 92*
Hullin, Tod R. 1943- *St&PR 93*
Hullin, Tod Robert 1943- *WhoAm 92*
Hull-Itkin, Nicole Karol 1964- *WhoAmW 93, WhoEmL 93*
Hullmandel, Nicolas-Joseph 1756-1823 *Baker 92*
Hullum, Anita Ruth 1925- *WhoSSW 93*
Hulme, Darlys Mae 1937- *WhoAmW 93*
Hulme, Denny *BioIn 17*
Hulme, Keri *BioIn 17*
Hulme, Keri 1947- *IntLitE, WhoWor 93*
Hulme, Patrick James 1944- *St&PR 93*
Hulme, Roy Allan 1954- *WhoEmL 93*
Huls, Harrison 1923- *WhoAm 92*
Hulse, Dale Edward *Law&B 92*
Hulse, Dexter Curtis 1952- *WhoEmL 93, WhoWor 93*
Hulse, Frank W. d1992 *NewYTBS 92*
Hulse, Frederick S. 1906-1990 *BioIn 17*
Hulse, George Althouse 1934- *WhoAm 92*
Hulse, James W. *Law&B 92*
Hulse, James William 1935- *St&PR 93*
Hulse, Jerry 1924- *WhoAm 92*
Hulse, Jesse Gifford 1955- *WhoEmL 93*
Hulse, Mary Jean 1935- *WhoAmW 93*
Hulse, Paul Stephen *St&PR 93*
Hulse, Richard E. 1931- *St&PR 93*
Hulse, Robert Douglas 1943- *WhoE 93, WhoWor 93*
Hulse, Stewart Harding, Jr. 1931- *WhoAm 92*
Hulsebosch, Charles Joseph 1933- *WhoAm 92*
Hulselmans, Jan L.J. 1937- *WhoScE 91-2*
Hulseman, Robert L. 1932- *WhoAm 92*
Hulsemann, Kuni 1927- *WhoScE 91-3*
Hulsey, Elizabeth Benbrook 1936- *WhoAmW 93*
Hulsey, John *BioIn 17*
Hulsey, Tammy Kaye 1961- *WhoAmW 93*
Hulsey, V. Michele *Law&B 92*
Hulslander, Richard T. 1937- *St&PR 93*
Hulst, John B. *WhoAm 92*
Hulstaert, Gustaaf 1900-1990 *IntDcAn*
Hulston, John K. 1915- *St&PR 93*
Hulston, John Kenton 1915- *WhoAm 92*
Hult, Jan A.H. 1927- *WhoScE 91-4*
Hult, Karen Marie 1956- *WhoEmL 93*
Hult, Matti Juhani 1933- *WhoScE 91-4*
Hultborn, Hans R.A. 1943- *WhoScE 91-2*
Hultgren, Dennis N. 1946- *St&PR 93*
Hultgren, Herbert Nils 1917- *WhoAm 92*
Hultgren, Warren Curtis 1920- *WhoAm 92*
Hultine, Carl J. 1947- *St&PR 93*
Hulting, Wayne Allan 1951- *St&PR 93*
Hultink, Albertus *Law&B 92*
Hultkrantz, Lars B. 1952- *WhoWor 93*
Hultman, Charles William 1930- *WhoAm 92*
Hultman, Eric H. 1925- *WhoScE 91-4*
Hultman, Evan Leroy 1925- *WhoAm 92*
Hulton, Leslie James *WhoScE 91-1*
Hultquist, Joshua Keith 1932- *St&PR 93*
Hultquist, Larry M. *Law&B 92*
Hultquist, Paul Fredrick 1920- *WhoAm 92*
Hultquist, Timothy Allen 1950- *WhoAm 92*
Hultqvist, Bengt Karl Gustaf 1927- *WhoScE 91-4*
Hultstrand, Donald Maynard 1927- *WhoAm 92*
Humaid ibn Rashid Al-Nuami, Sheikh 1930- *WhoWor 93*
Human, Mel 1954- *WhoEmL 93*
Humann, L. Phillip *WhoAm 92*
Humann, Walter Johann 1937- *WhoAm 92*
Humason, Sarah Waters Monroe *AmWomPl*
Humayun 1508-1556 *HarEnMi*
Humbel, Rene E. 1930- *WhoScE 91-4*
Humber, Richard Alan 1947- *WhoE 93*
Humberstone, H. Bruce 1903-1984 *BioIn 17*
Humberstone, H. Bruce (Lucky) 1903-1984 *MiSFD 9N*
Humbert c. 1000-1061 *OxDcByz*
Humbert, Georges 1870-1936 *Baker 92*
Humbert, James Ronald 1938- *WhoAm 92, WhoSSW 93*
Humbertson, Lisa Lou 1959- *WhoAmW 93*
Humble, Joseph Elgin 1953- *WhoEmL 93, WhoSSW 93*
Humble, (Leslie) Keith 1927- *Baker 92*
Humble, Richard 1945- *BioIn 17*
Humble, Roberta Mudge 1946- *WhoE 93*
Humboldt, Alexander, Freiherr von 1769-1859 *BioIn 17*
Humboldt, Alexander von 1769-1859 *Expl 93 [port], IntDcAn*
Humboldt, Friedrich Wilhelm Heinrich Alexander 1769-1859 *BioIn 17*
Humboldt, Karl Wilhelm von 1767-1835 *IntDcAn*
Humboldt, Wilhelm, Freiherr von 1767-1835 *BioIn 17*
Humbracht, Loyal Charles 1925- *St&PR 93*
Humburg, William Richard *Law&B 92*
Hume, Alexander Hamilton 1797-1873 *Expl 93*
Hume, David 1711-1776 *BioIn 17*
Hume, David Cady 1919- *St&PR 93*
Hume, David G. *Law&B 92*
Hume, Edward *MiSFD 9*
Hume, Ernest Harding 1924- *WhoAm 92*
Hume, F. *Law&B 92*
Hume, Fergus 1859-1932 *ScF&FL 92*
Hume, Frederick Raymond 1943- *WhoAm 92*
Hume, Horace Delbert 1898- *WhoWor 93*
Hume, Ivor Noel 1927- *BioIn 17*
Hume, James Borden 1950- *WhoAm 92*
Hume, Jaquelin Holliday d1991 *BioIn 17*
Hume, John L. 1939- *St&PR 93*
Hume, Kathryn 1945- *ScF&FL 92*
Hume, Michael H. 1955- *St&PR 93*

Hume, Paul (Chandler) 1915- Baker 92, WhoAm 92
Hume, Robert Alan 1936- WhoAm 92
Hume, Stephen 1947- WhoAm 92
Hume, Susan Rachel 1952- WhoEmL 93
Hume, William John WhoScE 91-1
Humel, Gerald 1931- Baker 92
Humenesky, Gregory 1951- St&PR 93, WhoAm 92
Humer, Philip Wilson 1932- WhoE 93
Humes, David Walker 1954- WhoEmL 93, WhoSSW 93
Humes, Edward WhoAm 92
Humes, Graham 1932- St&PR 93, WhoAm 92
Humes, Harold Louis d1992 NewYTBS 92
Humes, Helen 1913-1981 Baker 92, BioIn 17
Humes, James C. 1934- ScF&FL 92
Humes, James Calhoun 1934- WhoAm 92, WhoWor 93
Humes, John W., Jr. Law&B 92
Humes, Robert Ernest 1943- WhoAm 92, WhoE 93
Humes, Samuel, IV 1930- WhoWor 93
Humfrey, Pelham 1647-1674 Baker 92
Humi, Mayer 1944- WhoE 93
Humick, Thomas Charles Campbell 1947- WhoEmL 93
Humiston, Ronald Squier 1944- St&PR 93
Humke, Ramon L. 1932- St&PR 93, WhoAm 92
Huml, Donald Scott 1946- St&PR 93, WhoAm 92
Huml, Pavel 1937- WhoScE 91-4
Humlum, Ole 1949- WhoScE 91-2
Humm, Bernard 1936- WhoUN 92
Hummel, Andries 1936- WhoScE 91-3
Hummel, Berta 1909-1946 BioIn 17
Hummel, Carl William 1929- St&PR 93
Hummel, Charles Frederick 1932- WhoAm 92
Hummel, Dana D. Mallett WhoAmW 93
Hummel, Daryl G. 1948- St&PR 93
Hummel, Don W. 1933- St&PR 93
Hummel, Dorothy Kaye 1944- WhoAmW 93
Hummel, Ferdinand 1855-1928 Baker 92
Hummel, Franklin 1953- WhoE 93
Hummel, Fred Ernest 1927- WhoAm 92
Hummel, Gene Maywood 1926- WhoAm 92
Hummel, Herman 1953- WhoScE 91-3
Hummel, Jack L. Law&B 92
Hummel, Jacqueline Marie 1964- WhoAmW 93
Hummel, James Arthur 1942- St&PR 93
Hummel, Johann Nepomuk 1778-1837 Baker 92, OxDcOp
Hummel, Joseph OxDcOp
Hummel, Kay Jean 1943- WhoSSW 93
Hummel, Kermit 1954- St&PR 93
Hummel, Konrad 1923- WhoScE 91-3
Hummel, Margaret AmWomPl
Hummel, Marilyn Mae 1931- WhoAmW 93
Hummel, Mary Innocentia 1909-1946 BioIn 17
Hummel, Michael John 1949- St&PR 93
Hummel, Rita Cecile 1951- WhoSSW 93
Hummel, Robert Jensen 1935- St&PR 93
Hummel, Robert Paul 1928- WhoAm 92
Hummel, Rolf Erich 1934- WhoSSW 93
Hummel, Susan BioIn 17
Hummell, Burton Howard 1932- St&PR 93, WhoAm 92, WhoSSW 93
Hummell, Ross Bennett 1957- St&PR 93
Hummer, Paul F. 1941- St&PR 93
Hummer, Paul F., II 1941- WhoAm 92
Hummer, Paul Jacob, Jr. 1932- WhoWrEP 92
Hummer, T(erry) R. 1950- DcLB 120 [port]
Hummer, Thomas Michael 1942- St&PR 93
Hummer, William B. 1924- St&PR 93
Hummer-Miller, Susanne 1947- WhoEmL 93
Hummler, Richard J. d1990 BioIn 17
Humperdinck, Engelbert 1854-1921 Baker 92, IntDcOp [port], OxDcOp
Humperdinck, Engelbert 1936- Baker 92, WhoAm 92
Humperdinck, Wolfram 1893-1985 OxDcOp
Humpert, Hans 1901-1943 Baker 92
Humpert, John E. 1962- WhoWrEP 92
Humpf, Gregory Joseph 1939- St&PR 93
Humphrey, Alexander P., IV Law&B 92
Humphrey, Ann Gordon 1965- St&PR 93
Humphrey, Arthur Earl 1927- WhoAm 92
Humphrey, Carletta Sue 1954- WhoAmW 93
Humphrey, Charles Durham 1943- WhoAm 92
Humphrey, Charles Edward, Jr. 1943- WhoAm 92
Humphrey, Chester Bowden 1939- WhoE 93
Humphrey, Dennis Dewayne 1958- WhoWrEP 92
Humphrey, Donna Claire 1962- WhoEmL 93
Humphrey, Doris 1895-1958 BioIn 17
Humphrey, Edward William 1926- WhoAm 92
Humphrey, Edwin Lowell 1920- WhoWrEP 92
Humphrey, Faye L. 1939- St&PR 93
Humphrey, George Bennett 1934- WhoWor 93
Humphrey, George Edward 1949- WhoE 93
Humphrey, George Magoffin, II 1942- St&PR 93, WhoAm 92
Humphrey, Gwen 1934- WhoSSW 93
Humphrey, Howard Clark WhoIns 93
Humphrey, Hubert H. 1911-1978 ColdWar 1 [port], DcTwHis, PolPar
Humphrey, Hubert Horatio 1911-1978 BioIn 17, EncAACR [port]
Humphrey, Hubert Horatio, III 1942- WhoAm 92
Humphrey, J. Steven 1951- WhoEmL 93
Humphrey, James 1939- WhoE 93
Humphrey, Jayne Hulbert 1947- WhoAmW 93
Humphrey, John Julius 1926- WhoWor 93
Humphrey, John William 1937- St&PR 93
Humphrey, Judy Lucille 1949- WhoEmL 93, WhoSSW 93
Humphrey, Karen Michael 1945- WhoAm 92, WhoAmW 93
Humphrey, Lawrence Taylor 1962- WhoSSW 93
Humphrey, Louise Ireland 1918- WhoAmW 93, WhoWor 93
Humphrey, Lyman Underwood 1844-1915 BioIn 17
Humphrey, Margo 1942- BlkAuII 92
Humphrey, Maud(e) 1868- AmWomPl
Humphrey, Muriel BioIn 17
Humphrey, Neil Darwin 1928- WhoAm 92
Humphrey, Otis Dean 1942- WhoSSW 93
Humphrey, Paul 1915- WhoWrEP 92
Humphrey, Paul 1960- WhoWor 93
Humphrey, Paul Elmo 1913- St&PR 93
Humphrey, Philip Strong 1926- WhoAm 92
Humphrey, Ralph 1932-1990 BioIn 17
Humphrey, Robert 1903-1991 BioIn 17
Humphrey, Robert C. 1918- St&PR 93
Humphrey, Robert L. Law&B 92
Humphrey, Roger Cleveland 1940- St&PR 93
Humphrey, Ronald D. 1938- WhoSSW 93
Humphrey, Rosalie Anne 1947- WhoE 93
Humphrey, Roy A. BioIn 17
Humphrey, Samuel Stockwell 1923- WhoE 93
Humphrey, Shirley Joy 1937- WhoAmW 93
Humphrey, Thomas M. 1935- St&PR 93
Humphrey, Twyla Sharise 1961- WhoAmW 93
Humphrey, Watts Sherman 1927- WhoAm 92
Humphrey, William Albert 1927- St&PR 93, WhoAm 92
Humphrey, William Roland 1917- WhoE 93
Humphreys, Andrew Atkinson 1810-1883 HarEnMi
Humphreys, Benjamin Charles 1934- WhoAsAP 91
Humphreys, Charles E. 1952- St&PR 93
Humphreys, Colin John WhoScE 91-1
Humphreys, David Anderson 1956- WhoWor 93
Humphreys, David John 1936- WhoAm 92
Humphreys, Donald Lewis Law&B 92
Humphreys, Donald Robert 1923- WhoAm 92
Humphreys, E. WhoScE 91-1
Humphreys, Frank Jardine, II 1953- WhoSSW 93
Humphreys, Fred C. 1923- St&PR 93
Humphreys, Frederick John WhoScE 91-1
Humphreys, George G(ary) 1949- ConAu 138
Humphreys, Homer Alexander 1902- WhoSSW 93
Humphreys, J.R. 1918- ScF&FL 92
Humphreys, James W. 1915- WhoAm 92
Humphreys, John 1960- St&PR 93
Humphreys, John Richard Adams 1918- WhoWrEP 92
Humphreys, Josephine BioIn 17
Humphreys, Josephine 1945- WhoAm 92
Humphreys, Kenneth Jerome 1944- St&PR 93
Humphreys, Kenneth King 1938- WhoAm 92
Humphreys, Laud 1930-1988 BioIn 17
Humphreys, Leonard Ross 1927- WhoWor 93
Humphreys, Lloyd Girton 1913- WhoAm 92
Humphreys, Martha 1943- SmATA 71 [port]
Humphreys, Michael Edward 1953- WhoEmL 93, WhoSSW 93
Humphreys, Robert, Jr. 1932- WhoIns 93
Humphreys, Robert Edward 1942- WhoE 93
Humphreys, Robert Russell 1938- WhoAm 92
Humphreys, Robert T.C., Jr. 1932- St&PR 93
Humphreys, Roberta Marie 1944- WhoAmW 93
Humphreys, Trevor L. 1937- St&PR 93
Humphreys, Wayne BioIn 17
Humphries, Asa Alan, Jr. 1924- WhoSSW 93
Humphries, Barry BioIn 17
Humphries, Barry 1934- News 93-1 [port]
Humphries, Betty Bowers 1952- WhoAmW 93
Humphries, Beverly Nell 1930- WhoAm 92
Humphries, Bruce B. 1954- St&PR 93
Humphries, Charlotte Anne 1955- WhoAmW 93
Humphries, D. Keith 1943- St&PR 93
Humphries, Diane Mizerek 1963- WhoEmL 93
Humphries, Edward Francis 1957- WhoEmL 93
Humphries, Ervin Grigg 1936- WhoSSW 93
Humphries, Frederick S. 1935- WhoSSW 93
Humphries, Harold Lee 1931- St&PR 93
Humphries, Jefferson 1955- ScF&FL 92
Humphries, Joan Ropes 1928- WhoAmW 93, WhoSSW 93, WhoWor 93
Humphries, John O'Neal 1931- WhoAm 92
Humphries, Judy Lynn 1946- WhoEmL 93, WhoWor 93
Humphries, M. Clayton, Jr. Law&B 92
Humphries, Michael William 1940- St&PR 93
Humphries, P.J. 1955- St&PR 93
Humphries, Robert Lee, Jr. 1930- WhoSSW 93
Humphries, Rolfe 1894-1969 BioIn 17
Humphries, Steven Eugene 1952- WhoSSW 93
Humphries, Thomas Joel 1945- WhoE 93
Humphries, Weldon R. 1937- St&PR 93, WhoAm 92
Humphry, Ann Wickett BioIn 17
Humphry, Derek 1930- BioIn 17
Humphry, Derek c. 1931- News 92 [port]
Humphry, Derek John 1930- WhoWor 93, WhoWrEP 92
Humphry, James, III 1916- WhoAm 92
Humphry, John A. 1916-1989 BioIn 17
Humphrys, Leslie G. ScF&FL 92
Humpstone, John H. d1991 BioIn 17
Humway, Ronald Jimmie 1945- WhoSSW 93
Hun, Sen BioIn 17
Hunault, Joan Burton 1950- WhoAmW 93
Huncke, Herbert 1915- BioIn 17
Hund, Robert Arthur 1927- WhoWrEP 92
Hundere, Myriam Goldsmith 1933- St&PR 93
Hundertmark, Thad R. 1929- St&PR 93
Hundertwasser, Friedensreich 1928- WhoWor 93
Hundley, Crystal L. 1953- WhoAmW 93
Hundley, Frank T. 1932- WhoAm 92
Hundley, Garry Wayne 1951- WhoE 93, WhoWor 93
Hundley, John W. 1899-1990 BioIn 17
Hundley, Norris Cecil, Jr. 1935- WhoAm 92
Hundman, Robert Louis 1935- WhoWrEP 92
Hundsalz, Mathias Georg 1943- WhoUN 92
Hundt, Paul R. Law&B 92
Hundt, Paul Robert 1939- St&PR 93, WhoAm 92
Huneeus Cox, Pablo 1940- WhoWor 93
Huneke, John George 1931- WhoE 93
Huneke, Wayne R. 1951- St&PR 93
Huneker, James 1857-1921 GayN
Huneker, James Gibbons 1857-1921 Baker 92
Huneycutt, Alice Ruth 1951- WhoAmW 93, WhoEmL 93
Huneycutt, D.J. Law&B 92
Hung, Frederick 1906-1988 BioIn 17
Hung, George Wen-Chi 1932- WhoSSW 93
Hung, Jackson Yau-Bong 1948- WhoWor 93
Hung, James Chen 1929- WhoAm 92
Hung, Nguyen Dang 1941- WhoWor 93
Hung, Raymond Kin Sang 1948- WhoWor 93
Hung, Ru J. 1934- WhoAm 92, WhoSSW 93
Hung, Samo 1952- MiSFD 9
Hung, Tin-Kan 1936- WhoAm 92
Hung, Yen-Wan 1944- WhoAmW 93
Hung Ch'eng-ch'ou 1593-1665 HarEnMi
Hunger, Jack Edward 1934- St&PR 93
Hunger, W. Kingsley 1945- St&PR 93
Hungerford, Bruce 1922-1977 Baker 92
Hungerford, Charles Michael Law&B 92
Hungerford, David S. 1938- WhoAm 92
Hungerford, Ed Vernon, III 1939- WhoAm 92
Hungerford, Gary A. 1948- WhoE 93, WhoEmL 93, WhoIns 93
Hungerford, Mark C. St&PR 93
Hungerford, Pixie MajAI
Hungerland, Jacklyn Erlin 1930- WhoAmW 93
Hung Hsiu-ch'uan 1814-1864 HarEnMi
Hung Ki Hoon 1954- WhoAsAP 91
Hungler, Charles E. 1936- St&PR 93
Hungry Wolf, Adolf 1944- ConAu 38NR
Hungry Wolf, Beverly 1950- ConAu 38NR
Hung Ta-ch'uan 1823-1852 HarEnMi
Huniford, James BioIn 17
Huni-Mihacsek, Felice 1891-1976 Baker 92
Huning, Allan Arthur 1938- St&PR 93
Huning, Deborah Gray 1950- WhoAm 92, WhoAmW 93
Hunkele, Denise Diane Law&B 92
Hunkele, Lester Martin, III 1947- WhoAm 92
Hunker, Paul B., Jr. Law&B 92
Hunker, T(racy) Allen 1957- WhoWrEP 92
Hunkin, Mary Louise 1950- WhoEmL 93
Hunkins, Francis Peter 1938- WhoAm 92
Hunkins, Melinda W. Law&B 92
Hunkins-Hallinan, Hazel 1890-1982 BioIn 17
Hunley, Burt H. Law&B 92
Hunley, Charles Laudie, Jr. 1920- WhoSSW 93
Hunn, Fredric A. 1938- St&PR 93
Hunn, John Newton 1946- WhoSSW 93
Hunnewell, Julie Desloge Haggerty d1992 NewYTBS 92
Hunnewell, Ruthann Baffo 1954- WhoAmW 93, WhoEmL 93
Hunnicutt, Ann Sproule 1930- WhoE 93
Hunnicutt, Richard P. 1926- St&PR 93
Hunningher, Benjamin 1903-1991 BioIn 17
Hunnings, Wardie Giles 1929- St&PR 93
Hunsaker, Charles R. Law&B 92
Hunsaker, Floyd B. 1915- WhoWor 93
Hunsaker, Richard E. 1948- St&PR 93
Hunsaker, Richard Kendall 1960- WhoEmL 93, WhoWor 93
Hunsberger, Charles Wesley 1929- WhoAm 92
Hunsberger, Ruby Moore 1913- WhoAmW 93
Hunsburger, Ed ScF&FL 92
Hun Sen 1951- WhoAsAP 91
Hunsicker, Jackson MiSFD 9
Hunsicker, Scott Alan 1955- WhoEmL 93
Hunsinger, B. Frank 1943- St&PR 93
Hunsinger, Doyle J. 1947- WhoE 93
Hunstad, Robert Edward 1940- St&PR 93, WhoAm 92, WhoIns 93
Hunsucker, David Grey 1963- WhoSSW 93
Hunsucker, Robert Dean 1925- St&PR 93
Hunt, Albert Barker 1910- St&PR 93, WhoAm 92
Hunt, Albert Charles 1927- WhoWor 93
Hunt, Albert R. 1942- JrnUS
Hunt, Alvis T. 1923- WhoAm 92
Hunt, Andrew 1955- WhoScE 91-1
Hunt, Annice Elizabeth 1934- WhoWrEP 92
Hunt, Barbara 1907-1984 ScF&FL 92
Hunt, Barbara R. Law&B 92
Hunt, Bernice 1920- WhoE 93
Hunt, Bernice (Kohn) 1920- WhoWrEP 92
Hunt, Bob 1948- St&PR 93
Hunt, Bobby Ray 1941- WhoAm 92
Hunt, Bruce 1958- WhoWor 93
Hunt, Bruce J. 1956- ConAu 136
Hunt, Bryan 1947- BioIn 17, WhoAm 92
Hunt, Carl G. 1912- St&PR 93
Hunt, Caroline BioIn 17
Hunt, Caroline Collins 1941- WhoSSW 93
Hunt, Cathy Delise 1956- WhoSSW 93
Hunt, Charles Bernard 1957- WhoE 93
Hunt, Charles Brownlow, Jr. 1916- WhoAm 92
Hunt, Charles Butler 1906- WhoAm 92
Hunt, Charles E. Law&B 92
Hunt, Charlotte 1915- ScF&FL 92
Hunt, Craig A. Law&B 92

Hunt, Daniel S. 1938- St&PR 93
Hunt, Dave 1926- ScF&FL 92
Hunt, David 1913- BioIn 17
Hunt, David 1942- WhoWor 93
Hunt, David C(urtis) 1935- ConAu 38NR
Hunt, David Ford 1931- WhoAm 92
Hunt, David Kenneth 1946- St&PR 93
Hunt, David N. 1948- WhoSSW 93
Hunt, Deborah Lee 1960- WhoWrEP 92
Hunt, Dennie S. 1942- St&PR 93
Hunt, Diana Dilger 1953- WhoE 93, WhoEmL 93
Hunt, Donald G. 1950- St&PR 93
Hunt, Donald R. 1921- WhoAm 92
Hunt, Donald Samuel 1938- St&PR 93, WhoAm 92
Hunt, Donnell Ray 1926- WhoAm 92
Hunt, Earl Busby 1933- WhoAm 92
Hunt, Earl Stephen 1948- WhoE 93
Hunt, Effie Neva 1922- WhoAm 92
Hunt, Estelle AmWomPl
Hunt, Everett Clair 1928- WhoAm 92, WhoE 93
Hunt, Forrest L. 1947- St&PR 93
Hunt, Frances Elaine 1953- WhoAmW 93
Hunt, Francis Howard 1919- WhoE 93
Hunt, Frank Bouldin 1915- WhoAm 92
Hunt, Fred A. 1951- St&PR 93
Hunt, Gary Neil 1943- WhoSSW 93
Hunt, Gary Wayne 1961- WhoSSW 93
Hunt, George BioIn 17
Hunt, George 1854-1933 IntDcAn
Hunt, George Andrew 1949- WhoEmL 93
Hunt, George G. 1935- WhoIns 93
Hunt, George Laird 1918- WhoSSW 93
Hunt, George Pinney 1918-1991 BioIn 17
Hunt, George Wylie Paul 1859-1934 BioIn 17
Hunt, Gordon 1934- WhoAm 92
Hunt, Gregory Charles 1960- WhoSSW 93
Hunt, Gregory Lynn 1947- WhoAm 92, WhoWor 93
Hunt, Gregory Todd BioIn 17
Hunt, H. Guy 1933- WhoAm 92, WhoSSW 93, WhoWor 93
Hunt, H.L. 1889-1974 BioIn 17
Hunt, Harold E. 1931- St&PR 93
Hunt, Harold Keith 1938- WhoAm 92
Hunt, Helen 1949- WhoE 93
Hunt, Henry Carter 1952- St&PR 93
Hunt, Henry Jackson 1819-1889 HarEnMi
Hunt, Hilton Adair 1955- St&PR 93
Hunt, Howard Francis 1918- WhoAm 92, WhoE 93
Hunt, Irene 1907- BioIn 17, DcAmChF 1960, MajAI [port]
Hunt, Isobel Violet 1866-1942 BioIn 17
Hunt, J. Frank d1880 BioIn 17
Hunt, J. McVicker 1906-1991 BioIn 17
Hunt, Jack 1945- St&PR 93
Hunt, Jacob Tate 1916- WhoAm 92
Hunt, James B., Jr. 1937- PolPar
Hunt, James Baxter, Jr. 1937- WhoAm 92
Hunt, James Calvin 1925- WhoAm 92
Hunt, James D. 1939- St&PR 93
Hunt, James M. Law&B 92
Hunt, James Robert 1925- WhoAm 92
Hunt, Jane Jewett 1945- WhoWrEP 92
Hunt, Janet B. Law&B 92
Hunt, Jean 1932- WhoAm 92
Hunt, Jerry (Edward) 1943- Baker 92
Hunt, Joe Harold 1925- WhoAm 92
Hunt, John David 1925- WhoAm 92
Hunt, John Edwin 1918- WhoSSW 93
Hunt, John Edwin, Sr. 1918- St&PR 93
Hunt, John F. Law&B 92
Hunt, John Meacham 1918- WhoE 93
Hunt, John Miles 1932- St&PR 93
Hunt, John R. 1952- St&PR 93
Hunt, John Wesley 1927- WhoAm 92
Hunt, Johnnie B. 1924- WhoAm 92
Hunt, Jonathan 1938- WhoAsAP 91
Hunt, Joseph L. 1949- St&PR 93
Hunt, Joseph Raphael 1919-1945 BiDAMSp 1989
Hunt, Joyce F. Law&B 92
Hunt, Judith Mohsberg 1946- WhoAmW 93
Hunt, Julian B. 1940- WhoScE 91-1
Hunt, Julian Courtenay 1917- WhoSSW 93
Hunt, Karen Sue 1954- WhoEmL 93
Hunt, Katherine E. AmWomPl
Hunt, Lacy Harris, II 1942- St&PR 93
Hunt, Lamar 1932- WhoAm 92
Hunt, Lamar 1933- BioIn 17
Hunt, Larry Keith 1945- WhoSSW 93
Hunt, Laura AmWomPl
Hunt, Lawrence Halley, Jr. 1943- WhoWor 93
Hunt, Lawrence J. 1920- DcAmChF 1960
Hunt, Lawrence John 1946- WhoE 93
Hunt, Lee Philip 1939- WhoSSW 93
Hunt, Leigh 1784-1859 BioIn 17
Hunt, Linda BioIn 17
Hunt, Linda 1945- WhoAm 92, WhoAmW 93
Hunt, Linda Marie 1947- WhoAmW 93
Hunt, Lisa ScF&FL 92
Hunt, Lois A. 1947- St&PR 93
Hunt, Lynda Joyce 1951- WhoAmW 93
Hunt, M. Kelly 1965- WhoAmW 93
Hunt, Marion Paul 1926- St&PR 93
Hunt, Marjorie Kalteyer 1915- St&PR 93
Hunt, Mark Alan 1949- WhoAm 92
Hunt, Marsha 1946- ConLC 70 [port]
Hunt, Mary Elizabeth 1951- WhoAmW 93
Hunt, Mary-Ellen Law&B 92
Hunt, Mary Friedel 1940- WhoAmW 93
Hunt, Mary Reilly 1921- WhoAmW 93, WhoWor 93
Hunt, Maurice Arthur 1942- WhoWrEP 92
Hunt, Michie Irene 1951- WhoAmW 93
Hunt, Morton M(agill) 1920- WhoWrEP 92
Hunt, Nelson Bunker 1926- BioIn 17
Hunt, Oliver Joel 1905-1978 BiDAMSp 1989
Hunt, P.G. 1935- St&PR 93
Hunt, Patricia Jacqueline 1961- WhoAmW 93
Hunt, Patrick John 1935- WhoE 93
Hunt, Peter 1928- MiSFD 9
Hunt, Peter H. 1938- MiSFD 9
Hunt, Peter Huls 1938- WhoAm 92
Hunt, Peter James 1940- WhoSSW 93
Hunt, Peter Kevin 1946- St&PR 93
Hunt, Peter True 1951- WhoE 93
Hunt, Pfilip Gardnyr Law&B 92
Hunt, Philip W. 1921- St&PR 93
Hunt, Ralph 1765-1838 BioIn 17
Hunt, Ralph James Dunnet 1928- WhoAsAP 91
Hunt, Ray Lee BioIn 17
Hunt, Ray Lee 1943- WhoSSW 93
Hunt, Richard d1992 BioIn 17, NewYTBS 92
Hunt, Richard 1935- BioIn 17, WhoAm 92
Hunt, Richard B. 1948- St&PR 93
Hunt, Richard Carlton 1917- WhoAm 92
Hunt, Richard P. d1992 NewYTBS 92 [port]
Hunt, Richard (Patrick) 1938- ConAu 137
Hunt, Richard (Paul) 1921-1992 ConAu 139
Hunt, Robert Law&B 92
Hunt, Robert Chester 1923- St&PR 93, WhoAm 92
Hunt, Robert Cushman 1934- WhoE 93
Hunt, Robert J. 1949- St&PR 93
Hunt, Robert McPhail, Jr. 1943- WhoSSW 93
Hunt, Robert William Gainer WhoScE 91-1
Hunt, Robin Ray 1935- St&PR 93
Hunt, Roger B. St&PR 93
Hunt, Ronald Duncan 1935- WhoAm 92, WhoE 93
Hunt, Ronald Forrest 1943- St&PR 93, WhoAm 92
Hunt, Ross Stuart 1959- WhoEmL 93
Hunt, Ruth Cecelia 1923- WhoSSW 93
Hunt, S. Owen Law&B 92
Hunt, Samuel P., III Law&B 92
Hunt, Samuel Pancoast, III 1943- WhoAm 92
Hunt, Shelby Dean 1939- WhoSSW 93
Hunt, Shirley Sophia 1959- WhoAmW 93
Hunt, Sue Whittington 1952- WhoAmW 93, WhoEmL 93, WhoWor 93
Hunt, Timothy A. 1949- WhoWrEP 92
Hunt, Tommy 1933- SoulM
Hunt, V. William 1944- St&PR 93
Hunt, Vincent E. 1941- St&PR 93
Hunt, Vincent Robert 1934- WhoAm 92
Hunt, Violet 1866-1942 BioIn 17
Hunt, W. Kenneth 1953- St&PR 93
Hunt, Waller Staples, Jr. 1928- WhoSSW 93
Hunt, Walter ScF&FL 92
Hunt, Walter Kenneth, III 1953- WhoAm 92
Hunt, Walter L. 1941- St&PR 93, WhoAm 92
Hunt, Ward 1810-1886 OxCSupC [port]
Hunt, William 1934- WhoWrEP 92
Hunt, William Clay 1942- St&PR 93
Hunt, William Daniel 1954- WhoSSW 93
Hunt, William E., Sr. 1923- WhoAm 92
Hunt, William Edward 1921- WhoAm 92
Hunt, William Gibbes 1791-1833 JrnUS
Hunt, William H. Law&B 92
Hunt, William Herbert BioIn 17
Hunt, William Holman 1827-1910 BioIn 17
Hunt, William J. 1925- St&PR 93
Hunt, William J. 1946- WhoIns 93
Hunt, William John 1951- WhoEmL 93
Hunt, William Joseph, Jr. 1950- WhoE 93, WhoEmL 93
Hunt, William Morris 1824-1879 BioIn 17
Hunt, William O. 1933- St&PR 93
Hunt, William Pitt 1769-1797 BioIn 17
Hunt, Willis B., Jr. WhoSSW 93
Hunt, Wilson Price 1782-1842 & Stuart, Robert 1785-1848 Expl 93
Hunt-Clerici, Carol Elizabeth 1938- WhoE 93
Hunte, Beryl Eleanor WhoAmW 93
Hunte, Julian 1940- DcCPCAm
Hunten, Donald Mount 1925- WhoAm 92
Hunten, Franz 1793-1878 Baker 92
Hunter, Agnes Monk AmWomPl
Hunter, Alan F. 1939- St&PR 93
Hunter, Alan (James Herbert) 1922- ConAu 40NR
Hunter, Alastair G.M. 1946- WhoScE 91-1
Hunter, Alberta 1895-1984 Baker 92
Hunter, Anne Kathleen 1945- WhoE 93
Hunter, Beatrice Trum 1918- WhoWrEP 92
Hunter, Ben BioIn 17
Hunter, Bernice Thurman 1922- WhoCanL 92
Hunter, Betty Turner 1948- WhoEmL 93
Hunter, Bruce E. Law&B 92
Hunter, Buddy D. 1930- WhoAm 92
Hunter, Burton D. Law&B 92
Hunter, Bynum Merritt 1925- WhoAm 92
Hunter, Catfish 1946- BioIn 17
Hunter, Charles Alvin 1926- WhoSSW 93
Hunter, Charles David 1929- St&PR 93, WhoAm 92
Hunter, Charles J. Law&B 92
Hunter, Charles Norton 1906-1978 HarEnMi
Hunter, Christopher Stuart WhoScE 91-1
Hunter, Clarence H. 1925- St&PR 93
Hunter, Croil 1893-1970 EncABHB 8 [port]
Hunter, D. WhoScE 91-1
Hunter, D. Michael 1942- St&PR 93
Hunter, David 1802-1886 HarEnMi
Hunter, David A. 1951- St&PR 93
Hunter, David D. 1940- St&PR 93
Hunter, David D. 1941- WhoAm 92
Hunter, David J. 1945- St&PR 93
Hunter, David Wittmer 1928- WhoAm 92
Hunter, Dean Dwight, Jr. 1926- WhoSSW 93
Hunter, Donald 1934- St&PR 93, WhoAm 92
Hunter, Donald Forrest 1934- WhoWor 93
Hunter, Donnell Walker 1930- WhoWrEP 92
Hunter, Dorian 1932- WhoAm 92
Hunter, Duncan 1948- CngDr 91
Hunter, Duncan Lee 1948- WhoAm 92
Hunter, Durant Adams 1948- WhoWor 93
Hunter, Earle Leslie, III 1929- WhoAm 92
Hunter, Edgar Hayes 1914- WhoAm 92
Hunter, Edward A., Jr. Law&B 92
Hunter, Edwin Ford, Jr. 1911- WhoAm 92, WhoSSW 93
Hunter, Elizabeth Ives-Valsam 1945- WhoAm 92
Hunter, Elmo Bolton 1915- WhoAm 92, WhoWor 93
Hunter, Ernest B., Jr. 1924- St&PR 93
Hunter, Ervin J. 1941- St&PR 93
Hunter, Evan 1926- BioIn 17, ConAu 38NR, ScF&FL 92, WhoAm 92, WhoWrEP 92
Hunter, Frank A. Law&B 92
Hunter, Frank Herbert 1901- WhoAm 92
Hunter, Fred WhoAm 92
Hunter, Frederick Douglas Law&B 92
Hunter, Garrett B. 1937- St&PR 93
Hunter, George 1894-1978 BioIn 17
Hunter, George 1927- WhoIns 93
Hunter, Glenn S. BioIn 17
Hunter, Gordon James Allan 1965- WhoWor 93
Hunter, (James) Graham ConAu 136
Hunter, Harlen Charles 1940- WhoAm 92
Hunter, Harold Cooper, Jr. 1945- St&PR 93
Hunter, Harold Raymond 1956- WhoEmL 93, WhoSSW 93
Hunter, Holly 1958- WhoAm 92, WhoAmW 93
Hunter, Holly P. 1958- St&PR 93
Hunter, Howell Coolidge, Jr. 1952- WhoSSW 93
Hunter, Ian McLellan 1915-1991 BioIn 17
Hunter, Ivory Joe 1914-1974 SoulM
Hunter, J.D. St&PR 93
Hunter, Jack D. Law&B 92
Hunter, Jack Duval 1937- St&PR 93, WhoAm 92
Hunter, Jack Duval, II 1959- WhoEmL 93
Hunter, Jack Laird 1927- St&PR 93
Hunter, Jairy C., Jr. 1942- WhoSSW 93
Hunter, James Alexander 1928- WhoAm 92
Hunter, James C. 1942- St&PR 93
Hunter, James D. WhoAm 92
Hunter, James Galbraith, Jr. 1942- WhoAm 92, WhoWor 93
Hunter, James M., Jr. Law&B 92
Hunter, James Paul 1934- WhoAm 92
Hunter, Jeffrey Joseph 1941- WhoWor 93
Hunter, Jerry E. 1938- WhoAm 92, WhoSSW 93
Hunter, Jesse Thomas, Jr. 1924- St&PR 93
Hunter, Jill B. 1962- WhoEmL 93
Hunter, Jim BioIn 17
Hunter, Jim 1946- BioIn 17
Hunter, John WhoScE 91-1
Hunter, John Angus Alexander 1939- WhoWor 93
Hunter, John Harnden 1934- WhoAm 92
Hunter, John Leslie 1946- WhoEmL 93
Hunter, John M. Law&B 92
Hunter, John Robert 1936- WhoAm 92
Hunter, John Stuart 1923- WhoAm 92
Hunter, Jonas L., Jr. Law&B 92
Hunter, Judy Arlene 1956- WhoAmW 93
Hunter, Karen Ayd Law&B 92
Hunter, Karen Lynn 1963- WhoAmW 93
Hunter, Kathryn Motz 1925- St&PR 93
Hunter, Kathy 1944- WhoWrEP 92
Hunter, Kenneth 1946- WhoAm 92
Hunter, Kenneth James 1944- WhoAm 92
Hunter, Kermit Houston 1910- WhoAm 92
Hunter, Kim 1922- BioIn 17, WhoAm 92, WhoAmW 93
Hunter, Kristin WhoWrEP 92
Hunter, Kristin 1931- BlkAull 92
Hunter, Kristin (Eggleston) 1931- DcAmChF 1960, MajAI [port], WhoE 93
Hunter, Larry Dean 1950- WhoAm 92
Hunter, Leland Clair 1925- St&PR 93
Hunter, Leland Clair, Jr. 1925- WhoWor 93
Hunter, Lynette 1951- ScF&FL 92
Hunter, Lynn 1947- WhoAmW 93
Hunter, Madeline C. BioIn 17
Hunter, Malcolm Law&B 92
Hunter, Margaret Jenkins 1942- WhoSSW 93
Hunter, Margaret King 1919- WhoAm 92
Hunter, Marsha L. Law&B 92
Hunter, Marvin Thomas 1942- WhoE 93
Hunter, Mary Anderson 1949- WhoAmW 93
Hunter, Mary Jane 1919- WhoSSW 93
Hunter, Matthew 1934- St&PR 93, WhoAm 92, WhoE 93
Hunter, Maxcy P. 1927- St&PR 93
Hunter, Maxwell W., II BioIn 17
Hunter, Michael 1941- WhoAm 92
Hunter, Michael Bourne 1947- WhoWrEP 92
Hunter, Michael Thomas 1949- St&PR 93
Hunter, Minerva AmWomPl
Hunter, Mollie 1922- ConAu 37NR, MajAI [port], ScF&FL 92
Hunter, Nancy Donehoo 1956- WhoSSW 93
Hunter, Naomi Elizabeth 1916- WhoAm 92
Hunter, O. 1938- St&PR 93
Hunter, Olivia M. AmWomPl
Hunter, Pamela Irene 1955- WhoEmL 93
Hunter, Patricia Rae 1952- WhoAmW 93
Hunter, Paul 1954- WhoE 93
Hunter, Peter Alexander 1959- St&PR 93
Hunter, R.M. Law&B 92
Hunter, Richard A. 1930- St&PR 93
Hunter, Richard Davis 1950- WhoEmL 93
Hunter, Richard Edward 1919- WhoAm 92
Hunter, Richard Grant, Jr. 1938- WhoSSW 93, WhoWor 93
Hunter, Rita 1933- OxDcOp
Hunter, Rita (Nellie) 1933- Baker 92
Hunter, Robert Brinkley 1938- WhoWor 93
Hunter, Robert C. 1941- St&PR 93
Hunter, Robert Charles 1948- WhoSSW 93
Hunter, Robert Coleman 1941- WhoAm 92
Hunter, Robert Douglas 1928- BioIn 17
Hunter, Robert Frank 1923- WhoAm 92
Hunter, Robert Grams 1927- WhoAm 92
Hunter, Robert John 1933- WhoWor 93
Hunter, Robert M. T. 1809-1887 PolPar
Hunter, Robert Nelson 1930- St&PR 93, WhoAm 92
Hunter, Robert P., Jr. Law&B 92
Hunter, Robert P., Jr. 1935- St&PR 93
Hunter, Robert Paul 1964- WhoSSW 93
Hunter, Robert T. 1934- St&PR 93
Hunter, Robert Tweedy, Jr. 1934- WhoAm 92
Hunter, Rodney John 1940- WhoSSW 93
Hunter, Ronald E. Law&B 92
Hunter, Ronald L. 1936- St&PR 93
Hunter, Ronald V. 1944- St&PR 93, WhoAm 92
Hunter, Ross 1926- WhoAm 92, WhoWor 93
Hunter, Ross 1954- WhoWor 93
Hunter, Royce Glenn 1938- WhoIns 93
Hunter, S.L. ScF&FL 92

Hunter, Sally Irene 1936- *WhoWor 93*
Hunter, Sam *BioIn 17*
Hunter, Sam 1923- *WhoAm 92*
Hunter, Samuel Paul 1944- *St&PR 93*
Hunter, Sheryl Lynn 1958- *WhoWrEP 92*
Hunter, Stephanie Y. *Law&B 92*
Hunter, Sue Persons 1921- *WhoAmW 93*
Hunter, Susan Gail 1950- *St&PR 93*
Hunter, Teola P. *AfrAmBi*
Hunter, Thom Hugh 1918- *WhoAm 92*
Hunter, Thomas Harrison 1913- *WhoAm 92*
Hunter, Thomas O'D. *ScF&FL 92*
Hunter, Thomas R. *Law&B 92*
Hunter, Tim *MiSFD 9*
Hunter, Timothy M. 1962- *St&PR 93*
Hunter, Timothy W. *Law&B 92*
Hunter, Tony 1943- *WhoAm 92*
Hunter, Tracy Smith 1952- *WhoSSW 93*
Hunter, Wanda Sanborn 1904-1990 *BioIn 17*
Hunter, William Harry, III 1952- *WhoE 93*
Hunter, William Jay, Jr. *Law&B 92*
Hunter, William Jay, Jr. 1944- *WhoAm 92*
Hunter, William Mill, II 1949- *St&PR 93*
Hunter, William Morgan 1923- *WhoAm 92*
Hunter, William Schmidt 1931- *St&PR 93, WhoE 93, WhoWor 93*
Hunter Blair, Pauline Clarke 1921- *WhoAm 92*
Hunter-Bone, Maureen Claire 1946- *WhoAmW 93, WhoEmL 93*
Hunter-Duvar, John 1821-1899 *BioIn 17*
Hunter-Dyer, Kathryn Lynette 1946- *WhoEmL 93*
Hunter-Gault, Charlayne *BioIn 17*
Hunter-Gault, Charlayne 1942- *JrnUS, WhoWrEP 92*
Hunter-Stiebel, Penelope *WhoAm 92*
Hunt Family *BioIn 17*
Hunting, Anne Ritchie 1944- *WhoWor 93*
Hunting, D.D., Jr. 1926- *St&PR 93*
Hunting, Ema L. *AmWomPl*
Hunting, Ema M. *AmWomPl*
Hunting, Emma Suckow *AmWomPl*
Huntingdon, Countess of 1907- *BioIn 17*
Huntington, A. Ronald 1921- *WhoAm 92*
Huntington, Ada L. *AmWomPl*
Huntington, Charles Ellsworth 1919- *WhoAm 92*
Huntington, Collis P. 1821-1900 *GayN*
Huntington, Curtis Edward 1942- *St&PR 93, WhoAm 92*
Huntington, Cynthia 1951- *WhoWrEP 92*
Huntington, David Carew 1922-1990 *BioIn 17*
Huntington, David Mack Goode 1926- *WhoAm 92*
Huntington, Earl L. 1929- *St&PR 93*
Huntington, Earl Lloyd 1929- *WhoAm 92*
Huntington, Ellsworth 1876-1947 *GayN*
Huntington, Fred 1912- *BioIn 17*
Huntington, Henry E. 1850-1927 *DcLB Y92 [port]*
Huntington, Henry Edwards 1850-1927 *BioIn 17*
Huntington, James Cantine, Jr. 1928- *WhoAm 92*
Huntington, John 1940- *ScF&FL 92*
Huntington, Karen Rae 1945- *WhoWrEP 92*
Huntington, Lawrence S. 1935- *St&PR 93*
Huntington, Mary C. 1923- *WhoAmW 93*
Huntington, Peter Perit 1935- *WhoE 93*
Huntington, Robert Hubbard 1937- *St&PR 93, WhoE 93*
Huntington, S.W. 1947- *WhoScE 91-1*
Huntington, Samuel Phillips 1927- *WhoAm 92*
Huntington, William Reed d1990 *BioIn 17*
Huntley, Alice Mae 1917- *WhoAmW 93*
Huntley, Charles William 1913- *WhoAm 92*
Huntley, Chester Robert 1911-1974 *JrnUS*
Huntley, David Austin 1933- *St&PR 93*
Huntley, Diane E. 1946- *WhoAmW 93*
Huntley, Donald W. *Law&B 92*
Huntley, Frances *AmWomPl*
Huntley, Ian David *WhoScE 91-1*
Huntley, James Robert 1923- *WhoAm 92*
Huntley, Marcia Lynn 1951- *St&PR 93*
Huntley, Noel *ScF&FL 92*
Huntley, Raymond 1903-1990 *BioIn 17*
Huntley, Raymond 1904-1990 *ConTFT 10*
Huntley, Robert Edward Royall 1929- *WhoAm 92*
Huntley, Robert Joseph 1924- *WhoWor 93*
Huntley, Robert Ross 1926- *WhoAm 92*
Huntley, Robin S. 1948- *St&PR 93*
Huntley, Tim 1939- *ScF&FL 92*
Huntley, William Thomas, III 1935- *WhoSSW 93*
Hunton, Donald Bothen 1927- *WhoAm 92*
Huntoon, Carolyn Leach 1940- *WhoSSW 93*
Huntoon, Robert Brian 1927- *WhoE 93*
Huntoon, Robert D. d1992 *NewYTBS 92*
Huntress, Wesley Theodore, Jr. 1942- *WhoE 93*
Hunts, Barney D. *St&PR 93*
Huntsinger, Fritz Roy 1935- *WhoAm 92*
Huntsinger, Martha Elaine 1944- *WhoSSW 93*
Huntsman, John Robert 1951- *WhoEmL 93*
Huntsman, Jon M. 1937- *ConEn*
Huntsman, Jon Meade, Jr. 1960- *WhoAm 92*
Huntsman, Leslie D. 1948- *St&PR 93*
Huntting, Cynthia Cox 1936- *WhoAmW 93*
Huntzicker, Jon Noble 1939- *St&PR 93*
Hunyadi, Janos c. 1387-1456 *HarEnMi*
Hunyadi, Janos c. 1407-1456 *OxDcByz*
Hunyadi, Steve 1937- *St&PR 93*
Hunzicker, Warren John 1920- *WhoAm 92, WhoIns 93*
Hunziker, Christian Ulrich 1926-1991 *BioIn 17*
Hunziker, Don A. 1927- *WhoAm 92, WhoSSW 93*
Hunziker, Don Allen 1927- *St&PR 93*
Hunziker, Erich 1953- *WhoWor 93*
Hunziker, Frederick John, Jr. *Law&B 92*
Hunziker, Frederick John, Jr. 1928- *St&PR 93*
Hunziker, Robert M. *Law&B 92*
Hunziker, Robert McK. 1932- *St&PR 93*
Hunziker, Robert McKee 1932- *WhoAm 92*
Hunziker, Terry *BioIn 17*
Huo Ch'u-ping d115BC *HarEnMi*
Huon, Hubert John 1936- *WhoWor 93*
Huopaniemi, Tero-Pekka 1962- *WhoWor 93*
Huot, Lois Ann *Law&B 92*
Huot, Rachel Irene 1950- *WhoAm 92, WhoAmW 93, WhoEmL 93, WhoSSW 93*
Huot, William J. 1926- *St&PR 93*
Huovie, Curtis Oliver 1947- *St&PR 93*
Huovila, Seppo P. 1928- *WhoScE 91-4*
Hupalo, Meredith Topliff 1917- *WhoAmW 93*
Hupe, Dennis D. 1951- *St&PR 93*
Hupf, Robert Edmund 1948- *St&PR 93*
Hupfeld, Herman 1894-1951 *Baker 92*
Hupfeld, Stanley F. *BioIn 17*
Hupfeld, Stanley Francis 1944- *WhoAm 92*
Hupfer, L. Lee *St&PR 93*
Hu Ping 1930- *WhoAsAP 91*
Hupp, Jack Scott 1930- *St&PR 93, WhoAm 92*
Hupp, M. Theresa *Law&B 92*
Hupp, Patricia Ellen 1950- *WhoAmW 93, WhoWor 93*
Hupp, Terry L. 1941- *St&PR 93*
Huppe, Alex 1947- *WhoE 93, WhoEmL 93*
Huppe, Francis Frowin 1934- *WhoAm 92*
Huppenthal, Leslaw 1923- *WhoScE 91-4*
Hupper, John Roscoe 1925- *WhoAm 92*
Huppert, Caroline *MiSFD 9*
Huppert, Gary E. 1967- *St&PR 93*
Huppert, Isabelle *BioIn 17*
Huppert, Isabelle 1955- *IntDcF 2-3 [port]*
Huppert, Isabelle Anne 1953- *WhoWor 93*
Huppert, Norman K., Jr. 1959- *St&PR 93*
Hupperts, Paul (Henri Franciscus Marie) 1919- *Baker 92*
Huppi, G. *WhoScE 91-4*
Huppmann, Winfried J. 1945- *WhoScE 91-4*
Huppuch, Thomas Warner *Law&B 92*
Huq, Shamul 1931- *WhoAsAP 91*
Hu Qiaomu 1912-1992 *NewYTBS 92 [port]*
Hu Qili 1929- *WhoAsAP 91*
Hur, Sonja Vegdahl 1956- *WhoAmW 93*
Hur, Stephen Ponyi 1947- *WhoEmL 93*
Hura, Gurdeep Singh 1950- *WhoWor 93*
Huras, William David 1932- *WhoAm 92*
Hurault, J.P. *WhoScE 91-2*
Hurault, Jean-Paul 1941- *WhoScE 91-3*
Huray, Paul Gordon 1941- *WhoSSW 93*
Hurcomb, Thomas J. 1937- *St&PR 93*
Hurcombe, Wendy 1941- *WhoE 93*
Hurd, Byron Thomas 1933- *WhoWor 93*
Hurd, Charles W. 1927- *St&PR 93*
Hurd, Clara J. H. *AmWomPl*
Hurd, Clement 1908-1988 *BioIn 17*
Hurd, Clement (G.) 1908-1988 *MajAI [port]*
Hurd, Cuthbert C. 1911- *WhoAm 92*
Hurd, Douglas 1930- *BioIn 17*
Hurd, Douglas Richard 1930- *WhoWor 93*
Hurd, Edith Thacher 1910- *BioIn 17, MajAI*
Hurd, Eric Ray 1936- *WhoSSW 93, WhoWor 93*
Hurd, Florence 1918- *ScF&FL 92*
Hurd, Francine 1947- *See* Peaches & Herb *SoulM*
Hurd, G. David 1929- *St&PR 93, WhoIns 93*
Hurd, Gale Anne *BioIn 17*
Hurd, Gale Anne 1955- *WhoWor 93*
Hurd, Henriette Wyeth 1907- *BioIn 17*
Hurd, J. Nicholas 1942- *St&PR 93, WhoAm 92*
Hurd, Joseph E. 1942- *WhoAm 92*
Hurd, Marjorie *BioIn 17*
Hurd, Michael Edward William 1947- *WhoWrEP 92*
Hurd, Michael (John) 1928- *Baker 92*
Hurd, Paul Gemmill *Law&B 92*
Hurd, Peter 1904-1984 *BioIn 17*
Hurd, Richard M. 1924- *St&PR 93*
Hurd, Richard Nelson 1926- *WhoAm 92, WhoSSW 93*
Hurd, Shirley Dyer 1940- *WhoAmW 93, WhoWor 93*
Hurd, Suzanne Sheldon 1939- *WhoAm 92*
Hurd, (John) Thacher 1949- *MajAI [port]*
Hurd, Thomas Robert 1951- *WhoEmL 93*
Hurd, W. Russell 1946- *St&PR 93*
Hurdle, Patricia Ann 1946- *WhoAmW 93*
Hurdle, Thomas Gray 1919- *WhoSSW 93*
Hurduc, Neculai 1926- *WhoScE 91-4*
Hure, Jean 1877-1930 *Baker 92*
Huret, Barry S. 1938- *WhoE 93*
Huret, Louis Dominique 1944- *WhoWor 93*
Huret, Marilynn Joyce *WhoAmW 93*
Hurewitz, David *Law&B 92*
Hurewitz, Jacob Coleman 1914- *WhoAm 92, WhoE 93*
Hurewitz, Sharon Joy 1959- *WhoEmL 93*
Hurford, Christopher John 1931- *WhoAsAP 91*
Hurford, Gary T. 1936- *St&PR 93*
Hurford, Gary Thomas 1936- *WhoAm 92, WhoSSW 93*
Hurford, John Boyce 1938- *WhoAm 92*
Hurford, Peter (John) 1930- *Baker 92*
Hurford, William Edward 1955- *WhoE 93*
Hurford-Jones, David James 1933- *WhoWor 93*
Hur Jae Hong 1937- *WhoAsAP 91*
Hurkos, Peter 1911-1988 *BioIn 17*
Hurlbert, Clark D. 1941- *St&PR 93*
Hurlbert, Gordon C. 1924- *St&PR 93*
Hurlbert, Gordon Charles 1924- *WhoAm 92*
Hurlbert, Jane LaVerne 1944- *WhoAmW 93*
Hurlbert, Roger William 1941- *WhoAm 92*
Hurlbert, William Henry 1827-1895 *JrnUS*
Hurlburt, Charles Arthur 1963- *WhoE 93*
Hurlburt, Frances Alice 1937- *WhoSSW 93*
Hurlburt, Harley Ernest 1943- *WhoWor 93*
Hurlburt, Jack 1925- *St&PR 93*
Hurlbut, Chris Lakin *Law&B 92*
Hurlbut, Robert H. 1935- *St&PR 93*
Hurlbut, Robert Harold 1935- *WhoE 93, WhoWor 93*
Hurlbut, Robert St. Clair 1924- *St&PR 93, WhoAm 92*
Hurlbut, Stephen Augustus 1815-1882 *HarEnMi*
Hurlbutt, Guy G. *Law&B 92*
Hurley, Albert Rowe 1939- *St&PR 93*
Hurley, Alfred Francis 1928- *WhoAm 92, WhoSSW 93*
Hurley, Anne Irene 1958- *WhoE 93, WhoEmL 93*
Hurley, Augustus H., Jr. 1928- *St&PR 93*
Hurley, Bobby *BioIn 17*
Hurley, Brian Xavier 1951- *WhoAm 92*
Hurley, Cheryl Joyce 1947- *WhoAm 92, WhoAmW 93*
Hurley, Cornelius Keefe, Jr. 1945- *WhoAm 92*
Hurley, Daniel Patrick *Law&B 92*
Hurley, Dean C. 1954- *WhoE 93*
Hurley, Donald G. 1933- *St&PR 93*
Hurley, Francis T. 1927- *WhoAm 92*
Hurley, Frank Thomas, Jr. 1924- *WhoSSW 93*
Hurley, Grady Schell 1954- *WhoEmL 93*
Hurley, Graham *ScF&FL 92*
Hurley, Harry James, Jr. 1926- *WhoAm 92*
Hurley, James F. 1937- *St&PR 93*
Hurley, James J. 1946- *WhoE 93*
Hurley, John Neal 1951- *St&PR 93*
Hurley, John R. *Law&B 92*
Hurley, John William 1929- *St&PR 93*
Hurley, Laurel 1927- *Baker 92*
Hurley, Laurence Harold 1944- *WhoAm 92*
Hurley, Lawrence Joseph *Law&B 92*
Hurley, Lawrence Joseph 1946- *WhoEmL 93*
Hurley, Linda Joyce 1959- *WhoAmW 93*
Hurley, Linda Kay 1951- *WhoAm 92*
Hurley, Lisa *Law&B 92*
Hurley, Margaret Strickland *AmWomPl*
Hurley, Marjorie Bryan 1941- *WhoAmW 93*
Hurley, Mark Joseph 1919- *WhoAm 92*
Hurley, Marlene Emogene 1938- *WhoAmW 93, WhoWor 93*
Hurley, Mary Josephine 1956- *WhoSSW 93*
Hurley, Maureen O. *Law&B 92*
Hurley, Maureen Viola 1952- *WhoWrEP 92*
Hurley, Maxwell *ScF&FL 92*
Hurley, Melissa 1955- *St&PR 93*
Hurley, Michael Francis 1942- *WhoE 93*
Hurley, Michael Francis 1957- *WhoEmL 93*
Hurley, Morris Elmer, Jr. 1920- *WhoAm 92*
Hurley, Oliver Leon 1932- *WhoSSW 93*
Hurley, Patricia Bullock 1956- *WhoAmW 93*
Hurley, Patricia Wendy 1945- *WhoAmW 93*
Hurley, Patrick Mason 1912- *WhoAm 92*
Hurley, Peyton 1919- *St&PR 93*
Hurley, Richard J. 1906-1976? *ScF&FL 92*
Hurley, Robert Joseph 1932- *WhoAm 92*
Hurley, Rosalinde *WhoScE 91-1*
Hurley, Sabrina *Law&B 92*
Hurley, Samuel Clay, III 1936- *WhoAm 92*
Hurley, Samuel W., Jr. *AfrAmBi [port]*
Hurley, Steven Ray 1947- *WhoE 93, WhoEmL 93*
Hurley, Thaddeus Christopher 1945- *WhoWor 93*
Hurley, Thomas J. *Law&B 92*
Hurley, Thomas John 1960- *WhoEmL 93*
Hurley, Thomas O. 1951- *St&PR 93*
Hurley, Webster H. 1921- *St&PR 93*
Hurley, William E. d1992 *NewYTBS 92*
Hurley, William James, Jr. 1924- *WhoWor 93*
Hurley, William Joseph 1926- *WhoAm 92*
Hurley, William Joseph 1939- *WhoAm 92, WhoE 93*
Hurlimann, Theodor *WhoScE 91-4*
Hurlock, James Bickford 1933- *WhoAm 92*
Hurlock, Roger W. 1912- *St&PR 93*
Hurlow, John Philip 1945- *WhoWor 93*
Hurlstone, William (Yeates) 1876-1906 *Baker 92*
Hurmence, Belinda 1921- *DcAmChF 1985, ScF&FL 92*
Hurn, David 1934- *WhoWor 93*
Hurney, Lee Maurice 1950- *WhoE 93*
Hurni, Richard Jay 1934- *St&PR 93*
Hurnik, Ilja 1922- *Baker 92*
Hurok, Sol(omon Israelovich) 1888-1974 *Baker 92*
Hurok, Solomon Israelevich 1888-1974 *BioIn 17*
Huron, Roderick Eugene 1934- *WhoAm 92*
Hurr, Wanda L. 1955- *WhoAmW 93*
Hurrell, George *BioIn 17*
Hurrell, George d1992 *NewYTBS 92*
Hurrle, Jane *AmWomPl*
Hurry, Robert Otis 1938- *St&PR 93*
Hursch, James Alexander 1961- *WhoEmL 93*
Hursey, B. Edward 1927- *St&PR 93*
Hursey, Jeffrey M. 1951- *St&PR 93*
Hursh, Robert D. 1927- *St&PR 93*
Hurson, Daniel L. 1920- *St&PR 93*
Hurst, Amanda Cady 1951- *WhoAmW 93*
Hurst, Brian Desmond 1900-1986 *MiSFD 9N*
Hurst, Charles Jackson 1941- *WhoAm 92*
Hurst, Christina Marie 1955- *WhoAm 92, WhoAmW 93, WhoEmL 93*
Hurst, D.W. *WhoScE 91-1*
Hurst, Daniel Jay 1954- *WhoSSW 93*
Hurst, Derek Thomas 1938- *WhoWor 93*
Hurst, Ernest C. 1926- *St&PR 93*
Hurst, Fannie 1885-1968 *ScF&FL 92*
Hurst, Fannie 1889-1968 *AmWomPl, JeAmFiW*
Hurst, Frances Ethel Weekley 1919- *WhoAmW 93, WhoSSW 93*
Hurst, George 1926- *Baker 92*
Hurst, Gerald Palmer *Law&B 92*
Hurst, Gregory Squire 1947- *WhoAm 92, WhoWor 93*
Hurst, Guy *BioIn 17*
Hurst, H. Rex 1939- *WhoIns 93*
Hurst, Hal N. 1935- *St&PR 93*
Hurst, James Willard 1910- *WhoAm 92*
Hurst, Jeanne 1934- *WhoSSW 93*
Hurst, Jim *WhoScE 91-1*
Hurst, John Emory, Jr. 1928- *WhoAm 92*
Hurst, John L., III 1939- *WhoAm 92*
Hurst, John Phillip *Law&B 92*
Hurst, Josephine Marie 1938- *WhoAmW 93*
Hurst, Kenneth Landis 1949- *WhoE 93*

Hurst, Kenneth Thurston 1923- *WhoAm 92*
Hurst, Lawrence J. *Law&B 92*
Hurst, Leland L. 1930- *St&PR 93*
Hurst, Leland Lyle 1930- *WhoAm 92*
Hurst, Linda Gibson 1953- *WhoAmW 93*
Hurst, Lionel A. 1950- *WhoUN 92*
Hurst, Lulu fl. 19th cent.- *BioIn 17*
Hurst, Marlin *St&PR 93*
Hurst, Mary Jane 1952- *WhoAmW 93, WhoSSW 93*
Hurst, Michael Edward 1931- *WhoAm 92*
Hurst, Michael James 1947- *WhoSSW 93*
Hurst, Michael Patrick *Law&B 92*
Hurst, Michael William 1947- *WhoE 93, WhoEmL 93*
Hurst, Nicholas Richard 1938- *WhoAm 92*
Hurst, Richard L. *St&PR 93*
Hurst, Robert J. 1945- *St&PR 93*
Hurst, Robert Jay 1945- *WhoAm 92*
Hurst, Robert Philip 1930- *WhoE 93*
Hurst, Ronald D. *Law&B 92*
Hurst, Timothy Allen 1951- *WhoEmL 93*
Hurst, William S. *Law&B 92*
Hursthouse, Michael B. *WhoScE 91-1*
Hurston, Zora Neale 1891?-1960 *AmWomWr 92, ConBlB 3 [port], MagSAmL [port]*
Hurston, Zora Neale 1901?-1960 *AmWomPl, IntDcAn*
Hurston, Zora Neale 1906-1960 *EncAACR*
Hurston, Zora Neale 1907-1960 *BioIn 17*
Hurt, Charlie Deuel, III 1950- *WhoAm 92*
Hurt, James Riggins 1934- *WhoAm 92*
Hurt, Jennings Laverne, III 1952- *WhoEmL 93*
Hurt, John *BioIn 17*
Hurt, John 1940- *IntDcF 2-3 [port]*
Hurt, John Vincent 1940- *WhoAm 92*
Hurt, Michelle D. 1964- *WhoAmW 93*
Hurt, Robert C. 1909- *St&PR 93*
Hurt, Robert Glenn 1919- *WhoWor 93*
Hurt, Stan Charles 1939- *St&PR 93*
Hurt, Stephen Wayne 1951- *WhoE 93*
Hurt, William 1950- *BioIn 17, HolBB [port], IntDcF 2-3, WhoAm 92*
Hurt, William Holman 1927- *WhoAm 92*
Hurt, William Rollins *Law&B 92*
Hurta, Glenn R. 1942- *St&PR 93*
Hurta, Kaye Lynn 1961- *WhoSSW 93*
Hurtado-Donaldson, Ana Nora *WhoWor 93*
Hurt-Bacchetti, Pamela Denise 1964- *WhoEmL 93*
Hurteau, Gilles David 1928- *WhoAm 92*
Hurter, Arthur Patrick *WhoAm 92*
Hurtig, Mel *ConAu 137*
Hurtig, Serge 1927- *WhoWor 93*
Hurtt, Caleb Brown 1931- *St&PR 93*
Hurtubise, Paul *Law&B 92*
Hurtz, William T. *MiSFD 9*
Hurum, Alf (Thorvald) 1882-1972 *Baker 92*
Hurvell, Bengt O. 1935- *WhoScE 91-4*
Hurvich, Leo Maurice 1910- *WhoAm 92*
Hurvitz, Arthur Isaac 1939- *WhoAm 92*
Hurvitz, Carole Hughes 1942- *WhoAm 92*
Hurvitz, Ralph A. *Law&B 92*
Hurwich, Robert Allen 1941- *St&PR 93*
Hurwitch, John Edward 1942- *WhoAm 92*
Hurwitz, Bertha *AmWomPl*
Hurwitz, Charles E. 1940- *St&PR 93*
Hurwitz, Charles Edwin 1940- *WhoAm 92, WhoSSW 93*
Hurwitz, David L. 1928-1990 *BioIn 17*
Hurwitz, Ellen Stiskin 1942- *WhoAm 92*
Hurwitz, Emanuel (Henry) 1919- *Baker 92*
Hurwitz, Harry *MiSFD 9*
Hurwitz, Henry 1918-1992 *BioIn 17*
Hurwitz, Henry, Jr. d1992 *NewYTBS 92*
Hurwitz, Israel Samuel 1930- *WhoE 93*
Hurwitz, Jodie Linda 1955- *WhoAmW 93*
Hurwitz, Johanna 1937- *MajAI [port], ScF&FL 92, SmATA 71 [port], WhoWrEP 92*
Hurwitz, Johanna (Frank) 1937- *DcAmChF 1985, WhoAm 92*
Hurwitz, Lawrence Neal 1939 *WhoAm 92*
Hurwitz, Leo 1909-1991 *AnObit 1991, BioIn 17*
Hurwitz, Mark Henry 1951- *WhoE 93*
Hurwitz, Melvin H. 1932- *St&PR 93*
Hurwitz, Richard Michael 1963- *WhoWor 93*
Hurwitz, Robert M. *Law&B 92*
Hurwitz, Robert S. *Law&B 92*
Hurwitz, Sam 1965- *MiSFD 9*
Hurwitz, Sol 1932- *WhoE 93*
Hurwitz, Stephen Allen 1942- *St&PR 93*
Hurwood, Bernhardt J. 1926-1987 *ScF&FL 92*
Hurzeler, P. *WhoScE 91-4*
Hus, J.J. 1942- *WhoScE 91-2*
Hus, Jan 1369?-1415 *BioIn 17*
Husa, Karel 1921- *Baker 92, BioIn 17*
Husa, Karel Jaroslav 1921- *WhoAm 92, WhoWor 93*
Husain, M.F. 1915- *WhoAsAP 91*
Husain, Mir Asghar 1946- *WhoUN 92*
Husain, Mubarak 1939- *WhoUN 92*
Husain, Mukhtar 1950- *WhoWor 93*
Husain, Nasir 1957- *WhoWor 93*
Husain, Syed Shahid 1932- *WhoUN 92*
Husain, Syed Shahid 1935- *WhoUN 92*
Husain, Taqdir 1929- *WhoAm 92*
Husak, Gustav *BioIn 17*
Husak, Gustav 1913- *ColdWar 2 [port]*
Husak, Gustav 1913-1991 *AnObit 1991, CurBio 92N*
Husak, Vaclav 1938- *WhoScE 91-4*
Husar, Emile 1915- *WhoE 93*
Husar, John Paul 1937- *WhoAm 92*
Husayn, Saddam *BioIn 17*
Husayn, Taha 1889-1973 *BioIn 17*
Husband, Harold 1905- *St&PR 93*
Husband, James Francis, II 1946- *St&PR 93*
Husband, Richard Lorin, Sr. 1931- *WhoAm 92, WhoWor 93*
Husband, W. Wayne 1950- *St&PR 93*
Husbands, Humphrey Oliver 1929- *WhoE 93*
Husby, Anita Kay 1950- *WhoAmW 93*
Husby, Donald Evans 1927- *WhoAm 92*
Husch, Bertram 1923- *WhoWor 93*
Husch, Gerhard 1901-1984 *OxDcOp*
Husch, Gerhard (Heinrich Wilhelm Fritz) 1901-1984 *Baker 92*
Husch, Lawrence Stanislaus 1942- *WhoSSW 93*
Huschka, Martin F. 1949- *St&PR 93*
Huschka, Pius A. 1930- *St&PR 93*
Hus-Desforges, Pierre Louis 1773-1838 *Baker 92*
Huse, Frank Peter *Law&B 92*
Huse, Frank Peter 1948- *St&PR 93*
Huse, Stephen M. 1942- *St&PR 93*
Husebye, Eystein S. 1937- *WhoScE 91-4*
Husemann, Robert William 1931- *WhoAm 92*
Husemoller, Roger Paul 1939- *St&PR 93*
Hu Sepang *WhoAsAP 91*
Husfeld, Luciana 1956- *WhoScE 91-3*
Husfloen, Kyle Douglas 1949- *WhoAm 92*
Hushen, John W. 1935- *WhoAm 92*
Hushen, John Wallace 1935- *St&PR 93*
Hushing, William Collins 1918- *WhoAm 92*
Husk, G. Ronald 1937- *WhoAm 92, WhoSSW 93*
Huskey, Harry Douglas 1916- *WhoAm 92*
Huskey, Tom 1954- *St&PR 93*
Huskins, Arnold Martin 1959- *WhoSSW 93*
Huskins, Joseph Patterson 1908- *St&PR 93*
Huskinson, John C. 1955- *St&PR 93*
Husler, Jurg Rudolf 1947- *WhoWor 93*
Huslid, Martin Johannes 1931- *WhoUN 92*
Huslig, Mary Ann 1947- *WhoAmW 93*
Husman, Catherine Bigot 1943- *WhoAm 92, WhoIns 93*
Husman, Kaj R.H. 1944- *WhoScE 91-4*
Husmann, Don 1930- *St&PR 93*
Husmann, Heinrich 1908-1983 *Baker 92*
Husmann, Otto Karl 1923- *WhoWor 93*
Husnu, Seniha *IntDcAn*
Huson, George Roe 1929- *WhoE 93*
Huson, Paul 1942- *ScF&FL 92*
Huss, Allan M. *Law&B 92*
Huss, Edward Eugene 1932- *St&PR 93*
Huss, Henry Holden 1862-1953 *Baker 92*
Huss, John 1369?-1415 *BioIn 17*
Huss, John Anthony 1935- *St&PR 93*
Huss, John Jay 1936- *St&PR 93*
Huss, Lawrence D. *Law&B 92*
Huss, Sandy 1953- *ConAu 138*
Huss, Werner Rudolf Alois 1936- *WhoWor 93*
Hussain, A. *WhoUN 92*
Hussain, Abu Taher Mohammed Akhtar 1956- *WhoWor 93*
Hussain, Al 1949- *St&PR 93*
Hussain, Altaf 1955- *WhoWor 93*
Hussain, Nisar 1935- *WhoWor 93*
Hussain, Rashid *BioIn 17*
Hussain, Syed Asad 1928- *WhoWor 93*
Hussain, Tajammal 1941- *WhoWor 93*
Hussain Bin Pehin Orang Kaya Digadong, Yang Berhormat Pehin Jawatan Luar *WhoAsAP 91*
Hussainun, Salih Abu Bakr Bin *WhoWor 93*
Hussar, Daniel Alexander 1941- *WhoAm 92*
Hussar, John James 1960- *WhoE 93*
Hussein, King of Jordan 1935- *BioIn 17*
Hussein, Ahmed Dia 1941- *WhoAm 92, WhoE 93, WhoWor 93*
Hussein, Mohamed-Ali Faisal 1934- *WhoUN 92*
Hussein, Pattie Yu 1956- *WhoEmL 93*
Hussein, Saddam *BioIn 17*
Hussein, Saddam 1937- *ColdWar 2 [port], DcTwHis, WhoWor 93*
Hussein, Sayed Ahmed 1934- *WhoUN 92*
Hussein, Sayed Ali 1938- *WhoUN 92*
Hussein, Uday 1963?- *BioIn 17*
Hussein, Waris 1938- *MiSFD 9*
Hussein bin Onn 1922-1990 *BioIn 17*
Hussein Bin Talal 1935- *WhoWor 93*
Husseini, Faisal al- *BioIn 17*
Husseini, Hussein *WhoWor 93*
Husseini, Ishak Mousa d1990 *BioIn 17*
Hussein ibn Ali 1856-1931 *DcTwHis*
Hussein ibn Talal 1935- *DcTwHis*
Husselman, Grace 1923- *WhoAmW 93*
Hussey, Carol Ann 1955- *WhoAmW 93*
Hussey, Conleth D. 1955- *WhoScE 91-3*
Hussey, Edward Walter 1938- *WhoSSW 93*
Hussey, Eunice G. *AmWomPl*
Hussey, Gemma *BioIn 17*
Hussey, John Fleming 1940- *St&PR 93*
Hussey, Marmaduke James 1923- *WhoWor 93*
Hussey, Patricia *BioIn 17*
Hussey, Peter A. 1933- *St&PR 93*
Hussey, Philip W., Jr. 1931- *St&PR 93*
Hussey, Philip William, Jr. 1931- *WhoE 93*
Hussey, Robert F. *St&PR 93*
Hussey, Ward MacLean 1920- *WhoAm 92*
Hussey, William Bertrand 1915- *WhoAm 92*
Husson, Jean-Claude 1937- *WhoScE 91-2*
Hust, Bernard de Claviere d' *BioIn 17*
Hust, Bruce Kevin 1957- *WhoWor 93*
Hustache, Philippe *St&PR 93*
Hustad, Thomas Pegg 1945- *WhoWor 93*
Husted, John Edwin 1915- *WhoAm 92*
Husted, Marlin K. 1930- *St&PR 93*
Husted, Ralph Waldo 1911- *WhoAm 92*
Husted, Stewart Winthrop 1946- *WhoEmL 93, WhoSSW 93*
Husted-Andersen, Adda *BioIn 17*
Husti, Istvan 1949- *WhoScE 91-4*
Husting, E. Lee 1939- *WhoSSW 93*
Husting, Peter Marden 1935- *WhoAm 92*
Huston, Anjelica *BioIn 17*
Huston, Anjelica 1951- *IntDcF 2-3 [port], WhoAm 92, WhoAmW 93*
Huston, Anne Marshall *ConAu 40NR*
Huston, Annette Lynn 1963- *WhoEmL 93*
Huston, Beatrice Louise 1932- *WhoAm 92*
Huston, Bernard K. 1939- *St&PR 93*
Huston, Bo 1959- *ConGAN*
Huston, Claudius H. 1876-1952 *PolPar*
Huston, Claudius Hart 1876-1952 *BioIn 17*
Huston, D.M. *WhoScE 91-1*
Huston, Daniel Cliff 1955- *WhoEmL 93*
Huston, Danny *MiSFD 9*
Huston, Dennis Robert 1952- *St&PR 93*
Huston, DeVerille Anne 1947- *WhoAmW 93*
Huston, Dolores Haynes 1929- *WhoAmW 93*
Huston, Edwin Allen 1938- *St&PR 93, WhoAm 92*
Huston, Fred John 1929- *WhoSSW 93*
Huston, Harland Watson 1924- *St&PR 93*
Huston, Harris Hyde 1907- *WhoAm 92, WhoWor 93*
Huston, James d1992 *BioIn 17*
Huston, Jimmy *MiSFD 9*
Huston, John 1906-1987 *BioIn 17, MiSFD 9N*
Huston, John Charles 1927- *WhoAm 92, WhoWor 93*
Huston, John Dennis 1939- *WhoSSW 93*
Huston, John Leo 1944- *WhoAm 92*
Huston, John Lewis 1919- *WhoAm 92*
Huston, John Oliver 1945- *St&PR 93*
Huston, John Wilson 1925- *WhoAm 92*
Huston, Joseph P. 1940- *WhoScE 91-3*
Huston, Kathleen 1944- *WhoAm 92*
Huston, Larry L. *Law&B 92*
Huston, Margo 1943- *WhoAm 92, WhoAmW 93*
Huston, Michael E. 1948- *WhoIns 93*
Huston, Michael Everett 1959- *WhoEmL 93, WhoSSW 93*
Huston, Michelle Madeliene 1965- *WhoAmW 93*
Huston, Nancy Elizabeth 1947- *WhoSSW 93*
Huston, Norman Earl 1919- *WhoAm 92*
Huston, Phillip M., Jr. *Law&B 92*
Huston, Preston D. 1925- *St&PR 93*
Huston, Samuel Richard 1940- *WhoAm 92*
Huston, Scott 1916-1991 *BioIn 17*
Huston, (Thomas) Scott, (Jr.) 1916-1991 *Baker 92*
Huston, Stella Ethel 1951- *WhoAmW 93*
Huston, Steven C. *Law&B 92*
Huston, Steven Craig 1954- *WhoEmL 93*
Huston, Ted Laird 1943- *WhoAm 92*
Huston, Tom Charles 1941- *WhoAm 92*
Huston, Walter 1884-1950 *IntDcF 2-3 [port]*
Hustvedt, Siri 1955- *ConAu 137*
Huszar, Gabor Bela 1938- *WhoE 93*
Huszar, Istvan 1923- *WhoScE 91-4*
Huszar, Marta Jean 1953- *WhoE 93*
Huta, Henry Nicholaus 1947- *WhoEmL 93, WhoWor 93*
Hutabarat, Sans Soaloon 1936- *WhoUN 92*
Hutaff, William Rhett, III 1956- *St&PR 93*
Hutas, Imre 1926- *WhoScE 91-4*
Hutch, Willie *SoulM*
Hutchcraft, A. Stephen 1930- *St&PR 93*
Hutchence, Michael *BioIn 17*
Hutchenrider, Clarence B. 1908-1991 *BioIn 17*
Hutchens, Frank 1892-1965 *Baker 92*
Hutchens, Gail Rakes 1938- *St&PR 93*
Hutchens, John Kennedy 1905- *WhoAm 92*
Hutchens, John Oliver 1914- *WhoAm 92*
Hutchens, Judy Poplin 1952- *WhoAmW 93*
Hutchens, Teresa Ann 1954- *WhoSSW 93*
Hutchens, Timothy Rice 1938- *WhoE 93*
Hutchens, Trudy Pearce 1969- *WhoE 93*
Hutchens, Tyra Thornton 1921- *WhoAm 92*
Hutcheon, Duncan Elliot 1922- *WhoAm 92*
Hutcheon, Linda Ann 1947- *WhoAmW 93*
Hutcheon, Wallace Schoonmaker 1933- *WhoSSW 93*
Hutcher, Andrew M. *Law&B 92*
Hutcher, Andrew Mark *Law&B 92*
Hutcherson, Bobby 1941- *Baker 92, WhoAm 92*
Hutcherson, Karen Fulghum 1951- *WhoEmL 93*
Hutcherson, Reginald Kenneth 1929- *St&PR 93*
Hutcherson, William T. 1946- *St&PR 93*
Hutcheson, Carolyn Pirtle 1930- *WhoWrEP 92*
Hutcheson, Donald Wade 1933- *WhoSSW 93*
Hutcheson, Ernest 1871-1951 *Baker 92*
Hutcheson, Fritz 1915- *St&PR 93*
Hutcheson, Gregory Ellis 1956- *WhoSSW 93*
Hutcheson, Harold Leo 1916- *WhoAm 92*
Hutcheson, James Sterling 1919- *WhoAm 92, WhoWor 93*
Hutcheson, Janet Reid 1934- *WhoAm 92, WhoE 93*
Hutcheson, Jerry Dee 1932- *WhoWor 93*
Hutcheson, Joseph Chappell, III 1907- *WhoAm 92*
Hutcheson, Mark Andrew 1942- *WhoAm 92*
Hutcheson, Philip Charles 1948- *WhoEmL 93, WhoSSW 93, WhoWor 93*
Hutcheson, Thad T., Jr. 1941- *WhoAm 92*
Hutcheson, Zenas Willard, III 1953- *WhoE 93*
Hutchings, Alan Arthur 1944- *St&PR 93*
Hutchings, Arthur (James Bramwell) 1906- *Baker 92*
Hutchings, Brian LaMar 1915- *WhoAm 92*
Hutchings, G.J. 1951- *WhoScE 91-1*
Hutchings, George Henry 1922- *WhoAm 92*
Hutchings, Graham John *WhoScE 91-1*
Hutchings, John Barrie 1941- *WhoAm 92*
Hutchings, LeAnne von Neumeyer *WhoAmW 93*
Hutchings, Leo George 1924- *St&PR 93*
Hutchings, Nancy C. *Law&B 92*
Hutchings, Peter Lounsbery 1943- *WhoAm 92*
Hutchins, Carleen Maley 1911- *WhoAmW 93*
Hutchins, Collingwood 1936- *WhoWor 93*
Hutchins, Constantine, Jr. *Law&B 92*
Hutchins, Constantine, Jr. 1928- *St&PR 93*
Hutchins, David Leonard 1948- *WhoEmL 93*
Hutchins, Dexter Carleton 1938- *WhoE 93*
Hutchins, Dianne 1953- *WhoAmW 93, WhoEmL 93*
Hutchins, Donald B. 1948- *St&PR 93*
Hutchins, Elizabeth Leigh 1858-1935 *BioIn 17*
Hutchins, Frank McAllister 1922- *WhoAm 92*
Hutchins, Geraldine L. *ScF&FL 92*
Hutchins, Grover MacGregor 1932- *WhoE 93*
Hutchins, Henry Alexander 1944- *WhoSSW 93*
Hutchins, Henry Joseph 1773-1861 *BioIn 17*
Hutchins, Jeane M. 1947- *WhoWrEP 92*

Hutchins, Joan Morthland 1940- WhoAmW 93
Hutchins, John Osborne 1920- WhoAm 92
Hutchins, John Richard, III WhoAm 92
Hutchins, K. Grant Law&B 92
Hutchins, K. Grant 1942- St&PR 93
Hutchins, Michael George WhoScE 91-1
Hutchins, Pamela Elizabeth 1947- WhoAmW 93
Hutchins, Pat ChlBIID [port]
Hutchins, Pat 1942- BioIn 17, ChlFicS, MajAI [port], SmATA 70 [port], -16AS [port]
Hutchins, Ralph E. 1944- St&PR 93
Hutchins, Ralph Edwin, Jr. 1944- WhoAm 92
Hutchins, Richard B. 1918- St&PR 93
Hutchins, Robert Maynard 1899-1977 BioIn 17
Hutchins, Robert S. 1907-1990 BioIn 17
Hutchins, Shirley M. 1933- WhoWrEP 92
Hutchins, Thomas BioIn 17
Hutchins, Thomas Williams 1948- St&PR 93
Hutchins, W. James 1946- WhoEmL 93
Hutchins, William Bruce, III 1943- St&PR 93, WhoAm 92
Hutchins, William John 1939- WhoWor 93
Hutchinson, A.L., Jr. 1933- St&PR 93
Hutchinson, Albert Newhall 1939- WhoAm 92
Hutchinson, Allan Robert WhoScE 91-1
Hutchinson, Andrew James 1963- WhoSSW 93
Hutchinson, Ann 1950- WhoAmW 93
Hutchinson, Anne Marbury 1591-1643 BioIn 17
Hutchinson, B. Thomas 1934- WhoE 93
Hutchinson, Bruce 1901- WhoCanL 92
Hutchinson, C.A. WhoScE 91-1
Hutchinson, Carroll R. 1933- WhoIns 93
Hutchinson, Carroll Ray 1933- St&PR 93
Hutchinson, Cecil Clair 1934- St&PR 93
Hutchinson, Charles Edgar 1935- WhoAm 92
Hutchinson, Charles Kimball 1928- St&PR 93
Hutchinson, Charles Maxwell 1925- WhoE 93
Hutchinson, Charles Smith, Jr. 1930- WhoAm 92
Hutchinson, David 1960- ScF&FL 92
Hutchinson, Douglas 1960- St&PR 93
Hutchinson, Douglas Curtis 1957- WhoSSW 93
Hutchinson, Earl Ofari 1945- ConAu 138, WhoWrEP 92
Hutchinson, Edward Prince 1906-1990 BioIn 17
Hutchinson, Evelyn 1903-1991 AnObit 1991
Hutchinson, Everett 1915- WhoAm 92
Hutchinson, Frank David, III 1929- St&PR 93
Hutchinson, Frederick Edward 1930- WhoAm 92
Hutchinson, G. Evelyn 1903-1991 BioIn 17
Hutchinson, George Allen 1936- WhoE 93
Hutchinson, George Evelyn 1903-1991 BioIn 17
Hutchinson, George J. 1937- WhoIns 93
Hutchinson, George Joseph 1937- St&PR 93
Hutchinson, Gradystein Williams BioIn 17
Hutchinson, Harold David 1931- WhoAm 92
Hutchinson, Heidi Law&B 92
Hutchinson, Ian Farley 1938- WhoWor 93
Hutchinson, Jeanette 1951- See Emotions SoulM
Hutchinson, John H. St&PR 93
Hutchinson, John Neville WhoScE 91-1
Hutchinson, John Woodside 1939- WhoAm 92
Hutchinson, Julien Reay 1930- St&PR 93
Hutchinson, Julius Steven 1952- WhoEmL 93
Hutchinson, Loren Kelley 1916- St&PR 93
Hutchinson, M. Curry 1939- St&PR 93
Hutchinson, M.H.R. WhoScE 91-1
Hutchinson, Margaret L. AmWomPl
Hutchinson, Martha LuClare 1941- WhoE 93
Hutchinson, Martin Oliver 1950- WhoWor 93
Hutchinson, Maureen Pat 1956- WhoAmW 93
Hutchinson, Melvin J. 1918- St&PR 93
Hutchinson, Michael Peter 1947- WhoEmL 93
Hutchinson, Nancy Anne 1947- WhoAmW 93
Hutchinson, Olin Fulmer, Jr. 1943- WhoSSW 93
Hutchinson, Pemberton 1931- St&PR 93, WhoAm 92
Hutchinson, Philip A., Jr. Law&B 92
Hutchinson, Philip A., Jr. 1938- St&PR 93
Hutchinson, Raymond Alexander 1937- St&PR 93, WhoAm 92
Hutchinson, Richard Armstrong 1944- St&PR 93
Hutchinson, Richard William 1928- WhoAm 92
Hutchinson, Robert Joseph WhoScE 91-1
Hutchinson, Robert Joseph 1957- WhoWrEP 92
Hutchinson, Ronald Porter 1951- WhoEmL 93
Hutchinson, Sara Ann 1964- WhoAmW 93
Hutchinson, Sheila 1953- See Emotions SoulM
Hutchinson, Thomas 1711-1780 BioIn 17
Hutchinson, Thomas Cuthbert 1939- WhoAm 92
Hutchinson, Thomas D. 1954- St&PR 93
Hutchinson, Thomas Eugene 1936- WhoAm 92
Hutchinson, Tom WhoAm 92
Hutchinson, Tom 1930- ScF&FL 92
Hutchinson, Travis George 1942- St&PR 93
Hutchinson, Virginia Nettles 1936- WhoE 93
Hutchinson, W.B. 1944- WhoScE 91-4
Hutchinson, Wanda 1951- See Emotions SoulM
Hutchinson, William Burke 1909- WhoAm 92
Hutchinson, William David 1932- WhoAm 92, WhoE 93
Hutchinson, William J. Law&B 92
Hutchison, Alexander C. 1934- St&PR 93
Hutchison, Barbra Ann 1937- WhoAmW 93
Hutchison, Clyde Allen, Jr. 1913- WhoAm 92
Hutchison, Coe 1953- St&PR 93
Hutchison, Craig Austin 1952- St&PR 93
Hutchison, David 1946- ScF&FL 92
Hutchison, David A. 1946- WhoWrEP 92
Hutchison, Don 1931- ScF&FL 92
Hutchison, Donald Jay 1938- WhoSSW 93
Hutchison, Dorris Jeannette 1918- WhoAm 92
Hutchison, Douglas B. 1957- WhoEmL 93
Hutchison, Elizabeth May 1924- WhoAmW 93
Hutchison, Geoffrey Richard 1935- WhoAm 92
Hutchison, Gregg Hugh Law&B 92
Hutchison, James Arthur, Jr. 1917- WhoE 93
Hutchison, James Donald 1932- WhoE 93
Hutchison, Jane Campbell 1932- WhoAmW 93
Hutchison, Jane Eleanor Nelson 1959- WhoEmL 93
Hutchison, John Bower WhoScE 91-1
Hutchison, Joseph G., Jr. 1950- WhoWrEP 92
Hutchison, Kay Bailey 1943- WhoAm 92, WhoAmW 93, WhoSSW 93
Hutchison, Kenneth 1903-1989 BioIn 17
Hutchison, Loyd C., II 1952- St&PR 93
Hutchison, Michael S. WhoWrEP 92
Hutchison, Murray Hunter 1938- St&PR 93
Hutchison, Pat 1943- WhoAmW 93
Hutchison, Ralph Oswald 1923- WhoSSW 93
Hutchison, Richard Lee 1958- WhoEmL 93
Hutchison, Ron 1954- St&PR 93
Hutchison, Ronald Blaine 1950- WhoAm 92
Hutchison, Russell Edwin Law&B 92
Hutchison, Stanley Philip 1923- WhoAm 92
Hutchison, Theodore M. 1932- WhoIns 93
Hutchison, Theodore Murtagh 1932- St&PR 93, WhoAm 92
Hutchison, Victor Hobbs 1931- WhoAm 92
Hutchison, William Forrest 1925- WhoAm 92
Hutchison-Hall, William Ellsworth Henry, IV 1963- WhoE 93
Hutchman, Laurence 1948- WhoCanL 92
Huth, Edward Janavel 1923- WhoAm 92
Huth, John A. 1941- St&PR 93
Huth, John H. 1930- St&PR 93
Huth, John Harvey 1922- WhoE 93
Huth, Kenneth J. St&PR 93
Huth, Robert D. 1946- St&PR 93
Huth, William Edward 1931- WhoAm 92
Huther, George W., III St&PR 93
Huthnance, Robert Thompson 1942- St&PR 93
Hutier, Oskar von 1857-1934 HarEnMi
Hutka, Glenn 1939- St&PR 93
Hutley, H.T. WhoScE 91-1
Hutley, Michael C. 1944- WhoScE 91-1
Hutmacher, Janet Ann 1948- WhoAmW 93
Hutman, Norma Louise 1934- WhoE 93
Hutner, Herbert L. WhoAm 92
Hutner, Milton d1990 BioIn 17
Hutner, Penny 1960- St&PR 93
Hutner, Robert Wolf 1931- St&PR 93
Hutner, Seymour Herbert 1911- WhoAm 92
Hutnikiewicz, Artur Maria 1916- WhoWor 93
Hutomo, Mandela Putra BioIn 17
Hutsaliuk, Yarema 1960- WhoE 93
Hutschenreuter, Karl 1920- WhoScE 91-3
Hutschenruijter Baker 92
Hutschenruyter Baker 92
Hutschenruyter, Willem Jacob 1828-1889 Baker 92
Hutschenruyter, Wouter 1796-1878 Baker 92
Hutschenruyter, Wouter 1859-1943 Baker 92
Hutsell, Thomas Carlyle 1939- St&PR 93
Hutsenpiller, Charles William 1942- WhoSSW 93
Hutson, Charles Randolph 1949- St&PR 93
Hutson, Dan C., II 1953- St&PR 93
Hutson, Danny James 1957- WhoEmL 93, WhoSSW 93
Hutson, Don 1913- BioIn 17
Hutson, Don 1931- WhoAm 92
Hutson, Harry Marshall 1920- WhoSSW 93
Hutson, Keith Eugene 1925- St&PR 93
Hutson, Leroy SoulM
Hutson, Leroy 1945- BioIn 17
Hutson, Pamela R. Law&B 92
Hutson, Shaun 1958- ScF&FL 92
Hutson, William Richard 1936- WhoE 93
Hu Tsung-nan 1895-1962 HarEnMi
Hu Tsu Tau, Richard 1926- WhoAsAP 91, WhoWor 93
Hutt, Eric John Villette 1915- WhoWor 93
Hutt, Joanna Cravey 1943- WhoWrEP 92
Hutt, Peter Barton 1934- WhoAm 92
Hutt, Robert Jeffrey 1936- WhoAsAP 91
Huttar, Charles A. 1920- ScF&FL 92
Huttemann, K.-J. WhoScE 91-3
Hutten, Helmut 1936- WhoScE 91-3
Huttenback, Robert Arthur 1928- WhoAm 92
Huttenbrenner, Anselm 1794-1868 Baker 92
Huttenbrink, Karl-Bernd 1952- WhoScE 91-3
Huttenstine, Marian Louise 1940- WhoSSW 93
Hutter, Adolph Matthew, Jr. 1937- WhoAm 92
Hutter, David 1930-1990 BioIn 17
Hutter, Donald S. 1932-1990 BioIn 17
Hutter, Donald Stephen 1932- WhoWrEP 92
Hutter, George Frederick 1943- WhoSSW 93
Hutter, Heidi E. 1957- WhoIns 93
Hutter, James Risque 1924- WhoAm 92
Hutter, Ralf 1931- WhoScE 91-4
Hutter, Ralf 1946- See Kraftwerk ConMus 9
Hutter, Robert Law&B 92
Hutter, Robert Victor Paul 1929- WhoAm 92
Hutter, Rudolf Gustav Emil 1910- WhoAm 92
Hutterer, Ferenc 1929- WhoAm 92
Huttermann, Aloys WhoScE 91-3
Huttinger, Richard C. 1924- St&PR 93
Huttner, Manfred 1930- WhoWor 93
Huttner, Marian Alice 1920- WhoAm 92
Huttner, Richard M. 1947- WhoAm 92
Huttner, Wieland B. 1950- WhoScE 91-3
Hutto, Earl 1926- CngDr 91, WhoAm 92, WhoSSW 93
Hutto, J.B. d1983 BioIn 17
Hutto, James Calhoun 1931- WhoAm 92
Hutto, John L. 1941- St&PR 93
Hutto, Richard Jay 1952- WhoSSW 93
Hutto, Tommye Whitt 1939- WhoAm 92
Hutton, A.D. WhoScE 91-1
Hutton, Albert Edward 1925- St&PR 93
Hutton, Ann Hawkes 1909- WhoAm 92
Hutton, Betty 1921- IntDcF 2-3
Hutton, Brian G. 1935- MiSFD 9
Hutton, E. William Law&B 92
Hutton, Edward L. 1919- St&PR 93
Hutton, Edward Luke 1919- WhoAm 92, WhoWor 93
Hutton, Ernest Watson, Jr. 1944- WhoE 93
Hutton, George Norman, Jr. 1929- St&PR 93
Hutton, George Thompson 1946- WhoEmL 93
Hutton, Herbert J. 1937- WhoAm 92, WhoE 93
Hutton, Jack Gossett, Jr. 1931- WhoE 93
Hutton, James Brian Edward 1931- WhoWor 93
Hutton, James Morgan, III 1927- WhoAm 92
Hutton, Jerry Bob 1938- WhoSSW 93
Hutton, John Alexander 1868-1947 BioIn 17
Hutton, John Evans, Jr. 1931- WhoAm 92
Hutton, Joseph 1928- St&PR 93
Hutton, Lauren BioIn 17
Hutton, Linda Jo 1947- WhoWrEP 92
Hutton, Paul Andrew 1949- WhoWrEP 92
Hutton, Priscilla Metcalfe 1953- WhoAmW 93
Hutton, Richard 1561?-1639 BioIn 17
Hutton, Robert 1920- BioIn 17
Hutton, Robert William 1921- St&PR 93
Hutton, Robin R. 1945- St&PR 93
Hutton, S.P. WhoScE 91-1
Hutton, Thomas Hays 1921- St&PR 93
Hutton, Timothy 1960- HolBB [port]
Hutton, Timothy 1961- WhoAm 92
Hutton, Warwick ChlBIID [port]
Hutton, Warwick Blair 1939- WhoAm 92
Hutton, William Cochrane 1937- WhoSSW 93
Hutton, William Michael 1948- WhoE 93
Hutton, William S. 1943- WhoIns 93
Hutton, Winfield Travis 1935- WhoE 93, WhoWor 93
Huttrer, Gerald William 1939- St&PR 93
Hutts, Joseph Clair, Jr. 1941- St&PR 93
Huttunen, Jussi K. 1941- WhoScE 91-4
Hutz, James Alan 1949- St&PR 93
Hutzelman, Stephen H. 1942- St&PR 93
Hutzelman, Thomas H. 1944- St&PR 93
Huval, Barbara Jane 1936- WhoSSW 93
Huvos, Andrew 1930- WhoE 93, WhoWor 93
Huvos, Christopher L. 1946- WhoEmL 93
Huvos, Kornel 1913- WhoAm 92
Hux, Eugene L. 1927- St&PR 93
Hux, Robert C. St&PR 93
Hux, Ronald Wayne 1957- St&PR 93
Huxham, Christine Sylvia WhoScE 91-1
Hu Xiaoyun 1935- WhoAsAP 91
Huxley, Aldous 1894-1963 BioIn 17, MagSWL [port], ScF&FL 92, WorLitC [port]
Huxley, Andrew Fielding 1917- WhoAm 92, WhoWor 93
Huxley, David B. d1992 NewYTBS 92
Huxley, Elspeth 1907- BioIn 17
Huxley, Hugh Esmor 1924- WhoAm 92
Huxley, Julian 1887-1975 BioIn 17, ScF&FL 92
Huxley, Laura Archera 1914- ScF&FL 92
Huxley, Thomas Henry 1825-1895 BioIn 17
Huxman, Walter Augustus 1887-1972 BioIn 17
Huxsaw, Charles Law&B 92
Huxster, Howard Knight 1924- WhoE 93
Huxtable, Ada Louise WhoAm 92, WhoAmW 93
Huxtable, Peter Lees 1943- WhoWor 93
Hu Yaobang 1915-1989 ColdWar 2 [port], DcTwHis
Huybrechts, Albert 1899-1938 Baker 92
Huybrechts, Guy H.R. 1936- WhoScE 91-2
Huybrechts, Marc Alexander 1941- WhoWor 93
Huyck, Margaret Hellie 1939- WhoAmW 93
Huyck, Willard MiSFD 9, WhoAm 92
Huyck, Willard 1945- ScF&FL 92
Huyer, Adriana 1945- WhoAmW 93
Huyett, Daniel Henry, III 1921- WhoE 93
Huyett, Daniel Henry, 3rd 1921- WhoAm 92
Huyffer, Paul 1938- St&PR 93
Huygen, Wil 1922- ScF&FL 92
Huygens, R.J.J. 1930- WhoScE 91-2
Huygens, Remmert William 1932- WhoAm 92
Huyghe, Gilbert Francois 1924- WhoWor 93
Huyghe, Jacques Marcel 1943- WhoE 93
Huyghe, Patrick ScF&FL 92
Huyghe, Rene Louis 1906- WhoWor 93
Huyghue, Douglas Smith 1816-1891 BioIn 17
Huyler, Jean Wiley 1935- WhoAm 92, WhoWrEP 92
Huyler, William Creighton, Jr. 1944- WhoSSW 93
Huynh, Cao Tri 1936- WhoUN 92
Huynh, Tuan 1936- ConEn
Huynh Ngoc, Phien 1944- WhoWor 93
Huyser, Robert E(rnest) 1924- ConAu 139
Huyser, Robert Ernest 1924- WhoAm 92
Huyskens, Chris J. 1945- WhoScE 91-3
Huyskens, J. WhoScE 91-3
Huysman, Arlene Weiss 1929- WhoAm 92, WhoAmW 93, WhoSSW 93
Huysmans, Joris-Karl 1848-1907 DcLB 123 [port]

Huyssen, Andreas 1942- *WhoAm 92, WhoWor 93*
Huyuh Tan Phat 1913- *DcTwHis*
Huzar, Eleanor Goltz 1922- *WhoAm 92*
Huze, Cyril Michel 1949- *WhoWor 93*
Huzinec, Mary Suzanne 1956- *WhoE 93*
Huzvar, Barbara Jo 1950- *WhoWrEP 92*
Hvass, Charles Thomas, Jr. 1950- *WhoEmL 93*
Hvistendahl, Joyce Kilmer 1918- *WhoAm 92*
Hvorostovsky, Dmitri *BioIn 17*
Hvorostovsky, Dmitri 1962- *Baker 92*
Hvoslef (Saeverud), Ketil 1939- *Baker 92*
Hwa, Erh-Cheng 1945- *WhoE 93*
Hwa, Lee-Jinn 1924- *WhoWor 93*
Hwa, Stephen Chi-Ping 1933- *St&PR 93*
Hwang, Byong Ha 1954- *WhoWor 93*
Hwang, Byung-Ki 1936- *Baker 92*
Hwang, Cordelia Jong 1942- *WhoWor 93*
Hwang, David Henry *BioIn 17*
Hwang, David Henry 1957- *WhoAm 92*
Hwang, Eui-Gak 1940- *WhoWor 93*
Hwang, Grace Y. *Law&B 92*
Hwang, Ivy *Law&B 92*
Hwang, K. Philip 1936- *St&PR 93*
Hwang, Kijun 1949- *WhoWor 93*
Hwang, Li-San 1935- *St&PR 93*
Hwang, Peter Lam Hum 1945- *WhoWor 93*
Hwang, San-Bao 1946- *WhoE 93*
Hwang, Suk-Geun 1950- *WhoWor 93*
Hwang, Woei-Yann Pauchy 1948- *WhoWor 93*
Hwang, Woonbong 1958- *WhoWor 93*
Hwang Byung Tai 1936- *WhoAsAP 91*
Hwang Byung Woo 1932- *WhoAsAP 91*
Hwang Chul Su 1927- *WhoAsAP 91*
Hwang Dae Bong 1930- *WhoAsAP 91*
Hwang Myung Soo 1928- *WhoAsAP 91*
Hwang Nak-Joo 1931- *WhoAsAP 91*
Hwang Seung-Gyun, Dr. 1937- *WhoAsAP 91*
Hwang Yoon Ki 1936- *WhoAsAP 91*
Hwilka, John S. 1953- *St&PR 93*
Hyakinthos of Cyprus d1346 *OxDcByz*
Hyakutake, Haruyoshi 1888-1947 *HarEnMi*
Hyams, Bernard D. 1925- *WhoScE 91-4*
Hyams, Edward 1910-1975 *ScF&FL 92*
Hyams, Gerald Theodore 1933- *WhoE 93*
Hyams, Joe 1923- *WhoAm 92, WhoWrEP 92*
Hyams, Nessa *MiSFD 9*
Hyams, Peter 1943- *MiSFD 9, ScF&FL 92*
Hyatt, Carole 1935- *WhoAmW 93*
Hyatt, Christopher *Law&B 92*
Hyatt, Christopher Wayne *Law&B 92*
Hyatt, David d1992 *NewYTBS 92*
Hyatt, Dennis Michael *Law&B 92*
Hyatt, Dennis Michael 1940- *St&PR 93*
Hyatt, Felicia B. 1920- *BioIn 17*
Hyatt, Gilbert P. *BioIn 17, NewYTBS 92 [port]*
Hyatt, James *Law&B 92*
Hyatt, James V. 1951- *St&PR 93*
Hyatt, James Vescelius *Law&B 92*
Hyatt, Jerome Bowman, Jr. 1946- *WhoSSW 93*
Hyatt, Joel Z. 1950- *WhoAm 92*
Hyatt, Joel Zylberberg 1950- *ConEn*
Hyatt, John *BioIn 17*
Hyatt, Kenneth Ernest 1940- *St&PR 93, WhoAm 92*
Hyatt, Melvin Gene 1949- *WhoSSW 93*
Hyatt, Meredith R., Jr. *Law&B 92*
Hyatt, Phillip Steven 1935- *St&PR 93*
Hyatt-Smith, Ann Rose 1953- *WhoAmW 93, WhoE 93*
Hybasek, Ivan 1929- *WhoScE 91-4*
Hybl, William J. 1942- *St&PR 93*
Hycka Maruniak, Miguel 1924- *WhoScE 91-3*
Hyclak, Joseph Gerard 1957- *WhoEmL 93*
Hydatius c. 395-c. 470 *OxDcByz*
Hyde, Agnes *AmWomPl*
Hyde, Alan Litchfield 1928- *WhoAm 92*
Hyde, Alice Bach 1939- *WhoAmW 93*
Hyde, Allie Bargum 1926- *WhoAmW 93*
Hyde, Anthony 1946- *ConAu 136, WhoCanL 92*
Hyde, Barbara P. 1945- *WhoAmW 93*
Hyde, Charles F. 1920- *St&PR 93*
Hyde, Charles Henry, III 1952- *St&PR 93*
Hyde, Christopher 1949- *ScF&FL 92*
Hyde, Christopher 1950- *WhoCanL 92*
Hyde, Clarence Brodie, II 1937- *WhoAm 92, WhoSSW 93*
Hyde, David Rowley 1929- *WhoAm 92*
Hyde, Dawn Stauffer 1954- *WhoAmW 93, WhoEmL 93*
Hyde, Dayton O. 1925- *BioIn 17*
Hyde, Dorothy Gillette *AmWomPl*
Hyde, Doug 1946- *BioIn 17*
Hyde, Douglas *BioIn 17*
Hyde, Douglas G. 1943- *St&PR 93*
Hyde, Douglas Gaylord 1943- *WhoAm 92*
Hyde, Edward 1609-1674 *BioIn 17*
Hyde, Elizabeth Howe 1920- *WhoAm 92*
Hyde, Ella Mae 1938- *WhoAmW 93*
Hyde, Florence Elise *AmWomPl*
Hyde, Geoffrey 1930- *WhoWor 93*
Hyde, George H. 1922- *St&PR 93*
Hyde, Geraldine Veola 1926- *WhoAmW 93, WhoWor 93*
Hyde, Gregory R. *ScF&FL 92*
Hyde, Henry Baldwin 1915- *WhoE 93*
Hyde, Henry J. 1924- *CngDr 91*
Hyde, Henry John 1924- *WhoAm 92*
Hyde, Herbert Lee 1925- *WhoSSW 93*
Hyde, Howard Laurence 1957- *WhoE 93*
Hyde, Jack 1916- *WhoAm 92*
Hyde, John 1943- *ScF&FL 92*
Hyde, John Kenneth 1930-1986 *BioIn 17*
Hyde, John Michael 1930- *WhoAm 92*
Hyde, John Paul 1934- *WhoAm 92*
Hyde, Joseph R., III 1942- *St&PR 93*
Hyde, Kenneth R. 1944- *St&PR 93*
Hyde, Laurin E. d1991 *BioIn 17*
Hyde, Lawrence H. 1924- *St&PR 93*
Hyde, Lawrence Henry, Jr. 1924- *WhoAm 92*
Hyde, Lewis 1945- *WhoWrEP 92*
Hyde, Margaret O(ldroyd) 1917- *MajAI [port]*
Hyde, Mark Powell 1881-1952 *ScF&FL 92*
Hyde, Mary Morley Crapo 1912- *WhoAm 92*
Hyde, Michael Clarendon 1923- *WhoWor 93*
Hyde, Michael Joseph 1956- *WhoEmL 93*
Hyde, Michael Theodore *Law&B 92*
Hyde, Nina d1990 *BioIn 17*
Hyde, Pamela Suzon 1950- *WhoAmW 93*
Hyde, Peter Dawson 1924- *WhoSSW 93*
Hyde, Richard A. *Law&B 92*
Hyde, Richard Mark 1955- *WhoEmL 93, WhoSSW 93*
Hyde, Robert Burke, Jr. 1928- *WhoAm 92*
Hyde, Robert W., Jr. *Law&B 92*
Hyde, Robert William, Jr. 1956- *WhoEmL 93*
Hyde, Rosel H. d1992 *NewYTBS 92 [port]*
Hyde, Shelley *ScF&FL 92*
Hyde, Stuart Wallace 1923- *WhoAm 92*
Hyde, Thomas *WhoScE 91-1*
Hyde, Thomas D. 1948- *St&PR 93*
Hyde, Thomas Horace *WhoScE 91-1*
Hyde, Walter 1875-1951 *Baker 92, OxDcOp*
Hyde, William 1946- *WhoEmL 93*
Hyde-Chambers, Derek 1913-1980 *ScF&FL 92*
Hyde-Jackson, M. Deborah 1949- *WhoAm 92*
Hydell, Martin H. 1942- *St&PR 93*
Hyden, Dorothy Louise 1948- *WhoAmW 93, WhoEmL 93*
Hyden, Joe Bailey 1939- *WhoSSW 93*
Hyder, Jeanne McEachern 1962- *WhoAmW 93*
Hyder, Stuart J. *Law&B 92*
Hyde White, Wilfrid 1903-1991 *AnObit 1991, BioIn 17*
Hydok, Joseph Thomas 1928- *St&PR 93, WhoAm 92*
Hydrisko, Robert Emerson 1962- *St&PR 93*
Hydrisko, Stanley Joseph 1927- *WhoE 93*
Hyduk, Dennis Michael 1951- *St&PR 93*
Hydzik, Michael James 1950- *WhoE 93*
Hye-Knudsen, Johan 1896-1975 *Baker 92*
Hyer, Frank Sidney 1933- *St&PR 93*
Hyer, Frederick L., Jr. 1940- *St&PR 93, WhoIns 93*
Hyer, J. Walter, III *Law&B 92*
Hyer, Laura Jane 1956- *WhoAmW 93*
Hyer, Marsha Liles 1955- *WhoAmW 93*
Hyer, Martha *BioIn 17*
Hyer, Martha 1924?- *SweetSg C [port]*
Hyer, Michael Edward 1945- *WhoE 93, WhoWor 93*
Hyer, Michael H. *Law&B 92*
Hyers, Conrad 1933- *ScF&FL 92*
Hyers, Judith Gegenheimer 1945- *St&PR 93*
Hyers, Kemper Kent 1929- *St&PR 93*
Hyett, James d1990 *BioIn 17*
Hyjek, Walter John 1937- *St&PR 93*
Hykel, Richard Daniel 1944- *St&PR 93*
Hyken, Edward Jonathan 1967- *WhoE 93*
Hykes, David (Bond) 1953- *Baker 92*
Hykin, Douglas Harold William *WhoScE 91-1*
Hyla, James Franklin 1945- *WhoE 93, WhoWor 93*
Hyland, Anthony David Charles *WhoScE 91-1*
Hyland, Bruce 1931- *WhoUN 92*
Hyland, David F. *Law&B 92*
Hyland, Douglas K. S. 1949- *WhoAm 92, WhoSSW 93*
Hyland, Edward B. 1942- *St&PR 93*
Hyland, Geoffrey F. *St&PR 93*
Hyland, Geoffrey Fyfe *WhoAm 92*
Hyland, John P. 1928- *St&PR 93, WhoIns 93*
Hyland, John Roth, Jr. 1950- *WhoWor 93*
Hyland, Lawrence A. 1897-1989 *BioIn 17*
Hyland, Michael Pearson 1936- *WhoUN 92*
Hyland, Richard Francis 1937- *St&PR 93*
Hyland, Robert d1992 *NewYTBS 92*
Hyland, Robert E. *Law&B 92*
Hyland, Robert Francis d1992 *BioIn 17*
Hyland, Robert J., Jr. 1949- *St&PR 93*
Hyland, Thomas Patrick 1964- *WhoE 93*
Hyland, Thomas Robert 1932- *WhoSSW 93*
Hyland, William Francis 1923- *WhoAm 92*
Hylander, Walter Raymond, Jr. 1924- *WhoSSW 93, WhoWor 93*
Hyle, Charles Thomas 1961- *WhoEmL 93, WhoSSW 93*
Hyle, Jack Otto 1929- *WhoE 93, WhoWor 93*
Hyles, Vernon 1943- *ScF&FL 92*
Hylinski, Thomas E. 1953- *St&PR 93*
Hyllested, August 1856-1946 *Baker 92*
Hyltenius, Carl-Magnus G. 1940- *WhoUN 92*
Hylton, Hannelore Menke 1936- *WhoAm 92*
Hylton, Jane W. 1929- *St&PR 93*
Hylton, Jane Waller 1929- *WhoAmW 93*
Hylton, Kevin Earl 1956- *St&PR 93*
Hylton, Richard Maurice 1954- *WhoEmL 93*
Hylton, Thomas James 1948- *WhoAm 92, WhoE 93*
Hyman, Albert Lewis 1923- *WhoAm 92*
Hyman, Arnold 1931- *WhoE 93*
Hyman, Betty Harpole 1938- *WhoAmW 93*
Hyman, Bruce 1944- *St&PR 93*
Hyman, Bruce Malcolm 1943- *WhoAm 92, WhoE 93, WhoWor 93*
Hyman, David Nell 1943- *WhoWrEP 92*
Hyman, Dick 1927- *ConTFT 10*
Hyman, Earle 1926- *WhoAm 92*
Hyman, Flo *BioIn 17*
Hyman, Flora 1954-1986 *BiDAMSp 1989*
Hyman, Glenn Carter 1958- *WhoEmL 93*
Hyman, Irwin A. 1935- *WhoE 93*
Hyman, Isabelle 1930- *WhoE 93*
Hyman, Jackie 1949- *ScF&FL 92*
Hyman, James R., Jr. *Law&B 92*
Hyman, Jerome Elliot 1923- *WhoAm 92*
Hyman, John Adams 1840-1891 *BioIn 17*
Hyman, Laura 1927- *WhoE 93*
Hyman, Lawrence Robert 1940- *WhoE 93*
Hyman, Lester Samuel 1931- *WhoAm 92*
Hyman, Lloyd George 1928- *WhoAm 92*
Hyman, M. David 1934- *St&PR 93*
Hyman, Marshall Leonard 1924- *St&PR 93*
Hyman, Mary Bloom *WhoAmW 93, WhoE 93, WhoWor 93*
Hyman, Michael Richard 1954- *WhoEmL 93, WhoSSW 93*
Hyman, Milton 1905- *WhoAm 92*
Hyman, Morton P. 1936- *St&PR 93*
Hyman, Morton Peter 1936- *WhoAm 92, WhoWor 93*
Hyman, Patricia *St&PR 93*
Hyman, Paula Ellen *WhoAm 92*
Hyman, Phyllis *BioIn 17*
Hyman, Ralph Alan 1928- *WhoAm 92*
Hyman, Ray, Sr. *St&PR 93*
Hyman, Ray, Jr. *St&PR 93*
Hyman, Roger David 1957- *WhoEmL 93*
Hyman, Sarah Ellis *AmWomPl*
Hyman, Seymour 1927- *WhoAm 92*
Hyman, Seymour Charles 1919- *WhoAm 92*
Hyman, Stanley H. 1936- *BioIn 17*
Hyman, Stanley Herbert 1936- *WhoAm 92*
Hyman, Trina Schart *ChlBIID [port]*
Hyman, Trina Schart 1939- *MajAI [port]*
Hyman, W. Maier 1930- *St&PR 93*
Hyman, William 1958- *WhoE 93*
Hymel, Gary Gerard 1933- *WhoAm 92*
Hymer, Esther Juliette *WhoAmW 93*
Hymer, Stephen *BioIn 17*
Hymes, Dell Hathaway 1927- *WhoAm 92, WhoSSW 93*
Hymes, L. *WhoScE 91-3*
Hymes, Norma 1949- *WhoEmL 93*
Hymes, Viola 1906-1991 *BioIn 17*
Hymes, William Russell 1927- *WhoE 93*
Hymoff, Edward d1992 *NewYTBS 92*
Hymoff, Edward 1924- *WhoAm 92*
Hymowitz, Mitchell I. 1956- *St&PR 93*
Hymowitz, Theodore 1934- *WhoAm 92*
Hynam, John *ScF&FL 92*
Hynd, Noel 1947- *WhoEmL 93*
Hynde, Chrissie 1951- *See* Pretenders, The *ConMus 8*
Hyndman, Arnold Gene 1952- *WhoE 93*
Hyndman, Thomas M., Jr. 1924- *St&PR 93*
Hyne, James Bissett 1929- *WhoAm 92*
Hyne, Janet Elizabeth 1940- *WhoAmW 93*
Hyneman, Charles Shang 1900- *BioIn 17*
Hyneman, Esther F. 1939- *ScF&FL 92*
Hynes, Hugh Bernard Noel 1917- *WhoAm 92*
Hynes, James Thomas *Law&B 92*
Hynes, Jane F. *BioIn 17*
Hynes, John J. 1927- *St&PR 93*
Hynes, Mary Ann 1947- *St&PR 93, WhoAm 92, WhoAmW 93*
Hynes, Michael Kevin 1935- *WhoSSW 93*
Hynes, Neil John 1935- *St&PR 93*
Hynes, Richard Olding 1944- *WhoAm 92, WhoE 93*
Hynes, Samuel 1924- *ScF&FL 92, WhoAm 92*
Hynes, Terence Michael 1954- *WhoAm 92*
Hynninen, Jorma 1941- *Baker 92*
Hynninen, Jorma Kalervo 1941- *WhoWor 93*
Hynson, George Beswick 1932- *St&PR 93*
Hypatia c. 355-415 *OxDcByz*
Hypatios dc. 541 *OxDcByz*
Hypatios fl. 4th cent.- *OxDcByz*
Hypatios of Rouphinianai c. 366-466 *OxDcByz*
Hyre, Frank F. 1934- *St&PR 93*
Hyre, Rexford C. 1940- *St&PR 93*
Hyre, Ruth Starr 1923- *WhoAmW 93*
Hyrick, Marie Lynne 1954- *WhoE 93*
Hyrtakenos, Theodore fl. 14th cent.- *OxDcByz*
Hysaw, Guillermo L. *BioIn 17*
Hysinger, Vaughn G. 1943- *St&PR 93*
Hyslop, A.H. *Law&B 92*
Hyslop, Carol Dhu 1942- *WhoSSW 93*
Hyslop, James R. 1945- *St&PR 93*
Hyslop, Richard Michael 1949- *WhoEmL 93*
Hyslop, William Arthur 1946- *WhoSSW 93*
Hyson, Charles David 1915- *WhoAm 92*
Hyson, Frank J. 1932- *St&PR 93*
Hysong, James Wilson 1947- *St&PR 93*
Hyspecka, Ludmila 1934- *WhoScE 91-4*
Hytche, William Percy 1927- *WhoAm 92*
Hytes, Jason *ScF&FL 92*
Hytier, Adrienne Doris *WhoAm 92, WhoE 93*
Hytner, Nicholas 1955- *OxDcOp*
Hytonen, Jyrki Olavi 1956- *WhoScE 91-4*
Hytonen, Martii 1953- *WhoScE 91-4*
Hytower, Roy 1943- *BioIn 17*
Hyttinen, Lars Juhani 1939- *WhoUN 92*
Hyun, Hong Choo 1940- *WhoWor 93*
Hyun, Peter 1906- *ConAu 136*
Hyun, Wonbok 1929- *WhoWor 93*
Hyvarinen, Heikki P.E. 1938- *WhoScE 91-4*
Hyvarinen, Lauri *WhoScE 91-4*
Hyvarinen, Matti Jussi 1937- *WhoWor 93*
Hyvl, Daniel J. *Law&B 92*
Hyvnar, John K. *Law&B 92*
Hyvonen, C.W. 1946- *St&PR 93*
Hyvonen, Seppo Johannes 1939- *WhoWor 93*
Hyyppa, Jussi M.I. 1930- *WhoScE 91-4*
Hyyppa, Markku T. 1942- *WhoScE 91-4*
Hyytinen, Elene *St&PR 93*
Hyytinen, Niilo M. 1926- *St&PR 93*

I

Iaccarino, Maurizio 1938- *WhoScE 91-3*
Iaccarino, Ralph *BioIn 17*
Iaccheo, Armand R. 1923- *St&PR 93*
Iachetti, Rose Maria Anne 1931- *WhoAmW 93, WhoWor 93*
Iacob, Mihai 1933- *DrEEuF*
Iacobelli, Janet Elaine 1959- *WhoAmW 93*
Iacobelli, John Louis 1931- *WhoWor 93*
Iacobellis, Nicola Sante 1949- *WhoScE 91-3*
Iacobellis, Sam F. 1929- *St&PR 93*
Iacobellis, Sam Frank 1929- *WhoAm 92*
Iacobucci, Frank 1937- *WhoAm 92, WhoWor 93*
Iacobucci, Guillermo Arturo 1927- *WhoWor 93*
Iacocca, Lee 1924- *News 93-1 [port], WhoAm 92*
Iacocca, Lee A. *BioIn 17*
Iacocca, Lee A. 1924- *St&PR 93*
Iacocca, Lido Anthony 1924- *WhoAm 92*
Iacona, Lynn Ann 1958- *WhoE 93*
Iacona, Robert 1945- *St&PR 93*
Iacone, Marge 1943- *WhoAmW 93*
Iaconelli, William B. 1933- *St&PR 93*
Iaconianni, Frank Joseph 1954- *WhoE 93*
Iacono, Maggie *BioIn 17*
Iacopelli, Thomas John 1960- *St&PR 93*
Iacoponi, Michael Joseph 1959- *WhoSSW 93*
Iacovelli, Guido David 1923- *St&PR 93*
Iacoviello, Carolyn Hansen *WhoAmW 93*
Iacovo, Michael Jamaal 1955- *WhoEmL 93*
Iacovou, George 1938- *WhoWor 93*
Iadanza, Eugene Anthony 1948- *WhoE 93, WhoEmL 93*
Iadarola, Antoinette *WhoAmW 93*
Iadarola, Stephen J. 1958- *St&PR 93*
Iadavaia, Elizabeth Ann 1960- *WhoAmW 93, WhoEmL 93*
Iaderosa, Gina Marie 1960- *WhoE 93*
Iafe, William 1955- *WhoE 93*
Iakinf, Father *IntDcAn*
Iakovidis, Spyros Eustace 1923- *WhoAm 92*
IAkovlev, Vasilii Vasilevich 1886- *BioIn 17*
Iakovos, Archbishop 1911- *WhoAm 92*
Iakovos, Bishop *WhoAm 92*
Iamblichos c. 250-c. 325 *OxDcByz*
Iampieri, James F. 1945- *St&PR 93*
Iams, David Aveling 1938- *WhoAm 92*
Ianello, Stephen *Law&B 92*
Iangalio, Masket Gabriel 1949- *WhoAsAP 91*
Iannaccone, Adolph Carmine 1950- *WhoEmL 93*
Iannaccone, Anthony (Joseph) 1943- *Baker 92*
Iannarone, Anthony J. *Law&B 92*
Iannazzone, Ralph L. 1933- *St&PR 93*
Iannettoni, Louis 1924- *St&PR 93*
Ianni, Eomond M. *Law&B 92*
Ianni, Francis Alphonse 1931- *WhoAm 92*
Ianni, Francis Anthony James 1926- *WhoAm 92*
Ianni, Jerry Girolamo 1970- *WhoE 93*
Ianni, Ronald William 1935- *WhoAm 92*
Ianniello, Robert Michael 1954- *WhoEmL 93*
Ianno, Angela Marie 1958- *WhoAmW 93*
Ianno, Frank *Law&B 92*
Iannone, Bartholomew Charles 1945- *WhoE 93*
Iannone, Carol *BioIn 17*
Iannotti, Daniel V. *Law&B 92*
Iannotti, Joseph Patrick 1954- *WhoE 93*
Iannucci, Patricia J. 1953- *St&PR 93*
Iannuzzi, Daniel Andrew 1934- *WhoE 93*
Iannuzzi, John Nicholas 1935- *WhoAm 92, WhoE 93, WhoWor 93*
Ianosi, Ioan Sigismund 1943- *WhoScE 91-4*
Iantosca, Maryann 1958- *WhoAmW 93*
Ianuzzi, Ralph J. 1931- *St&PR 93*
Ianziti, Adelbert John 1927- *WhoWor 93*
Iaquinto, James J. 1947- *St&PR 93*
Iarossi, Nancy Semler 1949- *WhoAmW 93*
IAshvili, Paolo Dzhibrailovich 1895-1937 *BioIn 17*
Iasillo, Peter 1929- *WhoE 93*
Iasites *OxDcByz*
Iassemidis, George 1952- *WhoWor 93*
Iasvili, Paolo 1895-1937 *BioIn 17*
Iatesta, John Michael *Law&B 92*
Iatesta, John Michael 1944- *WhoE 93*
Iati, Anthony P. 1933- *St&PR 93*
Iatrides, John Orestes 1932- *WhoE 93*
Iatropoulos, Michael John 1938- *WhoE 93*
Iauco, David N. 1951- *St&PR 93*
Iavicoli, Mario Anthony 1939- *WhoAm 92*
Iba, Barbara Jean Young 1937- *WhoAmW 93, WhoE 93, WhoWor 93*
Iba, Lynn E. *Law&B 92*
Ibach, David Wynn *Law&B 92*
Ibach, Douglas Theodore 1925- *WhoE 93*
Ibach, Harold P.W. 1941- *WhoScE 91-3*
Ibach, Johannes Adolf 1766-1848 *Baker 92*
Iball, Kingsley *WhoScE 91-1*
Ibanez, Carlos 1877-1960 *DcTwHis*
Ibanez, Felix Marti- *ScF&FL 92*
Ibanez, Jane Bourguard 1947- *WhoAmW 93*
Ibanez, Jesus 1953- *WhoWor 93*
Ibanez, Manuel Luis 1935- *WhoAm 92, WhoSSW 93*
Ibanez, Michael Louis 1916- *HispAmA*
Ibanez, Sara de 1909-1971 *BioIn 17, SpAmA*
Ibanez, Silvia Safille 1952- *WhoAmW 93, WhoEmL 93*
Ibanez, Vicente Blasco 1867-1928 *BioIn 17*
Ibarbourou, Juana de 1892-1979 *SpAmA*
Ibarbourou, Juana de 1895-1979 *BioIn 17*
Ibarguen, Alberto 1944- *St&PR 93*
Ibarguen, Carlos 1951- *St&PR 93*
Ibarguengoitia, Jorge 1928-1983 *DcMexL*
Ibarruri, Delores 1895-1989 *DcTwHis*
Ibarruri, Dolores 1895-1989 *BioIn 17*
Ibas d457 *OxDcByz*
Ibata, Koichi 1947- *WhoWor 93*
Ibbett, Roland Norman *WhoScE 91-1*
Ibbotson, Eva 1925- *ScF&FL 92*
Ibbs, G.T. *WhoScE 91-1*
Ibbs, Patricia Johnson 1938- *WhoAmW 93*
Ibe, Chidi Adonis 1947- *WhoUN 92*
Ibele, Erik W. *Law&B 92*
Ibele, Erin C. 1961- *St&PR 93*
Iben, Icko, Jr. 1931- *WhoAm 92*
Iben, Miriam Genevieve Fett 1937- *WhoAmW 93*
Iberall, Arthur Saul 1918- *WhoAm 92*
Ibers, James Arthur 1930- *WhoAm 92*
Ibert, Jacques 1890-1962 *BioIn 17, OxDcOp*
Ibert, Jacques (Francois Antoine) 1890-1962 *Baker 92*
ibn Abdul-Aziz, Abdullah 1924- *WhoWor 93*
Ibn Al-'adim 1192-1262 *OxDcByz*
Ibn Al-Athir 1160-1233 *OxDcByz*
Ibn al-Nadim, Muhammad ibn Ishaq fl. 987- *BioIn 17*
Ibn Al-Qalanisi c. 1072-1160 *OxDcByz*
Ibn Battuta 1304-c. 1369 *OxDcByz*
Ibn Battuta 1304-1377 *BioIn 17*
Ibn Battuta, Abu Abdallah 1304-1369 *Expl 93*
Ibn Bibi fl. 13th cent.- *OxDcByz*
Ibn Fadlan, Ahmad fl. 10th cent.- *Expl 93*
Ibn Hawkal, Abu al-Kasim Ibn Ali al-Nasibi 920?-990? *Expl 93*
Ibn Hawqal dc. 988 *OxDcByz*
Ibni Al-Marhum Syed Putra, Raja of Perlis Hassan Jamalullail 1920- *WhoAsAP 91*
Ibn Idris, Ahmad d1837 *BioIn 17*
Ibn Jubayr 1145-1217 *OxDcByz*
Ibn Jubayr, Abu al-Hasan Muhammed 1145-1217 *Expl 93*
Ibn Khaldun 1332-1406 *BioIn 17*
Ibn Khurdadhbeh c. 825-c. 912 *OxDcByz*
Ibn Rusta *OxDcByz*
Ibn Sa'ud, King of Saudi Arabia 1880-1953 *BioIn 17*
Ibn Shaddad *OxDcByz*
Ibold, Charles J. *Law&B 92*
Ibragimov, Ildar Abdullovic 1932- *WhoWor 93*
Ibragimov, Vagif Rza Ogly 1947- *WhoWor 93*
Ibrahim, Anjum 1957- *WhoWor 93*
Ibrahim, Barbara Lethem 1949- *WhoAmW 93*
Ibrahim, Fayez Fares 1941- *St&PR 93*
Ibrahim, Izzat 1942- *WhoWor 93*
Ibrahim, Khaled 1960- *St&PR 93*
Ibrahim, Mohamed 1938- *St&PR 93*
Ibrahim, Mohamed T. *WhoScE 91-1*
Ibrahim, Nabil Mustafa 1938- *WhoWor 93*
Ibrahim, Waziri (Alhaji) 1926- *WhoAfr*
Ibrahim, Youssef Abdel-Aziz 1935- *WhoUN 92*
Ibrahim Bin Ali, Hon 1951- *WhoAsAP 91*
Ibrahim Ibn-Al Aghlab 756-812 *HarEnMi*
Ibrishimov, N. 1928- *WhoScE 91-4*
Ibscher, Lutz 1940- *WhoScE 91-4*
Ibsen, Henrik 1828-1906 *MagSWL [port], OxDcOp, WorLitC [port]*
Ibuka, Masaru *BioIn 17*
Ibuka, Masaru 1908- *WhoWor 93*
Ibuki, Bunmei 1938- *WhoAsAP 91*
Ibukun, Lawrence Olu 1932- *WhoUN 92*
Ibur, Jane Ellen 1950- *WhoWrEP 92*
Ibuse, Masuji 1898- *BioIn 17*
Icahn, Carl C. *BioIn 17*
Icahn, Carl C. 1936- *EncABHB 8 [port], WhoAm 92, WhoE 93*
Icaza, Francisco de Asis de 1863-1925 *DcMexL*
Icaza, Jorge 1906-1978 *SpAmA*
Icaza, Xavier 1892- *DcMexL*
Ice, Billie Oberta 1962- *WhoAmW 93, WhoEmL 93*
Ice, John Frederick 1927- *WhoSSW 93*
Ice, Rodney Dean 1937- *WhoSSW 93*
Ice, Ruth 1928- *WhoWrEP 92*
Ice Cube *BioIn 17*
Iceland, William Frederick 1924- *WhoWor 93*
Icenhower, David J. 1951- *WhoSSW 93*
Icenogle, Ronald Dean 1951- *WhoEmL 93*
Ice-T *BioIn 17*
Ice-T c. 195-?- *News 92 [port], -92-3 [port]*
Ichaso, Leon *MiSFD 9*
Ichido, Hyoe 1855-1931 *HarEnMi*
Ichihara, Akitami 1934- *WhoWor 93*
Ichihashi, Hidetoshi 1950- *WhoWor 93*
Ichii, Junji 1936- *WhoAsAP 91*
Ichiishi, Tatsuro 1943- *WhoAm 92*
Ichikawa, Hiroshi 1931- *WhoWor 93*
Ichikawa, Kon 1915- *MiSFD 9*
Ichikawa, Shoichi 1923- *WhoAsAP 91*
Ichikawa, Tadao 1936- *WhoWor 93*
Ichikawa, Yoshio 1914- *WhoWor 93*
Ichikawa, Yuichi 1935- *WhoAsAP 91*
Ichiki, Kiyono d1942 *BioIn 17*
Ichiki, Kiyono 1892-1942 *HarEnMi*
Ichim, Ionita 1940- *WhoScE 91-4*
Ichimura, Shinichi 1925- *WhoWor 93*
Ichimura, Tohju 1931- *WhoWor 93*
I-Ching 634-712? *Expl 93*
Ichino, Yoko *WhoAm 92, WhoAmW 93*
Ichinose, Masao 1952- *WhoWor 93*
Ichisaka, Shinichiro 1939- *St&PR 93*
Ichiyama, Dennis Yoshihide 1944- *WhoAm 92*
Ichiyanagi, Toshi 1933- *Baker 92*
Ichord, Richard H. 1926-1992 *NewYTBS 92 [port]*
Ichord, Richard Howard 1926- *WhoAm 92*
Ichtertz, Nanette B. 1959- *WhoAmW 93*
Ickes, Harold L. 1874-1952 *BioIn 17, EncAACR*
Ickes, Harold M. *NewYTBS 92 [port]*
Icole, Michel 1935- *WhoScE 91-2*
Icone, Joe Al 1942- *St&PR 93*
Iconoclast 1883-1966 *BioIn 17*
Ida, Shiroh 1940- *WhoWor 93*
Idanpaan-Heikkila, Juhana Eljas 1937- *WhoUN 92*
Idaszak, Jerome Joseph 1945- *WhoAm 92*
Iddings, Kathleen Ann *WhoWrEP 92*
Iddings, Roger Griffith 1930- *WhoSSW 93*
Iddrissu, Mahama (Alhaji) 1939- *WhoAfr*
Ide, Gary L. 1953- *St&PR 93*
Ide, Kamy Lorraine 1954- *WhoEmL 93*
Ide, Marcy 1962- *St&PR 93*
Ide, Patricia Louise 1935- *WhoWrEP 92*
Ide, Shoichi 1939- *WhoAsAP 91*
Ideker, Judith Shaivitz 1942- *WhoAmW 93*
Idel, Harlan W. 1943- *St&PR 93*
Idelsohn, Abraham Zevi 1882-1938 *Baker 92*
Idelsohn, Sergio Rodolfo 1947- *WhoWor 93*
Idelson, Janine H. *Law&B 92*
Idemen, M. Mithat 1935- *WhoScE 91-4*
Iding, Allan Earl 1939- *WhoWor 93*
Idle, Eric 1943- *MiSFD 9, QDrFCA 92 [port]*

Idleman, Jerry Gene 1939- *St&PR 93*
Idleman, Larry Lynn 1938- *St&PR 93, WhoAm 92*
Idleman, Lee H. 1933- *St&PR 93*
Idleman, Lee Hillis 1933- *WhoAm 92*
Idler, David Richard 1923- *WhoAm 92, WhoWor 93*
Idol, Billy *BioIn 17*
Idol, James Daniel, Jr. 1928- *WhoAm 92, WhoWor 93*
Idol, John Lane, Jr. 1932- *WhoSSW 93*
Idone, Christopher *BioIn 17*
Idoni, Timothy C. *BioIn 17*
Idris, I, King of Libya 1890-1983 *BioIn 17*
Idris, Ahmad ibn d1837 *BioIn 17*
Idris, Ali Ahmed 1937- *WhoUN 92*
Idris, Awad 1933- *WhoUN 92*
Idris, Yusuf 1927-1991 *BioIn 17*
Idrisi, Al- 1100-c. 1165 *OxDcByz*
Idrisi, Abu Abd-Allah Muhammed al-Sharif al- 1100-1166 *Expl 93*
Idriss, Farouk Salim 1928- *WhoAm 92*
Idrissu, Alhadj *WhoWor 93*
Idstein, James Richard 1953- *WhoEmL 93*
Iduarte Foucher, Andres 1907-1984 *DcMexL*
Idyll, Janice Leah 1947- *WhoAmW 93*
Idziak, Benjamin R. *Law&B 92*
Idzik, Daniel R. *Law&B 92*
Idzik, Daniel Ronald 1935- *WhoAm 92*
Idzik, Martin Francis 1942- *WhoAm 92*
Idzikowski, Ludwik 1891-1929 *PolBiDi*
Idzikowski, Stanislaw 1894-1977 *PolBiDi*
Iekawe, Jacques 1946- *WhoAsAP 91*
Ienaga, Kazuharu 1948- *WhoWor 93*
Ieng, Kounsaky 1929- *WhoUN 92*
Iengo, Valerie 1955- *WhoEmL 93*
Ierodiakonou, Charalambos 1930- *WhoScE 91-3*
Ieuter, Fredric E. 1938- *St&PR 93*
Ieuter, Fritz 1938- *St&PR 93*
Ievoli, Richard Joseph 1946- *WhoE 93*
Ieyoub, Richard Phillip 1944- *WhoAm 92*
Ifantis, Ioannis 1955- *WhoScE 91-3*
Ifeagwu, Sam Chukwudi 1952- *WhoWor 93*
Ifeanyi, Charles Cameme 1932- *WhoWor 93*
Iffland, August Wilhelm 1759-1814 *BioIn 17*
Iffy, Leslie 1925- *WhoAm 92, WhoWor 93*
Ifill, O. Urcille 1921-1991 *BioIn 17*
Ifkovic, Edward Joseph 1943- *WhoE 93*
Iftikar, Syed H. *St&PR 93*
Ifukube, Akira 1914- *Baker 92*
Igarashi, Hitoshi d1991 *BioIn 17*
Igarashi, Kozo 1926- *WhoAsAP 91*
Igarashi, Takenobu 1944- *BioIn 17*
Igasaki, Masao, Jr. 1925- *WhoAm 92*
Igasaki, Toshio 1925- *WhoWor 93*
Igdaloff, Susan Gail 1948- *WhoEmL 93*
Igel, George Joseph, Jr. 1924- *St&PR 93*
Iger, Robert *BioIn 17*
Iger, Robert A. *WhoAm 92*
Igesz, Bodo 1935- *WhoAm 92*
Iggers, Georg Gerson 1926- *WhoAm 92*
Iglehart, John K. 1939- *WhoAm 92*
Iglehart, Kenneth Robert 1951- *WhoSSW 93*
Igleheart, Elizabeth Robbin 1957- *WhoEmL 93*
Igleheart, James B. 1922- *St&PR 93*
Iglesias, Adriana T. 1957- *WhoWor 93*
Iglesias, Eduardo Hector 1936- *WhoWor 93*
Iglesias, Enrique V. 1930- *WhoAm 92, WhoWor 93*
Iglesias, Julio *BioIn 17*
Iglesias, Julio 1943- *WhoAm 92, WhoWor 93*
Iglesias (Buga), Julio 1943- *Baker 92*
Iglesias, Maria Adela 1950- *WhoEmL 93*
Iglesias Tomaz, Jose Antonio 1950- *WhoWor 93*
Igleski, Thomas R. *Law&B 92*
Igleski, Thomas Robert 1934- *St&PR 93, WhoAm 92*
Iglewicz, Boris 1939- *WhoAm 92*
Iglewicz, Raja 1945- *WhoAm 92*
Iglhaut, Ludwig E. 1936- *St&PR 93*
Ignaczak, Jozef 1935- *WhoScE 91-4*
Ignatakis, Christos 1949- *WhoScE 91-3*
Ignatiadis, Varvara 1955- *WhoE 93*
Ignatieff, Paul 1936- *WhoUN 92*
Ignatiev, Alexander Yurievich 1956- *WhoWor 93*
Ignatij of Smolensk fl. 1389-1405 *OxDcByz*
Ignatios c. 797- *OxDcByz*
Ignatios of Nicaea *OxDcByz*
Ignatios of Smolensk *OxDcByz*
Ignatios the Deacon c. 77-?-c. 845 *OxDcByz*
Ignatius, of Loyola, Saint 1491-1556 *BioIn 17*
Ignatius, Pseudo- *OxDcByz*
Ignatov, Petar *WhoScE 91-4*
Ignatow, David 1914- *WhoAm 92, WhoWrEP 92*
Ignazio, Fred d' *ScF&FL 92*
Ignoffo, Carlo Michael 1928- *WhoAm 92*
Ignoffo, Flori Frances 1928- *WhoWrEP 92*
Igoe, Michael Lambert, Jr. 1930- *WhoAm 92*
Igoe, Peter Michael 1942- *St&PR 93*
Igoe, William Joseph 1928- *St&PR 93*
Igor d945 *OxDcByz*
Igoshin, Vladimir Alexandrovich 1947- *WhoWor 93*
Iguchi, Ienari 1941- *WhoWor 93*
Iguiniz, Juan Bautista 1881- *DcMexL*
Igumnov, Konstantin (Nikolaievich) 1873-1948 *Baker 92*
Igusa, Jun-Ichi 1924- *WhoAm 92*
Ih, Charles Chung Sen 1933- *WhoE 93*
Ihamuotila, Jaakko Veikko Artturi *WhoWor 93*
Ihamuotila, Risto V.A. 1938- *WhoScE 91-4*
Ihantola, Heikki K.J. *WhoScE 91-4*
Ihara, Michio 1928- *WhoAm 92*
Ihara, Yoshinori 1924- *WhoWor 93*
Ihasz, Mihaly 1931- *WhoScE 91-4*
Ihde, Aaron John 1909- *WhoAm 92*
Ihde, Don 1934- *WhoAm 92*
Iheme, Ishmael Udeze 1941- *WhoWor 93*
Ihgari, Joseph C. *St&PR 93*
Ihimaera, Witi 1944- *IntLitE, IntvWPC 92 [port]*
Ihlanfeldt, William 1936- *WhoWor 93*
Ihle, H.A. *WhoScE 91-3*
Ihle, Herbert Duane 1939- *WhoAm 92*
Ihle, John Livingston 1925- *WhoAm 92*
Ihlefeld, August 1898-1991 *BioIn 17*
Ihler, Garret Martin 1939- *WhoSSW 93*
Ihling, Edward L. 1926- *St&PR 93*
Ihm, Stephen L. *Law&B 92*
Ihne, Robert W. *Law&B 92*
Ihrie, Robert 1925- *WhoAm 92*
Ihrig, Carolyn 1956- *WhoAmW 93*
Ihrig, Edwin Charles, Jr. 1947- *WhoWor 93*
Ihrig, Judson La Moure 1925- *WhoAm 92*
Ihrig, William Kent 1959- *WhoEmL 93*
Ii, Jack Morito 1926- *WhoWor 93*
Ii, Naomasa 1561-1602 *HarEnMi*
Iida, Minoru 1936- *WhoWor 93*
Iida, Shojiro 1888- *HarEnMi*
Iida, Shuichi 1926- *WhoWor 93*
Iida, Takeo 1943- *WhoWor 93*
Iida, Tsuneo 1939- *WhoAm 92*
Iida, Yukisato 1918- *WhoWor 93*
Iijima, Shigetaka 1919- *WhoWor 93*
Iijima, Toshiro 1927- *WhoWor 93*
Iinoya, Koichi 1917- *WhoWor 93*
Iinuma, Hiroichi 1931- *WhoWor 93*
Iizuka, Jugoro 1933- *WhoWor 93*
Ijape, Mathias 1954- *WhoAsAP 91*
Ijaz, Mujaddid Ahmed d1992 *NewYTBS 92*
Ijichi, Hikojiro 1859-1912 *HarEnMi*
Ijichi, Kosuke 1855-1917 *HarEnMi*
Ijiri, Yuji 1935- *WhoAm 92*
Ijuin, Goro 1852-1921 *HarEnMi*
Ijuin, Matsuji 1893-1944 *HarEnMi*
Ikada, Yoshito 1935- *WhoWor 93*
Ikagawa, Tadaichi 1939- *St&PR 93*
Ikangaa, Juma *BioIn 17*
Ikard, Frank N. 1913-1991 *BioIn 17*
Ikard, Frank Neville, Jr. 1942- *WhoAm 92*
Ikawa-Smith, Fumiko 1930- *WhoAm 92*
Ike, Robert William 1952- *WhoEmL 93*
Ikebe, Shin-Ichiro 1943- *Baker 92*
Ikeda, Donna Rika 1939- *WhoAmW 93*
Ikeda, Hayato 1899-1965 *DcTwHis*
Ikeda, Hideo 1930- *WhoWor 93*
Ikeda, Hisako *WhoScE 91-1*
Ikeda, Hisako 1928- *WhoWor 93*
Ikeda, Kazuyosi 1928- *WhoWor 93*
Ikeda, Moss Marcus Masanobu 1931- *WhoWor 93*
Ikeda, Motohisa 1940- *WhoAsAP 91*
Ikeda, Osamu 1931- *WhoAsAP 91*
Ikeda, Saburo 1940- *WhoWor 93*
Ikeda, Satoshi 1942- *WhoWor 93*
Ikeda, Shinichiro *St&PR 93*
Ikeda, Shizunori 1921- *WhoWor 93*
Ikeda, Tadashi 1928- *WhoWor 93*
Ikeda, Tatsuya *Law&B 92*
Ikeda, Terumasa 1564-1613 *HarEnMi*
Ikeda, Yoshio T. 1943- *WhoWor 93*
Ikeda, Yukihiko 1937- *WhoAsAP 91*
Ikegami, Toshiroh 1948- *WhoWor 93*
Ikegaya, Takashi 1930- *WhoWor 93*
Ikehara, Morio 1923- *WhoWor 93*
Ikehata, Seiichi 1929- *WhoAsAP 91*
Ikenberry, Don Kevin 1954- *WhoEmL 93*
Ikenberry, Henry Cephas, Jr. 1920- *WhoAm 92*
Ikenberry, Stanley Oliver 1935- *WhoAm 92, WhoWor 93*
Ikenouchi, Tomojiro 1906- *Baker 92*
Ikenoyama, Helen M. *St&PR 93*
Ikettes *SoulM*
Ikhnaton fl. c. 1388BC-1358BC *BioIn 17*
Ikic, Drago 1917- *WhoScE 91-4*
Ikimi, Tom Omoghegbe 1944- *WhoAfr*
Ikin, Van 1951- *ScF&FL 92*
Ikins, Rachael Zacov 1954- *WhoAmW 93*
Ikkos, Aris John 1960- *WhoWor 93*
Ikle, Doris Margret 1928- *WhoAmW 93*
Ikle, Fred Charles 1924- *ColdWar 1, WhoAm 92*
Ikle, Richard A. 1930- *WhoAm 92*
Ikonen, Juhani 1938- *WhoScE 91-4*
Ikonen, Lauri 1888-1966 *Baker 92*
Ikonomov, Boyan Georgiev 1900-1973 *Baker 92*
Ikuma, Yasuro 1948- *WhoWor 93*
Ikuo, Kyoichi 1934- *St&PR 93*
Ikuzawa, Masao 1927- *WhoWor 93*
Ila, Tony 1944- *WhoAsAP 91*
Ilacqua, Rosario S. 1927- *St&PR 93*
Ilangyi, Bya'ene Akulu *WhoAm 92*
Ilardi, Alfredo 1942- *WhoUN 92*
Ilardi, Terry J. *Law&B 92*
Ilarion *OxDcByz*
Ilavsky, Jan 1945- *WhoScE 91-4*
Ilberman, Barry 1950- *St&PR 93*
Ilchak, Christine Baird 1949- *WhoAmW 93*
Ilchman, Alice Stone *BioIn 17*
Ilchman, Alice Stone 1935- *WhoAm 92, WhoAmW 93, WhoE 93*
Ilchman, Warren F. *BioIn 17*
Ilchman, Warren Frederick 1933- *WhoAm 92, WhoE 93*
Ilchuk, Frank H. d1991 *BioIn 17*
Ildari, Hassan *MiSFD 9*
Ildefonso *BioIn 17*
Ilderton, Jane Wallace 1936- *WhoAmW 93, WhoSSW 93*
Ileana, Princess of Romania 1909-1991 *BioIn 17*
Ileana of Romania 1909-1991 *AnObit 1991*
Ilegems, Marc 1940- *WhoScE 91-4, WhoWor 93*
Il'enko, Jurij 1936- *DrEEuF*
Ileo, Songoamba (Joseph) 1921- *WhoAfr*
Iler, Arthur W. *Law&B 92*
Iler, Kirby James *Law&B 92*
Ilerici, Kemal 1910- *Baker 92*
Iles, Bertha L. *AmWomPl*
Iles, Ronald A. 1935- *St&PR 93*
Ileto, Rafael M. 1920- *WhoAsAP 91*
Ilett, Frank, Jr. 1940- *WhoAm 92*
Ilfrey, Jack *BioIn 17*
Ilg, John Herold 1926- *St&PR 93*
Ilg, Raymond Paul 1938- *WhoAm 92*
Ilg, Ruth Merkle 1945- *WhoWrEP 92*
Ilgen, Daniel Richard 1943- *WhoAm 92*
Ilhan, Ismail 1946- *WhoScE 91-4*
Ilhardt, Lora Schofield *Law&B 92*
Iliadis, Costantinos 1944- *WhoScE 91-3*
Iliadis, Nick 1951- *WhoEmL 93*
Ilic, Marija D. 1951- *WhoAmW 93*
Ilic, Vladeta 1922- *WhoScE 91-4*
Ilich, Daniel Frank 1931- *St&PR 93*
Ilich, Richard Joseph 1959- *St&PR 93*
Il'ichev, Vitaly Grigorievitch 1950- *WhoWor 93*
Ilie, Paul 1932- *WhoAm 92*
Iliescu, Constantin *WhoScE 91-4*
Iliescu, Ion *BioIn 17*
Iliescu, Ion 1930- *WhoWor 93*
Iliev, Georgi Ljubomirov 1953- *WhoWor 93*
Iliev, Ivan *WhoScE 91-4*
Iliev, Konstantin 1924-1988 *Baker 92*
Iliev, Ljubomir Georgiev 1913- *WhoScE 91-4*
Iliff, John Wesley 1831-1878 *BioIn 17*
Iliff, Nicholas Taylor 1947- *WhoE 93*
Iliff, Warren Jackson 1944- *WhoE 93*
Iliff, Warren Jolidon 1936- *WhoAm 92*
Ilijanic, Ljudevit 1928- *WhoScE 91-4*
Il'in, Vladimir Alexandrovich 1928- *WhoWor 93*
Ilitch, Michael *WhoAm 92*
Ilitch Lites, Denise *Law&B 92*
Ilitsch, Daniza 1914-1965 *Baker 92*
Ilizarov, Gavril A. d1992 *NewYTBS 92 [port]*
Ilkson, Atilla S. *Law&B 92*
Ill, Marton Jozsef 1930- *WhoScE 91-4*
Illakowiczowa, Kazimiera 1892-1983 *PolBiDi*
Ille, B.G. 1927- *St&PR 93*
Ille, Bernard G. 1927- *WhoIns 93*
Ille, Bernard Glenn 1927- *WhoAm 92*
Ille, Robert G. 1945- *St&PR 93*
Ille, Vasile 1925- *WhoScE 91-4*
Illescas, Carlos 1919?- *DcMexL*
Illescas, Jorge *DcCPCAm*
Illescas-Ortiz, Rafael 1944- *WhoWor 93*
Illian, C.R. 1941- *St&PR 93*
Illica, Luigi 1857-1919 *IntDcOp [port], OxDcOp*
Illich, Ivan 1926- *BioIn 17, DcTwHis, WhoAm 92*
Illick, Joseph E. *BioIn 17*
Illienko, Yuri *MiSFD 9*
Illig, Alvin A. d1991 *BioIn 17*
Illig, Carl 1909- *WhoAm 92*
Illig, James Michael 1913- *WhoAm 92*
Illiger, Hans Jochen 1939- *WhoWor 93*
Illingworth, Thomas 1870-c. 1923 *BioIn 17*
Illion, Larry Steven 1949- *St&PR 93*
Illman, Soren Arnold 1943- *WhoWor 93*
Illner-Canizaro, Hana 1939- *WhoAmW 93*
Illos d488 *OxDcByz*
Illson, Dorothy Spence d1990 *BioIn 17*
Illueca, Jorge Enrique 1945- *WhoUN 92*
Illuzzi, Vincent 1953- *WhoE 93*
Illyes, Andrew Earl 1949- *St&PR 93*
Ilmonen, Eino Ossian 1908- *WhoWor 93*
Ilnicka-Olejniczak, Olga 1933- *WhoScE 91-4*
Ilom, Gaspar *DcCPCAm*
Ilowiecki, Maciej Tadeusz 1935- *WhoWor 93*
Ilstad, Geir Are 1955- *WhoEmL 93*
Ilstrup, Thomas G. *Law&B 92*
Ilten, David Frederick 1938- *WhoWor 93*
Iltis, John Frederic 1940- *WhoAm 92*
Iltzsch, Henry H. 1929- *St&PR 93*
Ilutovich, Leon *WhoAm 92*
Ilyinsky, Alexander Alexandrovich 1859-1920 *Baker 92*
Im, Kwon-Taek *MiSFD 9*
Im, Yung Kook 1928- *WhoSSW 93*
'Imad Al-Din 1125-1201 *OxDcByz*
Imaeda, Norio 1924- *WhoAsAP 91*
Imagawa, David Tadashi 1922- *WhoAm 92*
Imagawa, Sadayo 1325-1420 *HarEnMi*
Imai, Dorothy Kuniye *WhoAmW 93*
Imai, Isamu 1919- *WhoAsAP 91*
Imai, Keiichiro *Law&B 92*
Imai, Mari Marlene 1950- *WhoAmW 93*
Imai, Masaaki 1930- *WhoWor 93*
Imai, Nobuko 1943- *Baker 92*
Imai, Noriyoshi 1933- *WhoWor 93*
Imai, Tadashi 1912-1991 *MiSFD 9N*
Imai, Takeo 1898- *HarEnMi*
Imai, Yasufumi 1945- *WhoWor 93*
Imaizumi, Takao 1930- *WhoAsAP 91*
Imaki, Kiyoyasu 1927- *WhoWor 93*
Imam, Ahmad Fahmy 1937- *WhoWor 93*
Imam, Syed Shaikhul 1951- *WhoWor 93*
Imam, Zafar 1941- *WhoAsAP 91*
Imamoglu, Kamil H. 1926- *WhoScE 91-4*
Imamoto, Tsuneo 1942- *WhoWor 93*
Imamoto, Yoshiko *BioIn 17*
Imamshah, Norman David 1942- *WhoE 93*
Imamura, Hitoshi 1886-1968 *HarEnMi*
Imamura, Kelly Kikuji *Law&B 92*
Imamura, Masashi 1924- *WhoWor 93*
Imamura, Shohei 1926- *MiSFD 9*
Imamura, Toru 1956- *WhoWor 93*
Imamura, Tsutomu 1927- *WhoWor 93*
Iman 1955- *ConBIB 4 [port]*
Imanaliyev, Muratbek *WhoWor 93*
Imanishi, Jiro 1947- *WhoWor 93*
Imanishi-Kari, Thereza *BioIn 17*
Imanyara, Gitobu *BioIn 17*
Imazu, Hiroshi 1946- *WhoAsAP 91*
Imbach, Jean-Louis 1936- *WhoWor 93*
Imbault, James Joseph 1944- *WhoAm 92, WhoWor 93*
Imbeau, Stephen Alan 1947- *WhoEmL 93, WhoSSW 93*
Imbembo, Anthony Louis 1942- *WhoWor 93*
Imber, Barry 1945- *St&PR 93, WhoE 93*
Imber, Jonathan 1950- *WhoE 93*
Imber, Naphtali Herz 1856-1909 *JeAmHC*
Imberman, Samuel *MiSFD 9*
Imbert, C. *WhoScE 91-2*
Imbert, Christian 1937- *WhoScE 91-2*
Imbert, Hugues 1842-1905 *Baker 92*
Imbert, Richard Conrad 1941- *WhoE 93*
Imbert Barrera, Antonio 1920- *DcCPCAm*
Imbleau, Claude 1957- *St&PR 93*
Imbler, C. Clarke 1933- *WhoIns 93*
Imboden, John Daniel 1823-1895 *HarEnMi*
Imboden, Ronald Gordon 1931- *WhoAm 92*
Imboden-Edwards, Patrica Altom 1961- *WhoEmL 93*
Imbriaco, James *Law&B 92*
Imbriani, Robert Peter, Sr. 1948- *WhoE 93*
Imbrie, Andrew (Welsh) 1921- *Baker 92, WhoAm 92*
Imbrie, Charity J. *Law&B 92*
Imbrie, John Zeller 1956- *WhoEmL 93*
Imbrogno, Edward Nicola 1922- *St&PR 93*
Imbruno, Kathleen Marguerite 1941- *WhoAmW 93*
Imbs, Jean Louis 1937- *WhoScE 91-2*
Imbusch, George F. 1935- *WhoScE 91-3*
Imbusch, George Francis 1935- *WhoWor 93*
Imdahl, Max 1925-1988 *BioIn 17*
Imel, John Michael 1932- *WhoSSW 93*

Imel, Priscilla Brown 1954- WhoEmL 93
Imershein, Betsy 1953- BioIn 17
Imershein, Charles J. 1923- St&PR 93
Imershein, William Leonard 1922- St&PR 93
Imes, James F. 1932- St&PR 93
Imes, Jeffrey Lynn 1947- WhoWor 93
Imesch, Joseph Leopold 1931- WhoAm 92
Imgrund, Bernadine Wojtanowski 1936- WhoAmW 93
Imhoff, Herbert F. 1926- St&PR 93
Imhoff, Herbert Franklin, Jr. 1950- St&PR 93
Imhoff, Irma B. AmWomPl
Imhoff, John Edward 1950- St&PR 93
Imhoff, Klaus R. WhoScE 91-3
Imhoff, Peter H. 1956- St&PR 93
Imhoff, W. Joseph 1940- St&PR 93
Imhoff, Walter Francis 1931- St&PR 93, WhoAm 92
Imhoof, Markus 1941- MiSFD 9
Imig, David Gregg 1939- WhoAm 92
Imig, Robert Adam, Jr. Law&B 92
Imlah, Peter WhoScE 91-1
Imlay, James Henderson 1764-1823 BioIn 17
Imlay, John Prescott, Jr. 1936- St&PR 93, WhoAm 92
Imle, John Fredrick, Jr. 1940- St&PR 93
Immel, Calvin Louis 1929- St&PR 93
Immel, Mary Blair 1930- WhoWrEP 92
Immel, Vincent Clare 1920- WhoAm 92
Immelmann, Max 1890-1916 HarEnMi
Immendorff, Jorg BioIn 17
Immerman, Paul Alan Law&B 92
Immerman, Paul Alan 1951- WhoEmL 93
Immesberger, Helmut 1934- WhoWor 93
Immke, Keith Henry 1953- WhoEmL 93
Immonen, Bror Krister Mauritz 1962- WhoWor 93
Immonen, Gerald Matthew 1936- WhoE 93
Immordino, Peter Anthony 1937- WhoE 93
Immroth, John Phillip 1936-1976 BioIn 17
Imondi, Deborah Ann 1952- WhoE 93
Imoto, Kumao 1903- HarEnMi
Imparato, Anthony Michael 1922- WhoAm 92
Imparator, Peter George 1930- St&PR 93
Impellizeri, Monica 1920- WhoAmW 93
Impens, Ivan 1935- WhoScE 91-2
Impens, Robert Andre Leon Frederic 1934- WhoScE 91-2
Imperato, F. Nicholas 1944- WhoE 93
Imperato, Pascal James 1937- WhoAm 92, WhoE 93, WhoWrEP 92
Imperatore, Nancy Theresa 1924- WhoAmW 93
Imperial, Carlos R. 1930- WhoAsAP 91
Imperial, Eduardo Law&B 92
Imperiali, Beatrice 1957- WhoAmW 93, WhoEmL 93
Imperiali, Giuseppe Renato 1651-1737 BioIn 17
Imperio, Angelito 1939- WhoWor 93
Impert, John Edward Law&B 92
Impey, Eugene Clutterbuck 1830-1904 BioIn 17
Impey, Rose 1947- ConAu 137, SmATA 69 [port]
Impoco, Laura Jo 1967- WhoE 93
Impoco, Tony BioIn 17
Impola, Richard A(arre) 1923- ConAu 139
Impressions SoulM
Imray, Thomas John 1939- WhoAm 92
Imre, Gyorgy 1927- WhoScE 91-4
Imre, Laszlo K. 1929- WhoScE 91-4
Imre, Paul David 1925- WhoE 93
Imrey, Frances Gloria 1927- WhoE 93
Imrhan, Sheik Nazir 1950- WhoEmL 93, WhoSSW 93
Imrie, Derek Charles WhoScE 91-1
Imru' al-Qays OxDcByz
Imse, Robert A. WhoIns 93
Imseng, Raoul A. 1930- WhoWor 93
Imura, Akiya BioIn 17
Imus, Don BioIn 17
Imus, Richard Howard 1938- WhoAm 92
Imus, Russel Walter 1935- St&PR 93
Imwinkelried, Edward John 1946- WhoAm 92, WhoEmL 93
In, Rachel Chiang 1938- WhoWor 93
Inaba, Gail M. Law&B 92
Inaba, Motokichi 1935- WhoWor 93
Inaba, Osamu d1992 NewYTBS 92
Inabinet, George Walker, Jr. 1927- WhoSSW 93
Inabinet, Rhett E. 1955- St&PR 93
Inabinette, Norma Bartin 1942- WhoAm 92
Inacio, Aldina Moreira 1942- WhoScE 91-3
Inacker, Charles John 1936- WhoAm 92
Inada, Kenneth Kameo 1923- WhoE 93
Inada, Masazumi 1896- HarEnMi
Inada, Susumu 1952- WhoWor 93
Inadomi, Robert John 1948- St&PR 93
Inagaki, Hiroshi 1905- MiSFD 9N
Inagaki, Norihiro 1942- WhoWor 93
Inagami, Tadashi 1931- WhoAm 92
Inagami, Takeshi 1944- WhoWor 93
Inaganti, Prasad V. 1945- St&PR 93
Inait, M. Yousaf 1935- WhoWor 93
Inalcik, Halil 1916- WhoAm 92
Inamori, Kazuo 1932- WhoWor 93
Inamoto, Megumu 1932- WhoWor 93
Inamoto, Yoshiyuki 1952- St&PR 93
Inamura, Toshio 1928- WhoAsAP 91
Inamura, Toshiyuki 1935- WhoAsAP 91
Inatome, Rick 1953- WhoAm 92
Inazumi, Hikoji 1923- WhoWor 93
Inbal, Eliahu 1936- Baker 92, WhoWor 93
Incalicchio, Mario 1936- St&PR 93
Incandela, Gerald Jean-Marie 1952- WhoEmL 93
Incaprera, Frank Philip 1928- WhoSSW 93
Incaudo, Claude J. 1933- St&PR 93
Incaudo, Joseph A. 1940- St&PR 93
Ince, A. Nejat WhoScE 91-4
Ince, Bill 1949- St&PR 93
Ince, Darrel WhoScE 91-1
Ince, Donald R. 1928- St&PR 93
Ince, Edward V. St&PR 93
Ince, Eugene St. Clair, Jr. 1926- WhoAm 92
Ince, George R. d1990 BioIn 17
Ince, Laurence Peter 1937- WhoSSW 93
Ince, Richard W. 1938- St&PR 93, WhoAm 92
Ince, Thomas H. 1882-1924 MiSFD 9N
Ince, Thomas Harper 1880-1924 BioIn 17
Inch, Herbert Reynolds 1904-1988 Baker 92
Inch, Kevin MiSFD 9
Inch, Maude Elizabeth AmWomPl
Inch, Morris Alton 1925- WhoAm 92
Inchaustegui Cabral, Hector 1912-1979 SpAmA
Inchbald, Mrs. 1753-1821 BioIn 17
Inchbald, Elizabeth Simpson 1753-1821 BioIn 17
Inclan, Federico Schroeder 1910-1981 DcMexL
Inclan, Hilda Marianne 1946- WhoWor 93
Inclan, Luis G. 1816-1875 DcMexL
Incropera, Frank Paul 1939- WhoAm 92
Inculet, Ion I. 1921- WhoAm 92
Incze, Kalman 1936- WhoScE 91-4
Inczedy, Janos 1923- WhoScE 91-4
Indacochea, Alfredo Guillermo 1951- WhoWor 93
Inda-Cunningham, Arturo Enrique 1950- WhoWor 93
Indahl, Dennis Deltyne 1935- St&PR 93
Indelen, Erdogan 1939- WhoScE 91-4
Indelicato, Albert D. 1950- St&PR 93
Indelicato, Dorothy L. 1933- St&PR 93
Indelicato, Venerando J. 1932- St&PR 93
Indelicato, Vincent 1933- St&PR 93
Inder Jit 1927- WhoAsAP 91
India, Bernardino c. 1528-1590 BioIn 17
India, Sigismondo d' c. 1582-c. 1629 Baker 92
Indiana, Robert 1928- BioIn 17, WhoAm 92
Indick, Ben P. 1923- ScF&FL 92
Indick, Janet 1932- WhoAmW 93
Indig, George S. Law&B 92
Indio BioIn 17
Indiveri, Francesco 1939- WhoWor 93
Indjoudjian, Dickran 1920- WhoWor 93
Indrabhakti, Indrasong 1922- WhoWor 93
Indrasutanta, Waskita 1954- WhoWor 93
Indulski, Janusz WhoScE 91-4
Indurante, Peter Joseph 1950- WhoEmL 93
Indursky, Arthur 1943- WhoE 93, WhoWor 93
Indusi, Joseph Paul 1942- WhoE 93
Indy, Vincent d' 1851-1931 Baker 92, OxDcOp
Indyk, Boleslaw WhoScE 91-1
Ines de la Cruz, Juana 1651-1695 BioIn 17
Iness, Jane Dale 1947- WhoAmW 93
Inez, Colette 1931- WhoAm 92, WhoWrEP 92
Infanger, Ann 1933- WhoAmW 93
Infantas, Fernando de las 1534-c. 1610 Baker 92
Infante, Christine Marie 1952- WhoWrEP 92
Infante, Daisy Inocentes 1946- WhoAmW 93
Infante, Ettore Ferrari 1938- WhoAm 92
Infante, G. Cabrera 1929- BioIn 17
Infante, Lindy 1940- WhoAm 92
Infante, Manuel 1883-1958 Baker 92
Infante, Pedro 1917-1956 IntDcF 2-3
Infantolino, Philip Louis 1942- WhoE 93
Infeld, Eryk 1940- WhoWor 93
Inferrera, Marie Antoinette 1958- WhoAmW 93, WhoEmL 93
Infinger, Glenn T. Law&B 92
Infosino, Anne Marie 1960- WhoAmW 93
Infusino, Jeffrey Scott 1950- WhoAm 92, WhoE 93, WhoEmL 93
Infuso, Joseph 1927- WhoWor 93
Ing, Dean 1931- ScF&FL 92
Ing, Dennis Roy 1947- WhoWor 93
Ing, Gloria Mae Law&B 92
Ing, M. Gordon Law&B 92
Ing, Samuel Wei 1932- WhoE 93
Ing, Sheridan C.F. 1923- St&PR 93
Ingaglio, Diego Augustus 1922- WhoE 93
Ingaglio, Michael Louis 1960- WhoEmL 93
Ingall, David 1930- WhoAm 92
Ingalls, Albert G. 1888-1958 BioIn 17
Ingalls, Daniel H.H. 1916- St&PR 93
Ingalls, Daniel H.H., Jr. 1944- St&PR 93
Ingalls, Everett Palmer, III 1947- WhoEmL 93
Ingalls, Harold W. 1947- St&PR 93
Ingalls, James BioIn 17
Ingalls, Jeremy 1911- WhoAm 92, WhoAmW 93, WhoWor 93, WhoWrEP 92
Ingalls, Laura AmWomPl
Ingalls, Lula E. AmWomPl
Ingalls, Marie Cecelie 1936- WhoAmW 93
Ingalls, Rachel BioIn 17
Ingalls, Rachel 1937- ScF&FL 92
Ingalls, Robert Lynn 1934- WhoAm 92
Ingalls, Roscoe C., Jr. 1920- St&PR 93
Ingalls, William G. 1930- St&PR 93
Ingalsbe, William James 1947- WhoEmL 93
Ingamells, Julia Irene 1945- WhoWrEP 92
Ingarden, Roman Stanislaw 1920- WhoScE 91-4, WhoWor 93
Ingarden, Roman (Witold) 1893-1970 Baker 92
Ingarra, Joseph P. St&PR 93
Ingato, Robert J. Law&B 92
Ingbar, Mary Lee 1926- WhoE 93
Ingber, Alix Sara 1945- WhoSSW 93
Ingber, Jeffrey Fred 1954- St&PR 93
Ingberg, Donald Dennis 1936- St&PR 93
Ingberg, Earl Eugene, Jr. 1947- St&PR 93
Inge, M. Thomas 1936- ScF&FL 92
Inge, Milton Thomas 1936- WhoAm 92, WhoSSW 93
Inge, Ronald Eugene 1956- St&PR 93
Inge, William 1913-1973 BioIn 17
Inge, William Bullock 1933- St&PR 93
Ingebrand, George B. 1927- St&PR 93
Ingebrigtsen, Catherine Williams 1955- WhoAmW 93
Ingegneri, Marc'Antonio c. 1547-1592 Baker 92
Ingelheim, Albrecht, Graf von BioIn 17
Ingelow, Jean 1820-1897 NinCLC 39 [port]
Ingels, Jack Edward 1942- WhoE 93, WhoWor 93
Ingels, Marty BioIn 17
Ingels, Marty 1936- WhoAm 92
Ingeman, Jerry Andrew 1950- WhoEmL 93, WhoWor 93
Ingenhoven, Jan 1876-1951 Baker 92
Ingenthron, Karen Barbara 1945- WhoAmW 93, WhoE 93
Ingerman, Michael Leigh 1937- WhoWor 93
Ingerman, Peter Zilahy 1934- WhoE 93, WhoWor 93
Ingerslev, Fritz H.B. 1912- WhoScE 91-2
Ingerslev, Fritz Halfdan Bent 1912- WhoWor 93
Ingersoll, Alfred Cajori 1920- WhoAm 92
Ingersoll, Earl George 1938- WhoE 93
Ingersoll, Helen Frances 1878- AmWomPl
Ingersoll, John Gregory 1948- WhoEmL 93
Ingersoll, Kenneth 1959- St&PR 93
Ingersoll, Patsy Grey AmWomPl
Ingersoll, Paul Mills 1928- WhoAm 92
Ingersoll, Ralph, II BioIn 17
Ingersoll, Ralph, II 1946- JrnUS
Ingersoll, Ralph M. 1900-1985 JrnUS
Ingersoll, Ralph (McAllister) 1900-1985 DcLB 127 [port]
Ingersoll, Robert Green 1833-1899 BioIn 17
Ingersoll, Robert Stephen 1914- WhoAm 92
Ingersoll, Roy WhoWrEP 92
Ingersoll, Thelma Saks Bradford d1992 BioIn 17
Ingersoll, William Boley 1938- WhoE 93, WhoWor 93
Ingervall, Bengt Filip 1934- WhoWor 93
Ingestad, Torsten 1927- WhoScE 91-4
Ingevaldson, Paul Martin 1945- St&PR 93
Ingham, Albert Joseph, Jr. 1934- St&PR 93
Ingham, Barbara Mary WhoScE 91-1
Ingham, Catherine Curtis 1951- WhoAmW 93
Ingham, Cranford A. Law&B 92, WhoAm 92
Ingham, Derek Binns WhoScE 91-1
Ingham, John N. 1939- ConAu 138
Inghelbrecht, D(esire)-E(mile) 1880-1965 Baker 92
Inghilleri, Giovanni 1894-1959 Baker 92, OxDcOp
Inghram, Brent J. 1955- WhoEmL 93
Inghram, Howell Arthur 1896-1990 BioIn 17
Inghram, Mark Gordon 1919- WhoAm 92
Ingimarsson, Ragnar G. 1934- WhoScE 91-4
Ingis, Gail 1935- WhoE 93
Ingle, Alexander W. 1942- St&PR 93
Ingle, H. Larry 1936- WhoSSW 93
Ingle, Henry Thomas 1943- WhoAm 92
Ingle, James Chesney, Jr. 1935- WhoAm 92
Ingle, John Ide 1919- WhoAm 92
Ingle, Joseph B. 1946- ConAu 136
Ingle, Linda 1937- St&PR 93
Ingle, Marcus David 1943- WhoE 93
Ingle, Marleen Bengel 1932- WhoSSW 93
Ingle, Morton Blakeman 1942- St&PR 93, WhoAm 92
Ingle, Richard Maurice 1946- WhoSSW 93
Ingle, Robert D. 1939- WhoAm 92
Ingle, Stephen James 1940- WhoWor 93
Ingledue, Elwood d1990 BioIn 17
Inglehart, Marita Rosch 1951- WhoEmL 93
Ingleman, John A. 1946- St&PR 93
Ingles, Luis I., Jr. 1942- St&PR 93
Inglett, Betty Lee 1930- WhoAmW 93
Inglezes, Demetrios Spyridonovich 1773-1844 BioIn 17
Inglis, Andrew Franklin 1920- WhoAm 92
Inglis, Brian 1916- BioIn 17
Inglis, David Rittenhouse 1905- WhoAm 92
Inglis, Esther 1571-1624 BioIn 17
Inglis, Ivan Leslie 1926- St&PR 93
Inglis, James WhoAm 92
Inglis, John B. 1901-1990 BioIn 17
Inglis, Pamela Ann 1965- WhoAmW 93
Inglis, Rewey Belle BioIn 17
Inglis, Robert Shepherd, Jr. 1929- WhoSSW 93
Inglis, Thomas Anderson WhoScE 91-1
Inglot, Anna Dubowska 1933- WhoWor 93
Inglot, Peter B. 1924- St&PR 93
Ingman, Folke 1933- WhoScE 91-4
Ingman, Richard Wilson 1944- St&PR 93
Ingold, Catherine White 1949- WhoAm 92
Ingold, Keith Usherwood 1929- WhoAm 92
Ingoldsby, Arthur W. 1907- St&PR 93
Ingoldsby, Roderick 1944- St&PR 93
Ingpen, Robert 1936- ScF&FL 92
Ingraham, Craig S. Law&B 92
Ingraham, David W. 1942- St&PR 93
Ingraham, Donald S. Law&B 92
Ingraham, Edward Clarke, Jr. 1922- WhoAm 92
Ingraham, Erick ChlBIID [port]
Ingraham, Hubert WhoWor 93
Ingraham, James H. 1954- St&PR 93
Ingraham, James Herbert Law&B 92
Ingraham, Janet 1954- WhoAmW 93
Ingraham, John Wright 1930- WhoAm 92, WhoE 93, WhoWor 93
Ingraham, Mary B. AmWomPl
Ingraham, Michael Lee 1930- St&PR 93
Ingraham, Samuel Cooke, III 1939- WhoE 93
Ingraham Dietzen, Carolyn Anne 1947- WhoEmL 93
Ingram, Alvin John 1914- WhoAm 92
Ingram, Alyce M. 1914- WhoWrEP 92
Ingram, Anne BioIn 17
Ingram, B.N. 1927- St&PR 93
Ingram, Benjamin Broderick 1957- WhoSSW 93
Ingram, Bruce G. St&PR 93
Ingram, Charles Clark, Jr. 1916- St&PR 93, WhoAm 92
Ingram, David 1944- WhoAm 92
Ingram, David S. WhoScE 91-1
Ingram, Denny Ouzts, Jr. 1929- WhoAm 92
Ingram, Derek George Woodward WhoScE 91-1
Ingram, Diana Joyce 1957- WhoAmW 93
Ingram, Don V. 1935- St&PR 93
Ingram, Dorothy Stamps 1946- WhoEmL 93
Ingram, E. Michael Law&B 92
Ingram, E. Michael 1952- St&PR 93
Ingram, Edgar W., Jr. 1910- St&PR 93, WhoAm 92
Ingram, Edgar W., III 1951- WhoAm 92
Ingram, Ernest M. 1926- St&PR 93
Ingram, Erskine Bronson 1931- St&PR 93
Ingram, George Conley 1930- WhoAm 92
Ingram, Gregory Keith 1944- WhoUN 92
Ingram, Helen Moyer 1937- WhoWrEP 92
Ingram, James SoulM, WhoAm 92

Ingram, James Allan *Law&B 92*
Ingram, James Charles 1928- *WhoScE 91-3, WhoUN 92*
Ingram, James E. *Law&B 92*
Ingram, James P. 1940- *St&PR 93*
Ingram, Jeffrey Charles 1953- *WhoEmL 93*
Ingram, John Henry 1842-1916 *ScF&FL 92*
Ingram, Johnnye Hughes 1904- *WhoAmW 93*
Ingram, Joy Louise 1953- *WhoAmW 93*
Ingram, Kenneth Frank 1929- *WhoAm 92, WhoSSW 93*
Ingram, Kenneth Lloyd 1948- *WhoSSW 93*
Ingram, Lawrence Warren 1921- *WhoAm 92*
Ingram, Luther 1944- *SoulM*
Ingram, Paul *BioIn 17*
Ingram, Rex 1892-1950 *MiSFD 9N*
Ingram, Rick E. *BioIn 17*
Ingram, Robert B. *AfrAmBi [port], Law&B 92*
Ingram, Robert Palmer 1917- *WhoAm 92*
Ingram, Samuel William, Jr. 1933- *WhoAm 92*
Ingram, Sheila *BlkAmWO*
Ingram, Shirley Jean 1946- *WhoAmW 93*
Ingram, Thomas H. *ScF&FL 92*
Ingram, Thomas Lewis 1913-1990 *BioIn 17*
Ingram, Tom 1924- *ScF&FL 92*
Ingram, Wallace Reeves 1960- *WhoSSW 93*
Ingram, William, Jr. 1961- *WhoWor 93*
Ingram, William P. *Law&B 92*
Ingrams, Richard 1937- *BioIn 17*
Ingrant, Richard S., Jr. 1956- *St&PR 93*
Ingrassia, Deborah Elizabeth *St&PR 93*
Ingrassia, Paul Joseph 1950- *WhoAm 92*
Ingrey, Paul Bosworth 1939- *WhoIns 93*
Ingri, Nils Herman 1929- *WhoScE 91-4*
Ingrid, Charles *ScF&FL 92*
Ingrum, Adrienne Gillette 1954- *WhoAmW 93*
Ingrum, Amaryllis June Hale 1938- *WhoWor 93*
Ings, Robert M.J. 1943- *WhoScE 91-1*
Ingulfsen, Charlene 1964- *WhoEmL 93*
Ingvar, David Henschen 1924- *WhoScE 91-4*
Ingvesgard, Ingmar *WhoScE 91-4*
Ingwersen, Martin Lewis 1919- *WhoAm 92*
Inhaber, Herbert 1941- *WhoWor 93*
Inhelder, Barbel 1913- *BioIn 17*
Inhofe, James M. 1934- *CngDr 91, WhoAm 92, WhoSSW 93*
Inigo, Martin *ConAu 139*
Inigo, Rafael Madrigal 1932- *WhoAm 92*
Inigo Leal, Baldomero *WhoScE 91-3*
Iniguez, Jaime 1931- *WhoScE 91-3*
Injac, Marko 1938- *WhoScE 91-4*
Ink, Dwight A. 1922- *WhoAm 92*
Inkeles, Alex 1920- *WhoAm 92*
Inkellis, Barbara G. *Law&B 92*
Inkellis, Steven A. *Law&B 92*
Inkley, Scott Russell 1921- *WhoAm 92*
Inkley, Scott Russell, Jr. 1952- *WhoAm 92*
Inkson, John Christopher *WhoScE 91-1*
Inkster, Norman David 1938- *WhoAm 92*
Inkster, Tim 1949- *WhoCanL 92*
Inlander, Charles Bennett 1946- *WhoE 93*
Inlow, David Ronald *BioIn 17*
Inlow, Edgar Burke 1915- *WhoAm 92*
Inlow, Lawrence W. *Law&B 92*
Inlow, Lawrence W. 1950- *St&PR 93*
Inman, Bobby R. 1931- *St&PR 93*
Inman, Bobby Ray 1931- *WhoAm 92*
Inman, D. *WhoScE 91-1*
Inman, Daniel John 1947- *WhoE 93*
Inman, Grant Muir 1941- *St&PR 93*
Inman, James Carlton, Jr. 1945- *WhoSSW 93, WhoWor 93*
Inman, John 1805-1850 *JrnUS*
Inman, John Edward 1947- *WhoSSW 93*
Inman, John Keith 1928- *WhoE 93*
Inman, Laura *Law&B 92*
Inman, Margaret Anne 1929- *St&PR 93*
Inman, Margie Yvonne 1952- *WhoAmW 93*
Inman, Peter T. 1948- *WhoWrEP 92*
Inman, Robert Frederick 1943- *WhoSSW 93*
Inman, Ross Banks 1931- *WhoAm 92*
Inman, Terry W. 1940- *WhoAm 92*
Inman, Will 1923- *WhoWrEP 92*
Inman, William Howard Wallace 1929- *WhoWor 93*
Inman, William Peter 1936- *WhoAm 92*
Inman, Yolanda Otero 1957- *WhoAmW 93*
Innamorati, Joseph E. *Law&B 92*
Innanen, Larry J. *Law&B 92*
Innanen, Larry John 1950- *WhoAm 92*
Innaurato, Albert *BioIn 17*
Innaurato, Albert Francis 1947- *WhoAm 92*
Innerst, Preston Eugene 1927- *WhoAm 92*
Innes, David Lyn 1941- *WhoAm 92, WhoSSW 93*
Innes, Donn 1927- *St&PR 93*
Innes, Evan *ScF&FL 92*
Innes, Georgette Meyer 1918- *WhoAmW 93, WhoWor 93*
Innes, Heather D. *Law&B 92*
Innes, J.W. Brodie- *ScF&FL 92*
Innes, John Phythian, II 1934- *WhoAm 92*
Innes, Kenneth William 1931- *WhoWor 93*
Innes, Lucy Mitchell- *BioIn 17*
Innes, Michael 1906- *BioIn 17*
Innes, Peter 1954- *WhoScE 91-1*
Innes, Peter Bruce 1941- *WhoAm 92*
Innes, Ruth 1929- *WhoWrEP 92*
Innes, Zondra F. 1953- *St&PR 93*
Inness-Brown, Elizabeth Ann 1954- *WhoWrEP 92*
Inness-Brown, Virginia Royall d1990 *BioIn 17*
Innis, Donald Q. 1924-1988 *BioIn 17*
Innis, Pauline *WhoAmW 93*
Innis, Roy 1934- *AfrAmBi*
Innis, Roy Emile Alfredo 1934- *WhoAm 92*
Innis, Yvonne Phyllis-Jean 1948- *WhoE 93*
Innocent, II *OxDcByz*
Innocent, III 1160?-1216 *OxDcByz*
Innocent, IV c. 1200-1254 *OxDcByz*
Innocent, Peter Robert *WhoScE 91-1*
Innocenti, Antonio Cardinal 1915- *WhoWor 93*
Innocenti, Mario 1951- *WhoSSW 93*
Innocenti, Ray D. 1935- *St&PR 93*
Innocenti, Robert Edward 1937- *St&PR 93*
Innokentii *IntDcAn*
Inns, Harry Douglas Ellis 1922- *WhoWor 93*
Inoguchi, Kuniko 1952- *WhoWor 93*
Inoguchi, Toshihira 1896-1944 *HarEnMi*
Inoki, Kanji 1943- *WhoAsAP 91*
Inokuchi, Tsugio 1940- *WhoWor 93*
Inokuma, Juji 1931- *WhoAsAP 91*
Inonga Lokonga L'Ome d1991 *BioIn 17*
Inonu, Ismet 1884-1973 *BioIn 17, DcTwHis*
Inonu, Rashid Ismet 1884-1973 *HarEnMi*
Inoue, Hikaru 1851-1908 *HarEnMi*
Inoue, Hironori 1925- *WhoAsAP 91*
Inoue, Ikutaro 1872-1965 *HarEnMi*
Inoue, Issei 1932- *WhoAsAP 91*
Inoue, Kei 1919- *WhoAsAP 91*
Inoue, Keichi 1935- *WhoUN 92*
Inoue, Kichio 1923- *WhoAsAP 91*
Inoue, Kiichi 1932- *WhoAsAP 91*
Inoue, Osamu 1940- *WhoWor 93*
Inoue, Shigeyoshi 1889- *HarEnMi*
Inoue, Shinya 1921- *WhoAm 92*
Inoue, Shohei 1929- *WhoAsAP 91*
Inoue, Shohei 1933- *WhoWor 93*
Inoue, Shun 1938- *WhoWor 93*
Inoue, Shunichi 1933- *WhoUN 92*
Inoue, Takao 1957- *WhoWor 93*
Inoue, Takashi 1925- *WhoAsAP 91*
Inoue, Takeshi 1932- *WhoWor 93*
Inoue, Tetsuo 1938- *WhoAsAP 91*
Inoue, Tomoyasu 1947- *WhoWor 93*
Inoue, Yasushi 1907-1991 *AnObit 1991, BioIn 17*
Inoue, Yoshihisa 1947- *WhoAsAP 91*
Inoue, Yoshihisa 1949- *WhoWor 93*
Inoue, Yoshio 1929- *WhoWor 93*
Inoue, Yutaka 1927- *WhoAsAP 91*
Inouye, Daniel 1924- *ConHero 2 [port]*
Inouye, Daniel K. *BioIn 17*
Inouye, Daniel K. 1924- *CngDr 91*
Inouye, Daniel Ken 1924- *WhoAm 92*
Inouye, Jon 1955- *ScF&FL 92*
Inouye, Wayne Michael 1951- *WhoEmL 93*
Inouye, Zuiken 1936- *WhoWor 93*
Insalaco, Joseph d1991 *BioIn 17*
Insanally, Samuel Rudolph 1936- *WhoUN 92*
Insanally, Sheik Riyak David 1959- *WhoWor 93*
Insanguine, Giacomo 1728-1795 *OxDcOp*
Insanguine, Giacomo (Antonio Francesco Paolo Michele) 1728-1795 *Baker 92*
Insani, John Louis 1925- *St&PR 93*
Inscho, Clyde Sylvester, Jr. 1927- *WhoSSW 93*
Inscho, Jean Anderson 1936- *WhoAmW 93*
Inselberg, Rachel 1934- *WhoAmW 93*
Inselbuch, Dora d1992 *BioIn 17*
Inselman, Laura Sue 1944- *WhoAm 92, WhoAmW 93*
Insinga, Aron K. *ScF&FL 92*
Insinga, Joanne Theresa 1954- *WhoE 93*
Insler, Stanley 1937- *WhoAm 92*
Insley, Richard S. 1945- *St&PR 93*
Insley, Will 1929- *BioIn 17, WhoAm 92*
Insolia, Kerry Anne 1964- *WhoAmW 93*
Insprucker, Nancy Rhoades 1959- *WhoAmW 93*
Instone, John Clifford 1924- *WhoAm 92*
Intemann, Robert Louis 1938- *WhoAm 92*
Inten, Ferdinand 1848-1918 *Baker 92*
Interrante, Leonard Vincent 1939- *WhoE 93*
Intilli, Sharon Marie 1950- *WhoAmW 93*
Intintolo, John Augustine 1962- *WhoE 93*
Intrater, Cheryl Watson Waylor 1943- *WhoAmW 93*
Intrator, Orna 1960- *WhoE 93*
Intrator, Richard L. 1952- *St&PR 93*
Intravia, John Andrew 1950- *WhoE 93*
Intrieri, Cesare Adriano 1938- *WhoWor 93*
Intriligator, Devrie Shapiro *WhoAm 92, WhoWor 93*
Intriligator, Marc Steven 1952- *WhoE 93*
Intriligator, Michael David 1938- *WhoAm 92*
Introvigne, Massimo 1955- *WhoWor 93*
Intruders *SoulM*
Inui, Harumi 1934- *WhoAsAP 91*
Inui, Thomas Spencer 1943- *WhoAm 92*
Inukai, Tsunehiko 1944- *WhoWor 93*
Invanowski, Sigismund 1874-1944 *PolBiDi*
Inverso, Denise Marie 1963- *WhoAmW 93*
Inwood, David Gerald 1946- *WhoEmL 93*
Inza, Julian R. 1961- *WhoWor 93*
Inzana, Barbara Ann 1939- *WhoAmW 93*
Inzana, Carolyn Marie 1966- *WhoAmW 93*
Inzenga (y Castellanos), Jose 1828-1891 *Baker 92*
Inzetta, Mark Stephen *Law&B 92*
Inzinga, Jacqueline Marie 1967- *WhoE 93*
Inzitari, Frank 1935- *St&PR 93*
Ioannides, E. 1942- *WhoScE 91-3*
Ioannides, Eustathios E. 1942- *WhoWor 93*
Ioannidis, Yannis 1930- *Baker 92*
Ioannikios c. 752-846 *OxDcByz*
Ioannou, Greg 1953- *ScF&FL 92*
Ioannou, Nicolaos 1946- *WhoScE 91-4*
Ioannou, Susan 1944- *WhoCanL 92*
Ioasaf of Vidin fl. c. 1375-1400 *OxDcByz*
Iodice, Elaine 1947- *WhoAmW 93*
Iodice, Emilio Francis 1946- *WhoEmL 93*
Iodice, Jody DiMeno 1953- *WhoAm 92*
Iodice, Ruth Genevieve Work 1925- *WhoWrEP 92*
Ioel *OxDcByz*
Ioffe, Adolf Abramovich 1883-1927 *BioIn 17*
Ioffe, Boris Lazarevich 1926- *WhoWor 93*
Ioku, Sadao 1925- *WhoAsAP 91*
Ioli, James Peter 1951- *WhoE 93*
Iommi, Tony 1948- See Black Sabbath *ConMus 9*
Ion, Nicolae 1932- *WhoUN 92*
Iona, Mario 1917- *WhoAm 92*
Ionas, Constantinos 1930- *WhoScE 91-3*
Ionascu, Gheorghita 1936- *WhoScE 91-4*
Ione *ConAu 137*
Ione, Carole 1937- *ConAu 137*
Ionel 1919-1982 *ScF&FL 92*
Ionesco, Eugene *BioIn 17*
Ionesco, Eugene 1912- *MagSWL [port], WhoAm 92, WhoWor 93, WorLitC [port]*
Ionescu, Anton 1939- *WhoScE 91-4*
Ionescu, Elisabeth 1948- *WhoWor 93*
Ionescu, Liviu 1944- *WhoScE 91-4*
Ionescu, Maria *WhoScE 91-4*
Ionescu, Virgil 1943- *WhoScE 91-4*
Ionescu Tulcea, Cassius 1923- *WhoAm 92, WhoWor 93*
Ioos, George F. 1931- *St&PR 93*
Ioppolo, Frank S. *Law&B 92*
Iordanou, Constantine P. 1950- *St&PR 93*
Iorgulescu, Jorge 1935- *WhoAm 92*
Iorillo, John R. 1935- *St&PR 93*
Iorillo, Mario Angelo 1939- *WhoAm 92*
Iorio, Edward J. 1911- *St&PR 93*
Iorio, Ralph A. 1925- *St&PR 93*
Iorio, Ralph Arthur 1925- *WhoAm 92*
Iosa Ghini, Massimo *BioIn 17*
Ioseliani, Otar 1934- *DrEEuF*
Ioselliani, Otar *MiSFD 9*
Iott, Richard B. 1951- *St&PR 93*
Iott, Timothy Lee 1950- *St&PR 93*
Iotti, Robert C. 1941- *St&PR 93*
Iouchkiavitchious, Henrikas Alguirdas 1935- *WhoUN 92*
Iovacchini, Eric Vincent 1947- *WhoSSW 93*
Iovanni, Nancy Jean 1962- *WhoAmW 93*
Iovenko, Michael 1930- *WhoAm 92, WhoE 93*
Iovine, Carmine P. 1943- *WhoAm 92*
Iovino, Charlyn Adlis *Law&B 92*
Ip, Chuen Ching 1959- *WhoWor 93*
Ip, Henrietta Man-Hing 1947- *WhoAsAP 91*
Ip, Matthew Wai-Fan 1951- *WhoEmL 93*
Ip, Rose Marie *Law&B 92*
Ip, Sunny 1941- *St&PR 93*
Ipaktschi, Junes *WhoScE 91-3*
Iparraguirre y Balerdi, Jose Maria de 1820-1881 *Baker 92*
Ipavec, Benjamin 1829-1909 *Baker 92*
Ipcar, Dahlov 1917- *ScF&FL 92, WhoAm 92*
Ipcar, Dahlov (Zorach) 1917- *MajAI [port]*
Ipe, J. Bruce *Law&B 92*
Iphicrates c. 412BC-353BC *HarEnMi*
Ipousteguy, Jean 1920- *WhoWor 93*
Ippel, Gerald L. 1927- *St&PR 93*
Ippen, Erich Peter 1940- *WhoAm 92*
Ippolito, Andrew V. 1932- *St&PR 93*
Ippolito, Angelo 1922- *WhoAm 92*
Ippolito, Ferdinando 1919- *WhoScE 91-3*
Ippolito, Joseph Victor *Law&B 92*
Ippolito, Michael 1955- *St&PR 93*
Ippolitov-Ivanov, Mikhail 1859-1935 *Baker 92, OxDcOp*
Ipsarides, Chazalambos *WhoScE 91-4*
Ipsen, Brad *St&PR 93*
Ipsen, Carol Anne 1951- *WhoEmL 93*
Ipuche-Riva, Pedro 1924- *Baker 92*
Iqbal, Muhammad 1876-1938 *DcTwHis*
Iqbal, Zafar 1946- *WhoAm 92*
Iqbal, Zubair 1944- *WhoUN 92*
Iradier, Sebastian de *Baker 92*
Irani, Farhad M. 1938- *WhoWor 93*
Irani, Joseph H. 1927- *St&PR 93*
Irani, Ray R. *BioIn 17*
Irani, Ray R. 1935- *St&PR 93, WhoAm 92*
Irani, Raymond Reza 1928- *WhoAm 92*
Irani, Sands Kenyon 1942- *WhoE 93*
Irby, Benjamin Freeman 1938- *WhoSSW 93*
Irby, Charles Lyons 1954- *St&PR 93*
Irby, Daphne Evangeline 1962- *WhoAmW 93*
Irby, E. Kay 1935- *WhoSSW 93*
Irby, Jack Daniel 1953- *St&PR 93*
Irby, James B. *BioIn 17*
Irby, Kenneth (Lee) 1936- *WhoWrEP 92*
Irby, Maura Mills *BioIn 17*
Irby, Richard *Law&B 92*
Irby, Stuart C., Jr. 1923- *St&PR 93*
Irby, Stuart Charles, Jr. 1923- *WhoAm 92*
Irby, Stuart M. 1953- *St&PR 93*
Iredale, John Arthur *WhoScE 91-1*
Iredale, P. *WhoScE 91-1*
Iredell, James 1751-1799 *OxCSupC [port]*
Iredell, Robert, IV 1941- *St&PR 93*
Irelan, Robert W. 1937- *St&PR 93*
Ireland, Andrew P. 1930- *WhoAm 92, WhoSSW 93*
Ireland, Andy 1930- *CngDr 91*
Ireland, Ann 1953- *WhoCanL 92*
Ireland, David 1927- *ScF&FL 92*
Ireland, Harry Bert 1938- *St&PR 93*
Ireland, Harry Bert, Jr. *Law&B 92*
Ireland, Herbert Orin 1919- *WhoAm 92*
Ireland, James Duane 1913-1991 *BioIn 17*
Ireland, James Duane, III 1950- *St&PR 93*
Ireland, Jill *BioIn 17*
Ireland, Joan E. 1949- *St&PR 93*
Ireland, John d1992 *NewYTBS 92 [port]*
Ireland, John 1914-1992 *BioIn 17*
Ireland, John (Nicholson) 1879-1962 *Baker 92*
Ireland, Kathy *BioIn 17*
Ireland, Kenneth 1929- *ScF&FL 92*
Ireland, Lee Wilson 1951- *WhoEmL 93*
Ireland, Lisa Diane 1961- *WhoAmW 93*
Ireland, Marvin Edwin 1947- *WhoEmL 93*
Ireland, Norman C. 1927- *St&PR 93*
Ireland, Patricia *BioIn 17, NewYTBS 92 [port], WhoAm 92*
Ireland, Patricia 1945- *CurBio 92 [port], WhoAmW 93*
Ireland, Patricia c. 1946- *News 92 [port]*
Ireland, Patrick 1935- *WhoAm 92*
Ireland, R.L., III 1920- *St&PR 93*
Ireland, Robert Livingston, III 1920- *WhoAm 92*
Ireland, Sandra L(eora) Jones 1942- *ConAu 137*
Irell, Lawrence Elliott 1912- *WhoAm 92*
Irene *OxDcByz*
Irene c. 752-803 *OxDcByz*
Irene, Eugene Arthur 1941- *WhoAm 92, WhoSSW 93*
Irene Doukaina c. 1066-1123 *OxDcByz*
Irene-Yolanda of Montferrat 1273?-1317 *OxDcByz*
Ireson, Barbara *ChlFicS*
Ireson, Barbara 1927- *ScF&FL 92*
Ireson, J.A. *WhoScE 91-1*
Ireton, Henry 1611-1651 *HarEnMi*
Ireton, John Francis, Jr. 1939- *WhoAm 92*
Ireton, Thomas F. *Law&B 92*
Ireton, Thomas Francis 1940- *St&PR 93, WhoAm 92*
Ireton-Hewitt, John H. 1937- *St&PR 93*

Ireton-Hewitt, John Howard 1937- WhoAm 92, WhoE 93
Irey, Charlotte York 1918- WhoAm 92
Irey, Nelson Sumner 1911- WhoAm 92
Ireys, Alice Recknagel 1911- WhoAm 92
Irfan, Muhammad 1928- WhoWor 93
Irgens Jensen, Ludvig (Paul) 1894-1969 Baker 92
Irgon, Joseph 1919- WhoWor 93
Iri, Masao 1933- WhoWor 93
Iria, Joaquim Alberto WhoScE 91-3
Irie, Setsujiro 1921- WhoWor 93
Irie, Sueo BioIn 17
Irigaray, Jean-Leon 1938- WhoScE 91-2
Irigaray, Luce BioIn 17
Irigoyen, Hipolito 1850-1933 DcTwHis
Irimajiri, Shoichiro BioIn 17
Irino, Yoshiro 1921-1980 Baker 92
Irion, Arthur Lloyd 1918- WhoAm 92
Irion, Georg Friedrich 1942- WhoScE 91-3
Irion, James V. 1950- St&PR 93
Irion, Mary Jean 1922- WhoWrEP 92
Irions, Charles Carter 1929- WhoAm 92
Irish, Chas. A. 1929- St&PR 93
Irish, Douglas Lynn 1939- WhoAm 92
Irish, Frank Sylvester 1932- St&PR 93
Irish, George Butler 1944- WhoAm 92
Irish, J. A. George 1942- DcCPCAm
Irish, Larry Gordon 1944- St&PR 93
Irish, Leon Eugene 1938- WhoAm 92
Irish, Marian D. 1909- BioIn 17
Irish, Marie AmWomPl
Irish, Marilyn Eleanor 1943- WhoE 93
Irish, R.W. Law&B 92
Iriye, Akira 1934- WhoAm 92
Irizarri-Lamela, Andres E. 1937- WhoSSW 93
Irlbeck, Dennis H. Law&B 92
Irmas, Audrey BioIn 17
Irmas, Matthew MiSFD 9
Irmas, Sydney BioIn 17
Irmelshausen, Charles Henneberg zu ScF&FL 92
Irmer, Manfred Wilhelm 1936- WhoUN 92
Irminger, Eldon R. 1947- St&PR 93
Irminger, Eugene H. 1929- St&PR 93
Irminger, Eugene Herman 1929- WhoAm 92
Irmscher, Wallace G. 1923- St&PR 93
Irngartinger, Hermann 1938- WhoScE 91-3, WhoWor 93
Irom, Daniel MiSFD 9
Irom, Larry H. Law&B 92
Iron, Ralph 1855-1920 BioIn 17
Irons, Alden Hatheway 1939- WhoE 93
Irons, Dennis Michael 1951- WhoEmL 93, WhoSSW 93
Irons, George Vernon 1902- WhoAm 92
Irons, Jack
See Red Hot Chili Peppers, The News 93-1
Irons, Jeremy NewYTBS 92 [port]
Irons, Jeremy 1948- BioIn 17, IntDcF 2-3 [port]
Irons, Jeremy John 1948- WhoAm 92
Irons, John 1942- ScF&FL 92
Irons, William George 1933- WhoAm 92
Ironside, H.A. 1876-1951 BioIn 17
Ironside, Henry Allan 1876-1951 BioIn 17
Ironside, Jetske 1940- BioIn 17
Ironside, Michael BioIn 17
Ironside, Virginia 1944- ScF&FL 92
Irretier, Horst D. 1949- WhoScE 91-3
Irretier, Horst Dieter 1949- WhoWor 93
Irrgang, Heinrich Bernhard 1869-1916 Baker 92
Irrthum, Henri Emile 1947- WhoWor 93
Irsay, James Steven 1959- WhoAm 92
Irsay, Robert 1923- WhoAm 92
Irsfeld, John Henry 1937- WhoWrEP 92
Irsigler, Karl WhoScE 91-4
Irurre-Perez, Jose 1940- WhoScE 91-3
Irvan, Robert P. WhoIns 93
Irvan, Robert P. 1937- St&PR 93
Irvin, Charles L. Law&B 92
Irvin, Charles Richard 1932- St&PR 93
Irvin, David Rand 1948- WhoEmL 93, WhoSSW 93
Irvin, Dona L. 1917- ConAu 138
Irvin, Eames 1928- St&PR 93
Irvin, George William 1940- WhoWor 93
Irvin, John 1940- MiSFD 9
Irvin, John Granville 1924- WhoSSW 93
Irvin, Lynda Elare 1950- WhoAmW 93
Irvin, Michael BioIn 17
Irvin, Michael Richard 1951- St&PR 93
Irvin, Patricia BioIn 17
Irvin, Patricia Gaeron 1944- WhoAmW 93
Irvin, Patricia Louise 1955- WhoAmW 93
Irvin, Robert Andrew 1948- WhoEmL 93
Irvin, Robert H. Law&B 92
Irvin, Robert H. 1952- St&PR 93
Irvin, Robert Joseph 1920- WhoAm 92
Irvin, Sam MiSFD 9
Irvin, Thomas J. Law&B 92
Irvin, Tinsley H. 1933- WhoIns 93
Irvin, Tinsley Hoyt 1933- St&PR 93, WhoAm 92
Irvin, W. Lynn 1935- St&PR 93
Irvine, George 1948- WhoAm 92
Irvine, George A. 1941- St&PR 93
Irvine, Georgeanne 1955- SmATA 72 [port]
Irvine, Gretchen Kranz 1946- WhoEmL 93
Irvine, Horace Hills, II 1937- WhoE 93
Irvine, J. Michael Law&B 92
Irvine, James Bosworth 1914- WhoSSW 93
Irvine, John Alexander 1947- WhoAm 92, WhoSSW 93
Irvine, John Henry 1951- WhoWor 93
Irvine, John Maxwell WhoScE 91-1
Irvine, John Michael 1954- WhoE 93, WhoEmL 93
Irvine, Louva Elizabeth 1939- WhoAm 92
Irvine, Mat ScF&FL 92
Irvine, Peter Bennington 1951- WhoE 93, WhoEmL 93
Irvine, Phyllis Eleanor Kuhnle 1940- WhoAmW 93
Irvine, Reed John 1922- WhoAm 92, WhoE 93
Irvine, Robert ScF&FL 92
Irvine, Roger Kenneth 1933- St&PR 93
Irvine, Rose Loretta Abernethy 1924- WhoAmW 93
Irvine, Stewart Edward 1950- St&PR 93
Irvine, Theodora Ursula AmWomPl
Irvine, Thomas Francis, Jr. 1922- WhoAm 92
Irvine, William Burriss 1925- WhoWor 93
Irving, A. Marshall 1929- WhoE 93
Irving, Adam, Jr. 1943- St&PR 93
Irving, Amy 1953- WhoAm 92
Irving, David MiSFD 9
Irving, Edmund 1910-1990 BioIn 17
Irving, Edward 1927- WhoAm 92
Irving, Edward M. 1928- St&PR 93
Irving, George Steven 1922- WhoAm 92
Irving, George Washington, Jr. 1910- WhoE 93
Irving, George Washington, III 1940- WhoAm 92, WhoE 93
Irving, Gitte Nielsen 1954- WhoE 93, WhoEmL 93, WhoWor 93
Irving, Glenn Alexander 1931- St&PR 93
Irving, I.A.L. 1938- St&PR 93
Irving, Jack Howard 1920- WhoAm 92
Irving, John 1942- BioIn 17, MagSAmL [port]
Irving, John K. 1953- St&PR 93
Irving, John Kenneth Law&B 92
Irving, John Winslow 1942- WhoAm 92, WhoWrEP 92
Irving, Joyce Arlene 1945- WhoAmW 93
Irving, Kenneth C. 1899-1992 NewYTBS 92 [port]
Irving, Michael Henry 1923- WhoAm 92
Irving, Miles Horsfall WhoScE 91-1
Irving, Richard BioIn 17
Irving, Richard d1990 BioIn 17
Irving, Richard 1917-1990 MiSFD 9N
Irving, Richard H., III Law&B 92
Irving, Robert BioIn 17, MajAI
Irving, Robert 1913-1991 AnObit 1991
Irving, Robert (Augustine) 1913- Baker 92
Irving, Robert Churchill 1928- WhoE 93
Irving, Robert J., Jr. Law&B 92
Irving, Robert McCardell 1930-1989 BioIn 17
Irving, Ronald 1931- St&PR 93
Irving, S.J. WhoScE 91-1
Irving, Stephanie (Jean) 1962- ConAu 139
Irving, Terry 1951- WhoAm 92, WhoE 93
Irving, Thomas Pitt d1818 BioIn 17
Irving, Tom L. 1956- St&PR 93
Irving, Washington 1783-1859 MagSAmL [port], ScF&FL 92, WorLitC [port]
Irving-Strain, Bonnie Ann 1946- WhoAmW 93
Irwin, Alice W. 1943- St&PR 93
Irwin, Ann(abelle Bowen) 1915- MajAI [port]
Irwin, Bessie AmWomPl
Irwin, Beverly Joan 1928- WhoAmW 93
Irwin, Bryan St&PR 93
Irwin, Byron 1941- WhoE 93, WhoWor 93
Irwin, Christopher Wayne 1948- St&PR 93
Irwin, Clare James Law&B 92
Irwin, David George 1933- WhoWor 93
Irwin, Deborah Jo 1952- WhoEmL 93, WhoWor 93
Irwin, Donald d1991 BioIn 17
Irwin, Fay WhoWrEP 92
Irwin, G. Stormy 1929- WhoAmW 93
Irwin, Gary R. Law&B 92
Irwin, George Rankin 1907- WhoAm 92
Irwin, Glenn Ward, Jr. 1920- WhoAm 92
Irwin, Grace Luce AmWomPl
Irwin, Graham W. 1920-1991 BioIn 17
Irwin, Gregory Matthew 1961- WhoEmL 93
Irwin, H. Thomas 1943- St&PR 93
Irwin, H. William 1920- WhoAm 92
Irwin, Hadley MajAI
Irwin, Hale 1945- BioIn 17
Irwin, Hale S. 1945- WhoAm 92
Irwin, Ira 1932- St&PR 93
Irwin, James 1930-1991 AnObit 1991, News 92
Irwin, James Benson 1930-1991 BioIn 17
Irwin, James Carson 1932- St&PR 93
Irwin, Jeanne E. Law&B 92
Irwin, Joe Robert 1936- St&PR 93, WhoAm 92
Irwin, John David 1939- WhoAm 92
Irwin, John Nichol, II 1913- WhoAm 92
Irwin, John Robert 1945- St&PR 93
Irwin, John Thomas 1940- WhoAm 92
Irwin, John Wesley 1937- WhoAm 92
Irwin, Joseph James 1908- ScF&FL 92
Irwin, Judith Westphal 1949- WhoE 93
Irwin, Lawrence Burton 1947- WhoEmL 93
Irwin, Leo Howard 1917- WhoAm 92
Irwin, Linda Belmore 1950- WhoAmW 93, WhoWor 93
Irwin, Margaret AmWomPl
Irwin, Margaret 1889-1967 BioIn 17, ScF&FL 92
Irwin, Margaret Hardinge d1940 BioIn 17
Irwin, Mark 1953- WhoWrEP 92
Irwin, Martin 1949- WhoE 93, WhoEmL 93
Irwin, Michael Henry Knox 1931- WhoWor 93
Irwin, Miriam Dianne Owen 1930- WhoAmW 93
Irwin, Miriam Owen 1930- WhoWrEP 92
Irwin, Myron Richard 1912- St&PR 93
Irwin, Pat 1921- WhoAm 92
Irwin, Patricia Kathleen Page 1916- BioIn 17
Irwin, Patrick H. 1923- St&PR 93
Irwin, Patti J. 1954- St&PR 93
Irwin, Peter Anthony Law&B 92
Irwin, Peter John 1934- St&PR 93
Irwin, Philip Donnan 1933- WhoAm 92
Irwin, R. Neil 1941- WhoWor 93
Irwin, Raymond Richard 1928- St&PR 93
Irwin, Richard Dorsey 1905-1989 BioIn 17
Irwin, Richard F. Law&B 92
Irwin, Richard Loren 1924- WhoAm 92
Irwin, Richard Stephen 1942- WhoE 93
Irwin, Robert 1946- ScF&FL 92
Irwin, Robert J.A. 1927- St&PR 93
Irwin, Robert James Armstrong 1927- WhoAm 92
Irwin, Robert Walter 1928- WhoAm 92
Irwin, Robert Wilson 1939- WhoWor 93
Irwin, Robin J. Law&B 92
Irwin, S. Macdonald 1927- St&PR 93
Irwin, Samuel Macdonald 1927- WhoAm 92
Irwin, Sarita ScF&FL 92
Irwin, Scott Arnold 1951- St&PR 93
Irwin, Theodore 1907- WhoAm 92
Irwin, Van C. 1944- St&PR 93
Irwin, W.R. 1915- ScF&FL 92
Irwin, Walter 1950- ScF&FL 92
Irwin, Will 1873-1948 JrnUS
Irwin, William Arthur BioIn 17
Irwin, William Richard 1944- St&PR 93
Irzykowski, Karol 1873-1944 PolBiDi
I.S. ScF&FL 92
Isaac BioIn 17
Isaac, Abravanel 1437-1508 BioIn 17
Isaac, Adele 1854-1915 Baker 92, OxDcOp
Isaac, Alberto MiSFD 9
Isaac, Bina Susan 1958- WhoAmW 93
Isaac, Charles D. 1932- St&PR 93
Isaac, David John Law&B 92
Isaac, George, Jr. 1923- St&PR 93
Isaac, George A., III 1953- St&PR 93
Isaac, Heinrich c. 1450-1517 Baker 92
Isaac, James MiSFD 9
Isaac, John Lansing Law&B 92
Isaac, John R., Jr. BioIn 17
Isaac, Paul Edward 1926- WhoSSW 93
Isaac, Rael Jean 1933- WhoE 93
Isaac, Rhys Llywelyn 1937- WhoWor 93
Isaac, Robert Michael 1928- WhoAm 92
Isaac, Rondall ScF&FL 92
Isaac, Sol Morton 1911- WhoAm 92
Isaac, Steven Richard 1947- WhoAm 92, WhoSSW 93
Isaac, Walter Lon 1956- WhoEmL 93, WhoSSW 93, WhoWor 93
Isaac, William Michael 1943- WhoAm 92
Isaac, Yvonne Renee 1948- WhoAmW 93
Isaac Angelos, II c. 1156-1204 OxDcByz
Isaac Komnenos c. 1155-1195? OxDcByz
Isaac Komnenos, I c. 1007-c. 1060 OxDcByz
Isaackson, Larry Dean 1951- WhoIns 93
Isaacman, Steven 1930- WhoE 93
Isaac Nash, Eva Mae 1936- WhoWor 93
Isaac of Antioch fl. 5th cent.- OxDcByz
Isaacoff, Dana Margolia 1960- WhoAmW 93
Isaac of Nineveh fl. c. 680- OxDcByz
Isaacs, Alvin Law&B 92
Isaacs, Amy Fay 1946- WhoAm 92
Isaacs, Arnold Robinson 1941- WhoE 93
Isaacs, Barbara Lynn 1955- WhoAmW 93
Isaacs, Byrna Rackel AmWomPl
Isaacs, David 1950- WhoWor 93
Isaacs, Dorna L. 1952- St&PR 93
Isaacs, Florence 1937- WhoWrEP 92
Isaacs, Gary BioIn 17
Isaacs, Gerald William 1927- WhoAm 92
Isaacs, Godfrey Leonard 1924- WhoSSW 93
Isaacs, Helen Coolidge Adams 1917- WhoAm 92, WhoAmW 93, WhoWor 93
Isaacs, John Henry 1949- WhoEmL 93, WhoSSW 93
Isaacs, Jon T. 1945- St&PR 93
Isaacs, Kendal 1925- DcCPCAm
Isaacs, Kenneth Lothaire 1904-1991 BioIn 17
Isaacs, Kenneth Sidney 1920- WhoAm 92, WhoWor 93
Isaacs, Leonard 1939-1988 ScF&FL 92
Isaacs, Leonard Bernard 1951- WhoEmL 93
Isaacs, Marion Margery Scranton d1992 BioIn 17, NewYTBS 92
Isaacs, Mark D. 1955- WhoWrEP 92
Isaacs, Michael Burton 1947- WhoEmL 93
Isaacs, Neil D. 1931-1988 ScF&FL 92
Isaacs, Patricia B. 1925- St&PR 93
Isaacs, R.J. 1905- St&PR 93
Isaacs, Roger David 1925- WhoAm 92, WhoWor 93
Isaacs, Russell L. 1932- St&PR 93
Isaacs, S.F. 1937- St&PR 93
Isaacs, S. Fred 1937- WhoAm 92
Isaacs, S. Ted 1914- WhoWor 93
Isaacs, Susan 1943- BioIn 17, WhoE 93
Isaacs, Thomas K. 1949- St&PR 93
Isaacs, William Russell 1923- WhoSSW 93
Isaacson, Arline Levine 1946- WhoAmW 93
Isaacson, Bernard 1936- St&PR 93
Isaacson, Burt M. 1929- St&PR 93
Isaacson, Diane Kathleen 1952- WhoWrEP 92
Isaacson, Edith Lipsig 1920- WhoAmW 93, WhoE 93
Isaacson, Gerald Sidney 1927- WhoAm 92
Isaacson, Jeffrey Law&B 92
Isaacson, John Magyar 1946- WhoAm 92
Isaacson, M.S. 1932- St&PR 93
Isaacson, Mark Jeffrey Law&B 92
Isaacson, Marvin Gerald 1918- WhoSSW 93, WhoWor 93
Isaacson, Melvin Stuart 1949- WhoE 93
Isaacson, Milton Stanley 1932- WhoAm 92
Isaacson, Norman Harry 1922- WhoE 93
Isaacson, Robert Lee 1928- WhoAm 92
Isaacson, Robert Louis 1944- WhoWor 93
Isaacson, Robert William 1942- WhoE 93
Isaacson, Steven C. Law&B 92
Isaacson, Walter Seff 1952- WhoAm 92
Isaak, Chris BioIn 17
Isaak, Gerhard Law&B 92
Isaak, Heinrich c. 1450-1517 Baker 92
Isaakidis, Anestis 1946- WhoScE 91-3
Isabell, Robert BioIn 17
Isabella, I, Queen of Spain 1451-1504 BioIn 17
Isabella, Thomas A. 1938- St&PR 93
Isabella d'Este 1474-1539 BioIn 17
Isabelle, Didier Bernard WhoScE 91-2
Isa Bin Pehin Datu Perdana Menteri Dato, Yang Berhormat Pehin Orang Kaya Laila WhoAsAP 91
Isa bin Salman Al-Khalifa, Sheikh 1933- WhoWor 93
Isac, Ilarie 1933- WhoScE 91-4
Isac, Maria 1946- WhoScE 91-4
Isadora, Rachel BioIn 17
Isadora, Rachel 1953?- ConAu 137, MajAI [port]
Isaiah BioIn 17
Isaias, Estefano 1948- St&PR 93
Isakoff, Janice Ann Law&B 92
Isakoff, Sheldon Erwin 1925- WhoAm 92
Isakow, Selwyn 1952- WhoAm 92
Isaksson, Ake G. 1926- WhoScE 91-4
Isamitt, Carlos 1887-1974 Baker 92
Isaurian Dynasty OxDcByz
Isautier, Bernard Francois 1942- WhoWor 93
Isay, Jane Franzblau 1939- WhoAm 92
Isay, Richard Alexander WhoAm 92
Isayama, Hiroshi 1921- WhoAsAP 91
Isbell, Cecily A. Law&B 92
Isbell, Charles Edwin 1931- St&PR 93
Isbell, David Bradford 1929- WhoAm 92

Iszard, Calvin Oscar, Jr. 1943- *WhoE 93, WhoWor 93*
Iszard, Robert French 1919- *St&PR 93*
Itabashi, Hideo Henry 1926- *WhoAm 92*
Itagaki, Seishiro 1885-1946 *HarEnMi*
Itagaki, Tadashi 1924- *WhoAsAP 91*
Itahara, Toshio 1949- *WhoWor 93*
Itahashi, Ikuo 1925- *WhoWor 93*
Itakura, Hiroshi 1934- *WhoWor 93*
Italos, John *OxDcByz*
Itam, Samuel Paul Orok 1952- *WhoUN 92*
Itameri-Kinter, Terry 1953- *St&PR 93*
Itami, Jinroh 1937- *WhoWor 93*
Itami, Juzo *BioIn 17*
Itami, Juzo 1933- *MiSFD 9*
Itani, Frances *WhoCanL 92*
Itani, Frances (Susan) 1942- *ConAu 138*
Itani, Reiko 1958- *WhoWor 93*
Itano, Harvey Akio 1920- *WhoAm 92*
Iten, C. John 1955- *St&PR 93*
Ites, William Jay 1950- *St&PR 93*
Ith, Lily Van *ScF&FL 92*
Ithakissios, Dionyssis S. 1941- *WhoScE 91-3*
Itin, James Richard 1933- *St&PR 93, WhoAm 92*
Itkin, Robert J. *Law&B 92*
Itnyre, Jacqueline Harriet 1941- *WhoAmW 93*
Ito, Chuji 1934- *WhoAsAP 91*
Ito, Eisei 1941- *WhoAsAP 91*
Ito, Fumio 1929- *WhoWor 93*
Ito, Hideko 1943- *WhoAsAP 91*
Ito, Hitashi *BioIn 17*
Ito, Kentaro 1939- *WhoWor 93*
Ito, Kiyosi 1915- *WhoWor 93*
Ito, Koji 1937- *WhoWor 93*
Ito, Kosuke 1941- *WhoAsAP 91*
Ito, Masatoshi 1947- *WhoAsAP 91*
Ito, Masayoshi 1913- *WhoAsAP 91*
Ito, Midori *BioIn 17*
Ito, Rikuma 1931- *St&PR 93*
Ito, Ryuta 1922- *Baker 92, WhoWor 93*
Ito, Seiichi 1890-1945 *HarEnMi*
Ito, Shigemasa 1942- *WhoWor 93*
Ito, Shigeru 1928- *WhoAsAP 91*
Ito, Sho 1924- *WhoWor 93*
Ito, Soichiro 1924- *WhoAsAP 91*
Ito, Sukemaro 1834-1906 *HarEnMi*
Ito, Takashi *Law&B 92*
Ito, Takeshi 1932- *WhoWor 93*
Ito, Toyo 1941- *BioIn 17*
Ito, Yasuki 1943- *WhoWor 93*
Ito, Yoshitada Zen 1917- *WhoWor 93*
Ito, Yuko 1843-1914 *HarEnMi*
Ito, Zenichi 1924- *WhoWor 93*
Itoh, Makoto 1936- *WhoWor 93*
Itoh, Seishichi 1935- *St&PR 93, WhoAm 92*
Itoh, Tatsuo 1940- *WhoAm 92*
Itohisa, Yaeko 1932- *WhoAsAP 91*
Itokawa, Yoshinori 1933- *WhoWor 93*
Itskovitz, Harold David 1929- *WhoAm 92*
Itson, Janice Marie 1962- *WhoAmW 93*
Itson, Sonja Patrice 1943- *WhoAmW 93*
Itsumi, Yoshitaka 1946- *WhoWor 93*
Itta, Emanuele 1944- *WhoWor 93*
Itta, Paul d1991 *BioIn 17*
Itten, Johannes 1888-1967 *BioIn 17*
Itter, Diane 1946-1989 *BioIn 17*
Itti, Roland 1940- *WhoScE 91-2*
Ittleson, Henry Anthony 1937- *WhoAm 92*
Ittner, Helen Louise 1935- *WhoAmW 93*
Ittner, Robert A. *Law&B 92*
Itts, Elizabeth Ann Dunham 1928- *WhoAm 92*
Itu, Daniel 1963- *WhoAsAP 91*
Iturbi, Amparo 1898-1969
See Iturbi, Jose 1895-1980 *Baker 92*
Iturbi, Amparo 1899-1969 *NotHsAW 93 [port]*
Iturbi, Jose 1895-1980 *Baker 92*
Iturriberry, Juan Jose 1936- *Baker 92*
Itzaina, Roberto 1950- *WhoWor 93*
Itzin, Charles Francis 1946- *WhoWrEP 92*
Itzkoff, Norman Jay *Law&B 92*
Itzkowitz, Murray 1928- *WhoE 93*
Itzkowitz, Norman 1931- *WhoAm 92*
Itzkowitz, Theodore D. *Law&B 92*
Iudica, Ross C. 1941- *St&PR 93*
Iuen, Frank John, III *Law&B 92*
IUldashev, Kh. M. *BioIn 17*
Iuliucci, John Domenic 1942- *WhoE 93*
IUrovskii, IAkov Mikhailovich 1878-1938 *BioIn 17*
Iuso, William R. 1942- *St&PR 93*
IUsupov, F.F. 1887-1967 *BioIn 17*
IUsupov, Feliks Feliksovich 1887-1967 *BioIn 17*
Iuta, Taomati Taurabakai 1939- *WhoAsAP 91*
Ivajlo *OxDcByz*
Ivan, III 1440-1505 *OxDcByz*
Ivan, Daniel J. 1940- *St&PR 93*
Ivan, Marian O'Loane 1956- *WhoAmW 93, WhoEmL 93*
Ivan, Mircea-Dumitru 1939- *WhoScE 91-4*
Ivan, Orejas Iban 1936- *WhoWor 93*
Ivan, Rosalyn *AmWomPl*
Ivan, Thomas Nathaniel 1911- *WhoAm 92*
Ivan Alexander *OxDcByz*
Ivancevic, Walter Charles 1920- *WhoAm 92*
Ivancic, Joanne M. *Law&B 92*
Ivanhoe, Herman 1908- *WhoE 93*
Ivanhoe, Mark *ScF&FL 92*
Ivanhoe, Ruth 1931- *St&PR 93*
Ivanick, Carol W. Trencher 1939- *WhoAm 92*
Ivanick, Joseph 1922- *St&PR 93*
Ivanier, Isin 1906- *WhoAm 92, WhoE 93*
Ivanier, Paul 1932- *WhoAm 92*
Ivanilov, Yury Pavlovich 1931- *WhoWor 93*
Ivanisevic, Boris 1921- *WhoScE 91-4*
Ivanisevic, Goran *BioIn 17*
Ivanko dc. 1200 *OxDcByz*
Ivanko, Kathleen *Law&B 92*
Ivanof, Antipa *WhoScE 91-4*
Ivanoff, Bernard 1939- *WhoUN 92*
Ivanoff, Joanne Marie 1931- *WhoAmW 93*
Ivanov, Alexandre Anatolij 1957- *WhoWor 93*
Ivanov, Alexey 1904-1988 *OxDcOp*
Ivanov, Andrei 1900-1970 *OxDcOp*
Ivanov, Chavdar Petkov 1915- *WhoScE 91-4*
Ivanov, D.D. 1896-1980 *BioIn 17*
Ivanov, Dmitrii Dmitrievich 1896-1980 *BioIn 17*
Ivanov, Georgi 1924- *Baker 92*
Ivanov, Ivan B. 1935- *WhoScE 91-4*
Ivanov, Ivan Borissov 1929- *WhoScE 91-4*
Ivanov, Konstantin 1907-1984 *Baker 92*
Ivanov, L. *WhoScE 91-4*
Ivanov, Lyuben Dimitrov 1941- *WhoScE 91-4, WhoWor 93*
Ivanov, Mikhail Mikhailovich 1849-1927 *Baker 92*
Ivanov, Nicholas Yudovich 1851-1919 *HarEnMi*
Ivanov, Nikolai (Kuzmich) 1810-1880 *Baker 92*
Ivanov, Nikolay 1810-1880 *OxDcOp*
Ivanov, Oleg Vladimirovich 1954- *WhoWor 93*
Ivanov, Radostin Petrov 1942- *WhoWor 93*
Ivanov, Sergei Alekseevich 1952- *WhoWor 93*
Ivanov, Sergey 1949- *WhoWor 93*
Ivanov, Stojan 1935- *WhoScE 91-4*
Ivanov, Valentin Konstantinovech 1908- *WhoWor 93*
Ivanov, Victor Vladimirovich 1929- *WhoWor 93*
Ivanov-Boretzky, Mikhail Vladimirovich 1874-1936 *Baker 92*
Ivanovich, Cristoforo 1628-1689 *OxDcOp*
Ivanovici, Ion 1845-1902 *Baker 92*
Ivanovitch, Michael Stevo 1939- *WhoE 93, WhoWor 93*
Ivanov-Radkevitch, Nikolai 1904-1962 *Baker 92*
Ivanovs, Janis 1906-1983 *Baker 92*
Ivans, W.S. 1920- *St&PR 93*
Ivans, Wayne W. 1915- *St&PR 93*
Ivans, William Stanley 1920- *WhoAm 92*
Ivan the Terrible 1530-1584 *OxDcOp*
Ivan, the Terrible, IV, Czar of Russia 1530-1584 *BioIn 17*
Ivanyi, J. *WhoScE 91-1*
Ivanyi, Ludmila *WhoScE 91-1*
Ivarato, Aita Ikirari 1953- *WhoAsAP 91*
Ivashko, Vladimir *BioIn 17*
Ivask, Ivar Vidrik 1927-1992 *ConAu 139*
Ivaska, Ari U. 1946- *WhoScE 91-4*
Iveagh, Lord 1937-1992 *NewYTBS 92 [port]*
Ivens, Gunther P. 1925- *WhoScE 91-3*
Ivens, Joris 1898-1989 *BioIn 17*
Ivens, Mary Sue 1929- *WhoAm 92, WhoAmW 93, WhoSSW 93*
Ivens, Roberto 1850-1898
See Capelo, Hermenegildo de Brito 1841-1917 & Ivens, Roberto 1850-1898 *Expl 93*
Iver, Robert Drew 1947- *WhoSSW 93*
Iveropoulos, John *OxDcByz*
Iveroth, Carl Axel 1914- *WhoWor 93*
Iveroth, T. *WhoScE 91-2*
Ivers, Donald Louis 1941- *WhoAm 92*
Iversen, Bendt 1933- *WhoWor 93*
Iversen, James Delano 1933- *WhoAm 92*
Iversen, L.L. *WhoScE 91-1*
Iversen, Nicholas Drake 1951- *WhoE 93*
Iversen, Ole-Jan 1946- *WhoScE 91-4*
Iverson, Alvin Arnold 1944- *WhoSSW 93*
Iverson, Ann Cummings 1941- *WhoAm 92*
Iverson, Betty L. 1934- *WhoSSW 93*
Iverson, Carl John 1940- *St&PR 93*
Iverson, Carol Jean 1937- *WhoAmW 93*
Iverson, Eric G. *ScF&FL 92*
Iverson, F. Kenneth *BioIn 17*
Iverson, F. Kenneth 1925- *St&PR 93*
Iverson, Francis Kenneth 1925- *WhoAm 92, WhoSSW 93*
Iverson, John B. 1946- *St&PR 93*
Iverson, John I. *Law&B 92*
Iverson, Lucille Karin 1925- *WhoWrEP 92*
Iverson, Peter James 1944- *WhoAm 92*
Iverson, Thomas Allen 1958- *WhoEmL 93*
Iverson, Wayne Dahl 1931- *WhoAm 92*
Iverson, Willard F. 1935- *WhoIns 93*
Ives, A.P. *WhoScE 91-1*
Ives, Adriene Diane 1951- *WhoAmW 93*
Ives, Alice Emma 1876-1930 *AmWomPl*
Ives, Anson Bradley 1964- *WhoE 93*
Ives, Burl 1909- *Baker 92, WhoAm 92*
Ives, Charles C. 1935- *St&PR 93*
Ives, Charles (Edward) 1874-1954 *Baker 92, BioIn 17*
Ives, Colta Feller 1943- *WhoAm 92, WhoAmW 93*
Ives, Cora Semmes *AmWomPl*
Ives, David Otis 1919- *WhoAm 92*
Ives, Dermod 1904- *WhoAm 92*
Ives, Edward Dawson 1925- *WhoAm 92*
Ives, George 1834-1863 *BioIn 17*
Ives, George Skinner 1922- *WhoAm 92*
Ives, J. Atwood 1936- *St&PR 93, WhoAm 92*
Ives, Jeanette Routh 1950- *WhoE 93*
Ives, John David 1931- *WhoAm 92*
Ives, Kenneth Holbrook 1916- *WhoWrEP 92*
Ives, Margaret 1903- *WhoAm 92*
Ives, Rich Lee 1951- *WhoWrEP 92*
Ives, Ronn Brian 1950- *WhoAm 92*
Ives, Scott S. *Law&B 92*
Ives, Simon 1600-1662 *Baker 92*
Ives, Timothy R. 1928- *St&PR 93*
Ives, Vernon A. 1908-1990 *BioIn 17*
Ives, W. Byron 1928- *St&PR 93*
Iveson, William Edward 1940- *WhoE 93*
Ivester, J. Harold 1940- *St&PR 93*
Ivester, Jim C. *St&PR 93*
Ivester, Melvin Douglas 1947- *WhoAm 92*
Ivey, Allen Eugene *WhoE 93*
Ivey, Anthony D. *St&PR 93*
Ivey, Christine *ScF&FL 92*
Ivey, Claude Tarlton 1933- *WhoAm 92*
Ivey, David Malcolm 1952- *WhoEmL 93, WhoSSW 93*
Ivey, Donald Glenn 1922- *WhoAm 92*
Ivey, Elizabeth S. 1935- *WhoAm 92*
Ivey, Ellis, II 1931- *WhoSSW 93*
Ivey, Harriet M. 1949- *St&PR 93*
Ivey, Henry Franklin 1921- *WhoE 93*
Ivey, James Burnett 1925- *WhoAm 92*
Ivey, James G. 1951- *St&PR 93*
Ivey, James Stephen 1955- *WhoSSW 93*
Ivey, Janet Ruth d1990 *BioIn 17*
Ivey, Jean Eichelberger 1923- *WhoAm 92*
Ivey, John Courtney 1903-1989 *BioIn 17*
Ivey, John E. 1919-1992 *BioIn 17*
Ivey, John E., Jr. d1992 *NewYTBS 92 [port]*
Ivey, John E(li), Jr. 1919-1992 *CurBio 92N*
Ivey, Judith 1951- *WhoAm 92, WhoAmW 93*
Ivey, Mary Bradford 1941- *WhoE 93*
Ivey, Merleen Denson 1949- *WhoAmW 93*
Ivey, Michael Wayne 1964- *WhoEmL 93, WhoSSW 93*
Ivey, Reanee Nanette 1957- *WhoEmL 93*
Ivey, Reef C., II *Law&B 92*
Ivey, Richard Macaulay 1925- *St&PR 93, WhoAm 92*
Ivey, Robert Carl 1939- *WhoAm 92*
Ivey, William Hamilton 1951- *WhoEmL 93*
Ivey, William James 1944- *WhoAm 92*
Ivic, Petar Krste 1946- *WhoWor 93*
Ivicevich, Helen Madelene 1951- *WhoAmW 93*
Ivie, Bryan *BioIn 17*
Ivie, Leslie Todd 1960- *WhoEmL 93*
Ivins, Marsha S. 1951- *WhoAmW 93*
Ivins, Molly *BioIn 17, WhoAmW 93*
Ivins, Molly c. 1944- *ConAu 138*
Ivins, Steven David 1937- *WhoE 93*
Ivins, Virginia Wilcox 1827?- *BioIn 17*
Ivochkina, Nina Mikhailovna 1941- *WhoWor 93*
Ivogun, Maria 1891-1987 *Baker 92, IntDcOp [port], OxDcOp*
Ivon, Daniel *Law&B 92*
Ivory, J. Angus 1932- *St&PR 93*
Ivory, James *BioIn 17, ScF&FL 92*
Ivory, James 1928- *MiSFD 9*
Ivory, James (Francis) 1928- *ConAu 139, WhoAm 92*
Ivory, Ming Marie 1949- *WhoAm 92, WhoEmL 93*
Ivory, Peter B. C. B. 1927- *WhoAm 92*
Ivry, Alfred Lyon 1935- *WhoAm 92*
Ivry, Patricia Weisman 1950- *WhoAmW 93*
Ivry, Richard d' 1829-1903 *Baker 92*
Ivsic, Mathieu Michel 1934- *WhoWor 93*
Ivy, Conway G. 1941- *St&PR 93*
Ivy, Conway Gayle 1941- *WhoAm 92, WhoWor 93*
Ivy, Edward Everett 1913- *WhoWor 93*
Ivy, L. H. 1930- *WhoSSW 93*
Ivy, Mary Ann 1947- *WhoSSW 93*
Ivy, Quin 1937- *SoulM*
Ivy, Robert Adams, Jr. 1947- *WhoSSW 93*
Ivy, Robert E. 1933- *St&PR 93*
Ivy, William 1949- *St&PR 93*
Iwahara, M. *Law&B 92*
Iwahori, Shuichi 1938- *WhoWor 93*
Iwaki, Hidehiro 1956- *WhoWor 93*
Iwaki, Hiroyuki 1932- *Baker 92*
Iwakuni, Tetsundo *BioIn 17*
Iwakura, Yoshio 1914- *WhoWor 93*
Iwakuro, Hideo 1897-1970 *HarEnMi*
Iwama, Kazuo 1936- *WhoWor 93*
Iwamatsu, Jun Atsushi 1908- *MajAI [port]*
Iwamoto, Atsushi 1938- *WhoWor 93*
Iwamoto, Hisato 1943- *WhoAsAP 91*
Iwamoto, Masakazu 1948- *WhoWor 93*
Iwamoto, Masamitsu 1929- *WhoAsAP 91*
Iwamoto, Toschitake 1935- *WhoWor 93*
Iwamura, Toshio 1934- *WhoWor 93*
Iwamura, Uichiro 1927- *WhoAsAP 91*
Iwan, Wilfred Dean 1935- *WhoAm 92*
Iwanami, Yujiro 1919- *WhoWor 93*
Iwanczyk, Jan Stanislaw 1947- *St&PR 93*
Iwaniuk, Wactaw 1915- *WhoCanL 92*
Iwanski, Marie Ida 1948- *WhoEmL 93*
Iwanyshyn, Deborah Luteran 1953- *WhoAmW 93*
Iwaoka, Teiki 1944- *WhoWor 93*
Iwarson, Sten A. 1940- *WhoScE 91-4*
Iwasaka, Dennis K. 1944- *St&PR 93*
Iwasaki, Junzo 1924- *WhoAsAP 91*
Iwasaki, Toshio 1921- *WhoWor 93*
Iwashimizu, Yukio 1943- *WhoWor 93*
Iwashita, Masahiro 1932- *WhoWor 93*
Iwashita, Shima 1941- *IntDcF 2-3 [port]*
Iwashita, Takeki 1931- *WhoWor 93*
Iwaszkiewicz, Jaroslaw 1894-1980 *PolBiDi*
Iwata, Junsuke 1937- *WhoAsAP 91*
Iwata, Yasuo 1932- *WhoWor 93*
Iwataki, Dale M. *Law&B 92*
Iwatani, Yoshinori 1952- *WhoWor 93*
Iwatare, Sukio 1929- *WhoAsAP 91*
Iwatsuki, Kunio 1934- *WhoWor 93*
Iwaya, Takeshi 1957- *WhoAsAP 91*
Iwersen, Alfred, Jr. 1939- *St&PR 93*
Iwicki, Stanley D. 1946- *St&PR 93*
Iworsley, Arthur W. 1946- *WhoEmL 93*
Ix, Douglas E. 1930- *St&PR 93*
Ix, Robert Edward 1929- *WhoAm 92*
Ixcan, Tiger of *DcCPCAm*
Iyad, Abu *BioIn 17*
Iyayi, Macaulay 1948- *WhoWor 93*
Iyer, B. Rajam 1922- *WhoAm 92*
Iyer, Chuck Balachandran 1939- *WhoSSW 93*
Iyer, Pico *BioIn 17*
Iyer, Ramasswamy Ramalingam 1929- *WhoWor 93*
Iyer, Ravishankar Krishnan 1949- *WhoWor 93*
Iyer, Sathasivaiyer Varatharaja 1960- *WhoWor 93*
Iyer, Subramaniam Narayana 1934- *WhoUN 92*
Izac, Edouard V.M. 1891-1990 *BioIn 17*
Izant, Robert James, Jr. 1921- *WhoAm 92*
Izard, Anne R. 1916-1990 *BioIn 17*
Izard, Daniel *WhoScE 91-2*
Izard, Jacques-Yves 1933- *WhoScE 91-2*
Izard, John 1923- *WhoAm 92*
Izard, Ralph 1742-1804 *PolPar*
Izard, Ralph Sidney 1935- *WhoSSW 93*
Izatt, James Alexander *WhoScE 91-1*
Izatt, Jerald Ray 1928- *WhoAm 92, WhoSSW 93*
Izco, Jesus 1940- *WhoWor 93*
Ize, Alain 1947- *WhoUN 92*
Izenour, George Charles 1912- *WhoAm 92*
Izenour, Steven 1940- *WhoAm 92*
Izenstark, Joseph Louis 1919- *WhoAm 92*
Izenstark, Robert C. *St&PR 93*
Izetbegovic, Alija *WhoWor 93*
Izikowitz, Karl Gustav 1903-1984 *IntDcAn*
Izlar, William Henry, Jr. 1931- *WhoAm 92*
Izquierdo de Albinana, Asuncion 1914- *DcMexL*
Izumi, Shuzo 1940- *WhoWor 93*
Izumi, Yoji 1942- *St&PR 93*
Izumi, Yoshio 1954- *WhoWor 93*
Izurieta, Fabian 1946- *WhoWor 93*
Izzi, Anthony J. 1947- *St&PR 93*
Izzi, Eileen C. 1942- *WhoAmW 93*
Izzi, Eugene *BioIn 17*
Izzi, John Donald 1931- *WhoE 93, WhoWor 93*
Izzi, Peter W., Jr. 1947- *St&PR 93*

Izzo, George Martin 1949- *WhoSSW 93*
Izzo, Henry J. 1935- *St&PR 93*
Izzo, Lucille Anne 1954- *WhoAmW 93*
Izzo, Richard S. 1951- *WhoE 93*

Izzo, George Martin 1949- *WhoSSW 93*
Izzo, Henry J. 1935- *St&PR 93*
Izzo, Lucille Anne 1954- *WhoAmW 93*
Izzo, Richard S. 1951- *WhoE 93*

J

J., D.N. ScF&FL 92
Jaafar, Mohamed Ali 1924- WhoWor 93
Ja'afar Ibni Al-Marhum Abdul Rahman 1922- WhoWor 93
Ja'afar Ibni Al-Marhum Tunku Abdul Rahman, Yang DiPertuan Besar Tunku 1922- WhoAsAP 91
Jaakkola, Hannu V.T. 1951- WhoScE 91-4
Jaakkola, J.E. Juhani 1935- WhoScE 91-4
Jaakkola, Sipi P. 1939- WhoUN 92
Jaakson, Ernst Rudolf 1905- WhoUN 92
Jaaskelainen, Paavo Mikko Pellervo 1931- WhoScE 91-4
Jabala dc. 528 OxDcByz
Jabalpurwala, Kaizer Esufali 1932- WhoWor 93
Jabar, Ramon J. 1930- WhoAsAP 91
Jabara, Francis Dwight 1924- WhoAm 92
Jabara, Michael Dean 1952- WhoAm 92
Jabara, Paul d1992 NewYTBS 92 [port]
Jabbar, Kareem Abdul ConAu 139
Jabbar, Kareem Abdul- 1947- BioIn 17
Jabbar-Malik, M.A. 1933- St&PR 93
Jabbour, Joseph Mitchell 1950- WhoE 93
Jabbour, Suzanne L. Law&B 92
Jaben, Edward 1926- St&PR 93, WhoAm 92
Jaben, Jan Elaine 1952- WhoWrEP 92
Jaber, Joyce Sarah Law&B 92
Jaber al-Ahmad al-Jaber al-Sabah 1926- BioIn 17
Jabes, Edmond BioIn 17
Jabez, Myran ScF&FL 92
Jabir al-Ahmad al-Jabir Al-Sabah, Sheikh 1926- WhoWor 93
Jablin, Fredric Mark 1952- WhoSSW 93
Jablokov, Alexander 1956- ScF&FL 92
Jablon, Claude Jacques 1946- WhoWor 93
Jablon, Elaine 1950- WhoEmL 93, WhoSSW 93
Jablon, Paul Christopher 1949- WhoE 93
Jabloner, Harold 1937- WhoE 93
Jablonka, Rafael BioIn 17
Jablons, Jane Ellen 1953- WhoAmW 93
Jablons, Joel Simeon 1920- WhoE 93
Jablonski, Boleslaw 1928- WhoScE 91-4
Jablonski, Carol Ann Law&B 92
Jablonski, Daniel Gary 1954- WhoE 93
Jablonski, David 1953- ScF&FL 92
Jablonski, Edward 1922- WhoWrEP 92
Jablonski, James Joseph 1944- St&PR 93
Jablonski, Jozef 1935- WhoScE 91-4
Jablonski, Leon 1931- WhoScE 91-4
Jablonski, Michal Wawrzyniec 1920- WhoScE 91-4
Jablonski, Richard J. 1939- St&PR 93
Jablonski, Ronald E. 1954- St&PR 93
Jablonski, Wanda 1920-1992 BioIn 17
Jablonski, Wanda M. d1992 NewYTBS 92 [port]
Jablonski, Wanda Mary WhoWor 93
Jablonsky, Stephen 1941- WhoE 93
Jablow, Alta d1992 NewYTBS 92
Jablow, Arnold 1942- St&PR 93
Jablow, George d1991 BioIn 17
Jablow, Jeffrey St&PR 93
Jablow, Peter Anthony 1950- WhoEmL 93
Jablowsky, Albert Isaac 1944- WhoWor 93
Jabotinsky, Vladimir 1880-1940 BioIn 17
Jabr, Ibrahim R. 1946- WhoUN 92
Jabs, Jacob 1930- St&PR 93
Jabu Ak Numpang, Alfred WhoAsAP 91
Jaccard, C. WhoScE 91-4
Jaccard, Claude F. 1929- WhoScE 91-4
Jaccard, Walter B. Law&B 92
Jaccard, Walter B. 1953- St&PR 93
Jacchia, Agide 1875-1932 Baker 92
Jaccoma, Richard 1943- ScF&FL 92
Jacey, Charles Frederick, Jr. 1936- WhoE 93
Jache, Albert William 1924- WhoAm 92
Jachera, J.T. 1930- St&PR 93
Jachet di Mantua 1483-1559 Baker 92
Jachimecki, Zdzislaw 1882-1953 Baker 92, PolBiDi
Jachino, Carlo 1887-1971 Baker 92
Jachna, Joseph D. 1935- WhoAm 92
Jachowicz, Stanislaw 1796-1857 PolBiDi
Jacic, Ljubomir 1955- WhoScE 91-4
Jacinto, George Anthony 1949- WhoEmL 93, WhoSSW 93
Jack, Charles R. 1935- St&PR 93
Jack, D. WhoScE 91-1
Jack, David Emmanuel 1918- WhoWor 93
Jack, Donald L. 1924- WhoCanL 92
Jack, Gary A. Law&B 92
Jack, George Peter William 1942- WhoWor 93
Jack, James Clyde, Jr. 1919- St&PR 93
Jack, James E. 1941- St&PR 93
Jack, Joy Lynne 1960- WhoAmW 93
Jack, Minta Sue 1935- WhoAmW 93
Jack, Nancy Rayford 1939- WhoAm 92
Jack, Phyllis Harris 1934- WhoAmW 93, WhoSSW 93
Jack, Richard 1941- WhoScE 91-1
Jack, William Irvine 1935- WhoAm 92
Jacka, Martin 1943- SmATA 72 [port]
Jackal, Thomas M. Law&B 92
Jackanin, Albina Veronica 1924- WhoWrEP 92
Jackee BioIn 17, ConTFT 10
Jackel, Lawrence WhoAm 92
Jackel, Simon Samuel 1917- WhoWor 93
Jackels, Curt R. 1946- St&PR 93
Jackendoff, Nathaniel 1919- WhoAm 92
Jackendoff, Ray Saul 1945- WhoAm 92
Jacker, Corinne Litvin 1933- WhoAm 92, WhoWrEP 92
Jacki, Jan 1924- WhoScE 91-4
Jackim, Janet E. Law&B 92
Jackins, Harvey 1916- ConAu 37NR
Jackins, Joseph A. 1947- St&PR 93
Jackiw, Roman 1939- WhoAm 92, WhoE 93
Jackle, Josef 1939- WhoScE 91-3
Jackle, Karen Dee 1945- WhoAmW 93
Jacklin, Carol Nagy 1939- WhoAmW 93
Jacklin, Tony 1944- WhoWor 93
Jacklitch, Thomas R. 1942- St&PR 93
Jackman, Christopher 1916-1991 BioIn 17
Jackman, David G. 1947- St&PR 93
Jackman, Edward F. Law&B 92
Jackman, Henry N.R. 1932- St&PR 93
Jackman, Henry Newton Rowell 1932- WhoAm 92, WhoE 93
Jackman, John S. 1841-1912 BioIn 17
Jackman, Lloyd Miles 1926- WhoAm 92
Jackman, Peter J. 1939- WhoScE 91-1
Jackman, Robert Alan 1939- WhoAm 92, WhoWor 93
Jackman, Roy P. 1924- St&PR 93
Jacko, Diane Newell WhoWrEP 92
Jacko, Robert Bertram 1940- WhoAm 92
Jackobs, Miriam Ann 1940- WhoAm 92
Jackowiak, Patricia 1959- WhoWor 93
Jackowitz, Carol 1944- St&PR 93
Jackowitz, Edward C. St&PR 93
Jackowitz, Sydney L. Law&B 92
Jackowski, Jo-Ann Theresa 1946- WhoAmW 93
Jackowski, Joseph P. Law&B 92
Jacks, Maston Thompson Law&B 92
Jacks, Neville St&PR 93
Jacks, Thomas Jerome 1938- WhoSSW 93
Jackson, Ada (Acraman) DcChlFi
Jackson, Adrian Ward- BioIn 17
Jackson, Al, Jr. 1935-1975 SoulM
Jackson, Alan BioIn 17, WhoScE 91-1
Jackson, Alan Anthony WhoScE 91-1
Jackson, Alastair John Law&B 92
Jackson, Albert Law&B 92
Jackson, Alfred George 1945- St&PR 93
Jackson, Alice Humbert 1914- WhoAmW 93
Jackson, Alison 1953- SmATA 73 [port]
Jackson, Alison Willis Law&B 92
Jackson, Allen Keith 1932- WhoAm 92
Jackson, Alma F. Law&B 92
Jackson, Alvin B., Jr. 1961- WhoSSW 93
Jackson, Andrew 1767-1845 BioIn 17, HarEnMi, OxCSupC, PolPar
Jackson, Andrew 1948- WhoEmL 93
Jackson, Andrew Walston Law&B 92
Jackson, Anne WhoAm 92, WhoAmW 93
Jackson, Arthur D., Jr. Law&B 92
Jackson, Arthur J. 1924- BioIn 17
Jackson, B.L., Jr. 1924- St&PR 93
Jackson, Barbara Bund 1944- WhoAmW 93
Jackson, Barbara W. 1929- WhoAmW 93, WhoSSW 93
Jackson, Bart 1941- St&PR 93
Jackson, Basil 1920- ScF&FL 92
Jackson, Benjamin Taylor 1929- WhoE 93
Jackson, Bennie, Jr. 1947- WhoWor 93
Jackson, Bernard Rex 1915- WhoSSW 93
Jackson, Bernice Hammond 1918- WhoE 93
Jackson, Betty A. Law&B 92
Jackson, Betty Eileen 1925- WhoWor 93
Jackson, Betty Jean 1932- WhoSSW 93
Jackson, Betty L. Deason 1927- WhoWor 93
Jackson, Bill D. 1937- WhoAm 92
Jackson, Billy Morrow 1926- WhoAm 92
Jackson, Blyden 1910- WhoAm 92, WhoSSW 93
Jackson, Bo BioIn 17
Jackson, Bo 1962- WhoAm 92
Jackson, Bobby Rand 1931- WhoAm 92
Jackson, Booker T. Law&B 92
Jackson, Brian J. 1956- St&PR 93
Jackson, Bruce L. 1946- St&PR 93
Jackson, Bruce Leslie WhoAm 92
Jackson, Byron Haden 1943- WhoE 93
Jackson, C. Robert 1939- St&PR 93
Jackson, Carl Robert 1928- WhoAm 92, WhoWor 93
Jackson, Carmault Benjamin, Jr. 1924- WhoAm 92
Jackson, Carol Law&B 92
Jackson, Carolyn Laughlin 1938- WhoSSW 93
Jackson, Carolyn Wittorff 1953- WhoEmL 93
Jackson, Catherine Galloway 1945- WhoAmW 93
Jackson, Charles Ian 1935- WhoAm 92
Jackson, Charles Neason, II 1931- WhoE 93
Jackson, Charles R. 1954- WhoSSW 93
Jackson, Charles Robert 1939- WhoAm 92
Jackson, Charles Wayne 1930- WhoSSW 93
Jackson, Charlotte E. 1903?-1989 BioIn 17
Jackson, Cheong Kim Hee 1958- WhoWor 93
Jackson, Cherie BioIn 17
Jackson, Chuck 1937- SoulM
Jackson, Chuck 1945- BioIn 17
Jackson, Clarice Brooks Law&B 92
Jackson, Claudine Edith 1934- WhoAm 92
Jackson, Clintona Law&B 92
Jackson, Cora AmWomPl
Jackson, Cordell 1923- News 92 [port]
Jackson, Curtis Maitland 1933- WhoAm 92
Jackson, Dale Edward 1950- WhoAm 92, WhoWor 93
Jackson, Daniel BioIn 17
Jackson, Daniel Francis 1925- WhoAm 92
Jackson, Daniel Wendell Law&B 92
Jackson, Daphne Frances WhoScE 91-1
Jackson, Darryl Robert 1957- St&PR 93
Jackson, Daryl Sanders 1937- WhoWor 93
Jackson, David BioIn 17
Jackson, David 1946- WhoAm 92
Jackson, David A. 1924- WhoWor 93
Jackson, David Allen 1955- St&PR 93
Jackson, David Gordon 1947- St&PR 93
Jackson, David H. 1930- St&PR 93
Jackson, David J. 1940- St&PR 93
Jackson, David Kelly, Jr. ScF&FL 92
Jackson, David Munro 1925- WhoAm 92
Jackson, David Pingree 1931- WhoAm 92
Jackson, David R. Law&B 92
Jackson, Deborah Cheryl 1955- WhoWor 93
Jackson, Deborah Eleanor 1959- WhoAmW 93
Jackson, Deborah J. 1958- St&PR 93
Jackson, Deborah Renate Charlotte 1962- WhoUN 92
Jackson, Della Rosetta Hayden 1905- WhoAmW 93, WhoSSW 93
Jackson, Dempster McKee 1930- WhoAm 92
Jackson, Diana Jean 1949- WhoEmL 93
Jackson, Dolly Joyce 1932- WhoAmW 93
Jackson, Don J. 1934- St&PR 93
Jackson, Don Merrill 1913- WhoAm 92
Jackson, Donald Brooks d1992 BioIn 17
Jackson, Donald G. MiSFD 9
Jackson, Donald J. 1943- BioIn 17
Jackson, Donald K. St&PR 93
Jackson, Donald Kenneth 1944- WhoAm 92, WhoE 93
Jackson, Donald Raymond 1928- St&PR 93
Jackson, Donald Richard 1938- WhoE 93
Jackson, Donald V. 1943- St&PR 93
Jackson, Donald W. St&PR 93

Jackson, Donna Ann 1951- WhoEmL 93, WhoSSW 93
Jackson, Douglas 1940- MiSFD 9
Jackson, Douglas R. 1941- St&PR 93
Jackson, Duane 1942- WhoWor 93
Jackson, Dudley Pennington 1924- WhoAm 92
Jackson, Dwayne Adrian 1955- WhoE 93
Jackson, E. WhoScE 91-1
Jackson, E.C. Law&B 92
Jackson, E. Rogers 1930- WhoAm 92
Jackson, Earl B. 1936- St&PR 93
Jackson, Eddie See Queensryche ConMus 8
Jackson, Edith Banfield 1895-1977 BioIn 17
Jackson, Edwin L. 1930- St&PR 93
Jackson, Elmer Joseph 1920- WhoAm 92
Jackson, Elmer Martin, Jr. 1906- WhoAm 92, WhoWor 93
Jackson, Ernestine ConTFT 10
Jackson, Ethan WhoAm 92
Jackson, Ethel Noland 1944- WhoE 93
Jackson, Eugene Bernard 1915- WhoAm 92
Jackson, Eugene D. St&PR 93
Jackson, Eugene Wesley 1928- WhoAm 92, WhoWor 93
Jackson, Everett Gee 1900- WhoAm 92
Jackson, F.H. 1927- St&PR 93
Jackson, Felix d1992 NewYTBS 92
Jackson, Fleda Brown 1944- WhoWrEP 92
Jackson, Frances Mitchell AmWomPl
Jackson, Francis (Alan) 1917- Baker 92
Jackson, Francis Charles 1917- WhoAm 92, WhoWor 93
Jackson, Francis Joseph 1932- St&PR 93, WhoAm 92
Jackson, Frank 1856- BioIn 17
Jackson, Frank Westley, III Law&B 92
Jackson, Fred 1952- WhoE 93
Jackson, Freda Lucille 1928- WhoAmW 93, WhoWrEP 92
Jackson, Freddie 1956- SoulM
Jackson, Frederick Herbert 1919- WhoAm 92
Jackson, Gabriel 1921- WhoAm 92
Jackson, Gaines Bradford 1943- WhoSSW 93
Jackson, George MiSFD 9, SoulM
Jackson, George A. 1931- St&PR 93
Jackson, George K(nowil) 1757-1822 Baker 92
Jackson, George Lyman 1923- WhoAm 92
Jackson, George Pullen 1874-1953 Baker 92
Jackson, Geraldine 1934- WhoAmW 93
Jackson, Glenda BioIn 17
Jackson, Glenda 1936- IntDcF 2-3 [port], WhoAm 92, WhoWor 93
Jackson, Glenn A. Law&B 92
Jackson, Glenn T. 1960- WhoIns 93
Jackson, Gordon 1923-1990 BioIn 17
Jackson, Grady Lee 1939- WhoAm 92
Jackson, Graeme St&PR 93
Jackson, Gregory Wayne 1950- WhoEmL 93, WhoWor 93
Jackson, Grover G. Law&B 92
Jackson, Guida M. 1930- ConAu 37NR, SmATA 71 [port]
Jackson, H. Clark 1944- WhoIns 93
Jackson, H. Girard Law&B 92
Jackson, Harold BioIn 17
Jackson, Harold 1953- WhoAm 92, WhoSSW 93
Jackson, Harold Milton 1953- WhoEmL 93, WhoSSW 93
Jackson, Harper Scales, Jr. 1951- WhoEmL 93, WhoSSW 93, WhoWor 93
Jackson, Harry Allen 1916- WhoE 93
Jackson, Harry Andrew 1924- WhoAm 92
Jackson, Harry D. 1926- St&PR 93
Jackson, Harry Thomas, Jr. 1939- WhoAm 92
Jackson, Hazel Brill 1894-1991 BioIn 17
Jackson, Helen Hunt 1830-1885 BioIn 17
Jackson, Henry F. BioIn 17
Jackson, Henry M. 1912-1983 ColdWar 1 [port], PolPar
Jackson, Henry Martin BioIn 17
Jackson, Herb 1945- WhoAm 92
Jackson, Hermoine Prestine 1945- WhoAm 92, WhoE 93
Jackson, Holbrook 1874-1948 BioIn 17
Jackson, Horatio Nelson BioIn 17
Jackson, Howard Lee 1957- WhoE 93, WhoEmL 93
Jackson, Howell Edmunds 1832-1895 OxCSupC [port]
Jackson, Inez AmWomPl
Jackson, Isaiah 1945- ConBlB 3 [port], WhoAm 92
Jackson, Isaiah (Allen) 1945- Baker 92
Jackson, J.B. WhoScE 91-1
Jackson, J. Christopher Law&B 92
Jackson, J. Des BioIn 17
Jackson, J.M., Jr. Law&B 92
Jackson, Jack 1928-1991 BioIn 17
Jackson, Jack Eldon 1928- St&PR 93
Jackson, Jackie 1951- See Jacksons SoulM
Jackson, Jacqueline 1928- BioIn 17, ScF&FL 92
Jackson, Jacqueline (Dougan) 1928- DcAmChF 1960
Jackson, James A. 1962- St&PR 93
Jackson, James F. 1939- WhoAm 92
Jackson, James J. 1944- St&PR 93
Jackson, James Karl Law&B 92
Jackson, James L. 1945- St&PR 93
Jackson, James Leonard 1932- WhoAm 92, WhoSSW 93
Jackson, James M. 1943- WhoIns 93
Jackson, James Montgomery 1950- WhoE 93
Jackson, James Robert 1922- WhoE 93
Jackson, James Sidney 1944- WhoAm 92
Jackson, Jane W. 1944- WhoAmW 93
Jackson, Janet BioIn 17
Jackson, Janet 1966- AfrAmBi, SoulM
Jackson, Janet Damita 1966- WhoAm 92
Jackson, Janet E. AfrAmBi [port]
Jackson, Janet Hosea 1933- WhoAmW 93
Jackson, Jay W. 1961- ConAu 139
Jackson, Jeffery M. 1949- St&PR 93
Jackson, Jeffrey E. Law&B 92
Jackson, Jeffrey Pendleton 1949- St&PR 93
Jackson, Jeffrey W. Law&B 92
Jackson, Jermaine 1954- SoulM
Jackson, Jerry Donald 1944- St&PR 93, WhoAm 92, WhoSSW 93
Jackson, Jerry Thomas 1941- St&PR 93
Jackson, Jesse 1908-1983 BlkAull 92, ChlLR 28 [port], MajAI [port]
Jackson, Jesse 1941- DcTwHis
Jackson, Jesse L. 1941- BioIn 17, EncAACR, PolPar
Jackson, Jesse L., Jr. BioIn 17
Jackson, Jesse Louis 1941- AfrAmBi, WhoAm 92
Jackson, Jimmie Lee 1938-1965 EncAACR
Jackson, Jimmy Joe 1947- WhoE 93
Jackson, Jimmy S. 1943- St&PR 93
Jackson, Jo Hutchinson 1919- WhoSSW 93
Jackson, Joan Holden 1941- WhoSSW 93
Jackson, Joe WhoAm 92
Jackson, Joe 1887?-1951 BioIn 17
Jackson, Joe Clarence 1911- WhoSSW 93
Jackson, Joe William, Jr. 1955- WhoSSW 93
Jackson, John A. 1943- ConAu 138
Jackson, John Arthur 1947- WhoWrEP 92
Jackson, John B. 1954- St&PR 93
Jackson, John Charles 1939- WhoWor 93
Jackson, John David Law&B 92
Jackson, John David 1925- WhoAm 92
Jackson, John E. 1945- St&PR 93
Jackson, John Earnest 1941- WhoE 93, WhoWor 93
Jackson, John Edgar 1942- WhoAm 92
Jackson, John Howard 1932- WhoAm 92
Jackson, John L. Law&B 92
Jackson, John T. 1921- St&PR 93
Jackson, John Taylor Law&B 92
Jackson, John Tillson 1921- WhoAm 92
Jackson, John Wyant 1944- WhoAm 92
Jackson, Jonathan Steven 1961- WhoSSW 93
Jackson, Jonathan Val 1934- WhoAm 92
Jackson, Joseph WhoWrEP 92
Jackson, Joseph H. BioIn 17
Jackson, Joy Juanita 1928- WhoAmW 93
Jackson, Judge 1883-1958 Baker 92
Jackson, Julian Ellis 1913- WhoAm 92
Jackson, June d1990 BioIn 17
Jackson, Karen Louise 1949- WhoE 93
Jackson, Karl Dion 1942- WhoAm 92
Jackson, Kate BioIn 17
Jackson, Katherine BioIn 17
Jackson, Kathryn Jean 1957- WhoSSW 93
Jackson, Keith Jerome 1965- WhoAm 92
Jackson, Keith MacKenzie 1928- BiDAMSp 1989
Jackson, Keith Manning 1958- WhoSSW 93
Jackson, Kenneth Arthur 1930- WhoAm 92
Jackson, Kenneth G. Law&B 92
Jackson, Kenneth M. Law&B 92
Jackson, Kenneth Terry 1939- WhoAm 92
Jackson, Kingsbury Temple 1917- WhoAm 92
Jackson, Laird Gray 1930- WhoAm 92
Jackson, Larry 1931-1990 BioIn 17
Jackson, Larry Artope 1925- WhoAm 92
Jackson, LaToya BioIn 17
Jackson, LaToya 1956- See Jacksons SoulM
Jackson, Laura 1901-1991 BioIn 17
Jackson, Laura Riding 1901-1991 ConLC 70
Jackson, Lawrence 1937- St&PR 93
Jackson, Lawrence 1940- WhoScE 91-1
Jackson, Lawrence Curtis 1931-1990 BiDAMSp 1989
Jackson, Lee WhoAm 92
Jackson, Leland Brooks 1940- WhoAm 92
Jackson, LeRoy Eugene 1933- WhoAm 92
Jackson, Leslie Ann 1958- WhoWrEP 92
Jackson, Lewis MiSFD 9
Jackson, Lewis Albert 1912- WhoAm 92
Jackson, Lewis Duane 1949- WhoAm 92
Jackson, Lola Hirdler 1942- WhoAmW 93
Jackson, Louise Anne 1948- WhoEmL 93
Jackson, Loyd Appleby 1946- WhoAmW 93
Jackson, Lynda Kay 1949- WhoAmW 93, WhoEmL 93
Jackson, M. Louise 1941- WhoSSW 93
Jackson, Mack Willie 1960- WhoSSW 93
Jackson, Mae Boger 1963- WhoAmW 93
Jackson, Mahalia 1911-1972 Baker 92, BioIn 17, ConMus 8 [port]
Jackson, Mamie Eva 1911- WhoAmW 93
Jackson, Marette McCauley 1931- WhoSSW 93
Jackson, Maria AmWomPl
Jackson, Marie Kathryn Davis 1954- WhoAmW 93
Jackson, Marilyn N. 1943- WhoAmW 93
Jackson, Marion Leroy 1914- WhoAm 92
Jackson, Mark WhoWrEP 92
Jackson, Marlene W. Law&B 92
Jackson, Marlon 1957- See Jacksons SoulM
Jackson, Martin Fredric 1946- WhoE 93
Jackson, Mary 1910- WhoAm 92
Jackson, Mary Anne 1953- WhoAmW 93
Jackson, Mary Foreman BioIn 17
Jackson, Mary L. 1938- WhoAmW 93
Jackson, Maude AmWomPl
Jackson, Maureen 1950- See Jacksons SoulM
Jackson, Max T. 1932- St&PR 93
Jackson, Maynard 1938- AfrAmBi [port], WhoAm 92, WhoSSW 93
Jackson, Maynard H. BioIn 17
Jackson, Maynard Holbrook, Jr. 1938- EncAACR
Jackson, Melbourne Leslie 1915- WhoAm 92
Jackson, Melissa Margaret 1962- WhoAmW 93
Jackson, Melvin W. 1913- St&PR 93
Jackson, Merryl S. Law&B 92
Jackson, Michael 1958- BioIn 17, SoulM
Jackson, Michael Barson WhoScE 91-1
Jackson, Michael Charles 1940- WhoAm 92
Jackson, Michael Christopher WhoScE 91-1
Jackson, Michael John 1938- WhoAm 92
Jackson, Michael Joseph 1958- AfrAmBi, Baker 92, WhoAm 92, WhoWor 93
Jackson, Michael Peart WhoScE 91-1
Jackson, Mick MiSFD 9
Jackson, Miles M. 1929- BioIn 17
Jackson, Miles Merrill 1929- WhoAm 92
Jackson, Millie 1943- SoulM
Jackson, Milt(on) 1923- Baker 92
Jackson, Milton 1923- WhoAm 92
Jackson, Muriel Grace 1929- WhoAmW 93
Jackson, Myron E. Law&B 92
Jackson, Myron Eaton 1927- St&PR 93
Jackson, Nell BlkAmWO [port]
Jackson, Nell 1929-1988 BioIn 17
Jackson, Noell Ross 1967- WhoAmW 93
Jackson, Norman Eugene 1937- St&PR 93
Jackson, Osborne A.Y. 1938- WhoUN 92
Jackson, O'Shea BioIn 17
Jackson, Patricia A. Law&B 92
Jackson, Patricia Lee 1916- WhoAm 92, WhoAmW 93, WhoE 93
Jackson, Patricia Pike 1960- WhoEmL 93
Jackson, Patrick John 1932- WhoE 93
Jackson, Paul E. Law&B 92
Jackson, Paul I. 1951- St&PR 93
Jackson, Paul Robert 1928- WhoAm 92
Jackson, Paulette White 1949- WhoAmW 93, WhoEmL 93
Jackson, Peggy Whittington 1947- WhoAmW 93
Jackson, Peter 1961- MiSFD 9
Jackson, Peter Charles WhoScE 91-1
Jackson, Peter J. 1929- WhoScE 91-1
Jackson, Peter Vorious, III 1927- WhoAm 92
Jackson, Phil BioIn 17, NewYTBS 92 [port]
Jackson, Phil 1945- CurBio 92 [port]
Jackson, Philip C. 1935- St&PR 93
Jackson, Philip Chappell 1928- BioIn 17
Jackson, Philip Chappell, Jr. 1928- St&PR 93
Jackson, Philip Douglas WhoAm 92
Jackson, Philip W. 1928- BioIn 17
Jackson, Phillip 1950- St&PR 93
Jackson, Quintin T. 1947- St&PR 93
Jackson, R.A. 1946- St&PR 93
Jackson, R. Graham 1913- WhoAm 92
Jackson, Rachel Donelson Robards 1767-1828 BioIn 17
Jackson, Randy 1962- See Jacksons SoulM
Jackson, Raymond SoulM
Jackson, Raymond Sidney, Jr. 1938- WhoAm 92
Jackson, Rebecca A. 1955- St&PR 93
Jackson, Reed McInnis 1950- WhoSSW 93
Jackson, Reggie BioIn 17
Jackson, Reginald Martinez 1946- WhoAm 92
Jackson, Reginald Sherman 1910- WhoAm 92
Jackson, Richard Delyn 1937- WhoAm 92, WhoSSW 93
Jackson, Richard G. Law&B 92
Jackson, Richard George 1940- WhoAm 92
Jackson, Richard K. Law&B 92
Jackson, Richard Lee 1931- St&PR 93
Jackson, Richard M., Jr. Law&B 92
Jackson, Richard Montgomery 1920- WhoAm 92
Jackson, Richard Paul 1946- WhoWrEP 92
Jackson, Richard Pharus 1948- WhoSSW 93
Jackson, Richard Seymour 1915- WhoE 93
Jackson, Richard Thomas 1930- WhoSSW 93
Jackson, Robert BioIn 17, ScF&FL 92
Jackson, Robert 1911-1991 AnObit 1991
Jackson, Robert Deverr, Jr. 1961- WhoEmL 93, WhoSSW 93
Jackson, Robert Eugene, Jr. 1949- WhoWor 93
Jackson, Robert Frederick 1947- WhoEmL 93, WhoSSW 93
Jackson, Robert G. BioIn 17
Jackson, Robert H. Law&B 92
Jackson, Robert Houghwout 1892-1954 DcTwHis, OxCSupC [port]
Jackson, Robert Keith 1943- WhoSSW 93
Jackson, Robert Michael 1959- WhoEmL 93
Jackson, Robert Russell 1953- WhoE 93
Jackson, Robert Scott 1946- WhoE 93
Jackson, Robert Sherwood 1945- WhoAm 92
Jackson, Robert Street 1943- WhoAm 92
Jackson, Robert W. 1930- St&PR 93
Jackson, Robert W. 1936- WhoIns 93
Jackson, Robert William 1930- WhoAm 92
Jackson, Roberta Plant WhoSSW 93, WhoWor 93
Jackson, Robins H. 1924- St&PR 93
Jackson, Robyn Nannette 1960- WhoSSW 93
Jackson, Rochelle H. Law&B 92
Jackson, Rollin Ashby, Jr. 1934- WhoSSW 93
Jackson, Ronald J. BioIn 17
Jackson, Ronald L. Law&B 92
Jackson, Ronald Lee 1936- St&PR 93
Jackson, Rosa Catherine 1948- WhoWrEP 92
Jackson, Rosemary 1917- ScF&FL 92
Jackson, Roy A. 1950- St&PR 93
Jackson, Roy V. Law&B 92
Jackson, Ruby Marie 1948- WhoAmW 93
Jackson, Rudolph Ellsworth 1935- WhoAm 92
Jackson, Russell E. 1948- St&PR 93
Jackson, Ruth 1902- WhoAm 92
Jackson, Ruth Robertson 1939- WhoAmW 93
Jackson, Ruthie Fay 1948- WhoEmL 93
Jackson, Samuel E., Jr. 1928- St&PR 93
Jackson, Samuel L. BioIn 17
Jackson, Samuel L. 1949?- ConTFT 10
Jackson, Samuel P. 1818-1885 Baker 92
Jackson, Sarah Jeanette 1924- WhoAm 92
Jackson, Sharon Broome 1952- WhoSSW 93
Jackson, Sharon Patrice 1958- WhoAmW 93
Jackson, Sharron Deniece 1959- WhoAmW 93
Jackson, Sheila Cathryn 1952- WhoE 93
Jackson, Sheldon BioIn 17
Jackson, Shirley 1916-1965 AmWomWr 92
Jackson, Shirley 1919-1965 Au&Arts 9 [port], ScF&FL 92, WorLitC [port]
Jackson, Shirley A. AfrAmBi
Jackson, Shirley A. 1943- WhoAmW 93
Jackson, Stanley Webber 1920- WhoE 93
Jackson, Stephanie Ann 1960- WhoEmL 93, WhoSSW 93
Jackson, Stephanie D. Law&B 92
Jackson, Stephen Eric 1946- WhoEmL 93

Jackson, Stephen Keith 1939- St&PR 93, WhoAm 92
Jackson, Steve 1951- ScF&FL 92
Jackson, Steve 1953- ScF&FL 92
Jackson, Steven L. Law&B 92
Jackson, Stonewall 1824-1863 BioIn 17
Jackson, Stu WhoAm 92
Jackson, Stuart ScF&FL 92
Jackson, Susan K. Law&B 92
Jackson, Susan Roberta 1949- WhoAm 92
Jackson, Susan Van Dyke 1947- WhoEmL 93
Jackson, Susanne Leora 1934- WhoAmW 93
Jackson, Sylvia WhoAmW 93
Jackson, Tara Brockway Law&B 92
Jackson, Ted M. 1928- St&PR 93
Jackson, Theodore Marshall 1928- WhoAm 92
Jackson, Theodore Warren Law&B 92
Jackson, Theresa Pittman 1945- WhoSSW 93
Jackson, Thomas Cline 1930- St&PR 93
Jackson, Thomas Clyde 1949- WhoE 93, WhoEmL 93
Jackson, Thomas E. Law&B 92
Jackson, Thomas Gene 1949- WhoEmL 93
Jackson, Thomas Goodlow 1943- WhoSSW 93
Jackson, Thomas H. 1930- WhoWrEP 92
Jackson, Thomas Harold, Jr. 1951- WhoSSW 93
Jackson, Thomas Humphrey 1950- WhoAm 92
Jackson, Thomas Jonathan 1824-1863 BioIn 17, HarEnMi
Jackson, Thomas Penfield 1937- CngDr 91, WhoAm 92
Jackson, Tito 1953- See Jacksons SoulM
Jackson, Tom d1990 BioIn 17
Jackson, Tommie Lee 1951- WhoWor 93
Jackson, Tommy Dave 1944- WhoSSW 93
Jackson, Toni L. 1946- St&PR 93
Jackson, Tonya Elishe 1965- WhoAmW 93
Jackson, Tracy 1962?- ScF&FL 92
Jackson, Velma Louise 1945- WhoE 93, WhoWor 93
Jackson, Vickie Wood 1950- WhoSSW 93
Jackson, Victor Louis 1933- WhoAm 92
Jackson, Vincent Edward 1962- AfrAmBi
Jackson, W. Bruce 1943- WhoAm 92
Jackson, W. Henry Law&B 92
Jackson, Walter 1938- BioIn 17
Jackson, Walter 1939- SoulM
Jackson, Ward 1928- WhoAm 92
Jackson, Wayne 1944- SoulM
Jackson, Wes BioIn 17
Jackson, Wes 1936- WhoWrEP 92
Jackson, William 1730-1803 Baker 92, OxDcOp
Jackson, William 1815-1866 Baker 92
Jackson, William 1917- ScF&FL 92
Jackson, William David 1927- WhoAm 92
Jackson, William E. 1956- St&PR 93
Jackson, William Eldred 1919- WhoAm 92
Jackson, William Franklin 1850-1936 BioIn 17
Jackson, William J(oseph) 1943- ConAu 139
Jackson, William Lawrence 1954- WhoEmL 93
Jackson, William MacLeod 1926- WhoAm 92
Jackson, William Paul, Jr. 1938- WhoAm 92, WhoWor 93
Jackson, William R. 1908- St&PR 93
Jackson, William Richard 1936- WhoWor 93
Jackson, William Roy 1935- WhoWor 93
Jackson, William Turrentine 1915- WhoAm 92
Jackson, William Vernon 1926- WhoAm 92
Jackson, William Ward 1913- WhoAm 92
Jackson, Willie Lee 1945- WhoE 93
Jackson-Bryant, Roni Law&B 92
Jackson Family BioIn 17
Jackson Five SoulM
Jackson Greene, Dorothy Faye 1947- WhoAmW 93
Jacksons SoulM
Jackwerth, Ewald 1932- WhoScE 91-3
Jacky, Doris Victoria 1928- WhoAmW 93
Jaclot, Francois Charles 1949- WhoAm 92
Jaco, C.D. BioIn 17
Jaco, Charles BioIn 17
Jaco, William Howard 1940- St&PR 93
Jacob BioIn 17
Jacob, Benjamin 1778-1829 Baker 92
Jacob, Bernard Michel 1930- WhoAm 92
Jacob, Bruce Robert 1935- WhoAm 92
Jacob, Charles Elmer 1931- WhoAm 92
Jacob, Christine Ann 1959- WhoAmW 93
Jacob, Edwin J. 1927- WhoAm 92
Jacob, Ellis 1953- St&PR 93, WhoAm 92
Jacob, Francois 1920- BioIn 17, WhoAm 92, WhoScE 91-2, WhoWor 93
Jacob, Fred Law&B 92
Jacob, Gary Steven 1949- WhoAm 92, WhoE 93
Jacob, George Prasad 1950- WhoWor 93
Jacob, Gerald Regis 1952- WhoEmL 93
Jacob, Gordon (Percival Septimus) 1895-1984 Baker 92
Jacob, Harry Myles 1913- WhoAm 92
Jacob, Harry Samuel 1933- WhoAm 92
Jacob, Helmut 1932- WhoScE 91-3
Jacob, Herbert 1933- WhoAm 92
Jacob, Ian 1899- BioIn 17
Jacob, Jean-Louis 1939- WhoScE 91-2
Jacob, Jerry R. 1933- St&PR 93
Jacob, Jerry Rowland 1933- WhoAm 92
Jacob, John C. 1950- WhoWrEP 92
Jacob, John E. 1934- BioIn 17
Jacob, John Edward 1934- AfrAmBi, WhoAm 92, WhoE 93
Jacob, Lawrence 1945- St&PR 93
Jacob, Louise Helen 1924- WhoAmW 93
Jacob, M.M. 1928- WhoAsAP 91
Jacob, Margaret C(andee) 1943- ConAu 37NR
Jacob, Marvin Eugene 1935- WhoAm 92
Jacob, Mary Ellen L. 1939- WhoWrEP 92
Jacob, Maurice R. 1933- WhoScE 91-4
Jacob, Maurice Rene 1933- WhoWor 93
Jacob, Maxime 1906-1977 Baker 92
Jacob, Nancy Louise 1943- WhoAm 92
Jacob, Nicholas David Grenville 1957- WhoWor 93
Jacob, Paul Bernard, Jr. 1922- WhoAm 92
Jacob, Piers ScF&FL 92
Jacob, Richard E. 1948- St&PR 93
Jacob, Richard J. 1919- St&PR 93
Jacob, Robert Allen 1941- WhoSSW 93
Jacob, Ruthard 1925- WhoScE 91-3
Jacob, Shirley Ann 1949- WhoE 93
Jacob, Stanley Wallace 1924- WhoAm 92
Jacob, Suzanne WhoCanL 92
Jacob, Thomas Bernard 1934- WhoAm 92
Jacob, Vincent J. 1933- St&PR 93
Jacob, William F. 1941- St&PR 93
Jacob Baradaeus c. 500-578 OxDcByz
Jacober, Dale Stuart 1962- St&PR 93
Jacober, Todd J. 1960- St&PR 93
Jacobey, John Arthur, III 1929- WhoAm 92, WhoE 93
Jacobi, Carl 1908- ScF&FL 92
Jacobi, Derek George 1938- WhoAm 92, WhoWor 93
Jacobi, Erwin R(euben) 1909-1979 Baker 92
Jacobi, Frederick 1891-1952 Baker 92
Jacobi, Friedrich Heinrich 1743-1819 BioIn 17
Jacobi, Georg 1840-1906 Baker 92
Jacobi, George T. 1922- St&PR 93
Jacobi, Johann Georg 1740-1814 BioIn 17
Jacobi, Lawrence Richard 1950- WhoSSW 93
Jacobi, Lotte 1896-1990 BioIn 17
Jacobi, Ole 1934- WhoScE 91-2
Jacobi, Paula AmWomPl
Jacobi, Peter Paul 1930- WhoAm 92, WhoWrEP 92
Jacobi, Renate Maria 1936- WhoWor 93
Jacobi, Robert V., Jr. WhoWrEP 92
Jacobi, Ronald N. Law&B 92
Jacobi, Ronald N. 1947- WhoAm 92
Jacobi, Susan M. Law&B 92
Jacobi, William Mallett 1930- WhoAm 92
Jacob of Sarug c. 451-521 OxDcByz
Jacoboni, Carlo 1941- WhoScE 91-3
Jacobovici, Simcha 1953- MiSFD 9
Jacobovitz, Donald Darius 1955- WhoSSW 93
Jacobowitz, Harold Saul 1950- St&PR 93
Jacobowitz, Henry George 1958- WhoE 93
Jacobowitz, Jan Law&B 92
Jacobowitz, John 1940- St&PR 93
Jacobowitz, Judah L. WhoWrEP 92
Jacobowitz, Ruth Scherr WhoAmW 93, WhoWor 93
Jacobs, Abigail Conway 1942- WhoAm 92
Jacobs, Alan 1947- WhoAm 92
Jacobs, Alan Martin 1932- WhoAm 92
Jacobs, Alicia Melvina 1955- WhoE 93
Jacobs, Amelia 1927- WhoAmW 93
Jacobs, Andrew 1932- BioIn 17
Jacobs, Andrew, Jr. 1932- CngDr 91, WhoAm 92
Jacobs, Anna C. 1939- WhoAmW 93
Jacobs, Arnold Stephen 1940- WhoAm 92
Jacobs, Arthur (David) 1922- Baker 92
Jacobs, Arthur Dietrich 1933- WhoWor 93
Jacobs, Arthur Russell 1947- WhoEmL 93
Jacobs, Augusta Adelle 1925- WhoAmW 93
Jacobs, Barbara Frank 1942- WhoE 93
Jacobs, Bella Hertzberg 1919- WhoAmW 93
Jacobs, Bernard 1924-1992 BioIn 17
Jacobs, Bernard B. 1916- St&PR 93, WhoAm 92
Jacobs, Bonita Cheryl 1949- WhoAmW 93, WhoSSW 93
Jacobs, Bradford McElderry 1920- WhoAm 92
Jacobs, Bruce Edmund 1947- St&PR 93
Jacobs, Burleigh E. 1920- St&PR 93
Jacobs, Burleigh Edmund 1920- WhoAm 92
Jacobs, C. Bernard 1918- WhoAm 92
Jacobs, Carl Henry 1948- WhoE 93
Jacobs, Charles M. 1933- WhoE 93
Jacobs, Charles Robinson 1918- WhoSSW 93
Jacobs, Christie Jean 1961- WhoEmL 93
Jacobs, Christopher Harry 1948- WhoE 93
Jacobs, Curtis M. Law&B 92
Jacobs, D.A.H. 1946- WhoScE 91-1
Jacobs, David BioIn 17
Jacobs, David 1939- ConTFT 10
Jacobs, David Alastair 1944- WhoWor 93
Jacobs, David H. d1992 NewYTBS 92
Jacobs, David Michael 1942- WhoE 93
Jacobs, Dawn Charlene Williams 1956- WhoAmW 93
Jacobs, Deborah Ann 1948- WhoSSW 93
Jacobs, Debra McQuaig 1950- WhoAmW 93
Jacobs, Dennis E. 1949- St&PR 93
Jacobs, Dennis Eric WhoScE 91-1
Jacobs, Diana Pietrocarli 1950- WhoEmL 93
Jacobs, Donald G. 1930- St&PR 93
Jacobs, Donald Paul 1942- WhoAm 92
Jacobs, Donald Warren 1932- WhoE 93
Jacobs, Douglas P. Law&B 92
Jacobs, Edith Roeder AmWomPl
Jacobs, Edwin Max 1925- WhoAm 92
Jacobs, Ehren David 1960- St&PR 93
Jacobs, Eleanor 1929- WhoAmW 93
Jacobs, Eleanor Alice 1923- WhoAm 92, WhoAmW 93, WhoE 93, WhoWor 93
Jacobs, Eli BioIn 17
Jacobs, Eli S. WhoE 93
Jacobs, Eli S. 1937- St&PR 93
Jacobs, Ella AmWomPl
Jacobs, Ellen Judy 1943- WhoSSW 93
Jacobs, Eugene Gardner 1926- WhoE 93
Jacobs, Eugene William 1933- St&PR 93
Jacobs, Flora Gill 1918- WhoE 93
Jacobs, Francis Albin 1918- WhoAm 92
Jacobs, Franklin A. 1932- St&PR 93
Jacobs, Frederick Carl 1946- St&PR 93
Jacobs, Gary G. 1941- WhoAm 92
Jacobs, George 1924- WhoAm 92
Jacobs, Gerald d1991 BioIn 17
Jacobs, Greg BioIn 17
Jacobs, Hans-Jurgen 1936- WhoWor 93
Jacobs, Harold Robert 1936- WhoAm 92, WhoWor 93
Jacobs, Harriet 1813?-1897 AmWomWr 92
Jacobs, Harriet A. 1813-1896? BioIn 17
Jacobs, Harry A., Jr. 1921- St&PR 93
Jacobs, Harry Milburn, Jr. 1928- WhoAm 92, WhoSSW 93, WhoWor 93
Jacobs, Harvey Collins 1915- WhoAm 92
Jacobs, Helen Hull 1908- WhoAm 92
Jacobs, Horace 1911- WhoWrEP 92
Jacobs, Howard A. 1925- St&PR 93
Jacobs, Ilene B. 1947- St&PR 93, WhoAm 92, WhoAmW 93
Jacobs, Ira 1931- WhoAm 92
Jacobs, Irene BioIn 17
Jacobs, Irwin L. BioIn 17
Jacobs, Irwin L. 1941- St&PR 93
Jacobs, Irwin Lawrence 1941- WhoAm 92
Jacobs, Irwin M. BioIn 17, St&PR 93
Jacobs, J. Ethan Law&B 92
Jacobs, Jack Edmond 1948- WhoE 93
Jacobs, Jack H. 1945- BioIn 17
Jacobs, Jacques 1919- St&PR 93
Jacobs, James BioIn 17
Jacobs, James B. 1947- ConAu 39NR
Jacobs, James Lamar 1947- WhoSSW 93
Jacobs, James P. 1952- St&PR 93
Jacobs, James Paul 1930- WhoSSW 93
Jacobs, James S. 1945- ScF&FL 92
Jacobs, Jan L. 1933- WhoIns 93
Jacobs, Jane 1916- WhoAmW 93
Jacobs, Jane Brand 1940- WhoE 93
Jacobs, Jane Breslin Law&B 92
Jacobs, Janna Iris 1955- WhoAmW 93
Jacobs, Jeffrey L. Law&B 92
Jacobs, Jeffrey Lee 1951- WhoE 93, WhoEmL 93
Jacobs, Jennifer 1952- WhoSSW 93
Jacobs, Jerald A. BioIn 17
Jacobs, Jeremy M. WhoAm 92, WhoE 93
Jacobs, Jim 1942- WhoAm 92
Jacobs, Jo Ellen 1952- WhoAmW 93
Jacobs, Jocelyn 1956- WhoAmW 93
Jacobs, John Edward 1920- WhoAm 92
Jacobs, John Howard 1925- WhoAm 92
Jacobs, John P. 1943- St&PR 93
Jacobs, John Patrick 1945- WhoAm 92
Jacobs, John R. Law&B 92
Jacobs, John William 1943- WhoE 93
Jacobs, Jon Robert 1950- WhoEmL 93
Jacobs, Joseph 1854-1916 ConAu 136, MajAI [port]
Jacobs, Joseph Donovan 1908- WhoAm 92
Jacobs, Joseph J. 1916- St&PR 93
Jacobs, Joseph James 1925- WhoE 93
Jacobs, Joseph John 1916- WhoAm 92
Jacobs, Judy 1952- ConAu 137, SmATA 69 [port]
Jacobs, Julian I. 1937- CngDr 91, WhoAm 92
Jacobs, Karen Louise 1943- WhoAmW 93
Jacobs, Kathleen Caldwell 1940- WhoAmW 93
Jacobs, Kenneth A. 1948- WhoSSW 93
Jacobs, Kenneth L. Law&B 92
Jacobs, Kent Frederick 1938- WhoAm 92
Jacobs, Kevin Eugene 1960- WhoSSW 93
Jacobs, Konrad 1928- WhoWor 93
Jacobs, Lambert W. 1931- St&PR 93
Jacobs, Laurence Stanton 1940- WhoAm 92, WhoE 93
Jacobs, Lawrence-Hilton MiSFD 9
Jacobs, Lawrence Ronald d1991 BioIn 17
Jacobs, Leanne S. Law&B 92
Jacobs, Leanne Sinclair Law&B 92
Jacobs, Leland B. d1992 NewYTBS 92 [port]
Jacobs, Leland B. 1907-1992 BioIn 17
Jacobs, Leland Blair 1907-1992 ConAu 137, SmATA 71
Jacobs, Leon 1915- WhoAm 92
Jacobs, Leonard John 1940- St&PR 93
Jacobs, Leonard S. 1946- St&PR 93
Jacobs, Leslie William 1944- WhoAm 92
Jacobs, Libby 1947- WhoAmW 93, WhoEmL 93
Jacobs, Linda Lee 1961- WhoEmL 93
Jacobs, Lois Jean 1947- WhoAmW 93
Jacobs, Lola Lynda 1949- WhoAmW 93
Jacobs, Lou 1903-1992 NewYTBS 92 [port]
Jacobs, Louis 1920- ConAu 38NR
Jacobs, Louis Sullivan WhoAm 92, WhoWor 93
Jacobs, Lowell L. Law&B 92
Jacobs, Maria 1930- WhoCanL 92
Jacobs, Marian Beckmann 1935- WhoE 93
Jacobs, Marie Stevens d1991 BioIn 17
Jacobs, Marilyn Susan 1952- WhoAm 92, WhoEmL 93
Jacobs, Marion Kramer WhoAm 92
Jacobs, Marisa Frances Law&B 92
Jacobs, Mark Anthony 1965- WhoSSW 93
Jacobs, Mark N. Law&B 92
Jacobs, Mark Neil 1946- St&PR 93, WhoAm 92, WhoEmL 93
Jacobs, Mary Kathryn 1947- WhoEmL 93
Jacobs, Matthew Stephen 1943- St&PR 93
Jacobs, Melville 1902-1971 IntDcAn
Jacobs, Melvin 1926- St&PR 93, WhoAm 92
Jacobs, Michael A. Law&B 92
Jacobs, Michael Aaron 1953- WhoE 93
Jacobs, Michael Edward Hyman 1948- WhoWor 93
Jacobs, Michael L. 1942- St&PR 93
Jacobs, Michael Lee 1957- WhoEmL 93
Jacobs, Michael T. 1958- ConAu 139
Jacobs, Michel 1936- WhoScE 91-2
Jacobs, Norman A. 1937- St&PR 93
Jacobs, Norman Allan 1937- St&PR 93
Jacobs, Norman Gabriel 1924- WhoAm 92
Jacobs, Norman Joseph 1932- WhoAm 92
Jacobs, Paul 1930-1983 Baker 92
Jacobs, Paul Eugene 1932- WhoSSW 93
Jacobs, Paul Robert 1948- WhoSSW 93
Jacobs, Paul Samuel DcAmChF 1985, ScF&FL 92
Jacobs, Peter Daniel Alexander 1939- WhoAm 92
Jacobs, Piers 1933- WhoAsAP 91
Jacobs, Rachel Isabelle 1945- WhoAmW 93
Jacobs, Ralph R. 1928- St&PR 93
Jacobs, Rene 1946- Baker 92
Jacobs, Reuven 1956- WhoEmL 93
Jacobs, Richard Alan 1934- WhoAm 92
Jacobs, Richard Allen 1936- St&PR 93, WhoAm 92
Jacobs, Richard E. WhoAm 92
Jacobs, Richard Emory Law&B 92
Jacobs, Richard James 1941- WhoAm 92
Jacobs, Richard Matthew 1924- WhoAm 92
Jacobs, Richard Michael 1955- WhoE 93, WhoEmL 93
Jacobs, Richard Moss 1925- WhoE 93
Jacobs, Rita Diane 1946- WhoE 93
Jacobs, Rita Goldman 1927- WhoAm 92, WhoAmW 93
Jacobs, Robert 1913- WhoAm 92
Jacobs, Robert Alan 1948- WhoE 93
Jacobs, Robert Durene 1918- WhoSSW 93

Jaczynowska, Katarzyna 1875-1920 *PolBiDi*
Jadach, Nella Emilia 1962- *WhoAmW 93*
Jadambaa, Shagalyn *WhoWor 93*
Jadassohn, Salomon 1831-1902 *Baker 92*
Jade, Symon *ScF&FL 92*
Jadhav 1937- *WhoAsAP 91*
Jadhav, Arvind Vithalrao 1942- *WhoWor 93*
Jadick, Harry J. 1956- *St&PR 93*
Jadin, Louis Emmanuel 1768-1853 *Baker 92*
Jadis, Donna *ScF&FL 92*
Jadlocki, Lawrence John 1949- *WhoAm 92*
Jadlow, Janice Wickstead 1945- *WhoSSW 93*
Jadlow, Joseph Martin 1942- *WhoAm 92, WhoSSW 93*
Jadlowker, Hermann 1877-1953 *Baker 92, IntDcOp, OxDcOp*
Jadlowski, Ann Michele *BioIn 17*
Jadot, Jean Lambert Octave 1909- *WhoAm 92*
Jadresic, Alfredo Arturo 1925- *WhoWor 93*
Jadwiga 1373-1399 *PolBiDi*
Jadwin, Jay E. *Law&B 92*
Jadwin, Linda F. 1943- *WhoAmW 93*
Jae 1947- *WhoAmW 93, WhoEmL 93*
Jaeck, Lois Marie 1946- *ConAu 137*
Jaeckel, Howard F. *Law&B 92*
Jaeckel, James Carl 1944- *WhoE 93*
Jaeckin, Just 1940- *MiSFD 9*
Jaeckle, Edwin F. d1992 *NewYTBS 92*
Jaeckle, Edwin F. 1894-1992 *BioIn 17*
Jaeckle, Fred William 1943- *St&PR 93*
Jaeckle, Harvey 1917- *St&PR 93*
Jaeger, Albert 1944- *WhoScE 91-2*
Jaeger, Ami Susan *Law&B 92*
Jaeger, Brenda Kay 1950- *WhoWrEP 92*
Jaeger, C.K. 1912- *ScF&FL 92*
Jaeger, Christoph T. 1935- *WhoUN 92*
Jaeger, David A. 1938- *St&PR 93*
Jaeger, David Arnold 1938- *WhoAm 92*
Jaeger, Heimo 1942- *WhoScE 91-4*
Jaeger, Howard Russell *Law&B 92*
Jaeger, James L. 1948- *St&PR 93*
Jaeger, Leonard Henry 1905- *WhoAm 92*
Jaeger, Lowell Larry 1951- *WhoWrEP 92*
Jaeger, Mark S. *Law&B 92*
Jaeger, Muriel 1893?- *ScF&FL 92*
Jaeger, Nils I. 1936- *WhoScE 91-3*
Jaeger, Richard Charles 1944- *WhoAm 92, WhoSSW 93*
Jaeger, Richard Morrow 1938- *WhoSSW 93*
Jaeger, Robert Gordon 1937- *WhoSSW 93*
Jaeger, Robert J. 1948- *St&PR 93*
Jaeger, Sharon Ann 1945- *WhoWrEP 92*
Jaeger, Stephen Owen 1944- *St&PR 93*
Jaeger-Found, Maria Ann 1965- *WhoAmW 93*
Jaegers, Beverly Carol 1935- *WhoWrEP 92*
Jaegers, Donna Marie 1958- *WhoAmW 93*
Jaeggi, Kenneth Vincent 1945- *WhoAm 92*
Jaehne, Richard Leroy 1946- *WhoSSW 93*
Jaekel, Chris Ellen 1962- *WhoAmW 93*
Jaell, Alfred 1832-1882 *Baker 92*
Jaell, Marie 1846-1925 *Baker 92*
Jae-Man, Lee 1930- *WhoWor 93*
Jaenicke, Lothar 1923- *WhoScE 91-3*
Jaenicke, Rainer 1930- *WhoScE 91-3*
Jaenike, William F. 1937- *St&PR 93*
Jaenke, Edwin August 1930- *St&PR 93*
Jaeschke, Frank 1951- *St&PR 93*
Jafek, Bruce William 1941- *WhoAm 92*
Jafelice, Ray *MiSFD 9*
Jaff, Alvin Martin 1931- *St&PR 93*
Jaffa, David 1929- *St&PR 93*
Jaffa, Kathleen de *AmWomPl*
Jaffa, Max 1911-1991 *AnObit 1991*
Jaffa, Minnie Suckerberg 1886- *AmWomPl*
Jaffan, Heather 1938- *St&PR 93*
Jaffe, Abraham 1932- *St&PR 93*
Jaffe, Alan Steven 1939- *WhoAm 92*
Jaffe, Andrew Mark 1938- *WhoWor 93*
Jaffe, Andrew Michael 1923- *WhoWor 93*
Jaffe, Arnold 1930- *St&PR 93*
Jaffe, Arthur Michael 1937- *WhoAm 92*
Jaffe, Austin Jay 1952- *WhoE 93*
Jaffe, Barbara Ann 1950- *WhoAmW 93*
Jaffe, Bernard Michael *WhoAm 92, WhoE 93*
Jaffe, Betsy Latimer 1935- *WhoWrEP 92*
Jaffe, Bruce M. 1944- *WhoAm 92*
Jaffe, Bruce Morgan 1944- *St&PR 93*
Jaffe, Caroline Ruth 1961- *WhoEmL 93*
Jaffe, Edward Ephraim 1928- *WhoAm 92*
Jaffe, Eileen Karen 1954- *WhoEmL 93*
Jaffe, Elizabeth Latimer 1935- *WhoE 93*
Jaffe, Eric Allen 1942- *WhoE 93*
Jaffe, Ernst Richard 1925- *WhoAm 92*
Jaffe, F. Filmore 1918- *WhoAm 92*
Jaffe, Felice 1924- *WhoScE 91-4*
Jaffe, Gary 1956- *St&PR 93*
Jaffe, Harold 1940- *WhoWrEP 92*
Jaffe, Harold W. 1946- *CurBio 92 [port]*
Jaffe, Henry d1992 *NewYTBS 92*
Jaffe, Herb d1991 *BioIn 17*
Jaffe, Herb 1921?-1991 *ConTFT 10*
Jaffe, Herbert J. 1934- *St&PR 93*
Jaffe, Herbert M. 1924- *St&PR 93*
Jaffe, Irma Blumenthal *WhoE 93*
Jaffe, Jay M. 1941- *St&PR 93*
Jaffe, Jeff Hugh 1920- *WhoSSW 93*
Jaffe, Jeffrey Martin 1954- *WhoAm 92*
Jaffe, Klaus W.B. Carbonell 1951- *WhoWor 93*
Jaffe, Leo 1909- *St&PR 93, WhoAm 92*
Jaffe, Leonard Sigmund 1916- *WhoAm 92*
Jaffe, Lewis 1956- *WhoEmL 93*
Jaffe, Louise 1936- *WhoAmW 93*
Jaffe, Maggie 1948- *WhoWrEP 92*
Jaffe, Marc *BioIn 17*
Jaffe, Mark Charles 1960- *WhoE 93*
Jaffe, Mark M. 1941- *WhoE 93*
Jaffe, Marvin Eugene 1936- *WhoAm 92*
Jaffe, Marvin I. 1924- *St&PR 93*
Jaffe, Maurice H. 1912- *St&PR 93*
Jaffe, Melvin 1919- *WhoAm 92*
Jaffe, Michael *BioIn 17*
Jaffe, Michael 1940- *St&PR 93, WhoAm 92*
Jaffe, Michael 1942- *WhoE 93*
Jaffe, Morry 1940- *WhoE 93*
Jaffe, Murray Sherwood 1926- *WhoAm 92*
Jaffe, Nora 1928- *WhoAm 92*
Jaffe, Nora Crow 1944- *ScF&FL 92*
Jaffe, Norman 1932- *WhoAm 92*
Jaffe, Otto 1846-1929 *BioIn 17*
Jaffe, Paul Lawrence 1928- *WhoAm 92, WhoE 93*
Jaffe, Richard Louis 1952- *WhoEmL 93*
Jaffe, Robert Benton 1933- *WhoAm 92*
Jaffe, Rona *BioIn 17*
Jaffe, Rona 1932- *WhoAm 92, WhoAmW 93, WhoWrEP 92*
Jaffe, Sam 1891?-1984 *IntDcF 2-3*
Jaffe, Sara 1950- *WhoAmW 93*
Jaffe, Sigmund 1921- *WhoAm 92*
Jaffe, Stanley 1940- *MiSFD 9*
Jaffe, Stanley R. 1940- *ConTFT 10*
Jaffe, Stanley Richard 1940- *WhoAm 92, WhoE 93*
Jaffe, Steven 1928- *WhoE 93*
Jaffe, Steven Charles *MiSFD 9*
Jaffe, Susan *WhoAm 92, WhoAmW 93*
Jaffe, Susan Lynn *WhoAmW 93*
Jaffe, Suzanne Denbo 1943- *WhoAmW 93*
Jaffe, Sylvia 1926- *WhoWrEP 92*
Jaffe, Sylvia Sarah 1917- *WhoAmW 93, WhoSSW 93*
Jaffe, William A. 1938- *WhoE 93*
Jaffe, William Julian 1910- *WhoWor 93*
Jaffee, Al 1921- *BioIn 17*
Jaffee, Annette Williams 1945- *WhoWrEP 92*
Jaffee, Irving 1906-1981 *ScF&FL 92*
Jaffee, Keith W. 1960- *St&PR 93*
Jaffee, Mary 1899-1985 *ScF&FL 92*
Jaffee, Michael 1938- *Baker 92, WhoAm 92*
Jaffee, Richard M. 1936- *St&PR 93*
Jaffee, Robert D. 1933- *St&PR 93*
Jaffee, Robert Isaac 1917- *WhoAm 92*
Jaffee, Sandra Schuyler 1943- *WhoAm 92*
Jaffer, Frances E. 1921- *WhoWrEP 92*
Jaffer, Navin 1958- *WhoEmL 93*
Jaffer Sharief, C.K. 1933- *WhoAsAP 91*
Jaffery, Sheldon 1934- *ScF&FL 92*
Jaffeson, Richard Charles 1947- *WhoE 93*
Jaffess, Judith S. *Law&B 92*
Jaffin, Charles Leonard 1928- *WhoAm 92*
Jaffiol, Claude 1933- *WhoScE 91-2*
Jafolis, Stephen Nicholas 1950- *WhoE 93*
Jagacinski, Carolyn Mary 1949- *WhoAmW 93*
Jagadish, Chennupati 1957- *WhoWor 93*
Jagan, Cheddi 1918- *BioIn 17*
Jagan, Janet 1920- *BioIn 17*
Jagel, Frederick 1897-1982 *Baker 92*
Jagel, Mildred Noble 1926- *WhoAmW 93*
Jagellonka, Anna 1523-1596 *PolBiDi*
Jagen, Edward Joseph 1949- *WhoE 93*
Jagendorf, Andre Tridon 1926- *WhoAm 92*
Jagendorf, M.A. 1888-1981 *ScF&FL 92*
Jager, Elizabeth Anne 1934- *WhoAmW 93*
Jager, H.J. *WhoScE 91-3*
Jager, Ronald *BioIn 17*
Jager, Tom *BioIn 17*
Jagerstad, Margaretha Ingeborg 1943- *WhoWor 93*
Jagerstatter, Franz *BioIn 17*
Jaggar, David Michael *WhoScE 91-1*
Jaggard, Keith W. 1947- *WhoScE 91-1*
Jaggears, Albert R. 1936- *St&PR 93*
Jagger, Bianca 1945- *BioIn 17*
Jagger, Bianca 1950- *WhoEmL 93*
Jagger, C. Thomas 1937- *St&PR 93*
Jagger, David Michael 1941- *St&PR 93*
Jagger, Dean 1903-1991 *AnObit 1991, BioIn 17*
Jagger, Jade *BioIn 17*
Jagger, Mick *BioIn 17*
Jagger, Mick 1943- *WhoAm 92, WhoWor 93*
Jagger, Mick 1944- *Baker 92*
Jagger, Robert Samuel 1943- *WhoWor 93*
Jaggers, Annielaura Mixon 1918- *WhoWrEP 92*
Jagid, Bruce 1940- *St&PR 93*
Jagiello 1348-1434 *PolBiDi*
Jagiello, Frederick 1468-1503 *PolBiDi*
Jagiellonczyk, Aleksander 1461-1506 *PolBiDi*
Jagiellonczyk, Ludwik d1526 *PolBiDi*
Jagiellonczyk, Wladyslaw 1456-1516 *PolBiDi*
Jagla, Frances Marie *Law&B 92*
Jaglom, Henry *BioIn 17*
Jaglom, Henry 1941- *MiSFD 9*
Jaglom, Jacob 1927- *St&PR 93*
Jagmetti, Marco Alessandro 1935- *WhoWor 93*
Jagninski, Tom 1935- *ConAu 137*
Jago, Deidre Ellen Berguson 1948- *WhoAmW 93*
Jago, Jeffrey John 1943- *WhoWor 93*
Jagoda, Barry Lionel 1944- *WhoAm 92*
Jagoda, Donald Robert 1929- *WhoAm 92*
Jagoda, Jerzy Antoni 1937- *WhoWor 93*
Jagoda, Leonard Joseph 1947- *St&PR 93*
Jagodzinski, Zbigniew Adam 1929- *WhoScE 91-4*
Jagoszewski, Eugeniusz Henryk 1929- *WhoWor 93*
Jagow, Charles Herman 1910- *WhoWor 93*
Jagow, Elmer 1922- *WhoAm 92*
Jagr, Jaromir *BioIn 17*
Jagsch, Albert 1947- *WhoScE 91-4*
Jagt, Jack 1942- *St&PR 93, WhoE 93*
Jagtiani, Julapa Rungkasiri 1957- *WhoE 93*
Jagus, Rosemary 1950- *WhoE 93*
Jahan, Marine 1958- *WhoEmL 93*
Jahau, Chalngura 1957- *WhoWor 93*
Jahde, Judy Ann 1949- *WhoAmW 93*
Jaher, Hannah Lavi 1946- *WhoAmW 93*
Jahiel, Rene Ino 1928- *WhoWor 93*
Jahier, Jean 1929- *WhoScE 91-2*
Jahkola, Kaarlo Antero 1931- *WhoScE 91-4*
Jahkola, Matti 1937- *WhoScE 91-4*
Jahn, Alfred 1915- *WhoWor 93*
Jahn, Billie Jane 1921- *WhoAmW 93, WhoSSW 93, WhoWor 93*
Jahn, Earl W. 1918- *St&PR 93*
Jahn, Ernest T. 1936- *ScF&FL 92*
Jahn, Evelyn Eleanor 1909- *St&PR 93*
Jahn, Friedrich 1935- *WhoScE 91-3*
Jahn, Helmut 1940- *WhoAm 92*
Jahn, Jerome J. *Law&B 92*
Jahn, Jerome J. 1936- *St&PR 93*
Jahn, Joseph M. *ScF&FL 92*
Jahn, Laurence Roy 1926- *WhoAm 92*
Jahn, Michael *ScF&FL 92*
Jahn, Mike 1943- *ScF&FL 92*
Jahn, Otto 1813-1869 *Baker 92*
Jahn, Patricia Lynn 1948- *St&PR 93*
Jahn, Paul Alfred 1937- *WhoWor 93*
Jahn, Paul Ronald 1942- *St&PR 93*
Jahn, Reinhard 1950- *WhoScE 91-3*
Jahn, Robert C. *St&PR 93*
Jahn, Robert G. *BioIn 17*
Jahn, Robert George 1930- *WhoAm 92*
Jahn, Virginia C. 1919- *St&PR 93*
Jahn, Wilhelm 1834-1900 *Baker 92*
Jahn, Wolfgang G. *St&PR 93*
Jahncke, Thomas Book 1946- *WhoEmL 93*
Jahnichen, Stefan 1947- *WhoScE 91-3*
Jahnig, Fritz Paul 1940- *WhoWor 93*
Jahnke, Bernd 1944- *WhoScE 91-3*
Jahnke, Erich W. 1946- *St&PR 93*
Jahnke, Robert A. 1944- *St&PR 93*
Jahnn, Hans Henny 1894-1959 *DcLB 124 [port]*
Jahns, Dorothy *St&PR 93*
Jahns, Friedrich Wilhelm 1809-1888 *Baker 92*
Jahoda, Marie *BioIn 17*
Jahr, Cliff *BioIn 17*
Jahr, John 1900-1991 *BioIn 17*
Jahr, Paul Kenneth 1950- *WhoSSW 93*
Jahr, R. *WhoScE 91-3*
Jahrling, Olimpia Daniele 1945- *WhoAmW 93*
Jahrling, Rolf 1913- *BioIn 17*
Jahrmarker, Hans 1921- *WhoScE 91-3*
Jaicks, Frederick Gillies 1918- *WhoAm 92*
Jaicks, Wilson A., Jr. 1922- *St&PR 93*
Jaicomo, Ronald James 1932- *St&PR 93*
Jaidah, Ali Mohammed 1941- *WhoWor 93*
Jaijongkit, Boonyasak 1933- *WhoUN 92*
Jaikaransingh, Ken 1951- *WhoWor 93*
Jaime, Adela 1955- *WhoWor 93*
Jaimes, M. Annette 1946- *ConAu 137*
Jain, Amolak C. 1929- *WhoSSW 93*
Jain, Ash 1950- *WhoE 93*
Jain, Dinesh Kumar 1952- *WhoUN 92*
Jain, Hari Krishan 1930- *WhoScE 91-3, WhoWor 93*
Jain, Jasbir 1937- *WhoWor 93*
Jain, Lalit K. *Law&B 92*
Jain, Piyare Lal 1921- *WhoAm 92*
Jain, Raj 1951- *WhoWrEP 92*
Jain, Sagar Chand 1930- *WhoAm 92*
Jain, Surendra Mohan 1947- *St&PR 93*
Jaini, Yolanda Marie Jimenez 1950- *WhoAmW 93, WhoEmL 93*
Jairazbhoy, Nazir (Ali) 1927- *Baker 92*
Jairrels, William H. *Law&B 92*
Jais, Richard Benjamin 1930- *WhoWor 93*
Jaiven, Jack 1946- *St&PR 93*
Jaivin, Linda 1955- *ConAu 139*
Jakab, Ferenc 1943- *WhoScE 91-4*
Jakab, Irene *WhoAm 92, WhoAmW 93, WhoE 93, WhoWor 93*
Jakab, Tivadar 1925- *WhoScE 91-4*
Jakala, Stanley H. 1926- *WhoWor 93*
Jakande, Lateef Kayode (Alhaji) 1929- *WhoAfr*
Jakes, Clifford Duncan 1942- *St&PR 93*
Jakes, Jean Ann 1956- *WhoWrEP 92*
Jakes, John 1932- *BioIn 17, ScF&FL 92, WhoAm 92*
Jakes, John William 1932- *WhoWrEP 92*
Jakes, Karen Sorkin 1947- *WhoAmW 93*
Jakes, Milos 1922- *ColdWar 2 [port]*
Jakes, Petr 1940- *WhoScE 91-4*
Jakes, William Chester 1922- *WhoAm 92*
Jaki, Stanley Ladislas 1924- *WhoAm 92*
Jakielo, David F. 1953- *St&PR 93*
Jakimiec, Jerzy 1935- *WhoScE 91-4*
Jakimov, Jakim 1925- *DrEEuF*
Jaklitsch, Donald John 1947- *WhoE 93*
Jakmas, Richard Gordon 1951- *St&PR 93*
Jakmauh, Edward 1942- *St&PR 93*
Jakob, Dennis H. 1948- *St&PR 93*
Jakob, Ludwig 1929- *WhoScE 91-3*
Jakob, Michel Alexandre 1962- *WhoWor 93*
Jakob, Robert Marshall *Law&B 92*
Jakobe, Virginia Ellis 1922- *WhoE 93*
Jakober, Marie 1941- *ScF&FL 92*
Jakobi, Paula *AmWomPl*
Jakoboski, Bethann *Law&B 92*
Jakobovits, Immanuel *BioIn 17*
Jakobowski, Thomas W. 1931- *St&PR 93*
Jakobs, Diane Marie 1956- *WhoSSW 93*
Jakobs, Kai 1957- *WhoWor 93*
Jakobs, Karl Heinrich 1941- *WhoWor 93*
Jakobs, Nancy Martha 1940- *St&PR 93*
Jakobsen, Carolyn Anne 1947- *WhoAsAP 91*
Jakobsen, Carolyn Edith 1947- *WhoAmW 93*
Jakobsen, Hans Jorgen *WhoScE 91-2*
Jakobsen, Hans Jorgen 1940- *WhoWor 93*
Jakobsen, Jakob Knudsen 1912- *WhoAm 92*
Jakobsen, Jan Robert 1932- *WhoScE 91-2*
Jakobsen, Jorgen 1940- *WhoScE 91-2*
Jakobsen, Karin 1954- *WhoScE 91-4*
Jakobson, Mark John 1923- *WhoAm 92*
Jakobsson, Ejler 1911-1986 *ScF&FL 92*
Jakobsson, Jakob 1931- *WhoScE 91-4*
Jakobsson, S.B. *WhoScE 91-2*
Jakobsson, Sveinn Peter 1939- *WhoScE 91-4*
Jakopcic, Kresimir 1930- *WhoScE 91-4*
Jakowicka-Friderici, Teodozja *Baker 92*
Jaksch, Hans Jurgen 1930- *WhoWor 93*
Jaksic, Danilo 1932- *WhoScE 91-4*
Jaksic, Milan M. 1932- *WhoScE 91-4*
Jaksic, Zelimir 1930- *WhoScE 91-4*
Jaksits, Dezso 1931- *WhoScE 91-4*
Jakstas, Alfred John 1916- *WhoAm 92*
Jaksy, Joseph J. 1900-1991 *BioIn 17*
Jakubauskas, Edward Benedict 1930- *WhoAm 92*
Jakubec, Vaclav 1930- *WhoScE 91-4*
Jakubiec, Marian 1923- *WhoScE 91-4*
Jakubiec, R. J. 1941- *WhoAm 92*
Jakubisko, Juraj 1938- *DrEEuF*
Jakubowics, Craig E.R. *Law&B 92*
Jakubowics, Craig Eugene Russell 1952- *WhoEmL 93*
Jakubowska, Wanda 1907- *DrEEuF*
Jakubowski, Augustyn 1927- *WhoScE 91-4*
Jakubowski, Donna Marie 1957- *WhoWrEP 92*
Jakubowski, Marek 1939- *WhoScE 91-4*
Jakubowski, Maxim 1944- *ScF&FL 92*
Jakubowski, Ryszard 1932- *WhoWor 93*
Jakubowski, W. 1933- *St&PR 93*
Jakubowsky, Frank R. 1931- *WhoWrEP 92*
Jakucs, Laszlo 1926- *WhoScE 91-4*
Jakucs, Pal 1928- *WhoScE 91-4*

Jalal, Ibrahim Mohammad 1943- *WhoWor 93*
Jalal, Kazi A.F.M. 1940- *WhoUN 92*
Jalal, Patricia Imrana 1960- *WhoWor 93*
Jalal al-Din Muhammad 1542-1605 *BioIn 17*
Jalal al-Din Rumi, Maulana 1207-1273 *BioIn 17*
Jalas, Jussi 1908- *Baker 92*
Jalayer, Behrooz 1938- *St&PR 93*
Jalbert, Eugene Roland 1951- *WhoEmL 93, WhoSSW 93*
Jalbert, Michael Eugene 1945- *St&PR 93*
Jalbert, Norman W. 1943- *St&PR 93*
Jalbert, Norman William 1943- *WhoE 93*
Jalbert, P.G.L. 1935- *WhoScE 91-2*
Jalbert, Ronald Richard 1938- *St&PR 93*
Jalbert, Susanne Elaine 1951- *WhoAmW 93*
Jaleel, George *St&PR 93*
Jales, Mark *ScF&FL 92*
Jaleski, Mary *ScF&FL 92*
Jalil, Abdul 1920- *St&PR 93*
Jalkanen, Risto Einari 1953- *WhoScE 91-4*
Jaller, Michael M. 1924- *WhoE 93*
Jallim, Collins *ScF&FL 92*
Jallins, Richard David 1957- *WhoWor 93*
Jalonen, John William 1922- *St&PR 93*
Jalongo, Mary Renck 1950- *WhoE 93*
Jalonick, George Washington, IV 1940- *WhoSSW 93, WhoWor 93*
Jalton, Frederic 1924- *DcCPCAm*
Jam, Jimmy & Lewis, Terry *SoulM*
Jama, Mohamed Abdi 1952- *WhoUN 92*
Jamagne, Marcel-Georges-Henri 1931- *WhoScE 91-2*
Jamail, Joseph Dahr, Jr. 1925- *WhoAm 92, WhoSSW 93*
Jamail, Randall *WhoAm 92*
Jamail, S. Shawn *Law&B 92*
Jamain, Patrick *MiSFD 9*
Jamal, Amir Habib 1922- *WhoUN 92*
Jamal, Jasim Yousof 1940- *WhoUN 92*
Jamal, Moez Ahamed 1955- *WhoEmL 93, WhoWor 93*
Jamar, Steven Dwight 1953- *WhoEmL 93*
Jambor, Aron 1933- *WhoScE 91-4*
Jambor, Imre 1946- *WhoScE 91-4*
Jambor, Pierre 1947- *WhoUN 92*
Jambor, Robert Vernon 1936- *WhoAm 92*
Jambrik, Rose 1947- *WhoScE 91-4*
Jameel, Fathulla *WhoWor 93*
Jamell, Jeanne 1933- *St&PR 93*
Jamero, Nilo Rodis- *ScF&FL 92*
Jamerson, James d1983 *SoulM*
James *OxDcByz*
James, I 1208-1276 *HarEnMi*
James, I 1394-1437 *LitC 20 [port]*
James, I, King of Great Britain 1566-1625 *BioIn 17*
James, II 1430-1460 *HarEnMi*
James, II 1633-1701 *HarEnMi*
James, II, King of Scotland 1430-1460 *BioIn 17*
James, VI, King of Scotland 1566-1625 *BioIn 17*
James, Alan D. 1950- *WhoScE 91-1*
James, Alesa Michelle *Law&B 92*
James, Alice 1848-1892 *BioIn 17*
James, Alice Archer 1870- *AmWomPl*
James, Allen 1945- *St&PR 93*
James, Allix Bledsoe 1922- *WhoAm 92, WhoSSW 93*
James, Amabel Boyce 1952- *WhoAmW 93*
James, Amy Lumsden 1962- *WhoAmW 93*
James, Anne Scott- 1913- *BioIn 17*
James, Annette L. *AmWomPl*
James, Anthony Septimus 1951- *WhoE 93*
James, Arthur Giangiacomo 1912- *WhoAm 92*
James, Arthur Horace 1883-1973 *BioIn 17*
James, Arthur Lawrence *WhoScE 91-1*
James, Artis Edward, Jr. 1946- *St&PR 93*
James, Austin 1924- *St&PR 93*
James, Barbara Woodward 1936- *WhoAmW 93*
James, Barry Nelson 1933- *St&PR 93*
James, Bernard J. *ScF&FL 92*
James, Betsy *ScF&FL 92*
James, Bill 1949- *BioIn 17*
James, Brian Robert 1936- *WhoAm 92*
James, Bruce B. *St&PR 93*
James, Bruce David 1942- *WhoWor 93*
James, Bruce M. 1935- *St&PR 93*
James, Byron S. 1932- *St&PR 93*
James, C.B. *WhoWrEP 92*
James, C.G. *WhoScE 91-1*
James, C.L.R. 1901-1989 *BioIn 17, DcCPCAm*
James, C(yril) L(ionel) R(obert) 1901-1989 *DcLB 125 [port]*
James, C. Shelton 1939- *St&PR 93*
James, Calvin d1886 *BioIn 17*
James, Calvin Ellington, Sr. 1937- *WhoAm 92*
James, Captain Lew *MajAI*
James, Carl G. 1952- *St&PR 93*
James, Carolyne Faye 1945- *WhoAm 92*
James, Cedric *BioIn 17*
James, Chappie 1920-1978 *BioIn 17*
James, Charles Franklin, Jr. 1931- *WhoAm 92*
James, Charles Griffin 1933- *WhoSSW 93*
James, Charles Leslie 1939- *St&PR 93*
James, Charles R. 1934- *St&PR 93*
James, Clive 1939- *BioIn 17*
James, Craig 1941- *WhoAm 92*
James, Craig T. 1941- *CngDr 91, WhoSSW 93*
James, Cyril Lionel Robert 1901-1989 *BioIn 17*
James, D.W.F. *WhoScE 91-1*
James, Dakota 1922- *ScF&FL 92*
James, Daniel 1920-1978 *BioIn 17*
James, Daniel, Jr. 1920-1978 *AfrAmBi*
James, Daniel J. 1920- *WhoAm 92*
James, David *ScF&FL 92*
James, David Edward 1935- *WhoAm 92*
James, David John Glyndwr *WhoScE 91-1*
James, David L. 1955- *WhoWrEP 92*
James, David Lee 1933- *WhoAm 92, WhoWor 93*
James, David Nicholas 1952- *WhoEmL 93*
James, David Paul 1952- *WhoSSW 93*
James, David Randolph, Jr. 1924- *WhoSSW 93*
James, David W. 1933- *St&PR 93*
James, Diane Louise 1965- *WhoWrEP 92*
James, Don *BioIn 17, WhoAm 92*
James, Donald 1931- *ScF&FL 92*
James, Donald E. *Law&B 92*
James, Donald K. *Law&B 92*
James, Donald William 1952- *St&PR 93*
James, Dorothy 1898-1982 *Baker 92*
James, Dorris Clayton 1931- *WhoAm 92*
James, Dot 1938- *WhoAmW 93*
James, Dynely *ConAu 37NR, MajAI*
James, Edward 1907-1984 *ScF&FL 92*
James, Edward 1947- *ScF&FL 92*
James, Edwin *WhoWrEP 92*
James, Edwin Clark 1932- *WhoAm 92*
James, Elmore 1918-1963 *ConMus 8 [port]*
James, Emlyn *WhoWrEP 92*
James, Estelle 1935- *WhoAm 92*
James, Etta *BioIn 17*
James, Etta 1938- *SoulM*
James, Evan Douglas *WhoScE 91-1*
James, Felicia Gay 1966- *WhoSSW 93*
James, Francis Edward, Jr. 1931- *WhoAm 92*
James, Frank 1844-1915 *BioIn 17*
James, Frank William 1946- *WhoWrEP 92*
James, Frederick Calhoun 1922- *WhoAm 92*
James, G.P.R. 1799-1860 *ScF&FL 92*
James, G. Peter 1946- *St&PR 93*
James, G. Robert 1961- *WhoE 93*
James, Garth Wilkinson 1845-1883 *BioIn 17*
James, Gary Douglas 1954- *WhoE 93*
James, Gene A. 1932- *St&PR 93*
James, Gene Albert 1932- *WhoAm 92*
James, Geneva Behrens 1942- *WhoAmW 93*
James, George Barker 1937- *St&PR 93*
James, George Barker, II 1937- *WhoAm 92*
James, George P. R. 1801-1860 *DcLB 116 [port]*
James, George Roosa 1866-1937 *BioIn 17*
James, George Wharton 1858-1923 *BioIn 17*
James, Gordon Douglas *WhoScE 91-1*
James, Gregory Jon 1960- *WhoSSW 93*
James, Hamilton Evans 1951- *WhoAm 92*
James, Harold *AfrAmBi*
James, Harold 1956- *WhoE 93*
James, Harold Arthur 1903- *WhoAm 92*
James, Harry (Haag) 1916-1983 *Baker 92*
James, Henry 1811-1882 *BioIn 17*
James, Henry 1843-1916 *BioIn 17, GayN, JrnUS, MagSAmL [port], OxDcOp, ScF&FL 92, TwCLC 47, WorLitC [port]*
James, Henry 1940- *St&PR 93*
James, Henry Thomas 1915- *WhoAm 92*
James, Herman Delano 1943- *WhoAm 92*
James, Howard P. *Law&B 92*
James, Howard P. 1923- *St&PR 93*
James, Howard Phillip 1948- *WhoEmL 93*
James, Hugh Neal 1952- *WhoSSW 93*
James, Hugh R. 1947- *St&PR 93*
James, I.M. *WhoScE 91-1*
James, Irving Arthur 1922- *WhoAm 92*
James, J. Alison *ScF&FL 92*
James, J. Douglas 1918- *St&PR 93*
James, Jack 1930- *St&PR 93*
James, Jamie *BioIn 17*
James, Jeannie Henrietta 1921- *WhoAmW 93*
James, Jennifer Austin 1943- *WhoWor 93*
James, Jerre Helen 1933- *WhoAmW 93*
James, Jesse 1847-1882 *BioIn 17*
James, Jessica d1990 *BioIn 17*
James, Jimmie, Jr. 1938- *WhoSSW 93*
James, Johannes 1928- *WhoWor 93*
James, John *ScF&FL 92*
James, John Alan 1927- *WhoAm 92*
James, John Delmar 1944- *WhoAm 92*
James, John Joseph *Law&B 92*
James, John Lewis *Law&B 92*
James, John William, Jr. 1930- *WhoSSW 93*
James, Joyce 1952- *St&PR 93*
James, Joyce Marie 1951- *WhoEmL 93*
James, Judith Vogel 1937- *WhoE 93*
James, Karyn MacKenzie 1962- *WhoAmW 93*
James, Katherine Harriett 1942- *WhoSSW 93*
James, Kathryn Kanarek 1949- *WhoAmW 93, WhoEmL 93*
James, Kelvin Christopher *ConAu 138*
James, Kenneth *Law&B 92*
James, L. Dean 1947- *ScF&FL 92*
James, Laurence 1942- *ScF&FL 92*
James, Lawrence D. 1914- *St&PR 93*
James, Lloyd E. *ConAu 138*
James, Lois Bradshaw 1939- *WhoAmW 93*
James, Louis Earl, II 1951- *WhoEmL 93*
James, Louis Meredith 1941- *WhoSSW 93*
James, M.R. 1862-1936 *ScF&FL 92*
James, Mabel 1908- *BioIn 17*
James, Magna Moriama 1961- *WhoSSW 93*
James, Marcia Hammond 1939- *WhoAmW 93*
James, Maria Beatriz *WhoAmW 93*
James, Marie Moody 1928- *WhoAmW 93*
James, Marie Ruppert 1942- *WhoAmW 93*
James, Marion Ray 1940- *WhoAm 92*
James, Mark *WhoWrEP 92*
James, Marquis 1891-1955 *JrnUS*
James, Martin *ScF&FL 92*
James, Marty d1991 *BioIn 17, NewYTBS 92*
James, Marty L. 1960- *St&PR 93*
James, Mary *BioIn 17, ConAu 37NR, MajAI*
James, Mary 1927- *ScF&FL 92*
James, Mary A. *AmWomPl*
James, Mary Lynn 1949- *WhoAmW 93*
James, Mary Robertson Walsh 1810-1882 *BioIn 17*
James, May F. *AmWomPl*
James, Michael A. *Law&B 92*
James, Michael A. 1943- *St&PR 93*
James, Michael Andrew 1953- *WhoE 93, WhoEmL 93*
James, Michael Henry 1943- *WhoWor 93*
James, Michael N. G. *WhoAm 92*
James, Michael Thames 1949- *WhoEmL 93*
James, Milton Garnet 1937- *WhoE 93*
James, Mona Hinkle 1935- *WhoAmW 93*
James, Nehemiah 1902-1969 *BioIn 17*
James, Norman L. *BioIn 17*
James, Oliver F.W. *WhoScE 91-1*
James, P.D. *BioIn 17*
James, P. D. 1920- *MagSWL [port]*
James, Patricia Ann 1933- *WhoAm 92*
James, Patrick J. 1910- *St&PR 93*
James, Paul *ScF&FL 92*
James, Paul Charles 1935- *WhoAm 92*
James, Peter 1948- *ScF&FL 92*
James, Peter Graham 1946- *St&PR 93*
James, Philip *ConAu 38NR, ScF&FL 92*
James, Philip 1890-1975 *Baker 92*
James, Philip 1932- *WhoSSW 93*
James, Phyllis Dorothy 1920- *WhoAm 92, WhoWor 93*
James, Phyllis P. 1947- *St&PR 93*
James, R. Alan *ScF&FL 92*
James, R.G. *WhoScE 91-1*
James, Richard Alan 1950- *WhoEmL 93*
James, Rick 1952- *SoulM*
James, Robert *ScF&FL 92*
James, Robert Charles 1943- *St&PR 93, WhoAm 92*
James, Robert Gamble 1933- *St&PR 93*
James, Robert Leo 1936- *WhoAm 92, WhoE 93*
James, Robert S. 1939- *St&PR 93*
James, Robert Scott 1943- *WhoAm 92*
James, Robertson 1846-1910 *BioIn 17*
James, Robyn Leonard 1953- *WhoE 93*
James, Ronald Bruce 1954- *St&PR 93*
James, Ronald William *WhoScE 91-1*
James, Russell 1942- *ConAu 137*
James, S.S. *WhoWrEP 92*
James, Scott 1960- *WhoWor 93*
James, Sean Christopher 1940- *St&PR 93*
James, Sharpe 1936- *AfrAmBi [port], WhoAm 92, WhoE 93*
James, Sheila Feagley 1925- *WhoAmW 93*
James, Sheryl Teresa 1951- *WhoAm 92, WhoAmW 93, WhoSSW 93*
James, Sidney 1913-1976 *QDrFCA 92 [port]*
James, Sidney Lorraine 1906- *WhoAm 92*
James, Skip 1902-1969 *BioIn 17*
James, Stanislaus Anthony 1919- *WhoWor 93*
James, Stephanie *ConAu 139*
James, Stephen John *WhoScE 91-1*
James, Susan *ScF&FL 92*
James, Sydney Vincent 1929- *WhoAm 92, WhoWrEP 92*
James, Theodore, Jr. 1934- *WhoWrEP 92*
James, Thomas 1572?-1629 *BioIn 17*
James, Thomas 1593-1635 *Expl 93*
James, Thomas Alan 1942- *BioIn 17, St&PR 93*
James, Thomas Naum 1925- *WhoAm 92, WhoWor 93*
James, Thomas S. *Law&B 92*
James, Valerie *ScF&FL 92*
James, Vivian Hector Thomas 1924- *WhoWor 93*
James, W.P.T. *WhoScE 91-1*
James, Walter 1915- *WhoWor 93*
James, Wayne Edward 1950- *WhoEmL 93*
James, Wayne Lamar 1934- *St&PR 93*
James, Will(iam Roderick) 1892-1942 *ConAu 137, MajAI [port]*
James, William 1771-1832 *BioIn 17*
James, William 1842-1910 *BioIn 17, GayN*
James, William 1929- *St&PR 93, WhoAm 92*
James, William Bruce 1958- *WhoSSW 93*
James, William Dobeian 1765- *BioIn 17*
James, William Hall 1910- *WhoE 93, WhoWor 93*
James, William Joseph 1922- *WhoAm 92*
James, William Kenneth *BioIn 17*
James, William M. 1931- *St&PR 93*
James, William N. *WhoWrEP 92*
James, William R. 1950- *St&PR 93*
James, William Ramsay 1933- *WhoAm 92*
James, William Stirling 1941- *WhoWor 93*
James, William W. 1931- *WhoAm 92*
James, Wilmot G. 1953- *ConAu 138*
James-French, Dayv *WhoCanL 92*
James Mayer, Susan Smyth 1955- *WhoAmW 93*
James of Kokkinobaphos fl. 12th cent.- *OxDcByz*
Jameson, A. Gregory d1992 *NewYTBS 92*
Jameson, A. Gregory 1915-1992 *BioIn 17*
Jameson, Anna Brownell 1794-1860 *BioIn 17*
Jameson, Charles Scott Kennedy 1925- *WhoWor 93*
Jameson, Craig E. *Law&B 92*
Jameson, David Alan 1952- *WhoEmL 93*
Jameson, Dorothea 1920- *WhoAm 92, WhoAmW 93*
Jameson, J. Larry 1937- *St&PR 93*
Jameson, James Larry 1937- *WhoAm 92*
Jameson, Jay Marshall 1943- *WhoE 93*
Jameson, Jerry *MiSFD 9*
Jameson, Julianne 1943- *WhoAmW 93*
Jameson, Kenneth D. 1950- *St&PR 93*
Jameson, Leander Starr 1852-1917 *HarEnMi*
Jameson, Leander Starr 1853-1917 *BioIn 17*
Jameson, Michael Hamilton 1924- *WhoAm 92*
Jameson, Patricia Marian 1945- *WhoAmW 93*
Jameson, Paul Vladimir 1929- *WhoE 93*
Jameson, Paula Ann 1945- *WhoAmW 93*
Jameson, Robert Benson Makeham 1933- *St&PR 93*
Jameson, Sam 1936- *ConAu 136*
Jameson, Sanford Chandler 1932- *WhoWor 93*
Jameson, Shirley Ann 1939- *WhoSSW 93*
Jameson, Storm 1891-1986 *ScF&FL 92*
Jameson, Vernon J. *St&PR 93*
Jameson, Victor Loyd 1924- *WhoAm 92*
Jameson, William Glen *Law&B 92*
Jami, Jacques *WhoScE 91-2*
Jamieson, Adele M. *Law&B 92*
Jamieson, Chris W. 1954- *WhoAm 92*
Jamieson, Christopher W. 1954- *St&PR 93*
Jamieson, David Donald 1926- *WhoAm 92*
Jamieson, David Norman 1958- *WhoWor 93*
Jamieson, Deborah A. *Law&B 92*
Jamieson, Donald Campbell 1921-1986 *BioIn 17*
Jamieson, Edward Leo 1929- *WhoAm 92*
Jamieson, Evan *ScF&FL 92*
Jamieson, Graham A. 1929- *WhoAm 92*
Jamieson, H.L. 1911- *St&PR 93*
Jamieson, Henry Louis 1911- *WhoAm 92*
Jamieson, Ian Miller *WhoScE 91-1*
Jamieson, J.B. 1933- *WhoScE 91-1*

Jamieson, James Phillips 1953- *WhoSSW 93*
Jamieson, Jeff S. *Law&B 92*
Jamieson, John B. 1940- *St&PR 93*
Jamieson, John Kenneth 1910- *WhoAm 92*
Jamieson, John Lawrence 1951 *WhoSSW 93*
Jamieson, Michael Lawrence 1940- *WhoAm 92, WhoSSW 93*
Jamieson, R. Bruce 1935- *WhoIns 93*
Jamieson, Reginald Mac 1927- *St&PR 93*
Jamieson, Robert, Jr. 1936- *St&PR 93*
Jamieson, Ronald Fraser 1931- *WhoWor 93*
Jamieson, Russell Ladeau, Jr. 1958- *WhoEmL 93, WhoSSW 93*
Jamieson, Stuart William 1947- *WhoAm 92, WhoWor 93*
Jamieson, Timm 1947- *St&PR 93*
Jamieson, W. Scott 1953- *St&PR 93*
Jamieson-Craig, Thomas Kern *WhoScE 91-1*
Jamilla, Bernardo B. 1934- *WhoUN 92*
Jamin, Christian Georges 1948- *WhoWor 93*
Jamin, G.A. 1941- *St&PR 93*
Jamin, Gerald Alan 1941- *WhoAm 92*
Jamir, S.C. 1931- *WhoAsAP 91*
Jamis, Fayad 1930-1988 *SpAmA*
Jamison, Charles H. 1940- *St&PR 93*
Jamison, Daniel Oliver 1952- *WhoEmL 93*
Jamison, Delos Cy 1949- *WhoAm 92*
Jamison, Earl *BioIn 17*
Jamison, Gary Lee 1942- *St&PR 93*
Jamison, Gary Stefan 1960- *WhoSSW 93*
Jamison, Harrison Clyde 1925- *WhoAm 92*
Jamison, Herbert L., Jr. 1924- *St&PR 93*
Jamison, Hubert Milton 1946- *WhoEmL 93*
Jamison, John Ambler 1916- *WhoAm 92, WhoSSW 93*
Jamison, John Vincent, III 1911- *St&PR 93*
Jamison, Judith *BioIn 17*
Jamison, Judith 1944- *WhoAm 92, WhoAmW 93, WhoE 93*
Jamison, Lorena Lucile *AmWomPl*
Jamison, Max Killian 1918- *WhoWor 93*
Jamison, Michael David 1955- *St&PR 93*
Jamison, Oliver Morton 1916- *WhoAm 92*
Jamison, Philip 1925- *WhoAm 92*
Jamison, Richard Bryan 1932- *WhoAm 92*
Jamison, Richard Melvin 1938- *WhoAm 92*
Jamison, Robert Irwin 1939- *St&PR 93*
Jamison, Sheila Ann English 1950- *WhoWor 93*
Jamison, Steven R. 1951- *WhoE 93*
Jamison, Susan Clapp 1929- *WhoAmW 93*
Jamison, Thomas Jefferson 1917- *St&PR 93*
Jamison, Zean, Jr. 1932- *St&PR 93*
Jamme, Albert Joseph 1916- *WhoAm 92*
Jammet, H. *WhoScE 91-1*
Jamplis, Robert Warren 1920- *WhoAm 92*
Jampol, Craig Brian 1957- *WhoAm 92*
Jampole, Diana Patricia 1958- *WhoAmW 93, WhoEmL 93*
Jampolis, Neil Peter 1943- *WhoAm 92*
Jampolsky, Gerald G. 1925- *BioIn 17*
Jamrich, John Xavier 1920- *WhoAm 92*
Jamrozy, Zygmunt 1928- *WhoScE 91-4*
Jamshidi, Simin 1956- *WhoEmL 93*
Jamuda 1943- *WhoAsAP 91*
Jan, Chenhuan Jack 1961- *WhoEmL 93*
Jan, George Pokung 1925- *WhoWor 93*
Janabil 1933- *WhoAsAP 91*
Janacek, Jim W. 1942- *St&PR 93*
Janacek, Leos 1854-1928 *Baker 92, BioIn 17, IntDcOp [port], OxDcOp*
Janacek, Leos 1950- *WhoScE 91-4*
Janas, Adam 1938- *St&PR 93*
Janausher, Francesca Romana Magdalena 1830-1904 *PolBiDi*
Janavey, Harry William 1959- *WhoE 93*
Janbazian, Movses Boqhos 1945- *WhoE 93*
Janberg, Klaus *WhoScE 91-3*
Janca, Josef 1944- *WhoScE 91-4*
Jancauskas, Don 1946- *WhoEmL 93*
Jancel, Raymond 1926- *WhoWor 93*
Janci, David F. *Law&B 92*
Janco, Howard L. *Law&B 92*
Jancso, Miklos 1921- *DrEEuF, MiSFD 9*
Jancu, Paul 1926- *WhoE 93*
Jancuk, Wilma Ann 1944- *WhoE 93*
Jancys, Eugenijus 1961- *WhoWor 93*
Janczewski, Janet L. *Law&B 92*
Janda, Krystyna 1952- *BioIn 17*
Janda, Linda *St&PR 93*
Jander, Owen (Hughes) 1930- *Baker 92*
Jandik, Linda Jean 1946- *WhoAmW 93*
Jandl, Ernst 1925- *BioIn 17*
Jandl, Henry Anthony 1910- *WhoAm 92*
Jandl, James Harriman 1925- *WhoAm 92*
Jandl, Richard Lowe 1924- *WhoE 93*
Jandrasits, James William *Law&B 92*
Jandura, Paula Eilese Davis 1952- *WhoAmW 93, WhoEmL 93*
Jane, John Anthony 1931- *WhoAm 92*
Janecek, Karel 1903-1974 *Baker 92*
Janecek, Lenore Elaine 1944- *WhoAmW 93*
Janecek, Miloslav 1941- *WhoScE 91-4*
Janecke, Ronald Brian 1939- *WhoAm 92*
Janecki, Slawomir 1931- *WhoScE 91-4*
Janeczek, Henryk 1950- *WhoWor 93*
Janeczko, Paul B. 1945- *Au&Arts 9 [port]*
Janeczko, Paul B(ryan) 1945- *WhoWrEP 92*
Janeczko, Stanislaw Tadeusz 1953- *WhoWor 93*
Janeicke, Rainer 1930- *WhoWor 93*
Janelidze, George 1952- *WhoWor 93*
Janelle, Louise Cecile 1949- *WhoE 93*
Janello, Amy (Elizabeth) 1962- *ConAu 136*
Janelsina, Veronica 1910- *WhoAmW 93*
Janenka, Stephen James 1960- *WhoEmL 93*
Janensch, Paul 1938- *WhoAm 92*
Janequin, Clement c. 1485-1558 *Baker 92*
Janer, Javier Manuel 1959- *WhoSSW 93*
Janert, Klaus Ludwig 1922- *WhoWor 93*
Janerus, Ingolf Valentin 1943- *St&PR 93*
Janes, Anton 1952- *WhoScE 91-4*
Janes, Clinton S., Jr. *Law&B 92*
Janes, George Sargent 1927- *WhoAm 92, WhoE 93*
Janes, J.F. *WhoScE 91-1*
Janes, J. Robert 1935- *WhoCanL 92*
Janes, Janice Judge *Law&B 92*
Janes, John Anthony 1943- *St&PR 93*
Janes, John Joseph, Jr. 1957- *St&PR 93*
Janes, Joseph Anthony, Jr. 1951- *WhoSSW 93*
Janes, Judy *WhoWrEP 92*
Janes, Percy 1922- *WhoCanL 92*
Janes, Robert James 1925- *WhoE 93*
Janes, Robert Roy 1948- *WhoAm 92*
Janes, Ross *WhoScE 91-1*
Janes, Steven M. 1954- *WhoWrEP 92*
Janes, William Sargent 1953- *WhoE 93, WhoEmL 93*
Janeshutz, Trish 1947- *ScF&FL 92*
Janetatos, Jack Peter 1934- *WhoAm 92, WhoWor 93*
Janetos, Andrew E. 1936- *St&PR 93*
Janetos, Paul E., Sr. 1931- *St&PR 93*
Janevski, Blagoja Kame 1934- *WhoWor 93*
Janeway, Eliot 1913- *WhoAm 92, WhoE 93*
Janeway, Elizabeth (Hall) 1913- *DcAmChF 1960, WhoAm 92, WhoAmW 93, WhoWrEP 92*
Janeway, Michael Charles 1940- *WhoAm 92, WhoWrEP 92*
Janeway, Richard 1933- *WhoAm 92, WhoSSW 93*
Jang, Lisa Lee 1955- *WhoAmW 93*
Jang, Song-Hyon 1939- *WhoWor 93*
Jangaard, Norman Olaf 1941- *St&PR 93, WhoAm 92*
Janger, Kathleen 1940- *BioIn 17*
Janggi Muyang, Andrew 1947- *WhoAsAP 91*
Jang-Ho, Lee 1945- *MiSFD 9*
Jangoux, Michel J.A.G. 1946- *WhoScE 91-2*
Jani, Allen A. 1946- *St&PR 93*
Jani, Jagadish 1921- *WhoAsAP 91*
Jani, Sushma Niranjan 1959- *WhoAmW 93, WhoE 93, WhoEmL 93, WhoWor 93*
Janiak, A. Richard 1946- *St&PR 93*
Janiak, Anthony Richard, Jr. 1946- *WhoAm 92*
Janiak, Jane Marie 1947- *WhoEmL 93*
Janicak, Philip Gregory 1946- *WhoEmL 93*
Janice, Barbara 1949- *WhoE 93*
Janick, Jules 1931- *WhoAm 92*
Janicki, Klemens 1516-1543 *PolBiDi*
Janicki, Robert Stephen 1934- *St&PR 93, WhoAm 92*
Janicki, Stanislaw 1836-1888 *PolBiDi*
Janicki, Thomas N. 1952- *WhoE 93*
Janifer, Laurence M. 1933- *ScF&FL 92*
Janigian, Bruce Jasper 1950- *WhoEmL 93*
Janigro, Antonio 1918-1989 *Baker 92*
Janik, Brigitte Edith 1948- *WhoWor 93*
Janik, Catherine J. *Law&B 92*
Janik, Janina M. 1925- *WhoScE 91-4*
Janik, Jerzy Antoni 1927- *WhoScE 91-4*
Janik, Jozsef 1928- *WhoScE 91-4*
Janik, Tadeusz Jacek 1954- *WhoSSW 93*
Janikovsky, Eva *BioIn 17*
Janikowski, Constance Janelle 1934- *St&PR 93*
Janin, J.-L. 1940- *WhoScE 91-2*
Janin, Joel 1943- *WhoScE 91-2*
Janin, Luc Francois 1958- *WhoWor 93*
Janin, Pierre Raymond 1941- *St&PR 93*
Janis, Allen Ira 1930- *WhoAm 92*
Janis, Anita Gail 1951- *WhoAmW 93*
Janis, Byron 1928- *Baker 92, WhoAm 92*
Janis, Conrad *WhoAm 92*
Janis, Donald E. 1942- *St&PR 93*
Janis, Donald Emil 1942- *WhoAm 92*
Janis, Elsie 1889-1956 *AmWomPl*
Janis, Irving Lester 1918-1990 *BioIn 17*
Janis, Jay d1992 *NewYTBS 92*
Janis, Marion Crystal 1958- *WhoSSW 93*
Janis, Sidney 1896-1989 *BioIn 17*
Janischewskyj, Wasyl 1925- *WhoAm 92*
Janiszewski, Edward J. 1928- *St&PR 93*
Janiszewski, Leszek 1925- *WhoScE 91-4, WhoWor 93*
Janitsch, Johann Gottlieb 1708-c. 1763 *Baker 92*
Janjic, Jevrem 1939- *WhoScE 91-4*
Janjic, Mile 1930- *WhoUN 92*
Janjic, Tomislav 1928- *WhoScE 91-4*
Janjigian, Albert Sarkis 1946- *WhoE 93*
Janjigian, Vahan 1956- *WhoEmL 93*
Janjua, Gulistan 1925- *WhoAsAP 91*
Janke, James F. *Law&B 92*
Janke, Kenneth 1934- *WhoWor 93*
Janke, Kenneth S., Jr. 1958- *St&PR 93*
Janke, Paul R. 1949- *St&PR 93*
Janke, Rhonda Rae 1958- *WhoAmW 93*
Janke, Tom Michael 1943- *St&PR 93*
Jankel, Annabel *MiSFD 9*
Jankelevich, Jaime Waisbein 1949- *WhoWor 93*
Jankelevitch, Vladimir 1903-1985 *Baker 92*
Janklow, Linda LeRoy 1938- *WhoAm 92, WhoE 93*
Janklow, Morton Lloyd 1930- *WhoAm 92, WhoWor 93*
Janknegt, R.A. 1934- *WhoScE 91-3*
Janko, May 1926- *WhoAm 92*
Janko, Paul von 1856-1919 *Baker 92*
Jankofsky, Klaus Peter 1938- *WhoAm 92*
Jankoski, Michael Edward *Law&B 92*
Jankousky, Angela Libby 1956- *WhoAmW 93*
Jankov, Aleksandar *WhoScE 91-4*
Jankovic, Joseph 1948- *WhoAm 92, WhoWor 93*
Jankovic, Radoslav 1933- *WhoScE 91-4*
Jankovic, Slobodan 1925- *WhoScE 91-4*
Jankovich, Sam 1934- *WhoAm 92*
Jankovits, Tibor 1940- *WhoScE 91-4*
Jankowicz, Eleonora 1923- *WhoScE 91-4*
Jankowicz, Stanislaw 1931- *WhoScE 91-4*
Jankowska, Danuta Jadwiga 1927- *WhoScE 91-4*
Jankowski, Gene F. 1934- *St&PR 93, WhoAm 92*
Jankowski, James Paul 1937- *WhoAm 92*
Jankowski, Jerzy *WhoScE 91-4*
Jankowski, Jerzy Adam 1933- *WhoScE 91-4*
Jankowski, Martin Sanchez 1945- *BioIn 17*
Jankowski, Phyllis Elaine 1938- *WhoAmW 93*
Jankowski, Theodore Andrew 1946- *WhoE 93*
Jankowski, Walter Joseph 1920- *St&PR 93*
Jankowski-Spennicchia, Irene 1938- *WhoAmW 93*
Jankowsky, Joseph Simon 1934- *St&PR 93*
Janku, Hana 1940- *Baker 92*
Janku, Ivo 1929- *WhoScE 91-4*
Jankura, Donald Eugene 1929- *St&PR 93, WhoAm 92*
Janky, Douglas Michael 1946-1991 *BioIn 17*
Janky, Gladyce O. 1953- *St&PR 93*
Janle, Peter 1943- *WhoScE 91-3*
Janmohamed, Salim 1950- *St&PR 93*
Jannaconi, Giuseppe 1741-1816 *Baker 92*
Janne, Juhani E. 1941- *WhoScE 91-4*
Janneh, Abdoulie 1944- *WhoUN 92*
Jannemin, Bernard *BioIn 17*
Jannen, Robert L. 1927- *St&PR 93*
Jannes, Georges 1946- *WhoScE 91-2*
Jannett, Ira Roger 1947- *WhoSSW 93*
Jannetta, Peter Joseph 1932- *WhoAm 92*
Janney, Craig *BioIn 17*
Janney, Kay Print 1938- *WhoAmW 93*
Janney, Oliver J. 1946- *St&PR 93*
Janney, Oliver James *Law&B 92*
Janney, Richard Neil 1941- *St&PR 93*
Jannicelli, Matteo 1935- *WhoWrEP 92*
Janning, Christopher Joseph 1964- *St&PR 93*
Janning, Mary Bernadette 1917- *WhoAm 92*
Jannings, Emil 1884-1950 *IntDcF 2-3 [port]*
Jannini, Ralph H. 1932- *St&PR 93*
Jannink, G. *WhoScE 91-2*
Jannis, Dorothy *WhoWrEP 92*
Jannone, Ottorino 1932- *WhoUN 92*
Jannoni, Richard F. 1935- *St&PR 93*
Jannotta, Edgar D. 1931- *St&PR 93*
Jannotti, Gene 1946- *WhoE 93*
Jannuzi, F. Tomasson 1934- *WhoAm 92*
Janochoski, Thomas Allen 1958- *St&PR 93*
Janock, Marcia Linda 1960- *WhoEmL 93*
Janoff, Charles J. *Law&B 92*
Janofsky, Arnold *Law&B 92*
Janofsky, Leonard S. 1909- *WhoAm 92*
Janos, Adam 1930- *WhoScE 91-4*
Janos, Joseph A. 1941- *St&PR 93*
Janosch *ConAu 38NR, MajAI, SmATA 72*
Janoschek, Rudolf 1939- *WhoScE 91-4*
Janoschek, Werner R. 1940- *WhoScE 91-4*
Janosdeak, Egon 1925- *WhoScE 91-4*
Janosik, Edward Gabriel 1918- *WhoAm 92*
Janoski, Debra H. *Law&B 92*
Janoski, Henry Valentine 1933- *WhoAm 92*
Janosko, Rudolph E. M. 1930- *WhoE 93*
Janossy, George *WhoScE 91-1*
Janot, Christian 1936- *WhoScE 91-2*
Janota, Martin 1939- *WhoScE 91-4*
Janousek, Vaclav 1929- *WhoScE 91-4*
Janov, Gwenellen P. 1948- *WhoAmW 93*
Janover, Michael D. 1946- *WhoEmL 93*
Janovich, Alvin C. 1946- *St&PR 93*
Janovitz, William Paul 1942- *St&PR 93*
Janovka, Thomas Balthasar 1669-1741 *Baker 92*
Janovszky, Janos 1942- *WhoScE 91-4*
Janow, Chris 1953- *WhoE 93, WhoEmL 93*
Janow, Lydia Frances 1957- *WhoAmW 93*
Janowiak, Jean Brooks- *ScF&FL 92*
Janowiec, Mieczyslaw Jan 1921- *WhoScE 91-4*
Janowitz, Gundula 1937- *Baker 92, IntDcOp, OxDcOp, WhoWor 93*
Janowitz, Henry David 1915- *WhoAm 92, WhoE 93*
Janowitz, Kathy Palestrant *Law&B 92*
Janowitz, Phyllis *WhoWrEP 92*
Janowitz, Tama *NewYTBS 92 [port]*
Janowitz, Tama 1957- *WhoWrEP 92*
Janowka, Thomas Balthasar 1669-1741 *Baker 92*
Janowski, Aleksander 1941- *WhoUN 92*
Janowski, Edward *St&PR 93*
Janowski, Marek 1939- *Baker 92*
Janowski, Max 1912-1991 *BioIn 17*
Janowski, Thaddeus Marian 1923- *WhoAm 92, WhoSSW 93*
Janowski, Ziporah *Law&B 92*
Janowsky, Carol 1939- *St&PR 93*
Janowsky, Sy 1928- *St&PR 93*
Jans, Candace 1952- *WhoEmL 93*
Jans, James Patrick 1927- *WhoAm 92*
Jansa, Janez *BioIn 17*
Jansa, Leopold 1795-1875 *Baker 92*
Jansa, Renate 1945- *WhoScE 91-4*
Jansen, A. 1960- *WhoScE 91-3*
Jansen, Adolf 1899-1989 *BioIn 17*
Jansen, Angela Bing 1929- *WhoAm 92*
Jansen, Ann Kealey *Law&B 92*
Jansen, Barbara 1954- *WhoEmL 93*
Jansen, Cornelius 1585-1638 *BioIn 17*
Jansen, Dan *BioIn 17*
Jansen, Dirk Adriaan 1956- *WhoWor 93*
Jansen, Donald Orville 1939- *WhoAm 92*
Jansen, Elizabeth Holt 1927- *WhoAmW 93*
Jansen, Erik Christian 1943- *WhoWor 93*
Jansen, F.P. *WhoScE 91-3*
Jansen, G. Thomas 1926- *WhoAm 92*
Jansen, Gerd 1928- *WhoScE 91-3*
Jansen, Gwendolyn Beth 1955- *WhoAmW 93*
Jansen, Heinz 1941- *WhoWor 93*
Jansen, Henry 1918- *St&PR 93, WhoAm 92*
Jansen, Jacques M.L. 1950- *WhoScE 91-3*
Jansen, Johannes Gerrit 1946- *WhoWor 93*
Jansen, John Carl 1947- *WhoEmL 93*
Jansen, Larry Joseph 1947- *St&PR 93*
Jansen, Patrick J. 1927- *St&PR 93*
Jansen, Peter-Jorg 1940- *WhoScE 91-4*
Jansen, Ralph 1927- *St&PR 93*
Jansen, Raymond A., Jr. 1939- *St&PR 93*
Jansen, Richard *St&PR 93*
Jansen, Robert Bruce 1922- *WhoAm 92*
Jansen, Robert Paul Siebrand 1946- *WhoWor 93*
Jansen, Ronald L. *Law&B 92*
Jansen, Walter B. 1945- *St&PR 93*
Jansing, John Curry 1925- *St&PR 93*
Jansky, Jeannette Jefferson 1927- *WhoAmW 93, WhoE 93*
Jansky, Russell *St&PR 93*
Jansky, Sandra W. 1949- *St&PR 93*
Janson, Alfred 1937- *Baker 92*
Janson, Anthony Frederick 1943- *WhoAm 92*
Janson, Barbara Jean 1942- *WhoAmW 93*

Janson, Greg F. *Law&B 92*
Janson, Hank *ScF&FL 92*
Janson, Jennifer Jo 1956- *WhoAmW 93*
Janson, Joseph Bror, II 1928- *WhoAm 92*
Janson, Nicolas dc. 1480 *BioIn 17*
Janson, Patrick F. 1967- *WhoAm 92*
Janson, Philippe A. 1949- *WhoScE 91-4*
Janson, Rainer 1942- *WhoWor 93*
Janson, Raymond Kenneth 1927- *St&PR 93*
Janson, Richard Wilford 1926- *St&PR 93*
Jansons, Arvid *Baker 92*
Jansons, Mariss 1943- *Baker 92*
Janss, William Cluff 1918- *WhoAm 92*
Janssen, Alfred Guthrie 1949- *WhoWrEP 92*
Janssen, Daniel 1936- *BioIn 17*
Janssen, Erwin T. 1936- *WhoAm 92*
Janssen, Gail Edwin 1930- *WhoAm 92*
Janssen, Herbert 1892-1965 *Baker 92, IntDcOp, OxDcOp*
Janssen, J.D. 1940- *WhoScE 91-3*
Janssen, Jerry Frederick *Law&B 92*
Janssen, Judith M. *Law&B 92*
Janssen, Jules 1824-1907 *BioIn 17*
Janssen, Lawrence Raymond 1943- *WhoSSW 93*
Janssen, Martin Christopher 1948- *WhoWor 93*
Janssen, P.A.E.M. 1951- *WhoScE 91-3*
Janssen, Paul Adriaan Jan 1926- *WhoScE 91-2*
Janssen, Peter Anton 1936- *WhoAm 92*
Janssen, R. *WhoScE 91-3*
Janssen, Richard J. 1936- *St&PR 93*
Janssen, Werner 1899-1990 *Baker 92, BioIn 17*
Janssens, Jean-Francois-Joseph 1801-1835 *Baker 92*
Janssens, Jessica Rolande Julienne 1962- *WhoWor 93*
Janssens, Jozef P.F. 1943- *WhoScE 91-2*
Jansson, Bengt I. 1932- *WhoScE 91-4*
Jansson, Bengt-Owe 1931- *WhoScE 91-4*
Jansson, Elli Jenny Margareta 1927- *WhoScE 91-4*
Jansson, Ingvar 1924- *WhoScE 91-4*
Jansson, John Phillip 1918- *WhoWor 93*
Jansson, Marja-Terttu Helena 1943- *WhoScE 91-4*
Jansson, Mikael 1960- *WhoScE 91-4*
Jansson, Tove 1914- *ScF&FL 92*
Jansson, Tove Marika 1914- *ConAu 38NR, MajAI [port]*
Jansz, H.S. 1927- *WhoScE 91-3*
Jansz, Luxman Graciyas 1960- *WhoWor 93*
Janszen, Wilbur John, Jr. 1940- *St&PR 93*
Janszky, Jozsef 1943- *WhoScE 91-4*
Janszoon, Willem 1570- *Expl 93*
Janta-Polczynski, Aleksander 1908-1975 *PolBiDi*
Janto, Armund M. 1944- *St&PR 93*
Jantsch, Robert Craig 1953- *WhoE 93*
Jantsch, Wolfgang Johannes 1946- *WhoWor 93*
Jantunen, Kauko Ilmari 1941- *WhoWor 93*
Jantunen, Matti J. 1946- *WhoScE 91-4*
Jantz, Cynthia Marie 1957- *WhoEmL 93*
Jantz, Kenneth M. 1942- *St&PR 93*
Jantzen, John Marc 1908- *WhoAm 92, WhoWor 93*
Jantzen, Ronald Edward 1946- *WhoSSW 93*
Jantzen, William J. 1909- *St&PR 93*
January, Anna Linton 1879- *AmWomPl*
January, Lewis Edward 1910- *WhoAm 92*
January, Lois *SweetSg C [port]*
Janura, Jan Arol 1949- *WhoEmL 93*
Janus, Julie *WhoAm 92*
Janus, Lincoln V. *Law&B 92*
Janus, Paul William 1939- *St&PR 93*
Janush, Joseph J. 1929- *St&PR 93*
Januzzi, James Louis 1941- *WhoE 93*
Januzzi, Lidercio 1954- *WhoWor 93*
Jan, van Brugge 1501?-1556 *BioIn 17*
Janvey, Abraham A. 1911- *St&PR 93*
Janvier, Thomas A. 1849-1913 *ScF&FL 92*
Janz, Milli *WhoE 93*
Janz, Wolfgang Dietrich 1920- *WhoScE 91-3*
Janzen, Daniel H. *BioIn 17*
Janzen, Daniel Hunt 1939- *WhoAm 92*
Janzen, Deborah K. 1952- *WhoAmW 93*
Janzen, Howard E. 1954- *St&PR 93*
Janzen, Jerry Lee 1936- *WhoSSW 93*
Janzen, Norine Madelyn Quinlan 1943- *WhoAmW 93*
Janzen, Peter S. *Law&B 92*
Janzon, Bo *WhoScE 91-4*
Janzow, Walter Theophilus 1918- *WhoAm 92*
Jao, Grace *St&PR 93*
Jaosolo, Bedo d1989 *BioIn 17*
Jaouni, Katherine Cook 1928- *WhoAmW 93*
Japha, Barbara *Law&B 92*
Japha, Daniel S. *Law&B 92*
Japhet, Ernest Israel 1921- *St&PR 93*
Japka, Roberta H. 1933- *WhoAmW 93*
Japlon, Howard E. *Law&B 92*
Jaqua, Frederick W. *Law&B 92*
Jaqua, Frederick W. 1921- *St&PR 93*
Jaqua, Richard Allen 1938- *WhoAm 92*
Jaques, E. Vernon 1942- *St&PR 93*
Jaques, Faith 1923- *MajAI [port], SmATA 69*
Jaques, Louis Barker 1911- *WhoAm 92*
Jaques, Thomas Francis 1938- *WhoAm 92, WhoSSW 93*
Jaques-Dalcroze, Emile 1865-1950 *Baker 92, BioIn 17*
Jaquet, James R. 1929- *St&PR 93*
Jaquette, John J. 1918- *St&PR 93*
Jaquette, John Joseph 1918- *WhoAm 92*
Jaquint, Robert W. 1925- *St&PR 93*
Jaquish, John E. 1937- *WhoAm 92*
Jaquish, Michael Paul 1934- *WhoSSW 93*
Jaquith, Donald S. 1925- *St&PR 93*
Jaquith, George Oakes 1916- *WhoWor 93*
Jaquith, Richard Herbert 1919- *WhoAm 92*
Jaquith, William Walter 1944- *St&PR 93*
Jaracz, Stefan 1883-1945 *PolBiDi*
Jara Diaz, Sergio R. 1951- *WhoWor 93*
Jara Gumucio, Victor 1918- *WhoWor 93*
Jaraiz, Eladio Maldonado 1952- *WhoWor 93*
Jaramillo, Arthur Lewis 1949- *WhoAm 92*
Jaramillo, Cleofas M. 1878-1956 *DcLB 122 [port]*
Jaramillo, Cleofas Martinez 1878-1956 *NotHsAW 93*
Jaramillo, Felipe 1940- *WhoUN 92*
Jaramillo, Hernan 1942- *WhoUN 92*
Jaramillo, Hernando Jose, III 1932- *WhoSSW 93*
Jaramillo, Mari-Luci 1928- *HispAmA, NotHsAW 93 [port]*
Jaramillo, Marino 1923- *WhoWor 93*
Jaramillo Levi, Enrique 1944- *SpAmA*
Jaran, John Robert 1952- *St&PR 93*
Jaras, Algis *BioIn 17*
Jarboe, J. Michael *Law&B 92*
Jarboe, John A. 1933- *WhoIns 93*
Jarc, Frank Robert 1942- *WhoAm 92*
Jarcho, Saul Wallenstein 1906- *WhoAm 92, WhoE 93*
Jarchow, Friedrich 1926- *WhoScE 91-3*
Jarchow, Hans-Joachim 1935- *WhoWor 93*
Jardanyi, Pal 1920-1966 *Baker 92*
Jardel, Jean-Paul Ernest 1936- *WhoUN 92*
Jardetzky, Oleg 1929- *WhoAm 92*
Jardillier, Jean-Claude 1939- *WhoScE 91-2*
Jardin, Craig Dennis *Law&B 92*
Jardine, David Henry 1947- *St&PR 93*
Jardine, Don L. 1926- *St&PR 93*
Jardine, G.C. *WhoScE 91-1*
Jardine, James Quintus 1954- *WhoSSW 93*
Jardine, John Wallace, Jr. 1927- *St&PR 93*
Jardine, Larry L. 1936- *St&PR 93*
Jardon, Claude Earl *Law&B 92*
Jardon, Claude Earl, Jr. 1941- *St&PR 93*
Jardot, Leo C. *Law&B 92*
Jarecke, George Walter *Law&B 92*
Jarecki, Henry George 1933- *WhoE 93*
Jarecki, Henryk 1846-1918 *Baker 92*
Jarecki, Janis Marie 1955- *WhoE 93*
Jarecki, Tadeusz 1888-1955 *Baker 92*
Jareckie, Stephen Barlow 1929- *WhoAm 92*
Jared, Robert P. *Law&B 92*
Jaresko, Natalie Ann 1965- *WhoAmW 93*
Jaret, Stanley 1929- *St&PR 93*
Jaric, Robert Ronald 1942- *WhoSSW 93*
Jaricot, Pauline 1799-1862 *BioIn 17*
Jarislowsky, Stephen Arnold 1925- *St&PR 93*
Jarke, Wayne *Law&B 92*
Jarkovsky, Isaac *Law&B 92*
Jarkovsky, Isaac 1926- *St&PR 93, WhoAm 92*
Jarmain, Edwin Roper 1907- *St&PR 93*
Jarman, Derek 1942- *BioIn 17, MiSFD 9*
Jarman, Joseph 1937- *WhoAm 92*
Jarman, Julia *ScF&FL 92*
Jarman, Kevin Richard 1965- *WhoWor 93*
Jarman, Mark Anthony 1952- *DcLB 120 [port]*
Jarman, Mark Foster 1952- *WhoEmL 93, WhoSSW 93*
Jarman, Michael *WhoScE 91-1*
Jarman, Richard Sinclair 1947- *St&PR 93*
Jarmi, Al- fl. 9th cent.- *OxDcByz*
Jarmie, Nelson 1928- *WhoAm 92*
Jarmon, Pamela Gayle 1961- *WhoAmW 93*
Jarmus, Stephan Onysym 1925- *WhoAm 92*
Jarmusch, Jim *BioIn 17, NewYTBS 92 [port]*
Jarmusch, Jim 1953- *MiSFD 9*
Jarmusch, Robert Thomas 1922- *St&PR 93*
Jarmusch, Roland J. 1945- *St&PR 93*
Jarmuth, Jeffrey Jackson *Law&B 92*
Jarnach, Philipp 1892-1982 *Baker 92*
Jarnefelt, (Edvard) Armas 1869-1958 *Baker 92*
Jarnholm, Arne R. *Law&B 92*
Jarno, Georg 1868-1920 *Baker 92*
Jarnowick, Giovanni *Baker 92*
Jarnowick, Pierre Louis Hus-Desforges *Baker 92*
Jarnuszkiewicz, Stanislaw 1921- *WhoScE 91-4*
Jaro, Zoltan 1921- *WhoScE 91-4*
Jaroch, Jiri 1920-1986 *Baker 92*
Jaroch, Margaret M. 1954- *St&PR 93*
Jaroch, Raymond *St&PR 93*
Jaroff, Leon Morton 1927- *WhoAm 92, WhoWor 93*
Jaroff, Sergei 1896-1985 *Baker 92*
Jaron, Dov 1935- *WhoAm 92, WhoE 93*
Jaronczyk, Robert C. 1951- *St&PR 93*
Jaroniec, Mieczyslaw 1949- *WhoScE 91-4*
Jaros, Arthur G. 1922- *St&PR 93*
Jaros, Dean 1938- *WhoAm 92*
Jaros, Erich Anton 1932- *WhoUN 92*
Jaros, Jerome Edward 1944- *WhoAm 92*
Jaros, Milan *WhoScE 91-1*
Jaros, Robert James 1939- *WhoE 93*
Jarosik, Gary Robert *Law&B 92*
Jaroski, Edward L. 1946- *St&PR 93, WhoIns 93*
Jaroslav 978-1054 *OxDcByz*
Jaroslawicz, David 1947- *WhoE 93*
Jarosz, Andrzej *WhoScE 91-4*
Jarosz, Frederick John 1929- *St&PR 93, WhoIns 93*
Jarosz, Jan 1939- *WhoScE 91-4*
Jarosz, Stanislaw Jan 1923- *WhoWor 93*
Jaroszewicz, Leokadia 1926- *WhoScE 91-4*
Jaroszewicz, Mark T. 1921- *WhoAm 92*
Jaroszewicz, Piotr d1992 *NewYTBS 92*
Jaroszewski, Jerzy W. 1950- *WhoWor 93*
Jaroszewski, Wojciech 1935- *WhoScE 91-4*
Jaroudi, Muhammad *WhoWor 93*
Jarowey, Peter M. 1952- *St&PR 93*
Jarowinsky, Werner 1927-1990 *BioIn 17*
Jarowski, Charles Ignatius 1946- *WhoEmL 93*
Jarquin, Agustin *DcCPCAm*
Jarrar, Adil Ahmad 1932- *WhoWor 93*
Jarrard, Clisby W. *Law&B 92*
Jarrard, Jerald Osborne 1917- *WhoAm 92*
Jarrard, Leonard Everett 1930- *WhoAm 92*
Jarrat, Henri Aaron 1938- *WhoAm 92*
Jarratt, Peter *WhoScE 91-1*
Jarrault, Alexandre *WhoCanL 92*
Jarre, Maurice 1924- *Baker 92*
Jarreau, Al 1940- *Baker 92, CurBio 92 [port], SoulM, WhoAm 92*
Jarred, Ada Delony 1937- *WhoWor 93*
Jarrell, Donald Ray 1963- *WhoSSW 93*
Jarrell, Iris Bonds 1942- *WhoAmW 93*
Jarrell, James A. *Law&B 92*
Jarrell, James Michael 1957- *St&PR 93*
Jarrell, John W. *WhoAm 92*
Jarrell, Myra Williams 1867-1937 *AmWomPl*
Jarrell, Paul Douglas 1944- *WhoWor 93*
Jarrell, Randall 1914-1965 *BioIn 17, DcAmChF 1960, MajAI [port]*
Jarrett, Alexis 1948- *WhoAmW 93, WhoEmL 93, WhoWor 93*
Jarrett, Amanda Jean *ConAu 39NR*
Jarrett, Anthony 1930- *WhoAm 92*
Jarrett, Cora 1877-1969 *ScF&FL 92*
Jarrett, David *ScF&FL 92*
Jarrett, Dennis Eugene 1946- *WhoAm 92*
Jarrett, Eugene Lawrence 1942- *WhoAm 92*
Jarrett, Graham Edmund 1935- *St&PR 93*
Jarrett, Harry Berton 1933- *St&PR 93*
Jarrett, James Warren 1944- *St&PR 93*
Jarrett, Jerry Vernon *BioIn 17*
Jarrett, Jerry Vernon 1931- *St&PR 93, WhoAm 92*
Jarrett, John David, Sr. 1947- *St&PR 93*
Jarrett, Keith *BioIn 17*
Jarrett, Keith 1945- *Baker 92, News 92 [port], WhoAm 92*
Jarrett, Kenny *BioIn 17*
Jarrett, Noel 1921- *WhoAm 92*
Jarrett, Oswald *WhoScE 91-1*
Jarrett, Phyllis Jean 1961- *WhoSSW 93*
Jarrett, Polly Hawkins 1929- *WhoSSW 93*
Jarrett, Randall F. 1943- *St&PR 93*
Jarrett, Richard John *WhoScE 91-1*
Jarrett, Richard M. 1947- *St&PR 93*
Jarrett, Richard Scott 1946- *St&PR 93*
Jarrett, Richard Steven 1955- *WhoE 93*
Jarrett, Robin Beth 1955- *WhoSSW 93*
Jarrett, Ruth 1942- *WhoE 93*
Jarrett, Ruth Frances 1958- *WhoWor 93*
Jarrett, Stephanie B. *Law&B 92*
Jarrett, Stephen William 1948- *WhoUN 92*
Jarrett, Steven P. 1954- *St&PR 93*
Jarrett, Teresa Yvonne 1953- *WhoAmW 93, WhoEmL 93*
Jarrett, William Fleming Hoggan *WhoScE 91-1*
Jarrick, Michael A. *Law&B 92*
Jarriel, Linda Byrd 1952- *WhoEmL 93*
Jarriel, Thomas Edwin 1934- *WhoAm 92*
Jarrott, Charles 1927- *MiSFD 9, WhoAm 92*
Jarrow, Robert Alan 1952- *WhoAm 92*
Jarrow, Stanley L. 1919- *St&PR 93*
Jarry, Alfred 1873-1907 *ScF&FL 92*
Jarry, Paul Rudger 1937- *WhoWrEP 92*
Jars, Pierre 1927- *St&PR 93*
Jart, Aage 1931- *WhoWor 93*
Jartman, Marc R. *St&PR 93*
Jarudi, Nabeel Izzat 1941- *WhoE 93*
Jaruzelski, Wojciech *BioIn 17*
Jaruzelski, Wojciech 1923- *ColdWar 2 [port], PolBiDi*
Jarvela, Dennis L. *Law&B 92*
Jarvenkyla, Jyri Jaakko 1947- *WhoWor 93*
Jarvi, Kenneth T. *Law&B 92*
Jarvi, Neeme *BioIn 17*
Jarvi, Neeme 1937- *Baker 92, WhoAm 92*
Jarvi, Timo H.J. 1942- *WhoScE 91-4*
Jarvie, Clodagh Gibson- *ScF&FL 92*
Jarvie, Lawrence L. 1906-1990 *BioIn 17*
Jarvik, Laurence 1956- *MiSFD 9*
Jarvik, Lissy F. *WhoAm 92*
Jarvik, Murray Elias 1923- *WhoAm 92*
Jarvik, Robert 1946- *WhoAm 92, WhoE 93, WhoWor 93*
Jarvilehto, Matti 1945- *WhoScE 91-4*
Jarvinen, Antero 1952- *WhoScE 91-4*
Jarvinen, Pentti A. 1923- *WhoScE 91-4*
Jarvis, Alfred Raymond, Jr. *Law&B 92*
Jarvis, Averill Rand *Law&B 92*
Jarvis, Barbara Ann 1946- *WhoAmW 93, WhoEmL 93, WhoWor 93*
Jarvis, Barbara Anne 1934- *WhoAmW 93*
Jarvis, Basil 1936- *WhoWor 93*
Jarvis, Billy Britt 1943- *WhoSSW 93*
Jarvis, Christopher L. 1948- *St&PR 93*
Jarvis, Daniel O. 1950- *St&PR 93*
Jarvis, Darrell E. *Law&B 92*
Jarvis, E. K. *MajAI*
Jarvis, Edward *ScF&FL 92*
Jarvis, Edward Curtis 1951- *St&PR 93, WhoE 93, WhoWor 93*
Jarvis, Frederick Gordon 1930- *WhoWrEP 92*
Jarvis, Gary Lee 1955- *WhoEmL 93*
Jarvis, Gilbert Andrew 1941- *WhoAm 92*
Jarvis, Gwen 1953- *WhoAmW 93*
Jarvis, James Howard, II 1937- *WhoAm 92, WhoSSW 93*
Jarvis, James M. 1912- *St&PR 93*
Jarvis, Jeffrey Scott 1952- *WhoEmL 93*
Jarvis, Joseph Boyer 1923- *WhoAm 92*
Jarvis, Lawrence F. 1917- *St&PR 93*
Jarvis, Mike *ScF&FL 92*
Jarvis, Morris O. 1940- *St&PR 93, WhoAm 92, WhoSSW 93*
Jarvis, Oscar T., Jr. 1930- *WhoAm 92*
Jarvis, Paul Gordon *WhoScE 91-1*
Jarvis, R. *WhoScE 91-1*
Jarvis, R.H. *WhoScE 91-1*
Jarvis, Rebecca Jane 1951- *WhoAmW 93*
Jarvis, Robert Mark 1959- *WhoEmL 93, WhoSSW 93, WhoWor 93*
Jarvis, Robin *ScF&FL 92*
Jarvis, Sharon 1943- *ScF&FL 92*
Jarvis, Terrance Carlyle 1943- *WhoAm 92*
Jarvis, Wayne Frederick, Jr. *Law&B 92*
Jarvis, William E. 1925- *St&PR 93*
Jarvis, William Esmond 1931- *WhoAm 92*
Jarvis, William Eugene 1925- *WhoAm 92*
Jarvis, William Hyde 1964- *WhoE 93*
Jarvis Family *BioIn 17*
Jary, Roland Saunders 1936- *St&PR 93*
Jarzebski, Adam 1590-1649 *PolBiDi*
Jarzyna, Henryk 1922- *WhoScE 91-4*
Jaschek, Carlos 1926- *WhoScE 91-2*
Jaschek, Carlos O.R. 1926- *WhoScE 91-2*
Jaschke, Dieter 1942- *WhoScE 91-3*
Jasen, Matthew Joseph 1915- *WhoAm 92*
Jasentuliyana, Nandasiri 1938- *BioIn 17, WhoUN 92*
Jasey, Neil N. *Law&B 92*
Jasica, Andrea Lynn 1945- *WhoAmW 93*
Jasienica, Pawel 1909-1970 *PolBiDi*
Jasienko, Stefan 1921- *WhoScE 91-4*
Jasinowski, Jerry Joseph 1939- *WhoAm 92*
Jasinski, Arnold Robert 1933- *WhoE 93*
Jasinski, Jan T. 1806-1879 *PolBiDi*
Jasinski, Jerry 1940- *WhoE 93*
Jasinski, Paul Carl *Law&B 92*
Jasinski, Roman d1991 *BioIn 17*
Jasinski, Wieslaw 1932- *WhoScE 91-4*
Jasinski, William *BioIn 17*

Jasinski-Caldwell, Mary L. 1959- WhoAmW 93, WhoEmL 93
Jasiorowski, H.A. WhoScE 91-3
Jasiorowski, Henryk A. 1926- WhoScE 91-4
Jaskanis, Jan Kazimierz 1932- WhoWor 93
Jaske, John B. Law&B 92
Jaskiewicz, Anne M. 1960- St&PR 93
Jaskiewicz, Leonard Albert 1927- WhoAm 92
Jaskiewicz, Ludwik Zbigniew 1921- WhoScE 91-4
Jaskol, Earl 1943- St&PR 93, WhoE 93
Jaskol, Leonard R. 1937- St&PR 93
Jaskol, Norman 1933- St&PR 93
Jasko/La, Marian 1932- WhoScE 91-4
Jaskot, John Joseph 1921- WhoAm 92
Jaskot, Marty J. 1937- St&PR 93
Jaskula, Marian Jozef 1948- WhoWor 93
Jaslow, Howard 1935- WhoE 93
Jaslow, Robert I. 1923-1990 BioIn 17
Jasman, Stefan 1927- WhoScE 91-4
Jasmin, Claude 1930- BioIn 17, WhoCanL 92, WhoWrEP 92
Jasmin, Claude 1938- WhoScE 91-2
Jasmin, Edwin Herard 1933- St&PR 93
Jasmin, Ernest A. AfrAmBi [port]
Jasmin, Gaetan 1924- WhoAm 92
Jasmund, Norman William 1956- WhoEmL 93
Jasnow, David Michael 1943- WhoAm 92
Jasny, George Roman 1924- WhoAm 92
Jasny, Vojtech 1925- DrEEuF
Jason, J. Julie Law&B 92
Jason, J. Julie 1949- WhoEmL 93
Jason, Jerry ScF&FL 92
Jason, Marilyn S. Law&B 92
Jason, Nathan Mitchel 1921-1990 BioIn 17
Jason, Philip Kenneth 1941- WhoWrEP 92
Jason, Stuart ConAu 39NR
Jaspard, J.-M. 1936- WhoScE 91-2
Jaspard, Jean-Marie 1936- WhoScE 91-2
Jaspen, Nathan 1917- WhoAm 92, WhoE 93, WhoWor 93
Jasper, Chris
See Isley Brothers, The ConMus 8
Jasper, Christopher Howard 1951- WhoEmL 93
Jasper, Donald Edward 1918- WhoAm 92
Jasper, Doris Jean Berry 1933- WhoAmW 93, WhoWor 93
Jasper, Herbert Henri 1906- WhoAm 92
Jasper, James M(acdonald) 1957- ConAu 138
Jasper, Mabel M. AfrAmBi [port]
Jasper, Margaret Catherine 1954- WhoEmL 93
Jasper, Paul Robert 1959- WhoWor 93
Jasper, Paul T. 1937- St&PR 93
Jasper, Paul Tucker 1937- WhoAm 92
Jasper, Seymour 1919- WhoE 93, WhoWor 93
Jaspers, Edmonde WhoScE 91-2
Jaspersen, Frederick Zarr 1938- WhoAm 92, WhoE 93
Jass, Herman Earl 1918- WhoE 93
Jassem, Marek A. 1926- WhoScE 91-4
Jassem, Wiktor 1922- WhoScE 91-4
Jasser, Ronald Maury 1948- St&PR 93, WhoEmL 93
Jasso, Joseph B. 1936- St&PR 93
Jasso, William Gattis 1953- WhoWor 93
Jasspon, Ethel Reed AmWomPl
Jassy, Everett Lewis 1937- WhoAm 92
Jastram, Roy W. 1915-1991 BioIn 17
Jastrow, Joseph 1863-1944 PolBiDi
Jastrow, Marie BioIn 17
Jastrow, Robert 1925- BioIn 17, WhoAm 92
Jastrow, Werner 1934- WhoE 93
Jastrun, Mieczyslaw 1903-1983 PolBiDi
Jastrzebska, Jadwiga 1929- WhoScE 91-4
Jastrzebski, Tadeusz 1937- WhoWor 93
Jaswant Singh 1938- WhoAsAP 91
Jaswell, Roy P. 1934- St&PR 93
Jaswon, M.A. WhoScE 91-1
Jaswon, Maurice Arthur 1922- WhoWor 93
Jaszczak, John 1947- St&PR 93
Jaszczak, Ronald Jack 1942- WhoAm 92, WhoWor 93
Jatene, Adib Domingos 1929- WhoWor 93
Jatila, E.J. 1939- WhoScE 91-4
Jatlow, Peter I. 1936- WhoAm 92
Jaton, Jean-Claude 1938- WhoScE 91-4
Jatras, Stephen James 1926- St&PR 93, WhoAm 92
Jatues, Ayresome ScF&FL 92
Jatzkewitz, Horst Waldemar 1912- WhoWor 93
Jaubert, Maurice 1900-1940 Baker 92
Jauch, Ronald R. 1945- St&PR 93
Jaudes, Robert Christian 1933- St&PR 93
Jaudes, William E. Law&B 92
Jaudes, William E. 1937- St&PR 93, WhoAm 92
Jaudon, Valerie 1945- WhoAm 92
Jauhiainen, Erkki E. 1938- WhoScE 91-4
Jauhiainen, Pertti Juhani 1960- WhoWor 93
Jauho, Pekka Antti Olavi 1923- WhoScE 91-4
Jaumot, Frank Edward, Jr. 1923- WhoAm 92
Jaunich, Robert, II 1940- St&PR 93
Jauquet-Kalinoski, Barbara 1948- WhoAmW 93, WhoEmL 93
Jauregui, Paul Luis 1941- St&PR 93
Jaures, Jean 1859-1914 BioIn 17
Jaus, William Currie 1920- WhoAm 92
Jausions, Paul 1834-1870 Baker 92
Jausoro, Gina Marie 1963- WhoAmW 93
Jauss, Anne Marie 1902?-1991 SmATA 69
Jauss, Anne Marie 1907-1991 BioIn 17
Jauss, David Russell 1951- WhoWrEP 92
Jauzein, Philippe 1953- WhoScE 91-2
Javacheff, Christo Vladimirov 1935- WhoAm 92
Javal, Camille 1934- WhoWor 93
Javali, J.P. 1931- WhoAsAP 91
Javan, Ali 1926- WhoAm 92
Javaras, Barbara Kariotis 1946- WhoEmL 93
Javed, Murid Hussain 1960- WhoWor 93
Javers, Ron WhoWrEP 92
Javid, Manucher J. 1922- WhoAm 92
Javier, Aileen Riego 1948- WhoWor 93
Javier, Exequiel B. 1946- WhoAsAP 91
Javier, Rufino S. 1934- WhoAsAP 91
Javierre Ortas, Antonio Maria Cardinal 1921- WhoWor 93
Javits, Eric BioIn 17
Javits, Jacob 1904-1986 ColdWar 1 [port]
Javits, Jacob Koppel 1904-1986 JeAmHC
Javits, Joshua Moses 1950- WhoAm 92
Javits, Michael D. 1937- St&PR 93
Javna, John ScF&FL 92
Javor, Frank A. 1916- ScF&FL 92
Javor, Kenneth D. 1948- WhoIns 93
Javor, Tibor 1926- WhoScE 91-4
Javorek, Judeth Newham 1950- WhoAmW 93, WhoEmL 93
Javoy, Marc 1937- WhoScE 91-2
Jawaharlal Nehru 1889-1964 BioIn 17
Jawara, Dawda Kairaba 1924- WhoAfr, WhoWor 93
Jawetz, Ernest 1916- WhoAm 92
Jawlensky, Alexej von c. 1864-1941 BioIn 17
Jaworiwsky, I. Stephen 1947- St&PR 93
Jaworowski, Zbigniew 1927- WhoScE 91-4
Jaworske, Mary Ann WhoAmW 93
Jaworski, Francis ScF&FL 92
Jaworski, Francis S. Law&B 92
Jaworski, Philip Joseph 1927- St&PR 93
Jay, Benny E. 1938- St&PR 93
Jay, Bruce John 1944- St&PR 93
Jay, Burton Dean 1937- St&PR 93, WhoAm 92, WhoIns 93
Jay, Charles Douglas 1925- WhoAm 92
Jay, David Jakubowicz 1925- WhoWor 93
Jay, Frank Peter 1922- WhoAm 92
Jay, Glenda Dorene 1946- WhoAmW 93
Jay, James Albert 1916- WhoSSW 93, WhoWor 93
Jay, John 1745-1829 OxCSupC [port]
Jay, Margaret AmWomPl
Jay, Mark H. Law&B 92
Jay, Michael Eliot 1949- WhoE 93
Jay, Nigel N. 1963- St&PR 93
Jay, Norma Joyce 1925- WhoAmW 93
Jay, Peter 1937- ScF&FL 92
Jay, Ralph WhoWrEP 92
Jay, Robert L. Law&B 92
Jay, Stephen Jordan 1941- WhoAm 92
Jay, Thelma Gertrude Allen 1923- WhoWrEP 92
Jay, Thomas G. 1915- St&PR 93
Jay, W. Walton Law&B 92
Jayabalan, Vemblaserry 1937- WhoAm 92
Jayalalitha Jayaram 1948- WhoAsAP 91
Jayant, Nuggehally Sampath 1946- WhoAm 92
Jayanta Mahapatra BioIn 17
Jayasekera, Thavatinsa Mendis 1947- WhoWor 93
Jayasena, Widanagamage 1948- WhoWor 93
Jayawant, Bhalchandra Vinayak WhoScE 91-1
Jayawardana, Obadage Charly 1941- WhoWor 93
Jayaweera, Shanath Amarasiri Arumabadu WhoScE 91-1
Jaycox, Edward Van Kleeck 1938- WhoAm 92
Jaycox, Elbert Ralph 1923- WhoWrEP 92
Jaycox, Robert Peter 1931- WhoE 93
Jaye, David Robert, Jr. 1930- WhoAm 92
Jayez, Jacques-Henri 1943- WhoScE 91-2
Jayjock, Michael Anthony 1946- WhoEmL 93
Jayme, William North 1925- BioIn 17
Jayne, Billy BioIn 17
Jayne, Cynthia Elizabeth 1953- WhoAmW 93, WhoE 93, WhoEmL 93
Jayne, Edward Randolph, II 1944- WhoAm 92
Jayne, Marcel Glyndwr WhoScE 91-1
Jayne, Theodore Douglas 1929- WhoAm 92
Jaynes, Barry S. Law&B 92
Jaynes, Donald O. Law&B 92
Jayo, Juan M. Law&B 92
Jayroe, Billie Jean 1929- WhoAmW 93
Jayson, Gerald Gert WhoScE 91-1
Jayson, Jeffrey Arthur 1949- WhoE 93
Jayson, Lester Samuel 1915- WhoAm 92
Jayson, Malcolm I V WhoScE 91-1
Jayson, Melinda Gayle 1956- WhoAmW 93
Jazairy, Idriss 1936- WhoUN 92
Jazayery, Mohammad Ali 1924- WhoAm 92
Jazdzewski, Krzysztof 1938- WhoScE 91-4
JB 1951- WhoEmL 93
Jbili, Abdelali 1949- WhoUN 92
Jea, Yu-Huei 1943- WhoWor 93
Jeakins, Dorothy 1914- ConTFT 10
Jean 1921- WhoWor 93
Jean, Grand Duke of Luxembourg 1921- BioIn 17
Jean, Gabrielle Lucille 1924- WhoAmW 93
Jean, Kenneth WhoAm 92
Jean, Melaga Djutitsa Fodoh, II 1938- WhoUN 92
Jean, Raymond 1933- WhoScE 91-2
Jean, Valerie 1953- WhoWrEP 92
Jean, Wilmer Francis 1915- WhoWor 93
Jean-Aubry, Georges 1882-1949 Baker 92
Jean-Baptiste, Chavannes DcCPCAm
Jeandin, Michel 1955- WhoScE 91-2
Jeanes, Joe W. 1927- WhoAm 92
Jeanes, Joe Wesley 1927- St&PR 93
Jeanes, Lincoln Douglas 1931- WhoSSW 93
Jeanette, Henry C. Law&B 92
Jeanfils, Joseph D.G. 1952- WhoScE 91-2
Jeanloz, Raymond 1952- WhoAm 92
Jeanloz, Roger William 1917- WhoAm 92
Jeanmaire, Jean-Louis d1992 NewYTBS 92
Jeanmaire, Jean-Louis 1910-1992 BioIn 17
Jeanmougin, David T. 1940- St&PR 93
Jeanne, Robert Lawrence 1942- WhoAm 92
Jeanne d'Arc, Saint 1412-1431 BioIn 17
Jeanneney, Jean-Marcel 1910- BioIn 17
Jeanneney, Jules 1864-1957 BioIn 17
Jeanneret, Albert 1886-1973 Baker 92
Jeanneret, Marsh 1917-1990 BioIn 17
Jeanneret, Olivier 1926- WhoScE 91-4
Jeanneret, Paul Richard WhoSSW 93
Jeanneret-Gris, Charles Edouard 1887-1965 BioIn 17
Jeannero, Douglas M. 1926- St&PR 93
Jeannero, Jane M. Law&B 92
Jeannerod, Marc 1935- WhoScE 91-2
Jeannette, Harry Edward 1917- BiDAMSp 1989
Jeannin, Jules Cecilien 1866-1933 Baker 92
Jeannin, Yves P. 1931- WhoScE 91-2
Jean Paul 1763-1825 BioIn 17
Jean-Pierre, Judith Hagans Law&B 92
Jeanrenaud, Bernard 1930- WhoScE 91-4
Jeanrenaud, Joan 1956-
See Kronos Quartet, The News 93-1
Jeans, Carl E. 1941- St&PR 93
Jeans, John Berger 1931- St&PR 93
Jeansonne, Angela Lynne 1961- WhoAmW 93
Jeansonne, Gloria Janelle 1946- WhoAmW 93
Jeansonne, Lawrence Bob 1938- St&PR 93
Jeansonne, Susanna BioIn 17
Jeanteur, Philippe Andre 1940- WhoWor 93
Jeas, William C. 1938- WhoAm 92, WhoE 93
Jeavons, John BioIn 17
Jeavons, Norman Stone 1930- WhoAm 92
Jeavons, Robert W. 1925- St&PR 93
Jebavy, Linda 1950- WhoAmW 93
Jebb, Alan WhoScE 91-1
Jebb, Eglantyne 1876-1928 BioIn 17
Jebb, Robert Dudley 1944- WhoWrEP 92
Jebsen, Jens Wohl 1919- WhoScE 91-4
Jecklin, G.D. 1935- St&PR 93
Jecklin, Lois Underwood 1934- WhoAm 92, WhoAmW 93
Jedel, Peter Harold 1939- WhoAm 92
Jedenoff, George Alexander 1917- WhoAm 92
Jedinak, Audrey Grace 1930- St&PR 93
Jedlicka, Joseph F., III Law&B 92
Jedlicka, Judith Ann 1944- WhoAm 92
Jedlicka, Michael Joseph 1947- WhoEmL 93
Jedliczka, Ernst 1855-1904 Baker 92
Jedlinski, Zbigniew Jan 1922- WhoScE 91-4
Jedruch, Jacek 1927- WhoE 93, WhoWor 93
Jedrychowski, Wieslaw Antoni 1932- WhoScE 91-4
Jedryka, Stanislaw 1933- DrEEuF
Jedrzejewski, Wlodzimierz 1923- WhoScE 91-4
Jedrzejowicz, Piotr 1942- WhoScE 91-4
Jedrzejowska, Hanna 1930- WhoScE 91-4
Jedwab, Jacques 1925- WhoScE 91-2
Jee, Justin Soonho 1951- WhoE 93, WhoEmL 93
Jeelof, Gerrit 1927- WhoAm 92
Jeep, Jeffery D. Law&B 92
Jeep, Johannes 1581?-1644 Baker 92
Jeevarathinam, R. 1921- WhoAsAP 91
Jeeves, Malcolm Alexander WhoScE 91-1
Jeeves, Terry 1922- ScF&FL 92
Jefcoat, James Robert 1943- St&PR 93
Jeff, Gloria Jean 1952- WhoAmW 93
Jeffares, A(lexander) Norman 1920- ConAu 39NR
Jeffares, Robert Travis 1935- St&PR 93
Jeffay, Henry 1927- WhoAm 92
Jeffcoat, Gaines R. 1922- St&PR 93
Jeffe, Huldah Cherry WhoAm 92
Jeffe, Sidney D. 1927- St&PR 93
Jeffe, Sidney David 1927- WhoAm 92
Jeffee, Saul d1991 BioIn 17
Jeffer, Edward Kenneth 1940- WhoSSW 93
Jefferds, Joseph Crosby, Jr. 1919- St&PR 93
Jefferds, Joseph Crosby, III 1944- St&PR 93
Jefferds, Mary Lee 1921- WhoAmW 93, WhoWor 93
Jefferds, Vincent H. 1916-1992 BioIn 17
Jefferds, Vincent Harris d1992 NewYTBS 92
Jefferies, D.G. WhoScE 91-1
Jefferies, Jack P. 1928- WhoAm 92
Jefferies, John Trevor 1925- WhoAm 92
Jefferies, Michael John 1941- WhoAm 92
Jefferies, Mike ScF&FL 92
Jefferies, Richard 1848-1887 BioIn 17, ScF&FL 92
Jefferies, Robert A., Jr. Law&B 92
Jefferies, Robert Aaron 1941- St&PR 93
Jefferies, Robert Aaron, Jr. 1941- WhoAm 92
Jefferis, Frank Dodgson 1952- WhoWor 93
Jeffers, Avanella Carmen 1922- WhoWrEP 92
Jeffers, Dale Welborn 1952- WhoSSW 93
Jeffers, Donald E. 1925- WhoAm 92
Jeffers, Gene 1948- WhoE 93
Jeffers, George W. 1897-1990 BioIn 17
Jeffers, H. Paul 1934- ScF&FL 92
Jeffers, Ida Pearle 1935- WhoAmW 93
Jeffers, J.N.R. WhoScE 91-1
Jeffers, Jerome L. Law&B 92
Jeffers, John James 1937- St&PR 93
Jeffers, John Robinson 1887-1962 BioIn 17
Jeffers, Michael Bogue 1940- St&PR 93, WhoAm 92
Jeffers, Robinson 1887-1962 BioIn 17, MagSAmL [port], WorLitC [port]
Jeffers, Susan ChlBIID [port]
Jeffers, Susan 1942- MajAI [port], SmATA 70 [port]
Jeffers, Suzanne 1949- WhoAmW 93
Jeffers, Velma M. BioIn 17
Jefferson, Beatrice W. AmWomPl
Jefferson, "Blind Lemon" 1897-1929 Baker 92
Jefferson, Carter BioIn 17
Jefferson, Cheryl May 1954- WhoAmW 93
Jefferson, D.A. WhoScE 91-1
Jefferson, Eddie 1918-1979 BioIn 17
Jefferson, Edward Graham 1921- St&PR 93
Jefferson, James Walter 1937- WhoAm 92
Jefferson, John Daniel 1948- WhoWor 93
Jefferson, John H. 1947- St&PR 93
Jefferson, Kristin Marie 1947- WhoAmW 93, WhoEmL 93
Jefferson, Letitia Gibson 1937- WhoAmW 93
Jefferson, Lila Rae 1953- WhoEmL 93
Jefferson, Martha Wayles Skelton 1748-1782 BioIn 17
Jefferson, Melvin Dorsey 1922- WhoAm 92
Jefferson, Paul Roger Law&B 92
Jefferson, Peter Augustus 1928- WhoAm 92
Jefferson, Roland MiSFD 9

Jefferson, Sandra Traylor 1942- WhoAmW 93, WhoSSW 93, WhoWor 93
Jefferson, Thomas 1743-1826 BioIn 17, OxCSupC, PolPar
Jefferson, Thomas 1941- DcCPCAm
Jefferson, Tommy Payton 1943- St&PR 93
Jefferson, Wayne 1948- WhoAm 92
Jefferson, William BioIn 17
Jefferson, William F. 1949- St&PR 93
Jefferson, William Harrison 1929- St&PR 93
Jefferson, William J. 1947- CngDr 91, WhoAm 92, WhoSSW 93
Jefferson, William Jackson 1929- St&PR 93
Jeffers Wikle, Margaret 1961- WhoAmW 93
Jeffery, A.M. Law&B 92
Jeffery, Alan G. 1938- St&PR 93
Jeffery, David Henry 1963- WhoEmL 93
Jeffery, Donald B. 1927- St&PR 93
Jeffery, G. ScF&FL 92
Jeffery, Geoffrey Marron 1919- WhoAm 92
Jeffery, George Harold 1909- WhoWor 93
Jeffery, Ivan L. 1946- St&PR 93
Jeffery, Jonathan WhoScE 91-1
Jeffery, Joseph 1907- St&PR 93
Jeffery, Maria Aoling Chea 1962- WhoAmW 93, WhoEmL 93, WhoSSW 93, WhoWor 93
Jeffery, Maurice Stanley 1932- St&PR 93
Jeffery, Peter Grant 1953- WhoAm 92
Jeffery, Richard P., Jr. 1932- St&PR 93
Jeffery, William D. Law&B 92
Jeffery, William Richard 1944- WhoAm 92
Jefferys, William Hamilton, III 1940- WhoAm 92
Jeffes, James Henry Elliston WhoScE 91-1
Jeffett, Frank Asbury 1927- WhoAm 92
Jeffett, Nancy Pearce 1928- WhoSSW 93
Jefford, Charles William 1929- WhoScE 91-4
Jeffords, Edward Alan 1945- WhoSSW 93
Jeffords, James M. 1934- CngDr 91
Jeffords, James Merrill 1934- WhoAm 92, WhoE 93
Jeffords, Walter M. d1990 BioIn 17
Jeffrey, Alan WhoScE 91-1
Jeffrey, Charles Alan 1950- WhoEmL 93
Jeffrey, Charles Cahill 1944- WhoE 93
Jeffrey, Clyde Grey, Jr. 1929- WhoSSW 93
Jeffrey, Francis 1773-1850 BioIn 17
Jeffrey, Glenn W. 1946- St&PR 93
Jeffrey, John Orval 1963- WhoWor 93
Jeffrey, Louis Robert 1927- St&PR 93
Jeffrey, Nan Coggeshall 1949- WhoWrEP 92
Jeffrey, Noela Mary 1941- WhoAmW 93
Jeffrey, Penelope S. 1944- WhoAmW 93
Jeffrey, Peter Law&B 92
Jeffrey, Robert Campbell 1927- WhoAm 92, WhoWor 93
Jeffrey, Robert George, Jr. 1933- WhoAm 92
Jeffrey, Shirley Ruthann 1936- WhoSSW 93
Jeffrey, Terry D. Law&B 92
Jeffrey, Thomas E. 1947- ConAu 136
Jeffrey, Thomas W. Law&B 92
Jeffrey, Walter Leslie 1908- WhoAm 92
Jeffrey, William Alan 1960- WhoEmL 93
Jeffreys, Alec John WhoScE 91-1
Jeffreys, Anne 1923- SweetSg C [port]
Jeffreys, Charles Wayne 1945- WhoSSW 93
Jeffreys, Elystan Geoffrey 1926- WhoAm 92, WhoSSW 93
Jeffreys, George c. 1610-1685 Baker 92
Jeffreys, Margaret Villar 1953- WhoAmW 93, WhoEmL 93, WhoSSW 93
Jeffries, Betty WhoWrEP 92
Jeffries, Carol Jean 1957- WhoAmW 93
Jeffries, Carson Dunning 1922- WhoAm 92
Jeffries, Charles Dean 1929- WhoAm 92
Jeffries, Don 1940- ConAu 137
Jeffries, Donald George 1934- St&PR 93
Jeffries, Donald James WhoScE 91-1
Jeffries, Essie Mae 1947- WhoAmW 93
Jeffries, Gary A. Law&B 92
Jeffries, Graham ScF&FL 92
Jeffries, Leonard, Jr. BioIn 17
Jeffries, Lionel 1926- MiSFD 9, QDrFCA 92 [port]
Jeffries, Marsha Denell 1954- WhoAmW 93
Jeffries, McChesney Hill 1922- WhoAm 92
Jeffries, Michael J. St&PR 93
Jeffries, R.J. 1923- St&PR 93
Jeffries, Robert Alan 1933- WhoAm 92
Jeffries, Robert Joseph 1923- WhoAm 92
Jeffries, Ross Edwin, Jr. Law&B 92
Jeffries, Shannon 1963- BioIn 17
Jeffries, Thomas A. 1954- St&PR 93
Jeffries, William Patrick WhoAsAP 91
Jeffris, Ronald Duane 1937- WhoAm 92
Jeffry, William A. Law&B 92
Jeffs, G.W. 1925- St&PR 93
Jeffs, Thomas Hamilton, II 1938- St&PR 93, WhoAm 92
Jeffs, Wallace E. 1926- WhoIns 93
Jeffus, James T. Law&B 92
Jeftic, Ljubomir Mile 1936- WhoUN 92, WhoWor 93
Jegasothy, Brian Vasanthakumar 1943- WhoAm 92
Jegede, Victor Adebayo 1944- St&PR 93
Jegen, Carol Frances 1925- WhoAmW 93
Jegen, Lawrence A., III 1934- WhoAm 92
Jegla, Dorothy Eldredge 1939- WhoAmW 93
Jeglitsch, Friedrich 1930- WhoScE 91-4
Jehan des Murs Baker 92
Jehin, Frantz 1839-1899 Baker 92
Jehin-Prume, Frantz 1839-1899 Baker 92
Jehl, Louis C. 1924- St&PR 93
Jehle, Michael Edward 1954- St&PR 93, WhoAm 92, WhoEmL 93
Jehlen, Patricia D. 1943- WhoAmW 93
Jehn, Hermann Alfred 1937- WhoWor 93
Jeitschko, Wolfgang K. 1936- WhoScE 91-3
Jeitschko, Wolfgang Karl 1936- WhoWor 93
Jekel, Benita D'Andrea 1934- St&PR 93
Jekel, James Franklin 1934- WhoAm 92
Jekel, Pamela L. 1948- WhoWrEP 92
Jeknavorian, Aram A. 1939- St&PR 93
Jekot, Edward Joseph, Sr. 1939- WhoE 93
Jekyll, Gertrude 1843-1932 BioIn 17
Jelalian, Albert V. 1933- WhoE 93, WhoWor 93
Jelasko, Michael Joseph 1949- WhoE 93
Jelavich, Barbara 1923- WhoAm 92
Jelen, Janos 1955- WhoUN 92
Jelenik, Otto John 1940- WhoE 93
Jelenski, Andrzej WhoScE 91-4
Jelensperger, Francis J. 1943- WhoAm 92
Jelic, Milan 1944- DrEEuF
Jelich, Vincenz 1596-c. 1636 Baker 92
Jelicic, Vincenz 1596-c. 1636 Baker 92
Jelin, Stephen Jacob 1934- WhoAm 92
Jelinek, Frantisek 1933- WhoScE 91-4
Jelinek, Frederick 1932- WhoAm 92
Jelinek, Hanns 1901-1969 Baker 92
Jelinek, Hans d1992 NewYTBS 92
Jelinek, Hans 1910-1992 BioIn 17
Jelinek, John Joseph 1955- WhoAm 92
Jelinek, Josef Emil 1928- WhoAm 92
Jelinek, Josef J. 1934- WhoScE 91-4
Jelinek, Otto John 1940- WhoAm 92
Jelinek, Patricia Boyd 1929- WhoAmW 93
Jelinek, Richard C. St&PR 93
Jelinek, Richard Jan 1934- WhoScE 91-4
Jelinek, Robert 1929- WhoAm 92
Jelinek-Fink, P. WhoScE 91-3
Jeljaszewicz, Janusz 1930- WhoScE 91-4
Jelks, Edward Baker 1922- WhoAm 92
Jellema, Rod(erick) Hartigh 1927- WhoWrEP 92
Jellenc, Lynn Pace 1958- WhoSSW 93
Jellet, James Morgan 1940- WhoAm 92
Jellett, Mainie 1897-1944 BioIn 17
Jelley, Annette Lisa 1961- St&PR 93
Jellicoe, Geoffrey Alan 1900- BioIn 17
Jellicoe, John Rushworth 1859-1935 DcTwHis, HarEnMi
Jellicorse, John Lee 1937- WhoAm 92
Jelliffe, Charles Gordon 1914- WhoAm 92
Jelliffe, Roger Woodham 1929- WhoAm 92
Jellinek, Adolf 1821-1893 BioIn 17
Jellinek, George 1919- Baker 92, WhoAm 92
Jellinek, Harry 1924- WhoScE 91-4
Jellinek, Roger 1938- WhoAm 92, WhoWrEP 92
Jellinger, Kurt 1931- WhoScE 91-4
Jellison, Anne Doherty 1950- WhoAmW 93
Jelloun, Tahar ben ScF&FL 92
Jelloun, Tahar ben 1944- BioIn 17
Jellovitz, John Charles 1942- St&PR 93
Jellows, Tracy Patrick 1951- WhoE 93
Jelyotte, Pierre 1713-1797 OxDcOp
Jemaa, Mohamed Ben BioIn 17
Jemelian, John Nazar 1933- WhoAm 92
Jemison, Cheryl Lynne 1959- WhoEmL 93
Jemison, Don Lee Law&B 92
Jemison, Frank Zimmerman, Jr. 1948- St&PR 93
Jemison, John Snow, III 1949- St&PR 93
Jemison, Mae C. BioIn 17
Jemison, Mae C. 1956- AfrAmBi [port], News 93-1 [port]
Jemison, Mae Carol 1956- NewYTBS 92 [port], WhoAmW 93
Jemison, Mary 1743-1833 BioIn 17
Jemison, Steven W. Law&B 92
Jemison, Theodore Judson 1918- WhoAm 92
Jemmott, Elizabeth Joy 1941- WhoSSW 93
Jemnitz, Sandor (Alexander) 1890-1963 Baker 92
Jemut Masing, James 1949- WhoAsAP 91
Jen, Enoch C. 1951- St&PR 93
Jen, Frank Chifeng 1931- WhoAm 92, WhoE 93
Jen, Gish 1955- ConLC 70 [port]
Jen, Kai-Lin Catherine 1949- WhoEmL 93
Jena, Ruth Michaelis- 1905-1989 BioIn 17
Jenckes, Joseph S. 1935- St&PR 93
Jenckes, Virginia Ellis 1877-1976 BioIn 17
Jencks, Christopher Sandys 1936- WhoAm 92
Jencks, Gardner 1907- Baker 92
Jencks, William Platt 1927- WhoAm 92
Jenco, Lawrence BioIn 17
Jenden, Donald James 1926- WhoAm 92
Jenders, Thomas 1942- St&PR 93
Jendritzky, Gerd 1940- WhoScE 91-3
Jene, Joanne 1935- WhoAmW 93
Jenefsky, Jack 1919- WhoWor 93
Jenes, Theodore George, Jr. 1930- WhoAm 92
Jeney, Andras 1934- WhoScE 91-4
Jeney, Zoltan 1943- Baker 92
Jeng, Chawn-Yaw 1956- WhoEmL 93
Jenifer, Franklyn G. BioIn 17
Jenifer, Franklyn Green WhoE 93
Jenior, Mary-Margaret WhoAmW 93
Jenkin, Douglas Alan 1932- WhoSSW 93
Jenkin, Graham Thomas 1947- WhoWor 93
Jenkin, Len ScF&FL 92
Jenkins, Adelbert Howard 1934- WhoE 93
Jenkins, Alan Bradford 1936- St&PR 93
Jenkins, Albert Felton, Jr. 1941- WhoAm 92
Jenkins, Alexander, III 1934- St&PR 93, WhoAm 92
Jenkins, Alice 1887-1967 BioIn 17
Jenkins, Allen 1890-1974 QDrFCA 92 [port]
Jenkins, Anne Elizabeth Green 1944- WhoAmW 93
Jenkins, Anthony Charles 1956- WhoE 93
Jenkins, Arthur D. 1897-1988 BioIn 17
Jenkins, Aubrey Dennis WhoScE 91-1
Jenkins, Aubrey Dennis 1927- WhoWor 93
Jenkins, B. Larry 1938- St&PR 93
Jenkins, Barry Glenn 1952- WhoSSW 93
Jenkins, Benjamin Larry 1938- WhoAm 92, WhoIns 93
Jenkins, Billie Beasley 1943- WhoAmW 93
Jenkins, Brenda Gwenetta 1949- WhoAmW 93
Jenkins, Britt 1943- St&PR 93
Jenkins, Bruce Sterling 1927- WhoAm 92
Jenkins, Carl Anthony 1958- WhoSSW 93
Jenkins, Carrell Ray 1930- WhoAm 92
Jenkins, Carson Lewis WhoScE 91-1
Jenkins, Charla R. 1947- WhoAmW 93
Jenkins, Charles Francis 1940- WhoSSW 93
Jenkins, Charles Lamont 1934- BiDAMSp 1989
Jenkins, Charles Steven 1948- WhoSSW 93
Jenkins, Clara Barnes 1943- WhoAm 92, WhoAmW 93, WhoSSW 93, WhoWor 93
Jenkins, Connie Webster 1955- WhoSSW 93
Jenkins, Cynthia BioIn 17
Jenkins, Daniel Edwards, Jr. 1916- WhoAm 92
Jenkins, David 1848-1915 Baker 92
Jenkins, David 1936- BioIn 17
Jenkins, David A. Law&B 92, WhoAm 92
Jenkins, David A. 1957- St&PR 93
Jenkins, David B. WhoAm 92
Jenkins, David George WhoScE 91-1
Jenkins, David L. 1931- ConAu 136
Jenkins, David Malvern 1936- WhoScE 91-3
Jenkins, Dennis Robert 1957- WhoSSW 93
Jenkins, Donald John 1931- WhoAm 92
Jenkins, E. Clark 1940- St&PR 93
Jenkins, Ed 1933- CngDr 91
Jenkins, Edgar Lanier 1933- WhoAm 92, WhoSSW 93
Jenkins, Edith A(rnstein) 1913- ConAu 137
Jenkins, Ernest B. 1934- St&PR 93
Jenkins, Everett Law&B 92
Jenkins, Everett Wilbur, Jr. 1953- WhoWor 93
Jenkins, Ferguson 1943- AfrAmBi, BioIn 17
Jenkins, Ferguson Arthur 1943- BiDAMSp 1989
Jenkins, Ferguson Arthur, Jr. 1943- WhoAm 92
Jenkins, Floyd T. 1942- St&PR 93
Jenkins, Frances Owens 1924- WhoAmW 93
Jenkins, Geoffrey 1920- ScF&FL 92
Jenkins, George 1908- ConTFT 10, WhoAm 92
Jenkins, George Charles 1927- WhoWor 93
Jenkins, George P. 1915- St&PR 93
Jenkins, Gerald R. Law&B 92
Jenkins, Glenna Glee 1918- WhoWrEP 92
Jenkins, Gloria Delores WhoAmW 93
Jenkins, Gordon 1910-1984 Baker 92
Jenkins, Harriet G. BioIn 17
Jenkins, Harry ScF&FL 92
Jenkins, Hayes Alan Law&B 92
Jenkins, Hayes Alan 1933- BioIn 17
Jenkins, Helen Ann 1945- WhoWor 93
Jenkins, Helen Heath 1952- WhoEmL 93
Jenkins, Helen Williams 1921- WhoSSW 93
Jenkins, Henry Alfred 1952- WhoAsAP 91
Jenkins, Herbert T. d1990 BioIn 17
Jenkins, Hester Donaldson 1869-1941 AmWomPl
Jenkins, Howard 1951- WhoSSW 93
Jenkins, Hugh Oliver WhoScE 91-1
Jenkins, J.M. 1942- St&PR 93
Jenkins, J.S.B. 1943- St&PR 93
Jenkins, James Allister 1923- WhoAm 92
Jenkins, James Jerome 1923- WhoSSW 93
Jenkins, James L. 1939- St&PR 93
Jenkins, James P. 1948- St&PR 93
Jenkins, James Pollock 1948- WhoAm 92
Jenkins, James Robert Law&B 92
Jenkins, James Robert 1945- WhoAm 92
Jenkins, James Sherwood, Jr. 1941- WhoSSW 93
Jenkins, James Thomas 1951- St&PR 93
Jenkins, James William 1953- WhoWor 93
Jenkins, Jane BioIn 17
Jenkins, Jane Amy 1965- WhoE 93
Jenkins, Jay Law&B 92
Jenkins, Jean Alice 1938- WhoAsAP 91
Jenkins, Jerry Bruce 1949- WhoWrEP 92
Jenkins, Jesse Frank 1918- St&PR 93
Jenkins, John BioIn 17
Jenkins, John 1592-1678 Baker 92
Jenkins, John A. 1950- ConAu 139
Jenkins, John Anthony 1926- WhoAm 92
Jenkins, John Curtis Law&B 92
Jenkins, John E. Law&B 92
Jenkins, John Edgar 1925- St&PR 93
Jenkins, John Edward, Sr. 1914- St&PR 93
Jenkins, John Reese 1952- WhoAm 92
Jenkins, John Smith 1932- WhoAm 92
Jenkins, John T. Law&B 92
Jenkins, John Tierce 1920- WhoWrEP 92
Jenkins, Johnny SoulM
Jenkins, Joy BioIn 17
Jenkins, Kenneth Vincent WhoAm 92, WhoE 93
Jenkins, Kevin J. WhoAm 92
Jenkins, Larry E. 1941- St&PR 93
Jenkins, Lawrence Eugene 1933- WhoAm 92
Jenkins, Len 1943- WhoWrEP 92
Jenkins, Leroy 1932- Baker 92, WhoAm 92
Jenkins, Lew BioIn 17
Jenkins, Lisa L. 1957- St&PR 93
Jenkins, Lorena Michelle BioIn 17
Jenkins, Louis 1947- WhoSSW 93
Jenkins, Louise Sherman 1943- WhoAmW 93
Jenkins, Lucy D. AmWomPl
Jenkins, Lyll Becerra De DcAmChF 1985
Jenkins, M. T. Pepper 1917- WhoAm 92
Jenkins, Mabel Pickford d1991 BioIn 17
Jenkins, Margaret Aikens 1925- WhoAmW 93
Jenkins, Margaret Bunting 1935- WhoAm 92, WhoSSW 93
Jenkins, Margaret L. BioIn 17
Jenkins, Marie Hooper 1929- WhoSSW 93
Jenkins, Marjorie C. 1911- WhoWrEP 92
Jenkins, Mark 1958- ConAu 137
Jenkins, Marshall Whitfield 1952- WhoEmL 93, WhoSSW 93
Jenkins, Mary B. Law&B 92
Jenkins, Maurice G. Law&B 92
Jenkins, Melody Stinson 1951- WhoEmL 93, WhoSSW 93
Jenkins, Michael MiSFD 9
Jenkins, Michael Austin 1942- WhoAm 92
Jenkins, Michael Glen Law&B 92
Jenkins, Michael Romilly Heald 1936- WhoWor 93
Jenkins, Myra Ellen 1916- WhoAmW 93

Jenkins, Neil E. Law&B 92
Jenkins, Neil Edmund 1949- St&PR 93, WhoAm 92
Jenkins, Newell (Owen) 1915- Baker 92
Jenkins, Orville Wesley 1913- WhoAm 92
Jenkins, Patrick 1955- SmATA 72 [port]
Jenkins, Paul 1923- WhoAm 92
Jenkins, Paul N. 1939- St&PR 93
Jenkins, Paul R. 1942- WhoWrEP 92
Jenkins, Peter d1992 NewYTBS 92
Jenkins, Peter 1934-1992 BioIn 17
Jenkins, Peter Edwin 1940- WhoAm 92
Jenkins, Phillip L. 1923- St&PR 93
Jenkins, R. St&PR 93, WhoScE 91-1
Jenkins, R.H. 1933- WhoScE 91-1
Jenkins, R. Lee 1929- St&PR 93
Jenkins, Rachel WhoScE 91-1
Jenkins, Rebecca Law&B 92
Jenkins, Richard Lee 1931- WhoAm 92
Jenkins, Richard N. 1944- St&PR 93
Jenkins, Robert Berryman 1950- WhoEmL 93, WhoSSW 93, WhoWor 93
Jenkins, Robert D. 1929- St&PR 93
Jenkins, Robert Ellsworth, Jr. 1942- WhoSSW 93
Jenkins, Robert Harrington 1943- St&PR 93
Jenkins, Robert Nesbit 1951- WhoE 93
Jenkins, Robert Spurgeon 1921- WhoAm 92
Jenkins, Rodger Kiley 1938- St&PR 93
Jenkins, Rowland Harris WhoScE 91-1
Jenkins, Roy 1920- ColdWar 1 [port]
Jenkins, Roy Harris 1920- DcTwHis, WhoWor 93
Jenkins, Ruben Lee 1929- WhoAm 92
Jenkins, Ruth L. AmWomPl
Jenkins, Sally BioIn 17
Jenkins, Samuel L. 1928- St&PR 93
Jenkins, Sandra L. 1946- St&PR 93
Jenkins, Scott R. 1949- St&PR 93
Jenkins, Shirley BioIn 17
Jenkins, Shirley d1991 NewYTBS 92
Jenkins, Simon David 1943- WhoWor 93
Jenkins, Speight 1937- WhoAm 92
Jenkins, Stephen C. 1937- St&PR 93
Jenkins, Stephen Carl 1937- WhoSSW 93
Jenkins, Steven Marvin 1949- WhoSSW 93
Jenkins, Thom d1991 BioIn 17
Jenkins, Thomas A. 1942- St&PR 93
Jenkins, Thomas Canfield, IV 1949- WhoEmL 93, WhoSSW 93
Jenkins, Thomas Joseph Law&B 92
Jenkins, Thomas Llewellyn 1927- WhoAm 92
Jenkins, Thomas M. Law&B 92
Jenkins, Thomas Michael 1951- St&PR 93
Jenkins, Timothy BioIn 17
Jenkins, W.M. Peter 1954- St&PR 93
Jenkins, Wardell Lewis 1940- WhoE 93
Jenkins, Warren C. 1925- St&PR 93
Jenkins, Warren Charles 1925- WhoAm 92
Jenkins, Wendell L. St&PR 93
Jenkins, Will F. ScF&FL 92
Jenkins, Will F. 1896-1975 BioIn 17
Jenkins, William 1920- St&PR 93
Jenkins, William Atwell 1922- WhoAm 92
Jenkins, William Kenneth 1947- WhoAm 92
Jenkins, William Lawrence 1943- St&PR 93
Jenkins, William Maxwell 1919- WhoAm 92
Jenkins, William McLaren WhoScE 91-1
Jenkins, William Nelson 1928- St&PR 93
Jenkins, William R. St&PR 93
Jenkins-Hadden, Julie Law&B 92
Jenkinson, Anthony d1611 Expl 93
Jenkinson, Judith Apsey 1943- WhoAmW 93, WhoWor 93
Jenko, Davorin 1835-1914 Baker 92
Jenko, Jerome J. Law&B 92
Jenks, Amabel AmWomPl
Jenks, Brenda 1943- WhoE 93
Jenks, Bruce F.E. WhoUN 92
Jenks, Carolyn Boyd 1935- WhoWrEP 92
Jenks, Downing Bland 1915- WhoAm 92
Jenks, George Merritt 1929- WhoE 93
Jenks, George S. 1927- St&PR 93
Jenks, George Schuyler 1927- WhoAm 92
Jenks, Homer Simeon 1914- WhoAm 92
Jenks, John Bernard 1937- St&PR 93
Jenks, Michael WhoScE 91-1
Jenks, Sarah Isabel 1913- WhoAmW 93
Jenks, Schuyler T. 1956- St&PR 93
Jenks, Stephen 1772-1856 Baker 92
Jenks, Thomas Edward 1929- WhoAm 92
Jenks, Tom 1950- ConAu 137
Jenks, William P. 1957- St&PR 93
Jenks-Davies, Kathryn Ryburn 1916- WhoAmW 93, WhoSSW 93
Jenne, Kirk Law&B 92
Jenneke, L.E. 1923- St&PR 93
Jennekens, Jon Hubert 1932- WhoUN 92
Jenner, Bruce 1949- WhoAm 92
Jenner, Edward Levant 1918- WhoE 93
Jenner, Frederick Alexander WhoScE 91-1
Jenner, Frederick Alexander 1927- WhoWor 93
Jenner, Gustav 1865-1920 Baker 92
Jenner, Janann V. ScF&FL 92
Jenner, Michael Ralph 1951- WhoWor 93
Jenner, Peter WhoScE 91-1
Jenner, Ray W. 1952- St&PR 93
Jenner, William Alexander 1915- WhoWor 93
Jennerich, Edward John 1945- WhoAm 92
Jenness, Diamond 1886-1969 IntDcAn
Jenness, Mary d1947 AmWomPl
Jenness, Phyllis 1922- WhoAm 92
Jennett, J. Charles 1940- WhoAm 92
Jennett, Sheila WhoScE 91-1
Jennett, Shirley Shimmick 1937- WhoAmW 93
Jennewein, James Joseph 1929- WhoAm 92
Jenney, Jack H. 1933- St&PR 93
Jenney, Neil 1945- BioIn 17
Jenney, Neil Franklin, Jr. 1945- WhoAm 92
Jenney, Robert M. 1918- St&PR 93
Jenney-West, Roxanne Elizabeth 1960- WhoAmW 93, WhoEmL 93
Jenni, Donald Alison 1932- WhoAm 92
Jenni, Leo WhoScE 91-4
Jennik, Susan Marie 1952- WhoE 93
Jennings, A. Drue WhoAm 92
Jennings, A. Drue 1946- St&PR 93
Jennings, Alan WhoScE 91-1
Jennings, Albert L. 1934- St&PR 93
Jennings, Alfred Higson, Jr. 1959- WhoE 93
Jennings, Alston 1917- WhoAm 92, WhoSSW 93, WhoWor 93
Jennings, Alvin R. d1990 BioIn 17
Jennings, Anne M. 1931- WhoAmW 93
Jennings, Barbara Jean 1951- WhoSSW 93
Jennings, Bruce 1949- WhoE 93
Jennings, Burgess Hill 1903- WhoAm 92
Jennings, Carl Anthony 1944- St&PR 93
Jennings, Carol 1945- WhoE 93
Jennings, Charles Richard 1941- WhoE 93
Jennings, Coleman A. 1933- BioIn 17
Jennings, Coleman Alonzo 1933- WhoAm 92
Jennings, David Harry WhoScE 91-1
Jennings, David S. 1942- St&PR 93
Jennings, David Sheldon 1959- WhoSSW 93
Jennings, Dean Thomas 1951- WhoEmL 93
Jennings, Dennis Raymond 1942- WhoSSW 93
Jennings, Diane B. 1953- St&PR 93
Jennings, Donald Edward 1948- WhoE 93
Jennings, Donald Erb 1939- WhoE 93
Jennings, E.C., Jr. 1946- St&PR 93
Jennings, E. Paul, Jr. 1932- St&PR 93
Jennings, Edward Harrington 1937- WhoAm 92, WhoWor 93
Jennings, Elizabeth 1926- BioIn 17, WhoWor 93
Jennings, Elizabeth (Joan) 1926- ConAu 39NR
Jennings, Eulora M. AmWomPl
Jennings, Frank Gerard 1915- WhoAm 92
Jennings, Frank Louis WhoAm 92
Jennings, Fred Edward 1954- WhoEmL 93
Jennings, Frederic Beach, Jr. 1945- WhoE 93
Jennings, Frederick G. 1950- St&PR 93
Jennings, Gary ScF&FL 92
Jennings, Gerald Douglas 1945- WhoSSW 93
Jennings, Glenn A., Jr. Law&B 92
Jennings, Glenn Andrew 1951- WhoWor 93
Jennings, Glenn Ray 1949- St&PR 93
Jennings, Herbert Spencer 1868-1947 BioIn 17
Jennings, Isabel Yumol 1932- WhoAmW 93
Jennings, James Burnett 1940- St&PR 93
Jennings, James J., Jr. Law&B 92
Jennings, James K., Jr. 1941- St&PR 93
Jennings, James L. St&PR 93
Jennings, Jan ScF&FL 92
Jennings, Jerry D. 1940- WhoAm 92
Jennings, Jesse David 1909- IntDcAn, WhoAm 92
Jennings, Joanne Griffin 1942- WhoAmW 93
Jennings, John Robert Rogers 1937- WhoE 93
Jennings, Joseph Ashby 1920- WhoAm 92
Jennings, Joseph Leslie 1937- St&PR 93
Jennings, Karla Kublin 1968- WhoAmW 93
Jennings, Keith Robert WhoScE 91-1
Jennings, Kelly Stephen Law&B 92
Jennings, Lee Byron 1927- WhoAm 92
Jennings, Lynn BioIn 17, WhoAmW 93
Jennings, Madelyn Pulver 1934- St&PR 93, WhoAm 92, WhoAmW 93, WhoWor 93
Jennings, Marcella Grady 1920- WhoAmW 93, WhoWor 93
Jennings, Michael Alan Law&B 92
Jennings, Michael E. 1945- St&PR 93, WhoAm 92
Jennings, Myron Kent 1934- WhoAm 92
Jennings, Nancy Ann 1932- WhoAmW 93
Jennings, Napoleon Augustus 1856-1919 BioIn 17
Jennings, Norman S. 1945- WhoUN 92
Jennings, Patricia Carol 1959- WhoEmL 93
Jennings, Paul Christian 1936- WhoAm 92
Jennings, Peter 1938- BioIn 17, JrnUS
Jennings, Peter Charles 1938- WhoAm 92
Jennings, Phillip C. 1946- ScF&FL 92
Jennings, Ralph Edward, Jr. 1958- WhoEmL 93
Jennings, Ralph Merwin 1938- WhoE 93
Jennings, Regina BioIn 17
Jennings, Robert Burgess 1926- WhoAm 92, WhoSSW 93
Jennings, Robert G. 1938- St&PR 93
Jennings, Robert Lee 1946- WhoE 93
Jennings, Robert Yewdall 1913- WhoWor 93
Jennings, Robyn E. Law&B 92
Jennings, Roger L. 1940- St&PR 93
Jennings, Roger Lee 1940- WhoE 93
Jennings, Royce Merlyn 1920- St&PR 93
Jennings, Rubye Cooley 1930- WhoAmW 93
Jennings, Sharon Elizabeth 1947- WhoAmW 93
Jennings, Stephen Grant 1946- WhoAm 92
Jennings, Thomas C. 1940- St&PR 93
Jennings, Thomas Joseph Law&B 92
Jennings, Thomas P. 1947- St&PR 93
Jennings, Thomas Parks Law&B 92
Jennings, Thomas Parks 1947- WhoAm 92
Jennings, Toni 1949- WhoAmW 93
Jennings, Vivien Ann 1934- WhoAmW 93
Jennings, Vivien Lee 1945- WhoAmW 93
Jennings, Wanda Beth 1947- WhoEmL 93
Jennings, Warren E., Jr. 1928- WhoIns 93
Jennings, Waylon (Arnold) 1937- Baker 92
Jennings, William Bryan, Jr. 1939- WhoSSW 93
Jennings, Wynne R. 1950- St&PR 93
Jennings-Crowe, Candace Ann 1952- WhoAmW 93
Jennische, Per 1943- WhoScE 91-4
Jennison, C. S. ConAu 38NR, MajAI
Jennison, James S. 1934- St&PR 93
Jennison, John W. d1969? ScF&FL 92
Jennison, Peter Saxe 1922- WhoE 93, WhoWrEP 92
Jennrich, William Frank 1940- St&PR 93
Jenny, Susan A. Law&B 92
Jenoff, Marvyne 1942- WhoCanL 92
Jenrette, Richard H. BioIn 17
Jenrette, Richard Hampton 1929- St&PR 93, WhoAm 92
Jenrette, Thomas Shepard, Jr. 1946- WhoEmL 93, WhoSSW 93, WhoWor 93
Jens, Elizabeth Lee Shafer 1915- WhoWor 93
Jens, Walter 1923- WhoWor 93
Jensch, Peter Jurgen 1940- WhoScE 91-3
Jensen, A. Kris 1927- St&PR 93
Jensen, Adolf 1837-1879 Baker 92
Jensen, Adolf Ellegard 1899-1965 IntDcAn
Jensen, Adolph Robert 1915- WhoAm 92
Jensen, Ais Egede 1948- WhoWor 93
Jensen, Alvin L. 1930- St&PR 93
Jensen, Andrew Oden 1920- WhoSSW 93
Jensen, Anne Turner 1926- WhoAmW 93
Jensen, Arne 1938- WhoScE 91-2
Jensen, Arne Wilhelm Oluf 1951- WhoScE 91-3
Jensen, Arthur Seigfried 1917- WhoAm 92
Jensen, Barbara Elizabeth A. 1948- WhoAmW 93
Jensen, Barbara Wood 1927- WhoWor 93
Jensen, Bard Uri 1963- WhoWor 93
Jensen, Bill G. 1933- St&PR 93
Jensen, Birthe 1938- WhoScE 91-2
Jensen, Bjarne Sloth 1942- WhoWor 93
Jensen, Bruce H. 1931- WhoAm 92
Jensen, Burl C. 1937- St&PR 93
Jensen, Carol Ann 1951- WhoAmW 93
Jensen, Charles Patrick 1931- WhoE 93
Jensen, Charles S. d1990 BioIn 17
Jensen, Christian Reid 1940- WhoSSW 93, WhoWor 93
Jensen, Clayne R. 1930- WhoAm 92
Jensen, Craig William 1951- WhoEmL 93
Jensen, D. Clifford St&PR 93
Jensen, D. Lowell 1928- WhoAm 92
Jensen, Dale Alan 1949- WhoWrEP 92
Jensen, Dale Martin 1949- St&PR 93
Jensen, Daniel Reuben 1947- St&PR 93
Jensen, Daryl D. 1939- St&PR 93
Jensen, David Alan 1946- St&PR 93
Jensen, David Elden 1921- St&PR 93
Jensen, David H. 1950- St&PR 93
Jensen, David R. 1942- St&PR 93
Jensen, David Warren 1956- WhoE 93
Jensen, Deborah Ann 1952- WhoAmW 93
Jensen, Delores 1944- WhoAmW 93
Jensen, Dick Leroy 1930- WhoAm 92
Jensen, Don A. Law&B 92
Jensen, Don Arlen 1935- St&PR 93, WhoAm 92
Jensen, Doris J. 1939- WhoAmW 93
Jensen, Douglas St&PR 93
Jensen, Dwight William 1934- WhoWrEP 92
Jensen, E. Henning 1933- WhoScE 91-2
Jensen, Eberhart 1922- WhoScE 91-4
Jensen, Edmund Paul 1937- St&PR 93, WhoAm 92
Jensen, Ejner J. 1937- ConAu 138, ScF&FL 92
Jensen, Elwood Vernon 1920- WhoAm 92
Jensen, Eric Finn 1927- WhoAm 92
Jensen, Erik Henning 1933- WhoUN 92
Jensen, Ernest 1915- WhoWor 93
Jensen, Floyd A. Law&B 92
Jensen, George Aaron 1934- St&PR 93
Jensen, Gerald L. 1940- St&PR 93
Jensen, Gerald Randolph 1924- WhoWrEP 92
Jensen, Grady Edmonds 1922- WhoAm 92
Jensen, Gustav 1843-1895 Baker 92
Jensen, Gwendolyn Evans 1936- WhoAm 92, WhoAmW 93
Jensen, H.E. Kresten 1939- WhoScE 91-2
Jensen, Hanne Margrete 1935- WhoAmW 93
Jensen, Hans Arne 1936- WhoScE 91-2
Jensen, Hans Jorgen 1929- WhoWor 93
Jensen, Hans-Peter 1921- WhoScE 91-3
Jensen, Hans Peter 1943- WhoScE 91-2
Jensen, Harlan Ellsworth 1915- WhoAm 92, WhoWor 93
Jensen, Harold Leroy 1926- WhoAm 92
Jensen, Harold Sherwood 1930- WhoAm 92
Jensen, Helen 1919- WhoAmW 93
Jensen, Helene Wickstrom 1929- WhoE 93
Jensen, Henning Holst 1944- WhoWor 93
Jensen, Homer 1914-1991 BioIn 17
Jensen, J. David 1948- St&PR 93
Jensen, J. Fris 1927- WhoScE 91-2
Jensen, Jack Eugene 1927-1982 BiDAMSp 1989
Jensen, Jack Michael 1951- WhoAm 92
Jensen, Jakki Renee 1959- WhoAmW 93
Jensen, James B. Law&B 92
Jensen, James Herbert 1906- WhoAm 92
Jensen, James Robert 1922- WhoAm 92
Jensen, Jens Karl 1938- WhoScE 91-2
Jensen, Jim 1958- BioIn 17
Jensen, Jodeen Marie 1964- WhoEmL 93
Jensen, Joel E. 1935- St&PR 93
Jensen, John E. 1928- St&PR 93
Jensen, John Eric Law&B 92
Jensen, Julius, III 1933- St&PR 93
Jensen, Kaj Frank 1947- WhoScE 91-2
Jensen, Karl Erik St&PR 93
Jensen, Katherine Kemp 1955- WhoAmW 93, WhoE 93, WhoEmL 93
Jensen, Kenneth R. 1914- St&PR 93
Jensen, Kent Charles 1962- WhoSSW 93
Jensen, Kris 1953- ScF&FL 92
Jensen, Lars Moller 1952- WhoScE 91-2
Jensen, Laura Linnea 1948- WhoWrEP 92
Jensen, Laust 1914- WhoWor 93
Jensen, Lester A. Law&B 92
Jensen, Loren Ann 1953- WhoAmW 93, WhoEmL 93, WhoWor 93
Jensen, Loren D. 1937- St&PR 93
Jensen, Louis 1943- BioIn 17
Jensen, Ludvig (Paul) Irgens Baker 92
Jensen, Marie AmWomPl
Jensen, Marilyn Moore 1935- St&PR 93
Jensen, Marlene F. 1947- WhoAm 92
Jensen, Marvin Eli 1926- WhoAm 92
Jensen, Maxine Elizabeth 1919- WhoWrEP 92
Jensen, Melody R.J. Law&B 92
Jensen, Michael Charles 1934- WhoAm 92
Jensen, Michael Cole 1939- WhoAm 92
Jensen, Muriel 1945- WhoWrEP 92
Jensen, Niels 1949- WhoWor 93
Jensen, Niels Peter 1802-1846 Baker 92
Jensen, Norman Peter 1938- WhoAm 92
Jensen, O.A. 1924- WhoScE 91-2
Jensen, Olaf Myhre 1931- WhoScE 91-2
Jensen, Ole Moller 1944- WhoScE 91-2
Jensen, Oliver 1914- BioIn 17

Jensen, Oliver Ormerod 1914- WhoAm 92
Jensen, Owen Franklin, Jr. St&PR 93
Jensen, Owen Franklin, III 1950- St&PR 93
Jensen, Pamela Marie 1962- WhoAmW 93
Jensen, Patricia Ann Hurley 1946- WhoAmW 93
Jensen, Paul M. 1944- ScF&FL 92
Jensen, Peter J. 1939- St&PR 93
Jensen, Philip Bailey 1922- WhoE 93
Jensen, Polly BioIn 17
Jensen, Poul BioIn 17
Jensen, Poul Vagn 1943- WhoScE 91-2
Jensen, Ralph D. 1950- St&PR 93
Jensen, Regina Brunhild 1951- WhoAmW 93, WhoEmL 93, WhoWor 93
Jensen, Reuben Rolland 1920- WhoAm 92
Jensen, Ricard 1954- WhoSSW 93
Jensen, Richard Gerald 1951- WhoSSW 93
Jensen, Robert 1938-1990 BioIn 17
Jensen, Robert Granville 1935- WhoAm 92, WhoE 93
Jensen, Robert L. 1928- St&PR 93
Jensen, Robert Trygve 1922- WhoAm 92
Jensen, Roger A. 1939- St&PR 93
Jensen, Roger W. Law&B 92
Jensen, Roland J. 1929- St&PR 93
Jensen, Roland Jens 1929- WhoAm 92
Jensen, Ronald Ralph 1937- St&PR 93
Jensen, Ronnie Blaine 1950- WhoEmL 93
Jensen, Ruby Jean ScF&FL 92
Jensen, Russell P. 1953- St&PR 93
Jensen, Sam 1935- WhoAm 92
Jensen, Scott D. 1952- St&PR 93
Jensen, Sheryl Rufenacht 1956- WhoAmW 93, WhoEmL 93
Jensen, Soren Stistrup 1956- WhoE 93, WhoEmL 93, WhoWor 93
Jensen, Stanley A. 1924- St&PR 93
Jensen, Steven R. 1955- St&PR 93
Jensen, Susan Ann 1946- WhoAm 92, WhoE 93
Jensen, Teresa Elaine 1948- WhoAmW 93
Jensen, Thomas 1898-1963 Baker 92
Jensen, Thomas Edward Law&B 92
Jensen, Thomas H. 1932- St&PR 93
Jensen, Thomas S. 1956- St&PR 93
Jensen, Walter Edward 1937- WhoAm 92, WhoSSW 93
Jensen, William M. 1950- St&PR 93
Jensen-Moran, Joan Mary 1952- WhoAmW 93
Jensen-Savoie, Gayle 1960- WhoSSW 93
Jensh, Ronald Paul 1938- WhoAm 92
Jenson, Edith M. AmWomPl
Jenson, Hal Brockbank 1954- WhoSSW 93
Jenson, Jan K. 1946- WhoWrEP 92
Jenson, Jon Eberdt 1934- WhoAm 92
Jenson, Kathy LaVon 1943- WhoAmW 93
Jenson (Lockington), Dylana (Ruth) 1961- Baker 92
Jenson, Martin ScF&FL 92
Jenson, Nicolas dc. 1480 BioIn 17
Jenson, Pauline Marie 1927- WhoE 93
Jenson, Ronald Allen 1948- WhoEmL 93
Jenson, Taylor R. 1938- St&PR 93
Jenssen, Arthur H. 1923- St&PR 93
Jenssen, George W. St&PR 93
Jenssen, Paul Harold 1956- WhoE 93
Jentes, William Robert 1932- WhoAm 92
Jentoft, Arthur Philip 1927- St&PR 93
Jentsch, Stefan P. 1955- WhoScE 91-3
Jentz, Gaylord Adair 1931- WhoAm 92, WhoSSW 93, WhoWor 93
Jentz, Katharina Marianne 1968- WhoAmW 93
Jentzsch, Ric 1947- WhoWor 93
Jeon, Bang Nam 1954- WhoE 93, WhoEmL 93
Jeon, Kwang Wu 1934- WhoSSW 93
Jephson, Robert 1736-1803 BioIn 17
Jepperson, Thomas C. Law&B 92
Jeppesen, Henrik 1937- WhoScE 91-2
Jeppesen, K. Tad 1938- St&PR 93
Jeppesen, Knud (Christian) 1892-1974 Baker 92
Jeppesen, Susan Quandt 1954- WhoAmW 93
Jeppson, Buckley Carlos 1948- WhoE 93
Jeppson, Calvin W. 1933- St&PR 93
Jeppson, J.O. ScF&FL 92
Jeppson, Jay Herald 1926- WhoAm 92
Jeppson, John 1916- WhoAm 92, WhoE 93
Jepsen, Dale Edward Law&B 92
Jepsen, Jane Barry 1934- WhoE 93
Jepsen, Jonathan M. 1945- St&PR 93
Jepsen, Ole Bent 1936- WhoScE 91-2
Jepsen, Peter Lee 1952- WhoEmL 93
Jepsen, Roger William 1928- WhoAm 92
Jepsen-Lozano, Lisa 1952- WhoE 93
Jepson, C.D. WhoScE 91-1
Jepson, Christopher Mark Law&B 92
Jepson, Hans Godfrey 1936- WhoAm 92, WhoWor 93
Jepson, Helen 1904- Baker 92
Jepson, Helen Anna 1947- WhoEmL 93
Jepson, John Willisford 1931- St&PR 93
Jepson, Michael Harrop WhoScE 91-1
Jepson, Robert Scott, Jr. 1942- WhoAm 92, WhoWor 93
Jepson, W.B. WhoScE 91-1
Jepson-Young, Peter d1992 NewYTBS 92
Jeram, Anita 1965- SmATA 71 [port]
Jerauld, Gordon Otis 1921- St&PR 93
Jerauld, Margie A. AmWomPl
Jerd, R. Frank St&PR 93
Jerdee, Thomas Harlan 1927- WhoAm 92
Jeremiah BioIn 17
Jeremiah, Barbara Susanne Law&B 92
Jeremiah, Brian Philip WhoScE 91-1
Jeremiah, David Elmer 1934- WhoAm 92
Jeremias, Bohuslav 1859-1918 Baker 92, OxDcOp
Jeremias, Jaroslav 1889-1919 Baker 92, OxDcOp
Jeremias, Otakar 1892-1962 Baker 92, OxDcOp
Jeren, Tatjana 1941- WhoScE 91-4
Jerezano 1867-1912 BioIn 17
Jerge, Dale Robert 1951- WhoE 93, WhoEmL 93
Jerge, Marie Charlotte 1952- WhoAmW 93, WhoEmL 93
Jergens, Adele 1917- SweetSg D [port]
Jergens, Andrew MacAoidh 1935- WhoSSW 93
Jergens, Phillip ScF&FL 92
Jerger, Alfred 1889-1976 Baker 92, OxDcOp
Jerger, Edward William 1922- WhoAm 92
Jeri, Federico Raul 1918- WhoWor 93
Jeris, John Stratis 1930- WhoE 93
Jeritza, Maria 1887-1982 Baker 92, IntDcOp, OxDcOp
Jerka-Dziadosz, Maria 1938- WhoScE 91-4
Jerkins, Catherine A. 1959- St&PR 93
Jerkins, Ken M. 1944- St&PR 93
Jerkku, Jorma Severi 1938- WhoWor 93
Jerlstrom, Bernard J. Law&B 92
Jermansky, Gary 1960- WhoE 93
Jermer, P. Joran A. 1950- WhoScE 91-4
Jermyn, Helen Williams 1957- WhoEmL 93, WhoSSW 93
Jermyn, John William, III 1951- WhoEmL 93
Jerndal, Jens 1934- WhoWor 93
Jerne, Niels Kaj 1911- WhoWor 93
Jerner, R. Craig 1938- WhoSSW 93
Jernigan, Antoinette D. 1959- WhoAmW 93
Jernigan, Bob 1928- WhoAm 92
Jernigan, Candy d1991 BioIn 17
Jernigan, Harry 1946- WhoEmL 93
Jernigan, Helen Chastain 1925- WhoAmW 93
Jernigan, Kenneth 1926- WhoAm 92
Jernigan, Marian Sue 1940- WhoAmW 93
Jernigan, Michael O'Neal 1953- WhoEmL 93
Jernigan, Ralph W. 1946- St&PR 93
Jernigan, Tamara E. 1959- WhoAmW 93
Jernigan, William Wade 1935- WhoSSW 93
Jernstedt, Richard Don 1947- WhoAm 92
Jerolimic, Nevio P. 1950- St&PR 93
Jerome 331?-420 OxDcByz
Jerome, Saint d419? BioIn 17
Jerome, Albert D. 1942- St&PR 93
Jerome, Albert David 1942- WhoAm 92
Jerome, Elizabeth Rose 1961- WhoAmW 93
Jerome, Fred Louis 1939- WhoAm 92
Jerome, Frederick S. Law&B 92
Jerome, Geraldine Peck 1931- WhoAmW 93
Jerome, James Alexander 1933- WhoAm 92, WhoE 93
Jerome, Jeff BioIn 17
Jerome, Jennie 1854-1921 BioIn 17
Jerome, Jerome K. 1859-1927 BioIn 17, ScF&FL 92
Jerome, Jerrold V. 1929- WhoAm 92
Jerome, Jerrold Vincent 1929- St&PR 93, WhoIns 93
Jerome, John James 1933- WhoAm 92
Jerome, Joseph Walter 1939- WhoAm 92
Jerome, Judson BioIn 17
Jerome, Norge Winifred 1930- WhoAm 92
Jerome, Norman A. 1925- St&PR 93
Jerome, Sandra Lee 1954- WhoAmW 93
Jerome, Timothy 1943- ConTFT 10
Jeromin, Leszek 1937- WhoScE 91-4
Jeromson, James Robert, Jr. 1924- St&PR 93
Jeronimo, Lawrence J. 1947- WhoIns 93
Jeroski, Anthony Joseph, Jr. 1948- WhoWor 93
Jeroslow, Steven L. Law&B 92
Jeroy, Frederick Daly 1937- WhoSSW 93
Jerrard, John Ralston 1930- St&PR 93
Jerrard, Richard Patterson 1925- WhoAm 92
Jerrard, Robert Neil WhoScE 91-1
Jerrel, Bryan 1927- BioIn 17
Jerrett, Cathy Louise 1953- WhoWrEP 92
Jerrett, Jack Edward Law&B 92
Jerritts, Stephen G. 1925- St&PR 93, WhoAm 92, WhoWor 93
Jerro, John L. d1991 BioIn 17
Jerrold, S. Harrison 1934- WhoE 93
Jerry, Robert Howard 1923- WhoAm 92
Jerrytone, Samuel Joseph 1947- WhoWor 93
Jersak, Jozef 1929- WhoScE 91-4
Jersey, Deirdre Irene 1946- WhoEmL 93
Jersild, Arthur T(homas) 1902- WhoWrEP 92
Jersild, James Law&B 92
Jersild, James L. Law&B 92
Jersild, Jorgen 1913- Baker 92
Jersild, P.C. 1935- ScF&FL 92
Jersild, Thomas Nielsen 1936- WhoAm 92, WhoWor 93
Jerstad, John L. 1918-1943 BioIn 17
Jeruc, Donald Joseph Law&B 92
Jerumanis, Aivars L. 1938- St&PR 93
Jerusalem, Siegfried 1940- Baker 92, CurBio 92 [port], IntDcOp, OxDcOp
Jervey, Edward Darrell 1936- WhoSSW 93
Jervey, Harold Edward, Jr. 1920- WhoAm 92
Jervey, Hilton M. 1939- St&PR 93
Jervis, Barrie William WhoScE 91-1
Jervis, Herbert Hunter Law&B 92
Jervis, John 1735-1823 HarEnMi
Jervis, Kimberley James 1954- WhoWor 93
Jervis, Robert 1940- WhoAm 92
Jervis, Robert E. 1927- WhoAm 92
Jervis, Sally Ann 1937- WhoAmW 93
Jervis, Santiago 1937- WhoWor 93
Jervis, Tabitha ScF&FL 92
Jervis-Read, Diana Isabel 1945- WhoWor 93
Jerz, Lawrence Robert Law&B 92
Jerzmanowski, Erasm 1844-1909 PolBiDi
Jerzmanska, Anna 1928- WhoScE 91-4
Jerzy, Marek, Antoni 1939- WhoScE 91-4
Jesanis, Peter Joseph 1958- WhoEmL 93
Jeschelnig, Charles Jeffery 1963- St&PR 93
Jeschelnig, Richard John 1951- St&PR 93
Jeschke, Channing Renwick 1927- WhoAm 92, WhoSSW 93
Jeschke, Wolf Dieter 1931- WhoScE 91-3
Jeschke, Wolfgang 1936- ScF&FL 92
Jesdinsky, H.J. 1931- WhoScE 91-3
Jeshuran, Winston Rajadural 1939- WhoE 93
Jesinghaus, Walter 1902-1966 Baker 92
Jesion, Paula J. Law&B 92
Jeske, Debora Rae 1952- WhoEmL 93
Jeske, Howard Leigh 1917- WhoAm 92
Jeske, Marc Richard Law&B 92
Jesky, T. J. 1947- WhoWor 93
Jespers, Paul G.A. 1929- WhoScE 91-2
Jespersen, Jorgen B. 1954- WhoScE 91-2
Jespersen, K.I. WhoScE 91-1
Jespersen, Neil David 1946- WhoE 93
Jespersen, Vagn 1918- WhoScE 91-2
Jess, Ellen AmWomPl
Jess, Jacquelyn Ann 1960- WhoEmL 93
Jess, Larry Elliott 1958- WhoSSW 93
Jess de Navarrete, Susan Barbara 1947- WhoSSW 93
Jesse, Nicole Marie 1962- WhoAmW 93
Jessee, Edgar Howard 1953- WhoSSW 93
Jessee, Lance 1943- St&PR 93
Jessee, Nina S. 1948- WhoSSW 93
Jessee, S. Lee 1954- WhoE 93
Jessee, Salley Sue 1948- WhoSSW 93
Jessee, William F. 1946- St&PR 93
Jessel, Leon 1871-1942 Baker 92
Jessel, M.J.M. 1921- WhoScE 91-2
Jesseman, Wendell William 1934- St&PR 93
Jessen, Barbara Eileen 1947- WhoAmW 93
Jessen, David Wayne 1950- WhoAm 92
Jessen, John Henry, Sr. 1923- St&PR 93
Jessenig, Werner Rainer 1943- WhoScE 91-4
Jesseph, Steven Austin 1951- WhoEmL 93, WhoSSW 93
Jesser, Benn Wainwright 1915- WhoAm 92
Jesser, Edward A., Jr. 1916- St&PR 93
Jesser, Roger Franklyn 1926- WhoAm 92
Jesser, William Augustus 1939- WhoSSW 93
Jesseramsing, Chitmansing 1933- WhoAm 92, WhoWor 93
Jessey, Karen C. Law&B 92
Jesshope, Christopher Roger WhoScE 91-1
Jessiman, Alistair 1957- WhoAm 92
Jessop, David Alan WhoScE 91-1
Jessop, Dorothy Emma 1929- WhoWrEP 92
Jessop, Jeanette Wanless Law&B 92
Jessua, Alain 1932- MiSFD 9
Jessup, Harley 1954- WhoAm 92
Jessup, Hillary Jeanne 1945- WhoSSW 93
Jessup, Joe Lee 1913- WhoAm 92, WhoSSW 93, WhoWor 93
Jessup, John Baker 1921- WhoAm 92
Jessup, Paul Frederick 1939- WhoAm 92
Jessup, Philip Caryl, Jr. 1926- WhoAm 92
Jessup, Richard Stotesbury d1990 BioIn 17
Jessup, Steve R. 1952- St&PR 93
Jessup, Steven Lee 1954- WhoEmL 93, WhoSSW 93
Jessup, Stewart E. 1924- WhoAm 92, WhoSSW 93, WhoWor 93
Jessup, W. Edgar, Jr. 1922- St&PR 93
Jessup, Warren T. 1916- WhoAm 92, WhoWor 93
Jessup, William McClellan, Jr. 1928- WhoE 93
Jessup, William Royall 1933- WhoSSW 93
Jessurun D'Oliveira, Hans Ulrich 1933- WhoWor 93
Jessye, Eva 1895-1992 BioIn 17
Jester, Dana Edward 1939- St&PR 93
Jester, David Linville 1930- WhoSSW 93
Jester, Guy Earlscourt 1929- St&PR 93
Jester, Mary George 1946- WhoEmL 93
Jester, Roberts Charles, Jr. 1917- WhoAm 92, WhoE 93, WhoWor 93
Jester, Tod Krueger 1942- St&PR 93
Jestin, Heimwarth B. 1918- WhoAm 92
Jesup, Morris Ketchum 1828-1908 BioIn 17
Jesurun, Harold Mendez 1915- WhoAm 92
Jesus, Jose Luis 1950- WhoUN 92
Jesus Christ BioIn 17
Jesweak, Clayton C. 1931- St&PR 93
Jeszensky, Zoltan 1931- WhoScE 91-4
Jeszenszky, Geza 1941- WhoWor 93
Jeter, Allen Hunter 1927- St&PR 93
Jeter, Clifton B., Jr. 1944- WhoE 93
Jeter, Dwight Eugene 1951- WhoSSW 93
Jeter, George W. 1935- St&PR 93
Jeter, K.W. 1950- ScF&FL 92
Jeter, Katherine Leslie Brash 1921- WhoAmW 93, WhoSSW 93
Jeter, Michael BioIn 17, WhoAm 92, WhoE 93
Jeter, Richard Alan 1951- WhoSSW 93
Jeter, Richard Wainwright 1940- WhoSSW 93
Jeter, Susan M. 1960- WhoAmW 93
Jethmalani, Ram 1923- WhoAsAP 91
Jethro Tull ConMus 8 [port]
Jetson, Raymond A. AfrAmBi
Jett, Bill 1944- St&PR 93
Jett, Charles Cranston 1941- WhoAm 92, WhoWor 93
Jett, Donn 1951- BioIn 17
Jett, Ernest C. Law&B 92
Jett, Marti WhoAmW 93
Jett, Stephen Clinton 1938- WhoAm 92
Jette, Lorraine Doris 1942- WhoAmW 93
Jetter, Arthur Carl, Jr. 1947- WhoEmL 93
Jetton, Girard Reuel, Jr. 1924- WhoAm 92
Jetton, Michael T. St&PR 93
Jett-Parmer, Jonathan Jackson 1965- WhoSSW 93
Jeub, Michael Leonard 1943- St&PR 93, WhoAm 92
Jeuda, Basil Simon 1938- WhoWor 93
Jeunet, Jean-Pierre MiSFD 9
Jeung Ill Young 1945- WhoAsAP 91
Jeuniaux, Charles E.L. 1928- WhoScE 91-2
Jeury, Michel 1934- ScF&FL 92
Jevtic, Stevan L. 1927- WhoScE 91-4
Jew, Henry 1950- WhoSSW 93
Jew, Jean BioIn 17
Jewel, Jimmy 1909- & Warriss, Ben 1909- QDrFCA 92 [port]
Jeweler, Susan Eileen 1947- WhoAmW 93
Jewelewicz, Raphael 1932- WhoE 93
Jewell, Ann Lynette 1959- WhoAmW 93
Jewell, Byron Frank 1946- WhoAm 92, WhoSSW 93
Jewell, David Morris 1950- WhoEmL 93
Jewell, Elizabeth S. AmWomPl
Jewell, George Benson 1944- WhoE 93
Jewell, George Hiram 1922- WhoAm 92
Jewell, Jan M. 1944- St&PR 93
Jewell, John J. 1954- WhoEmL 93
Jewell, John Nolan 1949- WhoSSW 93
Jewell, Marshall 1825-1883 BioIn 17, PolPar
Jewell, Nancy A. Law&B 92
Jewell, Peter Arundel WhoScE 91-1
Jewell, Richard 1949- WhoWrEP 92
Jewell, Robert B. 1906- St&PR 93
Jewell, Robert Burnett 1906- WhoAm 92
Jewell, Stanley R. 1946- St&PR 93

Jewell, Thomas Lawrence 1944- *St&PR 93*
Jewell, Timothy Powell 1939- *WhoSSW 93*
Jewell, William Sylvester 1932- *WhoAm 92*
Jewett, Charles Edgar 1952- *St&PR 93*
Jewett, Frank Sniffen 1932- *WhoE 93*
Jewett, G.F., Jr. 1927- *St&PR 93*
Jewett, George Frederick, Jr. 1927- *WhoAm 92*
Jewett, Gerald Anson, Jr. 1925- *St&PR 93*
Jewett, Gregory Lewis 1956- *WhoEmL 93*
Jewett, Harvey C., IV 1948- *WhoAm 92*
Jewett, John Persinger 1943- *WhoAm 92, WhoE 93*
Jewett, John Rhodes 1922- *WhoAm 92*
Jewett, Louise Rogers d1914 *AmWomPl*
Jewett, Louise Rogers 1859-1914 *BioIn 17*
Jewett, Lucille McIntyre 1929- *WhoWor 93*
Jewett, Paul King d1991 *BioIn 17*
Jewett, Raymond L. 1924- *St&PR 93*
Jewett, Rebecca Lee 1949- *WhoAm 92*
Jewett, Richard Kirk 1926- *St&PR 93*
Jewett, Robert William *Law&B 92*
Jewett, Robert William 1952- *St&PR 93*
Jewett, Sarah Orne 1849-1909 *AmWomWr 92, BioIn 17, GayN, MagSAmL [port]*
Jewett, Stephen Frank *Law&B 92*
Jewett, Truda Cleeves 1931- *WhoE 93*
Jewett, William Amory 1919- *WhoSSW 93*
Jewison, Norman *BioIn 17*
Jewison, Norman 1926- *MiSFD 9*
Jewison, Norman Frederick 1926- *WhoAm 92, WhoWor 93*
Jewitt, David Willard Pennock 1921- *WhoAm 92*
Jewitt, John Rodgers 1783-1821 *BioIn 17*
Jewitt, Terence S. 1931- *WhoScE 91-1*
Jewler, Allen Jerome 1935- *WhoSSW 93*
Jewsbury, Roger Alan 1947- *WhoWor 93*
Jeydel, Richard K. *Law&B 92*
Jeydel, Richard K. 1950- *St&PR 93, WhoAm 92*
Jeye, Peter Austin 1959- *WhoEmL 93, WhoSSW 93*
Jeynes, Mary Kay 1941- *WhoAmW 93*
Jez, John B. 1935- *St&PR 93*
Jezebel, Queen dc. 843BC *BioIn 17*
Jezek, Jaroslav 1906-1942 *Baker 92*
Jezek, Tomas *BioIn 17*
Jezek, Zdenek 1932- *WhoUN 92*
Jezer, Rhea 1940- *WhoAmW 93*
Jezerinac, Joseph 1936- *St&PR 93*
Jezierny, Susan C. 1949- *WhoAmW 93*
Jezierski, Edward 1948- *WhoWor 93*
Jeziorkowski, John G. 1952- *St&PR 93*
Jeziorski, Bogumil S. 1947- *WhoWor 93*
Jezl, Barbara Ann 1947- *WhoE 93*
Jezuin *WhoScE 91-2*
Jezuit, Leslie J. 1945- *St&PR 93*
Jezuit, Leslie James 1945- *WhoAm 92*
Jezyna, Czeslaw 1925- *WhoScE 91-4*
Jhabvala, Ruth Prawer *BioIn 17*
Jhabvala, Ruth Prawer 1927- *IntLitE, WhoAm 92, WhoWor 93, WhoWrEP 92*
Jhe, Wonho 1960- *WhoWor 93*
Jhikram, Mohan Lal 1919- *WhoAsAP 91*
Jhin, Michael Kontien 1950- *WhoAm 92, WhoSSW 93*
Ji, Chaozhu 1929- *WhoUN 92*
Ji, Li 1927- *WhoWor 93*
Ji, Peiding 1942- *WhoWor 93*
Ji, Shanyu 1955- *WhoEmL 93, WhoSSW 93*
Ji, Xinhua 1941- *WhoWor 93*
Jian Chunwang 1938- *WhoAsAP 91*
Jian Chunyun 1930- *WhoAsAP 91*
Jianfeng, Yuan 1963- *WhoWor 93*
Jiang, Boju 1937- *WhoWor 93*
Jiang, Fu Ru 1927- *WhoWor 93*
Jiang, Jian Ping 1958- *WhoWor 93*
Jiang, Jinchu 1940- *WhoWor 93*
Jiang, Long 1933- *WhoWor 93*
Jiang, Sheng 1941- *WhoWor 93*
Jiang, Shouli 1944- *WhoWor 93*
Jiang, Zhenghua 1937- *WhoWor 93*
Jiang Hongquan 1932- *WhoAsAP 91*
Jiang Jiehi 1887-1975 *DcTwHis*
Jiang Minkuan 1930- *WhoAsAP 91*
Jiang Qing 1914- *DcTwHis*
Jiang Qing 1914-1991 *AnObit 1991, BioIn 17, News 92*
Jiang Xiesheng 1928- *WhoAsAP 91*
Jiang Xinxiong 1931- *WhoAsAP 91*
Jiang Yangkun 1931- *BioIn 17*
Jiang Zemin *BioIn 17*
Jiang Zemin 1926- *WhoAsAP 91, WhoWor 93*
Jianxin, Huang 1952- *MiSFD 9*
Jiao Yulu *BioIn 17*
Jia-Yuan, Charlotte 1958- *WhoEmL 93*
Jia Zhijie 1936- *WhoAsAP 91*
Jibben, Laura Ann 1949- *WhoEmL 93*
Jibilian, Gerald A. *Law&B 92*
Jicha, Henry Louis, Jr. 1928- *WhoE 93*
Jickling, John Ward 1921- *WhoAm 92*
Jilcott, Rupert Wadsworth, III 1947- *WhoSSW 93*
Jilek, Frantisek 1913- *Baker 92*
Jilek, John P. 1952- *St&PR 93*
Jiler, William Laurence 1925- *WhoAm 92*
Jiles, Pam *BlkAmWO*
Jiles, Paulette 1943- *BioIn 17, WhoCanL 92*
Jilhewar, Ashok 1947- *WhoEmL 93, WhoWor 93*
Jillette, Arthur George, Jr. 1937- *WhoE 93*
Jillette, Penn 1955- See Penn & Teller *News 92*
Jillian, Ann *BioIn 17*
Jillian, Ann 1950- *WhoAm 92*
Jillian, Ann 1951- *HolBB [port]*
Jillson, Robert Lyman 1936- *WhoWor 93*
Jilot, Dennis L. 1947- *St&PR 93*
Jimbo, Ichiro 1929- *WhoWor 93*
Jimbo, Masato 1957- *WhoWor 93*
Jimbo, Michio 1951- *WhoWor 93*
Jimbo, Tetsuo Ted 1961- *WhoWor 93*
Jimenez, Beatrice Carolyn 1943- *WhoAmW 93*
Jimenez, Bettie Eileen 1932- *WhoAmW 93*
Jimenez, Edith *WhoScE 91-1*
Jimenez, Emilio S. 1933- *WhoWor 93*
Jimenez, Flaco 1939- See Texas Tornados, The *ConMus 8*
Jimenez, Francisco 1943- *WhoWrEP 92*
Jimenez, Jose Ramon 1944- *WhoWor 93*
Jimenez, Jose William *Law&B 92*
Jimenez, Juan Ignacio 1958- *WhoWor 93*
Jimenez, Juan Ramon *BioIn 17*
Jimenez, Luis 1940- *HispAmA*
Jimenez, Luis Alfonso, Jr. 1940- *WhoAm 92*
Jimenez, Neal *MiSFD 9*
Jimenez, Neal (Randall) 1960- *ConAu 138*
Jimenez, Rolando Daniel 1938- *WhoSSW 93*
Jimenez, Susan Ann 1943- *WhoAmW 93*
Jimenez De Cisneros, Francisco 1436-1517 *HarEnMi*
Jimenez de Quesada, Gonzalo 1501?-1579? *Expl 93 [port]*
Jimenez-Dianderas, Carlos Rolando 1962- *WhoWor 93*
Jimenez-Leal, Orlando *MiSFD 9*
Jimenez-Mabarak, Carlos 1916- *Baker 92*
Jimenez Maes, Petra *NotHsAW 93*
Jimenez Martinez, Victor Manuel 1949- *WhoWor 93*
Jimenez Morales, Guillermo *WhoWor 93*
Jimenez-Rueda, Julio 1896-1960 *DcMexL*
Jimenez-Wagenheim, Olga 1941- *HispAmA [port]*
Jimenez y Muro, Dolores 1848-1925 *BioIn 17*
Jimeno, Cheri Annette 1950- *WhoAmW 93*
Jimerson, Herman Lee 1957- *WhoEmL 93*
Jimeson, Robert Mackay, Jr. 1921- *WhoSSW 93*
Jimi, Shozaburo 1945- *WhoAsAP 91*
Jimirro, James P. 1937- *WhoAm 92*
Jimison, Z. Mae 1943- *AfrAmBi [port]*
Jimmu, Tenno dc. 585BC *HarEnMi*
Jin, Guofan 1929- *WhoWor 93*
Jin, Marvin Young-Jong 1946- *WhoEmL 93*
Jin, Xie 1923- *MiSFD 9*
Jin, Yongjian 1934- *WhoUN 92*
Jin, Zheng Da 1934- *WhoWor 93*
Jinchang, Lai 1964- *WhoWor 93*
Jindrak, Karel Francis 1926- *WhoE 93*
Jines, Michael Lee *Law&B 92*
Jing, Xuecheng 1945- *WhoWor 93*
Jing, Zhengfu 1938- *WhoWor 93*
Jinga 1582-1663 *BioIn 17*
Jingu, Empress of Japan 170-269 *BioIn 17*
Jin Jian 1953- *WhoAsAP 91*
Jinks, James Raymond *Law&B 92*
Jinks, Robert Larry 1929- *WhoAm 92*
Jinks, Sharon Jean 1947- *WhoAmW 93*
Jinnah, Muhammad Ali 1876-1948 *DcTwHis*
Jinnett, Pamela Callard 1949- *WhoAmW 93*
Jinnett, Robert Jefferson 1949- *WhoAm 92, WhoE 93, WhoWor 93*
Jinno, Yoh 1951- *WhoEmL 93*
Jinnouchi, Takao 1933- *WhoAsAP 91*
Jin Qingmin *BioIn 17*
Jinright, Marjorie Anne 1950- *WhoSSW 93*
Jipguep, Jean 1939- *WhoUN 92*
Jirak, K(arel) B(oleslav) 1891-1972 *Baker 92*
Jiral, Jeannine Carol 1955- *WhoEmL 93, WhoSSW 93*
Jiranek, Josef 1855-1940 *Baker 92*
Jiras, Robert *MiSFD 9*
Jirasek, Ivo 1920- *Baker 92*
Jirasek, Jiri 1933- *WhoScE 91-4*
Jires, Jaromil 1935- *DrEEuF*
Jiricna, Eva 1939- *BioIn 17*
Jirik, David T. 1950- *WhoEmL 93*
Jirikovec, Leroy Edward 1925- *St&PR 93*
Jirkans, Maribeth Joie 1945- *WhoAmW 93, WhoWor 93*
Jirko, Ivan 1926-1978 *Baker 92*
Jiro 1947- *WhoAsAP 91*
Jirousek, Jaroslav 1931- *WhoScE 91-4*
Jirovec, Ronald Arthur 1948- *St&PR 93*
Jirovec, Vojtech Matyas *Baker 92*
Jirran, Raymond Joseph 1934- *WhoSSW 93*
Jirsa, James Otis 1938- *WhoAm 92*
Jischa, Michael 1937- *WhoScE 91-3*
Jischke, Martin C. 1941- *WhoAm 92*
Ji-Shou, Ruan 1961- *WhoWor 93*
Jisland, Olof 1963- *WhoWor 93*
Jito, Empress of Japan 645-702 *BioIn 17*
Jittlov, Mike *MiSFD 9*
Jivasantikarn, Nirund 1945- *WhoWor 93*
Jivraj, Amin *BioIn 17*
Jiwkow, Wasil 1926- *WhoWor 93*
Jiyu, Ren 1916- *WhoWor 93*
Joachain, Charles J. 1937- *WhoScE 91-2*
Joachim, Amalie 1839-1899 *Baker 92*
Joachim, Joseph 1831-1907 *Baker 92*
Joachim, Miroslav Vaclav Jan 1919- *WhoWor 93*
Joachim, Otto 1910- *Baker 92*
Joachim, Richard Walter 1932- *WhoWor 93*
Joan *WhoWrEP 92*
Joanes, Juan de d1579 *BioIn 17*
Joannes, H. *WhoScE 91-2*
Joannes Duns, Scotus c. 1266-1308 *BioIn 17*
Joannette, Vianney 1940- *St&PR 93*
Joan of Arc c. 1412-1431 *HarEnMi, OxDcOp*
Joan, of Arc, Saint 1412-1431 *BioIn 17*
Joanou, Jennifer *BioIn 17*
Joanou, Phil *BioIn 17*
Joanou, Phil 1961- *MiSFD 9*
Joanou, Phillip 1933- *WhoAm 92*
Joans, Ted 1928- *BioIn 17*
Joao, IV 1604-1656 *Baker 92*
Joaquim, Richard Ralph 1936- *WhoWor 93*
Joaquin, Nereo R. 1939- *WhoAsAP 91*
Joaquin, Nick 1917- *IntLitE*
Joas, Hans 1948- *WhoWor 93*
Job *BioIn 17*
Job fl. 13th cent.- *OxDcByz*
Job, Anette Karls 1964- *WhoAmW 93*
Job, Ann Marie 1956- *WhoAmW 93*
Job, Donald D. 1942- *WhoWrEP 92*
Job, Jean-Claude 1922- *WhoScE 91-2*
Job, Reuben Philip 1928- *WhoAm 92*
Job, Vanessa Renee 1959- *WhoSSW 93*
Job, William James 1929- *WhoWor 93*
Jobarteh, Ebrima Kebba 1940- *WhoUN 92*
Jobe, Edward B. 1929- *WhoAm 92*
Jobe, Edward Blinn 1929- *WhoIns 93*
Jobe, Frank Wilson 1925- *WhoAm 92*
Jobe, G. David 1943- *St&PR 93*
Jobe, Jan S. 1950- *WhoIns 93*
Jobe, Jonathan Edward, Jr. *Law&B 92*
Jobe, Larry Alton 1940- *WhoAm 92*
Jobe, Mary Leonore 1886-1966 *BioIn 17*
Jobe, Muriel Ida 1931- *WhoAmW 93, WhoWor 93*
Jobe, Rebecca Fay 1962- *WhoAmW 93*
Jobe, Shirley A. 1946- *WhoAmW 93, WhoEmL 93*
Jobe, Warren Yancey 1940- *St&PR 93, WhoAm 92*
Jobert, Jean 1883-1957 *Baker 92*
Jobert, Michel 1921- *BioIn 17*
Jobes, James William, Jr. 1936- *WhoSSW 93*
Jobim, Antonio Carlos *BioIn 17*
Jobin, Raoul 1906-1974 *OxDcOp*
Jobin, Robert 1930- *St&PR 93*
Joblove, George *WhoAm 92*
Jobs, Steven *BioIn 17*
Jobs, Steven P. 1955- *ConEn*
Jobs, Steven Paul 1955- *WhoAm 92*
Jobson, Mareda Bell 1946- *WhoAmW 93*
Jobson, Thomas Wootten 1925- *WhoAm 92*
Jobst, Kazmer 1924- *WhoScE 91-4*
Jocelyn, Susan E. W. *AmWomPl*
Jochelson, Waldemar 1855-1937 *IntDcAn*
Jochem, Eberhard 1942- *WhoScE 91-3*
Jochen, James E. 1937- *St&PR 93*
Jochim, Michael Allan 1945- *WhoAm 92*
Jochim, Michael Eugene 1945- *WhoSSW 93*
Jochnowitz, Rose 1916- *WhoAmW 93*
Jochum, Eugen 1902-1987 *Baker 92, OxDcOp*
Jochum, Georg Ludwig 1909-1970 *Baker 92*
Jochum, Manfred *Law&B 92*
Jochum, Otto 1898-1969 *Baker 92*
Jochum, Veronica *WhoAm 92*
Jochum, Veronica 1932- *Baker 92*
Jock, Paul F., II 1943- *WhoAm 92*
Jocke, Ralph Edward 1953- *WhoEmL 93*
Jockers, Ethel Catherine 1932- *WhoAmW 93*
Jockers, Laurens R. 1940- *WhoIns 93*
Jockusch, Carl Groos, Jr. 1941- *WhoAm 92*
Jodal, Gabor 1913- *Baker 92*
Jode, (Wilhelm August Ferdinand) Fritz 1887-1970 *Baker 92*
Jodl, Alfred 1890-1946 *BioIn 17, HarEnMi*
Jodogne, J.-C. 1937- *WhoScE 91-2*
Jodoin, Luc *Law&B 92*
Jodoin, Maurice 1939- *St&PR 93*
Jodorowsky, Alejandro *MiSFD 9*
Jodorowsky, Alexandro 1929- *BioIn 17*
Jodorowsky, Raquel 1937- *SpAmA*
Jodra, L.G. *WhoScE 91-3*
Jodrell, Steve *MiSFD 9*
Jodsaas, Larry Elvin 1935- *St&PR 93, WhoAm 92*
Joeckel, Paul M. 1952- *St&PR 93*
Joel fl. 13th cent.- *OxDcByz*
Joel, Amos Edward, Jr. 1918- *WhoAm 92*
Joel, Benjamin Frank 1958- *WhoSSW 93*
Joel, Billy 1949- *Baker 92, BioIn 17, WhoAm 92*
Joel, Lydia d1992 *BioIn 17, NewYTBS 92*
Joel, William Lee, II 1933- *WhoAm 92*
Joels, Kerry Mark 1931- *ScF&FL 92*
Joels, Norman *WhoScE 91-1*
Joelson, Mark Rene 1934- *WhoAm 92*
Joelson, Nanette Biller 1928- *WhoAmW 93*
Joens, Michael *MiSFD 9*
Joensuu, Jyrki Ilmari 1948- *WhoWor 93*
Joergensen, Per Bay 1945- *WhoWor 93*
Joern, Charles Edward, Jr. 1951- *WhoEmL 93*
Joerschke, John David 1951- *WhoSSW 93*
Joest, David R. *Law&B 92*
Joest, Douglas P. 1953- *St&PR 93*
Joesting, Herbert W. 1905-1963 *BiDAMSp 1989*
Jofen, Jean *WhoAm 92*
Joffe, Arthur *MiSFD 9*
Joffe, Carl Herbert *Law&B 92*
Joffe, Charles 1929- *WhoAm 92*
Joffe, Mark *MiSFD 9*
Joffe, Robert David 1943- *WhoAm 92*
Joffe, Roland 1945- *MiSFD 9*
Joffe, Stephen Neal 1943- *WhoWor 93*
Joffre, Joseph Jacques Cesaire 1852-1931 *BioIn 17, DcTwHis, HarEnMi*
Joffre, Stephen Paul 1913- *WhoAm 92*
Joffroy, William *BioIn 17*
Joffroy-Black, Florence Helene 1965- *WhoE 93*
Jog, D.V. 1922- *ScF&FL 92*
Jogi, Ajit P.K. 1946- *WhoAsAP 91*
Joglekar, Prafulla Narayan 1947- *WhoE 93, WhoEmL 93*
Jogues, Isaac 1607-1646 *BioIn 17*
Joh, Hyon Jae 1947- *WhoWor 93*
Joh, Yasushi 1933- *WhoWor 93*
Johal, Darshan Singh 1933- *WhoUN 92*
Johan, Z. 1935- *WhoScE 91-2*
Johan, Zdenek 1935- *WhoScE 91-2*
Johanan ben Zakkai dc. 80 *BioIn 17*
Johan Bin O.T. Ghani *WhoAsAP 91*
Johann, Mark W. 1954- *St&PR 93*
Johann Adam Andreas, Furst Liechtenstein 1656-1712 *BioIn 17*
Johannes d425 *HarEnMi*
Johannes, George Robert 1938- *St&PR 93, WhoAm 92*
Johannes, John Roland 1943- *WhoAm 92*
Johannes, Ralph 1929- *WhoWor 93*
Johannes, Virgil Ivancich 1930- *WhoAm 92*
Johannes Chrysorrhoas c. 700-754 *Baker 92*
Johannesen, Grant 1921- *Baker 92*
Johannesen, Michael B. *Law&B 92*
Johannesen, Thomas M. 1946- *St&PR 93*
Johannes, Magnus, Archbishop of Uppsala 1488-1544 *BioIn 17*
Johanneson, Gerald Benedict 1940- *St&PR 93*
Johannessen, Dag O. 1932- *St&PR 93*
Johannessen, Per 1941- *WhoUN 92*
Johannesson, Magnus Gunnar 1964- *WhoWor 93*
Johannesson, Rolf 1946- *WhoScE 91-4*
Johannesson, Thomas Rolf 1943- *WhoWor 93*
Johannesson, Torkell *WhoScE 91-4*
Johanns, Charles F. 1936- *WhoAm 92, WhoIns 93*
Johanns, Michael O. 1950- *WhoAm 92*
Johannsen, Chris Jakob 1937- *WhoAm 92*
Johannsen, Lisa Sharidan Gaskill 1960- *WhoEmL 93*
Johannsen, Nicholas 1844-1928 *BioIn 17*
Johannsson, Axel 1951- *WhoScE 91-1*
Johannsson, Kjartan 1939- *WhoUN 92*

Johannsson, Magnus Blondal 1925- *Baker 92*
Johanos, Donald 1928- *Baker 92, WhoAm 92*
Johansen, David Monrad 1888-1974 *Baker 92*
Johansen, Eivind Herbert 1927- *WhoAm 92, WhoWor 93*
Johansen, Gunnar 1906-1991 *Baker 92, BioIn 17*
Johansen, Henry Kjell 1937- *WhoScE 91-4*
Johansen, Inge Johannes Tjernes 1928- *WhoScE 91-4*
Johansen, Iris 1938- *ScF&FL 92*
Johansen, Jan Rolf 1926- *WhoScE 91-4*
Johansen, John W. 1943- *St&PR 93*
Johansen, John Wesley 1943- *WhoAm 92*
Johansen, Josephine Lilliesta 1953- *WhoE 93*
Johansen, Kathleen Marie 1961- *WhoEmL 93*
Johansen, Keld 1950- *WhoWor 93*
Johansen, Lawrence Andrew 1950- *WhoE 93*
Johansen, Paul E. 1910- *St&PR 93*
Johansen, Peter 1938- *WhoScE 91-2*
Johansen, Poul 1946- *WhoScE 91-2*
Johansen, Reidar Flod 1946- *WhoWor 93*
Johansen, Richard W. 1951- *St&PR 93*
Johansen, Vagn 1941- *WhoScE 91-2*
Johanson, Bengt C.A. 1920- *WhoScE 91-4*
Johanson, Donald Carl 1943- *WhoAm 92*
Johanson, Karl J. 1932- *WhoScE 91-4*
Johanson, Norman Eric 1940- *St&PR 93*
Johanson, Patricia Maureen 1940- *WhoAm 92*
Johanson, Ralph Nathanael, Jr. *Law&B 92*
Johanson, Stanley Morris 1933- *WhoAm 92*
Johanson, Sven-Eric (Emanuel) 1919- *Baker 92*
Johanson, Waldemar G., Jr. 1937- *WhoAm 92*
Johanson, William Gary 1946- *WhoE 93*
Johansson, Allan Aki 1941- *WhoScE 91-4*
Johansson, Bengt (Viktor) 1914-1989 *Baker 92*
Johansson, Borje E.G. 1930- *WhoScE 91-4*
Johansson, Dicken 1926- *WhoWor 93*
Johansson, Elof Daniel Bertil 1936- *WhoAm 92*
Johansson, Ingvar 1935- *WhoScE 91-4*
Johansson, Kurt Y. 1938- *WhoScE 91-4*
Johansson, Nils A. 1948- *St&PR 93*
Johansson, Nils Alrik 1932- *WhoScE 91-4*
Johansson, P. Bertil 1919- *WhoScE 91-4*
Johansson, Risto Tapio 1948- *WhoScE 91-4*
Johansson, Stig Axel 1934- *WhoWor 93*
Johansson, Sven Vage Kenneth 1945- *WhoWor 93*
Johansson, Thomas Bernhard 1943- *WhoWor 93*
Johar Bin Dato Paduka Haji Noordin, Yang Berhormat Datu Paduka Haji *WhoAsAP 91*
Johard, Carl Olof 1951- *WhoWor 93*
Johari, Hamid 1961- *WhoE 93*
Johe, Sharon Doyle *Law&B 92*
John *OxDcByz*
John, Archduke of Austria 1782-1859 *HarEnMi*
John, King of England 1167-1216 *BioIn 17*
John, I *OxDcByz*
John, I dc. 630 *OxDcByz*
John, II *OxDcByz*
John, II c. 356- *OxDcByz*
John, III *OxDcByz*
John, VII *OxDcByz*
John, VIII *OxDcByz*
John, X d929 *OxDcByz*
John, XXIII 1881-1963 *DcTwHis*
John, XXIII, Pope 1881-1963 *BioIn 17, ConHero 2 [port]*
John, Andrew *ConAu 138*
John, Anthony *ScF&FL 92*
John, Cheryl Annette 1957- *St&PR 93*
John, Colin *ScF&FL 92*
John, Ctirad 1920- *WhoScE 91-4*
John, David Thomas *WhoScE 91-1*
John, Donald A. 1931- *St&PR 93*
John, Donas *WhoWrEP 92*
John, Doreen Ann 1949- *WhoEmL 93*
John, Elton *BioIn 17*
John, Elton 1947- *Baker 92*
John, Elton Hercules 1947- *WhoAm 92*
John, Eugene Allen, Jr. *Law&B 92*
John, Frank Herbert, Jr. 1961- *WhoE 93*
John, Frederick Elias 1946- *St&PR 93*
John, Hugo Herman 1929- *WhoAm 92*
John, James Edward Albert 1933- *WhoAm 92*
John, Jerome Francis 1940- *St&PR 93*
John, Joby 1957- *WhoE 93*
John, Joseph 1938- *St&PR 93*
John, Kenneth *DcCPCAm*
John, Leonard Keith 1949- *WhoWor 93*
John, Little Willie 1937-1968 *SoulM*
John, Olivia Newton- *BioIn 17*
John, Owen *ScF&FL 92*
John, Patrick 1937- *DcCPCAm*
John, Ralph Candler 1919- *WhoAm 92*
John, Richard Rodda 1929- *WhoAm 92*
John, Robert McClintock 1947- *WhoE 93, WhoEmL 93*
John, Robert St. 1941- *St&PR 93*
John, Russell T. 1946- *St&PR 93, WhoIns 93*
John, Tommy *BioIn 17*
John, Valampuri 1946- *WhoAsAP 91*
John, Yvonne Maree 1944- *WhoAmW 93*
John Aktouarios c. 1275-c. 1328 *OxDcByz*
John Alexios Komnenos, III *OxDcByz*
John Anagnostes fl. 15th cent.- *OxDcByz*
John Asen, II c. 1195-1241 *OxDcByz*
John Bekkos, XI 123-?-1297 *OxDcByz*
John Casimir, II 1609-1672 *PolBiDi*
John Chrysostom 34-?-407 *OxDcByz [port]*
John Chrysostom, Saint d407 *BioIn 17*
John Chrysostomites, VIII *OxDcByz*
Johncock, Gordon Walter 1936- *WhoAm 92*
John Comnenus, II 1088-1143 *HarEnMi*
John Doukas, I c. 1240-c. 1289 *OxDcByz*
John Duns, Scotus c. 1266-1308 *BioIn 17*
Johnee *WhoWrEP 92*
John Eleemon d619? *OxDcByz*
Johner, Dominicus 1874-1955 *Baker 92*
John Geometres fl. 10th cent.- *OxDcByz*
John Glykys, XIII c. 1260-1319 *OxDcByz*
John Grammatikos, VII dc. 867 *OxDcByz*
John Italos c. 1025-c. 1082 *OxDcByz*
John Joseph of Austria, the younger 1629-1679 *HarEnMi*
John Kalekas, XIV 1283-1347 *OxDcByz*
John Kamateros, X d1206 *OxDcByz*
John Kantakouzenos, VI c. 1295-1383 *OxDcByz*
John Katholikos, V dc. 925 *OxDcByz*
John Klimax c. 579-c. 650 *OxDcByz [port]*
John Komnenos, II 1087-1143 *OxDcByz [port]*
John Komnenos, II c. 1262-1297 *OxDcByz*
John Komnenos, IV c. 1403-1460 *OxDcByz*
John Laskaris, IV 1250-c. 1305 *OxDcByz*
Johnloz, Gregory Lee 1948- *St&PR 93*
John Lydos 490-c. 565 *OxDcByz*
John Merkouropoulos *OxDcByz*
John Nesteutes, IV *OxDcByz*
John of Amalfi fl. 11th cent.- *OxDcByz*
John of Antioch *OxDcByz*
John of Austria 1547-1578 *HarEnMi*
John of Biclar dc. 621 *OxDcByz*
John of Brienne c. 1170-1237 *OxDcByz*
John of Caesarea fl. 6th cent.- *OxDcByz*
John of Cappadocia c. 500-c. 548 *OxDcByz*
John of Damascus c. 675-c. 749 *OxDcByz*
John of Ephesus c. 507-586? *OxDcByz*
John of Epiphaneia fl. 6th cent.-7th cent. *OxDcByz*
John of Euboea fl. 8th cent.- *OxDcByz*
John of Gaza fl. 6th cent.- *OxDcByz*
John of Karpathos *OxDcByz*
John of Leyden *OxDcOp*
John, of London fl. 1267- *BioIn 17*
John of Marignolli fl. 14th cent.- *Expl 93*
John of Monte Corvino 1247?-1328 *Expl 93*
John of Naples fl. c. 900- *OxDcByz*
John of Nikiu fl. 7th cent.- *OxDcByz*
John of Poutze fl. 1120-1157 *OxDcByz*
John of Rila c. 876-946 *OxDcByz*
John of Sardis *OxDcByz*
John of Skythopolis *OxDcByz*
John Olbracht, I 1459-1501 *PolBiDi*
Johnopolos, Stephen Gary 1950- *WhoE 93, WhoEmL 93*
John Oxeites, IV dc. 1100 *OxDcByz*
John Palaiologos, V 1332-1391 *OxDcByz*
John Palaiologos, VII c. 1370-1408 *OxDcByz*
John Palaiologos, VIII 1392-1448 *OxDcByz*
John Patrikios dc. 698 *OxDcByz*
John Paul, II 1920- *DcTwHis, PolBiDi [port]*
John Paul, II, His Holiness Pope 1920- *WhoAm 92, WhoWor 93*
John Paul, II, Pope 1920- *BioIn 17, ColdWar 2 [port]*
John Petric'i dc. 1125 *OxDcByz*
John Roger *OxDcByz*
Johns, Albert Cameron 1914- *WhoAm 92*
Johns, Allan Thomas *WhoScE 91-1*
Johns, Beverley Anne Holden 1946- *WhoAmW 93*
Johns, Bibi Gun Birgit *WhoWor 93*
Johns, Carol E. 1956- *WhoAmW 93*
Johns, Carol Johnson 1923- *WhoAmW 93*
Johns, Catherine 1952- *WhoAmW 93*
Johns, Charley Jerome 1928- *St&PR 93*
Johns, Claude Jackson, Jr. 1930- *WhoAm 92*
Johns, Clayton 1857-1932 *Baker 92*
Johns, D. Malcolm, Jr. *Law&B 92*
Johns, David Lee 1951- *WhoEmL 93, WhoSSW 93*
Johns, Dianna Rose 1951- *WhoAmW 93*
Johns, Donna J. 1945- *WhoIns 93*
Johns, Douglas 1948- *WhoAm 92*
Johns, Douglas A. *Law&B 92*
Johns, Elizabeth Jane Hobbs 1941- *WhoAmW 93, WhoSSW 93*
Johns, Frances Sarra 1944- *WhoAmW 93*
Johns, Gary *BioIn 17*
Johns, Gary Thomas 1952- *WhoAsAP 91*
Johns, Horace Edward 1945- *WhoSSW 93*
Johns, James Edward 1938- *St&PR 93*
Johns, James Haight 1926- *St&PR 93*
Johns, James Kirkham *Law&B 92*
Johns, James S. 1933- *St&PR 93*
Johns, Jasper *BioIn 17*
Johns, Jasper 1930- *WhoAm 92, WhoWor 93*
Johns, Jeanine L. 1956- *WhoAmW 93*
Johns, John Dixon *Law&B 92*
Johns, John Edwin 1921- *WhoAm 92*
Johns, John Philip 1949- *WhoEmL 93*
Johns, John Richards 1952- *WhoE 93, WhoEmL 93*
Johns, Lee Rhea 1956- *WhoAmW 93, WhoEmL 93*
Johns, Lori *BioIn 17*
Johns, Mary E. 1953- *WhoEmL 93*
Johns, Michael Douglas 1964- *WhoE 93, WhoSSW 93*
Johns, Michael E. *BioIn 17*
Johns, Michael Marieb Edward 1942- *WhoE 93*
Johns, Norma N. *ScF&FL 92*
Johns, Paul Emile c. 1798-1860 *Baker 92*
Johns, R.W. 1948- *St&PR 93*
Johns, Ray E. d1991 *BioIn 17*
Johns, Ray L. 1932- *St&PR 93*
Johns, Raymond Edward 1943- *WhoSSW 93*
Johns, Richard Alan *WhoScE 91-1*
Johns, Richard James 1925- *WhoAm 92*
Johns, Richard Seth Ellis 1946- *WhoEmL 93*
Johns, Robert S. 1946- *St&PR 93*
Johns, Roger L. 1942- *St&PR 93*
Johns, Roy 1929- *WhoWrEP 92*
Johns, Susan Andersen 1950- *WhoAmW 93*
Johns, Susan D. 1954- *WhoAmW 93*
Johns, Ted 1942- *WhoCanL 92*
Johns, Thomas Alan 1961- *WhoEmL 93*
Johns, Thomas Charles 1951- *St&PR 93*
Johns, Varner Jay, Jr. 1921- *WhoAm 92*
Johns, W.E. 1893-1968 *ScF&FL 92*
Johns, W.E., Captain *MajAI*
Johns, W(illiam) E(arle) 1893-1968 *MajAI [port]*
Johns, Warren LeRoi 1929- *WhoE 93*
Johns, William Davis, Jr. 1925- *WhoAm 92*
Johns, William Patrick 1941- *WhoAm 92*
Johns, William Richard *WhoScE 91-1*
Johns, Willy *ScF&FL 92*
John Scholastikos *OxDcByz*
John Scholastikos, III c. 503- *OxDcByz*
Johnsen, Arvid *WhoScE 91-4*
Johnsen, Clifford Andrew 1941- *St&PR 93*
Johnsen, Edward Joseph *Law&B 92*
Johnsen, Erik Frithjof 1925- *WhoAm 92, WhoSSW 93*
Johnsen, Eugene Carlyle 1932- *WhoAm 92*
Johnsen, Gretchen Lynne 1952- *WhoWrEP 92*
Johnsen, Hallvard Olav 1916- *Baker 92*
Johnsen, Ib 1945- *WhoScE 91-2*
Johnsen, Jarl K. 1938- *WhoScE 91-4*
Johnsen, Joan Stearns *Law&B 92*
Johnsen, Niels Winchester 1922- *WhoSSW 93*
Johnsen, Ola M. 1943- *WhoScE 91-4*
Johnsen, Peter H. *Law&B 92*
Johnsen, Richard Alan 1946- *WhoAm 92, WhoEmL 93*
Johnsen, Ronald A. 1937- *St&PR 93*
Johnsen, Russell Harold 1922- *WhoAm 92*
Johnsen, Trevor Meldal- *ScF&FL 92*
Johnsen, Walter Craig 1950- *WhoE 93*
Johnsen, William A. 1955- *St&PR 93*
Johnsey, Walter F. 1924- *St&PR 93*
Johnsgard, Paul A(ustin) 1931- *ConAu 39NR*
John Sikeliotes *OxDcByz*
John Sikeliotes fl. c. 1000- *OxDcByz*
John Smbat *OxDcByz*
John Sobieski, III 1629-1696 *HarEnMi*
Johnson, A. *ConAu 37NR, MajAI, SmATA 72*
Johnson, A. Clark 1930- *St&PR 93*
Johnson, A. E. *ConAu 37NR, MajAI, SmATA 72*
Johnson, A. Gary 1950- *St&PR 93*
Johnson, A.J. *BioIn 17, Law&B 92*
Johnson, A. L. *WhoAm 92*
Johnson, A(rtemas) N(ixon) 1817-1892 *Baker 92*
Johnson, A. Paul 1955- *WhoWrEP 92*
Johnson, A. Rodman *Law&B 92*
Johnson, Abigail Chase 1953- *WhoAmW 93*
Johnson, Addie Collins *WhoAmW 93, WhoE 93*
Johnson, Alan *MiSFD 9*
Johnson, Alan Arthur 1930- *WhoAm 92*
Johnson, Alan B. 1939- *WhoAm 92*
Johnson, Alan G. 1934- *St&PR 93*
Johnson, Alan W. 1925- *St&PR 93*
Johnson, Albert Llewellyn, II 1960- *WhoE 93*
Johnson, Albert Madden 1943- *St&PR 93*
Johnson, Albert Wesley 1923- *WhoAm 92, WhoWor 93*
Johnson, Albert Zena 1952- *WhoSSW 93*
Johnson, Albin d1992 *NewYTBS 92*
Johnson, Alexander Chester 1932- *WhoE 93*
Johnson, Alfred Carl, Jr. 1930- *WhoSSW 93*
Johnson, Alice *BioIn 17*
Johnson, Allan H. 1950- *St&PR 93*
Johnson, Allan M. *Law&B 92*
Johnson, Allan R. 1947- *St&PR 93*
Johnson, Allen Dress 1941- *WhoAm 92*
Johnson, Allen Halbert 1922- *WhoAm 92*
Johnson, Allen Huggins 1937- *WhoAm 92*
Johnson, Allen J. 1939- *St&PR 93, WhoIns 93*
Johnson, Allen Madison, Jr. 1941- *WhoWor 93*
Johnson, Allen W. 1949- *WhoAm 92*
Johnson, Alonzo Bismark 1958- *WhoSSW 93*
Johnson, Alton Cornelius 1924- *WhoAm 92*
Johnson, Alva William 1936- *WhoSSW 93*
Johnson, Alvin Donnel 1940- *WhoE 93*
Johnson, Alvin Roscoe 1942- *WhoAm 92*
Johnson, Alyn William 1933- *WhoAm 92*
Johnson, Amy 1903-1941 *Expl 93*
Johnson, Andrea D. *Law&B 92*
Johnson, Andrew 1808-1875 *BioIn 17, PolPar*
Johnson, Andrew Emerson, III 1931- *WhoAm 92*
Johnson, Andrew Myron 1935- *WhoAm 92*
Johnson, Angela 1961- *ConAu 138, SmATA 69*
Johnson, Angela 1962- *BlkAull 92*
Johnson, Angela Claire 1960- *WhoEmL 93*
Johnson, Anita 1926- *WhoAm 92*
Johnson, Ann Nealous 1938- *WhoSSW 93*
Johnson, Anna *BioIn 17*
Johnson, Anna Gayle 1953- *WhoAmW 93*
Johnson, Anna Mae 1928- *WhoAmW 93*
Johnson, Annabel *ConAu 37NR, MajAI, SmATA 72*
Johnson, Annabel 1921- *ScF&FL 92*
Johnson, Annabel (Jones) 1921- *DcAmChF 1960*
Johnson, Annabell (Jones) 1921- *ConAu 37NR, MajAI [port], SmATA 72 [port]*
Johnson, Anne Elizabeth 1934- *WhoAmW 93*
Johnson, Anne Elizabeth 1955- *WhoAmW 93*
Johnson, Anne MarcoVecchio 1931- *WhoAm 92, WhoAmW 93*
Johnson, Anthony Francis *WhoScE 91-1*
Johnson, Anthony Keith 1943- *WhoWor 93*
Johnson, Anthony O'Leary 1957- *WhoWor 93*
Johnson, Anthony William 1936- *WhoSSW 93*
Johnson, Antonia Axson 1943- *WhoAm 92*
Johnson, Arlene Lytle 1937- *WhoAm 92*
Johnson, Arne Ivar 1924- *WhoScE 91-4*
Johnson, Arnold Ivan 1919- *WhoAm 92*
Johnson, Arnold William 1916- *WhoWor 93*
Johnson, Arthur Edward 1922- *St&PR 93*
Johnson, Arthur Eugene 1942- *WhoAm 92*
Johnson, Arthur Gilbert 1926- *WhoAm 92*
Johnson, Arthur Menzies 1921- *WhoAm 92*
Johnson, Arthur William, Jr. 1949- *WhoAm 92*
Johnson, Arvid Conrad, III 1964- *WhoEmL 93*
Johnson, Arvid M. 1938- *WhoAm 92*
Johnson, Ashmore Clark, Jr. 1930- *WhoAm 92, WhoSSW 93*
Johnson, Avis E. 1934- *St&PR 93*

Johnson, B.A. 1944- *St&PR 93*
Johnson, Badri Nahvi 1934- *WhoAmW 93*
Johnson, Barbara Ann 1948- *WhoWrEP 92*
Johnson, Barbara Anne 1939- *WhoSSW 93*
Johnson, Barbara Converse 1955- *WhoAmW 93*
Johnson, Barbara Ferry 1923- *ScF&FL 92*
Johnson, Barbara Sue 1952- *WhoEmL 93*
Johnson, Barry Douglas *Law&B 92*
Johnson, Barry Edward *WhoScE 91-1*
Johnson, Barry Lee 1938- *WhoAm 92*
Johnson, Barry Leigh 1947- *WhoE 93*
Johnson, Belinda *Law&B 92*
Johnson, Belton Kleberg d1991 *BioIn 17*
Johnson, Ben *WhoAm 92*
Johnson, Ben 1918- *IntDcF 2-3 [port]*
Johnson, Ben Eugene 1928- *St&PR 93*
Johnson, Bengt-Emil 1936- *Baker 92*
Johnson, Benj. F. *ConAu 137*
Johnson, Benjamin 1918- *WhoAm 92*
Johnson, Benjamin Edgar 1921- *WhoAm 92*
Johnson, Benjamin F. *ConAu 137*
Johnson, Benjamin Ford 1959- *WhoEmL 93*
Johnson, Benjamin Franklin, III 1943- *WhoAm 92*
Johnson, Benjamin J. *BioIn 17*
Johnson, Benjamin Leibold 1950- *WhoE 93, WhoEmL 93*
Johnson, Berkeley D. 1906-1990 *BioIn 17*
Johnson, Bernard G. 1915- *St&PR 93*
Johnson, Bernice A. *AmWomPl*
Johnson, Beth Exum 1952- *WhoAmW 93, WhoSSW 93, WhoWor 93*
Johnson, Beth Michael 1938- *WhoAmW 93*
Johnson, Betsey Lee 1942- *WhoAm 92, WhoAmW 93*
Johnson, Betsy Ancker- 1929- *BioIn 17*
Johnson, Betty Anne 1924- *WhoAmW 93*
Johnson, Betty June 1932- *WhoAmW 93*
Johnson, Betty Zschiegner 1933- *WhoAmW 93*
Johnson, Beverly *BioIn 17*
Johnson, Beverly Kaye *Law&B 92*
Johnson, Beverly Phillips 1963- *WhoAmW 93, WhoEmL 93*
Johnson, Bill *DcAmChF 1960*
Johnson, Bix McPhail 1946- *St&PR 93*
Johnson, Bob *BioIn 17*
Johnson, Bob 1931-1991 *AnObit 1991*
Johnson, Boine T., Jr. 1931- *St&PR 93*
Johnson, Boine Theodore 1931- *WhoAm 92*
Johnson, Bonnie Lee 1941- *WhoAmW 93*
Johnson, Boreham Boyd 1952- *WhoEmL 93, WhoSSW 93*
Johnson, Brad *BioIn 17*
Johnson, Brad Hart 1951- *WhoEmL 93*
Johnson, Bradford J. 1937- *St&PR 93*
Johnson, Braiden Rex *ConAu 139*
Johnson, Bram *BioIn 17*
Johnson, Brenda Faye 1953- *WhoEmL 93*
Johnson, Brenda Jean 1965- *WhoAmW 93*
Johnson, Brenda Kay 1946- *WhoAmW 93*
Johnson, Brenda Lee 1950- *WhoAmW 93, WhoEmL 93*
Johnson, Brian 1952- *WhoE 93, WhoEmL 93*
Johnson, Brian A. 1944- *WhoIns 93*
Johnson, Brian Robert 1960- *WhoE 93*
Johnson, Brooke Bailey *BioIn 17*
Johnson, Bruce 1932- *WhoAm 92*
Johnson, Bruce A. *Law&B 92*
Johnson, Bruce Edward 1959- *WhoE 93*
Johnson, Bruce L. *Law&B 92*
Johnson, Bruce Lynn 1969- *WhoE 93*
Johnson, Bruce Marvin 1933- *WhoAm 92, WhoE 93*
Johnson, Bryce G. 1953- *St&PR 93*
Johnson, Bryce M. *Law&B 92*
Johnson, "Bunk" (William Geary) 1889?-1949 *Baker 92*
Johnson, Burdette A. 1905- *St&PR 93*
Johnson, Byron 1915- *St&PR 93*
Johnson, Byron Jerald 1937- *WhoAm 92*
Johnson, Byron John *Law&B 92*
Johnson, C. Paul *BioIn 17*
Johnson, C. Richard 1941- *WhoAm 92*
Johnson, C. Scott 1944- *WhoAm 92*
Johnson, C. Terry 1937- *WhoAm 92*
Johnson, Calvert Berry 1949- *WhoEmL 93, WhoSSW 93*
Johnson, Calvin, Jr. 1951- *WhoE 93*
Johnson, Campbell Carrington 1895-1968 *EncAACR*
Johnson, Carl Anderson 1943- *WhoAm 92*
Johnson, Carl Earld 1936- *WhoE 93*
Johnson, Carl J. 1942- *St&PR 93*
Johnson, Carla Rae 1947- *WhoE 93*
Johnson, Carol Ann 1951- *WhoAmW 93*
Johnson, Carol Ann 1958- *WhoAmW 93*
Johnson, Carol Roxane 1929- *WhoAm 92*
Johnson, Carolyn C. 1931- *St&PR 93*
Johnson, Carroll Frye 1913- *WhoAm 92*
Johnson, Carroll O. 1929- *St&PR 93*
Johnson, Catherine Augusta Lewis 1937- *WhoAmW 93*
Johnson, Catherine Common 1914- *WhoAmW 93*
Johnson, Cathleen *WhoAm 92*
Johnson, Cathy 1942- *BioIn 17*
Johnson, Cathy 1953- *WhoAmW 93*
Johnson, Cecil L. *Law&B 92*
Johnson, Cecile Ryden *WhoWor 93*
Johnson, Celia 1908-1982 *IntDcF 2-3 [port]*
Johnson, Chad *BioIn 17*
Johnson, Charlene Elizabeth 1933- *WhoAmW 93*
Johnson, Charles 1679-1748 *BioIn 17*
Johnson, Charles 1948- *ScF&FL 92, WhoAm 92*
Johnson, Charles A. *Law&B 92*
Johnson, Charles Austin 1930- *WhoAm 92*
Johnson, Charles B. 1933- *St&PR 93*
Johnson, Charles Barris 1939- *WhoSSW 93*
Johnson, Charles Bartlett 1933- *WhoAm 92*
Johnson, Charles Blake 1952- *WhoWrEP 92*
Johnson, Charles Christopher, Jr. 1921- *WhoAm 92*
Johnson, Charles E., II *St&PR 93*
Johnson, Charles E., Jr. 1955- *WhoE 93*
Johnson, Charles Edward *WhoScE 91-1*
Johnson, Charles Edward 1941- *WhoSSW 93*
Johnson, Charles Ernest Arnold 1940- *WhoSSW 93*
Johnson, Charles Foreman 1929- *WhoWor 93*
Johnson, Charles John, Jr. 1932- *WhoAm 92*
Johnson, Charles K. *Law&B 92*
Johnson, Charles Knox 1913- *St&PR 93*
Johnson, Charles Lane 1938- *BiDAMSp 1989*
Johnson, Charles Lavon, Jr. 1954- *WhoSSW 93*
Johnson, Charles M. 1941- *WhoAm 92*
Johnson, Charles Michael 1965- *WhoE 93*
Johnson, Charles Owen 1926- *WhoSSW 93*
Johnson, Charles Patrick 1961- *WhoE 93*
Johnson, Charles Richard 1912- *WhoWor 93*
Johnson, Charles Richard 1948- *BioIn 17*
Johnson, Charles Royal 1948- *WhoSSW 93*
Johnson, Charles S. 1893-1956 *EncAACR*
Johnson, Charles Simons 1940- *WhoWor 93*
Johnson, Charles Spurgeon 1893-1956 *BioIn 17*
Johnson, Charles W. *WhoAm 92*
Johnson, Charlotte Verne 1944- *WhoAmW 93*
Johnson, Chas W. 1938- *St&PR 93*
Johnson, Chauncey Paul 1931- *St&PR 93, WhoAm 92*
Johnson, Cheryl Elizabeth 1952- *WhoAmW 93, WhoSSW 93*
Johnson, Cheryl June 1938- *WhoWrEP 92*
Johnson, Chic 1891-1962 *See* Olsen, Ole 1892-1965 & Johnson, Chic 1891-1962 *QDrFCA 92*
Johnson, Christine Marie 1952- *WhoEmL 93*
Johnson, Christopher Ralph 1947- *WhoWrEP 92*
Johnson, Cinda Hawks 1948- *WhoAmW 93*
Johnson, Cindee Lee 1960- *WhoAmW 93*
Johnson, Cindy Lou *MiSFD 9*
Johnson, Cindy Swan 1959- *WhoE 93*
Johnson, Ciri Diane 1956- *WhoAmW 93, WhoE 93*
Johnson, Claire M. 1912- *St&PR 93*
Johnson, Clarence 1942- *BioIn 17*
Johnson, Clarence Leonard 1910-1990 *BioIn 17*
Johnson, Clarence Traylor, Jr. 1929- *WhoSSW 93*
Johnson, Clark Allen 1931- *St&PR 93*
Johnson, Clark Eugene, Jr. 1930- *WhoAm 92*
Johnson, Clark Everette, Jr. 1923- *WhoAm 92*
Johnson, Clark H. 1935- *St&PR 93*
Johnson, Clark Hughes 1935- *WhoAm 92*
Johnson, Clark W. 1949- *St&PR 93*
Johnson, Clarke Courtney 1936- *WhoAm 92*
Johnson, Claudia Alta Taylor 1912- *BioIn 17*
Johnson, Claudia Durst 1938- *WhoAmW 93, WhoSSW 93*
Johnson, Clayton Errold 1921- *WhoWor 93*
Johnson, Clifford *Law&B 92*
Johnson, Clifford Andrew, III 1945- *WhoAm 92*
Johnson, Clifford Ivery 1944- *WhoAm 92*
Johnson, Clifford L. *Law&B 92*
Johnson, Clifford P. *Law&B 92*
Johnson, Clifford R. 1923- *WhoAm 92*
Johnson, Clifford Vincent 1936- *WhoSSW 93*
Johnson, Clifton Herman 1921- *WhoAm 92, WhoSSW 93, WhoWor 93*
Johnson, Clyde 1935- *St&PR 93*
Johnson, Clyde Ervin 1948- *WhoEmL 93*
Johnson, Colin 1938- *IntLitE*
Johnson, Conor Deane 1943- *WhoAm 92*
Johnson, Conrad A. d1991 *BioIn 17*
Johnson, Constance Ann Trillich 1949- *WhoAmW 93, WhoWor 93*
Johnson, Corwin Waggoner 1917- *WhoAm 92*
Johnson, Craig Norman 1942- *WhoAm 92*
Johnson, Craig R. 1951- *WhoAm 92*
Johnson, Crawford Toy, III 1925- *WhoAm 92*
Johnson, Crockett *MajAI*
Johnson, Crystal Duane 1954- *WhoAmW 93, WhoEmL 93, WhoSSW 93*
Johnson, Curt 1928- *WhoWrEP 92*
Johnson, Curtis 1946- *St&PR 93*
Johnson, Curtis B. *Law&B 92*
Johnson, Curtis Lee 1928- *WhoAm 92*
Johnson, Curtiss Sherman 1899- *WhoE 93, WhoWor 93*
Johnson, Cynthia L. *Law&B 92*
Johnson, Cyrus Edwin 1929- *WhoAm 92*
Johnson, D.G. *WhoScE 91-1*
Johnson, D.V. *Law&B 92*
Johnson, Dale A. 1937- *St&PR 93, WhoAm 92*
Johnson, Dale L. 1929- *WhoSSW 93*
Johnson, Dale R. 1944- *St&PR 93*
Johnson, Dana K. *Law&B 92*
Johnson, Daniel J. *Law&B 92*
Johnson, Daniel L., Jr. *Law&B 92*
Johnson, Daniel McDonald 1953- *WhoSSW 93*
Johnson, Daniel Milo 1940- *WhoSSW 93*
Johnson, Daniel Robert 1938- *WhoAm 92*
Johnson, Daniel Shahid 1954- *SmATA 73 [port]*
Johnson, Darlene *BioIn 17*
Johnson, Darlene Jean *Law&B 92*
Johnson, Daryl Diane 1953- *WhoE 93*
Johnson, Daryle G. 1936- *WhoIns 93*
Johnson, Dave *BioIn 17*
Johnson, Davey *BioIn 17*
Johnson, David *BioIn 17, WhoScE 91-1*
Johnson, David, III 1943- *WhoSSW 93*
Johnson, David Allen 1943- *BiDAMSp 1989*
Johnson, David Allen 1954- *WhoWor 93*
Johnson, David Blackwell 1954- *WhoE 93, WhoEmL 93*
Johnson, David Carl 1942- *St&PR 93*
Johnson, David Earl 1937- *St&PR 93*
Johnson, David Elliot 1933- *WhoAm 92*
Johnson, David Emanuel 1937- *WhoE 93*
Johnson, David F. *Law&B 92*
Johnson, David Gale 1916- *WhoAm 92*
Johnson, David H., III 1955- *St&PR 93*
Johnson, David Hayden *Law&B 92*
Johnson, David Howard 1956- *WhoSSW 93*
Johnson, David Jordan 1946- *St&PR 93*
Johnson, David L. *Law&B 92*
Johnson, David L. 1929- *WhoIns 93*
Johnson, David L. 1937- *St&PR 93*
Johnson, David Lee 1946- *WhoAm 92*
Johnson, David Lincoln *Law&B 92*
Johnson, David Lincoln 1929- *WhoAm 92*
Johnson, David Lynn 1934- *WhoAm 92*
Johnson, David Mathis 1947- *WhoAm 92*
Johnson, David N. *Law&B 92*
Johnson, David Owen 1918- *St&PR 93*
Johnson, David Peter 1945- *St&PR 93*
Johnson, David R 1953- *St&PR 93*
Johnson, David Scott *Law&B 92*
Johnson, David Simonds 1924- *WhoAm 92, WhoE 93*
Johnson, David Stafford *Law&B 92*
Johnson, David Terrence 1937- *WhoWor 93*
Johnson, David W. *BioIn 17*
Johnson, David W. 1959- *St&PR 93*
Johnson, David Willis 1932- *St&PR 93, WhoAm 92, WhoE 93, WhoWor 93*
Johnson, David Wolcott 1940- *WhoAm 92, WhoWor 93*
Johnson, Dawn Roe *Law&B 92*
Johnson, Dean Adams 1937- *WhoAm 92*
Johnson, Dean Conway 1934- *WhoAm 92*
Johnson, Dean E. 1931- *WhoIns 93*
Johnson, Dean Evan 1931- *St&PR 93*
Johnson, Dean R. *Law&B 92*
Johnson, Dean T. *St&PR 93*
Johnson, Deane Anne *Law&B 92*
Johnson, Deane Frank 1918- *St&PR 93, WhoE 93*
Johnson, Debbie *Law&B 92*
Johnson, Deborah L. *Law&B 92*
Johnson, Deborah Sue 1948- *WhoAmW 93*
Johnson, Debra Hunter *Law&B 92*
Johnson, Debra Steele 1957- *WhoSSW 93*
Johnson, d'Elaine Ann Herard 1932- *WhoAmW 93*
Johnson, Delores Fitzgerald 1953- *WhoAmW 93*
Johnson, Delos R., Jr. 1924- *St&PR 93*
Johnson, Denis 1949- *BioIn 17, DcLB 120 [port], ScF&FL 92*
Johnson, Denise Thorne *BioIn 17*
Johnson, DeNise Vick 1963- *WhoSSW 93*
Johnson, Dennis Burl 1949- *WhoEmL 93, WhoSSW 93*
Johnson, Dennis Duane 1938- *WhoAm 92*
Johnson, Dennis Lester 1938- *WhoAm 92*
Johnson, Dennis Ray 1946- *WhoEmL 93, WhoSSW 93*
Johnson, Dennis W. 1945- *St&PR 93*
Johnson, Deron d1992 *NewYTBS 92*
Johnson, Deron 1938-1992 *BioIn 17*
Johnson, Derrick *BioIn 17*
Johnson, Derrick Stuart 1934- *WhoWor 93*
Johnson, Dewey Edward 1935- *WhoSSW 93*
Johnson, Diana Bergin 1956- *WhoAmW 93*
Johnson, Diana Lynn 1954- *WhoAmW 93*
Johnson, Diane 1934- *BioIn 17, WhoWrEP 92*
Johnson, Diane Fisher 1959- *WhoSSW 93*
Johnson, Diane Kay 1937- *WhoWor 93*
Johnson, Diane (Lain) 1934- *ConAu 40NR, WhoAm 92*
Johnson, Diane Lynn 1945- *WhoAmW 93*
Johnson, Dolores *BlkAuII 92*
Johnson, Dolores 1949- *ConAu 137, SmATA 69 [port]*
Johnson, Don *BioIn 17*
Johnson, Don 1949- *HolBB [port]*
Johnson, Don Robert 1942- *WhoE 93*
Johnson, Don Wayne 1949- *WhoAm 92*
Johnson, Donald Allen 1926- *St&PR 93*
Johnson, Donald Arthur 1952- *WhoEmL 93*
Johnson, Donald B. 1915- *St&PR 93*
Johnson, Donald C. *Law&B 92*
Johnson, Donald D. 1917- *ConAu 137*
Johnson, Donald E. 1928- *St&PR 93*
Johnson, Donald Harry 1944- *WhoSSW 93*
Johnson, Donald Howard 1930- *St&PR 93*
Johnson, Donald Lee 1935- *WhoAm 92*
Johnson, Donald Lee 1947- *St&PR 93, WhoAm 92*
Johnson, Donald Rex 1938- *WhoAm 92*
Johnson, Donald Ross 1920- *WhoSSW 93*
Johnson, Donna J. *Law&B 92*
Johnson, Donna M. 1939- *WhoWrEP 92*
Johnson, Dora Myrtle Knudtson 1900- *WhoAmW 93*
Johnson, Dorothy 1905-1984 *ScF&FL 92*
Johnson, Dorothy Mae 1929- *WhoAmW 93*
Johnson, Dorothy Phyllis 1925- *WhoAmW 93*
Johnson, Dorothy Strathman Gullen 1931- *WhoWrEP 92*
Johnson, Dorothy Sutherland 1951- *WhoE 93*
Johnson, Doug *BioIn 17*
Johnson, Doug 1919- *WhoAm 92*
Johnson, Douglas Allen *Law&B 92*
Johnson, Douglas E. *WhoAm 92*
Johnson, Douglas V. *Law&B 92*
Johnson, Douglas W. 1955- *St&PR 93*
Johnson, Douglas W(ayne) 1934- *WhoWrEP 92*
Johnson, Douglass F. 1913- *St&PR 93*
Johnson, Duane Gordon 1943- *St&PR 93*
Johnson, Dwight N 1944- *St&PR 93*
Johnson, E. Christopher, Jr. *Law&B 92*
Johnson, E. Eric 1927- *St&PR 93, WhoWor 93*
Johnson, E.M. *ScF&FL 92*
Johnson, Earl 1958- *St&PR 93*
Johnson, Earl, Jr. 1933- *WhoAm 92, WhoWrEP 92*
Johnson, Earl L. 1930- *St&PR 93*
Johnson, Earl LeRoy 1932- *St&PR 93*
Johnson, Earle Bertrand 1914- *WhoAm 92*
Johnson, Eartha Jean *Law&B 92*
Johnson, Earvin *NewYTBS 92 [port]*
Johnson, Earvin 1959- *BioIn 17, ConBlB 3 [port], WhoAm 92*
Johnson, Earvin, Jr. 1959- *AfrAmBi*
Johnson, Eddie Bernice *AfrAmBi [port]*
Johnson, Eddie Bernice 1935- *WhoAmW 93*
Johnson, Edgar *BioIn 17*
Johnson, Edgar 1912- *ScF&FL 92*

Johnson, Edgar Ernest 1933- St&PR 93
Johnson, Edgar F. 1899-1991 BioIn 17
Johnson, Edgar M. 1941- WhoSSW 93
Johnson, Edgar (Raymond) 1912- DcAmChF 1960
Johnson, Edgar (Raymond) 1912-1990 ConAu 37NR, MajAI, SmATA 72 [port]
Johnson, Edith d1969 SweetSg A [port]
Johnson, Edna Beatrice 1951- WhoSSW 93
Johnson, Edna Ruth 1918- WhoSSW 93
Johnson, Edna Scott 1913- WhoAmW 93
Johnson, Edward 1767-1829 BioIn 17
Johnson, Edward 1878-1959 Baker 92, IntDcOp, OxDcOp
Johnson, Edward A. Law&B 92
Johnson, Edward A. 1917- WhoAm 92
Johnson, Edward Cecil 1944- WhoSSW 93
Johnson, Edward Crosby, III 1930- WhoAm 92
Johnson, Edward Elemuel 1926- WhoAm 92
Johnson, Edward Eric 1944- St&PR 93, WhoE 93
Johnson, Edward Fuller 1921- WhoE 93
Johnson, Edward L. 1923-1992 NewYTBS 92
Johnson, Edward Michael 1945- WhoE 93
Johnson, Edward Nayland 1948- WhoEmL 93, WhoSSW 93
Johnson, Edward Roy 1940- WhoAm 92
Johnson, Edway Richard 1927- WhoSSW 93
Johnson, Edwin C. ScF&FL 92
Johnson, Edwin F. 1934- St&PR 93
Johnson, Eileen Frances 1936- WhoAmW 93
Johnson, Elaine Bowe 1940- WhoAmW 93
Johnson, Elaine Glenn 1943- WhoAmW 93
Johnson, Elaine McDowell 1942- WhoAm 92, WhoAmW 93
Johnson, Eliza McCardle 1810-1876 BioIn 17
Johnson, Elizabeth A. Law&B 92
Johnson, Elizabeth Ann WhoAmW 93
Johnson, Elizabeth Ann 1936- WhoWor 93
Johnson, Elizabeth Diane Long 1945- WhoAmW 93
Johnson, Elizabeth Finn Law&B 92
Johnson, Elizabeth Gamble 1925- WhoAmW 93
Johnson, Elizabeth Hill 1913- WhoAmW 93
Johnson, Elizabeth Redmond 1956- WhoAmW 93
Johnson, Elizabeth V. 1923- St&PR 93
Johnson, Ella B. AmWomPl
Johnson, Ellen Christine 1948- WhoAmW 93
Johnson, Ellen H. 1910-1992 BioIn 17, NewYTBS 92
Johnson, Ellen H(ulda) 1910-1992 ConAu 137
Johnson, Ellen Irene 1948- WhoAmW 93
Johnson, Ellen Meyers 1949- WhoAmW 93
Johnson, Ellen Randel 1916- WhoAmW 93, WhoSSW 93
Johnson, Ellen Schultz 1918- WhoAmW 93
Johnson, Elliott Amos 1907- WhoAm 92
Johnson, Elliott M. 1929- St&PR 93
Johnson, Elliott Willard 1949- WhoEmL 93
Johnson, Ellis Lane 1938- WhoAm 92
Johnson, Elmer Marshall 1930- WhoAm 92
Johnson, Elmer William 1932- WhoAm 92
Johnson, Elsie Ernest WhoAmW 93
Johnson, Elvira Lanette 1964- WhoAmW 93
Johnson, Emery Allen 1929- WhoAm 92
Johnson, Emily Pauline 1861-1913 BioIn 17
Johnson, Emily Pauline 1862-1913 AmWomPl
Johnson, Eric BioIn 17
Johnson, Eric G. AfrAmBi [port]
Johnson, Eric Lynn 1949- St&PR 93
Johnson, Eric Norman St&PR 93
Johnson, Erik R. 1945- St&PR 93
Johnson, Ernest Frederick, (Jr.) 1918- WhoAm 92
Johnson, Ernest J. 1944- St&PR 93
Johnson, Ervin Albert 1931- St&PR 93
Johnson, Estelle Taylor 1941- WhoAmW 93
Johnson, Ethel Jean Law&B 92
Johnson, Eugene Clare 1940- WhoE 93
Johnson, Eugene Franklin, Jr. 1956- WhoSSW 93
Johnson, Eugene Joseph 1937- WhoE 93
Johnson, Eugene Laurence 1936- WhoAm 92
Johnson, Eugene R., Jr. 1924- St&PR 93
Johnson, Eugene Walter 1939- WhoAm 92
Johnson, Evans Combs 1922- WhoSSW 93
Johnson, Evelyn Bryan 1909- WhoAmW 93
Johnson, Evelyne 1922- WhoWrEP 92
Johnson, Everett Clark 1955- WhoEmL 93
Johnson, Everett Ramon 1915- WhoAm 92
Johnson, Ewell Calvin 1926- WhoAm 92
Johnson, Eyvind 1900-1976 ScF&FL 92
Johnson, F.A. WhoScE 91-1
Johnson, F. Ross BioIn 17
Johnson, F. Ross 1931- St&PR 93
Johnson, Fay Clarence 1928- WhoSSW 93
Johnson, Ferd 1905- WhoAm 92
Johnson, Fern L. WhoAm 92
Johnson, Fidelia Gale 1959- WhoSSW 93
Johnson, Florence AmWomPl
Johnson, Forrest B. ScF&FL 92
Johnson, Francis 1930- WhoE 93
Johnson, Francis S. 1925- St&PR 93
Johnson, Francis Severin 1918- WhoAm 92
Johnson, Frank BioIn 17
Johnson, Frank 1792-1844 Baker 92
Johnson, Frank Anthony 1962- WhoWor 93
Johnson, Frank Corliss 1927- WhoAm 92
Johnson, Frank Edward 1920- WhoAm 92
Johnson, Frank H. 1908-1990 BioIn 17
Johnson, Frank Minis 1918- EncAACR
Johnson, Frank Minis, Jr. 1918- WhoAm 92
Johnson, Frank Stanley, Jr. 1930- St&PR 93, WhoAm 92
Johnson, Frank William, Jr. 1952- WhoSSW 93
Johnson, Franklin Kevin 1954- WhoE 93
Johnson, Franklin Ridgway 1912- WhoAm 92, WhoWor 93
Johnson, Franklyn Arthur 1921- WhoAm 92
Johnson, Fred 1908-1982 BioIn 17
Johnson, Fred K. 1945- BioIn 17
Johnson, Freda S. 1947- St&PR 93, WhoAm 92
Johnson, Frederick Dean 1911- WhoSSW 93, WhoWor 93
Johnson, Frederick Ross 1931- WhoSSW 93
Johnson, Frederick W. Law&B 92
Johnson, Frederick William 1947- WhoWrEP 92
Johnson, Frosty 1935- ScF&FL 92
Johnson, G. Roberts 1940- WhoAm 92
Johnson, Gabriel Ampah 1930- WhoWor 93
Johnson, Gail Lynne 1953- WhoEmL 93
Johnson, Gary Alan 1957- WhoSSW 93
Johnson, Gary C. Law&B 92
Johnson, Gary E. Law&B 92
Johnson, Gary E. 1935- St&PR 93
Johnson, Gary Edward 1952- WhoWor 93
Johnson, Gary Keith 1951- WhoEmL 93
Johnson, Gary Lee 1933- St&PR 93
Johnson, Gary R. Law&B 92
Johnson, Gary Wayne 1940- WhoSSW 93
Johnson, Geneva Bolton WhoAm 92
Johnson, George 1920- WhoAm 92
Johnson, George 1953- See Brothers Johnson SoulM
Johnson, George, Jr. 1926- WhoAm 92
Johnson, George Andrew 1949- St&PR 93
Johnson, George Carl 1947- WhoEmL 93
Johnson, George Clayton 1929- ScF&FL 92
Johnson, George H. 1941- St&PR 93
Johnson, George Leonard 1931- WhoSSW 93
Johnson, George Leonard 1947- St&PR 93
Johnson, George P. 1948- St&PR 93
Johnson, George R. 1933- St&PR 93
Johnson, George Robert 1927- WhoWor 93
Johnson, George William 1928- WhoAm 92, WhoSSW 93
Johnson, Georgia Douglas 1877-1966 EncAACR
Johnson, Georgia Douglas 1886-1966 AmWomPl
Johnson, Georgia Douglas Camp 1886-1966 BioIn 17
Johnson, Gerald A. 1948- St&PR 93
Johnson, Gerald Donald 1931- St&PR 93
Johnson, Gerald Lee 1938- St&PR 93
Johnson, Gerald White 1890-1980 JrnUS
Johnson, Geraldine Esch 1921- WhoAmW 93
Johnson, Gerard G. 1941- WhoAm 92, WhoE 93
Johnson, Gerard Griffin 1941- St&PR 93
Johnson, Gifford Kenneth 1918- WhoSSW 93
Johnson, Gilbert Eugene 1933- St&PR 93
Johnson, Gilbert Fred 1931- St&PR 93
Johnson, Glen D. WhoSSW 93
Johnson, Glen Roger 1929- WhoAm 92
Johnson, Glendon E. 1924- St&PR 93, WhoIns 93
Johnson, Glenn B. 1922- St&PR 93
Johnson, Glenn S. 1958- St&PR 93
Johnson, Glenn Thompson 1917- WhoAm 92
Johnson, Gloria Busch 1942- WhoSSW 93
Johnson, Gloria Lee 1931- WhoAmW 93
Johnson, Gloria Tapscott AfrAmBi
Johnson, Gordon 1930- WhoWor 93
Johnson, Gordon O. 1933- St&PR 93
Johnson, Gordon Selby 1918- WhoAm 92, WhoSSW 93
Johnson, Grant D. 1930- St&PR 93
Johnson, Grant Lester 1929- St&PR 93, WhoAm 92
Johnson, Greg WhoWrEP 92
Johnson, Gregg Stephen 1960- WhoEmL 93
Johnson, Gregory E. 1961- St&PR 93
Johnson, Gregory L. Law&B 92
Johnson, Gregory Paul 1954- WhoE 93
Johnson, Gregory W. 1937- St&PR 93
Johnson, Gus LaRoy 1947- WhoAm 92, WhoSSW 93
Johnson, Gustav E. 1927- St&PR 93
Johnson, Guy Benton 1901-1991 BioIn 17
Johnson, Guy V. Law&B 92
Johnson, Gwenavere Anelisa 1909- WhoAmW 93
Johnson, H. Arvid Law&B 92
Johnson, H. Arvid 1936- WhoAm 92
Johnson, H. Fisk 1958- St&PR 93
Johnson, H. Richard 1926- St&PR 93
Johnson, Hal Harold Gustav 1915- WhoAm 92
Johnson, Hall 1887-1970 Baker 92
Johnson, Hansford Tillman 1936- WhoAm 92
Johnson, Hardwick Smith, Jr. 1958- WhoSSW 93
Johnson, Harold Arthur 1924- WhoE 93
Johnson, Harold Earl 1939- WhoAm 92
Johnson, Harold H., III 1952- St&PR 93
Johnson, Harold Keith 1912-1983 CmdGen 1991 [port]
Johnson, Harold R. 1923- St&PR 93
Johnson, Harold R. 1926- WhoAm 92
Johnson, Harold Timothy 1958- WhoEmL 93, WhoSSW 93
Johnson, Harrison F. 1904- St&PR 93
Johnson, Harry A., III Law&B 92
Johnson, Harry A., III 1949- WhoAm 92
Johnson, Harry C. 1932- St&PR 93
Johnson, Harry E. 1931- St&PR 93
Johnson, Hartley A. 1935- St&PR 93
Johnson, Haynes Bonner 1931- WhoAm 92, WhoE 93
Johnson, Helen Anita 1956- WhoAmW 93
Johnson, Helen D. d1990 BioIn 17
Johnson, Helen Marie 1943- WhoAmW 93
Johnson, Helene Mullins 1898-1991 BioIn 17
Johnson, Henry 1748-1835 HarEnMi
Johnson, Henry Arna 1919- WhoAm 92
Johnson, Henry Clay 1910- WhoAm 92
Johnson, Henry Clyde 1914- WhoWor 93
Johnson, Henry Eugene, III 1951- WhoSSW 93
Johnson, Henry Franklin, Mrs. 1922- St&PR 93
Johnson, Henry Parker 1951- St&PR 93
Johnson, Henry Samuel, Jr. 1914- St&PR 93
Johnson, Henry T. 1937- WhoAm 92
Johnson, Herbert Alan 1934- WhoAm 92
Johnson, Herbert C. 1909-1990 BioIn 17
Johnson, Herbert Frederick 1934- WhoAm 92
Johnson, Herbert M. 1936- St&PR 93
Johnson, Herbert Michael 1936- WhoAm 92
Johnson, Herbert O. 1918- St&PR 93
Johnson, Herschel Lee 1948- BlkAull 92
Johnson, Hervey 1839-1923 BioIn 17
Johnson, Hervey M. d1992 NewYTBS 92
Johnson, Hervey M. 1941-1992 BioIn 17
Johnson, Hester N. AmWomPl
Johnson, Hilary Kathleen Law&B 92
Johnson, Hillary Earnest Law&B 92
Johnson, Hiram W. 1886-1945 PolPar
Johnson, Hollis Eugene, III 1935- WhoAm 92
Johnson, Hollis Ralph 1928- WhoAm 92
Johnson, Horace 1893-1964 Baker 92
Johnson, Horace Richard 1926- WhoAm 92
Johnson, Horton Anton 1926- WhoAm 92, WhoE 93
Johnson, Howard D. Law&B 92
Johnson, Howard Eugene 1915- WhoWor 93
Johnson, Howard Michael 1960- WhoAm 92
Johnson, Howard Russell 1944- WhoSSW 93
Johnson, Howard Wesley 1922- WhoAm 92, WhoWor 93
Johnson, Hugh BioIn 17
Johnson, Hugh 1939- ConAu 39NR
Johnson, Hugh Bailey 1904- WhoAm 92
Johnson, Hugh E. 1929- St&PR 93
Johnson, Hulette M. 1943- St&PR 93
Johnson, Hunter 1906- Baker 92
Johnson, Ian Terence WhoScE 91-1
Johnson, Ingolf Birger 1913- WhoAm 92
Johnson, Irving McClure 1905-1991 BioIn 17
Johnson, Irving Stanley 1925- WhoAm 92
Johnson, Iver Christian 1928- WhoWor 93
Johnson, J. Albert 1933- WhoE 93
Johnson, J. Chester 1944- WhoAm 92, WhoE 93
Johnson, J. Fred 1951- St&PR 93
Johnson, J. J. WhoAm 92
Johnson, J.J. 1924- BioIn 17
Johnson, "J.J." (James Louis) 1924- Baker 92
Johnson, J.M. Hamlin 1925- St&PR 93, WhoAm 92
Johnson, J. Mitchell 1951- WhoEmL 93
Johnson, J(ohn) Rosamond 1873-1954 Baker 92
Johnson, J. Wayne St&PR 93
Johnson, J. William 1941- St&PR 93
Johnson, Jack BioIn 17
Johnson, Jack 1878-1946 BioIn 17
Johnson, Jack Leo 1933- St&PR 93, WhoIns 93
Johnson, Jack Thomas 1915- WhoAm 92
Johnson, Jacquelyn G. Law&B 92
Johnson, James A. 1943- WhoAm 92
Johnson, James Arnold 1939- WhoAm 92
Johnson, James B. 1944- ScF&FL 92
Johnson, James Bek, Jr. 1943- WhoAm 92, WhoSSW 93
Johnson, James Blair 1944- WhoWrEP 92
Johnson, James Clarence Law&B 92
Johnson, James Douglas 1950- WhoSSW 93
Johnson, James Earl 1938- BiDAMSp 1989
Johnson, James Edwin 1950- WhoSSW 93
Johnson, James Elver 1937- WhoSSW 93
Johnson, James Gann, Jr. 1915- WhoAm 92
Johnson, James Gibb 1937- WhoAm 92
Johnson, James Gordon 1929- WhoE 93
Johnson, James H. Law&B 92
Johnson, James H., Jr. 1944- St&PR 93
Johnson, James Harold 1944- WhoAm 92
Johnson, James Henry WhoScE 91-1
Johnson, James Hodge 1932- WhoSSW 93
Johnson, James Holbrook 1955- WhoWrEP 92
Johnson, James Hubert, Jr. Law&B 92
Johnson, James J. Law&B 92
Johnson, James L. 1927- St&PR 93
Johnson, James Lawrence 1927- WhoAm 92
Johnson, James Lawrence 1953- WhoWor 93
Johnson, James Louis 1924- BioIn 17
Johnson, James Myron 1927- WhoAm 92
Johnson, James P. 1891-1955 BioIn 17
Johnson, James P. 1894-1955 NewYTBS 92 [port]
Johnson, James P(rice) 1891-1955 Baker 92
Johnson, James Robert 1923- WhoAm 92
Johnson, James Terence 1942- WhoAm 92
Johnson, James Vernor 1923- St&PR 93
Johnson, James Walton 1916- St&PR 93
Johnson, James Waring 1959- WhoEmL 93
Johnson, James Weldon 1871-1938 Baker 92, BioIn 17, BlkAull 92, EncAACR
Johnson, James Wilburn, Jr. 1947- WhoSSW 93
Johnson, James Wiley 1940- St&PR 93
Johnson, James William 1927- WhoAm 92
Johnson, James William 1943- BiDAMSp 1989
Johnson, James Winston 1930- WhoAm 92
Johnson, Jane WhoWrEP 92
Johnson, Jane Penelope 1940- WhoAmW 93, WhoSSW 93, WhoWor 93
Johnson, Janet 1940- WhoAmW 93
Johnson, Janet A. 1940- WhoAm 92
Johnson, Janet Alayne 1961- WhoAmW 93
Johnson, Janet Gray Andrews 1956- WhoSSW 93
Johnson, Janet Helen 1944- WhoAm 92, WhoAmW 93
Johnson, Janet Lou 1939- WhoAmW 93
Johnson, Janet M. Law&B 92

Johnson, Janet Marie 1942- WhoSSW 93
Johnson, Janice Christine 1956- WhoEmL 93
Johnson, Janice Kay 1946- WhoEmL 93
Johnson, Janis 1956- St&PR 93
Johnson, Jay Francis 1934- WhoE 93
Johnson, Jean Elaine 1925- WhoAm 92, WhoAmW 93, WhoE 93
Johnson, Jeanne Patricia 1957- WhoAmW 93
Johnson, Jed BioIn 17, MiSFD 9
Johnson, Jed Joseph, Jr. 1939- WhoAm 92
Johnson, Jeffery Harold 1960- WhoEmL 93
Johnson, Jeffrey B. 1947- St&PR 93
Johnson, Jeffrey Michael 1962- WhoSSW 93
Johnson, Jeffrey Scott 1952- WhoEmL 93
Johnson, Jeh Vincent 1931- WhoAm 92
Johnson, Jennifer Anne 1963- WhoAmW 93
Johnson, Jere Macy 1954- St&PR 93, WhoE 93, WhoEmL 93
Johnson, Jerome Ben 1950- WhoEmL 93
Johnson, Jerome E. 1942- St&PR 93
Johnson, Jerome Edwin 1942- WhoE 93
Johnson, Jerome L. Jerry WhoAm 92
Johnson, Jerome Linne 1929- WhoWor 93
Johnson, Jerry A. 1931- WhoAm 92
Johnson, Jerry Lynn 1962- WhoEmL 93
Johnson, Jetsie White 1944- WhoAmW 93
Johnson, Jill Marie Kobus Law&B 92
Johnson, Jimmy SoulM
Johnson, Jimmy 1943- WhoAm 92, WhoSSW 93
Johnson, Jo Ann 1938- WhoAmW 93
Johnson, Joan 1943- WhoAmW 93
Johnson, Joan B. 1929- WhoAmW 93
Johnson, Joan Bray 1926- WhoAmW 93
Johnson, Joan E. Stout 1944- WhoWrEP 92
Johnson, Joan Marie 1954- WhoE 93
Johnson, JoAnn BioIn 17
Johnson, Joanne Mary 1947- WhoAmW 93
Johnson, Joe William 1908- WhoAm 92
Johnson, John c. 1540-c. 1594 Baker 92
Johnson, John 1742-1830 HarEnMi
Johnson, John 1926- WhoSSW 93
Johnson, John A. 1915- WhoAm 92
Johnson, John A. 1926- St&PR 93
Johnson, John Allen 1950- WhoEmL 93
Johnson, John Andrew Law&B 92
Johnson, John Andrew 1942- WhoWor 93
Johnson, John B. 1916- St&PR 93
Johnson, John Brayton 1916- WhoAm 92
Johnson, John E. 1942- St&PR 93
Johnson, John E., Jr. 1940- St&PR 93
Johnson, John Frank 1942- WhoAm 92
Johnson, John Gray 1924- WhoAm 92
Johnson, John H. BioIn 17
Johnson, John H. 1918- ConBlB 3 [port], WhoAm 92
Johnson, John Harold 1918- AfrAmBi, JrnUS
Johnson, John Henry 1929- BioIn 17
Johnson, John Irwin, Jr. 1931- WhoAm 92
Johnson, John J. Law&B 92
Johnson, John J. 1912- WhoAm 92
Johnson, John James 1932- St&PR 93
Johnson, John Lamar Law&B 92
Johnson, John Lowell 1926- WhoE 93
Johnson, John Prescott 1921- WhoAm 92
Johnson, John Richard WhoAsAP 91
Johnson, John Robert 1936- WhoWor 93
Johnson, John Warren 1929- WhoAm 92
Johnson, John William 1947- St&PR 93
Johnson, John William, Jr. 1932- WhoAm 92
Johnson, Johnnie D. 1938- St&PR 93
Johnson, Johnny BioIn 17
Johnson, Johnny 1938- WhoSSW 93
Johnson, Johnny Albert 1938- WhoSSW 93
Johnson, Johnny, & the Bandwagon SoulM
Johnson, Johnny Gayle 1948- WhoEmL 93
Johnson, Johnny Ray 1929- WhoAm 92
Johnson, Joia 1960- St&PR 93
Johnson, Jonas Talmadge 1947- WhoE 93
Johnson, Jonathan Edwin, II 1936- WhoAm 92
Johnson, Jory (F.) 1950- ConAu 137
Johnson, Joseph Andrew, III 1940- WhoSSW 93
Johnson, Joseph Benjamin 1934- WhoAm 92, WhoSSW 93
Johnson, Joseph Bernard 1919- WhoAm 92
Johnson, Joseph D. d1990 BioIn 17
Johnson, Joseph Edward 1932- WhoE 93
Johnson, Joseph Eggleston, III 1930- WhoAm 92
Johnson, Joseph Ernest 1942- WhoIns 93
Johnson, Joseph Esrey 1906-1990 BioIn 17
Johnson, Joseph Eversole 1930- St&PR 93
Johnson, Joseph H. BioIn 17
Johnson, Joseph H. 1943- St&PR 93
Johnson, Joseph H., Jr. 1925- WhoAm 92
Johnson, Joseph Henry St&PR 93
Johnson, Joseph L. 1895-1991 BioIn 17
Johnson, Joseph P. St&PR 93
Johnson, Josephine Ann 1938- St&PR 93
Johnson, Josephine Goode BioIn 17
Johnson, Josephine Powell 1941- WhoAmW 93
Johnson, Josephine W. BioIn 17
Johnson, Joy A. Law&B 92
Johnson, Joy Duvall 1932- WhoAmW 93
Johnson, Joyce 1935- BioIn 17
Johnson, Joyce 1936- St&PR 93
Johnson, Joyce Ann 1950- WhoEmL 93
Johnson, Judith A. ScF&FL 92
Johnson, Judith Ekberg St&PR 93
Johnson, Judith Evelyn 1936- WhoWrEP 92
Johnson, Judith Kay 1939- WhoAm 92, WhoSSW 93
Johnson, Judith Lynn 1955- WhoE 93
Johnson, Judy BioIn 17
Johnson, Judy Sherrill 1944- WhoAmW 93
Johnson, Julian Ernest 1925- St&PR 93
Johnson, Julian Ernest, III 1949- St&PR 93
Johnson, Julie West 1947- WhoEmL 93
Johnson, Julius Frank 1940- AfrAmBi [port], WhoAm 92
Johnson, K.C. Law&B 92
Johnson, K. Gail 1945- WhoAmW 93
Johnson, Karen Anne 1962- WhoEmL 93
Johnson, Karen Britton 1942- WhoAmW 93
Johnson, Karen Lee 1948- WhoAm 92
Johnson, Katharyn Price 1897- WhoAmW 93, WhoE 93
Johnson, Katherine Elizabeth BioIn 17
Johnson, Katherine Holthaus 1961- WhoAmW 93
Johnson, Kathleen Keane 1940- St&PR 93
Johnson, Kathryn BioIn 17
Johnson, Kathy BioIn 17
Johnson, Keith WhoScE 91-1
Johnson, Keith G. 1931- St&PR 93
Johnson, Keith Gilbert 1931- WhoAm 92
Johnson, Keith L. 1939- St&PR 93
Johnson, Keith P. St&PR 93
Johnson, Kenneth 1942- MiSFD 9
Johnson, Kenneth Alan Law&B 92
Johnson, Kenneth E. 1915- St&PR 93
Johnson, Kenneth H. Law&B 92
Johnson, Kenneth Harvey 1936- WhoAm 92
Johnson, Kenneth James Law&B 92
Johnson, Kenneth James 1935- St&PR 93
Johnson, Kenneth L. WhoScE 91-1
Johnson, Kenneth Langstreth 1925- WhoWor 93
Johnson, Kenneth Major, II 1957- WhoEmL 93
Johnson, Kenneth O. 1920- WhoAm 92
Johnson, Kenneth Odell 1922- WhoAm 92
Johnson, Kenneth Oscar 1920- WhoAm 92
Johnson, Kenneth Owen 1920- WhoAm 92
Johnson, Kenneth Peter 1932- WhoAm 92
Johnson, Kenneth R. ScF&FL 92
Johnson, Kenneth R. 1948- ScF&FL 92
Johnson, Kenneth Theodore 1918- WhoSSW 93
Johnson, Kennett Conrad 1927- WhoAm 92
Johnson, Kevin 1966- BioIn 17
Johnson, Kevin A. Law&B 92
Johnson, Kevin A. 1955- St&PR 93
Johnson, Kevin C. Law&B 92
Johnson, Kevin James Law&B 92
Johnson, Kristin Leigh 1965- WhoAm 92
Johnson, Kristine H. Law&B 92
Johnson, L. Elizabeth 1953- St&PR 93
Johnson, Lady Bird 1912- BioIn 17, WhoAm 92, WhoAmW 93, WhoSSW 93
Johnson, Lael F. Law&B 92
Johnson, Lael Frederic 1938- St&PR 93, WhoAm 92
Johnson, Lamont 1922- ConTFT 10, MiSFD 9
Johnson, Langston C., Jr. 1955- WhoSSW 93
Johnson, Larry BioIn 17
Johnson, Larry 1949- BioIn 17
Johnson, Larry C. St&PR 93
Johnson, Larry D. 1945- WhoUN 92
Johnson, Larry E. 1950- St&PR 93
Johnson, Larry Glenn 1948- St&PR 93
Johnson, Larry James 1949- WhoEmL 93, WhoSSW 93
Johnson, Larry Walter 1934- WhoAm 92
Johnson, Larry Wilson 1938- WhoAm 92
Johnson, Lars S. Law&B 92
Johnson, Laura BioIn 17
Johnson, Laura Ann 1959- WhoEmL 93
Johnson, Laura Elizabeth Deen 1958- WhoAmW 93
Johnson, Lavern Oscar 1935- WhoE 93
Johnson, Lawrence Alan 1947- WhoAm 92
Johnson, Lawrence C. Law&B 92
Johnson, Lawrence David 1937- WhoSSW 93
Johnson, Lawrence M. 1940- St&PR 93, WhoAm 92
Johnson, Lawrence Wilbur, Jr. 1955- WhoEmL 93
Johnson, Lee Harnie 1909- WhoAm 92
Johnson, Lee R. 1946- St&PR 93
Johnson, Lennart Ingemar 1924- WhoWor 93
Johnson, Leo Francis 1928- WhoE 93
Johnson, Leo Gordon 1933- WhoE 93
Johnson, Leonard C. d1991 BioIn 17
Johnson, Leonard Hjalma 1957- WhoEmL 93
Johnson, Leopoldo A. 1935- St&PR 93
Johnson, Leroy R. 1928- AfrAmBi
Johnson, Leslie WhoScE 91-1
Johnson, Lester Fredrick 1919- WhoAm 92
Johnson, Lester O. 1912- St&PR 93
Johnson, Lewis Brandon 1922- St&PR 93
Johnson, Lillian Beatrice 1922- WhoAmW 93
Johnson, Linda Arlene 1946- WhoAmW 93
Johnson, Linda Diane 1947- WhoEmL 93
Johnson, Linda Dianne 1954- AfrAmBi, WhoSSW 93
Johnson, Linda E. BioIn 17
Johnson, Linda Lee Davis 1947- WhoEmL 93
Johnson, Linda Southwick 1949- WhoAmW 93
Johnson, Linda Thelma 1954- WhoAmW 93
Johnson, Lindsay C.F. Law&B 92
Johnson, Linnea 1946- ConAu 138
Johnson, Lisa Gavazzi 1962- WhoSSW 93
Johnson, Lisa Webbe 1957- St&PR 93
Johnson, Lisabeth Anne 1958- WhoAmW 93
Johnson, Lissa H(alls) 1955- ConAu 136
Johnson, Lissa Halls 1955- BioIn 17
Johnson, Lizabeth Lettie 1957- WhoAmW 93, WhoEmL 93
Johnson, Lloyd Harlin 1928- WhoE 93
Johnson, Lloyd Newhall 1921- WhoSSW 93
Johnson, Lloyd Peter 1930- St&PR 93, WhoAm 92
Johnson, Lockrem 1924-1977 Baker 92
Johnson, Loering M. 1926- WhoAm 92
Johnson, Lois Walfrid 1936- WhoWrEP 92
Johnson, Lonnell Edward 1942- WhoSSW 93
Johnson, Lonnie L. Law&B 92
Johnson, Lori Ann 1959- WhoEmL 93
Johnson, Lorraine B. 1952- St&PR 93
Johnson, Lorraine Cimino Law&B 92
Johnson, LouAnne 1953- ConAu 138
Johnson, Louis 1955- See Brothers Johnson SoulM
Johnson, Louise Ellen French 1960- WhoEmL 93
Johnson, Louise Napier WhoScE 91-1
Johnson, Lowell Ferris 1912- WhoAm 92
Johnson, LuAn 1956- WhoAmW 93, WhoEmL 93
Johnson, Lucy M. Law&B 92
Johnson, Lyle R. 1931- St&PR 93
Johnson, Lyman Keating 1951- WhoEmL 93
Johnson, Lynda Bird 1943- BioIn 17
Johnson, Lyndon B. 1908-1973 BioIn 17, ColdWar 1 [port], DcTwHis, PolPar
Johnson, Lynn Law&B 92
Johnson, Lynne Lalor 1943- WhoAmW 93
Johnson, M. Alanson, II 1933- St&PR 93
Johnson, M.E. 1922- St&PR 93
Johnson, Mabel P. AmWomPl
Johnson, Madeline C. AmWomPl
Johnson, Madeline Mitchell 1930- WhoAmW 93
Johnson, Magic 1959- BioIn 17, WhoAm 92
Johnson, Malcolm Clinton, Jr. 1925- WhoAm 92
Johnson, Malcolm Lewis 1943- WhoWor 93
Johnson, Malcom Law&B 92
Johnson, Manuel H. BioIn 17
Johnson, Marc C. Law&B 92
Johnson, Margaret AmWomPl
Johnson, Margaret Ann 1948- WhoAmW 93
Johnson, Margaret Helen 1933- WhoAmW 93, WhoWor 93
Johnson, Margaret Hill 1923- WhoAmW 93
Johnson, Margaret Kathleen 1920- WhoAm 92
Johnson, Margaret Kinsley 1961- WhoAmW 93
Johnson, Maria Cannarozzi 1963- WhoSSW 93
Johnson, Maria E. 1955- St&PR 93
Johnson, Marian Ilene 1929- WhoAmW 93, WhoWor 93
Johnson, Marie W. AmWomPl
Johnson, Marietta BioIn 17
Johnson, Marijo Anne 1935- WhoE 93
Johnson, Marilyn Ann 1946- WhoEmL 93
Johnson, Marilyn Rae 1958- WhoEmL 93
Johnson, Marion Phillip 1931- WhoAm 92
Johnson, Mark Law&B 92
Johnson, Mark A. St&PR 93
Johnson, Mark Alan 1960- WhoAm 92
Johnson, Mark Allen Law&B 92
Johnson, Mark Eugene 1951- WhoEmL 93
Johnson, Mark Leonard 1954- St&PR 93
Johnson, Mark Matthew 1950- WhoSSW 93
Johnson, Mark Musgrave 1946- St&PR 93
Johnson, Mark Oliver 1945- St&PR 93
Johnson, Mark S. Law&B 92
Johnson, Mark Steven 1961- WhoSSW 93
Johnson, Mark W. Law&B 92
Johnson, Mark Wendell 1961- WhoSSW 93
Johnson, Markham P., III 1953- WhoWrEP 92
Johnson, Marlene 1946- WhoAm 92, WhoAmW 93, WhoWor 93
Johnson, Marlene A. 1935- WhoAm 92
Johnson, Marlene E. AfrAmBi [port]
Johnson, Marlin J.E. 1922- St&PR 93
Johnson, Marlys Dianne 1948- WhoAm 92
Johnson, Marques Kevin 1956- BiDAMSp 1989, WhoAm 92
Johnson, Marson Harry 1941- WhoSSW 93
Johnson, Martha Collins 1913- WhoAmW 93
Johnson, Martin Allen 1931- WhoAm 92
Johnson, Martin Earl 1929- WhoAm 92
Johnson, Martin Harry 1950- WhoEmL 93
Johnson, Marty Jo 1947- WhoWrEP 92
Johnson, Marv 1938- SoulM
Johnson, Marvin Donald 1928- St&PR 93, WhoAm 92, WhoWor 93
Johnson, Marvin Melrose 1925- WhoAm 92
Johnson, Marvin Richard Alois 1916- WhoAm 92
Johnson, Mary Alice 1942- WhoAmW 93
Johnson, Mary Alice 1958- WhoAmW 93
Johnson, Mary Ann Law&B 92
Johnson, Mary Elizabeth 1905- WhoAmW 93
Johnson, Mary Ellen 1946- St&PR 93
Johnson, Mary Frances 1951- WhoAmW 93
Johnson, Mary J. 1917- AfrAmBi [port]
Johnson, Mary Lea 1926- ConTFT 10
Johnson, Mary Louise 1932- WhoWrEP 92
Johnson, Mary Murphy 1940- WhoAmW 93, WhoSSW 93
Johnson, Mary Susan 1937- WhoAmW 93, WhoWor 93
Johnson, Mary Thomson AmWomPl
Johnson, Maryann Elaine 1943- WhoAmW 93
Johnson, Maryanna Morse 1936- WhoAmW 93
Johnson, Matthew Brian 1957- WhoEmL 93
Johnson, Maurice Glen 1936- WhoAm 92
Johnson, Maurice Joseph 1919- WhoE 93
Johnson, Max B. Law&B 92
Johnson, Maxine Frahm 1939- WhoAmW 93
Johnson, Maynard B. 1921- St&PR 93
Johnson, Maynard R. Law&B 92
Johnson, Melinda 1936- WhoWor 93
Johnson, Melinda Jean 1962- WhoAmW 93
Johnson, Melissa Bruce 1952- WhoAmW 93
Johnson, Melvin Edward 1939- St&PR 93
Johnson, Melvin Herbert 1938- St&PR 93
Johnson, Merle 1874-1935 ScF&FL 92
Johnson, Micah William 1963- WhoSSW 93
Johnson, Michael BioIn 17
Johnson, Michael Edward 1956- WhoSSW 93
Johnson, Michael Floyd 1945- WhoSSW 93
Johnson, Michael Kenneth 1953- WhoSSW 93
Johnson, Michael L. Law&B 92
Johnson, Michael O. 1946- St&PR 93
Johnson, Michael Olin Law&B 92

Johnson, Michael Paul 1941- *WhoAm 92*
Johnson, Michael Peter 1950- *WhoUN 92*
Johnson, Michael R. *Law&B 92*
Johnson, Michael Wallace *Law&B 92*
Johnson, Millard Wallace, Jr. 1928- *WhoAm 92*
Johnson, Miller Alanson, II 1933- *WhoAm 92*
Johnson, Milton Raymond, Jr. 1919- *WhoSSW 93*
Johnson, Mitchell Allen 1942- *St&PR 93*
Johnson, Mordecai Wyatt 1890-1976 *EncAACR*
Johnson, Murray C. 1959- *St&PR 93*
Johnson, Murray H. 1956- *WhoEmL 93, WhoSSW 93, WhoWor 93*
Johnson, N.W. *WhoScE 91-1*
Johnson, Nancy C. Pickles 1950- *WhoEmL 93*
Johnson, Nancy Elizabeth 1953- *WhoEmL 93*
Johnson, Nancy Faye 1951- *WhoEmL 93*
Johnson, Nancy Izzo 1947- *WhoAmW 93*
Johnson, Nancy Jill 1960- *WhoAmW 93*
Johnson, Nancy L. *BioIn 17*
Johnson, Nancy L. 1935- *CngDr 91*
Johnson, Nancy Lee 1935- *WhoAm 92, WhoAmW 93, WhoE 93*
Johnson, Nancy Lynn *Law&B 92*
Johnson, Nancy M. 1947- *WhoIns 93*
Johnson, Nancy Plattner 1938- *WhoSSW 93*
Johnson, Neal Curtis *Law&B 92*
Johnson, Ned 1926- *WhoAm 92*
Johnson, Neil 1954- *SmATA 73 [port]*
Johnson, Neil B. *Law&B 92*
Johnson, Neil Gordon 1927- *St&PR 93*
Johnson, Neil Richard 1945- *WhoE 93*
Johnson, Nelda Owens 1936- *WhoSSW 93*
Johnson, Nicholas 1934- *WhoAm 92, WhoWrEP 92*
Johnson, Nickolas O. 1935- *WhoSSW 93*
Johnson, Niel M. 1931- *ScF&FL 92*
Johnson, Nigel 1947- *WhoScE 91-1*
Johnson, Noble 1881-1957 *IntDcF 2-3 [port]*
Johnson, Noel Lars 1957- *WhoAm 92, WhoWor 93*
Johnson, Nora Toner 1952- *WhoAmW 93, WhoEmL 93*
Johnson, Norma Alice 1932- *WhoWrEP 92*
Johnson, Norma Holloway *CngDr 91, WhoAm 92, WhoAmW 93, WhoE 93*
Johnson, Norma J. 1925- *WhoAmW 93*
Johnson, Norma R. *Law&B 92*
Johnson, Norma Tadlock *ScF&FL 92*
Johnson, Norman *SoulM*
Johnson, Norman 1928- *WhoAm 92*
Johnson, Norman E. 1948- *St&PR 93*
Johnson, Norman James 1921- *WhoSSW 93*
Johnson, Norman Jeremy E. 1935- *WhoE 93*
Johnson, Noye Monroe 1930-1987 *BioIn 17*
Johnson, Nunnally 1897-1977 *BioIn 17, MiSFD 9N*
Johnson, Oliver 1957- *ScF&FL 92*
Johnson, Oliver Thomas, Jr. 1946- *WhoAm 92*
Johnson, Omotunde Evan George 1941- *WhoE 93, WhoSSW 93, WhoUN 92, WhoWor 93*
Johnson, Ora Mae 1944- *WhoWrEP 92*
Johnson, Orlin E. 1948- *St&PR 93*
Johnson, Orrin Wendell 1920- *WhoAm 92*
Johnson, Owen Verne 1946- *WhoEmL 93*
Johnson, Pamela 1949- *SmATA 71*
Johnson, Pamela Hansford 1912-1981 *BioIn 17*
Johnson, Pamela Tonn *Law&B 92*
Johnson, Patricia Altenbernd 1945- *WhoAmW 93*
Johnson, Patricia Anna 1938- *WhoWrEP 92*
Johnson, Patricia Burke 1941- *WhoAmW 93*
Johnson, Patricia Duren 1943- *WhoAmW 93*
Johnson, Patricia Hardy 1933- *WhoAmW 93, WhoWor 93*
Johnson, Patricia Joseph 1949- *WhoEmL 93*
Johnson, Patricia Mary 1937- *WhoAmW 93*
Johnson, Patrick, Jr. 1955- *WhoSSW 93*
Johnson, Patrick Arthur *Law&B 92*
Johnson, Patrick Read *MiSFD 9*
Johnson, Patti Lynn 1958- *WhoAmW 93*
Johnson, Paul *BioIn 17, SoulM, WhoAm 92*
Johnson, Paul A. 1919- *St&PR 93*
Johnson, Paul B. 1891-1991 *BioIn 17*
Johnson, Paul Christian 1928- *WhoAm 92*
Johnson, Paul Edwin 1933- *WhoSSW 93*
Johnson, Paul Howard 1924- *WhoAm 92*
Johnson, Paul Joseph 1923- *WhoAm 92*
Johnson, Paul K. *Law&B 92*
Johnson, Paul Lawrence 1952- *WhoEmL 93*
Johnson, Paul Oren 1937- *WhoAm 92*
Johnson, Paul Owen 1919- *WhoWor 93*
Johnson, Paul William 1958- *WhoE 93*
Johnson, Paula R. *Law&B 92*
Johnson, Pauline Benge 1932- *WhoAmW 93*
Johnson, Peggy *BioIn 17*
Johnson, Peggy Turner 1930- *WhoAmW 93*
Johnson, Pepper 1964- *WhoAm 92*
Johnson, Per-Olof 1928- *WhoWor 93*
Johnson, Perry H. 1946- *St&PR 93*
Johnson, Peter 1936- *WhoScE 91-1*
Johnson, Peter Christopher 1954- *WhoWrEP 92*
Johnson, Peter Dexter, Jr. 1945- *WhoSSW 93*
Johnson, Peter Forbes 1934- *WhoSSW 93*
Johnson, Peter K. *Law&B 92*
Johnson, Peter Malcolm *WhoScE 91-1*
Johnson, Peter R. *Law&B 92*
Johnson, Peter T. *Law&B 92*
Johnson, Philip A. 1915-1991 *BioIn 17*
Johnson, Philip Cortelyou 1906- *BioIn 17, WhoAm 92, WhoWor 93*
Johnson, Philip McBride 1938- *WhoAm 92*
Johnson, Phillip E. 1940- *ConAu 136*
Johnson, Phillip Eugene 1937- *WhoAm 92*
Johnson, Phyllis *BioIn 17*
Johnson, Phyllis Aileen 1955- *WhoAmW 93*
Johnson, Phyllis Kay 1955- *WhoEmL 93*
Johnson, Phyllis Marie *WhoE 93*
Johnson, Phyllis Michelle 1954- *WhoEmL 93*
Johnson, Pollyann 1948- *WhoAmW 93*
Johnson, Preston Lewis 1934- *St&PR 93*
Johnson, Quincy Lindell 1954- *WhoWor 93*
Johnson, R.C., Jr. 1920- *St&PR 93*
Johnson, R. Craig *Law&B 92*
Johnson, R.D. *St&PR 93*
Johnson, R.P. *WhoScE 91-1*
Johnson, Rachel Ramirez 1937- *WhoSSW 93*
Johnson, Rady A. *St&PR 93*
Johnson, Rady Alan 1936- *WhoAm 92*
Johnson, Ralph Raymond 1943- *WhoAm 92*
Johnson, Ralph S. 1943- *St&PR 93*
Johnson, Randy H. *Law&B 92*
Johnson, Raud Earl *Law&B 92*
Johnson, Ray Clifford 1927- *WhoAm 92*
Johnson, Raymond Ard 1942- *WhoE 93*
Johnson, Raymond Coles 1907- *WhoAm 92*
Johnson, Raymond Harold 1939- *St&PR 93*
Johnson, Raymond L. 1931- *St&PR 93*
Johnson, Raymond W. 1934- *WhoWor 93*
Johnson, Raymonda Theodora Greene 1939- *WhoAmW 93*
Johnson, Rebecca L. *BioIn 17*
Johnson, Rebecca L. 1956- *ConAu 136*
Johnson, Rebekah Terrell 1958- *WhoAm 92*
Johnson, Reid Stuart 1951- *WhoEmL 93*
Johnson, Rena *Law&B 92*
Johnson, Renee Grace 1962- *WhoEmL 93*
Johnson, Reverdy 1937- *WhoAm 92*
Johnson, Rheuben C. 1937- *WhoIns 93*
Johnson, Rhoda Ann Brown 1938- *WhoE 93*
Johnson, Richard *BioIn 17*
Johnson, Richard 1933- *St&PR 93*
Johnson, Richard A. 1936- *St&PR 93*
Johnson, Richard Abraham 1910- *WhoAm 92*
Johnson, Richard Alan 1955- *WhoSSW 93*
Johnson, Richard Arnold 1937- *WhoAm 92*
Johnson, Richard Arthur 1936- *WhoAm 92*
Johnson, Richard August 1937- *WhoAm 92*
Johnson, Richard Clark 1937- *WhoAm 92*
Johnson, Richard Clayton 1930- *WhoAm 92*
Johnson, Richard D. 1932- *St&PR 93*
Johnson, Richard Damerau 1934- *WhoAm 92*
Johnson, Richard David 1927- *WhoAm 92*
Johnson, Richard Dean 1936- *WhoWor 93*
Johnson, Richard E. 1929- *St&PR 93*
Johnson, Richard E. 1946- *St&PR 93*
Johnson, Richard Earles 1920- *WhoE 93*
Johnson, Richard Fred 1944- *WhoAm 92*
Johnson, Richard Frederick 1943- *WhoE 93*
Johnson, Richard H. *St&PR 93*
Johnson, Richard Hugh 1926- *WhoWor 93*
Johnson, Richard J.V. 1930- *St&PR 93*
Johnson, Richard James Vaughan 1930- *WhoSSW 93*
Johnson, Richard James Vaughn 1930- *WhoAm 92*
Johnson, Richard John 1947- *WhoEmL 93*
Johnson, Richard L. *Law&B 92*
Johnson, Richard Mentor 1780-1850 *HarEnMi, PolPar*
Johnson, Richard S. 1932- *St&PR 93*
Johnson, Richard T. 1931- *WhoAm 92*
Johnson, Richard Tenney 1930- *WhoAm 92*
Johnson, Richard Walter 1928- *WhoWor 93*
Johnson, Richard Warren 1939- *WhoAm 92*
Johnson, Richard William 1916- *WhoAm 92*
Johnson, Rick L. 1953- *St&PR 93*
Johnson, Rick Paul 1951- *St&PR 93*
Johnson, Ricky Leon 1952- *WhoEmL 93, WhoSSW 93*
Johnson, Rob *BioIn 17*
Johnson, Robbin M. *Law&B 92*
Johnson, Robert *BioIn 17*
Johnson, Robert d1938 *BioIn 17*
Johnson, Robert c. 1583-1633 *Baker 92*
Johnson, Robert 1931-1991 *BiDAMSp 1989*
Johnson, Robert A. *Law&B 92*
Johnson, Robert Alan 1933- *WhoSSW 93*
Johnson, Robert Alan 1944- *WhoAm 92, WhoWor 93*
Johnson, Robert Allison 1928- *WhoAm 92*
Johnson, Robert B. 1934- *St&PR 93*
Johnson, Robert Britten 1924- *WhoAm 92*
Johnson, Robert Bruce 1912- *WhoAm 92*
Johnson, Robert C. *Law&B 92*
Johnson, Robert Clyde 1919- *WhoAm 92*
Johnson, Robert Dale 1965- *WhoEmL 93, WhoWor 93*
Johnson, Robert David 1957- *WhoEmL 93*
Johnson, Robert Dudley 1945- *WhoSSW 93*
Johnson, Robert E. *Law&B 92*
Johnson, Robert E. 1926- *St&PR 93*
Johnson, Robert E. 1936- *WhoAm 92*
Johnson, Robert Edward 1922- *WhoAm 92*
Johnson, Robert Edward 1946- *WhoSSW 93*
Johnson, Robert Elmer 1947- *WhoEmL 93*
Johnson, Robert Eugene 1911- *WhoAm 92, WhoE 93*
Johnson, Robert G. 1928- *St&PR 93*
Johnson, Robert Gerald 1928- *WhoAm 92*
Johnson, Robert Gibbon 1771-1850 *BioIn 17*
Johnson, Robert H. *Law&B 92*
Johnson, Robert Henry 1921- *WhoAm 92*
Johnson, Robert Henry 1939- *WhoUN 92*
Johnson, Robert Hersel 1923- *WhoAm 92*
Johnson, Robert Ivar 1933- *WhoAm 92*
Johnson, Robert J. *Law&B 92*
Johnson, Robert Joseph 1938- *WhoAm 92*
Johnson, Robert L. 1946?- *ConBlB 3 [port]*
Johnson, Robert Lauren 1949- *WhoSSW 93*
Johnson, Robert Lawrence, Jr. 1945- *WhoAm 92*
Johnson, Robert Lewis, Jr. 1935- *WhoAm 92*
Johnson, Robert Louis *BioIn 17*
Johnson, Robert Louis 1946- *WhoAm 92*
Johnson, Robert Maurice 1945- *WhoAm 92*
Johnson, Robert Merrill 1926- *WhoAm 92*
Johnson, Robert Michael *Law&B 92*
Johnson, Robert Milton 1962- *WhoEmL 93*
Johnson, Robert P. 1945- *WhoIns 93*
Johnson, Robert Raymond 1917- *WhoAm 92*
Johnson, Robert Richard 1932- *St&PR 93*
Johnson, Robert Sherlaw 1932- *Baker 92*
Johnson, Robert T. 1923- *St&PR 93*
Johnson, Robert Thomas *WhoWrEP 92*
Johnson, Robert Underwood 1853-1937 *GayN*
Johnson, Robert Willard 1921- *WhoAm 92*
Johnson, Robert William *Law&B 92, WhoScE 91-1*
Johnson, Robert William, Jr. 1927- *WhoSSW 93*
Johnson, Rodney Marcum 1947- *WhoEmL 93, WhoSSW 93*
Johnson, Roger Allen *Law&B 92*
Johnson, Roger Dean 1935- *WhoIns 93*
Johnson, Roger J. 1936- *WhoIns 93*
Johnson, Roger N. 1939- *WhoWrEP 92*
Johnson, Roger Paul *WhoScE 91-1*
Johnson, Roger W. 1934- *St&PR 93*
Johnson, Roger W. 1935- *WhoAm 92*
Johnson, Roger Warren 1960- *WhoSSW 93*
Johnson, Rogers Bruce 1928- *WhoAm 92*
Johnson, Roland A. *WhoAm 92*
Johnson, Roland Edward 1933- *St&PR 93*
Johnson, Rolla L. 1916- *St&PR 93*
Johnson, Rolland Clair 1944- *WhoAm 92*
Johnson, Ronald 1935- *WhoWrEP 92*
Johnson, Ronald A. *St&PR 93*
Johnson, Ronald B. 1928- *St&PR 93*
Johnson, Ronald Bryan 1948- *WhoE 93*
Johnson, Ronald C. *BioIn 17*
Johnson, Ronald C. 1941- *WhoIns 93*
Johnson, Ronald Carl 1935- *WhoAm 92*
Johnson, Ronald Cecil *WhoScE 91-1*
Johnson, Ronald Cleve 1941- *St&PR 93*
Johnson, Ronald D. 1945- *St&PR 93*
Johnson, Ronald F. *Law&B 92*
Johnson, Ronald Kay 1939- *WhoWor 93*
Johnson, Ronald Keith 1957- *St&PR 93*
Johnson, Ronald Leroy 1943- *WhoWrEP 92*
Johnson, Ronald M. 1950- *St&PR 93*
Johnson, Ronald W. 1942- *St&PR 93*
Johnson, Rosalie E. *Law&B 92*
Johnson, Rose Marie 1964- *WhoAmW 93*
Johnson, Rosemary Wrucke 1924- *WhoAmW 93*
Johnson, Rosi K. 1951- *St&PR 93*
Johnson, Roxana Louise 1944- *WhoAmW 93*
Johnson, Roy *WhoScE 91-1*
Johnson, Roy M. 1947- *St&PR 93*
Johnson, Roy Ragnar 1932- *WhoAm 92*
Johnson, Roy W. 1945- *St&PR 93*
Johnson, Roy W. 1948- *St&PR 93*
Johnson, Ruby LaVerne 1917- *WhoAmW 93*
Johnson, Russell F. 1928- *St&PR 93*
Johnson, Russell Ward 1948- *WhoEmL 93*
Johnson, Ruth 1937- *WhoE 93*
Johnson, Ruth Ann Craig Goswick 1946- *WhoAmW 93*
Johnson, Ruth Brammer *Law&B 92*
Johnson, Ruth Marie 1917- *WhoAmW 93*
Johnson, Ryerson 1901- *ScF&FL 92*
Johnson, Sally Hope 1951- *WhoAmW 93*
Johnson, Sam *BioIn 17*
Johnson, Sam 1930- *BioIn 17, WhoAm 92*
Johnson, Sam D. 1920- *WhoSSW 93*
Johnson, Sammye La Rue 1946- *WhoWrEP 92*
Johnson, Sammye LaRue 1946- *WhoSSW 93*
Johnson, Samuel 1709-1784 *BioIn 17, MagSWL [port], WorLitC [port]*
Johnson, Samuel C. 1928- *St&PR 93*
Johnson, Samuel Curtis 1928- *WhoAm 92, WhoWor 93*
Johnson, Samuel Sam 1930- *WhoSSW 93*
Johnson, Sandy 1953- *MiSFD 9*
Johnson, Sanford A. 1918- *St&PR 93*
Johnson, Sankey Anton 1940- *WhoAm 92*
Johnson, Scott David 1955- *WhoSSW 93*
Johnson, Scott M. *Law&B 92*
Johnson, Scott W. *Law&B 92*
Johnson, Scott W. 1940- *St&PR 93*
Johnson, Scott William 1940- *WhoAm 92*
Johnson, Searcy Lee 1908- *WhoAm 92*
Johnson, Seddon *ScF&FL 92*
Johnson, Selina Pedersen 1954- *WhoAmW 93*
Johnson, Selina Tetzlaff 1906- *WhoAm 92*
Johnson, Shane 1959- *ScF&FL 92*
Johnson, Sharon Foster 1947- *WhoAmW 93*
Johnson, Sharon Kay 1944- *WhoAmW 93*
Johnson, Sheila C. *St&PR 93*
Johnson, Sheldon Ashley 1948- *WhoSSW 93*
Johnson, Sheldon Wayne 1947- *WhoEmL 93*
Johnson, Shelley A. 1951- *St&PR 93*
Johnson, Sherri Dale 1948- *WhoAmW 93, WhoEmL 93*
Johnson, Sherri Lynn 1956- *WhoE 93, WhoEmL 93*
Johnson, Sherry 1950- *St&PR 93*
Johnson, Shirley Elaine 1946- *WhoAmW 93, WhoEmL 93*
Johnson, Shirley Jeanne 1928- *WhoWrEP 92*
Johnson, Shirley Jenise 1955- *WhoAmW 93*
Johnson, Shirley Mae 1940- *WhoAmW 93*
Johnson, Sid 1939- *St&PR 93*
Johnson, Sidney George, II *Law&B 92*
Johnson, Sidney Keith 1942- *WhoAm 92*
Johnson, Sondra Lea 1952- *WhoAmW 93, WhoEmL 93*
Johnson, Sonia 1936- *BioIn 17*
Johnson, Sonjii *BioIn 17*
Johnson, Stanford Leland 1924- *WhoAm 92*

Johnson, Stanley David 1943- St&PR 93
Johnson, Stanley R. 1938- WhoAm 92
Johnson, Stanley Webster 1938- WhoSSW 93
Johnson, Stephanie Lynn 1962- WhoEmL 93
Johnson, Stephen Anthony 1947- St&PR 93
Johnson, Stephen C. 1942- St&PR 93
Johnson, Stephen L. 1944- St&PR 93
Johnson, Stephen R. Law&B 92
Johnson, Sterling Cornaby 1940- St&PR 93
Johnson, Steven J. 1936- St&PR 93
Johnson, Steven Lloyd 1954- WhoSSW 93
Johnson, Steven M. Law&B 92
Johnson, Steven M. 1951- St&PR 93
Johnson, Steven Nelson 1953- WhoE 93
Johnson, Stewart Willard 1933- WhoAm 92
Johnson, Sue Beth 1953- WhoE 93
Johnson, Susan Law&B 92
Johnson, Susan A. St&PR 93
Johnson, Susan E. Law&B 92
Johnson, Susan E. 1940- ConAu 138
Johnson, Susan (Ruth) 1956- ConAu 137
Johnson, Susanna Willard 1730-1810 BioIn 17
Johnson, Susanne Louise 1941- WhoAmW 93
Johnson, Suzanne Bennett 1948- WhoSSW 93
Johnson, Suzanne Curtis WhoAmW 93
Johnson, Suzanne D. Law&B 92
Johnson, Suzette Mason 1966- WhoAmW 93
Johnson, Syl 1936- BioIn 17
Johnson, T. Miles G. 1957- WhoWor 93
Johnson, Teresa H. Law&B 92
Johnson, Teresa J. 1962- WhoAmW 93
Johnson, Terry 1935- See Flamingos SoulM
Johnson, Terry Charles 1936- WhoAm 92
Johnson, Terry Lee 1950- WhoE 93
Johnson, Theodore Oliver, Jr. 1929- WhoAm 92
Johnson, Theodore R. BioIn 17, Law&B 92
Johnson, Theresa Mae 1949- WhoSSW 93
Johnson, Thomas 1732-1819 OxCSupC [port]
Johnson, Thomas Allibone Budd 1955- WhoSSW 93, WhoWor 93
Johnson, Thomas Buckley 1955- WhoE 93
Johnson, Thomas Edward 1953- WhoEmL 93
Johnson, Thomas Eugene 1948- WhoEmL 93
Johnson, Thomas F. 1949- St&PR 93
Johnson, Thomas Floyd 1943- WhoAm 92
Johnson, Thomas Francis 1942- WhoE 93
Johnson, Thomas H. WhoAm 92
Johnson, Thomas Hawkins 1943-1990 BioIn 17
Johnson, Thomas L., Jr. 1914- St&PR 93
Johnson, Thomas N.P., Jr. 1918- St&PR 93
Johnson, Thomas Paul 1950- St&PR 93
Johnson, Thomas Pershing 1940- St&PR 93
Johnson, Thomas Phillips 1914- St&PR 93
Johnson, Thomas Russell 1944- St&PR 93, WhoAm 92
Johnson, Thomas S. 1940- St&PR 93
Johnson, Thomas Stephen 1940- WhoAm 92, WhoE 93
Johnson, Thomas Stuart 1942- WhoWor 93
Johnson, Thomas W. 1957- WhoSSW 93
Johnson, Thomas Webber, Jr. 1941- WhoAm 92
Johnson, Thor 1913-1975 Baker 92
Johnson, Thruston Charles 1914- WhoE 93, WhoWor 93
Johnson, Tim 1946- CngDr 91
Johnson, Timothy BioIn 17
Johnson, Timothy Andrew 1968- WhoE 93
Johnson, Timothy Jay 1959- WhoWor 93
Johnson, Timothy P. Law&B 92
Johnson, Timothy Peter 1946- WhoAm 92
Johnson, Toby 1945- ScF&FL 92
Johnson, Tod Stuart 1944- WhoAm 92, WhoWor 93
Johnson, Todd ScF&FL 92
Johnson, Tom ScF&FL 92
Johnson, Tom 1939- Baker 92
Johnson, Tom 1941- BioIn 17
Johnson, Tom Milroy 1935- WhoAm 92
Johnson, Tor 1912-1971 BioIn 17
Johnson, Torrence Vaino 1944- WhoAm 92
Johnson, Tracey Denise 1966- WhoE 93
Johnson, Trebbe 1948- WhoWrEP 92
Johnson, U. Alexis 1908- WhoAm 92
Johnson, Uwe 1934-1984 BioIn 17, ConAu 39NR
Johnson, Van 1916- IntDcF 2-3, WhoAm 92
Johnson, Vassel 1922- DcCPCAm
Johnson, Vaughan 1962- WhoAm 92
Johnson, Velma Catherine Hannah 1960- WhoAmW 93
Johnson, Verna Mae 1930- WhoAmW 93
Johnson, Vernon A. Law&B 92, WhoAm 92
Johnson, Vernon Alfred 1928- St&PR 93
Johnson, Vernon Eugene 1930- WhoSSW 93
Johnson, Vernon Leroy 1929- St&PR 93
Johnson, Vicki Marie 1954- WhoAmW 93
Johnson, Vicki R. 1952- WhoAmW 93
Johnson, Vicky Lynn 1955- WhoEmL 93
Johnson, Victor Lawrence 1928- WhoAm 92
Johnson, Victoria Kaprielian 1959- WhoAmW 93
Johnson, Vincent Gregory 1956- WhoSSW 93
Johnson, Virgil Allen 1921- WhoAm 92
Johnson, Virginia 1950- BioIn 17
Johnson, Virginia Alma Fairfax 1950- WhoAm 92
Johnson, Virginia B. 1954- St&PR 93
Johnson, W. Barney 1911- St&PR 93
Johnson, W.E. 1923-1989 BioIn 17
Johnson, W.E. 1928- St&PR 93
Johnson, W. Loy 1929- WhoAm 92, WhoSSW 93
Johnson, W. Thomas 1941- BioIn 17
Johnson, W. Thomas, Jr. 1941- WhoSSW 93
Johnson, Waine Cecil 1928- WhoAm 92
Johnson, Walker Reed 1931- WhoAm 92
Johnson, Wallace 1939- WhoWor 93
Johnson, Walter 1887-1946 BioIn 17
Johnson, Walter 1939- WhoE 93
Johnson, Walter Curtis 1913- WhoAm 92
Johnson, Walter Harry 1938- WhoE 93
Johnson, Walter Henry, III 1948- WhoE 93
Johnson, Walter Kline 1923- WhoAm 92
Johnson, Walter L. 1927- WhoAm 92
Johnson, Walter Roland 1927- WhoE 93
Johnson, Warren Donald 1922- WhoAm 92
Johnson, Warren Richard 1928- WhoAm 92, WhoSSW 93, WhoWor 93
Johnson, Wayne D. 1932- WhoAm 92
Johnson, Wayne David 1932- St&PR 93
Johnson, Wayne Eaton 1930- WhoAm 92
Johnson, Wayne Harold 1942- WhoAm 92
Johnson, Wayne L. 1942- ScF&FL 92
Johnson, Wayne Leslie 1953- WhoSSW 93
Johnson, Wendell Norman AfrAmBi [port]
Johnson, Wendell Stacy 1927-1990 BioIn 17
Johnson, Weyman Thompson, Jr. 1951- WhoAm 92, WhoSSW 93
Johnson, Willard Raymond 1935- WhoAm 92
Johnson, William 1715-1774 HarEnMi
Johnson, William 1771-1834 BioIn 17, OxCSupC [port]
Johnson, William A., Jr. 1953- St&PR 93
Johnson, William Alexander 1934- WhoAm 92, WhoE 93
Johnson, William Benedict d1991 BioIn 17
Johnson, William Benjamin 1918- WhoAm 92
Johnson, William Bruce 1940- WhoWor 93
Johnson, William C. 1940- St&PR 93
Johnson, William Cumming, Jr. 1904- WhoWor 93
Johnson, William D., III St&PR 93
Johnson, William David 1924- WhoAm 92
Johnson, William Douglas 1928- WhoE 93
Johnson, William Douglas 1956- WhoSSW 93
Johnson, William E. 1933- St&PR 93
Johnson, William E. 1941- St&PR 93, WhoAm 92, WhoSSW 93
Johnson, William Edwin Law&B 92
Johnson, William G. 1947- St&PR 93
Johnson, William H. d1878 BioIn 17
Johnson, William Hall 1943- WhoAm 92
Johnson, William Henry 1901-1970 ConBlB 3 [port]
Johnson, William Howard 1922- WhoAm 92
Johnson, William Hugh, Jr. 1935- WhoAm 92
Johnson, William Jennings 1955- WhoWor 93
Johnson, William Joseph 1941- WhoAm 92, WhoE 93
Johnson, William Larry 1943- WhoSSW 93
Johnson, William Oscar ScF&FL 92
Johnson, William Potter 1935- WhoAm 92, WhoWor 93
Johnson, William R. 1930- WhoAm 92, WhoE 93
Johnson, William Ray 1930- WhoSSW 93
Johnson, William Richard 1947- WhoAm 92
Johnson, William Richard, Jr. 1942- St&PR 93, WhoAm 92
Johnson, William Rudolph 1933- WhoAm 92
Johnson, William Stewart 1933- WhoAm 92
Johnson, William Stuart 1958- WhoEmL 93
Johnson, William Summer 1913- WhoAm 92
Johnson, William Weber 1909-1992 ConAu 139
Johnson, Willie Joe 1947- WhoSSW 93
Johnson, Willis BioIn 17
Johnson, Wilma Harris 1942- WhoSSW 93
Johnson, Wilson S. d1990 BioIn 17
Johnson, Winston Conrad 1943- WhoSSW 93, WhoWor 93
Johnson, Wyatt Thomas 1941- BioIn 17, St&PR 93
Johnson, Wyatt Thomas, Jr. 1941- WhoAm 92
Johnson, Wylie Pierson 1919- WhoSSW 93
Johnson, Yormie 1959- WhoAfr
Johnson, Yvonne Marie 1950- WhoWrEP 92
Johnson, Zane Quentin 1924- WhoAm 92
Johnson, Zoe Ann 1960- WhoAmW 93, WhoEmL 93
Johnson Ben BioIn 17
Johnson-Brown, Hazel 1927- AfrAmBi [port]
Johnson-Champ, Debra Sue 1955- WhoAmW 93
Johnson-Cousin, Danielle Paulette 1943- WhoAmW 93
Johnson-Delaney, Cathy Anne 1956- WhoAmW 93
Johnson-Grayum, Jane Robin 1957- WhoEmL 93
Johnson-Lesson, Charleen Ann 1949- WhoAmW 93
Johnson-Masters, Virginia E. 1925- WhoAm 92
Johnson, of Boone, Benjamin F. MajAI
Johnson-Wolff, Christina Marie 1950- WhoAm 92
Johnsrud, Russell Lloyd 1909-1992 WhoAm 92
Johnsson, Anders C.G. 1939- WhoScE 91-4
Johnsson, Hillary Crute 1959- WhoE 93
Johnston, A. Sidney Law&B 92
Johnston, Agnes Christine AmWomPl
Johnston, Aimee Ann 1960- WhoAmW 93
Johnston, Alan Rogers 1914- WhoAm 92
Johnston, Alastair John Carmichael 1928- WhoWor 93
Johnston, Albert Sidney 1803-1862 BioIn 17, HarEnMi
Johnston, Alfred G. 1922- St&PR 93
Johnston, Alistair D. 1937- St&PR 93, WhoIns 93
Johnston, Andrew W.B. WhoScE 91-1
Johnston, Annie Fellows 1863-1931 AmWomPl
Johnston, Anthony Sudekum 1944- WhoSSW 93
Johnston, Barry Hasler 1954- WhoE 93
Johnston, Ben Earl 1938- WhoAm 92
Johnston, Ben(jamin Burwell) 1926- Baker 92
Johnston, Bill BioIn 17
Johnston, Brad L. 1940- St&PR 93
Johnston, Brenda Ann 1953- WhoAmW 93
Johnston, Bruce Foster 1919- WhoAm 92
Johnston, Carla Brooks 1940- WhoE 93
Johnston, Carol Elizabeth 1948- WhoSSW 93
Johnston, Carole Anne 1944- WhoWrEP 92
Johnston, Charles Bernie, Jr. 1931- WhoAm 92
Johnston, Charles Frederick 1933- St&PR 93
Johnston, Chester F., Mrs. AmWomPl
Johnston, Christina Jane 1952- WhoAmW 93, WhoEmL 93
Johnston, Cicely Anne 1912- WhoWrEP 92
Johnston, Cliff S. WhoScE 91-1
Johnston, Colin Ivor 1934- WhoWor 93
Johnston, Cyrus Conrad, Jr. 1929- WhoAm 92
Johnston, D.W. 1903- St&PR 93
Johnston, David Ian 1932- WhoAm 92, WhoWor 93
Johnston, David Lloyd 1941- WhoAm 92
Johnston, David Owen 1930- WhoSSW 93
Johnston, David Ritchey 1950- WhoE 93
Johnston, David White 1921- St&PR 93
Johnston, Desmond Geoffrey WhoScE 91-1
Johnston, Dolores Mae Mascik 1927- WhoAmW 93
Johnston, Don 1927- St&PR 93
Johnston, Donald Robert 1926- WhoAm 92
Johnston, Douglas Frederick 1930- WhoAm 92
Johnston, Edward Allan 1921- WhoAm 92
Johnston, Edward D. Law&B 92
Johnston, Edward Elliott 1918- WhoAm 92
Johnston, Edward Joseph 1935- WhoE 93
Johnston, Elizabeth Parr- BioIn 17
Johnston, Emma Louise 1863- AmWomPl
Johnston, Frances Benjamin 1864-1952 BioIn 17
Johnston, Frank C. 1955- WhoE 93
Johnston, Frank Marion 1928- WhoSSW 93
Johnston, Frank Thomas 1955- WhoSSW 93
Johnston, Fred B., II 1938- St&PR 93
Johnston, Fred William, Jr. 1933- WhoAm 92
Johnston, Freedy BioIn 17
Johnston, Gary 1946- WhoWrEP 92
Johnston, Gary R. 1942- St&PR 93
Johnston, George Benson 1913- WhoCanL 92
Johnston, George Gustin 1932- WhoAm 92
Johnston, George Sim 1924-1991 BioIn 17
Johnston, George W. Law&B 92
Johnston, Gerald Andrew 1931- WhoAm 92
Johnston, Gerald McArthur 1942- St&PR 93
Johnston, Gerald Samuel 1930- WhoE 93
Johnston, Ginny 1946- BioIn 17
Johnston, Gordon Robert 1928- WhoE 93
Johnston, Gordon Wolf 1951- WhoEmL 93
Johnston, Grace Eliette 1957- WhoEmL 93
Johnston, Gwinavere Adams 1943- WhoAmW 93
Johnston, H. Frederick 1927- St&PR 93
Johnston, Harold Sledge 1920- WhoAm 92
Johnston, Harry 1931- CngDr 91
Johnston, Harry A., II 1931- WhoAm 92, WhoSSW 93
Johnston, Harry M., III Law&B 92
Johnston, Hugh Buckner 1913- WhoWrEP 92
Johnston, Ian Alistair WhoScE 91-1
Johnston, J. Bennett 1932- CngDr 91
Johnston, J. Bruce 1930- St&PR 93
Johnston, J.M. ScF&FL 92
Johnston, J. Phillips L. 1939- St&PR 93
Johnston, James 1903-1991 OxDcOp
Johnston, James Cannon 1955- WhoE 93
Johnston, James D. 1930- St&PR 93, WhoAm 92
Johnston, James Jordon 1931- WhoAm 92
Johnston, James Monroe, III 1940- WhoAm 92
Johnston, James Stewart 1932- WhoScE 91-1
Johnston, James W. BioIn 17
Johnston, James Wesley 1946- WhoAm 92
Johnston, Janet 1944- SmATA 71 [port]
Johnston, Jeanette McCandless 1951- WhoAmW 93
Johnston, Jeffrey D. 1950- St&PR 93
Johnston, Jeffrey Monroe 1952- WhoEmL 93
Johnston, Jennifer Faye 1957- WhoAmW 93
Johnston, Jerry Wayne 1946- St&PR 93
Johnston, Jill N. Law&B 92
Johnston, Jim MiSFD 9
Johnston, Joe MiSFD 9, ScF&FL 92
Johnston, John Bennett, Jr. 1932- WhoAm 92, WhoSSW 93
Johnston, John Devereaux, Jr. 1932- WhoAm 92
Johnston, John Gerard, Jr. 1926- St&PR 93
Johnston, John J. 1931- St&PR 93
Johnston, John J. 1950- WhoAm 92
Johnston, John Martin 1923- WhoAm 92
Johnston, John Philip 1935- WhoAm 92
Johnston, John Thomas 1930- WhoSSW 93
Johnston, Joni Elizabeth 1960- WhoAmW 93, WhoEmL 93

Johnston, Joseph Eggleston 1807-1891 *BioIn 17, HarEnMi*
Johnston, Josephine Rose 1926- *WhoAmW 93, WhoE 93*
Johnston, Judy Ann 1951- *WhoAmW 93*
Johnston, Julie Ann *Law&B 92*
Johnston, Karen L. *BioIn 17*
Johnston, Katherine Fortino 1956- *St&PR 93*
Johnston, Kenneth Richard 1938- *WhoAm 92*
Johnston, Kevin R. *Law&B 92*
Johnston, Kurt M. 1954- *St&PR 93*
Johnston, Laurance Scott 1950- *WhoAm 92*
Johnston, Leonora *AmWomPl*
Johnston, Linda Joyce 1943- *WhoAmW 93*
Johnston, Linda Osgood *Law&B 92*
Johnston, Lloyd Douglas 1940- *WhoAm 92*
Johnston, Lynn Frances 1957- *WhoSSW 93*
Johnston, Lynn H. 1931- *WhoIns 93*
Johnston, Lynn Henry 1931- *St&PR 93*
Johnston, Malcolm Carlyle 1934- *WhoAm 92*
Johnston, Margaret Mims 1933- *WhoAmW 93, WhoSSW 93*
Johnston, Margie Anne 1957- *WhoAmW 93*
Johnston, Marguerite 1917- *ConAu 138, WhoAm 92*
Johnston, Marie E. *WhoWrEP 92*
Johnston, Marilyn *BioIn 17*
Johnston, Mark Byron *Law&B 92*
Johnston, Marshall William 1919- *St&PR 93, WhoAm 92*
Johnston, Mary 1870-1936 *AmWomPl*
Johnston, Mary Ellen 1951- *WhoEmL 93*
Johnston, Mary Hollis 1946- *WhoAmW 93*
Johnston, Mary Judith 1954- *WhoAmW 93*
Johnston, Michael Anthony 1947- *St&PR 93*
Johnston, Michael F. 1947- *St&PR 93*
Johnston, Michael Joseph 1938- *St&PR 93*
Johnston, Michael Richard 1946- *WhoAm 92*
Johnston, Michael T. 1949- *St&PR 93*
Johnston, Murray Lloyd, Jr. 1940- *St&PR 93, WhoAm 92*
Johnston, Murray R. 1949-1990 *BioIn 17*
Johnston, Nancy Dahl 1954- *WhoAmW 93, WhoEmL 93*
Johnston, Nancy Jean 1952- *WhoAmW 93*
Johnston, Norma *ScF&FL 92*
Johnston, Norman John 1918- *WhoAm 92*
Johnston, Ollie 1912- *BioIn 17*
Johnston, Pamela McEvoy 1937- *WhoAmW 93, WhoWor 93*
Johnston, Patricia Marie *Law&B 92*
Johnston, Paul P. 1944- *WhoAm 92*
Johnston, Paula Joan 1945- *WhoSSW 93*
Johnston, Paula May 1959- *WhoAmW 93*
Johnston, Pauline Kay 1951- *WhoSSW 93*
Johnston, Phillip Michael 1944- *WhoAm 92*
Johnston, R.D. *WhoScE 91-1*
Johnston, R(onald) J(ohn) 1941- *ConAu 40NR*
Johnston, Rhodes 1917- *St&PR 93*
Johnston, Richard Elton 1952- *WhoEmL 93*
Johnston, Richard Fourness 1925- *WhoAm 92*
Johnston, Richard L. *Law&B 92*
Johnston, Richard M. 1935- *St&PR 93*
Johnston, Richard Park 1930- *St&PR 93*
Johnston, Rita Margaret 1935- *WhoAm 92*
Johnston, Robert 1953- *WhoWor 93*
Johnston, Robert Addison 1936- *St&PR 93*
Johnston, Robert B. 1937- *BioIn 17, NewYTBS 92 [port]*
Johnston, Robert Chapman 1930- *WhoAm 92*
Johnston, Robert Cossin 1913- *WhoAm 92*
Johnston, Robert D., Jr. 1950- *St&PR 93*
Johnston, Robert Donaghy 1929- *WhoAm 92*
Johnston, Robert G. 1944- *WhoUN 92*
Johnston, Robert H. 1923- *St&PR 93*
Johnston, Robert L. 1931- *St&PR 93*
Johnston, Robert Lynn 1940- *WhoSSW 93*
Johnston, Roger A. *Law&B 92*
Johnston, Ronald Carlo 1943- *WhoSSW 93*
Johnston, Ronald John *WhoScE 91-1*
Johnston, Ronald Lee 1948- *WhoEmL 93*
Johnston, Roy G. 1914- *WhoAm 92*
Johnston, Ruby Charlotte 1918- *WhoAmW 93*
Johnston, S. Parker, Jr. 1915- *St&PR 93*
Johnston, Samuel Thomas 1924- *WhoAm 92*
Johnston, Sarah Virginia 1950- *St&PR 93*
Johnston, Sean A. *Law&B 92*
Johnston, Sean Francois 1956- *WhoWor 93*
Johnston, Shepherd D. 1947- *St&PR 93*
Johnston, Stanley H(oward), Jr. 1946- *ConAu 137*
Johnston, Stephen E. 1942- *St&PR 93*
Johnston, Summerfield K., Jr. *WhoSSW 93*
Johnston, Susan Kargol 1949- *WhoAmW 93*
Johnston, Thomas 1945- *ScF&FL 92*
Johnston, Thomas Gayle 1909- *WhoWor 93*
Johnston, Thomas J. 1922- *St&PR 93*
Johnston, Thomas John 1922- *WhoAm 92*
Johnston, Velda *ScF&FL 92*
Johnston, Virginia Anne 1966- *WhoE 93*
Johnston, Virginia Evelyn 1933- *WhoAmW 93*
Johnston, Waldo Cory Melrose 1913- *WhoAm 92*
Johnston, Walter Eugene, III 1936- *St&PR 93*
Johnston, Warren E. *BioIn 17*
Johnston, Warren Eugene 1933- *WhoAm 92*
Johnston, William Andrew 1871-1929 *JrnUS*
Johnston, William Arnold 1942- *WhoWrEP 92*
Johnston, William David 1944- *WhoAm 92*
Johnston, William E., Jr. 1940- *St&PR 93*
Johnston, William Francis Roche 1950- *WhoWor 93*
Johnston, William Freame 1808-1872 *BioIn 17*
Johnston, William M. 1946- *St&PR 93*
Johnston, William Noel 1919- *WhoAm 92*
Johnston, William O. d1990 *BioIn 17*
Johnston, William Raymond 1945- *WhoWor 93*
Johnston, William Webb 1933- *WhoAm 92*
Johnston, Ynez 1920- *WhoAm 92*
Johnstone, Alexander Henry *WhoScE 91-1*
Johnstone, Anna d1992 *NewYTBS 92*
Johnstone, Arthur Edward 1860-1944 *Baker 92*
Johnstone, Campbell 1929- *St&PR 93*
Johnstone, Chauncey Olcott 1943- *WhoAm 92*
Johnstone, D. Bruce 1941- *WhoAm 92, WhoE 93*
Johnstone, David Moore 1926- *WhoWrEP 92*
Johnstone, Edmund Frank 1909- *WhoAm 92*
Johnstone, Edward H. 1922- *WhoSSW 93*
Johnstone, Edward K., II 1936- *St&PR 93*
Johnstone, Eve Cordelia *WhoScE 91-1*
Johnstone, George 1730-1787 *HarEnMi*
Johnstone, George W. 1938- *St&PR 93, WhoAm 92*
Johnstone, Henry Webb, Jr. 1920- *WhoAm 92*
Johnstone, Homer 1935- *St&PR 93*
Johnstone, Iain 1943- *ConTFT 10*
Johnstone, James George 1920- *WhoAm 92*
Johnstone, Jay 1946- *BioIn 17*
Johnstone, John Wallace Claire 1931- *WhoAm 92*
Johnstone, John William, Jr. 1932- *St&PR 93, WhoAm 92*
Johnstone, Keith J. 1947- *St&PR 93*
Johnstone, Larry Anthony 1958- *WhoEmL 93*
Johnstone, Monica Carolyn 1959- *WhoE 93*
Johnstone, Neil Harvey 1946- *WhoUN 92*
Johnstone, Pat M. 1958- *WhoEmL 93*
Johnstone, Patrick Jan St. George 1938- *WhoWor 93*
Johnstone, Paula Sue 1947- *WhoAmW 93*
Johnstone, Philip MacLaren 1961- *WhoE 93, WhoEmL 93*
Johnstone, Quintin 1915- *WhoAm 92*
Johnstone, Robert Philip 1943- *WhoAm 92*
Johnstone, Rose Mamelak 1928- *WhoAm 92, WhoAmW 93*
Johnstone, Sally Mac 1949- *WhoAmW 93, WhoEmL 93*
Johnstone, Sandra 1936-1991 *BioIn 17*
Johnstone, William Mervyn 1946- *WhoWrEP 92*
Johnstone, William W. 1938- *ScF&FL 92*
Johnston-Feller, Ruth Marie 1923- *WhoAmW 93*
Johnston-O'Connor, Elizabeth J. 1952- *WhoE 93*
John the Almsgiver *OxDcByz*
John the Baptist *OxDcByz*
John the Exarch dc. 917 *OxDcByz*
John the Grammarian *OxDcByz*
John the Orphanotrophos d1043 *OxDcByz*
John Tzimiskes, I c. 925-976 *OxDcByz*
John Uglješa d1371 *OxDcByz*
John Vatatzes, III c. 1192-1254 *OxDcByz*
John Vladislav d1018 *OxDcByz*
Johnwick, Charles David 1950- *WhoEmL 93*
John Xiphilinos, VIII c. 1010- *OxDcByz*
John Zimisces, I 924-976 *HarEnMi*
Joho, Jean-Pierre 1939- *WhoScE 91-4*
Johsi, Sudha Vijay 1940- *WhoAsAP 91*
Johst, Hanns 1890-1978 *DcLB 124 [port]*
Joice, Nora Lee 1948- *WhoSSW 93*
Joiner, Burt L. 1919- *St&PR 93*
Joiner, Donald Lee 1935- *St&PR 93*
Joiner, Helen Lee 1952- *WhoSSW 93*
Joiner, James B. 1931- *St&PR 93*
Joiner, Larry J. 1939- *WhoAm 92*
Joiner, Lorell Howard 1945- *St&PR 93, WhoSSW 93*
Joiner, Marion Douglas 1947- *WhoSSW 93*
Joiner, Michael Charles 1954- *WhoScE 91-1*
Joiner, Stephen T. 1945- *St&PR 93*
Joiner, Webb F. 1933- *St&PR 93*
Joiner, Webb Francis 1933- *WhoAm 92*
Joinville, Patricia Kay 1955- *WhoEmL 93*
Joist, Johann Heinrich 1935- *WhoAm 92*
Jokay, Istvan 1928- *WhoScE 91-4*
Jokelainen, Jida Aili 1924- *WhoScE 91-4*
Jokinen, Erkki 1941- *Baker 92*
Jokinen, M.A. 1932- *WhoScE 91-4*
Jokinen, Tapani Veikko Juhani 1937- *WhoScE 91-4*
Jokisaari, Jukka Paavo 1944- *WhoScE 91-4*
Jokl, Ernst F. 1907- *WhoAm 92, WhoSSW 93*
Jokl, Georg 1896-1954 *Baker 92*
Jokl, Otto 1891-1963 *Baker 92*
Jokl, Vladimir 1926- *WhoScE 91-4*
Joklik, Gunther Franz 1928- *WhoAm 92*
Joklik, Wolfgang Karl 1926- *WhoAm 92*
Joksic, Dusan 1939- *WhoScE 91-4*
Jolankai, Marton 1949- *WhoScE 91-4*
Jolas, Betsy 1926- *Baker 92, BioIn 17*
Joley, Lisa Annette *Law&B 92*
Jolibois, Keith Edward 1954- *WhoSSW 93*
Jolicoeur, Louise 1953- *St&PR 93*
Jolicoeur, Paul 1945- *WhoAm 92*
Jolin, Peggy 1952- *WhoAmW 93*
Joliot, Jean Frederic 1900-1958 *BioIn 17*
Joliot-Curie, Frederic 1900-1958 *BioIn 17*
Joliot-Curie, Irene 1897-1956 *BioIn 17*
Jolis, Alan *BioIn 17*
Jolissaint, Stephen Lacy 1951- *WhoEmL 93, WhoSSW 93*
Jolivet, Andre 1905-1974 *Baker 92*
Jolivet, Emmanuel 1949- *WhoScE 91-2*
Jolivet, Jean-Loup 1945- *WhoScE 91-2*
Jolivet, Vincent 1930- *St&PR 93*
Jolivette, Thayer E. 1936- *St&PR 93*
Jolles, Francois Albert 1962- *WhoWor 93*
Jolles, Georges Edgar Rene 1929- *WhoWor 93*
Jolles, Ira H. *Law&B 92*
Jolles, Ira H. 1938- *St&PR 93*
Jolles, Ira Hervey 1938- *WhoAm 92*
Jolles, Pierre 1927- *WhoScE 91-2, WhoWor 93*
Jolles, Scott Alan 1960- *WhoEmL 93, WhoSSW 93*
Jolley, Brenda Jean 1957- *WhoEmL 93*
Jolley, David 1942- *WhoAm 92*
Jolley, Elizabeth 1923- *BioIn 17, IntLitE*
Jolley, Jack J. 1925- *WhoAm 92*
Jolley, John Kenneth 1945- *WhoE 93*
Jolley, Margaret Clark 1937- *WhoAmW 93*
Jolley, Mark *ScF&FL 92*
Jolley, Rhonda Sue 1956- *WhoSSW 93*
Jolley, Weldon B. 1926- *St&PR 93*
Jolley, William, Jr. 1937- *WhoAm 92*
Jollie, William Pucette 1928- *WhoSSW 93*
Jolliet, Louis 1645-1700 *Expl 93*
Jolliff, Carl R. 1926- *WhoAm 92*
Jolliff, Robert A. 1943- *St&PR 93*
Jolly, Alan Gordon 1930- *WhoSSW 93*
Jolly, Barbara Lee 1952- *WhoAmW 93*
Jolly, Bruce Dwight 1943- *WhoAm 92*
Jolly, Bruce Overstreet 1912- *WhoSSW 93*
Jolly, Charles N. *Law&B 92*
Jolly, Charles Nelson 1942- *St&PR 93*
Jolly, Daniel Ehs 1952- *WhoEmL 93, WhoWor 93*
Jolly, E. Grady 1937- *WhoAm 92, WhoSSW 93*
Jolly, J. Mel 1942- *St&PR 93*
Jolly, Lynda Sue *Law&B 92*
Jolly, Purshotam Lal 1949- *WhoEmL 93*
Jolly, Raymond A., Jr. *Law&B 92*
Jolly, Richard 1934- *WhoUN 92*
Jolly, Roy H. 1923- *St&PR 93*
Jolly, Shirley Elizabeth 1951- *WhoAmW 93*
Jolly, Sidney Joseph 1946- *WhoEmL 93*
Jolly, Stratford D. *ScF&FL 92*
Jolly, Wayne Travis 1940- *WhoAm 92, WhoWor 93*
Jolly, William Lee 1927- *WhoAm 92*
Jolly, William Thomas 1929- *WhoSSW 93*
Jollymore, Nicholas *Law&B 92*
Jollymore, Nicholas John 1946- *WhoE 93*
Jolson, Al d1950 *BioIn 17*
Jolson, Al 1886-1950 *Baker 92, IntDcF 2-3 [port]*
Jolson, Lois Rochelle 1959- *WhoE 93*
Joly, Andre 1951- *St&PR 93*
Joly, C. 1943- *WhoScE 91-3*
Joly, Jean-Gil 1940- *WhoAm 92, WhoWor 93*
Joly, Jean Robert 1950- *WhoAm 92*
Joly, Louis-Noel 1936- *WhoWor 93*
Joly, Luc J. *Law&B 92*
Jomarron, Will C. 1944- *WhoAm 92*
Jomini, Antoine Henri, Baron de 1779-1869 *HarEnMi*
Jommelli, Niccolo 1714-1774 *Baker 92, IntDcOp [port]*
Jommelli, Nicolo 1714-1774 *OxDcOp*
Jommellino *OxDcOp*
Jommersbach, Kristine 1955- *St&PR 93*
Jonah *BioIn 17*
Jonah, James O.C. *WhoUN 92*
Jonah, Margaret Martin 1942- *WhoAmW 93*
Jonaitis, Aldona 1948- *ConAu 139*
Jonaitis, Aldona Claire 1948- *WhoEmL 93*
Jonak, Zdenek 1917- *Baker 92*
Jonap, Lane 1923- *St&PR 93*
Jonas, Alberto 1868-1943 *Baker 92*
Jonas, Ana 1943- *WhoAmW 93*
Jonas, Ann *BioIn 17, ChlBID [port]*
Jonas, Ann 1919- *WhoWrEP 92*
Jonas, Ann 1932- *ConAu 136, MajAI [port]*
Jonas, Brian S. 1961- *St&PR 93*
Jonas, Edward M. 1938- *St&PR 93*
Jonas, Emile 1827-1905 *Baker 92*
Jonas, Gary Fred 1945- *WhoAm 92*
Jonas, George 1935- *BioIn 17, WhoCanL 92*
Jonas, Gilbert 1930- *WhoE 93*
Jonas, Harry S. 1926- *WhoAm 92*
Jonas, Jiri 1932- *WhoAm 92*
Jonas, Joan 1936- *WhoAm 92*
Jonas, John Joseph 1932- *WhoAm 92*
Jonas, Maryla 1911-1959 *Baker 92, PolBiDi*
Jonas, Oswald 1897-1978 *Baker 92*
Jonas, Ruth Haber 1935- *WhoAmW 93*
Jonas, Saran 1931- *WhoAm 92, WhoWor 93*
Jonas, Steven 1936- *WhoAm 92*
Jonas, Werner 1935- *St&PR 93*
Jonason, Jan G. 1938- *WhoScE 91-4*
Jonason, Pauline Marie 1928- *WhoE 93*
Jonassen, Gaylord D. 1932- *WhoE 93*
Jonassen, Gunvald Henning 1935- *WhoScE 91-4*
Jonassen, James O. 1940- *WhoAm 92*
Jonassohn, Kurt 1920- *WhoAm 92*
Jonatansson, Halldor 1932- *WhoWor 93*
Jonathan *BioIn 17*
Jonathan, Neville B.H. *WhoScE 91-1*
Jonaus, Laura J. *Law&B 92*
Joncieres, Victorin de 1839-1903 *Baker 92*
Jonckheer, Efrain *DcCPCAm*
Jonckheere, Alan Mathew 1947- *WhoAm 92*
Jonckheere, Edouard *WhoScE 91-2*
Jondahl, Terri Elise 1959- *WhoAmW 93, WhoEmL 93, WhoWor 93*
Jonderko, Krzysztof Pawel 1958- *WhoWor 93*
Joneja, Madan Gopal 1936- *WhoAm 92*
Joner, Bruno 1921- *WhoSSW 93*
Jones *Baker 92*
Jones, Aaron *BioIn 17*
Jones, Abbott C. 1934- *WhoAm 92*
Jones, Agnes Hamilton *AmWomPl*
Jones, Alan 1941- *WhoScE 91-1*
Jones, Alan 1943- *WhoScE 91-2*
Jones, Alan Hedrick 1937- *WhoWrEP 92*
Jones, Alan Michael *WhoScE 91-1*
Jones, Alan Porter, Jr. 1925- *St&PR 93*
Jones, Alan Pryce- 1908- *BioIn 17*
Jones, Alan V. *WhoScE 91-1*
Jones, Albert Cecil 1938- *WhoSSW 93*
Jones, Alex S. 1946- *WhoAm 92, WhoE 93*
Jones, Alexander Elvin 1920- *WhoAm 92*
Jones, Alfred Cookman, III *Law&B 92*
Jones, Alfred William, Jr. 1930- *St&PR 93*
Jones, Alice C. 1853-1933 *BioIn 17*
Jones, Allan *St&PR 93*
Jones, Allan d1992 *NewYTBS 92 [port]*
Jones, Allan Mervyn *WhoScE 91-1*
Jones, Allan W. 1929- *WhoIns 93*

Jones, Allen H. 1927- St&PR 93
Jones, Allen K. 1947- St&PR 93
Jones, Alphonso Casey 1959- WhoSSW 93
Jones, Alton 1899-1971 Baker 92
Jones, Alun Denry Wynn 1939- WhoWor 93
Jones, Alwyn Harris WhoScE 91-1
Jones, Amy MiSFD 9
Jones, Andrew Law&B 92
Jones, Andrew Nolan 1943- WhoAm 92
Jones, Andrew T. Law&B 92
Jones, Andrew T. 1939- St&PR 93
Jones, Angela 1959- WhoEmL 93
Jones, Ann 1935- WhoAmW 93
Jones, Ann (Maret) 1937- WhoWrEP 92
Jones, Ann Van Narter AmWomPl
Jones, Anne 1935- WhoWor 93
Jones, Anne Elizabeth 1945- WhoAmW 93, WhoSSW 93
Jones, Anne Hudson 1944- WhoSSW 93
Jones, Anne Patricia 1935- WhoAm 92
Jones, Annie Walton 1952- WhoEmL 93
Jones, Antonia BioIn 17
Jones, Aphrodite Alicia 1958- WhoSSW 93
Jones, Arthur Edwin, Jr. 1918- WhoAm 92
Jones, Arthur McDonald, Sr. 1947- St&PR 93, WhoAm 92
Jones, Arthur Stanley 1932- WhoWor 93
Jones, Audrey M.T. St&PR 93
Jones, B. Calvin 1925- WhoSSW 93
Jones, B. Rees 1937- St&PR 93, WhoIns 93
Jones, Bailey Armstrong 1961- WhoWrEP 92
Jones, Barbara BlkAmWO [port]
Jones, Barbara 1937- BioIn 17
Jones, Barbara Ann 1946- WhoAmW 93
Jones, Barbara Ann 1957- WhoEmL 93, WhoSSW 93
Jones, Barbara Ann Posey 1943- WhoAm 92, WhoAmW 93, WhoSSW 93
Jones, Barbara Archer 1945- WhoSSW 93
Jones, Barbara Carole 1953- WhoAmW 93
Jones, Barbara Christine 1942- WhoAmW 93
Jones, Barbara Dean 1931- WhoAmW 93
Jones, Barbara Pendleton 1947- WhoE 93
Jones, Barclay Gibbs 1925- WhoE 93
Jones, Barclay Gibbs 1960- St&PR 93
Jones, Barry Edward WhoScE 91-1
Jones, Barry Owen 1932- WhoWor 93
Jones, Barry Owens WhoAsAP 91
Jones, Beatrice 1953- WhoAmW 93
Jones, Ben DcCPCAm
Jones, Ben 1912- St&PR 93, WhoAm 92
Jones, Ben 1941- CngDr 91, WhoAm 92
Jones, Benjamin Ben 1941- WhoSSW 93
Jones, Benjamin F. 1824-1903 PolPar
Jones, Benjamin F. 1922- St&PR 93
Jones, Benjamin Franklin 1922- WhoAm 92
Jones, Benjamin H., II Law&B 92
Jones, Benjamin Joseph 1951- WhoE 93
Jones, Bernard 1957- WhoEmL 93
Jones, Bernt-E. V. 1946- WhoScE 91-4
Jones, Betty Jeanne 1946- WhoAmW 93
Jones, Betty Knight 1942- WhoAmW 93
Jones, Beverly Ann Miller 1927- WhoAmW 93
Jones, Beverly E. Law&B 92
Jones, Bill 1949- WhoE 93
Jones, Bill T. BioIn 17
Jones, Billy Ernest 1933- WhoAm 92, WhoSSW 93
Jones, Billy Mac 1925- WhoAm 92
Jones, Bob 1883-1968 BioIn 17
Jones, Bob, Jr. 1911- WhoAm 92
Jones, Bobby BioIn 17
Jones, Bobby 1902-1971 BioIn 17
Jones, Bobette 1928- St&PR 93
Jones, Boisfeuillet, Jr. Law&B 92
Jones, Bonnie B. Law&B 92
Jones, Bonnie Jean 1960- WhoAmW 93
Jones, Bonnie Yvette 1961- WhoSSW 93
Jones, Booker T SoulM
Jones, Booker T. 1944- Baker 92, ConMus 8 [port]
Jones, Boyd Marion, II 1953- WhoSSW 93
Jones, Boyd T. 1932- St&PR 93
Jones, Bradley Rex 1955- WhoEmL 93
Jones, Branson Coltrane 1927- St&PR 93
Jones, Brenda Anne 1943- WhoWor 93
Jones, Brenda Gail 1949- WhoAmW 93
Jones, Brenda Kay 1958- WhoAmW 93
Jones, Brennon 1945- ConAu 136
Jones, Brereton C. 1939- WhoAm 92, WhoWor 93
Jones, Brian 1942-1969 Baker 92
Jones, Brian 1943-1969 BioIn 17
Jones, Brian Joseph 1950- WhoE 93
Jones, Bruce ScF&FL 92
Jones, Bruce Hovey 1947- WhoWor 93
Jones, Bruce Stanley 1938- WhoWor 93
Jones, Bryan D(avidson) 1944- ConAu 139
Jones, Burton V. Law&B 92
Jones, Busta See Gang of Four ConMus 8
Jones, C. Goodman WhoIns 93
Jones, C.H. Tunnicliffe 1900-1991 BioIn 17
Jones, C. Kevin 1963- WhoEmL 93
Jones, C. Mark 1935- St&PR 93
Jones, C. Paul 1927- WhoAm 92
Jones, C. W. 1921- WhoWor 93
Jones, Calvin K. 1946- St&PR 93
Jones, Calvin Nichols 1947- WhoSSW 93
Jones, Candy d1990 BioIn 17
Jones, Cantwell BioIn 17
Jones, Carl A. 1912- St&PR 93
Jones, Carla Kay 1962- WhoAmW 93
Jones, Carleton Shaw 1942- WhoAm 92
Jones, Carol Ann 1950- WhoEmL 93, WhoSSW 93
Jones, Carol Dawn 1935- St&PR 93
Jones, Carol Leigh 1949- WhoWor 93
Jones, Caroline BioIn 17
Jones, Caroline Robinson WhoAmW 93
Jones, Carolyn BioIn 17
Jones, Carolyn B. Law&B 92
Jones, Carolyn Ellis 1928- WhoAmW 93
Jones, Carolyn Evans 1931- WhoAmW 93
Jones, Carolyn Pembroke 1945- WhoSSW 93
Jones, Catesby ap Roger 1821-1877 HarEnMi
Jones, Catesby Brooke 1925- WhoAm 92
Jones, Catherine Ann 1936- WhoAm 92
Jones, Catherine Quailes 1967- WhoSSW 93
Jones, Charles 1910- Baker 92
Jones, Charles Davis 1917- WhoWor 93
Jones, Charles Edward 1918- WhoAm 92
Jones, Charles Edward 1920- WhoAm 92
Jones, Charles Eric, Jr. 1957- WhoSSW 93
Jones, Charles F. 1911-1991 BioIn 17
Jones, Charles Frank 1927- St&PR 93
Jones, Charles Hill, Jr. 1933- WhoAm 92
Jones, Charles Irving 1943- WhoAm 92
Jones, Charles J. 1940- WhoWor 93
Jones, Charles M. 1912- MiSFD 9
Jones, Charles W. 1923- WhoAm 92
Jones, Charles Wesley 1850- BiDAMSp 1989
Jones, Charles Williams 1905-1989 BioIn 17
Jones, Charlie WhoAm 92
Jones, Charlott Ann 1927- WhoAm 92
Jones, Charlotte 1916-1992 NewYTBS 92 [port]
Jones, Cheri Lynn 1963- WhoAmW 93
Jones, Cherry 1956- ConTFT 10
Jones, Christian Trevor Law&B 92
Jones, Christine Elizabeth 1959- WhoEmL 93
Jones, Christine M. 1929- St&PR 93
Jones, Christine Massey 1929- WhoAm 92
Jones, Christopher K. 1951- St&PR 93
Jones, Chuck 1912- BioIn 17
Jones, Clara Stanton 1913- AfrAmBi
Jones, Clarence Morton 1954- WhoSSW 93
Jones, Clarence Raymond, Jr. 1946- WhoSSW 93
Jones, Claris Eugene, Jr. 1942- WhoAm 92
Jones, Clark David 1935- St&PR 93, WhoAm 92
Jones, Clarke Chastain 1948- St&PR 93
Jones, Claude E. 1907- ScF&FL 92
Jones, Clayton W. Law&B 92
Jones, Cliff L. 1950- WhoSSW 93
Jones, Clifford 1939- WhoSSW 93
Jones, Clifford A. 1912- St&PR 93
Jones, Clifford Aaron 1912- WhoAm 92
Jones, Clifford Bryn WhoScE 91-1
Jones, Clifton S., Jr. 1934- St&PR 93
Jones, Clive B. 1941- St&PR 93
Jones, Clyde Adam 1924- WhoE 93
Jones, Colin D. Law&B 92
Jones, Colin Howard 1937- WhoAm 92
Jones, Colin Hywel WhoScE 91-1
Jones, Colin John Francis Philip WhoScE 91-1
Jones, Compton Seth 1925- WhoSSW 93
Jones, Conrad d1992 NewYTBS 92
Jones, Corinne Mae 1947- WhoAmW 93
Jones, Corrine 1930- WhoAmW 93
Jones, Courtway 1923- ScF&FL 92
Jones, Craig R. 1946- St&PR 93
Jones, Cranston 1918-1991 BioIn 17
Jones, Cranston Edward 1918-1992 WhoAm 92
Jones, Curtis 1934- WhoSSW 93
Jones, Curtis Harvey 1929- St&PR 93
Jones, Curtis Westbrook Law&B 92
Jones, Cynthia Clarke 1938- WhoE 93
Jones, D. WhoScE 91-1
Jones, D.E. Law&B 92
Jones, D.F. 1918-1981 ScF&FL 92
Jones, D.G. 1929- WhoCanL 92
Jones, D.J. 1940- ScF&FL 92
Jones, D. Paul St&PR 93
Jones, D. Paul, Jr. 1942- WhoAm 92, WhoSSW 93
Jones, Dale C. 1948- St&PR 93
Jones, Dale Edwin 1948- WhoE 93
Jones, Dale P. 1936- St&PR 93, WhoSSW 93
Jones, Dallas Williams 1941- WhoE 93
Jones, Dan Lewis 1951- WhoEmL 93, WhoSSW 93
Jones, Daniel Elven 1943- WhoSSW 93
Jones, Daniel Hare 1949- WhoAm 92
Jones, Daniel (Jenkyn) 1912- Baker 92
Jones, Darryl F.O. 1953- St&PR 93
Jones, David BioIn 17, Law&B 92, WhoScE 91-1
Jones, David 1934- MiSFD 9
Jones, David 1953- BioIn 17
Jones, David A. BioIn 17
Jones, David A. 1931- St&PR 93
Jones, David Allan 1942- WhoSSW 93
Jones, David Allen 1931- WhoAm 92
Jones, David Anthony Law&B 92
Jones, David B. 1943- St&PR 93
Jones, David C. Law&B 92
Jones, David C. 1921- HarEnMi
Jones, David C. 1944- St&PR 93
Jones, David Charles 1921- WhoAm 92
Jones, David Charles 1935- WhoSSW 93, WhoWor 93
Jones, David Eugene 1942- WhoAm 92
Jones, David F. 1940- St&PR 93
Jones, David Galbraith 1938- WhoE 93
Jones, David Gareth WhoScE 91-1
Jones, David Gareth 1948- WhoWor 93
Jones, David Henry 1937- St&PR 93, WhoAm 92
Jones, David Hugh 1934- WhoAm 92
Jones, David John 1933- WhoIns 93
Jones, David John 1934- WhoAm 92
Jones, David Michael 1895-1974 BioIn 17
Jones, David Milton 1938- WhoAm 92
Jones, David P. Law&B 92
Jones, David R. 1937- St&PR 93, WhoSSW 93
Jones, David Rhodes 1932- WhoAm 92
Jones, David Robert 1941- WhoAm 92
Jones, David Spence 1941- WhoSSW 93
Jones, Deacon 1938- BioIn 17
Jones, Dean BioIn 17
Jones, Dean 1933- QDrFCA 92 [port]
Jones, Dean Carroll WhoAm 92
Jones, Dee 1949- WhoWor 93
Jones, Del 1946- WhoWrEP 92
Jones, Della 1946- OxDcOp
Jones, Denise 1939- BioIn 17
Jones, Denise Ann 1963- WhoAmW 93, WhoEmL 93
Jones, Dennis 1945- ScF&FL 92
Jones, Dennis M. 1938- St&PR 93
Jones, Dereck M. Law&B 92
Jones, Derek Charles 1946- WhoE 93
Jones, Devon BioIn 17
Jones, Devon A. Law&B 92
Jones, Dewey Michael Law&B 92
Jones, Diana Wynne BioIn 17
Jones, Diana Wynne 1934- ChlFicS, MajAI [port], ScF&FL 92, SmATA 70 [port], WhoAm 92
Jones, Diane Catherine 1938- WhoWrEP 92
Jones, Diane W. 1949- St&PR 93
Jones, Dianna Lynn 1954- WhoSSW 93
Jones, Dionne Juanita 1945- WhoE 93
Jones, Don 1938- WhoWrEP 92
Jones, Donald Esplin 1931- St&PR 93
Jones, Donald H. 1937- St&PR 93
Jones, Donald M. 1946- St&PR 93
Jones, Donna Joanne 1946- WhoAmW 93
Jones, Doris Mae 1938- WhoAmW 93
Jones, Dorothy R. d1992 NewYTBS 92
Jones, Dorothy V. 1927- ConAu 138
Jones, Doug BioIn 17
Jones, Douglas C. 1924- ScF&FL 92
Jones, Douglas Clyde 1924- WhoAm 92, WhoWrEP 92
Jones, Douglas Epps 1930- WhoAm 92
Jones, Douglas Samuel WhoScE 91-1
Jones, Douglas Samuel 1922- WhoWor 93
Jones, Dwain L. 1927- St&PR 93
Jones, Dwight W. 1931- St&PR 93
Jones, E. Bradley 1927- St&PR 93
Jones, E.D. WhoScE 91-1
Jones, E. Fay 1921- BioIn 17
Jones, E. Stanley 1884-1973 BioIn 17
Jones, E. Stewart, Jr. 1941- WhoE 93, WhoWor 93
Jones, Earl F., Jr. Law&B 92
Jones, Eben Lee 1949- WhoEmL 93
Jones, Ebon Richard 1944- WhoAm 92
Jones, Ed BioIn 17
Jones, Eddie 1926-1959 BioIn 17
Jones, Eddie J. WhoSSW 93
Jones, Edgar Allan, Jr. 1921- WhoAm 92
Jones, Edith Law&B 92
Jones, Edith Hollan 1949- BioIn 17, WhoAm 92, WhoAmW 93, WhoSSW 93
Jones, Edith Irby 1927- WhoAmW 93
Jones, Edith J. Law&B 92
Jones, Edloe Pendleton, III 1939- WhoSSW 93
Jones, Edna Ruth 1932- WhoSSW 93
Jones, Ednah WhoWrEP 92
Jones, Edward 1752-1824 Baker 92
Jones, Edward 1935- WhoAm 92
Jones, Edward A. 1939- St&PR 93
Jones, Edward Allen 1946- WhoE 93
Jones, Edward C. 1936- St&PR 93
Jones, Edward George 1939- WhoAm 92
Jones, Edward J. St&PR 93
Jones, Edward Lambert, Jr. 1936- St&PR 93
Jones, Edward Magruder 1928- WhoAm 92
Jones, Edward Powis 1919- WhoAm 92
Jones, Edward S. Law&B 92
Jones, Edward White, II 1921- WhoAm 92
Jones, Edwin Channing, Jr. 1934- WhoAm 92
Jones, Edwin Michael 1916- WhoAm 92
Jones, Edwin Rudolph, Jr. 1938- WhoSSW 93
Jones, Eldred Durosimi 1925- WhoWor 93
Jones, Eleanor Brodie AmWomPl
Jones, Elin Denise 1955- WhoE 93
Jones, Elizabeth Law&B 92
Jones, Elizabeth Ann 1945- WhoAmW 93
Jones, Elizabeth Kennedy St&PR 93
Jones, Elizabeth N. Law&B 92
Jones, Elizabeth Nordwall 1934- WhoAm 92
Jones, Elizabeth Winifred 1939- WhoAmW 93
Jones, Elmer Leroy 1935- St&PR 93
Jones, Elvin 1927- ConMus 9 [port]
Jones, Elvin (Ray) 1927- Baker 92
Jones, Emily Marie 1947- WhoAmW 93
Jones, Emlyn BioIn 17
Jones, Enoch Michael 1963- WhoSSW 93
Jones, Erika Ziebarth 1955- WhoAmW 93
Jones, Ernest 1879-1958 BioIn 17
Jones, Ernest A. d1992 NewYTBS 92
Jones, Ernest Austin, Jr. 1960- WhoSSW 93
Jones, Ernest Donald 1943- WhoAm 92
Jones, Ernest Edward 1931- WhoAm 92
Jones, Ernest L. 1950- St&PR 93
Jones, Ernest Paul 1952- St&PR 93
Jones, Esther Lloyd- 1901-1991 BioIn 17
Jones, Ethelene Dyer 1930- WhoWrEP 92
Jones, Etta WhoAm 92
Jones, Eugene D. 1925- St&PR 93
Jones, Eugene Gordon 1929- WhoWor 93
Jones, Eugene Kinckle 1885-1954 EncAACR
Jones, Eugene S. MiSFD 9
Jones, Euine Fay 1921- WhoAm 92
Jones, Eunice Li 1951- St&PR 93
Jones, Eva Joyce 1934- WhoSSW 93
Jones, F. Ben 1932- WhoAm 92
Jones, Fara Law&B 92
Jones, Fay 1921- BioIn 17
Jones, Felicia BioIn 17
Jones, Fielder Allison 1871-1934 BiDAMSp 1989
Jones, Francis Thomas 1933- WhoE 93
Jones, Francis Whitney 1944- WhoSSW 93
Jones, Frank 1856-1893 BioIn 17
Jones, Frank Cater 1925- WhoAm 92
Jones, Frank Earl ScF&FL 92
Jones, Frank Edward 1917- WhoAm 92
Jones, Frank Pierce, Jr. 1929- St&PR 93
Jones, Frank R. 1945- St&PR 93
Jones, Frank Ray 1945- WhoAm 92
Jones, Frank William 1915- WhoAm 92
Jones, Frank Wyman 1940- WhoAm 92
Jones, Franklin Ross 1921- WhoAm 92
Jones, Fred Eugene 1926- WhoAm 92
Jones, Fred Richard 1947- WhoAm 92, WhoE 93, WhoEmL 93
Jones, G.A.C. WhoScE 91-1
Jones, G. Russell WhoScE 91-1
Jones, Galen Everts 1928- WhoAm 92
Jones, Galen Ray 1948- WhoEmL 93
Jones, Garth Nelson 1925- WhoAm 92
Jones, Gary Law&B 92
Jones, Gary Lee 1966- WhoSSW 93
Jones, Gayl 1949- BioIn 17
Jones, Gene Stanley 1951- WhoE 93, WhoEmL 93
Jones, Genia Kay 1954- WhoAmW 93
Jones, Geoffrey John Charles 1927- St&PR 93
Jones, Geoffrey Melvill 1923- WhoAm 92
Jones, George BioIn 17
Jones, George 1931- Baker 92, NewYTBS 92 [port], WhoAm 92
Jones, George Bobby 1946- WhoEmL 93
Jones, George Bryan 1947- WhoE 93
Jones, George Edward 1916- WhoAm 92
Jones, George Fleming 1935- WhoAm 92
Jones, George Henry 1942- WhoAm 92
Jones, George Herbert 1922- WhoSSW 93

Jones, George J. 1942- *St&PR 93*
Jones, George L. *BioIn 17*
Jones, George L. 1950- *St&PR 93, WhoAm 92*
Jones, George L. 1957- *WhoSSW 93*
Jones, George William *WhoScE 91-1*
Jones, George Winford 1936- *WhoSSW 93*
Jones, Geraint (Iwan) 1917- *Baker 92*
Jones, Geraldine M. 1927- *WhoAmW 93*
Jones, Gerry Norman 1932- *WhoAsAP 91*
Jones, Gladys Hurt 1920- *WhoSSW 93*
Jones, Gladys Olivia *AmWomPl*
Jones, Glanville Rees Jeffreys *WhoScE 91-1*
Jones, Glenn Earle 1946- *WhoEmL 93*
Jones, Glenn R. 1930- *St&PR 93*
Jones, Gloria Ellen 1948- *WhoEmL 93*
Jones, Glower Whitehead 1936- *WhoWor 93*
Jones, Glyn *ScF&FL 92*
Jones, Gordon Rees *WhoScE 91-1*
Jones, Gordon Wayne 1930- *St&PR 93*
Jones, Grace 1952- *Baker 92, ConMus 9 [port]*
Jones, Grace 1953- *SoulM*
Jones, Grace Latimer 1879- *AmWomPl*
Jones, Graham S., II *Law&B 92*
Jones, Grant 1922- *WhoSSW 93*
Jones, Grant Richard 1938- *WhoAm 92*
Jones, Gregory G. 1955- *WhoEmL 93*
Jones, Gregory Vaughan *WhoScE 91-1*
Jones, Gregory W. *Law&B 92*
Jones, Gregory William 1949- *WhoSSW 93*
Jones, Gregory Wynn, Sr. 1948- *WhoAm 92*
Jones, Gurnos *WhoScE 91-1*
Jones, Gwenyth Ellen 1952- *WhoAm 92*
Jones, Gwyn *WhoScE 91-1*
Jones, Gwyneth 1936- *Baker 92, BioIn 17, IntDcOp [port], OxDcOp, WhoAm 92, WhoWor 93*
Jones, Gwyneth 1952- *ScF&FL 92*
Jones, H. Alan *Law&B 92*
Jones, H.G. *WhoScE 91-1*
Jones, Hank 1918- *Baker 92*
Jones, Harold 1904-1992 *ConAu 139, SmATA 72*
Jones, Harold A. 1938- *WhoSSW 93*
Jones, Harold Antony 1943- *WhoAm 92*
Jones, Harold Foy 1930- *St&PR 93*
Jones, Harold Gilbert, Jr. 1927- *WhoAm 92*
Jones, Harry Gordon 1950- *WhoEmL 93*
Jones, Harry Willmer 1911- *WhoAm 92*
Jones, Harvey C. *St&PR 93*
Jones, Harvey Davis 1939- *WhoSSW 93*
Jones, Harvey Royden d1991 *BioIn 17*
Jones, Harvey Royden, III 1963- *WhoEmL 93*
Jones, Harvie Paul 1930- *WhoAm 92*
Jones, Helen Carol 1933- *WhoSSW 93*
Jones, Helen Hart 1921- *WhoAm 92*
Jones, Henry 1912- *WhoAm 92*
Jones, Henry Arthur 1851-1929 *BioIn 17*
Jones, Henry Earl 1940- *WhoAm 92*
Jones, Henry V. 1938- *St&PR 93*
Jones, Herbert C. 1936- *AfrAmBi*
Jones, Herbert M. 1939- *St&PR 93*
Jones, Herman Otto, Jr. 1933- *WhoSSW 93*
Jones, Hilton Pressley, III 1948- *WhoWrEP 92*
Jones, Homer Walter, Jr. 1925- *WhoWor 93*
Jones, Horace Allyn 1906- *BiDAMSp 1989*
Jones, Horace C., II 1916- *St&PR 93*
Jones, Horace Charles 1910- *WhoAm 92*
Jones, Houston Gwynne 1924- *WhoAm 92, WhoSSW 93*
Jones, Howard *WhoScE 91-1*
Jones, Howard A. d1992 *NewYTBS 92 [port]*
Jones, Howard Eugene 1954- *WhoSSW 93*
Jones, Howard Langworthy 1917- *WhoAm 92*
Jones, Howard St. Claire, Jr. 1921- *WhoAm 92*
Jones, Howard Wilbur, Jr. 1910- *WhoAm 92*
Jones, Howard William 1935- *WhoE 93*
Jones, Hugh Alan 1950- *WhoE 93*
Jones, Hugh Bethune 1939- *WhoSSW 93*
Jones, Hugh H., Jr. 1930- *St&PR 93*
Jones, Hugh Richard 1914- *WhoAm 92*
Jones, Hugh Richard, Jr. 1938- *WhoAm 92*
Jones, Huw Roland *WhoScE 91-1*
Jones, Ian Frederick *WhoScE 91-1*
Jones, Ian Frederick 1952- *WhoEmL 93, WhoSSW 93*
Jones, Inigo 1573-1652 *BioIn 17, OxDcOp*
Jones, J.A. *ScF&FL 92*
Jones, J. Barry *Law&B 92*
Jones, J. Benton, Jr. 1930- *WhoAm 92*
Jones, J.C. *WhoScE 91-1*
Jones, J. Daniel 1948- *St&PR 93*
Jones, J. Fred *Law&B 92*
Jones, J. Gilbert 1922- *WhoWor 93*
Jones, J. Jeff *ScF&FL 92*
Jones, J. Kenley 1935- *WhoAm 92*
Jones, J. Kenneth 1945- *WhoAm 92*
Jones, J. Knox, Jr. 1929- *WhoAm 92*
Jones, J. Larry 1941- *St&PR 93*
Jones, J. Nicholas 1944- *WhoWrEP 92*
Jones, J. Raymond 1899-1991 *BioIn 17*
Jones, Jack 1938- *WhoAm 92*
Jones, Jack Benjamin 1944- *WhoAm 92*
Jones, Jack Dellis 1925- *WhoAm 92*
Jones, Jack Payne 1928- *WhoWrEP 92*
Jones, Jacqueline Laurette 1959- *WhoWrEP 92*
Jones, James 1921-1977 *BioIn 17, DcLB Y92 [port]*
Jones, James Allen 1957- *St&PR 93*
Jones, James Alton 1956- *WhoEmL 93*
Jones, James Andrew 1965- *WhoSSW 93*
Jones, James Arthur 1917- *WhoAm 92*
Jones, James Cellan *MiSFD 9*
Jones, James D. 1938- *St&PR 93*
Jones, James E.T. *WhoScE 91-1*
Jones, James Earl *BioIn 17*
Jones, James Earl 1931- *ConBlB 3 [port], IntDcF 2-3, WhoAm 92*
Jones, James Edward, Jr. 1924- *WhoAm 92*
Jones, James Fleming, Jr. 1947- *WhoAm 92*
Jones, James Joseph 1932- *St&PR 93*
Jones, James K. 1839-1908 *PolPar*
Jones, James Kimbrough 1839-1908 *BioIn 17*
Jones, James Landon, Jr. 1950- *St&PR 93*
Jones, James McKernon 1924- *WhoSSW 93*
Jones, James Ogden 1935- *WhoSSW 93*
Jones, James P. *Law&B 92*
Jones, James Parker 1940- *WhoSSW 93*
Jones, James R. 1935- *St&PR 93*
Jones, James R. 1939- *WhoAm 92, WhoE 93*
Jones, James Rees 1916- *WhoAm 92*
Jones, James Richard 1940- *WhoAm 92*
Jones, James Richard 1947- *WhoEmL 93, WhoSSW 93*
Jones, James Robert 1934- *WhoAm 92*
Jones, James T. *Law&B 92*
Jones, James Thomas 1949- *WhoSSW 93*
Jones, James Thomas, Jr. 1946- *WhoE 93, WhoEmL 93, WhoSSW 93, WhoWor 93*
Jones, James Tilford 1927- *WhoSSW 93*
Jones, James William 1946- *St&PR 93*
Jones, Jamie Denise 1955- *WhoAmW 93*
Jones, Jan Laverty *WhoAm 92*
Jones, Jane Lloyd- d1991 *BioIn 17*
Jones, Janet Dulin 1957- *WhoAmW 93*
Jones, Janet Marie 1958- *WhoAmW 93, WhoE 93*
Jones, Janet Sandona 1957- *St&PR 93*
Jones, Janet Sue 1946- *St&PR 93*
Jones, Jay D. *Law&B 92*
Jones, Jean Elizabeth Makini 1959- *WhoE 93*
Jones, Jean Melody 1949- *WhoAmW 93*
Jones, Jean R. 1919- *WhoWrEP 92*
Jones, Jean Souther 1937- *WhoSSW 93*
Jones, Jeanne Elise Dumas 1949- *WhoAmW 93, WhoEmL 93*
Jones, Jeanne Marie 1948- *WhoAmW 93*
Jones, Jeannine Ann 1936- *WhoAmW 93*
Jones, Jeff 1944- *ScF&FL 92*
Jones, Jeffery R. *Law&B 92*
Jones, Jeffery Richard 1956- *WhoEmL 93*
Jones, Jeffrey *BioIn 17*
Jones, Jeffrey A. 1946- *WhoAm 92*
Jones, Jeffrey David 1949- *WhoSSW 93*
Jones, Jeffrey W. 1962- *St&PR 93*
Jones, Jeffrey Walton 1953- *WhoAm 92*
Jones, Jenk, Jr. 1936- *WhoAm 92*
Jones, Jenkin Lloyd 1911- *DcLB 127 [port]*
Jones, Jennie *BioIn 17*
Jones, Jennifer 1919- *IntDcF 2-3 [port], WhoAm 92*
Jones, Jennifer Carolyn 1961- *WhoE 93*
Jones, Jennifer L. *Law&B 92*
Jones, Jennifer Lee 1949- *St&PR 93*
Jones, Jennings Hinch 1913- *WhoAm 92*
Jones, Jenny *BioIn 17*
Jones, Jenny 1954- *ScF&FL 92*
Jones, Jerral W. 1943- *WhoSSW 93*
Jones, Jerral Wayne Jerry 1942- *WhoAm 92*
Jones, Jerry L. *BioIn 17*
Jones, Jerry Lynn 1933- *WhoAm 92*
Jones, Jerry R. 1940- *St&PR 93*
Jones, Jerve Maldwyn 1918- *WhoAm 92*
Jones, Jesse Holman 1874-1956 *BioIn 17*
Jones, Jesse L. *BioIn 17*
Jones, Jim Dean 1942- *St&PR 93*
Jones, Jo(nathan) 1911-1985 *Baker 92*
Jones, Joan Megan 1933- *WhoAmW 93*
Jones, Joe 1947- *St&PR 93*
Jones, Joe A. 1938- *St&PR 93*
Jones, Joe Ellis 1949- *WhoEmL 93*
Jones, Joe Frank, III 1949- *WhoEmL 93, WhoSSW 93*
Jones, Joel Mackey 1937- *WhoAm 92*
Jones, John d1879 *BioIn 17*
Jones, John A. *ScF&FL 92*
Jones, John A. 1946- *St&PR 93*
Jones, John Arthur 1921- *WhoAm 92*
Jones, John Bailey 1927- *WhoAm 92*
Jones, John Barclay, Jr. 1928- *WhoAm 92*
Jones, John Charles 1921- *WhoAm 92*
Jones, John David 1951- *St&PR 93*
Jones, John David Stuart 1949- *WhoWor 93*
Jones, John E. 1934- *St&PR 93*
Jones, John Earl 1934- *WhoAm 92*
Jones, John Ellis 1941- *WhoSSW 93, WhoWor 93*
Jones, John Elsworth 1927- *WhoAm 92*
Jones, John Evan 1930- *WhoAm 92*
Jones, John Furness *WhoScE 91-1*
Jones, John G. *Law&B 92, ScF&FL 92*
Jones, John Gareth *WhoScE 91-1*
Jones, John Gornal 1938- *WhoAm 92*
Jones, John Gwynfryn *WhoScE 91-1*
Jones, John H. *BioIn 17*
Jones, John H., Jr. 1944- *St&PR 93, WhoIns 93*
Jones, John Harris 1922- *WhoAm 92, WhoWor 93*
Jones, John Harvey- *BioIn 17*
Jones, John Lou 1929- *WhoAm 92*
Jones, John Luther 1864?-1900 *GayN*
Jones, John Lynton 1944- *WhoWor 93*
Jones, John M., III *ScF&FL 92*
Jones, John Martin, Jr. 1928- *WhoAm 92*
Jones, John Paul 1747-1792 *HarEnMi*
Jones, John Paul 1946- *BioIn 17*
Jones, John Percival 1829-1912 *BioIn 17*
Jones, John R. 1943- *St&PR 93*
Jones, John Rees *WhoScE 91-1*
Jones, John Richards *WhoScE 91-1*
Jones, John Robert *ScF&FL 92*
Jones, John Stephen Phillips *WhoScE 91-1*
Jones, John T. 1940- *WhoIns 93*
Jones, John W. 1791-1848 *PolPar*
Jones, John Walker 1943- *WhoAm 92*
Jones, Johnie H. 1929- *WhoAm 92*
Jones, Johnnie A., III 1953- *WhoEmL 93*
Jones, Joie Pierce 1941- *WhoAm 92*
Jones, Jon Rex 1935- *St&PR 93*
Jones, Joseph 1833-1896 *IntDcAn*
Jones, Joseph A. *Law&B 92*
Jones, Joseph B. *Law&B 92*
Jones, Joseph Edward 1935- *WhoAm 92*
Jones, Joseph Hayward 1924- *WhoE 93*
Jones, Joseph Louis 1923- *St&PR 93, WhoAm 92*
Jones, Joseph M. 1908-1990 *BioIn 17*
Jones, Joseph S. 1913- *St&PR 93*
Jones, Joseph Wayne 1936- *WhoAm 92, WhoSSW 93*
Jones, Judith H. *Law&B 92*
Jones, Julia Faye Griggs 1945- *WhoAmW 93*
Jones, Julie 1935- *WhoAm 92*
Jones, K. C. 1932- *WhoAm 92*
Jones, Kalin *Law&B 92*
Jones, Karen Rene 1959- *WhoAmW 93*
Jones, Kathleen Ann 1964- *WhoAmW 93, WhoEmL 93*
Jones, Kathryn Cherie 1955- *WhoAmW 93*
Jones, Kathryn Kristy 1958- *WhoEmL 93*
Jones, Kathy Wilkins 1954- *WhoSSW 93*
Jones, Kay Dennis *Law&B 92*
Jones, Keith Alden 1941- *WhoAm 92*
Jones, Keith N. *Law&B 92*
Jones, Kelly G. *Law&B 92*
Jones, Kelsey 1922- *Baker 92*
Jones, Kelsey A. 1933- *WhoWor 93*
Jones, Kelvin I. *ScF&FL 92*
Jones, Kendor P. *Law&B 92*
Jones, Kenneth *Law&B 92*
Jones, Kenneth A. *Law&B 92*
Jones, Kenneth A. 1950- *St&PR 93*
Jones, Kenneth Bruce 1953- *WhoSSW 93*
Jones, Kenneth J. *Law&B 92*
Jones, Kenneth R. 1937- *St&PR 93*
Jones, Kenneth Robert *WhoScE 91-1*
Jones, Kenneth T. 1963- *St&PR 93*
Jones, Kensinger 1919- *WhoAm 92*
Jones, Kent Albert 1953- *WhoEmL 93*
Jones, Kevin C. *Law&B 92*
Jones, Kevin Doyle 1950- *WhoSSW 93*
Jones, Kevin K. *Law&B 92*
Jones, Kevin Raymond 1953- *WhoEmL 93, WhoWor 93*
Jones, Kevin Scott 1958- *WhoEmL 93, WhoSSW 93*
Jones, Kevin Timothy 1958- *WhoSSW 93*
Jones, L.L. *WhoScE 91-1*
Jones, L.Q. *MiSFD 9*
Jones, L. Q. 1927- *WhoAm 92*
Jones, L.Q. 1936- *ScF&FL 92*
Jones, Laird R. *Law&B 92*
Jones, Lamar S. *St&PR 93*
Jones, Lana J. 1951- *St&PR 93*
Jones, Lanyon *ScF&FL 92*
Jones, Larry Hudson 1948- *WhoEmL 93, WhoSSW 93*
Jones, Larry J. *Law&B 92*
Jones, Larry L. 1936- *St&PR 93*
Jones, Larry Martin 1952- *WhoE 93*
Jones, Laura Ann 1963- *WhoEmL 93*
Jones, Laura Ann 1968- *WhoAmW 93*
Jones, Laura Ellen 1944- *WhoE 93*
Jones, Lauren W. *Law&B 92*
Jones, Laurence 1933- *WhoWor 93*
Jones, Laurence B. *Law&B 92*
Jones, Laurence Baron 1950- *WhoEmL 93*
Jones, Lauretta Marie 1953- *WhoAm 92*
Jones, Laurie Lynn 1947- *WhoAm 92, WhoE 93*
Jones, Lawassa B. 1938- *WhoAmW 93, WhoSSW 93*
Jones, Lawrence Campbell 1913- *WhoAm 92*
Jones, Lawrence Kelly 1953- *WhoSSW 93*
Jones, Lawrence Marion 1931- *St&PR 93*
Jones, Lawrence McCeney, Jr. 1924- *WhoAm 92*
Jones, Lawrence N. 1921- *BioIn 17*
Jones, Lawrence Neale 1921- *WhoAm 92*
Jones, Lawrence Ryman 1921- *WhoSSW 93*
Jones, Lawrence T. 1940- *St&PR 93*
Jones, Lawrence Tunnicliffe 1950- *WhoE 93, WhoEmL 93, WhoWor 93*
Jones, Lawrence William 1925- *WhoAm 92*
Jones, Lee Bennett 1938- *WhoAm 92*
Jones, Lee O. 1940- *St&PR 93*
Jones, LeeAnn 1961- *WhoEmL 93*
Jones, Leland Carson 1946- *St&PR 93*
Jones, Leon 1936- *WhoE 93*
Jones, Leon 1936-1992 *ConAu 137*
Jones, Leon Herbert, Jr. 1923- *WhoAm 92, WhoSSW 93, WhoWor 93*
Jones, Leonade D. *BioIn 17*
Jones, Leonade Diane 1947- *AfrAmBi, St&PR 93, WhoAm 92*
Jones, LeRoi *ConAu 38NR*
Jones, LeRoi 1934- *BioIn 17, EncAACR, WhoAm 92*
Jones, Lesley Mitchell 1948- *St&PR 93*
Jones, Leslie A. 1939- *St&PR 93*
Jones, Leslie David 1946- *WhoWor 93*
Jones, Leslie E. *Law&B 92*
Jones, Leslie R. *Law&B 92*
Jones, Lewanna 1955- *WhoAmW 93*
Jones, Lewis Bevel, III 1926- *WhoAm 92*
Jones, Lillie Agnes 1910- *WhoAmW 93, WhoWor 93*
Jones, Lillie Mae 1929- *WhoAmW 93*
Jones, Lincoln, III 1933- *WhoAm 92*
Jones, Linda d1972 *SoulM*
Jones, Linda Morgan 1946- *WhoSSW 93*
Jones, Linda Quinton 1943- *WhoAmW 93*
Jones, Linda R. Wolf 1943- *WhoAmW 93*
Jones, Lisa Ann *BioIn 17*
Jones, Lisa Gail 1960- *WhoAmW 93*
Jones, Lisa Grantz 1958- *WhoSSW 93*
Jones, Lisa Mae 1961- *WhoAmW 93*
Jones, Lisa Taylor *BioIn 17*
Jones, Liz Lloyd- *BioIn 17*
Jones, Lloyd E. *BioIn 17*
Jones, Lloyd S. 1931- *ScF&FL 92*
Jones, Lloyd W. 1938- *St&PR 93*
Jones, Lois Mailou *WhoAm 92*
Jones, Loree Jon *BioIn 17*
Jones, Lorella Margaret 1943- *WhoAmW 93*
Jones, Loren Farquhar 1905- *WhoAm 92*
Jones, Lorna D. 1947- *WhoE 93*
Jones, Louis Clark 1908-1990 *BioIn 17*
Jones, Lowell Robert 1931- *WhoE 93*
Jones, Lyle Vincent 1924- *WhoAm 92*
Jones, M. Colleen 1950- *WhoEmL 93*
Jones, M. Hume 1950- *St&PR 93*
Jones, Madison Ralph, III 1938- *WhoSSW 93*
Jones, Madonna Mary 1940- *WhoWor 93*
Jones, Malinda Thiessen 1947- *WhoAmW 93, WhoEmL 93*
Jones, Mallory 1939- *WhoWor 93*
Jones, Marc Edmund 1888-1980 *ScF&FL 92*
Jones, Marcia Thornton *ScF&FL 92*
Jones, Marcia Thornton 1958- *SmATA 73*
Jones, Margaret *ScF&FL 92*
Jones, Margaret Bridwell 1939- *WhoWrEP 92*
Jones, Margaret Eileen Zee 1936- *WhoAm 92*
Jones, Margaret L. 1954- *St&PR 93*
Jones, Margaret Stone 1927- *WhoAmW 93*
Jones, Margaret Wandel 1952- *WhoAmW 93*
Jones, Marguerite Jackson 1949- *WhoAmW 93*
Jones, Marilee Kathleen 1933- *WhoAmW 93*
Jones, Marilyn Elaine 1930- *WhoAmW 93*
Jones, Marion *AmWomPl*

Jones, Marjorie Gillette 1924- WhoWrEP 92
Jones, Marjory Maffitt 1931- WhoSSW 93
Jones, Mark 1956- MiSFD 9
Jones, Mark E. 1939- St&PR 93
Jones, Mark Elmer, Jr. 1920- WhoAm 92
Jones, Mark L. Law&B 92
Jones, Mark Logan 1950- WhoE 93, WhoWor 93
Jones, Mark Mitchell 1951- WhoSSW 93
Jones, Marlynn Ruth 1963- WhoAmW 93
Jones, Marsha Ellis BioIn 17
Jones, Marshall Paul, Jr. 1947- WhoSSW 93
Jones, Martha Nyvall 1933- St&PR 93
Jones, Martin Kenneth WhoScE 91-1
Jones, Marvin Leroy 1937- St&PR 93
Jones, Mary Alice 1965- WhoEmL 93
Jones, Mary E. 1943- AfrAmBi [port]
Jones, Mary Elizabeth WhoSSW 93
Jones, Mary Elizabeth 1955- WhoAmW 93
Jones, Mary Ellen 1922- WhoAm 92, WhoAmW 93
Jones, Mary Holmes 1921- WhoWrEP 92
Jones, Mary J. 1938- ScF&FL 92
Jones, Mary S. Law&B 92
Jones, Mary Ulmer Law&B 92
Jones, Mason 1919- Baker 92
Jones, Mattie Saunders 1942- WhoSSW 93, WhoWor 93
Jones, Max L. 1937- St&PR 93
Jones, Maxine Holmes 1929- WhoAmW 93
Jones, McClure ScF&FL 92
Jones, Merris Lee, Jr. 1964- WhoE 93
Jones, Mervyn BioIn 17
Jones, Michael A. 1946- WhoAm 92
Jones, Michael Calhoun 1936- St&PR 93
Jones, Michael E. 1946- St&PR 93
Jones, Michael Earl 1950- WhoEmL 93
Jones, Michael Eric 1964- WhoSSW 93
Jones, Michael H. 1947- St&PR 93
Jones, Michael J. Law&B 92
Jones, Michael J. 1939- St&PR 93
Jones, Michael Kingston 1931- WhoScE 91-1
Jones, Michael Lynn Law&B 92
Jones, Michael Thomas Law&B 92
Jones, Mike d1990 BioIn 17
Jones, Milnor 1925- WhoWor 93
Jones, Milton Bennion 1926- WhoAm 92
Jones, Milton Thomas 1948- WhoEmL 93
Jones, Milton Wakefield 1930- WhoAm 92
Jones, Mimi BioIn 17
Jones, Molly Mason 1911- WhoAmW 93
Jones, Molly Mufich 1949- WhoE 93
Jones, Monte 1926- St&PR 93
Jones, Mother 1830-1930 ConHero 2 [port]
Jones, Nancy C. 1942- WhoAmW 93
Jones, Nancy Carol 1934- WhoAmW 93
Jones, Nancy E. ScF&FL 92
Jones, Nancy Gale 1940- WhoAmW 93
Jones, Nancy Joy 1939- WhoWrEP 92
Jones, Nathaniel Raphael 1926- WhoAm 92
Jones, Neal ScF&FL 92
Jones, Neil R. 1909-1988 ScF&FL 92
Jones, Nelson R. 1942- St&PR 93
Jones, Nettie (Pearl) 1941- ConAu 137
Jones, Nina Marie 1967- WhoAmW 93
Jones, Norah WhoScE 91-1
Jones, Norma Henry 1929- WhoWrEP 92
Jones, Norma Louise WhoAm 92
Jones, Norman WhoScE 91-1
Jones, Norman Barrie WhoScE 91-1
Jones, Norman M. 1930- St&PR 93
Jones, Norman T. 1936- St&PR 93
Jones, Norman Thomas 1936- WhoAm 92
Jones, O. K., III 1942- WhoAm 92
Jones, O. Steven Law&B 92
Jones, Oliver Hastings 1922- WhoAm 92
Jones, Orlo Law&B 92
Jones, Orlo D. 1938- St&PR 93
Jones, Orlo Dow 1938- WhoAm 92
Jones, Orville William WhoScE 91-1
Jones, Owen 1809-1874 BioIn 17
Jones, Owen 1931- WhoScE 91-1
Jones, Owen Craven, Jr. 1936- WhoAm 92
Jones, Owen John, III 1949- WhoE 93
Jones, Owen T.G. WhoScE 91-1
Jones, Pamela Lewis 1962- WhoAmW 93
Jones, Pamela Lorraine 1956- WhoWrEP 92
Jones, Parry 1891-1963 Baker 92, OxDcOp
Jones, Patricia Avera 1936- WhoAmW 93
Jones, Patricia Elsie 1949- WhoE 93
Jones, Patrick S. 1944- St&PR 93
Jones, Paul BioIn 17
Jones, Paul B. Law&B 92
Jones, Paul C. 1938- St&PR 93
Jones, Paul David 1942- WhoSSW 93
Jones, Paul H. 1928- St&PR 93
Jones, Paul Hastings 1918- WhoSSW 93
Jones, Paul M. 1950- WhoWrEP 92
Jones, Paula Faye Law&B 92
Jones, Pauline H. Law&B 92
Jones, Percy Coleman 1947- WhoEmL 93
Jones, Perry Thomas 1890-1970 BiDAMSp 1989
Jones, Peter A. 1941- WhoIns 93
Jones, Peter A. 1951- ScF&FL 92
Jones, Peter A. 1955- St&PR 93
Jones, Peter d'Alroy 1931- WhoAm 92, WhoWrEP 92
Jones, Peter Michael Seaton 1932- WhoWor 93
Jones, Philip WhoScE 91-1
Jones, Philip Davis 1932- WhoAm 92
Jones, Philip Howard 1937- WhoAm 92
Jones, Philip L. Law&B 92
Jones, Philip (Mark) 1928- Baker 92
Jones, Philip Newton 1924- WhoAm 92
Jones, Philip S. 1943- St&PR 93
Jones, Philip William WhoScE 91-1
Jones, Phillip Clarence 1942- St&PR 93
Jones, Phillip Ray Law&B 92
Jones, Phillip Sanford 1912- WhoAm 92
Jones, "Philly Joe" 1923-1985 Baker 92
Jones, Phyllis Atkins 1949- WhoEmL 93, WhoSSW 93
Jones, Phyllis Edith 1924- WhoAm 92
Jones, Pirkle 1914- WhoAm 92
Jones, Portia Lynn 1951- WhoAmW 93
Jones, Quincy BioIn 17
Jones, Quincy 1933- SoulM, WhoAm 92
Jones, Quincy Delight, Jr. 1933- AfrAmBi
Jones, Quincy (Delight, Jr.) 1933- Baker 92
Jones, R(ichard) P(reston) 1942- WhoWrEP 92
Jones, R.S. Law&B 92
Jones, R. Wray BioIn 17
Jones, Randall St&PR 93
Jones, Randall Dean 1953- WhoIns 93
Jones, Randle Garrett Law&B 92
Jones, Randy WhoAm 92
Jones, Ray Neil 1953- WhoEmL 93, WhoSSW 93
Jones, Rayford Scott 1936- WhoAm 92
Jones, Raymond E. 1941- WhoIns 93
Jones, Raymond Edward, Jr. 1927- WhoAm 92
Jones, Raymond F. 1915- ScF&FL 92
Jones, Raymond Harold 1926- St&PR 93
Jones, Raymond Moylan 1942- WhoE 93
Jones, Rebecca Alvina Patronis 1952- WhoEmL 93
Jones, Rebecca C(astaldi) 1947- WhoWrEP 92
Jones, Regina Nickerson 1942- WhoAm 92, WhoAmW 93
Jones, Reginald Lorrin 1951- WhoEmL 93
Jones, Reginald P. 1946- St&PR 93
Jones, Reginald Teague- 1889-1988 BioIn 17
Jones, Renee Kauerauf 1949- WhoAmW 93, WhoEmL 93, WhoSSW 93, WhoWor 93
Jones, Retha Simmons 1945- WhoE 93
Jones, Richard 1953- OxDcOp
Jones, Richard A. 1947- St&PR 93
Jones, Richard Abner, Jr. 1946- WhoEmL 93
Jones, Richard Allen Law&B 92
Jones, Richard Allen 1931- WhoE 93
Jones, Richard Andrew 1953- WhoWrEP 92
Jones, Richard C. Law&B 92
Jones, Richard Cyrus 1928- WhoAm 92
Jones, Richard E. Law&B 92
Jones, Richard Eugene 1937- St&PR 93
Jones, Richard Hutton 1914- WhoAm 92
Jones, Richard Lamar 1939- WhoAm 92
Jones, Richard M. Law&B 92
Jones, Richard M. 1926- St&PR 93, WhoAm 92
Jones, Richard Norman 1913- WhoAm 92
Jones, Richard P. St&PR 93
Jones, Richard T. 1946- St&PR 93
Jones, Richard Theodore 1929- WhoAm 92
Jones, Richard Wallace 1929- WhoAm 92
Jones, Richmond Addison 1937- WhoWor 93
Jones, Rickie Lee BioIn 17
Jones, Rita Ann 1947- WhoEmL 93, WhoSSW 93
Jones, Robert Law&B 92
Jones, Robert c. 1485-c. 1536 Baker 92
Jones, Robert c. 1570-c. 1615 Baker 92
Jones, Robert 1942- MiSFD 9
Jones, Robert A. WhoScE 91-1
Jones, Robert Allison 1935- St&PR 93
Jones, Robert Alonzo 1937- WhoWor 93
Jones, Robert C. Law&B 92
Jones, Robert C. 1943- WhoAm 92
Jones, Robert Doyne 1933- WhoAm 92
Jones, Robert Edmond 1887-1954 BioIn 17
Jones, Robert Edward 1927- WhoAm 92
Jones, Robert Emmet 1928- WhoAm 92
Jones, Robert Eugene Law&B 92
Jones, Robert Eugene 1926- WhoSSW 93
Jones, Robert F. 1934- ScF&FL 92
Jones, Robert Fredrick 1930- WhoWrEP 92
Jones, Robert G. 1948- St&PR 93
Jones, Robert Gean 1925- WhoAm 92
Jones, Robert Gerard Law&B 92
Jones, Robert Godwin ConAu 137
Jones, Robert H. 1925- St&PR 93
Jones, Robert Henry 1935- WhoAm 92, WhoWor 93
Jones, Robert Huhn 1927- WhoAm 92
Jones, Robert Kenneth 1926-1986 ScF&FL 92
Jones, Robert Lawton 1925- WhoAm 92, WhoSSW 93
Jones, Robert Lee 1920- WhoAm 92
Jones, Robert Lee 1944- WhoE 93
Jones, Robert Lee 1945- St&PR 93
Jones, Robert Lee, Jr. 1943- WhoAm 92
Jones, Robert Lyle 1959- WhoEmL 93
Jones, Robert Marion 1919- WhoAm 92
Jones, Robert McKittrick 1933- St&PR 93
Jones, Robert Quince 1930- WhoAm 92
Jones, Robert Russell 1927- WhoAm 92
Jones, Robert Sinclair 1929- St&PR 93
Jones, Robert Thomas 1910- WhoAm 92
Jones, Robert Trent, Sr. 1906- WhoAm 92
Jones, Robert Trent, Jr. 1939- WhoAm 92
Jones, Robert Wayne 1937- WhoSSW 93
Jones, Robert Wesley Law&B 92
Jones, Robert William Law&B 92
Jones, Robert William 1944- WhoSSW 93
Jones, Robertson Law&B 92
Jones, Robin BioIn 17
Jones, Robin Arbuckle 1962- WhoAmW 93, WhoEmL 93
Jones, Rocky WhoWrEP 92
Jones, Roderick John WhoScE 91-1
Jones, Rodney 1950- DcLB 120 [port]
Jones, Rodney G. 1950- WhoAm 92
Jones, Roger BioIn 17
Jones, Roger Alan 1947- WhoEmL 93
Jones, Roger C. 1947- St&PR 93
Jones, Roger Clyde 1919- WhoAm 92, WhoWor 93
Jones, Roger David 1941- WhoScE 91-1
Jones, Roger Lee 1954- WhoSSW 93
Jones, Roger W. 1920- St&PR 93
Jones, Roger Walton 1953- WhoWrEP 92
Jones, Roger Wayne 1939- WhoWor 93
Jones, Ronald Bamber 1952- WhoSSW 93
Jones, Ronald Conrad 1944- WhoE 93
Jones, Ronald D. 1948- St&PR 93
Jones, Ronald David 1930- WhoAm 92
Jones, Ronald G. 1935- St&PR 93
Jones, Ronald L. Law&B 92
Jones, Ronald Lee 1942- WhoAm 92
Jones, Ronald Lloyd 1938- St&PR 93
Jones, Ronald Mervyn WhoScE 91-1
Jones, Ronald Neu 1939- St&PR 93
Jones, Ronald Samuel WhoScE 91-1
Jones, Ronald Winthrop 1931- WhoAm 92
Jones, Ronald Woodbridge 1932- St&PR 93
Jones, Roosevelt, Jr. 1959- St&PR 93
Jones, Rosemarie Frieda 1950- WhoAmW 93
Jones, Rosie BioIn 17
Jones, Ross 1942- WhoAm 92, WhoE 93
Jones, Rowan Harrison WhoScE 91-1
Jones, Roxanne H. AfrAmBi [port]
Jones, Roxanne Harper 1928- WhoAmW 93, WhoE 93
Jones, Royal Maurice 1937- WhoSSW 93
Jones, Rufus E. 1940- AfrAmBi [port]
Jones, Rufus Parnell 1933- BiDAMSp 1989
Jones, Russ ScF&FL 92
Jones, Russel Cameron 1935- WhoAm 92
Jones, Russell H. 1944- St&PR 93
Jones, Russell L. WhoAm 92
Jones, Sally Daviess Pickrell 1923- WhoAmW 93, WhoE 93
Jones, Sam BioIn 17
Jones, Sam Houston 1897-1978 BioIn 17
Jones, Sam Willis, Jr. 1942- St&PR 93
Jones, Samantha BioIn 17
Jones, Samuel 1935- WhoAm 92
Jones, Samuel M. 1936- St&PR 93
Jones, Sandra 1946- WhoEmL 93
Jones, Sandra L. ConAu 137
Jones, Sandra LaVern 1948- WhoE 93
Jones, Sandra Lou 1944- WhoAmW 93
Jones, Sandra Rattray 1941- WhoAmW 93
Jones, Sarah Elizabeth Eggleston 1959- WhoAmW 93
Jones, Sarah J. 1940- St&PR 93
Jones, Scott A. 1957- St&PR 93
Jones, Scott T. 1955- St&PR 93
Jones, Seaborn Gustavus, Jr. 1942- WhoWrEP 92
Jones, Sharon June 1952- WhoAmW 93, WhoSSW 93
Jones, Sharon Kay 1952- WhoSSW 93
Jones, Sharon Lester 1944- WhoAmW 93
Jones, Sharyn M. 1955- WhoAmW 93
Jones, Sheila ScF&FL 92
Jones, Sheila Ruth 1956- WhoAmW 93
Jones, Shelby L. 1936- St&PR 93, WhoIns 93
Jones, Sheldon Atwell 1938- WhoAm 92, WhoE 93
Jones, Sheree Eileen 1961- WhoAmW 93
Jones, Sherman J. 1946- WhoAm 92
Jones, Shirley BioIn 17, WhoAm 92
Jones, Sidney 1861-1946 Baker 92
Jones, Sidney Francis, Jr. 1937- St&PR 93
Jones, Sidney Lewis 1933- WhoAm 92
Jones, Simmons 1920- ConAu 136
Jones, Sissieretta 1868-1933 Baker 92
Jones, Sonia Josephine 1945- WhoAmW 93
Jones, Sophia Lorraine 1967- WhoAmW 93
Jones, "Spike" (Lindley Armstrong) 1911-1965 Baker 92
Jones, Stan 1931- BioIn 17
Jones, Stanley Boyd 1938- WhoAm 92
Jones, Stanley Houston 1935- St&PR 93
Jones, Stanley Paul 1931- BiDAMSp 1989
Jones, Stephan L. 1935- WhoIns 93
Jones, Stephan Lowry 1935- St&PR 93
Jones, Stephanie Tubbs AfrAmBi [port]
Jones, Stephen ScF&FL 92
Jones, Stephen 1940- WhoSSW 93, WhoWor 93
Jones, Stephen 1953- ScF&FL 92
Jones, Stephen Brewster 1949- WhoEmL 93
Jones, Stephen Dunbar 1946- St&PR 93
Jones, Stephen Graf 1947- WhoEmL 93
Jones, Stephen James 1945- WhoIns 93
Jones, Stephen Lane 1945- WhoSSW 93
Jones, Stephen Yates 1958- WhoSSW 93
Jones, Steve BioIn 17
Jones, Steve 1948- St&PR 93
Jones, Steven Emrys 1957- WhoWor 93
Jones, Steven G. 1949- St&PR 93
Jones, Steven Gibb 1949- WhoSSW 93
Jones, Steven Lee Law&B 92
Jones, Steven Marlin 1942- St&PR 93
Jones, Stuart 1913-1938 BiDAMSp 1989
Jones, Stuart Lawrence Law&B 92
Jones, Susan Dorfman 1939- WhoAmW 93, WhoE 93, WhoWor 93
Jones, Susan Emily 1948- WhoAm 92
Jones, Suzanne P. 1946- WhoAmW 93
Jones, Suzanne Whitmore 1950- WhoEmL 93, WhoSSW 93
Jones, Sybil E. AmWomPl
Jones, Sydney Tucker, III 1944- St&PR 93
Jones, T. Lawrence WhoIns 93
Jones, T.M. WhoScE 91-1
Jones, Tammy Holsclaw 1962- WhoSSW 93
Jones, Tara BioIn 17
Jones, Ted ConAu 138
Jones, Terence WhoScE 91-1
Jones, Terence G. ScF&FL 92
Jones, Terri Alane 1957- WhoAmW 93
Jones, Terry 1942- BioIn 17, MiSFD 9, ScF&FL 92, WhoAm 92
Jones, Terry E. 1951- St&PR 93
Jones, Terry L. 1933- St&PR 93
Jones, Thad(deus Joseph) 1923-1986 Baker 92
Jones, Theador Edward 1937- ConAu 138
Jones, Theodore d1991 BioIn 17
Jones, Theodore Lawrence 1920- WhoAm 92
Jones, Theodore William 1924- WhoAm 92
Jones, Thomas A. 1820- BioIn 17
Jones, Thomas ap Catesby 1790-1858 HarEnMi
Jones, Thomas C. 1946- WhoIns 93
Jones, Thomas Charles 1934- St&PR 93
Jones, Thomas Chester 1946- WhoAm 92
Jones, Thomas Curtis 1939- WhoAm 92
Jones, Thomas E. 1938- St&PR 93
Jones, Thomas H. 1916- St&PR 93
Jones, Thomas M. 1946- St&PR 93
Jones, Thomas Maxfield 1938- WhoE 93
Jones, Thomas Neal 1930- WhoAm 92
Jones, Thomas Neil 1945- St&PR 93
Jones, Thomas W. Law&B 92
Jones, Thomas W. 1949- WhoIns 93
Jones, Thomas Wade 1949- WhoAm 92
Jones, Thomas Walter 1945- WhoAm 92
Jones, Thomas Wright 1947- WhoE 93
Jones, Tim Wynne- BioIn 17, ScF&FL 92
Jones, Timothy 1959- St&PR 93
Jones, Timothy Dale 1949- WhoWrEP 92
Jones, Tina M. 1936- WhoAmW 93
Jones, Tom 1940- Baker 92, WhoAm 92
Jones, Tommy Lee 1946- HolBB [port], WhoAm 92
Jones, Tony Armstrong- 1930- BioIn 17
Jones, Tracey Kirk, Jr. 1917- WhoAm 92
Jones, Trevor ScF&FL 92
Jones, Trevor 1947- WhoAm 92
Jones, Trevor Owen 1930- WhoAm 92, WhoWor 93
Jones, Tudor Bowden WhoScE 91-1

Jones, Ulysses S. Law&B 92
Jones, Valerie Kaye 1956- WhoAmW 93
Jones, Veda Boyd 1948- WhoWrEP 92
Jones, Veda Rae Boyd 1948- WhoAmW 93
Jones, Vernon T. 1929- St&PR 93
Jones, Vicki Sue 1957- WhoWrEP 92
Jones, Vickie S. Law&B 92
Jones, Vincent Starbuck 1906- WhoAm 92
Jones, Virgil Carrington 1906- WhoWrEP 92
Jones, Virginia Lacy 1912-1984 BioIn 17
Jones, W. WhoScE 91-1
Jones, W. Paul BioIn 17
Jones, Wallace Jude 1942- WhoE 93
Jones, Walter B. 1913- CngDr 91
Jones, Walter B. 1913-1992 NewYTBS 92 [port]
Jones, Walter Beaman 1913- WhoAm 92
Jones, Walter Charles 1959- WhoEmL 93
Jones, Walter Edward 1951- WhoSSW 93
Jones, Walter Harrison 1922- WhoAm 92, WhoWor 93
Jones, Walton Linton 1918- WhoAm 92, WhoWor 93
Jones, Wanda Carol 1956- WhoEmL 93, WhoWor 93
Jones, Wanda Faye 1949- WhoEmL 93
Jones, Ward E., II 1946- WhoSSW 93
Jones, Warren David 1914- WhoAm 92
Jones, Warren Rentz 1957- St&PR 93
Jones, Warren Thomas 1942- WhoAm 92
Jones, Warwick Linley 1943- WhoUN 92
Jones, Wayne Powell 1953- WhoSSW 93
Jones, Wellington Downing, III 1945- WhoAm 92
Jones, Weyman (B.) 1928- DcAmChF 1960
Jones, Weyman Beckett 1928- St&PR 93
Jones, Wilbur Boardman, Jr. 1915- WhoAm 92
Jones, Wilbur Stone 1945- St&PR 93
Jones, Wiley N. St&PR 93
Jones, Willard, II Law&B 92
Jones, William 1726-1800 Baker 92
Jones, William 1746-1794 BioIn 17
Jones, William 1824-1864 HarEnMi
Jones, William 1871-1909 IntDcAn
Jones, William A. Law&B 92
Jones, William Allen Law&B 92
Jones, William Allen 1941- St&PR 93, WhoAm 92
Jones, William Arnold 1924- WhoAm 92
Jones, William Augustus, Jr. 1927- WhoAm 92
Jones, William Benjamin, Jr. 1924- WhoAm 92
Jones, William Bowdoin 1928- WhoAm 92
Jones, William Catron 1926- WhoAm 92
Jones, William Charles 1944- WhoE 93
Jones, William Edward 1942- WhoAm 92
Jones, William Ernest 1936- WhoAm 92
Jones, William French, Jr. 1950- WhoAm 92
Jones, William Gareth WhoScE 91-1
Jones, William Henry, Jr. 1919- St&PR 93
Jones, William Jay Law&B 92
Jones, William Jeremy WhoScE 91-1
Jones, William Kenneth 1930- WhoAm 92
Jones, William Kinzy 1946- WhoEmL 93, WhoSSW 93
Jones, William Leicester 1906- St&PR 93
Jones, William McKendrey 1927- WhoAm 92
Jones, William N. 1926- St&PR 93
Jones, William Randall 1955- WhoAm 92
Jones, William Rex 1922- WhoAm 92
Jones, William Riley, Jr. 1947- WhoSSW 93
Jones, William W. Law&B 92
Jones, William Watt Law&B 92
Jones, William Wood, Jr. 1954- St&PR 93
Jones, Willis B., Jr. 1936- St&PR 93
Jones, Winona Nigels 1928- WhoAmW 93, WhoSSW 93, WhoWor 93
Jones, Winson 1925- St&PR 93
Jones, Yvonne Harris WhoAmW 93
Jones-Davis, Bettye Ann Law&B 92
Jones-McBeth, LeNora 1951- WhoAmW 93
Joneson, Michael G. 1946- St&PR 93
Jones-Orr, Regina Lynn 1951- WhoAmW 93
Jones-Shoemaker, Cynthia Cavenaugh 1938- WhoAm 92, WhoE 93
Jones-Smith, Jacqueline 1952- WhoAm 92, WhoAmW 93
Jones-Wilson, Faustine Clarisse 1927- WhoAm 92
Jong, Anthony W. d1992 NewYTBS 92
Jong, Erica BioIn 17
Jong, Erica 1942- JeAmFiW, ScF&FL 92
Jong, Erica Mann 1942- WhoAm 92, WhoWor 93, WhoWrEP 92
Jong, Marinus de 1891-1984 Baker 92
Jongbloed, A.W. 1944- WhoScE 91-3
Jongbloet, Piet Hein Leo Arthur Michiel 1933- WhoWor 93
Jonge, Gustaaf Adolf de 1924- WhoWor 93
Jongebreur, Aad A. 1941- WhoScE 91-3
Jongen, Joseph 1873-1953 Baker 92
Jongen, Leon (Marie-Victor-Justin) 1884-1969 Baker 92
Jonish, Arley Duane 1927- WhoAm 92
Jonish, James Edward 1941- WhoAm 92
Jonker, Pieter 1950- WhoWor 93
Jonkers, Martinus Karel Petrus 1924- WhoWor 93
Jonkouski, Jill Ellen WhoAmW 93
Jons, Timothy E. Law&B 92
Jonscher, Andrew K. WhoScE 91-1
Jonscher, John 1948- St&PR 93
Jonsdottir, Thorgunnur 1948- WhoWor 93
Jonsell, Bengt E. 1936- WhoScE 91-4
Jonsen, Albert R. 1931- WhoAm 92
Jonsen, Paul 1960- WhoWor 93
Jonson, Ben 1572?-1637 DcLB 121 [port], OxDcOp, WorLitC [port]
Jonson, Ben 1573?-1637 BioIn 17, MagSWL [port]
Jonson, Dan L. 1943- WhoIns 93
Jonson, Gunilla 1943- WhoScE 91-4
Jonson, Kerstin M.C. 1945- WhoScE 91-4
Jonsson, Bengt Goran 1944- WhoWor 93
Jonsson, Bror 1948- WhoScE 91-4
Jonsson, Carl R. 1935- St&PR 93
Jonsson, Gerd Margareta 1945- WhoWor 93
Jonsson, Goran B. 1929- WhoScE 91-4
Jonsson, Jan Ake 1948- WhoWor 93
Jonsson, Jens Johannes 1922- WhoAm 92
Jonsson, Jonas 1930- WhoScE 91-4
Jonsson, Josef Petrus 1887-1969 Baker 92
Jonsson, Kjartan A. 1940- WhoE 93, WhoWor 93
Jonsson, Lars Olov 1952- WhoWor 93
Jonsson, Lena 1947- WhoScE 91-4
Jonsson, Nils Inge Einar 1928- WhoWor 93
Jonsson, Richard Eugene Thomas 1935- WhoWrEP 92
Jonsson, Stephen Rapier 1951- WhoSSW 93
Jonsson, Ture 1934- WhoUN 92
Jontry, Richard 1942- WhoWor 93
Jontz, James Prather 1951- WhoAm 92
Jontz, Jim BioIn 17
Jontz, Jim 1951- CngDr 91
Joo, Arpad 1948- Baker 92
Joo, Ferenc 1938- WhoScE 91-4
Joo, Istvan 1928- WhoScE 91-4
Joo, Young Je 1949- WhoWor 93
Joos, David W. 1953- St&PR 93
Joos, Felipe Miguel 1952- WhoE 93
Joos, Patrick O.L. 1959- WhoScE 91-2
Joos, Paul 1936- WhoScE 91-2
Joosse, Barbara Monnot 1949- WhoWrEP 92
Joossens, Jozef Victor 1915- WhoWor 93
Jooste, Waldie 1947- St&PR 93
Joosten, Ferdinand Louis 1928- WhoWrEP 92
Joosten, Stef Mathias Maria 1959- WhoWor 93
Joplin, Albert Frederick 1919- WhoWor 93
Joplin, Frances Grigsby AmWomPl
Joplin, Janis 1943-1970 BioIn 17
Joplin, Janis (Lyn) 1943-1970 Baker 92
Joplin, John Francis 1924- St&PR 93
Joplin, Julian Mike 1936- WhoAm 92
Joplin, Scott 1868-1917 Baker 92, BioIn 17, GayN, IntDcOp, OxDcOp
Jopling, Jane 1932- WhoUN 92
Joppa, Glenn L. Law&B 92
Joppa, Robert Glenn 1922- WhoAm 92
Joppien, Gunter 1938- WhoScE 91-3
Jora, Mihail 1891-1971 Baker 92
Joralemon, Barbara Gail 1951- WhoEmL 93
Jorberg, Lennart Gustav 1927- WhoWor 93
Jorda, Enrique 1911- Baker 92
Jordahl, Robert Arnold 1926- WhoSSW 93
Jordal, Douglas R. Law&B 92
Jordan, Adrienne Gayle Law&B 92
Jordan, Albert Robert 1945- WhoE 93
Jordan, Alexander Joseph, Jr. 1938- WhoAm 92
Jordan, Amos Azariah, Jr. 1922- WhoAm 92
Jordan, Amy Beth 1961- WhoE 93
Jordan, Andrew Peter Habberley WhoScE 91-1
Jordan, Andrew Stephen 1936- WhoE 93
Jordan, Angel Goni 1930- WhoAm 92, WhoE 93
Jordan, Anne 1943- ScF&FL 92
Jordan, Armin 1932- Baker 92
Jordan, Arthur DePriest Law&B 92
Jordan, B. Everett 1896-1974 BioIn 17
Jordan, Barbara 1936- BioIn 17, ConBlB 4 [port]
Jordan, Barbara C. 1936- EncAACR, WhoAm 92, WhoAmW 93
Jordan, Barbara Charline 1936- AfrAmBi
Jordan, Barbara Leslie 1915- WhoWrEP 92
Jordan, Barbara Schwinn WhoAm 92, WhoWor 93
Jordan, Benjamin Everett 1896-1974 BioIn 17
Jordan, Benjamin Everett, Jr. 1926- St&PR 93
Jordan, Bertrand R. 1939- WhoScE 91-2
Jordan, Betty Sue 1920- WhoAmW 93
Jordan, Boyd E. 1937- St&PR 93
Jordan, Brenda ScF&FL 92
Jordan, Brian J. Law&B 92
Jordan, Bryce 1924- WhoAm 92, WhoWor 93
Jordan, Carina AmWomPl
Jordan, Carolyn Lucile 1932- WhoAmW 93
Jordan, Charles Milton 1949- WhoAm 92
Jordan, Charles Morrell 1927- WhoAm 92
Jordan, Clifford 1919- St&PR 93
Jordan, Clifford Henry 1921- WhoAm 92
Jordan, Crawford 1949- WhoScE 91-1
Jordan, Daniel Porter, Jr. 1938- WhoSSW 93
Jordan, Danny Clyde 1951- WhoEmL 93
Jordan, Darrell E. 1938- WhoAm 92
Jordan, David 1940- WhoE 93
Jordan, David Edward Law&B 92
Jordan, David Loran 1933- WhoAm 92
Jordan, David Starr 1851-1931 BioIn 17
Jordan, Dennis 1955- St&PR 93
Jordan, Don ConAu 139, SmATA 73
Jordan, Don D. 1932- St&PR 93, WhoSSW 93
Jordan, Dorian K. Law&B 92
Jordan, Douglas Saunders 1942- St&PR 93
Jordan, DuPree, Jr. 1929- WhoAm 92
Jordan, Earl Clifford 1916- WhoWor 93
Jordan, Edward 1945- St&PR 93
Jordan, Edward Conrad 1910- WhoAm 92
Jordan, Edward George 1929- WhoAm 92
Jordan, Elizabeth Garver 1867-1947 AmWomPl
Jordan, Elizabeth Goodrich AmWomPl
Jordan, Elke 1937- WhoAm 92, WhoAmW 93
Jordan, Ervin Leon, Jr. 1954- WhoSSW 93
Jordan, Ethel B. AmWomPl
Jordan, Eugene Fusz Law&B 92
Jordan, Frank M. WhoAm 92
Jordan, Fred WhoAm 92
Jordan, G. Gary 1940- St&PR 93
Jordan, G.P. ScF&FL 92
Jordan, Gene Morrison 1931- WhoWor 93
Jordan, George E. 1940- WhoE 93
Jordan, George Lyman, Jr. 1921- WhoAm 92
Jordan, George R., Jr. 1920- St&PR 93, WhoIns 93
Jordan, George Washington, Jr. 1938- WhoSSW 93
Jordan, Glenn 1936- MiSFD 9, WhoAm 92
Jordan, Grace C. AmWomPl
Jordan, Gregory Doty 1951- WhoSSW 93
Jordan, Hamilton NewYTBS 92
Jordan, Hamilton McWhorter 1944- WhoAm 92
Jordan, Henry Hellmut, Jr. 1921- WhoSSW 93
Jordan, Henry Kevin 1956- St&PR 93
Jordan, Henry Preston, Jr. 1926- WhoSSW 93
Jordan, Henry Wendell 1935-1977 BiDAMSp 1989
Jordan, Henryk 1842-1907 PolBiDi
Jordan, Herbert R. d1991 BioIn 17
Jordan, Howard Emerson 1926- WhoAm 92
Jordan, I. King BioIn 17
Jordan, Irene 1919- Baker 92
Jordan, J. J. 1946- WhoSSW 93
Jordan, J. Luther, Jr. 1921- St&PR 93
Jordan, Jack Gerald 1929- WhoSSW 93
Jordan, James Pinson 1925- St&PR 93
Jordan, James Ralph 1910-1980 BiDAMSp 1989
Jordan, Jane B.L. Law&B 92
Jordan, Jean Ann 1956- WhoAmW 93
Jordan, Jeanette Irene 1944- WhoAmW 93
Jordan, Jeffery Reid 1964- WhoSSW 93
Jordan, Jennifer BioIn 17
Jordan, Jerry Neville 1928- WhoAm 92
Jordan, Joan Kowalski 1941- WhoAmW 93
Jordan, Joe J. 1923- WhoAm 92
Jordan, John Albert Law&B 92
Jordan, John Allen, Jr. 1935- St&PR 93, WhoAm 92
Jordan, John Edward 1930- WhoSSW 93
Jordan, John Emory 1919- WhoAm 92
Jordan, John J. d1991 BioIn 17
Jordan, John Lester 1944- WhoE 93
Jordan, John Michael 1963- WhoE 93
Jordan, John Patrick 1934- WhoAm 92, WhoE 93
Jordan, John Richard, Jr. 1921- WhoAm 92
Jordan, John Trevarthen- BioIn 17
Jordan, John William 1912- WhoSSW 93
Jordan, Jonathan Fitzgerald 1963- WhoSSW 93
Jordan, Joseph d1992 NewYTBS 92
Jordan, Joseph 1919- WhoAm 92
Jordan, Joseph 1927- St&PR 93
Jordan, Joseph Michael 1922- WhoAm 92
Jordan, Joseph Rembert 1947- WhoAm 92
Jordan, Joseph William 1948- St&PR 93
Jordan, Juanita BioIn 17
Jordan, Judith Victoria 1943- WhoAmW 93, WhoE 93
Jordan, Jules 1850-1927 Baker 92
Jordan, June 1936- BioIn 17, BlkAuII 92, DcAmChF 1960, MajAI [port]
Jordan, June M. 1936- WhoAm 92
Jordan, Karen Leigh 1954- WhoSSW 93
Jordan, Kate 1862-1926 AmWomPl
Jordan, Kathleen Anne Finn 1940- WhoE 93
Jordan, Kathleen Smith 1949- WhoE 93
Jordan, Kenneth U. AfrAmBi [port]
Jordan, Kurt 1930- WhoScE 91-3
Jordan, Larry Clinton 1943- St&PR 93
Jordan, Laura ConAu 139
Jordan, Lawrence E. 1958- St&PR 93
Jordan, Lennon Douglas, Jr. 1953- WhoEmL 93
Jordan, Leo C. 1943- St&PR 93
Jordan, Leo Clayton 1943- WhoAm 92
Jordan, Leo F. 1932- St&PR 93
Jordan, Leo John 1931- WhoAm 92
Jordan, Linda Eastridge 1954- WhoSSW 93
Jordan, Lise H. Law&B 92
Jordan, Lorna 1958- WhoAmW 93, WhoEmL 93
Jordan, Louis 1908-1975 Baker 92
Jordan, Louis Hampton 1922- WhoAm 92
Jordan, Lucas 1632-1705 BioIn 17
Jordan, Luis Perez 1955- WhoWor 93
Jordan, M. Alice AmWomPl
Jordan, Margaret H. BioIn 17
Jordan, Margaret R. 1937- WhoAmW 93
Jordan, Mark Henry 1915- WhoAm 92
Jordan, Mark W. Law&B 92
Jordan, Marlon BioIn 17
Jordan, Marvin Evans, Jr. 1944- WhoWor 93
Jordan, Marvin Wesley, Jr. 1949- WhoSSW 93
Jordan, Michael BioIn 17
Jordan, Michael 1963- AfrAmBi, ConHero 2 [port]
Jordan, Michael Adrian, II 1947- WhoEmL 93
Jordan, Michael F. Law&B 92
Jordan, Michael Hugh 1936- WhoAm 92, WhoSSW 93
Jordan, Michael Jeffery 1963- WhoAm 92
Jordan, Michael Lee McAdams 1946- WhoEmL 93
Jordan, Michelle Denise 1954- WhoAmW 93
Jordan, Michelle Henrietta 1948- WhoAm 92
Jordan, Millicent Dobbs BioIn 17
Jordan, Monica M. WhoScE 91-1
Jordan, Morris Reginald, Jr. 1951- WhoEmL 93, WhoSSW 93
Jordan, Nancy Youngblood 1947- WhoSSW 93
Jordan, Narelle BioIn 17
Jordan, Neil 1950- MiSFD 9
Jordan, Neil 1951- BioIn 17
Jordan, Nicholas Theodore 1940- St&PR 93
Jordan, Pat BioIn 17
Jordan, Patrice Marie 1957- St&PR 93
Jordan, Paul Howard, Jr. 1919- WhoAm 92
Jordan, Paul Richard 1926- WhoWrEP 92
Jordan, Peter Colin 1936- WhoAm 92
Jordan, Peter Friedrich 1911- WhoE 93
Jordan, Peter Wilson 1943- WhoWrEP 92
Jordan, Philip Harding, Jr. 1931- WhoAm 92
Jordan, Randall Warren 1952- WhoSSW 93
Jordan, Richard A. 1946- WhoIns 93
Jordan, Richard Charles 1909- WhoAm 92
Jordan, Richard Thomas 1948- WhoEmL 93
Jordan, Robert WhoWrEP 92
Jordan, Robert 1940- WhoAm 92
Jordan, Robert 1948- ScF&FL 92

Jordan, Robert Andrew 1955- *WhoEmL 93, WhoSSW 93*
Jordan, Robert Elijah, III 1936- *WhoAm 92*
Jordan, Robert Hadley *Law&B 92*
Jordan, Robert Leon 1928- *WhoAm 92*
Jordan, Robert Leon 1934- *WhoAm 92, WhoSSW 93*
Jordan, Robert Maynard 1924- *WhoAm 92*
Jordan, Robert Smith 1929- *WhoAm 92*
Jordan, Robert T. 1937- *St&PR 93*
Jordan, Rodney W. *Law&B 92*
Jordan, Roger 1933- *St&PR 93*
Jordan, Ronald E. 1943- *St&PR 93*
Jordan, Ronald Lee 1939- *St&PR 93*
Jordan, Roy Wilcox 1911- *WhoAm 92*
Jordan, Russell Wood, III *Law&B 92*
Jordan, Sally *BioIn 17*
Jordan, Sandra 1952- *WhoAmW 93*
Jordan, Sandra Dickerson 1951- *WhoAmW 93*
Jordan, Sherryl *ScF&FL 92*
Jordan, Sherryl 1949- *SmATA 71 [port]*
Jordan, Shirley Drake 1935- *WhoAmW 93*
Jordan, Stanley 1960- *WhoAm 92*
Jordan, Steven Jeffrey 1945- *St&PR 93*
Jordan, Sverre 1889-1972 *Baker 92*
Jordan, Sydney F. *Law&B 92*
Jordan, Terry Gilbert 1938- *WhoAm 92*
Jordan, Theodore Wayne 1950- *WhoSSW 93*
Jordan, Theresa Joan 1949- *WhoAmW 93, WhoE 93*
Jordan, Thomas Fredrick 1936- *WhoAm 92*
Jordan, Thomas Hillman 1948- *WhoAm 92*
Jordan, Thomas Richard 1928- *WhoAm 92*
Jordan, Tom *BioIn 17*
Jordan, V. Craig 1947- *WhoAm 92*
Jordan, Vernon E. *NewYTBS 92 [port]*
Jordan, Vernon E., Jr. 1935- *ConBlB 3 [port], St&PR 93*
Jordan, Vernon Eulion, Jr. 1935- *AfrAmBi, EncAACR [port], WhoAm 92, WhoWor 93*
Jordan, Victor Walter Lennard *WhoScE 91-1*
Jordan, Wayne Clifford 1949- *St&PR 93*
Jordan, Wayne Robert 1940- *WhoAm 92, WhoSSW 93*
Jordan, William *Law&B 92*
Jordan, William Bryan, Jr. 1940- *WhoAm 92*
Jordan, William Chester 1948- *WhoAm 92*
Jordan, William J(ohnston) 1924- *ConAu 39NR*
Jordan, William James 1942- *St&PR 93*
Jordan, William McLendon 1944- *St&PR 93*
Jordan, William Randall *Law&B 92*
Jordan, William Reynier Van Evera, Sr. *WhoAm 92, WhoSSW 93*
Jordan, Winthrop Donaldson 1931- *WhoAm 92*
Jordan, Wrenza Lou 1929- *WhoAm 92*
Jordana, Rafael 1941- *WhoScE 91-3, WhoWor 93*
Jordanes d552? *OxDcByz*
Jordan Haight, Mary Ellen 1927- *ConAu 136*
Jordan-Holmes, Clark 1946- *WhoEmL 93*
Jordania, Vakhtang 1942- *WhoAm 92, WhoSSW 93*
Jordano, Joan Karen 1938- *WhoAmW 93*
Jordanov, Dimcho 1924- *WhoScE 91-4*
Jordanus of Severac 1290-1354 *Expl 93*
Jorda-Olives, Marta 1953- *WhoWor 93*
Jorden, Doris Marie 1943- *WhoWrEP 92*
Jorden, Edwin William, Jr. 1947- *WhoAm 92*
Jorden, Eleanor Harz *WhoAm 92*
Jorden, James Roy 1934- *WhoAm 92*
Jorden, William John 1923- *WhoAm 92*
Jordon, David Lewis 1937- *St&PR 93*
Jordon, Deborah E. *Law&B 92*
Jordon, Deborah Elizabeth 1951- *WhoAm 92, WhoAmW 93, WhoE 93*
Jordon, Leo J. *Law&B 92*
Jordon, Robert Earl 1938- *WhoAm 92*
Jordovic, Mitar 1923- *WhoScE 91-4*
Jordy, William Henry 1917- *WhoAm 92*
Jorge, Nuno Maria Roque 1947- *WhoWor 93*
Jorge Blanco, Salvador 1926- *DcCPCAm*
Jorge Cardoso, Onelio 1914- *SpAmA*
Jorgensen, Alfred H. 1934- *WhoWor 93*
Jorgensen, Anders Fjendbo 1950- *WhoWor 93*
Jorgensen, Bo Barker 1946- *WhoWor 93*
Jorgensen, Charles Everett 1932- *St&PR 93*
Jorgensen, Chester Neil 1925- *St&PR 93*
Jorgensen, Christian Klixbull 1931- *WhoScE 91-4*
Jorgensen, Earle M. 1899- *BioIn 17*
Jorgensen, Edvard 1950- *WhoEmL 93*
Jorgensen, Erik 1912- *Baker 92*
Jorgensen, Erik 1921- *WhoAm 92*
Jorgensen, Evelyn 1910- *St&PR 93*
Jorgensen, Gail 1947- *WhoAmW 93*
Jorgensen, Gordon D. 1932- *WhoIns 93*
Jorgensen, Gordon David 1921- *WhoAm 92*
Jorgensen, Gordon Dean 1932- *St&PR 93*
Jorgensen, Gunnar 1933- *WhoScE 91-2*
Jorgensen, Ivar *ScF&FL 92*
Jorgensen, James Douglas 1948- *WhoAm 92*
Jorgensen, Janet L. 1957- *St&PR 93*
Jorgensen, Jens Anker 1940- *WhoUN 92*
Jorgensen, Johannes 1927- *WhoScE 91-2*
Jorgensen, Judith Ann *WhoAmW 93*
Jorgensen, Judith Strong 1959- *WhoE 93*
Jorgensen, Karsten Ejsing 1937- *WhoWor 93*
Jorgensen, Katherine *BioIn 17*
Jorgensen, Langdon Jon 1957- *WhoEmL 93*
Jorgensen, Les *BioIn 17*
Jorgensen, Mogens Hugo 1943- *WhoWor 93*
Jorgensen, Niels O. 1931- *WhoScE 91-2*
Jorgensen, Paul Alfred 1916- *WhoAm 92, WhoWor 93*
Jorgensen, Paul J. 1930- *St&PR 93, WhoAm 92*
Jorgensen, Per Magnus 1944- *WhoScE 91-4*
Jorgensen, Poul 1934- *Baker 92*
Jorgensen, Richard Edward 1948- *WhoWrEP 92*
Jorgensen, Robert K. 1921- *St&PR 93*
Jorgensen, Robert Westengaard 1907- *WhoWor 93*
Jorgensen, Ron 1957- *St&PR 93*
Jorgensen, Tina 1942- *WhoUN 92*
Jorgensen, Villy *WhoScE 91-2*
Jorgensen, William Ernest 1913- *WhoAm 92*
Jorgensen, William L. 1949- *WhoAm 92*
Jorgensen-Kornman, Karen Virginia 1953- *WhoEmL 93*
Jorgenson, Dale K. 1939- *St&PR 93*
Jorgenson, Dale Weldeau 1933- *WhoAm 92*
Jorgenson, Ivar *BioIn 17, MajAI*
Jorgenson, Joan Mary 1959- *WhoAmW 93*
Jorgenson, William Lloyd 1942- *WhoE 93*
Jorgeson, Brent Wilson 1950- *WhoEmL 93, WhoWor 93*
Jori, Armanda 1933- *WhoScE 91-3*
Jori, J. Istvan 1943- *WhoScE 91-4*
Joris, David 1501?-1556 *BioIn 17*
Joris, Francoise Mallet- 1930- *BioIn 17*
Jorisz, Jan 1501?-1556 *BioIn 17*
Jorjorian, Thomas 1957- *WhoSSW 93*
Jork, Hellmut 1934- *WhoScE 91-3*
Jorkasky, Richard Joseph 1929- *St&PR 93*
Jormark, Susan Carole 1949- *WhoAmW 93*
Jorn, Karl 1876-1947 *Baker 92*
Jorn, Linda Maree 1961- *WhoAmW 93*
Jorndt, L. Daniel 1941- *St&PR 93*
Jorne, Jacob 1941- *WhoAm 92*
Jorns, David Lee 1944- *WhoAm 92*
Jornvall, Hans 1942- *WhoScE 91-4*
Jornvall, Hans Evert 1942- *WhoWor 93*
Jorrand, Philippe 1941- *WhoScE 91-2*
Jorsater, Steven Bertil 1955- *WhoWor 93*
Jortner, Alan Jeffery 1951- *St&PR 93*
Jortner, Joshua 1933- *WhoWor 93*
Jorve, Barry M. *WhoIns 93*
Jory, David C. *Law&B 92*
Jory, Howard R. 1931- *WhoAm 92*
Jory, Jon *BioIn 17*
Josca, Natalia *BioIn 17*
Joscelyn, Kent Buckley 1936- *WhoAm 92*
Joscelyn, Robert G. 1923- *St&PR 93*
Jose, Amaro fl. 19th cent.- See Baptista, Pedro Joao fl. 19th cent.- & Jose, Amaro fl. 19th cent.- *Expl 93*
Jose, Calavera Ruiz 1931- *WhoWor 93*
Jose, Donald Edwin 1947- *WhoEmL 93*
Jose, F. Sionil 1924- *BioIn 17*
Jose, Francisco Sionil 1924- *BioIn 17*
Jose, Shirley Ann 1934- *WhoAmW 93*
Jose, Victor Caballero 1949- *WhoSSW 93*
Joseff, J.C. *BioIn 17*
Joseffy, Rafael 1852-1915 *Baker 92*
Josefowitz, Natasha 1926- *ConAu 40NR*
Josefsen, Arent Bak 1947- *WhoScE 91-2*
Josefsson, Bjorn O. 1942- *WhoScE 91-4*
Josefsson, Lars 1931- *WhoScE 91-2*
Josefsson, Lars O. 1953- *WhoScE 91-4*
Joselson, Tedd 1954- *Baker 92*
Joselyn, Jo Ann 1943- *WhoAm 92*
Josendale, James E. 1917- *St&PR 93*
Josenhans, Paul J. 1936- *St&PR 93*
Josenhans, Paul John *Law&B 92*
Josens, Guy R.M. 1945- *WhoScE 91-2*
Joseph *BioIn 17*
Joseph 1840-1904 *BioIn 17*
Joseph, Chief c. 1840-1904 *HarEnMi*
Joseph, Metropolitan Bishop 1942- *WhoAm 92*
Joseph, pere 1577-1638 *BioIn 17*
Joseph, I d1283 *OxDcByz*
Joseph, II c. 1360-1439 *OxDcByz*
Joseph, II, Holy Roman Emperor 1741-1790 *BioIn 17*
Joseph, A. David 1932- *St&PR 93*
Joseph, Alex *BioIn 17*
Joseph, Allan Jay 1938- *WhoAm 92*
Joseph, Allison *BioIn 17*
Joseph, Andrew Hamilton 1930- *WhoWor 93*
Joseph, Ann *Law&B 92*
Joseph, Anne *ScF&FL 92, SmATA 73*
Joseph, Anthony Barnett 1955- *WhoEmL 93*
Joseph, Babu 1950- *WhoEmL 93*
Joseph, Bernard Michel 1962- *WhoE 93*
Joseph, Burton *Law&B 92*
Joseph, Burton M. 1921- *St&PR 93, WhoAm 92*
Joseph, Celia M. *Law&B 92*
Joseph, Daniel Donald 1929- *WhoAm 92*
Joseph, Danielle Yvette 1968- *WhoAmW 93*
Joseph, David J., Jr. 1916- *WhoAm 92*
Joseph, Edith Hoffman 1928- *WhoAmW 93*
Joseph, Edward 1919-1991 *BioIn 17*
Joseph, Eleanor Ann 1944- *WhoAmW 93*
Joseph, Frank Samuel 1940- *WhoWrEP 92*
Joseph, Franz 1914- *ScF&FL 92*
Joseph, Fred, Jr. 1942- *WhoSSW 93, WhoWrEP 92*
Joseph, Frederick Harold 1937- *WhoAm 92*
Joseph, Georgann *Law&B 92*
Joseph, George 1921- *St&PR 93*
Joseph, Geri Mack 1923- *WhoAm 92*
Joseph, Gregory Paul 1951- *WhoAm 92, WhoE 93*
Joseph, Harriet 1919- *WhoAmW 93*
Joseph, Helen 1905-1992 *NewYTBS 92 [port]*
Joseph, Helen Haiman *AmWomPl*
Joseph, J. Jonathan 1932- *WhoE 93*
Joseph, Jack *WhoWrEP 92*
Joseph, Jacob 1848-1902 *JeAmHC*
Joseph, Jacques 1943- *WhoScE 91-2*
Joseph, James Alfred 1935- *WhoAm 92*
Joseph, Jennifer 1961- *WhoWrEP 92*
Joseph, Jerome 1918- *St&PR 93*
Joseph, Jerry 1945- *St&PR 93*
Joseph, John 1923- *WhoAm 92*
Joseph, John James 1953- *WhoEmL 93*
Joseph, John Lawrence 1945- *WhoAm 92*
Joseph, Jon A. *Law&B 92*
Joseph, Jon A. 1947- *St&PR 93*
Joseph, Joyce Marie 1947- *WhoAmW 93*
Joseph, Judith R. 1948- *WhoAm 92*
Joseph, Jules K. 1927- *WhoAm 92*
Joseph, Lawrence M. *Law&B 92*
Joseph, Leonard 1919- *WhoAm 92*
Joseph, Linda Hoffmann 1959- *WhoAmW 93*
Joseph, Lura Ellen 1947- *WhoEmL 93, WhoSSW 93*
Joseph, M.K. 1914-1981 *ScF&FL 92*
Joseph, Marc F. *Law&B 92*
Joseph, Marc W. *Law&B 92*
Joseph, Marcel Paul 1935- *WhoAm 92*
Joseph, Marilyn Susan 1946- *WhoEmL 93*
Joseph, Mark 1946- *ScF&FL 92*
Joseph, Mathai *WhoScE 91-1*
Joseph, Matthew Alan *Law&B 92*
Joseph, Michael *ScF&FL 92*
Joseph, Michael Anthony 1944- *St&PR 93, WhoAm 92*
Joseph, O.F. *WhoScE 91-1*
Joseph, P. A. 1944- *WhoWor 93*
Joseph, Paul Christopher, Jr. *WhoSSW 93*
Joseph, Phyllis Freedman 1938- *WhoAmW 93*
Joseph, Ramon Rafael 1930- *WhoAm 92*
Joseph, Richard Michael 1937- *St&PR 93*
Joseph, Richard S. 1937- *WhoE 93*
Joseph, Robert George 1948- *WhoEmL 93*
Joseph, Robert L. 1948- *St&PR 93*
Joseph, Rodney Randy 1945- *WhoE 93*
Joseph, Roger David 1941- *St&PR 93*
Joseph, Ronald 1910- *BioIn 17*
Joseph, Ronald K. 1962- *WhoWrEP 92*
Joseph, Rosaline Resnick 1929- *WhoAmW 93*
Joseph, Ruth Rhodes 1916- *WhoWrEP 92*
Joseph, Sammy William 1934- *WhoE 93*
Joseph, Sharon Jean 1950- *WhoE 93*
Joseph, Stanley *BioIn 17*
Joseph, Stephanie R. *Law&B 92*
Joseph, Stephanie R. 1946- *WhoAm 92*
Joseph, Stephen Laurence 1954- *WhoE 93*
Joseph, Susan B. 1958- *WhoAmW 93, WhoE 93*
Joseph, Thomas G. 1936- *St&PR 93*
Joseph, Thomas George 1936- *WhoWor 93*
Joseph ben Mattathias *BioIn 17*
Josephine, Empress 1763-1814 *BioIn 17*
Josephi Wellmann, Martin 1942- *WhoWor 93*
Joseph-Nathan, Pedro 1941- *WhoWor 93*
Joseph Rhakendytes c. 1260-c. 1330 *OxDcByz*
Josephs, Arthur *ConAu 137*
Josephs, Babette 1940- *WhoAmW 93*
Josephs, Eileen Sherle *WhoAmW 93*
Josephs, James David 1925- *WhoSSW 93*
Josephs, Jess J. 1917- *WhoE 93*
Josephs, John P. 1936- *St&PR 93*
Josephs, Larry *BioIn 17*
Josephs, Lois B. 1956- *St&PR 93*
Josephs, Melvin Jay 1926- *WhoAm 92, WhoE 93*
Josephs, Ray 1912- *WhoAm 92*
Josephs, Wilfred 1927- *Baker 92*
Josephson, Alan Samuel 1930- *WhoE 93*
Josephson, Brian David 1940- *WhoWor 93*
Josephson, Diana Hayward 1936- *WhoAm 92*
Josephson, Donna L. *Law&B 92*
Josephson, Edward H. 1938- *St&PR 93*
Josephson, Erland 1923- *IntDcF 2-3, WhoWor 93*
Josephson, Jacob Axel 1818-1880 *Baker 92*
Josephson, John E. 1947- *St&PR 93*
Josephson, Karen *WhoAmW 93*
Josephson, Kenneth Bradley 1932- *WhoAm 92*
Josephson, Lisa Broida *Law&B 92*
Josephson, Mark Eric 1943- *WhoAm 92*
Josephson, Marvin 1927- *St&PR 93, WhoAm 92*
Josephson, Michael *BioIn 17*
Josephson, Sarah *WhoAmW 93*
Josephson, Warren *Law&B 92*
Josephson, William Howard 1934- *WhoAm 92, WhoE 93*
Joseph the Hymnographer c. 812-c. 886 *OxDcByz*
Joseph the Philosopher *OxDcByz*
Josephus, Flavius *BioIn 17*
Josephus Flavius fl. c. 38-100 *OxDcByz*
Josey, Deborah K. 1949- *WhoEmL 93*
Josey, Elonnie Junius 1924- *WhoAm 92, WhoWor 93*
Josh *MajAI*
Joshi, Arun Dattatraya 1937- *WhoSSW 93*
Joshi, Jagmohan 1933- *WhoWor 93*
Joshi, Krishan K. 1936- *St&PR 93*
Joshi, Narahari 1941- *WhoWor 93*
Joshi, Niharika *DcChlFi*
Joshi, S.T. 1958- *ScF&FL 92*
Joshi, Sadanand Dattatray 1950- *WhoEmL 93, WhoSSW 93*
Joshi, Satish Devdas 1950- *WhoWor 93*
Joshi, Suresh Meghashyam *WhoAm 92, WhoSSW 93*
Joshi, Vijay S. 1939- *WhoSSW 93*
Joshua *BioIn 17*
Joshua, Ebenezer 1908- *DcCPCAm*
Joshua, Ivy *DcCPCAm*
Joshua the Stylite *OxDcByz*
Josiah, Walter James 1933- *St&PR 93*
Josiak, Jerzy Roman 1936- *WhoScE 91-4*
Josie, Peter 1941- *DcCPCAm*
Josien, Jean-Pierre 1942- *WhoScE 91-2*
Josif, Enriko 1924- *Baker 92*
Josifovic, Mirko 1922- *WhoScE 91-4*
Josipovici, Gabriel 1940- *BioIn 17*
Joskow, Jules *WhoAm 92*
Joskow, Paul Lewis 1947- *WhoAm 92, WhoWor 93*
Joskow, Renee W. 1960- *WhoAmW 93*
Joslin, Alfred H. 1914-1991 *BioIn 17*
Joslin, Charles A.F. *WhoScE 91-1*
Joslin, David Alan *WhoScE 91-1*
Joslin, John E. *Law&B 92*
Joslin, Lois Anne Fetters 1934- *WhoAmW 93*
Joslin, Rodney D. 1944- *St&PR 93*
Joslin, Roger 1936- *St&PR 93, WhoIns 93*
Joslin, Roger Scott 1936- *WhoAm 92*
Joslyn, Catherine Ruth 1950- *WhoE 93*
Joslyn, Jay Thomas 1923- *WhoAm 92*
Joslyn, Lee W. 1955- *St&PR 93*
Joslyn, Robert Bruce 1945- *WhoWor 93*
Joslyn, Veronica Joan 1920- *WhoWrEP 92*
Joson, Eduardo N. 1950- *WhoAsAP 91*
Josovitz, Michael S. 1961- *WhoE 93*
Jospe, Jack D. 1920- *St&PR 93*
Jospe, Joseph Lewis 1951- *St&PR 93*
Jospin, Lionel *BioIn 17*
Jospin, Lionel Robert 1937- *WhoWor 93*
Josquin des Prez *Baker 92*
Joss, Addie 1880-1911 *BioIn 17*
Joss, Andrzej 1939- *WhoScE 91-4*
Joss, Diana May 1938- *WhoSSW 93*
Joss, George Smith 1926- *WhoWor 93*
Joss, Paul Christopher 1945- *WhoAm 92*

Josselin de Jong, J.P.B. de 1886-1964 *IntDcAn*
Josselson, Diana 1921- *WhoWor 93*
Josselson, Jack Bernard 1905- *WhoAm 92*
Josselson, Ruthellen (Lefkowitz) 1946- *ConAu 139*
Josso, Nathalie 1934- *WhoScE 91-2*
Jost, Barbara Dinger 1947- *WhoEmL 93*
Jost, Erica Elisabeth *WhoAmW 93*
Jost, H. Peter 1921- *WhoWor 93*
Jost, Helen Christine 1944- *St&PR 93*
Jost, Jon 1943- *MiSFD 9*
Jost, Lawrence John 1944- *WhoAm 92*
Jost, Lou *BioIn 17*
Jost, Peter 1955- *WhoEmL 93*
Jost, Wesley William 1930- *WhoE 93, WhoWor 93*
Jostad, Debra Jean Anna 1952- *WhoEmL 93*
Josten, Werner (Erich) 1885-1963 *Baker 92*
Josuke, Tsunetsugu 1937- *WhoWor 93*
Jotcham, Thomas Denis 1918- *WhoE 93*
Joteyko, Tadeusz 1872-1932 *Baker 92*
Jou, Bing 1955- *WhoWor 93*
Jou, David 1953- *WhoWor 93*
Jouan, Bernard *WhoScE 91-2*
Jouandet, Virginia Chin *Law&B 92*
Jouannet, Pierre 1942- *WhoScE 91-2*
Jouany, Jean-Pierre 1944- *WhoScE 91-2*
Joubert, Gerhard Robert 1937- *WhoWor 93*
Joubert, John 1927- *OxDcOp*
Joubert, John (Pierre Herman) 1927- *Baker 92*
Joubert, Louis Marcel 1922- *WhoScE 91-2*
Joubert, Petrus Jacobus 1831-1900 *HarEnMi*
Joudrie, Herbert Earl 1934- *St&PR 93*
Joudry, Patricia 1921- *WhoCanL 92*
Jouffret, Michel L. 1941- *WhoScE 91-2*
Joughin, Louis d1991 *BioIn 17*
Jouguelet, Pierre *ScF&FL 92*
Jouhaux, Leon 1879-1954 *BioIn 17*
Jouin, Henri Auguste 1841-1913 *BioIn 17*
Joukowsky, Artemis A. W. 1930- *WhoAm 92, WhoE 93, WhoWor 93*
Joule, James Prescott 1818-1889 *BioIn 17*
Jour, J.M. *WhoScE 91-2*
Jourdain, Alice Marie 1923- *WhoAm 92*
Jourdain, Eleanor 1864-1924 *BioIn 17*
Jourdain, Francis 1876-1958 *BioIn 17*
Jourdain, Frantz 1847-1935 *BioIn 17*
Jourdain, Frantz-Philippe 1906- *BioIn 17*
Jourdain, Margaret d1951 *BioIn 17*
Jourdan, Claude 1934- *WhoScE 91-2*
Jourdan, Jean-Baptiste 1762-1833 *HarEnMi*
Jourdan, Louis 1919?- *IntDcF 2-3 [port]*
Jourdan, Louis 1921- *WhoAm 92*
Jourden, Lewis E. 1938- *St&PR 93*
Jourdheuil, Pierre 1926- *WhoScE 91-2*
Jourdian, George William 1929- *WhoAm 92*
Jourdren, Marc Henri 1960- *WhoWor 93*
Jouret, Bernard P.J.M. 1945- *WhoScE 91-2*
Jouret, Leon 1828-1905 *Baker 92*
Journeau, Christophe 1963- *WhoWor 93*
Journeay, Glen Eugene 1925- *WhoSSW 93*
Journel, Hubert 1954- *WhoWor 93*
Journell, Elizabeth Ann 1963- *WhoAmW 93*
Journet, Marcel 1867-1933 *Baker 92, IntDcOp, OxDcOp*
Journet, Michel 1931- *WhoScE 91-2*
Journey, Drexel Dahlke 1926- *WhoAm 92, WhoE 93, WhoWor 93*
Jourquin, Lucien 1928- *WhoScE 91-2*
Jousset, Jean-Claude 1938- *WhoScE 91-2*
Jouve, Daniel Gabriel 1938- *WhoWor 93*
Jouve, Nicolas 1944- *WhoScE 91-3*
Jouvenceaux, Andre 1923- *WhoScE 91-2*
Jouventin, Pierre 1942- *WhoScE 91-2*
Jouvet, Louis 1887-1951 *IntDcF 2-3 [port]*
Jouvet, Michel Valentin 1925- *WhoScE 91-2*
Jouy, Etienne de 1764-1846 *OxDcOp*
Jouzel, Jean Ce'festin 1947- *WhoWor 93*
Jova, Henri Vatable 1919- *WhoAm 92*
Jovancicevic, Vladimir 1947- *WhoE 93*
Jovane, Francesco *WhoScE 91-3*
Jovanovic, Jovan 1934- *WhoScE 91-4*
Jovanovic, Milan 1918- *WhoScE 91-4*
Jovanovic, Milan Miodrag 1952- *WhoSSW 93*
Jovanovic, Miodrag 1936- *WhoAm 92*
Jovanovic, Miroslav N. 1957- *WhoWor 93*
Jovanovic, Momir 1927- *WhoScE 91-4*
Jovanovic, Savo 1935- *WhoScE 91-4*
Jovanovic, Zarko *WhoScE 91-4*
Jovanovich, Peter *BioIn 17*
Jovanovich, Peter William 1949- *WhoAm 92*
Jovanovich, William 1920- *WhoAm 92, WhoWrEP 92*
Jovanovitch, Milena 1951- *WhoAmW 93*
Jovellanos, Jose Jesus Salas, Jr. 1954- *WhoWor 93*
Jovellanos, Jose Urtula 1917- *WhoWor 93*
Jover, Moyano Amador 1936- *WhoScE 91-3*
Jovian c. 331-364 *HarEnMi, OxDcByz*
Jovic, Djordje *WhoScE 91-4*
Jovin, Thomas M. 1939- *WhoScE 91-3*
Jovine, Giuseppe 1922- *DcLB 128 [port]*
Jowdy, Jeffrey William 1959- *WhoEmL 93, WhoSSW 93, WhoWor 93*
Jowers, Jerry Earl 1949- *WhoSSW 93*
Jowers, Lawrence Victor 1921- *WhoWrEP 92*
Jowers, Ronnie Lee 1951- *WhoSSW 93*
Jowett, John Martin 1954- *WhoWor 93*
Jowitt, Paul William *WhoScE 91-1*
Joxe, Louis 1901-1991 *AnObit 1991, BioIn 17*
Joxe, Pierre 1934- *BioIn 17*
Joxe, Pierre Daniel 1934- *WhoWor 93*
Joy, Carrol d1990 *BioIn 17*
Joy, Charles Richard 1952- *WhoEmL 93*
Joy, David Anthony 1957- *WhoSSW 93*
Joy, Edward Bennett 1941- *WhoAm 92, WhoSSW 93*
Joy, Genevieve 1919- *Baker 92*
Joy, Marilyn D. 1956- *WhoAmW 93*
Joy, Mary B. 1908-1990 *BioIn 17*
Joy, Patrick Francis 1943- *WhoE 93*
Joy, Paul W. 1924- *St&PR 93*
Joy, Perihan Dursun *WhoWrEP 92*
Joy, Robert 1951- *ConTFT 10*
Joy, Robert John Thomas 1929- *WhoAm 92, WhoE 93*
Joy, William *ScF&FL 92*
Joyaux, Alain Georges 1950- *WhoAm 92*
Joyaux, Georges Jules 1923-1990 *BioIn 17*
Joyce, Andrea *BioIn 17*
Joyce, Anne Raine 1942- *WhoAmW 93, WhoE 93*
Joyce, Arthur E. *Law&B 92*
Joyce, Bernita Anne *WhoAmW 93*
Joyce, Bill *SmATA 72*
Joyce, Bridget *Law&B 92*
Joyce, Bruce Arthur *WhoScE 91-1*
Joyce, Burton M. 1942- *St&PR 93*
Joyce, Burton Montgomery 1942- *WhoAm 92*
Joyce, Charles Vincent, III 1942- *WhoE 93*
Joyce, Christopher P. 1949- *St&PR 93*
Joyce, Claude Clinton 1931- *St&PR 93*
Joyce, Davis Darrell 1940- *WhoSSW 93*
Joyce, Diana Lee 1957- *WhoAmW 93*
Joyce, Donald Franklin 1938- *ConAu 139*
Joyce, Edward F. 1944- *St&PR 93*
Joyce, Edward J., Jr. *Law&B 92*
Joyce, Edward Rowen 1927- *WhoSSW 93*
Joyce, Eileen 1912-1991 *AnObit 1991*
Joyce, Ellenmarie *BioIn 17*
Joyce, Florence V. Mienert 1923- *WhoAmW 93*
Joyce, Glenn Russell 1939- *WhoE 93*
Joyce, Graham 1954- *ScF&FL 92*
Joyce, Helen Marie 1938- *St&PR 93*
Joyce, Jack R. 1942- *St&PR 93*
Joyce, James 1882-1941 *BioIn 17, MagSWL [port], WorLitC [port]*
Joyce, James Daniel 1921- *WhoAm 92*
Joyce, James E. 1926- *St&PR 93*
Joyce, James Edward, Sr. 1926- *WhoIns 93*
Joyce, James J., Jr. *Law&B 92*
Joyce, Jeannette *AmWomPl*
Joyce, Joan 1940- *BioIn 17*
Joyce, Jocelyn *ScF&FL 92*
Joyce, John J. 1943- *St&PR 93*
Joyce, John J., Jr. *Law&B 92*
Joyce, John Joseph 1930- *WhoE 93*
Joyce, John Robert 1951- *WhoScE 91-3*
Joyce, Joseph J. *Law&B 92*
Joyce, Joseph James 1943- *WhoAm 92*
Joyce, Joseph M. *Law&B 92*
Joyce, Joseph Michael 1951- *St&PR 93*
Joyce, Joseph Patrick 1951- *WhoEmL 93*
Joyce, Joyce Ann 1949- *ConAu 137*
Joyce, Kevern R. 1946- *St&PR 93*
Joyce, Manya *BioIn 17*
Joyce, Marian *Law&B 92*
Joyce, Michael A. *Law&B 92*
Joyce, Michael J. 1942- *WhoAm 92*
Joyce, Michael Ray 1950- *WhoEmL 93*
Joyce, Michael Stewart 1942- *WhoAm 92*
Joyce, Neal A. 1940- *St&PR 93*
Joyce, Patrick J. *Law&B 92*
Joyce, Paul Roberts 1947- *St&PR 93*
Joyce, Peter Leonard 1946- *WhoUN 92*
Joyce, Philip Halton 1928- *WhoAm 92*
Joyce, Robert F. 1896-1990 *BioIn 17*
Joyce, Robert J. 1948- *St&PR 93*
Joyce, Robert Joseph 1948- *WhoAm 92*
Joyce, Rosemary Alexandria 1956- *WhoE 93*
Joyce, Stephen F. 1941- *St&PR 93*
Joyce, Stephen Francis 1941- *WhoAm 92*
Joyce, Suzanne Mills 1946- *WhoSSW 93*
Joyce, Terence Thomas 1946- *WhoWor 93*
Joyce, Thomas C. 1937- *St&PR 93*
Joyce, Thomas J. *Law&B 92*
Joyce, Tom *ScF&FL 92*
Joyce, Walter d1991 *BioIn 17*
Joyce, William *ChlBIID [port]*
Joyce, William 1906-1946 *BioIn 17*
Joyce, William 1957- *SmATA 72*
Joyce, William B. 1932- *WhoE 93*
Joyce, William H. *St&PR 93*
Joyce, William James *Law&B 92*
Joyce, William Leonard 1942- *WhoAm 92*
Joyce, William Michael 1865-1941 *BiDAMSp 1989*
Joye, Afrie Songco 1942- *WhoAmW 93*
Joye, Donald David 1946- *WhoE 93*
Joye, E. Michael 1944- *WhoAm 92*
Joyner, Billy N. 1932- *St&PR 93*
Joyner, Billy Norris 1932- *WhoIns 93*
Joyner, Claude Reuben, Jr. 1925- *WhoAm 92, WhoWor 93*
Joyner, Delorez Florence Griffith 1959- *AfrAmBi*
Joyner, Earl Scarboro 1934- *St&PR 93*
Joyner, Edd Ray 1948- *WhoSSW 93*
Joyner, Ferris Kimball, Jr. *Law&B 92*
Joyner, Florence Griffith *BioIn 17*
Joyner, Floyd T., Jr. 1927- *St&PR 93*
Joyner, Gordon L. *AfrAmBi [port]*
Joyner, Henry Curtis 1954- *WhoAm 92*
Joyner, John Brooks 1944- *WhoAm 92*
Joyner, John Erwin 1935- *WhoAm 92*
Joyner, Leon Felix 1924- *WhoAm 92*
Joyner, Michael Tyson 1948- *WhoSSW 93*
Joyner, Nancy Carol 1936- *WhoSSW 93*
Joyner, Richard W. 1944- *WhoScE 91-1*
Joyner, Richard William 1944- *WhoWor 93*
Joyner, Roy Elton 1922- *WhoAm 92*
Joyner, Suzanne DiMascio 1942- *WhoE 93*
Joyner, Tom *BioIn 17*
Joyner, Walton Kitchin 1933- *WhoAm 92*
Joyner, Weyland Thomas 1929- *WhoAm 92*
Joyner, William Maughan, Jr. 1953- *WhoSSW 93*
Joyner-Kersee, Jackie *BioIn 17*
Joyner-Kersee, Jackie 1962- *BlkAmWO [port], News 93-1 [port]*
Joyner-Kersee, Jacqueline 1962- *AfrAmBi, WhoAm 92, WhoAmW 93*
Joynt, James E. 1945- *St&PR 93*
Joynt, Robert James 1925- *WhoAm 92*
Jozefek, J.M. *Law&B 92*
Jozefowicz, Wlodzimierz 1932- *WhoScE 91-4*
Jozoff, Malcolm 1939- *St&PR 93*
Jozwiak, Ronald D. 1947- *St&PR 93*
Jozwik, Francis Xavier 1940- *WhoWor 93, WhoWrEP 92*
Jreige, Heny Gebran 1958- *WhoWor 93*
Jsomaki, Heikki *WhoScE 91-4*
Ju, Chester 1949- *St&PR 93*
Ju, Chow-Soon Chuang 1924- *WhoWrEP 92*
Juan, Alfredo 1963- *WhoWor 93*
Juan, Don *BioIn 17*
Juana Ines de la Cruz 1651-1695 *BioIn 17*
Juan Carlos, I 1938- *News 93-1 [port], WhoWor 93*
Juanes, Juan de d1579 *BioIn 17*
Juang, Jer-Nan 1945- *WhoSSW 93*
Juanita d1851 *BioIn 17*
Juarez, Antonio 1952- *WhoEmL 93, WhoSSW 93*
Juarez, Benito 1806-1872 *BioIn 17*
Juarez, Jorge Ramon 1907?- *DcMexL*
Juarez Inglesias, Manuela *WhoScE 91-3*
Juarroz, Roberto 1925- *SpAmA*
Juba, Dorothy Virginia Margaret d1990 *BioIn 17*
Juba, Robert David 1948- *WhoWrEP 92*
Jubany Arnau, Narcisco Cardinal 1913- *WhoWor 93*
Jubb, Kendahl Jan *BioIn 17*
Jube, Edward H. 1929- *St&PR 93*
Jubelirer, Robert C. 1937- *WhoE 93*
Juberg, Richard Kent 1929- *WhoWor 93*
Juberthie, Christian 1931- *WhoScE 91-2*
Jubinville, Alain Maurice Joseph 1928- *WhoAm 92*
Jubinville, Luc A. 1935- *St&PR 93*
Jubitz, Monroe A. 1916- *St&PR 93*
Jubitz, Monroe Albin, Jr. 1944- *St&PR 93*
Juby, Michael Leroy 1957- *WhoEmL 93*
Juceam, Eleanor Pam 1936- *WhoE 93*
Juceam, Robert E. 1940- *WhoAm 92, WhoWor 93*
Juch, Emma 1863-1939 *OxDcOp*
Juch, Emma (Antonia Joanna) 1863-1939 *Baker 92*
Juchatz, Wayne W. *Law&B 92*
Juchelka, Miroslav 1922- *Baker 92*
Juchniewicz, Jaroslaw R. 1928- *WhoScE 91-4*
Juchniewicz, Romuald 1925- *WhoScE 91-4*
Juckem, Wilfred Philip 1915- *WhoAm 92*
Jucys, Algimantas Adolfas 1936- *WhoWor 93*
Jud, Rudolf 1923- *WhoWor 93*
Juda, Walter 1916- *St&PR 93*
Judah, Douglas Fraser 1942- *St&PR 93*
Judah, Janeen Sue 1959- *WhoAmW 93, WhoEmL 93*
Judah, Jay Stillson 1911- *WhoAm 92*
Judah, ha-Levi 12th cent.- *BioIn 17*
Judas, MacCabeus d161BC *BioIn 17*
Judas Iscariot *BioIn 17*
Judd, A.M. *ScF&FL 92*
Judd, Alan 1946- *ConAu 139*
Judd, Alice Gay *AmWomPl*
Judd, Ardon B., Jr. *Law&B 92*
Judd, Arnold Walter, Jr. 1942- *St&PR 93*
Judd, Brian Raymond 1931- *WhoAm 92*
Judd, Burke Haycock 1927- *WhoSSW 93*
Judd, Cyril *ConAu 37NR, ScF&FL 92, WhoCanL 92*
Judd, Donald 1928- *BioIn 17*
Judd, Frances K. *MajAI*
Judd, Frank Ashcroft 1935- *WhoWor 93*
Judd, Frederick Lee 1957- *St&PR 93, WhoAm 92*
Judd, Gary 1942- *WhoAm 92*
Judd, Granville E. *BioIn 17*
Judd, Jacob 1929- *WhoE 93*
Judd, James 1949- *Baker 92*
Judd, James Thurston 1938- *WhoAm 92*
Judd, John E. 1930- *St&PR 93*
Judd, John William 1930- *St&PR 93*
Judd, Kim K. *Law&B 92*
Judd, Leonard R. 1939- *WhoAm 92*
Judd, Leonard Robert 1939- *St&PR 93*
Judd, Naomi *WhoAm 92, WhoAmW 93*
Judd, Naomi 1948- *BioIn 17*
Judd, Neil Merton 1887-1976 *IntDcAn*
Judd, Norman R. 1948- *St&PR 93*
Judd, O'Dean P. 1937- *WhoAm 92*
Judd, Ralph Waverly 1930- *WhoWrEP 92*
Judd, Raymond Earl, Jr. 1934- *WhoSSW 93*
Judd, Richard Louis 1937- *WhoE 93*
Judd, Robert 1939- *ConAu 38NR*
Judd, Robert Carpenter 1921- *WhoAm 92*
Judd, Robert L. *Law&B 92*
Judd, Ron *BioIn 17*
Judd, Walter Henry 1898- *BioIn 17*
Judd, William Reid 1951- *WhoEmL 93, WhoSSW 93*
Judd, William Robert 1917- *WhoAm 92*
Judd, Wynonna 1964- *WhoAm 92, WhoAmW 93*
Judd, Wynonna 1966- *BioIn 17*
Jude, James Roderick 1928- *WhoAm 92*
Judell, Cynthia N. 1924- *WhoAmW 93*
Judell, Robert B. 1923- *St&PR 93*
Judelson, David N. 1928- *WhoAm 92*
Judelson, Stephen B. d1992 *BioIn 17, NewYTBS 92 [port]*
Judge, Carol Lynn 1956- *WhoAmW 93*
Judge, Cathleen Charlotte 1953- *WhoAmW 93*
Judge, Charles W. 1931- *St&PR 93*
Judge, Christopher John *WhoScE 91-1*
Judge, David Allen 1964- *WhoE 93*
Judge, David Howard 1928- *St&PR 93*
Judge, Dolores Barbara *WhoAmW 93*
Judge, Edward Henry 1945- *WhoE 93*
Judge, Frank T., III *Law&B 92*
Judge, Hugh Gordon 1939- *St&PR 93*
Judge, Jack 1878-1938 *Baker 92*
Judge, Jane *AmWomPl*
Judge, Joanne M. *BioIn 17*
Judge, John Emmet 1912- *WhoAm 92, WhoWor 93*
Judge, K. *WhoScE 91-1*
Judge, Laurie 1946- *WhoAmW 93*
Judge, Norman R. *St&PR 93*
Judge, R.P. *St&PR 93*
Judge, Rosemary Ann *WhoAm 92*
Judge, Stanley J. 1927- *St&PR 93*
Judge, Thomas J. 1927- *St&PR 93*
Judin, Vesa-Pekka S. 1951- *WhoScE 91-4*
Judis, Barry D. *St&PR 93*
Judis, Gary K. *St&PR 93*
Judith *OxDcOp*
Judith, D.B. *Law&B 92*
Judkiewicz, Luba 1921- *WhoScE 91-4*
Judkins, Bennett Mallory 1947- *WhoSSW 93*
Judkins, David Cummins 1938- *WhoSSW 93*
Judkins, Dean R. 1949- *St&PR 93*
Judkins, Donald Ward 1912- *WhoAm 92*
Judkins, Jack *Law&B 92*
Judo Husodo, Siswono 1943- *WhoAsAP 91*
Judson, Adoniram 1788-1850 *BioIn 17*
Judson, Arnold Sidney 1927- *WhoAm 92, WhoE 93*
Judson, Arthur, II 1930- *St&PR 93*
Judson, Arthur (Leon) 1881-1975 *Baker 92*
Judson, Charles James 1944- *WhoAm 92*
Judson, Clara Ingram 1879-1960 *ConAu 137, MajAI [port]*

Judson, Donald Rae 1948- St&PR 93
Judson, Franklyn N. 1942- WhoUN 92
Judson, Franklyn Sylvanus 1915- WhoAm 92
Judson, Horace Freeland 1931- WhoAm 92
Judson, Jeannette Alexander 1912- WhoAm 92
Judson, Margaret Atwood 1899-1991 BioIn 17
Judson, Philip Livingston 1941- WhoAm 92
Judson, Ray Warner 1926- St&PR 93
Judson, Robert William 1947- WhoSSW 93
Judson, Sheldon 1918- WhoAm 92
Judson, Whitcomb L. GayN
Judson, William Lees 1842-1928 BioIn 17
Judy, David William 1960- WhoE 93
Judy, John Morris 1940- WhoSSW 93
Judy, John Wayne, Jr. 1931- WhoAm 92
Judy, John William, Jr. 1938- WhoAm 92
Judy, S. Wade 1934- WhoAm 92
Judy, Shirley Jean 1948- WhoAmW 93
Judy, William Jerome 1931- St&PR 93
Judywhite WhoWrEP 92
Jue, Gary St&PR 93
Jue, Susan Lynne 1956- WhoAmW 93, WhoEmL 93
Juel, Niels 1629-1697 HarEnMi
Juel, Twila Eileen 1948- WhoAmW 93
Juelich, Richard James 1950- WhoEmL 93
Juell, Dagny 1867-1901 BioIn 17
Juelsgaard, Stephen Glen Law&B 92
Juenemann, Jean 1936- WhoAmW 93
Juenemann, Julie Ann 1956- WhoAmW 93
Juengel, Eugene Thomas 1932- St&PR 93
Juenger, Friedrich Klaus 1930- WhoAm 92, WhoWor 93
Juerchko, Jack 1938- St&PR 93
Juergens, Bonnie Kay 1947- WhoSSW 93
Juergens, George Ivar 1932- WhoAm 92
Juergens, Rainer 1941- St&PR 93
Juette-Braun, Giselle C. 1931- WhoAmW 93
Juettner, Paul J. Law&B 92
Juffa, Michael Richard 1952- WhoEmL 93
Jugan, Jeanne 1792-1879 BioIn 17
Jugdutt, Bodh Indrakumar 1943- WhoWor 93
Juge, Charles Francois 1939- WhoUN 92
Jugenheimer, Donald Wayne 1943- WhoAm 92, WhoE 93
Jugnauth, Anerood 1930- WhoAfr, WhoWor 93
Juhan, Alexander 1765-1845 Baker 92
Juhan, James Baker 92
Juhan-Vague, Irene 1945- WhoScE 91-2
Juhase, Kathleen Anne Law&B 92
Juhase, Kim Steven 1953- WhoE 93
Juhasz, A. Zoltan 1929- WhoScE 91-4
Juhasz, C. WhoScE 91-1
Juhasz, Joseph St&PR 93
Juhasz, Paul R. Law&B 92
Juhl, Daniel Leo 1935- St&PR 93, WhoAm 92
Juhl, Harold Alexander 1950- WhoSSW 93
Juhl, Loren Earl 1918- WhoAm 92
Juhl, Paulgeorg 1950- WhoWor 93
Juhlin, Doris Arlene 1942- WhoAmW 93
Juhlin, Lennart 1926- WhoScE 91-4
Juhn, David W. 1959- WhoEmL 93
Juhnke, H. Richard Law&B 92
Juhre, Harold William, Jr. 1932- WhoE 93
Juillet, Chantal 1960- WhoAm 92
Juillet, Pierre Armand 1921- BioIn 17
Juillet, Yves Marie 1946- WhoWor 93
Juilliard, Augustus D. 1836-1919 Baker 92
Jukes, Betty C. 1932- WhoSSW 93
Jukes, Mavis 1947- MajAI [port], SmATA 72 [port]
Jukes, Terence Douglas 1952- WhoE 93
Jukes, Thomas Hughes 1906- WhoAm 92
Jukofsky, S. Lawrence 1925- WhoSSW 93
Jukola-Sulonen, Eeva-Liisa 1943- WhoScE 91-4
Julander, Paula Foil 1939- WhoAmW 93
Julao, Liza Calbay 1951- WhoAmW 93
Jule, Thomas 1959- St&PR 93
Julen, Donald L. 1943- St&PR 93
Jules-Verne, Jean 1892- ScF&FL 92
Julesz, Bela 1928- WhoAm 92, WhoWor 93
Julesz, Janos 1943- WhoScE 91-4
Julia, Marc Yves 1922- WhoScE 91-2
Julia, Raul BioIn 17
Julia, Raul 1940- HispAmA [port]
Julia, Raul 1944- WhoAm 92
Julian 332-363 HarEnMi, OxDcByz
Julian, Alexander, II 1948- WhoAm 92
Julian, Alfred WhoWrEP 92
Julian, Courtney Chauncey BioIn 17
Julian, Desmond G. 1926- WhoScE 91-1
Julian, Ellen Ruth 1957- WhoEmL 93
Julian, George M. 1931- St&PR 93
Julian, Ida 1945- WhoE 93
Julian, Jerry B. 1933- WhoAm 92
Julian, John Thomas 1946- St&PR 93
Julian, K. WhoScE 91-1
Julian, Kimm David 1954- WhoAm 92
Julian, Marsha Roanne 1936- WhoAmW 93
Julian, Maurice BioIn 17
Julian, Michael 1951- WhoAm 92
Julian, Michele Denise 1954- WhoAmW 93
Julian, Percy L. BioIn 17
Julian, Rupert 1889-1943 MiSFD 9N
Juliana, James Nicholas 1922- WhoAm 92
Juliani, Giovanni 1927- WhoScE 91-3
Juliani, Hector Ramon 1931- WhoWor 93
Juliano, Albert Joseph 1929- St&PR 93
Juliano, Bienvenido Ochoa 1936- WhoWor 93
Juliano, Edward F., Jr. Law&B 92
Juliano, Michael St&PR 93
Julian of Askalon fl. 6th cent.- OxDcByz
Julian of Halikarnassos dc. 527 OxDcByz
Julian the Egyptian fl. 6th cent.- OxDcByz
Julianus Argentarius fl. 6th cent.- OxDcByz
Juliber, Lois BioIn 17
Julich, Marvin Milam 1941- WhoSSW 93
Julie, David B. Law&B 92
Julie, David Brian 1939- St&PR 93
Julie, Loebe 1920- St&PR 93
Julie, Ora McBride 1939- St&PR 93, WhoAmW 93
Julien, Gail Leslie 1940- WhoAmW 93
Julien, Isaac BioIn 17, MiSFD 9
Julien, Isaac 1960- ConBlB 3 [port]
Julien, JoElla L. 1942- WhoAmW 93
Julien, Michel WhoScE 91-2
Juliff, Peter Laurence 1938- WhoWor 93
Julifs, Sandra Jean 1939- WhoAmW 93
Julin, Joseph Richard 1926- WhoAm 92, WhoWor 93
Julius, E. Haldeman- ScF&FL 92
Julius, H.W. WhoScE 91-3
Julius, Leslie 1917-1990 BioIn 17
Julius, Nancy 1955- WhoAmW 93
Julius, Stevo 1929- WhoAm 92
Julius Caesar 100?BC-44BC OxDcOp
Julius Nepos d480 HarEnMi, OxDcByz
Juliusson, Marguerite 1956- WhoAmW 93
Juliusson, Steinthor 1938- WhoWor 93
Jull, David Francis 1944- WhoAsAP 91
Jullian, Serge WhoScE 91-2
Jullien, Adolphe 1845-1932 Baker 92
Jullien, Gilles c. 1650-1703 Baker 92
Jullien, Jean-Francois 1942- WhoScE 91-2
Jullien, Louis 1812-1860 Baker 92, OxDcOp
Julshamn, Kare 1943- WhoScE 91-4
July, Serge 1942- BioIn 17
Jumao-as, Alex Baronda 1961- WhoEmL 93
Jumayyil, Amin 1942- DcTwHis
Jumayyil, Pierre 1905-1984 DcTwHis
Jumblat, Kamal 1917-1977 DcTwHis
Jumblatt, Kamal d1977 BioIn 17
Jumblatt, Walid BioIn 17
Jumean, Fawwaz Hanna 1942- WhoWor 93
Jumilhac, Pierre-Benoit de 1611-1682 Baker 92
Jumonville, Felix Joseph, Jr. 1920- WhoAm 92
Jumonville, George R. 1942- St&PR 93
Jump, Bernard, Jr. 1938- WhoAm 92, WhoE 93
Jump, Chester Jackson, Jr. 1918- WhoAm 92
Jump, Gordon WhoAm 92
Jump, Linda Gail 1949- WhoEmL 93, WhoWor 93
Jumper, Cindy Ann 1954- WhoEmL 93
Jumper, John Phillip 1945- WhoAm 92
Junchang, Shen 1939- WhoWor 93
Junchen, David Lawrence 1946- WhoEmL 93, WhoWor 93
Junck, Benedetto 1852-1903 Baker 92
Junckerstorff-Venuto, Sarah Jewelene 1956- WhoAmW 93
Junco, Alfonso 1896-1975 DcMexL
Juncos, Jorge Luis 1952- WhoEmL 93
Jund, Daniel Edward 1946- St&PR 93
Jundzis, Talavs 1951- WhoWor 93
June, Franz E. 1934- St&PR 93
June, Joan Yvonne WhoE 93
Juneau, John Bradley 1959- St&PR 93
Juneau, Pierre 1922- WhoE 93
Juneau, Richard James 1933- St&PR 93
Juneja, Satish K. 1946- St&PR 93
Junek, John C. Law&B 92
Junell, Robert Frank 1914- St&PR 93
Junemann, R. WhoScE 91-3
Jung, Andre 1939- WhoWor 93
Jung, Artur 1930- WhoScE 91-3
Jung, C.G. 1875-1961 BioIn 17
Jung, Carl Gustav 1875-1961 BioIn 17
Jung, Carl Gustav 1885-1961 DcTwHis
Jung, Chang-Ju 1932- WhoWor 93
Jung, Charlotte Jeanne 1924- St&PR 93
Jung, Doranne 1948- WhoEmL 93
Jung, Doris 1924- WhoAm 92, WhoAmW 93
Jung, Edgar J. 1894-1934 BioIn 17
Jung, Franz 1888-1963 DcLB 118
Jung, George Henry 1938- St&PR 93
Jung, Greg Mark 1963- WhoEmL 93, WhoSSW 93
Jung, Hilda Ziifle WhoAmW 93
Jung, Horst 1937- WhoScE 91-3
Jung, Hugo Max 1928- WhoScE 91-3
Jung, Ivan 1941- WhoScE 91-4
Jung, James D. 1942- St&PR 93
Jung, Jan MiSFD 9
Jung, Jeffrey George 1952- WhoSSW 93
Jung, Jerrold Mark 1953- St&PR 93
Jung, Jin Hwa 1960- WhoWor 93
Jung, John Bernard 1926- St&PR 93
Jung, Kaitee M. Law&B 92
Jung, LaDonna 1960- WhoAmW 93
Jung, Laramie Jane 1951- WhoEmL 93
Jung, Manfred 1945- Baker 92
Jung, Michel J. 1943- WhoScE 91-2
Jung, Peter U. 1937- St&PR 93
Jung, Philipp C. d1992 NewYTBS 92
Jung, Rana Krishna 1933- WhoUN 92
Jung, Reinhard Paul 1946- WhoWor 93
Jung, Rodney C. 1920- WhoAm 92, WhoSSW 93
Jung, Samson Pang 1963- WhoEmL 93, WhoWor 93
Jung-Alsen, Kurt 1915-1976 DrEEuF
Jungalwala, Firoze Bamanshaw 1936- WhoE 93
Jungbauer, Mary Ann 1934- WhoAmW 93
Jungblut, Peter W. WhoScE 91-3
Jungbluth, Connie Carlson 1955- WhoAmW 93, WhoEmL 93
Jungbluth, Georg 1928- WhoScE 91-3
Jungbluth, John A. 1920- St&PR 93
Jungbluth, Kirk E. 1949- WhoWor 93
Junge, Billy Wayne 1945- WhoSSW 93
Junge, Charlotte Ella Maria 1927- WhoScE 91-3
Junge, Klaus 1926- WhoScE 91-3
Jungeberg, Thomas D. Law&B 92
Jungeberg, Thomas D. 1950- St&PR 93
Jungel, Eberhard BioIn 17
Junger, Miguel Chapero 1923- WhoAm 92
Junger, Zdenek WhoScE 91-4
Jungerman, John Albert 1921- WhoAm 92
Jungermann, Eric 1923- St&PR 93
Jungers, Charles S. 1943- St&PR 93
Jungers, Francis 1926- WhoAm 92
Junghaene, Joan L. 1924- St&PR 93
Junghans, Paula Marie 1949- WhoEmL 93
Jungholm, Sven Johan 1921- WhoWor 93
Jungk, Robert Baum 1913- WhoWor 93
Jungkind, Walter 1923- WhoAm 92
Jungkuntz, Richard Paul 1918- WhoAm 92
Jungling, Henry C., Jr. St&PR 93
Jungman, Ann ScF&FL 92
Jungman, Robert Peter 1937- WhoSSW 93, WhoWor 93
Jungmann, Frederick Arthur 1936- WhoE 93
Jungnickel, Christa BioIn 17
Jungnickel, Dieter 1952- WhoWor 93
Jung-Stilling, Johann Heinrich 1740-1817 BioIn 17
Jungwirth, Manfred 1919- Baker 92
Junia, Edward Xavier 1948- WhoEmL 93
Junid Bin Megat Ayob, Dato' Megat 1942- WhoAsAP 91
Junius, Daniel M. 1952- St&PR 93
Junius, Ralph W. 1923- St&PR 93
Junius Pera, Marcus fl. c. 230BC-216BC HarEnMi
Junk, Wolfgang Johannes 1942- WhoScE 91-3
Junker, Christine Rosetta 1953- WhoAmW 93, WhoEmL 93
Junker, Detlef 1939- WhoWor 93
Junker, Edward Philip, III 1937- St&PR 93
Junker, George E. St&PR 93
Junker, Kirk William 1959- WhoEmL 93
Junker, Martha E. Law&B 92
Junker, Sandra Jean 1947- WhoAmW 93
Junkin, Joseph Swan 1939- St&PR 93
Junkins, Carole Anne 1950- WhoSSW 93
Junkins, Jerry R. 1937- St&PR 93
Junkins, Jerry Ray 1937- WhoAm 92, WhoSSW 93
Junkunc, Charles A. 1942- St&PR 93
Juno, Gary Peter Law&B 92
Junod, Alain 1939- WhoScE 91-4
Junod, Henri-Alexandre 1863-1934 IntDcAn
Junor, John 1919- BioIn 17
Junot, Jean Andoche 1771-1813 HarEnMi
Junsela, Jyrhi WhoScE 91-4
Juntereal, F.A., Jr. 1934- WhoIns 93
Junttila, Olavi 1942- WhoScE 91-4
Junya, Yano 1932- WhoWor 93
Junz, Helen B. WhoAm 92, WhoUN 92
Juokslahti, Tapio 1948- WhoScE 91-4
Juon, Lester Allen 1938- St&PR 93, WhoAm 92
Juon, Paul (Pavel Fedorovich) 1872-1940 Baker 92
Juon, Sharon Lee 1947- WhoAmW 93
Juovenen, Risto Juhani 1927- WhoScE 91-4
Juozapaitis, Jurgis 1942- Baker 92
Jupin, Charles-Francois 1805-1839 Baker 92
Jupiter, Mary Greta 1947- WhoEmL 93
Jupp, Michael John d1989 BioIn 17
Juppe, Alain 1945- BioIn 17
Juppin de Fondaumiere, Bertrand 1945- WhoUN 92
Juptner, Werner Paul Otto 1941- WhoWor 93
Juquin, Pierre 1930- BioIn 17
Jur, Jan 1922- WhoScE 91-4
Jura, Czeslaw 1927- WhoScE 91-4
Jura, James J. 1942- WhoAm 92
Juracek, Pavel 1935-1989 DrEEuF
Jurado, Alicia 1922- SpAmA
Jurado, Katy 1927- HispAmA, SweetSg D
Jurado, Ramon H. 1922-1978 SpAmA
Juran, Joseph M. 1904- BioIn 17
Juran, Joseph Moses 1904- WhoAm 92
Juran, Nathan 1907- MiSFD 9
Juras, JuliAnn Berg WhoAm 92
Jurasek, Kris Charles 1947- St&PR 93
Juraska, Janice Marie 1949- WhoEmL 93
Jurczak, Patricia Jean 1962- WhoEmL 93
Jurczyk, Irene Donohue 1949- WhoWrEP 92
Jurczyk, Joanne Monica 1958- WhoAmW 93
Jurczyk, Witold Jerzy 1931- WhoScE 91-4
Jurdana, Ernest J. 1944- WhoAm 92
Jurecic, Robert Louis 1950- WhoE 93
Juredine, David G. 1937- St&PR 93
Juren, Dennis Franklin 1935- WhoAm 92
Jurewicz, Lisa Marie 1955- WhoAmW 93
Jurgemeyer, Donald William 1920- WhoAm 92
Jurgens, Conrad R. 1947- WhoIns 93
Jurgens, Conrad Robert 1947- St&PR 93
Jurgens, E.L. 1905- St&PR 93
Jurgens, Fritz 1888-1915 Baker 92
Jurgens, Hans W. 1932- WhoScE 91-3
Jurgens, James B. Law&B 92
Jurgens, John F.B., III 1945- St&PR 93
Jurgens, Jurgen 1925- Baker 92
Jurgens, Rainer 1941- St&PR 93
Jurgensen, Barbara 1928- WhoAmW 93
Jurgensen, Carl 1925- WhoScE 91-3
Jurgensen, Delbert Frederick 1909- St&PR 93
Jurgensen, John H., III 1939- WhoAm 92
Jurgensen, Sonny 1934- BioIn 17
Jurgensen, Thomas Einar Law&B 92
Jurgensen, Warren Peter 1921- WhoAm 92
Jurgensen, William Gerald 1951- St&PR 93
Jurgenson, Pyotr (Ivanovich) 1836-1904 Baker 92
Juriansz, Frank 1919- St&PR 93
Jurica, A.R. 1942- St&PR 93
Jurich, Julie Ann 1946- WhoEmL 93
Jurick, Marilyn Lou 1929- WhoAmW 93, WhoE 93
Jurick, Robert Rudolph 1942- WhoSSW 93
Jurij Dolgorukij c. 1090-1157 OxDcByz
Jurik, Paul 1937- WhoSSW 93
Jurimae, Endel 1931- WhoWor 93
Jurin, Eric William 1952- WhoE 93, WhoEmL 93
Jurin, Mislav 1939- WhoScE 91-4
Jurinac, Sena 1921- Baker 92, IntDcOp, OxDcOp
Jurist, James Alfred WhoAm 92
Jurjans, Andrejs 1856-1922 Baker 92
Jurji, Edward J. 1907-1990 BioIn 17
Jurkans, Janis 1946- WhoWor 93
Jurkat, Martin Peter 1935- WhoAm 92
Jurkevich, Gayana 1953- ConAu 139, WhoE 93
Jurkiewicz, Maurice John 1923- WhoAm 92
Jurkmen, Serif 1941- WhoScE 91-4
Jurkoic, Paul N. Law&B 92
Jurkowski, Boleslaw 1940- WhoWor 93
Jurmain, Suzanne 1945- SmATA 72 [port]
Jurman, Claudia Lynne 1956- WhoEmL 93
Jurman Howard, Patricia Dianne Law&B 92
Jurney, Dorothy Misener 1909- WhoAm 92
Jurock, Oswald Erich 1944- WhoAm 92
Jurovsky, Simon 1912-1963 Baker 92
Jurras, Mark Ivan 1924- St&PR 93

Jurriens, Marinus 1943- *WhoScE 91-3*
Jurrist, Charles 1944-1991 *BioIn 17*
Jurtshuk, Peter, Jr. 1929- *WhoAm 92*
Jury, Eliahu Ibraham 1923- *WhoAm 92*
Jury, John Robert 1930- *St&PR 93*
Jurzykowski, Alfred 1899-1966 *PolBiDi*
Juska, Andrew Joseph 1955- *WhoSSW 93*
Juskewycz, Stephan R. *St&PR 93*
Jusko, William Joseph 1942- *WhoE 93*
Jussim, Estelle 1927- *WhoE 93*
Jussim, Jared *Law&B 92*
Jussup, W. John *Law&B 92*
Just, Arnold 1932- *WhoScE 91-2*
Just, Ernest Everett 1883-1941 *ConBlB 3 [port]*
Just, Gemma Rivoli 1921- *WhoAmW 93, WhoWor 93*
Just, Jennifer Ramsay 1958- *WhoEmL 93*
Just, Lesley Lynn 1957- *WhoEmL 93*
Just, Marion Rebecca 1943- *WhoE 93*
Just, Philip Ray 1955- *WhoEmL 93, WhoSSW 93*
Just, Richard E. *BioIn 17*
Just, Richard Eugene 1948- *WhoAm 92, WhoEmL 93*
Just, Thomas 1932- *WhoScE 91-3*
Just, Ward S. *BioIn 17*
Just, Ward Swift 1935- *WhoAm 92, WhoWrEP 92*
Juste, Christian 1931- *WhoScE 91-2*
Juster, Kenneth Ian 1954- *WhoEmL 93*
Juster, Norton 1929- *DcAmChF 1960, MajAI [port]*
Juster, Ronald Samuel 1943- *St&PR 93*
Justesen, Don Robert 1930- *WhoAm 92*
Justesen, Wayne Q., Jr. *Law&B 92*
Justesen, Wayne Quay, Jr. 1946- *St&PR 93*
Justice, Blair 1927- *WhoAm 92*
Justice, Brady R., Jr. 1930- *St&PR 93*
Justice, Brady Richmond, Jr. 1930- *WhoAm 92*
Justice, Charles Richard 1930- *St&PR 93*
Justice, David Christopher 1966- *WhoAm 92*
Justice, Denise Hurn 1956- *WhoAmW 93*
Justice, Donald Rodney 1925- *WhoAm 92, WhoWrEP 92*
Justice, Franklin P. 1938- *St&PR 93*
Justice, Franklin Pierce, Jr. 1938- *WhoAm 92*
Justice, Gary A. 1946- *St&PR 93*
Justice, Jack Burton 1931- *WhoAm 92*
Justice, Jack G. 1932- *St&PR 93*
Justice, Jack Ronald 1940- *WhoWrEP 92*
Justice, James Robertson *QDrFCA 92*
Justice, Kathleen Murphy *WhoAmW 93*
Justice, Keith L. 1949- *ScF&FL 92*
Justice, Lincoln *BioIn 17*
Justice, Ora Lynn 1942- *WhoWor 93*
Justice, Paula Susanne 1953- *WhoWrEP 92*
Justice, Phyllis C. 1915- *WhoAmW 93*
Justice, Rose Marie *BioIn 17*
Justice, William Wayne *BioIn 17*
Justice, William Wayne 1920- *WhoAm 92, WhoSSW 93*
Justin, I c. 450-527 *HarEnMi, OxDcByz*
Justin, II d578 *OxDcByz*
Justin, John, Jr. 1917- *News 92*
Justin, John S., Jr. 1917- *St&PR 93, WhoAm 92*
Justinger, Amy Lynn 1967- *WhoAmW 93*
Justinger, Maryann Elizabeth 1951- *WhoAmW 93, WhoEmL 93*
Justinian c. 525-582 *OxDcByz*
Justinian, I c. 482-565 *OxDcByz*
Justinian, II c. 668-711 *OxDcByz*
Justiniano, Alberto *WhoScE 91-3*
Justinian Rhinometus, II 669-711 *HarEnMi*
Justinian the Great, I 483-565 *HarEnMi*
Justinianus c. 525-582 *HarEnMi*
Justis, L. Ellis, Jr. *Law&B 92*
Justman, Paul *MiSFD 9*
Justo, Agustin Pedro 1876-1943 *DcTwHis*
Justo, Juan Bautista 1865-1928 *BioIn 17*
Justus, Buddy Earl d1990 *BioIn 17*
Justus, Carl Gerald 1939- *WhoSSW 93*
Justus, George Richard 1939- *St&PR 93*
Justus, Leslie *Law&B 92*
Justus, Wayne 1952- *BioIn 17*
Justynski, Janusz 1941- *WhoWor 93*
Jusu-Sheriff, Salia 1929- *WhoAfr*
Jusyp, Serge M. *Law&B 92*
Juszkiewicz, Henry Edward 1953- *St&PR 93, WhoSSW 93*
Juszkiewicz, Teodor 1922- *WhoScE 91-4, WhoWor 93*
Jutard, A. *WhoScE 91-2*
Jute, Andre *ScF&FL 92*
Juterbock, Richard E. *Law&B 92*
Juthani, Nalini Virendra 1946- *WhoEmL 93*
Jutila, Edwin J. *Law&B 92*
Jutila, Simo Antero 1957- *WhoE 93*
Jutkevic, Sergej 1904-1985 *DrEEuF*
Jutkins, J. Ronn *St&PR 93*
Jutra, Claude 1930-1987 *MiSFD 9N*
Jutras, Michel L. *Law&B 92*
Jutras, Thomas Henry, Jr. 1968- *WhoE 93*
Jutterstrom, Christina 1940- *WhoWor 93*
Jutz, Jakob Johann 1942- *WhoWor 93*
Jutze, George A. 1927- *St&PR 93*
Jutzler, Gustav Adolf 1925- *WhoScE 91-3*
Juvan, Frank T. 1946- *St&PR 93*
Juve, Arthur James 1951- *WhoSSW 93*
Juve, Richard Henry 1920- *St&PR 93*
Juvelis, Priscilla Catherine 1945- *WhoAmW 93*
Juvenal *OxDcByz*
Juventin, Jean 1928- *WhoAsAP 91*
Juvet, Richard Spalding, Jr. 1930- *WhoAm 92*
Juvik, Lars Hansen *BioIn 17*
Juviler, Peter Henry 1926- *WhoAm 92, WhoWor 93*
Jux, Ulrich 1929- *WhoScE 91-3*
Ju Ying *BioIn 17*
Juzbasic, Miriam 1926- *WhoScE 91-4*
Juzeliunas, Julius 1916- *Baker 92*
Juzumas, Richard E. *Law&B 92*
Juzwik, Frank L. 1922- *St&PR 93*
Jyrkiainen, Reijo (Einari) 1934- *Baker 92*
Jyrkila, Faina 1917- *WhoWor 93*
Jywook, Sam M. 1947- *St&PR 93*

K

Ka, Djibo Laity *WhoWor 93*
Kaaber, Henning 1932- *WhoScE 91-2*
Kaack, Karl 1938- *WhoScE 91-2*
Kaaf, Kathy 1945- *WhoWor 93*
Kaake, Norman Bradford 1954- *WhoEmL 93*
Kaan, Jindrich z Albestu 1852-1926 *Baker 92*
Kaan, Miklos 1937- *WhoScE 91-4*
Kaan-Albest, Heinrich 1852-1926 *Baker 92*
Kaapcke, Wallace Letcher 1916- *WhoWor 93*
Kaas, Donald G. *Law&B 92*
Kaas, Jon H. *WhoAm 92*
Kaase, Kristopher Jerome 1966- *WhoSSW 93*
Kaatz, Rebecca Sue 1954- *WhoAmW 93*
Kaatz, Ronald B. 1934- *WhoAm 92*
Kaba-Camara, Dienebou 1946- *WhoUN 92*
Kabachnik, Martin Israilevich 1908- *WhoWor 93*
Kabacik, Pawel 1963- *WhoWor 93*
Kabacinski, Mary M. *St&PR 93*
Kaback, Elaine 1939- *WhoAmW 93*
Kaback, Stuart Mark 1934- *WhoE 93*
Kabaila, Vytenis Kazimieras 1929- *WhoWor 93*
Kabaivanska, Raina 1934- *OxDcOp*
Kabaivanska, Raina (Yakimova) 1934- *Baker 92*
Kabak, Douglas Thomas 1957- *WhoE 93, WhoEmL 93, WhoWor 93*
Kabak, Edward M. *Law&B 92*
Kabak, Irwin William 1936- *WhoE 93*
Kabaker, Richard A. *Law&B 92*
Kabakibo, Abdul Wahab Chaban 1932- *WhoUN 92*
Kabakov, Alexander *ScF&FL 92*
Kabakov, Ilya 1933- *BioIn 17, NewYTBS 92 [port]*
Kabal, A.M. *WhoCanL 92*
Kabala, Edward John 1942- *WhoE 93, WhoWor 93*
Kabalevsky, Dimitry Borisovich 1904- *IntDcOp*
Kabalevsky, Dmitri (Borisovich) 1904-1987 *Baker 92*
Kabalevsky, Dmitry 1904-1987 *OxDcOp*
Kabalka, George Walter 1943- *WhoSSW 93*
Kaballarios *OxDcByz*
Kaballaropoulos *OxDcByz*
Kabamba, Nkamany 1939- *WhoUN 92*
Kabanov, Leonid Pavlovich 1937- *WhoUN 92*
Kabasilas *OxDcByz*
Kabasilas, Neilos c. 1300-1363 *OxDcByz*
Kabasilas, Nicholas Chamaetos c. 1322-c. 1391 *OxDcByz*
Kabasta, Oswald 1896-1946 *Baker 92*
Kabat, Elvin Abraham 1914- *WhoAm 92, WhoE 93*
Kabateck, Gladys Irene 1930- *WhoAmW 93*
Kabay, John K. 1942- *St&PR 93*
Kabaya, Tsuruhiko *BioIn 17*
Kabayama, Sukenori 1837-1922 *HarEnMi*
Kabbah, Ahmad Tejan 1932- *WhoUN 92*
Kabbah, Patricia Lucy 1933- *WhoUN 92*
Kabbaj, Salah Eddine 1959- *WhoWor 93*
Kabbert, William J., II *Law&B 92*
Kabel, Robert James 1946- *WhoAm 92*
Kabel, Robert Lynn 1932- *WhoAm 92*
Kabela, Frank, Jr. 1938- *WhoE 93*
Kabelac, Miloslav 1908-1979 *Baker 92*
Kabele, William Charles 1947- *St&PR 93*
Kabelitz, Dieter 1951- *WhoWor 93*
Kabelka, J. *WhoScE 91-4*
Kabemba, Mukoka K. *Law&B 92*
Kabengele, Ntanda 1942- *WhoWor 93*
Kaber, Steven Carl 1951- *WhoEmL 93*
Kaberry, Phyllis Mary 1910-1977 *IntDcAn*
Kabia, Estina A. 1940- *WhoUN 92*
Kabiq, Marie 1955- *WhoAmW 93*
Kable, Edward E. *Law&B 92*
Kable, Lawrence Philip 1926- *WhoIns 93*
Kable, Mark 1948- *St&PR 93*
Kabore, Gaston 1951- *MiSFD 9*
Kabos, Ilona 1893-1973 *Baker 92*
Kabotie, Fred 1900-1986 *BioIn 17*
Kabriel, Marcia Gail 1938- *WhoAmW 93*
Kabua, Amata *WhoWor 93*
Kabureck, George Richard 1939- *St&PR 93, WhoAm 92*
Kabwasa, Nsang-O'Khan Antoine 1939- *WhoUN 92*
Kac, Victor G. 1943- *WhoAm 92*
Kacalak, Wojciech 1945- *WhoScE 91-4*
Kacek, Don J. 1936- *St&PR 93, WhoAm 92*
Kacer, Peter 1957- *St&PR 93*
Kachadoorian, Zubel 1924- *WhoAm 92*
Kachadurian, K. *St&PR 93*
Kachajian, George Simon 1927- *St&PR 93*
Kachaunov, Stephan *WhoScE 91-4*
Kachel, Harold Stanley 1928- *WhoSSW 93*
Kachele, Andrew Reynolds 1947- *WhoE 93*
Kachele, Horst *WhoScE 91-3*
Kachka, Larry 1950- *St&PR 93*
Kachlein, George F., III 1934- *St&PR 93*
Kachlein, Mark R. 1961- *St&PR 93*
Kachlev, Yuri B. 1934- *WhoWor 93*
Kachlik, Antonin 1923- *DrEEuF*
Kachline, James Edward *Law&B 92*
Kachmar, Jessie K. 1913- *WhoWrEP 92*
Kachmar, Lori A. *Law&B 92*
Kachmarik, George Steven, VI 1953- *WhoSSW 93*
Kachru, Braj Behari 1932- *WhoAm 92*
Kachru, Yamuna 1933- *WhoAm 92*
Kachuck, Beatrice 1926- *WhoE 93*
Kachur, Betty Rae 1930- *WhoAmW 93*
Kachurak, Susan Ellen 1962- *WhoAmW 93*
Kachyna, Karel 1924- *DrEEuF*
Kacic, Ivo 1929- *WhoScE 91-4*
Kacillas, JoAnne *Law&B 92*
Kacin, Joanne V. *Law&B 92*
Kacin, William L. 1932- *St&PR 93*
Kacinskas, Jerome 1907- *Baker 92*
Kacir, Barbara Brattin 1941- *WhoAm 92, WhoAmW 93*
Kacira, Niyazi 1943- *St&PR 93*
Kacki, Edward 1925- *WhoScE 91-4*
Kackley, James R. *WhoAm 92*
Kaclik, Debi Louise 1953- *WhoAmW 93*
Kacmarcik, Thomas 1925- *WhoWor 93*
Kacmarik, Elaine Dorothy 1938- *WhoAmW 93*
Kacoha, Margie 1955- *WhoWrEP 92*
Kacos, Dean G. 1957- *St&PR 93*
Kacprowski, Janusz 1916- *WhoScE 91-4*
Kacprzyk, Janusz A. 1947- *WhoWor 93*
Kacser, Claude 1934- *WhoE 93*
Kacvinsky, Raymond C. 1949- *St&PR 93*
Kacyzne, Alter 1885-1941 *PolBiDi*
Kaczanowski, Carl Henry 1948- *WhoEmL 93*
Kaczender, George 1933- *MiSFD 9*
Kaczer, Jan 1919- *WhoScE 91-4*
Kaczkowski, Jerzy Piotr 1925- *WhoWor 93*
Kaczkowski, Karol 1797-1867 *PolBiDi*
Kaczkowski, Zbigniew 1921- *WhoWor 93*
Kaczmarczyk, Darlene Ann 1950- *WhoAmW 93*
Kaczmarek, Jan 1920- *WhoScE 91-4*
Kaczmarek, Jan M.Z. *Law&B 92*
Kaczmarek, Jane *WhoAm 92*
Kaczmarek, Kenneth Kasimer 1939- *St&PR 93*
Kaczmarek, Kenneth W. 1946- *St&PR 93*
Kaczmarek, Zdzislaw 1928- *WhoWor 93*
Kaczmarski, Michael J. 1953- *St&PR 93*
Kaczmarski, Michael John 1953- *WhoAm 92, WhoE 93*
Kaczor, Linda Marie 1961- *WhoAmW 93*
Kaczorek, Tadeusz 1932- *WhoWor 93*
Kaczorowski, Gregory John 1949- *WhoAm 92*
Kaczur, Jerry John 1951- *WhoSSW 93*
Kad, Surinder Kumar 1950- *WhoEmL 93*
Kadaba, Murali Parthsarathy 1949- *WhoE 93*
Kadaba, Prasanna Venkatarama 1931- *WhoSSW 93*
Kadak, Andrew C. 1945- *St&PR 93*
Kadakia, Shailesh Chandrakant 1952- *WhoEmL 93, WhoSSW 93*
Kadan, Ranjit Singh 1935- *WhoSSW 93*
Kadane, David K. 1914-1991 *BioIn 17*
Kadane, Joseph B. 1941- *WhoAm 92*
Kadanoff, Leo Philip 1937- *WhoAm 92*
Kadar, Anna 1935- *WhoScE 91-4*
Kadar, Bela 1919- *WhoScE 91-4*
Kadar, Gyula 1930- *WhoScE 91-4*
Kadar, Jan 1918-1979 *DrEEuF, MiSFD 9N*
Kadar, Janos 1912-1989 *ColdWar 2 [port], DcTwHis*
Kadare, Ismail *BioIn 17*
Kadare, Ismail 1936- *CurBio 92 [port]*
Kadavy, Paul Dean 1943- *St&PR 93*
Kaddafi, Muammar 1942- *BioIn 17*
Kaddah, Naim Mohamed 1930- *WhoUN 92*
Kaddaras, James Chris, Jr. *Law&B 92*
Kaddu, John Baptist 1945- *WhoWor 93*
Kade, Otto 1819-1900 *Baker 92*
Kadel, William H. d1990 *BioIn 17*
Kaden, Allen R. 1943- *St&PR 93*
Kaden, Ellen Oran *Law&B 92, WhoAmW 93*
Kaden, R.E. Heiner 1938- *WhoWor 93*
Kadenbach, Bernhard 1933- *WhoScE 91-3*
Kader, Jac B. 1931- *WhoSSW 93*
Kaderbhoy, Asgar A. *Law&B 92*
Kaderli, Dennis Wayne 1946- *St&PR 93*
Kades, Charles Louis 1906- *WhoAm 92*
Kadets, Michael 1923- *WhoWor 93*
Kadets, Vladimir Michailovitch 1960- *WhoWor 93*
Kadey, Frederic Lionel, Jr. 1918- *WhoSSW 93*
Kadharsha 1935- *WhoAsAP 91*
Kadin, Fred Martin 1942- *WhoAm 92*
Kadin, Howard Gene *Law&B 92*
Kadin, Marshall Edward 1939- *WhoAm 92*
Kadir bin Haji Sheikh Fadzir, Dato' Bin Haji Sheikh Abdul 1939- *WhoAsAP 91*
Kadish, Avni Samuel 1954- *WhoEmL 93*
Kadish, David A. *Law&B 92*
Kadish, Joshua David 1951- *WhoEmL 93*
Kadish, Jules Edgar 1922- *WhoWor 93*
Kadish, Lori Gail 1962- *WhoAmW 93, WhoE 93*
Kadish, Michael L. *Law&B 92*
Kadish, Reuben 1913-1992 *NewYTBS 92*
Kadish, Richard L. 1943- *St&PR 93, WhoAm 92*
Kadish, Sanford Harold 1921- *WhoAm 92*
Kadison, Richard Vincent 1925- *WhoAm 92*
Kadison, Stuart L. 1923- *WhoAm 92*
Kadle, JoAnne Coyle 1953- *WhoAmW 93*
Kadlec, Rudolph Joseph 1932- *St&PR 93, WhoAm 92*
Kadleck, Joseph J. 1936- *St&PR 93*
Kadlub, Leonard Allen 1951- *WhoEmL 93*
Kadlubek, Wincenty 1160-1223 *PolBiDi*
Kadlubowski, Marian F. *Law&B 92*
Kadlubowski, Roscislaw 1921- *WhoScE 91-4*
Kadner, Robert Joseph 1942- *WhoAm 92*
Kado, Clarence Isao 1936- *WhoAm 92*
Kadobyanskii, Roman 1949- *WhoWor 93*
Kadoh Agundong Ferdinand, Datuk *WhoAsAP 91*
Kadokawa, Haruki *BioIn 17, MiSFD 9*
Kadonada, George 1942- *St&PR 93*
Kadosa, Pal 1903-1983 *Baker 92*
Kadota, Takashi Theodore 1930- *WhoAm 92*
Kadowaki, Joe G. 1919- *St&PR 93*
Kadowaki, Takuji 1925- *WhoWor 93*
Kadoya, Tetsuo 1949- *St&PR 93*
Kadoyi, Aloys 1945- *WhoAfr*
Kadrey, Richard 1957- *ScF&FL 92*
Kadry, Ahmed d1990 *BioIn 17*
Kady, Michael S. 1949- *St&PR 93*
Kady, Michael Stanley 1949- *WhoE 93*
Kaechele, David Paul 1940- *St&PR 93*
Kaechele, Diane J. 1952- *WhoAmW 93, WhoEmL 93*
Kaefer, Christian E. 1945- *St&PR 93*
Kaefer, Gene J. 1928- *St&PR 93*
Kaegel, Ray Martin 1925- *WhoWor 93*
Kaegel, Richard James 1939- *WhoAm 92*
Kaegi, Richard John 1948- *St&PR 93*
Kaehler, James A. *Law&B 92*
Kael, Pauline *BioIn 17*
Kael, Pauline 1919- *WhoAm 92, WhoAmW 93, WhoE 93, WhoWrEP 92*
Kaelber, Don Edward 1933- *St&PR 93*
Kaelin, Eugene Francis 1926- *WhoAm 92*
Kaelin, Jeannette Jill 1956- *WhoEmL 93*
Kaelin, Kerry John 1950- *WhoSSW 93*
Kaelin, LeeAnn Jenee 1965- *WhoAmW 93*
Kaelin, Pamela Marie 1965- *WhoWrEP 92*
Kaemmerlen, Cathy June 1949- *WhoSSW 93*
Kaempe, Bent P. 1934- *WhoScE 91-2*
Kaempfert, Bert(hold) 1923-1980 *Baker 92*
Kaempfert, Max 1871-1941 *Baker 92*
Kaenzig, Joseph G., Jr. 1945- *St&PR 93*
Kaep, Louis J. 1903-1991 *BioIn 17*

Kaercher, Marilyn Anita 1924- *WhoAmW 93*
Kaercher, Robert Lloyd 1924- *St&PR 93*
Kaericher, C.W. 1921- *St&PR 93*
Kaerjae, Juhani 1934- *WhoWor 93*
Kaesberg, Paul Joseph 1923- *WhoAm 92*
Kaesche, Helmut 1928- *WhoScE 91-3*
Kaeser, Clifford Richard 1936- *St&PR 93, WhoAm 92*
Kaeser, Heinrich E. 1924- *WhoScE 91-4*
Kaeser, Kurt R. 1962- *St&PR 93*
Kaeser, Steven Dale *Law&B 92*
Kaeslin, Laura M. 1917- *St&PR 93*
Kaessner, Michael L. 1950- *St&PR 93*
Kaestner, Erich 1899-1974 *ConAu 40NR, MajAI [port]*
Kaeter, Gene J. *St&PR 93*
Kaeter, Margaret 1957- *WhoWrEP 92*
Kaever, Matthias J. 1929- *WhoScE 91-3*
Kafadar, Ahmed D. 1915- *St&PR 93*
Kafadar, Charles Bell 1945- *St&PR 93, WhoAm 92*
Kafalas, Constantinos 1922- *St&PR 93*
Kafali, Kemal *WhoScE 91-4*
Kafarski, Mitchell I. 1917- *WhoAm 92*
Kafenda, Frico 1883-1963 *Baker 92*
Kaferstein, Friedrich Karl 1938- *WhoUN 92*
Kafes, William O. *Law&B 92*
Kafes, William O. 1935- *St&PR 93*
Kafes, William Owen 1935- *WhoAm 92*
Kaff, Albert Ernest 1920- *WhoAm 92, WhoWor 93*
Kaffenberger, Ernst Wilhelm 1931- *WhoWor 93*
Kaffenberger, Wilfried Ernst 1944- *St&PR 93*
Kaffer, Roger Louis 1927- *WhoAm 92*
Kaffer, William John 1929- *St&PR 93*
Kafferlin, William H. 1923- *St&PR 93*
Kaffka, Johann Christoph 1754-1815 *Baker 92*
Kaffka, Karoly J. 1927- *WhoScE 91-4*
Kafka, Barbara *BioIn 17*
Kafka, Barbara 1933- *ConAu 136*
Kafka, F(rancis) L. 1926- *ConAu 139*
Kafka, Franz 1883-1924 *BioIn 17, DcTwHis, MagSWL [port], ScF&FL 92, TwCLC 47 [port], WorLitC [port]*
Kafka, Gerhard Johannes 1943- *WhoWor 93*
Kafka, Johann Nepomuk 1819-1886 *Baker 92*
Kafka, Joseph A. *St&PR 93*
Kafka, Marian Stern 1927- *WhoAmW 93, WhoE 93*
Kafka-Barron, Eva 1926- *WhoAmW 93*
Kafka-Lutzow, Astrid 1937- *WhoScE 91-4*
Kafle, Deepak Raj 1953- *WhoWor 93*
Kafoury, Michael A. *Law&B 92*
Kagami, Manabu 1959- *WhoWor 93*
Kagan, Arthur Myron 1919- *St&PR 93*
Kagan, Carolyn *WhoScE 91-1*
Kagan, David Bruce *Law&B 92*
Kagan, Donald 1932- *WhoAm 92*
Kagan, George Irwin 1939- *WhoWor 93*
Kagan, Henri 1930- *WhoScE 91-2*
Kagan, Irving 1928- *St&PR 93*
Kagan, Janet 1946- *ScF&FL 92*
Kagan, Jeremy Paul 1945- *MiSFD 9, WhoAm 92*
Kagan, Jerome *BioIn 17*
Kagan, Jerome 1929- *WhoAm 92*
Kagan, Julia Lee 1948- *WhoAm 92, WhoE 93*
Kagan, Nelson 1960- *WhoWor 93*
Kagan, Norman *ScF&FL 92*
Kagan, Patricia Amanda 1949- *WhoSSW 93*
Kagan, Peter *BioIn 17*
Kagan, Rory Lynn *Law&B 92*
Kagan, Sioma 1907- *WhoAm 92, WhoWor 93*
Kagan, Spencer S. 1961- *St&PR 93*
Kagan, Stephen Bruce 1944- *St&PR 93, WhoAm 92*
Kaganovich, L.M. 1893-1991 *BioIn 17*
Kaganovich, Lazar 1893-1991 *AnObit 1991*
Kaganovich, Lazar' Moiseevich 1893-1991 *BioIn 17*
Kagarakis, Constantine 1933- *WhoScE 91-3*
Kagarlitsky, Yuli 1926- *ScF&FL 92*
Kagawa, Kyoko 1931- *IntDcF 2-3 [port]*
Kagaya, Hiroshi Kan 1930- *WhoWor 93*
Kagel, Diego Roberto 1952- *WhoWor 93*
Kagel, Mauricio 1931- *Baker 92, IntDcOp, WhoAm 92*
Kagen, Sergius 1909-1964 *Baker 92*
Kagesa, Sadaaki 1893-1948 *HarEnMi*
Kagey, F. Eileen 1925- *WhoAmW 93*
Kageyama, Kiichi 1936- *WhoWor 93*
Kageyama, Sanpei 1945- *WhoWor 93*
Kaggen, Lois 1944- *WhoAmW 93*
Kagi, Jeremias H.R. 1930- *WhoScE 91-4*
Kagiwada, Harriet Hatsune Natsuyama 1937- *WhoAmW 93*
Kagiwada, Reynold Shigeru 1938- *WhoAm 92*
Kagle, Joseph Louis, Jr. 1932- *WhoAm 92*
Kagler, Robert Wayne 1951- *WhoEmL 93*
Kahalas, Harvey 1941- *WhoE 93*
Kahan, Aaron *BioIn 17*
Kahan, Al E. 1922- *St&PR 93*
Kahan, Alan S. 1959- *ConAu 139*
Kahan, Barry Donald 1939- *WhoAm 92*
Kahan, Herman L. 1954- *WhoEmL 93*
Kahan, James Paul 1942- *WhoAm 92*
Kahan, Leonard H. 1924- *St&PR 93*
Kahan, Marlene 1952- *WhoAm 92, WhoE 93*
Kahan, Mitchell Douglas 1951- *WhoAm 92*
Kahan, Samuel D. 1947- *WhoAm 92*
Kahan, William M. 1933- *WhoAm 92*
Kahana, Aron 1921- *WhoAm 92*
Kahana, David 1903- *BioIn 17*
Kahana, Eva Frost 1941- *WhoAm 92*
Kahana, Kalman 1910-1991 *BioIn 17*
Kahane, Dennis Spencer 1947- *WhoAm 92*
Kahane, Henry 1902- *WhoAm 92*
Kahane, Jean-Pierre 1926- *WhoWor 93*
Kahane, Jeffrey (Alan) 1956- *Baker 92*
Kahane, Matthew Graham 1948- *WhoUN 92*
Kahane, Meir *BioIn 17*
Kahari, Jorma 1941- *WhoScE 91-4*
Kaharl, Victoria A(nn) 1952- *ConAu 137*
Kahelin, William J. *Law&B 92*
Kahen, Harold I. 1918- *St&PR 93, WhoAm 92*
Kahin, George McTurnan 1918- *WhoAm 92*
Kahl, Alfred Louis, Jr. 1932- *WhoE 93*
Kahl, Gordon *BioIn 17*
Kahl, Gunter 1936- *WhoScE 91-3*
Kahl, Jeffrey Brian 1950- *St&PR 93*
Kahl, M.W. 1930- *St&PR 93*
Kahl, Michael F. *Law&B 92*
Kahl, Willi 1893-1962 *Baker 92*
Kahl, William Frederick 1922- *WhoAm 92*
Kahle, Daniel A. *Law&B 92*
Kahle, Douglas *St&PR 93*
Kahle, G. Kent 1951- *St&PR 93*
Kahle, Hans Gert 1944- *WhoScE 91-4*
Kahle, Heinz Gerhard J. 1925- *WhoScE 91-3*
Kahle, Jack E. 1929- *St&PR 93*
Kahle, John H. *Law&B 92*
Kahle, Roger Raymond 1943- *WhoWor 93*
Kahlenbeck, Howard 1929- *St&PR 93*
Kahlenberg, Jeannette Dawson 1931- *WhoE 93*
Kahlenberg, John B. 1915- *St&PR 93*
Kahlenberg, Karl W. 1933- *St&PR 93*
Kahlenberg, Richard D(awson) 1963- *ConAu 138*
Kahler, Dorothy Stirling 1955- *WhoAmW 93*
Kahler, Elizabeth Sartor 1911- *WhoAm 92*
Kahler, Herbert Frederick 1936- *WhoAm 92*
Kahler, Jack *ScF&FL 92*
Kahler, Mark P. *Law&B 92*
Kahler, Mary Ellis 1919-1990 *BioIn 17*
Kahler, Richard M. 1935- *St&PR 93*
Kahler, Rick S. 1955- *St&PR 93*
Kahler, Willibald 1866-1938 *Baker 92*
Kahlert, Hartmut W. 1940- *WhoScE 91-4*
Kahlert, Vera Ines 1956- *WhoEmL 93*
Kahles, John Frank 1914- *WhoAm 92*
Kahlmann, H.C. *WhoScE 91-3*
Kahlo, Frida 1907-1954 *BioIn 17*
Kahlow, Barbara Fenvessy 1946- *WhoAmW 93, WhoEmL 93*
Kahlweit, Manfred 1928- *WhoScE 91-3*
Kahm, Steven Elliot *Law&B 92*
Kahmann, Anthony Robert 1921- *WhoSSW 93*
Kahn, Ada Paskind 1934- *WhoAmW 93*
Kahn, Alan Edwin 1929- *WhoE 93*
Kahn, Albert Michael 1917- *WhoAm 92, WhoSSW 93, WhoWor 93*
Kahn, Alex 1931- *St&PR 93*
Kahn, Alfred *ScF&FL 92*
Kahn, Alfred, Jr. 1916- *WhoSSW 93*
Kahn, Alfred E. 1917- *EncABHB 8 [port]*
Kahn, Alfred Edward 1917- *WhoAm 92*
Kahn, Alfred Joseph 1919- *WhoAm 92*
Kahn, Anna L. 1923- *St&PR 93*
Kahn, Annette 1941- *BioIn 17*
Kahn, Arnold N. 1941- *St&PR 93*
Kahn, Arnold Sanford 1942- *WhoSSW 93*
Kahn, Arthur H. 1931- *WhoAm 92*
Kahn, Axel 1944- *WhoScE 91-2*
Kahn, B. Franklin 1925- *St&PR 93*
Kahn, Bernd 1928- *WhoAm 92*
Kahn, Bernhard 1876-1955 *BioIn 17*
Kahn, Carl Ronald 1944- *WhoAm 92, WhoE 93*
Kahn, Carole 1937- *WhoE 93*
Kahn, Charles Howard 1926- *WhoAm 92*
Kahn, Daniel Gerald 1955- *WhoE 93*
Kahn, David 1912- *WhoAm 92*
Kahn, David 1930- *WhoAm 92*
Kahn, David L. *St&PR 93*
Kahn, Debra Johnson 1950- *St&PR 93*
Kahn, Doris Chilton 1928- *WhoE 93*
Kahn, Douglas Allen 1934- *WhoAm 92*
Kahn, Douglas Gerard 1946- *WhoAm 92*
Kahn, Edwin Leonard 1918- *WhoAm 92*
Kahn, Elliot 1920- *St&PR 93*
Kahn, Ellis Irvin 1936- *WhoSSW 93*
Kahn, Ely Jacques, Jr. 1916- *WhoAm 92, WhoE 93*
Kahn, Erich Itor 1905-1956 *Baker 92*
Kahn, Faith-Hope 1921- *WhoAmW 93, WhoE 93*
Kahn, Florence Prag 1866-1948 *BioIn 17*
Kahn, Frank J. 1921- *St&PR 93*
Kahn, Franz Daniel *WhoScE 91-1*
Kahn, Fred A. 1932- *WhoE 93*
Kahn, Gerald J. 1926- *St&PR 93*
Kahn, Gordon Barry 1931- *WhoAm 92*
Kahn, H. Bernard 1923- *St&PR 93*
Kahn, Harry 1916- *WhoAm 92*
Kahn, Harry H. *Law&B 92*
Kahn, Harry H. 1943- *St&PR 93*
Kahn, Herbert 1922- *St&PR 93*
Kahn, Herman 1922-1983 *ColdWar 1 [port]*
Kahn, Herman Bernard 1923- *WhoAm 92*
Kahn, Herman H. 1909-1991 *BioIn 17*
Kahn, Herta Hess 1919- *WhoAm 92*
Kahn, Hugo 1932- *St&PR 93*
Kahn, I.B. 1917- *St&PR 93*
Kahn, Irving 1905- *St&PR 93*
Kahn, Irving B. 1917- *WhoAm 92*
Kahn, Irving I. 1916- *St&PR 93*
Kahn, Irwin William 1923- *WhoWor 93*
Kahn, Isadore J. 1914- *St&PR 93*
Kahn, James 1947- *ScF&FL 92*
Kahn, James Stanley 1947- *WhoE 93*
Kahn, James Steven 1931- *WhoAm 92*
Kahn, Jeff *MiSFD 9*
Kahn, Jeffrey Hay 1939- *WhoAm 92*
Kahn, Jenette Sarah 1947- *WhoAm 92, WhoE 93*
Kahn, Joan 1914- *ScF&FL 92*
Kahn, Jocelyn D. d1990 *BioIn 17*
Kahn, Joel Ira 1952- *WhoEmL 93*
Kahn, Joseph Gabriel 1913- *WhoAm 92*
Kahn, Judith Michael 1943- *WhoAm 92*
Kahn, Judy *BioIn 17*
Kahn, Laurence Howard 1943- *WhoE 93*
Kahn, Leonard Richard 1926- *WhoAm 92*
Kahn, Leslie Ruth 1947- *WhoE 93*
Kahn, Linda McClure *WhoAmW 93, WhoWor 93*
Kahn, Lisa Margarete *WhoSSW 93*
Kahn, Louis I. *BioIn 17*
Kahn, Ludwig Werner 1910- *WhoE 93*
Kahn, M. *WhoScE 91-1*
Kahn, Madeleine (H.) 1955- *ConAu 137*
Kahn, Madeline Gail *WhoAm 92*
Kahn, Marcel-Francis 1929- *WhoScE 91-2, WhoWor 93*
Kahn, Mark Bennet 1957- *WhoE 93*
Kahn, Mehr 1945- *WhoUN 92*
Kahn, Michael *WhoAm 92*
Kahn, Michael A. 1952- *ConAu 138*
Kahn, Muriel Joan 1933- *WhoAmW 93*
Kahn, Myron 1930- *St&PR 93*
Kahn, Nancy Valerie 1952- *WhoAmW 93, WhoEmL 93*
Kahn, Nathan Samuel 1954- *St&PR 93*
Kahn, Neil 1957- *St&PR 93*
Kahn, Norman 1932- *WhoAm 92*
Kahn, Obie *ScF&FL 92*
Kahn, Olivier 1942- *WhoScE 91-2*
Kahn, Otto Hermann 1867-1934 *Baker 92*
Kahn, Paul 1949- *WhoWrEP 92*
Kahn, Paul Frederick 1935- *WhoAm 92*
Kahn, Paul Markham 1935- *WhoIns 93, WhoWor 93*
Kahn, Paula 1940- *WhoWor 93*
Kahn, Peggy *ConAu 37NR*
Kahn, Peter B. 1935- *WhoAm 92*
Kahn, Peter C. 1940- *WhoE 93*
Kahn, Philippe *BioIn 17*
Kahn, Richard Dreyfus 1931- *WhoAm 92*
Kahn, Richard Ferdinand 1905-1989 *BioIn 17*
Kahn, Richard M. *Law&B 92*
Kahn, Richard Paul 1926- *WhoE 93*
Kahn, Robert 1865-1951 *Baker 92, BioIn 17*
Kahn, Robert H., Jr. 1923- *WhoAm 92*
Kahn, Robert Irving 1918- *WhoAm 92, WhoWor 93*
Kahn, Robert Jean 1935- *WhoScE 91-2*
Kahn, Robert Theodore 1933- *WhoAm 92*
Kahn, Robin Phoebe 1961- *WhoE 93*
Kahn, Roger 1927- *BiDAMSp 1989, WhoAm 92, WhoWrEP 92*
Kahn, Roy J. 1932- *St&PR 93*
Kahn, S. Carroll, Jr. 1924- *St&PR 93*
Kahn, Sanford *BioIn 17*
Kahn, Sigmund Benham 1933- *WhoAm 92*
Kahn, Susan Beth 1924- *WhoAm 92, WhoAmW 93*
Kahn, Sy Myron 1924- *WhoWrEP 92*
Kahn, Thomas 1938- *WhoAm 92*
Kahn, Tom d1992 *NewYTBS 92*
Kahn, Tom 1938-1992 *BioIn 17*
Kahn, Walter 1917- *St&PR 93, WhoAm 92*
Kahn, Walter Kurt 1929- *WhoAm 92*
Kahn, Wolf 1927- *WhoAm 92*
Kahnberg, Karl-Erik A. 1941- *WhoScE 91-4*
Kahne, Hilda 1922- *WhoE 93*
Kahne, Stephen James 1937- *WhoAm 92, WhoSSW 93*
Kahng, Dawon *BioIn 17*
Kahng, Dawon d1992 *NewYTBS 92*
Kahng, Dawon 1931- *WhoAm 92, WhoWor 93*
Kahn-Goldfarb, Anna Lee 1923- *St&PR 93*
Kahnke, Jean Bernadette 1959- *WhoAmW 93*
Kahnt, Christian Friedrich 1823-1897 *Baker 92*
Kahnt, Gunter A. 1929- *WhoScE 91-3*
Kahnweiler, Daniel Henry 1884-1979 *BioIn 17*
Kahnweiler, William Mark 1950- *WhoSSW 93*
Kahoun, Jindrich 1929- *WhoScE 91-4*
Kahowez, Gunter 1940- *Baker 92*
Kahr, Toby Yale 1932- *WhoSSW 93*
Kahrel, Ate Nicolaas 1948- *WhoWor 93*
Kahrs, Cynthia Anne 1948- *WhoEmL 93*
Kahssay, Haile-Mariam 1942- *WhoUN 92*
Kai, Robert T. 1944- *St&PR 93*
Kaiba, Kaus *WhoScE 91-3*
Kaic, Zvonimir *WhoScE 91-4*
Kaida, Ikuo 1931- *WhoWor 93*
Kaiden, Richard Louis 1941- *WhoE 93*
Kaido, Bonnell Dolores 1951- *WhoAmW 93, WhoEmL 93*
Kaifu, Toshiki *BioIn 17*
Kaifu, Toshiki 1931- *WhoAsAP 91, WhoWor 93*
Kaige, Alice Tubb 1922- *WhoAmW 93*
Kaige, Chen 1952- *MiSFD 9*
Kaija, Judith Nanyonga 1953- *WhoUN 92*
Kaijser, Lennart 1937- *WhoScE 91-4*
Kaikow, Rita Ellen 1947- *WhoAmW 93*
Kail, Daniel R. 1935- *St&PR 93*
Kail, Jack *Law&B 92*
Kail, Robert Lee *WhoWrEP 92*
Kaila, Ermo 1923- *WhoScE 91-4*
Kaila, Martti M. 1933- *WhoScE 91-4*
Kaila, Martti Mikael 1933- *WhoWor 93*
Kailasanath, Kazhikathra 1953- *WhoEmL 93*
Kailashpati 1913- *WhoAsAP 91*
Kailath, Thomas 1935- *St&PR 93, WhoAm 92*
Kailian, Aram Harry 1949- *WhoE 93, WhoEmL 93*
Kailian, Vaughn M. *St&PR 93*
Kaim, Franz 1856-1935 *Baker 92*
Kaiman, David S. 1955- *St&PR 93*
Kaiman, Marvin 1930- *St&PR 93*
Kaiman, Stan C. *Law&B 92*
Kaiman, Stan C. 1938- *St&PR 93*
Kain, Clayton A. 1946- *St&PR 93*
Kain, Jack Allan 1929- *St&PR 93*
Kain, Karen Alexandria 1951- *WhoAm 92, WhoWor 93*
Kain, Mike E. 1955- *St&PR 93*
Kain, Richard M. 1908-1990 *BioIn 17*
Kain, Richard Yerkes 1936- *WhoAm 92*
Kain, Susan Lane 1946- *St&PR 93*
Kain, Virginia Rose *WhoWrEP 92*
Kain, William H. 1912- *St&PR 93*
Kainen, Jacob 1909- *WhoAm 92*
Kainen, Paul Chester 1943- *WhoE 93*
Kainlauri, Eino Olavi 1922- *WhoAm 92*
Kains, Josephine *ScF&FL 92*
Kaintz, Robert Lee *Law&B 92*
Kainuma, Jiro 1933- *WhoAsAP 91*
Kainz, Erich 1940- *WhoScE 91-4*
Kaioumos fl. 7th cent.- *OxDcByz*
Kaipainen, Jouni (Ilari) 1956- *Baker 92*
Kaipainen, Wilhelm J. 1918- *WhoScE 91-4*
Kairey, Mindy Sue 1963- *WhoEmL 93*
Kairis, Paul J. 1957- *St&PR 93*
Kairisalo, Pekka 1951- *WhoScE 91-4*
Kairoff, Joshua David 1964- *WhoEmL 93*
Kaisarios, Pseudo- *OxDcByz*
Kaisel, Stanley F. 1922- *WhoAm 92*
Kaiser, Adrian E., Jr. 1928- *St&PR 93*
Kaiser, Albert Farr 1933- *WhoAm 92*
Kaiser, Alfred 1872-1917 *Baker 92*
Kaiser, Amy Jo 1959- *WhoAmW 93*
Kaiser, Bo Paul 1917- *WhoWor 93*
Kaiser, Colin F. 1933- *St&PR 93*
Kaiser, Diane 1946- *WhoE 93*
Kaiser, Edgar Fosburgh, Jr. 1942- *WhoAm 92, WhoWor 93*
Kaiser, Eric J. *Law&B 92*
Kaiser, Erich 1925- *WhoScE 91-4*
Kaiser, Ernest Daniel 1915- *WhoWrEP 92*
Kaiser, F.E. *St&PR 93*
Kaiser, Fred 1906- *WhoAm 92*

Kaiser, Georg 1878-1945 *DcLB 124 [port]*
Kaiser, Grace H. *BioIn 17*
Kaiser, Harvey Harold 1936- *WhoE 93*
Kaiser, Henry 1952- *Baker 92*
Kaiser, Henry John 1882-1967 *BioIn 17*
Kaiser, James B. 1934- *WhoUN 92*
Kaiser, James G. *BioIn 17*
Kaiser, James G. 1943- *St&PR 93*
Kaiser, James M. 1937- *St&PR 93*
Kaiser, James W. 1946- *St&PR 93*
Kaiser, Jean Morgan 1932- *WhoSSW 93*
Kaiser, Jill Adler 1948- *WhoE 93*
Kaiser, John Atwood 1951- *WhoEmL 93*
Kaiser, Joseph P., Jr. 1948- *St&PR 93*
Kaiser, Karen Elizabeth 1957- *WhoEmL 93*
Kaiser, Lloyd Eugene 1927- *WhoAm 92*
Kaiser, Mark Alexander 1957- *WhoSSW 93*
Kaiser, Marshall J. 1947- *St&PR 93*
Kaiser, Marvin Kent 1941- *St&PR 93*
Kaiser, Michael J. 1946- *St&PR 93*
Kaiser, Nicholas Thomas 1933- *St&PR 93*
Kaiser, Norman Stanley 1949- *St&PR 93*
Kaiser, Philip Mayer 1913- *WhoAm 92, WhoSSW 93*
Kaiser, Richard 1952- *WhoWor 93*
Kaiser, Richard G. 1949- *St&PR 93*
Kaiser, Robert 1934- *WhoE 93*
Kaiser, Robert Greeley 1943- *WhoAm 92*
Kaiser, Robert Lee 1935- *WhoSSW 93*
Kaiser, Rudolf Franz Josef 1927- *WhoWor 93*
Kaiser, Saamir 1964- *WhoE 93*
Kaiser, Sandra June Leana 1948- *WhoSSW 93*
Kaiser, Seth Alan 1956- *WhoE 93*
Kaiser, Shawna *Law&B 92*
Kaiser, Steven Craig 1953- *WhoEmL 93*
Kaiser, Susan F. *Law&B 92*
Kaiser, Thomas G. *WhoIns 93*
Kaiser, Walter Ronald 1933- *St&PR 93*
Kaiser, Werner *Law&B 92*
Kaiser, Werner M. 1944- *WhoScE 91-3*
Kaiser, Wolfgang A. 1923- *WhoScE 91-3*
Kaiser-Botsai, Sharon Kay 1941- *WhoAmW 93*
Kaiserlian, Penelope Jane 1943- *WhoAm 92*
Kaiserman, Constance *MiSFD 9*
Kaisev, Rostislav Atanasov *WhoScE 91-4*
Kaish, Luise Clayborn 1925- *WhoAm 92*
Kaish, Morton 1927- *WhoAm 92, WhoE 93*
Kaishev, Rostislav Atanasov 1908- *WhoScE 91-4*
Kaising, Elmer A. 1933- *St&PR 93*
Kaissling, Karl-Ernst *WhoScE 91-3*
Kaita, Robert 1952- *WhoE 93*
Kaitai, Li 1937- *WhoWor 93*
Kaitner, Bruce Edmund 1927- *St&PR 93*
Kaitson, E. Chris *Law&B 92*
Kaity, Stephen 1954- *St&PR 93*
Kaiulani, Princess of Hawaii 1875-1899 *BioIn 17*
Kaizaki, Sumio 1943- *WhoWor 93*
Kaizer, Arleen Niezgodzki 1939- *WhoAmW 93*
Kaizuki, Kiyonori 1950- *SmATA 72 [port]*
Kaj, Stanislaw Hubert 1951- *WhoWor 93*
Kajak, Zdzislaw 1929- *WhoScE 91-4*
Kajander, R.J. 1939- *WhoScE 91-4*
Kajantie, Keijo Olavi 1940- *WhoScE 91-4*
Kajanus, Robert 1856-1933 *Baker 92*
Kajencki, Francis C(asimir) 1918- *ConAu 38NR*
Kajfasz, Stanislaw 1925- *WhoScE 91-4*
Kaji, Akira 1930- *WhoE 93*
Kaji, Gautam S. 1941- *WhoUN 92*
Kaji, Hideko Katayama 1932- *WhoAmW 93, WhoE 93*
Kaji, Kiyoshi 1928- *WhoAsAP 91*
Kajiji, Zoyeb Taherali 1913- *WhoWor 93*
Kajitani, Ban 1941- *BioIn 17*
Kajiwara, Kagetoki d1200 *HarEnMi*
Kajiwara, Keigi 1937- *WhoAsAP 91*
Kajiwara, Kiyoshi 1921- *WhoAsAP 91*
Kajiyama, Seiroku 1926- *WhoAsAP 91*
Kajiyama, Tisato 1940- *WhoWor 93*
Kajkowski, Ray 1948- *BioIn 17*
Kajoi, Michael Steven 1950- *WhoE 93*
Kajornprasart, Sanan 1935- *WhoAsAP 91*
Kajosaari, Eero Tapio 1927- *WhoScE 91-4*
Kajrunajtys, Kasjan Antoni 1964- *WhoWor 93*
Kakabadse, Andrew P. *WhoScE 91-1*
Kakari, Sophia Anastasiou *WhoWor 93*
Kakas, George J. 1910- *St&PR 93*
Kakati, Dinesh Chandra 1941- *WhoWor 93*
Kakaty, Kenneth Joseph 1944- *St&PR 93*
Kakehi, Akikazu 1946- *WhoWor 93*
Kakehi, Kazuaki 1947- *WhoWor 93*
Kakichev, Valentin Andreevich 1926- *WhoWor 93*
Kakiichi, Yoshiaki 1934- *WhoWor 93*
Kakish, Stephen 1922- *St&PR 93*
Kakizawa, Koji 1933- *WhoAsAP 91*
Kakkar, S. 1938- *St&PR 93*
Kakkar, Vijay Vir 1937- *WhoWor 93*
Kakkuri, Juhani 1933- *WhoScE 91-4*
Kako, Cris T. *Law&B 92*
Kakodkar, Purushottam 1913- *WhoAsAP 91*
Kakol, Jerzy Marian 1952- *WhoWor 93*
Kakol, Mieczyslaw 1920- *WhoScE 91-4*
Kakowski, Aleksander 1862-1938 *PolBiDi*
Kaku, Michio 1947- *WhoE 93, WhoWor 93*
Kaku, Ryuzaburo 1926- *WhoE 93*
Kakuma, Yasumasa 1927- *WhoAsAP 91*
Kakusa, Cathy Jean 1949- *St&PR 93*
Kakuta, Kakuji 1890-1944 *HarEnMi*
KAL *BioIn 17*
Kalaba, Robert Edwin 1926- *WhoAm 92*
Kalabinski, Jacek Michal 1938- *WhoE 93*
Kalabis, Viktor 1923- *Baker 92*
Kalabza, Jack F. 1928- *St&PR 93*
Kalachevsky, Mikhail 1851-c. 1910 *Baker 92*
Kalaf, Jack *St&PR 93*
Kalaf, Walter Nadeem 1925- *WhoSSW 93*
Kalafati, Vasili (Pavlovich) 1869-1942 *Baker 92*
Kalafut, George Wendell 1934- *St&PR 93, WhoAm 92, WhoSSW 93*
Kalafut, Mark A. *Law&B 92*
Kalahar, William L. 1941- *St&PR 93*
Kalaher, Richard A. *Law&B 92*
Kalaher, Richard Alan 1940- *St&PR 93, WhoAm 92*
Kalai, Ehud 1942- *WhoAm 92*
Kalaidjian, Berj Boghos 1936- *WhoWor 93*
Kalaidjian, Emma M. *Law&B 92*
Kalainov, Sam Charles 1930- *St&PR 93, WhoAm 92, WhoIns 93*
Kalajian, Adolfo 1926- *WhoWor 93*
Kalakau Bin Untol 1954- *WhoAsAP 91*
Kalal, Jaroslav 1930- *WhoScE 91-4*
Kalamanos *OxDcByz*
Kalamaras, Paul 1958- *St&PR 93*
Kalamaros, Edward Nicholas 1934- *WhoAm 92*
Kalamotousakis, George John 1936- *WhoAm 92, WhoWor 93*
Kalan, George Richard 1944- *WhoAm 92, WhoE 93*
Kalangis, Ike 1937- *St&PR 93*
Kalangula, Peter Tanyangenge 1926- *WhoAfr*
Kalanquin, Patricia Cathryn 1959- *WhoAmW 93*
Kalant, Harold 1923- *WhoAm 92*
Kalanta, James John 1953- *St&PR 93*
Kalapos, George J., Jr. *Law&B 92*
Kalas, Frank Joseph, Jr. 1943- *WhoE 93, WhoWor 93*
Kalas, Julius 1902-1967 *Baker 92*
Kalas, Melvyn R. 1934- *St&PR 93*
Kalaska, Ann *Law&B 92*
Kalaska, Vernon W. 1931- *St&PR 93*
Kalaski, Robert John 1941- *WhoWrEP 92*
Kalasky, James F. *Law&B 92*
Kalasz, Huba 1941- *WhoScE 91-4*
Kalata, John Joseph 1947- *St&PR 93*
Kalatozov, Mihail 1903-1973 *DrEEuF*
Kalatozov, Mikhail 1903-1973 *MiSFD 9N*
Kala'un d1290 *HarEnMi*
Kalawski, Eva M. *Law&B 92*
Kalayjian, Anie Sanentz *WhoAmW 93*
Kalb, Christian J. 1934- *St&PR 93*
Kalb, Elizabeth Ann 1957- *WhoAmW 93*
Kalb, Jennifer Johnson *Law&B 92*
Kalb, Johann 1721-1780 *HarEnMi*
Kalb, Martin 1942- *WhoAm 92*
Kalb, Marvin *WhoAm 92*
Kalb, Marvin 1930- *JrnUS*
Kalban, Lawrence S. *Law&B 92*
Kalbeck, Max 1850-1921 *Baker 92*
Kalberer, Dolletta Ann 1951- *WhoE 93*
Kalberkamp, Carl H. 1930- *St&PR 93*
Kalbfeld, Brad Marshall 1954- *WhoAm 92*
Kalbfleisch, George Randolph 1931- *WhoSSW 93*
Kalbfleisch, John McDowell 1930- *WhoAm 92, WhoSSW 93, WhoWor 93*
Kalbfleisch, Laura B. 1967- *St&PR 93*
Kalcevic, Timothy Francis 1950- *WhoWor 93*
Kalck, Craig W. 1948- *WhoIns 93*
Kalckar, Herman Moritz 1908-1991 *BioIn 17*
Kalckreuth, Leopold Karl Walter, Graf von 1855-1928 *BioIn 17*
Kaldate, Bapu 1929- *WhoAsAP 91*
Kalden, Joachim Robert 1937- *WhoScE 91-3*
Kalderen, Erik Erland 1931- *WhoWor 93*
Kalderen, Lars Gunnar 1928- *WhoWor 93*
Kaldewaij, Anne 1947- *WhoWor 93*
Kaldewey, Harald E.M. 1921- *WhoScE 91-3*
Kaldi, Pal 1927- *WhoScE 91-4*
Kaldis, Guy Constantine 1937- *WhoE 93*
Kaldor, Mihaly 1924- *WhoScE 91-4*
Kaldor, Nicholas 1908-1986 *BioIn 17*
Kale *OxDcByz*
Kale, Herbert William, II 1931- *WhoSSW 93*
Kalechofsky, Roberta 1931- *ScF&FL 92, WhoWrEP 92*
Kalecki, Michal *BioIn 17*
Kalecki, Michal 1889-1970 *PolBiDi*
Kaledo, Grace Lucille 1928- *WhoAmW 93*
Kaleem, Muhammad 1964- *WhoWor 93*
Kalekas *OxDcByz*
Kalekas, Manuel d1410 *OxDcByz*
Kalelkar, Ashok Satish 1943- *St&PR 93, WhoAm 92, WhoE 93*
Kalellis, William 1917- *St&PR 93*
Kalember, Patricia *BioIn 17*
Kalensky, Zdenek Denny 1931- *WhoUN 92*
Kaler, Anne K(atherine) 1935- *ConAu 138*
Kaler, Emile T., Jr. 1935- *St&PR 93*
Kaler, Eric William 1956- *WhoE 93*
Kales, Anthony 1934- *WhoAm 92*
Kales, Christopher P. *BioIn 17*
Kales, Christopher P. d1992 *NewYTBS 92*
Kales, Paul Albert 1937- *WhoE 93*
Kaleta, Paul J. *Law&B 92*
Kalette, Stephen R. *Law&B 92*
Kalette, Stephen Richard 1950- *St&PR 93*
Kalev, Ljubomir Tzonev 1921- *WhoScE 91-4*
Kalevras, Vladimir 1936- *WhoScE 91-3*
Kaley, Arthur Warren 1921- *St&PR 93, WhoAm 92*
Kalezic, Zarko 1931- *WhoScE 91-4*
Kalfelz, Roque Antonio 1945- *WhoWor 93*
Kalfon, Frederick 1941- *St&PR 93*
Kalhauge, Sophus Viggo Harald 1840-1905 *Baker 92*
Kalhorn, Gene Edward 1944- *St&PR 93*
Kalian, Robert P. 1939- *WhoWrEP 92*
Kalib, David Leonard 1940- *WhoIns 93*
Kalib, Goldie Szachter 1931- *BioIn 17*
Kalicharran, Judith 1955- *WhoE 93*
Kalichstein, Joseph 1946- *Baker 92, WhoEmL 93*
Kalicki, Patricia Ann 1954- *WhoAmW 93*
Kalicki, Robert J. 1958- *St&PR 93*
Kalidasa fl. c. 400- *ClMLC 9*
Kaliff, Joseph d1992 *NewYTBS 92*
Kaliff, Joseph Alfred 1922- *WhoAm 92*
Kaliher, Michael Dennis 1947- *WhoWor 93*
Kalik, Vaclav 1891-1951 *Baker 92*
Kalikow, Peter Steven 1942- *WhoAm 92*
Kalikow, Theodora J. 1941- *WhoAm 92*
Kalil, Farris G. 1938- *St&PR 93*
Kalil, Farris George 1938- *WhoAm 92*
Kalil, Margaret d1991 *BioIn 17*
Kalil, Michael *BioIn 17*
Kalim, Muhammad Siddiq 1921- *WhoWor 93*
Kalimo, Esko Antero 1937- *WhoWor 93*
Kalin, Boris Alexandrovich 1935- *WhoWor 93*
Kalin, Jesse Gene 1940- *WhoE 93*
Kalin, Karin Bea 1943- *WhoAmW 93*
Kalin, Richard S. *St&PR 93*
Kalin, Robert 1921- *WhoAm 92, WhoSSW 93, WhoWor 93*
Kalin, Tom *MiSFD 9*
Kalin, Tomaz *WhoScE 91-4*
Kalin, Tomaz 1936- *WhoScE 91-4*
Kalina, Mike d1992 *BioIn 17*
Kalina, Richard 1946- *WhoAm 92*
Kalina, Robert Edward 1936- *WhoAm 92*
Kalinger, Daniel Jay 1952- *WhoAm 92*
Kalings, Lars Olof 1930- *WhoUN 92*
Kaliniak, Catherine Mary 1958- *WhoEmL 93*
Kalinin, Mikhail Ivanovich 1875-1946 *DcTwHis*
Kalinin, Victor Alexandrovich 1951- *WhoWor 93*
Kalinnikov, Vasili (Sergeievich) 1866-1901 *Baker 92*
Kalinoski, Henry Thomas 1957- *WhoE 93*
Kalinowski, Eugeniusz 1927- *WhoScE 91-4*
Kalinowski, Jan 1938- *WhoScE 91-4*
Kalinowski, Jozef 1835-1907 *PolBiDi*
Kalinowski, Jozef 1947- *WhoWor 93*
Kalinowski, Marek K. 1936- *WhoScE 91-4*
Kalinowski, Marek Wojciech 1950- *WhoWor 93*
Kalinowski, Rosemarie 1952- *St&PR 93*
Kalinowsky, Lothar B. d1992 *NewYTBS 92*
Kalinowsky, Lothar B. 1899- *WhoAm 92*
Kalins, Dorothy 1942- *WhoAm 92, WhoWrEP 92*
Kalinski, David E. *Law&B 92*
Kalinsky, George *BioIn 17*
Kalipolites, June Turner 1932- *WhoAmW 93, WhoE 93, WhoWor 93*
Kalisa, Ruti 1948- *WhoUN 92*
Kalisch, Beatrice Jean 1943- *WhoAm 92, WhoAmW 93*
Kalisch, Paul 1855-1946 *Baker 92*
Kalisch, Philip A. 1942- *WhoAm 92*
Kalischer, Alfred 1842-1909 *Baker 92*
Kalischer, Peter d1991 *BioIn 17*
Kalish, Alexander Edward 1953- *WhoEmL 93, WhoSSW 93*
Kalish, Arthur 1930- *WhoAm 92*
Kalish, Bernard 1937- *St&PR 93*
Kalish, Bertha 1875-1939 *PolBiDi*
Kalish, Carl M. *St&PR 93*
Kalish, Donald 1919- *WhoAm 92*
Kalish, Gilbert 1935- *Baker 92*
Kalish, Harry Alexander 1907- *WhoAm 92*
Kalish, Herbert S. 1922- *St&PR 93*
Kalish, Myron 1919- *St&PR 93, WhoAm 92*
Kalish, Paddy 1955- *WhoWor 93*
Kalish, Ronald G. 1940- *St&PR 93*
Kalish, Tom Michael 1931- *St&PR 93*
Kalisher, Sheila Lynn 1944- *WhoE 93*
Kalishman, Jerome 1927- *St&PR 93*
Kalishman, Reesa Joan 1959- *WhoAmW 93, WhoEmL 93, WhoSSW 93*
Kalish-Weiss, Beth Isaacs 1933- *WhoAmW 93*
Kaliski, Alan Edward 1947- *WhoIns 93*
Kaliski, Mary 1938- *WhoAmW 93*
Kaliski, Stephan Felix 1928- *WhoAm 92*
Kaliszewski, Ignacy Stanislaw 1949- *WhoWor 93*
Kaliszewski, Leo Robert 1935- *St&PR 93*
Kaliszky, Sandor 1927- *WhoScE 91-4*
Kalita, Bhubaneswar 1951- *WhoAsAP 91*
Kalivas, Nickolas George 1960- *WhoWor 93*
Kalka, Robert Alois, Jr. 1966- *WhoEmL 93*
Kalkandelen, Ayla 1939- *WhoScE 91-4*
Kalkbrenner, Christian 1755-1806 *Baker 92*
Kalkbrenner, Frederic 1785-1849 *Baker 92*
Kalkhof, Thomas Corrigan 1919- *WhoE 93, WhoWor 93*
Kalkhoff, Pamela Marie 1966- *WhoAmW 93*
Kalkin, Adam *BioIn 17*
Kalkman, C. *WhoScE 91-3*
Kalkman, Donald Alfred 1927- *St&PR 93*
Kalksma, Peter F. 1933- *St&PR 93*
Kalkstein, Joshua A. *Law&B 92*
Kalkstein, Laurence Saul 1948- *WhoE 93*
Kalkus, Stanley 1931- *WhoAm 92*
Kalkwarf, Kenneth Lee 1946- *WhoSSW 93*
Kalkwarf, Leonard V. 1928- *WhoAm 92*
Kall, Gayle Ann 1954- *WhoEmL 93*
Kall, Janice Elena 1960- *WhoEmL 93*
Kall, Patricia Anne *Law&B 92*
Kallaher, Michael Joseph 1940- *WhoAm 92*
Kalland, Lloyd Austin 1914- *WhoAm 92*
Kallas, Phillip G. 1946- *WhoWrEP 92*
Kallas, Siim 1948- *WhoWor 93*
Kallas, William E. 1946- *St&PR 93*
Kallaugher, Kevin *BioIn 17*
Kallel, Abdallah 1943- *WhoWor 93*
Kallem, Anne d1990 *BioIn 17*
Kallembach, Larry J. 1958- *St&PR 93*
Kallen, A.J. Bengt 1929- *WhoScE 91-4, WhoWor 93*
Kallen, Erland 1954- *WhoScE 91-4*
Kallen, Horace Meyer 1882-1974 *BioIn 17*
Kallen, Thomas E. 1928- *St&PR 93*
Kallenberg, John Kenneth 1942- *WhoAm 92*
Kallenberg, Siegfried Garibaldi 1867-1944 *Baker 92*
Kallenberger, Werner E. 1947- *WhoScE 91-3*
Kallend, Anthony Stewart 1937- *WhoScE 91-1*
Kallendorf, Craig William 1954- *WhoEmL 93, WhoSSW 93*
Kallenekos, Constantine *Law&B 92*
Kalleres, Arthur Peter 1941- *WhoAm 92*
Kalleres, Michael Peter 1939- *WhoAm 92*
Kallergis, George 1936- *WhoScE 91-3*
Kallerud, Sheron Gayle 1938- *WhoAmW 93*
Kalley, Gordon Stewart 1953-1992 *WhoE 93*
Kallfelz, Francis A. 1938- *WhoAm 92*
Kallfelz, Hans Carlo 1933- *WhoWor 93*
Kallgren, Edward Eugene 1928- *WhoAm 92*
Kallgren, Joyce Kislitzin 1930- *WhoAm 92*
Kallgren, Theodore R. 1962- *St&PR 93*
Kalli, Seppo T. 1953- *WhoScE 91-4*
Kallierges, George *OxDcByz*
Kallikles, Nicholas fl. 12th cent.- *OxDcByz*
Kallina, Emanuel John, II 1948- *WhoE 93*
Kallings, Lar Olof *WhoScE 91-4*
Kallinikos *OxDcByz*
Kallio, Alpo Johannes 1935- *WhoScE 91-4*
Kallio, Heikki Olavi 1937- *WhoScE 91-4*
Kallio, Paavo P. 1914- *WhoScE 91-4*
Kalliokoski, Pentti J. 1947- *WhoScE 91-4*

Kalliomaki, Kalevi *WhoScE 91-4*
Kallir, Francisca d1992 *NewYTBS 92*
Kallir, Jane Katherine *WhoAm 92, WhoEmL 93*
Kallir, John 1923- *WhoAm 92, WhoE 93*
Kallir, Lilian *BioIn 17*
Kallir, Lilian 1931- *Baker 92*
Kallis, Jack A. 1919- *St&PR 93*
Kallison, Perry M. 1934- *St&PR 93*
Kallisthenes, Pseudo- *OxDcByz*
Kallistos, I d1363 *OxDcByz*
Kallistratos, George 1927- *WhoScE 91-3*
Kallivoda, Johann Wenzel 1801-1866 *Baker 92*
Kalliwoda, Johann Wenzel 1801-1866 *Baker 92*
Kalliwoda, Wilhelm 1827-1893 *Baker 92*
Kallman, Donald Harry 1930- *St&PR 93*
Kallman, Ernest A. 1936- *St&PR 93*
Kallman, Kathleen Barbara 1952- *WhoAmW 93*
Kallmann, Helmut (Max) 1922- *Baker 92, WhoAm 92, WhoWrEP 92*
Kallmann, Stanley Walter 1943- *WhoAm 92*
Kallmyer, C. Gregory 1950- *St&PR 93*
Kallmyer, Jerry Doane 1955- *WhoEmL 93*
Kallner, Anders B. 1938- *WhoScE 91-4*
Kallne-Rachlew, Elisabeth 1944- *WhoWor 93*
Kallo, Denes 1931- *WhoScE 91-4*
Kallock, Roger W. *BioIn 17*
Kallock, Roger William 1938- *WhoAm 92*
Kallok, Michael John 1948- *WhoAm 92*
Kallop, William M. 1943- *St&PR 93*
Kallos, Bruce Oliver 1935- *WhoE 93*
Kalls, K.A. 1947- *St&PR 93*
Kallsen, Theodore John 1915- *WhoAm 92, WhoSSW 93*
Kallstenius, Edvin 1881-1967 *Baker 92*
Kallstrand, Bo Gosta 1949- *WhoWor 93*
Kallstrom, Robert Elvir 1938- *St&PR 93*
Kalltorp, L. Ove 1940- *WhoScE 91-4*
Kallweit, Viola Esther 1919- *WhoAmW 93*
Kalm, Arne 1936- *St&PR 93*
Kalm, Ernst 1940- *WhoScE 91-3*
Kalmadi, Suresh 1944- *WhoAsAP 91*
Kalman, Alajos 1935- *WhoScE 91-4*
Kalman, Andrew 1919- *WhoAm 92*
Kalman, Bela 1944- *WhoScE 91-4*
Kalman, Bobbie 1947- *BioIn 17*
Kalman, C. Arnold 1919- *St&PR 93*
Kalman, Calvin Shea 1944- *WhoWor 93*
Kalman, Charles 1929- *OxDcOp*
Kalman, Emmerich 1882-1953 *Baker 92, OxDcOp*
Kalman, John Arnold 1928- *WhoWor 93*
Kalman, Laszlo 1946- *WhoScE 91-4*
Kalman, Maira *BioIn 17*
Kalman, Rudolf Emil 1930- *WhoAm 92, WhoWor 93*
Kalman, Thomas Ivan 1936- *WhoE 93*
Kalmanir, Karen Ann 1958- *WhoEmL 93*
Kalmanoff, Martin 1920- *WhoAm 92*
Kalmar, Laszlo 1931- *Baker 92*
Kalmbach, Charles Frederic 1920- *St&PR 93*
Kalmbach, Gudrun 1937- *WhoWor 93*
Kalmbach, L.D. 1951- *St&PR 93*
Kalmoukos, P.E. *WhoScE 91-3*
Kalmus, Allan Henry 1917- *WhoAm 92*
Kalmus, Ellin *WhoAmW 93, WhoE 93*
Kalmus, Geoffrey M. 1934- *WhoAm 92*
Kalmus, George E. 1935- *WhoScE 91-1*
Kalmus, George Ernest 1935- *WhoWor 93*
Kalmus, Gerhard Wolfgang 1942- *WhoSSW 93*
Kalmus, Peter I.P. *WhoScE 91-1*
Kalmus, Peter Ignaz Paul 1933- *WhoWor 93*
Kalnins, Alfreds 1879-1951 *Baker 92, OxDcOp*
Kalnins, Imants 1941- *Baker 92*
Kalnins, Janis 1904- *Baker 92*
Kalnins, Janis 1904-1951 *OxDcOp*
Kalnins, Ojars Eriks 1949- *WhoUN 92*
Kalogerou, Byron Stephen *Law&B 92*
Kalojan d1207 *OxDcByz*
Kalomirakis, Theodore *BioIn 17*
Kalomiris, Manolis 1883-1962 *Baker 92, OxDcOp*
Kalomodios fl. c. 1200- *OxDcByz*
Kalopheros, John Laskaris c. 1325-1392 *OxDcByz*
Kalos, Malvin Howard 1928- *WhoAm 92*
Kalothetos, Joseph dc. 1355 *OxDcByz*
Kalou, Joeli *WhoAsAP 91*
Kaloudis, George Stergiou 1952- *WhoE 93*
Kalous, Vratislav 1935- *WhoScE 91-4*
Kaloustian, Chahe Khatcher 1945- *WhoWor 93*
Kaloustian, David Joel Levon 1960- *WhoWor 93*
Kalow, Werner 1917- *WhoAm 92*
Kaloyanides, Michael George 1950- *WhoEmL 93*
Kaloyanova-Simeonova, Fina Petrova 1926- *WhoScE 91-4*
Kalpage, Stanley 1925- *WhoUN 92, WhoWor 93*
Kalpakian, Laura Anne 1945- *WhoWrEP 92*
Kalpokas, Donald 1943- *WhoAsAP 91*
Kalra, Anil 1951- *WhoWor 93*
Kalsi, Swadesh S. *Law&B 92*
Kalsner, Stanley 1936- *WhoAm 92, WhoE 93*
Kalsow, Carolyn Marie 1943- *WhoE 93*
Kalsow, Kathryn Ellen 1938- *WhoAmW 93*
Kalstrup, P.R. 1934- *St&PR 93*
Kalt, Howard Michael 1943- *WhoAm 92*
Kalt, Kathy Andrew 1950- *St&PR 93*
Kalt, Marvin Robert 1945- *WhoAm 92*
Kaltenbach, Frederick Wilhelm 1895-1945? *BioIn 17*
Kaltenbach, Hubert Leonard 1922- *WhoAm 92*
Kaltenbach, Jane Couffer 1922- *WhoE 93*
Kaltenbach, Shirley Jean 1948- *WhoAmW 93, WhoEmL 93*
Kaltenbacher, Philip D. *Law&B 92*
Kaltenbacher, Philip David 1937- *St&PR 93, WhoAm 92*
Kaltenborn, Hans Von 1878-1965 *JrnUS*
Kaltenborn, Rolf 1915- *WhoSSW 93*
Kalter, Alan *WhoAm 92*
Kalter, Edmond Morey 1950- *WhoAm 92*
Kalter, Sabine 1889-1957 *Baker 92*
Kalter, Seymour Sanford 1918- *WhoAm 92*
Kalthoff, Jorg F. 1940- *WhoScE 91-3*
Kalthoff, Klaus Otto 1941- *WhoAm 92*
Kaltinick, Paul R. 1932- *WhoAm 92*
Kaltman, Eric 1942- *St&PR 93*
Kaltman, Florence D. *St&PR 93*
Kaltofen, Erich 1955- *WhoE 93*
Kalton, Graham 1936- *WhoAm 92*
Kalton, Robert Rankin 1920- *WhoAm 92*
Kaltsos, Angelo John 1930- *WhoE 93, WhoWor 93*
Kaludis, George 1938- *WhoAm 92*
Kalugin, Lloyd 1926- *WhoE 93*
Kalugin, Oleg *BioIn 17*
Kalupa, Frank B. 1935- *WhoSSW 93*
Kalus, Susan Lynn 1958- *WhoEmL 93*
Kalushev, George Ivanov 1944- *WhoWor 93*
Kalussowski, Henryk Korwin 1806-1894 *PolBiDi*
Kaluszka, Marek 1959- *WhoWor 93*
Kaluza, William J. *Law&B 92*
Kaluza, William J. 1954- *St&PR 93*
Kalvala, Prabhakar Rao 1938- *WhoAsAP 91*
Kalvaria, Leon 1958- *WhoAm 92*
Kalver, Gail Ellen 1948- *WhoAm 92*
Kalvius, Georg Michael 1933- *WhoScE 91-3*
Kalvoda, Robert 1926- *WhoScE 91-4*
Kalvviotis-Gazelas, Cl. *WhoScE 91-3*
Kalwajtys, Ronald R. 1938- *St&PR 93*
Kalwinsky, Charles Knowlton 1946- *WhoAm 92*
Kalyabin, Gennadiy Anatolievich 1947- *WhoWor 93*
Kalyanpur, Manohar Gopal *WhoWor 93*
Kalyn, Wayne *BioIn 17*
Kam, Denis C.H. 1935- *St&PR 93*
Kam, Lydia B. 1952- *WhoIns 93*
Kama, Pierre Babacar 1942- *WhoWor 93*
Kamada, Kaname 1921- *WhoAsAP 91*
Kamada, Noriyuki 1940- *WhoWor 93*
Kamai, Gordon M. *Law&B 92*
Kamakahi, Jeffrey J(on) 1960- *ConAu 139*
Kamal, Ahmad 1938- *WhoUN 92*
Kamal, Aroona Mian 1954- *WhoWor 93*
Kamal Al-Din *OxDcByz*
Kamali, Norma 1945- *WhoAm 92, WhoAmW 93*
Kaman, Charles Huron 1919- *St&PR 93, WhoE 93*
Kaman, Robert Lawrence 1941- *WhoSSW 93*
Kamana, Dunstan Weston 1937- *WhoAfr*
Kamara, Abu Bakr 1929- *WhoAfr*
Kamara, Joseph Andrew 1945- *WhoUN 92*
Kamaras, Katalin 1953- *WhoWor 93*
Kamarck, Lawrence 1927- *ScF&FL 92*
Kamarck, Lawrence Norbert 1927- *WhoE 93*
Kamarinos, Georges 1940- *WhoScE 91-2*
Kamariotes, Matthew d1490 *OxDcByz*
Kamateros *OxDcByz*
Kamateros, John fl. 12th cent.- *OxDcByz*
Kamath, Padmanabh Manjunath 1937- *WhoWor 93*
Kamatoy, Lourdes Aguas 1945- *WhoAmW 93, WhoWor 93*
Kamb, Walter Barclay 1931- *WhoAm 92*
Kambara, George Kiyoshi 1916- *WhoAm 92*
Kamber, Victor Samuel 1944- *WhoAm 92*
Kamberg, Kenneth Edward 1915- *St&PR 93*
Kamble, Arvind Kamble 1952- *WhoAsAP 91*
Kambour, Roger Peabody 1932- *WhoAm 92*
Kambourian, James Stewart 1944- *WhoSSW 93*
Kamdar, Raj N. 1946- *St&PR 93*
Kameda, Masumi 1957- *WhoWor 93*
Kameen, John Paul 1941- *WhoE 93*
Kameese, Suzanne C. 1952- *St&PR 93*
Kamei, Hisaoki 1939- *WhoAsAP 91*
Kamei, Shizuka 1933- *WhoAsAP 91*
Kamei, Yoshiyuki 1936- *WhoAsAP 91*
Kamejima, Kohji 1949- *WhoWor 93*
Kamel, Wafa I. 1940- *WhoUN 92*
Kamemoto, Fred Isamu 1928- *WhoAm 92*
Kamemoto, Haruyuki 1922- *WhoAm 92*
Kamen, D. Jonathan 1953- *WhoEmL 93*
Kamen, Gary Paul *WhoE 93*
Kamen, Harry P. *Law&B 92*
Kamen, Harry P. 1933- *St&PR 93*
Kamen, Harry Paul 1933- *WhoAm 92*
Kamen, Jay 1953- *MiSFD 9*
Kamen, Madelyn Jean 1942- *WhoAmW 93, WhoSSW 93*
Kamen, Martin David 1913- *WhoAm 92*
Kamen, Milton 1921- *WhoE 93*
Kamen, Paula 1967- *ConAu 137*
Kamenar, Boris 1929- *WhoScE 91-4*
Kamenear, Elliot B. *Law&B 92*
Kamenetz, Rodger Lee 1950- *WhoWrEP 92*
Kamenetzky, Ricardo Daniel 1954- *WhoEmL 93*
Kamenev, Lev Borisovich 1883-1936 *DcTwHis*
Kamenka, Hippolyte 1897-1990 *BioIn 17*
Kamen-Kaye, Maurice 1905- *WhoE 93*
Kamenos, Olivia Andrew 1950- *WhoAmW 93*
Kamenske, Bernard Harold 1927- *WhoAm 92*
Kamensky, Alexander 1900-1952 *Baker 92*
Kamentsky, Louis Aaron 1930- *WhoAm 92*
Kameny, Nat 1923- *WhoE 93*
Kamer, Joel Victor 1942- *St&PR 93, WhoAm 92*
Kameras, David Howard 1952- *WhoE 93*
Kamerer, Bruce Edward *Law&B 92*
Kamerick, Eileen A. *Law&B 92*
Kamerman, Jack B. 1940- *WhoE 93*
Kamerman, Sheila Brody 1928- *WhoAm 92, WhoAmW 93*
Kamerow, Martin Laurence 1931- *WhoAm 92*
Kamerschen, David Roy 1937- *WhoAm 92*
Kamerschen, Karen Sue 1943- *WhoAmW 93, WhoSSW 93*
Kamerschen, Robert Jerome 1936- *WhoAm 92*
Kames, Henry Home 1696-1782 *BioIn 17*
Kames, Kenneth F. 1935- *St&PR 93, WhoAm 92*
Kamesar, Daniel I. d1990 *BioIn 17*
Kametani, Hideki 1951- *WhoWor 93*
Kametches, Chris L. 1935- *St&PR 93*
Kam Foon Wing 1939- *WhoWor 93*
Kamhi, Samuel Vitali 1922- *WhoWor 93*
Kamholz, Stephan L. 1947- *WhoAm 92*
Kami, Michael John 1922- *St&PR 93*
Kamide, Kenji 1934- *WhoWor 93*
Kamiel, Max d1990 *BioIn 17*
Kamien, Marcia 1940- *WhoWrEP 92*
Kamienski, Linda Ciccarelli 1960- *WhoAmW 93*
Kamienski, Lucian 1885-1964 *Baker 92*
Kamienski, Lucjan 1885-1964 *PolBiDi*
Kamienski, Maciej 1734-1821 *Baker 92, OxDcOp, PolBiDi*
Kamii, Constance Kazuko 1931- *WhoAmW 93*
Kamijo, Fumihiko 1934- *WhoWor 93*
Kamikamica, Josevata Nakausabaria 1934- *WhoAsAP 91*
Kamikawa, Alden Tanemitsu 1940- *WhoE 93*
Kamil, Harvey 1944- *St&PR 93*
Kamil, Mohammed Abdallah 1936- *WhoAfr*
Kamimura, Hikonojo 1849-1916 *HarEnMi*
Kamin, Amy Rose 1960- *WhoE 93*
Kamin, Ben *BioIn 17*
Kamin, Benjamin Alon 1953- *WhoAm 92*
Kamin, Chester Thomas 1940- *WhoAm 92*
Kamin, Robert Jay 1933- *St&PR 93*
Kamin, Sherwin 1927- *WhoAm 92*
Kamineni, Pitcheswara Rao 1953- *WhoWor 93*
Kaminer, Benjamin 1924- *WhoAm 92*
Kaminer, Debbie Nadine *Law&B 92*
Kaminer, Peter H. 1915- *WhoAm 92*
Kaminetzky, Harold Alexander 1923- *WhoAm 92*
Kaminiates, John *OxDcByz*
Kaminker, Paul Andre 1933- *WhoE 93*
Kaminow, Ira Paul 1940- *St&PR 93*
Kaminow, Ivan Paul 1930- *WhoAm 92*
Kamins, Barry Michael 1943- *WhoE 93*
Kamins, Bruce *Law&B 92*
Kaminska, Alina 1929- *WhoScE 91-4*
Kaminska, Esther R. 1868-1925 *PolBiDi*
Kaminska, Ida 1899-1980 *PolBiDi*
Kaminski, Abraham Isaac 1867-1918 *PolBiDi*
Kaminski, Andre 1923-1991 *BioIn 17*
Kaminski, Andrzej 1946- *WhoWor 93*
Kaminski, David L. *Law&B 92*
Kaminski, Donald Leon 1940- *WhoAm 92*
Kaminski, Eugeniusz 1923- *WhoScE 91-4*
Kaminski, Eva M.C. *Law&B 92*
Kaminski, Gerhard 1925- *WhoWor 93*
Kaminski, Heinrich 1886-1946 *Baker 92*
Kaminski, Joanne 1961- *WhoEmL 93*
Kaminski, John *WhoAm 92*
Kaminski, Joseph 1903-1972 *Baker 92*
Kaminski, Joseph C. 1943- *WhoIns 93*
Kaminski, Julian 1929- *WhoScE 91-4*
Kaminski, Lech M. 1931- *WhoScE 91-4*
Kaminski, Linda J. 1950- *WhoE 93*
Kaminski, Raymond *ScF&FL 92*
Kaminski, Robert Stanley 1936- *St&PR 93*
Kaminski, Wieslaw Andrzej 1949- *WhoWor 93*
Kaminski, Wlodzimierz 1924- *WhoScE 91-4*
Kaminsky, Alice R. *WhoWrEP 92*
Kaminsky, Alice Richkin *WhoAm 92*
Kaminsky, Allan L. *St&PR 93*
Kaminsky, Arthur Charles 1946- *WhoAm 92*
Kaminsky, George 1906-1991 *BioIn 17*
Kaminsky, Gerhard 1919- *WhoScE 91-3*
Kaminsky, Howard 1940- *ScF&FL 92, WhoAm 92*
Kaminsky, Joan Conn 1946- *WhoAmW 93*
Kaminsky, John R. *Law&B 92*
Kaminsky, Judith Gerson 1942- *WhoAmW 93, WhoSSW 93*
Kaminsky, Larry E. 1938- *St&PR 93*
Kaminsky, Larry Michael *Law&B 92*
Kaminsky, Laura 1956- *WhoAmW 93, WhoEmL 93*
Kaminsky, Manfred Stephan 1929- *WhoAm 92*
Kaminsky, Marc 1943- *WhoWrEP 92*
Kaminsky, Nancy Fran 1959- *St&PR 93*
Kaminsky, Peter *Law&B 92*
Kaminsky, Ray 1950- *St&PR 93*
Kaminsky, Richard Alan 1951- *WhoEmL 93*
Kaminsky, Seth 1940- *St&PR 93*
Kaminsky, Susan Stanwood *ScF&FL 92*
Kaminsky, Walter 1941- *WhoScE 91-3*
Kaminsky, Yury George 1938- *WhoWor 93*
Kaminstein, Philip 1928- *WhoE 93*
Kamionsky, Oscar (Isaievich) 1869-1917 *Baker 92*
Kamis, Edward Joseph 1927- *WhoE 93*
Kamisar, Jonathan R. *Law&B 92*
Kamisar, Sandra Lee 1937- *WhoAmW 93*
Kamisar, Yale 1929- *WhoAm 92, WhoWor 93*
Kamitani, Shinnosuke 1924- *WhoAsAP 91*
Kamitses, Zoe 1941- *ScF&FL 92*
Kamitses, Zoe Karen 1941- *WhoAmW 93*
Kamiya, Fuji 1927- *WhoWor 93*
Kamiya, Noriaki 1948- *WhoWor 93*
Kamke, Paul Burton 1959- *WhoE 93*
Kamlani, Deirdre Shay 1959- *WhoWor 93*
Kamler, Frantisek 1948- *WhoScE 91-4*
Kamlet, Barbara Lynn 1949- *WhoEmL 93*
Kamlot, Robert 1926- *WhoAm 92*
Kamm, Ervin *St&PR 93*
Kamm, Henry 1925- *WhoAm 92*
Kamm, Herbert 1917- *WhoAm 92*
Kamm, Jacob Oswald 1918- *WhoAm 92, WhoWor 93*
Kamm, Kris *BioIn 17*
Kamm, Laurence Richard 1939- *WhoAm 92*
Kamm, Linda Heller 1939- *WhoAm 92*
Kamm, Peter 1957- *BioIn 17*
Kamm, Robert B. 1919- *WhoAm 92*
Kamm, Robert E. *Law&B 92*
Kamm, Roger Dale 1950- *WhoE 93*
Kamm, Thomas Allen 1925- *WhoAm 92*
Kamm, William Edward 1900-1988 *BiDAMSp 1989*
Kamma, F.C. 1906-1987 *IntDcAn*
Kamman, Alan Bertram 1931- *WhoAm 92, WhoWor 93*
Kamman, Curtis Warren 1939- *WhoAm 92, WhoWor 93*
Kamman, William 1930- *WhoAm 92*
Kammasch, Gudrun 1942- *WhoWor 93*
Kammeier, Frederick A. 1936- *St&PR 93*
Kammen, Michael 1936- *WhoAm 92*
Kammen, Michael G. *BioIn 17*
Kammer, Harry Samuel 1954- *St&PR 93*
Kammer, Max L. 1920- *St&PR 93*
Kammer, Raymond Gerard, Jr. 1947- *WhoAm 92*

Kammer, Robert A. *Law&B 92*
Kammer, Roselyn 1921- *St&PR 93*
Kammerer, Edward H. *Law&B 92*
Kammerer, G. *WhoScE 91-3*
Kammerer, Harry S. 1951- *St&PR 93*
Kammerer, John A. 1942- *St&PR 93*
Kammerer, Richard Craig 1943- *WhoAm 92*
Kammerer, Stephen P. 1946- *St&PR 93*
Kammerer, William G. 1950- *St&PR 93*
Kammerer, William Henry 1912- *WhoAm 92*
Kammerman, Arthur C. 1915- *St&PR 93*
Kammerman, Arthur Charles Cyril 1915- *WhoE 93*
Kammermeier, Helmut Karl 1932- *WhoScE 91-3*
Kammeyer, Sonia Margaretha 1942- *WhoAmW 93*
Kammholz, Theophil C. d1992 *NewYTBS 92*
Kammholz, Theophil Carl 1909- *WhoAm 92*
Kammlade, William Garfield 1892-1988 *BioIn 17*
Kammueller, Reiner 1931- *WhoScE 91-3*
Kamnikar, Michael A. 1951- *St&PR 93*
Kamod, Paul 1939- *WhoAsAP 91*
Kamoen, Oswald A.F.R. 1932- *WhoScE 91-2*
Kamogawa, Hiroshi 1913- *WhoWor 93*
Kamon, Effie H. 1925- *St&PR 93*
Kamon, Robert B. 1927- *St&PR 93*
Kamoun, Pierre 1936- *WhoScE 91-2*
Kamowitz, Herbert Meyer 1931- *WhoE 93*
Kamp, Caspar Jan 1936- *WhoUN 92*
Kamp, George Hamil 1934- *WhoSSW 93*
Kamp, Martin Werner 1959- *WhoWor 93*
Kamp, Reiner 1958- *St&PR 93*
Kamp, Ronald Carl *Law&B 92*
Kamp, Thomas G. 1925- *St&PR 93*
Kampa, Mary Frances *Law&B 92*
Kampe, Lawrence 1935- *St&PR 93*
Kampelmacher, Erwin H. 1920- *WhoScE 91-3*
Kampelman, Max M. 1920- *BioIn 17, WhoAm 92, WhoWor 93*
Kampen, Emerson *BioIn 17*
Kampen, Emerson 1928- *St&PR 93, WhoAm 92*
Kamper-Jorgensen, Finn *WhoScE 91-2*
Kampf, Cindy Alise 1961- *WhoE 93, WhoEmL 93*
Kampf, Joel *St&PR 93*
Kampf, Karl 1874-1950 *Baker 92*
Kampf, Philip L. 1931- *St&PR 93*
Kampfer, Thomas *Law&B 92*
Kamph, Patricia Ann 1956- *WhoEmL 93*
Kamphoefner, Walter D. 1948- *ConAu 137*
Kampits, Eva Ida 1946- *WhoAmW 93, WhoE 93*
Kampler, Nina L. *Law&B 92*
Kampmann, Bernhard 1949- *WhoWor 93*
Kampmann, Steven *MiSFD 9*
Kampmeier, Curtis Neil 1941- *WhoWor 93*
Kampmeier, Donald G. 1944- *St&PR 93*
Kampmeier, Jack August 1935- *WhoAm 92*
Kampouris, A. Emmanuel *St&PR 93*
Kampouris, Emmanuel 1928- *WhoScE 91-3*
Kampouris, Emmanuel Andrew 1934- *WhoAm 92, WhoE 93*
Kamran, Abid Adam 1953- *WhoSSW 93*
Kamrath, Bradley Greg, Sr. 1961- *St&PR 93*
Kamrow, Catherine M. *Law&B 92*
Kamrowski, Gerome 1914- *WhoAm 92*
Kamsky, Gata *BioIn 17*
Kamsky, Leonard 1918- *WhoAm 92*
Kamsky, Rustam *BioIn 17*
Kamson, Mei-Jin-Lung 1939- *WhoAsAP 91*
Kamsteeg, Arie 1940- *WhoWor 93*
Kamstra, Garrett Allen 1954- *St&PR 93*
Kamu, Okko (Tapani) 1946- *Baker 92*
Kamuda, Karen Bilsbury 1939- *WhoE 93*
Kamunanwire, Perezi Karukubiro 1937- *WhoUN 92*
Kamuri, Rose T. *St&PR 93*
Kamykowski, Daniel Louis 1945- *WhoSSW 93*
Kamytzes *OxDcByz*
Kamzan, Stephen 1949- *St&PR 93*
Kan, Diana Artemis Mann Shu 1926- *WhoAm 92, WhoWor 93*
Kan, Kit-Keung 1943- *WhoSSW 93*
Kan, Lydia A. 1962- *WhoEmL 93*
Kan, Michael 1933- *WhoAm 92*
Kan, Naoto 1946- *WhoAsAP 91*
Kan, Paul Man-Lok 1947- *WhoEmL 93, WhoWor 93*
Kan, Sergei 1953- *ConAu 137*
Kan, Yuet Wai 1936- *WhoAm 92*
Kana, Said Mohidine 1936- *WhoWor 93*
Kanaan, George Elias 1946- *WhoWor 93*
Kanaboutzes, John fl. 15th cent.- *OxDcByz*
Kanabus, Henry 1949- *WhoWrEP 92*
Kanaday, Joseph, Jr. 1926- *St&PR 93*
Kanady, Mary Jo *Law&B 92*
Kanagawa, Diane Wiltshire 1955- *WhoWor 93*
Kanagy, James *Law&B 92*
Kanak, April *Law&B 92*
Kanakoudi-Tsakalidou, Florence 1940- *WhoWor 93*
Kanal, Laveen N. 1931- *WhoAm 92*
Kanaly, Steven Francis 1946- *WhoAm 92*
Kanamori, Hiroo 1936- *WhoAm 92*
Kananack, William J. *Law&B 92*
Kananos, John *OxDcByz*
Kananos, Laskaris fl. 15th cent.- *OxDcByz*
Kananowitz, Anna Gilson 1924- *WhoWrEP 92*
Kanapa, Jean 1924-1978 *BioIn 17*
Kanari, Norimichi 1946- *St&PR 93*
Kanaris, Konstantinos 1790-1877 *HarEnMi*
Kanarkowski, Edward Joseph 1947- *WhoAm 92, WhoE 93, WhoEmL 93*
Kanarowski, Stanley Martin 1912- *WhoE 93, WhoWor 93*
Kanary, Richard Lincoln 1934- *St&PR 93*
Kanas, John Adam 1946- *St&PR 93, WhoAm 92*
Kanaseki, Takeo 1897-1983 *IntDcAn*
Kanasewich, Ernest Roman 1931- *WhoAm 92*
Kanavos, Panagiotis Grigoriou 1964- *WhoWor 93*
Kanawa, Kiri Te *OxDcOp*
Kanazir, Dusan 1921- *WhoScE 91-4*
Kanber, Riza 1944- *WhoScE 91-4*
Kanbur, Ravi *WhoScE 91-1*
Kancelbaum, Joshua Jacob 1936- *WhoAm 92*
Kancheli, Giya (Alexandrovich) 1935- *Baker 92*
Kanchev, L.N. 1936- *WhoScE 91-4*
Kanchi, Rama Moorthy Venkata 1937- *WhoUN 92*
Kanda, Atsushi 1941- *WhoAsAP 91*
Kanda, Motohisa 1943- *WhoAm 92*
Kanda, Seiichi 1927- *WhoWor 93*
Kandalaft, Marlene Mary 1952- *St&PR 93*
Kandall, Richard D. *St&PR 93*
Kandaras, Homer Michael 1929- *WhoAm 92*
Kandasamy, Sallepan 1943- *WhoUN 92*
Kandel, A.M. 1949- *St&PR 93*
Kandel, Christopher Nelson 1960- *WhoWor 93*
Kandel, Denise Bystryn 1933- *WhoAmW 93*
Kandel, Michael 1941- *ScF&FL 92*
Kandel, Nelson Robert 1929- *WhoE 93, WhoWor 93*
Kandel, Paul David 1944- *WhoE 93*
Kandel, Sue Ellen 1951- *WhoAmW 93*
Kandel, William Lloyd 1939- *WhoAm 92*
Kandeler, Riklef 1927- *WhoScE 91-4*
Kandell, Leonard S. d1992 *BioIn 17*
Kander, John (Harold) 1927- *Baker 92, WhoAm 92, WhoE 93*
Kander, Nadav *BioIn 17*
Kandhal, Prithvi Singh 1935- *WhoSSW 93*
Kandiah, Gunaratnam 1941- *WhoWor 93*
Kandidos fl. 5th cent.-6th cent. *OxDcByz*
Kandinsky, Wassily 1866-1944 *BioIn 17*
Kandl, Mark David Dorn 1968- *WhoE 93*
Kandler, Joseph Rudolph 1921- *WhoWor 93*
Kandor, Joseph Robert 1960- *WhoE 93*
Kandra, Gyorgy *WhoScE 91-4*
Kandravy, John 1935- *WhoE 93*
Kandutsch, Andrew August 1926- *WhoE 93*
Kane, Agnes Brezak 1946- *WhoEmL 93*
Kane, Alex *ScF&FL 92*
Kane, Alice *Law&B 92*
Kane, Alice T. 1948- *WhoIns 93*
Kane, Alice Theresa 1948- *St&PR 93, WhoAm 92*
Kane, Amanda Bryan d1990 *BioIn 17*
Kane, Art 1925- *WhoAm 92*
Kane, Barbara Stewart *Law&B 92*
Kane, Bartholomew Aloysius 1945- *WhoAm 92*
Kane, Big Daddy *BioIn 17*
Kane, Carol 1952- *BioIn 17, WhoAm 92, WhoAmW 93*
Kane, Carolyn 1944- *WhoAmW 93*
Kane, Cecelia Drapeau 1915- *WhoAmW 93*
Kane, Charles Fairweather, Jr. 1950- *WhoE 93*
Kane, Daniel 1915- *St&PR 93*
Kane, Daniel 1957- *ScF&FL 92*
Kane, Daniel Hipwell 1908- *WhoAm 92*
Kane, Daniel Patrick 1957- *WhoSSW 93*
Kane, David C. 1949- *St&PR 93*
Kane, David Edward 1952- *St&PR 93*
Kane, David N. 1945- *St&PR 93, WhoIns 93*
Kane, Donald Barrett 1932- *St&PR 93*
Kane, E. Leonard 1929- *St&PR 93*
Kane, Edward J. 1930- *St&PR 93*
Kane, Edward James 1935- *WhoAm 92*
Kane, Edward Joseph 1951- *WhoEmL 93*
Kane, Edward K. 1929- *St&PR 93*
Kane, Edward Konrad *Law&B 92*
Kane, Edward Leonard 1929- *WhoAm 92*
Kane, Edward Robert Michael 1929- *WhoWor 93*
Kane, Edward Rynex 1918- *WhoAm 92*
Kane, Elizabeth 1942- *ConAu 136*
Kane, Frank H. *Law&B 92*
Kane, Frederick E. 1958- *St&PR 93*
Kane, Gary Allen 1936- *St&PR 93*
Kane, Geoffrey Peter 1944- *WhoE 93*
Kane, George 1943- *St&PR 93*
Kane, George Joseph 1916- *WhoAm 92*
Kane, Gil 1926- *ScF&FL 92*
Kane, Gordon Philo 1925- *WhoSSW 93*
Kane, Harry Joseph 1923- *WhoAm 92*
Kane, Helen Pooke 1851- *AmWomPl*
Kane, Herman William 1939- *WhoAm 92*
Kane, Howard Edward 1927- *WhoAm 92*
Kane, Howard Jay 1947- *WhoE 93, WhoEmL 93*
Kane, Ira Owen 1946- *St&PR 93*
Kane, Jack Allison 1921- *WhoWor 93*
Kane, Jacqueline Jones 1917- *WhoE 93*
Kane, James G. 1926- *St&PR 93*
Kane, James Golden 1926- *WhoAm 92*
Kane, James T. *Law&B 92*
Kane, Jay Brassler 1931- *WhoAm 92, WhoE 93*
Kane, Jeffrey 1952- *WhoE 93*
Kane, Jeffrey W. *Law&B 92*
Kane, Jerry Robert 1941- *St&PR 93*
Kane, John Dandridge Henley, Jr. 1921- *WhoAm 92*
Kane, John F. *Law&B 92*
Kane, John William, Jr. *Law&B 92*
Kane, Joseph Charles 1935- *WhoAm 92, WhoE 93*
Kane, Joseph Thomas *Law&B 92*
Kane, Joseph Thomas 1933- *St&PR 93*
Kane, Julia Kim *Law&B 92*
Kane, Julie M. *Law&B 92*
Kane, Karen A. *Law&B 92*
Kane, Kathleen Elizabeth 1961- *WhoEmL 93*
Kane, Larry d1991 *BioIn 17*
Kane, Louis Isaac 1931- *WhoAm 92*
Kane, Lucile Marie 1920- *WhoAm 92*
Kane, Manuel Edward 1920- *St&PR 93*
Kane, Marcia Susan 1959- *WhoE 93*
Kane, Margaret Brassler 1909- *WhoAm 92, WhoAmW 93, WhoE 93, WhoWor 93*
Kane, Marilyn Elizabeth 1941- *WhoAmW 93*
Kane, Maryanne *BioIn 17*
Kane, Matthew A., Jr. *Law&B 92*
Kane, Melissa 1957- *WhoEmL 93*
Kane, Michael E. *St&PR 93*
Kane, Michael Joel 1951- *WhoE 93*
Kane, Michele C. *Law&B 92*
Kane, Norman A. 1947- *St&PR 93*
Kane, Pamela 1946- *WhoAmW 93*
Kane, Patricia 1955- *WhoWrEP 92*
Kane, Patricia A. *Law&B 92*
Kane, Patricia Lanegran 1926- *WhoAm 92*
Kane, Peter 1918-1991 *AnObit 1991*
Kane, Peter Gerard 1962- *WhoE 93*
Kane, Peter Harold *Law&B 92*
Kane, Racquel E. 1929- *St&PR 93*
Kane, Racquel Elona 1932- *WhoE 93, WhoWor 93*
Kane, Richard 1928- *WhoAm 92*
Kane, Richard Stephen 1937- *St&PR 93*
Kane, Robert B. 1940- *St&PR 93*
Kane, Robert Francis 1926- *WhoAm 92*
Kane, Robert J. d1992 *NewYTBS 92*
Kane, Robert Joseph 1912-1992 *BioIn 17*
Kane, Robert Louis 1940- *WhoAm 92*
Kane, Ronald 1944- *WhoAm 92*
Kane, Sam 1919- *WhoWor 93*
Kane, Stanley B. 1920- *St&PR 93*
Kane, Stanley Bruce 1920- *WhoAm 92, WhoE 93*
Kane, Stanley Phillip 1930- *WhoAm 92*
Kane, Stratton J. 1938- *St&PR 93, WhoIns 93*
Kane, Thomas J. 1938- *St&PR 93*
Kane, Thomas Patrick 1942- *WhoAm 92*
Kane, Thomas Reif 1924- *WhoAm 92*
Kane, Walter Reilly 1926- *WhoE 93*
Kane, Warren F. 1923- *St&PR 93*
Kane, William James 1933- *WhoAm 92*
Kane, William L. 1938- *WhoWrEP 92*
Kanefsky, Joel 1947- *St&PR 93*
Kanegsberg, Henry S. 1945- *WhoE 93*
Kanehl, Hot Rod *BioIn 17*
Kaneko, Genjiro 1944- *WhoAsAP 91*
Kaneko, Haruo 1929- *WhoWor 93*
Kaneko, Hisashi 1933- *WhoAm 92*
Kaneko, Kazuyoshi 1942- *WhoAsAP 91*
Kaneko, Masao 1942- *WhoWor 93*
Kaneko, Mitsuharu 1895-1975 *BioIn 17*
Kaneko, Mitsuhiro 1924- *WhoAsAP 91*
Kaneko, Mitsuru *WhoAm 92*
Kaneko, Takasuke 1942- *St&PR 93*
Kaneko, Tokunosuke 1932- *WhoAsAP 91*
Kaneko, Yoshihiro 1922- *WhoWor 93*
Kanelakos, Linda Kay 1945- *WhoAmW 93*
Kanellopoulos, Charalambos Constantinos 1941- *WhoWor 93*
Kanellos, Margaret Carrol 1946- *WhoAmW 93*
Kanellos, Nicolas 1945- *WhoSSW 93*
Kanely, James R. 1941- *St&PR 93*
Kanemaru, Shin *NewYTBS 92*
Kanemaru, Shin 1914- *BioIn 17, WhoAsAP 91*
Kanemaru, Shin 1915- *WhoWor 93*
Kanemitsu, Matsumi 1922- *WhoAm 92*
Kanemitsu, Matsumi 1922-1992 *BioIn 17, NewYTBS 92*
Kanemoto, Erv *BioIn 17*
Kanengiser, Amy D. *Law&B 92*
Kaner, H. d1970? *ScF&FL 92*
Kaner, Harvey *Law&B 92*
Kaner, Harvey Sheldon 1930- *St&PR 93, WhoAm 92*
Kanerva, Pekka 1939- *WhoScE 91-4*
Kanerviko, Arthur W., Jr. *Law&B 92*
Kanes, Karen L. 1962- *WhoAmW 93*
Kanesa-Thasan, Saravanamuttu 1928- *WhoUN 92*
Kanet, Roger Edward 1936- *WhoAm 92*
Kaneta, Kiyoshi 1930- *WhoWor 93*
Kaneta, Sidney 1945- *St&PR 93*
Kanev, Dinyo Dimitrov 1922- *WhoScE 91-4*
Kanev, Stefan *WhoScE 91-4*
Kane-Vanni, Patricia Ruth *Law&B 92*
Kane-Vanni, Patricia Ruth 1954- *WhoAmW 93*
Kanevski, Vitali 1937- *BioIn 17*
Kanew, Jeff *MiSFD 9*
Kanfer, Frederick H. *WhoAm 92*
Kanfer, Julian Norman 1930- *WhoAm 92*
Kanfer, Ruth *BioIn 17*
Kanfer, Ruth 1955- *WhoEmL 93*
Kanfer, Stefan *BioIn 17*
Kang, Bann C. 1939- *WhoAmW 93*
Kang, Bin Goo 1936- *WhoWor 93*
Kang, Edward Paotai 1942- *WhoE 93, WhoWor 93*
Kang, Ho Ryun d1990 *BioIn 17*
Kang, Ji Ding 1935- *WhoWor 93*
Kang, Joong-Woong 1948- *WhoWor 93*
Kang, Juliana Haeng-Cha 1941- *WhoAmW 93*
Kang, Jung Il 1942- *WhoWor 93*
Kang, Kyoung Sook 1942- *WhoAmW 93*
Kang, Kyungsik 1936- *WhoAm 92*
Kang, Ming-Chang 1948- *WhoWor 93*
Kang, Pongshik 1923- *WhoWor 93*
Kang, Seong-Mo 1946- *WhoWor 93*
Kang, Shin Il 1955- *WhoWor 93*
Kang, Sukhi 1934- *Baker 92*
Kang, Sung Kyew 1941- *WhoWor 93*
Kang, Sung-Mo 1945- *WhoAm 92*
Kang, Yoon-Se 1934- *WhoWor 93*
Kang, Young-Hee 1930- *WhoWor 93*
Kanga, Firdaus *BioIn 17*
Kangas, James Richard 1944- *WhoWrEP 92*
Kangas, Jukka A. 1946- *WhoScE 91-4*
Kangas, Julie Elizabeth 1956- *WhoAmW 93*
Kangas, Ronald Clinton 1941- *St&PR 93*
Kang Bo Seung 1931- *WhoAsAP 91*
K'ang-Hsi 1654-1722 *HarEnMi*
Kangilaski, Jaan 1936- *ScF&FL 92*
Kang Jae Sup 1948- *WhoAsAP 91*
Kang Keqing 1911-1992 *BioIn 17, NewYTBS 92*
Kang Kum Sik 1942- *WhoAsAP 91*
Kangles, Nick J. *Law&B 92*
Kang Sam Jae 1953- *WhoAsAP 91*
Kang Sheng 1899-1975 *BioIn 17*
Kang Sin Ok 1937- *WhoAsAP 91*
Kang Sung Mo 1934- *WhoAsAP 91*
Kangwarnjit, Suchart 1953- *WhoWor 93*
Kang Woo Hyuk 1939- *WhoAsAP 91*
Kang Young Hoon, His Excellency 1922- *WhoAsAP 91*
Kani, Takeo 1932- *St&PR 93, WhoWor 93*
Kania, Antoinette Mary 1943- *WhoE 93*
Kania, Edwin M. 1927- *St&PR 93*
Kanian, Mark A. *Law&B 92*
Kaniaru, Donald W. 1942- *WhoUN 92*
Kanick, Robert W. 1962- *St&PR 93*
Kanick, Virginia 1925- *WhoAmW 93*
Kanidinc, Salahattin 1927- *WhoAm 92*
Kaniecki, Michael Joseph 1935- *WhoAm 92*
Kaniecki, Thaddeus John 1931- *WhoE 93*
Kanievska, Marek *MiSFD 9*
Kaniewska, Irena 1914-1963 *PolBiDi*
Kanigan, William S. 1944- *St&PR 93*
Kanigel, Robert 1946- *WhoWrEP 92*
Kanigel, Robert Joseph 1946- *WhoEmL 93*
Kanin, Dennis Roy 1946- *WhoAm 92*
Kanin, Fay *WhoAm 92*

Kanin, Garson 1912- *BioIn 17, MiSFD 9, WhoAm 92*
Kanin, Kotoshito 1865-1945 *HarEnMi*
Kanipe, Gary R. *St&PR 93*
Kanis, Frank H. 1911- *St&PR 93*
Kanitz, Ernest 1894-1978 *Baker 92*
Kanitz, Terry Wayne 1941- *St&PR 93*
Kanjanapas, Mongkul *BioIn 17*
Kanjana-Vanit, Rachan 1921- *WhoWor 93*
Kanjani, Mulchand Assandas 1937- *WhoWor 93*
Kanji, Abe 1939- *WhoWor 93*
Kanji, Gopal Kishore *WhoScE 91-1*
Kanjorski, Paul E. 1937- *CngDr 91*
Kanjorski, Paul Edmund 1937- *WhoAm 92, WhoE 93*
Kanka, Allena *AmWomPl*
Kankare, Esko *WhoScE 91-4*
Kankare, Jouko Juhani 1940- *WhoScE 91-4*
Kankel, Keith Victor 1942- *St&PR 93*
Kann, Hans 1927- *Baker 92*
Kann, Peter R. *BioIn 17, St&PR 93*
Kann, Peter Robert 1942- *WhoAm 92, WhoE 93*
Kannabos, Nicholas *OxDcByz*
Kanne, Friedrich August 1778-1833 *OxDcOp*
Kanne, Gerald M. 1930- *St&PR 93*
Kanne, Marvin George 1937- *St&PR 93*
Kanne, Michael Stephen 1938- *WhoAm 92*
Kannel, William Bernard 1923- *WhoAm 92, WhoE 93*
Kannenberg, Mark E. 1947- *St&PR 93*
Kannengiesser, Charles A. 1926- *WhoAm 92*
Kanner, Abraham Pascal 1911- *St&PR 93*
Kanner, Alexis 1952- *MiSFD 9*
Kanner, Allan *BioIn 17*
Kanner, Bernice *BioIn 17*
Kanner, Brian G. *Law&B 92*
Kanner, Edwin B. 1922- *St&PR 93*
Kanner, Ellen 1961- *WhoEmL 93*
Kanner, Ellen Barbara 1950- *WhoEmL 93*
Kanner, Helena Levine 1953- *WhoIns 93*
Kanner, Jerome Herbert 1903- *Baker 92*
Kanner, Lawrence Theodore 1929- *WhoE 93*
Kanner, Leo 1894-1981 *BioIn 17*
Kanner, Robert Howard 1947- *St&PR 93*
Kanner-Rosenthal, Hedwig 1882-1959 *Baker 92*
Kanninen, Markku 1952- *WhoScE 91-4*
Kanninen, Melvin Fred 1935- *WhoAm 92*
Kanning, Christopher James 1965- *WhoSSW 93*
Kanno, Hisashi 1923- *WhoAsAP 91*
Kannry, Sybil 1931- *WhoAmW 93, WhoE 93*
Kano, Akio 1934- *WhoAsAP 91*
Kano, Hiroshi 1934- *WhoWor 93*
Kano, Masaru 1935- *WhoAsAP 91*
Kano, Michihiko 1942- *WhoAsAP 91*
Kano, Noriaki 1940- *WhoWor 93*
Kano, Susan Leslie 1959- *WhoWrEP 92*
Kanode, Delno G. *Law&B 92*
Kanofsky, Alvin Sheldon 1939- *WhoAm 92, WhoE 93*
Kanofsky, Jacob Daniel 1948- *WhoEmL 93, WhoWor 93*
Kanofsky, Myron Ross 1952- *WhoEmL 93*
Kanon, Joseph A. 1946- *St&PR 93*
Kanorr, Russell Daniel 1956- *WhoSSW 93*
Kanost, Harold Sheldon 1934- *WhoWor 93*
Kanouse, Thomas John 1936- *St&PR 93*
Kanovei, Vladimir Grigorievitch 1951- *WhoWor 93*
Kanovitz, Howard 1929- *WhoAm 92, WhoE 93*
Kanovsky, Helen R. *Law&B 92*
Kanovsky, Sharon Rachel 1964- *WhoAmW 93*
Kanowski, Siegfried *WhoScE 91-3*
Kansakar, Sunil Ratna 1960- *WhoWor 93*
Kansala, Kari A. 1948- *WhoScE 91-4*
Kansanen, Pekka Heikki 1949- *WhoScE 91-4*
Kansara, Suryakant Ratilal *WhoWor 93*
Kansky, Lawrence Joseph, Jr. 1957- *WhoE 93*
Kansu, Sevket Aziz 1903-1983 *IntDcAn*
Kant, Douglas *Law&B 92*
Kant, Gloria Jean 1944- *WhoAm 92*
Kant, Immanuel 1724-1804 *BioIn 17*
Kant, Kenneth James 1935- *WhoSSW 93*
Kant, Krishan 1927- *WhoAsAP 91*
Kantabutra, Bundhit 1916- *WhoWor 93*
Kantakouzenos *OxDcByz*
Kanten, Mary Jean 1953- *WhoAmW 93*
Kanter, Alla 1957- *St&PR 93*
Kanter, Ann Rawson 1938- *WhoE 93*
Kanter, Arnold Lee 1945- *WhoAm 92*
Kanter, Benny *Law&B 92*
Kanter, Bonnie M. *Law&B 92*
Kanter, Carl Irwin 1932- *St&PR 93, WhoAm 92*
Kanter, Donald Richard 1951- *WhoWor 93*
Kanter, Gerald Alan 1931- *St&PR 93*
Kanter, Gerald Leonard 1935- *WhoAm 92*
Kanter, Hal 1918- *MiSFD 9, WhoAm 92*
Kanter, Irving 1924- *WhoAm 92*
Kanter, James I. 1920- *St&PR 93*
Kanter, Jay Ira 1926- *WhoAm 92*
Kanter, Joel Stephen 1956- *WhoEmL 93*
Kanter, Joseph Hyman 1923- *WhoAm 92*
Kanter, Kenneth R. 1935- *WhoE 93*
Kanter, Lorna Joan 1931- *WhoE 93*
Kanter, Rosabeth Moss 1943- *WhoAm 92, WhoAmW 93*
Kanthal, Jeffrey Michael 1946- *WhoE 93*
Kanthamneni, Sudhakar 1947- *St&PR 93*
Kanthasamy, K. 1930-1988 *BioIn 17*
Kanthasamy, Kandiah 1930-1988 *BioIn 17*
Kantner, Paul 1941- *WhoAm 92*
Kantner, Paul 1942- *Baker 92*
Kantoch, Miroslaw 1928- *WhoScE 91-4*
Kantoff, Sidney Michael d1991 *BioIn 17*
Kantor, Andrea D. *Law&B 92*
Kantor, Csaba 1945- *WhoScE 91-4*
Kantor, David 1915- *WhoSSW 93*
Kantor, Edwin 1932- *WhoAm 92*
Kantor, Gabriella *BioIn 17*
Kantor, Hal 1924- *ScF&FL 92*
Kantor, Lawrence 1947- *St&PR 93*
Kantor, MacKinlay 1904-1977 *BioIn 17*
Kantor, Mark Neil 1956- *St&PR 93*
Kantor, Marvin 1934- *WhoAm 92*
Kantor, Nathan 1942- *St&PR 93, WhoAm 92*
Kantor, Richard H. 1955- *St&PR 93*
Kantor, Seth 1926- *WhoAm 92*
Kantor, Simon William 1925- *WhoAm 92*
Kantor, Tadeusz 1893-1969 *PolBiDi*
Kantor, Tadeusz 1915-1990 *BioIn 17, PolBiDi*
Kantorek, Sandra Schwahl 1952- *WhoAmW 93, WhoEmL 93*
Kantorksi, Alan Lloyd 1947- *St&PR 93*
Kantorowitz-Shaffer, Thelma Doris 1931- *WhoAmW 93*
Kantounis, Stratos George 1931- *WhoE 93*
Kantrowitz, Adrian 1918- *WhoAm 92*
Kantrowitz, Allen S. *Law&B 92*
Kantrowitz, Arthur 1913- *WhoAm 92*
Kantrowitz, Jonathan Daniel 1945- *WhoAm 92*
Kantrowitz, Stan *Law&B 92*
Kanty, Charles W. 1950- *St&PR 93*
Kantzenbach, Erhard 1931- *WhoWor 93*
Kantzler, George William 1924- *WhoSSW 93*
Kanuit, Robert B. 1944- *St&PR 93*
Kanuk, Leslie Lazar *WhoAm 92*
Kanuth, James Gordan 1953- *WhoSSW 93*
Kanwit, Glen Harris 1943- *WhoAm 92*
Kany, Donald J. 1944- *St&PR 93*
Kany, Donald Joseph 1944- *WhoAm 92*
Kany, Judy Casperson 1937- *WhoAmW 93, WhoE 93*
Kany, Steven C. *Law&B 92*
Kany, Steven C. 1943- *St&PR 93*
Kan Ying fl. c. 94- *HarEnMi*
Kanyomozi, Yonasani Bankobeza 1940- *WhoWor 93*
Kanzaki, Takenori 1943- *WhoAsAP 91*
Kanze, Edward (J.), III 1956- *ConAu 139*
Kanzer, Larry 1942- *WhoE 93*
Kanzer, Mark 1908- *WhoE 93*
Kanzig, Werner 1922- *WhoWor 93*
Kanzinger, Russell Christian 1940- *St&PR 93*
Kanzler, Walter Wilhelm 1938- *WhoE 93*
Kao, Charles Kuen 1933- *WhoAm 92*
Kao, Ching-Yuan *BioIn 17*
Kao, Karl S.Y. *ScF&FL 92*
Kao, Pai Chih 1934- *WhoAm 92*
Kao, Race Li-Chan 1943- *WhoE 93*
Kao, William Chishon 1952- *WhoEmL 93*
Kao, Winfun 1958- *WhoWor 93*
Kao Chiung 555-607 *HarEnMi*
Kao Hsien-chih d755 *HarEnMi*
Kaonis, Donna Christine 1949- *WhoWrEP 92*
Kaoru, Inoue 1926- *WhoWor 93*
Kapadia, Haresh K. 1950- *St&PR 93*
Kapadia, Mehernosh Minocheher 1960- *WhoE 93*
Kapanci, Yusuf 1929- *WhoScE 91-4*
Kapandji, Adalbert Ibrahim 1928- *WhoWor 93*
Kapania, Rakesh Kumar 1956- *WhoEmL 93*
Kapas, Sandor 1922- *WhoScE 91-4*
Kapatkin, Fred 1927- *WhoE 93*
Kapche, Ronald Anthony 1941- *WhoSSW 93, WhoWor 93*
Kapcsandy, Louis E. 1936- *St&PR 93*
Kapcsandy, Louis Endre 1936- *WhoAm 92*
Kapczynski, Helmut Hermann 1946- *WhoE 93*
Kapecki, Walter Joseph 1933- *St&PR 93*
Kapei, Abraham 1945- *WhoAsAP 91*
Kapel, Kirk Frederick 1956- *St&PR 93*
Kapell, Bernard L. 1926- *St&PR 93*
Kapell, William 1922-1953 *Baker 92*
Kapella, Bohdan Wojciech 1943- *WhoWor 93*
Kaper, Bronislaw 1902-1983 *Baker 92, PolBiDi*
Kapetanadis, Ilias 1930- *WhoScE 91-4*
Kapetanakis, Evangelos George 1950- *WhoScE 91-3*
Kaphan, Gerard Claude 1932- *WhoScE 91-2*
Kaphan, Robert C. 1944- *St&PR 93*
Kapica, Jack 1946- *WhoCanL 92*
Kapikian, Albert Zaven 1930- *WhoE 93, WhoWor 93*
Kapilevich, Mendel Berkovich 1923- *WhoE 93*
Kapioltas, John 1927- *St&PR 93, WhoAm 92, WhoWor 93*
Kapitaniak, Bronislaw 1943- *WhoScE 91-2*
Kapitaniak, Tomasz 1959- *WhoWor 93*
Kapitany, Sandor 1938- *WhoScE 91-4*
Kapitonov, Boris Viktorovich 1951- *WhoWor 93*
Kapitsa, Lairssa Mikhaylovna 1942- *WhoUN 92*
Kapitsa, P.L. 1894-1984 *BioIn 17*
Kapitsa, Petr Leonidovich 1894-1984 *BioIn 17*
Kapko, Jerzy 1921- *WhoScE 91-4*
Kapko, Jerzy Ludwik 1921- *WhoWor 93*
Kaplan, Abraham 1918- *St&PR 93*
Kaplan, Alan 1941- *St&PR 93*
Kaplan, Alan Michael 1951- *WhoEmL 93*
Kaplan, Albert 1932- *WhoE 93*
Kaplan, Aline Boucher 1947- *ScF&FL 92*
Kaplan, Allen Stanford 1939- *WhoE 93*
Kaplan, Alvin 1941- *St&PR 93*
Kaplan, Alvin Irving 1925- *WhoAm 92*
Kaplan, Amy Louise 1950- *WhoAmW 93*
Kaplan, Andrew R. 1957- *WhoE 93*
Kaplan, Ann *St&PR 93*
Kaplan, Arnold H. 1939- *St&PR 93*
Kaplan, Barbara Elaine 1950- *WhoAmW 93*
Kaplan, Barnard Alan 1949- *WhoE 93*
Kaplan, Ben Augustus 1952- *WhoEmL 93*
Kaplan, Benjamin 1911- *WhoAm 92*
Kaplan, Bernard Joseph 1918- *WhoE 93, WhoWor 93*
Kaplan, Bernice Antoville 1923- *WhoAm 92*
Kaplan, Bess 1927- *DcChlFi, WhoCanL 92*
Kaplan, Bradley S. 1960- *WhoEmL 93*
Kaplan, Bruce D. d1992 *NewYTBS 92*
Kaplan, Carl E. 1939- *St&PR 93*
Kaplan, Carl Eliot 1939- *WhoAm 92*
Kaplan, Carol Olive 1961- *WhoE 93*
Kaplan, Carolyn Sue 1944- *WhoAmW 93*
Kaplan, Cora 1940- *ScF&FL 92*
Kaplan, Daile 1950- *WhoAmW 93*
Kaplan, Daniel I. *BioIn 17*
Kaplan, Daniel I. 1943- *St&PR 93, WhoAm 92*
Kaplan, David L. *Law&B 92*
Kaplan, David Michael 1946- *ScF&FL 92, WhoWrEP 92*
Kaplan, Debra Lee 1951- *WhoAmW 93*
Kaplan, Diane Susan 1957- *WhoEmL 93*
Kaplan, Donald David 1930- *St&PR 93*
Kaplan, Ed *MiSFD 9*
Kaplan, Edith Freund 1924- *WhoE 93*
Kaplan, Edna Engelman 1948- *WhoE 93*
Kaplan, Edward L. 1942- *St&PR 93*
Kaplan, Ellen Lasher 1943- *WhoAmW 93*
Kaplan, Elliot S. 1936- *WhoAm 92*
Kaplan, Erica Lynn 1955- *WhoAmW 93*
Kaplan, Evan Keith *Law&B 92*
Kaplan, Fania 1887-1918 *BioIn 17*
Kaplan, Fred 1937- *BioIn 17, WhoE 93*
Kaplan, Frederic Clark 1948- *WhoE 93*
Kaplan, Gail Carol 1949- *WhoAm 92*
Kaplan, Gary 1939- *WhoAm 92*
Kaplan, George Harry 1948- *WhoE 93*
Kaplan, George R. 1919- *St&PR 93*
Kaplan, Georges d1990 *BioIn 17*
Kaplan, Gilbert B. 1951- *WhoAm 92*
Kaplan, Gilbert M. *Law&B 92*
Kaplan, Gustave 1920- *St&PR 93*
Kaplan, Harley B. 1954- *St&PR 93*
Kaplan, Harley Lance 1961- *WhoE 93*
Kaplan, Harold 1916- *WhoAm 92*
Kaplan, Harold 1918- *WhoAm 92*
Kaplan, Harold Edward 1950- *WhoEmL 93*
Kaplan, Harold Irving 1921- *WhoAm 92*
Kaplan, Harold Irwin 1927- *WhoAm 92*
Kaplan, Harold Paul 1939- *WhoE 93*
Kaplan, Harriet 1934- *WhoE 93*
Kaplan, Helen Singer 1929- *BioIn 17*
Kaplan, Helene Lois 1933- *WhoAm 92, WhoAmW 93*
Kaplan, Henry David 1945- *WhoSSW 93*
Kaplan, Henry Jerrold 1942- *WhoAm 92*
Kaplan, Hillary G. *Law&B 92*
Kaplan, Howard Fred 1941- *St&PR 93*
Kaplan, Huette Myra 1933- *WhoAmW 93*
Kaplan, Isaac Raymond 1929- *WhoAm 92*
Kaplan, James I. *Law&B 92*
Kaplan, James Lee 1939- *WhoE 93*
Kaplan, Janet M. *St&PR 93*
Kaplan, Jared 1938- *WhoWor 93*
Kaplan, Jean Gaither 1927- *WhoAmW 93*
Kaplan, Jeremiah 1926- *St&PR 93, WhoAm 92*
Kaplan, Joan Davidson 1943- *WhoE 93*
Kaplan, Jocelyn Rae 1952- *WhoAmW 93*
Kaplan, Joe 1902-1991 *BioIn 17*
Kaplan, John *BioIn 17*
Kaplan, John 1959- *WhoAm 92*
Kaplan, Jonathan *NewYTBS 92 [port]*
Kaplan, Jonathan 1947- *MiSFD 9*
Kaplan, Jonathan Harris 1957- *WhoE 93, WhoEmL 93, WhoWor 93*
Kaplan, Jonathan Stewart 1947- *WhoAm 92*
Kaplan, Joseph 1902-1991 *BioIn 17*
Kaplan, Judith 1938- *ConEn*
Kaplan, Judith Helene 1938- *St&PR 93, WhoAmW 93*
Kaplan, Justin *BioIn 17*
Kaplan, Justin 1925- *WhoAm 92, WhoWrEP 92*
Kaplan, Kenneth F. 1945- *St&PR 93*
Kaplan, Kristen A. *Law&B 92*
Kaplan, Laura Garcia 1957- *WhoAmW 93*
Kaplan, Lawrence H. *Law&B 92*
Kaplan, Lawrence J. *Law&B 92*
Kaplan, Lawrence R. 1950- *St&PR 93*
Kaplan, Lee Michael 1954- *WhoE 93*
Kaplan, Leo Sylvan 1924- *WhoAm 92*
Kaplan, Leonard Eugene 1940- *WhoAm 92, WhoSSW 93*
Kaplan, Leonard L. 1928- *WhoE 93*
Kaplan, Lewis A. 1944- *WhoAm 92*
Kaplan, Linda Faye 1951- *WhoAmW 93*
Kaplan, Lloyd Arthur 1934- *WhoAm 92*
Kaplan, Madeline 1944- *WhoAmW 93, WhoE 93, WhoWor 93*
Kaplan, Manuel E. 1928- *WhoAm 92*
Kaplan, Marilyn Flashenberg *WhoAm 92*
Kaplan, Mark 1953- *Baker 92*
Kaplan, Mark N. 1930- *St&PR 93*
Kaplan, Mark Norman 1930- *WhoAm 92*
Kaplan, Mark Steven 1947- *WhoEmL 93*
Kaplan, Marshall Harvey 1939- *WhoSSW 93*
Kaplan, Maureen Flynn 1951- *WhoAmW 93*
Kaplan, Melvin Hyman 1920- *WhoAm 92, WhoE 93*
Kaplan, Michael Jay 1951- *St&PR 93*
Kaplan, Michael L.B. 1934- *St&PR 93*
Kaplan, Michael Lewis Bernard 1934- *WhoE 93*
Kaplan, Milton 1910- *WhoWrEP 92*
Kaplan, Mitchell Alan 1954- *WhoE 93, WhoWor 93*
Kaplan, Mordecai Menahem 1881-1983 *BioIn 17, JeAmHC*
Kaplan, Morton A. 1921- *WhoAm 92*
Kaplan, Muriel Sheerr 1924- *WhoAm 92, WhoSSW 93*
Kaplan, Mustafa 1961- *WhoScE 91-4*
Kaplan, Neal 1951- *WhoEmL 93*
Kaplan, Neil Alan 1947- *WhoEmL 93*
Kaplan, Nelly 1931- *MiSFD 9*
Kaplan, Nolan Scott 1951- *WhoEmL 93*
Kaplan, Norman C. 1952- *St&PR 93*
Kaplan, Norman Mayer 1931- *WhoAm 92*
Kaplan, Oscar Joel 1915- *WhoAm 92*
Kaplan, Paul A. d1991 *BioIn 17*
Kaplan, Peter Benjamin 1939- *WhoAm 92*
Kaplan, Peter James 1943- *WhoAm 92*
Kaplan, Peter Jay 1954- *St&PR 93*
Kaplan, Peter Roy 1949- *WhoSSW 93*
Kaplan, Philip Larry 1950- *WhoE 93*
Kaplan, R.W. 1924- *St&PR 93*
Kaplan, Randy Kaye 1954- *WhoEmL 93*
Kaplan, Richard *BioIn 17*
Kaplan, Richard 1929- *WhoAm 92*
Kaplan, Richard David 1951- *WhoEmL 93*
Kaplan, Richard Jay *Law&B 92*
Kaplan, Richard Michael *Law&B 92*
Kaplan, Robert B. 1928- *ScF&FL 92*
Kaplan, Robert B. 1929- *WhoAm 92*
Kaplan, Robert Malcolm 1947- *WhoAm 92*
Kaplan, Robert Marshall 1936- *WhoWor 93*
Kaplan, Robert Phillip 1936- *WhoAm 92*
Kaplan, Ronald Alan 1943- *St&PR 93*
Kaplan, Ronald V. 1930- *St&PR 93, WhoAm 92, WhoE 93*
Kaplan, Ronald W. 1951- *St&PR 93*
Kaplan, Samuel 1922- *WhoAm 92, WhoWor 93*
Kaplan, Sandra Lee 1956- *WhoEmL 93*
Kaplan, Sandra Solon 1934- *WhoAmW 93*
Kaplan, Sanford 1916- *St&PR 93*

Karkowksi, Ellen Faye 1959- *WhoAmW 93*
Karkowski, Zdzislaw 1925- *WhoScE 91-4*
Karkus, Theodore W. 1959- *St&PR 93*
Karkut, Bonnie Lee 1934- *WhoAmW 93*
Karkut, Emil Joseph 1916- *WhoAm 92*
Karkut, Richard Theodore 1948- *WhoWor 93*
Karl, V, Emperor of Germany 1500-1558 *BioIn 17*
Karl, Barry Dean 1927- *WhoAm 92*
Karl, Dennis R. d1992 *NewYTBS 92*
Karl, Dennis (R.) 1954-1992 *ConAu 139*
Karl, Eric Alan 1956- *WhoE 93*
Karl, Gabriel 1937- *WhoAm 92*
Karl, George 1951- *WhoAm 92*
Karl, Gregory Paul 1950- *WhoEmL 93*
Karl, Helen Weist 1948- *WhoAmW 93, WhoEmL 93*
Karl, Herb 1938- *SmATA 73 [port]*
Karl, Jean E. 1927- *ScF&FL 92*
Karl, Jean Edna 1927- *WhoWrEP 92*
Karl, Justin Joseph *Law&B 92*
Karl, Kurt Erskine 1952- *WhoE 93*
Karl, Leo Emil, Jr. 1929- *WhoE 93*
Karl, Malcolm *St&PR 93*
Karl, Martin S. 1954- *St&PR 93*
Karl, Max Henry 1910- *WhoAm 92*
Karl, Michael *WhoWrEP 92*
Karl, Robert Harry 1947- *WhoEmL 93, WhoSSW 93*
Karl, Stephanie Kay 1963- *WhoAmW 93*
Karl, Tom 1846-1916 *Baker 92*
Karlak, Laura Carroll *Law&B 92*
Karlan, Andrew Warren 1944- *WhoE 93*
Karlan, LuAnn Florio 1954- *WhoE 93, WhoWor 93*
Karlberg, Bengt E. 1933- *WhoScE 91-4*
Karlberg, John R. 1941- *St&PR 93*
Karle, Isabella 1921- *WhoAm 92, WhoAmW 93*
Karle, James J. 1950- *St&PR 93*
Karle, Jerome 1918- *WhoAm 92, WhoE 93, WhoWor 93*
Karlen, John Adam 1933- *WhoAm 92*
Karlen, Peter Hurd 1949- *WhoWor 93*
Karlen, Robert Edwin 1947- *WhoEmL 93*
Karlen, Wibjorn 1937- *WhoScE 91-4*
Karlin, Barbara *BioIn 17*
Karlin, Bernie 1927- *BioIn 17, ConAu 136*
Karlin, Daniel 1953- *ConAu 139*
Karlin, Elyse Zorn 1950- *WhoWrEP 92*
Karlin, Lynn *BioIn 17*
Karlin, Michael Jonathan Abraham 1952- *WhoEmL 93*
Karlin, Miriam R. *Law&B 92*
Karlin, Nurit *BioIn 17*
Karlin, Robert Lowell 1929- *St&PR 93*
Karlin, Samuel 1924- *WhoAm 92*
Karlin, Susan Coffin 1953- *WhoSSW 93*
Karlinger, Janos 1943- *WhoScE 91-4*
Karlins, M(artin) William 1932- *Baker 92*
Karlins, Martin William 1932- *WhoAm 92*
Karlins, Marvin 1941- *ScF&FL 92*
Karlinsky, Simon 1924- *WhoAm 92*
Karlinszki, Edit 1930- *WhoScE 91-4*
Karll, Jo Ann 1948- *WhoAmW 93*
Karloff, Alvin J. 1931- *St&PR 93*
Karloff, Boris 1887-1969 *BioIn 17, IntDcF 2-3 [port]*
Karlovec, Lucien B., Jr. 1936- *St&PR 93*
Karlovec, Robert V. 1922- *St&PR 93*
Karlowicz, Jan 1836-1903 *See* Karlowicz, Mieczyslaw 1876-1909 *Baker 92*
Karlowicz, Jan Aleksander Ludwik 1836-1903 *IntDcAn*
Karlowicz, Mieczyslaw 1876-1909 *Baker 92, PolBiDi*
Karlquist, Anders Sten 1944- *WhoWor 93*
Karlqvist, S. Anders 1944- *WhoScE 91-4*
Karls, John Spencer 1942- *WhoAm 92*
Karlsen, Asbjorn *WhoScE 91-4*
Karlson, Cindy Lee 1961- *WhoAmW 93*
Karlson, David J. *St&PR 93*
Karlson, Dixie D. 1941- *WhoAmW 93*
Karlson, Elizabeth G.J. *Law&B 92*
Karlson, Karl Eugene 1920- *WhoAm 92, WhoE 93*
Karlson, Kevin W. 1952- *WhoSSW 93*
Karlson, Phil 1908-1986 *MiSFD 9N*
Karlson, Ulrich 1956- *WhoWor 93*
Karlsson, Bengt Olog 1937- *WhoUN 92*
Karlsson, Bjorn G. 1946- *WhoScE 91-4*
Karlsson, Christer B. 1944- *WhoWor 93*
Karlsson, Erik B. 1931- *WhoScE 91-4*
Karlsson, Henry *WhoScE 91-4*
Karlsson, Henry 1933- *WhoScE 91-4*
Karlsson, Ingemar Harry 1944- *WhoWor 93*
Karlsson, Kaj Hakan 1935- *WhoScE 91-4*
Karlsson, Linda Marie 1949- *WhoEmL 93*
Karlsson, Per Wennerberg 1936- *WhoWor 93*
Karlstrom, Paul Johnson 1941- *WhoAm 92*
Karlstromer, Axel Christer 1942- *WhoWor 93*
Karlton, Lawrence K. 1935- *WhoAm 92*
Karma, Erol 1936- *WhoScE 91-4*
Karma, Pekka Heikki 1944- *WhoScE 91-4*
Karmaker, Ratneswar 1938- *WhoWor 93*
Karman, James A. 1937- *St&PR 93*
Karman, James Anthony 1937- *WhoAm 92*
Karman, Janice *MiSFD 9*
Karmazin, J. Donald 1941- *St&PR 93*
Karmazin, John, Jr. 1924- *St&PR 93*
Karmazin, Mel *BioIn 17*
Karmazin, Sharon Elyse 1946- *WhoAmW 93*
Karmeier, Delbert Fred 1935- *WhoAm 92*
Karmel, Leslie 1923- *St&PR 93*
Karmel, Roberta S. 1937- *WhoAm 92, WhoAmW 93*
Karmelin, Michael Allen 1947- *WhoE 93*
Karmen, Arthur 1930- *WhoAm 92*
Karmin, Monroe William 1929- *WhoAm 92*
Karmoul, Akram Jamil 1939- *WhoUN 92*
Karn, Dennis D. 1923- *St&PR 93*
Karn, Richard Wendall 1927- *WhoAm 92*
Karnakis, Andrew T. *Law&B 92*
Karnath, Joan Edna 1947- *WhoAmW 93, WhoEmL 93, WhoWor 93*
Karnatz, William E. 1937- *St&PR 93*
Karnaugh, Maurice 1924- *WhoAm 92*
Karner, Helmut Franz 1947- *WhoWor 93*
Karnes, Evan Burton, II *WhoWor 93*
Karnes, John *Law&B 92*
Karnes, Lucia Rooney 1921- *WhoAmW 93*
Karnes, Timothy Joseph 1956- *WhoEmL 93*
Karney, James Terrence 1944- *WhoSSW 93*
Karney, Joe D. 1933- *St&PR 93*
Karney, Joe Dan 1933- *WhoAm 92*
Karni, Edi 1944- *WhoAm 92*
Karni, Michaela Jordan 1941- *WhoWrEP 92*
Karni, Shlomo 1932- *WhoAm 92*
Karnick, Loren *Law&B 92*
Karnicki, Zbigniew Stefan 1940- *WhoScE 91-4*
Karniewicz, Jan 1928- *WhoScE 91-4*
Karnitz, Jane Connie 1958- *St&PR 93*
Karnkowski, Stanislaw 1520-1603 *PolBiDi*
Karnovsky, Manfred L. 1918- *WhoAm 92*
Karnovsky, Morris 1926- *BioIn 17*
Karnovsky, Morris John 1926- *WhoAm 92*
Karnow, Stanley *BioIn 17*
Karnow, Stanley 1925- *WhoAm 92, WhoE 93*
Karnowsky, Deborah *WhoAm 92, WhoAmW 93*
Karns, B. Lee 1930- *St&PR 93*
Karns, Barry Wayne 1946- *WhoSSW 93*
Karns, Jeanne Ann 1951- *WhoAmW 93*
Karns, John Marshall 1928-1990 *BioIn 17*
Karns, Paul A. *Law&B 92*
Karnsund, Georg *WhoScE 91-4*
Karny, Alfons 1902- *PolBiDi*
Karo, Albert 1945- *WhoAsAP 91*
Karo, Douglas Paul 1947- *WhoEmL 93*
Karoff, Richard Martin 1929- *WhoE 93*
Karol, Catherine M. *Law&B 92*
Karol, Frederick John 1933- *WhoAm 92*
Karol, John Jacob, Jr. 1935- *WhoE 93*
Karol, Joseph E. 1940- *St&PR 93*
Karol, Meryl Helene 1940- *WhoAmW 93*
Karol, Nathaniel H. 1929- *WhoAm 92*
Karol, Pamala Marie 1950- *WhoAmW 93*
Karol, Reuben Hirsh 1922- *WhoAm 92, WhoE 93, WhoWor 93*
Karolevitz, Robert Francis 1922- *WhoWrEP 92*
Karoly, Gyula 1941- *WhoScE 91-4*
Karolyi, Mihaly 1875-1955 *DcTwHis*
Karon, Robert Allen 1949- *WhoEmL 93*
Karos, Gus 1923- *St&PR 93*
Karoui, Hamed 1927- *WhoWor 93*
Karow, Alann F. 1939- *St&PR 93*
Karow, Charles Stanley 1954- *WhoE 93, WhoEmL 93*
Karp, Abraham J. 1921- *ConAu 40NR*
Karp, Abraham Joseph 1921- *WhoAm 92, WhoE 93*
Karp, Allen 1940- *St&PR 93, WhoE 93*
Karp, Angela *WhoScE 91-1*
Karp, Carl 1954- *ConAu 139*
Karp, David 1922- *WhoAm 92*
Karp, Donald M. 1937- *St&PR 93*
Karp, Donald Mathew 1937- *WhoAm 92*
Karp, Harvey Lawrence 1927- *WhoAm 92*
Karp, Herbert Rubin 1921- *WhoAm 92*
Karp, Howard M. 1941- *WhoE 93*
Karp, Jack A. 1944- *St&PR 93*
Karp, Jack Lee 1936- *WhoAm 92*
Karp, Jeffrey Randall *Law&B 92*
Karp, Jeffrey Randall 1951- *WhoEmL 93*
Karp, Judith Esther 1946- *WhoAmW 93*
Karp, Mark Edward 1946- *St&PR 93*
Karp, Martin Everett 1922- *WhoAm 92*
Karp, Marylou *Law&B 92*
Karp, Natalie Lynn 1962- *WhoAmW 93*
Karp, Nathan 1915- *WhoAm 92*
Karp, Peter Simon 1935- *WhoE 93*
Karp, Richard M. 1929- *St&PR 93, WhoAm 92*
Karp, Richard Manning 1935- *WhoAm 92*
Karp, Rick Alvin 1954- *WhoEmL 93*
Karp, Robert 1934- *WhoAm 92*
Karp, Sherman 1935- *WhoAm 92*
Karp, Stanley Robert *Law&B 92*
Karp, Steven C. *Law&B 92*
Karpa, Jay Norman 1935- *WhoE 93*
Karpacs, Joanne Mary 1945- *WhoWrEP 92*
Karpal Singh 1940- *WhoAsAP 91*
Karpan, Kathleen Marie 1942- *WhoAm 92, WhoAmW 93*
Karpas, Abraham *WhoScE 91-1*
Karpas, Alan K. 1940- *St&PR 93*
Karpath, Ludwig 1866-1936 *Baker 92*
Karpati, Istvan 1924- *WhoScE 91-4*
Karpati, Janos 1932- *Baker 92*
Karpatkin, Margaret 1932- *WhoAm 92*
Karpe, Niklas Johan 1962- *WhoWor 93*
Karpe, Richard 1929- *WhoE 93*
Karpel, Craig S. 1944- *WhoAm 92*
Karpel, Richard Leslie 1944- *WhoE 93*
Karpeles, Leopold *BioIn 17*
Karpeles, Maud 1885-1976 *Baker 92*
Karpen, Marian Joan 1944- *WhoAm 92, WhoAmW 93, WhoE 93, WhoWor 93*
Karpen, Richard L. 1926- *St&PR 93*
Karpenski, Martin J. *Law&B 92*
Karpeshina, Yulia 1956- *WhoWor 93*
Karpf, Ilene P. *Law&B 92*
Karpf, Ronald Jay 1948- *WhoEmL 93*
Karpfel, Zdenek *WhoScE 91-4*
Karpiel, Doris Catherine 1935- *WhoAmW 93*
Karpinski, Franciszek 1741-1825 *PolBiDi*
Karpinski, Jacek 1927- *WhoWor 93*
Karpinski, Karol Jan 1934- *WhoScE 91-4*
Karpinski, Kenneth Lee 1947- *WhoE 93*
Karpinski, Lawrence Walter 1952- *St&PR 93*
Karpinski, Patricia Anne 1948- *WhoEmL 93, WhoSSW 93*
Karpinski, Richard Henry Stephen 1945- *WhoE 93*
Karpinski, Stanislaw 1892-1982 *PolBiDi*
Karpinski, Tadeusz 1936- *WhoScE 91-4*
Karpinsky, Len Vyacheslavovich 1929- *BioIn 17*
Karpiscak, John, III 1957- *WhoEmL 93*
Karplus, Esteban J. 1937- *St&PR 93*
Karplus, Martin 1930- *WhoAm 92*
Karplus, Robert 1927-1990 *BioIn 17*
Karplus, Walter J. 1927- *WhoAm 92*
Karpman, Harold Lew 1927- *WhoAm 92*
Karpman, Laura 1959- *Baker 92*
Karpman, Scott 1958- *St&PR 93*
Karpouzas, John 1927- *WhoScE 91-3*
Karpov, Anatoly 1951- *BioIn 17*
Karpov, Anatoly Yevgenievich 1951- *WhoWor 93*
Karpovich, Eugene J. 1946- *St&PR 93*
Karpowich, Leonard H. *Law&B 92*
Karpowicz, Joseph Raymond *Law&B 92*
Karppi, Risto A.J. 1946- *WhoScE 91-4*
Karppinen, Martti *WhoScE 91-4*
Karpuzov, D.S. 1940- *WhoScE 91-4*
Karr, Alan Francis 1947- *WhoAm 92*
Karr, Beverly Ann 1967- *WhoAmW 93*
Karr, Bruce R. *Law&B 92*
Karr, David Maurice 1932- *St&PR 93*
Karr, Deborah Lynn 1964- *WhoAmW 93*
Karr, Elizabeth McRae 1953- *WhoAmW 93*
Karr, Gary (Michael) 1941- *Baker 92*
Karr, Howard Henry 1943- *St&PR 93*
Karr, James d1989 *BioIn 17*
Karr, Jay Miles 1926- *WhoWrEP 92*
Karr, John H. 1950- *St&PR 93*
Karr, Kari Bethany Ward 1951- *WhoAmW 93*
Karr, Norman 1927- *WhoAm 92*
Karr, Patti 1932- *ConTFT 10*
Karr, Phyllis Ann 1944- *ConAu 40NR, ScF&FL 92*
Karr, Richard Lloyd 1947- *WhoEmL 93*
Karr, Robert Irving 1924- *St&PR 93*
Karr, Susan Schott 1954- *WhoAmW 93*
Karr, William Lee 1951- *WhoWor 93*
Karraker, Katherine Hildebrandt 1951- *WhoAmW 93*
Karran, John Henry *WhoScE 91-1*
Karras, Alex 1935- *WhoAm 92*
Karre, Kathleen Mary 1957- *WhoEmL 93*
Karre, Mary E. *Law&B 92*
Karre, Richard A. *Law&B 92*
Karren, Brad Lewis *Law&B 92*
Karren, Keith J(ohn) 1943- *ConAu 40NR*
Karrer, Carol Converse 1940- *WhoAmW 93*
Karrer, Gerhard 1955- *WhoScE 91-4*
Karres, Matthew Steven *Law&B 92*
Karrh, Bruce Wakefield 1936- *WhoAm 92*
Karr-Kidwell, P. J. 1952- *WhoSSW 93*
Karron, Allen *St&PR 93*
Karrys, William G. 1923- *St&PR 93*
Kars, Jean-Rodolphe 1947- *Baker 92*
Karsai, Karoly 1926- *WhoScE 91-4*
Karsan, Nooruddin 1957- *WhoEmL 93*
Karsch, Anna Louisa 1722-1791 *BioIn 17*
Karsch, Daniel Selwyn 1923- *WhoAm 92*
Karsen, Sonja Petra 1919- *WhoAm 92, WhoAmW 93, WhoE 93, WhoWor 93*
Karsh, Brice *BioIn 17*
Karsh, Richard Bruce 1944- *WhoSSW 93*
Karsh, Yousuf 1908- *WhoAm 92, WhoWor 93*
Karshner, Roger Kay 1928- *WhoWrEP 92*
Karsk, Bruce 1952- *St&PR 93*
Karski, Jan 1914- *PolBiDi*
Karsner, Michael S. 1958- *St&PR 93*
Karson, Allen Ronald 1947- *WhoEmL 93, WhoWor 93*
Karson, Burton Lewis 1934- *WhoAm 92*
Karson, Catherine June 1956- *WhoAmW 93*
Karson, Daniel E. *Law&B 92*
Karson, Emile 1921- *WhoAm 92*
Karson, Eric *MiSFD 9*
Karson, Michael J. *Law&B 92*
Karst, Francis 1947- *WhoScE 91-2*
Karst, Kenneth Leslie 1929- *WhoAm 92*
Karst, Marilyn Grace 1936- *WhoAmW 93*
Karsten, David W. 1947- *St&PR 93*
Karsten, John Alan 1932- *St&PR 93*
Karsten, Kenneth Stephen 1913- *WhoSSW 93*
Karstien, Diana C. 1946- *WhoAmW 93*
Karszes, Arthur J. 1936- *St&PR 93*
Karta, Glenn E. *Law&B 92*
Kartalia, Mitchell P. 1913- *WhoAm 92*
Kartalov, Paskal 1936- *WhoScE 91-4*
Kartanowicz, John Joseph 1939- *St&PR 93*
Kartasasmita, Ginandjar 1941- *WhoAsAP 91*
Kartchner, Gene B. *Law&B 92*
Kartchner, Kenner Casteel 1886-1970 *BioIn 17*
Karten, Harvey Jules 1935- *WhoAm 92*
Karten, Terry 1947- *WhoAm 92*
Karter, Jerome 1937- *WhoIns 93*
Karthaios, Rena *BioIn 17*
Karthauser, Brad C. 1957- *St&PR 93*
Kartiganer, Joseph 1935- *WhoAm 92*
Kartje, Jean Van Landuyt 1953- *WhoEmL 93*
Kartman, K. 1958- *St&PR 93*
Kartman, Marc G. *Law&B 92*
Kartnig, Theodor Karl 1931- *WhoScE 91-4*
Kartomi, Margaret Joy 1940- *WhoWor 93*
Kartsev, Alexander 1883-1953 *Baker 92*
Kartsev, Vladimir Petrovich 1938- *WhoUN 92*
Karttunen, Frances 1942- *ConAu 138*
Karttunen, Simo T.P. 1939- *WhoScE 91-4*
Kartzinel, Ronald 1945- *WhoAm 92*
Karu, Gilda M. 1951- *WhoAmW 93*
Karube, Isao 1942- *BioIn 17*
Karukstis, Kerry Kathleen 1955- *WhoEmL 93*
Karunarathne, Vickramabahu Bandara 1948- *WhoWor 93*
Karunatilake, Halwalage Neville Sepala 1930- *WhoWor 93*
Karve, Irawati 1905-1970 *IntDcAn*
Karvelis, Leon J., Jr. 1942- *WhoAm 92*
Karwan, Tadeusz Jan 1925- *WhoScE 91-4*
Karwatzki, John Michael *WhoScE 91-1*
Karwoski, Glenn John 1955- *WhoEmL 93*
Kary, Jodi Heflin *St&PR 93*
Karybakas, C.A. 1934- *WhoScE 91-3*
Karyotakis, Theodore 1903-1978 *Baker 92*
Karzel, Karlfried H.E. 1929- *WhoScE 91-3*
Kasa, Mustafa 1939- *WhoScE 91-4*
Kasa, Pamela D. 1943- *WhoAm 92, WhoAmW 93*
Kasa, Pamela Dorothy *Law&B 92*
Kasa, Pamela Dorothy 1943- *St&PR 93*
Kasacks, Sally Frame *St&PR 93*
Kasahara, Susumu 1940- *WhoWor 93*
Kasahara, Yasushi 1941- *WhoWor 93*
Kasai, Kazuhiko 1937- *WhoWor 93*
Kasakove, Susan 1938- *WhoAmW 93, WhoE 93*
Kasandrenos *OxDcByz*
Kasanin, Mark Owen 1929- *WhoAm 92*
Kasanof, Robert 1929-1991 *BioIn 17*
Kasap, Halil 1949- *WhoScE 91-4*
Kasap, Mulkiye 1947- *WhoScE 91-4*
Kasarda, John Dale 1945- *WhoAm 92*
Kasarjian, Levon, Jr. *Law&B 92*
Kasarjian, Levon, Jr. 1937- *St&PR 93*
Kasarskis, Edward Joseph 1946- *WhoSSW 93*
Kasatkina, Natalya Dmitriyevna 1934- *WhoWor 93*
Kasavubu, Joseph 1910-1969 *DcTwHis*
Kasaya, Yukio *BioIn 17*
Kasbeer, Stephen Frederick 1925- *WhoAm 92*
Kasch, Jame E. 1934- *St&PR 93*
Kasch, James Alan 1946- *St&PR 93*

Kasch, Jeffrey Clark 1942- St&PR 93
Kasch, Rick Darrel 1950- WhoE 93
Kaschak, Ellyn 1943- ConAu 139
Kasche, Volker 1939- WhoWor 93
Kaschmann, Giuseppe 1847-1925 Baker 92
Kaschub, William John 1942- St&PR 93
Kascus, Marie Annette 1943- WhoAmW 93
Kasdan, Lawrence BioIn 17
Kasdan, Lawrence 1949?- CurBio 92 [port], MiSFD 9, ScF&FL 92
Kasdan, Lawrence Edward 1949- WhoAm 92
Kasden, Allen J. 1949- St&PR 93
Kasdin, Mark Benjamin 1944- St&PR 93
Kasdon, Solomon Charles 1912- WhoE 93
Kasdorf, Julia 1962- ConAu 139
Kase, Nathan Ginden 1930- WhoAm 92
Kase, Paul St&PR 93
Kase, Stephen A. Law&B 92
Kaseda, Hiroshi 1943- WhoWor 93
Kaseff, Fred 1957- St&PR 93
Kaseff, Gary WhoAm 92
Kasem, Casey 1932- BioIn 17
Kasem, Casey 1933- WhoAm 92
Kasemets, Udo 1919- Baker 92
Kasemo, Bengt H. 1942- WhoScE 91-4
Kasen, Donald Michael 1946- St&PR 93
Kasen, Martin 1934- St&PR 93
Kasen, Stewart M. 1939- St&PR 93
Kasen, Stewart Michael 1939- WhoAm 92
Kasenberg, Darlene Frances 1951- WhoAmW 93
Kasenene, Peter K. 1946- WhoWor 93
Kasenter, Robert Albert 1946- WhoAm 92
Kasenter, Robert Albert 1946- St&PR 93
Kase-Polisini, Judith Baker 1932- WhoAmW 93
Kaser, David 1924- WhoAm 92
Kaser, Michael Charles 1926- WhoWor 93
Kaser, Peter G. 1945- St&PR 93
Kaser, Wayne M. 1938- St&PR 93
Kash, Don Eldon 1934- WhoAm 92
Kash, Graham Stephens 1937- WhoSSW 93
Kash, Wyatt Keith 1955- WhoWrEP 92
Kasha, Kenneth John 1933- WhoAm 92
Kasha, Lawrence 1933-1990 BioIn 17
Kasha, Michael 1920- BioIn 17
Kashani, Javad Hassan-Nejad 1937- WhoAm 92
Kashdin, Gladys Shafran 1921- WhoAmW 93
Kashdin, Laurence M. 1947- St&PR 93
Kasher, Asa 1940- WhoWor 93
Kashgarian, Michael 1933- WhoAm 92
Kashima, Kathleen Joyce 1959- WhoAmW 93
Kashimba, Paul T. Law&B 92
Kashin, Daniil Nikitich 1769-1841 Baker 92
Kashinski, Gerald J. Law&B 92
Kashiwa, Sukekata 1907- WhoWor 93
Kashiwabara, Hisatsugu 1928- WhoWor 93
Kashiwagi, Yusuke 1917- St&PR 93, WhoWor 93
Kashiwaya, Koji 1939- WhoUN 92
Kashkashian, Kim 1952- Baker 92
Kashkin, Nikolai Dmitrievich 1839-1920 Baker 92
Kashmeri, Sarwar Aghajani 1942- WhoWor 93
Kashnow, R.A. 1942- St&PR 93
Kashou, Jean Lee 1945- WhoAmW 93
Kashperov, Vladimir (Nikitich) 1826-1894 Baker 92
Kashuba, Jane Elizabeth 1945- WhoAmW 93
Kashul, Deborah Anne Law&B 92
Kashyap, Rangasami Lakshmi Narayan 1938- WhoAm 92
Kasi, Leela Peshkar 1939- WhoAmW 93, WhoSSW 93
Kasianchuk, Walter St&PR 93
Kasianov, Alexander 1891-1982 Baker 92
Kasich, John R. 1952- CngDr 91, WhoAm 92
Kasik, John 1943- St&PR 93
Kasimer, Eli 1926 St&PR 93
Kasimir, Marin BioIn 17
Kasimos, John Nicholas 1955- WhoWor 93
Kasindorf, Blanche Robins 1925- WhoAmW 93, WhoE 93
Kasinec, Edward 1945- WhoAm 92
Kasinitz, Philip 1957- ConAu 137
Kasinoff, Bernard Herman 1920- WhoAm 92
Kasior, Serjit Kaur 1949- WhoAmW 93
Kasitah Gaddam, Datuk 1947- WhoAsAP 91
Kaskarelis, Dionysios Vassilios 1915- WhoWor 93
Kaske, Robert Earl 1921-1989 BioIn 17
Kaskel, Edward 1910- St&PR 93
Kaskel, Karl von 1866-1943 Baker 92
Kaskel, Murry 1915- St&PR 93
Kaskel, Rick Harlan 1954- WhoSSW 93
Kaskell, Peter Howard 1924- WhoAm 92
Kaskey, Dale Edward 1944- St&PR 93
Kaskey, Richard A. 1921- St&PR 93
Kaskinen Riesberg, Barbara Kay 1952- WhoAmW 93, WhoEmL 93
Kasko, Marilyn Jean 1945- WhoAmW 93
Kasko, William Paul 1942- St&PR 93
Kaskowitz, Edwin 1936- WhoAm 92
Kasky, Rita 1940- WhoE 93
Kasle, Richard L. 1927- St&PR 93
Kasle, Roger H. WhoAm 92
Kasle, Thomas Ross 1953- St&PR 93
Kasler, Paula Law&B 92
Kasley, Helen Mary 1951- St&PR 93
Kaslick, Ralph Sidney 1935- WhoAm 92
Kaslik, Bob BioIn 17
Kaslik, Vaclav 1917- OxDcOp
Kaslik, Vaclav 1917-1989 Baker 92
Kaslow, Florence W. WhoAm 92, WhoSSW 93
Kaslow, Florence Whiteman BioIn 17
Kaslow, John Francis 1932- St&PR 93, WhoAm 92
Kaslow, Richard Alan 1943- WhoE 93
Kaslusky, Anne 1948- WhoE 93
Kasman, Andrew Todd Law&B 92
Kasmer, Irene 1926- WhoAmW 93
Kasmir, Gail Alice 1958- WhoAmW 93, WhoEmL 93
Kasner, Michael ScF&FL 92
Kasnowski, Chester Nelson 1944- WhoE 93
Kasonde, Joseph Mwenya 1938- WhoUN 92
Kasowicz, Jan 1922- WhoScE 91-4
Kasowitz, Marc Elliot 1952- WhoAm 92
Kaspar, Anne Pamela 1960- WhoE 93
Kaspar, Don G. 1928- St&PR 93
Kaspar, James E. 1935- St&PR 93
Kaspar, Jean 1941- BioIn 17
Kaspar, Robert Stephen 1958- St&PR 93
Kaspar, Valfrids R. 1939- St&PR 93
Kasparian, Kaspar 1940- St&PR 93
Kasparov, G. K. ConAu 139
Kasparov, Gari ConAu 139
Kasparov, Garri Kimovich 1963- WhoWor 93
Kasparov, Garry ConAu 139
Kasparov, Gary BioIn 17
Kasparov, Gary (Kimovich) 1963- ConAu 139
Kasper, Carol Katherine 1936- WhoAmW 93
Kasper, Casimir W. 1919- St&PR 93
Kasper, Connie Jo Irvin 1955- St&PR 93
Kasper, Erik 1940- WhoScE 91-2
Kasper, H. WhoScE 91-4
Kasper, Herbert 1926- WhoAm 92
Kasper, Horst Manfred 1939- WhoE 93, WhoWor 93
Kasper, Leslie James Law&B 92
Kasper, M. 1947- WhoWrEP 92
Kasper, Ronald Wayne 1944- WhoAm 92
Kasper, Shirl(ey Elaine) 1948- ConAu 137
Kasper, Siegfried Ferdinand 1950- WhoWor 93
Kasper, Stanley Frank 1920- WhoWrEP 92
Kasper, Susan Kathryn 1944- WhoAmW 93
Kasper, Timothy C. 1956- St&PR 93
Kasper, Vancy DcChlFi
Kasperbauer, Michael John 1929- WhoAm 92, WhoSSW 93
Kasperczyk, Jurgen 1941- WhoWor 93
Kasperson, Jeanne Xanthakos 1938- WhoAmW 93
Kasperson, Richard Willet 1927- WhoAm 92
Kaspin, Jeffrey Marc 1948- WhoE 93
Kasprenski, Matthew Anthony 1932- WhoE 93
Kasprick, Lyle Clinton 1932- St&PR 93, WhoAm 92, WhoWor 93
Kasprowicz, Betty M. 1941- WhoIns 93
Kasprowicz, Jan 1860-1926 PolBiDi
Kasprzak, Joyce Ann 1946- WhoAmW 93
Kasprzak, Kenneth Eugene 1953- WhoE 93
Kasprzak, Lucian Alexander 1943- WhoAm 92
Kasprzak, Waclaw A. 1932- WhoScE 91-4
Kasprzak, Wojciech Pawel 1946- WhoScE 91-4
Kasprzycki, Wincenty 1802-1849 PolBiDi
Kasprzyk, Donald C. 1951- St&PR 93
Kasputys, Joseph E. 1936- St&PR 93
Kasputys, Joseph Edward 1936- WhoAm 92, WhoSSW 93
Kasriel, Bernard L. 1946- WhoAm 92
Kass, Alan Paul Law&B 92
Kass, Benny Lee 1936- WhoAm 92
Kass, Bernard St&PR 93
Kass, Edward J. 1928- St&PR 93
Kass, Fredrik J. 1929- St&PR 93
Kass, Jeffrey F. 1943- St&PR 93
Kass, Jerome Allan 1937- WhoWor 93
Kass, Joseph G. 1936- St&PR 93
Kass, Julius 1905-1989 BioIn 17
Kass, Leon Richard 1939- WhoAm 92
Kass, Linda Stern 1953- ConAu 138
Kass, Marshall I. 1929- St&PR 93
Kass, Matthew Anthony 1937- St&PR 93
Kass, R.E. Law&B 92
Kass, R. Robert 1925- WhoE 93
Kass, Steven R. St&PR 93
Kass, Wayne E. St&PR 93
Kass, William Alan 1932- WhoE 93
Kassab, Damian S. Law&B 92
Kassab, Sara Jane Law&B 92
Kassabov, Jordan Dimitrov 1928- WhoScE 91-4
Kassai, Tibor 1930- WhoScE 91-4
Kassam, Amirali Hassanali 1943- WhoWor 93
Kassan, Stuart S. 1946- WhoWor 93
Kassander, Arno Richard, Jr. 1920- WhoAm 92
Kassapoglou, Christos 1959- WhoE 93
Kassar, Mario BioIn 17
Kassar, Richard A. 1947- St&PR 93
Kassatly, Sam Antoine Law&B 92
Kassaye, Moulatou M.K. 1932- WhoUN 92
Kassebaum, Donald Gene 1931- WhoAm 92
Kassebaum, John Philip 1932- WhoE 93, WhoWor 93
Kassebaum, Nancy Landon BioIn 17
Kassebaum, Nancy Landon 1932- CngDr 91, WhoAm 92, WhoAmW 93
Kassees, Joanne Massad 1951- WhoE 93
Kassel, Barbara 1952- WhoEmL 93
Kassel, James E. 1930- WhoIns 93
Kassel, Kenneth 1955- St&PR 93
Kassel, Miriam 1930- St&PR 93
Kassel, Robert 1927- St&PR 93
Kassel, Terry Law&B 92
Kassel, Tichi Wilkerson 1932- WhoAm 92
Kassel, Virginia Weltmer WhoAm 92
Kassell, Neal Frederic 1946- WhoAm 92
Kassem, Abdul Karim 1914-1963 BioIn 17, DcTwHis
Kassem, Lou BioIn 17
Kassem, Lou 1931- ScF&FL 92
Kassenaar, John D.C. 1929- St&PR 93
Kassenoff, Melvyn Mark Law&B 92
Kassern, Tadeusz (Zygfrid) 1904-1957 Baker 92
Kassern, Tadeusz Zygfryd 1904-1957 PolBiDi
Kasses, Kenneth George 1945- WhoAm 92
Kassevgari, Roman ScF&FL 92
Kassewitz, Ruth Eileen Blower 1928- WhoAmW 93
Kassia 800?-c. 843 OxDcByz
Kassiano, Dominic Gitwawa Bakhit WhoAfr
Kassim-Momodu, Momodu Law&B 92
Kassing, Rainer 1938- WhoScE 91-3
Kassinger, Theodore William 1953- WhoE 93
Kassirer, Jerome P. BioIn 17
Kassis, George 1942- WhoUN 92
Kassis, Raymond 1937- WhoSSW 93
Kassler, Michael 1941- WhoWor 93
Kassman, Andrew Lance 1950- WhoEmL 93
Kassman, Herbert Seymour 1924- WhoAm 92
Kassmayer, Moritz 1831-1884 Baker 92
Kassmeier, Randolf Frank Law&B 92
Kassof, Allen H. 1930- WhoE 93, WhoWor 93
Kassoff, Hal 1943- WhoE 93
Kasson, Helen Finch AmWomPl
Kasson, James Matthews 1943- WhoAm 92
Kasson, John Franklin 1944- WhoSSW 93
Kassor, Gerd S.J. 1935- St&PR 93
Kassos, T. George 1935- St&PR 93
Kass-Simon, Gabriele 1936- WhoAmW 93
Kassum, Saleem 1944- WhoUN 92
Kast, Dallas d1991 BioIn 17
Kast, George F. 1946- St&PR 93
Kast, Nancy Lea 1955- WhoAmW 93
Kast, Peter A. Law&B 92
Kast, Pierre 1920-1984 ScF&FL 92
Kastalsky, Alexander (Dmitrievich) 1856-1926 Baker 92
Kastamonites OxDcByz
Kastel, August Paul 1936- St&PR 93
Kastel, Warren MajAI
Kastelic, Patricia A. 1937- St&PR 93
Kastelic, Robert Frank 1934- St&PR 93, WhoAm 92
Kastell, Leonard I. BioIn 17
Kastellec, Philip R. Law&B 92
Kasten, Fritz 1929- WhoScE 91-3
Kasten, Karl Albert 1916- WhoAm 92
Kasten, Paul Rudolph 1923- WhoAm 92
Kasten, Richard John 1938- WhoAm 92
Kasten, Robert W., Jr. 1942- CngDr 91, WhoAm 92
Kasten, Stanley Harvey 1952- WhoAm 92, WhoSSW 93
Kasten, William Arthur 1956- WhoE 93
Kastenholz, James Peter 1963- WhoE 93
Kastenholz, Mary Ellen Connelly 1958- WhoAmW 93
Kastening, Bertel 1929- WhoScE 91-3, WhoWor 93
Kaster, Leonard Albert 1947- WhoEmL 93
Kaster, Lewis Ross 1932- WhoE 93
Kastiel, Ray William 1926- St&PR 93
Kastigar, Elizabeth A. Law&B 92
Kastin, Abba Jeremiah 1934- WhoAm 92, WhoSSW 93
Kastl, Dian Evans 1953- WhoAmW 93
Kastle, Herbert D. 1924-1987 ScF&FL 92
Kastle, Leonard (Gregory) 1929- Baker 92
Kastler, Bonnie Lou 1956- WhoEmL 93
Kastli, Rene Anton 1942- WhoWor 93
Kastner, Alfred 1870-1948 Baker 92
Kastner, Barbara WhoAmW 93
Kastner, Christine Kriha 1951- WhoWrEP 92
Kastner, Cynthia Law&B 92
Kastner, Elliott 1933- MiSFD 9
Kastner, Elwood Curt d1992 BioIn 17, NewYTBS 92
Kastner, Erich 1899-1974 ScF&FL 92
Kastner, Georges Frederic Eugene 1852-1882 Baker 92
Kastner, Jean-Georges 1810-1867 Baker 92
Kastner, Jill (Marie) 1964- SmATA 70 [port]
Kastner, (Macario) Santiago 1908- Baker 92
Kastner, Sid St&PR 93
Kastner, Thomas Mortimer 1926- WhoSSW 93
Kaston, Sanford 1957- St&PR 93
Kastor, Frank Sullivan 1933- WhoAm 92
Kastor, John Alfred 1931- WhoAm 92
Kastor, Ross Lowell 1922- WhoSSW 93
Kastorsky, Vladimir 1871-1948 OxDcOp
Kastorsky, Vladimir (Ivanovich) 1871-1948 Baker 92
Kastovsky, Dieter 1940- WhoWor 93
Kastriner, Lawrence George Law&B 92
Kastrinsky, Howard Mark 1952- WhoSSW 93
Kastrop, Robert R. St&PR 93
Kastrup, H.S. Allan d1991 BioIn 17
Kastrup, Niels Hove 1951- St&PR 93
Kasuya, Kimiko BioIn 17
Kasuya, Koichi 1943- WhoWor 93
Kasuya, Minoru 1936- WhoWor 93
Kasuya, Shigeru 1926- WhoAsAP 91
Kasuya, Terumi 1924- WhoAsAP 91
Kasworm, Carol Edith 1944- WhoAmW 93, WhoSSW 93
Kasyanov, Victor Nikolaevich 1948- WhoWor 93
Kaszniak, Alfred Wayne 1949- WhoAm 92
Kaszubowski, Martin John 1960- WhoE 93
Kata, Edward John 1941- St&PR 93
Katagiri, Akiyasu 1933- WhoWor 93
Katahn, T.L. 1955- WhoWrEP 92
Katai, Andrew A. 1937- St&PR 93
Katai, Andrew Andras 1937- WhoAm 92
Kataja, Eero I. 1927- WhoScE 91-4
Katakalon OxDcByz
Katakalon Kekaumenos dc. 1057 OxDcByz
Katakami, Kojin 1939- WhoAsAP 91
Katakura, Tadashi 1898- HarEnMi
Kataoka, Shichiro 1854-1920 HarEnMi
Kataoka, Takeshi 1949- WhoAsAP 91
Kataphloron OxDcByz
Katarincic, Joseph Anthony 1931- WhoAm 92
Kataskepenos, Nicholas fl. 12th cent.- OxDcByz
Katayama, Arthur Shoji 1927- WhoAm 92
Katayama, Robert Nobuichi 1924- WhoAm 92
Katayama, Sadao 1930- WhoWor 93
Katayama, Tetsuya 1953- WhoWor 93
Katayama, Tohru 1930- WhoWor 93
Katayama, Toranosuke WhoAsAP 91
Katayama, Toshihiro 1928- WhoAm 92
Katchalova, Lidia 1929- WhoScE 91-4
Katchalski, Ephraim 1916- BioIn 17
Katcharoff, Michel d1990 BioIn 17
Katchen, Julius 1926-1969 Baker 92
Katcher, Avrum Labe 1925- WhoAm 92
Katcher, Jerome Fred 1933- St&PR 93
Katcher, Leo d1991 BioIn 17
Katcher, Lewis H. 1942- St&PR 93
Katcher, Philip Martin 1944- WhoE 93
Katcher, Richard 1918- WhoAm 92
Katcher, Robert J. Law&B 92
Katchever, Joanne Mae 1929- WhoAmW 93
Katchman, Ross N. Law&B 92
Katchor, Ben BioIn 17

Katchur, Edward George 1951- WhoEmL 93
Katchur, Marlene Martha 1946- WhoEmL 93
Kate, Herman F.C. ten 1858-1931 IntDcAn
Kate, Stephan St&PR 93
Kateb, George Anthony 1931- WhoAm 92
Kategaya, Eriya 1945- WhoAfr
Katelus, Gary G. 1954- St&PR 93
Kateman, Gerrit 1930- WhoWor 93
Katen, Gloriann Law&B 92
Kater, Louis 1938- WhoScE 91-3
Kates, Charles O. d1992 NewYTBS 92
Kates, George Norbert 1895-1990 BioIn 17
Kates, Henry E. 1939- St&PR 93, WhoAm 92
Kates, Josef 1921- St&PR 93
Kates, Morris 1923- WhoAm 92
Kates, Peggy Jean 1950- WhoAmW 93
Kates, Phillip Brown 1919- St&PR 93
Kates, Robert William 1929- WhoAm 92
Kates, Sam BioIn 17
Kates, Stephen (Edward) 1943- Baker 92
Kates, Susan Prentky WhoAmW 93, WhoE 93
Kates, Victor 1915- St&PR 93
Katgerman, Laurens 1945- WhoWor 93
Kath, Birgitte BioIn 17
Kath, Ruth Robert 1948- WhoAmW 93
Kathe, Barbara Ann 1931- WhoE 93
Katheder, Thomas Law&B 92
Kathenes, Brian G. 1956- WhoE 93
Katherine, Robert Andrew 1941- WhoAm 92
Kathka, David Arlin WhoAm 92
Kathol, Lea A. St&PR 93
Kathol, Robert F. 1941- St&PR 93
Kathuria, Nirmal Bhatia 1948- WhoEmL 93
Kathwari, M. Farooq 1944- St&PR 93, WhoAm 92
Katila, Ronald Harvey Law&B 92
Katims, Jason Alexander 1960- WhoE 93
Katims, Milton 1909- Baker 92
Katims, Nancy Klastorin Naron 1949- WhoAmW 93
Katin, Peter (Roy) 1930- Baker 92, WhoWor 93
Katjiuongua, Moses Katjikuru 1942- WhoAfr
Katkat, Ali Vahap 1950- WhoScE 91-4
Katke, Mary Lou 1959- WhoEmL 93
Katkin, Edward Samuel 1937- WhoAm 92, WhoE 93
Katkin, Pamela E. ScF&FL 92
Katkin, S.B. Law&B 92
Katko, Charles 1926- WhoAm 92
Katkovnik, Vladimir Yakovlevich 1937- WhoWor 93
Katleman, Harris L. WhoAm 92
Katlic, John E. 1928- St&PR 93
Katlic, John Edward 1928- WhoAm 92
Kato, Daisuke 1942- WhoWor 93
Kato, Eileen A. 1950- WhoEmL 93
Kato, Hidetoshi 1930- WhoWor 93
Kato, Kanji 1870-1939 HarEnMi
Kato, Ken 1950- ScF&FL 92
Kato, Kiyomasa 1562-1611 HarEnMi
Kato, Koichi 1939- WhoAsAP 91, WhoWor 93
Kato, Mankichi 1940- WhoAsAP 91
Kato, Masakatsu 1942- WhoUN 92
Kato, Masanobu 1946- WhoAm 92
Kato, Michinobu 1926- WhoWor 93
Kato, Minobu 1953- St&PR 93
Kato, Morihiro 1936- WhoWor 93
Kato, Mutsuki 1926- WhoAsAP 91
Kato, Pamela Kiyomi 1964- WhoAmW 93
Kato, Peter Eiichi 1934- WhoWor 93
Kato, Ryuichi 1930- WhoWor 93
Kato, Shigeaki 1947- WhoAsAP 91
Kato, Shuji 1948- WhoWor 93
Kato, Shunsaku 1923- WhoWor 93
Kato, Tadaya 1938- WhoWor 93
Kato, Takenori 1915- WhoAsAP 91
Kato, Tomohiko 1941- WhoWor 93
Kato, Tomosaburo 1861-1923 HarEnMi
Kato, Tukuji 1926- WhoAsAP 91
Kato, Walter Yoneo 1924- WhoAm 92
Kato, Yasuhisa 1945- WhoUN 92
Katoh, Arthur Kow 1933- WhoE 93
Katon, John Edward 1929- WhoAm 92
Katona, Peter Geza 1937- WhoAm 92
Katona, Raymond Michael Law&B 92
Katona-Apte, Judit 1943- WhoAmW 93
Katope, Christopher George 1918- WhoAm 92
Katopes, Peter James 1947- WhoWrEP 92
Katopis, Anthony 1944- WhoE 93
Kator, Steven W. 1948- St&PR 93
Kato Takaaki 1860-1926 DcTwHis
Katovic, Zvonimir 1933- WhoScE 91-4
Katovich, John C. 1953- St&PR 93
Katovich, John Charles Law&B 92
Katovich, Kathleen Law&B 92
Katrantzos, Vlassis N. 1938- WhoWor 93
Katrares, John fl. 1309-1322 OxDcByz
Katritzky, Alan Roy 1928- WhoAm 92
Katritzky, Linde 1928- WhoSSW 93
Kats, Boris Aleksandrovich 1952- WhoWor 93
Kats, James Stephan 1948- WhoEmL 93
Katsahnias, Thomas George 1928- WhoAm 92
Katsampes, Theodore Peter 1949- St&PR 93
Katsanos, Nicholas A. 1930- WhoScE 91-3
Katsaragakis, Elisseos Stavrou 1943- WhoWor 93
Katsaris, Cyprien 1951- Baker 92
Katsaros, Constantine 1926- WhoAm 92
Katsch, Kurt 1893-1958 BioIn 17
Katschnig, Heinz 1942- WhoScE 91-4
Katselas, Milton 1933- MiSFD 9
Katsh, Abraham Isaac 1908- WhoAm 92
Katsianis, John Nick 1960- WhoEmL 93, WhoWor 93
Katsikadelis, John Theodore 1937- WhoWor 93
Katsikas, Sokratis Konstantine 1960- WhoWor 93
Katsiotis, Paul 1927- WhoScE 91-3
Katskee, Melvin Robert Law&B 92
Katski, Antoine 1817-1899 PolBiDi
Katson, Roberta Marina 1947- WhoAmW 93
Katsonis, Michael George 1951- WhoSSW 93
Katsonov, Florence Jean WhoWrEP 92
Katsoulis, Larry N. 1945- St&PR 93
Katsoyannos, Panayotis 1939- WhoWor 93
Katsu, Awa 1823-1899 HarEnMi
Katsu, Kokichi 1802-1850 BioIn 17
Katsuki, Hirohiko 1921- WhoWor 93
Katsuki, Kenji 1943- WhoAsAP 91
Katsuki, Takeshi 1937- WhoWor 93
Katsumi, Masayuki 1933- WhoWor 93
Katsuno, Angela Tamao 1966- WhoAmW 93
Katsuno, Masatsune 1941- WhoUN 92
Katsura, Fumiko 1944- WhoWor 93
Katsura, Kohshoh 1934- WhoWor 93
Katsura, Taro 1847-1913 HarEnMi
Katsushika, Hokusai 1760-1849 BioIn 17
Katsuyama, Y. Glen Law&B 92
Katsuyama, Yutaka 1949- WhoWor 93
Katt, Elliot BioIn 17
Katt, Elmer A. 1917- St&PR 93
Kattan, Naim 1928- WhoCanL 92
Kattan, Olga 1928-1991 BioIn 17
Kattan, Peter Issa 1961- WhoSSW 93
Kattas, Paula Louise 1959- WhoAmW 93
Katten, Richard L. 1946- WhoIns 93
Kattenstroth, Christian 1937- WhoWor 93
Katter, Nafe Edmund 1926- WhoE 93
Katter, Robert Cummin 1918- WhoAsAP 91
Katterman, Grace Lenore 1935- WhoAmW 93
Kattos, Tina 1968- WhoAmW 93
Kattus, James Robert 1922- WhoSSW 93
Kattwinkel, John 1941- WhoAm 92
Katungi, Charles Kakuru 1942- WhoUN 92
Katushi, Sakai 1935- WhoWor 93
Katutaro, Kuge 1937- WhoWor 93
Katwijk, Paul van 1885-1974 Baker 92
Katz, Abraham 1926- WhoAm 92, WhoE 93, WhoWor 93
Katz, Adam BioIn 17
Katz, Adrian Izhack 1932- WhoAm 92
Katz, Alan R. 1942- St&PR 93
Katz, Alex 1927- BioIn 17, WhoAm 92
Katz, Alix Martha 1948- WhoE 93, WhoEmL 93
Katz, Allan Jack 1947- WhoSSW 93
Katz, Allan Robert 1942- WhoSSW 93
Katz, Amnon 1935- WhoWrEP 92
Katz, Anne Harris WhoAmW 93
Katz, Arnold 1930- WhoAm 92
Katz, Arnold M. 1954- St&PR 93
Katz, Arnold Martin 1932- WhoAm 92
Katz, Arnold Martin 1940- WhoE 93, WhoWor 93
Katz, Aya 1960- WhoEmL 93
Katz, Barry Michael Law&B 92
Katz, Bennett Lee Law&B 92
Katz, Bennett R. Law&B 92
Katz, Bernard WhoScE 91-1
Katz, Bernard 1911- WhoWor 93
Katz, Bernard 1936- WhoE 93
Katz, Bobbi 1933- ConAu 37NR
Katz, Candace Kaufman 1947- WhoE 93
Katz, Carlos 1934- WhoAm 92
Katz, Carol Hecht Law&B 92
Katz, Charles L. Law&B 92
Katz, Cindi Robin 1954- WhoAmW 93
Katz, Colleen WhoAm 92
Katz, Colleen Burke 1936- WhoWrEP 92
Katz, Daniel Barry 1948- WhoEmL 93
Katz, Daniel Roger 1961- WhoE 93
Katz, David Allan 1933- St&PR 93
Katz, David Carey 1940- St&PR 93
Katz, Dolores 1924- WhoAmW 93
Katz, Donald Paul 1947- St&PR 93
Katz, Doug MiSFD 9
Katz, Douglas Jeffrey 1942- WhoAm 92
Katz, Earl L. 1918- St&PR 93
Katz, Edward M. BioIn 17
Katz, Edward Morris 1921- WhoAm 92
Katz, Edward Petroff 1933- St&PR 93
Katz, Elaine Marcia 1942- WhoAmW 93
Katz, Eliot 1957- WhoWrEP 92
Katz, Elizabeth A. 1959- St&PR 93
Katz, Ephraim d1992 NewYTBS 92
Katz, Eric Stephen 1946- WhoEmL 93
Katz, Erwin I. St&PR 93
Katz, Eugene Yurii 1952- WhoWor 93
Katz, Fred N. 1941- WhoSSW 93
Katz, Frederick 1898-1989 BioIn 17
Katz, Gerald 1938- St&PR 93
Katz, Gerald 1939- WhoAm 92, WhoIns 93
Katz, Glenn Lawrence Law&B 92
Katz, Gloria WhoAm 92
Katz, Gloria 1945- ScF&FL 92
Katz, Gregory 1950- St&PR 93
Katz, Hadrian Ronald 1949- WhoEmL 93
Katz, Hanns 1892-1940 BioIn 17
Katz, Harold 1937- WhoAm 92
Katz, Harold Ambrose 1921- WhoAm 92
Katz, Harvey A. 1927- ScF&FL 92, St&PR 93
Katz, Henry 1937- WhoAm 92, WhoIns 93
Katz, Herman d1990 BioIn 17
Katz, Hilda 1909- WhoAm 92, WhoAmW 93, WhoE 93, WhoWor 93
Katz, Hilliard Joel 1918- WhoAm 92
Katz, Hope N. 1964- WhoAmW 93
Katz, Howard G. Law&B 92
Katz, Irwin Howard 1927- St&PR 93
Katz, Israel J(oseph) 1930- Baker 92
Katz, Jack 1934- WhoAm 92
Katz, Jacob BioIn 17
Katz, James M. Law&B 92
Katz, James Martin 1942- St&PR 93
Katz, Jane 1943- WhoAmW 93
Katz, Jason L. 1947- St&PR 93
Katz, Jason Lawrence 1947- WhoAm 92
Katz, Jay 1922- WhoAm 92
Katz, Jeffrey Harvey 1947- WhoE 93, WhoEmL 93
Katz, Jeffrey Owen 1950- WhoE 93
Katz, Jerrold Pinya 1939- WhoE 93
Katz, Jerry 1961- WhoE 93
Katz, Joanne Seffens 1955- WhoAmW 93
Katz, John 1938- WhoAm 92
Katz, Jonathan Garber 1950- WhoAm 92
Katz, Jose 1944- WhoE 93
Katz, Joseph 1952- WhoEmL 93
Katz, Joseph Jacob 1912- WhoAm 92
Katz, Joseph Louis 1938- WhoAm 92
Katz, Joseph M. 1913-1991 BioIn 17
Katz, Judith 1951- ConAu 139
Katz, Judith Helen 1950- WhoAmW 93
Katz, Judith T. 1946- St&PR 93
Katz, Julian 1937- WhoAm 92, WhoE 93, WhoWor 93
Katz, Kathy Silver 1947- WhoEmL 93
Katz, Laurence Barry 1954- WhoAm 92
Katz, Lawrence Allen 1942- WhoAm 92
Katz, Lawrence Andrew 1948- St&PR 93
Katz, Lawrence Edward 1947- WhoEmL 93
Katz, Lawrence W. Law&B 92
Katz, Leon 1921- WhoAm 92
Katz, Leonard William 1938- WhoE 93
Katz, Leslie George 1918- ScF&FL 92
Katz, Lewis Robert 1938- WhoAm 92
Katz, Lillian Vernon BioIn 17
Katz, Lillian Vernon 1927- St&PR 93
Katz, Lois Anne 1941- WhoE 93
Katz, Lorraine Walters d1991 BioIn 17
Katz, M.D. Law&B 92
Katz, Marc P. Law&B 92
Katz, Marc Paul 1953- St&PR 93
Katz, Marcia 1950- WhoAm 92, WhoAmW 93
Katz, Mariann 1948- St&PR 93
Katz, Marilyn Faye 1945- WhoAmW 93
Katz, Marjorie A. Law&B 92
Katz, Mark Norman 1954- WhoSSW 93
Katz, Marshall Paul 1939- WhoAm 92
Katz, Martha Lessman 1952- WhoAmW 93
Katz, Martin Howard 1931- WhoAm 92
Katz, Martin Jay 1943- St&PR 93
Katz, Marvin 1930- WhoE 93
Katz, Maurice Harry 1937- WhoAm 92
Katz, Maurice Joseph 1937- WhoAm 92
Katz, Menke 1906- WhoWrEP 92
Katz, Menke 1906-1991 BioIn 17
Katz, Michael 1928- WhoAm 92
Katz, Michael A. Law&B 92
Katz, Michael Alan 1963- WhoE 93
Katz, Michael J. 1950- St&PR 93
Katz, Michael Jeffery 1950- WhoEmL 93
Katz, Michael Ray 1944- ConAu 39NR, WhoAm 92
Katz, Michael S. 1947- WhoEmL 93
Katz, Michael S. 1953- St&PR 93
Katz, Milton 1907- WhoAm 92
Katz, Mindru 1925-1978 Baker 92
Katz, Morris 1915- St&PR 93
Katz, Morton H. 1934- St&PR 93
Katz, Morton Norris 1919- WhoE 93
Katz, Murray L. 1932- WhoAm 92
Katz, Nancy S. Law&B 92
Katz, Nancy Sue 1954- WhoAmW 93
Katz, Nestor Eduardo 1952- WhoWor 93
Katz, Norman 1925- WhoAm 92, WhoE 93
Katz, Norman 1942- St&PR 93
Katz, Paul R. Law&B 92
Katz, Peter 1947- WhoAm 92
Katz, Peter Christopher 1953- St&PR 93
Katz, Phyllis Alberts WhoAmW 93
Katz, Phyllis Pollak 1939- WhoAm 92
Katz, Richard Alan 1950- WhoE 93
Katz, Richard C. Law&B 92
Katz, Richard Jon 1932- WhoE 93
Katz, Richard Steven Law&B 92
Katz, Richard W. Law&B 92
Katz, Robert A. d1992 NewYTBS 92
Katz, Robert Arvin 1927- WhoAm 92
Katz, Robert H. 1925- St&PR 93
Katz, Robert Herman 1925- WhoIns 93
Katz, Robert Irwin 1924- WhoSSW 93
Katz, Robert J. Law&B 92
Katz, Robert James 1947- WhoAm 92
Katz, Robert Langdon 1917- WhoAm 92
Katz, Robert Lee 1926- WhoAm 92
Katz, Robert Mathias 1949- WhoE 93
Katz, Robert Nathan 1939- WhoE 93
Katz, Robin K. Law&B 92
Katz, Roger A. Law&B 92
Katz, Ronald Alan 1949- St&PR 93
Katz, Ronald Levy 1938- WhoWor 93
Katz, Ronald Lewis 1932- WhoAm 92
Katz, Ronald S. 1946- WhoEmL 93
Katz, Samuel 1914- St&PR 93
Katz, Samuel 1923- WhoAm 92
Katz, Samuel Lawrence 1927- WhoAm 92, WhoSSW 93
Katz, Sanford Noah 1933- WhoAm 92
Katz, Saul Milton 1915- WhoAm 92
Katz, Sharon F. 1955- WhoEmL 93
Katz, Sheldon 1934- WhoE 93
Katz, Shelley ScF&FL 92
Katz, Sol 1913- WhoAm 92
Katz, Stanley BioIn 17
Katz, Stanley Nider 1934- WhoAm 92, WhoWor 93
Katz, Stephen Robert 1945- WhoUN 92
Katz, Steve 1935- JeAmFiW
Katz, Steve Robert 1935- WhoWrEP 92
Katz, Steven Edward 1937- WhoAm 92, WhoWor 93
Katz, Steven Jay Law&B 92
Katz, Steven Martin 1941- WhoWor 93
Katz, Steven Theodore 1944- WhoAm 92
Katz, Stuart 1964- WhoEmL 93
Katz, Stuart Charles 1937- WhoAm 92
Katz, Susan A. 1939- WhoWrEP 92
Katz, Susan Audrey 1956- WhoAmW 93
Katz, Susan J. 1935- St&PR 93
Katz, Susan R. 1950- WhoAmW 93
Katz, Susan Stanton 1951- WhoEmL 93
Katz, Sydney L. 1941- St&PR 93
Katz, Victoria Manuela 1941- WhoAmW 93
Katz, Vincent BioIn 17
Katz, Welwyn Wilton BioIn 17
Katz, Welwyn Wilton 1948- DcChlFi, ScF&FL 92, WhoAm 92, WhoCanL 92
Katz, Wendy R. 1945- ScF&FL 92
Katz, William 1940- ScF&FL 92
Katz, William Armstrong 1928- WhoAm 92
Katz, William David 1915- WhoAm 92, WhoSSW 93
Katz, William E. 1924- St&PR 93
Katz, William Emanuel 1924- WhoAm 92
Katz, William Loren 1927- WhoAm 92, WhoWrEP 92
Katzakian, Bozant 1915- St&PR 93
Katzberg, Jane Michaels 1940- WhoE 93
Katzel, Jeanine Alma 1948- WhoAmW 93
Katzell, Raymond A. 1919- WhoAm 92
Katzen, Jack 1921-1991 BioIn 17
Katzen, Jay Kenneth 1936- WhoAm 92
Katzen, Lila Pell 1932- WhoAm 92
Katzen, Raphael 1915- WhoAm 92
Katzen, Sally 1942- WhoAm 92, WhoAmW 93
Katzenbach, John Strong Miner 1950- WhoE 93
Katzenbach, Nicholas deB 1922- BioIn 17, St&PR 93
Katzenbach, Nicholas deBelleville 1922- WhoAm 92
Katzenbach, Shirley Steinman d1991 BioIn 17
Katzenberg, Jeffrey BioIn 17, NewYTBS 92 [port]
Katzenberg, Jeffrey 1950- ConTFT 10, WhoAm 92
Katzenstein, Barbara Jane 1943- WhoAmW 93
Katzenstein, Gary Jay 1956- WhoE 93, WhoEmL 93
Katzenstein, Thea 1927- WhoAmW 93, WhoSSW 93

Katzer, Georg 1935- *Baker 92*
Katz Froning, Susan *Law&B 92*
Katzianer, Johann 1480-1539 *HarEnMi*
Katzin, Jerome S. 1918- *St&PR 93*
Katzin, Lee H. 1935- *MiSFD 9*
Katzir, Ephraim 1916- *BioIn 17, WhoWor 93*
Katzir, Levy 1934- *WhoAm 92*
Katzka, Gabriel d1990 *BioIn 17*
Katzman, Elaine Menter 1927- *WhoAmW 93*
Katzman, Elliot M. 1956- *St&PR 93*
Katzman, Herbert Henry 1923- *WhoAm 92*
Katzman, John *BioIn 17*
Katzman, Lawrence 1922- *St&PR 93*
Katzman, Leonard *ConTFT 10*
Katzman, Melvin S. *Law&B 92*
Katzman, Mitchell Ronald *Law&B 92*
Katzman, Randi Michele 1964- *WhoE 93*
Katzman, Robert 1925- *WhoAm 92*
Katzmann, Gary Stephen 1953- *WhoE 93, WhoEmL 93*
Katzmann, Robert Allen 1953- *WhoE 93, WhoEmL 93*
Katzowitz, Lauren *WhoE 93*
Katzper, Meyer 1936- *WhoE 93*
Kau, Lawrie Elizabeth 1942- *WhoWrEP 92*
Kauachi, Jose 1939- *St&PR 93*
Kauahi, Ethel N. 1943- *WhoAmW 93*
Kaub, Peter 1955- *St&PR 93*
Kauder, Hugo 1888-1972 *Baker 92*
Kauder, Knut Hans-Jurgen 1940- *WhoScE 91-3*
Kauderer, Bernard Marvin 1931- *WhoAm 92*
Kaudewitz, Fritz 1921- *WhoWor 93*
Kauer, Erhard 1928- *WhoScE 91-3*
Kauer, Ferdinand 1751-1831 *Baker 92*
Kauer, Ferdinand August 1751-1831 *OxDcOp*
Kauf, David K. 1933- *WhoIns 93*
Kauf, David Karl 1933- *St&PR 93*
Kauf, Gary D. 1943- *St&PR 93*
Kauf, Tom K. *Law&B 92*
Kaufelt, David A. *WhoWrEP 92*
Kaufelt, David A. 1939- *ScF&FL 92*
Kaufelt, David Allan 1939- *ConAu 38NR*
Kaufelt, Stanley Philip 1920- *St&PR 93, WhoAm 92*
Kaufer, Howard *St&PR 93*
Kaufer, Jonathan 1955- *MiSFD 9*
Kauffman, Andrew John 1920- *WhoE 93*
Kauffman, Bruce William 1934- *WhoAm 92, WhoE 93, WhoWor 93*
Kauffman, Dean R., Jr. *St&PR 93*
Kauffman, Dean Ronald 1921- *St&PR 93*
Kauffman, Ellwood 1928- *St&PR 93*
Kauffman, Erle Galen 1933- *WhoAm 92*
Kauffman, Ewing Marion 1916- *WhoAm 92*
Kauffman, George Bernard 1930- *WhoAm 92*
Kauffman, Gordon Lee, Jr. 1946- *WhoAm 92*
Kauffman, James Harold 1944- *St&PR 93*
Kauffman, James Milton 1940- *WhoAm 92*
Kauffman, Janet 1945- *WhoWrEP 92*
Kauffman, Jeffrey Michael 1942- *WhoE 93*
Kauffman, John Thomas 1926- *St&PR 93, WhoAm 92*
Kauffman, Juanita Eileen 1946- *St&PR 93*
Kauffman, Kathy Coventon 1948- *WhoAmW 93*
Kauffman, Kenneth Lee 1943- *WhoSSW 93*
Kauffman, Laura Tavel 1956- *WhoEmL 93*
Kauffman, Leon A. 1934- *WhoE 93*
Kauffman, Luke Edward 1941- *WhoE 93, WhoWor 93*
Kauffman, Marjorie Ann 1928- *St&PR 93*
Kauffman, Marvin Earl 1933- *WhoAm 92*
Kauffman, Richard N. 1916- *St&PR 93*
Kauffman, Robert Craig 1932- *WhoAm 92*
Kauffman, Robert Louis 1926- *St&PR 93*
Kauffman, Robert R. 1940- *St&PR 93*
Kauffman, Sandra Daley 1933- *WhoAmW 93*
Kauffman, Stanley Chester 1924- *WhoAm 92*
Kauffman, Timothy Jay 1949- *St&PR 93*
Kauffman, William Ray 1947- *WhoAm 92*
Kauffmann, Angelica 1741-1807 *BioIn 17*
Kauffmann, Emil 1836-1909 *Baker 92*
Kauffmann, Ernst Friedrich 1803-1856 *Baker 92*
Kauffmann, Fritz 1855-1934 *Baker 92*
Kauffmann, Howard C. 1923- *St&PR 93*
Kauffmann, Leo Justinus 1901-1944 *Baker 92*
Kauffmann, Samuel Hay 1898-1971 *DcLB 127 [port]*
Kauffmann, Stanley 1916- *BioIn 17*
Kauffmann, Stanley Jules 1916- *WhoAm 92, WhoWrEP 92*
Kauffmann, Thomas 1924- *WhoScE 91-3*
Kaufinger, George 1934- *St&PR 93*
Kaufman, Alan Joel 1943- *St&PR 93*
Kaufman, Albert Nick 1924- *WhoWor 93*
Kaufman, Alex 1924- *WhoAm 92*
Kaufman, Allan M. *Law&B 92*
Kaufman, Allan M. 1948- *WhoAm 92*
Kaufman, Amy Rebecca 1951- *WhoWrEP 92*
Kaufman, Andrew Lee 1931- *WhoAm 92*
Kaufman, Andrew Michael 1949- *WhoAm 92*
Kaufman, Antoinette D. 1939- *WhoAm 92*
Kaufman, Armin 1925- *St&PR 93*
Kaufman, Arnold M. 1935- *St&PR 93*
Kaufman, Arnold Marvin 1935- *WhoAm 92*
Kaufman, Bart D. 1945- *St&PR 93*
Kaufman, Bel *WhoAm 92, WhoWrEP 92*
Kaufman, Benjamin 1894?-1981 *BioIn 17*
Kaufman, Charles *MiSFD 9*
Kaufman, Charles 1937- *WhoE 93*
Kaufman, Charles R. 1908-1990 *BioIn 17*
Kaufman, Charlotte King 1920- *WhoAmW 93*
Kaufman, Daniel I. 1922- *St&PR 93*
Kaufman, David A. 1915- *St&PR 93*
Kaufman, David Joseph 1931- *WhoE 93, WhoWor 93*
Kaufman, Debra Ellen 1959- *WhoAmW 93*
Kaufman, Debra Gammell *Law&B 92*
Kaufman, Debra Jane 1951- *WhoWrEP 92*
Kaufman, Denise Norma 1954- *WhoAmW 93*
Kaufman, Donald Leroy 1931- *WhoAm 92*
Kaufman, Donald Saul 1945- *WhoE 93*
Kaufman, Douglas *ScF&FL 92*
Kaufman, Edward Lewis *Law&B 92*
Kaufman, Elaine Sue Sommers 1933- *WhoAmW 93*
Kaufman, Erwin R. *St&PR 93*
Kaufman, Frank Albert 1916- *WhoAm 92*
Kaufman, Frank J. 1944- *St&PR 93*
Kaufman, Frank Joseph 1944- *WhoAm 92*
Kaufman, George S. 1889-1961 *BioIn 17*
Kaufman, Gerald A. 1941- *St&PR 93*
Kaufman, Glen 1932- *BioIn 17*
Kaufman, Gordon Dester 1925- *WhoAm 92*
Kaufman, Gustavo A. *Law&B 92*
Kaufman, Harold Richard 1926- *WhoAm 92*
Kaufman, Harry 1894-1961 *Baker 92*
Kaufman, Harry 1937- *WhoE 93, WhoWor 93*
Kaufman, Hazel Sharrard *AmWomPl*
Kaufman, Henry 1927- *WhoAm 92*
Kaufman, Herbert 1922- *ConAu 137*
Kaufman, Herbert 1928- *St&PR 93*
Kaufman, Herbert Edward 1931- *WhoAm 92*
Kaufman, Herbert Mark 1946- *WhoWor 93*
Kaufman, Howard Jack *Law&B 92*
Kaufman, Howard Jack 1942- *WhoAm 92*
Kaufman, Ira Gladstone 1909- *WhoWor 93*
Kaufman, Ira Jeffrey 1928- *WhoAm 92*
Kaufman, Irene S. 1933- *WhoAmW 93*
Kaufman, Irving 1925- *WhoAm 92*
Kaufman, Irving N. 1924- *WhoAm 92, WhoE 93*
Kaufman, Irving R. *BioIn 17*
Kaufman, Irving R. 1910-1992 *NewYTBS 92 [port]*
Kaufman, Irving R(obert) 1910-1992 *CurBio 92N*
Kaufman, Isaac 1947- *St&PR 93*
Kaufman, Jackie *BioIn 17*
Kaufman, James E. 1950- *St&PR 93*
Kaufman, James Henry 1953- *WhoEmL 93*
Kaufman, Jane 1938- *WhoAm 92*
Kaufman, Janice Horner 1949- *WhoAmW 93*
Kaufman, Jeffrey Allen 1952- *WhoEmL 93, WhoWor 93*
Kaufman, Jeffrey Hugh 1952- *WhoEmL 93*
Kaufman, Jerome J. 1917- *WhoAm 92*
Kaufman, Jerome L. 1933- *WhoAm 92*
Kaufman, Jess 1920- *WhoE 93*
Kaufman, Jim 1949- *MiSFD 9*
Kaufman, Joe 1911- *WhoE 93*
Kaufman, Joel 1960- *WhoEmL 93*
Kaufman, John E. 1927- *WhoAm 92*
Kaufman, John Gilbert, Jr. 1931- *WhoAm 92*
Kaufman, John Pearse 1944- *WhoSSW 93*
Kaufman, John Robert 1931- *WhoE 93*
Kaufman, Judith 1942- *WhoE 93*
Kaufman, Jules P. *Law&B 92*
Kaufman, Julian Mortimer 1918- *WhoAm 92*
Kaufman, Karl Lincoln 1911- *WhoAm 92*
Kaufman, Laura Phyllis 1947- *WhoAmW 93*
Kaufman, Leon I. 1927- *St&PR 93*
Kaufman, Linda Ruth 1960- *WhoAmW 93*
Kaufman, Lloyd 1945- *MiSFD 9*
Kaufman, Louis 1905- *Baker 92*
Kaufman, Lynne Levin *Law&B 92*
Kaufman, Malvin 1929- *St&PR 93*
Kaufman, Marcus Maurice 1929- *WhoAm 92*
Kaufman, Mark David 1949- *WhoEmL 93*
Kaufman, Martin 1940- *WhoWrEP 92*
Kaufman, Martin M. 1921- *St&PR 93*
Kaufman, Martin Theodore 1945- *St&PR 93*
Kaufman, Melvin 1939- *St&PR 93*
Kaufman, Menahem 1921- *ConAu 138*
Kaufman, Mervyn Douglas 1932- *WhoAm 92*
Kaufman, Michael David 1941- *WhoAm 92*
Kaufman, Monica *AfrAmBi [port]*
Kaufman, Nathan 1915- *WhoAm 92*
Kaufman, Paul 1923- *WhoAm 92*
Kaufman, Paul Albert 1915- *St&PR 93*
Kaufman, Paul Michael 1949- *WhoEmL 93*
Kaufman, Paula T. 1946- *WhoAm 92, WhoAmW 93*
Kaufman, Perry Jay 1943- *WhoWor 93*
Kaufman, Peter Bishop 1928- *WhoAm 92*
Kaufman, Philip 1936- *MiSFD 9, WhoAm 92*
Kaufman, Phyllis Cynthia 1945- *WhoAmW 93*
Kaufman, Ray G. 1944- *St&PR 93*
Kaufman, Raymond Henry 1925- *WhoAm 92*
Kaufman, Richard d1991 *BioIn 17*
Kaufman, Richard 1936-1990 *BioIn 17*
Kaufman, Richard 1959- *St&PR 93*
Kaufman, Richard A. *Law&B 92*
Kaufman, Richard A. 1951- *St&PR 93*
Kaufman, Richard Louis 1955- *St&PR 93*
Kaufman, Robert *BioIn 17*
Kaufman, Robert Edward 1934- *St&PR 93*
Kaufman, Robert Jules 1921- *WhoAm 92*
Kaufman, Robert Lester *Law&B 92*
Kaufman, Robert Max 1929- *WhoAm 92, WhoE 93*
Kaufman, Robert Perry 1949- *St&PR 93*
Kaufman, Roger 1932- *WhoSSW 93*
Kaufman, Roger Wayne 1938- *WhoAm 92*
Kaufman, Rolf 1930- *St&PR 93*
Kaufman, Ron *BioIn 17*
Kaufman, Ronald Paul 1929- *WhoAm 92*
Kaufman, Russell Eugene 1946- *WhoEmL 93*
Kaufman, Sanford Paul 1928- *WhoAm 92*
Kaufman, Scott Wayne 1949- *WhoAm 92*
Kaufman, Shelley S. 1953- *WhoEmL 93*
Kaufman, Sol 1916- *St&PR 93*
Kaufman, Stanley N. *St&PR 93*
Kaufman, Stephen Carl *Law&B 92*
Kaufman, Stephen E. 1932- *WhoE 93*
Kaufman, Stephen Lawrence 1942- *WhoSSW 93*
Kaufman, Stephen P. 1941- *St&PR 93*
Kaufman, Stuart J. 1950- *WhoWrEP 92*
Kaufman, Terry *Law&B 92*
Kaufman, Theodore D. *Law&B 92*
Kaufman, Thomas Frederick 1949- *WhoAm 92, WhoEmL 93*
Kaufman, Victor A. *St&PR 93*
Kaufman, Walter J. 1917- *St&PR 93*
Kaufman, William 1910- *WhoAm 92, WhoWor 93*
Kaufman, William Michael *Law&B 92*
Kaufman, William Michael 1958- *WhoEmL 93*
Kaufman, William Morris 1931- *WhoAm 92*
Kaufmann, Armin 1902-1980 *Baker 92*
Kaufmann, D.B. 1934- *St&PR 93*
Kaufmann, Edgar 1910-1989 *BioIn 17*
Kaufmann, Friedrich 1785-1866 *Baker 92*
Kaufmann, Fritz 1896-1991 *BioIn 17*
Kaufmann, George 1931-1990 *BioIn 17*
Kaufmann, Guillermo Hector 1947- *WhoWor 93*
Kaufmann, Hans 1923- *WhoIns 93*
Kaufmann, Helen 1887-1978 *Baker 92*
Kaufmann, Henry Mark 1929- *WhoAm 92, WhoE 93, WhoWor 93*
Kaufmann, Herbert 1941- *WhoScE 91-3*
Kaufmann, Jack 1942- *WhoAm 92*
Kaufmann, James A. 1923- *WhoAm 92*
Kaufmann, Joe *ScF&FL 92*
Kaufmann, Joseph Gregory, Jr. 1953- *WhoWrEP 92*
Kaufmann, Kenneth K. *Law&B 92*
Kaufmann, Kenneth K. 1930- *St&PR 93*
Kaufmann, Mark S. 1932- *St&PR 93*
Kaufmann, Mark Steiner 1932- *WhoAm 92, WhoE 93, WhoWor 93*
Kaufmann, Marta E. 1947- *WhoAmW 93*
Kaufmann, Michael *WhoScE 91-3*
Kaufmann, Michael Myron 1940- *WhoE 93*
Kaufmann, Paul T. 1936- *St&PR 93*
Kaufmann, Peter 1942- *WhoScE 91-3*
Kaufmann, Robert W. 1949- *St&PR 93*
Kaufmann, Stephan 1926- *St&PR 93*
Kaufmann, Sylvia Nadeau 1940- *WhoAmW 93*
Kaufmann, Thomas DaCosta 1948- *WhoE 93*
Kaufmann, Thomas David 1922- *WhoAm 92*
Kaufmann, Walter 1907-1984 *Baker 92*
Kaufmann, Werner 1924- *WhoScE 91-3*
Kaufmann, Yehuda 1886-1976 *BioIn 17*
Kaufold, Leroy 1924- *WhoAm 92*
Kaufthal, Ilan 1947- *St&PR 93*
Kauger, Yvonne 1937- *WhoAm 92, WhoAmW 93, WhoSSW 93*
Kaukonen, Esko Olavi 1941- *WhoWor 93*
Kaukovirta, Erkki J. 1934- *WhoScE 91-4*
Kaukovirta, Erkki Johannes 1934- *WhoWor 93*
Kaul, Alexander *WhoScE 91-3*
Kaul, Calvin J. E., Jr. 1947- *WhoSSW 93*
Kaul, Chand Narain 1936- *WhoUN 92*
Kaul, Inge 1944- *WhoUN 92*
Kaul, Oskar 1885-1968 *Baker 92*
Kaul, Sheila *WhoAsAP 91*
Kaul, Udo 1939- *St&PR 93, WhoAm 92*
Kaula, P.N. 1924- *BioIn 17*
Kaula, Prithvi Nath 1924- *BioIn 17*
Kaula, William Mason 1926- *WhoAm 92*
Kaulakis, Arnold Francis 1916- *WhoAm 92*
Kaulbach, Kenneth George *Law&B 92*
Kaulkin, Donna Brookman 1943- *WhoAm 92*
Kaull, George H. 1931- *St&PR 93*
Kaumeyer, Linda Louise 1950- *WhoEmL 93*
Kaun, Hugo 1863-1932 *Baker 92*
Kaunda, Kenneth 1924- *ColdWar 2 [port], DcTwHis*
Kaunda, Kenneth D. 1924- *BioIn 17*
Kaunda, Kenneth David 1924- *WhoAfr, WhoWor 93*
Kaunda, Wezi Chizuma Burukutu 1951- *WhoAfr*
Kaune, Charles Robert 1943- *WhoE 93*
Kaung, Thomas T.S. 1937- *St&PR 93*
Kaung, William Hsueh Ping 1945- *WhoAm 92*
Kaunisto, Seppo Jori Juhani 1941- *WhoScE 91-4*
Kaunitz, Hans 1905- *WhoE 93*
Kaunitz, Karen Rose Koppel 1951- *WhoSSW 93*
Kaup, David Earle 1952- *WhoSSW 93*
Kaup, Edmund Raymond 1932- *WhoSSW 93*
Kaup, Ludger 1939- *WhoWor 93*
Kauper, Thomas Eugene 1935- *WhoAm 92*
Kaupp, Gerd 1940- *WhoScE 91-3, WhoWor 93*
Kaupp, Janine Gail 1958- *WhoAmW 93*
Kauppi, Lea H. 1952- *WhoScE 91-4*
Kauppila, Veikko Aulis 1937- *WhoWor 93*
Kauppinen, Kauko Kalervo 1940- *WhoScE 91-4*
Kauppinen, Risto Antero 1955- *WhoWor 93*
Kauppinen, Veijo Antero 1941- *WhoScE 91-4*
Kauppinen, Veli S. 1933- *WhoScE 91-4*
Kaur, Prabhjot 1927- *WhoWor 93*
Kaur, Simren 1940- *DcChlFi*
Kauranen, Pentti M. 1930- *WhoScE 91-4*
Kauranne, L. Kalevi *WhoScE 91-4*
Kaurene, Bruce Richard 1955- *WhoE 93*
Kaurismaki, Aki *BioIn 17*
Kaurismaki, Aki 1957- *MiSFD 9*
Kaurismaki, Mika 1955- *MiSFD 9*
Kaus, Kristian *WhoScE 91-4*
Kaus, Otto Michael 1920- *WhoAm 92*
Kausay, Tibor 1934- *WhoScE 91-4*
Kauscher, Dorothy *AmWomPl*
Kaushal, Swaraj 1952- *WhoAsAP 91*
Kaushik, Purushottam 1930- *WhoAsAP 91*
Kaushik, Sadasivam J. 1949- *WhoScE 91-2*
Kausler, Donald Harvey 1927- *WhoAm 92*
Kauth, Benjamin 1913- *WhoE 93*
Kautsky, Gunnar F.H. 1921- *WhoScE 91-4*
Kautsky, Karl 1854-1938 *BioIn 17, DcTwHis*
Kautt, Glenn Gregory 1948- *WhoEmL 93, WhoWor 93*
Kautter, David John 1948- *WhoAm 92, WhoEmL 93*
Kautz, August V. 1828-1895 *HarEnMi*
Kautz, James C. 1931- *St&PR 93*
Kautz, John Terry 1945- *St&PR 93*
Kautz, Richard C. 1916- *St&PR 93*
Kautz, Richard Carl 1916- *WhoAm 92*
Kautzleben, H. *WhoScE 91-3*
Kautzman, Edward J. 1935- *St&PR 93*
Kautzmann, Dwight Clarence Harry 1945- *WhoAm 92*

Kauvar, Abraham J. 1915- *WhoAm 92*
Kauzlarich, James Joseph 1927- *WhoAm 92*
Kauzlarich, Richard Dale 1944- *WhoAm 92*
Kauzmann, Walter Joseph 1916- *WhoAm 92, WhoE 93*
Kavad 449-531 *OxDcByz*
Kavadas-Pappas, Iphigenia Katherine 1958- *WhoAmW 93, WhoEmL 93*
Kavad-Shiruya *OxDcByz*
Kavafian, Ani 1948- *Baker 92*
Kavafian, Ida 1952- *Baker 92*
Kavage, William 1940- *St&PR 93*
Kavalek, Lubomir 1943- *WhoAm 92*
Kavaler, Lucy 1930- *WhoWrEP 92*
Kavaler, Lucy E. *St&PR 93*
Kavaler, Rebecca *WhoWrEP 92*
Kavaler-Alder, Susan 1950- *WhoAmW 93*
Kavalsky, Basil Gerald 1941- *WhoUN 92*
Kavan, Anna 1901-1968 *BioIn 17*
Kavan, Anna 1904-1968 *ScF&FL 92*
Kavanagh, Dan 1946- *WhoWor 93*
Kavanagh, David John *Law&B 92*
Kavanagh, Herminie Templeton *AmWomPl*
Kavanagh, J. Daniel 1949- *WhoSSW 93*
Kavanagh, James A. 1937- *WhoScE 91-3*
Kavanagh, John Patrick 1950- *WhoEmL 93*
Kavanagh, John Paul 1956- *WhoUN 92*
Kavanagh, P.J. 1931- *BioIn 17*
Kavanagh, Patrick 1904-1967 *BioIn 17*
Kavanagh, Patrick Joseph 1931- *BioIn 17*
Kavanagh, Paul M. 1928- *St&PR 93*
Kavanagh, Richard 1945- *WhoScE 91-3*
Kavanagh, Thomas 1924- *WhoScE 91-3*
Kavanaugh, Carol T. *Law&B 92*
Kavanaugh, David K. *Law&B 92*
Kavanaugh, Everett Edward, Jr. 1941- *WhoAm 92*
Kavanaugh, Frank James 1934- *WhoSSW 93*
Kavanaugh, James Francis, Jr. 1949- *WhoEmL 93*
Kavanaugh, James J(oseph) 1934- *ConAu 38NR*
Kavanaugh, Katharine 1875- *AmWomPl*
Kavanaugh, Timothy Sebastian *Law&B 92*
Kavee, Robert Charles 1934- *WhoAm 92*
Kaveney, Andrew J. *ScF&FL 92*
Kaveney, Roz 1949- *ScF&FL 92*
Kaverman, Donald Lee 1952- *WhoWrEP 92*
Kavesh, Robert A. 1927- *WhoAm 92*
Kavett, Hyman d1992 *BioIn 17*
Kavey, Richard Plaut 1947- *WhoEmL 93*
Kavka, Gregory Stephen 1947- *WhoAm 92*
Kavkewitz, Michael 1950- *WhoSSW 93*
Kavlakoglu, Sirri Sinan 1925- *WhoScE 91-4*
Kavli, Fred 1927- *St&PR 93*
Kavlie, Dag 1939- *WhoScE 91-4*
Kavner, Julie *BioIn 17*
Kavner, Julie 1950- *NewYTBS 92 [port]*
Kavner, Julie 1951- *CurBio 92 [port], News 92 [port], -92-3 [port], WhoAm 92*
Kavner, Nora B. *Law&B 92*
Kavori, Jerry Stanley 1950- *WhoAsAP 91*
Kavrakoglu, Ibrahim 1941- *WhoScE 91-4*
Kavulic, Richard A. 1950- *St&PR 93*
Kavzanjian, John Daniel 1951- *St&PR 93*
Kaw, Autar Krishen 1960- *WhoEmL 93, WhoSSW 93*
Kaw, Edgar Lawrence 1898-1971 *BiDAMSp 1989*
Kawa, Nancy Ann 1967- *WhoAmW 93*
Kawabata, Nariyoshi 1935- *WhoWor 93*
Kawabata, Tutsuo 1945- *WhoAsAP 91*
Kawabata, Yasunari 1899-1972 *MagSWL [port]*
Kawabe, Ichiro 1960- *WhoWor 93*
Kawabe, Masakazu 1886-1965 *HarEnMi*
Kawabe, Torashiro 1890-1960 *HarEnMi*
Kawabe, Yutaka 1958- *WhoWor 93*
Kawachika, James Akio 1947- *WhoWor 93*
Kawadri, Anwar 1953- *MiSFD 9*
Kawaguchi, Kiyotake 1892-1961 *HarEnMi*
Kawaguchi, Tsuyoshi 1952- *WhoWor 93*
Kawahara, Fred Katsumi 1921- *WhoWor 93*
Kawahara, Haruyuki 1919- *WhoWor 93*
Kawahara, Mutsuto 1942- *WhoWor 93*
Kawahara, Shinjiro 1917- *WhoAsAP 91*
Kawahara, Tatuo 1916- *WhoWor 93*
Kawai, Iroku 1928- *WhoWor 93*
Kawai, Joshua Yoshitaka 1952- *WhoWor 93*
Kawai, Tokutaro 1930- *WhoWor 93*
Kawaja, Kaleem Ullah 1941- *WhoE 93*
Kawaja, Terence Gerard 1962- *WhoE 93*
Kawakami, Hajime 1879-1946 *BioIn 17*
Kawakami, Hiromi 1938- *St&PR 93*
Kawakami, Nobuo 1946- *WhoAsAP 91*
Kawakami, Soroku 1848-1899 *HarEnMi*
Kawakami, Yusuke 1945- *WhoWor 93*
Kawakubo, Keisuke 1935- *WhoWor 93*
Kawakubo, Rei *BioIn 17*
Kawalerowicz, Jerzy 1922- *DrEEuF*
Kawamata, Kenjiro 1926- *WhoAsAP 91*
Kawamata, Motoo 1936- *WhoWor 93*
Kawamitsu, Isao 1944- *WhoWor 93*
Kawamoto, Edwin H. *Law&B 92*
Kawamoto, Nobuhiko *BioIn 17*
Kawamoto, Yoji 1942- *WhoWor 93*
Kawamura, Eric K. *Law&B 92*
Kawamura, Hirofumi 1929- *WhoWor 93*
Kawamura, Hiroshi 1936- *WhoAm 92*
Kawamura, Kageaki 1850-1926 *HarEnMi*
Kawamura, Mitsunori 1939- *WhoWor 93*
Kawamura, Sumiyoshi 1836-1904 *HarEnMi*
Kawamura, Takeo 1942- *WhoAsAP 91*
Kawanishi, Susumu 1931- *WhoWor 93*
Kawano, Hiroshi 1925- *WhoWor 93*
Kawano, James Conrad *WhoE 93*
Kawano, Randall Toshio 1959- *WhoEmL 93*
Kawara, Riki 1937- *WhoAsAP 91*
Kawarabayashi, Yusuke Carl 1939- *WhoWor 93*
Kawasaki, Kanji 1922- *WhoAsAP 91*
Kawasaki, Kenji 1947- *WhoWor 93*
Kawasaki, Ryo 1947- *WhoEmL 93*
Kawashima, Kiko *BioIn 17*
Kawashima, Masao 1929- *WhoWor 93*
Kawashima, Minoru 1936- *WhoAsAP 91*
Kawashima, Takeshi 1930- *WhoE 93*
Kawata, Paul Akio *WhoE 93*
Kawata, Tadashi 1925- *WhoWor 93*
Kawatski, Deanna *BioIn 17*
Kawauchi, Hiroshi 1940- *WhoWor 93*
Kawawa, Rashidi Mfaume 1926- *WhoAfr*
Kawazura, Hiroshi 1928- *WhoWor 93*
Kawczynski, Diane Marie 1959- *WhoAmW 93*
Kawecki, Arkadiusz Marian 1929- *WhoScE 91-4, WhoWor 93*
Kawer, Dina Rochelle 1957- *WhoAmW 93*
Kawitzky, Ronald David 1953- *St&PR 93*
Kawmy, Susan Yost 1950- *WhoAmW 93*
Kawski, Alfons 1927- *WhoScE 91-4*
Kawuki, Joseph Nsanusi 1934- *WhoUN 92*
Kawula, John Michael 1947- *WhoE 93*
Kay, A.B. 1939- *WhoScE 91-1*
Kay, Alan Cooke *WhoAm 92*
Kay, Allen Steven 1945- *WhoAm 92*
Kay, Andrew F. 1919- *St&PR 93*
Kay, Anthony Barrington *WhoScE 91-1*
Kay, Arnold Melvin 1933- *St&PR 93*
Kay, Barry S. *St&PR 93*
Kay, Bernard Melvin 1932- *WhoAm 92*
Kay, Carol McGinnis 1941- *WhoAm 92*
Kay, Charles D. 1950- *WhoEmL 93, WhoSSW 93*
Kay, Charline Bockhold *ScF&FL 92*
Kay, Christina *BioIn 17*
Kay, Cyril Max 1931- *WhoAm 92*
Kay, David d1991 *BioIn 17*
Kay, David A. 1940- *BioIn 17*
Kay, Douglas *WhoAm 92*
Kay, Douglas Casey 1932- *WhoAm 92*
Kay, Elizabeth Alison 1928- *WhoAmW 93*
Kay, Felix Ross 1927- *WhoSSW 93*
Kay, Gersil Newmark *St&PR 93*
Kay, Gilbert Lee *MiSFD 9*
Kay, Guy Gavriel 1954- *ScF&FL 92, WhoCanL 92*
Kay, H.-M. *WhoScE 91-3*
Kay, Hans Werner 1927- *WhoScE 91-3*
Kay, Helen 1912- *WhoAmW 93, WhoE 93, WhoWor 93, WhoWrEP 92*
Kay, Herbert 1924- *St&PR 93, WhoAm 92*
Kay, Herma Hill *NewYTBS 92 [port]*
Kay, Herma Hill 1934- *WhoAm 92, WhoAmW 93*
Kay, Hershy 1919-1981 *Baker 92*
Kay, Irvin William 1924- *WhoSSW 93*
Kay, J. Douglas 1953- *St&PR 93*
Kay, Jack Garvin 1930- *WhoAm 92*
Kay, James Fredrick 1922- *WhoAm 92*
Kay, Jane Holtz 1938- *WhoWrEP 92*
Kay, Jeffrey Robert 1952- *St&PR 93*
Kay, Jerome 1920- *WhoAm 92*
Kay, Jerome Harold 1921- *WhoAm 92*
Kay, Jim *BioIn 17*
Kay, Joel Phillip 1936- *WhoAm 92*
Kay, John David 1937- *WhoSSW 93*
Kay, Jonathon *MiSFD 9*
Kay, Karen Rahnasto *Law&B 92*
Kay, Kelly *Law&B 92*
Kay, Kenneth *ScF&FL 92*
Kay, Kenneth J. 1955- *St&PR 93*
Kay, Kenneth Jeffrey 1955- *WhoAm 92*
Kay, Larry Alan *Law&B 92*
Kay, Larry Alan 1947- *St&PR 93*
Kay, Larry David 1954- *St&PR 93*
Kay, M. Jane 1925- *St&PR 93*
Kay, Margaret J. 1951- *WhoE 93*
Kay, Marguerite M. Boyle 1947- *WhoAmW 93*
Kay, Marsha Helen 1961- *WhoAmW 93*
Kay, Mary Ellen *SweetSg C [port]*
Kay, Mary Patricia 1947- *WhoEmL 93*
Kay, Michael *WhoScE 91-1*
Kay, Michelle Suzanne 1954- *WhoAm 92*
Kay, Paul A. 1951- *St&PR 93*
Kay, Paul de Young 1934- *WhoAm 92*
Kay, Robert Nigel *WhoScE 91-1*
Kay, Robert William Anthony 1952- *WhoE 93*
Kay, Ronald James 1947- *WhoAm 92*
Kay, Sandra Irene 1952- *WhoAmW 93*
Kay, Sanford 1942- *St&PR 93*
Kay, Saul 1914- *WhoAm 92*
Kay, Stanley B. *Law&B 92*
Kay, Stanley R. d1990 *BioIn 17*
Kay, Stephen B. 1934- *St&PR 93*
Kay, Steven R. 1954- *St&PR 93*
Kay, Susan *ScF&FL 92*
Kay, Suzanne Mahlburg 1947- *WhoEmL 93*
Kay, Thomas E. 1947- *St&PR 93*
Kay, Thomas Oliver 1929- *WhoAm 92*
Kay, Thomas Robert 1960- *WhoEmL 93*
Kay, Ulysses 1917- *WhoAm 92*
Kay, Ulysses Simpson 1917- *Baker 92*
Kay, Vicki M. 1937- *St&PR 93*
Kay, W. Richard, Jr. *Law&B 92*
Kay, Walter Anthony 1945- *St&PR 93*
Kay, William Gemmill, Jr. 1930- *WhoAm 92*
Kaya, Robert Masayoshi 1914- *WhoWor 93*
Kaya, Rustem 1947- *WhoScE 91-4*
Kayaalp, Suleyman Oguz 1931- *WhoScE 91-4*
Kayalar, Aksit 1937- *WhoUN 92*
Kayar, Susan Rennie 1953- *WhoE 93*
Kayayan, Agop K. 1943- *WhoUN 92*
Kayden, Jerold S. 1953- *WhoEmL 93*
Kayden, Mimi R. 1933- *St&PR 93*
Kaye, Andrew W. 1948- *WhoIns 93*
Kaye, Bernard 1930- *St&PR 93*
Kaye, Danny 1913-1987 *Baker 92, IntDcF 2-3 [port], QDrFCA 92 [port]*
Kaye, Deborah Hollis *Law&B 92*
Kaye, Diane L. *Law&B 92*
Kaye, Donald 1931- *WhoAm 92*
Kaye, Elizabeth Ann 1951- *WhoEmL 93*
Kaye, Evelyn 1937- *WhoWrEP 92*
Kaye, Evelyn Patricia 1937- *WhoAm 92*
Kaye, Frances Bagdol 1947- *WhoAmW 93*
Kaye, G. Roland *WhoScE 91-1*
Kaye, Gail Leslie 1955- *WhoAmW 93*
Kaye, Gene Warren 1950- *WhoSSW 93*
Kaye, George M. 1931- *St&PR 93*
Kaye, Geraldine 1925- *ChlFicS*
Kaye, Gordon Israel 1935- *WhoAm 92*
Kaye, Harvey N. 1940- *St&PR 93*
Kaye, Janet Miriam 1937- *WhoAmW 93, WhoE 93*
Kaye, Jerome 1923- *WhoSSW 93*
Kaye, Jerome R. 1928- *St&PR 93, WhoAm 92*
Kaye, Judith Smith 1938- *WhoAmW 93*
Kaye, Judy *BioIn 17, SmATA 71*
Kaye, Judy 1948- *WhoAmW 93*
Kaye, Lenard Wayne 1950- *WhoEmL 93*
Kaye, Leonard B. *Law&B 92*
Kaye, M.M. 1908- *BioIn 17*
Kaye, M.M. 1909- *ScF&FL 92*
Kaye, Maggie *ScF&FL 92*
Kaye, Marilyn 1949- *ScF&FL 92*
Kaye, Marvin 1938- *ScF&FL 92*
Kaye, Mary Margaret 1908- *BioIn 17*
Kaye, Melanie Fern 1960- *WhoEmL 93*
Kaye, Merlin *ScF&FL 92*
Kaye, Nancy Weber 1929- *WhoAmW 93, WhoE 93*
Kaye, Neil Scott 1958- *WhoE 93, WhoEmL 93*
Kaye, Paul Henry 1951- *WhoScE 91-1*
Kaye, Rasa *WhoWrEP 92*
Kaye, Robert 1917- *WhoAm 92*
Kaye, Robert Charles 1947- *WhoEmL 93*
Kaye, Sammy 1910-1987 *Baker 92*
Kaye, Saralee *ScF&FL 92*
Kaye, Stanley Bernard *WhoScE 91-1*
Kaye, Stephen Frederick 1946- *St&PR 93*
Kaye, Stephen J. 1943- *St&PR 93*
Kaye, Stephen Rackow 1931- *WhoAm 92*
Kaye, Stuart Martin 1946- *WhoEmL 93*
Kaye, Stubby 1918- *QDrFCA 92 [port]*
Kaye, Sylvia Fine d1991 *BioIn 17*
Kaye, Terry *ScF&FL 92*
Kaye, Tony *BioIn 17*
See Also Yes *ConMus 8*
Kaye, Walter 1927- *WhoAm 92, WhoE 93*
Kaye, Wilbur Irving 1922- *WhoAm 92*
Kaye, William Greenwood 1931- *WhoScE 91-1*
Kaye, William R. 1952- *St&PR 93*
Kaye, William Samuel 1953- *WhoAm 92*
Kayes, Evan R. 1949- *St&PR 93*
Kayes, Robert P. *St&PR 93*
Kayhart, Marion 1926- *WhoE 93*
Kayitah, Austin *BioIn 17*
Kayitmazbatir, Nurettin 1942- *WhoScE 91-4*
Kay-Khusraw, I d1211 *OxDcByz*
Kaylie, Harvey *BioIn 17*
Kaylin, Samuel O. d1991 *BioIn 17*
Kaylor, Barbara Brotman 1959- *St&PR 93, WhoAmW 93, WhoEmL 93*
Kaylor, Jefferson Daniel, Jr. 1947- *WhoE 93*
Kaylor, Robert *MiSFD 9*
Kaynard, Meryl R. *Law&B 92*
Kaynes, Robert J., Jr. 1956- *St&PR 93*
Kaynes, Robert Jacob 1927- *St&PR 93*
Kaynor, Sanford Bull 1926- *WhoAm 92*
Kays, B. Thomas 1944- *WhoSSW 93*
Kays, Eloise Claire *WhoAmW 93*
Kays, James William 1924- *St&PR 93*
Kays, William Morrow 1920- *WhoAm 92*
Kaysen, Carl 1920- *WhoAm 92, WhoWor 93*
Kaysen, David Brookes 1949- *St&PR 93*
Kayser, Arnd F. 1932- *WhoScE 91-3*
Kayser, Arnd Frederik 1932- *WhoWor 93*
Kayser, Donald R. 1930- *St&PR 93*
Kayser, Donald Robert 1930- *WhoAm 92*
Kayser, Fritz Hermann 1933- *WhoScE 91-4*
Kayser, Hans Josef 1927- *WhoScE 91-3*
Kayser, Heinrich Ernst 1815-1888 *Baker 92*
Kayser, Kenneth Wayne 1947- *WhoE 93*
Kayser, Kraig 1960- *St&PR 93*
Kayser, Leif 1919- *Baker 92*
Kayser, Louis E. *Law&B 92*
Kayser, Philipp Christoph 1755-1823 *Baker 92*
Kayser, Robert Justin 1946- *WhoEmL 93*
Kayser, Stephen S. 1900-1988 *BioIn 17*
Kayser, Terry M. 1957- *St&PR 93*
Kayser, Thomas Arthur 1935- *WhoAm 92*
Kayser, Verne S. 1943- *St&PR 93*
Kaysone Phomvihan 1920- *WhoWor 93*
Kayton, Howard H. 1936- *WhoIns 93*
Kayton, Myron 1934- *WhoAm 92*
Kaz, Nathaniel 1917- *WhoAm 92*
Kazachenko, Grigori 1858-1938 *Baker 92*
Kazakoff, Michael 1923- *St&PR 93*
Kazakov, Yuri Pavlovich 1927- *BioIn 17*
Kazala, Michael J. 1952- *St&PR 93*
Kazan, Basil Gibran 1914- *WhoE 93, WhoWor 93*
Kazan, Benjamin 1917- *WhoAm 92*
Kazan, Chris d1991 *BioIn 17*
Kazan, Elia *BioIn 17*
Kazan, Elia 1909- *MiSFD 9, WhoAm 92*
Kazan, Kathryn Lukins 1957- *WhoEmL 93*
Kazan, Lainie 1940- *BioIn 17*
Kazan, Lainie 1942- *WhoAm 92*
Kazan, Molly Day Thacher d1963 *AmWomPl*
Kazan, Nicholas *ConTFT 10*
Kazan, Richard 1945- *St&PR 93*
Kazan, Robert Peter 1947- *WhoEmL 93*
Kazancigil, Ali 1942- *WhoUN 92*
Kazandjiev, Vasil 1934- *Baker 92*
Kazanly, Nikolai (Ivanovich) 1869-1916 *Baker 92*
Kazanocigil, Ali 1942- *WhoWor 93*
Kazantzakis, Nikos 1883-1957 *BioIn 17, MagSWL [port], ScF&FL 92*
Kazaras, Peter *BioIn 17*
Kazarian, Paul 1955- *WhoE 93*
Kazazis, Kostas 1934- *WhoAm 92*
Kazda, Louis Frank 1916- *WhoAm 92*
Kazee, Norman Bruce *Law&B 92*
Kazee, Paul Michael 1956- *WhoE 93*
Kazem, Ismail 1931- *WhoE 93*
Kazemi, Abbas Ashtiani 1956- *WhoE 93*
Kazemi, Farhad 1943- *WhoAm 92*
Kazemi, Homayoun 1934- *WhoAm 92*
Kazemi, Hossein 1938- *WhoAm 92*
Kazemzadeh, Firuz 1924- *WhoAm 92*
Kazen, George Philip 1940- *WhoAm 92, WhoSSW 93*
Kazenas, Susan Jean 1956- *WhoAmW 93*
Kazezski, Stanley G. 1934- *St&PR 93*
Kazhdan, Alexander P. 1922- *ConAu 138*
Kazhdan, David 1946- *WhoAm 92*
Kazic, Danilo M. 1930- *WhoScE 91-4*
Kazik, John S. 1942- *St&PR 93*
Kazim, Victor 1942- *WhoWor 93*
Kazimierski, Zbyszko 1936- *WhoScE 91-4*
Kazimir, Edward Oliver 1943- *St&PR 93*
Kazin, Alfred 1915- *BioIn 17, JeAmHC, WhoAm 92, WhoWor 93, WhoWrEP 92*
Kazin, Alice Rene 1949- *WhoAmW 93*
Kazle, Elynmarie 1958- *WhoAmW 93*
Kazmann, Hollis Beem *Law&B 92*
Kazmayer, Robert d1991 *BioIn 17*
Kazmerski, Lawrence Lee 1945- *WhoAm 92*
Kazmierczak, Andrzej 1950- *WhoWor 93*
Kazmierski, Kurt P. *St&PR 93*
Kazon, Bernard 1924- *St&PR 93*
Kazoora, Joseph 1958- *WhoWor 93*
Kazor, Walter Robert 1922- *WhoSSW 93, WhoWor 93*
Kazu *BioIn 17*
Kazuro, Stanislaw 1881-1961 *Baker 92*

Kazuro, Stanislaw 1882-1961 *PolBiDi*
Kazuteru, Matsuda 1939- *St&PR 93*
Kazynski, Wiktor 1812-1867 *Baker 92*
KC & the Sunshine Band *SoulM*
K-Doe, Ernie 1936- *SoulM*
Ke, Gang 1950- *WhoE 93*
Kea, Neville *ScF&FL 92*
Keach, James *MiSFD 9*
Keach, Margaret Sally 1903- *WhoAmW 93*
Keach, Stacy, Sr. 1914- *WhoAm 92*
Keach, Stacy, Jr. 1941- *WhoAm 92*
Keadle, W. Glenn 1950- *St&PR 93*
Keady, George Cregan, Jr. 1924- *WhoAm 92*
Keady, Michael J. 1926- *St&PR 93*
Keagle, Douglas Lee 1946- *WhoE 93*
Keagle, Susan Jane 1940- *WhoE 93*
Keagle, William Aloysius, Jr. 1952- *WhoE 93*
Keairns, Yvonne Ewing 1939- *WhoAmW 93*
Keal, Minna 1909- *BioIn 17*
Keala, Francis Ahloy 1930- *WhoAm 92*
Kealey, Beth Ann 1962- *WhoAmW 93*
Kealy, Patrick John 1943- *WhoAm 92*
Keammerer, Warren Roy 1946- *WhoEmL 93*
Keamy, Donald George 1930- *WhoE 93*
Kean, B.H. 1912- *BioIn 17*
Kean, Benjamin Harrison 1912- *BioIn 17, WhoAm 92*
Kean, Bernard Peter 1948- *WhoUN 92*
Kean, Charles Thomas 1941- *WhoAm 92*
Kean, Hamilton Fish 1925- *WhoAm 92*
Kean, John 1929- *St&PR 93, WhoAm 92*
Kean, John Vaughan 1917- *WhoE 93, WhoWor 93*
Kean, Marshall Lee 1957- *WhoWor 93*
Kean, Robert W., Jr. 1922- *St&PR 93*
Kean, Steve *Law&B 92*
Kean, Thomas H. 1935- *WhoAm 92, WhoE 93*
Kean, Thomas Joseph 1933- *St&PR 93*
Keanan, Staci *BioIn 17*
Keane, Anthony John 1961- *WhoEmL 93*
Keane, Bil 1922- *WhoAm 92*
Keane, Christopher *ScF&FL 92*
Keane, Colleen Ann 1949- *WhoAmW 93*
Keane, Daniel J. 1939- *St&PR 93, WhoAm 92*
Keane, David L. 1952- *St&PR 93*
Keane, Denise F. *Law&B 92*
Keane, Edmund J., Jr. 1933- *WhoAm 92*
Keane, George Michael, Jr. 1947- *WhoEmL 93*
Keane, Gustave Robert 1914- *WhoAm 92*
Keane, J. Timothy *Law&B 92*
Keane, John B. *Law&B 92*
Keane, John F. 1931- *St&PR 93*
Keane, John K., Jr. *Law&B 92*
Keane, Katherine Walker *Law&B 92*
Keane, Kevin P. 1954- *St&PR 93*
Keane, Kevin Thomas 1933- *St&PR 93*
Keane, Louis H. 1944- *St&PR 93*
Keane, Mark Edward 1919- *WhoAm 92*
Keane, Mary Elizabeth 1953- *WhoAmW 93, WhoE 93, WhoEmL 93*
Keane, Michael G. 1944- *WhoScE 91-3*
Keane, Michael G. 1955- *WhoScE 91-3*
Keane, Molly *BioIn 17*
Keane, Nancyellen *Law&B 92*
Keane, Patricia M. *Law&B 92*
Keane, Peter Leo 1917- *WhoAm 92*
Keane, Raymond Thomas *Law&B 92*
Keane, Simon M. *WhoScE 91-1*
Keane, Stephen Edward 1943- *St&PR 93*
Keane, Thomas F. 1932-1991 *BioIn 17*
Keane, William Francis 1942- *WhoAm 92*
Keaney, John Joseph 1932- *WhoAm 92*
Keaney, William Regis 1937- *WhoAm 92*
Keany, Sutton 1943- *WhoAm 92*
Kear, Arthur Thomas 1934- *St&PR 93*
Kear, Bernard Henry 1931- *WhoAm 92*
Kear, David 1923- *WhoWor 93*
Kear, Frank E. *Law&B 92*
Kear, Kenneth Emery 1948- *WhoEmL 93*
Kear, Maria Martha Ruscitella 1954- *WhoEmL 93*
Kearins, Michael J. 1946- *St&PR 93*
Kearl, Bryant Eastham 1921- *WhoAm 92*
Kearl, Greg L. *St&PR 93*
Kearney, Christopher J. *Law&B 92*
Kearney, Connie W. 1938- *WhoWrEP 92*
Kearney, Daniel Patrick 1939- *WhoAm 92*
Kearney, Dennis Ferrell 1959- *WhoSSW 93*
Kearney, Edward Rutledge 1931- *St&PR 93*
Kearney, Gretchen Warner 1955- *WhoEmL 93*
Kearney, Hugh Francis 1924- *WhoAm 92*
Kearney, John Bernard 1951- *WhoEmL 93*
Kearney, John F. 1951- *St&PR 93*
Kearney, John Joseph, Jr. 1924- *WhoAm 92*
Kearney, John Peters 1940- *WhoE 93*
Kearney, John Walter 1924- *WhoAm 92*
Kearney, Joseph Laurence 1927- *WhoAm 92*
Kearney, Karen Marie 1951- *WhoAmW 93*
Kearney, Kevin Emmett 1929- *WhoSSW 93*
Kearney, Kevin Joseph Patrick 1935- *WhoWor 93*
Kearney, Lawrence Michael 1948- *WhoWrEP 92*
Kearney, Margaret Victoria 1938- *WhoAmW 93*
Kearney, Matthew Bernard 1940- *St&PR 93*
Kearney, Michael C. 1949- *St&PR 93*
Kearney, Michael John 1940- *WhoWor 93*
Kearney, Michelle 1945- *NotHsAW 93*
Kearney, Milo Edward 1938- *WhoSSW 93*
Kearney, Patricia Ann 1943- *WhoAmW 93*
Kearney, Peter James 1943- *WhoScE 91-3*
Kearney, Richard Craig 1946- *WhoE 93*
Kearney, Richard David 1914- *WhoAm 92*
Kearney, Richard James 1927- *WhoSSW 93, WhoWor 93*
Kearney, Robert Edward 1958- *WhoEmL 93*
Kearney, Rose Theresa 1951- *WhoAmW 93, WhoEmL 93*
Kearney, Sheila J. *Law&B 92*
Kearney, Stephen M. 1956- *St&PR 93*
Kearney, Stephen Michael 1956- *WhoAm 92*
Kearney, Stephen P. *Law&B 92*
Kearney, Thomas B. 1956- *WhoIns 93*
Kearney, Timothy Francis 1958- *WhoWor 93*
Kearney-Cooke, Ann M. 1956- *WhoAmW 93*
Kearns, Amos R., Jr. 1935- *St&PR 93*
Kearns, Burtsell J. *Law&B 92*
Kearns, C. Richard *St&PR 93*
Kearns, David E. *Law&B 92*
Kearns, David Todd 1930- *BioIn 17, St&PR 93, WhoE 93, WhoWor 93*
Kearns, Francis Emner 1905- *WhoAm 92*
Kearns, James Frances 1928- *St&PR 93*
Kearns, James Joseph 1924- *WhoAm 92*
Kearns, James T. 1938- *WhoIns 93*
Kearns, James Thomas 1938- *St&PR 93*
Kearns, Janet Catherine 1940- *WhoAm 92*
Kearns, John W. 1933- *WhoSSW 93*
Kearns, John William 1935- *WhoSSW 93*
Kearns, Josephine Anna 1954- *WhoWrEP 92*
Kearns, Lionel 1937- *WhoCanL 92*
Kearns, Merle Grace 1938- *WhoAmW 93*
Kearns, Robert Francis 1945- *St&PR 93*
Kearns, Robert W. *BioIn 17*
Kearns, Ruth Mary Schiller 1946- *WhoSSW 93*
Kearns, Terrance Brophy 1946- *WhoAm 92, WhoEmL 93, WhoSSW 93*
Kearns, Thomas W. *Law&B 92*
Kearns, Vincent E. 1939- *St&PR 93*
Kearns, Virginia L. *Law&B 92*
Kearns, Warren Kenneth 1929- *St&PR 93, WhoAm 92*
Kearns, William Michael, Jr. 1935- *WhoAm 92*
Kearns, William R. d1992 *NewYTBS 92*
Kearns, William Stanley 1941- *WhoE 93*
Kearny, Philip 1814-1862 *HarEnMi*
Kearny, Stephen Watts 1794-1848 *HarEnMi*
Kearse, Amalya Lyle 1937- *AfrAmBi, WhoAm 92, WhoAmW 93, WhoE 93*
Kearsley, Steven N. 1941- *St&PR 93*
Kearton, Reginald R. 1910- *St&PR 93*
Keasbey, Victoria Irene 1955- *WhoAmW 93*
Keasler, George Morris 1938- *WhoSSW 93*
Keasling, Dale A. 1943- *St&PR 93*
Keasling, John F. 1931- *St&PR 93*
Keat, James Eldred 1932- *WhoE 93*
Keat, James Sussman 1929- *WhoE 93*
Keath, Martin Travis 1966 *WhoSSW 93*
Keath, Melaine Louise 1969- *WhoAmW 93*
Keathley, Frank Maben, Jr. 1947- *WhoEmL 93, WhoSSW 93*
Keathley, Michael N. 1957- *St&PR 93*
Keathley, Naymond Haskins 1940- *WhoSSW 93*
Keating, Anne Fraser 1955- *WhoEmL 93*
Keating, Charles H., Jr. *BioIn 17*
Keating, Charles H., III 1955- *WhoAm 92*
Keating, Charles N. 1942- *St&PR 93*
Keating, Cornelius F. 1925- *St&PR 93*
Keating, Cornelius Francis 1925- *WhoAm 92*
Keating, Daniel Joseph, III 1949- *WhoAm 92*
Keating, Diane *WhoCanL 92*
Keating, E. Lyle *Law&B 92*
Keating, Eugene Kneeland 1928- *WhoAm 92*
Keating, Francis Anthony, II 1944- *WhoAm 92*
Keating, Frank J. 1928- *WhoWor 93*
Keating, H.R.F. 1912- *ScF&FL 92*
Keating, H.R.F. 1926- *BioIn 17*
Keating, Henry Reymond Fitzwalter 1926- *BioIn 17*
Keating, James Bernard 1935- *WhoAm 92*
Keating, Joe Francis 1947- *WhoEmL 93*
Keating, John Honan 1919-1990 *BioIn 17*
Keating, John McLeod 1830-1906 *JrnUS*
Keating, John Richard 1934- *WhoAm 92, WhoSSW 93*
Keating, John Roderick 1941- *WhoWrEP 92*
Keating, Joseph T. 1952- *St&PR 93*
Keating, Joseph William 1939- *St&PR 93*
Keating, Karen Rupert 1954- *WhoAm 92*
Keating, Kerry W. 1935- *St&PR 93*
Keating, Laurel 1924- *WhoAmW 93*
Keating, Lawrence J. *Law&B 92*
Keating, Lynne Hoffman 1944- *WhoSSW 93*
Keating, Margaret Joan 1944- *WhoAmW 93*
Keating, Martin Joseph *Law&B 92*
Keating, Michael Burns 1940- *WhoAm 92*
Keating, Michael J. *Law&B 92*
Keating, Michael L. 1952- *St&PR 93*
Keating, Nancy L. *Law&B 92*
Keating, Pamela *Law&B 92*
Keating, Patrick 1937- *St&PR 93*
Keating, Paul *BioIn 17*
Keating, Paul 1944- *CurBio 92 [port], WhoWor 93*
Keating, Paul John 1944- *WhoAsAP 91*
Keating, Paul Raynor 1958- *WhoEmL 93*
Keating, Pearl M. *AmWomPl*
Keating, Penny *BioIn 17*
Keating, Richard Joseph *WhoE 93*
Keating, Richard P. 1935- *St&PR 93, WhoIns 93*
Keating, Richard Pierre *Law&B 92*
Keating, Robert B. 1924- *WhoAm 92*
Keating, Robert Edward 1937- *WhoAm 92*
Keating, Robert J. 1918- *St&PR 93*
Keating, Sarah Peachey 1963- *WhoAmW 93*
Keating, Shonah *BioIn 17*
Keating, Stephen J. *Law&B 92*
Keating, Terry Michael 1958- *WhoWor 93*
Keating, Thomas E. *WhoIns 93*
Keating, Thomas E. 1933- *St&PR 93*
Keating, Thomas Patrick 1949- *WhoSSW 93*
Keating, Timothy James 1946- *WhoE 93*
Keating, Tristan Jack 1917- *WhoWor 93*
Keating, William H. *Law&B 92*
Keating, William John 1927- *St&PR 93*
Keating, William S. *Law&B 92*
Keating, William Warren, III 1966- *WhoEmL 93*
Keatinge, Richard Harte 1919- *WhoAm 92, WhoWor 93*
Keatinge, William Richard *WhoScE 91-1*
Keaton, Buster 1895-1966 *BioIn 17, MiSFD 9N, QDrFCA 92 [port]*
Keaton, Charles Howard 1937- *WhoSSW 93*
Keaton, David L. 1939- *St&PR 93*
Keaton, Diane *BioIn 17*
Keaton, Diane 1946- *HolBB [port], IntDcF 2-3 [port], WhoAm 92*
Keaton, Diane 1949- *MiSFD 9*
Keaton, Frances Marlene 1944- *WhoAmW 93*
Keaton, Joseph Francis 1895-1966 *BioIn 17*
Keaton, Lawrence Cluer 1924- *WhoSSW 93, WhoWor 93*
Keaton, Michael *BioIn 17*
Keaton, Michael 1951- *CurBio 92 [port], HolBB [port], QDrFCA 92 [port], WhoAm 92*
Keator, Carol Lynne 1945- *WhoAmW 93*
Keats, Donald (Howard) 1929- *Baker 92, WhoAm 92*
Keats, Douglas Edward 1950- *St&PR 93*
Keats, Emma *BioIn 17*
Keats, Ezra Jack 1916-1983 *ChlBIID [port], MajAI [port]*
Keats, Glenn Arthur 1920- *WhoWor 93*
Keats, Harold Alan 1913- *WhoAm 92*
Keats, Joe *WhoWrEP 92*
Keats, John 1795-1821 *BioIn 17, MagSWL [port], WorLitC [port]*
Keats, Matthew Mason 1952- *WhoSSW 93*
Keats, Patricia Hart 1946- *WhoSSW 93*
Keats, Theodore Eliot 1924- *WhoAm 92, WhoSSW 93*
Keats, William Frank 1941- *WhoE 93*
Keaty, Robert Burke 1949- *WhoEmL 93, WhoSSW 93, WhoWor 93*
Keaveney, David Michael 1935- *St&PR 93*
Keaveney, John C. d1991 *BioIn 17*
Keaveny, Denis James 1946- *St&PR 93, WhoAm 92, WhoEmL 93*
Keays, Anne C. *Law&B 92*
Keays, Ethelyn Emery *AmWomPl*
Keays, Wayne Chesley 1940- *St&PR 93*
Kebabian, Paul Blakeslee 1917- *WhoAm 92*
Kebarle, Paul 1946- *WhoAm 92*
Kebblish, John Basil 1925- *WhoAm 92, WhoWor 93*
Kebel, Keith N. 1946- *St&PR 93*
Kebel, Keith Nelsen 1946- *WhoE 93*
Kebich, Vyacheslav *WhoWor 93*
Kebric, Robert Barnett 1946- *WhoSSW 93*
Kececioglu, Dimitri Basil 1922- *WhoAm 92*
Kechagias, Epaminondas Nondas 1960- *WhoWor 93*
Kecherid, Aly-Bey 1936- *WhoUN 92*
Keck, Ann I. *Law&B 92*
Keck, David Randal 1950- *St&PR 93*
Keck, Donald Bruce 1941- *WhoAm 92*
Keck, Elizabeth K. 1959- *St&PR 93*
Keck, James Moulton 1921- *WhoAm 92*
Keck, Leander Earl 1928- *WhoAm 92*
Keck, Merel Fogg 1928- *WhoAm 92*
Keck, Richard Joseph 1963- *WhoEmL 93*
Keck, Robert Clifton 1914- *WhoAm 92, WhoWor 93*
Keck, Rudolf Wilhelm 1935- *WhoWor 93*
Keck, William 1908- *WhoAm 92*
Keckel, Peter J. 1942- *WhoSSW 93*
Kecki, Zbigniew 1926- *WhoScE 91-4*
Keckley, James D. 1924- *St&PR 93*
Keddam, Michel H. 1940- *WhoScE 91-2*
Keddar, Ahmed 1934- *WhoUN 92*
Kedderis, Pamela Jean 1956- *WhoAmW 93*
Keddie, Peter *St&PR 93*
Keddie, Roland Thomas 1928- *WhoAm 92, WhoE 93*
Keddy, Wayne Richard 1945- *WhoAm 92*
Keding, Ann Maxwell 1944- *WhoAmW 93*
Kedourie, Elie d1992 *NewYTBS 92*
Kedourie, Elie 1926-1992 *ConAu 139*
Kedrenos, George fl. 12th cent.- *OxDcByz*
Kedrinskii, Valery Kirillovich 1938- *WhoWor 93*
Kedryna, Zbigniew M. 1931- *WhoScE 91-4*
Kedves, Ferenc Janos 1932- *WhoScE 91-4*
Kedzie, Daniel P. 1930- *WhoIns 93*
Kedzior, Janusz 1937- *WhoWor 93*
Kee, Cornelis 1900- *Baker 92*
Kee, Deborah Lau *Law&B 92*
Kee, Howard Clark 1920- *WhoAm 92*
Kee, Joseph L. 1942- *St&PR 93*
Kee, Maude Elizabeth 1895-1975 *BioIn 17*
Kee, Piet(er Willem) 1927- *Baker 92*
Kee, Sharon Phillips 1950- *WhoEmL 93*
Kee, Shirley Ann 1935- *WhoAmW 93*
Kee, Walter Andrew 1914- *WhoAm 92*
Keeble, John Robert 1944- *WhoWrEP 92*
Keeble, Kezia *BioIn 17*
Keebler, Lois Marie 1955- *WhoWor 93*
Keech, Ian Arthur 1934- *WhoWor 93*
Keedwell, Anthony Donald 1928- *WhoWor 93*
Keedwell, Douglas Robert 1920- *St&PR 93*
Keedy *BioIn 17*
Keedy, Mervin L. 1920- *WhoAm 92*
Keefauver, Timothy Gary 1958- *WhoWor 93*
Keefe, Carolyn 1928- *ScF&FL 92*
Keefe, Denis 1930-1990 *BioIn 17*
Keefe, Edward Francis 1910- *WhoE 93*
Keefe, Harry Victor, Jr. 1922- *WhoAm 92*
Keefe, James Vincent 1936- *St&PR 93*
Keefe, Mary Patricia *Law&B 92*
Keefe, Michael C. *Law&B 92*
Keefe, Richard E. 1936- *WhoAm 92, WhoWor 93*
Keefe, Roger Manton 1919- *WhoAm 92*
Keefe, Roger Manton 1919-1992 *BioIn 17*
Keefe, Stanley A. 1933- *St&PR 93*
Keefe, Susan Emley 1947- *WhoAmW 93*
Keefe, Todd *BioIn 17*
Keefe, William Joseph 1925- *WhoAm 92*
Keefe, William Lee 1937- *WhoE 93*
Keefer, Christine Ann 1962- *WhoWrEP 92*
Keefer, David A. 1948- *St&PR 93*
Keefer, David Knight 1949- *WhoEmL 93*
Keefer, Ivan Earl 1944- *St&PR 93*
Keefer, J. Michael *Law&B 92*
Keefer, J. Michael 1947- *WhoAm 92*
Keefer, Janice Kulyk 1952- *WhoCanL 92*
Keefer, Karen W. 1944- *St&PR 93*
Keefer, Lowell B. 1884-1971 *ScF&FL 92*
Keefer, R. Scott 1947- *St&PR 93*
Keefer, Robert Edward 1925- *St&PR 93*
Keefer, Thomas Anthony John 1945- *WhoUN 92*
Keefover, Marvin Dale 1944- *St&PR 93*
Keegan, Brian S. 1939- *WhoIns 93*
Keegan, David Lloyd 1939- *WhoAm 92*
Keegan, Frank Joseph *Law&B 92*
Keegan, George Joseph, Jr. 1921- *WhoAm 92*
Keegan, Gerald *BioIn 17*

Keegan, James B. 1941- *St&PR 93*
Keegan, James Joseph 1947- *WhoEmL 93*
Keegan, Jane 1956- *WhoAm 92*
Keegan, Jane Ann 1950- *WhoAmW 93, WhoEmL 93*
Keegan, John 1934- *BioIn 17*
Keegan, John Aloysius, Jr. 1941- *WhoE 93*
Keegan, John (Desmond Patrick) 1934- *ConAu 136*
Keegan, John Robert 1950- *WhoEmL 93*
Keegan, K. Brian 1959- *WhoEmL 93*
Keegan, Kathleen M. 1951- *St&PR 93*
Keegan, Kenneth Donald 1927- *WhoAm 92*
Keegan, Mark *Law&B 92*
Keegan, Mel *ScF&FL 92*
Keegan, Peter William 1944- *St&PR 93*
Keegan, Richard John 1924- *WhoAm 92*
Keegan, Robert Henry 1944- *WhoE 93*
Keegel, Blase Anthony 1965- *WhoSSW 93*
Keehan, Michael B. *Law&B 92*
Keehan, Terence M. *BioIn 17*
Keehley, Susan Jean 1962- *WhoAmW 93*
Keehn, David C. *Law&B 92*
Keehn, Neil Francis 1948- *WhoEmL 93*
Keehn, Sally M. 1947- *ConAu 137*
Keehn, Silas 1930- *St&PR 93, WhoAm 92*
Keehner, Michael Arthur Miller 1943- *WhoAm 92*
Keekley, Patricia Ann 1958- *WhoSSW 93*
Keel, Donald Stephen 1946- *WhoSSW 93*
Keel, Howard 1917- *IntDcF 2-3*
Keel, John A. 1930- *ScF&FL 92*
Keel, Lee 1953- *WhoSSW 93*
Keel, Michael C. *St&PR 93*
Keel, Michael Clarence 1940- *WhoAm 92*
Keel, Page Clark, Jr. 1946- *St&PR 93*
Keel, W.J. *Law&B 92*
Keel, William Clifford 1957- *WhoEmL 93, WhoSSW 93*
Keel, Yvette Ferguson 1960- *WhoSSW 93*
Keelan, Mary Eileen 1965- *WhoAmW 93*
Keele, Luqman *ScF&FL 92*
Keele, Lyndon A. 1928- *St&PR 93*
Keelean, John S. 1939- *St&PR 93*
Keeler 1952- *WhoE 93*
Keeler, Dennis Crossin 1953- *WhoEmL 93*
Keeler, Fred Ashmead 1925- *St&PR 93*
Keeler, Frederic S., Jr. *Law&B 92*
Keeler, George E. 1929- *St&PR 93*
Keeler, James L. 1935- *St&PR 93*
Keeler, James Leonard 1935- *WhoAm 92*
Keeler, Janet Bradford 1947- *WhoAm 92, WhoAmW 93*
Keeler, John F. 1956- *St&PR 93*
Keeler, John Montgomery 1933- *WhoE 93*
Keeler, Kathleen Marie 1957- *WhoAmW 93*
Keeler, Lynne Livingston Mills 1934- *WhoAmW 93*
Keeler, Robert B. *Law&B 92*
Keeler, Ross Vincent 1948- *WhoWor 93*
Keeler, Ruby 1910- *BioIn 17, IntDcF 2-3 [port]*
Keeler, Theodore Edwin 1945- *WhoAm 92*
Keeler, William Henry 1931- *WhoAm 92, WhoE 93*
Keeley, A.H. *WhoWrEP 92*
Keeley, Alvin William 1937- *St&PR 93*
Keeley, Doris Barbara *Law&B 92*
Keeley, Edmund 1928- *WhoWrEP 92*
Keeley, Edmund LeRoy 1928- *WhoAm 92*
Keeley, George Paul 1930- *WhoAm 92*
Keeley, James 1867-1934 *JrnUS*
Keeley, John Lemuel 1904- *WhoAm 92*
Keeley, Leah R. 1967- *WhoSSW 93*
Keeley, Leslie Enraught 1834-1900 *GayN*
Keeley, Mary Gentry Paxton *AmWomPl*
Keeley, Philip Max 1941- *St&PR 93*
Keeley, Robert Vossler 1929- *WhoAm 92*
Keeley, Timothy W. 1949- *WhoE 93*
Keeley, Wayne Joseph 1956- *WhoE 93, WhoEmL 93*
Keeling, Charles David 1928- *WhoAm 92*
Keeling, Edward J. *Law&B 92*
Keeling, Joe Keith 1936- *WhoAm 92*
Keeling, John Michael 1947- *WhoEmL 93*
Keeling, Terry Lee 1950- *WhoEmL 93*
Keels, Martha Ann 1957- *WhoAmW 93*
Keelser, James Martin 1935- *WhoSSW 93*
Keel-Williams, Mildred Yvonne 1954- *WhoWrEP 92*
Keely, Eugene Joseph 1935- *St&PR 93*
Keely, George Clayton 1926- *WhoAm 92*
Keem, Michael Dennis 1950- *WhoE 93, WhoEmL 93*
Keen, Alan Robert 1941- *WhoWor 93*
Keen, Alice A. *AmWomPl*
Keen, Andrew Nick *Law&B 92*
Keen, Arnold Ralph 1918- *WhoE 93*
Keen, Benjamin 1913- *ConAu 136*
Keen, Charlotte Elizabeth 1943- *WhoAm 92*
Keen, Colleen Elizabeth 1945- *WhoAmW 93*
Keen, Constantine 1925- *WhoAm 92*
Keen, Constantine 1926- *St&PR 93*
Keen, D. Michael *Law&B 92*
Keen, Fred Jacob 1935- *St&PR 93*
Keen, James Parker 1946- *WhoE 93*
Keen, James Stephen 1934- *St&PR 93*
Keen, Joseph 1907- *St&PR 93*
Keen, Joseph Walter *Law&B 92*
Keen, Lamont J. 1952- *St&PR 93*
Keen, Malcolm Deller *Law&B 92*
Keen, Maria Elizabeth 1918- *WhoAmW 93*
Keen, Michael John 1935- *WhoAm 92*
Keen, Paul R. *Law&B 92*
Keen, Peter *WhoScE 91-1*
Keen, Rebecca Ann 1960- *WhoAmW 93*
Keen, Robert Charles *WhoScE 91-1*
Keen, Sam *BioIn 17, ConAu 137*
Keen, Susan Atkinson *ScF&FL 92*
Keena, Kevin T. *Law&B 92*
Keenan, Anthony *WhoScE 91-1*
Keenan, Anthony Harold Brian 1940- *WhoE 93*
Keenan, Anthony Lee 1949- *WhoEmL 93, WhoWor 93*
Keenan, April Lori 1954- *WhoAmW 93*
Keenan, Barbara 1941- *WhoAmW 93*
Keenan, Barbara Milano *WhoAmW 93, WhoSSW 93*
Keenan, Brett R. *Law&B 92*
Keenan, Brian *NewYTBS 92 [port]*
Keenan, Brian 1950- *BioIn 17*
Keenan, Clarke Meredith 1946- *St&PR 93*
Keenan, David L. *Law&B 92*
Keenan, Edmund Terrence 1965- *WhoE 93*
Keenan, Edward Louis 1935- *WhoAm 92*
Keenan, Elizabeth Louise 1932- *WhoE 93*
Keenan, Florence *Law&B 92*
Keenan, Gerald John 1927- *WhoE 93*
Keenan, Gerard Patrick 1945- *WhoWrEP 92*
Keenan, Hugh Thomas 1936- *WhoSSW 93*
Keenan, Jack A. 1915- *St&PR 93*
Keenan, James Augustine, Jr. 1932- *WhoE 93*
Keenan, James F. *Law&B 92*
Keenan, James George 1944- *WhoAm 92*
Keenan, James Ignatius, Jr. *Law&B 92*
Keenan, James Ignatius, Jr. 1932- *St&PR 93, WhoIns 93*
Keenan, James Joseph 1931- *WhoE 93*
Keenan, James L. 1937- *St&PR 93*
Keenan, James Lee 1937- *WhoAm 92*
Keenan, James Robert 1950- *St&PR 93*
Keenan, Joe *BioIn 17*
Keenan, Joe 1958- *ConGAN*
Keenan, John F. 1945- *St&PR 93*
Keenan, John Fontaine 1929- *WhoE 93*
Keenan, John H. 1938- *St&PR 93*
Keenan, Joseph T. 1944- *St&PR 93*
Keenan, Kathleen Gloria 1955- *WhoE 93*
Keenan, Kevin Patrick 1951- *WhoEmL 93*
Keenan, Mary Ann 1950- *WhoAm 92*
Keenan, Michael Edgar 1934- *WhoAm 92*
Keenan, Michael John 1946- *WhoSSW 93*
Keenan, Mike *BioIn 17, WhoAm 92*
Keenan, Nancy A. *WhoAm 92*
Keenan, P.J. 1932- *St&PR 93*
Keenan, Peter Francis, Jr. 1949- *WhoEmL 93*
Keenan, Randall H. 1932?-1969? *ScF&FL 92*
Keenan, Retha Ellen Vornholt 1934- *WhoAmW 93*
Keenan, Richard Lawrence 1923- *St&PR 93*
Keenan, Robert Anthony 1930- *WhoAm 92*
Keenan, Robert J. 1956- *WhoE 93*
Keenan, T.J. *St&PR 93*
Keenan, Terrance 1924- *WhoAm 92*
Keenan, Thomas R. 1952- *St&PR 93*
Keenan, Timothy J. *Law&B 92*
Keenan, Willis J. 1918- *St&PR 93*
Keenan-Abilay, Georgia Ann 1936- *WhoAmW 93*
Keenan-Beusmann, Patricia 1952- *WhoAmW 93*
Keene, Carolyn *BioIn 17, ConAu 37NR, MajAI, ScF&FL 92*
Keene, Charles Thornton 1945- *WhoE 93*
Keene, Christopher 1946- *Baker 92, BioIn 17, WhoAm 92, WhoE 93*
Keene, Clifford Henry 1910- *WhoAm 92, WhoWor 93*
Keene, Constance 1921- *Baker 92*
Keene, Daniel Ward 1947- *WhoAm 92*
Keene, Day 1904-1969 *ScF&FL 92*
Keene, Floyd S. *Law&B 92*
Keene, Floyd Stanley 1949- *St&PR 93*
Keene, Howard B. 1942- *St&PR 93*
Keene, Irene 1953- *WhoWrEP 92*
Keene, John Clark 1931- *WhoAm 92*
Keene, Joseph E. 1938- *ScF&FL 92*
Keene, Laura 1826?-1873 *BioIn 17*
Keene, Linda Baker *BioIn 17*
Keene, Margaret Girthel 1915- *WhoAmW 93*
Keene, Michelle Lasalle 1965- *WhoE 93*
Keene, Nietzchka *MiSFD 9*
Keene, Pamela A. 1952- *WhoSSW 93*
Keene, Paul Farwell 1920- *WhoE 93*
Keene, Richard C. *Law&B 92*
Keene, Stephen Winslow 1938- *St&PR 93, WhoIns 93*
Keene, Susie Miller Horne 1929- *WhoAmW 93*
Keene, William Blair 1933- *WhoAm 92*
Keene, William Patrick 1938- *St&PR 93*
Keene-Burgess, Ruth Frances 1948- *WhoAmW 93*
Keenen, Bruce G. 1949- *St&PR 93*
Keener, Charles Richard 1939- *WhoAm 92*
Keener, Craig Steven 1960- *WhoSSW 93*
Keener, E. Barlow *Law&B 92*
Keener, Frederick M. 1937- *ScF&FL 92*
Keener, Gaither *Law&B 92*
Keener, Hazel *SweetSg B [port]*
Keener, Jefferson W., Jr. 1932- *St&PR 93*
Keener, Kenneth C. *Law&B 92*
Keener, Marvin Stanford 1943- *WhoSSW 93*
Keener, Polly Leonard 1946- *WhoAmW 93*
Keener, Robert W. 1931- *St&PR 93*
Keener, Sara *AmWomPl*
Keener, Stephen T. 1957- *St&PR 93*
Keeney, Arthur Hail 1920- *WhoAm 92*
Keeney, Cecil Madison 1927- *St&PR 93*
Keeney, Dennis Raymond 1937- *WhoAm 92*
Keeney, Edmund Ludlow 1908- *WhoAm 92*
Keeney, John Christopher 1922- *WhoAm 92*
Keeney, L. Douglas 1951- *WhoEmL 93*
Keeney, Lafayette 1926- *St&PR 93*
Keeney, Marisa Gesina 1927- *WhoAmW 93*
Keeney, Michael D. *St&PR 93*
Keeney, Philip Gregory 1925- *WhoE 93*
Keeney, Richard A. *Law&B 92*
Keeney, Richard M. *St&PR 93*
Keen-Schwartz, Brenda Denniston 1949- *WhoAmW 93*
Keeny, Spurgeon Milton, Jr. 1924- *WhoAm 92*
Keep, Judith N. 1944- *WhoAmW 93*
Keepers, William L. 1938- *WhoAm 92*
Keepin, George Robert, Jr. 1923- *WhoAm 92*
Keeping, Cecil E. 1948- *St&PR 93*
Keeping, Charles 1924-1988 *ScF&FL 92, SmATA 69 [port]*
Keeping, Charles (William James) 1924-1988 *MajAI [port]*
Keepman, Marc P. *St&PR 93*
Keepnews, Orrin *BioIn 17*
Keeports, David Dale 1951- *WhoEmL 93*
Keer, Kathleen *WhoWrEP 92*
Keer, Leon Morris 1934- *WhoAm 92*
Keerthisena, Hewa Henipelle Jeevananda 1945- *WhoWor 93*
Keery, Paul A. *Law&B 92*
Kees, Beverly 1941- *WhoAmW 93*
Keesee, Allen Randolph Key 1919- *St&PR 93*
Keesee, Christian Kirkpatrick 1961- *WhoSSW 93*
Keesee, Frances M. 1924- *St&PR 93*
Keesee, Patricia Hartford 1928- *WhoE 93*
Keesee, Thomas Woodfin, Jr. 1915- *WhoAm 92*
Keesen, Susan *Law&B 92*
Keesey, Richard L. 1948- *St&PR 93*
Keesey, Ulker Tulunay 1932- *WhoAm 92*
Keeshan, Bob 1927- *WhoAm 92*
Keeshan, William Francis, Jr. 1934- *WhoAm 92*
Keeshen, Kathleen Kearney 1937- *WhoAmW 93*
Keeshin, Scott A. *Law&B 92*
Keeshin, Scott Avery 1952- *St&PR 93*
Keesing, Wouter *Law&B 92*
Keeslar, Don *MiSFD 9*
Keesler, Allen John, Jr. 1938- *St&PR 93*
Keesling, Francis Valentine, Jr. 1908- *WhoAm 92*
Keesling, James Edgar 1942- *WhoSSW 93*
Keesling, Karen Ruth 1946- *WhoAm 92, WhoAmW 93*
Keeter, James Edwin, Sr. 1933- *WhoAm 92*
Keeton, James Hamilton 1910- *St&PR 93*
Keeton, Kathy 1939- *BioIn 17*
Keeton, Kathy Merle 1939- *WhoE 93*
Keeton, Morris Teuton 1917- *WhoAm 92*
Keeton, Robert Ernest 1919- *WhoAm 92*
Keever, Cynthia Douglas 1956- *WhoAmW 93*
Keever, Herbert Weller 1927- *St&PR 93*
Keevert, Sandra Lynn 1955- *WhoAmW 93*
Keevil, N.B. 1938- *St&PR 93*
Keevil, Norman Bell 1938- *WhoAm 92, WhoWor 93*
Keevil, Philip C. 1946- *St&PR 93*
Keevil, Philip Clement 1946- *WhoAm 92*
Keevins, Marianne Dorothy 1941- *WhoAmW 93*
Keezer, Dexter M. 1895-1991 *BioIn 17*
Kefalides, Nicholas Alexander 1927- *WhoE 93*
Kefalonitis, Andrew 1949- *St&PR 93*
Kefauver, Carey Estes 1903-1963 *DcTwHis*
Kefauver, Estes 1903-1963 *PolPar*
Kefauver, Weldon Addison 1927- *WhoAm 92*
Kefer, Paul 1875-1941 *Baker 92*
Keffer, Charles Joseph 1941- *WhoAm 92*
Keffer, Mark A. *Law&B 92*
Keffer, W.R. *Law&B 92*
Kefor, Thomas Paul 1950- *St&PR 93*
Kegan, Stephanie *ScF&FL 92*
Kegel, Herbert 1920-1990 *Baker 92*
Kegel, Scott R. 1956- *St&PR 93*
Kegel, William George 1922- *WhoAm 92*
Kegeles, Gerson 1917- *WhoAm 92*
Kegeles, Lawrence Steven 1947- *WhoE 93*
Kegeles, S. Stephen 1925- *WhoE 93*
Kegelman, Matthew Roland 1928- *WhoE 93*
Kegen d1050 *OxDcByz*
Kegerreis, Robert James 1921- *WhoAm 92*
Keggi, Julia Quarles 1935- *WhoE 93*
Kegley, Jacquelyn Ann 1938- *WhoAmW 93*
Kegley, James Henry 1912- *St&PR 93*
Kegley, John Franklin 1944- *WhoE 93*
Kegley, Morris W. *Law&B 92*
Kehaya, Ery W. 1923- *WhoSSW 93*
Kehl, Randall Herman 1954- *WhoEmL 93*
Kehle, Ralph O. 1934- *St&PR 93*
Kehler, Philip Leroy 1936- *WhoSSW 93*
Kehm, Raymond A. 1936- *St&PR 93*
Kehm, Walter Howard 1937- *WhoAm 92*
Kehnle, Jeffrey Bill 1941- *St&PR 93*
Kehoe, Dennis M. 1949- *St&PR 93*
Kehoe, John Edward 1947- *WhoEmL 93*
Kehoe, John P. 1938- *WhoAm 92*
Kehoe, Joseph M., Jr. *Law&B 92*
Kehoe, L. Paul 1938- *WhoE 93*
Kehoe, Susan 1947- *WhoAmW 93*
Kehoe, Thomas J. *Law&B 92*
Kehoe, William Francis 1933- *WhoAm 92*
Kehoe, William Joseph 1941- *WhoSSW 93*
Kehr, Elizabeth McNeely *AmWomPl*
Kehr, Gunter 1920-1989 *Baker 92*
Kehr, Henning 1958- *WhoWor 93*
Kehr, Pierre Henri 1937- *WhoWor 93*
Kehrer, Daniel M. 1953- *WhoAm 92, WhoWrEP 92*
Kehret, Margaret A. *ScF&FL 92*
Kehret, Peg 1936- *ScF&FL 92, SmATA 73 [port], WhoAm 92*
Kehrli, Paula Jean 1960- *WhoAmW 93*
Kehrwald, Daniel J. 1943- *St&PR 93*
Kehrwald, Frank J. *Law&B 92*
Keib, John W. *Law&B 92*
Keible, Edward A. 1943- *St&PR 93*
Keicher, Werner Alex 1944- *WhoWor 93*
Keicher, William Eugene 1947- *WhoE 93*
Keider, Norman B. 1931- *St&PR 93*
Keifer, J. W. 1836-1932 *PolPar*
Keifetz, Corey J. 1951- *St&PR 93*
Keiffer, E. Gene 1929- *St&PR 93*
Keiffer, Edwin Gene 1929- *WhoAm 92, WhoSSW 93*
Keiffer, Edwin Paul 1956- *WhoEmL 93*
Keiffer, Thomas M. *Law&B 92*
Keighley, Michael Robert Burch *WhoScE 91-1*
Keighley, William 1889-1986 *MiSFD 9N*
Keightley, Mabel S. *AmWomPl*
Keigler, John E. 1929- *WhoAm 92*
Keii, Tominaga 1920- *WhoWor 93*
Keijbets, M.J.H. 1944- *WhoScE 91-3*
Keijiro, Kubota 1925- *WhoWor 93*
Keil, Alfred Adolf Heinrich 1913- *WhoAm 92*
Keil, Alfredo 1850-1907 *Baker 92, OxDcOp*
Keil, Beverly 1946- *WhoAmW 93*
Keil, Erwin 1938- *WhoScE 91-4*
Keil, Gerhard 1926- *WhoScE 91-3*
Keil, Herbert M. 1940- *St&PR 93*
Keil, Jeffrey C. 1943- *WhoAm 92*
Keil, Jeffrey Craig 1943- *St&PR 93*
Keil, John Mullan 1922- *WhoAm 92*
Keil, Klaus 1934- *WhoAm 92*
Keil, M. David 1931- *WhoAm 92*
Keil, Ulrich 1943- *WhoScE 91-3, WhoWor 93*
Keilberth, Joseph 1908-1968 *Baker 92, IntDcOp, OxDcOp*
Keilholtz, Patricia Diane 1950- *WhoE 93*
Keilholtz, Scott R. 1936- *St&PR 93*
Keilin, Eugene Jacob 1942- *WhoAm 92*
Keill, Stuart Langdon 1927- *WhoAm 92*
Keiller, James Bruce 1938- *WhoSSW 93*
Keillor, Garrison *BioIn 17*
Keillor, Garrison 1942- *MagSAmL [port]*
Keillor, Garrison Edward 1942- *WhoAm 92, WhoE 93, WhoWrEP 92*
Keillor, Sharon Ann 1945- *WhoAm 92*

Keilman, Louis, II 1960- *WhoEmL 93, WhoSSW 93*
Keilman, Robert E. 1945- *St&PR 93*
Keilp, Judith Catherine *Law&B 92*
Keilson, Julian 1924- *WhoAm 92*
Keilstrup, Margaret 1945- *ConAu 138*
Keim, Barbara Howell 1946- *WhoAmW 93*
Keim, Betty Adele T. 1935- *WhoAmW 93*
Keim, John D. 1945- *St&PR 93*
Keim, Judith Marie 1948- *WhoAmW 93*
Keim, Lewis P. 1930- *St&PR 93*
Keim, Peter De Graaf 1941- *WhoE 93*
Keim, Robert Phillip 1920- *WhoAm 92*
Keim, Thomas Paul 1942- *WhoSSW 93*
Keim, Wayne Franklin 1923- *WhoAm 92*
Keim, Willi 1934- *WhoScE 91-3*
Keimer, Samuel 1688-1739 *JrnUS*
Keimig, Scott David 1953- *WhoE 93*
Kein, Sybil *BioIn 17*
Keiner, Robert Bruce, Jr. 1942- *WhoAm 92*
Keir, Hamish MacDonald *WhoScE 91-1*
Keir, Thelma Cazalet- 1899-1989 *BioIn 17*
Keirns, Harry D. 1938- *St&PR 93*
Keirns, James Jeffrey 1947- *WhoAm 92*
Keirns, Janelle Ray 1949- *WhoAmW 93*
Keirstead, Allan Guy 1944- *St&PR 93*
Keirstead, Phillip Owen 1938- *WhoSSW 93*
Keiser, A. Kay 1936- *WhoAmW 93*
Keiser, Bernhard Edward 1928- *WhoAm 92*
Keiser, Charles Arthur 1943- *St&PR 93*
Keiser, Donald Matson 1939- *St&PR 93*
Keiser, Edmund Davis, Jr. 1934- *WhoAm 92, WhoSSW 93*
Keiser, Ellwood 1929- *BioIn 17*
Keiser, Harry Robert 1933- *WhoAm 92*
Keiser, Henry Bruce 1927- *WhoAm 92, WhoE 93, WhoWor 93*
Keiser, Ingrid J. *Law&B 92*
Keiser, Morton 1918- *St&PR 93*
Keiser, Nancy Eyman 1947- *WhoEmL 93*
Keiser, Norman Michael 1919- *St&PR 93*
Keiser, Paul Harold 1927- *WhoAm 92*
Keiser, Reinhard 1674-1739 *Baker 92, IntDcOp, OxDcOp*
Keiser, Robert L. 1942- *St&PR 93*
Keiser, Ross Edward 1951- *WhoSSW 93*
Keiser-Jenkins, Karen Lynne 1960- *WhoAmW 93*
Keishiro, Maeda 1926- *WhoWor 93*
Keisler, Ben L. *Law&B 92*
Keisler, Howard Jerome 1936- *WhoAm 92*
Keisler, Lynda DuBose 1947- *WhoSSW 93*
Keisler, William B. *Law&B 92*
Keisling, Gary M. 1951- *St&PR 93*
Keisling, Judy C. 1936- *St&PR 93*
Keisling, Mary West *WhoSSW 93*
Keisling, Phillip *BioIn 17*
Keisling, Phillip A. 1955- *WhoAm 92*
Keisman, Howard I. *Law&B 92*
Keiss, Isabelle 1931- *WhoAmW 93*
Keister, Donald Lee 1933- *WhoE 93*
Keister, George Benjamin 1928- *WhoAm 92*
Keister, Lawrence D. 1950- *St&PR 93*
Keistler, Betty Lou 1935- *WhoAmW 93, WhoSSW 93*
Keitel, David C. *Law&B 92*
Keitel, Harvey 1947- *WhoAm 92*
Keitel, Wilhelm 1882-1946 *BioIn 17, HarEnMi*
Keiter, Dale H. 1952- *WhoE 93*
Keiter, John W. *Law&B 92*
Keiter, Les 1919- *BioIn 17*
Keith, Alexander MacDonald 1928- *WhoAm 92*
Keith, Andrew 1958- *ScF&FL 92*
Keith, Arthur Berriedale 1879-1944 *BioIn 17*
Keith, Barry Harold 1954- *WhoE 93, WhoEmL 93*
Keith, Brandon *ScF&FL 92*
Keith, Brian Michael 1921- *WhoAm 92*
Keith, Brian Thomas 1951- *WhoSSW 93*
Keith, Camille Tigert 1945 *WhoAmW 93*
Keith, Carlton *ConAu 37NR, MajAI, SmATA 69*
Keith, Caroline H(elen) 1940- *ConAu 139*
Keith, Charles 1957- *WhoSSW 93*
Keith, Charles L. *Law&B 92*
Keith, Clyde H. 1912- *St&PR 93*
Keith, Dale Martin 1940- *WhoWor 93*
Keith, Damon J. 1922- *AfrAmBi*
Keith, Damon Jerome 1922- *WhoAm 92*
Keith, Darielle *ScF&FL 92*
Keith, David 1906- *BioIn 17*
Keith, David 1954- *MiSFD 9*
Keith, David Box 1934- *WhoSSW 93*
Keith, Debra Lynn 1956- *WhoAmW 93*
Keith, Dennis Collins, Sr. 1937- *WhoSSW 93*
Keith, Dennis Dalton 1943- *WhoE 93*
Keith, Donald Raymond 1927- *WhoAm 92*
Keith, Donald Wayne 1947- *WhoEmL 93*
Keith, Edna G. *AmWomPl*
Keith, Edward Oliver 1951- *WhoEmL 93, WhoSSW 93*
Keith, Elmer 1899-1983 *BioIn 17*
Keith, Garnett Lee, Jr. 1935- *St&PR 93, WhoAm 92*
Keith, Gordon 1908- *WhoWor 93*
Keith, Harold (Verne) 1903- *DcAmChF 1960, MajAI [port]*
Keith, Harvey *MiSFD 9*
Keith, Hugh 1950- *St&PR 93*
Keith, James E. 1924- *St&PR 93*
Keith, Jennie 1942- *WhoAm 92*
Keith, Jerome A. *Law&B 92*
Keith, John Ray 1948- *WhoEmL 93*
Keith, Juanita Orton 1917- *WhoAmW 93*
Keith, Kent Marsteller 1948- *WhoAm 92, WhoEmL 93*
Keith, Leroy, Jr. 1939- *WhoAm 92*
Keith, Marian 1874?-1961 *BioIn 17*
Keith, Marilyn *ConTFT 10*
Keith, Mary Agnes 1947- *WhoAmW 93*
Keith, Nancy *BioIn 17*
Keith, Nancy 1916-1990 *ConAu 138*
Keith, Nora *AmWomPl*
Keith, Pauline Mary 1924- *WhoAmW 93*
Keith, Penny Sue 1949- *WhoAmW 93*
Keith, Quentin Gangewere 1919- *WhoE 93, WhoWor 93*
Keith, Rhonda Cheryl 1947- *WhoAmW 93*
Keith, Robert Drake 1935- *St&PR 93*
Keith, Robert E. 1941- *St&PR 93*
Keith, Robert R. 1941- *WhoAm 92*
Keith, Robert Ralph 1941- *St&PR 93*
Keith, Robin Elizabeth 1959- *WhoSSW 93*
Keith, Roy W. *Law&B 92*
Keith, Simon *BioIn 17*
Keith, Slim *BioIn 17, ConAu 138*
Keith, Susan S. *Law&B 92*
Keith, Thomas Jeffery 1944- *WhoSSW 93*
Keith, Timothy Jones 1948- *St&PR 93*
Keith, Timothy Zook 1952- *WhoSSW 93*
Keith, W.J. 1934- *WhoCanL 92*
Keith, William H., Jr. 1950- *ScF&FL 92*
Keith, William John 1934- *WhoWrEP 92*
Keithley, Bradford Gene 1951- *St&PR 93, WhoAm 92, WhoSSW 93*
Keithley, David Arvin, Jr. 1954- *WhoSSW 93*
Keithley, Erwin M. 1905-1991 *BioIn 17*
Keithley, George 1935- *WhoAm 92, WhoWrEP 92*
Keithley, Jay Clark *Law&B 92*
Keithley, Joseph Faber 1915- *WhoAm 92*
Keith-Lucas, Alan 1910- *WhoSSW 93*
Keith-Spiegel, Patricia Cosette *WhoAm 92*
Keitner, Kerstin 1945- *WhoUN 92*
Keitz, Steve J. *Law&B 92*
Keizer, Joel Edward 1942- *WhoAm 92*
Keizo, Ishii 1920- *WhoWor 93*
Kej, Asger *WhoScE 91-2*
Kejik, Cyril 1932- *WhoScE 91-4*
Kejlhof, John 1942- *WhoWor 93*
Kejoa, George *WhoAsAP 91*
Kekaumenos c. 1020-c. 1070 *OxDcByz*
Keke, Leo 1947- *WhoAsAP 91*
Kekes, John 1936- *WhoAm 92*
Kekich, Mike *BioIn 17*
Kekki, Pertti 1940- *WhoScE 91-4*
Keko, Xhanfize 1927- *DrEEuF*
Kelada, Asaad *MiSFD 9*
Kelaiditis, George Emmanuel 1951- *WhoWor 93*
Kelalis, Panayotis 1932- *WhoAm 92*
Kelbaugh, Douglas Stewart 1945- *WhoAm 92*
Kelberer, John Jacob 1926-1991 *BioIn 17*
Kelberine, Alexander 1903-1940 *Baker 92*
Kelbley, Stephen P. 1942- *St&PR 93*
Kelbley, Stephen Paul 1942- *WhoAm 92*
Kelby, David E. 1937- *St&PR 93*
Kelch, James Raymond 1952- *WhoSSW 93*
Kelch, Robert Paul 1942- *WhoAm 92*
Kelder, Diane 1934- *ConAu 40NR*
Kelder, Maarten Albert 1963- *WhoEmL 93*
Kelder, William Richard 1948- *St&PR 93*
Keldorfer, Robert 1901-1980 *Baker 92*
Keldorfer, Viktor (Josef) 1873-1959 *Baker 92*
Keldysh, Yuri 1907- *Baker 92*
Kele, Roger Alan 1943- *WhoE 93*
Kelehear, Carole Marchbanks Spann 1945- *WhoAmW 93*
Keleher, Brendan 1954- *WhoEmL 93*
Keleher, Gary J. *Law&B 92*
Keleher, James P. 1931- *WhoAm 92*
Keleher, Michael Cassat 1955- *WhoSSW 93*
Keleinikov, Andrei 1924- *BioIn 17*
Kelejian, Harry Herand 1937- *WhoAm 92, WhoE 93*
Kelemen, Arpad 1932- *WhoScE 91-4*
Kelemen, Charles F. 1943- *WhoAm 92*
Kelemen, Endre 1921- *WhoScE 91-4*
Kelemen, Karoly 1930- *WhoScE 91-4*
Kelemen, Milko 1924- *Baker 92*
Kelemen, Zoltan 1926-1979 *Baker 92, OxDcOp*
Kelen, Erwin Anton 1935- *St&PR 93*
Kelen, Joyce Arlene 1949- *WhoEmL 93*
Kelen, Tibor 1930- *WhoScE 91-4*
Kelenyi, Gabor 1926- *WhoScE 91-4*
Keler dc. 520 *OxDcByz*
Keler, Adalbert Paul von 1820-1882 *Baker 92*
Keler, Marianne M. *Law&B 92*
Keler, Marianne Martha 1954- *WhoAmW 93*
Keler-Bela 1820-1882 *Baker 92*
Keles, Aynur 1941- *WhoScE 91-4*
Keleti, Georg 1925- *WhoE 93*
Keleti, Marton 1905-1973 *DrEEuF*
Keleti, Tamas 1927- *WhoScE 91-4*
Kelevedzhiev, Emil Stoykov 1953- *WhoWor 93*
Kelha, Vaino *WhoScE 91-4*
Kelinsky, Allen E. *Law&B 92*
Kelkar, Subhash Govind 1946- *WhoEmL 93*
Kelkar, Vijay Laxman 1942- *WhoUN 92*
Kell, Alan Blair 1920- *WhoWor 93*
Kell, Gary H. 1940- *St&PR 93*
Kell, George 1922- *BioIn 17*
Kell, George C. 1922- *WhoAm 92*
Kell, Jean Bruyere 1909- *WhoWrEP 92*
Kell, John F., Jr. 1937- *St&PR 93*
Kell, Mary Kate *Law&B 92*
Kell, Reginald (Clifford) 1906-1981 *Baker 92*
Kell, Tom 1949- *St&PR 93*
Kellaigh, Kathleen 1955- *WhoAmW 93, WhoEmL 93*
Kellam, Diane Celine Fidi 1950- *WhoAmW 93*
Kellam, Elizabeth *AmWomPl*
Kellam, Lucius James 1911- *St&PR 93*
Kellam, Lucius James, Jr. 1911- *WhoWor 93*
Kellam, Marla Ann 1955- *St&PR 93*
Kellam, Sarah White 1944- *WhoSSW 93*
Kellam, Sidney S. 1903-1986 *PolPar*
Kelland, Michael B. 1943- *St&PR 93*
Kelland, Michael Buckner 1943- *WhoAm 92*
Kelland, Robert Pope, Jr. 1955- *WhoSSW 93*
Kellar, Charlotte Avrutis *WhoAmW 93, WhoWrEP 92*
Kellar, Jeff Frederick 1949- *WhoE 93*
Kellar, Lorrence T. 1937- *St&PR 93*
Kellar, Lorrence Theodore 1937- *WhoAm 92*
Kellar, Marshal M. 1932- *St&PR 93*
Kellar, Marshal McGee 1932- *WhoSSW 93*
Kellar, Mary L. 1920- *WhoSSW 93*
Kellar, Steven Marshal 1956- *St&PR 93*
Kellar, Von *ScF&FL 92*
Kellaway, Frank 1922- *DcChlFi*
Kellaway, Ian Walter *WhoScE 91-1*
Kellaway, Peter 1920- *WhoAm 92, WhoWor 93*
Kelleam, Joseph E. 1913-1975 *ScF&FL 92*
Kellegrew, Robert W., Jr. *Law&B 92*
Kelleher, Brian M. *Law&B 92*
Kelleher, Bryan John 1924- *WhoWor 93*
Kelleher, Carolyn Virginia 1943- *WhoAmW 93*
Kelleher, Debra Lee 1958- *WhoAmW 93*
Kelleher, Ed *ScF&FL 92*
Kelleher, Herbert David *BioIn 17*
Kelleher, Herbert David 1931- *St&PR 93, WhoAm 92, WhoSSW 93*
Kelleher, James F. *Law&B 92*
Kelleher, James P. 1914- *WhoWrEP 92*
Kelleher, James Raymond 1948- *WhoEmL 93*
Kelleher, John J. *Law&B 92*
Kelleher, John M. *WhoAm 92*
Kelleher, Karen A. 1948- *St&PR 93*
Kelleher, Kathleen 1951- *WhoEmL 93, WhoWor 93*
Kelleher, Ken 1933- *St&PR 93*
Kelleher, Kevin John 1953- *WhoEmL 93*
Kelleher, Mary 1962- *WhoAmW 93*
Kelleher, Patricia A. *Law&B 92*
Kelleher, Philip Conboy 1928- *WhoE 93*
Kelleher, Richard Cornelius 1949- *WhoEmL 93, WhoWor 93*
Kelleher, Robert Jeffrey 1945- *WhoWor 93*
Kelleher, Robert Joseph 1913- *WhoAm 92*
Kelleher, Thomas M. *Law&B 92*
Kelleher, Thomas M. 1953- *St&PR 93*
Kelleher, Timothy John 1940- *St&PR 93, WhoAm 92*
Kelleher, Timothy Joseph 1954- *WhoEmL 93*
Kelleher, Victor 1939- *ScF&FL 92*
Kelleher, Victor (Michael Kitchener) 1939- *DcChlFi*
Kelleher, William Eugene, Jr. 1953- *WhoEmL 93*
Kelleher, William Gordon 1942- *WhoE 93*
Kellem, Milton d1992 *NewYTBS 92*
Kellem, Milton 1911-1992 *BioIn 17*
Kellen, Michael L. 1948- *WhoIns 93*
Kellen, Michael Leo 1948- *St&PR 93*
Kellen, Stephen Max 1914- *St&PR 93, WhoAm 92*
Kellenberg, Bill 1929- *St&PR 93*
Kellenberger, Eduard 1920- *WhoScE 91-4*
Kellenter, Sigrid 1938- *WhoAmW 93*
Keller, Alan Buchanan 1942- *WhoUN 92*
Keller, Alex Stephen 1928- *WhoAm 92*
Keller, Alfred Zelma *WhoScE 91-1*
Keller, Alvin G. 1909- *St&PR 93*
Keller, Arthur Michael 1957- *WhoWor 93*
Keller, Ben Robert, Jr. 1936- *WhoSSW 93, WhoWor 93*
Keller, Bernd *BioIn 17*
Keller, Beverly *ConAu 38NR*
Keller, Beverly 1929?- *ScF&FL 92*
Keller, Bill *BioIn 17*
Keller, Bryan J. *Law&B 92*
Keller, C. Graden, Jr. 1949- *WhoEmL 93, WhoWor 93*
Keller, Charlean 1930- *St&PR 93*
Keller, Charles Ernest 1916-1990 *BiDAMSp 1989*
Keller, Charles Henry 1947- *WhoWrEP 92*
Keller, Charles R. 1901-1990 *BioIn 17*
Keller, Charlie 1916-1990 *BioIn 17*
Keller, Christoph, Jr. 1915- *WhoAm 92*
Keller, Clarence Cornelius 1930- *St&PR 93*
Keller, Cornelius 1931- *WhoWor 93*
Keller, Cynthia Susan 1958- *St&PR 93*
Keller, Daniel R. 1949- *St&PR 93*
Keller, Daniel Whittemore 1947- *WhoEmL 93*
Keller, Darla Lynn 1956- *WhoEmL 93*
Keller, David 1941- *ScF&FL 92*
Keller, David H. 1880-1966 *ScF&FL 92*
Keller, David King 1948- *WhoWor 93*
Keller, David M. 1941- *WhoWrEP 92*
Keller, Dawn Susan 1962- *WhoAmW 93*
Keller, Deane 1901-1992 *BioIn 17, NewYTBS 92*
Keller, Dennis J. *St&PR 93*
Keller, Dennis James 1941- *WhoWor 93*
Keller, Diane Joy 1959- *WhoE 93*
Keller, Diane Marie 1950- *WhoAmW 93*
Keller, Don *BioIn 17*
Keller, Donald H. 1933- *St&PR 93*
Keller, Donald John 1932- *WhoAm 92*
Keller, Donald S. 1939- *St&PR 93*
Keller, Donna Cheryl *WhoAmW 93*
Keller, Dorothy Margaret Miller 1910- *WhoAmW 93*
Keller, Edward Clarence, Jr. 1932- *WhoAm 92*
Keller, Edward Lowell 1939- *WhoAm 92*
Keller, Eliot Aaron 1947- *WhoAm 92*
Keller, Ellen L. *Law&B 92*
Keller, Eric 1945- *WhoWor 93*
Keller, Frederick King *MiSFD 9*
Keller, Frederick W. 1955- *St&PR 93*
Keller, Gary 1941- *St&PR 93*
Keller, George Henrik 1931- *WhoAm 92*
Keller, George M. 1923- *St&PR 93*
Keller, George Matthew 1923- *WhoAm 92*
Keller, George R. 1951- *St&PR 93, WhoIns 93*
Keller, Glen Elven, Jr. 1938- *WhoAm 92*
Keller, Glenn Walter 1944- *St&PR 93*
Keller, Gottfried d1704 *Baker 92*
Keller, Gregory James 1960- *WhoSSW 93*
Keller, Hans Erich 1927- *WhoScE 91-3*
Keller, Hans (Heinrich) 1919-1985 *Baker 92*
Keller, Helen 1880-1968 *BioIn 17, DcTwHis*
Keller, Henry Fredrick 1933- *St&PR 93*
Keller, Hermann 1885-1967 *Baker 92*
Keller, Homer 1915- *Baker 92*
Keller, Jack 1928- *WhoAm 92*
Keller, Jackie 1940- *St&PR 93*
Keller, Jaime *BioIn 17*
Keller, Jaime Roberto 1936- *WhoWor 93*
Keller, James B. 1944- *St&PR 93*
Keller, James J. 1948- *St&PR 93*
Keller, James LeRoy 1947- *WhoE 93*
Keller, James T. *St&PR 93*
Keller, James Wesley 1958- *WhoEmL 93, WhoWor 93*
Keller, Jay A. 1939- *St&PR 93*
Keller, Jay Arthur 1939- *WhoAm 92*
Keller, Jimmie Ellis 1948- *WhoSSW 93*
Keller, John Francis 1925- *WhoAm 92*
Keller, John Greenway, Jr. 1958- *WhoAm 92*
Keller, John J. 1918- *St&PR 93*
Keller, John Paul 1939- *St&PR 93*
Keller, John Richard 1924- *WhoAm 92, WhoE 93*
Keller, John Vanderveer 1941- *WhoSSW 93*
Keller, Jorgen Rothe Keith 1924- *WhoWor 93*
Keller, Joseph A. 1926- *St&PR 93*
Keller, Joseph Bishop 1923- *WhoAm 92*
Keller, Joseph Steve 1935- *St&PR 93*

Keller, Judith A. *Law&B 92*
Keller, Juergen U. 1938- *WhoScE 91-3*
Keller, Karen H. *Law&B 92*
Keller, Karl 1784-1855 *Baker 92*
Keller, Katherine A. *Law&B 92*
Keller, Kenneth Harrison 1934- *WhoAm 92*
Keller, Kevin John 1957- *WhoE 93*
Keller, Kurt Joseph 1925- *St&PR 93*
Keller, Larry Jay 1941- *St&PR 93*
Keller, Lawrence P. *St&PR 93*
Keller, Lee James *Law&B 92*
Keller, LeRoy 1905- *WhoAm 92*
Keller, Linda Rahlmann 1955- *WhoAmW 93*
Keller, Louis William 1931- *St&PR 93*
Keller, Margaret Gilmer 1911- *WhoE 93*
Keller, Margaret Marie 1944- *WhoAmW 93*
Keller, Mario *St&PR 93*
Keller, Mark 1907- *WhoE 93, WhoWor 93*
Keller, Matthias 1813-1875 *Baker 92*
Keller, Michael Goldwyn 1947- *St&PR 93*
Keller, Michael John 1966- *WhoSSW 93*
Keller, Nancy Joan *WhoE 93*
Keller, Neil Richard 1954- *St&PR 93*
Keller, Otto 1861-1928 *Baker 92*
Keller, Paul 1921- *WhoAm 92*
Keller, Paul David 1943- *St&PR 93*
Keller, Pearl Josephson 1923- *WhoE 93*
Keller, R. *WhoScE 91-2*
Keller, Ralph Alance 1956- *WhoSSW 93*
Keller, Raymond F. *Law&B 92*
Keller, Renee Susan 1960- *WhoAmW 93, WhoEmL 93*
Keller, Richard B. 1929- *St&PR 93*
Keller, Robert Alexander 1930- *St&PR 93*
Keller, Robert Alexander, III 1930- *WhoAm 92*
Keller, Robert Joseph 1930- *St&PR 93*
Keller, Robert L. 1946- *St&PR 93*
Keller, Robert R. 1913- *St&PR 93*
Keller, Robert Scott 1945- *WhoWor 93*
Keller, Robert W. *Law&B 92*
Keller, Roger A. *Law&B 92*
Keller, Ronald E. 1936- *WhoIns 93*
Keller, Ross W. 1940- *St&PR 93*
Keller, Rudolf 1933- *WhoE 93*
Keller, Samuel William 1930- *WhoAm 92*
Keller, Shelly B. 1948- *WhoEmL 93*
Keller, Stanley 1938- *WhoAm 92*
Keller, Stephen P. 1942- *St&PR 93*
Keller, Steven Ray 1947- *WhoEmL 93, WhoSSW 93*
Keller, Susan Agnes 1952- *WhoAmW 93*
Keller, Teresa Diane 1951- *WhoAmW 93*
Keller, Teresa Gale 1958- *WhoEmL 93*
Keller, Theodor 1927- *WhoScE 91-4*
Keller, Thomas Clements 1938- *St&PR 93, WhoAm 92*
Keller, Thomas Franklin 1931- *WhoAm 92, WhoSSW 93*
Keller, Thomas J. *St&PR 93*
Keller, Thomas Martin 1937- *WhoUN 92*
Keller, Thomas Walter, II 1952- *WhoE 93, WhoEmL 93*
Keller, Tillman J., III 1941- *St&PR 93*
Keller, Tim A. 1942- *St&PR 93*
Keller, Walter 1873-1940 *Baker 92*
Keller, Walter 1942- *WhoScE 91-4*
Keller, William Francis 1922- *WhoAm 92*
Keller, William G. 1915- *St&PR 93*
Keller, William Martin, Jr. 1940- *St&PR 93*
Kellerer, Helmut G. 1937- *WhoScE 91-3*
Kellerhals-Stewart, Heather 1937- *ScF&FL 92*
Kellerman, Christopher Allan 1942- *St&PR 93*
Kellerman, David 1918- *St&PR 93*
Kellerman, Faye Marder 1952- *WhoEmL 93*
Kellerman, Hillel 1956- *St&PR 93*
Kellerman, Jonathan Seth 1949- *WhoAm 92*
Kellerman, Sally Claire 1937- *WhoAm 92, WhoAmW 93*
Kellerman, Sylvia 1920- *St&PR 93*
Kellermann, Christian 1815-1866 *Baker 92*
Kellermann, Donald S. *St&PR 93*
Kellermann, Francois Etienne Christophe 1735-1820 *HarEnMi*
Kellermann, Hope Patricia Iversen 1924- *WhoAmW 93*
Kellermann, Kenneth Irwin 1937- *WhoAm 92, WhoSSW 93*
Kellermann, Robert F. 1948- *St&PR 93*
Kellermeyer, Donald V. 1939- *St&PR 93*
Kellermeyer, Robert William 1929- *WhoAm 92*
Kellerth, Jan-Olof 1940- *WhoScE 91-4*
Kelletat, Dieter Hanns 1941- *WhoWor 93*
Kellett, Brian 1922- *St&PR 93*
Kellett, David William *WhoScE 91-1*
Kellett, Michael T. *Law&B 92*
Kellett, Morris C. 1935- *WhoAm 92*
Kellett, William Hiram, Jr. 1930- *WhoAm 92*
Kelley, Abby 1811-1887 *BioIn 17*
Kelley, Aimee T. *AmWomPl*
Kelley, Albert Benjamin 1936- *WhoAm 92*
Kelley, Albert Joseph 1924- *St&PR 93, WhoAm 92, WhoE 93, WhoWor 93*
Kelley, Allen Charles 1937- *WhoAm 92*
Kelley, Aloysius Paul 1929- *WhoAm 92, WhoE 93*
Kelley, Ami Phillips *Law&B 92*
Kelley, B.G. *WhoWrEP 92*
Kelley, Beth Maureen 1949- *WhoAmW 93*
Kelley, Betty Marie 1955- *WhoAmW 93, WhoEmL 93*
Kelley, Birdie Mae 1956- *WhoSSW 93*
Kelley, Bruce Gunn 1954- *St&PR 93, WhoIns 93*
Kelley, Charles *ScF&FL 92*
Kelley, Christine Ruth 1951- *WhoAmW 93*
Kelley, Christopher Donald 1957- *WhoEmL 93*
Kelley, Dale *BioIn 17*
Kelley, Dan B. 1938- *St&PR 93*
Kelley, Daniel M. 1925- *St&PR 93*
Kelley, Daniel McCann 1925- *WhoAm 92*
Kelley, David Charles 1957- *WhoE 93*
Kelley, David Forest 1949- *WhoEmL 93*
Kelley, David Lee 1936- *St&PR 93, WhoAm 92*
Kelley, Dawn Elizabeth 1961- *WhoAmW 93*
Kelley, Dean Maurice 1926- *WhoAm 92*
Kelley, Deborah Maria 1963- *WhoAmW 93*
Kelley, Delores Goodwin 1936- *WhoAmW 93*
Kelley, Donald Reed 1931- *WhoAm 92*
Kelley, Douglas Eaton 1960- *WhoEmL 93*
Kelley, Douglas Paul *Law&B 92*
Kelley, Edgar Stillman 1857-1944 *Baker 92*
Kelley, Edward Allen 1927- *WhoE 93*
Kelley, Edward W. 1927- *BioIn 17*
Kelley, Edward Watson, Jr. 1932- *WhoAm 92, WhoWor 93*
Kelley, Estel W. 1917- *St&PR 93*
Kelley, Estella *AmWomPl*
Kelley, Ethel May 1878- *AmWomPl*
Kelley, Eugene John 1922- *WhoAm 92, WhoSSW 93*
Kelley, Everette Eugene 1938- *WhoAm 92*
Kelley, Florence 1859-1932 *BioIn 17*
Kelley, Frank Joseph 1924- *WhoAm 92*
Kelley, Frederick M., Jr. 1948- *St&PR 93*
Kelley, G. Daniel, Jr. 1940- *WhoAm 92*
Kelley, G. Richard 1932- *St&PR 93*
Kelley, Gaynor N. *BioIn 17*
Kelley, Gaynor N. 1931- *St&PR 93*
Kelley, George Edmund 1925- *WhoSSW 93*
Kelley, George Edward 1940- *WhoE 93*
Kelley, Georgia 1947- *WhoEmL 93*
Kelley, Glen P. 1948- *St&PR 93*
Kelley, Guy J. *Law&B 92*
Kelley, Harold H. *BioIn 17*
Kelley, Harold Harding 1921- *WhoAm 92*
Kelley, Jack *BioIn 17*
Kelley, Jack H. 1932- *WhoIns 93*
Kelley, Jackson DeForest 1920- *WhoAm 92*
Kelley, James Charles, III 1940- *WhoAm 92*
Kelley, James Francis 1941- *WhoAm 92*
Kelley, James G. 1948- *St&PR 93*
Kelley, James H. 1939- *St&PR 93*
Kelley, James J., Jr. 1949- *WhoWrEP 92*
Kelley, James Kevin 1955- *WhoSSW 93*
Kelley, Jennifer Lock 1965- *WhoAmW 93*
Kelley, Jessie A. *AmWomPl*
Kelley, Jessie Stillman 1866-1949 *Baker 92*
Kelley, John A. 1907- *BiDAMSp 1989*
Kelley, John A. 1949- *St&PR 93*
Kelley, John Allen *Law&B 92*
Kelley, John Carleton 1947- *WhoUN 92*
Kelley, John Dennis 1900- *WhoAm 92*
Kelley, John Gary 1954- *WhoE 93*
Kelley, John H. 1941- *St&PR 93*
Kelley, John Joseph 1930- *BiDAMSp 1989*
Kelley, John Joseph, Jr. 1936- *WhoAm 92*
Kelley, John L. 1918- *St&PR 93*
Kelley, John Paul 1919- *WhoAm 92*
Kelley, John R., Jr. 1949- *St&PR 93*
Kelley, Joseph Cosgrove 1949- *St&PR 93*
Kelley, Joseph George, Jr. 1924- *St&PR 93*
Kelley, Joseph V. 1922- *St&PR 93*
Kelley, Kara Jane 1968- *WhoAmW 93*
Kelley, Kate 1955- *WhoWrEP 92*
Kelley, Kathryn 1949- *WhoE 93*
Kelley, Kerri Burns 1963- *WhoAmW 93*
Kelley, Kevin Charles *Law&B 92*
Kelley, Kitty *BioIn 17*
Kelley, Kitty 1942- *CurBio 92 [port], WhoWrEP 92*
Kelley, Laura Frances *AmWomPl*
Kelley, Leo P. 1928- *ScF&FL 92*
Kelley, Linda D. *Law&B 92*
Kelley, Linda Eileen 1950- *WhoAmW 93*
Kelley, Lisa Nicole 1964- *WhoAmW 93*
Kelley, Lyn Schraff 1956- *WhoAmW 93, WhoEmL 93*
Kelley, Margaret Ann 1950- *WhoUN 92*
Kelley, Margaret Northern 1937- *WhoAmW 93*
Kelley, Marian Herbst 1959- *St&PR 93, WhoEmL 93, WhoSSW 93*
Kelley, Marsha Christine 1965- *WhoAmW 93*
Kelley, Martha Maywood 1947- *St&PR 93*
Kelley, Mary Burnett *WhoAmW 93*
Kelley, Mary Elizabeth 1947- *WhoAmW 93*
Kelley, Maurice Leslie, Jr. 1924- *WhoAm 92, WhoWor 93*
Kelley, (Minnie) May *AmWomPl*
Kelley, Michael Curtis 1947- *WhoWor 93*
Kelley, Michael Dwaine 1945- *St&PR 93*
Kelley, Michael J. 1951- *St&PR 93*
Kelley, Michael John 1942- *WhoAm 92*
Kelley, Michael Robert 1940- *WhoSSW 93*
Kelley, Michael Stephen 1952- *St&PR 93*
Kelley, Michael T. 1952- *St&PR 93*
Kelley, Noble Henry 1901- *WhoAm 92*
Kelley, Patricia Hagelin 1953- *WhoAmW 93, WhoEmL 93*
Kelley, Paul Joseph 1941- *St&PR 93*
Kelley, Paul Xavier 1928- *WhoAm 92*
Kelley, Peggy Elaine 1960- *WhoEmL 93*
Kelley, Phil O. 1950- *St&PR 93*
Kelley, Philip E. 1929- *BioIn 17*
Kelley, Richard Alan 1952- *WhoAm 92*
Kelley, Richard Gilbert 1931- *St&PR 93*
Kelley, Richard Roy 1933- *WhoAm 92*
Kelley, Robb Beardsley 1917- *St&PR 93, WhoAm 92, WhoIns 93*
Kelley, Robert 1945- *St&PR 93*
Kelley, Robert C. 1932- *WhoSSW 93*
Kelley, Robert Douglas 1942- *WhoSSW 93*
Kelley, Robert E. 1938- *WhoAm 92*
Kelley, Robert L. *Law&B 92*
Kelley, Robert Lloyd 1925- *WhoAm 92*
Kelley, Robert Lynn 1950- *St&PR 93*
Kelley, Robert Otis 1944- *WhoAm 92*
Kelley, Royden Krueger 1911- *WhoE 93*
Kelley, Sean Patrick 1957- *St&PR 93*
Kelley, Shannon *BioIn 17*
Kelley, Sheila Seymour *St&PR 93, WhoAm 92, WhoAmW 93*
Kelley, Stafford K. 1932- *St&PR 93*
Kelley, Susan Elaine 1952- *WhoSSW 93*
Kelley, Terry *WhoSSW 93*
Kelley, Thomas Francis 1932- *WhoE 93*
Kelley, Thomas J. *Law&B 92*
Kelley, Thomas P. 1905-1982 *ScF&FL 92*
Kelley, Timothy Joseph 1950- *St&PR 93*
Kelley, Vincent Charles 1916- *WhoAm 92*
Kelley, Virginia *NewYTBS 92 [port]*
Kelley, W. Michael *Law&B 92*
Kelley, W. Michael 1947- *St&PR 93*
Kelley, Wayne Plumbley, Jr. 1933- *WhoAm 92*
Kelley, Wendell J. 1926- *St&PR 93, WhoAm 92*
Kelley, William Melvin *BioIn 17*
Kelley, William Nimmons 1939- *WhoAm 92, WhoWor 93*
Kelley, William Thomas 1917- *WhoAm 92*
Kelley-Kinyon, Jamie Michele 1954- *WhoEmL 93*
Kellgren, George Lars 1943- *WhoSSW 93, WhoWor 93*
Kellgren, John 1940- *WhoE 93*
Kellie, Lawrence 1862-1932 *Baker 92*
Kelliher, Daniel Joseph, Jr. 1944- *St&PR 93*
Kelliher, Donald J. 1943- *St&PR 93*
Kelliher, John M. 1951- *St&PR 93*
Kelliher, Peter Maurice 1912- *WhoAm 92*
Kelliomaa, Jill F. *Law&B 92*
Kellison, Donna Louise George 1950- *WhoAmW 93*
Kellison, James Bruce 1922- *WhoAm 92*
Kellison, Stephen George 1942- *WhoAm 92*
Kellman, Arthur 1913- *WhoSSW 93*
Kellman, Barnet 1947- *MiSFD 9*
Kellman, Barnet Kramer 1947- *WhoAm 92*
Kellman, Ira Stuart 1940- *WhoAm 92*
Kellman, Jerold L. 1945- *WhoWrEP 92*
Kellman, Jessie Rebecca 1960- *WhoAmW 93, WhoEmL 93*
Kellman, Joseph 1920- *WhoAm 92*
Kellman, Steven G. 1947- *WhoAm 92, WhoEmL 93, WhoSSW 93*
Kellner, Aaron d1992 *NewYTBS 92 [port]*
Kellner, Aaron 1914- *WhoAm 92*
Kellner, Allen 1915- *St&PR 93*
Kellner, Douglas Ernest 1956- *WhoE 93, WhoEmL 93*
Kellner, George Andrew 1942- *St&PR 93*
Kellner, Irwin L. 1938- *St&PR 93, WhoAm 92*
Kellner, Jamie *BioIn 17, WhoAm 92*
Kellner, Lawrence W. *St&PR 93*
Kellner, Richard George 1943- *WhoWor 93*
Kellner, Robert *WhoScE 91-4*
Kellner, Robert Dean 1956- *WhoEmL 93, WhoSSW 93*
Kellner, Robert G. 1953- *St&PR 93*
Kellner, Robert Scott 1941- *WhoAm 92*
Kellock, Alan d1992 *NewYTBS 92*
Kellock, Alan 1914-1992 *BioIn 17*
Kellock, Alan Converse 1942- *WhoAm 92*
Kellock, Sally H. 1936- *WhoUN 92*
Kelloe, Jane *Law&B 92*
Kellogg, Alice D. 1862-1900 *BioIn 17*
Kellogg, Ann Marie 1939- *WhoAmW 93*
Kellogg, Ansel Nash 1832-1886 *JrnUS*
Kellogg, C. Burton, II 1934- *St&PR 93*
Kellogg, C.T. 1931- *St&PR 93*
Kellogg, Cal Stewart *BioIn 17*
Kellogg, Cal Stewart, II 1947- *WhoAm 92*
Kellogg, Carol Kay 1941- *WhoAm 92*
Kellogg, Chester M. *BioIn 17*
Kellogg, Clara (Louise) 1842-1916 *Baker 92, OxDcOp*
Kellogg, Claude Carroll 1935- *St&PR 93*
Kellogg, David *MiSFD 9*
Kellogg, David 1950- *WhoAm 92*
Kellogg, David Wayne 1941- *WhoSSW 93*
Kellogg, Douglas Elliott 1919- *St&PR 93*
Kellogg, Dwight Alva 1940- *St&PR 93*
Kellogg, Elizabeth Rockey 1870- *AmWomPl*
Kellogg, Frederic Hartwell 1904- *WhoAm 92*
Kellogg, Frederic Rogers 1942- *WhoAm 92*
Kellogg, Gary Lee 1950- *WhoEmL 93*
Kellogg, Harry E. 1923- *St&PR 93*
Kellogg, Herbert Humphrey 1920- *WhoAm 92*
Kellogg, Kathleen Langenbeck 1953- *WhoAmW 93*
Kellogg, M. Bradley 1946- *ScF&FL 92*
Kellogg, Marion Schuyler 1920- *WhoE 93*
Kellogg, Mark Wentworth 1942- *St&PR 93*
Kellogg, Martin Nykes 1930- *St&PR 93*
Kellogg, Mercedes *BioIn 17*
Kellogg, Peter Newman 1956- *WhoEmL 93*
Kellogg, Rebecca Ross Small 1960- *WhoAmW 93*
Kellogg, Robert Kent 1962- *WhoSSW 93*
Kellogg, Robert Leland 1928- *WhoAm 92*
Kellogg, Stella Leal 1919- *WhoAmW 93*
Kellogg, Steven 1941- *WhoAm 92*
Kellogg, Steven (Castle) 1941- *MajAI [port]*
Kellogg, Thomas L. 1936- *WhoIns 93*
Kellogg, Tom N. 1936- *WhoIns 93*
Kellogg, Tommy Nason 1936- *St&PR 93, WhoAm 92*
Kellogg, William K., III 1930- *St&PR 93*
Kellogg, William Welch 1917- *WhoAm 92*
Kellogg-Smith, Peter 1920- *WhoWor 93*
Kellokumpu-Lehtinen, Pirkko-Liisa I. *WhoScE 91-4*
Kellor, Frances Alice 1873-1952 *BioIn 17*
Kellough, Cheryl *BioIn 17*
Kell-Smith, Carla Sue 1952- *WhoAmW 93*
Kellum, Carmen Kaye 1952- *WhoAmW 93*
Kellum, David 1936- *ScF&FL 92*
Kelly, Alonzo Hyatt, Jr. 1922- *WhoAm 92*
Kelly, Amelia Jean *Law&B 92*
Kelly, Amy Ruth 1878- *AmWomPl*
Kelly, Andrew Dighton 1926- *St&PR 93*
Kelly, Angel *BioIn 17*
Kelly, Angela 1950- *BioIn 17*
Kelly, Anne C. 1916- *WhoAmW 93*
Kelly, Annie *BioIn 17*
Kelly, Anthony 1929- *WhoWor 93*
Kelly, Anthony Odrian 1935- *WhoAm 92*
Kelly, Armandine Frances 1947- *WhoWrEP 92*
Kelly, Arthur Lloyd 1937- *WhoAm 92*
Kelly, Arthur Paul 1938- *WhoAm 92*
Kelly, Aurel Maxey 1923- *WhoAm 92*
Kelly, Austin Patrick, Jr. 1935- *St&PR 93*
Kelly, Barbara Anne 1949- *WhoAmW 93*
Kelly, Bernard J. 1936- *St&PR 93*
Kelly, Beverly Beebe Grimes 1930- *WhoAmW 93*
Kelly, Brian C. *Law&B 92*
Kelly, Brian Christopher 1951- *St&PR 93*
Kelly, Brian J. 1934- *St&PR 93*
Kelly, Brian J. 1954- *WhoAm 92*
Kelly, Brian Matthew 1956- *WhoEmL 93*
Kelly, Bryan 1934- *Baker 92*
Kelly, Burton Vincent 1932- *WhoAm 92*
Kelly, Carol White 1946- *WhoAmW 93, WhoEmL 93*
Kelly, Carolyn Sue 1952- *WhoAm 92*
Kelly, Carter B. 1937- *St&PR 93*
Kelly, Catherine Makem 1948- *WhoEmL 93*

Kelly, Charles Arthur 1932- WhoAm 92, WhoWor 93
Kelly, Charles Brian 1935- WhoSSW 93
Kelly, Charles E. 1920?-1985 BioIn 17
Kelly, Charles J., Jr. 1929- WhoAm 92
Kelly, Cheryl Ann 1956- WhoEmL 93
Kelly, Chris NewYTBS 92 [port]
Kelly, Christine Ann 1952- WhoAmW 93, WhoEmL 93
Kelly, Christine Evans 1952- St&PR 93
Kelly, Christopher P. Law&B 92
Kelly, Colleen Law&B 92
Kelly, Colleen Adele 1934- WhoAmW 93
Kelly, Coriene 1926- St&PR 93
Kelly, Craig Edward Law&B 92
Kelly, Craig J. 1945- WhoAm 92
Kelly, Dan Michael 1946- St&PR 93
Kelly, Daniel 1936-1989 BiDAMSp 1989
Kelly, Daniel Grady, Jr. 1951- WhoAm 92
Kelly, Daniel John 1940- WhoWor 93
Kelly, Daniel Martin 1906- WhoE 93
Kelly, Daniel William Kevin 1936- WhoWor 93
Kelly, David Austin 1938- St&PR 93, WhoAm 92
Kelly, David H. 1944- St&PR 93
Kelly, David Hilary 1929- WhoE 93
Kelly, David Hoover 1944- WhoAm 92
Kelly, David J. ScF&FL 92
Kelly, David Michael 1938- WhoE 93, WhoWrEP 92
Kelly, David Roy 1955- WhoWor 93
Kelly, Deborah Elise 1946- St&PR 93
Kelly, Dee J. 1929- WhoAm 92, WhoSSW 93
Kelly, Dennis D. 1938-1991 BioIn 17
Kelly, Dennis H. 1937- St&PR 93
Kelly, Dennis John Law&B 92
Kelly, Dennis Ray 1948- WhoEmL 93
Kelly, Donald F. 1945- St&PR 93
Kelly, Donald Francis WhoScE 91-1
Kelly, Donald Philip 1922- WhoAm 92
Kelly, Donovan Patrick WhoScE 91-1
Kelly, Dorothy Ann 1929- WhoAm 92, WhoAmW 93
Kelly, Douglas 1934- WhoAm 92
Kelly, Eamon Michael 1936- WhoAm 92, WhoSSW 93, WhoWor 93
Kelly, Earletha BioIn 17
Kelly, Ed O. d1904 BioIn 17
Kelly, Edmund Joseph 1937- WhoAm 92
Kelly, Edna Flannery 1906- BioIn 17
Kelly, Edward Francis 1932- WhoAm 92
Kelly, Edward J. 1876-1950 PolPar
Kelly, Edward John, V 1936- WhoSSW 93
Kelly, Edward Thomas 1957- St&PR 93
Kelly, Eileen Anne 1965- WhoE 93
Kelly, Eileen Patricia 1955- WhoAmW 93, WhoEmL 93, WhoSSW 93, WhoWor 93
Kelly, Eileen Patricia 1958- WhoAmW 93
Kelly, Elizabeth Walt Baker 1908-1991 BioIn 17
Kelly, Ellsworth 1923- BioIn 17, News 92 [port], WhoAm 92
Kelly, Eric Damian 1947- WhoEmL 93, WhoWor 93
Kelly, Eric P(hilbrook) 1884-1960 MajAI [port]
Kelly, Erin Marie 1967- WhoAmW 93
Kelly, Eugene 1961- WhoEmL 93
Kelly, Eugene Walter, Jr. 1936- WhoAm 92
Kelly, Fanny 1845-1904 BioIn 17
Kelly, Francis Daniel 1909- WhoAm 92
Kelly, Francis J., Jr. 1929- St&PR 93, WhoAm 92
Kelly, Francis J., III Law&B 92
Kelly, Francis P. 1946- St&PR 93
Kelly, Frank WhoScE 91-1
Kelly, Frank K. 1914- ConAu 39NR, ScF&FL 92
Kelly, Franklin (Wood) 1953- ConAu 139, WhoAm 92, WhoEmL 93
Kelly, Fred 1916- BioIn 17
Kelly, Frederick W. 1937- St&PR 93
Kelly, Gail Paradise BioIn 17
Kelly, Gary Clayton 1955- St&PR 93
Kelly, Gary M. 1934- St&PR 93
Kelly, Gene 1912- BioIn 17, IntDcF 2-3 [port], MiSFD 9
Kelly, Gene Curran 1912- WhoAm 92
Kelly, Geoffrey James Law&B 92
Kelly, George Anthony 1916- BioIn 17, WhoAm 92, WhoWrEP 92
Kelly, George E. 1908- St&PR 93
Kelly, George G. 1955- St&PR 93
Kelly, George J., Jr. Law&B 92
Kelly, George S. Law&B 92
Kelly, Gerald Joseph 1947- WhoEmL 93
Kelly, Gerald Wayne 1944- WhoSSW 93, WhoWor 93
Kelly, Glenda Marie 1944- WhoAmW 93
Kelly, Grace 1929-1982 BioIn 17, IntDcF 2-3 [port]
Kelly, Grace R. 1949- WhoAmW 93
Kelly, Graham D. 1941- WhoAsAP 91
Kelly, Gregory Lewis Law&B 92
Kelly, Gregory Maxwell 1930- WhoWor 93
Kelly, H. Vincent 1933- WhoE 93
Kelly, Harold Ernest 1885?-1970? ScF&FL 92
Kelly, Helen Mayo 1933- St&PR 93
Kelly, Henry Ansgar 1934- WhoAm 92
Kelly, Herman Floyd, Jr. 1938- WhoSSW 93
Kelly, Hugh 1739-1777 BioIn 17
Kelly, Hugh Padraic 1931- WhoAm 92
Kelly, Hugh Rice Law&B 92
Kelly, Hugh Rice 1942- WhoAm 92
Kelly, J. Fredrick, Jr. 1950- St&PR 93
Kelly, J.J., III 1945- St&PR 93
Kelly, J. Michael Law&B 92
Kelly, J. Michael 1947- St&PR 93
Kelly, Jack d1992 NewYTBS 92 [port]
Kelly, James 1913- WhoAm 92
Kelly, James A. 1932- St&PR 93
Kelly, James Andrew 1936- WhoAm 92
Kelly, James Anthony 1949- WhoE 93
Kelly, James Arthur, Jr. 1934- WhoAm 92
Kelly, James Burton 1931- WhoIns 93
Kelly, James C. St&PR 93
Kelly, James C. 1937- WhoScE 91-3
Kelly, James Christopher 1939- St&PR 93
Kelly, James Dewitt 1918- St&PR 93
Kelly, James E. Law&B 92
Kelly, James Edward 1944- St&PR 93
Kelly, James Edward Jim 1960- WhoAm 92
Kelly, James F. 1922- St&PR 93
Kelly, James J. Law&B 92
Kelly, James Joseph, Jr. 1951- WhoAm 92
Kelly, James McGirr WhoE 93
Kelly, James Patrick 1946- WhoWor 93
Kelly, James Patrick 1951- ScF&FL 92
Kelly, James Patrick 1952- WhoE 93
Kelly, James Patrick, Jr. 1933- WhoAm 92
Kelly, James Thomas 1942- WhoE 93
Kelly, Jane Law&B 92
Kelly, Janet Langford 1957- WhoAmW 93
Kelly, Jay Thomas 1950- WhoAm 92
Kelly, Jeff ConAu 136
Kelly, Jeff 1944- BioIn 17
Kelly, Jeffrey 1946- BioIn 17, ConAu 136
Kelly, Jeffrey Stephen 1947- St&PR 93
Kelly, Jennifer Faye 1957- WhoSSW 93
Kelly, Jerrold J. 1930- St&PR 93
Kelly, Jim 1960- CurBio 92 [port]
Kelly, Joel 1944- St&PR 93
Kelly, John 1822-1885 PolPar
Kelly, John C. Law&B 92
Kelly, John C., Jr. 1936- St&PR 93
Kelly, John Charles 1928- WhoWor 93
Kelly, John David, Jr. 1941- St&PR 93
Kelly, John E. Law&B 92
Kelly, John F. Law&B 92
Kelly, John F. 1938- WhoIns 93
Kelly, John Fleming 1926- WhoAm 92
Kelly, John Forsyth Law&B 92
Kelly, John Francis 1938- WhoAm 92
Kelly, John Fredrick 1933- St&PR 93
Kelly, John G. Law&B 92
Kelly, John G. 1927- St&PR 93, WhoIns 93
Kelly, John Hubert 1939- WhoAm 92, WhoWor 93
Kelly, John J. 1935- WhoScE 91-3
Kelly, John Joseph, Jr. 1940- WhoAm 92
Kelly, John Michael Law&B 92
Kelly, John P. 1935- St&PR 93
Kelly, John Patrick 1933- WhoAm 92
Kelly, John Patrick 1952- WhoEmL 93
Kelly, John Paul, Jr. 1941- AfrAmBi
Kelly, John Thomas 1925- WhoAm 92
Kelly, John W. Law&B 92
Kelly, Jon Ferguson Law&B 92
Kelly, Joseph C. Law&B 92
Kelly, Joseph Edward 1937- WhoAm 92
Kelly, Joseph Elton, III 1927- St&PR 93
Kelly, Joseph Francis, Jr. 1938- WhoAm 92
Kelly, Joseph Gordon WhoScE 91-1
Kelly, Joseph I. Law&B 92
Kelly, Joseph John 1948- WhoWrEP 92
Kelly, Josephine Kaye 1944- WhoAmW 93
Kelly, Joyce Marie 1940- WhoE 93
Kelly, Katherine C. AmWomPl
Kelly, Katherine Wick 1887-1937 AmWomPl
Kelly, Kathleen Anne 1955- WhoWor 93
Kelly, Kathleen C. 1947- St&PR 93
Kelly, Kathleen M. 1964- SmATA 71 [port]
Kelly, Kathleen Mary 1964- WhoE 93
Kelly, Kathleen Sue 1943- WhoAmW 93
Kelly, Katie BioIn 17
Kelly, Keith John 1954- WhoE 93
Kelly, Ken 1946- ScF&FL 92
Kelly, Kenneth Constantine 1928- WhoAm 92
Kelly, Kenneth J. Law&B 92
Kelly, Kenneth James 1932- St&PR 93
Kelly, Kenneth James 1940- WhoAm 92
Kelly, Kevin 1934- WhoAm 92
Kelly, Kevin 1945- See Byrds, The ConMus 8
Kelly, Kevin Gerard 1956- WhoSSW 93
Kelly, L. Kevin 1953- WhoAm 92
Kelly, L. Thomas 1945- WhoAm 92, WhoE 93
Kelly, Lawrence Joseph 1933- St&PR 93
Kelly, Lee F. 1942- St&PR 93
Kelly, Leo B., Jr. 1921- St&PR 93
Kelly, Lillian Darlene 1957- WhoSSW 93
Kelly, Linda Law&B 92
Kelly, Lucie Stirm Young 1925- WhoAm 92
Kelly, Luther Wrentmore, Jr. 1925- WhoAm 92
Kelly, Lynn C. 1947- WhoE 93
Kelly, M.T. 1947- WhoCanL 92
Kelly, Maeve 1930- ScF&FL 92
Kelly, Margaret Flanagan Law&B 92
Kelly, Marguerite Lelong 1932- WhoE 93
Kelly, Marguerite Stehli 1931- WhoAmW 93
Kelly, Marjorie Helen 1953- WhoAmW 93
Kelly, Mark E. 1947- St&PR 93
Kelly, Mark Hamilton 1953- WhoEmL 93
Kelly, Mark S. BioIn 17
Kelly, Martin J. 1937- St&PR 93
Kelly, Martin Paul 1955- WhoWor 93
Kelly, Mary Ann BioIn 17
Kelly, Mary Elin 1949- WhoAmW 93
Kelly, Mary Jo 1947- WhoWrEP 92
Kelly, Mary Lee 1949- WhoWrEP 92
Kelly, Mary Louise 1952- WhoEmL 93
Kelly, Matthew Edward 1928- WhoAm 92
Kelly, Mattie Caroline May 1912- WhoAmW 93, WhoWor 93
Kelly, Maureen Ann 1965- WhoWor 93
Kelly, Maureen C. 1944- St&PR 93
Kelly, Maureen Patricia 1955- WhoAmW 93
Kelly, Maxine Ann 1931- WhoAmW 93
Kelly, Michael WhoScE 91-1
Kelly, Michael 1762-1826 Baker 92, IntDcOp [port], OxDcOp
Kelly, Michael A. Law&B 92
Kelly, Michael A. 1936- St&PR 93
Kelly, Michael C. Law&B 92
Kelly, Michael Garcin 1946- WhoEmL 93, WhoSSW 93
Kelly, Michael George 1959- WhoE 93
Kelly, Michael J. Law&B 92
Kelly, Michael J. d1990 BioIn 17
Kelly, Michael John 1952- WhoEmL 93
Kelly, Michael Roberts 1947- WhoSSW 93
Kelly, Michael Thomas Law&B 92
Kelly, Mollie AmWomPl
Kelly, Nancy 1953- MiSFD 9
Kelly, Nancy Folden 1951- WhoAm 92
Kelly, Neil Joseph 1940- St&PR 93
Kelly, Pamela Davis 1947- WhoAmW 93
Kelly, Pat 1967- BioIn 17
Kelly, Patricia WhoWrEP 92
Kelly, Patricia 1932- WhoAmW 93
Kelly, Patrick BioIn 17, MiSFD 9
Kelly, Patrick 1954?-1990 ConBlB 3 [port]
Kelly, Patrick Chastain 1947- WhoSSW 93
Kelly, Patrick F. 1929- WhoAm 92
Kelly, Patrick J. 1926- WhoAm 92
Kelly, Patrick T. 1935- St&PR 93
Kelly, Patsy 1910-1981 QDrFCA 92 [port]
Kelly, Paul Charles, Jr. 1948- WhoE 93
Kelly, Paul E. 1912- St&PR 93
Kelly, Paul J., Jr. Law&B 92
Kelly, Paul Knox 1940- WhoAm 92, WhoE 93, WhoWor 93
Kelly, Paul L. 1956- St&PR 93
Kelly, Paul Lance 1939- St&PR 93
Kelly, Paul Thomas 1936- St&PR 93
Kelly, Paula Campbell Law&B 92
Kelly, Peter Galbraith 1937- WhoAm 92
Kelly, Peter J. Law&B 92
Kelly, Peter Joseph Law&B 92
Kelly, Peter M. 1941- St&PR 93
Kelly, Petra 1947-1992 NewYTBS 92
Kelly, Preston W. 1936- St&PR 93
Kelly, R. Richard Dennis 1945- WhoE 93
Kelly, Raymond Boone, III 1947- WhoSSW 93
Kelly, Raymond Case 1942- WhoWor 93
Kelly, Raymond Francis 1939- St&PR 93, WhoAm 92
Kelly, Raymond M. 1939- WhoIns 93
Kelly, Richard BioIn 17, Law&B 92, ScF&FL 92
Kelly, Richard 1937- WhoWrEP 92
Kelly, Richard L. 1938- St&PR 93
Kelly, Richard Leo 1938- WhoIns 93
Kelly, Richard S. 1951- St&PR 93
Kelly, Richard Smith 1925- WhoAm 92
Kelly, Robert ScF&FL 92
Kelly, Robert 1916- Baker 92
Kelly, Robert 1934- WhoWrEP 92
Kelly, Robert 1935- BioIn 17, WhoAm 92
Kelly, Robert Donald 1929- WhoAm 92
Kelly, Robert E. 1926- WhoWrEP 92
Kelly, Robert Edward, Jr. Law&B 92
Kelly, Robert Edward, Jr. 1950- WhoEmL 93
Kelly, Robert Emmett 1929- WhoAm 92
Kelly, Robert Emmett 1952- WhoE 93
Kelly, Robert F. d1992 NewYTBS 92 [port]
Kelly, Robert F. 1917-1992 BioIn 17
Kelly, Robert F. 1930- St&PR 93
Kelly, Robert F. 1935- WhoAm 92, WhoE 93
Kelly, Robert H. Law&B 92
Kelly, Robert H. 1929- St&PR 93
Kelly, Robert J. Law&B 92
Kelly, Robert Lynn 1939- WhoAm 92, WhoE 93
Kelly, Robert Thomas 1924- WhoAm 92
Kelly, Robert Vincent, Jr. 1938- St&PR 93, WhoAm 92, WhoWor 93
Kelly, Robert Vincent, III 1962- WhoEmL 93
Kelly, Robert Weber 1916- St&PR 93
Kelly, Roger 1946- WhoScE 91-1
Kelly, Ronald ScF&FL 92
Kelly, Ronald James 1950- WhoSSW 93
Kelly, Ros 1948- WhoAsAP 91
Kelly, Ruth Eileen 1921- St&PR 93
Kelly, Ruthanne St&PR 93
Kelly, Sandra K. Law&B 92
Kelly, Sandra L. 1957- St&PR 93
Kelly, Sean 1940- ScF&FL 92
Kelly, Shane 1956?-1986? ScF&FL 92
Kelly, Sharon Pratt BioIn 17
Kelly, Sharon Pratt 1944- CurBio 92 [port], WhoAm 92, WhoAmW 93, WhoE 93
Kelly, Sheryl K. Law&B 92
Kelly, Stanley C. 1947- St&PR 93
Kelly, Stanley Conway 1947- WhoAm 92
Kelly, Stephen John 1940- WhoAm 92
Kelly, Susan Croce 1947- WhoEmL 93
Kelly, Susan E. 1962- WhoAmW 93
Kelly, Susan Lynley 1965- WhoAmW 93
Kelly, Susan Sorrell Law&B 92
Kelly, Suzanne Woodward 1946- WhoAmW 93
Kelly, Sylvia Hayden Neahr 1938- WhoWrEP 92
Kelly, Theodore A. 1920-1990 BioIn 17
Kelly, Thomas 1950- WhoIns 93
Kelly, Thomas A. 1951- St&PR 93
Kelly, Thomas Brooke 1943- WhoAm 92
Kelly, Thomas Cajetan 1931- WhoAm 92, WhoSSW 93
Kelly, Thomas F. Law&B 92
Kelly, Thomas Francis 1942- St&PR 93
Kelly, Thomas H. 1942- WhoIns 93
Kelly, Thomas J. d1988 BioIn 17
Kelly, Thomas J. 1927- St&PR 93
Kelly, Thomas James 1931- WhoAm 92
Kelly, Thomas Jesse, Jr. 1941- WhoAm 92
Kelly, Thomas Joseph 1953- WhoSSW 93
Kelly, Thomas Joseph, III 1947- WhoAm 92
Kelly, Thomas Mortimer 1953- WhoEmL 93
Kelly, Thomas Paine, Jr. 1912- WhoAm 92
Kelly, Tim Donahue 1944- WhoAm 92
Kelly, Timothy G. Law&B 92
Kelly, Timothy Michael 1947- WhoAm 92, WhoSSW 93
Kelly, Tom BioIn 17
Kelly, Tom 1950- WhoAm 92
Kelly, Viana Eileen 1953- WhoEmL 93
Kelly, Victor Clayton, Jr. 1943- St&PR 93
Kelly, Vincent Michael, Jr. 1933- WhoSSW 93
Kelly, W.M. 1949- WhoScE 91-3
Kelly, W. Richard, Jr. 1929- St&PR 93
Kelly, Walter M., II Law&B 92
Kelly, Walter R. 1926- St&PR 93
Kelly, William 1914- WhoAm 92, WhoSSW 93
Kelly, William A. BioIn 17
Kelly, William Bernard 1955- WhoEmL 93
Kelly, William Bret 1922- WhoWor 93
Kelly, William Clark 1922- WhoAm 92
Kelly, William F., III 1951- St&PR 93
Kelly, William Franklin, Jr. 1938- WhoAm 92
Kelly, William Harold 1926- WhoAm 92
Kelly, William P. Law&B 92
Kelly, William Patrick 1848-1916 ScF&FL 92
Kelly, William Russell 1906- BioIn 17
Kelly, William Scott 1948- St&PR 93
Kelly, William Watkins 1928- WhoAm 92
Kelly, Winfield M. 1935- WhoAm 92, WhoE 93
Kelly-Pizarro, Patricia Ann 1961- WhoAmW 93
Kelm, Bonnie G. 1947- WhoAmW 93, WhoWor 93
Kelm, George 1928- St&PR 93
Kelm, Linda 1944- WhoAm 92
Kelmachter, Barry Lee 1946- WhoEmL 93
Kelman, Arthur 1918- WhoAm 92
Kelman, Charles 1930- WhoAm 92, WhoWor 93
Kelman, David 1934- St&PR 93

Kelman, Edward Michael 1943- *WhoE 93*
Kelman, Gary Allen 1951- *WhoE 93, WhoEmL 93*
Kelman, Herbert Chanoch 1927- *WhoAm 92*
Kelman, J. Brent 1942- *St&PR 93*
Kelman, John Matheson 1938- *St&PR 93*
Kelman, Judith 1945- *ScF&FL 92*
Kelman, Mark Gregory 1951- *WhoAm 92*
Kelman, Wolfe 1923-1990 *BioIn 17*
Kelmenson, Leo-Arthur 1927- *WhoAm 92*
Kelne, Nathan 1918- *WhoAm 92*
Kelnhofer, F. *WhoScE 91-4*
Kelsall, Charles 1782-1857 *BioIn 17*
Kelsay, Royal Edward 1930- *St&PR 93*
Kelsey, Clyde Eastman, Jr. 1924- *WhoAm 92, WhoSSW 93*
Kelsey, Darrel A. *Law&B 92*
Kelsey, Floyd Lamar, Jr. 1925- *WhoAm 92*
Kelsey, Frances Oldham 1914- *WhoAmW 93*
Kelsey, Jarel Robert 1937- *St&PR 93*
Kelsey, John Edward 1942- *WhoSSW 93*
Kelsey, John L. 1925- *St&PR 93*
Kelsey, John Walter 1910- *WhoAm 92*
Kelsey, Mary F. 1925- *St&PR 93*
Kelsey, Maynard James 1939- *St&PR 93*
Kelsey, Michael David *Law&B 92*
Kelsey, Robert Randall 1951- *WhoEmL 93*
Kelsey, Sara A. *Law&B 92*
Kelsey, Susan Evans *Law&B 92*
Kelsh, John Conley *Law&B 92*
Kelshaw, Terence 1936- *WhoAm 92*
Kelso, Alec John 1930- *WhoAm 92*
Kelso, Ann Breeding 1945- *WhoAmW 93, WhoSSW 93, WhoWor 93*
Kelso, Ben *BioIn 17*
Kelso, David Mark *Law&B 92*
Kelso, Frank Benton, II 1933- *WhoAm 92*
Kelso, Gwendolyn Lee 1935- *WhoAmW 93, WhoWor 93*
Kelso, Harold Glen 1929- *WhoAm 92*
Kelso, James Richard 1949- *St&PR 93*
Kelso, John Glover, Sr. 1932- *WhoE 93*
Kelso, John Hodgson 1925- *WhoAm 92*
Kelso, John Morris 1922- *WhoAm 92*
Kelso, Louis 1913-1991 *AnObit 1991*
Kelso, Louis O. *BioIn 17*
Kelso, Richard Wallace 1937- *St&PR 93*
Kelso, Terry A. 1948- *St&PR 93*
Kelson, Allen Howard 1940- *WhoAm 92, WhoWrEP 92*
Kelson, Irwin S. 1932- *WhoIns 93*
Kelterborn, Rudolf 1931- *Baker 92*
Keltner, J. Robert 1921- *St&PR 93*
Keltner, Karen Lee 1947- *WhoAmW 93*
Keltner, Ken 1916-1991 *BioIn 17*
Keltner, Kenneth Frederick 1916-1991 *BiDAMSp 1989*
Keltner, Raymond Marion, Jr. 1929- *WhoAm 92*
Kelton, Arthur Marvin, Jr. 1939- *WhoWor 93*
Kelton, David J. 1925- *St&PR 93*
Kelton, Richard *BioIn 17*
Kelton, William A. 1939- *WhoIns 93*
Kelton, William Jackson 1932- *WhoSSW 93*
Kelts, Susan Margaret 1949- *WhoEmL 93*
Keltsch, Donald Robert 1924- *St&PR 93*
Keltsch, Maurice Carl 1927- *St&PR 93*
Kelty, Michael P. 1950- *St&PR 93*
Kelty, Miriam Carol 1938- *WhoAmW 93*
Kelty, Ruth Ann *WhoAmW 93*
Kelty, Wlliam John 1948- *WhoAsAP 91*
Kelty-Kople, Karen Ann 1946- *St&PR 93*
Keltz, Martin J. 1944- *St&PR 93*
Keltz, Michael J. 1946- *St&PR 93*
Kelvin, Baron 1824-1907 *BioIn 17*
Kelvin, Jeffrey Barnett 1948- *WhoEmL 93*
Kelvington, Wilbur Lee 1929- *WhoWor 93*
Kelzer, John B. 1936- *St&PR 93*
Kem, Richard Samuel 1934- *WhoAm 92*
Kemakeza, Allen 1951- *WhoAsAP 91*
Kemal, Mustafa *DcTwHis*
Kemal, Yasar 1923- *WhoWor 93*
Kemali, Milena 1928- *WhoScE 91-3*
Kemball, Christopher 1946- *WhoAm 92*
Kemball, Christopher Ross 1946- *St&PR 93*
Kembel, David A. *Law&B 92*
Kemble, Adelaide 1814-1879 *Baker 92, OxDcOp*
Kemble, Ernest Dell 1935- *WhoAm 92*
Kemble, John Hasking 1912-1990 *BioIn 17*
Kemble, Katie *BioIn 17*
Kemble, Stephen A. 1932- *St&PR 93*
Kemelhor, Robert Elias 1919- *WhoE 93*
Kemelman, Harry 1908- *WhoAm 92, WhoWrEP 92*
Kemeny, John G. 1926-1992 *NewYTBS 92 [port]*
Kemenyffy, Steven 1943- *WhoE 93*
Kemerling, James Lee 1939- *St&PR 93*
Kemezys, K. Peter *Law&B 92*
Kemhadjian, Henri Antoine *WhoScE 91-1*
Kemler, Robert Michael 1945- *WhoE 93*
Kemmel, William A., Jr. *Law&B 92*
Kemmel, William Anthony, Jr. 1930- *St&PR 93*
Kemmer, Dennis J. *Law&B 92*
Kemmer, Richard Julius 1945- *WhoAm 92*
Kemmer, Suzanne Elizabeth 1959- *WhoAmW 93*
Kemmerer, Donald Lorenzo 1905- *WhoAm 92*
Kemmerer, John L., Jr. 1911- *St&PR 93*
Kemmerer, Kathleen Mary 1952- *WhoE 93*
Kemmerer, Peter Ream 1942- *WhoE 93, WhoWor 93*
Kemmerer, Sharon Jean 1956- *WhoAmW 93*
Kemmerer, Terry *St&PR 93*
Kemmerly, Guy Tristan 1960- *WhoSSW 93*
Kemmerly, Jack Dale 1936- *WhoAm 92*
Kemmet, Gerald William 1939- *St&PR 93*
Kemmett, William J. *WhoWrEP 92*
Kemmis, Daniel Orra 1945- *WhoAm 92*
Kemmler, Eric L. *Law&B 92*
Kemner, Mark H. 1945- *St&PR 93*
Kemner, Rudolf 1937- *WhoWor 93*
Kemnitz, Charles Frederick 1954- *WhoSSW 93*
Kemnitz, D.H. 1926- *St&PR 93*
Kemnitz, Josef Blazek 1943- *WhoWor 93*
Kemnitz, Thomas Milton *WhoAm 92*
Kemp, Alexander George *WhoScE 91-1*
Kemp, Aubrey L. 1939- *St&PR 93*
Kemp, Barbara 1881-1959 *Baker 92*
See Also Schillings, Max von 1868-1933 *OxDcOp*
Kemp, Betty Ruth 1930- *WhoAm 92, WhoAmW 93, WhoSSW 93*
Kemp, Brian Richard C. 1943- *WhoWor 93*
Kemp, Bruce E. 1946- *WhoWor 93*
Kemp, Danial Schaeffer 1936- *WhoAm 92*
Kemp, Daniel W. *Law&B 92*
Kemp, David d1935? *BioIn 17*
Kemp, Deborah Joan 1951- *WhoEmL 93*
Kemp, Diane Legge 1949- *WhoAm 92*
Kemp, Dick Douglas 1939- *St&PR 93*
Kemp, Earl 1929- *ScF&FL 92*
Kemp, Edgar Ray, Jr. 1924- *St&PR 93*
Kemp, Edward H. 1908-1989 *BioIn 17*
Kemp, Ejvind 1929- *WhoScE 91-2, WhoWor 93*
Kemp, Eugene Thomas 1930- *WhoE 93*
Kemp, Evan Jennings, Jr. 1937- *WhoAm 92, WhoE 93*
Kemp, "Father" (Robert J.) 1820-1897 *Baker 92*
Kemp, Francis 1940-1990 *BioIn 17*
Kemp, Frank 1927- *St&PR 93*
Kemp, Gary *BioIn 17*
Kemp, Gene 1926- *ChlFicS, ChlLR 29 [port], MajAI*
Kemp, Geoffrey Thomas Howard 1939- *WhoAm 92*
Kemp, Gina Christine 1968- *WhoSSW 93*
Kemp, Harold Robert 1931- *WhoWor 93*
Kemp, Harris Atteridge 1912- *WhoAm 92*
Kemp, J. Robert 1920- *WhoAm 92*
Kemp, Jack *BioIn 17*
Kemp, Jack 1935- *CngDr 91*
Kemp, Jack F. 1935- *PolPar*
Kemp, Jack French 1935- *WhoAm 92, WhoE 93, WhoWor 93*
Kemp, James 1942- *WhoSSW 93*
Kemp, John Daniel 1940- *WhoAm 92*
Kemp, John French 1935- *BiDAMSp 1989*
Kemp, John Randolph 1945- *WhoSSW 93*
Kemp, Joseph 1778-1824 *Baker 92*
Kemp, Judy Vantrease 1958- *WhoAmW 93*
Kemp, June 1933- *WhoWor 93*
Kemp, K. Thomas 1940- *St&PR 93*
Kemp, Ken *ScF&FL 92*
Kemp, Mae Wunder *WhoAmW 93*
Kemp, Martin *BioIn 17*
Kemp, Martin John 1942- *WhoWor 93*
Kemp, Maury Page 1929- *WhoAm 92*
Kemp, Nancy *ScF&FL 92*
Kemp, Nettie Emmerine 1908- *WhoWrEP 92*
Kemp, Patrick Samuel 1932- *WhoAm 92*
Kemp, Paul *BioIn 17*
Kemp, Penn 1944- *WhoCanL 92*
Kemp, Peter 1942- *ScF&FL 92*
Kemp, Peter Warren 1948- *WhoEmL 93*
Kemp, Ralph Gene, Jr. 1944- *WhoAm 92*
Kemp, Robert Bowers, Jr. 1941- *St&PR 93*
Kemp, Robert William 1943- *St&PR 93*
Kemp, Robin *ScF&FL 92*
Kemp, Sally Rush 1933- *WhoAmW 93*
Kemp, Samuel Leon 1945- *WhoSSW 93*
Kemp, Suzanne Leppart 1929- *WhoAmW 93*
Kemp, Terence James *WhoScE 91-1*
Kemp, Theresa Anne 1956- *WhoE 93*
Kemp, Thomas Dupre, Jr. 1903- *WhoSSW 93*
Kemp, Thomas Jay *WhoE 93*
Kemp, Thomas L. 1951- *St&PR 93*
Kemp, Walter Robert *Law&B 92*
Kemp, Wesley Barton 1946- *St&PR 93*
Kemp, William J., Jr. *Law&B 92*
Kempa, Edward Stanislaus 1927- *WhoScE 91-4*
Kempa, Gerald 1934- *WhoAm 92, WhoE 93*
Kempainen, Robert *BioIn 17*
Kempe, Frederick 1954- *ConAu 138*
Kempe, Lloyd Lute 1911- *WhoAm 92*
Kempe, Margery c. 1373- *BioIn 17*
Kempe, Robert A. 1922- *St&PR 93*
Kempe, Rudolf 1910-1976 *Baker 92, IntDcOp, OxDcOp*
Kempe, Volker 1939- *WhoScE 91-3*
Kempema, James L. 1931- *St&PR 93*
Kempen, Gerard A.M. 1943- *WhoWor 93*
Kempen, H.J.M. 1947- *WhoScE 91-3*
Kempen, Paul van 1893-1955 *Baker 92*
Kempener, Pieter de c. 1503-c. 1580 *BioIn 17*
Kempenfelt, Richard 1718-1782 *HarEnMi*
Kempenich, William J. *Law&B 92*
Kemper, Casey Randolph 1947- *WhoAm 92*
Kemper, David W. 1950- *St&PR 93*
Kemper, David Woods, II 1950- *WhoAm 92*
Kemper, Dorla Dean 1929- *WhoAmW 93*
Kemper, Fritz H. 1927- *WhoScE 91-3*
Kemper, Gertrude Ziesing d1991 *BioIn 17*
Kemper, Han C.G. 1941- *WhoScE 91-3*
Kemper, Jackson, Jr. 1935- *St&PR 93*
Kemper, James Dee 1947- *WhoAm 92*
Kemper, James M., Jr. 1921- *St&PR 93*
Kemper, James Madison, Jr. 1921- *WhoAm 92*
Kemper, James Willard 1927- *WhoSSW 93*
Kemper, John Dustin 1924- *WhoAm 92*
Kemper, Jonathan McBride 1953- *St&PR 93, WhoAm 92*
Kemper, Lee H. 1921- *WhoIns 93*
Kemper, Lee Howard 1921- *St&PR 93*
Kemper, Pamela Diane 1960- *WhoAmW 93*
Kemper, Richard F. 1947- *St&PR 93*
Kemper, Robert Van 1945- *WhoSSW 93*
Kemper, Rufus Crosby, Jr. 1927- *St&PR 93, WhoAm 92*
Kemper, Sallie *AmWomPl*
Kemper, Steven Edward 1951- *WhoWrEP 92*
Kemper, Thomas W. 1947- *St&PR 93*
Kemper, Troxey 1915- *ConAu 136, WhoWrEP 92*
Kemper, Walker Warder, Jr. 1924- *WhoWor 93*
Kemper Littman, Marlyn 1943- *WhoAm 92, WhoAmW 93, WhoSSW 93*
Kemperman, Albert Frederik 1955- *WhoWor 93*
Kempers, Roger Dyke 1928- *WhoAm 92*
Kempf, Cecil Joseph 1927- *WhoAm 92*
Kempf, Donald G., Jr. 1937- *WhoAm 92*
Kempf, Douglas Paul 1954- *WhoEmL 93*
Kempf, Ivan 1928- *WhoScE 91-2*
Kempf, Joseph John, Jr. *Law&B 92*
Kempf, Martine 1958- *WhoAmW 93, WhoEmL 93, WhoWor 93*
Kempf, Paul Stuart 1918- *WhoAm 92*
Kempf, Reva Ann 1947- *WhoEmL 93*
Kempf, Wolfgang 1925- *WhoScE 91-3*
Kempfer, Homer 1911- *WhoAm 92*
Kempff, Wilhelm 1895-1991 *AnObit 1991, BioIn 17*
Kempff, Wilhelm (Walter Friedrich) 1895-1991 *Baker 92*
Kempher, Ruth Moon 1934- *WhoSSW 93*
Kempin, Frederick Gustav, Jr. 1922- *WhoAm 92*
Kempin, Linda Jeanne 1951- *WhoE 93*
Kempinen, LaVerne M. *Law&B 92*
Kempken, D.W. 1945- *St&PR 93*
Kempkes, Michael Alan 1960- *WhoE 93*
Kemple, Joseph Nephi 1921- *WhoAm 92*
Kempler, Roger *Law&B 92*
Kempley, Rita A. 1945- *WhoAm 92*
Kemplin, Richard D. 1929- *St&PR 93*
Kempner, Isaac Herbert, III 1932- *WhoAm 92, WhoSSW 93*
Kempner, James Carroll 1939- *WhoAm 92*
Kempner, Joseph 1923- *WhoAm 92*
Kempner, Maximilian Walter 1929- *WhoAm 92*
Kempner, Michael W. 1958- *WhoAm 92*
Kempner, Robert Max Wasilii 1899- *WhoAm 92, WhoE 93, WhoWor 93*
Kempner, T. *WhoScE 91-1*
Kempner, Thomas, Jr. *BioIn 17*
Kempner, Thomas Lenox 1927- *St&PR 93*
Kempner, Walter 1903- *WhoAm 92*
Kemp-Orino, Sylvia *Law&B 92*
Kempowski, Walter 1929- *BioIn 17*
Kempski, Ralph Aloisius 1934- *WhoAm 92*
Kempson, John Edwin *WhoScE 91-1*
Kempster, Norman Roy 1936- *WhoAm 92*
Kempthorne, Dirk Arthur 1951- *WhoAm 92*
Kempthorne, Oscar 1919- *WhoAm 92*
Kempton, George Roger 1934- *St&PR 93, WhoAm 92*
Kempton, Greta 1903-1991 *BioIn 17*
Kempton, James Murray 1918- *WhoAm 92*
Kempton, Karl 1943- *WhoWrEP 92*
Kempton, Murray 1918- *JrnUS*
Kemske, Floyd Steven 1947- *WhoWrEP 92*
Kemsley, Arthur *BioIn 17*
Kemsley, William d1990 *BioIn 17*
Kenady, James S. 1946- *St&PR 93*
Kenaga, Eugene Ellis 1917- *WhoWor 93*
Kenagy, John Warner 1945- *WhoAm 92*
Kenagy, Robert C. 1931- *St&PR 93*
Kenagy, Robert Thornton *Law&B 92*
Kenan, Frank H. 1912- *St&PR 93*
Kenan, James G., III 1945- *St&PR 93*
Kenan, Owen Graham 1943- *St&PR 93*
Kenan, Randall 1963- *ConGAN*
Kenan, Thomas Stephen, III 1937- *WhoSSW 93*
Kenan, Wilfred Mills 1930- *St&PR 93*
Kenar, Antoni 1906-1959 *PolBiDi*
Kenas, Jane Hamilton 1951- *WhoAmW 93*
Kenchelian, Mark L. *Law&B 92*
Kenczewicz, Timothy 1953- *St&PR 93*
Kenda, Margaret 1942- *SmATA 71*
Kendal, Felicity 1946- *WhoWor 93*
Kendall, Albert F. d1991 *BioIn 17*
Kendall, Carol 1917- *ScF&FL 92*
Kendall, Carol (Seeger) 1917- *DcAmChF 1960, MajAI [port]*
Kendall, Christopher 1949- *WhoAm 92*
Kendall, Clifford M. 1931- *St&PR 93*
Kendall, Cynthia *WhoAmW 93*
Kendall, David Andrew *WhoScE 91-1*
Kendall, David George *WhoScE 91-1*
Kendall, David Nelson 1916- *WhoSSW 93*
Kendall, David R. 1958- *St&PR 93*
Kendall, Dolores Diane Pisapia 1946- *WhoAmW 93*
Kendall, Donald McIntosh 1921- *BioIn 17, WhoAm 92, WhoE 93*
Kendall, Donald Roderick, Jr. 1952- *WhoE 93*
Kendall, Donald Sargent 1948- *St&PR 93*
Kendall, Earline Doak 1935- *WhoAmW 93*
Kendall, George P., Jr. 1934- *WhoAm 92*
Kendall, Gordon *ScF&FL 92*
Kendall, Henry Way 1926- *BioIn 17, WhoAm 92, WhoE 93, WhoWor 93*
Kendall, J. Christine 1947- *WhoAmW 93*
Kendall, Jane (F.) 1952- *ConAu 137*
Kendall, Jillian D. 1949- *WhoSSW 93*
Kendall, John *ScF&FL 92*
Kendall, John Seedoff 1928- *WhoAm 92*
Kendall, John Walker, Jr. 1929- *WhoAm 92*
Kendall, Julie Ellen 1952- *WhoWor 93*
Kendall, Julius 1919- *St&PR 93, WhoAm 92*
Kendall, Katherine Anne 1910- *WhoAm 92*
Kendall, Kay *BioIn 17*
Kendall, Kay 1927-1959 *IntDcF 2-3 [port]*
Kendall, Kay Lynn 1950- *WhoAmW 93*
Kendall, Keith Edward 1958- *WhoEmL 93*
Kendall, Kenneth Edward 1948- *WhoWor 93*
Kendall, Kim Elizabeth 1952- *WhoEmL 93*
Kendall, Laurel Ann 1956- *WhoAmW 93, WhoEmL 93*
Kendall, Leigh Wakefield 1937- *WhoE 93*
Kendall, Leon T. 1928- *WhoIns 93*
Kendall, Leon Thomas 1928- *WhoAm 92*
Kendall, Marion Doris *WhoScE 91-1*
Kendall, Mark 1942- *ScF&FL 92*
Kendall, Martha G. *AmWomPl*
Kendall, Peter Landis 1936- *WhoAm 92*
Kendall, Phillip Alan 1942- *WhoWor 93*
Kendall, Richard H. 1930- *St&PR 93*
Kendall, Robert Louis, Jr. 1930- *WhoAm 92*
Kendall, Robert McCutcheon 1931- *St&PR 93*
Kendall, Ronald Edward 1942- *St&PR 93*
Kendall, Sara Schreiner *Law&B 92*
Kendall, Scipiaruth 1955- *WhoAmW 93*
Kendall, Steven Walter 1947- *WhoSSW 93*
Kendall, Thomas Lee 1946- *WhoEmL 93*
Kendall, Wilfed Iroaki 1943- *WhoUN 92*
Kendall, William Denis 1903- *WhoAm 92*
Kendall, William E. 1914- *St&PR 93*
Kendall, William H. 1943- *St&PR 93*
Kendall, William R. *Law&B 92*
Kendall-Taylor, Pat *WhoScE 91-1*
Kende, Andrew Steven 1932- *WhoAm 92*
Kende, Hans Janos 1937- *WhoAm 92*

Kende, Stephen James 1947- *WhoWor 93*
Kendeigh, Donald Charles 1939- *St&PR 93*
Kendell, Robert Evan *WhoScE 91-1*
Kendell, Ross Ezra 1934- *St&PR 93, WhoAm 92*
Kender, Walter John 1935- *WhoAm 92*
Kenderdine, John Marshall 1912- *WhoAm 92*
Kendig, Diane Lyn 1950- *WhoWrEP 92*
Kendig, Edwin Lawrence, Jr. 1911- *WhoAm 92, WhoWor 93*
Kendig, Ellsworth Harold, Jr. 1922- *WhoAm 92*
Kendig, Joan Johnston 1939- *WhoAm 92*
Kendig, Robert Ellsworth 1949- *WhoEmL 93*
Kendle, Keith E. *WhoScE 91-1*
Kendle, Nick Warren 1950- *WhoEmL 93*
Kendler, Bernhard 1934- *WhoAm 92, WhoWrEP 92*
Kendler, Howard Harvard 1919- *WhoAm 92*
Kendrew, John Cowdery 1917- *WhoAm 92, WhoWor 93*
Kendrick, Alexander d1991 *BioIn 17*
Kendrick, Budd Leroy 1944- *WhoAm 92*
Kendrick, Carol *Law&B 92*
Kendrick, Cheryl Donofrio 1948- *WhoAmW 93*
Kendrick, Clinton J. 1943- *St&PR 93*
Kendrick, Darryl D. 1956- *WhoEmL 93*
Kendrick, David Andrew 1937- *WhoAm 92*
Kendrick, Deborah Keefer 1950- *WhoAmW 93*
Kendrick, Donald Clive *WhoScE 91-1*
Kendrick, Edmund H. 1921- *St&PR 93*
Kendrick, James B. 1920-1989 *BioIn 17*
Kendrick, James Earl 1940- *WhoAm 92, WhoE 93, WhoWor 93*
Kendrick, John A. *Law&B 92*
Kendrick, John Whitefield 1917- *WhoAm 92*
Kendrick, Joseph Trotwood 1920- *WhoAm 92*
Kendrick, Katherine S. *Law&B 92*
Kendrick, Kenneth L. d1992 *NewYTBS 92*
Kendrick, Mark C. 1957- *WhoEmL 93*
Kendrick, Matthew James *Law&B 92*
Kendrick, Mel *BioIn 17*
Kendrick, Nona Caroline 1932- *WhoWrEP 92*
Kendrick, Peter Murray 1936- *WhoAm 92*
Kendrick, Richard Lofton 1944- *WhoSSW 93, WhoWor 93*
Kendrick, Robert Lawrence 1963- *WhoSSW 93*
Kendrick, Robert Warren 1946- *WhoSSW 93*
Kendrick, Ronald Edward 1935- *WhoAm 92*
Kendrick, Ronald H. 1941- *WhoAm 92*
Kendrick, Stephanie Bird 1953- *WhoEmL 93*
Kendrick, Steven Thomas 1949- *WhoSSW 93*
Kendrick, Thomas Rudolph 1933- *WhoAm 92*
Kendrick, Walter 1947- *ScF&FL 92*
Kendrick, William Bryce 1933- *WhoAm 92*
Kendrick, William J. 1932- *St&PR 93*
Kendrick, William Marvin *WhoAm 92*
Kendricks, Eddie d1992 *NewYTBS 92 [port]*
Kendricks, Eddie 1939- *SoulM*
Kendricks, Eddie 1939-1992 *News 93-2*
Kendro, Maria Angela *Law&B 92*
Kendry, Adrian Philip *WhoScE 91-1*
Kendyl, Sharice *ScF&FL 92*
Keneally, Michael Edward 1955- *St&PR 93*
Keneally, Thomas *BioIn 17*
Keneally, Thomas 1935- *IntLitE, ScF&FL 92*
Keneally, Thomas Michael 1935- *WhoWor 93*
Kenealy, Matthew H., III 1956- *WhoE 93, WhoEmL 93*
Kenealy, Patrick 1959- *WhoWrEP 92*
Kenedi, Robert 1931- *St&PR 93*
Kenedy, Reid 1938- *St&PR 93*
Kenefick, James L. 1929- *St&PR 93*
Kenefick, John Henry, Jr. 1921- *WhoAm 92*
Kenefick, Mary Helen *Law&B 92*
Kenehan, Edward F., Jr. *Law&B 92*
Kenelly, John Willis, Jr. 1935- *WhoAm 92, WhoSSW 93*
Keneman, Feodor 1873-1937 *Baker 92*
Kenemore, Max J. *Law&B 92*
Kenen, Peter Bain 1932- *WhoAm 92*
Kenerleber, A.J. 1923- *St&PR 93*
Kenesey, John William *Law&B 92*
Kenesi, Claude 1930- *WhoScE 91-2*
Kenessey, Jeno 1905-1976 *Baker 92*
Kenet, Monica S. *Law&B 92*
Kenevan, Edward D. *Law&B 92*
Kenfield, Dexter L. *Law&B 92*
Kenfield, Thomas L. *St&PR 93*
Keng Chi-mao d1671 *HarEnMi*
Keng Chung-ming d1649 *HarEnMi*
Kengo Wa Dondo, Lobitsh Leon 1934- *WhoAfr*
Kenig, Marvin Jerry 1936- *WhoE 93*
Kenig, Noe 1923- *WhoWor 93*
Kenilorea, Peter 1943- *WhoAsAP 91*
Ke-Ning, Zhang 1933- *WhoWor 93*
Kenins, Talivaldis 1919- *Baker 92*
Kenison, Katrina 1958- *ConAu 138*
Kenison, Raymond Robert 1932- *WhoWor 93*
Kenitzer, Terri Marie 1962- *WhoAmW 93*
Kenji, Asakawa 1938- *WhoWor 93*
Kenji, Makino 1934- *WhoWor 93*
Kenjo, Takashi 1940- *ConAu 137*
Kenkel, James Lawrence 1944- *WhoWor 93*
Kenkel, Joel Nicklas 1941- *WhoIns 93*
Kenley, Elizabeth Sue 1945- *WhoAmW 93, WhoSSW 93, WhoWor 93*
Kenly, Granger Farwell 1919- *WhoAm 92*
Kenly, John 1818-1891 *HarEnMi*
Kenmare, Enid Lindeman Cameron Cavendish Furness *BioIn 17*
Kenmore, Frank J. *ScF&FL 92*
Kenmore, Robert H. *St&PR 93*
Kenna, Diane Elizabeth Goodrich 1951- *WhoEmL 93*
Kenna, E. Douglas 1924- *St&PR 93*
Kenna, Edgar Douglas 1924- *WhoAm 92*
Kenna, Edward F. 1945- *St&PR 93*
Kenna, Frank 1923- *St&PR 93*
Kenna, Gary Franklin 1954- *St&PR 93*
Kenna, James Joseph 1932- *St&PR 93*
Kenna, James Joseph, Jr. 1932- *WhoAm 92*
Kennamer, Lorrin Garfield, Jr. 1924- *WhoAm 92*
Kennan, Elizabeth Topham 1938- *WhoAm 92, WhoAmW 93, WhoE 93*
Kennan, George F. 1904- *ColdWar 1 [port]*
Kennan, George Frost 1904- *BioIn 17, ConAu 39NR, WhoAm 92*
Kennan, Joan Elisabeth 1936- *WhoE 93*
Kennan, Kent Wheeler 1913- *Baker 92, WhoAm 92*
Kennard, Clyde *BioIn 17*
Kennard, Francis M. 1929- *St&PR 93*
Kennard, Jean E. 1936- *ScF&FL 92*
Kennard, Joyce *WhoAm 92, WhoAmW 93*
Kennard, Marietta C. *AmWomPl*
Kennard, Olga *WhoScE 91-1*
Kennaway, Adrienne 1945- *BioIn 17*
Kennaway, Alexander *WhoScE 91-1*
Kenne, David C. 1947- *St&PR 93*
Kenneally, Dennis Michael 1946- *WhoAm 92*
Kenneally, William 1951- *St&PR 93*
Kenneally, William G. *BioIn 17*
Kenneally, William J. *Law&B 92*
Kennealy, Patricia 1946- *ScF&FL 92*
Kenneday, Elizabeth Anne 1950- *WhoAmW 93*
Kennedy, A. *Law&B 92*
Kennedy, Adele Pattin 1936- *WhoWrEP 92*
Kennedy, Adrienne Lita 1931- *WhoAm 92*
Kennedy, Alex 1933- *WhoIns 93*
Kennedy, Alexander John 1931- *WhoAm 92*
Kennedy, Alfred Doby 1939- *WhoAm 92, WhoSSW 93*
Kennedy, Alison Durden *Law&B 92*
Kennedy, Anna R. *AmWomPl*
Kennedy, Anthony Arnold 1939- *WhoUN 92*
Kennedy, Anthony M. *BioIn 17*
Kennedy, Anthony M. 1936- *CngDr 91*
Kennedy, Anthony McLeod 1936- *OxCSupC [port], WhoAm 92, WhoE 93*
Kennedy, Arthur 1914-1990 *BioIn 17, ConTFT 10, IntDcF 2-3*
Kennedy, Barbara Ellen Perry 1937- *WhoAmW 93*
Kennedy, Barbara Joan 1929- *St&PR 93*
Kennedy, Barton *WhoWrEP 92*
Kennedy, Berenice Connor *WhoAm 92*
Kennedy, Bernard J. *Law&B 92*
Kennedy, Bernard J. 1931- *St&PR 93*
Kennedy, Bernard Joseph 1931- *WhoAm 92*
Kennedy, Bernard P. *Law&B 92*
Kennedy, Beverly Kleban Burris 1943- *WhoAmW 93, WhoSSW 93*
Kennedy, Bill 1923- *BioIn 17*
Kennedy, Bob *BioIn 17*
Kennedy, Brian James 1941- *St&PR 93, WhoAm 92*
Kennedy, Burt 1922- *MiSFD 9*
Kennedy, Burt Raphael 1922- *WhoAm 92*
Kennedy, Byrl James 1921- *WhoAm 92*
Kennedy, Caroline *BioIn 17*
Kennedy, Carver Gager 1930- *WhoSSW 93*
Kennedy, Catherine *BioIn 17*
Kennedy, Cecilia Margarita 1953- *WhoAmW 93*
Kennedy, Charles E. *Law&B 92*
Kennedy, Charles G. 1954- *WhoAm 92*
Kennedy, Charles H. *Law&B 92*
Kennedy, Cheryl Cole 1961- *WhoAmW 93*
Kennedy, Cheryl Lynn 1946- *WhoAmW 93, WhoAmW 93*
Kennedy, Chester Ralph, Jr. 1926- *WhoAm 92, WhoE 93, WhoWor 93*
Kennedy, Christie Ann 1950- *WhoAmW 93*
Kennedy, Christina Kay *WhoScE 91-1*
Kennedy, Christopher Neal *Law&B 92*
Kennedy, Christopher Robin 1948- *WhoAm 92*
Kennedy, Clarice Evelyn 1931- *WhoAmW 93*
Kennedy, Clive Russell *WhoScE 91-1*
Kennedy, Colleen Geralyn 1955- *WhoAmW 93, WhoEmL 93*
Kennedy, Cornelia Groefsema 1923- *WhoAm 92, WhoAmW 93*
Kennedy, Cornelius Bryant 1921- *WhoAm 92, WhoWor 93*
Kennedy, Craig M. 1959- *St&PR 93*
Kennedy, D. James 1930- *BioIn 17*
Kennedy, Dan W., III 1945- *St&PR 93*
Kennedy, David *BioIn 17*
Kennedy, David Boyd 1933- *WhoAm 92*
Kennedy, David D. *Law&B 92*
Kennedy, David E. 1939- *St&PR 93*
Kennedy, David Michael 1941- *WhoAm 92*
Kennedy, David Michael 1951- *WhoE 93*
Kennedy, David Woodford 1941- *WhoE 93*
Kennedy, Davis Lee 1938- *WhoE 93*
Kennedy, Debra Joyce 1955- *WhoAmW 93*
Kennedy, Dennis James 1930- *BioIn 17*
Kennedy, Donald *BioIn 17*
Kennedy, Donald 1931- *WhoAm 92, WhoWor 93*
Kennedy, Donald A. 1927- *St&PR 93*
Kennedy, Donald D., Jr. *Law&B 92*
Kennedy, Donald Davidson, Jr. 1931- *St&PR 93*
Kennedy, Donald Parker 1918- *St&PR 93, WhoAm 92*
Kennedy, Dorothy M(intzlaff) 1931- *ConAu 40NR*
Kennedy, Doug *BioIn 17*
Kennedy, Duncan *BioIn 17*
Kennedy, Edgar 1890-1948 *QDrFCA 92 [port]*
Kennedy, Edgar Rees *ScF&FL 92*
Kennedy, Edmund 1818-1848 *Expl 93*
Kennedy, Edward G. *Law&B 92*
Kennedy, Edward M. *NewYTBS 92 [port]*
Kennedy, Edward M. 1932- *CngDr 91, PolPar*
Kennedy, Edward Moore 1932- *BioIn 17, WhoAm 92, WhoE 93, WhoWor 93*
Kennedy, Edward Moore 1961- *BioIn 17*
Kennedy, Edward S. *St&PR 93*
Kennedy, Edwin Lust 1904- *WhoAm 92*
Kennedy, Eileen *Law&B 92*
Kennedy, Elizabeth Mae 1949- *WhoAmW 93, WhoEmL 93*
Kennedy, Ellen Woodman 1950- *WhoE 93*
Kennedy, Ethel *BioIn 17*
Kennedy, Eugene Cullen 1928- *WhoAm 92*
Kennedy, Eugene Patrick 1919- *WhoAm 92*
Kennedy, Eugene Richard 1919- *WhoAm 92*
Kennedy, Evelyn Siefert 1927- *WhoAmW 93*
Kennedy, F. Frederick, Jr. 1943- *WhoWor 93*
Kennedy, Francis 1926- *WhoAm 92*
Kennedy, Frank Robert 1914- *WhoAm 92*
Kennedy, G. Alfred 1940- *WhoAm 92*
Kennedy, Gary L. *Law&B 92*
Kennedy, Gavin 1940- *WhoWor 93*
Kennedy, George 1926- *WhoAm 92*
Kennedy, George Alexander 1928- *WhoAm 92*
Kennedy, George D. 1926- *St&PR 93, WhoAm 92*
Kennedy, George Hunt 1936- *WhoAm 92*
Kennedy, Gersham J.A. 1949- *WhoScE 91-1*
Kennedy, Harold David 1945- *St&PR 93*
Kennedy, Harold E. *Law&B 92*
Kennedy, Harold Edward 1927- *St&PR 93, WhoAm 92, WhoWor 93*
Kennedy, Harriet Forte 1939- *WhoE 93*
Kennedy, Harriet L. *AmWomPl*
Kennedy, Harvey Edward 1928- *WhoAm 92*
Kennedy, Ian Glen 1945- *WhoAm 92*
Kennedy, J. Arthur *ConTFT 10*
Kennedy, J. Gerald 1947- *ScF&FL 92*
Kennedy, J. Jack, Jr. 1956- *WhoEmL 93, WhoSSW 93*
Kennedy, Jack Leland 1924- *WhoAm 92*
Kennedy, Jack W. 1924- *St&PR 93*
Kennedy, James A. *Law&B 92*
Kennedy, James Andrew 1937- *St&PR 93, WhoAm 92*
Kennedy, James C. *Law&B 92*
Kennedy, James C. 1947- *WhoAm 92, WhoSSW 93*
Kennedy, James Drake, Jr. 1924- *St&PR 93*
Kennedy, James F. *Law&B 92*
Kennedy, James Harrington 1924- *WhoE 93, WhoWrEP 92*
Kennedy, James J. 1933- *St&PR 93*
Kennedy, James L. 1937- *WhoAm 92*
Kennedy, James Waite 1937- *WhoAm 92*
Kennedy, Jay Richard 1904-1991 *BioIn 17*
Kennedy, Jayne *BioIn 17*
Kennedy, Jeanine F. *St&PR 93*
Kennedy, Jimmy 1902-1984 *BioIn 17*
Kennedy, Joan *BioIn 17*
Kennedy, Joan Canfield 1931- *WhoAmW 93*
Kennedy, JoAnne 1957- *WhoEmL 93*
Kennedy, Joe David, Jr. 1956- *WhoSSW 93*
Kennedy, Joey David, Jr. 1956- *WhoAm 92*
Kennedy, John *ConTFT 10*
Kennedy, John A. 1921- *St&PR 93*
Kennedy, John C. *St&PR 93*
Kennedy, John David *WhoScE 91-1*
Kennedy, John Elmo, Jr. 1932- *WhoSSW 93*
Kennedy, John F. *DcCPCAm*
Kennedy, John F. 1917-1963 *BioIn 17, PolPar*
Kennedy, John F. 1919-1963 *ColdWar 1 [port]*
Kennedy, John F. 1960- *BioIn 17*
Kennedy, John Fisher 1933- *WhoAm 92*
Kennedy, John Fitzgerald 1917-1963 *DcTwHis*
Kennedy, John H. 1930- *WhoAm 92*
Kennedy, John H., Jr. 1954- *WhoAm 92, WhoSSW 93*
Kennedy, John Hollingsworth 1951- *WhoWrEP 92*
Kennedy, John J. 1949- *St&PR 93*
Kennedy, John Joseph 1914- *WhoAm 92*
Kennedy, John M. 1921- *WhoWrEP 92*
Kennedy, John Oliver Stevenson 1947- *WhoWor 93*
Kennedy, John O'Loughlin 1932- *WhoWor 93*
Kennedy, John P. *Law&B 92*
Kennedy, John Patrick 1966- *WhoSSW 93*
Kennedy, John Raymond 1930- *WhoAm 92*
Kennedy, John Wesley 1920- *WhoAm 92*
Kennedy, John William 1956- *WhoE 93*
Kennedy, Jon Reid 1942- *WhoWrEP 92*
Kennedy, Joseph C. *ScF&FL 92*
Kennedy, Joseph Charles 1929- *ConAu 40NR*
Kennedy, Joseph P. 1888-1969 *BioIn 17, PolPar*
Kennedy, Joseph P., II 1952- *CngDr 91*
Kennedy, Joseph Patrick 1932- *WhoSSW 93*
Kennedy, Joseph Patrick, II *BioIn 17*
Kennedy, Joseph Patrick, II 1952- *WhoAm 92, WhoE 93*
Kennedy, Joseph Paul 1928- *WhoAm 92*
Kennedy, Josepha Marie 1928- *WhoWrEP 92*
Kennedy, Judith M. 1939- *St&PR 93*
Kennedy, Kara *BioIn 17*
Kennedy, Karen Syence 1943- *WhoAmW 93, WhoSSW 93*
Kennedy, Karol Estelle 1932- *BiDAMSp 1989*
Kennedy, Kathleen *BioIn 17*
Kennedy, Kathy Irene 1956- *WhoEmL 93*
Kennedy, Keith F. *Law&B 92*
Kennedy, Keith Furnival 1925- *St&PR 93, WhoAm 92*
Kennedy, Kenneth Adrian Raine 1930- *WhoAm 92*
Kennedy, Kenneth W., Jr. 1945- *WhoAm 92*
Kennedy, Kerry *BioIn 17*
Kennedy, Kevin d1992 *BioIn 17, NewYTBS 92*
Kennedy, L. James 1927- *St&PR 93*
Kennedy, Lawrence Allan 1937- *WhoAm 92*
Kennedy, Leigh 1951- *ScF&FL 92*
Kennedy, Leo 1907- *WhoCanL 92*
Kennedy, Lisa Gayle 1964- *WhoAmW 93*
Kennedy, Lucille A. 1923- *St&PR 93*
Kennedy, Ludovic 1919- *BioIn 17*
Kennedy, Marc J. *Law&B 92*
Kennedy, Marc J. 1945- *WhoAm 92, WhoSSW 93*
Kennedy, Margaret Swierz 1941- *WhoWrEP 92*

Kennedy, Maria I. *Law&B 92*
Kennedy, Marion *AmWomPl*
Kennedy, Mark 1952- *WhoSSW 93*
Kennedy, Mark Raymond 1957- *WhoAm 92*
Kennedy, Mary *AmWomPl, St&PR 93*
Kennedy, Mary Elizabeth 1934- *WhoAmW 93*
Kennedy, Matthew Washington 1921- *WhoAm 92*
Kennedy, May Grabbe 1951- *WhoE 93*
Kennedy, Michael *BioIn 17*
Kennedy, Michael 1954- *MiSFD 9*
Kennedy, Michael Edward, III 1927- *BiDAMSp 1989*
Kennedy, (George) Michael (Sinclair) 1926- *Baker 92*
Kennedy, Michael John 1940- *WhoScE 91-3*
Kennedy, Michael LeMoyne 1958- *BioIn 17*
Kennedy, Michael Paul *Law&B 92*
Kennedy, Michael William *Law&B 92*
Kennedy, Moorhead 1930- *WhoAm 92*
Kennedy, Nancy Devlin d1991 *BioIn 17*
Kennedy, Nigel *BioIn 17*
Kennedy, Nigel 1956- *CurBio 92 [port]*
Kennedy, Nigel 1957- *ConMus 8 [port]*
Kennedy, Nigel (Paul) 1956- *Baker 92*
Kennedy, Patrick J. *BioIn 17*
Kennedy, Patrick W. 1956- *St&PR 93*
Kennedy, Paul *BioIn 17*
Kennedy, Paul Henry *Law&B 92*
Kennedy, Paul J. *Law&B 92*
Kennedy, Paul Michael 1945- *WhoAm 92*
Kennedy, Paula E. *Law&B 92*
Kennedy, Peggy *ScF&FL 92*
Kennedy, Peter *Law&B 92*
Kennedy, Peter Graham Edward *WhoScE 91-1*
Kennedy, Philip L. 1932- *St&PR 93*
Kennedy, Phillip J. *WhoAm 92*
Kennedy, Quentin J. 1933- *St&PR 93*
Kennedy, Quentin J., Sr. 1933- *WhoAm 92*
Kennedy, Quentin James *Law&B 92*
Kennedy, R. Michael, Jr. 1943- *St&PR 93*
Kennedy, Raoul Dion 1944- *WhoAm 92, WhoWor 93*
Kennedy, Rebecca J. Miller 1949- *WhoAmW 93*
Kennedy, Rebecca Lee 1941- *WhoAmW 93*
Kennedy, Richard 1910-1989 *BioIn 17*
Kennedy, Richard 1932- *ScF&FL 92*
Kennedy, Richard A. 1938- *WhoAm 92*
Kennedy, Richard D. 1940- *St&PR 93*
Kennedy, Richard Frederick 1933- *WhoAm 92*
Kennedy, (Jerome) Richard 1932- *DcAmChF 1985, WhoAm 92, WhoWrEP 92*
Kennedy, Richard S. 1920- *BioIn 17*
Kennedy, Richard Thomas 1919- *WhoAm 92*
Kennedy, Robert 1925-1968 *DcTwHis*
Kennedy, Robert 1938- *BioIn 17*
Kennedy, Robert 1939- *WhoSSW 93*
Kennedy, Robert A. 1948- *St&PR 93*
Kennedy, Robert Alan *WhoScE 91-1*
Kennedy, Robert D. *BioIn 17*
Kennedy, Robert Delmont 1932- *St&PR 93, WhoAm 92, WhoE 93*
Kennedy, Robert Emmet 1910- *WhoAm 92, WhoWor 93*
Kennedy, Robert Emmet, Jr. 1941- *WhoAm 92*
Kennedy, Robert Eric 1955- *WhoEmL 93*
Kennedy, Robert Eugene 1942- *WhoAm 92*
Kennedy, Robert F. 1925-1968 *BioIn 17, ColdWar 1 [port], ConHero 2 [port], PolPar*
Kennedy, Robert Francis 1954- *BioIn 17*
Kennedy, Robert J. 1913- *St&PR 93*
Kennedy, Robert M. *Law&B 92*
Kennedy, Robert Marlo *Law&B 92*
Kennedy, Robert Meyer 1933- *St&PR 93*
Kennedy, Robert Norman 1932- *WhoAm 92*
Kennedy, Robert Samuel 1924- *WhoSSW 93*
Kennedy, Robert Spayde 1933- *WhoAm 92, WhoE 93*
Kennedy, Robert William 1931- *WhoAm 92*
Kennedy, Roger, Jr. 1937- *WhoWor 93*
Kennedy, Roger G. 1940- *St&PR 93*
Kennedy, Roger George 1926- *WhoAm 92*
Kennedy, Rose Fitzgerald 1890- *BioIn 17, WhoAm 92*
Kennedy, Royd *BioIn 17*
Kennedy, Sandra Hays 1945- *WhoWrEP 92*
Kennedy, Sean *Law&B 92*
Kennedy, Sheila Grace 1949- *WhoEmL 93*
Kennedy, Shelia Walters 1969- *WhoSSW 93*
Kennedy, Shirley Duglin 1951- *WhoSSW 93*
Kennedy, Stanley C. 1890-1968 *EncABHB 8 [port]*
Kennedy, Stephen Dandridge 1942- *St&PR 93, WhoAm 92*
Kennedy, T. Richard 1935- *WhoIns 93*
Kennedy, Tamyra Machele 1958- *WhoAmW 93*
Kennedy, Ted 1932- *BioIn 17*
Kennedy, Ted, Jr. 1961- *BioIn 17*
Kennedy, Teresa J. 1956- *WhoAmW 93*
Kennedy, Terry 1941- *WhoWrEP 92*
Kennedy, Theodore Clifford 1930- *WhoAm 92*
Kennedy, Thomas *WhoAm 92*
Kennedy, Thomas B. *St&PR 93*
Kennedy, Thomas Chester 1940- *St&PR 93*
Kennedy, Thomas Edgar 1958- *WhoEmL 93*
Kennedy, Thomas Eugene 1944- *WhoWrEP 92*
Kennedy, Thomas Franklin 1941- *WhoSSW 93*
Kennedy, Thomas H. 1946- *WhoEmL 93*
Kennedy, Thomas Leo 1936- *WhoAm 92*
Kennedy, Thomas Patrick 1932- *WhoAm 92, WhoE 93, WhoSSW 93, WhoWor 93*
Kennedy, Thomas Riley 1934- *St&PR 93*
Kennedy, Timothy J. *Law&B 92*
Kennedy, Tom *MiSFD 9*
Kennedy, Traver Hall 1952- *WhoE 93, WhoEmL 93*
Kennedy, Vans 1784-1846 *BioIn 17*
Kennedy, Veronica Mary Sylvia 1930- *WhoE 93*
Kennedy, Victoria Reggie *NewYTBS 92 [port]*
Kennedy, W. Craig, Jr. 1935- *St&PR 93*
Kennedy, W. Keith 1943- *St&PR 93*
Kennedy, W. M. 1924- *WhoAm 92*
Kennedy, Warren Charles 1941- *WhoE 93*
Kennedy, Wilbert Keith, Sr. 1919- *WhoAm 92*
Kennedy, Wilbert Keith, Jr. 1943- *WhoAm 92*
Kennedy, William 1928- *BioIn 17, MagSAmL [port], ScF&FL 92, WhoWrEP 92*
Kennedy, William Bean 1926- *WhoAm 92*
Kennedy, William Burton 1928- *WhoE 93*
Kennedy, William E., Jr. 1919- *St&PR 93*
Kennedy, William Edward 1955- *St&PR 93*
Kennedy, William Francis 1918- *WhoAm 92*
Kennedy, William H., Jr. *BioIn 17*
Kennedy, William Henry Joseph d1990 *BioIn 17*
Kennedy, William James 1944- *WhoE 93*
Kennedy, William Jesse, III 1922- *St&PR 93*
Kennedy, William Joseph 1928- *WhoAm 92*
Kennedy, William Joseph 1952- *WhoSSW 93*
Kennedy, William P. *Law&B 92, ScF&FL 92*
Kennedy, William S. 1926- *WhoWrEP 92*
Kennedy, William Thomas 1938- *WhoE 93*
Kennedy, X. J. *ConAu 40NR*
Kennedy, X. J. 1929- *ChILR 27 [port], ScF&FL 92, WhoAm 92, WhoWor 93, WhoWrEP 92*
Kennedy Family *BioIn 17*
Kennedy-Fraser, Marjorie 1857-1930 *Baker 92*
Kennedy-Glans, Donna M. *Law&B 92*
Kennedy-Minott, Rodney *WhoAm 92*
Kennedy-Takahashi, Charlotte Aline 1946- *WhoWor 93*
Kennedy-Verbel, Jeanne Marie 1965- *WhoWrEP 92*
Kennel, Charles Frederick 1939- *WhoAm 92*
Kennel, Robert Philip 1936- *St&PR 93*
Kennell, Arthur C. 1931- *St&PR 93*
Kennell, Kevin J. 1961- *St&PR 93*
Kennell, Richard Wayne 1952- *WhoEmL 93*
Kennelly, Anne Marie *Law&B 92*
Kennelly, Barbara B. *BioIn 17*
Kennelly, Barbara B. 1936- *CngDr 91, WhoAm 92, WhoAmW 93, WhoE 93*
Kennelly, Cheryl C. *Law&B 92*
Kennelly, John Jerome 1918- *WhoWor 93*
Kennelly, Karen Margaret 1933- *WhoAm 92, WhoAmW 93*
Kennelly, Laura Ballard 1941- *WhoSSW 93*
Kennely, Patricia *ScF&FL 92*
Kenner, Bruce Bell 1940- *St&PR 93*
Kenner, Carol J. 1950- *WhoAmW 93*
Kenner, Carole Ann 1953- *WhoEmL 93*
Kenner, Chris 1929-1976 *SoulM*
Kenner, Fred A. 1952- *St&PR 93*
Kenner, Hugh *BioIn 17*
Kenner, Laurel 1954- *WhoAmW 93*
Kenner, Lynn Edward *Law&B 92*
Kenner, Mary Ellen 1941- *WhoSSW 93*
Kenner, Thomas 1932- *WhoScE 91-4*
Kenner, William Hugh 1923- *WhoWrEP 92*
Kennerley, John Atkinson 1933- *WhoUN 92*
Kennerley, John Randall 1939- *WhoWor 93*
Kennerly, David Hume 1947- *WhoEmL 93*
Kennerly, James Edward 1924- *St&PR 93*
Kennerly, Rosa Waymyers 1949- *WhoAmW 93*
Kennett, James Peter 1940- *WhoAm 92*
Kennett, Jiyu 1924- *WhoWrEP 92*
Kennett, Rick *ScF&FL 92*
Kennett, Robert L. *WhoAm 92*
Kennett, William Alexander 1932- *WhoAm 92*
Kennett-Charles, Ann Jean 1951- *WhoAmW 93*
Kennevan, Walter James 1912- *WhoE 93*
Kenney, Daniel B. *Law&B 92*
Kenney, Donald J. 1947- *St&PR 93*
Kenney, Donald James 1947- *WhoAm 92*
Kenney, Donna Denise 1960- *WhoE 93*
Kenney, Douglas C. 1947-1980 *ScF&FL 92*
Kenney, Edward P. *Law&B 92*
Kenney, Eileen Geralyn 1964- *WhoAmW 93*
Kenney, F. Donald 1918- *WhoWor 93*
Kenney, Francis Joseph 1925- *St&PR 93*
Kenney, Frank Deming 1921- *WhoAm 92*
Kenney, George Churchill 1889-1977 *HarEnMi*
Kenney, Gregory T. *Law&B 92*
Kenney, Harry Wesley, Jr. 1926- *WhoAm 92*
Kenney, Howard Washington 1917- *WhoAm 92*
Kenney, James Francis 1921- *WhoAm 92*
Kenney, Jerome P. 1941- *WhoAm 92*
Kenney, John A., Jr. *Law&B 92*
Kenney, John Michel 1938- *WhoE 93, WhoWor 93*
Kenney, John Patrick 1946- *WhoEmL 93*
Kenney, Joseph A., Jr. *Law&B 92*
Kenney, Karen Marie 1965- *WhoAmW 93*
Kenney, Lawrence J. d1990 *BioIn 17*
Kenney, Louis Augustine 1917- *WhoAm 92*
Kenney, Mary Elizabeth 1960- *WhoEmL 93*
Kenney, Mary Whitney *Law&B 92*
Kenney, Neil Patrick 1932- *WhoAm 92*
Kenney, Patricia A. *Law&B 92*
Kenney, Patrick Joseph *BioIn 17*
Kenney, Raymond Joseph, Jr. 1932- *WhoAm 92*
Kenney, Richard Alec 1924- *WhoAm 92*
Kenney, Richard J. 1941- *WhoAm 92*
Kenney, Richard Laurence 1948- *WhoAm 92*
Kenney, Robert P. 1934- *St&PR 93*
Kenney, Scott Robert 1956- *WhoEmL 93*
Kenney, Susan (McIlvaine) 1941- *ConAu 37NR*
Kenney, Thomas F. 1941- *St&PR 93*
Kenney, Thomas Frederick 1941- *WhoAm 92*
Kenney, Thomas H. 1942- *St&PR 93*
Kenney, W. John 1904-1992 *BioIn 17*
Kenney, Walter T. 1930- *WhoSSW 93*
Kenney, William J. d1990 *BioIn 17*
Kenney-Wallace, Geraldine 1943- *WhoAmW 93*
Kennickell, Ralph E., Jr. *BioIn 17*
Kennicott, Robert 1835-1866 *IntDcAn*
Kenniff, James A. 1951- *St&PR 93*
Kenniff, James M. *St&PR 93*
Kenniff, T. Charles *Law&B 92*
Kennington, Robert E., II 1932- *St&PR 93*
Kennis, Robert Howard *Law&B 92*
Kennish, Katharine *WhoWrEP 92*
Kennison, James Dudley 1920- *St&PR 93*
Kennon, Alfred W. 1941- *St&PR 93*
Kennon, John David 1917- *WhoIns 93*
Kennon, Nancy Jones 1943- *WhoSSW 93*
Kennon, Paul 1934-1990 *BioIn 17*
Kennon, Peter G. 1947- *St&PR 93*
Kennon, Randall H. *Law&B 92*
Kenny, Adele M. 1948- *WhoWrEP 92*
Kenny, Alexander Donovan 1925- *WhoAm 92*
Kenny, Brian *WhoScE 91-1*
Kenny, Charles D. 1945- *St&PR 93*
Kenny, Dennis James *Law&B 92*
Kenny, Dennis James 1935- *St&PR 93*
Kenny, Douglas Timothy 1923- *WhoAm 92, WhoWor 93*
Kenny, Edmund Joyce 1920- *WhoAm 92*
Kenny, F.W. 1938- *WhoScE 91-3*
Kenny, Herbert A. 1912- *WhoWrEP 92*
Kenny, Herbert C. d1992 *NewYTBS 92*
Kenny, James C. 1926- *St&PR 93*
Kenny, Jane A. 1945- *WhoAm 92, WhoAmW 93*
Kenny, John J. 1938- *St&PR 93*
Kenny, John Logan 1938- *WhoIns 93*
Kenny, John Thomas 1938- *St&PR 93*
Kenny, Kathryn *WhoWrEP 92*
Kenny, Maurice F. 1929- *WhoWrEP 92*
Kenny, Michael Antony *Law&B 92*
Kenny, Michael H. 1937- *WhoAm 92*
Kenny, Mike *BioIn 17*
Kenny, Raymond P. 1933- *St&PR 93*
Kenny, Robert Martin *WhoE 93*
Kenny, Robert Wayne 1932- *WhoAm 92*
Kenny, Roger Michael 1938- *WhoAm 92*
Kenny, Shirley Strum 1934- *WhoAm 92, WhoAmW 93, WhoE 93*
Kenny, Teresa Marie *Law&B 92*
Kenny, Thomas Henry 1918- *WhoAm 92*
Kenny, Yvonne 1950- *Baker 92, OxDcOp*
Keno, Robert Peter 1924- *St&PR 93*
Kenoyer, Willa 1933- *WhoAmW 93*
Kenrich, John Lewis 1929- *WhoAm 92*
Kensel, Neven Michael 1940- *WhoSSW 93*
Kensett, John Frederick 1816-1872 *BioIn 17*
Kenshalo, Daniel Ralph 1922- *WhoAm 92*
Kensik, Roman P. 1931- *WhoScE 91-4*
Kensing, Henry V. *Law&B 92*
Kensing, Henry V. 1933- *St&PR 93*
Kensinger, Richard Gerald 1947- *WhoE 93*
Kensinger, Tina R. 1961- *WhoEmL 93*
Kensit, Patsy *BioIn 17*
Kensky, James Francis 1946- *St&PR 93*
Kent *BioIn 17*
Kent, Alan Joseph 1954- *WhoSSW 93*
Kent, Allen 1921- *ConAu 39NR, WhoAm 92, WhoE 93*
Kent, Amy L. *Law&B 92*
Kent, Arthur *BioIn 17, ScF&FL 92*
Kent, Arthur E. 1936- *St&PR 93*
Kent, Bartis Milton 1925- *WhoSSW 93, WhoWor 93*
Kent, Bill *WhoAm 92*
Kent, Brad C. 1949- *St&PR 93*
Kent, Calvin Albert 1941- *WhoAm 92*
Kent, Carol 1944- *WhoWrEP 92*
Kent, Charles E. *Law&B 92*
Kent, Dennis Vladimir 1946- *WhoAm 92*
Kent, Donald Charles 1923- *WhoAm 92*
Kent, Donald Paul 1954- *WhoE 93*
Kent, Earl B. 1921- *St&PR 93*
Kent, Edgar Robert, Jr. 1941- *WhoAm 92*
Kent, Edward F. *St&PR 93*
Kent, Fortune *ScF&FL 92*
Kent, Frank R. 1877-1958 *JrnUS*
Kent, Frederick Heber 1905- *WhoAm 92, WhoWor 93*
Kent, Gail *AmWomPl*
Kent, Gary *MiSFD 9*
Kent, Gary Warner 1933- *WhoSSW 93*
Kent, Gayle Steverson 1938- *WhoSSW 93*
Kent, Geoffrey *Law&B 92*
Kent, Geoffrey 1914- *WhoAm 92*
Kent, George Cantine, Jr. 1914- *WhoAm 92*
Kent, Gordon Donald 1920- *WhoE 93*
Kent, Greg B. 1947- *St&PR 93*
Kent, Howard Lees 1930- *WhoE 93*
Kent, Irwin I. 1923- *WhoE 93*
Kent, Jack Thurston 1908- *WhoSSW 93*
Kent, James 1700-1776 *Baker 92*
Kent, James A. 1922- *WhoAm 92*
Kent, James Howard 1923- *St&PR 93*
Kent, James M. 1956- *ConAu 139*
Kent, Jan Georg 1942- *WhoWor 93*
Kent, Jeanne Yvonne 1947- *WhoE 93*
Kent, Jesse Gaston, Jr. 1946- *St&PR 93*
Kent, Jill Elspeth 1948- *WhoAm 92, WhoAmW 93*
Kent, Joan 1935- *WhoSSW 93*
Kent, Joan Ruth *WhoSSW 93*
Kent, John Francis 1950- *WhoWor 93*
Kent, John Telford *WhoScE 91-1*
Kent, Judith Philliber 1946- *WhoSSW 93*
Kent, Kenneth Mitchell 1938- *WhoE 93, WhoWor 93*
Kent, Kristin H. *Law&B 92*
Kent, Lewis 1927- *WhoAsAP 91*
Kent, Linda Gail 1946- *WhoAm 92*
Kent, Lorraine Ruth *Law&B 92*
Kent, Melvin Floyd 1953- *WhoSSW 93*
Kent, Mollie 1933- *WhoWrEP 92*
Kent, Nancy Lee 1956- *WhoAmW 93*
Kent, Nicolas *MiSFD 9*
Kent, Paul *ScF&FL 92*
Kent, Paula *WhoAm 92*
Kent, Peter *Law&B 92*
Kent, Peter Blodget 1948- *St&PR 93*
Kent, Peter J. 1946- *St&PR 93*
Kent, Raymond Knezevich 1929- *WhoAm 92*
Kent, Richard Vincent 1949- *WhoWrEP 92*
Kent, Robert A. *Law&B 92*
Kent, Robert Brydon 1921- *WhoAm 92*
Kent, Robert John 1948- *WhoE 93*
Kent, Robert W. *Law&B 92*

Kent, Robert Warren 1935- *St&PR 93, WhoAm 92*
Kent, Roberta B. 1945- *WhoAmW 93*
Kent, Rockwell 1882-1971 *BioIn 17*
Kent, Rolly 1946- *WhoWrEP 92*
Kent, Ronald S. *Law&B 92*
Kent, Roy Norman 1944- *St&PR 93*
Kent, Sally Litherland 1937- *WhoAmW 93*
Kent, Samuel B. 1949- *WhoSSW 93*
Kent, Sandra Lee 1946- *WhoWrEP 92*
Kent, Sheila Kelly 1932- *WhoAmW 93*
Kent, Sherman B. 1927- *St&PR 93*
Kent, Simon *ConAu 137*
Kent, Sophia Morris *AmWomPl*
Kent, Stephen *ScF&FL 92*
Kent, Steven Peter 1950- *St&PR 93*
Kent, Terry Jeanne 1962- *WhoEmL 93*
Kent, Theodore Charles *WhoWor 93*
Kent, Thomas Frederick 1940- *St&PR 93*
Kent, Timothy Donovan 1955- *WhoSSW 93*
Kent, Warren T. 1925- *St&PR 93*
Kent, Wayne 1966- *St&PR 93*
Kent, William B. 1955- *St&PR 93*
Kent, William J. *Law&B 92*
Kentgens, Arnold Peter Maria 1959- *WhoWor 93*
Kentish, John William 1938- *St&PR 93*
Kent-Marshall, Piper *Law&B 92*
Kentner, Louis 1905-1987 *Baker 92*
Kenton, Ann Yvonne 1951- *WhoScE 91-1*
Kenton, Egon 1891-1987 *Baker 92*
Kenton, Frank Joseph 1950- *WhoEmL 93*
Kenton, James A. 1955- *St&PR 93*
Kenton, James Alan 1955- *WhoAm 92*
Kenton, L.P. *ScF&FL 92*
Kenton, Stan 1912-1979 *BioIn 17*
Kenton, Stan(ley Newcomb) 1911-1979 *Baker 92*
Kenton Smith, Wanda Gayle 1957- *WhoAmW 93*
Kentros, Arthur G. *Law&B 92*
Kentz, Frederick Clement, III *Law&B 92*
Kenward, James 1908- *ScF&FL 92*
Kenward, John A. 1956- *St&PR 93*
Kenward, Robert Eyres *WhoScE 91-1*
Kenworthy, Harry William 1947- *WhoEmL 93*
Kenworthy, Joan Margaret *WhoScE 91-1*
Kenyatta, Jomo c. 1891-1978 *BioIn 17*
Kenyatta, Jomo c. 1893-1978 *ColdWar 2 [port], DcTwHis*
Kenyatta, Jomo c. 1894-1978 *IntDcAn*
Kenyatta, Muhammad d1992 *BioIn 17, NewYTBS 92 [port]*
Kenyon, Bernice Lesbia 1883?-1935 *AmWomPl*
Kenyon, Bruce Davis 1943- *St&PR 93, WhoAm 92*
Kenyon, Bruce Guy 1929- *WhoWrEP 92*
Kenyon, Charles Lincoln 1933- *WhoE 93*
Kenyon, Charles Moir 1916- *WhoAm 92*
Kenyon, Daphne Anne 1952- *WhoAmW 93, WhoEmL 93*
Kenyon, David V. 1930- *WhoAm 92*
Kenyon, Doris Margaret 1898- *AmWomPl*
Kenyon, Edward Tipton 1929- *WhoAm 92*
Kenyon, Ernest M. 1920-1980? *ScF&FL 92*
Kenyon, Frances S. *AmWomPl*
Kenyon, Gary Michael 1949- *WhoAm 92*
Kenyon, Jane 1947- *DcLB 120 [port]*
Kenyon, Jane Jennifer 1947- *WhoAm 92*
Kenyon, Jerome M. 1925- *St&PR 93*
Kenyon, John Michael 1949- *St&PR 93*
Kenyon, Julia Caroline 1919- *WhoAmW 93*
Kenyon, Karen Beth 1938- *WhoWrEP 92*
Kenyon, Lloyd 1732-1802 *BioIn 17*
Kenyon, Michael *Law&B 92, WhoCanL 92*
Kenyon, Paul *ScF&FL 92*
Kenyon, Peter 1940- *St&PR 93*
Kenyon, Regan Clair 1949- *WhoE 93*
Kenyon, Richard Albert 1933- *WhoAm 92*
Kenyon, Richard John 1943- *St&PR 93*
Kenyon, Robert Edwin, Jr. 1908- *WhoAm 92*
Kenyon, Roger Alan 1953- *WhoE 93*
Kenyon, Rosemary Gill *Law&B 92*
Kenyon, Sidney Eugene 1959- *WhoEmL 93, WhoSSW 93*
Kenyon, Thomas Leo 1938- *WhoAm 92*
Kenzie, Ross Bruce 1931- *WhoAm 92*
Kenzo *BioIn 17*
Kenzo, Itoh 1947- *WhoWor 93*
Keochakian, Simon V. 1935- *WhoE 93*
Keogh, Frank T. 1927- *St&PR 93*
Keogh, Heidi Helen Dake 1950- *WhoAmW 93, WhoEmL 93*
Keogh, James 1916- *WhoAm 92*
Keogh, Judy Irene 1952- *WhoAmW 93*
Keogh, Myles Walter 1840-1876 *BioIn 17*
Keogh, Patrick James 1944- *WhoE 93*
Keogh, Raymond 1947- *WhoScE 91-3*
Keogh, Tracy Suitt 1961- *WhoEmL 93*
Keohane, Nannerl Overholser 1940- *WhoAm 92, WhoAmW 93, WhoE 93*
Keohane, Robert Owen 1941- *WhoAm 92*
Keohane, Stephen Thomas *Law&B 92*
Keon, Thomas Peter 1936- *WhoE 93*
Keonjian, Edward 1909- *WhoE 93*
Keosajan, Edmond 1936- *DrEEuF*
Keosseian, Charles Joseph 1929- *St&PR 93*
Keough, Donald L. 1941- *St&PR 93*
Keough, Donald Raymond 1926- *St&PR 93, WhoAm 92, WhoSSW 93*
Keough, Francis Paul 1917- *WhoAm 92*
Keough, James Gillman, Jr. 1947- *WhoEmL 93*
Keough, James Gordon 1946- *WhoAm 92*
Keough, William H. 1937- *St&PR 93*
Keoun, L. Craig 1939- *St&PR 93*
Keowen, Sheralee June 1939- *St&PR 93*
Keown, Don G. 1932- *St&PR 93*
Keown, Donald G. 1932- *WhoIns 93*
Kepa, Sailosi Wai 1939- *WhoAsAP 91*
Kepecs, Alex *St&PR 93*
Kepecs, Joseph Goodman 1912- *WhoAm 92*
Kepes, Gyorgy 1906- *WhoWor 93*
Kepets, Hugh Michael 1946- *WhoAm 92*
Kephalas *OxDcByz*
Kephalas, Constantine fl. c. 900- *OxDcByz*
Kephart, Darlene 1955- *WhoAmW 93*
Kephart, Larry Robert 1949- *WhoEmL 93*
Kephart, Lori Maureen Du'Mont 1968- *WhoAmW 93*
Kephart, William Milton 1919- *WhoAm 92*
Kepke, Robert Joe *Law&B 92*
Kepler, Elise Anne 1964- *WhoEmL 93*
Kepler, Johannes 1571-1630 *Baker 92, BioIn 17*
Kepler, Raymond Glen 1928- *WhoAm 92*
Kepley, Thomas Alvin 1928- *WhoAm 92*
Keplinger, Duane 1926- *WhoSSW 93*
Keplinger, Robert B., Jr. 1932- *St&PR 93*
Keplinger, Tab A. 1960- *St&PR 93*
Kepner, Kevin R. *Law&B 92*
Kepner, Rita Marie 1944- *WhoAmW 93, WhoWor 93*
Kepner, Tyler *BioIn 17*
Kepner, Woody 1920- *WhoAm 92*
Keppard, Freddie 1889-1933 *Baker 92*
Keppel, Alice 1869-1947 *BioIn 17*
Keppel, Augustus 1725-1786 *HarEnMi*
Keppel, Francis C. *BioIn 17*
Keppel, James D. 1944- *St&PR 93*
Keppel, John 1917- *WhoAm 92*
Keppel, Robert F. 1918- *St&PR 93*
Kepple, J.B. 1936- *St&PR 93*
Kepple, Ronald Lee 1934- *St&PR 93*
Kepple, Thomas Ray, Jr. 1948- *WhoAm 92, WhoWor 93*
Keppler, Billie Jo 1949- *WhoEmL 93*
Keppler, Dietrich 1940- *WhoScE 91-3*
Keppler, E. *WhoScE 91-4*
Keppler, Herbert 1925- *WhoAm 92*
Keppler, Jodell Anne 1959- *St&PR 93*
Keppler, Johannes 1571-1630 *BioIn 17*
Keppler, William Edmund 1922- *WhoAm 92*
Ker, Frank G. *Law&B 92*
Ker, Oliver Livermore 1765-1797 *BioIn 17*
Keramas, James George 1928- *WhoE 93*
Kerameos-Foroglou, Chryssi 1935- *WhoScE 91-3*
Keran, Jerry E. 1941- *St&PR 93*
Keran, Michael William 1931- *St&PR 93*
Keranen, Antti J. 1946- *WhoScE 91-4*
Keranen, Gary John 1948- *St&PR 93*
Kerbel, John J. 1944- *St&PR 93*
Kerbel, Robert Norton 1931- *WhoE 93*
Kerbel, Robert Stephen 1945- *WhoWor 93*
Kerber, Andrew G. *Law&B 92*
Kerber, Hubert 1957- *WhoScE 91-4*
Kerber, John L. 1926- *St&PR 93*
Kerber, Linda Kaufman 1940- *WhoAm 92*
Kerber, Ronald Lee 1943- *WhoAm 92*
Kerbis, Gertrude Lempp *WhoAm 92*
Kerbow, Odis Doyce 1932- *St&PR 93*
Kerby, Robert Browning 1938- *WhoSSW 93, WhoWor 93*
Kerby, Stewart L. 1936- *St&PR 93*
Kerby, Stewart Lawrence 1936- *WhoAm 92*
Kerch, John G., Jr. 1931- *St&PR 93*
Kercher, Edwin C. 1946- *St&PR 93*
Kercher, Mary Horgan *Law&B 92*
Kercheval, Ken 1935- *WhoAm 92*
Kerchkhove, Claude 1933- *WhoScE 91-2*
Kerchner, Charles F., Jr. 1945- *St&PR 93*
Kerchner, Charles Frederick, Jr. 1945- *WhoAm 92*
Kercho, Randy S. 1956- *St&PR 93*
Kerckhoff, John D., Jr. *Law&B 92*
Kerckhoff, Richard Daniel 1905- *St&PR 93*
Kerckhoff, Richard Karl 1921- *WhoSSW 93*
Kerebel, Bertrand 1921- *WhoScE 91-2*
Kerekou, Mathieu *BioIn 17*
Kerekou, Mathieu Ahmed 1933- *WhoAfr*
Keremedjiev, George *BioIn 17*
Keremes, Constance Andrea 1958- *WhoWrEP 92*
Keremitsis, Eileen 1952- *WhoAmW 93*
Kerensky, Aleksandr Fyodorovich 1881-1970 *BioIn 17*
Kerensky, Alexander Feodorovich 1881-1970 *DcTwHis*
Kerenyi, Ervin 1928- *WhoScE 91-4*
Keres, Paul 1916- *BioIn 17*
Keresey, Richard Michael 1945- *St&PR 93, WhoAm 92*
Keresey, Thomas M. 1931- *St&PR 93*
Kerester, Charles John 1927- *WhoAm 92*
Kerestes, Joseph 1957- *St&PR 93*
Kerestes, Michael C. 1946- *St&PR 93*
Keresztesi, Bela 1922- *WhoScE 91-4*
Keresztesi, Zoltan 1936- *WhoScE 91-4*
Kerfanto, Michel 1926- *WhoScE 91-2*
Kerfoot, Glenn Warren 1921- *WhoWrEP 92*
Kerfoot, William Buchanan, Jr. 1944- *WhoAm 92*
Kergosien, Harold A. 1947- *St&PR 93*
Kerguelen, Michel 1928- *WhoScE 91-2*
Kerich, J. Patrick 1938- *St&PR 93*
Kerich, James Patrick 1938- *WhoAm 92*
Kerigan, Florence *AmWomPl*
Kerillis, Henri de 1889-1958 *BioIn 17*
Kerimaddin of Aksaray *OxDcByz*
Kerimov, Alexander 1947- *WhoWor 93*
Kerin, Barbara Lee 1943- *WhoAmW 93*
Kerin, Beth *BioIn 17*
Kerin, John 1938- *St&PR 93*
Kerin, John Charles 1937- *WhoAsAP 91*
Kerins, Francis Joseph 1927- *WhoAm 92*
Kerins, Paul T. 1943- *St&PR 93*
Kerins, Thomas Edward 1945- *St&PR 93*
Kerivan, William Robert 1945- *WhoSSW 93*
Kerker, Leonard J. *St&PR 93*
Kerker, Milton 1920- *WhoAm 92*
Kerkhoff, Maria A.T. 1948- *WhoScE 91-3*
Kerkhove, Jim Van *St&PR 93*
Kerkorian, Kirk *BioIn 17*
Kerkorian, Kirk 1917- *EncABHB 8 [port], WhoAm 92*
Kerkut, G.A. *WhoScE 91-1*
Kerl, Johann Kaspar 1627-1693 *Baker 92*
Kerle, Jacobus de 1531?-1591 *Baker 92*
Kerler, William R. 1929- *St&PR 93*
Kerley, Gary Lee 1949- *WhoWrEP 92*
Kerley, Jane *AmWomPl*
Kerley, Janice Johnson 1938- *WhoAmW 93*
Kerley, Nicholas William 1945- *WhoScE 91-1*
Kerley, Rosialee *AmWomPl*
Kerley, Thomas O. 1941- *St&PR 93*
Kerlin, Gilbert 1909- *St&PR 93*
Kerlin, Paul 1947- *WhoWor 93*
Kerll, Johann Kaspar 1627-1693 *Baker 92*
Kerman, Edward R. 1943- *St&PR 93*
Kerman, Joseph 1924- *BioIn 17, OxDcOp*
Kerman, Joseph (Wilfred) 1924- *Baker 92, WhoAm 92*
Kerman, Judith B. 1945- *ScF&FL 92*
Kerman, Judith Berna 1945- *WhoAmW 93, WhoWrEP 92*
Kerman, Lucy Whitcomb *Law&B 92*
Kerman, Thea 1949- *WhoWor 93*
Kermani-Arab, Vali 1939- *WhoAm 92*
Kermanshachi, Phillip 1962- *St&PR 93*
Kermeen, J.S. 1930- *St&PR 93*
Kermode, Frank 1919- *WhoAm 92*
Kern, Adele 1901-1980 *Baker 92, OxDcOp*
Kern, Angeline Frazier 1939- *WhoAmW 93*
Kern, Barbara J. *Law&B 92*
Kern, Barbara Patricia 1935- *WhoAmW 93*
Kern, Bernard Donald 1919- *WhoAm 92*
Kern, Byron Mehl 1921- *WhoAm 92*
Kern, Canyon *WhoWrEP 92*
Kern, Charles William 1935- *WhoAm 92, WhoWor 93*
Kern, Constance Elizabeth 1937- *WhoAmW 93*
Kern, Daniel Edmund 1965- *WhoE 93*
Kern, Edith 1912- *WhoWrEP 92*
Kern, Ellis 1940- *WhoAm 92*
Kern, Ellyn R. 1938- *WhoWrEP 92*
Kern, Frank Norton 1920- *WhoAm 92, WhoE 93, WhoWor 93*
Kern, Franklin Lorenz 1932- *WhoAm 92*
Kern, Fred, Jr. 1918- *WhoAm 92*
Kern, Fred Robert, Jr. 1943- *WhoAm 92*
Kern, Gary 1938- *ScF&FL 92*
Kern, Geof *BioIn 17*
Kern, George C. 1926- *St&PR 93*
Kern, George Calvin, Jr. 1926- *WhoAm 92, WhoWor 93*
Kern, Gerald N. 1938- *St&PR 93*
Kern, Gregory *ScF&FL 92*
Kern, Harry Frederick 1911- *WhoAm 92*
Kern, Irving John 1914- *WhoAm 92*
Kern, Jean 1930- *WhoScE 91-4*
Kern, Jeffrey Alan 1962- *WhoSSW 93*
Kern, Jerome 1885-1945 *BioIn 17, OxDcOp*
Kern, Jerome (David) 1885-1945 *Baker 92*
Kern, Jerome H. 1937- *WhoAm 92*
Kern, Jill Phelps 1956- *WhoAmW 93, WhoEmL 93*
Kern, John W. 1849-1917 *PolPar*
Kern, John Worth 1849-1917 *BioIn 17*
Kern, Kevin W. 1958- *St&PR 93*
Kern, Kevin Walsh *Law&B 92*
Kern, Lorena J. *Law&B 92*
Kern, Mark Sherwood 1959- *WhoSSW 93*
Kern, Martin Harold 1941- *WhoAm 92*
Kern, Nancy Welton 1946- *St&PR 93*
Kern, Patricia 1927- *Baker 92, OxDcOp*
Kern, Patricia Joan 1933- *WhoAmW 93*
Kern, Paul Alfred 1958- *WhoEmL 93, WhoWor 93*
Kern, Paul R. 1926- *St&PR 93*
Kern, R. *WhoScE 91-2*
Kern, Regina Flora 1948- *WhoEmL 93*
Kern, Richard E. 1932- *WhoScE 91-3*
Kern, Ruth G. *Law&B 92*
Kern, Scott C. *Law&B 92*
Kern, Timothy Lynn 1956- *WhoEmL 93*
Kern, Werner 1925- *WhoE 93*
Kern, William Ira 1938- *St&PR 93*
Kernaghan, Eileen 1939- *ScF&FL 92, WhoCanL 92*
Kernaghan, John Thomas 1953- *WhoE 93*
Kernahan, Dennis Arthur 1948- *St&PR 93*
Kernan, Barbara Desind 1939- *WhoAm 92, WhoAmW 93, WhoE 93, WhoWor 93*
Kernan, John T. 1946- *WhoAm 92*
Kernan, Mary Catherine 1957- *WhoEmL 93*
Kernan, Richard M., Jr. 1940- *WhoIns 93*
Kernan, William *BioIn 17*
Kernen, Jules Alfred 1929- *WhoAm 92*
Kerner, Daniella 1952- *WhoE 93*
Kerner, Fred 1921- *WhoAm 92, WhoE 93, WhoWor 93, WhoWrEP 92*
Kerner, Howard Alex 1951- *WhoWor 93*
Kerner, Justinus Andreas Christian 1786-1862 *BioIn 17*
Kerner, Martin 1947- *WhoEmL 93*
Kerner, Otto 1908-1976 *EncAACR*
Kerner, William J., Sr. *Law&B 92*
Kerner-Wheelock, Tamara Lynn 1965- *WhoAmW 93*
Kernes, Susan Paula 1952- *WhoAmW 93*
Kerney, Thomas Lincoln, II 1950- *WhoE 93, WhoEmL 93, WhoWor 93*
Kern-Foxworth, Marilyn Louise 1954- *WhoAmW 93, WhoSSW 93, WhoWor 93*
Kernochan, John Marshall 1919- *WhoAm 92*
Kernodle, Una Mae 1947- *WhoAmW 93*
Kerns, Christianne Finch 1958- *WhoAmW 93*
Kerns, Cindy Greenawalt 1956- *WhoAmW 93*
Kerns, David G. 1955- *WhoSSW 93*
Kerns, Ed 1945- *WhoE 93*
Kerns, Gertrude Yvonne 1931- *WhoAmW 93, WhoWor 93*
Kerns, Joanna *BioIn 17*
Kerns, Joseph E. *BioIn 17*
Kerns, Paula Irene 1950- *WhoE 93*
Kerns, Robert Louis 1929- *WhoAm 92*
Kerns, Robert M. *Law&B 92*
Kerns, Robert Owen 1933- *St&PR 93*
Kerns, Rodney L. 1954- *WhoSSW 93*
Kerouac, Jack 1922-1969 *AmWrS3, BioIn 17, MagSAmL [port], WorLitC [port]*
Keroularios *OxDcByz*
Kerpchar, Michael 1924- *WhoE 93, WhoWor 93*
Kerpelman, Larry C. 1939- *St&PR 93*
Kerpelman, Larry Cyril 1939- *WhoAm 92*
Kerper, Duane J. 1939- *St&PR 93*
Kerper, Meike 1929- *WhoAmW 93*
Kerr, Adam J. 1933- *WhoScE 91-4*
Kerr, Alasdair Russell 1948- *WhoWor 93*
Kerr, Alex Arthur, Jr. 1952- *WhoWor 93*
Kerr, Alva Rae 1926- *WhoSSW 93*
Kerr, Anthony Robert 1941- *WhoAm 92*
Kerr, Arnold D. 1928- *WhoE 93*
Kerr, Baine Perkins 1919- *St&PR 93, WhoAm 92, WhoWor 93*
Kerr, Banks D. 1922- *St&PR 93*
Kerr, Blair M. 1930- *St&PR 93*
Kerr, Charles Randall 1933- *WhoSSW 93*
Kerr, Chester Brooks 1913- *WhoAm 92, WhoWor 93*
Kerr, Clarence William 1923- *WhoAm 92*
Kerr, Clark 1911- *WhoAm 92*
Kerr, David Nicol Sharp *WhoScE 91-1*
Kerr, David Wylie 1943- *WhoAm 92, WhoWor 93*
Kerr, Deborah 1921- *IntDcF 2-3 [port]*
Kerr, Deborah Jane 1921- *WhoWor 93*
Kerr, Deborah MacPhail 1951- *WhoAmW 93*
Kerr, Donald Jon 1938- *St&PR 93*
Kerr, Donald MacLean, Jr. 1939- *WhoAm 92, WhoE 93*

Kerr, Dorothy Marie Burmeister 1935- *WhoAm 92*
Kerr, Douglas *Law&B 92*
Kerr, Duncan James Colquhoun 1952- *WhoAsAP 91*
Kerr, E. Bartlett 1924- *ConAu 139*
Kerr, Edmund H. 1924- *St&PR 93*
Kerr, Edmund Hugh 1924- *WhoAm 92*
Kerr, Edward Lawrence 1934- *St&PR 93*
Kerr, Edwin L. *Law&B 92*
Kerr, Emily Susan 1957- *WhoEmL 93*
Kerr, Ewing T. d1992 *NewYTBS 92*
Kerr, Ewing Thomas 1900- *WhoAm 92*
Kerr, Frank John 1918- *WhoAm 92, WhoE 93*
Kerr, Fred 1947- *St&PR 93*
Kerr, G. 1963- *WhoScE 91-1*
Kerr, Gordon J. 1953- *St&PR 93*
Kerr, Graham *BioIn 17*
Kerr, Gregory Alan 1950- *WhoWor 93*
Kerr, Harrison 1897-1978 *Baker 92*
Kerr, Helen *AmWomPl*
Kerr, Howard 1931- *ScF&FL 92*
Kerr, Howard J. 1947- *WhoAm 92*
Kerr, Hugh *BioIn 17*
Kerr, Hugh Douglas 1950- *WhoAm 92*
Kerr, Hugh T. 1909-1992 *BioIn 17*
Kerr, Hugh Thomson 1909- *ConAu 137*
Kerr, Hugh Thomson, Jr. d1992 *NewYTBS 92*
Kerr, James Harold 1948- *WhoSSW 93*
Kerr, James Joseph 1926- *St&PR 93, WhoAm 92*
Kerr, James W. 1914- *WhoAm 92*
Kerr, Janet K. *Law&B 92*
Kerr, Jean 1923- *WhoAm 92, WhoWrEP 92*
Kerr, Joan Namahana *Law&B 92*
Kerr, John 1914-1991 *AnObit 1991, BioIn 17*
Kerr, John, Jr. 1925- *St&PR 93*
Kerr, John E. 1940- *St&PR 93*
Kerr, John Martin 1934- *WhoSSW 93*
Kerr, John Robert 1914- *DcTwHis*
Kerr, John Wellington 1950- *WhoE 93*
Kerr, Katharine 1944- *ScF&FL 92*
Kerr, Kathleen Ann 1949- *St&PR 93*
Kerr, Kathryn Ann 1946- *WhoWrEP 92*
Kerr, Kleon Harding 1911- *WhoWor 93*
Kerr, Leslie Ann 1949- *WhoWrEP 92*
Kerr, Lisa Ann 1963- *WhoAmW 93*
Kerr, Lorin E. 1909-1991 *BioIn 17*
Kerr, Louise Ano Nuevo 1938- *NotHsAW 93*
Kerr, M. D. 1934- *WhoAm 92*
Kerr, M.E. *BioIn 17, ConAu 37NR, MajAI*
Kerr, M. E. 1927- *ChlLR 29 [port], DcAmChF 1960*
Kerr, Mabel Dorothea *WhoAmW 93*
Kerr, Mary Price 1943- *WhoAmW 93*
Kerr, Merle Duane 1947- *St&PR 93*
Kerr, Michael *ScF&FL 92*
Kerr, Michael C. 1826-1876 *PolPar*
Kerr, Nancy Helen 1947- *WhoAmW 93, WhoEmL 93*
Kerr, Nancy Karolyn 1934- *WhoAmW 93*
Kerr, Pamela Marianne 1953- *WhoE 93*
Kerr, Patrick Corbitt 1950- *WhoAm 92*
Kerr, Paul William 1930- *St&PR 93*
Kerr, Phyllis Forbes 1942- *SmATA 72 [port]*
Kerr, Rhonda Ann 1964- *WhoAmW 93*
Kerr, Robert Benjamin 1943- *WhoE 93*
Kerr, Robert S. 1896-1963 *PolPar*
Kerr, Robert Samuel 1896-1963 *BioIn 17*
Kerr, Robert William 1945- *WhoAm 92*
Kerr, Sandria Neidus 1940- *WhoAmW 93, WhoSSW 93*
Kerr, Stanley B. 1928- *WhoAm 92*
Kerr, Stephen R. 1946- *St&PR 93*
Kerr, Stephen Robert *WhoAm 92*
Kerr, Sylvia Joann 1941- *WhoAmW 93*
Kerr, Theodore William, Jr. 1912- *WhoE 93*
Kerr, Thomas Adolphus 1923- *WhoAm 92*
Kerr, Thomas E. *Law&B 92*
Kerr, Thomas Henderson, III 1945- *WhoE 93*
Kerr, Thomas J. 1945- *St&PR 93*
Kerr, Thomas Jefferson, IV 1933- *WhoAm 92*
Kerr, Tim 1960- *WhoAm 92*
Kerr, Virginia Grille 1935- *WhoAmW 93*
Kerr, Walter F. 1913- *WhoAm 92, WhoWrEP 92*
Kerr, Walter H. 1914- *WhoWrEP 92*
Kerr, Walter Hughes 1927- *St&PR 93*
Kerr, William 1919- *WhoAm 92*
Kerr, William Andrew 1934- *WhoAm 92*
Kerr, William Byron 1932- *WhoAm 92*
Kerr, William Donald 1948- *St&PR 93*
Kerr, William T. 1941- *WhoAm 92*
Kerr, William Turnbull 1941- *St&PR 93*
Kerrebijn, Karel Ferdinand 1929- *WhoWor 93*
Kerrebrock, Jack Leo 1928- *WhoAm 92*
Kerrey, Bob 1943- *WhoAm 92*
Kerrey, J. Robert 1943- *CngDr 91*
Kerrey, Robert *BioIn 17*
Kerrick, Jill Maureen 1964- *WhoEmL 93*
Kerrick, Jon Paul 1939- *St&PR 93*
Kerridge, Isaac C., Jr. 1924- *St&PR 93*
Kerridge, Isaac Curtis, Jr. 1924- *WhoAm 92*
Kerrigan, Anthony *BioIn 17*
Kerrigan, Anthony 1918- *WhoAm 92*
Kerrigan, (Thomas) Anthony 1918- *WhoWrEP 92*
Kerrigan, J. Warren 1879-1947 *BioIn 17*
Kerrigan, James W. 1936- *St&PR 93*
Kerrigan, Juanita Irene 1946- *St&PR 93*
Kerrigan, Nancy *BioIn 17*
Kerrigan, Patrick J. 1952- *St&PR 93*
Kerrigan, Walter W., II 1953- *WhoEmL 93*
Kerrine, T. Michael *Law&B 92*
Kerruish, Jessie Douglas d1949 *ScF&FL 92*
Kerry, Brian Robert *WhoScE 91-1*
Kerry, John F. 1943- *CngDr 91*
Kerry, John Forbes 1943- *BioIn 17, WhoAm 92, WhoE 93, WhoWor 93*
Kerry, Lois *MajAI*
Kerry, Norman 1894-1956 *BioIn 17*
Kersavage, Carol Joan 1934- *WhoWrEP 92*
Kersbergen, Robert J.D. 1951- *WhoIns 93*
Kersch, Robert Stanley 1928- *St&PR 93*
Kerschbaum, Thomas 1943- *WhoScE 91-3*
Kerscher, Daniel J. *Law&B 92*
Kerscher, Rudolf *WhoScE 91-3*
Kerschner, Barry J. *Law&B 92*
Kerschner, Joan Gentry 1945- *WhoAm 92*
Kerschner, Lee Ronald 1931- *WhoAm 92*
Kersee, Bob *BioIn 17*
Kersee, Jackie Joyner- *BioIn 17*
Kersey, Jerry *BioIn 17*
Kersey, Katharine C(lark) 1935- *ConAu 38NR*
Kersey, Tanya-Monique 1961- *ConAu 138, WhoAmW 93, WhoWrEP 92*
Kersey, Terry Lee 1947- *WhoEmL 93, WhoWor 93*
Kershaw, Carol Jean 1947- *WhoAmW 93, WhoEmL 93*
Kershaw, Ian 1943- *ConAu 137*
Kershaw, Kenneth Andrew 1930- *WhoAm 92*
Kershaw, Nellie 1891-1924 *BioIn 17*
Kershaw, R.A. 1947- *St&PR 93*
Kershaw, Robert Alan 1947- *WhoAm 92*
Kershaw, Stephen John 1954- *WhoWor 93*
Kershaw, Stewart 1941- *WhoAm 92*
Kershbaumer, Louis August 1931- *St&PR 93*
Kershenbaum, Richard Mendel 1951- *WhoEmL 93*
Kershman, Susan *BioIn 17*
Kershner, Irvin 1923- *ConTFT 10, MiSFD 9*
Kershner, Richard Brandon, Jr. 1944- *WhoSSW 93*
Kershner, Thomas Gordon 1941- *St&PR 93*
Kershner, William Robert 1952- *WhoSSW 93*
Kersic, Nikolaj 1925- *WhoScE 91-4*
Kersjes, A.W. 1928- *WhoScE 91-3*
Kersjes, Anton (Frans Jan) 1923- *Baker 92, WhoWor 93*
Kerslake, Kenneth Alvin 1930- *WhoAm 92*
Kerslake, Rosaleen C. *Law&B 92*
Kerst, Donald William 1911- *WhoAm 92*
Kerst, Vanda E. *AmWomPl*
Kerstein, Lawrence 1922- *St&PR 93*
Kerstein, Philip M. *Law&B 92*
Kersten, Christian George 1949- *WhoE 93*
Kersten, Geert R. 1958- *St&PR 93*
Kersten, Walter H. 1926- *WhoScE 91-3*
Kersters, Willem 1929- *Baker 92*
Kerstetter, Guinevere Anne *WhoAmW 93*
Kerstetter, Michael James 1936- *WhoAm 92*
Kerstetter, Raymond John, Jr. 1936- *St&PR 93*
Kerstetter, William Edward *Law&B 92*
Kerstetter-Hull, Joanne Rita 1952- *WhoE 93, WhoEmL 93, WhoWor 93*
Kersting, Edwin Joseph 1919- *WhoAm 92*
Kersting, Joan M. *Law&B 92*
Kersting, Kees 1943- *WhoScE 91-3*
Kersting, Nelle F. *AmWomPl*
Kersting, Wolfgang 1939- *WhoScE 91-3*
Kerstner, Ralph Melvin 1932- *St&PR 93*
Kert, Larry 1930-1991 *AnObit 1991, BioIn 17, ConTFT 10*
Kertess, Hans William 1939- *St&PR 93*
Kertesz, Adam 1948- *WhoScE 91-4*
Kertesz, Andre *BioIn 17*
Kertesz, George Joseph 1928- *St&PR 93*
Kertesz, Istvan 1929-1973 *Baker 92, OxDcOp*
Kertesz, Louis R. 1947- *St&PR 93*
Kerth, Leroy T. 1928- *WhoAm 92*
Kerton, Nick Anthony 1950- *WhoWor 93*
Kertz, Hubert Leonard 1910- *WhoAm 92, WhoWor 93*
Kervina-Thompson, Mimi 1945- *WhoAmW 93*
Ker Wilson, Barbara *ScF&FL 92*
Ker Wilson, Barbara 1929- *SmATA 70 [port]*
Kerwin, Carolyn Ann 1950- *WhoEmL 93*
Kerwin, Cornelius Martin 1949- *WhoE 93*
Kerwin, Finian d1991 *BioIn 17*
Kerwin, John Michael 1920- *St&PR 93*
Kerwin, Joseph Peter 1932- *WhoAm 92*
Kerwin, Larkin 1924- *WhoAm 92, WhoWor 93*
Kerwin, Lawrence J., Jr. 1927- *St&PR 93*
Kerwin, Patrick Joseph 1947- *St&PR 93*
Kerwin, Thomas Hugh 1930- *WhoAm 92*
Kerwin, William James 1922- *WhoAm 92*
Kerwood, Gary Scott *Law&B 92*
Kerwood, Lewis O. 1917- *WhoAm 92*
Kerxton, Alan Smith 1938- *WhoAm 92*
Keryczynskyj, Leo Ihor 1948- *WhoEmL 93*
Keryk, Wendy Margaret 1951- *St&PR 93*
Kerze, Allan Richard 1946- *WhoEmL 93*
Kes, Pieter Hendrik 1944- *WhoWor 93*
Kes, Willem 1856-1934 *Baker 92*
Keschl, Constance Frances 1949- *WhoAmW 93*
Kesegi, Pamela Lynne Tawney 1951- *WhoEmL 93*
Kesel, George F. 1932- *WhoAm 92*
Keseru, Janos 1926- *WhoScE 91-4*
Kesey, Ken *BioIn 17*
Kesey, Ken 1935- *MagSAmL [port], WhoAm 92, WorLitC [port]*
Kesey, Ken (Elton) 1935- *ConAu 38NR, WhoWrEP 92*
Keshishian, Alek *BioIn 17, MiSFD 9*
Keshishian, Rose Setrag 1922- *WhoSSW 93*
Keshwani, Rajesh Lokchand 1962- *WhoWor 93*
Kesici, Vehbi 1929- *WhoScE 91-4*
Kesik, Tadeusz 1942- *WhoScE 91-4*
Kesisoglu, Garbis 1936- *WhoWor 93*
Keska, Jerry Kazimierz 1945- *WhoWor 93*
Kesl, W.J. 1951- *St&PR 93*
Kesler, Clyde Ervin 1922- *WhoAm 92*
Kesler, Jay *BioIn 17*
Kesler, Jay Lewis 1935- *WhoAm 92*
Kesler, Larry Badger 1938- *WhoAm 92*
Kesler, Larry Dean 1944- *WhoE 93*
Kesler, Olivia 1939- *St&PR 93, WhoAm 92*
Kesler, Robert Milton, Jr. *Law&B 92*
Kesler, Stan *SoulM*
Kesler, Stephen Edward 1940- *WhoAm 92*
Kesler, Susannah E. *Law&B 92*
Kesler-Corneil, Dian *St&PR 93*
Kesling, Willard Ray, Jr. 1948- *WhoEmL 93*
Kesner, Harvey J. *Law&B 92*
Kesri, Sitaram 1919- *WhoAsAP 91*
Kesse, G.O. *WhoScE 91-2*
Kesseba, Abbas Mostafa 1937- *WhoUN 92*
Kessedjian, Catherine *WhoWor 93*
Kessel, Dagobert G. 1935- *WhoScE 91-3*
Kessel, Jeffrey Brian 1960- *WhoWrEP 92*
Kessel, John 1950- *ScF&FL 92*
Kessel, John Howard 1928- *WhoWrEP 92*
Kessel, John Joseph 1950- *WhoSSW 93*
Kessel, Kathy L. 1951- *WhoE 93*
Kessel, Laura Elizabeth 1969- *WhoAmW 93*
Kessel, Renee F. *Law&B 92*
Kessel, Richard Glen 1931- *WhoAm 92*
Kessel, Roger H. *Law&B 92*
Kesseler, Roger L. 1936- *St&PR 93*
Kesseler, Simone Elizabeth 1962- *WhoWor 93*
Kesselhaut, Arthur 1935- *St&PR 93*
Kesselhaut, Arthur M. 1935- *WhoIns 93*
Kesselhaut, Arthur Melvyn 1935- *WhoAm 92*
Kesselly, Edward Binyah *WhoWor 93*
Kesselman, Bernard A. *Law&B 92*
Kesselman, Bruce Alan 1951- *WhoAm 92, WhoE 93*
Kesselman, Frederic B. 1942- *St&PR 93*
Kesselman, Jonathan Rhys 1946- *WhoAm 92*
Kesselman, Judi R. *ConAu 37NR*
Kesselman, Theodore Leonard 1932- *WhoAm 92*
Kesselman-Turkel, Judi 1934- *ConAu 37NR*
Kesselring, Albert 1885-1960 *BioIn 17*
Kesselring, Albert von 1885-1960 *HarEnMi*
Kesselring, Albrecht 1885-1960 *DcTwHis*
Kesselring, Kathleen Joan 1962- *WhoAmW 93*
Kesselring, Robert Lawrence 1950- *WhoSSW 93*
Kessen, William 1925- *WhoAm 92*
Kessinger, John Roy 1940- *St&PR 93*
Kessinger, Margaret Anne 1941- *WhoAmW 93*
Kessinger, Tom G. 1941- *WhoE 93*
Kessinger, Tom George 1941- *WhoAm 92*
Kesslen, Sheldon Robert 1936- *St&PR 93*
Kessler, A. D. 1923- *WhoAm 92, WhoWor 93*
Kessler, Alan Craig 1950- *WhoWor 93*
Kessler, Alan Lee 1950- *WhoE 93*
Kessler, Alan S. *ScF&FL 92*
Kessler, Barbara Milgram *Law&B 92*
Kessler, Barbara Milgram 1950- *WhoEmL 93*
Kessler, Bruce 1936- *MiSFD 9*
Kessler, Bruce J. 1937- *St&PR 93*
Kessler, Carol Farley 1936- *ScF&FL 92*
Kessler, Daniel T. *Law&B 92*
Kessler, David 1951- *News 92 [port]*
Kessler, David A. *BioIn 17*
Kessler, David A. 1951- *WhoAm 92*
Kessler, David S. *Law&B 92*
Kessler, Dennis Jules 1951- *St&PR 93*
Kessler, Dietrich 1936- *WhoAm 92*
Kessler, Edwin 1928- *WhoAm 92, WhoSSW 93*
Kessler, Erich 1927- *WhoScE 91-3*
Kessler, Frank 1932- *St&PR 93*
Kessler, Franz Rudolf 1927- *WhoScE 91-3*
Kessler, Frederick Melvyn 1932- *WhoE 93*
Kessler, Gerald 1922- *St&PR 93*
Kessler, Guenther 1934- *WhoScE 91-3*
Kessler, Hal Ross *Law&B 92*
Kessler, Harold David 1945- *WhoE 93*
Kessler, Herbert Josef 1943- *WhoWor 93*
Kessler, Herbert Leon 1941- *WhoAm 92*
Kessler, Horst 1940- *WhoScE 91-3*
Kessler, Irving Isar 1931- *WhoAm 92*
Kessler, Irving Kenneth 1919- *WhoAm 92*
Kessler, Jacques Isaac 1929- *WhoAm 92*
Kessler, Jascha Frederick 1929- *WhoWrEP 92*
Kessler, Joachim 1930- *WhoScE 91-3*
Kessler, Joan F. 1943- *WhoAmW 93*
Kessler, John Henry 1945- *St&PR 93*
Kessler, John L. *Law&B 92*
Kessler, John Otto 1928- *WhoAm 92*
Kessler, John Whitaker 1936- *WhoAm 92*
Kessler, Joseph Christoph 1800-1872 *Baker 92*
Kessler, Karl Gunther 1919- *WhoAm 92*
Kessler, Lawrence B. *Law&B 92*
Kessler, Lawrence Bert 1946- *WhoAm 92, WhoWor 93*
Kessler, Lawrence Devlin 1936- *WhoSSW 93*
Kessler, Lawrence P. *Law&B 92*
Kessler, Leizer R. 1939- *St&PR 93*
Kessler, Leona Hanover 1925- *WhoAmW 93*
Kessler, Leonard M. *Law&B 92*
Kessler, Lutz Robert 1936- *WhoScE 91-3*
Kessler, Manfred 1934- *WhoScE 91-3*
Kessler, Mark Keil 1936- *WhoAm 92*
Kessler, Maureen Conners *Law&B 92*
Kessler, Mike *St&PR 93*
Kessler, Milton 1917- *St&PR 93*
Kessler, Milton 1930- *WhoAm 92, WhoWrEP 92*
Kessler, Morris H. 1920- *St&PR 93*
Kessler, Nathan 1923- *WhoAm 92*
Kessler, Otto H. 1910- *St&PR 93*
Kessler, Paul Buckley 1953- *St&PR 93*
Kessler, Pete William 1949- *WhoE 93*
Kessler, Peter Lawrence *ScF&FL 92*
Kessler, Peter Otto 1948- *WhoWor 93*
Kessler, Philip Joel 1947- *WhoWor 93*
Kessler, Phyllis Jane 1947- *WhoAmW 93*
Kessler, Phyllis K. 1956- *WhoAmW 93*
Kessler, Ralph Kenneth 1943- *WhoAm 92*
Kessler, Richard John 1948- *WhoE 93*
Kessler, Risa *ScF&FL 92*
Kessler, Robert Jack 1933- *WhoAm 92*
Kessler, Robert Richard 1935- *St&PR 93*
Kessler, Rod 1949- *WhoWrEP 92*
Kessler, Ronald Borek 1943- *WhoAm 92*
Kessler, Sheila *WhoAmW 93*
Kessler, Sidney H. 1926- *WhoE 93*
Kessler, Stephen *BioIn 17*
Kessler, Stephen Lee 1943- *St&PR 93*
Kessler, Steven L. *Law&B 92*
Kessler, Steven Leigh 1957- *WhoEmL 93*
Kessler, Thomas 1937- *Baker 92*
Kessler, Wallace Frank 1938- *WhoE 93*
Kessler, William Eugene 1944- *WhoAm 92*
Kessler, William Henry 1924- *WhoAm 92*
Kessler, Wirt Duane 1911- *WhoWrEP 92*
Kessler-Hodgson, Lee Gwendolyn 1947- *WhoAmW 93, WhoEmL 93*
Kesslin, Howard 1931- *St&PR 93*
Kessman, Alan 1947- *ConEn*
Kessmann, Roy William 1941- *WhoSSW 93*
Kessner, Daniel (Aaron) 1946- *Baker 92*
Kessner, Ronald Joseph 1942- *WhoSSW 93*
Kessock, John, Jr. *St&PR 93*

Kest, John Marshall 1948- *WhoEmL 93*
Kesteloot, Hugo E.C. 1927- *WhoScE 91-2*
Kesten, Larry *BioIn 17*
Kesten, Ronald E. 1942- *WhoE 93*
Kestenbaum, Harold L. 1949- *St&PR 93*
Kestenbaum, Leon Marvin *Law&B 92*
Kestenbaum, M. Robert *Law&B 92*
Kestenbaum, Mel 1937- *St&PR 93*
Kestenbaum, Stuart Jon 1951- *WhoE 93*
Kestenbaum, William Wolf 1921- *WhoE 93*
Kestenberg, Leo 1882-1962 *Baker 92*
Kestenberg, Milton d1991 *BioIn 17*
Kester, Dale Emmert 1922- *WhoAm 92*
Kester, Howard 1904-1977 *BioIn 17*
Kester, Howard Anderson 1904-1977 *EncAACR*
Kester, John Gordon 1938- *WhoAm 92*
Kester, Katharine E. *AmWomPl*
Kester, Laurel Gaye 1950- *WhoAmW 93*
Kester, Mary Martha Irene 1913- *WhoE 93*
Kester, Randall Blair 1916- *WhoAm 92*
Kester, Stewart Randolph 1927- *WhoAm 92*
Kesterke, Norman W. 1934- *St&PR 93*
Kesterman, Frank Raymond 1937- *WhoAm 92, WhoE 93*
Kesterson, David Bert 1938- *WhoAm 92*
Kesterson, Jeffery Doyle 1955- *WhoSSW 93*
Kesterson, Michael Denis 1932- *St&PR 93*
Kesterton, David 1948- *ScF&FL 92*
Kesteven, G.R. 1911- *ScF&FL 92*
Kestin, Howard H. 1937- *WhoAm 92*
Kestin, Joan B. 1944- *WhoAmW 93*
Kestin, Joseph 1913- *WhoAm 92*
Kesting, Theodore 1918- *WhoAm 92*
Kestle, Wendell Russell 1935- *WhoSSW 93*
Kestler, Francis J. 1944- *St&PR 93*
Kestler, Hans 1944- *St&PR 93*
Kestler, Jeffrey L. *Law&B 92*
Kestler, Jeffrey Lewis 1947- *WhoAm 92, WhoEmL 93*
Kestnbaum, Albert S. 1939- *WhoAm 92*
Kestnbaum, Robert Dana 1932- *WhoAm 92*
Kestner, Auguste Scheurer- 1833-1899 *BioIn 17*
Keston, Albert S. d1992 *NewYTBS 92*
Keston, Albert S. 1911-1992 *BioIn 17*
Keston, Joan Balboul 1937- *WhoAmW 93*
Kesty, Robert Edward 1941- *WhoE 93*
Kesy, Andrzej 1953- *WhoScE 91-4*
Kesy, Zbigniew 1953- *WhoScE 91-4*
Keszler, Jozef *WhoScE 91-4*
Keszthelyi, Lajos 1927- *WhoScE 91-4*
Ketcham, Alfred Schutt 1924- *WhoAm 92*
Ketcham, Geoffrey C. 1951- *St&PR 93*
Ketcham, Hank 1920- *BioIn 17*
Ketcham, Henry King 1920- *WhoAm 92*
Ketcham, Jeffrey H. 1942- *St&PR 93*
Ketcham, Max 1953- *WhoSSW 93*
Ketcham, Orman Weston 1918- *WhoAm 92*
Ketcham, Ralph 1927- *WhoAm 92*
Ketchen, Gavin Leo 1962- *WhoE 93*
Ketchen-Elmore, Jacqueline Lillian 1952- *WhoSSW 93*
Ketcher, Greg Alan 1963- *WhoSSW 93*
Ketchersid, Wayne Lester, Jr. 1946- *WhoEmL 93, WhoWor 93*
Ketcherside, James L. 1935- *WhoIns 93*
Ketcherside, James Lee 1935- *St&PR 93*
Ketchmark, Daniel E. 1931- *St&PR 93*
Ketchum, Alton Harrington 1904- *WhoAm 92, WhoWor 93*
Ketchum, Black Jack 1866-1901 *BioIn 17*
Ketchum, Chandler Griswold 1922- *WhoWor 93*
Ketchum, David Storey 1920- *WhoAm 92*
Ketchum, Ezekiel Sargent 1935- *St&PR 93, WhoAm 92*
Ketchum, Harold A. 1912- *St&PR 93*
Ketchum, Irene Frances 1914- *WhoAmW 93*
Ketchum, Jack 1946- *ScF&FL 92*
Ketchum, Jack B. 1907- *St&PR 93*
Ketchum, James Roe 1939- *WhoAm 92, WhoE 93*
Ketchum, John Bunten 1955- *WhoEmL 93, WhoSSW 93*
Ketchum, Linda Ellen 1956- *WhoWrEP 92*
Ketchum, Richard Malcolm 1922- *WhoAm 92*
Ketchum, Robert Glenn *BioIn 17*
Ketchum, Robert Glenn 1947- *WhoAm 92*
Ketchum, Robert Scott 1937- *WhoAm 92*
Ketchum, Thomas 1866-1901 *BioIn 17*
Ketchum, William Clarence, Jr. 1931- *WhoE 93*
Ketelbey, Albert (William) 1875-1959 *Baker 92*
Ketelhohn, Werner 1940- *WhoWor 93*
Ketelhut, Marcella *Law&B 92*
Ketelsen, James L. 1930- *St&PR 93*
Ketelsen, James Lee 1930- *WhoAm 92, WhoSSW 93*
Ketema, Yifru 1930- *WhoUN 92*
Ketkar, Suhas Laxman 1943- *WhoAm 92*
Ketner, Kenneth Laine 1939- *WhoAm 92*
Ketner, Kenneth Laine, (Sr.) 1939- *ConAu 139*
Ketner, Ralph W. 1920- *St&PR 93*
Ketner, Ralph Wright 1920- *WhoAm 92*
Keto, C. Tsehloane 1941- *WhoE 93, WhoWor 93*
Keto, John Edwin 1909- *WhoAm 92*
Ketonen, Arvo Mikko Olavi 1945- *WhoWor 93*
Ketover, Richard 1935- *St&PR 93*
Ketrow, Sandra Marie 1949- *WhoAmW 93*
Ketrzynski, Wojciech 1835-1876 *BioIn 17*
Kets de Vries, Manfred Florian 1942- *WhoWor 93*
Ketskemety, Istvan 1927- *WhoScE 91-4*
Kett, Herbert Joseph 1933- *St&PR 93, WhoAm 92*
Kett, Joseph Francis 1938- *WhoAm 92*
Kettaneh, Tarek Michael 1947- *WhoAm 92*
Kettelkamp, Donald Benjamin 1930- *WhoAm 92*
Kettell, Leedom 1939- *St&PR 93*
Kettell, Russell Willard 1944- *WhoAm 92*
Ketteman, Helen 1945- *SmATA 73*
Ketten, Darlene R. 1947- *WhoE 93*
Kettenbach, Lawrence J., Jr. *Law&B 92*
Kettenis, Jacobus Josef 1938- *WhoScE 91-3*
Kettenus, Aloys 1823-1896 *Baker 92*
Ketter, David Lee 1929- *WhoAm 92*
Ketter, Pam *WhoWrEP 92*
Ketterer, David 1942- *ScF&FL 92*
Ketterer, David (Anthony Theodor) 1942- *WhoWrEP 92*
Ketterer, Eugene 1831-1870 *Baker 92*
Ketterer, Kenneth C. 1939- *St&PR 93*
Kettering, G.L. 1954- *St&PR 93*
Kettering, Glen Lee 1954- *WhoAm 92*
Ketterl, Werner 1925- *WhoScE 91-3*
Ketterman, Grace H(orst) 1926- *WhoWrEP 92*
Ketterman, Myra Lee 1952- *WhoAmW 93*
Ketting, Otto 1935- *Baker 92*
Ketting, Piet 1904-1984 *Baker 92*
Kettinger, David John 1954- *WhoE 93*
Kettinger, Robert R. 1942- *St&PR 93*
Kettle, Leroy *ScF&FL 92*
Kettle, Pamela 1934- *ScF&FL 92*
Kettle, Roger John *WhoScE 91-1*
Kettle, Roger John 1943- *WhoWor 93*
Kettle, Sally Anne 1938- *WhoAmW 93*
Kettler, Carl Frederick 1936- *WhoAm 92*
Kettler, Dietrich 1936- *WhoScE 91-3*
Kettlewell, Gail Biery 1939- *WhoAmW 93*
Kettlewell, James K. 1930- *WhoE 93*
Kettlewell, Peter John *WhoScE 91-1*
Kettlewood, Bea Card 1929- *WhoAmW 93*
Kettrup, Antonius A.F. 1938- *WhoScE 91-3*
Kettrup, Antonius August Franz 1938- *WhoWor 93*
Kettunen, Algot Eero 1940- *WhoWor 93*
Kettunen, Kauko 1926- *WhoScE 91-4*
Kettunen, Lauri 1935- *WhoScE 91-4*
Kettunen, Pentti O. *WhoScE 91-4*
Kety, Seymour Solomon 1915- *WhoAm 92*
Ketyi, Ivan 1926- *WhoScE 91-4*
Ketzner, J.A. 1951- *St&PR 93*
Keulegan, Emma Pauline 1930- *WhoAmW 93, WhoSSW 93, WhoWor 93*
Keulen, Margarete 1961- *ScF&FL 92*
Keuler, Roland Leo 1933- *St&PR 93, WhoAm 92*
Keulks, George William 1938- *WhoAm 92*
Keune, Hartmut 1945- *WhoUN 92*
Keune, John K. 1948- *St&PR 93*
Keung, John Lee Chi *St&PR 93*
Keuning, Patricia Dubrava 1944- *WhoWrEP 92*
Keuppens, Bert Emiel 1949- *WhoUN 92*
Keuris, Tristan 1946- *Baker 92*
Keurvels, Edward (Hubertus Joannes) 1853-1916 *Baker 92*
Keusch, Michael 1955- *MiSFD 9*
Keussler, Gerhard von 1874-1949 *Baker 92*
Keuthen, Catherine J. *Law&B 92*
Kevan, Douglas Keith McEwan 1920- *WhoAm 92*
Kevan, Larry 1938- *WhoAm 92*
Kevany, Michael J. *St&PR 93*
Kevenides, Herve Arnaud 1938- *WhoAm 92*
Keves, Gyorgy 1935- *WhoWor 93*
Keviczky, Laszlo 1945- *WhoScE 91-4*
Kevill, Dennis Neil 1935- *WhoAm 92*
Kevill-Davies, Sally 1945- *ConAu 138*
Kevles, Daniel Jerome 1939- *WhoAm 92*
Kevlin, Dean 1949- *WhoEmL 93*
Kevlin, Terry Lynn 1957- *WhoSSW 93*
Kevorkian, Aram Trevor *St&PR 93*
Kevorkian, Jack *BioIn 17*
Kevorkian, Richard 1937- *WhoAm 92, WhoSSW 93*
Kew, Robert James 1938- *St&PR 93*
Kewal, Narendra Krishan 1952- *WhoWor 93*
Kewish, Dean A. *Law&B 92*
Kewley, Sharon Lynn 1958- *WhoAmW 93, WhoEmL 93*
Key, Alexander 1904-1979 *ScF&FL 92*
Key, Alexander (Hill) 1904-1979 *DcAmChF 1960*
Key, Ann Blackmore 1942- *WhoAmW 93*
Key, Chapin 1922- *WhoAm 92*
Key, Charles Christopher 1948- *WhoEmL 93*
Key, David E. 1960- *St&PR 93*
Key, Derrick N. 1947- *St&PR 93*
Key, Donald 1923- *WhoWrEP 92*
Key, Francis Scott 1779-1843 *Baker 92*
Key, J. Louise 1949- *WhoAmW 93*
Key, Jack Brien 1930- *WhoSSW 93*
Key, Jack Dayton 1934- *WhoAm 92*
Key, James Everett 1944- *WhoSSW 93*
Key, Jerry Wayne *Law&B 92*
Key, John W., II 1960- *St&PR 93*
Key, Karen Letisha 1957- *WhoSSW 93*
Key, Kenneth James 1962- *WhoEmL 93*
Key, L.J. *ScF&FL 92*
Key, Martha V. 1929- *St&PR 93*
Key, Mary Etna 1944- *WhoAmW 93*
Key, Mary Ritchie 1924- *ConAu 38NR, WhoAm 92, WhoAmW 93*
Key, Phillip 1940- *WhoWor 93*
Key, Pierre van Rensselaer 1872-1945 *Baker 92*
Key, Rutherford Lyle, Jr. *Law&B 92*
Key, Samuel M. *ScF&FL 92*
Key, Sarah *BioIn 17*
Key, Stephen Lewis 1943- *WhoAm 92*
Key, Ted 1912- *ScF&FL 92, WhoAm 92*
Key, Theodore *ScF&FL 92*
Key, Thomas H. 1937- *St&PR 93*
Key, V.O., Jr. 1908-1963 *PolPar*
Keyan, Masoud 1949- *St&PR 93*
Keydel, Frederick Reid 1928- *WhoAm 92*
Keydel, Wolfgang 1936- *WhoScE 91-3*
Keye, Don *ScF&FL 92*
Keyes, A. Vincent 1932- *St&PR 93*
Keyes, Alan L. 1950- *WhoAm 92*
Keyes, Arthur Hawkins, Jr. 1917- *WhoAm 92*
Keyes, Carol Ruth 1935- *WhoE 93*
Keyes, Carolyn Stacy 1961- *WhoAmW 93*
Keyes, Christopher Michael *Law&B 92*
Keyes, Daniel 1927- *BioIn 17, WhoAm 92, WhoWrEP 92*
Keyes, Darlynn Ladd 1948- *WhoAmW 93, WhoEmL 93, WhoWor 93*
Keyes, David Elliot 1956- *WhoE 93*
Keyes, David Taylor 1947- *WhoSSW 93*
Keyes, Edward Lawrence, Jr. 1929- *St&PR 93, WhoAm 92*
Keyes, Emilie *AmWomPl*
Keyes, Emmalou 1931- *WhoAmW 93*
Keyes, Erasmus Darwin 1810-1895 *HarEnMi*
Keyes, Evelyn 1917- *BioIn 17*
Keyes, Fenton 1915- *WhoAm 92*
Keyes, Fenton George 1916- *St&PR 93*
Keyes, Geoffrey 1886-1967 *HarEnMi*
Keyes, Gordon Lincoln 1920- *WhoAm 92*
Keyes, James H. 1940- *St&PR 93*
Keyes, James Henry 1940- *WhoAm 92*
Keyes, James L., Jr. 1928- *St&PR 93*
Keyes, James Lyman, Jr. 1928- *WhoWor 93*
Keyes, James Willard 1955- *WhoSSW 93*
Keyes, Joan Ross Rafter 1924- *WhoAmW 93*
Keyes, Lee Nathan 1959- *WhoSSW 93*
Keyes, Margaret M. *Law&B 92*
Keyes, Margaret Naumann 1918- *WhoAm 92*
Keyes, Marion Alvah, IV 1938- *WhoAm 92, WhoWor 93*
Keyes, Mary Willard *AmWomPl*
Keyes, R.A., Jr. 1952- *St&PR 93*
Keyes, Ralph Jeffry 1945- *WhoWrEP 92*
Keyes, Robert William 1921- *WhoAm 92*
Keyes, Roger John Brownlow 1872-1945 *HarEnMi*
Keyes, Saundra Elise 1945- *WhoAm 92*
Keyes, Steven Richard *Law&B 92*
Keyes, Thom 1943- *ScF&FL 92*
Keyfitz, Nathan 1913- *WhoAm 92, WhoWor 93*
Keyhoe, Donald E. 1897-1988 *ScF&FL 92*
Keyishian, Harry 1932- *ScF&FL 92*
Keyishian, M. Deiter *WhoWrEP 92*
Keyko, David Andrew 1946- *WhoEmL 93*
Keyles, Claire G. *Law&B 92*
Keyles, Sidney Alan *Law&B 92*
Keylon, Charles David 1947- *WhoEmL 93*
Keymer, David King 1936- *WhoE 93*
Keymeulen, H. *WhoScE 91-2*
Keynes, John Maynard 1883-1946 *BioIn 17, DcLB DS10, DcTwHis*
Keys, Alfred John *WhoScE 91-1*
Keys, Clement M. 1876-1952 *EncABHB 8 [port]*
Keys, David N. 1956- *St&PR 93*
Keys, Desley Kay 1951- *St&PR 93*
Keys, Gloria Pack 1929- *WhoAmW 93*
Keys, Kerry Shawn 1946- *WhoWrEP 92*
Keys, Lloyd Kenneth 1939- *WhoSSW 93*
Keys, Lucy Stearns *AmWomPl*
Keys, Marshall Theodore 1945- *WhoE 93*
Keys, Martha Elizabeth 1930- *BioIn 17*
Keys, Paul Ross 1940- *WhoE 93*
Keys, Sandra Bailey 1944- *WhoAmW 93*
Keys, Thomas Edward 1908- *WhoAm 92*
Keys, W. David *Law&B 92*
Keyser, David Richard 1941- *WhoE 93*
Keyser, F. Ray, Jr. 1927- *St&PR 93*
Keyser, Frank Ray, Jr. 1927- *WhoAm 92*
Keyser, John Alden, Jr. 1943- *St&PR 93*
Keyser, John J. *St&PR 93*
Keyser, Martin Alan *Law&B 92*
Keyser, Mary Clark 1918- *WhoAmW 93*
Keyser, Robert N. 1934- *St&PR 93*
Keyser, Samuel Jay 1935- *WhoAm 92*
Keyser, Stephen Allen 1948- *St&PR 93*
Keyser, Steven H. 1950- *WhoAm 92*
Keyserling, Mary Dublin 1910- *WhoAm 92, WhoE 93, WhoWor 93*
Keysor, Allan L. *Law&B 92*
Keyston, Stephani Ann 1955- *WhoAmW 93, WhoEmL 93*
Keyt, David 1930- *WhoAm 92*
Keytes, Lou 1881-1926 *BioIn 17*
Keyton, James W. 1932- *WhoSSW 93*
Keyum Bawudun 1939- *WhoAsAP 91*
Keyworth, George Albert, II 1939- *WhoAm 92*
Keyworth, Richard Charles Anthony *WhoWor 93*
Kezdi-Kovacs, Zsolt 1936- *DrEEuF*
Kezer, Claude Dean 1933- *WhoSSW 93*
Kezer, John C. *St&PR 93*
Kezer, Laura Effingham 1938- *WhoAm 92*
Kezer, Pauline Ryder 1942- *WhoAm 92, WhoAmW 93, WhoE 93*
Kezha, Maria *BioIn 17*
Kezios, George 1957- *WhoEmL 93*
Kezlarian, Nancy Kay 1948- *WhoAmW 93, WhoEmL 93*
Kezysiak, William F. *St&PR 93*
Kgabo, Englishman M.K. 1925- *WhoAfr*
Khabarov, Yerofey Pavlovich 1610?-1670? *Expl 93*
Khabbaz, Abdallah Morris 1941- *WhoWor 93*
Khacatur d1072? *OxDcByz*
Khachadurian, Avedis 1926- *WhoAm 92*
Khachaturian, Aram (Ilich) 1903-1978 *Baker 92*
Khachaturian, Karen (Surenovich) 1920- *Baker 92*
Khachigian, Kenneth Larry 1944- *WhoAm 92*
Khadafy, Moammar 1942- *BioIn 17*
Khaddam, Abdulhalim 1932- *WhoWor 93*
Khadduri, Farid Majid 1945- *WhoSSW 93*
Khadduri, Majid 1909- *WhoAm 92*
Khader, Basem F. 1938- *WhoUN 92*
Khadra, Sandra Beckley 1948- *WhoAmW 93*
Khadzhiev, Parashkev 1912- *Baker 92*
Khaikin, Boris 1904-1978 *OxDcOp*
Khaikin, Boris (Emmanuilovich) 1904-1978 *Baker 92*
Khain, Victor 1914- *WhoWor 93*
Khairullah, Zahid Yahya 1945- *WhoAm 92, WhoE 93, WhoWor 93*
Khakee, Lois Lynette 1939- *WhoSSW 93*
Khaketla, Bennett Makalo 1914- *WhoAfr*
Khakhlyutin-Tsvetov, Victor Petrovitch 1960- *WhoWor 93*
Khalaf, Ali Ali 1933- *WhoWor 93*
Khalaf, Maria Eugenia 1954- *WhoAmW 93*
Khaldun, Ibn 1332-1406 *BioIn 17*
Khalef, Bachir 1937- *WhoWor 93*
Khalid *OxDcByz*
Khalid, Abdus Samad 1928- *WhoWor 93*
Khalid ibn Abd al-Aziz 1913-1982 *DcTwHis*
Khalifa, Isa bin Sulman Al- *BioIn 17*
Khalifa bin Salman Al-Khalifa, Sheikh 1935- *WhoWor 93*
Khalifah ibn Hamad Al Thani, Amir of Qatar 1932?- *BioIn 17*
Khalil, Hassan Kamal 1950- *WhoAm 92*
Khalil, Khazem el- d1990 *BioIn 17*
Khalil, Michael O. 1954- *WhoAm 92*
Khalil, Samir *BioIn 17*
Khalil, Tarek Mohamed 1941- *WhoAm 92*
Khalique, Abdul 1949- *St&PR 93*
Khalsa, Dayal Kaur *BioIn 17*
Khalsa, Dayal Kaur 1943-1989 *ConAu 137, MajAI [port]*
Khaltaev, Nicolai Gavrilovitch 1947- *WhoUN 92*
Khama, Seretse 1921-1980 *BioIn 17, DcTwHis*
Khambaty, Moiz B. 1934- *St&PR 93*

Khamenei, Hojatoleslam Ali 1940- BioIn 17
Khamenei, Hojatoleslam Ali Hoseini 1940- WhoWor 93
Khamsy, Saly 1931- WhoUN 92, WhoWor 93
Khamtai Siphandon WhoWor 93
Khan, Abdul Haleem 1936- WhoWor 93
Khan, Abdul Jabbar 1937- WhoWor 93
Khan, Abdul Rahim 1953- WhoWor 93
Khan, Abrar Ahmed 1965- WhoAsAP 91
Khan, Adalat 1937- WhoUN 92
Khan, Afaq Husain 1930-1990 BioIn 17
Khan, Ahmed Asghar 1932- WhoUN 92
Khan, Ahmed M. 1955- WhoWor 93
Khan, Akbar Ali 1953- WhoWor 93
Khan, Akhtar Hameed 1913- BioIn 17
Khan, Al-Sameen Tewfik 1961- WhoE 93
Khan, Alamzaib Abdullah 1956- WhoWor 93
Khan, Aman 1958- WhoWor 93
Khan, Amanullah 1940- WhoAm 92
Khan, Amir U. 1927- WhoAm 92
Khan, Arif Mohammad 1951- WhoAsAP 91
Khan, Atiqur Rahman 1937- WhoUN 92
Khan, Chaka 1953- ConMus 9 [port], SoulM, WhoAm 92, WhoAmW 93
Khan, Chaudhry Nasir Ali 1954- WhoWor 93
Khan, Dilawar Ali 1940- WhoUN 92
Khan, Ghani Mohammad 1936- WhoWor 93
Khan, Ghulam Ishaq 1915- WhoAsAP 91, WhoWor 93
Khan, Hamid Hasan 1954- WhoWor 93
Khan, Hamid Raza 1942- WhoWor 93
Khan, Hussain Ahmad 1936- St&PR 93
Khan, Ishrat Husain 1938- St&PR 93
Khan, Ismith 1925- DcLB 125 [port]
Khan, Jamil Akber 1952- WhoE 93
Khan, Jawaid Tariq 1936- WhoWor 93
Khan, Jehangir Alam 1958- WhoEmL 93
Khan, Kalim Ullah 1937- St&PR 93
Khan, Karen Parrott 1955- WhoSSW 93
Khan, Kunwar Aftab Ahmed 1951- WhoWor 93
Khan, Kunwar Mehmood Ali 1920- WhoAsAP 91
Khan, Lutfor Rahman 1950- WhoWor 93
Khan, Mirza Hussain 1952- WhoUN 92
Khan, Mirza Taqi c. 1798-1852 BioIn 17
Khan, Mohammad Asad 1940- WhoAm 92, WhoWor 93
Khan, Mohammad Sayeedur Rahman 1946- WhoWor 93
Khan, Mohammed Nasser 1957- WhoWor 93
Khan, Muhammad Ataullah 1921- WhoWor 93
Khan, Muhammad Ishtiaq 1934- WhoUN 92
Khan, Muhammad Jamil 1932- WhoUN 92
Khan, Mustapha MiSFD 9
Khan, Nazir F. 1945- St&PR 93
Khan, Nurul Islam 1946- WhoAsAP 91
Khan, Obaidullah A.Z.M. 1934- WhoUN 92
Khan, Sadruddin Aga 1933- BioIn 17
Khan, Sahabzada Yaqub 1920- WhoAsAP 91
Khan, Salim Akhtar 1953- WhoWor 93
Khan, Sarbuland 1945- WhoUN 92
Khan, Shahrukh Rafi 1952- WhoE 93
Khan, Sirajul Hossain 1926- WhoAsAP 91
Khan, Sultan Zaman 1932- WhoUN 92
Khanayev, Nikandr 1890-1974 OxDcOp
Khandker Sayeed, Nazmul Hasan 1958- WhoWor 93
Khandoshkin, Ivan (Yevstafievich) 1747-1804 Baker 92
Khandpur, Roshan Lal 1946- WhoEmL 93
Khandwala, Atul S. 1942- St&PR 93
Khang, Chulsoon 1935- WhoAm 92
Khanga, Yelena BioIn 17
Khanin, Yakov Izraelovich 1931- WhoWor 93
Khanna, Deepak Kumar 1944- WhoWor 93
Khanna, Kailash C. 1938- St&PR 93
Khanna, Prabha 1927- WhoAmW 93
Khanna, Sumedha 1938- WhoUN 92
Khanwalkar, Arundhati Law&B 92
Khanzada, Abdul Wahab Khan 1939- WhoWor 93
Khanzadian, Vahan 1939- WhoAm 92
Khaparde, Saroj 1941- WhoAsAP 91
Khaqani 1121?-1199 OxDcByz
Kharasch, Virginia Sison 1956- WhoAmW 93, WhoEmL 93
Khare, Mohan 1942- WhoAm 92, WhoE 93, WhoWor 93
Kharrazi, Kamal 1944- WhoUN 92
Kharrazi, Kamal A. 1944- WhoWor 93
Kharuzin, A.N. 1864-1933 IntDcAn
Kharuzin, M.N. 1860-1888 IntDcAn
Kharuzin, N.N. 1865-1900 IntDcAn
Kharuzina, V.N. 1866-1931 IntDcAn
Khasbulatov, Ruslan WhoWor 93
Khashoggi, Adnan BioIn 17
Khatami, Elizabeth Cabral 1964- WhoEmL 93
Khatami, Mahin 1943- WhoAmW 93
Khatchadourian, George M. 1937- WhoUN 92
Khatena, Joe ConAu 39NR
Khatena, Joe 1925- WhoSSW 93
Khatena, Joseph 1925- ConAu 39NR
Khatib, Ghassan 1962- WhoE 93, WhoEmL 93
Khattab, Carol Fults d1990 BioIn 17
Khattak, Chandra P. 1944- St&PR 93
Khattak, Jehangir Khan 1937- WhoWor 93
Khattak, Tariq Ali 1962- WhoWor 93
Khatun, Kumari Sayeeda 1944- WhoAsAP 91
Khayat, Azeez Victor 1933- WhoE 93
Khayatt, Shaker Albert 1935- WhoAm 92
Khazan, Lorraine 1947- WhoEmL 93
Khazarian, Roxanne Law&B 92
Khazeh, Khashayar 1948- WhoE 93
Khazei, Amir Moshen 1928- WhoE 93
Khedouri, Marc Mitchell 1963- WhoSSW 93
Kheel, Theodore Woodrow 1914- WhoAm 92
Kheifits, Alexander Israelevitch 1944- WhoWor 93
Kheireddin, Khideiwi Hussein 1949- WhoWor 93
Kher, Bal Gangadhar 1888-1957 BioIn 17
Kheradi, Sohrab 1938- WhoUN 92
Kherdian, David 1931- BioIn 17, ConAu 39NR, MajAI [port], WhoAm 92, WhoWrEP 92
Khevenhuller, Ludwig Andreas von 1683-1744 HarEnMi
Khieu, Samphan 1932- WhoAsAP 91
Khiev, Virak BioIn 17
Khilnani, Jashan Rewachand F. 1930- WhoWor 93
Khim, Jay Wook 1940- WhoAm 92, WhoWor 93
Khimjee, Mohamed Suleman 1930- WhoWor 93
Khlebnikov, K.T. 1784-1838 IntDcAn
Khlebnikov, Nikolai Nikolaevich 1947- WhoUN 92
Khleifi, Michel MiSFD 9
Khlobystov, Vladimir Vladmirovich 1939- WhoWor 93
Khmelevskaja-Plotnikova, Galina 1936- WhoScE 91-2
Khng, Thomas Hong-Choon 1939- WhoWor 93
Kho, Chin Seng 1956- WhoWor 93
Kho, Eusebio 1933- WhoWor 93
Khodr, Khalil Ortiz, Jr. 1950- WhoWor 93
Khodzha-Einatov, Leon 1904-1954 Baker 92
Khoe, Giok-djan 1946- WhoWor 93
Khoei, Abolqassem al- d1992 NewYTBS 92 [port]
Khokhlov, Pavel 1854-1919 OxDcOp
Khokhlov, Pavel (Akinfievich) 1854-1919 Baker 92
Khokhlov, Vitaly Sergeyevich 1938- WhoWor 93
Khol, Josef 1928- WhoScE 91-4
Khol, Ronald 1935- WhoAm 92
Kholoussy, A. Mohsen 1947- WhoAm 92
Khomeini, Ruholla 1900-1989 DcTwHis
Khomeini, Ruholla Musavi 1902-1989 ColdWar 2 [port]
Khomeini, Ruhollah BioIn 17
Khoo, Boon-Hor WhoScE 91-1
Khoraiche, Antoine Pierre Cardinal 1907- WhoAm 92, WhoWor 93
Khorana, Har Gobind 1922- WhoAm 92, WhoE 93, WhoWor 93
Khorana, Satish C. 1953- WhoUN 92
Khoroche, Peter (Andrew) 1947- ConAu 136
Khosh, Mary Sivert 1942- WhoAmW 93
Khoshdel, Ezat 1949- WhoWor 93
Khosla, Rajinder Paul 1933- WhoAm 92
Khosla, Sheelkumar Lalchand 1934- WhoWor 93
Khosla, Ved Mitter 1926- WhoAm 92, WhoWor 93
Khosrovi, Behzad 1944- St&PR 93
Khouadja, Habib 1930- WhoUN 92
Khoudonazarov, Doviat BioIn 17
Khoueiri, Sami C. 1960- St&PR 93
Khouini, Hamadi 1943- WhoUN 92
Khouri, Callie BioIn 17
Khouri, Callie Ann 1957- WhoAmW 93
Khouri, Charles Hanna 1942- WhoSSW 93
Khouri, Clifford Philip 1961- WhoSSW 93
Khouri, Fred John 1916- WhoAm 92, WhoWor 93
Khouri, Margaret Rose 1949- WhoAmW 93
Khouri, Michael A. Law&B 92
Khoury, Admin J. St&PR 93
Khoury, Henry B. 1947- WhoEmL 93
Khoury, Kale Charles 1942- WhoSSW 93
Khoury, Kenneth Law&B 92
Khoury, Kenneth F. Law&B 92
Khoury, Nancy Litaker 1943- WhoAmW 93
Khouw, Boen Tie 1934- WhoWor 93
Khouzam, Hani Raoul 1950- WhoEmL 93, WhoSSW 93
Khouzani, Michel 1929- WhoUN 92
Khrennikov, Andrew Yurievich 1958- WhoWor 93
Khrennikov, Tikhon 1913- OxDcOp
Khrennikov, Tikhon (Nikolaievich) 1913- Baker 92
Khrennikov, Tikhon Nikolayevich 1913- WhoWor 93
Khrissanoff, Sergey Mark 1948- WhoWor 93
Khromchenko, Solomon 1907- OxDcOp
Khruschev, Nikita 1894-1971 BioIn 17
Khrushchev, Nikita S. 1894-1971 ColdWar 2 [port]
Khrushchev, Nikita Sergeevich 1894-1971 BioIn 17
Khrushchev, Nikita Sergeyevich 1894-1971 DcTwHis
Khrushchev, Sergei (Nikitich) 1935- ConAu 136
Khubeis, Isa George 1934- WhoWor 93
Khubov, Georgi (Nikitich) 1902-1981 Baker 92
Khudonazarov, Dovlat BioIn 17
Khuhro, Shafiq Ahmed 1943- WhoWor 93
Khun Sa BioIn 17
Khurana, Sat Pal 1942- St&PR 93
Khuri, Nicola Najib 1933- WhoAm 92
Khusainov, Denis Yakhjevich 1946- WhoWor 93
Khush, Gurdev Singh 1935- WhoWor 93
Khvorostiany, Igor M. 1945- WhoUN 92
Ki, M.F. Leonie 1949- WhoWor 93
Kiam, Victor K., II BioIn 17
Kiam, Victor K., II 1926- St&PR 93
Kiam, Victor Kermit, II 1926- WhoAm 92
Kiang, Assumpta 1939- WhoWor 93
Kiang, Lindsey Law&B 92
Kiang, Nelson Yuan-Sheng 1929- WhoAm 92
Kiang, Robert L. 1939- WhoE 93
Kiang, Tao 1928- WhoScE 91-3
Kiani, Rukhsana J. Law&B 92
Kias, Thomas Nelson 1942- WhoSSW 93
Kibaki, Mwai 1931- WhoAfr, WhoWor 93
Kibasi, K.T. WhoScE 91-1
Kibbe, James William 1926- WhoAm 92, WhoE 93
Kibbe, Margaret AmWomPl
Kibbe, Pat BioIn 17
Kibbee, Chandler H. 1907-1992 BioIn 17
Kibble, Thomas Walter Bannerman WhoScE 91-1
Kibble-Smith, Brian Law&B 92
Kibblewhite, Edward James 1944- WhoAm 92
Kibblewhite, M. 1952- WhoScE 91-1
Kibby, Claude Anson 1949- WhoEmL 93
Kibe, Yoshiaki 1926- WhoAsAP 91
Kibiloski, Floyd Terry 1946- WhoSSW 93
Kibler, Craig Morton 1952- WhoSSW 93
Kibler, Gary Albin 1943- St&PR 93
Kibler, James Everett, Jr. 1944- WhoWrEP 92
Kibler, Larry R. 1952- WhoSSW 93
Kibler, Larry Warren 1947- St&PR 93
Kibler, Virginia Elaine 1951- WhoAmW 93, WhoEmL 93
Kibler, Virginia Mary 1960- WhoAmW 93
Kibler, Wallace Edward 1936- WhoWrEP 92
Kibor, Joseph BioIn 17
Kibria, Shah A.M.S. 1931- WhoUN 92
Kibrick, Anne 1919- WhoAm 92, WhoAmW 93
Kice, James V. 1925- St&PR 93
Kice, John Edward 1949- St&PR 93
Kicher, Thomas Patrick 1937- WhoAm 92
Kichler, Benita K. Law&B 92
Kichline, Diane Donchez 1957- WhoEmL 93
Kickbusch, Ilona Senta 1948- WhoUN 92
Kickham, Michael Francis 1929- St&PR 91
Kicking Bear BioIn 17
Kickish, Margaret Elizabeth 1949- WhoAmW 93
Kickler, James A. WhoIns 93
Kickler, James Arnold 1927- St&PR 93, WhoAm 92
Kicklighter, Claude Milton 1933- WhoAm 92
Kicklighter, Clois Earl 1939- WhoAm 92
Kicklighter, Tina WhoAmW 93
Kicknosway, Faye 1936- WhoWrEP 92
Kid BioIn 17
Kida, Eugene 1944- St&PR 93
Kida, Teruhiko 1941- WhoWor 93
Kidalowski, Raymond John 1946- WhoE 93
Kid Antrim BioIn 17
Kidawa, Anthony Stanley 1942- WhoE 93
Kid Capri BioIn 17
Kid Curry c. 1867-c. 1910 BioIn 17
Kidd, A. Duncan 1931- WhoAm 92
Kidd, A.F. 1953- ScF&FL 92
Kidd, A. Paul 1939- WhoAm 92
Kidd, Adam 1802-1831 BioIn 17
Kidd, Agnes Juanita 1918- WhoAmW 93
Kidd, Cecil WhoScE 91-1
Kidd, Charles Vincent 1914- WhoAm 92
Kidd, David C. Law&B 92
Kidd, Debra Jean 1956- WhoAmW 93, WhoWor 93
Kidd, Doug 1941- WhoAsAP 91
Kidd, Douglas Law&B 92
Kidd, Gerald Steele, II 1945- WhoAm 92
Kidd, James F. 1939- St&PR 93
Kidd, James M., Jr. St&PR 93
Kidd, Jocelyn Denise 1958- WhoSSW 93
Kidd, John Edward 1936- WhoAm 92
Kidd, John F. 1931- St&PR 93
Kidd, John Graydon 1908-1991 BioIn 17
Kidd, John W. BioIn 17
Kidd, Langford 1931- WhoAm 92
Kidd, Lawrie K. 1931- St&PR 93
Kidd, Mary Frix AmWomPl
Kidd, Michael WhoAm 92
Kidd, Michael 1919- ConTFT 10, MiSFD 9
Kidd, Nancy Van Tries 1933- WhoAmW 93, WhoSSW 93
Kidd, Patricia Eileen 1952- WhoEmL 93
Kidd, Rebecca Montgomery 1942- WhoAm 92, WhoWor 93
Kidd, Rita Carolyn 1943- WhoAmW 93
Kidd, Rita Gail 1947- WhoAmW 93
Kidd, Robert H. 1944- St&PR 93
Kidd, Robert Hugh 1944- WhoAm 92
Kidd, Ronald 1948- ConAu 39NR, DcAmChF 1985, ScF&FL 92
Kidd, Rosemary 1945- WhoAmW 93
Kidd, Sandra B. Law&B 92
Kidd, Sandra Karen 1958- WhoSSW 93
Kidd, Vallee Melvina 1918- WhoSSW 93
Kidd, Virginia 1921- ScF&FL 92
Kidd, Walter L. d1990 BioIn 17
Kidd, William 1803-1867 BioIn 17
Kidd, William Matthew 1918- WhoAm 92
Kidd, Wilmot Higgins, III 1941- St&PR 93
Kidde, Janet ScF&FL 92
Kidde, John Lyon 1934- St&PR 93, WhoAm 92
Kidder, Alfred V. 1885-1963 IntDcAn
Kidder, Augusta Raymond d1939 AmWomPl
Kidder, C. Robert 1943- WhoE 93
Kidder, C. Robert 1944- St&PR 93
Kidder, Charles Louis Law&B 92
Kidder, Fred D. Law&B 92
Kidder, Fred Dockstater 1922- WhoAm 92
Kidder, John Newell 1932- WhoAm 92
Kidder, Jonathan Edward, Jr. 1922- WhoWor 93
Kidder, Margot BioIn 17
Kidder, Margot 1948- WhoAm 92, WhoAmW 93
Kidder, Nancy Louise 1945- WhoAmW 93
Kidder, Norman Kent 1951- St&PR 93
Kidder, Priscilla St&PR 93
Kidder, Rex E. Law&B 92
Kidder, Tracy BioIn 17
Kidder, Tracy 1945- ConAu 40NR
Kidder, Virelle Fransecky 1945- WhoWrEP 92
Kiddoo, Richard Clyde 1927- WhoSSW 93
Kideckel, Arnold 1939- WhoIns 93
Kideckel, David Arthur 1948- WhoE 93
Kidera, George Jerome 1913- WhoAm 92
Kidera, Geralyn Ann Law&B 92
Kiderlen-Waechter, Alfred von 1852-1912 BioIn 17
Kidman, Nicole BioIn 17
Kidman, Nicole 1967- News 92 [port]
Kidman, Nicole 1968?- ConTFT 10
Kidner, John 1923- ScF&FL 92
Kidnie, B. St&PR 93
Kidron, Beeban MiSFD 9
Kidson, Frank 1855-1926 Baker 92
Kidston, Alan R. Law&B 92
Kidston, Alan R. 1928- St&PR 93
Kidwai, Mohd. Hashim 1921- WhoAsAP 91
Kidwell, C. Harold d1991 BioIn 17
Kidwell, Carl James Law&B 92
Kidwell, David Stephen 1940- WhoAm 92
Kidwell, Eric Allen 1961- WhoSSW 93
Kidybinski, Antoni 1934- WhoScE 91-4
Kiebala, Susan Marie 1952- WhoAmW 93
Kiechlin, Robert Jerome 1919- WhoAm 92
Kieckhaefer, William Frederick 1950- WhoEmL 93
Kieckhafer, Thomas William 1938- St&PR 93
Kieckhefer, Guy Norton 1926- St&PR 93
Kieckhefer, James R. Law&B 92
Kiedaisch, Howard G. 1945- St&PR 93
Kiedis, Anthony BioIn 17

Kiedis, Anthony c. 1963- *See* Red Hot Chili Peppers, The *News 93-1*
Kiedrowski, Dale Michael 1950- *St&PR 93*
Kiedrowski, P. Jay 1949- *St&PR 93*
Kief, Horst Rolf 1931- *WhoUN 92*
Kief, Paul Allan 1934- *WhoAm 92*
Kiefaber, John McReynolds 1950- *St&PR 93*
Kiefaber, Warner H., Jr. 1917- *St&PR 93*
Kiefaber, Warner H., III 1942- *St&PR 93*
Kiefer, Alfons *BioIn 17*
Kiefer, Alfred G., Jr. *Law&B 92*
Kiefer, Alfred W. 1912- *St&PR 93*
Kiefer, Allen E. 1943- *St&PR 93*
Kiefer, Anselm 1945- *BioIn 17*
Kiefer, Carl Omer 1942- *St&PR 93*
Kiefer, Charles F. 1950- *St&PR 93*
Kiefer, Daniel M. 1954- *St&PR 93*
Kiefer, George Gerard 1942- *WhoSSW 93*
Kiefer, J. Richard, Jr. 1928- *WhoE 93*
Kiefer, Juergen 1936- *WhoWor 93*
Kiefer, Jurgen 1936- *WhoScE 91-3*
Kiefer, Kit Annette 1958- *WhoAmW 93, WhoEmL 93*
Kiefer, Klaus Heinrich 1947- *WhoWor 93*
Kiefer, Lawrence B. *Law&B 92*
Kiefer, Peter Charles 1964- *WhoSSW 93*
Kiefer, Raymond H. 1927- *WhoAm 92, WhoIns 93*
Kiefer, Renata Gertrud 1946- *WhoAmW 93*
Kiefer, Richard Otto 1937- *St&PR 93*
Kiefer, Stanley Clarence 1941- *St&PR 93*
Kiefer, Walter G. 1911- *St&PR 93*
Kiefer, William Ray *Law&B 92*
Kiefer, Wolfgang 1941- *WhoScE 91-3, WhoWor 93*
Kiefert, Alice Stockwell 1929- *WhoAmW 93*
Kieff, Elliott Dan 1943- *WhoAm 92*
Kieffer, Barbara 1952- *St&PR 93*
Kieffer, Burton L. 1919- *St&PR 93*
Kieffer, Donald Frederic 1934- *WhoSSW 93*
Kieffer, James Milton 1921- *WhoAm 92*
Kieffer, Jarold Alan 1923- *WhoAm 92*
Kieffer, Joyce Loretta 1940- *WhoAm 92*
Kieffer, Patrick M. 1922- *WhoAm 92*
Kieffer, Richard William 1937- *St&PR 93*
Kieffer, Robert C. *Law&B 92*
Kieffer, Stephen Aaron 1935- *WhoAm 92, WhoE 93*
Kieffer, Susan Werner 1942- *WhoAm 92, WhoAmW 93*
Kieffer, Townsend T. d1990 *BioIn 17*
Kieffer, William Franklinn 1915- *WhoAm 92*
Kieffer-Andrews, Marilyn Joanne 1947- *WhoEmL 93*
Kiefner, John Robert, Jr. 1946- *WhoEmL 93*
Kieft, Gerald Nelson 1946- *WhoEmL 93*
Kiegiel, Christina Theresa 1965- *WhoAmW 93*
Kiehl, Victoria A. *Law&B 92*
Kiehle, John A. *ScF&FL 92*
Kiehne, Anna Marie 1947- *WhoEmL 93*
Kiehne, Frank Charles, Jr. 1925- *WhoWor 93*
Kiehne, Thomas Merill 1947- *WhoSSW 93*
Kiekel, William Edward 1939- *St&PR 93*
Kiel, Edward J. 1938- *St&PR 93*
Kiel, Frederick Orin 1942- *WhoAm 92*
Kiel, Friedrich 1821-1885 *Baker 92*
Kiel, Geoffrey Charles 1949- *WhoWor 93*
Kiel, Paul N. *Law&B 92*
Kiel, Paul N. 1942- *St&PR 93*
Kielbas, Robert S. 1950- *St&PR 93*
Kielbasa, Richard Francois 1947- *WhoScE 91-2*
Kielholz, Paul 1916-1990 *BioIn 17*
Kielland, Axel 1951- *WhoWor 93*
Kielland, Olav 1901-1985 *Baker 92*
Kielland-Brandt, Morten C. 1944- *WhoScE 91-2*
Kielsky, Michael Gerd 1964- *WhoEmL 93*
Kielsmeier, Catherine Jane *WhoAmW 93*
Kielty, Edward Robert 1945- *St&PR 93*
Kielty, John Lawrence, III 1943- *WhoAm 92*
Kielty, William R. 1937- *St&PR 93*
Kiely, Dan R. 1944- *St&PR 93*
Kiely, Dan Ray 1944- *WhoAm 92, WhoE 93*
Kiely, Julia Anne *WhoScE 91-1*
Kiely, Michael Hughes 1944- *WhoE 93*
Kiely, Patrick J. 1951- *St&PR 93*
Kiely, Philip G. *Law&B 92*
Kiely, William L. 1942- *St&PR 93*
Kiemle, Fred William, Jr. 1934- *WhoSSW 93*
Kien, Truong Thai 1933- *WhoScE 91-2*
Kienast, Bill 1931-1984 *BioIn 17*
Kienast, Wallace Frank Elliott 1923- *St&PR 93*
Kienast Family *BioIn 17*
Kienbaum, Karen Smith *Law&B 92*
Kienbaum, Thomas Gerd 1942- *WhoAm 92*
Kiener, Eduard *WhoScE 91-4*
Kiener, Eduard 1938- *WhoScE 91-4*
Kiener, Mary Elaine 1950- *WhoAmW 93, WhoEmL 93*
Kieninger, Richard George 1927- *WhoWrEP 92*
Kienitz, Karl Heinz 1961- *WhoWor 93*
Kienle, Paul 1931- *WhoScE 91-3*
Kienle, Richard W. *Law&B 92*
Kientz, Roland Charles 1956- *WhoWor 93*
Kieny, Albert Joseph, Jr. 1924- *St&PR 93*
Kienzl, Wilhelm 1857-1941 *Baker 92, OxDcOp*
Kienzle, Susan Smart *Law&B 92*
Kienzle, William X. 1928- *BioIn 17*
Kieper, David Glenn 1959- *WhoEmL 93*
Kiepert, Donniece Ann 1957- *WhoEmL 93, WhoSSW 93*
Kiepper, James Julius 1933- *WhoE 93*
Kiepura, Jan 1902-1966 *Baker 92, IntDcOp, OxDcOp, PolBiDi [port]*
Kier, Ann B. 1949- *WhoEmL 93*
Kier, Kearney Kay 1936- *St&PR 93*
Kier, Lady Miss *BioIn 17*
Kier, Porter Martin 1927- *WhoAm 92*
Kier, Porter Sawyer 1935- *WhoAm 92*
Kierans, Thomas *BioIn 17*
Kieren, Thomas Henry 1941- *St&PR 93, WhoAm 92*
Kierig, Paul Nicholas *Law&B 92*
Kierkegaard, Carl Peder J.H. 1928- *WhoScE 91-4*
Kierkegaard, Peter 1932- *WhoScE 91-2*
Kierkegaard, Søren 1813-1855 *BioIn 17*
Kierman, Steven Wayne 1950- *St&PR 93*
Kiermayer, Oswald 1930- *WhoScE 91-4*
Kiernan, Christopher 1960- *St&PR 93*
Kiernan, Edwin A., Jr. 1926- *WhoAm 92*
Kiernan, Henry Gerard 1951- *WhoE 93*
Kiernan, Jerald Robert 1945- *St&PR 93*
Kiernan, John E. *Law&B 92*
Kiernan, John Edward 1967- *WhoE 93*
Kiernan, John J. 1926- *St&PR 93*
Kiernan, Marmy C. G. 1956- *WhoAmW 93, WhoEmL 93*
Kiernan, Michael James 1963- *WhoE 93*
Kiernan, Owen Burns 1914- *WhoAm 92*
Kiernan, Peter DeLacy, III 1953- *WhoAm 92*
Kiernan, Peter Joseph 1939- *St&PR 93*
Kiernan, Richard Francis 1935- *WhoAm 92*
Kiernan, Sarah A. *Law&B 92*
Kiernan, William Joseph, Jr. 1932- *WhoAm 92, WhoSSW 93*
Kierniesky, Nicholas Charles 1943- *WhoE 93*
Kieronska, Dorota Helena 1965- *WhoWor 93*
Kiersch, Fritz 1951- *MiSFD 9*
Kiersch, George Alfred 1918- *WhoAm 92, WhoWor 93*
Kierscht, Charles Mason 1939- *St&PR 93*
Kierscht, Marcia Selland *WhoAmW 93*
Kierski, Jozef 1935- *WhoUN 92, WhoWor 93*
Kierstan, M.P.J. *WhoScE 91-1*
Kierulff, Charles Taylor 1919- *WhoWrEP 92*
Kierulff, Stephen 1942- *WhoWrEP 92*
Kierzkowski, John Philip 1939- *St&PR 93*
Kies, Constance Virginia 1934- *WhoAmW 93*
Kies, Cosette 1936- *ScF&FL 92*
Kies, Cosette Nell 1936- *WhoAm 92*
Kies, Frederick Karl 1941- *St&PR 93*
Kieschnick, Michael Hall 1953- *ConAu 139*
Kieselmann, Gerhard Maria 1956- *WhoWor 93*
Kieselstein-Cord, Barry *BioIn 17*
Kieser, Ellwood E. 1929- *ConTFT 10*
Kieser, Nita Irene 1960- *St&PR 93*
Kieser, William 1926- *St&PR 93*
Kiesewetter, Raphael Georg 1773-1850 *Baker 92*
Kiesewetter, Tomasz 1911 *Baker 92*
Kiesinger, Kurt Georg 1904-1988 *ColdWar 1 [port], DcTwHis*
Kiesler, Charles A. 1934- *BioIn 17*
Kiesler, Charles Adolphus 1934- *WhoAm 92, WhoSSW 93*
Kieslich, F.O. Klaus 1929- *WhoScE 91-3*
Kiesling, Ernst Willie 1934- *WhoAm 92*
Kiesling, Gerald K. 1933- *St&PR 93*
Kiesling, Gerald Kenneth 1933- *WhoIns 93*
Kiesling, Walt 1903-1962 *BioIn 17*
Kieslowski, Krzysztof 1941- *BioIn 17, DrEEuF, MiSFD 9*
Kiest, Alan Scott 1949- *WhoEmL 93, WhoWor 93*
Kiest, Lauren J. 1932- *St&PR 93*
Kieule, Paul *WhoScE 91-3*
Kiever, Paul K. 1946- *St&PR 93*
Kievman, Louis 1910-1990 *BioIn 17*
Kiewra, Gustave Paul 1943- *WhoSSW 93*
Kifer, Alan Craig 1952- *WhoWor 93*
Kiffney, V. Robert *Law&B 92*
Kiflom, Adiam *BioIn 17*
Kifner, John William 1941- *WhoAm 92*
Kift, Philip S. *Law&B 92*
Kiger, Joseph Charles 1920- *WhoAm 92, WhoWor 93*
Kiger, Patrick Joseph 1957- *WhoE 93*
Kiggen, James D. 1932- *St&PR 93*
Kiggins, Gilbert M. 1931- *WhoAm 92*
Kiggins, Gilbert Macgillivray 1931- *St&PR 93*
Kiggins, Mildred L. 1927- *WhoAmW 93*
Kight, Charles Walter, III 1938- *St&PR 93*
Kight, Douglas Paul *Law&B 92*
Kight, Edward H. 1935- *St&PR 93*
Kight, Edward Hill 1935- *WhoAm 92*
Kight, James Alan 1950- *St&PR 93*
Kight, Peter J. *St&PR 93*
Kight, Robert Wallace 1947- *WhoSSW 93*
Kightlinger, Ray Milton 1931- *St&PR 93*
Kigin, Thomas Edward 1928- *St&PR 93*
Kigin, Thomas John *Law&B 92*
Kigoshi, Kunihiko 1919- *WhoWor 93*
Kigoshi, Yasutsama 1854-1932 *HarEnMi*
Kiguchi, Hiroko 1958- *St&PR 93*
Kihara, Yasuki 1955- *WhoWor 93*
Kihira, Teiko 1928- *WhoAsAP 91*
Kihlborg, Lars H.E. 1930- *WhoScE 91-4*
Kihle, Donald Arthur 1934- *WhoSSW 93, WhoWor 93*
Kihlman, Bengt Anders 1922- *WhoScE 91-4*
Kihlman, Tor Staffan Daniel 1934- *WhoScE 91-4*
Kihlstrom, Jan Erik 1928- *WhoScE 91-4*
Kihn, Harry 1912- *WhoAm 92, WhoWor 93*
Kiil, Fredrik 1921- *WhoScE 91-4*
Kiil, Leevi 1940- *St&PR 93*
Kijac, Peter 1932- *St&PR 93*
Kijanka, Theodore H. 1942- *St&PR 93*
Kijima, Hideo 1946- *WhoAsAP 91*
Kijima, Kiyohiko 1917- *Baker 92*
Kijiner, Thomas D. *WhoWor 93*
Kijko, Andrzej 1948- *WhoScE 91-4*
Kijlstra, Aize 1950- *WhoScE 91-3*
Kijowski, Janusz 1948- *DrEEuF*
Kijowski, Jerzy 1943- *WhoScE 91-4*
Kikel, Rudy John 1942- *WhoWrEP 92*
Kiken, Norman Paul 1942- *St&PR 93*
Kiker, Billy Frazier 1936- *WhoAm 92*
Kiker, Douglas *BioIn 17*
Kiki de Montparnasse 1901-1953? *BioIn 17*
Kikiewicz, Zbigniew 1924- *WhoScE 91-4*
Kikkawa, Akikazu 1937- *St&PR 93*
Kikkawa, Jiro 1929- *WhoWor 93*
Kikkawa, Motoharu 1530-1586 *HarEnMi*
Kikkawa-Ward, Carol Hiroko 1938- *WhoAmW 93*
Kiko, Princess of Japan *BioIn 17*
Kiko, Philip George 1951- *WhoAm 92*
Kikoine, Gerard *MiSFD 9*
Kikol, John Charles 1944- *St&PR 93*
Kikuchi, Kazuhiro 1934- *WhoWor 93*
Kikuchi, Makoto 1925- *BioIn 17*
Kikuchi, Takemitsu d1373 *HarEnMi*
Kikuchi, Taketomo 1363-1407 *HarEnMi*
Kikuchi, Toru 1944- *St&PR 93*
Kikutake, Kiyonori 1928- *WhoWor 93*
Kilachand, Rajen Arvind 1950- *WhoWor 93*
Kiladze, Grigori 1902-1962 *Baker 92*
Kilambi, Raghu 1965- *St&PR 93*
Kilanowski, Michael C., Jr. *Law&B 92*
Kilanowski, Michael Charles, Jr. 1948- *WhoAm 92*
Kilar, Wojciech 1932- *Baker 92*
Kilarski, Wincenty Michal 1931- *WhoScE 91-4*
Kilb, Jenny 1952- *WhoAmW 93*
Kilbane, Mary Ellen 1953- *WhoAmW 93*
Kilbane, Thomas Stanton 1941- *WhoAm 92*
Kilberg, James Anthony 1956- *WhoSSW 93*
Kilberg, William Jeffrey 1946- *WhoAm 92*
Kilbinger, Heinz 1939- *WhoScE 91-3*
Kilbom, Asa 1938- *WhoScE 91-4*
Kilborn, Gary Lee 1947- *WhoE 93*
Kilborne, Frances McDonald *Law&B 92*
Kilborne, William Skinner 1912- *WhoAm 92*
Kilbourne, Barbara Jean 1941- *WhoAmW 93*
Kilbourne, Clara Anne 1939- *WhoWrEP 92*
Kilbourne, Douglas M. 1948- *St&PR 93*
Kilbourne, Edwin Dennis 1920- *WhoAm 92*
Kilbourne, John Dwight 1926- *WhoAm 92*
Kilbourne, John Halliday *Law&B 92*
Kilbourne, Lewis Buckner 1947- *WhoAm 92*
Kilbourne, R. Stewart d1992 *NewYTBS 92 [port]*
Kilbourne, William Truman 1934- *St&PR 93, WhoAm 92*
Kilbride, Beryl Smith 1938- *WhoAmW 93*
Kilbride, James J. 1934- *WhoIns 93*
Kilbuck, John H. 1920- *St&PR 93*
Kilburg, Carol Sue 1956- *St&PR 93*
Kilburn, Bettina Baechtold 1956- *WhoAmW 93*
Kilburn, Donald C. 1956- *WhoAm 92, WhoE 93*
Kilburn, Edwin A. *Law&B 92*
Kilburn, Edwin A. 1933- *St&PR 93*
Kilburn, Edwin Allen 1933- *WhoAm 92*
Kilburn, H. Thomas, Jr. 1931- *St&PR 93*
Kilburn, Henry Thomas, Jr. 1931- *WhoAm 92*
Kilburn, Mary Helen 1945- *WhoAmW 93*
Kilburn, Penelope White 1940- *WhoE 93*
Kilby, Clyde S. 1902-1986 *ScF&FL 92*
Kilby, Jack St. Clair *BioIn 17*
Kilby, Jack St. Clair 1923- *WhoAm 92*
Kilby, Marilyn Frances 1940- *WhoSSW 93*
Kilcarr, J. Kenneth 1918- *WhoAm 92*
Kilcline, Thomas John 1925- *WhoAm 92*
Kilcoyne, John Francis 1922- *St&PR 93*
Kilcup, Clara Griego 1960- *WhoEmL 93*
Kilcur, James Francis *Law&B 92*
Kildare, Earl of d1513 *BioIn 17*
Kildare, H. Bernard 1919- *St&PR 93*
Kilde, Jeanne Halgren 1957- *WhoAmW 93*
Kildeberg, Poul 1930- *WhoScE 91-2*
Kildee, Dale E. 1929- *CngDr 91*
Kildee, Dale Edward 1929- *WhoAm 92*
Kildreff, John P. *Law&B 92*
Kildsig, Nancy Evaline 1936- *WhoAmW 93*
Kilduff, Brian Lawrence 1945- *St&PR 93*
Kile, Carol Ann 1946- *WhoAmW 93*
Kile, Deborah Ann *Law&B 92*
Kile, James Frederick *Law&B 92*
Kile, James Kevin 1957- *St&PR 93*
Kile, Laura Kellers 1967- *WhoAmW 93*
Kile, Raymond Lawrence 1946- *WhoEmL 93*
Kile, Thomas Charles 1946- *St&PR 93*
Kileen, Charles Michel 1942- *St&PR 93*
Kilenyi, Edward, Sr. 1884-1968 *Baker 92*
Kilenyi, Edward, Jr. 1910- *Baker 92*
Kiley, Constance Schrader 1939- *St&PR 93*
Kiley, Daniel Urban 1912- *WhoAm 92*
Kiley, James William 1944- *WhoAm 92*
Kiley, Kristina *Law&B 92*
Kiley, Matthew Peter 1965- *WhoSSW 93*
Kiley, Richard Paul 1922- *WhoAm 92*
Kilfiger, Marcel Ernest 1924- *WhoWor 93*
Kilga, Rainer 1934- *WhoScE 91-4*
Kilgore, Axel *ScF&FL 92*
Kilgore, Bernard 1908-1967 *DcLB 127 [port]*
Kilgore, Donald Gibson, Jr. 1927- *WhoAm 92, WhoSSW 93, WhoWor 93*
Kilgore, Edwin Carroll 1923- *WhoAm 92*
Kilgore, Eugene Sterling, Jr. 1920- *WhoAm 92*
Kilgore, Jeffrey Harper 1948- *WhoSSW 93*
Kilgore, Jerry G. 1945- *St&PR 93*
Kilgore, Joe Madison 1918- *WhoAm 92*
Kilgore, John Edward, Jr. 1921- *WhoAm 92*
Kilgore, Jon W. 1943- *St&PR 93*
Kilgore, Kathleen 1946- *ScF&FL 92*
Kilgore, Marion Dewey 1936- *WhoSSW 93*
Kilgore, Mary Catherine 1965- *WhoAmW 93*
Kilgore, Sarah Elizabeth 1961- *WhoAmW 93*
Kilgore, William Jackson 1917- *WhoAm 92, WhoWor 93*
Kilgour, Alistair C. *WhoScE 91-1*
Kilgour, Frederick Gridley 1914- *WhoAm 92, WhoWor 93*
Kilgriff, Stephen P. *Law&B 92*
Kilgus, Edward Louis 1920- *St&PR 93*
Kilgus, Lowell Keith 1945- *St&PR 93*
Kilguss, George E. 1934- *St&PR 93*
Kilgust, Mary Lynn 1955- *WhoAm 92*
Kilham, Walter H., Jr. 1904- *WhoAm 92*
Kilhenny, Valerie J. *Law&B 92*
Kilian, Crawford 1941- *ScF&FL 92, WhoCanL 92, WhoWrEP 92*
Kilian, David P. *Law&B 92*
Kilian, Jurgen E. 1937- *WhoScE 91-3*
Kilian, Michael D. 1939- *WhoAm 92*
Kilian, Walter 1932- *WhoScE 91-4*
Kilic, A. Ulvi 1927- *WhoScE 91-4*
Kilic Arslan, I d1107 *OxDcByz*
Kilic Arslan, II c. 1115-1192 *OxDcByz*
Kilimnik, Kenneth S. *Law&B 92*
Kilimnik, Robert F. 1947- *St&PR 93*
Kilinski, Jan 1760-1819 *PolBiDi*
Kilkeary, John 1932- *WhoIns 93*
Kilkeary, Martin J. *Law&B 92*
Kilkeary, Nan 1943- *WhoWrEP 92*
Kilkeary, Nan M. 1943- *WhoWor 93*
Kilkelly, Brian Holten 1943- *WhoSSW 93*

Kilkelly, Marjorie Lee 1954- *WhoAmW 93*
Kilkenny, John F. 1901- *WhoAm 92*
Kilkenny, John J. *Law&B 92*
Kilkenny, John Jude 1950- *WhoEmL 93*
Kilkka, Kenneth M. 1952- *St&PR 93*
Kilkki, Pekka Juhani *WhoScE 91-4*
Kill, Lawrence 1935- *WhoAm 92*
Kill, Lisa Karen *Law&B 92*
Kill, Robert H. 1947- *St&PR 93*
Killaly, Laurence MacDonald *Law&B 92*
Killam, Candis Louise 1956- *WhoAmW 93*
Killam, Eva King 1921- *WhoAm 92*
Killander, Dick C.F. 1937- *WhoScE 91-4*
Killanin, Lord 1914- *WhoWor 93*
Kille, C.A. 1929- *St&PR 93*
Kille, Mary Jean 1937- *WhoAmW 93*
Kille, Willard Bronson, III 1946- *WhoEmL 93, WhoSSW 93, WhoWor 93*
Killea, Lucy Lytle 1922- *WhoAmW 93*
Killebrew, Ellen Jane 1937- *WhoAmW 93*
Killebrew, Flavius Charles 1949- *WhoSSW 93*
Killebrew, George Buckley 1939- *St&PR 93*
Killebrew, Gwendolyn 1939- *Baker 92*
Killebrew, Harmon 1936- *BioIn 17*
Killebrew, Harmon Clayton 1936- *WhoAm 92*
Killebrew, James Robert 1918- *WhoAm 92, WhoSSW 93*
Killeen, Alan R. 1934- *St&PR 93*
Killeen, Claire Favrot 1931- *WhoAmW 93*
Killeen, Edward F. 1930- *St&PR 93*
Killeen, Luann G. 1938- *St&PR 93*
Killeen, Melissa Helen 1955- *WhoE 93, WhoWor 93*
Killefer, Tom 1917- *WhoAm 92*
Killelea, Michael Joseph *Law&B 92*
Killen, Buddy *SoulM*
Killen, Carroll Gorden 1919- *St&PR 93, WhoAm 92*
Killen, Kathleen Elizabeth 1953- *WhoAmW 93*
Killenberg, George Andrew 1917- *WhoAm 92*
Killens, John Oliver 1916-1987 *EncAACR*
Killen-Wolf, Anne 1959- *WhoAmW 93*
Killgallon, Christine Behrens 1958- *WhoAmW 93*
Killgallon, William C. 1939- *St&PR 93*
Killgore, Andrew Ivy 1919- *WhoAm 92*
Killgore, Le 1926- *WhoSSW 93*
Killheffer, T.F. *Law&B 92*
Killhour, William Gherky 1925- *WhoE 93*
Killian, George Ernest 1924- *WhoAm 92*
Killian, Kevin 1952- *ConGAN*
Killian, Lewis Martin 1919- *WhoAm 92, WhoSSW 93*
Killian, Michael F. 1952- *WhoAm 92*
Killian, Miriam *St&PR 93*
Killian, Nathan Rayne 1935- *WhoSSW 93, WhoWor 93*
Killian, Patrick O. *Law&B 92*
Killian, Robert James 1954- *WhoSSW 93*
Killian, Robert Kenneth 1919- *WhoAm 92*
Killian, Ruth Selvey 1921- *WhoAmW 93*
Killian, William Paul 1935- *St&PR 93, WhoAm 92*
Killian-Faith, Joan 1947- *St&PR 93*
Killias, Martin 1948- *WhoScE 91-4*
Killien, Christi 1956- *SmATA 73 [port]*
Killilea, Ann Irene *Law&B 92*
Killilea, Jane Bernadette 1950- *WhoAmW 93*
Killin, Charles Clark 1923- *WhoAm 92*
Killingback, Julia *BioIn 17*
Killinger, George Glenn 1908- *WhoAm 92*
Killinger, Kerry Kent 1949- *WhoAm 92*
Killinger, Pam *BioIn 17*
Killingsworth, Charles Clinton 1917- *WhoAm 92*
Killingsworth, Kay 1942- *WhoUN 92*
Killingsworth, Mark Edwin 1951- *St&PR 93*
Killingsworth, Ted E. *Law&B 92*
Killion, Redley 1951- *WhoAsAP 91*
Killion, Thomas K. 1941- *St&PR 93*
Killion, Wayne Worden 1925- *St&PR 93*
Killip, Ian *WhoScE 91-1*
Killips, Danforth 1918- *WhoAm 92*
Killkelley, Robert P. 1934- *St&PR 93*
Killmayer, Wilhelm 1927- *Baker 92*
Killoran, Dermot Eugene 1952- *WhoWor 93*
Killoran, Neil 1956- *WhoScE 91-1*
Killoran, William V., Jr. *Law&B 92*
Killoren, Glenn Arthur 1935- *St&PR 93*
Killoren, Jack K. 1952- *St&PR 93*
Killoren, Robert 1950- *WhoWrEP 92*
Killorin, Edward Wylly 1928- *WhoSSW 93, WhoWor 93*
Killorin, Robert Ware 1959- *WhoSSW 93, WhoWor 93*
Killory, Diane Silberstein 1954- *WhoAm 92, WhoAmW 93*
Killough, Jack Christopher 1948- *WhoEmL 93*
Killough, James Stuart 1940- *St&PR 93*
Killough, Larry Neil 1932- *WhoAm 92*
Killough, Lee 1942- *BioIn 17, ScF&FL 92*
Killough, R.B. 1948- *St&PR 93*
Killough, Stephen P. *Law&B 92*
Killough, Stephen Pinckney 1935- *St&PR 93*
Killpack, J. Robert 1922- *St&PR 93*
Killpack, James Robert 1922- *WhoAm 92*
Killus, James 1950- *ScF&FL 92*
Killworth, Steven J. *Law&B 92*
Killy, Jean Claude 1943- *BioIn 17*
Kilmain, George F. 1933- *St&PR 93*
Kilmain, William Henry 1936- *WhoE 93*
Kilman, James William 1931- *WhoAm 92*
Kilmann, Ralph Herman 1946- *WhoAm 92, WhoE 93, WhoEmL 93, WhoWor 93*
Kilmartin, Cynthia A.H. 1956- *St&PR 93*
Kilmartin, Edward John 1923- *WhoAm 92*
Kilmartin, Joseph Francis, Jr. 1924- *WhoE 93*
Kilmartin, Marianne Penelope 1946- *WhoWor 93*
Kilmartin, Robert C. d1990 *BioIn 17*
Kilmartin, Terence 1922-1991 *AnObit 1991*
Kilmartin, Thomas John, III 1939- *WhoAm 92*
Kilmer, James E. 1940- *WhoIns 93*
Kilmer, Joanne Whalley- *BioIn 17*
Kilmer, John Henry 1917- *St&PR 93*
Kilmer, Karen Lynn 1951- *WhoAmW 93*
Kilmer, Kenton 1909- *WhoWrEP 92*
Kilmer, Sally Jean 1936- *WhoAmW 93*
Kilmer, Val *BioIn 17*
Kilmer, Val 1959- *WhoAm 92*
Kilminister, Neal *Law&B 92*
Kilnapp, George L., Sr. 1931- *St&PR 93*
Kilodney, Crad 1948- *ConAu 37NR, WhoCanL 92*
Kilov, Haim Israel 1946- *WhoEmL 93*
Kilpatric, Jim G. *Law&B 92*
Kilpatrick, Adele *AmWomPl*
Kilpatrick, Bill J. 1928- *St&PR 93*
Kilpatrick, Carolyn Cheeks 1945- *AfrAmBi [port], WhoAmW 93*
Kilpatrick, Charles Otis 1922- *WhoAm 92*
Kilpatrick, Gary John 1943- *St&PR 93*
Kilpatrick, George H. 1936- *WhoAm 92*
Kilpatrick, Heather *Law&B 92*
Kilpatrick, Hugh Judson 1836-1881 *HarEnMi*
Kilpatrick, Jack (Frederick) 1915-1967 *Baker 92*
Kilpatrick, James J. 1920- *JrnUS*
Kilpatrick, James Jackson, Jr. 1920- *WhoAm 92*
Kilpatrick, James Lowe 1931- *WhoAm 92*
Kilpatrick, John Reed 1889-1960 *BiDAMSp 1989*
Kilpatrick, Lester L. 1923- *St&PR 93*
Kilpatrick, Mark Kevin 1955- *WhoSSW 93*
Kilpatrick, Robert David *Law&B 92*
Kilpatrick, Robert Donald 1924- *WhoAm 92*
Kilpatrick, Robert Edward 1952- *WhoWor 93*
Kilpatrick, Ronald Wade 1945- *St&PR 93*
Kilpatrick, Weston *BioIn 17*
Kilpinen, Yrjo (Henrik) 1892-1959 *Baker 92*
Kilreon, Beth *ConAu 38NR*
Kilroy, John Muir 1918- *WhoAm 92*
Kilroy, Maura A. *Law&B 92*
Kilroy, Patrick J., Jr. *Law&B 92*
Kilroy, R.J. 1942- *St&PR 93*
Kilroy-Silk, Robert 1942- *ScF&FL 92*
Kilsdonk, John A. 1954- *St&PR 93*
Kilsdonk-Biggs, Rachel Constance 1915- *WhoWrEP 92*
Kilshaw, Peter John *WhoScE 91-1*
Kilsheimer, John Robert 1923- *WhoSSW 93*
Kilson, Martin Luther, Jr. 1931- *WhoAm 92*
Kilts, Albert F. 1945- *St&PR 93*
Kilts, Douglas Walter 1946- *WhoAm 92, WhoE 93*
Kilty, Jerome Timothy 1922- *WhoAm 92*
Kilty, S. Timothy 1933- *St&PR 93*
Kilvert, Francis 1840-1879 *BioIn 17*
Kilvert, Roy 1933- *WhoAsAP 91*
Kilwien-Meck, Sherri Rae 1960- *WhoEmL 93*
Kilworth, Garry 1941- *ScF&FL 92*
Kilzer, Louis Charles 1951- *WhoAm 92*
Kim, Andrew Byongsoo 1936- *St&PR 93*
Kim, Brian Hyung 1965- *WhoE 93*
Kim, Byong-Kak 1934- *WhoWor 93*
Kim, Byong-kon 1929- *Baker 92*
Kim, Byung-Dong 1943- *WhoWor 93*
Kim, Candace Junghyun 1967- *WhoAmW 93*
Kim, Chan-Jin 1941- *WhoWor 93*
Kim, Charles Wesley 1926- *WhoAm 92, WhoWor 93*
Kim, Chin-Woo 1936- *WhoAm 92*
Kim, Chong Il *BioIn 17*
Kim, Chong Soong 1945- *WhoSSW 93*
Kim, Choong Sun *WhoWor 93*
Kim, Chung Wook 1934- *WhoAm 92*
Kim, David Sang Chul 1915- *WhoE 93*
Kim, Dong Ik 1933- *WhoWor 93*
Kim, Doo Sik 1951- *WhoWor 93*
Kim, Doohie 1935- *WhoWor 93*
Kim, E. Han 1946- *WhoAm 92, WhoWor 93*
Kim, Earl 1920- *Baker 92, WhoAm 92*
Kim, Edward William 1949- *WhoAm 92, WhoEmL 93*
Kim, Elizabeth Jeesook 1960- *WhoAmW 93*
Kim, Esther Y. *Law&B 92*
Kim, Eun-Sook 1937- *BioIn 17*
Kim, Hack Hyun 1942- *WhoAm 92*
Kim, Heemong 1957- *WhoE 93, WhoEmL 93*
Kim, Hyong Chun 1929- *WhoUN 92*
Kim, Hyong Sok 1962- *WhoE 93*
Kim, Ih Chin 1925- *WhoE 93*
Kim, Jaegwon 1934- *WhoAm 92*
Kim, Jai Soo 1925- *WhoAm 92, WhoE 93, WhoWor 93*
Kim, James J. 1936- *St&PR 93*
Kim, James Joo-Jin 1936- *WhoAm 92*
Kim, Jin Hi 1958- *Baker 92*
Kim, Jin-Keun 1952- *WhoWor 93*
Kim, Jin Seok 1948- *WhoWor 93*
Kim, John Ho 1949- *WhoWor 93*
Kim, Jong Il *BioIn 17*
Kim, Jun Young 1951- *WhoWor 93*
Kim, Jung-Hoo *BioIn 17*
Kim, Kathleen 1958- *WhoE 93*
Kim, Ke Chung 1934- *WhoAm 92*
Kim, Ki Hoon 1933- *WhoE 93*
Kim, Kwang Sik 1947- *WhoEmL 93*
Kim, Kwang Soo 1950- *WhoWor 93*
Kim, Kyong-Won 1939- *WhoWor 93*
Kim, Kyu-Won 1952- *WhoWor 93*
Kim, Leo 1942- *St&PR 93*
Kim, Lillie Ann 1960- *WhoAmW 93*
Kim, Michael Charles 1950- *WhoEmL 93*
Kim, Moon Hyun 1934- *WhoAm 92*
Kim, Moon-Il 1929- *WhoWor 93*
Kim, Myung Suk 1943- *WhoWor 93*
Kim, Myunghee 1932- *WhoE 93*
Kim, Oscar 1934- *WhoE 93*
Kim, Pan Soo 1947- *WhoE 93*
Kim, Po *WhoE 93*
Kim, Rhyn Hyun 1936- *WhoAm 92, WhoSSW 93*
Kim, Richard E. 1932- *WhoWrEP 92*
Kim, Sandra *Law&B 92*
Kim, Sang-Ha 1926- *WhoWor 93*
Kim, Sang-Min 1931- *WhoWor 93*
Kim, Sang Yong 1935- *WhoWor 93*
Kim, Sangduk 1930- *WhoAmW 93*
Kim, Seong-Jun 1937- *WhoE 93*
Kim, Seunghwan *WhoWor 93*
Kim, Soo-Ryong 1951- *WhoEmL 93*
Kim, Stephan Sou-Hwan Cardinal 1922- *WhoWor 93*
Kim, Sun Hong *BioIn 17*
Kim, Sung-Hoon 1958- *WhoWor 93*
Kim, Sung-Hou 1937- *WhoAm 92*
Kim, Sung Soon 1945- *WhoWor 93*
Kim, Synja P. *WhoAmW 93, WhoE 93*
Kim, Theresa Ki-ja 1933- *WhoE 93*
Kim, Thomas Kunhyuk 1929- *WhoAm 92*
Kim, Unsup 1934- *WhoE 93*
Kim, Wan Hee 1926- *WhoAm 92*
Kim, Willa *WhoAm 92, WhoAmW 93, WhoE 93*
Kim, Won Kyung 1931- *WhoWor 93*
Kim, Woo-Ki 1942- *WhoWor 93*
Kim, Yong Choon 1935- *WhoAm 92*
Kim, Yong Hwa 1951- *St&PR 93*
Kim, Yong-Ik *DcAmChF 1960*
Kim, Yongmin 1953- *WhoWor 93*
Kim, Yoon Berm 1929- *WhoAm 92*
Kim, Yoon-Won 1955- *WhoWor 93*
Kim, Young Ho 1927- *WhoE 93*
Kim, Young-Ho 1945- *WhoWor 93*
Kim, Young Ho 1953- *WhoWor 93*
Kim, Young Kil 1956- *WhoSSW 93*
Kim, Young-Su 1945- *WhoWor 93*
Kim, Young-Uck 1947- *Baker 92*
Kim, Youngho 1959- *WhoWor 93*
Kim, Yuhn-Bok 1942- *WhoWor 93*
Kima, Akira 1930- *WhoAsAP 91*
Kimario, Muhiddin Mfaume 1937- *WhoAfr*
Kimata, Hiroaki 1942- *WhoUN 92*
Kimati, Valerian Pius 1936- *WhoUN 92*
Kimatian, Stephen H. 1941- *WhoAm 92, WhoE 93*
Kimball, Allyn Winthrop 1921- *WhoAm 92*
Kimball, Anna May *AmWomPl*
Kimball, Astrid *AmWomPl*
Kimball, Bruce Arnold 1941- *WhoAm 92*
Kimball, Charles Arthur 1939- *WhoWrEP 92*
Kimball, Charles Henry Gallwey 1909- *St&PR 93*
Kimball, Charles Newton 1911- *WhoAm 92*
Kimball, Clyde William 1928- *WhoAm 92*
Kimball, Connie E. *WhoWrEP 92*
Kimball, Daniel Webster 1946- *WhoEmL 93*
Kimball, David T. 1927- *St&PR 93*
Kimball, Dorothy Jean 1927- *WhoAmW 93*
Kimball, Edward H. 1905-1990 *BioIn 17*
Kimball, Edward Lawrence 1930- *WhoAm 92*
Kimball, Gayle 1953- *WhoAmW 93*
Kimball, Irving S. 1918- *St&PR 93*
Kimball, Jacob, Jr. 1761-1826 *Baker 92*
Kimball, James L. 1919- *St&PR 93*
Kimball, Janus *ScF&FL 92*
Kimball, Justin H. *Law&B 92*
Kimball, Kathryn *AmWomPl*
Kimball, Leo Robert 1923- *St&PR 93*
Kimball, Lindsley F. d1992 *NewYTBS 92*
Kimball, Lindsley F(iske) 1894-1992 *CurBio 92N*
Kimball, Lindsley Fiske 1894- *WhoAm 92*
Kimball, Natalie D. 1951- *St&PR 93*
Kimball, Raymond Alonzo 1918- *WhoAm 92*
Kimball, Raymond Joel 1948- *WhoEmL 93*
Kimball, Reid Roberts 1926- *WhoAm 92*
Kimball, Richard A., Jr. *St&PR 93*
Kimball, Richard Arthur, Jr. 1930- *WhoAm 92*
Kimball, Richard Wilson 1938- *WhoWrEP 92*
Kimball, Robert Bartus *Law&B 92*
Kimball, Robert Eric 1939- *WhoAm 92, WhoWrEP 92*
Kimball, Roger 1953- *ConAu 136*
Kimball, Roland Baldwin 1921- *WhoAm 92*
Kimball, Rosamond *AmWomPl*
Kimball, Ruth Putnam *AmWomPl*
Kimball, Spencer W(oolley) 1895-1985 *ConAu 39NR*
Kimball, Sue Laslie *WhoWrEP 92*
Kimball, Sue Laslie 1921- *WhoSSW 93*
Kimball, Walter Henry 1953- *WhoEmL 93*
Kimbel, Karl Heinz 1924- *WhoWor 93*
Kimbel, Virginia *Law&B 92*
Kimbell, Charles William, III 1943- *WhoE 93*
Kimbell, David Alan 1929- *St&PR 93*
Kimbell, Edith Maria 1945- *WhoAmW 93*
Kimber, William John 1931- *WhoE 93*
Kimberland, Kendall Graham 1907- *WhoE 93*
Kimberlin, Greg K. *Law&B 92*
Kimberlin, John H. 1943- *St&PR 93*
Kimberlin, Sam Owen, Jr. 1928- *WhoSSW 93*
Kimberling, C. Ronald 1950- *St&PR 93*
Kimberly, Gail *ScF&FL 92*
Kimberly, John R. d1992 *NewYTBS 92 [port]*
Kimberly, John Robert 1942- *WhoAm 92*
Kimberly, Robert Parker 1946- *WhoE 93*
Kimberly, William Essick 1933- *WhoAm 92, WhoWor 93*
Kimble, Allan Wayne 1960- *WhoSSW 93*
Kimble, Barry William 1961- *WhoEmL 93*
Kimble, Dale Mitchell 1955- *WhoSSW 93*
Kimble, Gladys Augusta Lee 1906- *WhoAmW 93*
Kimble, Gregory Adams 1917- *WhoAm 92*
Kimble, Marilyn Cecelia 1946- *WhoAmW 93*
Kimble, Michael d1990 *BioIn 17*
Kimble, Reeva Jacobson 1937- *WhoAmW 93*
Kimble, Robert P. 1946- *St&PR 93*
Kimble, William Earl 1926- *WhoAm 92*
Kimbler, Larry Bernard 1938- *WhoSSW 93*
Kim Bong Ho 1934- *WhoAsAP 91*
Kim Bong Jo 1939- *WhoAsAP 91*
Kim Bong Wook 1930- *WhoAsAP 91*
Kimbrel, Monroe 1916- *St&PR 93*
Kimbrell, Grady Ned 1933- *WhoWrEP 92*
Kimbrell, Jack Ezzell 1926- *WhoWor 93*
Kimbrell, Murvin Jackson 1930- *WhoSSW 93*
Kimbrell, Odell C., Jr. 1927- *St&PR 93*
Kimbrell, Odell Culp, Jr. 1927- *WhoAm 92*
Kimbrell, W. David 1951- *ConEn*
Kimbrell, W. Duke 1924- *BioIn 17, St&PR 93*
Kimbrell, Willard Duke 1924- *WhoAm 92*
Kimbriel, Katharine Eliska 1956- *ScF&FL 92*
Kimbro, Jean *ScF&FL 92*
Kimbro, John M. 1929- *ScF&FL 92*
Kimbrough, A. Charles, Sr. 1939- *St&PR 93*

Kimbrough, Allen Wayne 1953- *WhoAm 92*
Kimbrough, Charles *WhoAm 92*
Kimbrough, Elaine McClain 1953- *WhoSSW 93*
Kimbrough, Emily 1899-1989 *BioIn 17*
Kimbrough, John Clifton 1925- *WhoWrEP 92*
Kimbrough, Katheryn *ScF&FL 92*
Kimbrough, Larry D. 1948- *St&PR 93*
Kimbrough, Larry Keith 1960- *WhoSSW 93*
Kimbrough, Marjorie L. 1937- *BioIn 17*
Kimbrough, Marvin Gordon 1932- *WhoSSW 93*
Kimbrough, Mary Alice 1932- *WhoSSW 93*
Kimbrough, Ralph Bradley, Sr. 1922- *WhoAm 92*
Kimbrough, Sally Ann 1964- *WhoSSW 93*
Kimbrough, Ted *BioIn 17*
Kimbrough, William Adams, Jr. 1935- *WhoAm 92*
Kimbrough, William Walter, III 1928- *WhoAm 92, WhoWor 93*
Kimbrough Davis, Carolyn *Law&B 92*
Kim Byung Yong 1932- *WhoAsAP 91*
Kimchi, Dan *St&PR 93*
Kim Chong Kon 1931- *WhoAsAP 91*
Kim Choong Jo 1943- *WhoAsAP 91*
Kim Chung Ho 1936- *WhoAsAP 91*
Kim Chung Yul d1992 *NewYTBS 92*
Kim Dae Jung 1925- *WhoWor 93*
Kim Dae Jung 1927- *WhoAsAP 91*
Kim Deog-Ryong 1942- *WhoAsAP 91*
Kim Deuk So 1939- *WhoAsAP 91*
Kim Dong In 1928- *WhoAsAP 91*
Kim Dong-Joo 1945- *WhoAsAP 91*
Kim Dong Kyu 1933- *WhoAsAP 91*
Kim Dong Young 1937- *WhoAsAP 91*
Kim Doo-Yoon 1927- *WhoAsAP 91*
Kim Duk Kyu 1942- *WhoAsAP 91*
Kime, Bradley J. 1960- *St&PR 93*
Kime, Robert C. *Law&B 92*
Kime, Wayne Raymond 1941- *WhoSSW 93*
Kimel, Jacob Daniel 1937- *WhoSSW 93*
Kimelberg, Harold Keith 1941- *WhoE 93*
Kimelman, Donald Bruce 1947- *WhoAm 92*
Kimelman, Henry L. 1921- *WhoAm 92*
Kimen, Thomas W. *St&PR 93*
Kimenyi, Alexandre 1948- *WhoEmL 93*
Kimerer, Neil Banard, Sr. 1918- *WhoAm 92, WhoWor 93*
Kimes, Beverly Rae 1939- *WhoAmW 93*
Kimes, Don Mark 1950- *WhoEmL 93*
Kimes, Sheryl Elaine 1954- *WhoEmL 93*
Kim-Farley, Robert James 1948- *WhoUN 92*
Kim Geong Jil 1937- *WhoAsAP 91*
Kim Hay Kyu 1941- *WhoAsAP 91*
Kim Hong Man 1944- *WhoAsAP 91*
Kim Hyun 1950- *WhoAsAP 91*
Kim Hyun-Uk 1940- *WhoAsAP 91*
Kim Il Dong 1940- *WhoAsAP 91*
Kim Il-Sung 1912- *ColdWar 2 [port], DcTwHis, WhoAsAP 91, WhoWor 93*
Kim Il Yun 1939- *WhoAsAP 91*
Kiminami, Takahiko *St&PR 93*
Kim In-Ki 1934- *WhoAsAP 91*
Kim In-Kon 1929- *WhoAsAP 91*
Kim In Young 1940- *WhoAsAP 91*
Kim Jae Kwang 1923- *WhoAsAP 91*
Kim Jae Tai 1936- *WhoAsAP 91*
Kim Jaison 1936- *WhoAsAP 91*
Kim Jang Sook 1935- *WhoAsAP 91*
Kim Jeun Soo 1939- *WhoAsAP 91*
Kim Jim Jae 1944- *WhoAsAP 91*
Kim Jin Young 1940- *WhoAsAP 91*
Kim Jong Ki 1940- *WhoAsAP 91*
Kim Jong Pil 1927- *WhoAsAP 91*
Kim Jong Shik 1936- *WhoAsAP 91*
Kim Jong Wan 1933- *WhoAsAP 91*
Kim Joo Ho 1933- *WhoAsAP 91*
Kim Joong Kwon 1940- *WhoAsAP 91*
Kim Jung Kil 1946- *WhoAsAP 91*
Kimker, Klaholt P. 1945- *St&PR 93*
Kim Keun Soo 1936- *WhoAsAP 91*
Kim Ki-Bae 1937- *WhoAsAP 91*
Kim Kil Hong 1943- *WhoAsAP 91*
Kim Kil Kon 1932- *WhoAsAP 91*
Kim Kwang Hyop c. 1910- *HarEnMi*
Kim Kwang Il 1941- *WhoAsAP 91*
Kimm, Barbara Chandler 1936- *WhoAmW 93*
Kimmage, Paul *BioIn 17*
Kimmel, Allan Jeffrey 1952- *WhoE 93*
Kimmel, Bruce 1947- *MiSFD 9*
Kimmel, Bruce Lee 1945- *WhoSSW 93*
Kimmel, Carol Frances 1917- *WhoAm 92*
Kimmel, Ellen Bishop 1939- *WhoSSW 93*
Kimmel, Gary Dean 1937- *St&PR 93*
Kimmel, George Stuart 1934- *St&PR 93*
Kimmel, H. Steven 1946- *WhoAm 92*
Kimmel, Husband Edward 1882-1968 *HarEnMi*
Kimmel, Irvine 1918- *St&PR 93*
Kimmel, Jerold 1946- *St&PR 93*
Kimmel, Jesse A. 1916- *St&PR 93*
Kimmel, Joyce Frances 1948- *WhoEmL 93*
Kimmel, Marek 1953- *WhoSSW 93*
Kimmel, Mark 1940- *WhoWor 93*
Kimmel, Mark Edward *Law&B 92*
Kimmel, Mark J. 1959- *St&PR 93*
Kimmel, Michael S. *BioIn 17*
Kimmel, Patricia Temple 1930- *St&PR 93*
Kimmel, Paul Robert 1947- *WhoE 93*
Kimmel, Peter Scott 1947- *WhoE 93, WhoWor 93*
Kimmel, Robert Irving 1922- *WhoAm 92, WhoE 93*
Kimmel, Troy Max, Jr. 1957- *WhoSSW 93*
Kimmel, Victor 1921- *St&PR 93*
Kimmel, William J. 1947- *St&PR 93*
Kimmell, Garman Oscar 1913- *St&PR 93*
Kimmell, J. Kachen *Law&B 92*
Kimmelman, Burt Joseph 1947- *WhoWrEP 92*
Kimmelman, Gary A. *Law&B 92*
Kimmelman, Joan E. *Law&B 92*
Kimmelman, Michael Simon 1958- *WhoAm 92*
Kimmelman, Peter 1944- *St&PR 93*
Kimmelman, Seth 1951-1991 *BioIn 17*
Kimmerling, Karl Paul *Law&B 92*
Kimmey, James Richard, Jr. 1935- *WhoAm 92*
Kimmich, Christoph Martin 1939- *WhoAm 92*
Kimmich, Sara Jane 1963- *WhoAmW 93*
Kimmitt, Robert M. 1947- *BioIn 17*
Kimmitt, Robert Michael 1947- *WhoAm 92, WhoWor 93*
Kimmle, Manfred 1942- *WhoAm 92*
Kim Moon Ki 1933- *WhoAsAP 91*
Kim Moon Won 1943- *WhoAsAP 91*
Kim Myung Sup 1939- *WhoAsAP 91*
Kimnach, Myron William 1922- *WhoAm 92*
Kim Nam 1931- *WhoAsAP 91*
Kimoto, Hiroshi 1943- *WhoWor 93*
Kimpel, Benjamin Franklin 1905- *WhoAm 92*
Kimpel, John Martin *Law&B 92*
Kimple, Scott Carlisle 1966- *WhoEmL 93, WhoSSW 93*
Kimpton, Bill *BioIn 17*
Kimrey, Gregory Scott 1955- *WhoSSW 93*
Kim Sung, II 1910- *HarEnMi*
Kim Sung Yong 1928- *WhoAsAP 91*
Kim Tae Ho 1936- *WhoAsAP 91*
Kim Tai Shik 1940- *WhoAsAP 91*
Kim Ung c. 1910- *HarEnMi*
Kimura, Akira 1936- *WhoWor 93*
Kimura, Doreen *BioIn 17, WhoAm 92, WhoAmW 93*
Kimura, Heitaro 1888-1948 *HarEnMi*
Kimura, Kenji 1961- *WhoWor 93*
Kimura, Kimi Takeuchi 1936- *WhoE 93*
Kimura, Kunihiko 1927- *WhoWor 93*
Kimura, Lillian Chiyeko 1929- *WhoAmW 93*
Kimura, Mary S. 1928- *St&PR 93*
Kimura, Masatomi 1891-1960 *HarEnMi*
Kimura, Minoru 1935- *WhoWor 93*
Kimura, Mitsuhiko 1951- *WhoWor 93*
Kimura, Morio 1938- *WhoAsAP 91*
Kimura, Shigenobu 1925- *WhoWor 93*
Kimura, Tetsuya 1959- *WhoWor 93*
Kimura, Yoshio 1948- *WhoAsAP 91*
Kimura, Yoshitsugu 1936- *WhoWor 93*
Kim Won Ki 1938- *WhoAsAP 91*
Kim Woon Hwan 1947- *WhoAsAP 91*
Kim Woo Suk 1937- *WhoAsAP 91*
Kim Yong Chae 1933- *WhoAsAP 91*
Kim Yong Hwan 1933- *WhoAsAP 91*
Kim Yong-nam *WhoWor 93*
Kim Yong-Tae 1937- *WhoAsAP 91*
Kim Yoon Whan 1933- *WhoAsAP 91*
Kim Young Bae 1933- *WhoAsAP 91*
Kim Young Do 1930- *WhoAsAP 91*
Kim Young Jin 1947- *WhoAsAP 91*
Kim Young Sam 1927- *NewYTBS 92 [port]*
Kim Young Sam 1929- *WhoAsAP 91*
Kim Young Sun 1931- *WhoAsAP 91*
Kim Yung Koo 1940- *WhoAsAP 91*
Kimzey, Carol Eugenia 1947- *WhoAmW 93*
Kimzey, Jackie R. 1952- *St&PR 93*
Kimzey, James R. 1938- *St&PR 93*
Kim Zoong-Wie 1940- *WhoAsAP 91*
Kinaci, Ilhan 1932- *St&PR 93*
Kinaci, Selman R. 1926- *WhoScE 91-4*
Kinahan, Cami Sacco *Law&B 92*
Kinahan, James Joseph *Law&B 92*
Kinal, Hilary Andrew 1960- *WhoEmL 93*
Kinard, Agnes Dodds *WhoAmW 93*
Kinard, Bruiser 1914-1985 *BioIn 17*
Kinard, Frank Efird 1924- *WhoSSW 93*
Kinard, Frank M. 1914-1985 *BioIn 17*
Kinard, Fredrick William 1906- *WhoSSW 93*
Kinard, Glenn E. 1947- *St&PR 93*
Kinard, Hargett Yingling 1912- *WhoAm 92*
Kinard, Jack Dalton 1930- *WhoSSW 93*
Kinard, Mike 1939- *St&PR 93*
Kinard, William Carlton 1919- *St&PR 93*
Kinariwala, Bharat 1926- *WhoAm 92*
Kinashi, Takakzu 1902-1944 *HarEnMi*
Kinber, Efim 1949- *WhoWor 93*
Kinberg, Judy 1948- *WhoAm 92*
Kincade, Gary Brent 1942- *WhoSSW 93*
Kincade, H. Patricia 1930- *St&PR 93*
Kincade, John *MiSFD 9*
Kincade, William Hadley 1939- *WhoE 93*
Kincaid, Bradley 1895-1989 *Baker 92*
Kincaid, David P. *Law&B 92*
Kincaid, Elsie Elizabeth 1929- *WhoSSW 93*
Kincaid, Hugh Reid 1934- *WhoAm 92*
Kincaid, Jamaica *BioIn 17*
Kincaid, Jamaica 1949- *ConBlB 4 [port], WhoAm 92, WhoAmW 93*
Kincaid, James Alan 1930- *St&PR 93*
Kincaid, Joe Kaylor 1948- *WhoWor 93*
Kincaid, Owings Wilson 1921- *WhoAm 92*
Kincaid, Paul 1952- *ScF&FL 92*
Kincaid, Paul P. *St&PR 93*
Kincaid, Ray L. 1935- *St&PR 93*
Kincaid, Robin *ScF&FL 92*
Kincaid, Rodney Lyle 1933- *WhoWor 93*
Kincaid, Sandra Kathleen *Law&B 92*
Kincaid, Steven Randall 1953- *WhoE 93, WhoEmL 93*
Kincaid, Tim *MiSFD 9*
Kincaid, William 1895-1967 *Baker 92*
Kincaid-Washington, Carrie Jacqueline 1955- *WhoAmW 93*
Kincannon, Felice *WhoAm 92*
Kincannon, Jack F. 1918-1991 *BioIn 17*
Kincannon, Karen Courtney 1945- *WhoSSW 93*
Kincart, Robert Owen 1949- *WhoEmL 93, WhoSSW 93, WhoWor 93*
Kincel, David F. 1946- *St&PR 93*
Kinch, Dalphine Nora 1953- *WhoE 93*
Kinch, Martin 1943- *WhoCanL 92*
Kincheloe, R.L. 1930- *St&PR 93*
Kinchen, Robert P. 1933-1991 *BioIn 17*
Kinchen, Thomas Alexander 1946- *WhoSSW 93*
Kind, Dieter 1929- *WhoScE 91-3*
Kind, Phyllis Dawn 1933- *WhoAmW 93*
Kind, Richard John 1941- *WhoAm 92*
Kind, Stephen Joseph 1936- *St&PR 93*
Kindall, Charlotte Eloise 1944- *WhoAmW 93*
Kindel, H. Stephanie 1944- *WhoAmW 93*
Kindel, James Horace, Jr. 1913- *WhoAm 92*
Kindel, Robert James 1947- *WhoWrEP 92*
Kinder, Ira 1942- *WhoSSW 93*
Kinder, Ralph 1876-1952 *Baker 92*
Kinder, Richard Dan 1944- *WhoAm 92, WhoSSW 93*
Kinder, Stuart 1924- *ScF&FL 92*
Kinder, Terry L. 1958- *St&PR 93*
Kinder, Thomas Marshall 1942- *WhoSSW 93*
Kindermann, August *OxDcOp*
Kindermann, August 1817-1891 *Baker 92, OxDcOp*
Kindermann, Franziska *OxDcOp*
Kindermann, Johann Erasmus 1616-1655 *Baker 92*
Kindermann, Marie *OxDcOp*
Kindermann, Markus Karl 1961- *WhoWor 93*
Kinderwater, Joseph C. 1922- *WhoAm 92*
Kindig, Everett William 1936- *WhoSSW 93*
Kindig, Fred Eugene 1920- *WhoAm 92*
Kindig, Karl K. *Law&B 92*
Kindiger, Wayde Scott *Law&B 92*
Kindl, Ralph J. 1939- *St&PR 93*
Kindleberger, Charles P., II 1910- *WhoAm 92*
Kindleberger, Charles Poor 1910- *BioIn 17*
Kindler, Hans 1892-1949 *Baker 92*
Kindler, Janusz 1934- *WhoScE 91-4*
Kindler, Jeffery B. *Law&B 92*
Kindlund, Joanne M. 1949- *St&PR 93*
Kindlund, Newton C. 1940- *St&PR 93*
Kindness, Kathleen *WhoScE 91-1*
Kindness, Thomas Norman 1929- *WhoAm 92*
Kindred, George Charles 1898- *WhoE 93*
Kindrick, Charles Henry 1951- *St&PR 93*
Kindrick, Robert LeRoy 1942- *WhoAm 92*
Kinds, Herbert Eugene 1933- *WhoWor 93*
Kindschi, John P. *Law&B 92*
Kindsvater, John H. *St&PR 93*
Kindt, John Warren, Sr. 1950- *WhoAm 92*
Kindt, Thomas James 1939- *WhoAm 92*
Kindt-Larsen, Ture 1940- *WhoScE 91-2*
Kiner, Grace *AmWomPl*
Kiner, Ralph 1922- *BioIn 17*
Kines, Joan Elaine 1949- *WhoEmL 93*
King, Adele Cockshoot 1932- *WhoAmW 93*
King, Alan 1927- *WhoAm 92*
King, Alan C. 1951- *St&PR 93*
King, Alan Jonathan 1954- *WhoEmL 93*
King, Albert *BioIn 17*
King, Albert d1992 *NewYTBS 92 [port]*
King, Albert 1923- *SoulM*
King, Albert 1924- *ScF&FL 92*
King, Albert Daniel Williams 1930-1969 *EncAACR*
King, Alec Hyatt 1911- *Baker 92*
King, Alexander Harvey 1954- *WhoE 93*
King, Alexander Vernon 1956- *WhoEmL 93*
King, Algin Braddy 1926- *WhoAm 92, WhoSSW 93, WhoWor 93*
King, Allan 1930- *MiSFD 9*
King, Alvin Thomas 1944- *WhoWrEP 92*
King, Amy Cathryne Patterson 1928- *WhoAmW 93, WhoSSW 93*
King, Andre Richardson 1931- *WhoAm 92*
King, Ann Ottoson 1946- *WhoEmL 93*
King, (Maria) Anna 1964- *SmATA 72 [port]*
King, Annette Faye 1947- *WhoAsAP 91*
King, Anthony Gabriel 1953- *WhoAm 92*
King, Arnold Kimsey 1901- *WhoAm 92*
King, Arthur Hood 1927- *St&PR 93, WhoAm 92*
King, Arthur M. *Law&B 92*
King, Augusta Ada Byron 1815-1852 *BioIn 17*
King, B.B. *BioIn 17*
King, "B.B." 1925- *Baker 92, SoulM, WhoAm 92*
King, B.M. *WhoScE 91-1*
King, Barbara Lewis 1930- *AfrAmBi*
King, Barrett Taylor 1947- *WhoEmL 93*
King, Ben E. 1938- *SoulM*
King, Bernard *BioIn 17*
King, Bernard 1944- *WhoScE 91-1*
King, Bernard 1946- *ScF&FL 92*
King, Bernard 1956- *WhoAm 92*
King, Bernard David 1949- *WhoE 93*
King, Bernice *BioIn 17*
King, Bernice 1963- *ConBlB 4 [port]*
King, Bert Edward, Jr. 1945- *WhoSSW 93*
King, Betsy *BioIn 17, WhoAm 92, WhoAmW 93*
King, Betty 1948- *ScF&FL 92*
King, Beulah Brown 1892- *AmWomPl*
King, Beverly Edwards 1951- *WhoSSW 93*
King, Billi H. *WhoCanL 92*
King, Billie Jean *BioIn 17*
King, Billie Jean 1938- *WhoAm 92*
King, Billie Jean Moffitt 1943- *WhoAm 92, WhoAmW 93*
King, Bobby *BioIn 17*
King, Brian J. *Law&B 92*
King, Brian Pierce 1948- *St&PR 93*
King, Bruce 1924- *WhoAm 92*
King, Bruce 1933- *ScF&FL 92*
King, Bruce Donald 1947- *St&PR 93*
King, Carl B. *Law&B 92*
King, Carol Soucek 1943- *WhoWrEP 92*
King, Carole *BioIn 17*
King, Carole 1941- *Baker 92*
King, Carole 1942- *WhoAm 92*
See Also Goffin & King *SoulM*
King, Carolyn Dineen 1938- *WhoAm 92, WhoAmW 93, WhoSSW 93*
King, Carolyn Mae 1946- *WhoAmW 93*
King, Cary Judson, III 1934- *WhoAm 92*
King, Charles 1844-1933 *BioIn 17*
King, Charles Conaway 1929- *St&PR 93*
King, Charles D. 1953- *St&PR 93*
King, Charles Glyn *Law&B 92*
King, Charles H., Jr. *BioIn 17*
King, Charles L. 1926- *St&PR 93*
King, Charles Mark 1952- *WhoEmL 93, WhoSSW 93*
King, Charles McDonald, Jr. 1934- *WhoAm 92*
King, Charles R. 1955- *St&PR 93*
King, Charles Ross 1925- *WhoAm 92, WhoWor 93*
King, Charles Thomas 1911- *WhoE 93, WhoWor 93*
King, Chester Harding, Jr. 1913- *WhoAm 92*
King, Christine Ledesma 1945- *WhoAmW 93*
King, Christine Paran 1949- *WhoAmW 93*
King, Christopher *ScF&FL 92*
King, Christopher Davis 1948- *WhoSSW 93*
King, Christopher French 1950- *WhoScE 91-1*
King, Cindy Lynn 1956- *WhoAmW 93*
King, Clarence 1842-1901 *BioIn 17*
King, Clark E. 1934- *St&PR 93*
King, Claudia Louan 1940- *WhoAmW 93*
King, Clennon 1921- *EncAACR*
King, Clive 1924- *ScF&FL 92*
King, (David) Clive 1924- *ChlFicS*
King, Clyde Richard 1924- *WhoAm 92*
King, Coretta Scott 1927- *AfrAmBi, BioIn 17, WhoAm 92, WhoAmW 93, WhoSSW 93*
King, Coretta Scott 1929- *ConBlB 3 [port], EncAACR [port]*

King, Craig S. *WhoAm 92*
King, Cynthia 1925- *ScF&FL 92*
King, Cynthia Bregman 1925- *WhoWrEP 92*
King, Cynthia Remington 1956- *WhoE 93*
King, Cyril *DcCPCAm*
King, Dan E. 1952- *St&PR 93*
King, Daniel J. 1952- *St&PR 93*
King, Dave W. *Law&B 92*
King, David 1940- *WhoWrEP 92*
King, David 1960- *ScF&FL 92*
King, David Alderson 1936- *St&PR 93*
King, David Anthony *WhoScE 91-1*
King, David C. *WhoScE 91-1*
King, David Edgar 1936- *WhoAm 92*
King, David L. *Law&B 92*
King, David Louis John 1948- *WhoUN 92*
King, David P. 1949- *St&PR 93*
King, David W. 1946- *WhoAm 92*
King, Dennis Eugene 1936- *St&PR 93*
King, Dennis Michael 1946- *St&PR 93*
King, Diana Hanbury *BioIn 17*
King, Diane R. 1950- *St&PR 93*
King, Dominic B. *Law&B 92*
King, Dominic Benson 1928- *St&PR 93, WhoAm 92*
King, Don 1929- *BioIn 17*
King, Don 1932- *AfrAmBi, WhoAm 92*
King, Donald C. 1930- *WhoAm 92*
King, Donald G. 1925- *St&PR 93*
King, Donita M. *Law&B 92*
King, Douglas Lohr 1941- *St&PR 93, WhoAm 92, WhoWor 93*
King, Douglas Willard 1959- *WhoEmL 93*
King, Doyle D. 1936- *St&PR 93*
King, Duane C. *Law&B 92*
King, Dwight Lyman 1917- *St&PR 93*
King, Earl *SoulM*
King, Edmund Ludwig 1914- *WhoE 93*
King, Edward 1794-1873 *OxCSupC*
King, Edward H. *Law&B 92*
King, Edward J. *Law&B 92*
King, Edward Louis 1920- *WhoAm 92*
King, Edward Postell, Jr. 1884-1958 *HarEnMi*
King, Edward William 1923- *WhoAm 92*
King, Elaine A. 1947- *WhoAm 92*
King, Eleanor 1906-1991 *BioIn 17*
King, Elizabeth Chiu 1935- *WhoWrEP 92*
King, Elizabeth Kim *Law&B 92*
King, Elizabeth Maureen 1957- *WhoAmW 93*
King, Emmett Alonzo, III 1942- *WhoE 93, WhoWor 93*
King, Ernest Joseph 1878-1956 *BioIn 17, HarEnMi*
King, Ernest Wade 1959- *WhoEmL 93*
King, Evans 1954- *WhoUN 92*
King, Evelyn 1960- *SoulM*
King, F.C. *Law&B 92*
King, Florence *AmWomPl, BioIn 17*
King, Frances Rockefeller *AmWomPl*
King, Francine Ellen 1946- *St&PR 93*
King, Francis A. *Law&B 92*
King, Francis Henry 1923- *BioIn 17, WhoWor 93*
King, Frank *ScF&FL 92*
King, Frank Theodore 1923- *St&PR 93*
King, Freddie 1934-1976 *BioIn 17*
King, Frederick Alexander 1925- *WhoAm 92*
King, Gail Marie *Law&B 92*
King, Geoffrey Stephen Douglas 1924- *WhoScE 91-2*
King, George Edward 1931- *WhoAm 92*
King, George F. 1938- *St&PR 93*
King, George Gerard 1940- *WhoAm 92*
King, George H. *St&PR 93*
King, George Harold 1920- *BioIn 17*
King, George M. *St&PR 93*
King, George S. 1938- *St&PR 93*
King, George Smith, Jr. 1928- *WhoAm 92*
King, George W. 1932- *St&PR 93*
King, George William *Law&B 92*
King, Georgiana Goddard 1871-1939 *AmWomPl*
King, Gerald 1951- *St&PR 93*
King, Gerald Simon 1948- *WhoIns 93*
King, Gerard Francis 1935- *St&PR 93*
King, Gladys Dorman 1960- *WhoAmW 93*
King, Glenn Richard 1928- *St&PR 93*
King, Gloria Reed 1946- *WhoAmW 93*
King, Glynda B. 1946- *WhoAmW 93*
King, Grace Elizabeth 1852-1932 *AmWomPl*
King, Gundar Julian 1926- *WhoAm 92, WhoWor 93*
King, Gwendolyn Bair 1915- *WhoAmW 93*
King, Gwendolyn S. *WhoAm 92, WhoAmW 93*
King, H. Joe, Jr. 1932- *St&PR 93*
King, Harold 1899-1990 *BioIn 17*
King, Harold 1945- *ScF&FL 92*
King, Harold Charles 1895-1984 *Baker 92*
King, Harold D. 1932- *St&PR 93*
King, Harold Raymond 1945- *WhoSSW 93*
King, Harold Thomas, Jr. 1949- *WhoAm 92*
King, Harriette Collins 1935- *WhoSSW 93*
King, Harry Warnock 1942- *St&PR 93*
King, Harvey Bills 1929- *St&PR 93*
King, Hazel Caudle 1947- *WhoWrEP 92*
King, Helen Emori 1936- *WhoAmW 93*
King, Henry 1592-1669 *DcLB 126 [port]*
King, Henry 1842-1915 *JrnUS*
King, Henry c. 1888-1982 *BioIn 17, MiSFD 9N*
King, Henry Lawrence 1928- *WhoAm 92*
King, Hilary 1949- *WhoUN 92*
King, Hiram Bronson 1931- *WhoE 93*
King, Howard J. 1933- *St&PR 93*
King, I.C. *WhoScE 91-1*
King, Imogene Martina 1923- *WhoAm 92, WhoAmW 93*
King, Indle Gifford 1934- *WhoAm 92*
King, Ivan Robert 1927- *WhoAm 92*
King, J.B. *Law&B 92*
King, J.D. *BioIn 17*
King, Jack A. 1936- *WhoIns 93*
King, Jack Howell 1952- *WhoEmL 93, WhoSSW 93, WhoWor 93*
King, Jack L. 1939- *WhoAm 92*
King, James 1925- *Baker 92, BioIn 17, IntDcOp, OxDcOp*
King, James A. 1948- *St&PR 93*
King, James A., Jr. *Law&B 92*
King, James Albert, Jr. *Law&B 92*
King, James Arthur 1920- *St&PR 93*
King, James B. 1935- *WhoAm 92, WhoE 93*
King, James Cecil 1924- *WhoAm 92*
King, James Claude 1924- *WhoAm 92*
King, James Edward 1940- *WhoAm 92, WhoE 93*
King, James Lawrence 1927- *WhoAm 92, WhoSSW 93*
King, James N. 1937- *WhoScE 91-1*
King, James Nedwed 1947- *St&PR 93, WhoAm 92*
King, James Russell 1954- *WhoEmL 93*
King, James W. *BioIn 17*
King, Jamie 1954- *St&PR 93*
King, Jane Cudlip Coblentz 1922- *WhoAmW 93*
King, Jennifer Carolyn 1960- *WhoAmW 93*
King, Jerry D. *Law&B 92*
King, Jerry P. 1935- *ConAu 139*
King, Jessie Marion 1875-1949 *BioIn 17*
King, Jimmie Leo 1938- *WhoSSW 93*
King, Jody W. *Law&B 92*
King, John *ScF&FL 92, WhoScE 91-1*
King, John Allison 1935- *WhoE 93, WhoWor 93*
King, John Anderson 1951- *WhoEmL 93*
King, John Barton 1873-1965 *BiDAMSp 1989*
King, John Charles Peter 1949- *WhoAm 92*
King, John D. 1913- *St&PR 93*
King, John Earl 1946- *WhoIns 93*
King, John Ethelbert, Jr. 1913- *WhoAm 92*
King, John Francis 1925- *WhoAm 92*
King, John Joseph 1938- *St&PR 93*
King, John Lane 1924- *WhoAm 92*
King, John P. 1938- *St&PR 93*
King, John P. 1951- *St&PR 93*
King, John Paul 1941- *WhoE 93*
King, John Quill Taylor 1921- *WhoAm 92*
King, John Robert 1948- *ScF&FL 92*
King, John Ronald Beresford 1942- *WhoWor 93*
King, John Stuart 1927- *WhoE 93*
King, John Talbott, Jr. 1945- *WhoAm 92*
King, Jon
See Gang of Four *ConMus 8*
King, Jon J. 1940- *St&PR 93*
King, Jonathan 1925- *WhoAm 92*
King, Joni D. *Law&B 92, St&PR 93*
King, Joseph Bertram 1924- *WhoAm 92*
King, Joseph E. 1941- *WhoIns 93*
King, Joseph Edward 1941- *St&PR 93*
King, Joseph Lloyd 1946- *WhoEmL 93*
King, Joseph Paul 1941- *WhoAm 92*
King, Joseph Willet 1934- *WhoSSW 93*
King, Joy Dent 1946- *WhoAmW 93*
King, Joyce *ConAu 37NR*
King, Joyce Calistri 1927- *WhoAmW 93*
King, Julia Marion 1939- *WhoWor 93*
King, Kamau J. *Law&B 92*
King, Karen Jeanne 1953- *WhoWrEP 92*
King, Karen K. *Law&B 92*
King, Karl L(awrence) 1891-1971 *Baker 92*
King, Katherine Chungho 1937- *WhoE 93*
King, Kathleen Marie *WhoE 93*
King, Kathryn Elizabeth 1926- *WhoWrEP 92*
King, Kathryn J. *Law&B 92*
King, Kathryn Theresa 1960- *WhoAmW 93*
King, Keith *Law&B 92*
King, Keith M. *ScF&FL 92*
King, Kelly Stuart 1948- *St&PR 93*
King, Kenneth Vernon, Jr. 1950- *WhoSSW 93*
King, Kernan Francis *Law&B 92*
King, Kernan Francis 1944- *St&PR 93, WhoAm 92*
King, Kimberly Nelson 1953- *WhoSSW 93*
King, L. Dianne 1958- *WhoAmW 93*
King, L. Ellis 1939- *WhoAm 92, WhoSSW 93*
King, Larry 1933- *BioIn 17, ConAu 139, ConTFT 10, News 93-1 [port], WhoAm 92*
King, Larry Dale *Law&B 92*
King, Larry Dale 1949- *St&PR 93*
King, Larry L. *BioIn 17*
King, Larry L. 1929- *ConTFT 10, WhoAm 92, WhoE 93*
King, Larry Peyton d1990 *BioIn 17*
King, Larry R. 1939- *St&PR 93*
King, Laura Jane 1947- *WhoAmW 93*
King, Laurel Luise *Law&B 92*
King, Lauren Juanita 1951- *WhoAmW 93, WhoEmL 93*
King, Lawrence E. *Law&B 92*
King, Lawrence E., Jr. *BioIn 17*
King, Lawrence Philip 1929- *WhoAm 92*
King, Lawrence Wayne 1940- *WhoE 93*
King, Lea Elise 1963- *WhoAmW 93*
King, Lee *WhoAm 92*
King, Leland W. 1907- *WhoAm 92*
King, Leon 1921- *WhoAm 92*
King, Leonard Henry 1940- *WhoWor 93*
King, Leroy A., Jr. 1940- *St&PR 93*
King, LeRoy Francis 1928- *St&PR 93*
King, Leslie John 1934- *WhoAm 92*
King, Linda Marie 1952- *WhoAmW 93*
King, Linda Orr 1948- *WhoAmW 93, WhoSSW 93*
King, Lis Sonder 1932- *WhoAmW 93*
King, Llewellyn Willings 1939- *WhoE 93*
King, Lorenz 1945- *WhoScE 91-3*
King, Lowell Restell 1932- *WhoAm 92*
King, Lyndel Irene Saunders 1943- *WhoAm 92*
King, M.S. *WhoScE 91-1*
King, Marcia 1940- *WhoAm 92, WhoAmW 93*
King, Marcia Gygli 1931- *WhoAmW 93*
King, Marcia Jones 1934- *WhoAmW 93, WhoE 93*
King, Marcia Louise 1950- *WhoWrEP 92*
King, Margaret Ann 1936- *WhoAmW 93*
King, Margaret Carolyn 1943- *WhoE 93*
King, Margaret Leah 1947- *WhoAm 92*
King, Margaret Mary *Law&B 92*
King, Margaret Mary 1953- *St&PR 93*
King, Marian A. *Law&B 92*
King, Marjorie Jean 1928- *WhoSSW 93*
King, Mark A. 1951- *St&PR 93*
King, Mark Charles 1961- *St&PR 93*
King, Marquita Juanita 1957- *WhoAmW 93*
King, Marsha K. *Law&B 92*
King, Marsha Krieger *Law&B 92*
King, Martin Luther 1929-1968 *BioIn 17*
King, Martin Luther, Jr. 1929-1968 *DcTwHis, EncAACR [port], PolPar*
King, Mary-Claire *BioIn 17*
King, Mary-Claire 1946- *WhoAmW 93*
King, Mary Jane 1950- *WhoAmW 93, WhoEmL 93*
King, Mary Kathleen Teresa 1939- *WhoWor 93*
King, Mary Margaret 1946- *WhoSSW 93*
King, Mary Perry 1865- *AmWomPl*
King, Mary Smothers 1937- *WhoAmW 93*
King, Marylee Hansen 1946- *WhoEmL 93*
King, Matthew c. 1733-1823 *OxDcOp*
King, Matthew L. *Law&B 92*
King, Matthew Peter c. 1773-1823 *Baker 92*
King, Maurice Athelstan 1936- *WhoWor 93*
King, Max A. *Law&B 92*
King, Maxwell E. P. *WhoAm 92, WhoE 93*
King, Melvin *Law&B 92*
King, Michael *NewYTBS 92 [port]*
King, Michael C. 1940- *St&PR 93*
King, Michael Dumont 1949- *WhoEmL 93*
King, Michael Gordon 1948- *St&PR 93*
King, Michael James 1957- *WhoE 93*
King, Michael John 1938- *St&PR 93*
King, Michael Lewis 1949- *WhoSSW 93*
King, Micki 1944- *BioIn 17*
King, Mike *BioIn 17*
King, Mike 1947- *St&PR 93*
King, Monica Kayla 1962- *WhoAmW 93, WhoEmL 93*
King, Morgana 1930- *WhoAm 92*
King, Morris Kenton 1924- *WhoAm 92*
King, Nadine Ronnie 1946- *WhoSSW 93*
King, Nancy 1936- *WhoAmW 93*
King, Nancy 1945- *WhoAmW 93*
King, Ned P. 1919- *St&PR 93*
King, Nicelma Johnson 1947- *WhoAmW 93*
King, Nicholas L. d1992 *NewYTBS 92*
King, Nina Davis 1941- *WhoAm 92*
King, Norman A. *ConAu 40NR*
King, Olin B. 1934- *St&PR 93, WhoSSW 93*
King, Oliver A. 1855-1923 *Baker 92*
King, Ordie Herbert, Jr. 1933- *WhoAm 92*
King, Pamela Ann 1951- *WhoE 93, WhoEmL 93*
King, Pamela Vernay 1965- *WhoAmW 93*
King, Patricia 1941- *WhoAm 92*
King, Patricia Ann 1942- *WhoAm 92*
King, Patricia Anne 1945- *WhoAmW 93*
King, Patricia Miller 1937- *WhoAm 92*
King, Patrick *WhoAm 92*
King, Paul Hamilton 1936- *WhoAm 92*
King, Paul Harvey 1941- *WhoSSW 93*
King, Paul L. 1934- *St&PR 93*
King, Paul Louis 1934- *WhoIns 93*
King, Paula *ScF&FL 92*
King, Perry 1948- *HolBB [port], WhoAm 92*
King, Pete 1914-1982 *Baker 92*
King, Peter Cotterill 1930- *WhoAm 92*
King, Peter J. 1938- *WhoE 93, WhoWor 93*
King, Peter J., Jr. 1921- *St&PR 93*
King, Peter Joseph, Jr. 1921- *WhoAm 92*
King, Phil John 1940- *WhoWrEP 92*
King, Philip 1872-1938 *BiDAMSp 1989*
King, Philip Gordon 1922- *WhoE 93, WhoWor 93*
King, Phillip 1934- *WhoWor 93*
King, Preston 1806-1865 *PolPar*
King, R. Edwin, Jr. 1936- *EncAACR*
King, Ray John 1933- *WhoAm 92*
King, Reatha Clark 1938- *AfrAmBi*
King, Renita D. *Law&B 92*
King, Rey Reginald 1954- *WhoWrEP 92*
King, Richard Allen 1944- *WhoAm 92*
King, Richard Allen, Sr. 1939- *WhoWrEP 92*
King, Richard Arthur 1940- *St&PR 93*
King, Richard Eugene 1948- *WhoE 93, WhoEmL 93, WhoWor 93*
King, Richard H. 1942- *ConAu 40NR*
King, Richard Harding 1925- *WhoAm 92*
King, Richard Hood 1934- *St&PR 93, WhoAm 92*
King, Richard Hugg 1767-1835 *BioIn 17*
King, Rick *MiSFD 9*
King, Robert *ScF&FL 92*
King, Robert Allen *BioIn 17*
King, Robert Augustin 1910- *WhoAm 92, WhoWor 93*
King, Robert B. 1950- *WhoIns 93*
King, Robert Bainton 1922- *WhoAm 92*
King, Robert Bennett 1928- *WhoSSW 93*
King, Robert Bruce 1938- *WhoAm 92*
King, Robert Charles 1928- *WhoAm 92*
King, Robert Cotton 1931- *WhoAm 92*
King, Robert D. 1936- *WhoAm 92*
King, Robert D. 1950- *St&PR 93*
King, Robert David 1950- *WhoAm 92*
King, Robert Harlen 1935- *WhoSSW 93*
King, Robert Howard 1941- *St&PR 93*
King, Robert J. 1946- *St&PR 93*
King, Robert J., Jr. *Law&B 92*
King, Robert John 1935- *WhoAm 92*
King, Robert L. 1938- *St&PR 93*
King, Robert Leonard 1904- *WhoAm 92*
King, Robert Leroy 1931- *WhoAm 92*
King, Robert Lewis, Sr. 1940- *AfrAmBi [port]*
King, Robert Lucien 1936- *WhoAm 92, WhoWor 93*
King, Robert M. 1945- *St&PR 93*
King, Robert N. *Law&B 92*
King, Robert Royal *WhoIns 93*
King, Robert Thomas 1930- *WhoAm 92*
King, Robert W., Jr. 1946- *WhoEmL 93, WhoSSW 93*
King, Rodney *BioIn 17*
King, Roger *NewYTBS 92 [port]*
King, Roger (Frank Graham) 1947- *ConAu 139*
King, Roger J. *St&PR 93*
King, Roger J.B. 1933- *WhoScE 91-1*
King, Roger Leo 1945- *St&PR 93*
King, Rollin White 1931- *St&PR 93*
King, Rona I. 1947- *St&PR 93*
King, Ronald Curtis *WhoScE 91-1*
King, Ronold Wyeth Percival 1905- *WhoAm 92, WhoWor 93*
King, Rosalyn Mercita 1948- *WhoAmW 93, WhoEmL 93*
King, Ruby Thompson *WhoAmW 93, WhoWor 93*
King, Rufus 1893-1966 *ScF&FL 92*
King, Rufus 1917- *WhoAm 92*
King, Russell C., Jr. 1934- *WhoSSW 93*
King, Ruth *BioIn 17*
King, Sam *BioIn 17*
King, Sam S. 1924- *St&PR 93*
King, Samuel 1847-1882 *BioIn 17*
King, Samuel Pailthorpe 1916- *WhoAm 92*
King, Sandra 1944- *WhoAmW 93*
King, Sandra Lee 1942- *WhoAmW 93*

King, Sanford MacCallum 1926- *WhoAm 92*
King, Sarah Christine *Law&B 92*
King, Scottow Atherton *Law&B 92*
King, Sharon Mulrooney 1938- *WhoSSW 93*
King, Sheldon Selig 1931- *WhoAm 92*
King, Sheri-Lee 1964- *WhoAmW 93*
King, SherriJoyce 1948- *WhoAmW 93*
King, Sheryl Jayne 1945- *WhoAmW 93, WhoWor 93*
King, Sidsel Elizabeth Beth 1932- *WhoAmW 93*
King, Spencer Taft 1938- *WhoWor 93*
King, Stephen 1944- *WhoSSW 93*
King, Stephen 1947- *BioIn 17, MagSAmL [port], MiSFD 9, ScF&FL 92*
King, Stephen E. *Law&B 92*
King, Stephen Edwin 1947- *WhoAm 92, WhoE 93, WhoWrEP 92*
King, Stephen Scott 1937- *WhoAm 92*
King, Stephen William Pearce 1947- *WhoWor 93*
King, Steve Mason 1951- *WhoEmL 93, WhoSSW 93*
King, Steven 1960- *WhoE 93*
King, Steven Alan 1951- *WhoEmL 93*
King, Steven Bruce 1949- *WhoAm 92*
King, Steven Ray 1960- *WhoSSW 93*
King, Susan B. 1940- *St&PR 93*
King, Susan Bennett 1940- *WhoAm 92, WhoAmW 93*
King, Susan Elizabeth 1947- *WhoEmL 93*
King, Susan M. *Law&B 92*
King, T. Jackson 1948- *ScF&FL 92*
King, Tabitha 1949- *ScF&FL 92*
King, Tammy Lynn 1964- *WhoE 93*
King, Tappan 1950- *ScF&FL 92*
King, Teresita Lim 1952- *WhoAmW 93, WhoWor 93*
King, Thea 1925- *Baker 92*
King, Thomas 1934- *WhoE 93*
King, Thomas 1944- *WhoWor 93*
King, Thomas A. 1942- *St&PR 93*
King, Thomas Allen 1942- *WhoAm 92*
King, Thomas B. *St&PR 93*
King, Thomas Creighton 1928- *WhoAm 92*
King, Thomas H. 1934- *WhoAm 92*
King, Thomas Howard 1955- *St&PR 93, WhoEmL 93*
King, Thomas Jeremy 1933- *WhoWor 93*
King, Thomas L. 1930- *St&PR 93, WhoE 93*
King, Thomas Lawrence 1953- *WhoE 93*
King, Thomas R. *St&PR 93*
King, Thomas Syme 1946- *St&PR 93*
King, Timothy Allen *Law&B 92*
King, Tom 1946- *WhoSSW 93*
King, Toni Holly 1954- *WhoSSW 93*
King, Vincent 1935- *ScF&FL 92*
King, W. Russell 1949- *St&PR 93, WhoAm 92*
King, Walter Barnett, Jr. 1959- *WhoSSW 93*
King, Walter Clair 1927- *St&PR 93*
King, Walter Francis, III 1932- *WhoWor 93*
King, Walter Wing-Keung 1950- *WhoWor 93*
King, Warren R. 1950- *St&PR 93*
King, Wayne Lynn 1948- *WhoSSW 93*
King, Weldon 1911- *WhoWor 93*
King, Wilhelmenia Ormond 1933- *WhoSSW 93*
King, Willard Fahrenkamp 1924- *WhoAm 92*
King, William Bruce 1932- *WhoAm 92*
King, William Carl 1944- *WhoAm 92*
King, William Collins 1921- *WhoAm 92*
King, William Douglas 1941- *WhoAm 92, WhoE 93*
King, William Joseph 1929- *St&PR 93*
King, William Lyon MacKenzie 1874-1950 *BioIn 17, DcTwHis*
King, William Patrick 1947- *St&PR 93*
King, William Patrick 1962- *WhoE 93*
King, William R. D. 1786-1853 *PolPar*
King, William Richard 1938- *WhoAm 92*
King, William T. *Law&B 92*
King, William Terry 1943- *WhoAm 92*
King, William Warren 1944- *WhoWrEP 92*
King, William Wonderly 1918- *WhoSSW 93*
King, Woodie, Jr. 1937- *WhoAm 92*
King, Woods, Jr. 1928- *St&PR 93, WhoAm 92*
King, Yvonne Marcella 1939- *WhoE 93*
King, Yvonne Nyoka 1952- *WhoEmL 93*
King, Zalman *MiSFD 9*
Kingcaid, Raymond L. 1924- *St&PR 93*
King Calkins, Carol Coleman 1949- *WhoAmW 93, WhoEmL 93*
King Curtis 1934-1971 *SoulM*
Kingdom, Roger 1962- *BiDAMSp 1989*
Kingdon, Henry Shannon 1934- *WhoAm 92*
Kingdon, John Wells 1940- *WhoAm 92*
Kingdon, Robert McCune 1927- *WhoAm 92*
Kingdon, V. Scott *Law&B 92*
Kinge, Sadik Aziz 1931- *WhoUN 92*
Kingery, John *BioIn 17*
Kingery, John C. *Law&B 92*
Kingery, John C. d1992 *NewYTBS 92*
Kingery, William David 1926- *WhoAm 92*
Kinget, G. Marian 1910- *WhoAm 92*
Kinget, R.D. 1938- *WhoScE 91-2*
King-Ettema, Elizabeth Dorothy 1953- *WhoAmW 93*
King Family *BioIn 17*
King Floyd *SoulM*
King-Griswold, Kathy Ann 1957- *WhoEmL 93*
King-Haden, Kelly Louise 1959- *WhoAmW 93*
King-Hall, Magdalen 1904-1971 *ScF&FL 92*
Kingham, Richard Frank 1946- *WhoAm 92, WhoE 93, WhoWor 93*
Kinghorn, Carol Ann *WhoAmW 93*
Kinghorn, Curtis D. *Law&B 92*
Kinghorn, Frank C. 1943- *WhoScE 91-1*
Kingibe, Baba Gana 1945- *WhoAfr*
Kingma, Stanley George 1937- *WhoSSW 93*
Kingma, Todd W. *Law&B 92*
Kingman, David Arthur 1948- *BiDAMSp 1989*
Kingman, Dong 1911- *BioIn 17, WhoAm 92*
Kingman, Joseph Ramsdell, III 1927- *WhoAm 92*
Kingman, Lee 1919- *BioIn 17*
Kingman, (Mary) Lee 1919- *DcAmChF 1960*
Kingman, William Lockwood 1930- *WhoAm 92*
Kingsberg, Alan *MiSFD 9*
Kingsberg, Harold J. 1927- *St&PR 93*
Kingsberg, Harold Joseph 1927- *WhoAm 92*
Kingsbery, Walton Waits, Jr. 1928- *WhoAm 92*
Kingsbury, Arthur F. 1948- *St&PR 93*
Kingsbury, Carolyn Ann 1938- *WhoAmW 93*
Kingsbury, Charles Herbert 1932- *WhoE 93*
Kingsbury, David T. 1940- *WhoAm 92*
Kingsbury, Debra L. *Law&B 92*
Kingsbury, Donald 1929- *ScF&FL 92, WhoCanL 92*
Kingsbury, Dorothy Louise 1946- *WhoWrEP 92*
Kingsbury, Frederick Hutchinson 1907-1989 *BioIn 17*
Kingsbury, Gale N. 1935- *St&PR 93*
Kingsbury, Herbert Brenneis 1934- *WhoE 93*
Kingsbury, John Merriam 1928- *WhoAm 92, WhoWor 93*
Kingsbury, Kathleen A. *Law&B 92*
Kingsbury, Mary Melinda 1867-1951 *BioIn 17*
Kingsbury, Read Austin 1925- *WhoAm 92*
Kingsbury, Richard F. 1941- *St&PR 93*
Kingsbury, Sara 1876- *AmWomPl*
Kingsbury, Susan 1870-1949 *BioIn 17*
Kingsbury-Smith, Joseph 1908- *St&PR 93, WhoAm 92*
Kingseed, C. Mark *Law&B 92*
Kingsford, Barbara A. *Law&B 92*
Kingsford, William C. 1946- *St&PR 93*
Kingsford, William Charles 1946- *WhoAm 92*
Kingslake, Rudolf 1903- *WhoAm 92*
Kingsley, Alvin B. 1936- *St&PR 93*
Kingsley, Ben *BioIn 17*
Kingsley, Ben 1943- *WhoAm 92, WhoWor 93*
Kingsley, Charles 1819-1875 *NinCLC 35 [port]*
Kingsley, Daniel Thain 1932- *WhoAm 92*
Kingsley, Darwin Pearl, III 1927- *WhoE 93*
Kingsley, Dorothy 1909- *BioIn 17*
Kingsley, Emily Perl 1940- *WhoAmW 93*
Kingsley, Frederick William 1932- *St&PR 93*
Kingsley, James Gordon 1933- *WhoAm 92*
Kingsley, Jean-Pierre 1943- *WhoAm 92*
Kingsley, John M., Jr. 1931- *St&PR 93*
Kingsley, John McCall, Jr. 1931- *WhoAm 92*
Kingsley, Lawrence Scott 1955- *WhoEmL 93*
Kingsley, Mary 1862-1900 *Expl 93 [port]*
Kingsley, Mary Henrietta 1862-1900 *BioIn 17*
Kingsley, Oliver Dowling, Jr. 1942- *WhoAm 92*
Kingsley, Patricia 1932- *WhoAm 92*
Kingsley, Sarah Du Bois 1958- *WhoE 93*
Kingsley, Sidney 1906- *WhoAm 92*
Kingsley, Thomas Drowne 1916- *WhoAm 92*
Kingsley, Walter Ingalls 1923- *WhoAm 92*
Kingsley, William E. 1934- *WhoIns 93*
Kingsley, William Earl 1944- *St&PR 93*
Kingsley Linfoot, Catherine Priscilla 1948- *WhoAmW 93*
Kingsmill, A.S. 1927- *St&PR 93*
Kingsmill, Suzanne Foster 1952- *WhoWrEP 92*
King-Smith, Dick 1922- *ChlFicS, MajAI [port], ScF&FL 92*
Kings of Rhythm *SoulM*
Kingsolver, Barbara *BioIn 17*
Kingsolver, Barbara Ellen 1955- *WhoAm 92*
Kingson, Charles I. 1938- *WhoAm 92*
Kingson, Eric Roger 1946- *WhoEmL 93*
Kingston, Arthur Edward *WhoScE 91-1*
Kingston, Cecelia M. *WhoWrEP 92*
Kingston, David George Ian 1938- *WhoSSW 93*
Kingston, George *WhoAm 92*
Kingston, James Burke 1953- *WhoEmL 93, WhoSSW 93*
Kingston, Jeremy *ScF&FL 92*
Kingston, John Vincent 1937- *WhoUN 92*
Kingston, Mary F. *AmWomPl*
Kingston, Maurice David 1937- *WhoWor 93*
Kingston, Maxine Hong *BioIn 17*
Kingston, Maxine Hong 1940- *AmWomWr 92, MagSAmL [port], WhoAm 92, WhoAmW 93*
Kingston, Maxine (Ting Ting) Hong 1940- *ConAu 38NR*
Kingston, Neal Martin 1951- *WhoE 93*
Kingston, Paul Frederick *WhoScE 91-1*
Kingston, Robert Hildreth 1928- *WhoAm 92*
Kingston, Winifred 1894-1967 *SweetSg A*
Kingston Trio, The *ConMus 9 [port]*
Kington, Barry Clark 1942- *WhoWor 93*
Kingwill, David G. 1940- *St&PR 93*
Kinigakis, Panagiotis 1949- *WhoE 93, WhoWor 93*
Kinion, Darrell G. 1954- *St&PR 93*
Kinion, Mark Anthony 1956- *WhoSSW 93*
Kinirons, John J. *Law&B 92*
Kinison, Sam *BioIn 17*
Kinison, Sam d1992 *NewYTBS 92 [port]*
Kinison, Sam c. 1954-1992 *News 93-1*
Kinkade, Arlie *AmWomPl*
Kinkade, Edgar D. 1950- *St&PR 93*
Kinkade, Maurice Edward 1942- *St&PR 93*
Kinkaid, Thomas Cassin 1888-1972 *HarEnMi*
Kinkead, Eugene d1992 *NewYTBS 92*
Kinkead, Verda Christine 1931- *WhoAmW 93*
Kinkel, Anne Jackson 1961- *WhoAmW 93*
Kinkel, Johanna 1810-1858 *Baker 92*
Kinkel, Klaus 1936- *WhoWor 93*
Kinkeldey, Otto 1878-1966 *Baker 92, BioIn 17*
Kinkle, George Phillip, Jr. 1925- *WhoAm 92*
Kinkoku 1761-1832 *BioIn 17*
Kinlaw, Dennis Franklin 1922- *WhoAm 92, WhoSSW 93*
Kinlaw, Elizabeth Davis 1919- *WhoAmW 93*
Kinler, Robert J. *Law&B 92*
Kinloch, Johnny 1936- *St&PR 93*
Kinloch, Robert Francis 1937- *WhoUN 92*
Kinlow, Eugene 1940- *WhoAm 92*
Kinman, James Walter 1930- *St&PR 93*
Kinmartin, Paul D., Sr. 1946- *St&PR 93*
Kinmouth, Margy *MiSFD 9*
Kinn, John Matthias 1925- *WhoAm 92, WhoE 93, WhoWor 93*
Kinnaird, Charles Roemler 1932- *WhoAm 92*
Kinnaird, John 1924-1980 *ScF&FL 92*
Kinnaird, Margaret Mary 1949- *WhoEmL 93*
Kinnaird, Michael Gates 1956- *WhoSSW 93*
Kinnaird, W.H. 1923- *St&PR 93*
Kinnaman, C. F., Mrs. *AmWomPl*
Kinnaman, David L. 1938- *St&PR 93*
Kinnaman, William Andrew *Law&B 92*
Kinnamon, David Lucas 1941- *WhoAm 92*
Kinnamon, Jay Brian 1959- *WhoIns 93*
Kinnamon, Keneth 1932- *WhoAm 92, WhoSSW 93*
Kinnamon, Kenneth Ellis 1934- *WhoAm 92*
Kinnamos, John c. 1143-c. 1185 *OxDcByz*
Kinnan, Brent E. *Law&B 92*
Kinnan, David E. *Law&B 92*
Kinnan, Roy Doug 1951- *WhoIns 93*
Kinnard, David B. 1951- *St&PR 93*
Kinnard, Roy 1952- *ScF&FL 92*
Kinnard, William James, Jr. 1932- *WhoAm 92*
Kinnari, Markus Juhani 1943- *WhoScE 91-4*
Kinne, David Weir 1936- *WhoWor 93*
Kinne, Frances Bartlett *WhoAm 92, WhoAmW 93*
Kinne, Jack Robert 1948- *St&PR 93*
Kinne, Morris Y., Jr. *Law&B 92*
Kinne, Otto 1923- *WhoScE 91-3*
Kinne, Rolf K.-H. 1941- *WhoScE 91-3*
Kinnear, George E.R., II 1928- *St&PR 93, WhoAm 92*
Kinnear, James W. 1898-1990 *BioIn 17*
Kinnear, James W. 1928- *St&PR 93*
Kinnear, James Wesley, III 1928- *WhoAm 92, WhoE 93*
Kinnear, Mary 1898-1991 *BioIn 17*
Kinnear, Susan Jenkins d1992 *NewYTBS 92*
Kinneberg, Arthur Hempton 1921- *WhoAm 92*
Kinnebrew, Guy Forrest 1949- *WhoEmL 93*
Kinnebrew, Jackson Metcalfe 1941- *WhoAm 92*
Kinnell, Galway 1927- *AmWrS3, BioIn 17, WhoWrEP 92*
Kinnen, Edwin 1925- *WhoAm 92*
Kinner, Albert Vernon 1927- *St&PR 93*
Kinner, Peter Cummings 1947- *WhoEmL 93*
Kinnerley, Lynne *ScF&FL 92*
Kinnersly, Philip *Law&B 92*
Kinney, A.M., Jr. *Law&B 92*
Kinney, Abbott Ford 1909- *WhoWor 93*
Kinney, Aldon M., Jr. 1921- *St&PR 93*
Kinney, Aldon Monroe, Jr. 1921- *WhoAm 92*
Kinney, Allan G. 1951- *St&PR 93*
Kinney, Arthur Frederick 1933- *WhoAm 92, WhoE 93*
Kinney, Bernard E. 1929- *St&PR 93*
Kinney, Bill *BioIn 17*
Kinney, Charles 1906-1991 *BioIn 17*
Kinney, Dale Francis 1930- *St&PR 93*
Kinney, Daniel *Law&B 92*
Kinney, Daniel Earl 1961- *WhoEmL 93*
Kinney, Dennis M. *Law&B 92*
Kinney, Donal *Law&B 92*
Kinney, Earl Robert 1917- *WhoAm 92*
Kinney, Francis L. 1932- *St&PR 93*
Kinney, George Patrick 1959- *WhoEmL 93*
Kinney, Jack d1992 *BioIn 17, NewYTBS 92*
Kinney, James Raymond 1951- *WhoSSW 93*
Kinney, John Francis 1937- *WhoAm 92*
Kinney, Joseph Allen 1949- *WhoEmL 93*
Kinney, Karin Margaret *Law&B 92*
Kinney, Kenneth Parrish 1921- *WhoAm 92*
Kinney, Kristi LeAnn 1957- *WhoAmW 93*
Kinney, Linford Nelson 1937- *WhoWor 93*
Kinney, Lisa Frances 1951- *WhoAmW 93*
Kinney, Marjorie Sharon 1940- *WhoAmW 93*
Kinney, Mary Anne *Law&B 92*
Kinney, Pamela *BioIn 17*
Kinney, Robert Bruce 1937- *WhoAm 92*
Kinney, William Burnet 1799-1880 *JrnUS*
Kinney, William Light, Jr. 1933- *WhoAm 92, WhoSSW 93*
Kinney, William Rudolph, Jr. 1942- *WhoAm 92*
Kinney Hanson, Sharon D. 1942- *WhoWrEP 92*
Kinniburgh, Alan James 1951- *WhoE 93*
Kinnick, Nile 1919?-1943 *BioIn 17*
Kinnicutt, Philip Heywood 1941- *St&PR 93*
Kinniment, David John *WhoScE 91-1*
Kinning, Ronald Lee 1939- *St&PR 93*
Kinninger, Terance A. 1956- *St&PR 93*
Kinnison, William Andrew 1932- *WhoAm 92*
Kinnock, Neil *BioIn 17*
Kinnock, Neil 1942- *NewYTBS 92 [port]*
Kinnock, Neil Gordon 1942- *WhoWor 93*
Kino, Carol *BioIn 17*
Kino, Gordon Stanley 1928- *WhoAm 92*
Kino, Isamu 1932- *WhoWor 93*
Kinoe, Yosuke 1961- *WhoWor 93*
Kinon, Richard *MiSFD 9*
Kinoshita, Etsuji 1920- *WhoWor 93*
Kinoshita, Isaac Shinichi 1933- *St&PR 93*
Kinoshita, Kay 1954- *WhoEmL 93*
Kinoshita, Keisuke 1912- *MiSFD 9*
Kinoshita, Shigeru 1950- *WhoWor 93*
Kinoshita, Shinji 1931- *WhoWor 93*
Kinoshita, Toichiro 1925- *WhoAm 92*
Kinoshita, Tomio 1944- *WhoWor 93*
Kinosian, Janet Marie 1957- *WhoAmW 93*
Kinosita, Seiiti 1924- *WhoWor 93*
Kinoy, Sarah Jane d1991 *BioIn 17*
Kinra, Vikram Kumar 1946- *WhoSSW 93*
Kins, Tonya *Law&B 92*
Kinsbury, Arthur F. 1948- *St&PR 93*

Kinsell, Jeffrey Clift 1951- *WhoEmL 93*
Kinsell, Robert Patrick 1951- *WhoSSW 93*
Kinsella, Daniel John 1952- *WhoE 93*
Kinsella, Dorothy M. 1944- *WhoScE 91-3*
Kinsella, John Degan 1941- *WhoE 93*
Kinsella, John Edward 1938- *WhoAm 92*
Kinsella, Marco Antonio 1954- *WhoE 93*
Kinsella, Ralph Aloysius, Jr. 1919- *WhoAm 92*
Kinsella, Thomas 1928- *BioIn 17, WhoWor 93*
Kinsella, W.P. *BioIn 17*
Kinsella, W.P. 1935- *ScF&FL 92*
Kinsella, W(illiam) P(atrick) 1935- *WhoWrEP 92*
Kinsella, William P. 1935- *WhoCanL 92*
Kinsella, William Patrick 1935- *WhoAm 92*
Kinser, Dennis 1944- *St&PR 93*
Kinser, Donald Leroy 1941- *WhoSSW 93*
Kinser, Nicole LaMarr 1962- *WhoAmW 93*
Kinser, Richard Edward 1936- *WhoWor 93*
Kinsey, Helen E. 1906-1990 *BioIn 17*
Kinsey, James Andrew 1945- *WhoE 93*
Kinsey, James Lloyd 1934- *WhoAm 92*
Kinsey, Madalyn Suzann *Law&B 92*
Kinsey, Norman Victor 1921- *St&PR 93*
Kinsey, Raymond Alexander 1929- *St&PR 93*
Kinsey, Wayne R. 1942- *St&PR 93*
Kinsey, William Charles 1935- *St&PR 93, WhoAm 92*
Kinsey-Warnock, Natalie 1956- *SmATA 71 [port]*
Kinsinger, David Lester *Law&B 92*
Kinsinger, Jack Burl 1925- *WhoAm 92*
Kinsinger, Robert Earl 1923- *WhoAm 92*
Kinski, Klaus 1926- *IntDcF 2-3 [port]*
Kinski, Klaus 1926-1991 *AnObit 1991, BioIn 17, ConTFT 10, News 92*
Kinski, Nastassia *BioIn 17*
Kinski, Nastassia 1961- *IntDcF 2-3*
Kinski, Nastassja *WhoAm 92*
Kinsky, Georg Ludwig 1882-1951 *Baker 92*
Kinsler, Bruce Whitney 1947- *WhoEmL 93*
Kinsley, Michael *BioIn 17*
Kinsley, Michael E. 1951- *WhoAm 92, WhoE 93*
Kinsley, Terrence D. 1952- *St&PR 93*
Kinsley, William Benton 1934- *WhoAm 92, WhoWrEP 92*
Kinslow, William Edward 1938- *St&PR 93*
Kinsman, David Bailey 1953- *WhoE 93*
Kinsman, Donald Markham 1923- *WhoE 93*
Kinsman, Frank William 1925- *WhoE 93*
Kinsman, Lawrence Charles 1953- *WhoWrEP 92*
Kinsman, Robert Donald 1929- *WhoAm 92*
Kinsman, Robert Preston 1949- *WhoEmL 93, WhoWor 93*
Kinsolving, Augustus B. *Law&B 92*
Kinsolving, Augustus Blagden 1940- *St&PR 93, WhoAm 92*
Kinsolving, Charles McIlvaine, Jr. 1927- *WhoAm 92*
Kinsolving, Laurence Edwin 1941- *WhoAm 92, WhoSSW 93*
Kinstler, Bradley Dean 1953- *WhoIns 93*
Kinstler, Everett Raymond 1926- *WhoAm 92, WhoWor 93*
Kinstlick, Riva F. *Law&B 92*
Kinstlinger, Jack 1931- *St&PR 93, WhoAm 92, WhoE 93*
Kint, Andre 1929- *WhoScE 91-2*
Kintanar, Thomas Artuz 1955- *WhoEmL 93*
Kinter, Bruce Timothy 1949- *WhoEmL 93*
Kintigh, Allen Ellis 1924- *St&PR 93*
Kintigh, William Thomas 1946- *St&PR 93*
Kintisch, Nancy *BioIn 17*
Kintner, Earl W. *BioIn 17*
Kintner, Earl W. d1991 *NewYTBS 92*
Kintner, Earl W(ilson) 1912-1991 *CurBio 92N*
Kintner, Jerome Worthy 1915- *St&PR 93*
Kintner, Treva Carpenter 1920- *WhoAmW 93, WhoWor 93*
Kintner, William Roscoe 1915- *WhoAm 92, WhoWor 93*
Kintup 1849?- *Expl 93*
Kintz, George Jerome 1931- *St&PR 93*
Kintz, Virginia J. 1917- *St&PR 93*
Kintzele, John Alfred 1936- *WhoAm 92*
Kintzing, Donald C. 1929- *WhoIns 93*
Kinukawa, Masakiti 1929- *WhoWor 93*
Kinunda, Michael Joseph 1934- *WhoUN 92*
Kinyon, Grace V. *AmWomPl*
Kinzel, Helmut 1925- *WhoScE 91-4*
Kinzel, Richard L. 1940- *St&PR 93*
Kinzel, Wolfgang 1949- *WhoScE 91-3*
Kinzelbach, Ragnar K. 1941- *WhoScE 91-3*
Kinzelberg, Harvey 1945- *WhoAm 92*
Kinzer, Debra Anne 1959- *WhoAmW 93*
Kinzer, Donald Louis 1914- *WhoAm 92*
Kinzer, Donald Marshall 1943- *St&PR 93*
Kinzer, James R. *Law&B 92*
Kinzer, James Raymond 1928- *WhoAm 92*
Kinzer, William Luther 1929- *WhoAm 92*
Kinzey, Bertram York, Jr. 1921- *WhoSSW 93*
Kinzey, Ouida Blackerby 1922- *WhoAmW 93*
Kinzey, Ruth Ellen 1955- *WhoAmW 93*
Kinzey, Warren Glenford 1935- *WhoAm 92, WhoE 93*
Kinzie, Jeannie Jones 1940- *WhoAmW 93*
Kinzie, Mary 1944- *WhoWrEP 92*
Kinzie, Miriam Annette 1953- *WhoAmW 93*
Kinzie, Pamela L. 1953- *WhoAmW 93*
Kinzie, Raymond Wyant 1930- *St&PR 93, WhoAm 92*
Kinzie, Robert William 1933- *St&PR 93*
Kinzig, Raymond Charles 1946- *WhoEmL 93*
Kinzinger, Hector 1927- *WhoScE 91-2*
Kinzinger, Laura Lee 1951- *WhoAmW 93*
Kinzler, Alexander C. 1958- *St&PR 93*
Kinzler, Kennard A. 1943- *St&PR 93*
Kinzler, Morton H. 1925- *St&PR 93*
Kinzler, Thomas M. *Law&B 92*
Kinzly, Robert Edward 1939- *WhoAm 92*
Kioka, Jun 1952- *WhoAsAP 91*
Kiolbasa, Charles G., Jr. 1951- *St&PR 93*
Kiolbassa, Peter 1837-1905 *PolBiDi*
Kionka, Edward James 1939- *WhoAm 92*
Kiousis, Martin John 1930- *St&PR 93*
Kip, Richard deR. 1913- *WhoIns 93*
Kip, Ruloff F., Jr. *Law&B 92*
Kip, Terri Skinner 1955- *WhoAmW 93*
Kipalan, Albert 1948- *WhoAsAP 91*
Kiper, Ali Muhlis 1924- *WhoAm 92*
Kiper, Florence *AmWomPl*
Kiperman, IAkov Efimovich 1893-1938 *BioIn 17*
Kipka, Ross A. *Law&B 92*
Kipke, Harry George 1899-1972 *BiDAMSp 1989*
Kipling, Rudyard 1865-1936 *BioIn 17, MagSWL [port], ScF&FL 92, WorLitC [port]*
Kipling, (Joseph) Rudyard 1865-1936 *MajAI [port]*
Kiplinger, Austin Huntington 1918- *St&PR 93, WhoAm 92, WhoWrEP 92*
Kiplinger, Christina Louise 1957- *WhoWrEP 92*
Kiplinger, Glenn Francis 1930- *WhoAm 92*
Kiplinger, Knight A. 1948- *WhoAm 92*
Kiplinger, Knight Austin 1948- *St&PR 93*
Kiplinger, LaVerne Colwell d1990 *BioIn 17*
Kiplinger, Willard Monroe d1967 *BioIn 17*
Kipnis, Aaron R. 1948- *ConAu 137*
Kipnis, Alexander 1891-1978 *Baker 92, BioIn 17, IntDcOp [port], OxDcOp*
Kipnis, David Morris 1927- *WhoAm 92*
Kipnis, Howard Alan *Law&B 92*
Kipnis, Igor 1930- *Baker 92, WhoAm 92*
Kipnis, Levin 1894-1990 *BioIn 17*
Kipniss, Robert 1931- *WhoAm 92*
Kipp, Donald Bogart 1905-1991 *BioIn 17*
Kipp, Egbert Mason 1914- *WhoWor 93*
Kipp, John H. 1943- *St&PR 93*
Kipp, Lyman 1929- *WhoSSW 93*
Kipp, Robert Almy 1932- *WhoAm 92*
Kippax, John 1915-1974 *ScF&FL 92*
Kippel, Gary M. *WhoAm 92, WhoE 93*
Kippels, Steven Loren 1950- *WhoSSW 93*
Kippenhahn, Rudolf 1926- *WhoScE 91-3*
Kippenhan, Charles Jacob 1919- *WhoAm 92*
Kipper, Barbara Levy 1942- *St&PR 93, WhoAmW 93*
Kipper, Judith *BioIn 17*
Kippert, Robert John, Jr. 1952- *WhoEmL 93*
Kippes, Otto *BioIn 17*
Kipphardt, Heinar 1922-1982 *DcLB 124 [port]*
Kipphut, W. Michael 1953- *St&PR 93*
Kipping, Hans F. 1924- *WhoE 93*
Kipping, Vernon Louis 1921- *WhoWor 93*
Kipple, C. Wayne 1942- *St&PR 93*
Kiprian c. 1330-1406 *OxDcByz*
Kipriyanov, Ivan Alexandrovich 1923- *WhoWor 93*
Kira, Mitsuo 1943- *WhoWor 93*
Kiracofe, Barbara Elaine 1934- *WhoAmW 93*
Kiraly, Erno 1919- *Baker 92*
Kiraly, James Francis 1933- *St&PR 93*
Kiraly, Laszlo 1930- *WhoScE 91-4*
Kiraly, Thomas E. 1960- *St&PR 93*
Kiraly, Zoltan 1925- *WhoScE 91-4*
Kiran, Yurcell *Law&B 92*
Kirban, Lloyd 1931- *WhoAm 92*
Kirban, Salem *ScF&FL 92*
Kirbo, Bruce, Sr. 1930- *St&PR 93*
Kirbo, Charles Hughes 1917- *WhoAm 92*
Kirby, Allan Price, Jr. 1931- *St&PR 93, WhoAm 92*
Kirby, Brian J. *WhoScE 91-1*
Kirby, Brian John 1936- *WhoWor 93*
Kirby, Bruce Robert William 1929- *WhoE 93*
Kirby, C.E. *WhoScE 91-1*
Kirby, Carol Eller *Law&B 92*
Kirby, Charles Hoyt, III 1945- *WhoSSW 93*
Kirby, Charles William, Jr. 1926- *WhoAm 92*
Kirby, Dan L. *Law&B 92*
Kirby, Dan L. 1946- *St&PR 93*
Kirby, Daniel B. 1950- *St&PR 93*
Kirby, Deborah MacDonald 1948- *WhoAmW 93*
Kirby, Emily Baruch 1929- *WhoAm 92*
Kirby, Francis L. 1944- *St&PR 93*
Kirby, Frank N. 1925- *St&PR 93*
Kirby, Fred M., II 1919- *St&PR 93*
Kirby, Fred Morgan, II 1919- *WhoAm 92*
Kirby, Gary L. 1942- *St&PR 93, WhoIns 93*
Kirby, Gordon William *WhoScE 91-1*
Kirby, Gordon William 1934- *WhoWor 93*
Kirby, Harriet Griswold *AmWomPl*
Kirby, Herbert Weldon 1933- *St&PR 93*
Kirby, Howard Roland *WhoScE 91-1*
Kirby, Ian John 1934- *WhoWor 93*
Kirby, Jackie 1947- *WhoSSW 93*
Kirby, James Edmund, Jr. 1933- *WhoAm 92*
Kirby, James Wallace 1947- *WhoEmL 93, WhoSSW 93*
Kirby, Jane Crocker 1953- *WhoAmW 93*
Kirby, Jeri Patricia Hall 1947- *WhoAmW 93*
Kirby, Joe F. 1953- *WhoAm 92*
Kirby, Joe P. 1953- *St&PR 93*
Kirby, Joe Patrick 1953- *WhoIns 93*
Kirby, John *BioIn 17*
Kirby, John 1908-1952 *Baker 92*
Kirby, John Joseph, Jr. 1939- *WhoAm 92*
Kirby, John P., Jr. *Law&B 92*
Kirby, Kathleen M. *Law&B 92*
Kirby, Kenneth Bruce 1957- *WhoEmL 93*
Kirby, Kent Bruce 1934- *WhoAm 92*
Kirby, Kerry J. 1946- *St&PR 93*
Kirby, Kier *BioIn 17*
Kirby, Lillian Margaret Bruno 1953- *WhoAmW 93*
Kirby, Margaret *SmATA 72*
Kirby, Mary Weeks 1947- *WhoAmW 93*
Kirby, Maurice Helm, Jr. 1926- *St&PR 93*
Kirby, Michael Donald 1939- *WhoWor 93*
Kirby, Patricia Charlotte 1949- *WhoAmW 93*
Kirby, Percival Robson 1887-1970 *Baker 92*
Kirby, Philip Dorsey 1931- *St&PR 93*
Kirby, Preston R. 1950- *St&PR 93*
Kirby, Priscilla Crosby 1955- *WhoSSW 93*
Kirby, Richard C. 1922- *WhoScE 91-4*
Kirby, Robert Lanham 1930- *WhoSSW 93*
Kirby, Robert S., Jr. *Law&B 92*
Kirby, Ron *WhoScE 91-1*
Kirby, Ron P. *WhoScE 91-1*
Kirby, Russell Stephen 1954- *WhoSSW 93*
Kirby, Stephen C. 1951- *St&PR 93*
Kirby, Steve Thomas 1952- *St&PR 93*
Kirby, Susan E. 1949- *BioIn 17*
Kirby, T.J. *ScF&FL 92*
Kirby, Thomas Wesley 1950- *WhoEmL 93*
Kirby, Tom *WhoWrEP 92*
Kirby, Turner E. 1931- *St&PR 93*
Kirby, Ward Nelson 1939- *St&PR 93, WhoAm 92*
Kirby, William 1817-1906 *BioIn 17*
Kirby, William Joseph 1937- *St&PR 93, WhoAm 92*
Kirby, William Murray Maurice 1914- *WhoAm 92*
Kirby, William T. 1911-1990 *BioIn 17*
Kirbye, George c. 1565-1634 *Baker 92*
Kirby-Smith, Edmund 1824-1893 *BioIn 17, HarEnMi*
Kirby-Swift, Colleen Kay 1948- *WhoEmL 93*
Kirby Welch, Suzanne *Law&B 92*
Kirch, Deborah Mobray 1956- *WhoAmW 93*
Kirch, Eugene 1933- *St&PR 93*
Kirch, Max Samuel 1915- *WhoAm 92*
Kirch, Michael 1905- *St&PR 93*
Kirch, Murray Robert 1940- *WhoWor 93*
Kirch, Rebecca A. 1965- *St&PR 93*
Kirch, Wilhelm 1947- *WhoWor 93*
Kirchem, Kenneth William 1942- *WhoSSW 93*
Kirchen, Elaine D. 1942- *St&PR 93*
Kirchen, Karen J. *Law&B 92*
Kirchen, Richard Henry 1945- *St&PR 93*
Kircher, Athanasius 1601-1680 *Baker 92*
Kircher, Dudley P. 1934- *St&PR 93*
Kircher, Joyce Megginson 1928- *WhoWrEP 92*
Kircher, Robert E. 1933- *WhoAm 92*
Kircher, Sally Joy *Law&B 92*
Kirchgessner, Kenenth Francis 1936- *WhoSSW 93*
Kirchgessner, Manfred 1929- *WhoScE 91-3*
Kirchhausen, Tomas 1952- *WhoE 93*
Kirchheimer, Arthur Edward 1931- *WhoAm 92*
Kirchhof, Anton Conrad *Law&B 92*
Kirchhof, Anton Conrad 1945- *St&PR 93*
Kirchhof, Charles I.H.I. 1963- *WhoScE 91-3*
Kirchhof, Rolf 1956- *WhoScE 91-3*
Kirchhofer, John A. 1937- *St&PR 93*
Kirchhoff, Bruce C. *Law&B 92*
Kirchhoff, Charles L. *St&PR 93*
Kirchhoff, Frederick 1942- *ScF&FL 92*
Kirchhoff, Helga 1930- *WhoScE 91-3*
Kirchhoff, Keith Erwin 1954- *St&PR 93*
Kirchhoff, Paul 1900-1972 *IntDcAn*
Kirchhoff, Walter 1879-1951 *Baker 92*
Kirchick, Howard Jason 1949- *WhoSSW 93*
Kirchknopf, Erin 1963- *WhoEmL 93, WhoWor 93*
Kirchknopf, Erin Massie 1963- *WhoAmW 93*
Kirchman, Charles Vincent 1935- *WhoE 93*
Kirchmann, Jacob 1710-1792 *Baker 92*
Kirchmayer, Leon Kenneth 1924- *WhoAm 92*
Kirchmayer-Hilprecht, Martin 1923- *WhoWor 93*
Kirchmayr, Hans R. 1935- *WhoScE 91-4*
Kirchmier, Edward T. 1939- *St&PR 93*
Kirchner, Bruce McH. 1948- *St&PR 93*
Kirchner, Bruce McHarg 1948- *WhoAm 92, WhoEmL 93*
Kirchner, Edwin James 1924- *WhoAm 92*
Kirchner, Ernst Ludwig *BioIn 17*
Kirchner, James William 1920- *WhoAm 92, WhoWor 93*
Kirchner, John Albert 1915- *WhoAm 92*
Kirchner, King P. 1927- *St&PR 93*
Kirchner, Kurt 1926- *WhoScE 91-3*
Kirchner, Leon 1919- *Baker 92, WhoAm 92*
Kirchner, Louis John 1942- *St&PR 93*
Kirchner, Lynn 1956- *WhoEmL 93*
Kirchner, Noel 1931- *St&PR 93*
Kirchner, Patrick A. *Law&B 92*
Kirchner, Suzanne Cornelia 1955- *WhoAmW 93*
Kirchner, Theodor (Furchtegott) 1823-1903 *Baker 92*
Kirchner, Theodore Harry 1947- *WhoEmL 93*
Kirchner, Thomas 1952- *WhoE 93*
Kirchner, William G. 1916- *St&PR 93*
Kirchner, William Louis, Jr. 1926- *St&PR 93*
Kirchoff, Marsha Denise 1953- *WhoAmW 93*
Kirchoff, Mary L. 1959- *ScF&FL 92*
Kirchoff, Michael Joseph 1945- *St&PR 93*
Kirckman, Jacob 1710-1792 *Baker 92*
Kircos, George *Law&B 92*
Kircos, Louis A. 1953- *St&PR 93*
Kirdar, Nemir *BioIn 17*
Kirdar, Nemir Amin 1936- *WhoAm 92, WhoWor 93*
Kirdar, Uner 1934- *WhoUN 92*
Kireeff, Ivan Nickolaievich 1902-1991 *BioIn 17*
Kirgis, Frederic L. 1907- *WhoAm 92*
Kirgis, Frederic Lee, Jr. 1934- *WhoAm 92*
Kirhofer, Walter Joseph 1925- *St&PR 93*
Kiriac-Georgescu, Dumitru 1866-1928 *Baker 92*
Kiriakopoulos, Kostas Marios 1960- *WhoWor 93*
Kiricuta, Ion 1918- *WhoScE 91-4*
Kirigin, Ivo 1914-1964 *Baker 92*
Kirik of Novgorod 1110- *OxDcByz*
Kirikos, Nick 1916- *WhoE 93*
Kirikoski, Markku *WhoScE 91-4*
Kirilenko, Andrei Pavlovich 1906-1990 *BioIn 17*
Kirill dc. 1182 *OxDcByz*
Kirilov, Marko 1923- *WhoScE 91-4*
Kiripolsky, Ronald George 1940- *St&PR 93*
Kirjassoff, Gordon Louis 1922- *WhoAm 92*
Kirk, Alexander 1948- *WhoE 93*
Kirk, Alexis Vemian 1938- *WhoAm 92*
Kirk, "Andy" 1898- *Baker 92*
Kirk, Andy 1898-1992 *NewYTBS 92 [port]*
Kirk, Artemis *BioIn 17*
Kirk, Billy Don 1930- *WhoSSW 93*
Kirk, Chester Howard 1917- *WhoAm 92*
Kirk, Colin Leslie *WhoScE 91-1*
Kirk, Colleen Jean 1918- *WhoAm 92*
Kirk, Daniel Lee 1919- *WhoAm 92*

Kirk, David WhoScE 91-1
Kirk, David Guertin 1941- St&PR 93
Kirk, David Neville WhoScE 91-1
Kirk, David Shelby 1941- WhoE 93
Kirk, David Starr 1943- WhoE 93
Kirk, Diane Loraine 1957- St&PR 93
Kirk, Donald 1938- WhoAm 92, WhoWor 93
Kirk, Donald James 1932- WhoAm 92, WhoE 93
Kirk, Douglas ScF&FL 92
Kirk, Douglas John Law&B 92
Kirk, Earl, Jr. 1927- WhoAm 92
Kirk, Edgar Lee 1923- WhoAm 92
Kirk, Flora Kay Stude 1944- WhoAmW 93
Kirk, Frank C. 1889-1963 BioIn 17
Kirk, Gerald Arthur 1940- WhoAm 92
Kirk, Gerald E. 1941- St&PR 93
Kirk, Graham WhoScE 91-1
Kirk, Grayson Louis 1903- WhoAm 92
Kirk, Harold Mark 1950- WhoE 93
Kirk, Jack Lewis 1947- WhoSSW 93
Kirk, Jackson A. 1941- St&PR 93
Kirk, James Eric 1942- St&PR 93
Kirk, James F. Law&B 92
Kirk, James Gerald 1939- St&PR 93
Kirk, James John Law&B 92
Kirk, James Robert 1941- WhoAm 92
Kirk, Jeffrey Lloyd Law&B 92
Kirk, Jeffrey W. 1953- St&PR 93
Kirk, Jenny N. 1945- WhoAsAP 91
Kirk, Jerry Worth 1946- St&PR 93
Kirk, John Mark 1951- WhoSSW 93
Kirk, John Monfries 1952- WhoWor 93
Kirk, John N. 1949- WhoScE 91-1
Kirk, Larry G. 1940- St&PR 93
Kirk, Larry Wayne 1957- St&PR 93
Kirk, Laura Gail 1940- WhoAmW 93
Kirk, Lisa d1990 BioIn 17
Kirk, Lynda Pounds 1946- WhoAm 92, WhoAmW 93, WhoSSW 93, WhoWor 93
Kirk, Marguerite 1894-1991 BioIn 17
Kirk, Mark A. 1957- St&PR 93
Kirk, Mary d1990 BioIn 17
Kirk, Maurice Blake 1921- WhoAm 92
Kirk, Norm BioIn 17
Kirk, Norman 1923-1974 DcTwHis
Kirk, Norman Andrew 1937- WhoWrEP 92
Kirk, Paul 1914- WhoAm 92
Kirk, Paul Grattan, Jr. 1938- PolPar, WhoAm 92
Kirk, Pearl Louise 1930- WhoWrEP 92
Kirk, Peter Francis 1953- WhoEmL 93
Kirk, Philip ScF&FL 92
Kirk, Rahsaan 1936-1977 Baker 92
Kirk, Richard ScF&FL 92
Kirk, Richard A. 1930- BioIn 17, St&PR 93
Kirk, Richard Augustus 1930- WhoAm 92
Kirk, Rita Sue 1949- WhoAmW 93
Kirk, Robert MiSFD 9
Kirk, Robert L. 1929- St&PR 93
Kirk, Robert Leonard 1929- WhoSSW 93
Kirk, Robley Gordon 1944- WhoSSW 93
Kirk, Roger E. 1930- WhoSSW 93
Kirk, Russell BioIn 17
Kirk, Russell 1918- ScF&FL 92
Kirk, Russell Amos 1918- WhoAm 92, WhoWrEP 92
Kirk, Samuel Alexander 1904- WhoAm 92
Kirk, Samuel Joseph 1946- St&PR 93
Kirk, Sara E. AmWomPl
Kirk, Sherwood 1924- WhoAm 92, WhoWor 93
Kirk, Stuart Champion 1943- WhoSSW 93
Kirk, Susan St&PR 93
Kirk, Susan L. Law&B 92
Kirk, Thomas Garrett, Jr. 1943- WhoAm 92
Kirk, Thomas Kent 1940- WhoAm 92
Kirk, Thomas L. St&PR 93
Kirk, Tim 1947- ScF&FL 92
Kirk, Timothy W. Law&B 92
Kirk, Wilber Wolfe 1932- WhoSSW 93
Kirk, William E., III Law&B 92
Kirk, William Smith 1928- WhoSSW 93
Kirkbride, Chalmer Gatlin 1906- WhoAm 92
Kirkbride, Walter Terry 1946- St&PR 93
Kirkby, Emma 1949- Baker 92
Kirkby, Maurice Anthony 1929- WhoAm 92
Kirkby, Michael John WhoScE 91-1
Kirkby, Wayne A. Law&B 92
Kirkby Lunn, Louise OxDcOp
Kirkby-Lunn, Louise 1873-1930 Baker 92
Kirk-Duggan, Michael Allan 1931- WhoSSW 93, WhoWor 93
Kirke, David 1596-1656 HarEnMi
Kirke, Peadar N. 1945- WhoScE 91-3
Kirkeby, Per 1938- BioIn 17
Kirkegaard, Jens WhoScE 91-2
Kirkegaard, Raymond Lawrence, Jr. 1937- WhoAm 92
Kirkeide, John M. 1955- St&PR 93
Kirkemo, Elizabeth Ellen 1962- WhoAmW 93
Kirkendall, Donald Eugene 1939- WhoAm 92
Kirkendall, Jeffrey Lawrence 1954- WhoEmL 93
Kirkendall, Judith Midgley 1931- WhoAmW 93
Kirkendall, Lester Allen 1903-1991 BioIn 17
Kirkendall, Richard Stewart 1928- WhoAm 92
Kirkendall, Walter Murray 1917- WhoAm 92
Kirker, Constance Louise 1949- WhoAmW 93
Kirker, Jack M. WhoAm 92
Kirker, Katherine AmWomPl
Kirkey, Jaclyn Hilliard 1951- WhoAmW 93
Kirkham, Aileen Imogene 1951- WhoSSW 93
Kirkham, Don 1908- WhoAm 92
Kirkham, Francis Robison 1904- WhoAm 92
Kirkham, James Alvin 1935- St&PR 93
Kirkham, John Anthony 1943- St&PR 93
Kirkham, M. B. WhoAm 92, WhoAmW 93, WhoWor 93
Kirkham, Shirley A. 1935- St&PR 93
Kirkham-Sandy, Christopher 1949- WhoWor 93
Kirkhart, Karen Eileen 1948- WhoAmW 93
Kirkhoff, James Bruce 1921- St&PR 93
Kirkiacharian, Serge B. 1933- WhoScE 91-2
Kirkien-Rzeszotarski, Alicia Maria WhoAmW 93
Kirkland, Alfred Younges 1917- WhoAm 92
Kirkland, Bertha Theresa WhoAmW 93
Kirkland, Bryant Mays 1914- WhoAm 92, WhoWor 93
Kirkland, David J. 1949- WhoScE 91-1
Kirkland, Douglas BioIn 17
Kirkland, Gelsey BioIn 17
Kirkland, Gelsey 1953- WhoAm 92
Kirkland, Hunter Moss Fry 1956- St&PR 93
Kirkland, James Alvin 1959- WhoSSW 93
Kirkland, John Clarence 1963- WhoWor 93
Kirkland, John Cyril St&PR 93
Kirkland, John David 1933- WhoAm 92
Kirkland, Joseph 1830-1894 GayN
Kirkland, Joseph J. 1925- WhoAm 92
Kirkland, Joseph Lane 1922- WhoAm 92
Kirkland, Kenny BioIn 17
Kirkland, Ladye Hillis 1956- WhoEmL 93
Kirkland, Malcolm 1943- St&PR 93
Kirkland, Mary Jane 1937- WhoAmW 93
Kirkland, N.L. 1946- WhoWrEP 92
Kirkland, Randall Lee 1952- WhoWor 93
Kirkland, Russell Kermit 1942- WhoSSW 93
Kirkland, Steven E. Law&B 92
Kirkland, Virgil Wayne 1939- WhoWor 93
Kirkland, William George 1922- St&PR 93
Kirkle, Diane Luise 1944- WhoWrEP 92
Kirklin, John W. 1917- BioIn 17
Kirkman, Cindi Harper 1960- WhoSSW 93
Kirkman, Elwood F. 1904- St&PR 93
Kirkman, James A. 1942- St&PR 93
Kirkman, James A., III Law&B 92
Kirkman, Raymon Lee 1941- St&PR 93
Kirkman, Reymond F. Law&B 92
Kirkman, Roger Norman 1949- St&PR 93
Kirkman, Stacy Norman 1924- St&PR 93
Kirkner, James Norman 1935- WhoE 93
Kirkov, Ljudmil 1933- DrEEuF
Kirkpatrick, Andrew Booth, Jr. 1929- WhoAm 92
Kirkpatrick, Anne Saunders 1938- WhoAmW 93
Kirkpatrick, Charles Harvey 1931- WhoAm 92
Kirkpatrick, Clayton 1915- DcLB 127 [port], WhoAm 92
Kirkpatrick, Colin Hunter WhoScE 91-1
Kirkpatrick, David Lawson Irwin 1939- WhoScE 91-1
Kirkpatrick, Edward Scott 1941- WhoAm 92
Kirkpatrick, Edward Thomson 1925- WhoAm 92
Kirkpatrick, Eleanor Blake 1909- WhoAmW 93
Kirkpatrick, Evron Maurice 1911- WhoAm 92
Kirkpatrick, Forrest H. 1905- St&PR 93
Kirkpatrick, Forrest Hunter 1905- WhoAm 92
Kirkpatrick, Francis Hubbard, Jr. 1943- WhoAm 92, WhoE 93
Kirkpatrick, Jean BioIn 17
Kirkpatrick, Jeane Duane Jordan 1926- WhoAm 92, WhoAmW 93, WhoWor 93, WhoWrEP 92
Kirkpatrick, Jeane J. 1926- BioIn 17, ColdWar 1 [port], PolPar
Kirkpatrick, John 1905- Baker 92
Kirkpatrick, John 1905-1991 BioIn 17, ConAu 136
Kirkpatrick, John Alton 1933- WhoAm 92
Kirkpatrick, John E. 1929- St&PR 93
Kirkpatrick, John Elson 1908- WhoAm 92, WhoSSW 93
Kirkpatrick, John Gildersleeve 1917- WhoAm 92
Kirkpatrick, Joycelyn 1947- WhoAmW 93, WhoEmL 93
Kirkpatrick, L.F. 1916- St&PR 93
Kirkpatrick, Marianne O'Neil 1956- WhoAmW 93
Kirkpatrick, Nancy Foster 1933- WhoAm 92
Kirkpatrick, Oliver Austin 1911-1988 BlkAull 92
Kirkpatrick, Patricia Kay 1950- WhoAmW 93
Kirkpatrick, Paul d1992 NewYTBS 92
Kirkpatrick, Philip R. 1947- WhoEmL 93
Kirkpatrick, Ralph (Leonard) 1911-1984 Baker 92
Kirkpatrick, Richard Alan 1947- WhoEmL 93
Kirkpatrick, Robert Hugh 1954- WhoEmL 93
Kirkpatrick, Robert James 1946- WhoAm 92
Kirkpatrick, Roger N. Law&B 92
Kirkpatrick, Samuel Alexander WhoAm 92, WhoSSW 93
Kirkpatrick, Sidney D(ale) 1955- ConAu 136
Kirkpatrick, Thaddeus D. Law&B 92
Kirkpatrick, Thomas M. 1938- St&PR 93
Kirkpatrick, Vicki Karen 1952- WhoAmW 93, WhoEmL 93
Kirkpatrick, William 1769-1832 BioIn 17
Kirkpatrick, William Edward 1940- St&PR 93
Kirkpatrick, William Michael 1953- WhoSSW 93
Kirksey, Avanelle 1926- WhoAm 92
Kirksey, John Edward 1957- St&PR 93
Kirksey, John Morgan 1946- WhoSSW 93
Kirksey, Robert Frederick 1959- WhoEmL 93
Kirksey, Terrie Lynn 1958- WhoAmW 93
Kirkup, James 1918- BioIn 17
Kirkup, Sandra Lynne 1963- WhoAmW 93
Kirkwood, Byron D. 1949- St&PR 93
Kirkwood, Catherine 1949- WhoAmW 93
Kirkwood, Connie Lou 1943- WhoAmW 93
Kirkwood, Daniel WhoScE 91-1
Kirkwood, David Herbert Waddington 1924- WhoAm 92
Kirkwood, Eileen Janet 1942- WhoAmW 93
Kirkwood, G.W. 1937- St&PR 93
Kirkwood, Gene 1945- WhoAm 92
Kirkwood, James 1930-1989 BioIn 17, ConAu 40NR
Kirkwood, James Mace 1942- WhoE 93
Kirkwood, Jim ConAu 40NR
Kirkwood, Kathleen AmWomPl
Kirkwood, Maurice Richard 1920- WhoAm 92
Kirkwood, Richard Edwin 1927- WhoSSW 93
Kirkwood, Thomas Burton Loram WhoScE 91-1
Kirkyla, Viktoras Antanas 1940- WhoE 93
Kirley, Paul O. 1947- St&PR 93
Kirlin, John A. 1918- St&PR 93
Kirlin, Priscilla R. 1922- St&PR 93
Kirman, Charles Gary 1949- WhoAm 92
Kirmani, Naheed 1946- WhoUN 92
Kirmani, Zaheer Ali 1940- WhoSSW 93
Kirmse, Anne-Marie Rose 1941- WhoAmW 93, WhoE 93
Kirmse, Wolfgang 1930- WhoScE 91-3
Kirmser, Michelle Skarbnik Law&B 92
Kirmser, Philip George 1919- WhoAm 92
Kirn, Andre 1931- WhoScE 91-2
Kirn, Bob Joseph 1947- St&PR 93
Kirn, John J., Jr. Law&B 92
Kirn, Marda BioIn 17
Kirn, Walter N., Jr. Law&B 92
Kirnan, Jean Powell 1956- WhoE 93
Kirnberger, Johann Philipp 1721-1783 Baker 92
Kirouac, Joseph-Louis-Conrad 1885-1944 BioIn 17
Kirousis, Lefteris Miltiades 1951- WhoWor 93
Kirov, Sergey Mironovich 1886-1934 DcTwHis
Kirsanow, Peter Nicholas Law&B 92
Kirsch, Alan D. Law&B 92
Kirsch, Anthony Thomas 1930- WhoAm 92
Kirsch, Arthur W. 1941- St&PR 93
Kirsch, Arthur William 1941- WhoAm 92
Kirsch, Christine Jo 1950- WhoAmW 93, WhoEmL 93
Kirsch, David Alan 1933- WhoE 93
Kirsch, Donald 1931- St&PR 93, WhoWor 93
Kirsch, E. Achim Law&B 92
Kirsch, Elaine B. Law&B 92
Kirsch, Emily Jordan 1933- WhoAmW 93
Kirsch, Irving 1943- ConAu 136
Kirsch, Jack Frederick 1934- WhoAm 92
Kirsch, James Stephen 1946- WhoEmL 93
Kirsch, Karen Jill 1957- WhoE 93
Kirsch, Kenneth C. 1943- St&PR 93
Kirsch, Laurence Stephen 1957- WhoE 93, WhoEmL 93, WhoWor 93
Kirsch, Leonard David Law&B 92
Kirsch, Nancy Law&B 92
Kirsch, Neville 1911-1991 BioIn 17
Kirsch, Pamela Law&B 92
Kirsch, Philippe 1947- WhoUN 92
Kirsch, Ralph M. 1928- St&PR 93
Kirsch, Robert R. 1922-1980 ScF&FL 92
Kirsch, Ronald Arthur 1938- St&PR 93
Kirsch, Steven J. 1951- ScF&FL 92
Kirsch, William Joseph 1956- WhoE 93
Kirschbaum, Alan Ira 1948- WhoEmL 93, WhoSSW 93
Kirschbaum, Gerald S. Law&B 92
Kirschbaum, James Louis 1940- WhoAm 92
Kirschbaum, Joel Jerome 1935- WhoE 93
Kirschberg, Nancy Jeanne Miller 1948- WhoSSW 93
Kirschberg, Reva Godlove 1921- WhoE 93
Kirschbrown, Lita Bryna 1952- WhoAmW 93, WhoEmL 93, WhoWor 93
Kirschenbaum, Louis Jean 1943- WhoE 93
Kirschenbaum, Paulenne Roeske 1936- WhoAmW 93
Kirschenbaum, Peter C. Law&B 92
Kirschenbaum, Peter Charles Law&B 92
Kirschenbaum, Richard H. 1939- St&PR 93
Kirschenbaum, Susan Schulman 1943- WhoAmW 93
Kirschenbaum, Walter L. d1992 NewYTBS 92
Kirschenbaum, William 1944- St&PR 93, WhoAm 92, WhoWor 93
Kirschenmann, Henry George, Jr. 1930- WhoAm 92
Kirscher, John C. 1934- St&PR 93
Kirschman, Ellen Freeman 1939- WhoAmW 93
Kirschner, Ahron ben Moscheh 1827- BioIn 17
Kirschner, Barbara Starrels 1941- WhoAm 92
Kirschner, David WhoAm 92
Kirschner, Henryk Wladyslaw 1929- WhoScE 91-4
Kirschner, James Edward 1945- St&PR 93
Kirschner, Karen Marie 1956- WhoAmW 93
Kirschner, Kenneth M. 1942- St&PR 93
Kirschner, Leon C. 1940- St&PR 93
Kirschner, Richard D. St&PR 93
Kirschner, Richard Michael 1949- WhoWor 93
Kirschner, Ronald Allen 1942- WhoE 93, WhoWor 93
Kirschner, Ruth Brin 1924- WhoAmW 93
Kirschner, Sidney 1934- St&PR 93, WhoAm 92, WhoSSW 93
Kirschner, Stanley 1927- WhoAm 92
Kirschner, William Steven 1950- WhoEmL 93
Kirschstein, Ruth Lillian 1926- WhoAm 92, WhoAmW 93, WhoE 93
Kirscht, Judith Mary (Kenyon) 1933- WhoWrEP 92
Kirschten, Barbara Louise 1950- WhoEmL 93
Kirsh, Andrea M. Law&B 92
Kirsh, Ellen M. Law&B 92
Kirsh, James T., Jr. 1953- St&PR 93
Kirsh, James Theodore 1925- St&PR 93
Kirsh, M. Eli 1950- WhoE 93
Kirsh, Michael Alan 1952- WhoWor 93
Kirshbaum, Howard M. 1938- WhoAm 92
Kirshbaum, Ralph (Henry) 1946- Baker 92
Kirshbaum, Ronald Michael 1938- St&PR 93
Kirshenbaum, David I. Law&B 92
Kirshenbaum, William Albert 1936- St&PR 93
Kirshner, Alan I. 1935- WhoIns 93
Kirshner, Jacob 1927- WhoE 93
Kirshner, Norman 1923- WhoAm 92
Kirshner, Robert 1949- WhoE 93
Kirsner, Joseph Barnett 1909- WhoAm 92
Kirsner, Kenneth S. Law&B 92
Kirsner, Laura T. 1945- St&PR 93

Kirsner, Robert 1921- *WhoAm 92*
Kirst, Hans Hellmut 1914-1989 *ScF&FL 92*
Kirst, Michael W. *BioIn 17*
Kirstein, George G. 1909-1986 *BioIn 17*
Kirstein, Lincoln 1907- *BioIn 17, WhoAm 92*
Kirstein, Naomi Wagman 1937- *WhoAmW 93*
Kirstein, Peter Thomas *WhoScE 91-1*
Kirstein, Philip L. *Law&B 92*
Kirstein, Rosemary *ScF&FL 92*
Kirsten, Dorothy 1910-1992 *NewYTBS 92 [port]*
Kirsten, Dorothy 1915- *Baker 92, WhoAm 92*
Kirsten, Dorothy 1917- *OxDcOp*
Kirsten, Frederick K. 1885-1952 *BioIn 17*
Kirsten, Ralf 1930- *DrEEuF*
Kirsteuer, Ernst Karl Eberhart 1933- *WhoAm 92*
Kirszbaum, Rene 1940- *WhoUN 92*
Kirtley, Bacil F. 1924- *ScF&FL 92*
Kirtley, Donald R. 1938- *St&PR 93*
Kirtley, Hattie Mae 1934- *WhoAmW 93*
Kirtley, Jane Elizabeth 1953- *WhoAmW 93, WhoEmL 93, WhoWor 93*
Kirtley, Olivia Faulkner 1950- *St&PR 93*
Kirtley, Phyllis *WhoWrEP 92*
Kirtley, Stephanie Michelle 1959- *WhoAmW 93*
Kirtoka, Nicolae *WhoWor 93*
Kirudja, Charles M. 1946- *WhoUN 92*
Kirven, Gerald 1922- *WhoAm 92, WhoSSW 93*
Kirven, J.D., Jr. 1917- *St&PR 93*
Kirven, Peyton Edward 1924- *WhoAm 92*
Kirwan, Betty-Jane 1947- *WhoAmW 93*
Kirwan, Frances Clare 1959- *WhoWor 93*
Kirwan, Katharyn Grace 1913- *WhoAmW 93*
Kirwan, R.A. *WhoScE 91-3*
Kirwan, Ray Henry 1923- *WhoSSW 93*
Kirwan, Thomas M. d1992 *BioIn 17*
Kirwan, Thomas M. 1940- *St&PR 93*
Kirwan, William English, II 1938- *WhoAm 92*
Kirwan-Vogel, Anna *ScF&FL 92*
Kirwin, Kenneth F. 1941- *WhoAm 92*
Kiryu, Keiji 1935- *WhoWor 93*
Kis, Danilo *BioIn 17*
Kis, John 1928- *St&PR 93*
Kisaichi, Yasuhiko 1933- *WhoWor 93*
Kisak, Paul Francis 1956- *WhoEmL 93, WhoSSW 93, WhoWor 93*
Kisberg, Franklin 1960- *St&PR 93*
Kisch, Horst 1942- *WhoWor 93*
Kisch, Louis U.C. 1935- *St&PR 93*
Kisch, Raymond R. *WhoIns 93*
Kischel, Beatrice 1920- *WhoWor 93*
Kischuk, Richard Karl 1949- *WhoAm 92*
Kise, James Nelson 1937- *WhoAm 92, WhoE 93*
Kisekka, Samson Babi Mululu 1912- *WhoAfr*
Kiselev, Yuri Nikolaevich 1940- *WhoWor 93*
Kiselica, Winifred Theresa 1929- *WhoE 93*
Kiselik, Paul Howard 1937- *WhoAm 92, WhoE 93*
Kiselman, Christer Oscar 1939- *WhoWor 93*
Kiser, Arthur George 1943- *St&PR 93*
Kiser, Clyde Vernon 1904- *WhoAm 92*
Kiser, Donald L. 1933- *St&PR 93*
Kiser, Glenn, Jr. 1951- *WhoEmL 93, WhoSSW 93*
Kiser, Glenn Augustus 1917- *WhoSSW 93, WhoWor 93*
Kiser, Jackson L. 1929- *WhoSSW 93*
Kiser, James W. 1934- *St&PR 93*
Kiser, James Webb 1934- *WhoAm 92*
Kiser, Jerry W. 1950- *St&PR 93*
Kiser, John L. *Law&B 92*
Kiser, Karen Jean 1946- *WhoAmW 93*
Kiser, Lisa Jean 1949- *WhoAmW 93*
Kiser, Mose, III 1956- *WhoEmL 93, WhoSSW 93*
Kiser, Nagiko Sato 1923- *WhoAmW 93, WhoWor 93*
Kiser, William Francis 1935- *St&PR 93*
Kiser, William Sites 1928- *WhoAm 92*
Kish, Eleanor M(ary) 1924- *SmATA 73 [port]*
Kish, Ely *SmATA 73*
Kish, George Franklin 1944- *WhoE 93*
Kish, Joseph Laurence, Jr. 1933- *WhoAm 92*
Kish, Leslie 1910- *WhoAm 92*
Kish, Michael Stephen 1961- *WhoEmL 93*
Kishel, Gregory Francis 1951- *WhoEmL 93*
Kishi, Hachiro 1930- *WhoAsAP 91*
Kishi, Yoshito 1937- *WhoAm 92*
Kishibe, Shigeo 1912- *Baker 92*
Kishida, Fumitake 1926- *WhoAsAP 91*
Kishimori, Phillip T. 1936- *St&PR 93*
Kishimoto, Kazuo 1952- *WhoWor 93*
Kishimoto, Keishi 1961- *WhoWor 93*
Kishimoto, Uichiro 1922- *WhoWor 93*
Kishimoto, Yasuo 1925- *WhoAm 92*
Kishimoto, Yuji 1938- *WhoSSW 93, WhoWor 93*
Kishino, Katsumi 1952- *WhoWor 93*
Kishi Nobusuke 1896-1987 *DcTwHis*
Kishon, Ephraim *MiSFD 9*
Kisida, Elek 1936- *WhoScE 91-4*
Kisiel, Henry Francis, Jr. 1950- *WhoE 93*
Kisiel, Wanda 1946- *WhoScE 91-4*
Kisielewicz, Michal 1939- *WhoWor 93*
Kisielewski, Stefan 1911- *Baker 92*
Kisielow, Wlodzimierz 1914- *WhoScE 91-4*
Kisielowski, Eugene 1932- *WhoE 93*
Kiska, Timothy Olin 1952- *WhoAm 92*
Kislak, Jean Hart 1931- *WhoAmW 93*
Kislevitz, Joshua Luther 1957- *St&PR 93*
Kisliakov, N.A. 1901-1973 *IntDcAn*
Kisliakov, Sava 1934- *WhoScE 91-4*
Kislik, Louis A. 1931- *WhoAm 92*
Kislik, Richard William 1927- *WhoAm 92, WhoWor 93*
Kislowski, Richard John 1942- *St&PR 93*
Kisluk, Eileen W. *Law&B 92*
Kismaric, Carole Lee 1942- *WhoAm 92*
Kisnad, Hiten Vithal 1958- *WhoE 93, WhoEmL 93*
Kisner, Jacob 1926- *WhoAm 92, WhoE 93, WhoWor 93*
Kisner, James 1947- *ScF&FL 92*
Kisner, Ronald Harris 1948- *St&PR 93*
Kiso, Yoshiaki 1945- *WhoWor 93*
Kisor, Henry 1940- *BioIn 17*
Kisor, Henry Du Bois 1940- *WhoAm 92*
Kisoyama, Kane 1917- *WhoWor 93*
Kispert, Lowell Donald 1940- *WhoSSW 93*
Kiss, Dezso 1929- *WhoScE 91-4*
Kiss, Erno 1929- *WhoScE 91-4*
Kiss, Istvan 1944- *WhoScE 91-4*
Kiss, Istvan Ferenc 1934- *WhoScE 91-4*
Kiss, Janos 1920- *Baker 92*
Kiss, Janos 1921- *WhoScE 91-4*
Kiss, John B. 1948- *St&PR 93*
Kiss, Stefan 1926- *WhoScE 91-4*
Kissa, Erik 1923- *WhoAm 92*
Kissane, James Donald 1930- *WhoAm 92*
Kissane, Jean Charlotte 1946- *WhoE 93, WhoEmL 93*
Kissane, John J. *Law&B 92*
Kissane, Mary Elizabeth *WhoE 93*
Kissane, Michael J. *Law&B 92*
Kissane, Richard F. 1951- *St&PR 93*
Kissane, Thomas *WhoE 93*
Kissane, William F. 1933- *St&PR 93*
Kisseberth, Paul Barto 1932- *WhoAm 92*
Kissel, E.U. 1928- *St&PR 93*
Kissel, Howard William 1942- *WhoAm 92*
Kissel, Jacques 1946- *WhoScE 91-2*
Kissel, Joseph F. 1947- *St&PR 93*
Kissel, Lester 1903- *St&PR 93*
Kissel, Michael Case *WhoE 93, WhoWor 93*
Kissel, Walter J. 1933- *St&PR 93*
Kissel, William Thorn, Jr. 1920- *WhoE 93, WhoWor 93*
Kissick, Gary Richard 1946- *WhoWrEP 92*
Kissick, Jennifer *BioIn 17*
Kissick, W. Norman *St&PR 93*
Kissick, William Lee 1932- *WhoAm 92, WhoE 93, WhoWor 93*
Kissick, William Lee, Jr. 1958- *WhoE 93*
Kissiloff, William 1929- *WhoAm 92*
Kissin, Evgeny *BioIn 17*
Kissin, Evgeny 1971- *Baker 92*
Kissin, Irving d1991 *BioIn 17*
Kissin, Yevgeny 1971- *NewYTBS 92 [port]*
Kissinger, Harold Arthur 1922- *WhoAm 92*
Kissinger, Henry *DcCPCAm*
Kissinger, Henry 1923- *BioIn 17, ColdWar 1 [port]*
Kissinger, Henry Alfred 1923- *DcTwHis, JeAmHC, WhoAm 92, WhoWor 93*
Kissinger, John C. 1942- *St&PR 93*
Kissinger, John Calvin 1925- *WhoE 93*
Kissinger, Scott VerBryck *Law&B 92*
Kissinger, Walter Bernhard 1924- *St&PR 93*
Kissling, Dorothy H. *ScF&FL 92*
Kissling, Frances *BioIn 17*
Kissling, Grace Elizabeth 1955- *WhoSSW 93*
Kissling, John R., Jr. 1945- *St&PR 93*
Kissling, Walter 1931- *St&PR 93*
Kisslinger, Leonard Sol 1930- *WhoAm 92*
Kissner, Mary Jean 1957- *St&PR 93*
Kister, James Milton 1930- *WhoAm 92*
Kisters, Gerry 1919-1986 *BioIn 17*
Kistiakowsky, Vera 1928- *WhoAm 92, WhoAmW 93*
Kistler, Alan Lee 1928- *WhoAm 92*
Kistler, Aline *AmWomPl*
Kistler, Beth Ann *Law&B 92*
Kistler, Cyrill 1848-1907 *Baker 92*
Kistler, Darci *BioIn 17*
Kistler, Darci 1964- *News 93-1 [port]*
Kistler, Darci Anna 1964- *WhoAm 92*
Kistler, George Clifford 1934- *St&PR 93*
Kistler, James Donald 1949- *WhoE 93*
Kistner, Carl Friedrich 1797-1844 *Baker 92*
Kistner, David Harold 1931- *WhoAm 92, WhoWor 93*
Kistner, Jennifer Ruth 1957- *WhoEmL 93*
Kistner, Jerry Lee 1950- *WhoE 93*
Kistruck, S.M. 1945- *St&PR 93*
Kisvarsanyi, Eva Bognar 1935- *WhoAmW 93*
Kisynski, Jan Maria 1933- *WhoWor 93*
Kisza, Adolf 1934- *WhoScE 91-4*
Kiszel, Janos 1928- *WhoScE 91-4*
Kiszka, Sonia Ann 1938- *WhoAmW 93*
Kit, Saul 1920- *WhoAm 92, WhoSSW 93*
Kita, Jean Claude 1948- *WhoScE 91-2*
Kita, Jerzy Marian 1931- *WhoScE 91-4*
Kita, Shuji 1925- *WhoAsAP 91*
Kitabatake, Akiie 1317-1338 *HarEnMi*
Kitabatake, Akinobu dc. 1380 *HarEnMi*
Kitabatake, Chikafusa 1293-1354 *HarEnMi*
Kitada, Shinichi 1948- *WhoEmL 93, WhoWor 93*
Kitagami, Yasuharu 1939- *St&PR 93*
Kitagawa, Audrey Emiko 1951- *WhoAmW 93*
Kitagawa, Ishimatsu 1919- *WhoAsAP 91*
Kitagawa, Joseph M. 1915-1992 *NewYTBS 92*
Kitagawa, Kazuo 1953- *WhoAsAP 91*
Kitagawa, Masanori 1931- *WhoAsAP 91*
Kitagawa, Masayasu 1944- *WhoAsAP 91*
Kitagawa, Norio 1940- *WhoWor 93*
Kitagawa, Tokujiro 1942- *WhoWor 93*
Kitagawa, Toshikazu 1958- *WhoWor 93*
Kitagawa, Tosio 1909- *WhoWor 93*
Kitagawa-Otsuru, Chieko 1958- *WhoWor 93*
Kitahara, Chiaki *BioIn 17*
Kitahara, Satoko 1929-1958 *BioIn 17*
Kita Ikki d1937 *DcTwHis*
Kitaj, R.B. *BioIn 17*
Kitaj, Ronald B. *BioIn 17*
Kitaj, Torben Peter 1950- *WhoWor 93*
Kitajima, Heiichiro 1925- *WhoWor 93*
Kitajima, Yoshitoshi 1933- *St&PR 93*
Kitamura, Fumio 1932- *WhoWor 93*
Kitamura, Naofo 1947- *WhoAsAP 91*
Kitamura, Ryuji 1937- *St&PR 93*
Kitamura, Satoshi *BioIn 17*
Kitamura, Tetsuo 1938- *WhoAsAP 91*
Kitamura, Toshinori 1947- *WhoWor 93*
Kitani, Osamu 1935- *WhoWor 93*
Kitano, Hirohisa 1931- *WhoWor 93*
Kitano, Kazuaki 1939- *WhoWor 93*
Kitanow, William 1948- *BioIn 17*
Kitaoka, Beverly Jo 1953- *WhoAmW 93*
Kitaro *BioIn 17*
Kitatani, Katsuhide 1931- *WhoUN 92*
Kitayama, Katsuhiko 1937- *WhoWor 93*
Kitayama, Mitch W. 1956- *St&PR 93*
Kitayenko, Dimitri Georgievitch 1940- *WhoWor 93*
Kitayenko, Dmitri 1940- *Baker 92*
Kitazaki, Jeanne Durnford 1940- *WhoAmW 93*
Kitazawa, Eiichi 1942- *WhoWor 93*
Kitazawa, Kiyonori 1927- *WhoAsAP 91*
Kitazawa, Masakuni 1929- *WhoWor 93*
Kitbunchu, Michael Michai Cardinal 1929- *WhoWor 93*
Kitch, Edmund Wells 1939- *WhoAm 92*
Kitch, Frederick David 1928- *St&PR 93, WhoAm 92*
Kitch, Gerald C. 1937- *St&PR 93*
Kitchel, Denison 1908- *WhoAm 92*
Kitchell, James Wallace 1927- *WhoSSW 93*
Kitchell, Joyce *BioIn 17*
Kitchell, Kenneth Francis, Jr. 1947- *WhoEmL 93, WhoSSW 93*
Kitchell, Samuel Farrand 1921- *WhoAm 92*
Kitchen, Bert *ChlBIID [port], ConAu 138, SmATA 70*
Kitchen, C.A. *WhoScE 91-1*
Kitchen, Dorothy 1912-1989 *SweetSg B*
Kitchen, Herbert Thomas 1940- *ConAu 138, SmATA 70 [port]*
Kitchen, James Edward 1931- *St&PR 93*
Kitchen, John Howard 1957- *WhoE 93, WhoEmL 93*
Kitchen, John Martin 1936- *WhoAm 92, WhoWrEP 92*
Kitchen, John Milton 1912- *WhoAm 92, WhoWor 93*
Kitchen, Lawrence O. 1923- *St&PR 93*
Kitchen, Lawrence Oscar 1923- *WhoAm 92*
Kitchen, Michael B. 1945- *St&PR 93*
Kitchen, Paul Howard 1937- *WhoAm 92*
Kitchen, Stephen E. *Law&B 92*
Kitchen, Steven L. 1945- *St&PR 93*
Kitchen, Susan Treffeisen 1948- *WhoAmW 93*
Kitchener, Horatio Herbert 1850-1916 *DcTwHis, HarEnMi*
Kitchener, S. Alan 1932- *St&PR 93*
Kitchens, Clarence Wesley, Jr. 1943- *WhoAm 92*
Kitchens, Fred B., Jr. *Law&B 92*
Kitchens, Frederick Lynton, Jr. 1940- *WhoSSW 93, WhoWor 93*
Kitchens, Larry Edwin 1940- *WhoSSW 93*
Kitchens, Leonard H. 1943- *St&PR 93*
Kitchens, Sherri Carp 1954- *WhoEmL 93*
Kitchens, William Charlie 1945- *WhoSSW 93*
Kitcher, Philip Stuart 1947- *WhoAm 92*
Kitchin, Christopher Robert *WhoScE 91-1*
Kitchin, Frank David d1990 *BioIn 17*
Kitchin, James D., III 1931- *WhoAm 92*
Kitchin, Laurence Tyson 1913- *WhoAm 92*
Kitchin, Peter William 1948- *WhoScE 91-2*
Kitchin, Rosemarie A. 1939- *WhoWrEP 92*
Kitching, Peter 1938- *WhoAm 92*
Kitching, Richard Paul *WhoScE 91-1*
Kitching, Ronald *WhoScE 91-1*
Kitchings, A. Langley *Law&B 92*
Kite, Alvin E., Jr. 1933- *St&PR 93*
Kite, J. Sellers 1928- *St&PR 93*
Kite, Mary E. 1959- *WhoAmW 93*
Kite, Steven B. 1949- *WhoEmL 93*
Kite, Thomas O., Jr. 1949- *BiDAMSp 1989*
Kite, Thomas O. Tom, Jr. 1949- *WhoAm 92*
Kite, William McDougall 1923- *WhoAm 92*
Kite-Powell, Stephen M. *Law&B 92*
Kitingan, Jeffrey Gapari 1947- *WhoWor 93*
Kito, Shiro 1934- *WhoWor 93*
Kito, Shozo 1927- *WhoWor 93*
Kitovani, Tengiz *WhoWor 93*
Kitsch, Hieronymous 1953- *ScF&FL 92*
Kitscha, Hector 1930- *St&PR 93*
Kitska, Susan Ann 1946- *WhoAmW 93*
Kitson, Charles Herbert 1874-1944 *Baker 92*
Kitsopoulos, Sotirios C. 1930- *WhoWor 93*
Kits van Heyningen, Robert W.B. 1957- *St&PR 93*
Kitt, A.J. *BioIn 17, NewYTBS 92 [port]*
Kitt, Eartha *BioIn 17*
Kitt, Eartha 1928- *Baker 92, ConMus 9 [port]*
Kitt, Eartha Mae 1928- *WhoAm 92*
Kitt, Edith Stratton 1878- *BioIn 17*
Kitt, Loren Wayne 1941- *WhoAm 92*
Kitt, Tamara *MajAI*
Kittaka, Atsushi 1959- *WhoWor 93*
Kittani, Hala 1940- *WhoUN 92*
Kittas, Joel Richard 1936- *St&PR 93*
Kittel, Bruno 1870-1948 *Baker 92*
Kittel, Charles 1916- *WhoAm 92*
Kittel, Gerhard 1925- *WhoScE 91-3*
Kittel, Hermine 1879-1948 *Baker 92*
Kittel, Johann Christian 1732-1809 *Baker 92*
Kittell, Donald D. 1937- *WhoAm 92*
Kittelson, David Burnelle 1942- *WhoAm 92*
Kittides, Christopher P. 1940- *St&PR 93*
Kittinger, Erwin Magnus 1941- *WhoWor 93*
Kittinger, Joseph *BioIn 17*
Kittl, Johann Friedrich 1806-1868 *Baker 92*
Kittle, Cecil W. 1945- *St&PR 93*
Kittle, Charles Frederick 1921- *WhoAm 92*
Kittle, Dennis Dean 1959- *WhoSSW 93*
Kittleson, Henry Marshall 1929- *WhoAm 92*
Kittlitz, Linda Gale 1949- *WhoAmW 93*
Kittlitz, Rudolf Gottlieb, Jr. 1935- *WhoAm 92*
Kittner, Marc R. *Law&B 92*
Kittner, Paul *St&PR 93*
Kitto, Armand E. 1927- *St&PR 93*
Kitto, Thomas C. 1955- *St&PR 93*
Kittredge, Annette *AmWomPl*
Kittredge, Chessman 1918- *St&PR 93*
Kittredge, John Kendall 1927- *WhoAm 92*
Kittredge, John Williamson 1956- *WhoEmL 93*
Kittredge, Mary 1949- *ScF&FL 92*
Kittredge, Robert P. 1925- *St&PR 93*
Kittredge, Sidney 1932- *St&PR 93*
Kittredge, Thelma *AmWomPl*
Kittrell, Barbara Cluck 1947- *WhoAmW 93*
Kittrie, Nicholas Norbert Nehemiah 1930- *WhoAm 92, WhoE 93*
Kittross, John Michael 1929- *WhoAm 92*
Kitts, Dean Carson 1934- *WhoAm 92*

Kitts, James Joseph 1943- WhoE 93
Kitts, Mark BioIn 17
Kittson, Augustan Daniel 1955- St&PR 93
Kittson, Myrna Ann 1925- St&PR 93
Kituomba MajAI
Kitz, Richard John 1929- WhoAm 92
Kitz, Steven Leonard 1953- WhoEmL 93
Kitzic, John, Jr. 1954- St&PR 93, WhoAm 92
Kitzing, Llona S. St&PR 93
Kitzing, R. WhoScE 91-1
Kitzinger, Uwe 1928- WhoWor 93
Kitzke, Eugene David 1923- WhoAm 92
Kitzler, Elroy B. 1926- St&PR 93
Kitzler, Otto 1834-1915 Baker 92
Kitzmiller, Dirk W. Law&B 92
Kitzmiller, Howard Lawrence 1930- St&PR 93
Kitzmiller, William Michael 1931- WhoAm 92
Kiuchi, Nobutsuna 1951- WhoWor 93
Kiuner, N.V. 1877-1955 IntDcAn
Kiurina, Berta 1882-1933 Baker 92
Kiurkchiysky, Krasimir 1936- Baker 92
Kivel, Maxine Nancy 1934- WhoAmW 93
Kivelson, Margaret Galland 1928- WhoAm 92, WhoAmW 93
Kivenko, Kenneth WhoAm 92, WhoE 93
Kives, Harold St&PR 93
Kives, Raymond St&PR 93
Kivett, Clarence 1905- St&PR 93
Kivett, Marvin Franklin 1917- WhoAm 92
Kivette, Ruth Montgomery 1926- WhoAm 92
Kiviat, Abel 1892-1991 AnObit 1991, BioIn 17
Kiviat, Abel Richard 1892-1991 BiDAMSp 1989
Kiviat, Philip Jay 1937- WhoAm 92
Kiviat, Stephen Howard WhoE 93
Kiviat, Stephen Howard 1941- WhoAm 92
Kivikas, Toivelemb 1937- WhoScE 91-4, WhoWor 93
Kivinen, Seppo Tapio 1946- WhoWor 93
Kiviniemi, Jaakko Pekka 1926- WhoScE 91-4
Kivisakk, Enn 1937- WhoScE 91-4
Kivisto, Torsti WhoScE 91-4
Kivy, Peter 1934- Baker 92
Kiwi, Miguel German 1938- WhoWor 93
Kiwior, Carla Marie 1964- WhoE 93
Kiwitt, Sidney 1928- St&PR 93, WhoAm 92
KixMiller, Richard Wood 1920- WhoWor 93
Kiyan, Shinei 1911- WhoAsAP 91
Kiyono, Kenji 1885-1955 IntDcAn
Kiyose, Yasuji 1900-1981 Baker 92
Kizer, Carolyn Ashley 1925- WhoAm 92, WhoWrEP 92
Kizer, John Oscar 1913- WhoAm 92
Kizer, Kenneth Wayne 1951- WhoAm 92
Kizer, R.J. 1952- MiSFD 9
Kizer, William M. 1925- WhoIns 93
Kizziar, Janet Wright WhoAm 92
Kjaer, Anders C. 1919- WhoScE 91-2
Kjaergaard, Leif 1946- WhoWor 93
Kjaersdam, Finn 1943- WhoScE 91-2
Kjaerulff, Erling 1936- WhoScE 91-2
Kjartansson, Kristjan Georg 1934- WhoWor 93
Kjeldaas, Terje, Jr. 1924- WhoAm 92
Kjelgaard, James A. ScF&FL 92
Kjelgaard, James Arthur 1910-1959 ConAu 137, MajAI [port]
Kjelgaard, Jim ConAu 137, MajAI
Kjelgaard, Jim 1910-1959 ScF&FL 92
Kjellberg, Uno Law&B 92
Kjellen, Bo John 1933- WhoWor 93
Kjellmark, Eric William, Jr. 1928- WhoE 93
Kjellsby, Erling 1901-1976 Baker 92
Kjellstrom, Elving Joel 1922- St&PR 93
Kjellstrom, Sven 1875-1950 Baker 92
Kjelmyr, John Peter Law&B 92
Kjelsberg, Ronald Maurice Law&B 92
Kjems, Jorgen WhoScE 91-2
Kjerulf, Halfdan 1815-1868 Baker 92
Kjessler, S.O. Berndt 1934- WhoScE 91-4
Kjos, Otto Dennis 1946- WhoSSW 93
Kjos, Victoria Ann 1953- WhoAmW 93
Klaas, Nicholas Paul 1925- WhoAm 92
Klaas, Richard Lee 1945- WhoSSW 93, WhoWor 93
Klaassen, Carol S. 1951- WhoWrEP 92
Klaassens, Jan Berend 1942- WhoWor 93
Klabbatz, Chester George 1933- St&PR 93
Klaben, Arthur S. 1937- St&PR 93
Klabo, Lincoln C. 1937- St&PR 93
Klabosh, Charles Joseph 1920- WhoSSW 93, WhoWor 93
Klabunde, Florence Alice 1938- WhoWrEP 92
Klacsmann, John Anthony 1921- WhoAm 92
Klaczko, Julian 1825-1906 PolBiDi
Klaczynski, Joseph Charles 1930- St&PR 93
Kladas, John fl. 14th cent.-15th cent. OxDcByz
Kladder, Stephen James Law&B 92
Kladney, David 1948- WhoEmL 93
Kladnik, Silvester 1942- WhoScE 91-4
Klaeren, Herbert Aloysius 1950- WhoWor 93
Klaerner, C.M. 1920- St&PR 93
Klaerner, Curtis Maurice 1920- WhoAm 92
Klaetke, Fritz 1966- WhoE 93
Klafehn, Lynn Marie Law&B 92
Klaffke, Stephan Joseph 1958- WhoEmL 93
Klafsky, Anton Maria 1877-1965 Baker 92
Klafsky, Katharina 1855-1896 Baker 92, OxDcOp
Klaghofer, Eduard 1944- WhoScE 91-4
Klagsbrun, Samuel C. 1932- St&PR 93
Klagsbrunn, Hans Alexander 1909- WhoAm 92
Klaholz, Larry Robert 1946- St&PR 93
Klahr, Aryeh Leslie 1952- WhoE 93
Klahr, Michael W. 1943- WhoSSW 93
Klahr, Myra Blossom 1933- WhoWrEP 92
Klahr, Saulo 1935- WhoAm 92
Klaiber, Mark Jeffrey Law&B 92
Klaiber, Teresa Lynn Martin 1949- WhoWrEP 92
Klainer, Albert S. 1935- ScF&FL 92
Klainer, Jo-Ann ScF&FL 92
Klaja, Cynthia Marie 1961- WhoAmW 93
Klajbor, Dorothea M. 1915- WhoAmW 93
Klak, Stjepan 1920- WhoScE 91-4
Klamer, Jane Ferguson Law&B 92
Klamerus, Karen Jean 1957- WhoAmW 93
Klami, Uuno (Kalervo) 1900-1961 Baker 92
Klamka, Jerzy Andrzej 1944- WhoWor 93
Klammer, Franz 1954?- BioIn 17
Klammer, Joseph Francis 1925- WhoWor 93
Klamon, Lawrence P. 1937- St&PR 93
Klamon, Lawrence Paine 1937- WhoAm 92, WhoSSW 93
Klamut, Jan 1936- WhoScE 91-4
Klancer, Richard 1937- St&PR 93
Klancnik, Louis 1910- St&PR 93
Klanda, Betty A. 1958- WhoAmW 93
Klane, Robert MiSFD 9
Klang, Ove WhoScE 91-4
Klaoudatos, Spiros 1944- WhoScE 91-3
Klaper, Martin Jay 1947- WhoAm 92
Klaper, Steven ScF&FL 92
Klaperman, Gilbert 1921- St&PR 93, WhoAm 92
Klapes, Nancy Arlene 1955- WhoEmL 93
Klapinsky, Raymond J. Law&B 92
Klapinsky, Raymond Joseph Law&B 92
Klapinsky, Raymond Joseph 1938- St&PR 93
Klapoetke, Thomas Matthias 1961- WhoWor 93
Klapper, Carol Lorraine 1923- WhoAm 92
Klapperich, Frank Lawrence, Jr. 1934- St&PR 93, WhoAm 92
Klappert, Peter 1942- WhoWrEP 92
Klapps, James P. Law&B 92
Klaptocz, Bronislaw 1926- WhoScE 91-4
Klar, Arthur d1991 BioIn 17
Klare, George Roger 1922- WhoAm 92
Klare, Michael Thomas 1942- WhoAm 92
Klarenbeck, Justin WhoAm 92
Klarfeld, Jonathan Michael 1937- WhoE 93
Klarich, Nina Marie WhoAm 92
Klaristenfeld, Harry I. 1950- St&PR 93, WhoIns 93
Klarman, Herbert Elias 1916- WhoAm 92
Klarr, James Law&B 92
Klas, Robert C. 1928- St&PR 93
Klasen, Karl 1909-1991 BioIn 17
Klasnic, John Charles 1939- WhoWor 93
Klass, Irene 1916- St&PR 93
Klass, Jacob 1945- St&PR 93
Klass, Judith A. ScF&FL 92
Klass, Judy 1967- ScF&FL 92
Klass, Kathie J. 1951- WhoAmW 93, WhoEmL 93
Klass, Morton 1927- WhoAm 92
Klass, Paul Mitchell 1959- WhoEmL 93
Klass, Perri 1958- BioIn 17, News 93-2 [port]
Klass, Philip 1920- BioIn 17
Klass, Philip Julian 1919- WhoAm 92
Klass, Phyllis Constance 1927- WhoAmW 93
Klass, Rosanne Traxler WhoE 93
Klass, Sheila Solomon 1927- ConAu 37NR, WhoWrEP 92
Klass, Sidney 1916- St&PR 93
Klassen, Cornelius 1894-1954 BioIn 17
Klassen, David Morris 1939- WhoSSW 93
Klassen, Elmer Theodore 1908-1990 BioIn 17
Klassen, Peter James 1930- WhoAm 92
Klasson, Charles R., Jr. 1958- St&PR 93
Klastersky, Jean 1940- WhoScE 91-2
Klastorin, Michael ScF&FL 92
Klastrup, Kim 1954- WhoWor 93
Klatell, Jack 1918- WhoAm 92
Klatell, Robert E. Law&B 92
Klatell, Robert Edward 1945- St&PR 93, WhoAm 92
Klatsky, Bruce J. 1948- WhoE 93
Klatt, Bebbe 1938-1990 BioIn 17
Klatt, David Frederick 1948- WhoAm 92
Klatt, Gordon Roy 1942- WhoAm 92
Klatt, Kenneth A. Law&B 92
Klatte, Diethard W. 1950- WhoWor 93
Klatte, Wilhelm 1870-1930 Baker 92
Klatzkin Bochner, Robin Jane 1960- WhoEmL 93
Klatzow, Peter (James Leonard) 1945- Baker 92
Klaube, Joerg Herbert 1941- St&PR 93
Klauber, Amy Josephine AmWomPl
Klauber, Steven 1947- St&PR 93
Klauberg, W.J. 1926- St&PR 93
Klauberg, William Joseph 1926- WhoAm 92
Klauder, Gerard John 1946- WhoEmL 93
Klauder, John Rider 1932- WhoAm 92, WhoSSW 93
Klauer, Robert E. 1943- St&PR 93
Klauer, William J. 1909- St&PR 93
Klauer, William R. 1942- St&PR 93
Klaui, Wolfgang WhoScE 91-3
Klaus, Barbara BioIn 17
Klaus, Carl Hanna 1932- WhoAm 92
Klaus, Charles 1935- WhoAm 92
Klaus, Damian MiSFD 9
Klaus, Elmer Erwin 1921- WhoAm 92
Klaus, Francois WhoWor 93
Klaus, George Leonard 1924- WhoE 93
Klaus, Kenneth Blanchard 1923-1980 Baker 92
Klaus, Kim Matthews 1955- WhoEmL 93
Klaus, Philip W. 1915- St&PR 93
Klaus, Suzanne Lynne 1956- WhoEmL 93
Klaus, Vaclav BioIn 17, NewYTBS 92 [port]
Klauschie, Jack Arthur, Jr. 1952- WhoEmL 93
Klause, Annette Curtis BioIn 17, ScF&FL 92
Klause, Annette Curtis 1953- WhoAm 92
Klausen, Ray 1939- ConTFT 10
Klausen, Raymond 1939- WhoAm 92
Klauser, William Karl, Jr. 1952- WhoSSW 93
Klausewitz, Wolfgang 1922- WhoScE 91-3
Klaushofer, Hans 1920- WhoScE 91-4
Klausing, Lavern H. 1928- St&PR 93
Klausler, Alfred P. BioIn 17
Klausman, Michael St&PR 93
Klausmann, Walter J. 1937- St&PR 93
Klausmann, Walter Joseph 1937- WhoAm 92
Klausmeier, Herbert John 1915- WhoAm 92
Klausmeyer, David Michael 1934- St&PR 93, WhoSSW 93, WhoWor 93
Klausmeyer, Thomas Henry 1921- WhoWor 93
Klausner, Bennett 1939- WhoE 93
Klausner, Lawrence David 1939- ScF&FL 92
Klausner, Robert J. d1991 BioIn 17
Klausner, Samuel Zundel 1923- WhoAm 92
Klauwell, Otto (Adolf) 1851-1917 Baker 92
Klavanidis, John 1922- WhoScE 91-3
Klaveness, Dag 1945- WhoScE 91-4
Klaveness, Jan O'Donnell ScF&FL 92
Klaveness, Jan O'Donnell 1939- DcAmChF 1960
Klavins, Janis Viliberts 1921- WhoE 93
Klaviter, Helen Lothrop 1944- WhoAm 92
Klaw, Barbara Van Doren 1920- WhoAm 92
Klaw, Spencer 1920- WhoAm 92
Klawiter, Donald Casimir 1950- WhoEmL 93
Klawitter, Andrew L. Law&B 92
Klawitter, George Albert 1942- WhoWrEP 92
Klawonn, William Edward 1954- WhoWor 93
Klay, Andor C. 1912- WhoE 93
Klayman, Norman S. 1936- St&PR 93
Kleb, Kathryn 1945- St&PR 93
Kleb, Mary Jane 1917- St&PR 93
Kleb, Melvin E. 1917- St&PR 93
Kleb, William E. 1939- St&PR 93
Kleba, Louise Mary 1953- WhoSSW 93
Kleback, Lisa Lynn 1963- WhoAmW 93
Klebanoff, Philip Samuel 1918- WhoAm 92
Klebanoff, Seymour Joseph 1927- WhoAm 92
Klebanoff, Susan M. Law&B 92
Klebanov, Dmitri 1907- Baker 92
Klebansky, Victor 1930- St&PR 93
Klebba, Robert H. 1928- St&PR 93
Klebba, Robert Harold 1928- WhoAm 92
Klebba-Duffy, Lorraine Marie 1969- WhoAmW 93
Klebe, Giselher 1925- OxDcOp
Klebe, Giselher (Wolfgang) 1925- Baker 92
Klebelsberg, Dieter 1928- WhoScE 91-4
Kleber, Dale Elliott Law&B 92
Kleber, Hans-Peter 1937- WhoWor 93
Kleber, Jean-Baptiste 1753-1800 HarEnMi
Kleber, Leonhard c. 1490-1556 Baker 92
Kleberg, Jack Carl 1930- WhoAm 92
Kleberger, Ilse 1921- ConAu 39NR
Klebosky, Laura Byrne 1963- WhoAmW 93
Kleck, Robert Eldon 1937- WhoAm 92
Klecki, Pawel Baker 92
Kleckner, Robert George, Jr. Law&B 92
Kleckner, Willard Richards 1937- WhoE 93
Kleczka, Gerald D. 1943- CngDr 91, WhoAm 92
Kleczka, John Casimir, III 1943- St&PR 93
Kleczkowski, Antoni Stanislaw 1922- WhoScE 91-4
Kleczkowski, Kazimierz 1924- WhoScE 91-4
Kleczynski, Jan 1837-1895 PolBiDi
Klee, Bernhard 1936- Baker 92
Klee, Doreen Patricia 1966- WhoAmW 93
Klee, Harvey H. Law&B 92
Klee, Karl Heinz WhoWor 93
Klee, Kenneth Nathan 1949- WhoAm 92
Klee, Marc Howard 1955- St&PR 93
Klee, Paul 1879-1940 BioIn 17
Klee, Paul F. 1944- WhoUN 92
Klee, Thomas Alan Law&B 92
Klee, Victor La Rue 1925- WhoAm 92
Kleeberg, Irene Cumming BioIn 17
Kleefeld, Wilhelm 1868-1933 Baker 92
Kleeman, Michael Jeffrey 1949- WhoAm 92
Kleeman, Walter Benton, Jr. 1918- WhoAm 92, WhoSSW 93
Kleemann, Wolfgang 1942- WhoScE 91-3
Kleemola, Heikki J. 1941- WhoScE 91-4
Kleemola, S.R. Mariaana 1941- WhoScE 91-4
Kleene, Alice Cole AmWomPl
Kleene, Stephen Cole 1909- WhoAm 92
Kleerekoper, Michael 1944- WhoAm 92
Kleffel, Arno 1840-1913 Baker 92
Kleffman, Carolee Schafer 1937- St&PR 93
Klefsjo, Bengt 1943- WhoWor 93
Klega, Miroslav 1929- Baker 92
Klehm, Karen Isabel 1957- WhoEmL 93
Klehn, Henry, Jr. 1936- St&PR 93
Kleiber, Carlos BioIn 17
Kleiber, Carlos 1930- Baker 92, IntDcOp, OxDcOp
Kleiber, Erich 1890-1956 Baker 92, IntDcOp, OxDcOp
Kleiber, James William 1934- St&PR 93
Kleier, George O. Law&B 92
Kleier, Kenneth J. Law&B 92
Kleihues, Josef Paul 1933- WhoAm 92
Kleihues, Paul 1936- WhoScE 91-4
Kleiler, James Robert 1949- WhoEmL 93
Kleiman, Alan Boyd 1930- WhoAm 92
Kleiman, Ansel 1925- WhoAm 92
Kleiman, Bernard 1928- WhoAm 92
Kleiman, Carol WhoAm 92
Kleiman, David Harold 1934- WhoAm 92
Kleiman, Gary Howard 1952- WhoAm 92, WhoE 93, WhoWor 93
Kleiman, Gary Neil 1960- WhoE 93
Kleiman, George Gershon 1942- WhoWor 93
Kleiman, Howard 1929- WhoE 93
Kleiman, Ida 1914- St&PR 93
Kleiman, Joseph 1919- WhoAm 92
Kleiman, Macklen 1913- St&PR 93
Kleiman, Mark A. R. 1951- ConAu 138
Kleiman, Mark Albert Robert 1951- WhoE 93
Kleiman, Stanley 1938- St&PR 93
Kleiman, Steven Lawrence 1942- WhoAm 92
Kleimann, H. WhoScE 91-2
Kleimola, M.E. 1946- WhoScE 91-4
Klein, Aaron 1948- WhoE 93
Klein, Abraham 1927- WhoAm 92
Klein, Alan Howard 1957- WhoEmL 93
Klein, Albrecht 1939- WhoScE 91-3
Klein, Amy S. Law&B 92
Klein, Andrew Manning 1941- WhoAm 92
Klein, Anne 1923?-1974 BioIn 17
Klein, Anne Carolyn 1947- WhoSSW 93
Klein, Anne Sceia 1942- WhoAmW 93, WhoE 93, WhoWor 93
Klein, Anthony George 1935- WhoWor 93
Klein, Arnold William 1945- WhoWor 93
Klein, Arthur 1934- WhoE 93
Klein, Arthur Deo 1944- WhoSSW 93
Klein, Arthur Luce 1916- WhoAm 92
Klein, Barbara Diane 1963- WhoAmW 93
Klein, Barbara Ward WhoE 93
Klein, Barry 1936- St&PR 93

Klein, Benjamin 1943- *WhoAm 92*
Klein, Benjamin Garrett 1942- *WhoSSW 93*
Klein, Bernard 1921- *WhoAm 92, WhoSSW 93, WhoWor 93*
Klein, Bernard Elliot 1947- *St&PR 93*
Klein, Bernard Robert 1941- *WhoE 93*
Klein, Bernd 1947- *WhoScE 91-3*
Klein, Bernhard (Joseph) 1793-1832 *Baker 92, BioIn 17*
Klein, Bert *Law&B 92*
Klein, Bertram W. 1930- *St&PR 93*
Klein, Bruce M. *Law&B 92*
Klein, Bruce Peter 1933- *St&PR 93*
Klein, Bruno Oscar 1858-1911 *Baker 92*
Klein, C. Robert 1923- *St&PR 93*
Klein, Calvin *BioIn 17*
Klein, Calvin Richard 1942- *WhoAm 92*
Klein, Carol J. 1951- *St&PR 93*
Klein, Charles H. 1908- *St&PR 93*
Klein, Charlotte Conrad 1923- *WhoAmW 93*
Klein, Cornelius 1946- *WhoUN 92*
Klein, Dana *Law&B 92*
Klein, Daniel M. 1939- *ScF&FL 92*
Klein, Daniel W. 1942- *St&PR 93*
Klein, David 1919- *ConAu 40NR, WhoAm 92, WhoWor 93*
Klein, David H. *Law&B 92*
Klein, David M. 1946- *WhoIns 93*
Klein, David Mark 1946- *St&PR 93*
Klein, Deborah *Law&B 92*
Klein, Deborah Cheryl 1953- *WhoEmL 93, WhoSSW 93*
Klein, Dennis *MiSFD 9*
Klein, Dennis Burton 1948- *WhoE 93*
Klein, Dona 1953- *WhoAmW 93*
Klein, Dona Vellek 1955- *WhoAmW 93*
Klein, Donald Franklin 1928- *WhoAm 92*
Klein, Donald H. d1991 *BioIn 17*
Klein, Doris Elaine 1929- *WhoAmW 93*
Klein, Douglas Jay 1942- *WhoSSW 93*
Klein, Dusan 1939- *DrEEuF*
Klein, Dyann Leslie 1951- *WhoAmW 93*
Klein, E. Gary 1931- *St&PR 93*
Klein, Edith Miller 1915- *WhoAmW 93*
Klein, Edward 1936- *ScF&FL 92*
Klein, Edward Joel 1936- *WhoAm 92*
Klein, Edward Robert 1950- *WhoSSW 93*
Klein, Elaine 1929- *WhoAmW 93, WhoE 93*
Klein, Elisabeth 1911- *Baker 92*
Klein, Elizabeth Archer 1963- *WhoEmL 93*
Klein, Emery I. 1928- *St&PR 93*
Klein, Esther E. *Law&B 92*
Klein, Esther Moyerman 1907- *WhoAmW 93*
Klein, Eva 1925- *WhoScE 91-4*
Klein, Fay Magid 1929- *WhoAmW 93*
Klein, Frank J. 1942- *St&PR 93*
Klein, Freda 1920- *WhoAmW 93*
Klein, Frederic Lee *Law&B 92*
Klein, Frederic William 1922- *St&PR 93, WhoAm 92, WhoE 93*
Klein, Fritz Heinrich 1892-1977 *Baker 92*
Klein, Gail Beth Marantz 1946- *WhoAmW 93*
Klein, Gene *BioIn 17*
Klein, George 1925- *WhoScE 91-4*
Klein, George deVries 1933- *WhoAm 92, WhoWor 93*
Klein, George Robert 1909- *WhoWor 93*
Klein, Gerald E. *Law&B 92*
Klein, Gerard 1937- *ScF&FL 92*
Klein, Gerd *WhoScE 91-4*
Klein, Gerhard 1920-1970 *DrEEuF*
Klein, Gordon Leslie 1946- *WhoSSW 93*
Klein, Gregory Alan 1950- *St&PR 93*
Klein, H.-F. 1940- *WhoScE 91-3*
Klein, H. Joseph 1942- *St&PR 93*
Klein, Hans Emil 1939- *WhoE 93*
Klein, Hans-Udo Manfred 1952- *WhoWor 93*
Klein, Harold 1910-1991 *BioIn 17*
Klein, Harold Charles 1937- *St&PR 93*
Klein, Harriet Farber 1948- *WhoAmW 93*
Klein, Harvey Allen 1947- *WhoSSW 93*
Klein, Heinz Guenter 1939- *WhoWor 93*
Klein, Helmut Hermann 1940- *St&PR 93*
Klein, Henry d1990 *BioIn 17*
Klein, Henry 1920- *WhoAm 92*
Klein, Herbert Alan 1936- *WhoE 93*
Klein, Herbert George 1918- *St&PR 93, WhoAm 92*
Klein, Herbert Sanford 1936- *ConAu 37NR, WhoAm 92*
Klein, Herman 1856-1934 *Baker 92, OxDcOp*
Klein, Hilton James 1950- *WhoE 93*
Klein, Howard Bruce 1950- *WhoE 93*
Klein, Ilona 1956- *WhoE 93*
Klein, Ira Paul *Law&B 92*
Klein, Irma Frances 1936- *WhoAmW 93*
Klein, Irving 1954- *St&PR 93*
Klein, Ivy Frances 1895- *Baker 92*
Klein, James A. 1963- *St&PR 93*
Klein, James B. *St&PR 93*
Klein, James Ronald 1936- *WhoWor 93*
Klein, Jan 1936- *WhoScE 91-3*
Klein, Jay Barry 1946- *WhoSSW 93*
Klein, Jean-Claude 1942- *WhoScE 91-2*
Klein, Jean-Marc Yves 1941- *WhoWor 93*
Klein, Jean-Paul 1947- *WhoScE 91-2*
Klein, Jean-Pierre 1931- *WhoUN 92*
Klein, Jeffrey *ScF&FL 92*
Klein, Jeffrey Alan *Law&B 92*
Klein, Jeffrey S. 1953- *WhoAm 92*
Klein, Jo Ann Martucci 1947- *WhoAmW 93, WhoEmL 93*
Klein, Joan Dempsey 1924- *WhoAm 92*
Klein, John 1915-1981 *Baker 92*
Klein, John H. 1946- *St&PR 93*
Klein, Jon
See Siouxsie and the Banshees *ConMus 8*
Klein, Jonas B. 1922- *St&PR 93*
Klein, Josef 1802-1862
See Klein, Bernhard (Joseph) 1793-1832 *Baker 92*
Klein, Joseph M. 1931- *St&PR 93*
Klein, Joseph Mark 1921- *St&PR 93, WhoAm 92*
Klein, Joseph Michelman 1936- *WhoAm 92*
Klein, Julia Meredith 1955- *WhoAm 92*
Klein, Karen 1955- *St&PR 93*
Klein, Karen Helene 1960- *WhoAmW 93*
Klein, Karl-E. 1926- *WhoScE 91-3*
Klein, Kay Janis 1942- *WhoAmW 93, WhoSSW 93*
Klein, Keith Lawrence *Law&B 92*
Klein, Kelly *BioIn 17, NewYTBS 92 [port]*
Klein, Kenneth 1939- *Baker 92*
Klein, Kenneth H. *Law&B 92*
Klein, Lauren Marsha 1957- *WhoEmL 93*
Klein, Lawrence Robert *BioIn 17*
Klein, Lawrence Robert 1920- *WhoAm 92, WhoE 93, WhoWor 93*
Klein, Leslie A. *Law&B 92*
Klein, Lothar 1932- *Baker 92*
Klein, Luella 1924- *WhoAm 92*
Klein, Manfred 1948- *WhoScE 91-3*
Klein, Marilyn Weiland 1928- *WhoAm 92*
Klein, Marion Ann 1926- *St&PR 93*
Klein, Marjorie Hanson 1933- *WhoAmW 93*
Klein, Mark *BioIn 17*
Klein, Marshall S. 1926- *WhoAm 92*
Klein, Martha M. *Law&B 92*
Klein, Martin *BioIn 17, WhoWor 93*
Klein, Martin I. 1947- *WhoEmL 93*
Klein, Martin Jesse 1924- *WhoAm 92*
Klein, Marymae E. 1917- *ConAu 40NR*
Klein, Maurice J. 1908- *WhoAm 92*
Klein, Melanie 1882-1960 *BioIn 17*
Klein, Melvyn Norman 1941- *WhoAm 92*
Klein, Michael D. 1949- *St&PR 93*
Klein, Michael Elihu 1946- *WhoE 93, WhoEmL 93*
Klein, Michael Jay 1947- *WhoE 93*
Klein, Michael Lawrence 1940- *WhoAm 92*
Klein, Michael Roger 1942- *WhoAm 92, WhoWor 93*
Klein, Michael Sherman 1951- *WhoAm 92*
Klein, Michael Tully 1955- *WhoAm 92*
Klein, Michael William 1931- *WhoAm 92*
Klein, Miles M. 1927- *St&PR 93*
Klein, Miles Vincent 1933- *WhoAm 92*
Klein, Milton Martin 1917- *WhoSSW 93*
Klein, Miriam Borgenicht *BioIn 17*
Klein, Miriam Borgenicht d1992 *NewYTBS 92*
Klein, Morton 1925- *WhoAm 92, WhoE 93*
Klein, Morton Joseph 1928- *WhoAm 92*
Klein, Nancy *BioIn 17*
Klein, Naomi *St&PR 93*
Klein, Norma 1938- *DcAmChF 1960*
Klein, Norma 1938-1989 *ConAu 37NR, MajAI [port]*
Klein, Norman J. 1935- *St&PR 93*
Klein, Oscar Roy, Jr. 1927- *St&PR 93*
Klein, Otakar 1931- *WhoScE 91-4*
Klein, Paul *Law&B 92*
Klein, Paul E. 1934- *WhoAm 92, WhoE 93*
Klein, Peter 1907- *Baker 92, OxDcOp*
Klein, Peter M. *Law&B 92*
Klein, Peter Martin 1934- *St&PR 93, WhoAm 92*
Klein, Peter W. *Law&B 92*
Klein, Peter William 1955- *St&PR 93*
Klein, Philip A. *BioIn 17*
Klein, Philip Alexander 1927- *WhoAm 92, WhoE 93*
Klein, Phyllis Katz *St&PR 93*
Klein, Randall 1962- *WhoSSW 93*
Klein, Raymond Maurice 1938- *WhoAm 92*
Klein, Richard 1923- *WhoE 93*
Klein, Richard B. 1938- *St&PR 93*
Klein, Richard D. 1932- *St&PR 93*
Klein, Richard Dean 1932- *WhoAm 92*
Klein, Richard Grant 1942- *St&PR 93*
Klein, Richard Harold 1940- *WhoSSW 93*
Klein, Richard J. *Law&B 92*
Klein, Richard L. 1933- *St&PR 93*
Klein, Richard Lee 1933- *WhoAm 92*
Klein, Richard Stephen 1938- *WhoAm 92, WhoWor 93*
Klein, Richard Temple, Jr. 1956- *St&PR 93, WhoAm 92*
Klein, Robert 1924- *WhoAm 92*
Klein, Robert 1942- *WhoAm 92*
Klein, Robert Allan 1944- *WhoAm 92*
Klein, Robert Dale 1951- *WhoWor 93*
Klein, Robert Edward 1926- *WhoWor 93*
Klein, Robert H., Jr. *Law&B 92*
Klein, Robert S. 1926- *St&PR 93*
Klein, Roberta Phyllis 1934- *WhoSSW 93, WhoWor 93*
Klein, Robin 1936- *ConAu 40NR, DcChlFi, MajAI [port], ScF&FL 92*
Klein, Robin Cathy *Law&B 92*
Klein, Ronald Lloyd 1939- *WhoAm 92*
Klein, Rudolf 1935- *WhoScE 91-3*
Klein, Rudolf Ewald *WhoScE 91-1*
Klein, Ruth B. *St&PR 93*
Klein, Ruth B. 1908- *WhoAmW 93*
Klein, Sami Weiner 1939- *WhoAm 92*
Klein, Samuel H. 1925- *St&PR 93*
Klein, Sheldon 1935- *WhoAm 92*
Klein, Sheldon 1951- *St&PR 93*
Klein, Shirley Ann 1953- *WhoEmL 93*
Klein, Stanley H. d1992 *NewYTBS 92*
Klein, Stanley H. 1908-1992 *BioIn 17*
Klein, Steffen *WhoScE 91-2*
Klein, Stephanie *Law&B 92*
Klein, Stephen Thomas 1947- *WhoE 93*
Klein, Steve A. 1951- *WhoEmL 93*
Klein, Steven Gary 1948- *WhoE 93*
Klein, Susan *Law&B 92*
Klein, Susan E. 1942- *St&PR 93*
Klein, Susan Lynn 1967- *WhoE 93*
Klein, Susan Marsha 1953- *WhoAmW 93, WhoE 93*
Klein, T.E.D. 1947- *ScF&FL 92*
Klein, Ted 1926- *St&PR 93*
Klein, Theo 1929- *WhoScE 91-2*
Klein, Theodore Eibon Donald 1947- *WhoAm 92*
Klein, Thomas A. *Law&B 92*
Klein, Thomas James 1947- *WhoWrEP 92*
Klein, Thomas P. 1953- *St&PR 93*
Klein, Tom Chaim 1951- *WhoE 93*
Klein, Verle Wesley 1933- *WhoAm 92*
Klein, Victoria Lynn 1946- *WhoAmW 93*
Klein, Viola 1908-1973 *BioIn 17*
Klein, Virginia S. 1936- *WhoWrEP 92*
Klein, Walter C. *BioIn 17*
Klein, Werner 1936- *WhoScE 91-3*
Klein, William 1926- *MiSFD 9*
Klein, William 1928- *BioIn 17*
Klein, William, II 1919- *WhoE 93*
Klein, William Harry 1951- *WhoWrEP 92*
Klein, Wolfgang 1946- *WhoScE 91-3*
Klein, Yetta *AmWomPl*
Klein, Yvonne Mathews 1933- *WhoCanL 92*
Kleinbard, Joan *ScF&FL 92*
Kleinbaum, N.H. *ScF&FL 92*
Kleinbaum, Wendy Slote *Law&B 92*
Kleinberg, David Lewis 1943- *WhoAm 92*
Kleinberg, Fredric Laufer 1949- *WhoWrEP 92*
Kleinberg, Howard J. 1932- *WhoAm 92*
Kleinberg, Israel 1930- *WhoAm 92*
Kleinberg, Jacob 1914- *WhoAm 92*
Kleinberg, Judith G. 1946- *WhoAmW 93*
Kleinberg, Lawrence 1943- *WhoAm 92*
Kleinberg, Marvin H. 1927- *WhoAm 92*
Kleinberg, Norman Charles 1946- *WhoEmL 93*
Kleinberg, Robert I. *Law&B 92*
Kleinberg, Robert I. 1937- *St&PR 93*
Kleindienst, Richard Gordon 1923- *WhoAm 92*
Kleine, Herman 1920- *WhoAm 92*
Kleine, Richard Allen 1946- *WhoEmL 93*
Kleine, Tilmann Otto 1936- *WhoScE 91-3*
Kleinelp, William Charles, III 1948- *WhoE 93*
Kleiner, Aaron 1947- *St&PR 93, WhoEmL 93*
Kleiner, Arnold Joel 1943- *WhoE 93*
Kleiner, Darlene D. *Law&B 92*
Kleiner, Diana Elizabeth Edelman 1947- *WhoAmW 93*
Kleiner, Diethelm 1938- *WhoScE 91-3*
Kleiner, Fred Scott 1948- *WhoAm 92*
Kleiner, Henry Thomas 1922- *WhoE 93*
Kleiner, Joel Howard 1949- *St&PR 93*
Kleiner, Kathleen Allen 1958- *WhoEmL 93*
Kleiner, Mark 1946- *WhoEmL 93*
Kleiner, Richard Arthur 1921- *WhoAm 92, WhoWrEP 92*
Kleinert, Harold Earl 1922- *WhoAm 92*
Kleinert, Robert William 1923- *St&PR 93*
Kleinfeld, Andrew Jay 1945- *WhoAm 92*
Kleinfeld, Erwin 1927- *WhoAm 92*
Kleinfeldt, Richard C. 1941- *St&PR 93*
Kleingartner, Archie 1936- *WhoAm 92*
Kleinhans, Theodore John 1924- *WhoWrEP 92*
Kleinhans-Kelleher, Joan Mary 1954- *WhoAmW 93*
Kleinhanz, Frank J. 1932- *St&PR 93*
Kleinheinz, Franz Xaver 1765-1832 *Baker 92*
Kleinhenz, Christopher 1941- *WhoAm 92*
Kleinhenz, Karen R. 1954- *St&PR 93*
Kleinhenz, Michael J. 1955- *St&PR 93*
Kleinkauf, Horst 1930- *WhoWor 93*
Kleinknecht, Christian Frederick 1924- *WhoAm 92*
Kleinknecht, Jakob Friedrich 1722-1794 *Baker 92*
Kleinknecht, Kenneth Samuel 1919- *WhoAm 92*
Kleinknecht, Konrad 1940- *WhoScE 91-3*
Kleinknecht, Konrad Albert 1940- *WhoWor 93*
Kleinkort, Joseph Alexius 1946- *WhoSSW 93*
Klein-Kurland, Pamela M. *Law&B 92*
Kleinlein, Kathy Lynn 1950- *WhoAmW 93, WhoEmL 93*
Kleinman, Arthur Michael 1941- *WhoAm 92, WhoE 93*
Kleinman, Ava Beth *Law&B 92*
Kleinman, George 1951- *WhoEmL 93, WhoWor 93*
Kleinman, Hynda Karen 1947- *WhoAm 92, WhoE 93, WhoEmL 93*
Kleinman, Joel C. 1946-1991 *BioIn 17*
Kleinman, L. Frank 1945- *St&PR 93*
Kleinman, Laurence V. 1942- *St&PR 93*
Kleinman, Leon Paul 1940- *WhoWor 93*
Kleinman, Leonard Israel 1935- *WhoE 93*
Kleinman, Martin 1952- *WhoE 93*
Kleinman, Marvin E. 1925- *St&PR 93*
Kleinman, Milton E. *Law&B 92*
Kleinman, Philip 1925- *St&PR 93*
Kleinman, Randall *Law&B 92*
Kleinman, Randall 1952- *WhoIns 93*
Kleinman, Robert *Law&B 92*
Kleinman, Stuart Bruce 1959- *WhoEmL 93*
Kleinman, Susan Phyllis 1947- *WhoEmL 93*
Kleinmann, Richard *Law&B 92*
Kleinmanns, Robert Harry 1928- *St&PR 93*
Kleinmichel, Richard 1846-1901 *Baker 92*
Kleinn, Volker 1939- *St&PR 93*
Kleinow, Walter 1936- *WhoScE 91-3*
Kleinpoppen, Hans *WhoScE 91-1*
Kleinpoppen, Hans Johann Willi 1928- *WhoWor 93*
Kleinrath, Hans Friedrich 1928- *WhoScE 91-4*
Kleinrock, Leonard 1934- *WhoAm 92*
Kleinrock, Virginia Barry 1947- *WhoE 93*
Kleinrok, Zdzislaw Michal 1928- *WhoScE 91-4*
Kleinschmidt, Edward Joseph 1951- *WhoWrEP 92*
Kleinschmidt, Georg 1938- *WhoScE 91-3*
Kleinschnitz, Barbara Joy 1944- *WhoAmW 93*
Kleinschrod, Walter Andrew 1928- *WhoAm 92, WhoWrEP 92*
Kleinschuster, Stephen John 1939- *WhoAm 92*
Kleinsinger, George 1914-1982 *Baker 92*
Kleinsmith, Harry *BioIn 17*
Kleinsmith, Lewis Joel 1942- *WhoAm 92*
Kleinsorge, William Peter 1941- *WhoSSW 93*
Klein-Szanto, Andres J. P. 1943- *WhoE 93*
Kleintop, Ronald Lee 1945- *WhoSSW 93*
Kleinzeller, Arnost 1914- *WhoAm 92*
Kleis, John Dieffenbach 1912- *WhoE 93*
Kleis, Sandra E. *St&PR 93*
Kleisbauer, J.P. 1940- *WhoScE 91-2*
Kleiser, John Randal 1946- *WhoAm 92*
Kleiser, Leonhard 1949- *WhoWor 93*
Kleiser, Peter *BioIn 17*
Kleiser, Randal 1946- *MiSFD 9*
Kleist, Ewald Christian von 1715-1759 *BioIn 17*
Kleist, Ewald von 1881-1954 *BioIn 17*
Kleist, Heinrich von 1777-1811 *BioIn 17, NinCLC 37 [port]*
Kleist, Peter D. 1918- *St&PR 93*
Kleist, Robert A. *St&PR 93*
Kleist-Retzow, Ruth von 1867-1945 *BioIn 17*
Kleitsch, Joseph 1885-1931 *BioIn 17*
Kleitz, Michel 1937- *WhoScE 91-2*
Klekoda-Baker, Antonia Marie 1939- *WhoAmW 93*
Klekowski, Romuald Zdzislaw 1924- *WhoScE 91-4*
Klem, Joseph J. *Law&B 92*
Klema, Ernest Donald 1920- *WhoAm 92*
Klemann, Gilbert L., II *Law&B 92*
Klemas, Stephen Alan 1947- *WhoEmL 93*
Klembeth, John P. 1926- *St&PR 93*
Klemens, Eberhard Rudolf 1950- *WhoWor 93*
Klemens, Paul Gustav 1925- *WhoAm 92*
Klemens, Roney W. 1938- *St&PR 93*

Klement, Jerry Charles 1940- St&PR 93
Klement, Jonathan Joseph 1939- St&PR 93
Klement, Timothy J. 1946- St&PR 93
Klement, Vera 1929- WhoAm 92
Klement, Zoltan 1926- WhoScE 91-4
Klements, Joseph Michael 1953- WhoE 93
Klementyev, Lev (Mikhailovich) 1868-1910 Baker 92
Klemetti, Heikki 1876-1953 Baker 92
Klemin, Diana BioIn 17
Klemm, Amy S. Law&B 92
Klemm, Brian W. Law&B 92
Klemm, Johann Gottlob Baker 92
Klemm, Richard Henry 1931- WhoAm 92, WhoE 93
Klemm, William Robert 1934- WhoSSW 93
Klemme, Carl William 1928- St&PR 93, WhoAm 92
Klemme, Donald D. 1945- St&PR 93
Klemme, Howard Charles 1930- WhoAm 92
Klemmensen, Per Dausell WhoScE 91-2
Klemmer, Konrad Gerhardt 1930- WhoWor 93
Klemow, Kenneth Mark 1953- WhoEmL 93
Klemp, Gordon V. 1948- St&PR 93
Klemperer, Leslie P. Law&B 92
Klemperer, Otto 1885-1973 Baker 92, IntDcOp [port], OxDcOp
Klemperer, William 1927- WhoAm 92, WhoE 93
Klempin, Rosemary Catherine 1960- WhoAmW 93
Klempner, Diane Yon 1953- WhoAmW 93
Klempner, Mark Steven Joel 1949- WhoE 93
Klen, Tapio 1945- WhoScE 91-4
Klenau, Paul von 1883-1946 OxDcOp
Klenau, Paul (August) von 1883-1946 Baker 92
Klenda, L.D. 1937- St&PR 93
Klene, Roger Ralph 1949- WhoE 93
Klengel, August (Stephen) Alexander 1783-1852 Baker 92
Klengel, Julius 1859-1933 Baker 92
Klengel, Paul 1854-1935 Baker 92
Kleniewski, Nancy 1948- WhoAmW 93
Klenoff, Bruce Howard 1944- WhoE 93
Klenotich, Joseph M. 1946- St&PR 93
Klenovsky, Nikolai (Semyonovich) 1853-1915 Baker 92
Klenovsky, Paul Baker 92
Klenow, Hans 1923- WhoScE 91-2
Klens, Rick 1952- WhoEmL 93
Klensch, Elsa BioIn 17
Klepac, Dusan 1917- WhoScE 91-4
Klepac, Glenn E. Law&B 92
Klepac, Robert Karl 1943- WhoAm 92
Kleper, Michael Laurence 1947- WhoEmL 93
Klepinski, Robert J. Law&B 92
Kleponis, Jerome Albert 1955- WhoE 93
Klepp, Susan Edith 1943- WhoAmW 93
Kleppe, John Arthur 1939- St&PR 93, WhoAm 92
Kleppe, Jon 1946- WhoScE 91-4
Klepper, Anne 1920- WhoE 93
Klepper, Cheryl Ann Law&B 92
Klepper, Elizabeth Lee 1936- WhoAm 92
Klepper, Lawrence R. 1928- St&PR 93
Klepper, Lesa Kay 1961- WhoEmL 93
Klepper, William M., II 1944- WhoE 93
Klepple, Horst ScF&FL 92
Kleppner, Daniel 1932- WhoAm 92
Klepzig, James K. 1943- St&PR 93
Klerer, Melvin 1926- WhoE 93
Klerk, Albert de 1917- Baker 92
Klerkx, Jean M.M. 1936- WhoScE 91-2
Klerman, Gerald L. d1992 NewYTBS 92
Klerman, Gerald L. 1928-1992 BioIn 17
Klesius, Phillip Harry 1938- WhoAm 92
Kleskovic, Peter Z. 1925- St&PR 93
Klesper, Ernst 1927- WhoScE 91-3
Klespies, Linda Sue 1952- WhoAmW 93, WhoEmL 93
Klesse, William R. 1946- St&PR 93
Klessig, Daniel Frederick 1949- WhoE 93
Klessinger, Martin 1934- WhoScE 91-3
Klestil, Thomas 1932- WhoWor 93
Klestzick, Karen Rea 1954- WhoAmW 93
Kletke, Marilyn Graves 1945- WhoAmW 93
Kletschka, Harold Dale 1924- WhoAm 92
Kletsky, Earl Justin 1930- WhoE 93
Klett, Edwin Lee 1935- WhoAm 92, WhoE 93
Klett, Gordon A. 1925- WhoAm 92
Klettke, William August 1952- St&PR 93
Kletzki, Paul 1900-1973 Baker 92
Kletzki, Pawel 1900-1973 PolBiDi
Klevana, Leighton Quentin Joseph 1934- WhoE 93
Klevatt, Steve WhoAm 92
Kleve, Keith E. 1953- St&PR 93
Kleven, Arvid 1899-1929 Baker 92
Kleven, Clifford Ingemar 1930- St&PR 93
Kleven, Max J. MiSFD 9
Klevenhagen, Stanley Christopher WhoScE 91-1
Klevering, Loren L. 1940- St&PR 93
Klevins, Richard A. 1946- St&PR 93
Klevit, Alan Barre 1935- WhoWor 93
Klewin, Jane Elizabeth Law&B 92
Kley, Doe Annette 1963- WhoAmW 93
Kley, John Arthur 1921- WhoAm 92, WhoWor 93
Kley, Juergen 1944- St&PR 93
Kleyman, Greta 1967- WhoE 93
Kleyn, Edward Gerald 1947- St&PR 93
Kleypas, Lisa 1964- ScF&FL 92
Kliban, B. 1935-1990 BioIn 17
Klibanov, Alexander Maxim 1949- WhoAm 92
Klick, Jean E. 1943- WhoAm 92, WhoAmW 93
Klick, Ronald C. St&PR 93
Klicka, Josef 1855-1937 Baker 92
Klide, Robert 1949- WhoE 93
Kliebert, Bradley Joseph 1946- WhoSSW 93
Kliebhan, Jerome L. 1932- WhoWrEP 92
Kliebhan, Mary Camille 1923- WhoAm 92
Kliefoth, Arthur Bernhard, III 1942- WhoAm 92, WhoSSW 93, WhoWor 93
Kliegl, Eugene F. 1926- St&PR 93
Kliegl, John H. St&PR 93
Kliegman, Jeanne Lisa 1965- WhoAmW 93
Kliem, Peter O. 1938- St&PR 93
Kliem, Peter Otto 1938- WhoAm 92
Klien, Walter 1928-1991 Baker 92, BioIn 17
Kliesch, William Frank 1928- WhoSSW 93
Kliesmet, Mary H. Law&B 92
Kliesmet, Mary Honzik Law&B 92
Klieve, Otto K. St&PR 93
Kliewer, Kenneth Lee 1935- WhoAm 92
Kliewer, Warren 1931- WhoWrEP 92
Kliger, Brian Norman 1938- WhoWor 93
Kliger, Jack WhoE 93
Kliger, Milton Richard 1922- WhoAm 92
Kligerman, Morton M. 1917- WhoAm 92
Kligfield, Paul David 1945- WhoAm 92
Kligge, Joseph C. 1947- St&PR 93
Klijn, Anton 1937- St&PR 93
Klika, Eduard 1928- WhoScE 91-4
Klika, Karel 1915- WhoWor 93
Klika, Steven Charles 1954- WhoSSW 93
Klima, Alois 1905-1980 Baker 92
Klima, Dennis P. St&PR 93
Klima, Ivan BioIn 17
Klima, Jiri 1930- WhoScE 91-4
Klima, Karen Ann 1960- WhoEmL 93
Klima, Martha Scanlan 1938- WhoAmW 93
Kliman, Merwin 1932- St&PR 93
Kliman, Susan Schaefer 1963- WhoAmW 93, WhoEmL 93
Klimara, Ronald J. St&PR 93
Klimas, Antanas 1924- WhoAm 92
Klimashousky, William J. Law&B 92
Klimaszewski, Sedzimir Maciej 1937- WhoScE 91-4
Klimczak, Janice Beverly 1944- WhoE 93
Klimczak, R. Steven Law&B 92
Klimek, Kazimierz 1934- WhoScE 91-4
Klimek, Miros WhoScE 91-4
Klimek, Rudolf 1932- WhoScE 91-4, WhoWor 93
Klimek, Sandra Christina 1948- WhoAmW 93
Kliment, Charles Karel 1932- WhoE 93
Kliment, Robert Michael 1933- WhoAm 92, WhoWor 93
Kliment, Stephen A. BioIn 17
Kliment, Stephen Alexander 1930- WhoAm 92
Kliment of Ohrid fl. 9th cent.-10th cent. OxDcByz
Klimentova, Maria 1857-1946 OxDcOp
Klimisch, Richard Leo 1938- WhoAm 92
Klimkowski, Ann Francis 1931- WhoAmW 93
Klimo, Emil 1930- WhoScE 91-4
Klimo, R.G. 1936- St&PR 93
Klimov, Elem BioIn 17
Klimov, Elem 1933- DrEEuF, MiSFD 9
Klimov, Mikhail 1881-1937 Baker 92
Klimov, Valery (Alexandrovich) 1931- Baker 92
Klimova, Rita BioIn 17
Klimova, Rita 1931- WhoWor 93
Klim Smoljatic OxDcByz
Klimstra, Paul Dale 1933- WhoAm 92
Klimstra, Willard David 1919- WhoAm 92
Klimusko, Allan Jon 1961- St&PR 93
Klimut, David A. Law&B 92
Klimyk, Anatoli Uljanovich 1939- WhoWor 93
Klinck, Carl Frederick 1908- WhoCanL 92
Klinck, Harold Rutherford 1922- WhoAm 92
Klinck, Julia M. AmWomPl
Klinck, Patricia Ewasco 1940- WhoAm 92, WhoAmW 93
Klindt, Steven 1947- WhoE 93
Klindworth, Karl 1830-1916 Baker 92
Kline, Alan David 1949- St&PR 93
Kline, Alan H. 1934- St&PR 93
Kline, Allen Haber, Jr. 1954- WhoEmL 93
Kline, Arnold Wolfe 1932- St&PR 93
Kline, Arthur Jonathan 1928- WhoWor 93
Kline, Barry L. 1946- St&PR 93
Kline, Bernard Herman 1916- St&PR 93
Kline, Bernard Melvin 1925- St&PR 93
Kline, Bruce L. 1926- St&PR 93
Kline, Charles Howard d1992 NewYTBS 92
Kline, Charles Howard 1918-1992 BioIn 17
Kline, Claire Ellen 1955- WhoAmW 93
Kline, David C. Law&B 92
Kline, David Gellinger 1934- WhoAm 92, WhoWor 93
Kline, David Lamar 1947- St&PR 93, WhoAm 92, WhoEmL 93
Kline, Denny Lee 1939- WhoSSW 93
Kline, Donald 1933- St&PR 93
Kline, Donald 1948- WhoAm 92, WhoEmL 93
Kline, Edmund 1935- St&PR 93
Kline, Edward A. 1946- St&PR 93
Kline, Edward Charles, Jr. 1925- WhoSSW 93
Kline, Edward Mahon 1909-1990 BioIn 17
Kline, Emanuel 1921- WhoE 93
Kline, Frank Robert, Jr. 1950- WhoEmL 93
Kline, Gary A. Law&B 92
Kline, Gary Dean 1949- St&PR 93
Kline, George Leonard 1945- St&PR 93
Kline, George Louis 1921- WhoAm 92
Kline, George William, II 1949- WhoSSW 93
Kline, Gordon Mabey 1903- WhoAm 92, WhoWor 93
Kline, Gregory Chisholm 1945- St&PR 93
Kline, H. Charles 1929- WhoE 93
Kline, Harry Byrd WhoAm 92, WhoSSW 93
Kline, Herbert 1909- MiSFD 9
Kline, Jacob 1917- WhoAm 92
Kline, Jacques Howard 1940- St&PR 93
Kline, James E. 1941- St&PR 93
Kline, James Edward Law&B 92
Kline, James Edward 1941- WhoAm 92
Kline, James Freeman 1939- WhoSSW 93
Kline, James L. 1933- St&PR 93
Kline, Jane Eileen 1943- WhoAmW 93
Kline, John Alvin 1939- WhoAm 92
Kline, John Anthony 1938- WhoAm 92
Kline, John William 1919- WhoAm 92
Kline, Joyce Sheryl 1965- WhoEmL 93
Kline, Katherine 1945- WhoE 93
Kline, Keith Lawrence 1925- St&PR 93
Kline, Kenneth Alan 1939- WhoAm 92
Kline, Kevin BioIn 17
Kline, Kevin 1947- ConTFT 10, HolBB [port]
Kline, Kevin Delaney 1947- WhoAm 92
Kline, Lee B. 1914- WhoAm 92
Kline, Linda 1940- WhoAmW 93
Kline, Lloyd Warfel 1931- WhoWrEP 92
Kline, Lois Darlene 1926- St&PR 93
Kline, Louise Brayton d1991 BioIn 17
Kline, Lucy-Carole 1933- WhoSSW 93
Kline, Mable Cornelia Page 1928- WhoAmW 93, WhoWor 93
Kline, Marlene E. Law&B 92
Kline, Martin Scott 1948- WhoEmL 93
Kline, Mary Frances 1961- WhoEmL 93
Kline, Milton Vance 1923- WhoAm 92, WhoE 93
Kline, Morris d1992 NewYTBS 92 [port]
Kline, Morris 1908-1992 ConAu 139
Kline, Norman Charles 1946- WhoSSW 93
Kline, Otis Adelbert 1891-1946 ScF&FL 92
Kline, Paul WhoScE 91-1
Kline, Paul W.M. 1928- St&PR 93
Kline, Raymond Adam 1926- WhoAm 92
Kline, Richard BioIn 17
Kline, Richard Dethoff 1941- WhoE 93
Kline, Richard H. 1927- St&PR 93
Kline, Richard Stephen 1948- WhoAm 92
Kline, Rija BioIn 17
Kline, Robert C. Law&B 92
Kline, Robert Joseph 1944- WhoSSW 93
Kline, Robert Samuel 1938- WhoSSW 93
Kline, Robert Y. ScF&FL 92
Kline, Ronald Alan 1952- WhoEmL 93
Kline, Ronald Steven 1947- WhoEmL 93
Kline, Sanford E. 1928- St&PR 93
Kline, Sharon Jeanne 1940- WhoSSW 93
Kline, Stephen Jay 1922- WhoAm 92
Kline, Stephen Parks 1954- WhoEmL 93
Kline, Suzy 1943- BioIn 17
Klineberg, John Michael 1938- BioIn 17
Klineberg, Otto d1992 NewYTBS 92 [port]
Klineberg, Otto 1899-1992 BioIn 17
Klinedinst, Pamela Liane 1948- WhoAmW 93
Klinefelter, Danny Allen 1947- WhoSSW 93
Klinefelter, Gary V. Law&B 92
Klinefelter, Hylda Catharine 1929- WhoAmW 93
Klinefelter, James Louis 1925- WhoAm 92
Klinefelter, Sarah Stephens 1938- WhoAmW 93
Klineman, Ronald Bruce 1933- WhoE 93
Klinetob, Darwin Dana, Jr. WhoSSW 93
Kling, David G. 1949- St&PR 93
Kling, Doris Ruth 1933- WhoAmW 93
Kling, Gloria S. 1923- St&PR 93
Kling, John J. 1912- St&PR 93
Kling, Kenneth Raymond 1947- St&PR 93
Kling, Mark A. Law&B 92
Kling, Merle 1919- WhoAm 92
Kling, Phradie 1933- WhoAmW 93, WhoE 93
Kling, Richard W. 1940- WhoIns 93
Kling, Richard William 1940- St&PR 93, WhoAm 92
Kling, S. Lee 1928- St&PR 93, WhoAm 92
Kling, Sandra Christine 1950- WhoAmW 93
Kling, Simcha 1922-1991 BioIn 17
Kling, Vincent George 1916- WhoAm 92
Kling, Wiley B., Jr. 1947- St&PR 93
Kling, William 1915- WhoAm 92, WhoWor 93
Kling, William Hugh 1942- WhoAm 92
Klingaman, Robert LeRoy 1914- WhoWor 93
Klingauf, F. WhoScE 91-3
Klingberg, Alice Lillian 1914- WhoAmW 93
Klingbiel, Paul Herman 1919- WhoSSW 93
Klinge, Charles W. 1931- St&PR 93
Klinge, Hans 1928- WhoScE 91-3
Klinge, Henrik 1952- St&PR 93
Klinge, Valerie 1940- WhoAmW 93
Klingebiel, Albert Arnold 1910- WhoE 93
Klingel, Hans 1932- WhoWor 93
Klingel, Patti Jean 1955- WhoAmW 93
Klingelsmith, Sharon Lee 1948- WhoEmL 93
Klingeman, Ellis Dudley 1932- St&PR 93
Klingen, Leo H. 1926- WhoWor 93
Klingenberg, Friedrich Wilhelm 1809-1888 Baker 92
Klingenberg, Hans Hermann 1940- WhoWor 93
Klingenberg, Martin 1928- WhoScE 91-3
Klingenberg, Martin Ernst 1928- WhoWor 93
Klingenberg, Wilhelm P.A. 1924- WhoWor 93
Klingenburg, Anne Louise 1935- WhoAmW 93
Klingenheben, Hermann August 1886-1967 IntDcAn
Klingenmeyer, Ralph 1942- WhoAm 92
Klingensmith, Arthur Paul 1949- WhoEmL 93, WhoWor 93
Klingensmith, Harvey R. 1952- St&PR 93
Klingensmith, Thelma Hyde 1904- WhoAmW 93
Klingenstein, Andrew Davis 1957- WhoEmL 93
Klingenstein, Frederick Adler 1931- WhoAm 92
Klinger, Allen 1937- WhoAm 92
Klinger, Ernest T. 1935- St&PR 93
Klinger, Friedrich Maximilian 1752-1831 BioIn 17
Klinger, Harry Ernest WhoWrEP 92
Klinger, Jeffery L. Law&B 92
Klinger, Joseph R. 1942- St&PR 93
Klinger, Judith Ann 1943- WhoAmW 93
Klinger, Kurt 1928- BioIn 17
Klinger, Linda Anne 1949- WhoAmW 93
Klinger, Martin Ernst Christoph 1935- WhoWor 93
Klinger, Oliver Cecil 1910- WhoAm 92
Klinger, Philip W. 1935- St&PR 93
Klingerman, Richard W. BioIn 17
Klingerman, Robert Harvey 1939- St&PR 93
Klinges, David Henry 1928- St&PR 93
Klinghoffer, June Florence 1921- WhoAmW 93
Klingler, David BioIn 17
Klingler, Eugene Herman 1932- WhoAm 92
Klingler, Gwendolyn Walbolt 1944- WhoAmW 93
Klingler, Raymond P. 1947- St&PR 93
Klingler, Rolf J. 1944- WhoWor 93
Klingman, Darwin 1944-1989 BioIn 17
Klingman, Jack Dennis 1927- WhoE 93
Klingman, John Philip 1947- WhoSSW 93
Klingman, Lynzee WhoAm 92
Klingmuller, Walter 1929- WhoScE 91-3

Klingsberg, David 1934- WhoAm 92
Klingspor, Per C.-O. 1948- WhoScE 91-4
Klinhormhual, Everlida Llamas 1950- WhoEmL 93
Klink, Al 1915-1991 BioIn 17
Klink, Bruce C. 1950- St&PR 93
Klink, Harold Anthony 1942- St&PR 93
Klink, Karin Elizabeth 1937- WhoAmW 93
Klink, Kurt 1954- WhoWor 93
Klinke, Erhard D. 1934- WhoScE 91-3
Klinke, Rainer H.H. 1936- WhoScE 91-3
Klinkenberg, Hilka Elisabeth 1946- WhoE 93
Klinkenberg, John O. 1949- St&PR 93
Klinkenborg, Verlyn BioIn 17
Klinkenborg, Verlyn 1953?- ConAu 139
Klinkert, Anthony Jacob 1957- WhoSSW 93
Klinkmuller, Erich 1928- WhoWor 93
Klinkowitz, Jerome 1943- ScF&FL 92, WhoWrEP 92
Klinkowitz, Julie Huffman- ScF&FL 92
Klinkowski, Pete R. 1947- WhoE 93
Klinksiek, Klaus E. 1934- WhoScE 91-3
Klinman, Judith Pollock 1941- WhoAm 92
Klinman, Norman Ralph 1937- WhoAm 92
Klinsky, Arnold 1944- WhoE 93
Klinsky, Steven Bruce 1956- WhoEmL 93
Klint, Douglas Earl 1950- St&PR 93
Klint, Kenneth 1936- WhoWor 93
Klinzing, George Engelbert 1938- WhoE 93
Klinzman, Frank W. 1928- WhoIns 93
Klion, Stanley Ring 1923- WhoAm 92
Klipfell, John Martin 1949- St&PR 93
Kliphardt, Raymond A. 1917- WhoAm 92
Kliphouse, Everett A. 1941- St&PR 93
Klipp, Todd Lamont Causey 1950- WhoE 93, WhoEmL 93
Klipp, William J. 1955- St&PR 93
Klippel, Charles Hamilton Law&B 92
Klippel, Terry J. 1952- St&PR 93
Klippenberg, Erik 1926- WhoScE 91-4
Klipper, Joseph 1913- St&PR 93
Klipper, S. Ida 1920- St&PR 93
Klippert, Richard Hobdell, Jr. 1940- WhoWor 93
Klippstatter, Kurt L. 1934- WhoAm 92
Klipsch, M. David 1941- St&PR 93
Klipstein, Harold D. 1908-1990 BioIn 17
Klipstein, Kenneth Hampton 1900-1991 BioIn 17
Klipstine, Geo. L. 1925- St&PR 93
Klipstine, John L. 1947- St&PR 93
Klir, George Jiri 1932- WhoAm 92
Klisart, Luke H. 1930- St&PR 93
Klitgaard, Robert J. 1916- St&PR 93
Klitgaard, Thomas J. Law&B 92
Klitzing, Klaus von 1943- WhoWor 93
Klitzke, Theodore Elmer 1915- WhoAm 92
Klitzman, Abraham R. 1907-1991 BioIn 17
Klitzman, Robert Lloyd 1958- WhoE 93, WhoEmL 93
Klitzsch, Karl Emanuel 1812-1889 Baker 92
Klivans, Norman R. 1918- St&PR 93
Klivans, Robert L. Law&B 92
Klix, Friedhart 1927- WhoScE 91-3
Klobasa, Edward Alan Law&B 92
Klobasa, John Anthony 1951- WhoAm 92, WhoEmL 93
Klobucar, Berislav 1924- Baker 92
Klobusicky, Koloman 1937- WhoScE 91-4
Klobusicky, Tibor Bela 1911- St&PR 93
Kloc, Clifford John 1946- St&PR 93
Klocek, Gary R. 1950- St&PR 93
Klock, Benny Leroy 1934- WhoSSW 93
Klock, Joseph Peter, Jr. 1949- WhoAm 92
Klock, Mark Steven 1958- WhoE 93
Klocke, Mary Margaret 1961- WhoEmL 93
Klockenkamper, Reinhold 1937- WhoScE 91-3
Klocko, John J., III Law&B 92
Klodnicki, Z. George 1923- St&PR 93
Klodowski, Harry Francis, Jr. 1954- WhoEmL 93
Klodt, Henning 1952- WhoWor 93
Klodzinski, Beatrice Davis 1950- WhoAmW 93, WhoEmL 93
Klodzinski, Joseph Anthony 1942- WhoWor 93
Kloecker, John F. 1923- St&PR 93
Kloepfer, Marguerite 1916- ScF&FL 92
Kloepfer, Marguerite Fonnesbeck 1916- WhoAmW 93, WhoWor 93
Kloepfer, Richard Donald 1942- WhoIns 93
Kloepffer, Walter 1938- WhoWor 93
Kloeppel, Robert T. Law&B 92
Kloepper, David Alan 1945- WhoE 93, WhoWor 93
Kloer, Philip Baldwin 1955- WhoSSW 93
Kloesel, George W. 1950- St&PR 93
Kloesel, Gregory Bernard 1964- WhoSSW 93
Kloesel, Mark Anthony 1953- St&PR 93
Kloesmeyer, Iliana Marisa 1958- WhoE 93
Kloetzel, John Arthur 1941- WhoE 93
Kloft, Werner 1925- WhoScE 91-3
Klohn, Earle Jardine 1927- WhoAm 92
Kloiber, Lawrence A. St&PR 93
Klokner, James R. 1934- St&PR 93
Klombers, Norman 1923- WhoAm 92
Klomburg, Albert Henry 1933- St&PR 93
Klomp, Aad. J. 1927- WhoWor 93
Klonaris, Mary 1928- WhoAmW 93
Klong, Lawrence Alan 1938- St&PR 93
Klonglan, Gerald Edward 1936- WhoAm 92
Klonoff, Harry 1924- WhoAm 92
Klonski, Teri Alyson 1961- WhoSSW 93
Klontz, Marsha Ann Law&B 92
Klontz, Virgil 1916- WhoWor 93
Kloos, Jeanette Doris Burns 1950- WhoEmL 93
Kloos, Marguerite Julie 1958- WhoAmW 93
Klooster, Judson 1925- WhoAm 92
Klooster, Willem Gerrit 1935- WhoWor 93
Klopcic, Matjaz 1934- DrEEuF
Klopf, Gordon John 1917- WhoAm 92, WhoWor 93
Klopf, Lynne B. Law&B 92
Klopfenstein, Edward Lee 1941- St&PR 93
Klopfenstein, Melinda Lee 1944- WhoAmW 93
Klopfenstein, Philip Arthur 1937- WhoAm 92
Klopfenstein, Timothy J. 1956- WhoIns 93
Klopfer, Michel L. 1952- WhoWor 93
Klopffer, Walter 1938- WhoScE 91-3
Klopfleisch, Stephanie Squance 1940- WhoAmW 93
Klopman, Gilles 1933- WhoAm 92
Klopott, Zvi Simcha 1948- WhoEmL 93
Kloppel, Gunter K.P. 1943- WhoScE 91-2, -91-3
Kloppel, Gunter Karl Paul 1943- WhoWor 93
Klopper, Arnold I. WhoScE 91-1
Klopper, Arnold Ilardus 1922- WhoWor 93
Klopper, James Joseph Law&B 92
Klopper, Walter J. 1925- WhoScE 91-3
Klopping, Martin Louis 1953- St&PR 93
Klopsch, Heinz Peter 1941- WhoWor 93
Klopsteg, Paul 1889-1991 AnObit 1991
Klopsteg, Paul Ernest 1889-1991 BioIn 17
Klopstock, Friedrich Gottlieb 1724-1803 BioIn 17
Klopstock, Meta 1728-1758 BioIn 17
Klos, Elmar 1910- DrEEuF
Klos, Jerome John 1927- WhoAm 92
Klose, Friedrich (Karl Wilhelm) 1862-1942 Baker 92
Klose, Hyacinthe-Eleonore 1808-1880 Baker 92
Klose, Jules Zeiser 1927- WhoE 93
Klose, Karl W. 1924- St&PR 93
Klose, Margarete 1902-1968 Baker 92, OxDcOp
Klose, Patsy Mae Ellen 1941- WhoAmW 93
Klose, Randall M. d1992 NewYTBS 92 [port]
Klose, Roger E. St&PR 93
Klose, Thomas Joseph 1949- WhoSSW 93
Klose, Uwe 1957- WhoWor 93
Klose, Wolfgang D. 1930- WhoScE 91-3
Klose, Wolfgang Dietrich 1930- WhoWor 93
Klosk, Steven M. Law&B 92
Klosk, Steven Mark 1957- St&PR 93, WhoAm 92
Kloska, Bonnie BioIn 17
Kloska, Ronald Frank 1933- St&PR 93, WhoAm 92
Kloske, Dennis BioIn 17
Kloskowska, Antonina 1919- WhoWor 93
Kloskowski, Vincent John, Jr. 1934- WhoE 93
Klosner, Jerome Martin 1928- WhoAm 92, WhoE 93
Klosowski, Jerome M. 1940- BioIn 17
Kloss, Erich 1863-1910 Baker 92
Kloss, Gene 1903- WhoAm 92, WhoWor 93
Kloss, Henry E. St&PR 93
Kloss, John J. 1949- St&PR 93
Kloss, Richard C. 1954- St&PR 93
Kloss, Robert William 1949- WhoAm 92, WhoWor 93
Kloss, William 1937- WhoE 93
Klosson, Boris H. 1919-1990 BioIn 17
Klosson, Michael 1949- WhoAm 92
Klossowski, Michel Balthazar 1908- BioIn 17
Klossowski, Thadee BioIn 17
Kloster, Burton J., Jr. Law&B 92
Kloster, Burton J., Jr. 1931- St&PR 93
Kloster, Burton John, Jr. 1931- WhoAm 92
Klosterman, Albert L. 1942- St&PR 93
Klosterman, Albert Leonard 1942- WhoAm 92
Klosterman, Ken BioIn 17
Klostermann, Roy J. Law&B 92
Klostermeyer, Henning 1933- WhoScE 91-3
Klosty, Marylin Law&B 92
Kloth, Rachell Darden 1939- WhoAmW 93
Klotman, Robert Howard 1918- WhoAm 92
Klots, Alexander Barrett 1903-1989 BioIn 17
Klots, Cornelius Ephraim 1933- WhoSSW 93
Klott, David Lee 1941- WhoAm 92
Klott, Klaus 1952- WhoWor 93
Klotter, James C. 1947- WhoSSW 93
Klotter, John Charles 1918- WhoAm 92
Klotz Baker 92
Klotz, Arthur Paul 1913- WhoAm 92
Klotz, Charles Rodger 1942- WhoAm 92
Klotz, David Wayne 1952- WhoEmL 93, WhoSSW 93
Klotz, Florence WhoAm 92
Klotz, Howard J. 1934- WhoIns 93
Klotz, Howard S. 1939- St&PR 93
Klotz, Irving Myron 1916- WhoAm 92
Klotz, John Wesley 1919- WhoAm 92
Klotz, Linda Katherine 1948- WhoEmL 93
Klotz, Mathias 1653-1743 Baker 92
Klotz, Richard G. 1954- St&PR 93
Klotz, Sebastian 1696-1775 Baker 92
Klotz, Susanne BioIn 17
Klotz, William Henry 1919- St&PR 93
Klotzbach, Willis O'Brien 1915- WhoE 93
Klotzek, Benno 1937- WhoWor 93
Klotzer, Charles Lothar 1925- WhoWrEP 92
Klouda, Naomi Gladys 1960- WhoWrEP 92
Klove, Hallgrim 1927- WhoWor 93
Klove, Torleiv 1943- WhoWor 93
Kloves, Steve MiSFD 9
Kloz Baker 92
Klozotsky, John E. 1937- St&PR 93
Kluba, Henryk 1931- DrEEuF
Klubnikin, Kheryn 1951- WhoEmL 93
Klucas, Donna Marie 1956- WhoAmW 93
Klucevsek, Guy 1947- Baker 92
Klucher, Nancy Jackson Law&B 92
Kluchin, Philip 1916- St&PR 93
Kluchnikoff, Boris Kamir 1935- WhoUN 92
Klucis, Gustav Gustavovich 1895-1944 BioIn 17
Kluck, Alexander von 1846-1934 HarEnMi
Kluck, Robert Allen 1936- WhoSSW 93
Kluckhohn, Clyde Kay Maben 1905-1960 IntDcAn
Kluckhohn, Karl F. 1930- St&PR 93
Kluckko, Thomas M. 1940- St&PR 93
Kluczek, Julian Piotr 1930- WhoScE 91-4
Kluczynski, J. WhoScE 91-4
Kluczynski, Janet 1955- WhoAmW 93
Kluegel, Arthur Ernest Law&B 92
Klueh, Kenneth Cyril 1937- St&PR 93, WhoAm 92
Klueh, Ronald Lloyd 1936- WhoSSW 93
Kluepfel, Dieter 1930- WhoAm 92
Kluessendorf, Joanne WhoAmW 93
Klueting, Harm 1949- WhoWor 93
Kluewer, Jeffery Dane 1947- WhoE 93
Kluff, Barry WhoWrEP 92
Kluft, Cornelis 1946- WhoScE 91-3
Kluft, Gerald McElroy 1947- WhoEmL 93, WhoSSW 93
Klug, Aaron WhoScE 91-1
Klug, Aaron 1926- WhoAm 92, WhoWor 93
Klug, Dieter M. 1937- WhoScE 91-3
Klug, Mark William 1926- St&PR 93
Klug, Richard Paul 1934- St&PR 93, WhoAm 92
Klug, Robert Bruce 1947- WhoSSW 93
Klug, Ronald Allan 1939- WhoWrEP 92
Klug, Scott 1953- CngDr 91
Klug, Scott Leo 1953- WhoAm 92
Klug, Thomas Loren 1949- WhoE 93
Klug, William A. 1932- St&PR 93
Klug, William Frederick, IV 1939- St&PR 93
Kluge, Alexander 1932- MiSFD 9
Kluge, Dorothea M. C. AmWomPl
Kluge, Gunther von 1882-1944 BioIn 17, HarEnMi
Kluge, H. 1942- St&PR 93
Kluge, J. Hans 1928- WhoAm 92, WhoE 93
Kluge, John Werner BioIn 17
Kluge, John Werner 1914- WhoAm 92
Kluge, Len H. 1945- WhoWor 93
Kluge, P(aul) F(rederick) 1942- ConAu 37NR
Kluge, Patricia BioIn 17
Kluge, Richard Manfred 1936- WhoScE 91-3
Kluger, Joseph Harris 1955- WhoE 93
Kluger, Ruth 1931- WhoAm 92
Kluger, Steve 1952- ConAu 138
Klughardt, August (Friedrich Martin) 1847-1902 Baker 92
Klugheit, Mark A. 1948- WhoAm 92
Klugiewicz, Jan 1937- WhoScE 91-4
Klugman, Debra E. Law&B 92
Klugman, Jack BioIn 17
Klugman, Jack 1922- WhoAm 92
Klugman, Peter Jay 1942- WhoE 93
Klugman, Richard Emanuel 1924- WhoAsAP 91
Klugman, Robert 1947- St&PR 93
Klugman, Werner 1920- St&PR 93
Klugmann, E. 1933- WhoScE 91-4
Kluk, Cheryl Rossell 1954- WhoAmW 93
Kluk, Nada 1946- WhoAmW 93, WhoEmL 93
Kluka, Darlene Ann 1950- WhoAmW 93, WhoSSW 93
Klukan, John 1953- WhoSSW 93
Klumas, Karen Elyse Law&B 92
Klumb, Richard A. 1931- St&PR 93
Klumpp, Donald K. 1943- St&PR 93
Klumpp, Larry Carl 1944- St&PR 93
Klumpp, Missy Beck 1963- WhoSSW 93
Klumpp, Stephen Paul 1952- WhoEmL 93
Klumpp, Theodore G. 1903- St&PR 93
Klunk, Walter Edward 1924- St&PR 93
Klunzinger, Dwight L. 1954- St&PR 93
Klus, S.E. 1946- St&PR 93
Klusak, Jan 1934- Baker 92
Klussmann, Friedrick W. 1929- WhoScE 91-3
Klutsis, Gustav Gustavovich 1895-1944 BioIn 17
Kluttz, John L. 1942- St&PR 93
Klutz, Anthony Aloysius, Jr. 1954- WhoEmL 93, WhoSSW 93, WhoWor 93
Klutznick, Philip M. 1907- BioIn 17
Kluver, Billy 1927- BioIn 17
Kluver, Kent Robert Law&B 92
Kluwin, William James Law&B 92
Kluxen, Herman Anthony, III 1950- St&PR 93
Kluz, Zofia 1939- WhoScE 91-4
Kluzak, Gord BioIn 17
Kluzniak, Feliks 1951- WhoWor 93
Klyatskin, Valery Isaakovich 1940- WhoWor 93
Klyberg, Albert Thomas 1940- WhoAm 92, WhoE 93
Klyman, Anne Griffiths 1936- WhoWrEP 92
Klyne, Karl ScF&FL 92
Kman, Sharon Louise 1945- WhoAmW 93
Kmentt, Waldemar 1929- Baker 92
Kmet, Rebecca Eugenia 1948- WhoAmW 93
Kmetz, Donald R. WhoAm 92
Kmiec, Bogumil Leon 1944- WhoWor 93
Kmiec, Douglas William 1951- WhoAm 92
Kmieciak, D. Lee 1950- WhoE 93
Kmiecik, Marian 1930- WhoScE 91-4
Kmiecik, Thomas T. 1959- St&PR 93
Kmiotek, Jacqueline J. Law&B 92
Kmiotek, Jacqueline J. 1959- WhoEmL 93
Kmita, Jan 1922- WhoScE 91-4
Knaack, Howard 1924- St&PR 93
Knaack, Susan F. 1942- St&PR 93
Knaak, Richard A. 1961- ScF&FL 92
Knab, Armin 1881-1951 Baker 92
Knab, Donald Ralph 1922- WhoAm 92
Knabb, Albert Stanley 1937- St&PR 93
Knabe, George William, Jr. 1924- WhoAm 92
Knabe, James Lloyd 1946- St&PR 93
Knabe, William 1803-1864 Baker 92
Knachel, Philip Atherton 1926- WhoAm 92
Knachel, Robert Eugene 1936- St&PR 93
Knack, Arnold O. 1935- WhoE 93
Knackstedt, George T. 1947- St&PR 93
Knackstedt, Gunter 1929- WhoWor 93
Knackstedt, Mary V. 1940- WhoE 93
Knaebel, Ernest 1872-1947 OxCSupC
Knaebel, John Ballantine 1906-1991 BioIn 17
Knafo, Danielle Sylvia 1953- WhoAmW 93, WhoEmL 93
Knafou, Remy WhoScE 91-2
Knaggs, Nelson Stuart 1907- WhoAm 92
Knaifel, Alexander 1943- Baker 92
Knak, Gunter 1935- WhoScE 91-3
Knake, Ellery Louis 1927- WhoAm 92
Knap, Anna Krystyna 1961- WhoAmW 93
Knap, Rolf 1937- Baker 92
Knape, Anthony Brian 1953- WhoSSW 93
Knape, Raymond E. 1931- St&PR 93
Knape, Walter 1906- Baker 92
Knapen, Robert 1946- St&PR 93
Knapheide, Harold W., III 1945- St&PR 93

Knapowski, Jan Boleslaw 1933- *WhoWor 93*
Knapp, Amanda 1955- *BioIn 17*
Knapp, Arthur, Jr. d1992 *NewYTBS 92 [port]*
Knapp, Bettina L. 1926- *ScF&FL 92*
Knapp, Bettina Liebowitz 1926- *WhoWrEP 92*
Knapp, Candace Louise 1948- *WhoAmW 93*
Knapp, Charles B. 1946- *WhoAm 92, WhoSSW 93*
Knapp, Charles Harris 1931- *WhoE 93*
Knapp, Clement B., Jr. 1942- *St&PR 93*
Knapp, Cleon Talboys 1937- *WhoAm 92, WhoWor 93*
Knapp, Cliff 1950- *St&PR 93*
Knapp, Clifford J. *WhoIns 93*
Knapp, David Allan 1938- *WhoE 93*
Knapp, David Arthur 1960- *WhoSSW 93*
Knapp, David Hebard 1938- *WhoAm 92*
Knapp, David L. 1939- *St&PR 93*
Knapp, David W. 1936- *St&PR 93*
Knapp, David Wayne 1936- *WhoE 93*
Knapp, Dennis Raymond 1912- *WhoAm 92*
Knapp, Donna M. 1956- *WhoAmW 93*
Knapp, Edward Alan 1932- *WhoAm 92*
Knapp, Edward D. 1934- *St&PR 93*
Knapp, Frederick J. 1944- *WhoAm 92*
Knapp, Gary Lee 1953- *WhoSSW 93*
Knapp, Gary W. 1956- *St&PR 93*
Knapp, George 1814-1883 *JrnUS*
Knapp, George G.P. 1923- *WhoIns 93*
Knapp, George Griff Prather 1923- *WhoAm 92*
Knapp, George O., III 1940- *St&PR 93*
Knapp, Gregory Peter 1942- *St&PR 93*
Knapp, Harold A. d1989 *BioIn 17*
Knapp, Horst Herbert 1925- *WhoWor 93*
Knapp, Ilana A. 1952- *St&PR 93*
Knapp, James Ian Keith 1943- *WhoAm 92*
Knapp, John M. 1936- *St&PR 93*
Knapp, John Raymond 1954- *WhoAm 92*
Knapp, John Williams 1932- *WhoAm 92*
Knapp, Joseph Palmer 1864-1951 *BioIn 17*
Knapp, Judith P. *Law&B 92*
Knapp, Jules F. 1928- *St&PR 93*
Knapp, Lawrence J. *ScF&FL 92*
Knapp, Lee A. 1958- *St&PR 93*
Knapp, Leonard Kennedy, Jr. 1945- *WhoSSW 93*
Knapp, Lloyd W. 1931- *St&PR 93*
Knapp, Louis Harold 1942- *St&PR 93*
Knapp, Madonna Faye 1933- *WhoAmW 93*
Knapp, Marc Steven 1944- *WhoAm 92*
Knapp, Michael d1992 *BioIn 17, NewYTBS 92*
Knapp, Michael 1946- *St&PR 93*
Knapp, Mildred Florence 1932- *WhoAmW 93*
Knapp, Nancy Hay 1922- *WhoAmW 93, WhoE 93*
Knapp, Patricia Ann 1943- *WhoE 93*
Knapp, Patrick William 1951- *WhoEmL 93*
Knapp, Paul Raymond 1945- *St&PR 93*
Knapp, Peter H. 1962- *St&PR 93*
Knapp, Peter Hobart d1992 *NewYTBS 92*
Knapp, Peter Hobart 1916-1992 *BioIn 17*
Knapp, Peter O. 1930- *St&PR 93*
Knapp, Peter Osborn 1930- *WhoAm 92*
Knapp, Phebe Palmer 1839-1908 *Baker 92*
Knapp, Philip 1916-1991 *BioIn 17*
Knapp, Philip Bernard 1923- *WhoE 93*
Knapp, Richard Bruce 1933- *WhoAm 92*
Knapp, Richard Elliott *Law&B 92*
Knapp, Richard Elwood 1928- *St&PR 93*
Knapp, Richard Maitland 1941- *WhoAm 92*
Knapp, Robert Charles 1927- *WhoAm 92*
Knapp, Sherry Lynn 1958- *WhoE 93*
Knapp, Thomas Edwin 1925- *WhoAm 92*
Knapp, Thomas Joseph 1952- *WhoEmL 93*
Knapp, Tillmann Wilhelm 1941- *WhoWor 93*
Knapp, Virginia Estella 1919- *WhoAmW 93*
Knapp, Whitman 1909- *WhoAm 92*
Knapp, William d1990 *BioIn 17*
Knapp, William Bernard 1921- *WhoWor 93*
Knapp, William Howard *Law&B 92*
Knapp, William J. *Law&B 92*
Knapp, Wolfgang 1945- *WhoWor 93*
Knappe, Joachim A. 1934- *WhoScE 91-3*
Knappenberger, Dorothy Lavina 1906- *WhoAmW 93*
Knappenberger, Paul Henry, Jr. 1942- *WhoAm 92*
Knappertsbusch, Hans 1888-1965 *Baker 92, IntDcOp, OxDcOp*
Knappman, Elizabeth Frost 1943- *WhoWrEP 92*
Knapp-Steen, Sue *WhoE 93*
Knapton, Paul Michael 1958- *WhoWor 93*
Knarr, Shirley A. 1951- *St&PR 93*
Knarr, Willard A., Jr. *WhoIns 93*
Knaub, Donald Edward 1936- *WhoAm 92*
Knauer, Carl 1940- *St&PR 93*
Knauer, Edward 1934- *St&PR 93*
Knauer, Georg Nicolaus 1926- *WhoAm 92*
Knauer, Hermes *BioIn 17*
Knauer, Velma Stanford 1918- *WhoAmW 93*
Knauer, Virginia Dare *AmWomPl*
Knauer, Virginia Harrington 1915- *WhoAm 92*
Knauf, Albert E. 1943- *St&PR 93*
Knaur, John Sherman, Jr. 1924- *St&PR 93*
Knaus, Ronald L. 1937- *WhoSSW 93*
Knaus, Ronald Mallen 1937- *WhoSSW 93*
Knauss, Bernhard *BioIn 17*
Knauss, Emma *AmWomPl*
Knauss, John Atkinson 1925- *WhoAm 92*
Knauss, Robert H. *Law&B 92*
Knauss, Robert Lynn 1931- *WhoAm 92*
Knauss, Walter W., Jr. 1921- *St&PR 93*
Knauth, Stephen Craig 1950- *WhoWrEP 92*
Kneale, Nigel 1922- *ScF&FL 92*
Kneale, W.C. 1906-1990 *BioIn 17*
Kneale, William Calvert 1906-1990 *BioIn 17*
Kneavel, Thomas Charles, Jr. 1941- *WhoE 93*
Knebel, Fletcher 1911- *WhoAm 92*
Knebel, Henry A. *Law&B 92*
Knebel, Iosif Nikolaevich 1854-1926 *BioIn 17*
Knebel, Jack Gillen 1939- *WhoAm 92*
Knebel, John Albert 1936- *WhoAm 92*
Knecht, Charles Daniel 1932- *WhoAm 92*
Knecht, Dennis Fred 1943- *St&PR 93*
Knecht, James Herbert 1925- *WhoAm 92*
Knecht, Julia Ann 1959- *WhoAmW 93*
Knecht, Justin Heinrich 1752-1817 *Baker 92*
Knecht, Raymond L. 1948- *St&PR 93*
Knecht, Rita Marie *WhoWrEP 92*
Knecht, Roland Edward 1929- *St&PR 93, WhoAm 92*
Knechtges, David Richard 1942- *WhoAm 92*
Knee, Ruth Irelan 1920- *WhoAmW 93*
Knee, Stephen H. 1940- *WhoAm 92*
Kneedler, Alvin Richard 1943- *WhoAm 92, WhoE 93*
Kneeland, Bruce Franklin 1947- *WhoEmL 93*
Kneeland, Bryan E. 1952- *St&PR 93*
Kneeland, Douglas Eugene 1929- *WhoAm 92*
Kneeland, Robert *St&PR 93*
Kneeland, Samuel 1697-1769 *JrnUS*
Kneen, G. 1949- *WhoScE 91-1*
Kneen, Geoffrey 1949- *WhoWor 93*
Kneen, James Russell 1955- *WhoEmL 93, WhoWor 93*
Kneen, Russell Packard 1923- *WhoAm 92*
Kneer, Joseph 1949- *WhoWor 93*
Kneer, Thomas T. 1921- *St&PR 93*
Kneezel, Ronald D. *Law&B 92*
Knefelkamp, Ulrich 1951- *WhoWor 93*
Knego, Frank Michael 1929- *St&PR 93*
Kneib, Joseph A. 1948- *St&PR 93*
Kneifel, Hans *ScF&FL 92*
Kneip, Robert Charles 1948- *St&PR 93*
Kneipp, Sara 1944- *WhoSSW 93*
Kneisel, Franz 1865-1926 *Baker 92*
Kneisel, Henrietta 1767-1801 *See* Righini, Vincenzo 1756-1812 *OxDcOp*
Kneiser, Richard John 1938- *WhoAm 92, WhoWor 93*
Kneissl, William Lee 1936- *St&PR 93, WhoAm 92*
Kneitel, Thomas Stephen 1933- *WhoAm 92, WhoWrEP 92*
Knell, Gary E. *Law&B 92*
Knell, Gary Evan 1954- *WhoAm 92, WhoE 93*
Knell, Walter Lee 1953- *St&PR 93*
Kneller, Eckart F. 1928- *WhoScE 91-3*
Kneller, John William 1916- *WhoAm 92*
Kneller, William Arthur 1929- *WhoAm 92*
Knepler, Gail Orit 1959- *WhoE 93*
Knepler, Henry 1922- *WhoAm 92*
Knepp, Virginia Lee Hahn 1946- *WhoAmW 93*
Knepp, Wallace R., Jr. 1924- *St&PR 93*
Knepper, Barry Michael 1950- *St&PR 93*
Knepper, George W. 1926- *WhoAm 92*
Knepper, Jimmy 1927- *BioIn 17*
Knepper, Mike 1952- *BioIn 17*
Knepper, Teresa Rachel 1962- *WhoAmW 93*
Knepper, William E. 1909- *WhoIns 93*
Knepper, William Edward 1909- *WhoAm 92*
Kner, Andrew Peter 1935- *WhoAm 92, WhoE 93*
Knerly, Mary Johnson 1925- *WhoAmW 93, WhoWor 93*
Knerly, Vicky W. 1961- *WhoEmL 93*
Knerr, George Francis 1921- *WhoE 93*
Knerr, M.E. *ScF&FL 92*
Knerr, Reinhard H. 1939- *WhoAm 92*
Knerr, Thomas T. 1921- *St&PR 93*
Knesel, Ernest Arthur, Jr. 1945- *WhoAm 92, WhoSSW 93*
Knesel, Patricia Louise 1949- *WhoSSW 93*
Kness, Darlene Mara 1948- *WhoAmW 93*
Kness, Richard Maynard 1937- *WhoAm 92, WhoE 93, WhoWor 93*
Knetzer, Thelma T. 1927- *St&PR 93*
Kneubuhl, Fritz K. 1931- *WhoScE 91-4*
Kneucker, Raoul F. *WhoScE 91-4*
Kneuer, Paul Joseph 1960- *WhoE 93*
Kneuper, Heinz-Josef 1959- *WhoWor 93*
Knevel, Adelbert Michael 1922- *WhoAm 92*
Knevels, Gertrude 1881- *AmWomPl*
Kney, Kevin John *Law&B 92*
Knez, Eugene Irving 1916- *IntDcAn*
Knezevic, Goran *WhoScE 91-4*
Knezevic, Peter F. 1927- *WhoScE 91-4*
Knezo, Genevieve Johanna 1942- *WhoAmW 93*
Kniaziewicz, Karol 1762-1842 *PolBiDi*
Kniaznin, Franciszek 1750-1807 *PolBiDi*
Knibb, David *WhoScE 91-1*
Knibb, Grace B. 1931- *St&PR 93*
Knicely, H.V. 1936- *St&PR 93*
Knicely, Howard V. 1936- *WhoAm 92*
Knickerbocker, Christina Mary 1959- *WhoE 93*
Knickerbocker, Daniel Candee, Jr. 1919- *WhoAm 92*
Knickerbocker, Idola Newberry 1935- *WhoSSW 93*
Knickerbocker, Robert Platt, Jr. 1944- *WhoAm 92*
Knickerbocker, Vera *AmWomPl*
Knickrehm, Glenn Allen 1948- *WhoWor 93*
Kniepkamp, Linda Marie *Law&B 92*
Knier, Frederick Wallis 1943- *St&PR 93*
Knieriem, Roger William 1943- *St&PR 93*
Knierim, Kim Phillip 1945- *WhoAm 92*
Knierim, Thomas Patrick 1963- *WhoE 93*
Knies, Paul Henry 1918- *WhoAm 92*
Kniese, Julius 1848-1905 *Baker 92*
Kniesler, Frederick Cornelius, Jr. 1954- *WhoE 93, WhoEmL 93*
Kniess, H.G. *WhoScE 91-3*
Kniess, Terry L. 1950- *WhoEmL 93, WhoSSW 93*
Knievel, Arthur William 1920- *St&PR 93*
Kniewasser, Andrew Graham 1926- *WhoAm 92*
Kniffen, Jan R. 1948- *St&PR 93*
Kniffen, Jan Rogers 1948- *WhoAm 92*
Knigge, Adolf, Freiherr von 1752-1796 *BioIn 17*
Knigge, Wolfgang M.H. 1920- *WhoScE 91-3*
Knight, Alan Edward Whitmarsh 1946- *WhoWor 93*
Knight, Alfred Crocker *Law&B 92*
Knight, Alice Dorothy Tirrell 1903- *WhoAmW 93*
Knight, Alison Kay 1961- *WhoAmW 93*
Knight, Allen M. 1949- *St&PR 93*
Knight, Alvin Raleigh 1941- *WhoSSW 93*
Knight, Andrew Charles *WhoScE 91-1*
Knight, Arthur Lee, Jr. 1937- *St&PR 93*
Knight, Arthur Robert 1938- *WhoAm 92*
Knight, Arthur Winfield 1937- *WhoWrEP 92*
Knight, Athelia Wilhelmenia 1950- *WhoAm 92*
Knight, Barbara M. *Law&B 92*
Knight, Bernard *WhoScE 91-1*
Knight, C. Foster *Law&B 92*
Knight, Carla Kay 1959- *WhoEmL 93*
Knight, Carolyn Stephanie 1953- *WhoAmW 93*
Knight, Carolyn Williams 1943- *WhoSSW 93*
Knight, Charles 1791-1873 *BioIn 17*
Knight, Charles Anthony 1937- *WhoE 93*
Knight, Charles F. 1936- *St&PR 93*
Knight, Charles Field 1936- *WhoAm 92*
Knight, Charles Frasuer 1932- *WhoAm 92*
Knight, Charles Robert 1874-1953 *BioIn 17*
Knight, Charlotte A. *Law&B 92*
Knight, Chet 1939- *St&PR 93*
Knight, Christopher 1950- *WhoAm 92*
Knight, Christopher 1957- *BioIn 17*
Knight, Colin S. *St&PR 93*
Knight, Corabelle 1876-1952 *BioIn 17*
Knight, Damon 1922- *ScF&FL 92*
Knight, Damon Francis 1922- *BioIn 17*
Knight, Dan Phillip 1941- *WhoSSW 93*
Knight, David Bates 1939- *WhoSSW 93*
Knight, Debra Ann Mizer 1960- *WhoAmW 93*
Knight, Delos Lavern, III 1956- *WhoSSW 93*
Knight, Denis 1921- *ConAu 137*
Knight, Donald W. 1940- *St&PR 93*
Knight, Douglas Allan 1943- *WhoSSW 93*
Knight, Douglas Maitland 1921- *St&PR 93, WhoAm 92, WhoWor 93*
Knight, Douglas Walker 1952- *St&PR 93*
Knight, Edward Howden 1933- *WhoAm 92*
Knight, Edward R. 1917- *WhoE 93*
Knight, Elizabeth 1870-1933 *BioIn 17*
Knight, Eric Lee 1959- *WhoWor 93*
Knight, Eric (Mowbray) 1897-1943 *ConAu 137, MajAI [port]*
Knight, Etheridge *BioIn 17*
Knight, Etheridge 1931-1991 *ConLC 70*
Knight, Frank Bardsley 1933- *WhoAm 92*
Knight, Fred Barrows 1925- *WhoAm 92*
Knight, Frederick 1944- *SoulM*
Knight, Freida Herndon 1943- *WhoAmW 93*
Knight, Gareth 1930- *ScF&FL 92*
Knight, Gary 1939- *WhoAm 92*
Knight, Gary Douglas 1948- *WhoAm 92*
Knight, George B. *Law&B 92*
Knight, George Blanchard 1923- *St&PR 93*
Knight, George Fredrick 1943- *St&PR 93*
Knight, George Marlin *Law&B 92*
Knight, George Preston 1950- *WhoEmL 93*
Knight, Gerald 1948- *St&PR 93*
Knight, Gillian 1934- *OxDcOp*
Knight, Gladys *BioIn 17*
Knight, Gladys 1944- *Baker 92* *See Also* Knight, Gladys, & the Pips *SoulM*
Knight, Gladys, & the Pips *SoulM*
Knight, Gladys M. 1944- *AfrAmBi*
Knight, Gladys Maria 1944- *WhoAm 92, WhoAmW 93*
Knight, Grace Parker 1951- *WhoE 93*
Knight, Graham John *WhoScE 91-1*
Knight, H. Stuart 1921- *WhoAm 92*
Knight, Harold Edwin Holm, Jr. 1930- *St&PR 93, WhoAm 92*
Knight, Harry Adam *ScF&FL 92*
Knight, Harry W. 1909- *WhoAm 92, WhoWor 93*
Knight, Haven A. 1929- *St&PR 93*
Knight, Herbert B. 1928- *St&PR 93*
Knight, Herbert Borwell 1928- *WhoAm 92*
Knight, Hilary 1926- *MajAI [port], SmATA 69 [port]*
Knight, Howard Atwood 1942- *WhoAm 92, WhoE 93*
Knight, Howard Audway, Jr. 1943- *WhoAm 92*
Knight, Ida Brown 1918- *WhoAmW 93*
Knight, Ione Kemp 1922- *WhoSSW 93*
Knight, J.A. 1927- *St&PR 93*
Knight, James A. 1927- *WhoAm 92*
Knight, James Allen 1918- *WhoAm 92*
Knight, James Atwood 1954- *WhoWor 93*
Knight, James H. 1939- *St&PR 93*
Knight, James L. 1909-1991 *AnObit 1991*
Knight, James Landon 1909-1991 *BioIn 17*
Knight, James P. 1929- *St&PR 93*
Knight, Jane *BioIn 17*
Knight, Janet Susan 1950- *WhoWrEP 92*
Knight, Jean A. *SoulM*
Knight, Jeffrey Richard 1962- *WhoEmL 93, WhoWor 93*
Knight, Jeffrey William 1949- *WhoAm 92*
Knight, Jerry Glenn 1938- *WhoSSW 93*
Knight, Joan Aldrich 1948- *WhoAmW 93*
Knight, John Allan 1931- *WhoAm 92*
Knight, John Francis 1919- *WhoAm 92*
Knight, John Phillips, Jr. 1944- *St&PR 93*
Knight, John S. 1894-1981 *JrnUS*
Knight, Jon 1968- *BioIn 17*
Knight, Jordan 1970- *BioIn 17*
Knight, Joseph Adams 1930- *WhoAm 92*
Knight, Joseph Philip 1812-1887 *Baker 92*
Knight, Judith Marie 1950- *WhoAmW 93*
Knight, June Elizabeth 1920- *WhoWrEP 92*
Knight, June Juanita 1935- *St&PR 93*
Knight, K. Coffield 1931- *St&PR 93*
Knight, Kathleen Dotzel *Law&B 92*
Knight, Kathryn L. *ScF&FL 92*
Knight, Kathryn Lasky *MajAI, SmATA 69*
Knight, Kathy 1950- *WhoAmW 93*
Knight, Katie *ScF&FL 92*
Knight, Keith Desmond St. Aubyn *WhoWor 93*
Knight, Kenneth George 1949- *WhoE 93*
Knight, Linda Mayo *Law&B 92*
Knight, Malcolm Donald 1944- *WhoUN 92*
Knight, Margarett Lee 1923- *WhoAmW 93, WhoWor 93*
Knight, Marietta *AmWomPl*
Knight, Marilyn *ScF&FL 92*
Knight, Martha Vestal 1949- *WhoEmL 93, WhoSSW 93*
Knight, Max 1909- *ConAu 40NR*
Knight, Merrill D., III 1930- *WhoIns 93*
Knight, Merrill Donnaldson, III 1930- *St&PR 93*
Knight, Michael J. 1951- *WhoE 93*
Knight, Myra Gregory 1951- *WhoSSW 93*

Knight, Nancy Carol 1947- *WhoWrEP 92*
Knight, Norman 1924- *WhoAm 92, WhoE 93*
Knight, Norman L. 1895-1972 *ScF&FL 92*
Knight, Paul Ford 1947- *St&PR 93*
Knight, Peter Leonard *WhoScE 91-1*
Knight, Philip *St&PR 93*
Knight, Philip H. *BioIn 17*
Knight, Philip H. 1938- *St&PR 93*
Knight, Philip Hampson 1938- *WhoAm 92*
Knight, Rebecca R. 1941- *WhoWrEP 92*
Knight, Richard 1955- *WhoE 93*
Knight, Richard G.H., III 1949- *WhoE 93*
Knight, Richard Holmes, Jr. *Law&B 92*
Knight, Rick Jay 1956- *St&PR 93*
Knight, Robert *ScF&FL 92*
Knight, Robert 1945- *SoulM*
Knight, Robert Edward 1941- *WhoWor 93*
Knight, Robert Huntington 1919- *WhoAm 92, WhoWor 93*
Knight, Robert Jackson, Jr. 1926- *WhoAm 92*
Knight, Robert Joseph 1945- *WhoWor 93*
Knight, Robert Kingston 1932- *WhoWor 93*
Knight, Robert Montgomery 1940- *WhoAm 92*
Knight, Sam L. 1936- *St&PR 93*
Knight, Samuel Nicholas 1948- *WhoE 93*
Knight, Sarah Kemble 1666-1727 *BioIn 17*
Knight, Shirley 1936- *WhoAm 92, WhoAmW 93*
Knight, Shirley M. 1908- *St&PR 93*
Knight, Stephen 1938- *WhoAm 92*
Knight, Stephen 1940-1985 *ScF&FL 92*
Knight, Stephen James, III 1947- *St&PR 93*
Knight, T.E. 1939- *St&PR 93*
Knight, Thomas J., Jr. 1955- *WhoEmL 93*
Knight, Toni Cecille Frye 1949- *WhoEmL 93*
Knight, Tony *ScF&FL 92*
Knight, Townsend Jones 1928- *WhoAm 92*
Knight, V. C. 1904- *WhoAm 92*
Knight, Verne C. 1904- *St&PR 93*
Knight, Vick R(alph), Jr. 1928- *ConAu 37NR*
Knight, W. Thomas *Law&B 92*
Knight, Walker Leigh 1924- *WhoAm 92*
Knight, Walter Early 1911- *WhoAm 92*
Knight, Warren Van Horn 1945- *WhoE 93*
Knight, Wendell Morgan 1936- *WhoSSW 93*
Knight, William *BioIn 17*
Knight, William Henry, III 1956- *WhoEmL 93*
Knight, William J. 1929- *WhoAm 92*
Knight, William Thomas 1937- *St&PR 93*
Knight, Wm. David 1942- *WhoIns 93*
Knighten, James M. 1938- *WhoIns 93*
Knightg, Jeffrey A. *Law&B 92*
Knight-Kymer, Jean Elizabeth 1946- *WhoAmW 93*
Knighton, David Reed 1949- *WhoAm 92*
Knighton, Robert Syron 1914- *WhoAm 92*
Knight-Patterson, W. M. *ConAu 37NR*
Knights, Bryan *BioIn 17*
Knights, Edwin Munroe 1924- *WhoAm 92*
Knights, Peter Roger 1938- *WhoE 93*
Knights, Robert 1942- *MiSFD 9*
Knight-Weiler, Rene Margaret 1953- *WhoWrEP 92*
Kniker, William Theodore 1929- *WhoSSW 93*
Knilans, Kyleen Hale 1953- *St&PR 93*
Knilans, Michael Jerome 1927- *WhoAm 92*
Knill, John Lawrence *WhoScE 91-1*
Knill, John Lawrence 1934- *WhoWor 93*
Knill, Ronald John 1935- *WhoSSW 93*
Knip, Mikael 1950- *WhoScE 91-4*
Knipe, Anthony Christopher *WhoScE 91-1*
Knipe, Anthony Christopher 1942- *WhoWor 93*
Knipe, Robert W. 1939- *St&PR 93, WhoAm 92*
Knipe, W. Stan 1935- *WhoAm 92*
Knipel, David N. *Law&B 92*
Knipp, Fred M. 1931- *St&PR 93*
Knipp, Helmut 1943- *WhoAm 92, WhoSSW 93*
Knipp, Richard Henry 1914- *WhoWor 93*
Knipp, Stephen S. 1933- *St&PR 93*
Knippenberg, Angela Uther 1948- *WhoUN 92*
Knippenburg, Tracy 1962- *WhoEmL 93*
Knipper, John David 1961- *WhoSSW 93*
Knipper, Lev 1898-1974 *OxDcOp*
Knipper, Lev (Konstantinovich) 1898-1974 *Baker 92*
Knippers, Rolf 1936- *WhoScE 91-3*
Knipschild, Robert 1927- *WhoAm 92*
Knisel, Russell Henry 1933- *St&PR 93*
Knisel, Timothy Steven 1952- *WhoSSW 93*
Knisely, Anne Marie 1955- *WhoAmW 93*
Knisely, Beth Ann 1959- *WhoAmW 93*
Knisely, Charles William, Jr. 1952- *WhoE 93*
Knisely, Gary T. *Law&B 92*
Knisely, Gary Theodore 1948- *St&PR 93*
Knisely, Jay Wallace 1947- *WhoEmL 93*
Knisely, Jo Ann 1958- *St&PR 93*
Knisely, Marjorie L. 1924- *St&PR 93*
Knisely, Robert August 1940- *WhoAm 92*
Knisely, Robert D. 1922- *St&PR 93*
Knisely, William Hagerman 1922- *WhoSSW 93*
Kniskern, Gary Dale 1945- *St&PR 93*
Kniskern, Joseph Warren 1951- *WhoEmL 93, WhoSSW 93*
Kniskern, Maynard 1912- *WhoAm 92, WhoWor 93*
Knisley, Larry Ray 1942- *St&PR 93*
Knisley, Sylvia Jo *BioIn 17*
Knispel, Barry 1944- *St&PR 93*
Knister, James Alan 1937- *St&PR 93*
Knittl, Karel 1853-1907 *Baker 92*
Knittle, Frank Edward 1942- *St&PR 93*
Knizak, Milan 1940- *BioIn 17*
Knizeski, Justine Estelle 1954- *WhoAmW 93*
Knobel, Dale Thomas 1949- *WhoEmL 93, WhoSSW 93*
Knobel, J. Wallace *Law&B 92*
Knobel, Philip 1929?-1982? *ScF&FL 92*
Knobil, Ernst 1926- *WhoAm 92*
Knoblauch, Joel Philip 1955- *WhoEmL 93*
Knoblauch, Leo Charles 1909- *St&PR 93*
Knoblauch, Mark George 1947- *WhoAm 92*
Knobler, Alfred Everett 1915- *WhoAm 92*
Knobler, Peter Stephen 1946- *WhoAm 92, WhoWrEP 92*
Knobloch, Carl W., Jr. 1930- *St&PR 93*
Knobloch, Carl William, Jr. 1930- *WhoAm 92, WhoSSW 93*
Knobloch, Erwin 1934- *WhoScE 91-4*
Knobloch, Ferdinand J. 1916- *WhoAm 92*
Knoblowitz, Martin 1949- *St&PR 93*
Knoch, Robert H. 1932- *St&PR 93*
Knoche, Donald Irving 1931- *St&PR 93*
Knoche, Douglas Andrew 1951- *WhoSSW 93*
Knoche, Everett, Jr. 1930- *St&PR 93*
Knock, Corky John 1933- *St&PR 93*
Knock, Peter Benjamin 1948- *WhoAm 92*
Knockaert, Cyreen Marcel 1947- *WhoScE 91-2*
Knodell, Clayton William 1927- *St&PR 93*
Knoebel, David Jon 1949- *WhoEmL 93*
Knoebel, Richard Henry 1927- *St&PR 93*
Knoebel, Suzanne Buckner 1926- *WhoAm 92*
Knoedler, Elmer L. 1912- *WhoAm 92*
Knoedler, Gunther H. 1929- *St&PR 93, WhoAm 92*
Knoell, William H. 1924- *St&PR 93*
Knoepfle, John *BioIn 17*
Knoepfle, John 1923- *WhoWrEP 92*
Knoepfler, Peter Tamas 1929- *WhoAm 92*
Knoepflmacher, U.C. 1931- *ScF&FL 92*
Knoepflmacher, Ulrich Camillus 1931- *WhoAm 92*
Knof, Hans Kurt 1933- *WhoWor 93*
Knoflacher, H. Markus *WhoScE 91-4*
Knoke, David Harmon 1947- *WhoAm 92*
Knoles, George Harmon 1907- *WhoAm 92*
Knoll, Andrew Herbert 1951- *WhoAm 92*
Knoll, Bruce Evans 1953- *WhoAm 92*
Knoll, Christopher M. 1955- *St&PR 93*
Knoll, David E. 1944- *St&PR 93, WhoE 93*
Knoll, Erwin 1931- *WhoAm 92, WhoWrEP 92*
Knoll, Florence Schust 1917- *WhoAm 92*
Knoll, Frank J. 1948- *St&PR 93*
Knoll, Fred 1955- *St&PR 93*
Knoll, Glenn Frederick 1935- *WhoAm 92*
Knoll, Herman Joseph 1934- *WhoIns 93*
Knoll, Jacqueline Sue 1932- *WhoAmW 93*
Knoll, James B. *St&PR 93*
Knoll, Jerry 1924- *WhoAm 92*
Knoll, Joseph 1925- *WhoScE 91-4*
Knoll, Rose Ann 1954- *WhoAmW 93*
Knoll, Samuel H. 1940- *St&PR 93*
Knolle, Mary Anne Ericson 1941- *WhoSSW 93*
Knolle, Peter 1931- *WhoWor 93*
Knollenberg, Walter Thomas 1945- *St&PR 93*
Knoller, Guy David 1946- *WhoEmL 93*
Knook, Dick L. 1941- *WhoScE 91-3*
Knoop, Lisa Stevens *Law&B 92*
Knoor, Raymond R. 1918- *St&PR 93*
Knop, Gerhard 1923- *WhoScE 91-3*
Knopf, Alfred, Jr. 1918- *WhoAm 92*
Knopf, Irwin Jay 1924- *WhoSSW 93*
Knopf, Karen L. *Law&B 92*
Knopf, Kenyon Alfred 1921- *WhoAm 92*
Knopf, Paul Mark 1936- *WhoAm 92, WhoE 93*
Knopf, Robert John 1932- *WhoSSW 93*
Knopf, William Lee 1954- *WhoEmL 93*
Knopman, David S. 1950- *WhoAm 92*
Knopoff, Leon 1925- *WhoAm 92*
Knopow, Gary Alan 1947- *WhoWor 93*
Knopp, John *St&PR 93*
Knopp, Marvin Isadore 1933- *WhoAm 92, WhoE 93*
Knopp, Stephanie Ann 1950- *WhoAmW 93*
Knopp, Stephen Gene 1949- *St&PR 93*
Knops, R.J. *WhoScE 91-1*
Knops, Robin John 1932- *WhoWor 93*
Knorozov, IUrii V. *BioIn 17*
Knorr, Annette E. *Law&B 92*
Knorr, Daniel B. 1942- *St&PR 93*
Knorr, Ernst-Lothar von 1896-1973 *Baker 92*
Knorr, Gerard K. *Law&B 92*
Knorr, Gerard K. 1939- *St&PR 93*
Knorr, Iwan (Otto Armand) 1853-1916 *Baker 92*
Knorr, Judith R. 1941- *WhoWrEP 92*
Knorr, Julius 1807-1861 *Baker 92*
Knorr, Klaus Eugen 1911-1990 *BioIn 17*
Knortz, Herbert Charles 1921- *WhoAm 92*
Knortz, Walter Robert 1919- *WhoAm 92*
Knosalla, Lynda Sue 1963- *WhoAmW 93*
Knospe, Elizabeth Ann *Law&B 92*
Knospe, William Herbert 1929- *WhoAm 92*
Knost, Tony Alan 1961- *WhoEmL 93*
Knote, Heinrich 1870-1953 *Baker 92, OxDcOp*
Knotek, Stanislav 1936- *WhoScE 91-4*
Knott, Andre J. 1938- *WhoWor 93*
Knott, Douglas Ronald 1927- *WhoAm 92*
Knott, Gray Smithwick 1954- *WhoSSW 93*
Knott, Henry Joseph 1906- *WhoAm 92*
Knott, James Robert 1910- *WhoAm 92*
Knott, John Frederick *WhoScE 91-1*
Knott, John Ray, Jr. 1937- *WhoAm 92*
Knott, Joseph F. d1991 *BioIn 17*
Knott, Mark D. 1948- *St&PR 93*
Knott, Martin 1943- *WhoWor 93*
Knott, Martin E. 1926- *St&PR 93*
Knott, Philip Martin *WhoScE 91-1*
Knott, Robert H. 1939- *St&PR 93*
Knott, Steven E. *Law&B 92*
Knott, Tara Davis 1943- *WhoAmW 93*
Knott, Wiley Eugene 1938- *WhoWor 93*
Knott, William C(ecil), Jr. *WhoWrEP 92*
Knottenbelt, Hans Jorgen 1934- *WhoWor 93*
Knotts, Don 1924- *QDrFCA 92 [port], WhoAm 92*
Knotts, Glenn Richard 1934- *WhoAm 92, WhoSSW 93*
Knotts, Max L. 1922- *St&PR 93*
Knotts, Robert Lee 1942- *WhoSSW 93*
Knotts, Sarah April 1952- *WhoAmW 93, WhoEmL 93*
Knotts, William Norman 1940- *St&PR 93*
Knour, Arthur *WhoE 93*
Knowland, William F. 1908-1974 *PolPar*
Knowler, John T. *WhoScE 91-1*
Knowles, Alison 1933- *WhoAm 92*
Knowles, Anne 1933- *ScF&FL 92*
Knowles, Asa S. 1909-1990 *BioIn 17*
Knowles, Ava Beatrice *AmWomPl*
Knowles, Barbara Bang 1937- *WhoAmW 93*
Knowles, Brian J. 1956- *WhoE 93*
Knowles, Catherine Francis 1959- *WhoAmW 93*
Knowles, Christopher Allan 1949- *WhoE 93, WhoEmL 93*
Knowles, Christopher G. 1943- *St&PR 93*
Knowles, Christopher John *WhoScE 91-1*
Knowles, Cyril 1944-1991 *AnObit 1991*
Knowles, David 1896-1974 *BioIn 17*
Knowles, David K. *Law&B 92*
Knowles, Edward Frank 1929- *WhoAm 92*
Knowles, Elizabeth Anne 1948- *WhoAmW 93*
Knowles, F.E. *WhoScE 91-1*
Knowles, Gregory Adams 1947- *WhoE 93, WhoEmL 93*
Knowles, Jack Oliver 1916- *WhoAm 92*
Knowles, Jack W. 1945- *St&PR 93*
Knowles, James Kenyon 1931- *WhoAm 92*
Knowles, Jeremy Randall 1935- *WhoAm 92, WhoE 93*
Knowles, Jocelyn Wagner 1918- *WhoE 93*
Knowles, John 1926- *Au&Arts 10 [port], BioIn 17, ConAu 40NR, MagSAmL [port], WhoAm 92, WhoWrEP 92*
Knowles, Leo A. 1930- *St&PR 93*
Knowles, Lynda Hettich 1959- *WhoEmL 93*
Knowles, Malcolm Shepherd *BioIn 17*
Knowles, Malcolm Shepherd 1913- *WhoAm 92*
Knowles, Marie Wells 1940- *WhoAmW 93*
Knowles, Marjorie Fine 1939- *WhoAm 92*
Knowles, Michael *WhoScE 91-1*
Knowles, Nancy Welch 1930- *St&PR 93*
Knowles, Peter James 1960- *WhoWor 93*
Knowles, Phyllis Bradfute 1927- *WhoAmW 93, WhoSSW 93*
Knowles, Rebecca *Law&B 92*
Knowles, Richard Alan John 1935- *WhoAm 92*
Knowles, Richard James Robert 1943- *WhoE 93, WhoWor 93*
Knowles, Richard Norris 1935- *WhoSSW 93, WhoWor 93*
Knowles, Robert Barry 1944- *WhoWor 93*
Knowles, Robert E. 1950- *St&PR 93*
Knowles, Robert G. *WhoIns 93*
Knowles, Robert Gordon, Jr. 1943- *WhoSSW 93*
Knowles, Sheila Jeanette 1954- *WhoAmW 93*
Knowles, Stephen G. 1946- *St&PR 93*
Knowles, Stephen Howard 1940- *WhoWor 93*
Knowles, Susan Christine 1951- *WhoAsAP 91*
Knowles, Thomas George 1928- *WhoSSW 93, WhoWor 93*
Knowles, Vernon 1899-1968 *ScF&FL 92*
Knowles, W.P. 1891- *ScF&FL 92*
Knowles, Warren P. 1908- *St&PR 93*
Knowles, Warren Perley 1908- *WhoAm 92*
Knowles, William Leroy 1935- *WhoAm 92*
Knowles, William Townsend 1935- *St&PR 93*
Knowles Sorokin, Cheryl A. *Law&B 92*
Knowlton, Anne Apperly 1952- *WhoAmW 93*
Knowlton, Annie Rogers *AmWomPl*
Knowlton, Austin E. *WhoAm 92*
Knowlton, Beatrice *AmWomPl*
Knowlton, Edgar Colby, Jr. 1921- *WhoAm 92, WhoWrEP 92*
Knowlton, Jack W. 1926- *St&PR 93*
Knowlton, Joseph Smith 1931- *St&PR 93*
Knowlton, Nancy 1949- *WhoAmW 93*
Knowlton, Peter J. *Law&B 92*
Knowlton, Richard L. 1932- *St&PR 93, WhoAm 92*
Knowlton, Robert Charles 1929- *WhoSSW 93*
Knowlton, Sam D., II *Law&B 92*
Knowlton, Thomas A. 1946- *St&PR 93, WhoAm 92*
Knowlton, Thomas Anson d1992 *NewYTBS 92*
Knowlton, William Allen 1920- *St&PR 93, WhoAm 92, WhoSSW 93, WhoWor 93*
Knowlton, Winthrop 1930- *St&PR 93*
Knox, Ann Brewer 1926- *WhoWrEP 92*
Knox, Arthur Lloyd 1932- *St&PR 93*
Knox, Barbara Ruth Snyder 1924- *WhoAmW 93*
Knox, Bernard MacGregor Walker 1914- *WhoAm 92*
Knox, Bernie *St&PR 93*
Knox, C. Neal 1935- *WhoAm 92*
Knox, Calvin M. *MajAI*
Knox, Charles Henry 1950- *WhoSSW 93*
Knox, Charles Robert Chuck 1932- *WhoAm 92*
Knox, Donald E(dward) 1936-1986 *ConAu 39NR*
Knox, Douglas Richard 1951- *St&PR 93*
Knox, (Mary) Eleanor Jessie 1909- *MajAI [port]*
Knox, Ernest George *WhoScE 91-1*
Knox, Ernest Rudder 1916- *WhoAm 92*
Knox, Ethel L. *AmWomPl*
Knox, Florence Clay *AmWomPl*
Knox, Frank 1874-1944 *JrnUS*
Knox, Frank M. 1902-1990 *BioIn 17*
Knox, Frank R. *Law&B 92*
Knox, Frederick J. 1930- *St&PR 93*
Knox, George 1922- *ConAu 138*
Knox, George L. 1943- *St&PR 93*
Knox, George Levi, III 1943- *WhoAm 92*
Knox, Gertrude Leverich *AmWomPl*
Knox, Glenda Jane 1939- *WhoAmW 93*
Knox, Havolyn Crocker 1937- *WhoAmW 93*
Knox, Henry 1750-1806 *CmdGen 1991 [port], HarEnMi*
Knox, Hubbard Allen, III 1940- *WhoAm 92*
Knox, Jack Dill 1937- *St&PR 93, WhoSSW 93*
Knox, James *MajAI*
Knox, James David Edgar *WhoScE 91-1*
Knox, James E. 1937- *St&PR 93*
Knox, James Edwin *Law&B 92*
Knox, James Edwin 1937- *WhoAm 92*
Knox, James Lester 1919- *WhoAm 92*
Knox, Janet *AmWomPl*
Knox, Jessie A. *AmWomPl*
Knox, John 1900-1990 *BioIn 17*
Knox, John, Jr. 1932- *WhoAm 92*
Knox, John Armoy 1850-1906 *JrnUS*
Knox, John Keith *Law&B 92*
Knox, Lance Lethbridge 1944- *WhoAm 92, WhoWor 93*
Knox, Margaret 1866- *AmWomPl*
Knox, Michael Dennis 1946- *WhoSSW 93*

Kocher, Juanita Fay 1933- *WhoAmW 93, WhoWor 93*
Kocher, Paul H. 1907- *ScF&FL 92*
Kocher, Robert Conrad 1941- *St&PR 93*
Kocher, Walter W. *Law&B 92*
Kocher, Walter W. 1934- *St&PR 93*
Kocher, Walter William 1934- *WhoAm 92*
Kocherthaler, Mina *WhoE 93*
Kochhar, Devendra M. 1938- *WhoE 93*
Kochhar, Sunir 1958- *St&PR 93*
Kochheiser, Keith Allen 1950- *WhoEmL 93*
Kochi, Jay Kazuo 1927- *WhoAm 92, WhoSSW 93*
Kochis, Gail Marie Elizabeth 1952- *WhoAmW 93*
Kochka, Al 1928- *WhoAm 92*
Kochler, Keith W. *Law&B 92*
Kochman, Edward 1948- *St&PR 93*
Kochman, Paula B. *Law&B 92*
Kochman, Serge *WhoScE 91-2*
Kochno, Boris 1904-1990 *BioIn 17*
Kocho, Mirijana *Law&B 92*
Kochs, Heinz-Josef 1949- *WhoScE 91-3*
Kochs, Herbert William 1903- *WhoAm 92*
Koch-Sheras, Phyllis Rebecca 1944- *WhoSSW 93*
Kochsiek, Manfred 1941- *WhoScE 91-3*
Kochta, Ruth Martha 1924- *WhoAmW 93*
Kochubey, Youri N. 1932- *WhoUN 92*
Kochubka, Gary Paul 1962- *St&PR 93*
Koci, Ludvik F. 1936- *St&PR 93*
Koci, Ludvik Frank 1936- *WhoAm 92*
Kocian, James J. 1935- *St&PR 93*
Kocian, Jaroslav 1883-1950 *Baker 92*
Kociecki, Stefan Witold 1922- *WhoScE 91-4*
Kocienski, Philip Joseph *WhoScE 91-1*
Kocin, Sidney 1914- *WhoWrEP 92*
Kocinski, John *BioIn 17*
Kociol, Stephen M. *Law&B 92*
Kocisko, Stephen John 1915- *WhoAm 92, WhoE 93*
Kocjan, Antoni 1902-1944 *PolBiDi*
Kock, Lars Anders Wolfram 1913- *WhoWor 93*
Kock, Leonhard 1924- *WhoScE 91-4*
Kock, Robert Marshall 1942- *WhoSSW 93, WhoWor 93*
Kockberg, Mats Borje 1950- *WhoWor 93*
Kockelmans, Joseph J. 1923- *WhoAm 92*
Kockenmeister, Bill H. *Law&B 92*
Kockler, Norbert 1944- *WhoScE 91-3*
Kocks, Patrick J. *Law&B 92*
Koco, Linda Gale 1945- *WhoAmW 93, WhoWrEP 92*
Kocour, Ruth Anne 1947- *WhoAmW 93*
Kocourek, Paul F. 1950- *St&PR 93*
Kocourek, Wayne C. 1937- *St&PR 93*
Kocsar, Miklos 1933- *Baker 92*
Kocsis, Anne 1961- *WhoAmW 93*
Kocsis, James Paul 1936- *WhoAm 92*
Kocsis, Patrick James *BioIn 17*
Kocsis, Zoltan 1952- *WhoWor 93*
Kocsis, Zoltan (Gyorgy) 1952- *Baker 92*
Kocurek, Mary Jane 1939- *WhoAmW 93*
Kocurek, Patricia Terrazas 1935- *WhoAmW 93, WhoSSW 93*
Kocurko, Michael John 1945- *WhoSSW 93*
Koczalski, Raoul 1884-1948 *Baker 92, PolBiDi*
Koczirz, Adolf 1870-1941 *Baker 92*
Koczorowski, Boguslaw 1930- *WhoScE 91-4*
Koczorowski, Zbigniew K. 1933- *WhoScE 91-4*
Koczur, Leslie Ann *Law&B 92*
Koczur, Paula Marchewka 1949- *St&PR 93*
Koczwara, Christine Joy 1945- *WhoAmW 93*
Koczwara, Christine Joy Trella 1945- *WhoSSW 93*
Koczwara, Frantisek c. 1750-1791 *Baker 92*
Koczy, Alojzy 1931- *WhoScE 91-4*
Koda, Harold Jyun 1950- *WhoAm 92*
Koda-Callan, Elizabeth *BioIn 17*
Koda-Callan, Elizabeth 1944- *ConAu 136*
Kodaira, Kunihiko 1915- *WhoWor 93*
Kodaira, Tadamasa 1942- *WhoAsAP 91*
Kodaka, Kunio 1932- *St&PR 93, WhoE 93*
Kodalli, Nevit 1924- *Baker 92*
Kodaly, Zoltan 1882-1967 *Baker 92, IntDcOp [port], OxDcOp*
Kodama, Gentaro 1852-1906 *HarEnMi*
Kodama, James Hisao 1923- *WhoWor 93*
Kodama, Kenji 1933- *WhoAsAP 91*
Kodama, Shinjiro 1906- *WhoWor 93*
Kodama, Shinzo 1932- *WhoWor 93*
Kodani, Hiroyuki 1940- *WhoWor 93*
Kodar, Oja *MiSFD 9*
Kodet, Albert Charles 1958- *WhoE 93, WhoEmL 93*
Kodinos, Pseudo- *OxDcByz*
Kodis, Mary Caroline 1927- *WhoAmW 93*
Koditschek, Daniel Eliezar 1954- *WhoE 93*
Kodiyalam, Srinivas 1960- *WhoE 93*
Kodosky, Jeffrey Leo 1949- *WhoAm 92*
Kodousek, Kim Robert *Law&B 92*
Kodym, Miloslav 1930- *WhoScE 91-4, WhoWor 93*
Koe, Robert Edwards 1945- *St&PR 93*
Koebel, Wayne Robert 1947- *St&PR 93*
Koeberg, Frits Ehrhardt Adriaan 1876-1961 *Baker 92*
Koechler, Hans 1948- *WhoWor 93*
Koechlin, Charles (Louis Eugene) 1867-1950 *Baker 92*
Koeckert, Robert A. 1947- *St&PR 93*
Koedel, John G., Jr. 1937- *St&PR 93*
Koedel, John Gilbert, Jr. 1937- *WhoAm 92, WhoE 93*
Koedel, Robert Craig 1927- *WhoAm 92*
Koefoed, Nils 1959- *WhoScE 91-2*
Koegel, Albert J. 1926- *St&PR 93*
Koegel, William Fisher 1923- *WhoAm 92*
Koegel-Knabner, Ingrid 1958- *WhoWor 93*
Koehl, Camille Joan 1943- *WhoAmW 93, WhoWor 93*
Koehl, Mimi *BioIn 17*
Koehler, Albert Max 1935- *St&PR 93*
Koehler, Daniel Walter 1950- *St&PR 93*
Koehler, David Gerard 1958- *WhoEmL 93*
Koehler, George Applegate 1921- *WhoAm 92*
Koehler, George F. *St&PR 93*
Koehler, George Richard 1932- *WhoE 93*
Koehler, Hugh Gladstone d1990 *BioIn 17*
Koehler, Jane Ellen 1944- *WhoAm 92*
Koehler, Jo Ann M. 1951- *WhoWrEP 92*
Koehler, John Edget 1941- *WhoAm 92*
Koehler, Pawel Andrzej 1959- *WhoWor 93*
Koehler, Peter J. 1955- *WhoWor 93*
Koehler, Reginald Stafford, III 1932- *WhoAm 92*
Koehler, Rudolph August 1934- *St&PR 93*
Koehler, T. James 1935- *St&PR 93*
Koehler, T. Richard 1933- *St&PR 93*
Koehler, Wolfgang H. 1941- *WhoScE 91-3*
Koehn, George Waldemar 1943- *St&PR 93, WhoAm 92*
Koehn, Ilse 1929-1991 *BioIn 17*
Koehn, John Edward 1932- *St&PR 93*
Koehn, Lala *WhoCanL 92*
Koehn, Nancy Fowler 1959- *WhoAmW 93*
Koehn, Thomas K. 1949- *St&PR 93*
Koehn, William James 1936- *WhoWor 93*
Koehne, Heinrich H. 1939- *WhoScE 91-3*
Koehnke, Janet Del 1954- *WhoE 93*
Koehr, James Elmer 1937- *WhoAm 92*
Koekoek, Roelof 1963- *WhoWor 93*
Koelb, Clayton 1942- *ScF&FL 92, WhoSSW 93*
Koelb, Clayton T. 1920- *St&PR 93*
Koelb, Clayton Talmadge 1920- *WhoAm 92*
Koelemay, James Martin, Jr. *Law&B 92*
Koelle, George Brampton 1918- *WhoAm 92*
Koeller, Wilhelm 1941- *WhoWor 93*
Koelliker, Angela *AmWomPl*
Koelling, Herbert Lee 1932- *WhoAm 92*
Koellreutter, Hans Joachim 1915- *Baker 92*
Koelsch, M. Oliver 1912- *WhoAm 92*
Koelsch, William Alvin 1933- *WhoWrEP 92*
Koeltl, John George 1945- *WhoAm 92, WhoWor 93*
Koelz, Anne Marie 1942- *WhoWor 93*
Koelzer, Victor Alvin 1914- *WhoAm 92*
Koelzer, Winfried 1937- *WhoScE 91-3*
Koeman, J.H. 1936- *WhoScE 91-3*
Koempe, Carsten 1957- *WhoWor 93*
Koen, Benjamin Lawrence 1942- *St&PR 93*
Koen, Billy Vaughn 1938- *WhoAm 92*
Koen, Clifford Mock, Jr. 1949- *WhoSSW 93*
Koen, Fanny Blankers- 1918- *BioIn 17*
Koenck, David Neal 1948- *St&PR 93*
Koeneke, Karl Herbert 1929- *St&PR 93*
Koeneke, Michael S. 1947- *St&PR 93*
Koeneman, Alvin Berthold 1933- *WhoAm 92*
Koeneman, James P. 1948- *St&PR 93, WhoAm 92, WhoEmL 93*
Koenemann, Theodore *Baker 92*
Koenen, Austin Voorhees 1941- *WhoE 93*
Koenen, Friedrich 1829-1887 *Baker 92*
Koenen, Jane Yvonne 1930- *WhoAmW 93*
Koenen, Tilly 1873-1941 *Baker 92*
Koenhen, Dirk Marinus 1949- *WhoWor 93*
Koenig, A. Bertram 1910- *St&PR 93*
Koenig, Allen Edward 1939- *WhoAm 92*
Koenig, Angela C. *St&PR 93*
Koenig, Brian Edward 1948- *WhoSSW 93*
Koenig, Diane G. 1940- *WhoAmW 93*
Koenig, Dolores Barbara 1950- *WhoAmW 93*
Koenig, Eleanor Constance *AmWomPl*
Koenig, Elizabeth Barbara 1937- *WhoAmW 93*
Koenig, Elliott Joseph 1928- *St&PR 93*
Koenig, Erl August 1935- *WhoE 93*
Koenig, Franz Cardinal 1905- *WhoWor 93*
Koenig, Gay Pennington 1956- *WhoAmW 93*
Koenig, George W. 1929- *St&PR 93*
Koenig, Giovanni Klaus 1924-1989 *BioIn 17*
Koenig, Gottfried Michael 1926- *Baker 92*
Koenig, Harold Martin 1940- *WhoAm 92*
Koenig, Harold P. 1926- *St&PR 93*
Koenig, Harold Paul 1926- *WhoSSW 93*
Koenig, James E. 1947- *St&PR 93*
Koenig, James Edward 1947- *WhoAm 92*
Koenig, John Richard 1946- *WhoEmL 93, WhoSSW 93*
Koenig, Judith Ellen 1954- *WhoAmW 93*
Koenig, Kim Diane 1956- *WhoEmL 93*
Koenig, Maria L. 1966- *WhoAmW 93*
Koenig, Maryjane 1947- *WhoE 93*
Koenig, Michael Edward Davison 1941- *WhoAm 92*
Koenig, Renate 1934- *WhoScE 91-3*
Koenig, Richard Michael 1942- *WhoAm 92*
Koenig, Robert August 1933- *WhoWor 93*
Koenig, Robert John 1935- *WhoAm 92*
Koenig, Robert W. 1932- *St&PR 93*
Koenig, Rodney Curtis 1940- *WhoAm 92*
Koenig, Thomas L. 1940- *St&PR 93*
Koenig, Walter 1936- *ScF&FL 92*
Koenig, William C. 1947- *St&PR 93*
Koenig, Wolfgang W. 1936- *St&PR 93*
Koeniger, Nikolaus 1941- *WhoScE 91-3*
Koenig-Macko, Joanne Frances 1949- *WhoE 93*
Koenigs, Rita Scales 1952- *WhoAmW 93*
Koenigsberg, Martin 1912- *St&PR 93*
Koenigsberg, Moses 1879-1945 *JrnUS*
Koenigsknecht, Roy A. *BioIn 17*
Koenigsknecht, Roy A. 1942- *WhoAm 92*
Koenigstein, Francois Claudius 1859-1892 *BioIn 17*
Koeninger, Edward Calvin 1930- *WhoAm 92*
Koeninger, George 1940- *St&PR 93*
Koeninger, Kay 1951- *WhoWrEP 92*
Koenis, J.P. *WhoScE 91-3*
Koenitzer, Jane C. *Law&B 92*
Koenner, Alfred 1921- *ConAu 40NR*
Koepchen, Hans-Peter 1924- *WhoScE 91-3*
Koepcke, Elizabeth Russell 1961- *WhoEmL 93*
Koepcke, F. Kristen *Law&B 92*
Koepcke, F. Kristen 1935- *St&PR 93, WhoAm 92*
Koepeczi-Deak, Bajan 1945- *St&PR 93*
Koepf, Michael 1940- *WhoWrEP 92*
Koepf, Werner Karl 1942- *WhoWor 93*
Koepfinger, Joseph Leo 1925- *WhoAm 92*
Koepfler, Edward R. 1948- *St&PR 93*
Koepke, Allen C. 1945- *St&PR 93*
Koepke, Jack Edward 1942- *WhoIns 93*
Koepke, John Arthur 1929- *WhoAm 92*
Koepke, John D. 1935- *St&PR 93*
Koepke, Peter Christian 1944- *WhoWor 93*
Koepke, Wulf 1928- *ConAu 39NR*
Koepnick, Donald Joseph 1945- *St&PR 93, WhoSSW 93*
Koepp, Donald William 1929- *WhoAm 92*
Koepp, Donna Pauline Petersen 1941- *WhoAmW 93*
Koepp, Leila Haddad 1945- *WhoE 93*
Koeppe, Eugene Charles, Jr. 1955- *WhoWor 93*
Koeppe, Patsy Poduska 1932- *WhoSSW 93*
Koeppel, Andrew E. 1943- *St&PR 93*
Koeppel, Gary Merle 1938- *WhoWor 93*
Koeppel, Sanford E. *Law&B 92*
Koeppen, Albert W. 1930- *St&PR 93*
Koepsell, Gilmore John 1925- *St&PR 93*
Koerber, Dirk 1940- *St&PR 93*
Koerber, Joan C. 1929- *WhoAmW 93, WhoE 93, WhoWor 93*
Koerber, Marilynn Eleanor 1942- *WhoAmW 93*
Koerber, Marvin Alfred 1934- *WhoSSW 93*
Koerble, Barbara Lee 1957- *WhoSSW 93*
Koering, Marilyn Jean 1938- *WhoAm 92*
Koering, Rene 1940- *Baker 92*
Koering, Ursula 1921-1976 *BioIn 17*
Koermer, Fred G. *BioIn 17*
Koerner, Beverly Lynn 1948- *WhoAmW 93*
Koerner, Ernest Lee 1931- *St&PR 93*
Koerner, Henry 1915-1991 *BioIn 17*
Koerner, Irving d1991 *BioIn 17*
Koerner, James David 1923- *WhoAm 92*
Koerner, Jerry Lynn 1950- *WhoAmW 93, WhoEmL 93, WhoWor 93*
Koerner, Philip Donald 1946- *St&PR 93, WhoIns 93*
Koerner, Stephen George *Law&B 92*
Koert, Dorothy Lucile 1908- *WhoAmW 93*
Koertge, Noretta 1935- *WhoWrEP 92*
Koertge, Ronald *BioIn 17*
Koertge, Ronald Boyd 1940- *WhoWrEP 92*
Koerting, Richard J. 1937- *St&PR 93*
Koeslag, Gerhardus Johannes 1943- *WhoWor 93*
Koessel, Donald Ray 1929- *WhoAm 92*
Koessler, Hans 1853-1926 *Baker 92*
Koessler, James W. *Law&B 92*
Koessler, Paul J. 1937- *St&PR 93*
Koestenblatt, Marlene Phylis 1945- *WhoAmW 93*
Koester, Doris Juanita 1964- *WhoAmW 93*
Koester, Fred William 1936- *St&PR 93*
Koester, Helmut Heinrich 1926- *WhoAm 92*
Koester, James A. *Law&B 92*
Koester, James A. 1941- *St&PR 93*
Koester, Robert Gregg 1932- *WhoAm 92*
Koester, Robert H. *Law&B 92*
Koester, Ronald 1956- *St&PR 93*
Koester, Ronald Dean 1935- *St&PR 93*
Koesterer, Ralph J. 1926- *St&PR 93*
Koestler, Arthur 1905-1983 *BioIn 17, ScF&FL 92*
Koestler, Frances A. *BioIn 17*
Koestler, Frances Adlerstein d1992 *NewYTBS 92*
Koestner, Adalbert 1920- *WhoAm 92*
Koeth, Leonard Alfred 1937- *WhoSSW 93*
Koether, Bernard Gustave, II 1937- *St&PR 93*
Koether, Paul Otto 1936- *St&PR 93*
Koether, Philip 1956- *WhoE 93*
Koets, Erico 1942- *WhoWor 93*
Koetsch, Philip 1935- *St&PR 93*
Koetsier, Jan 1911- *Baker 92*
Koetters, Michael Charles 1943- *WhoAm 92*
Koetters, Thomas Joseph 1943- *St&PR 93*
Koevenig, James L. *BioIn 17*
Koevenig, James Louis 1931- *WhoSSW 93*
Koewler, James L., Jr. *Law&B 92*
Koff, Richard M. 1926- *BioIn 17, ScF&FL 92*
Koff, Richard Myram 1926- *St&PR 93*
Koff, Robert Hess 1938- *WhoAm 92, WhoE 93*
Koffel, Martin M. 1939- *St&PR 93*
Koffi, Aoussou 1924- *WhoAfr*
Koffi, Leon Konan *WhoWor 93*
Koffigoh, Joseph Kokou *WhoWor 93*
Koffigoh, Koku 1943- *WhoAfr*
Koffler, Irving 1932- *St&PR 93*
Koffler, Jozef 1896-1943 *Baker 92, PolBiDi*
Koffler, Peter D. *Law&B 92*
Koffler, Russell 1937- *WhoE 93*
Koffman, Burton I. *WhoAm 92*
Koffman, Milton Aaron 1923- *St&PR 93, WhoAm 92*
Koffman, Morley 1930- *St&PR 93*
Koffman, Neill Austin 1962- *St&PR 93*
Koffsky, Robert Michael 1937- *WhoE 93*
Kofke, William Andrew 1952- *WhoE 93*
Kofler, Hansjorg *WhoScE 91-4*
Kofler, Valentine Mathew 1927- *St&PR 93*
Kofmehl, William Earl, Jr. 1943- *WhoE 93*
Kofnovec, Gary S. *St&PR 93*
Kofoed, William Carl 1934- *WhoSSW 93*
Koford, James Shingle 1938- *St&PR 93*
Koford, Stuart Keith 1953- *WhoEmL 93*
Kofranek, Anton Miles 1921- *WhoAm 92*
Kofsky, Kipp Scott 1962- *St&PR 93*
Kofstad, Per K. 1929- *WhoScE 91-4*
Koga, Elaine 1942- *WhoAmW 93*
Koga, Issei 1947- *WhoAsAP 91*
Koga, Makoto 1940- *WhoAsAP 91*
Koga, Mary 1920- *WhoAm 92*
Koga, Masahiro 1934- *WhoAsAP 91*
Koga, Mineichi 1885-1944 *HarEnMi*
Kogalovskii, Sergei 1934- *WhoWor 93*
Kogan, David Seth 1964- *St&PR 93*
Kogan, Elizabeth Gilels
See Kogan, Leonid (Borisovich) 1924-1982 *Baker 92*
Kogan, Gerald 1933- *WhoAm 92, WhoSSW 93*
Kogan, Jay *Law&B 92*
Kogan, Leonid (Borisovich) 1924-1982 *Baker 92*
Kogan, Pavel 1952-
See Kogan, Leonid (Borisovich) 1924-1982 *Baker 92*
Kogan, Ray *WhoWrEP 92*
Kogan, Richard Jay 1941- *St&PR 93, WhoAm 92, WhoE 93*
Koganei, Yoshikiyo 1859-1944 *IntDcAn*
Kogawa, Joy 1935- *WhoCanL 92*
Kogel, Gustav Friedrich 1849-1921 *Baker 92*

Kogel, Marcus David 1903-1989 *BioIn 17*
Kogelnik, Herwig Werner 1932- *WhoAm 92*
Koger, Fred 1924- *BioIn 17*
Koger, Ira M. 1912- *St&PR 93, WhoAm 92*
Koger, Marsha Kay 1962- *WhoAmW 93*
Koggan, Arthur H. 1928- *St&PR 93*
Kogge, Peter Michael 1946- *WhoAm 92*
Kogi, Hiroko 1955- *WhoAmW 93*
Kogitz, Jeffrey Michael 1947- *St&PR 93*
Kogovsek, Conrad J. 1951- *St&PR 93*
Kogure, Hiroaki 1952- *WhoWor 93*
Kogure, Yamato 1928- *WhoAsAP 91*
Kogut, John Anthony 1942- *St&PR 93, WhoAm 92*
Kogut, Maurice David 1930- *WhoAm 92*
Koh, Boon Piang Laurence 1927- *WhoWor 93*
Koh, Hesung Chun 1929- *WhoAm 92*
Koh, Jai-Sang 1956- *WhoWor 93*
Koh, Kern 1948- *WhoWor 93*
Koh, Severino Legarda 1927- *WhoAm 92*
Koh, Tong Chui 1946- *WhoEmL 93*
Kohalmy, Tamas 1936- *WhoScE 91-4*
Kohan, Dennis Lynn 1945- *WhoWor 93*
Kohan, Mark Anthony 1960- *WhoE 93, WhoEmL 93*
Kohan, Melvin Ira 1921- *WhoE 93*
Kohan, Theodore S. 1940- *St&PR 93*
Kohana, Sidney 1928- *St&PR 93*
Kohel, Russell James 1934- *WhoAm 92*
Kohila, Tarja Tuulikki 1947- *WhoWor 93*
Kohill, Malcolm *ScF&FL 92*
Kohin, Roger P. 1931- *WhoE 93*
Kohl, Atlee Mitchell 1945- *St&PR 93*
Kohl, Benedict M. 1931- *WhoAm 92*
Kohl, Ernst 1935- *WhoWor 93*
Kohl, Helmut *NewYTBS 92*
Kohl, Helmut 1930- *BioIn 17, ColdWar 1 [port], DcTwHis, WhoWor 93*
Kohl, Herbert 1935- *WhoAm 92*
Kohl, Herbert H. 1935- *CngDr 91*
Kohl, Jacques T. 1930- *WhoScE 91-2*
Kohl, Johannes *WhoScE 91-3*
Kohl, John Clayton 1908- *WhoAm 92*
Kohl, Marvin 1932- *WhoE 93*
Kohl, Peter 1925- *St&PR 93*
Kohl, Shelley Jo 1967- *WhoE 93*
Kohl, Steven 1947- *St&PR 93*
Kohl, Stewart Allen 1955- *WhoAm 92*
Kohl, Theresa Welch 1950- *WhoSSW 93*
Kohl, Werner 1928- *WhoScE 91-4*
Kohlberg, Jerome, Jr. 1925- *WhoAm 92*
Kohlberger, Richard A. *Law&B 92*
Kohlbrugge, J.H.F. 1865-1941 *IntDcAn*
Kohlbry, S.T. 1928- *St&PR 93*
Kohlenberg, Stanley 1932- *WhoE 93*
Kohler, Charlotte *AmWomPl*
Kohler, Charlotte 1908- *WhoAm 92*
Kohler, Claus 1928- *WhoWor 93*
Kohler, Claus O. 1935- *WhoScE 91-3*
Kohler, Eberhart Karl 1929- *WhoScE 91-3, WhoWor 93*
Kohler, Ernesto 1849-1907 *Baker 92*
Kohler, Ernst 1799-1847 *Baker 92*
Kohler, Foy David 1908-1990 *BioIn 17*
Kohler, Fred 1888-1938 *BioIn 17*
Kohler, Friedrich 1924- *WhoWor 93*
Kohler, Georges J.F. 1946- *WhoScE 91-3, WhoWor 93*
Kohler, Hans 1941- *WhoWor 93*
Kohler, Hans Dirk 1946- *WhoWor 93*
Kohler, Harro Wolfgang 1918- *WhoScE 91-4*
Kohler, Herbert Vollrath, Jr. 1939- *St&PR 93, WhoAm 92*
Kohler, Hubert Stephan 1937- *WhoScE 91-3*
Kohler, Jeffrey Martin 1956- *WhoAm 92*
Kohler, Jerry L. 1944- *St&PR 93*
Kohler, John Charles 1944- *WhoE 93*
Kohler, John Michael, Jr. 1934- *St&PR 93*
Kohler, Kathryn D. *Law&B 92*
Kohler, Klaus Jurgen 1945- *WhoWor 93*
Kohler, Larry R. 1946- *WhoUN 92*
Kohler, Louis 1820-1886 *Baker 92*
Kohler, Martha Hansen 1947- *WhoEmL 93*
Kohler, Mary Antoinette 1964- *WhoAmW 93*
Kohler, Max Adam 1915- *WhoAm 92*
Kohler, Michael X. 1937- *St&PR 93*
Kohler, Niklaus 1941- *WhoScE 91-4*
Kohler, Peter G. 1934- *St&PR 93*
Kohler, Peter Ogden 1938- *WhoAm 92*
Kohler, Richard Allen 1950- *WhoEmL 93*
Kohler, Ruth DeYoung *BioIn 17*
Kohler, Ruth DeYoung 1941- *WhoAm 92*
Kohler, Saul 1928- *WhoE 93*
Kohler, Sheila (May) 1941- *ConAu 137*
Kohler, Siegfried 1923- *Baker 92*
Kohler, Terry Jodok 1934- *St&PR 93*
Kohler, William John *Law&B 92*
Kohler, William R. 1940- *St&PR 93*
Kohlhof, L.L. 1929- *WhoIns 93*
Kohlhof, Lavern Louis 1929- *St&PR 93*
Kohlhorst, Gail Lewis 1946- *WhoAm 92*
Kohlman, David Leslie 1937- *WhoAm 92*
Kohlman, Louis Freddie 1915-1990 *BioIn 17*
Kohlmann, Henry George 1939- *WhoAm 92*
Kohlmann, Phyllis Beth 1948- *WhoE 93*
Kohlmeier, Daniel Kimbrell 1960- *WhoEmL 93*
Kohlmeier, Lenore 1953- *WhoScE 91-3*
Kohlmeier, Louis Martin, Jr. 1926- *WhoAm 92*
Kohlmeyer, Ida Rittenberg 1912- *WhoAm 92*
Kohl-Moszczyc, DoreeAnn 1958- *WhoAmW 93*
Kohloss, Frederick Henry 1922- *WhoAm 92*
Kohls, Robert A., Jr. *Law&B 92*
Kohls, William Richard 1957- *St&PR 93*
Kohls Stehman, Betty 1952- *WhoEmL 93*
Kohlstaedt, Anne Thoburn 1952- *WhoAmW 93*
Kohlstedt, Sally Gregory 1943- *WhoAm 92*
Kohn, A. Eugene 1930- *WhoAm 92*
Kohn, Anne Frankenthaler d1992 *BioIn 17*
Kohn, Arthur *BioIn 17*
Kohn, Bruce A. *Law&B 92*
Kohn, Clyde Frederick 1911-1989 *BioIn 17*
Kohn, Daniel Reuben *Law&B 92*
Kohn, Daniel Reuben 1952- *St&PR 93*
Kohn, David 1940- *St&PR 93*
Kohn, Dennis Fredrich 1940- *WhoAm 92*
Kohn, Erin *AmWomPl*
Kohn, Erwin 1923- *WhoSSW 93*
Kohn, Gerhard 1928- *WhoScE 91-3*
Kohn, Harold Elias 1914- *WhoAm 92, WhoE 93, WhoWor 93*
Kohn, Harry Jeremy 1943- *St&PR 93*
Kohn, Henry 1917- *St&PR 93, WhoAm 92*
Kohn, Henry L. *Law&B 92*
Kohn, Immanuel 1926- *WhoAm 92, WhoWor 93*
Kohn, James Paul 1924- *WhoAm 92*
Kohn, Joachim Benjamin 1952- *WhoE 93*
Kohn, John Peter, Jr. 1902- *WhoAm 92*
Kohn, Joseph John 1932- *WhoAm 92*
Kohn, Julieanne 1946- *WhoAmW 93, WhoEmL 93*
Kohn, Julius 1906- *St&PR 93*
Kohn, Karen Josephine 1951- *WhoAmW 93*
Kohn, Karl (Georg) 1926- *Baker 92*
Kohn, Larry Michael 1953- *WhoEmL 93*
Kohn, Leonore 1911- *St&PR 93*
Kohn, Livia 1956- *ConAu 139*
Kohn, Louis R. *Law&B 92*
Kohn, Mary Louise Beatrice 1920- *WhoAmW 93, WhoWor 93*
Kohn, Melvin L. 1928- *WhoAm 92*
Kohn, Michael 1953- *WhoSSW 93*
Kohn, Peter R. *Law&B 92*
Kohn, Richard *Law&B 92*
Kohn, Richard H. 1940- *WhoAm 92*
Kohn, Richard H(enry) 1940- *ConAu 37NR*
Kohn, Rik 1948- *St&PR 93*
Kohn, Robert David 1950- *St&PR 93*
Kohn, Robert H. 1957- *St&PR 93*
Kohn, Robert N. *Law&B 92*
Kohn, Robert Samuel, Jr. 1949- *WhoEmL 93, WhoWor 93*
Kohn, Roger 1938- *WhoUN 92*
Kohn, Sara Gunn 1938- *WhoSSW 93*
Kohn, Walter 1923- *WhoAm 92*
Kohne, Richard Edward 1924- *WhoAm 92*
Kohnen, Heinz 1938- *WhoScE 91-3*
Kohnen, Robert Eugene 1933- *St&PR 93*
Kohner, Eva Maria *WhoScE 91-1*
Kohner, Pancho 1939- *MiSFD 9*
Kohner, Peter 1948- *St&PR 93*
Kohnhorst, Earl Eugene 1947- *St&PR 93*
Kohnke, Mary Florence 1932- *WhoSSW 93*
Kohnstamm, Lee W. 1936- *St&PR 93*
Kohonen, Teuvo Kalevi 1934- *WhoScE 91-4*
Kohout, Pavel 1928- *ScF&FL 92*
Kohoutek, Ctirad 1929- *Baker 92*
Kohoutek, Richard 1943- *WhoWor 93*
Kohr, Glenn Earl 1928- *St&PR 93*
Kohr, Leopold *BioIn 17*
Kohr, Robert Leon 1952- *WhoE 93*
Kohring, Dagmar Luzia 1951- *WhoE 93, WhoEmL 93*
Kohrman, Arthur Fisher 1934- *WhoAm 92*
Kohrt, Carl F. 1943- *St&PR 93*
Kohrt, Carl Fredrick 1943- *WhoAm 92*
Kohrt, Iona J. 1930- *St&PR 93*
Kohs, Ellis Bonoff 1916- *Baker 92*
Koh Se Jin 1934- *WhoAsAP 91*
Kohser, Russell *St&PR 93*
Kohser, Russell Norman, II 1953- *St&PR 93*
Kohsiek, H. *WhoScE 91-3*
Kohut, Dawn Page *Law&B 92*
Kohut, J.M. *St&PR 93*
Kohut, John Walter 1946- *WhoAm 92, WhoE 93, WhoEmL 93, WhoWor 93*
Kohut, Rebekah Bettelheim 1864-1951 *BioIn 17*
Kohut, Stephen 1939- *St&PR 93*
Koi, Andrew Z. 1931- *St&PR 93*
Koibaev, Vladimir 1955- *WhoWor 93*
Koide, Frank Takayuki 1935- *WhoAm 92*
Koike, Kay 1940- *SmATA 72 [port]*
Koile, Earl 1917- *WhoAm 92*
Koinis, Steven W. 1956- *WhoE 93, WhoEmL 93*
Koirala, Girija Prasad *WhoAsAP 91, WhoWor 93*
Koiro, Beverly Ann 1948- *WhoAmW 93*
Koirtyohann, Samuel Roy 1930- *WhoAm 92*
Koischwitz, Max Otto 1902-1944 *BioIn 17*
Koiso, Kuniaki 1880-1950 *HarEnMi*
Koistinen, Jukka Lauri K. 1942- *WhoUN 92*
Koithan, Mary Susan 1956- *WhoEmL 93*
Koivisto, Erkki Lauri Matias 1927- *WhoWor 93*
Koivisto, Erkki M. 1927- *WhoScE 91-4*
Koivisto, Heikki Juha 1945- *WhoWor 93*
Koivisto, Mauno Henrik 1923- *WhoWor 93*
Koivistoinen, Pekka E. 1932- *WhoScE 91-4*
Koivo, Heikki Niilo 1943- *WhoScE 91-4*
Koivusalo, Martti Johannes 1930- *WhoWor 93*
Koiwai, Kiyoshi 1935- *WhoAsAP 91*
Koizumi, Fumio 1927- *Baker 92*
Koizumi, Junichiro 1942- *WhoAsAP 91*
Koizumi, Kazuhiro 1949- *Baker 92*
Koizumi, Shunzo 1946- *WhoWor 93*
Koizumi, Yakumo 1850-1904 *BioIn 17*
Koj, Aleksander 1935- *WhoScE 91-4, WhoWor 93*
Koja, Kathe 1960- *ScF&FL 92*
Kojian, Varujan (Haig) 1935- *Baker 92, WhoAm 92*
Kojima, Kenichi 1942- *WhoWor 93*
Kojima, Mitsuko 1924- *WhoWor 93*
Kojima, N. *WhoScE 91-3*
Kojima, Ryuichi O. 1949- *WhoWor 93*
Kojima, Shusaku *St&PR 93*
Kojima, Takemasa 1935- *WhoWor 93*
Kojo, Makato *Law&B 92*
Kojo, Shosuke 1948- *WhoWor 93*
Kojori, Hassan Ali 1956- *WhoWor 93*
Kok, Frans Johan 1943- *WhoE 93*
Kok, Willem 1938- *WhoWor 93*
Kokai, Rezso 1906-1962 *Baker 92*
Kokal, Joseph J. 1942- *St&PR 93*
Kokal, Leon H. 1947- *St&PR 93*
Kokalj, Daniejl 1941- *WhoScE 91-4*
Kokaska, Charles James 1937- *WhoAm 92*
Koke, Jeffrey David 1957- *WhoEmL 93, WhoSSW 93*
Koke, Richard Joseph 1916- *WhoAm 92*
Koken, Bernd Krafft 1926- *WhoWor 93*
Koken, M. Diane *Law&B 92*
Kokenda, Robert Earl 1932- *St&PR 93*
Koker, Bernhard Chomse-B. 1949- *WhoWor 93*
Koki, Alois 1932- *WhoAsAP 91*
Kokjer, Serena Strazzulla 1939- *St&PR 93, WhoAmW 93*
Kokke, Robert 1931- *WhoScE 91-3*
Kokkinakis, George 1937- *WhoScE 91-3*
Kokkinobaphos, James of *OxDcByz*
Kokko, Juha Pekka 1937- *WhoAm 92, WhoSSW 93*
Kokkonen, Joonas 1921- *Baker 92, WhoWor 93*
Kokmeyer, Edward W. 1937- *St&PR 93*
Kokocki, Stanley Peter 1956- *WhoSSW 93*
Kokola, Melody Bacsko 1947- *WhoEmL 93*
Kokorev, Alexsandr A. 1935- *WhoUN 92*
Kokoschka, Oskar 1886-1980 *BioIn 17, DcLB 124 [port]*
Kokoszczynski, Ryszard Zbigniew 1954- *WhoWor 93*
Kokot, Franciszek 1929- *WhoScE 91-4*
Kokot, Franciszek Jozef 1929- *WhoWor 93*
Kokotovich, Nick M. 1948- *St&PR 93*
Koksal, Fatma Zeynep 1951- *WhoScE 91-4*
Koksal, Orhan 1922- *WhoScE 91-4*
Koksoy, Mumin 1934- *WhoScE 91-4*
Kokt, Gerard Johannes 1953- *WhoWor 93*
Kokten, Ismail Kilic 1904-1974 *IntDcAn*
Kokubo, Toshio 1955- *WhoWor 93*
Kok Wee Kiat, Dato' 1940- *WhoAsAP 91*
Kol, Jacob 1947- *WhoWor 93*
Kolachevsky, Mikhail *Baker 92*
Kolacke, F. Robert *Law&B 92*
Kolacz, Michael David 1963- *WhoEmL 93*
Kolaff, Kevin *Law&B 92*
Kolakofsky, Daniel 1943- *WhoScE 91-4*
Kolakosky, Mary B. *Law&B 92*
Kolakowska, Anna 1938- *WhoScE 91-4*
Kolakowska, Anna Zofia Alicja 1938- *WhoWor 93*
Kolakowski, Edward 1938- *WhoScE 91-4*
Kolanowski, Jaroslaw 1935- *WhoScE 91-2*
Kolansky, Harold 1924- *WhoAm 92*
Kolar, Donna L. *Law&B 92*
Kolar, John Joseph 1927- *WhoWrEP 92*
Kolar, Mary Jane *BioIn 17*
Kolar, Mary Jane 1941- *WhoAm 92, WhoWor 93*
Kolar, Milton Anton 1916- *WhoAm 92*
Kolar, Victor 1888-1957 *Baker 92*
Kolarik, Jaromir C. 1930- *WhoScE 91-4*
Kolarik, William Joel 1949- *WhoSSW 93*
Kolarov, Dobromir Krastev 1930- *WhoScE 91-4*
Kolarow, Iwan 1934- *WhoScE 91-4*
Kolarsick, Leroy D. 1921- *St&PR 93*
Kolarzyk, K. *WhoScE 91-4*
Kolasa, Ann Cathryn 1960- *WhoAmW 93*
Kolasa, Kathryn Marianne Kelly 1949- *WhoAmW 93*
Kolash, Helen Anna 1908- *WhoAmW 93*
Kolaskar, Ashok Sadanand 1950- *WhoWor 93*
Kolata, Gina 1948- *WhoAmW 93*
Kolatch, Alfred Jacob 1916- *WhoAm 92*
Kolatch, Myron 1929- *WhoAm 92*
Kolb, Barbara 1939- *Baker 92, BioIn 17*
Kolb, Barbara Konheim 1937- *WhoAmW 93*
Kolb, Bertha Mae 1925- *WhoAmW 93*
Kolb, Charles Edward Mealey 1950- *WhoAm 92*
Kolb, Charles Eugene 1945- *WhoAm 92*
Kolb, David Allen 1939- *WhoAm 92*
Kolb, David L. 1939- *St&PR 93*
Kolb, Dietmar 1940- *WhoScE 91-3*
Kolb, Frances Arick 1937-1991 *BioIn 17*
Kolb, Frederick John, Jr. 1917- *WhoE 93*
Kolb, Frederick T. *Law&B 92*
Kolb, Gwin Jackson 1919- *WhoAm 92, WhoWrEP 92*
Kolb, Harold H., Jr. 1933- *WhoAm 92, WhoSSW 93*
Kolb, Henry G. *Law&B 92*
Kolb, Henry Karl 1936- *St&PR 93*
Kolb, Ilona 1938- *St&PR 93*
Kolb, Jerry Wilbert 1935- *WhoAm 92*
Kolb, Keith Robert 1922- *WhoAm 92*
Kolb, Ken Lloyd 1926- *WhoAm 92*
Kolb, Kenneth Lloyd 1926- *WhoWrEP 92*
Kolb, Lawrence Coleman 1911- *WhoAm 92*
Kolb, Leonard 1931- *St&PR 93*
Kolb, Marilyn K. *Law&B 92*
Kolb, Marsha *Law&B 92*
Kolb, Mary Lorraine 1947- *WhoAmW 93, WhoEmL 93*
Kolb, Mignon G. 1934- *St&PR 93*
Kolb, Nancy Dwyer 1940- *WhoE 93*
Kolb, Nathaniel Key, Jr. 1933- *WhoAm 92*
Kolb, Noel Joseph 1930- *WhoWor 93*
Kolb, Philip 1907-1992 *ConAu 139*
Kolb, Theodore Alexander 1920- *WhoAm 92*
Kolb, Thomas A. 1951- *St&PR 93*
Kolb, Vera M. 1948- *WhoAmW 93, WhoEmL 93*
Kolb, Wade S., Jr. 1949- *WhoEmL 93*
Kolb, Walter A. 1926- *WhoScE 91-3*
Kolbe, Fritz *BioIn 17*
Kolbe, Hellmuth Walter 1926- *WhoWor 93*
Kolbe, James Thomas 1942- *WhoAm 92*
Kolbe, Jane Boegler 1944- *WhoAm 92, WhoAmW 93*
Kolbe, Jim 1942- *CngDr 91*
Kolbe, Karl William, Jr. 1926- *WhoAm 92*
Kolbe, Maximilian, Saint 1894-1941 *BioIn 17*
Kolbe, Oskar 1836-1878 *Baker 92*
Kolbe, Sherry Lynn 1957- *WhoE 93*
Kolbeck, Gustavo A. Romero 1923- *WhoWor 93*
Kolbeinsson, Arni *WhoScE 91-4*
Kolbenheyer, Erwin Guido 1878-1962 *DcLB 124 [port]*
Kolber, Daniel Hackner 1953- *WhoEmL 93, WhoSSW 93*
Kolber, Mark Joel 1951- *WhoEmL 93*
Kolberg, Antoni 1815-1891 *PolBiDi*
Kolberg, Curt 1959- *St&PR 93*
Kolberg, Elizabeth Anne *Law&B 92*
Kolberg, Henryk Oskar 1814-1890 *IntDcAn*
Kolberg, Oskar 1814-1890 *PolBiDi*
Kolberg, (Henryk) Oskar 1814-1890 *Baker 92*
Kolbert, Kathryn 1952- *WhoEmL 93*
Kolbeson, Marilyn Hopf 1930- *WhoAmW 93*
Kolbin, Vyacheslav V. 1941- *WhoWor 93*
Kolbl, Otto R. 1940- *WhoScE 91-4*
Kolbye, Albert Christian, Jr. 1935- *WhoAm 92*
Kolch, Walter 1960- *WhoWor 93*

Kolchak, Aleksandr Vasiliyevich 1874-1920 HarEnMi
Kolchak, Alexander Vasileyvich 1874-1920 DcTwHis
Kolchin, E.R. 1916-1991 BioIn 17
Kolchin, Ellis Robert 1916-1991 BioIn 17
Kold, Per 1942- WhoWor 93
Kolditz, Gottfried 1922-1982 DrEEuF
Kolditz, L. WhoScE 91-3
Kolditz, Lothar 1929- WhoWor 93
Koldobsky, Alexander Lvovich 1955- WhoWor 93
Koldunov, Andrej Vitalievich 1948- WhoWor 93
Koldyke, Mike WhoAm 92
Kole, Janet Stephanie 1946- WhoAmW 93
Kole, Jeffrey Holitser 1960- WhoE 93
Kole, John William 1934- WhoAm 92
Koledo, Thomas John 1935- St&PR 93
Kole-Harf, Patricia Jean 1937- WhoAmW 93, WhoWor 93
Kolehmainen, Jan Waldroy 1940- WhoAm 92
Kolehmainen, John Ilmari 1910- WhoAm 92
Kolehouse, Bobbie Lee Susan 1954- WhoWrEP 92
Kolenc, Koleen M. 1951- WhoAmW 93
Kolencik, Richard Joseph Law&B 92
Kolenda, Christopher George 1963- WhoSSW 93
Koler, Berk S. 1938- WhoUN 92
Koles, Terrie BioIn 17
Kolesar, Andrew B. 1941- St&PR 93
Kolesar, Peter John 1936- WhoAm 92
Koleske, Joseph Victor 1930- WhoSSW 93
Kolesnick, Rustam Erick 1957- WhoWor 93
Kolesnikov, Sergey Ivanovich 1950- WhoWor 93
Kolessa, Filaret (Mikhailovich) 1871-1947 Baker 92
Kolesza, Wiktor 1947- WhoWor 93
Kolettis, Miltiades 1923- WhoWor 93
Kolev, Gancho 1935- WhoWor 93
Kolevzon, Peter Stephen 1942- WhoAm 92
Koley, James Lawrence 1930- St&PR 93
Kolff, J. van Santen 1848-1896 Baker 92
Kolhoff, David J. Law&B 92
Kolibash, William Anthony 1944- WhoAm 92
Kolich, Kathy J. Law&B 92
Kolikoff, Arnold D. Law&B 92
Kolin, Jan 1925- WhoScE 91-4
Kolingba, Andre 1935- WhoAfr
Kolingba, Andre-Dieudonne 1936- WhoWor 93
Kolins, Wayne Alan 1944- WhoAm 92
Kolinski, Mieczyslaw 1901-1981 Baker 92
Kolisch, Rudolf 1896-1978 Baker 92
Kolitz, Sally Lynn 1943- WhoSSW 93
Kolizeras, Kostas 1943- St&PR 93
Kolk, Henricus Johannes 1947- WhoWor 93
Kolk, Nancy S. Law&B 92
Kolker, Allan Erwin 1933- WhoAm 92
Kolker, Bonnie Lynne 1953- WhoE 93, WhoEmL 93
Kolker, James David 1947- St&PR 93
Kolker, Raymond F. 1942- St&PR 93
Kolker, Roger Russell 1929- WhoAm 92
Kolker, Sondra G. 1938- WhoAmW 93
Kolkey, Daniel Miles 1952- WhoAm 92, WhoEmL 93
Kolkhorst, Kathryn Mackay 1949- WhoEmL 93
Kolkman, Paul F. 1946- WhoIns 93
Kolko, Gabriel 1932- WhoAm 92, WhoWrEP 92
Koll, Donald M. St&PR 93
Koll, Peter 1941- WhoScE 91-3
Koll, Richard Leroy 1925- WhoAm 92
Kollar, Axel 1935- WhoWor 93
Kollar, Joanne Marie 1949- WhoAmW 93
Kollas, John G. 1946- WhoScE 91-3
Kollat, David Truman 1938- WhoAm 92
Kollataj, Hugo 1750-1812 PolBiDi
Kollberg, Erik L. 1937- WhoScE 91-4
Kolle, Barbara Kay 1959- WhoAmW 93
Kolle, George Frederic 1927- St&PR 93
Kolleeny, Glenn Scott Law&B 92
Kollegger, James G. 1942- WhoWor 93
Kollek, Amos MiSFD 9
Kollek, Teddy BioIn 17
Kollen, Melissa Susan 1954- WhoE 93
Kolleng, John L. Law&B 92
Kollentz, Anton Dan 1929- St&PR 93
Koller, Alan Manuel 1945- WhoE 93
Koller, Alexander Joseph 1957- WhoE 93, WhoEmL 93
Koller, Alice BioIn 17
Koller, Alois J. 1910- St&PR 93
Koller, Arnold 1933- WhoWor 93
Koller, Fritz 1906- WhoWor 93
Koller, George Aloysius 1947- WhoSSW 93
Koller, Jackie French 1948- ScF&FL 92, SmATA 72 [port]
Koller, James 1936- ConAu 39NR
Koller, James Anthony 1936- WhoWrEP 92
Koller, John Dryden 1942- WhoE 93
Koller, Loren D. 1940- WhoAm 92
Koller, Marita A. 1955- WhoEmL 93
Koller, Martin Frank 1948- WhoE 93
Koller, Marvin Robert 1919- WhoAm 92
Koller, Paul Johannes 1952- WhoWor 93
Koller, Rudolf 1934- WhoScE 91-3
Koller, Werner 1931- WhoScE 91-3
Koller, Xavier MiSFD 9
Kollevoll, Kristan George 1954- WhoE 93
Kollias, George Van, Jr. 1947- WhoAm 92
Kollmann, Augustus Frederic Christopher 1756-1829 Baker 92
Kollmann, Heinz A. 1939- WhoScE 91-4
Kollmann, Hilda Hanna 1913- WhoAm 92
Koll-Nesher, Uri 1949- St&PR 93
Kollo, Rene 1937- Baker 92, IntDcOp, OxDcOp
Kollo, Walter 1878-1940 Baker 92, OxDcOp
Kollock, David Hall 1916- WhoE 93
Kollock, James Paul 1951- WhoEmL 93
Kollock, Shepard 1750-1839 JrnUS
Kollodzieyski, Rene 1937- Baker 92
Kollodzieyski, Walter 1878-1940 Baker 92
Kollontai, A. 1872-1952 BioIn 17
Kollontai, Aleksandra 1872-1952 BioIn 17
Kollouthos fl. 5th cent.-6th cent. OxDcByz
Kollur, M.L. WhoAsAP 91
Kollwitz, Kathe 1867-1945 BioIn 17
Kolm, Harvard Brown 1929- St&PR 93
Kolm, Henry Herbert 1924- St&PR 93, WhoAm 92
Kolman, Helen Theresa 1958- WhoEmL 93
Kolman, Mark Herbert 1946- WhoEmL 93
Kolman, Petr 1937- Baker 92
Kolman, Richard L. Law&B 92
Kolman, Romuald Stanislaw Antoni 1922- WhoScE 91-4
Kolmar, Wendy K. 1950- ScF&FL 92
Kolmer, John H. 1945- St&PR 93
Kolmos, Hans Jorn Jepsen 1948- WhoWor 93
Kolneder, Walter 1910- Baker 92
Kolno, Jan of c. 1430-c. 1477 PolBiDi
Kolodey, Fred James 1936- WhoAm 92
Kolodie, Lucien Pierre 1933- WhoScE 91-2
Kolodin, Irving 1908-1988 Baker 92
Kolodner, Ignace Izaak 1920- WhoAm 92
Kolodner, Richard David 1951- WhoEmL 93
Kolodny, Abraham Lewis 1917- WhoE 93
Kolodny, Annette 1941- WhoAmW 93
Kolodny, Edwin Hillel 1936- WhoAm 92
Kolodny, Nancy Joan 1946- WhoEmL 93
Kolodny, Richard Law&B 92
Kolodny, Richard 1943- WhoAm 92
Kolodny, Robert Alan 1943- WhoSSW 93
Kolodny, Stanley Charles 1923- WhoAm 92
Kolody, John T. 1920-1990 BioIn 17
Kolodziej, Edward Albert 1935- WhoAm 92
Kolodziej, Krysia 1948- WhoWrEP 92
Kolodziejczyk, Aleksander Marian 1942- WhoScE 91-4
Kolok, Kenneth George 1938- St&PR 93
Kolokowsky, Henry S. 1939- St&PR 93
Kololo, Jean-Blaise WhoWor 93
Kolombatovic, Vadja Vadim 1924- WhoAm 92, WhoE 93, WhoWor 93
Kolomiets, Victor Grigorievich 1936- WhoWor 93
Kolomytsev, Valery Dmitrievich 1944- WhoUN 92
Kolonel, Laurence Norman 1942- WhoAm 92
Kolopsky, Jerry 1926- St&PR 93
Kolor, Michael Garrett 1934- WhoE 93
Kolos, Chris Nicholas 1959- WhoEmL 93
Kolos, Wlodzimierz 1928- WhoScE 91-4
Koloski, Diane Carol 1965- WhoE 93
Koloski, Richard F. 1944- St&PR 93
Koloskov, Valentin Yurievich 1961- WhoWor 93
Kolotyrkin, Yakov Mikhailovich 1910- WhoWor 93
Kolovat, David Victor Law&B 92
Kolowich, Patricia Ann 1958- WhoAmW 93
Kolpakova, Irina WhoAm 92
Kolpin, Marc A. 1932- St&PR 93
Kolsch, Eckehart 1937- WhoScE 91-3
Kolsky, Allan 1932- St&PR 93
Kolsky, Herbert d1992 NewYTBS 92
Kolsky, Herbert 1916-1992 BioIn 17
Kolson, Richard Jay 1948- St&PR 93
Kolstad, Charles Durgin 1948- WhoEmL 93
Kolstad, Chester James 1926- St&PR 93
Kolstad, George Andrew 1919- WhoWor 93
Kolstad, James L. 1939- WhoAm 92
Kolstad, Nils 1930- WhoScE 91-4
Kolstadt, Allen C. 1931- WhoWor 93
Koltai, Ralph 1924- IntDcOp, OxDcOp
Koltai, Stephen Miklos 1922- WhoWor 93
Koltay, E. WhoScE 91-4
Kolter, Joe 1926- CngDr 91
Kolter, Joseph Paul 1926- WhoAm 92, WhoE 93
Kolterjahn, Paul Henry 1924- St&PR 93, WhoAm 92
Koltes, Thomas G. 1928- St&PR 93
Koltnow, Peter Gregory 1929- WhoAm 92
Kolton, Paul 1923- St&PR 93, WhoAm 92
Kolton-Schneider, Lynne 1957- WhoAmW 93
Koltonski, Waclaw 1920- WhoScE 91-4
Koltsaty, Arkady 1905- BioIn 17
Koltun, Frances Lang WhoE 93
Koltun, Stanley Phelps 1925- WhoSSW 93
Koltz, Tony ScF&FL 92
Kolumban, Nicholas 1940- WhoWrEP 92
Kolupaev, Victor 1936- ScF&FL 92
Kolve, V. A. 1934- WhoAm 92
Kolvek, Janice Annas 1953- WhoAmW 93
Kolvenbach, Donald M. 1934- St&PR 93, WhoAm 92
Kolvenbach, Peter-Hans BioIn 17
Kolvenbach, Peter Hans 1928- WhoWor 93
Kolvin, Israel WhoScE 91-1
Kolyada, Viktor Ivanovics 1947- WhoWor 93
Kolybas, Sergios fl. 12th cent.- OxDcByz
Kolybine, Victor 1936- WhoUN 92
Kolyer, John (McNaughton) 1933- ConAu 39NR
Kolyn, Adriana S. AmWomPl
Kolz, Beverly Anne 1946- WhoAmW 93
Kolzak, Stephen F. d1990 BioIn 17
Kolze, Jack Thomas Law&B 92
Komack, James 1930- MiSFD 9
Komae, Hisashi 1927- WhoWor 93
Komai, Akira 1931- WhoWor 93
Koman, Victor 1944- ScF&FL 92
Komandi, Gyorgy 1924- WhoScE 91-4
Komando, Kimberly Ann 1964- WhoAmW 93, WhoEmL 93
Komar, Arthur B. 1931- WhoAm 92
Komar, Kathleen Lenore 1949- WhoAmW 93
Komar, Paul 1938- WhoAm 92
Komarek, Luke Raymond 1953- WhoAm 92
Komarek, Peter 1941- WhoScE 91-3
Komarin, Gary 1951- WhoEmL 93
Komarnicki, Edward Rafal 1912- WhoWor 93
Komaroff, Stanley 1935- WhoAm 92
Komarovsky, Mirra WhoAm 92
Komarovsky, Mirra 1906- BioIn 17
Komatina, Miljan 1922- WhoUN 92
Komatsu, S. Richard 1916- WhoAm 92
Komatsu, Sadao 1930- WhoAsAP 91
Komatsu, Sakyo 1931- ScF&FL 92
Komatsubara, Michitaro 1886-1940 HarEnMi
Komeda, Krzystof Trzcinski 1932-1969 PolBiDi
Komejan, Maryam St&PR 93
Komen, John Denis 1936- St&PR 93
Komenda, Pamela 1953- St&PR 93
Komenda, Stanislav 1936- WhoScE 91-4
Komenich, Kim 1956- WhoAm 92
Komensky, Alan Michael Law&B 92
Komentiolos d602 OxDcByz
Komer, Robert W. 1922- ColdWar 1 [port]
Komer, Robert William 1922- WhoAm 92
Komer, Stuart 1926- St&PR 93
Komesu, Okifumi 1931- WhoWor 93
Kometopouloi OxDcByz
Komi, Pauli Kyosti 1936- WhoWor 93
Komidar, Joseph Stanley 1916- WhoAm 92
Komie, Stephen Mark 1949- WhoEmL 93
Komins, Burton L. 1930- St&PR 93
Komins, Roger A. 1964- St&PR 93
Kominsky, Randall G. Law&B 92
Komisar, Arnold 1947- WhoAm 92, WhoE 93, WhoWor 93
Komisar, David Daniel 1917- WhoAm 92
Komisar, Jerome Bertram 1937- WhoAm 92
Komitas 1869-1935 Baker 92
Komito, Edward 1958- St&PR 93
Komito, Sanford 1931- St&PR 93
Komitowski, Dymitr 1932- WhoScE 91-3
Komiyama, Jushiro 1927- WhoAsAP 91
Komkov, Vadim 1919- WhoAm 92
Komlev, Lev Ivanovich WhoUN 92
Komline, Elizabeth Marlow 1917- St&PR 93
Komline, Russell Marlow 1948- St&PR 93
Komline, Thomas Raymond 1944- St&PR 93
Komlos, Peter 1935- WhoWor 93
Kommandeur, Jan 1929- WhoScE 91-3
Kommedahl, Thor 1920- WhoAm 92
Komnene, Anna 1083-c. 1153 OxDcByz
Komnene, Irene c. 1110-c. 1151 OxDcByz
Komnene, Maria 1152-1182? OxDcByz
Komnenian Dynasty OxDcByz
Komnenodoukas OxDcByz
Komnenos OxDcByz
Komnenos, Isaac c. 1050-c. 1102 OxDcByz
Komnenos, Isaac fl. 12th cent.- OxDcByz
Komnenos, Isaac the Porphyrogennetos 1093-c. 1152 OxDcByz
Komnenos, John OxDcByz
Komnick, Hans 1934- WhoScE 91-3
Komodore, Bill G. 1932- WhoAm 92
Komori, Hiroo 1925- WhoWor 93
Komori, Tatsukuni 1932- WhoAsAP 91
Komoroski, Richard Andrew 1947- WhoSSW 93
Komorous, Rudolf 1931- Baker 92
Komorowski, Cheryl Ann 1956- WhoAmW 93, WhoEmL 93
Komorzynski, Egon 1878-1963 Baker 92
Komoto, Toshio 1911- WhoAsAP 91
Komp, Barbara Ann 1954- WhoAmW 93
Komp, Diane Marilyn 1940- WhoAm 92
Komp, Richard Joseph 1938- WhoE 93
Kompas, John George BioIn 17
Kompass, Edward John 1926- WhoAm 92
Kompfner, Rudolph 1909-1977 BioIn 17
Komplektov, Viktor BioIn 17
Komppa, Veikko WhoScE 91-4
Komulainen, Hannu 1952- WhoScE 91-4
Komunyakaa, Yusef 1947- DcLB 120 [port]
Komura, Masahiko 1942- WhoAsAP 91
Kon, Beno R. 1932- St&PR 93
Kon, Fannong 1933- WhoUN 92
Kon, Mark Andrew 1952- WhoEmL 93
Kon, Mitchell Allen 1957- WhoE 93
Kon, Richard 1952- St&PR 93
Kon, Stella Lim Sing Po 1944- WhoWor 93
Kona, Martha Mistina WhoAmW 93
Konan-Bedie, Henri 1934- WhoWor 93
Konarske, Gary L. 1947- St&PR 93
Konarski, Stanislaw 1700-1773 PolBiDi
Koncel, James E. 1929- St&PR 93
Koncelik, Joseph Arthur 1940- WhoAm 92
Konchalovsky, Andrei 1937- MiSFD 9
Konchanin, Lynn Marie 1957- WhoEmL 93
Konchar, Jerry 1949- St&PR 93
Konczal, Dennis R. 1950- St&PR 93
Konczalski, Ronald Louis 1935- St&PR 93
Kondakis, X. Gerasimos 1932- WhoScE 91-3
Kondakov, Alexander Konstantinovich 1928- WhoWor 93
Kondas, Nicholas Frank 1929- St&PR 93, WhoAm 92, WhoWor 93
Konde, Sangbana 1944- WhoUN 92
Kondelik, John P. 1942- WhoAm 92
Kondelin, George John, Jr. 1949- WhoEmL 93, WhoSSW 93
Kondo, Chuko 1932- WhoAsAP 91
Kondo, Kenneth S. 1950- St&PR 93
Kondo, Kiroki 1941- WhoUN 92
Kondo, Masatoshi Stephan 1940- WhoAm 92
Kondo, Morio 1932- WhoWor 93
Kondo, Motoji 1930- WhoAsAP 91
Kondo, Nobutake 1886-1953 HarEnMi
Kondo, Peter H. Law&B 92
Kondo, Shunsuke 1942- WhoWor 93
Kondo, Takahiko 1944- WhoWor 93
Kondo, Takeo 1922- WhoAm 92
Kondo, Tetsuo 1929- WhoAsAP 91
Kondo, Vala BioIn 17
Kondo, Yasuo BioIn 17
Kondo, Yoji ScF&FL 92
Kondonassis, Alexander John 1928- WhoAm 92
Kondorosi, Adam 1946- WhoScE 91-4
Kondorossy, Leslie 1915- Baker 92
Kondos, George Michael 1948- St&PR 93
Kondra, Douglass Emil 1946- St&PR 93
Kondra, Emil Paul 1917- St&PR 93
Kondracki, Michal 1902- Baker 92
Kondrashin, Anatoli Victorovich 1940- WhoUN 92
Kondrashin, Kirill (Petrovich) 1914-1981 Baker 92
Kondrashov, Stanislav (Nikolaevich) 1928- ConAu 40NR
Kondratas, Skirma Anna 1944- WhoAm 92, WhoAmW 93
Kondratiuk, Andrzej 1936- DrEEuF
Kondratowicz, Frank John 1927- St&PR 93
Kondylis, Theophanis 1949- WhoScE 91-3
Kondziela, Joseph Richard 1954- WhoE 93, WhoEmL 93, WhoWor 93
Kone, Abdoulaye 1933- WhoAfr
Kone, James S. 1912- St&PR 93
Kone, James S., Jr. 1949- St&PR 93
Kone, Kafougouna WhoWor 93
Kone, Russell Joseph 1929- WhoAm 92
Konecky, Gary 1957- WhoE 93, WhoEmL 93
Konecky, Nathan 1943- St&PR 93
Konecsni, John-Emery 1946- WhoE 93
Koneczny, Henryk 1927- WhoScE 91-4

Konefal, Janet 1947- *WhoSSW 93*
Konek, Bernie John 1940- *St&PR 93*
Konen, Harry Paul 1940- *WhoSSW 93*
Koner, Pauline 1912- *WhoAm 92*
Kones, Richard 1948- *WhoAm 92, WhoE 93, WhoWor 93*
Konetzni, Anny 1902-1968 *Baker 92, IntDcOp, OxDcOp*
Konetzni, Hilde 1905-1980 *Baker 92, IntDcOp, OxDcOp*
Koneval, William Paul 1934- *St&PR 93*
Konevsky, Anatoly A. 1937- *WhoUN 92*
Konezny, Lorette M. Sobol 1948- *WhoAmW 93, WhoEmL 93*
Kong, Andy Wong Chi *St&PR 93*
Kong, Jackie *MiSFD 9*
Kong, Jin Au 1942- *WhoAm 92*
Kong, King *ScF&FL 92*
Kongabel, H. Fred 1929- *WhoAm 92*
Konguetsof, Leonidas 1931- *WhoScE 91-3*
Konicek, Michael Richard 1952- *St&PR 93*
Konicz, Tadeusz 1733-1793 *PolBiDi*
Koniecko, Edward Stanley 1913- *WhoAm 92*
Koniecpolski, Stanislaw 1591-1646 *HarEnMi, PolBiDi*
Konieczny, Marian 1930- *PolBiDi*
Konieczny, Scott J. 1965- *St&PR 93*
Konieczny, Sharon Louise 1952- *WhoWor 93*
Konietzko, J.K. 1934- *WhoScE 91-3*
Konietzko, Kurt O. 1924- *WhoE 93*
Koniev, Ivan Stepanovich 1897-1973 *DcTwHis*
Konig, Edgar 1929- *WhoWor 93*
Konig, Giovanni Klaus 1924-1989 *BioIn 17*
Konig, Heinz Johannes Erdmann 1929- *WhoWor 93*
Konig, Johann Ulrich von 1688-1744 *OxDcOp*
Konig, Klaus Dietrich 1934- *WhoWor 93*
Konig, Klaus G. 1931- *WhoScE 91-3*
Konig, Walther *BioIn 17*
Konig, Wilfried 1928- *WhoScE 91-3*
Konig, Wolfgang 1943- *WhoScE 91-3*
Konig, Wolfgang 1949- *WhoWor 93*
Konigsberg, Richard Lee 1953- *WhoE 93*
Konigsburg, E.L. *BioIn 17*
Konigsburg, E(laine) L(obl) 1930- *ConAu 39NR, DcAmChF 1960, DcAmChF 1985, MajAI [port]*
Konigsburg, Elaine Lobl 1930- *WhoAm 92*
Konigslow, Johann Wilhelm Cornelius von 1745-1833 *Baker 92*
Konigslow, Otto Friedrich von 1824-1898 *Baker 92*
Konigsson, Lars-Konig A. 1933- *WhoScE 91-4*
Konikiewicz, Leonard Wieslaw 1928- *WhoSSW 93*
Koning, David 1820-1876 *Baker 92*
Koning, Hans 1921- *BioIn 17*
Koning, Hans 1924- *WhoAm 92, WhoWrEP 92*
Koning, J. *WhoScE 91-3*
Koning, Patricia Sonders *Law&B 92*
Koning, Ross Edward 1953- *WhoE 93*
Koning, Tako 1949- *St&PR 93*
Koningsberger, Hans 1921- *BioIn 17*
Koningsberger, Hans 1924- *WhoAm 92*
Konior-Zelasko, Lynne Bartlett 1953- *WhoAmW 93*
Konishi, Hiroyuki 1936- *WhoAsAP 91*
Konishi, Kenji 1929- *WhoWor 93*
Konishi, Masakazu 1933- *WhoAm 92*
Konishi, Yukinaga d1600 *HarEnMi*
Konishiki *BioIn 17*
Konisky, Jordan 1941- *WhoAm 92*
Konitz, Lee 1927- *Baker 92*
Konius, Georgi *Baker 92*
Konjhodzic, Faruk 1936- *WhoScE 91-4*
Konjovic, Petar 1882-1970 *Baker 92*
Konkel, Richard Steven 1950- *WhoE 93*
Konkle, B.L. 1931- *St&PR 93*
Konkle, Henry R. 1929- *St&PR 93*
Konkle, Janet Marie Everest 1917- *WhoWrEP 92*
Konkler, Tim J. 1947- *St&PR 93*
Konkol, Chris P. *Law&B 92*
Konkol, George 1923- *St&PR 93*
Konkol, Robert Anthony 1951- *WhoE 93*
Konlges, Christopher L. *St&PR 93*
Konner, Joan Weiner 1931- *WhoAm 92*
Konner, Kenneth Lloyd *Law&B 92*
Konney, Paul E. *Law&B 92*
Konney, Paul E. 1944- *St&PR 93*
Konney, Paul Edward 1944- *WhoAm 92*
Konnick, Dianne Cheryl 1961- *WhoEmL 93*
Konn McCormick, Susan 1953- *St&PR 93*
Konnyu, Ernest Leslie 1937- *WhoAm 92*
Kono, Kristo 1907- *Baker 92*
Kono, Tetsuro 1925- *WhoAm 92*
Kono, Toshihiko 1930- *WhoWrEP 92*
Kono, Yohei 1937- *WhoAsAP 91*
Konobeev, Iouri Vasiljevich 1934- *WhoWor 93*
Konoe Fumimaro 1891-1945 *DcTwHis*
Konoike, Yoshitada 1940- *WhoAsAP 91*
Konoma, Kazuhisa 1942- *St&PR 93*
Konomi, Ujitsura 1942- *WhoWor 93*
Konon, Neena Nicholai 1951- *WhoAmW 93, WhoEmL 93*
Kononiuk, Stephen John 1946- *St&PR 93*
Konop, Thomas Francis *Law&B 92*
Konopel'chenko, Boris Georgievich 1948- *WhoWor 93*
Konopinski, Emil J. 1911-1990 *BioIn 17*
Konopisos, Konstantine Andrew 1919- *WhoAm 92*
Konopka, Gisela Peiper 1910- *WhoAm 92*
Konopka, Janusz Franciszek 1931- *WhoWor 93*
Konopka, Jozef 1940- *WhoScE 91-4*
Konopka, Lech Jerzy 1938- *WhoScE 91-4*
Konopko, Elliot 1953- *St&PR 93*
Konopnicka, Maria 1842-1910 *PolBiDi*
Konover, Vicki 1951- *WhoE 93*
Konowalczyk, Jean S. *Law&B 92*
Konoye, Hidemaro 1898-1973 *Baker 92*
Konrad, Adolf Ferdinand 1915- *WhoAm 92*
Konrad, Agnes Crossman 1921- *WhoAmW 93*
Konrad, Alfons *BioIn 17*
Konrad, Alison Marie 1960- *WhoAmW 93*
Konrad, Dusan 1935- *WhoAm 92*
Konrad, G. Gregory 1951- *WhoWrEP 92*
Konrad, Gyorgy 1933- *ConLC 73 [port]*
Konrad, Michael T. 1960- *St&PR 93*
Konrad, Michael Warren 1936- *WhoAm 92*
Konrad, Victor Alexander 1947- *WhoE 93*
Konrat'ev, Anatolii Semenovich 1948- *WhoWor 93*
Konselman, Douglas Derek 1958- *WhoEmL 93, WhoSSW 93, WhoWor 93*
Konshin, Valentin Arkadjevich 1936- *WhoUN 92*
Konsis, Kenneth Frank 1952- *WhoWor 93*
Konski, James Louis 1917- *WhoAm 92*
Konsowa, Mokhtar Hassan 1953- *WhoWor 93*
Konstam, Aaron Harry 1936- *WhoSSW 93*
Konstand, Robert *Law&B 92*
Konstantin Kostenecki c. 1380-c. 1431 *OxDcByz*
Konstantin Mihailovic of Ostrovica *OxDcByz*
Konstantin of Preslav fl. 9th cent.-10th cent. *OxDcByz*
Konstantinov, Tzvetan Krumov *WhoSSW 93, WhoWor 93*
Konstantinovic, Zoran Vladimir 1920- *WhoWor 93*
Konstanty, James Casimir 1917-1976 *BiDAMSp 1989*
Konstantynowicz, Erast 1919- *WhoScE 91-4*
Kont, Paul 1920- *Baker 92*
Kontarsky, Alfons 1932- *Baker 92*
Kontarsky, Aloys 1931- *Baker 92*
Kontarsky, Bernhard 1937- *Baker 92*
Kontich, Michael James 1949- *St&PR 93*
Kontnier, Robert D. 1941- *St&PR 93*
Kontny, Vincent L. 1937- *St&PR 93*
Kontogouris, Venetia Gerarismos 1951- *WhoAmW 93*
Kontopidis, George D. 1954- *St&PR 93*
Kontorovich, Vladimir 1951- *WhoEmL 93*
Kontos, John 1937- *WhoScE 91-3*
Kontostathis, Kyriakos 1959- *WhoE 93*
Kontostephanos *OxDcByz*
Kontski, Antonie de 1817-1899 *Baker 92*
Kontski, Apollinaire de 1825-1879 *Baker 92*
Kontski, Charles de 1815-1867 *Baker 92*
Konttinen, Sirkka-Liisa 1948- *BioIn 17*
Kontz, Robert J. 1952- *St&PR 93*
Konuma, Mitsuharu 1950- *WhoWor 93*
Konvitz, Arthur H. d1991 *BioIn 17*
Konvitz, Jeffrey 1944- *ScF&FL 92*
Konvitz, Josef Wolf 1946- *WhoAm 92*
Konvitz, Milton Ridbaz 1908- *WhoAm 92*
Konwicki, Tadeusz *BioIn 17*
Konwicki, Tadeusz 1926- *ConAu 39NR, DrEEuF, WhoWor 93*
Konwin, Thor W. 1943- *St&PR 93*
Konwin, Thor Warner 1943- *WhoWor 93*
Konwitschny, Franz 1901-1962 *Baker 92, OxDcOp*
Konya, Sandor 1923- *Baker 92, OxDcOp*
Konyha, Stephen Michael 1940- *WhoE 93*
Konyukhova, Nadejda Borisovna 1941- *WhoWor 93*
Konyves, Tom 1947- *WhoCanL 92*
Konz, D.A. *St&PR 93*
Konz, Gerald Keith 1932- *WhoAm 92*
Konz, Helen Katherine 1910- *WhoAmW 93*
Konzal, Joseph Charles 1905- *WhoAm 92*
Konzen, Jon L. 1934- *St&PR 93*
Konzo, Seichi d1992 *NewYTBS 92*
Koo, Antonio Yin Lun 1961- *WhoWor 93*
Koo, George Ping Shan 1938- *WhoAm 92*
Koo, M.K. 1944- *St&PR 93*
Koo, Reginald Chewyat 1949- *WhoEmL 93*
Koo, Samuel 1941- *WhoUN 92*
Koob, Raymond Joseph 1947- *WhoWrEP 92*
Koob, Robert Duane 1941- *WhoAm 92*
Koocher, Gerald Paul 1947- *WhoEmL 93*
Koock, Victor I. *Law&B 92*
Koock, Victor I. 1940- *St&PR 93*
Koock, Victor Ivan 1940- *WhoAm 92*
Koogle, Effie Louise *AmWomPl*
Koogler, Candace Kay 1960- *WhoAmW 93*
Koogler, Mark B. *Law&B 92*
Koogler, Robert Foster 1933- *St&PR 93*
Kooiker, Leonie 1927- *ScF&FL 92*
Kooistra, E. *WhoScE 91-3*
Koo Ja Choon 1933- *WhoAsAP 91*
Kook, Abraham Isaac 1865-1935 *BioIn 17*
Kook, Edward Frankel 1903-1990 *BioIn 17*
Kooken, John Frederick 1931- *WhoAm 92*
Kool, Lawrence Bernard 1952- *WhoE 93, WhoEmL 93*
Kool, Timothy Jay 1959- *St&PR 93*
Kool & the Gang *SoulM*
Koole, Arend (Johannes Christiaan) 1908- *Baker 92*
Koolen, A.J. 1944- *WhoScE 91-3*
Kool Moe Dee *BioIn 17*
Kool Moe Dee c. 1963- *ConMus 9 [port]*
Kooloian, Elizabeth 1931- *WhoAmW 93*
Koomen, Cornelis Jan 1947- *WhoWor 93*
Koomen, Martin John 1917- *WhoE 93*
Koomey, Paul Clifton 1927- *St&PR 93*
Koomey, Richard Alan *Law&B 92*
Koon, Ann Bourn Marks 1952- *WhoAmW 93*
Koon, Dennis H. 1947- *WhoUN 92*
Koon, Man-Kay 1951- *WhoWor 93*
Koon, Norman Carroll 1938- *WhoAm 92*
Koon, Vivian Jenkins 1947- *WhoEmL 93*
Koonce, Alexander Eben 1958- *WhoEmL 93*
Koonce, Gene C. 1932- *St&PR 93*
Koonce, John Peter 1932- *WhoWor 93*
Koonce, K. Max, II *Law&B 92*
Koonce, Kenneth Lowell 1939- *WhoSSW 93*
Koonce, Kenneth Terry 1938- *WhoAm 92, WhoE 93*
Koonce, Mary Ann 1962- *WhoAmW 93*
Koonce, Neil Wright *Law&B 92*
Koonce, Neil Wright 1947- *WhoAm 92*
Koonce, Rodney Llewellyn 1947- *WhoEmL 93*
Koono, Zenya 1936- *WhoWor 93*
Koons, Betsy Jeanne 1953- *WhoE 93*
Koons, Carolyn *ConAu 136*
Koons, Charles A. 1943- *St&PR 93*
Koons, Charles Bruce 1929- *WhoSSW 93*
Koons, Donaldson 1917- *WhoAm 92*
Koons, Irvin Louis 1922- *WhoAm 92*
Koons, Jeff 1955- *BioIn 17*
Koons, Linda Gleitsman 1954- *WhoAm 92*
Koons, Michael Jon 1939- *St&PR 93*
Koons, Robert Charles 1957- *WhoEmL 93, WhoSSW 93*
Koons, Robert Henry 1956- *WhoE 93*
Koons, Susan Ann 1949- *WhoAmW 93*
Koonts, Jones Calvin 1924- *WhoAm 92*
Koonts, Robert Henry *Law&B 92*
Koonts, Robert Henry 1927- *St&PR 93, WhoAm 92*
Koontz, Alfred Joseph, Jr. 1942- *WhoAm 92*
Koontz, David Stuart 1958- *WhoSSW 93*
Koontz, Dean R. 1945- *Au&Arts 9 [port], BioIn 17, ScF&FL 92*
Koontz, Dean Ray 1945- *WhoAm 92*
Koontz, Edward Larry 1946- *St&PR 93, WhoEmL 93*
Koontz, Eldon Ray 1913- *WhoE 93*
Koontz, Eva Isabelle 1935- *WhoAmW 93, WhoWor 93*
Koontz, Raymond 1912- *St&PR 93, WhoAm 92*
Koontz, Richard H. 1940- *St&PR 93*
Koontz, Richard Harvey 1940- *WhoAm 92*
Koontz, Robin Michal 1954- *ConAu 138, SmATA 70 [port]*
Koontz, Ronald David 1943- *St&PR 93*
Koontz, Thomas Wayne 1939- *WhoWrEP 92*
Koontz, Warren Woodson, Jr. 1932- *WhoAm 92*
Koonz, Claudia *WhoAmW 93*
Koop, C. Everett *BioIn 17*
Koop, Charles Everett 1916- *WhoAm 92*
Koop, Chris R. 1960- *St&PR 93*
Koop, Dale Wayne 1939- *St&PR 93*
Kooper, Al 1944- *Baker 92*
Kooper, Bernard 1925- *St&PR 93*
Kooper, Laurence Stanley 1957- *WhoE 93*
Kooper, Sybil Hart 1925-1991 *BioIn 17*
Koopersmith, Jeffrey MacArthur 1948- *WhoEmL 93, WhoWor 93*
Koopman, Cheryl Ann 1950- *WhoEmL 93*
Koopman, Jacques d1991 *BioIn 17*
Koopman, Ton 1944- *Baker 92*
Koopman, William James 1945- *WhoAm 92*
Koopmann, Reta Collene 1944- *WhoAmW 93, WhoSSW 93, WhoWor 93*
Koopmans, Cheryl Bette 1950- *WhoAmW 93*
Koornstra, M.J. *WhoScE 91-3*
Koos, Russell L. 1942- *St&PR 93*
Kooser, Ted *BioIn 17*
Koot, Hank M. *WhoIns 93*
Kooyker-Romijn, Hanna Maria *ScF&FL 92*
Koozin, Kristine Lynn 1950- *WhoAmW 93*
Kopac, Andrew Joseph 1947- *WhoEmL 93*
Kopachevskii, Nikolai Dmitrievich 1940- *WhoWor 93*
Kopack, Laura Reyes *Law&B 92*
Kopack, Pamela Lee 1951- *WhoAmW 93*
Kopacz, Stanislaw 1938- *WhoScE 91-4*
Kopala, E. Wayne 1947- *St&PR 93*
Kopala, Jan *WhoScE 91-4*
Kopald, Larry S. 1954- *WhoAm 92*
Kopanski, Bruce Dexter 1957- *St&PR 93*
Kopar, Mark W. 1947- *St&PR 93*
Kopcak, Drema M. *Law&B 92*
Kopcha, Joseph 1906-1986 *BiDAMSp 1989*
Kopcha, Stephen Christopher 1941- *St&PR 93*
Kopchik, Jeffrey M. 1954- *St&PR 93*
Kopcke, Karl-Heinz d1991 *BioIn 17*
Kopcke, Richard William 1947- *St&PR 93*
Kopcych, Anthony, Jr. 1971- *WhoEmL 93*
Kopec, Frank John 1943- *WhoAm 92*
Kopec, Jack 1945- *WhoAm 92*
Kopec, Joseph Arthur 1946- *WhoEmL 93*
Kopec, Michael Joseph 1939- *St&PR 93*
Kopech, Joseph I. 1923- *St&PR 93*
Kopech, Robert Irving 1951- *WhoAm 92*
Kopecky, Kenneth John 1943- *WhoAm 92*
Kopecky, Mary Jo Ellen 1946- *WhoAmW 93*
Kopecky, Miloslav 1928- *WhoScE 91-4*
Kopecky, Pavel 1949- *Baker 92*
Kopel, David 1910- *WhoAm 92*
Kopel, David Benjamin 1960- *WhoEmL 93*
Kopel, Kenneth Fred 1947- *WhoSSW 93*
Kopelent, Marek 1932- *Baker 92*
Kopell, Bernard Morton 1933- *WhoAm 92*
Kopell, Bernie 1933- *BioIn 17*
Kopelman, Arie L. 1938- *St&PR 93, WhoAm 92*
Kopelman, Leonard 1940- *WhoAm 92*
Kopelman, Paul 1929- *St&PR 93*
Kopelman, Richard Eric 1943- *WhoAm 92, WhoE 93*
Kopelman, Susan Anderson 1964- *WhoAmW 93*
Kopelson, Arnold 1935- *ConTFT 10*
Kopen, Dan Francis 1948- *WhoE 93*
Kopen, Doris K. 1914- *St&PR 93*
Kopen, Jack R. 1953- *St&PR 93*
Kopen, Oscar J. 1911- *St&PR 93*
Kopenhaver, Lillian Lodge 1941- *WhoAmW 93, WhoSSW 93*
Kopenhaver, Patricia Ellsworth *WhoAm 92, WhoAmW 93, WhoE 93*
Koperski, Nanci Carol 1962- *WhoAmW 93*
Koperwas, Sam Earl 1948- *WhoWrEP 92*
Kopetski, Mike 1949- *CngDr 91, WhoAm 92*
Kopetz, Vinette Nadine 1935- *WhoAmW 93*
Kopf, Alfred Walter 1926- *WhoAm 92*
Kopf, Benjamin 1956- *WhoE 93*
Kopf, Eugene Herbert 1937- *WhoAm 92*
Kopf, Janet Carolyn 1946- *WhoAmW 93*
Kopf, Kenneth A. *Law&B 92*
Kopf, Peter William 1944- *WhoE 93*
Kopf, R.E. 1940- *St&PR 93*
Kopff, Matthew J. 1957- *St&PR 93*
Kopidlansky, Victor Raymond 1931- *St&PR 93*
Kopietz, Peter 1961- *WhoWor 93*
Kopiloff, George 1939- *WhoAm 92*
Kopin, Irwin Jerome 1929- *WhoAm 92*
Kopins, John Louis 1934- *St&PR 93*
Kopinski, Dale M. *St&PR 93*
Kopischke, G.L. 1931- *St&PR 93*
Kopit, Arthur 1937- *WhoAm 92, WhoE 93*
Kopit, Arthur L. *BioIn 17*
Kopke, Russell W. 1947- *St&PR 93*
Kopke, Val K. 1941- *St&PR 93*
Kopko, Edward M. 1954- *St&PR 93*
Koplan, Jeffrey Powell 1945- *WhoAm 92*
Koplan, Sharon W. *Law&B 92*
Koplewicz, Harold Samuel 1953- *WhoE 93, WhoEmL 93, WhoWor 93*
Koplewski, Andrzej *St&PR 93*

Koplin, Anne Irene 1957- *WhoAmW 93*
Koplin, Donald Leroy 1932- *WhoWor 93*
Koplin, Merton Y. d1992 *BioIn 17, NewYTBS 92 [port]*
Koplitz, Richard A. 1937- *St&PR 93*
Koplovitz, Kay *BioIn 17*
Koplovitz, Kay 1945- *WhoAm 92, WhoAmW 93*
Koplovitz, Sholom *Law&B 92*
Kopman, Benjamin 1887-1965 *BioIn 17*
Kopman, Elizabeth Suzanne 1950- *WhoAmW 93*
Kopnisky, James Richard 1938- *St&PR 93*
Kopp, Anatole 1915-1990 *BioIn 17*
Kopp, B.E. 1930- *St&PR 93*
Kopp, Bradford B. 1951- *WhoAm 92*
Kopp, Byron E. *Law&B 92*
Kopp, Carolyn Sue 1940- *WhoAmW 93*
Kopp, Charles Gilbert 1933- *WhoAm 92, WhoE 93, WhoWor 93*
Kopp, Claire Joan Bernstein 1931- *WhoAmW 93*
Kopp, David Charles 1945- *St&PR 93, WhoAm 92*
Kopp, David Eugene 1951- *WhoEmL 93*
Kopp, Eugene Howard 1929- *WhoAm 92*
Kopp, Eugene Paul 1934- *WhoAm 92*
Kopp, Frederick Philip 1949- *WhoEmL 93*
Kopp, Hans Eberhard 1935- *WhoUN 92*
Kopp, Harriet Green 1917- *WhoAm 92*
Kopp, James K. 1944- *St&PR 93*
Kopp, James W. *Law&B 92*
Kopp, John Louis 1940- *St&PR 93*
Kopp, Melvin 1930- *St&PR 93*
Kopp, Nancy Kornblith 1943- *WhoAmW 93*
Kopp, Richard Edgar 1931- *WhoAm 92*
Kopp, Robert Walter 1935- *WhoAm 92*
Kopp, Troy *BioIn 17*
Kopp, Veniamin Gersh-Leibovitsh 1914- *WhoWor 93*
Kopp, Virginia Ann 1959- *WhoAmW 93, WhoEmL 93*
Kopp, W. Brewster *WhoAm 92*
Kopp, W. Brewster 1925- *St&PR 93*
Kopp, William H. 1949- *St&PR 93*
Koppa, Patricia Ann 1960- *WhoEmL 93*
Koppang, Hanna Stromme 1938- *WhoScE 91-4*
Koppany, George 1932- *WhoScE 91-4*
Koppe, George Maceo *BiDAMSp 1989*
Koppekin, Stephen M. *Law&B 92*
Koppel, Andrea Roth 1942- *WhoE 93*
Koppel, Audrey Feiler 1944- *WhoAmW 93*
Koppel, Barbara Sue 1952- *WhoE 93*
Koppel, Edward James 1940- *JrnUS*
Koppel, Elliott Louis 1944- *St&PR 93*
Koppel, Erwin *Law&B 92*
Koppel, Gary Allen 1943- *WhoAm 92*
Koppel, Herman D(avid) 1908- *Baker 92*
Koppel, Sheree Powers 1951- *WhoAmW 93, WhoWrEP 92*
Koppel, Ted *BioIn 17*
Koppel, Ted 1940- *WhoAm 92*
Koppel, Thomas Herman 1944- *Baker 92*
Koppel, Thomas Paul 1943- *WhoWrEP 92*
Koppel-Duran, Patricia 1944- *WhoUN 92*
Koppelman, Chaim 1920- *WhoAm 92*
Koppelman, Charles *WhoAm 92*
Koppelman, David V. 1940- *St&PR 93*
Koppelman, Jeffrey Roy 1953- *St&PR 93*
Koppelman, Julius 1916- *St&PR 93*
Koppelman, Kim Arden 1956- *WhoEmL 93*
Koppelman, Stephen *St&PR 93*
Koppelmann, David V. 1940- *St&PR 93*
Koppen, Jerry L. 1945- *St&PR 93*
Koppen, Jerry Lynn 1945- *WhoIns 93*
Koppen, Kristin K. 1953- *St&PR 93*
Koppen, Rudiger *BioIn 17*
Koppenaal, Richard John 1930- *WhoAm 92*
Kopper, Hilmar 1935- *WhoWor 93*
Kopper, James L. 1945- *St&PR 93*
Kopper, Laszlo 1942- *WhoScE 91-4*
Koppers, Wilhelm 1886-1961 *IntDcAn*
Koppett, Leonard 1923- *WhoAm 92*
Koppien, Kim Lee 1951- *St&PR 93*
Koppinen, Ilpo Ilmari 1944- *WhoWor 93*
Koppinger, Thomas J. 1941- *WhoIns 93*
Koppitz, Hans-Joachim 1924- *WhoWor 93*
Kopple, Barbara *MiSFD 9*
Kopple, Kenneth D. 1930- *WhoAm 92*
Koproski, Alexander Robert 1934- *WhoE 93*
Koprowska, Irena 1917- *WhoAmW 93, WhoE 93*
Koprowski, Donald Joseph *Law&B 92*
Koprowski, Hilary *WhoAm 92, WhoE 93*
Koprowski, Kenneth Mitchell 1949- *WhoEmL 93*
Koprowski, Wayne M. *Law&B 92*
Koprowski, Wayne M. 1947- *St&PR 93*
Koprulu, Abdulla d1735 *HarEnMi*
Koprulu, Murat Nafiz 1957- *WhoEmL 93*
Kops, Paul F. 1937- *St&PR 93*
Kopsch, Heinz 1925- *WhoScE 91-3*
Kopsiaftis, C. 1920- *WhoScE 91-3*
Koptuck, Anthony Edward 1926- *St&PR 93*
Kopylov, Alexander 1854-1911 *Baker 92*
Kopytman, Mark 1929- *Baker 92*
Kor, Rose Mary 1950- *WhoAmW 93*
Korab, William H. 1942- *St&PR 93*
Korabljov, Igor Georgievich 1937- *WhoUN 92*
Korabov, Nikola 1928- *DrEEuF*
Korach, Dan 1937- *St&PR 93*
Korach, Jeffrey L. 1941- *St&PR 93*
Korach, Kenneth Steven 1946- *WhoSSW 93*
Korach, Lawrence I. 1915- *St&PR 93*
Korach, William Mark 1945- *WhoAm 92*
Koralek, Jenny 1934- *SmATA 71 [port]*
Koran, Connie Jean 1953- *WhoWrEP 92*
Koranda, Kenneth A. *Law&B 92*
Koranda, William F. 1950- *St&PR 93*
Koranyi, Adam 1932- *WhoAm 92*
Korayem, Essam Ali 1941- *WhoWor 93*
Korb, Donald Baird 1923- *St&PR 93*
Korb, Jack Lionel 1927- *St&PR 93*
Korb, Kenneth Allan 1932- *WhoAm 92, WhoE 93*
Korb, Linda Ann 1948- *WhoSSW 93*
Korb, William Brown, Jr. 1940- *WhoAm 92, WhoWor 93*
Korban Ali, M. 1924- *WhoAsAP 91*
Korbar, Marcia Marie 1955- *WhoWrEP 92*
Korbay, Francis Alexander 1846-1913 *Baker 92*
Korbecki, Thomas Anthony 1928- *St&PR 93*
Korbel, Edward 1929- *St&PR 93*
Korben, Donald Lee 1948- *WhoE 93, WhoWor 93*
Korber, Christoph 1952- *WhoScE 91-3*
Korber, Michael Bruce 1946- *St&PR 93*
Korbitz, Bernard Carl 1935- *WhoAm 92, WhoWor 93*
Korbmann, Reiner Karl-Heinz 1946- *WhoWor 93*
Korbut, Olga 1955- *BioIn 17*
Korcelli, Piotr 1939- *WhoScE 91-4*
Korcha, Lynda Lee 1952- *WhoAmW 93*
Korchagin, Anatolii Borisovich 1952- *WhoWor 93*
Korchilov, Igor D. 1941- *WhoUN 92*
Korchin, Sheldon J. *BioIn 17*
Korchmar, Don 1922- *St&PR 93*
Korchmarev, Klimenti (Arkadievich) 1899-1958 *Baker 92*
Korchmaros, Gabor Gabriele 1948- *WhoWor 93*
Korchowsky, George William 1955- *St&PR 93*
Korchun, Walter M. *Law&B 92*
Korchynsky, Michael 1918- *WhoAm 92*
Korczak, Cezary Wlodzimierz 1925- *WhoScE 91-4*
Korczak, Dieter 1948- *WhoScE 91-3*
Korczak, Janusz 1878-1942 *BioIn 17, PolBiDi*
Korczewski, Aleksander Olgierd 1922- *WhoWor 93*
Korczynski, Andrzej 1935- *WhoScE 91-4*
Kord, Kazimierz 1930- *Baker 92*
Kord, Victor George 1935- *WhoE 93*
Korda, Alexander 1893-1956 *MiSFD 9N*
Korda, Carol S. *Law&B 92*
Korda, Michael (Vincent) 1933- *ConAu 39NR, WhoWrEP 92*
Korda, Reva 1926- *WhoAm 92*
Korda, Zoltan 1895-1961 *MiSFD 9N*
Kordac, Vaclav 1937- *WhoScE 91-4*
Kordalski, Anthony Tadausz 1926- *WhoAm 92*
Kordecki, Augustyn 1603-1673 *PolBiDi*
Kordek, Kathleen Ann *Law&B 92*
Kordell, Peter *BioIn 17*
Kordes, Hagen 1942- *WhoWor 93*
Kordesch, Karl V. 1922- *WhoScE 91-4, WhoWor 93*
Kordich, Jay *BioIn 17*
Kordich, Jay 1923- *News 93-2 [port]*
Kordon, Bernardo 1915- *SpAmA*
Kordon, Claude *WhoScE 91-2*
Kordons, Uldis 1941- *St&PR 93, WhoAm 92*
Kordulla, Wilhelm *WhoScE 91-3*
Korec, Jan Chryzostom Cardinal 1924- *WhoWor 93*
Korein, Sarah *BioIn 17*
Korek, Joan Susan 1957- *WhoEmL 93*
Korel, Charles *ScF&FL 92*
Koreleski, Krzysztof Jan 1942- *WhoScE 91-4, WhoWor 93*
Korell, Steven W. *Law&B 92*
Koren, Edward Benjamin 1935- *WhoAm 92*
Koren, Edward Franz 1946- *WhoAm 92*
Koren, Mary Elaine 1950- *WhoAmW 93*
Koren, R. 1945- *St&PR 93*
Koren, Samuel M. 1941- *St&PR 93, WhoIns 93*
Korenaga, Takashi 1949- *WhoWor 93*
Korenberg, Rosanne *Law&B 92*
Korenman, Stanley George *WhoAm 92*
Korenman, Victor 1937- *WhoE 93*
Koreshchenko, Arseni 1870-1921 *Baker 92*
Koret, Sydney *WhoE 93*
Koretz, Jane Faith 1947- *WhoAmW 93*
Koretz, Leo 1881-1926 *BioIn 17*
Koretzki, Paul Richard 1940- *WhoE 93, WhoWor 93*
Koretzky, David B. *Law&B 92*
Korey, Lois 1933-1990 *BioIn 17*
Korey, Stanley M. 1930- *St&PR 93*
Korey-Krzeczowski, George J. M. Kniaz 1921- *WhoAm 92*
Korf, Richard Paul 1925- *WhoE 93*
Korfanty, Wojciech 1873-1939 *PolBiDi*
Korfel, Jerzy T. 1942- *St&PR 93*
Korff, David *BioIn 17*
Korff, Donald Henry 1925- *St&PR 93*
Korff, Ira A. 1949- *St&PR 93, WhoAm 92*
Korff, John *BioIn 17*
Korff, Serge A. 1906-1989 *BioIn 17*
Korg, Jacob 1922- *WhoAm 92*
Korganov, Genari 1858-1890 *Baker 92*
Korhonen, Aarno Heikki Mikael 1924- *WhoScE 91-4*
Korhonen, Antti Samuli 1950- *WhoWor 93*
Korhonen, Kalle-Heikki 1926- *WhoScE 91-4*
Korhonen, L. Kalevi 1933- *WhoScE 91-4*
Korhonen, Timo K. 1949- *WhoScE 91-4*
Kori, Kiyotaka *BioIn 17*
Kori, Tosiaki 1941- *WhoWor 93*
Korinek, Miroslav 1925- *Baker 92*
Korins, Leopold *WhoAm 92*
Koris, David J. *Law&B 92*
Koriun *OxDcByz*
Koriyama, Naoshi 1926- *WhoWor 93*
Korkegi, Robert Hani 1925- *WhoE 93*
Korkman, Johan F. 1943- *WhoScE 91-4*
Korkolonis, Robert Stephen 1960- *St&PR 93*
Korman, Barbara 1938- *WhoAm 92, WhoE 93*
Korman, Barry S. *Law&B 92*
Korman, Bernard J. 1931- *St&PR 93*
Korman, David L. *Law&B 92*
Korman, Edward R. 1942- *WhoAm 92, WhoE 93*
Korman, Gerd 1928- *WhoAm 92*
Korman, Gordon 1963- *Au&Arts 10 [port], WhoCanL 92*
Korman, Gordon (Richard) 1963- *MajAI [port]*
Korman, Harvey Herschel 1927- *WhoAm 92*
Korman, Ira Bruce 1944- *WhoAm 92*
Korman, James William 1943- *WhoAm 92, WhoSSW 93*
Korman, Jess J. 1933- *WhoAm 92*
Korman, Justine 1958- *ConAu 138, SmATA 70 [port]*
Korman, Lewis J. 1945- *WhoAm 92*
Korman, Louis Yves 1947- *WhoE 93*
Korman, Nathaniel Irving 1916- *WhoAm 92*
Korman, Paul *Law&B 92*
Korman, Robert 1947- *St&PR 93*
Korman, Timothy J. 1952- *St&PR 93*
Kormano, Martti J. 1941- *WhoScE 91-4*
Kormes, John Winston 1935- *WhoE 93, WhoWor 93*
Kormi, Kazem *WhoScE 91-1*
Kormondy, Edward John 1926- *WhoAm 92*
Kormos, Keith J. 1947- *St&PR 93*
Korn, Adolfo 1932- *WhoUN 92*
Korn, Alan Martin 1944- *St&PR 93*
Korn, Barry Paul 1944- *WhoE 93*
Korn, Bennet d1989 *BioIn 17*
Korn, Bernard 1925- *St&PR 93, WhoAm 92*
Korn, Candy Lee 1942- *WhoAmW 93*
Korn, Carl 1921- *St&PR 93*
Korn, Claire Vedensky 1933- *WhoAmW 93*
Korn, Clara Anna 1866-1940 *Baker 92*
Korn, David 1933- *WhoAm 92*
Korn, David 1934- *WhoAm 92*
Korn, David A(dolph) 1930- *ConAu 139*
Korn, Donald Louis 1933- *St&PR 93*
Korn, Edward David 1928- *WhoAm 92*
Korn, Henri 1934- *WhoScE 91-2*
Korn, Henry 1945- *WhoWrEP 92*
Korn, Howard L. 1932- *St&PR 93*
Korn, Hyman 1902-1991 *BioIn 17*
Korn, Janos *WhoScE 91-1*
Korn, Joel 1946- *St&PR 93*
Korn, Joseph Howard 1947- *WhoE 93*
Korn, Judith Ann 1947- *WhoAmW 93*
Korn, Laurence Jay *St&PR 93*
Korn, Lester B. 1936- *St&PR 93*
Korn, Lester Bernard 1936- *WhoAm 92*
Korn, Mel R. 1929- *St&PR 93*
Korn, Michael d1991 *BioIn 17*
Korn, Peter 1944- *St&PR 93*
Korn, Peter A. 1939- *WhoAm 92*
Korn, Peter Jona 1922- *Baker 92*
Korn, Rachel 1898-1982 *WhoCanL 92*
Korn, Stephen 1945- *St&PR 93*
Korn, Steven Eric 1944- *WhoE 93*
Korn, Steven W. *Law&B 92, WhoAm 92*
Korn, Walter 1908- *WhoWor 93*
Kornacki, Richard Alfred 1952- *WhoEmL 93*
Kornadt, Hans-Joachim Kurt 1927- *WhoWor 93*
Kornahrens, Herman 1927- *St&PR 93*
Kornas, Jan 1923- *WhoScE 91-4*
Kornauth, Egon 1891-1959 *Baker 92*
Kornberg, Arthur 1918- *BioIn 17, News 92 [port], WhoAm 92, WhoWor 93*
Kornberg, Fred 1936- *St&PR 93, WhoE 93*
Kornberg, Hans (Leo) *WhoScE 91-1*
Kornberg, Hans Leo 1928- *WhoWor 93*
Kornberg, James Philip 1947- *WhoEmL 93*
Kornberg, Mindy *Law&B 92*
Kornberg, Warren Stanley 1927- *WhoAm 92*
Kornbichler, Heinz 1925- *WhoScE 91-3*
Kornblatt, David W. 1927- *St&PR 93*
Kornblatt, Marc *ScF&FL 92*
Kornbleet, Lynda Mae 1951- *WhoAmW 93*
Kornblet, Donald Ross 1943- *WhoAm 92*
Kornblit, Sandra Cohen *Law&B 92*
Kornblith, Hilary Stuart 1954- *WhoE 93*
Kornblith, John H. d1992 *NewYTBS 92*
Kornblith, John Howard 1924- *WhoAm 92*
Kornbluh, Joyce S. *Law&B 92*
Kornbluh, Mark *BioIn 17*
Kornbluh, Myron *Law&B 92*
Kornbluh, Walter 1931- *St&PR 93*
Kornblum, Allan *BioIn 17*
Kornblum, Carl B. 1938- *St&PR 93*
Kornblut, Gerri L. *Law&B 92*
Kornbluth, C.M. 1923-1958 *BioIn 17, ScF&FL 92*
Kornbluth, Cyril M. 1923-1958 *BioIn 17*
Kornbluth, Ralph Ross 1938- *WhoE 93*
Kornbluth, Sandra Joan 1951- *WhoAmW 93*
Kornbrekke, H.N. 1944- *St&PR 93*
Korndoerfer, Claus Wolfgang 1925- *St&PR 93*
Korndorf, Nikolai 1947- *Baker 92*
Korndorffer, William Earl 1930- *WhoSSW 93*
Kornecki, Andrew Jan 1946- *WhoEmL 93, WhoSSW 93*
Kornegay, Cecilia Christina 1951- *WhoAmW 93*
Kornegay, H.R. 1952- *St&PR 93*
Kornegay, Horace Robinson 1924- *WhoAm 92*
Kornegay, Patricia A. *Law&B 92*
Kornegay, Robert Madrid 1952- *WhoWrEP 92*
Kornegay, Roy Aubry, Jr. 1937- *WhoSSW 93*
Kornel, Ludwig 1923- *WhoAm 92*
Korner, Anthony David 1939- *WhoAm 92*
Korner, Carol Ann 1960- *WhoAmW 93*
Korner, Christian Gottfried 1756-1831 *Baker 92*
Korner, Horst 1938- *WhoScE 91-3*
Korner, Jules G., III 1922- *CngDr 91*
Korner, Jules Gilmer, III 1922- *WhoAm 92*
Korner, Stephan 1913- *WhoWor 93*
Korner, Theodor 1791-1813 *BioIn 17*
Kornerup, Peter 1939- *WhoWor 93*
Korney, Arthur Francis, Jr. 1933- *St&PR 93*
Kornfeld, Alan David 1942- *WhoWor 93*
Kornfeld, Allan 1937- *St&PR 93*
Kornfeld, Allan A. 1937- *WhoAm 92*
Kornfeld, Gary Lloyd 1955- *WhoEmL 93*
Kornfeld, Itzchak Ehud 1953- *WhoEmL 93*
Kornfeld, Joseph Alton 1907- *WhoSSW 93*
Kornfeld, Marvin William 1928- *St&PR 93*
Kornfeld, Paul 1889-1942 *DcLB 118 [port]*
Kornfeld, Rosalind Hauk 1935- *WhoAmW 93*
Kornfield, Alfred Theodore 1918- *WhoAm 92*
Korngold, Alvin Leonard 1924- *WhoAm 92, WhoWor 93*
Korngold, Erich 1897-1957 *OxDcOp*
Korngold, Erich Wolfgang 1897-1957 *Baker 92, IntDcOp [port]*
Korngold, Julius 1860-1945 *Baker 92*
Kornhauser, Arthur 1896-1990 *BioIn 17*
Kornhauser, Henry 1932- *WhoAm 92*
Kornhauser, Kenneth Richard 1947- *WhoE 93*
Kornhauser, Stanley Henry 1934- *WhoE 93*
Kornheiser, Anthony I. 1948- *WhoAm 92*
Kornheiser, Martin H. *Law&B 92*
Kornheiser, Tony 1948- *ConAu 138*

Kornick, Nancy S. *Law&B 92*
Korniczky, Paul John 1961- *WhoEmL 93*
Korniewicz, Helen M. *Law&B 92*
Kornilov, Lavr Georgievich 1870-1918 *BioIn 17*
Kornish, Doris *BioIn 17*
Kornman, Kay Adele *Law&B 92*
Kornmeyer, Robin A. 1948- *St&PR 93*
Kornmuller, Otto 1824-1907 *Baker 92*
Kornobis, Stefan 1947- *WhoScE 91-4*
Kornosky, Christine 1955- *WhoEmL 93*
Kornreich, Donald Bruce 1937- *St&PR 93*
Kornreich, Joel Craig 1948- *St&PR 93*
Kornreich, Morton Alan 1924- *WhoAm 92*
Kornsey, Robert J. 1937- *St&PR 93*
Kornstad, Leif 1926- *WhoScE 91-4*
Kornstein, Don Robert 1952- *St&PR 93, WhoAm 92*
Kornstein, Edward 1929- *St&PR 93, WhoE 93*
Kornwise, Robert 1971?-1987 *ScF&FL 92*
Kornylak, Harold John 1950- *WhoSSW 93*
Kornylak, Thomas Andrew 1945- *St&PR 93*
Korobeinik, Yuri Fyodorovitch 1930- *WhoWor 93*
Korodi, Andras 1922-1986 *Baker 92*
Korogiannakis, Antonios *WhoScE 91-3*
Korohoda, Wlodzimierz 1937- *WhoScE 91-4*
Korolev, Alexej Gennadjevich 1959- *WhoWor 93*
Korolev, Sergei *BioIn 17*
Korolewicz-Wayda, Janina 1880-1955 *PolBiDi*
Korolkiewicz, Edward *WhoScE 91-1*
Korolko, Vicki *BioIn 17*
Korologos, Tom Chris 1933- *WhoAm 92*
Koroltchouk, Valentin Pavlovich 1939- *WhoUN 92*
Koroly, Michael Vincent 1949- *WhoEmL 93*
Korolyuk, Vladimir Semenovich 1925- *WhoWor 93*
Koroma, Abdul Karim 1945- *WhoAfr*
Koropatkin, Nicholas 1946- *St&PR 93*
Koros, Aurelia Marie Carissimo 1934- *WhoAmW 93*
Koros, William John 1947- *WhoAm 92*
Korotich, Vitaly *BioIn 17*
Korotkin, Audrey Rhona 1957- *WhoAmW 93*
Korotkin, Dmitriy Alexandrovich 1965- *WhoWor 93*
Korotkin, Fred 1917- *WhoWor 93*
Korotyaev, Evgeni Leonidovich 1952- *WhoWor 93*
Korovin, Sergey Konstantinovitch 1945- *WhoWor 93*
Korowi, Wiwa *WhoWor 93*
Korowi, Wiwa 1948- *WhoAsAP 91*
Korp, Patricia Anne 1942- *WhoAmW 93*
Korpal, Eugene Stanley 1931- *WhoAm 92*
Korpel, Adrian 1932- *WhoAm 92*
Korpela, Jon E. 1953- *St&PR 93*
Korpela, Kauko Mauno 1927- *WhoScE 91-4*
Korpela, Richard Allan 1943- *St&PR 93*
Korphage, George J. 1947- *St&PR 93*
Korpinen, Pekka Juha Tapio 1944- *WhoWor 93*
Korpinen, Sakari Otto Johannes 1946- *WhoWor 93*
Korres, George 1962- *WhoWor 93*
Kors, Michael *BioIn 17*
Kors, R. Paul 1935- *WhoAm 92*
Korsakov, Allan B. 1942- *St&PR 93*
Korschot, Benjamin Calvin 1921- *WhoAm 92, WhoWor 93*
Korschot, John C. 1951- *St&PR 93*
Korsen, Elliott *Law&B 92*
Korsgaard, Christine Marion 1952- *WhoAm 92*
Korsgaard, Vagn 1921- *WhoScE 91-2*
Korshak, Yvonne 1936- *WhoAmW 93*
Korshunov, Aleksej Dmitrievich 1936- *WhoWor 93*
Korsmo, Charlie *BioIn 17*
Korsnack, J.J. 1954- *St&PR 93*
Korson, Roy 1922- *WhoE 93*
Korst, Christopher A. *Law&B 92*
Korstad, John Edward 1949- *WhoSSW 93*
Korsten, Mary Ann 1957- *WhoAmW 93*
Korsu, Kenneth W. 1943- *St&PR 93*
Korsyn, Irene Hahne 1927- *WhoAm 92*
Korszewski, Nina 1967- *WhoWor 93*
Kort, Rosemary 1951- *WhoAmW 93*
Kortan, Josef 1946- *WhoScE 91-4*
Korte, Bernhard Hermann 1938- *WhoWor 93*
Korte, Ernst Heiner 1943- *WhoScE 91-3*
Korte, Friedhelm 1923- *WhoScE 91-3*
Korte, Karl (Richard) 1928- *Baker 92, WhoAm 92*
Korte, Loren A. *WhoAm 92*
Korte, Loren A. 1933- *St&PR 93*
Korte, Martin Roland 1947- *St&PR 93*
Korte, Oldrich Frantisek 1926- *Baker 92*
Korte, Stephan Wilhelm 1957- *WhoWor 93*
Korte, Werner 1906-1982 *Baker 92*
Kortekangas, Olli 1955- *Baker 92*
Korten, Thomas C. 1947- *St&PR 93*
Kortenhaus, William James 1934- *St&PR 93*
Kortenhorst, Louis F. 1928- *WhoScE 91-3*
Kortenhorst, Peter Jan Philip 1950- *WhoWor 93*
Kortepeter, Carl Max 1928- *WhoAm 92, WhoWrEP 92*
Korth, Charlotte Brooks *WhoAmW 93, WhoWor 93*
Korth, Charlotte Williams *St&PR 93*
Korth, Eugene H. 1917-1987 *BioIn 17*
Korth, Fred 1909- *St&PR 93, WhoAm 92, WhoWor 93*
Korth, Fritz-Alan 1938- *St&PR 93, WhoAm 92*
Korth, Penne Percy 1942- *WhoAm 92, WhoAmW 93, WhoWor 93*
Korth, Philip A. 1936- *ConAu 137*
Korthals, Robert Willem 1933- *WhoAm 92*
Korthoff, Herbert William 1944- *WhoAm 92*
Korting, Wolfgang 1940- *WhoScE 91-3*
Kortman, Bob 1887-1967 *BioIn 17*
Kortman, Joyce Elaine 1935- *WhoAmW 93*
Kortner, Fritz 1892-1970 *IntDcF 2-3 [port]*
Kortright, Suzanne Alaine Lawless 1954- *WhoEmL 93*
Kortschak, Hugo 1884-1957 *Baker 92*
Kortschak, Sepp August 1933- *St&PR 93, WhoSSW 93*
Kortsen, Bjarne 1930- *Baker 92*
Korttila, Kari 1948- *WhoScE 91-4*
Korty, David Joseph 1950- *WhoEmL 93*
Korty, John 1936- *MiSFD 9*
Korver, P.K. *WhoScE 91-3*
Korwek, Alexander D. 1932- *St&PR 93*
Korwek, Alexander Donald 1932- *WhoAm 92, WhoSSW 93*
Korylak, John Raymond 1953- *St&PR 93*
Korytowski, Adam Witold 1946- *WhoWor 93*
Korzec, Arthur *Law&B 92*
Korzec, Zdzislaw 1929- *WhoScE 91-4*
Korzenik, Armand Alexander 1927- *WhoAm 92*
Korzeniowski, Aleksander Marian 1924- *WhoWor 93*
Korzeniowski, Apollo Nalecz 1820-1869 *PolBiDi*
Korzeniowski, Jozef 1797-1863 *PolBiDi*
Korzeniowsky, Waldemar *MiSFD 9*
Korzybski, Alfred 1879-1950 *PolBiDi*
Kos, Alexander Joachim 1946- *WhoWor 93*
Kosa, Andras 1932- *WhoScE 91-4*
Kosa, Ferenc 1937- *DrEEuF*
Kosa, Gyorgy 1897-1984 *Baker 92*
Kosacoff-Karp, Phyllis Joyce 1944- *WhoAmW 93*
Kosak, Anthony James 1934- *WhoAm 92*
Kosaka, Kenji 1946- *WhoAsAP 91*
Kosakoff, Reuven 1898-1987 *Baker 92*
Kosakow, James Matthew 1954- *WhoE 93, WhoEmL 93, WhoWor 93*
Kosar, Bernie *BioIn 17*
Kosar, Bernie, Jr. 1963- *WhoAm 92*
Kosar, Robert W. 1929- *St&PR 93*
Kosaraju, S. Rao 1943- *WhoAm 92*
Kosarin, Jonathan Henry 1951- *WhoAm 92*
Kosary, Domokos 1913- *WhoWor 93*
Kosasky, Harold Jack 1927- *WhoE 93, WhoWor 93*
Kosbab, F(rederic) Paul 1922- *WhoWrEP 92*
Kosc, Jean Rochelle 1936- *WhoE 93*
Koscelnick, Jeanne 1960- *WhoAmW 93*
Kosch, Richard Patrick 1947- *St&PR 93*
Kosch, Walter T. *Law&B 92*
Koschat, Thomas 1845-1914 *Baker 92*
Kosche, Tatiana 1966- *WhoAmW 93*
Koscianski, Leonard Joseph 1952- *WhoE 93*
Koscielak, Jerzy 1930- *WhoScE 91-4, WhoWor 93*
Koscielniak, Audrey A. 1944- *WhoE 93*
Koscielniak, Bruce *BioIn 17*
Kosciuk, Lisa Marie 1965- *WhoEmL 93*
Kosciusko, Jacques Antoine 1943- *WhoWor 93*
Kosciusko, Tadeusz Andrezj Bonawentura 1746-1817 *HarEnMi*
Kosciuszko, Stefan Henry 1959- *WhoWor 93*
Kosciuszko, Tadeusz 1746-1817 *PolBiDi [port]*
Koscs-Fleming, Mary Ellen *Law&B 92*
Kose, Volkmar E. 1936- *WhoScE 91-3*
Kosel, Howard E. 1931- *St&PR 93*
Kosel, Ulrich 1939- *WhoWor 93*
Koselitz, Johann Heinrich 1854-1918 *Baker 92*
Koselke, Georgette Marion 1947- *WhoEmL 93*
Koser, Gary Richard 1950- *WhoEmL 93*
Kosh, Zelda Horner 1913- *WhoWrEP 92*
Koshan, Jeremy Michael *Law&B 92*
Koshar, Herbert Bernard 1917- *St&PR 93*
Koshar, Louis David 1928- *WhoAm 92*
Kosheff, Martin Joel 1938- *WhoAm 92*
Koshelev, Yuriy Grigoryevich 1947- *WhoWor 93*
Koshetz, Nina (Pavlovna) 1894-1965 *Baker 92*
Koshi, Masaki 1934- *WhoWor 93*
Koshiishi, Azuma *WhoAsAP 91*
Koshimoto, Edwin Takuzo 1966- *WhoSSW 93*
Koshio, Genya 1933- *WhoWor 93*
Koshiro, Kazutoshi 1932- *WhoWor 93*
Koshland, Daniel Edward 1892-1979 *BioIn 17*
Koshland, Daniel Edward, Jr. 1920- *WhoAm 92*
Koshland, Marian Elliott 1921- *WhoAm 92, WhoAmW 93*
Koshland, William A. 1906- *St&PR 93*
Koshuta, Monica *BioIn 17*
Kosiba, Bradley Everett 1953- *WhoEmL 93, WhoSSW 93*
Kosich, George J. 1934- *WhoAm 92*
Kosich, George John 1934- *WhoE 93, WhoWor 93*
Kosidlo, Stanley P. *St&PR 93*
Kosiek, Lawrence J. 1947- *St&PR 93*
Kosik, Edwin Michael 1925- *WhoAm 92, WhoE 93*
Kosikowski, Frank Vincent 1916- *WhoAm 92*
Kosina, Zdenek 1938- *WhoScE 91-4*
Kosinar, William James 1944- *St&PR 93*
Kosinski, Dennis Steven 1946- *WhoWrEP 92*
Kosinski, Jerzy 1933-1991 *AnObit 1991, ConLC 70 [port], JeAmHC*
Kosinski, Jerzy N. 1933-1991 *BioIn 17, PolBiDi*
Kosinski, Jozef 1753-1821 *PolBiDi*
Kosinsky, Barbara Timm 1942- *WhoAmW 93, WhoWrEP 92*
Kosisky, Shelley Ann 1959- *WhoAmW 93*
Kosiver, Jeffrey M. 1943- *St&PR 93*
Koskas, Yvan David 1934- *WhoWor 93*
Koske, Richard A. *Law&B 92*
Koskela, Aarni *WhoScE 91-4*
Koski, Ann Louise 1951- *WhoAm 92*
Koski, Conrad W. 1945- *St&PR 93*
Koski, Deanna Eleanor 1941- *WhoAmW 93*
Koski, Linda Mae 1947- *WhoAm 92*
Koski, Veikko Ensio 1937- *WhoScE 91-4*
Koski, Walter David 1933- *WhoAm 92*
Koskie, R. Edward 1930- *St&PR 93*
Koskimies, Kai Evert 1950- *WhoWor 93*
Koskinas, Stephan Aristotle 1946- *WhoAm 92*
Koskinen, Ari Mauri Petri 1956- *WhoWor 93*
Koskinen, Donald Steward 1928- *St&PR 93*
Koskinen, Esko Hugo 1938- *WhoWor 93*
Koskinen, Heikki *WhoScE 91-4*
Koskinen, John Andrew 1939- *WhoAm 92*
Kosko, John Joseph 1951- *WhoE 93*
Kosleck, Julius 1825-1904 *Baker 92*
Koslen, Joel M. 1957- *St&PR 93*
Kosler, Zdenek 1928- *Baker 92, OxDcOp, WhoWor 93*
Kosloff, Alexander d1991 *BioIn 17*
Kosloff, Andrew Robert *Law&B 92*
Koslosky, Adam Martin 1956- *St&PR 93*
Koslosky, Pierce Andrew, Jr. 1950- *St&PR 93*
Koslow, Diane Ruth 1942- *WhoE 93*
Koslow, Esther *Law&B 92*
Koslow, Harold 1926- *St&PR 93*
Koslow, Myron Alan 1936- *WhoE 93*
Koslow, Stephen Hugh 1940- *WhoE 93*
Koslow, Trudy Ruth 1955- *WhoSSW 93*
Koslowski, Peter Franziskus Theodor 1952- *WhoWor 93*
Kosma, Joseph 1905-1969 *Baker 92*
Kosma, Zbigniew Jozef 1949- *WhoScE 91-4*
Kosmahl, Henry G. 1919- *WhoAm 92*
Kosmala, Witold Aleksander Jan 1953- *WhoEmL 93, WhoSSW 93*
Kosman, John G. 1930- *St&PR 93*
Kosman, John George 1930- *WhoE 93*
Kosmas, I d768 *OxDcByz*
Kosmas, Christos 1961- *WhoWor 93*
Kosmas Indikopleustes fl. 6th cent.- *OxDcByz*
Kosmas Magistros dc. 946 *OxDcByz*
Kosmas the Hymnographer c. 675-c. 752 *OxDcByz*
Kosmas the Priest fl. 10th cent.- *OxDcByz*
Kosmas Vestitor 730?-850? *OxDcByz*
Kosmatopoulos, Konstadinos 1950- *WhoScE 91-2*
Kosmicke, Sterling Ralph 1941- *St&PR 93*
Kosmidou-Dimitropoulou, Kiratso I. 1943- *WhoScE 91-3*
Kosminsky, Peter *MiSFD 9*
Kosmo, Jeffrey D. 1942- *St&PR 93*
Kosner, Edward Alan 1937- *WhoAm 92, WhoE 93*
Kosnett, Jeffrey Russell 1955- *WhoEmL 93*
Kosnik, Edward Francis 1944- *St&PR 93*
Kosniowska, G. Ann 1947- *WhoWor 93*
Kosniowski, Czes 1947- *WhoWor 93*
Kosof, Anna Clara *WhoE 93*
Kosoff, Flora May 1926- *WhoWrEP 92*
Kosoff, Richard *St&PR 93*
Kosolosky, Roland 1948- *WhoWor 93*
Kosovich, Dushan Radovan 1926- *WhoAm 92*
Kosovych, Bohdan S. *Law&B 92*
Kosow, Alan L. 1949- *St&PR 93*
Kosow, Irving Lionel 1919- *WhoSSW 93*
Kosowsky, David I. 1930- *WhoAm 92*
Kosowsky, Nina 1946- *WhoEmL 93*
Koss, David B. *Law&B 92*
Koss, Joel E. 1954- *St&PR 93*
Koss, John C. 1930- *St&PR 93*
Koss, John Charles 1930- *WhoAm 92*
Koss, Leopold G. 1920- *WhoAm 92, WhoWor 93*
Koss, Mary Lyndon Pease 1948- *WhoAmW 93*
Koss, Michael *St&PR 93*
Koss, Michael Leonard 1948- *St&PR 93*
Koss, Peter 1932- *WhoScE 91-4, WhoWor 93*
Koss, Raoul M. 1930- *St&PR 93*
Koss, Rosabel *BioIn 17*
Koss, Rosabel Steinhauer 1913- *WhoAmW 93*
Kossack, Carl Frederick 1915- *WhoSSW 93*
Kossacoff, Sandra E. *Law&B 92*
Kossak, Juliusz 1824-1899 *PolBiDi*
Kossak, Wojciech 1856-1942 *PolBiDi*
Kossakowski, Jozef 1771-1840 *PolBiDi*
Kossakowski, Stefan 1921- *WhoScE 91-4*
Kossak-Szczucka, Zofia 1890-1968 *PolBiDi*
Kossar, Bernard R. *St&PR 93*
Kossel, Clifford George 1916- *WhoAm 92*
Kossen, N.W.F. *WhoScE 91-3*
Kossiakoff, Alexander 1914- *WhoAm 92*
Kossick, Robert M. 1940- *St&PR 93*
Kossila, Vappu Leonara 1927- *WhoScE 91-4*
Kossl, Thomas *Law&B 92*
Kossl, Thomas Leonard 1952- *St&PR 93*
Kossler, Hans *Baker 92*
Kossler, J.R. 1943- *St&PR 93*
Kosslyn, Stephen Michael 1948- *ConAu 40NR*
Kossmaly, Carl 1812-1893 *Baker 92*
Kossman, Paul 1926- *St&PR 93*
Kossoff, Burton 1923- *St&PR 93*
Kossoff, Leon 1926- *BioIn 17*
Kossoff, Phyllis L. 1936- *St&PR 93*
Kossoff, Stanley M. 1925- *St&PR 93*
Kossou, Basile Toussaint 1944- *WhoUN 92*
Kossover, Herb Allan 1948- *WhoEmL 93*
Kossow, Sophia 1910- *WhoAm 92*
Kossowski, Henryk 1855-1921 *PolBiDi*
Kossuth, Lajos 1802-1894 *BioIn 17*
Kossuth, Selwyn Barnett 1937- *WhoAm 92*
Kost, Wayne L. 1951- *WhoAm 92*
Kosta, Louise Anne 1949- *WhoWrEP 92*
Kostabi, Mark *BioIn 17*
Kostabi, Mark 1960- *WhoE 93*
Kostak, Mira Anna 1954- *WhoAmW 93*
Kostaki, Georgii Dionisevich 1912-1990 *BioIn 17*
Kostal, John Alexander 1960- *WhoEmL 93*
Kostallari, Androkli Hari 1922- *WhoWor 93*
Kostanecki, Stanislaw 1860-1910 *PolBiDi*
Kostant, Bertram 1928- *WhoAm 92*
Kostar, Ronald Edward 1950- *WhoWrEP 92*
Kostarchuk, Yuri Victor 1946- *WhoWor 93*
Kostas, Evans 1935- *St&PR 93*
Kostash, Myrna 1944- *WhoCanL 92*
Kostecke, B. William 1925- *WhoAm 92*
Kostecki, Andrzej 1938- *WhoScE 91-4*
Kostecki, Mikolaj 1924- *WhoWor 93*
Kostecky, James Frank 1943- *WhoE 93*
Kostek, Bozena 1959- *WhoWor 93*
Kostek, James R. 1947- *St&PR 93*
Kostel, Laura Everitt 1934- *WhoSSW 93*
Kostelanetz, Andre 1901-1980 *Baker 92*
Kostelanetz, Boris 1911- *WhoAm 92*
Kostelanetz, Richard 1940- *Baker 92, WhoAm 92, WhoE 93, WhoWrEP 92*
Kostelanetz, Richard (Cory) 1940- *ConAu 38NR*

Kosteleba, Nancy Ann 1947- *WhoAmW 93, WhoE 93*
Kostelni, James C. 1935- *St&PR 93*
Kostelnik, Thomas M. 1943- *St&PR 93*
Kostelny, Albert Joseph, Jr. 1951- *WhoEmL 93*
Kosten, Harold W. 1937- *St&PR 93*
Kosten, Jeffrey Thomas *Law&B 92*
Kosten, Richard M. 1945- *St&PR 93*
Kostenko, Yury Vassilievich 1945- *WhoUN 92*
Koster, Andries Sjoerd 1952- *WhoWor 93*
Koster, Elaine Landis *St&PR 93*
Koster, Eugene S. 1942- *WhoIns 93*
Koster, Eugene Stanley 1942- *St&PR 93*
Koster, H. 1933- *WhoScE 91-3*
Koster, Henry 1905-1988 *MiSFD 9N*
Koster, James 1948- *St&PR 93, WhoAm 92, WhoE 93, WhoEmL 93*
Koster, Johan F. 1940- *WhoScE 91-3*
Koster, John Peter, Jr. 1945- *WhoAm 92*
Koster, Karen Anne *Law&B 92*
Koster, Michael Jay 1954- *St&PR 93*
Koster, Noreen Catherine 1953- *WhoAmW 93*
Koster, R.M. 1934- *ScF&FL 92*
Koster, Richard B. 1950- *St&PR 93*
Koster, William P. 1929- *BioIn 17, St&PR 93*
Koster, William Pfeiffer 1929- *WhoAm 92*
Kosterlitz, Amy Louise 1953- *WhoAmW 93*
Kosterlitz, Hans Walter *WhoScE 91-1*
Kostic, Dusan 1925- *Baker 92*
Kostic, Vojislav 1931- *Baker 92*
Kostiha, Kenneth James 1930- *St&PR 93*
Kostilainen, Valter 1928- *WhoScE 91-4*
Kostin, Ilya Nickolayevich 1966- *WhoWor 93*
Kostin, Michele G. *Law&B 92*
Kostin, Vladimir Alexeevich 1939- *WhoWor 93*
Kostiner, Eileen T. 1938- *WhoWrEP 92*
Kostinsky, Harvey 1949- *WhoAm 92*
Kostis, John Basil 1936- *WhoE 93*
Kostka, Frantisek 1945- *WhoScE 91-4*
Kostka, Heather Sharkey *WhoE 93*
Kostka, Krzysztof Jan 1930- *WhoScE 91-4*
Kostka, Vladimir 1930- *WhoScE 91-4*
Kostka-Potocki, Stanislaw 1755-1821 *PolBiDi*
Kostlin, Heinrich Adolf 1846-1907 *Baker 92*
Kostmayer, Peter H. 1946- *CngDr 91*
Kostmayer, Peter Houston 1946- *WhoAm 92, WhoE 93*
Kostner, Gerhard M. 1940- *WhoScE 91-4*
Kostochka, Alexandr Vasily 1951- *WhoWor 93*
Kostof, Spiro 1936-1991 *AnObit 1991, BioIn 17*
Kostolansky, David John 1943- *St&PR 93*
Kostolansky, Joseph P. 1933- *St&PR 93*
Kostorz, Gernot 1941- *WhoScE 91-4, WhoWor 93*
Kostoulas, Katina Kay 1953- *WhoAmW 93*
Kostov, Georgi 1941- *Baker 92*
Kostov, Ivan 1913- *WhoScE 91-4*
Kostrowicki, Andrzej Samuel 1921- *WhoScE 91-4*
Kostrowicki, Jerzy *WhoScE 91-4*
Kostrykin, Vadim Valentinovich 1963- *WhoWor 93*
Kostrzewa, Joseph Gerald 1941- *St&PR 93*
Kostrzewski, Andrzej 1939- *WhoWor 93*
Kostrzewski, Jan *WhoScE 91-4*
Kostuch, Dorothy Ann 1935- *WhoAmW 93*
Kostuch, Martha *BioIn 17*
Kostuch, Mitchell John 1931- *WhoAm 92, WhoE 93*
Kostyniak, Paul John 1947- *WhoE 93*
Kostyniuk, Allan J. 1940- *St&PR 93*
Kostyo, Jack Lawrence 1931- *WhoAm 92*
Kostyra, Richard *BioIn 17*
Kostyra, Richard Joseph 1940- *WhoAm 92, WhoE 93*
Kosugi, Takashi 1935- *WhoAsAP 91*
Kosugi, Takehisa 1938- *Baker 92*
Kosut, Kenneth Paul 1949- *WhoAm 92, WhoSSW 93*
Kosuth, Joseph 1945- *BioIn 17, WhoAm 92*
Kosutic, Zvonimir 1924- *WhoScE 91-4*
Kos'yan, Ruben Derenikovich 1946- *WhoWor 93*
Kosygin, Alexei Nikolayevich 1904-1981 *DcTwHis*
Kosygin, Alexsei Nikolaevich 1904-1980 *ColdWar 2 [port]*
Koszarski, Richard 1947- *WhoAm 92*
Koszewski, Bohdan Julius 1918- *WhoWor 93*
Koszinowski, Ulrich H. 1944- *WhoScE 91-3*
Koszka, Joseph Edward 1923- *St&PR 93*
Koszkul, Josef 1938- *WhoWor 93*
Kosztolnyik, Zoltan Joseph 1930- *WhoSSW 93*
Koszulinski, Georg W. 1948- *St&PR 93*
Kot, S. *WhoScE 91-4*
Kot, Sarina Ying-Lai 1962- *WhoEmL 93*
Kotadiya, Manubhai *WhoAsAP 91*
Kotaite, Assad 1924- *WhoUN 92*
Kotalac, Russell T. 1964- *St&PR 93*
Kotali, Caleb 1945- *WhoAsAP 91*
Kotani, Eric 1933- *ScF&FL 92*
Kotani, Teruji 1926- *WhoAsAP 91*
Kotani, Tom *MiSFD 9*
Kotani, Tsuneyuki 1924- *WhoWor 93*
Kotansky, William J. *Law&B 92*
Kotarba, Adam 1938- *WhoScE 91-4*
Kotarbinski, Tadeusz 1886-1981 *PolBiDi*
Kotaru, Satyanarayana 1944- *WhoE 93*
Kotas, John Peter 1955- *St&PR 93*
Kotas, Robert Vincent 1938- *WhoAm 92*
Kotch, Alex 1926- *WhoAm 92*
Kotch, John E. 1927- *St&PR 93*
Kotch, Thomas *ScF&FL 92*
Kotcheff, Ted 1931- *ConTFT 10, MiSFD 9*
Kotcheff, William T. *ConTFT 10*
Kotcheff, William Theodore 1931- *WhoAm 92*
Kotcher, Ezra 1903-1990 *BioIn 17*
Kotcher, Raymond Lowell 1951- *WhoAm 92, WhoE 93*
Kotchetkov, Vladislav Pavlovich 1936- *WhoUN 92*
Kotchian, A. Carl 1914- *St&PR 93*
Kotecha, Kishor Champaklal 1958- *WhoWor 93*
Kotecha, Mahesh Kanjibhai 1947- *WhoAm 92*
Kotek, Freddie Mark 1956- *St&PR 93*
Kotek, (Eduard) Joseph 1855-1885 *Baker 92*
Kotelba-Witkowska, Barbara Adela 1930- *WhoScE 91-4*
Koteles, Gyorgy J. 1934- *WhoScE 91-4*
Koteles, William John 1953- *St&PR 93*
Kotelko, Barbara 1927- *WhoScE 91-4*
Kotelko, Krystyna 1920- *WhoScE 91-4*
Kotelly, George Vincent 1931- *WhoAm 92, WhoWrEP 92*
Koten, John A. 1929- *St&PR 93, WhoAm 92*
Kotera, Nobuo 1938- *WhoWor 93*
Kotermanski, Mitchell L. 1941- *St&PR 93*
Koteskey, Ronald Lynn 1942- *WhoSSW 93*
Koth, David N. *Law&B 92*
Koth, Erika 1925-1989 *Baker 92, IntDcOp*
Kothari, Ajay Prasannajit 1954- *WhoE 93, WhoEmL 93*
Kothari, Bijay Singh 1928- *WhoWor 93*
Kothari, Kiron U. 1956- *St&PR 93*
Kothari, Kul Bhushan 1937- *WhoUN 92*
Kothe, Aloys 1828-1868 *Baker 92*
Kothe, Bernhard 1821-1897 *Baker 92*
Kothe, Charles Aloysius 1912- *WhoAm 92*
Kothe, Charles Donald 1922- *St&PR 93*
Kothe, Gerd 1941- *WhoScE 91-3*
Kothe, Wilhelm 1831-1897 *Baker 92*
Kotheimer, William Conrad 1925- *WhoAm 92*
Kothen, Karl Axel 1871-1927 *Baker 92*
Kothera, Lynne M. 1938- *WhoAmW 93, WhoE 93*
Kothmann, Bruce P. *St&PR 93*
Kothmann, Jamie R. 1928- *St&PR 93*
Koths, Jay Sanford 1926- *WhoAm 92*
Koths, Kirston Edward 1948- *WhoEmL 93*
Kotidis, Petros Anestis 1960- *WhoE 93*
Kotik, Charlotta 1940- *BioIn 17*
Kotik, Petr 1942- *Baker 92, WhoE 93*
Kotilainen, Otto 1868-1936 *Baker 92*
Kotilainen, Risto 1940- *WhoScE 91-4*
Kotin, Gabriel Gary 1933- *St&PR 93*
Kotite, Rich 1942- *WhoAm 92, WhoE 93*
Kotiuga, Peter Robert 1958- *WhoEmL 93*
Kotker, Norman Richard 1931- *WhoWrEP 92*
Kotker, Zane 1934- *WhoWrEP 92*
Kotkin, David 1956- *WhoAm 92*
Kotkin, Roberta Beth *Law&B 92*
Kotkins, Henry Louis, Jr. 1948- *St&PR 93*
Kotkowski, Andrzej 1940- *DrEEuF*
Kotlan, C.M. *ScF&FL 92*
Kotler, Barry L. *Law&B 92*
Kotler, Milton 1935- *WhoAm 92*
Kotler, Philip *BioIn 17*
Kotler, Philip 1931- *WhoAm 92*
Kotler, Richard Lee 1952- *WhoEmL 93*
Kotler, Steven 1947- *St&PR 93, WhoAm 92*
Kotliar, Vladimir S. 1933- *WhoUN 92*
Kotlikoff, Barbara *BioIn 17*
Kotlowitz, Alex c. 1955- *ConAu 138*
Kotlowitz, Dan 1957- *WhoAm 92*
Kotlowitz, Robert 1924- *JeAmFiW, WhoAm 92*
Kotnik, France 1882-1955 *IntDcAn*
Kotonski, Wlodzimierz 1925- *Baker 92, WhoWor 93*
Kotoske, Roger Allen 1933- *WhoAm 92*
Kotouc, John F. 1946- *St&PR 93*
Kotoulas, Othon B. 1932- *WhoScE 91-3*
Kotov, Victor Nikolayevich 1947- *WhoWor 93*
Kotovnikov, Felix 1948- *St&PR 93*
Kotovsky, Kenneth 1939- *WhoE 93*
Kotowski, Christine Anne 1947- *WhoAmW 93*
Kotrlik, Joe Wayne 1948- *WhoSSW 93*
Kotrschal, Kurt Michael 1953- *WhoWor 93*
Kotsch, Hildreth *AmWomPl*
Kotsiopulos, Peter George 1947- *WhoEmL 93*
Kotsis, Aleksander 1836-1877 *PolBiDi*
Kotsonis, Frank Nick 1943- *WhoAm 92*
Kotsovinos, Nikolas E. 1944- *WhoScE 91-3*
Kott, Alan 1948- *WhoEmL 93*
Kott, Beverly Parat 1936- *WhoAmW 93*
Kott, Gary Lynn 1942- *St&PR 93*
Kott, Jan K. 1914- *WhoAm 92*
Kott, Josef Jan 1932- *WhoWor 93*
Kott, Laurent *WhoScE 91-2*
Kott, Mike *ScF&FL 92*
Kotta, Joseph Robert 1939- *WhoUN 92*
Kotta, ulle 1948- *WhoWor 93*
Kottamasu, Mohan Rao 1947- *WhoE 93*
Kottapalli, Sesi Bhushan Rao 1951- *WhoEmL 93*
Kottaridis, Stavros D. 1933- *WhoWor 93*
Kottas, John Frederick 1940- *WhoAm 92*
Kotter, Hans c. 1485-1541 *Baker 92*
Kotter, John Paul 1947- *WhoAm 92*
Kotthaus, Jorg Peter 1944- *WhoScE 91-3*
Kottiath, Mathew T. *BioIn 17*
Kottick, Edward Leon 1930- *WhoAm 92*
Kottick, Gloria 1930- *WhoWrEP 92*
Kottis, Athena Petraki *WhoWor 93*
Kottis, George Christopher 1933- *WhoWor 93*
Kottis, Nick C. *Law&B 92*
Kottkamp, John Harlan 1930- *WhoAm 92*
Kottke, Alan P. 1958- *St&PR 93*
Kottke, Frederick Edward 1926- *WhoWor 93*
Kottler, Jeffrey A. 1951- *ConAu 136*
Kottler, Joan Lynn 1943- *WhoSSW 93*
Kottlitz, Adolf 1820- *Baker 92*
Kottlowski, Frank Edward 1921- *WhoAm 92, WhoWor 93*
Kottman, Roy Milton 1916- *WhoAm 92*
Kottmann, Heinz 1930- *St&PR 93*
Kottmeier, Charles Augustus, II 1937- *WhoSSW 93*
Kottmeyer, John David 1950- *WhoAm 92*
Kotto, Yaphet 1937- *MiSFD 9*
Kottom, Paul Wayne 1954- *WhoEmL 93*
Kottucz, Heinz *WhoScE 91-3*
Kotuk, Andrea Mikotajuk 1948- *WhoAmW 93, WhoE 93*
Kotula, Franciszek 1900-1983 *IntDcAn*
Kotula, Gloria Anne 1946- *WhoEmL 93*
Kotulak, Richard M. *Law&B 92*
Kotulak, Ronald 1935- *WhoAm 92*
Kotulka, Franks S. 1943- *St&PR 93*
Kotun, Henry Paul 1931- *WhoAm 92*
Kotvis, Jill Alison *Law&B 92*
Kotwal, Deepak Atmaram 1948- *St&PR 93*
Kotyk, Joann Theresa 1952- *WhoEmL 93*
Kotz, David Michael 1943- *WhoAm 92*
Kotz, John Carl 1937- *WhoE 93*
Kotz, Kathryn Lego *Law&B 92*
Kotz, Nathan Kallison 1932- *WhoAm 92*
Kotz, Richard F. *Law&B 92*
Kotz, Richard P. 1941- *St&PR 93*
Kotz, Samuel 1930- *WhoAm 92*
Kotz, Steven W. 1950- *St&PR 93*
Kotz, Suzanne 1951- *WhoAmW 93*
Kotzebue, August von 1761-1819 *BioIn 17, OxDcOp*
Kotzen, Marshall Jason 1942- *WhoE 93*
Kotzler, Jurgen F. 1940- *WhoScE 91-3*
Kotzmann, Warren C. *Law&B 92*
Kotzolt, Heinrich 1814-1881 *Baker 92*
Kotzschmar, Hermann 1829-1909 *Baker 92*
Kotzwinkle, William 1938- *MajAI [port], ScF&FL 92, SmATA 70 [port], WhoAm 92*
Kouba, Sandra Louise 1941- *WhoWrEP 92*
Kouba, Vaclav 1929- *WhoScE 91-3*
Koubek, Edward 1937- *WhoE 93*
Koublanova, Elena M. 1944- *WhoWor 93*
Kouchoukos, Nicholas Thomas 1936- *WhoAm 92*
Koucky, John Richard 1934- *WhoAm 92*
Koudela, Karel 1933- *WhoScE 91-4*
Koudelka, Josef 1938- *WhoWor 93*
Koudrjachov, Oleg 1932- *BioIn 17*
Kouf, Jim *MiSFD 9*
Koufax, Sandy 1935- *BioIn 17*
Koughan, Francis Michael 1943- *St&PR 93*
Kouguell, Arkadie 1898-1985 *Baker 92*
Kouinis, John 1931- *WhoScE 91-3*
Koukouzeles, Joannes c. 1280-1360? *Baker 92*
Koukouzeles, John dc. 1341 *OxDcByz*
Koul, M.K. 1941- *St&PR 93*
Koulamas, Christos Panagiotis 1959- *WhoEmL 93*
Koulax, Tommy d1992 *BioIn 17*
Koulischer, Georges 1936- *WhoUN 92*
Kouloumdjian, Jacques 1938- *WhoScE 91-2*
Koumaras, Terence J. *ScF&FL 92*
Koumare, Mamadou Falley 1936- *WhoUN 92*
Kounadis, Arghyris 1924- *Baker 92*
Kounchev, Ognyan Ivanov 1956- *WhoWor 93*
Koundakjian, Stephen J. *Law&B 92*
Kounellis, Jannis *BioIn 17*
Koupf, Gary I. 1950- *WhoIns 93*
Kourakos, Tina 1955- *WhoEmL 93*
Kouremenos, Dimitris 1936- *WhoScE 91-3*
Kouri, Donald Jack 1938- *WhoAm 92, WhoSSW 93*
Kourides, P. Nicholas *Law&B 92*
Kourides, Peter Theologos 1910- *WhoAm 92*
Kouril, Irene 1935- *WhoAmW 93*
Kourilsky, Philippe *WhoScE 91-2*
Kouris, Michael *BioIn 17*
Kouris, Paul A. *Law&B 92*
Kouris, Paul Andrew 1949- *WhoAm 92*
Kouris, Stamatis 1933- *WhoScE 91-3*
Kourkouas *OxDcByz*
Kourkouas, John dc. 946 *OxDcByz*
Kournikova, Anna *NewYTBS 92 [port]*
Kourogenis, Constantine Nicolas 1935- *WhoScE 91-3*
Kourouma, Ahmadou *BioIn 17*
Kourouma, Malamine 1954- *WhoUN 92*
Kourtikios *OxDcByz*
Koury, Aleah George 1925- *WhoAm 92*
Koury, George Eli 1921- *WhoSSW 93*
Koury, George John 1930- *St&PR 93*
Koury, Leo J. d1991 *BioIn 17*
Koury, Thomas Leo 1923- *WhoE 93*
Koussa, Harold Alan 1947- *WhoE 93, WhoEmL 93*
Kousser, Joseph Morgan 1943- *WhoAm 92*
Koussevitsky, Sergey 1874-1951 *OxDcOp*
Koussevitzky, Serge (Alexandrovich) 1874-1951 *Baker 92*
Koutecky, Jaroslav 1922- *WhoWor 93*
Koutitas, Christopher 1947- *WhoScE 91-3*
Koutras, Demetrios A. 1930- *WhoWor 93*
Koutras, Phoebus 1932- *WhoAm 92*
Koutrelakos, William *BioIn 17*
Koutroulis, Aris George 1938- *WhoE 93*
Kouts, Herbert John Cecil 1919- *WhoAm 92*
Koutselinis, Antonios 1935- *WhoWor 93*
Koutsika-Sotiriou, Metaxia 1946- *WhoWor 93*
Koutsis, James 1949- *St&PR 93*
Koutsky, Dean Roger 1935- *WhoAm 92*
Koutsogeorgas, Agamemnon d1991 *BioIn 17*
Koutzen, Boris 1901-1966 *Baker 92*
Kouvalainen, Kauko Einari 1930- *WhoScE 91-4*
Kouvel, James Spyros 1926- *WhoAm 92*
Kouvelas, Elias D. 1938- *WhoScE 91-3*
Kouvelos, K. *WhoScE 91-3*
Kouw, Willy Alexander 1932- *WhoSSW 93*
Kouwenhoven, Jan Karel 1935- *WhoScE 91-3*
Kouwenhoven, John Atlee 1909-1990 *BioIn 17*
Kouymjian, Dickran 1934- *WhoAm 92*
Kouyoumjian, Charles H. 1940- *WhoAm 92, WhoE 93, WhoWor 93*
Kouzel, Alfred d1990 *BioIn 17*
Kouzmanoff, Alexander 1915- *WhoAm 92*
Kouzminov, Vladimir Alekseevitch 1944- *WhoUN 92*
Kovac, Frederick James 1930- *St&PR 93, WhoAm 92*
Kovac, Gary W. 1956- *St&PR 93*
Kovac, John Nicholas 1950- *WhoEmL 93*
Kovacevic, Cynthia S. *Law&B 92*
Kovacevic, Kresimir 1913- *Baker 92*
Kovacevic, Petko 1937- *WhoScE 91-4*
Kovacevich, Christopher 1928- *WhoAm 92*
Kovacevich, Richard M. *WhoAm 92*
Kovach, Andrew Louis 1948- *WhoE 93, WhoEmL 93, WhoWor 93*
Kovach, Arisztid 1920- *WhoScE 91-4*
Kovach, Barbara Ellen 1941- *WhoAm 92, WhoAmW 93, WhoE 93*
Kovach, Barbara Jeanne *Law&B 92*
Kovach, Bernard C. 1934-1990 *BioIn 17*
Kovach, Bill 1932- *WhoAm 92*
Kovach, Deanna Kay 1946- *St&PR 93*
Kovach, Dennis J. *Law&B 92*
Kovach, Edward T. 1941- *St&PR 93*
Kovach, Eugene George 1922- *WhoAm 92*
Kovach, James P. 1936- *St&PR 93*

Kovach, John Richard 1943- *St&PR 93*
Kovach, John Stephen 1936- *WhoAm 92*
Kovach, Stephen R. 1949- *St&PR 93*
Kovach, Thomas Allen 1949- *WhoSSW 93*
Kovachev, Bogomil Zhivkov 1932- *WhoScE 91-4*
Kovachev, Metodi *WhoScE 91-4*
Kovachevich, Elizabeth Anne 1936- *WhoAmW 93, WhoSSW 93*
Kovacic, William Evan 1952- *WhoEmL 93, WhoWor 93*
Kovacik, Neal Stephen 1952- *WhoWor 93*
Kovack, Nancy *BioIn 17*
Kovack, Roger F. 1948- *St&PR 93*
Kovacs, Adam 1940- *WhoScE 91-4*
Kovacs, Andras 1925- *DrEEuF*
Kovacs, B. *WhoScE 91-4*
Kovacs, Beatrice 1945- *WhoSSW 93*
Kovacs, Denes 1930- *WhoWor 93*
Kovacs, Diane Kaye 1962- *WhoAmW 93*
Kovacs, Elizabeth Ann 1944- *WhoAm 92*
Kovacs, Ernie 1919-1962 *QDrFCA 92 [port]*
Kovacs, Ferenc 1921- *WhoScE 91-4*
Kovacs, Ferenc 1938- *WhoScE 91-4*
Kovacs, Gabor 1938- *WhoUN 92*
Kovacs, Gabor 1939- *WhoWor 93*
Kovacs, Gabor 1940- *WhoScE 91-4*
Kovacs, George 1926- *St&PR 93*
Kovacs, Imre *WhoScE 91-4*
Kovacs, Kalman 1920- *WhoScE 91-4*
Kovacs, Katherine Singer 1946-1989 *BioIn 17*
Kovacs, Laszlo 1933- *WhoAm 92*
Kovacs, Laszlo 1934- *WhoScE 91-4*
Kovacs, Louis Edward 1915- *St&PR 93*
Kovacs, Margit 1930- *WhoScE 91-4*
Kovacs, Marian Kuhn 1932- *WhoAmW 93*
Kovacs, Mate 1941- *WhoUN 92*
Kovacs, Robert 1930- *WhoScE 91-4*
Kovacs, Steven *MiSFD 9*
Kovacs, Tibor F. 1929- *WhoScE 91-4*
Kovacs, William F. 1955- *St&PR 93*
Kovacs, William Lawrence 1947- *WhoEmL 93*
Kovago, Katalin *BioIn 17*
Koval, Bernard C. 1935- *St&PR 93*
Koval, Charles Francis 1938- *WhoAm 92*
Koval, Don O. 1942- *WhoAm 92*
Koval, George Carl 1936- *WhoIns 93*
Koval, Jennifer Amy 1965- *WhoE 93*
Koval, Marian (Viktorovich) 1907-1971 *Baker 92*
Kovalak, Drew *Law&B 92*
Kovalchuk, Mikhail *ScF&FL 92*
Kovalcik, Kenneth John 1946- *WhoAm 92, WhoE 93*
Kovalefsky, Edward W. 1953- *St&PR 93*
Kovaleski, John David 1962- *WhoEmL 93*
Kovalev, Pavel 1890-1951 *Baker 92*
Kovalevich, Donald 1950- *WhoAm 92*
Kovalevsky, Maxim Alexejevich 1938- *WhoWor 93*
Kovalevsky, Vladimir Antonovich 1927- *WhoWor 93*
Kovalik, Oliver Peter 1947- *WhoWor 93*
Kovalsky, George Brian 1950- *WhoE 93*
Kovaly, John Joseph 1928- *WhoAm 92*
Kovar, Dan Rada 1934- *WhoSSW 93*
Kovar, Jiui-George 1930- *WhoScE 91-4*
Kovar, Karl-Artur 1938- *WhoScE 91-3*
Kovar, Milo 1926- *WhoWrEP 92*
Kovar, Pavel 1942- *WhoScE 91-4*
Kovari, Viktor 1936- *WhoScE 91-4*
Kovaricek, Frantisek 1924- *Baker 92*
Kovarik, Daniel Charles 1958- *WhoE 93*
Kovarik, Eugene J. 1931- *St&PR 93*
Kovarovic, Karel 1862-1920 *Baker 92, OxDcOp*
Kovaru, Frantisek 1943- *WhoScE 91-4*
Kovary, Laura Yvette 1957- *WhoWor 93*
Kovatch, Denise Beebe 1952- *WhoEmL 93*
Kovatch, Jak Gene 1929- *WhoAm 92*
Kovatcheva, Stefka Evstatieva 1947- *WhoAm 92*
Kovats, Andras 1924- *WhoScE 91-4*
Koved, Lance J. 1949- *St&PR 93*
Kovel, Lee Ralph 1951- *WhoAm 92*
Kovel, Ralph M. *WhoAm 92, WhoWrEP 92*
Kovel, Ronald J. 1957- *St&PR 93*
Kovel, Terry Horvitz 1928- *WhoAm 92, WhoWrEP 92*
Koveleski, Kathryn Delane 1925- *WhoAmW 93*
Kovell, Alfred J. *Law&B 92*
Koven, Andrew Ian *Law&B 92*
Koven, Howard Richard 1921- *WhoAm 92*
Koven, Kathryn Marie Lewis 1963- *WhoSSW 93*
Koven, Reginald de *Baker 92*
Kovens, Irvin d1989 *BioIn 17*
Kovens, Michael Lee 1942- *St&PR 93*
Kovenya, Victor Mikhailovitch 1940- *WhoWor 93*
Kover, George 1931- *WhoScE 91-4*
Koves, Arpad 1956- *WhoScE 91-4*
Kovi, Ati 1960- *WhoEmL 93*
Kovic, Ron *BioIn 17*
Kovic, Ron 1946- *ConAu 138, ConHero 2 [port]*
Kovich, Ann E. 1952- *St&PR 93*
Kovich, Robert 1950-1991 *BioIn 17*
Kovin, Joel Bruce 1944- *St&PR 93*
Kovitz, Alan Marc 1957- *WhoSSW 93*
Kovner, Joel Wyatt 1941- *St&PR 93*
Kovner, Matthew Robert 1955- *WhoEmL 93*
Kovner, Richard Stephen 1936- *WhoE 93*
Kovrig, Bennett 1940- *WhoAm 92*
Kovtynovich, Dan 1952- *WhoWor 93*
Kowacic, Joseph Peter 1919- *WhoWrEP 92*
Kowack, Paul 1945- *St&PR 93*
Kowal, Charles Thomas 1940- *WhoAm 92*
Kowal, David Martin 1950- *WhoEmL 93, WhoSSW 93*
Kowal, George Michael 1952- *WhoEmL 93*
Kowal, Karen L. *Law&B 92*
Kowal, Peter M. 1957- *St&PR 93*
Kowal, Ruth Elizabeth 1948- *WhoAmW 93*
Kowal, Zbigniew 1928- *WhoScE 91-4*
Kowalak, Wladyslaw 1933- *WhoWor 93*
Kowalchik, Walter *Law&B 92*
Kowalchik, Walter 1937- *St&PR 93*
Kowalczewski, Doreen Mary Thurlow 1926- *WhoAmW 93*
Kowalczyk, David Theodore 1952- *WhoWrEP 92*
Kowalczyk, Jeanne Stuart 1942- *WhoAmW 93*
Kowalczyk, Jerzy Stephen John 1923- *WhoScE 91-4*
Kowalczyk, John T. *Law&B 92*
Kowalczyk, Maciej Stanislaw 1956- *WhoWor 93*
Kowalczyk, Mary Beth *Law&B 92*
Kowalczyk, Richard Leon 1935- *WhoAm 92*
Kowalewicz, Andrzej 1932- *WhoScE 91-4*
Kowalewski, Jan Kazimierz 1921- *WhoScE 91-4, WhoWor 93*
Kowalewski, Jozef 1947- *WhoScE 91-4*
Kowalewski, Keith 1950- *St&PR 93*
Kowalewski, Rich *Law&B 92*
Kowalewski, Susan Jane 1959- *WhoAmW 93*
Kowalik, Piotr Jan 1939- *WhoScE 91-4*
Kowaliw, Steven Joseph 1952- *St&PR 93*
Kowalke, Kim H. 1948- *WhoAm 92*
Kowalkowski, Martha Jean 1939- *St&PR 93*
Kowallik, Wolfgang 1931- *WhoScE 91-3*
Kowalska, Teresa 1946- *WhoScE 91-4*
Kowalski, Bernard L. 1929- *MiSFD 9*
Kowalski, Christine Marie 1949- *WhoE 93*
Kowalski, Henri 1841-1916 *Baker 92*
Kowalski, James Andrew 1938- *St&PR 93*
Kowalski, Janie Mae 1951- *WhoEmL 93*
Kowalski, John 1928- *WhoWrEP 92*
Kowalski, Julius 1912- *Baker 92*
Kowalski, Kathleen Madland 1944- *WhoE 93*
Kowalski, Kazimierz 1925- *WhoScE 91-4*
Kowalski, Kenneth Lawrence 1932- *WhoAm 92*
Kowalski, Lynn Mary 1955- *WhoE 93*
Kowalski, Max 1882-1956 *Baker 92*
Kowalski, Michael Francis 1961- *WhoE 93*
Kowalski, Michael L. 1953- *St&PR 93*
Kowalski, Neal Anthony 1945- *WhoWor 93*
Kowalski, Robert Anthony *WhoScE 91-1*
Kowalski, Robin Marie 1964- *WhoAmW 93, WhoSSW 93*
Kowalski, Stephen Wesley 1931- *WhoAm 92*
Kowalski, Suzanne Gross *Law&B 92*
Kowalski, Wayne W. 1948- *St&PR 93*
Kowalski, Witold Cezariusz 1919- *WhoScE 91-4*
Kowalski, Zbigniew 1927- *WhoScE 91-4*
Kowalsky, Adrian Dion 1947- *WhoEmL 93*
Kowaluk, Ralph S. 1941- *St&PR 93*
Kowalyshyn, Theodore Jacob 1935- *WhoE 93*
Kowarski, Allen Avinoam 1927- *WhoAm 92*
Kowarski, Felicjan Szczesny 1890-1948 *PolBiDi*
Kowbel, Lawrence James 1937- *WhoAm 92*
Kowel, Stephen Thomas 1942- *WhoAm 92, WhoSSW 93*
Kowert, Gregory Clarence 1946- *St&PR 93*
Kowieski, Thomas Edward 1949- *St&PR 93*
Kowing, Klaus Norbert 1930- *WhoScE 91-3*
Kowit, Steve Mark 1938- *WhoWrEP 92*
Kowlessar, Muriel 1926- *WhoAmW 93*
Kownacki, Andrzej 1938- *WhoScE 91-4*
Kowzan, Tadeusz 1922- *WhoWor 93*
Kox, Hans 1930- *Baker 92*
Koya, B.V. Abdulla 1914- *WhoAsAP 91*
Koyama, Hachiro 1922- *WhoAm 92*
Koyama, Hiromi Maria 1937- *WhoWor 93*
Koyama, Hitoshi 1931- *WhoWor 93*
Koyama, Ippei 1914- *WhoAsAP 91*
Koyama, Kiyoshige 1914- *Baker 92*
Koyama, Shin-ya 1962- *WhoWor 93*
Koyama, Yasushi 1941- *WhoWor 93*
Koyano, Eiichi 1923- *WhoWor 93*
Koyano, Keiichirou 1953- *WhoEmL 93*
Koza, Christian Klaus 1963- *WhoWor 93*
Koza, Joan Lorraine 1941- *WhoAmW 93*
Kozak, Alfred W. *Law&B 92*
Kozak, Christa H. 1961- *WhoAmW 93*
Kozak, Ellen M. 1944- *ScF&FL 92, WhoWrEP 92*
Kozak, Fedor Vasilievich 1938- *WhoUN 92*
Kozak, Harley Jane *BioIn 17*
Kozak, Imre 1930- *WhoScE 91-4*
Kozak, Josef 1942- *WhoScE 91-4*
Kozak, Marlene Galante 1952- *WhoAmW 93*
Kozak, Michael Joseph 1952- *WhoE 93*
Kozakis, Ernest 1927- *St&PR 93*
Kozakowski, Jennifer Lyn 1960- *WhoAmW 93*
Kozameh, Carlos Nicholas 1956- *WhoWor 93*
Kozar, Bradley Kenneth 1958- *WhoEmL 93*
Kozar, Ferenc 1943- *WhoScE 91-4*
Kozar, William C. 1941- *St&PR 93*
Kozarich, John W. *St&PR 93*
Kozarsky, Bruce Lyle 1957- *WhoE 93*
Kozarzewski, Bohdan 1937- *WhoScE 91-4*
Kozbelt, Laurie 1963- *WhoWrEP 92*
Kozberg, Donna Walters 1952- *WhoAmW 93, WhoE 93, WhoEmL 93, WhoWor 93*
Kozberg, Steven Freed 1953- *WhoEmL 93*
Kozel, Frank Joseph, Jr. 1945- *St&PR 93*
Kozel, John A. 1954- *St&PR 93*
Kozel, Katherine Jean 1957- *WhoAmW 93*
Kozel, Robert W. 1921- *St&PR 93*
Kozel, Thomas Randall 1946- *WhoAm 92*
Kozeliski, Anthony 1912- *St&PR 93*
Kozeliski, Frank Anthony 1944- *St&PR 93*
Kozeluch, Johann Antonin 1738-1814 *Baker 92*
Kozeluch, Leopold (Jan Antonin) 1747-1818 *Baker 92*
Kozeluh, Johann Antonin 1738-1814 *Baker 92*
Kozeluh, Leopold (Jan Antonin) 1747-1818 *Baker 92*
Kozer, Jose 1940- *WhoWrEP 92*
Kozer, Stephen Louis 1951- *WhoEmL 93*
Kozera, A. *WhoScE 91-4*
Kozera, Ryszard *WhoScE 91-4*
Kozera, Wienczyslawa 1927- *WhoScE 91-4*
Kozerski, Bohdan 1932- *WhoScE 91-4*
Kozhedub, Ivan N. 1920-1991 *BioIn 17*
Kozhev Angel, Petrov 1933- *WhoWor 93*
Kozhevnikova, Irina N. 1959- *WhoWor 93*
Kozhuharov, Christophor 1946- *WhoEmL 93*
Koziakin, Vladimir *ScF&FL 92*
Koziar, Stephen F., Jr. *Law&B 92*
Koziarski, Andrzej Kazimierz 1932- *WhoScE 91-4*
Kozicki, Stephen Michael 1955- *WhoWor 93*
Kozicki, Zvi Elazar 1950- *St&PR 93*
Koziej, Eugeniusz 1926- *WhoScE 91-4*
Kozik, James S. *Law&B 92*
Kozik, Patricia Jane 1931- *WhoAmW 93*
Kozik, Renee Dallam 1957- *WhoAmW 93*
Kozikowski, Janusz *BioIn 17*
Kozikowski, Mitchell 1935- *St&PR 93, WhoAm 92*
Kozikowski, Nancy *BioIn 17*
Kozikowski, Stanley John *WhoE 93*
Kozina, Irene *Law&B 92*
Kozina, Marjan 1907-1966 *Baker 92*
Kozincev, Grigorij 1905-1973 *DrEEuF*
Kozinski, Alex 1950- *WhoAm 92*
Kozinski, Andrzej Wladyslaw 1925- *WhoAm 92*
Kozintsev, Grigori 1905-1973 *MiSFD 9N*
Koziorowska, Jadwiga Hanna 1921- *WhoScE 91-4*
Koziorowski, Antoni Edward 1924- *WhoScE 91-4*
Kozitka, Richard Eugene 1934- *St&PR 93, WhoAm 92*
Koziy, Bohdan *BioIn 17*
Kozlak, Michael Joseph 1953- *St&PR 93*
Kozloff, Lloyd M. 1923- *WhoAm 92*
Kozlov, Leonid 1947- *WhoAm 92*
Kozlov, Vladimir Vassilievich 1936- *WhoUN 92*
Kozlova, Valentina 1957- *WhoAm 92*
Kozlovsky, Ivan 1900- *OxDcOp*
Kozlovsky, Ivan (Semyonovich) 1900- *Baker 92*
Kozlow, Jeffrey Scott *Law&B 92*
Kozlowiecki, Henryk 1935- *WhoScE 91-4*
Kozlowska, Czeslawa Anna 1921- *WhoScE 91-4*
Kozlowski, Alex J. 1949- *St&PR 93*
Kozlowski, Andrzej R. 1938- *WhoScE 91-4*
Kozlowski, Candid 1836-1922 *PolBiDi*
Kozlowski, Donna Maureen 1946- *WhoSSW 93*
Kozlowski, Edmund Wojciech 1932- *WhoScE 91-4*
Kozlowski, Edward W. 1925- *St&PR 93*
Kozlowski, Ellen Rhoda 1953- *WhoEmL 93*
Kozlowski, Grzegorz 1942- *WhoScE 91-4*
Kozlowski, Jan Andrzej 1928- *WhoScE 91-4*
Kozlowski, Jan Przemyslaw 1926- *WhoScE 91-4*
Kozlowski, John R. 1939- *St&PR 93*
Kozlowski, Jozef Antonovitch 1757-1831 *PolBiDi*
Kozlowski, Julie *Law&B 92*
Kozlowski, Kazimierz 1928- *WhoScE 91-4*
Kozlowski, Krzysztof *BioIn 17*
Kozlowski, L. Dennis 1946- *WhoAm 92, WhoE 93*
Kozlowski, Linda *BioIn 17*
Kozlowski, Paul G. 1938- *St&PR 93*
Kozlowski, Raymond F., Jr. *Law&B 92*
Kozlowski, Richard Walter 1931- *St&PR 93*
Kozlowski, Ronald Stephan 1937- *WhoAm 92*
Kozlowski, Ryszard *WhoScE 91-4*
Kozlowski, Susan 1952- *St&PR 93*
Kozlowski, Susan M. *Law&B 92*
Kozlowski, Tadeusz 1926- *St&PR 93*
Kozlowski, Theodore Thomas 1917- *WhoAm 92*
Kozlowski, Thomas Joseph, Jr. 1950- *WhoAm 92*
Kozlowski, Walter George 1934- *St&PR 93*
Kozma, Adam 1928- *WhoAm 92*
Kozma, Andras 1937- *WhoScE 91-4*
Kozma, M.J. 1929- *St&PR 93*
Kozma, Matei 1929- *Baker 92*
Kozma, Pal 1920- *WhoScE 91-4*
Kozmian, Stanislaw Egbert 1811-1885 *PolBiDi*
Kozminske, Ronald L. *Law&B 92*
Kozminski, Czeslaw 1932- *WhoScE 91-4*
Kozminski, Stefan Stanislaw 1920- *WhoWor 93*
Kozodoy, Neal 1942- *WhoAm 92*
Kozofsky, Linda J. 1951- *St&PR 93*
Kozol, George B. *Law&B 92, St&PR 93*
Kozol, Jonathan *BioIn 17*
Kozol, Jonathan 1936- *News 92 [port], WhoAm 92, WhoWrEP 92*
Kozub, Michael Victor 1943- *St&PR 93*
Kozubowski, Tadeusz 1921- *WhoScE 91-4*
Kozyreff, Vladimir Nikolaevitch 1943- *WhoWor 93*
Kozyrev, A.V. *BioIn 17*
Kozyrev, Andrei *WhoWor 93*
Kozyrev, Andrei V. 1951- *CurBio 92 [port]*
Kozyrev, Andrei Vladimirovich *BioIn 17*
Kozyris, Phaedon John 1932- *WhoAm 92*
Kpakpo, Ayite Jean-Claude 1942- *WhoUN 92*
K. Pathmanaban, Dato' 1937- *WhoAsAP 91*
Kpodo-Tay, Daniel Sydney 1934- *WhoWor 93*
Kra, Ethan Emanuel 1948- *WhoE 93, WhoWor 93*
Kra, Irwin 1937- *WhoAm 92*
Kra, Pauline Skornicki 1934- *WhoAmW 93, WhoE 93, WhoWor 93*
Kraabel, Stephen Edward 1941- *St&PR 93*
Kraai, A.R. 1929- *WhoScE 91-3*
Kraak, Henriette Louise 1950- *WhoScE 91-3*
Kraak, Myron L. 1933- *St&PR 93*
Kraar, Louis 1934- *WhoE 93*
Kraatz, David Charles 1954- *WhoE 93*
Krabbe, Jacob Jan 1928- *WhoScE 91-3*
Krabbe, Katrin *BioIn 17*
Krabbenhoft, Kenneth Lester 1923- *WhoAm 92*
Kraber, Robert L. 1940- *St&PR 93*
Krach, Mitchell Peter 1924- *WhoAm 92, WhoE 93*
Kracht, Carol L. *Law&B 92*
Kracht, Uwe 1941- *WhoUN 92*
Kracht, William Glen 1962- *WhoWor 93*
Kracke, Robert Russell 1938- *WhoSSW 93*
Kracke, Rolf 1932- *WhoScE 91-3*
Krackow, Kenneth Alan 1944- *WhoE 93*
Krader, Barbara 1922- *Baker 92*
Kradjel, Richard J. *Law&B 92*

Kraegel, Frederick G. 1948- St&PR 93
Kraehe, Enno Edward 1921- WhoAm 92, WhoWor 93
Kraehenbuhl, Jean-Pierre 1941- WhoScE 91-4
Kraeling, Robert Russell 1942- WhoSSW 93
Kraemer, Clarice T. d1990 BioIn 17
Kraemer, David R. 1941- St&PR 93
Kraemer, Friedrich Wilhelm 1907-1990 BioIn 17
Kraemer, Honey 1921- WhoAmW 93
Kraemer, J.G. 1942- St&PR 93
Kraemer, James Paul 1964- WhoE 93
Kraemer, Johannes 1941- WhoScE 91-3
Kraemer, Kenneth Leo 1936- WhoAm 92
Kraemer, Lillian Elizabeth 1940- WhoAm 92, WhoAmW 93
Kraemer, Philipp 1931- WhoE 93, WhoWor 93
Kraemer, Richard A. St&PR 93, WhoAm 92
Kraemer, Sandy Frederick 1937- WhoAm 92, WhoWor 93
Kraenzle, Anton I. 1931- WhoScE 91-3
Kraetzer, Mary C. 1943- WhoAmW 93
Kraeusslich, Horst Erich 1926- WhoWor 93
Kraeutler, Jacqueline M. Law&B 92
Krafft, Bertrand 1940- WhoScE 91-2
Krafft, Geoffrey Arthur 1958- WhoSSW 93
Krafft, Helen AmWomPl
Krafft, Marie Elizabeth 1956- WhoAmW 93
Krafft, Remco 1940- WhoUN 92
Kraft, Alan Myron 1925- WhoAm 92
Kraft, Anton 1749-1820 Baker 92
Kraft, Arthur 1944- WhoAm 92
Kraft, Burnell D. 1931- St&PR 93, WhoAm 92
Kraft, C. William, Jr. 1903- WhoAm 92
Kraft, Cari 1963- WhoAmW 93
Kraft, Carl David Law&B 92
Kraft, David Anthony 1952- ScF&FL 92
Kraft, David Christian 1937- WhoAm 92
Kraft, David Marvin, Jr. 1937- WhoWrEP 92
Kraft, Debra J. Law&B 92
Kraft, Donald B. 1927- St&PR 93
Kraft, Donald Bowman 1927- WhoAm 92
Kraft, Donna M. Law&B 92
Kraft, Elaine Joy 1951- WhoAmW 93
Kraft, Elisabeth Allen 1937- WhoAmW 93
Kraft, Elizabeth 1957- WhoAmW 93
Kraft, Friedrich Anton 1807-1874 See Kraft, Nikolaus 1778-1853 Baker 92
Kraft, Gary D. 1954- St&PR 93
Kraft, George Howard 1936- WhoAm 92
Kraft, Gerald 1935- WhoAm 92
Kraft, Gerald G. St&PR 93
Kraft, Harry 1947- St&PR 93
Kraft, Herbert Arnold 1923- St&PR 93
Kraft, Horst W. 1929- WhoScE 91-3
Kraft, Irma AmWomPl
Kraft, James Allen Law&B 92
Kraft, John C. WhoAm 92
Kraft, John F. 1941- St&PR 93
Kraft, Joseph 1924-1986 JrnUS
Kraft, Joseph M. Law&B 92
Kraft, Julius B. Law&B 92
Kraft, Kathleen Coleman WhoAmW 93
Kraft, Kenneth Houston, Jr. 1934- WhoWor 93
Kraft, Klaus Herbert 1934- St&PR 93
Kraft, Leo (Abraham) 1922- Baker 92, WhoAm 92
Kraft, Marcijane Law&B 92
Kraft, Mary Law&B 92
Kraft, Nikolaus 1778-1853 Baker 92
Kraft, Richard A. BioIn 17
Kraft, Robert Alan 1934- WhoAm 92
Kraft, Robert G., Jr. 1950- St&PR 93
Kraft, Steven Richard Law&B 92
Kraft, Sumner Charles 1928- WhoAm 92
Kraft, Volker 1941- WhoScE 91-3
Kraft, Walter 1905-1977 Baker 92
Kraft, Walter H. 1938- St&PR 93
Kraft, Wilfried 1937- WhoScE 91-3
Kraft, William 1923- Baker 92
Kraft, William Frederick 1938- WhoE 93
Kraft, Wolfgang S. 1939- St&PR 93
Krafte, Jill H. Law&B 92
Krafthefer, Kerry M. 1941- St&PR 93
Kraft-Kitaj, Dana Leslie 1964- WhoAm 92
Kraftman, Michael Benjamin 1957- WhoWor 93
Kraftson, Raymond H. 1940- St&PR 93, WhoAm 92, WhoE 93
Kraftwerk ConMus 9 [port]
Krag, Donald Richards 1927- WhoAm 92
Krag, Olga 1937- WhoAmW 93, WhoWor 93
Krage, Patricia Ann Sheridan 1952- WhoEmL 93
Kragen, Jules Mark 1954- WhoEmL 93
Krages, Bert P., II Law&B 92
Kraggerud, Egil 1939- WhoWor 93
Kragh-Jacobsen, Soren 1947- MiSFD 9
Kragler, Robert 1943- WhoWor 93
Krah, John Guest Neale 1953- WhoE 93
Krahelski, Michael A. Law&B 92
Krahl, Enzo 1924- WhoAm 92
Krahn, Agnes 1925- St&PR 93
Krahulec, James Eugene Law&B 92
Kraig, Thomas Lee, Jr. Law&B 92
Kraijenhoff, Gualtherus 1922- WhoWor 93
Krailing, Tessa 1935- ScF&FL 92
Kraines, Maurice H. 1920- St&PR 93
Krainev, Vladimir (Vsevolodovich) 1944- Baker 92
Krainik, Ardis BioIn 17
Krainik, Ardis 1929- WhoAm 92, WhoAmW 93
Krainin, Julian 1941- MiSFD 9
Krainin, Julian Arthur 1941- WhoAm 92
Krainski, Joanna Donna 1947- WhoEmL 93
Kraisinger, Jerome J. Law&B 92
Kraiss, Glenn S. 1933- WhoAm 92
Kraiss, Glenn Stephen 1933- St&PR 93
Kraiza, Edward Anthony 1947- St&PR 93
Krajca, Kenneth Edward 1944- WhoSSW 93
Krajci, Joseph R., Jr. Law&B 92
Krajcsik, George Charles 1938- WhoWor 93
Krajec, Richard A. 1929- St&PR 93
Krajewski, Adriano 1947- WhoScE 91-3
Krajewski, Joel Alan 1965- WhoE 93
Krajewski, Ryszard Norbert 1955- WhoE 93
Krajicek, Mark Andrew Law&B 92
Krajka, Andrzej Antoni 1958- WhoWor 93
Krakau, C.E.T. 1921- WhoScE 91-4
Krakauer, Albert Alexander 1937- St&PR 93, WhoAm 92
Krakauer, Barbara 1931- WhoE 93
Krakauer, John L. 1941- St&PR 93
Krakauer, Lawrence Jay 1942- St&PR 93
Krakauer, Randall Sheldon 1949- WhoEmL 93
Krakauer, Rosalind J. Law&B 92
Krakauer, Sidney d1989 BioIn 17
Krakauer, Thomas Henry 1942- WhoAm 92, WhoSSW 93
Krakoff, Irwin Harold 1923- WhoAm 92
Krakoff, Robert L. 1935- St&PR 93
Krakoff, Robert Leonard 1935- WhoAm 92, WhoE 93
Krakora-Looby, Janice Marie 1951- WhoAmW 93, WhoEmL 93
Krakow, Amy Ginzig 1950- WhoAmW 93, WhoE 93
Krakow, Barbara Levy 1936- WhoAm 92
Krakow, Dennis W. Law&B 92
Krakower, Bernard Hyman 1935- WhoWor 93
Krakower, Ira J. Law&B 92
Krakowiak, Edward Thomas 1928- St&PR 93
Krakowiak, Sacha M. 1937- WhoScE 91-2
Krakowka, Pawel 1918- WhoScE 91-4
Krakowski, Frank M. 1946- St&PR 93
Krakowski, Maciej Romuald 1924- WhoScE 91-4
Krakowski, Mary Frances Law&B 92
Krakowski, Richard John 1946- WhoEmL 93
Krakusin, Roger K. Law&B 92
Kral, Frank 1940- WhoAm 92
Kral, Nancy Bolin 1958- WhoAmW 93
Kral, Pavel 1944- WhoUN 92
Kral, Vaclav 1924- WhoScE 91-4
Kralicek, Jaroslav 1925- WhoScE 91-4
Kralick, Charles 1953- St&PR 93
Kralik, Juraj 1926- WhoUN 92
Kralik, Miroslav WhoScE 91-4
Kralj, Alojz 1937- WhoScE 91-4
Kralj, Milan 1921- WhoScE 91-4
Kraljevic, Kresimir WhoScE 91-4
Kraljevic, Svetozar BioIn 17
Krall, Cathy Ann 1954- WhoEmL 93
Krall, George F. 1936- St&PR 93
Krall, John Morton 1938- WhoE 93
Krall, Patricia Mary 1953- WhoEmL 93
Krallinger, Joseph Charles 1931- WhoAm 92
Kralova, Marie 1933- WhoScE 91-4
Kralovec, Josef 1940- WhoScE 91-4
Kram, Guenther Reinhard 1957- WhoEmL 93
Kram, Michael Arnold 1950- WhoSSW 93
Kram, Shirley Wohl 1922- WhoAm 92, WhoE 93
Kraman, Cynthia 1950- WhoWrEP 92
Kramaric, Peter S. Law&B 92
Kramarsky, Lola Popper d1991 BioIn 17
Kramarsky, Wynn 1926- BioIn 17
Krambeck, Robert Harold 1943- WhoAm 92
Kramer BioIn 17
Kramer, A(rthur) Walter 1890-1969 Baker 92
Kramer, Aaron 1921- WhoAm 92, WhoWrEP 92
Kramer, Alan Sharfsin 1934- WhoAm 92
Kramer, Albert D. Law&B 92
Kramer, Albert Hartman 1955- St&PR 93
Kramer, Alex-Ann 1957- WhoEmL 93
Kramer, Allan Franklin, II 1950- WhoE 93, WhoEmL 93
Kramer, Amanda BioIn 17
Kramer, Andrea R. Law&B 92
Kramer, Andrew Michael 1944- WhoAm 92
Kramer, Anne Pearce 1926- WhoAmW 93, WhoWor 93
Kramer, Barnett Sheldon 1948- WhoE 93
Kramer, Barry Alan 1948- WhoEmL 93
Kramer, Barry Allen 1949- WhoEmL 93
Kramer, Bernard 1922- WhoAm 92
Kramer, Bernhard 1942- WhoScE 91-3
Kramer, Brian John Law&B 92
Kramer, Burton 1932- WhoAm 92
Kramer, Carl U. 1928- WhoScE 91-4
Kramer, Carol Gertrude 1939- WhoAmW 93
Kramer, Carol L. 1928- St&PR 93
Kramer, Cecile E. 1927- WhoAm 92
Kramer, Charlene Kahlor 1951- St&PR 93
Kramer, Charles Henry 1922- WhoAm 92
Kramer, Charles R. St&PR 93
Kramer, Charles William 1942- St&PR 93
Kramer, Cheryl J. Law&B 92
Kramer, Corrinnie A. 1937- St&PR 93
Kramer, Dale 1936- ScF&FL 92
Kramer, Dale P. St&PR 93
Kramer, Dale Vernon 1936- WhoAm 92
Kramer, Dana ScF&FL 92
Kramer, Deirdre Anne 1954- WhoAmW 93
Kramer, Diana 1928- WhoAm 92, WhoAmW 93
Kramer, Diana R. 1949- WhoAmW 93, WhoE 93
Kramer, Donald 1937- St&PR 93, WhoAm 92
Kramer, Donald A. 1942- St&PR 93
Kramer, Donald W. 1938- WhoAm 92
Kramer, Donovan Mershon, Sr. 1925- St&PR 93
Kramer, Dorothy d1991 BioIn 17
Kramer, Dorothy Gloria 1925- WhoAmW 93
Kramer, Douglas 1950- ConAu 138
Kramer, Douglas C. 1942- St&PR 93
Kramer, Earl 1933- St&PR 93, WhoAm 92
Kramer, Edward George 1950- WhoEmL 93
Kramer, Edward John 1939- WhoAm 92
Kramer, Eleanor 1939- WhoWor 93
Kramer, Elizabeth Maria 1954- WhoAmW 93
Kramer, Eugene L. 1939- WhoAm 92
Kramer, Ferdinand 1901- WhoAm 92
Kramer, Frank Raymond 1908- WhoAm 92
Kramer, Franklin 1923- WhoE 93
Kramer, Fred Russell 1942- WhoAm 92
Kramer, G. Alan Law&B 92
Kramer, George P. 1927- WhoAm 92
Kramer, George Rudolph 1958- WhoEmL 93
Kramer, Gerhardt Theodore 1909- WhoAm 92
Kramer, Gert-Jan 1942- WhoWor 93
Kramer, Gert Jan 1961- WhoWor 93
Kramer, Harry 1914- St&PR 93
Kramer, Harry 1939- WhoE 93
Kramer, Harry John 1925- WhoWrEP 92
Kramer, Harvey Merrill 1952- WhoE 93
Kramer, Helmut WhoScE 91-4
Kramer, Henry WhoAm 92
Kramer, Henry Herman 1930- St&PR 93
Kramer, Herbert J. 1939- WhoScE 91-3
Kramer, Hilton BioIn 17
Kramer, Horst Emil Adolf 1936- WhoWor 93
Kramer, Irvin Raymond 1912- WhoAm 92
Kramer, Irving St&PR 93
Kramer, Ivan Law&B 92
Kramer, James M. Law&B 92
Kramer, James Matthew 1942- St&PR 93
Kramer, James Randall Law&B 92
Kramer, Jane 1938- WhoAm 92, WhoWrEP 92
Kramer, Jerome 1948- St&PR 93
Kramer, Jerry MiSFD 9
Kramer, Joan Whitney 1914-1990 BioIn 17
Kramer, Joel 1937- St&PR 93
Kramer, Joel Roy 1948- WhoAm 92
Kramer, John Paul 1928- WhoAm 92
Kramer, John S. 1931- St&PR 93
Kramer, Jonathan 1942- Baker 92
Kramer, Jorg-Dietrich 1938- WhoWor 93
Kramer, Joseph 1924- WhoE 93
Kramer, Karen Sue 1942- WhoAmW 93
Kramer, Kathryn ScF&FL 92
Kramer, Keith 1959- WhoWrEP 92
Kramer, Kenneth Bentley 1942- WhoAm 92
Kramer, Kenneth James Law&B 92
Kramer, Kenneth Robert 1945- St&PR 93
Kramer, Lance 1941- St&PR 93
Kramer, Larry BioIn 17, NewYTBS 92
Kramer, Larry 1935- ConGAN
Kramer, Lawrence Eliot 1946- WhoE 93
Kramer, Leonie Judith 1924- ConAu 39NR
Kramer, Loren 1929- St&PR 93
Kramer, Lynne Adair 1952- WhoAmW 93
Kramer, Marc B. 1944- WhoE 93
Kramer, Marc D. 1961- WhoE 93
Kramer, Mark W. Law&B 92
Kramer, Mary Eleanor AmWomPl
Kramer, Mary Vincent 1957- WhoAmW 93, WhoEmL 93
Kramer, Melinda Gamble 1946- WhoAmW 93
Kramer, Meyer 1919- WhoAm 92
Kramer, Michael Paul 1945- St&PR 93
Kramer, Morton 1914- WhoAm 92
Kramer, Nora 1896?-1984 ScF&FL 92
Kramer, Ole 1940- WhoScE 91-2
Kramer, Paul Allyn Law&B 92
Kramer, Paul Jackson 1904- WhoAm 92
Kramer, Paul L. 1944- St&PR 93
Kramer, Paul R. 1936- WhoE 93
Kramer, Paula Villar 1957- WhoAmW 93
Kramer, Peter David 1948- WhoEmL 93
Kramer, Peter Joseph 1953- St&PR 93
Kramer, Peter Robin 1951- WhoEmL 93
Kramer, Philip 1921- WhoAm 92
Kramer, Philip Earl 1940- WhoWrEP 92
Kramer, Phillip D. 1956- St&PR 93
Kramer, Randall Joseph Law&B 92
Kramer, Reuben Robert 1909- WhoAm 92
Kramer, Richard Elwin 1934- St&PR 93
Kramer, Richard L. 1945- St&PR 93
Kramer, Richard Mario 1950- WhoE 93
Kramer, Richard P. 1942- St&PR 93
Kramer, Robert 1913- WhoAm 92
Kramer, Robert 1939- MiSFD 9
Kramer, Robert G. 1953- St&PR 93
Kramer, Robert Ivan 1933- WhoAm 92
Kramer, Robert Lee Law&B 92
Kramer, Ruth 1925- WhoAmW 93
Kramer, Samuel Noah 1897-1990 BioIn 17
Kramer, Sandra 1943- WhoAmW 93
Kramer, Sherri Marcelle 1954- WhoAmW 93, WhoEmL 93
Kramer, Sidney B. 1915- WhoAm 92
Kramer, Simon 1919- WhoAm 92
Kramer, Stanley 1913- BioIn 17, MiSFD 9
Kramer, Stanley E. 1913- WhoAm 92
Kramer, Steven David 1948- WhoSSW 93
Kramer, Thomas 1944- WhoScE 91-3
Kramer, Thomas E. 1921- St&PR 93
Kramer, Timothy Eugene Law&B 92
Kramer, Wayne 1948- See MC5, The ConMus 9
Kramer, William 1924- St&PR 93
Kramer, William David 1944- WhoAm 92
Kramer, William Edward 1952- WhoE 93
Kramer, William J., Jr. 1940- St&PR 93
Kramer, William Joseph 1939- WhoAm 92
Kramer, Winifred Anita 1946- WhoEmL 93
Kramer-Ganz, Kim Allison 1965- WhoE 93
Kramer-Rolls, Dana ScF&FL 92
Kramish, Arnold 1923- WhoAm 92
Kramish, Marc Eric 1958- WhoSSW 93
Kramm, Deborah Lucille Law&B 92, WhoAmW 93, WhoE 93, WhoWor 93
Kramm, Kenneth Roger 1945- WhoSSW 93
Kramme, Paul Edgar, Jr. 1923- St&PR 93
Kramme, Richard Grover 1933- St&PR 93
Krammer, Josef WhoScE 91-4
Kramnick, Isaac 1938- ConAu 139, WhoAm 92
Kramp, Jeffery B. Law&B 92
Kramp, Mark L. Law&B 92
Kramp, Richard William 1945- WhoAm 92
Kramp, Ronald Arthur 1938- WhoScE 91-2
Kramsztyk, Roman 1885-1942 PolBiDi
Kramvis, Andreas Constantinos 1952- WhoE 93
Kranda, Michael L. 1953- St&PR 93
Krane, Robert A. 1933- St&PR 93
Krane, Robert Alan 1933- WhoAm 92
Krane, Stephen Martin 1927- WhoAm 92
Krane, Steven Charles 1957- WhoEmL 93
Krane, Susan 1954- WhoSSW 93
Kranenburg, Hendrik J. 1955- St&PR 93
Kranepool, Ed 1944- BioIn 17
Kranepool, Harry Anthony 1941- WhoE 93
Kraner, Madeline R. WhoWrEP 92
Kranich, Helmuth, Sr. 1833-1902 Baker 92
Kranich, Margaret Mansley 1925- WhoAmW 93
Kranich, Wilmer LeRoy 1919- WhoAm 92
Kranich & Bach Baker 92
Kranick, Lewis Girard 1914- St&PR 93

Kranig, Carol Ann 1947- *WhoSSW 93*
Kranig, K.J. 1946- *St&PR 93*
Kranitz, Michael L. *Law&B 92*
Kranitz, Theodore Mitchell 1922- *WhoAm 92*
Kranitzky, Mary Lisa 1955- *WhoAmW 93*
Kranjec, Velimir 1930- *WhoScE 91-4*
Kranking, Margaret Graham 1930- *WhoAmW 93, WhoE 93*
Krannich, Beverley Turner *Law&B 92*
Krannich, Beverley Turner 1951- *St&PR 93*
Kranovich, Nancy 1957- *St&PR 93*
Krans, Th.F. 1936- *WhoScE 91-3*
Kransdorf, Ronald Joseph 1935- *St&PR 93*
Kranseler, Arthur Sheldon 1934- *St&PR 93*
Kranser, Leonard Samuel 1932- *St&PR 93*
Krantz, David S. 1949- *WhoE 93*
Krantz, Eugen 1844-1898 *Baker 92*
Krantz, Hazel (Newman) *ConAu 40NR*
Krantz, Jeffry Ostler 1952- *St&PR 93*
Krantz, Jerome 1955- *WhoE 93*
Krantz, Judith *BioIn 17*
Krantz, Judith Tarcher 1928- *WhoAm 92*
Krantz, Kermit Edward 1923- *WhoAm 92, WhoWor 93*
Krantz, Melissa Marianne 1954- *WhoAm 92*
Krantz, Palmer Eric 1950- *WhoAm 92*
Krantz, Robert E. 1946- *St&PR 93*
Krantz, Sanford Burton 1934- *WhoAm 92*
Krantz, Stanley H. *Law&B 92*
Krantz, Stephen Falk 1923- *WhoAm 92*
Krantzman, Irving Emanuel 1916- *WhoAm 92*
Kranyik, Elizabeth Ann 1957- *WhoAmW 93, WhoE 93*
Kranz, Albert Richard 1928- *WhoScE 91-3*
Kranz, Audie M. 1954- *St&PR 93*
Kranz, Eugene F. 1933- *BioIn 17*
Kranz, Harry 1923- *WhoE 93*
Kranz, Jakob F.J. 1922- *WhoScE 91-3*
Kranz, Janet Lee 1947- *WhoEmL 93*
Kranz, Jerry K. *BioIn 17*
Kranz, Jurgen F. 1925- *WhoScE 91-3*
Kranz, Kenneth Louis, Jr. 1946- *WhoWor 93*
Kranz, Norman 1924- *WhoAm 92*
Kranz, Wilbur Joseph 1927- *St&PR 93*
Kranzberg, Kenneth 1937- *St&PR 93*
Kranzberg, Melvin 1917- *WhoAm 92, WhoSSW 93*
Kranzdorf, Jeffrey Paul *Law&B 92*
Kranzdorf, Norman M. 1930- *St&PR 93*
Kranz Johnson, Maureen Ann 1956- *St&PR 93*
Kranzler, John Harold 1960- *WhoSSW 93*
Kranzler, Myles Mitchell 1928- *St&PR 93*
Kranzley, Arthur S. 1927- *St&PR 93*
Kranzow, Ronald R. *Law&B 92*
Kranzow, Ronald Roy 1931- *St&PR 93, WhoAm 92*
Krapek, Karl J. 1948- *St&PR 93*
Krapf, Gerhard 1924- *Baker 92*
Krapf, Ludwig 1810-1881 *Expl 93*
Krapf, Norbert 1943- *WhoWrEP 92*
Krapf, Richard Clarence 1930- *St&PR 93*
Krapohl, James Roy 1945- *St&PR 93*
Krapp, Edgar 1947- *Baker 92*
Krappinger, Herbert Ernst 1950- *WhoWor 93*
Krappinger, Odo 1928- *WhoScE 91-3*
Krappman, Andrew J., Jr. *Law&B 92*
Kraprayoon, Suchinda *BioIn 17*
Kraras, Gust C. 1921- *WhoE 93, WhoWor 93*
Krarup, Jakob 1936- *WhoWor 93*
Krasa, Hans 1899-1944 *Baker 92*
Krasavage, Kenneth William 1942- *St&PR 93*
Krash, Abe 1927- *WhoAm 92*
Krash, Ronald D. 1933-1990 *BioIn 17*
Krashna, Robert William 1956- *WhoE 93*
Krasicki, Ignacy 1735-1801 *PolBiDi*
Krasilovsky, Alexis 1950- *MiSFD 9*
Krasilovsky, Phyllis 1926- *MajAI [port]*
Krasinski, Leon Gerard *Law&B 92*
Krasinski, Zygmunt 1812-1859 *PolBiDi*
Krask, Sylvia Jo *Law&B 92*
Kraska, Jan 1928- *WhoScE 91-4*
Kraske, Bonny Kathleen 1954- *WhoAmW 93*
Kraske, Karl V. 1935- *St&PR 93*
Kraske, Karl Vincent 1935- *WhoAm 92*
Krasko, Michael John 1943- *WhoAm 92*
Kraskouskas, Kathleen Dawn 1962- *WhoAmW 93*
Kraslow, David 1926- *WhoAm 92, WhoSSW 93*
Krasna, Alvin Isaac 1929- *WhoAm 92*
Krasnansky, Marvin L. 1930- *St&PR 93*
Krasnapolsky, Yuri 1934- *Baker 92*
Krasne, Albert S. *Law&B 92*
Krasne, Betty 1933- *WhoAmW 93*
Krasner, Herbert *St&PR 93*
Krasner, Louis 1903- *Baker 92, WhoAm 92*
Krasner, Oscar Jay 1922- *WhoWor 93*
Krasner, Robert Charles Jeffrey 1947- *WhoAm 92*
Krasner, Sidney D. 1932- *St&PR 93*
Krasney, Josephine *St&PR 93*
Krasney, Josephine Rachel 1924- *WhoAmW 93*
Krasney, Samuel A. 1924- *St&PR 93*
Krasney, Samuel Joseph 1925- *St&PR 93, WhoAm 92*
Krasno, Richard Michael 1942- *WhoE 93*
Krasnoff, Abraham *WhoAm 92, WhoE 93*
Krasnoff, Barbara 1954- *ScF&FL 92*
Krasnoff, Jeffrey Paul 1955- *St&PR 93*
Krasnohorska, Eliska 1847-1926 *OxDcOp*
Krasnov, Guennadi A. 1937- *WhoUN 92*
Krasnow, David M. *Law&B 92*
Krasnow, Marvin L. 1938- *St&PR 93*
Krasnow, Michael Arthur 1945- *WhoSSW 93*
Krasnow, Ronald S. *Law&B 92*
Krasnow, Sheryl Edith 1934- *WhoAmW 93*
Krasnow, Todd J. 1957- *St&PR 93*
Krasnow, Willard *Law&B 92*
Krasny, Leslie Tilzer *Law&B 92*
Krasny, Paul 1935- *MiSFD 9*
Krasova, Marta 1901-1970 *Baker 92, OxDcOp*
Krass, Marc S. *Law&B 92*
Krass, Peter J. 1956- *WhoE 93*
Krass, Robert Peter 1936- *St&PR 93*
Krassas, Gerasimos Efthimios 1943- *WhoWor 93*
Krasse, Bo 1922- *WhoScE 91-4*
Krasser, Hans Wolfgang 1937- *WhoWor 93*
Krassner, Jerry 1953- *WhoSSW 93*
Krassner, Michael L. *Law&B 92*
Krasso, Gyorgy d1991 *BioIn 17*
Krastev, Ivan Manolov 1951- *WhoScE 91-4*
Krastev, Krastjo 1923- *WhoScE 91-4*
Krasts, Aivars 1938- *St&PR 93*
Krasucki, Henri 1924- *BioIn 17*
Kraszewski, Jozef Ignacy 1812-1887 *PolBiDi*
Kraszna-Krausz, Andor 1904-1989 *BioIn 17*
Krat, Gary Walden 1947- *St&PR 93, WhoAm 92*
Kratena, Jiri *BioIn 17*
Krathen, David Howard 1946- *WhoEmL 93*
Krathwohl, David Reading 1921- *WhoAm 92, WhoE 93*
Kratochvil, Byron George 1932- *WhoAm 92*
Kratochvil, Jiri 1929- *WhoScE 91-4*
Kratochvil, Louis Glen 1922- *WhoAm 92*
Kratochvil, Pavel 1930- *WhoScE 91-4*
Kratochvill, James P. *Law&B 92*
Kratochwil, Klaus 1937- *WhoScE 91-4*
Kratovil, Edward D. 1944- *St&PR 93*
Kratoville, Harry J. 1930- *St&PR 93*
Kratt, Peter G. *Law&B 92*
Kratt, Peter George 1940- *St&PR 93, WhoAm 92*
Kratter, Leslie Michael 1945- *St&PR 93*
Kratz, Hans Lewis 1938- *St&PR 93*
Kratz, Jens Volker 1944- *WhoScE 91-3*
Kratz, Marilyn June 1938- *WhoWrEP 92*
Kratz, Paul James 1941- *WhoSSW 93*
Kratz, Teresa Stettner 1956- *WhoAmW 93*
Kratzel, Ekkehard 1935- *WhoWor 93*
Kratzer, Guy Livingston 1911- *WhoAm 92, WhoE 93, WhoWor 93*
Kratzig, Wilfried B. 1932- *WhoScE 91-3*
Krauch, Carl Heinrich 1931- *WhoWor 93*
Krauchick, Dale Zobal 1955- *WhoAmW 93*
Krauer, Felix 1934- *WhoScE 91-4*
Krauk, Elsie Alexandria 1919- *WhoAmW 93, WhoE 93*
Kraulis, Olaf Ernest 1943- *St&PR 93*
Kraupp, Otto 1920- *WhoScE 91-4*
Kraus, Albert Andrew, Jr. 1948- *WhoEmL 93*
Kraus, Alfred 1957 *WhoWor 93*
Kraus, Alfredo *BioIn 17*
Kraus, Alfredo 1924- *WhoAm 92, WhoWor 93*
Kraus, Alfredo 1927- *Baker 92, IntDcOp [port], OxDcOp*
Kraus, Arie *St&PR 93*
Kraus, Auguste 1853-1939
See Seidl, Anton 1850-1898 *OxDcOp*
Kraus, Bruce R. 1954- *ScF&FL 92*
Kraus, Carl E. 1947- *St&PR 93*
Kraus, David 1930- *WhoSSW 93*
Kraus, Detlef 1919- *Baker 92*
Kraus, Eileen S. *WhoAm 92*
Kraus, Elena *Law&B 92*
Kraus, Ernst 1863-1941 *Baker 92, OxDcOp*
Kraus, Felix von 1870-1937 *Baker 92*
Kraus, Frederick H. *Law&B 92*
Kraus, Gary Paul 1953- *WhoEmL 93, WhoSSW 93*
Kraus, Hans 1905- *BioIn 17*
Kraus, Helen Antoinette 1909- *WhoWrEP 92*
Kraus, Herbert Myron 1921- *WhoAm 92*
Kraus, James Robert 1926- *St&PR 93*
Kraus, Jean Elizabeth Grau 1932- *WhoSSW 93, WhoWor 93*
Kraus, Joanna Halpert 1937- *WhoWrEP 92*
Kraus, John Daniel 1910- *BioIn 17*
Kraus, Joseph M. *Law&B 92*
Kraus, Joseph M. 1955- *St&PR 93*
Kraus, Joseph Martin 1756-1792 *Baker 92, OxDcOp*
Kraus, Karl 1874-1936 *DcLB 118 [port]*
Kraus, Lawrence B. 1950- *St&PR 93*
Kraus, Lili 1903-1986 *Baker 92*
Kraus, Merrie Beth 1954- *WhoAmW 93*
Kraus, Michael 1901-1990 *BioIn 17*
Kraus, N.J., Sr. 1928- *St&PR 93*
Kraus, Nancy Jane *Law&B 92*
Kraus, Norma Jean 1931- *WhoAm 92, WhoAmW 93, WhoE 93*
Kraus, Otakar 1909-1980 *Baker 92, OxDcOp*
Kraus, Otto 1930- *WhoScE 91-3*
Kraus, Pansy Daegling 1916- *WhoAmW 93, WhoWor 93*
Kraus, Richard 1902-1978 *OxDcOp*
Kraus, Richard Carl 1946- *St&PR 93*
Kraus, Robert 1925- *BioIn 17*
Kraus, Robert D. *Law&B 92*
Kraus, Robert David 1957- *WhoAm 92*
Kraus, (Herman) Robert 1925- *MajAI [port]*
Kraus, Roland M. 1921- *St&PR 93*
Kraus, Steven M. *Law&B 92*
Kraus, Thayne L. 1933- *St&PR 93*
Kraus, W.F. 1931- *WhoScE 91-3*
Krause, Alan M. 1929- *St&PR 93*
Krause, Albert 1938- *WhoWor 93*
Krause, Anton 1834-1907 *Baker 92*
Krause, Arthur B. 1941- *St&PR 93*
Krause, Benjamin D. 1936- *St&PR 93*
Krause, Bernard Leo 1938- *WhoAm 92*
Krause, Bernie *BioIn 17*
See Also Weavers, The *ConMus 8*
Krause, Brian *BioIn 17*
Krause, C.J. 1924- *St&PR 93*
Krause, Carolyn Diane Hay 1945- *WhoSSW 93*
Krause, Charles Joseph 1937- *WhoAm 92*
Krause, Charles W. 1929- *St&PR 93*
Krause, Chester Lee 1923- *WhoAm 92*
Krause, Curtis Stuart *Law&B 92*
Krause, Daphne Hylda 1927- *WhoWor 93*
Krause, David James 1953- *WhoAm 92*
Krause, David John 1941- *St&PR 93*
Krause, Donald L. 1939- *St&PR 93*
Krause, Ed d1992 *NewYTBS 92 [port]*
Krause, Edward J. 1955- *WhoSSW 93*
Krause, Egon 1933- *WhoScE 91-3*
Krause, Emil 1840-1916 *Baker 92*
Krause, Eugene Franklin 1937- *WhoAm 92*
Krause, Frank-Lothar 1942- *WhoScE 91-3*
Krause, Gunther 1935- *WhoScE 91-3*
Krause, H. Werner 1934- *St&PR 93*
Krause, Harry Dieter 1932- *WhoAm 92*
Krause, Heather Dawn 1956- *WhoAmW 93*
Krause, Heinz Werner 1934- *WhoAm 92, WhoWor 93*
Krause, Helen Fox 1932- *WhoE 93*
Krause, Helmut 1927- *WhoScE 91-3*
Krause, Jerry 1939- *WhoAm 92*
Krause, John F. 1945- *St&PR 93*
Krause, John L. 1917- *WhoWor 93*
Krause, John M. *St&PR 93*
Krause, Judith 1952- *WhoCanL 92*
Krause, Karen Ratigan 1950- *WhoAmW 93*
Krause, Kathryn M. *Law&B 92*
Krause, L. William 1942- *WhoAm 92*
Krause, Laurence Alan 1956- *WhoE 93*
Krause, Lawrence Allen 1939- *WhoAm 92*
Krause, Lester W. 1947- *St&PR 93*
Krause, Lois Ruth Breur 1946- *WhoAmW 93, WhoEmL 93, WhoWor 93*
Krause, Manfred Otto 1931- *WhoAm 92*
Krause, Martin 1853-1918 *Baker 92*
Krause, Martine Anne Marie 1962- *WhoE 93*
Krause, Mary Alice 1950- *WhoSSW 93*
Krause, Michael D. 1952- *WhoIns 93*
Krause, Michael S. 1940- *St&PR 93*
Krause, Nina 1932- *WhoWrEP 92*
Krause, Norman L. 1917- *St&PR 93*
Krause, Pat 1930- *ConAu 37NR, WhoCanL 92*
Krause, Patricia Ann 1941- *WhoAmW 93*
Krause, Paul 1951- *ConAu 139*
Krause, Paul Edward 1956- *WhoEmL 93*
Krause, Philip C. 1920- *St&PR 93*
Krause, Raymond A. *Law&B 92*
Krause, Raymond R. 1951- *St&PR 93*
Krause, Richard D. 1930- *St&PR 93*
Krause, Richard J. 1932- *St&PR 93*
Krause, Richard James 1942- *WhoAm 92*
Krause, Richard Michael 1925- *WhoAm 92*
Krause, Richard William 1936- *WhoAm 92*
Krause, Robert Frederick 1926- *St&PR 93, WhoAm 92*
Krause, Robert M. 1950- *St&PR 93*
Krause, Sonja 1933- *WhoAm 92, WhoAmW 93*
Krause, Susan D. *Law&B 92*
Krause, Susan D. 1953- *St&PR 93*
Krause, Suzanne Louise 1946- *WhoAmW 93*
Krause, Theodor 1833-1910 *Baker 92*
Krause, Tom 1934- *Baker 92, OxDcOp*
Krause, Walter 1919- *WhoAm 92*
Krause, Werner William 1937- *St&PR 93*
Krause, William Austin 1930- *WhoAm 92*
Krausen, Anthony Sharnik 1944- *WhoWor 93*
Krause-Stetson, Diane *Law&B 92*
Kraus-Friedmann, Naomi 1933- *WhoAmW 93*
Kraushaar, Antoinette M. 1902-1992 *NewYTBS 92*
Kraushaar, John Florence 1932- *WhoAm 92*
Kraushaar, William Lester 1920- *WhoAm 92*
Krauskopf, Konrad Bates 1910- *WhoAm 92*
Krauskopf, Kurt Jeffrey 1954- *St&PR 93*
Krauskopf, Mark D. *Law&B 92*
Krauss, Alan Robert 1943- *WhoAm 92, WhoWor 93*
Krauss, Charles A., Jr. 1931- *St&PR 93*
Krauss, Charles Anthony, Jr. 1931- *WhoAm 92*
Krauss, Clemens 1893-1954 *IntDcOp [port], OxDcOp*
Krauss, Clemens (Heinrich) 1893-1954 *Baker 92*
Krauss, Clifford 1953- *ConAu 136*
Krauss, Clifford Hans 1954- *St&PR 93*
Krauss, Gabrielle 1842-1906 *OxDcOp*
Krauss, (Marie) Gabrielle 1842-1906 *Baker 92*
Krauss, Geoffrey H. *Law&B 92*
Krauss, Geoffrey Howard *Law&B 92*
Krauss, George 1933- *WhoAm 92*
Krauss, Hans L. 1927- *WhoScE 91-3*
Krauss, Herbert Harris 1940- *WhoAm 92*
Krauss, Herbert N. 1932- *St&PR 93*
Krauss, James *Law&B 92*
Krauss, Janet 1935- *WhoWrEP 92*
Krauss, Janet Hentoff 1935- *WhoE 93*
Krauss, Jeffrey M. 1953- *St&PR 93*
Krauss, Judith Belliveau 1947- *WhoAm 92*
Krauss, Kevin Brian 1953- *St&PR 93*
Krauss, Lawrence Maxwell 1954- *WhoE 93*
Krauss, Lynn D. *Law&B 92*
Krauss, Marlene 1945- *WhoAm 92*
Krauss, Michael Edward 1934- *WhoAm 92*
Krauss, Michael Ian 1951- *WhoE 93, WhoEmL 93*
Krauss, Michael J. 1943- *St&PR 93*
Krauss, Nathan Harry 1908- *St&PR 93*
Krauss, Ray Herbert 1949- *WhoAm 92*
Krauss, Robert Aron 1946- *St&PR 93*
Krauss, Robert Wallfar 1921- *WhoAm 92*
Krauss, Ruth (Ida) 1911- *MajAI [port]*
Krauss, Steven James 1942- *WhoAm 92, WhoE 93*
Krauss, Sue Elizabeth 1951- *WhoAmW 93, WhoEmL 93, WhoWor 93*
Krauss, Werner 1884-1959 *IntDcF 2-3 [port]*
Krausslich, Horst 1926- *WhoScE 91-3*
Kraus Trujillo, Alfredo 1924- *WhoAm 92, WhoWor 93*
Krausz, Andor Kraszna- 1904-1989 *BioIn 17*
Krausz, Michael 1942- *WhoAm 92*
Kraut, Gerald Anthony 1951- *WhoAm 92*
Kraut, Jeffrey Alan 1956- *WhoE 93*
Kraut, Joanne Lenora 1949- *WhoAmW 93*
Kraut, Joel Arthur 1937- *WhoE 93, WhoWor 93*
Krautblatt, Charles John 1950- *WhoEmL 93*
Krauter, Thomas F. 1927- *WhoAm 92*
Krauter, Thomas Francis 1927- *St&PR 93*
Krauth, Joachim 1941- *WhoScE 91-3*
Krauth, Norman Lee 1929- *St&PR 93*
Krauthammer, Charles 1950- *WhoAm 92, WhoE 93*
Krautman, Harvey *St&PR 93*
Krautman, Jeff *St&PR 93*
Krautter, Elisa Bialk 1912-1990 *BioIn 17*
Krautz, Erich 1906- *WhoScE 91-4*
Krauza, Joanne M. *WhoAmW 93*
Krauze, Antoni 1940- *DrEEuF*
Krauze, Zygmunt 1938- *Baker 92*
Krauzer, Steven M. 1948- *ScF&FL 92*

Kravchenko, Leonid P. 1938- WhoWor 93
Kravchuk, Leonid BioIn 17
Kravchuk, Leonid Makarorovich 1934- WhoWor 93
Kravchuk, Robert Sacha 1955- WhoEmL 93
Kravec, Cynthia Vallen 1951- WhoWor 93
Kravets, Barbara Zeitlin 1935- WhoAmW 93
Kravetz, Alexander A. 1962- WhoUN 92
Kravetz, Beth 1949- WhoEmL 93
Kravetz, Stanley BioIn 17
Kravis, Harrison S. d1991 BioIn 17
Kravis, Henry R. BioIn 17, WhoAm 92
Kravis, Irving B. BioIn 17
Kravis, Irving B. d1992 NewYTBS 92
Kravis, Nathan Mark 1957- WhoEmL 93
Kravitc, David C. St&PR 93
Kravitch, Phyllis A. 1920- WhoAm 92, WhoAmW 93
Kravitt, Gregory Ian 1950- St&PR 93
Kravitz, Bernard L. 1933- St&PR 93
Kravitz, Ellen King 1929- WhoAm 92
Kravitz, Ian Hunter Law&B 92
Kravitz, John Jay 1946- WhoE 93
Kravitz, Lawrence Charles 1932- WhoAm 92
Kravitz, Lenny BioIn 17
Kravitz, Linda BioIn 17
Kravitz, Linda Delanne 1947- WhoAmW 93
Kravitz, Marjorie Ruth 1937- WhoE 93
Kravitz, Martha Sandra 1951- WhoAmW 93
Kravitz, Rhonda A. Rios 1949- BioIn 17
Kravitz, Richard 1949- St&PR 93
Kravitz, Rubin 1928- WhoAm 92, WhoWor 93
Kravitz, William N. BioIn 17
Kravjansky, Mikulas 1928- WhoWor 93
Kraw, George Martin 1949- WhoEmL 93, WhoWor 93
Krawchuk, Mary Ann Law&B 92
Krawczyk, Charles C. Law&B 92
Krawczyk, Gerard 1953- MiSFD 9
Krawczyk, Joan Marie 1951- WhoAmW 93
Krawinkel, Michael Bernhardt 1950- WhoWor 93
Krawitz, Arnold S. 1937- St&PR 93
Krawitz, Herman Everett 1925- WhoAm 92
Krawitz, Rhoda Nayor 1925- WhoE 93
Kray, Eugene John 1935- WhoE 93
Kraybill, Henry Lawrence 1918- WhoE 93
Kraybill, Paul Nissley 1925- WhoAm 92
Krayenbuehl, Thomas Ernst 1936- WhoWor 93
Krayer, William L. Law&B 92
Kraynak, Michael, Jr. 1930- St&PR 93
Kraysler, Stephen F. 1942- WhoIns 93
Krc, Ivo 1932- WhoScE 91-4
Krchma, Stephen P. Law&B 92
Krcmar, Helmut Alfred Otto 1954- WhoWor 93
Kreaden, Gerald 1935- WhoE 93
Kreader, Barbara Barlow 1946- WhoWrEP 92
Kreager, Eileen Davis 1924- WhoAmW 93, WhoWor 93
Kreager, H. Dewayne 1912- St&PR 93
Kreager, Heather Law&B 92
Kreager, Henry Dewayne 1912- WhoAm 92
Kreamer, John Harrison 1922- WhoAm 92
Krebs Baker 92
Krebs, Aloysia Michalesi 1826-1904 See Krebs, Carl August 1804-1880 Baker 92
Krebs, Arno William, Jr. 1942- WhoAm 92
Krebs, Bernt 1938- WhoScE 91-3
Krebs, Calvin J. Law&B 92
Krebs, Carl August 1804-1880 Baker 92
Krebs, E. Michael St&PR 93
Krebs, Edwin Gerhard 1918- WhoAm 92
Krebs, Elizabeth Louise 1968- WhoAmW 93
Krebs, Frederick John 1949- WhoE 93
Krebs, Gary Lynn 1943- WhoSSW 93
Krebs, Hans Adolf 1900-1981 BioIn 17
Krebs, Helmut 1913- Baker 92
Krebs, James Arthur, Jr. 1948- WhoE 93
Krebs, Johann Gottfried 1741-1814 Baker 92
Krebs, Johann Ludwig 1713-1780 Baker 92
Krebs, Johann Tobias 1690-1762 Baker 92
Krebs, John H. 1926- WhoAm 92
Krebs, John Richard WhoScE 91-1
Krebs, John Richard 1945- WhoWor 93
Krebs, Joseph Jackson, Jr. 1930- St&PR 93
Krebs, Julia Elizabeth 1943- WhoAmW 93
Krebs, Lois Ponnock 1938- WhoAmW 93, WhoE 93
Krebs, Margaret Eloise 1927- WhoAmW 93, WhoE 93
Krebs, Marie 1851-1900 See Krebs, Carl August 1804-1880 Baker 92
Krebs, Max Vance 1916- WhoAm 92
Krebs, Robert D. 1942- St&PR 93
Krebs, Robert Duncan 1942- WhoAm 92
Krebs, Ronald Edward 1938- St&PR 93
Krebs, Serge Antoine Pierre 1957- WhoWor 93
Krebs, Sylvia Ann 1942- WhoAmW 93
Krebs, T.J. Andrew 1953- St&PR 93
Krebs, William A. Wallace 1916-1991 BioIn 17
Krebs, William E. 1946- St&PR 93
Krebsbach, Karen K. WhoAmW 93
Krebsbach, Renita Allene 1960- WhoAmW 93
Krebsbach, Sandra Gehlen 1947- WhoAmW 93
Krebsbach, Theodore A. Law&B 92
Krechel, Roger N. 1936- St&PR 93
Krechevsky, Curtis Law&B 92
Krechman, Carole Sumner 1940- WhoAmW 93
Krecke, Charles Francis 1926- WhoAm 92
Kreczmar, Antoni Florian 1945- WhoScE 91-4
Krediet, Piet 1919- WhoScE 91-3
Kreeb, K.H. 1927- WhoScE 91-3
Kreeft, Peter 1937- ScF&FL 92
Kreeger, David 1909-1990 BioIn 17
Kreeger, M.R. Law&B 92
Kreeger, Susan L. Law&B 92
Kreek, Mary Jeanne WhoWor 93
Kreer, Irene Overman 1926- WhoAmW 93
Kreer, John Belshaw 1927- WhoAm 92
Krefman, Stephen D. Law&B 92
Kreft, Anthony Frank, III 1948- WhoE 93
Krefting, Carol Lee 1948- WhoAmW 93
Krefting, Robert John 1944- WhoAm 92, WhoE 93
Kregel, Jon BioIn 17
Kregel, Kathleen Marie 1948- WhoAmW 93
Kregel, Robert Louis 1919- WhoAm 92
Kreger, Brian F. Law&B 92
Kreger, Elwyn L. 1924- St&PR 93
Kreger, Ronald Eugene 1952- St&PR 93
Kreger, Steve W. Law&B 92
Kreglow, Amanda Byington 1948- WhoAmW 93
Kregstein, Stephen P. Law&B 92
Kreh, Kent Q. 1935- St&PR 93
Krehbiel, Clarice Weekley 1929- St&PR 93
Krehbiel, Constance Miller 1944- WhoAmW 93
Krehbiel, Floyd Harold 1923- St&PR 93
Krehbiel, Frederick A. 1941- St&PR 93
Krehbiel, Frederick August, II 1941- WhoAm 92
Krehbiel, Henry (Edward) 1854-1923 Baker 92
Krehbiel, John H. 1906- WhoAm 92
Krehbiel, Peter W. 1929- St&PR 93
Krehbiel, Robert C. 1921- St&PR 93
Krehbiel, William R. 1932- St&PR 93
Krehel, Roberta Mae 1927- WhoAmW 93
Krehl, Stephan 1864-1924 Baker 92
Kreibich, Herbert WhoScE 91-3
Kreick, John R. 1944- St&PR 93
Kreider, Gary L. 1949- St&PR 93
Kreidler, Robert N. d1992 NewYTBS 92 [port]
Kreidler, Robert Neil 1929- WhoAm 92
Kreienkamp, Raymond S. 1960- WhoEmL 93
Kreifeldt, John Gene 1934- WhoE 93
Kreifels, Frank Anthony 1951- WhoAm 92
Kreig, James J. Law&B 92
Kreig, Raymond R. 1922- St&PR 93
Kreiger, Barbara Sue 1948- WhoE 93
Kreiger, Bruce Dennis Law&B 92
Kreiger, Geoffrey W. 1950- St&PR 93
Kreiger, Harold d1992 NewYTBS 92
Kreighbaum, John Scott 1946- WhoAm 92
Kreighbaum, William Eugene 1934- WhoE 93
Kreil, Gunther 1934- WhoScE 91-4
Kreil, Walter Nelson, Jr. 1947- St&PR 93, WhoEmL 93
Kreilein, Robert Lee 1943- St&PR 93
Kreilick, Robert W. 1938- WhoAm 92
Kreiman, Robert Theodore 1924- St&PR 93
Kreimer, Richard BioIn 17
Krein, Alexander (Abramovich) 1883-1951 Baker 92
Krein, Grigori (Abramovich) 1879-1955 Baker 92
Krein, Julian (Grigorievich) 1913- Baker 92
Krein, William A. 1940- WhoAm 92
Kreinbrook, Dennis Wehrle 1951- WhoE 93
Kreindler, Jerry Law&B 92
Kreindler, Peter Michael Law&B 92
Kreiner, Andres Juan 1950- WhoWor 93
Kreiner, Jerzy M. 1940- WhoScE 91-4
Kreiner, Philip 1950- WhoCanL 92
Kreiniker, Thomas J. 1952- St&PR 93
Kreinin, Mordechai Eliahu 1930- WhoAm 92
Kreis, Eliahu Simha 1936- WhoUN 92
Kreis, Gene S. 1939- St&PR 93
Kreis, Robert R. 1926- St&PR 93
Kreis, Ronald W. 1942- St&PR 93
Kreis, Willi 1924- WhoAm 92
Kreisberg, Neil Ivan 1945- St&PR 93, WhoAm 92
Kreische, Werner 1935- WhoScE 91-3
Kreische, Werner Rudolf 1935- WhoWor 93
Kreisel, Henry 1922-1991 WhoCanL 92
Kreisel, Wilfried 1942- WhoUN 92
Kreisinger, Vladimir 1929- WhoScE 91-4
Kreisky, Bruno BioIn 17
Kreisky, Bruno 1911-1990 DcTwHis
Kreisl, Gary M. 1954- St&PR 93
Kreisler, Fritz 1875-1962 Baker 92
Kreisler, Kathi St&PR 93
Kreisler, Larry St&PR 93
Kreisler, Stuart L. St&PR 93
Kreisman, Arthur 1918- WhoAm 92
Kreisman, Barbara Ann BioIn 17
Kreisman, Herbert 1912- St&PR 93
Kreisselmeier, Gerhard WhoScE 91-3
Kreissl, J. Scott 1946- St&PR 93
Kreissle von Hellborn, Heinrich 1822-1869 Baker 92
Kreiter, Harry 1917- St&PR 93
Kreiter, Herbert M. 1928- St&PR 93
Kreitler, Thomas S. 1957- St&PR 93
Kreitman, Benjamin Zvi 1920- WhoAm 92
Kreitman, Jill BioIn 17
Kreitman, N.B. WhoScE 91-1
Kreitzberg, Charles Barry 1947- WhoE 93
Kreitzberg, Fred Charles 1934- WhoAm 92, WhoWor 93
Kreitzberg, Richard Anthony 1934- St&PR 93
Kreitzer, Gary A. 1955- St&PR 93
Kreitzer, J. Karl 1942- St&PR 93
Kreitzer, Jack 1949- WhoWrEP 92
Kreitzer, Lois Helen 1933- WhoAmW 93, WhoE 93, WhoWor 93
Kreitzer, Stuart Sherman 1959- WhoSSW 93
Kreizel, William J. 1921- St&PR 93
Kreja, Ludwik 1935- WhoScE 91-4
Krejci, Isa 1904-1968 Baker 92
Krejci, Josef 1821-1881 Baker 92
Krejci, Miroslav 1891-1964 Baker 92
Krejcik, Jiri 1918- DrEEuF
Krejcova, Hana 1931- WhoScE 91-4
Krejcsi, Cynthia Ann 1948- WhoAmW 93
Krejs, Guenter J. 1945- WhoScE 91-4
Krek, Uros 1922- Baker 92
Krekeler, Heinz Ludwig 1906- WhoWor 93
Krekorian, Elizabeth Anne 1928- WhoAmW 93
Krelitz, Philip James 1911- St&PR 93
Kremberg, Marvin Roy 1951- WhoEmL 93
Kremen, David F. Law&B 92
Kremenitzer, Janet Pickard 1949- WhoAmW 93
Kremenliev, Boris 1911-1988 Baker 92
Krementz, Edward Thomas 1917- WhoAm 92
Krementz, Jill 1940- MajAI [port], SmATA 71 [port], WhoAm 92, WhoAmW 93, WhoWrEP 92
Krementz, Walter, Jr. d1992 NewYTBS 92
Kremer, Alvin W. 1904-1990 BioIn 17
Kremer, Alvin Webster, Jr. 1939- WhoSSW 93
Kremer, Eugene R. 1938- WhoAm 92
Kremer, Fred, Jr. 1926- WhoAm 92
Kremer, Gidon 1947- Baker 92
Kremer, H. Michel 1935- WhoScE 91-2
Kremer, Hans 1934- WhoScE 91-3
Kremer, Honor Frances 1939- WhoAmW 93
Kremer, Isa 1885-1956 Baker 92
Kremer, J. Eric 1933- St&PR 93
Kremer, John Frederick 1949- WhoWrEP 92
Kremer, Jonny Simon 1942- WhoWor 93
Kremer, Merle W. 1916-1991 BioIn 17
Kremer, Mervin Carl 1930- St&PR 93
Kremer, Peter BioIn 17
Kremer, Remy Peter 1893-1965 BiDAMSp 1989
Kremer, Rudiger ConAu 139
Kremer, Ruediger 1942- ConAu 139
Kremer, Russell Eugene 1954- WhoEmL 93
Kremer, Sarah Frances 1953- WhoAmW 93, WhoSSW 93
Kremers, Al Henry 1934- St&PR 93
Kreminec, Kathleen Elizabeth 1959- WhoAmW 93
Kreml, Franklin Martin 1907- WhoAm 92, WhoWor 93
Kremlev, Yuli (Anatolyevich) 1908-1971 Baker 92
Kremmel, Donn A. Law&B 92
Kremmin, Thomas Rudi Franz 1950- St&PR 93
Kremp, Herbert 1928- WhoWor 93
Krempa, Frank Stanley 1935- St&PR 93
Krempasky, Julius 1931- WhoScE 91-4
Krempel, Ralf Hugo Bernhard 1935- WhoWor 93
Krempels, Ronald Keith 1963- WhoSSW 93
Krempelsetzer, Georg 1827-1871 Baker 92
Krempl, Erhard 1934- WhoAm 92, WhoE 93
Krems, Susan Alexander 1940- WhoAmW 93
Kremser, Eduard 1838-1914 Baker 92
Kren, Emil 1935- WhoScE 91-4
Kren, Thomas John 1950- WhoAm 92
Krendel, Ezra Simon 1925- WhoAm 92
Krenek, Ernst 1900- Baker 92
Krenek, Ernst 1900-1991 AnObit 1991, BioIn 17, ConAu 136, CurBio 92N, IntDcOp [port], OxDcOp
Krenek, Wilfred M. 1953- St&PR 93
Krengel, Ulrich 1937- WhoWor 93
Krenitsky, Michael V. 1915- WhoAm 92
Krenitsky, Thomas Anthony 1938- St&PR 93, WhoAm 92, WhoSSW 93
Krenkel, Peter Ashton 1930- WhoAm 92
Krenkel, Roy G. 1918-1983 ScF&FL 92
Krenmayr, Peter 1932- WhoWor 93
Krenn, Franz 1816-1897 Baker 92
Krenn, Fritz 1897-1964 Baker 92, OxDcOp
Krenn, Werner 1943- Baker 92
Krens, Thomas 1946- WhoAm 92, WhoE 93
Krensky, Harold 1912- WhoAm 92
Krensky, Stephen 1953- ScF&FL 92
Krents, Milton Ellis 1911- WhoAm 92
Krentz, Eugene Leo 1932- WhoAm 92
Krentz, Jayne Ann ScF&FL 92
Krentz, Jayne Ann 1948- ConAu 139
Krentz, Kristine Jo 1949- WhoAmW 93
Krentz, Michael L. 1958- St&PR 93
Krentz, Richard D. 1942- St&PR 93
Krentzlin, Richard 1864-1956 Baker 92
Krenz, Dean Albert 1930- WhoAm 92
Krenz, Donald A. 1936- WhoAm 92
Krenz, Egon BioIn 17
Krenz, Frank Edgar 1933- WhoUN 92
Krenz, Jan 1926- Baker 92, WhoWor 93
Krepinevich, Kevin W. 1954- WhoAm 92
Krepky, Cynthia D. 1956- WhoAmW 93
Kreppel, Milton Mark 1951- WhoEmL 93
Kreppel, Robert John Law&B 92
Kreps, David Marc 1950- WhoAm 92
Kreps, Juanita Morris 1921- WhoAm 92, WhoAmW 93
Kreps, Robert Wilson 1946- WhoAm 92
Kresa, Helmy 1904-1991 BioIn 17
Kresa, Kent 1938- St&PR 93, WhoAm 92
Kresak, Lubor 1927- WhoScE 91-4
Kresanek, Jozef 1913-1986 Baker 92
Kresch, Scott E. Law&B 92
Krese, Michael Joseph 1956- WhoEmL 93
Kresge, Alexander Jerry 1926- WhoAm 92
Kresge, Bruce Anderson 1931- WhoAm 92
Kresh, J. Yasha 1948- WhoAm 92
Kresh, Michael D. 1954- WhoE 93
Kresh, Paul BioIn 17
Kresh, Paul 1919- WhoAm 92
Kresic, Mladen D. Law&B 92
Kresivo, Miriam Law&B 92
Kreski, Edward J. 1912- St&PR 93
Kreskin 1935- WhoAm 92
Kresko, Daniel Andrew 1929- St&PR 93
Kresky, Michael 1954- St&PR 93
Kresl, Miles L., Jr. 1939- St&PR 93
Kresloff, Richard Stephen 1944- WhoE 93
Kress, Agnes Irene 1947- WhoWrEP 92
Kress, Donald F. 1938- St&PR 93
Kress, Edward C. 1944- St&PR 93
Kress, Edward Marshall 1949- St&PR 93
Kress, George 1903- St&PR 93
Kress, George F. 1903- WhoAm 92
Kress, Jean-Jacques 1933- WhoScE 91-2
Kress, Nancy 1948- ScF&FL 92
Kress, Paul Frederick 1935- WhoAm 92
Kress, Ralph Herman 1904- WhoAm 92
Kress, Robert Frederick 1941- St&PR 93
Kress, Roy Alfred 1916- WhoE 93
Kress, Samuel H. 1863-1955 BioIn 17
Kresse, Hans 1940- WhoScE 91-3
Kressel, Henry 1934- WhoAm 92
Kressin, Lori Lee 1959- WhoAmW 93
Kressler, James Phillip 1931- WhoAm 92
Kressman, Annabelle BioIn 17
Kressman, Hank BioIn 17
Kreston, Martin Howard 1931- WhoAm 92
Kresze, Gunter 1921- WhoScE 91-3
Kretch, Albert J. 1943- St&PR 93
Kretchman, Christina BioIn 17

Kretchmar, Barbara S.M. Law&B 92
Kretchmer, Norman 1923- WhoAm 92
Kretchmer, Richard Allan Law&B 92
Kretchmer, Valerie Sandler 1953- WhoEmL 93
Kreter, Charles R. 1956- St&PR 93
Kretowicz, Janusz Jozef 1939- WhoUN 92
Kretschmer, Edmund 1830-1908 Baker 92
Kretschmer, Frank F., Jr. 1930- WhoAm 92
Kretschmer, Keith Hughes 1934- WhoAm 92
Kretschmer, Paul Robert 1929- WhoAm 92
Kretsinger, Robert H. 1937- WhoSSW 93
Krett, Vasil 1931- WhoUN 92
Kretzenbacher, Leopold 1912- IntDcAn
Kretzer, William T. WhoSSW 93
Kretzmann, Justus Paul 1913- WhoAm 92
Kretzmann, Walter John 1943- St&PR 93
Kretzschmar, (August Ferdinand) Hermann 1848-1924 Baker 92
Kretzschmar, John R. 1933- St&PR 93
Kretzschmar, William Addison, Jr. 1953- WhoSSW 93
Kreube, Charles Frederic 1777-1846 Baker 92
Kreuch, Paul C., Jr. 1938- St&PR 93
Kreuder, Ernst 1903-1972 ScF&FL 92
Kreuder, Peter Paul 1905-1981 Baker 92
Kreuger, Ralph W. BioIn 17
Kreuger, Ralph Walter 1942- St&PR 93
Kreuscher, Ronald H. 1935- St&PR 93
Kreutel, Randall William, Jr. 1934- WhoSSW 93
Kreuter, Charles R. 1950- St&PR 93
Kreuter, Eric Anton 1959- WhoE 93
Kreuter, Gretchen V. 1934- WhoAm 92
Kreuter, Jorg 1948- WhoScE 91-3
Kreuter, Jorg Wilhelm Rudolf 1948- WhoWor 93
Kreuter, Konrad Franz 1939- WhoWor 93
Kreutz, Arthur 1906-1991 Baker 92
Kreutz, Arthur R. 1906-1991 BioIn 17
Kreutz, Austin Thomas 1952- WhoE 93
Kreutz, Werner 1931- WhoScE 91-3
Kreutzberg, Georg W. 1932- WhoScE 91-3
Kreutzberger, Alfred 1922- WhoScE 91-3
Kreutzberger, Mario BioIn 17
Kreutzer, Allan C. 1943- St&PR 93
Kreutzer, Conrad 1780-1849 OxDcOp
Kreutzer, Conradin 1780-1849 Baker 92
Kreutzer, Franklin David 1940- WhoAm 92, WhoWor 93
Kreutzer, Jean Nicolas Auguste 1778-1832 Baker 92
Kreutzer, Leon Charles Francois 1817-1868 Baker 92
Kreutzer, Leonid 1884-1953 Baker 92
Kreutzer, Louis G. 1929- St&PR 93
Kreutzer, Louis G., Jr. 1929- WhoAm 92
Kreutzer, Rodolphe 1766-1831 Baker 92, OxDcOp
Kreutzer, S. Stanley 1907- WhoAm 92, WhoWor 93
Kreutzjans, Michael J. 1954- St&PR 93
Kreuz, Roger James 1961- WhoSSW 93
Kreuzer, Theodore Robert 1947- WhoAm 92
Kreuziger, Frederick A. ScF&FL 92
Krevans, Julius Richard 1924- WhoAm 92, WhoWor 93
Krevans, Rachel 1957- WhoAmW 93
Krevitsky, Nik 1914-1991 BioIn 17
Krevsky, Benjamin 1952- WhoEmL 93
Krewson, Lorraine Wilma 1930- WhoAmW 93
Krewson, Walter Irwin 1925- St&PR 93
Krey, Mary Ann Reynolds 1947- WhoAm 92, WhoEmL 93
Krey, Robert Dean 1929- WhoAm 92
Krey, Uwe 1938- WhoScE 91-3
Kreyche, Gerald Francis 1927- WhoAm 92
Kreye, Volker A.W. 1940- WhoScE 91-3
Kreykes, William 1937- WhoAm 92
Kreyling, Edward George, Jr. 1923- WhoAm 92
Kreysa, G. 1945- WhoScE 91-3
Kriezel, Alexander A. Law&B 92
Krezelewski, Mieczyslaw 1926- WhoScE 91-4
Krga, Joan S. 1943- St&PR 93
Kriak, John Michael 1947- St&PR 93, WhoAm 92
Kriaris, Karyn Law&B 92
Kribbs, D. Lee 1941- St&PR 93
Kribel, Robert Edward 1937- WhoAm 92
Kricheff, Robert S. St&PR 93
Kricheldorf, Hans R. 1942- WhoScE 91-3
Krichevskii, Grigorii Grigor'evich 1910- BioIn 17
Krichilsky, Tina 1964- WhoSSW 93
Krick, Irving Parkhurst 1906- WhoAm 92, WhoWor 93
Krick, John 1947- St&PR 93
Krick, Kenneth A. 1934- St&PR 93, WhoAm 92
Krick, Marilyn A. 1952- WhoEmL 93
Kricka, Jaroslav 1882-1969 Baker 92
Krickeberg, Walter 1885-1962 IntDcAn
Krickstein, Aaron BioIn 17
Krida, Jeffrey D. 1946- St&PR 93
Kridel, James S. 1940- WhoAm 92
Kridel, William J. 1916-1991 BioIn 17
Krider, Patricia Ann 1956- WhoAmW 93
Kridler, J.W. 1927- St&PR 93
Kridner, L. Kirk Law&B 92
Kriebel, Charles H. 1933- St&PR 93
Kriebel, Charles Hosey 1933- WhoAm 92
Kriebel, Robert I. St&PR 93
Krieble, Robert H. 1916- WhoAm 92, WhoWor 93
Kriechbaum, Michael 1941- WhoWor 93
Krief, Alain 1942- WhoScE 91-2
Krieg, Adrian H. 1938- St&PR 93
Krieg, Adrian Henry 1938- WhoE 93
Krieg, Arthur Frederick 1930- WhoAm 92, WhoE 93
Krieg, Audrey 1942- St&PR 93
Krieg, Harry J. 1924- St&PR 93
Krieg, Martha Fessler 1948- WhoAmW 93
Krieg, Phyllis Cheek 1960- WhoEmL 93
Krieg, Rebecca Jane 1953- WhoAmW 93
Krieg, Steven David Law&B 92
Kriegel, Beth Ann 1961- WhoAmW 93, WhoEmL 93
Kriegel, Jay L. BioIn 17
Kriegel, Jay L. 1940- WhoAm 92
Kriegel, Leonard 1933- WhoWrEP 92
Kriegel, Samuel Law&B 92
Krieger, Abbott Joel 1939- WhoAm 92
Krieger, Adam 1634-1666 Baker 92
Krieger, Armando 1940- Baker 92
Krieger, Benjamin William 1937- St&PR 93
Krieger, Carl 1928- St&PR 93
Krieger, Dolores Esther 1935- WhoAmW 93
Krieger, Edino 1928- Baker 92
Krieger, Gary A. Law&B 92
Krieger, Gary Robert 1951- WhoEmL 93
Krieger, Harvey 1933- St&PR 93
Krieger, Herbert William 1889-1970 IntDcAn
Krieger, Howard P. d1992 NewYTBS 92
Krieger, Irvin Mitchell 1923- WhoAm 92
Krieger, Johann 1651-1735 Baker 92
Krieger, Johann Philipp 1649-1725 Baker 92, OxDcOp
Krieger, Joseph Bernard 1937- WhoE 93
Krieger, Kurt L. Law&B 92
Krieger, Leonard 1918-1990 BioIn 17
Krieger, Leonard P. 1936- St&PR 93
Krieger, Leslie Herbert 1938- WhoSSW 93
Krieger, Martin H. 1944- ConAu 138
Krieger, Murray 1923- WhoAm 92, WhoWrEP 92
Krieger, Nancy Jane 1958- WhoAmW 93
Krieger, Nora Jane 1946- WhoE 93
Krieger, Paul Edward 1942- WhoAm 92, WhoSSW 93, WhoWor 93
Krieger, Philip Sheridan 1947- St&PR 93
Krieger, Robert Edward 1925- WhoAm 92
Krieger, Robert Lee, Jr. 1946- WhoSSW 93, WhoWor 93
Krieger, Simon 1954- WhoWor 93
Krieger, Stanley L. 1942- St&PR 93
Krieger, Stuart A. 1918- St&PR 93
Krieger, Stuart E. Law&B 92
Krieger, Theodore Kent 1950- WhoWrEP 92
Krieger, William Carl 1946- WhoEmL 93
Krieger-Olsen, Joyce 1950- WhoE 93
Krieger Vasena, Adalbert 1920- WhoWor 93
Kriegler, Arnold Matthew 1932- WhoSSW 93
Kriegler, Connie BioIn 17
Kriegshaber, Victor H. BioIn 17
Kriegsman, Edward Michael 1965- WhoE 93
Kriegsman, Kay Harris 1943- WhoAmW 93
Kriegsman, Martin I. 1942- St&PR 93
Kriegsman, William Edwin 1932- WhoAm 92
Kriek, Erik 1931- WhoScE 91-3
Kriendler, Jeannette E. d1991 BioIn 17
Kriendler, Jeffrey Feller 1946- St&PR 93
Krienke, Carol Belle Manikowske 1917- WhoAmW 93, WhoWor 93
Krienke, Kendra Cliver WhoE 93
Kriens, Christian 1881-1934 Baker 92
Krier, James Edward 1939- WhoAm 92
Krier, Jeanne Dwyer 1944- WhoE 93
Krier, Joseph Roland 1946- WhoAm 92
Krier, Ruth Weaver 1948- WhoAmW 93
Kries, Harold H. 1933- St&PR 93
Kriesberg, Irving 1919- WhoE 93
Kriesberg, Louis 1926- WhoE 93
Kriesberg, Simeon M. 1951- WhoEmL 93
Krietemeyer, George O. 1936- St&PR 93
Krietzberg, David H. 1955- St&PR 93
Kriezis, Epaminondas 1930- WhoWor 93
Krigsman, Naomi 1930- WhoE 93
Krikelas, James 1932- BioIn 17
Krikelis, Nicholas 1944- WhoScE 91-3
Krikelis, Nicholas J. 1944- WhoWor 93
Krikelis, Vassilis 1947- WhoScE 91-3
Kriken, John Lund 1938- WhoAm 92
Krikorian, Abraham Der 1937- WhoE 93
Krikos, George Alexander 1922- WhoAm 92, WhoWor 93
Krill, Arthur Melvin 1921- WhoAm 92
Krim, Arthur B. 1910- BioIn 17, WhoAm 92, WhoE 93
Krim, Mathilde 1926- BioIn 17, WhoAmW 93
Krimen, Richard A. Law&B 92
Krimendahl, H. Frederick 1928- St&PR 93
Krimendahl, Herbert Frederick, II 1928- WhoAm 92
Krimezis, Cynthia Evangelou 1951- WhoAm 92, WhoAmW 93
Krimigis, Stamatios Mike 1938- WhoAm 92
Krimm, Martin Christian 1921- WhoSSW 93
Krimmer, Matthew H. Law&B 92
Krims, Leslie Robert 1942- WhoE 93
Krims, Marvin Bennett 1928- WhoE 93
Krimsky, L.C. 1940- St&PR 93
Kriner, Sally Gladys Pearl 1911- WhoAmW 93
Kriney, Marilyn W. 1938- WhoAmW 93
Kring, C.I. 1926- St&PR 93
Kring, Maurice W. 1936- St&PR 93
Kring, Michael K. 1952- ScF&FL 92
Kring, Walter Donald 1916- WhoAm 92
Kringel, John G. 1939- St&PR 93, WhoAm 92
Krinick, Cathy Ellen 1953- WhoEmL 93
Krinsky, Carol Herselle 1937- WhoAm 92, WhoAmW 93
Krinsky, Fredda Susan 1952- WhoWor 93
Krinsky, Paul Lewis 1928- WhoAm 92
Krinsky, Robert D. 1937- St&PR 93
Krinsky, Robert Daniel 1937- WhoAm 92
Krinsley, David Henry 1927- WhoAm 92
Krinsley, Dick BioIn 17
Krinsly, Stuart Z. Law&B 92
Krinsly, Stuart Z. 1917- St&PR 93, WhoAm 92
Kripke, Kenneth Norman 1920- WhoAm 92
Kripke, Margaret Louise 1943- WhoAmW 93
Krippendorff, Klaus Herbert 1932- WhoE 93
Krippner, Stanley Curtis 1932- WhoAm 92
Krips, Henry (Joseph) 1912-1987 Baker 92
Krips, Josef 1902-1974 Baker 92, IntDcOp, OxDcOp
Kris, Edward Joseph 1923- WhoAm 92, WhoE 93
Krisak, Annette 1957- WhoAmW 93
Krisch, Alan David 1939- WhoAm 92
Krisch, Joel 1924- St&PR 93
Krisch, Samuel J., II 1958- WhoAm 92
Krischner, Harald 1930- WhoScE 91-4
Krisciokaitis, Raymond John 1937- WhoAm 92
Krisciunas, Joseph P. 1939- St&PR 93
Kriscunas, Robert A. Law&B 92
Krise, Patricia Love 1959- WhoAmW 93, WhoWor 93
Kriser, Anka Angelowa 1931- WhoE 93
Krish, John MiSFD 9
Krishamoorthy, P.S. ScF&FL 92
Krishan, Shrikant 1960- WhoWor 93
Krishchenko, Alexander Petrovich 1948- WhoWor 93
Krishen, Kumar 1939- WhoAm 92, WhoSSW 93, WhoWor 93
Krisher, Bernard 1931- WhoAm 92
Krisher, Lawrence Charles 1933- WhoE 93
Krisher, Ralph E., Jr. Law&B 92
Krisher, William K. 1931- WhoAm 92
Krishnadasan, Vishakan 1931- WhoUN 92
Krishnakumar, Kalmanje Srinivas 1960- WhoSSW 93
Krishnakumar, S. 1939- WhoAsAP 91
Krishnamra, Toemsakdi 1927- WhoWor 93
Krishnamurthi, Cackalani Ramalingam 1934- WhoUN 92
Krishnamurthy, Gerbail Thimmegowda 1937- WhoAm 92
Krishnamurti, G. ScF&FL 92
Krishnamurti, J. 1895-1986 BioIn 17
Krishnamurti, Jiddu 1895-1986 BioIn 17, ConAu 39NR
Krishnan, Bharathi 1939- ScF&FL 92
Krishnan, Palaniappa 1953- WhoE 93, WhoEmL 93
Krishnayya, Chandra Pasupulati 1932- WhoAm 92
Krislov, Samuel 1929- WhoAm 92
Krismanth, Kenneth A. St&PR 93
Krisnan, Raman Bala 1943- WhoWor 93
Krispin, Jacob 1952- WhoE 93
Kriss, Anthony 1946- WhoWor 93
Kriss, Debra Lynn Law&B 92
Kriss, Dorothy Jean 1947- WhoE 93, WhoEmL 93
Kriss, Eric BioIn 17
Kriss, Ronald WhoAm 92
Krisst, Raymond John 1937- WhoAm 92
Krist, Betty Jane 1946- WhoAmW 93, WhoE 93, WhoEmL 93
Krist, Martin Allan 1961- WhoEmL 93
Kristal, Mark Bennett 1944- WhoE 93
Kristel, Ira B. 1927- St&PR 93
Kristeller, Paul Oskar WhoAm 92
Kristen, Udo 1937- WhoScE 91-3
Kristensen, Charles BioIn 17
Kristensen, Henning Gjelstrup 1939- WhoScE 91-2
Kristensen, Kristian 1945- WhoScE 91-2
Kristensen, Michael K. Law&B 92
Kristensen, Richard E. 1946- St&PR 93
Kristensson, Gerhard Sven 1949- WhoWor 93
Kristeva, Julia 1941- BioIn 17
Kristiansen, Ingrid BioIn 17
Kristiansen, Magne 1932- WhoAm 92
Kristina, Queen of Sweden 1626-1689 BioIn 17
Kristinsson, Hordur 1937- WhoWor 93
Kristjansson, Elias 1938- WhoWor 93
Kristjansson, Leo 1943- WhoScE 91-4
Kristof, Dennis Robert 1943- WhoSSW 93
Kristof, Frank S. d1991 BioIn 17
Kristof, Jane 1932- WhoAmW 93
Kristof, Ladis Kris Donabed 1918- WhoAm 92
Kristof, Nicholas Donabet 1959- WhoAm 92
Kristofco, Thomas John 1960- St&PR 93
Kristoferson, Lars A. 1942- WhoScE 91-4
Kristoff, James WhoAm 92
Kristoff, James Christopher 1957- WhoEmL 93
Kristofferson, Karl Eric 1929- WhoAm 92
Kristofferson, Kris BioIn 17
Kristofferson, Kris 1936- Baker 92, WhoAm 92
Kristoffersson, Eeva Riitta 1929- WhoScE 91-4
Kristol, Irving BioIn 17
Kristol, Irving 1920- WhoAm 92
Kristol, William 1952- NewYTBS 92 [port], WhoAm 92
Kriston, Michael E. 1940- St&PR 93
Kristopeit, Donald Julius 1926- St&PR 93
Kristwald-Kallefelz, Elfriede Hildegarde 1938- WhoWrEP 92
Krit, Robert Lee 1920- WhoWor 93
Kritchevsky, David 1920- WhoAm 92, WhoE 93
Kritoboulos, Michael dc. 1470 OxDcByz
Kritselis, William Nicholas 1931- WhoWor 93
Kritsick, Stephen Mark 1951- WhoAm 92
Krittman, Irwin M. Law&B 92
Kritz, Ernesto H. 1943- WhoUN 92
Kritz, Mary M. ConAu 138
Kritzer, Donald L. 1934- St&PR 93
Kritzer, Howard S. Law&B 92
Kritzer, Paul E. Law&B 92
Kritzer, Paul E. 1942- St&PR 93
Kritzer, Paul Eric 1942- WhoAm 92
Kritzman, Jeffrey D. 1954- St&PR 93
Kriukov, Nikolai 1908-1961 Baker 92
Kriukov, Vladimir 1902-1960 Baker 92
Krivchenya, Alexey 1910-1974 OxDcOp
Krivine, Alain 1941- BioIn 17
Krivine, Emmanuel 1947- Baker 92
Krivinka, Gustav 1928- Baker 92
Krivisky, Barry M. Law&B 92
Krivitzky, Jerrold S. Law&B 92
Krivkovich, Peter George 1946- WhoAm 92
Krivosha, Norman M. Law&B 92
Krivosha, Norman M. 1934- WhoIns 93
Krivosha, Norman Marvin 1934- St&PR 93
Krivoshia, Eli, Jr. Law&B 92
Krivoshia, Eli, Jr. 1935- WhoAm 92
Krivoy, Kathy Lynn 1956- WhoEmL 93
Krivsky, Ivan Yuriyovich 1932- WhoWor 93
Krivsky, William A. 1929- St&PR 93, WhoAm 92
Kriyananda 1926- WhoWor 93
Kriz, George James 1936- WhoAm 92, WhoSSW 93
Kriz, Miroslav A. 1908-1991 BioIn 17
Kriz, Vilem Francis 1921- WhoAm 92
Kriz, Wilhelm 1936- WhoScE 91-3
Krizan, Karen BioIn 17
Krizanc, John 1956- WhoCanL 92
Krizek, Randall E. 1951- St&PR 93
Krizek, Raymond John 1932- WhoAm 92
Krizek, Thomas Joseph 1932- WhoAm 92, WhoWor 93
Krizkovsky, Pavel 1820-1885 Baker 92
Kriznar, Mirko 1923- WhoScE 91-4
Krmpotic, Ivica WhoScE 91-4
Krmpotic-Nemanic, Jelena 1921- WhoScE 91-4
Kroc, Ray BioIn 17

Kroch, Carl A. 1914- *St&PR 93*
Kroch, Carl Adolph 1914- *WhoAm 92*
Krochka, James J. *Law&B 92*
Krochmal, Arnold 1919- *WhoSSW 93*
Krock, Arthur 1886-1974 *JrnUS*
Krocka, Richard J. *Law&B 92*
Krockman, Arnold Francis 1945- *WhoE 93*
Krodel, William Joseph 1928- *St&PR 93*
Kroebel, Reinhard Heinrich Walter 1934- *WhoScE 91-3*
Kroeber, Alfred L. 1876-1960 *IntDcAn*
Kroeber, C. Kent 1939- *St&PR 93, WhoAm 92*
Kroeber, Clifton Brown 1921- *WhoAm 92*
Kroeber, Karl 1926- *ScF&FL 92, WhoAm 92*
Kroeger, Arthur 1932- *WhoAm 92*
Kroeger, Arthur F. 1912- *St&PR 93*
Kroeger, Berry 1912-1991 *BioIn 17*
Kroeger, Ernest Richard 1862-1934 *Baker 92*
Kroeger, Hans 1928- *WhoScE 91-3*
Kroeger, Harold K. *Law&B 92*
Kroeger, John F. *Law&B 92*
Kroeger, Karl 1932- *Baker 92*
Kroeger, N. Bernard 1945- *St&PR 93*
Kroeger, Susan Jean 1961- *WhoE 93*
Kroeger, William C. d1991 *BioIn 17*
Kroehling, John H. 1923- *St&PR 93*
Kroekel, Juliette Ann 1947- *WhoWrEP 92*
Kroeker, Allen 1951- *MiSFD 9*
Kroemer, Henrike Beate 1961- *WhoAmW 93*
Kroener, Peter H. 1942- *St&PR 93*
Kroener, William Frederick, III 1945- *WhoAm 92*
Kroening, Robert *St&PR 93*
Kroeplin, Karla Joan 1961- *WhoEmL 93*
Kroes, Ralph Stephen 1931- *WhoWor 93*
Kroes, Robert 1940- *WhoScE 91-3*
Kroese, Chris Coyle 1959- *St&PR 93*
Kroesen, Frederick James 1923- *WhoAm 92*
Kroesen, Jill Anne 1949- *WhoWrEP 92*
Kroetch, James E. *Law&B 92*
Kroetch, Patricia Ann Robinson 1935- *WhoWor 93*
Kroetsch, Robert 1927- *BioIn 17, ConAu 38NR, WhoCanL 92*
Kroetsch, Robert Paul 1927- *WhoAm 92*
Kroetz, Deanna Lynn 1961- *WhoAmW 93*
Kroez, Harold 1937- *St&PR 93, WhoE 93*
Kroft, Steve Frederick 1945- *WhoAm 92*
Kroger, Achim 1937- *WhoScE 91-3*
Kroger, Althea 1946- *WhoAmW 93*
Kroger, Dawn Virginia 1941- *WhoSSW 93*
Kroger, Joan A. 1954- *St&PR 93*
Kroger, Joseph J. 1934- *St&PR 93*
Kroger, William Saul 1906- *WhoAm 92*
Krogh, David L. *Law&B 92*
Krogh, Lester Christensen 1925- *WhoAm 92*
Krogh, Peter 1941- *WhoWor 93*
Krogh, Peter Frederic 1937- *WhoAm 92*
Krogh, Stein 1935- *WhoScE 91-4*
Krogh-Jensen, Mogens 1935- *WhoWor 93*
Krogius, Tristan Ernst Gunnar 1933- *WhoAm 92*
Krogstad, Jack Lynn 1944- *WhoAm 92*
Krogstad, Olaf 1929- *WhoScE 91-4*
Krogulski, John Leo 1927- *WhoE 93*
Kroh, Jerzy 1924- *WhoScE 91-4*
Kroha, Bradford King 1926- *WhoAm 92*
Kroha, Elizabeth *BioIn 17*
Kroha, Johann 1961- *WhoWor 93*
Kroha, Vaclav 1935- *WhoScE 91-4*
Krohg, Christian 1852-1925 *BioIn 17*
Krohg, Oda 1860-1935 *BioIn 17*
Krohn, Barbara Rapchak 1954- *WhoWor 93*
Krohn, Carole A. *Law&B 92*
Krohn, Claus Dankertsen 1923- *WhoAm 92, WhoWor 93*
Krohn, Conrad *WhoScE 91-4*
Krohn, Duane Ronald 1946- *WhoAm 92*
Krohn, Ernst C(hristopher) 1888-1975 *Baker 92*
Krohn, Felix (Julius Theofil) 1898-1963 *Baker 92*
Krohn, Hans-Joachim 1943- *St&PR 93*
Krohn, Ilmari (Henrik Reinhold) 1867-1960 *Baker 92*
Krohn, Josephine Elliott *AmWomPl*
Krohn, Karsten 1944- *WhoWor 93*
Krohn, Kenneth Robert 1946- *WhoEmL 93*
Krohn, Lisa *BioIn 17*
Krohn, Robert F. 1933- *St&PR 93*
Krohn, William Eugene 1932- *St&PR 93*
Krok, Robert L. 1945- *St&PR 93*
Krokar, James Paul 1948- *WhoEmL 93*
Krol, B. *WhoScE 91-3*
Krol, John A. 1936- *WhoAm 92*
Krol, John Cardinal 1910- *WhoAm 92, WhoWor 93*
Krol, John Casimir 1949- *WhoE 93, WhoEmL 93*
Krol, Kazimierz 1954- *WhoScE 91-4*
Krol, Rosemary 1955- *WhoAmW 93*
Krolak, Marian 1929- *WhoScE 91-4*
Krolikiewicz, Grzegorz 1939- *DrEEuF*
Krolikowska, Maria Janina 1922- *WhoScE 91-4*
Krolikowski, Czeslaw 1926- *WhoScE 91-4*
Krolikowski, Wojciech 1926- *WhoScE 91-4*
Krolikowski, Zbigniew 1923- *WhoScE 91-4*
Krolis, K.E. *WhoScE 91-3*
Kroll, Alexander *BioIn 17*
Kroll, Alexander S. 1937- *WhoAm 92, WhoE 93*
Kroll, Arthur Herbert 1939- *WhoAm 92*
Kroll, Barry Lewis 1934- *WhoAm 92*
Kroll, Boris 1913-1991 *BioIn 17*
Kroll, Ernest 1914- *WhoAm 92*
Kroll, Erwin 1886-1976 *Baker 92*
Kroll, Herbert 1940- *WhoScE 91-3*
Kroll, John Ernest 1940- *WhoSSW 93*
Kroll, Jules *BioIn 17, NewYTBS 92 [port]*
Kroll, Jules B. *Law&B 92*
Kroll, Leon 1884-1974 *BioIn 17*
Kroll, Leonard Joseph 1935- *WhoE 93*
Kroll, Martin Harris 1952- *WhoE 93*
Kroll, Michael Joseph 1948- *St&PR 93*
Kroll, Michael Robert *Law&B 92*
Kroll, Norman Myles 1922- *WhoAm 92*
Kroll, Richard 1952- *WhoE 93*
Kroll, Robert James 1928- *WhoAm 92*
Kroll, Rohan Gerhard *WhoScE 91-1*
Kroll, Sharon Ruth Hecker 1958- *WhoAmW 93, WhoEmL 93*
Kroll, Stephen R. 1946- *St&PR 93*
Kroll, Steven *BioIn 17*
Kroll, Thomas Robert 1947- *St&PR 93*
Kroll, Walter *WhoScE 91-3*
Kroll, William 1901-1980 *Baker 92*
Kroloff, George Michael 1935- *WhoAm 92*
Kroloff, Steven J. *Law&B 92*
Krolopp, Rudolph William 1930- *WhoAm 92*
Krolopp, Wlodzimierz Jan 1928- *WhoWor 93*
Krolow, Karl *BioIn 17*
Krolyk, Christina Cuthbert *Law&B 92*
Krom, George Charles 1930- *St&PR 93*
Krom, Judith Sue 1942- *WhoAmW 93*
Krom, Ruud Arne Finco 1941- *WhoAm 92*
Krombein, Karl vonVorse 1912- *WhoAm 92*
Kromberg, Morten John 1962- *WhoWor 93*
Kromberg, William A. 1945- *St&PR 93*
Krombholc, Jaroslav 1918-1983 *Baker 92, OxDcOp*
Krombholc, Karlo 1905- *Baker 92*
Kromenhoek, J.P. 1942- *St&PR 93*
Kromer, Istvan 1944- *WhoScE 91-4*
Kromer, Martin 1515-1589 *PolBiDi*
Kromer, Michael Charles 1945- *WhoE 93*
Kromer, Wolfram 1935- *WhoWor 93*
Krominga, Lynn 1950- *WhoAm 92*
Kromka, James Thomas Michael 1954- *WhoEmL 93, WhoWor 93*
Krommenacker, Raymond 1947- *WhoUN 92*
Krommer, Franz Vincez 1759-1831 *Baker 92*
Kromolicki, Joseph 1882-1961 *Baker 92*
Krompecher, Stephen John 1947- *WhoSSW 93*
Kromphardt, Jurgen A.J. 1933- *WhoWor 93*
Kron, Jo Anne L. *Law&B 92*
Kronast, Benedikt 1929- *WhoScE 91-3*
Kronbach, Thomas 1952- *WhoWor 93*
Kronberg, Bengt 1949- *WhoScE 91-4*
Krone, Andrew Joseph 1952- *WhoEmL 93*
Krone, Chester 1935- *ScF&FL 92*
Krone, Frank 1928- *St&PR 93*
Krone, Gerald Sidney 1933- *WhoAm 92*
Krone, Helmut 1925- *WhoAm 92*
Krone, Irene 1940- *WhoE 93*
Krone, Joan E. 1941- *WhoAmW 93*
Krone, Julie *BioIn 17*
Krone, Julie 1963- *WhoAmW 93*
Krone, Philip Sand 1948- *St&PR 93*
Krone, W. *WhoScE 91-3*
Krone, Wolfgang 1935- *WhoUN 92*
Kronegger, Maria Elisabeth 1932- *ScF&FL 92, WhoAm 92, WhoAmW 93, WhoE 93*
Kronen, Jerilyn 1947- *WhoAmW 93*
Kronen, Peter Heinrich 1921- *WhoWor 93*
Kronenberg, Franklin W. *Law&B 92*
Kronenberg, Inez V. 1937- *WhoAmW 93*
Kronenberg, Marvin Lee 1929- *WhoE 93*
Kronenberg, Mindy H. 1954- *WhoWrEP 92*
Kronenberg, Norman 1936- *St&PR 93*
Kronenberg, Richard Samuel 1938- *WhoAm 92, WhoSSW 93*
Kronenberg, Robert B. *Law&B 92*
Kronenberg, Susan L. 1948- *WhoWrEP 92*
Kronenfeld, David Brian 1941- *WhoAm 92*
Kronenfeld, Jennie Jacobs 1949- *WhoAmW 93*
Kronenthal, Richard Leonard 1928- *WhoE 93*
Kronenwett, Frederick Rudolph 1923- *WhoE 93*
Kronenwetter, Jeffrey Alan 1962- *WhoE 93*
Kronenwetter, Michael *BioIn 17*
Kronenwetter, Timothy J. *St&PR 93*
Kroner, Alfred 1939- *WhoScE 91-3*
Kroner, Walter Manfred 1934- *WhoE 93*
Kronestedt, O. Torbjorn 1942- *WhoScE 91-4*
Kronewitter, Joseph Ray 1949- *St&PR 93*
Kronfeld, Alan C. 1930- *St&PR 93*
Kronfeld, David Schultz 1928- *WhoAm 92*
Kronfeld, Fred N. 1929- *St&PR 93*
Kronfeld, Gary H. 1955- *St&PR 93*
Kronfeld, Leopold James 1941- *WhoE 93*
Kronfellner-Kraus, Gottfried *WhoScE 91-4*
Kronfol, Fuad Mohammed 1936- *WhoUN 92*
Krongard, Alvin *BioIn 17*
Krongard, Alvin B. 1936- *St&PR 93*
Krongard, Howard J. *Law&B 92*
Kronholm, Martha Mary 1952- *WhoAmW 93*
Kronick, David A. 1917- *WhoAm 92*
Kronick, Jane Collier 1932- *WhoAmW 93*
Kronick, William *MiSFD 9*
Kronik, John William 1931- *WhoAm 92*
Kroning, Michael H.A.W. 1944- *WhoScE 91-3*
Kroninger, Luther H., Jr. 1930- *St&PR 93*
Kroninger, Stephen *BioIn 17*
Kroninger, Timothy K. *Law&B 92*
Kronish, Richard Mark 1961- *WhoE 93*
Kronk, Catherine *Law&B 92*
Kronk, Courtney *BioIn 17*
Kronke, Dorene Emma 1950- *WhoAmW 93*
Kronke, Emil 1865-1938 *Baker 92*
Kronman, Anthony Townsend 1945- *WhoAm 92*
Kronman, Carol Jane 1944- *WhoWor 93*
Kronman, Joseph Henry 1931- *WhoAm 92*
Kronmuller, Helmut Friedrich 1931- *WhoScE 91-3*
Kronner, Joan Marie 1960- *WhoEmL 93*
Kronold, Hans 1872-1922 *Baker 92, PolBiDi*
Kronold, Selma 1861-1920 *Baker 92, PolBiDi*
Kronos Quartet, The *News 93-1 [port]*
Kronovich, Thomas *Law&B 92*
Kronrad, Robert B. 1951- *St&PR 93*
Kronsberg, Jeremy Joe *MiSFD 9*
Kronschnabel, George J. 1925- *St&PR 93*
Kronschnabel, Robert James 1935- *St&PR 93, WhoAm 92*
Kronstadt, Arnold Mayo 1919- *WhoAm 92*
Kronstadt, Nat 1923- *St&PR 93*
Kronstein, Werner J. 1930- *WhoAm 92*
Kronvall, Goran 1938- *WhoScE 91-4*
Kronvall, Johnny 1948- *WhoScE 91-4*
Kroo, Gyorgy 1926- *Baker 92*
Kroo, Norbert 1934- *WhoScE 91-4, WhoWor 93*
Krook, Bertil Olof 1932- *WhoAm 92*
Kroon, Ciro *DcCPCAm*
Kroon, John C. 1939- *St&PR 93*
Kroon, Reinout P. d1992 *NewYTBS 92*
Kroos, Arthur G., III *Law&B 92*
Krooss, Barbara Lee 1948- *WhoAmW 93*
Krop, Pamela S. *Law&B 92*
Kropas, Claudia Victoria 1957- *WhoAmW 93, WhoEmL 93*
Kropf, Carol Ann 1941- *WhoAmW 93*
Kropf, Richard Thomas 1909- *St&PR 93*
Kropilak, Mark J. *Law&B 92*
Kroposki, Michael G. *Law&B 92*
Kropp, Charles August 1937- *St&PR 93*
Kropp, David Arthur 1933- *WhoAm 92*
Kropp, David Edward 1941- *St&PR 93*
Kropp, Norman W. *Law&B 92*
Kropp, Paul 1948- *WhoCanL 92*
Kropp, Regina C. *WhoE 93*
Kropp, Richard P. 1940- *WhoIns 93*
Kropp, Stacy Anne 1964- *WhoAmW 93*
Kropp, Werner 1923- *WhoWor 93*
Kropper, Jon Franklin 1933- *WhoAm 92*
Kropschot, Richard H. 1927- *WhoAm 92*
Kroschel, Kristian 1942- *WhoWor 93*
Kroser, Albert S. 1930- *WhoE 93*
Kroskey, Douglas W. 1953- *St&PR 93*
Krosner, Fred 1935- *St&PR 93*
Krosnick, Annette Susan 1948- *WhoEmL 93*
Krosnick, Joel 1941- *WhoAm 92*
Krosoczka, Joseph D. 1928- *St&PR 93*
Krossner, Rhonda Parrella 1951- *WhoAmW 93*
Krostich, Henry J. 1950- *WhoEmL 93*
Kroszel, Janusz *WhoScE 91-4*
Kroszner, Randall Scott 1962- *WhoEmL 93*
Kroth, Jeannie Mae 1944- *WhoAmW 93*
Krothapalli, Radha Krishna 1951- *WhoEmL 93*
Krotinger, Jonathan H. *Law&B 92*
Krotiuk, William John 1948- *WhoE 93, WhoEmL 93*
Krotki, Karol Jozef 1922- *WhoAm 92*
Kroto, Harold *WhoScE 91-1*
Krotseng, Richard Van Marter *Law&B 92*
Krotter, John R. 1910- *St&PR 93*
Krotter, Robert J. 1930- *St&PR 93*
Kroulek, Jack James 1931- *St&PR 93*
Kroupa, Sharon A. *Law&B 92*
Krouse, Diane Murray 1954- *WhoEmL 93*
Krouse, George Raymond, Jr. 1945- *WhoAm 92*
Krouskop, Janice Louise 1953- *WhoAmW 93, WhoEmL 93*
Krout, W. Vincent 1924- *St&PR 93*
Krovatin, William *Law&B 92*
Krovetz, L. Jerome 1929- *WhoSSW 93*
Krovina, P.P. *WhoScE 91-1*
Krow, Josef Theodor 1797-1859 *Baker 92*
Krowczynski, Leszek 1925- *WhoScE 91-4*
Krowe, Allen Julian 1932- *WhoAm 92*
Krown, Susan Ellen 1946- *WhoAmW 93*
Kroyer, Bill *MiSFD 9*
Kroyer, Theodor 1873-1945 *Baker 92*
Krpan, Daniel R. 1938- *St&PR 93*
Krpata, Anne Marie 1933- *WhoAmW 93*
Krsek, George 1920- *St&PR 93*
Krsiak, Miloslav 1939- *WhoScE 91-4*
Krsinic, Frano 1947- *WhoScE 91-4*
Krska, Vaclav 1900-1969 *DrEEuF*
KRS-One *BioIn 17*
KRS-One c. 1965- *ConMus 8 [port]*
Krstic, Petar 1877-1957 *Baker 92*
Krsul, John Aloysius, Jr. 1938- *WhoAm 92, WhoWor 93*
Krubeck, Richard 1945- *St&PR 93*
Krubiner, Alan Martin *Law&B 92*
Krucenski, Leonard Joseph 1931- *WhoE 93*
Kruchina, Nikolai E. 1928-1991 *BioIn 17*
Kruchkow, Diane 1947- *WhoWrEP 92*
Kruchten, Marcia 1932- *ScF&FL 92*
Kruchten, Marcia Helen 1932- *WhoWrEP 92*
Kruck, Werner H. 1933- *St&PR 93*
Kruckeberg, Arthur R(ice) 1920- *ConAu 137*
Kruckeberg, Arthur Rice 1920- *WhoAm 92*
Kruckenberg, Wayne Leonard 1950- *WhoWor 93*
Krucker, Werner 1925- *WhoScE 91-4*
Kruckl, Franz 1841-1899 *Baker 92*
Kruckmeyer, Erna *AmWomPl*
Krucks, William 1918- *St&PR 93, WhoAm 92*
Kruczkowski, Leon 1900-1962 *PolBiDi*
Krudener, Juliane von 1764-1824 *BioIn 17*
Krueger, Alan Douglas 1937- *WhoWor 93*
Krueger, Betty Jane 1923- *WhoWor 93*
Krueger, Betty L. 1929- *St&PR 93*
Krueger, Bonnie Lee 1950- *WhoAm 92, WhoAmW 93, WhoEmL 93, WhoWor 93*
Krueger, Carl Alan 1951- *St&PR 93*
Krueger, Caryl Waller 1929- *WhoWrEP 92*
Krueger, Charles Alvin 1951- *WhoEmL 93*
Krueger, Charles Z. *Law&B 92*
Krueger, Darrell William 1943- *WhoAm 92*
Krueger, David Wayne 1947- *WhoWrEP 92*
Krueger, Douglas Herbert 1944- *St&PR 93*
Krueger, Eric Eugene 1958- *WhoE 93*
Krueger, Eugene Rex 1935- *WhoAm 92*
Krueger, Francis Lee, III 1955- *WhoE 93*
Krueger, Gerhard Richard Franz 1936- *WhoWor 93*
Krueger, Gretchen Marie Dewailly 1952- *WhoEmL 93, WhoSSW 93*
Krueger, Harvey M. 1929- *St&PR 93*
Krueger, Harvey Mark 1929- *WhoAm 92*
Krueger, Helmut 1939- *WhoScE 91-4*
Krueger, James 1938- *WhoAm 92*
Krueger, James A. 1938- *St&PR 93*
Krueger, James Elwood 1926- *WhoE 93*
Krueger, Jeffrey A. 1954- *St&PR 93*
Krueger, Karl (Adalbert) 1894-1979 *Baker 92*
Krueger, Ken 1926- *ScF&FL 92*
Krueger, Kenneth John 1946- *WhoAm 92*
Krueger, Kevin Paul 1959- *WhoEmL 93*
Krueger, Kurt Donn 1952- *WhoWor 93*
Krueger, Lorenz 1932- *ConAu 136*
Krueger, Margery *ScF&FL 92*
Krueger, Marlis 1940- *WhoWor 93*
Krueger, Maynard August, Jr. 1931- *St&PR 93*
Krueger, Myron W. *BioIn 17*

Krueger, Nancy Asta 1947- *WhoAmW 93, WhoEmL 93*
Krueger, Patricia Marie 1960- *WhoAmW 93*
Krueger, Paul 1949- *St&PR 93*
Krueger, Ralph Arthur 1952- *WhoE 93*
Krueger, Ralph Ray 1927- *WhoAm 92*
Krueger, Robert A. 1935- *St&PR 93*
Krueger, Robert Allen 1935- *WhoE 93*
Krueger, Robert Blair 1928- *WhoAm 92*
Krueger, Robert Charles 1935- *WhoAm 92*
Krueger, Robert Kenneth 1941- *WhoSSW 93*
Krueger, Robert W. 1916- *St&PR 93*
Krueger, Robert William 1916- *WhoAm 92*
Krueger, Rolf 1937- *WhoSSW 93*
Krueger, Terry *ScF&FL 92*
Krueger, Thomas H. *Law&B 92*
Krueger, Thomas Lynn 1952- *WhoEmL 93*
Krueger, Vernon L. 1956- *WhoSSW 93*
Krueger, Walter 1881-1967 *HarEnMi*
Kruegler, Nancy Alice 1946- *WhoEmL 93*
Kruer, William L. *BioIn 17*
Kruesi, Paul R. 1928- *St&PR 93*
Kruess, James 1926- *MajAI [port]*
Kruft, Stephen R. *Law&B 92*
Krug, A.E. *Law&B 92*
Krug, Anthony Earle 1938- *St&PR 93*
Krug, David John 1949- *St&PR 93*
Krug, Friedrich 1812-1892 *Baker 92*
Krug, Hartman H. 1937- *St&PR 93*
Krug, Helmut 1925- *WhoScE 91-3*
Krug, John Carleton 1951- *WhoEmL 93, WhoSSW 93*
Krug, Joseph 1858-1915 *Baker 92*
Krug, Joseph C. d1990 *BioIn 17*
Krug, Joseph H. 1916-1991 *BioIn 17*
Krug, Judith Fingeret 1940- *WhoAmW 93*
Krug, Karen-Ann 1951- *WhoAmW 93, WhoEmL 93*
Krug, Maurice F. 1929- *St&PR 93*
Krug, Walter Carl, Jr. 1938- *WhoSSW 93*
Kruger, Andrzej 1940- *WhoScE 91-4*
Kruger, Arthur Martin 1932- *WhoAm 92*
Kruger, Arthur Newman 1916- *WhoAm 92*
Kruger, Barbara *BioIn 17*
Kruger, Bonny Beatrice 1950- *WhoEmL 93*
Kruger, Charles Herman, Jr. 1934- *WhoAm 92*
Kruger, Curtis Frank 1930- *St&PR 93*
Kruger, Dennis George 1946- *WhoSSW 93*
Kruger, Eduard 1807-1885 *Baker 92*
Kruger, Eric 1954- *St&PR 93*
Kruger, Frederick B. *Law&B 92*
Kruger, Gary I. *Law&B 92*
Kruger, Gary Iver 1946- *WhoEmL 93*
Kruger, Gustav Otto, Jr. 1916- *WhoAm 92*
Kruger, Jeffrey 1950- *St&PR 93*
Kruger, Jerome 1927- *WhoAm 92*
Kruger, Kally Karlene *Law&B 92*
Kruger, Kenneth Charles 1930- *WhoAm 92*
Kruger, Lawrence 1929- *WhoAm 92*
Kruger, Lorenz *ConAu 136*
Kruger, Marc L. *Law&B 92*
Kruger, Melvin I. 1929- *St&PR 93*
Kruger, Mollee Coppel 1929- *WhoAmW 93, WhoWrEP 92*
Kruger, Nell *AmWomPl*
Kruger, Otto 1885-1974 *BioIn 17*
Kruger, Patricia Regina *Law&B 92*
Kruger, Paul 1825-1904 *BioIn 17*
Kruger, Paul Robert 1957- *WhoWor 93*
Kruger, Peggy Ann Mullen 1942- *WhoAmW 93*
Kruger, Reto 1953- *WhoEmL 93*
Kruger, Richard Hunt 1953- *WhoEmL 93*
Kruger, Stephanus Johannes Paulus 1825-1904 *BioIn 17*
Kruger, Steven L. 1956- *St&PR 93*
Kruger, Tristram Coffin 1951- *WhoE 93, WhoEmL 93, WhoWor 93*
Kruger, Weldon Dale 1931- *WhoAm 92*
Kruger, Wilhelm 1820-1883 *Baker 92*
Krugliak, Samuel 1917- *St&PR 93*
Kruglov, Victor Makarovich 1937- *WhoWor 93*
Krugman, Jeff *St&PR 93*
Krugman, Paul Robin 1953- *WhoAm 92*
Krugman, Saul 1911- *WhoAm 92*
Krugman, Stanley L. 1925- *St&PR 93*
Krugman, Stanley Lee 1925- *WhoAm 92*
Krug-Waldsee 1858-1915 *Baker 92*
Kruh, Daniel 1934- *WhoE 93*
Kruh, David (S.) 1956- *ConAu 138*
Kruh, Jacques 1922- *WhoScE 91-2*
Kruh, Louis 1923- *ConAu 138*
Kruh, Robert F. 1925- *WhoAm 92*
Kruhoeffer, Volker 1930- *St&PR 93*
Kruidenier, David 1921- *St&PR 93, WhoAm 92*
Kruiderink, Anton 1939- *WhoUN 92*
Kruis, M.H. van't 1861-1919 *Baker 92*
Kruithof, Egbert K.O. 1949- *WhoScE 91-4*
Kruizenga, Richard John 1930- *St&PR 93, WhoAm 92*
Kruk, Donald Nicholas *Law&B 92*
Kruk, J.W. 1940- *St&PR 93*
Kruk, Katherine *Law&B 92*
Krukiel, Charles E. *Law&B 92*
Kruklitis, A. 1941- *St&PR 93*
Krukowski, Lucian 1929- *WhoAm 92*
Krul, Eli 1926-1971 *Baker 92*
Krul, Joseph E. 1945- *St&PR 93*
Krulak, Charles Chandler 1942- *WhoAm 92*
Krulak, Victor Harold 1913- *WhoAm 92*
Krulewich, Helen D. 1948- *WhoAmW 93, WhoE 93*
Krulfeld, Ruth Marilyn 1931- *WhoAm 92*
Krulich, Joseph R. 1936- *St&PR 93*
Krulik, Barbara S. 1955- *WhoAm 92*
Krulik, Nancy E. *ScF&FL 92*
Krulik, Stephanie Miriam 1943- *WhoWrEP 92*
Krulik, Theodore 1948- *ScF&FL 92*
Krulitz, Leo M. 1938- *St&PR 93*
Krulitz, Leo Morrion 1938- *WhoAm 92*
Krulitz, Pamela Ristau 1964- *WhoAmW 93*
Krull, Annie 1876-1947 *OxDcOp*
Krull, Charles Fred 1933- *WhoAm 92*
Krull, Donald Scott 1963- *WhoSSW 93*
Krull, Edward Alexander 1929- *WhoWor 93*
Krull, Ira Stanley 1940- *WhoE 93*
Krull, James Sargent 1948- *WhoE 93*
Krull, Joy Denise 1950- *WhoAmW 93*
Krull, Kevin Charles 1952- *WhoAm 92*
Krull, Manfred 1940- *WhoUN 92*
Krulwich, Terry Ann 1943- *WhoAmW 93*
Krum d814 *OxDcByz*
Krum, Joseph C. 1937- *St&PR 93*
Krum, Paul R. 1912- *St&PR 93*
Kruman, Mark Steven 1953- *WhoEmL 93, WhoWor 93*
Krumb, P.P. 1942- *St&PR 93*
Krumbein, Charles Harvey 1944- *St&PR 93, WhoAm 92*
Krumboltz, John Dwight 1928- *WhoAm 92*
Krumeich, Elizabeth Kneisel *Law&B 92*
Krumgold, Joseph (Quincy) 1908-1980 *DcAmChF 1960, MajAI [port]*
Krumhansl, Bernice Rosemary 1922- *WhoWrEP 92*
Krumholz, Alfred F., Jr. 1921- *St&PR 93*
Krumholz, Steve 1949- *St&PR 93*
Krumholz, Wilhelm Vilem 1915- *WhoE 93*
Krumins, Girts 1932- *WhoAm 92*
Krumm, Charles Ferdinand 1941- *WhoAm 92*
Krumm, Daniel John 1926- *St&PR 93, WhoAm 92*
Krumm, John McGill 1913- *WhoAm 92*
Krumm, Nancy Marakas *Law&B 92*
Krumm, William Frederick 1923- *WhoAm 92*
Krummacher, Johann-Henrich Karl 1946- *WhoWor 93*
Krumme, Donald P. 1931- *St&PR 93*
Krumme, George W. 1922- *St&PR 93*
Krummel, Donald William 1929- *WhoAm 92*
Krumov, I. *WhoScE 91-4*
Krump, Jeffrey R. 1952- *WhoEmL 93*
Krumpholtz, Anne-Marie c. 1755-c. 1824 *Baker 92*
Krumpholtz, Jean-Baptiste 1742-1790 *Baker 92*
Krumpholtz, Wenzel c. 1750-1817 *See* Krumpholtz, Jean-Baptiste 1742-1790 *Baker 92*
Krungvong, Niyut 1957- *WhoWor 93*
Krupa, Gene 1909-1973 *Baker 92*
Krupansky, Blanche 1925- *WhoAm 92*
Krupat, Arnold 1941- *WhoAm 92*
Krupa-Wojciechowska, Barbara 1930- *WhoScE 91-4*
Krupcale, Jeffrey David 1966- *WhoSSW 93*
Krupinska, Jolanta 1928- *WhoScE 91-4*
Krupinski, Jedrzej 1939- *WhoScE 91-4*
Krupinski, Loretta *BioIn 17*
Krupinsky, Jacquelyn Stowell 1932- *WhoWrEP 92*
Krupka, Laura June 1961- *WhoAmW 93*
Krupka, Robert George 1949- *WhoAm 92*
Krupkat, Ann Katherine 1926- *WhoAmW 93*
Krupman, William Allan 1936- *WhoAm 92*
Krupnick, Elizabeth Rachel 1949- *WhoAmW 93*
Krupnick, Janice Lee 1950- *WhoAmW 93, WhoEmL 93*
Krupnick, Jerold Barry 1943- *St&PR 93*
Krupnick, Steven Barry 1949- *St&PR 93*
Krupnik, Tadeusz Ignacy 1925- *WhoScE 91-4*
Krupnik, Vee M. *WhoAm 92, WhoAmW 93*
Krupp, Clarence William 1929- *WhoAm 92*
Krupp, Edward J. 1940- *St&PR 93*
Krupp, Edwin Charles 1944- *WhoAm 92, WhoWrEP 92*
Krupp, Fred David 1954- *WhoAm 92*
Krupp, Frederic D. *BioIn 17*
Krupp, Gustav 1869-1950 *DcTwHis*
Krupp, Helmar *WhoScE 91-3*
Krupp, Iames Arthur Gustave 1944- *WhoE 93*
Krupp, Judy-Arin 1937- *WhoE 93*
Krupp, Marcus Abraham 1913- *WhoAm 92*
Krupp, Margaret Ann 1956- *WhoEmL 93*
Kruppa, Joel 1948- *WhoScE 91-2*
Krupsha, Andrew John 1946- *St&PR 93*
Krupska, Danya 1921- *WhoAm 92, WhoE 93*
Krupsky, Joseph F. *Law&B 92*
Krus, David James 1940- *WhoAm 92*
Krus, John F. 1949- *St&PR 93*
Krus, Lech 1945- *WhoScE 91-4*
Krus, Stefan 1926- *WhoScE 91-4*
Krusceniski, Salomea 1873-1952 *OxDcOp*
Krusch, Karl Wilhelm 1951- *WhoWor 93*
Kruse, Alan G. *Law&B 92*
Kruse, Ann Gray 1941- *WhoAmW 93*
Kruse, Becky Ann 1949- *WhoAmW 93*
Kruse, Cathy Callahan 1960- *St&PR 93*
Kruse, Cathy L. 1954- *St&PR 93*
Kruse, Christine G. 1952- *WhoAmW 93*
Kruse, David L. 1944- *St&PR 93*
Kruse, David Louis, II 1944- *WhoAm 92*
Kruse, Donna Hynes 1956- *WhoEmL 93*
Kruse, Edgar Christ 1912- *WhoAm 92*
Kruse, Edward H. 1918- *St&PR 93*
Kruse, F. Michael *WhoAm 92*
Kruse, Hans Jakob *BioIn 17*
Kruse, Heeren Samuel Eilts 1911- *WhoAm 92*
Kruse, Heidi Lee 1962- *WhoAmW 93*
Kruse, Howard L. *Law&B 92*
Kruse, James Joseph 1932- *WhoAm 92*
Kruse, John Allen, Jr. *Law&B 92*
Kruse, John Alphonse 1926- *WhoAm 92*
Kruse, Lise Fiaux 1947- *WhoWor 93*
Kruse, Marlin L. 1936- *St&PR 93*
Kruse, Paul Robert 1912- *WhoAm 92*
Kruse, Paul Walters, Jr. 1927- *WhoAm 92*
Kruse, Regina Beth 1948- *WhoE 93*
Kruse, Richard J., Jr. *Law&B 92*
Kruse, Richard K. 1938- *St&PR 93*
Kruse, Richard Kareth, Jr. 1938- *WhoAm 92*
Kruse, Thomas Joseph 1946- *WhoSSW 93*
Kruse, Virginia Gilda 1921- *WhoAmW 93*
Krusen, Henry Stanley 1907- *WhoAm 92*
Krush, Beth 1918- *MajAI [port]*
Krush, Joe 1918- *MajAI*
Krushchev, Nikita *DcCPCAm*
Krushchev, Nikita 1894-1971 *BioIn 17*
Krushelnitskaya, Salomea (Ambrosivna) 1872-1952 *Baker 92*
Krushelnytska, Salomea 1873-1952 *OxDcOp*
Krushenick, John 1927- *WhoE 93*
Krushenick, Nicholas 1929- *WhoAm 92*
Krusick, Margaret Ann 1956- *WhoAmW 93*
Krusie, Kathleen Rose 1960- *WhoEmL 93*
Kruska, Kenneth John 1936- *St&PR 93*
Kruskal, Martin David 1925- *WhoAm 92*
Kruskal, William Henry 1919- *WhoAm 92*
Kruskemper, Gertrud M. 1930- *WhoScE 91-3*
Krus Krus, Petu' *BioIn 17*
Krusky, J. Roger 1941- *St&PR 93*
Krusos, Denis Angelo 1927- *WhoAm 92, WhoE 93*
Kruss, James 1926- *ScF&FL 92*
Krussmann, Helmut 1938- *WhoScE 91-3*
Kruszewski, Jan 1929- *WhoScE 91-4*
Krut, Stephen Frank 1943- *WhoE 93*
Krutan, George 1924- *St&PR 93*
Krutch, Joseph Wood 1893-1970 *ScF&FL 92*
Krutchkoff, Richard Gerald 1953- *WhoAm 92, WhoEmL 93, WhoSSW 93*
Krutenat, Richard Carroll 1934- *WhoWrEP 92*
Kruth, Harold E. *Law&B 92*
Krutilek, D.R. 1942- *St&PR 93*
Krutilek, Daniel Ray 1942- *WhoIns 93*
Kruus, Harri Kullervo 1950- *WhoWor 93*
Kruy, Joseph F. 1931- *St&PR 93*
Kruyf, Ton de 1937- *Baker 92*
Kruyt, A.C. 1869-1949 *IntDcAn*
Kruza, J. A. 1940- *WhoE 93*
Krvavac, Hajrudin 1926- *DrEEuF*
Kry, Stig Adolf 1929- *St&PR 93*
Kryczynski, Selim 1941- *WhoScE 91-4*
Kryder, Mark Howard 1943- *WhoAm 92*
Krygel, Barbara Ann 1947- *WhoAmW 93, WhoEmL 93*
Krygell, Johan Adam 1835-1915 *Baker 92*
Kryger Jensen, Peter 1957- *WhoScE 91-2*
Krygier, Stanley James 1903- *WhoE 93*
Krygowski, Tadeusz Marek 1937- *WhoScE 91-4*
Kryle, Sanford I. *Law&B 92*
Krylov, Pavel 1885-1935 *Baker 92*
Krymskii, Victor 1883-1927 *BioIn 17*
Krys, Sheldon Jack 1934- *WhoAm 92*
Krysakowski, John M. 1943- *St&PR 93*
Kryshak, Thaddeus Francis 1930- *WhoAm 92*
Kryshak, Thomas E. 1935- *WhoIns 93*
Krysiak, Joseph Francis 1915- *St&PR 93*
Krysiak, Julian A., Mrs. 1920- *St&PR 93*
Krysinski, Jan Eugeniusz 1935- *WhoScE 91-4*
Krysinski, Linda Ann 1957- *WhoAm 92*
Krysinski, Thomas Frank 1945- *WhoSSW 93*
Krysl, Marilyn 1942- *WhoWrEP 92*
Krystal, John Harrison 1958- *WhoEmL 93*
Krystek, Ryszard 1941- *WhoScE 91-4*
Krystowski, John C. *St&PR 93*
Krystyniak, Franklin Dominic 1942- *WhoSSW 93*
Kryszewski, Wojciech Marian 1958- *WhoWor 93*
Krysztoforski, Joseph Theodore 1953- *WhoE 93*
Kryter, Karl David 1914- *WhoAm 92*
Kryuchkov, Vladimir Aleksandrovich 1924- *BioIn 17*
Kryza, Elmer Gregory 1922- *WhoAm 92*
Kryzhanovsky, Ivan 1867-1924 *Baker 92*
Kryzius, Zigmantas 1953- *WhoWor 93*
Krzanowska, Halina 1926- *WhoScE 91-4*
Krzanowski, Joseph John, Jr. 1940- *WhoAm 92, WhoSSW 93*
Krzanowski, Wojtek Janusz *WhoScE 91-1*
Krzemien, Louis J., Jr. *Law&B 92*
Krzeminska-Pakula, Maria 1938- *WhoWor 93*
Krzeminski, Janusz 1928- *WhoScE 91-4*
Krzeminski-Freda, Henryk Leon 1933- *WhoScE 91-4*
Krzesinski, Felix 1823-1905 *PolBiDi*
Krzos, Joseph T. 1944- *St&PR 93*
Krzykowski, Dennis Lee 1951- *St&PR 93*
Krzymanski, Jan Antoni 1929- *WhoScE 91-4*
Krzyminski, Janet Restivo 1948- *WhoAmW 93*
Krzymowski, Tadeusz 1927- *WhoScE 91-4*
Krzynowek, S. Theodore 1943- *WhoE 93*
Krzysch, Gunter 1929- *WhoScE 91-3*
Krzysztofowicz, Roman 1947- *WhoAm 92*
Krzywanek, Hansdieter 1935- *WhoScE 91-3*
Krzywicki, Ludwik 1859-1941 *IntDcAn*
Krzyzan, Judy Lynn 1951- *WhoAmW 93, WhoEmL 93*
Krzyzanowski, Eve 1951- *WhoAm 92, WhoE 93*
Krzyzanowski, Jerzy A. 1927- *WhoScE 91-4*
Krzyzanowski, Julian 1892-1976 *PolBiDi*
Krzyzanowski, Konrad 1871-1922 *PolBiDi*
Krzyzanowski, Maciej Tadeusz 1920- *WhoScE 91-4*
Krzyzanowski, Richard L. *Law&B 92*
Krzyzanowski, Richard L. 1932- *St&PR 93*
Krzyzanowski, Richard Lucien 1932- *WhoAm 92*
Krzyzanowski, Wladimir B. 1824-1887 *PolBiDi*
Krzyzewski, Michael William 1947- *BiDAMSp 1989*
Krzyzewski, Mike 1947- *News 93-2 [port]*
Ksansnak, James E. 1940- *St&PR 93, WhoAm 92*
Kshessinska, Mathilda Maria 1872-1971 *PolBiDi*
Ksienski, Aharon Arthur 1924- *WhoAm 92*
Ksiezarek, Stanislaw 1938- *WhoScE 91-4*
Ksoll, Christina Maria 1964- *WhoEmL 93*
K-Solo *BioIn 17*
Kszepka, Joseph Anthony 1931- *WhoE 93*
Ktenas, Theodore Basil 1937- *WhoWor 93*
Ktorides, Stanley *Law&B 92*
K-Turkel, Judi *ConAu 37NR*
K-Turkel, Judi 1934- *WhoAmW 93, WhoWrEP 92*
Ku, Jentung *WhoE 93, WhoWor 93*
Ku, R. Fashun 1949- *WhoE 93*
Ku, Thomas Hsiu-Heng 1948- *WhoWor 93*
Ku, Y. H. 1902- *WhoAm 92, WhoE 93, WhoWor 93*
Kua, Teck-Guan 1961- *WhoSSW 93*
Kuan, Shia Shiong 1933- *WhoSSW 93*
Kuang, Zhiquan 1935- *WhoWor 93*
Kuang Wu-Ti d57 *HarEnMi*
Kuba, James F. 1948- *St&PR 93*
Kubach, Hans Erich 1909- *BioIn 17*

Kubacki, Krzysztof Stefan 1953- *WhoWor 93*
Kubacki, Stanislaw J. 1939- *WhoScE 91-4*
Kubal, David L. 1936-1982 *ScF&FL 92*
Kubale, Bernard Stephen 1928- *St&PR 93*
Kubale, Marek Edward 1946- *WhoWor 93*
Kuball, Hans-Georg 1931- *WhoScE 91-3*
Kuban, Ronald J. 1934- *St&PR 93*
Kubanek, Vladimir *WhoScE 91-4*
Kubarski, Jan Antoni 1950- *WhoWor 93*
Kubasch, Heike *ScF&FL 92*
Kubasek, Anthony Joseph 1963- *WhoE 93*
Kubasick, Chris *ScF&FL 92*
Kubasiewicz, Marian 1921- *WhoScE 91-4*
Kubat, Cynthia M. *Law&B 92*
Kubba, Ali Abdullah *WhoScE 91-1*
Kube, Harold Deming 1910- *WhoWor 93*
Kubeczka, Karl-Heinz 1935- *WhoScE 91-3*
Kubeja, Judith Wallace 1948- *WhoAmW 93, WhoE 93*
Kubek, Anthony Christopher 1935- *BiDAMSp 1989, WhoAm 92*
Kubelik, Jan 1880-1940 *Baker 92*
Kubelik, Rafael 1914- *IntDcOp, OxDcOp*
Kubelik, (Jeronym) Rafael 1914- *Baker 92*
Kubelka, Richard Preston 1952- *WhoEmL 93*
Kube-McDowell, Michael P. 1954- *ScF&FL 92*
Kubena, Karen Sidell 1945- *WhoSSW 93*
Kuberski, Frank J. 1941- *St&PR 93*
Kubersky, Zave 1936- *St&PR 93*
Kubiak, John Michael 1935- *WhoE 93*
Kubiak, Jon S. *Law&B 92*
Kubiak, Jon S. 1935- *St&PR 93*
Kubiak, Robert J. 1952- *St&PR 93*
Kubiak, Tadeusz 1924-1979 *PolBiDi*
Kubiak, Teresa 1937- *Baker 92*
Kubicek, Christian Peter 1951- *WhoScE 91-4*
Kubicek, David 1944-1990 *ScF&FL 92*
Kubicek, Herbert Theodor 1946- *WhoWor 93*
Kubicek, Peter John 1930- *St&PR 93*
Kubicek, R.T. 1942- *St&PR 93*
Kubicek, Robert Vincent 1935- *WhoAm 92, WhoWrEP 92*
Kubicek, Yvonne Jean 1958- *WhoAmW 93*
Kubicke, George John 1944- *St&PR 93*
Kubicki, Stanislaw 1926- *WhoScE 91-3*
Kubicz, Aleksandra Anna 1932- *WhoWor 93*
Kubicz, Lawrence 1947- *WhoEmL 93*
Kubiczky, Stephen Ralph 1947- *WhoEmL 93*
Kubida, William Joseph *Law&B 92*
Kubida, William Joseph 1949- *WhoEmL 93, WhoWor 93*
Kubiet, Leo Lawrence 1924- *WhoAm 92*
Kubik, Jack Roy 1929- *St&PR 93*
Kubik, Matthew 1950- *WhoEmL 93*
Kubik, Richard J. 1953- *St&PR 93*
Kubik, Robert L. *Law&B 92*
Kubik, Stanislav 1930- *WhoScE 91-4*
Kubilius, Jonas 1921- *WhoWor 93*
Kubilus, Norbert John 1948- *St&PR 93, WhoAm 92, WhoEmL 93, WhoWor 93*
Kubin, Charles Calvin 1932- *St&PR 93*
Kubin, Eero Johannes 1948- *WhoScE 91-4*
Kubin, Michael Ernest 1951- *WhoAm 92*
Kubin, Rudolf 1909-1973 *Baker 92*
Kubinski, Henry Anthony 1933- *WhoAm 92*
Kubinszky, Mihaly 1927- *WhoScE 91-4*
Kubis, Edward A. *Law&B 92*
Kubisen, Steven Joseph, Jr. 1952- *WhoAm 92*
Kubiske, David Arthur 1954- *WhoEmL 93*
Kubistal, Patricia Bernice 1938- *WhoAmW 93, WhoWor 93*
Kubiszyn, Irydion 1930- *WhoScE 91-4*
Kubiszyn, Lucy Stallworth 1936- *WhoSSW 93*
Kubitschek, Juscelino 1902-1976 *DcTwHis*
Kubitz, Kermit R. *Law&B 92*
Kubitzki, Klaus 1933- *WhoScE 91-3*
Kublai Khan 1215-1294 *HarEnMi*
Kublai Khan 1216-1294 *BioIn 17*
Kublanov, Anya *BioIn 17*
Kublanov, Simon *BioIn 17*
Kubler, Bernard 1930- *WhoScE 91-4*
Kubler, Fred C., Jr. 1929- *St&PR 93*
Kubler, M. *WhoScE 91-3*
Kubler, Werner Wolf 1927- *WhoScE 91-3*
Kubler-Ross, Elisabeth 1926- *WhoAm 92, WhoAmW 93, WhoWrEP 92*
Kubli, Eric 1940- *WhoScE 91-4*
Kublik, Gail (Thompson) 1914-1984 *Baker 92*
Kubly, Dale A. *Law&B 92*
Kubly, Herbert 1915- *WhoAm 92*
Kubly, Herbert Oswald 1915- *WhoWrEP 92*
Kubo, Souichi 1928- *WhoWor 93*
Kubo, Takashi 1935- *WhoUN 92*
Kubo, Wataru 1929- *WhoAsAP 91*
Kubota, Joe *WhoAm 92*
Kubota, Manae 1924- *WhoAsAP 91*
Kubr, Milan 1930- *WhoUN 92, WhoWor 93*
Kubrick, Kenneth W. *Law&B 92*
Kubrick, Stanley *BioIn 17*
Kubrick, Stanley 1928- *MiSFD 9, WhoAm 92, WhoWor 93*
Kubrusly, Carlos 1947- *WhoWor 93*
Kubu, F. *WhoScE 91-4*
Kubuabola, Ratu Inoke 1948- *WhoAsAP 91*
Kubuj, Krystyna 1945- *WhoScE 91-4*
Kuby, Barbara Eleanor 1944- *WhoAmW 93*
Kuby, Edward R. 1938- *WhoIns 93*
Kuby, Edward Raymond 1938- *St&PR 93, WhoAm 92*
Kuby, Lolette Beth 1943- *WhoWrEP 92*
Kubzansky, Philip Eugene 1928- *WhoAm 92*
Kuc, Joseph A. 1929- *WhoSSW 93*
Kucan, Milan *WhoWor 93*
Kucan, Zeljko 1934- *WhoScE 91-4*
Kucera, Daniel Jerome 1939- *WhoAm 92*
Kucera, Daniel William 1923- *WhoAm 92*
Kucera, Edna Lee 1948- *WhoAmW 93*
Kucera, Henry 1925- *WhoAm 92*
Kucera, Janice 1950- *BioIn 17*
Kucera, Janice Ann 1971- *WhoSSW 93*
Kucera, Louis Stephen 1935- *WhoSSW 93*
Kucera, Philip E. *Law&B 92*
Kucera, Vaclav 1929- *Baker 92*
Kucera, Vladimir 1943- *WhoScE 91-4*
Kuchak, Joann M. 1949- *St&PR 93*
Kuchak, JoAnn Marie 1949- *WhoAmW 93*
Kuchar, Jeffrey Andrew 1954- *St&PR 93*
Kuchar, Johann Baptist 1751-1829 *Baker 92*
Kuchar, Kathleen Ann 1942- *WhoAmW 93*
Kucharavy, Robert M. 1946- *WhoE 93, WhoEmL 93*
Kucharski, John Michael 1936- *St&PR 93, WhoAm 92*
Kucharski, Kathy Jo *Law&B 92*
Kucharski, Kathy Jo 1948- *St&PR 93*
Kucharski, Lisa Marie 1964- *WhoWrEP 92*
Kucharski, Mieczyslaw 1931- *WhoScE 91-4*
Kucharski, Robert Joseph 1932- *St&PR 93, WhoAm 92*
Kucharski, Stanislaw H. 1941- *WhoScE 91-4*
Kucharsky, David Eugene 1931- *WhoAm 92*
Kucharz, Johann Baptist 1751-1829 *Baker 92*
Kuchel, Maria *Law&B 92*
Kuchel, Thomas H. 1910- *PolPar*
Kucheman, Clark Arthur 1931- *WhoAm 92*
Kuchen, W. 1926- *WhoScE 91-3*
Kucher, Eckhard 1952- *WhoWor 93*
Kuchera, Michael Louis 1955- *WhoWor 93*
Kuchler, William 1947- *St&PR 93*
Kuchner, Eugene Frederick 1945- *WhoE 93, WhoWor 93*
Kuchta, John Andrew 1943- *WhoE 93*
Kuchta, Ronald Andrew 1935- *WhoAm 92, WhoE 93*
Kuchta, Thomas Walter 1942- *WhoAm 92*
Kucic, Joseph 1964- *WhoE 93, WhoEmL 93, WhoWor 93*
Kucij, Timothy Michael 1954- *WhoEmL 93, WhoWor 93*
Kucinski, Paul Wesley 1955- *WhoEmL 93*
Kuck, David Jerome 1937- *WhoAm 92*
Kuck, John Howland 1932- *St&PR 93*
Kuck, Marie Elizabeth Bukovsky 1910- *WhoAmW 93*
Kuck, Timothy William *Law&B 92*
Kucken, Friedrich Wilhelm 1810-1882 *Baker 92*
Kuckertz, Josef 1930- *Baker 92*
Kuckhoff, Carl, Jr. 1930- *St&PR 93*
Kuckro, Lee G. *Law&B 92*
Kuckro, Lee Gerard 1941- *St&PR 93*
Kucler, Edward Alan 1942- *St&PR 93*
Kucserik, Mary Anne 1958- *WhoWor 93*
Kucsman, Arpad 1927- *WhoScE 91-4*
Kucy, Lawrence J. *Law&B 92*
Kuczinski, Paul 1846-1897 *Baker 92*
Kuczkir, Mary 1933- *ScF&FL 92*
Kuczmarski, Susan Smith 1951- *WhoWor 93*
Kuczwanski, John S. 1945- *St&PR 93*
Kuczwara, Thomas Paul 1951- *WhoEmL 93*
Kuczynski, John R. *Law&B 92*
Kuczynski, John Raymond 1953- *St&PR 93*
Kuczynski, Pedro Pablo 1938- *WhoE 93*
Kudat, Ayse 1944- *WhoAmW 93*
Kuddes, John R. *Law&B 92*
Kudelko, David Gerald 1948- *WhoSSW 93*
Kudelski, Karl Matthias 1805-1877 *Baker 92*
Kuder, Beryl M. *Law&B 92*
Kudesh, Stephen B. 1944- *St&PR 93*
Kudia, Frank A. *Law&B 92*
Kudish, David J. 1943- *WhoAm 92*
Kudlicz, Bonawentura 1780-1848 *PolBiDi*
Kudlik, Mary Catherine 1938- *WhoAmW 93*
Kudlow, Lawrence Alan 1947- *WhoAm 92, WhoWor 93*
Kudner, Richard Don 1927- *St&PR 93*
Kudo 1951- *BioIn 17*
Kudo, Emiko Iwashita 1923- *WhoWor 93*
Kudo, Iwao 1921- *WhoAsAP 91*
Kudo, Tetsuichi 1940- *WhoWor 93*
Kudrick, Lloyd Joseph 1936- *WhoE 93*
Kudrle, William Alan 1954- *WhoEmL 93*
Kudrna, Chris 1954- *WhoIns 93*
Kudrna, Christopher R. 1954- *St&PR 93*
Kudrnac, I.K. 1926- *St&PR 93*
Kudrnac, Kristian Ivoj 1949- *WhoAm 92*
Kudryashov, Oleg 1932- *BioIn 17*
Kudryavtsev, Eduard Victor 1931- *WhoUN 92*
Kudryk, Oleg 1912- *WhoAm 92*
Kudsk, Per 1957- *WhoScE 91-2*
Kudzma, Elizabeth Anne Connelly 1946- *WhoAmW 93*
Kudzma, J.C. *St&PR 93*
Kuebeler, Glenn Charles 1935- *WhoE 93*
Kuebler, David Wayne 1947- *WhoEmL 93, WhoSSW 93, WhoWor 93*
Kuebler, Thomas L. 1923- *St&PR 93*
Kuechenmeister, Karl Thomas 1946- *WhoAm 92, WhoE 93, WhoEmL 93*
Kuechler, Karl 1946- *St&PR 93*
Kuehl, Hal C. 1923- *WhoAm 92*
Kuehl, Hal Charles 1923- *St&PR 93*
Kuehl, Hans Henry 1933- *WhoAm 92*
Kuehl, John E. 1958- *St&PR 93*
Kuehl, John Richard 1928- *WhoWrEP 92*
Kuehler, Jack Dwyer 1932- *WhoE 93*
Kuehn, Andrew J. *MiSFD 9*
Kuehn, Carol Ann 1954- *St&PR 93*
Kuehn, Charlotte *Law&B 92*
Kuehn, D.A. 1943- *St&PR 93*
Kuehn, David Laurance 1940- *WhoAm 92*
Kuehn, Edmund Karl 1916- *WhoAm 92*
Kuehn, George E. *Law&B 92*
Kuehn, George E. 1946- *St&PR 93, WhoAm 92*
Kuehn, James H. 1918- *St&PR 93*
Kuehn, James Marshall 1926- *WhoAm 92*
Kuehn, Nancy H. *Law&B 92*
Kuehn, Philip G. d1992 *NewYTBS 92*
Kuehn, Raymond Kenneth 1929- *St&PR 93*
Kuehn, Robert E. 1932-1986? *ScF&FL 92*
Kuehn, Ronald L., Jr. 1935- *St&PR 93, WhoAm 92, WhoSSW 93*
Kuehne, Donald James 1930- *St&PR 93*
Kuehnel, Kathi A. *Law&B 92*
Kuehneman, Gene George, Jr. 1953- *WhoE 93*
Kuehner, Horst Karl 1937- *St&PR 93*
Kuehner, John Alan 1931- *WhoAm 92*
Kuehnert, Deborah Anne 1949- *WhoAmW 93, WhoEmL 93*
Kuehnle, Emery Charles, Jr. 1928- *St&PR 93*
Kuehnle, Norman Bruce 1940- *WhoE 93*
Kuelbs, John T. *Law&B 92*
Kuelbs, John Thomas 1942- *WhoAm 92*
Kuemmel, Reiner 1939- *WhoWor 93*
Kuemmerle, John F. 1925- *St&PR 93*
Kuendig, Silvano 1925- *WhoScE 91-4*
Kuenemann, Wesley Ben 1937- *St&PR 93*
Kuenen, J.G. 1940- *WhoScE 91-3*
Kuenne, Robert Eugene 1924- *WhoE 93*
Kuenneth, John Robert 1932- *WhoSSW 93*
Kuenster, John Joseph 1924- *WhoAm 92, WhoWrEP 92*
Kuentz, Bruce J. 1953- *St&PR 93*
Kuentz, John Charles 1925- *St&PR 93*
Kueny, Mary Ellen 1955- *WhoEmL 93*
Kueny, Michel 1949- *WhoScE 91-2*
Kuenzler, Edward Julian 1929- *WhoAm 92*
Kueper, Clement John 1928- *St&PR 93*
Kuerten, Ludwig 1955- *WhoWor 93*
Kuerti, Anton (Emil) 1938- *Baker 92, WhoAm 92*
Kues, Mary Carolyn 1936- *WhoE 93*
Kuesel, Thomas Robert 1926- *St&PR 93, WhoAm 92*
Kuester, D.J. *St&PR 93*
Kuethe, Peggy Sue 1958- *WhoWrEP 92*
Kuether, Ronald Clarence 1934- *St&PR 93*
Kuever, Nancy Jeanne 1947- *WhoAmW 93*
Kufaev, Mikhail Nikolaevich 1888- *BioIn 17*
Kufeld, Jack 1907-1990 *BioIn 17*
Kufeld, William Manuel 1922- *WhoAm 92*
Kufeldt, James 1938- *WhoSSW 93*
Kuffel, Edmund 1924- *WhoAm 92*
Kufferath, Hubert Ferdinand 1818-1896 *Baker 92*
Kufferath, Johann Hermann 1797-1864 *Baker 92*
Kufferath, Louis 1811-1882 *Baker 92*
Kufferath, Maurice 1852-1919 *Baker 92*
Kuffler, Laura Ann 1965- *St&PR 93*
Kuffner, Joseph 1776-1856 *Baker 92*
Kuffner-Hirt, Mary Jane 1951- *WhoEmL 93*
Kufic, Pseudo- *OxDcByz*
Kuflik, Madeline B. *Law&B 92*
Kufner, Josef 1924- *WhoScE 91-4*
Kufner, Max 1920- *WhoScE 91-3*
Kuftin, B.A. 1892-1953 *IntDcAn*
Kugell, Robert Herbert 1935- *St&PR 93*
Kugeman, Patricia McEwen 1941- *WhoAmW 93*
Kugle, J. Alan *Law&B 92*
Kuglen, Francesca Bernadette 1961- *WhoEmL 93*
Kugler, Andrej 1953- *WhoScE 91-4*
Kugler, Anthony W. 1955- *St&PR 93*
Kugler, Daniel Edward 1947- *WhoE 93*
Kugler, Deborah Karen 1950- *WhoAmW 93*
Kugler, Frank J., Jr. 1934- *St&PR 93*
Kugler, Hans Jurgen 1953- *WhoWor 93*
Kugler, Henry C.F. *Law&B 92*
Kugler, Lawrence Dean 1941- *WhoAm 92*
Kugler, Robert 1946- *WhoScE 91-3*
Kugler, Robert J. 1930- *St&PR 93*
Kugler, Seymour 1936- *St&PR 93*
Kugler, William Charles 1935- *St&PR 93*
Kuh, Ernest Shiu-Jen 1928- *WhoAm 92*
Kuh, George Dennis 1946- *WhoEmL 93*
Kuh, Richard Henry 1921- *WhoAm 92*
Kuhac, Franz Xaver 1834-1911 *Baker 92*
Kuhagen, Lawrence K. 1954- *St&PR 93*
Kuhajek, Eugene James 1934- *WhoAm 92*
Kuhar, Frank 1946- *St&PR 93*
Kuhar, June Carolynn 1935- *WhoAmW 93*
Kuhar, Michael Joseph 1944- *WhoAm 92*
Kuhar, Timothy 1955- *St&PR 93*
Kuharic, Franjo Cardinal 1919- *WhoWor 93*
Kuharich, Joseph Lawrence 1917-1981 *BiDAMSp 1989*
Kuharsky, Andrew Sergius 1957- *WhoSSW 93*
Kuhbach, Robert *Law&B 92*
Kuhbauch, Walter 1942- *WhoScE 91-3*
Kuhe, Wilhelm 1823-1912 *Baker 92*
Kuhfeld, Mary Pulvar *ScF&FL 92*
Kuhfeld, Peter *BioIn 17*
Kuhi, Leonard Vello 1936- *WhoAm 92*
Kuhl, David Edmund 1929- *WhoAm 92*
Kuhl, Ernest Peter 1881-1981 *ConAu 39NR*
Kuhl, Herbert 1940- *WhoScE 91-3*
Kuhl, Margaret Helen Clayton *WhoAmW 93*
Kuhl, Norman Ernest 1940- *St&PR 93*
Kuhl, Paul Beach 1935- *WhoAm 92*
Kuhl, Thomas J. 1936- *St&PR 93*
Kuhlau, Friedrich 1786-1832 *OxDcOp*
Kuhlau, (Daniel) Friedrich (Rudolph) 1786-1832 *Baker 92*
Kuhle, Shirley Jean 1936- *WhoWor 93*
Kuhler, Renaldo Gillet 1931- *WhoSSW 93, WhoWor 93*
Kuhlman, Augustus Frederick 1889-1986 *BioIn 17*
Kuhlman, Elmer George 1934- *WhoSSW 93*
Kuhlman, John Michael 1948- *WhoSSW 93*
Kuhlman, Kathryn 1907-1976 *BioIn 17*
Kuhlman, Kerry J. *Law&B 92*
Kuhlman, Robert Alan 1955- *WhoEmL 93*
Kuhlman, Susan *WhoAmW 93*
Kuhlman, Walter Egel 1918- *WhoAm 92*
Kuhlmann, Arkadi 1946- *St&PR 93*
Kuhlmann, F. Mark *Law&B 92*
Kuhlmann, Fred L. 1916- *St&PR 93, WhoAm 92*
Kuhlmann, Fred Mark 1948- *St&PR 93*
Kuhlmann, Judith Grace 1949- *WhoAmW 93*
Kuhlmann, Kathleen 1950- *Baker 92*
Kuhlmann, Rolf F.W. 1937- *St&PR 93*
Kuhlmann, Stephen William *WhoScE 91-1*
Kuhlmann, Susan *ConAu 37NR*
Kuhlmann, William Carl 1950- *St&PR 93*
Kuhlmann-Wilsdorf, Doris 1922- *WhoAm 92, WhoAmW 93, WhoSSW 93*
Kuhlmeijer, Heinrich Johannes 1916- *WhoWor 93*
Kuhlmey, Walter Trowbridge 1918- *WhoAm 92*
Kuhlthau, John Suydam 1937- *WhoE 93*
Kuhmstedt, Friedrich Karl 1809-1858 *Baker 92*

Kuhn, Albert Joseph 1926- *WhoAm 92*
Kuhn, Alfred 1914-1981 *ConAu 37NR*
Kuhn, Arthur Richard 1931- *St&PR 93*
Kuhn, Bowie K. 1926- *WhoAm 92*
Kuhn, Clifford *BioIn 17*
Kuhn, David A. *Law&B 92*
Kuhn, David A. 1929- *St&PR 93*
Kuhn, David Alan 1929- *WhoAm 92*
Kuhn, Debbie *WhoAmW 93*
Kuhn, Eduard 1940- *WhoScE 91-2*
Kuhn, Eleanor Adele 1922- *WhoAmW 93*
Kuhn, Eleanor G. 1922- *St&PR 93*
Kuhn, Endre 1928- *WhoScE 91-4*
Kuhn, Frank Rudolf 1962- *WhoE 93*
Kuhn, Frantisek 1931- *WhoScE 91-4*
Kuhn, Gretchen 1951- *WhoEmL 93*
Kuhn, Gunther 1941- *WhoScE 91-3*
Kuhn, Gustav 1947- *Baker 92*
Kuhn, Hans Heinrich *WhoSSW 93*
Kuhn, Hansjoerg Karl 1939- *WhoE 93*
Kuhn, Heinrich *WhoScE 91-3*
Kuhn, Heinz-Wolfgang 1934- *WhoWor 93*
Kuhn, Howard Arthur 1940- *WhoAm 92*
Kuhn, Irene Corbally 1900- *BioIn 17*
Kuhn, Irvin Nelson 1928- *WhoAm 92*
Kuhn, James E. 1946- *WhoSSW 93*
Kuhn, James Paul 1937- *St&PR 93, WhoAm 92*
Kuhn, Johann 1660-1722 *Baker 92*
Kuhn, John Mark 1955- *WhoSSW 93*
Kuhn, Josef Leonz 1926- *WhoAm 92*
Kuhn, Karl F(rancis) 1939- *ConAu 37NR*
Kuhn, Kathleen Jo 1947- *WhoAmW 93*
Kuhn, Klaus 1927- *WhoScE 91-3*
Kuhn, Lan 1939- *ScF&FL 92*
Kuhn, Lucille Ross 1927- *WhoAmW 93*
Kuhn, Maggie *BioIn 17*
Kuhn, Maggie 1905- *ConHero 2 [port]*
Kuhn, Margaret 1905- *WhoAm 92, WhoAmW 93*
Kuhn, Mary Croughan 1914- *WhoAmW 93*
Kuhn, Matthew 1936- *WhoAm 92*
Kuhn, Michael 1943- *WhoScE 91-4*
Kuhn, Nino Karl 1936- *WhoScE 91-4*
Kuhn, Paul Hubert, Jr. 1943- *WhoAm 92, WhoSSW 93*
Kuhn, Peter Mouat 1920- *WhoAm 92*
Kuhn, Raymond E. 1942- *St&PR 93*
Kuhn, Richard John Alois 1936- *WhoE 93*
Kuhn, Robert Belden *Law&B 92*
Kuhn, Robert Mitchell 1942- *St&PR 93, WhoAm 92*
Kuhn, Robert P. 1926- *St&PR 93*
Kuhn, Roland J. 1912- *St&PR 93*
Kuhn, Ronald Joseph 1944- *St&PR 93*
Kuhn, Ronald Joseph 1957- *WhoAm 92*
Kuhn, Roy C. 1936- *St&PR 93*
Kuhn, Sherman M. *BioIn 17*
Kuhn, Siegfried 1935- *DrEEuF*
Kuhn, Stephen L. *Law&B 92*
Kuhn, Stephen L. 1947- *St&PR 93*
Kuhn, Thomas S. *BioIn 17*
Kuhn, Warren Boehm 1924- *WhoAm 92*
Kuhn, Werner d1990 *BioIn 17*
Kuhn, William Frederick 1930- *WhoSSW 93*
Kuhnau, Johann 1660-1722 *Baker 92*
Kuhnau, Johann Christoph 1735-1805 *Baker 92*
Kuhnau, Johann Friedrich Wilhelm 1780-1848
See Kuhnau, Johann Christoph 1735-1805 *Baker 92*
Kuhnau, Reiner 1936- *WhoWor 93*
Kuhne, Friedrich 1938- *WhoScE 91-3*
Kuhne, Sharon Anglin 1951- *WhoWrEP 92*
Kuhnen, Frithjof M. 1927- *WhoScE 91-3*
Kuhnen, Michael d1991 *BioIn 17*
Kuhnen, Wolfgang *WhoScE 91-4*
Kuhner, Arlene Elizabeth 1939- *WhoAmW 93*
Kuhner, Basil 1840-1911 *Baker 92*
Kuhnert, Robert Richard 1925- *St&PR 93*
Kuhnke, Thomas J. 1943- *St&PR 93*
Kuhnl, Reinhard 1936- *WhoWor 93*
Kuhnley, Edward John 1951- *WhoEmL 93*
Kuhnly, Barry Scott 1966- *WhoE 93*
Kuhnmuench, John R. 1944- *St&PR 93*
Kuhnmuench, John R., Jr. *Law&B 92*
Kuhnmuesuench, John Richard, Jr. *Law&B 92*
Kuhnreich, George A. d1991 *BioIn 17*
Kuhns, Barbara Anne 1948- *WhoEmL 93*
Kuhns, F.L. 1946- *St&PR 93*
Kuhns, John Farrell 1947- *WhoEmL 93*
Kuhns, Polly 1947- *WhoE 93*
Kuhns, Roger James 1922- *St&PR 93*
Kuhns, Sally Nelson 1952- *WhoEmL 93*
Kuhns, William G. 1922- *St&PR 93*
Kuhns, William George 1922- *WhoAm 92*
Kuhr, H.A. *WhoScE 91-3*
Kuhr, James R. *WhoIns 93*
Kuhr, James R. 1941- *St&PR 93*
Kuhr, Michael S. 1949- *St&PR 93*
Kuhrmeyer, Carl Albert 1928- *St&PR 93, WhoAm 92*
Kuhrt, Sharon Lee 1957- *WhoAmW 93, WhoEmL 93*
Kuhse, Hanne-Lore 1925- *Baker 92*
Kuhule, Kenneth R. *St&PR 93*
Kuijken *Baker 92*
Kuijken, Barthold 1949- *Baker 92*
Kuijken, Sigiswald 1944- *Baker 92*
Kuijken, Wieland 1938- *Baker 92*
Kuik, Maarten 1954- *WhoEmL 93*
Kuiken, G.D.C. 1940- *WhoScE 91-3*
Kuiper, Frederick Daniel 1955- *St&PR 93*
Kuiper, Luitsen 1936-1989 *BioIn 17*
Kuiper, Willem Gustaaf 1949- *WhoWor 93*
Kuiperi, Hans Cornelis 1939- *WhoWor 93*
Kuipers, A. 1947- *WhoScE 91-3*
Kuipers, Simon Klaas 1943- *WhoWor 93*
Kuitca, Guillermo 1961- *BioIn 17*
Kuitert, H(arminus) Martinus 1924- *ConAu 37NR*
Kuivila, Henry Gabriel 1917- *WhoAm 92*
Kuivila, Ron 1955- *Baker 92*
Kujala, Veli Topi 1951- *WhoWor 93*
Kujala, Walfrid Eugene 1925- *WhoAm 92*
Kujansuu, Raimo *WhoScE 91-4*
Kujau, Konrad *BioIn 17*
Kujawa, Charles C. d1991 *BioIn 17*
Kujawa, Henry Richard 1959- *WhoE 93*
Kujawa, John A. *Law&B 92*
Kujawa, Thomas Leon 1940- *WhoSSW 93*
Kujraoka, Hyosuke 1915- *WhoAsAP 91*
Kujszczyk, Szczesny 1939- *WhoScE 91-4*
Kukal, Zdenek 1932- *WhoScE 91-4*
Kukan, Eduard 1939- *WhoUN 92*
Kukanskis, Peter E. 1946- *St&PR 93*
Kukec, Anna Marie 1958- *WhoAmW 93*
Kukihara, Shizuka *BioIn 17*
Kukihara, Tetsuo *BioIn 17*
Kukin, Alexander 1920- *WhoScE 91-4*
Kukin, Ira 1924- *St&PR 93*
Kukla, Cynthia Mary 1951- *WhoAmW 93*
Kukla, Judi Ann 1945- *St&PR 93*
Kukla, Robert John 1932- *WhoAm 92*
Kuklin, Anthony Bennett 1929- *WhoAm 92*
Kuklin, Bailey Howard 1941- *WhoE 93*
Kuklin, Jeffrey P. *Law&B 92*
Kuklin, Susan *BioIn 17*
Kuklinski, T.F. 1932- *St&PR 93*
Kukovics, Sandor 1950- *WhoScE 91-4*
Kukuk, Karen Eloise 1938- *WhoAmW 93*
Kukuk, Terry Lee 1946- *WhoEmL 93*
Kukula, Tadeusz 1923- *WhoScE 91-4*
Kukulech, Virginia Linn 1957- *WhoAmW 93*
Kukulin, Vladimir Iosiphovich 1939- *WhoWor 93*
Kukulinsky, Nancy Elaine 1950- *WhoAmW 93*
Kukura, Rita Anne 1947- *WhoAmW 93, WhoEmL 93, WhoSSW 93, WhoWor 93*
Kukush, Alexander Georgiyevich 1957- *WhoWor 93*
Kulachote, Anchaneekorn Prachuabmoh 1943- *WhoWor 93*
Kulak, Theodore Joseph 1958- *St&PR 93*
Kulakowski, Andrzej 1929- *WhoScE 91-4*
Kulakowski, Jan 1930- *WhoWor 93*
Kularb, Narong 1937- *WhoWor 93*
Kulasiri, Gamalathge Don 1957- *WhoWor 93*
Kulason, Robert Alexander 1928- *St&PR 93*
Kulbertus, Henri E. 1938- *WhoScE 91-2*
Kulcsar, Andras 1922- *WhoScE 91-4*
Kulcsar, Bela 1944- *WhoScE 91-4*
Kulcsar, Ferenc 1935- *WhoScE 91-4*
Kulda, Jiri 1925- *WhoScE 91-4*
Kule, Christopher Anthony *Law&B 92*
Kulenkampff, Georg 1898-1948 *Baker 92*
Kulenkampff, Gustav 1849-1921 *Baker 92*
Kulesha, Gary 1954- *Baker 92*
Kulesza, Frank W. 1920- *St&PR 93*
Kulesza, Frank William 1920- *WhoE 93*
Kulesza, Jacek 1931- *WhoScE 91-4*
Kulharya, Himmat Singh 1945- *St&PR 93*
Kulhawy, Fred Howard 1943- *WhoE 93*
Kulich, Nicholas A. 1943- *St&PR 93*
Kulick, Bob *BioIn 17*
Kulick, Richard John 1949- *WhoE 93*
Kulicke, Charles Scott 1949- *St&PR 93, WhoAm 92*
Kulidzanov, Lev 1924- *DrEEuF*
Kulik, Boles *WhoWrEP 92*
Kulik, Buzz 1923- *MiSFD 9*
Kulik, Debra Rose 1960- *WhoAmW 93*
Kulik, Joseph P. *Law&B 92*
Kulik, Rosalyn Franta 1951- *WhoAm 92*
Kulikov, Viktor Georgiyevich 1921- *WhoWor 93*
Kulikowska, Teresa 1933- *WhoScE 91-4*
Kulikowski, J.J. *WhoScE 91-1*
Kulikowski, Juliusz Lech 1931- *WhoScE 91-4*
Kulikowski, Roman *WhoScE 91-4*
Kulild, James Clinton 1947- *WhoEmL 93, WhoSSW 93*
Kulin, Keith David 1948- *WhoE 93, WhoEmL 93*
Kulinski, Edward Zenon *Law&B 92*
Kulinski, Ronald Francis 1958- *WhoSSW 93*
Kulinski, Stephen Edward 1955- *WhoSSW 93*
Kulis, Savva 1936- *DrEEuF*
Kulisch, Ulrich Walter 1933- *WhoWor 93*
Kuliscioff, Anna 1857-1925 *BioIn 17*
Kulisic, Petar 1940- *WhoScE 91-4*
Kuliyev, Avdy *WhoWor 93*
Kuljanic, Elso 1936- *WhoScE 91-4*
Kulka, Dan 1938-1979 *BioIn 17*
Kulka, Frigyes 1925- *WhoScE 91-4*
Kulka, Janos 1929- *Baker 92*
Kulkarni, Arun Digambar 1947- *WhoEmL 93, WhoSSW 93*
Kulkarni, Arvind Ganesh 1917- *WhoAsAP 91*
Kulkarni, Dattatraya Vishnu *WhoScE 91-1*
Kulkarni, Prabhu Balkrishna *WhoWor 93*
Kulkarni, Venkatesh *WhoSSW 93*
Kulkin, Mary-Ellen *ConAu 40NR*
Kull, A. Stoddard *ConAu 138*
Kull, Andrew 1947- *ConAu 138*
Kull, Bryan Paul 1960- *WhoEmL 93*
Kull, Carolyn Jane 1959- *WhoAmW 93*
Kull, Francis Raymond 1921- *WhoE 93*
Kull, Lorenz A. 1937- *WhoAm 92*
Kull, Lorenz Anthony 1937- *St&PR 93*
Kull, Ulrich O. 1938- *WhoScE 91-3*
Kulla, Michael 1929- *WhoE 93*
Kulla, Raymond J. *Law&B 92*
Kullak, Adolf 1823-1862 *Baker 92*
Kullak, Franz 1844-1913 *Baker 92*
Kullak, Theodor 1818-1882 *Baker 92*
Kullander, Sven 1936- *WhoScE 91-4*
Kullas, Albert John 1917- *WhoAm 92*
Kullberg, Duane Reuben 1932- *WhoAm 92, WhoWor 93*
Kullberg, Gary Walter 1941- *WhoAm 92, WhoE 93*
Kullberg, John Francis 1939- *WhoAm 92*
Kullberg, Rolf Evert 1930- *WhoWor 93*
Kulle, Victor *MiSFD 9*
Kullen, Barbara C. *Law&B 92*
Kullen, Richard C., Jr. *Law&B 92*
Kullenberg, Bertil Johan Fredrik 1913- *WhoWor 93*
Kullenberg, Gunnar E.B. 1938- *WhoScE 91-2*
Kullenberg, Roger Dale 1930- *WhoAm 92*
Kuller, Alan S. *Law&B 92*
Kuller, Lewis Henry 1934- *WhoAm 92*
Kuller, Mark David *Law&B 92*
Kullgren, Elwood M. 1911- *St&PR 93*
Kullick, Ronald H. 1942- *St&PR 93*
Kullman, Charles 1903-1983 *Baker 92*
Kullman, Harry 1919-1982 *ConAu 39NR*
Kullman, Mary Caola *Law&B 92*
Kullman, Wilfred M. 1936- *St&PR 93*
Kulmala, Elmer Pete 1951- *WhoEmL 93*
Kulmburg, Alfred 1934- *WhoScE 91-4*
Kulmer, Morris H. 1945- *St&PR 93*
Kulok, William Allan 1940- *WhoE 93, WhoWor 93*
Kulorodin-Hedman, Birgitta 1937- *WhoScE 91-4*
Kulp, F. Bruce *Law&B 92*
Kulp, J. Robert 1935- *WhoE 93, WhoWor 93*
Kulp, Jonathan B. 1937- *WhoE 93*
Kulp, Nancy 1921-1991 *AnObit 1991, BioIn 17, ConTFT 10*
Kulp, Philip Masterton 1929- *WhoAm 92*
Kulp, Richard Wayne 1943- *WhoSSW 93*
Kulpa, John Edward 1929- *WhoAm 92*
Kulpa, Karen Joan 1965- *WhoAmW 93, WhoEmL 93*
Kulpa, Paula Ann 1963- *WhoAmW 93*
Kulper, Perry Dean 1953- *WhoAm 92*
Kulski, Julian Eugeniusz 1929- *WhoAm 92*
Kulski, Julian S. c. 1895-1976 *PolBiDi*
Kulski, Wladyslaw W(szebor) 1903- *ConAu 37NR*
Kulstad, George Arthur 1935- *WhoE 93*
Kulstad, Guy Charles 1930- *WhoWor 93*
Kult, Robert Phillip 1940- *St&PR 93*
Kultermann, Udo 1927- *WhoAm 92*
Kultgen, David B. *Law&B 92*
Kuluva, Will d1990 *BioIn 17*
Kulvinskas, Victor P. 1950- *WhoWrEP 92*
Kulwin, David Samuel 1964- *WhoSSW 93*
Kulwin, Herbert 1930- *St&PR 93*
Kulynych, Petro 1921- *St&PR 93*
Kulzick, Kenneth Edmund 1927- *WhoAm 92*
Kumagai, Hiroshi 1940- *WhoAsAP 91*
Kumagai, Hiroyuki 1954- *WhoEmL 93*
Kumagai, Takenobu 1937- *WhoWor 93*
Kumagai, Tasaburo *WhoAsAP 91*
Kumai, Kei *MiSFD 9*
Kumamoto, Chukei 1925- *WhoWor 93*
Kuman, Peter 1954- *WhoAsAP 91*
Kumaniecki, Kazimierz 1905-1977 *PolBiDi*
Kumanski, Krassimir *WhoScE 91-4*
Kumar, Akhil 1956- *WhoE 93*
Kumar, Ashwani 1928- *WhoAsAP 91*
Kumar, Birendra 1954- *St&PR 93*
Kumar, Dilip *IntDcF 2-3*
Kumar, Harinath V. 1938- *WhoE 93*
Kumar, Kaplesh 1947- *WhoWor 93*
Kumar, Krishan 1942- *ScF&FL 92*
Kumar, Krishna 1936- *WhoWor 93*
Kumar, Marko 1949- *WhoScE 91-4*
Kumar, Martha Joynt 1941- *WhoAmW 93*
Kumar, Panganamala Ramana 1952- *WhoAm 92*
Kumar, Prem. 1945- *WhoWrEP 92*
Kumar, Rajendra 1947- *St&PR 93*
Kumar, Rajendra 1948- *WhoWor 93*
Kumar, Ram N. *St&PR 93*
Kumar, Ramesh Pal 1948- *WhoWor 93*
Kumar, Romesh 1944- *WhoAm 92*
Kumar, Smita Rajeev 1959- *WhoEmL 93*
Kumar, Sudhir 1942- *WhoWor 93*
Kumar, Surendra 1935- *St&PR 93*
Kumar, Surinder 1944- *WhoAm 92*
Kumar, Surinder 1945- *WhoAm 92*
Kumar, Tobi Jeanne *WhoE 93*
Kumar, Vijay 1945- *WhoE 93*
Kumarakulasinghe, Prabha 1935- *WhoUN 92*
Kumaramangalam, Rangarajan 1952- *WhoAsAP 91*
Kumashiro, Masato *St&PR 93*
Kumbaro, Saimir 1945- *DrEEuF*
Kumberg, Wolf J. *Law&B 92*
Kumble, Steven *BioIn 17*
Kumble, Steven Jay 1933- *WhoAm 92, WhoWor 93*
Kume, Hiroshi *BioIn 17*
Kume, Hitoshi 1937- *WhoWor 93*
Kume, Tadashi *BioIn 17*
Kume, Yutaka *BioIn 17*
Kumel, Harry 1940- *MiSFD 9*
Kumer, Roy L. 1908- *St&PR 93*
Kumer, Zmaga 1924- *Baker 92*
Kumermann, Daniel *BioIn 17*
Kumin, Libby Barbara 1945- *WhoAmW 93*
Kumin, Maxine 1925- *BioIn 17, WhoWrEP 92*
Kumin, Maxine Winokur 1925- *WhoAm 92, WhoAmW 93*
Kumler, Kipton Cornelius 1940- *WhoAm 92*
Kumm, Henry William 1901-1991 *BioIn 17*
Kummann, William *ScF&FL 92*
Kummel, Eugene H. 1923- *WhoAm 92*
Kummel, Hermann Gerhard Heinrich 1922- *WhoWor 93*
Kummer, Clare 1888-1958 *AmWomPl*
Kummer, Daniel William *WhoAm 92*
Kummer, Fred S. 1929- *WhoAm 92*
Kummer, Frederic Arnold 1873-1943 *ScF&FL 92*
Kummer, Friedrich August 1797-1879 *Baker 92*
Kummer, Kaspar 1795-1870 *Baker 92*
Kummer, Robert W., Jr. 1936- *St&PR 93*
Kummer, Wolfgang 1935- *WhoScE 91-4*
Kummerer, Karl R. 1928- *WhoScE 91-3*
Kummerfeld, Donald David 1934- *WhoAm 92*
Kummerle, Salomon 1838-1896 *Baker 92*
Kummert, Jean *WhoScE 91-2*
Kummert, Richard Osborne 1932- *WhoAm 92*
Kummler, Ralph H. 1940- *WhoAm 92*
Kummroh, Richard *WhoScE 91-4*
Kumorowski, Victoria McKay 1947- *WhoEmL 93*
Kumosani, Taha A. 1955- *WhoWor 93*
Kump, Ernest Joseph 1911- *WhoAm 92*
Kump, Peter Clark 1937- *WhoE 93*
Kump, Scott Anthony 1956- *St&PR 93*
Kump, Theresa *BioIn 17*
Kump, Thomas George 1962- *WhoEmL 93*
Kumpe, David E. *Law&B 92*
Kumpulainen, Jorma T. 1947- *WhoScE 91-4*
Kun, Bela 1886-1938 *DcTwHis*
Kun, Kenneth A. 1930- *WhoAm 92*
Kun, Tibor Halasi- 1914-1991 *BioIn 17*
Kuna, Henryk 1885-1945 *PolBiDi*
Kunad, Rainer 1936- *Baker 92*
Kunar, David Joseph 1953- *WhoEmL 93*
Kunast, Hendrik Muller- *BioIn 17*
Kunc, Bozidar 1903-1964 *Baker 92*
Kunc, Jan 1883-1976 *Baker 92*
Kunc, Seref 1944- *WhoScE 91-4*
Kuncewicz, Maria 1897- *PolBiDi*
Kuncl, Lawrence G. 1938- *St&PR 93*
Kundahl, George Gustavus 1940- *WhoAm 92*
Kundakci, Vace 1952- *WhoEmL 93*
Kundel, Harold Louis 1933- *WhoAm 92*
Kundent, Nancy A. *Law&B 92*
Kundera, Ludvik 1891-1971 *Baker 92*
Kundera, Milan *BioIn 17*
Kundera, Milan 1929- *MagSWL [port], WhoWor 93*

Kundert, Alice E. 1920- *WhoAm 92*
Kundert, David Jon 1942- *St&PR 93*
Kundig, Walter 1932- *WhoScE 91-4, WhoWor 93*
Kundinger, Mathew Hermann 1955- *WhoEmL 93*
Kundrat, Douglas Andrew *Law&B 92*
Kundrat, Stephanie L. 1962- *WhoAmW 93, WhoE 93*
Kundsin, Ruth Blumfeld 1916- *WhoE 93*
Kundt, Wolfgang 1931- *WhoScE 91-3*
Kundtz, John Andrew 1933- *WhoAm 92*
Kundtz, Lee R. 1932- *St&PR 93*
Kundur, Prabha Shankar 1939- *WhoAm 92*
Kunel, Larry Gene 1938- *St&PR 93*
Kunen, James L. d1991 *BioIn 17*
Kunen, Seth 1949- *WhoSSW 93*
Kunene, Mazisi (Raymond) 1930- *DcLB 117 [port]*
Kunert, Joachim 1929- *DrEEuF*
Kunes, Daniel Joseph 1937- *St&PR 93*
Kunes, John Charles 1949- *WhoE 93*
Kunes, Steven Mark 1956- *WhoEmL 93*
Kunetka, James 1944- *ScF&FL 92*
Kung, Alice *Law&B 92*
Kung, Edward Y. 1934- *St&PR 93*
Kung, Frank F.C. 1948- *St&PR 93*
Kung, Hans 1928- *BioIn 17, WhoWor 93*
Kung, Ling-Yang 1944- *WhoWor 93*
Kung, Patrick C. 1947- *St&PR 93*
Kung, Patrick Chung-Shu 1947- *WhoAm 92, WhoE 93*
Kung, Shien Woo 1909- *WhoAm 92*
Kung, Sun-Yuan 1950- *WhoAm 92*
Kung Gong Pin-Mei, Ignatius Cardinal 1901- *WhoWor 93*
Kunhardt, Dorothy Meserve 1901-1979 *BioIn 17*
Kunhardt, Edith *BioIn 17*
Kunhardt, Erich Enrique 1949- *WhoAm 92*
Kunhardt, Philip B(radish), Jr. 1928- *ConAu 37NR*
Kuniansky, Richard Ben 1953- *WhoEmL 93*
Kunicki-Goldfinger, Wladyslaw Jerzy Henry 1916- *WhoScE 91-4*
Kunieda, Hironobu 1948- *WhoWor 93*
Kunihiro, Masao 1930- *WhoAsAP 91*
Kuniholm, John G. *Law&B 92*
Kunin, Madeleine *BioIn 17*
Kunin, Madeleine May 1933- *WhoAm 92, WhoAmW 93, WhoE 93*
Kunin, Myron *St&PR 93*
Kunis, Abraham Maxwell 1914- *WhoIns 93*
Kunis, Solomon d1991 *BioIn 17*
Kunisch, Robert Dietrich 1941- *WhoAm 92, WhoE 93*
Kunisch, Robert Dietrict 1941- *St&PR 93*
Kunishi, Tadao 1936- *St&PR 93*
Kunitake, Tatsuro 1928- *WhoWor 93*
Kunits, Luigi von 1870-1931 *Baker 92*
Kunitz, Stanley 1905- *AmWrS3, BioIn 17*
Kunitz, Stanley Jasspon 1905- *WhoAm 92*
Kuniya, Joji 1952- *WhoWor 93*
Kunjachen, P.K. 1925- *WhoAsAP 91*
Kunjufu, Jawanza 1953- *ConBlB 3 [port], SmATA 73 [port]*
Kunjukunju, Pappy 1939- *WhoE 93*
Kunkel, Charles 1840-1923 *Baker 92*
Kunkel, David Nelson 1943- *WhoAm 92*
Kunkel, Eleanore L. 1927- *St&PR 93*
Kunkel, Georgie Myrtia *WhoAmW 93*
Kunkel, Jacob 1846-1882 *Baker 92*
Kunkel, Kenneth Edward 1949- *WhoEmL 93*
Kunkel, Louis Martens 1949- *WhoAm 92*
Kunkel, Russell J. 1942- *St&PR 93*
Kunkel, Russell Jeffrey 1942- *WhoAm 92*
Kunkel, Sherman 1919-1991 *BioIn 17*
Kunkel, William Albert 1952- *BioIn 17*
Kunkemueller, A. Henry 1935- *St&PR 93*
Kunkemueller, Henry 1935- *WhoIns 93*
Kunkle, George M. 1953- *St&PR 93*
Kunkle, John H., Jr. 1927- *St&PR 93*
Kunkler, Arnold William 1921- *WhoAm 92*
Kunko, Richard F. 1954- *St&PR 93*
Kunnas, Martta Aino Kyllikki 1928- *WhoScE 91-4*
Kunneke, Eduard 1885-1953 *Baker 92*
Kuno, H. John 1938- *WhoAm 92*
Kuno, Toichiro 1937- *WhoAsAP 91*
Kunos, George 1942- *WhoAm 92*
Kunov, Hans 1938- *WhoAm 92*
Kunreuther, Howard Charles 1938- *ConAu 37NR*
Kuns, Nancy Lee 1960- *WhoAmW 93, WhoEmL 93*
Kunsch, Louis 1937- *WhoE 93*
Kunsemuller, Ernst 1885-1918 *Baker 92*
Kunst, Jaap (Jakob) 1891-1960 *Baker 92*
Kunst, Jos 1936- *Baker 92*
Kunstadt, George H. 1922- *St&PR 93*
Kunstadter, Geraldine S. 1928- *WhoAmW 93, WhoE 93, WhoWor 93*
Kunstadter, John W. 1927- *St&PR 93*
Kunstler, David B. 1934- *WhoAm 92*
Kunstler, David Bruce 1934- *St&PR 93*
Kunstler, James Howard 1948- *ScF&FL 92*
Kunstler, William c. 1920- *News 92 [port], -92-3 [port]*
Kunstler, William Moses 1919- *WhoAm 92*
Kunstmann, Rudolf 1941- *WhoWor 93*
Kunter, K. *WhoScE 91-4*
Kunter, Manfred 1940- *WhoScE 91-3*
Kuntz, Barbara M.E. 1944- *WhoScE 91-3, WhoWor 93*
Kuntz, Carolyn Jean 1955- *WhoAmW 93*
Kuntz, Edward L. *St&PR 93*
Kuntz, Hal Goggan 1937- *WhoSSW 93, WhoWor 93*
Kuntz, John David Kenneth *Law&B 92*
Kuntz, John F. *Law&B 92*
Kuntz, L.G. 1950- *St&PR 93*
Kuntz, Marion Lucile Leathers 1924- *WhoAm 92*
Kuntz, Paul Grimley 1915- *WhoAm 92*
Kuntz, Robert *ScF&FL 92, St&PR 93*
Kuntz, William Francis, II 1950- *WhoE 93*
Kuntz, William R. 1949- *St&PR 93*
Kuntz, William R., Jr. *Law&B 92*
Kuntze, C. Donald 1922-1991 *BioIn 17*
Kuntze, Herbert 1930- *WhoScE 91-3*
Kuntze, Karl 1817-1883 *Baker 92*
Kuntze-Konicz, Tadeusz 1731-1795 *PolBiDi*
Kuntzleman, Charles Thomas 1940- *WhoWrEP 92*
Kuntzman, Ronald 1933- *WhoAm 92*
Kunulilo, Kilongola Jumbe 1950- *WhoWor 93*
Kunwald, Ernst 1868-1939 *Baker 92*
Kunz, Alfred 1929- *Baker 92*
Kunz, Charles Alan 1945- *WhoSSW 93*
Kunz, Edith *AmWomPl*
Kunz, Eric Gibson 1940- *St&PR 93*
Kunz, Erich 1909- *Baker 92, IntDcOp, OxDcOp*
Kunz, Ernst 1891-1980 *Baker 92*
Kunz, George Frederick 1856-1932 *BioIn 17*
Kunz, Gerald Keith 1932- *St&PR 93*
Kunz, Harold Russell 1931- *WhoE 93*
Kunz, Horst 1940- *WhoScE 91-3*
Kunz, Janet Alice 1956- *WhoAmW 93, WhoEmL 93*
Kunz, John B. 1931- *St&PR 93*
Kunz, John Edward, Jr. 1964- *WhoE 93*
Kunz, John P. 1934- *WhoAm 92*
Kunz, Lawrence Joseph *St&PR 93*
Kunz, Margaret McCarthy *WhoSSW 93*
Kunz, Michelle Beth 1955- *WhoEmL 93, WhoSSW 93*
Kunz, Phillip Ray 1936- *WhoAm 92*
Kunz, Rino Ernst 1946- *WhoWor 93*
Kunz, Sharon Kay 1951- *St&PR 93*
Kunz, Ulrich H. 1935- *WhoScE 91-3*
Kunz, Virgina B(rainard) 1921- *ConAu 37NR*
Kunz, William Edward 1939- *St&PR 93*
Kunze, Carol A. *Law&B 92*
Kunze, Caroline Ryan 1961- *WhoAmW 93*
Kunze, George William 1922- *WhoAm 92*
Kunze, Hans-Joachim D. 1935- *WhoScE 91-3*
Kunze, Klaus 1933- *WhoScE 91-3*
Kunze, Peter 1931- *WhoScE 91-3*
Kunze, Ralph Carl 1925- *WhoAm 92*
Kunze, Reiner 1933- *BioIn 17*
Kunze, Richard Spencer 1948- *WhoE 93*
Kunzel, Erich 1935- *Baker 92*
Kunzel, Erich, Jr. 1935- *WhoAm 92*
Kunzel, Wolfgang 1936- *WhoScE 91-3*
Kunzen *Baker 92*
Kunzen, Adolph Carl 1720-1781 *Baker 92*
Kunzen, Adolph Karl 1720-1781 *OxDcOp*
Kunzen, Friedrich Ludwig Aemilius 1761-1817 *Baker 92, OxDcOp*
Kunzen, Johann Paul 1696-1757 *Baker 92*
Kunzen, Louise Friederica Ulrica 1765-1839 *Baker 92*
Kunzendorf, Robert Godfrey 1951- *WhoE 93*
Kunzig, Anne Ellen 1952- *WhoAmW 93*
Kunzler, John Eugene 1923- *WhoAm 92*
Kunzler, Ron R. *Law&B 92*
Kunzli, H. *WhoScE 91-4*
Kunzmann, Horst 1940- *WhoScE 91-3*
Kunz-Ramsay, Yvette W. 1928- *WhoWor 93*
Kuo, Chih-Cheng 1956- *WhoE 93*
Kuo, Franklin F. 1934- *WhoAm 92*
Kuo, John Tsungfen 1922- *WhoE 93*
Kuo, Nan-hung 1936- *WhoWor 93*
Kuo, Penny May 1969- *WhoAmW 93*
Kuo, Ping-chia 1908- *WhoAm 92, WhoWor 93*
Kuo, Shirley 1930- *WhoAsAP 91*
Kuo, Shirley Wan Yong 1930- *WhoWor 93*
Kuo, Tung-Yao 1926- *WhoWor 93*
Kuok, Robert *BioIn 17*
Kuo Nan-Hung 1936- *WhoAsAP 91*
Kuonen, V. *WhoScE 91-4*
Kuo Sung-lin d1925 *HarEnMi*
Kuo Wei-Fan 1937- *WhoAsAP 91*
Kupal, James K. 1949- *WhoAsAP 91*
Kupchak, Kenneth Roy 1942- *WhoWor 93*
Kupchella, Charles Edward 1942- *WhoSSW 93*
Kupchick, Alan Charles 1942- *WhoAm 92*
Kupcinet, Essee Solomon *WhoAmW 93*
Kupcinet, Irv 1912- *WhoAm 92*
Kupel, Frederick John 1929- *WhoAm 92*
Kuper, Adam Jonathan *WhoScE 91-1*
Kuper, Adam Jonathan 1941- *WhoAm 92*
Kuper, Dennis L. 1947- *St&PR 93*
Kuper, Dennis Lee 1947- *WhoAm 92*
Kuper, George Henry 1940- *WhoAm 92*
Kuper, Hilda Beemer 1911- *IntDcAn*
Kuperberg, Frederick *Law&B 92*
Kuperberg, Sidney R. *Law&B 92*
Kuperen, Fransua 1668-1733 *BioIn 17*
Kuperman, Robert Ian 1941- *St&PR 93, WhoAm 92*
Kupersmith, A. Harry 1925- *WhoAm 92*
Kuperus, M. *WhoScE 91-3*
Kupfer, Carl 1928- *WhoAm 92, WhoE 93*
Kupfer, David J. 1942- *WhoAm 92*
Kupfer, Harry 1935- *IntDcOp, OxDcOp*
Kupfer, Jerome Alan 1929- *WhoSSW 93*
Kupfer, Ruth Joan Irwin 1954- *WhoAmW 93*
Kupfer, Sherman 1926- *WhoAm 92*
Kupferberg, Herbert 1918- *Baker 92*
Kupferman, Harvey S. 1935- *St&PR 93*
Kupferman, Meyer 1926- *Baker 92, WhoAm 92*
Kupferman, Theodore R. 1920- *WhoAm 92*
Kupfermann, Irving 1938- *WhoE 93*
Kupferschmid, Owen M. d1991 *BioIn 17*
Kuphal, John Edward 1945- *St&PR 93*
Kupiainen, Cindy Jo 1968- *WhoAmW 93*
Kupiec-Weglinski, Jerzy Wojciech 1951- *WhoE 93*
Kupietz, Roberta 1953- *WhoAmW 93*
Kupila-Ahvenniemi, Sirkka L. 1927- *WhoScE 91-4*
Kupjack, Eugene J. d1991 *BioIn 17*
Kupka, Frantisek 1871-1957 *BioIn 17*
Kupke, Christian 1939- *WhoScE 91-3*
Kupkovic, Ladislav 1936- *Baker 92*
Kuplicki, Francis Philip *Law&B 92*
Kuppenheimer, John Daniel 1941- *WhoE 93*
Kupper, Alice 1942- *WhoAmW 93*
Kupper, Annelies 1906-1988 *OxDcOp*
Kupper, Annelies (Gabriele) 1906-1987 *Baker 92*
Kupper, Cathy Marie 1962- *WhoAmW 93*
Kupper, Leo 1935- *WhoWor 93*
Kupper, Philip Lloyd 1940- *WhoWor 93*
Kupper, Tassilo Georg 1947- *WhoWor 93*
Kupperberg, Paul *ScF&FL 92*
Kupperman, Charles M. 1950- *St&PR 93*
Kupperman, Helen Slotnick *WhoAmW 93*
Kupperman, Karen Ordahl 1939- *WhoAmW 93*
Kupperman, Louis Brandeis 1946- *WhoAm 92, WhoEmL 93*
Kupperman, Mitchell J. 1951- *WhoAm 92*
Kupperman, Robert Harris 1935- *WhoAm 92*
Kupperman, Stephen Henry 1953- *WhoEmL 93*
Kuppers, Horst 1933- *WhoScE 91-3*
Kuppig, C.J. *ScF&FL 92*
Kuppuswamy, C.K. 1932- *WhoAsAP 91*
Kupras, Lucjan Krystyn 1928- *WhoScE 91-3*
Kupris, Eleanor Marie 1941- *St&PR 93*
Kuprowicz, Rebecca Jane 1958- *WhoEmL 93*
Kupsch, Walter Oscar 1919- *WhoAm 92*
Kupst, Mary Jo 1945- *WhoAmW 93*
Kurahara, Koreyoshi *MiSFD 9*
Kural, Ilhan 1959- *WhoScE 91-4*
Kural, Orhan 1950- *WhoScE 91-4*
Kuralt, Charles 1934- *BioIn 17, JrnUS*
Kuralt, Charles Bishop 1934- *WhoAm 92, WhoE 93*
Kuralt, Thomas *St&PR 93*
Kuramata, Shiro 1934-1991 *BioIn 17*
Kuramoto, June 1948- *BioIn 17*
Kuramoto, Kizuku 1927- *WhoWor 93*
Kuramoto, Roy 1927- *St&PR 93*
Kuranari, Tadashi 1918- *WhoAsAP 91*
Kurant, Martin J. *St&PR 93*
Kuras, Jean Mary 1944- *WhoAmW 93*
Kuras, Thomas Francis 1947- *WhoE 93*
Kurasawa, Muan Yukihiro 1934- *WhoWor 93*
Kurasch, Teri J. 1956- *St&PR 93*
Kurasch, Teri Joyce *Law&B 92*
Kurata, Eiki 1949- *WhoAsAP 91*
Kurata, Hiroyuki 1938- *WhoAsAP 91*
Kurata, Tsutom 1933- *WhoWor 93*
Kurata, Yasushi 1946- *St&PR 93*
Kurath, Gertrude Prokosch (Tula) 1903- *Baker 92*
Kurau, Robert James 1918- *St&PR 93*
Kurbatov, Vitalii Gennadievich 1952- *WhoWor 93*
Kurc, Georges 1929- *WhoScE 91-2*
Kurcharz, Eugene Joseph 1951- *WhoScE 91-4*
Kurcman, Metin 1937- *WhoScE 91-4*
Kurcman, Seyhan 1941- *WhoScE 91-4*
Kurczewski, Walter W. *Law&B 92*
Kurdachenko, Leonid 1949- *WhoWor 93*
Kurdyla, Ronald H. *Law&B 92*
Kurdziel, Joseph 1938- *St&PR 93*
Kureishi, Hanif *BioIn 17, MiSFD 9*
Kureishi, Hanif 1954?- *ConAu 139, ConTFT 10, CurBio 92 [port]*
Kurek, Dolores Bodnar 1935- *WhoAmW 93*
Kurek, Jalu 1904-1983 *PolBiDi*
Kurelec, Branko 1935- *WhoScE 91-4*
Kurelek, William 1927-1977 *MajAI [port]*
Kurepa, Alexandra 1956- *WhoSSW 93*
Kures, Ken M. 1948- *St&PR 93*
Kuret, Niko 1906- *IntDcAn*
Kurfees, Donald Bryson 1933- *St&PR 93*
Kurfman, Dana 1925-1990 *BioIn 17*
Kuri-Aldana, Mario 1931- *Baker 92*
Kurian, George *BioIn 17*
Kurian, George Thomas 1931- *WhoAm 92*
Kurian, Verghese 1934- *WhoWor 93*
Kurianski, Jerzy 1955- *WhoWor 93*
Kuriansky, Judy 1947- *WhoAmW 93, WhoE 93, WhoEmL 93*
Kuribayashi, Tadamichi 1891-1945 *HarEnMi*
Kurie, Andrew Edmunds 1932- *WhoSSW 93*
Kurien, P.J. 1941- *WhoAsAP 91*
Kurien, Santha T. 1945- *WhoE 93*
Kurihara, Yuko 1920- *WhoAsAP 91*
Kuriki, Kyoichi 1935- *WhoWor 93*
Kurimoto, Kazuo 1935- *WhoUN 92*
Kurimura, Kazuo 1924- *WhoAsAP 91*
Kurina, Galina Alekseevna 1949- *WhoWor 93*
Kurinsky, Emil Matthew 1948- *St&PR 93*
Kurisaqila, Apenisa 1933- *WhoAsAP 91*
Kurisky, George A. 1937- *St&PR 93*
Kurisu, Hironori 1927- *WhoWor 93*
Kurisu, Kojiro 1937- *WhoWor 93*
Kurit, Neil 1940- *WhoAm 92*
Kurita, Chushiro 1910- *WhoWor 93*
Kurita, Osamu 1930- *WhoWor 93*
Kurita, Takeo 1889-1977 *HarEnMi*
Kuritzkes, Beth Manes *Law&B 92*
Kuriyama, Constance Brown 1942- *WhoSSW 93*
Kuriyama, Takakazu *BioIn 17, NewYTBS 92*
Kurk, Mitchell 1931- *WhoE 93*
Kurka, Robert 1921-1957 *IntDcOp*
Kurka, Robert (Frank) 1921-1957 *Baker 92*
Kurkcuoglu, M. *WhoScE 91-4*
Kurke, Kathleen Tighe 1958- *WhoAmW 93*
Kurke, Lance Brownson 1952- *WhoE 93*
Kurke, Martin Ira 1924- *WhoSSW 93*
Kurkela, Timo T. 1937- *WhoScE 91-4*
Kurki-Suonio, Eero Juho Ilmari 1929- *WhoScE 91-4*
Kurki-Suonio, Kaarle V.J. 1933- *WhoScE 91-4*
Kurkjian, Ann L. 1946- *WhoAmW 93*
Kurkjian, Gregory Arthur, Jr. 1936- *St&PR 93*
Kurkjian, Kathy P. *Law&B 92*
Kurkjian, Louis H. 1935- *WhoAm 92*
Kurkjian, Tim *BioIn 17*
Kurko, Michael C. 1942- *St&PR 93*
Kurkul, Stephan H. 1946- *St&PR 93*
Kurl, Daya Nath 1952- *WhoWor 93*
Kurlan, Marvin Zeft 1934- *WhoE 93, WhoWor 93*
Kurland, Geoffrey *BioIn 17*
Kurland, Gerald A. *Law&B 92*
Kurland, Harold Arthur 1952- *WhoEmL 93*
Kurland, Jeffrey *BioIn 17*
Kurland, Jonathan Joshua 1939- *WhoSSW 93*
Kurland, Lawrence R. *Law&B 92*
Kurland, Leonard J. 1925- *St&PR 93*
Kurland, Leonard Terry 1921- *WhoAm 92*
Kurland, Lewis Stewart *Law&B 92*
Kurland, Michael 1938- *ScF&FL 92*
Kurland, Philip B. 1921- *WhoAm 92*
Kurland, Richard M. 1953- *St&PR 93*
Kurland, Sheryl Paula 1957- *WhoE 93*
Kurlander, Honey Wachtel *WhoE 93*
Kurlander, Neale 1924- *WhoE 93, WhoWor 93*
Kurlandzki, Jerzy 1931- *WhoScE 91-4*
Kurman, Mitch *BioIn 17*
Kurman, Rochelle G. 1954- *WhoSSW 93*
Kurmann, Robert C. 1947- *St&PR 93*
Kurnick, Nathaniel Bertrand 1917- *WhoAm 92*

Kurnit, Paul David 1948- *WhoAm 92*
Kurnit, Shepard 1924- *WhoAm 92*
Kurnow, Ernest 1912- *WhoAm 92*
Kurobane, Itsuo 1944- *WhoWor 93*
Kuroda, Nagamasa 1568-1623 *HarEnMi*
Kuroda, Rokuro 1926- *WhoWor 93*
Kuroda, Teruhiko 1930- *WhoWor 93*
Kuroda, Toshiro 1926- *WhoWor 93*
Kuroda, Yoichi *BioIn 17*
Kuroda, Yoshitaka 1546-1604 *HarEnMi*
Kuroiwa, Yutaka 1910- *WhoWor 93*
Kurokawa, Akito 1928- *WhoWor 93*
Kurokawa, Kisho 1934- *WhoWor 93*
Kuroki, Nobuhiko 1921- *WhoWor 93*
Kuroki, Takemoti 1844-1923 *HarEnMi*
Kuron, Jacek 1934- *ColdWar 2 [port]*
Kuron, Klaus *BioIn 17*
Kuropatkin, Aleksei Nikolaevich 1848-1925 *HarEnMi*
Kurosaki, Yasuo 1936- *WhoWor 93*
Kurosawa, Akira *NewYTBS 92 [port]*
Kurosawa, Akira 1910- *BioIn 17, MiSFD 9, WhoWor 93*
Kurosawa, Kazukiyo 1926- *WhoWor 93*
Kuroshima Kameto 1893-1965 *HarEnMi*
Kurosky, Alexander 1938- *WhoAm 92*
Kurowski, Theodore G. 1929- *St&PR 93*
Kurowski, Tomasz Christopher *Law&B 92*
Kuroyanagi, Akira 1931- *WhoAsAP 91*
Kuroyanagi, Tetsuko 1934- *WhoWor 93*
Kurpinski, Karol 1785-1857 *OxDcOp*
Kurpinski, Karol (Kazimierz) 1785-1857 *Baker 92, PolBiDi*
Kurppa, Sirpa L.A. 1953- *WhoScE 91-4*
Kurras, Herbert L. 1932- *St&PR 93*
Kurre, James Anthony 1951- *WhoEmL 93*
Kurrelmeyer, Louis Hayner 1928- *WhoAm 92, WhoWor 93*
Kurren, Faye W. *Law&B 92*
Kurri, Jari 1960- *WhoAm 92*
Kurry, Joseph R. 1950- *St&PR 93*
Kurschner, Lisa Marie 1964- *WhoAmW 93*
Kurschner, Richard Carl 1958- *WhoEmL 93*
Kurschner, Robert Rudolph 1935- *St&PR 93*
Kursel, Marcy Ann 1953- *WhoWrEP 92*
Kursh, H. David 1952- *St&PR 93*
Kursh, Raymond J. *St&PR 93*
Kurshan, Barbara Lynn 1948- *WhoAmW 93*
Kurska, Daniel Grotta- *ScF&FL 92*
Kursman, Jerome 1921- *St&PR 93*
Kursman, Peter Jed 1952- *St&PR 93*
Kursteiner, Jean Paul 1864-1943 *Baker 92*
Kursten, Martin O.C. *WhoScE 91-3*
Kursunoglu, Behram N. 1922- *WhoAm 92, WhoWor 93*
Kurt, Melanie 1880-1941 *Baker 92, OxDcOp*
Kurtag, Gyorgy 1926- *Baker 92*
Kurten, Bjorn *BioIn 17*
Kurten, Bjorn 1924-1988 *ScF&FL 92*
Kurtenbach, Nancy 1959- *St&PR 93*
Kurtev, Bogdan Jordanov *WhoScE 91-4*
Kurth, Carl Ferdinand 1928- *WhoAm 92*
Kurth, Ernst 1886-1946 *Baker 92*
Kurth, Karlheinz 1940- *WhoScE 91-3*
Kurth, Lieselotte 1923- *WhoAm 92*
Kurth, Peter 1953- *ConAu 139*
Kurth, Reinhard 1942- *WhoScE 91-3*
Kurth, Ronald James 1931- *WhoAm 92, WhoSSW 93*
Kurth, Sidney Charles 1955- *WhoWor 93*
Kurth, Walter Richard 1932- *WhoAm 92, WhoE 93*
Kurtis, William Horton 1940- *WhoAm 92*
Kurtz, Anthony D. 1929- *St&PR 93*
Kurtz, Barbara Brandon 1941- *WhoAmW 93*
Kurtz, Bruce Edward 1936- *WhoAm 92*
Kurtz, Carol Deanne 1956- *WhoAmW 93*
Kurtz, Charles Jewett, III 1940- *WhoWor 93*
Kurtz, Cora Sweigart 1940- *WhoSSW 93*
Kurtz, David Merrill, Jr. *Law&B 92*
Kurtz, Diana Stella 1966- *WhoEmL 93*
Kurtz, Dolores May 1933- *WhoAmW 93*
Kurtz, Donald R. 1930- *St&PR 93*
Kurtz, Edward Frampton 1881-1965 *Baker 92*
Kurtz, Edwin Bernard 1926- *WhoWor 93*
Kurtz, Efrem 1900- *Baker 92*
Kurtz, Elaine 1928- *WhoE 93*
Kurtz, F. Anthony 1941- *St&PR 93*
Kurtz, Gary Douglas 1940- *WhoAm 92*
Kurtz, Grant Wilson 1942- *St&PR 93*
Kurtz, Harvey A. 1950- *WhoAm 92*
Kurtz, Jerome 1931- *WhoAm 92*
Kurtz, Joel Barry 1944- *WhoE 93, WhoWor 93*
Kurtz, John H. 1949- *St&PR 93*
Kurtz, John R. 1930- *St&PR 93*
Kurtz, Jules 1914- *St&PR 93*
Kurtz, Karen Barbara 1948- *WhoAmW 93, WhoEmL 93*
Kurtz, Katherine 1944- *ScF&FL 92*
Kurtz, Kenneth R. 1946- *St&PR 93*
Kurtz, Leonard D. 1915-1991 *BioIn 17*
Kurtz, Lloyd Sherer, Jr. 1934- *WhoAm 92*
Kurtz, Mark Edward 1946- *WhoSSW 93*
Kurtz, Maurice E. 1922- *St&PR 93*
Kurtz, Max 1920- *WhoE 93, WhoWor 93*
Kurtz, Maxine 1921- *WhoAmW 93*
Kurtz, Melvin H. *Law&B 92*
Kurtz, Melvin H. 1936- *St&PR 93, WhoAm 92*
Kurtz, Michael *Law&B 92*
Kurtz, Michael L. 1941- *WhoSSW 93*
Kurtz, Myers Richard 1924- *WhoAm 92, WhoSSW 93*
Kurtz, Nancy C. *Law&B 92*
Kurtz, Nat *Law&B 92*
Kurtz, Patricia A. *Law&B 92*
Kurtz, Patti Joan 1957- *WhoWrEP 92*
Kurtz, Paul 1925- *WhoAm 92, WhoE 93, WhoWor 93*
Kurtz, Paul Michael 1946- *WhoEmL 93*
Kurtz, Quentin Eugene *Law&B 92*
Kurtz, Robert Arthur 1943- *WhoSSW 93*
Kurtz, Robert Gary 1952- *WhoE 93*
Kurtz, Robert James 1941- *WhoSSW 93*
Kurtz, Sheldon Francis 1943- *WhoAm 92*
Kurtz, Sheldon Ian 1938- *WhoE 93*
Kurtz, Stephen J. 1936- *St&PR 93*
Kurtz, Stewart K. 1931- *WhoAm 92*
Kurtz, Swoosie *WhoAm 92, WhoAmW 93*
Kurtz, T.S. 1948- *St&PR 93*
Kurtz, Theodore Stephen 1944- *WhoE 93*
Kurtz, Thomas Gordon 1941- *WhoAm 92*
Kurtz, William A. *Law&B 92*
Kurtzberg, Evelyn Claire 1942- *WhoE 93*
Kurtze, Crystal Catherine Gard 1949- *WhoWrEP 92*
Kurtzig, Sandra *St&PR 93*
Kurtzig, Sandra L. *BioIn 17*
Kurtzig, Sandra L. 1946- *WhoAm 92, WhoAmW 93*
Kurtzke, John Francis, Sr. 1926- *WhoAm 92*
Kurtzman, Allan Roger 1933- *WhoAm 92*
Kurtzman, Benita Pam 1959- *WhoAmW 93*
Kurtzman, Clifford Roger 1959- *WhoEmL 93*
Kurtzman, Myron Bernard *Law&B 92*
Kurtzman, Neil A. 1936- *WhoAm 92, WhoWor 93*
Kurtzman, Zvi 1947- *St&PR 93*
Kurtzon, Lawrence *St&PR 93*
Kuruc, Alvin Ronald 1957- *WhoE 93*
Kurucz, Donald Michael 1939- *St&PR 93*
Kurucz, Gyula 1927- *WhoScE 91-4*
Kurumado, Hiroshi 1947- *WhoWor 93*
Kurumado, Minoru 1919- *WhoWor 93*
Kury, Franklin Leo 1936- *WhoAm 92*
Kuryk, David Neal 1947- *WhoEmL 93*
Kurylev, Yaroslav Vadimovich 1952- *WhoWor 93*
Kurylko, Bohdan I. 1928- *St&PR 93*
Kurylo, Carolyn Kreiter 1946- *WhoWrEP 92*
Kurys, Diane 1948- *MiSFD 9*
Kuryu, Masao 1920- *WhoWor 93*
Kurz, Desi Halban- 1912- *OxDcOp*
Kurz, Diana *BioIn 17*
Kurz, Edward A. 1926- *St&PR 93*
Kurz, Edward Philip 1921- *WhoWor 93*
Kurz, Edward V. *Law&B 92*
Kurz, Hans D. 1938- *WhoUN 92*
Kurz, Hans-Rudolf d1990 *BioIn 17*
Kurz, Heinrich 1943- *WhoScE 91-3*
Kurz, Herbert 1920- *St&PR 93*
Kurz, Isolde *Law&B 92*
Kurz, Joseph Felix von 1717-1784 *OxDcOp*
Kurz, Joseph Louis 1933- *WhoAm 92*
Kurz, Kathy Ann 1956- *WhoAmW 93*
Kurz, Kelli McDonald. 1955- *WhoAm 92*
Kurz, Kenneth William 1955- *St&PR 93*
Kurz, Manfred 1936- *WhoScE 91-3*
Kurz, Michael J. 1952- *WhoIns 93*
Kurz, Mitchell Howard 1951- *WhoAm 92*
Kurz, Mordecai 1934- *WhoAm 92*
Kurz, Richard 1935- *WhoScE 91-3*
Kurz, Richard Michael 1942- *WhoIns 93*
Kurz, Ron 1940- *WhoWrEP 92*
Kurz, Selma 1874-1933 *Baker 92, IntDcOp, OxDcOp*
Kurz, Siegfried 1930- *Baker 92*
Kurz, Thomas Patrick *Law&B 92*
Kurz, Thomas Patrick 1951- *WhoAm 92*
Kurz, Warren W. *Law&B 92*
Kurz, William Charles Frederick 1942- *WhoAm 92*
Kurz, William W. *St&PR 93*
Kurzawa, Zbigniew 1924- *WhoScE 91-4*
Kurzeja, Ronald 1949- *St&PR 93*
Kurzina, Stanley B. d1990 *BioIn 17*
Kurzinger, Ignaz Franz Xaver 1724-1797 *Baker 92*
Kurzinger, Paul Ignaz 1750-c. 1820 *Baker 92*
Kurzman, Dan 1927- *WhoWor 93*
Kurzman, Harold Philip 1936- *WhoSSW 93*
Kurzman, Stephen Alan 1945- *WhoE 93*
Kurzrock, Razelle 1954- *WhoAmW 93*
Kurzweg, Ulrich Hermann 1936- *WhoAm 92, WhoSSW 93*
Kurzweil, Edith *WhoAm 92, WhoAmW 93*
Kurzweil, Judith *Law&B 92*
Kurzweil, Raymond *BioIn 17*
Kurzweil, Raymond C. 1948- *ConEn*
Kus, Henryk Jozef 1925- *WhoWor 93*
Kusaka, Jin'ichi 1889-1972 *HarEnMi*
Kusaka, Kazumasa *BioIn 17*
Kusaka, Ryunosuke 1892-1971 *HarEnMi*
Kusakabe, Kiyoko 1935- *WhoAsAP 91*
Kusakawa, Shozo 1928- *WhoAsAP 91*
Kusama, Yayoi 1929- *WhoAm 92*
Kusano, Motohiko 1947- *WhoWor 93*
Kusano, Takeshi 1928- *WhoAsAP 91*
Kusano, Yasushi 1932- *WhoWor 93*
Kusar, Daniel D. 1928- *St&PR 93*
Kusch, Polykarp 1911- *WhoAm 92, WhoSSW 93, WhoWor 93*
Kusche, Benno 1916- *Baker 92, OxDcOp*
Kusche, Herbert R. 1921- *St&PR 93*
Kuschinsky, Klaus 1939- *WhoScE 91-3*
Kuse, James Russell 1930- *WhoAm 92, WhoSSW 93*
Kusek, Carol Joan 1955- *WhoAmW 93, WhoEmL 93*
Kuser, Daniel M. 1944- *St&PR 93*
Kuserk, Frank Thomas 1951- *WhoEmL 93*
Kusevitsky, Moshe 1899-1966 *Baker 92*
Kush, Charles Andrew, III 1964- *WhoE 93, WhoEmL 93*
Kushawaha, Ran Naresh 1929- *WhoAsAP 91*
Kushel, Gerald 1930- *WhoE 93*
Kusheloff, David Leon 1917- *WhoAm 92*
Kushen, Allan Stanford 1929- *St&PR 93, WhoAm 92*
Kushen, Betty Sandra 1933- *WhoE 93*
Kushi, Francis Xavier 1938- *WhoAm 92*
Kushi, Yoshihiko 1937- *WhoWor 93*
Kushida, Takashi 1935- *WhoWor 93*
Kushihara, Yoshinao 1926- *WhoAsAP 91*
Kushlan, Samuel Daniel 1912- *WhoAm 92*
Kushmeider, Rose Marie 1956- *WhoEmL 93*
Kushner, David Zakeri 1935- *WhoAm 92*
Kushner, Donald *St&PR 93*
Kushner, Donn 1927- *ScF&FL 92, WhoCanL 92*
Kushner, Donn 1929- *DcChlFi*
Kushner, Ellen 1955- *ScF&FL 92*
Kushner, Eva 1929- *WhoAm 92, WhoAmW 93*
Kushner, Gail Lori 1953- *WhoEmL 93*
Kushner, Harold Joseph 1933- *WhoAm 92*
Kushner, Harvey D. 1930- *St&PR 93*
Kushner, Harvey David 1930- *WhoAm 92*
Kushner, Harvey Wolf 1941- *WhoE 93*
Kushner, Jeffrey L. 1948- *St&PR 93, WhoAm 92*
Kushner, Jill Menkes 1951- *BioIn 17*
Kushner, Lawrence Maurice 1924- *WhoAm 92*
Kushner, Michael James 1951- *WhoEmL 93*
Kushner, Robert Arnold *Law&B 92*
Kushner, Robert Arnold 1935- *St&PR 93, WhoAm 92*
Kushner, Robert Ellis 1949- *WhoAm 92*
Kushner, Shari *Law&B 92*
Kushner, Sidney Ralph 1943- *WhoSSW 93*
Kushner, Sylvia Deutscher d1990 *BioIn 17*
Kushnick, Helen Gorman 1945- *WhoAmW 93*
Kushul', Aleksandra IAkovlevna 1907-1985 *BioIn 17*
Kushwaha, Manvir Singh 1951- *WhoWor 93*
Kusi, Jonathan Atta 1944- *WhoUN 92*
Kusiak, Phil 1954- *St&PR 93*
Kusi-Appiah, Samuel Okyere 1952- *WhoWor 93*
Kusisto, Kathryn Haas 1958- *WhoEmL 93*
Kusisto, Oscar Perry 1915- *WhoWor 93*
Kuska, John Joseph, Jr. 1953- *WhoE 93*
Kuske, Edward Alan 1940- *WhoAm 92*
Kuskin, Debi F. 1956- *St&PR 93*
Kuskin, Gary S. 1950- *St&PR 93*
Kuskin, Karla *BioIn 17*
Kuskin, Karla 1932- *MajAI [port], WhoAm 92, WhoWrEP 92*
Kusler, James O'Dell 1947- *WhoAm 92*
Kusler, Mary-Margaret 1945- *WhoAmW 93*
Kusler, Rex Ernest 1952- *WhoWrEP 92*
Kusma, Taissa Turkevich *WhoAm 92*
Kusnerus, Wendell G. *Law&B 92*
Kusnetzov, Howard 1942- *WhoE 93*
Kusnick, Barry A. 1910- *ConAu 37NR*
Kusocinski, Janusz 1907-1940 *PolBiDi*
Kuspan, Joseph F. 1925- *St&PR 93*
Kuspit, Donald B(urton) 1935- *ConAu 37NR*
Kuspit, Donald Burton 1935- *WhoAm 92*
Kuss, Henry J. 1922-1990 *BioIn 17*
Kuss, Richard L. 1923- *WhoAm 92*
Kussel, William Ferdinand, Jr. 1957- *WhoEmL 93, WhoWor 93*
Kusser, Johann Sigismund 1660-1727 *Baker 92, OxDcOp*
Kusserow, Richard Phillip 1940- *WhoAm 92*
Kussevitsky, Serge (Alexandrovich) *Baker 92*
Kussman, David Alan 1952- *WhoEmL 93*
Kuster, Hermann 1817-1878 *Baker 92*
Kustes, John Thomas 1950- *St&PR 93*
Kustes, William Anthony 1946- *WhoSSW 93*
Kustica, Douglas E. 1946- *St&PR 93*
Kustin, Kenneth 1934- *WhoAm 92, WhoE 93*
Kustka, Christine May 1949- *WhoAmW 93*
Kustra, Robert W. 1943- *WhoAm 92*
Kustron, Konnie Gerlyn 1954- *WhoEmL 93*
Kusturica, Emir *BioIn 17*
Kusturica, Emir 1955- *DrEEuF, MiSFD 9*
Kusuhara, Tomoko Saito 1935- *WhoWor 93*
Kusulas, Elias P. 1940- *St&PR 93*
Kusumaatmadja, Sarwono 1943- *WhoAsAP 91*
Kusumi, Akihiro 1952- *WhoWor 93*
Kusumo, Sardono W. *BioIn 17*
Kusumoto, Isao 1943- *St&PR 93*
Kusumoto, Sadahei *BioIn 17*
Kusunoki, Masanori c. 1330-1390 *HarEnMi*
Kusunoki, Masashige 1294-1336 *HarEnMi*
Kusunoki, Masatsura 1326-1348 *HarEnMi*
Kusy, Andrzej 1942- *WhoScE 91-4*
Kusy, Lynn Francis 1946- *WhoEmL 93*
Kusy, Robert Peter 1947- *WhoAm 92, WhoEmL 93, WhoSSW 93*
Kusz, Natalie *BioIn 17*
Kuszelewski, Leszek 1922- *WhoScE 91-4*
Kuszell, Antoni F. 1935- *WhoScE 91-4*
Kuta, Kathleen M. *Law&B 92*
Kutas, Ferenc 1930- *WhoScE 91-4*
Kutasi, Katalin Erzsebet 1956- *WhoAmW 93, WhoE 93*
Kutateladze, Semen Samsonovich 1945- *WhoWor 93*
Kutavicius, Bronislovas 1932- *Baker 92*
Kutcher, Steve *BioIn 17*
Kutchin, Jill 1952- *St&PR 93*
Kutchin, Jill Caryn 1952- *WhoAmW 93*
Kutchin, Joseph William 1928- *St&PR 93*
Kutchins, Michael Joseph 1941- *WhoAm 92*
Kutemeyer, Peter Martin 1938- *WhoWor 93*
Kuter, Joseph J. *Law&B 92*
Kutev, Filip 1903-1982 *Baker 92*
Kuthiravattom, Thomas 1945- *WhoAsAP 91*
Kuthy, Arnold Robert 1932- *WhoE 93*
Kutko, Rostyslaw 1944- *St&PR 93*
Kutler, Stanley Ira 1934- *WhoAm 92*
Kutler, Stephen C. 1935- *WhoAm 92*
Kutlina, Mary Louise 1963- *WhoE 93*
Kutner, Malcolm J. 1921- *BiDAMSp 1989*
Kutner, Wlodzimierz 1948- *WhoWor 93*
Kutney, James Peter 1932- *WhoAm 92*
Kutrzeba, Joseph Stanislaw 1927- *WhoAm 92*
Kutsch, Clifford Dale 1930- *St&PR 93*
Kutschbach, James William, Sr. 1923- *St&PR 93*
Kutscher, Eugene Bernard 1947- *WhoE 93, WhoEmL 93*
Kutsukake, Tetsuo 1929- *WhoAsAP 91*
Kutsunugi, Takeko 1922- *WhoAsAP 91*
Kutten, Lawarence Joseph 1953- *WhoE 93*
Kuttler, Carl Martin, Jr. 1940- *WhoAm 92*
Kuttner, Bernard A. 1934- *WhoWor 93*
Kuttner, Catherine *ScF&FL 92*
Kuttner, Henry 1915-1958 *BioIn 17, ScF&FL 92*
Kuttner, Ludwig Georg 1946- *St&PR 93*
Kuttner, Paul 1931- *WhoWrEP 92*
Kuttruff, Karl Heinrich 1930- *WhoScE 91-3*
Kutuzov *OxDcOp*
Kutuzov, Mikhail Ilarionovich Golenischev 1745-1813 *HarEnMi*
Kutyna, Donald Joseph 1933- *WhoAm 92*
Kutz, Henry Douglas 1946- *WhoSSW 93*
Kutz, John A. *Law&B 92*
Kutz, Kazimierz 1929- *DrEEuF*
Kutz, Kenneth John 1926- *WhoAm 92*
Kutz, Myer Paul 1939- *WhoWrEP 92*
Kutzbach, Heinz Dieter 1940- *WhoScE 91-3*
Kutzelnigg, Werner 1933- *WhoScE 91-3, WhoWor 93*
Kutzen, Jerome Jefferies 1923- *St&PR 93*
Kutzen, Peggy Duke 1951- *St&PR 93*
Kutzin, Lawrence M. 1952- *St&PR 93*
Kutzin, Milton 1917- *St&PR 93*

Kutzmark, George F. 1928- *St&PR 93*
Kuugka, Peter 1949- *WhoAsAP 91*
Kuula, Toivo (Timoteus) 1883-1918 *Baker 92*
Kuulasmaa, Karl A. 1954- *WhoScE 91-4*
Kuusipalo, Jussi 1952- *WhoScE 91-4*
Kuusisto, Ilkka Taneli 1933- *Baker 92*
Kuusisto, Taneli 1905- *Baker 92*
Kuvrat dc. 642 *OxDcByz*
Kuwahara, Hidechika 1955- *WhoWor 93*
Kuwahara, Mitsunori 1936- *WhoWor 93*
Kuwahara, Yasue 1957- *WhoSSW 93*
Kuwano, Koichi 1954- *WhoWor 93*
Kuwano, Yukinori 1941- *WhoWor 93*
Kuwata, Kazuhiro 1942- *WhoWor 93*
Kuwatly, Shukri el- 1891-1967 *BioIn 17*
Kuwayama, George 1925- *ConAu 39NR, WhoAm 92*
Kuyama, Sumihiro 1936- *WhoUN 92*
Kuyath, Richard Norman *Law&B 92*
Kuyath, Richard Norman 1948- *WhoEmL 93*
Kuyatt, Chris Ernie Earl 1930- *WhoAm 92*
Kuyers, David J. 1949- *St&PR 93*
Kuyk, Willem 1934- *WhoScE 91-2, WhoWor 93*
Kuykendall, Crystal Arlene 1949- *WhoAmW 93, WhoEmL 93*
Kuykendall, John Wells 1938- *WhoAm 92, WhoSSW 93*
Kuykendall, Ronald Edward *Law&B 92*
Kuykendall, Theodore Cramor 1947- *St&PR 93*
Kuylenstjerna, C. Goran J. 1932- *WhoScE 91-4*
Kuyper, Elisabeth 1877-1953 *Baker 92*
Kuyper, Joan Carolyn 1941- *WhoAmW 93, WhoE 93*
Kuyper, Vicki Jean 1956- *WhoWrEP 92*
Kuypers, H.G.J.M. *BioIn 17*
Kuyt, Ernie *BioIn 17*
Kuzdo, Victor 1859-1966 *Baker 92*
Kuze, Kimitaka 1928- *WhoAsAP 91*
Kuzel, Hans-Jurgen *WhoScE 91-3*
Kuzel, Radomir 1931- *WhoScE 91-4*
Kuzell, William Charles 1914- *WhoAm 92*
Kuzhamyarov, Kuddus 1918- *OxDcOp*
Kuzichkin, Vladimir Andreyevich 1947- *BioIn 17*
Kuzin, Ilya Aleksandrovich 1961- *WhoWor 93*
Kuzma, David R. *St&PR 93*
Kuzma, Gregory Paul 1950- *WhoE 93*
Kuzmak, Lubomyr Ihor 1931- *WhoWor 93*
Kuzmichev, Valentin Evdokimovich 1945- *WhoWor 93*
Kuzmin, Edward Leonidovitch 1941- *WhoWor 93*
Kuzmin, Mikhail Ivanovich 1938- *WhoWor 93*
Kuzminski, Lawrence N. 1941- *St&PR 93*
Kuzminski, Zbigniew 1921- *DrEEuF*
Kuznetsov, (Edward) 1939- *ConAu 39NR*
Kuznetsov, Michael Ivanovich 1949- *WhoWor 93*
Kuznetsov, Vasilii Vasil'evich 1901-1990 *BioIn 17*
Kuznetsova, Maria 1880-1966 *OxDcOp*
Kuznetsova, Maria (Nikolaievna) 1880-1966 *Baker 92*
Kuznetsova, Olga Ivanovna 1950- *WhoWor 93*
Kuznetzov, Konstantin (Alexeievich) 1883-1953 *Baker 92*
Kuzniarski, Andrzej 1938- *WhoScE 91-4*
Kuznik, Susan Marie 1956- *WhoEmL 93*
Kuznitsky, Susan *BioIn 17*
Kuzoe, Felix Ahli Stanislaus 1936- *WhoUN 92*
Kuzora-Ziarno, Irena 1928- *WhoScE 91-4*
Kuzsel, Karen Barbara 1949- *WhoAmW 93*
Kuzui, Fran Rubel *MiSFD 9*
Kvalheim, Olav Martin 1951- *WhoWor 93*
Kvalseth, Tarald Oddvar 1938- *WhoAm 92*
Kvam, Einar 1933- *WhoScE 91-4*
Kvam, Oddvar S(chirmer) 1927- *Baker 92*
Kvamme, Peder 1918- *St&PR 93*
Kvandal, (David) Johan 1919- *Baker 92*
Kvapil, Jaroslav 1892-1958 *Baker 92*
Kvaran, Agust 1952- *WhoWor 93*
Kvasnica, Jozef 1930- *WhoScE 91-4*
Kvasnicka, Lad 1944- *St&PR 93*
Kvasov, Boris Il'ich 1946- *WhoWor 93*
Kvech, Timothy Jerry 1967- *WhoSSW 93*
Kveder, Sergije 1924- *WhoScE 91-4*
Kvederis, Paul Mark *WhoE 93*
Kvenvold, Tony Mark 1956- *WhoE 93, WhoEmL 93*
Kvernadze, Bidzina 1928- *Baker 92*
Kvetina, Jaroslav 1930- *WhoScE 91-4*
Kvitka, Klyment 1880-1953 *Baker 92*
Kvitsinsky, Andrei Anatolievich 1958- *WhoWor 93*
Kviyn, Adriana *AmWomPl*
Kviz, Boris 1931- *WhoScE 91-4*
Kwa, Raymond Pain-Boon 1944- *WhoE 93, WhoWor 93*
Kwack, Beyoung Hwa 1930- *WhoWor 93*
Kwak, Sung 1941- *WhoAm 92*
Kwak, Won-mo 1935- *WhoWor 93*
Kwakernaak, Huibert 1937- *WhoScE 91-3*
Kwalwasser, Amy Sue 1956- *WhoWrEP 92*
Kwalwasser, Helen 1927- *Baker 92*
Kwalwasser, Jacob 1894-1977 *Baker 92*
Kwame *BioIn 17*
Kwan, Elaine Isa 1950- *WhoAmW 93*
Kwan, Frank T.Y. 1949- *St&PR 93*
Kwan, Simon Hon Tak 1961- *WhoWor 93*
Kwan, Stanley 1957- *MiSFD 9*
Kwandt, Joanne 1944- *WhoAmW 93*
Kwapil, William Joseph, Jr. 1943- *St&PR 93*
Kwapis, Ken *MiSFD 9*
Kwapisz, Marian 1935- *WhoWor 93*
Kwapiszewski, Wincenty 1927- *WhoScE 91-4*
Kwapulinski, Jerzy Henryk 1940- *WhoWor 93*
Kwarara, Galeva 1942- *WhoAsAP 91*
Kwasizur, John Michael 1939- *St&PR 93*
Kwasnick, Paul Jack 1925- *WhoAm 92*
Kwasnicki, Stanley F. 1936- *St&PR 93*
Kwasniewski, Aleksander 1954- *WhoWor 93*
Kwasnik, Joseph Robert 1951- *St&PR 93*
Kwass, Sidney J. 1908- *WhoSSW 93*
Kwast, James 1852-1927 *Baker 92*
Kwast, Tomasz Tadeusz 1942- *WhoScE 91-4*
Kwei, Gloria Yung Ching 1943- *WhoAmW 93*
Kweit, Robert W(illiam) 1946- *ConAu 37NR*
Kweller, Goldie Bober 1920-1991 *BioIn 17*
Kwiat, Arthur *St&PR 93*
Kwiat, Joseph J. *WhoAm 92*
Kwiat, Kenneth Bernard 1939- *St&PR 93*
Kwiatek, Harlan Jay *Law&B 92*
Kwiatkowska-Korczak, Janina 1926- *WhoWor 93*
Kwiatkowski, Alan Paul 1940- *St&PR 93*
Kwiatkowski, Aleksander W. 1925- *WhoScE 91-4*
Kwiatkowski, Diana J. 1958- *WhoWrEP 92*
Kwiatkowski, Edward Louis 1950- *St&PR 93*
Kwiatkowski, Edwin John 1933- *WhoAm 92*
Kwiatkowski, Henryk 1932- *WhoScE 91-4*
Kwiatkowski, Jozef Stanislaw 1936- *WhoScE 91-4*
Kwiatkowski, Ryszard 1931- *Baker 92*
Kwiatkowski, Thomas David 1941- *St&PR 93*
Kwiatkowski, Waldemar 1937- *WhoScE 91-4*
Kwiatkowski, Zbigniew Adam 1929- *WhoScE 91-4*
Kwicien, John Martin 1950- *WhoIns 93*
Kwiecinski, Andrzej Robert 1940- *WhoScE 91-4*
Kwiecinski, Marek W. 1929- *WhoScE 91-4*
Kwik, K.H. 1935- *WhoScE 91-3*
Kwiker, Louis A. 1935- *WhoAm 92*
Kwiram, Alvin L. 1937- *WhoAm 92*
Kwiterovich, Peter Oscar, Jr. 1940- *WhoE 93*
Kwitny, Jeff *MiSFD 9*
Kwitter, Karen Beth 1951- *WhoAmW 93*
Kwitz, Mary DeBall *ScF&FL 92*
Kwock, Laureen C. 1951- *WhoWrEP 92*
Kwoh, Daniel S. *BioIn 17*
Kwok, Raymond Hung Fai 1963- *WhoWor 93*
Kwok, Tak-seng *BioIn 17*
Kwolek, Julian A. 1941- *St&PR 93*
Kwon, Dae Young 1957- *WhoWor 93*
Kwon, Dong-sook 1932- *WhoWor 93*
Kwon, Joon Taek 1935- *WhoWor 93*
Kwon Dal Soo 1938- *WhoAsAP 91*
Kwong, Chi-Hung Maurice 1960- *WhoWor 93*
Kwong, Gordon P. 1958- *St&PR 93*
Kwong, James Kin-Ping 1954- *WhoWor 93*
Kwong, Peter Kong Kit 1936- *WhoWor 93*
Kwong, Stephen T. *St&PR 93*
Kwon Hae Ok 1936- *WhoAsAP 91*
Kwon Hun-Sung 1959- *WhoAsAP 91*
Kwon Roh Kap 1931- *WhoAsAP 91*
Kwon-Taek, Im 1936- *MiSFD 9*
Ky, Nguyen Cao 1930- *DcTwHis*
Kybal, Dalimil 1916- *WhoE 93*
Kyburg, Henry Guy Ely, Jr. 1928- *WhoAm 92, WhoE 93*
Kyd, Charles William 1948- *WhoWrEP 92*
Kyd, Margot A. 1953- *St&PR 93*
Kyd, Marilyn Gratton 1948- *WhoWrEP 92*
Kyd, Thomas 1558-1594 *DramC 3*
Kyd, Warren J. 1939- *WhoAsAP 91*
Kydones, Demetrios c. 1324-c. 1398 *OxDcByz*
Kydones, Prochoros c. 1333-1369? *OxDcByz*
Kyees, John Edward 1946- *WhoEmL 93*
Kyes, Robert L(ange) 1933- *ConAu 37NR*
Kyger, Joanne 1934- *ConAu 16AS [port]*
Kyger, Joanne (Elizabeth) 1934- *ConAu 40NR*
Kyhl, Curtis Daniel 1937- *St&PR 93*
Kyhl, Robert Louis 1917- *WhoAm 92*
Kyker, Christine White 1925- *WhoSSW 93*
Kyker, Claude J. 1942- *St&PR 93*
Kyl, John Henry 1919- *WhoAm 92*
Kyl, Jon 1942- *CngDr 91*
Kyl, Jon Llewellyn 1942- *WhoAm 92*
Kylavaara, Ilkka Uolevi 1946- *WhoWor 93*
Kyle, Alastair Boyd 1931- *WhoWor 93*
Kyle, Andrew Crockett, III 1945- *WhoSSW 93*
Kyle, David A. 1919- *ScF&FL 92*
Kyle, Donald Gordon 1950- *WhoEmL 93, WhoSSW 93*
Kyle, Gary W. *Law&B 92*
Kyle, Glenna Maxey *Law&B 92*
Kyle, Harold K. *Law&B 92*
Kyle, James H. *BioIn 17*
Kyle, Jerry L. 1941- *St&PR 93*
Kyle, John Hamilton 1925- *WhoAm 92*
Kyle, Keith 1925- *ConAu 137*
Kyle, Mary J. *WhoWrEP 92*
Kyle, Penelope Ward *Law&B 92*
Kyle, Penelope Ward 1947- *WhoAmW 93*
Kyle, Richard Erwin 1905- *WhoAm 92*
Kyle, Robert Arthur 1928- *WhoAm 92*
Kyle, Robert Campbell, II 1935- *WhoAm 92, WhoWor 93*
Kyle, Terrence W. 1950- *St&PR 93*
Kyle, Terrence Wayne 1950- *WhoAm 92*
Kyle, William Davidson, Jr. 1915- *St&PR 93*
Kyle, William L., Jr. 1927- *St&PR 93*
Kyle, William Walsh 1946- *St&PR 93*
Kyle, Willis B. 1914- *St&PR 93*
Kylian, Jiri *BioIn 17*
Kylian, Jiri 1947- *WhoAm 92, WhoWor 93*
Kyllonen, Timo-Juhani 1955- *Baker 92*
Kylstra, Johannes Arnold 1925- *WhoAm 92*
Kyman, Alexander L. 1929- *St&PR 93*
Kyman, Alexander Leon 1929- *WhoAm 92*
Kyman, Lawrence *St&PR 93*
Kyman, Wendy 1947- *WhoAmW 93, WhoEmL 93*
Kyne, Mary Theresa 1953- *WhoE 93*
Kynoch, James Brent 1959- *WhoAm 92, WhoE 93, WhoEmL 93*
Kyo, Machiko 1924- *IntDcF 2-3 [port]*
Kyotani, Yoshihiro 1926- *WhoWor 93*
Kyparissiotes *OxDcByz*
Kyparissiotes, John c. 1310-c. 1378 *OxDcByz*
Kyprianou, Spyros 1932- *WhoWor 93*
Kypta, Richard J. *Law&B 92*
Kyriakis, Nickolas 1954- *WhoScE 91-3*
Kyriakopoulou, P.E. *WhoScE 91-3*
Kyriakos fl. 6th cent.?- *OxDcByz*
Kyriakou, Linda G. *St&PR 93*
Kyriakou, Linda Grace 1943- *WhoAmW 93*
Kyriakou, Rena 1918- *Baker 92*
Kyriazis, Arthur John 1958- *WhoE 93, WhoEmL 93, WhoWor 93*
Kyriazis, Basil 1932- *WhoScE 91-3*
Kyrill of Pittsburgh, Bishop *WhoAm 92*
Kyrklund, B. *WhoScE 91-3*
Kyrkos, Leonidas *WhoWor 93*
Kyros d457 *OxDcByz*
Kyros and John *OxDcByz*
Kyser, Kay 1906-1985 *Baker 92, BioIn 17*
Kysor, Daniel Francis 1956- *WhoE 93*
Kyst, Kaare 1944- *WhoWor 93*
Kyte, William S. 1942- *WhoScE 91-1*
Kytle, Ray 1941- *ScF&FL 92*
Kytmanov, Alexander 1949- *WhoWor 93*
Kytzler, Bernhard Peter Paul 1929- *WhoWor 93*
Kyuchukov, Nedko G. 1921- *WhoScE 91-4*
Kyuma, Fumio *WhoAsAP 91*
Kyuma, Kazutake 1931- *WhoWor 93*
Kyung, Koo Ja 1925- *WhoWor 93*
Kyzar, Kent Como 1953- *WhoEmL 93*
Kyzar, Ollie Jeanette 1933- *WhoAmW 93*

L

Laabs, Peter 1948- *St&PR 93*
Laajoki, Kauko V.O. 1940- *WhoScE 91-4*
Laaksonen, Donna J. 1949- *WhoWrEP 92*
Laaksonen, Reino 1924- *WhoScE 91-4*
Laaly, Heshmat Ollah 1927- *WhoWor 93*
Laamanen, Arvo Taavetti 1929- *WhoScE 91-4*
Laan, Hans van der 1904-1991 *BioIn 17*
LA & Babyface *SoulM*
Laane, Jaan 1942- *WhoSSW 93*
Laane, Tiiu Virkhaus 1940- *WhoSSW 93*
Laano, Archie Bienvenido Maano 1939- *WhoAm 92, WhoE 93, WhoWor 93*
Laapas, Heikki R. 1949- *WhoScE 91-4*
Laarmans, John 1960- *WhoWor 93*
Laartz, Esther Elizabeth 1913- *WhoAm 92*
Laas, Virginia J(eans) 1943- *ConAu 139*
Laaser, Ulrich 1941- *WhoScE 91-3*
Laatsch, Audrey Frieda 1929- *WhoAmW 93*
Laba, Marvin 1928- *WhoAm 92*
Labaki, Georges T. 1955- *WhoE 93*
Labalme, Patricia Hochschild 1927- *WhoAm 92*
LaBan, Myron Miles 1936- *WhoAm 92*
Laban, Philip 1933- *St&PR 93*
Laban, Robert Y. 1935- *St&PR 93*
Laband, Paul Alexander 1948- *WhoWor 93*
Labanick, George Michael 1950- *WhoSSW 93*
Labanowski, Elizabeth Jacobs *Law&B 92*
Labanowski, Gabriel Szczepan 1947- *WhoScE 91-4*
Labanowsky, Charles Joseph *Law&B 92*
Labant, Cynthia Jean 1963- *WhoAmW 93*
LaBant, Robert James 1945- *WhoAm 92*
LaBar, Flora M. 1931- *St&PR 93*
LaBar, John R. 1931- *St&PR 93*
La Barbara, Joan 1947- *Baker 92, BioIn 17*
LaBarbera, Nicole Alexandra 1966- *WhoAmW 93*
Labardi, Jillian Gay 1945- *WhoSSW 93*
Labaree, Benjamin Woods 1927- *WhoE 93*
LaBarge, Karin Peterson 1953- *WhoAmW 93, WhoE 93*
Labarge, Margaret Wade 1916- *WhoAmW 93*
LaBarge, Pierre L., Jr. 1925- *St&PR 93*
LaBarge, Richard Allen 1934- *WhoE 93*
Labaria, Violeta T. 1934- *WhoAsAP 91*
Labarowski, John Victor 1941- *St&PR 93*
LaBarre, Carl Anthony 1918- *WhoAm 92*
Labarre, Jean-Francois Rene 1936- *WhoScE 91-2*
Labarre, Theodore (Francois-Joseph) 1805-1870 *Baker 92*
La Barre, Weston 1911- *IntDcAn, WhoWrEP 92*
Labash, Elizabeth Baker 1944- *St&PR 93*
Labastida, Fernando 1936- *WhoUN 92*
Labastida, Jaime 1939- *DcMexL*
Labat, Jean Paul 1939- *WhoScE 91-2*
Labath, Octave 1941- *St&PR 93*
Labato, Joseph R. 1946- *St&PR 93*
Labaton, Stephen 1961- *WhoE 93*
Labatt, Leonard 1838-1897 *Baker 92*
Labatt, Sheila *Law&B 92*
LaBauve, Minette Benard 1959- *WhoSSW 93*
Labaw, Jeffrey Scott *Law&B 92*
Labbadia, Lewis Reynold 1953- *WhoEmL 93*
Labbauf, Farsad Reza 1965- *WhoE 93*
L'Abbe *Baker 92*
Labbe, Armand Joseph 1944- *WhoWor 93*
Labbe, Donald 1930- *St&PR 93*
Labbe, Elise E. 1956- *WhoAmW 93, WhoSSW 93*
L'abbe, Gerrit Karel 1940- *WhoWor 93*
Labbe, Paul 1939- *St&PR 93*
Labbe, Romeo J. 1935- *St&PR 93*
L'Abbe l'aine c. 1700-1768 *Baker 92*
L'Abbe le cadet c. 1710-1777 *Baker 92*
L'Abbe le fils 1727-1803 *Baker 92*
Labbett, John Edgar 1950- *St&PR 93, WhoAm 92*
Labe, Louise 1526?-1566 *BioIn 17*
La Beaume, Edmond, Mrs. *AmWomPl*
Labedz, Chester Stephen, Jr. *Law&B 92*
La Beet, Octave d1991 *BioIn 17*
LaBelle, Edward Francis 1948- *WhoE 93*
Labelle, Eugene Jean-Marc 1941- *WhoAm 92*
LaBelle, Gary Lee 1944- *St&PR 93*
LaBelle, Michael Maurice 1951- *WhoE 93*
LaBelle, Patti *BioIn 17*
Labelle, Patti 1944- *AfrAmBi, Baker 92, ConMus 8 [port], SoulM, WhoAm 92, WhoAmW 93*
LaBelle, Stephen F. 1948- *St&PR 93*
LaBelle, Thomas Jeffrey 1941- *WhoAm 92*
Laben, Nancy Jill *Law&B 92*
Labenskyj, Ihor Nicholas 1946- *WhoEmL 93*
Labeque, Katia 1950- *Baker 92*
Labeque, Marielle 1952- *Baker 92*
Laber, Heinz 1937- *WhoWor 93*
Laber, Jeri Lidsky 1931- *WhoE 93*
Laberge, Albert 1871-1960 *BioIn 17*
LaBerge, Ellen T. *Law&B 92*
LaBerge, Ellen Therese 1958- *St&PR 93*
Laberge, Marie 1929- *WhoCanL 92*
La Berge, Walter Barber 1924- *WhoAm 92*
Labernik, Mary Sue 1937- *WhoAmW 93*
Laberrigue, Andre 1924- *WhoScE 91-2*
Labey, Marcel 1875-1968 *Baker 92*
Labeyrie, Vincent 1924- *WhoScE 91-2*
Labhart, Alexis 1916- *WhoWor 93*
Labhart, Cecil W. 1933- *St&PR 93*
Labia, Fausta 1870-1935 *Baker 92, OxDcOp*
Labia, Gianna Perea- 1908- *OxDcOp*
Labia, Maria 1880-1953 *Baker 92, OxDcOp*
La Bianca, Cory Jane 1948- *WhoAmW 93*
Labie, Charles Francois 1926- *WhoScE 91-2*
Labine, Clem 1926- *BioIn 17*
Labinger, Jay Alan 1947- *WhoEmL 93*
Labisky, Ronald Frank 1934- *WhoSSW 93*
Labitzky, August 1832-1903 *Baker 92*
Labitzky, Joseph 1802-1881 *Baker 92*
Lablache, Federico *OxDcOp*
Lablache, Francesca *OxDcOp*
Lablache, Luigi 1794-1858 *Baker 92, OxDcOp*
Lablache, Luigi 1795-1858 *IntDcOp [port]*
Lablache-Combier, Alain Jacques Dominique 1937- *WhoScE 91-2*
La Blanc, Charles Wesley, Jr. 1925- *WhoAm 92*
La Blanc, Elizabeth Anne 1940- *WhoAmW 93*
LaBlanc, Robert Edmund 1934- *St&PR 93, WhoAm 92*
Labmeier, John Francis *Law&B 92*
Laboda, Amy Sue 1962- *WhoAm 92, WhoAmW 93*
Laboda, Gerald 1936- *WhoSSW 93*
Laboe, Norman J. 1940- *WhoAm 92*
Laboisse, Christian L. 1950- *WhoScE 91-2*
Labombarde, Peter Michael 1954- *WhoE 93*
LaBonia, Michael J. 1936- *St&PR 93*
Labonne, Beatrice Marie 1943- *WhoUN 92*
La Bonte, Clarence Joseph 1939- *WhoAm 92*
LaBonte, Eugene Edward, Jr. 1945- *St&PR 93*
Labonte, John Joseph 1939- *WhoWrEP 92*
LaBonte, Jovite 1933- *St&PR 93, WhoAm 92, WhoIns 93*
Labonte, Lisa Anne J. *Law&B 92*
Labonte, Michel 1945- *St&PR 93*
LaBoon, Lawrence Joseph 1938- *WhoE 93, WhoWor 93*
LaBoon, Robert Bruce 1941- *WhoAm 92*
Labor, Josef 1842-1924 *Baker 92*
Laborda Martin, Juan Jose 1947- *WhoWor 93*
Laborde, Alden James 1915- *WhoAm 92*
LaBorde, Charles B. 1949- *WhoEmL 93, WhoSSW 93*
Laborde, George P. 1908- *St&PR 93*
Laborde, Hernan *DcCPCAm*
La Borde, Jean-Benjamin de 1734-1794 *OxDcOp*
La Borde, Jean-Benjamin (-Francois) de 1734-1794 *Baker 92*
Laborde, John P. 1923- *St&PR 93*
Laborde, John Peter 1923- *WhoAm 92, WhoSSW 93*
Laborde, Ronald Anthony 1956- *St&PR 93*
LaBorde, Terrence Lee 1947- *WhoE 93*
Laborne, George P. 1908- *St&PR 93*
Labota, Dolores Bernadette 1954- *WhoEmL 93*
LaBounty, David Edward 1937- *St&PR 93*
Labounty, James Philip 1943- *St&PR 93*
Labousier, Susan Evelyn 1954- *WhoAmW 93*
Labovitz, Harry 1950- *St&PR 93*
Labovitz, Israel M. d1992 *BioIn 17, NewYTBS 92*
Labovitz, Laurence Brian 1946- *WhoEmL 93*
Labowsky, Dorothy 1920- *St&PR 93*
Labra, George P. 1928- *St&PR 93*
La Brack, Kenneth Alan 1947- *WhoE 93*
Labrador, Enrique 1902- *SpAmA*
LaBrant, Lou 1888-1991 *BioIn 17*
LaBreche, George Joseph, Jr. 1945- *St&PR 93*
Labreck, Gerald R. 1944- *St&PR 93*
LaBrecque, John Joseph 1948- *WhoWor 93*
Labrecque, Paul Gerard 1946- *WhoE 93*
Labrecque, Raymond Roger 1932- *St&PR 93*
Labrecque, Richard Joseph 1938- *St&PR 93, WhoAm 92*
Labrecque, Theodore Joseph 1903- *WhoAm 92, WhoE 93, WhoWor 93*
Labrecque, Thomas G. 1938- *St&PR 93, WhoAm 92*
Labrenz, Shari K. 1950- *St&PR 93*
Labrie, Fernand 1937- *WhoAm 92*
LaBrie, J. Roland 1948- *WhoE 93*
Labrie, Lawrence James *Law&B 92*
LaBriola, Peter 1947- *St&PR 93*
Labro, Pierre Jean 1920- *WhoWor 93*
Labroca, Mario 1896-1973 *Baker 92, OxDcOp*
Labrosse, Leo E. 1925- *St&PR 93*
LaBruna, Vincent Francis 1958- *WhoE 93*
Labs, Richard J. 1956- *St&PR 93*
Labsker, Lev Grigoryevich 1936- *WhoWor 93*
Labuda, Iwo Maria 1945- *WhoSSW 93*
La Budde, Kenneth James 1920- *WhoAm 92*
LaBudde, Sam *BioIn 17*
Labunski, Felix 1892-1979 *Baker 92, PolBiDi*
Labunski, Stephen Bronislaw 1924- *WhoAm 92*
Labunski, Wiktor 1895-1974 *Baker 92*
Laburda, Jiri 1931- *Baker 92*
Labusch, Reiner 1935- *WhoScE 91-3*
Labussiere, Jacques 1935- *WhoScE 91-2*
Labuz, Ronald Matthew 1953- *WhoE 93, WhoEmL 93, WhoWor 93*
Laby, Henri Georges 1923- *WhoScE 91-2*
Lac, Ming Q. 1948- *St&PR 93, WhoEmL 93*
Lacagnina, Michael Anthony 1932- *WhoAm 92*
Lacaillade, Raymond H. 1944- *St&PR 93*
Lacalle Herrera, Luis Alberto 1941- *WhoWor 93*
Lacan, Jacques 1901-1981 *BioIn 17, ConLC 75 [port]*
Lacanlale, Agerico O. 1949- *WhoUN 92*
LaCapra, Dominick Charles 1939- *WhoAm 92*
Lacasse, Gilbert 1940- *St&PR 93*
LaCasse, James Phillip 1948- *WhoEmL 93*
Lacasse, Lise *WhoCanL 92*
LaCastro, Diane M. *St&PR 93*
Lacattiva, Claire Antoinette 1931- *WhoE 93*
Lacatus, Victor 1941- *WhoScE 91-4*
Lacau, Georges Loustaunau- 1894-1955 *BioIn 17*
La Cava, Donald Leon 1928- *WhoWor 93*
La Cava, Gregory 1892-1952 *MiSFD 9N*
Lacayo, Antonio *BioIn 17*
Lacayo, Carmela Gloria 1943- *NotHsAW 93 [port], WhoAmW 93*
Lacayo, Gonzalo *DcCPCAm*
Lacaze, Jean-Francois 1929- *WhoScE 91-2*
Lacaze, Xavier Emile 1952- *WhoWor 93*
Lacaz-Vieira, Francisco 1935- *WhoWor 93*
Laccetti, Guido 1879-1943 *Baker 92*
Lacci, John Vincent *Law&B 92*
Lace, Kathryn *AmWomPl*
Lace, William Worley 1942- *WhoSSW 93*
Lacefield, Carole Rose 1958- *WhoEmL 93*
Lacefield, David W. 1954- *St&PR 93*
La Celle, Paul Louis 1929- *WhoAm 92*

Lacer, Kathryn Lorene 1930- *WhoAmW 93, WhoSSW 93*
Lacerda, Francisco de 1869-1934 *Baker 92*
Lacerenza, Joseph P. *Law&B 92*
Lacerra, Ronald J. 1939- *WhoIns 93*
Lacey, Alan *ScF&FL 92*
Lacey, Beatrice Cates 1919- *WhoAm 92, WhoAmW 93*
Lacey, Cloyd Eugene 1918- *WhoAm 92*
Lacey, Cynthia Ann 1958- *WhoAmW 93*
Lacey, Dan d1992 *NewYTBS 92 [port]*
Lacey, Dane Eugene 1932- *WhoSSW 93*
Lacey, Daniel Alfred 1939- *St&PR 93*
Lacey, David E. 1946- *St&PR 93*
Lacey, E. Ralph d1990 *BioIn 17*
Lacey, Frank M. *Law&B 92*
Lacey, Frederick B. *BioIn 17*
Lacey, Howard Elton 1937- *WhoAm 92, WhoSSW 93*
Lacey, Hugh Matthew 1939- *WhoAm 92*
Lacey, J.A. *WhoScE 91-1*
Lacey, J. Michael 1945- *St&PR 93*
Lacey, Joan Mary 1920- *WhoWrEP 92*
Lacey, John *WhoScE 91-1*
Lacey, John Irving 1915- *WhoAm 92*
Lacey, John S. *St&PR 93*
Lacey, John William Charles 1930- *WhoAm 92*
Lacey, Pamela Anne 1955- *WhoE 93*
Lacey, Peeler Grayson 1954- *WhoSSW 93*
Lacey, Ron *St&PR 93*
Lacey, Ronald 1935-1991 *AnObit 1991*
Lacey, Sally C. 1949- *St&PR 93*
Lacey, Stanley Lenwood 1958- *St&PR 93*
Lacey, William H. 1940- *WhoAm 92*
Lach, Alma *WhoWrEP 92*
Lach, Alma Elizabeth *WhoAm 92, WhoAmW 93, WhoWor 93*
Lach, Eileen M. *Law&B 92*
Lach, Eileen Marie 1950- *WhoAm 92*
Lach, Joseph Theodore 1934- *WhoAm 92*
Lach, Robert 1874-1958 *Baker 92*
Lach, Stephanie Lynn-Arnold 1960- *WhoAmW 93*
LaChance, Denise *Law&B 92*
Lachance, Gerard R. 1941- *St&PR 93*
Lachance, Janice Rachel 1953- *WhoAm 92, WhoAmW 93*
Lachance, Leo Emery 1931- *WhoUN 92*
Lachance, Paul Albert 1933- *WhoAm 92, WhoE 93*
Lachance, Roger William 1944- *WhoE 93*
Lachanodrakon, Michael d792 *OxDcByz*
Lachapelle, Andre 1931- *WhoAm 92*
Lachapelle, Anthony D. 1948- *St&PR 93*
Lachapelle, Cleo Edward 1925- *WhoE 93*
Lachapelle, Jean-Marie 1937- *WhoScE 91-2*
Lachenauer, Eckhard Walter 1949- *WhoWor 93*
Lachenbruch, Arthur Herold 1925- *WhoAm 92*
Lachenbruch, David 1921- *WhoAm 92, WhoWrEP 92*
Lachenicht-Berkeley, Angela Marie 1955- *WhoAmW 93*
Lachenmann, Helmut Friedrich 1935- *Baker 92*
Lacher, Carolyn Harper 1959- *WhoAmW 93*
Lacher, Gunther 1929- *WhoScE 91-3*
Lacher, Joseph P. 1945- *WhoAm 92*
Lacher, Peggy A. 1952- *St&PR 93*
Lachica Garrido, Manuel 1929- *WhoScE 91-3*
Lachman, Andrea *BioIn 17*
Lachman, Ed 1948- *MiSFD 9*
Lachman, Lawrence 1916- *St&PR 93, WhoAm 92*
Lachman, Marguerite Leanne 1943- *WhoAm 92*
Lachman, Mort 1918- *MiSFD 9*
Lachman, Morton 1918- *WhoAm 92*
Lachman, Roy E. *Law&B 92*
Lachmann, Peter Julius *WhoScE 91-1*
Lachmann, Robert 1892-1939 *Baker 92*
Lachmund, Carl (Valentine) 1857-1928 *Baker 92*
Lachner *Baker 92*
Lachner, Franz 1803-1890 *OxDcOp*
Lachner, Franz Paul 1803-1890 *Baker 92*
Lachner, Ignaz 1807-1895 *Baker 92, OxDcOp*
Lachner, Marshall Smith 1914-1991 *BioIn 17*
Lachner, Theodor 1788-1877 *Baker 92*
Lachner, Vincenz 1811-1893 *Baker 92, OxDcOp*
Lachnit, Bob *BioIn 17*
Lachnith, Ludwig 1746-1820 *OxDcOp*
Lachnith, Ludwig Wenzel 1746-1820 *Baker 92*
Lachow, Alisa 1967- *WhoAmW 93*
Lachowicz, Franciszek 1908- *WhoE 93*
Lachowicz, Henryk Konrad 1933- *WhoWor 93*
Lachowicz, Tadeusz Michal 1930- *WhoWor 93*
Lachowski, Andrzej 1937- *WhoScE 91-4*
Lachowski, Jamie Edward 1955- *WhoEmL 93*
Lachowski, Wlodzimierz Mieczyslaw 1957- *WhoWor 93*
Lachs, John 1934- *WhoAm 92, WhoSSW 93*
Lachs, Manfred 1914- *WhoUN 92, WhoWor 93*
Lachter, Gerald David 1941- *WhoE 93*
Lacirignola, C. *WhoScE 91-3*
Lack, Charles David 1950- *WhoSSW 93*
Lack, Hans-Walter 1949- *WhoScE 91-3*
Lack, Helen 1949- *St&PR 93*
Lack, James J. 1944- *WhoE 93*
Lack, Larry Henry 1952- *WhoEmL 93, WhoWor 93*
Lack, Leon 1922- *WhoAm 92*
Lack, Stanley A. 1942- *St&PR 93*
Lackamp, Gregory E. 1949- *St&PR 93*
Lackas, John C. 1904-1990 *BioIn 17*
Lackenbauer, G.S. *St&PR 93*
Lackenmier, James Richard 1938- *WhoAm 92*
Lackens, John Wendell, Jr. 1934- *WhoAm 92*
Lackey, Dorothy Dunaway 1955- *WhoAmW 93*
Lackey, James Edward 1953- *WhoE 93, WhoEmL 93*
Lackey, Julia Faye 1960- *WhoAmW 93*
Lackey, Kris Lee 1953- *WhoSSW 93*
Lackey, Larry Alton, Sr. 1940- *WhoWor 93*
Lackey, Lawrence Bailis, Jr. 1914- *WhoAm 92*
Lackey, Leon Agee, Jr. 1945- *St&PR 93*
Lackey, Marcus Hughes, Jr. 1954- *WhoEmL 93*
Lackey, Mary Michele 1955- *WhoAmW 93*
Lackey, Melissa *Law&B 92*
Lackey, Mercedes 1950- *ScF&FL 92*
Lackey, Paul K. 1943- *St&PR 93*
Lackey, R. Douglas *Law&B 92*
Lackey, S. Allen *Law&B 92, WhoAm 92*
Lackey, S. Allen 1942- *St&PR 93*
Lackey, Virginia Louise 1941- *WhoAmW 93*
Lackey, Walter Jackson 1940- *WhoSSW 93*
Lackland, John 1167-1216 *BioIn 17*
Lackland, John 1939- *WhoAm 92*
Lackland, Theodore Howard 1943- *WhoAm 92*
Lackman, Jack Gene 1939- *St&PR 93*
Lackman, Milton 1947- *St&PR 93*
Lackmann, Kathryn Ficklin *Law&B 92*
Lackmeyer, Suzy Beth Davidson 1945- *WhoSSW 93*
Lackner, Henriette 1922- *WhoAmW 93*
Lackner, James Robert 1940- *WhoAm 92*
Lackner, Karl 1942- *WhoScE 91-3*
Lacks, John P. 1904- *St&PR 93*
Lacks, Kurt *St&PR 93*
Lacks, Sanford Abraham 1934- *WhoE 93*
LaClair, Bruce A. 1953- *St&PR 93*
LaClair, Richard Jay 1942- *WhoE 93*
Laclotte, Michel *BioIn 17*
Lacob, Joseph S. *St&PR 93*
Lacoe, Bruce E. 1950- *St&PR 93*
Lacoeuilhe, J.J. 1937- *WhoScE 91-2*
Lacolla, John Anthony 1932- *St&PR 93*
Lacombe, Joseph-Patrice Truillier- 1807-1863 *BioIn 17*
Lacombe, Louis (Trouillon) 1818-1884 *Baker 92*
Lacombe, Paul 1837-1927 *Baker 92*
Lacombe, Richard George 1945- *St&PR 93*
LaComb-Williams, Linda Lou 1948- *WhoAmW 93*
Lacome, Paul (-Jean-Jacques) 1838-1920 *Baker 92*
Lacome d'Estalenx, Paul (-Jean-Jacques) 1838-1920 *Baker 92*
Lacomis, Bernard J. *Law&B 92*
La Condamine, Charles-Marie de 1701-1774 *Expl 93*
LaConde, Kenneth V. 1940- *St&PR 93*
LaConte, Ellen *ScF&FL 92*
Laconte, Pierre 1934- *WhoScE 91-2*
Laconte, Robert James 1950- *St&PR 93*
LaConte, Ronald T. *ScF&FL 92*
Lacore, Suzanne 1875-1975 *BioIn 17*
La Corte, John N. d1991 *BioIn 17*
Lacoste, Jacques H. 1920- *WhoScE 91-2*
LaCoste, Lilly *ConAu 138*
Lacoste, Paul 1923- *WhoAm 92*
Lacoste, Robert 1898-1989 *BioIn 17*
Lacoume, Jean-Louis 1940- *WhoScE 91-2*
LaCount, David William 1961- *St&PR 93*
La Counte, Max E. 1941- *St&PR 93*
La Cour, Jorgen 1932- *WhoScE 91-2*
Lacouture, Felipe Ernesto 1928- *WhoAm 92*
Lacouture, Jean *BioIn 17*
Lacouture, Leonard D. 1949- *St&PR 93*
Lacouture, Richard James *Law&B 92*
Lacovara, Philip A. *Law&B 92*
Lacovara, Philip Allen 1943- *WhoAm 92*
La Creta, John Joseph 1932- *St&PR 93*
La Croix, Arda *AmWomPl*
Lacroix, Arild 1943- *WhoScE 91-3*
Lacroix, Christian *BioIn 17*
Lacroix, Christian Marie Marc 1951- *WhoAm 92*
Lacroix, Daniel R. 1942- *St&PR 93*
LaCroix, Dennis J. *Law&B 92*
Lacroix, Didier 1952- *WhoScE 91-2*
Lacroix, Georgette 1921- *WhoCanL 92*
Lacroix, Jean-Pierre 1929- *WhoWor 93*
LaCroix, M. Steven *Law&B 92*
LaCroix, M. Steven 1948- *St&PR 93*
LaCroix, Marcel 1930- *St&PR 93*
Lacroix, Mary 1937- *WhoWrEP 92*
Lacroix, Pierre 1947- *St&PR 93*
Lacroix, Robert Veyron- 1922-1991 *BioIn 17*
Lacroix, Roger Louis 1928- *WhoWor 93*
Lacson, Jose Carlos V. 1942- *WhoAsAP 91*
Lactantius c. 240-c. 325 *OxDcByz*
Lacter, Barry 1945- *St&PR 93*
Lactilla 1752-1806 *BioIn 17*
Lacy, Alan Jasper 1953- *WhoAm 92*
Lacy, Alexander Shelton 1921- *WhoAm 92*
Lacy, Andre B. 1939- *St&PR 93*
Lacy, Ann Matthews 1932- *WhoAmW 93*
Lacy, Antonio M. 1957- *WhoWor 93*
Lacy, Bert *BioIn 17*
Lacy, Bill 1933- *WhoAm 92*
Lacy, Bill N. *BioIn 17*
Lacy, Carol Angela 1943- *WhoAmW 93*
Lacy, Elizabeth Bermingham 1945- *WhoAmW 93, WhoSSW 93*
Lacy, Glyn L. 1957- *St&PR 93*
Lacy, Gordon R. 1940- *St&PR 93*
Lacy, Herman Edgar 1935- *WhoAm 92*
Lacy, James Daniel 1947- *WhoAm 92*
Lacy, James Harris 1940- *St&PR 93*
Lacy, James Vincent 1952- *WhoAm 92*
Lacy, Jerry 1936- *WhoAm 92*
Lacy, Joseph Newton 1905- *WhoAm 92*
Lacy, Josephine Wipior 1917- *WhoAmW 93*
Lacy, Kenneth E. 1956- *WhoEmL 93*
Lacy, Margriet Bruyn 1943- *WhoAmW 93*
Lacy, Norris Joiner 1940- *WhoAm 92*
Lacy, Paul 1947- *St&PR 93*
Lacy, Paul Eston 1924- *WhoAm 92*
Lacy, Peter Dempsey 1920- *WhoAm 92*
Lacy, Ronald Lynn 1956- *WhoEmL 93*
Lacy, Rose Ann 1945- *St&PR 93*
Lacy, Steve 1934- *WhoAm 92*
Lacy, Steven R. *Law&B 92*
Lacy, William Howard 1945- *St&PR 93*
Lacz, Stanley John 1938- *WhoE 93*
Laczay, Peter W. 1934- *St&PR 93*
Laczi, Ferenc 1945- *WhoScE 91-4*
Laczko, Brian John 1952- *WhoSSW 93*
LaDage, Janet Lee 1949- *WhoAmW 93*
Lada-Mocarski, Laura 1902- *BioIn 17*
Lada-Mocarski, Polly 1902- *BioIn 17*
Ladany, L. *BioIn 17*
Ladany, Laszlo *BioIn 17*
Ladanyi, Branka Maria 1947- *WhoAmW 93*
Ladanyi, Branko 1922- *WhoAm 92*
Ladar, Jerrold Morton 1933- *WhoAm 92*
Ladas, Alice Kahn *WhoE 93*
Ladau, Robert Francis 1940- *WhoAm 92*
Laday, Jerome Michael 1953- *WhoE 93*
Ladbetter, Ronald M. 1944- *St&PR 93*
Ladd, A. Earl 1935- *St&PR 93*
Ladd, Alan 1913-1969 *IntDcF 2-3 [port]*
Ladd, Alan, Jr. *BioIn 17*
Ladd, Alan Walbridge, Jr. 1937- *WhoAm 92*
Ladd, Barton Dyer 1936- *WhoAm 92*
Ladd, Brian 1957- *ConAu 137*
Ladd, Charles Cushing, III 1932- *WhoAm 92*
Ladd, Cheryl *BioIn 17*
Ladd, Cynthia J. *Law&B 92*
Ladd, David L. 1931- *St&PR 93*
Ladd, David Niven 1938- *St&PR 93*
Ladd, Delano Wood, Jr. 1925- *WhoAm 92*
Ladd, Diane 1939- *WhoAm 92*
Ladd, Everett Carll 1937- *WhoAm 92, WhoE 93*
Ladd, Everett Carll, Jr. 1937- *WhoWrEP 92*
Ladd, J.B. 1923- *St&PR 93*
Ladd, James Roger 1943- *WhoAm 92*
Ladd, Joan Ruth LeTourneur *WhoAmW 93*
Ladd, Joseph C. 1927- *St&PR 93*
Ladd, Joseph Carroll 1927- *WhoAm 92*
Ladd, Lawrence R. 1949- *WhoE 93*
Ladd, Marcia Lee 1950- *St&PR 93*
Ladd, Robert Dwinell 1918- *St&PR 93*
Ladd, Robert T. 1956- *St&PR 93*
Ladd, Sandra Lee *BioIn 17*
Ladden, Linda Lee 1957- *WhoAmW 93*
Ladd-Franklin, Christine 1847-1930 *BioIn 17*
Laddon, Warren M. *Law&B 92*
Laddon, Warren Milton 1933- *WhoAm 92*
Laddu, Atul Ramchandra 1940- *WhoAm 92*
Ladefoged, Peter Nielsen 1925- *WhoAm 92*
Ladehoff, Leo William 1932- *St&PR 93, WhoAm 92*
Ladehoff, Robert Louis 1932- *WhoAm 92*
Ladeira, Eduardo Antonio 1939- *WhoWor 93*
Laden, Ben Ellis 1942- *WhoAm 92*
Laden, Karl 1932- *WhoAm 92*
Laden, Patrick Robert *Law&B 92*
Ladenheim, Harry 1932- *WhoE 93*
Ladenheim, Kala Evelyn 1950- *WhoWrEP 92*
Ladensack, John P. 1950- *St&PR 93*
Lader, Lawrence 1919- *WhoAm 92, WhoWrEP 92*
Lader, Malcolm Harold *WhoScE 91-1*
Lader, Melvin Paul 1947- *WhoEmL 93*
Lader, Philip 1946- *WhoAm 92*
Lader, Wendy Friedman 1952- *WhoAmW 93*
Laderach, Paul A. 1933- *WhoIns 93*
Laderman, David M. 1944- *St&PR 93*
Laderman, Ezra 1924- *Baker 92, WhoAm 92*
Laderman, Gabriel 1929- *WhoAm 92*
Laderman, Louis Nathan 1951- *WhoEmL 93*
Laderoute, Charles David 1948- *WhoE 93, WhoEmL 93*
Laderoute, Laurin L., Jr. *Law&B 92*
Laderoute, Laurin L., Jr. 1941- *St&PR 93*
Laderoute, Laurin Leroy, Jr. 1941- *WhoAm 92*
La De Route, Robert Wayne 1945- *St&PR 93*
Ladeveze, Pierre 1945- *WhoScE 91-2*
Ladewig, Adelheid Gertrud d1990 *BioIn 17*
Ladewig, Brock Lorenz 1953- *St&PR 93*
Ladewig, Jan 1946- *WhoScE 91-3*
Ladewig, Marion 1914- *BioIn 17*
Ladik, Janos 1929- *WhoScE 91-3*
Ladik, Janos Jozsef 1929- *WhoWor 93*
Ladin, Eugene 1927- *WhoAm 92*
Ladin, Leonard Irwin 1933- *WhoE 93*
Lading, Lars 1943- *WhoScE 91-2*
Ladinsky, Herbert 1935- *WhoScE 91-3, WhoWor 93*
Ladisch, Stephan 1947- *WhoEmL 93*
Ladish, John H. 1924- *St&PR 93*
Ladizinsky, Dinah L. 1948- *St&PR 93*
Ladjevardi, Hamid 1948- *WhoAm 92, WhoE 93, WhoEmL 93, WhoWor 93*
Ladky, Frank Jack 1921- *St&PR 93*
Ladly, Frederick B. 1930- *St&PR 93*
Ladly, Frederick Bernard 1930- *WhoAm 92*
Ladman, Aaron Julius 1925- *WhoAm 92*
Ladman, Jerry R. 1935- *WhoAm 92*
Ladmirault, Paul (-Emile) 1877-1944 *Baker 92*
Ladner, Charles L. 1938- *St&PR 93*
Ladner, Charles Leon 1938- *WhoAm 92*
Ladner, Frank S. 1927- *WhoAm 92*
Ladner, Lee Russell 1934- *St&PR 93*
Ladner, Thomas E. 1916- *WhoAm 92*
Ladner, Thomas Ellis 1916- *St&PR 93*
Ladnier, Tommy 1900-1939 *Baker 92*
Ladouceur, Karen Marie 1970- *WhoAmW 93*
LaDow, C. Stuart 1925- *WhoAm 92*
La Du, Bert Nichols, Jr. 1920- *WhoAm 92*
La Duca, Nicholas 1951- *WhoEmL 93*
LaDue, Eddy Lorain 1939- *WhoE 93*
Ladue, William Stuart 1955- *WhoE 93*
LaDuke, Nancie *WhoAmW 93*
Laduke, Nancie Wright *Law&B 92*
Ladunka, Naum 1730-1782 *Baker 92*
Ladurie, Emmanuel Le Roy 1929- *BioIn 17*
Ladurner, Ignace Antoine (Francois Xavier) 1766-1839 *Baker 92*
Laduron, Dominique 1941- *WhoScE 91-2*
Laduron, Pierre M. 1936- *WhoScE 91-2*
Ladwig, Alan Michael 1948- *WhoAm 92*
Lady, Larry G. 1940- *St&PR 93*
Lady, Larry Gene 1940- *WhoAm 92*
Lady Ashton d1990 *BioIn 17*
Lady Miss Kier *BioIn 17*
Lady Miss Kier c. 1960- See Deee-Lite *ConMus 9*
Lady of Quality, A *MajAI*
Lady of Quality, A. *ConAu 40NR*
Ladzinski, Gerard Robert 1962- *WhoE 93*
Laekeman, Gert 1951- *WhoScE 91-2*
Laemmli, Olrich 1940- *WhoScE 91-4*
Laenas, Marcus Popillius fl. c. 180BC-160BC *HarEnMi*
Laengrich, Arthur Richard 1933- *St&PR 93*
Laeri, Franco Giulio 1949- *WhoWor 93*
Laermans, Christiane Clemence 1944- *WhoWor 93*
Laerum, Ole Didrik 1940- *WhoScE 91-4*
Laessig, Robert H. 1913- *WhoAm 92*

Laidlaw, Anna Robena 1819-1901 *Baker 92*
Laidlaw, George R. 1954- *St&PR 93*
Laidlaw, George Ross *Law&B 92*
Laidlaw, H. Daniel 1949- *WhoSSW 93*
Laidlaw, Harry Hyde, Jr. 1907- *WhoAm 92*
Laidlaw, Laura Anne 1931- *WhoSSW 93*
Laidlaw, Marc 1960- *ScF&FL 92*
Laidlaw, Robert Richard 1923- *WhoAm 92, WhoSSW 93*
Laidlaw, William Samuel Hugh 1956- *WhoAm 92*
Laidler, David Ernest William 1938- *WhoAm 92*
Laidman, Harvey 1942- *MiSFD 9*
Lai In-Jaw 1946- *WhoAsAP 91*
Laikari, Hannu Tapani 1933- *WhoScE 91-4*
Laiken, Tiffany J. 1962- *WhoSSW 93*
Laikin, George J. 1910- *St&PR 93*
Laikin, George Joseph 1910- *WhoAm 92*
Laimbeer, Bill *BioIn 17*
Laimbeer, Bill 1957- *WhoAm 92*
Laimbeer, William 1934- *WhoAm 92*
Laine, Cleo *BioIn 17*
Laine, Cleo 1927- *Baker 92, WhoAm 92, WhoAmW 93*
Laine, Derek Charles *WhoScE 91-1*
Laine, Erick J. 1933- *St&PR 93*
Laine, Francois Bloch- 1912- *BioIn 17*
Laine, Gerard Henri 1947- *WhoScE 91-2*
Laine, Jaakko Einari 1945- *WhoScE 91-4*
Laine, Jorma *WhoScE 91-4*
Laine, Katie Myers 1947- *WhoAmW 93, WhoEmL 93*
Laine, Kimmo Kalevi Edvard 1968- *WhoWor 93*
Laine, Lalli Kalervo 1930- *WhoScE 91-4*
Laine, Seppo Kalevi 1939- *WhoScE 91-4*
Lainez, Manuel Mujica *ScF&FL 92*
Laing, Aileen Hyland 1936- *WhoSSW 93*
Laing, Alan Kemp 1902- *WhoAm 92*
Laing, Alexander 1903-1976 *ScF&FL 92*
Laing, Ernest William *WhoScE 91-1*
Laing, (Alexander) Gordon 1793-1826 *Expl 93*
Laing, Joann Mills 1957- *WhoE 93*
Laing, John 1948- *MiSFD 9*
Laing, John Wailon 1937- *WhoE 93*
Laing, Karel Ann 1939- *WhoAm 92, WhoAmW 93*
Laing, Malcolm Brian 1955- *WhoEmL 93, WhoSSW 93*
Laing, R.D. 1927-1989 *BioIn 17*
Laing, Robert S. 1948- *St&PR 93*
Laing, Robert Scott 1952- *WhoEmL 93*
Laing, Ronald David 1927-1989 *BioIn 17*
Laingen, L(owell) Bruce 1922- *ConAu 139*
Laingen, Lowell Bruce 1922- *WhoAm 92*
Laino, Robert T. 1947- *St&PR 93*
Lainson, Gretchen Hollman 1916- *St&PR 93*
Lainson, Hal 1912- *St&PR 93*
Lainson, John Jennings 1920- *St&PR 93*
Lainus Ak Andrew Luak *WhoAsAP 91*
Laiou, Angeliki E. 1941- *WhoAm 92, WhoAmW 93, WhoE 93*
Lair, Helen May 1918- *WhoWor 93*
Lair, Jesse K. 1926- *WhoWrEP 92*
Lair, Judith Anne Trevvett 1942- *WhoE 93*
Lair, Robert Louis 1921- *WhoAm 92*
Lair, Thomas E. 1931- *St&PR 93*
Laird, Alan Douglas Kenneth 1914- *WhoAm 92*
Laird, Barbara J. *Law&B 92*
Laird, Charles David 1939- *WhoAm 92*
Laird, David 1927- *WhoAm 92*
Laird, E. Ruth 1921- *WhoAm 92*
Laird, Edward DeHart, Jr. 1952- *WhoEmL 93*
Laird, Elizabeth W. 1936- *WhoWrEP 92*
Laird, Elmer *BioIn 17*
Laird, Evalyn Walsh 1902- *WhoWor 93*
Laird, Fiona C. *Law&B 92*
Laird, Jack 1923-1991 *ConTFT 10*
Laird, James Craig 1923- *St&PR 93*
Laird, James H. 1958- *St&PR 93*
Laird, Jean Elouise Rydeski 1930- *WhoAmW 93*
Laird, Jo Backer *Law&B 92*
Laird, John Evans, III 1947- *St&PR 93*
Laird, John Robert 1942- *St&PR 93, WhoAm 92*
Laird, Lindsay Margaret *WhoScE 91-1*
Laird, Marlena 1949- *MiSFD 9*
Laird, Mary *WhoAm 92, WhoAmW 93, WhoWor 93*
Laird, Melvin 1922- *ColdWar 1 [port]*
Laird, Melvin R. 1922- *PolPar*
Laird, Melvin Robert 1922- *WhoAm 92*
Laird, Morris E. 1908- *St&PR 93*
Laird, Pamela Paxson 1940- *WhoAmW 93*
Laird, Peter D. 1944- *St&PR 93*
Laird, Richard H. 1951- *WhoE 93*
Laird, Robert Edward 1958- *WhoSSW 93*
Laird, Robert Winslow 1936- *WhoAm 92*
Laird, Roy Dean 1925- *WhoAm 92*
Laird, Samuel 1944- *WhoUN 92*
Laird, Sherry Susan *Law&B 92*
Laird, Shirley Eder *WhoAmW 93*
Laird, Steven Ray *Law&B 92*
Laird, W.F. 1919- *St&PR 93*
Laird, Walter Jones, Jr. 1926- *WhoAm 92*
Laird, Wilbur David, Jr. 1937- *WhoAm 92*
Laird, William Everette, Jr. 1934- *WhoAm 92*
Laird, William Ronald Edwards *WhoScE 91-1*
Laird, William Winder d1989 *BioIn 17*
Laires, Fernando 1925- *WhoAm 92*
Laise, Caroline Clendening 1917-1991 *BioIn 17*
Laisy, Albert W. *Law&B 92*
Laitakari, Ilkka 1929- *WhoScE 91-4*
Laitala, Jerry E. 1938- *St&PR 93*
Laithwaite, Eric Roberts *WhoScE 91-1*
Laiti, Dominic Aldo 1931- *St&PR 93*
Laitin, David Dennis 1945- *WhoAm 92*
Laitin, Joseph 1914- *ConAu 136, WhoAm 92*
Laitinen, Heikki Juhani 1950- *WhoScE 91-4*
Laitinen, Herbert A. 1917-1991 *BioIn 17*
Laitinen, Reino *WhoScE 91-4*
Laitinen, Richard A. 1944- *St&PR 93*
Lajarte, Theodore (-Edouard Dufaure de) 1826-1890 *Baker 92*
Lajeunesse, Claude 1941- *WhoAm 92*
Lajeunesse, Marcel 1942- *WhoAm 92*
Lajeunesse, Marie Louise Cecilia Emma *Baker 92*
Lajoie, Antoine Gerin 1824-1882 *BioIn 17*
Lajoie, Brian Alan 1946- *St&PR 93*
Lajoie, James Robert *Law&B 92*
Lajoie, Roland 1936- *WhoAm 92, WhoE 93*
Lajoie, William Richard 1934- *WhoAm 92*
Lajoie-Mazenc, Michel 1938- *WhoScE 91-2*
Lajoinie, Andre 1929- *BioIn 17*
Lajos, Judith 1941- *WhoScE 91-4*
Lajos, Tamas 1944- *WhoScE 91-4*
Lajous, Roberta 1954- *WhoWor 93*
Lajtha, Gyorgy 1930- *WhoScE 91-4*
Lajtha, Laszlo 1892-1963 *Baker 92*
Lajunen, Lauri H.J. 1950- *WhoScE 91-4*
Lakapenos, George fl. c. 1297-1310 *OxDcByz*
Lakas, Demetrios *DcCPCAm*
Lakatos, Bela 1946- *WhoScE 91-4*
Lakatos, Istvan Janos 1943- *WhoScE 91-4*
Lake, Ann Winslow 1919- *WhoAm 92*
Lake, Arthur 1905- *QDrFCA 92 [port]*
Lake, Barbara Lee 1934- *WhoAmW 93*
Lake, Blair Moody 1932- *WhoAmW 93*
Lake, Carol Lee 1944- *WhoAmW 93*
Lake, Charles William, Jr. 1918- *WhoAm 92*
Lake, Christopher Robert 1952- *WhoE 93*
Lake, Dale Fletcher 1936- *St&PR 93*
Lake, David *BioIn 17*
Lake, David J. 1929- *ScF&FL 92*
Lake, David S. 1938- *WhoAm 92*
Lake, David Sanders 1938- *St&PR 93*
Lake, Elizabeth Shawn 1946- *WhoWrEP 92*
Lake, F. Edward 1934- *St&PR 93*
Lake, Finley Edward 1934- *WhoAm 92*
Lake, George H. 1933- *St&PR 93*
Lake, Hobart 1934- *St&PR 93*
Lake, Hubert, Jr. 1948- *WhoSSW 93*
Lake, I. Beverly, Jr. *WhoSSW 93*
Lake, Jane Burford 1937- *WhoAmW 93*
Lake, Jerome Glen 1932- *WhoWor 93*
Lake, Joseph Edward 1941- *WhoAm 92, WhoWor 93*
Lake, Joseph Frank 1933- *St&PR 93*
Lake, Kathleen C. 1955- *WhoAmW 93*
Lake, Keithley Fitzroy T. *Law&B 92*
Lake, Michael Smith 1941- *St&PR 93*
Lake, Ralph B. *Law&B 92*
Lake, Richard Arthur 1946- *St&PR 93, WhoIns 93*
Lake, Ricki *BioIn 17*
Lake, Robert D. *Law&B 92*
Lake, Robert R. 1944- *St&PR 93*
Lake, Ross Duane 1937- *St&PR 93*
Lake, Ruth Elaine 1954- *WhoAmW 93*
Lake, Sally Lu *Law&B 92*
Lake, Scott A. 1960- *St&PR 93*
Lake, Simeon Timothy, III 1944- *WhoAm 92, WhoSSW 93*
Lake, Suzanne Philena 1929- *WhoAmW 93*
Lake, Veronica 1919-1973 *IntDcF 2-3*
Lake, Virginia D'Albert- *BioIn 17*
Lake, William Thomas 1910- *WhoAm 92*
Lake, William Truman 1943- *WhoAm 92*
Lake, Willis Wayne 1927- *St&PR 93*
Lakeland, Paul 1946- *ConAu 137*
Lakeman, Paul Eric 1950- *WhoE 93*
Lakenbach, Cary 1946- *St&PR 93*
Laker, Irving 1928- *St&PR 93*
Lakervi, Erkki O. 1945- *WhoScE 91-4*
Lakey, Arnold Neil 1937- *St&PR 93*
Lakey, Brian Roy *WhoScE 91-1*
Lakey, J.R.A. *WhoScE 91-3*
Lakey, Keith David *Law&B 92*
Lakhani, Julia Mary 1961- *WhoSSW 93*
Lakhanpal, Sharad 1951- *WhoEmL 93, WhoSSW 93, WhoWor 93*
Lakhmids *OxDcByz*
Laki, Philip 1941- *WhoAsAP 91*
Lakier, Alexander Borisovich *BioIn 17*
Lakin, Deborah Anne 1947- *WhoAmW 93*
Lakin, James Dennis 1945- *WhoAm 92*
Lakin, Judy Shelton 1958- *WhoEmL 93*
Lakin, Rita *ScF&FL 92*
Lakin, Thomas J. 1942- *St&PR 93*
Laklan, Carli 1907- *DcAmChF 1960*
Lakner, Yehoshua 1924- *Baker 92*
Lakos, Marcille Harris 1917- *WhoAmW 93*
Lakritz, Isaac 1952- *WhoAm 92*
Lakritz, Seymour 1921-1990 *BioIn 17*
Laks, Joseph J. *Law&B 92*
Laks, Simon 1901-1983 *Baker 92*
Lakshmanna, C. 1935- *WhoAsAP 91*
Lakshmikantham, Vangipuram 1926- *WhoAm 92*
Lakshminarayana, Budugur 1935- *WhoAm 92, WhoE 93*
Laksov, Dan 1940- *WhoWor 93*
Laky, Anthony Joseph 1941- *WhoE 93*
Laky, Joseph E. 1941- *St&PR 93*
Laky, Marcia 1945- *WhoAmW 93*
Lal, Brij V. 1952- *ConAu 139*
Lal, Deepak Kumar *WhoScE 91-1*
Lal, Deepak Kumar 1940- *WhoWor 93*
Lal, Devendra 1929- *WhoAm 92*
Lal, Devi *BioIn 17*
Lal, Jayant Saran 1944- *WhoWor 93*
Lala, Dominick J. 1928- *St&PR 93, WhoAm 92*
Lala, Jaynarayan Hotchand 1951- *WhoEmL 93*
Lala, Peeyush Kanti 1934- *WhoAm 92*
Lala, Petr 1942- *WhoUN 92*
Lalach, Joanne J.D. *Law&B 92*
Lalak, John Anthony, III 1942- *St&PR 93*
Laland, Soren G. 1922- *WhoScE 91-4*
Lalande, Henriette *OxDcOp*
Lalande, Michel-Richard *Baker 92*
Lalani, Salim 1945- *WhoWor 93*
Lalanne, C. *WhoScE 91-2*
Lalanne, Jean-Louis Georges 1938- *WhoWor 93*
Lalanne, Michel 1936- *WhoScE 91-2*
La Laurencie, Lionel de 1861-1933 *Baker 92*
Lalayants, Igor Ervandovich 1945- *WhoWor 93*
Lale, Cissy Stewart 1924- *WhoAmW 93*
LaLena, John Charles 1931- *WhoAm 92*
Laliberte, (Joseph Francois) Alfred 1882-1952 *Baker 92*
La Liberte, Ann Gillis 1942- *WhoAmW 93*
La Liberte, Clarence Emory 1917- *St&PR 93*
Laliberte, Normand Julien, Jr. 1951- *WhoEmL 93*
Lalich, Gayle L. *Law&B 92*
Lalicki, Barbara *BioIn 17*
Laliker, Richard Henry 1945- *WhoSSW 93*
La Lima, Salvatore John 1931- *WhoE 93*
Lalji, Phil *St&PR 93*
Lalka, Judith C. *Law&B 92*
Lalka, Judith Candelor 1947- *St&PR 93, WhoAm 92*
Lalla, Barbara Ann 1949- *WhoWor 93*
Lalla, Thomas R., Jr. *Law&B 92*
Lalla Abla, Queen 1910-1992 *BioIn 17*
Lallana, Victor Hugo 1951- *WhoWor 93*
Lallemand, A. *WhoScE 91-2*
Lallemand, J.Y. 1943- *WhoScE 91-2*
Lalley, Frank Edward 1944- *WhoAm 92*
Lalley, Paul *ScF&FL 92*
Lalli, Cele Goldsmith 1933- *WhoAm 92*
Lalli, Domenico 1679-1741 *OxDcOp*
Lalli, Frank *BioIn 17*
Lalli, John M. 1942- *St&PR 93*
Lalli, Michael Anthony 1955- *WhoEmL 93*
L'Allier, James Joseph 1945- *WhoE 93*
L'Allier, Jean-Paul *WhoAm 92, WhoE 93*
Lallinger, E. Michael 1915- *WhoAm 92*
Lally, Ann Marie 1914- *WhoAmW 93, WhoWor 93*
Lally, Daniel Joseph 1963- *WhoWor 93*
Lally, Daniel W. *Law&B 92*
Lally, David E. 1941- *St&PR 93*
Lally, Douglas Robert 1962- *St&PR 93, WhoE 93*
Lally, Eileen Marie 1943- *WhoAmW 93*
Lally, Elizabeth H. 1936- *St&PR 93*
Lally, Margaret M. *WhoWrEP 92*
Lally, Michael David 1942- *WhoAm 92, WhoWrEP 92*
Lally, Norma Ross 1932- *WhoAmW 93*
Lally, Richard Francis 1925- *WhoAm 92*
Lally, T.M. *ScF&FL 92*
Lally, Thomas Arthur, Count de 1702-1766 *HarEnMi*
Lally, Thomas Michael 1936- *St&PR 93*
Lally, Tim Douglas Patrick 1942- *WhoSSW 93*
Lally, William Joseph 1937- *WhoE 93, WhoWor 93*
Lal Mandal, Dhanik 1932- *WhoAsAP 91*
Lalo, Charles 1877-1953 *Baker 92*
Lalo, Edouard 1823-1892 *IntDcOp, OxDcOp*
Lalo, Edouard (-Victoire-Antoine) 1823-1892 *Baker 92*
Lalo, Pierre 1866-1943 *Baker 92, OxDcOp*
La Loca, (Pamala Marie Karol) 1950- *WhoWrEP 92*
LaLoggia, Frank *MiSFD 9*
Lalonde, Brice 1946- *BioIn 17*
Lalonde, Jeffrey A. 1947- *St&PR 93*
Lalonde, John Stephen, Sr. 1948- *WhoEmL 93, WhoWor 93*
Lalonde, Marc 1929- *WhoAm 92*
Lalonde, Marcel 1935- *St&PR 93*
Lalonde, Thomas J. 1951- *St&PR 93*
Lalonde, Venant *BioIn 17*
Lalor, Brian 1941- *BioIn 17*
Lalor, James Fintan 1807-1849 *BioIn 17*
Lalor, Michael Joseph *WhoScE 91-1*
Lalor, R. Peter 1950- *St&PR 93*
Laloy, Louis 1874-1944 *Baker 92*
Lalumia, Carl Risley 1928- *St&PR 93*
LaLumiere, Andre 1949- *St&PR 93*
Lalumiere, Catherine 1935- *WhoWor 93*
La Lupe d1992 *BioIn 17, NewYTBS 92 [port]*
Lalwani, Narendra Dhanraj 1952- *WhoEmL 93*
Lam, Alec *St&PR 93*
Lam, Billy 1960- *WhoWor 93*
Lam, Chun-Ming Gordon 1964- *WhoE 93*
Lam, Daniel Wai-Keung 1949- *WhoAsAP 91*
Lam, David *BioIn 17, WhoAm 92*
Lam, Izabel *BioIn 17*
Lam, Judy Wai-Chun 1963- *WhoAmW 93*
Lam, Kai-Luan Helen 1963- *WhoAmW 93*
Lam, Mike H. *St&PR 93*
Lam, Ngo Van 1944- *WhoUN 92*
Lam, Nora *BioIn 17*
Lam, Richard C. *Law&B 92*
Lam, Sau-Hai 1930- *WhoAm 92*
Lam, Sau-Wing 1952- *St&PR 93*
Lam, Simon Shin-Sing 1947- *WhoAm 92*
Lam, Tony *NewYTBS 92 [port]*
Lam, Wendy Wing Chuen 1964- *WhoWor 93*
Lama, Patrick J. 1939- *St&PR 93*
LaMacchia, John Thomas 1941- *WhoAm 92*
Lamachia, Joseph James 1946- *WhoEmL 93*
Lamade, Barbara Spencer *Law&B 92*
Lamagra, Anthony James 1935- *WhoAm 92*
Lamaina, Francis C. 1939- *St&PR 93*
LaMaina, Lawrence J., Jr. 1935- *St&PR 93*
LaMaina, Lawrence Joseph, Jr. 1934- *WhoAm 92*
Lamaison, Peter Laurens 1941- *St&PR 93*
Lamalie, Robert Eugene 1931- *WhoAm 92*
Laman, Jene Terry 1932- *WhoSSW 93*
Laman, Jerry T. 1947- *St&PR 93*
Laman, Karl Edvard 1867-1944 *IntDcAn*
Lamand, Michel *WhoScE 91-2*
Lamand, Michel 1935- *WhoScE 91-2*
Lamanec, Tracy 1941- *WhoAm 92*
Lamanna, John Joseph 1951- *WhoSSW 93*
Lamanno, Richard Carl 1960- *WhoEmL 93*
Lamantia, Angelo 1960- *St&PR 93*
LaMantia, Charles Robert 1939- *St&PR 93, WhoAm 92*
Lamantia, Victor A. *Law&B 92*
Lamar, Charles Wilbur, III 1948- *WhoEmL 93*
Lamar, Dwight 1951- *BiDAMSp 1989*
Lamar, Jacob V., Jr. *BioIn 17*
Lamar, Jake 1961- *ConAu 137*
Lamar, Joseph Rucker 1857-1916 *OxCSupC [port]*
Lamar, Lucius Quintus Cincinnatus 1825-1893 *OxCSupC [port]*
Lamar, Ola Sylvia 1958- *WhoAmW 93*
Lamar, Patricia Werner *Law&B 92*
Lamar, Richard E. 1931- *St&PR 93*
Lamar, Thomas Allen, Jr. 1936- *WhoAm 92*
LaMar, Timothy J. *Law&B 92*
La Mara *Baker 92*
La Marche, Michel *WhoScE 91-2*
Lamare, Jacques-Michel-Hurel de 1772-1823 *Baker 92*
La Marmora, Alfonso Ferrero di 1804-1878 *HarEnMi*
Lamaro, Emilia 1940- *WhoWor 93*

Lamarque, Maurice P. St&PR 93
Lamarr, Hedy 1914- IntDcF 2-3 [port]
Lamarre, Bernard 1931- BioIn 17, WhoAm 92, WhoE 93, WhoWor 93
La Marre, Jacques-Michel-Hurel de 1772-1823 Baker 92
LaMarre, Mark F. Law&B 92
La Marre, Mildred Holtz 1917- WhoAmW 93
Lamarre, Paul Ronald 1950- WhoE 93
Lamas, Carlos Eduardo 1951- WhoEmL 93
Lamas, Fernando 1915-1982 HispAmA
Lamas, Lorenzo 1958- WhoAm 92
Lamason, Jerry Lynn 1927- St&PR 93
La Massese, Claude Scotto WhoScE 91-2
Lamattina, Lawrence E. 1945- WhoAm 92
LaMay, Joseph Charles 1947- WhoEmL 93
Lamb, Alan F. 1941- St&PR 93
Lamb, Andrew (Martin) 1942- ConAu 137, WhoWor 93
Lamb, Anthony Peter 1950- St&PR 93
Lamb, Antony Hamilton 1939- WhoAsAP 91
Lamb, Bob G. 1931- St&PR 93
Lamb, Caroline 1785-1828 DcLB 116 [port], NinCLC 38 [port]
Lamb, Charles 1775-1834 BioIn 17, WorLitC [port]
Lamb, Charles G. Law&B 92
Lamb, Charles Guy 1949- WhoSSW 93
Lamb, Connie 1947- ConAu 139
Lamb, Darlis Carol WhoAmW 93
Lamb, Dean Coleman 1956- WhoSSW 93
Lamb, Dorrance Winfield 1947- St&PR 93
Lamb, Douglas Booth 1918- St&PR 93
Lamb, Edgar Andrew 1958- WhoE 93
Lamb, Elizabeth Searle 1917- WhoWrEP 92
Lamb, Frederic D. Law&B 92
Lamb, Frederic Davis 1931- St&PR 93, WhoAm 92
Lamb, G. Nash Law&B 92
Lamb, George A. 1906- WhoAm 92, WhoWor 93
Lamb, George Richard 1928- WhoAm 92
Lamb, Gil 1904- QDrFCA 92 [port]
Lamb, Girard E. 1923- St&PR 93
Lamb, Gordon Howard 1934- WhoAm 92
Lamb, Harry 1942- WhoWor 93
Lamb, Henry Grodon 1906- WhoE 93
Lamb, Henry James 1949- WhoSSW 93
Lamb, Hugh 1946- ScF&FL 92
Lamb, Isabelle Smith St&PR 93
Lamb, Jack Richard 1934- WhoSSW 93
Lamb, James R. 1941- St&PR 93
Lamb, Jamie Parker, Jr. 1933- WhoAm 92
Lamb, Janice B. 1945- St&PR 93
Lamb, Joan Marie 1958- WhoEmL 93
Lamb, John WhoScE 91-1
Lamb, John F.P. Law&B 92
Lamb, John G., Jr. Law&B 92
Lamb, Jonathan Robert WhoScE 91-1
Lamb, Joseph F(rancis) 1887-1960 Baker 92
Lamb, Joseph Fairweather WhoScE 91-1
Lamb, Joseph Peter 1927- St&PR 93
Lamb, Joseph Stephen 1934- St&PR 93, WhoAm 92
Lamb, Karl Allen 1933- WhoE 93
Lamb, Kenneth Edward 1952- WhoSSW 93
Lamb, Marcus N. Law&B 92
Lamb, Marilyn Freeman 1933- WhoAmW 93
Lamb, Michael Ernest 1953- WhoEmL 93
Lamb, Michael R. 1944- St&PR 93
Lamb, Natalie Sesto Law&B 92
Lamb, Norman Arthur 1936- St&PR 93
Lamb, Patricia Frazer 1931- WhoAmW 93
Lamb, Phillip Allen 1947- WhoSSW 93
Lamb, Raymond Augustus 1940- WhoAm 92
Lamb, Rex McNaughton, III 1949- WhoAm 92
Lamb, Robert E. 1940- St&PR 93
Lamb, Robert Edward 1936- WhoAm 92, WhoWor 93
Lamb, Robert Lewis 1932- WhoAm 92
Lamb, Sandra E. 1946- WhoAmW 93
Lamb, Sydney MacDonald 1929- WhoAm 92
Lamb, Thomas Howard 1929- St&PR 93
Lamb, Tim 1947- St&PR 93
Lamb, Ursula Schaefer 1914- WhoAm 92
Lamb, W. Scott BioIn 17
Lamb, Walter c. 1450-1499 Baker 92
Lamb, Warren G. 1943- St&PR 93
Lamb, William Michael Law&B 92
Lamb, Willis Eugene, Jr. 1913- WhoAm 92, WhoWor 93
Lamballe, princesse de 1749-1792 BioIn 17
Lambard, Creede ScF&FL 92
Lambard, Sharleen ScF&FL 92
Lambardi, Camillo c. 1560-1634 Baker 92
Lambardi, Francesco c. 1587-1642 Baker 92
Lambden, R.J. Law&B 92
Lambden, Ronald J. Law&B 92
Lambdin, Craig Haskell 1958- WhoE 93
Lambdin, Laura Cooner 1961- WhoSSW 93
Lambdin, Robert Thomas 1958- WhoSSW 93
Lambe, Catherine van de Velde 1950- WhoEmL 93
Lambe, Dean R. 1943- ScF&FL 92
Lambe, Sean Francis Anthony 1940- WhoWor 93
Lambe, Thomas William 1920- WhoAm 92
Lambeau, Curly 1898-1965 BioIn 17
Lambeck, Debra T. 1958- St&PR 93
Lambek, Jules K. Law&B 92
Lambelet, Geroge 1875-1945 Baker 92
Lamberechts, Luc J.J. 1944- WhoWor 93
Lamberg, Arnold 1934- St&PR 93
Lamberg, Joan Bernice 1935- WhoAmW 93
Lamberg, Stanley Lawrence 1933- WhoAm 92
Lamberg, Walter Jerome 1942- WhoWrEP 92
Lamberg-Allardt, Christel J.E. 1949- WhoScE 91-4
Lamberg-Karlovsky, Clifford Charles 1937- WhoAm 92, WhoWor 93
Lambergs, Guntis J. 1956- WhoE 93
Lamberson, John Roger 1933- St&PR 93, WhoAm 92, WhoWor 93
Lambert, Abbott Lawrence 1919- WhoE 93
Lambert, Alan G. 1934- St&PR 93
Lambert, Allen Thomas 1911- St&PR 93
Lambert, Allison Stith 1959- WhoAmW 93
Lambert, Angela Maria 1940- ConAu 138
Lambert, Anne Haskins 1932- WhoSSW 93
Lambert, Benjamin Franklin Law&B 92
Lambert, Benjamin Joseph, III 1937- WhoSSW 93
Lambert, Betsy Holaday 1945- WhoAmW 93
Lambert, Betty 1933-1983 WhoCanL 92
Lambert, Blanche 1960- WhoAmW 93
Lambert, Bo 1943- WhoScE 91-4
Lambert, Carol A. 1941- WhoAmW 93
Lambert, Carol Ann 1947- WhoAmW 93, WhoWor 93
Lambert, Charles F., Jr. 1931- St&PR 93
Lambert, Charles G. Law&B 92
Lambert, Constant 1905-1951 Baker 92, OxDcOp
Lambert, Daniel Michael 1941- WhoAm 92
Lambert, Dave 1917-1966 BioIn 17
Lambert, David Richard 1951- WhoSSW 93
Lambert, Deborah Ketchum 1942- WhoAmW 93, WhoE 93
Lambert, Deborah Sue 1952- WhoAmW 93
Lambert, Dennis SoulM
Lambert, Derek 1929- BioIn 17, ScF&FL 92
Lambert, Didier Charles 1957- WhoWor 93
Lambert, Douglas Harold 1949- WhoEmL 93, WhoSSW 93
Lambert, Edythe Rutherford 1921- WhoSSW 93
Lambert, Eleanor BioIn 17, WhoAm 92
Lambert, Eugene Louis 1948- St&PR 93, WhoE 93, WhoEmL 93
Lambert, Frederick William 1943- WhoAm 92
Lambert, George R. Law&B 92
Lambert, George Robert 1933- St&PR 93, WhoAm 92
Lambert, Georgia Lynn 1948- WhoWrEP 92
Lambert, Henry A. 1935- St&PR 93
Lambert, Howard R. Law&B 92
Lambert, Ian 1946- St&PR 93, WhoAm 92
Lambert, J.L. 1930- WhoScE 91-2
Lambert, Jack BioIn 17
Lambert, James A. 1956- St&PR 93
Lambert, James Aloysius, II 1956- WhoAm 92
Lambert, Jane E. 1950- WhoAmW 93
Lambert, Jane K. 1924- WhoWrEP 92
Lambert, Jean Marjorie 1943- WhoAmW 93
Lambert, Jeremiah Daniel 1934- WhoAm 92
Lambert, John Alexander 1930- WhoWor 93
Lambert, John Bernard 1948- WhoE 93, WhoEmL 93
Lambert, John Boyd 1929- WhoAm 92
Lambert, John Denholm WhoScE 91-1
Lambert, John Phillip 1944- WhoAm 92, WhoWor 93
Lambert, Joseph Buckley 1940- WhoAm 92
Lambert, Joseph Earl 1948- WhoSSW 93
Lambert, Juan Bautista 1884-1945 Baker 92
Lambert, Julie Louise 1953- WhoEmL 93
Lambert, LaDoyce 1935- St&PR 93
Lambert, Lee R. 1942- St&PR 93
Lambert, Lionel d1990 BioIn 17
Lambert, Lon Keith Law&B 92
Lambert, Lucien 1858-1945 Baker 92
Lambert, Lyn Dee 1954- WhoEmL 93
Lambert, M. WhoScE 91-2
Lambert, Madeline AmWomPl
Lambert, Martha Lowery 1937- WhoAmW 93
Lambert, Mary MiSFD 9
Lambert, Mary Pulliam 1944- WhoAmW 93
Lambert, Michael Gerard 1952- WhoEmL 93
Lambert, Michael Malet 1930- WhoAm 92
Lambert, Michel 1610-1696 Baker 92
Lambert, Nadine Murphy WhoAm 92
Lambert, Nigel WhoScE 91-1
Lambert, Olaf Cecil 1920- WhoAm 92
Lambert, Paul Christopher 1928- WhoAm 92, WhoWor 93
Lambert, Paul Henri 1938- WhoScE 91-4, WhoUN 92
Lambert, Paula Wynne Stephens 1943- WhoAmW 93
Lambert, Pauline Averil Roy 1938- WhoSSW 93
Lambert, Peggy Lynne Bailey 1948- WhoAmW 93
Lambert, Philip 1925- WhoAm 92
Lambert, Philip 1946- WhoWor 93
Lambert, Phyllis 1927- BioIn 17
Lambert, Raymond E. 1925- St&PR 93
Lambert, Richard G. 1936- St&PR 93
Lambert, Robert F. 1959- St&PR 93
Lambert, Robert Frank 1924- WhoAm 92
Lambert, Robert Gilbert 1930- WhoAm 92
Lambert, Robert Graham, Jr. 1934- WhoSSW 93
Lambert, Robert Lowell 1923- WhoAm 92
Lambert, Rollins E. BioIn 17
Lambert, S.K. St&PR 93
Lambert, Samuel M. 1913-1991 BioIn 17
Lambert, Sanders R., Jr. 1931- St&PR 93
Lambert, Thomas Wayne 1942- St&PR 93, WhoAm 92
Lambert, Tony d1990 BioIn 17
Lambert, W., III 1948- ScF&FL 92
Lambert, Wallace E. BioIn 17
Lambert, William D. Law&B 92
Lambert, William E., III Law&B 92
Lambert, William G. 1920- WhoAm 92
Lambert, William H. 1936- St&PR 93
Lambert, William Martin 1929- St&PR 93
Lambert, William Wilson 1919- WhoAm 92
Lamberth, Edwin Eugene 1931- WhoSSW 93
Lamberth, Ella Ruth Wheeler 1927- WhoAmW 93
Lamberth, Marcus Hughes 1949- WhoSSW 93
Lamberth, Royce C. 1943- CngDr 91, WhoAm 92, WhoE 93
Lamberth, Victoria Renee 1968- WhoSSW 93
Lamberti, Corrado Rolando 1947- WhoWor 93
Lamberti, Franco 1937- WhoScE 91-3
Lamberti, Judith Ann 1951- WhoEmL 93
Lamberti, Marjorie 1937- WhoAm 92
Lamberti, Nicholas 1944- St&PR 93
Lamberton, Eva G. AmWomPl
Lamberts, Emile Louis 1941- WhoWor 93
Lamberts, Luc G.G. 1939- WhoScE 91-2
Lambertsen, Christian James 1917- WhoAm 92
Lambertsen, Georg WhoScE 91-4
Lambertsen, Mary Ann 1939- St&PR 93, WhoAmW 93
Lambertson, David Floyd 1940- WhoWor 93
Lambertson, Larry Hall 1950- WhoSSW 93
Lambertson, Wingate Augustus, Jr. 1920- WhoSSW 93
Lambertz, Richard H. 1940- St&PR 93
Lambeth, Deborah Hayes 1956- WhoAm 92
Lambeth, E. Julia Law&B 92
Lambeth, Ellen Smith WhoSSW 93
Lambeth, Thomas Willis 1935- WhoSSW 93
Lambeth, Victor Neal 1920- WhoAm 92
Lambie, James K. 1928- St&PR 93
Lambie, James T. 1942- St&PR 93
Lambie, Kerry G. St&PR 93
Lambillotte, Louis 1796-1855 Baker 92
Lambing, Steven Jay 1957- WhoSSW 93
Lambinon, Jacques E.J. 1936- WhoScE 91-2
Lambird, Mona Salyer 1938- WhoAm 92, WhoAmW 93
Lambirth, Frank ScF&FL 92
Lambjerg-Hansen, Harry 1934- WhoScE 91-2
Lambkin, Jeanne Theresa 1961- WhoAmW 93
Lambkin, Nina B. AmWomPl
Lambly, Sharon A. 1940- St&PR 93
Lambly, Sharon Ann 1940- WhoAmW 93
Lambo, Jerry Dean 1935- WhoAm 92
Lambo, Thomas Adeoye 1923- WhoScE 91-4, WhoWor 93
Lamboite, Joao Lourenco 1952- WhoWor 93
Lamboley, Catherine A. Law&B 92
Lamboley, Harold Joseph, Jr. Law&B 92
Lambooy, E. 1947- WhoScE 91-3
Lambord, Benjamin 1879-1915 Baker 92
Lamborn, Arthur H. 1929-1990 BioIn 17
Lamborn, Earle 1934- St&PR 93
Lamborn, LeRoy Leslie 1937- WhoAm 92
Lambos, William Andrew 1956- WhoSSW 93
Lambotte, Hendrik R.M.E. 1925- WhoScE 91-2
Lambotte, Luc 1937- WhoScE 91-2
Lambotte, Rene Edgard 1931- WhoWor 93
Lambotte, Rene Edgard Eugene 1931- WhoScE 91-2
Lambourne, David ScF&FL 92
Lambourne, Robert ScF&FL 92
Lambowitz, Sheila 1947- WhoAmW 93
Lambrakos, Michael 1946- St&PR 93
Lambrecht, Francis Hubert 1895-1978 IntDcAn
Lambrecht, Gunter 1941- WhoScE 91-3
Lambrecht, Luc Johan 1951- WhoWor 93
Lambrecht, Sally Borcher 1960- WhoAmW 93
Lambrechts, Catherine L. 1923- St&PR 93
Lambrechts, Herbert William 1923- St&PR 93
Lambremont, Edward Nelson, Jr. 1928- WhoAm 92
Lambright, Stephen Kirk 1942- St&PR 93, WhoAm 92
Lambrix, Robert John 1939- St&PR 93
Lambro, Donald Joseph 1940- WhoAm 92
Lambro, Philip 1935- Baker 92
Lambro, Phillip 1935- WhoAm 92
Lambros, Lambros John 1935- WhoAm 92
Lambroussis, Harry G. 1934- St&PR 93
Lambroussis, Harry George 1934- WhoAm 92
LaMear, Danielle Rae 1963- WhoAmW 93
Lameiro, Gerard Francis 1949- WhoEmL 93, WhoWor 93
Lameko, Pule 1939- WhoAsAP 91
Lamel, Linda H. 1943- St&PR 93, WhoIns 93
Lamel, Linda Helen 1943- WhoAm 92, WhoAmW 93
Lamendola, Jennifer Joyce 1962- WhoEmL 93
Lamendola, Michael John 1953- WhoE 93
Lamendola, Ronald N. 1947- St&PR 93
Lamer, Antonio BioIn 17
Lamer, Antonio 1933- WhoAm 92
Lamere, David F. 1960- St&PR 93
Lamere, Robert Kent 1926- WhoAm 92
Lamerigts, A.G.A. 1947- WhoScE 91-3
Lamers, William Francis 1951- St&PR 93
Lamesch, Fernand L. 1934- St&PR 93
Lamey, William Daniel Alexander 1953- WhoAm 92
Lamhut, Phyllis BioIn 17
Lami, Charles Nicholas 1954- WhoE 93
Lami, Gyula 1922- WhoScE 91-4
Lamia, Thomas Roger 1938- WhoWor 93
Lamie, Theresa St&PR 93
Lamirande, Emilien 1926- WhoAm 92
Lamis, Leroy 1925- WhoAm 92
Lamishaw, Matthew I. Law&B 92
Lamison, Donald R. 1940- St&PR 93
Lamka, Philip Charles 1947- WhoAm 92
Lamkin, Bill Dan 1929- WhoAm 92
Lamkin, Billy M. 1945- St&PR 93
Lamkin, Grace AmWomPl
Lamkin, Martha D. 1942- St&PR 93
Lamkin, Nina B. AmWomPl
Lamkin, Selma Hoffman 1925- WhoE 93
Lamkin, William Pierce 1919- WhoAm 92
Lamm, Carolyn Beth 1948- WhoAm 92, WhoAmW 93, WhoE 93, WhoEmL 93, WhoWor 93
Lamm, Donald Stephen 1931- St&PR 93, WhoAm 92
Lamm, Harolene Willerman 1957- WhoAmW 93
Lamm, Jeffrey A. St&PR 93
Lamm, Kathi Lynn 1950- WhoAmW 93
Lamm, Lester Paul 1934- WhoAm 92

Lamm, Michael 1936- *WhoWrEP 92*
Lamm, Michael Emanuel 1934- *WhoAm 92*
Lamm, Richard 1935- *ScF&FL 92*
Lamm, Robert B. *Law&B 92*
Lamm, Robert B. 1947- *St&PR 93*
Lamm, Robert E. *Law&B 92*
Lamm, Robert Earl 1955- *WhoEmL 93*
Lamm, Roderick William 1929- *St&PR 93*
Lammasniemi, Jorma Paavo Juhani 1948- *WhoScE 91-4*
Lammens, Edmond Marie 1928- *WhoScE 91-2*
Lammens, Pierre 1944- *WhoWor 93*
Lammers, Bea Mearlyn 1938- *WhoAmW 93*
Lammers, Edward August 1923- *St&PR 93*
Lammers, Gerda 1915- *Baker 92, OxDcOp*
Lammers, Julius 1829-1888 *Baker 92*
Lammers, Lennis Larry 1937- *WhoE 93*
Lammert, Richard Alan *Law&B 92*
Lammert, Thomas Edward 1947- *WhoEmL 93, WhoWor 93*
Lammertsma, Koop 1949- *WhoEmL 93*
Lammey, Guinn Crestman *Law&B 92*
Lammie, James Michael 1949- *WhoEmL 93, WhoSSW 93*
Lamming, George 1927- *BioIn 17, IntLitE*
Lamming, George Eric *WhoScE 91-1*
Lamming, George (William) 1927- *DcLB 125 [port]*
Lamming, Robert Love 1910- *WhoWor 93*
Lammon, Katherine Rae 1956- *WhoAmW 93*
Lammons, J. Howard 1929- *St&PR 93*
Lammot, Brooke W. 1931- *St&PR 93*
Lamneck, David Arthur 1952- *WhoIns 93*
Lamnidis, Alexander 1955- *WhoWor 93*
Lamon, Eddie William 1939- *WhoSSW 93*
Lamon, Harry Vincent, Jr. 1932- *WhoAm 92*
Lamonaca, Inga Jennifer 1952- *St&PR 93*
Lamond, Frederic(k Archibald) 1868-1948 *Baker 92*
Lamond, Gaylord Marvin 1923- *WhoAm 92*
Lamond, James *BioIn 17*
Lamond, John Patrick 1937- *St&PR 93*
Lamond, Pierre R. *St&PR 93*
Lamond, R.W. *St&PR 93*
Lamonds, Harold A. 1924- *St&PR 93*
Lamone, Rudolph Philip 1931- *WhoAm 92*
Lamonica, Filippo 1928- *St&PR 93*
Lamonica, John 1954- *WhoEmL 93*
LaMonica, Michael Samuel, Jr. 1941- *St&PR 93*
Lamonica, Paul Raymond 1944- *WhoAm 92*
LaMonica, Thomas Edward 1945- *WhoE 93*
Lamons, John Edward 1948- *WhoSSW 93*
Lamons, Robert G. 1932- *St&PR 93*
Lamons, Robert P. 1923- *St&PR 93*
Lamont, Alice *WhoAmW 93*
LaMont, Andre 1957- *WhoSSW 93*
Lamont, Barbara 1939- *WhoE 93, WhoSSW 93*
LaMont, Barbara Gibson 1925- *WhoAm 92*
Lamont, Billy 1962- *WhoE 93*
Lamont, Bridget Later 1948- *WhoAm 92*
Lamont, Colleen A. *Law&B 92*
Lamont, Corliss 1902- *WhoAm 92, WhoWor 93, WhoWrEP 92*
Lamont, Deni 1932-1991 *BioIn 17*
Lamont, Donald B. 1919- *St&PR 93*
Lamont, Gene 1946- *WhoAm 92*
Lamont, Howard Marsden *Law&B 92*
Lamont, Katharine *AmWomPl*
Lamont, Lansing 1930- *WhoAm 92*
Lamont, Lee *WhoAm 92*
Lamont, M.H. *WhoScE 91-1*
Lamont, Norman 1942- *CurBio 92 [port]*
Lamont, Norman Stewart Hughson 1942- *WhoWor 93*
Lamont, Peter Hubert *WhoScE 91-1*
Lamont, Rosette Clementine *WhoAm 92*
Lamontagne, David Edward 1948- *St&PR 93*
LaMontagne, Kirsten Krueger 1940- *WhoAmW 93*
Lamontagne, Myrna Lynne 1950- *WhoWrEP 92*
LaMontagne, Theresa Ann 1963- *WhoAmW 93*
La Montaine, John 1920- *Baker 92*
La Monte, Angela Mae 1944- *WhoE 93*
Lamont-Havers, Ronald William 1920- *WhoAm 92*
Lamorde, Abubakar Gofolo 1944- *WhoWor 93*
LaMoreaux, Philip Elmer 1920- *WhoAm 92*
Lamorena, Alberto C., III 1949- *WhoAm 92*
LaMoreux, Frederick Holmes 1941- *St&PR 93, WhoAm 92*
Lamoreux, Lary Gene 1952- *WhoEmL 93*
Lamorey, D.H. *Law&B 92*
Lamorie, Clarence Carl 1928- *St&PR 93*
Lamoriello, Francine Cynthia 1957- *WhoE 93*
Lamoriello, Louis Anthony 1942- *WhoAm 92*
Lamorisse, Albert 1922-1970 *MiSFD 9N*
Lamos, Mark 1946- *WhoAm 92*
Lamote de Grignon, Juan 1872-1949 *Baker 92*
Lamote de Grignon y Ribas, Ricardo 1899-1962 *Baker 92*
Lamothe, Georges 1837-1894 *Baker 92*
Lamothe, Irene Elise 1949- *WhoWor 93*
LaMothe, William Edward 1926- *St&PR 93, WhoAm 92*
Lamott, Anne *BioIn 17*
La Motta, Emanuel P. 1907-1991 *BioIn 17*
La Motta, Stephanie *BioIn 17*
Lamotte, Alain *WhoScE 91-2*
La Motte, Antoine Houdar de 1672-1731 *OxDcOp*
Lamotte, Kevin *BioIn 17*
LaMotte, William Mitchell 1938- *WhoAm 92*
La Motte-Fouque, Friedrich Heinrich Karl, Freiherr von 1777-1843 *BioIn 17*
La Motte-Fouque, Karoline Auguste, Freiin de 1773-1831 *BioIn 17*
Lamour, Dorothy 1914- *IntDcF 2-3*
Lamour, Henry M. *Law&B 92*
L'Amour, Louis 1908-1988 *BioIn 17, MagSAmL [port], ScF&FL 92*
L'Amour, Louis (Dearborn) 1908-1988 *ConAu 40NR*
Lamoureux, Charles 1834-1899 *Baker 92*
Lamoureux, Gloria Kathleen 1947- *WhoAmW 93, WhoEmL 93*
Lamoureux, Paul A. 1947- *St&PR 93*
Lamoureux, William A. 1938- *WhoSSW 93*
Lamp, John Ernest 1943- *WhoAm 92*
Lamp, Karen Jean *Law&B 92*
Lamp, Robert Alexander 1951- *St&PR 93*
Lamp, Robert Harry 1936- *St&PR 93*
Lamp, Sandra Graft *Law&B 92*
Lamp, Walter *Law&B 92*
Lampard-Naccari, Catherine Ann 1951- *WhoEmL 93*
Lampariello, Paolo 1944- *WhoWor 93*
Lamparski, Richard *WhoWrEP 92*
Lampart, Abe *Law&B 92*
Lamparter, William C. 1929- *WhoAm 92*
Lampathakis, James Dean 1961- *WhoEmL 93*
Lampe, Annacarol 1951- *WhoAmW 93*
Lampe, David Alan 1960- *WhoE 93*
Lampe, David Elwood 1941- *WhoE 93*
Lampe, Frederick Walter 1927- *WhoAm 92*
Lampe, Guy Lee 1956- *St&PR 93*
Lampe, Harriett Richmond 1906- *WhoAmW 93*
Lampe, Henry Oscar 1927- *WhoSSW 93*
Lampe, Istvan 1932- *WhoScE 91-4*
Lampe, John Frederick c. 1703-1751 *OxDcOp*
Lampe, Laszlo 1929- *WhoScE 91-4*
Lampe, Linda M. *Law&B 92*
Lampe, Robert C. *Law&B 92*
Lampedusa, Giuseppe di Tomasi 1896-1957 *BioIn 17*
Lam Pei, Peggy 1928- *WhoAsAP 91*
Lampel, Anita Kay 1946- *WhoAmW 93, WhoEmL 93*
Lampel, Gerolf C. 1932- *WhoScE 91-4*
Lamperski, Mark Anthony 1951- *WhoSSW 93*
Lampert, Fritz H. 1933- *WhoScE 91-3*
Lampert, Hope *BioIn 17*
Lampert, Joseph A. 1941- *St&PR 93, WhoIns 93*
Lampert, Lawrence D. 1952- *WhoSSW 93*
Lampert, Leonard Franklin 1919- *WhoWor 93*
Lampert, Richard H. 1947- *St&PR 93*
Lampert, Sidney 1931- *St&PR 93*
Lampert, Winfried 1941- *WhoScE 91-3*
Lamperti, Claudia 1934- *ScF&FL 92*
Lamperti, Francesco 1811-1892 *Baker 92, OxDcOp*
Lamperti, Giovanni 1839-1910 *OxDcOp*
Lamperti, Giovanni Battista 1839-1910 *Baker 92*
Lamperti, Giuseppe 1834-1898 *OxDcOp*
Lamperti, John Williams 1932- *WhoAm 92*
Lampeter, Kathleen Mary 1961- *WhoEmL 93*
Lamphear, Vivian Shaw 1954- *WhoAmW 93, WhoEmL 93*
Lamphere, Gilbert H. *St&PR 93*
Lamphere, James Joseph 1935- *St&PR 93*
Lamphier, Blaise Michael 1963- *WhoE 93*
Lamping, Kathryn S. *Law&B 92*
Lamping, William Jay 1954- *WhoEmL 93*
Lampio, Teppo Sakari 1921- *WhoScE 91-4*
Lampitt, Dinah 1937- *ScF&FL 92*
Lampkin, Barbara Jo 1947- *WhoEmL 93*
Lampkin, Lillian C. d1990 *BioIn 17*
Lampkin, Nicolas *WhoScE 91-1*
Lampl, Jack W., Jr. 1921- *St&PR 93*
Lampl, Jack Willard, Jr. 1921- *WhoAm 92*
Lampl, Michael Scott 1962- *WhoSSW 93*
Lampl, Peggy Ann 1930- *WhoAm 92*
Lamplugh, Mary Beth 1948- *WhoEmL 93*
Lampman, Archibald 1861-1899 *BioIn 17*
Lampman, Evelyn Sibley 1907-1980 *DcAmChF 1960, ScF&FL 92*
Lampman, George James 1945- *WhoE 93*
Lampman, Susan M. *St&PR 93*
Lampo, Valerie Simokso 1949- *WhoAmW 93*
Lamport, Allan Howard 1942- *St&PR 93*
Lamport, Anthony Matthew 1935- *WhoAm 92*
Lamport, Bernard 1930-1991 *BioIn 17*
Lamport, Felicia 1916- *WhoAm 92*
Lamport, Leslie B. 1941- *WhoAm 92*
Lamport, W.H., Mrs. *AmWomPl*
Lampos, James 1962- *WhoE 93*
Lamprecht, Dorothy McCoy 1950- *WhoSSW 93*
Lamprecht, Ingolf H.D. 1933- *WhoScE 91-3*
Lampreia, Jose d1991 *BioIn 17*
Lamprich, Julie E. *Law&B 92*
Lampropoulos, F.P. 1949- *St&PR 93*
Lampros-Klein, Francine Demetra 1948- *WhoEmL 93*
Lampson, John E. 1936- *St&PR 93*
Lampson, Marilyn 1937- *St&PR 93*
Lampson, Mary *MiSFD 9*
Lamptey, Jonathan Charles 1950- *WhoEmL 93, WhoWor 93*
Lampton, Chris *ConAu 37NR*
Lampton, Christopher *BioIn 17, ConAu 37NR*
Lampton, Christopher 1950- *ScF&FL 92*
Lampton, Christopher F. *ConAu 37NR*
Lampton, Dinwiddie, Jr. 1914- *St&PR 93*
Lampton, Nancy 1942- *WhoIns 93*
Lampugnani, Giovanni Battista 1706-c. 1786 *Baker 92, OxDcOp*
Lampugnani, Vittorio Magnago 1951- *BioIn 17*
Lamsdorff-Galagane, Vladimir 1938- *WhoWor 93*
Lam-Seng, Koh 1946- *WhoWor 93*
Lamson, David Frank 1924- *St&PR 93*
Lamson, Evonne Viola 1946- *WhoEmL 93*
Lamson, George Herbert 1940- *WhoAm 92*
Lamson, Joan E. 1937- *St&PR 93*
Lamson, Wade P. 1929- *St&PR 93*
Lamson, Wade S. *Law&B 92*
Lamstein, Shari R. *Law&B 92*
Lamster, Ira Barry 1950- *WhoE 93*
Lamvik, Jono 1929- *WhoScE 91-4*
Lamy, Jean N. 1941- *WhoScE 91-2*
Lamy, John Baptist 1814-1888 *BioIn 17*
Lamy, Mary Rebecca 1929- *WhoSSW 93*
Lamy, Maurice L.F.J. 1942- *WhoScE 91-2*
Lamy, Paul 1949- *WhoUN 92*
Lamy, Peter Paul 1925- *WhoAm 92*
Lamy, Rose Marie Gaudio 1936- *WhoAmW 93*
Lan, Chin-Mou 1932- *WhoWor 93*
Lanahan, John A. 1935- *St&PR 93*
Lanahan, John Stevenson 1922- *WhoAm 92*
Lanahan, William Wallace, III 1943- *St&PR 93*
Lanam, Linda L. *Law&B 92*
Lanam, Linda L. 1948- *WhoIns 93*
Lanam, Linda Lee 1948- *WhoAmW 93*
Lanardonne, Carlos *Law&B 92*
Lanari, Alessandro 1790-1862 *OxDcOp*
LaNasa, Marion Anthony, Jr. 1953- *WhoSSW 93*
La Natra, Jodi Ann 1943- *WhoE 93*
Lancashire, Ben John 1928- *St&PR 93*
Lancaster, Alden 1956- *WhoE 93*
Lancaster, Beaufort Marion 1945- *WhoSSW 93*
Lancaster, Bruce Morgan 1923- *WhoAm 92*
Lancaster, Burt 1913- *BioIn 17, IntDcF 2-3 [port], MiSFD 9*
Lancaster, Burton 1913- *WhoAm 92*
Lancaster, Carroll Townes, Jr. 1929- *WhoSSW 93, WhoWor 93*
Lancaster, Donald Gene 1943- *St&PR 93*
Lancaster, Edwin Beattie 1916- *WhoAm 92*
Lancaster, Frederick Wilfrid 1933- *WhoAm 92*
Lancaster, Gary L. *Law&B 92*
Lancaster, H. Martin 1943- *CngDr 91*
Lancaster, Harold Martin 1943- *WhoAm 92, WhoSSW 93*
Lancaster, Henry Oliver 1913- *WhoWor 93*
Lancaster, Janette Boyd *Law&B 92*
Lancaster, John C. *Law&B 92*
Lancaster, John Thomas 1931- *WhoAm 92*
Lancaster, Joseph Lawrence, Jr. 1925- *WhoAm 92*
Lancaster, Kelvin John 1924- *WhoAm 92, WhoE 93*
Lancaster, Kendell Rene Quesenberry 1956- *WhoSSW 93*
Lancaster, Lisa Marie 1966- *WhoAmW 93*
Lancaster, Louise B. *Law&B 92*
Lancaster, Nina Marie 1943- *WhoAmW 93*
Lancaster, Osbert 1908-1986 *BioIn 17, OxDcOp*
Lancaster, Otis Ewing 1909- *WhoE 93*
Lancaster, Patrick S. *Law&B 92*
Lancaster, Peggy *WhoAmW 93*
Lancaster, Peter 1929- *WhoAm 92*
Lancaster, Ralph Ivan, Jr. 1930- *WhoAm 92*
Lancaster, Ray H. 1935- *St&PR 93*
Lancaster, Richard Andrew 1943- *WhoE 93*
Lancaster, Robert Charles 1946- *St&PR 93*
Lancaster, Robert Samuel 1909- *WhoAm 92*
Lancaster, Roy 1948- *WhoAm 92*
Lancaster, Roy G. 1923- *St&PR 93*
Lancaster, Thomas, Earl of c. 1277-1322 *HarEnMi*
Lance, Bert 1931- *BioIn 17*
Lance, Charles Eugene 1954- *WhoSSW 93*
Lance, Daniel Francois 1960- *WhoWor 93*
Lance, David Jackson 1954- *WhoSSW 93*
Lance, Dennis L. 1944- *St&PR 93*
Lance, E. Christopher *WhoScE 91-1*
Lance, George Milward 1928- *WhoAm 92*
Lance, Glenda Rosanna Margaret 1933- *WhoWor 93*
Lance, James Alan 1948- *St&PR 93*
Lance, James Waldo 1926- *WhoWor 93*
Lance, James Winslow 1943- *WhoSSW 93*
Lance, Jeanne Louise 1945- *WhoWrEP 92*
Lance, Jill Ann 1945- *St&PR 93*
Lance, Kathryn 1943- *ScF&FL 92*
Lance, Larry K. 1941- *St&PR 93, WhoIns 93*
Lance, Major 1941- *BioIn 17*
Lance, Rosemary Hope 1938- *WhoAmW 93*
Lance, Steven *WhoE 93*
Lance, Thomas Allan *Law&B 92*
Lance, Thomas Bertram 1931- *WhoAm 92*
Lance, Tim *BioIn 17*
Lance, Walter C. 1934- *St&PR 93*
Lance, William Campbell 1944- *St&PR 93*
Lancen, Serge Jean Mathieu 1922- *Baker 92*
Lanchbery, John (Arthur) 1923- *Baker 92*
Lanchester, Edith 1871-1966 *BioIn 17*
Lanchester, Elsa 1902-1986 *BioIn 17, IntDcF 2-3*
Lanchester, Peter Compton *WhoScE 91-1*
Lanchner, Bertrand M. *Law&B 92*
Lanchner, Bertrand Martin 1929- *St&PR 93, WhoAm 92*
Lanci, Michel 1949- *WhoScE 91-2*
Lanci, Vincent 1945- *St&PR 93*
Lancia, Frederick Nicholas 1938- *St&PR 93*
Lancie, John (Sherwood) de *Baker 92*
Lancione, Gregory 1928- *St&PR 93*
Lanciotti, Don 1956- *St&PR 93*
Lanciotti, Michael A. 1956- *St&PR 93*
Lancit, Laurence A. *St&PR 93*
Lancour, Gene 1947- *ScF&FL 92*
Lancour, Harold 1908-1981 *BioIn 17*
Lancour, Karen Louise 1946- *WhoAmW 93*
Lancz, Alan Bruce 1957- *WhoEmL 93*
Land, Ailsa *WhoScE 91-1*
Land, Alan E. *Law&B 92*
Land, Allan H. 1922- *St&PR 93*
Land, Betty Lou Jackson 1947- *WhoEmL 93, WhoSSW 93*
Land, Dinah K. *Law&B 92*
Land, Douglas S. *Law&B 92*
Land, Edwin 1909-1991 *AnObit 1991*
Land, Edwin H. *BioIn 17*
Land, Frank 1911-1990 *BioIn 17*
Land, Frank Henry 1945- *WhoUN 92*
Land, Jan Pieter Nicholaas 1834-1897 *Baker 92*
Land, John Gerald 1939- *WhoSSW 93*
Land, Jon *ScF&FL 92*
Land, Judith Ann 1938- *WhoWrEP 92*
Land, Judith Broten 1951- *WhoAmW 93*
Land, Judy M. 1945- *WhoWor 93*
Land, Kenneth Carl 1942- *WhoAm 92*
Land, Kenneth Dean 1931- *WhoWor 93*
Land, Michael Francis *WhoScE 91-1*
Land, Ming Huey 1940- *WhoSSW 93*
Land, Rebekah Ruth 1946- *WhoEmL 93, WhoSSW 93*
Land, Reginald Brian 1927- *WhoAm 92*
Land, Richard Dale 1946- *WhoSSW 93*

Land, Roland John 1936- *WhoE 93*
Land, Stephen Britton 1954- *WhoEmL 93*
Land, Thomas Paul 1948- *WhoSSW 93*
Land, Thornton Reddoch 1941- *WhoIns 93*
Landa, Alfonso Beaumont, II 1961- *WhoEmL 93, WhoSSW 93, WhoWor 93*
Landa, Howard M. *Law&B 92*
Landa, Howard Martin 1943- *WhoAm 92*
Landa, Michelle Annette 1955- *WhoEmL 93*
Landa, Ruth Kaplan 1934- *WhoAmW 93*
Landa, Vladimir 1923- *WhoScE 91-4*
Landa, William Robert 1919- *WhoAm 92*
Landaal, Thomas Green 1954- *St&PR 93*
Landahl, Herbert Daniel 1913- *WhoAm 92*
Landahl, Marten T. 1927- *WhoScE 91-4*
Landais, Hubert 1921- *WhoWor 93*
Landale, Thomas David 1927- *St&PR 93*
Landale, Zoe 1952- *WhoCanL 92*
Landa Munarriz, Gisela Ivonne 1958- *WhoWor 93*
Landau, Annette Henkin 1921- *WhoWrEP 92*
Landau, Arthur Norman 1948- *WhoE 93*
Landau, Bernard Robert 1926- *WhoAm 92*
Landau, Caroline H. *Law&B 92*
Landau, Edmund 1877-1938 *BioIn 17*
Landau, Edward F. 1916-1990 *BioIn 17*
Landau, Edwin 1890-1975 *BioIn 17*
Landau, Ellis 1944- *St&PR 93, WhoAm 92*
Landau, Ely 1920- *WhoAm 92*
Landau, Gabriela Josefa 1927- *WhoAmW 93*
Landau, George L. 1928- *St&PR 93*
Landau, Harriet I. *Law&B 92*
Landau, Howard Charles 1945- *WhoAm 92*
Landau, Ioan Dore 1938- *WhoScE 91-2*
Landau, Irwin *WhoAm 92, WhoE 93*
Landau, Jacob 1917- *WhoAm 92*
Landau, Julie 1956- *St&PR 93*
Landau, Lauri Beth 1952- *WhoAmW 93*
Landau, Lev Davidovich 1908-1968 *BioIn 17*
Landau, Mark M. 1952- *St&PR 93*
Landau, Martin 1921- *WhoAm 92*
Landau, Martin 1934- *WhoAm 92*
Landau, Mary Jane 1953- *WhoAmW 93*
Landau, Michael R. 1946- *St&PR 93*
Landau, Michael Roy 1946- *WhoAm 92*
Landau, Nathaniel I. 1935- *St&PR 93*
Landau, Norma Beatrice 1942- *WhoAm 92*
Landau, Paul Howard 1934- *St&PR 93*
Landau, Peter Edward 1933- *WhoAm 92, WhoWrEP 92*
Landau, Philippine 1869-1964 *BioIn 17*
Landau, Ralph 1916- *WhoAm 92*
Landau, Rhona L. *Law&B 92*
Landau, Richard L. 1916- *WhoAm 92*
Landau, Richard S. 1946- *St&PR 93*
Landau, Robert 1940- *BioIn 17*
Landau, Robert I. 1933- *St&PR 93*
Landau, Robert Irwin 1933- *WhoAm 92*
Landau, Roy Neil 1931- *St&PR 93*
Landau, Saul 1936- *WhoAm 92*
Landau, Shelly 1956- *WhoAmW 93*
Landau, Sidney I. 1933- *WhoAm 92*
Landau, Siegfried 1921- *Baker 92*
Landau, Sonia 1937- *WhoAm 92*
Landau, Sybil Harriet 1937- *WhoAm 92*
Landau, Walter Loeber 1931- *WhoAm 92*
Landau, William Milton 1924- *WhoAm 92*
Landau-Crawford, Dorothy Ruth 1957- *WhoAmW 93, WhoEmL 93*
Landauer, Jay Paul 1935- *WhoAm 92*
Landauer, Jeramy Lanigan 1939- *WhoAm 92, WhoAmW 93*
Landauer, Rolf William 1927- *WhoAm 92*
Landauer, Walter E. 1923- *St&PR 93*
Landaverde, Alfredo *DcCPCAm*
Landaw, Stephen Arthur 1936- *WhoAm 92*
Landazuri Ricketts, Juan Cardinal 1913- *WhoWor 93*
Landberg, Ann Laurel 1926- *WhoAmW 93*
Landberg, George Gustaf 1939- *St&PR 93*
Lande, Alexander 1936- *WhoWor 93*
Lande, James Avra 1930- *WhoAm 92*
Lande, Jonathon G. *Law&B 92*
Lande, Lawrence Montague 1906- *WhoE 93*
Lande, Mia 1928- *St&PR 93*
Lande, Patricia Alison 1960- *WhoAmW 93*
Lande, Ruth Harriet 1929- *WhoE 93*
Landefeld, E. Kent 1933- *St&PR 93*
Landefeld, Edward Kent 1933- *WhoIns 93*
Landegger, Carl Clement 1930- *BioIn 17, WhoAm 92*
Landegger, Carl M. 1953- *St&PR 93*
Landel, Robert Davis 1940- *WhoAm 92*
Landel, Robert Franklin 1925- *WhoAm 92*
Landells, Michael B. *Law&B 92*
Landels, Shirley Marie 1952- *WhoAmW 93*
Landen, Laura L. 1945- *WhoAmW 93*
Landen, Leslie Scott 1952- *WhoEmL 93*
Landen, Robert Geran 1930- *WhoAm 92, WhoWor 93*
Landen, Sandra Joyce 1960- *WhoAmW 93*
Landenberger, Keith U. *Law&B 92*
Landeo, Luis Amador 1933- *WhoE 93*
Lander, Charles Allen 1937- *St&PR 93*
Lander, Diane *BioIn 17*
Lander, James Rollin, Jr. 1943- *WhoSSW 93*
Lander, Kathleen Mary 1932- *WhoAmW 93*
Lander, Raymond A., Jr. 1920- *St&PR 93*
Lander, Richard 1804-1834 *Expl 93*
Lander, Richard Leon 1928- *WhoAm 92*
Lander, Roy Pascoe 1935- *WhoWor 93*
Landero, Victor *BioIn 17*
Landers, Andy *BioIn 17*
Landers, Ann *BioIn 17*
Landers, Ann 1918- *WhoAm 92, WhoAmW 93*
Landers, Florence E. *AmWomPl*
Landers, James A. *St&PR 93*
Landers, Lew 1901-1962 *MiSFD 9N*
Landers, Mary K. 1905-1990 *BioIn 17*
Landers, Michael Gene 1966- *WhoSSW 93*
Landers, Michael R. 1942- *St&PR 93*
Landers, Patrick J. 1956- *St&PR 93*
Landers, Susan Mae *WhoAmW 93*
Landers, Thomas J. 1929- *WhoAm 92*
Landers, Vernette Trosper 1912- *WhoAmW 93, WhoWor 93*
Landerson, Louis d1990 *BioIn 17*
Landes, Arlene Augusta 1944- *WhoAmW 93*
Landes, David S(aul) 1924- *WhoWrEP 92*
Landes, George Miller 1928- *WhoAm 92*
Landes, John B. *St&PR 93*
Landes, John David 1942- *WhoSSW 93*
Landes, Robert N. *Law&B 92*
Landes, Robert Nathan 1930- *St&PR 93, WhoAm 92*
Landes, Ruth 1908-1991 *BioIn 17*
Landes, Sonia 1925- *WhoWrEP 92*
Landes, William-Alan 1945- *WhoWrEP 92*
Landes, William M. 1939- *WhoAm 92*
Landesberg, Janet Rubin 1952- *WhoEmL 93*
Landesberg, Joseph M. 1939- *WhoE 93*
Landesberg, Lee Jay 1948- *WhoEmL 93*
Landesberg, Steve *BioIn 17, WhoAm 92*
Landesman, Fredric Rocco 1947- *WhoAm 92*
Landesman, Heidi *WhoAmW 93*
Landesman, Linda Young 1949- *WhoE 93*
Landess, Fred S. 1933- *WhoAm 92*
Landeta, Matilde 1913- *BioIn 17*
Landfair, Billy Lou 1933- *St&PR 93*
Landgarten, Nathan 1918- *St&PR 93*
Landgraf, David C. *Law&B 92*
Landgraf, Susan Manning 1961- *WhoEmL 93*
Landgraver, Kenneth R., Jr. 1940- *St&PR 93*
Landgrebe, David Allen 1934- *WhoAm 92*
Landgrebe, George William 1941- *St&PR 93*
Landgrebe, John Allan 1937- *WhoAm 92*
Landgren, Craig Randall 1947- *WhoAm 92*
Landgren, George Lawrence 1919- *WhoAm 92*
Landgrover, John Joseph 1943- *St&PR 93*
Landguth, Daniel P. 1946- *WhoAm 92*
Landhage, Gaby *BioIn 17*
Landherr, Robert F. 1938- *St&PR 93*
Landi, Aldo G. 1950- *WhoUN 92*
Landi, Dale Michael 1938- *WhoAm 92*
Landi, Stefano 1586?-1639 *Baker 92, OxDcOp*
Landin, Myron W. 1948- *St&PR 93*
Landin, P.J. *WhoScE 91-1*
Landin, Thomas Milton 1937- *WhoAm 92, WhoE 93*
Landine, Michael J. *St&PR 93*
Landine, Robert C. *BioIn 17*
Landing, Benjamin Harrison 1920- *WhoAm 92*
Landini, Benedetto 1858-1938 *Baker 92*
Landini, Francesco c. 1325-1397 *Baker 92*
Landini, Richard George 1929- *WhoAm 92*
Landino, Franciscus c. 1325-1397 *Baker 92*
Landino, Paul *BioIn 17*
Landino, Richard Earl 1959- *WhoEmL 93*
Landino, Rita Ann 1942- *WhoAmW 93, WhoE 93*
Landis, Arthur H. 1917-1986 *ScF&FL 92*
Landis, Brenda Reinhart 1960- *WhoWrEP 92*
Landis, Carole 1919-1948 *BioIn 17*
Landis, Donald Howard 1929- *St&PR 93*
Landis, Edgar David 1932- *St&PR 93, WhoAm 92*
Landis, Elwood Winton 1928- *WhoAm 92, WhoWrEP 92*
Landis, Fred 1923- *WhoAm 92*
Landis, Fred Simon 1943- *WhoWor 93*
Landis, Frederick 1912-1990 *BioIn 17*
Landis, Gary Dean 1940- *WhoAm 92*
Landis, Geoffrey A. *ScF&FL 92*
Landis, George Arthur 1940- *WhoAm 92*
Landis, James David *BioIn 17*
Landis, James David 1942- *WhoAm 92*
Landis, James Richard, Jr. 1930- *WhoWrEP 92*
Landis, Jay L. 1930- *St&PR 93*
Landis, John 1950- *MiSFD 9*
Landis, John David 1950- *WhoAm 92*
Landis, John William 1917- *WhoAm 92*
Landis, Keith Allen 1964- *WhoE 93*
Landis, Lynn Lamberton 1949- *WhoEmL 93, WhoSSW 93*
Landis, Marie 1935?- *ScF&FL 92*
Landis, Mark Glenn 1942- *St&PR 93*
Landis, Pamela Ann Youngman 1941- *WhoE 93*
Landis, Peggy June 1964- *WhoAmW 93*
Landis, Richard Gordon 1920- *WhoWor 93*
Landis, Robert Kumler, III 1953- *WhoE 93, WhoEmL 93*
Landis, Robert M. 1920- *WhoAm 92*
Landis, Sharyn Branscome 1942- *WhoAmW 93*
Landis, Thomas Shepler 1927- *St&PR 93*
Landis-Groom, Eileen Elinor 1952- *WhoAmW 93*
Landisman, Mark 1928- *WhoAm 92, WhoSSW 93, WhoWor 93*
Landivar, Rafael 1731-1793 *DcMexL*
Landman, Bette Emeline 1937- *WhoAm 92, WhoAmW 93*
Landman, Lou 1927- *St&PR 93*
Landmann, Axel W. 1929- *WhoScE 91-1*
Landmark, P. *WhoScE 91-4*
Lando, Barbara Marcino 1940- *WhoAmW 93*
Lando, Jerome Burton 1932- *WhoAm 92*
Lando, Joe *BioIn 17*
Lando, Robert 1915- *St&PR 93*
Lando, Robert N. 1915- *WhoAm 92*
Landolfi, Tommaso 1908-1979 *ScF&FL 92*
Landolphi, Suzi *BioIn 17*
Landolt, Arlo Udell 1935- *WhoAm 92, WhoSSW 93*
Landolt, Dieter 1938- *WhoScE 91-4*
Landolt, Elias 1926- *WhoScE 91-4*
Landolt, Robert George 1939- *WhoAm 92, WhoSSW 93*
Landolt-Bohus, Eleanor Ruth 1954- *WhoEmL 93*
Landon, Alf *BioIn 17*
Landon, Alfred M. 1887-1987 *PolPar*
Landon, Christa 1921-1977 *Baker 92*
Landon, Cindy *BioIn 17*
Landon, D.N. 1936- *WhoScE 91-1*
Landon, Forrest M. 1933- *WhoAm 92*
Landon, Forrest Malcolm 1933- *St&PR 93*
Landon, Fred Barry 1951- *WhoE 93*
Landon, H(arold) C(handler) Robbins 1926- *Baker 92*
Landon, H. Ray 1935- *St&PR 93*
Landon, John Campbell 1937- *St&PR 93, WhoAm 92*
Landon, John William 1937- *WhoAm 92, WhoSSW 93, WhoWor 93*
Landon, Letitia Elizabeth 1802-1838 *BioIn 17*
Landon, Michael *BioIn 17*
Landon, Michael 1936-1991 *AnObit 1991, ConTFT 10, News 92*
Landon, Michael 1937-1991 *MiSFD 9N*
Landon, Pierre Albert 1932- *WhoWor 93*
Landon, R. Kirk 1929- *St&PR 93*
Landon, Robert Gray 1928- *WhoAm 92*
Landon, Robert Kirkwood 1929- *WhoAm 92, WhoIns 93*
Landon, Sealand Whitney 1896- *WhoAm 92*
Landon, Stuart *St&PR 93*
Landor, Walter Savage 1775-1864 *BioIn 17*
Landormy, Paul (Charles-Rene) 1869-1943 *Baker 92*
Landovsky, Rosemary Reid 1933- *WhoAmW 93, WhoWor 93*
Landow, George Paul 1940- *WhoAm 92*
Landowne, Robert A. 1931- *WhoE 93*
Landowska, Wanda 1879-1959 *PolBiDi*
Landowska, Wanda (Alexandra) 1879-1959 *Baker 92*
Landowski, Marcel 1915- *OxDcOp*
Landowski, Marcel (Francois Paul) 1915- *Baker 92*
Landowski, W.-L. 1899-1959 *Baker 92*
Landram, Christina Louella 1922- *WhoAmW 93*
Landre, Guillaume (Louis Frederic) 1905-1968 *Baker 92*
Landre, Willem 1874-1948 *Baker 92*
Landreneau, Janis Suchand 1948- *WhoEmL 93, WhoSSW 93*
Landreneau, Rodney Edmund, Jr. 1929- *WhoSSW 93, WhoWor 93*
Landres, Linda Grey *Law&B 92*
Landres, Paul 1912- *BioIn 17*
Landreth, Bill 1964- *ConAu 138*
Landreth, Charles Burnet 1947- *St&PR 93*
Landreth, Delia 1938- *WhoAmW 93*
Landreth, Kenneth Samuel 1947- *WhoSSW 93*
Landreth, Mark Duane 1954- *WhoSSW 93*
Landrey, Margaret M. *Law&B 92*
Landriault, Jacques Emile 1921- *WhoAm 92*
Landrieu, Mary 1955- *WhoAm 92*
Landrieu, Mary L. 1955- *WhoAmW 93, WhoSSW 93*
Landrieu, Pierre Raoul Henri 1941- *St&PR 93*
Landrigan, Philip John 1942- *WhoAm 92*
Landriscina, Ben 1944- *St&PR 93*
Landron, Michel John 1946- *WhoE 93*
Landrum, Diedra Gansloser 1952- *WhoEmL 93*
Landrum, Larry James 1943- *WhoWor 93*
Landrum, Phil M. 1907-1990 *BioIn 17*
Landrum, Rufus Jackson 1943- *WhoSSW 93*
Landrum-Brummund, Frances Ann 1918- *WhoAmW 93*
Landry, Alfred Ronald 1936- *WhoE 93*
Landry, Andrew *Law&B 92*
Landry, Brenda Lee 1942- *WhoAmW 93*
Landry, Connie P. 1946- *St&PR 93*
Landry, Debby Ann 1963- *WhoAmW 93*
Landry, Donald Camille 1938- *WhoSSW 93*
Landry, Dorothy Autry 1949- *WhoAmW 93*
Landry, Esther Frances 1935- *WhoE 93*
Landry, G.Y. 1938- *St&PR 93*
Landry, Jane Lorenz 1936- *WhoAm 92*
Landry, Janie Pool 1951- *WhoAmW 93*
Landry, Jean Eda 1950- *WhoE 93*
Landry, Jerome A. 1943- *WhoAm 92*
Landry, Joan Adele 1933- *St&PR 93*
Landry, Joan Adell 1933- *WhoAmW 93*
Landry, John T., Jr. *Law&B 92*
Landry, Keith G. *Law&B 92*
Landry, Lawrence S. 1956- *St&PR 93*
Landry, Monique 1937- *WhoAm 92, WhoAmW 93*
Landry, Napoleon-P. 1884-1956 *BioIn 17*
Landry, Rebecca Tucker 1960- *WhoAmW 93*
Landry, Rejean 1952- *St&PR 93*
Landry, Robert Edward 1929- *WhoAm 92*
Landry, Robert J. 1946- *St&PR 93*
Landry, Robert James 1950- *WhoEmL 93*
Landry, Robert John 1913-1991 *BioIn 17*
Landry, Robert Raymond 1947- *WhoEmL 93*
Landry, Roger D. 1934- *WhoWor 93*
Landry, Ronald Jude 1943- *WhoSSW 93*
Landry, Sara Griffin 1920- *WhoAmW 93*
Landry, Thomas Henry 1946- *St&PR 93, WhoAm 92*
Landry, Tom *BioIn 17*
Landry, Tom 1924- *WhoAm 92*
Landry, Yves 1947- *WhoScE 91-2*
Landsberg, Dennis Robert 1948- *WhoAm 92, WhoWor 93*
Landsberg, Donnamarie A. *Law&B 92*
Landsberg, Helmut Erich 1906-1985 *BioIn 17*
Landsberg, Jerry 1933- *WhoAm 92*
Landsberg, Johanna Dobrot 1940- *WhoAmW 93*
Landsberg, Marc *BioIn 17*
Landsberg, Margaretha Elizabeth 1925- *WhoWor 93*
Landsberg, Peter Theodore *WhoScE 91-1*
Landsberger, David 1948- *St&PR 93*
Landsberger, Henry A. 1926- *WhoAm 92*
Landsberger, Kurt 1920- *St&PR 93*
Landsbergis, Vytautas *BioIn 17*
Landsburg, Alan 1933- *ConTFT 10, MiSFD 9*
Landsiedel, William James *Law&B 92*
Landske, Dorothy Suzanne 1937- *WhoAmW 93*
Landsman, Joseph K. 1934- *WhoWrEP 92*
Landsman, Samuel N.B. *ScF&FL 92*
Landsman, Samuel N.B. 1950- *WhoWrEP 92*
Landsman, Sandy 1950- *ScF&FL 92*
Landsman, Theodore 1922-1990 *BioIn 17*
Landsmann, Leanna 1946- *WhoAm 92, WhoWrEP 92*
Landstrom, Mark R. *Law&B 92*
Landt, Myrna Rivers 1944- *WhoAmW 93*
Landtman, Gunnar 1878-1940 *IntDcAn*
Landua, Herman H., Jr. 1945- *WhoSSW 93*

Landureth, Lewis James 1943- WhoSSW 93
Landuyt, Bernard Francis 1907- WhoAm 92, WhoWor 93
Land-Weber, Ellen 1943- WhoAm 92
Landwehr, Arthur John 1934- WhoWor 93
Landwehr, Gottfried 1929- WhoWor 93
Landwehr, William Charles 1941- WhoAm 92
Landy, Burton Aaron 1929- WhoAm 92
Landy, Eugene BioIn 17
Landy, Eugene W. 1933- St&PR 93
Landy, Joseph P. 1932- St&PR 93, WhoAm 92
Landy, Marcia 1931- WhoE 93
Landy, Maurice 1913- WhoAm 92
Landy, Richard Allen 1931- WhoAm 92
Landzberg, Joel Serge 1958- WhoE 93
Landzettel, Robert W. 1935- St&PR 93
Lane, Adelaide Irene 1939- WhoE 93
Lane, Alvin Huey, Jr. 1942- WhoAm 92
Lane, Alvin S. 1918- WhoAm 92
Lane, Andrew MiSFD 9
Lane, Angela Gail 1955- St&PR 93
Lane, Ann J. 1931- ScF&FL 92
Lane, Ann Judith 1931- WhoAmW 93
Lane, Arthur Alan 1945- WhoAm 92
Lane, Barbara Miller 1934- WhoAm 92
Lane, Bensonetta Tipton AfrAmBi [port]
Lane, Bernard Paul 1938- WhoE 93
Lane, Bertha Palmer AmWomPl
Lane, Brian M. 1951- St&PR 93, WhoEmL 93
Lane, Bridget 1953- WhoWrEP 92
Lane, Bruce Stuart 1932- WhoAm 92
Lane, Burton 1912- Baker 92, BioIn 17, WhoAm 92
Lane, Carol Elaine 1935- WhoAmW 93
Lane, Carol Martin 1957- WhoAmW 93
Lane, Carolyn 1926- ScF&FL 92
Lane, Carolyn Blocker 1926- WhoWrEP 92
Lane, Charles BioIn 17, MiSFD 9
Lane, Charles 1953- ConBlB 3 [port]
Lane, Charles R. Law&B 92
Lane, Charles Stuart 1924- WhoWor 93
Lane, Chris AmWomPl
Lane, Clinton F. 1944- St&PR 93
Lane, Dana Ellis 1946- St&PR 93
Lane, Daniel McNeel 1936- WhoSSW 93
Lane, Daryl ScF&FL 92
Lane, David Alan 1958- WhoEmL 93
Lane, David Oliver 1931- WhoAm 92
Lane, David (Stuart) ConAu 39NR
Lane, Debi BioIn 17
Lane, Dianne Rhea 1950- WhoAmW 93
Lane, Dick 1928- BioIn 17
Lane, Donald Scott 1958- WhoSSW 93
Lane, Eastwood 1879-1951 Baker 92
Lane, Edward Alphonso Richard 1953- WhoEmL 93
Lane, Edward Wood, Jr. 1911- WhoAm 92
Lane, Elizabeth Ann 1959- WhoE 93, WhoEmL 93
Lane, Eric 1954- St&PR 93
Lane, Ernest Edward, III 1948- WhoE 93
Lane, Eugene Numa 1936- WhoAm 92
Lane, Fielding H. 1926- WhoAm 92
Lane, Fitz Hugh 1804-1865 BioIn 17
Lane, Frank Charles 1896-1981 BiDAMSp 1989
Lane, Frederick Carpenter 1949- WhoAm 92
Lane, Frederick Stanley 1915- WhoAm 92
Lane, G. William 1921- St&PR 93
Lane, Gary Law&B 92
Lane, Gary L. Law&B 92
Lane, Gary Stephen 1941- WhoE 93
Lane, Geoffrey Dawson 1918- BioIn 17
Lane, George Edward Law&B 92
Lane, Gertrude Battles BioIn 17
Lane, Gilbert Manuel 1938- WhoE 93
Lane, Gloria Julian 1932- WhoAmW 93, WhoWor 93
Lane, Grace Prevost 1937- WhoAmW 93
Lane, Hana Umlauf 1946- WhoAm 92
Lane, Harold Edwin 1913- WhoAm 92
Lane, Harriet 1830-1903 BioIn 17
Lane, Iris Mary 1934- WhoAmW 93
Lane, J. Gary Law&B 92
Lane, James A. 1924- BioIn 17
Lane, James Franklin 1931- WhoAm 92
Lane, James G., Jr. 1934- St&PR 93
Lane, James Garland, Jr. 1934- WhoAm 92
Lane, James Hamilton 1945- WhoSSW 93
Lane, James M. 1929- St&PR 93
Lane, James McConkey 1929- WhoAm 92
Lane, James Weldon 1926- WhoE 93, WhoWor 93
Lane, Jan-Erik 1946- ConAu 138
Lane, Jane 1905-1978 ScF&FL 92
Lane, Jani BioIn 17
Lane, Jean Mary 1950- WhoAmW 93
Lane, Jennifer Ruth 1954- WhoAm 92
Lane, Jerry ConAu 37NR, MajAI
Lane, John ScF&FL 92
Lane, John Dennis 1921- WhoAm 92
Lane, John M. 1941- St&PR 93
Lane, John Rodger 1944- WhoAm 92
Lane, John S. 1935- St&PR 93, WhoIns 93
Lane, John Thomas 1942- WhoAm 92
Lane, Joseph C. 1953- St&PR 93
Lane, Jules V. WhoIns 93
Lane, Julia A. 1927- WhoAmW 93
Lane, Kathleen Margaret 1946- WhoAmW 93
Lane, Keith 1945- WhoIns 93
Lane, Kelly Flemming 1964- WhoE 93
Lane, Kenneth Edwin 1928- WhoAm 92
Lane, Kenneth Jay BioIn 17
Lane, Kenneth Jay 1932- WhoAm 92
Lane, Kenneth Robert 1942- WhoE 93, WhoWor 93
Lane, Kevin Gordon 1964- WhoSSW 93
Lane, Kim BioIn 17
Lane, Laura A. Law&B 92
Lane, Laurence William 1890-1967 BioIn 17
Lane, Laurence William, Jr. 1919- WhoAm 92
Lane, Lawrence Jubin 1927- WhoAm 92, WhoWor 93
Lane, Leonard C. 1919- St&PR 93
Lane, Leonard Charles 1919- WhoAm 92
Lane, Lois M. White 1914- WhoWrEP 92
Lane, Lois N. 1948- WhoAm 92
Lane, Louis 1923- Baker 92, WhoAm 92
Lane, Loyd Carlton 1944- St&PR 93
Lane, Lupino 1892-1959 QDrFCA 92 [port]
Lane, M. Travis 1934- WhoCanL 92
Lane, Magda SweetSg A [port]
Lane, Malcolm Daniel 1930- WhoAm 92
Lane, Malia WhoWrEP 92
Lane, Marc J(ay) 1946- WhoWrEP 92
Lane, Margaret 1907- BioIn 17
Lane, Margaret Anna Smith 1918- WhoAmW 93
Lane, Margaret Beynon Taylor 1919- WhoAmW 93
Lane, Marie Irene 1944- WhoAmW 93
Lane, Marilyn E. 1931- St&PR 93
Lane, Marilyn Edith 1931- WhoAm 92
Lane, Marion Sue 1944- WhoWrEP 92
Lane, Mark 1927- WhoAm 92, WhoWrEP 92
Lane, Marvin Maskall, Jr. 1934- WhoAm 92
Lane, Marvin Maskell, Jr. 1934- St&PR 93
Lane, Mary Frances 1955- WhoAmW 93
Lane, Mary Hill 1943- WhoAmW 93
Lane, Mary Winston 1923- WhoAmW 93
Lane, Maureen Dorothea 1943- WhoAmW 93
Lane, Megan ScF&FL 92
Lane, Melvin B. 1922- St&PR 93
Lane, Melvin Bell 1922- WhoAm 92
Lane, Michael H. 1943- St&PR 93
Lane, Mills 1912-1989 BioIn 17
Lane, Montague 1929- WhoAm 92
Lane, Morgan E. 1907-1990 BioIn 17
Lane, Nancy 1938- WhoAm 92, WhoWrEP 92
Lane, Nancy Erica 1954- WhoAmW 93
Lane, Nancy Jane WhoScE 91-1
Lane, Nancy L. BioIn 17
Lane, Nathan 1921- WhoE 93
Lane, Nathan 1956- ConTFT 10
Lane, Neal Francis 1938- WhoAm 92
Lane, Neil A. 1931- St&PR 93
Lane, Newton A. 1915- St&PR 93
Lane, Newton Alexander 1915- WhoAm 92
Lane, Nora SweetSg B [port]
Lane, Patricia Louise 1950- WhoEmL 93
Lane, Patricia Nadine 1939- St&PR 93
Lane, Patricia S. 1932- WhoSSW 93
Lane, Patrick 1939- WhoAm 92, WhoCanL 92
Lane, Paul G. Law&B 92
Lane, Pinkie Gordon WhoWrEP 92
Lane, R. Richard Law&B 92
Lane, Randy 1952- WhoWrEP 92
Lane, Rebecca Massie WhoSSW 93
Lane, Richard Spencer 1935- WhoScE 91-1
Lane, Robert B. 1938- St&PR 93
Lane, Robert Casey Law&B 92
Lane, Robert Casey 1932- WhoAm 92
Lane, Robert Edwards 1917- WhoE 93
Lane, Robert Gerhart 1931- WhoAm 92
Lane, Robert L., Jr. Law&B 92
Lane, Robert Myers 1939- St&PR 93
Lane, Robin 1947- WhoAmW 93
Lane, Robyn Law&B 92
Lane, Ronald A. 1950- St&PR 93
Lane, Ronald Alan Law&B 92
Lane, Rose Wilder 1886-1968 AmWomPl, BioIn 17
Lane, Sarah Marie 1946- WhoAmW 93
Lane, Shari Lea 1950- WhoAmW 93
Lane, Sherry 1942- WhoE 93
Lane, Steve Allen 1935- WhoSSW 93
Lane, Steven E. Law&B 92
Lane, Susan Okamoto 1952- WhoAmW 93
Lane, Sylvia WhoAm 92
Lane, Terence James WhoScE 91-1
Lane, Thomas John 1933- WhoSSW 93
Lane, Vicki 1949- WhoSSW 93
Lane, Vincent BioIn 17
Lane, Virginia Carolyn Gay 1951- WhoAmW 93, WhoEmL 93
Lane, Warren C., Jr. 1923- WhoAm 92
Lane, Wendy Evrard 1951- WhoAm 92
Lane, Wendy M. Law&B 92
Lane, William Arthur 1958- WhoEmL 93, WhoSSW 93, WhoWor 93
Lane, William Carr Law&B 92
Lane, William Henry 1825?-1852 BioIn 17
Lane, William Kenneth 1922- WhoWor 93
Lane, William M. WhoAm 92
Lane, William Noble, III 1943- WhoAm 92
Lane, William Robert 1948- St&PR 93
Lane, William W. 1934- St&PR 93, WhoAm 92
Lane-Arrons, Marion Jean 1928- WhoE 93
Lanegran, David A(ndrew) 1941- ConAu 37NR
Lanegran, Virginia Eleanor 1930- WhoAmW 93
Lane-Oreiro, Laverne Teresa 1951- WhoAmW 93, WhoWor 93
Laner, Richard Warren 1933- WhoAm 92
Lane-Reticker, Edward 1926- St&PR 93, WhoAm 92
Lanes, David R. St&PR 93
Lanes, Selma Gordon 1929- WhoAm 92
Lanese, Anthony L., Jr. 1928- St&PR 93
Lanese, Herbert Joseph 1945- St&PR 93
Lanese, Jill Renee 1952- WhoE 93
Lane Stone, Nancy Ann 1945- WhoAmW 93
Laneuville, Eric MiSFD 9
Laney, D. Randy 1954- St&PR 93
Laney, David Randy 1954- WhoAm 92
Laney, Donna Jean 1959- WhoAmW 93
Laney, Frances T. ScF&FL 92
Laney, James Thomas 1927- WhoAm 92, WhoSSW 93
Laney, Landy B. 1932- WhoAm 92
Laney, Michael L. 1945- WhoAm 92
Laney, Sandra Eileen 1943- WhoAmW 93
Lanfeld, Alvin Jerome 1927- St&PR 93
Lanferman, Walter R. Law&B 92
Lanfield, Sidney 1898-1972 MiSFD 9N
Lanford, John C. 1930- St&PR 93
Lanford, Luke Dean 1922- WhoAm 92
Lanford, Oscar Erasmus, Jr. 1914- WhoAm 92
Lanford, Oscar Erasmus, III 1940- WhoAm 92, WhoWor 93
Lanford, William Armistead 1944- WhoE 93
Lanford, William Ernest, II 1945- WhoSSW 93
Lanford, William H. 1935- WhoIns 93
Lanfranchi, Giorgio A. 1938- WhoScE 91-3
Lanfranchi, Ronald Gregory 1953- WhoE 93
Lang, A. Heikki 1933- WhoScE 91-4
Lang, Abigail Sills 1944- WhoAmW 93
Lang, Alan E. 1933- St&PR 93
Lang, Andrew 1844-1912 BioIn 17, ConAu 137, IntDcAn, MajAI [port]
Lang, Benjamin (Johnson) 1837-1909 Baker 92
Lang, Bernard Albert 1936- St&PR 93
Lang, Bruce T. 1944- St&PR 93
Lang, C. Max 1937- WhoAm 92, WhoE 93
Lang, Cecil Yelverton 1920- WhoAm 92, WhoWrEP 92
Lang, Charles B. 1902- BioIn 17
Lang, Charles B. 1940- St&PR 93
Lang, Charles William 1943- WhoE 93
Lang, Christian Bernd 1948- WhoWor 93
Lang, Clyde Everett 1943- St&PR 93
Lang, Colin M. 1935- St&PR 93
Lang, Daniel 1935- BioIn 17
Lang, Daniel S. 1935- WhoAm 92
Lang, David 1957- Baker 92
Lang, David Wayne 1954- WhoE 93, WhoEmL 93
Lang, Donald F. 1930- WhoIns 93
Lang, Eddie 1902-1933 Baker 92
Lang, Edith AmWomPl
Lang, Edward J. 1937- St&PR 93
Lang, Ellen Frances Law&B 92
Lang, Erich Karl 1929- WhoAm 92
Lang, Eugene M. 1919- BioIn 17, WhoAm 92
Lang, Eugene Michael 1919- St&PR 93
Lang, Francis Harover 1907- WhoAm 92
Lang, Frank Alexander 1934- St&PR 93
Lang, Frederick Webber 1924- St&PR 93
Lang, Fritz BioIn 17
Lang, Fritz 1890-1976 MiSFD 9N
Lang, Galen 1947- WhoAsAP 91
Lang, Garland Herbert 1922- WhoSSW 93
Lang, George 1924- WhoAm 92
Lang, George A., Jr. 1925- St&PR 93
Lang, Gerhard 1925- WhoE 93
Lang, Gernot 1936- WhoScE 91-4
Lang, Gregor 1900-1988 ScF&FL 92
Lang, H. Jack 1904- WhoAm 92
Lang, H. Warren, Jr. 1928- St&PR 93
Lang, Hans 1908- Baker 92
Lang, Hans Joachim 1912- WhoAm 92
Lang, Helga M. Therese 1928- WhoAmW 93
Lang, Henry Spencer 1947- St&PR 93
Lang, I. Ward Law&B 92
Lang, I. Ward 1929- St&PR 93
Lang, Ian WhoScE 91-1
Lang, Ian Bruce 1940- WhoWor 93
Lang, Istvan 1933- Baker 92
Lang, Istvan 1946- WhoScE 91-4
Lang, Jack BioIn 17
Lang, Jacques 1938- WhoScE 91-2
Lang, James F. 1934- St&PR 93
Lang, James Robert 1943- St&PR 93, WhoAm 92
Lang, Jean McKinney 1921- WhoAmW 93
Lang, Jeffrey 1941- WhoSSW 93
Lang, Jeffrey Francis 1942- St&PR 93
Lang, Jenifer Harvey 1951- ConAu 138
Lang, John Calvin 1942- WhoSSW 93
Lang, John Cleveland 1940- WhoAm 92
Lang, John Francis 1915- WhoE 93, WhoWor 93
Lang, John S. BioIn 17
Lang, Josephine 1815-1880 BioIn 17
Lang, Josephine (Caroline) 1815-1880 Baker 92
Lang, K.D. BioIn 17, NewYTBS 92 [port]
lang, k.d. 1961- Baker 92, WhoAm 92, WhoAmW 93
Lang, K. D. 1962?- CurBio 92 [port]
Lang, Katherine Anne 1947- WhoAmW 93
Lang, King ScF&FL 92
Lang, Lanny R. 1958- St&PR 93
Lang, Leonard W. 1932- St&PR 93
Lang, Lillian Owen 1915- WhoSSW 93
Lang, Margaret Charles WhoSSW 93
Lang, Margaret Florence 1953- WhoAmW 93
Lang, Margaret Mary 1959- WhoSSW 93
Lang, Margaret Ruthven 1867-1972 Baker 92, BioIn 17
Lang, Margo Terzian WhoAm 92
Lang, Mary Elizabeth 1947- WhoE 93
Lang, Mary Louise Otto 1955- WhoAmW 93
Lang, Miriam 1915- WhoWrEP 92
Lang, Neil Stephan 1942- St&PR 93
Lang, Norton David 1940- WhoAm 92
Lang, Otto E. 1932- WhoAm 92
Lang, Patricia K. 1947- St&PR 93
Lang, Paul Henry 1901- Baker 92
Lang, Paul Henry 1901-1991 BioIn 17
Lang, Paul Joseph 1947- WhoE 93
Lang, Paul Louis 1940- St&PR 93, WhoAm 92
Lang, Pearl 1922- WhoAm 92
Lang, Perry MiSFD 9
Lang, Philip David 1929- WhoAm 92
Lang, Richard MiSFD 9
Lang, Richard David Law&B 92
Lang, Richard Lewis Law&B 92
Lang, Richard V. Law&B 92
Lang, Richard W., Jr. 1950- St&PR 93
Lang, Richard Warren 1949- WhoAm 92
Lang, Robert E. 1941- St&PR 93
Lang, Robert Howard, Jr. 1935- St&PR 93
Lang, Robert Todd 1924- St&PR 93, WhoAm 92
Lang, Rocky MiSFD 9
Lang, Ronald Anthony 1936- WhoAm 92
Lang, Ronald J. 1943- St&PR 93
Lang, Scott H. 1946- St&PR 93
Lang, Scott William 1959- WhoE 93, WhoEmL 93
Lang, Serge 1927- WhoAm 92
Lang, Simon 1934- ScF&FL 92
Lang, Stanley Albert 1944- WhoE 93
Lang, Stephen BioIn 17
Lang, Susan S. BioIn 17
Lang, Susan S. 1950- ConAu 136
Lang, T.T. ConAu 38NR, MajAI
Lang, Terence Henry 1937- St&PR 93
Lang, Thompson Hughes 1946- WhoAm 92
Lang, Todd Brentley 1960- WhoSSW 93
Lang, Victor John, Jr. 1936- St&PR 93
Lang, Victoria Winifred 1955- WhoEmL 93
Lang, Walter 1896-1966 Baker 92
Lang, Walter 1898-1972 MiSFD 9N
Lang, William Charles 1944- WhoAm 92
Lang, William Edward 1952- WhoWor 93
Lang, William Joseph 1932- St&PR 93
Lang, William Warner 1926- WhoAm 92
Lang, Winfried 1941- WhoUN 92
Langacker, Paul George 1946- WhoE 93
Langacker, Ronald Wayne 1942- WhoAm 92

Langan, Glenn 1917-1991 *BioIn 17*
Langan, John Patrick 1940- *WhoAm 92*
Langan, Keith E. *Law&B 92*
Langan, Kevin J. 1955- *WhoAm 92*
Langan, Marie A. 1943- *WhoAmW 93*
Langan, Roger Flemming 1961- *WhoE 93*
Langan, Timothy J. *Law&B 92*
Langaney, Andre 1942- *WhoScE 91-4*
Langauer-Lewowicka, Henryka Ludmila 1922- *WhoScE 91-4*
Langbacka, Ralf Runar 1932- *WhoWor 93*
Langbaum, Robert Woodrow 1924- *WhoAm 92, WhoSSW 93, WhoWrEP 92*
Langbein, John Harriss 1941- *WhoAm 92, WhoE 93*
Langberg, Diane Mandt 1948- *WhoAmW 93*
Langbien, Fred Henry 1952- *WhoAm 92*
Langbo, Arnold Gordon 1937- *St&PR 93, WhoAm 92*
Langbort, Polly 1933- *WhoAmW 93*
Langdale, Harley, Jr. 1914- *St&PR 93*
Langdale, John J. 1927- *St&PR 93*
Langdale, Noah Noel, Jr. 1920- *WhoAm 92*
Langdale, Robert Harley 1948- *St&PR 93*
Langdale, W.P. 1921- *St&PR 93*
Langdana, Farrokh Keki 1958- *WhoE 93*
Lang Dazhong *WhoAsAP 91*
Langdell, Robert Dana 1924- *WhoAm 92*
Langdon, Barbara Jane 1947- *St&PR 93*
Langdon, Edward A. 1951- *St&PR 93*
Langdon, Frank Corriston 1919- *WhoAm 92*
Langdon, George Dorland, Jr. 1933- *WhoAm 92, WhoE 93*
Langdon, Glen George, Jr. 1936- *WhoAm 92*
Langdon, Harry 1884-1944 *IntDcF 2-3 [port], QDrFCA 92 [port]*
Langdon, Herschel Garrett 1905- *WhoAm 92*
Langdon, Ina M. 1920- *St&PR 93*
Langdon, James Lloyd 1918- *St&PR 93*
Langdon, James Robert 1919- *St&PR 93*
Langdon, John O. *Law&B 92*
Langdon, Karen Sims 1951- *WhoAmW 93*
Langdon, Larry 1940- *WhoWrEP 92*
Langdon, Marion *AmWomPl*
Langdon, Michael 1920-1991 *Baker 92, OxDcOp*
Langdon, Molly Jean 1950- *WhoAmW 93*
Langdon, Norman E. 1888-1967 *ScF&FL 92*
Langdon, Richard c. 1729-1803 *Baker 92*
Langdon, Vicki N. 1960- *WhoSSW 93*
Lange *Baker 92*
Lange, Alan B. 1932- *St&PR 93*
Lange, Aloysia *OxDcOp*
Lange, Arthur Ernest 1920- *St&PR 93*
Lange, Carl G. 1954- *St&PR 93*
Lange, Carl James 1925- *WhoAm 92*
Lange, Chadwick Stephens 1938- *St&PR 93*
Lange, Clifford E. 1935- *WhoAm 92*
Lange, Daniel de 1841-1918 *Baker 92*
Lange, David 1938- *WhoAm 92*
Lange, David O. 1939- *St&PR 93*
Lange, David Russell 1942- *DcTwHis, WhoAsAP 91*
Lange, Deborah Ann 1962- *WhoSSW 93*
Lange, Dieter Ernst 1933- *WhoScE 91-3*
Lange, Dwaine Charles 1950- *WhoSSW 93*
Lange, Edward 1931- *WhoScE 91-4*
Lange, Edward Niles 1935- *WhoAm 92*
Lange, Francisco Curt 1903- *Baker 92*
Lange, Fred J., Jr. *Law&B 92*
Lange, Fred Joseph, Jr. 1950- *St&PR 93*
Lange, Frederick Edward, Jr. 1946- *WhoEmL 93*
Lange, Gerald William 1946- *WhoWrEP 92*
Lange, Gustav 1830-1889 *Baker 92*
Lange, Helmut 1940- *WhoWor 93*
Lange, Hope 1938- *WhoAm 92*
Lange, Jack Damgaard 1906- *WhoWor 93*
Lange, James Braxton 1937- *WhoAm 92*
Lange, Jane Louise 1947- *WhoAmW 93*
Lange, Jerzy Zygmunt 1923- *WhoScE 91-4*
Lange, Jessica *BioIn 17*
Lange, Jessica 1949- *HolBB [port], IntDcF 2-3 [port], WhoAm 92, WhoAmW 93*
Lange, John *ConAu 40NR*
Lange, John F. *ScF&FL 92*
Lange, Joseph 1751-1831 See Weber, Aloysia 1759?-1839 *OxDcOp*
Lange, Joseph 1855-1935 *BioIn 17*
Lange, Karen Ellen 1938- *St&PR 93*
Lange, Katherine JoAnn 1957- *WhoAmW 93, WhoWor 93*
Lange, Krister Y. 1945- *WhoScE 91-4*
Lange, Kurt Hermann 1919- *WhoWor 93*
Lange, Lawrence Robert 1955- *WhoEmL 93*
Lange, Lene 1948- *WhoScE 91-2*
Lange, Lester Henry 1924- *WhoAm 92*
Lange, Lois Jean 1931- *WhoSSW 93*
Lange, Lowell William 1928- *BiDAMSp 1989*
Lange, Lynette Patricia 1964- *WhoAmW 93*
Lange, Michael *MiSFD 9*
Lange, Morten 1919- *WhoScE 91-2*
Lange, Nancy Post 1950- *WhoE 93*
Lange, Norman 1951- *St&PR 93*
Lange, Oliver 1927- *ScF&FL 92*
Lange, Oscar Richard 1904-1965 *BioIn 17*
Lange, Oskar 1904-1965 *PolBiDi*
Lange, Otto Ludwig 1927- *WhoScE 91-3*
Lange, Phil C. 1914- *WhoAm 92*
Lange, Phillip F. 1947- *St&PR 93*
Lange, Rainer Horst 1937- *WhoScE 91-3*
Lange, Ralph A. *BioIn 17*
Lange, Reinhardt J. 1949- *St&PR 93*
Lange, Richard P. *Law&B 92*
Lange, Robert Dale 1920- *WhoAm 92, WhoSSW 93*
Lange, Samuel de 1811-1884 *Baker 92*
Lange, Samuel de 1840-1911 *Baker 92*
Lange, Stephan Charles 1950- *WhoE 93*
Lange, Stephen Mark 1957- *WhoEmL 93*
Lange, Steven Donald 1955- *WhoEmL 93*
Lange, Susan Alice 1947- *WhoAmW 93*
Lange, Ted *MiSFD 9, WhoAm 92*
Lange, Victor 1908- *WhoAm 92*
Lange, William J. *Law&B 92*
Lange, Wouter 1937- *WhoScE 91-3*
Lange, Wulfhard 1940- *WhoScE 91-3*
Lange-Asschenfeldt, Henning *WhoScE 91-3*
Langel, Robert Allan, III 1937- *WhoAm 92*
Langel, Vernon Peter 1931- *St&PR 93*
Langelaar, J. *WhoScE 91-3*
Langella, Frank 1940- *WhoAm 92*
Langella, Timothy J. *Law&B 92*
Lange-Muller, Peter Erasmus 1850-1926 *Baker 92*
Langenbeck, Konrad H. 1932- *WhoScE 91-3*
Langenberg, Christopher Melvin 1946- *St&PR 93*
Langenberg, Donald Newton 1932- *WhoAm 92, WhoE 93, WhoWor 93*
Langenberg, Frederick Charles 1927- *St&PR 93, WhoAm 92*
Langenderfer, Harold Quentin 1925- *WhoAm 92*
Langenderfer, Randall Lee 1957- *WhoEmL 93*
Langendoen, Donald Terence 1939- *WhoAm 92*
Langendorff, Frieda 1868-1947 *Baker 92*
Langeneck, Wolfgang 1962- *WhoWor 93*
Langenfeld, Douglas Eugene 1952- *WhoAm 92*
Langenfeld, Marian Stanislaw 1938- *WhoWor 93*
Langenfeld, Michel 1946- *WhoScE 91-2*
Langenfeld-Minasian, Christine M. *Law&B 92*
Langenhahn, Lyle E. 1933- *St&PR 93*
Langenheim, Edward Priest 1940- *St&PR 93*
Langenheim, Jean Harmon 1925- *WhoAmW 93*
Langenheim, Ralph Louis, Jr. 1922- *WhoAm 92*
Langenheim, Roger A. *Law&B 92*
Langenskiold, Tord 1955- *WhoScE 91-4*
Langenthal, Stephen R. *Law&B 92*
Langenus, Gustave 1883-1957 *Baker 92*
Langenwalter, Paul Edward, II 1948- *WhoEmL 93*
Langenwalter, Robert George 1924- *St&PR 93*
Langer, Alan S. *Law&B 92*
Langer, Alfred C. 1928- *St&PR 93*
Langer, Amy Schiffman 1954- *WhoE 93*
Langer, Andrew J. *WhoAm 92*
Langer, Arthur Mark 1936- *WhoAm 92, WhoE 93, WhoWor 93*
Langer, Bruce Alden 1953- *WhoEmL 93*
Langer, Carlton E. *Law&B 92*
Langer, Carlton Earl 1954- *St&PR 93*
Langer, David 1935- *St&PR 93*
Langer, Dennis Henry 1951- *WhoEmL 93, WhoWor 93*
Langer, E.W. 1927- *WhoScE 91-2*
Langer, Ebbe Wang 1927- *WhoWor 93*
Langer, Edward L. 1936- *WhoAm 92*
Langer, Edward Leo 1936- *St&PR 93*
Langer, Ellen Jane 1947- *WhoAm 92, WhoAmW 93*
Langer, Erick D. 1955- *ConAu 137*
Langer, Eva Marie 1958- *WhoEmL 93*
Langer, Frantisek 1888-1965 *BioIn 17*
Langer, Gayle Marlene 1937- *WhoAmW 93*
Langer, George Edward 1936- *WhoAm 92*
Langer, Helmut G. 1930- *WhoScE 91-3*
Langer, Horst *WhoAm 92*
Langer, James Stephen 1934- *WhoAm 92*
Langer, Jerk Wang 1960- *WhoWor 93*
Langer, Jim 1948- *BioIn 17*
Langer, Jiri 1894-1943 *BioIn 17*
Langer, Judith 1941- *WhoAmW 93*
Langer, Judith A. *Law&B 92*
Langer, Karen G. *WhoAmW 93*
Langer, Lawrence Lee 1929- *WhoAm 92*
Langer, Michael F.B. 1933- *WhoScE 91-3*
Langer, Morton 1941- *St&PR 93*
Langer, Patricia J. *Law&B 92*
Langer, Peter H. 1931- *St&PR 93*
Langer, Ralph Ernest 1937- *WhoAm 92, WhoSSW 93*
Langer, Robert Samuel 1948- *WhoAm 92*
Langer, S.W. 1909- *St&PR 93*
Langer, Sandra Lois 1941- *WhoE 93*
Langer, Seppo Wang 1963- *WhoWor 93*
Langer, Simon Hrimes 1952- *WhoEmL 93*
Langer, Steve Hall 1941- *St&PR 93*
Langer, Susanne Katherina Knauth 1895-1985 *BioIn 17*
Langer, Suzanne K(atherina) 1895-1985 *Baker 92*
Langer, Ulf W. 1932- *WhoScE 91-2*
Langer, Victor 1842-1902 *Baker 92*
Langer, William L. 1886-1959 *PolPar*
Langerak, Cornelis J. 1947- *WhoScE 91-3*
Langerak, Esley Oren 1920- *WhoAm 92*
Langerman, Peter A. 1955- *St&PR 93*
Langerman, Wayne Richard 1952- *WhoSSW 93*
Langeron, Jean-Paul 1928- *WhoScE 91-2*
Langert, Johann August Adolf 1836-1920 *Baker 92*
Langert, Nancy *BioIn 17*
Langert, Richard *BioIn 17*
Langerwerf, J.S.A. *WhoScE 91-3*
Langeveld, Dirk 1951- *St&PR 93*
Langevin, Andre 1927- *BioIn 17*
Langevin, Gilbert 1938- *WhoCanL 92*
Langevin, Jacques P. *Law&B 92*
Langevin, Louis-de-Gonzague 1921- *WhoAm 92*
Langevin, Mark E. *Law&B 92*
Langevin, R. *Law&B 92*
Langewiesche, William *BioIn 17*
Langfield, Raymond Lee 1921- *WhoWor 93*
Langfitt, D. Richard 1933- *St&PR 93*
Langfitt, Thomas William 1927- *WhoAm 92*
Langford, Arthur, Jr. 1949- *AfrAmBi [port]*
Langford, Daniel C. 1945- *St&PR 93*
Langford, David 1953- *ScF&FL 92*
Langford, David Anthony *WhoScE 91-1*
Langford, Dean T. 1939- *St&PR 93*
Langford, Dean Ted 1939- *WhoAm 92*
Langford, Donovan Albert, III 1950- *WhoAm 92*
Langford, Gerald Talmadge 1935- *WhoSSW 93*
Langford, Herbert G. 1922-1991 *BioIn 17*
Langford, James Rouleau 1937- *WhoAm 92*
Langford, Michele K. *ScF&FL 92*
Langford, Rick C. 1953- *WhoWrEP 92*
Langford, Robert D. 1936- *St&PR 93, WhoAm 92*
Langford, Robert E. 1912- *St&PR 93*
Langford, Robert L. 1950- *St&PR 93*
Langford, Roland Everett 1945- *WhoWor 93*
Langford, Thomas L. 1941- *St&PR 93*
Langford, Walter Martin 1931- *St&PR 93, WhoAm 92*
Langgaard, Rued (Immanuel) 1893-1952 *Baker 92*
Langgaard, Siegfried 1852-1914 See Langgaard, Rued (Immanuel) 1893-1952 *Baker 92*
Langgard, Leo B. 1942- *WhoScE 91-2*
Langguth, A.J. 1933- *WhoWrEP 92*
Langham, Barbara Dee 1938- *WhoWrEP 92*
Langham, Charles George, Jr. 1941- *WhoSSW 93*
Langham, Joan *WhoWrEP 92*
Langham, Michael 1919- *WhoAm 92*
Langham, Norma *WhoAmW 93, WhoE 93, WhoWor 93*
Langham-Coe, Joan *WhoWrEP 92*
Langhanke, Helen *AmWomPl*
Langhans, Edward Allen 1923- *WhoAm 92*
Langhans, Lester Frank, III 1948- *WhoE 93*
Langhans, Richard A. 1945- *St&PR 93*
Langhans, (Friedrich) Wilhelm 1832-1892 *Baker 92*
Langhart, Joseph Sidney, Jr. 1937- *WhoSSW 93*
Langhauser, John J. *Law&B 92*
Langheinrich, Werner Alfred 1934- *WhoScE 91-3*
Langheld, Christian *WhoUN 92*
Langhenry, John Godfred, Jr. 1933- *WhoAm 92*
Langhoff, Norbert *WhoScE 91-3*
Langholm, A.D. *ScF&FL 92*
Langholz, Robert Wayne 1930- *WhoAm 92*
Langhorne, Chiswell Dabney, Jr. 1940- *St&PR 93*
Langhorne, Elizabeth (Coles) 1909- *ConAu 40NR*
Langhorne, John 1735-1779 *BioIn 17*
Langhout-Nix, Nelleke 1939- *WhoAmW 93*
Langie, Louis A., Jr. 1928- *St&PR 93*
Langille, Harold James 1943- *St&PR 93*
Langille, Keri Kae 1961- *WhoAmW 93*
Langille-Mattei, Suzanne Yvonne 1954- *WhoWrEP 92*
Langkilde, N.E. 1923- *WhoScE 91-2*
Langlais, Arthur R. 1935- *St&PR 93*
Langlais, Catherine Renee 1955- *WhoWor 93*
Langlais, Jean 1907-1991 *AnObit 1991, Baker 92, BioIn 17*
Langlais, Patricia Ann 1949- *WhoWrEP 92*
Langland, Elizabeth 1948- *WhoSSW 93*
Langland, Joseph Thomas 1917- *WhoAm 92, WhoWrEP 92*
Langland, William 1330?-1400? *LitC 19*
Langlands, Ian Holmes 1926- *St&PR 93*
Langlands, Robert Phelan 1936- *WhoAm 92*
Langle, Honore (Francois Marie) 1741-1807 *Baker 92*
Langleben, Manuel Phillip 1924- *WhoAm 92*
Langley, Anthony H. 1947- *St&PR 93*
Langley, Bob 1936- *ScF&FL 92*
Langley, Christopher Kenneth 1950- *WhoWor 93*
Langley, Cynthia Murray 1954- *WhoEmL 93*
Langley, David *BioIn 17*
Langley, David Lee, Jr. 1951- *WhoEmL 93*
Langley, Desmond 1930- *WhoWor 93*
Langley, Dorothy 1904-1969 *ScF&FL 92*
Langley, Ellis Bradford 1923- *WhoAm 92*
Langley, Eugene Loyle 1924- *St&PR 93*
Langley, George Ross 1931- *WhoAm 92*
Langley, Hugh F. 1954- *St&PR 93*
Langley, Jerry L. 1947- *St&PR 93*
Langley, Jim *BioIn 17*
Langley, John J. 1932- *St&PR 93*
Langley, Katherine Gudger 1888-1948 *BioIn 17*
Langley, Kenneth H. 1935- *WhoE 93*
Langley, Marcia H. *Law&B 92*
Langley, MaryBeth 1950- *WhoAmW 93*
Langley, Meg *BioIn 17*
Langley, Noel 1911-1980 *ScF&FL 92*
Langley, Patricia Ann 1938- *WhoAmW 93*
Langley, Patricia Coffroth 1924- *WhoE 93*
Langley, Robert *ScF&FL 92*
Langley, Robert Archie 1937- *WhoSSW 93*
Langley, Roger Richard 1930- *WhoE 93*
Langley, Rolland Ament, Jr. 1931- *WhoWor 93*
Langley, William Robert 1940- *St&PR 93*
Langlinais, Joseph Willis 1922- *WhoAm 92, WhoSSW 93*
Langlois, Emile Auguste 1935- *WhoSSW 93*
Langlois, Fannie Myers *AmWomPl*
Langlois, Marie Jean 1942- *St&PR 93*
Langlois, Michael Arthur 1956- *WhoEmL 93*
Langlois, Robert J. 1929- *St&PR 93*
Langlois, Walter Gordon 1925- *WhoAm 92*
Langmaid, Bruce R. 1950- *St&PR 93*
Langman, Louis 1903-1991 *BioIn 17*
Langman, Michael J.G. *WhoScE 91-1*
Langman-Dorwart, Nancy 1948- *WhoAmW 93*
Langmann, Hans Joachim 1924- *WhoWor 93*
Langmore, John Henley *Law&B 92*
Langmore, John Preston 1947- *WhoAm 92*
Langmore, John Vance 1939- *WhoAsAP 91*
Langmuir, Alexander Duncan 1910- *WhoAm 92*
Langmuir, Charles Herbert 1950- *WhoE 93*
Langmuir, Leona Baumgartner 1902-1991 *BioIn 17*
Langmuir, Margaret Elizabeth 1935- *WhoAmW 93*
Langner, Kevan K. *St&PR 93*
Langner, Kevan Kellogg *Law&B 92*
Langner, Lola E. *Law&B 92*
Lango, Paul James 1956- *WhoE 93*
Langon *WhoScE 91-2*
Langowski, Horst-Christian 1954- *WhoWor 93*
Langpape, Reinhart 1928- *WhoScE 91-3*
Langren, Daniel David 1938- *St&PR 93*

Langridge, Philip 1939- OxDcOp
Langridge, Philip (Gordon) 1939- Baker 92
Langridge, Robert 1933- WhoAm 92
Langrock, Karl Frederick 1927- WhoAm 92
Langsam, Devra M. 1945- ScF&FL 92
Langsam, Gertrude Feinstein 1918- WhoAmW 93, WhoE 93
Langsdorf, Alexander, Jr. 1912- WhoAm 92
Langsdorf, Roger W. Law&B 92
Langsdorf, Thomas Kline 1947- St&PR 93
Langsdorff, Georg Heinrich 1774-1852 IntDcAn
Langseder, Dorothy L. 1928- WhoAmW 93
Langseth, Muriel Avonne 1939- WhoWrEP 92
Langseth-Christensen, Lillian BioIn 17
Langsford, A. WhoScE 91-1
Lang-Sims, Lois BioIn 17
Langsley, Donald Gene 1925- WhoAm 92
Langson, Nancy 1947- St&PR 93
Langstaff, Eleanor Marguerite 1934- WhoAmW 93
Langstaff, Elliot Kennedy 1923- WhoAm 92
Langstaff, Gary L. 1948- St&PR 93
Langstaff, Gary Lee 1948- WhoAm 92
Langstaff, George Quigley, Jr. 1925- WhoAm 92
Langstaff, Janis Jacobsen 1949- WhoAmW 93
Langstaff, John M. 1920- BioIn 17
Langstaff, John Meredith 1920- MajAI [port], WhoAm 92
Langston, Barbara Rice 1942- WhoAmW 93
Langston, Charles Adam 1949- WhoE 93
Langston, Charles C., Jr. 1937- St&PR 93
Langston, H.A., Jr. Law&B 92
Langston, Hiram Thomas 1912- WhoAm 92
Langston, John M. 1829-1897 PolPar
Langston, John Mercer 1829-1897 BioIn 17, EncAACR [port]
Langston, Mark 1960- WhoAm 92
Langston, Michael Allen 1950- WhoEmL 93
Langston, Michael Densmore 1945- St&PR 93
Langston, Murray MiSFD 9
Langston, Paul T. 1928- WhoAm 92
Langston, Roy A. 1912- WhoAm 92
Langston, Sally J. 1947- WhoEmL 93
Langston, William G. 1935- St&PR 93
Langston, William Gilbert Law&B 92
Langstrom, Bo Erik 1945- WhoScE 91-4
Langton, Anne 1804-1893 BioIn 17
Langton, Christopher G. BioIn 17
Langton, Daniel J. 1927- WhoWrEP 92
Langton, David George 1940- WhoSSW 93
Langton, Jane BioIn 17
Langton, Jane 1922- ScF&FL 92
Langton, Jane (Gillson) 1922- ConAu 40NR, DcAmChF 1960, MajAI [port]
Langton, Kenneth Patrick 1933- WhoAm 92
Langton, Raymond Benedict, III 1944- WhoE 93
Langton, Simon 1941- MiSFD 9
Langtry, Lillie 1853-1929 BioIn 17
Langtry, Philip S. 1934- St&PR 93
Langum, John Kenneth 1913- St&PR 93, WhoAm 92
Langum, W. Sue 1934- WhoAmW 93
Langus, Alan L. Law&B 92
Langwasser, George August 1938- St&PR 93
Langway, Richard Merritt 1939- WhoAm 92
Langweiler, Mark Jay 1952- WhoE 93
Langwig, John Edward 1924- WhoAm 92
Langwinski, Romuald Andrzej 1933- WhoScE 91-4
Langworthy, Audrey Hansen 1938- WhoAmW 93
Langworthy, Everett Walter 1918- WhoAm 92
Langworthy, J. Baird 1939- St&PR 93
Langworthy, James Brian 1934- WhoE 93
Langworthy, Keith Charles 1956- WhoE 93
Langworthy, Robert Burton 1918- WhoAm 92
Langworthy, William Clayton 1936- WhoAm 92
Lanham, Ben T., III 1945- St&PR 93
Lanham, Betty Bailey 1922- WhoAm 92
Lanham, Elizabeth 1912- WhoAm 92
Lanham, Howard Mitchell 1934- WhoIns 93
Lanham, Kenneth E. 1952- St&PR 93
Lanham, Logan Everett 1926- WhoAm 92
Lanham, Margaret Mary 1921- WhoAmW 93
Lanham, Scott Ayres 1958- WhoEmL 93
Lanham, Urless Norton 1918- WhoAm 92
Laniak, David Konstantyn 1935- St&PR 93, WhoAm 92
Laniel, Joseph 1889-1975 BioIn 17
Lanier, Albert G. d1992 NewYTBS 92
Lanier, Anita Suzanne 1946- WhoAmW 93, WhoEmL 93, WhoSSW 93
Lanier, Cathy Gibson 1957- WhoAmW 93
Lanier, Gerald N. 1937-1990 BioIn 17
Lanier, Geraldine Fe 1951- WhoWrEP 92
Lanier, James Newton 1939- WhoSSW 93
Lanier, Jaron BioIn 17
Lanier, John Hicks 1940- St&PR 93, WhoSSW 93
Lanier, Joseph Lamar, Jr. 1932- WhoSSW 93
Lanier, Joseph Vaughan 1928- St&PR 93
Lanier, Julian E. 1931- St&PR 93
Lanier, Louis-G. 1929- WhoScE 91-2
Lanier, Louis Guy 1929- WhoScE 91-2
Lanier, Lyle Hicks BioIn 17
Lanier, Michael Edward 1958- WhoSSW 93
Lanier, Nicholas 1588-1666 Baker 92
Lanier, Pattie Pelton 1938- WhoAm 92
Lanier, Raymond Hunter, Jr. 1949- WhoEmL 93
Lanier, Richard Blackburn 1958- WhoE 93, WhoWor 93
Lanier, Robert C. 1931- WhoAm 92
Lanier, Sidney 1842-1881 MajAI [port]
Lanier, Sidney (Clopton) 1842-1881 Baker 92
Lanier, Sterling E. 1927- ScF&FL 92
Lanier, Thomas 1923- WhoAm 92, WhoE 93, WhoWor 93
Lanier, Thomas F. 1942- St&PR 93
Lanier, W. Greg 1938- WhoSSW 93
Lanier, Willie BioIn 17
Lanier Miles, Barbara Jean WhoAmW 93
Lanigan, Charles Frederic 1940- St&PR 93
Lanigan, Denis George 1926- WhoAm 92
Lanigan, Edward J. 1928- St&PR 93
Lanigan, George Thomas 1845-1886 JrnUS
Lanigan, James Joseph 1924- WhoE 93
Lanigan, Jeramy E. BioIn 17
Lanigan, Kevin John 1946- St&PR 93
Lanigan, Robert J. 1928- St&PR 93, WhoAm 92
Lanin, Howard d1991 BioIn 17
Lanin, Lester BioIn 17
Lanin, Thomas Kenneth 1943- St&PR 93
Laning, J. Halcombe 1920- WhoAm 92
Laning, Richard Boyer 1918- WhoSSW 93
Laning, Robert Comegys 1922- WhoAm 92
Lanitis, Nicholas Constantine 1917- WhoWor 93
Lanitis, Tony Andrew 1926- WhoAm 92
Lanius, Carl E. 1944- St&PR 93
Lanius, Gloria Helene 1917- WhoWrEP 92
Lanius, Karl 1927- WhoScE 91-3
Lank, Edith Handleman 1926- WhoAmW 93
Lankamp, Herman 1939- WhoScE 91-3
Lanker, Brian BioIn 17
Lankester, Charles John 1938- WhoUN 92
Lankester, Michael (John) 1944- Baker 92
Lankford, Alana Frances 1948- WhoWrEP 92
Lankford, Charles A. St&PR 93
Lankford, Francis Greenfield, Jr. 1906- WhoAm 92
Lankford, Fred, III 1951- WhoEmL 93, WhoSSW 93
Lankford, John Llewellyn 1920- WhoE 93
Lankford, Mary Angeline Gruver 1964- WhoSSW 93
Lankford, Nelson D. 1948- ConAu 138
Lankford, Patricia Ann 1960- WhoAmW 93
Lankford, Ronald B. 1935- St&PR 93
Lankford, Ronald Sovey 1952- St&PR 93
Lankiewicz, Donald Phillip 1952- WhoSSW 93
Lankow, Anna 1850-1908 Baker 92
Lankowsky, Zenon P. Law&B 92
Lanks, Karl William 1942- WhoE 93
Lankton, Gordon B. 1931- St&PR 93
Lankton, Stephen Ryan 1947- WhoAm 92
Lanly, Jean-Paul 1938- WhoScE 91-3, WhoUN 92
Lanmon, Dwight Pierson 1938- WhoAm 92
Lann, John W. Law&B 92
Lanna, Robert A. 1934- St&PR 93
Lannamann, Richard Stuart 1947- WhoAm 92, WhoE 93, WhoWor 93
Lanner, August (Joseph) 1834-1855 Baker 92
Lanner, Joseph (Franz Karl) 1801-1843 Baker 92
Lannert, Robert C. 1940- St&PR 93
Lannert, Robert Cornelius 1940- WhoAm 92
Lannes, Jean 1769-1809 HarEnMi
Lannes, William Joseph, III 1937- WhoAm 92
Lanni, Joseph Terrence 1943- St&PR 93
Lanni, Richard A. St&PR 93
Lannie, P. Anthony Law&B 92
Lannigan, Julie Beth 1953- WhoWrEP 92
Lannigan, Peter Stuart 1960- St&PR 93
Lanning, James J. 1928- St&PR 93
Lanning, Michael Lee 1946- WhoWrEP 92
Lanning, Sereta ScF&FL 92
Lannon, Edward Hicks, Jr. 1924- St&PR 93
Lannon, John Joseph 1937- St&PR 93, WhoAm 92
Lannon, Kathleen Maria 1949- WhoE 93
Lannoo, Godfried Joseph 1927- WhoWor 93
Lannoy, Charles de c. 1487-1527 HarEnMi
L'Annunziata, Michael Frank 1943- WhoUN 92
Lano, Charles Jack 1922- WhoAm 92
Lano, James Dejerold Law&B 92
Lanoff, Samuel M. 1907- St&PR 93
Lanois, Daniel 1951- ConMus 8 [port]
LaNoue, Alcide Moodie 1934- WhoAm 92
Lanoue, Blaze Allen 1960- WhoEmL 93
La Noue, Terence David 1941- WhoAm 92
Lanouette, William (John) 1940- ConAu 136, WhoAm 92
Lanphear, Charles Edward 1947- St&PR 93
Lanphear, Shawna Rae 1957- WhoAmW 93
Lanphere, Don BioIn 17
Lanrezac, Charles Louis Marie 1852-1925 HarEnMi
Lans, Allan M. BioIn 17
Lansaw, Judy W. 1951- St&PR 93, WhoAm 92
Lansbury, Angela BioIn 17
Lansbury, Angela 1925- IntDcF 2-3, News 93-1 [port]
Lansbury, Angela Brigid 1925- WhoAm 92, WhoAmW 93
Lansbury, Coral 1929-1991 BioIn 17
Lansbury, Edgar George 1930- WhoAm 92
Lansbury, George 1859-1940 BioIn 17, DcTwHis
Lansbury, Russell Duncan 1945- WhoWor 93
Lansche, John E. Law&B 92
Lansdale, Daryl L. 1940- St&PR 93
Lansdale, Edward G. 1908-1987 BioIn 17
Lansdale, Joe R. 1951- ScF&FL 92
Lansdale, Phil 1906-1990 BioIn 17
Lansdown, Anthony Richard 1928- WhoWor 93
Lansdown, Brenda d1990 BioIn 17
Lansdown, Scott Law&B 92
Lansdowne, Henry Charles Keith Petty-Fitzmaurice, Marquess of 1845-1927 DcTwHis
Lansdowne, Henry Petty-Fitzmaurice, Marquis of 1845-1927 BioIn 17
Lansdowne, Karen Myrtle 1926- WhoAmW 93
Lansdowne, Peter W. 1938- WhoScE 91-1
Lanselle, Lee Penn 1954- WhoEmL 93
Lansford, L.R. 1946- St&PR 93
Lanshe, James Clement 1946- WhoEmL 93
Lansing, Allan Meredith 1929- WhoAm 92
Lansing, Andrew J. Law&B 92
Lansing, James W. 1946- St&PR 93
Lansing, Karen E. 1954- SmATA 71 [port]
Lansing, Marion Florence 1883- AmWomPl
Lansing, Robert 1928- ConTFT 10
Lansing, Robert Howell 1928- WhoAm 92, WhoWor 93
Lansing, Sherry BioIn 17
Lansing, Sherry Lee 1944- WhoAm 92, WhoAmW 93
Lansipuro, Yrjo Juhani 1940- WhoWor 93
Lanska, Mary Jo 1958- WhoEmL 93
Lansky, Aaron BioIn 17
Lansky, Aaron Jonathan 1955- WhoE 93
Lansky, Meyer 1902-1983 BioIn 17
Lansky, Mitchell I. Law&B 92
Lansky, Vicki Lee 1942- WhoWrEP 92
Lansky, Zdenek John 1922- WhoSSW 93
Lansky, Zena 1942- WhoAmW 93
Lansley, Peter Reginald WhoScE 91-1
Lansner, Kermit Irvin 1922- WhoAm 92
Lanson, Snooky 1914-1990 BioIn 17
Lanstein, Ronald J. St&PR 93
Lant, Carol Jane 1943- St&PR 93
Lant, Jeffrey Ladd 1947- WhoWrEP 92
Lant, T.P.R. WhoScE 91-1
Lantay, George Charles Wagner 1942- WhoAm 92
Lanteri, Antonio 1949- WhoWor 93
Lanterman, Elma Jeannette 1917- WhoAmW 93
Lanterman, Joseph Barney 1914-1991 BioIn 17
Lanternari, Vittorio 1918- IntDcAn
Lanthier, Jonh Spencer 1940- WhoAm 92
Lanthier, Ronald Ross 1926- WhoAm 92
Lanthorn, William Richard 1926- St&PR 93
Lantieri, Brenda Jean 1944- WhoAmW 93
Lantin, Emmanuel Macasaet 1934- WhoWor 93
Lantins, Arnold de c. 1400- Baker 92
Lantins, Hugo de c. 1399- Baker 92
Lanton, Sandy WhoWrEP 92
Lantos, Geoffrey Paul 1952- WhoE 93
Lantos, Peter Laszlo WhoScE 91-1
Lantos, Thomas Peter 1928- WhoAm 92
Lantos, Tom 1928- CngDr 91
Lantto, Marcia Mabel 1944- WhoAmW 93
Lantuh, Nicholas 1964- WhoSSW 93
Lantz, Billie Joanne 1956- WhoEmL 93
Lantz, David B. 1946- St&PR 93
Lantz, David Carson 1946- WhoE 93
Lantz, Eric John 1951- WhoEmL 93
Lantz, Fran ConAu 39NR
Lantz, Fran 1952- ScF&FL 92
Lantz, Francess L(in) 1952- ConAu 39NR
Lantz, Francess Lin 1952- BioIn 17
Lantz, George Benjamin, Jr. 1936- WhoAm 92
Lantz, Gracie d1992 BioIn 17, NewYTBS 92
Lantz, J.R. 1911- St&PR 93
Lantz, Jerry Allan 1954- WhoSSW 93
Lantz, Joanne Baldwin 1932- WhoAm 92, WhoAmW 93
Lantz, Kenneth Eugene 1934- WhoAm 92
Lantz, Phillip Edward 1938- WhoAm 92, WhoWor 93
Lantz, Robert Lynn 1939- St&PR 93
Lantz, Walter 1900- WhoAm 92
Lanus, Juan Archibaldo Archibaldo 1938- WhoUN 92
Lany, Mary Ambler Law&B 92
Lanyer, Aemilia 1569-1645 DcLB 121
Lanyi, Janos Karoly 1937- WhoAm 92
Lanyi, William David Law&B 92
Lanyon, Ellen 1926- WhoAm 92
Lanyon, J. Ken 1940- St&PR 93
Lanyon, Wesley Edwin 1926- WhoAm 92
Lanz, Egon 1941- WhoScE 91-3
Lanz, John Edwin, Jr. Law&B 92
Lanz, Robert Francis 1942- St&PR 93
Lanz, Robert H. 1922- St&PR 93
Lanza, Felice 1924- WhoScE 91-3
Lanza, Kenneth Anthony 1953- WhoE 93
Lanza, Mario 1921-1959 Baker 92
Lanza, Shelley Brown 1956- WhoAmW 93
Lanzafame, Raymond Joseph 1952- WhoE 93
Lanzano, Ralph Eugene 1926- WhoAm 92, WhoE 93, WhoWor 93
Lanzarotta, Santo Anthony 1928- St&PR 93
Lanza Tomasi, Gioacchino BioIn 17
Lanzel, Jerome E., Jr. 1931- St&PR 93
Lanzerotti, Louis John 1938- WhoAm 92
Lanzetti, James N. d1991 BioIn 17
Lanzetti, Salvatore c. 1710-c. 1760 Baker 92
Lanzi, Ray J. 1938- St&PR 93
Lanzillotta, A. Paul 1931- St&PR 93, WhoAm 92
Lanzillotti, Robert Franklin 1921- WhoAm 92
Lanzilotti, Thomas Anthony 1953- WhoE 93
Lanzit, Stephen Ray 1931- WhoAm 92
Lanzkowsky, Philip 1932- WhoAm 92
Lanzkron, Carolyn Kahn 1964- WhoAmW 93, WhoEmL 93
Lanzkron, Rolf Wolfgang 1929- WhoE 93
Lanzl, Lawrence Herman 1921- WhoAm 92
Lanzmann, Claude MiSFD 9
Lanzmann, Claude 1925- ConAu 139
Lanzon, Richard D., Jr. Law&B 92
Lanzoni, Vincent 1928- WhoAm 92
Lanzotti, Bill Andrew 1950- St&PR 93
Laouyane, Ahmed 1933- WhoUN 92
Lapacek, James Victor Law&B 92
Lapadat, Stephen C. Law&B 92
Lapadot, Sonee Spinner 1936- WhoAmW 93
Lapadula, Robert Mauro 1938- WhoE 93
Lapage, Stephen P. d1990 BioIn 17
LaPaglia, Anthony 1959?- ConTFT 10
La Paglia, Joseph Thomas 1943- St&PR 93
LaPaglia, S. Russell Law&B 92
La Palma, Marina de Bellagente 1949- WhoWrEP 92
LaPalombara, Joseph 1925- WhoAm 92
Lapanje, Savo 1925- WhoScE 91-4
Laparra, Raoul 1876-1943 Baker 92

La Pasionaria 1895-1989 *BioIn 17*
Lapatsanis, Petros D. 1927- *WhoScE 91-3*
Lapautre, Rene 1930- *WhoWor 93*
Lapayowker, Andrew *Law&B 92*
Lapayowker, Marc Spencer 1927- *WhoAm 92*
Lapchick, Elizabeth d1992 *BioIn 17*
Lapchick, Joe 1900-1970 *BioIn 17*
Lapchick, Richard Edward 1945- *WhoE 93*
Lapczynski, Susan Agnes 1960- *WhoEmL 93*
Lapedes, Clarence 1909- *St&PR 93*
La Penta, Robert Vincent 1945- *WhoAm 92*
La Perchia, Alexander *BioIn 17*
la Perouse, Jean Francois de Galaup, Comte de 1741-1788 *Expl 93 [port]*
Lapetina, Eduardo Gerardo 1940- *WhoAm 92*
Lapeyrie, Frederic Francois Pacicon 1956- *WhoWor 93*
Lapeyrolerie, Frank M. d1992 *NewYTBS 92*
Lapeyrolerie, Frank M. 1929-1992 *BioIn 17*
Lapham, John Edward 1936- *St&PR 93*
Lapham, Lewis A. 1909- *St&PR 93*
Lapham, Lewis Henry 1935- *WhoAm 92, WhoWrEP 92*
Lapham, Lowell Winship 1922- *WhoE 93*
Lapic, Jeffrey R. *Law&B 92*
Lapicola, John J. 1946- *St&PR 93*
Lapides, Jack 1914- *WhoAm 92*
Lapides, Jeffrey Rolf 1954- *WhoAm 92*
Lapides, Julian Lee 1931- *WhoE 93*
Lapides, Morton M. 1929- *St&PR 93*
Lapides, Robert E. 1918- *St&PR 93*
Lapidus, Arnold 1933- *WhoE 93, WhoWor 93*
Lapidus, Herbert 1931- *St&PR 93*
Lapidus, Jacqueline 1941- *WhoWrEP 92*
LaPidus, Jules Benjamin 1931- *WhoAm 92*
Lapidus, Leah Blumberg 1938- *WhoAmW 93, WhoE 93*
Lapidus, Leonard 1929- *St&PR 93, WhoE 93*
Lapidus, Morris 1902- *WhoAm 92, WhoWor 93*
Lapidus, Norman Israel 1930- *WhoAm 92, WhoE 93*
Lapiedra, Ramon 1940- *WhoScE 91-3*
Lapierre, Dominique *BioIn 17*
Lapierre, Dominique 1931- *WhoAm 92*
LaPierre, John L. *Law&B 92*
LaPierre, Robert 1927- *St&PR 93*
Lapietra, Gianfranco 1936- *WhoScE 91-3*
Lapin, Abraham 1923- *WhoE 93*
Lapin, Byron Richard 1941- *St&PR 93*
Lapin, Harvey I. 1937- *WhoAm 92*
Lapin, Jay F. *Law&B 92*
Lapin, Jay Forman 1945- *WhoAm 92*
Lapin, Jeffrey C. 1956- *St&PR 93*
Lapin, Robert 1930- *St&PR 93*
Lapin, Sergei G. 1912-1990 *BioIn 17*
Lapin, Sharon Joyce Vaughn 1938- *WhoAmW 93*
Lapine, James *MiSFD 9*
Lapine, James Elliot 1949- *WhoAm 92*
Lapinski, Frances Constance 1950- *WhoE 93*
Lapinski, Miroslaw 1932- *WhoScE 91-4*
Lapinski, Tadeusz Andrew 1928- *WhoAm 92*
Lapis, Karoly 1926- *WhoScE 91-4*
Lapithes, George fl. c. 1340-1349 *OxDcByz*
Lapithis, Aristides George 1921- *WhoScE 91-4*
Lapka, Fay S. *ScF&FL 92*
Lapka, Thomas L. *Law&B 92*
Lapke, John H. *Law&B 92*
Lapkin, Milton 1929- *WhoAm 92*
LaPlaca, David S. 1929- *St&PR 93*
La Placa, Michele 1931- *WhoScE 91-3*
Laplante, (Joseph) Andre (Roger) 1949- *Baker 92*
Laplante, Jerry *ScF&FL 92*
LaPlante, John Baptiste 1940- *WhoAm 92*
LaPlante, Joseph A. 1923-1990 *BioIn 17*
LaPlante, Laura 1904- *SweetSg B [port]*
la Plante, Richard *ScF&FL 92*
LaPlante, William A. 1930- *St&PR 93*
La Plata, George 1924- *HispAmA [port]*
LaPoe, Wayne Gilpin 1924- *WhoAm 92*
Lapof, Ray Charles 1932- *St&PR 93*
Lapointe, Dawn Dunaway 1955- *WhoEmL 93*
Lapointe, Edward Joseph 1942- *St&PR 93*
Lapointe, Gatien 1931-1983 *WhoCanL 92*
Lapointe, J.R. 1946- *St&PR 93*
Lapointe, Marc *Law&B 92*
Lapointe, Paul-Marie 1929- *WhoCanL 92*
Lapointe, Philippe *St&PR 93*
Lapointe, Ron d1992 *BioIn 17*
LaPointe-Peterson, Kittie Vadis 1915- *WhoAmW 93*
Laponce, Jean Antoine 1925- *WhoAm 92*
LaPorta, Ralph *St&PR 93*
LaPorta, Robert A. *Law&B 92*
La Porta, Robert Louis 1941- *St&PR 93*
Laporte, Andre 1931- *Baker 92*
Laporte, Cloyd, Jr. *Law&B 92*
Laporte, Cloyd, Jr. 1925- *St&PR 93, WhoAm 92*
La Porte, James 1931- *St&PR 93*
Laporte, Joseph de 1713-1779 *Baker 92*
LaPorte, Joseph James 1931- *St&PR 93*
Laporte, Leo Frederic 1933- *WhoAm 92*
Laporte, Lucien Kirsch d1991 *BioIn 17*
La Porte, Mary Helen 1944- *WhoAmW 93*
La Porte, Michael J. 1937- *St&PR 93*
LaPorte, Nicholas d1990 *BioIn 17*
Laporte, Pierre Francois 1799-1841 *OxDcOp*
Laporte, Richard G. *Law&B 92*
LaPorte, Robert Paul, Jr. 1947- *WhoEmL 93*
LaPorte, Ronald J. *Law&B 92*
Laporte, Thomas B. 1940- *St&PR 93*
LaPorte, William F. 1913- *St&PR 93*
LaPorte, William Francis 1933- *WhoE 93*
Laporte, Willy P.R. 1932- *WhoScE 91-2*
Laporte, Yves Frederic 1920- *WhoScE 91-2*
Laporte, Yves M.F. 1920- *WhoScE 91-2*
Laposata, Joseph Samuel 1938- *WhoAm 92*
Lapotaire, Robert Louis 1959- *WhoSSW 93*
La Poupliniere, Alexandre-Jean-Joseph Le Riche de 1693-1762 *Baker 92*
Lapovsky, Lucie *WhoAmW 93*
Lapp, Eleanor J. 1936- *BioIn 17*
Lapp, J. Parker 1953- *St&PR 93*
Lapp, Philip Alexander 1928- *WhoAm 92*
Lapp, Roger James 1933- *WhoSSW 93, WhoWor 93*
Lapp, Susan Bolster 1945- *WhoAmW 93*
Lappalainen, Eino 1939- *WhoScE 91-4*
Lappalainen, Pentti 1941- *WhoScE 91-4*
Lappalainen, Veikko 1932- *WhoScE 91-4*
Lappas, Spero Thomas 1952- *WhoEmL 93*
Lappat, Hans-Juergen Vinzenz 1953- *WhoWor 93*
Lappe, Frances Moore *BioIn 17*
Lappe, Frances Moore 1944- *WhoAm 92, WhoAmW 93, WhoWrEP 92*
Lappen, Chester I. 1919- *WhoAm 92*
Lappert, Michael Franz *WhoScE 91-1*
Lappert, Michael Franz 1928- *WhoWor 93*
Lappert, Walter *BioIn 17*
Lappi, Juha Veli 1951- *WhoScE 91-4*
Lappin, Gerald David 1910- *St&PR 93*
Lappin, Richard C. 1944- *WhoAm 92*
Lappin, Robert I. 1922- *St&PR 93*
Laprade, Barbara 1925- *St&PR 93*
La Prade, Ernest 1889-1969 *Baker 92, ScF&FL 92*
LaPrade, James Nicholas 1956- *WhoE 93, WhoEmL 93, WhoWor 93*
La Prade, Robert Timothy 1952- *St&PR 93*
Lapras, Michel 1932- *WhoScE 91-2*
La Pre, Lisa Marie 1968- *WhoE 93*
La Presle, Jacques de 1888-1969 *Baker 92*
Laprie, Jean-Claude 1944- *WhoScE 91-2*
Laprime, Jean-Henri Antonin 1952- *WhoE 93*
Lapsley, James Norvell, Jr. 1930- *WhoAm 92, WhoE 93*
Lapsley, Michael *BioIn 17*
Lapsley, Peter *WhoScE 91-1*
Lapsley, William Winston 1910- *WhoAm 92*
Laptad, Maria Nita Ramirez 1947- *WhoEmL 93*
Laptev, Ghennady Ivanovich 1938- *WhoWor 93*
Laptook, Eric J. *Law&B 92*
La Puma, Salvatore 1929- *ConAu 136*
Laputz, Leslie J. 1955- *St&PR 93*
Laqua, Wolfgang 1935- *WhoScE 91-3*
Laquai, Reinhold 1894-1957 *Baker 92*
Laquatra, Lisa Ann 1962- *WhoEmL 93*
Laqueur, Peter 1941- *WhoAm 92*
Laqueur, Walter 1921- *BioIn 17, WhoAm 92*
Laquian, Aprodicio Arcilla 1935- *WhoUN 92*
Laquinta, Fred John 1949- *WhoEmL 93*
Lara, Augustin 1897-1970 *Baker 92*
Lara, Gerardo Antonio 1947- *WhoWor 93*
Lara, Isidore de *Baker 92*
Lara, Jan *ScF&FL 92*
Lara, Jesus 1898-1980 *SpAmA*
Lara, Juan Jose 1947- *WhoWor 93*
Lara, Lucio Barreti de 1929- *WhoAfr*
Lara, Manuel 1867-1912 *BioIn 17*
Lara-Bareiro, Carlos 1914- *Baker 92*
Larabie, Eugene 1936- *St&PR 93*
Larach, Marilyn Green 1952- *WhoEmL 93*
Laragh, Brian Gerard 1929- *WhoAm 92*
Laraia, Michele 1949- *WhoUN 92*
La Raia, Robert F. *Law&B 92*
Laraki, Azedine 1929- *WhoWor 93*
Laramey, Mark S. 1950- *St&PR 93*
Laramore, Susan Ann 1963- *WhoAmW 93*
Laramy, James E. *Law&B 92*
Larance, Charles Larry 1938- *WhoIns 93*
Laranjeira, Manuel Fernandes 1928- *WhoScE 91-3*
LaRavia, Dennis Alson 1946- *WhoSSW 93*
Laraya-Cuasay, Lourdes Redublo 1941- *WhoAmW 93*
Larberg, John Frederick 1930- *WhoWor 93*
Larcan, Alain 1931- *WhoScE 91-2*
Larch, Patricia Lee 1952- *WhoAmW 93*
Larche, James Clifford, II 1946- *WhoSSW 93*
Larcher, Walter 1929- *WhoScE 91-4*
Larco Hoyle, Rafael 1901-1966 *IntDcAn*
Larcom, Lucy 1824-1893 *BioIn 17*
Larcombe, Mary *AmWomPl*
Lard, Charles Walter 1946- *St&PR 93*
Lard, Edwin Webster 1921- *WhoE 93*
Lard, William R. *Law&B 92*
Lardas, Konstantinos N. 1927- *WhoWrEP 92*
Larde, Enrique Roberto 1934- *WhoIns 93*
Larde-Arthes, Enrique Rafael 1899- *WhoE 93, WhoWor 93*
Lardennois, Bertrand 1936- *WhoScE 91-2*
Lardner, Breck Surbrug 1937- *St&PR 93*
Lardner, Henry Petersen 1932- *WhoAm 92*
Lardner, James F. 1924- *St&PR 93*
Lardner, Peter 1932- *St&PR 93, WhoIns 93*
Lardner, Ring 1885-1933 *BioIn 17, JrnUS*
Lardner, Ring Wilmer, Jr. 1915- *WhoAm 92, WhoWrEP 92*
Lardy, Barbara Dawe 1946- *WhoEmL 93*
Lardy, Henry Arnold 1917- *WhoAm 92*
Lareal, Pierre 1938- *WhoScE 91-2*
Lareau, Marybeth Bass 1941- *WhoE 93*
Lareau, Richard G. 1928- *St&PR 93*
Lareau, Richard George 1928- *WhoAm 92*
Laredo, Estrella Abecassis 1940- *WhoWor 93*
Laredo, Ruth 1937- *Baker 92, BioIn 17*
Laredo (y Unzueta), Jaime (Eduardo) 1941- *Baker 92*
la Ree, Gerry de *ScF&FL 92*
La Regina, Adriano 1937- *WhoWor 93*
Laren, Kuno 1924- *St&PR 93, WhoAm 92, WhoWor 93*
Larena, Alicia 1947- *WhoScE 91-3*
Lareng, Louis 1923- *WhoScE 91-2*
Larese, Edward John 1935- *WhoAm 92*
Laret, Robert L. 1946- *St&PR 93*
Larew, Karl Garret 1936- *WhoE 93*
Largay, Vincent B. 1930- *St&PR 93*
Large, Darlene Dintino 1935- *WhoAmW 93*
Large, Dewey Edmund, Jr. 1949- *WhoSSW 93*
Large, E.C. d1976 *ScF&FL 92*
Large, Edward Wilson 1930- *St&PR 93*
Large, G. Gordon M. 1940- *WhoAm 92*
Large, James M. *St&PR 93*
Large, James Mifflin, Jr. 1932- *WhoAm 92*
Large, John Andrew 1947- *WhoAm 92*
Large, John Barry 1930- *WhoScE 91-1*
Large, Robert Harris 1935- *St&PR 93*
Largen, Cheryl Renee 1957- *WhoAmW 93, WhoEmL 93*
Largen, Joseph 1940- *WhoAm 92*
Largen, Robert Glenn 1947- *St&PR 93*
Largent, R. Karl *ScF&FL 92*
Largent, Steve 1954- *WhoAm 92*
Largey, Joseph Charles 1952- *WhoE 93*
Largman, Kenneth 1949- *WhoWor 93*
Largo Caballero, Francisco 1869-1946 *DcTwHis*
Larheim, Tore A. 1948- *WhoScE 91-4*
Larher, Francois 1938- *WhoScE 91-2*
Laric, Frank *ScF&FL 92*
Laric, Michael Victor 1945- *WhoE 93*
Larifla, Dominique 1936- *DcCPCAm*
Larime, Michael W. 1943- *St&PR 93*
Larimer, David George 1944- *WhoAm 92, WhoE 93*
Larimer, Jake Arthur *Law&B 92*
Larin, Anne T. *Law&B 92*
Larin, Vladimir Borisovich 1936- *WhoWor 93*
Larini, Lourival 1941- *WhoWor 93*
Larish, John Joseph 1928- *WhoE 93*
Laris Stevens, Guillermo 1951- *WhoWor 93*
La Riviere, J.W.M. *WhoScE 91-2*
Lariviere, Lawrence Joseph 1938- *WhoE 93*
Lariviere, Maurice Joseph, Jr. 1949- *WhoEmL 93*
Lariviere, Susan Marie 1967- *WhoE 93*
Larizadeh, Mohammed Reza 1947- *WhoEmL 93*
Larjavaara, Tuomas Vaino Olavi 1943- *WhoWor 93*
Lark, Raymond 1939- *WhoAm 92, WhoWor 93*
Larkam, Beverley McCosham 1928- *WhoSSW 93*
Larkin, Alfred Sinnott, Jr. 1947- *WhoAm 92*
Larkin, Anthony C. 1942- *St&PR 93*
Larkin, Anya 1945- *WhoE 93*
Larkin, Barry 1964- *WhoAm 92*
Larkin, Dale C. *St&PR 93*
Larkin, David 1944- *ScF&FL 92*
Larkin, David J., Jr. *Law&B 92*
Larkin, Deirdre Ann 1960- *WhoAmW 93*
Larkin, Donald W. 1947- *WhoSSW 93*
Larkin, Edward W. *Law&B 92*
Larkin, Emmet 1927- *WhoAm 92, WhoWrEP 92*
Larkin, Eugene David 1921- *WhoAm 92*
Larkin, Felix Edward 1909-1991 *BioIn 17*
Larkin, George 1887?-1946 *BioIn 17*
Larkin, George Richard 1950- *WhoSSW 93*
Larkin, Henry 1820-1899 *BioIn 17*
Larkin, James 1876-1947 *BioIn 17*
Larkin, James P. *Law&B 92*
Larkin, James Thomas 1931- *WhoAm 92, WhoE 93*
Larkin, Jeffrey H. 1950- *St&PR 93*
Larkin, Joan 1939- *WhoAm 92*
Larkin, John Montague 1936- *WhoAm 92, WhoSSW 93*
Larkin, John Victor 1946- *WhoSSW 93*
Larkin, June Noble 1922- *WhoAm 92*
Larkin, Kevin Timothy 1957- *WhoSSW 93*
Larkin, Lee Roy 1928- *WhoAm 92*
Larkin, Leo Paul, Jr. 1925- *WhoAm 92*
Larkin, Lynne E. *Law&B 92*
Larkin, Margaret 1899-1967 *AmWomPl*
Larkin, Mary Ann *WhoWrEP 92*
Larkin, Mary Sue 1948- *WhoAmW 93*
Larkin, Mayo 1916- *WhoE 93*
Larkin, Michael Howard 1951- *WhoE 93*
Larkin, Michael J. 1941- *St&PR 93*
Larkin, Michael John 1950- *WhoAm 92*
Larkin, Michael Joseph 1941- *WhoAm 92*
Larkin, Nelle Jean 1925- *WhoAmW 93, WhoWor 93*
Larkin, Patrick G. 1929- *St&PR 93*
Larkin, Patty c. 1951- *ConMus 9 [port]*
Larkin, Paul L. 1947- *St&PR 93*
Larkin, Peter Anthony 1924- *WhoAm 92*
Larkin, Philip *BioIn 17*
Larkin, Philip 1922-1985 *MagSWL [port]*
Larkin, Richard Peter 1951- *St&PR 93*
Larkin, Robert Hayden 1946- *WhoE 93*
Larkin, Rufus 1958- *WhoSSW 93*
Larkin, Thomas Oliver 1802-1858 *BioIn 17*
Larkin, Tippy 1917-1991 *BioIn 17*
Larkins, Ernest Radford 1955- *WhoEmL 93, WhoSSW 93*
Larkins, Francis Patrick 1942- *WhoWor 93*
Larkins, Gary L. 1943- *St&PR 93*
Larkins, Gary Thomas 1956- *WhoAm 92*
Larkins, Grover Lamar 1926- *WhoSSW 93*
Larkins, Nelson J. 1961- *WhoEmL 93*
Larkins, Patricia Gail 1950- *WhoAmW 93*
Larkins, William L., Jr. *Law&B 92*
Larlee, William M. 1912- *St&PR 93*
Larmande, John Claude 1943- *WhoWor 93*
Larmande, Pierre 1950- *WhoScE 91-2*
Larmas, Markku A. 1943- *WhoScE 91-4*
Larmi, Teuvo K.I. 1924- *WhoScE 91-4*
Larmie, Walter Esmond 1920- *WhoE 93*
Larmon, Michael H. *Law&B 92*
Larmon, Robert Edwards 1927- *St&PR 93*
Larmouth, John *WhoScE 91-1*
Larn, John M. 1849-1878 *BioIn 17*
Larnaudie de Ferrand, Xavier Jean-Paul 1954- *WhoWor 93*
Larned, Michael Chouteau 1945- *St&PR 93*
Larned, Phyllis Quinn 1926- *WhoAmW 93*
Larned, William Edmund, Jr. 1919- *WhoAm 92*
Larner, Joseph 1921- *WhoAm 92*
Larney, Dennis P. 1935- *St&PR 93*
Laro, David 1942- *St&PR 93*
La Rocca, Aldo Vittorio 1926- *WhoWor 93*
Larocca, James Lawrence 1943- *WhoAm 92*
La Rocca, Nick (Dominick James) 1889-1961 *Baker 92*
LaRocca, Patricia Darlene McAleer 1951- *WhoEmL 93*
La Rocca, Renato V. 1957- *WhoWor 93*
LaRocca, Robert Kenneth 1943- *St&PR 93*
LaRocco, Joseph Donald, Jr. 1948- *WhoEmL 93*

LaRocco, Larry 1946- *CngDr 91, WhoAm 92*
Laroche, Giles 1956- *SmATA 71 [port]*
Laroche, Gilles 1937- *St&PR 93*
LaRoche, Gloria Rosemarie 1946- *WhoAmW 93*
Laroche, Hermann 1845-1904 *Baker 92*
Laroche, J.R. *Law&B 92*
LaRoche, Laurent Pierrepont 1921- *WhoSSW 93*
La Roche, Marie-Elaine 1949- *WhoAm 92, WhoAmW 93*
LaRoche, Richard Frederick, Jr. *Law&B 92*
LaRoche, Richard Frederick, Jr. 1945- *St&PR 93*
La Roche, Sophie von 1731-1807 *BioIn 17*
LaRoche-Lando, Michelle B. *Law&B 92*
LaRochelle, Diane Racine 1945- *WhoAm 92, WhoSSW 93*
LaRochelle, Philip Nicholas 1958- *WhoSSW 93*
La Rochelle, Pierre Drieu 1893-1945 *BioIn 17*
La Rochelle, Pierre-Louis 1928- *WhoAm 92*
Larochelle, Richard C. 1945- *St&PR 93*
La Rocque, Eugene Philippe 1927- *WhoAm 92*
La Rocque, Francois de 1886?-1946 *BioIn 17*
La Rocque, Gene Robert 1918- *WhoAm 92*
La Rocque, Gilbert 1943-1984 *WhoCanL 92*
LaRocque, Judith Anne 1956- *WhoAm 92*
La Rocque, Rod 1898-1959 *BioIn 17*
La Rocque, Stephen *MiSFD 9*
LaRoe, Edward Terhune, III 1943- *WhoE 93*
LaRosa, Christopher 1958- *St&PR 93*
LaRosa, Daniel Carmel 1949- *WhoE 93*
LaRosa, Dominic Joseph 1942- *St&PR 93*
LaRosa, Julius 1956- *WhoE 93, WhoEmL 93*
LaRosa, Mario F. 1947- *St&PR 93*
LaRosa, Paul S. 1942- *St&PR 93*
LaRosa, Robert A. 1938- *WhoE 93*
La Rosa, Roseann J. *Law&B 92*
La Rosa Parodi, Armando 1904-1977 *Baker 92*
Larose, Arthur P. 1932- *St&PR 93*
LaRose, David E. *Law&B 92*
Larose, Jean-Francois 1946- *WhoScE 91-2*
Larose, Juanita M. 1931- *St&PR 93*
LaRose, Keith Vernon 1953- *WhoEmL 93*
Larose, Lawrence Alfred 1958- *WhoE 93, WhoEmL 93, WhoWor 93*
Larose, Roger 1910- *WhoAm 92*
Larosiere de Champfeu, Jacques 1929- *WhoWor 93*
La Rossa, James Michael 1931- *WhoAm 92*
La Rotella, Pasquale 1880-1963 *Baker 92*
LaRouche, Lyndon 1923- *PolPar*
LaRouche, Lyndon H. *BioIn 17*
LaRouche, Lyndon H., Jr. 1922- *WhoAm 92*
LaRouche, Lyndon H(ermyle), Jr. 1922- *ConAu 138*
Larounis, George Philip 1928- *WhoAm 92, WhoWor 93*
Larousse, Jean 1937- *WhoScE 91-2*
Laroux, Carmen *SweetSg C*
Larovere, Ralph W. 1935- *St&PR 93*
Larowe, Nina Churchman 1838-1921 *BioIn 17*
Larpenteur, James Albert, Jr. 1935- *WhoAm 92*
Larr, Peter 1939- *St&PR 93, WhoAm 92*
Larra, F. *WhoScE 91-2*
Larrabee, Constance Stuart *BioIn 17*
Larrabee, Donald Richard 1923- *WhoAm 92*
Larrabee, Eric *BioIn 17*
Larrabee, June Hansen 1946- *WhoEmL 93, WhoSSW 93*
Larrabee, Leonard P., III *Law&B 92*
Larrabee, Martin Glover 1910- *WhoAm 92*
Larrabee, Richard M. *WhoE 93*
Larrabee, Robert 1907- *St&PR 93*
Larrabee, Susan B. *Law&B 92*
Larrabeiti, Michael de *ScF&FL 92*
Larrabure, Juan Luis 1949- *WhoUN 92*
Larraga, Vicente 1948- *WhoScE 91-3*
Larrauri, Agustin A. 1942- *WhoUN 92*
Larrazabal Antezana, Erik 1958- *WhoWor 93*
Larre, James G. *Law&B 92*
Larreamendy Joerns, Alejandro 1960- *WhoWor 93*
Larrecq, Anthony James 1908- *St&PR 93*
Larrenaga, Alfred V. *St&PR 93*
Larriba, German 1949- *WhoScE 91-3*
Larrick, James William 1950- *WhoAm 92*
Larrick, Michael Paul 1943- *WhoE 93*
Larrick, Nancy *BioIn 17*
Larrick, Nancy 1910- *WhoAmW 93*
Larrick, Warren Edward 1933- *St&PR 93*
Larrier, Renee Brenda 1950- *WhoAmW 93*
Larrieu Smith, Francie 1953?- *BioIn 17*
Larrimer, Mary *AmWomPl*
Larrimore, James A. 1934- *WhoUN 92*
Larrimore, Lida *AmWomPl*
Larrimore, Patsy Gadd 1933- *WhoAmW 93, WhoWor 93*
Larrimore, Randall Walter 1947- *WhoAm 92*
Larrivee, Henri 1737-1802 *Baker 92, OxDcOp*
Larrivee, Marie Jeanne 1733-1786 *Baker 92*
Larroca, Raymond G. 1930- *WhoAm 92, WhoWor 93*
Larrocha (y de la Calle), Alicia de 1923- *Baker 92*
L'Arronge, Adolf 1838-1908 *Baker 92*
Larroquette, John Bernard 1947- *WhoAm 92*
Larrouilh, Michel 1935- *St&PR 93, WhoAm 92*
Larrouturou, Bernard Jean 1958- *WhoWor 93*
Larrouy, David Ralph *Law&B 92*
Larrowe, Charles Patrick 1916- *WhoAm 92*
Larrue, Jacky *WhoScE 91-2*
Larry, R. Heath 1914- *WhoAm 92*
Larry, Sheldon 1949- *MiSFD 9*
Lars, Claudia 1889-1974 *SpAmA*
Lars, Claudia 1899-1974 *BioIn 17*
Larsen, Andrew J. 1947- *St&PR 93*
Larsen, Anita Margaret 1960- *WhoE 93*
Larsen, Annabelle *BioIn 17*
Larsen, Anne 1941- *WhoAm 92*
Larsen, Annette 1951- *WhoE 93*
Larsen, Arild *WhoScE 91-4*
Larsen, Arne 1936- *WhoScE 91-2*
Larsen, Arthur David 1925- *BiDAMSp 1989*
Larsen, B. Ahrenst *WhoScE 91-2*
Larsen, Barbara Kay *Law&B 92*
Larsen, Christian-Jacques 1938- *WhoScE 91-2*
Larsen, Don *BioIn 17*
Larsen, Donna Kay *WhoAmW 93*
Larsen, Edgar Robert, Jr. 1950- *WhoE 93*
Larsen, Edward G. 1951- *St&PR 93*
Larsen, Edwin Merritt 1915- *WhoAm 92*
Larsen, Elizabeth B. 1950- *WhoAmW 93*
Larsen, Eric *BioIn 17*
Larsen, Eric 1941- *WhoE 93*
Larsen, Eric Lyle 1954- *WhoSSW 93*
Larsen, Erik 1911- *WhoAm 92, WhoWor 93*
Larsen, Erik Allan 1968- *WhoE 93*
Larsen, Ethel Paulson 1918- *WhoAmW 93*
Larsen, Gary Loy 1945- *WhoAm 92*
Larsen, Hans 1945- *WhoScE 91-2, WhoWor 93*
Larsen, Hans Jorgen 1935- *WhoScE 91-2*
Larsen, Helge 1922- *WhoScE 91-4, WhoWor 93*
Larsen, Helge Kristen 1944- *WhoUN 92*
Larsen, Howard R. 1929- *St&PR 93*
Larsen, J. Bo 1949- *WhoScE 91-3*
Larsen, Jack Lenor *BioIn 17*
Larsen, Jan Martin *WhoScE 91-4*
Larsen, Janine Louise 1959- *WhoAmW 93*
Larsen, Jeanne 1950- *ScF&FL 92*
Larsen, Jeanne Louise 1950- *WhoWrEP 92*
Larsen, Jeffrey R. *Law&B 92*
Larsen, Jens Peter 1902-1988 *Baker 92*
Larsen, Jerry *BioIn 17*
Larsen, Jesper Kampmann 1950- *WhoWor 93*
Larsen, John Christian 1929- *WhoE 93*
Larsen, John Mathue, Jr. 1922- *WhoSSW 93*
Larsen, John S. 1939- *St&PR 93*
Larsen, John W. 1914-1990 *BioIn 17*
Larsen, Jonathan Zerbe 1940- *WhoAm 92*
Larsen, Jorgen *WhoScE 91-2*
Larsen, Jorgen Skou 1951- *WhoWor 93*
Larsen, Kai 1926- *WhoScE 91-2*
Larsen, Kent W. 1938- *St&PR 93*
Larsen, Larry Lee 1937- *WhoE 93*
Larsen, Laurence Putnam 1955- *WhoWor 93*
Larsen, Leif Andreas 1906-1990 *BioIn 17*
Larsen, Leo B. 1946- *WhoScE 91-2*
Larsen, Libby 1950- *Baker 92, BioIn 17*
Larsen, Lis Olesen 1933- *WhoScE 91-2*
Larsen, Mark Arvid 1948- *WhoE 93, WhoEmL 93*
Larsen, Mike 1944- *BioIn 17*
Larsen, Morgens Esrom 1942- *WhoWor 93*
Larsen, Neil Allyn 1952- *WhoE 93*
Larsen, Nella *BioIn 17*
Larsen, Nella 1891-1964 *EncAACR*
Larsen, Nels C. 1929- *St&PR 93*
Larsen, Niels Ove 1938- *WhoAm 92*
Larsen, Nils 1888-1937 *Baker 92*
Larsen, Ole Naesbye 1947- *WhoScE 91-2*
Larsen, Ole Nymark 1935- *WhoScE 91-2*
Larsen, Ole Stevens 1934- *WhoWor 93*
Larsen, Patricia Jane 1933- *WhoAmW 93*
Larsen, Paul A. 1949- *St&PR 93*
Larsen, Paul Emanuel 1933- *WhoAm 92*
Larsen, Peder Olesen 1934- *WhoScE 91-2, WhoWor 93*
Larsen, Per Arne 1944- *St&PR 93*
Larsen, Per Kristian 1940- *WhoScE 91-4*
Larsen, Phillip Nelson 1929- *WhoAm 92*
Larsen, Poul S. 1933- *WhoScE 91-2*
Larsen, R. Sinding *WhoScE 91-4*
Larsen, Ralph Irving 1928- *WhoAm 92, WhoSSW 93, WhoWor 93*
Larsen, Ralph S. 1938- *St&PR 93*
Larsen, Ralph Stanley 1938- *WhoAm 92, WhoE 93, WhoWor 93*
Larsen, Richard Gary 1948- *WhoAm 92*
Larsen, Richard Lee 1934- *WhoAm 92*
Larsen, Robert Dhu 1922- *WhoAm 92*
Larsen, Robert LeRoy 1934- *WhoAm 92*
Larsen, Ronald John 1937- *WhoE 93*
Larsen, Severin Olesen *WhoScE 91-2*
Larsen, Steve *BioIn 17*
Larsen, Susan Carol 1946- *WhoAm 92*
Larsen, Ted L. 1935- *St&PR 93*
Larsen, Terrence A. 1946- *St&PR 93*
Larsen, Thor *WhoScE 91-4*
Larsen, Torben 1942- *WhoScE 91-2*
Larsen, Ture Kindt *WhoScE 91-2*
Larsen, Wayne E. 1954- *St&PR 93*
Larsen, Wendy Wilder 1940- *WhoWrEP 92*
Larsen, William Lawrence 1926- *WhoAm 92*
Larsen-Todsen, Nanny 1884-1982 *Baker 92, OxDcOp*
Larsh, Howard William 1914- *WhoAm 92*
Larsimont, Charles Henri 1938- *WhoUN 92*
Larsomneur, Lee *St&PR 93*
Larson, Alan Andrew 1955- *WhoAm 92*
Larson, Alan Philip 1949- *WhoAm 92*
Larson, Alan W. 1938- *St&PR 93*
Larson, Allan Bennett 1943- *WhoE 93*
Larson, Allan Louis 1932- *WhoAm 92, WhoWor 93*
Larson, Anthony Lyle 1943- *WhoSSW 93*
Larson, April U. *WhoAmW 93*
Larson, Arthur Stanley 1925- *WhoWor 93*
Larson, Bennett Charles 1941- *WhoAm 92*
Larson, Bradley E. 1954- *St&PR 93*
Larson, Brent T. 1942- *WhoAm 92*
Larson, Brian Keith 1958- *St&PR 93*
Larson, Bruce Robert 1955- *WhoSSW 93*
Larson, Carl Everett 1939- *WhoAm 92*
Larson, Carol Lynn 1963- *WhoAmW 93*
Larson, Charles 1968- *WhoWrEP 92*
Larson, Charles Fred 1936- *WhoAm 92*
Larson, Charles Lester 1922- *WhoAm 92*
Larson, Charles Robert 1936- *WhoAm 92*
Larson, Christine *SweetSg C*
Larson, Clarence Edward 1909- *WhoAm 92*
Larson, Craig E. *Law&B 92*
Larson, Cynthia M. 1957- *St&PR 93*
Larson, Dale Irving 1937- *WhoAm 92*
Larson, Daniel N. 1954- *St&PR 93*
Larson, Daniel William 1954- *WhoWrEP 92*
Larson, David Bruce 1947- *WhoAm 92*
Larson, David Miles 1948- *WhoSSW 93*
Larson, Deborah Compel 1955- *WhoEmL 93*
Larson, Deborah Lynn 1952- *WhoAmW 93*
Larson, Diane LaVerne Kusler 1942- *WhoAmW 93*
Larson, Donald Clayton 1934- *WhoAm 92, WhoE 93*
Larson, Donald Dumford 1951- *WhoIns 93*
Larson, Donald Vernon 1934- *St&PR 93*
Larson, Doyle Eugene 1930- *WhoAm 92*
Larson, Earl Richard 1911- *WhoAm 92*
Larson, Earnie *BioIn 17*
Larson, Elizabeth Ann 1954- *WhoAmW 93*
Larson, Ellen Ruth 1960- *WhoWor 93*
Larson, Elwin S. 1926- *St&PR 93*
Larson, Emilie Gustava 1919- *WhoAmW 93*
Larson, Emma Mauritz *AmWomPl*
Larson, Eric L. *Law&B 92*
Larson, Eric Martin 1950- *WhoE 93*
Larson, Fred A. 1940- *St&PR 93*
Larson, Gary *BioIn 17*
Larson, Gary 1950- *WhoAm 92*
Larson, Gayle Elizabeth 1942- *WhoAmW 93*
Larson, Gaylen Nevoy 1940- *St&PR 93, WhoAm 92*
Larson, George Charles 1942- *WhoAm 92*
Larson, Glen A. *MiSFD 9*
Larson, Glen A. 1937- *ScF&FL 92*
Larson, Gordon *St&PR 93*
Larson, Gregg Michael *Law&B 92*
Larson, Harry Robert 1945- *WhoAm 92*
Larson, Harry Thomas 1921- *WhoAm 92*
Larson, Howard Bruce 1953- *WhoEmL 93, WhoWor 93*
Larson, Howard James 1931- *WhoAm 92*
Larson, Jacqueline S. *Law&B 92*
Larson, Jacquelynne Borst 1938- *WhoAmW 93*
Larson, James Robert 1950- *St&PR 93*
Larson, James Roger 1947- *St&PR 93*
Larson, Jane Arline 1948- *WhoEmL 93*
Larson, Jane Warren 1922- *WhoE 93*
Larson, Jean Ann 1959- *WhoAmW 93*
Larson, Jean Russell 1930- *DcAmChF 1960*
Larson, Jerry L. 1936- *WhoAm 92*
Larson, John August 1945- *St&PR 93*
Larson, John Barry 1948- *WhoAm 92*
Larson, John David 1941- *St&PR 93, WhoAm 92, WhoIns 93*
Larson, John Hyde 1930- *WhoAm 92*
Larson, John William 1935- *WhoAm 92*
Larson, Jonathan I. *Law&B 92*
Larson, Joseph A. 1920- *St&PR 93*
Larson, Joseph Stanley 1933- *WhoAm 92*
Larson, Julia Louise Fink 1950- *WhoAmW 93, WhoEmL 93, WhoWor 93*
Larson, Karen Ann 1949- *WhoAmW 93*
Larson, Karen Elaine 1947- *WhoEmL 93, WhoWor 93*
Larson, Karin Louise 1938- *St&PR 93*
Larson, Keith Willis 1942- *St&PR 93*
Larson, Kenneth Duane 1940- *St&PR 93*
Larson, Kermit Dean 1939- *WhoAm 92*
Larson, L.G. 1931- *St&PR 93*
Larson, Larry 1940- *WhoAm 92*
Larson, Lawrence John 1904- *WhoAm 92*
Larson, Lawrence Milton 1903- *St&PR 93*
Larson, Lee 1937- *BioIn 17*
Larson, Lee Ercell *Law&B 92*
Larson, Leonard Louis 1936- *WhoAm 92*
Larson, Linda K. 1942- *WhoE 93*
Larson, Lloyd Jack 1931- *St&PR 93*
Larson, Lloyd Warren 1920- *WhoE 93*
Larson, Lorell Vincent 1918- *WhoSSW 93*
Larson, Majliss *ScF&FL 92*
Larson, Marc William *Law&B 92*
Larson, Marc William 1953- *WhoEmL 93*
Larson, Margareta Glas- 1911- *BioIn 17*
Larson, Marjorie Marie 1922- *WhoWrEP 92*
Larson, Mark Allan 1948- *WhoAm 92*
Larson, Marlene Louise 1952- *WhoEmL 93*
Larson, Martin Alfred 1897- *WhoAm 92*
Larson, Mary E. 1944- *St&PR 93*
Larson, Maureen Inez 1955- *WhoWor 93*
Larson, Maurice Allen 1927- *WhoAm 92*
Larson, Mel 1929- *WhoAm 92*
Larson, Melinda Sue 1954- *WhoAmW 93*
Larson, Melvin Leon 1929- *St&PR 93*
Larson, Meria Ellena 1942- *WhoAmW 93*
Larson, Merlin L. 1937- *St&PR 93*
Larson, Michael J. 1941- *St&PR 93*
Larson, Mitchell Euray 1957- *WhoEmL 93*
Larson, Nancy Celeste 1951- *WhoAmW 93, WhoEmL 93, WhoWor 93*
Larson, Ove 1954- *WhoScE 91-4*
Larson, Paul E. 1952- *St&PR 93*
Larson, Paul Edward 1952- *WhoAm 92*
Larson, Randall D. 1954- *ScF&FL 92, WhoWrEP 92*
Larson, Randy *WhoWrEP 92*
Larson, Ray B. 1923- *St&PR 93*
Larson, Rebecca Lee 1958- *WhoEmL 93*
Larson, Reed Eugene 1922- *WhoAm 92*
Larson, Richard Albert 1930- *St&PR 93*
Larson, Richard Bondo 1941- *WhoAm 92*
Larson, Richard Charles 1943- *WhoAm 92*
Larson, Richard E. 1924- *St&PR 93*
Larson, Richard Gustaf 1942- *WhoAm 92*
Larson, Richard William 1948- *St&PR 93*
Larson, Robert Craig 1934- *WhoAm 92*
Larson, Robert Edward 1938- *WhoAm 92*
Larson, Robert Frederick 1930- *WhoAm 92*
Larson, Robert Roland 1931- *St&PR 93*
Larson, Roberta *ScF&FL 92*
Larson, Rolf J. 1934- *St&PR 93*
Larson, Roma Barksdale *Law&B 92*
Larson, Ronald Alan 1948- *St&PR 93*
Larson, Ronald Charles 1936- *St&PR 93*
Larson, Ronald Dale 1935- *St&PR 93*
Larson, Ronald G. 1930- *St&PR 93*
Larson, Ronald K. 1945- *St&PR 93*
Larson, Ronald L. 1953- *St&PR 93*
Larson, Rosamond Winterton 1932- *WhoWrEP 92*
Larson, Ross 1935- *ScF&FL 92*
Larson, Roy 1929- *WhoAm 92*
Larson, Roy B. *Law&B 92*
Larson, Russell Edward 1917- *WhoAm 92*
Larson, Ryan 1950- *WhoIns 93*
Larson, Ryan R. 1950- *St&PR 93*
Larson, Sidney 1923- *WhoAm 92*

Larson, Stanley E. 1925- St&PR 93
Larson, Stephen R. Law&B 92
Larson, Steve 1944- St&PR 93
Larson, Todd L. 1961- St&PR 93
Larson, Trudy Elizabeth 1966- WhoAmW 93
Larson, Virginia Mary 1912- WhoAmW 93
Larson, Ward Jerome 1924- WhoAm 92
Larson, Wilfred Joseph 1927- WhoAm 92
Larson, William Beckwith 1937- St&PR 93
Larson, Wolf BioIn 17
Larson-Asplund, Shelley Beth 1966- WhoAmW 93
Larsonneur, Claude WhoScE 91-2
Larsonneur, Lee 1933- St&PR 93
Larsson, Agne G. 1939- WhoScE 91-4
Larsson, Ake L. 1944- WhoScE 91-4
Larsson, Anders 1956- WhoScE 91-4
Larsson, Anders Lars 1952- WhoWor 93
Larsson, Bo Gunnar Torbjorn 1959- WhoWor 93
Larsson, Hans Lennart 1942- WhoAm 92
Larsson, Karl-Erik Axel 1923- WhoScE 91-4
Larsson, Kent 1946- WhoScE 91-4
Larsson, Kjell 1947- WhoScE 91-4
Larsson, Knut Bertil 1922- WhoWor 93
Larsson, Lars-Erik (Vilner) 1908-1986 Baker 92
Larsson, Lars-Inge WhoScE 91-2
Larsson, Olle BioIn 17
Larsson, William Dean 1945- St&PR 93
La Rue, Arlene Catherine 1912- WhoWrEP 92
La Rue, Carl Forman 1929- WhoAm 92
LaRue, Denise Carol 1947- WhoAmW 93
La Rue, Dorie Ann 1948- WhoSSW 93
Larue, Frank DcCPCAm
La Rue, Henry Aldred 1927- WhoAm 92
La Rue, James Albert 1941- WhoSSW 93
La Rue, (Adrian) Jan (Pieters) 1918- Baker 92
La Rue, Jan Pieters 1918- WhoAm 92
LaRue, Janis M. Law&B 92
LaRue, Molly d1990 BioIn 17
La Rue, Monique 1948- WhoCanL 92
LaRue, Paul Hubert 1922- WhoAm 92
La Rue, Pierre de c. 1460-1518 Baker 92
LaRue, Ray 1945- St&PR 93
LaRue, Richard Law&B 92
Laruette, Jean-Louis 1731-1792 OxDcOp
LaRussa, Anthony, Jr. 1944- BiDAMSp 1989
La Russa, Anthony Tony, Jr. 1944- WhoAm 92
LaRussa, Joseph Anthony 1925- WhoAm 92
LaRussa, Luann 1954- WhoE 93
LaRussa, Tony BioIn 17
LaRusso, Anthony Carl 1949- WhoEmL 93
La Russo, Marianne Elizabeth 1949- WhoAmW 93
Larvor, Pierre A. 1930- WhoScE 91-2
Larwood, Laurie 1941- WhoAmW 93
Lary, Yale 1930- BioIn 17
Larzelere, Harry J. 1941- WhoIns 93
Larzelere, William E., Jr. 1949- St&PR 93
Lasa, Jose M. 1946- WhoScE 91-3
Lasa, Luis R. 1949- St&PR 93
Lasaga, Antonio C. 1949- WhoAm 92
LaSage, John David 1937- WhoAm 92
Lasage, Michel J.P. 1936- WhoUN 92
Lasagna, Louis Cesare 1923- WhoAm 92
Lasak, John Joseph 1944- WhoE 93
LaSala, Joseph Anthony 1923- St&PR 93
LaSala, Samuel Philip 1949- WhoAm 92
Lasala, Stephen R. Law&B 92
La Salette, Joubert de 1743-1833 Baker 92
LaSalla, Susan 1943- WhoSSW 93
Lasalle, Antoine Charles Louis 1775-1809 HarEnMi
La Salle, Arthur Edward 1930- WhoAm 92, WhoSSW 93
LaSalle, Denise 1939- BioIn 17
LaSalle, Jean-Louis Baker 92
Lasalle, Karen Frances F. 1944- WhoAmW 93
La Salle, Peter 1947- WhoWrEP 92
La Salle, Rene Robert Cavelier 1643-1687 BioIn 17, Expl 93 [port]
La Salle, Robert Cavelier, sieur de 1643-1687 BioIn 17
la Salle, Victor ScF&FL 92
Lasalle, William J. Law&B 92
Lasan, Dolores Baja 1935- WhoUN 92
Lasaro, Iairo 1952- WhoAsAP 91
Lasarow, William Julius 1922- WhoAm 92
LaSarre, William Jolly 1931- St&PR 93
Lasater, Charles W. 1936- St&PR 93
Lasater, Garland M., Jr. 1938- St&PR 93
Lasater, Sandra Jo 1948- WhoAmW 93
LaScala, Anthony Charles 1924- St&PR 93
Lascara, Vincent Alfred 1919- WhoAm 92
Lascaux, Patrick 1943- WhoScE 91-2
Lasch, Christopher BioIn 17
Lasch, Christopher 1932- WhoAm 92, WhoWrEP 92
Lasch, Moira BioIn 17
Lasch, Robert 1907- WhoAm 92
Laschenski, John Patrick 1937- WhoE 93
Laschuk, Andrew Law&B 92
Laschuk, Roy Bogdan 1932- WhoAm 92
Lasdun, Denys Louis 1914- WhoWor 93
Lasdun, James 1958- ConAu 137
Lasek, Andre 1926- WhoScE 91-2
Lasek, Margaret Anne 1962- WhoAmW 93
Lasell, Chester Krum 1936- St&PR 93
Lasell, Raymond E. 1935- St&PR 93
Laselle, Mary Augusta 1860- AmWomPl
Lasenby, Jack 1931- BioIn 17
Laser, Charles, Jr. 1933- WhoSSW 93
Laser, Robert Redman, Jr. Law&B 92
Laserna, Blas de 1751-1816 Baker 92
Laserson, Lillian J. Law&B 92
Lasezkay, George M. Law&B 92
Lash, Douglas Steven 1948- WhoEmL 93
Lash, Fred 1945- St&PR 93
Lash, Irving d1991 BioIn 17
Lash, James William 1929- WhoE 93
Lash, Jeffrey N. 1949- ConAu 136
Lash, Linda Marie 1948- WhoWor 93
Lash, Mary Elizabeth 1928- WhoAmW 93
Lash, Myles Perry 1946- WhoAm 92
Lash, Nathaniel Robert 1922- WhoE 93
Lash, Richard Anthony 1961- WhoEmL 93, WhoSSW 93, WhoWor 93
Lash, Stephen Sycle 1940- WhoAm 92
Lashar, Walter Benjamin 1929- St&PR 93
Lashbrooke, Elvin Carroll, Jr. 1939- WhoAm 92
Lashelle, Charles S. 1947- St&PR 93
LaShelle, Charles Stanton 1947- WhoAm 92, WhoWor 93
Lasher, Donald R. 1929- WhoIns 93
Lasher, Donald Rex 1929- WhoAm 92
Lasher, Donna Maria 1948- WhoAmW 93, WhoEmL 93
Lasher, John A. 1951- St&PR 93
Lasher, Michael WhoWrEP 92
Lasher, Russell J. 1918- St&PR 93
Lashlee, JoLynne Van Marsdon 1948- WhoAmW 93
Lashley, Barbara Theresa 1944- WhoE 93
Lashley, Curtis Dale 1956- WhoEmL 93, WhoWor 93
Lashley, Kara Michele 1965- WhoSSW 93
Lashley, Mark Alan 1959- WhoE 93, WhoEmL 93
Lashley, Mary Ellen 1959- WhoAmW 93
Lashley, Virginia Stephenson Hughes 1924- WhoAmW 93
Lashman, Terrence O. 1944- St&PR 93
Lashman, Yvonne P. St&PR 93
Lashmit, Douglas A. Law&B 92
Lashner, Howard Bruce 1962- WhoEmL 93
Lashner, Marilyn Auerbach 1929- WhoE 93
Lashnits, Thomas Peter 1948- WhoWrEP 92
Lashof, Joyce C. WhoAmW 93
Lashoones, Richard H. 1950- St&PR 93
Lashutka, Gregory S. 1944- WhoAm 92
Lasiecka, Irena M. 1948- WhoAmW 93, WhoEmL 93, WhoSSW 93
Las Infantas, Fernando de Baker 92
Lasjaunias, Pierre Louis 1948- WhoScE 91-2
Laska, Gustav 1847-1928 Baker 92
Laska, John L. 1941- St&PR 93
Laskar, Amulya L. 1931-1991 BioIn 17
Laskari, Kerry Rusi 1958- WhoSSW 93
Laskaris OxDcByz
Laskaris, John fl. 15th cent.- OxDcByz
Laskay, Patricia Joann 1942- WhoAmW 93
Lasker, Bernard J. 1910-1992 BioIn 17, NewYTBS 92 [port]
Lasker, Edward 1912- WhoAm 92
Lasker, Emanuel 1868-1941 BioIn 17
Lasker, Gabriel Ward 1912- WhoAm 92
Lasker, Joan BioIn 17
Lasker, Joe ConAu 38NR
Lasker, Joel M. Law&B 92
Lasker, Joel Marc 1946- St&PR 93
Lasker, Jonathan Lewis 1948- WhoAm 92
Lasker, Joseph L. 1919- WhoAm 92
Lasker, Joseph Leon 1919- ConAu 38NR
Lasker, Martin 1932- St&PR 93
Lasker, Mary WhoAm 92
Lasker, Mary 1900- BioIn 17
Lasker-Schuler, Else 1869-1945 DcLB 124 [port]
Laskey, Lawrence A. Law&B 92
Laskey, Richard Anthony 1936- WhoAm 92
Laski, Frank Joseph 1929- WhoAm 92
Laski, Frida 1885- BioIn 17
Laski, Marghanita 1915-1988 ScF&FL 92
Laskiewicz, Larry K. Law&B 92
Laskin, Arthur James 1927- St&PR 93
Laskin, Bruce Steven 1956- St&PR 93
Laskin, Carol Rubin 1948- WhoE 93
Laskin, Daniel M. 1924- WhoAm 92
Laskin, Emily Jane 1953- WhoAmW 93
Laskin, Lee B. 1936- WhoE 93
Laskin, Richard Sheldon 1940- WhoWor 93
Laskine, Lily 1893-1988 Baker 92
Lasko, Allen Howard 1941- WhoWor 93
Lasko, John C. St&PR 93
Lasko, Richard P. Law&B 92
Laskow, Lynda Therese 1947- WhoEmL 93
Laskow, Mark J. Law&B 92
Laskowski, Irma Williams 1943- WhoAmW 93
Laskowski, Janusz Stanislaw 1936- WhoAm 92
Laskowski, Joanne Frances 1954- WhoAmW 93
Laskowski, Leonard Francis, Jr. 1919- WhoAm 92
Laskowski, Michael, Jr. 1930- WhoAm 92
Laskowski, Robert A. 1951- St&PR 93, WhoAm 92
Lasky, Barry St&PR 93
Lasky, David Law&B 92
Lasky, David 1932- St&PR 93, WhoAm 92
Lasky, Elizabeth Marchelewicz 1945- WhoE 93
Lasky, Jack Samuel 1930- St&PR 93
Lasky, Janet Louise 1955- WhoWrEP 92
Lasky, Jesse Louis 1880-1958 BioIn 17
Lasky, Kathryn BioIn 17
Lasky, Kathryn 1944- DcAmChF 1985, MajAI [port], ScF&FL 92, SmATA 69 [port]
Lasky, Marc Evan 1945- St&PR 93
Lasky, Melvin J. 1920- ColdWar 1 [port]
Lasky, Moses 1907- WhoAm 92
Lasky, Victor 1918-1990 BioIn 17
Lasley, John 1927- St&PR 93
Lasley, Thomas Terrell Law&B 92
Laslo, Ruth G. Law&B 92
Lasner, Ignaz 1815-1883 Baker 92
Lasner, Mark Samuels 1952- WhoE 93
Lasner, Russell Paul 1956- WhoE 93
Lasnick, Julius 1929- WhoAm 92
Lasnier, Rina 1915- WhoCanL 92
Lasoff, Mark WhoAm 92
Lason, Sandra Woolman 1934- WhoAmW 93
Lasonde, Marilynn Joy 1956- WhoWrEP 92
La Sor, William Sanford 1911- WhoAm 92
Lasorda, Thomas Charles 1927- BiDAMSp 1989
Lasorda, Thomas Charles Tom 1927- WhoAm 92
Lasorda, Tom BioIn 17
Lasota, Wanda Marta 1926- WhoScE 91-4
LaSpagnoletta, Benjamin Joseph 1946- WhoE 93, WhoEmL 93
la Spina, Greye 1880-1969 ScF&FL 92
Laspina, Peter Joseph 1951- WhoE 93, WhoEmL 93
Lasry, Claude 1956- WhoE 93
Lasry, Jean-Michel 1947- WhoWor 93
Lass, E. Donald 1938- St&PR 93
Lass, Ernest Donald 1938- WhoAm 92
Lass, Norman Jay 1943- WhoSSW 93
Lassalle, Jean 1847-1909 OxDcOp
Lassalle, Jean (-Louis) 1847-1909 Baker 92
Lassalle, Jean Michel 1947- WhoScE 91-2
Lassally, Walter 1926- ConTFT 10
Lassaw, Ibram 1913- WhoAm 92
Lasselle, Richard Charles 1946- WhoWor 93
Lassen, Arne Christian 1938- St&PR 93
Lassen, Eduard 1830-1904 Baker 92
Lassen, John Kai 1942- WhoE 93
Lassen, John Richard 1922- St&PR 93
Lassen, Lars 1929- WhoScE 91-3
Lassen, Pamela J. Sykes 1957- WhoAmW 93
Lassen, Peter d1859 BioIn 17
Lassen, Stuart Allan 1932- St&PR 93
Lassen, Ulrik V. 1930- WhoScE 91-2
Lasser, Alyse I. Law&B 92
Lasser, Brian d1992 NewYTBS 92
Lasser, Dustin ScF&FL 92
Lasser, Harold H. 1928- St&PR 93
Lasser, Joseph R. 1923- St&PR 93
Lasser, Joseph Robert 1923- WhoAm 92
Lasser, Louise WhoAm 92
Lasserre, Jean Bernard 1953- WhoWor 93
Lasserre, Jean Paul 1942- WhoE 93
Lasserre, Pierre 1940- WhoScE 91-2
Lasserre, Pierre Rene Jean 1940- WhoScE 91-2
Lassers, Willard J. 1919- WhoAm 92
Lassesen, Catherine Clay 1961- WhoAmW 93
Lasseter, Charles Erwin 1932- St&PR 93
Lasseter, Earle Forrest 1933- WhoAm 92
Lasseter, James, Jr. 1939- WhoSSW 93
Lasseter, Kenneth Carlyle 1942- WhoAm 92, WhoSSW 93
Lassettre, Edwin N. 1911-1990 BioIn 17
Lassick, Sydney 1922- WhoAm 92
Lassiter, Barbara Ann 1960- WhoEmL 93
Lassiter, Catherine Sparks 1922- WhoSSW 93
Lassiter, Edward M. 1935- St&PR 93
Lassiter, Isaac Steele 1941- WhoWrEP 92
Lassiter, James Harrison 1940- St&PR 93
Lassiter, James Morris, Jr. 1941- WhoSSW 93
Lassiter, John Douglas 1941- WhoSSW 93
Lassiter, John Wells Law&B 92
Lassiter, Joseph Baker, III 1947- St&PR 93
Lassiter, Kenneth T. 1935- WhoAm 92
Lassiter, Phillip B. 1943- St&PR 93
Lassiter, Reynolds B. H. 1963- WhoSSW 93
Lassiter, Ronald Corbett 1932- St&PR 93, WhoAm 92
Lassiter, Sybil Mae 1928- WhoAmW 93
Lasslo, Andrew 1922- WhoAm 92, WhoSSW 93, WhoWor 93
Lassman, Adrienne 1933- WhoAmW 93
Lassner, Franz George 1926- WhoAm 92
Lassner, Keith Michael 1949- WhoAm 92, WhoEmL 93
Lasso, Orlando di 1532-1594 Baker 92
Lasson, Mathieu d1553? BioIn 17
Lasson, Sally Ann BioIn 17
Lassonde, Richard Law&B 92
Lassou, Gouara 1948- WhoAfr
Lassus, Ferdinand de c. 1560-1609 Baker 92
Lassus, Rudolph de c. 1563-1625 Baker 92
Lasswell, Marcia Lee 1927- WhoAm 92
Lasswell, Thomas Ely 1919- WhoAm 92
Last, Alvin I. 1932- St&PR 93
Last, John Murray 1926- WhoWor 93
Last, Jurgen Friedrich 1956- WhoWor 93
Last, Marian Helen 1953- WhoAmW 93
Last, Martin 1929- ScF&FL 92
Last, Norman H. 1962- St&PR 93
Last, Sondra Carole 1932- WhoAmW 93
LaStaiti, Ronald Scott 1941- WhoAm 92
Laster, Atlas, Jr. 1948- WhoEmL 93, WhoWor 93
Laster, Elizabeth 1928- St&PR 93
Laster, Judith Eve 1959- WhoEmL 93
Laster, LaMar Frederick 1951- St&PR 93
Laster, Leonard 1928- WhoAm 92, WhoE 93
Laster, Oliver 1921- St&PR 93
Laster, Paul Alan 1951- WhoE 93
Laster, Ralph W. 1951- St&PR 93
Laster, Ralph William, Jr. 1951- WhoAm 92
Laster, Richard 1923- St&PR 93, WhoAm 92, WhoWor 93
Lastinger, Allen L. 1942- St&PR 93
Lastinger, Allen Lane, Jr. 1942- WhoSSW 93
Lastman, Melvin D. 1933- WhoAm 92, WhoWor 93
Lastowka, James Anthony 1951- WhoAm 92
Lastra, Idalia 1953- WhoSSW 93
Lastra, Jose Ramon 1939- WhoWor 93
Lastrapes, J. Stephen Law&B 92
Lasuchin, Michael 1923- WhoE 93
Lasusa, Barbara E. Law&B 92
LaSusa, Lawrence R. Law&B 92
Laswell, Bette Dowdell 1937- WhoAmW 93
Laswell, Harry Reginald 1940- WhoSSW 93
Laswell, Lucien Kroll 1939- St&PR 93
Laswell, Troy James 1920- WhoAm 92
Laszczka, Andrzej Konstanty 1930- WhoScE 91-4
Laszewski, Ronald Thomas 1949- WhoEmL 93
Laszewski, Ryszard Stanislaw 1941- WhoWor 93
Laszlo, I 1046?-1095 OxDcByz
Laszlo, Alexander 1895-1970 Baker 92
Laszlo, Aranka 1934- WhoScE 91-4
Laszlo, Janos 1922- WhoScE 91-4
Laszlo, Magda 1919- OxDcOp
Laszlo, Pierre 1938- WhoScE 91-2
Laszlo, Zoltan 1916- WhoScE 91-4
Lasztity, Radomir 1929- WhoScE 91-4
Lat, Emelyn Cruz BioIn 17
Latacz, Joachim 1934- WhoWor 93
Lataif, Lawrence P. 1943- WhoAm 92
Lataille, Ronald J. St&PR 93
Latalski, Maciej 1936- WhoScE 91-4
Latane, Bibb 1937- WhoAm 92, WhoSSW 93
Latane, David Eaton 1952- WhoSSW 93
Latanich, Terry S. 1950- St&PR 93
Latanision, Ronald Michael 1942- WhoAm 92, WhoE 93
Latcham, Franklin Chester 1922- WhoAm 92
Latchford, James J. 1944- St&PR 93
Latchford, Paul Carroll Law&B 92

Latchis, Kenneth Spero 1935- *WhoE 93*
Latchman, David Seymour *WhoScE 91-1*
Latchum, James Levin 1918- *WhoAm 92, WhoE 93*
Lateef, Noel V. *Law&B 92*
Lateef, Noel V. 1956- *St&PR 93*
Lateef, Tolens. *ConAu 139*
Lateef, Yusef 1920- *WhoAm 92*
Lateiner, Jacob 1928- *Baker 92*
Latek, Stanislaw Jan 1938- *WhoWor 93*
Latella, Robert N. *Law&B 92*
Latella, Robert N. 1942- *St&PR 93*
Latella, Robert Natale 1942- *WhoAm 92*
Latella, Salvatore Philip 1919- *WhoE 93*
Laterza, Vito 1926- *WhoWor 93*
Latham, Alfred William 1937- *St&PR 93*
Latham, Allen, Jr. 1908- *St&PR 93, WhoAm 92, WhoE 93*
Latham, Christopher Daniel 1951- *WhoE 93*
Latham, Daniel Walter *Law&B 92*
Latham, David 1950- *ScF&FL 92*
Latham, Diana Karnes 1934- *WhoAmW 93*
Latham, Edward Michael Locks 1930- *WhoWor 93*
Latham, Eleanor Ruth Earthrowl 1924- *WhoAmW 93*
Latham, Eunice Stunkard 1923- *WhoE 93*
Latham, James D. 1942- *St&PR 93*
Latham, James David *Law&B 92*
Latham, James David 1942- *WhoAm 92*
Latham, James Parker 1918- *WhoSSW 93*
Latham, Jean Lee 1902- *AmWomPl, BioIn 17, MajAI [port], WhoAm 92*
Latham, John *WhoScE 91-1*
Latham, Larry Lee 1945- *WhoAm 92, WhoSSW 93*
Latham, Lyndon Clint 1943- *WhoSSW 93*
Latham, Mavis *ConAu 37NR, MajAI*
Latham, Nanci Joan 1952- *WhoEmL 93*
Latham, Robert 1959- *ScF&FL 92*
Latham, Robert Jesse 1942- *St&PR 93*
Latham, Sandra Ann 1946- *WhoAmW 93*
Latham, Sheila 1950- *ScF&FL 92*
Latham, Tommye Paul 1945- *WhoSSW 93*
Latham, William Anthony 1948- *WhoUN 92*
Latham, William B. 1925- *St&PR 93*
Latham, William C. 1933- *St&PR 93*
Latham, William P(eters) 1917- *Baker 92*
Latham, William Peters 1917- *WhoAm 92*
Lathan, Roamey A. 1943- *St&PR 93*
Lathan, Samuel Robert, Jr. 1938- *WhoSSW 93*
Lathan, Stan 1945- *MiSFD 9*
Lathbury, Roger 1945- *WhoSSW 93, WhoWrEP 92*
Lathem, Edward Connery 1926- *WhoAm 92*
Lather, Mohinder Singh 1932- *WhoAsAP 91*
Lathi, Bhagawandas Pannalal 1933- *WhoWor 93*
Lathlaen, Robert Frank 1925- *St&PR 93, WhoAm 92*
Lathrop, Arthur Lester 1938- *St&PR 93*
Lathrop, Dean Allen 1937- *St&PR 93*
Lathrop, Denice Davis *Law&B 92*
Lathrop, Dorothy P(ulis) 1891-1980 *MajAI [port]*
Lathrop, Francis *ConAu 40NR, SmATA 73*
Lathrop, Gertrude Adams 1921- *WhoAm 92, WhoAmW 93*
Lathrop, Irvin T(unis) 1927- *WhoWrEP 92*
Lathrop, Irvin Tunis 1927- *WhoAm 92*
Lathrop, Jaime D. 1931- *St&PR 93*
Lathrop, Joyce Keen 1939- *WhoAmW 93*
Lathrop, Katherine Austin 1915- *WhoAm 92*
Lathrop, Kaye Don 1932- *WhoAm 92*
Lathrop, Mitchell Lee 1937- *WhoAm 92, WhoWor 93*
Lathrop, Roger Alan 1951- *WhoEmL 93*
Lathrop, Rose Hawthorne 1851-1926 *BioIn 17*
Lathrop, Thomas Albert 1941- *WhoWor 93*
Lathrop, Walter William, Jr. 1933- *St&PR 93*
Lathrop, William Hamilton 1939- *WhoAm 92*
Laties, Victor Gregory 1926- *WhoAm 92*
Latif, Abdul 1942- *WhoUN 92*
Latif, Mary Koon *WhoE 93*
Latifah, Queen c. 1970- *News 92 [port]*
Latiff, Ligia 1953- *WhoAmW 93*
Latigo Hernandez, Maria *NotHsAW 93*
Latilla, Gaetano 1711-1788 *Baker 92*
Latimer, B.A. *Law&B 92*
Latimer, Clay Louis *Law&B 92*
Latimer, Douglas Hamilton 1937- *WhoAm 92*
Latimer, George 1935- *WhoAm 92*
Latimer, George W. 1900-1990 *BioIn 17*
Latimer, Helen *WhoAmW 93*
Latimer, James Dunlap 1938- *St&PR 93*
Latimer, James Harold 1934- *WhoWor 93*
Latimer, James Hearn 1941- *WhoE 93*
Latimer, Jeffrey Allan 1958- *WhoSSW 93*
Latimer, Joanna *ConAu 39NR*
Latimer, John A., III 1950- *St&PR 93*
Latimer, John Francis 1903-1991 *WhoAm 92*
Latimer, Jonathan Peabody 1942- *WhoE 93*
Latimer, Lewis H. 1848-1928 *ConBlB 4 [port]*
Latimer, Lewis Howard 1848-1928 *BioIn 17*
Latimer, Lorenzo Palmer 1857-1941 *BioIn 17*
Latimer, Margaret Petta 1932- *WhoAmW 93*
Latimer, Matthew Parks 1964- *St&PR 93*
Latimer, Paul Jerry 1943- *WhoSSW 93*
Latimer, Roy Truett 1928- *WhoAm 92*
Latimer, Stephen Paul 1957- *WhoE 93*
Latimer, Wilbur Scott 1938- *WhoAm 92*
Latimer, William Perot 1935- *St&PR 93*
Latini, Anthony A. 1942- *WhoAm 92*
Latiolais, Ken Dale 1946- *St&PR 93*
Latiolais, Rene Louis 1942- *St&PR 93, WhoAm 92*
Latkovic, Goran 1959- *WhoWor 93*
Latno, Arthur Clement 1929- *St&PR 93*
Latno, Arthur Clement, Jr. 1929- *WhoAm 92*
Latocha, Eryk Oskar 1942- *WhoScE 91-4*
La Tombelle, Fernand de 1854-1928 *Baker 92*
Latona, Raymond W. 1936- *St&PR 93*
Latone, Anthony 1897-1975 *BiDAMSp 1989*
Latore, Daniel J. 1939- *WhoIns 93*
Latore, Daniel Joseph 1939- *St&PR 93*
LaTores, Santo Joseph 1949- *WhoAm 92*
LaTorre, L. Donald 1937- *St&PR 93, WhoAm 92*
Latorre, Mariano 1886-1955 *SpAmA*
Latorre, Robert George 1949- *WhoAm 92, WhoEmL 93, WhoSSW 93, WhoWor 93*
Latortue, Reegine Alta Grace 1952- *WhoE 93*
Latos, Hubert 1937- *WhoScE 91-4*
Latouche, John 1914-1956 *BioIn 17*
LaTouf, Larry 1939- *St&PR 93, WhoAm 92*
Latour, Ignace Henri Jean Theodore Fantin- 1836-1904 *BioIn 17*
Latour, Pierre Richard 1940- *WhoSSW 93*
Latour, Sharon Mary 1955- *WhoAmW 93*
Latour, Stanislaw 1927- *WhoWor 93*
Latour, Wallace Charles 1924- *WhoAm 92*
La Tour du Pin Chambly de la Charce, Rene-Charles-Humbert, marquis de 1834-1924 *BioIn 17*
la Tourette, Aileen 1946- *ScF&FL 92*
Latourette, Harry Hewes 1915- *St&PR 93*
La Tourette, John Ernest 1932- *WhoAm 92*
la Tourrette, Jacqueline *ScF&FL 92*
LaTourrette, James Thomas 1931- *WhoAm 92*
Latow, (Muriel) Roberta 1931- *ConAu 40NR*
la Tremoille, Louis de, II c. 1460-1525 *HarEnMi*
Latrenta, Nicholas D. 1952- *St&PR 93*
Latrobe, Benjamin Henry 1764-1820 *BioIn 17*
Latrouite, Daniel 1946- *WhoScE 91-2*
Latshaw, David Rodney 1939- *WhoE 93*
Latshaw, John 1921- *St&PR 93, WhoAm 92*
Latshaw, Patricia Joan Herget 1930- *WhoAmW 93*
Latsios, Barbara Lynn 1954- *WhoAmW 93, WhoEmL 93*
Latsko-Lockhart, Linda *BioIn 17*
Latta, Dorothy Mae 1955- *WhoAmW 93*
Latta, Jennie Davidson 1961- *WhoEmL 93*
Latta, John Alex 1954- *WhoWrEP 92*
Latta, Jonathan Kane 1955- *WhoWrEP 92*
Latta, Rick 1959- *WhoSSW 93*
Lattal, Alice Darnell 1943- *WhoSSW 93*
Lattany, Kristin Eggleston 1931- *WhoWrEP 92*
Lattanzi, Robert Marc 1958- *WhoEmL 93*
Lattanzio, David Albert 1942- *St&PR 93*
Lattavo, Philip Errol 1941- *St&PR 93*
Lattergrass, Izetta *BioIn 17*
Lattes, Armand 1934- *WhoScE 91-2*
Lattes, Jean-Claude J. 1941- *WhoAm 92*
Lattes, Raffaele 1910- *WhoAm 92*
Lattimer, Gary Lee 1939- *WhoAm 92*
Lattimer, John Kingsley 1914- *WhoAm 92, WhoWor 93*
Lattimore, Everett C. 1927-1991 *BioIn 17*
Lattimore, Jessie *ConAu 136*
Lattimore, Linda L. *Law&B 92*
Lattimore, Owen 1900-1989 *BioIn 17*
Lattimore, Vera R. *Law&B 92*
Lattin, Albert Floyd 1950- *WhoAm 92, WhoE 93*
Lattman, Laurence Harold 1923- *WhoAm 92*
Lattman, Norman S. 1936- *St&PR 93*
Lattman, Stanley 1940- *St&PR 93*
Latto, Lewis M., Jr. 1940- *WhoAm 92*
Latto, Richard Matheson *WhoScE 91-1*
Latto, Thymie Sam 1933- *WhoSSW 93*
Lattof, Caryl Elaine 1954- *St&PR 93*
Lattof, Mitchell George, Jr. 1956- *WhoEmL 93*
Lattre De Tassigny, Jean de 1889-1952 *HarEnMi*
Lattuada, Alberto 1914- *MiSFD 9*
Lattuada, Felice 1882-1962 *Baker 92*
Latture, James Paul, Jr. 1946- *WhoSSW 93*
Latu, Penisimani Loseli 1948- *WhoWor 93*
Latus, Timothy Dexter 1946- *WhoSSW 93, WhoWor 93*
Latvala, Eino Kenneth 1922- *WhoSSW 93*
Latz, G. Irving, II 1920- *WhoAm 92*
Latz, Gary W. 1949- *St&PR 93*
Latz, Jeanie Sell *Law&B 92*
Latz, Jeanie Sell 1951- *St&PR 93*
Latz, Rudolf 1953- *WhoWor 93*
Latzer, Richard N. 1937- *WhoIns 93*
Latzer, Richard Neal 1937- *St&PR 93, WhoAm 92*
Latzko, D.G.H. 1924- *WhoScE 91-3*
Lau, Adolfo 1939- *WhoWor 93*
Lau, Bobby Wai-Man 1944- *WhoWor 93*
Lau, Cheryl *WhoAm 92, WhoAmW 93*
Lau, Constance H. 1952- *St&PR 93*
Lau, Daniel B.T. 1919- *WhoIns 93*
Lau, Elizabeth Martinez 1951- *WhoEmL 93*
Lau, Eugene Wing Iu 1931- *WhoWor 93*
Lau, Evelyn 1970- *WhoCanL 92*
Lau, Harry Hung-Kwan 1939- *WhoE 93, WhoWor 93*
Lau, Henry Yan-Chung 1943- *WhoE 93*
Lau, Ian Van 1950- *WhoAm 92*
Lau, Jack Kim-Hung 1955- *WhoWor 93*
Lau, Jark Chong 1935- *WhoSSW 93*
Lau, Jeffrey Daniel 1948- *WhoEmL 93*
Lau, Johnny *BioIn 17*
Lau, Lawrence Juen-Yee 1944- *WhoAm 92*
Lau, Maureen Treacy 1946- *WhoEmL 93*
Lau, Michele Denise 1960- *WhoAmW 93, WhoEmL 93, WhoWor 93*
Lau, Miriam Kin-Yee 1947- *WhoAsAP 91*
Lau, Pauline Young 1943- *WhoAmW 93*
Lau, Phillip M. 1946- *St&PR 93*
Lau, Richard *Law&B 92*
Lau, Richard John 1939- *St&PR 93*
Lau, Ricky Yusing *BioIn 17*
Lau, Robert Keith 1958- *WhoE 93, WhoWor 93*
Lau, Susan *Law&B 92*
Lau, Tat Ching 1948- *WhoUN 92*
Lau, Tenda 1947- *WhoAsAP 91*
Lau, Victor Ngai Kwong 1949- *WhoWor 93*
Lau, Wah-Sum 1928- *WhoAsAP 91*
Laub, Alan John 1948- *WhoAm 92*
Laub, Ferdinand 1832-1875 *Baker 92*
Laub, Patricia Dillon 1958- *WhoEmL 93*
Laub, Ronald J. 1943- *St&PR 93*
Laub, Stephen W. 1945- *WhoE 93*
Laub, Thomas (Linnemann) 1852-1927 *Baker 92*
Laub, Vasa 1857-1911 *See* Laub, Ferdinand 1832-1875 *Baker 92*
Laub, William Murray 1924- *WhoAm 92*
Laubach, David Clair *WhoE 93*
Laubach, Frank Charles 1884-1970 *BioIn 17*
Laubach, Gerald David 1926- *St&PR 93*
Laubach, L.R. 1930- *St&PR 93*
Laubach, Rene 1948- *WhoEmL 93*
Laubach, Roger Alvin 1922- *WhoAm 92*
Laubach, Susan Ann 1940- *WhoAmW 93*
Laubaugh, Frederick 1926- *WhoWor 93*
Laube, David R. 1948- *St&PR 93*
Laube, Heinrich 1938- *WhoScE 91-3*
Laube, Lois Ruth 1946- *WhoEmL 93*
Laube, Roger Gustav 1921- *WhoAm 92*
Laube, Thomas 1952- *WhoWor 93*
Laube, William Tell 1940- *St&PR 93*
Laube-Morgan, Jerri 1928- *WhoAmW 93, WhoSSW 93*
Laubenstein, Linda J. d1992 *NewYTBS 92*
Laubenstein, William H., III *Law&B 92*
Laubenthal, Horst 1939- *OxDcOp*
Laubenthal, Horst (Rudiger) 1939- *Baker 92*
Laubenthal, Rudolf 1886-1971 *Baker 92, OxDcOp*
Lauber, Christopher Joseph 1958- *WhoEmL 93, WhoSSW 93*
Lauber, John K. 1942- *WhoAm 92, WhoE 93*
Lauber, Joseph 1864-1952 *Baker 92*
Lauber, Mignon Diane *WhoAmW 93, WhoWor 93*
Lauber, Patricia (Grace) 1924- *ConAu 38NR, MajAI [port], WhoAmW 93*
Lauber, Peg Carlson 1938- *WhoWrEP 92*
Lauber, Susanne L. *Law&B 92*
Laubereau, Alfred 1942- *WhoScE 91-3*
Laubgross, Janet Rebecca 1956- *WhoSSW 93*
Laubhan, Laura Jean 1962- *WhoAmW 93*
Laubich, Arnold 1929- *St&PR 93*
Laubier, Lucien Claude 1936- *WhoScE 91-2*
Laubjerg, Kristian 1948- *WhoUN 92*
Laubner, Martha Lee 1945- *WhoAmW 93*
Laubscher, Louis E. 1944- *St&PR 93*
Laubscher, William Roy 1943- *St&PR 93*
Lauby, Donald Ervin 1949- *WhoSSW 93*
Lauchert, John Joseph, Jr. 1956- *St&PR 93*
Laucirica, Louis Frank *St&PR 93*
Laucius, Stephanie Eve 1915- *WhoAmW 93*
Lauck, Anthony Joseph 1908- *WhoAm 92*
Lauck, Kevin Dale 1950- *St&PR 93*
Lauck, Sheila Renee 1961- *WhoEmL 93*
Lauda, Donald Paul 1937- *WhoAm 92*
Laudano, William B. 1953- *St&PR 93*
Laudano, William Bonaventura, Jr. 1953- *WhoE 93*
Laudati, Robert 1935- *St&PR 93*
Laude, Anthony *ScF&FL 92*
Laude, Bernard J. 1938- *WhoScE 91-2*
Lauder, Charles Houlton *Law&B 92*
Lauder, Dan *BioIn 17*
Lauder, Estee *BioIn 17, WhoAm 92, WhoAmW 93, WhoE 93*
Lauder, Estee c. 1908- *News 92 [port]*
Lauder, George Dick- *ScF&FL 92*
Lauder, Karen *BioIn 17*
Lauder, Kathryn Renee 1965- *WhoAmW 93*
Lauder, Leonard Alan 1933- *WhoAm 92*
Lauder, Norma J. 1949- *WhoAm 92, WhoEmL 93*
Lauder, R. William 1949- *St&PR 93*
Lauder, Ronald S. 1944- *BioIn 17*
Lauder, Ronald Stephen 1944- *WhoE 93*
Lauder, Valarie Anne 1926- *WhoAmW 93, WhoWor 93*
Lauder, William *ScF&FL 92*
Lauder, William P. *BioIn 17*
Lauderdale, Beverly Anne 1937- *WhoAmW 93*
Lauderdale, Clint Arlen 1932- *WhoAm 92*
Lauderdale, Gary D. 1945- *St&PR 93*
Lauderdale, James Sidney 1911- *St&PR 93*
Lauderdale, Katherine Sue 1954- *WhoEmL 93*
Lauderdale, Ronald A. *Law&B 92*
Lauderdale, Teresa Jean 1962- *WhoAmW 93*
Laudermilk, Jack *Law&B 92*
Laudicina, Eleanor V. 1942- *WhoAmW 93*
Laudick, Lawrence A. 1947- *St&PR 93*
Laudise, Robert Alfred 1930- *WhoAm 92*
Laudon, Richard B. 1934- *St&PR 93*
Laudone, Anita Helene 1948- *WhoAm 92*
Laue, Reinhard 1945- *WhoWor 93*
Lauener, P.-A. 1948- *WhoScE 91-4*
Lauenstein, Ann Gail 1949- *SmATA 73, WhoAmW 93, WhoEmL 93, WhoWor 93*
Lauenstein, Helmut 1937- *WhoScE 91-3, WhoWor 93*
Lauenstein, Milton Charles 1926- *St&PR 93, WhoAm 92*
Lauer, Bruce A. 1952- *St&PR 93*
Lauer, Bruce H. 1957- *St&PR 93*
Lauer, Gerald Joseph 1934- *St&PR 93*
Lauer, Gordon A. 1940- *St&PR 93*
Lauer, Harry Curtis 1927- *WhoSSW 93*
Lauer, James Lothar 1920- *WhoAm 92*
Lauer, Jeanette Carol 1935- *WhoAmW 93*
Lauer, Jerry Lee 1943- *St&PR 93*
Lauer, Joletta C. *Law&B 92*
Lauer, Keith G. 1953- *St&PR 93*
Lauer, Mark Wayne 1951- *WhoEmL 93, WhoSSW 93*
Lauer, Robert Lee 1933- *St&PR 93, WhoAm 92*
Lauer, Ronald Martin 1930- *WhoAm 92*
Lauer, Ruth Carol 1954- *WhoAmW 93*
Lauer, Stephen John 1947- *WhoEmL 93*
Lauer, Steven A. *Law&B 92*
Lauer, Steven K. 1949- *WhoIns 93*
Lauer, Wilhelm *WhoScE 91-3*
Lauerman, Henry Joseph, Jr. 1936- *St&PR 93*
Lauerman, James L. 1933- *St&PR 93*
Lauermann, Ernst *WhoScE 91-4*
Lauersen, Niels Helth 1939- *WhoAm 92*
Lauesen, Soren 1942- *WhoWor 93*
Laufenberg, Terre Lynn 1951- *WhoAmW 93*
Laufer, Allan Henry 1936- *WhoE 93*

Laufer, Beatrice *WhoAm 92, WhoAmW 93, WhoWor 93*
Laufer, Berthold 1874-1934 *IntDcAn*
Laufer, David D. *Law&B 92*
Laufer, Hans 1929- *WhoAm 92*
Laufer, Hilda *WhoE 93*
Laufer, Igor 1944- *WhoAm 92*
Laufer, Ira Jerome 1928- *WhoE 93*
Laufer, Joel 1933- *St&PR 93*
Laufer, Joseph *BioIn 17*
Laufer, Leonard Justin 1965- *WhoEmL 93*
Lauff, George Howard 1927- *WhoAm 92*
Lauffer, Alice A. 1919- *WhoAm 92*
Lauffer, Max Augustus, Jr. 1914- *WhoE 93*
Laufke, Hans G.A. 1935- *WhoScE 91-4*
Laufman, Harold 1912- *WhoAm 92, WhoE 93*
Lauge, Ginette 1935- *WhoScE 91-2*
Laugeri, Louis P.E. 1937- *WhoUN 92*
Laugerud Garcia, Kjell *DcCPCAm*
Laughead, G. Ross *Law&B 92*
Laughead, George Ross 1953- *St&PR 93, WhoEmL 93*
Laughery, Jack Arnold 1935- *St&PR 93, WhoSSW 93*
Laughery, Kenneth R. 1935- *WhoAm 92*
Laughlin, Ann Frances 1956- *WhoAmW 93*
Laughlin, Bob 1932- *St&PR 93*
Laughlin, C.B. 1953- *St&PR 93*
Laughlin, Charles William 1939- *WhoSSW 93*
Laughlin, Charlotte 1951- *ScF&FL 92*
Laughlin, Clara Elizabeth 1873-1941 *AmWomPl*
Laughlin, D.L. 1935- *St&PR 93*
Laughlin, David Eugene 1947- *WhoAm 92*
Laughlin, Frank *ConAu 138, MiSFD 9*
Laughlin, Greg 1942- *CngDr 91, WhoAm 92*
Laughlin, Gregory Greg 1942- *WhoSSW 93*
Laughlin, Henry Prather 1916- *WhoAm 92*
Laughlin, James *Law&B 92*
Laughlin, James 1914- *BioIn 17, WhoAm 92*
Laughlin, James Patrick 1951- *WhoEmL 93*
Laughlin, James Rodney 1946- *St&PR 93, WhoAm 92*
Laughlin, John Seth 1918- *WhoAm 92*
Laughlin, Louis Gene 1937- *WhoSSW 93*
Laughlin, Margaret Ann *WhoAmW 93*
Laughlin, Michael *MiSFD 9*
Laughlin, Monique Myrtle Weant 1924- *WhoSSW 93*
Laughlin, Otis William 1949- *WhoEmL 93*
Laughlin, Philip Daniel 1907- *St&PR 93*
Laughlin, Philip R. *BioIn 17*
Laughlin, Robert Arthur 1939- *WhoAm 92, WhoE 93*
Laughlin, Robert Scott 1945- *St&PR 93*
Laughlin, Stanley Ira 1924- *WhoE 93*
Laughlin, Terry Xavier 1936- *WhoWor 93*
Laughlin, Tom *BioIn 17*
Laughlin, Tom 1938?- *ConAu 138, MiSFD 9*
Laughlin, William Bedford 1955- *WhoWor 93*
Laughlin, William Eugene 1936- *WhoSSW 93, WhoWor 93*
Laughlin, William G. *Law&B 92*
Laughlin, William G. 1944- *St&PR 93*
Laughman, Clyde R. *St&PR 93*
Laughon, F.E. 1937- *St&PR 93*
Laughren, Judith 1951- *WhoAm 92*
Laughren, Terry 1940- *WhoAm 92*
Laughter, Benjamin *Law&B 92*
Laughter, Ron D. 1948- *WhoEmL 93*
Laughton, Anthony *WhoScE 91-1*
Laughton, Charles 1899-1962 *BioIn 17, IntDcF 2-3 [port], MiSFD 9N*
Laughton, John Charles 1946- *WhoE 93*
Laughton, M.A. *WhoScE 91-1*
Laughton, Marie *AmWomPl*
Laugier, Andre 1938- *WhoScE 91-2*
Laugier, C. *WhoScE 91-2*
Laugier, R. 1922- *WhoScE 91-2*
Laugier, Yvette Marie 1961- *WhoSSW 93*
Lauhanen, Risto Ensio 1965- *WhoScE 91-4*
Lauher, O. Don 1942- *St&PR 93*
Lauhoff, Jeanne Alexandrae 1965- *WhoSSW 93*
Lauinger, Frank Thomas 1940- *St&PR 93*
Lauinger, Philip C., Jr. 1935- *St&PR 93*
Laukaitis, Brenda Ann 1963- *WhoAmW 93*
Laukhuff, Perry 1906- *WhoSSW 93*
Laukien, Dirk Daniel 1964- *WhoWor 93*
Laul, Linda Barbara 1949- *WhoAmW 93*
Lauldi, Maner 1912- *OxDcOp*
Laulhere, Bernard M. 1914- *St&PR 93*
Laulicht, Murray Jack 1940- *WhoE 93*
Lauman, Richard H., Jr. 1956- *WhoE 93*
Lauman, Robert Milton 1925- *St&PR 93*
Lauman, Vona Weger 1929- *St&PR 93*
Laumann, Dennis James 1941- *St&PR 93*
Laumann, Edward Otto 1938- *WhoAm 92*
Laumann, Richard David *Law&B 92*
Laumann, Silken *BioIn 17*
Laumbach, Ronald L. *Law&B 92*
Laumer, Keith 1925- *BioIn 17, ScF&FL 92*
Laumont, Philippe Emile 1944- *WhoE 93*
Laun, Arthur Henry, Jr. 1930- *WhoAm 92*
Laun, Hans Martin 1944- *WhoWor 93*
Laun, Harold George 1905- *WhoAm 92*
Laun, Louis Frederick 1920- *WhoAm 92*
Laun, Max Walter *Law&B 92*
Launay, Andre 1930- *ScF&FL 92*
Launder, Arthur William 1939- *St&PR 93*
Launder, Brian Edward *WhoScE 91-1*
Launder, Brian Edward 1939- *WhoWor 93*
Launder, William H. 1954- *St&PR 93*
Launders, Michele *BioIn 17*
Laundon, Averill 1938- *St&PR 93*
Launer, Dale *MiSFD 9*
Launiainen, Jouko Olavi 1945- *WhoScE 91-4*
Launiala, Kari Antero 1934- *WhoScE 91-4*
Launis, Armas (Emanuel) 1884-1959 *Baker 92*
Lauper, Cyndi *BioIn 17*
Lauper, Cyndi 1953- *Baker 92, WhoAm 92*
Lauppi, Urs Victor 1943- *WhoWor 93*
Laupus, William Edward 1921- *WhoAm 92*
Laura, Charles Philip 1919- *St&PR 93*
Laura, Patricio Adolfo Antonio 1935- *WhoWor 93*
Laurance, Alfred D. *ConAu 40NR*
Laurance, Alice 1938- *ScF&FL 92*
Laurance, Andrew *ScF&FL 92*
Laurance, Dale R. 1945- *WhoAm 92*
Laurance, David *BioIn 17*
Laurance, Leonard Clark 1932- *WhoWor 93*
Laurans, Patricia Webster 1939- *WhoE 93*
Laurash, Jayme J. 1959- *St&PR 93*
Laure, Esther L. 1912- *St&PR 93*
Laure, George R. 1912- *St&PR 93*
Laure, Maurice Fernand 1917- *St&PR 93*
Laurea, Susan Annette *Law&B 92*
Laurel, Brenda Kay 1950- *WhoAmW 93*
Laurel, Salvador Hidalgo 1928- *WhoAsAP 91*
Laurel, Sotero Hidalgo 1918- *WhoAsAP 91*
Laurel, Stan 1890-1965 *BioIn 17*
Laurel, Stan 1890-1965 & Hardy, Oliver 1892-1957 *QDrFCA 92 [port]*
Laurel-Trinidad, Milagros 1941- *WhoAsAP 91*
Lauren, Hakan 1941- *WhoWor 93*
Lauren, Leonard 1932- *St&PR 93*
Lauren, Linda 1952- *WhoWrEP 92*
Lauren, Ralph *BioIn 17, NewYTBS 92*
Lauren, Ralph 1939- *WhoAm 92*
Laurence, Aurelie T. 1944- *WhoAmW 93*
Laurence, Christian 1944- *WhoScE 91-2*
Laurence, Dan H. 1920- *ScF&FL 92, WhoAm 92*
Laurence, David Ernst 1947- *WhoE 93*
Laurence, Elaine S. *Law&B 92*
Laurence, Margaret 1926- *DcChlFi*
Laurence, Margaret 1926-1987 *BioIn 17, IntLitE, MagSWL [port], WhoCanL 92*
Laurence, Marilyn Ligon 1933- *St&PR 93*
Laurence, Michael M. 1940- *St&PR 93*
Laurence, Michael Marshall 1940- *WhoAm 92*
Laurence, Nancy *BioIn 17*
Laurence, Robert Lionel 1936- *WhoAm 92*
Laurence, Ronald B. 1938- *St&PR 93*
Laurence, Sydney M. 1865-1940 *BioIn 17*
Laurencie, Lionel de la *Baker 92*
Laurencin, Marie 1885?-1956 *BioIn 17*
Laurendi, Nat 1923- *WhoE 93*
Laurens, Edmond 1852-1925 *Baker 92*
Laurens, Henri 1885-1954 *BioIn 17*
Laurens, Nicholas Joseph 1924- *St&PR 93*
Laurenson, Charles Philip 1927- *St&PR 93*
Laurenson, Robert Mark 1938- *WhoAm 92*
Laurent, Andre 1937- *WhoWor 93*
Laurent, Andre L.J. 1939- *WhoScE 91-2*
Laurent, Christian L.M.R.Gh. 1954- *WhoScE 91-2*
Laurent, Daniel 1953- *WhoWor 93*
Laurent, Daniel N.L. 1926- *WhoScE 91-2*
Laurent, Hector Francis 1947- *WhoEmL 93*
Laurent, Holly C. *Law&B 92*
Laurent, Lawrence Bell 1925- *WhoAm 92*
Laurent, Michel P. 1940- *WhoScE 91-2*
Laurent, Paul 1925-1990 *BioIn 17*
Laurent, Pierre 1925- *WhoScE 91-2*
Laurent, Pierre-Henri 1933- *WhoAm 92, WhoE 93*
Laurent, Robert Louis, Jr. 1955- *St&PR 93, WhoAm 92*
Laurent, Torvard C. 1930- *WhoScE 91-4*
Laurenti, Bartolomeo Girolamo c. 1644-1726 *Baker 92*
Laurents, Arthur 1917- *WhoAm 92*
Laurents, Arthur 1918- *BioIn 17*
Laurents, Renee Joan 1939- *WhoAmW 93*
Laurentz, Friedrich *BioIn 17*
Laurenzano, Robert Salvatore 1946- *WhoEmL 93*
Laurenzo, Vince D. 1939- *St&PR 93*
Laurenzo, Vincent Dennis 1939- *WhoAm 92*
Laures, Gerald M. 1947- *St&PR 93*
Lauret, Curtis Bernard, Jr. 1945- *WhoAm 92, WhoIns 93*
Lauret, Ronald Wayne 1941- *St&PR 93*
Laurgeau, Claude 1942- *WhoScE 91-2*
Lauria, Dan *BioIn 17*
Lauria, Frank 1935- *ScF&FL 92*
Lauria, Jorge Osvaldo 1925- *WhoWor 93*
Lauricella, Janet May 1944- *WhoAmW 93*
Lauricella, Leonard John 1948- *WhoE 93*
Lauridsen, Jan 1948- *WhoWor 93*
Laurie, Clayton David 1954- *WhoEmL 93*
Laurie, Gordon William 1953- *WhoSSW 93*
Laurie, Irving d1992 *BioIn 17, NewYTBS 92*
Laurie, James Andrew 1947- *WhoAm 92*
Laurie, John Veldon 1952- *St&PR 93, WhoAm 92*
Laurie, Margaret Sanders 1926- *WhoWrEP 92*
Laurie, Marilyn *St&PR 93, WhoAm 92, WhoAmW 93*
Laurie, Patricia D. *Law&B 92*
Laurie, Piper 1932- *BioIn 17, ConTFT 10, WhoAmW 93*
Laurier, Wilfred 1841-1919 *DcTwHis*
Laurila, Harold L. 1932- *St&PR 93*
Laurila, Norman Thomas Edward 1955- *WhoE 93*
Laurin, Francis Thomas 1916- *St&PR 93*
Laurin, Pierre *BioIn 17*
Laurin, Pierre 1939- *WhoAm 92*
Laurin, Richard King, Jr. 1960- *WhoEmL 93*
Laurincikas, Antanas 1948- *WhoWor 93*
Laurino, John Alan 1949- *WhoE 93*
Laurino, O.F. *Law&B 92*
Laurino, Robert Dennis 1951- *WhoEmL 93*
Laurins, Alex *BioIn 17*
Laurins, Janis John *BioIn 17*
Laurins, Zigurds *BioIn 17*
Lauriot-Prerost, H. *WhoScE 91-2*
Lauritsen, Jill Ann 1959- *WhoAmW 93*
Lauritsen, John P. *WhoWrEP 92*
Lauritsen, Kenneth Bruce 1942- *St&PR 93*
Lauritsen, Poul Halfdan 1933- *WhoWor 93*
Lauritzan, Laura Ann M. *Law&B 92*
Lauritzen, Bruce Ronnow 1943- *St&PR 93, WhoAm 92*
Lauritzen, Christian 1923- *WhoScE 91-3*
Lauritzen, Frederick 1921-1990 *BioIn 17*
Lauritzen, John Ronnow 1917- *WhoAm 92, WhoWor 93*
Lauritzen, Peter Owen 1935- *WhoAm 92*
Lauritzen, Steffen Lilholt 1947- *WhoWor 93*
Lauri-Volpi, Giacomo 1892-1979 *Baker 92, IntDcOp [port], OxDcOp*
Lauro, Antonio 1909-1986 *Baker 92*
Lauro, Mary Viola 1926- *WhoE 93*
Laurow, Zbigniew 1932- *WhoWor 93*
Laurs, J.J. 1940- *WhoScE 91-3*
Laursen, Arne Mosfeldt 1928- *WhoScE 91-2*
Laursen, Finn 1944- *WhoWor 93*
Laursen, Mogens 1931- *WhoWor 93*
Laursen, Paul Herbert 1929- *WhoAm 92*
Laursen, Soren N.S. 1935- *St&PR 93, WhoIns 93*
Laurus, Archbishop 1928- *WhoAm 92*
Lausch, Hans 1941- *WhoWor 93*
Lausche, Frank John 1895-1990 *BioIn 17*
Laush, Mary *St&PR 93*
Lausier, Ernest Alexander 1945- *St&PR 93*
Lauska, Franz (Seraphinus Ignatius) 1764-1825 *Baker 92*
Laustriat, Gilbert 1929- *WhoScE 91-2*
Laut, Agnes Christina 1871-1936 *BioIn 17*
Laut, Harold W. 1933- *St&PR 93*
Laut, Harold William 1933- *WhoIns 93*
Lauten, John Andrew 1954- *WhoSSW 93*
Lautenbach, Alfred Robert 1932- *WhoSSW 93*
Lautenbacher, Conrad Charles, Jr. 1942- *WhoAm 92*
Lautenbacher, Susanne 1932- *Baker 92*
Lautenberg, Frank *BioIn 17*
Lautenberg, Frank R. 1924- *CngDr 91, WhoAm 92, WhoE 93*
Lautenschlager, Eugene Louis 1926- *St&PR 93*
Lautenschlager, Garrett Brian 1955- *WhoSSW 93*
Lautenschlager, Gary Joseph 1949- *WhoEmL 93, WhoSSW 93*
Lautenschlager, Peggy A. 1955- *WhoAmW 93*
Lautenschlager, Sally Ann 1930- *St&PR 93*
Lauterbach, Melvin L. 1946- *St&PR 93*
Lauterbach, R.A. 1947- *St&PR 93*
Lauterbach, Robert Emil 1918- *WhoAm 92*
Lauterbach, Shirley Susan Pfeiffer 1955- *WhoAmW 93, WhoEmL 93, WhoSSW 93*
Lauterberg, Robert Wayne 1957- *WhoSSW 93*
Lauterborn, Robert F. 1936- *WhoAm 92*
Lauterbur, Paul Christian 1929- *WhoAm 92*
Lauterio, Thomas John 1956- *WhoSSW 93*
Lautermilch, John *Law&B 92*
Lauth, Richard Joseph 1935- *St&PR 93*
Lauther, Sidney J. 1948- *St&PR 93*
Lautin, Everett Marc 1946- *WhoE 93*
Lautman, Don A. 1930-1991 *BioIn 17*
Lautner, John *BioIn 17*
Lautrec, Henri de Toulouse- 1864-1901 *BioIn 17*
Lautrec, Odet de Foix, Count of 1485-1528 *HarEnMi*
Lautridou, Jean-Pierre 1938- *WhoScE 91-2*
Lautrup, Carlos B. *BioIn 17*
Lautz, Gunter 1923- *WhoScE 91-3*
Lautz, Henry Williams 1941- *St&PR 93*
Lautz, Lindsay Allan 1947- *WhoAm 92*
Lautzenheiser, Barbara J. 1938- *St&PR 93, WhoIns 93*
Lautzenheiser, Barbara Jean 1938- *WhoAm 92, WhoAmW 93*
Lautzenheiser, Dennis K. 1951- *St&PR 93*
Lautzenheiser, Karen Read 1946- *St&PR 93*
Lauven, Peter Michael 1948- *WhoWor 93*
Lauver, David Alan 1947- *WhoE 93*
Lauver, E. Eugene 1947- *St&PR 93*
Lauwers, Albert R. 1932- *WhoScE 91-2*
Lauwers, Ludwig H. 1957- *WhoScE 91-2*
Lauwers, Peter 1937- *WhoWor 93*
Lauwers, Peter M.J.T. 1937- *WhoScE 91-2*
Lauwers, Steven Joseph *Law&B 92*
Lauweryns, Joseph 1933- *WhoScE 91-2*
Lauweryns, Joseph Marie 1933- *WhoWor 93*
Lauwerys, Robert R. 1938- *WhoScE 91-2*
Lau-Wong, Mamie May-Ming, Sr. 1954- *WhoWor 93*
Lau Wong-Fat, Andrew 1936- *WhoAsAP 91*
Laux, Hans 1929- *WhoWor 93*
Laux, Ingrid Charlotte Regina 1938- *WhoUN 92*
Laux, Karl 1896-1978 *Baker 92*
Laux, Russell Frederick 1918- *WhoE 93*
Laux, Wolfrudolf 1934- *WhoScE 91-3*
Lauzier, Gerard *MiSFD 9*
Lauzon, Jean-Claude 1953- *MiSFD 9*
Lauzon, Normand Robert 1944- *WhoUN 92*
Lauzon, Rodrigue Vincent 1937- *WhoE 93*
Lauzon, Theophile A. 1929- *St&PR 93*
Lauzun-Stoney, Virginia 1911- *WhoAmW 93*
Lauzzana, Gail Anne 1945- *St&PR 93*
Lauzzana, Raymond Guido 1941- *WhoWor 93*
Lavagetto, Cookie 1912-1990 *BioIn 17*
Lavagne, Andre 1913- *Baker 92*
Lavagnino, Angelo Francesco 1909-1987 *Baker 92*
LaVail, Jennifer Hart 1943- *WhoAm 92, WhoAmW 93*
Laval, Joseph d1992 *NewYTBS 92*
Laval, Joseph 1902-1992 *BioIn 17*
Laval, Pierre 1883-1945 *BioIn 17, DcTwHis*
Lavalair *BioIn 17*
Lavalee, Leo P. 1933- *St&PR 93*
La Valette, Jean Parisot de 1494-1568 *HarEnMi*
Lavalle, Calixa 1842-1891 *Baker 92*
LaValle, Edith 1919- *WhoAmW 93*
LaValle, Irving Howard 1939- *WhoAm 92, WhoSSW 93*
Lavalle, Roberto 1932- *WhoUN 92*
LaValle, Sharlene Hartle 1949- *WhoE 93*
Lavallee, Charles Phillip 1928- *WhoWor 93*
Lavallee, Deirdre Justine 1962- *WhoAmW 93*
Lavallee, Joseph Andre 1956- *St&PR 93*
Lavallee, Roderick Leo 1936- *St&PR 93, WhoWor 93*
LaVallee, Theresa C. 1935- *St&PR 93*
Lavalle-Garcia, Armando 1924- *Baker 92*

LaValley, Al 1935- *ScF&FL 92*
Lavalou, Michel Jean 1930- *WhoWor 93*
Lavanchy, Philippe 1948- *WhoUN 92*
Lavandeira, Barbara A. *Law&B 92*
La Vanish, George Ronald 1953- *WhoE 93*
Lavarch, Michael Hugh 1961- *WhoAsAP 91*
Lavarnway, Gerard Thomas 1956- *WhoEmL 93*
Lavatelli, Leo Silvio 1917- *WhoSSW 93*
Lavater, Johann Caspar 1741-1801 *BioIn 17*
Lavau, Marcelle *WhoScE 91-2*
Lave, Charles Arthur 1938- *WhoAm 92*
Lave, Judith Rice *WhoAm 92, WhoAmW 93*
Lave, Lester Bernard 1939- *WhoAm 92*
LaVean, Michael Gilbert 1954- *WhoWor 93*
Laveccia, Benjamin L. 1935- *St&PR 93*
LaVeck, Gerald DeLoss 1927- *WhoAm 92*
La Vee, Katie *WhoWrEP 92*
La Veglia, Geri 1943- *WhoWrEP 92*
La Vela, Joseph A. *Law&B 92*
Lavell, Thomas Eugene 1928- *WhoE 93*
Lavelle, Alice Elizabeth *AmWomPl*
LaVelle, Arthur 1921- *WhoAm 92*
LaVelle, Betty Sullivan Dougherty 1941- *WhoAmW 93*
Lavelle, Brian Francis David 1941- *WhoSSW 93*
Lavelle, Charles Joseph 1950- *WhoEmL 93*
Lavelle, Michael Joseph 1934- *WhoAm 92*
Lavelle, Patrick Brian, Jr. 1961- *WhoE 93*
Lavelle, Paul M. 1949- *St&PR 93*
Lavelle, Paul Michael 1956- *WhoAm 92*
Lavelle, Robert E. 1922- *St&PR 93*
Lavelle, Sean Marius 1928- *WhoScE 91-3, WhoWor 93*
Lavelle, Sheila *ChlFicS*
Lavelle, Thomas *Law&B 92*
Lavelle, Thomas 1946- *St&PR 93*
Lavelle, W.J. 1944- *St&PR 93*
Lavelli, Anthony, Jr. 1926- *BiDAMSp 1989*
Lavelli, Dante *BioIn 17*
Lavelli, Jorge *BioIn 17*
Lavely, Joe Alan 1937- *WhoSSW 93*
Laven, Arnold 1922- *BioIn 17, MiSFD 9*
Laven, David Lawrence 1953- *WhoSSW 93*
Lavenas, Suzanne 1942- *WhoAmW 93, WhoE 93, WhoWor 93*
Lavenda, Bernard Howard 1945- *WhoWor 93*
Lavendel, Giuliana Avanzini *WhoAm 92*
Lavender, Adele 1924- *St&PR 93*
Lavender, Anthony 1953- *WhoWor 93*
Lavender, Carol King *Law&B 92*
Lavender, David Sievert 1910- *BioIn 17, ConAu 40NR*
Lavender, Fred Charles 1934- *St&PR 93*
Lavender, Robert Eugene 1926- *WhoAm 92, WhoSSW 93*
Lavengood, Lawrence Gene 1924- *WhoAm 92*
Lavenson, James H. 1919- *WhoAm 92*
Lavenson, Susan Barker 1936- *WhoAmW 93, WhoE 93*
Laventhol, David A. *BioIn 17*
Laventhol, David A. 1933- *St&PR 93*
Laventhol, David Abram 1933- *WhoAm 92*
Laventhol, Henry Lee 1927- *WhoAm 92*
Laver, Edith Gresham *Law&B 92*
Laver, Gerald Eby 1924- *WhoSSW 93*
Laver, John *WhoScE 91-1*
Laver, Peter John 1940- *WhoWor 93*
Laver, Rod *BioIn 17*
Laver, Rodney George 1938- *WhoAm 92*
Laver, Steven George 1941- *WhoE 93*
Laverack, Michael Stuart *WhoScE 91-1*
Laverdi, Barbara Joy *Law&B 92*
Laverdiere, Camille 1927- *WhoCanL 92*
La Verdiere, William 1902-1991 *BioIn 17*
La Verendrye, Pierre de 1685-1749 *Expl 93*
Laverge, Hendrik Johannes 1941- *St&PR 93*
Laverge, Jan 1909- *WhoAm 92*
Lavergne, Melanie Frances 1960- *WhoAmW 93*
Lavergne, Michel 1932- *WhoScE 91-2*
La Verne, Lucille *AmWomPl*
Laverne, Michel Marie-Jacques 1928- *WhoAm 92*
Laverriere, Lorraine Moreau 1938- *WhoWrEP 92*
Lavers, Norman 1935- *ScF&FL 92, WhoWrEP 92*
Laversin, Robert W. 1947- *St&PR 93*
Laverty, William E. 1951- *St&PR 93*
Lavery, Barry 1944- *WhoE 93*
Lavery, John 1856-1941 *BioIn 17*
Lavery, Richard Joseph 1953- *St&PR 93*
Lavery, Robert Creighton 1954- *WhoE 93*
Lavery, Thomas Francis 1945- *St&PR 93*
Laves, Benjamin Samuel 1946- *WhoEmL 93*
LaVette, Betty *SoulM*
Lavette, Teri E. *Law&B 92*
LaVey, Anton Szandor *BioIn 17*
Lavey, Gilbert L. 1934- *St&PR 93*
Lavey, Kenneth Henry 1923- *WhoAm 92*
Lavey, Stewart Evan 1945- *WhoAm 92*
La Via, Mariano Francis 1926- *WhoAm 92, WhoSSW 93*
Lavid, Jean Stern 1943- *WhoAmW 93, WhoWor 93*
Lavidge, Robert James 1921- *WhoAm 92*
Laviena, Luis R. 1955- *WhoE 93*
Lavier, Bertrand *BioIn 17*
Laviera, Tato 1950- *HispAmA [port]*
Lavieri, John N. 1944- *St&PR 93*
Lavietes, Marc Harry 1941- *WhoE 93*
Lavigerie, Charles Martial Allemand *BioIn 17*
LaVigna, Michael Paul 1940- *St&PR 93*
Lavigna, Vincenzo 1776-1836 *Baker 92*
Lavignac, (Alexandre Jean) Albert 1846-1916 *Baker 92*
Lavigne, Constance Woodard 1941- *WhoAmW 93*
LaVigne, Gregory Paul 1943- *St&PR 93*
LaVigne, Harland K. 1940- *St&PR 93*
Lavigne, John J. *Law&B 92*
Lavigne, Laurent J. 1938- *St&PR 93*
Lavigne, Louis J., Jr. 1948- *St&PR 93*
Lavigne, Louis James, Jr. 1948- *WhoAm 92*
Lavigueur, Guy A. 1937- *WhoAm 92*
Laville, Etienne Yves 1931- *WhoScE 91-2*
Lavin, Bernice E. 1925- *WhoAm 92, WhoAmW 93*
Lavin, Bernice Elizabeth 1925- *St&PR 93*
Lavin, Charles Blaise, Jr. 1940- *WhoAm 92*
Lavin, Gerard M. 1942- *St&PR 93*
Lavin, John Halley 1932- *WhoAm 92, WhoWrEP 92*
Lavin, Justin Paul, Jr. 1947- *WhoEmL 93*
Lavin, Leonard H. 1919- *St&PR 93, WhoAm 92*
Lavin, Linda *BioIn 17*
Lavin, Linda 1937- *WhoAm 92, WhoAmW 93*
Lavin, Mary 1912- *BioIn 17*
Lavin, Nancy Jean 1952- *WhoAmW 93*
Lavin, Philip Todd 1946- *WhoE 93*
Lavin, Rachel Lynn 1956- *WhoAmW 93*
Lavin, Richard P. *Law&B 92*
Lavin, Richard William *Law&B 92*
Lavin, Thomas J.A. 1949- *St&PR 93*
Lavin, William Kane 1944- *St&PR 93, WhoAm 92*
Lavina, Nelson Diaz 1937- *WhoUN 92*
Lavin Cerda, Hernan 1939- *SpAmA*
Lavin-Corti, Rose Maureen 1952- *WhoAmW 93*
Lavine, Adam 1967- *WhoE 93*
Lavine, Charles Ira 1947- *WhoE 93*
Lavine, David Arthur 1925- *St&PR 93*
Lavine, Eileen Martinson 1924- *WhoE 93*
Lavine, Gary J. *Law&B 92, WhoAm 92*
LaVine, Glen Edward 1932- *St&PR 93*
Lavine, Jerrold Lewis *WhoE 93*
Lavine, John M. 1941- *WhoAm 92*
Lavine, Judith Bazarsky 1945- *WhoE 93*
Lavine, Lawrence Neal 1951- *WhoAm 92*
Lavine, Marlaine 1946- *WhoE 93*
Lavine, Michael David 1948- *WhoEmL 93*
Lavine, Steven D(avid) 1947- *ConAu 139*
Lavine, Steven David 1947- *WhoAm 92*
Lavine, Thelma Zeno *WhoAm 92*
Lavington, Michael Richard 1943- *WhoAm 92*
Lavington, Simon Hugh *WhoScE 91-1*
Laviolette, Bruce Edward 1949- *WhoEmL 93, WhoSSW 93, WhoWor 93*
La Violette, Wesley 1894-1978 *Baker 92*
Laviron, Etienne G. 1930- *WhoScE 91-2*
Lavista, Mario 1943- *Baker 92*
La Vita, Roberto 1950- *WhoE 93, WhoEmL 93*
Lavitola, Maria Stella 1952- *WhoWor 93*
Lavitt, Mel S. 1937- *WhoAm 92*
Lavoie, Charles J. 1945- *St&PR 93*
Lavoie, Dennis James 1955- *WhoE 93*
Lavoie, Lionel A. 1937- *WhoAm 92*
Lavoie, Noella 1953- *WhoAmW 93*
Lavoie, Roger 1928- *WhoAm 92*
Lavoie, Serge 1963- *WhoAm 92*
Lavoisier, Antoine Laurent 1743-1794 *BioIn 17*
Lavoix, Henri-Marie-Francois 1846-1897 *Baker 92*
Lavond, Paul Dennis *ConAu 37NR*
Lavorata, Sue Lorraine 1962- *WhoAmW 93*
Lavoy, Peter R. 1941- *St&PR 93*
Lavoy, Thomas C. 1959- *St&PR 93*
Lavrangas, Dionysios 1860?-1941 *OxDcOp*
Lavrangas, Dionyssios 1860?-1941 *Baker 92*
Lavrovskaya, Elizaveta Andreievna 1845-1919 *Baker 92*
Lavry, Marc 1903-1967 *Baker 92*
Lavut, Martin 1939- *MiSFD 9*
Law, Andrew 1749-1821 *Baker 92*
Law, Andrew Bonar 1858-1923 *DcTwHis*
Law, Barry Arnold *WhoScE 91-1*
Law, Benjamin 1947- *St&PR 93*
Law, Bernard Francis 1931- *WhoE 93*
Law, Bernard Francis Cardinal 1931- *WhoAm 92, WhoWor 93*
Law, Brian John 1943- *WhoE 93*
Law, Carol Judith 1940- *WhoAmW 93*
Law, Clara *MiSFD 9*
Law, Colin Nigel *WhoScE 91-1*
Law, Cursey Shelby 1933- *WhoAm 92*
Law, David Holbrook 1946- *WhoAm 92*
Law, Diane A. 1949- *St&PR 93*
Law, Edwin B. 1924- *WhoSSW 93*
Law, Frederick Masom 1934- *WhoAm 92*
Law, Gale 1945- *St&PR 93*
Law, Hugh Toner 1922- *WhoWrEP 92*
Law, Janice *WhoWrEP 92*
Law, Joe Keith 1949- *WhoSSW 93*
Law, John Harold 1931- *WhoAm 92*
Law, John Manning 1927- *WhoAm 92*
Law, Kenneth S.K. 1943- *St&PR 93*
Law, Kevin M. 1952- *St&PR 93*
Law, L. William 1945- *St&PR 93*
Law, L. William, Jr. *Law&B 92*
Law, Lloyd William 1910- *WhoAm 92*
Law, Louise Disosway 1935- *WhoAmW 93*
Law, Madelyn C. *Law&B 92*
Law, Marvin A. 1938- *St&PR 93*
Law, Maureen Margaret 1940- *WhoAm 92*
Law, Michael R. 1947- *WhoEmL 93*
Law, Phillip Garth 1912- *WhoWor 93*
Law, R.D. 1933- *St&PR 93*
Law, R.G. *Law&B 92*
Law, R. Warren *Law&B 92*
Law, Richard d1991 *BioIn 17*
Law, Richard 1933- *ScF&FL 92*
Law, Robert *Law&B 92*
Law, Robert 1930- *WhoAm 92*
Law, Sylvia A. 1942- *WhoAm 92*
Law, Terence R. 1960- *WhoE 93*
Law, Thomas Hart 1918- *WhoAm 92*
Law, Tom *MiSFD 9*
Law, Wallace Vincent 1906- *WhoSSW 93*
Law, William Theodore 1922- *WhoSSW 93*
Lawacz, W.P. 1937- *WhoScE 91-4*
LaWare, John Kevin 1956- *St&PR 93*
LaWare, John P. *BioIn 17*
LaWare, John Patrick 1928- *WhoAm 92, WhoE 93, WhoWor 93*
LaWarre, William Michael 1941- *St&PR 93*
Lawatsch, Frank E., Jr. 1944- *St&PR 93*
Lawatsch, Frank Emil, Jr. 1944- *WhoAm 92*
Lawbaugh, Penelope 1945- *WhoWrEP 92*
Lawber, Harold Ernest, Jr. 1950- *WhoE 93*
Lawder, Douglas Ward, Jr. 1934- *WhoWrEP 92*
Lawes, Charles O., II *Law&B 92*
Lawes, Henry 1596-1662 *Baker 92, DcLB 126 [port]*
Lawes, James Sidney 1926- *WhoE 93*
Lawes, William 1602-1645 *Baker 92*
Lawford, Christopher *BioIn 17*
Lawford, G. Ross 1941- *WhoAm 92*
Lawford, Patricia Kennedy 1924- *BioIn 17*
Lawford, Peter 1923-1984 *BioIn 17*
Lawford, Peter Eugene *Law&B 92*
Lawford, Valentine *BioIn 17*
Lawhead, Stephen 1950- *ScF&FL 92*
Law Hieng Ding 1935- *WhoAsAP 91*
Lawhon, Charles Watson 1922- *St&PR 93*
Lawhon, Jim *BioIn 17*
Lawhon, John E., III 1934- *WhoAm 92*
Lawhon, Joseph Richard *Law&B 92*
Lawhon, Robert A. *Law&B 92*
Lawhorn, Jess S. 1933- *St&PR 93*
Lawi, David S. 1935- *St&PR 93*
Lawi, David Steven 1935- *WhoAm 92*
Lawin, Bruce A. 1934- *St&PR 93*
Lawin, Peter 1930- *WhoWor 93*
Lawing, Alvin L., Jr. 1933- *St&PR 93*
Lawing, Jack L. *Law&B 92*
Lawing, Jack Lee 1938- *St&PR 93*
Lawing, Sarah *BioIn 17*
Lawiri, Ezra d1991 *BioIn 17*
Lawlah, Gloria Gary 1939- *WhoAmW 93*
Lawler, Alice Bonzi 1914- *WhoAmW 93, WhoWor 93*
Lawler, Ann 1944- *WhoAmW 93*
Lawler, Barbara Byrd- *BioIn 17*
Lawler, Beverley Rhea 1925- *WhoAm 92*
Lawler, Charles W. 1949- *St&PR 93*
Lawler, Donald L. 1935- *ScF&FL 92*
Lawler, Evelyn *BlkAmWO*
Lawler, Geoffrey John 1954- *WhoWor 93*
Lawler, J.L. *Law&B 92*
Lawler, James P. 1934- *St&PR 93*
Lawler, James Ronald 1929- *WhoAm 92*
Lawler, John Kevin 1948- *WhoE 93*
Lawler, Karen Strand 1939- *WhoAmW 93*
Lawler, Kathleen Ann 1963- *WhoAmW 93*
Lawler, Lawrence Thomas, Jr. 1949- *St&PR 93*
Lawler, Lillian Beatrice 1898- *AmWomPl*
Lawler, Michael Gerard 1933- *WhoAm 92*
Lawler, Patrick 1948- *ConAu 136*
Lawler, Sylvia D. *WhoScE 91-1*
Lawler, Thomas Aquin 1953- *St&PR 93*
Lawler, Thomas M. *Law&B 92*
Lawler, William Greshan, Jr. *Law&B 92*
Lawless, Clive John *WhoScE 91-1*
Lawless, Gary Cameron 1951- *WhoWrEP 92*
Lawless, Gregory B. 1940- *St&PR 93*
Lawless, John C. 1958- *St&PR 93*
Lawless, John Craig 1958- *WhoEmL 93*
Lawless, John W. *St&PR 93*
Lawless, K. Gordon 1924- *St&PR 93*
Lawless, Robert 1937- *WhoSSW 93*
Lawless, Robert William 1937- *WhoAm 92, WhoSSW 93*
Lawless, Ronald Edward 1924- *WhoAm 92*
Lawley, Alan 1933- *WhoAm 92*
Lawley, Karen R. 1947- *WhoAmW 93, WhoEmL 93*
Lawley, Robert W. 1954- *St&PR 93*
Lawley, Susan Marc 1951- *WhoAmW 93, WhoE 93, WhoEmL 93, WhoWor 93*
Lawlis, Patricia Kite 1945- *WhoAmW 93*
Lawlor, Andrea M. *Law&B 92*
Lawlor, Christopher Luke *Law&B 92*
Lawlor, David William *WhoScE 91-1*
Lawlor, Declan Joseph 1952- *WhoWor 93*
Lawlor, Helen Anne 1944- *St&PR 93, WhoAmW 93*
Lawlor, Richard Patrick *Law&B 92*
Lawlor, Rob 1936- *WhoAm 92*
Lawlor, Robert James 1936- *St&PR 93*
Lawlor, Tom *BioIn 17*
Lawn, Christopher James 1944- *WhoScE 91-1*
Lawn, Gregory T. 1950- *WhoE 93*
Lawn, Ian David 1947- *WhoWor 93*
Lawn, John C. 1935- *WhoAm 92*
Lawn, Richard John 1949- *WhoAm 92, WhoEmL 93*
Lawner, Leslie J. *Law&B 92*
Lawner, Lynne 1935- *WhoWrEP 92*
Lawnicki, Mary 1940- *St&PR 93*
Lawniczak, Andrzej 1939- *WhoScE 91-4*
Lawniczak, James Michael 1951- *WhoAm 92*
Lawniczak, Maciej Jan 1926- *WhoScE 91-4*
Lawrance, Anthony James *WhoScE 91-1*
Lawrance, Charles Holway 1920- *WhoAm 92*
Lawrance, Scott 1947- *WhoCanL 92*
Lawrance, Sue Ann d1991 *BioIn 17*
Lawrence, Lady 1878-1976 *BioIn 17*
Lawrence, A.W. 1900-1991 *AnObit 1991*
Lawrence, Albert James 1947- *WhoAm 92*
Lawrence, Albert W. 1928- *St&PR 93*
Lawrence, Albert Weaver 1928- *WhoAm 92, WhoE 93, WhoIns 93, WhoWor 93*
Lawrence, Aletta Ann 1966- *WhoAmW 93*
Lawrence, Alice Louise 1928- *WhoAmW 93*
Lawrence, Andrea Mead 1932- *BioIn 17*
Lawrence, Ann 1942-1987 *ScF&FL 92*
Lawrence, Annabal *AmWomPl*
Lawrence, Anne 1945- *WhoAmW 93*
Lawrence, Arabella Susan 1871-1947 *BioIn 17*
Lawrence, Ariadne *ConAu 137*
Lawrence, Arthur Peter 1937- *WhoWrEP 92*
Lawrence, Ashley 1934-1990 *BioIn 17*
Lawrence, Audrey Beth 1954- *WhoE 93*
Lawrence, Barbara 1944- *WhoAm 92*
Lawrence, Barbara Ann 1951- *WhoEmL 93*
Lawrence, Barbara C. 1927- *St&PR 93*
Lawrence, Barbara Corell 1927- *WhoAmW 93*
Lawrence, Barbara Lu 1943- *WhoSSW 93*
Lawrence, Betsy Ellen 1947- *WhoAmW 93, WhoEmL 93*
Lawrence, Brian David 1958- *WhoE 93*
Lawrence, Bryan H. 1942- *St&PR 93*
Lawrence, Bryan Hunt 1942- *WhoAm 92*
Lawrence, Charles A. *Law&B 92*
Lawrence, Charles Edmund 1927- *WhoAm 92*
Lawrence, Charles Stephen *Law&B 92*
Lawrence, Christopher Rueckert 1953- *WhoAm 92*
Lawrence, D.H. 1885-1930 *BioIn 17, MagSWL [port], TwCLC 48 [port], WorLitC [port]*
Lawrence, David 1888-1973 *JrnUS*
Lawrence, David 1889-1966 *PolPar*
Lawrence, David, Jr. 1942- *WhoAm 92, WhoSSW 93*

Lawrence, David A. *Law&B 92*
Lawrence, David Herbert 1885-1930 *BioIn 17*
Lawrence, David K. *Law&B 92*
Lawrence, David Leo d1966 *BioIn 17*
Lawrence, David Michael 1943- *WhoAm 92*
Lawrence, David Paul 1961- *WhoEmL 93, WhoSSW 93*
Lawrence, David Stephen 1959- *WhoE 93*
Lawrence, Dean Grayson 1901- *WhoAmW 93*
Lawrence, Deborah Jean 1960- *WhoAmW 93*
Lawrence, Diantha Fitch *AmWomPl*
Lawrence, Donald R. *Law&B 92*
Lawrence, Donald Walter 1936- *St&PR 93*
Lawrence, Donna Marie 1953- *WhoAmW 93*
Lawrence, Dorothea Dix 1899-1979 *Baker 92*
Lawrence, E.A. *WhoWrEP 92*
Lawrence, Edgar 1944- *WhoE 93*
Lawrence, Ellis Fuller 1879-1946 *BioIn 17*
Lawrence, Ernest Orlando 1901-1958 *BioIn 17*
Lawrence, Ernest Richard 1944- *WhoE 93*
Lawrence, Estelene Yvonne 1933- *WhoAmW 93*
Lawrence, Ethel G. *AmWomPl*
Lawrence, Everett Dean 1934- *St&PR 93*
Lawrence, Florence 1886?-1938 *IntDcF 2-3 [port]*
Lawrence, Francis Leo 1937- *WhoE 93, WhoWor 93*
Lawrence, Garland R. 1933- *St&PR 93*
Lawrence, George D. 1950- *St&PR 93*
Lawrence, George D., Jr. *Law&B 92*
Lawrence, George Durwood, Jr. 1950- *WhoAm 92*
Lawrence, George H.C. 1937- *St&PR 93*
Lawrence, George Hubbard Clapp 1937- *WhoAm 92*
Lawrence, George John *Law&B 92*
Lawrence, George R. d1938 *BioIn 17*
Lawrence, Gerald 1939- *WhoAm 92*
Lawrence, Gerri G. *Law&B 92*
Lawrence, Gertrude 1898-1952 *Baker 92*
Lawrence, Glenn Robert 1930- *WhoAm 92*
Lawrence, Gloria Jean 1954- *WhoAmW 93*
Lawrence, Gordon Grant 1931- *WhoAm 92*
Lawrence, Harding Luther 1920- *EncABHB 8 [port]*
Lawrence, Henry Sherwood 1916- *WhoAm 92, WhoE 93*
Lawrence, Herbert Gordon 1939- *St&PR 93*
Lawrence, Howard Ray 1936- *WhoE 93*
Lawrence, Hugh *Law&B 92*
Lawrence, Isabel *AmWomPl*
Lawrence, J.A. *ScF&FL 92*
Lawrence, J.M. 1939- *St&PR 93*
Lawrence, J.R. *WhoScE 91-1*
Lawrence, Jacob 1917- *BlkAuII 92, ConBlB 4 [port], WhoAm 92*
Lawrence, James 1781-1813 *HarEnMi*
Lawrence, James Bland 1947- *WhoAm 92*
Lawrence, James D. *ScF&FL 92*
Lawrence, James Francis 1932- *St&PR 93*
Lawrence, James Huckabee 1953- *WhoSSW 93*
Lawrence, James Kaufman Lebensburger 1940- *WhoAm 92*
Lawrence, James Michael 1941- *St&PR 93*
Lawrence, Jean Hope 1944- *WhoAmW 93, WhoWrEP 92*
Lawrence, Jeff 1957- *St&PR 93*
Lawrence, Jerome 1915- *BioIn 17, WhoAm 92*
Lawrence, Jim 1918- *ScF&FL 92*
Lawrence, Joe A. 1934- *St&PR 93*
Lawrence, John 1904-1991 *AnObit 1991*
Lawrence, John Charles 1943- *WhoWor 93*
Lawrence, John E.S. 1938- *WhoUN 92*
Lawrence, John H. 1904-1991 *BioIn 17*
Lawrence, John Kidder 1949- *WhoEmL 93*
Lawrence, John M. *Law&B 92*
Lawrence, John Malcolm, Jr. 1934- *St&PR 93*
Lawrence, John Warren 1928- *St&PR 93*
Lawrence, Joseph D. 1924- *St&PR 93*
Lawrence, Josephine 1890?-1978 *ScF&FL 92*
Lawrence, Judiana 1936- *WhoE 93*
Lawrence, Karen *WhoCanL 92*
Lawrence, Kathleen Rockwell 1945- *ConAu 136*
Lawrence, Kathryn Ann 1946- *WhoSSW 93*
Lawrence, Ken 1942- *WhoSSW 93*
Lawrence, Kennard T. *Law&B 92*
Lawrence, Larry *Law&B 92*
Lawrence, Larry James 1944- *WhoE 93*
Lawrence, Lawrence Shubert, Jr. d1992 *NewYTBS 92*
Lawrence, Leanne 1961- *WhoAmW 93*
Lawrence, Lee Arthur *BioIn 17*
Lawrence, Les 1940- *WhoAm 92*
Lawrence, Leslie Gail 1961- *WhoE 93, WhoEmL 93*
Lawrence, Lillian Nixon *AmWomPl*
Lawrence, Linwood G., III *Law&B 92*
Lawrence, Lisa Marie 1961- *WhoAmW 93*
Lawrence, Lorraine Denise 1968- *WhoAmW 93*
Lawrence, Louise *ConAu 38NR*
Lawrence, Louise 1943- *ScF&FL 92*
Lawrence, Lucile 1907- *Baker 92*
Lawrence, Lynn *SmATA 73*
Lawrence, Madalena Joan Vignocchi 1952- *WhoEmL 93*
Lawrence, Marc A. 1946- *St&PR 93*
Lawrence, Margery 1896?-1969 *ScF&FL 92*
Lawrence, Marjorie 1909-1979 *IntDcOp, OxDcOp*
Lawrence, Marjorie (Florence) 1907-1979 *Baker 92*
Lawrence, Mark 1921-1991 *BioIn 17*
Lawrence, Martha Alice 1956- *WhoAmW 93*
Lawrence, Mary 1918-1991 *BioIn 17*
Lawrence, Mary Georgene Wells 1928- *WhoAm 92, WhoAmW 93*
Lawrence, Mary Wells *BioIn 17*
Lawrence, Melinda *BioIn 17*
Lawrence, Merle 1915- *WhoAm 92*
Lawrence, Merloyd Ludington 1932- *WhoAm 92*
Lawrence, Michael Andrew 1948- *WhoSSW 93*
Lawrence, Mickey Jo *Law&B 92*
Lawrence, Nancy Ann 1959- *WhoAmW 93, WhoEmL 93*
Lawrence, Nancy Morrison 1952- *WhoAmW 93*
Lawrence, Patricia Ann 1926- *WhoAmW 93*
Lawrence, Paul Roger 1922- *WhoAm 92*
Lawrence, Paula Denise 1959- *WhoAmW 93*
Lawrence, Peggy Laverne 1944- *WhoAmW 93*
Lawrence, Pelham Bissell 1945- *WhoAm 92*
Lawrence, Peter Anthony *WhoScE 91-1*
Lawrence, Peter J. 1956- *St&PR 93*
Lawrence, Phenis Joseph 1926- *WhoSSW 93*
Lawrence, Philip James 1919- *St&PR 93*
Lawrence, Ralph Waldo 1941- *WhoWor 93*
Lawrence, Randolph Thomas 1949- *WhoE 93*
Lawrence, Randy Bernard 1953- *WhoSSW 93*
Lawrence, Ray *MiSFD 9*
Lawrence, Ray Vance 1910- *WhoSSW 93*
Lawrence, Richard Cromwell 1933- *WhoWor 93*
Lawrence, Richard E. 1939- *St&PR 93*
Lawrence, Richard Sellers 1934- *WhoE 93*
Lawrence, Richard W., Jr. 1909- *St&PR 93*
Lawrence, Richard Wesley, Jr. 1909- *WhoAm 92*
Lawrence, Robert Ashton 1926- *St&PR 93, WhoE 93*
Lawrence, Robert Cutting, III 1938- *WhoAm 92*
Lawrence, Robert G. 1932- *WhoIns 93*
Lawrence, Robert Swan 1938- *WhoAm 92*
Lawrence, Robert W. 1924- *St&PR 93*
Lawrence, Roderick John 1949- *WhoWor 93*
Lawrence, Ronald *Law&B 92*
Lawrence, Ronald Eugene 1942- *WhoSSW 93*
Lawrence, Ruddick C. 1912- *St&PR 93*
Lawrence, Ruddick Carpenter 1912- *WhoAm 92, WhoWor 93*
Lawrence, Ruth Anderson *WhoAmW 93*
Lawrence, Sally Clark 1930- *WhoAmW 93*
Lawrence, Seymour 1926- *WhoAm 92*
Lawrence, Sherman S. 1918- *St&PR 93*
Lawrence, Sidney Smith 1948- *WhoEmL 93*
Lawrence, Sigmund Joseph 1918- *WhoE 93*
Lawrence, Simon *ScF&FL 92*
Lawrence, Stephen Reid 1921- *WhoE 93*
Lawrence, Steve *NewYTBS 92 [port]*
Lawrence, Steve 1935- *Baker 92, WhoAm 92*
Lawrence, Stewart D. 1948- *St&PR 93*
Lawrence, Stringer 1697-1775 *HarEnMi*
Lawrence, Susan Elizabeth 1945- *WhoAmW 93*
Lawrence, Sylvia Yvonne 1937- *WhoAmW 93*
Lawrence, T.E. 1888-1935 *BioIn 17, BritWr S2*
Lawrence, Telete Zorayda 1910- *WhoAm 92, WhoAmW 93, WhoWor 93*
Lawrence, Thomas Edward 1888-1935 *BioIn 17, DcTwHis, HarEnMi*
Lawrence, Thomas Eldredge d1990 *BioIn 17*
Lawrence, Thomas Patterson 1946- *WhoAm 92*
Lawrence, Troy *BioIn 17*
Lawrence, Vera Brodsky 1909- *Baker 92*
Lawrence, Vernon Elliott 1938- *WhoSSW 93*
Lawrence, Vicki Schultz 1949- *WhoAm 92*
Lawrence, Vickie Lee 1958- *WhoAmW 93*
Lawrence, W.H.C. *ScF&FL 92*
Lawrence, Wagner *WhoAsAP 91*
Lawrence, Walter, Jr. 1925- *WhoAm 92*
Lawrence, Walter Thomas 1950- *WhoEmL 93, WhoSSW 93*
Lawrence, Wayne Allen 1938- *WhoAm 92*
Lawrence, Willard Earl 1917- *WhoAm 92*
Lawrence, William Charles 1922- *WhoSSW 93*
Lawrence, William J., Jr. 1918- *St&PR 93*
Lawrence, William Joseph, Jr. 1918- *WhoAm 92*
Lawrence, William Louis, Jr. 1951- *St&PR 93*
Lawrence, William Porter 1930- *WhoAm 92*
Lawrence, William S. 1943- *St&PR 93*
Lawrence, William Walter 1929- *WhoE 93*
Lawrence, Winifred Gillen 1935- *WhoE 93*
Lawrenson, Peter John *WhoScE 91-1*
Lawrenz, Donald R. 1923- *WhoIns 93*
Lawrie, Caroline S. 1932- *St&PR 93*
Lawrie, Duncan H. 1943- *WhoAm 92*
Lawrie, Gerald Murray 1945- *WhoAm 92*
Lawrie, Peter 1945- *WhoIns 93*
Lawrie, Ralston Andrew *WhoScE 91-1*
Lawrie, Robert F.C. *Law&B 92*
Lawrie, Robert George *Law&B 92*
Lawroski, Harry 1928- *WhoAm 92*
Lawrowski, Zbigniew Henryk 1925- *WhoWor 93*
Lawry, Sylvia *WhoAm 92*
Lawryniuk, Viktor 1953- *WhoWrEP 92*
Laws, Anna Cantrell d1929 *AmWomPl*
Laws, David Garrard 1930- *St&PR 93, WhoAm 92*
Laws, Donald M. *Law&B 92*
Laws, Donald M. 1935- *St&PR 93*
Laws, Edward Raymond 1938- *WhoAm 92*
Laws, Hubert 1939- *Baker 92*
Laws, Jay B. *ScF&FL 92*
Laws, Judith Ann 1937- *WhoAmW 93*
Laws, Marjorie E. 1940- *St&PR 93*
Laws, Priscilla Watson 1940- *WhoAmW 93*
Laws, Richard Maitland 1926- *WhoWor 93*
Laws, Robert E. 1921-1990 *BioIn 17*
Laws, Robert E. 1927- *WhoAm 92*
Laws, Stephen 1952- *ScF&FL 92*
Laws, Susan Elizabeth 1967- *WhoAmW 93*
Lawshe, George Michael, III 1961- *WhoSSW 93*
Law-Smith, David John 1940- *St&PR 93*
Laws-Moseley, Barbara Lee 1946- *WhoE 93*
Lawson, Abram Venable 1922- *WhoAm 92*
Lawson, Alfred W. 1869-1954 *BioIn 17*
Lawson, Amy Elizabeth 1966- *WhoAmW 93*
Lawson, Andrew Lowell, Jr. 1938- *St&PR 93*
Lawson, Ann Marie McDonald *WhoAmW 93*
Lawson, Benjamin Samuel, Jr. 1949- *St&PR 93*
Lawson, Bryan Russell *WhoScE 91-1*
Lawson, Carroll D. 1956- *St&PR 93*
Lawson, Charlene Ann 1948- *WhoAmW 93*
Lawson, Charles Edmond 1935- *St&PR 93*
Lawson, Charles Joseph *Law&B 92*
Lawson, Conor 1943- *St&PR 93*
Lawson, Craig M. *Law&B 92*
Lawson, Cynthia Elizabeth 1961- *WhoAmW 93*
Lawson, David E. 1937- *WhoAm 92*
Lawson, David R. 1947- *WhoEmL 93*
Lawson, Deborah Davis *Law&B 92*
Lawson, Eugene K. 1939- *St&PR 93*
Lawson, Ferd O., Jr. 1925- *St&PR 93*
Lawson, Francis Colin 1917- *WhoAm 92*
Lawson, Frederick Hebel 1927- *St&PR 93, WhoAm 92*
Lawson, Gary Dean *Law&B 92*
Lawson, Gayla Hughes 1940- *WhoSSW 93*
Lawson, Harold D. 1947- *WhoEmL 93*
Lawson, Harold W. 1937- *WhoScE 91-4*
Lawson, Harry J. *Law&B 92*
Lawson, Hugh Harold 1927- *WhoSSW 93*
Lawson, J. Evelyn 1952- *WhoAmW 93*
Lawson, J. Frederick *Law&B 92*
Lawson, J. Jenice Evelyn 1952- *WhoWor 93*
Lawson, Jack *ScF&FL 92*
Lawson, James A. 1936- *St&PR 93*
Lawson, James Drew *Law&B 92*
Lawson, James Lee 1949- *WhoWor 93*
Lawson, James M., Jr. 1928- *EncAACR*
Lawson, James Thomas, Jr. 1935- *St&PR 93*
Lawson, Jane E. *St&PR 93*
Lawson, Jane Elizabeth *WhoAm 92*
Lawson, Janet Ann 1940- *WhoE 93*
Lawson, Jean Kerr 1941- *WhoAmW 93, WhoWor 93*
Lawson, Jean-Louis 1941- *WhoUN 92*
Lawson, Jennifer *BioIn 17*
Lawson, Jennifer 1946- *WhoAm 92, WhoAmW 93, WhoE 93*
Lawson, Jerry Edward 1936- *St&PR 93*
Lawson, Jimmie Don 1942- *WhoSSW 93*
Lawson, Joel Smith, III 1947- *WhoAm 92, WhoE 93*
Lawson, John *DcAmChF 1960*
Lawson, John c. 1610-1665 *HarEnMi*
Lawson, John H. *WhoAm 92*
Lawson, John Howard 1894-1977 *BioIn 17*
Lawson, John K. 1940- *St&PR 93*
Lawson, John Quinn 1940- *WhoAm 92*
Lawson, John Robert 1947- *St&PR 93*
Lawson, Jonathan Nevin 1941- *WhoE 93*
Lawson, Karyl M. *Law&B 92*
Lawson, Lawyer *AfrAmBi*
Lawson, Mark 1962- *ConAu 139*
Lawson, Mary J. 1940- *WhoAmW 93*
Lawson, Nancy P. 1926- *St&PR 93*
Lawson, Neils Vinton 1922- *WhoAm 92*
Lawson, NewAvery Glover 1922- *WhoE 93*
Lawson, Norman Clyde 1938- *St&PR 93*
Lawson, Pauline Price 1923- *St&PR 93*
Lawson, R. William *Law&B 92*
Lawson, Randall Clayton, II 1948- *WhoAm 92, WhoEmL 93*
Lawson, Regina Fern 1938- *WhoSSW 93*
Lawson, Robert 1892-1957 *ConAu 137, MajAI [port]*
Lawson, Robert Bernard 1940- *WhoAm 92*
Lawson, Robert Davis 1926- *WhoAm 92*
Lawson, Robert Eugene 1944- *WhoWor 93*
Lawson, Robert N. 1873-1945 *ScF&FL 92*
Lawson, Robert William, Jr. 1908- *WhoAm 92*
Lawson, Rodger S. 1943- *WhoIns 93*
Lawson, Rose Mary 1929- *WhoAmW 93*
Lawson, Ruth Catherine 1911-1990 *BioIn 17*
Lawson, Sam 1949- *St&PR 93*
Lawson, Susan *ScF&FL 92*
Lawson, Sybil *ScF&FL 92*
Lawson, T.J. *WhoScE 91-1*
Lawson, Thomas Cheney 1955- *WhoEmL 93, WhoWor 93*
Lawson, Thomas Richard 1940- *WhoAm 92*
Lawson, Thomas Walker 1940- *WhoSSW 93*
Lawson, Victor F. 1850-1925 *JrnUS*
Lawson, Vola *BioIn 17*
Lawson, W. Alan 1925- *WhoScE 91-3*
Lawson, Warren Glenn 1933- *WhoAm 92*
Lawson, Willard Francis, Jr. 1947- *WhoEmL 93, WhoSSW 93*
Lawson, William Burton 1930- *WhoE 93*
Lawson, William David, III 1924- *WhoAm 92, WhoSSW 93*
Lawson, William Hogan 1937- *St&PR 93*
Lawson, William Hogan, III 1937- *WhoAm 92*
Lawson, William Howard, Jr. 1946- *WhoEmL 93*
Lawson Donadio, Carolina Anna 1920- *WhoSSW 93*
Lawson-Johnston, Peter O. 1927- *St&PR 93*
Lawson-Johnston, Peter Orman 1927- *WhoAm 92, WhoE 93*
Lawton, Annie M. *AmWomPl*
Lawton, Bettina Mary 1954- *WhoAm 92*
Lawton, Brigitta 1948- *St&PR 93*
Lawton, Charles *WhoWrEP 92*
Lawton, Charles 1913- *WhoAm 92*
Lawton, Charles B. 1920- *St&PR 93*
Lawton, Cheryl Koris *Law&B 92*
Lawton, Cheryl Koris 1960- *WhoAmW 93*
Lawton, Dorothy 1874-1960 *BioIn 17*
Lawton, Edgar Herbert, Jr. 1929- *St&PR 93, WhoAm 92*
Lawton, Eric 1947- *WhoEmL 93*
Lawton, Eugene A. 1936- *St&PR 93*
Lawton, Eugene Alfred 1936- *WhoAm 92*
Lawton, Frank J. 1943- *St&PR 93*
Lawton, Gregory Moss 1958- *WhoEmL 93, WhoWor 93*
Lawton, Henry Ware 1843-1899 *HarEnMi*

Lawton, Henry William 1941- *WhoE 93*
Lawton, Jacqueline Agnes 1933- *WhoAmW 93*
Lawton, Jean Margaret 1930- *WhoAmW 93*
Lawton, John Hartley *WhoScE 91-1*
Lawton, John Hartley 1943- *WhoWor 93*
Lawton, John William Magarey 1939- *WhoWor 93*
Lawton, Jonathan *MiSFD 9*
Lawton, Joseph Benjamin, IV 1941- *WhoSSW 93*
Lawton, Kenneth Alan 1940- *St&PR 93*
Lawton, Lorilee Ann 1947- *WhoAmW 93, WhoE 93*
Lawton, Marcia Jean 1937- *WhoAmW 93, WhoSSW 93*
Lawton, Mary Cecilia 1935- *WhoAmW 93*
Lawton, Mary R. *Law&B 92*
Lawton, Michael James 1953- *WhoEmL 93*
Lawton, Patrick S. 1956- *St&PR 93*
Lawton, Randall W. 1945- *St&PR 93*
Lawton, Raymond M. 1954- *St&PR 93*
Lawton, Richard Stanley 1931- *St&PR 93*
Lawton, Thomas Gerard Samuel 1962- *WhoWrEP 92*
Lawton, Thomas P. *Law&B 92*
Lawton, Wesley Willingham, Jr. 1943- *WhoSSW 93*
Lawton, William Burton 1927- *St&PR 93, WhoAm 92*
Lawton, William John Penson 1950- *WhoE 93*
Lawwill, Theodore 1937- *WhoAm 92*
Lawyer, Vivian Jury 1932- *WhoAmW 93*
Lawyer, Vivian Moore 1946- *WhoE 93*
Lax, Alistair John *WhoScE 91-1*
Lax, David 1939- *St&PR 93*
Lax, Eric 1944- *ConAu 138*
Lax, Eugene H. 1949- *St&PR 93*
Lax, Gerald B. *Law&B 92*
Lax, Henry 1894-1990 *BioIn 17*
Lax, James David 1954- *WhoE 93*
Lax, Kathleen Thompson *WhoAmW 93*
Lax, Melvin 1922- *WhoAm 92, WhoE 93*
Lax, Peter David 1926- *WhoAm 92, WhoWor 93*
Lax, Philip 1920- *WhoAm 92, WhoWor 93*
Lax, Sharon M. *Law&B 92*
Laxalt, Paul 1922- *WhoWor 93*
Laxalt, Robert P(eter) 1923- *ConAu 38NR*
Laxalte Terra, Elbio Edgardo 1950- *WhoWor 93*
Laxer, Marc Alan 1947- *WhoEmL 93*
Laxmi Narain 1927- *WhoAsAP 91*
Laxness, Halldor 1902- *BioIn 17, WhoWor 93*
Laxo, Olav 1930- *St&PR 93*
Lay, Bernice Lay 1940- *WhoAmW 93*
Lay, Chris Andrew 1927- *St&PR 93*
Lay, Christine Ann 1957- *WhoAmW 93*
Lay, Christopher David 1946- *WhoE 93*
Lay, Donald Pomeroy 1926- *WhoAm 92*
Lay, Elizabeth Atkinson *AmWomPl*
Lay, Joseph Lafayette 1952- *St&PR 93*
Lay, K. Edward 1932- *WhoSSW 93*
Lay, Kenneth Lee 1942- *St&PR 93, WhoAm 92, WhoSSW 93*
Lay, Nancy Duke S. 1938- *WhoWrEP 92*
Lay, Norvie Lee 1940- *WhoAm 92*
Lay, Richard Michael 1961- *WhoSSW 93*
Lay, Russell Alan 1956- *WhoEmL 93, WhoSSW 93*
Lay, William Ellsworth 1862-1934 *BioIn 17*
Lay, William Sherman 1939- *St&PR 93*
Layamon fl. c. 1200- *CIMLC 10*
Layard, John 1891-1972 *IntDcAn*
Layard, Peter Richard Grenville *WhoScE 91-1*
Laybourn, Peter John Robert *WhoScE 91-1*
Laybourne, Everett Broadstone 1911- *WhoAm 92*
Laybourne, Gerry Bond *BioIn 17*
Laycock, Anita Simon 1940- *WhoAmW 93*
Laycock, Evelyn Elizabeth 1926- *WhoSSW 93*
Laycock, Fred 1926- *St&PR 93*
Laycock, Harold Douglas 1948- *WhoAm 92*
Laycock, John Field 1921- *WhoWor 93*
Laycock, Michael 1954- *St&PR 93*
Laycraft, George H. 1924- *St&PR 93*
Laycraft, James Herbert 1924- *WhoAm 92*
Layda, Louis J. 1944- *St&PR 93*
Layde, Durward Charles 1912- *WhoAm 92*
Layden, Andrew James 1930- *WhoAm 92*
Layden, Francis Patrick 1932- *WhoAm 92*
Layden, William Edward 1937- *WhoSSW 93*
Lay-Dopyera, Margaret Zoe 1931- *WhoE 93*
Laye, Camara 1928-1980 *BioIn 17*
Layer, Daniel Paul, Jr. *BioIn 17*
Layer, Eulalie Cross *AmWomPl*
Layer, Meredith Mitchum 1946- *WhoAm 92, WhoAmW 93*
Layhon, Christine Marie 1955- *WhoEmL 93*
Layiq, Sulaiman 1930- *WhoAsAP 91*
Layman, Caleb Maynard 1943- *St&PR 93*
Layman, Clifford Paul 1946- *WhoE 93*
Layman, David J. 1945- *St&PR 93*
Layman, David Michael 1955- *WhoSSW 93*
Layman, Elizabeth W. *Law&B 92*
Layman, Emma McCloy 1910- *WhoAm 92*
Layman, J. Allen 1952- *St&PR 93*
Layman, Jason *BioIn 17*
Layman, Lawrence 1930- *WhoAm 92*
Layman, Linda Anne 1936- *WhoAmW 93*
Layman, Richard Lawrence 1947- *WhoSSW 93*
Layman, Robert Eugene 1921- *St&PR 93*
Layman, William Arthur 1929- *WhoAm 92*
Layman, William R. 1950- *St&PR 93*
Laymon, Carl *ScF&FL 92*
Laymon, Cynthia J. 1948- *WhoSSW 93*
Laymon, Harold James 1951- *WhoWrEP 92*
Laymon, John L. 1917- *St&PR 93*
Laymon, Richard 1947- *ScF&FL 92*
Layne, Bobby 1929-1986 *BioIn 17*
Layne, David W. *Law&B 92*
Layne, Donna *WhoWrEP 92*
Layne, Edward Noel 1947- *St&PR 93*
Layne, James Nathaniel 1926- *WhoAm 92*
Layne, John Francis 1928- *WhoSSW 93*
Layson, Ruby Lee 1927- *WhoSSW 93*
Layson, William McIntyre 1934- *St&PR 93, WhoAm 92*
Layson, Zed Clark, Jr. 1937- *St&PR 93*
Laystrom, Robert Arnold 1952- *St&PR 93*
Layt, Herbert William 1932- *WhoWor 93*
Laytham, William Brown 1931- *St&PR 93*
Layton, Bill R. *Law&B 92*
Layton, Billy Jim 1924- *Baker 92, WhoAm 92*
Layton, David *MiSFD 9*
Layton, Donald Harvey 1950- *St&PR 93, WhoAm 92*
Layton, Edwin Thomas, Jr. 1928- *WhoAm 92*
Layton, Geoffrey 1884-1964 *BioIn 17*
Layton, Harry Christopher 1938- *WhoWor 93*
Layton, Irving 1912- *BioIn 17, WhoCanL 92*
Layton, James P. d1992 *NewYTBS 92 [port]*
Layton, Jean Carol 1951- *WhoAmW 93*
Layton, Joe 1931- *MiSFD 9, WhoAm 92*
Layton, John C. 1944- *WhoAm 92*
Layton, Karen Elaine 1960- *WhoEmL 93*
Layton, Kenneth A. 1940- *St&PR 93*
Layton, Leon H. 1930- *St&PR 93*
Layton, Lynne Bonnie 1950- *WhoAmW 93*
Layton, M.R. 1947- *St&PR 93*
Layton, Marjorie Rebecca 1928- *WhoE 93*
Layton, Molly Collins 1943- *WhoAmW 93*
Layton, Robert 1930- *Baker 92*
Layton, Robert Glenn 1946- *WhoEmL 93*
Layton, Robert L. *Law&B 92*
Layton, Thomas Ralph 1947- *WhoWrEP 92*
Layton, William George 1931- *St&PR 93, WhoAm 92*
Layton, William Isaac 1913- *WhoAm 92, WhoSSW 93*
Layzer, David 1925- *WhoAm 92*
Lazar c. 1329-1389 *OxDcByz*
Lazar, Abraham 1924- *St&PR 93*
Lazar, Donald A. *St&PR 93*
Lazar, Elysa *BioIn 17*
Lazar, Filip 1894-1936 *Baker 92*
Lazar, George Theodore 1931- *WhoE 93*
Lazar, Irving *BioIn 17*
Lazar, Irving Paul 1907- *WhoAm 92*
Lazar, Jamie Rothman *Law&B 92*
Lazar, Jay L. *Law&B 92*
Lazar, Kenneth Stuart 1948- *WhoEmL 93*
Lazar, Lawrence William 1954- *WhoAm 92*
Lazar, Lucia 1940- *WhoScE 91-4*
Lazar, Maciej Alan 1957- *WhoWor 93*
Lazar, Mark Howard 1952- *WhoE 93*
Lazar, Norman Donald 1942- *WhoE 93*
Lazar, Philippe *WhoScE 91-2*
Lazar, Rande Harris 1951- *WhoWor 93*
Lazar, S. Alan *Law&B 92*
Lazar, Swifty *BioIn 17*
Lazar, Virginia M. 1951- *St&PR 93*
Lazar, Zoe L. 1948- *WhoEmL 93*
Lazarchick, Michael Cox 1947- *WhoE 93*
Lazard, Jacques C. 1951- *St&PR 93*
Lazare, Aaron 1936- *WhoAm 92*
Lazare, Alick Bernard 1934- *WhoWor 93*
Lazare, Arthur B. *St&PR 93*
Lazare, Barbara R. *St&PR 93*
Lazare, Edward J. d1991 *BioIn 17*
LaZare, Howard Ted 1936- *St&PR 93*
Lazare, Martin 1829-1897 *Baker 92*
Lazareff, Jorge Antonio 1953- *WhoWor 93*
Lazarescu, Alan Edward *Law&B 92*
Lazarev, Alexandre 1945- *WhoWor 93*
Lazarev, Gregory L. 1936- *WhoUN 92*
Lazarev, Gregory Leivik 1946- *WhoE 93*
Lazarev, Nikolai Nikolaevich 1951- *WhoWor 93*
Lazarewicz, Jerzy W. 1940- *WhoScE 91-4*
Lazaridis, Stephanos 1944- *OxDcOp*
Lazarini, Gary Leo 1941- *St&PR 93*
Lazaris, Nicholas G. 1950- *WhoE 93*
Lazaris, Nicholas George 1950- *St&PR 93*
Lazaris, Pamela Adriane 1956- *WhoAmW 93*
Lazarkiewicz, Bogdan 1929- *WhoScE 91-4*
Lazaro, Hipolito 1887-1974 *OxDcOp*
Lazaro, Hippolito 1887-1974 *Baker 92*
Lazaro, Oscar 1963- *WhoWor 93*
Lazarof, Henri 1932- *Baker 92*
Lazaroff, Joseph L. *Law&B 92*
Lazar of P'arpi fl. 5th cent.- *OxDcByz*
Lazaron, Pauline H. *AmWomPl*
Lazaros dc. 865 *OxDcByz*
Lazaros d1368 *OxDcByz*
Lazaroski, Trajce *WhoScE 91-4*
Lazaros of Mount Galesios d1053 *OxDcByz*
Lazarovic, Karen 1947- *WhoAm 92*
Lazarow, David 1945- *St&PR 93*
Lazarre, Justin Joseph, Jr. 1939- *St&PR 93*
Lazarski, Joanne Louise 1946- *WhoWor 93*
Lazaruk, Lillie Margaret 1926- *WhoAmW 93*
Lazarus, A(rnold) L(eslie) 1914- *WhoWrEP 92*
Lazarus, Allan Matthew 1927- *WhoAm 92*
Lazarus, Arnold Allan 1932- *WhoAm 92*
Lazarus, Arnold Leslie 1914- *WhoAm 92*
Lazarus, Arnold M. 1950- *St&PR 93*
Lazarus, Arthur, Jr. 1926- *WhoAm 92*
Lazarus, Arthur Louis 1954- *WhoE 93, WhoEmL 93*
Lazarus, Ashley *MiSFD 9*
Lazarus, Barbara Beth 1946- *WhoEmL 93*
Lazarus, Barry A. 1942- *WhoE 93*
Lazarus, Charles *BioIn 17*
Lazarus, Charles 1923- *News 92 [port], WhoAm 92*
Lazarus, Charles P. 1923- *St&PR 93*
Lazarus, Charles Y. 1914- *St&PR 93*
Lazarus, Colin Royston *WhoScE 91-1*
Lazarus, Daniel 1898-1964 *Baker 92*
Lazarus, David 1921- *WhoAm 92*
Lazarus, Edward Hal 1959- *WhoEmL 93*
Lazarus, Emma 1849-1887 *BioIn 17, JeAmHC*
Lazarus, Fred 1884-1973 *BioIn 17*
Lazarus, Fred, IV 1942- *WhoAm 92*
Lazarus, George Milton 1932- *WhoAm 92*
Lazarus, Gerald Sylvan 1939- *WhoAm 92, WhoE 93*
Lazarus, Gustav 1861-1920 *Baker 92*
Lazarus, Harold 1927- *WhoAm 92, WhoWor 93*
Lazarus, Jerome B. 1922- *St&PR 93*
Lazarus, Jerrold *St&PR 93*
Lazarus, Joan A. 1929- *WhoE 93*
Lazarus, John 1947- *WhoCanL 92*
Lazarus, Kenneth Anthony 1942- *WhoAm 92*
Lazarus, Keo Felker 1913- *WhoWrEP 92*
Lazarus, Maurice 1915- *WhoAm 92*
Lazarus, Mell *WhoAm 92*
Lazarus, Richard S. *BioIn 17*
Lazarus, Richard Stanley 1922- *WhoAm 92*
Lazarus, Rochelle Braff 1947- *WhoAm 92, WhoE 93*
Lazarus, Sara Louise 1948- *WhoAmW 93, WhoEmL 93*
Lazarus, Shelly *BioIn 17*
Lazarus, William P. 1949- *WhoSSW 93*
Lazatin, Carmelo F. 1934- *WhoAsAP 91*
Lazay, Paul D. 1939- *St&PR 93*
Lazdunski, Claude J. 1940- *WhoScE 91-2*
Lazear, Edward Paul 1948- *WhoAm 92*
Lazear, Jonathan *BioIn 17*
Lazechko, Dorothy Molly 1926- *WhoAmW 93*
Lazenby, Fred Wiehl 1932- *St&PR 93, WhoAm 92, WhoIns 93*
Lazenby, Gail R. 1947- *WhoAmW 93*
Lazenby, Glenda Fay 1946- *WhoAmW 93*
Lazenby, James O. 1925- *St&PR 93*
Lazenby, Norman 1914- *ScF&FL 92*
Lazenby, Pender Jordan 1950- *St&PR 93*
Lazenby, Robert E. 1940- *St&PR 93*
Lazerow, Norman 1926- *St&PR 93*
Lazerson, Earl Edwin 1930- *WhoAm 92*
Lazerson, Jack 1936- *WhoAm 92*
Lazerwitz, Alison R. *Law&B 92*
Lazic, Milan 1927- *WhoScE 91-4*
Lazic, Zora *Law&B 92*
Lazich, Daniel 1941- *WhoWor 93*
Lazinsky, Jo Anne Marie *WhoE 93*
Lazio, Enrico A. 1958- *WhoEmL 93*
Lazo, Agustin 1898- *DcMexL*
Lazo, Ignacio Jesus 1955- *WhoEmL 93*
Lazo, Ralph d1992? *BioIn 17*
Lazo Arrasco, Jorge 1928- *WhoWor 93*
Lazo Barra, Florencio 1942- *WhoWor 93*
Lazor, Patricia Ann 1936- *WhoAmW 93*
Lazor, Theodosius 1933- *WhoAm 92*
Lazorchak, Joseph Michael 1957- *WhoE 93, WhoEmL 93*
Lazorik, Michael Raymond 1945- *St&PR 93*
Lazorwitz, Elaine Sherri 1954- *WhoEmL 93*
Lazovick, Paul B. 1935- *St&PR 93*
Lazowski, Yurek 1917-1980 *PolBiDi*
Lazroff, J.J. 1946- *St&PR 93*
Lazrus, Julian 1919- *St&PR 93*
Lazuta, Eugene M. *ScF&FL 92*
Lazuta, Gene 1959- *ScF&FL 92*
Lazutka, Juozas Rimantas 1960- *WhoWor 93*
Lazutkin, Vladimir Feodorovitch 1941- *WhoWor 93*
Lazz, MaryJane Vernon 1948- *WhoEmL 93*
Lazzara, Joseph John 1951- *St&PR 93*
Lazzari, Sylvio 1857-1944 *Baker 92*
Lazzari, Virgilio 1887-1953 *Baker 92*
Lazzarini, Ennio Vittorio Antonio 1929- *WhoWor 93*
Lazzaro, Anthony Derek 1921- *WhoAm 92*
Lazzaro, Judy Ann *Law&B 92*
Lazzaro-Weis, Carole Marie 1949- *WhoSSW 93*
Lazzelle, Laura Jane Monica 1952- *WhoAmW 93*
Lazzio, Emily Patricia 1941- *WhoAmW 93*
Lazzo, Michael Eugene *Law&B 92*
L. De Preville, Yves Paul Francois 1951- *WhoWor 93*
Le, Ai-Lan Thi 1960- *WhoSSW 93*
Le, Dao Mau 1939- *WhoWor 93*
Le, Duc Tho *BioIn 17*
Le, Mao Hua 1952- *WhoWor 93*
Le, Phi N. 1962- *WhoSSW 93*
Le, Tomoo 1929- *WhoAsAP 91*
Le, Triet *BioIn 17*
Lea, Clyde Wain *Law&B 92*
Lea, Colin 1944- *WhoScE 91-1, WhoWor 93*
Lea, David Alan *WhoScE 91-1*
Lea, Eleanor Lucille 1916- *WhoAmW 93*
Lea, F. Kay Amend 1941- *WhoAmW 93*
Lea, Fanny Heaslip 1884-1955 *AmWomPl*
Lea, Francis Carey d1991 *BioIn 17*
Lea, George A., Jr. 1950- *St&PR 93*
Lea, Helen *BioIn 17*
Lea, Homer 1876-1912 *GayN, ScF&FL 92*
Lea, Joan *ConAu 37NR, MajAI*
Lea, John C. *Law&B 92*
Lea, John Edward *Law&B 92*
Lea, Lola Stendig 1934- *WhoAm 92*
Lea, Lorenzo Bates 1925- *WhoAm 92*
Lea, Pamela Ann 1958- *WhoAmW 93*
Lea, Peter John *WhoScE 91-1*
Lea, Peter Leonard 1929- *WhoWor 93*
Lea, Scott Carter 1931- *St&PR 93, WhoAm 92*
Lea, Stanley E. 1930- *WhoAm 92*
Lea, Sydney 1942- *WhoWrEP 92*
Lea, Sydney L.W., Jr. 1942- *ScF&FL 92*
Lea, Sydney (L. Wright, Jr.) 1942- *DcLB 120 [port]*
Lea, Warren E. 1941- *St&PR 93*
Leab, Daniel Josef 1936- *WhoE 93*
Leabman, Gary Stuart 1949- *WhoEmL 93*
Leach, Anthony Raymond 1939- *St&PR 93, WhoAm 92*
Leach, Barney H. 1944- *St&PR 93*
Leach, Carl M. 1945- *St&PR 93*
Leach, Catherine Frances 1956- *WhoEmL 93, WhoSSW 93*
Leach, Cheryll Jean 1947- *WhoAmW 93*
Leach, Christopher 1925- *ScF&FL 92*
Leach, Cynthia Diane 1958- *WhoAmW 93*
Leach, David 1911- *BioIn 17*
Leach, Debra Ann 1952- *WhoAmW 93*
Leach, Edmund Ronald 1910-1989 *IntDcAn*
Leach, Edwin F. 1947- *St&PR 93*
Leach, Elizabeth A. Bieryla 1949- *WhoEmL 93*
Leach, Franklin Rollin 1933- *WhoAm 92*
Leach, Gladys Hodson *AmWomPl*
Leach, H. *WhoScE 91-1*
Leach, Harold Hunter 1926- *St&PR 93, WhoAm 92*
Leach, Harrison Langford 1923- *WhoE 93*
Leach, Howard H. 1930- *WhoAm 92*
Leach, J. Frank 1921- *St&PR 93*

Leach, James Albert Smith 1942- *WhoAm 92*
Leach, James Francis 1953- *WhoEmL 93, WhoSSW 93*
Leach, James Lindsay 1918- *WhoAm 92*
Leach, James Stuart Llewelyn *WhoScE 91-1*
Leach, Jeffrey Edward 1956- *St&PR 93*
Leach, Jim 1942- *CngDr 91*
Leach, Joan Genevieve 1941- *WhoE 93*
Leach, John Frank 1921- *WhoAm 92*
Leach, John Sanders 1937- *St&PR 93*
Leach, Joseph Lee 1921- *WhoAm 92, WhoWrEP 92*
Leach, Lois D. 1941- *WhoAmW 93*
Leach, Lynne E. 1949- *WhoE 93*
Leach, Mark P. *Law&B 92*
Leach, Mary Moynihan 1943- *WhoE 93*
Leach, Maurice Derby, Jr. 1923- *WhoAm 92*
Leach, Max Russell 1935- *St&PR 93*
Leach, Michael *Law&B 92*
Leach, Michael Glen 1940- *WhoAm 92*
Leach, P. *WhoScE 91-1*
Leach, Penelope 1937- *News 92 [port]*
Leach, Ralph F. 1917- *St&PR 93, WhoAm 92*
Leach, Richard Heald 1922- *WhoAm 92*
Leach, Rick *BioIn 17*
Leach, Robert Earl 1943- *WhoAm 92*
Leach, Robert Ellis 1931- *WhoAm 92, WhoE 93*
Leach, Robin *BioIn 17*
Leach, Rodney Edward 1928- *St&PR 93*
Leach, Ronald George 1938- *WhoAm 92*
Leach, Ronald L. *Law&B 92*
Leach, Ronald Lee 1934- *St&PR 93, WhoAm 92*
Leach, Ronald W. 1944- *WhoIns 93*
Leach, Russell 1922- *WhoAm 92*
Leach, Sandra Sinsel 1946- *WhoEmL 93*
Leach, Steve Alan 1943- *WhoSSW 93*
Leach, Sydney Minturn 1951- *WhoEmL 93*
Leach, Wilford d1988 *MiSFD 9N*
Leach, William B. *Law&B 92*
Leachman, Cloris 1930- *WhoAm 92, WhoAmW 93*
Leachman, Jennifer *BioIn 17*
Leachman, Karen L. 1942- *WhoSSW 93*
Leachman, Roger Mack 1942- *WhoAm 92*
Leacock, Philip 1917-1990 *BioIn 17, ConTFT 10, MiSFD 9N*
Leacock, Stephen 1869-1944 *MagSWL [port]*
Leacock, Stephen Butler 1869-1944 *BioIn 17*
Leadabrand, Ray L. 1927- *WhoAm 92*
Leadbelly 1885-1949 *BioIn 17*
Leadbetter, Alan J. 1934- *WhoScE 91-1*
Leadbetter, Danville 1811-1866 *BioIn 17*
Leadbetter, Mark Renton, Jr. 1944- *WhoWor 93*
Leader, Alan H. 1938- *St&PR 93, WhoE 93*
Leader, Bernice Kramer 1938- *WhoE 93*
Leader, Carl *WhoWrEP 92*
Leader, Elliot *WhoScE 91-1*
Leader, George Michael 1918- *BioIn 17*
Leader, Mary *ScF&FL 92*
Leader, Patricia Laureen 1955- *WhoAmW 93*
Leader, Robert Wardell 1919- *WhoAm 92*
Leader, Zachary 1946- *ConAu 138*
Leader Charge, Doris *BioIn 17*
Leadon, Bernard Matthew, Jr. 1917- *WhoSSW 93*
Leaf, Alexander 1920- *WhoAm 92, WhoE 93*
Leaf, Frederick Peter 1946- *WhoEmL 93*
Leaf, Harold E. d1991 *BioIn 17*
Leaf, Howard Westley 1923- *WhoAm 92*
Leaf, June 1929- *BioIn 17*
Leaf, Mindy Glass 1952- *WhoWrEP 92*
Leaf, (Wilbur) Munro 1905-1976 *MajAI [port]*
Leaf, Paul 1929- *MiSFD 9, WhoAm 92, WhoWrEP 92*
Leaf, Robert Stephen 1931- *WhoAm 92*
Leaf, Roger W. 1946- *St&PR 93*
Leaf, Roger Warren 1946- *WhoAm 92*
Leafe, Joseph A. *WhoAm 92*
League, Alice P. *Law&B 92*
League, Daniel Noel, Jr. 1936- *St&PR 93*
League, David *Law&B 92*
League, David Warren 1939- *St&PR 93*
League, Patricia Gordon 1948- *St&PR 93*
Leah *BioIn 17*
Leahey, Harry d1990 *BioIn 17*
Leahey, Jack M., Jr. *Law&B 92*
Leahey, Miles Cary 1952- *WhoEmL 93*
Leahey, T. Burke 1943- *St&PR 93*
Leahigh, Alan Kent 1944- *WhoAm 92*
Leahy, Arthur Stephen 1951- *WhoEmL 93*
Leahy, Arthur T. 1949- *St&PR 93*
Leahy, Charles Farrington 1935- *WhoE 93*
Leahy, David E. *Law&B 92*
Leahy, Denis J. 1925- *St&PR 93*
Leahy, Edward Joseph *Law&B 92*
Leahy, Harold Robert 1953- *WhoEmL 93*
Leahy, James E. 1919- *ConAu 138*
Leahy, John Edward *Law&B 92*
Leahy, John J. 1931- *St&PR 93*
Leahy, John Jacob 1921- *WhoAm 92*
Leahy, John Martin 1886-1967 *ScF&FL 92*
Leahy, Keith W. 1961- *WhoE 93*
Leahy, Larry *MiSFD 9*
Leahy, Lawrence Marshall 1949- *WhoSSW 93*
Leahy, Maurice Lewis 1920- *WhoWor 93*
Leahy, Michael J. 1901-1979 *BioIn 17, Expl 93*
Leahy, Michael Joseph 1939- *WhoAm 92*
Leahy, Michael Vincent *Law&B 92*
Leahy, Patrick J. *BioIn 17*
Leahy, Patrick J. 1940- *CngDr 91*
Leahy, Patrick Joseph 1940- *WhoAm 92, WhoE 93*
Leahy, Robert David 1952- *WhoE 93*
Leahy, Robert Louis 1946- *WhoE 93*
Leahy, Robert Maurice 1947- *WhoSSW 93*
Leahy, Sidney M., Jr. 1930- *WhoAm 92*
Leahy, Thomas Francis 1937- *St&PR 93, WhoAm 92, WhoE 93*
Leahy, Vincent P.J. 1943- *St&PR 93*
Leahy, Virginia Klein 1910- *St&PR 93*
Leahy, William F. 1913- *St&PR 93, WhoAm 92*
Leahy, William Joseph 1933- *WhoWrEP 92*
Leak, Allison G. 1938- *WhoAm 92*
Leak, Hazel Lucille Murray 1905- *WhoAmW 93*
Leak, Lee Virn 1932- *WhoE 93*
Leak, Lorie Kay 1953- *WhoAmW 93*
Leak, Margaret Elizabeth 1946- *St&PR 93, WhoAm 92, WhoAmW 93, WhoEmL 93*
Leak, Robert E. 1934- *WhoAm 92*
Leak, Sarah Elizabeth 1936- *WhoSSW 93*
Leake, Bernard Elgey *WhoScE 91-1*
Leake, Brenda Gail 1950- *WhoEmL 93*
Leake, Donald Lewis 1931- *WhoAm 92, WhoWor 93*
Leake, Donna Rose 1955- *WhoAmW 93*
Leake, John Espie 1946- *WhoWor 93*
Leake, Larry Bruce 1950- *WhoEmL 93*
Leake, Lucille Perkins 1913- *WhoSSW 93*
Leake, Preston Hildebrand 1929- *WhoAm 92, WhoSSW 93*
Leake, Sidney E. 1940- *St&PR 93*
Leake, Thomas J. *Law&B 92*
Leake, William D. 1929- *St&PR 93, WhoAm 92*
Leakey, L.S.B. 1903-1972 *IntDcAn*
Leakey, Louis 1903-1972 & Leakey, Mary 1913- & Leakey, Richard 1944- *ConHero 2 [port]*
Leakey, Louis Seymour Bazett 1903-1972 *BioIn 17*
Leakey, Mary 1913- *See* Leakey, Louis 1903-1972 & Leakey, Mary 1913- & Leakey, Richard 1944- *ConHero 2*
Leakey, Mary D. 1913- *IntDcAn*
Leakey, Mary Douglas 1913- *WhoAm 92, WhoWor 93*
Leakey, Richard 1944- *See* Leakey, Louis 1903-1972 & Leakey, Mary 1913- & Leakey, Richard 1944- *ConHero 2*
Leakey, Richard E. 1944- *BioIn 17*
Leakey, Richard Erskine 1944- *WhoWor 93*
Leakey, Roger Richard Bazett *WhoScE 91-1*
Leal, Alan G. *Law&B 92*
Leal, Barbara Jean Peters 1948- *WhoAmW 93, WhoSSW 93*
Leal, Ernesto *WhoWor 93*
Leal, Herbert Allan Borden 1917- *WhoAm 92*
Leal, Jose Luis *BioIn 17*
Leal, Juan de Valdes 1622-1690 *BioIn 17*
Leal, Leslie Gary 1943- *WhoAm 92*
Leal, Luis 1907- *DcMexL, HispAmA [port]*
Leal, Marianne Miles 1946- *WhoAmW 93, WhoSSW 93*
Leal, Peter R. *Law&B 92*
Leal Cortes, Alfredo 1931- *DcMexL*
Leaman, David Martin 1935- *WhoAm 92*
Leaman, Donna *Law&B 92*
Leaman, J. Richard, Jr. 1934- *St&PR 93, WhoAm 92, WhoE 93*
Leaman, Jack Ervin 1932- *WhoAm 92*
Leaman, Lily M. *AmWomPl*
Leaman, Stephen J. 1947- *St&PR 93*
Leaman, Stephen James 1947- *WhoIns 93*
Leambeau, Earl Louis 1898-1965 *BioIn 17*
Leamer, Laurence Allen 1941- *WhoAm 92*
Leamon, Dorothy *AmWomPl*
Leamy, Cameron J.D. 1932- *WhoIns 93*
Lean, David *BioIn 17*
Lean, David 1908-1991 *AnObit 1991, ConTFT 10, MiSFD 9N*
Lean, Eric Gung-Hwa 1938- *WhoAm 92*
Lean, Jerome Howard 1945- *WhoE 93*
Lean, Ralph E. 1945- *St&PR 93*
Leana, Carrie Renee 1953- *WhoAmW 93, WhoEmL 93*
Leander, Jussi Lasse Juhani 1945- *WhoScE 91-4*
Leandri, Giuseppe *WhoScE 91-3*
Leandri, William V. 1947- *St&PR 93, WhoAm 92*
Leandro, Paula Costa Pereira 1961- *WhoScE 91-3*
Leaness, Charles Gabriel 1950- *St&PR 93*
Leanse, Lloyd *St&PR 93*
Leao, Nara *BioIn 17*
Leape, Martha Palmer 1929- *WhoAmW 93*
Leaper, Eric John 1953- *WhoWrEP 92*
Leapley, Albert Otto 1924- *WhoSSW 93*
Leapley, Patricia Murray *WhoSSW 93*
Leapor, Mary 1722-1746 *BioIn 17*
Lear, David Calvin 1957- *WhoSSW 93*
Lear, Dorothy Bennett 1935- *WhoAmW 93*
Lear, Edward 1812-1888 *BioIn 17, MajAI [port]*
Lear, Erwin 1924- *WhoAm 92, WhoWor 93*
Lear, Evelyn 1926- *Baker 92, IntDcOp, OxDcOp*
Lear, Evelyn 1930- *WhoAm 92*
Lear, Frances *BioIn 17*
Lear, Frances Loeb 1923- *WhoAmW 93*
Lear, Gail Hollenbeck 1951- *WhoE 93*
Lear, John 1909- *WhoAm 92*
Lear, Norman *BioIn 17*
Lear, Norman 1922- *MiSFD 9*
Lear, Norman Milton 1922- *WhoAm 92*
Lear, Peter *BioIn 17*
Lear, Peter 1936- *ScF&FL 92*
Lear, Phillip Ephrian 1905- *WhoE 93*
Lear, Robert D. 1946- *St&PR 93*
Lear, Robert William 1917- *St&PR 93, WhoAm 92*
Lear, William Dennis 1960- *WhoEmL 93, WhoSSW 93*
Lear, William Edward 1918- *WhoAm 92*
Lear, William H. *Law&B 92*
Lear, William Henry 1939- *St&PR 93*
Learey, Fred Don 1906- *WhoAm 92, WhoSSW 93*
Learn, Doris Lynn 1949- *WhoEmL 93*
Learn, Elmer Warner 1929- *WhoAm 92*
Learn, Richard Leland 1955- *WhoE 93*
Learn, Richard Lisle 1935- *WhoE 93*
Learnard, William Ewing 1935- *WhoAm 92*
Learned, Michael 1939- *WhoAm 92*
Learoyd, Simon B.B. 1946- *WhoScE 91-1*
Leary, Arthur Pearson 1949- *WhoEmL 93*
Leary, Carol Ann 1947- *WhoE 93*
Leary, Clifford Clarence 1930- *St&PR 93*
Leary, Edward Andrew 1913- *WhoWrEP 92*
Leary, Genevieve Loesch 1927- *WhoE 93*
Leary, James Francis 1930- *St&PR 93*
Leary, James Francis 1948- *WhoE 93*
Leary, James Henry 1950- *WhoE 93*
Leary, Jane S. *Law&B 92*
Leary, Kathryn D. *BioIn 17*
Leary, Kevin Michael 1955- *WhoE 93*
Leary, Leo William 1919- *WhoAm 92*
Leary, Lewis Gaston 1906-1990 *BioIn 17*
Leary, Michael Joseph 1939- *St&PR 93*
Leary, Michael Warren 1949- *WhoAm 92*
Leary, Nancy Jane 1952- *WhoAmW 93, WhoSSW 93*
Leary, Robert Graham *Law&B 92*
Leary, Robin Janell 1954- *WhoAmW 93, WhoWor 93*
Leary, Thomas Barrett 1931- *WhoAm 92*
Leary, Thomas Patrick 1951- *WhoE 93*
Leary, Timothy 1920- *WhoAm 92*
Leary, Timothy Francis 1920- *BioIn 17*
Leary, Virginia Anne 1926- *WhoAmW 93, WhoE 93*
Leary, William James 1931- *WhoAm 92*
Leary Jones, Barbara Jean 1955- *WhoEmL 93, WhoSSW 93*
Leas, Dorothy Randall 1950- *WhoE 93*
Lease, Daniel H. 1926- *St&PR 93*
Lease, Daniel W. 1948- *St&PR 93*
Lease, Gary 1940- *ConAu 38NR*
Lease, Jane Etta 1924- *WhoAmW 93, WhoWor 93*
Lease, Maria C. *MiSFD 9*
Lease, Martin Harry, Jr. 1927- *WhoAm 92*
Lease, Mary Elizabeth Clyens 1853-1933 *GayN*
Lease, Richard Jay 1914- *WhoWor 93*
Lease, Ronald Charles 1940- *WhoAm 92*
Lease, Shari J. *Law&B 92*
Leasia, Richard S. 1923- *St&PR 93*
Leasia, Stephen H. *Law&B 92*
Leask, Ian Graham 1951- *ConAu 138*
Leaska, Mitchell A(lexander) 1934- *ConAu 39NR*
Leason, Robert W. 1930- *WhoE 93*
Leason, Robert Wales 1930- *St&PR 93*
Leasor, Jane 1922- *WhoAmW 93*
Least Heat Moon *BioIn 17*
Lea-Stokes, Michele Joanne 1956- *WhoAmW 93*
Leasure, Frederick H. 1948- *WhoE 93*
Leasure, Janet Lynn 1949- *WhoWrEP 92*
Leasure, Judith Ann 1947- *WhoAmW 93*
Leasure, June N. Ruff 1951- *WhoEmL 93*
Leasure, Mary Louise 1956- *WhoEmL 93*
Leath, Charles Alexander, Jr. 1944- *WhoSSW 93*
Leath, James Marvin 1931- *WhoAm 92*
Leath, Jerry L. 1941- *St&PR 93*
Leath, Kenneth Thomas 1931- *WhoE 93*
Leath, Paul Larry 1941- *WhoAm 92, WhoE 93*
Leatham, John Tonkin 1936- *WhoAm 92*
Leatham, Kate 1951- *St&PR 93*
Leathard, Helen Louise 1947- *WhoWor 93*
Leather, Agatha Moran d1990 *BioIn 17*
Leather, Richard Brenk 1932- *St&PR 93, WhoAm 92*
Leather, Victoria Potts 1947- *WhoSSW 93*
Leatherberry, Anne Knox Clark 1953- *WhoAmW 93, WhoEmL 93*
Leatherby, Russell E. *Law&B 92*
Leatherby, Russell E. 1953- *St&PR 93*
Leatherdale, Clive 1949- *ScF&FL 92*
Leatherdale, Douglas West 1936- *St&PR 93, WhoAm 92*
Leatherdale, Marcus Andrew 1952- *WhoE 93*
Leatherland, M.J. 1961- *WhoScE 91-1*
Leatherman, Allen H. 1935- *WhoIns 93*
Leatherman, Carolyn Hall 1946- *WhoAmW 93*
Leatherman, Charles Junior 1928- *WhoE 93*
Leatherman, John B. 1939- *St&PR 93*
Leatherman, Steven E. 1947- *St&PR 93*
Leathers, Bill F. *Law&B 92*
Leathers, James C. 1934- *St&PR 93*
Leathers, Margaret Weil 1949- *WhoAmW 93*
Leathers, Marvin Lionel 1954- *WhoEmL 93*
Leathers, Nancy Joan 1941- *WhoAmW 93*
Leathers, Robert *BioIn 17*
Leatherwood, Lillie *BlkAmWO*
Leaton, Edward K. 1928- *WhoAm 92*
Leaton, Marcella Kay 1952- *WhoAmW 93, WhoEmL 93*
Leaud, Jean-Pierre 1944- *IntDcF 2-3 [port]*
Leavell, Chuck *BioIn 17*
Leavell, Joanne Bernadette 1946- *WhoAmW 93*
Leavell, Landrum Pinson, II 1926- *WhoSSW 93*
Leavell, Michael Ray 1955- *WhoSSW 93*
Leavell, William A. 1923- *WhoSSW 93*
Leavengood, Victor Price 1924- *WhoAm 92*
Leavens, Patricia Ann 1933- *WhoAmW 93*
Leaventon, Barry Howard 1947- *St&PR 93*
Leaventon, Marc 1955- *St&PR 93*
Leavenworth, Donald H. 1930- *St&PR 93*
Leaver, Christopher John *WhoScE 91-1*
Leaver, Gardener 1921-1990 *BioIn 17*
Leaver, John David *WhoScE 91-1*
Leavey, John Peter, Jr. 1951- *WhoSSW 93*
Leavey, Thomas E. 1934- *St&PR 93*
Leavill, Otis 1941- *BioIn 17*
Leavis, F.R. 1895-1978 *BioIn 17*
Leavis, Frank Raymond 1895-1978 *BioIn 17*
Leavis, Q.D. 1906-1981 *BioIn 17*
Leavis, Queenie Dorothy 1906-1981 *BioIn 17*
Leavitt, A. Leroy 1943- *St&PR 93*
Leavitt, Arnold Keith 1932- *St&PR 93*
Leavitt, Audrey Faye Cox 1932- *WhoAm 92*
Leavitt, Caroline Susan 1952- *WhoWrEP 92*
Leavitt, Charles Loyal 1921- *WhoAm 92, WhoE 93*
Leavitt, Chase L. 1944- *St&PR 93*
Leavitt, Dana G. 1925- *St&PR 93*
Leavitt, Dana Gibson 1925- *WhoAm 92*
Leavitt, David 1961- *BioIn 17, ConGAN*
Leavitt, David Adam 1961- *WhoAm 92*
Leavitt, Donna Marzee 1958- *WhoEmL 93, WhoWrEP 92*
Leavitt, Gordon Hodsdon 1931- *St&PR 93*
Leavitt, H. Huntington 1947- *St&PR 93*
Leavitt, Harold Jack 1922- *WhoAm 92*
Leavitt, Horace M. 1929- *St&PR 93*
Leavitt, Jeffrey Stuart 1946- *WhoAm 92, WhoEmL 93*
Leavitt, Jerome Edward 1916- *WhoAm 92*
Leavitt, Joan Kazanjian 1926- *WhoAm 92, WhoAmW 93*

Leavitt, Joseph d1990 *BioIn 17*
Leavitt, Joshua 1794-1873 *BioIn 17*
Leavitt, Julian Jacob 1918- *WhoE 93*
Leavitt, Lawrence Ronald 1943- *St&PR 93*
Leavitt, Mary Janice Deimel 1924- *WhoAmW 93, WhoSSW 93, WhoWor 93*
Leavitt, Michael Okerlund 1951- *WhoEmL 93*
Leavitt, Michele Jolie 1957- *WhoE 93*
Leavitt, Paul B. 1942- *St&PR 93*
Leavitt, Paul Daniel *Law&B 92*
Leavitt, Robert David *Law&B 92*
Leavitt, Ronald 1934- *St&PR 93*
Leavitt, Sheldon Joseph 1922- *WhoSSW 93*
Leavitt, Sophie d1992 *NewYTBS 92*
Leavitt, Thomas Whittlesey 1930- *WhoAm 92, WhoE 93*
Leavitt, William D. 1941- *WhoWrEP 92*
Leavy, Brian David 1951- *WhoEmL 93*
Leavy, Edward 1929- *WhoAm 92*
Leavy, Herbert Theodore 1927- *WhoAm 92, WhoWor 93*
Leavy, Roger S. 1957- *St&PR 93*
Leax, John *BioIn 17*
Leazer, Richard H. 1941- *St&PR 93*
Leback, Warren G. 1924- *WhoAm 92*
Leballo, Potlako Kitchener *BioIn 17*
Lebamoff, Ivan Argire 1932- *WhoAm 92*
Le Bar, Michael Lewis 1945- *St&PR 93*
LeBaron, Bradley Dean 1960- *WhoSSW 93*
Lebaron, C. Steven *Law&B 92*
LeBaron, Dean *BioIn 17*
LeBaron, Ervil Morerel d1981 *BioIn 17*
LeBarron, Roger Melvyn 1940- *St&PR 93*
LeBarron, Suzanne Jane 1945- *WhoAm 92*
Le Bars, Yves 1941- *WhoScE 91-2*
Le Bas, Edward 1904-1966 *BioIn 17*
Lebas, Francois 1942- *WhoScE 91-2*
Le Bas, J.F. 1947- *WhoScE 91-2*
Lebas, Jean 1878-1944 *BioIn 17*
Le Baut, Guillaume Yves Marie 1940- *WhoScE 91-2*
Lebbin, Carole Sue 1948- *WhoEmL 93*
Lebby, Andrew Miller 1946- *WhoEmL 93*
Le Be, Guillaume 1525-1598 *Baker 92*
LeBeau, Bernard G. 1921- *St&PR 93*
LeBeau, Charles Paul 1944- *WhoAm 92*
LeBeau, Edward Charles 1929- *WhoAm 92*
LeBeau, Hector Alton, Jr. 1931- *WhoAm 92*
Lebeau, L.B. 1945- *WhoScE 91-2*
LeBeau, Paul Andrew 1950- *WhoE 93*
Lebeau, Robert Max *Law&B 92*
LeBeau, Roy *ConAu 136*
Lebeau, Suzanne 1948- *WhoCanL 92*
LeBeauf, Sabrina *WhoAm 92*
Lebec, Alain 1950- *WhoAm 92*
Lebeck, Robert 1929- *WhoWor 93*
Lebeck, Warren Wells 1921- *WhoAm 92*
Lebed, Hartzel Zangwill 1928- *WhoAm 92*
Lebedeff, Sergej A. d1990 *BioIn 17*
Lebedev, Leonid Petrovich 1946- *WhoWor 93*
Lebedeva, N.A. 1894-1978 *IntDcAn*
Lebedoff, David M. 1938- *WhoAm 92*
Lebedoff, Randy Miller *Law&B 92*
Lebedow, Aaron L. 1935- *St&PR 93*
Lebedow, Aaron Louis 1935- *WhoAm 92*
Lebed-Rofes, Ruth J. *Law&B 92*
Lebegue, Nicolas-Antoine c. 1631-1702 *Baker 92*
Lebel, Andre 1950- *St&PR 93*
Lebel, Gregory Galen 1950- *WhoE 93, WhoEmL 93*
Lebel, Pierre B. 1949- *St&PR 93*
Lebens, Jeffrey Kent 1944- *St&PR 93*
Lebens, Susan *Law&B 92*
Lebensbaum, Henry 1948- *WhoE 93*
Lebensfeld, Harry 1904- *St&PR 93*
Lebensohn, Zigmond Meyer 1910- *WhoAm 92*
Leber, Lester 1913- *WhoAm 92*
Leber, Ralph Eric 1949- *WhoE 93*
Leber, Steven Edward 1941- *WhoAm 92*
Leberer, Leslie Theodore 1948- *St&PR 93*
Le Berre, Rene Francois Michel 1932- *WhoUN 92*
Lebert, Sigmund 1821-1884 *Baker 92*
Lebeuf, Jean 1687-1760 *Baker 92*
LeBey, Barbara Sydell 1939- *WhoAmW 93*
Lebischak, J. Doris 1954- *WhoAmW 93*
LeBlanc, Aileen Louise 1952- *WhoSSW 93*
Leblanc, Alain 1931- *WhoScE 91-2*
LeBlanc, Alvin Louis 1931- *WhoAm 92*
LeBlanc, Annette 1965- *BioIn 17*
Leblanc, Barry D. 1954- *St&PR 93*
Leblanc, Bertrand 1929- *WhoCanL 92*
LeBlanc, Bryan 1946- *St&PR 93*
Le Blanc, Douglas R. *St&PR 93*
Leblanc, Edward *DcCPCAm*
LeBlanc, George T. 1930- *St&PR 93*
LeBlanc, Hugh Linus 1927- *WhoAm 92*
Leblanc, Hugues 1924- *WhoAm 92*
LeBlanc, James E. 1942- *WhoAm 92*
LeBlanc, Jean Leopold 1946- *WhoWor 93*
LeBlanc, Jeanette Amy 1968- *WhoAmW 93*
Le Blanc, Jesse E., II *WhoSSW 93*
LeBlanc, John Leslie 1941- *WhoSSW 93*
Le Blanc, Joy Comeaux 1937- *WhoWrEP 92*
LeBlanc, Laurie Alison 1964- *WhoAmW 93*
Leblanc, Leonard J. 1941- *St&PR 93*
LeBlanc, Leonard Joseph 1941- *WhoAm 92, WhoWor 93*
LeBlanc, Lillian Mary 1959- *WhoEmL 93*
LeBlanc, Paul Joseph 1947- *WhoE 93*
LeBlanc, Raymond Albert 1930- *St&PR 93*
Leblanc, Raymond P. *Law&B 92*
LeBlanc, Raymond Paul 1945- *St&PR 93*
LeBlanc, Richard *ScF&FL 92*
LeBlanc, Richard Philip 1946- *WhoEmL 93*
LeBlanc, Robert Bruce 1925- *WhoSSW 93*
Leblanc, Roger Maurice 1942- *WhoAm 92*
LeBlanc, Ronald P. *BioIn 17*
Leblanc, Roy F. *St&PR 93*
LeBlanc, Rufus J., Sr. 1917- *WhoAm 92*
LeBlanc, Tina *BioIn 17, WhoAm 92*
Le Blanc Bellevaux, Hubert 1941- *WhoWor 93*
LeBlanc-Daviault, A. *Law&B 92*
Leblang, Russell D. *Law&B 92*
Leblebici, Duran 1935- *WhoScE 91-4*
Leblique, Leopold Benjamin 1926- *WhoSSW 93*
Leblond, Charles *BioIn 17*
Leblond, Charles Philippe 1910- *WhoAm 92*
LeBlond, Paul Henri 1938- *WhoAm 92*
LeBlond, Richard K., II 1920- *St&PR 93*
LeBlond, Richard Knight, II 1920- *WhoAm 92*
Lebman, Robert Richard 1945- *WhoE 93*
Lebo, Marie 1941- *WhoAmW 93*
Lebo, William C. 1944- *St&PR 93*
Lebo, William C., Jr. *Law&B 92, WhoAm 92*
Le Bodic, Louis 1932- *WhoScE 91-2*
Leboeuf, Michel 1938- *WhoScE 91-2*
LeBoeuf, R.W. 1946- *St&PR 93*
Leboeuf, Steven J. 1948- *St&PR 93*
Lebofsky, Larry Allen 1947- *WhoEmL 93*
Lebold, John W. *Law&B 92*
Lebon, Alan Eliot *Law&B 92*
Lebon, Georgy Pierre 1937- *WhoWor 93*
Lebon, Pierre *WhoScE 91-2*
Lebor, John Francis 1906- *WhoAm 92*
Le Borg, Reginald 1902-1989 *MiSFD 9N*
Le Borgne, Yves F. 1942- *WhoUN 92*
Leborne, Aime-Ambroise-Simon 1797-1866 *Baker 92*
Leborne, Fernand 1862-1929 *Baker 92*
Lebos, Leo, Jr. 1942- *WhoAm 92*
Lebotsa, Mohomane Masimole 1927- *WhoAfr*
Lebouc, Charles-Joseph 1822-1893 *Baker 92*
Lebouitz, Martin F. 1946- *WhoAm 92, WhoE 93, WhoEmL 93, WhoWor 93*
LeBourgeois, Cynthia Carrie 1962- *WhoEmL 93*
Le Bourhis, Katell *BioIn 17*
LeBoutillier, John *BioIn 17, ScF&FL 92*
Lebovich, William Louis 1948- *ConAu 37NR*
LeBovidge, Richard Nathaniel 1937- *St&PR 93*
Lebovitz, Donna Rudnick 1943- *WhoWrEP 92*
Lebovitz, Harold Paul 1916- *WhoAm 92*
LeBow, Bennett S. 1938- *WhoAm 92*
Lebow, Fred *BioIn 17*
Lebow, Irwin Leon 1926- *WhoAm 92*
Lebow, Jeanne *WhoWrEP 92*
Lebow, Kenneth D. 1944- *St&PR 93*
Lebow, Laurel Mary Lavin 1956- *WhoEmL 93, WhoSSW 93*
Lebowitz, Abraham I. 1931- *WhoUN 92*
Lebowitz, Albert 1922- *WhoAm 92, WhoWrEP 92*
Lebowitz, Catharine Koch 1915- *WhoAmW 93*
Lebowitz, Fran *BioIn 17*
Lebowitz, Harvey M. 1929- *WhoAm 92*
Lebowitz, Joel Louis 1930- *WhoAm 92*
Lebowitz, Marshall 1923- *WhoAm 92, WhoE 93*
Lebowitz, Michael 1953- *WhoEmL 93*
Lebowitz, Michael David 1939- *WhoAm 92*
Lebowitz, Steven Mark 1965- *WhoE 93*
Lebow-Shepard, Jeanne Swift Gregory 1951- *WhoWrEP 92*
Lebrato, Mary Theresa 1950- *WhoAmW 93*
LeBrecht, Thelma Jane Mossman 1946- *WhoAmW 93, WhoE 93*
LeBreton, Jean Marie Rene 1927- *WhoWor 93*
Lebreton, Joseph 1932- *WhoScE 91-2*
Lebreton, Philippe 1933- *WhoScE 91-2*
LeBreton, Walter Joseph, Jr. 1961- *WhoEmL 93, WhoSSW 93*
Lebro, Theodore Peter 1910- *WhoWor 93*
le Brocguy, Louis 1916- *WhoWor 93*
Lebron, Jim *BioIn 17*
Lebrun, Albert 1871-1950 *BioIn 17*
LeBrun, Andrzej 1737-1811 *PolBiDi*
Lebrun, Claude 1929- *BioIn 17, ConAu 136*
Lebrun, Franziska 1756?-1791 *OxDcOp*
Lebrun, Franziska (Dorothea) 1756-1791 *Baker 92*
Lebrun, Jean 1759-c. 1809 *Baker 92*
Lebrun, Louis-Sebastien 1764-1829 *Baker 92, OxDcOp*
Lebrun, Louise-Elisabeth Vigee- 1755-1842 *BioIn 17*
Lebrun, Ludwig August 1752-1790 *Baker 92*
Lebrun, Paul Henri Joseph 1863-1920 *Baker 92*
Lebrun Moratinos, Jose Ali Cardinal 1919- *WhoWor 93*
Lebsack, Phyllis Jean 1921- *WhoAmW 93*
Lebsack, Todd D. *Law&B 92*
Lebson, Evan Michael 1943- *St&PR 93*
LeBuhn, Anne Mitchell 1958- *WhoAmW 93*
Le Buhn, Robert 1932- *WhoAm 92*
Lebwohl, Harold Benjamin 1954- *St&PR 93*
Lec, Ryszard Marian 1945- *WhoScE 91-4*
Lec, Stanislaw Jerzy 1909-1966 *PolBiDi*
Leca, Armando Lopes 1893-1977 *Baker 92*
Lecacheux, Bernard Louis Celestin 1930- *WhoScE 91-2*
Le Cain, Errol 1941-1989 *BioIn 17*
Le Cain, Errol (John) 1941-1989 *MajAI [port]*
Le Caine, Hugh 1914-1977 *Baker 92*
Lecale, Errol *ScF&FL 92*
Le Cam, Lucien Marie 1924- *WhoAm 92*
LeCamu, Gary Christopher 1963- *WhoSSW 93*
Lecanuet, Jean 1920- *BioIn 17*
Le Carpentier, Adolphe-Clair 1809-1869 *Baker 92*
Lecarpentier, Yves *WhoScE 91-2*
Le Carre, John 1931- *BioIn 17, BritWr S2, MagSWL [port], WhoAm 92, WhoWor 93*
Lecash, Leon Paul 1951- *WhoE 93*
Lecavalier, Raynald *Law&B 92*
Lecce, Frank Anthony 1947- *WhoE 93, WhoEmL 93*
Leccia, Ange 1952- *BioIn 17*
Lecerf, Olivier Maurice Marie 1929- *WhoAm 92*
Leceta, Juan de 1911-1991 *BioIn 17*
Lechat, Michel F. 1927- *WhoScE 91-2*
Lechat, Michel Francois 1927- *WhoWor 93*
Lechay, James 1907- *WhoAm 92*
Lechelt, Eugene Carl 1942- *WhoAm 92*
Lecher, Richard Clinton 1945- *WhoE 93*
Lechevalier, Hubert Arthur 1926- *WhoAm 92*
Lechini De Alvarez, Gladys Teresita 1951- *WhoWor 93*
Lechman, Wolodymr Bohdan 1932- *St&PR 93*
Lechner, Alfred James, Jr. 1948- *WhoAm 92*
Lechner, Bernard Joseph 1932- *WhoAm 92, WhoE 93*
Lechner, Herbert Dean 1932- *St&PR 93*
Lechner, Jane Ann 1949- *WhoAmW 93*
Lechner, Leonhard c. 1550-1606 *Baker 92*
Lechner, M. Dieter 1940- *WhoWor 93*
Lechner, Thomas Paul 1924- *St&PR 93*
Lechnowsky, Orest J. *Law&B 92*
Lechon, Jan 1899-1956 *PolBiDi*
Lechowski, Tadeusz Zygmunt 1928- *WhoScE 91-4*
Lechtenberg, Michael F. 1938- *St&PR 93*
Lechter, George Steve 1954- *WhoE 93, WhoEmL 93*
Lechthaler, Josef 1891-1948 *Baker 92*
Lechuga, Antonio 1946- *WhoScE 91-3*
Leciejewicz, Janusz 1928- *WhoScE 91-4*
Leck, Harris H. *Law&B 92*
Leck, Ian Maxwell *WhoScE 91-1*
Leckar, Stephen Craig 1948- *WhoEmL 93*
Leckenby, Nancy L. 1936- *WhoWrEP 92*
Lecker, Abraham 1916- *WhoAm 92*
Leckerling, Jon P. *Law&B 92*
Leckerling, Jon P. 1948- *WhoAm 92*
Leckey, Kenneth Paul, Jr. 1945- *WhoAm 92*
Leckie, Carol Mavis 1929- *WhoAmW 93*
Leckie, Frederick Alexander 1929- *WhoAm 92*
Leckie, George Gallie 1936- *WhoWor 93*
Leckie, James Edward 1953- *St&PR 93*
Leckie, Robert B. *Law&B 92*
Leckie, Robert B. 1947- *St&PR 93*
Leckie, Robert Bedford 1947- *WhoAm 92*
Lecklider, Jerry A. 1952- *St&PR 93*
Leckner, Bo Gunnar 1936- *WhoScE 91-4*
Leckner, Carole Hannah 1946- *WhoWrEP 92*
Leclair *Baker 92*
Le Clair, Charles George 1914- *WhoAm 92*
Leclair, Daniel *St&PR 93*
LeClair, D'Arcy Harrison 1947- *WhoAm 92*
Le Clair, Douglas Marvin 1955- *WhoEmL 93*
Le Clair, J.G. 1928- *St&PR 93*
Leclair, Jean-Benoit 1714-1759? *Baker 92*
Leclair, Jean-Marie 1697-1764 *Baker 92, OxDcOp*
Leclair, Jean-Marie 1703-1777 *Baker 92*
LeClair, Paul L. *Law&B 92*
Le Clair, Richard Alfred, Jr. 1943- *WhoE 93*
Le Claire, Charles J. *Law&B 92*
Le Claire, Harry Walter 1914- *WhoAm 92*
LeClaire, Robert William 1956- *WhoIns 93*
LeClaire, Ronald H. 1957- *St&PR 93*
Leclant, Francois 1934- *WhoScE 91-2*
Leclerc, Felix 1914-1988 *WhoCanL 92*
Leclerc, Gerard Albert 1942- *WhoWor 93*
Leclerc, Ginette 1912-1992 *BioIn 17, NewYTBS 92*
Leclerc, Henri 1929- *WhoScE 91-2*
LeClerc, Paul 1941- *WhoAm 92, WhoE 93*
Leclerc, Rachel 1955- *WhoCanL 92*
Leclerc de Hauteclocque, Philippe 1902-1947 *DcTwHis*
Leclercq, Guy 1944- *WhoScE 91-2*
Leclercq, Jean 1921- *WhoScE 91-2*
LeClere, David Anthony 1954- *WhoEmL 93*
Leclere, Georges Bernard 1944- *WhoUN 92*
Leclerq *WhoScE 91-2*
Le Clezio, J.-M.G. 1940- *BioIn 17*
Le Clezio, Jean-Marie Gustave 1940- *BioIn 17*
Lecno, John Ronald 1938- *St&PR 93*
Lecoanet, Andre 1937- *WhoScE 91-2*
Lecoca, Janice M. *St&PR 93*
Lecocq, Charles 1832-1918 *OxDcOp*
Lecoeur, Auguste d1992 *NewYTBS 92*
Lecoin, Louis 1888-1971 *BioIn 17*
Le Comber, Peter George *WhoScE 91-1*
Lecompte, Jan Gabriel Noel 1961- *WhoWor 93*
LeCompte, Malcolm Aaron 1946- *WhoAm 92, WhoEmL 93*
Lecompte, Michel 1939- *WhoScE 91-2*
le Comte, Corstiaan 1911- *WhoWor 93*
Lecomte, Didier 1943- *WhoWor 93*
Le Comte, Edward 1916- *ScF&FL 92*
Le Comte, Edward Semple 1916- *WhoAm 92, WhoWrEP 92*
Lecomte, Eugene Lucien 1929- *WhoIns 93*
Lecomte du Nouy, Patricia Jill 1938- *WhoUN 92*
Leconey, Douglas E. 1956- *St&PR 93*
Leconte, Patrice 1947- *MiSFD 9*
Lecoq, (Alexandre) Charles 1832-1918 *Baker 92*
LeCoq, John *BioIn 17*
Lecoq, Michel Henri 1940- *WhoWor 93*
Le Corbusier 1887-1965 *BioIn 17, ModArCr 3 [port]*
Le Corbusier, Charles-Edouard Jeanneret 1887-1966 *DcTwHis*
LeCount, Roscoe Dale, Jr. 1940- *WhoE 93*
Lecount, Vernon Roe 1948- *WhoEmL 93*
Le Count, Virginia G. 1917- *WhoAmW 93*
Le Couppey, Felix 1811-1887 *Baker 92*
LeCours, Harry Joseph 1932- *St&PR 93*
Lecours, Michel 1940- *WhoAm 92*
Lecourt, Nancy (Hoyt) 1951- *SmATA 73 [port]*
Le Coze, Jean 1942- *WhoScE 91-2*
LeCroissette, Dennis H. *BioIn 17*
Lecroy, Hoyt Franklin 1941- *WhoSSW 93*
Lecuna, Juan Vicente 1891-1954 *Baker 92*
Lecuona, Ernesto 1896-1963 *Baker 92*
Lecuyer, Ellen Delphine 1956- *WhoAmW 93*
Le Dain, Gerald Eric 1924- *WhoAm 92*
Ledakis, Gust Angelo 1931- *WhoUN 92*
Ledbetter, Barbara *St&PR 93*
Ledbetter, Beverly Elizabeth *WhoAm 92*
Ledbetter, Bureon E., Jr. *Law&B 92*
Ledbetter, Calvin Reville, Jr. *WhoAm 92*
Ledbetter, Connie Maxine 1951- *WhoAmW 93*
Ledbetter, Donald L. 1926- *St&PR 93*
Ledbetter, Eleanor *BioIn 17*
Ledbetter, Ernest Wayne, Jr. 1957- *WhoSSW 93*
Ledbetter, Huddie 1885-1949 *Baker 92, BioIn 17*
Ledbetter, J. Lee 1931- *WhoAm 92*
Ledbetter, Jeffrey Lee *Law&B 92*

Ledbetter, John William, Jr. 1937- *WhoSSW 93*
Ledbetter, Ken(neth Lee) 1931- *ConAu 40NR*
Ledbetter, Mary Lee Stewart 1944- *WhoAmW 93, WhoE 93*
Ledbetter, Patricia Lou 1931- *St&PR 93*
Ledbetter, Paul Mark 1947- *WhoEmL 93, WhoWor 93*
Ledbetter, Sharon Faye Welch 1941- *WhoAmW 93, WhoSSW 93*
Ledbetter, Sherry L. 1958- *St&PR 93*
Ledbetter, Suzanne Kay 1961- *WhoSSW 93*
Ledbury, Diana Gretchen 1931- *WhoAmW 93*
Leddicotte, George Comer 1947- *WhoAm 92, WhoE 93, WhoEmL 93, WhoWor 93*
Ledding, Mary S. *Law&B 92*
Leddy, John Henry 1929- *WhoAm 92*
Leddy, John Thomas 1949- *WhoEmL 93*
Leddy, Susan 1939- *WhoAmW 93*
Ledebur, Gary William 1949- *WhoE 93*
Ledebur, Linas Vockroth, Jr. 1925- *WhoAm 92*
Ledeen, Robert Wagner 1928- *WhoAm 92*
Ledel, David Gary 1947- *WhoSSW 93*
Ledenev, Roman (Semyonovich) 1930- *Baker 92*
Ledent, Felix-Etienne 1816-1886 *Baker 92*
Leder, Geraldine Daly 1956- *WhoEmL 93*
Leder, Jane Mersky *BioIn 17*
Leder, John Thomas 1963- *WhoSSW 93*
Leder, Mimi *MiSFD 9*
Leder, Norbert P.E. 1943- *WhoScE 91-4*
Leder, Paul *MiSFD 9*
Leder, Philip 1934- *WhoAm 92*
Lederberg, Joshua 1925- *WhoAm 92, WhoE 93, WhoWor 93*
Lederer, Bruno *Law&B 92*
Lederer, David B. 1939- *St&PR 93*
Lederer, Edith Madelon 1943- *WhoAm 92*
Lederer, Esther Pauline *BioIn 17*
Lederer, Esther Pauline 1918- *JrnUS*
Lederer, Jack Lawrence 1940- *WhoAm 92*
Lederer, Jerome 1902- *WhoAm 92*
Lederer, John Martin 1930- *WhoWor 93*
Lederer, Katherine Gay 1932- *WhoWrEP 92*
Lederer, Klaus *WhoScE 91-4*
Lederer, Leslie T. *Law&B 92, WhoAm 92*
Lederer, Lillian Day 1893-1991 *BioIn 17*
Lederer, Louis Franklin 1935- *St&PR 93*
Lederer, Marion Irvine 1920- *WhoAm 92*
Lederer, Max Donald, Jr. 1960- *WhoEmL 93*
Lederer, Norman 1938- *WhoE 93*
Lederer, Paul Edward 1942- *WhoSSW 93*
Lederer, Paul J. *ScF&FL 92*
Lederer, Paul R. 1939- *St&PR 93*
Lederer, Peter David 1930- *WhoAm 92*
Lederer, William J. 1912- *BioIn 17*
Lederer, William Julius 1912- *WhoAm 92, WhoWrEP 92*
Lederer-Antonucci, Yvonne 1958- *WhoE 93, WhoEmL 93*
Lederis, Karolis Paul 1920- *WhoAm 92*
Lederle, Trudpert 1922- *WhoScE 91-3*
Lederleitner, Joseph Benedict 1922- *WhoAm 92*
Lederman, Allen 1952- *St&PR 93*
Lederman, Deborah Hope 1963- *WhoAmW 93*
Lederman, Frank L. 1949- *WhoAm 92*
Lederman, Ira S. *Law&B 92*
Lederman, Ira S. 1953- *St&PR 93*
Lederman, J. Mark *Law&B 92*
Lederman, Leon Max 1922- *WhoAm 92, WhoWor 93*
Lederman, Leonard Lawrence 1931- *WhoAm 92*
Lederman, Luis 1948- *WhoUN 92*
Lederman, Marie Jean 1935- *WhoAm 92*
Lederman, Michael G. *Law&B 92*
Lederman, Michael Wainwright 1948- *WhoWor 93*
Lederman, Peter B. 1931- *St&PR 93*
Lederman, Peter Bernd 1931- *WhoAm 92*
Ledesma, Rolando Severino 1939- *WhoWor 93*
Ledesma, Romy 1935- *NotHsAW 93*
Ledesma, Vanetta Hall *Law&B 92*
Ledet, Grace Domingue 1943- *WhoAmW 93*
Ledet, Tina Carol 1964- *WhoAmW 93*
Ledeur, Jean-Paul 1933- *BioIn 17*
Ledez, Pierre 1927- *WhoScE 91-2*
Ledford, David Brian 1967- *WhoSSW 93*
Ledford, Gerald Edward, Jr. 1951- *WhoEmL 93*
Ledford, Jack Clarence 1920- *WhoAm 92*
Ledford, Marie Smalley 1951- *WhoEmL 93, WhoSSW 93*
Ledford, Richard Allison 1931- *WhoAm 92*
Ledford, Stephen *WhoSSW 93*
Ledford, Toni Dandridge 1942- *WhoAmW 93*
Ledford, William Lester 1935- *WhoSSW 93*
Ledger, Philip (Stevens) 1937- *Baker 92, WhoWor 93*
Ledger, William Joe *WhoAm 92*
Ledgerwood, Jeffrey Thomas 1957- *WhoSSW 93*
Ledgerwood, Joe Allen 1954- *St&PR 93*
Ledgerwood, Thomas P. *Law&B 92*
Ledic, Michele 1951- *WhoWor 93*
Ledig-Rowohlt, Heinrich Maria d1992 *NewYTBS 92*
Ledig-Rowohlt, Heinrich Maria 1908-1992 *BioIn 17*
Ledingham, John Gerard Garvin *WhoScE 91-1*
Ledion, Jean *WhoScE 91-2*
Ledley, Christian Salvesen 1925- *WhoE 93*
Ledley, Fred David 1954- *WhoEmL 93, WhoSSW 93*
Ledley, Robert Steven 1926- *WhoAm 92*
Ledley, Tamara Shapiro 1954- *WhoAmW 93*
Ledlie, Joseph Maurice Antony 1943- *WhoSSW 93*
Ledlow, Verla *St&PR 93*
Ledman, Robert Earl 1949- *WhoSSW 93*
Lednicer, Oliver 1934- *St&PR 93*
Ledochowska, Mary Theresa 1863-1922 *PolBiDi*
Ledochowski, Miecislaus 1822-1902 *PolBiDi*
Ledochowski, Wladimir 1866-1942 *PolBiDi*
Ledogar, Robert J. 1933- *WhoUN 92*
Ledon, Henry Jean 1945- *WhoWor 93*
LeDonne, Robert J. 1929- *WhoAm 92, WhoE 93*
Le Douarin, Nicole Marthe 1930- *WhoScE 91-2*
Ledoux, Andre 1919- *WhoScE 91-2*
Ledoux, Emmanuel 1948- *WhoScE 91-2*
LeDoux, Harold Anthony 1926- *WhoAm 92*
Ledoux, Jean-Louis 1947- *WhoScE 91-2*
LeDoux, John Clarence 1944- *WhoSSW 93*
Ledoux, Paul 1949- *WhoCanL 92*
Ledoux, Paul Wayne 1937- *WhoSSW 93*
Ledoux, Robert Bruce, Jr. *Law&B 92*
Ledoyen, Charles Eric 1943- *St&PR 93*
Ledsinger, Charles Albert, Jr. 1950- *St&PR 93, WhoAm 92*
Ledsome, John Russell 1932- *WhoAm 92*
LeDu, Bradley J. *Law&B 92*
LeDuBois, Jacques-Laurent 1943- *WhoSSW 93*
Le Duc, Albert Louis, Jr. 1937- *WhoSSW 93*
Leduc, Alphonse 1804-1868 *Baker 92*
Leduc, Alphonse, II 1844-1892 *Baker 92*
Leduc, B.V. 1950- *WhoScE 91-2*
Leduc, Bernard Maurice 1935- *St&PR 93*
Leduc, Claude-Alphonse *See* Leduc, Alphonse, II 1844-1892 *Baker 92*
Le Duc, Don Raymond 1933- *WhoAm 92*
Leduc, Emile-Alphonse, III 1878-1951 *See* Leduc, Alphonse, II 1844-1892 *Baker 92*
Leduc, Eugene Joseph 1953- *WhoE 93*
Leduc, Gilbert-Alphonse *See* Leduc, Alphonse, II 1844-1892 *Baker 92*
Leduc, Jacques *MiSFD 9*
Leduc, Jacques 1932- *Baker 92*
Leduc, Paul 1942- *MiSFD 9*
Leduc, Renato 1897- *DcMexL*
Leduc, Simon 1742-1777 *Baker 92*
Le Duc, Tho 1911-1990 *DcTwHis*
Leduc, Violette 1907-1972 *BioIn 17*
Ledward, David A. 1943- *WhoScE 91-1*
Ledwidge, Patrick Joseph 1928- *WhoAm 92*
Ledwig, Donald Eugene 1937- *WhoAm 92*
Ledwin, William F. 1937- *WhoIns 93*
Ledwin, William Francis 1937- *St&PR 93*
Ledwith, A. *WhoScE 91-1*
Ledwith, Anthony 1933- *WhoScE 91-1*
Ledwith, Douglas Thomas 1949- *St&PR 93*
Ledwith, Walter Andrew 1918- *WhoSSW 93*
Ledyard, John Odell 1940- *WhoAm 92*
Ledyard, Lewis Cass d1990 *BioIn 17*
Ledyard, Robins Heard 1939- *WhoAm 92*
Lee, A. Robert 1941- *ScF&FL 92*
Lee, Adrian Iselin, Jr. 1920- *WhoAm 92*
Lee, Agnes Rand 1868-1939 *AmWomPl*
Lee, Alan *ScF&FL 92*
Lee, Alan John Clive *WhoScE 91-1*
Lee, Albert Shawshan 1955- *WhoWor 93*
Lee, Alexandra H. *Law&B 92*
Lee, Alexis Anne 1956- *WhoAmW 93*
Lee, Alfred McClung d1992 *NewYTBS 92*
Lee, Alfred McClung 1906-1992 *BioIn 17, ConAu 137*
Lee, Alfred T. d1992 *NewYTBS 92*
Lee, Alfred Theodore 1946- *WhoEmL 93*
Lee, Alison Ann 1950- *WhoAmW 93*
Lee, Allan Wren 1924- *WhoAm 92, WhoSSW 93*
Lee, Allen Peng-Fei 1940- *WhoAsAP 91*
Lee, Alvin A. 1930- *WhoAm 92*
Lee, Amy Freeman 1914- *WhoSSW 93*
Lee, Amy Shiu 1947- *WhoAmW 93*
Lee, Anita Combs 1945- *WhoSSW 93*
Lee, Ann 1736-1784 *BioIn 17*
Lee, Ann McKeighan 1939- *WhoAmW 93*
Lee, Ann On-Yee *Law&B 92*
Lee, Anna *BioIn 17*
Lee, Anna 1914- *BioIn 17*
Lee, Anne Natalie *WhoAmW 93, WhoSSW 93*
Lee, Anthony Asa 1947- *WhoWrEP 92*
Lee, Arthur Lawrence *Law&B 92*
Lee, Arthur Virgil, III 1920- *WhoAm 92*
Lee, Audrey 1968- *WhoWrEP 92*
Lee, B. Kyun 1952- *WhoEmL 93, WhoSSW 93*
Lee, Barbara Catherine 1931- *WhoAmW 93*
Lee, Benny 1944- *St&PR 93*
Lee, Bernard 1935-1991 *BioIn 17*
Lee, Bernard S. 1934- *St&PR 93*
Lee, Bernard Scott 1935-1991 *AfrAmBi*
Lee, Bernard Shing-Shu 1934- *WhoAm 92*
Lee, Bertram M., Sr. *WhoAm 92*
Lee, Bette Galloway 1927- *WhoSSW 93*
Lee, Betty Jane 1928- *WhoE 93*
Lee, Betty Redding 1919- *WhoAm 92, WhoAmW 93*
Lee, Bob *BioIn 17*
Lee, Bob 1930- *BioIn 17*
Lee, Brandon *BioIn 17*
Lee, Brenda 1944- *Baker 92, WhoAm 92, WhoAmW 93*
Lee, Brian Edward 1952- *WhoAm 92*
Lee, Bruce 1941-1973 *IntDcF 2-3 [port]*
Lee, Bruce L. *St&PR 93*
Lee, Burns Wells 1913- *WhoAm 92*
Lee, Burton *BioIn 17*
Lee, Burton James, III 1930- *WhoAm 92*
Lee, Burtrand Insung 1952- *WhoEmL 93, WhoSSW 93*
Lee, Byron, Jr. 1929- *WhoAm 92*
Lee, Candie Ching Wah 1950- *WhoWor 93*
Lee, Carla Ann Bouska 1943- *WhoAmW 93*
Lee, Carol Ann 1953- *WhoAmW 93*
Lee, Carol Mon 1947- *St&PR 93*
Lee, Carroll Russell 1949- *St&PR 93*
Lee, Charleme Esma 1949- *WhoAmW 93*
Lee, Charles 1731-1782 *HarEnMi*
Lee, Charles 1913- *WhoAm 92*
Lee, Charles C. 1943- *St&PR 93*
Lee, Charles Ray 1934- *WhoSSW 93*
Lee, Charles Robert 1939- *WhoAm 92*
Lee, Chaur Shyan 1941- *WhoWor 93*
Lee, Che H. *Law&B 92*
Lee, Chee Sung 1950- *WhoUN 92*
Lee, Chen Hsi 1923- *WhoE 93*
Lee, Cheryl Lynne *Law&B 92*
Lee, Chester Maurice 1919- *WhoAm 92*
Lee, Chester T. 1951- *St&PR 93*
Lee, Chi-Hung 1955- *WhoWor 93*
Lee, Chi-Jen 1936- *WhoE 93*
Lee, Chi-Woo 1954- *WhoWor 93*
Lee, Chin-Min 1940- *WhoUN 92*
Lee, Chong-Sik 1931- *WhoAm 92*
Lee, Christopher 1922- *BioIn 17, IntDcF 2-3 [port], ScF&FL 92*
Lee, Christopher Frank Carandini 1922- *WhoAm 92*
Lee, Chung Keel 1940- *WhoWor 93*
Lee, Cinque *BioIn 17*
Lee, Clement William Khan 1938- *WhoE 93, WhoWor 93*
Lee, Clifford Leon, II 1957- *WhoSSW 93*
Lee, Clive Howard 1942- *WhoWor 93*
Lee, Connie Louise 1948- *WhoEmL 93*
Lee, Corinne Adams 1910- *WhoAmW 93*
Lee, Curtis Howard 1928- *WhoWor 93*
Lee, Curtis W. *Law&B 92*
Lee, Cynthia Hutchens 1956- *WhoAmW 93*
Lee, D. William 1927- *St&PR 93*
Lee, Dae Joo 1954- *WhoWor 93*
Lee, Dai-Keong 1915- *Baker 92, WhoAm 92, WhoWor 93*
Lee, Dan E. *Law&B 92*
Lee, Dan M. 1926- *WhoAm 92, WhoSSW 93*
Lee, Daniel Andrew 1951- *WhoEmL 93*
Lee, Daniel Kuhn 1946- *WhoWor 93*
Lee, Daniel Yong-geun 1954- *WhoE 93, WhoEmL 93*
Lee, Darryl J. *Law&B 92*
Lee, David *BioIn 17, ScF&FL 92*
Lee, David Bailey 1944- *WhoAm 92*
Lee, David Bierly 1937- *St&PR 93*
Lee, David C. 1930- *St&PR 93*
Lee, David Collins *Law&B 92*
Lee, David George 1947- *WhoEmL 93*
Lee, David Harold 1947- *WhoEmL 93*
Lee, David Morris 1931- *WhoAm 92*
Lee, David Sen-Lin 1937- *St&PR 93*
Lee, David Spence 1948- *St&PR 93*
Lee, David Stoddart 1934- *St&PR 93, WhoAm 92*
Lee, Deane Marks d1992 *BioIn 17*
Lee, Debra L. *St&PR 93*
Lee, Dennis 1939- *WhoCanL 92*
Lee, Dennis A. *Law&B 92*
Lee, Dennis (Beynon) 1939- *MajAI [port]*
Lee, Diana *St&PR 93*
Lee, Dominic 1942- *WhoAm 92*
Lee, Don Chang 1929- *WhoSSW 93*
Lee, Don L. *BioIn 17*
Lee, Donald *WhoScE 91-1*
Lee, Donald John 1927- *WhoAm 92, WhoE 93*
Lee, Donald Lewis *WhoScE 91-1*
Lee, Donald Soule 1933- *WhoSSW 93*
Lee, Donna *Law&B 92*
Lee, Doo-Yong *MiSFD 9*
Lee, Doris Emrick 1905-1983 *BioIn 17*
Lee, Drun-sun John 1944- *WhoE 93*
Lee, Duane Edward 1955- *WhoEmL 93*
Lee, E. Bruce 1932- *WhoAm 92*
Lee, E.W. *WhoScE 91-1*
Lee, Earl Victory 1929- *St&PR 93*
Lee, Edna Pritchard 1923- *WhoAmW 93*
Lee, Edward 1957- *ScF&FL 92*
Lee, Edward Brooke, Jr. 1917- *WhoWor 93*
Lee, Edward King Pang 1929- *WhoWor 93*
Lee, Elaine 1963- *WhoAmW 93*
Lee, Elizabeth Bobbitt 1928- *WhoAm 92, WhoAmW 93*
Lee, Elizabeth Briant 1908- *BioIn 17, WhoE 93*
Lee, Elizabeth Sosenheimer 1941- *WhoE 93*
Lee, Elsie 1912- *ScF&FL 92*
Lee, Emma McCain 1948- *WhoAmW 93*
Lee, Eric Kin-Lam 1948- *WhoE 93*
Lee, Ernest Markham 1874-1956 *Baker 92*
Lee, Eugene Canfield 1924- *WhoAm 92*
Lee, Eugene Stanley 1930- *WhoAm 92*
Lee, Evelyn Marie 1931- *WhoAmW 93*
Lee, Fitzhugh 1835-1905 *HarEnMi*
Lee, Frances Helen 1936- *WhoAmW 93*
Lee, Frank W. 1924- *WhoSSW 93*
Lee, Frederick Yuk Leong 1937- *WhoAm 92*
Lee, Gary Albert 1941- *WhoAm 92*
Lee, Gary Edward 1951- *St&PR 93*
Lee, Geddy 1953- *See* Rush *ConMus 8*
Lee, Gene F. 1960- *WhoE 93, WhoEmL 93*
Lee, Genevieve Bruggeman 1928- *WhoE 93*
Lee, Gentry 1942- *ScF&FL 92*
Lee, George C. 1933- *WhoAm 92*
Lee, George Hamor, II 1939- *WhoSSW 93*
Lee, George L. 1906- *AfrAmBi [port]*
Lee, George L., III 1956- *St&PR 93*
Lee, George Ludlow, Jr. 1926- *St&PR 93*
Lee, George Oscar 1930- *St&PR 93*
Lee, George Teck Guan 1959- *WhoWor 93*
Lee, George Tom 1933- *WhoWor 93*
Lee, Gerald Eugene 1958- *WhoSSW 93*
Lee, Gil Sik 1953- *WhoEmL 93*
Lee, Gilbert W. *Law&B 92*
Lee, Glen K. 1950- *WhoEmL 93, WhoWor 93*
Lee, Glenn Richard 1932- *WhoAm 92*
Lee, Gloria L. *WhoScE 91-1*
Lee, Gordon F. *St&PR 93*
Lee, Grace Tze 1953- *WhoEmL 93*
Lee, Graeme John 1945- *St&PR 93*
Lee, Greame Ernest 1935- *WhoAsAP 91*
Lee, Gregory Price 1952- *WhoSSW 93*
Lee, Griff Calicutt 1926- *WhoAm 92*
Lee, Hak-Sung 1936- *WhoWor 93*
Lee, Hamilton H. 1921- *WhoWor 93*
Lee, Hamilton Hangtao 1921- *WhoWrEP 92*
Lee, Hanchow 1935- *WhoWor 93*
Lee, Harold Philip 1944- *St&PR 93*
Lee, Harper 1926- *BioIn 17, MagSAmL [port], WorLitC [port]*
Lee, Harper Baylor 1884-1941 *BioIn 17*
Lee, Harry Andre *WhoScE 91-1*
Lee, Helen 1908-1991 *BioIn 17*
Lee, Henry 1756-1818 *HarEnMi*
Lee, Henry 1952- *WhoEmL 93*
Lee, Henry Lawrence, Jr. 1926- *St&PR 93*
Lee, Heo-Peh 1931- *WhoWor 93*
Lee, Herbert 1912-1961 *EncAACR*
Lee, Honkon 1920- *WhoWor 93*
Lee, Howard Douglas 1943- *WhoAm 92, WhoSSW 93*
Lee, Hugh T. *Law&B 92*
Lee, Hung Jung 1947- *WhoUN 92*
Lee, Hwa-Wei 1933- *WhoAm 92*
Lee, Hyman J., Jr. 1942- *St&PR 93*
Lee, Hyung Mo 1926- *WhoAm 92*
Lee, Ik-Hwan 1943- *WhoWor 93*
Lee, Ik-Mo 1956- *WhoWor 93*
Lee, Ikchoon 1929- *WhoWor 93*

Lee, Ingram, III Law&B 92
Lee, Irving Allen d1992 NewYTBS 92
Lee, Isaiah Chong-Pie 1934- WhoAm 92
Lee, J. Daniel, Jr. 1938- WhoAm 92, WhoIns 93
Lee, J. Manning Law&B 92
Lee, J. Patrick 1942- WhoSSW 93
Lee, J. Terrence 1942- St&PR 93
Lee, J. Tyler 1951- WhoIns 93
Lee, Jack 1936- WhoAm 92
Lee, Jackie SoulM
Lee, Jackson Frederick, Jr. 1942- WhoSSW 93
Lee, James A. 1939- St&PR 93
Lee, James Bernard 1927- WhoAm 92
Lee, James Douglas 1954- WhoEmL 93
Lee, James E. 1932- St&PR 93
Lee, James Matthew 1937- WhoAm 92
Lee, James Michael 1931- WhoAm 92
Lee, James Robert 1938- WhoAm 92
Lee, Jan Wai-Tsun 1940- WhoWor 93
Lee, Jane Tennyson 1954- St&PR 93
Lee, Janet Arlene 1931- WhoAmW 93
Lee, Jang-Ho MiSFD 9
Lee, Janie C. BioIn 17
Lee, Janie C. 1937- WhoAm 92
Lee, Janis 1945- WhoAmW 93
Lee, Jason Davis 1949- WhoWor 93
Lee, Jeanne Kit Yew 1959- WhoAmW 93
Lee, Jeannette BioIn 17
Lee, Jeannine Anne 1957- WhoEmL 93
Lee, Jen-shih 1940- WhoAm 92
Lee, Jennette Barbour Perry 1860-1951 AmWomPl
Lee, Jennifer BioIn 17
Lee, Jerome Beauchamp 1937- WhoAm 92
Lee, Jerome G. 1924- WhoAm 92
Lee, Jerry Carlton 1941- WhoAm 92
Lee, Jerry K., Sr. 1935- St&PR 93
Lee, Jimmy Che-Yung 1946- WhoEmL 93, WhoSSW 93
Lee, Jimmy Ray 1957- WhoEmL 93
Lee, Jo Ann Law&B 92
Lee, Joan Sarles Law&B 92
Lee, Joanna MiSFD 9
Lee, Joe MiSFD 9
Lee, Joe R. 1940- WhoAm 92
Lee, John ScF&FL 92, WhoScE 91-3
Lee, John 1948- WhoEmL 93
Lee, John A. WhoScE 91-1
Lee, John Alexander 1891-1982 DcTwHis
Lee, John Chonghoon, Sr. 1928- WhoAm 92, WhoE 93, WhoWor 93
Lee, John D. 1943- St&PR 93
Lee, John E., Jr. 1947- BioIn 17
Lee, John Edward, Jr. 1933- WhoAm 92
Lee, John Francis 1918- WhoAm 92
Lee, John Franklin 1927- WhoAm 92, WhoWor 93
Lee, John J. 1933- WhoE 93
Lee, John Jin Law&B 92
Lee, John Jin 1948- WhoAm 92
Lee, John Jongjin 1933- WhoE 93
Lee, Johnson Y. 1955- WhoWor 93
Lee, Joie BioIn 17
Lee, Jonas Phillip 1966- WhoEmL 93
Lee, Jonathan O. 1951- St&PR 93
Lee, Jonathan Owen 1951- WhoAm 92, WhoEmL 93
Lee, Jong-Hyeon 1966- WhoWor 93
Lee, Joseph David 1938- St&PR 93
Lee, Joseph Edward 1953- WhoSSW 93
Lee, Joseph William 1943- St&PR 93, WhoE 93
Lee, Josephine Patricia 1924- WhoE 93
Lee, Judith Anne 1950- WhoAmW 93, WhoE 93, WhoEmL 93
Lee, Judith Yaross 1949- ConAu 137
Lee, Judy Faye 1963- WhoSSW 93
Lee, Julian MajAI
Lee, Julie Jeanine Law&B 92
Lee, June Warren 1952- WhoAmW 93, WhoEmL 93
Lee, Kam Shing 1947- WhoWor 93
Lee, Karen Elizabeth 1956- WhoWor 93
Lee, Karen Elizabeth 1964- WhoAmW 93
Lee, Karl Olsen 1936- St&PR 93
Lee, Katharine Caecilia 1941- WhoAmW 93
Lee, Katherine Ann 1947- WhoAmW 93, WhoEmL 93
Lee, Kathleen Mary 1948- WhoEmL 93, WhoSSW 93
Lee, Kathryn Adele Bunding 1949- WhoEmL 93
Lee, Kathryn Ellen Law&B 92
Lee, Kathy 1949- St&PR 93
Lee, Kenneth Duane 1949- St&PR 93
Lee, Kenneth Stuart 1955- WhoEmL 93, WhoSSW 93, WhoWor 93
Lee, Kent L. 1923- BioIn 17
Lee, Kermit James, Jr. 1934- WhoAm 92
Lee, Keun Sok 1954- WhoE 93
Lee, Khoon Choy BioIn 17
Lee, Ki Chang 1950- WhoWor 93
Lee, Kimary Law&B 92
Lee, Kimun 1946- WhoEmL 93
Lee, Kok Ming Eric 1960- WhoWor 93
Lee, Kuan Yew BioIn 17
Lee, Kwan Il 1943- WhoE 93
Lee, Kwang 1941- St&PR 93
Lee, Kwang-Kyu 1932- WhoWor 93
Lee, Lance 1942- WhoWrEP 92
Lee, Lansing Burrows, Jr. 1919- WhoWor 93
Lee, Laura SoulM
Lee, Laura 1945- BioIn 17
Lee, Laura Eileen 1950- WhoWor 93
Lee, Laurel 1945- ConAu 138
Lee, Laurence Raymond 1928- WhoAm 92
Lee, Laurie BioIn 17
Lee, Lawrence Cho 1953- WhoWor 93
Lee, Lawrence W. 1938- St&PR 93
Lee, Lawrence Winston 1938- WhoAm 92
Lee, Leo Ou-fan 1939- WhoAm 92
Lee, Leon H., Jr. Law&B 92
Lee, Leonard 1935-1976
See Shirley & Lee SoulM
Lee, Leslie 1935- ConTFT 10
Lee, Lester L. 1933- St&PR 93
Lee, Lillian Vanessa 1951- WhoE 93
Lee, Lily Kiang 1946- WhoAmW 93, WhoEmL 93
Lee, Linda Hope WhoWrEP 92
Lee, Linda Luke Law&B 92
Lee, Linda Mae 1948- WhoEmL 93
Lee, Lisa Colleen 1963- WhoAmW 93
Lee, Lon Charles BioIn 17
Lee, Long Chi 1940- WhoWor 93
Lee, Loretta M. Law&B 92
Lee, Louis 1819-1896 Baker 92
Lee, Low Kee 1916- WhoAm 92
Lee, Lucille Lady 1942- WhoAmW 93
Lee, Lydia 1944- WhoWrEP 92
Lee, Lynda Mills 1944- WhoAmW 93
Lee, M.J. WhoScE 91-1
Lee, Margaret Anne 1930- WhoAmW 93
Lee, Margaret Norma 1928- WhoAmW 93
Lee, Marianna 1930- WhoAmW 93
Lee, Marietta Y.W.T. 1943- WhoAmW 93
Lee, Marilyn Irma Modarelli 1934- WhoE 93
Lee, Mark H. WhoScE 91-1
Lee, Martha 1946- WhoAmW 93, WhoWor 93
Lee, Martin 1923- St&PR 93
Lee, Martin Chu-Ming 1938- WhoAsAP 91
Lee, Marva Jean 1938- WhoAmW 93
Lee, Mary 1924- SweetSg C
Lee, Mary Caroline AmWomPl
Lee, Mary Elizabeth AmWomPl
Lee, Mary Margaret 1947- WhoSSW 93
Lee, Mary Paik 1900- BioIn 17
Lee, Maurice 1821-1895 Baker 92
Lee, Maurice (Du Pont), Jr. 1925- WhoWrEP 92
Lee, Maurice Wing Woo 1950- WhoWor 93
Lee, May Dean-Ming Lu 1949- WhoEmL 93
Lee, Megan Law&B 92
Lee, Michael B.K. Law&B 92
Lee, Michael G. W. 1947- WhoEmL 93
Lee, Michael John 1957- WhoAsAP 91
Lee, Michael Radcliffe WhoScE 91-1
Lee, Michael Radcliffe 1934- WhoWor 93
Lee, Michael U. Law&B 92
Lee, Michele 1942- WhoAm 92, WhoAmW 93
Lee, Michele Zaro 1943- WhoAmW 93
Lee, Michelle Un-Kyung 1962- WhoAmW 93
Lee, Mildred 1908- DcAmChF 1960
Lee, Ming Cho 1930- WhoAm 92, WhoWor 93
Lee, Murlin E. 1957- WhoEmL 93, WhoWor 93
Lee, Myung-Bak BioIn 17
Lee, Myung Bak 1941- WhoWor 93
Lee, Nancy Law&B 92
Lee, Nancy Francine 1956- WhoAmW 93
Lee, Naomi Pearl 1948- WhoEmL 93
Lee, Nelda S. 1941- WhoAm 92, WhoAmW 93
Lee, Norman Hubbard 1929- St&PR 93
Lee, Oi Hian 1951- WhoWor 93
Lee, Oliver Milton 1866-1941 BioIn 17
Lee, Oscar 1953- WhoWor 93
Lee, Pamela ScF&FL 92
Lee, Pamela Anne 1960- WhoAmW 93
Lee, Parkin Law&B 92
Lee, Patricia H. Law&B 92
Lee, Patrick A. Law&B 92
Lee, Patrick A. 1946- WhoAm 92
Lee, Patrick Christopher 1955- WhoE 93
Lee, Patrick P. 1938- St&PR 93
Lee, Patrick Paul 1938- WhoE 93
Lee, Paul D. 1942- St&PR 93
Lee, Paul King-lung 1942- WhoWor 93
Lee, Paulette Wang Law&B 92
Lee, Peggy BioIn 17
Lee, Peggy 1920- Baker 92, ConMus 8 [port]
Lee, Peggy Joyce 1940- WhoAmW 93
Lee, Peter Alan WhoScE 91-1
Lee, Peter Bernard 1959- WhoE 93
Lee, Peter Redvers 1960- WhoSSW 93
Lee, Philip Justice 1948- WhoEmL 93
Lee, Phillip Dukeal Kwaiyuen 1956- WhoSSW 93
Lee, Ping Hei 1934- WhoWor 93
Lee, R.E., Jr. Law&B 92
Lee, R. H. 1932- WhoAm 92
Lee, R. W., Mrs. AmWomPl
Lee, R. William, Jr. 1930- St&PR 93
Lee, Ramona Carmen 1959- WhoEmL 93
Lee, Raymond William, Jr. 1930- WhoAm 92
Lee, Rebecca WhoE 93
Lee, Richard C. 1916- PolPar
Lee, Richard D. 1940- St&PR 93
Lee, Richard Kenneth 1942- WhoAm 92
Lee, Richard Steward 1941- WhoE 93
Lee, Richard Vaille 1937- WhoAm 92, WhoWor 93
Lee, Richard Vincent 1924- WhoSSW 93
Lee, Robert 1929- WhoAm 92
Lee, Robert A. 1934- ScF&FL 92
Lee, Robert B. 1944- WhoE 93
Lee, Robert C. 1931- ScF&FL 92
Lee, Robert Dorwin 1939- WhoE 93
Lee, Robert E. 1807-1870 BioIn 17
Lee, Robert E.A. 1921- WhoWrEP 92
Lee, Robert Earl 1928- WhoAm 92
Lee, Robert Edward 1807-1870 HarEnMi
Lee, Robert Edward, Jr. Law&B 92
Lee, Robert Edward, Jr. 1941- WhoE 93
Lee, Robert Edwin 1918- BioIn 17, WhoAm 92
Lee, Robert Erwin, Jr. 1940- St&PR 93
Lee, Robert Hugh 1950- WhoEmL 93
Lee, Robert J.E. 1933- St&PR 93
Lee, Robert John 1929- WhoAm 92
Lee, Robert John 1956- WhoEmL 93
Lee, Robert Justin 1945- WhoSSW 93, WhoWor 93
Lee, Robert Sanford 1924- WhoAm 92, WhoE 93
Lee, Robert Wesley 1928- St&PR 93
Lee, Roberta d1984 BioIn 17
Lee, Ronald Barry 1932- WhoAm 92
Lee, Ronald D. 1948- St&PR 93
Lee, Ronald Demos 1941- WhoAm 92
Lee, Ronald E. Law&B 92
Lee, Ronald George 1952- St&PR 93
Lee, Rose Hum 1904-1964 BioIn 17
Lee, Rosetta Arintha 1958- WhoAmW 93
Lee, Rowland V. 1891-1975 MiSFD 9N
Lee, Roy Noble 1915- WhoAm 92, WhoSSW 93
Lee, Roy S. 1938- WhoUN 92
Lee, Sally BioIn 17
Lee, Samantha ScF&FL 92
Lee, Sammie French 1928- WhoAm 92
Lee, Sammy, I 1920- WhoAm 92
Lee, Samuel Dennis 1958- WhoE 93, WhoEmL 93
Lee, Samuel K. Law&B 92
Lee, Sanboh 1948- WhoWor 93
Lee, Sang Hak 1949- WhoWor 93
Lee, Sang Moon 1939- WhoAm 92
Lee, Sara
See Gang of Four ConMus 8
Lee, Sarah Tomerlin BioIn 17, WhoAm 92
Lee, Sean F. 1940- WhoAm 92
Lee, Sebastian 1805-1887 Baker 92
Lee, Seng Chean 1953- WhoWor 93
Lee, Sharon ScF&FL 92
Lee, Sharon Gail 1953- WhoEmL 93
Lee, Sheng Yen 1924- WhoE 93
Lee, Shepard 1926- St&PR 93
Lee, Sherman Emery 1918- WhoAm 92
Lee, Sheryl BioIn 17
Lee, Shew Kuhn 1923- WhoWor 93
Lee, Shih-Ying 1918- WhoAm 92
Lee, Shirley St&PR 93
Lee, Shuishih Sage 1948- WhoAm 92
Lee, Shyi-Long 1955- WhoWor 93
Lee, Sidney P. 1920- St&PR 93
Lee, Sidney Phillip 1926- WhoAm 92
Lee, Sidney Seymour 1921- WhoAm 92
Lee, Silas, III 1954- WhoSSW 93
Lee, Spike BioIn 17
Lee, Spike 1956- MiSFD 9
Lee, Spike 1957- AfrAmBi, WhoAm 92
Lee, Spike (Shelton Jackson) c. 1957- WhoWrEP 92
Lee, Stan 1922- ScF&FL 92, WhoAm 92
Lee, Stanley 1919- WhoAm 92
Lee, Stephen Dill 1833-1908 HarEnMi
Lee, Stephen E. St&PR 93
Lee, Stephen Randall 1952- WhoSSW 93
Lee, Steven 1950- WhoEmL 93
Lee, Sul Hi 1936- WhoAm 92
Lee, Sun-Ock 1943- WhoE 93
Lee, Sung Bok 1950- WhoWor 93
Lee, Sung Gun 1951- WhoWor 93
Lee, Susan WhoAmW 93
Lee, Susan 1943- WhoAmW 93
Lee, T. Jerry 1937- WhoIns 93
Lee, Tak Hong 1951- WhoScE 91-1
Lee, Tanith BioIn 17
Lee, Tanith 1947- ChlFicS, ScF&FL 92
Lee, Ted Choong Kil 1940- WhoE 93
Lee, Terrance H.M. 1940- St&PR 93
Lee, Terrence Allan 1955- WhoSSW 93
Lee, Terry 1946- WhoScE 91-3
Lee, Thai T. 1958- St&PR 93
Lee, Theresa K. Law&B 92
Lee, Thomas d1601 BioIn 17
Lee, Thomas Alexander 1941- WhoWor 93
Lee, Thomas B. 1925- St&PR 93
Lee, Thomas Dongho 1940- WhoWor 93
Lee, Thomas Henry 1923- WhoAm 92
Lee, Thomas Joseph, Jr. 1921- WhoAm 92, WhoWor 93
Lee, Thomas Patrick 1938- St&PR 93
Lee, Thomas Roy 1955- WhoWrEP 92
Lee, Thomas Way 1943- WhoWor 93
Lee, Tien Pei 1933- WhoAm 92
Lee, Timothy Earl 1947- WhoEmL 93, WhoWor 93
Lee, Timothy Guy 1939- WhoAm 92
Lee, Tok Eng 1953- WhoWor 93
Lee, Tom Stewart 1941- WhoAm 92, WhoSSW 93
Lee, Tong Hun 1931- WhoAm 92
Lee, Tony WhoScE 91-1
Lee, Tsu Tian 1949- WhoWor 93
Lee, Tsung-Dao 1926- WhoAm 92, WhoE 93, WhoWor 93
Lee, Tuck B. 1929- St&PR 93
Lee, Tunney Fee 1931- WhoAm 92
Lee, Vera G. WhoAmW 93
Lee, Vernon 1856-1935 ScF&FL 92
Lee, Vernon Roy 1952- WhoSSW 93
Lee, Virginia Marie 1954- WhoAmW 93
Lee, W.S. 1929- St&PR 93
Lee, Wallace Williams, Jr. 1915- WhoAm 92
Lee, Walt 1931- ScF&FL 92
Lee, Wanda Darlene 1951- WhoE 93
Lee, Warner ScF&FL 92
Lee, Warrick Edward, Jr. Law&B 92
Lee, Wayne 1945- St&PR 93
Lee, Wayne Floyd 1952- St&PR 93
Lee, William ConTFT 10
Lee, William 1911- BiDAMSp 1989
Lee, William Anthony 1946- St&PR 93
Lee, William Chien-Yeh 1932- WhoAm 92
Lee, William Clement, III Law&B 92
Lee, William Crutcher 1909-1977 BiDAMSp 1989
Lee, William D., Jr. Law&B 92
Lee, William David 1944- WhoWrEP 92
Lee, William David 1947- WhoEmL 93
Lee, William Franklin, III 1929- WhoAm 92
Lee, William I. 1952- St&PR 93
Lee, William John 1936- WhoAm 92
Lee, William Lamborn 1947- WhoE 93
Lee, William Marshall 1922- WhoAm 92
Lee, William Paul 1949- WhoSSW 93
Lee, William Robert WhoScE 91-1
Lee, William S. St&PR 93
Lee, William Saul 1938- WhoAm 92
Lee, William States 1929- WhoAm 92, WhoSSW 93
Lee, William Swain 1935- WhoE 93
Lee, Willis Augustus, Jr. 1888-1945 HarEnMi
Lee, Wo Yen 1932- WhoUN 92
Lee, Woong Man 1938- WhoE 93
Lee, Yau-Tat 1931- WhoUN 92
Lee, Yien-Hwei 1937- WhoWor 93
Lee, Yoon Joon 1954- WhoWor 93
Lee, Young Jack 1942- WhoAm 92
Lee, Young Ki 1946- WhoWor 93
Lee, Young Kil 1947- WhoWor 93
Lee, Young Moo 1954- WhoWor 93
Lee, Yuan Tseh 1936- WhoAm 92, WhoWor 93
Lee, Yung Dug 1926- WhoWor 93
Lee, Yung-Keun 1929- WhoAm 92
Lee, Yung N. 1956- WhoSSW 93
Lee, Yvonne A. 1933- St&PR 93
Lee, Yvonne Alberta 1933- WhoAm 92
Lee, Zuk-Nae 1940- WhoWor 93
Leeb, Bruce Harvey 1941- WhoE 93
Leeb, Charles Samuel 1945- WhoWor 93
Leeb, Diane Cheryl 1946- WhoAmW 93
Leeb, Wilhelm Ritter von 1876-1956 HarEnMi
Lee Boon Yang, Dr. 1947- WhoAsAP 91
Leebow, Steven B. 1947- ConEn
Leeby, L.R. St&PR 93
Lee Byoung Heui 1927- WhoAsAP 91
Lee Byun Yong 1927- WhoAsAP 91
Leece, William Alfred 1912- WhoE 93
Leece, William Joseph WhoWrEP 92
Leech, Charles Russell, Jr. 1930- WhoAm 92
Leech, Geoffrey Neil WhoScE 91-1
Leech, James C. Law&B 92
Leech, James William 1947- St&PR 93, WhoAm 92
Leech, John 1925- ConAu 139
Leech, John Dale 1939- WhoAm 92
Leech, Mike BioIn 17
Leech, Noyes Elwood 1921- WhoAm 92
Lee Chan Koo 1942- WhoAsAP 91
Lee Choon Koo 1935- WhoAsAP 91

Lefranc, Frederick Armand 1956- WhoAm 92
Lefranc, Gerard Marie Andre 1934- WhoScE 91-2
Le Franc, Jean-Daniel 1933- WhoWor 93
Lefrant, Serge Roger 1947- WhoScE 91-2
Lefschetz, Solomon 1884-1972 BioIn 17
Lefstein, Norman 1937- WhoAm 92
Left, Barbara Lynn 1968- WhoAmW 93
Leftin, Barton Bennett 1949- WhoE 93
Lefton, Al Paul, Jr. 1928- St&PR 93, WhoAm 92
Lefton, Harvey Bennett 1944- WhoE 93
Lefton, Joel M. St&PR 93
Lefton, Lester Alan 1946- WhoAm 92
Lefton, Lew Edward 1960- WhoSSW 93
Lefton, Norman Barry 1934- St&PR 93
Leftwich, James Stephen 1956- WhoWor 93
Leftwich, John Thomas, II 1946- WhoEmL 93
Leftwich, Richard Henry 1920- WhoAm 92
Le Fur, Jean-Yves BioIn 17
Le Gac, Jean BioIn 17
Legacy, Earl G. 1933- St&PR 93
Legagneur, Serge 1937- WhoCanL 92
Le Gall, Jean Louis 1940- WhoWor 93
Le Gall, Jean-Roger 1939- WhoWor 93
Le Gallienne, Dorian 1915-1963 Baker 92
Le Gallienne, Eva 1899-1991 AnObit 1991, BioIn 17, ConTFT 10
Legan, Richard N. 1937- St&PR 93
Legan, Thomas Lee 1933- St&PR 93
Legarda, Donato 1936- WhoWor 93
LeGardeur, Armand 1929- St&PR 93
Legaspi, Pilar F. ScF&FL 92
Legaspi, Ramon B. 1927- WhoAsAP 91
Legaspi, Rufino Encarnacion 1921- WhoE 93
Legasse, David Stephen 1949- WhoE 93
Legat, Ingrid Hildegard 1938- WhoWor 93
LeGates, John Crews 1940- WhoAm 92, WhoE 93, WhoWor 93
Legatti, Raymond 1932- St&PR 93
Legault, Jean-Francois Law&B 92
Legay, Jean-Marie 1925- WhoScE 91-2
Legel, Zero WhoCanL 92
Legendre, Louis 1945- WhoAm 92
LeGendre-Purse, Laurette Michele 1954- WhoEmL 93
Legenza, Richard A. Law&B 92
Leger, Cardinal 1904-1991 AnObit 1991
Leger, Alexis Saint-Leger 1887-1975 BioIn 17
Leger, Fernand 1881-1955 BioIn 17
Leger, Jean-Francois Law&B 92
Leger, Jean J. 1941- WhoScE 91-2
Leger, Jean-Marie 1934- WhoScE 91-2
Leger, Lubert James 1940- WhoSSW 93
Leger, Paul-Emile 1904-1991 CurBio 92N
Leger, Paul-Emile 1906-1991 BioIn 17
Leger, Richard Roubine 1935- WhoWor 93
Leger, Saint-Leger 1887-1975 BioIn 17
Leger, Walter John, Jr. 1951- WhoAm 92
Legere, Laurence Joseph 1919- WhoAm 92
Legeret, M. WhoScE 91-4
Legerton, Clarence William, Jr. 1922- WhoAm 92, WhoSSW 93
Legg, Allan Douglas 1942- WhoUN 92
Legg, Brian James WhoScE 91-1
Legg, Brian James 1945- WhoWor 93
Legg, James S. Law&B 92
Legg, Larry Barnard 1941- WhoSSW 93
Legg, Lawrence George Law&B 92
Legg, Linda S. Law&B 92
Legg, Louis E., Jr. 1928- St&PR 93
Legg, Mark William 1955- St&PR 93
Legg, Mary Nell 1947- WhoAmW 93
Legg, Robert H. 1917- St&PR 93
Legg, Robert Henry 1917- WhoAm 92
Legg, Thomas Charles 1956- St&PR 93
Legg, William Jefferson 1925- WhoAm 92
Leggat, Janet Cochrane 1954- WhoE 93
Leggat, John William, III 1942- St&PR 93
Leggat, Richard Durning 1927- WhoAm 92
Leggat, Thomas E. 1926- St&PR 93
Leggatt, Alison 1904-1990 BioIn 17
Legge, Christopher Howatson 1957- St&PR 93
Legge, Jacqueline Crosby 1961- WhoAm 92
Legge, Robert Scott 1951- WhoE 93
Legge, Rupert St&PR 93
Legge, Thomas Christopher 1951- WhoWrEP 92
Legge, Walter 1906-1979 Baker 92
Legge Kemp, Diane 1949- WhoAmW 93
Legget, Robert Ferguson 1904- WhoAm 92
Leggett, Anne Marie 1947- WhoAmW 93
Leggett, Donald Yates 1935- WhoSSW 93
Leggett, Glenn 1918- WhoAm 92
Leggett, Jeremy Kendal WhoScE 91-1
Leggett, John Carl 1930- WhoE 93
Leggett, John Ward 1917- WhoWrEP 92
Leggett, Malcolm H. 1937- WhoIns 93
Leggett, Roberta Jean 1926- WhoAm 92
Leggett, Sonyia Elizabeth 1936- WhoAmW 93
Leggett, Stephen Charles 1949- WhoWrEP 92
Leggett, William C. 1939- WhoAm 92
Leggette, Lemire Law&B 92
Leggiere, Philip Samuel 1926- WhoE 93
Leggitt, Don C., Sr. 1938- St&PR 93
Legien, Dariusz 1968- WhoWor 93
Leginska, Ethel 1886-1970 Baker 92
Legler, Donald Wayne 1931- WhoAm 92
Legler, Jennifer Onaitis 1952- WhoE 93
Legler, John Anthony 1952- WhoE 93
Legler, Kenneth Charles 1936- St&PR 93
Legler, Paul Kevin 1955- WhoEmL 93
Legler, Philip 1928- WhoWrEP 92
Legler, Theodore Rex, II 1946- WhoWor 93
Legley, Victor 1915- Baker 92
Legleye, Bernard 1937- WhoWor 93
Legnani, (Rinaldo) Luigi 1790-1877 Baker 92
Legnard, James M. Law&B 92
Lego, P.E. 1930- St&PR 93
Lego, Paul Edward 1930- WhoAm 92, WhoE 93
Le Goff, Jacques 1924- BioIn 17
Le Goffic, Francois 1936- WhoScE 91-2, WhoWor 93
Legomsky, Joanne St&PR 93
Legon, Anthony Charles WhoScE 91-1
LeGon, Jeni 1916- BioIn 17
Legorreta, Eduardo Antonio 1943- St&PR 93
Legorreta, Ricardo 1931- WhoWor 93
Legorreta, Ricardo 1960- WhoWor 93
Legowski, Claire Elise 1951- WhoAmW 93
Legrand WhoScE 91-2
Le Grand, Clay 1911- WhoAm 92
Legrand, Fred R. St&PR 93
Le Grand, Julian WhoScE 91-1
leGrand, Maria Hendrika 1948- WhoAmW 93
Legrand, Michel MiSFD 9
Legrand, Michel 1932- Baker 92
Le Grand, Nicholas W. Law&B 92
LeGrand, Patrick Arthur 1951- WhoWor 93
LeGrand, Susan Eles Schmidt 1967- WhoSSW 93
Legrand, Theo 1940- WhoWor 93
Legrand, Yves J. WhoScE 91-2
LeGrange, Ulyesse John 1931- WhoAm 92
Legrenzi, Giovanni 1626-1690 Baker 92, OxDcOp
Legros, Alphonse J.A. 1921- WhoScE 91-2
Legros, Auguste 1922- WhoAsAP 91
Legros, Jean-Claude 1942- WhoScE 91-2
Legros, Jean Jacques 1942- WhoScE 91-2
Le Gros, John Edward 1923- St&PR 93, WhoAm 92
Legros, Joseph 1739-1793 Baker 92, OxDcOp
Legros, L.J. 1937- St&PR 93
LeGros, Peter Arthur 1939- St&PR 93
Legros, Robert R. Law&B 92
Legters, Lyman Howard 1928- WhoAm 92
Legue, Laura Elizabeth 1954- WhoAmW 93
Le Guen, Veronique BioIn 17
Leguia y Salcedo, Augusto Bernardino 1863-1932 DcTwHis
Leguillon, Rolande Lucienne 1924- WhoAmW 93
LeGuin, Ursula 1929- BioIn 17
Le Guin, Ursula K. 1929- Au&Arts 9 [port], BioIn 17, ConLC 71 [port], MagSAmL [port], ScF&FL 92
Le Guin, Ursula K(roeber) 1929- ChlLR 28 [port], DcAmChF 1960, MajAI [port]
Le Guin, Ursula Kroeber 1929- WhoAm 92, WhoAmW 93, WhoWrEP 92
Leguizamo, John BioIn 17
Legum, Jeffrey A. 1941- St&PR 93
Legum, Jeffrey Alfred 1941- WhoAm 92, WhoE 93, WhoWor 93
Legum, Leslie 1911- St&PR 93
Legutki, John C. Law&B 92
Legwaila, Legwaila Joseph 1937- WhoUN 92
Lehan, Jonathan Michael 1947- WhoEmL 93
Lehan, Patricia Ellen 1960- WhoE 93
Lehan, Richard D'Aubin 1930- WhoAm 92, WhoWrEP 92
LeHand, Marguerite Alice d1944 BioIn 17
LeHand, Missy d1944 BioIn 17
Lehar, Franz 1838-1898 See Lehar, Franz 1870-1948 Baker 92
Lehar, Franz 1870-1948 Baker 92, OxDcOp
Lehe, James Eugene WhoSSW 93
Lehecka, Scott Alan Law&B 92
Lehel, Gyorgy 1926-1989 Baker 92
Le Heuzey, Jean-Yves 1951- WhoScE 91-2
Lehew, Willette Lewis 1935- WhoSSW 93
Lehey, Gregory Francis 1948- WhoWor 93
Lehfeldt, Maria Eisner d1991 BioIn 17
Lehfeldt, Martin Christopher 1940- WhoSSW 93
Lehigh, Earl F. 1930- St&PR 93
Lehigh, George Edward 1927- WhoSSW 93
Lehiste, Ilse 1922- WhoAm 92
Lehl, Jurgen BioIn 17
Lehmacher, Walter 1949- WhoScE 91-3
Lehman, Albert E. 1915- St&PR 93
Lehman, Angela Marie 1937- WhoAmW 93
Lehman, Arnold Lester 1944- WhoAm 92, WhoE 93
Lehman, Charles d1990 BioIn 17
Lehman, Christopher M. 1948- WhoAm 92
Lehman, David 1948- WhoWrEP 92
Lehman, David A. Law&B 92
Lehman, David R. 1940- WhoIns 93
Lehman, Dennis L. 1956- St&PR 93
Lehman, Donald Richard 1940- WhoE 93
Lehman, Edgar R. 1933- WhoIns 93
Lehman, Edward 1925- St&PR 93
Lehman, Edward William 1936- WhoAm 92
Lehman, Edwin WhoAm 92
Lehman, Ernest 1920- MiSFD 9
Lehman, Harold L. 1935- St&PR 93
Lehman, Harry Jac 1935- WhoAm 92
Lehman, Herbert H. 1878-1963 PolPar
Lehman, Herbert Henry 1878-1963 BioIn 17
Lehman, Howard M. 1927- St&PR 93
Lehman, Hyla Beroen WhoWor 93
Lehman, Jack Henry, Jr. 1918- St&PR 93
Lehman, Jackson R. 1931- St&PR 93
Lehman, James Luther 1929- WhoSSW 93
Lehman, John 1942- ColdWar 1 [port]
Lehman, John F., Jr. 1942- WhoAm 92
Lehman, Joseph Mann 1924- WhoSSW 93
Lehman, Kevin C. WhoIns 93
Lehman, Lawrence Brad 1953- WhoE 93
Lehman, Lawrence Herbert 1929- WhoAm 92
Lehman, Lawrence John Law&B 92
Lehman, Lois Joan 1932- WhoAm 92
Lehman, M.M. WhoScE 91-1
Lehman, Mark E. Law&B 92
Lehman, Mary BioIn 17
Lehman, Meir Manny 1925- WhoWor 93
Lehman, Neal Fowler Law&B 92
Lehman, Orin 1922- WhoAm 92, WhoWor 93
Lehman, Pamela Kay 1963- WhoEmL 93
Lehman, Richard H. 1948- CngDr 91
Lehman, Richard Henry 1948- WhoAm 92
Lehman, Richard Leroy 1930- WhoAm 92, WhoWor 93
Lehman, Robert 1924- WhoAm 92
Lehman, Robert G. 1933- St&PR 93
Lehman, Robert Nathan 1911- WhoAm 92
Lehman, Ronald Frank, II 1946- WhoAm 92
Lehman, Ruth Gillespie 1924- St&PR 93
Lehman, Seth Harold 1965- St&PR 93
Lehman, Sherelynn 1941- WhoAmW 93
Lehman, Shirley Yvonne 1936- WhoWrEP 92
Lehman, Valerie Robertson 1895- AmWomPl
Lehman, Wayne 1949- St&PR 93
Lehman, Wayne Eric 1949- WhoE 93
Lehman, William CngDr 91
Lehman, William 1913- WhoAm 92, WhoSSW 93
Lehmann, Alan Robert WhoScE 91-1
Lehmann, Alexander R. 1935- St&PR 93
Lehmann, Ascher 1796-1858 BioIn 17
Lehmann, Bruce Neal 1955- WhoEmL 93
Lehmann, Charles Henry 1924- St&PR 93
Lehmann, Doris Elizabeth 1933- WhoE 93
Lehmann, Edgar 1909- BioIn 17
Lehmann, Elizabeth Ann Ayotte 1952- WhoEmL 93
Lehmann, Erich Leo 1917- WhoAm 92
Lehmann, Esther Strauss 1944- WhoAmW 93
Lehmann, Ewald St&PR 93
Lehmann, Frederick Giessmann 1930- WhoE 93, WhoWor 93
Lehmann, Fritz 1904-1956 Baker 92
Lehmann, Hans G. BioIn 17
Lehmann, Hans Ulrich 1937- Baker 92
Lehmann, Heiner 1939- WhoScE 91-3
Lehmann, Heinz Edgar 1911- WhoAm 92
Lehmann, Heinz R. 1929- St&PR 93
Lehmann, Herbert Henry 1878-1963 JeAmHC
Lehmann, Ingrid A. 1948- WhoUN 92
Lehmann, Janet Comey 1947- WhoAmW 93
Lehmann, Jean 1956- WhoScE 91-2
Lehmann, John 1907-1987 BioIn 17
Lehmann, Leann R. 1950- WhoAmW 93
Lehmann, Lilli 1848-1929 Baker 92, IntDcOp [port], OxDcOp
Lehmann, Liza 1862-1918 Baker 92
Lehmann, Lotte 1888-1976 Baker 92, IntDcOp [port], OxDcOp
Lehmann, Manfred Roderich 1942- St&PR 93
Lehmann, Marie 1851-1931 Baker 92, OxDcOp
Lehmann, Maurice 1895-1974 OxDcOp
Lehmann, Michael MiSFD 9
Lehmann, Nolan 1944- St&PR 93
Lehmann, Phyllis Williams 1912- WhoAm 92
Lehmann, Richard J. WhoAm 92
Lehmann, Richard J. 1944- St&PR 93
Lehmann, Rolf Richard 1934- WhoWor 93
Lehmann, Rosamond 1901-1990 BioIn 17
Lehmann, Rudolph John Frederick 1907-1987 BioIn 17
Lehmann, Ruth Preston Miller 1912- WhoAm 92, WhoSSW 93, WhoWrEP 92
Lehmann, Thomas G. Law&B 92
Lehmann, Volker 1939- WhoScE 91-3
Lehmann, Walter 1878-1939 IntDcAn
Lehmann, William Leonardo 1924- WhoAm 92
Lehmann, Winfred Philipp 1916- WhoAm 92, WhoSSW 93
Lehmann-Carssow, Nancy Beth 1949- WhoAmW 93
Lehmann-Haupt, Christopher Charles Herbert 1934- WhoAm 92, WhoWrEP 92
Lehmann-Haupt, Hellmut 1903-1992 BioIn 17
Lehmann-Haupt, Hellmut E(mil) 1903-1992 CurBio 92N
Lehmann-Haupt, Hellmut (Emile) 1903-1992 ConAu 137
Lehmann-Nitsche, Robert 1872-1938 IntDcAn
Lehmberg, Stanford Eugene 1931- WhoAm 92
Lehmbruck, Wilhelm 1881-1919 BioIn 17
Lehmer, David Lawrence 1942- St&PR 93
Lehmer, Donald J. 1918-1975 IntDcAn
Lehmkuhl, Donald ScF&FL 92
Lehmkuhl, Lawrence A. 1937- St&PR 93
Lehn, Clifford A. 1930- St&PR 93
Lehn, Jean-Marie Pierre 1939- WhoAm 92, WhoScE 91-2, WhoWor 93
Lehn, Kenneth Matthew 1954- WhoAm 92
Lehner, Christine Reine 1952- WhoWrEP 92
Lehner, Gerhard Hans 1924- WhoWor 93
Lehner, Karlheinz J. 1956- WhoWor 93
Lehner, Paul Michael 1941- WhoSSW 93
Lehner, Peter MiSFD 9
Lehner, Richard Anthony 1946- WhoEmL 93
Lehner, Theo 1947- WhoScE 91-4
Lehner, Thomas WhoScE 91-1
Lehner, Urban Charles 1947- WhoAm 92
Lehnerd, Alvin P. 1928- St&PR 93
Lehnert, Bo P. 1926- WhoScE 91-4
Lehnert, Herbert Hermann 1925- WhoAm 92
Lehnert, J.H. Law&B 92
Lehnert, Lawrence A., Jr. 1957- St&PR 93
Lehnert, Rick 1957- St&PR 93
Lehnertz, Klaus 1960- WhoScE 91-3
Lehning, Herve Robert 1948- WhoWor 93
Lehnus, Gary Lee 1945- St&PR 93
Lehoczky, Dezso 1927- WhoScE 91-4
Lehoczky, John Paul 1943- WhoAm 92
Lehoczky, Laszlo 1921- WhoScE 91-4
Lehr, Barbara Augusta 1924- WhoE 93
Lehr, David 1910- WhoE 93
Lehr, Dwight Arden 1935- St&PR 93
Lehr, Ellen Delores 1920- WhoWrEP 92
Lehr, Erwin W. 1928- St&PR 93
Lehr, Gustav J. 1929- WhoIns 93
Lehr, Harvey Glenn 1937- St&PR 93
Lehr, Janet 1937- WhoAm 92
Lehr, Lewis Wylie 1921- St&PR 93, WhoAm 92
Lehr, Meredith L. Law&B 92
Lehr, Norma 1930- SmATA 71 [port]
Lehr, Rodger W., Jr. Law&B 92
Lehr, Roland 1912- St&PR 93
Lehr, Sheila M. Law&B 92
Lehr, Susan E. Law&B 92
Lehr, William, Jr. 1940- St&PR 93, WhoAm 92
Lehrach, Hans 1946- WhoScE 91-1
Lehrack, Otto J(ohn), III 1938- ConAu 139

Lehrer, James 1934- JrnUS
Lehrer, James Charles 1934- WhoAm 92, WhoWrEP 92
Lehrer, James M. Law&B 92
Lehrer, Joel Fredric 1941- WhoE 93
Lehrer, Kate 1939- ConAu 138
Lehrer, Kenneth Eugene 1946- WhoAm 92, WhoSSW 93
Lehrer, Leonard 1935- WhoAm 92
Lehrer, Merrill Clark 1955- WhoEmL 93
Lehrer, Paul Michael 1941- WhoE 93
Lehrer, Paulette M. 1949- WhoAmW 93
Lehrer, Stanley 1929- WhoAm 92, WhoWrEP 92
Lehrer, Thomas Andrew 1928- WhoAm 92
Lehrer, Warren I. 1955- WhoWrEP 92
Lehrer, William M. 1925- St&PR 93
Lehrhaupt, Charles M. Law&B 92
Lehritter, Anna Maria 1762-1783 See Righini, Vincenzo 1756-1812 OxDcOp
Lehrkind, H. Thompson Law&B 92
Lehrle, Roy Sherwin 1930- WhoWor 93
Lehrling, Terry James 1950- WhoEmL 93
Lehrman, Carol Anne 1955- WhoAmW 93
Lehrman, David 1936- WhoSSW 93
Lehrman, Irving 1911- WhoAm 92
Lehrman, Joseph 1924- St&PR 93
Lehrman, Leonard J(ordan) 1949- Baker 92
Lehrman, Lewis Edward 1938- WhoAm 92
Lehrman, Margaret McBride 1944- WhoAm 92
Lehrman, Maurice Allen 1925- St&PR 93
Lehrman, Michael L. 1932- St&PR 93
Lehrman, Nat 1929- WhoAm 92
Lehrman, Roy Edward 1953- WhoSSW 93, WhoWor 93
Lehtinen, Ileana Ros- BioIn 17, NotHsAW 93
Lehtinen, Pentti U. WhoScE 91-4
Lehtinen, Seppo Ilmari 1937- WhoWor 93
Lehto, Arto Juhani 1941- WhoWor 93
Lehto, Jukka Pekka 1944- WhoScE 91-4
Lehto, O. WhoScE 91-4
Lehto, Olli Erkki 1925- WhoWor 93
Lehtokangas, Martti WhoScE 91-4
Lehtonen, Maija Helena Maria 1924- WhoWor 93
Lehtonen, P.O. Johannes B. 1942- WhoScE 91-4
Lei, Jose 1930- WhoAsAP 91
Lei, Kuan-Shaur 1955- WhoEmL 93, WhoSSW 93
Leib, David Law&B 92
Leib, Franklin A(llen) 1944- ConAu 138
Leib, Joseph M. 1909- St&PR 93
Leibacher, John William 1941- WhoAm 92
Leibel, Dennis R. Law&B 92
Leibell, John J. Law&B 92
Leibenguth, Friedrich 1939- WhoScE 91-3
Leiber, Deborah Weiss Law&B 92
Leiber, Fritz 1910- WhoWrEP 92
Leiber, Fritz 1910-1992 BioIn 17, ScF&FL 92
Leiber, Fritz, Jr. d1992 NewYTBS 92
Leiber, Fritz, Jr. 1910- WhoAm 92
Leiber, Fritz (Reuter, Jr.) 1910-1992 ConAu 139, -40NR, SmATA 73
Leiber, Gerson August 1921- WhoAm 92
Leiber, Jerry 1933- BioIn 17 See Also Leiber & Stoller SoulM
Leiber, Judith BioIn 17
Leiber, Judith Maria 1921- WhoAm 92
Leiber, Justin 1938- ScF&FL 92
Leiber, Justin Fritz 1938- ConAu 39NR
Leiber & Stoller SoulM
Leibert, Karen Ann 1947- WhoAmW 93
Leibert, Richard William 1948- WhoEmL 93
Leibetseder, Josef 1934- WhoScE 91-4
Leibfritz, Dieter W. 1944- WhoScE 91-3, WhoWor 93
Leibholz, Stephen Wolfgang 1932- WhoAm 92
Leibig, Gloria Ann 1943- WhoAmW 93
Leibler, Isi Joseph 1934- WhoWor 93
Leibler, Jack Law&B 92
Leibler, Kenneth R. 1949- St&PR 93
Leibler, Kenneth Robert 1949- WhoAm 92
Leiblum, Mark David 1938- WhoWor 93
Leiblum, Sandra Risa 1943- WhoE 93
Leibman, Morris I. 1911-1992 BioIn 17
Leibman, Neil M. 1960- WhoEmL 93
Leibman, Ron 1937- WhoAm 92
Leibniz, Gottfried Wilhelm, Freiherr von 1646-1716 BioIn 17
Leibold, Arthur William, Jr. 1931- WhoAm 92
Leibold, Charles Howard 1954- St&PR 93
Leibold, Jay 1957- ScF&FL 92
Leibovit, Arnold 1950- MiSFD 9
Leibovit, Arnold L. 1950- St&PR 93
Leibovitz, Annie BioIn 17
Leibovitz, Annie 1949- WhoAm 92, WhoAmW 93
Leibovitz, Jehoshwa 1931- St&PR 93
Leibovitz, Maury 1917-1992 BioIn 17
Leibovitz, Maury P. 1917-1992 NewYTBS 92
Leibovitz, Mitchell G. BioIn 17
Leibovitz, Mitchell G. 1945- St&PR 93, WhoAm 92
Leibovitz, Morris Phillip 1917- St&PR 93
Leibow, Catherine Ann 1956- WhoAmW 93
Leibow, Lois May 1937- WhoAmW 93
Leibow, Ronald Louis 1939- WhoAm 92
Leibowitz, Ann G. Law&B 92
Leibowitz, Bernard 1930- St&PR 93
Leibowitz, Bernice 1929- WhoE 93
Leibowitz, George 1937- St&PR 93
Leibowitz, Herbert Akiba 1935- WhoAm 92, WhoWrEP 92
Leibowitz, Howard Allan 1941- St&PR 93
Leibowitz, Irwin 1906-1991 BioIn 17
Leibowitz, Jack Richard WhoAm 92
Leibowitz, Judith BioIn 17
Leibowitz, Marvin 1950- WhoWor 93
Leibowitz, Melvin Law&B 92
Leibowitz, Mitchell J. 1943- St&PR 93
Leibowitz, Norman 1947- WhoE 93
Leibowitz, Paul Jason 1941- WhoE 93
Leibowitz, Rene 1913-1972 Baker 92
Leibowitz, Sam St&PR 93
Leibowitz, Sidney WhoScE 91-1
Leibowitz, Yeshayahu 1903- BioIn 17
Leibrecht, John Joseph 1930- WhoAm 92
Leibsohn, Jacqueline Wendy 1961- WhoAmW 93
Leibsohn, Ludwig 1939- WhoE 93
Leibson, Charles M. 1929- WhoAm 92, WhoSSW 93
Leibson, Irving 1926- St&PR 93, WhoAm 92
Leibson, Mitchell H. 1952- St&PR 93
Leibtag, Bernard 1950- WhoE 93
Leibu, Henry Joachim 1921- WhoE 93
Leiby, Bruce Richard 1947- WhoE 93, WhoEmL 93, WhoWor 93
Leiby, Jack Leroy 1942- St&PR 93
Leiby, Richard Arthur 1954- WhoE 93
Leiby, Rodney Lloyd 1950- St&PR 93
Leicester, Robert Dudley, Earl of 1532?-1588 BioIn 17
Leich, H. 1941- WhoScE 91-2
Leich, John Foster 1920- WhoE 93
Leich, Mildred C. 1912- St&PR 93
Leich, Robert M., Jr. 1943- St&PR 93
Leich, Roland (Jacobi) 1911- Baker 92
Leicher, Bruce Law&B 92
Leichhardt, Ludwig 1813-1848 Expl 93 [port]
Leichliter, Van H., Jr. Law&B 92
Leichnitz, Kurt 1932- WhoScE 91-3
Leicht, R. T. 1951- WhoE 93
Leicht, Theodore M. 1927- St&PR 93
Leicht, Thomas E. 1950- WhoIns 93
Leichtentritt, Hugo 1874-1951 Baker 92
Leichter, Larry R. ScF&FL 92
Leichtling, Michael Alfred 1943- WhoAm 92
Leichtman, Harry MacGregor 1949- WhoE 93
Leick, Frederick William 1943- St&PR 93, WhoAm 92
Leidel, Frederick Otto 1916- WhoAm 92
Leidel, Peter A. 1956- St&PR 93
Leiden, Carl 1922- WhoAm 92
Leiden, Leo 1934- St&PR 93
Leiden, Warren Robert 1949- WhoAm 92
Leider, Frida 1888-1975 Baker 92, IntDcOp, OxDcOp
Leider, Gerald J. 1931- WhoAm 92
Leidesdorf, Arthur 1918-1991 BioIn 17
Leidheiser, Henry, Jr. 1920- WhoAm 92
Leidiger, Mary Lou 1927- WhoAmW 93
Leidner, Harold Edward 1937- WhoAm 92
Leidy, Bonnie Carol 1960- WhoWor 93
Leidy, Joseph 1823-1891 IntDcAn
Leidy, Katherine Anne Brown 1967- WhoAmW 93
Leidy, William Austin 1948- St&PR 93
Leier, Peter Michael Law&B 92
Leies, John Alex 1926- WhoAm 92
Leifer, Calvin 1929- WhoAm 92
Leifer, Jane A. Law&B 92
Leifer, Marvin William 1945- WhoE 93
Leifer, Neil MiSFD 9
Leifer, Neil 1943- BioIn 17
Leifer, Richard 1942- WhoE 93
Leiferkus, Sergey 1946- OxDcOp
Leiferman, Silvia Weiner WhoWor 93
Leiferman, Sylvia Weiner d1991 BioIn 17
Leifield, Albert Peter 1883-1970 BiDAMSp 1989
Leifman, Howard David 1956- WhoE 93
Leifs, Jon 1899-1968 Baker 92
Leigh, B. 1939- WhoScE 91-3
Leigh, Beverly E., Mr. 1924- St&PR 93
Leigh, David John WhoScE 91-1
Leigh, Fredric Homer 1940- AfrAmBi
Leigh, George Jeffery WhoScE 91-1
Leigh, James Ronald WhoScE 91-1
Leigh, Janet BioIn 17
Leigh, Janet 1927- IntDcF 2-3, WhoAm 92
Leigh, Jennifer Jason BioIn 17
Leigh, Jennifer Jason 1958- WhoAm 92
Leigh, Jennifer Jason 1962- CurBio 92 [port], WhoAmW 93
Leigh, Linda BioIn 17
Leigh, Linda Diane 1946- WhoAmW 93
Leigh, Lynn Laverne 1925- St&PR 93
Leigh, Marlisa Kay MacLeod 1965- WhoEmL 93
Leigh, Michael I. 1952- St&PR 93
Leigh, Mike 1943- BioIn 17, MiSFD 9
Leigh, Mitch 1928- Baker 92
Leigh, Monroe 1919- WhoAm 92
Leigh, Penny 1963- WhoSSW 93
Leigh, Penny Ruth WhoAmW 93, WhoE 93
Leigh, Peter Nigel WhoScE 91-1
Leigh, Robert 1949- WhoUN 92
Leigh, Roger Allen WhoScE 91-1
Leigh, Shari Greer 1959- WhoAmW 93, WhoEmL 93
Leigh, Sherren 1942- WhoAm 92, WhoAmW 93
Leigh, Stephen 1931- WhoAm 92, WhoE 93, WhoWor 93
Leigh, Stephen 1951- ScF&FL 92
Leigh, Vivien 1913-1967 IntDcF 2-3 [port]
Leigh, W. Colston d1992 NewYTBS 92 [port]
Leigh, W(illiam) Colston 1901-1992 CurBio 92N
Leigh, Walter 1905-1942 Baker 92, OxDcOp
Leigh, Wendy 1950- BioIn 17
Leigh-Hunt, Barbara 1935- ConTFT 10
Leigh-Manuell, Robert Allen 1942- WhoSSW 93
Leighninger, Sally Heinz 1950- WhoEmL 93
Leigh-Pemberton, Robert Robin 1927- WhoWor 93
Leight, Betsy Levy 1946- WhoEmL 93
Leighten, Edward Henry 1914- WhoAm 92
Leighten, Patricia 1946- WhoE 93, WhoEmL 93
Leightner, Joseph F. Law&B 92
Leighton, Charles M. 1935- St&PR 93
Leighton, David Struan Robertson 1928- WhoAm 92
Leighton, Dorothea C. 1908-1989 IntDcAn
Leighton, Edward ScF&FL 92
Leighton, Etta Veronica 1880- AmWomPl
Leighton, Frances Spatz WhoAm 92, WhoWor 93, WhoWrEP 92
Leighton, George Neves 1912- WhoAm 92
Leighton, Grace R. AmWomPl
Leighton, Isabel AmWomPl
Leighton, John Crichton 1925- WhoAm 92
Leighton, Joseph 1921- WhoAm 92
Leighton, Kenneth 1929-1988 Baker 92
Leighton, Kim Gregory 1952- WhoSSW 93
Leighton, Lawrence Ward 1934- WhoAm 92, WhoE 93
Leighton, Leslie Steven 1952- WhoEmL 93, WhoSSW 93
Leighton, Miriam WhoAmW 93
Leighton, Nancy L. Law&B 92
Leighton, Paul J. 1933- St&PR 93
Leighton, Paul Joe 1953- WhoAm 92
Leighton, Robert Benjamin 1919- WhoAm 92
Leighton, William c. 1565-1622 Baker 92
Leigner, Joseph William, III 1946- WhoSSW 93
Leih, Grace Janet 1936- WhoWrEP 92
Leijonhufvud, Axel Stig Bengt 1933- WhoAm 92
Leiken, Earl Murray 1942- WhoAm 92
Leikin, William F. Law&B 92
Leikola, Matti E.H. 1935- WhoScE 91-4
Leiman, Brad 1955- WhoCanL 92
Leiman, Herbert M. Law&B 92
Leiman, Joan Maisel 1934- WhoE 93
Leiman, Sid Zalman 1941- WhoAm 92
Leimas, Brooke ScF&FL 92
Leimbach, Marti BioIn 17
Leimer, Jacqueline A. Law&B 92
Leimer, Kurt 1920-1974 Baker 92
Leimer, Phyllis Hancock 1936- WhoAmW 93, WhoE 93
Leimert, Judith Hane Law&B 92
Lei Mingqiu WhoAsAP 91
Leimkuehler, Jon P. 1948- St&PR 93
Leimkuhler, Ferdinand Francis 1928- WhoAm 92
Leimkuhler, Gerard Joseph 1948- St&PR 93
Leimkuhler, Gerard Joseph, Jr. 1948- WhoAm 92
Leimon, Rebecca Oglesby 1949- WhoSSW 93
Lein, Charles D. 1941- WhoAm 92
Lein, Hebe Beatriz 1945- WhoAmW 93
Lein, John Nave 1926- WhoAm 92
Lein, Malcolm Emil 1913- WhoAm 92
Lein, R.P. 1931- St&PR 93
Leinbach, Joseph K. 1934- St&PR 93
Leinbach, Peter T. 1951- St&PR 93
Leinbach, Philip Eaton 1935- WhoAm 92
Leinberger, Christopher Brown 1951- WhoWor 93
Leindler, Laszlo 1935- WhoScE 91-4
Leinenkugel, Krista Silar Law&B 92
Leinenweber, Harry Daniel 1937- WhoAm 92
Leiner, Murray J. 1929- WhoE 93
Leiner, Wolfgang 1925- WhoWor 93
Leing, George Law&B 92
Leingang, Henry J. 1949- St&PR 93
Leinhardt, Jeanne E. Law&B 92
Leinhart, Philip H. 1960- St&PR 93
Leinieks, Valdis 1932- WhoAm 92, WhoWor 93
Leinikki, Pauli O. 1941- WhoScE 91-4
Leininger, Alan R. 1955- St&PR 93
Leininger, Barbara Burke 1944- WhoAmW 93
Leininger, Kenneth Alan 1924- St&PR 93
Leininger, Madeleine WhoAmW 93
Leininger, Madeleine Monica 1925- WhoAm 92
Leininger, Robert 1946- ScF&FL 92
Leininger, Robert E. Law&B 92
Leino, Deanna Rose 1937- WhoAmW 93
Leinonen, Tatu E. 1938- WhoScE 91-4
Leinonen, Tatu Einari 1938- WhoWor 93
Leinsdorf, Erich 1912- Baker 92, IntDcOp, OxDcOp, WhoAm 92
Leinss, Edward Albert 1941- St&PR 93
Leinster, Colin Ronald 1939- WhoWrEP 92
Leinster, Murray 1896-1975 BioIn 17, ScF&FL 92
Leinweber, Bruce Kornblatt 1935- WhoE 93
Leiper, Esther M. 1946- WhoWrEP 92
Leipertz, Alfred 1946- WhoWor 93
Leipham, Jay Edward 1946- WhoEmL 93
Leipold, Paul Arthur Law&B 92
Leipold, William Charles, Jr. 1949- WhoEmL 93
Leiponen, Hannu WhoScE 91-4
Leipper, Dale Frederick 1914- WhoAm 92
Leipsner, Steven BioIn 17
Leipzig, Arthur 1918- WhoAm 92
Leipzig, Libby Black 1925- WhoAmW 93
Leiris, Michel 1901-1990 BioIn 17, IntDcAn
Leis, Brian Norman 1947- WhoEmL 93
Leis, Henry Patrick, Jr. 1914- WhoAm 92, WhoE 93, WhoWor 93
Leis, Philip Edward 1931- WhoAm 92
Leis, Winogene B. 1919- WhoAmW 93, WhoSSW 93, WhoWor 93
Leisching, Eduard 1858-1938 BioIn 17
Leisen, Mitchell 1898-1972 MiSFD 9N
Leisenring, Edward B., Jr. 1926- St&PR 93
Leiser, Burton Myron 1930- WhoAm 92
Leiser, Clara d1991 BioIn 17
Leiser, Ernest Stern 1921- WhoAm 92
Leiser, Thomas Edward 1938- St&PR 93
Leisewitz, Johann Anton 1752-1806 BioIn 17
Leish, Kenneth William 1936- WhoAm 92
Leisher, George Loy, Jr. 1945- WhoAm 92
Leisher, William R. 1941-1992 NewYTBS 92
Leisher, William Rodger 1941- WhoAm 92
Leishman, John Gordon 1958- WhoE 93
Leishman, Judy Dean Law&B 92
Leishman, Marista Muriel 1932- WhoWor 93
Leishman, Thomas W. Law&B 92
Leising, Jean WhoAmW 93
Leisinger, Thomas 1936- WhoScE 91-4
Leisk, David (Johnson) 1906-1975 MajAI [port]
Leisler, Jacob 1640-1691 HarEnMi
Leisman, Gerald 1947- WhoE 93
Leisner, David 1953- Baker 92
Leisola, Matti Sipi Antero 1947- WhoScE 91-4
Leiss, Michael Thomas 1964- WhoSSW 93
Leiss, Peter 1939- St&PR 93
Leissa, Arthur William 1931- WhoAm 92, WhoWor 93
Leist, Elisabeth Pasek 1927- WhoAmW 93
Leist, Joseph Anthony 1945- WhoE 93
Leist, Ronald Robert 1937- St&PR 93
Leisten, Arthur G. Law&B 92
Leisten, Arthur Gaynor 1941- St&PR 93, WhoAm 92
Leister, Kenneth W. 1921- St&PR 93
Leister, Lori Ann 1962- WhoE 93

Leister, Mary McFarland 1917- *WhoWrEP 92*
Leister, Thomas A. 1959- *St&PR 93*
Leistner, Dieter 1952- *BioIn 17*
Leistner, Eckhard W. 1941- *WhoScE 91-3*
Leistner, Lothar E.E. 1927- *WhoScE 91-3*
Leisure, David 1950?- *ConTFT 10*
Leisure, George Stanley, Jr. 1924- *WhoAm 92*
Leisure, Peter Keeton 1929- *WhoAm 92*
Leisy, William Bernard 1957- *WhoSSW 93*
Leisz, George Webster 1923- *St&PR 93*
Leisz, Stuart Joseph 1931- *St&PR 93*
Leitao Da Cunha, Pedro Horacio J.M. 1933- *St&PR 93*
Leitch, Alma May 1924- *WhoAm 92, WhoSSW 93*
Leitch, Christopher *MiSFD 9*
Leitch, Daniel, III 1933- *St&PR 93*
Leitch, Donovan *Baker 92*
Leitch, Gordon James 1937- *WhoAm 92*
Leitch, John D. 1921- *St&PR 93*
Leitch, John Daniel 1921- *WhoAm 92*
Leitch, Maurice 1933- *ConAu 40NR*
Leitch, Monty Simmons 1950- *WhoSSW 93*
Leitch, Patricia 1933- *ScF&FL 92*
Leitch, Robert E. 1918- *St&PR 93*
Leitch, Robert Roy *WhoScE 91-1*
Leite, Alberto 1944- *WhoScE 91-3*
Leite, Antonio (Joaquim) da Silva 1759-1833 *Baker 92*
Leite, Carlos Alberto 1939- *WhoWor 93*
Leite, Eduardo Cerqueira 1950- *WhoAm 92*
Leite, Yolanda A.C. *Law&B 92*
Leite de Faria, Hernani J. Schwinghammer 1955- *WhoWor 93*
Leiter, Daniel N. 1940- *WhoAm 92*
Leiter, Daniel Norman 1940- *St&PR 93*
Leiter, Donald Eugene 1932- *WhoE 93*
Leiter, Elliot 1933- *WhoAm 92*
Leiter, Michael *St&PR 93*
Leiter, Peter *Law&B 92*
Leiter, Richard Allen 1952- *WhoEmL 93*
Leiter, Robert Allen 1949- *WhoAm 92*
Leiter, William C. 1939- *St&PR 93, WhoAm 92*
Leitereg, Elizabeth E. *Law&B 92*
Leitereg, Theodore J. *Law&B 92*
Leiterer, Jurgen 1945- *WhoWor 93*
Leiterstein, Steven Jay 1947- *WhoE 93*
Leites, Dimitry Alexander 1951- *WhoWor 93*
Leith, Cecil Eldon, Jr. 1923- *WhoAm 92*
Leith, Donald W. *St&PR 93*
Leith, Emmett Norman 1927- *WhoAm 92*
Leith, James Clark 1937- *WhoAm 92*
Leith, John Haddon 1919- *WhoAm 92*
Leith, Robert Morrison *St&PR 93*
Leith, Roderick Gordon 1928- *WhoAm 92*
Leith, William T. *St&PR 93*
Leithauser, Brad *BioIn 17*
Leithauser, Brad 1953- *DcLB 120 [port], ScF&FL 92*
Leithliter, H.T. 1949- *St&PR 93*
Leithold, Becky Jean 1961- *WhoAmW 93*
Leitmann, George 1925- *WhoAm 92*
Leitner, Alfred 1921- *WhoAm 92*
Leitner, Anthony J. *Law&B 92*
Leitner, David Larry 1956- *WhoEmL 93*
Leitner, Elliot 1930- *St&PR 93, WhoIns 93*
Leitner, Ferdinand 1912- *Baker 92, OxDcOp*
Leitner, Gerhard Wolfgang 1944- *WhoWor 93*
Leitner, Gregory Marc 1957- *WhoEmL 93*
Leitner, Isabella *BioIn 17*
Leitner, Mary Hathaway 1914- *St&PR 93*
Leitner, Melinda Jo 1958- *WhoE 93*
Leitner, Paul R. 1928- *WhoAm 92*
Leitner, Wilhelm 1926- *WhoScE 91-4*
Leitschuh, Cheryl Ann 1955- *WhoEmL 93*
Leitz, Jerry 1957- *St&PR 93*
Leitzbach, Adeline M. *AmWomPl*
Leitzell, Terry Lee 1942- *WhoAm 92*
Leitzinger, Sandra Mayes 1936- *WhoAmW 93*
Leitzmann, Albert 1867-1950 *Baker 92*
Leitzmann, Claus 1933- *WhoScE 91-3*
Leiva, Raul 1916- *DcMexL*
Leivesley, Thomas Leonard, Jr. 1923- *St&PR 93*
Leivick, David *MiSFD 9*
Leiviska, Helvi (Lemmikki) 1902-1982 *Baker 92*
Leizear, Charles William 1922- *WhoAm 92*
Leja, Joseph R., Jr. 1953- *St&PR 93*
Lejarraga, Pablo 1948- *WhoSSW 93*
Lejeune, Andree *WhoCanL 92*
Le Jeune, Claude c. 1528-1600 *Baker 92*
LeJeune, Dennis Edward 1942- *WhoAm 92*
Lejeune, Ferdy J. 1939- *WhoScE 91-2*
Le Jeune, Francis Ernest, Jr. 1929- *WhoAm 92*
Lejeune, Jerome Jean Louis 1926- *WhoScE 91-2*
LeJeune, Joseph Guillaume 1914- *WhoWor 93*
Lejeune, Pierre M.G.R. 1937- *WhoScE 91-2*
Lejins, Peter Pierre 1909- *WhoAm 92, WhoWor 93*
Lejnieks, L. Arno 1928- *St&PR 93*
Lejuez, Robert Michel 1933- *WhoScE 91-2*
Leka, Donald G. *Law&B 92*
Leka, George T. *St&PR 93*
Lekan, Thomas J. *BioIn 17*
Lekapenos *OxDcByz*
Lekapenos, George *OxDcByz*
Lekas, Mary Despina 1930- *WhoAmW 93*
Lekas, Mitchell Achilles 1922- *St&PR 93*
Lekes, J. *WhoScE 91-4*
Lekes, Jaroslav 1928- *WhoScE 91-4*
Lekeu, Guillaume (Jean Joseph Nicolas) 1870-1894 *Baker 92*
Lekeux, Pierre 1954- *WhoScE 91-2*
Lekhanya, Justin Metsing 1938- *WhoAfr*
Lekis, Lisa 1917- *WhoSSW 93*
Lekkala, Jukka Olavi 1952- *WhoScE 91-4*
Lekki, Walter J. 1938- *St&PR 93*
Lekse, Lynn *BioIn 17*
Lekse, William John 1947- *WhoE 93*
Lekstutis, John Paul 1943- *St&PR 93*
Lekus, Diana Rose 1948- *WhoAmW 93, WhoEmL 93*
Lekven, Jon 1941- *WhoScE 91-4*
L.E.L. 1802-1838 *BioIn 17*
Lelak, John Michael 1934- *St&PR 93*
Leland, Albert Wetmore 1954- *St&PR 93*
Leland, Carol Lynn *BioIn 17*
Leland, Christopher Towne 1951- *WhoWrEP 92*
Leland, David 1947- *MiSFD 9*
Leland, David D. 1935- *WhoAm 92*
Leland, David Dale 1935- *St&PR 93*
Leland, Emily *AmWomPl*
Leland, Harold Robert 1931- *St&PR 93, WhoAm 92*
Leland, Jo 1917- *WhoAmW 93*
Leland, John S. *Law&B 92*
Leland, Joy Hanson 1927- *WhoAm 92*
Leland, Lawrence 1915- *WhoAm 92*
Leland, Leslie *St&PR 93*
Leland, Lowell P. 1907- *ScF&FL 92*
Leland, Marc Ernest 1938- *WhoAm 92*
Leland, Mickey *BioIn 17*
Leland, Paula Susan 1953- *WhoAmW 93, WhoEmL 93*
Leland, Pound 1945- *St&PR 93*
Leland, Richard G. 1949- *WhoAm 92*
Leland, Sara *WhoAm 92*
Leland, Timothy 1937- *WhoAm 92*
Leland, Warren Hanan 1915- *WhoAm 92*
Lelart, Michel Jean 1933- *WhoWor 93*
Lelchuk, Alan 1938- *JeAmFiW, WhoAm 92, WhoWrEP 92*
Lele, Padmakar Pratap 1927- *WhoAm 92*
Leleu, Michel 1938- *WhoScE 91-2*
Lelewel, Joachim 1786-1861 *PolBiDi*
Lelewer, David Kann 1940- *WhoAm 92*
Lelie, P.N. 1955- *WhoScE 91-3*
Lelieveld, Peter 1942- *WhoScE 91-3*
Lelievre, Francois 1951- *WhoScE 91-2*
Lelkes, Janos 1945- *WhoScE 91-4*
Lella, Joseph William 1936- *WhoAm 92*
Lellinger, David Bruce 1937- *WhoE 93*
Lellouch, Joseph *WhoScE 91-2*
Lelogeais, Jean-Louis 1958- *St&PR 93*
Leloglu, N. *WhoScE 91-4*
Lelord, Gilbert Francois 1927- *WhoScE 91-2*
Lelouch, Claude 1937- *BioIn 17, MiSFD 9*
Leloudis, James Linwood, II 1955- *WhoSSW 93*
Lely, James A. *ScF&FL 92*
Lelyveld, Arthur Joseph 1913- *WhoAm 92*
Lelyveld, Gail Annick 1948- *WhoAmW 93, WhoE 93, WhoWor 93*
Lelyveld, Joseph Salem 1937- *WhoAm 92, WhoE 93*
Lem, Richard Douglas 1933- *WhoWor 93*
Lem, Robert K. *Law&B 92*
Lem, Stanislaw *BioIn 17*
Lem, Stanislaw 1921- *PolBiDi, ScF&FL 92*
Lema, Arnold H. 1938- *St&PR 93*
Lema, George R. 1924- *St&PR 93*
Lema, Jo-Anne S. 1947- *WhoE 93*
Lema, Mark Joseph 1949- *WhoE 93*
Lemacher, Heinrich 1891-1966 *Baker 92*
Lemagny, Jean-Claude 1931- *ConAu 136*
LeMahieu, James Joseph 1936- *WhoE 93*
Lemaignan, Clement 1949- *WhoWor 93*
Lemaire, Christian Jacques 1957- *WhoWor 93*
Lemaire, Gilles Joseph 1945- *WhoScE 91-2*
Le Maire, Jacob 1585-1616 *See* Schouten, Willem 1567-1625 & Le Maire, Jacob 1585-1616 *Expl 93*
Lemaire, Jacques E. 1936- *WhoScE 91-2*
Lemaire, Jean c. 1581-c. 1650 *Baker 92*
Lemaire, Jean Eugene Gaston 1854-1928 *Baker 92*
Lemaire, Joseph J. 1928- *St&PR 93*
Lemaire, Luc 1950- *WhoWor 93*
Lemaire, Maurice 1946- *WhoScE 91-2*
Lemaire, Remy 1937- *WhoScE 91-2*
Lemaire, Roger G. 1937- *WhoScE 91-2*
Le Maire, William Jan 1933- *WhoAm 92*
Le Maistre, Charles Aubrey 1924- *WhoSSW 93*
Le Maistre, Christopher William 1938- *WhoAm 92*
Le Maistre, David Joseph 1946- *St&PR 93*
Le Maistre, Mattheus c. 1505-1577 *Baker 92*
Lemaitre, J. *WhoScE 91-2*
Lemaitre, Jean 1934- *WhoScE 91-2*
Le Maitre, Mattheus c. 1505-1577 *Baker 92*
Leman, Eugene D. 1942- *St&PR 93*
Leman, Gerard Mathieu 1851-1920 *HarEnMi*
Leman, Samuel Earl, Jr. 1952- *WhoEmL 93*
Lemanek, Kathleen Lynn 1958- *WhoEmL 93*
Lemann, Bernard 1905- *WhoWrEP 92*
Lemann, Nancy 1956- *ConAu 136*
Lemann, Nicholas *BioIn 17*
Lemann, Nicholas 1954- *ConAu 138*
Lemann, Thomas B. 1926- *St&PR 93*
Lemann, Thomas Berthelot 1926- *WhoAm 92*
Lemanski, D.B. *St&PR 93*
Lemanski, Larry Fredrick 1943- *WhoAm 92, WhoWor 93*
LeMar, Bruce Richard 1946- *St&PR 93*
Lemarbe, Edward Stanley 1952- *St&PR 93, WhoE 93, WhoEmL 93*
Lemarchal, Philippe 1932- *WhoScE 91-2*
Lemarchand, Guillermo Andres 1963- *WhoWor 93*
Lemare, Edwin (Henry) 1865-1934 *Baker 92*
Lemass, Sean 1899-1971 *BioIn 17*
Lemaster, Arthur James 1933- *WhoE 93*
Le Master, Brenda Joyce 1952- *WhoAmW 93*
Le Master, Dennis Clyde 1939- *WhoAm 92*
LeMaster, Jimmie Ray 1934- *WhoSSW 93, WhoWrEP 92*
Lemaster, Kenneth L. *Law&B 92*
Lemaster, Richard L. 1925- *St&PR 93*
LeMaster, Robert Allen 1953- *WhoSSW 93*
LeMaster, Sherry Renee 1953- *WhoAmW 93*
LeMaster, Susan M. 1953- *WhoAmW 93*
Lemasters, John N. *WhoAm 92, WhoSSW 93*
Lemasters, John N. 1933- *St&PR 93*
Lemasters, John Nelson, III 1933- *WhoAm 92*
Lemasters, Steven Craig *WhoIns 93*
Lemattre, Pierre 1931- *WhoScE 91-2*
Le Maure, Catherine-Nicole 1704-1787 *OxDcOp*
Lemay, Andre 1936- *WhoUN 92*
LeMay, Charlotte Zihlman 1919- *WhoAmW 93*
LeMay, Curtis 1906-1990 *ColdWar 1 [port]*
LeMay, Curtis E. 1906- *PolPar*
LeMay, Curtis E. 1906-1990 *BioIn 17*
LeMay, Curtis Emerson 1906- *HarEnMi*
Lemay, Frank M. 1957- *NewYTBS 92 [port]*
Lemay, Harding 1922- *WhoWrEP 92*
Lemay, Helen Lillian Schneider 1947- *WhoAmW 93, WhoSSW 93*
LeMay, Jacques 1940- *WhoAm 92*
LeMay, James Charles *Law&B 92*
LeMay, John L. *BioIn 17*
Le May, Moira Kathleen 1934- *WhoAmW 93, WhoE 93*
LeMay, Nancy 1956- *WhoAmW 93*
LeMay, Nancy Cochran 1955- *WhoAmW 93*
Lemay, Pamphile 1837-1918 *BioIn 17*
Lemay, Phil 1935- *St&PR 93*
Lemay, Raymond 1927- *WhoAm 92*
Lemay, Robert C. 1950- *St&PR 93*
LeMay, Ronald *St&PR 93*
LeMay, Ronald T. *WhoAm 92*
Lembcke, Paul Anthony *BioIn 17*
Lembeck, William Jacobs 1928- *WhoSSW 93*
Lemberg, Louis 1916- *WhoAm 92*
Lemberg, Thomas M. *Law&B 92*
Lemberg, Thomas Michael 1946- *WhoAm 92, WhoEmL 93*
Lemberger, August Paul 1926- *WhoAm 92*
Lemberger, Louis 1937- *WhoAm 92*
Lemberger, Nancy Lee 1947- *WhoAmW 93, WhoEmL 93*
Lemberger, Norma 1944- *WhoE 93*
Lembitz, Edward Lawrence 1926- *WhoAm 92*
Lembke, A. *WhoScE 91-3*
Lembke, Janet 1933- *WhoWrEP 92*
Lembke, Janet Nutt 1933- *WhoSSW 93*
Lembo, Francine Elizabeth 1942- *St&PR 93*
Lembo, Gloria Ann 1949- *St&PR 93, WhoE 93*
Lembo, Keith *Law&B 92*
Lembo, Keith Douglas *Law&B 92*
Lembo, Michele Manzo 1961- *WhoAmW 93*
Lembo, Susan Ann 1961- *WhoAmW 93*
Lembong, Johannes Tarcicius 1930- *WhoWor 93*
Lemboris, Eric 1955- *WhoSSW 93*
Lemco, Jonathan 1956- *ConAu 139*
Lemco, Jonathan Martin 1956- *WhoE 93*
Lemcoe, M. Marshall 1921- *WhoAm 92*
LeMehaute, Bernard Jean 1927- *WhoAm 92*
Lemeki, Jacob 1941- *WhoAsAP 91*
Lemelin, Roger 1919- *BioIn 17*
Lemelin, Roger 1919-1992 *WhoCanL 92*
Le Melle, Gerald Anthony 1962- *WhoWor 93*
LeMelle, Tilden John 1929- *WhoAm 92*
Lemelman, Bernard *Law&B 92*
Lemelson, Jerome *WhoAm 92*
Lemelson, Jerome H. *NewYTBS 92 [port]*
Lemen, Deborah Jean 1959- *WhoAmW 93*
Le Men, Jean-Francois 1941- *WhoScE 91-2*
Lemen, Richard Alan 1943- *WhoAm 92*
Lemeni, Nicola Makedon Rossi- 1920-1991 *BioIn 17*
Lemens, William Vernon, Jr. 1935- *WhoSSW 93, WhoWor 93*
LeMense, Rodney Anthony 1937- *St&PR 93*
Lementowski, Michal 1943- *WhoE 93, WhoWor 93*
Lemer, Albert 1926- *St&PR 93*
Lemer, Jeanne fl. 1845- *BioIn 17*
Lemerise, Elizabeth Ann 1952- *WhoSSW 93*
Lemerle, Paul 1903-1989 *BioIn 17*
Lemert, James Bolton 1935- *WhoAm 92*
Lemery, Francis Patton 1939- *St&PR 93*
Lemery, J.L. 1941- *St&PR 93*
Lemesh, Nicholas Thomas 1946- *WhoAm 92*
Lemeshev, Sergei (Yakovlevich) 1902-1977 *Baker 92*
Lemeshev, Sergey 1902-1977 *OxDcOp*
Lemessurier, William James 1926- *St&PR 93*
le Mesurier, John 1912-1983 *QDrFCA 92 [port]*
Lemesurier, Peter *ConAu 40NR*
LeMesurier, Stuart William *Law&B 92*
Lemeur, Henry E. 1931- *St&PR 93*
Lemeur, Patricia McGrath 1932- *St&PR 93*
Lemeur, William T. 1956- *St&PR 93*
Le Mevel, B.P. *WhoScE 91-2*
LeMiere, Marie Jeanne 1733-1786 *See* Larrivee, Henri 1737-1802 *OxDcOp*
Lemieux, Annette Rose 1957- *WhoAmW 93*
LeMieux, Guy Frederic 1929- *St&PR 93*
Lemieux, John Napoleon *Law&B 92*
Lemieux, Joseph H. 1931- *St&PR 93*
Lemieux, Joseph Henry 1931- *WhoAm 92*
LeMieux, Linda Dailey 1953- *WhoAmW 93*
Lemieux, Mario *BioIn 17*
Lemieux, Mario 1965- *WhoAm 92*
Lemieux, Pamela 1959- *St&PR 93*
Lemieux, Raymond Urgel 1920- *WhoAm 92*
Lemieux-Levesque, Alice 1910-1983 *WhoCanL 92*
Leming, Christopher Edward 1956- *WhoSSW 93*
Leming, Donna Faye 1957- *WhoSSW 93*
Leming, Marcia Lou 1934- *St&PR 93*
Leming, William Vaughn 1945- *WhoSSW 93*
Le Minor, L. *WhoScE 91-2*
Lemire, Daniel J. *Law&B 92*
Lemire, David H. 1947- *St&PR 93*
Lemire, David Stephen 1949- *WhoEmL 93*
Lemire, James H. 1948- *St&PR 93*
Lemire, Jerome Albert 1947- *WhoEmL 93*
Lemkau, Paul V. d1992 *NewYTBS 92*
Lemkau, Paul Victor 1909-1992 *BioIn 17*
Lemke, Carlton Edward 1920- *WhoWrEP 92*
Lemke, Clark Elliott 1946- *WhoEmL 93*
Lemke, Corrine LaRue 1934- *WhoAmW 93*
Lemke, Donald Ervin 1948- *St&PR 93*
Lemke, James Underwood 1929- *WhoAm 92*
Lemke, Jay Lawrence 1946- *WhoE 93*

Lemke, John R. Law&B 92
Lemke, John Raymond 1941- St&PR 93
Lemke, Judith A. 1952- WhoEmL 93
Lemke, Michael Alois 1951- WhoEmL 93
Lemke, Paul Arenz 1937- WhoAm 92, WhoSSW 93
Lemke, Peter William 1941- St&PR 93
Lemke, Richard Warren 1953- WhoEmL 93, WhoSSW 93
Lemke, Ted St&PR 93
Lemke, Todd C. Law&B 92
Lemke, William 1878-1950 PolPar
Lemle, Robert S. Law&B 92
Lemle, Robert Spencer 1953- WhoAm 92, WhoE 93, WhoEmL 93, WhoWor 93
Lemley, Barbara Wink 1930- WhoE 93
Lemley, Douglas Edwin 1956- WhoSSW 93
Lemley, Jack K. BioIn 17
Lemley, Jack Kenneth 1935- St&PR 93, WhoAm 92
Lemley, Steven Smith 1945- WhoAm 92
Lemley, Thomas Blair 1945- St&PR 93
Lemli, Joseph 1928- WhoScE 91-2
Lemm, Richard 1946- WhoCanL 92
Lemme, Charles D. Law&B 92
Lemmens, Jacques Nicolas 1823-1881 Baker 92
Lemmens-Sherrington, Helen 1834-1906 Baker 92
Lemmer, Bjorn 1942- WhoScE 91-3
Lemmer, William C. Law&B 92
Lemmermen, Jay Charles 1948- WhoEmL 93, WhoSSW 93
Lemmert, D. Gail 1942- WhoSSW 93
Lemmo, James MiSFD 9
Lemmon, Harry Thomas 1930- WhoSSW 93
Lemmon, Jack BioIn 17
Lemmon, Jack 1925- IntDcF 2-3 [port], MiSFD 9, QDrFCA 92 [port], WhoAm 92
Lemmon, Marcia Hilary 1958- WhoEmL 93
Lemmon, Marilyn Sue 1939- WhoAmW 93, WhoWor 93
Lemmon, William Thomas, Jr. 1934- WhoE 93
Lemmond, Charles D., Jr. WhoE 93
Lemmond, Mary Sheldon 1945- WhoSSW 93
Lemmonds, Douglas Harper 1947- WhoE 93
Lemmons, James Curtis 1948- St&PR 93
Lemmons, Jerry A. 1937- St&PR 93
Lemmons, Miriam Elise 1932- WhoAmW 93
Lemmons, Patricia Katherine 1957- WhoAmW 93
Lemna, Thomas Edwin 1947- WhoEmL 93
Lemnios, Andrew Zachery 1931- WhoAm 92
Lemnios, William Zachary 1925- WhoE 93
Lemnitz, Tiana 1897- IntDcOp, OxDcOp
Lemnitz, Tiana (Luise) 1897- Baker 92
Lemnitzer, Lyman L. 1899-1988 HarEnMi
Lemnitzer, Lyman Louis 1899-1988 CmdGen 1991 [port]
Le Moal, Michel 1934- WhoScE 91-2
Le Moigne, Albert 1932- WhoScE 91-2
Lemoine, Antoine-Marcel 1753-1816 Baker 92
LeMoine, David Hartley BioIn 17
LeMoine, Fannie J. 1940- WhoAmW 93
LeMoine, Frank Eugene 1953- WhoEmL 93
Lemoine, Henry 1786-1854 Baker 92
Lemoine, Jacques G. 1938- WhoScE 91-2
Le Moine, James MacPherson 1825-1912 BioIn 17
Lemoine, Maurice Jean-Pierre 1947- WhoWor 93
Lemoine, Yves 1943- WhoScE 91-2
Lemoine-Sebastian, Cecile 1931- WhoScE 91-2
Lemole, Gerald Michael 1936- WhoAm 92
Lemon, Ann 1962- BioIn 17
Lemon, Charles Richard 1925- St&PR 93
Lemon, David W. 1945- St&PR 93
Lemon, David William 1945- WhoAm 92
Lemon, George Edward 1907- WhoWrEP 92
Lemon, Henry Martyn 1915- WhoAm 92
Lemon, J.R. 1942- St&PR 93
Lemon, Jerry Wayne 1935- WhoSSW 93
Lemon, L. Gene Law&B 92
Lemon, Leslie Gene 1940- St&PR 93, WhoAm 92
Lemon, Loren J. Law&B 92
Lemon, P.H.R.B. WhoScE 91-1
Lemon, Ralph BioIn 17
Lemon, Robert A., Jr. 1961- St&PR 93
Lemoncelli, John Joseph 1948- WhoE 93
LeMond, Greg 1961?- BioIn 17, ConHero 2 [port]
LeMond, Gregory James 1961- BiDAMSp 1989, WhoAm 92, WhoWor 93
Lemond, Xavier C. Law&B 92
Lemonias, Peter J. 1952- St&PR 93
Lemonick, Aaron 1923- WhoAm 92
Lemonnier, Daniel WhoScE 91-2
Lemons, Albert Lee 1944- WhoSSW 93
Lemons, Jamie BioIn 17
Lemons, Keith David 1954- WhoEmL 93, WhoSSW 93
Lemons, Russell 1939- St&PR 93
Lemons, Thomas F., Jr. Law&B 92
Lemons, Thomas Lowell 1949- WhoSSW 93
Lemont, Cedric Wilmont 1879-1954 Baker 92
Lemont, Paul Edwin 1940- St&PR 93
Lemor, Isaac 1951- St&PR 93
Lemor, Pierre Charles 1933- WhoE 93
Lemorande, Rusty MiSFD 9
Lemos, Carlos Miguel 1962- WhoWor 93
Lemos, Fernando A. 1957- St&PR 93
Lemos, Gloria Elliott 1946- WhoAm 92, WhoAmW 93
Lemos, Ramon Marcelino 1927- WhoAm 92
Lemos, Robert Anthony 1941- St&PR 93
Lemos De Sousa, Manuel Joao 1937- WhoScE 91-3
Le Mouel, Jean-Louis WhoScE 91-2
Lemoyne, Gabriel 1772-1815 See Lemoyne, Jean-Baptiste 1751-1796 Baker 92
LeMoyne, Irve Charles 1939- WhoAm 92
Lemoyne, Jean-Baptise 1751-1796 OxDcOp
Lemoyne, Jean-Baptiste 1751-1796 Baker 92
Lemp, Michael Albert 1937- WhoE 93
Lemperle, Edmund 1933- WhoScE 91-3
Lempert, Karoly 1924- WhoScE 91-4
Lempert, Richard A. 1932- St&PR 93, WhoAm 92
Lempert, Richard Owen 1942- WhoAm 92
Lempert, Spencer N. Law&B 92
Lempicki, Alexander 1922- WhoE 93
Lempicki, Chester P.J. 1947- St&PR 93
Le Muisit, Gilles 1272-1353? BioIn 17
Lemures, Ben ScF&FL 92
Lemuth, Richard F. Law&B 92
Lemyre, Joseph C. 1956- St&PR 93
Lena, Adolph John 1925- WhoE 93
Lenaerts, Lieven A. J. 1943- WhoWor 93
Lenaerts, Rene Bernard (Maria) 1902- Baker 92
Lenaghan, James Michael Law&B 92
Lenahan, Henry J. d1991 BioIn 17
Lenahan, James J. Law&B 92
Lenahan, John T. Law&B 92
Lenahan, Mea Lorraine 1932- WhoWrEP 92
Lenahan, Walter Clair 1934- WhoAm 92
Lenander, Melbert A. 1932- St&PR 93
Lenard, John 1937- WhoE 93
Lenard, Joseph Arvid 1946- WhoSSW 93
Le Nard, Marcel WhoScE 91-2
Lenard, Pal 1925- WhoScE 91-4
Lenard, Patricia M. Law&B 92
Lenardon, Robert Joseph 1928- WhoAm 92
Lenart, Raymond J. 1941- St&PR 93
Lenart, Robert P. Law&B 92
Lenartowicz, Henryk 1939- WhoScE 91-4
Lenartowicz, Stanislaw 1921- DrEEuF
Lenarz, Larry Rudolph 1924- St&PR 93
Le Nay, J. WhoScE 91-2
LeNay, Tom W. 1927- St&PR 93
Lencastre, Eduardo A.C. 1925- WhoScE 91-3
Lence, Robert B. Law&B 92
Lencek, Rado L. 1921- WhoAm 92, WhoWor 93
Lenchin Chetrick, Julianne 1956- WhoEmL 93
Lenclos, Jean Philippe BioIn 17
Lenczewski, Romuald Jozef 1957 WhoWor 93
Lenczowski, Mark Law&B 92
Lendaris, George Gregory 1935- WhoAm 92
Lende, Karen BioIn 17
Lender, Adam 1921- WhoAm 92
Lender, Herman Joseph 1923- WhoAm 92
Lenderking, William Raymond 1934- WhoE 93
Lenderman, Gaynell St&PR 93
Lending, Stephen A. Law&B 92
Lendl, Ivan BioIn 17
Lendl, Ivan 1960- WhoAm 92, WhoWor 93
Lendl, Jennifer Lynn 1951- WhoAmW 93
Lendman, Ernest Martin 1938- St&PR 93
Lendrum, James Thoburn 1907- WhoAm 92
Lendrum, John T. 1927- St&PR 93
Lendvai, Erno 1925- Baker 92
Lendvai, Erwin 1882-1949 Baker 92
Lendvay, Kamillo 1928- Baker 92
Lenehan, Pamela F. 1952- St&PR 93
Lenehan, William Thurman 1930- WhoAm 92
Leneman, Nina Kriz 1943- WhoUN 92
Lenepveu, Charles (Ferdinand) 1840-1910 Baker 92
Lener, Jeno 1894-1948 Baker 92
Lenero, Vicente 1933- DcMexL, SpAmA
Leney, George Willard 1927- WhoE 93, WhoWor 93
Lenfant, Claude Jean-Marie 1928- WhoAm 92
Lenfant, Jacques 1947- WhoScE 91-2
Lenfest, Harold Fitz Gerald 1930- WhoAm 92, WhoWor 93
Leng, Alfonso 1884-1974 Baker 92
Leng, Marc 1935- WhoScE 91-2
Leng, Marguerite Lambert 1926- WhoAmW 93
Leng, Shao Chuan 1921- WhoAm 92
Lengacher, Edward Victor 1942- WhoAm 92
Lengauer, Patricia Gale 1941- WhoAmW 93
Lengel, Diane 1962- WhoE 93
Lengel, Jerome Kenneth 1933- WhoE 93
Lengel, John Robert 1929- St&PR 93
Lengeler, Joseph W. 1937- WhoWor 93
Lengemann, Frederick William 1925- WhoAm 92
Lengemann, Robert Allen 1934- St&PR 93
Lenger, Charlene Jean 1957- WhoEmL 93
L'Engle, Madeleine 1918- BioIn 17, DcAmChF 1960, ScF&FL 92, SmATA 15AS [port], WhoAm 92, WhoAmW 93, WhoWrEP 92
L'Engle, Madeleine (Camp Franklin) 1918- ConAu 39NR, MajAI [port]
Lenglen, Suzanne 1899-1938 BioIn 17
Lengrand, Jean-Claude 1945- WhoScE 91-2
Lengyel, Alfonz 1921- WhoAm 92
Lengyel, Attila 1946- WhoScE 91-4
Lengyel, Cornel Adam 1915- WhoAm 92, WhoWrEP 92
Lengyel, Imre Andras 1934- WhoScE 91-4
Lengyel, Lajos 1937- WhoScE 91-4
Lengyel, Peter Emery 1940- St&PR 93
Lengyel, Tamas 1931- WhoScE 91-4
Lengyel, Zoltan 1949- WhoScE 91-4
Lenhard, John E. Law&B 92
Lenhard, Joseph Andrew 1929- WhoSSW 93
Lenhardt, Alfonso Emanual 1943- AfrAmBi, WhoAm 92
Lenhardt, Benjamin F., Jr. 1940- St&PR 93
Lenhart, Edward R. Law&B 92
Lenhart, Janet Marie 1959- WhoEmL 93
Lenhart, Katharine B. d1992 NewYTBS 92
Lenhart, Peter J. Law&B 92
Lenharth, William Howard 1946- WhoE 93
Lenher, Samuel d1992 NewYTBS 92
Lenher, Samuel 1905- WhoAm 92
Lenherr, Donald William 1940- WhoIns 93
Lenherr, Frederick Keith 1943- WhoAm 92
Lenhoff, Howard Maer 1929- WhoAm 92
Lenich, Martin J. 1959- St&PR 93
Lenig, Larry E., Jr. 1948- St&PR 93
Lenihan, Brian Joseph 1930- BioIn 17
Lenihan, Judith Ann 1939- St&PR 93
Lenihan, Rita 1914-1989 BioIn 17
Lenihan, Robert Joseph, II 1947- WhoEmL 93
Lenihan, Thomas F. Law&B 92
Lenihan, William Farringer 1930- WhoAm 92
Lenihan, William Joseph 1956- WhoEmL 93
Lenihan, Winifred AmWomPl
Le Nihouannen, Jean-Claude 1934- WhoScE 91-2
Lenin, Vladimir Il'ich 1870-1924 BioIn 17, DcTwHis
Lenk, Robert E. 1917- St&PR 93
Lenka, Kahnu Charan 1939- WhoAsAP 91
Lenkaitis, Lewis F. 1943- St&PR 93
Lenke, George H., Jr. 1924- St&PR 93
Lenke, Joanne Marie 1938- WhoAm 92
Lenker, Floyd William 1933- WhoWor 93
Lenker, Robert E. 1928- St&PR 93
Lenkey, Susan Vilma 1910- WhoAmW 93
Lenkiewicz, Robert O. 1942- BioIn 17
Lenkin, Harvey St&PR 93
Lenkoski, Leo Douglas 1925- WhoAm 92
Lenkowicz, Stanley M. Law&B 92
Lenkszus, Donald J. Law&B 92
Lenman, Bruce Philip 1938- WhoAm 92
Lennard, John (Chevening) 1964- ConAu 137
Lennarz, William Joseph 1934- WhoAm 92
Lennerlof, N.O. Lennart 1927- WhoScE 91-4
Lennerstrand, Gunnar 1938- WhoScE 91-4
Lennert, Karl 1921- WhoScE 91-3
Lennes, Gregory 1947- St&PR 93, WhoAm 92
Lennette, Edwin Herman 1908- WhoAm 92
Lennig, Edward Nicholas, III Law&B 92
Lennon, A. Max 1940- WhoAm 92, WhoSSW 93
Lennon, Amelia Oles 1949- WhoAmW 93
Lennon, Anne Marie St&PR 93
Lennon, Anthony G. Law&B 92
Lennon, Brooke Daniel 1939- St&PR 93
Lennon, Cynthia BioIn 17
Lennon, Dennis 1918-1991 AnObit 1991
Lennon, Donald R. 1938- ConAu 139
Lennon, Edward Joseph 1927- WhoAm 92
Lennon, Frank M. 1938- WhoAm 92
Lennon, Frank T. 1942- St&PR 93
Lennon, Harry WhoScE 91-1
Lennon, Harry K. 1917-1990 BioIn 17
Lennon, Jeanne Passante 1958- WhoAmW 93
Lennon, Jimmy d1992 BioIn 17
Lennon, Jimmy, Sr. d1992 NewYTBS 92
Lennon, John 1940-1980 BioIn 17, ConMus 9 [port]
Lennon, John (Winston) 1940-1980 Baker 92
Lennon, Joseph Luke 1919- WhoAm 92
Lennon, Kathleen Anne Law&B 92
Lennon, Marilyn Ellen 1954- WhoAm 92, WhoE 93
Lennon, Michael Anthony WhoScE 91-1
Lennon, Paul Edward St&PR 93
Lennon, Rose T. Law&B 92
Lennon, Sean BioIn 17
Lennon, Terry MiSFD 9
Lennon, Thomas Michael 1942- WhoAm 92
Lennox, Annie 1954- Baker 92
Lennox, Donald D. 1918- St&PR 93
Lennox, Donald Duane 1918- WhoAm 92
Lennox, Edward Newman 1925- WhoSSW 93
Lennox, Gregory P. 1955- St&PR 93
Lennox, Shirley Ann 1931- WhoAmW 93
Lennox, Vincent Joseph, Jr. 1947- WhoEmL 93
Lennox Fisch, Carol Jeanine 1952- WhoAmW 93
Leno, Jay BioIn 17
Leno, Jay 1950- WhoAm 92
Lenoard, Donald G. 1941- St&PR 93
Lenoch, Theodore James 1929- WhoSSW 93
Lenoir, Gloria Cisneros 1951- WhoAmW 93
Lenoir, Gloria Taylor 1928- WhoAmW 93
Lenoir, William Benjamin 1939- WhoAm 92
Lenon, Richard A. 1920- St&PR 93
Lenon, Richard Allen 1920- WhoAm 92
Lenormand, Rene 1846-1932 Baker 92
Le Notre, Andre 1613-1700 BioIn 17
Lenowitz, Arthur BioIn 17
Lenox, Angela Cousineau 1946- WhoAmW 93
Lenox, Kimberly 1965- WhoWrEP 92
Lenox, Mary Frances 1944- WhoAm 92, WhoAmW 93
Lenroot, Katherine F. BioIn 17
Lenrow, Jay Laurence Law&B 92
Lensbower, Jeffrey Lynn 1957- WhoE 93
Lensch, George Edward 1925- St&PR 93
Lenschow, Rolf Johan 1928- WhoWor 93
Lense, Edward Louis 1945- WhoWrEP 92
Lense, Frederick Thomas 1917- St&PR 93
Lensing, Charles Edmond 1930- St&PR 93
Lenski, Gerhard Emmanuel 1924- WhoSSW 93
Lenski, Lois 1893-1974 MajAI [port]
Lenskold, Richard K. 1937- St&PR 93
Lensky, Leib d1991 BioIn 17
Lenson, David 1945- WhoWrEP 92
Lent, Berkeley 1921- WhoAm 92
Lent, Blair 1930- MajAI
Lent, Evangeline M. AmWomPl
Lent, John Anthony 1936- WhoAm 92, WhoWrEP 92
Lent, Norman F. 1931- CngDr 91
Lent, Norman Frederick, Jr. 1931- WhoAm 92, WhoE 93
Lentczner, Bennett 1938- WhoSSW 93
Lente, Shenan BioIn 17
Lenthall, Franklyn 1919- WhoAm 92
Lenton, John Robert WhoScE 91-1
Lents, Don Glaude 1949- St&PR 93
Lents, Peggy Iglauer 1950- WhoEmL 93
Lentsch, Eugene J. 1924- St&PR 93
Lentsch, Karen Lee 1952- WhoAmW 93
Lentz, Bernard Frederic 1948- WhoEmL 93
Lentz, Daniel (Kirkland) 1941- Baker 92
Lentz, Edward T. Law&B 92

Lentz, Harold James 1947- WhoEmL 93
Lentz, Harris M., III ScF&FL 92
Lentz, Kay Shackelford 1946- WhoSSW 93
Lentz, Kevin Thomas 1958- St&PR 93
Lentz, L. Charles 1945- St&PR 93
Lentz, Robert Allen 1950- WhoEmL 93
Lentz, Robert H. Law&B 92
Lentz, Robert Raines 1943- St&PR 93
Lentz, Stanislaw 1861-1920 PolBiDi
Lentz, Susan G. Law&B 92
Lentz, Thomas N. 1948- St&PR 93
Lentz, Vernon E., Jr. St&PR 93
Lenya, Lotte 1898-1981 Baker 92, OxDcOp
Lenyashin, Vladimir Alexeyevich 1940- WhoWor 93
Lenz, Bruce C. 1943- St&PR 93
Lenz, Charles Wangelin 1942- St&PR 93
Lenz, Cynthia Lowe 1951- WhoAmW 93
Lenz, Edward Arnold 1942- WhoAm 92, WhoSSW 93
Lenz, Fred William 1947- St&PR 93
Lenz, Frederick Spalding, Jr. Law&B 92
Lenz, Friedrich A. 1922- WhoScE 91-3
Lenz, Heinz-Josef 1959- WhoWor 93
Lenz, Henry Paul 1925- WhoAm 92
Lenz, Jakob Michael Reinhold 1751-1792 BioIn 17
Lenz, John Joseph 1934- St&PR 93
Lenz, Jurgen WhoScE 91-4
Lenz, Kay 1953- WhoAm 92
Lenz, Millicent ScF&FL 92
Lenz, Otto WhoScE 91-3
Lenz, Robert H. WhoAm 92
Lenz, Robert H. 1939- St&PR 93
Lenz, Siegfried 1926- WhoWor 93
Lenz, Wilhelm von 1809-1883 Baker 92
Lenz, William Harding 1953- WhoE 93, WhoEmL 93
Lenza, Andrew Joseph 1962- St&PR 93
Lenze, Kevin George 1958- WhoSSW 93
Lenzen, Glenn H., Jr. Law&B 92
Lenzen, Louis C. Law&B 92
Lenzen, Wolfgang Mathias 1946- WhoWor 93
Lenzi, Guido 1941- WhoUN 92
Lenzi, Mauro 1933- WhoScE 91-3
Lenzi, Stephen Ernest Law&B 92
Lenzie, Charles A. 1937- St&PR 93
Lenzing, Helmut 1939- WhoWor 93
Lenzini, Arthur Lee 1927- WhoAm 92
Lenzlinger, Hans BioIn 17
Lenzmeier, Allen 1943- St&PR 93
Lenzmeier, Michelle S. Law&B 92
Leo, I c. 400-474 OxDcByz
Leo, II OxDcByz
Leo, II c. 467-474 OxDcByz
Leo, III OxDcByz
Leo, III c. 685-741 OxDcByz
Leo, VI 866-912 OxDcByz
Leo, IX 1002-1054 OxDcByz
Leo, Douglas William 1951- WhoE 93
Leo, Edmund K. 1936- WhoUN 92
Leo, Leonardo 1694-1744 Baker 92, OxDcOp
Leo, Malcolm 1944- MiSFD 9
Leo, Michael S. Law&B 92
Leo, Richard C. 1952- ConAu 139
Leo, Robert G., Jr. Law&B 92
Leo, Robert Joseph 1939- WhoAm 92
Leo, Victor J. Law&B 92
Leodas, Costa G. 1933- St&PR 93
Leodolter, Sepp WhoScE 91-4
Leodora, Anthony E. 1951- WhoE 93
Leo Grammatikos OxDcByz
LeoGrande, William Mark 1949- WhoAm 92
Leokum, Leonard ScF&FL 92
Leon, Arthur Sol 1931- WhoAm 92
Leon, Benjamin Joseph 1932- WhoAm 92
Leon, Bernard S. Law&B 92
Leon, Bruce Frederick 1952- WhoEmL 93, WhoSSW 93
Leon, Bruno 1924- WhoAm 92
Leon, Corinne D. Law&B 92
Leon, Craig L. Law&B 92
Leon, Dennis 1933- WhoAm 92
Leon, Donald Francis 1932- WhoAm 92
Leon, Edward 1925- WhoWor 93
Leon, Edward J. 1899-1991 BioIn 17
Leon, Eric Y. 1947- St&PR 93
Leon, Geoffrey d1990 BioIn 17
Leon, Jack Paul 1930- WhoAm 92
Leon, James Robert 1922- St&PR 93
Leon, Juan van der Hamen y 1596-c. 1632 BioIn 17
Leon, Judene Marie 1931- WhoWrEP 92
Leon, Lucrecia de 1568- BioIn 17
Leon, Luis Alfonso 1959- WhoWor 93
Leon, Luis E. 1952- St&PR 93
Leon, Marjorie Roth 1952- WhoEmL 93
Leon, Mary Ann 1947- WhoAmW 93
Leon, Robert Leonard 1925- WhoAm 92
Leon, Steve 1948- WhoWrEP 92
Leon, Tania J. 1943- HispAmA [port]
Leon, Tania (Justina) 1943- Baker 92, WhoAm 92
Leon, Terrence Thomas 1950- St&PR 93
Leon, Tomas Carlos 1951- WhoSSW 93
Leonard, Alison 1944- ConAu 138, SmATA 70 [port]
Leonard, Angeline Jane 1940- WhoAmW 93
Leonard, Arthur Sherman 1952- WhoEmL 93
Leonard, Bill d1881 BioIn 17
Leonard, Bill J. 1946- WhoSSW 93
Leonard, Bobby Frank 1932- St&PR 93
Leonard, Brett MiSFD 9
Leonard, Brian E. 1936- WhoScE 91-3
Leonard, Brian Edmund 1936- WhoWor 93
Leonard, Cheryl Martschink 1952- WhoAmW 93
Leonard, Craig E. 1949- St&PR 93
Leonard, Daniel Gerard 1962- WhoE 93
Leonard, David A. Law&B 92
Leonard, David A. 1942- St&PR 93
Leonard, David Arthur 1928- WhoAm 92
Leonard, David Heerwald Law&B 92
Leonard, David R. Law&B 92
Leonard, Debi Lynn 1955- WhoAmW 93
Leonard, Diana 1941- ConAu 137
Leonard, Donald J. 1933- St&PR 93
Leonard, Donald L. 1946- St&PR 93
Leonard, Donna K. Law&B 92
Leonard, Dorothy Louise 1932- WhoAmW 93
Leonard, Earl Rex 1939- St&PR 93
Leonard, Eason Harris 1920- WhoAm 92
Leonard, Edward Charles 1927- St&PR 93
Leonard, Edward F. 1932- WhoAm 92
Leonard, Edward Paul 1935- WhoAm 92
Leonard, Edwin Deane 1929- WhoAm 92, WhoE 93
Leonard, Elizabeth Ann 1950- WhoAmW 93
Leonard, Elizabeth Lipman 1947- WhoAmW 93
Leonard, Ellen Falek 1951- WhoEmL 93
Leonard, Ellis P. d1991 BioIn 17
Leonard, Elmore 1925- BioIn 17, ConLC 71 [port], ConTFT 10, ScF&FL 92
Leonard, Elmore John 1925- WhoAm 92, WhoWrEP 92
Leonard, Emily 1928- WhoE 93
Leonard, Emma Jane Carr 1851- AmWomPl
Leonard, Eugene Albert 1935- WhoAm 92
Leonard, Francis M., Jr. Law&B 92
Leonard, George Burr 1923- BioIn 17
Leonard, George Edmund 1940- WhoAm 92, WhoWor 93
Leonard, George Edmund, Jr. 1940- St&PR 93
Leonard, George H. 1921- ScF&FL 92
Leonard, George Jay 1946- WhoAm 92, WhoWor 93
Leonard, Gerald Dennis 1937- St&PR 93
Leonard, Gilbert Stanley 1941- WhoSSW 93, WhoWor 93
Leonard, Graham BioIn 17
Leonard, Graham Douglas 1921- WhoWor 93
Leonard, Gregory E. 1948- WhoIns 93
Leonard, H. Skipton 1945- WhoSSW 93
Leonard, Harry E. 1922- St&PR 93
Leonard, Herbert B. 1922- MiSFD 9
Leonard, Herman Beukema 1952- WhoAm 92
Leonard, Hubert 1819-1890 Baker 92
Leonard, Hugh BioIn 17
Leonard, Irvin 1921- St&PR 93
Leonard, Jack D'Artagnan 1937- St&PR 93
Leonard, James Law&B 92
Leonard, James Fulton 1920- WhoUN 92
Leonard, James Joseph 1924- WhoAm 92
Leonard, James O. 1942- St&PR 93
Leonard, James Stanley 1947- WhoSSW 93
Leonard, James T. d1991 BioIn 17
Leonard, Joan BioIn 17
Leonard, Joanne 1940- WhoAm 92
Leonard, John WhoE 93
Leonard, John 1954- WhoWor 93
Leonard, John Burford WhoScE 91-1
Leonard, John Clay, III 1950- WhoE 93
Leonard, John Dunbar 1933- St&PR 93
Leonard, John Francis 1935- WhoAm 92
Leonard, John Harry 1922- WhoAm 92
Leonard, John William, Jr. 1925- WhoAm 92
Leonard, Joseph Howard 1952- WhoE 93, WhoEmL 93
Leonard, Juanita BioIn 17
Leonard, Juanita Louise Evans 1939- WhoAmW 93
Leonard, Kenneth Carl Law&B 92
Leonard, Laurence 1932- WhoE 93
Leonard, Laurence B., Jr. 1930- St&PR 93
Leonard, Lawrence ScF&FL 92
Leonard, Lawrence Edwards 1934- WhoAm 92
Leonard, Lee 1959- St&PR 93
Leonard, Leo Donald 1938- WhoE 93
Leonard, M. David Law&B 92
Leonard, Marc 1945- St&PR 93
Leonard, Martha A. 1957- St&PR 93
Leonard, Martha Gail 1954- WhoSSW 93
Leonard, Martia AmWomPl
Leonard, Michael 1941- WhoAm 92
Leonard, Michael A. 1937- WhoWor 93
Leonard, Michael Steven 1947- WhoAm 92
Leonard, Nelson Jordan 1916- WhoAm 92
Leonard, Norman J. 1941- St&PR 93
Leonard, Pamela Kay 1962- WhoAmW 93
Leonard, Patrick J. 1934- St&PR 93
Leonard, Paul Haralson 1925- WhoAm 92
Leonard, Phyllis G(rubbs) 1924- WhoWrEP 92
Leonard, Pierre 1943- St&PR 93
Leonard, Ray Charles BioIn 17
Leonard, Raymond WhoScE 91-1
Leonard, Raymond 1941- ScF&FL 92
Leonard, Raymond Wesley 1909- WhoSSW 93
Leonard, Richard D., Jr. 1931- WhoIns 93
Leonard, Richard E. 1931- St&PR 93
Leonard, Richard Hart 1921- WhoAm 92
Leonard, Richard Manning 1908- WhoAm 92
Leonard, Robert d1990 BioIn 17
Leonard, Robert B. Law&B 92
Leonard, Robert Cowan 1931- WhoSSW 93
Leonard, Robert Sean BioIn 17
Leonard, Robert Warren 1926- WhoAm 92
Leonard, Robert Z. 1889-1968 MiSFD 9N
Leonard, Roy Junior 1929- WhoAm 92
Leonard, Ruth AmWomPl
Leonard, Sheldon 1907- WhoAm 92
Leonard, Stanley Strenger 1931- WhoAm 92
Leonard, Sugar Ray BioIn 17
Leonard, Sugar Ray 1956- WhoAm 92
Leonard, Susan Burden Law&B 92
Leonard, Susan Ruth 1955- WhoAmW 93, WhoSSW 93
Leonard, Terry MiSFD 9
Leonard, Thomas Aloysius 1946- WhoAm 92, WhoE 93, WhoEmL 93, WhoWor 93
Leonard, Timothy Dwight 1940- WhoAm 92, WhoSSW 93
Leonard, Virginia Kathryn 1944- WhoAmW 93
Leonard, Walter Raymond 1923- WhoAm 92, WhoSSW 93
Leonard, Wilford A. 1927- St&PR 93
Leonard, Will Ernest, Jr. 1935- WhoAm 92
Leonard, William G. 1946- St&PR 93
Leonard, William Samuel 1929- St&PR 93
Leonard-Dent, Marva J. AfrAmBi
Leonardi, Alfredo 1928- WhoScE 91-3
Leonardi, Leonardo 1936- WhoUN 92
Leonardi, Maurice 1942- St&PR 93, WhoAm 92
Leonardi, Robert M. Law&B 92
Leonardi, Samuel Joseph 1940- St&PR 93
Leonard-Nichols, Ruth Ann 1946- WhoEmL 93
Leonardo, Ann Adamson 1944- WhoAmW 93
Leonardo, Jose c. 1605-1656 BioIn 17
Leonardo, Lawrence J. 1948- St&PR 93
Leonardo, Louis Charles 1953- WhoEmL 93
Leonardo Bastos, Maria Helena Law&B 92
Leonardo, da Vinci 1452-1519 BioIn 17
Leonard of Chios 1395?-1459 OxDcByz
Leonardos, Gregory 1935- WhoE 93
Leonards, David 1946- WhoEmL 93
Leonards, Kenneth Stanley 1950- WhoEmL 93
Leonberger, Frederick John 1947- WhoAm 92
Leoncavallo, Ruggero 1857-1919 Baker 92, IntDcOp [port], OxDcOp
Leondar, Arnold Jerome 1924- WhoSSW 93
Leondar, Barbara 1928- WhoAmW 93, WhoE 93
Leon Dub, Marcelo 1946- WhoWor 93
Leone, Alfredo Mario 1951- WhoUN 92
Leone, Carole Anne 1946- WhoEmL 93
Leone, Charles Russell, Jr. 1935- WhoSSW 93
Leone, Daniel Cesidio 1932- WhoE 93
Leone, Esterino B. 1907- St&PR 93
Leone, George Frank 1926- St&PR 93, WhoAm 92
Leone, Jennifer G. Law&B 92
Leone, John MiSFD 9
Leone, John A. 1934- St&PR 93
Leone, Joseph Michael 1953- St&PR 93
Leone, Judith Gibson 1945- WhoAmW 93
Leone, Louis J. 1936- WhoE 93
Leone, Norma Leonardi 1935- WhoWrEP 92
Leone, Richard Carl 1941- WhoAm 92
Leone, Robert M. Law&B 92
Leone, Sergio 1921-1989 BioIn 17
Leone, Sergio 1929-1990 MiSFD 9N
Leone, Stephan Robert 1939- St&PR 93
Leone, Stephen Robert 1948- WhoAm 92
Leone, Ugo WhoUN 92
Leone, Vincent John 1937- St&PR 93
Leone, William C. 1924- St&PR 93
Leone, William Charles 1924- WhoAm 92
Leonenko, Nikolay Nikolayevich 1951- WhoWor 93
Leonett, Anthony Arthur 1929- WhoAm 92
Leonetti, B.V. 1944- St&PR 93
Leonetti, Matthew BioIn 17
Leonetti, Matthew Frank WhoAm 92
Leonetti, Michael Edward 1955- WhoEmL 93, WhoWor 93
Leonetti, Philip BioIn 17
Leon Felipe DcMexL
Leong, Ann Keet 1959- WhoWor 93
Leong, Carol Jean 1942- WhoAmW 93
Leong, Clara Jo 1955- WhoAmW 93
Leong, Edith L. 1925- St&PR 93
Leong, Edward Che-Hung 1939- WhoAsAP 91
Leong, G. Keong 1950- WhoWor 93
Leong, J.Y.H. 1925- St&PR 93
Leong, Jo-Ann Ching 1942- WhoAmW 93
Leong, Mang Su 1960- WhoWor 93
Leong, Martha Jo Edwards 1942- WhoAmW 93
Leong, Po-Chih 1939- MiSFD 9
Leong, Samuel 1956- WhoWor 93
Leong Khee Seong, Paul 1939- WhoAsAP 91
Leon-Guerrero, David Mesa 1955- WhoEmL 93
Leonhard, D.F. 1924- St&PR 93
Leonhard, William E. 1914- St&PR 93
Leonhard, William Edward 1914- WhoAm 92
Leonhardt, Frederick Wayne 1949- WhoAm 92
Leonhardt, Gustav (Maria) 1928- Baker 92
Leonhardt, Harry J. Law&B 92
Leonhardt, Jerald Lee 1948- St&PR 93
Leonhardt, Rudolf Walter 1921- WhoWor 93
Leonhardt, William Stroup 1916- WhoAm 92
Leon Herrera, Santos DcCPCAm
Leoni, Angelo Vincent 1929- St&PR 93
Leoni, Carlo 1942- WhoScE 91-3
Leoni, Edgar (Hugh) 1925- ConAu 38NR
Leoni, Franco 1864-1949 Baker 92
Leoni, Leone c. 1560-1627 Baker 92
Leoni, Mark Anthony 1961- WhoE 93
Leoni, Roberto 1943- WhoWor 93
Leonidas d480BC HarEnMi
Leonini, Magister c. 1135-c. 1201 Baker 92
Leoninus c. 1135-c. 1201 Baker 92
Leonis, Magister c. 1135-c. 1201 Baker 92
Leonis, John Michael 1933- WhoAm 92
Leonoff, L.E. 1943- St&PR 93
Leonora, John 1928- WhoAm 92
Leonov, Aleksei BioIn 17
Leonov, Leonid 1899- BioIn 17
Leonova, Darya 1829-1896 OxDcOp
Leonova, Darya (Mikhailovna) 1829-1896 Baker 92
Leonow, Alexander Sereyevitch 1948- WhoWor 93
Leonowens, Anna Harriette 1834-1914 BioIn 17
Leonowicz, Andrzej 1933- WhoScE 91-4, WhoWor 93
Leon-Portilla, Miguel 1926- WhoWor 93
Leon-Sanz, Miguel 1957- WhoWor 93
Leonte, Mircea 1930- WhoScE 91-4
Leontiadas, L.I. WhoScE 91-4
Leontic, Boran A. 1928- WhoScE 91-4
Leontief, Wassily 1906- WhoAm 92, WhoE 93, WhoWor 93
Leontios d706 OxDcByz
Leontios fl. 5th cent.-6th cent. OxDcByz
Leontios, Eugenia Georgia 1942- WhoAmW 93
Leontios of Byzantium dc. 543 OxDcByz
Leontios of Jerusalem c. 485-c. 543 OxDcByz
Leontios of Neapolis fl. 7th cent.- OxDcByz
Leontios Scholastikos fl. 6th cent.- OxDcByz
Leon Valenzuela, Juan Guillermo 1937- WhoWor 93
Leo of Catania OxDcByz
Leo of Chalcedon OxDcByz
Leo of Ohrid fl. 11th cent.- OxDcByz
Leo of Synada c. 940- OxDcByz
Leo of Tripoli OxDcByz
Leopard, Grady Bailey 1936- WhoSSW 93
Leopold, I 1640-1705 Baker 92
Leopold, III 1901-1983 DcTwHis
Leopold, Aldo 1886-1948 BioIn 17
Leopold, George William, Jr. Law&B 92
Leopold, George William, Jr. 1947- St&PR 93

Leopold, Hans A. 1937- WhoScE 91-4
Leopold, Irving Henry 1915- WhoAm 92
Leopold, Luna Bergere 1915- WhoAm 92
Leopold, M. Edwin 1934- St&PR 93, WhoIns 93
Leopold, Mark F. Law&B 92
Leopold, Mark F. 1950- WhoEmL 93
Leopold, Robert Livingston 1922- WhoAm 92
Leopold, Robert M. 1926- St&PR 93
Leopold, Susan Elizabeth 1960- WhoE 93
Leopold, Warren Edward 1953- WhoIns 93
Leopold-Wildburger, Ulrike 1949- WhoWor 93
Leo Sakellarios dc. 943 OxDcByz [port]
Leotard, Francois 1942- BioIn 17
Leotard, Francois Gerard Marie 1942- WhoWor 93
Leo the Armenian, V d820 HarEnMi, OxDcByz
Leo the Deacon c. 950-c. 992 OxDcByz
Leo the Great, I d461 OxDcByz
Leo the Isaurian, III c. 680-741 HarEnMi
Leo the Khazar, IV 750-780 OxDcByz
Leo the Kouropalates OxDcByz
Leo the Mathematician c. 790-c. 869 OxDcByz
Leo the Philosopher OxDcByz
Leo the Physician OxDcByz
Leo the Wise, the Philosopher, VI 866-912 HarEnMi
Leotta, Patricia A. Law&B 92
Leo Tuscus fl. 1160-1182 OxDcByz
Leoty, Claude 1942- WhoScE 91-2
Leotychidas c. 545BC-469BC HarEnMi
Leous, Stephen Francis 1958- WhoE 93
Leovey, Andras 1926- WhoScE 91-4
Leow, Ngee Fui 1935- WhoWor 93
Lepage, Alain Louis 1952- WhoWor 93
Lepage, George Edward 1938- St&PR 93
Le Page, Rand ScF&FL 92
Lepage, Robert J. 1932- St&PR 93
LePage, Wilbur Reed 1911- WhoAm 92, WhoE 93
Lepage, Yves 1928- WhoScE 91-2
Lepan, Douglas V. 1914- WhoCanL 92
Lepany, Jerome Law&B 92
Lepape, Harry L. 1930- St&PR 93
Lepape, Harry Leonard 1930- WhoAm 92
Le Parc, Jean-Marie 1946- WhoScE 91-2
Leparulo, Angelo 1928- St&PR 93
Lepawsky, Albert 1908-1992 WhoAm 92, WhoWor 93
Le Pecq, Jean-Bernard WhoScE 91-2
Le Pecq, Jean-Bernard 1939- WhoScE 91-2
Le Pen, Jean-Marie BioIn 17
Le Pensec, Louis 1937- WhoWor 93
Le Perchec, Pierre WhoScE 91-2
Leperco, Xavier Berard 1950- St&PR 93
Leperi, Karin Alexander 1952- WhoAmW 93
LePeron, Serge MiSFD 9
Lepesant, Jean-Antoine 1943- WhoScE 91-2
Lepeska, Will J. 1932- St&PR 93
Lepiane, Donald Carl Law&B 92
Le Pichon, Xavier T. 1937- WhoScE 91-2
Le Pichon, Xavier Thaddee 1937- WhoWor 93
Lepick, Fred C. 1925- St&PR 93
Lepidi, Lawrence John Law&B 92
Lepidus, Marcus Aemilius d77BC HarEnMi
L'Epine, Margherita de OxDcOp
L'Epine, (Francesca) Margherita de c. 1683-1746 Baker 92
Lepingle WhoScE 91-2
Lepinoy, Pierre Jean-Marie 1950- WhoWor 93
LePire, Joe H. 1892-1973 ScF&FL 92
Lepisto, Martti 1941- WhoScE 91-4
Lepisto, Toivo K. 1947- WhoScE 91-4
Lepkowski, Wil 1934- WhoAm 92
Leplawy, Miroslaw Tomasz 1924- WhoScE 91-4
Lepler, Carolyn St&PR 93
Lepler, Shirley M. Law&B 92
Lepley, Russell L. 1917- St&PR 93
Lepley, William WhoAm 92
Leplin, Emanuel 1917-1972 Baker 92
Lepman, Jella 1891-1970 BioIn 17
Le Poac, Philippe Jacques 1952- WhoWor 93
Lepofsky, Robert Jerry 1944- St&PR 93
Lepoivre, Philippe 1953- WhoScE 91-2
LePome, Penelope Marie 1945- WhoAmW 93
Le Poncin Lafitte, Monique WhoScE 91-2
Lepone, Donald E. 1944- St&PR 93
Lepore, Anna Maria 1948- WhoWor 93
Lepore, Dominick James 1911- WhoWrEP 92
Lepore, John Anthony 1935- WhoE 93
Lepore, Michael Joseph 1910- WhoAm 92, WhoE 93
Le Pors, Anicet 1931- BioIn 17
Leporte, James L. 1954- St&PR 93
Lepow, Leslie Hugh 1949- WhoAm 92
Lepowsky, James 1944- WhoE 93
Leppakoski, Erkki WhoScE 91-4
Leppaluoto, Juhani P. 1939- WhoScE 91-4
Leppard, Raymond 1927- IntDcOp, OxDcOp
Leppard, Raymond (John) 1927- Baker 92, WhoAm 92
Leppavuori, Seppo Ilmari 1939- WhoScE 91-4
Lepper, Mark Roger 1944- WhoAm 92
Leppert, Charles A. Law&B 92
Leppert, Phyllis Carolyn 1938- WhoAmW 93, WhoE 93
Leppert, Richard David 1943- WhoAm 92
Leppik, Margaret White 1943- WhoAmW 93
Leppin, Juergen 1932- WhoScE 91-3
Lepping, George WhoWor 93
Leppington, Francis Godfrey WhoScE 91-1
Leppla, Bruce W. 1949- St&PR 93
Leppman, Wolfgang Arthur 1922- ConAu 37NR
Leppo, Sheldon Sydney 1934- St&PR 93
Le Prestre, Sebastien 1633-1707 BioIn 17
Lepri, Daniel B. 1953- St&PR 93
Le Prince, Louis Aime Augustin 1841-1890 BioIn 17
Leprohon, Rosanna Eleanor 1829-1879 BioIn 17
Lepry, Louis A., Jr. 1954- St&PR 93
Leps, Thomas MacMaster 1914- WhoAm 92
Leps, Wassili 1870-1942 Baker 92
Lepschy, Antonio M. 1931- WhoScE 91-3
Lepshitz, W.M. Law&B 92
Leptich, Ronny Joseph 1943- St&PR 93
Le Quang Dao 1921- WhoWor 93
Lequerica, Martha WhoE 93
Le Querler, Jean-Francois 1943- WhoScE 91-2
LeQuesne, James Richard 1957- WhoWor 93
Le Quesne, Philip William 1939- WhoAm 92
Le Queux, William 1864-1927 ScF&FL 92
Lequien, Jean Germain Adrien 1933- WhoUN 92
Lequient, Guy 1941- St&PR 93
Lera, Thomas A. 1926- St&PR 93
Lerach, Richard F. Law&B 92
Lerangis, Peter ScF&FL 92
Lerangis, Peter 1955- SmATA 72 [port]
Lerat, Jean-Marie 1930- WhoWor 93
Le Ray, Dominique 1940- WhoScE 91-2
LeRay, Margaret May 1954- WhoE 93
Lerch, Beth Ann 1965- WhoE 93
Lerch, Carol 1938- St&PR 93
Lerch, Dana T. 1938- St&PR 93
Lerch, Irving Abram 1938- WhoE 93
Lerch, Jeffrey Walter 1948- WhoEmL 93
Lerch, John Albert 1950- WhoAm 92
Lerch, Justine Fredericks 1948- WhoSSW 93
Lerch, Richard Heaphy 1924- WhoAm 92
Lerch, Sharon 1940- WhoWrEP 92
Lerchen, George 1922- BioIn 17
Lercher, Johannes August 1954- WhoScE 91-4
Lerda, Daniel Enrique 1947- WhoWor 93
Lerdahl, (Al)Fred (Whitford) 1943- Baker 92
Leren, Martin W. 1950- St&PR 93
Leren, Nancy M. 1952- St&PR 93
Lerescu, Nick 1948- WhoE 93
Lerheim, Magne 1929- WhoWor 93
Lerigier, Mark Laurence 1951- St&PR 93
Lerin, Manuel 1915- DcMexL
Leritte, Jennifer Jones 1953- WhoSSW 93
Leritz, Lawrence Robert 1952- WhoAm 92, WhoEmL 93
Lerma, duque de 1552-1625 BioIn 17
Lerma, Roberto 1938- WhoWor 93
Lerma, Rosanna 1963- WhoEmL 93
Lerman, Albert 1936- WhoWrEP 92
Lerman, David Louis 1940- St&PR 93
Lerman, Eileen R. 1947- WhoAmW 93, WhoEmL 93
Lerman, Gerald Frederick 1941- St&PR 93
Lerman, Hannah 1936- WhoAmW 93
Lerman, Israel Cesar 1940- WhoWor 93
Lerman, Jeanette Paula 1948- St&PR 93, WhoAm 92
Lerman, Leo 1914- BioIn 17
Lerman, Leonard Solomon 1925- WhoAm 92
Lerman, Rhoda 1936- ScF&FL 92, WhoWrEP 92
Lerman, Robert Allan 1935- WhoE 93
Lerman, Stephen 1944- WhoWor 93
Lerman, Steven Ira 1944- WhoE 93
Lerman, Terry Allen Law&B 92
Lermontov, Mikhail 1814-1841 OxDcOp
Lerner, Abram 1913- WhoAm 92, WhoE 93
Lerner, Alan Burton 1930- St&PR 93, WhoAm 92
Lerner, Alan Jay 1918-1986 Baker 92, BioIn 17
Lerner, Alexander Robert 1946- WhoWor 93
Lerner, Alfred 1933- St&PR 93, WhoAm 92
Lerner, Arnold Stanley 1930- WhoAm 92
Lerner, Arthur 1915- ScF&FL 92
Lerner, Barbara 1935- WhoAmW 93, WhoE 93, WhoWor 93
Lerner, Beatrice I. d1992 BioIn 17, NewYTBS 92
Lerner, Bennett 1944- Baker 92
Lerner, Betsy BioIn 17
Lerner, Carl Michael Law&B 92
Lerner, Carol Menzel 1945- WhoAmW 93
Lerner, Dan MiSFD 9
Lerner, Daniel Merril 1932- WhoWor 93
Lerner, Dennis S. Law&B 92
Lerner, Edward M. ScF&FL 92
Lerner, Eric John 1947- WhoEmL 93
Lerner, Fred S. Law&B 92
Lerner, Frederic Howard 1957- WhoEmL 93
Lerner, Frederick Andrew 1945- ScF&FL 92, WhoE 93
Lerner, Gerald Michael 1943- WhoE 93
Lerner, Gerda 1920- BioIn 17, WhoWrEP 92
Lerner, Harry 1939- WhoAm 92
Lerner, Harry Jonas 1932- WhoAm 92
Lerner, Herbert J. 1938- WhoAm 92
Lerner, Hershey 1920- St&PR 93
Lerner, Howard 1927- St&PR 93
Lerner, Irving d1991 BioIn 17
Lerner, Irving 1909-1976 MiSFD 9N
Lerner, Irwin WhoAm 92
Lerner, Isadore Michael 1910-1977 BioIn 17
Lerner, Isidor AmWomPl
Lerner, Jill Law&B 92
Lerner, Joel D. Law&B 92
Lerner, Joel Samuel 1953- St&PR 93
Lerner, Jonathan 1948- ScF&FL 92
Lerner, Kenny BioIn 17
Lerner, Laurence BioIn 17
Lerner, Leonard Joseph WhoE 93
Lerner, Linda WhoWrEP 92
Lerner, Linda Joyce 1944- St&PR 93, WhoAmW 93, WhoE 93
Lerner, Liza Ann 1951- WhoWor 93
Lerner, Martin 1936- WhoAm 92
Lerner, Max 1902- JrnUS
Lerner, Max 1902-1992 BioIn 17, CurBio 92N, NewYTBS 92 [port]
Lerner, Max(well Alan) 1902-1992 ConAu 137
Lerner, Michael Albers 1943- WhoAm 92
Lerner, Moisey Yephimovich 1932- WhoWor 93
Lerner, Murray MiSFD 9
Lerner, Nathan Bernard 1913- WhoAm 92
Lerner, Paul Jerome Law&B 92
Lerner, Ralph 1949- WhoAm 92
Lerner, Richard Alan 1938- WhoAm 92
Lerner, Rita Guggenheim 1929- WhoAmW 93, WhoE 93
Lerner, Robert Earl 1940- WhoAm 92
Lerner, Samuel Law&B 92
Lerner, Sheldon 1939- WhoWor 93
Lerner, Stuart L. 1930- St&PR 93, WhoIns 93
Lerner, Teena L. 1957- WhoAmW 93
Lerner, Warren 1929- WhoAm 92
Lerner, William 1933- St&PR 93
Lerner-Lam, Eva I-Hwa 1954- WhoAmW 93, WhoEmL 93, WhoWor 93
Lernet-Holenia, Alexander 1897-1976 ScF&FL 92
Lernoux, Penny 1940-1989 BioIn 17
Le Rochois, Marthe OxDcOp
Leroe, Ellen 1949- BioIn 17, ScF&FL 92
Leroe, Ellen W(hitney) 1949- ConAu 40NR
Le Rossignol, James 1866-1969 BioIn 17
LeRoux, David Bain 1951- WhoIns 93
Leroux, Gaston 1868-1927 BioIn 17, ConAu 136, ScF&FL 92
Leroux, Hubert Law&B 92
Leroux, Jean-Paul WhoScE 91-2
Leroux, Lisa Marie 1966- WhoSSW 93
Leroux, Louise Zulme 1804-1877 See Dabadie, Henri-Bernard 1797-1853 OxDcOp
Le Roux, Maurice 1923- Baker 92
Leroux, Sylvain Guy 1956- WhoE 93
Leroux, Xavier (Henry Napoleon) 1863-1919 Baker 92
Le Roy, Andre F. 1933- WhoAm 92
Le Roy, Bruce Murdock 1920- WhoAm 92
Leroy, Claude 1947- WhoAm 92
Leroy, David Henry 1947- WhoAm 92
Leroy, E. WhoScE 91-2
LeRoy, Edward Carwile 1933- WhoAm 92
LeRoy, G. Palmer 1929- WhoAm 92
Leroy, Georges Lionel 1934- WhoWor 93
Leroy, Georges Lionel Etienne 1934- WhoScE 91-2
LeRoy, Isabel Hernandez 1951- WhoAmW 93, WhoEmL 93
Leroy, Jean-Louis 1937- WhoScE 91-2
Leroy, Jean-Paul 1939- WhoScE 91-2
LeRoy, Kitty d1877 BioIn 17
Le Roy, L. David 1920- WhoAm 92
Leroy, Mervyn 1900-1987 MiSFD 9N
LeRoy, Oswald Jozef 1936- WhoWor 93
Leroy, P.L.F. 1951- WhoScE 91-2
Leroy, Pierre Elie 1948- St&PR 93, WhoAm 92
Le Roy, Rene 1898-1985 Baker 92
LeRoy, Shirley Faucette 1951- WhoSSW 93
Leroy, Yves 1931- WhoScE 91-2
Le Royer, Eric 1963- WhoEmL 93
Le Roy Ladurie, Emmanuel 1929- BioIn 17
Lerski, Richard Anthony WhoScE 91-1
Lert, A.J. ScF&FL 92
Lert, Ernst (Josef Maria) 1883-1955 Baker 92
Lert, Richard (Johanes) 1885-1980 Baker 92
Lertora, Joanne Marie 1960- WhoAmW 93
Lerud, Joanne Van Ornum 1949- WhoAmW 93
Lerud-Chubb, DiAnne Kay 1942- WhoAmW 93
Lerum, Eileen Burns Law&B 92
Lerys, Steven H. 1949- WhoWor 93
Lerza, Ruth 1939- St&PR 93
Lesaar, Heinz Bernhard 1930- WhoWor 93
Lesaffre, Benoit 1952- WhoScE 91-2
LeSage, Janet Billings 1947- WhoAmW 93
LeSage, Joan M. Law&B 92
LeSage, William A. 1949- St&PR 93
Le Sage, William Alexander 1949- WhoAm 92
Lesak, David Michael 1952- WhoE 93
Lesar, Hiram Henry 1912- WhoAm 92
Lesauvage, J.R. St&PR 93
Lescarbot, Marc c. 1570-1642 BioIn 17
Lesch, George Henry 1909- WhoAm 92
Lesch, Michael 1939- WhoAm 92
Lesch, Michael Oscar 1938- WhoAm 92
Leschak, Peter Max 1951- WhoWrEP 92
Leschetizky, Theodor 1830-1915 Baker 92, PolBiDi
Lescroart, Emmett James 1951- St&PR 93
Lesdiguieres, Francois de Bonne, Duke of 1543-1626 HarEnMi
Lese, Alan E. 1943- St&PR 93
Lese, William M. 1925- St&PR 93
Leseberg, Detlef 1951- WhoWor 93
Leseman, Robert G. 1940- St&PR 93, WhoIns 93
Lesemann, Arvid Reenstjerna 1964- WhoWor 93
Lesemann, Pamela Louise 1955- WhoSSW 93
Leser, Bernard H. WhoE 93
Leser, Lawrence Arthur 1935- St&PR 93
Leserman, Lee Daniel 1946- WhoScE 91-2
Lesesne, Joab Mauldin, Jr. 1937- WhoAm 92
Lesh, Angela Dawn 1947- WhoEmL 93
Lesh, Newton D. Law&B 92
Lesh, Norman 1930- St&PR 93
Lesh, Olga AmWomPl
Lesh, Philip Chapman 1940- WhoAm 92
Le Shan, Eda J(oan) 1922- WhoWrEP 92
LeShan, Lawrence L. 1920- WhoAm 92
Le Shan, Lawrence L(ee) 1920- WhoWrEP 92
Le Shana, David Charles 1932- WhoAm 92
Leshaw, Jay 1925- St&PR 93
Lesher, Donald M. 1915- St&PR 93
Lesher, Donald Miles 1915- WhoAm 92
Lesher, Frank M. Law&B 92
Lesher, George Y. 1926-1990 BioIn 17
Lesher, John Lee 1934- St&PR 93
Lesher, John Lee, Jr. 1934- WhoAm 92
Lesher, Richard Lee 1933- WhoAm 92, WhoE 93
Lesher, Robert Overton 1921- WhoAm 92
Lesher, Stephen Harrison 1953- WhoEmL 93
Lesher, William Richard 1924- WhoAm 92
Leshinski, John J. Law&B 92
Leshinski, Linda 1952- WhoWrEP 92
Lesh-Laurie, Georgia Elizabeth 1938- WhoAmW 93
Leshner, Alan Irvin 1944- WhoAm 92
Leshner, Henry 1950- St&PR 93
LeShock, Edward 1949- WhoSSW 93
Lesiak, Lucille Ann 1946- WhoAmW 93
Lesiak, Tadeusz 1925- WhoScE 91-4, WhoWor 93
Le Sieg, Theo BioIn 17, MajAI
Lesieur, Marcel R.E. 1945- WhoScE 91-2
Lesieur, Roland Moses, Jr. 1950- WhoEmL 93
Lesieutre, George Andre 1958- WhoE 93

Lesiewicz, Witold 1922- DrEEuF
Lesiger, Ilene Gloria 1943- WhoAmW 93
Lesikar, James Daniel, II 1954- WhoE 93, WhoWor 93
Lesikar, Raymond Vincent 1922- WhoAm 92
Lesinski, Roger John 1949- St&PR 93
Lesjak, Lisa Mary 1963- WhoAmW 93
Lesjak, V. James 1934- WhoAm 92
Leske, Michael E. 1948- St&PR 93
Leskela, Markku Antero 1950- WhoScE 91-4, WhoWor 93
Leski, Antor R. 1913- St&PR 93
Leski, Michel 1934- WhoScE 91-4
Leskiewicz, Henryk J. 1919- WhoWor 93
Lesko, Betty Hardt 1945- WhoSSW 93
Lesko, Harry Joseph 1920- WhoAm 92
Lesko, James Joseph 1939- WhoE 93
Lesko, Leonard Henry 1938- WhoAm 92
Lesko, Wendy ConAu 136
Leskow, Olive 1919- WhoAmW 93
Leslie, Alexander c. 1740-1794 HarEnMi
Leslie, Allan Roy 1948- St&PR 93
Leslie, Bobby 1972- BioIn 17
Leslie, Buckskin Frank d1925? BioIn 17
Leslie, Cheryl Lees 1947- WhoAmW 93, WhoEmL 93
Leslie, Christopher Hugh Law&B 92
Leslie, David 1601-1682 HarEnMi
Leslie, David C. WhoScE 91-1
Leslie, David Stephen 1930- St&PR 93
Leslie, Donald A. BioIn 17
Leslie, Donald Wilmot 1942- WhoAm 92
Leslie, Frank 1821-1880 BioIn 17, JrnUS
Leslie, Frank, Mrs. 1836-1914 BioIn 17
Leslie, Frank Matthews WhoScE 91-1
Leslie, Frank Matthews 1935- WhoWor 93
Leslie, Gerrie Allen 1941- WhoAm 92
Leslie, Gordon A. 1946- WhoIns 93
Leslie, Helen Whitney Law&B 92
Leslie, Henry Arthur 1921- WhoAm 92, WhoSSW 93
Leslie, Henry (David) 1822-1896 Baker 92
Leslie, Jacques Robert, Jr. 1947- WhoAm 92
Leslie, James H. 1930- St&PR 93
Leslie, James Hill 1930- WhoAm 92
Leslie, James K. 1944- St&PR 93
Leslie, Janis Ethlyn 1960- WhoE 93
Leslie, John 1923- WhoE 93
Leslie, John Ethelbert 1910-1991 BioIn 17
Leslie, John Hampton 1914- WhoAm 92
Leslie, John Walter 1929- WhoAm 92
Leslie, John William 1923- WhoAm 92
Leslie, Josephine 1898-1979 ScF&FL 92
Leslie, Karl Edward Law&B 92
Leslie, Lisa BioIn 17
Leslie, Lottie Lyle 1930- WhoWrEP 92
Leslie, Marc C. Law&B 92
Leslie, Miriam Florence Folline 1836-1914 BioIn 17
Leslie, Nan 1926- SweetSg C [port]
Leslie, Peter 1922- ScF&FL 92
Leslie, Peter M. 1942- WhoUN 92
Leslie, Robert Lorne 1947- WhoEmL 93
Leslie, Royal Conrad 1923- WhoAm 92
Leslie, S.T. 1940- WhoScE 91-1
Leslie, Seymour Marvin 1922- WhoAm 92
Leslie, Suzanne C. Law&B 92
Leslie, William 1918-1990 BioIn 17
Leslie, William Cairns 1920- WhoAm 92
Lesly, Philip 1918- St&PR 93, WhoAm 92, WhoWor 93
Lesman, Michael Steven 1953- WhoE 93, WhoEmL 93, WhoWor 93
Lesmian, Boleslaw 1877-1937 PolBiDi
Lesnau, Marilyn Michele 1953- St&PR 93
Lesne, Michel 1943- WhoWor 93
Lesnek-Cooper, Carol H. Law&B 92
Lesnett, Thomas Jay 1948- St&PR 93
Lesniak, Robert John 1936- WhoE 93
Lesniak, Rose 1955- WhoWrEP 92
Lesnik, Steven Harris 1940- St&PR 93
Lesnikowski, Jan Marek 1936- WhoWor 93
Lesok, Eddie Monroe 1948- St&PR 93
Lesokhin, Mikhail Moiseevich 1933- WhoWor 93
Lesonsky, Rieva 1952- WhoAm 92, WhoAmW 93
Lesourne, Jacques-Francois 1928- WhoWor 93
Lesowitz, Marsha 1955- WhoAmW 93
Lesperance, John 1835?-1891 BioIn 17
L'Esperance, Robert P. 1946- St&PR 93
Lespinasse, Julie de 1732-1776 BioIn 17
Lespreance, Faye Love 1954- WhoSSW 93
Less, Theodore D. 1930- St&PR 93
Lessa, William Armand 1908- IntDcAn
Lessac, Frane BioIn 17
Lessac, Michael MiSFD 9
Lessack, Ronald D. 1947- St&PR 93
Lessaer, Stanislaw 1924- WhoScE 91-4
Lessard, John (Ayres) 1920- Baker 92
Lessard, Lynn Marie 1953- WhoAmW 93
Lessard, Michel M. 1939- WhoAm 92
Lessard, Pierre H. 1942- St&PR 93
Lessard, Pierre Henri 1942- WhoAm 92
Lessard, Raymond W. 1930- WhoAm 92, WhoSSW 93
Lesse, Etta Gordon WhoE 93
Lesse, Stanley 1922-1990 BioIn 17
Lessel, B. WhoScE 91-1
Lessel, Franciszek 1790-1838 PolBiDi
Lessel, Franz c. 1780-1838 Baker 92
Lessell, Simmons 1933- WhoE 93
Lessells, J. WhoScE 91-1
Lessen, Martin 1920- WhoAm 92
Lessenden, Edith Ann Fleming 1922- WhoAmW 93
Lesser, Aleksander 1814-1884 PolBiDi
Lesser, Alexander 1902-1982 IntDcAn
Lesser, Allen 1907- WhoE 93
Lesser, David Law&B 92
Lesser, David 1955- St&PR 93
Lesser, Edward Arnold 1934- St&PR 93, WhoAm 92
Lesser, Erwin 1929- WhoSSW 93
Lesser, Gilbert 1935-1990 BioIn 17
Lesser, Henry 1947- WhoAm 92
Lesser, Joseph M. 1928- WhoAm 92
Lesser, Joseph S. 1928- St&PR 93
Lesser, Laurence 1938- WhoAm 92, WhoE 93, WhoWor 93
Lesser, Lawrence J. 1939- WhoAm 92, WhoE 93
Lesser, Mark Elliott 1951- WhoSSW 93
Lesser, Marshall W. 1931- St&PR 93
Lesser, Milton ScF&FL 92
Lesser, Patricia Roth 1953- WhoEmL 93
Lesser, Rhoda Sharon 1929- WhoAmW 93
Lesser, Rika Ellen 1953- WhoWrEP 92
Lesser, Ruth WhoScE 91-1
Lesser, Stanford J. 1940- St&PR 93
Lesser, Walter Hunter 1957- WhoEmL 93, WhoSSW 93
Lesser, Wendy 1952- WhoAm 92
Lesser, Wendy Celia 1952- WhoWrEP 92
Lesses, Maurice F. 1932- St&PR 93
Lesses, Maurice Falcon 1932- WhoAm 92
Lesshafft, Hans Joachim 1934- WhoWor 93
Lessick, Mira Lee 1949- WhoAmW 93, WhoEmL 93
Lessin, Andrew R. 1942- St&PR 93
Lessin, Andrew Richard 1942- WhoAm 92
Lessin, Joan Kelly 1944- WhoAmW 93
Lessin, Lawrence Stephen 1937- WhoAm 92
Lessing, Doris 1919- IntLitE, MagSWL [port], ScF&FL 92, WhoAm 92, WhoWor 93
Lessing, Doris May 1919- BioIn 17
Lessing, E. WhoScE 91-3
Lessing, Fred W. 1915- St&PR 93
Lessing, Gotthold Ephraim 1729-1781 BioIn 17
Lessing, Heinz Walter 1910- WhoWor 93
Lessing, Katherine Bleecker WhoSSW 93
Lessing, Peter 1938- WhoSSW 93
Lessiter, Frank Donald 1939- WhoAm 92, WhoWrEP 92
Lessler, Richard Sigmund 1924- WhoAm 92
Lessman, Hope Miller d1992 NewYTBS 92
Lessman, Jac d1990 BioIn 17
Lessman, Robert Edward 1947- WhoEmL 93
Lessner, Harold J. 1943- St&PR 93
Lessner, Mark M. 1948- WhoEmL 93
Lessner, Sidney F. 1926- St&PR 93
Lessner, Stephan 1957- WhoWor 93
Lessnoff, Michael Harry 1940- WhoWor 93
Lessof, Maurice Hart WhoScE 91-1
Lessy, Roy Paul, Jr. 1944- WhoAm 92
Lestage, Daniel Barfield 1939- WhoAm 92
Lestage, Donald, III 1939- St&PR 93
Lester, Andrew ScF&FL 92
Lester, Barnett Benjamin 1912- WhoAm 92
Lester, Bijou Yang 1950- WhoE 93
Lester, Carolyn Sneed 1946- WhoAmW 93
Lester, Charles Theodore, Jr. 1954- WhoEmL 93
Lester, Colin ScF&FL 92
Lester, D. Nelson 1939- St&PR 93
Lester, D.W. 1953- St&PR 93
Lester, David 1916-1990 BioIn 17
Lester, Dorothy Mae 1943- WhoAmW 93
Lester, Edward 1831-1905 ScF&FL 92
Lester, Edwin 1895-1990 BioIn 17
Lester, Elenore 1919-1990 BioIn 17
Lester, George S. 1905- St&PR 93
Lester, Gerald Eugene Law&B 92
Lester, Hazen Russell, Jr. 1929- St&PR 93
Lester, Helen 1936- ConAu 38NR
Lester, James Dudley 1935- WhoSSW 93
Lester, Jerry Wayne 1944- WhoSSW 93
Lester, John Ernest 1888-1959 BioIn 17
Lester, John James Nathaniel, II 1952- WhoEmL 93
Lester, John Seerey- 1945- BioIn 17
Lester, Julius 1939- BlkAuII 92
Lester, Julius B. 1939- WhoAm 92, WhoWrEP 92
Lester, Julius Bernard 1939- EncAACR, MajAI [port]
Lester, Louise 1867-1932 SweetSg A
Lester, Major 1951- WhoWor 93
Lester, Malcolm 1924- WhoAm 92
Lester, Malcolm Coltrane 1967- WhoE 93
Lester, Mark Charles 1952- WhoE 93
Lester, Mark L. 1948- MiSFD 9
Lester, Michael B. 1940- WhoSSW 93
Lester, Pamela R. Law&B 92
Lester, Raymond J. Law&B 92
Lester, Richard 1932- MiSFD 9, WhoAm 92, WhoWor 93
Lester, Richard Allan Law&B 92
Lester, Richard Allan 1947- St&PR 93
Lester, Richard Garrison 1925- WhoAm 92
Lester, Robert A. Law&B 92
Lester, Robert Carlton 1933- WhoAm 92
Lester, Rodney St&PR 93
Lester, Sean 1888-1959 BioIn 17
Lester, Steven Burt 1954- WhoE 93
Lester, Susan E. 1956- St&PR 93
Lester, Tanya 1956- ConAu 138
Lester, Tilden Jackson 1933- St&PR 93
Lester, Virginia Laudano 1931- WhoAm 92
Lester, William Alexander, Jr. 1937- WhoAm 92
Lester, William Bernard 1939- WhoSSW 93
Lester, William Fredrick 1952- WhoSSW 93
Lester, William L.G. 1943- St&PR 93, WhoAm 92
Lester-Wolfe, Anita L. 1960- WhoAmW 93
Lesti, Mary Lynn WhoWrEP 92
Lestienne, Francis Gervais 1941- WhoWor 93
Lestin, Eric Hugh 1950- WhoSSW 93
Lestingi, Joseph Francis 1935- WhoE 93
Leston, Kristine E. Law&B 92
LeStourgeon, Diana Elizabeth 1927- WhoE 93
Lestrade, Swinburne A.S. 1947- WhoUN 92
Lestradet, Henri 1921- WhoScE 91-2
Lestradet, Henri Georges 1921- WhoWor 93
Lestrange, Kenneth J. 1957- St&PR 93
LeSuer, Kenneth R. 1935- WhoSSW 93
Lesueur, Claude Jean 1941- WhoScE 91-2
LeSueur, Elizabeth Fontaine 1947- St&PR 93
Le Sueur, Jean Francois 1760-1837 Baker 92, OxDcOp
Le Sueur, Meridel BioIn 17
LeSueur, Meridel 1900- AmWomWr 92
LeSueur, William Dawson 1840-1917 BioIn 17
Lesuisse, Roland Leon 1946- WhoWor 93
Lesur, Daniel (Jean Yves) 1908- Baker 92
Lesure, Francois 1923- Baker 92
Lesure, John B. 1933- St&PR 93
Leszak, James Paul 1960- WhoEmL 93
Leszczynska, Maria 1703-1768 PolBiDi
Leszczynski, Stanislaw 1677-1766 PolBiDi
Leszczynski, Witold 1933- DrEEuF
Leszczynski, Zbigniew Edward 1950- WhoWor 93
Leszczynski, Zbigniew Kazimierz 1927- WhoScE 91-4
Leta, Frances Banas 1937- WhoAmW 93
Le Tacon, Francois WhoScE 91-2
Letaconnoux, Calleen King 1948- St&PR 93
Le Talaer, Jean Yves 1932- WhoScE 91-2
LeTart, Laurin Harold 1942- St&PR 93
LeTart, Phyllis A. Law&B 92
Letaw, Harry, Jr. 1926- St&PR 93
Letcher, C. Scott Law&B 92
Letcher, Tina H. 1938- WhoWrEP 92
Letchworth, Ruth A. AmWomPl
Letelier (-Llonas), Alfonso 1912- Baker 92
LeTellier, Carroll Nance 1928- St&PR 93
Letellier, Phyllis Mortensen 1931- WhoWrEP 92
LeTellier, Scott Parks 1951- BioIn 17
LeTerneau, Susan Marie 1945- WhoAmW 93
Leterrier, J. WhoScE 91-2
Letesson, Jean-Jacques 1955- WhoScE 91-2
Letey, John Joseph, Jr. 1933- WhoAm 92
Leth, Steven Arthur 1948- WhoEmL 93
Letham, Dennis J. 1951- St&PR 93
Lethbridge, Francis Donald 1920- WhoAm 92
Lethbridge, George Tempest 1919- WhoWor 93
Lethiers, Francis 1943- WhoScE 91-2
Letiche, John Marion 1918- WhoAm 92
Letizia, B. 1936- St&PR 93
Letizio, Albert 1940- St&PR 93
Letko, Stephen George 1939- St&PR 93
Leto, Francis Joseph 1959- WhoEmL 93
Letofsky, Alan R. Law&B 92
Letofsky, Alan R. 1941- St&PR 93
Letokhov, Vladilen Stepanovich 1939- WhoWor 93
Letorey, Omer 1873-1938 Baker 92
Letourneau, Deborah Kay BioIn 17
LeTourneau, Duane John 1926- WhoAm 92
Letourneau, Peter D. 1947- St&PR 93
LeTourneau, Richard Howard 1925- WhoAm 92
Letowsky, Martin Elliot 1951- WhoEmL 93
Le Troquer, Andre 1884-1963 BioIn 17
LeTrung, Q. 1943- St&PR 93
Letscher, John F. 1931- St&PR 93
Letsie, III 1963- WhoWor 93
Letsie, Joshua Sekhobe 1947- WhoAfr
Letsie, Thaabe 1940- WhoAfr
Letsinger, Robert Lewis 1921- WhoAm 92
Letsou, George Vasilios 1958- WhoE 93
Lett, Austin Sherwood, Jr. 1941- St&PR 93
Lett, Cynthia Ellen Wein 1957- WhoAmW 93, WhoEmL 93
Lett, Gerald L. Law&B 92
Lett, James Chancey 1957- WhoSSW 93
Lett, James William 1955- WhoEmL 93, WhoSSW 93
Lett, Philip Wood, Jr. 1922- WhoAm 92
Lett, Sherri J. 1949- WhoAmW 93
Lettau, Reinhard 1929- BioIn 17
Lette, Kathy 1958- ConAu 136
Lettell, John S. ScF&FL 92
Letterman, David BioIn 17
Letterman, David 1947- Au&Arts 10 [port], WhoAm 92, WhoE 93
Letterman, David (Michael) 1947- ConAu 139
Letterman, Ronald M. 1942- St&PR 93
Letters, Robert 1933- WhoScE 91-3
Lettich, Sheldon MiSFD 9
Lettie, Ben 1937- St&PR 93
Lettieri, Richard Joseph 1947- WhoEmL 93
Lettieri, Ronald John 1950- WhoE 93
Lettmann, John William 1942- St&PR 93
Lettner, Kurt 1938- WhoScE 91-4
Letton, Alva Hamblin 1916- WhoAm 92
Lettow, Charles Frederick 1941- WhoAm 92, WhoE 93
Lettow-Vorbeck, Paul Emil von 1870-1964 HarEnMi
Lettrich, Jeffrey J. Law&B 92
Letts, Barry ScF&FL 92
Letts, Don MiSFD 9
Letts, J. Spencer 1934- WhoAm 92
Letts, Lindsay Gordon 1948- WhoE 93
Letts, Nancy Barlow 1942- WhoE 93
Letts, Thomas Clinton 1911- WhoWor 93
Lettvin, Theodore 1926- Baker 92, WhoAm 92, WhoE 93
Letuli, Olo Uluao Misilagi 1919- WhoAm 92
Letulle, Joan Ann 1933- WhoAmW 93
Letvin, Casey BioIn 17
Letvinchuk, John Michael 1953- WhoSSW 93
Letwin, Leon 1929- WhoAm 92
Letwin, Oliver 1956- BioIn 17
Leu, Leslyn Law&B 92
Leu, Walter 1934- WhoWor 93
Leubert, Alfred O.P. 1922- St&PR 93
Leubert, Alfred Otto Paul 1922- WhoAm 92, WhoE 93
Leuchtag, Hans Richard 1927- WhoSSW 93
Leuchter, Fred A. BioIn 17
Leuckart, F. Ernst Christoph 1748-1817 Baker 92
Leuckel, Wolfgang 1932- WhoScE 91-3
Leuelling, Julie Rose Weber Law&B 92
Leuenberger, Philippe 1944- WhoScE 91-4
Leugers, William J., Jr. 1942- St&PR 93
Leukefeld, Carl George 1943- WhoSSW 93, WhoWor 93
Leule, Richard K. St&PR 93
Leung, Calvin Yat-chor 1959- WhoWor 93
Leung, Christopher Chung Kit 1939- WhoE 93
Leung, Ernest C. 1939- WhoAsAP 91
Leung, George W. 1952- St&PR 93
Leung, Kenneth C. 1944- St&PR 93
Leung, Louis Man Lay 1956- WhoWor 93
Leung, Louis Man Tat 1965- WhoWor 93
Leung, Man Yat Kenny 1951- WhoWor 93
Leung, Raymond Chung-chun 1952- WhoSSW 93
Leung, Roderick Chi-tak 1949- WhoEmL 93, WhoWor 93
Leung, Ted Tit-Hung 1941- WhoAm 92

Leung, Wai-Tung 1946- *WhoAsAP 91*
Leung, Wing Hai 1937- *WhoSSW 93*
Leung Man-Kin, Michael 1938- *WhoAsAP 91*
Leunig, Mark W. *Law&B 92*
Leunissen, Dorothy Ann Piatnek 1928- *WhoE 93*
Leuos, Bob 1943- *St&PR 93*
Leupena, Tupua-Samoa 1922- *WhoAsAP 91*
Leupp, Alex Max 1939- *St&PR 93*
Leupp, Francis Ellington 1849-1918 *JrnUS*
Leurion, Remi 1957- *WhoWor 93*
Leuschner Fernandes, Rui 1933- *WhoScE 91-3*
Leusen, Isidoor Roger 1923- *WhoScE 91-2*
Leusink, Frederik Jan 1939- *WhoScE 91-3*
Leussing, Joanne Gilbert 1932- *WhoAmW 93*
Leute, Volkmar 1938- *WhoScE 91-3*
Leute, W.R., III 1945- *St&PR 93*
Leute, William Russell, III 1945- *WhoAm 92*
Leutenegger, Marc 1931- *WhoScE 91-2*
Leuterio, Mercedes Mabbun 1926- *WhoWor 93*
Leutgeb, Joseph (Ignaz) c. 1745-1811 *Baker 92*
Leuthauser, Klaus-Dieter 1937- *WhoScE 91-3*
Leuthold, David 1932- *WhoAm 92*
Leuthold, Raymond Martin 1940- *WhoAm 92*
Leutscher, Hendrik J. 1935- *WhoScE 91-3*
Leuty, Gerald Johnston 1919- *WhoWor 93*
Leutzbach, Wilhelm 1922- *WhoScE 91-3*
Leutze, James Richard 1935- *WhoAm 92, WhoSSW 93*
Leuver, Robert Joseph 1927- *WhoAm 92*
Leuzzi, Paul William, II *Law&B 92*
Lev, Abraham David *Law&B 92*
Lev, Alexander Shulim 1945- *WhoE 93*
Lev, Arthur Jason *Law&B 92*
Lev, Baruch Itamar 1938- *WhoAm 92*
Lev, Eliat 1949- *St&PR 93*
Lev, Ray 1912-1968 *Baker 92*
Leva, Charles R. 1914- *St&PR 93*
Leva, Donn W. 1927- *St&PR 93*
Leva, Enrico de 1867-1955 *Baker 92*
Leva, James Robert 1932- *St&PR 93, WhoAm 92*
Leva, Marx 1915- *WhoAm 92*
Leva, Neil Irwin 1929- *WhoE 93*
Levack, Arthur Paul 1909- *WhoAm 92*
Levack, Daniel J.H. *ScF&FL 92*
Levada, William Joseph 1936- *WhoAm 92*
Levade, Charles (Gaston) 1869-1948 *Baker 92*
Levai, Imre 1924- *WhoScE 91-4*
Levai, Julia Szilagyi 1942- *WhoAmW 93*
Levai, Pierre Alexandre 1937- *WhoAm 92*
Levai, Zoltan 1929- *WhoScE 91-4*
Leval, Pierre Nelson 1936- *WhoE 93*
Levalier, Dotian 1943- *WhoAm 92*
LeValley, Guy Glenn 1942- *WhoE 93*
LeValley, Joan Catherine 1931- *WhoAmW 93, WhoWor 93*
Levallois, M. *WhoScE 91-2*
Levan, B.W. 1941- *St&PR 93*
Levan, Curt W. *Law&B 92*
Le Van, Daniel Hayden 1924- *WhoE 93, WhoSSW 93, WhoWor 93*
Levan, David M. 1945- *St&PR 93*
Levan, Jack Alan 1954- *St&PR 93*
Levan, Larry d1992 *NewYTBS 92*
LeVander, Harold 1910-1992 *BioIn 17*
Levandoski, Kristine Louise 1959- *WhoAmW 93*
Levandowski, Barbara Sue 1948- *WhoAmW 93*
Levandowski, Donald William 1927- *WhoAm 92*
Levandowsky, Michael 1935- *WhoE 93*
Levant, Brian *MiSFD 9*
Levant, Oscar 1906-1972 *Baker 92, BioIn 17*
Levari, Henry K. 1948- *St&PR 93*
Levarie, Siegmund 1914- *Baker 92*
Levasseur, Jean-Henri 1764-c. 1826 *Baker 92*
Levasseur, Nicolas 1791-1871 *OxDcOp*
Levasseur, Nicolas (-Prosper) 1791-1871 *Baker 92*
LeVasseur, Richard Arthur 1942- *St&PR 93*
Levasseur, Rosalie 1749-1826 *Baker 92, OxDcOp*
Levasseur, William Ryan 1935- *WhoAm 92*
Levatino, Anthony Samuel 1940- *St&PR 93*
Levato, Joseph Anthony 1941- *WhoAm 92*
Levaux, Paul *WhoScE 91-2*
Levav, Itzhak 1939- *WhoUN 92*
LeVay, John Paul 1941- *St&PR 93*
LeVay, Simon 1943- *News 92 [port]*
Levcuk, Timofej 1912- *DrEEuF*
Leve, Alan Donald 1927- *WhoAm 92*
Levee, Didier Alain 1954- *WhoWor 93*
Levee, Harris Harold 1919- *WhoE 93*
Levee, John Harrison 1924- *WhoAm 92*
Leveen, Pauline 1925- *WhoE 93*
LeVeen, Robert Frederick 1946- *WhoEmL 93*
Levegood, Lynne L. *AmWomPl*
Leveille, Gilbert Antonio 1934- *WhoAm 92*
Leveille, Walter Henry, Jr. 1945- *WhoSSW 93*
Level, Leon Jules 1940- *St&PR 93, WhoAm 92*
Level, Randall Lee *Law&B 92*
Levelt, Willem J.M. 1938- *WhoScE 91-3*
Levelt Sengers, Johanna Maria Henrica 1929- *WhoAm 92, WhoAmW 93*
Leven, Alexander Leslie, Earl of c. 1580-1661 *HarEnMi*
Leven, Ann Ruth 1940- *WhoAm 92, WhoE 93*
Leven, Charles Louis 1928- *WhoAm 92, WhoWor 93*
Leven, Harris S. *Law&B 92*
Leven, Jeremy 1941- *ScF&FL 92*
Leven, Richard Michael 1940- *St&PR 93*
Levenberg, Alvin 1944- *St&PR 93*
Levenberg, Nathan 1919- *St&PR 93*
Levendorskii, Serge Zakhar 1951- *WhoWor 93*
Levendosky, Charles Leonard 1936- *WhoWrEP 92*
Levendusky, Philip George 1946- *WhoAm 92*
Levene, David A. 1939- *St&PR 93*
Levene, Malcolm *WhoScE 91-1*
Levene, Philip *ScF&FL 92*
Levenfeld, Milton Arthur 1927- *WhoAm 92*
Levenfeld, Richard B. *Law&B 92*
Levengood, William C. 1925- *WhoAm 92*
Levens, Charles 1689-1764 *Baker 92*
Levensaler, Walter Louis 1934- *WhoE 93*
Levenson, Alan Bradley 1935- *WhoAm 92, WhoE 93, WhoWor 93*
Levenson, Alan Ira 1935- *WhoAm 92*
Levenson, Barbara Sue 1942- *WhoAmW 93*
Levenson, Bill *BioIn 17*
Levenson, Boris 1884-1947 *Baker 92*
Levenson, Carl 1905-1990 *BioIn 17*
Levenson, Christopher 1934- *WhoCanL 92*
Levenson, Ethel Coppelman 1931- *WhoAmW 93*
Levenson, Harvey S. 1940- *St&PR 93*
Levenson, Harvey Stuart 1940- *WhoAm 92, WhoE 93*
Levenson, Jacob Clavner 1922- *WhoAm 92*
Levenson, Jordan *WhoWrEP 92*
Levenson, Lewis 1934- *St&PR 93*
Levenson, Linda *Law&B 92*
Levenson, M.J. *St&PR 93*
Levenson, Marc David 1945- *WhoAm 92*
Levenson, Maria Nijole 1940- *WhoSSW 93*
Levenson, Mark R. 1947- *St&PR 93*
Levenson, Mark S. *Law&B 92*
Levenson, Milton 1923- *WhoAm 92*
Levenson, Nathan S. 1916- *WhoE 93*
Levenson, Richard Neil 1942- *WhoAm 92*
Levenson, Robert J. 1941- *St&PR 93*
Levenson, Stanley Richard 1933- *WhoAm 92*
Levenson, Stanley Sanford 1920- *St&PR 93*
Levenson, Steven G. 1940- *St&PR 93*
Levenstein, Alan Peter 1936- *WhoAm 92*
Levenstein, Arnold 1930- *St&PR 93*
Levenstein, Harold 1923- *WhoE 93*
Levenstein, Henry 1950- *St&PR 93*
Levenstein, Robert 1926- *WhoAm 92*
Leventakis, John 1935- *WhoWor 93*
Levental, Harry E. 1916- *St&PR 93*
Levental, Valery Yakovlevich 1942- *WhoWor 93*
Leventer, Richard J. 1930- *St&PR 93*
Leventer, Terri *WhoAmW 93*
Leventhal, Alice Walker 1944- *BioIn 17*
Leventhal, Ann Z. 1936- *WhoWrEP 92*
Leventhal, Carl M. 1933- *WhoAm 92*
Leventhal, Cyndi 1963- *WhoEmL 93*
Leventhal, David 1958- *St&PR 93*
Leventhal, Edwin H. 1930- *St&PR 93*
Leventhal, Harriet Bonnie 1951- *WhoAmW 93*
Leventhal, Harry E. 1916- *St&PR 93*
Leventhal, Julius d1990 *BioIn 17*
Leventhal, Lionel *ScF&FL 92*
Leventhal, Lionel 1937- *BioIn 17*
Leventhal, Marvin 1937- *WhoE 93*
Leventhal, Morton 1924- *WhoSSW 93*
Leventhal, Nathan 1943- *WhoE 93*
Leventhal, Ruth 1940- *WhoAmW 93, WhoE 93*
Leventhal, Stuart Gary 1947- *WhoE 93*
Leventhal, Teri V. 1932- *WhoAmW 93*
Leventon, Aileen R. *Law&B 92*
Le Veque, Matthew Kurt 1958- *WhoEmL 93*
Lever, A.F. *WhoScE 91-1*
Lever, Andrew Michael Lindsay 1953- *WhoWor 93*
Lever, (Tresham) Christopher (Arthur Lindsay) 1932- *ConAu 136*
Lever, James Jefferson, III 1947- *WhoEmL 93, WhoSSW 93*
Lever, Jeffrey Darcy *WhoScE 91-1*
Lever, Walter Frederick 1909- *WhoAm 92, WhoWor 93*
Lever, William Fred *WhoScE 91-1*
Levere, Jane Lois 1950- *WhoAmW 93*
Levere, Richard David 1931- *WhoAm 92, WhoWor 93*
Leverenz, Anthony John 1946- *WhoWor 93*
Leverett, Miles Corrington 1910- *WhoAm 92*
Leverett, Thomas DeWitt 1956- *WhoSSW 93*
Leverette, Gary 1956- *WhoSSW 93*
Leverette, Mary Marlowe 1955- *WhoSSW 93*
Leverich, Kathleen 1948- *ConAu 137*
Leveridge, Richard c. 1670-1758 *Baker 92*
Levering, Bas 1947- *WhoWor 93*
Levering, Donald Warren 1949- *WhoWrEP 92*
Leverington, John James 1951- *WhoEmL 93*
Leverkuhn, Wayne Edward 1935- *WhoSSW 93*
Leverkus, Gertrude 1898-1989 *BioIn 17*
Levernier, Thomas John 1930- *St&PR 93*
Leveroos, John Prescott 1949- *WhoSSW 93*
Leversee, Gordon Jepson 1944- *WhoE 93*
LeVert, Francis Edward 1940- *WhoAm 92*
Levert, John Bertels, Jr. 1931- *WhoAm 92, WhoSSW 93*
Leverton, John William 1940- *WhoSSW 93*
Levertov, Denise 1923- *AmWrS3, BioIn 17, WhoAm 92, WhoWrEP 92*
Leveson, Irving Frederick 1939- *WhoAm 92*
Levesque, Allen Henry 1936- *WhoE 93*
Levesque, Donald Roger 1941- *St&PR 93*
Levesque, Louis 1908- *WhoAm 92*
Levesque, Lucien C. 1930- *St&PR 93*
Levesque, Marc *Law&B 92*
Levesque, Pascal 1923- *St&PR 93*
Levesque, Raymond 1928- *WhoCanL 92*
Levesque, Rene 1922-1987 *DcTwHis*
Levesque, Rene Jules Albert 1926- *WhoAm 92*
Leveto-Jabr, Paula Denise 1950- *WhoSSW 93*
Levetown, Robert A. *Law&B 92*
Levetown, Robert Alexander 1935- *WhoAm 92*
Levett, Mark A. 1949- *St&PR 93*
Levett, Michael John 1939- *St&PR 93*
Levey, Brigid Brophy 1929- *BioIn 17*
Levey, Gerald Saul 1937- *WhoAm 92*
Levey, Gregory D. d1991 *BioIn 17*
Levey, Harold Abram 1924- *WhoE 93*
Levey, J. Gerald *St&PR 93*
Levey, Jay *MiSFD 9*
Levey, Lisa D. *Law&B 92*
Levey, Merton David 1925- *St&PR 93*
Levey, Michael Vincent 1927- *WhoWor 93*
Levey, Richard C. 1833-c. 1904 *Baker 92*
Levey, Richard Michael 1811-1899 *Baker 92*
Levey, Robert Frank 1945- *WhoAm 92*
Levey, Samuel 1932- *WhoAm 92*
Levey, Sanford Norman 1929- *WhoSSW 93*
Levey, William A. 1943- *MiSFD 9*
Levey, William Charles 1837-1894 *Baker 92*
Levi, Alan J. *MiSFD 9*
Levi, Arlo Dane 1933- *St&PR 93, WhoAm 92*
Levi, Barbara Goss 1943- *WhoAmW 93*
Levi, C. *WhoScE 91-2*
Levi, Carlo 1902-1975 *BioIn 17*
Levi, David F. 1951- *WhoAm 92*
Levi, Doro 1898-1991 *BioIn 17*
Levi, Dorothy 1942- *WhoWrEP 92*
Levi, Edward Hirsch 1911- *WhoAm 92*
Levi, Enrico 1918- *WhoE 93*
Levi, Franco Achille 1919- *WhoWor 93*
Levi, Hans Wolfgang 1924- *WhoScE 91-3*
Levi, Herbert Walter 1921- *WhoAm 92*
Levi, Hermann 1839-1900 *Baker 92, IntDcOp, OxDcOp*
Levi, Ilan Mosche 1943- *WhoAm 92*
Levi, James Harry 1939- *WhoAm 92*
Levi, Jan Heller 1954- *WhoWrEP 92*
Levi, Josef Alan 1938- *WhoAm 92*
Levi, Julian Hirsch 1909- *WhoAm 92*
Levi, Kurt 1910- *WhoAm 92*
Levi, Lennart 1930- *WhoScE 91-4*
Levi, Malcolm A. 1916- *St&PR 93*
Levi, Mark 1951- *WhoE 93*
Levi, Maurice David 1945- *WhoAm 92*
Levi, Primo 1919-1987 *BioIn 17, ScF&FL 92*
Levi, Robert Henry 1915- *WhoAm 92*
Levi, Roy Elliott 1945- *WhoE 93*
Levi, Ruth E. *AmWomPl*
Levi, Salvator 1934- *WhoScE 91-2*
Levi, Samuel Gershon 1908-1990 *BioIn 17*
Levi, Steven C. 1948- *WhoWrEP 92*
Levi, Theodore 1924- *St&PR 93*
Levi, Toni Mergentime 1941- *WhoWrEP 92*
Levi, Vicki Gold 1941- *WhoE 93*
Levi, Wayne *BioIn 17*
Levi, Werner 1912- *ConAu 37NR*
Levi, Yoel 1950- *Baker 92, WhoAm 92, WhoSSW 93*
Levichev, Alexandr Vladimir 1951- *WhoWor 93*
Levick, Bruce W. 1954- *St&PR 93*
Levick, Stephen Eric 1951- *WhoEmL 93*
Levicki, John S. 1940- *St&PR 93*
Levicki, John Sullivan 1940- *WhoAm 92*
Levicky, Allen Paul 1948- *St&PR 93*
Levidis, Dimitri 1885?-1951 *Baker 92*
Levie, Howard Sidney 1907- *WhoAm 92*
Levie, Joseph Henry *WhoAm 92*
Levie, Rex Dean 1937?- *ScF&FL 92*
Le Vien, John Douglas 1918- *WhoAm 92*
Levien, Joy *Law&B 92, WhoAm 92*
Levien, Roger E. 1935- *St&PR 93*
Levi-Montalcini, Rita 1909- *BioIn 17, WhoAm 92, WhoWor 93*
Levin, A. Leo 1919- *WhoAm 92*
Levin, Aaron Reuben 1929- *WhoAm 92*
Levin, Adam L. *Law&B 92*
Levin, Alan M. 1926- *WhoAm 92*
Levin, Alan Michael 1948- *St&PR 93*
Levin, Amy Beth 1942- *WhoWrEP 92*
Levin, Barton John 1944- *WhoAm 92*
Levin, Bernard 1942- *WhoAm 92*
Levin, Bertha d1992 *NewYTBS 92*
Levin, Betsy 1935- *WhoAm 92*
Levin, Betty 1927- *ScF&FL 92*
Levin, Bruce Alan 1939- *St&PR 93, WhoAm 92*
Levin, Burton 1930- *WhoAm 92, WhoWor 93*
Levin, Carl *WhoAm 92*
Levin, Carl 1934- *WhoAm 92*
Levin, Carl M. 1934- *CngDr 91*
Levin, Carol Arlene 1945- *WhoAmW 93*
Levin, Dan 1914- *WhoWrEP 92*
Levin, David 1924- *WhoWrEP 92*
Levin, David Harold 1928- *WhoSSW 93*
Levin, David L. *Law&B 92*
Levin, David S. *Law&B 92*
Levin, David Saul 1934- *St&PR 93*
Levin, Debbe Ann 1954- *WhoAmW 93*
Levin, Diana Phyllis Karasik 1938- *WhoAmW 93*
Levin, Ed 1921- *BioIn 17*
Levin, Edward M. 1934- *WhoE 93*
Levin, Ellen Barrett *Law&B 92*
Levin, Elliot M. *St&PR 93*
Levin, Emil 1946- *WhoEmL 93*
Levin, Evanne Lynn *Law&B 92*
Levin, Ezra Gurion 1934- *WhoAm 92, WhoWor 93*
Levin, Felice Michaels 1928- *WhoAmW 93*
Levin, Flora Jean 1942- *WhoAmW 93*
Levin, Fredrick 1944- *WhoE 93*
Levin, Geoffrey Arthur 1955- *WhoAm 92*
Levin, Gerald M. 1939- *St&PR 93*
Levin, Gerald Manuel 1939- *WhoAm 92, WhoE 93*
Levin, Gilbert Victor 1924- *St&PR 93*
Levin, Harris 1906-1990 *BioIn 17*
Levin, Harry 1912- *BioIn 17, ScF&FL 92*
Levin, Harry 1925- *WhoAm 92*
Levin, Harry Tuchman 1912- *WhoAm 92*
Levin, Harvey J(oshua) 1924-1992 *ConAu 137*
Levin, Harvey Joshua 1924-1992 *BioIn 17*
Levin, Henry 1909-1980 *MiSFD 9N*
Levin, Herman d1990 *BioIn 17*
Levin, Howard S. 1924- *St&PR 93*
Levin, Hugh Lauter 1951- *WhoEmL 93*
Levin, Ira *BioIn 17*
Levin, Ira 1929- *ScF&FL 92, WhoAm 92, WhoWrEP 92*
Levin, Ira S. *Law&B 92*
Levin, Jack 1932- *WhoAm 92*
Levin, Jack G. 1947- *St&PR 93*
Levin, Jack S. 1936- *WhoAm 92*
Levin, Jacob Joseph 1926- *WhoAm 92*
Levin, James Ely *Law&B 92*
Levin, Janice H. *Law&B 92*
Levin, Jeffrey D. *St&PR 93*
Levin, Jeffrey K. *Law&B 92*
Levin, Jennifer Dawn d1986 *BioIn 17*
Levin, Jerry Wayne 1944- *St&PR 93, WhoAm 92, WhoSSW 93*
Levin, Joan Ellen 1947- *WhoE 93*
Levin, Joel H. *Law&B 92*

Levin, John 1944?- ScF&FL 92
Levin, John D. Law&B 92
Levin, John S. Law&B 92
Levin, Jonathan Vigdor 1927- WhoUN 92
Levin, Joseph W. 1939- WhoIns 93
Levin, Juan Alberto 1941- WhoWor 93
Levin, Jules Fred 1940- WhoAm 92
Levin, Kenneth Sherman 1937- WhoAm 92
Levin, Kerry 1951- WhoEmL 93
Levin, Lawrence Adam Law&B 92
Levin, Lawrence D. 1952- St&PR 93
Levin, Leslie H. 1925- St&PR 93
Levin, Lev Abramovich BioIn 17
Levin, Lois Ann 1941- WhoE 93
Levin, M.G. 1904-1963 IntDcAn
Levin, M. Penny 1956- WhoE 93, WhoEmL 93
Levin, Marc MiSFD 9
Levin, Marc S. Law&B 92
Levin, Marcia Alison WhoE 93
Levin, Mario 1953- WhoEmL 93
Levin, Mark Law&B 92
Levin, Mark Jay 1957- WhoWor 93
Levin, Marshall Abbott 1920- WhoAm 92
Levin, Martin Paul 1918- WhoAm 92
Levin, Marvin E. 1924- WhoAm 92
Levin, Meyer 1905-1981 BioIn 17, JeAmFiW, JeAmHC, ScF&FL 92
Levin, Michael David 1943- WhoWor 93
Levin, Michael Joseph 1943- WhoE 93, WhoWor 93
Levin, Michael S. 1950- St&PR 93
Levin, Mitchell Allan 1944- St&PR 93
Levin, Morton David 1923- WhoAm 92
Levin, Murray Simon 1943- WhoAm 92
Levin, Norman Cyril 1949- WhoAm 92, WhoE 93
Levin, Paul F. Law&B 92
Levin, Peggy Neumann 1949- WhoSSW 93
Levin, Peter MiSFD 9
Levin, Peter J. 1939- WhoAm 92
Levin, Phillip T. St&PR 93
Levin, Richard Charles 1947- WhoAm 92, WhoEmL 93
Levin, Richard I. 1948- St&PR 93
Levin, Richard J. 1946- St&PR 93
Levin, Richard Louis 1922- WhoAm 92
Levin, Robert Alan 1957- WhoEmL 93, WhoWor 93
Levin, Robert Daniel 1930- WhoAm 92
Levin, Robert Edmond 1931- WhoE 93
Levin, Robert Jeffrey Law&B 92
Levin, Robert Joseph 1928- WhoAm 92
Levin, Robert L. Law&B 92
Levin, Rona F. 1945- WhoE 93
Levin, Sam 1923- WhoScE 91-2
Levin, Samuel 1929- St&PR 93
Levin, Sander 1931- WhoAm 92
Levin, Sander M. 1931- CngDr 91
Levin, Sheldon L. 1935- St&PR 93
Levin, Sidney MiSFD 9
Levin, Sidney H. 1935- WhoSSW 93
Levin, Simon 1942- WhoAm 92
Levin, Simon Asher 1941- WhoAm 92
Levin, Stanley d1991 BioIn 17
Levin, Steve WhoWrEP 92
Levin, Tobe 1948- WhoWor 93
Levin, William Cohn 1917- WhoAm 92
Levin, William Edward 1954- WhoWor 93
Levina, Ol'ga Ivanovna 1908-1991 BioIn 17
Levina, Zara 1906-1976 Baker 92
Levinas, Emmanuel BioIn 17
Levinberg, Phyllis D. Law&B 92
Levine, Aaron 1917- WhoAm 92
Levine, Alan 1948- WhoEmL 93
Levine, Alan Hillel 1937- WhoE 93
Levine, Alan J. 1947- WhoAm 92
Levine, Alan M. St&PR 93
Levine, Alan Neal 1960- WhoEmL 93, WhoSSW 93
Levine, Alan Stuart 1958- WhoEmL 93
Levine, Albert Bernard 1922- St&PR 93
Levine, Allan St&PR 93
Levine, Allen 1929- St&PR 93, WhoAm 92
Levine, Allen A. 1912- St&PR 93
Levine, Alvin J. 1925- St&PR 93
Levine, Amy Janet Law&B 92
Levine, Andrew Scott Law&B 92
Levine, Arnold Eugene 1921- St&PR 93
Levine, Arnold Jay 1939- WhoAm 92
Levine, Arnold Leslie 1948- WhoAm 92
Levine, Arthur Elliott 1948- WhoAm 92
Levine, Arthur Samuel 1936- WhoAm 92
Levine, Barbara Hoberman 1937- ConAu 139
Levine, Barbara J. Law&B 92
Levine, Barry R. 1953- WhoWor 93
Levine, Beatrice Harris 1917- WhoAmW 93
Levine, Benjamin 1931- WhoE 93, WhoWor 93
Levine, Bernard B. 1918- St&PR 93
Levine, Bertram A. 1906-1991 BioIn 17
Levine, Beryl Joyce 1935- WhoAmW 93
Levine, Beth M. Law&B 92
Levine, Betty K. 1933- BioIn 17
Levine, Burton I. Law&B 92
Levine, Carl Morton 1931- WhoAm 92
Levine, Caroline 1929- WhoAmW 93
Levine, Charles A. 1897-1991 BioIn 17
Levine, Charles D. Law&B 92
Levine, Charles Michael 1942- WhoAm 92
Levine, Daniel 1934- WhoAm 92
Levine, David 1926- WhoAm 92
Levine, David Barry 1932- WhoAm 92
Levine, David Barry 1939- St&PR 93
LeVine, David E. 1933- WhoAm 92
Levine, David Lawrence 1919- WhoAm 92
Levine, David M. 1949- WhoE 93
Levine, David Michael 1950- St&PR 93
Levine, David P. 1948- BioIn 17
Levine, Dennis B. BioIn 17
Levine, Diana Maisel 1914- WhoAmW 93
Levine, Donald Nathan 1931- WhoAm 92
Le Vine, Duane Gilbert 1933- WhoAm 92, WhoWor 93
Levine, Edna Simon d1992 NewYTBS 92
Levine, Edna Simon 1910-1992 BioIn 17
Levine, Edward L. Law&B 92
Levine, Edwin Burton 1920- WhoAm 92
Levine, Ellen 1939- WhoWrEP 92
Levine, Ellen R. 1943- WhoAm 92, WhoAmW 93
Levine, Ellis B. Law&B 92
Levine, Ellis B. 1938- St&PR 93
Levine, Ernest Stephen 1944- St&PR 93
Levine, Eugene 1925- WhoE 93
Levine, Faith Laurel 1939- WhoE 93
Levine, Fred Andrew Law&B 92
Levine, Geoffrey 1942- WhoE 93
Levine, George 1931- ScF&FL 92
Levine, George H. 1928- St&PR 93
Levine, George Lewis 1931- WhoAm 92
Levine, George Richard 1929- WhoAm 92
Levine, Gerald Richard 1936- WhoAm 92, WhoE 93, WhoWor 93
Levine, Gilbert 1948- Baker 92
Levine, Harold 1921- WhoAm 92
Levine, Harold 1931- WhoAm 92, WhoSSW 93, WhoWor 93
Levine, Harold Grumet 1931- WhoSSW 93
Levine, Harry 1922- WhoAm 92
Levine, Harvey Robert 1931- WhoE 93
Levine, Helen Dorothy 1957- WhoAmW 93
Levine, Herbert 1916-1991 BioIn 17
Levine, Herbert Malcolm 1933- WhoWrEP 92
Levine, Herbert Samuel 1928- WhoAm 92
Levine, Howard Arnold 1932- WhoAm 92
Levine, Howard Harris 1949- WhoAm 92
Levine, I. Robert 1932- St&PR 93
Levine, I. Stanley 1928- WhoAm 92
Levine, Ira Noel 1937- WhoE 93
Levine, Ira S. Law&B 92
Levine, Ira S. 1960- St&PR 93
Levine, Irvin 1921- St&PR 93
Levine, Irving M. 1935- St&PR 93
Levine, Irving Raskin WhoAm 92
Levine, Israel E. 1923- WhoAm 92
Levine, Jack 1915- BioIn 17, WhoAm 92
Levine, Jack 1932- St&PR 93
Levine, Jack B. 1941- St&PR 93
Levine, James BioIn 17
Levine, James 1943- ConMus 8 [port], IntDcOp [port], News 92 [port], -92-3 [port], OxDcOp, WhoAm 92
Levine, James (Lawrence) 1943- Baker 92
Levine, Jane Rue 1944- WhoWor 93
Levine, Jane Sheila 1946- WhoEmL 93
Levine, Janet 1945- WhoWrEP 92
Levine, Janice R. 1954- WhoAmW 93, WhoE 93
Levine, Janis E. 1953- WhoAmW 93
Le Vine, Jerome Edward 1923- WhoWor 93
Levine, Jerome Fredric 1949- WhoE 93, WhoEmL 93
Levine, Jerome Paul 1937- WhoAm 92
Levine, Jesse E. 1951- St&PR 93
Levine, Jill 1958- WhoE 93
Levine, Joan Barbara 1942- WhoAmW 93
Levine, John David 1936- WhoAm 92
Levine, Jon M. 1958- St&PR 93
Levine, Jonathan B. Law&B 92
Levine, Jonathan B. 1943- St&PR 93
Levine, Joseph 1912- WhoAm 92
Levine, Joshua 1916- St&PR 93
Levine, Judith 1952- ConAu 139, WhoWrEP 92
Levine, Judith Dee 1950- WhoEmL 93
Levine, Julian Robert 1933- St&PR 93
Levine, Julie Gorchow 1956- WhoE 93
Levine, Ken BioIn 17
Levine, Kenneth M. 1946- St&PR 93
Levine, Lainie 1942- WhoAm 92
Levine, Larry 1933- St&PR 93
Levine, Laura BioIn 17
Levine, Laurence B. 1941- WhoE 93, WhoWor 93
Levine, Laurence E. 1941- WhoAm 92
Levine, Laurence Harvey 1946- WhoAm 92
Levine, Laurence William 1931- WhoAm 92
Levine, Lawrence E. Law&B 92
Levine, Lawrence J. St&PR 93
Levine, Lawrence Steven 1934- WhoAm 92
Levine, Lawrence William 1933- WhoAm 92
Levine, Leo M. 1930- St&PR 93
Levine, Leon 1937- St&PR 93, WhoSSW 93
Levine, Les 1935- BioIn 17, WhoE 93
Levine, Linda Jane 1943- WhoAmW 93
Levine, Linda N. 1942- WhoAmW 93
Levine, Lois Jaffin 1934- WhoAmW 93
Levine, Louis David 1940- WhoAm 92
Levine, Lowell J. 1937- WhoAm 92
Levine, Madeline Geltman 1942- WhoAm 92
Levine, Marilyn Markovich 1930- WhoAmW 93, WhoE 93
Levine, Mark Leonard 1945- WhoAm 92, WhoWrEP 92
Levine, Martin 1925- WhoSSW 93
Levine, Martin 1944- WhoAm 92
Levine, Martin David 1938- WhoAm 92
Levine, Martin Robert 1943- WhoAm 92
Levine, Marva M. Law&B 92
Levine, Marvin 1924- WhoE 93
Levine, Max H. St&PR 93
Levine, Mel 1943- CngDr 91
Levine, Meldon Edises 1943- WhoAm 92
Levine, Melvin Charles 1930- WhoE 93, WhoWor 93
Levine, Melvin J. 1925- St&PR 93
Levine, Michael BioIn 17
Levine, Michael 1954- WhoAm 92
Levine, Michael David 1955- St&PR 93
Levine, Michael Elias 1941- WhoAm 92
Levine, Michael Lawrence 1947- WhoEmL 93
Levine, Milton A. 1925- St&PR 93
Levine, Naomi B. 1923- BioIn 17
Levine, Naomi Bronheim 1923- WhoAm 92
Levine, Neal T. 1952- St&PR 93
Levine, Neil H. Law&B 92
Levine, Noel 1920- St&PR 93
Levine, Norman 1924- WhoCanL 92
Levine, Norman D. 1937- St&PR 93
Levine, Norman Dion 1912- WhoAm 92
Levine, Norman G. WhoIns 93
Levine, Norman Gene 1926- WhoAm 92
Levine, Norman M. St&PR 93
Levine, Oscar 1923- WhoE 93
Levine, Pat Golden d1991 BioIn 17
Levine, Paul 1948- ConAu 137
Levine, Paul Howard 1937- WhoE 93
Levine, Paul J. 1936- St&PR 93
Levine, Paul Michael 1934- WhoAm 92
Levine, Peter S. Law&B 92
Levine, Philip 1922- WhoAm 92
Levine, Philip 1928- ConAu 37NR, WhoAm 92, WhoWrEP 92
Levine, Rachmiel 1910- WhoAm 92
Levine, Ralph Law&B 92
Levine, Ralph 1936- St&PR 93
Levine, Randy Lewis 1955- WhoAm 92
Levine, Raphael David 1938- WhoAm 92, WhoWor 93
Levine, Rebecca-Sue 1946- WhoEmL 93
Levine, Rhea Joy Cottler 1939- WhoAm 92, WhoAmW 93
Levine, Richard 1933- WhoSSW 93
Levine, Richard Albert 1935- St&PR 93
Levine, Richard James 1942- WhoAm 92
Levine, Richard Steven 1947- WhoEmL 93
Levine, Richard Stewart 1952- WhoEmL 93
Levine, Robert BioIn 17
LeVine, Robert Alan 1932- WhoAm 92
Levine, Robert Arthur 1930- WhoAm 92
Levine, Robert Bernard 1933- St&PR 93
Levine, Robert Jeffrey 1956- WhoEmL 93
Levine, Robert John 1934- WhoAm 92, WhoE 93
Levine, Robert L. d1992 NewYTBS 92
Levine, Robert L. 1905-1992 BioIn 17
Levine, Robert Sidney 1921- WhoAm 92
Levine, Robert Sidney 1944- St&PR 93
Levine, Robin S. Law&B 92
Levine, Roger A. 1956- St&PR 93
Levine, Ronald H. 1935- WhoAm 92, WhoSSW 93
Levine, Ronald Jay 1953- WhoAm 92, WhoE 93, WhoEmL 93
Levine, Rosemary T. Law&B 92
Levine, Ruth Ellen 1959- WhoAmW 93
Levine, Ruth Rothenberg WhoAm 92
Levine, Samuel Harold 1925- WhoE 93
Levine, Samuel J. 1934- WhoE 93
Levine, Samuel Paul 1911- WhoWrEP 92
Levine, Sarah Loewenberg WhoAmW 93
Levine, Scott Alan 1949- WhoAm 92
Levine, Seymour St&PR 93
Levine, Seymour 1924- WhoAm 92
Levine, Sharon Gail 1961- WhoAmW 93
Levine, Sherrie 1947- BioIn 17
Levine, Sidney ScF&FL 92
Levine, Sol 1922- WhoAm 92
Levine, Solomon Bernard 1920- WhoAm 92
Levine, Stanley A. 1936- WhoAm 92, WhoE 93
Levine, Stephen Barry 1942- WhoSSW 93
Levine, Steven Alan 1951- WhoEmL 93
Levine, Steven L. Law&B 92
Levine, Stuart George 1932- WhoAm 92
Levine, Stuart Robert 1958- St&PR 93
Levine, Sumner Norton 1923- WhoAm 92
Levine, Susan A. Law&B 92
Levine, Susan B. 1958- WhoAmW 93
Levine, Suzanne Braun 1941- WhoAm 92
Levine, Suzanne M. BioIn 17
Levine, Suzanne Marin 1951- WhoE 93
Levine, Thomas Mark 1949- WhoE 93
Levine, Vicki Lucille 1927- WhoWrEP 92
Le Vine, Victor Theodore 1928- WhoAm 92
LeVine, Walter Daniel 1941- WhoE 93
Levine, William A. 1924- St&PR 93
Levine, William H. 1941- St&PR 93
Levine, William Silver 1941- WhoAm 92
Levine, Yari WhoAmW 93
Levine-Battista, Sandra 1935- WhoAmW 93
Levine-Calvi, Margaret 1954- St&PR 93
Levine-Freidus BioIn 17
Levine-Goffman, Laura Amy 1959- WhoEmL 93
Levine-Provost, Gail BioIn 17
Levine-Shneidman, Conalee 1930- WhoE 93
Levinger, Beryl Beth 1947- WhoAm 92, WhoE 93
Levinger, Elma Ehrlich 1887-1958 AmWomPl
Levinger, Jack 1922- St&PR 93
Levinger, Joseph Solomon 1921- WhoAm 92
Levinger, Moshe BioIn 17
Levinger, Moshe 1935- News 92 [port]
Levinger, Samuel 1945- St&PR 93
Levings, Charles Sandford, III 1930- WhoAm 92
Levings, Theresa Lawrence 1952- WhoEmL 93
Levingston, Ernest Lee 1921- St&PR 93, WhoSSW 93, WhoWor 93
Levingston, Jon Stuart 1958- WhoEmL 93
Levin-Rice, Patricia Oppenheim 1932- WhoAmW 93, WhoWor 93
Levins, Ilyssa 1958- WhoAm 92
Levins, Richard Francis Law&B 92
Levinsky, Barry Law&B 92
Levinsky, Norman George 1929- WhoAm 92
Levinsohn, Florence Hamlish WhoWrEP 92
Levinson, Alfred Linden 1933- WhoE 93
Levinson, Arthur D. 1950- St&PR 93
Levinson, Arthur David 1950- WhoAm 92
Levinson, Barry BioIn 17
Levinson, Barry 1932- MiSFD 9
Levinson, Barry 1942- WhoWrEP 92
Levinson, Barry L. 1932- WhoAm 92
Levinson, Barry Lewis 1955- WhoE 93
Levinson, Bruce 1950- St&PR 93
Levinson, Charles 1916- St&PR 93
Levinson, Daniel Ronald 1949- WhoAm 92
Levinson, David J. Law&B 92
Levinson, David Judah 1934- St&PR 93
Levinson, Deborah Joy 1957- WhoE 93
Levinson, Deborah Sue 1946- WhoE 93
Levinson, Eric Douglas Law&B 92
Levinson, Fred 1928- St&PR 93
Levinson, Gilbert E. 1928- WhoAm 92
Levinson, Harry St&PR 93
Levinson, Harry 1922- WhoAm 92
Levinson, Harvey 1929- St&PR 93
Levinson, Jeffrey Alan 1959- WhoSSW 93
Levinson, Jodi L. Law&B 92
Levinson, John Milton 1927- WhoAm 92
Levinson, Julie Carolyn 1967- WhoAmW 93
Levinson, Julius 1925- St&PR 93
Levinson, Kenneth Lee 1953- WhoWor 93
Levinson, Lawrence Edward 1930- St&PR 93, WhoAm 92
Levinson, Lawrence M. 1918- St&PR 93
Levinson, Leonard 1935- ScF&FL 92
Levinson, Leslie Harold 1929- WhoAm 92
Levinson, Luisa Mercedes 1914-1988 SpAmA
Levinson, Mark Bradley 1956- WhoEmL 93
Levinson, Max L. 1915- St&PR 93
Levinson, Morton I. 1930- St&PR 93
Levinson, Peter Joseph 1943- WhoWor 93
Levinson, Richard BioIn 17
Levinson, Riki ConAu 37NR, MajAI [port]
Levinson, Robert A. 1925- St&PR 93
Levinson, Robert Alan 1925- WhoAm 92

Levinson, Rochelle Fox 1949- *WhoAmW 93*
Levinson, Salmon O. 1865-1941 *JeAmHC*
Levinson, Sanford Victor 1941- *WhoAm 92*
Levinson, Sara *BioIn 17*
Levinson, Stephen Eliot 1944- *WhoAm 92*
Levinson, Sunni Roberta 1949- *WhoAmW 93*
Levinstein, Mark Steven 1958- *WhoEmL 93*
Levinstone, Bertram 1921- *WhoE 93*
Levinthal, Charles Frederick 1945- *WhoE 93*
Levinthal, Cyrus 1922-1990 *BioIn 17*
Levinthal, Elliott Charles 1922- *WhoAm 92*
Levinton, Jeffrey S. 1946- *WhoAm 92*
Levintow, Leon 1921- *WhoAm 92*
Levin-Wixman, Irene Staub 1928- *WhoAmW 93*
Levis, Art *BioIn 17*
Levis, Donald James 1936- *WhoAm 92*
Levis, Larry 1946- *DcLB 120 [port]*
Levis, Marjorie Rice *AmWomPl*
Levis, William J. *Law&B 92*
Levisalles, Jacques E.D. 1928- *WhoScE 91-2*
LeViseur, Suzanne 1958- *WhoAmW 93*
Levison, David Annan *WhoScE 91-1*
Levison-Marcus, Peggy Lee 1942- *WhoAmW 93*
Levi-Strauss, Claude *BioIn 17*
Levi-Strauss, Claude 1908- *IntDcAn, WhoWor 93*
Levit, Edithe Judith 1926- *WhoAm 92, WhoAmW 93*
Levit, Ginger 1937- *WhoAmW 93*
Levit, Heloise B. 1937- *WhoAmW 93*
Levit, Jay Joseph 1934- *WhoSSW 93*
Levit, Victor B. 1930- *WhoIns 93*
Levit, Victor Bert 1930- *WhoAm 92*
Levit, William Harold, Jr. 1938- *WhoAm 92*
Levitan, Dan 1957- *WhoAm 92*
Levitan, David Maurice 1915- *WhoAm 92*
Levitan, Herbert 1939- *WhoE 93*
Levitan, Kenneth Mark 1946- *WhoEmL 93*
Levitan, Laurence 1933- *WhoE 93*
Levitan, Paula Lee *Law&B 92*
Levitan, Robert Eugene 1933- *St&PR 93*
Levitan, Ruth *BioIn 17*
Levitan, Sar A. 1914- *WhoAm 92*
Levitan, Shari J. *Law&B 92*
Levitan, Steve 1960- *WhoEmL 93*
Levitas, Andrew Stephen 1948- *WhoE 93*
Levitas, Gloria B(arach) 1931- *WhoWrEP 92*
Levitas, Martin James *Law&B 92*
Levitas, Miriam C. Strickman 1936- *WhoAmW 93*
Levitas, Tamara B. 1948- *WhoEmL 93*
Levitch, Harry Herman 1918- *WhoSSW 93, WhoWor 93*
Levite, Laurence Allen 1940- *WhoE 93*
Levites, Gail Carol 1943- *St&PR 93*
Levitin, Lloyd Alan 1932- *St&PR 93*
Levitin, Michael Jay 1960- *WhoEmL 93*
Levitin, Sonia 1934- *BioIn 17, DcAmChF 1960*
Levitin, Sonia (Wolff) 1934- *DcAmChF 1985, MajAI [port]*
Levitine, George 1916-1989 *BioIn 17*
Leviton, Adina Platt 1962- *WhoEmL 93*
Leviton, Alan Edward 1930- *WhoAm 92*
Leviton, Fred J. 1953- *WhoEmL 93*
Leviton, Jay Bennet 1923- *WhoSSW 93*
Levitsky, Asher S. 1943- *St&PR 93*
Levitsky, Melvyn 1938- *WhoAm 92*
Levitsky, Neal Jonathan 1956- *WhoEmL 93*
Levitsky, Walter Simeon, Jr. 1932- *WhoE 93*
Levitt, Aaron 1938- *St&PR 93*
Levitt, Alfred d1991 *BioIn 17*
Levitt, Andrea J. *Law&B 92*
Levitt, Annette Shandler *WhoE 93*
Levitt, Arthur, Jr. 1931- *St&PR 93, WhoAm 92*
Levitt, B. Blake 1948- *ConAu 139*
Levitt, Barry Adnoff 1950- *WhoEmL 93*
Levitt, Brian M. *Law&B 92*
Levitt, Brian Michael 1947- *WhoE 93*
Levitt, Dana N. *Law&B 92*
Levitt, Daniel Philip 1936- *WhoAm 92*
Levitt, Gene 1920- *MiSFD 9*
Levitt, Gerald Steven 1944- *WhoAm 92*
Levitt, Irving Francis 1915- *WhoAm 92*
Levitt, Israel Monroe 1908- *WhoAm 92, WhoWor 93*
Levitt, Jesse 1919- *WhoE 93*
Levitt, John Lawrence 1951- *WhoEmL 93*
Levitt, Joshua G. *Law&B 92*
Levitt, Julian S. *Law&B 92*
Levitt, Leigh 1933- *WhoAmW 93*
Levitt, LeRoy Paul 1918- *WhoAm 92*
Levitt, Mark Howard 1952- *WhoE 93, WhoEmL 93*
Levitt, Miriam 1946- *WhoAmW 93*
Levitt, Mortimer 1907- *St&PR 93*
Levitt, Morton 1929- *WhoE 93*
Levitt, Patricia Evans 1965- *WhoSSW 93*
Levitt, Peter 1946- *WhoWrEP 92*
Levitt, Richard H. 1936- *St&PR 93*
Levitt, Richard S. 1930- *St&PR 93*
Levitt, Ruby d1992 *NewYTBS 92*
Levitt, Ruby 1907-1992 *BioIn 17*
Levitt, Russell David 1958- *WhoEmL 93*
Levitt, Seymour Herbert 1928- *WhoAm 92, WhoWor 93*
Levitt, Sidney 1947- *BioIn 17*
Levitt, Steven Charles 1945- *WhoAm 92*
Levitt, Susan B. 1953- *WhoWrEP 92*
Levitt, Theodore 1925- *St&PR 93, WhoAm 92*
Levittan, Shirley 1918-1992 *BioIn 17*
Levittan, Shirley R. 1918-1992 *NewYTBS 92 [port]*
Levitz, Paul Elliot 1956- *WhoAm 92*
Levitz, Richard Jay 1946- *St&PR 93*
Levitz, William Lawrence 1943- *WhoAm 92*
Levitzki, Mischa 1898-1941 *Baker 92*
Levitzky, Michael Gordon 1947- *WhoEmL 93, WhoSSW 93*
Levkoff, Henry S. 1923- *St&PR 93*
Levkowitz, Haim 1953- *WhoE 93*
Levlin, Jan-Erik 1938- *WhoScE 91-4*
Levner, Louis Jules 1951- *WhoE 93, WhoEmL 93*
Levon, O. U. *ConAu 38NR*
Levoni, Sergio 1939- *WhoScE 91-3*
Levorson, Kathryn Grace 1931- *WhoAmW 93*
Levos, Robert Wayne 1943- *St&PR 93*
Levovitz, Pesach Zechariah 1922- *WhoAm 92*
Levoy, Katherine A. *Law&B 92*
Levoy, Myron *ConAu 40NR, DcAmChF 1960*
Levoy, Myron 1930- *WhoAm 92*
Levrat, Bernard 1936- *WhoScE 91-4*
Levrero, Mario 1940- *SpAmA*
Levsen, Virginia Louise 1925- *WhoAmW 93*
Levshin, Linda Jean 1953- *WhoAmW 93*
Levsink, F.J. *WhoScE 91-3*
Levstek, Igor *WhoScE 91-4*
Levy, A. *Law&B 92*
Levy, Aaron 1742-1815 *BioIn 17*
Levy, Aharon 1940- *WhoWor 93*
Levy, Alain M. 1946- *WhoAm 92*
Levy, Alan D. 1938- *St&PR 93*
Levy, Alan Joel 1937- *WhoAm 92*
Levy, Alan Joseph 1932- *WhoAm 92, WhoWor 93, WhoWrEP 92*
Levy, Alan Richard 1957- *WhoEmL 93*
Levy, Alan Stephen 1948- *WhoEmL 93*
Levy, Alexandre 1864-1892 *Baker 92*
Levy, Alfred W. 1919- *St&PR 93*
Levy, Andrew P. 1951- *St&PR 93*
Levy, Andrew S. 1949- *St&PR 93*
Levy, Anne S. *Law&B 92*
Levy, Arnold Stuart 1941- *WhoAm 92*
Levy, Arthur J. *Law&B 92*
Levy, Arthur James 1947- *WhoE 93, WhoWor 93*
Levy, Arthur Theodore 1926- *WhoE 93*
Levy, Asser c. 1628-1682 *BioIn 17*
Levy, B. Joseph *Law&B 92*
Levy, Barbara A. *Law&B 92*
Levy, Barbara Jo 1949- *WhoEmL 93*
Levy, Barnet M. 1917- *WhoAm 92*
Levy, Benjamin 1903- *WhoE 93*
Levy, Benjamin 1937- *WhoE 93*
Levy, Benjamin 1940- *WhoAm 92, WhoE 93*
Levy, Bennett S. 1929- *St&PR 93*
Levy, Bernard I. 1946- *WhoScE 91-2*
Levy, Birdie 1918- *St&PR 93*
Levy, Bruce Farrell 1951- *WhoE 93*
Levy, Burt (Jerome) 1936- *Baker 92*
Levy, Burton 1912- *WhoAm 92*
Levy, Carol 1931- *WhoWrEP 92*
Levy, Chava Willing *BioIn 17*
Levy, Constance 1931- *SmATA 73 [port]*
Levy, Dan *WhoWor 93*
Levy, Daniel 1957- *WhoWor 93*
Levy, David *Law&B 92, WhoAm 92, WhoScE 91-2*
Levy, David 1937- *St&PR 93*
Levy, David 1938- *WhoWor 93*
Levy, David Alfred 1930- *WhoAm 92*
Levy, David B. *Law&B 92*
Levy, David C. *BioIn 17*
Levy, David Corcos 1938- *WhoE 93*
Levy, Deborah Marian 1957- *WhoEmL 93*
Levy, Donald 1935- *WhoWor 93*
Levy, Donald Harris 1939- *WhoAm 92*
Levy, Donna Marie *Law&B 92*
Levy, Edith M. *AmWomPl*
Levy, Edmond 1929- *MiSFD 9*
Levy, Edward *ScF&FL 92*
Levy, Edward C., Jr. 1931- *St&PR 93*
Levy, Edward Charles, Jr. 1931- *WhoAm 92*
Levy, Elizabeth 1942- *MajAI [port], ScF&FL 92, SmATA 69 [port]*
Levy, Emanuel 1918- *WhoIns 93*
Levy, Ernst 1895-1981 *Baker 92*
Levy, Etienne Paul Louis 1922- *WhoWor 93*
Levy, Eugene 1926-1990 *BioIn 17*
Levy, Eugene 1946- *MiSFD 9*
Levy, Eugene Howard 1944- *WhoAm 92*
Levy, Eugene Pfeifer 1936- *WhoAm 92*
Levy, Frank 1930- *Baker 92*
Levy, Franklin R. d1992 *BioIn 17, NewYTBS 92*
Levy, Fred d1991 *BioIn 17*
Levy, Gaston Raymond 1928- *St&PR 93*
Levy, George Aaron 1933- *WhoSSW 93*
Levy, George Charles 1944- *WhoAm 92*
Levy, Gerald Arnold 1933- *St&PR 93*
Levy, Gerard G. 1939- *St&PR 93*
Levy, Gerhard 1928- *WhoAm 92*
Levy, Harold David 1938- *WhoE 93*
Levy, Harold James 1925- *WhoE 93*
Levy, Harold M. *Law&B 92*
Levy, Harry Alan 1944- *WhoE 93*
Levy, Harry Dale 1923- *St&PR 93*
Levy, Heniot 1879-1946 *Baker 92*
Levy, Henry 1927- *WhoSSW 93*
Levy, Herbert Joel 1949- *WhoEmL 93*
Levy, Herbert Monte 1923- *WhoE 93, WhoWor 93*
Levy, Howard I. 1939- *WhoAm 92*
Levy, Irvin L. 1929- *St&PR 93, WhoAm 92, WhoSSW 93*
Levy, Isaac A. *St&PR 93*
Levy, Ivan Marshall 1937- *WhoE 93*
Levy, Jack *WhoScE 91-1*
Levy, Jacques B. 1937- *WhoScE 91-2*
Levy, James Peter 1940- *WhoAm 92*
Levy, Janet L. 1955- *St&PR 93*
Levy, Janet Wolf d1992 *BioIn 17, NewYTBS 92*
Levy, Jean Paul D. 1934- *WhoScE 91-2*
Levy, Jean-Pierre 1935- *WhoUN 92*
Levy, Jefery *MiSFD 9*
Levy, Jerome E. 1918- *WhoE 93*
Levy, Jerre Marie 1938- *WhoAm 92, WhoAmW 93*
Levy, Joan Lia *Law&B 92*
Levy, Joel 1947- *WhoAm 92*
Levy, Joel Howard 1938- *WhoWor 93*
Levy, Joel N. 1941- *St&PR 93, WhoE 93*
Levy, John 1941- *St&PR 93*
Levy, John Feldberg 1947- *WhoE 93*
Levy, John S. 1935- *St&PR 93*
Levy, Jonathan A. *Law&B 92*
Levy, Jonathan Michael 1946- *WhoEmL 93*
Levy, Jordan 1943- *St&PR 93, WhoAm 92, WhoE 93*
Levy, Joseph 1928- *St&PR 93, WhoAm 92*
Levy, Joseph W. 1932- *St&PR 93*
Levy, Joseph William 1932- *WhoAm 92*
Levy, Jules 1930- *Baker 92*
Levy, Julia 1935- *WhoAm 92*
Levy, Kathy Ann 1951- *WhoEmL 93*
Levy, Kenneth 1927- *WhoAm 92*
Levy, Kenneth James 1949- *WhoAm 92*
Levy, Kenneth Jay 1946- *WhoAm 92*
Levy, Larry 1947- *WhoWrEP 92*
Levy, Lazare 1882-1964 *Baker 92*
Levy, Leah Garrigan 1947- *WhoAmW 93*
Levy, Leo J. 1925- *St&PR 93*
Levy, Leon 1925- *St&PR 93, WhoAm 92*
Levy, Leon Bruce 1937- *WhoSSW 93*
Levy, Leon Sholom *WhoE 93*
Levy, Leonard Williams 1923- *WhoAm 92, WhoWrEP 92*
Levy, Lester A. 1922- *St&PR 93, WhoAm 92, WhoSSW 93*
Levy, Lewis 1938- *St&PR 93*
Levy, Lewis Lawrence 1922- *WhoE 93*
Levy, Liza 1951- *WhoAmW 93*
Levy, Louis 1921- *WhoAm 92*
Levy, Louis Edward 1932- *WhoAm 92*
Levy, Lynn Gail *Law&B 92*
Levy, Marc H. *WhoSSW 93*
Levy, Marguerite Elizabeth 1925- *WhoAmW 93, WhoE 93*
Levy, Marilyn *BioIn 17*
Levy, Marilyn 1922- *WhoE 93*
Levy, Marjorie *BioIn 17*
Levy, Mark 1948- *WhoE 93*
Levy, Mark A. 1952- *St&PR 93*
Levy, Mark Allan 1939- *WhoAm 92*
Levy, Mark Allan 1950- *WhoEmL 93*
Levy, Mark Barry 1948- *St&PR 93*
Levy, Mark F. 1955- *St&PR 93*
Levy, Mark Ray 1946- *WhoEmL 93*
Levy, Mark S. 1948- *St&PR 93*
Levy, Marvin B. 1935- *St&PR 93*
Levy, Marvin Daniel 1929- *WhoAm 92*
Levy, Marvin David 1932- *Baker 92, WhoAm 92*
Levy, Matthew Degen 1958- *WhoE 93*
Levy, Matthys 1929- *ConAu 139*
Levy, Maurice *ScF&FL 92*
Levy, Maurice Marc 1922- *WhoScE 91-2*
Levy, Max M. 1926- *St&PR 93*
Levy, Maxine Beitel 1940- *WhoAmW 93*
Levy, Maxine Kessie 1939- *WhoAmW 93*
Levy, Michael 1946- *St&PR 93*
Levy, Michael A. *Law&B 92*
Levy, Michael Howard 1947- *WhoEmL 93, WhoSSW 93*
Levy, Michael Richard 1946- *WhoAm 92*
Levy, Michael Scott 1953- *WhoE 93*
Levy, Michel-Maurice 1883-1965 *Baker 92*
Levy, Milton P., Jr. 1925- *St&PR 93*
Levy, Mordechai *BioIn 17*
Levy, Morris *BioIn 17*
Levy, Nathan 1945- *BioIn 17*
Levy, Nazila *Law&B 92*
Levy, Nelson Louis 1941- *WhoAm 92*
Levy, Nessim 1942- *St&PR 93*
Levy, Norman B. 1931- *WhoAm 92*
Levy, Norman Jay 1942- *WhoAm 92*
Levy, Olivier 1949- *WhoWor 93*
Levy, Paul Frederick 1937- *WhoSSW 93*
Levy, Penelope Ann 1942- *WhoWor 93*
Levy, Peter *Law&B 92*
Levy, Peter A. *Law&B 92*
Levy, Phil *WhoIns 93*
Levy, Philip *Law&B 92*
Levy, Ralph *MiSFD 9*
Levy, Ralph 1932- *St&PR 93, WhoAm 92*
Levy, Richard Bruce *Law&B 92*
Levy, Richard C. 1947- *WhoEmL 93*
Levy, Richard D. 1930- *St&PR 93*
Levy, Richard G. 1937- *St&PR 93*
Levy, Richard M. 1938- *St&PR 93*
Levy, Richard Philip 1923- *WhoAm 92*
Levy, Richard S. *St&PR 93*
Levy, Robert *Law&B 92*
Levy, Robert 1926- *WhoAm 92, WhoWrEP 92*
Levy, Robert Aaron 1926- *WhoSSW 93*
Levy, Robert Alan 1946- *WhoWor 93*
Levy, Robert B. *Law&B 92*
Levy, Robert B. 1911- *St&PR 93*
Levy, Robert E. 1939- *St&PR 93*
Levy, Robert Edward 1939- *WhoAm 92*
Levy, Robert G. d1991 *BioIn 17*
Levy, Robert Halle 1953- *St&PR 93*
Levy, Robert Isaac 1937- *WhoAm 92*
Levy, Robert Jeffrey 1956- *WhoWrEP 92*
Levy, Robert M. 1932- *St&PR 93*
Levy, Robert Marquis 1949- *WhoEmL 93*
Levy, Robert S. *Law&B 92*
Levy, Rochelle Feldman 1937- *WhoAmW 93, WhoE 93, WhoWor 93*
Levy, Roger B. *Law&B 92*
Levy, Ron Karl *Law&B 92*
Levy, Ronald K. *Law&B 92*
Levy, Ronald Stewart 1948- *St&PR 93*
Levy, Ross Stuart 1951- *WhoE 93*
Levy, Ruth A. 1958- *WhoAmW 93*
Levy, S. William 1920- *WhoAm 92*
Levy, Salomon 1926- *WhoAm 92*
Levy, Shuki *MiSFD 9*
Levy, Sidney 1909- *WhoE 93, WhoWor 93*
Levy, Stanley H. 1922- *St&PR 93*
Levy, Stanley Herbert 1922- *WhoAm 92*
Levy, Stephen 1947- *WhoWrEP 92*
Levy, Stephen Raymond 1940- *St&PR 93, WhoAm 92*
Levy, Steven B. 1954- *WhoEmL 93*
Levy, Susan 1949- *WhoAmW 93, WhoE 93, WhoEmL 93*
Levy, Susan Naomi 1948- *WhoAmW 93*
Levy, Sy 1929- *WhoAm 92*
Levy, Tracy *WhoSSW 93*
Levy, Uriah P. 1792-1862 *BioIn 17*
Levy, Walter James 1911- *WhoAm 92*
Levy, Warren P. 1952- *St&PR 93*
Levy, William Auerbach- 1889-1964 *BioIn 17*
Levy, William G. 1912- *St&PR 93*
Levy, William N. 1941- *St&PR 93*
Levy, Yacov 1945- *WhoAm 92*
Levy-Bruhl, Lucien 1857-1939 *IntDcAn*
Levy-Lang, Andre 1937- *WhoWor 93*
Levy-Leblond, Jean Marc 1940- *WhoScE 91-2*
Levy-Leboyer, Claude 1928- *WhoScE 91-2*
Levys, Isaac A. 1911- *St&PR 93*
Levy-Schoen, Ariane 1927- *WhoScE 91-2*
Lew, Amy Deborah 1948- *WhoAmW 93*
Lew, Edwin Wayne 1950- *WhoEmL 93, WhoSSW 93*
Lew, Fran *WhoE 93*
Lew, Mela *Law&B 92*
Lew, Richard S. *Law&B 92*
Lew, Roger A. 1941- *St&PR 93*
Lew, Roger Alan 1941- *WhoAm 92*
Lew, Ronald S. W. 1941- *WhoAm 92*
Lew, Salvador 1929- *WhoSSW 93*
Lew, Syn Pau 1954- *WhoAsAP 91*
Lew, Wayne W. *Law&B 92*
Lewack, Larry 1958- *WhoE 93*
Lewak, Stanislaw Jozef 1930- *WhoScE 91-4*
Lewallen, Tim *St&PR 93*
Lewan, Douglas 1957- *WhoE 93*
Lewand, F. Thomas 1946- *WhoEmL 93*
Lewando, Alfred Gerard, Jr. 1945- *WhoSSW 93*

Lewandowski, Andrew Anthony 1946- *WhoE 93, WhoEmL 93, WhoWor 93*
Lewandowski, Chester T. 1948- *St&PR 93*
Lewandowski, Humberto 1939- *WhoWor 93*
Lewandowski, Jan Lech 1926- *WhoScE 91-4*
Lewandowski, John Kazimierz 1935- *WhoSSW 93*
Lewandowski, Jozef Bogumil 1930- *WhoScE 91-4*
Lewandowski, Louis 1821-1894 *Baker 92, PolBiDi*
Lewandowski, Michalene Maria 1920- *WhoAmW 93, WhoWor 93*
Lewandowski, Robert Z. 1920- *PolBiDi*
Lewandowski, Seweryn 1920- *WhoScE 91-4*
Lewandowski, Stanley R., Jr. 1937- *St&PR 93*
Lewandowski, Thomas P. *Law&B 92*
Lewarne, Peter J. *Law&B 92*
Lewbel, Arthur Harris 1956- *WhoEmL 93*
Lewcock, Ronald Bentley 1929- *WhoAm 92, WhoWor 93*
Lewees, John *ConAu 137, MajAI*
Lewellen, Ted Charles 1940- *WhoSSW 93*
Lewellen, Verne C. 1901-1980 *BiDAMSp 1989*
Lewellen, Wilbur Garrett 1938- *WhoAm 92*
Lewelling, Lorenzo Dow 1846-1900 *BioIn 17*
Lewellyan, Ronald Lee 1946- *WhoEmL 93*
Lewent, Judy C. *BioIn 17, St&PR 93*
Lewent, Judy C. 1949- *WhoAm 92, WhoAmW 93*
Lewenthal, Raymond 1926-1988 *Baker 92*
Lewerenz, Joan Stuhlsatz 1946- *WhoEmL 93*
Lewers, Cornett L. *Law&B 92*
Lewers, Leigh Edward 1927- *St&PR 93*
Lewes, George Henry 1817-1878 *BioIn 17*
Lewi, Paul J. 1938- *WhoScE 91-2*
Lewicke, Bette 1952- *WhoAmW 93*
Lewicki, Gregory David 1951- *St&PR 93*
Lewicki, Piotr P. 1937- *WhoScE 91-4*
Lewin, Alan Charles 1945- *St&PR 93*
Lewin, Albert 1894-1968 *MiSFD 9N*
Lewin, Anne *BioIn 17*
Lewin, Ben 1946- *MiSFD 9*
Lewin, Bradford A. *Law&B 92*
Lewin, Bruce Roger 1947- *St&PR 93*
Lewin, Christopher George 1940- *WhoWor 93*
Lewin, Dasha 1929- *St&PR 93*
Lewin, David (Benjamin) 1933- *Baker 92*
Lewin, Frank Edmund 1953- *WhoEmL 93*
Lewin, George Farley 1912- *WhoWor 93*
Lewin, George Forest 1916- *WhoAm 92*
Lewin, Hugh 1939- *ConAu 38NR, MajAI [port], SmATA 72 [port]*
Lewin, John *WhoScE 91-1*
Lewin, John Richard 1946- *WhoEmL 93*
Lewin, Leif I. 1936- *WhoWor 93*
Lewin, Leonard 1919- *WhoAm 92*
Lewin, Leonard C. 1916- *WhoWrEP 92*
Lewin, Luis Eduardo 1946- *WhoWor 93*
Lewin, Michael L. 1909-1991 *BioIn 17*
Lewin, Miguel J.M. 1938- *WhoScE 91-2*
Lewin, Moshe 1921- *WhoAm 92*
Lewin, Pearl Goldman 1923- *WhoAmW 93*
Lewin, Ralph Arnold 1921- *WhoAm 92*
Lewin, Rebecca 1954- *WhoWrEP 92*
Lewin, Renee G. 1953- *WhoAm 92*
Lewin, Seymour Zalman 1921- *WhoAm 92*
Lewin, Theodore Edwin 1933- *WhoAm 92*
Lewin, Walter H. G. 1936- *WhoE 93*
Lewine, Robert F. 1913- *WhoAm 92*
Lewinger, Max 1870-1908 *Baker 92, PolBiDi*
Lewins, Anna 1956- *ScF&FL 92*
Lewinska, Maria Krystyna 1924- *WhoScE 91-4*
Lewinson, Sam 1914- *St&PR 93*
Lewinstein, Stephen R. 1941- *St&PR 93*
Lewinter, David J. *Law&B 92*
LeWinter, Nancy Nadler *BioIn 17*
Lewis, Lord *WhoScE 91-1*
Lewis, A. Duff, Jr. 1939- *WhoAm 92*
Lewis, Aaron Bryce 1965- *WhoEmL 93*
Lewis, Ada *St&PR 93*
Lewis, Al d1992 *NewYTBS 92*
Lewis, Alan d1991 *BioIn 17*
Lewis, Alan Gerber 1946- *St&PR 93*
Lewis, Alan M. *Law&B 92*
Lewis, Alan Wayne 1943- *WhoAm 92*
Lewis, Albert Buell 1867-1940 *IntDcAn*
Lewis, Albert M. *Law&B 92*
Lewis, Albert Ray *BioIn 17*
Lewis, Alexander, Jr. 1916- *St&PR 93, WhoAm 92*
Lewis, Alexander C. 1932- *St&PR 93*
Lewis, Alexander Ingersoll, III 1946- *WhoE 93, WhoEmL 93*
Lewis, Alfred H. 1857-1914 *JrnUS*
Lewis, Alice Norris *AmWomPl*
Lewis, Allan *WhoAm 92*
Lewis, Allan A. 1908-1991 *BioIn 17*
Lewis, Allen *DcCPCAm*
Lewis, Alvin Bower, Jr. 1932- *WhoE 93, WhoWor 93*
Lewis, Andrew Lindsay, Jr. 1931- *WhoAm 92*
Lewis, Ann *WhoWrEP 92*
Lewis, Ann Elizabeth *Law&B 92*
Lewis, Ann Frank 1937- *WhoAm 92*
Lewis, Anna *WhoWrEP 92*
Lewis, Anne Harrison *Law&B 92*
Lewis, Anne McCutcheon 1943- *WhoAmW 93*
Lewis, Anthony 1927- *JrnUS, WhoAm 92*
Lewis, Anthony (Carey) 1915-1983 *Baker 92*
Lewis, Anthony R. 1941- *ScF&FL 92*
Lewis, Archibald Ross 1914-1990 *BioIn 17*
Lewis, Arlene Jane Quiring 1934- *WhoAmW 93*
Lewis, Arnold Leroy, II 1952- *WhoWor 93*
Lewis, Arthur 1915- *DcCPCAm*
Lewis, Arthur 1915-1991 *AnObit 1991*
Lewis, Arthur Dee 1918- *WhoAm 92*
Lewis, Arthur O. 1920- *ScF&FL 92*
Lewis, Arthur R. 1931- *St&PR 93*
Lewis, Aubrey 1935- *St&PR 93*
Lewis, Audrey Gersh 1933- *WhoAmW 93*
Lewis, Austin William Russell 1932- *WhoAsAP 91*
Lewis, Barbara 1944- *SoulM*
Lewis, Barbara A. 1943- *SmATA 73*
Lewis, Barbara Ann 1945- *WhoWor 93*
Lewis, Benn E. 1908-1979 *ScF&FL 92*
Lewis, Bernard 1916- *WhoAm 92*
Lewis, Bernard Leroy 1923- *WhoAm 92*
Lewis, Bernard M. 1925- *WhoScE 91-3*
Lewis, Boyd De Wolf 1905- *WhoAm 92*
Lewis, Brenda J. Early 1955- *AfrAmBi*
Lewis, Brenda Joyce 1946- *WhoSSW 93*
Lewis, Brenda Ralph 1932- *SmATA 72 [port]*
Lewis, Brent Renault 1958- *WhoEmL 93, WhoWor 93*
Lewis, Bryan *Law&B 92*
Lewis, Butch *BioIn 17*
Lewis, C. Day 1904-1972 *BioIn 17*
Lewis, C.J. *WhoScE 91-1*
Lewis, C.S. 1898-1963 *BioIn 17, MagSWL [port], ScF&FL 92, WorLitC [port]*
Lewis, C(live) S(taples) 1898-1963 *ChlLR 27 [port], MajAI [port]*
Lewis, Canella *ScF&FL 92*
Lewis, Carl *BioIn 17, NewYTBS 92 [port]*
Lewis, Carl 1961- *ConBlB 4 [port], WhoAm 92*
Lewis, Carol *BlkAmWO*
Lewis, Carol Anne 1937- *WhoAmW 93*
Lewis, Carol Bowden 1938- *WhoSSW 93*
Lewis, Caroline *AmWomPl*
Lewis, Carrie Bullard 1865- *AmWomPl*
Lewis, Catherine J. *BioIn 17*
Lewis, Cecil Dwain 1929- *WhoSSW 93*
Lewis, Cecil Paul *WhoWrEP 92*
Lewis, Ceylon Smith, Jr. 1920- *WhoAm 92, WhoWor 93*
Lewis, Charles 1930- *ScF&FL 92*
Lewis, Charles A. 1942- *WhoAm 92*
Lewis, Charles Edwin 1928- *WhoAm 92*
Lewis, Charles J. 1927- *St&PR 93*
Lewis, Charles John 1927- *WhoAm 92*
Lewis, Charles Joseph 1940- *WhoAm 92, WhoE 93*
Lewis, Charles Leonard 1926- *WhoAm 92*
Lewis, Charles R., IV *Law&B 92*
Lewis, Charles Thomas 1956- *WhoE 93*
Lewis, Charlie P. *WhoSSW 93*
Lewis, Cheryl Ann 1959- *WhoSSW 93*
Lewis, Chester 1914-1990 *BioIn 17*
Lewis, Christine Lynne 1950- *WhoE 93*
Lewis, Christopher *MiSFD 9*
Lewis, Christopher Alan 1955- *WhoAm 92, WhoE 93*
Lewis, Cindy Anne *Law&B 92*
Lewis, Claire Ellen 1952- *WhoEmL 93*
Lewis, Claude, Jr. 1924- *WhoAm 92*
Lewis, Claude H. 1943- *St&PR 93*
Lewis, Clayman 1947- *WhoEmL 93*
Lewis, Clayton Wilson 1936- *WhoE 93*
Lewis, Clifford, III 1904- *WhoE 93*
Lewis, Clifford Fuller 1955- *WhoWrEP 92*
Lewis, Clifford S. 1954- *St&PR 93*
Lewis, Clive Staples 1898-1963 *BioIn 17*
Lewis, Clyde A. 1913- *WhoWor 93*
Lewis, Colin David *WhoScE 91-1*
Lewis, Connie *Law&B 92*
Lewis, Coraltha Omega *Law&B 92*
Lewis, Courtland Stanley 1949- *WhoE 93*
Lewis, Craig Graham David 1930- *WhoAm 92*
Lewis, Craig H. *Law&B 92*
Lewis, Craig Meredith 1956- *WhoEmL 93*
Lewis, Curtis Larry 1951- *WhoSSW 93*
Lewis, Cynthia Ann 1953- *WhoEmL 93*
Lewis, D.J. *WhoScE 91-1*
Lewis, Dale Kenton 1937- *WhoAm 92*
Lewis, Daniel 1925- *Baker 92*
Lewis, Daniel Day- *BioIn 17*
Lewis, Darrell L. 1931- *WhoAm 92*
Lewis, David *MiSFD 9*
Lewis, David 1944- *WhoAm 92*
Lewis, David A. *Law&B 92*
Lewis, David B. 1947- *St&PR 93*
Lewis, David Carleton 1935- *WhoAm 92*
Lewis, David Eldridge 1924- *WhoAm 92*
Lewis, David James 1920- *WhoWor 93*
Lewis, David John 1948- *WhoEmL 93*
Lewis, David Kellogg 1941- *WhoAm 92*
Lewis, David L. *BioIn 17*
Lewis, David L. 1954- *WhoEmL 93*
Lewis, David Lanier 1927- *WhoWrEP 92*
Lewis, David Malcolm *WhoScE 91-1*
Lewis, David Raymond 1956- *WhoEmL 93*
Lewis, David Sloan, Jr. 1917- *St&PR 93*
Lewis, David W. *St&PR 93*
Lewis, Dean Sumter 1933- *WhoAm 92*
Lewis, Delano E. 1938- *AfrAmBi [port]*
Lewis, Delano Eugene 1938- *WhoAm 92*
Lewis, Deloris Asynthia 1936- *WhoAmW 93*
Lewis, Dennis A. *WhoScE 91-1*
Lewis, Dennis R. *Law&B 92*
Lewis, Dianne Lynn 1953- *WhoAmW 93*
Lewis, Dickson W. 1948- *St&PR 93*
Lewis, Donald C. *Law&B 92*
Lewis, Donald Emerson 1950- *WhoAm 92, WhoE 93*
Lewis, Donald Ernest 1943- *WhoAm 92*
Lewis, Donald Everett 1931- *WhoSSW 93*
Lewis, Donald Joseph 1922- *WhoAm 92*
Lewis, Donald Ray 1946- *WhoWor 93*
Lewis, Donna Cunningham 1945- *WhoE 93*
Lewis, Douglas 1938- *WhoAm 92, WhoE 93, WhoWrEP 92*
Lewis, Douglas Grinslade 1938- *WhoE 93*
Lewis, Drew 1931- *St&PR 93*
Lewis, Duane L. 1934- *St&PR 93*
Lewis, Earnest W.B. 1909-1990 *BioIn 17*
Lewis, Eben Thaddeus *Law&B 92*
Lewis, Edna *BioIn 17*
Lewis, Edward 1940- *WhoAm 92, WhoE 93*
Lewis, Edward Alan 1942- *St&PR 93*
Lewis, Edward B. 1918- *WhoAm 92*
Lewis, Edward David 1953- *WhoEmL 93*
Lewis, Edward E. d1991 *BioIn 17*
Lewis, Edward J. *Law&B 92*
Lewis, Edward M. 1923- *St&PR 93*
Lewis, Edward Sheldon 1920- *WhoAm 92*
Lewis, Edward T. 1940- *BioIn 17*
Lewis, Edward Van Vliet 1914- *WhoAm 92*
Lewis, Edwin A. 1942- *WhoAm 92*
Lewis, Edwin Alvin 1942- *St&PR 93*
Lewis, Edwin L. *Law&B 92*
Lewis, Edwin Reynolds 1934- *WhoAm 92*
Lewis, Elizabeth Bowers 1956- *WhoAmW 93, WhoSSW 93*
Lewis, Elizabeth Foreman 1892-1958 *ConAu 137, MajAI [port]*
Lewis, Elizabeth May *AmWomPl*
Lewis, Ellen Terry 1959- *WhoEmL 93*
Lewis, Elliot R. *Law&B 92*
Lewis, Emanuel Raymond 1928- *WhoAm 92*
Lewis, Emily Jane 1955- *WhoEmL 93*
Lewis, Emily Sargent *AmWomPl*
Lewis, Evelyn 1946- *WhoAmW 93, WhoEmL 93*
Lewis, Everett *MiSFD 9*
Lewis, Father Al 1903-1992 *BioIn 17*
Lewis, Felice Flanery 1920- *WhoE 93*
Lewis, Flora *WhoAm 92, WhoAmW 93*
Lewis, Floyd Wallace 1925- *WhoAm 92*
Lewis, Frances Aaronson 1922- *WhoAm 92*
Lewis, Francine *ConAu 37NR, MajAI*
Lewis, Francis James 1930- *WhoAm 92*
Lewis, Frank Harlan 1919- *WhoAm 92*
Lewis, Frank J. 1930- *St&PR 93*
Lewis, Frank T. *Law&B 92*
Lewis, Franklin C. *Law&B 92*
Lewis, Frederick Carlton 1961- *WhoAm 92*
Lewis, G. Gregory *Law&B 92*
Lewis, Gail Dianne 1956- *WhoAmW 93, WhoEmL 93*
Lewis, Gareth David 1967- *WhoWor 93*
Lewis, Gary W. *Law&B 92*
Lewis, Gene Dale 1931- *WhoAm 92*
Lewis, Gene Evans 1928- *WhoAm 92*
Lewis, Geoffrey W. d1992 *NewYTBS 92*
Lewis, George Edward 1888-1979 *BiDAMSp 1989*
Lewis, George Ralph 1941- *WhoAm 92*
Lewis, George Withrow 1929- *WhoAm 92*
Lewis, Gerald 1924- *St&PR 93*
Lewis, Gerald A. 1934- *WhoAm 92*
Lewis, Geraldine Susan 1964- *WhoAmW 93*
Lewis, Gething Morgan 1912- *WhoWor 93*
Lewis, Gibson Donald 1936- *WhoSSW 93*
Lewis, Gladys Sherman 1933- *WhoAmW 93, WhoSSW 93*
Lewis, Gogo *ScF&FL 92*
Lewis, Goldy S. 1921- *St&PR 93*
Lewis, Goldy Sarah 1921- *WhoAm 92*
Lewis, Gordon E. 1938- *St&PR 93*
Lewis, Gordon Earl 1938- *WhoSSW 93*
Lewis, Gordon K. *BioIn 17*
Lewis, Grant Stephen 1942- *WhoAm 92*
Lewis, Gregg Allan 1951- *WhoAm 92, WhoWrEP 92*
Lewis, Gregory Williams 1940- *WhoWor 93*
Lewis, H. Gregg *BioIn 17*
Lewis, H. Gregg d1992 *NewYTBS 92*
Lewis, H. Nelson, Jr. 1934- *St&PR 93*
Lewis, Harmon Stanton 1947- *St&PR 93*
Lewis, Harold Alexander 1953- *WhoEmL 93*
Lewis, Harold Eugene 1933- *WhoSSW 93, WhoWor 93*
Lewis, Harrie F. 1917- *St&PR 93*
Lewis, Harriet Gerber 1919- *St&PR 93*
Lewis, Harriet Gerbert 1919- *WhoAm 92*
Lewis, Harry 1942- *WhoWrEP 92*
Lewis, Hartwell Arthur 1927- *WhoSSW 93*
Lewis, Helen Elizabeth 1951- *WhoEmL 93*
Lewis, Helen Natalie 1946- *WhoAmW 93, WhoEmL 93*
Lewis, Helen Phelps Hoyt 1902- *WhoAm 92*
Lewis, Henry 1932- *Baker 92*
Lewis, Henry Donald 1941- *WhoE 93*
Lewis, Henry Hicks 1940- *St&PR 93*
Lewis, Henry R. 1925- *St&PR 93*
Lewis, Henry Rafalsky 1925- *WhoAm 92*
Lewis, Henry Wilkins 1916- *WhoAm 92*
Lewis, Herbert Samuel 1934- *WhoAm 92*
Lewis, Herbie 1905-1991 *BioIn 17*
Lewis, Herschell Gordon *MiSFD 9*
Lewis, Hilda 1896-1974 *ScF&FL 92*
Lewis, Hiram Carson, Jr. 1930- *WhoSSW 93*
Lewis, Huey 1951- *ConMus 9 [port]*
Lewis, Hugh B. 1940- *WhoAm 92*
Lewis, Hunter 1947- *WhoAm 92, WhoSSW 93*
Lewis, I.A. 1921-1990 *BioIn 17*
Lewis, Irwin Albert 1921-1990 *BioIn 17*
Lewis, J. Gordon *Law&B 92*
Lewis, J. James 1939- *St&PR 93, WhoAm 92*
Lewis, J. Owen 1946- *WhoScE 91-3*
Lewis, J. Patrick 1942- *ConAu 138, SmATA 69 [port]*
Lewis, J.W. *WhoScE 91-1*
Lewis, Jack 1924- *WhoAm 92*
Lewis, Jack (Cecil Paul Lewis) 1924- *WhoWrEP 92*
Lewis, Jack N. 1947- *St&PR 93*
Lewis, Jack P. *BioIn 17*
Lewis, James B. 1947- *AfrAmBi [port]*
Lewis, James Beliven 1947- *WhoAm 92*
Lewis, James Berton 1911- *WhoAm 92*
Lewis, James David 1947- *WhoEmL 93*
Lewis, James Douglas *Law&B 92*
Lewis, James Earl 1939- *WhoE 93, WhoWor 93*
Lewis, James Edward 1927- *WhoAm 92*
Lewis, James Eldon 1938- *WhoAm 92*
Lewis, James Histed 1912- *WhoAm 92*
Lewis, James Owen 1946- *WhoWor 93*
Lewis, James Palmer 1941- *WhoSSW 93*
Lewis, James Pettis 1933- *WhoSSW 93*
Lewis, James Richard *Law&B 92*
Lewis, James Richard 1950- *St&PR 93*
Lewis, James Ross, Sr. 1919- *WhoSSW 93*
Lewis, Janet *WhoWrEP 92*
Lewis, Janet 1899- *BioIn 17*
Lewis, Janet Ruth 1952- *WhoAmW 93, WhoEmL 93*
Lewis, Janice Ann *Law&B 92*
Lewis, Janice Marie 1961- *WhoSSW 93*
Lewis, Janiece Alfreida 1956- *WhoAmW 93*
Lewis, Jason Alvert, Jr. 1941- *WhoWor 93*
Lewis, Jay Warren *Law&B 92*
Lewis, Jay Warren 1946- *St&PR 93*
Lewis, Jean 1924- *BioIn 17*
Lewis, Jean Sara Mechlouitz 1926- *WhoAmW 93*
Lewis, Jeanne Gerlach 1944- *WhoAmW 93*
Lewis, Jed Steven 1956- *WhoSSW 93*
Lewis, Jeffrey E. *Law&B 92*
Lewis, Jeffrey George 1956- *WhoWor 93*
Lewis, Jeffrey J. *Law&B 92*
Lewis, Jerald Paul 1938- *St&PR 93*
Lewis, Jerome A. 1927- *WhoAm 92*
Lewis, Jerome Xavier, II *Law&B 92*
Lewis, Jerome Xavier, II 1938- *WhoE 93*
Lewis, Jerrold 1928- *WhoAm 92*
Lewis, Jerry 1926- *BioIn 17, MiSFD 9, QDrFCA 92 [port], WhoAm 92, WhoWor 93*
Lewis, Jerry 1934- *CngDr 91, WhoAm 92*

Lewis, Jerry Lee *BioIn 17*
Lewis, Jerry Lee 1935- *Baker 92, WhoAm 92*
Lewis, Jerry M. 1924- *WhoAm 92*
Lewis, Jerry Michael 1953- *WhoEmL 93*
Lewis, Jerry Middleton 1937- *BioIn 17*
Lewis, Jessica Helen 1917- *WhoAm 92, WhoAmW 93*
Lewis, Joan Joel *St&PR 93*
Lewis, Joan Mendenhall 1929- *WhoAmW 93, WhoWor 93*
Lewis, Jocelya 1953- *WhoE 93*
Lewis, Joe *Law&B 92*
Lewis, Joe Emery 1934- *WhoSSW 93*
Lewis, Joe Ollin 1935- *WhoSSW 93*
Lewis, John *BioIn 17*
Lewis, John 1940- *AfrAmBi [port], BioIn 17, CngDr 91, EncAACR [port]*
Lewis, John (Aaron) 1920- *Baker 92*
Lewis, John Arthur 1940- *WhoUN 92*
Lewis, John C., Jr. 1935- *St&PR 93*
Lewis, John Clark, Jr. 1935- *WhoAm 92*
Lewis, John Earl 1931- *WhoWrEP 92*
Lewis, John Edgar 1944- *WhoSSW 93*
Lewis, John Elliott 1953- *St&PR 93*
Lewis, John Francis 1932- *WhoAm 92*
Lewis, John Furman *Law&B 92*
Lewis, John Furman 1934- *WhoAm 92*
Lewis, John Gregory *Law&B 92*
Lewis, John H. *Law&B 92*
Lewis, John Hardy, Jr. 1936- *WhoAm 92*
Lewis, John L. 1880-1969 *PolPar*
Lewis, John Leeman, Jr. 1929- *WhoAm 92*
Lewis, John Llewellyn 1880-1969 *DcTwHis*
Lewis, John Milton 1931- *WhoAm 92*
Lewis, John R. 1940- *PolPar, WhoAm 92, WhoSSW 93*
Lewis, John Raymond 1918- *WhoE 93*
Lewis, John Robert *BioIn 17*
Lewis, John Robert 1952- *WhoAm 92*
Lewis, John Samuel 1929- *WhoSSW 93*
Lewis, John Stuart 1946- *St&PR 93*
Lewis, John Thomson Condell 1955- *WhoEmL 93*
Lewis, John Wilson 1930- *WhoAm 92*
Lewis, Jon Andrew *Law&B 92*
Lewis, Jon Richard 1947- *WhoEmL 93*
Lewis, Jonathan Joseph 1958- *WhoWor 93*
Lewis, Jordan David 1937- *WhoAm 92*
Lewis, Joseph Brady 1946- *WhoEmL 93, WhoSSW 93*
Lewis, Joseph D. d1991 *BioIn 17*
Lewis, Joseph H. 1900?- *ConTFT 10, MiSFD 9*
Lewis, Joseph W. 1918- *St&PR 93*
Lewis, Josephine Miles 1865-1959 *BioIn 17*
Lewis, Josephine Victoria 1936- *WhoAmW 93*
Lewis, Joyce Marie Kienzle 1926- *WhoAmW 93*
Lewis, Joyce Staat 1952- *WhoAmW 93, WhoEmL 93*
Lewis, Judith *Law&B 92*
Lewis, Judith A. 1945- *WhoAmW 93*
Lewis, Judy Jones 1956- *WhoWrEP 92*
Lewis, Julian B. 1932- *St&PR 93*
Lewis, Julianne 1949- *WhoEmL 93*
Lewis, Juliette *BioIn 17*
Lewis, Julius 1931- *WhoAm 92*
Lewis, Justina *AmWomPl*
Lewis, Kathleen L. 1951- *St&PR 93*
Lewis, Kathryn Monica 1936- *WhoAmW 93, WhoWor 93*
Lewis, Ken *BioIn 17*
Lewis, Kenneth 1934- *WhoWor 93*
Lewis, Kenneth D. 1947- *WhoSSW 93*
Lewis, Kenneth Edward 1929- *WhoAm 92*
Lewis, Kristin Anitra 1949- *WhoEmL 93*
Lewis, Larry N. 1941- *St&PR 93*
Lewis, Lassie Marie *Law&B 92*
Lewis, Lawrence T., III 1948- *St&PR 93*
Lewis, Leona Johnson 1909- *WhoAm 92*
Lewis, Leonard D. 1910- *St&PR 93*
Lewis, Leonard J. 1923- *WhoAm 92*
Lewis, Leonard W. *Law&B 92*
Lewis, Leroy L., Jr. 1929- *St&PR 93*
Lewis, Leslie *BioIn 17*
Lewis, Leslie George *Law&B 92*
Lewis, Lila Irene *AmWomPl*
Lewis, Lillian *AmWomPl*
Lewis, Linda *BioIn 17*
Lewis, Linda Christine 1949- *St&PR 93*
Lewis, Linda Maureen 1948- *WhoAmW 93*
Lewis, Linda Sue 1947- *WhoAmW 93*
Lewis, Linda Ward 1945- *WhoWrEP 92*
Lewis, Lionel Stanley 1933- *WhoAm 92, WhoE 93*
Lewis, Lois Fuller 1930- *WhoWrEP 92*
Lewis, Lou 1929- *St&PR 93*
Lewis, Lucie Kaye 1951- *WhoEmL 93*
Lewis, Lucy M. d1992 *BioIn 17, NewYTBS 92*
Lewis, Lynn Owens 1957- *WhoSSW 93*
Lewis, M.H. *WhoScE 91-1*
Lewis, M. Leonard 1928- *St&PR 93*
Lewis, Margaret *AmWomPl*
Lewis, Margaret Mary 1959- *WhoAmW 93, WhoEmL 93*
Lewis, Margaret Reddick 1930- *St&PR 93*
Lewis, Margaret Shively 1925- *WhoAm 92*
Lewis, Marilyn Ware 1943- *St&PR 93*
Lewis, Marilyn Ware 1944- *WhoAm 92*
Lewis, Marion W., III 1922- *St&PR 93*
Lewis, Marisa Ann 1956- *WhoSSW 93*
Lewis, Marjorie 1929- *WhoWrEP 92*
Lewis, Mark *ScF&FL 92*
Lewis, Mark E. 1942- *St&PR 93*
Lewis, Mark Earldon 1951- *WhoWor 93*
Lewis, Mark Eliot 1926- *St&PR 93*
Lewis, Mark Stuart *Law&B 92*
Lewis, Martha Anne 1942- *WhoAmW 93*
Lewis, Martha Nell 1944- *WhoAmW 93*
Lewis, Martin E. 1941- *WhoAm 92*
Lewis, Martin Edward 1958- *WhoEmL 93, WhoWor 93*
Lewis, Martin R. 1929- *St&PR 93, WhoAm 92*
Lewis, Martin R., Jr. 1938- *St&PR 93*
Lewis, Martin W. 1956- *ConAu 139*
Lewis, Marvin E. 1907-1991 *BioIn 17*
Lewis, Mary Anita 1950- *WhoAmW 93*
Lewis, Mary Christianna *ScF&FL 92*
Lewis, Mary Christianna Milne 1907-1988 *BioIn 17*
Lewis, Mary Frances 1956- *WhoAmW 93*
Lewis, Mary Therese 1951- *WhoEmL 93*
Lewis, Meade (Anderson) 1905-1964 *Baker 92*
Lewis, Mel *BioIn 17*
Lewis, Melinda Marie 1966- *WhoAmW 93*
Lewis, Melvin 1926- *WhoAm 92*
Lewis, Melvin Wayne 1950- *St&PR 93*
Lewis, Meriwether 1774-1809 *BioIn 17, HarEnMi*
Lewis, Meriwether 1774-1809 & Clark, William 1770-1838 *Expl 93 [port]*
Lewis, Mervyn Keith *WhoScE 91-1*
Lewis, Mervyn Keith 1941- *WhoWor 93*
Lewis, Michael *WhoScE 91-1*
Lewis, Michael 1937- *WhoE 93*
Lewis, Michael 1950- *WhoE 93*
Lewis, Michael A. 1939- *St&PR 93*
Lewis, Michael John 1944- *WhoAm 92*
Lewis, Michael Seth 1953- *WhoE 93, WhoEmL 93*
Lewis, Milton F. 1913- *St&PR 93*
Lewis, Milton S. 1922- *St&PR 93*
Lewis, Mitchell Brain *Law&B 92*
Lewis, Monte Ross 1937- *WhoWrEP 92*
Lewis, Morris, Jr. 1911- *WhoAm 92*
Lewis, Muslima *Law&B 92*
Lewis, Nanci Vicedomini 1962- *WhoAmW 93*
Lewis, Nancy Redd *Law&B 92*
Lewis, Naome d1992 *BioIn 17, NewYTBS 92*
Lewis, Naomi *ScF&FL 92*
Lewis, Neil Phillip 1942- *WhoSSW 93*
Lewis, Nita Aries 1949- *WhoAmW 93, WhoSSW 93*
Lewis, Noah Wellington d1990 *BioIn 17*
Lewis, Norman *BioIn 17*
Lewis, Norman 1912- *WhoAm 92*
Lewis, Norman 1940- *ConAu 136*
Lewis, Norman Albert 1936- *St&PR 93*
Lewis, Norman Edward *Law&B 92*
Lewis, Orme, Jr. 1935- *WhoAm 92*
Lewis, Oscar d1992 *NewYTBS 92*
Lewis, Oscar 1893-1992 *ConAu 139, ScF&FL 92*
Lewis, Oscar 1914-1970 *IntDcAn*
Lewis, Owen Donald 1925- *WhoSSW 93*
Lewis, Owen John *WhoScE 91-1*
Lewis, Paddy Sandra 1945- *WhoAmW 93*
Lewis, Paige Fields 1946- *WhoAmW 93*
Lewis, Paul, Jr. 1939- *WhoSSW 93*
Lewis, Paul Le Roy 1925- *WhoAm 92, WhoE 93*
Lewis, Peggy Sue 1957- *WhoAmW 93*
Lewis, Peirce Fee 1927- *WhoAm 92*
Lewis, Perry Joshua 1938 *WhoAm 92*
Lewis, Peter 1928- *ScF&FL 92*
Lewis, Peter A. 1938- *WhoAm 92*
Lewis, Peter B. 1933- *St&PR 93, WhoIns 93*
Lewis, Peter Benjamin 1933- *WhoAm 92*
Lewis, Peter C. *Law&B 92*
Lewis, Peter Cushman 1934- *St&PR 93*
Lewis, Peter J. 1944- *WhoScE 91-2*
Lewis, Philip 1913- *WhoAm 92*
Lewis, Philip M. 1931- *WhoAm 92*
Lewis, Philip Patrick 1952- *WhoSSW 93*
Lewis, Phillip Harold 1922- *WhoAm 92*
Lewis, R. Gregory 1952- *St&PR 93*
Lewis, R. Mack, Jr. *Law&B 92*
Lewis, R.W.B. *BioIn 17*
Lewis, Ralph Jay, III 1942- *WhoWor 93*
Lewis, Ralph M. 1919- *St&PR 93*
Lewis, Ralph Milton 1919- *WhoAm 92, WhoWor 93*
Lewis, Ramsey 1935- *Baker 92, SoulM*
Lewis, Ramsey Emanuel, Jr. 1935- *WhoAm 92*
Lewis, Randall W. 1951- *St&PR 93*
Lewis, Randi J. 1955- *St&PR 93*
Lewis, Rebecca L. 1938- *WhoAmW 93*
Lewis, Regina Marie 1954- *WhoAmW 93, WhoEmL 93*
Lewis, Reginald F. *BioIn 17*
Lewis, Reginald F. 1942- *WhoAm 92*
Lewis, Rena *AmWomPl*
Lewis, Rhoda Haber 1932- *WhoE 93*
Lewis, Richard *BioIn 17, WhoAm 92*
Lewis, Richard 1914-1990 *Baker 92, BioIn 17, IntDcOp, OxDcOp*
Lewis, Richard 1945- *ScF&FL 92*
Lewis, Richard c. 1948- *News 92 [port]*
Lewis, Richard 1949?- *ConTFT 10*
Lewis, Richard A. 1944- *St&PR 93*
Lewis, Richard Alan 1943- *WhoSSW 93*
Lewis, Richard Allan 1952- *WhoAm 92, WhoE 93, WhoEmL 93*
Lewis, Richard Jay 1933- *WhoAm 92*
Lewis, Richard Lafayette 1923- *St&PR 93*
Lewis, Richard Neil 1953- *St&PR 93*
Lewis, Richard Newburn 1951- *WhoEmL 93*
Lewis, Richard Phelps 1936- *WhoAm 92*
Lewis, Richard Stanley 1916- *WhoAm 92, WhoWrEP 92*
Lewis, Richard Warren 1951- *WhoAm 92*
Lewis, Richard Warrington Baldwin *BioIn 17*
Lewis, Richard Warrington Baldwin 1917- *WhoWrEP 92*
Lewis, Ricki 1954- *WhoWrEP 92*
Lewis, Ricki Barbara 1954- *WhoAmW 93*
Lewis, Rita Hoffman 1947- *St&PR 93, WhoAm 92, WhoAmW 93, WhoEmL 93*
Lewis, Rob 1962- *SmATA 72 [port]*
Lewis, Robert *WhoScE 91-1*
Lewis, Robert A. *Law&B 92*
Lewis, Robert Alan 1933- *WhoAm 92*
Lewis, Robert Arnold 1958- *WhoWor 93*
Lewis, Robert E. 1945- *St&PR 93*
Lewis, Robert Edwin, Jr. 1947- *WhoAm 92, WhoSSW 93, WhoWor 93*
Lewis, Robert Enzer 1934- *WhoAm 92*
Lewis, Robert G. 1916- *St&PR 93*
Lewis, Robert Hall 1926- *Baker 92*
Lewis, Robert Harry 1947- *WhoEmL 93*
Lewis, Robert Henry 1949- *WhoEmL 93*
Lewis, Robert J. 1946- *St&PR 93*
Lewis, Robert John Cornelius Koons 1938- *WhoWor 93*
Lewis, Robert L. 1947- *St&PR 93*
Lewis, Robert Lawrence 1919- *WhoAm 92*
Lewis, Robert M. 1934- *MiSFD 9*
Lewis, Robert Owen 1927- *WhoAm 92*
Lewis, Robert Q. 1920-1991 *BioIn 17*
Lewis, Robin Richardson 1952- *WhoSSW 93*
Lewis, Roderic W. *Law&B 92*
Lewis, Roger 1912-1987 *ScF&FL 92*
Lewis, Roger Franklin 1936- *St&PR 93*
Lewis, Roger G. 1948- *St&PR 93*
Lewis, Roger Kutnow 1941- *WhoAm 92*
Lewis, Roland Wynne *WhoScE 91-1*
Lewis, Ronald Chapman 1950- *WhoSSW 93*
Lewis, Rone 1944- *St&PR 93*
Lewis, Rosa *AmWomPl*
Lewis, Roy Roosevelt 1935- *WhoWor 93*
Lewis, Russell Baugh 1926- *St&PR 93*
Lewis, S. Mitchell 1924- *WhoScE 91-1*
Lewis, Sabrina LaVerne 1963- *WhoEmL 93*
Lewis, Sally Jo *Law&B 92*
Lewis, Sally Sirkin *BioIn 17*
Lewis, Sam *ScF&FL 92*
Lewis, Samella Sanders 1924- *WhoAm 92*
Lewis, Samuel Winfield 1930- *WhoAm 92*
Lewis, Seymour D. d1992 *NewYTBS 92*
Lewis, Shari *BioIn 17*
Lewis, Shari 1934- *News 93-1 [port], WhoAm 92*
Lewis, Sheila Muriel 1937- *WhoAmW 93*
Lewis, Sheldon Noah 1934- *WhoAm 92*
Lewis, Sherman Richard 1936- *St&PR 93*
Lewis, Sherman Richard, Jr. 1936- *WhoAm 92, WhoWor 93*
Lewis, Sheryl Rae 1945- *WhoAmW 93*
Lewis, Sidney A. 1917- *St&PR 93*
Lewis, Simon 1953- *WhoE 93*
Lewis, Sinclair 1885-1951 *BioIn 17, MagSAmL [port], WorLitC [port]*
Lewis, Smiley 1913-1966 *SoulM*
Lewis, Stan *SoulM*
Lewis, Stephen *BioIn 17*
Lewis, Stephen B. *Law&B 92*
Lewis, Stephen Richmond, Jr. 1939- *WhoAm 92*
Lewis, Steven *BioIn 17*
Lewis, Steven C. 1948- *St&PR 93*
Lewis, Steven Mark 1949- *WhoEmL 93*
Lewis, Steven Richard 1953- *WhoWrEP 92*
Lewis, Stuart Weslie 1938- *WhoE 93*
Lewis, Suford 1943- *ScF&FL 92*
Lewis, Susan M. *ScF&FL 92*
Lewis, Sydney 1919- *St&PR 93, WhoAm 92*
Lewis, Sylvia 1945- *WhoWrEP 92*
Lewis, T. *WhoScE 91-1*
Lewis, Ted D. *Law&B 92*
Lewis, Terrell Paul *Law&B 92*
Lewis, Terry
See Jam, Jimmy & Lewis, Terry *SoulM*
Lewis, Theodore E. 1926- *WhoIns 93*
Lewis, Theodore Radford, Jr. 1946- *WhoSSW 93*
Lewis, Thomas B. 1938- *WhoAm 92*
Lewis, Thomas F., Jr. 1924- *WhoAm 92, WhoSSW 93*
Lewis, Thomas John 1952- *WhoAm 92*
Lewis, Thomas Proctor 1930- *WhoAm 92*
Lewis, Thomasine Elizabeth 1958- *WhoWrEP 92*
Lewis, Tim *ScF&FL 92*
Lewis, Timothy Edward 1956- *WhoE 93*
Lewis, Tola Ethridge, Jr. 1945- *WhoSSW 93*
Lewis, Tom 1924- *CngDr 91*
Lewis, Tony *ScF&FL 92*
Lewis, Trevor *WhoScE 91-1*
Lewis, Trisha Alisha 1953- *WhoAmW 93*
Lewis, Vernita Ann Wickliffe 1955- *WhoAmW 93*
Lewis, Victor *BioIn 17*
Lewis, Villa *AmWomPl*
Lewis, Vincent Joseph 1944- *St&PR 93*
Lewis, Virginia Elnora 1907- *WhoAm 92*
Lewis, Virginia Lorraine 1960- *WhoAmW 93*
Lewis, W. Arthur 1915-1991 *BioIn 17*
Lewis, W. Walker 1944- *St&PR 93*
Lewis, Walden John 1936- *St&PR 93*
Lewis, Walter David 1931- *WhoAm 92*
Lewis, Walter Laughn 1924- *WhoAm 92, WhoSSW 93*
Lewis, Welbourne Walker, Jr. 1915- *WhoAm 92*
Lewis, Wendy Suzanne 1965- *WhoAmW 93*
Lewis, Wilbur Curtis 1930- *WhoAm 92, WhoSSW 93, WhoWor 93*
Lewis, Wilbur H. 1930- *WhoAm 92*
Lewis, William A.J., III 1950- *St&PR 93*
Lewis, William Arthur 1915-1991 *BioIn 17*
Lewis, William Barrett 1909-1990 *BioIn 17*
Lewis, William D. 1950- *St&PR 93*
Lewis, William H. 1902-1990 *BioIn 17*
Lewis, William Headley, Jr. 1934- *WhoSSW 93, WhoWor 93*
Lewis, William Henry 1868-1949 *EncAACR*
Lewis, William J. 1766-1828 *BioIn 17*
Lewis, William J. 1947- *St&PR 93*
Lewis, William Leonard 1946- *WhoAm 92*
Lewis, William Mark 1952- *WhoE 93*
Lewis, William R. 1942- *St&PR 93*
Lewis, William Richard 1942- *WhoAm 92*
Lewis, William Scheer 1927- *WhoAm 92, WhoE 93, WhoWor 93*
Lewis, William V., Jr. 1959- *WhoE 93*
Lewis, William Walker 1942- *WhoAm 92*
Lewis, Williams G. *Law&B 92*
Lewis, Winfield Ellsworth 1924- *WhoE 93*
Lewis, Wyndham 1882-1957 *MagSWL [port]*
Lewis-Bogdan, Donna 1963- *WhoAmW 93*
Lewis-Brent, Lana Jane 1946- *St&PR 93, WhoAm 92, WhoAmW 93*
Lewis Carpin, Beverly Ann 1954- *WhoSSW 93*
Lewis-Kolbus, Melinda Anne 1958- *WhoAmW 93, WhoWor 93*
Lewisohn, Adolph 1849-1938 *Baker 92*
Lewisohn, Irene 1892-1944 *AmWomPl*
Lewisohn, Ludwig 1882-1955 *BioIn 17, JeAmFiW*
Lewisohn, Ludwig 1883-1955 *JeAmHC*
Lewison, J.E. Paul 1936- *St&PR 93*
Lewison-Singer, Rita 1939- *WhoAmW 93*
Lewit, Eugene Myron 1946- *WhoEmL 93*
Lewitch, Joseph 1926- *BioIn 17*
Lewitt, Maurice 1931- *St&PR 93*
LeWitt, Michael Herman 1948- *WhoE 93*
Lewitt, Miles Martin 1952- *WhoEmL 93, WhoWor 93*
Lewitt, S.N. 1954- *ScF&FL 92*
Lewitt, Shariann *ScF&FL 92*
LeWitt, Sol 1928- *WhoAm 92*
Lewittes, Don Jordan 1950- *WhoWor 93*
Lewittes, Mordecai Henry 1911-1990 *BioIn 17*
Lewittes, Morton H. 1911-1990 *BioIn 17*
Lewitzky, Bella 1916- *BioIn 17, WhoAm 92, WhoAmW 93*
Lewkowitch, Bernhard 1927- *Baker 92*
Lewkowitz, Karen Helene 1956- *WhoAmW 93*
Lewnes, Peter A. 1929- *WhoE 93*

Lewnes, Tula 1921- *WhoAmW 93*
Lewond fl. 8th cent.- *OxDcByz*
Lewsley, David A. *Law&B 92*
Lewter, Billy Ray 1936- *WhoSSW 93, WhoWor 93*
Lewy, Edgar d1991 *BioIn 17*
Lewy, Guenter 1923- *WhoWrEP 92*
Lewy, John Edwin 1935- *WhoAm 92*
Lewy, Ralph I. 1931- *St&PR 93, WhoAm 92*
Lewy, Robert Ira 1943- *WhoSSW 93*
Lewyn, Thomas Mark 1930- *WhoAm 92*
Lexau, Joan M. *DcAmChF 1960*
Lexsee, Richar *BioIn 17*
Le Xuan Hy 1957- *WhoE 93*
Ley, Andrew James 1945- *WhoAm 92*
Ley, Herbert Leonard, Jr. 1923- *WhoAm 92*
Ley, James M. 1958- *WhoWrEP 92*
Ley, Klaus Friedrich 1957- *WhoWor 93*
Ley, Linda Sue 1949- *WhoAmW 93*
Ley, Lothar 1943- *WhoScE 91-3*
Ley, Margaretha *BioIn 17*
Ley, Margaretha d1992 *NewYTBS 92 [port]*
Ley, Robert E. 1940- *WhoScE 91-2*
Ley, Ronald 1929- *WhoE 93*
Ley, Salvador 1907-1985 *Baker 92*
Ley, Sandra 1944- *ScF&FL 92*
Ley, Steven Victor *WhoScE 91-1*
Ley, Willy 1906-1969 *BioIn 17*
Leybach, Ignace (Xavier Joseph) 1817-1891 *Baker 92*
Leybold, Dennis 1954- *WhoEmL 93*
Leybourn, Carol 1933- *WhoAmW 93*
Leycuras, Yvonne A.M. 1931- *WhoScE 91-2*
Leyda, Margaret Larue 1923- *WhoAmW 93*
Leyden, Dennis Roger 1933- *WhoAm 92*
Leyden, Donald Elliott 1938- *WhoAm 92*
Leyden, Joan Marie 1944- *WhoWrEP 92*
Leyden, Michael Joseph, II 1950- *WhoWor 93*
Leyden, Norman 1917- *Baker 92*
Leyden, Raymond W., Jr. *Law&B 92*
Leydet, Francois Guillaume 1927- *WhoWor 93*
Leydhecker, Wolfgang 1919- *WhoWor 93*
Leydorf, Frederick Leroy 1930- *WhoAm 92*
Leyen, Robert Fitzwater 1924- *WhoSSW 93*
Leyerle, Betsy Smith 1950- *St&PR 93*
Leygonie, Robert 1923- *WhoScE 91-2*
Leygraf, Hans 1920- *Baker 92*
Leygues, Jean Claude Georges 1857-1933 *BioIn 17*
Leyh, George Francis 1931- *WhoAm 92*
Leyh, Richard Edmund, Sr. 1930- *WhoAm 92*
Leyhow, Sharon A. *Law&B 92*
Leyk, R.A. 1946- *St&PR 93*
Leyko, Wanda 1921- *WhoScE 91-4, WhoWor 93*
Leyland, James Richard 1944- *WhoAm 92*
Leyland, Jim *BioIn 17*
Leymaster, Glen R. 1915- *WhoAm 92*
Leyner, Mark *BioIn 17, NewYTBS 92 [port]*
Leyner, Mark 1956- *ScF&FL 92*
Leypoldt, Donald F. 1932- *St&PR 93*
Leypoldt, Frederick, III 1929- *St&PR 93*
Leys, Donald M. 1930- *St&PR 93*
Leyse, Walter Carlton 1932- *St&PR 93*
Leyser, Karl Joseph 1920-1992 *ConAu 137*
Leyssac, Paul P. 1929- *WhoScE 91-2*
Leyster, Judith 1609-1660 *BioIn 17*
Leyton, E.K. *ScF&FL 92*
Leyva, Jason Fernand 1953- *WhoEmL 93, WhoWor 93*
Leyva, Ricardo *ConAu 38NR*
Lezak, Cheryl C. 1950- *St&PR 93*
Lezak, Daniel S. 1933- *St&PR 93*
Lezama Lima, Jose 1910-1976 *SpAmA*
Lezama Serrano, Jose Oswaldo 1956- *WhoWor 93*
Lezcano, Margarita Maria 1948- *WhoAmW 93*
Lezdey, John 1931- *WhoE 93*
Lherie, Paul 1844-1937 *OxDcOp*
Lheritier, Jean c. 1480-c. 1552 *Baker 92*
Lhermitte, Rebecca Goodsell 1943- *WhoAmW 93*
L'Heureux, Dennis Paul 1950- *WhoE 93*
L'Heureux, Diane 1957- *WhoAmW 93*
L'Heureux, Jo Anne 1944- *WhoAmW 93*
L'Heureux, John Clarke 1934- *WhoAm 92, WhoWrEP 92*
L'Heureux, Willard John 1947- *WhoAm 92*
L'Heureux-Dube, Claire 1927- *WhoAm 92, WhoAmW 93*
Lhevine, Dave Bernard 1922- *WhoAm 92, WhoSSW 93*
Lhevinne, Josef 1874-1944 *Baker 92, BioIn 17*
Lhevinne, Rosina 1880-1976 *Baker 92*
Lhin, Erik van *ScF&FL 92*
L'Hoir, Jean-Xavier 1941- *WhoWor 93*
Lhomme, Jean 1938- *WhoScE 91-2*
L'Hommedieu, Marcial B. *St&PR 93*
Lhoste, J.M. 1936- *WhoScE 91-2*
Lhoste, Philippe 1941- *WhoScE 91-2*
Lhotka, Fran 1883-1962 *Baker 92*
Lhotka, John Francis 1921- *WhoAm 92, WhoSSW 93*
Lhotka-Kalinski, Ivo 1913-1987 *Baker 92*
L'Huillier, Peter 1926- *WhoAm 92*
Li, An-Min 1946- *WhoWor 93*
Li, Bing Xi 1934- *WhoWor 93*
Li, Chi-Kwong 1959- *WhoSSW 93*
Li, Chia-yu 1941- *WhoSSW 93*
Li, Chin-Hsien 1944- *WhoWor 93*
Li, Ching-Chung 1932- *WhoAm 92*
Li, Choh-Ming 1912-1991 *BioIn 17*
Li, Chou Hsiung 1923- *WhoE 93*
Li, Chu-Tsing 1920- *WhoAm 92*
Li, Chun-Fei 1938- *WhoWor 93*
Li, Chun Wah 1955- *WhoWor 93*
Li, Daoyu 1932- *WhoUN 92*
Li, David K.P. *BioIn 17*
Li, David Kwok-Po 1939- *WhoAsAP 91*
Li, Florence Tim Oi 1907-1992 *BioIn 17*
Li, Gao Wan 1929- *WhoWor 93*
Li, Guanghua 1938- *WhoWor 93*
Li, Huishi 1955- *WhoWor 93*
Li, James Chen Min 1925- *WhoAm 92*
Li, Jane Chiao 1939- *WhoAmW 93*
Li, Jane-Yu Ho 1946- *WhoEmL 93*
Li, Jia 1945- *WhoSSW 93*
Li, Jiahao 1944- *WhoUN 92*
Li, Jiye 1904- *WhoWor 93*
Li, K'o-Jan 1907-1988 *BioIn 17*
Li, Kui Wai 1952- *WhoWor 93*
Li, Li 1928- *WhoWor 93*
Li, Norman N. 1933- *WhoAm 92*
Li, Pearl Nei-Chien 1946- *WhoE 93*
Li, P'eng 1928- *BioIn 17*
Li, Qiao 1938- *WhoWor 93*
Li, Ronglu 1943- *WhoWor 93*
Li, Shanji *ScF&FL 92*
Li, Shoufu 1935- *WhoWor 93*
Li, Shude 1927- *WhoWor 93*
Li, Steven Shoei-lung 1938- *WhoSSW 93*
Li, Sze Bay Albert 1936- *WhoWor 93*
Li, Tie Cai 1950- *WhoWor 93*
Li, Ting-Kuo 1937- *WhoScE 91-2*
Li, Tingye 1931- *WhoAm 92*
Li, Tze-chung 1927- *WhoAm 92*
Li, Wen Rong 1941- *WhoWor 93*
Li, Wenlin 1942- *WhoWor 93*
Li, Wu 1958- *WhoSSW 93*
Li, Xiang 1942- *WhoWor 93*
Li, Yang-cheng 1940- *WhoWor 93*
Li, Yao 1958- *WhoWor 93*
Li, Ying 1961- *WhoWor 93*
Li, Yiping Y.P. 1943- *WhoWor 93*
Li, Yuan Zu 1923- *WhoWor 93*
Lia, Gary Peter 1941- *St&PR 93, WhoIns 93*
Liaaen-Jensen, Synnove 1932- *WhoScE 91-4*
Liacopoulos, Panayotis 1919- *WhoScE 91-2*
Liacos, L.G. 1922- *WhoScE 91-3*
Liacos, Paul Julian 1929- *WhoAm 92*
Liadov, Anatoli (Konstantinovich) 1855-1914 *Baker 92*
Liadov, Konstantin (Nikolaievich) 1820-1868 *Baker 92*
Liakos, Aris 1932- *WhoScE 91-3*
Liakos, Shirley Atchison 1953- *WhoEmL 93*
Liang, Can-Bin 1938- *WhoWor 93*
Liang, Chang-seng 1941- *WhoE 93*
Liang, Charles Chi 1934- *WhoE 93*
Liang, Elisa Lee 1961- *WhoEmL 93*
Liang, Hung 1920- *St&PR 93*
Liang, Isabella Yee-Shan *WhoE 93*
Liang, Jason Chia 1935- *WhoWor 93*
Liang, Jeffrey Der-Shing 1915- *WhoWor 93*
Liang, Kai Tien 1941- *WhoWor 93*
Liang, Michael Thean-Chong 1942- *WhoE 93*
Liang, Nian Ci 1940- *WhoWor 93*
Liang, Nong 1958- *WhoWor 93*
Liang, Vera Beh-Yuin Tsai 1946- *WhoAmW 93, WhoEmL 93*
Liang, Xi-ting 1937- *WhoWor 93*
Liang, Zhishun 1920- *WhoWor 93*
Liang Buting 1921- *WhoAsAP 91*
Liang Dongcai 1932- *WhoAsAP 91*
Liange, Kenneth *Law&B 92*
Liang Guanglie *WhoAsAP 91*
Liang Qichao 1873-1929 *DcTwHis*
Liang Su-Yung 1920- *WhoAsAP 91*
Liano, Anthony D. 1947- *St&PR 93*
Lianos, William P. 1936- *St&PR 93*
Lian-Sheng, Wang 1953- *WhoUN 92*
Liantonio, Julia Ann Mary 1950- *WhoEmL 93*
Liantonio, Thomas Victor 1951- *WhoEmL 93*
Liao, Chung Min 1957- *WhoWor 93*
Liao, Eric Nan-Kang 1938- *WhoWor 93*
Liao, Gong Fu 1945- *WhoWor 93*
Liao, Karen Anne 1945- *WhoE 93*
Liao, Kevin Chii Wen 1937- *WhoWor 93*
Liao, Mei-June *WhoAm 92*
Liao, Paul Foo-Hung 1944- *WhoAm 92*
Liao, Shutsung 1931- *WhoAm 92*
Liao, Tony Tung Lin 1929- *WhoWor 93*
Liao Hansheng, Lt.-Gen 1911- *WhoAsAP 91*
Liao Hui 1941- *WhoAsAP 91*
Liao Wenhai *WhoAsAP 91*
Liapunov, Sergei (Mikhailovich) 1859-1924 *Baker 92*
Liaquat Ali Khan, Nawabzada 1895-1951 *DcTwHis*
Liardon, Remy 1944- *WhoScE 91-4*
Liatoshinsky, Boris (Nikolaievich) 1895-1968 *Baker 92*
Liau, Mary Chong-Chin *WhoE 93*
Liba, Peter Michael 1940- *WhoAm 92*
Libadarios *OxDcByz*
Libadenos, Andrew c. 1308-c. 1361 *OxDcByz*
Libanios 314-c. 393 *OxDcByz*
Libassi, F. Peter 1930- *St&PR 93, WhoIns 93*
Libassi, Frank Peter *Law&B 92*
Libassi, Frank Peter 1930- *WhoAm 92*
Libbert, Eike 1928- *WhoWor 93*
Libbin, Anne Edna 1950- *WhoAm 92*
Libby, Bruce A. 1939- *St&PR 93*
Libby, Gary Russell 1944- *WhoAm 92, WhoSSW 93*
Libby, Gwynne Margaret 1958- *WhoAmW 93*
Libby, Henry Grady 1940- *St&PR 93*
Libby, John Kelway 1926- *WhoAm 92, WhoE 93, WhoWor 93*
Libby, Julianna 1956- *WhoAmW 93, WhoE 93*
Libby, Paul Langford 1948- *St&PR 93*
Libby, Paul Marc 1947- *WhoE 93*
Libby, Peter 1947- *WhoAm 92*
Libby, Ronald Theodore 1941- *WhoAm 92*
Libby, Sandra Chiavaras 1949- *WhoAmW 93*
Libby, Theodore Israel 1920- *St&PR 93*
Libchaber, Albert Joseph 1934- *WhoAm 92*
Libelt, Karol 1807-1875 *PolBiDi*
Liben, Michael Paul 1954- *WhoAm 92*
Libenson, Amy *Law&B 92*
Liber, Hillary Selese Jacobs 1953- *WhoEmL 93*
Liber, Jeffrey Mark 1952- *St&PR 93*
Liberace 1919-1987 *Baker 92, ConMus 9 [port]*
Liberator, John Dominick *Law&B 92*
Liberatore, Antonino 1929- *WhoScE 91-3*
Liberatore, James Howard 1933- *St&PR 93*
Liberatore, Nicholas Alfred 1916- *WhoAm 92*
Liberatori, Ronald Peter 1938- *St&PR 93*
Liberia-Peters, Maria *WhoWor 93*
Liberia-Peters, Maria 1941- *DcCPCAm*
Liberius d366 *OxDcByz*
Liberman, Alexander 1912- *BioIn 17, WhoAm 92, WhoWrEP 92*
Liberman, Alvin Meyer 1917- *WhoAm 92*
Liberman, Anatoly 1937- *ConAu 40NR*
Liberman, Arthur L. *Law&B 92*
Liberman, Clara *St&PR 93*
Liberman, Gail Jeanne 1951- *WhoAmW 93, WhoEmL 93*
Liberman, Ira L. 1926- *WhoAm 92*
Liberman, Isabelle Y. *BioIn 17*
Liberman, Lee Marvin 1921- *St&PR 93, WhoAm 92*
Liberman, Lee Sarah 1956- *WhoAm 92, WhoAmW 93*
Liberman, Manual *St&PR 93*
Liberman, Michael 1938- *WhoSSW 93*
Liberman, Michael Ira 1944- *St&PR 93*
Liberman, Robert Paul 1937- *WhoAm 92*
Liberman, Roni *St&PR 93*
Liberman, Samuel 1926- *St&PR 93, WhoAm 92*
Liberman, Silvain *WhoScE 91-2*
Liberman, Sylvain 1934-1988 *BioIn 17*
Liberman, Tatiana du Plessix 1906-1991 *BioIn 17*
Liberman-Cline, Nancy 1958- *BioIn 17*
Liberski, Benon 1926-1983 *PolBiDi*
Libert, Donald Joseph 1928- *WhoAm 92*
Libert, Gaetan Anselme 1953- *WhoWor 93*
Libert, Henri 1869-1937 *Baker 92*
Liberti, Arnaldo 1917- *WhoScE 91-3*
Liberti, Daniel J. *Law&B 92*
Liberti, Lorenzo 1942- *WhoScE 91-3*
Liberti, Paul A. 1936- *WhoAm 92*
Libertiny, Attila G. 1948- *St&PR 93*
Libertiny, George Zoltan 1934- *WhoAm 92*
Liberto, Carl 1949- *WhoAm 92*
Liberto, Joseph Salvatore 1929- *WhoAm 92*
Liberto, P. Frank *Law&B 92*
Liberty, Leona Helen 1940- *WhoE 93*
Liberty, Sharon Wakeman 1953- *WhoAmW 93*
Liberzon, Mark Rahmil 1948- *WhoWor 93*
Libeskind, Daniel 1946- *BioIn 17*
Libhart, Bonni 1935- *WhoWrEP 92*
Libin, Jerome B. 1936- *WhoAm 92*
Libin, Laurence Elliot 1944- *WhoAm 92*
Libin, Paul 1930- *WhoAm 92*
Libkind, Jean Sue Johnson 1944- *WhoAmW 93*
Libman, Alan David 1943- *WhoWor 93*
Libman, Carol 1928- *WhoCanL 92*
Libman, Gary *ScF&FL 92*
Libman, George H. *Law&B 92*
Libman, Lillian d1992 *NewYTBS 92 [port]*
Liboff, Richard Lawrence 1931- *WhoAm 92*
Libon, Philippe 1775-1838 *Baker 92*
Libonati, Michael Ernest 1944- *WhoAm 92*
Liboro-Tan, Regina Kaluag *WhoAmW 93*
Libove, Charles 1923- *WhoAm 92*
Librande, Laura 1958- *WhoEmL 93*
Librando, Gaetano 1953- *WhoUN 92*
Librizzi, Joseph *St&PR 93*
Libros, John F. 1954- *St&PR 93*
Libus, Zofia 1930- *WhoScE 91-4*
Licad, Cecile 1961- *Baker 92*
Licario *OxDcByz*
Licastri, Cheryl Lynne 1960- *WhoWrEP 92*
Licata, Anthony J. 1931- *St&PR 93*
Licata, Regina A. *Law&B 92*
Licciardi, Thomas S. 1949- *St&PR 93*
Liccione, Irma *AmWomPl*
Liccione, Maureen Therese 1953- *WhoAmW 93*
Licette, Miriam 1892-1969 *OxDcOp*
Lich, G(len) E(rnst) 1948- *ConAu 139*
Lich, Glen Ernst 1948- *WhoAm 92, WhoSSW 93*
Li Changchun 1945- *WhoAsAP 91*
Lichard, Milan 1853-1935 *Baker 92*
Licharowicz, Johanna Fe 1963- *WhoAmW 93*
Lichauer, Robert William 1947- *St&PR 93*
Lichey, Reinhold 1879-1957 *Baker 92*
Lichine, Alexis 1913-1989 *BioIn 17*
Lichine, Sacha *BioIn 17*
Lichko, Joseph 1955- *WhoAm 92*
Lichnevski, Mikhail S. 1940- *WhoUN 92*
Lichnowsky, Karl von 1761-1814 *Baker 92*
Lichnowsky, Moritz von 1771-1837 *See* Lichnowsky, Karl von 1761-1814 *Baker 92*
Lichstein, Edgar 1936- *WhoE 93, WhoWor 93*
Lichstein, Herman Carlton 1918- *WhoAm 92*
Licht, Alice Vess 1937- *WhoAmW 93*
Licht, Janice B. 1954- *WhoAmW 93*
Licht, Lilla Giles McKnight *WhoWrEP 92*
Licht, Paul 1938- *WhoAm 92*
Licht, Richard A. 1948- *WhoAm 92*
Licht, Stuart Lawrence 1954- *WhoE 93*
Lichtblau, John H. 1921- *WhoAm 92*
Lichtblau, Myron Ivor 1925- *WhoAm 92, WhoE 93*
Lichtenauer, Dixon Ann 1934- *WhoAmW 93*
Lichtenbaum, Stephen 1939- *WhoE 93*
Lichtenberg, Benjamin d1991 *BioIn 17*
Lichtenberg, Byron K. 1948- *WhoAm 92*
Lichtenberg, Georg Christoph 1742-1799 *BioIn 17*
Lichtenberg, Hans Robert *BioIn 17*
Lichtenberg, Jacqueline 1942- *ScF&FL 92*
Lichtenberg, Kurt 1947- *WhoEmL 93*
Lichtenberg, Margaret Klee 1941- *WhoAm 92*
Lichtenberg, Myles Louis 1960- *WhoEmL 93*
Lichtenberg, Philip 1926- *WhoE 93*
Lichtenberger, Arthur T. 1928- *St&PR 93*
Lichtenberger, Cheryl Lee 1951- *WhoAmW 93*
Lichtenberger, Frank H. 1937- *St&PR 93, WhoIns 93*
Lichtenberger, Horst William 1935- *WhoE 93*
Lichtenberger, Robert 1945- *St&PR 93*
Lichtenberger, William Robert 1925- *WhoIns 93*
Lichtendorf, Susan Siegel 1941- *WhoAmW 93*
Lichtenfels, Joanna Loraine 1940- *WhoWrEP 92*
Lichtenheld, Frank Robert 1923- *WhoWor 93*
Lichtenstadter, Ilse d1991 *BioIn 17*
Lichtensteiger, Walter 1936- *WhoScE 91-4*

Lichtenstein, Elissa Charlene 1954- *WhoAm 92, WhoAmW 93*
Lichtenstein, Harvey 1929- *WhoAm 92*
Lichtenstein, Karl August, Freiherr von 1767-1845 *Baker 92*
Lichtenstein, Lawrence Mark 1934- *WhoAm 92*
Lichtenstein, Michael B. *Law&B 92*
Lichtenstein, Pauline d1990 *BioIn 17*
Lichtenstein, Robert Jay 1948- *WhoEmL 93*
Lichtenstein, Robin O'Brien *Law&B 92*
Lichtenstein, Roy 1923- *BioIn 17, WhoAm 92*
Lichtenstein, Seymour 1926- *St&PR 93*
Lichtenstein, Seymour 1927- *WhoAm 92*
Lichtenstein, Stephen F. *Law&B 92*
Lichtenthal, Peter 1780-1853 *Baker 92*
Lichtenthaler, Frieder W. 1932- *WhoScE 91-3*
Lichtenthaler, Frieder Wilhelm 1932- *WhoWor 93*
Lichtenthaler, Hartmut Karl 1934- *WhoScE 91-3*
Lichtenwanger, William (John) 1915- *Baker 92*
Lichter, Edward Arthur 1928- *WhoAm 92*
Lichter, Paul Richard 1939- *WhoAm 92*
Lichter, Robert Louis 1941- *WhoE 93*
Lichter-Heath, Laurie Jean 1951- *WhoEmL 93*
Lichterman, Brian 1955- *WhoSSW 93*
Lichterman, Harold R. *Law&B 92*
Lichterman, Martin 1918- *WhoAm 92*
Lichterman, Scott Howard 1957- *St&PR 93*
Lichti, Allan *WhoWrEP 92*
Lichti, Barbara Jean 1942- *WhoAmW 93*
Lichtig, Leo Kenneth 1953- *WhoE 93*
Lichtiger, Monte 1939- *WhoSSW 93*
Lichtin, J. Leon 1924- *WhoAm 92*
Lichtin, Norman Nahum 1922- *WhoAm 92*
Lichtinger, Pedro 1954- *WhoWor 93*
Lichtman, Cecil 1913- *St&PR 93*
Lichtman, David Michael 1942- *WhoAm 92*
Lichtman, Howard 1955- *St&PR 93*
Lichtman, L. Savannah 1949- *St&PR 93*
Lichtman, Louis *BioIn 17*
Lichtman, Ronald Eugene 1956- *WhoSSW 93*
Lichtsinn, Robert W. 1929- *St&PR 93*
Lichtveld, Lou 1903- *Baker 92*
Lichty, Glenna Kelly *Law&B 92*
Lichty, Mark Edward 1949- *St&PR 93*
Lichty, Michael Jay *Law&B 92*
Licinius c. 265-325 *OxDcByz*
Licinius, Valerius Licinianus d325 *HarEnMi*
Licitra, Salvatore M. 1919- *WhoIns 93*
Lick, Dale Wesley 1938- *WhoAm 92, WhoE 93, WhoSSW 93*
Lick, Wilbert James 1933- *WhoAm 92*
Licke, W. John 1945- *St&PR 93*
Licke, Wallace John *Law&B 92*
Lickem, Conni Leebidow 1960- *WhoE 93*
Licker, Kenneth Ira 1944- *WhoSSW 93*
Lickerman, Howard Wayne 1927- *St&PR 93*
Lickiss, Mike *BioIn 17*
Lickl, Aegidius (Ferdinand) Karl 1803-1864
See Lickl, Johann Georg 1769-1843 *Baker 92*
Lickl, Johann Georg 1769-1843 *Baker 92*
Lickl, Karl Georg 1801-1877
See Lickl, Johann Georg 1769-1843 *Baker 92*
Lickle, William C. 1929- *St&PR 93*
Lickle, William Cauffiel 1929- *WhoAm 92*
Licklider, J.C.R. 1915-1990 *BioIn 17*
Licklider, Joseph Carl Robnett 1915-1990 *BioIn 17*
Licklider, Roy Eilers 1941- *WhoE 93*
Lickteig, Klaus E. 1938- *WhoScE 91-3*
Licopantis, Dean Peter 1961- *WhoE 93*
Licoscos, Andree Jeanne 1943- *WhoAmW 93*
Liday, Judy Anne 1939- *WhoAmW 93*
Li Dazhao 1888-1927 *DcTwHis*
Lidberg, Lars G. 1935- *WhoScE 91-4*
Liddell, Donald C. *Law&B 92*
Liddell, Donald Macy, Jr. 1907- *WhoWor 93*
Liddell, Gary W. 1950- *St&PR 93*
Liddell, Heather Mary *WhoScE 91-1*
Liddell, Jane Hawley Hawkes 1907- *WhoE 93, WhoWor 93*
Liddell, Ken E. 1912-1975 *BioIn 17*
Liddell, Leon Morris 1914- *WhoAm 92, WhoWor 93*
Liddell, Robert 1908- *BioIn 17*
Liddell, (John) Robert 1908-1992 *ConAu 139*
Liddell, Sharen 1945- *WhoWrEP 92*
Liddell, W. Kirk 1949- *St&PR 93, WhoAm 92*
Liddell, William A. *BioIn 17*
Liddell Hart, Basil Henry 1895-1970 *BioIn 17, HarEnMi*
Liddell-Moonan, Cynthia Ann 1951- *WhoAmW 93*
Liddicoat, Brian 1944- *WhoE 93*
Liddicoat, Richard Thomas, Jr. 1918- *WhoAm 92*
Liddle, Alan Curtis 1922- *WhoAm 92*
Liddle, Ernest Victor 1923- *WhoSSW 93*
Liddle, George R. 1927- *St&PR 93*
Liddle, Robert Howard, Jr. *Law&B 92*
Liddle, William David 1937- *WhoSSW 93*
Liddy, David G. *Law&B 92*
Liddy, G. Gordon *BioIn 17*
Liddy, James 1934- *WhoWrEP 92*
Liddy, Terence Cullerton 1944- *St&PR 93*
Lide, D.R., Jr. *WhoScE 91-2*
Lide, David Reynolds 1928- *WhoE 93*
Lide, Mary *ScF&FL 92*
Lide, Neoma Jewell Lawhon 1926- *WhoAmW 93*
Liden, Gunnar Knut 1918- *WhoWor 93*
Liden, S. Sture 1933- *WhoScE 91-4*
Lider, Carl L. 1941- *WhoSSW 93*
Lider, Robert Y. *Law&B 92*
Li Dezhu 1944- *WhoAsAP 91*
Lidgate, D. *WhoScE 91-1*
Lidgey, Francis John *WhoScE 91-1*
Lidholm, Ingvar (Natanael) 1921- *Baker 92*
Lidicker, William Zander, Jr. 1932- *WhoAm 92*
Lidke, Wilmer, II 1950- *St&PR 93*
Lidl, Vaclav 1922- *Baker 92*
Lidon, Jean Sih 1961- *WhoEmL 93*
Lidon, Jose 1748-1827 *Baker 92*
Li Donnici, Kenneth 1925- *St&PR 93*
Lidov, Arthur 1917-1990 *BioIn 17*
Lidow, Alan E. 1942- *St&PR 93*
Lidow, Eric 1912- *St&PR 93*
Lidstone, David J. *Law&B 92*
Lidstone, Herrick Kenley, Jr. 1949- *WhoWor 93*
Lidstrom, Esther Marie 1947- *WhoE 93*
Lidtke, Doris Keefe 1929- *WhoAmW 93*
Lidtke, Vernon LeRoy 1930- *WhoAm 92*
Lidvall, Christine Alma 1947- *WhoEmL 93*
Lidz, Carol Schneider 1941- *WhoAmW 93*
Lidz, Charles Wilmanns 1946- *WhoAm 92*
Lidz, Franz *BioIn 17*
Lie, Erika *Baker 92*
Lie, Harald 1902-1942 *Baker 92*
Lie, Oyvind 1956- *WhoScE 91-4*
Lie, Sigurd 1871-1904 *Baker 92*
Lie, Sverre O. 1938- *WhoScE 91-4*
Lie, Trygve Halvdan 1896-1968 *DcTwHis*
Lie, Ulf *WhoScE 91-2*
Lieb, Andrew Marc 1955- *WhoE 93*
Lieb, Carl Sears 1949- *WhoSSW 93*
Lieb, Elliott Hershel 1932- *WhoAm 92*
Lieb, Fred L. *Law&B 92*
Lieb, Irwin C. 1925-1992 *BioIn 17*
Lieb, Klaus Peter 1939- *WhoScE 91-3*
Lieb, Mark 1950- *St&PR 93*
Liebaers, Ingehorg 1945- *WhoScE 91-2*
Liebau, Friedrich K.F. 1926- *WhoScE 91-3*
Liebe, Eduard Ludwig 1819-1900 *Baker 92*
Liebeck, William W. *St&PR 93*
Liebeler, Susan Wittenberg 1942- *WhoAm 92, WhoAmW 93*
Liebelt, Arthur H. *WhoIns 93*
Liebel-Weckowicz, Helen Pauline Grit 1930- *WhoAm 92*
Liebenow, J. Gus 1925- *WhoAm 92*
Liebenow, Larry A. 1943- *St&PR 93*
Liebenow, Larry Albert 1943- *WhoAm 92*
Liebenson, Gloria Krasnow 1922- *WhoE 93*
Liebenson, Herbert 1920- *WhoAm 92*
Liebenson, Sidney Charles 1951- *WhoAm 92*
Lieber, Anna 1947- *WhoEmL 93*
Lieber, Carol N. *Law&B 92*
Lieber, Charles Donald 1921- *WhoAm 92*
Lieber, Charles Saul 1931- *WhoAm 92*
Lieber, Dalia Rofe 1937- *St&PR 93*
Lieber, David Leo 1925- *WhoAm 92*
Lieber, David Leslie 1957- *WhoAm 92*
Lieber, Edward Joseph *Law&B 92*
Lieber, Edward Joseph 1921- *St&PR 93*
Lieber, Francis 1800-1872 *BioIn 17*
Lieber, Franz 1800-1872 *BioIn 17*
Lieber, Jerome B. 1920- *St&PR 93*
Lieber, Jill *BioIn 17*
Lieber, Michael W. 1940- *St&PR 93*
Lieber, Oscar Montgomery 1830-1862 *BioIn 17*
Lieber, Stephen Andrew 1925- *WhoAm 92*
Lieber, Tood Michael 1944- *WhoWrEP 92*
Lieber, William *BioIn 17*
Lieberfarb, D.L. 1916- *St&PR 93*
Lieberfarb, James David 1955- *St&PR 93*
Lieberg, Godo Herbert Traugott 1929- *WhoWor 93*
Liebergall, Gordon S. 1934- *WhoE 93*
Liebergen, David A. *St&PR 93*
Lieberman, A. Robert *WhoScE 91-1*
Lieberman, Anne Marie 1946- *WhoEmL 93*
Lieberman, Archie 1926- *WhoAm 92*
Lieberman, Barry Louis 1952- *WhoEmL 93*
Lieberman, Bernard *Law&B 92*
Lieberman, Bruce R. *Law&B 92*
Lieberman, Charles 1948- *WhoAm 92*
Lieberman, David Ira 1941- *WhoAm 92*
Lieberman, Douglas Mark 1960- *WhoEmL 93*
Lieberman, E. James 1934- *BioIn 17*
Lieberman, E(dwin) James 1934- *WhoWrEP 92*
Lieberman, Edwin James 1934- *WhoE 93*
Lieberman, Elizabeth R. *Law&B 92*
Lieberman, Eugene 1918- *WhoWor 93*
Lieberman, Florence 1918- *WhoAmW 93*
Lieberman, Fredric 1940- *WhoAm 92*
Lieberman, Gail Forman 1943- *WhoAm 92*
Lieberman, Gerald J. 1925- *WhoAm 92*
Lieberman, Harvey 1945- *St&PR 93*
Lieberman, Harvey Joel 1943- *WhoE 93*
Lieberman, Harvey Michael 1949- *WhoE 93*
Lieberman, Henry Richard *WhoE 93*
Lieberman, Herbert H. 1933- *WhoWrEP 92*
Lieberman, Hillel 1942- *St&PR 93, WhoAm 92*
Lieberman, Ilene 1956- *WhoEmL 93*
Lieberman, James 1921- *WhoE 93*
Lieberman, Jeff *MiSFD 9*
Lieberman, Jethro Koller 1943- *WhoE 93*
Lieberman, John Joseph 1948- *WhoEmL 93*
Lieberman, Joseph I. 1942- *CngDr 91, WhoAm 92, WhoE 93*
Lieberman, Laurence 1935- *WhoAm 92, WhoWrEP 92*
Lieberman, Leonard 1929- *WhoAm 92*
Lieberman, Lester Zane 1930- *St&PR 93, WhoAm 92*
Lieberman, Louis 1944- *WhoAm 92*
Lieberman, Melvyn 1938- *WhoAm 92*
Lieberman, Morris Baruch 1925- *WhoAm 92*
Lieberman, Myron 1919- *WhoAm 92*
Lieberman, Nancy Strauman 1936- *WhoAmW 93*
Lieberman, Philip Alden 1948- *WhoWrEP 92*
Lieberman, Robert *MiSFD 9, St&PR 93*
Lieberman, Robert 1941- *ScF&FL 92*
Lieberman, Robert H. 1941- *MiSFD 9*
Lieberman, Robert I. 1954- *St&PR 93*
Lieberman, Rosalie 1907?-1979? *ScF&FL 92*
Lieberman, Seymour 1916- *WhoAm 92*
Lieberman, Shari 1958- *WhoAmW 93, WhoEmL 93*
Lieberman, Steven Paul *Law&B 92*
Lieberman, Stuart T. 1952- *St&PR 93*
Liebermann, Max 1847-1935 *BioIn 17*
Liebermann, Rolf 1910- *Baker 92, OxDcOp*
Liebermann, Thomas R. 1949- *St&PR 93*
Liebersbach, John W. *Law&B 92*
Lieberson, Goddard 1911-1977 *Baker 92, BioIn 17*
Lieberson, Peter 1946- *Baker 92*
Lieberson, Stanley 1933- *ConAu 38NR, WhoAm 92, WhoWrEP 92*
Lieberstein, Edward 1938- *St&PR 93*
Lieberstein, Eugene *Law&B 92*
Lieberthal, Mike *BioIn 17*
Liebes, Raquel 1938- *WhoAmW 93, WhoE 93, WhoWor 93*
Liebeskind, Donald R. 1931- *St&PR 93*
Liebeskind, Herbert 1921- *WhoAm 92*
Liebetreu, Mark Ernest 1962- *WhoSSW 93*
Liebhafsky, Erwin Eugene 1922- *WhoSSW 93*
Liebich, Hartmut Manfred 1940- *WhoWor 93*
Liebich, Marcia Trathen 1942- *WhoAmW 93, WhoE 93*
Liebig, Karl 1808-1872 *Baker 92*
Liebig, Richard Arthur 1923- *WhoAm 92*
Liebig, Siegfried 1938- *WhoWor 93*
Liebing, Howard C. 1921- *St&PR 93*
Liebknecht, Karl 1871-1919 *DcTwHis*
Liebl, Arthur Fredrick 1928- *St&PR 93*
Liebl, Thomas A. 1960- *St&PR 93*
Liebler, Elisabeth M. 1960- *WhoWor 93*
Liebling, A.J. 1904-1963 *BioIn 17*
Liebling, Abbott Joseph 1904-1963 *BioIn 17, JrnUS*
Liebling, Emil 1851-1914 *Baker 92*
Liebling, Estelle 1880-1970 *Baker 92*
Liebling, Georg 1865-1946 *Baker 92*
Liebling, Jerome 1924- *WhoAm 92*
Liebling, Leonard 1874-1945 *Baker 92*
Liebling, Norman Robert 1917- *WhoWor 93*
Liebman, Anita 1931- *WhoAmW 93*
Liebman, Arthur 1926- *ScF&FL 92*
Liebman, Burt H. *Law&B 92*
Liebman, Dave *BioIn 17*
Liebman, H. Burton 1934- *St&PR 93*
Liebman, Howard Mark 1952- *WhoWor 93*
Liebman, Jerome 1927- *WhoAm 92*
Liebman, Joel Fredric 1947- *WhoE 93*
Liebman, Jon Charles 1934- *WhoAm 92*
Liebman, Lance Malcolm 1941- *WhoAm 92*
Liebman, Lawrence Howard 1957- *WhoE 93*
Liebman, Lawrence M. 1930- *St&PR 93*
Liebman, Milton 1928- *WhoAm 92*
Liebman, Norman S. 1928- *St&PR 93*
Liebman, Paul *Law&B 92*
Liebman, Paul Robert 1945- *WhoSSW 93*
Liebman, Priscilla May d1990 *BioIn 17*
Liebman, Ronald Stanley 1943- *WhoAm 92, WhoE 93, WhoWor 93*
Liebman, Theodore 1939- *WhoAm 92*
Liebmann, Bernhard *WhoScE 91-3*
Liebmann, George William 1939- *WhoAm 92*
Liebmann, Herman 1918- *St&PR 93*
Liebmann, Richard 1950- *St&PR 93*
Liebmann, Seymour W. 1928- *WhoSSW 93*
Liebo, Stephen Lance 1948- *WhoEmL 93*
Liebovich, Samuel David 1946- *St&PR 93*
Liebovich, Sheldon Bernard 1937- *WhoAm 92*
Liebovich, Sidney 1939- *WhoE 93*
Liebovitch, Larry S. *WhoE 93*
Liebow, Charles 1944- *WhoE 93*
Liebowitz, Alan F. *Law&B 92*
Liebowitz, Alan F. 1948- *St&PR 93*
Liebowitz, Alan L. *Law&B 92*
Liebowitz, Harold 1924- *WhoAm 92*
Liebowitz, Leo 1927- *St&PR 93*
Liebowitz, Michael E. 1936- *St&PR 93*
Liebowitz, Neil Robert 1956- *WhoEmL 93*
Liebrecht, H. *WhoScE 91-3*
Liebscher, Hans Jurgen 1936- *WhoScE 91-3*
Liebscher, Walt 1918-1985 *ScF&FL 92*
Liebson, Donald Charles 1952- *WhoEmL 93*
Liebson, Milt 1923- *WhoE 93*
Liebson, S.D. *Law&B 92*
Liebson, Sidney Harold 1920- *WhoE 93*
Liebtag, Benford Gustav, III 1941- *WhoSSW 93*
Liechtenstein, Johann Adam Andreas, Furst 1656-1712 *BioIn 17*
Liechty, Craig 1959- *St&PR 93*
Liechty, John F. 1948- *St&PR 93*
Liechty, Jon D. 1949- *St&PR 93*
Lied, Einar *WhoScE 91-4*
Lieder, Rainer Michael 1938- *WhoWor 93*
Liederman, Al 1911- *WhoAm 92*
Liederman, David Samuel 1935- *WhoAm 92*
Liedtke, Guenter J. 1941- *St&PR 93*
Liedtke, J. Hugh 1922- *St&PR 93*
Liedtke, John Hugh 1922- *WhoAm 92, WhoSSW 93*
Liedtke, Russell Charles 1945- *St&PR 93*
Liedtke, William C. 1924-1991 *BioIn 17*
Lief, Evelyn *ScF&FL 92*
Lief, Harold Isaiah 1917- *WhoAm 92*
Lief, Inez H. *WhoAmW 93*
Lief, Leonard 1924- *WhoAm 92*
Lief, Ruth Ann *ScF&FL 92*
Lief, Stephen Jay 1956- *WhoEmL 93*
Lief, Thomas Parrish 1931- *WhoSSW 93*
Liefeld, Olive Fleming *BioIn 17*
Lieff, Ann *BioIn 17*
Lieff, Ann Spector 1952- *St&PR 93*
Lieff, Erwin 1926- *St&PR 93*
Lieflander, Manfred 1930- *WhoScE 91-3*
Liefooghe, Jacques 1926- *WhoScE 91-2*
Liegel, Reinald David 1942- *St&PR 93*
Liegey, Jean Richard 1928- *WhoSSW 93*
Liehl, Ekke 1941- *WhoScE 91-4*
Liekar, John P. 1951- *St&PR 93*
Liekar, John P., Jr. *Law&B 92*
Liem, Annie 1941- *WhoAmW 93*
Liem, Channing 1909- *WhoWor 93*
Liem, Khian Kioe 1942- *WhoWor 93*
Liem, Sioe Liong *BioIn 17*
Lien, Bruce Hawkins 1927- *St&PR 93*
Lien, Charles H. 1925- *St&PR 93*
Lien, Eric Jung-chi 1937- *WhoAm 92*
Lien, Eric L. 1946- *WhoE 93*
Lien, Jere H. 1932- *St&PR 93*
Lien, Leif 1940- *WhoScE 91-4*
Lien, Neil 1925- *St&PR 93*
Lien, Peter C. 1958- *St&PR 93*
Lien, Warren H. 1935- *St&PR 93*
Lienau, Emil Robert 1838-1920 *Baker 92*
Lienau, Friedrich Wilhelm 1876-1973
See Lienau, Emil Robert 1838-1920 *Baker 92*
Lienau, Robert Heinrich 1866-1949
See Lienau, Emil Robert 1838-1920 *Baker 92*

Liendecker, Edgar Merrill 1925- St&PR 93
Lienenbrugger, Herbert Gene 1942- St&PR 93
Lienhard, John Henry 1930- WhoAm 92
Lienhart, David Arthur 1939- WhoAm 92
Lienhart, James Lee 1935- WhoAm 92
Lie-Nissen, Erika 1845-1903 Baker 92
Lientz, Gerald ScF&FL 92
Liepa, Andris WhoAm 92
Liepe, Emil 1860-1940 Baker 92
Liepkalns, Vis Argots 1945- WhoWor 93
Liepke, Malcolm T. BioIn 17
Liepke, Skip BioIn 17
Liepmann, Hans Wolfgang 1914- WhoAm 92
Liepsch, Dieter Walter 1940- WhoWor 93
Lier, Bertus van Baker 92
Lier, Gregory C. 1952- St&PR 93
Lier, Jacques van Baker 92
Lierhammer, Theodor 1866-1937 Baker 92
Lierley, Earl 1917- St&PR 93
Liesch, Joseph R. Law&B 92
Liese, Bernhard H. 1942- WhoUN 92
Liese, Walter K.F. 1926- WhoScE 91-3
Liesenfeld, Vincent Joseph 1947- WhoEmL 93, WhoSSW 93
Lieser, David LeRoy Law&B 92
Lieser, Karl Heinrich 1921- WhoScE 91-3, WhoWor 93
Liesman, Francis Xavier, II Law&B 92
Liess, Bernd G.A. 1930- WhoScE 91-3
Liestman, Vicki 1961- SmATA 72
Lieth, William Law&B 92
Lietoila, Arto 1950- WhoScE 91-4
Lietzke, Milton Henry 1920- WhoAm 92
Lieu, Hou-Shun 1921- WhoAm 92
Lieurance, Floyd Oscar 1939- St&PR 93
Lieurance, Thurlow (Weed) 1878-1963 Baker 92
Lieury, Alain 1946- WhoScE 91-2
Lieuvin, Marcel 1940- WhoScE 91-2
Lieuwen, John N. 1951- WhoEmL 93
Lieuwma, Alex S. WhoE 93
Lieux, Meredith Hoag 1939- WhoAmW 93
Lievano, Fernando Law&B 92
Lievens, Edward Julius, Jr. 1933- WhoSSW 93
Lievense, William C. 1947- St&PR 93
Lieverman, Theodore Mark 1949- WhoEmL 93
Liew, Fah Pow 1960- WhoE 93
Liew Ah Kim WhoAsAP 91
Li Fang-Kuei 1902-1987 IntDcAn
Lifchitz, Max 1948- WhoEmL 93
Lifeson, Alex 1953- See Rush ConMus 8
Liff, Adam Joseph 1960- St&PR 93
Liff, Noah 1929- St&PR 93
Liffers, William A. 1929- St&PR 93
Liffers, William Albert 1929- WhoAm 92
Liffman, Kurt 1960- WhoWor 93
Lifgren, Derwood Keith 1927- St&PR 93
Lifgren, Martin William 1953- WhoEmL 93
Lifka, Mary Lauranne 1937- WhoAmW 93
Lifka, William Joseph 1929- St&PR 93
Lifland, John C. 1933- WhoAm 92, WhoE 93
Lifland, William Thomas 1928- WhoAm 92
Lifsey Portes, Susan A. Law&B 92
Lifshin, Lyn Diane 1949- WhoWrEP 92
Lifshitz, Aliza NotHsAW 93 [port]
Lifshitz, Leatrice H. 1933- WhoWrEP 92
Lifson, Burton S. 1923- St&PR 93
Lifson, Kalman A. 1926- St&PR 93
Lifson, Kalman Alan 1926- WhoAm 92
Liftin, John M. Law&B 92
Liftin, John Matthew 1943- WhoAm 92
Lifton, Betty Jean WhoAm 92
Lifton, Betty Jean (Kirschner) 1926- DcAmChF 1960
Lifton, Robert Jay 1926- BioIn 17, WhoAm 92, WhoWrEP 92
Lifton, Robert K. 1928- St&PR 93
Lifton, Robert Kenneth 1928- WhoAm 92
Lifton, Walter M. 1918- WhoAm 92
Lifton-Zoline, Pamela ScF&FL 92
Ligachev, Yegor K. BioIn 17
Ligare, Kathleen Meredith 1950- WhoAm 92
Ligas, Henry W. 1936- St&PR 93
Lige, Peter 1941- WhoAm 92
Ligendza, Catarina 1937- Baker 92
Li Genshen 1931- WhoAsAP 91
Ligeti, Gyorgy BioIn 17
Ligeti, Gyorgy 1923- IntDcOp [port], OxDcOp
Ligeti, Gyorgy Sandor WhoWor 93
Ligeti, Gyorgy (Sandor) 1923- Baker 92
Ligett, Waldo Buford 1916- WhoAm 92
Liggett, Bonnie Johnstone 1960- WhoE 93
Liggett, Hiram Shaw, Jr. 1932- WhoAm 92
Liggett, Hunter 1857-1935 HarEnMi
Liggett, J.L. 1957- St&PR 93
Liggett, Lawrence Melvin 1917- WhoAm 92
Liggett, Malcolm Hugh 1929- WhoE 93
Liggett, Thomas E. Law&B 92
Liggett, Thomas Jackson 1919- WhoAm 92
Liggett, Twila Marie Christensen 1944- WhoE 93
Liggio, Carl D. Law&B 92
Liggio, Carl Donald 1943- WhoAm 92
Liggio, Jean Vincenza 1927- WhoAmW 93, WhoE 93, WhoWor 93
Light, Albert 1927- WhoAm 92
Light, Arthur Heath WhoAm 92, WhoSSW 93
Light, Betty Jensen Pritchett 1924- WhoAm 92
Light, Cheryl Ellen Law&B 92
Light, Christopher Upjohn 1937- WhoAm 92, WhoWor 93
Light, Donald Eugene 1933- St&PR 93
Light, Dorothy K. 1937- St&PR 93
Light, Dorothy Kaplan 1937- WhoAm 92, WhoAmW 93
Light, Elliott D. Law&B 92
Light, Ernest Isaac 1931- WhoE 93
Light, Henry D. Law&B 92
Light, James Floyd, Jr. Law&B 92
Light, James Forest 1921- WhoAm 92
Light, Jeremy James 1943- WhoScE 91-1
Light, John 1943- ScF&FL 92
Light, John Caldwell 1934- WhoAm 92
Light, John Ralph 1955- WhoIns 93
Light, Judith BioIn 17
Light, Judith 1949?- ConTFT 10
Light, Kenneth B. Law&B 92
Light, Kenneth B. 1932- St&PR 93, WhoAm 92
Light, Kenneth Freeman 1922- WhoAm 92
Light, Lawrence 1941- WhoAm 92, WhoE 93
Light, Marion Jessel 1915- WhoAmW 93
Light, Mark Joseph 1952- WhoEmL 93
Light, Murray Benjamin 1926- St&PR 93, WhoAm 92, WhoE 93
Light, Pamela Delamaide 1950- WhoEmL 93
Light, Richard Jay 1942- WhoAm 92, WhoE 93
Light, Richard Todd 1948- WhoE 93
Light, Robert M. 1911- WhoAm 92
Light, Robley Jasper 1935- WhoAm 92
Light, Russell Jeffers Law&B 92
Light, Russell Jeffers 1949- WhoEmL 93
Light, Sheldon Neal 1951- WhoEmL 93
Light, Theodore Blaine, Jr. 1951- WhoEmL 93
Light, Timothy 1938- WhoAm 92
Light, Truman S. 1922- WhoE 93
Light, Walter Frederick 1923- St&PR 93, WhoAm 92
Light, Will WhoWrEP 92
Light, William Allan 1950- WhoWor 93
Light, William Randall 1958- WhoEmL 93
Lightbody, George Phillips 1962- WhoE 93
Lightbody, James Davies 1918- St&PR 93
Lightbourne, Robert Edward Arthur 1944- WhoE 93
Lightburn, Jeffrey Caldwell 1947- WhoWrEP 92
Lightcap, Royal Mansfield 1927- St&PR 93
Lightcap, Shirley M. 1927- St&PR 93
Lightcap, William T. 1937- St&PR 93
Lightdale, Charles J. 1940- WhoE 93
Lightel, Donna Gang 1939- WhoAmW 93
Lighter, Eric Aaron 1950- WhoWor 93
Lightfoot, Connie Dae 1952- WhoAmW 93
Lightfoot, D. J. ConAu 138
Lightfoot, David William 1945- WhoAm 92
Lightfoot, Gordon 1938- Baker 92
Lightfoot, Gordon Meredith 1938- WhoAm 92
Lightfoot, James Ross 1938- WhoAm 92
Lightfoot, Jan Linda 1949- WhoAmW 93
Lightfoot, Jim 1938- CngDr 91
Lightfoot, Jim Ross BioIn 17
Lightfoot, John 1735-1788 BioIn 17
Lightfoot, Marion F. 1931- St&PR 93
Lightfoot, Mark F. Law&B 92
Lightfoot, Mark Francis 1958- St&PR 93
Lightfoot, Teddi 1946- WhoAmW 93, WhoEmL 93
Lighthall, William Douw 1857-1954 BioIn 17
Lightheart, Kim WhoAm 92
Lightle, D. WhoScE 91-1
Lightman, Harold Allen 1925- WhoE 93, WhoWor 93
Lightner, A.M. 1904-1988 ScF&FL 92
Lightner, Ardyce Leah Stevens 1932- WhoE 93
Lightner, Candy BioIn 17
Lightner, Candy Lynne 1946- WhoAm 92, WhoAmW 93
Lightner, Drew Warren 1948- WhoEmL 93
Lightner, Edwin Allan 1907-1990 BioIn 17
Lightner, Frances AmWomPl
Lightner, James Edward 1937- WhoE 93
Lightner, James Richmond 1922- St&PR 93
Lightner, Kevin Wayne 1954- St&PR 93
Lightner, Robert P(aul) 1931- ConAu 37NR
Lightner, Robert Paul 1931- WhoSSW 93
Lightner, Robert Theodore, Jr. 1954- WhoSSW 93
Lightner, Ruth H. 1940- WhoAmW 93
Lightowlers, Edward Charles WhoScE 91-1
Lightsey, Harry M., III Law&B 92
Lightsey, Johnnie Mack 1932- St&PR 93
Lightstone, Ronald 1938- St&PR 93, WhoAm 92
Lightstone, Stephen A. 1945- St&PR 93
Lightwood, Carol Wilson 1941- WhoAmW 93
Lighty, Cynthia M. Law&B 92
Lighty, Paul Bruce 1944- St&PR 93
Ligi, Barbara Jean 1959- WhoE 93
Ligler, Frances Smith 1951- WhoAmW 93
Lignel, Jean Charles St&PR 93
Ligomenides, Panos Aristides 1928- WhoAm 92
Ligon, Cynthia Sandusky Law&B 92
Ligon, Ed D., Jr. 1933- St&PR 93
Ligon, Patti-Lou E. 1953- WhoAmW 93
Ligon, William Austin 1951- St&PR 93
Ligonde, Francois Wolf DcCPCAm
Ligorner, Karyn Lesli 1969- WhoAmW 93
Ligorski, Mark William Lloyd 1956- WhoEmL 93
Ligotti, Eugene Ferdinand 1936- WhoE 93
Ligotti, Thomas BioIn 17
Ligotti, Thomas 1953- ScF&FL 92
Li Guixian 1937- WhoAsAP 91
Liguori, Frank Nicholas 1946- St&PR 93
Liguori, Frank Nickolas 1946- WhoAm 92
Liguori, Fred 1930- WhoAm 92
Liguori, Henry August 1940- WhoSSW 93
Liguori, James Joseph 1948- St&PR 93
Lihani, John 1927- WhoSSW 93
Lihn, Enrique 1929-1988 SpAmA
Lihota, G.M. 1948- St&PR 93
Lihotz, Marie Elaine 1955- WhoEmL 93
Li Hsiu-ch'eng 1824-1864 HarEnMi
Li Hsu-pin 1817-1858 HarEnMi
Li Huifen 1941- WhoAsAP 91
Liiceanu, Gabriel BioIn 17
Liimatainen, Bruce Carl 1956- St&PR 93
Liimatainen, Heikki WhoScE 91-4
Liipfert, Christian E. Law&B 92
Liisberg, Eilif 1931- WhoUN 92
Liiv, H. Henry 1933- St&PR 93
Liiv, Tiina M. 1937- St&PR 93
Li Ji 1896-1979 IntDcAn
Li Jijun 1934- WhoAsAP 91
Lijinsky, William 1928- WhoAm 92
Li Jiulong 1929- WhoAsAP 91
Lijklema, Lambertus 1935- WhoScE 91-3
Lijoi, Christine Confroy 1954- WhoE 93
Lijoi, Peter Bruno 1953- WhoE 93, WhoEmL 93
Lijoodi, Japeth Livasia 1936- WhoAfr
Li Kanong 1898-1962 BioIn 17
Like, Steven 1956- WhoEmL 93
Likens, Gene E. 1935- BioIn 17
Likens, Gene Elden 1935- WhoAm 92
Likens, James Dean 1937- WhoWor 93
Li Keran 1907-1988 BioIn 17
Likhachev, Dmitriy Sergeyevich 1906- WhoWor 93
Liking, Werewere BioIn 17
Likins, Jeanne Marie 1953- WhoEmL 93
Likins, Peter William 1936- WhoAm 92
Likkel, Craig Francis 1953- St&PR 93
Likness, Lawrence Richard 1929- WhoAm 92
Li Kuang d119BC HarEnMi
Li Kuang-li d90BC HarEnMi
Lilagan, Maria Nieves WhoAmW 93
Li-Lancaster, Sharon 1949- St&PR 93
Li Lanqing WhoWor 93
Li Lanqing 1932- WhoAsAP 91
Lilar, Francoise 1930- WhoWor 93
Lilburn, Douglas (Gordon) 1915- Baker 92
Lilburn, Eileen ScF&FL 92
Lile, Charles Alan 1952- WhoEmL 93
Lile, James B. d1991 BioIn 17
Liles, Betty Kathleen 1944- WhoAmW 93
Liles, Catharine Burns 1944- WhoAmW 93
Liles, Davis Hudson 1948- WhoSSW 93
Liles, Elaine Bruce 1924- WhoSSW 93
Liles, Jack S. 1928- WhoAm 92
Liles, Joseph Marshall, III 1950- WhoSSW 93
Liles, Richard Desmond 1960- WhoWor 93
Liles, Robert, Jr. Law&B 92
Liles, W.J. 1925- St&PR 93
Liley, Arthur 1924- St&PR 93
Liley, Peter Edward 1927- WhoAm 92
Lilford, Richard James WhoScE 91-1
Lilien, Copie BioIn 17
Lilien, Mark Ira 1953- WhoAm 92
Liliencron, Rochus (Traugott Ferdinand), Freiherr von 1820-1912 Baker 92
Lilienfeld, David Eugene 1957- WhoEmL 93
Lilienfield, Lawrence Spencer 1927- WhoAm 92, WhoE 93
Lilienstern, O. Clayton 1943- WhoAm 92
Lilientalowa, Regina 1877-1924 IntDcAn
Lilienthal, Alfred M. 1915- WhoAm 92
Lilienthal, Julie Anne 1957- WhoEmL 93
Lilienthal, Peter MiSFD 9
Li Ligong 1925- WhoAsAP 91
Li Ling d74BC HarEnMi
Li Lisan 1900-1967 BioIn 17
Lili'uokalani 1838-1917 Baker 92
Lilius, Irmelin Sandman ScF&FL 92
Liljebeck, Roy C. 1937- WhoAm 92
Liljebeck, Roy C., Jr. 1937- St&PR 93
Liljeblad, Ingeborg 1887-1942 Baker 92
Liljeblom, Eva Helena Maria 1958- WhoWor 93
Liljedahl, Lars-Erik 1933- WhoScE 91-4
Liljefors, Ingemar (Kristian) 1906-1981 Baker 92
Liljefors, Ruben (Mattias) 1871-1936 Baker 92
Liljegren, Frank Sigfrid 1930- WhoAm 92
Liljegren, Jan Ragnar Gustaf 1929- WhoWor 93
Liljequist, David 1946- WhoScE 91-4
Lill, John (Richard) 1944- Baker 92
Lill, John William 1951- St&PR 93
Lillard, Charles 1944- WhoCanL 92
Lillard, John Franklin, III 1947- WhoAm 92
Lillard, Laura Lee 1957- WhoAmW 93
Lillard, Linda Faye 1953- WhoAmW 93
Lillard, Mark Hill, III 1943- WhoAm 92
Lillard, R. Dale 1950- St&PR 93
Lillard, R. Stewart 1940- WhoSSW 93
Lillard, Ross W. 1931- WhoAm 92
Lillehammer, Albert 1930- WhoScE 91-4
Lillehaugen, L. Meroy Law&B 92
Lillehei, Clarence Walton 1918- WhoAm 92
Lilleleht, Lembit Uno 1930- WhoSSW 93
Lillelund, Bent Hoyer 1933- WhoWor 93
Lillemoe, Kent O. 1958- St&PR 93
Lillesand, John Walter 1938- St&PR 93
Lillestol, Jane Marie 1936- WhoAm 92
Lillevang, Omar Johansen 1914- WhoAm 92
Lilley, Albert Frederick 1932- WhoAm 92
Lilley, D.M.J. WhoScE 91-1
Lilley, David Malcolm James 1948- WhoWor 93
Lilley, Geoffrey Michael WhoScE 91-1
Lilley, James Roderick 1928- WhoAm 92, WhoWor 93
Lilley, John Mark 1939- WhoAm 92
Lilley, John Robert, II 1929- WhoAm 92
Lilley, Leonard W. BioIn 17
Lilley, Mili Della WhoAmW 93, WhoSSW 93
Lilley, Peter Bruce 1943- WhoWor 93
Lilley, Robert Francis 1939- WhoAm 92
Lilley, Theodore Robert 1923- WhoAm 92
Lilley, William, III 1938- WhoAm 92
Lillian, Simone 1938- WhoAmW 93
Lillibridge, G.D. 1921- BioIn 17
Lillibridge, George Donald 1921- BioIn 17
Lillibridge, J.L. 1939- St&PR 93
Lillibridge, John Lee 1924- WhoAm 92
Lillibridge, Rhoal Duane 1929- St&PR 93
Lillich, Alice Louise 1940- WhoAmW 93
Lillich, Wayne J. 1928- St&PR 93
Lillicrap, Stephen C. WhoScE 91-1
Lillie, Beatrice 1894-1989 QDrFCA 92 [port]
Lillie, Charisse Ranielle 1952- WhoAmW 93, WhoEmL 93
Lillie, John M. 1937- St&PR 93
Lillie, John Mitchell 1937- WhoAm 92
Lillie, Mashall Sherwood 1953- WhoE 93
Lilliehook, Johan Bjorn Olof 1945- WhoWor 93
Lillien, Jeffrey S. Law&B 92
Lillienstein, Maxwell Julius 1927- WhoAm 92
Lillington, Kenneth 1916- ScF&FL 92
Lillios, Anna 1948- WhoSSW 93
Lillis, Arline 1935- St&PR 93
Lillis, William G. 1930- WhoAm 92
Lillo, George 1693-1739 BioIn 17
Lillo, Giuseppe 1814-1863 Baker 92
Lilly, Ben BioIn 17
Lilly, Bob BioIn 17
Lilly, Charles BlkAull 92
Lilly, David Maher 1917- BioIn 17
Lilly, Doris d1991 BioIn 17
Lilly, Doris 1930-1991 AnObit 1991
Lilly, Douglas K. 1929- WhoAm 92

Lilly, Edward G., Jr. 1925- *St&PR 93*
Lilly, Edward Guerrant, Jr. 1925- *WhoAm 92*
Lilly, Edward Paul, Jr. 1940- *St&PR 93*
Lilly, Eli 1885-1977 *IntDcAn*
Lilly, Elizabeth Giles 1916- *WhoAmW 93*
Lilly, Frank 1930- *WhoAm 92, WhoE 93*
Lilly, Geoffrey Bernard 1934- *WhoWor 93*
Lilly, George David 1934- *St&PR 93*
Lilly, James V. *Law&B 92*
Lilly, John C. *Law&B 92*
Lilly, John Cunningham 1915- *WhoAm 92*
Lilly, John R. 1928- *St&PR 93*
Lilly, John Russell 1929- *WhoAm 92*
Lilly, Joseph H., III *Law&B 92*
Lilly, Les J. 1950- *WhoWor 93*
Lilly, Leslie Bjerg 1953- *WhoEmL 93*
Lilly, Lynn L. 1926- *St&PR 93*
Lilly, M.D. *WhoScE 91-1*
Lilly, Mark 1950- *ConAu 136*
Lilly, Martin Stephen 1944- *WhoAm 92*
Lilly, Michael Alexander 1946- *WhoAm 92*
Lilly, Nancy Cobb 1930- *WhoSSW 93*
Lilly, Peter Byron 1948- *WhoAm 92, WhoEmL 93*
Lilly, Shannon Jeanne 1966- *WhoAm 92*
Lilly, Thelma Maxine 1925- *WhoAmW 93*
Lilly, Thomas Gerald 1933- *WhoAm 92, WhoSSW 93*
Lilly, Thomas More 1942- *WhoE 93*
Lilly, William Eldridge 1921- *WhoAm 92*
Lillya, Clifford Peter 1910- *WhoAm 92*
Lillydahl, Earl D., Jr. 1930- *St&PR 93*
Lillyman, William Brendan, Sr. 1928- *St&PR 93*
Lillyman, William John 1937- *WhoAm 92*
Lillywhite, Harvey Burr 1943- *WhoSSW 93*
Lilo, Reuben 1951- *WhoAsAP 91*
Liloia, Peter, Jr. 1926- *St&PR 93*
Lilwall, Nicholas B. 1937- *WhoScE 91-1*
Lilyquist, Christine 1940- *WhoAm 92*
Lim, Alexander Rufasta 1942- *WhoSSW 93*
Lim, Alexander Te 1942- *WhoSSW 93*
Lim, Alfredo *BioIn 17*
Lim, Alvin Kiat Hwee 1965- *WhoWor 93*
Lim, Anna *Law&B 92*
Lim, Chee Then 1930- *WhoWor 93*
Lim, Chin Lam 1937- *WhoWor 93*
Lim, Chong-Kiat 1956- *WhoWor 93*
Lim, Chun Kong 1945- *WhoWor 93*
Lim, Daniel Van 1948- *WhoSSW 93*
Lim, David Jang Jai 1935- *WhoAm 92*
Lim, Edgar Uy 1960- *WhoWor 93*
Lim, Elena *BioIn 17*
Lim, Genny 1946- *ConAu 39NR*
Lim, Grace Ya-Leng 1964- *WhoAmW 93*
Lim, Guan Eng *WhoAsAP 91*
Lim, Joseph Dy 1948- *WhoWor 93*
Lim, Jung-Duk 1945- *WhoWor 93*
Lim, Kit Siang 1941- *WhoAsAP 91*
Lim, Larry Kay 1948- *WhoEmL 93*
Lim, Louis *WhoScE 91-1*
Lim, Meng Kee 1951- *WhoWor 93*
Lim, Ooi-Kong 1950- *WhoWor 93*
Lim, Peng Kin 1936- *WhoUN 92*
Lim, Peter Beng Moh 1951- *WhoWor 93*
Lim, Poh Aun 1958- *WhoWor 93*
Lim, Ralph Wei Hsiong 1953- *WhoE 93*
Lim, Ramon Khe-Siong 1933- *WhoWor 93*
Lim, Robert Cheong, Jr. 1933- *WhoAm 92*
Lim, Shun Ping 1947- *WhoEmL 93, WhoWor 93*
Lim, Tae Wook 1959- *WhoSSW 93*
Lim, Teong Wah 1932- *WhoUN 92*
Lim, Thuan Woon John 1946- *WhoWor 93*
Lim, Tillie *Law&B 92*
Lim, Victor Chee Ping 1961- *WhoWor 93*
Lim, Youngil 1932- *WhoUN 92, WhoWor 93*
Lima, Bruno Russomano 1951- *WhoEmL 93*
Lima, Donald Allan 1953- *WhoEmL 93, WhoWor 93*
Lima, Joseph A. 1940- *St&PR 93*
Lima, Louis Martin, III 1962- *WhoSSW 93*
Lima, Luis Eduardo 1950- *WhoAm 92*
Lima, Manuel Bravo *WhoScE 91-3*
Lima, Margaret Mary Pawlowicz 1949- *WhoAmW 93*
Lima, Michael J. 1963- *St&PR 93*
Lima, Robert 1935- *WhoAm 92, WhoWrEP 92*
Lima, Salvo d1992 *BioIn 17*
Lima-De-Faria, Jose 1925- *WhoScE 91-3*
Lim Ah Lek, Dato' 1943- *WhoAsAP 91*
Liman, Arthur L. *BioIn 17*
Liman, Arthur L. 1932- *WhoAm 92*
Liman, Claude 1943- *WhoCanL 92*
LiMandri, Charles Salvatore 1955- *WhoWor 93*
Liman Von Sanders, Otto 1855-1929 *HarEnMi*
Limar, Nick *Law&B 92*
Limato, Edward Frank 1936- *WhoAm 92*
Limauro, Stephen L. *WhoIns 93*
Limb, Ben Quincy 1936- *WhoWor 93*
Limb, Han Hui 1937- *WhoWor 93*
Limb, Sue 1946- *ConAu 37NR*
Limbach, E.W. 1939- *St&PR 93*
Limbach, Walter F. 1924- *WhoAm 92*
Limbaugh, Rush *BioIn 17*
Limbaugh, Stephen Nathaniel 1927- *WhoAm 92*
Limberg, Allen L. *Law&B 92*
Limberg, Larry Randall 1951- *WhoEmL 93*
Limbert, Paul Mark 1947- *St&PR 93*
Lim Choo Won 1939- *WhoAsAP 91*
Lime, James Craig 1951- *WhoE 93*
Limehouse, Harry Bancroft, Jr. 1938- *WhoSSW 93*
Li Menghua 1922- *WhoAsAP 91*
Limentani, Ricordo di Alberto 1935-1986 *BioIn 17*
Lim Heng Tee 1940- *WhoAsAP 91*
Li Ming 1928- *WhoAsAP 91*
Liming, George Francis 1923- *St&PR 93*
Lim In Kyu 1940- *WhoAsAP 91*
Limjuco, Ruth D. Samonte *WhoUN 92*
Lim Keng Yaik, Dato' Seri 1939- *WhoAsAP 91*
Lim King Guan *WhoAsAP 91*
Lim Moo Woong 1943- *WhoAsAP 91*
Limmroth, Karin Leigh 1949- *WhoAmW 93, WhoEmL 93*
Limnander de Nieuwenhove, Armand Marie Ghislain 1814-1892 *Baker 92*
Limondin, Jacques 1928- *St&PR 93*
Limoni, Uri 1937- *St&PR 93*
Limonov, Edward 1944- *ConAu 137*
Limpel, Ivan 1932- *WhoScE 91-4*
Limperes, Donna *Law&B 92*
Limpert, John A. *BioIn 17*
Limpert, John Arthur 1934- *WhoAm 92, WhoE 93*
Limpert, Robert James 1939- *St&PR 93*
Limpitlaw, John Donald 1935- *WhoAm 92*
Limpo Gil, J.L. *WhoScE 91-3*
Limprecht, Hollis Joyce 1920- *WhoAm 92*
Limpus, Jane E. 1945- *St&PR 93*
Limpus, Lawrence L. *Law&B 92*
Limpus, Sharon Lynn *WhoEmL 93, WhoSSW 93*
Lin, A.D. 1948- *St&PR 93*
Lin, Alice Lee Lan 1937- *WhoAmW 93, WhoE 93, WhoWor 93*
Lin, Augustine Yee-Tharn 1953- *WhoWor 93*
Lin, Bo-In *Law&B 92*
Lin, Chao-Qiang 1933- *WhoWor 93*
Lin, Chin-Chu 1935- *WhoAm 92*
Lin, Cho-Liang 1960- *Baker 92*
Lin, Christina Yi-Ting 1968- *WhoAmW 93*
Lin, Donald J.L. 1924- *St&PR 93*
Lin, Edgar Jun-Yi 1938- *WhoWor 93*
Lin, Eva 1958- *St&PR 93*
Lin, Fang-Jen 1937- *WhoWor 93*
Lin, Fei-Jann 1934- *WhoWor 93*
Lin, Frank W. *St&PR 93*
Lin, Hun-Chi 1953- *WhoEmL 93*
Lin, J.T. *St&PR 93*
Lin, Jack 1932- *St&PR 93*
Lin, James Chih-I 1942- *WhoAm 92*
Lin, Jen-Kun 1935- *WhoWor 93*
Lin, Jia-tih 1937- *WhoWor 93*
Lin, Jin Kun 1943- *WhoWor 93*
Lin, Joseph Pen-Tze 1932- *WhoAm 92*
Lin, Justin Yifu 1952- *WhoWor 93*
Lin, Kuang Farn 1936- *WhoE 93*
Lin, Kuo-Chung 1940- *WhoUN 92*
Lin, Li-Min 1944- *WhoWor 93*
Lin, Liang Yu 1943- *WhoWor 93*
Lin, Long Wei 1932- *WhoWor 93*
Lin, Maya 1959- *ConHero 2 [port], WhoAmW 93*
Lin, Maya Ying *BioIn 17*
Lin, Min-Chung 1944- *WhoE 93*
Lin, Newman Kunti 1951- *WhoEmL 93*
Lin, Otto Chui Chau 1938- *WhoWor 93*
Lin, Peifen 1935- *WhoWor 93*
Lin, Pen-Min 1928- *WhoAm 92*
Lin, Qiguang 1962- *WhoWor 93*
Lin, Sammy *St&PR 93*
Lin, Shin 1945- *WhoAm 92*
Lin, Shu 1936- *WhoAm 92*
Lin, Shyi-Jang 1951- *WhoWor 93*
Lin, Sung Piau 1937- *WhoE 93*
Lin, Susan Tu 1923- *WhoE 93*
Lin, Tao 1958- *WhoEmL 93, WhoWor 93*
Lin, Thomas Fu Yuan 1954- *WhoE 93*
Lin, Thomas Wen-shyoung 1944- *WhoWor 93*
Lin, Tung Hua 1911- *WhoAm 92*
Lin, Tung Yen 1911- *WhoAm 92, WhoWor 93*
Lin, Tungching 1965- *WhoWor 93*
Lin, Tzong-biau 1936- *WhoWor 93*
Lin, Weizhu 1939- *WhoWor 93*
Lin, William Wen-Rong 1942- *WhoAm 92*
Lin, Wuu-Long 1939- *WhoAm 92, WhoUN 92*
Lin, Y. K. 1923- *WhoAm 92, WhoSSW 93*
Lin, Yixun 1937- *WhoWor 93*
Lin, Yuh Meei 1951- *WhoWor 93*
Lina, Jose David, Jr. 1951- *WhoAsAP 91*
Linaker, Michael R. *ScF&FL 92*
Linakis, John S. d1990 *BioIn 17*
Linander, Nils Otto 1925- *WhoAm 92*
Linane, William Edward 1928- *WhoWor 93*
Linarelli, John 1958- *WhoEmL 93*
Linares, Jose 1935- *WhoScE 91-3*
Linaweaver, Brad 1952- *ScF&FL 92*
Linaweaver, F. Pierce 1934- *WhoE 93*
Lin Baio 1907-1971 *DcTwHis*
Lin Biao 1907-1971 *ColdWar 2 [port]*
Lin Biao 1908-1971 *BioIn 17*
Linchitz, Richard Michael 1947- *WhoAm 92*
Lincicome, Bernard Wesley *ConAu 136*
Lincicome, Bernard Wesley 1941- *WhoAm 92*
Lincicome, Bernie 1941- *ConAu 136*
Lincicum, Michael Scott 1946- *WhoEmL 93*
Linck, Charles Edward 1923- *WhoSSW 93*
Linck, Ernestine Porcher 1918- *WhoSSW 93*
Linck, Michael Andrew 1926- *WhoWor 93*
Lincke, Joseph 1783-1837 *Baker 92*
Lincke, Lester Walter 1933- *St&PR 93*
Lincke, (Carl Emil) Paul 1866-1946 *Baker 92*
Lincks, Linda Sue *WhoAmW 93*
Linclau, Denise Marie 1951- *WhoEmL 93*
Lincoln, Abbey *BioIn 17, WhoAm 92*
Lincoln, Abbey 1930- *ConBlB 3 [port], ConMus 9 [port]*
Lincoln, Abraham 1809-1865 *BioIn 17, HarEnMi, OxCSupC, PolPar*
Lincoln, Adrian *WhoScE 91-1*
Lincoln, Alexander, III 1943- *WhoWor 93*
Lincoln, Ashby A. 1942- *St&PR 93*
Lincoln, Benjamin 1733-1810 *HarEnMi*
Lincoln, Bruce 1948- *WhoWrEP 92*
Lincoln, C(harles) Eric 1924- *WhoWrEP 92*
Lincoln, Carl Clifford, Jr. 1928- *WhoE 93, WhoWor 93*
Lincoln, Carol Ann 1949- *WhoSSW 93*
Lincoln, Caryl *SweetSg C [port]*
Lincoln, Charles Eric 1924- *WhoAm 92*
Lincoln, Christopher Scott 1956- *WhoEmL 93*
Lincoln, Crawford 1928- *St&PR 93*
Lincoln, D.W. *WhoScE 91-1*
Lincoln, David C. 1925- *St&PR 93*
Lincoln, David Lee 1949- *WhoEmL 93*
Lincoln, Edmond Lynch 1949- *WhoAm 92*
Lincoln, Edward John 1949- *WhoAm 92, WhoEmL 93*
Lincoln, Edward W., Jr. *Law&B 92*
Lincoln, Edwin Hale 1848-1938 *BioIn 17*
Lincoln, Florence *AmWomPl*
Lincoln, Flynt Colby 1957- *St&PR 93*
Lincoln, Franklin Benjamin, Jr. 1908- *WhoAm 92*
Lincoln, G.A. *WhoScE 91-1*
Lincoln, George Arthur 1907-1975 *BioIn 17*
Lincoln, Gordon A. 1928- *St&PR 93*
Lincoln, Ignatius Timothy Trebitsch- 1879-1943 *BioIn 17*
Lincoln, Jeannette Virginia 1915- *WhoAmW 93*
Lincoln, Larry Edward 1947- *WhoSSW 93*
Lincoln, Levi 1749-1820 *OxCSupC*
Lincoln, Lucian Abraham 1926- *WhoAm 92*
Lincoln, Lucy Cook 1934- *WhoSSW 93*
Lincoln, Mary Kathleen 1949- *WhoAmW 93*
Lincoln, Mary Todd 1818-1882 *BioIn 17*
Lincoln, Maurice 1887- *ScF&FL 92*
Lincoln, Raynard C., Jr. 1934- *St&PR 93*
Lincoln, Robert Allen 1946- *St&PR 93*
Lincoln, Rosamond Hadley 1924- *WhoAmW 93*
Lincoln, Rose Marie Davis 1925- *WhoAmW 93*
Lincoln, Sandy 1945- *WhoAm 92, WhoWor 93*
Lincoln, Sarah Bush Johnston 1788-1869 *BioIn 17*
Lincoln, Stanley Vincent *WhoScE 91-1*
Lincoln, Victor D. 1941- *St&PR 93, WhoIns 93*
Lincoln, Wayne Kaui 1946- *St&PR 93*
Lincoln Family *BioIn 17*
Lind, Carl Bradley 1929- *WhoAm 92*
Lind, Carol Johnson 1926- *WhoAmW 93*
Lind, Chester Carl 1918- *WhoAm 92*
Lind, Henry Curtis 1921- *OxCSupC*
Lind, Inga *WhoScE 91-2*
Lind, James Forest 1925- *WhoAm 92*
Lind, Jenny 1820-1887 *Baker 92, IntDcOp [port], OxDcOp*
Lind, Jon Robert 1935- *WhoWor 93*
Lind, Jose *BioIn 17*
Lind, Karen G. *Law&B 92*
Lind, Klaus *WhoScE 91-2*
Lind, Larry Frederick *WhoScE 91-1*
Lind, Lew *BioIn 17*
Lind, Niels Christian 1930- *WhoAm 92*
Lind, Norman P. *Law&B 92*
Lind, Robert Clarence 1937- *WhoE 93*
Lind, Robert G. 1927- *St&PR 93*
Lind, Sven-Gunnar 1954- *WhoWor 93*
Lind, T. *WhoScE 91-1*
Lind, Terrie Lee 1948- *WhoEmL 93*
Lind, Thomas O. *Law&B 92*
Lind, Thomas Otto 1937- *St&PR 93, WhoAm 92, WhoSSW 93*
Linda, Gerald 1946- *WhoAm 92*
Linda, Gustav 1937- *St&PR 93*
Lindabury, Harrison P., III 1938- *St&PR 93*
Lindahl, Barry Adair 1946- *WhoEmL 93*
Lindahl, Helen Gertrude 1917- *WhoWrEP 92*
Lindahl, Herbert Winfred 1927- *WhoAm 92*
Lindahl, Kai Curry- *BioIn 17*
Lindahl, Kevin Bruce 1961- *WhoEmL 93*
Lindahl, Roger Mathews 1955- *WhoWrEP 92*
Lindahl, Tomas 1938- *WhoScE 91-1*
Lindahl-Kiessling, Kerstin M. 1924- *WhoScE 91-4*
Lindal, Douglas Frederick 1950- *St&PR 93*
Lindal, Robert Walter 1947- *St&PR 93*
Lindal, S. Walter 1919- *St&PR 93*
Lindale, Donald Leslie 1938- *WhoWor 93*
Lindamood, George Edward 1938- *WhoE 93*
Lindamood, Judy Beth 1948- *WhoEmL 93*
Lindamood, Monty John 1968- *WhoSSW 93*
Lindars, Laurence Edward 1922- *St&PR 93, WhoAm 92*
Lindau, James H. 1933- *St&PR 93, WhoAm 92*
Lindau, Philip J. 1936- *St&PR 93*
Lindau, William Wade 1952- *WhoSSW 93*
Lindauer, John Howard, II 1937- *WhoAm 92*
Lindauer, M. *WhoScE 91-3*
Linday, Linda Anne 1949- *WhoEmL 93*
Lindberg, Ben A. d1991 *BioIn 17*
Lindberg, Charles David 1928- *WhoAm 92*
Lindberg, Dennis N. 1941- *St&PR 93*
Lindberg, Donald Allan Bror 1933- *WhoAm 92*
Lindberg, Erik 1937- *WhoScE 91-2*
Lindberg, Garry Martin 1941- *WhoAm 92*
Lindberg, Gary William *Law&B 92*
Lindberg, George W. 1932- *WhoAm 92*
Lindberg, Gosta Carl Herbert 1927- *St&PR 93*
Lindberg, J. Mark 1950- *St&PR 93*
Lindberg, Janice B. 1936- *WhoAmW 93*
Lindberg, Jean Melville 1918- *WhoAm 92*
Lindberg, K. Martin 1934- *WhoScE 91-4*
Lindberg, Karl-Egon 1927- *WhoAm 92, WhoWor 93*
Lindberg, Lars-Axel 1941- *WhoScE 91-4*
Lindberg, Leif Erik 1944- *WhoWor 93*
Lindberg, Magnus 1958- *Baker 92*
Lindberg, Oskar (Fredrik) 1887-1955 *Baker 92*
Lindberg, Pamela Jan 1963- *WhoAmW 93*
Lindberg, R.E. 1924- *St&PR 93*
Lindberg, Rosemarie 1925- *St&PR 93*
Lindberg, Stanley William 1939- *WhoAm 92, WhoWrEP 92*
Lindberg, Terrance L. 1942- *St&PR 93*
Lindberg, Theodore L., Jr. *Law&B 92*
Lindberg, Tod Marshall 1960- *WhoAm 92*
Lindberg, Tor 1932- *WhoScE 91-4*
Lindberg, Wenonah *BioIn 17*
Lindbergh, Anne 1940- *ScF&FL 92*
Lindbergh, Anne Morrow 1906- *BioIn 17*
Lindbergh, Anne Spencer Morrow 1906- *WhoAm 92*
Lindbergh, Charles 1902-1974 *BioIn 17*
Lindbergh, Charles A. 1902-1974 *EncABHB 8 [port], Expl 93 [port]*
Lindbergh, Charles Augustus 1902-1974 *DcTwHis*
Lindbergh, Diana St. Leger 1957- *WhoWor 93*
Lindblad, Adolf Fredrik 1801-1878 *Baker 92*
Lindblad, Bo Sigurd 1932- *WhoWor 93*
Lindblad, John Paul 1952- *WhoEmL 93*
Lindblad, Otto (Jonas) 1809-1864 *Baker 92*
Lindblad, Richard Arthur 1937- *WhoAm 92*
Lindblad, William John 1929- *St&PR 93*

Lindblade, Robert O. 1940- *St&PR 93*
Lindblom, Gerhard K. 1887-1969 *IntDcAn*
Lindblom, Lance Edmund 1948- *WhoWor 93*
Lindblom, Marlow E. 1939- *St&PR 93*
Lindblom, Ronald Carl 1942- *St&PR 93*
Lindbo, Larry Allen 1947- *St&PR 93*
Lindboe, Christian Fredrik 1945- *WhoScE 91-4*
Lindborg, Lennart U.R. 1942- *WhoScE 91-4*
Linde, (Anders) Bo (Leif) 1933-1970 *Baker 92*
Linde, Hans Arthur 1924- *WhoAm 92*
Linde, Hans-Martin 1930- *Baker 92*
Linde, Lucille Mae Jacobson 1919- *WhoAmW 93*
Linde, Lucinda 1960- *WhoAmW 93*
Linde, Maxine Helen 1939- *WhoAm 92, WhoAmW 93*
Linde, Robert Hermann 1944- *WhoWor 93*
Linde, Ronald Keith 1940- *WhoAm 92*
Lindeberg, Anders Johan 1958- *WhoWor 93*
Lindeborg, E.G. Lennart 1933- *WhoScE 91-4*
Lindeen, Gorden R., III *Law&B 92*
Lindeen, Larry Wayne *Law&B 92*
Lindegard, Bengt 1927- *WhoScE 91-4*
Lindegren, Johan 1842-1908 *Baker 92*
Lindeke, Marjorie Irene 1954- *WhoAmW 93*
Lindell, Andrea Regina 1943- *WhoAmW 93*
Lindell, Deborah Kay 1959- *WhoEmL 93*
Lindell, Edward Albert 1928- *WhoAm 92*
Lindell, John G. 1932- *St&PR 93*
Lindelof, Poul Erik 1938- *WhoScE 91-2*
Lindelof, Robert B. 1945- *St&PR 93*
Lindelof, William Christian, Jr. 1946- *WhoEmL 93, WhoSSW 93*
Lindem, Thomas Jules 1928- *St&PR 93*
Lindeman *Baker 92*
Lindeman, Carol Ann 1935- *WhoAmW 93*
Lindeman, Eduard 1885-1953 *BioIn 17*
Lindeman, Fredrik Christian 1803-1868 *Baker 92*
Lindeman, Just Riddervold 1822-1894 *Baker 92*
Lindeman, Kristian Theodor Madsen 1870-1934 *Baker 92*
Lindeman, Louis H., Jr. *Law&B 92*
Lindeman, Ludvig Mathias 1812-1887 *Baker 92*
Lindeman, Ole Andreas 1769-1857 *Baker 92*
Lindeman, Osmo (Uolevi) 1929-1987 *Baker 92*
Lindeman, Peter Brynie 1858-1930 *Baker 92*
Lindeman, Sherrill Rae 1948- *WhoAmW 93*
Lindeman, Warren Charles 1924- *St&PR 93*
Lindemann, A. Bernard *St&PR 93*
Lindemann, Donald Lee 1936- *St&PR 93, WhoAm 92*
Lindemann, Erika Caroline Dorothea 1946- *WhoSSW 93*
Lindemann, George Lyle 1936- *St&PR 93*
Lindemann, Glen 1939- *St&PR 93*
Lindemann, James Arthur 1942- *WhoWrEP 92*
Lindemann, Kate 1935- *WhoE 93*
Lindemann, Stephen William 1939- *WhoWor 93*
Lindemann, Willi 1921- *WhoScE 91-3*
Lindemer, Arthur Kent 1963- *WhoEmL 93*
Lindemer, George Geoffrey 1953- *WhoEmL 93*
Lindemer, Lawrence Boyd 1921- *WhoAm 92*
Linden, Ake Sten-Oscar 1926- *WhoUN 92*
Linden, Anthony 1957- *WhoWor 93*
Linden, Barnard Jay 1943- *WhoE 93*
Linden, David John 1951- *WhoSSW 93*
Linden, Edwin James 1933- *St&PR 93*
Linden, Eric Steven *MiSFD 9*
Linden, Eugene *BioIn 17*
Linden, Hal *BioIn 17*
Linden, Hal 1931- *WhoAm 92*
Linden, Harold Arthur 1941- *WhoE 93*
Linden, Harto Hannu Herbert 1948- *WhoScE 91-4*
Linden, Henry Robert 1922- *St&PR 93, WhoAm 92*
Linden, Kurt Joseph 1936- *WhoE 93*
Linden, Lynette Lois 1951- *WhoWor 93*
Linden, Marta d1990 *BioIn 17*
Linden, P.F. *WhoScE 91-1*
Linden, R.W. *Law&B 92*
Linden, Ronald A. 1948- *St&PR 93*
Linden, Thomas Charles 1959- *WhoEmL 93*
Lindenau, Judith Wood 1941- *WhoWrEP 92*
Lindenauer, Arthur 1937- *St&PR 93*
Lindenbach, Patrick D. 1955- *St&PR 93*
Lindenbaum, Seymour Joseph 1925- *WhoAm 92*
Lindenberg, Arthur Jay 1942- *WhoWrEP 92*
Lindenberg, Mary Jean 1952- *WhoEmL 93*
Lindenberg, Sherri Korfin 1962- *WhoEmL 93, WhoSSW 93*
Lindenberg, Steven Phillip 1945- *WhoE 93*
Lindenberger, George Ferdinand 1924- *WhoE 93*
Lindenberger, Herbert Samuel 1929- *WhoAm 92, WhoWrEP 92*
Lindenberger, Richard Brent *Law&B 92*
Lindenfeld, Peter 1925- *WhoAm 92*
Lindenmayer, Elaine Ackerman *Law&B 92*
Lindenmeyer, Mark Robert *Law&B 92*
Lindenmoyer, Alan John 1960- *WhoSSW 93*
Lindenmuth, Elise Bell 1945- *WhoE 93*
Lindenmuth, Noel Charles 1940- *WhoWor 93*
Lindenmuth, Richard Alan 1944- *WhoSSW 93*
Lindenmuth, Thomas W. 1948- *St&PR 93*
Lindenthal, Gustav 1850-1935 *BioIn 17*
Lindenthal, Jacob Jay 1941- *WhoE 93*
Linder, Harvey Ronald 1949- *WhoEmL 93, WhoSSW 93*
Linder, James Benjamin 1925- *WhoAm 92*
Linder, Joseph C. 1886-1948 *BiDAMSp 1989*
Linder, Lionel 1932- *WhoAm 92*
Linder, Max 1882?-1925 *IntDcF 2-3 [port]*
Linder, Max 1883-1925 *QDrFCA 92 [port]*
Linder, Norman West 1928- *WhoCanL 92*
Linder, P. Scott 1923- *WhoSSW 93*
Linder, Paul Scott 1921- *St&PR 93*
Linder, Richard M. 1931- *St&PR 93*
Linder, Sune *WhoScE 91-4*
Linder, Walter C. *Law&B 92*
Linder-Aronson, Sten Yngve 1930- *WhoScE 91-4*
Linderberg, Jan Erik 1934- *WhoScE 91-2*
Linderman, Dean 1943- *WhoSSW 93*
Linderman, Earl W. 1931- *BioIn 17*
Linderman, Jeanne Herron 1931- *WhoAmW 93, WhoWor 93*
Linderman, Robert 1952- *St&PR 93*
Linderman, Russell John 1955- *WhoSSW 93*
Linders, Howard D. 1932- *St&PR 93*
Lindesay, William *BioIn 17*
Lindfors, Lars-Eric 1937- *WhoScE 91-4*
Lindfors, Lars-Gunnar 1944- *WhoScE 91-4*
Lindfors, Viveca *WhoAm 92*
Lindfors, Viveca 1920- *MiSFD 9, WhoWrEP 92*
Lindgaard, Gitte 1946- *WhoWor 93*
Lindgren, Arne Sigfrid 1932- *WhoAm 92*
Lindgren, Astrid 1907- *BioIn 17, ChlFicS*
Lindgren, Astrid (Ericsson) 1907- *ConAu 39NR, MajAI [port]*
Lindgren, Barbro 1937- *BioIn 17*
Lindgren, Carl Edwin 1949- *WhoSSW 93*
Lindgren, Charlotte Holt 1924- *WhoWrEP 92*
Lindgren, Dag 1942- *WhoScE 91-4*
Lindgren, Derbin Kenneth, Jr. 1932- *WhoAm 92*
Lindgren, Donald R. 1933- *St&PR 93*
Lindgren, Georg 1940- *WhoScE 91-4, WhoWor 93*
Lindgren, Gerry 1946- *St&PR 93*
Lindgren, Goran Stig Henrik 1927- *WhoWor 93*
Lindgren, Ingvar P.K. 1931- *WhoScE 91-4*
Lindgren, Jan 1933- *WhoScE 91-4*
Lindgren, Jan B.R. 1941- *WhoScE 91-4*
Lindgren, John Ralph 1933- *WhoAm 92*
Lindgren, John Raymond, Jr. 1935- *St&PR 93*
Lindgren, Leslie B. *Law&B 92*
Lindgren, Richard Thomas 1927- *St&PR 93*
Lindgren, Robert *BioIn 17*
Lindgren, Timothy Joseph 1937- *St&PR 93, WhoAm 92*
Lindgren, Tore A. 1941- *St&PR 93*
Lindgren, Torgny 1938- *ConAu 136*
Lindh, Allan G. *BioIn 17*
Lindh, Anders 1944- *WhoScE 91-4*
Lindh, E. Gunnar 1922- *WhoScE 91-4*
Lindh, Henry C.B. 1930- *St&PR 93*
Lindh, Hilary *WhoAmW 93*
Lindh, Patricia Sullivan 1928- *WhoAm 92*
Lindh, Thomas Perolof 1952- *WhoWor 93*
Lindhagen, Gosta 1928- *WhoScE 91-4, WhoWor 93*
Lindhard, Jens 1922- *WhoScE 91-2*
Lindhard, Morten *BioIn 17*
Lindheim, Denise Rae 1964- *WhoAmW 93*
Lindheim, James Bruce 1945- *WhoAm 92*
Lindheim, Richard David 1939- *WhoAm 92*
Lindhjem, Jon Alan 1946- *St&PR 93*
Lindholdt, Paul J. 1954- *ConAu 137*
Lindholm, Arne C. 1938- *WhoScE 91-4*
Lindholm, Berit 1934- *Baker 92*
Lindholm, Charles Thomas 1946- *WhoE 93*
Lindholm, Clifford F., II 1930- *St&PR 93*
Lindholm, Clifford Falstrom, II 1930- *WhoE 93*
Lindholm, Devern Wayne 1948- *St&PR 93*
Lindholm, Dwight Henry 1930- *WhoAm 92, WhoWor 93*
Lindholm, Fredrik Arthur 1936- *WhoAm 92*
Lindholm, John Victor 1934- *WhoAm 92*
Lindholm, Margaret A. *ScF&FL 92*
Lindholm, Megan 1952- *ScF&FL 92*
Lindholm, Oddvar G. 1944- *WhoScE 91-4*
Lindholm, Stig Olof 1947- *WhoScE 91-4*
Lindholm, Tenny Albert 1948- *WhoEmL 93*
Lindholm, Ulric Svante 1931- *St&PR 93, WhoAm 92*
Lindhout, Pim 1953- *WhoScE 91-3*
Lindig, Bill M. 1936- *WhoSSW 93*
Lindkvist, Goran 1943- *WhoScE 91-4*
Lindl, Bruce J. *Law&B 92*
Lindland, H. Thomas 1927- *St&PR 93*
Lindland, Roger Kyle 1932- *St&PR 93*
Lindlau, Douglas W. 1946- *St&PR 93*
Lindle, Rosemary Schaffner 1951- *WhoAmW 93*
Lindley, Curtis Price 1924- *WhoAm 92*
Lindley, David Keith *WhoScE 91-1*
Lindley, Denise Michelle 1961- *WhoAmW 93*
Lindley, Ernest K. 1899-1979 *BioIn 17*
Lindley, James Gunn 1931- *St&PR 93, WhoAm 92, WhoSSW 93*
Lindley, Mary Ann *BioIn 17*
Lindley, Nancy Long 1954- *WhoAmW 93*
Lindley, Norman Dale 1937- *WhoWor 93*
Lindley, Robert 1776-1855 *Baker 92*
Lindley, Ronald David 1954- *St&PR 93*
Lindley, Todd James 1960- *WhoEmL 93*
Lindley-Anderson, Brenda Lee 1958- *WhoAmW 93*
Lindman, Bjorn 1942- *WhoScE 91-4*
Lindmayer, Joseph 1929- *WhoE 93*
Lindner, Albrecht L. 1935- *WhoScE 91-3*
Lindner, Carl H. *St&PR 93*
Lindner, Carl H. 1919- *WhoIns 93*
Lindner, Carl H., III 1953- *WhoIns 93*
Lindner, Carl Henry 1919- *WhoAm 92*
Lindner, Charlotte K. 1922- *WhoE 93*
Lindner, Elizabeth M. 1951- *St&PR 93, WhoIns 93*
Lindner, Erna Caplow 1928- *WhoAmW 93*
Lindner, Frank 1957- *BioIn 17*
Lindner, Isaac Newton 1921- *WhoE 93*
Lindner, Joachim 1938- *WhoWor 93*
Lindner, Joseph, Jr. 1929- *WhoAm 92*
Lindner, Kenneth Edward 1922- *WhoAm 92*
Lindner, Kenneth Robert, Jr. 1949- *WhoEmL 93*
Lindner, Kurt Julius 1922- *WhoAm 92*
Lindner, Luther Edward 1942- *WhoSSW 93*
Lindner, Maria Christina 1960- *WhoE 93, WhoEmL 93*
Lindner, Philip G. 1943- *St&PR 93*
Lindner, Robert David 1920- *St&PR 93, WhoAm 92, WhoIns 93*
Lindner, Ronald John 1934- *WhoAm 92*
Lindner, William R. 1945- *St&PR 93*
Lindner, Wulf Volker 1938- *WhoWor 93*
Lindo, David Kenneth 1936- *WhoWrEP 92*
Lindo, Dean *DcCPCAm*
Lindo, Hugo 1917-1985 *SpAmA*
Lindon, Jerome 1925- *WhoWor 93*
Lindon, John Arnold 1924- *WhoAm 92*
Lindon, Vincent *BioIn 17*
Lindop, Edmund 1925- *ConAu 38NR*
Lindop, George Black McMeekin 1945- *WhoWor 93*
Lindow, Donald A. 1916- *St&PR 93*
Lindow, Donald August 1916- *WhoAm 92*
Lindow, John Wesley 1910- *WhoAm 92*
Lindow, Lester William 1913- *WhoWor 93*
Lindow, Wayne Edwin 1926- *St&PR 93*
Lindow, Wesley 1910- *St&PR 93*
Lindpaintner, Peter Joseph von 1791-1856 *Baker 92*
Lindpaintner, Peter von 1791-1856 *OxDcOp*
Lindquist, Anders G. 1942- *WhoScE 91-4*
Lindquist, Anders Gunnar 1942- *WhoWor 93*
Lindquist, Armin 1928- *WhoScE 91-3*
Lindquist, Armin Hellmut 1928- *WhoUN 92*
Lindquist, Barbara Louise 1930- *WhoWrEP 92*
Lindquist, Emory Kempton 1908-1992 *ConAu 136*
Lindquist, Everett Carlton 1912- *WhoWor 93*
Lindquist, Fred H. 1926- *St&PR 93*
Lindquist, Jack B. 1927- *St&PR 93*
Lindquist, Jane Ingrid 1953- *WhoAmW 93*
Lindquist, John Theodore, II 1950- *WhoWor 93*
Lindquist, Kurt Eric, II 1957- *WhoEmL 93*
Lindquist, Mark 1959- *ConAu 136*
Lindquist, Peter Arthur 1957- *St&PR 93*
Lindquist, Raymond Irving 1907- *WhoAm 92*
Lindquist, Richard J. 1960- *St&PR 93*
Lindquist, Robert John 1948- *WhoSSW 93, WhoWor 93*
Lindquist, Susan P. 1940- *WhoAm 92*
Lindquist, William Brent 1953- *WhoEmL 93*
Lindqvist, Jens Harry 1967- *WhoWor 93*
Lindqvist, Ossi V. 1939- *WhoScE 91-4*
Lindqvist, Ulf E. 1947- *WhoScE 91-4*
Lindqvist, William F. 1942- *St&PR 93*
Lindroos, Michael E. *Law&B 92*
Lindroos, Veikko Kalervo 1938- *WhoScE 91-4*
Lindros, Bonnie *BioIn 17*
Lindros, Eric *BioIn 17*
Lindros, Eric 1973- *News 92 [port]*
Lindroth, John G. 1937- *St&PR 93*
Lindroth, Linda *BioIn 17*
Lindroth, Linda Hammer 1946- *WhoE 93*
Lindsay, Alan C. 1932- *St&PR 93*
Lindsay, Bertha d1990 *BioIn 17*
Lindsay, Bruce George 1947- *WhoEmL 93*
Lindsay, Bryan Eugene 1931- *WhoAm 92*
Lindsay, Carolyn Patricia 1953- *WhoAmW 93, WhoEmL 93*
Lindsay, Catherine Coffin 1950- *WhoEmL 93*
Lindsay, Charles Joseph 1922- *WhoAm 92*
Lindsay, Dale Richard 1913- *WhoAm 92*
Lindsay, David 1876-1945 *ScF&FL 92*
Lindsay, David Breed, Jr. 1922- *WhoAm 92*
Lindsay, Dianna Marie 1948- *WhoAmW 93, WhoEmL 93*
Lindsay, Donald Gene 1922- *WhoAm 92*
Lindsay, Donald J. 1941- *WhoAm 92, WhoE 93*
Lindsay, Donald Parker 1915- *WhoAm 92*
Lindsay, Eamon John 1942- *WhoAsAP 91*
Lindsay, Edward Williams 1950- *St&PR 93*
Lindsay, Elizabeth *ScF&FL 92*
Lindsay, Franklin Anthony 1916- *WhoAm 92, WhoE 93*
Lindsay, Franklin Daniel 1929- *St&PR 93*
Lindsay, Freda Theresa 1914- *WhoAmW 93*
Lindsay, George Carroll 1928- *WhoAm 92*
Lindsay, George Edmund 1916- *WhoAm 92*
Lindsay, George Nelson 1919- *WhoAm 92, WhoE 93*
Lindsay, Gereon d1991 *BioIn 17*
Lindsay, Gilbert 1900-1990 *BioIn 17*
Lindsay, Harold A(rthur) 1900- *DcChlFi*
Lindsay, J. Arthur 1930- *St&PR 93*
Lindsay, James Wiley 1934- *WhoAm 92*
Lindsay, Jeanne H. *BioIn 17*
Lindsay, Jill Kathleen 1946- *WhoAmW 93*
Lindsay, John Martin *WhoScE 91-1*
Lindsay, John Robert, Jr. 1925- *WhoAm 92*
Lindsay, John V. 1921- *PolPar, ScF&FL 92*
Lindsay, John Vliet 1921- *WhoAm 92, WhoE 93*
Lindsay, John W. 1926- *St&PR 93*
Lindsay, June Campbell McKee 1920- *WhoWor 93*
Lindsay, Kathleen *ScF&FL 92*
Lindsay, Leslie 1960- *WhoAmW 93*
Lindsay, Lionel O. *BioIn 17*
Lindsay, Maud McKnight 1874- *AmWomPl*
Lindsay, Michael Francis Morris 1909- *WhoWor 93*
Lindsay, Nancy A. 1943- *St&PR 93*
Lindsay, Nancy L. 1949- *St&PR 93*
Lindsay, Nathan James 1936- *WhoAm 92*
Lindsay, Norman 1879-1969 *BioIn 17*
Lindsay, Norman Roy 1936- *WhoWor 93*
Lindsay, Peter Alexander *WhoScE 91-1*
Lindsay, Richard *ScF&FL 92*
Lindsay, Richard Clark 1905-1990 *BioIn 17*
Lindsay, Robert 1924- *WhoAm 92*
Lindsay, Robert Mark 1960- *WhoWor 93*
Lindsay, Robert V. 1926- *St&PR 93*

Lindsay, Robert Van Cleef 1926- *WhoAm 92*
Lindsay, Roger Alexander 1941- *WhoAm 92*
Lindsay, Roger O. *WhoScE 91-1*
Lindsay, Ronald Thomas *Law&B 92*
Lindsay, Sharon W. *Law&B 92*
Lindsay, Suzanne 1963- *WhoAmW 93*
Lindsay, Vachel 1879-1931 *BioIn 17, WorLitC [port]*
Lindsay, William Dennis 1950- *WhoWrEP 92*
Lindsay, William Kerr 1920- *WhoAm 92*
Lindsay, William Neish, III 1947- *WhoEmL 93*
Lindsay-Hogg, Michael *BioIn 17*
Lindsay-Hogg, Michael 1940- *MiSFD 9*
Lindsell, Harold 1913- *WhoAm 92, WhoWor 93*
Lindseth, Richard Emil 1935- *WhoAm 92, WhoWor 93*
Lindseth, Roy Oliver 1925- *WhoAm 92*
Lindsey, Alfred Walter 1942- *WhoAm 92*
Lindsey, Ann Kendrick 1945- *WhoAmW 93*
Lindsey, Bonnie Joan 1935- *WhoAmW 93*
Lindsey, Casimir Charles 1923- *WhoAm 92*
Lindsey, Cynthia M. *Law&B 92*
Lindsey, David Hosford 1950- *WhoAm 92*
Lindsey, Dottye Jean 1929- *WhoAmW 93*
Lindsey, Elizabeth Dawn 1962- *WhoAmW 93*
Lindsey, Frank Irwin 1947- *St&PR 93*
Lindsey, H. Edward, Jr. 1926- *WhoWor 93*
Lindsey, Hal *BioIn 17*
Lindsey, James Darryl 1944- *St&PR 93*
Lindsey, James L. 1940- *St&PR 93*
Lindsey, Jan B. *Law&B 92*
Lindsey, Joanne Meredith *WhoE 93*
Lindsey, Johanna 1952- *ScF&FL 92, WhoWrEP 92*
Lindsey, (Helen) Johanna 1952- *ConAu 40NR*
Lindsey, John Horace 1922- *WhoAm 92*
Lindsey, John Morton 1930- *St&PR 93, WhoAm 92*
Lindsey, Jonathan Asmel 1937- *WhoAm 92*
Lindsey, Joy Felder 1960- *WhoAmW 93*
Lindsey, Kate Curtin 1954- *WhoAmW 93*
Lindsey, Keith 1957- *WhoScE 91-1*
Lindsey, Lawrence Benjamin 1954- *WhoAm 92, WhoE 93, WhoWor 93*
Lindsey, Robert (Hughes) 1935- *WhoWrEP 92*
Lindsey, Robert Sours 1913-1991 *WhoAm 92*
Lindsey, S. Mark *Law&B 92*
Lindsey, Selden 1854-1939 *BioIn 17*
Lindsey, Susan Jane 1949- *WhoAmW 93*
Lindsey, Victor Ewart 1950- *WhoSSW 93*
Lindsey, William Fuselle 1923- *WhoWrEP 92*
Lindskog, David Richard 1936- *WhoAm 92*
Lindskog, Marjorie Otilda 1937- *WhoAmW 93, WhoWor 93*
Lindskog, Mary Anne 1950- *WhoSSW 93*
Lindskog, Norbert F. 1932- *WhoWor 93*
Lindskoog, Kathryn 1934- *ScF&FL 92*
Lindsley, Donald B. *BioIn 17*
Lindsley, Donald Benjamin 1907- *WhoAm 92*
Lindstedt, R. Goran 1937- *WhoScE 91-4*
Lindstedt, Sven T. 1927- *WhoScE 91-4*
Lindstedt-Siva, June 1941- *WhoAm 92, WhoAmW 93*
Lindsten, Jan E. 1935- *WhoScE 91-4*
Lindstrand, Kai 1937- *WhoScE 91-4*
Lindstroem, Bo S. 1939- *WhoScE 91-4*
Lindstrom, Audray S. *WhoAmW 93*
Lindstrom, Daniel Lee 1960- *WhoEmL 93*
Lindstrom, Eric Everett 1936- *WhoSSW 93, WhoWor 93*
Lindstrom, Eugene Shipman 1923- *WhoAm 92*
Lindstrom, Janet Elena 1934- *WhoE 93*
Lindstrom, John A. 1950- *St&PR 93*
Lindstrom, Jon Martin 1945- *WhoE 93*
Lindstrom, Joyce Leah Evans 1931- *WhoWrEP 92*
Lindstrom, Kari Juhani 1946- *WhoScE 91-4*
Lindstrom, Marilyn Martin 1946- *WhoAmW 93*
Lindstrom, Marla Sue *WhoSSW 93*
Lindstrom, Maurits 1932- *WhoScE 91-4*
Lindstrom, Naomi Eva 1950- *WhoSSW 93*
Lindstrom, Olle 1924- *WhoScE 91-4*
Lindstrom, Philip Martin 1917- *St&PR 93*
Lindstrom, Raymond W. *BioIn 17*
Lindstrom, Robert J. 1918- *St&PR 93*
Lindstrom, Sandra M. 1957- *WhoAmW 93*
Lindstrom, Tom S.C. 1948- *WhoScE 91-4*
Linduska, Joseph Paul 1913- *WhoAm 92*
Lindvall, Michael Lloyd 1947- *WhoE 93*
Lindvall, Torgny 1945- *WhoWor 93*
Lindy, Linus R. 1940- *St&PR 93*
Lindzen, Richard Siegmund 1940- *WhoAm 92, WhoE 93*
Line, David *ScF&FL 92*
Line, Kimberly Campbell 1961- *WhoEmL 93*
Lineback, Charles D. 1948- *St&PR 93*
Lineback, Charles David 1948- *WhoIns 93*
Lineback, Harvey Lee 1946- *WhoE 93, WhoWor 93*
Linebarger, James Morris 1934- *WhoSSW 93, WhoWrEP 92*
Linebarger, Paul M.A. *ScF&FL 92*
Linebaugh, Mack Starks, Jr. 1938- *St&PR 93*
Lineberger, Donald R. 1933- *St&PR 93*
Lineberger, Henry Otis, Jr. 1927- *WhoSSW 93*
Lineberger, James R. 1946- *St&PR 93*
Lineberger, Samira M. *Law&B 92*
Lineberger, William Carl 1939- *WhoAm 92*
Lineen, Edward M. *Law&B 92*
Linehan, D.L. *WhoScE 91-3*
Linehan, Helen M. 1939- *WhoAmW 93*
Linehan, James B. 1957- *St&PR 93*
Linehan, James Richard 1956- *WhoSSW 93*
Linehan, John Charles 1939- *St&PR 93*
Linehan, Karen M. *Law&B 92*
Linehan, L. *ScF&FL 92*
Linek, Henry 1947- *WhoE 93*
Linemeyer, David Lee 1949- *WhoAm 92*
Linen, Jonathan S. *WhoAm 92*
Liner, David B. *Law&B 92*
Liner, Jack G. 1940- *St&PR 93*
Linert, Susan Marie 1949- *WhoAmW 93, WhoEmL 93*
Lines, Jeffrey Andrew *WhoScE 91-1*
Lines, Kathleen 1902-1988 *BioIn 17, ScF&FL 92*
Lines, L. Joseph, III *Law&B 92*
Lines, Tim 1932- *WhoUN 92*
Linet, Beverly 1929- *WhoWrEP 92*
Linett, Deena 1938- *WhoWrEP 92*
Linett, Robert Allen 1947- *St&PR 93*
Lineva, Evgenia 1854-1919 *Baker 92*
Lineweaver, Paul Kelton 1925- *WhoE 93*
Lin Feng-hsiang d1855 *HarEnMi*
Linfield, Deborah R. *Law&B 92*
Linfield, Deborah R. d1992 *BioIn 17, NewYTBS 92*
Linfield, James C.T. *St&PR 93*
Linford, James C. 1944- *St&PR 93*
Linford, Mary Suzanne 1935- *WhoAmW 93*
Linford, Roger Geoffrey *WhoScE 91-1*
Ling, Amy 1939- *ConAu 137*
Ling, Christopher Charles Junmin 1965- *WhoWor 93*
Ling, Daniel 1926- *WhoAm 92*
Ling, Douglas Chih-Yen 1960- *WhoE 93*
Ling, Dwight L. 1923- *WhoAm 92*
Ling, Edwin Rodger 1931- *WhoWrEP 92*
Ling, Jack Chieh-Sheng *WhoSSW 93*
Ling, Joseph Tso-Ti 1919- *WhoAm 92*
Ling, Kathryn Wrolstad 1943- *WhoAmW 93*
Ling, Lily Hsu-Chiang 1952- *WhoSSW 93*
Ling, Mathew S. 1963- *St&PR 93*
Ling, Matthew Keith 1965- *WhoWor 93*
Ling, Paul G. 1936- *St&PR 93*
Ling, Peter *ScF&FL 92*
Ling, Robert F. 1939- *WhoSSW 93*
Ling, Suilin 1930- *WhoAm 92, WhoE 93, WhoWor 93*
Ling, William H. 1951- *St&PR 93*
Lingad, Emigdio L. 1953- *WhoAsAP 91*
Lingafelter, Edward Clay, Jr. 1914- *WhoAm 92*
Lingama-Toleque, Christian *WhoWor 93*
Lingamneni, Jaganmohan Rao 1942- *WhoAm 92*
Lingappa, Yamuna 1929- *WhoE 93*
Lingard, Joan 1932- *ConAu 40NR, MajAI [port]*
Lingard, Kevin 1942- *WhoAsAP 91*
Lingard, Steven W. *Law&B 92*
Lingbeck, Gary L. 1955- *St&PR 93*
Lingelbach, David Charles 1961- *WhoE 93, WhoEmL 93*
Lingeman, Richard Roberts 1931- *WhoAm 92*
Lingemann, Bernd Julius 1943- *WhoWor 93*
Lingenfelser, Catherine Theresa 1952- *WhoAmW 93*
Lingenfelter, Sherwood Galen 1941- *WhoAm 92*
Lingens, Franz 1925- *WhoScE 91-3*
Linger, Gerald H. 1937- *St&PR 93*
Linger, Marcella Hall 1946- *WhoAmW 93*
Lingg, Joseph Frederick 1945- *St&PR 93*
Lingjaerde, R. *WhoScE 91-4*
Lingl, Friedrich Albert 1927- *WhoAm 92*
Lingle, Jennet Burnell *WhoAmW 93*
Lingle, Kathleen McCall 1944- *WhoAmW 93*
Lingle, Marilyn Felkel 1932- *WhoAmW 93*
Lingle, Sarah Elizabeth 1955- *WhoAmW 93, WhoEmL 93, WhoSSW 93*
Lingle, Scott David 1953- *WhoEmL 93*
Ling Leong Sik, Dato' 1943- *WhoAsAP 91*
Linglin, Denis *WhoScE 91-2*
Lingman, Goran Krispin 1949- *WhoWor 93*
Lingnell, A. William 1942- *St&PR 93*
Lingnert, Hans 1947- *WhoScE 91-4*
Lingo, Bradley William *Law&B 92*
Lingoes, James Charles 1923- *WhoAm 92*
Lingris, John 1923- *St&PR 93*
Ling Shun-Sheng 1901-1978 *IntDcAn*
Lin Hanxiong 1929- *WhoAsAP 91*
Linhares, Phil 1939- *BioIn 17*
Linhart, Joseph J. d1992 *BioIn 17, NewYTBS 92*
Linhart, Letty Lemon 1933- *WhoAmW 93*
Lini, Walter Hadye 1942- *WhoAsAP 91*
Liniecki, Julian 1930- *WhoScE 91-4*
Liniger, Dave *BioIn 17*
Linjama, Jouko (Sakari) 1934- *Baker 92*
Link, Andrew Durant 1952- *WhoSSW 93*
Link, Anthony Edward 1932- *WhoE 93*
Link, Arthur Stanley 1920- *WhoAm 92*
Link, Carolyn Crosby Wilson *AmWomPl*
Link, Charles Dale 1939- *WhoAm 92*
Link, David E. *BioIn 17*
Link, David M. 1930- *WhoAm 92*
Link, Deborah Ann 1954- *WhoAmW 93*
Link, Dennis William 1953- *WhoEmL 93*
Link, E. G. 1952- *WhoEmL 93*
Link, Eugene Michael *Law&B 92*
Link, Frank Albert 1930- *WhoWor 93*
Link, Fred Motter 1904- *WhoAm 92*
Link, George Hamilton 1939- *WhoAm 92*
Link, Gerhard 1948- *WhoScE 91-3*
Link, Hans 1935- *WhoScE 91-4*
Link, James E. 1943- *St&PR 93*
Link, Jerome Edward 1931- *WhoAm 92*
Link, John Daniel 1953- *WhoSSW 93*
Link, Kurt 1937- *WhoSSW 93*
Link, Mae Mills 1915- *WhoAm 92, WhoAmW 93*
Link, Margaret Ann 1934- *WhoSSW 93*
Link, Nina Beth 1943- *WhoAm 92*
Link, Norman 1908- *St&PR 93*
Link, Perry 1931- *St&PR 93*
Link, Peter Karl 1930- *WhoAm 92*
Link, Raymond Roger 1943- *WhoSSW 93*
Link, Richard Jay 1954- *WhoSSW 93*
Link, Robert A. *Law&B 92*
Link, Robert Allen 1932- *St&PR 93, WhoAm 92*
Link, Robert U. 1920- *St&PR 93*
Link, Ron *MiSFD 9*
Link, Roy H. 1944- *St&PR 93*
Link, Shirley Ann 1946- *WhoAmW 93*
Link, Thomas 1946- *St&PR 93*
Link, William *BioIn 17*
Link, William P. 1947- *St&PR 93*
Link, William Theodore 1933- *WhoAm 92*
Linke, Bronislaw Wojciech 1906-1962 *PolBiDi*
Linke, Harald A.B. 1936- *WhoE 93*
Linke, Ray E. 1947- *St&PR 93*
Linkenauger, James Edward 1944- *St&PR 93*
Linkens, Derek Arthur *WhoScE 91-1*
Linker, Diane S. *Law&B 92*
Linker, Jonathan Steven 1949- *WhoAm 92*
Linkin, Robert E. *Law&B 92*
Linkin, Robert Edward 1952- *St&PR 93*
Linklater, Elizabeth Mary 1959- *WhoAmW 93*
Linklater, Eric 1899-1974 *ScF&FL 92*
Linklater, Richard *MiSFD 9*
Linklater, William Joseph 1942- *WhoAm 92*
Linkletter, Arthur Gordon 1912- *WhoAm 92*
Linko, E. Pekka K. 1930- *WhoScE 91-4*
Linko, Ernst 1889-1960 *Baker 92*
Linko, Lauri Tapani 1931- *WhoWor 93*
Linko, Matti 1932- *WhoScE 91-4*
Linkous, Thomas L. *Law&B 92*
Linkous, William Joseph, Jr. 1929- *WhoAm 92*
Links, Robert David 1949- *WhoEmL 93*
Linksz, James Joseph 1941- *WhoE 93*
Linkwitz, Klaus W. 1927- *WhoScE 91-3*
Linley, Elizabeth 1754-1792 *OxDcOp*
Linley, Elizabeth Ann 1754-1792 *See* Linley, Thomas, Sr. 1733-1795 *Baker 92*
Linley, George 1798-1865 *Baker 92*
Linley, Jane *OxDcOp*
Linley, Maria 1763-1784 *OxDcOp*
Linley, Mary 1758-1787 *OxDcOp* *See Also* Linley, Thomas, Sr. 1733-1795 *Baker 92*
Linley, Ozias 1765-1831 *OxDcOp*
Linley, Ozias Thurston 1765-1831 *See* Linley, Thomas, Sr. 1733-1795 *Baker 92*
Linley, Thomas 1733-1795 *OxDcOp*
Linley, Thomas 1756-1778 *OxDcOp*
Linley, Thomas, Sr. 1733-1795 *Baker 92*
Linley, Thomas, Jr. 1756-1778 *See* Linley, Thomas, Sr. 1733-1795 *Baker 92*
Linley, William 1771-1835 *OxDcOp* *See Also* Linley, Thomas, Sr. 1733-1795 *Baker 92*
Lin Liyun 1933- *WhoAsAP 91*
Linman, E.K. *Law&B 92*
Linman, James William 1924- *WhoAm 92*
Linn, Ann Marie 1937- *WhoE 93*
Linn, Anthony Blane 1951- *WhoE 93, WhoEmL 93*
Linn, Bjorn G. 1933- *WhoScE 91-4*
Linn, Brian James 1947- *WhoEmL 93, WhoWor 93*
Linn, Carole Anne 1945- *WhoAmW 93, WhoWor 93*
Linn, Deborah A. *Law&B 92*
Linn, Edward Allen 1922- *WhoAm 92, WhoWrEP 92*
Linn, Eldon R. 1934- *WhoIns 93*
Linn, James Herbert 1925- *WhoAm 92*
Linn, Jay George, Jr. 1916- *WhoAm 92*
Linn, John J. 1935- *WhoIns 93*
Linn, Karen 1957- *ConAu 139*
Linn, Milman H., III 1931- *St&PR 93*
Linn, Nellie Meader *AmWomPl*
Linn, Richard Thomas 1953- *WhoE 93*
Linn, Robert 1925- *Baker 92*
Linn, Robert A. 1931- *St&PR 93*
Linn, Robert Allen *Law&B 92*
Linn, Robert Allen 1932- *WhoE 93*
Linn, Robert Bruce 1943- *WhoIns 93*
Linn, Robert Joseph 1926- *WhoSSW 93*
Linn, Steven R. *Law&B 92*
Linn, Stuart Michael 1940- *WhoAm 92*
Linn, T.F. *Law&B 92*
Linn, Thomas Frank 1947- *WhoEmL 93*
Linna, Timo Juhani 1937- *WhoAm 92*
Linna, Vaino d1992 *NewYTBS 92*
Linna, Vaino 1920-1992 *BioIn 17*
Linnaeus, Carl 1707-1778 *BioIn 17*
Linnala, Eino (Mauno Aleksanteri) 1896-1973 *Baker 92*
Linnane, Anthony William 1930- *WhoWor 93*
Linnane, James Joseph 1941- *WhoE 93*
Linnansalo, Vera 1950- *WhoAmW 93*
Linnas, Karl *BioIn 17*
Linn-Baker, Mark *WhoAm 92*
Linne, Carl von 1707-1778 *BioIn 17*
Linne, Marty Marie *Law&B 92*
Linne, Ralph William 1951- *WhoEmL 93*
Linne, Sigvald 1899-1986 *IntDcAn*
Linnekin, Damaris Jocelyn 1963- *WhoAmW 93*
Linnell, James Edward 1931- *St&PR 93*
Linnell, John 1792-1882 *BioIn 17*
Linnell, Robert Hartley 1922- *WhoAm 92*
Linneman, Jerome Robert 1941- *St&PR 93*
Linnemeier, Thomas Jay 1936- *St&PR 93*
Linnen, Thomas Francis 1925- *WhoAm 92, WhoE 93*
Linnenberg, Clem Charles, Jr. 1912- *WhoE 93*
Linner, Donald 1939- *WhoE 93*
Linnert, Terrence G. *Law&B 92*
Linnert, Terrence Gregory 1946- *WhoAm 92*
Linney, Beverly 1923- *WhoAm 92, WhoAmW 93*
Linney, Romulus 1930- *ConAu 40NR, ConTFT 10, WhoWrEP 92*
Linnhoff, B. *WhoScE 91-1*
Linnik, Victor *BioIn 17*
Linn Kent, Debra *Law&B 92*
Linnstaedter, J. Susan *Law&B 92*
Lino, Hector, Jr. *BioIn 17*
Linomarl *WhoWrEP 92*
Linowes, David F. 1917- *St&PR 93*
Linowes, David Francis 1917- *WhoAm 92, WhoWor 93*
Linowes, Harry Michael 1928- *WhoAm 92*
Linowitz, Sol Myron 1913- *WhoAm 92*
Lin Piao 1907-1971 *HarEnMi*
Lins, Delbert Edwin 1933- *WhoAm 92*
Lins, Marcos Correia 1939- *WhoUN 92*
Lins, Michael Earl 1951- *WhoEmL 93*
Lins, Robert Louis 1949- *WhoWor 93*
Linschoten, Jan Huyghen van 1563-1611 *Expl 93 [port]*
Linsenbard, William E. *Law&B 92*
Linsenbarth, Adam 1931- *WhoScE 91-4*
Linsenmair, K. Eduard 1940- *WhoScE 91-3*
Linsenmann, William Michael 1919- *St&PR 93, WhoAm 92*
Linsenmeyer, John Michael 1940- *WhoAm 92*
Linser, Paul William 1939- *WhoWrEP 92*
Lin Shui-Hwu 1926- *WhoAsAP 91*
Linsk, Michael Stephen 1940- *WhoAm 92*

Linskill, William Thomas ScF&FL 92
Linsky, Edward W. 1935- St&PR 93
Linsky, Fannie Barnett AmWomPl
Linsley, Julia W. 1950- St&PR 93
Linsley, Robert Martin 1930- WhoAm 92
Linsmayer, J. Nicholas 1950- St&PR 93
Linsmayer, Robert Michael 1922- St&PR 93
Linsner, Kenneth BioIn 17
Linson, Art ConTFT 10, MiSFD 9
Linson, Corwin Knapp 1864-1934 GayN
Linssen, John ScF&FL 92
Linstead, George (Frederick) 1908-1974 Baker 92
Linstedt, Walter G. Law&B 92
Linstone, Clark Raymond 1958- WhoEmL 93
Lint, Charles de ScF&FL 92
Lint, Lewis E. 1926- WhoSSW 93
Lintag, Romualdo Mendoza 1962- WhoWor 93
Lintel, Albert G., Jr. 1930- St&PR 93
Linthicum, James Harold 1944- WhoSSW 93
Lintner, Robert D. 1929- St&PR 93
Linton, Arlene Mae 1949- WhoEmL 93
Linton, Barbara J. 1952- WhoAmW 93
Linton, Bonnie Lou Maples 1944- WhoAmW 93
Linton, David C. Law&B 92
Linton, Douglas Edward 1947- St&PR 93
Linton, F. Leroy 1937- St&PR 93
Linton, Frederick M. 1932- WhoAm 92
Linton, George Howard 1924- St&PR 93
Linton, Heather Smith 1956- WhoEmL 93
Linton, Jeffrey D. Law&B 92
Linton, John R. Law&B 92
Linton, Michael Alan 1956- WhoEmL 93
Linton, Michael Manley BioIn 17
Linton, Ralph 1893-1953 IntDcAn
Linton, Renee BioIn 17
Linton, Richard William 1951- WhoSSW 93
Linton, Robert D. 1954- WhoIns 93
Linton, Robert David 1954- WhoAm 92
Linton, Robert E. 1925- St&PR 93
Linton, Robert M. 1946- St&PR 93
Linton, Roy Nathan 1918- WhoAm 92
Linton, Steven Jay 1949- WhoEmL 93
Linton, Thomas A. Law&B 92
Lints, Frederic A. 1932- WhoScE 91-2
Lintunen, A. Law&B 92
Lintz, Leroy Devan 1929- St&PR 93
Lintz, Robert C. 1933- St&PR 93
Lintz, Robert Carroll 1933- WhoAm 92
Lintz, Robert Harry 1927- St&PR 93
Linvill, John Grimes 1919- WhoAm 92
Linville, Larry 1939- BioIn 17
Linville, Larry Lavon 1939- WhoAm 92
Linville, Lewis Frederick 1935- St&PR 93
Linville, Thomas Merriam 1904- WhoAm 92
Linwick, Philip C. 1931- St&PR 93
Linwood, James George 1940- WhoWor 93
Lin Xiangao BioIn 17
Linxwiler, James David 1949- WhoEmL 93
Lin Yincai 1930- WhoAsAP 91
Lin Yuehua 1910- IntDcAn
Linz, Anthony James 1948- WhoEmL 93, WhoWor 93
Linz, Arthur 1938- St&PR 93
Linz, Gerhard David 1927- WhoSSW 93
Linz, Thomas David 1959- WhoSSW 93
Linzalone, Mary Jane 1928- WhoAmW 93, WhoWor 93
Linzer, Elliot 1946- WhoE 93
Linzer, Ruth 1921- St&PR 93
Linzer, Wladimir H. 1936- WhoScE 91-4
Lin Zhenhua 1921- WhoAsAP 91
Linzner, Charles Law&B 92
Linzner, Charles 1948- WhoE 93, WhoEmL 93
Linzner, Gordon 1949- ScF&FL 92, WhoWrEP 92
Lin Zongtang 1926- WhoAsAP 91
Liolios, J. Scott 1965- St&PR 93
Lion, Bruno BioIn 17
Lion, Garrett E. 1945- St&PR 93
Lion, Paul Michel, III 1934- WhoAm 92
Lionakis, George 1924- WhoAm 92
Lionarons, Joyce Tally 1952- WhoE 93
Lionberger, John Shepley, Jr. 1927- St&PR 93
Lionberger, Lyle Jene 1948- WhoEmL 93
Lioncourt, Guy de 1885-1961 Baker 92
Lione, Susan Garrett 1945- WhoAmW 93
Lionette, Dominick John 1922- St&PR 93
Lionetti, Frank Carmine 1947- WhoEmL 93
Lionni, Leo 1910- BioIn 17, ChlBIID [port], WhoAm 92
Lionni, Leo(nard) 1910- ConAu 38NR, MajAI [port], SmATA 72 [port]
Lions, Jacques Louis 1928- WhoWor 93
Liontos Finnell, Anthea L. 1961- WhoAmW 93, WhoEmL 93
Lior, Itzhak 1938- WhoUN 92
Lioret WhoScE 91-2
Liotta, P. H. 1956- ConAu 136
Liotta, Peter Hearns 1956- WhoWrEP 92
Liotta, Ray BioIn 17
Liotta, Ray 1955- WhoAm 92
Liou, Juin Jei 1954- WhoSSW 93
Liou, Ming-Lei 1935- WhoAm 92
Liouville, Joseph 1809-1882 BioIn 17
Lioz, Lawrence Stephen 1945- WhoAm 92
Lipa, Jerzy J. 1932- WhoScE 91-4
Lipani, John F. Law&B 92
LiPari, Joseph L. 1955- WhoE 93
Lipari, Paul A. 1947- St&PR 93
Liparites OxDcByz
Lipatti, Dinu 1917-1950 Baker 92
Lipavsky, Joseph 1769-1810 Baker 92
Lipawsky, Joseph 1769-1810 Baker 92
Lipchitz, Jacques 1891-1973 BioIn 17
Lipczuk, Ryszard 1948- WhoWor 93
Lipe, Michael Alexander 1944- WhoWrEP 92
Lipeles, Enid Sandra 1942- WhoAmW 93
Lipeles, Jay Laurence 1938- WhoSSW 93
Lipeles, Maxine Ina 1953- WhoAm 92
Lipely, Gary B. 1954- St&PR 93
Lipely, Kim Renee 1955- WhoEmL 93
Li Peng 1928- BioIn 17, WhoAsAP 91, WhoWor 93
Lipetz, Cathy Law&B 92
Lipford, John V. 1940- St&PR 93
Lipford, Mack Donald 1960- WhoSSW 93
Lipford, Rocque Edward 1938- WhoAm 92
Lipham, James B. 1948- St&PR 93
Lipic, Joseph G. 1935- St&PR 93
Lipicky, Raymond John 1933- WhoE 93
Lipin, Joan Carol 1947- WhoEmL 93
Lipin, S. Barry 1920- WhoWor 93
Lipinski, Ann Marie WhoAm 92
Lipinski, Edward R. 1943- WhoE 93
Lipinski, Jamie Lynne 1962- WhoE 93
Lipinski, Janusz Stefan 1935- WhoScE 91-4
Lipinski, Karol Jozef 1790-1861 PolBiDi
Lipinski, Krzysztof 1930- WhoScE 91-4
Lipinski, William O. 1937- CngDr 91
Lipinski, William Oliver 1937- WhoAm 92
Lipinski, Wojciech Antoni 1944- WhoWor 93
Lipinsky, Carl 1790-1861 Baker 92
Lipinsky, Edward Solomon 1929- WhoAm 92
Lipinsky de Orlov, Lucian Christopher 1962- WhoE 93, WhoEmL 93
Lipira, Robert Dominic 1946- St&PR 93, WhoEmL 93
Lipitz, Elaine Kappel 1924- WhoAmW 93
Lipizzi, Carlo 1957- WhoWor 93
Lipka, Arkadiusz Krzysztof 1959- WhoWor 93
Lipka, Bernard J. 1948- St&PR 93
Lipka, David H. St&PR 93
Lipka, Jerzy 1917- WhoScE 91-4
Lipka, Judy Ann 1960- WhoEmL 93, WhoSSW 93
Lipke, Brian Jeffery 1951- St&PR 93, WhoAm 92
Lipke, Ken 1929- St&PR 93
Lipkin, Caren Rubinson 1958- WhoE 93
Lipkin, Charles d1991 BioIn 17
Lipkin, David 1913- WhoAm 92
Lipkin, David B. Law&B 92
Lipkin, Gerald Howard 1941- St&PR 93
Lipkin, Jerome J. 1933- St&PR 93
Lipkin, Mack, Jr. 1943- WhoAm 92
Lipkin, Malcolm (Leyland) 1932- Baker 92
Lipkin, Martin 1926- WhoAm 92
Lipkin, Mary Castleman Davis 1907- WhoWor 93
Lipkin, Seymour 1927- Baker 92, WhoAm 92
Lipkind, Marvin Lee 1926- St&PR 93
Lipkind, William 1904-1974 IntDcAn
Lipking, Lawrence 1934- WhoWrEP 92
Lipkovic, Peter 1934- WhoSSW 93
Lipkovska, Lydia (Yakovlevna) 1882-1955 Baker 92
Lipkovski, T. Aleksandar 1955- WhoWor 93
Lipkowitz, Zena St&PR 93
Lipkowska, Lydia 1882-1958 OxDcOp
Lipman, Annette Law&B 92
Lipman, Bernard 1920- WhoAm 92
Lipman, Burton E. 1931- WhoWrEP 92
Lipman, Carol Koch 1960- WhoAmW 93
Lipman, Clara 1869- AmWomPl
Lipman, Daniel Gordon 1912- WhoWor 93
Lipman, David 1931- WhoAm 92, WhoWrEP 92
Lipman, Elinor 1950- ConAu 136
Lipman, Eugene Jay 1919- WhoAm 92, WhoE 93
Lipman, Frederick D. 1935- WhoAm 92
Lipman, Howard W. d1992 NewYTBS 92
Lipman, Ira A. 1940- St&PR 93
Lipman, Ira Ackerman 1940- WhoAm 92, WhoE 93, WhoSSW 93, WhoWor 93
Lipman, Jack 1920- WhoE 93
Lipman, Joel Abelman 1942- WhoWrEP 92
Lipman, Martin S. Law&B 92
Lipman, Michael 1934- St&PR 93
Lipman, Richard Paul 1935- WhoE 93
Lipman, Samuel BioIn 17
Lipman, Samuel 1934- Baker 92, WhoAm 92
Lipman, Wynona M. AfrAmBi [port], WhoAmW 93, WhoE 93
Lipmanowicz, Henri 1938- St&PR 93
Lipnack, Jessica Pauli 1947- WhoE 93
Lipner, Alan J. Law&B 92
Lipner, Alan J. 1938- WhoAm 92
Lipner, Arthur Charles 1958- WhoE 93
Lipner, Harry 1922- WhoAm 92
Lipner, Jay C. 1945-1991 BioIn 17
Lipner, Maxine 1961- WhoWrEP 92
Lipnick, Rob BioIn 17
Lipnik, Alvin Law&B 92
Li Po 701-762 MagSWL [port]
Lipof, Irene Doris 1946- WhoSSW 93
Lipoff, Alvin 1930- St&PR 93
Lipoff, Deborah Law&B 92
Lipoff, Stuart J. 1947- St&PR 93
Lipofsky, Marvin 1938- BioIn 17
Lipow, Jason Law&B 92
Lipowczan, Adam 1937- WhoScE 91-4
Lipowski, Zbigniew Jerzy 1924- WhoAm 92
Lipowsky, Felix Joseph 1764-1842 Baker 92
Lipowsky, Thaddaus Ferdinand 1738-1767 Baker 92
Lipp, Donald Ralph 1935- St&PR 93
Lipp, Maria Magdalena 1745-1827 See Haydn, Michael 1737?-1806 OxDcOp
Lipp, Susan Klotz 1947- WhoE 93
Lipp, Wilma 1925- Baker 92, IntDcOp
Lippa, Allan J. Law&B 92
Lippa, Erik Alexander 1945- WhoE 93
Lippai, Steven Edward WhoIns 93
Lippard, Emma Gerberding AmWomPl
Lippard, Lucy Rowland 1937- WhoWrEP 92
Lippard, Stephen James 1940- WhoAm 92
Lippe, Barbara Mildred 1942- WhoAmW 93
Lippe, Melvin Karl 1933- WhoAm 92
Lippe, Pamela BioIn 17
Lippe, Pamela Towen 1952- WhoAmW 93
Lippe, Philipp Maria 1929- WhoAm 92, WhoWor 93
Lippe, Richard ScF&FL 92
Lippe, W.-M. 1945- WhoScE 91-3
Lipper, Arthur, III 1931- St&PR 93
Lipper, Jerome 1936-1991 BioIn 17
Lipper, Kenneth 1941- WhoAm 92
Lipperman, Robert L. 1954- WhoIns 93
Lippert, Albert 1925- St&PR 93, WhoE 93
Lippert, Allan Leonard 1941- WhoSSW 93
Lippert, Carl R. Law&B 92
Lippert, Felice Mark 1930- WhoAmW 93
Lippert, Felice Sally 1930- St&PR 93
Lippert, Herbert Karl 1930- WhoScE 91-3
Lippert, Lawrence John 1937- St&PR 93
Lippert, Richard J. 1935- St&PR 93
Lippert, Ronald Steven 1949- WhoWrEP 92
Lippert, Thomas Joseph 1932- St&PR 93
Lippes, Gerald Sanford 1940- WhoAm 92
Lipphardt, Walther 1906-1981 Baker 92
Lippi, D.M. 1914- St&PR 93
Lippincott, David 1924-1984 ScF&FL 92
Lippincott, Gary A. 1953- SmATA 73 [port]
Lippincott, Helen Zabriskie 1921- WhoE 93
Lippincott, James Andrew 1930- WhoAm 92
Lippincott, Jonathan Ramsay 1946- WhoEmL 93
Lippincott, Joseph Wharton, III 1951- St&PR 93
Lippincott, Marion W. AmWomPl
Lippincott, Philip Edward 1935- St&PR 93, WhoAm 92, WhoWor 93
Lippincott, Robert, III 1947- WhoIns 93
Lippincott, Ruth B. Law&B 92
Lippincott, Sara Jane Clarke 1823-1904 JrnUS
Lippincott, Sarah Lee 1920- WhoAm 92
Lippincott, Walter Heulings, Jr. 1939- WhoAm 92
Lippincott, William J. d1992 NewYTBS 92
Lippincott, William J. 1919-1992 BioIn 17
Lippitt, Elizabeth Charlotte WhoAmW 93, WhoWor 93
Lippitz, Richard Allen, Sr. 1936- St&PR 93
Lippitz, Wilfried 1945- WhoWor 93
Lippman, Adam Bart 1965- WhoE 93
Lippman, Alfred Julian 1900- WhoSSW 93
Lippman, Barry 1949- WhoAm 92, WhoE 93
Lippman, Craig Harris 1949- WhoE 93
Lippman, David Henry 1962- WhoE 93
Lippman, Edward A(rthur) 1920- Baker 92
Lippman, John A. 1949- St&PR 93
Lippman, Julie Mathilde 1864- AmWomPl
Lippman, Lee 1937- St&PR 93
Lippman, Lee Rubin 1937- WhoAm 92
Lippman, Marcia BioIn 17
Lippman, Neal 1962- WhoE 93
Lippman, William Jennings 1925- WhoAm 92
Lippman, William O., Jr. 1935- St&PR 93
Lippmann, Heinz Israel 1908- WhoE 93
Lippmann, Horst P.W. 1931- WhoWor 93
Lippmann, Janet Gurian 1936- WhoE 93
Lippmann, Michael 1944- WhoE 93
Lippmann, Walter 1889-1974 BioIn 17, ColdWar 1 [port], JeAmHC, JrnUS, PolPar
Lippner, Lewis Alan 1948- WhoE 93
Lippold, B.C. WhoScE 91-3
Lippold, Richard 1915- WhoAm 92
Lippon, Larry St&PR 93
Lipps, Patricia E. 1952- WhoIns 93
Lipps, Theodor 1851-1914 Baker 92
Lippson, Robert Lloyd 1931- WhoE 93
Lippy, Charles H(oward) 1943- ConAu 138
Lippy, Charles Howard 1943- WhoSSW 93
Lippy, Stephen Richard 1956- WhoEmL 93
Lips OxDcByz
Lips, Jozef Hendrick Gaston 1934- WhoScE 91-2
Lips, Julius Ernst 1895-1950 IntDcAn
Lipschitz, Louis 1945- St&PR 93
Lipschultz, Bess AmWomPl
Lipschultz, Frederick Phillip 1937- WhoE 93
Lipschultz, Howard Elliott 1947- WhoEmL 93
Lipschultz, William H. 1930- St&PR 93
Lipschutz, Ilse Hempel 1923- WhoAm 92
Lipschutz, Michael Elazar 1937- WhoAm 92
Lipscomb, Anna Rose Feeny 1945- WhoAmW 93
Lipscomb, Barbara Wilkerson 1951- WhoAmW 93
Lipscomb, James L. Law&B 92
Lipscomb, John Bailey 1950- WhoSSW 93
Lipscomb, Linda A. Law&B 92
Lipscomb, M. A., Mrs. AmWomPl
Lipscomb, Mance 1895-1976 BioIn 17
Lipscomb, Michael S. 1946- St&PR 93
Lipscomb, Oscar Hugh 1931- WhoAm 92, WhoSSW 93
Lipscomb, Paul Rogers 1914- WhoAm 92
Lipscomb, Sally T. 1948- WhoEmL 93
Lipscomb, Sylvester Hirram 1958- WhoE 93
Lipscomb, William Nunn, Jr. 1919- WhoAm 92, WhoE 93, WhoWor 93
Lipscomb, William O., Jr. 1939- St&PR 93
Lipscomb-Brown, Edra Evadean 1919- WhoAm 92
Lipscombe, Robert 1952- ScF&FL 92
Lipset, Seymour Martin 1922- WhoAm 92, WhoWrEP 92
Lipsett, Julius d1990 BioIn 17
Lipsett, Suzanne 1943- ScF&FL 92
Lipsett, W. John Law&B 92
Lipsey, John C. 1930- WhoAm 92
Lipsey, Joseph, Jr. 1934- WhoWor 93
Lipsey, Michael Ross 1959- WhoSSW 93
Lipsey, Richard Allan 1930- WhoWor 93
Lipsey, Richard George 1928- WhoAm 92
Lipsey, Robert E(dward) 1926- ConAu 40NR
Lipsey, Robert Edward 1926- WhoAm 92, WhoE 93
Lipsey, Stanford 1927- St&PR 93, WhoAm 92, WhoE 93
Lipsher, Molly Barbara 1952- WhoE 93
Lipshie, Joseph 1911- WhoAm 92
Lipshutz, Robert Jerome 1921- WhoAm 92
Lipsig, Robert J. 1942- St&PR 93
Lipsitt, Lewis Paeff 1929- WhoAm 92
Lipsitt, Martin Frederic 1934- WhoAm 92, WhoE 93
Lipsitz, Lawrence Irwin 1937- WhoE 93
Lipsitz, Michael Law&B 92
Lipsitz, Robert Joel 1949- WhoE 93
Lipsitz, Steven H. Law&B 92
Lipsius, Marie 1837-1927 Baker 92
Lipsker, Eileen Franklin BioIn 17
Lipski, Jan Jozef BioIn 17
Lipski, Jan Jozef 1926-1991 AnObit 1991
Lipski, Sharyn Ann 1945- WhoE 93
Lipski, Tadeusz 1925- WhoScE 91-4
Lipsky, Ian David 1957- WhoEmL 93
Lipsky, Lawrence J. 1926- St&PR 93

Lipsky, Leonard 1936- WhoE 93
Lipsky, Linda Ethel 1939- WhoAmW 93
Lipsky, Oldrich 1924-1986 DrEEuF
Lipsky, Robert David 1956- St&PR 93
Lipsky, Stephen Edward 1932- St&PR 93, WhoAm 92
Lipsky, W. Robert 1938- WhoAm 92
Lipsman, Paulee 1947- WhoEmL 93
Lipsman, Richard Marc 1946- WhoE 93, WhoEmL 93
Lipsman, William S. Law&B 92
Lipson, Abigail 1956- WhoE 93
Lipson, Allen S. Law&B 92
Lipson, Allen S. 1942- St&PR 93
Lipson, Avis Ruth 1951- WhoAmW 93
Lipson, Barry David 1936- WhoWor 93
Lipson, Bernice B. 1933- St&PR 93
Lipson, David R. Law&B 92
Lipson, Herbert George 1925- WhoE 93
Lipson, Herbert Harold 1924- St&PR 93
Lipson, Leon 1921- WhoAm 92
Lipson, Leslie Michael 1912- WhoAm 92
Lipson, Marjorie Youmans 1947- WhoE 93
Lipson, Melvin Alan 1936- WhoAm 92
Lipson, Merek E. Law&B 92
Lipson, Michael H. Law&B 92
Lipson, Paul S. 1915- WhoAm 92
Lipstadt, Aaron 1952- MiSFD 9
Lipstate, Eugene Jacob 1927- WhoSSW 93
Lipstate, Jo Ann 1930- WhoAmW 93
Lipstein, Owen BioIn 17
Lipstein, Sidney D. Law&B 92
Lipstone, Howard Harold 1928- St&PR 93, WhoAm 92
Lipsyte, Robert BioIn 17
Lipsyte, Robert 1938- DcAmChF 1960
Lipsyte, Robert (Michael) 1938- MajAI [port]
Liptak, Gregory J. 1940- St&PR 93
Liptak, Irene Frances 1926- WhoAmW 93
Liptak, John Frank 1945- St&PR 93
Liptak, Jozsef J. 1941- WhoScE 91-4
Liptak, Mark Ramone 1958- WhoEmL 93
Liptak, Michelle Ann 1954- WhoAmW 93
Liptay, Wolfgang 1928- WhoScE 91-3
Lipthratt, Charles Vernon 1937- St&PR 93
Lipton, Allan 1938- WhoAm 92
Lipton, Allen David 1940- WhoSSW 93
Lipton, Alvin Elliot 1945- WhoAm 92
Lipton, Amy N. Law&B 92
Lipton, Barbara WhoAmW 93
Lipton, Benjamin d1991 BioIn 17
Lipton, Bronna Jane 1951- WhoAm 92
Lipton, Charles 1928- St&PR 93, WhoAm 92, WhoE 93
Lipton, Daniel Bernard WhoAm 92
Lipton, Jeffrey M. 1942- St&PR 93
Lipton, Jeffrey Marc 1942- WhoAm 92
Lipton, Joan Elaine WhoAm 92
Lipton, John M. 1936- WhoSSW 93
Lipton, Leah 1928- WhoAmW 93
Lipton, Lester 1936- WhoWor 93
Lipton, Lois J. Law&B 92
Lipton, Lorian 1957- WhoEmL 93
Lipton, Marc I. Law&B 92
Lipton, Mark Daniel 1947- WhoEmL 93
Lipton, Mark K. St&PR 93
Lipton, Martha 1913- Baker 92
Lipton, Martin 1931- WhoAm 92
Lipton, Mildred Ceres 1921- WhoAmW 93
Lipton, Nina Anne 1959- WhoAmW 93
Lipton, Peggy BioIn 17
Lipton, Peter 1954- ConAu 138
Lipton, Robert Steven 1946- WhoEmL 93
Lipton, Steven E. Law&B 92
Lipton, Stuart Arthur 1950- WhoAm 92
Lipton, William Lawrence 1944- WhoWrEP 92
Lipton, Zelda 1923- St&PR 93
Liptser, Robert Shevilevich 1936- WhoWor 93
Liptzin, Benjamin 1945- WhoAm 92
Liput, James Anthony, Sr. 1955- St&PR 93
Lipworth, Stephen 1939- St&PR 93
Li Qianyuan WhoAsAP 91
Liquido, Nicanor Javier 1953- WhoEmL 93
Liquori, Martin William, Jr. 1949- WhoAm 92
Liquori, Sal ScF&FL 92
Lira Alvarez, Miguel Nicolas 1905-1961 DcMexL
Liria, Peter, Jr. Law&B 92
Li Rosi, Angelo C. 1941- WhoIns 93
Lirou, Jean Francois Espic, Chevalier de 1740-1806 Baker 92
Li Ruihua 1924- BioIn 17
Li Ruihuan 1934- WhoAsAP 91
Li Ruihuan 1935- WhoWor 93
Lis, Anthony Stanley 1918- WhoAm 92, WhoWor 93
Lis, Daniel T. Law&B 92
Lis, Daniel T. 1940- WhoAm 92
Lis, Daniel T. 1946- St&PR 93
Lis, Edward Francis 1918- WhoAm 92
Lisa, Claire Jeannette WhoE 93
Lisa, Isabelle O'Neill 1934- WhoAmW 93
Lisa, Joseph P. Law&B 92
Lisa, Luigi 1930- WhoScE 91-3
Lisa Lisa NotHsAW 93
Lisan, Amha Tume 1949- WhoEmL 93
Lisanby, James Walker 1928- WhoAm 92
Lisanke, Vincent P. WhoAm 92
Lisante, Stephen James 1950- WhoE 93
Lisauskas, Anthony J. 1940- St&PR 93
Lisberger, Steven 1951- MiSFD 9
Lisboa, Antonio Francisco 1730-1814 BioIn 17
Lisboa-Farrow, Elizabeth Oliver 1947- WhoEmL 93
Lisby, Gregory Carroll 1952- WhoEmL 93, WhoSSW 93
Liscano, Juan 1915- SpAmA
Lisch, Howard 1950- WhoE 93
Lischer, Ludwig Frederick 1915- WhoAm 92
Lischewski, Hans-Christian 1944- WhoE 93
Lischke, Gerhard 1948- WhoWor 93
Liscic, Bozidar 1929- WhoScE 91-4
Liscom, Clayton Lee 1947- St&PR 93, WhoAm 92
Liscow, Andrew S. 1956- St&PR 93
Liscow, Christian Ludwig 1701-1760 BioIn 17
Lise, Claude 1941- DcCPCAm
Lisenbee, Alvis Lee 1940- WhoAm 92
Lisenby, Michael B. Law&B 92
Lisenby, Sadie Johnson 1933- WhoAmW 93
Lisenko, Emilie Dierking 1955- WhoAmW 93
Lisenko, Nikolay OxDcOp
Li-Senmao 1929- WhoAsAP 91
Lish, Gerald Jonathan 1931- St&PR 93
Lish, Gordon 1934- WhoAm 92
Lish, Gordon Jay 1934- WhoWrEP 92
Lish, Jennifer Dawn 1957- WhoE 93
Li Sheng 727-793 HarEnMi
Lisher, John Leonard 1950- WhoEmL 93
Li Shih-min 598-649 HarEnMi
Lishin, Grigori 1854-1888 Baker 92
Lishka, Edward Joseph 1949- WhoEmL 93, WhoWor 93
Li Shoushan 1929- WhoAsAP 91
Li Shuzheng 1930- WhoAsAP 91
Lisi, Lorenzo Law&B 92
Lisi, Michael Angelo Law&B 92
Lisi, Penelope Leitner 1951- WhoAmW 93, WhoEmL 93
Lisi, Virna 1937- BioIn 17
Lisicki, Andrzej B. 1930- WhoScE 91-4
Lisicki, Zygmunt 1923- WhoScE 91-4
Lisimachio, Jean Louis 1945- St&PR 93
Lisinski, Vatroslav 1819-1854 Baker 92, OxDcOp
Lisio, Donald John 1934- WhoAm 92
Lisitsian, S.D. 1865-1947 IntDcAn
Lisitsian, S.S. 1893-1979 IntDcAn
Lisitski, Jon Louis 1939- St&PR 93
Lisitsyan, Pavel 1911- OxDcOp
Lisitsyan, Pavel (Gerasimovich) 1911- Baker 92
Lisitzky, Ephraim E. 1885-1962 BioIn 17
Lisk, Franklyn Athanasius 1946- WhoUN 92, WhoWor 93
Lisk, Pamela Konieczka Law&B 92
Lisk, Penelope Tsaltas 1959- WhoE 93
Lisk, Thomas David 1947- WhoSSW 93
Liska, Eileen Marguerite 1948- WhoEmL 93
Liska, George 1922- WhoAm 92
Liska, Ivan WhoWor 93
Liska, Marian 1926- WhoScE 91-4
Liska, Zdenek 1922-1983 Baker 92
Liskamm, William Hugo 1931- WhoAm 92
Lisker, Arthur 1929- St&PR 93
Lisker, Deborah J. Law&B 92
Lisker, Harvey 1955- St&PR 93
Lisker, Larry 1927- St&PR 93
Lisker, Leo 1924- St&PR 93
Lisker, Martin 1951- St&PR 93
Lisker, Phyllis 1931- St&PR 93
Liskey, A. Keith 1944- St&PR 93
Liskin, Barbara Ann 1952- WhoE 93, WhoEmL 93
Liskov, Barbara Huberman 1939- WhoAmW 93
L'Isle, Lord De 1909-1991 AnObit 1991
Lisle, Janet Taylor 1947- DcAmChF 1985, ScF&FL 92
Lisle, John C. 1941- St&PR 93
Lisle, Robert Walton 1927- WhoAm 92
Lisle, Vernon John 1939- WhoSSW 93
L'Isle Adam, Auguste Villiers de ScF&FL 92
Lisman, Gerard William 1955- WhoE 93
Lisnek, Paul Michael 1958- WhoWor 93
Lison, Arno-E. 1944- WhoScE 91-3
Lisovik, Leonid Petrovich 1948- WhoWor 93
Lisowski, Joseph Anthony 1944- WhoWrEP 92
Lisowski, Jozef 1928- WhoScE 91-4
Lisowski, Zbigniew Stanisklaw 1923- WhoScE 91-4
Lispector, Clarice 1925-1977 BioIn 17, ConAu 139
Liss, Alan R. d1992 NewYTBS 92
Liss, Daniel G. 1949- WhoWrEP 92
Liss, Herbert Myron 1931- WhoAm 92
Liss, Mark Jay 1956- WhoEmL 93
Liss, Norman 1932- WhoWor 93
Liss, Peter Simon WhoScE 91-1
Liss, Victor 1937- St&PR 93
Lissa, Zofia 1908-1980 Baker 92, PolBiDi
Lissack, Michael 1958- St&PR 93
Lissack, Michael Robert 1958- WhoAm 92
Lisse, Allan 1926- St&PR 93
Lisse, Stephen Dennis 1950- WhoSSW 93
Lissenko, Nikolai (Vitalievich) 1842-1912 Baker 92
Lissinna, Manfred St&PR 93
Lissit, Scott Alan 1960- WhoSSW 93
Lissitz, Robert Wooster 1941- WhoAm 92
Lissman, Barry Alan 1952- WhoAm 92
Lissner, Jorgen 1945- WhoUN 92
Lissner, Lance Michael 1950- St&PR 93
Lisson, Deborah ScF&FL 92
Lisson, Deborah 1941- SmATA 71 [port]
Lissy, David H. Law&B 92
List, David Patton 1920- WhoAm 92
List, Diane Ruth 1948- WhoAmW 93
List, Douglass William 1955- WhoE 93, WhoEmL 93, WhoWor 93
List, Emanuel 1886-1967 OxDcOp
List, Emanuel 1888-1967 Baker 92
List, Ericson John 1939- WhoAm 92
List, Eugene 1918-1985 Baker 92
List, Garrett 1943- Baker 92
List, Hans WhoScE 91-4
List, Herbert 1903-1975 BioIn 17
List, Irwin 1932- St&PR 93
List, John DeWitt 1935- WhoAm 92
List, John E. 1925?- BioIn 17
List, John Jay Law&B 92
List, John Jay 1946- St&PR 93
List, Kurt 1913-1970 Baker 92
List, Lawrence I. 1938-1991 BioIn 17
List, Michael H. 1942- St&PR 93
List, Philip L. 1953- St&PR 93
List, Raymond Edward 1944- WhoAm 92
Lista, Paolo 1964- WhoWor 93
Listemann, Bernhard 1841-1917 Baker 92
Listemann, Franz 1873-1930 Baker 92
Listemann, Fritz 1839-1909 Baker 92
Listemann, Paul 1871-1950 Baker 92
Lister, Carol 1935- WhoAmW 93
Lister, D. WhoScE 91-1
Lister, David 1947- MiSFD 9
Lister, Elena Goldstein 1957- WhoEmL 93
Lister, Harry Joseph 1936- St&PR 93, WhoAm 92, WhoSSW 93
Lister, Louise Merbe 1937- WhoAmW 93
Lister, Lydia Warren AmWomPl
Lister, Margot Ruth Aline WhoScE 91-1
Lister, Mary 1950- ChlFicS
Lister, Sandie BioIn 17
Lister, Stephen L. 1942- St&PR 93
Lister, Sue Ann 1950- WhoEmL 93
Lister, Thomas Mosie 1921- WhoAm 92
Listerud, Mark Boyd 1924- WhoWor 93
Listgarten, Max Albert 1935- WhoAm 92
Listi, Frank Joseph 1945- St&PR 93
Listinsky, Jay John 1951- WhoEmL 93, WhoSSW 93
Listner, Chem J. 1948- St&PR 93
Liston, Alan A. Law&B 92
Liston, Alan A. 1946- WhoAm 92, WhoE 93
Liston, Charles 1932-1971 BioIn 17
Liston, Edward 1900-1986 ScF&FL 92
Liston, Mary Frances 1920- WhoAm 92
Liston, Ronald Argyle 1926- WhoE 93
Liston, Sonny 1932-1971 BioIn 17
Listov, Konstantin 1900-1983 Baker 92
Listwa, Leslie P. 1957- St&PR 93
Li Su 773-821 HarEnMi
Liszi, Janos 1940- WhoScE 91-4
Liszka, Ludwik WhoScE 91-4
Liszka, Tadeusz 1950- WhoScE 91-4
Liszt, Franz 1811-1886 Baker 92, BioIn 17, OxDcOp
Liszt, Howard Paul 1946- WhoAm 92
Litaize, Gaston (Gilbert) 1909- Baker 92
Litan, Robert Eli 1950- WhoAm 92
Litchard, Mary Jane 1951- WhoEmL 93
Litchfield, Ada Bassett 1916- WhoWrEP 92
Litchfield, Carol Darline 1936- WhoAmW 93
Litchfield, Grace Denio 1849- AmWomPl
Litchfield, Jean Anne 1942- WhoAmW 93, WhoWor 93
Litchfield, Stephen A. Law&B 92
Litchfield, Thompson Dumont 1917- St&PR 93
Litchman, Joseph F. 1927- St&PR 93
Lite, Victor 1937- St&PR 93
Literes Carrion, Antonio 1673?-1747 Baker 92
Literes Montalbo, Antonio d1768 See Literes Carrion, Antonio 1673?-1747 Baker 92
Lites, James WhoAm 92
Litewka, Jack 1945- WhoWrEP 92
Litewka, Julko d1991 BioIn 17
Litfin, Richard Albert 1918- WhoAm 92
Litherland, Albert Edward 1928- WhoAm 92
Lithgow, John BioIn 17
Lithgow, John Arthur 1945- WhoAm 92
Lithgow, Theodore T. 1932- WhoAm 92
Lithgow, William Carroll 1920- WhoSSW 93
Lithner, Folke 1930- WhoScE 91-4
Lithwick, Norman Harvey 1938- WhoAm 92
Li Tieying BioIn 17
Li Tieying 1936- WhoAsAP 91, WhoWor 93
Litinsky, Genrik 1901-1985 Baker 92
Litke, Arthur Ludwig 1922- WhoAm 92
Litke, Bruce William 1928- St&PR 93
Litke, Donald Paul 1934- WhoAm 92
Litke, James W. 1955- St&PR 93
Litke, Jean A. 1929- St&PR 93
Litke, John David 1944- WhoE 93
Litke, Steven H. 1955- St&PR 93
Litle, Robert Forgie 1924- WhoSSW 93
Litman, Armand C. d1991 BioIn 17
Litman, Bernard 1920- WhoAm 92
Litman, Bert 1917- St&PR 93
Litman, Helena D. Law&B 92
Litman, James L. 1936- St&PR 93
Litman, Mark Alan Law&B 92
Litman, Peter E. Law&B 92
Litman, Peter E. 1951- St&PR 93
Litman, Raymond S. 1936- St&PR 93
Litman, Raymond Stephen 1936- WhoAm 92
Litman, Robert Barry 1947- WhoAm 92, WhoE 93, WhoEmL 93, WhoWrEP 92
Litman, Ruth Ann 1959- WhoEmL 93
Litmer, Jack L. Law&B 92
Litner, Mark Steven 1959- WhoEmL 93
Litoff, Judy Barrett 1944- WhoE 93
Litolff, Henry 1818-1891 OxDcOp
Litolff, Henry Charles 1818-1891 Baker 92
Litolff, Theodor 1839-1912 See Litolff, Henry Charles 1818-1891 Baker 92
Litow, Mark I. Law&B 92
Litow, Merrill 1927- WhoAm 92
Litrides, Lindy 1952- WhoEmL 93
Litrownik, Alan Jay 1945- WhoAm 92
Litschauer, Charles A. 1928- St&PR 93
Litschgi, A. Byrne 1920- St&PR 93, WhoAm 92
Litschgi, Richard John 1937- WhoAm 92
Litsey, Jana Jones Law&B 92
Litsey, Sarah WhoWrEP 92
Litsios, Socrates 1937- WhoUN 92
Litsky, Warren 1924- WhoAm 92
Litster, James David 1938- WhoAm 92
Li Tsung-jen 1890- DcTwHis
Li Tsung-jen 1891-1969 HarEnMi
Litt, Bonnie S. Law&B 92
Litt, Francois-Xavier 1941- WhoScE 91-2
Litt, Iris 1928- WhoWrEP 92
Litt, Iris F. 1940- WhoAm 92
Litt, Mitchell 1932- WhoAm 92
Litt, Morton Herbert 1926- WhoAm 92
Litt, Nahum 1935- WhoAm 92
Litta, Giulio 1822-1891 Baker 92
Littaua, Ferdinand Zabala 1942- WhoUN 92
Littauer, Robert M. 1948- St&PR 93
Littbrand, Bo G.R. 1936- WhoScE 91-4
Litteken, John Dan 1948- St&PR 93
Littel, Therese AmWomPl
Littell, Danny Lane 1941- St&PR 93
Littell, Franklin Hamlin 1917- WhoAm 92
Littell, Jeffrey D. 1954- WhoEmL 93
Littell, Jessica Fuller 1958- WhoEmL 93
Littell, Jonathan 1969?- ScF&FL 92
Littell, Noble Kieth 1920- WhoSSW 93
Littell, Phillip A. 1938- St&PR 93
Littell, Randall Alan 1956- WhoSSW 93
Littell, Robert 1935?- ScF&FL 92
Littell, Wallace William 1922- WhoAm 92
Litten, H. Randall 1937- St&PR 93, WhoSSW 93
Litten, Julian (William Sebastian) 1947- ConAu 136
Litteneker, Randall J. Law&B 92
Litteneker, Rebecca U. Law&B 92
Litterer, Joseph August 1926- WhoE 93
Litterini, Donald E. 1938- St&PR 93
Littig, Lawrence William 1927- WhoAm 92
Littin, Miguel 1942- MiSFD 9
Littke, Lael 1929- ScF&FL 92
Littky, Dennis BioIn 17
Little, Alan Brian 1925- WhoAm 92
Little, Alex Graham 1943- WhoAm 92
Little, Ann 1891-1984 SweetSg A [port]

Little, Anna Denise 1954- *WhoAmW 93, WhoWor 93*
Little, Arthur Dehon 1944- *St&PR 93, WhoAm 92*
Little, Bentley *ScF&FL 92*
Little, Berkeley Haynsworth 1948- *WhoSSW 93*
Little, Bradley A. 1951- *St&PR 93*
Little, Brenda Joyce 1945- *WhoSSW 93*
Little, Brian F. *Law&B 92*
Little, Brian F. 1943- *St&PR 93, WhoAm 92*
Little, Carl Maurice 1924- *WhoAm 92*
Little, Charles Curtis 1954- *WhoEmL 93*
Little, Charles Edward 1926- *WhoAm 92*
Little, Charles Gordon 1924- *WhoAm 92*
Little, Christopher Bradford 1961- *WhoSSW 93*
Little, Christopher Mark 1941- *St&PR 93, WhoAm 92, WhoE 93*
Little, Cleavon 1939- *BioIn 17*
Little, Cleavon 1939-1992 *NewYTBS 92 [port], News 93-2*
Little, Cleavon Jake 1939- *WhoAm 92*
Little, David Clark 1952- *WhoWor 93*
Little, David Robert *Law&B 92*
Little, Deborah A. 1960- *WhoAmW 93*
Little, Debra Krueger 1960- *WhoAmW 93*
Little, Delbert M. 1898-1991 *BioIn 17*
Little, Dennis Gage 1935- *St&PR 93, WhoAm 92*
Little, Dianne Ruth *WhoAmW 93*
Little, Douglas B. *Law&B 92*
Little, Douglas Jonathan 1945- *WhoSSW 93*
Little, Dwight H. *MiSFD 9*
Little, Edmund *ScF&FL 92*
Little, Elbert Luther, Jr. 1907- *WhoAm 92, WhoSSW 93*
Little, Eunice K. 1954- *WhoAmW 93*
Little, F. A., Jr. 1936- *WhoSSW 93*
Little, Francis J. 1934-1990 *BioIn 17*
Little, George Daniel 1929- *WhoAm 92*
Little, Geraldine Clinton 1923- *WhoWrEP 92*
Little, Henri Bayliffe 1924- *St&PR 93, WhoAm 92*
Little, Jack Edward 1938- *St&PR 93, WhoAm 92*
Little, James B. 1935- *St&PR 93*
Little, James Morris 1952- *WhoAm 92, WhoE 93*
Little, James N. 1940- *St&PR 93*
Little, James S. 1941- *St&PR 93*
Little, James Stuart 1941- *WhoAm 92*
Little, Jean 1932- *BioIn 17, WhoAm 92, WhoCanL 92*
Little, (Flora) Jean 1932- *ChlFicS, DcChlFi, MajAI [port]*
Little, Jill Ann 1940- *WhoE 93*
Little, Jo-Ann Christine 1959- *WhoAmW 93*
Little, John *BioIn 17*
Little, John Andrew 1937- *St&PR 93*
Little, John Bertram 1929- *WhoAm 92*
Little, John Dutton Conant 1928- *WhoAm 92, WhoWor 93*
Little, John Hadley 1941- *WhoAm 92*
Little, John Wesley 1935- *WhoAm 92*
Little, John William 1944- *WhoAm 92*
Little, Jon Warren 1952- *WhoSSW 93*
Little, Joseph G. *Law&B 92*
Little, Kenneth E. *Law&B 92*
Little, Kenneth E. 1929- *St&PR 93*
Little, Kerry *WhoWrEP 92*
Little, Kim Gerald 1947- *WhoSSW 93*
Little, Larry Chatmon 1945- *BiDAMSp 1989*
Little, Lessie Jones 1906-1986 *BioIn 17, BlkAuII 92*
Little, Lester Knox 1935- *WhoAm 92*
Little, Loren Everton 1941- *WhoWor 93*
Little, Loyd Harry, Jr. 1940- *WhoAm 92, WhoWrEP 92*
Little, Malcolm *EncAACR*
Little, Malcolm 1925-1965 *BioIn 17*
Little, Margaret Ann 1954- *WhoEmL 93*
Little, Mary Eva 1934- *WhoAmW 93*
Little, Michael F. 1943- *St&PR 93*
Little, Michael Frederick 1943- *WhoSSW 93*
Little, Michael S. *Law&B 92*
Little, Ned Allen 1940- *WhoE 93*
Little, O. Grant 1950- *St&PR 93*
Little, P.F. *ScF&FL 92*
Little, Pamela Anne 1954- *St&PR 93*
Little, Patricia Chavez de 1952- *WhoAmW 93*
Little, Patrick *ScF&FL 92*
Little, Paul H. *ScF&FL 92*
Little, R. Donald 1937- *WhoE 93, WhoWor 93*
Little, Richard Allen 1939- *WhoWor 93*
Little, Richard Caruthers 1938- *WhoAm 92*
Little, Richard J. *Law&B 92*
Little, Richard L. *St&PR 93*
Little, Richard Le Roy 1944- *WhoAm 92*
Little, Robert Andrews 1915- *WhoAm 92*
Little, Robert Colby 1920- *WhoAm 92*
Little, Robert David 1937- *WhoAm 92*
Little, Robert Eugene 1933- *WhoAm 92*
Little, Robert L. 1938- *BioIn 17*
Little, Rodney Darren 1966- *WhoSSW 93*
Little, Sylvia Ford *WhoAmW 93*
Little, Thomas Edward 1948- *WhoE 93*
Little, Thomas Malcolm 1932- *St&PR 93*
Little, Thomas Mayer 1935- *WhoAm 92*
Little, W.J. Knox 1839-1918 *ScF&FL 92*
Little, W. S., Mrs. *AmWomPl*
Little, W.T. *WhoScE 91-1*
Little, William Arthur 1930- *WhoAm 92*
Little, William E. d1991 *BioIn 17*
Little, William G. 1942- *St&PR 93*
Little, William Henry 1948- *WhoEmL 93*
Little, William Norris 1931- *St&PR 93*
Little Anthony & the Imperials *SoulM*
Littlechild, Stephen 1943- *BioIn 17*
Littledale, Freya Lota *WhoWrEP 92*
Littledale, Freya Lota Brown *WhoAm 92, WhoAmW 93*
Little David *SoulM*
Little Esther *SoulM*
Little Eva 1945- *SoulM*
Littlefeather, Sacheen *BioIn 17*
Littlefield, Baker R. 1907- *St&PR 93*
Littlefield, Bill 1948- *WhoWrEP 92*
Littlefield, David H. 1944- *St&PR 93*
Littlefield, Donald Bruce 1946- *St&PR 93*
Littlefield, Edmund Wattis 1914- *WhoAm 92*
Littlefield, Hazel 1931- *ScF&FL 92*
Littlefield, Joan Kohler 1936- *WhoAmW 93*
Littlefield, John Walley 1925- *WhoAm 92*
Littlefield, Paul Damon 1920- *St&PR 93, WhoAm 92*
Littlefield, Raymond S. 1945- *St&PR 93*
Littlefield, Richard Wells, Jr. 1948- *WhoSSW 93*
Littlefield, Roy Everett, III 1952- *WhoE 93, WhoWor 93*
Littlefield, T. *WhoScE 91-1*
Littlefield, Vivian Moore 1938- *WhoAm 92, WhoAmW 93*
Littlefield, Warren *BioIn 17, WhoAm 92*
Littlefield, Woodrow Wilson, III 1963- *WhoSSW 93*
Littleford, William D. 1914- *St&PR 93*
Littlehale, John D. 1954- *St&PR 93*
Littlejohn, Angus C. d1992 *NewYTBS 92*
Littlejohn, Broadus, III 1960- *St&PR 93*
Littlejohn, Broadus Richard, Jr. 1925- *WhoAm 92*
Littlejohn, David *WhoScE 91-1*
Littlejohn, David 1937- *WhoAm 92*
Littlejohn, Gavin Stuart *WhoScE 91-1*
Littlejohn, John Price 1949- *WhoSSW 93*
Littlejohn, Mark Hays 1936- *WhoSSW 93*
Littlejon, Jon *WhoWrEP 92*
Little Milton 1934- *BioIn 17, SoulM*
Littler, Dale Anthony *WhoScE 91-1*
Littler, Gene Alec 1930- *WhoAm 92*
Littler, John *WhoScE 91-1*
Little Richard *Baker 92, BioIn 17*
Little Richard 1932- *WhoAm 92*
Little Richard 1935- *SoulM*
Littleton, Charles Thomas 1938- *WhoE 93*
Littleton, Harvey Kline 1922- *WhoAm 92*
Littleton, Isaac Thomas, III 1921- *WhoAm 92*
Littleton, Jeffre *BioIn 17*
Littleton, Jesse Talbot, III 1917- *WhoAm 92*
Littleton, John Edward 1943- *WhoSSW 93*
Littleton, John Martin *WhoScE 91-1*
Littleton, Joseph Cook 1920- *WhoE 93*
Littleton, Sarah Elizabeth 1965- *WhoWor 93*
Littleton, Taylor Dowe 1930- *WhoAm 92*
Littleton, Wayne H. 1948- *St&PR 93*
Little Walter *Baker 92*
Little Willie John *Baker 92*
Littlewood, B. *WhoScE 91-1*
Littlewood, Douglas Burden 1922- *WhoAm 92*
Littlewood, Janet D. 1954- *WhoScE 91-1*
Littlewood, Joan *BioIn 17*
Littlewood, Stephen *WhoScE 91-1*
Littlewood, Thomas Benjamin 1928- *WhoAm 92*
Littman, Bruce Henry 1944- *WhoE 93*
Littman, Earl 1927- *St&PR 93, WhoAm 92*
Littman, Howard 1927- *WhoAm 92*
Littman, Irving 1940- *WhoAm 92*
Littman, Jules Sanford 1946- *WhoE 93*
Littman, Lawrence, Jr. 1937- *St&PR 93*
Littman, Lynne *MiSFD 9*
Littman, Lynne 1941- *WhoAmW 93*
Littman, Richard Anton 1919- *WhoAm 92*
Littman, Richard G. *St&PR 93*
Littman, Rosemary Cheris *BioIn 17*
Littmann, Mark Evan 1939- *WhoSSW 93*
Littner, Ner 1915- *WhoAm 92*
Litton, Andrew 1959- *Baker 92*
Litton, Robert Clifton 1934- *WhoSSW 93*
Littrell, Billy R. 1934- *St&PR 93*
Litvack, Mark Davis *Law&B 92*
Litvack, Sanford M. *Law&B 92*
Litvack, Sanford Martin 1936- *WhoAm 92*
Litvak, Anatole 1902-1974 *MiSFD 9N*
Litvak, Leonard L. 1922- *St&PR 93*
Litvak King, Jaime 1933- *WhoWor 93*
Litvinchev, Igor Semionovich 1956- *WhoWor 93*
Litvinchuk, Alexander Petrovich 1958- *WhoWor 93*
Litvinne, Felia 1860?-1936 *Baker 92, OxDcOp*
Litvinov, Gregory Lazarevich 1944- *WhoWor 93*
Litvinov, Maxim Maximovich 1876-1951 *DcTwHis*
Litvinov, William Grigorievich 1934- *WhoWor 93*
Litwack, Gerald 1929- *WhoAm 92, WhoE 93*
Litwack, Leon Frank 1929- *WhoAm 92, WhoWrEP 92*
Litwaitis, Jim Michael 1942- *St&PR 93*
Litwak, Eileen Kane 1941- *WhoAmW 93*
Litwak, Leo 1924- *WhoWrEP 92*
Litwak, Manuel 1938- *WhoE 93*
Litwak, Michael Anatol 1902-1974 *MiSFD 9N*
Litwak, Paul R. 1948- *St&PR 93*
Litweiler, John Berkey 1940- *WhoAm 92, WhoWrEP 92*
Litwin, Donald L. 1934- *St&PR 93*
Litwin, Harry 1907- *St&PR 93*
Litwin, Lawrence Theodore 1927- *St&PR 93*
Litwin, Linda Joan 1944- *WhoAmW 93*
Litwin, Martin Stanley 1930- *WhoAm 92, WhoSSW 93*
Litwin, Michael J. 1947- *St&PR 93*
Litwin, Michael Joseph 1947- *WhoAm 92*
Litwin, Paul Jeffrey 1955- *WhoEmL 93*
Litwin, Valerie Lee *Law&B 92*
Litwiniszyn, Jerzy 1914- *WhoScE 91-4*
Litwinka, Michael *Law&B 92*
Litwinowicz, Manfred Siegmund 1950- *WhoEmL 93*
Litz, Arthur Walton, Jr. 1929- *WhoAm 92, WhoWrEP 92*
Litz, Marla Bennett 1959- *WhoSSW 93*
Litz, Robert D. *Law&B 92*
Litzau, Johannes Barend 1822-1893 *Baker 92*
Litzenberg, Robert Goldsborough 1910- *BioIn 17*
Litzinger, Jerrold J. *Law&B 92*
Litzmann, Berthold 1857-1926 *Baker 92*
Litzsinger, Orville Jack 1936- *WhoE 93*
Litzsinger, Paul Richard 1932- *WhoAm 92*
Li Tzu-ch'eng 1606-1645 *HarEnMi*
Liu, Alan Fong-Ching 1933- *WhoWor 93*
Liu, Alice Yee-Chang 1948- *WhoAmW 93, WhoEmL 93*
Liu, Bai-Xin 1935- *WhoWor 93*
Liu, Baw-Lin 1945- *WhoSSW 93*
Liu, Ben-chieh 1938- *WhoAm 92*
Liu, Benjamin Young-hwai 1934- *WhoAm 92*
Liu, Bo Lian 1944- *WhoWor 93*
Liu, Chao-Han 1939- *WhoAm 92, WhoWor 93*
Liu, Charles Chung-Cha 1953- *WhoE 93*
Liu, Chieh 1906-1991 *BioIn 17*
Liu, Chung-Chiun 1936- *WhoAm 92*
Liu, Ernest K. H. 1950- *WhoAm 92*
Liu, Frank *BioIn 17*
Liu, Gui Zhen 1944- *WhoWor 93*
Liu, Guo-Qing 1933- *WhoWor 93*
Liu, Han-Shou 1930- *WhoWor 93*
Liu, Hao-wen 1926- *WhoAm 92*
Liu, Joseph T. C. 1934- *WhoAm 92*
Liu, Khang-Lee 1939- *WhoWor 93*
Liu, Laifu 1938- *WhoWor 93*
Liu, Lee 1933- *St&PR 93, WhoAm 92*
Liu, Liquan 1926- *WhoWor 93*
Liu, Mei (Michael) *Law&B 92*
Liu, Ming-Chit 1937- *WhoWor 93*
Liu, Minggang 1944- *WhoWor 93*
Liu, Morris *St&PR 93*
Liu, Nancy *Law&B 92*
Liu, Pak Wai 1948- *WhoWor 93*
Liu, Pamela Pei-Ling 1951- *WhoE 93*
Liu, Patricia Kay 1955- *WhoEmL 93*
Liu, Paul *BioIn 17*
Liu, Pin-Yen 1925- *BioIn 17*
Liu, Qizhong 1938- *WhoWor 93*
Liu, Ralph Yieh-Min 1958- *WhoE 93, WhoEmL 93*
Liu, Ray Ho 1942- *WhoSSW 93*
Liu, Roger Kim Sing 1934- *WhoWor 93*
Liu, Ruey-Wen 1930- *WhoAm 92*
Liu, Sarah 1943- *ConAu 38NR*
Liu, Stephen Shu-Ning 1930- *WhoWrEP 92*
Liu, Ta-Jen 1919- *WhoWor 93*
Liu, Tally C. 1950- *St&PR 93*
Liu, Ti Lang 1932- *WhoWor 93*
Liu, Vi-Cheng 1917- *WhoAm 92*
Liu, Warren Kuo-Tung 1952- *St&PR 93*
Liu, Wen *Law&B 92*
Liu, Xianqiu 1941- *St&PR 93*
Liu, Xiaoyan 1957- *WhoSSW 93*
Liu, Yick Wah Edmund 1953- *WhoWor 93*
Liu, Young King 1934- *WhoAm 92*
Liu, Yu-Jih 1948- *WhoWor 93*
Liu, Zhuo Jun 1958- *WhoWor 93*
Liu Anyuan 1927- *WhoAsAP 91*
Liu Binyan 1925- *BioIn 17, ConAu 136*
Liu Chih 1892- *HarEnMi*
Liu Chih-tan 1902-1936 *HarEnMi*
Liu Fangren 1936- *WhoAsAP 91*
Liu Guofan 1930- *WhoAsAP 91*
Liu Guoguang 1923- *WhoAsAP 91*
Liu Haisu 1896- *WhoWor 93*
Liu Hongru 1931- *WhoAsAP 91*
Liu Jingsong 1933- *WhoAsAP 91*
Liukkonen, Matti Antero 1945- *WhoWor 93*
Liukkonen, Simo Sakari 1940- *WhoScE 91-4*
Liuksila, Aarno Olavi 1943- *WhoUN 92*
Liu K'un-yi 1830-1902 *HarEnMi*
Liu Ronghui 1939- *WhoAsAP 91*
Liu Shaoqi 1898-1969 *ColdWar 2 [port]*
Liu Shaoqi 1898-1974? *DcTwHis*
Liu Suinian 1929- *WhoAsAP 91*
Liu Sung-Pan 1931- *WhoAsAP 91*
Liutprand of Cremona c. 920-c. 972 *OxDcByz*
Liu Xiang *BioIn 17*
Liu Xiao *BioIn 17*
Liu Yi 1930- *WhoAsAP 91*
Liu Yuan d310 *HarEnMi*
Liu Yujie *WhoAsAP 91*
Liu Yuxi *BioIn 17*
Liu Zhengwei 1930- *WhoAsAP 91*
Liu Zhongdong *BioIn 17*
Liuzzi, Dominic E. 1932- *St&PR 93*
Liuzzi, Fernando 1884-1940 *Baker 92*
Liuzzi, Robert C. 1944- *St&PR 93, WhoAm 92*
Liuzzo, Joseph Anthony 1926- *WhoAm 92*
Liuzzo, Viola Fauver Gregg 1925-1965 *EncAACR*
Liva, Janice B. *Law&B 92*
Livadaras, Nikolaos 1933- *WhoWor 93*
Livadas, R.J. 1931- *WhoScE 91-4*
Livage, Jacques 1938- *WhoScE 91-2*
Livasy, Ray G. 1929- *St&PR 93*
Livaudais, Herbert Syme 1917- *St&PR 93*
Livaudais, Marcel, Jr. 1925- *WhoSSW 93*
Live, Israel 1907- *WhoAm 92*
Lively, Adam 1961- *ScF&FL 92*
Lively, Carol A. 1935- *WhoAm 92*
Lively, Edwin Lester 1930- *WhoAm 92*
Lively, Edwin Lowe 1920- *WhoAm 92*
Lively, Elizabeth Anne 1953- *WhoAmW 93*
Lively, Howard Randolph, Jr. 1934- *WhoAm 92*
Lively, James Keeton *Law&B 92*
Lively, John Pound 1945- *St&PR 93, WhoAm 92*
Lively, Norman E. 1929- *St&PR 93*
Lively, Penelope 1933- *BioIn 17, ScF&FL 92*
Lively, Penelope (Margaret) 1933- *ChlFicS, MajAI [port], WhoWor 93*
Lively, Pierce 1921- *WhoAm 92*
Livengood, Richard Vaughn 1934- *WhoSSW 93*
Livengood, T.C. 1955- *St&PR 93*
Livengood, Victoria Ann 1959- *WhoAm 92*
Liverati, Giovanni 1772-1846 *Baker 92*
Livergant, Harold Leonard 1924- *St&PR 93, WhoAm 92*
Livermore, Donald Raymond 1947- *WhoEmL 93*
Livermore, Jeanne M. 1948- *St&PR 93*
Livermore, Joseph McMaster 1937- *WhoAm 92*
Liversage, Richard Albert 1925- *WhoAm 92*
Livesay, Dorothy 1909- *BioIn 17, WhoCanL 92*
Livesay, Florence Randal 1874-1953 *BioIn 17*
Livesay, Ron 1950- *St&PR 93*
Livesay, Thomas Andrew 1945- *WhoAm 92*
Livesey, Geoffrey *WhoScE 91-1*
Livesey, James Lawrence *WhoScE 91-1*
Livesey, John *ScF&FL 92*
Livesey, Michael J. d1990 *BioIn 17*
Livey, D.T. *WhoScE 91-1*
Livezey, Tracy A. *Law&B 92*
Livi, Ivan David 1920- *WhoE 93*
Livia, Anna 1955- *ScF&FL 92*
Liviabella, Lino 1902-1964 *Baker 92*
Livick, Malcolm Harris 1929- *WhoAm 92*
Livigisitone, Tanuvasa 1929- *WhoAsAP 91*
Livigni, Filippo fl. 1773-1785 *OxDcOp*
Livigni, Rosemarie 1957- *WhoAmW 93*

Livigni, Russell A. 1934- St&PR 93
Livingood, Clarence S. 1911- WhoAm 92, WhoWor 93
Livingood, Suzanne Hubbuch 1948- WhoSSW 93
Livingston, Ann Chambliss 1952- WhoEmL 93
Livingston, Berkeley 1909-1975 ScF&FL 92
Livingston, Bob 1943- CngDr 91
Livingston, Bradford Lee 1954- WhoEmL 93
Livingston, Brian BioIn 17
Livingston, Calvin J. Law&B 92
Livingston, Colleen M. 1946- WhoE 93, WhoEmL 93
Livingston, Coy R. 1946- St&PR 93
Livingston, David Morse 1941- WhoAm 92
Livingston, Don R. 1947- St&PR 93
Livingston, Edmund W., Jr. 1943- St&PR 93
Livingston, Edward Michael 1948- WhoEmL 93
Livingston, Edward Walter 1932- St&PR 93
Livingston, Ethel AmWomPl
Livingston, Gideon Eleazar 1927- WhoE 93
Livingston, Gordon Stuart 1938- WhoE 93
Livingston, Henry Brockholst 1757-1823 OxCSupC [port]
Livingston, Homer J., Jr. 1935- St&PR 93
Livingston, James Craig 1930- WhoWrEP 92
Livingston, James Evertte 1940- WhoAm 92
Livingston, James L. 1954- St&PR 93
Livingston, Jane Shelton 1944- WhoAm 92
Livingston, Jay Carl WhoWrEP 92
Livingston, Jay Harold 1915- WhoAm 92
Livingston, Jayson 1965- ConAu 136
Livingston, Jennie MiSFD 9
Livingston, John H., II Law&B 92
Livingston, Johnston R. 1923- WhoAm 92
Livingston, Joseph A. 1905-1989 BioIn 17
Livingston, Karen Dean 1948- WhoWrEP 92
Livingston, Kaye Laurel 1965- WhoAmW 93
Livingston, Lee Franklin 1942- WhoE 93
Livingston, Lorton Stoy, Jr. 1942- St&PR 93
Livingston, Louis Bayer 1941- WhoAm 92
Livingston, Luther Wakefield, Jr. 1936- WhoSSW 93
Livingston, M. Jay 1934- ScF&FL 92
Livingston, Margaret Morrow Gresham 1924- WhoAmW 93
Livingston, Mark Verile Law&B 92
Livingston, Maturin 1769-1847 BioIn 17
Livingston, Mollie Parnis WhoAm 92
Livingston, Myra Cohn BioIn 17
Livingston, Myra Cohn 1926- MajAI [port], WhoAm 92, WhoAmW 93, WhoWrEP 92
Livingston, Myran J. ScF&FL 92
Livingston, Myran Jabez, Jr. 1934- WhoWrEP 92
Livingston, Myrtle Athleen Smith 1902- AmWomPl
Livingston, Paisley 1951- ConAu 136
Livingston, Pamela Anna 1930- WhoAmW 93
Livingston, Patrick Murray 1920- WhoAm 92, WhoWrEP 92
Livingston, Peter 1766-1847 BioIn 17
Livingston, Peter Shuyler 1772-1809 BioIn 17
Livingston, Peter William 1767-1826 BioIn 17
Livingston, Randall Murch 1949- WhoEmL 93
Livingston, Robert Burr 1918- WhoAm 92
Livingston, Robert Gerald 1927- WhoE 93, WhoWor 93
Livingston, Robert L. 1937- St&PR 93
Livingston, Robert J. 1942- St&PR 93
Livingston, Robert Jean 1932- St&PR 93
Livingston, Robert Linlithgow, Jr. 1943- WhoAm 92, WhoSSW 93
Livingston, Ruby Erwin AmWomPl
Livingston, Terrance K. Law&B 92
Livingston, Thomas Eugene 1948- WhoAm 92
Livingston, W.P. Law&B 92
Livingston, William 1723-1790 BioIn 17
Livingston, William Curtis, III 1943- St&PR 93
Livingston, William Harold WhoSSW 93
Livingston, William Lafayette 1932- WhoE 93
Livingston, William M. 1913- St&PR 93
Livingston, William M., Jr. 1946- St&PR 93
Livingston, William Samuel 1920- WhoSSW 93
Livingstone, Charleen Thompson 1929- WhoAmW 93
Livingstone, Daniel Archibald 1927- WhoAm 92
Livingstone, David 1813-1873 BioIn 17, Expl 93 [port]
Livingstone, Donald 1924- WhoWor 93
Livingstone, Frank Brown 1928- WhoAm 92
Livingstone, Harrison Edward 1937- WhoE 93, WhoWrEP 92
Livingstone, Ian 1949- ScF&FL 92
Livingstone, James McCardle WhoScE 91-1
Livingstone, John Leslie 1932- WhoAm 92
Livingstone, Mark J. ScF&FL 92
Livingstone, Susan Morrisey 1946- WhoAm 92, WhoAmW 93
Livingstone, Trudy Dorothy Zweig 1946- WhoAmW 93, WhoEmL 93, WhoSSW 93, WhoWor 93
Livingston Hindman, Mary M. 1948- WhoSSW 93
Livingston-White, Deborah Joyce Halemah 1947- WhoWrEP 92
Livingston-Wilson, Karen E. Law&B 92
Livinov, Maxim Maximovich 1876-1951 BioIn 17
Livius Salinator, Gaius fl. c. 188BC- HarEnMi
Livius Salinator, Marcus 254BC-c. 204BC HarEnMi
Livolsi, Santo 1938- WhoWor 93
LiVolsi, Virginia Anne 1943- WhoE 93
Livoni, Cathy 1956- ScF&FL 92
Livornese, Linda M. 1951- St&PR 93
Livsey, Barbara 1946- BioIn 17
Livsey, Robert Callister 1936- WhoAm 92
Livy c. 59BC-17AD HarEnMi
Lix, Terry J. 1951- St&PR 93
Li Xiannian 1909- ColdWar 2 [port]
Li Xiannian 1909-1992 NewYTBS 92 [port]
Li Ximing 1926- WhoAsAP 91
Li Xinjian BioIn 17
Li Xinliang 1936- WhoAsAP 91
Lixl-Purcell, Andreas 1951- WhoEmL 93, WhoSSW 93
Li Xueqin 1933- ConAu 136
Li Xuge 1927- WhoAsAP 91
Li Yanping BioIn 17
Li Yuan fl. 618-627 HarEnMi
Li Yuan-hung 1864-1928 HarEnMi
Lizalde, Eduardo 1929- DcMexL
Lizanich-Aro, Suzanne 1953- WhoE 93
Lizano, Gerardo 1948- WhoUN 92
Lizarraga, Juan J. Law&B 92
Li Zemin 1934- WhoAsAP 91
Lizenby, Linda Lee 1956- WhoEmL 93
Li Zhaoli 1926- BioIn 17
Li Zhen d1990 BioIn 17
Li Zhenqian 1937- WhoAsAP 91
Li Ziqi 1923- WhoAsAP 91
Li Zongren 1890- BioIn 17
Lizzani, Carlo 1917- MiSFD 9
Lizzi, Frank BioIn 17
Ljarja, Rikard 1943- DrEEuF
Ljones, Torbjorn 1943- WhoScE 91-4
Ljubenko, Dusan J. 1927- St&PR 93
Ljubesic, Nikola 1940- WhoScE 91-4
Ljubicic, Ante 1938- WhoScE 91-4
Ljubicic Drozdowski, Miladin Peter 1921- WhoWor 93
Ljundquist, Kent 1948- ScF&FL 92
Ljung, Greta Marianne WhoAmW 93
Ljung, Lennart 1946- WhoScE 91-4
Ljung, Viveka 1935- WhoWor 93
Ljungberg, Gota 1893-1955 OxDcOp
Ljungberg, Gota (Albertina) 1893-1955 Baker 92
Ljungberg, Michael Hans 1957- WhoWor 93
Ljunggren, Hans-Gustaf 1961- WhoWor 93
Ljungman, Lennart S. 1940- WhoUN 92
Ljungstrom, Goran 1933- WhoWor 93
L.L. Cool J BioIn 17
L. L. Cool J. 1968- SoulM
Llaca, Juan Sanchez St&PR 93
Llado, Jesus M. 1941- WhoWor 93
Llamas, Vicente Jose 1944- HispAmA
Llanos, Fernando fl. 1506-1513 BioIn 17
Llanos, Manuel Company WhoScE 91-3
Llaurado, Josep G. 1927- WhoAm 92
Llaurado, Joseph 1927- HispAmA
Llauro, Roberto Alejandro 1954- WhoWor 93
Llera Moravia, Carmen 1954- BioIn 17
Lleras Camargo, Alberto 1906- DcTwHis
Lleras Camargo, Alberto 1906-1990 BioIn 17
Llewellyn, Betty Halff 1911- WhoAmW 93, WhoWor 93
Llewellyn, Edward 1917-1984 ScF&FL 92
Llewellyn, Frederick Eaton 1917- St&PR 93, WhoWor 93
Llewellyn, Irene Beatrice 1940- WhoE 93
Llewellyn, J. Bruce BioIn 17
Llewellyn, J.J. ScF&FL 92
Llewellyn, Jim O. Law&B 92
Llewellyn, John Schofield, Jr. 1935- St&PR 93, WhoAm 92, WhoE 93
Llewellyn, Leonard Frank 1933- WhoWor 93
Llewellyn, Michael John 1939- WhoWor 93
Llewellyn, Ralph Alvin 1933- WhoAm 92
Llewellyn, Thomas Sylvester, III 1936- WhoSSW 93
Llewellyn Smith, Christopher Hubert WhoScE 91-1
Llewellyn Smith, Christopher Hubert 1942- WhoWor 93
Llewellyn-Smith, Michael John 1942- WhoWor 93
Llewellyn-Thomas, Edward ScF&FL 92
Lliboutry, Louis A. 1922- WhoScE 91-2
Llimona, Joan 1860-1926 BioIn 17
Llimona, Josep 1864-1934 BioIn 17
Llinas, Rodolfo 1934- HispAmA
Llinas, Rodolfo Riascos 1934- WhoAm 92
Llobet, Miguel 1875-1938 Baker 92
Llongueras, Luis BioIn 17
Llongueras y Badia, Juan 1880-1953 Baker 92
Llopis, Blanca 1956- WhoWor 93
Llorca, James Pingul 1958- WhoWor 93
Llorens Duran, Josep Ignasi de 1946- WhoScE 91-3
Llorente, Segundo 1906-1989 BioIn 17
Llorente Del Moral, Vicenta 1930- WhoScE 91-3
Lloret Morancho, Antonio 1955- WhoScE 91-3
Llosa, Luis MiSFD 9
Llosa, Mario Vargas 1936- BioIn 17
Llovio-Menendez, Jose Luis BioIn 17
Lloyd, A(lbert) L(ancaster) 1908-1982 Baker 92
Lloyd, A.R. 1927- ScF&FL 92
Lloyd, Albert Lawrence, Jr. 1930- WhoAm 92
Lloyd, Angelica D. Law&B 92
Lloyd, Anne Gladys 1889- AmWomPl
Lloyd, Arthur G. Law&B 92
Lloyd, Arthur Leonard 1925- St&PR 93
Lloyd, Boardman 1942- WhoAm 92
Lloyd, Bruce WhoAsAP 91
Lloyd, Caroline ScF&FL 92
Lloyd, Cecil Rhodes 1930- WhoSSW 93
Lloyd, Celeste Scalise 1959- WhoSSW 93, WhoWor 93
Lloyd, Charles BioIn 17
Lloyd, Charles Harford 1849-1919 Baker 92
Lloyd, Charles R. 1932- St&PR 93
Lloyd, Christopher 1938- QDrFCA 92 [port], WhoAm 92
Lloyd, Clive Wayne WhoScE 91-1
Lloyd, D.R. WhoScE 91-1
Lloyd, D.R. 1937- WhoScE 91-3
Lloyd, David WhoScE 91-1
Lloyd, David 1920- Baker 92
Lloyd, David A. WhoScE 91-1
Lloyd, David Hubert 1948- WhoWrEP 92
Lloyd, David Richard 1947- WhoEmL 93
Lloyd, Debra Wood 1951- WhoAmW 93
Lloyd, Don Keith 1944- St&PR 93
Lloyd, Douglas Seward 1939- WhoAm 92
Lloyd, E. James ConAu 138
Lloyd, Edward 1815-1890 BioIn 17
Lloyd, Edward, IV 1744-1796 BioIn 17
Lloyd, Elisabeth A. 1956- ConAu 139
Lloyd, Elizabeth ScF&FL 92
Lloyd, Elizabeth Ellen 1949- WhoEmL 93
Lloyd, Elizabeth Jeanine 1936- WhoAmW 93
Lloyd, Elliott 1947- WhoEmL 93
Lloyd, Errol 1943- BioIn 17, BlkAuII 92
Lloyd, Eugene Walter 1943- St&PR 93, WhoAm 92
Lloyd, Francis Leon, Jr. 1955- WhoEmL 93
Lloyd, Frank 1888-1960 MiSFD 9N
Lloyd, Gary E. St&PR 93
Lloyd, George 1913- Baker 92
Lloyd, Gretchen Law&B 92
Lloyd, Harold 1893-1971 IntDcF 2-3 [port], QDrFCA 92 [port]
Lloyd, Harold 1894-1971 BioIn 17
Lloyd, Harold Sidney 1953- St&PR 93
Lloyd, Harris Horton 1937- WhoSSW 93
Lloyd, Henry Demarest 1847-1903 PolPar
Lloyd, Hugh 1876-1950 BioIn 17
Lloyd, Hugh Adams 1918- WhoAm 92
Lloyd, Ian BioIn 17
Lloyd, Irene Brown 1945- WhoAmW 93
Lloyd, J.A.T. 1870-1956 ScF&FL 92
Lloyd, Jacqueline 1950- WhoSSW 93
Lloyd, James A. 1946- St&PR 93
Lloyd, James Norman 1962- WhoSSW 93
Lloyd, James T. 1941- WhoAm 92
Lloyd, Jeffrey Hywel 1946- WhoWor 93
Lloyd, Joan Elizabeth 1941- WhoWrEP 92
Lloyd, Joe Thomas, Jr. 1945- WhoSSW 93
Lloyd, John Beckwith WhoScE 91-1
Lloyd, John Eugene 1940- WhoE 93
Lloyd, John Raymond 1942- WhoAm 92
Lloyd, John S. 1945- WhoUN 92
Lloyd, John Wylie WhoScE 91-1
Lloyd, Jonathan 1948- Baker 92
Lloyd, Jonathan David 1952- St&PR 93
Lloyd, Joseph Wesley 1914- WhoWor 93
Lloyd, Judith Ann 1945- WhoAmW 93
Lloyd, Julian Edward 1953- WhoWor 93
Lloyd, June Dickson 1936- WhoE 93
Lloyd, Kate Rand 1923- WhoAm 92, WhoAmW 93
Lloyd, Kent 1931- WhoAm 92
Lloyd, Leona Loretta 1949- WhoEmL 93
Lloyd, Lewis Keith, Jr. 1941- WhoAm 92, WhoSSW 93
Lloyd, Lewis L. Law&B 92
Lloyd, Linda Marie 1941- WhoWrEP 92
Lloyd, Lisa ConAu 139
Lloyd, Malcolm Russell 1939- St&PR 93, WhoAm 92
Lloyd, Margaret Ann 1942- WhoSSW 93
Lloyd, Maria Bioren 1966- WhoAmW 93
Lloyd, Marilyn 1929- BioIn 17, CngDr 91, WhoAm 92, WhoAmW 93, WhoSSW 93
Lloyd, Markland Gale 1948- WhoE 93
Lloyd, Mary Ellen 1947- WhoAmW 93
Lloyd, Mary Kazaleh Law&B 92
Lloyd, Michael 1948- ConTFT 10
Lloyd, Michael Jeffrey 1948- WhoAm 92
Lloyd, Morris, Jr. 1937- St&PR 93
Lloyd, Noel ScF&FL 92
Lloyd, Noel Glynne WhoScE 91-1
Lloyd, Norman 1909-1980 Baker 92
Lloyd, Owen Ll. WhoScE 91-1
Lloyd, Pamela Lynne 1948- WhoAmW 93
Lloyd, Raymond Grann WhoAm 92
Lloyd, Raymond Joseph 1942- St&PR 93
Lloyd, Richard Edmund 1954- WhoEmL 93
Lloyd, Robert 1940- OxDcOp
Lloyd, Robert Albert 1930- WhoE 93
Lloyd, Robert (Andrew) 1940- Baker 92, WhoWor 93
Lloyd, Robert Glanville WhoScE 91-1
Lloyd, Robert Jabez 1918- St&PR 93
Lloyd, Robert Michael 1945- WhoSSW 93
Lloyd, Robert V. 1938- St&PR 93
Lloyd, Robert William 1954- St&PR 93
Lloyd, Roger B. 1901- ScF&FL 92
Lloyd, Rosemarie 1960- WhoAmW 93
Lloyd, Selwyn 1904-1978 ColdWar 1 [port]
Lloyd, Ted BioIn 17
Lloyd, Terrie John 1958- WhoWor 93
Lloyd, Thomas E. 1952- St&PR 93
Lloyd, Thomas R. Law&B 92
Lloyd, Timothy Charles 1951- WhoAm 92
Lloyd, Trevor Owen 1934- WhoWrEP 92
Lloyd, Wanda Smalls 1949- WhoAm 92
Lloyd, William Demarest 1847-1903 GayN
Lloyd, William Hunter, Sr. 1948- WhoEmL 93, WhoWor 93
Lloyd da Silva, Deolinda Maria 1958- WhoAmW 93
Lloyd-Davies, Peter R. 1943- WhoE 93
Lloyde, Robert S. 1946- St&PR 93
Lloyd Evans, Barbara 1924- ConAu 37NR
Lloyd George, David 1863-1945 BioIn 17, DcTwHis
Lloyd-Jones, David 1934- OxDcOp
Lloyd-Jones, David (Mathias) 1934- Baker 92, WhoWor 93
Lloyd-Jones, Donald J. 1931- WhoAm 92
Lloyd-Jones, Esther 1901-1991 BioIn 17
Lloyd-Jones, Hugh Jefferd 1922- WhoWor 93
Lloyd-Jones, J.G. WhoScE 91-1
Lloyd-Jones, Jane d1991 BioIn 17
Lloyd-Jones, Jean G. Hall 1929- WhoAmW 93
Lloyd-Jones, Liz BioIn 17
Lloyd-Smith, Allan 1945- ScF&FL 92
Lloyd-Stanger, Carol Ann 1963- WhoAmW 93
Lloyd Webber, Andrew 1948- Baker 92, BioIn 17, OxDcOp, WhoAm 92, WhoWor 93
Lloyd Webber, Julian 1951- Baker 92, ScF&FL 92
Llull, Ramon 1235?-1315 BioIn 17
Llywelyn, Morgan 1937- ScF&FL 92
Lo, Bruce Wai 1944- WhoWor 93
Lo, Chu Shek 1936- WhoE 93
Lo, Eddy Kong Chuan 1937- WhoWor 93
Lo, Eileen Yin-Fei 1937- WhoAmW 93
Lo, Fu-Chen 1935- WhoUN 92
Lo, Jeannie Pui Ching 1965- WhoAmW 93
Lo, Kai-Yin BioIn 17
Lo, Patrick Punchuk 1952- WhoSSW 93
Lo, Quinn WhoWrEP 92
Lo, Ron 1956- WhoE 93
Lo, Ronald Ping Wong 1936- WhoAm 92, WhoWor 93
Lo, Saved WhoSSW 93
Lo, Theresa Nong 1945- WhoAmW 93
Lo, Yuen-Tze 1920- WhoAm 92
Loach, Kenneth 1936- MiSFD 9
Loach, Kenneth William 1934- WhoE 93

Loader, Jay Gordon 1923- WhoAm 92
Loader, John James WhoScE 91-1
Loadman, Michael John Russell 1939- WhoScE 91-1
Loaharanu, Paisan 1942- WhoUN 92
Loar, Peggy A. 1948- WhoSSW 93
Loasby, Brian John WhoScE 91-1
Loats, John Timothy 1954- WhoEmL 93
Lob, Horst W. 1932- WhoScE 91-3
Lobachevski, N.I. 1792-1856 BioIn 17
Lobaczewska, Stefania 1888-1963 Baker 92
Lobanov-Rostovsky, Oleg 1934- WhoAm 92
Lobato, LeAnn Mary Law&B 92
Lobato, Mary Lee 1961- St&PR 93
Lobato-Sanchez, Dorothy 1938- WhoAmW 93
Lobaugh, Leslie E. Law&B 92
LoBaugh, Leslie E., Jr. WhoAm 92
Lobb, James W. 1932- St&PR 93
Lobb, John C. 1914-1990 BioIn 17
Lobb, William Atkinson 1951- WhoEmL 93
Lobban, Richard Andrew, Jr. 1943- WhoE 93
Lobbia, John E. 1941- St&PR 93, WhoAm 92
Lobdell, David 1941-1991 WhoCanL 92
Lobdell, Jared 1937- ScF&FL 92
Lobdell, Kate Laffey Law&B 92
Lobdell, Leighton M. 1927- St&PR 93
Lobdell, Robert Charles 1926- WhoAm 92
Lobdell, Warren Lamson Law&B 92
Lobe, Johann Christian 1797-1881 Baker 92
Lobeck, Charles Champlin, Jr. 1926- WhoAm 92
Lobeck, Daniel John 1951- WhoEmL 93, WhoSSW 93
Lobeck, Linda Marie 1960- WhoAmW 93
Lobel, Anita ChlBIID [port]
Lobel, Anita (Kempler) 1934- MajAI [port]
Lobel, Arnold 1933-1987 ChlBIID [port]
Lobel, Arnold (Stark) 1933-1987 MajAI [port]
Lobel, Brana 1942- ScF&FL 92
Lobel, Charles Irving 1921- WhoWor 93
Lobel, David S. 1953- St&PR 93
Lobel, Leonard J. 1940- St&PR 93
Lo Bello, Anthony Joseph 1947- WhoEmL 93
Lo Bello, Joseph D. 1940- St&PR 93
Lo Bello, Joseph David 1940- WhoAm 92
Lo Bello, Nino 1921- WhoAm 92
Lobenfeld, Eric J. Law&B 92
Lobenfeld, Eric J. 1950- St&PR 93
Lober, Gregory Wayne 1948- WhoEmL 93
Lober, Paul Hallam 1919- WhoAm 92
Lober, Richard O. 1932- St&PR 93
Loberg, Bengt E.H. 1928- WhoScE 91-4
Lobert, John C. Law&B 92
LoBianco, Robert d1991 BioIn 17
Lo Bianco, Tony MiSFD 9
Lobig, Janie Howell 1945- WhoAmW 93
Lobillo, Jorge 1943- DcMexL
Lobingier, Elizabeth Erwin Miller 1889- AmWomPl
Lobisser, George J. 1927- St&PR 93
Lobitz, Walter Charles, Jr. 1911- WhoAm 92
Lobkowitz Baker 92
Lobkowitz, Ferdinand Joseph Johann 1797-1868 Baker 92
Lobkowitz, Ferdinand Philipp Joseph 1724-1784 Baker 92
Lobkowitz, Joseph Franz Maximilian 1772-1816 Baker 92
Lobkowitz, Philipp Hyacinth 1680-1734 Baker 92
Lobl, Herbert Max 1932- WhoAm 92
Lobl, Victor MiSFD 9
Loblack, E. C. DcCPCAm
Loble, Lester H., II Law&B 92
Loble, Lester H., II 1941- St&PR 93
Lobley, Alan Haigh 1927- WhoAm 92
Lobley, James D. 1946- St&PR 93
Lobley, James Richard 1932- St&PR 93
Lobliner, Sanford M. 1936- St&PR 93
Lobman, Harry L. 1920- St&PR 93
Lobman, Helaine Felice Law&B 92
Lobner, Joyce E. AmWomPl
Lobo, Alonso c. 1555-1617 Baker 92
Lobo, Angelo Peter 1939- WhoE 93
Lobo, Antonio Ataide 1925- WhoWor 93
Lobo, Duarte c. 1565-1646 Baker 92
Lobo, Pio Caetano 1936- WhoWor 93
Lobo, Victor Manuel 1940- WhoScE 91-3
Lobo e Silva Filho, Roberto Leal 1938- WhoWor 93
Lobos, Heitor Villa- BioIn 17
Lobosco, Louis William 1952- WhoEmL 93, WhoWor 93
Lobregat, Ma. Clara L. 1921- WhoAsAP 91
Lobron, Barbara L. 1944- WhoAm 92, WhoAmW 93, WhoE 93
LoBrutto, Patrick ScF&FL 92
Lobsang Rampa, T. BioIn 17
Lobsang Rampa, T. 1911?-1981 ScF&FL 92
Lobsang Rampa, Tuesday BioIn 17
Lobsenz, Amelia WhoAm 92, WhoE 93
Lobsenz, Herbert M. 1932- St&PR 93
Lobsenz, Herbert Munter 1932- WhoAm 92
Lobstein, Timothy Allen Law&B 92
Lobue, Philip Joseph 1937- St&PR 93
Lobur, Julia Marie 1955- WhoAmW 93, WhoE 93
Lobus, Jorg-Uwe Richard 1957- WhoWor 93
Localio, S. Arthur 1911- WhoAm 92
Locasale, Edward Joseph 1947- St&PR 93
Locascio, Joan M. 1957- St&PR 93
Locascio, Salvadore Joseph 1933- WhoAm 92
Locastro, Dominic James 1941- WhoSSW 93
Locatelli, Paul Leo 1938- WhoAm 92
Locatelli, Pietro Antonio 1695-1764 Baker 92
Locey, Martin Lawrence 1953- WhoSSW 93
Loch, Edward James 1939- WhoSSW 93
Loch, Jakab 1932- WhoScE 91-4
Lochak, Georges 1930- WhoWor 93
Lochan, F.N.C. 1940- St&PR 93
Lochanko, Elizabeth Alexandra 1957- WhoAmW 93
Locher, Duane 1947- WhoEmL 93
Locher, Edward P. 1951- St&PR 93
Locher, Ellis K., Jr. Law&B 92
Locher, Gottfried Wilhelm 1911- WhoWor 93
Locher, Marianne 1959- WhoE 93
Locher, Paul Raymond, Jr. 1957- WhoEmL 93
Locher, Ralph Sidney 1915- WhoAm 92
Locher, Richard Earl 1929- WhoAm 92
Lochhead, Douglas 1922- WhoCanL 92
Lochhead, Douglas (Grant) 1922- ConAu 39NR
Lochhead, Jack Van Slyke 1944- WhoE 93
Lochhead, Marion 1902-1985 ScF&FL 92
Lochlan, Helen Beatrice AmWomPl
Lochman, Daniel Thomas 1953- WhoSSW 93
Lochman, William H., Jr. 1947- St&PR 93
Lochman, William Hershey, Jr. 1947- WhoE 93
Lochmann, Ernst-Heinrich 1926- WhoScE 91-3
Lochmann, Ernst-Randolf 1931- WhoScE 91-3
Lochmiller, Kurtis L. 1952- WhoEmL 93, WhoWor 93
Lochner, Conrad, III 1954- WhoSSW 93
Lochner, John M. 1946- St&PR 93
Lochner, Philip R. 1943- St&PR 93
Lochner, Philip Raymond, Jr. 1943- WhoAm 92
Lochovsky, Frederick Horst 1949- WhoWor 93
Lochte, Richard Samuel 1946- WhoEmL 93
Lochtenberg, Bernard Hendrik 1931- St&PR 93, WhoAm 92, WhoE 93
LoCicero, Alice Katherine 1945- WhoAmW 93
Lock, Albert Larry, Jr. 1947- WhoEmL 93, WhoWor 93
Lock, Andrew Raymond WhoScE 91-1
Lock, Dale C. Law&B 92
Lock, Gerald Seymour Hunter 1935- WhoAm 92
Lock, James Curtis 1928- WhoSSW 93
Lock, Joseph Henry 1932- St&PR 93
Lock, Matthew c. 1621-1677 Baker 92
Lock, Richard William 1931- St&PR 93, WhoAm 92
Lock, Robert (Robin) Christopher WhoScE 91-1
Lock, Teri Lyn 1964- WhoAmW 93
Lockard, Charles Wesley 1952- WhoSSW 93
Lockard, John Allen 1944- WhoAm 92
Lockard, K. Wayne 1934- St&PR 93
Lockard, Steven Hartley 1950- St&PR 93
Lockard, Wm. Thomas 1957- St&PR 93
Lockavitch, Joseph Francis 1947- WhoSSW 93
Locke, Alain Leroy 1885-1954 EncAACR
Locke, Alain LeRoy 1886-1954 BioIn 17
Locke, Ashley ScF&FL 92
Locke, Belle Marshall AmWomPl
Locke, Bernadette BioIn 17
Locke, Bryan M.C. 1940- WhoUN 92
Locke, Carl Edwin, Jr. 1936- WhoAm 92
Locke, Charles Stanley 1929- St&PR 93, WhoAm 92
Locke, Christian David 1969- WhoSSW 93
Locke, D. Allan d1990 BioIn 17
Locke, David Ross 1833-1888 JrnUS
Locke, Don Cary 1943- WhoSSW 93
Locke, Donald Tillman Law&B 92
Locke, Edward 1928- WhoWrEP 92
Locke, Edwin Allen, Jr. 1910- WhoAm 92
Locke, Edwin Allen, III 1938- WhoAm 92, WhoWor 93
Locke, Elizabeth Hughes 1939- WhoSSW 93
Locke, George 1936- ScF&FL 92
Locke, Gordon 1938- St&PR 93
Locke, Harold Ogden 1931- WhoE 93
Locke, James Craig 1951- St&PR 93
Locke, John 1632-1704 BioIn 17, IntDcAn
Locke, John Whiteman, III 1936- WhoAm 92
Locke, John William 1933- WhoE 93
Locke, Joseph ScF&FL 92
Locke, L.W. BioIn 17
Locke, L.W. 1934- St&PR 93
Locke, Mary G. 1954- WhoAmW 93
Locke, Matthew c. 1621-1677 Baker 92, OxDcOp
Locke, Maury D. Law&B 92
Locke, Michael 1929- WhoAm 92
Locke, Nicke C. St&PR 93
Locke, Norton 1927- WhoAm 92
Locke, Patricia Anne 1946- WhoSSW 93
Locke, Patricia Marie 1955- WhoAmW 93
Locke, Ralph P. 1949- WhoE 93, WhoEmL 93
Locke, Randy Lee 1944- WhoWor 93
Locke, Richard Adams 1800-1871 JrnUS
Locke, Richard F. Law&B 92
Locke, Robert Albert 1940- St&PR 93
Locke, Robert O. 1918- St&PR 93
Locke, Sondra 1947- MiSFD 9, WhoAm 92
Locke, Stanley 1934- WhoE 93
Locke, Stephen Charles 1953- WhoEmL 93, WhoSSW 93
Locke, Steven Elliot 1945- WhoAm 92
Locke, Susan S. Law&B 92
Locke, Thomas Bernard 1948- WhoEmL 93, WhoSSW 93
Locke, Virginia Otis 1930- WhoAmW 93
Locke, W. Timothy 1955- WhoAm 92
Locke, Wendell Vernon 1924- WhoAm 92
Locke, William Henry 1947- WhoEmL 93
Locke, William Wesley 1935- St&PR 93, WhoAm 92
Locke Berger, Kathleen Carol 1963- WhoE 93
Lockemann, Peter C. 1935- WhoScE 91-3
Lockemann, Peter Christian 1935- WhoWor 93
Locker, J. Gary 1937- WhoAm 92
Locker, Laurence David 1940- WhoSSW 93
Locker, Lois Serota 1960- WhoEmL 93
Locker, Thomas 1937- MajAI [port]
Lockerby, A. Wayne 1942- St&PR 93
Lockerman, Bradley 1955- WhoEmL 93
Lockett, Alan Geoffrey WhoScE 91-1
Lockett, Barbara Ann 1936- WhoAm 92
Lockett, Donna Alcorn 1941- St&PR 93
Lockett, F.J. WhoScE 91-1
Lockett, James Kenneth 1953- WhoWor 93
Lockett, James L. 1930- St&PR 93
Lockett, Pierre WhoAm 92
Lockett, Reginald Franklin 1947- WhoWrEP 92
Lockett-Egan, Marian Workman 1931- WhoAmW 93
Lockey, Richard Funk 1940- WhoAm 92
Lockhart, Aileene Simpson 1911- WhoAm 92
Lockhart, Alain 1929- WhoScE 91-2
Lockhart, Anita May 1934- WhoWrEP 92
Lockhart, Ann June 1945- WhoAmW 93
Lockhart, Bette Jayne 1936- St&PR 93
Lockhart, Brooks Javins 1920- WhoAm 92
Lockhart, Charles David 1953- St&PR 93
Lockhart, Colleen Marie 1964- WhoEmL 93
Lockhart, J.G. 1794-1854 BioIn 17
Lockhart, James 1930- OxDcOp
Lockhart, James B. BioIn 17
Lockhart, James Bicknell, III 1946- WhoEmL 93
Lockhart, James Blakely 1936- WhoAm 92
Lockhart, James Blakley 1936- St&PR 93
Lockhart, James H. Stewart BioIn 17
Lockhart, James (Lawrence) 1930- Baker 92
Lockhart, John Gibson 1794-1854 BioIn 17, DcLB 116 [port]
Lockhart, John M. 1911- St&PR 93
Lockhart, John Mallery 1911- WhoAm 92
Lockhart, Joyce Colquhoun 1932- WhoWor 93
Lockhart, Linda Latsko- BioIn 17
Lockhart, M.E. Law&B 92
Lockhart, Madge Clements 1920- WhoAmW 93
Lockhart, Mary Ellen S. 1963- WhoAmW 93
Lockhart, Mary Guy 1947- WhoEmL 93
Lockhart, Michael D. 1949- WhoAm 92
Lockhart, Richard David 1936- St&PR 93
Lockhart, Robert Ray, III 1939- St&PR 93
Lockhart, Ronald Wayne 1931- St&PR 93
Lockhart, Russel A(rthur) 1938- WhoWrEP 92
Lockhead, Gregory Roger 1931- WhoAm 92, WhoSSW 93
Lock-King, Virginia Sunderland 1959- WhoAmW 93
Locklair, Dan Steven 1949- WhoEmL 93, WhoSSW 93
Lockledge, Ann 1932- WhoAmW 93
Lockley, Jane Law&B 92
Locklin, Allen C. 1929- St&PR 93
Locklin, N.S. 1934- St&PR 93
Locklin, Wilbert Edwin 1920- St&PR 93, WhoAm 92
Lockman, Norman Alton 1938- WhoAm 92, WhoE 93
Lockmiller, Carlotta Elizabeth 1942- WhoSSW 93
Lockmiller, David Alexander 1906- WhoAm 92
Lockridge, Ernest Hugh 1938- WhoWrEP 92
Lockridge, Richard 1898-1982 ScF&FL 92
Lockroy, Edouard Etienne Antoine 1840-1913 BioIn 17
Lockspeiser, Edward 1905-1973 Baker 92
Lockton, David B. St&PR 93
Lockton, John D., Jr. St&PR 93
Lockway, Julia Lai-Ngan WhoAmW 93
Lockwood, Annea 1939- Baker 92
Lockwood, Carol Marie 1943- WhoAmW 93
Lockwood, Charles H. Law&B 92
Lockwood, David John 1942- WhoWor 93
Lockwood, Deborah Jane 1956- WhoAmW 93
Lockwood, Don L. 1932- St&PR 93
Lockwood, Dorothy Pyle C.H. St&PR 93
Lockwood, Eileen Chamberlain 1934- WhoAmW 93, WhoWrEP 92
Lockwood, Frances Ellen 1950- WhoAm 92
Lockwood, Frances Mann 1946- WhoSSW 93
Lockwood, Frank C. 1864-1948 BioIn 17
Lockwood, Gerald A. 1946- St&PR 93
Lockwood, Helshi 1941- WhoE 93
Lockwood, James C. Law&B 92
Lockwood, John LeBaron 1924- WhoAm 92
Lockwood, Julianne Louise 1929- WhoAmW 93
Lockwood, Kenneth Paul 1942- St&PR 93
Lockwood, Kent 1960- St&PR 93
Lockwood, Lewis C. EncAACR
Lockwood, Lewis (Henry) 1930- Baker 92, WhoAm 92
Lockwood, Luther A., II 1966- WhoSSW 93
Lockwood, Margaret 1916-1990 BioIn 17, IntDcF 2-3 [port]
Lockwood, Mark A. 1954- St&PR 93
Lockwood, Molly Ann 1936- WhoAm 92, WhoE 93, WhoWor 93
Lockwood, Normand 1906- Baker 92
Lockwood, Paul D. d1990 BioIn 17
Lockwood, Paul W. 1951- St&PR 93
Lockwood, Rhodes Greene 1919- WhoAm 92
Lockwood, Robert Philip 1949- WhoAm 92
Lockwood, Robert W. Law&B 92
Lockwood, Robert W. 1924- WhoAm 92
Lockwood, Stephen Chapman 1941- WhoAm 92
Lockwood, Theodore Davidge 1924- WhoAm 92
Lockwood, Victoria BioIn 17
Lockwood, Willard Atkinson 1924- WhoAm 92
Lockwood, William A. 1923- St&PR 93
Lockwood Hourani, Laurel Lee 1950- WhoAmW 93
Lockyer, Charles Warren, Jr. 1944- St&PR 93, WhoAm 92
Lockyer, John A. 1934- St&PR 93
Lockyer, Judith 1949- ConAu 138
Lockyer, Michael Alan WhoScE 91-1
LoCoco, Veronica 1934- WhoAmW 93
Loconto, Peter R. 1942- St&PR 93
Locs, Gyula 1936- WhoScE 91-4
Locsin, Carmelo J. 1944- WhoAsAP 91
Lodato, Doug MiSFD 9
Lodde, Barbara Lynn 1949- WhoEmL 93
Lodder, Adrianus 1939- WhoWor 93
Lodder, Robert Andrew 1959- WhoEmL 93, WhoSSW 93
Lodding, Alexander R. E. 1930- WhoWor 93
Loden, Erle van ScF&FL 92
Loden, Lars Olof 1930- WhoScE 91-4
Loder, Edward 1813-1865 OxDcOp
Loder, Kate 1825-1904 OxDcOp
Loder, Lorraine Lee 1952- WhoEmL 93
Loder, Michael Wescott 1945- WhoE 93

Loderhose, Richard E. St&PR 93
Loderstedt, Robert L. St&PR 93
Lodewick, Philip Hughes 1944- WhoE 93, WhoWor 93
Lodewycks, Karel Axel 1910-1990 BioIn 17
Lodewyk, Eric 1940- WhoAm 92
Lodge, Arthur Scott 1922- WhoAm 92
Lodge, David 1935- BioIn 17
Lodge, David Williams 1941- St&PR 93, WhoAm 92
Lodge, Edward J. 1933- WhoAm 92
Lodge, George Cabot 1873-1909 GayN
Lodge, George Cabot 1927- WhoAm 92
Lodge, H. Cabot St&PR 93
Lodge, Henry Cabot DcCPCAm
Lodge, Henry Cabot 1850-1924 BioIn 17, DcTwHis, PolPar
Lodge, Henry Cabot, Jr. 1902-1985 PolPar
Lodge, Jack W., Jr. 1912- St&PR 93
Lodge, James Robert 1925- WhoAm 92
Lodge, John W., III 1947- St&PR 93
Lodge, Juliet WhoScE 91-1
Lodge, Thomas Russell, Sr. 1943- WhoAm 92, WhoE 93
Lodi, Giovanni Agostino da fl. c. 1500- BioIn 17
Lodish, Harvey Franklin 1941- WhoAm 92
Lodish, Leonard Melvin 1943- WhoAm 92
Lodmell, Dean Walter 1959- WhoE 93
Lodowski, Ruth Ellen 1951- WhoAmW 93, WhoSSW 93
Lodwick, Gwilym Savage 1917- WhoAm 92, WhoWor 93
Lodwick, Sheila Anne Ramerman 1956- WhoEmL 93
Lodwick, Teresa Jane 1959- WhoWrEP 92
Lodzinska, Alicja 1925- WhoScE 91-4
Lodzinski, Kazimierz 1922- WhoScE 91-4
Loe, Donn E. 1935- St&PR 93
Loe, Emmett Baxter 1924- WhoSSW 93
Loe, Raymond A. 1931- St&PR 93
Loeb, Alice Pentlarge d1990 BioIn 17
Loeb, Andrew Gothard Law&B 92
Loeb, Andrew Gothard 1944- St&PR 93
Loeb, Barry L. 1941- St&PR 93
Loeb, Ben Fohl, Jr. 1932- WhoAm 92
Loeb, Carlo WhoScE 91-3
Loeb, Charles Walter 1921- WhoScE 91-3
Loeb, David S. 1924- St&PR 93
Loeb, Emiko Toda BioIn 17
Loeb, Frances Lehman 1906- WhoAmW 93, WhoE 93, WhoWor 93
Loeb, Gerard Serge 1949- WhoWor 93
Loeb, Henry d1992 NewYTBS 92
Loeb, James I. d1992 NewYTBS 92 [port]
Loeb, James I. 1908-1992 BioIn 17
Loeb, James (Isaac), Jr. 1908-1992 CurBio 92N
Loeb, Jane Rupley 1938- WhoAmW 93
Loeb, Jeanette Winter 1952- WhoAmW 93
Loeb, Jennifer Susan 1958- WhoEmL 93
Loeb, Jerome T. 1940- St&PR 93
Loeb, Jerome Thomas 1940- WhoAm 92
Loeb, John Hilder d1991 BioIn 17
Loeb, John Jacob 1910-1970 Baker 92
Loeb, John L., Jr. 1930- St&PR 93
Loeb, John Langeloth 1902- WhoAm 92, WhoWor 93
Loeb, John Langeloth, Jr. 1930- WhoAm 92, WhoE 93
Loeb, Larry M. Law&B 92
Loeb, Marshall Robert 1929- WhoAm 92
Loeb, Marvin Phillip 1926- St&PR 93
Loeb, Nackey S. 1924- St&PR 93
Loeb, Nackey Scripps 1924- WhoAm 92, WhoAmW 93, WhoE 93
Loeb, Nancy 1939- WhoAmW 93
Loeb, Nancy Wasserman 1948- WhoAmW 93
Loeb, Olga d1992 NewYTBS 92 [port]
Loeb, Peter Kenneth 1936- WhoAm 92
Loeb, Robert Burris 1948- WhoSSW 93
Loeb, Ronald Marvin 1932- WhoAm 92
Loeb, Timothy Allan 1950- St&PR 93, WhoWrEP 92
Loeb, Virgil, Jr. 1921- WhoAm 92
Loeb, Walter Ferdinand 1925- WhoAm 92
Loeb, William 1905-1981 DcLB 127 [port], PolPar
Loeb, William 1905-1985 JrnUS
Loebbecke, Ernest J. 1911- St&PR 93
Loebell, Diane A. Law&B 92
Loebelsohn, Carol 1931- WhoAmW 93
Loebenstein, William Vaille 1914- WhoE 93
Loeblich, Helen Nina Tappan 1917- WhoAm 92
Loeb-Munson, Stella Marie 1943- WhoAmW 93
Loebus, Fritz Hans 1943- WhoUN 92
Loecy, Nancy 1955- WhoAmW 93
Loedding, Peter Alfred 1934- WhoE 93
Loef, Paul Theodore Law&B 92
Loef, Sarah Ruth Gottlieb 1905- WhoAmW 93
Loeffel, Bruce 1943- WhoAm 92, WhoE 93
Loeffel, Robert L. 1926- St&PR 93
Loeffelbein, Roger 1942- WhoSSW 93
Loeffelholz, J.R. 1929- St&PR 93
Loeffke, Bernard 1934- WhoAm 92
Loeffler, Carl Eugene 1946- WhoWrEP 92
Loeffler, Charles Martin (Tornow) 1861-1935 Baker 92
Loeffler, David E. 1946- WhoAm 92
Loeffler, David Karl 1959- WhoEmL 93
Loeffler, Frank Joseph 1928- WhoAm 92
Loeffler, Hans William 1916- WhoWor 93
Loeffler, Heinrich 1938- WhoWor 93
Loeffler, James Joseph 1931- WhoAm 92
Loeffler, Richard Harlan 1932- WhoAm 92
Loeffler, William George, Jr. 1939- WhoSSW 93
Loeffler, William Robert 1949- WhoEmL 93, WhoWor 93
Loeh, Herbert W. 1932- St&PR 93
Loehle, Betty Barnes 1923- WhoAm 92
Loehlin, John Clinton 1926- WhoAm 92
Loehr, Dean Verner 1952- St&PR 93
Loehr, James E. BioIn 17
Loehr, Johannes-Matthias 1959- WhoWor 93
Loehr, Marla 1937- WhoAm 92, WhoAmW 93
Loehr, Robert A. Law&B 92
Loehrke, Christine Carol 1950- WhoAmW 93, WhoEmL 93
Loeillet Baker 92
Loeillet, Jacques 1685-c. 1748 Baker 92
Loeillet, Jean Baptiste 1680-1730 Baker 92
Loeillet, Jean Baptiste 1688-c. 1720 Baker 92
Loeillet, John Baker 92
Loeillet de Gant 1688-c. 1720 Baker 92
Loeillet of London, John 1680-1730 Baker 92
Loeliger, David A. 1939- WhoWor 93
Loeliger, Jon Frederick 1955- St&PR 93
Loengard, John Borg 1934- WhoAm 92
Loening, Peter B. 1957- St&PR 93
Loening, Regina B. Law&B 92
Loeper, F. Joseph 1944- WhoE 93
Loepfe, Edmund Felix 1937- WhoScE 91-4
Loepp, Fred Edward 1940- St&PR 93
Loeppert, H. Verne 1921- St&PR 93
Loeppert, Richard Henry, Jr. 1944- WhoSSW 93
Loer, David W. 1944- St&PR 93
Loerakker, Jo Ann Katherine 1941- WhoSSW 93
Loerch, Kay Jeanine 1957- WhoSSW 93
Loerch, Russel D. 1926- St&PR 93
Loerke, William Carl 1920- WhoAm 92
Loers, Deborah Lynn 1951- WhoAmW 93
Loertscher, Alfred 1915- WhoWor 93
Loes, David Anthony 1927- St&PR 93
Loesberg, Richard Scott 1953- St&PR 93
Loesch, Harold C. 1926- WhoSSW 93
Loesch, Harrison 1916- WhoAm 92
Loesch, Judith Ann 1946- WhoAmW 93
Loesch, Katharine Taylor 1922- WhoAmW 93
Loesche, Walter Joseph 1935- WhoAm 92
Loesche, William P. Law&B 92
Loescher, Barbara Ann 1953- WhoAmW 93, WhoSSW 93
Loescher, Edward M. 1943- St&PR 93
Loescher, Robert W. 1947- St&PR 93
Loescher, Robert Wayne 1947- WhoAm 92
Loeschhorn, Albert Baker 92
Loeschner, Ray B. 1931- WhoAm 92
Loeschorn, Carol Anne Law&B 92
Loeser, David 1950- St&PR 93
Loeser, Hans F. 1920- St&PR 93
Loeser, Hans Ferdinand 1920- WhoAm 92
Loeser, John David 1935- WhoAm 92
Loeser, Julius L. Law&B 92
Loeser, Katinka 1913-1991 BioIn 17
Loess, Henry Bernard 1924- WhoAm 92
Loesser, Arthur 1894-1969 Baker 92
Loesser, Emily BioIn 17
Loesser, Frank 1910-1969 BioIn 17
Loesser, Frank (Henry) 1910-1969 Baker 92
Loessner, G. Arno, III 1942- WhoE 93
Loev, Arthur 1934- St&PR 93
Loev, Bernard 1928- WhoAm 92
Loev, Gerald 1947- St&PR 93
Loeve, W. 1936- WhoScE 91-3
Loevendie, Theo 1930- Baker 92
Loevenguth, John R. 1952- St&PR 93
Loevi, Francis Joseph, Jr. 1945- WhoAm 92
Loevinger, Lee 1913- WhoAm 92, WhoE 93, WhoWor 93
Loevy, Sandor A. 1940- St&PR 93
Loew, Charles Elwood 1913- St&PR 93
Loew, Charles Williams 1953- St&PR 93
Loew, David N. 1949- WhoEmL 93, WhoWor 93
Loew, Franklin Martin 1939- WhoAm 92
Loew, Mildred Falk d1990 BioIn 17
Loew, Ralph William 1907- WhoAm 92
Loewe, Carl 1796-1869 Baker 92, OxDcOp
Loewe, Ferdinand Baker 92
Loewe, Frederick 1901-1988 Baker 92
Loewe, Frederick 1904-1988 BioIn 17
Loewe, Leslie F. 1921- St&PR 93, WhoAm 92
Loewe, Sophie 1815-1866 OxDcOp
Loewe, Sophie (Johanna) 1815-1866 Baker 92
Loewe Maraj, Elaine Hilda 1955- WhoAm 92
Loewen, Erwin G. 1921- WhoAm 92
Loewen, Raymond 1940- St&PR 93
Loewenbaum, G. Walter, II 1945- WhoAm 92, WhoSSW 93
Loewenberg, Alfred 1902-1949 Baker 92, OxDcOp
Loewenberg, Ernst 1896-1987 BioIn 17
Loewenberg, Gerhard 1928- WhoAm 92
Loewengard, Max Julius 1860-1915 Baker 92
Loewenheim, Harold Arthur 1911- WhoE 93
Loewenstein, Benjamin S. 1912- St&PR 93
Loewenstein, Benjamin Steinberg 1912- WhoAm 92
Loewenstein, George Wolfgang 1890- WhoSSW 93
Loewenstein, Gerard 1930- St&PR 93
Loewenstein, Walter Bernard 1926- WhoAm 92
Loewenstern, Kenneth M. 1944- St&PR 93
Loewenthal, Nessa Parker 1930- WhoAmW 93
Loewenthal, Stanley 1947- WhoE 93
Loewer, Henry Peter 1934- WhoSSW 93
Loewer, Peter 1934- ConAu 138
Loewer, (Henry) Peter 1934- ConAu 136
Loewus, David Ivan 1952- WhoWor 93
Loewus, Mary Walz 1923- WhoAmW 93
Loewy, Arthur F. 1929- St&PR 93
Loewy, David Michael 1955- WhoEmL 93, WhoSSW 93
Loewy, Erich H. 1927- ConAu 139
Loewy, Henry M. 1910- St&PR 93
Loewy, Raymond Fernand 1893-1986 BioIn 17
Loewy, Robert Gustav 1926- WhoAm 92
Loewy, Steven A. 1952- WhoEmL 93
Lofaro, Raymond Anthony 1936- WhoAm 92
Lofaro, Rocco, Jr. 1950- WhoSSW 93
Lofaso, Fred J. 1932- St&PR 93
Lo Faso, Fred Joseph 1932- WhoE 93
Lofberg, Hans Allan S. 1938- WhoScE 91-4
Lofberg, Per G.H. 1947- St&PR 93
Loferski, Joseph John 1925- WhoAm 92
Lofficier, Jean-Marc ScF&FL 92
Loffler, Anton Wilhelm 1927- WhoWor 93
Loffler, Hans D. 1927- WhoScE 91-3
Lofgren, Charles Augustin 1939- WhoAm 92
Lofgren, Karl Adolph 1915- WhoAm 92
Lofgren, Nils BioIn 17
Lofland, John Franklin 1936- WhoAm 92
Lofland, Lyn Hebert 1937- WhoAm 92
Loflin, William Eugene, Jr. 1959- WhoE 93
Lo Forti, Vernon Allen 1953- St&PR 93, WhoAm 92
Lofquist, William Spencer 1936- WhoE 93
Lofstedt, Bengt Torkel Magnus 1931- WhoAm 92
Lofstrom, Mark D. 1953- WhoEmL 93
Loftfield, Robert Berner 1919- WhoAm 92
Lofthouse, Robert Ellis 1950- WhoEmL 93
Lofthouse, Stephen 1945- WhoWor 93
Loftin, Courtney BioIn 17
Loftin, Marion Theo 1915- WhoAm 92
Loftin, Michael L. 1941- St&PR 93
Loftin, Nancy Carol 1954- St&PR 93
Loftin, Raymond Victor, Jr. 1927- WhoAm 92
Loftin, Richard Bowen 1949- WhoSSW 93
Lofting, Hugh 1886-1947 ScF&FL 92
Lofting, Hugh (John) 1886-1947 ConAu 137, MajAI [port]
Loftis, Curtis Bryant 1952- WhoEmL 93
Loftis, Gary Don 1944- WhoSSW 93
Loftis, John Clyde, Jr. 1919- WhoAm 92
Loftis, Joseph Michael 1941- St&PR 93, WhoE 93
Lofton, James David 1956- WhoAm 92
Lofton, Mellanese S. Law&B 92
Lofton, Michael W. 1946- St&PR 93
Lofton, Otmara 1959- WhoAmW 93
Lofton, Randall Hampton 1947- WhoEmL 93
Lofts, Norah 1904-1983 ScF&FL 92
Loftus, Andrew John 1961- WhoE 93
Loftus, Brendan Gerard 1955- WhoWor 93
Loftus, Cecilia AmWomPl
Loftus, James T. Law&B 92
Loftus, Janice Bland 1938- WhoAmW 93
Loftus, Kevin Law&B 92
Loftus, Linda Mary 1950- WhoAmW 93
Loftus, Mary Eileen Law&B 92
Loftus, Michael J. 1928- St&PR 93
Loftus, Mitchell John 1951- WhoEmL 93
Loftus, Peter G. 1940- St&PR 93
Loftus, Rita Celestine 1938- WhoAmW 93
Loftus, Stephen Francis 1933- WhoAm 92
Loftus, Thomas J. Law&B 92
Loftus, William 1927- St&PR 93
Loftus, William Frederick 1938- St&PR 93
Loftus, William George 1926- St&PR 93
Loftus, William Michael 1944- WhoIns 93
Loftus, William Peter 1963- WhoE 93
Lofty, Charles F. 1945- St&PR 93
Lofty, Donald A. Law&B 92
Lofwall, Clas 1944- WhoWor 93
Loga, Sanda 1932- WhoAm 92
Logachev, Dmitry Yur'evich 1954- WhoWor 93
Logan, April Charise 1952- WhoEmL 93
Logan, Barbara Jean 1932- WhoAmW 93
Logan, Bob MiSFD 9
Logan, Brent F. Law&B 92
Logan, Bruce MiSFD 9
Logan, Bruce David 1945- WhoE 93
Logan, Carolyn F. ScF&FL 92
Logan, Charles 1930- ScF&FL 92
Logan, Charles Wilbur 1934- WhoSSW 93
Logan, Clay S. St&PR 93
Logan, Dan 1946- WhoE 93, WhoEmL 93, WhoWor 93
Logan, Denise Patricia 1958- WhoEmL 93
Logan, Francis D., Jr. 1945- St&PR 93
Logan, Francis Donald 1930- WhoE 93
Logan, Francis Dummer 1931- WhoAm 92
Logan, Frank Henderson 1936- WhoAm 92
Logan, Frederick Knight 1871-1928 Baker 92
Logan, Frieda BioIn 17
Logan, Gail Kathryn 1945- WhoAmW 93
Logan, George H. 1916- St&PR 93
Logan, Gordon Baker 1946- WhoSSW 93
Logan, Grace Eleanor Miller 1908- WhoAmW 93, WhoE 93
Logan, Harold Roy 1921- WhoAm 92
Logan, Harvey c. 1867-c. 1910 BioIn 17
Logan, Henry Vincent 1942- St&PR 93, WhoAm 92
Logan, Howard M. 1925- St&PR 93
Logan, James C. 1914- WhoAm 92
Logan, James Kenneth 1929- WhoAm 92
Logan, Jane ConAu 136
Logan, Janet Ruth 1941- WhoAmW 93
Logan, Jean Shipley 1943- WhoAmW 93
Logan, John A. 1826-1887 PolPar
Logan, John Alexander 1826-1886 HarEnMi
Logan, John Arthur, Jr. 1923- WhoAm 92
Logan, John F. 1938- St&PR 93
Logan, John Francis 1938- WhoAm 92
Logan, Joseph Granville, Jr. 1920- WhoAm 92
Logan, Joshua 1908-1988 MiSFD 9N
Logan, Joyce Polley 1935- WhoSSW 93
Logan, Kathryn Vance 1946- WhoEmL 93, WhoSSW 93
Logan, Les ScF&FL 92
Logan, Liz BioIn 17
Logan, Lonie 1871-1900 BioIn 17
Logan, Lorretta Gail 1960- WhoEmL 93
Logan, Lowell Arthur 1929- St&PR 93
Logan, Lox Albert, Jr. 1954- WhoAm 92
Logan, Lynnette Ann 1966- WhoAmW 93
Logan, Margaret Colston 1942- WhoSSW 93
Logan, Mary Calkin 1941- WhoSSW 93
Logan, Mathew Kuykendall 1933- WhoAm 92, WhoSSW 93
Logan, Maurice George 1886-1977 BioIn 17
Logan, Michael 1955- St&PR 93
Logan, Michael James 1953- WhoSSW 93
Logan, Nesta Adean 1951- WhoAmW 93
Logan, Nicki Lea Bruce 1943- WhoSSW 93
Logan, Nora ScF&FL 92
Logan, Oran F. 1943- St&PR 93
Logan, Peter Stephen, Sr. 1925- St&PR 93
Logan, Ralph Andre 1926- WhoAm 92
Logan, Rayford Whittingham 1897-1982 EncAACR
Logan, Raymond F. 1923- St&PR 93
Logan, Richard Leo 1941- St&PR 93
Logan, Robert 1939- WhoIns 93
Logan, Robert E., Jr. 1957- St&PR 93
Logan, Robert F. B. 1932- WhoAm 92
Logan, Rodman Emmason 1922- WhoAm 92
Logan, Ronald McKinley 1935- WhoUN 92

Logan, Sandra Jean 1940- *WhoAmW 93*
Logan, Sharon Brooks 1945- *WhoAmW 93*
Logan, Stephen Bean, III 1932- *WhoSSW 93*
Logan, Sylvia Isabelle 1956- *WhoAmW 93*
Logan, Terence 1949- *WhoE 93*
Logan, Teresa 1961- *WhoSSW 93*
Logan, Terry James 1943- *WhoAm 92*
Logan, Veryle Jean *WhoAmW 93*
Logan, Vincent *BioIn 17*
Logan, W.A. 1903- *St&PR 93*
Logan, Walter C., II *St&PR 93*
Logan, William 1950- *ConAu 136, DcLB 120 [port]*
Logan, William Edmond 1798-1875 *BioIn 17*
Loganbill, G. Bruce 1938- *WhoAm 92*
Logar, Mihovil 1902- *Baker 92*
Logeman, John Donald 1939- *WhoAm 92*
Logeman, R.M. 1927- *St&PR 93*
Logemann, Jerilyn Ann 1942- *WhoAmW 93*
Loggem, Manuel van 1916- *ScF&FL 92*
Loggia, Robert *BioIn 17*
Loggia, Robert 1930- *WhoAm 92*
Loggie, Jennifer Mary Hildreth 1936- *WhoAm 92*
Loggins, Bobby Gene 1955- *WhoEmL 93*
Loggins, David Harold 1957- *WhoEmL 93*
Loggins, Donald Anthony 1951- *WhoE 93*
Loggins, Edward M. 1930- *WhoAm 92*
Loggins, Kenny 1947- *WhoAm 92*
Loggins, Kenny 1948- *Baker 92*
Loghry, Gerald Jay 1937- *St&PR 93*
Logi, Piero 1933- *WhoScE 91-3*
Logie, Elma M. *AmWomPl*
Logier, Johann Bernhard 1777-1846 *Baker 92*
Logigian, John Douglas 1952- *WhoEmL 93*
Loginow, Wlodzimierz 1927- *WhoScE 91-4*
Logio, Thomas 1941- *WhoE 93*
Logofet, Dmitrii Olegovich 1947- *WhoWor 93*
Logothetis, Anestis 1921- *Baker 92*
Logothetis, Dimitri *MiSFD 9*
Logothetis, E.N. *St&PR 93*
Logothetis, John 1925- *WhoScE 91-3*
Logothetis, Steven 1955- *St&PR 93*
Logreco, Gerard Ernest 1951- *WhoEmL 93, WhoSSW 93*
Logroscino, Nicola 1698?-1765 *OxDcOp*
Logroscino, Nicola Bonifacio 1698?-1765? *Baker 92*
Logsdon, James C. *Law&B 92*
Logsdon, John M. *BioIn 17*
Logsdon, Kay Lynne 1955- *WhoWrEP 92*
Logsdon, Richard Henry 1912- *WhoAm 92*
Logsdon, Robert Lester 1947- *WhoEmL 93*
Logsdon, Syd 1950?- *ScF&FL 92*
Logsdon, Thomas S(tanley) 1937- *WhoWrEP 92*
Logston, Anne *ScF&FL 92*
Logue, Courtland L., Jr. *St&PR 93*
Logue, Dennis Emhardt 1944- *WhoAm 92*
Logue, Edward Joseph 1921- *WhoAm 92, WhoE 93*
Logue, Frank 1924- *WhoAm 92*
Logue, John Joseph 1929- *WhoE 93*
Logue, Joseph Carl 1920- *WhoAm 92*
Logue, Judith R. 1942- *WhoAmW 93*
Logue, Peter Calvin 1958- *WhoEmL 93*
Logue, Toni Elisabeth 1961- *WhoAmW 93*
Logue-Kinder, Joan 1943- *WhoAm 92, WhoAmW 93, WhoE 93*
Loguinov, Evgueni Nickolaevitch 1937- *WhoUN 92*
Logvinenko, Vladimir 1943- *WhoWor 93*
Loh, Arthur Tsung Yuan 1923- *WhoE 93*
Loh, Hoon Sun *BioIn 17*
Loh, Hung Chee 1947- *WhoWor 93*
Loh, Keng-Aun 1936- *WhoUN 92*
Loh, Morag 1935- *SmATA 73 [port]*
Loh, Robert Nan-Khang *WhoAm 92*
Loh, Toon Seng Michael 1957- *WhoWor 93*
Loh, Wallace D. *BioIn 17*
Lohafer, Douglas Allen 1949- *WhoEmL 93, WhoWor 93*
Lohafer, Susan 1942- *ConAu 37NR*
Lohan, Dirk 1938- *WhoAm 92*
Lohan, William Denis 1931- *WhoWrEP 92*
Lohaus, Judith D. *Law&B 92*
Lohaus, Judith Dora 1951- *WhoAmW 93, WhoEmL 93*
Lohden, William P. 1932- *St&PR 93*
Loher, Brian H. 1951- *St&PR 93*
Lohest, Max 1857-1926 *IntDcAn*
Lohf, Kenneth A. 1925- *WhoAm 92*
Lohlein, Georg Simon 1725-1781 *Baker 92*
Lohm, Ulrik 1943- *WhoScE 91-4*
Lohman, Anna 1812-1878 *BioIn 17*
Lohman, Gordon Russell 1934- *St&PR 93*
Lohman, Janette Massie *Law&B 92*
Lohman, John Frederick 1935- *WhoAm 92*
Lohman, Loretta Cecelia 1944- *WhoAmW 93*
Lohman, Walter Rearick 1917- *WhoAm 92*
Lohman, William Francis 1948- *St&PR 93*
Lohmann, George Young, Jr. 1947- *WhoE 93*
Lohmann, James Glen 1955- *WhoSSW 93*
Lohmann, Janet Cynthia 1939- *St&PR 93*
Lohmann, Janet K. *Law&B 92*
Lohmann, Jeanne Ruth Ackley 1923- *WhoWrEP 92*
Lohmann, Keith Henry 1955- *WhoE 93*
Lohmann, Margaret Ann 1952- *WhoAmW 93*
Lohmann, Virginia Elisabeth 1962- *WhoEmL 93*
Lohmann, Wolfgang 1930- *WhoScE 91-3*
Lohmeier, Stanley F. 1951- *St&PR 93*
Lohmeyer, Douglas Edward 1948- *WhoE 93*
Lohmeyer, Lyle S. 1953- *St&PR 93*
Lohmuller, Martin Nicholas 1919- *WhoAm 92*
Lohmus, Jaak Hermann-Karl 1937- *WhoWor 93*
Lohn, Alois Josef 1934- *WhoAm 92*
Lohner, Rainald 1959- *WhoE 93*
Lohnes, Walter F. W. 1925- *WhoAm 92*
Lohoff, Randy K. *Law&B 92*
Lohr, Benjamin Franklin, Mrs. 1928- *WhoSSW 93, WhoWor 93*
Lohr, Charles Henry 1925- *WhoWor 93*
Lohr, Donald Russell 1933- *St&PR 93*
Lohr, George E. 1931- *WhoAm 92*
Lohr, Harold Russell 1922- *WhoAm 92*
Lohr, John H. 1946- *WhoEmL 93*
Lohr, Mary Margaret *WhoAm 92*
Lohr, Richard Theodore 1941- *St&PR 93*
Lohr, Theodore R. 1911- *St&PR 93*
Lohr, William James 1949- *WhoIns 93*
Lohre, John William 1947- *St&PR 93*
Lohrentz, Donald William 1936- *WhoAm 92*
Lohrer, George *BioIn 17*
Lohrer, Richard Baker 1932- *St&PR 93, WhoAm 92*
Lohrman, John J. 1920- *St&PR 93, WhoAm 92*
Lohrman, William Walter 1954- *WhoEmL 93, WhoSSW 93*
Lohrmann, Erich 1931- *WhoScE 91-3*
Lohs, Karlheinz 1929- *WhoScE 91-3*
Lohse, Austin Webb 1926- *WhoAm 92*
Lohse, David John 1952- *WhoE 93*
Lohse, James E. 1945- *St&PR 93*
Lohse, Otto 1858-1925 *Baker 92*
Lohse, Ray George 1923- *St&PR 93*
Lohse, William 1952- *St&PR 93*
Lohsen, Robert A. 1955- *St&PR 93*
Loibl, Judith Watson 1939- *WhoAmW 93*
Loibner, Hans 1947- *WhoScE 91-4*
Loid, Hans Peder 1941- *WhoScE 91-4*
Loiederman, A. Mario 1934- *WhoE 93*
Loiello, John Peter 1943- *WhoE 93*
Loigman, Harold 1930- *St&PR 93, WhoAm 92*
Loikkanen, Jouko 1932- *WhoScE 91-4*
Loikkanen, Pentti J. 1935- *WhoScE 91-4*
Loinger, Angelo 1923- *WhoScE 91-3*
Lois, George *BioIn 17*
Lois, George 1931- *St&PR 93, WhoAm 92*
Loisance, Daniel Y. 1945- *WhoScE 91-2*
Loiseau, Maurice Joseph 1945- *WhoSSW 93*
Loiseau, Philippe 1941- *WhoScE 91-2*
Loiseau, Richard *Law&B 92*
Loiseaux, Jean Marie 1939- *WhoScE 91-2*
Loiselle, Arthur A., Jr. *Law&B 92*
Loiselle, Gilles *BioIn 17*
Loiselle, Gilles 1929- *WhoAm 92, WhoE 93*
Loitiere, Bernard *WhoScE 91-2*
Loiyd, James T. *Law&B 92*
Lojas, Jozef 1923- *WhoScE 91-4*
Lojczyk-Krolikiewicz, Irena Danuta 1922- *WhoWor 93*
Lojo, Manuel A. *Law&B 92*
Lokar, Marco *BioIn 17*
Loken, Barbara Jean 1951- *WhoAmW 93*
Loken, James Burton 1940- *WhoAm 92*
Loker, Beau 1953- *St&PR 93*
Lokey, Hamilton 1910- *WhoAm 92*
Lokey, Irene Raye 1946- *WhoAmW 93, WhoEmL 93*
Loke Yuen Yow, Datuk 1952- *WhoAsAP 91*
Lokhandwala, Fakhrudin Akberali 1932- *St&PR 93*
Lokhaug, Karin Elise 1943- *WhoUN 92*
Lokiec, Liora 1946- *WhoE 93*
Lokin, D.H.A.C. *WhoWor 93*
Lokio, Ari H. Johannes 1940- *WhoScE 91-4*
Lokis, Marianna 1967- *WhoE 93*
Lokke, Virgil L. 1915- *ScF&FL 92*
Lokken, Eva Tryti 1964- *WhoEmL 93*
Lokker, Laura *Law&B 92*
Lokocy, Jacqueline Marie 1961- *WhoAmW 93*
Lokos, Laszlo 1929- *WhoScE 91-4*
Lokshin, Alexander 1920- *Baker 92*
Lola, Joe William 1928- *WhoSSW 93*
Lolich, Mickey *BioIn 17*
Loliger, Hans-Christoph 1923- *WhoScE 91-3*
Loliger, Jurg 1943- *WhoScE 91-4*
Lolis, Demetrios 1935- *WhoScE 91-3*
Lolla, John Joseph, Jr. 1953- *WhoEmL 93*
Lollar, Coleman Aubrey 1946- *WhoWrEP 92*
Lollar, Coleman Aubrey, Jr. 1946- *WhoAm 92*
Lollar, John H. 1938- *St&PR 93*
Lollar, John Sherman 1924-1977 *BiDAMSp 1989*
Lollar, Robert Miller 1915- *WhoWor 93*
Lollar, Thomas William 1951- *WhoE 93*
Lollar, Thurman Ray 1940- *St&PR 93*
Lolley, William Randall 1931- *WhoAm 92*
Lollgen, Herbert 1943- *WhoWor 93*
Lolli, Antonio c. 1725-1802 *Baker 92*
Lolli, Don Ray 1949- *WhoEmL 93*
Lollobrigida, Gina 1927- *BioIn 17, WhoWor 93*
Lollobrigida, Gina 1928?- *IntDcF 2-3 [port]*
Loloma, Charles 1921-1991 *BioIn 17*
Lolwing, Alfred James 1929- *St&PR 93*
Lom, Herbert 1917- *BioIn 17, IntDcF 2-3*
Lomakin, Gavriil Yakimovich 1812-1885 *Baker 92*
Loman, Diane Louise Moore 1948- *WhoAmW 93*
Loman, Mary LaVerne 1928- *WhoAmW 93, WhoSSW 93*
Lomans, Frans P. 1955- *WhoWor 93*
Lomas, Bernard Tagg 1924- *WhoAm 92, WhoWor 93*
Lomas, Beverly *St&PR 93*
Lomas, Nigel Paul 1958- *WhoWor 93*
LoMascolo, Angelo Romualdo 1946- *WhoEmL 93*
Lomas Garza, Carmen *NotHsAW 93*
Lomas Garza, Carmen 1948- *HispAmA*
Lomask, Milton Nachman 1909- *WhoAm 92, WhoWrEP 92*
Lomask, Morton Rubin 1930- *St&PR 93*
Lomasney, Mark T. 1957- *St&PR 93*
Lomasney, Martin 1859-1933 *PolPar*
Lomason, Harry Austin, II 1934- *St&PR 93, WhoAm 92*
Lomason, William Keithledge 1910- *WhoAm 92*
Lomax, Alan 1915- *Baker 92, BioIn 17*
Lomax, Derek W(illiam) 1933-1992 *ConAu 137*
Lomax, Donald P. 1934- *St&PR 93*
Lomax, Gary T. 1951- *St&PR 93*
Lomax, Harvard 1922- *WhoAm 92*
Lomax, J.J.S. 1932- *WhoScE 91-1*
Lomax, John Avery 1867-1948 *Baker 92*
Lomax, John Avery 1875-1948 *BioIn 17*
Lomax, John Frank 1939- *St&PR 93*
Lomax, John H. 1924- *St&PR 93, WhoAm 92, WhoSSW 93*
Lomax, Louise E. 1922-1970 *EncAACR*
Lomax, Lunsford 1835-1913 *HarEnMi*
Lomax, Margaret Irene 1938- *WhoAmW 93*
Lomax, Michael L. 1947- *AfrAmBi [port]*
Lomax, Peggy Jean 1960- *WhoE 93*
Lomax, Suzanne Quillen 1958- *WhoAmW 93*
Lomba, F.J.G. 1933- *WhoScE 91-2*
Lombard, Alain 1940- *Baker 92*
Lombard, Carole 1908-1942 *BioIn 17, IntDcF 2-3 [port]*
Lombard, Guy 1940- *WhoWor 93*
Lombard, James Anthony, III 1955- *WhoEmL 93*
Lombard, James Raymond 1942- *WhoE 93*
Lombard, Lynn Marie 1951- *WhoAmW 93*
Lombard, Marcie Nan 1962- *WhoAmW 93*
Lombard, Mitchell Monte 1951- *WhoEmL 93, WhoSSW 93*
Lombard, Richard S. *Law&B 92*
Lombard, Richard Spencer 1928- *WhoAm 92*
Lombardi, Bonnell M. *Law&B 92*
Lombardi, Carl A. 1943- *St&PR 93*
Lombardi, Cornelius Ennis, Jr. 1926- *WhoAm 92*
Lombardi, Curtis Jay 1952- *WhoEmL 93*
Lombardi, David Richard 1949- *WhoEmL 93*
Lombardi, Elizabeth 1958- *WhoAmW 93*
Lombardi, Eugene Patsy 1923- *WhoAm 92*
Lombardi, Felipe Rojas- d1991 *BioIn 17*
Lombardi, Jeffrey 1962- *St&PR 93*
Lombardi, John Barba-Linardo 1915- *WhoAm 92*
Lombardi, John Joseph 1940- *St&PR 93*
Lombardi, John V. 1942- *WhoAm 92, WhoSSW 93*
Lombardi, Johnny *BioIn 17*
Lombardi, Louis, Jr. 1946- *St&PR 93, WhoIns 93*
Lombardi, Luca 1945- *Baker 92*
Lombardi, Menotti J., Jr. *Law&B 92*
Lombardi, Patrick Arnold 1950- *WhoEmL 93*
Lombardi, Vince *BioIn 17*
Lombardini-Sirmen, Maddalena Laura 1735-c. 1785 *Baker 92*
Lombardi-Stanko, Donna M. *Law&B 92*
Lombardo, Bonnie Jane 1941- *WhoAmW 93*
Lombardo, Catherine M. *Law&B 92*
Lombardo, Charles J. 1943- *St&PR 93*
Lombardo, Drew A. 1947- *St&PR 93*
Lombardo, Eugene Vincent 1938- *WhoAm 92*
Lombardo, Frank, Jr. 1936- *St&PR 93*
Lombardo, Gaetano 1940- *WhoAm 92, WhoWor 93*
Lombardo, Gary Anthony 1948- *WhoEmL 93*
Lombardo, Guy 1902-1977 *Baker 92*
Lombardo, Irene E. 1944- *WhoWrEP 92*
Lombardo, Jay Frank 1963- *WhoEmL 93*
Lombardo, Joe d1990 *BioIn 17*
Lombardo, John N. 1942- *WhoIns 93*
Lombardo, John Richard 1933- *St&PR 93*
Lombardo, Louis *MiSFD 9*
Lombardo, Michael John 1927- *WhoE 93, WhoWor 93*
Lombardo, N. *WhoScE 91-3*
Lombardo, Philip Joseph 1935- *WhoAm 92, WhoWor 93*
Lombardo, Robin Ann 1956- *WhoE 93*
Lombardo, Sisto 1948- *WhoScE 91-3*
Lombardo, Stephen John 1952- *WhoE 93*
Lombardo de Caso, Maria 1905-1964 *DcMexL*
Lombardo Toledano, Vicente *DcCPCAm*
Lombardo Trostorff, Danielle Maria 1951- *WhoEmL 93*
Lombino, Joseph *Law&B 92*
Lombolou, Edouard 1939- *WhoUN 92*
Lombra, Raymond Eugene 1946- *WhoAm 92*
Lombroso, Cesare 1835-1909 *IntDcAn*
L'Ome, Inonga Lokonga d1991 *BioIn 17*
Lomeli, Ann *Law&B 92*
Lomeli, Francisco A. 1947- *HispAmA*
Lomeli, Marta 1952- *WhoAmW 93, WhoEmL 93, WhoWor 93*
Lo Menzo, Mario *BioIn 17*
Lomicka, William Henry 1937- *WhoAm 92*
Lomma, Anthony C. 1958- *St&PR 93*
Lomma, Ralph J. 1926- *St&PR 93*
Lommatzsch, Ruth Myrtle 1913- *WhoWrEP 92*
Lommel, Ulli *MiSFD 9*
Lommel Halpern, Marsha 1947- *WhoAmW 93*
Lomnicki, Adam 1935- *WhoScE 91-4*
Lomnicki, Jan 1929- *DrEEuF*
Lomnicki, Tadeusz 1927- *IntDcF 2-3*
Lomnicki, Tadeusz Jan 1927- *WhoWor 93*
Lomo, Leif 1929- *St&PR 93, WhoAm 92*
Lomon, Earle Leonard 1930- *WhoAm 92*
Lomon, Ruth 1930- *Baker 92*
Lomonaco, Robert Anthony 1940- *St&PR 93*
Lomonosoff, James Marc 1951- *WhoAm 92*
Lomov, Boris Fiodorovich 1927-1989 *BioIn 17*
Lomov, Sergej Alecksandrovich 1922- *WhoWor 93*
Lompe, Klaus 1937- *WhoWor 93*
Lomurro, Donald Michael 1950- *WhoEmL 93*
Lonabocker, Louise Madore 1948- *WhoE 93*
Lonardo, Carmen Giuseppe 1963- *WhoE 93*
Lonati, Carlo Ambrogio c. 1645-c. 1710 *Baker 92*
Lonati, John, Jr. 1933- *St&PR 93*
Lonborg, James Reynold 1942- *WhoAm 92*
Loncraine, Richard 1946- *MiSFD 9*
Lond, Harley Weldon 1946- *WhoWrEP 92*
Londen, Jack 1929- *St&PR 93*
Londo, Ger 1935- *WhoScE 91-3*
London, Anne McKee 1955- *WhoAmW 93*
London, Barry Joseph 1946- *WhoAm 92*
London, Charles Stuart 1946- *WhoE 93, WhoEmL 93*
London, Charlotte Isabella 1946- *WhoEmL 93*
London, Cheryl Ann 1957- *WhoAmW 93, WhoEmL 93*

London, David Bruce 1948- *WhoE 93, WhoEmL 93*
London, Edwin 1929- *Baker 92*
London, Eleanor 1955- *WhoE 93*
London, Ephraim 1911-1990 *BioIn 17*
London, Eric S. 1952- *St&PR 93*
London, Fran 1950- *WhoWrEP 92*
London, George 1919-1985 *Baker 92, IntDcOp [port], OxDcOp*
London, Herbert Ira 1939- *WhoAm 92*
London, Irving Myer 1918- *WhoAm 92*
London, J. Phillip 1937- *St&PR 93, WhoAm 92*
London, Jack *MajAI*
London, Jack 1876-1916 *BioIn 17, GayN, MagSAmL [port], ScF&FL 92, WorLitC [port]*
London, Jack Edward 1949- *WhoEmL 93*
London, Jerry 1937- *MiSFD 9*
London, Jill Abbey 1953- *WhoEmL 93*
London, Joan 1901-1971 *BioIn 17*
London, John *ScF&FL 92*
London, John C. *Law&B 92*
London, John Griffith 1876-1916 *MajAI [port]*
London, Jonathan Paul 1947- *WhoWrEP 92*
London, Joseph J. *Law&B 92*
London, Leslie H. 1945- *St&PR 93*
London, Liz E. *WhoWrEP 92*
London, Lloyd Llewellyn 1920- *St&PR 93, WhoSSW 93*
London, Marina 1956- *WhoEmL 93*
London, Martin 1934- *WhoAm 92*
London, Meyer 1871-1926 *JeAmHC*
London, Michael Jeffrey 1952- *WhoE 93, WhoEmL 93*
London, Mimi *BioIn 17*
London, Perry d1992 *NewYTBS 92*
London, Perry 1931-1992 *ConAu 139*
London, Philip 1932- *St&PR 93*
London, Rhoda A. *Law&B 92*
London, Robin Sigman 1963- *WhoAmW 93*
London, Roy *MiSFD 9*
London, Stefanie L. *Law&B 92*
London, Theodore 1933- *St&PR 93*
London, W. Boyd, Jr. 1952- *St&PR 93*
London, W. Thomas 1944- *St&PR 93*
Londonderry, Marchioness of 1878-1959 *BioIn 17*
Londoner, David Jay 1937- *WhoAm 92*
Londre, Felicia Hardison 1941- *WhoWrEP 92*
Londrie, Barbara Sisson 1963- *WhoEmL 93*
Londroche, Gerald Clifford 1938- *WhoSSW 93*
Londynsky, Samuel 1921- *WhoE 93*
Lone, Jacqueline V. 1935- *WhoAmW 93*
Lone, M. Salim 1943- *WhoUN 92*
Lone, Mohammed Salim 1943- *WhoE 93*
Lone, Rita Joan 1938- *WhoAmW 93*
Lonegan, Thomas Lee 1932- *WhoWor 93*
Loneman, Richard Eugene 1953- *WhoEmL 93*
Lonergan, Francis d1991 *BioIn 17*
Lonergan, Grace E. *AmWomPl*
Lonergan, James D. 1925- *St&PR 93*
Lonergan, Mary Carolyn 1952- *WhoEmL 93*
Lonergan, Thomas Francis, III 1941- *WhoWor 93*
Lones, Gregory Sanford *Law&B 92*
Lones, Gregory Sanford 1959- *WhoEmL 93*
Lones, Robert Ian 1945- *WhoWor 93*
Loney, David *Law&B 92*
Loney, David Allen 1945- *WhoIns 93*
Loney, Glenn Meredith 1928- *WhoAm 92*
Loney, Robert Treulieb 1932- *St&PR 93*
Long, Adrian Ernest *WhoScE 91-1*
Long, Alfred B. 1909- *WhoSSW 93*
Long, Alvin W. 1923- *St&PR 93*
Long, Alvin William 1923- *WhoAm 92*
Long, Amelia Rose 1944- *WhoAmW 93*
Long, Andre Edwin 1957- *WhoEmL 93*
Long, Anna Maribeth 1960- *WhoEmL 93*
Long, Anthony Arthur 1937- *WhoAm 92*
Long, Bernard Jackson 1941- *St&PR 93*
Long, Bettye Virginia 1924- *WhoAmW 93*
Long, Beverly Glenn 1923- *WhoAm 92*
Long, Big Steve d1868 *BioIn 17*
Long, Brian *WhoScE 91-1*
Long, Bruce C. 1945- *St&PR 93*
Long, Carl Dean 1938- *WhoE 93*
Long, Carl Ferdinand 1928- *WhoAm 92*
Long, Catherine Small 1924- *BioIn 17*
Long, Cecil Lanier 1938- *WhoSSW 93*
Long, Cedric William 1937- *WhoE 93*
Long, Charles E. 1940- *WhoAm 92*
Long, Charles Farrell 1933- *WhoSSW 93*
Long, Charles Franklin 1938- *WhoAm 92, WhoWrEP 92*
Long, Charles Houston 1926- *WhoAm 92*
Long, Charles R. 1904-1978 *ScF&FL 92*
Long, Charles Thomas 1942- *WhoAm 92*
Long, Charles Walter 1931- *WhoSSW 93*
Long, Ciel M. 1936- *WhoE 93*
Long, Clarence E., III 1943- *St&PR 93*
Long, Clarence William 1917- *WhoAm 92*
Long, Dale 1926-1991 *BioIn 17*
Long, Dale Hawkins 1952- *WhoEmL 93*
Long, Dallas Crutcher, III 1940- *BiDAMSp 1989*
Long, David G. 1948- *WhoScE 91-1*
Long, David J. *Law&B 92*
Long, David Russell 1942- *WhoE 93*
Long, Diane Kathryn 1963- *WhoAmW 93*
Long, Donald Charles 1923- *St&PR 93*
Long, Donald E. *St&PR 93*
Long, Donald J. 1951- *St&PR 93*
Long, Donlin Martin 1934- *WhoAm 92*
Long, Dorothy ValJean Shepherd 1928- *WhoAmW 93*
Long, Doug *ScF&FL 92*
Long, Douglas Clark 1932- *WhoAm 92*
Long, Dreama Ann 1959- *WhoEmL 93*
Long, Duncan 1949- *ScF&FL 92*
Long, Durward 1930- *WhoAm 92*
Long, Earl K. *BioIn 17*
Long, Earl K. 1895-1960 *PolPar*
Long, Earlene Roberta 1938- *WhoWrEP 92*
Long, Edward A. 1927- *St&PR 93*
Long, Edward Arlo 1927- *WhoAm 92*
Long, Elizabeth Ann 1961- *WhoAmW 93*
Long, Enid Hammerman 1930- *WhoAmW 93*
Long, Erik L. 1951- *WhoSSW 93*
Long, Eugene Hudson 1908- *WhoWrEP 92*
Long, Eugene Thomas, III 1935- *WhoAm 92*
Long, Flynn Vincent, Jr. 1928- *WhoSSW 93*
Long, Francis Mark 1929- *WhoAm 92*
Long, Frank Belknap 1903- *ScF&FL 92*
Long, Frank Weathers 1906- *WhoWrEP 92*
Long, Franklin A. 1910- *WhoAm 92*
Long, Frederick Daniel 1946- *WhoSSW 93*
Long, G.E. 1944- *St&PR 93*
Long, G. Gordon 1953- *WhoWrEP 92*
Long, Gabrielle *ScF&FL 92*
Long, Gabrielle Gibbs 1942- *WhoAmW 93*
Long, Gary L. 1942- *St&PR 93*
Long, Gary Marvin 1949- *WhoEmL 93*
Long, Gertrude D. 1941- *WhoUN 92*
Long, Gilbert A. 1928- *WhoScE 91-2*
Long, Gretchen 1937- *St&PR 93*
Long, Harry W., Jr. *Law&B 92*
Long, Helen Halter *WhoAm 92*
Long, Helen Halter 1906- *WhoWrEP 92*
Long, Helen Simester 1929- *WhoAmW 93*
Long, Henry K., Jr. 1936- *St&PR 93*
Long, Herbert Strainge 1919- *WhoAm 92*
Long, Howard Charles 1918- *WhoAm 92*
Long, Huey 1893-1935 *PolPar*
Long, Huey Pierce 1893-1935 *BioIn 17, DcTwHis*
Long, I. A. *WhoAm 92*
Long, J. Craig *Law&B 92*
Long, Jackie B. 1956- *St&PR 93*
Long, James Alfred 1942- *WhoAm 92*
Long, James Alvin 1917- *WhoSSW 93*
Long, James Duncan 1925- *WhoSSW 93*
Long, James Sidney 1941- *WhoSSW 93*
Long, Janet Louise 1954- *WhoE 93*
Long, Jefferson Franklin 1836-1900 *BioIn 17*
Long, Jennifer Cervenka 1967- *WhoAmW 93*
Long, Jill 1952- *BioIn 17, CngDr 91*
Long, Jill Lynette 1952- *WhoAm 92, WhoAmW 93*
Long, Jim R. *Law&B 92*
Long, Joan Hazel 1952- *WhoE 93, WhoEmL 93*
Long, Joann Morey *WhoSSW 93*
Long, Joanna Ormiston 1922- *WhoWrEP 92*
Long, John *BioIn 17*
Long, John Allen 1919- *St&PR 93*
Long, John Arthur *ScF&FL 92*
Long, John Brian *WhoScE 91-1*
Long, John Broaddus, Jr. 1944- *WhoAm 92*
Long, John D. 1920- *WhoAm 92*
Long, John Douglas 1920- *WhoIns 93*
Long, John Franklin, Jr. 1953- *WhoSSW 93*
Long, John Holmes 1947- *WhoEmL 93*
Long, John Maloy 1925- *WhoAm 92*
Long, John Paul 1926- *WhoAm 92*
Long, Joseph Francis, II 1963- *WhoE 93*
Long, Joseph M. 1912-1990 *BioIn 17*
Long, Karen Marple *Law&B 92*
Long, Kathleen Ann 1947- *WhoAmW 93*
Long, Kathleen G. 1961- *St&PR 93*
Long, Kenneth Hammond 1946- *WhoSSW 93*
Long, Kenneth R. *Law&B 92*
Long, Kenneth Robert 1940- *St&PR 93, WhoAm 92*
Long, Kerry Blair 1950- *WhoEmL 93*
Long, Kerry Jean 1948- *WhoEmL 93*
Long, Kim 1949- *SmATA 69 [port]*
Long, Larry Clark 1950- *St&PR 93*
Long, Laura Louise 1951- *WhoEmL 93, WhoSSW 93*
Long, Lily Augusta d1927 *AmWomPl*
Long, Linda Ann 1952- *WhoEmL 93*
Long, Linda Ann 1953- *WhoEmL 93*
Long, Linnea *Law&B 92*
Long, Lorna E. 1944- *St&PR 93*
Long, Louise Chatel 1938- *WhoAmW 93*
Long, Lucinda Herron 1946- *WhoEmL 93*
Long, Lucinda P. *Law&B 92*
Long, Lyda Belknap *ScF&FL 92*
Long, Madeleine J. *WhoAm 92*
Long, Margaret Elaine 1947- *WhoEmL 93*
Long, Margaret S. 1947- *St&PR 93*
Long, Marguerite (Marie Charlotte) 1874-1966 *Baker 92*
Long, Marie Katherine 1925- *WhoAmW 93*
Long, Marilyn *WhoWrEP 92*
Long, Mark Alexander Dietterich 1954- *WhoSSW 93*
Long, Mark Earl 1950- *WhoSSW 93*
Long, Martha Ardelia 1913- *WhoWrEP 92*
Long, Maurice Wayne 1925- *WhoAm 92*
Long, Melvin Durward 1931- *WhoAm 92*
Long, Meredith J. 1928- *St&PR 93, WhoAm 92*
Long, Michael Howard 1956- *WhoE 93, WhoEmL 93*
Long, Michael T. *Law&B 92*
Long, Michael Thomas 1942- *St&PR 93, WhoAm 92*
Long, Mildred B. 1923- *St&PR 93*
Long, Molly A. 1945- *St&PR 93*
Long, Monroe W. 1921- *St&PR 93*
Long, Nancy Suttle 1935- *WhoSSW 93*
Long, Nichola Y. 1955- *WhoAmW 93*
Long, Norman Ernest 1936- *WhoScE 91-3*
Long, Norton Enneking 1910- *WhoAm 92*
Long, Opal Virginia 1945- *WhoSSW 93*
Long, Patricia Ann 1947- *WhoAmW 93*
Long, Patricia Irene 1946- *WhoAmW 93*
Long, Patrick Brien 1943- *St&PR 93, WhoAm 92*
Long, Patrick Kevin 1950- *St&PR 93*
Long, Perrin H., Jr. *WhoAm 92*
Long, Peter P. 1928- *St&PR 93*
Long, Peter Robert 1946- *WhoWor 93*
Long, Phillip Clifford 1942- *St&PR 93, WhoAm 92*
Long, Phyllis W. *Law&B 92*
Long, R. Gregory 1960- *WhoEmL 93*
Long, R. Kenneth 1922- *St&PR 93*
Long, Raiford N. 1925- *St&PR 93*
Long, Randall G. 1958- *St&PR 93*
Long, Richard 1945- *BioIn 17*
Long, Richard A. 1949- *St&PR 93*
Long, Richard Allan 1940- *WhoWor 93*
Long, Richard Brian 1966- *WhoSSW 93*
Long, Richard C. 1953- *WhoEmL 93*
Long, Richard John 1942- *St&PR 93*
Long, Richard Louis, Jr. 1947- *WhoEmL 93*
Long, Richard Paul 1934- *WhoAm 92*
Long, Robert 1954- *WhoWrEP 92*
Long, Robert A., Jr. *Law&B 92*
Long, Robert D. *St&PR 93*
Long, Robert Douglas *WhoAm 92*
Long, Robert Emmet 1934- *WhoAm 92*
Long, Robert Eugene 1931- *WhoAm 92*
Long, Robert G. 1912- *St&PR 93*
Long, Robert Hill 1952- *WhoWrEP 92*
Long, Robert J. 1927- *St&PR 93*
Long, Robert L. 1937- *St&PR 93*
Long, Robert Lyman John 1920- *WhoAm 92*
Long, Robert Merrill 1938- *St&PR 93, WhoAm 92*
Long, Robert Radcliffe 1919- *WhoAm 92*
Long, Ronald Alex 1948- *WhoE 93*
Long, Rose McConnell 1892-1970 *BioIn 17*
Long, Ruilin 1939- *WhoWor 93*
Long, Russell B. 1918- *PolPar*
Long, Russell E. 1959- *St&PR 93*
Long, Russell S. *Law&B 92*
Long, Samuel Byron 1951- *WhoEmL 93, WhoSSW 93*
Long, Sarah Ann 1943- *WhoAm 92*
Long, Sarah Elizabeth Brackney 1926- *WhoAmW 93*
Long, Sarah Patricia 1954- *WhoAmW 93*
Long, Shari Denise 1968- *WhoAmW 93*
Long, Sharon Hope 1946- *WhoAmW 93*
Long, Sharon R. *BioIn 17*
Long, Sharon Rugel 1951- *WhoAm 92, WhoAmW 93*
Long, Sheila Ann 1955- *WhoAmW 93*
Long, Shelley *WhoAm 92*
Long, Shelley 1949- *HolBB [port], QDrFCA 92 [port], WhoAmW 93*
Long, Shirley Dobbins 1943- *WhoWrEP 92*
Long, Stephen 1784-1864 *Expl 93*
Long, Stephen D. *Law&B 92*
Long, Steven K. *Law&B 92*
Long, Susan Bea 1961- *WhoAmW 93*
Long, Susan Grafeld 1951- *WhoWrEP 92*
Long, Susan Osborne 1959- *WhoSSW 93*
Long, Susan Webb 1946- *WhoEmL 93, WhoSSW 93*
Long, Suzanna Maupin 1961- *WhoAmW 93*
Long, Thad Gladden 1938- *WhoWor 93*
Long, Theodore T. *Law&B 92*
Long, Thomas E. 1944- *WhoIns 93*
Long, Thomas G. 1935- *St&PR 93*
Long, Thomas J. 1910- *St&PR 93*
Long, Thomas J. 1915- *St&PR 93*
Long, Thomas R. *Law&B 92*
Long, Thomas R. 1930- *St&PR 93*
Long, Thomas Ross 1929- *WhoSSW 93*
Long, Tim *Law&B 92*
Long, Tom 1932- *St&PR 93, WhoAm 92*
Long, Vicki *BioIn 17*
Long, Vonda Olson 1947- *WhoAmW 93*
Long, Walter 1927- *St&PR 93*
Long, Walter Edward 1935- *WhoAm 92*
Long, William A. 1950- *St&PR 93*
Long, William Allan 1928- *St&PR 93, WhoAm 92*
Long, William Artee, Jr. 1950- *WhoEmL 93*
Long, William B. *Law&B 92*
Long, William Everett 1919- *WhoAm 92*
Long, William McMurray 1948- *WhoWor 93*
Long, William Michael 1952- *St&PR 93*
Long, William Penuel, Jr. 1944- *WhoE 93*
Long, Willis Franklin 1934- *WhoAm 92*
Long, Yiming 1948- *WhoWor 93*
Longabaugh, Harry 1861?-1908 *BioIn 17*
Longacre, Daniel E. 1912- *St&PR 93*
Longacre, David Evans 1958- *WhoEmL 93*
Longacre, William 1963- *St&PR 93*
Longair, Malcolm S. 1941- *WhoScE 91-1*
Longair, Malcolm Sim 1941- *WhoWor 93*
Longaker, D. Garry 1941- *St&PR 93*
Longaker, Richard Pancoast 1924- *WhoAm 92*
Longaker, Robert George, II *Law&B 92*
Longar, Mark William 1950- *WhoEmL 93*
Longardner, Craig Theodor 1955- *WhoEmL 93*
Longarzo, Jerry A., Jr. *Law&B 92*
Longas, Federico 1893-1968 *Baker 92*
Longbrake, William A. 1943- *St&PR 93*
Longbrake, William Arthur 1943- *WhoAm 92*
Longchampt, Michel Jean-Marie 1934- *St&PR 93*
Longcope, Christopher 1928- *WhoE 93*
Longden, Albert Teshon 1946- *St&PR 93*
Longden, Claire Suzanne 1938- *WhoAmW 93*
Longe, Kevin Thomas 1959- *St&PR 93*
Longenecker, Herbert Eugene 1912- *WhoAm 92*
Longenecker, John Oakley 1947- *WhoEmL 93*
Longenecker, Justin G. 1917- *WhoSSW 93*
Longenecker, Margaret Ann 1925- *WhoAmW 93*
Longenecker, Mark H. *Law&B 92*
Longer, Janice Martino 1955- *St&PR 93*
Longest-Slaughter, Helen Vezelma 1944- *WhoSSW 93*
Longeteig, Iver J. 1941- *WhoWrEP 92*
Longeval, Emile 1947- *WhoScE 91-2*
Long Family *BioIn 17*
Longfellow, Harold E. 1927- *St&PR 93*
Longfellow, Henry Wadsworth 1807-1882 *MagSAmL [port]*
Longfield, Bradley J(ames) 1955- *ConAu 139*
Longfield, Craig N. 1945- *St&PR 93*
Longfield, John W. 1949- *St&PR 93*
Longfield, Ross Nicol 1940- *St&PR 93*
Longfield, William Herman 1938- *WhoAm 92*
Longford, Countess of 1906- *BioIn 17*
Longhofer, Ronald Stephen 1946- *WhoEmL 93*
Longhurst, Robert R., III 1927- *St&PR 93*
Longhurst, Robert Russell 1921- *WhoSSW 93, WhoWor 93*
Longhurst, Suzanne Elizabeth 1958- *WhoWrEP 92*
Longin, Thomas Charles 1939- *WhoAm 92*
Longino, Grady Estes 1923- *WhoSSW 93*
Longinotti, Mary Angela 1949- *WhoAmW 93*
Longinovic, Tomislav Z. 1955- *WhoWrEP 92*
Longinus, Flavius d499 *HarEnMi*
Long-Jeffries, Angela Sue 1964- *WhoAmW 93*
Longland, Jean Rogers 1913- *WhoWrEP 92*
Longley, Alice Beebe 1948- *WhoEmL 93*
Longley, Bernique 1923- *BioIn 17, WhoAm 92*

Longley, Christopher Quentin Mori 1961- *WhoWor 93*
Longley, Diane Gene 1937- *WhoWrEP 92*
Longley, J. *WhoScE 91-1*
Longley, James B. 1925-1980 *PolPar*
Longley, James Wildon 1913- *WhoE 93, WhoWor 93*
Longley, Laura Ann 1948- *WhoWrEP 92*
Longley, Luc *BioIn 17*
Longley, Marjorie Watters 1925- *WhoAm 92, WhoWor 93*
Longley, Michael 1939- *BioIn 17*
Longley, Mitch *BioIn 17*
Longley, Robert Benton, Jr. 1964- *WhoSSW 93*
Longley, William P. 1851-1877? *BioIn 17*
Longman, Gary Lee 1948- *WhoAm 92*
Longman, Kenneth Alan *WhoScE 91-1*
Longman, P.A. 1945- *WhoScE 91-1*
Longman, Richard Winston 1943- *WhoAm 92*
Longmire, Paul *BioIn 17*
Longmire, William Polk, Jr. 1913- *WhoAm 92*
Longmoore, John T. 1934- *St&PR 93*
Longmore, George 1793?-1867 *BioIn 17*
Longnaker, John L. 1926- *St&PR 93*
Longnaker, John Leonard 1926- *WhoAm 92*
Longnecker, Beth Anne 1956- *WhoAmW 93, WhoEmL 93*
Longnecker, David E. 1939- *WhoAm 92*
Longnecker, Edna B. *AmWomPl*
Longnion, Bonnie Lee 1948- *WhoAmW 93, WhoSSW 93*
Longo, Achille 1900-1954 *Baker 92*
Longo, Alessandro 1864-1945 *Baker 92*
Longo, Charles Michael 1942- *St&PR 93*
Longo, Chris *ScF&FL 92*
Longo, Dan Louis 1949- *WhoE 93*
Longo, Dennis 1945- *St&PR 93*
Longo, Joseph Thomas 1942- *WhoAm 92*
Longo, Kathryn Milani 1946- *WhoE 93*
Longo, Lawrence Daniel 1926- *WhoAm 92*
Longo, Patti Jean 1954- *WhoSSW 93*
Longo, Paul 1934- *WhoE 93*
Longo, Richard Anthony 1952- *WhoE 93*
Longo, Robert *BioIn 17*
Longo, Robin Weisbarth 1954- *WhoE 93*
Longo, Ronald Anthony 1952- *WhoEmL 93*
Longo, Vincenzo G. 1925- *WhoScE 91-3*
Longobardi, AnitaRose Teresa 1961- *WhoEmL 93*
Longobardi, Joseph J. *WhoAm 92, WhoE 93*
Longobardi, Nino 1953- *BioIn 17*
Longobardi, Patrizia G. 1954- *WhoWor 93*
Longobardo, Guy Alfred 1961- *WhoEmL 93*
Longo-Muth, Linda Louise 1948- *WhoE 93*
Longone, Daniel Thomas 1932- *WhoAm 92*
Longoria, Felix *BioIn 17*
Longoria, Malvina *Law&B 92*
Longridge, John Charles 1937- *St&PR 93*
Longrigg, Roger *ScF&FL 92*
Longsderff, Richard William 1934- *St&PR 93*
Longshore, June Usry 1934- *WhoAmW 93*
Longson, Donald E. 1941- *WhoIns 93*
Longstreet, James 1821-1904 *BioIn 17, HarEnMi*
Longstreet, Roxanne *ScF&FL 92*
Longstreet, Stephen 1907- *WhoAm 92*
Longstreet, Victor Mendell 1907- *WhoAm 92*
Longstreth, Susan 1946- *WhoAmW 93, WhoEmL 93*
Longstreth, T. Morris 1886-1975 *ScF&FL 92*
Longstreth, Thacher *BioIn 17*
Longstreth, William Thacher 1920- *St&PR 93*
Longsworth, Charles R. 1929- *WhoAm 92*
Longsworth, Charles Robert 1929- *St&PR 93*
Longsworth, Eileen Catherine 1950- *WhoAmW 93*
Longsworth, Ellen Louise 1949- *WhoAmW 93, WhoEmL 93*
Longsworth, Gerald Grant 1959- *WhoEmL 93*
Long-Tims, Marilyn Virginia 1940- *WhoWrEP 92*
Longtin, Cheryl Joy 1948- *St&PR 93, WhoEmL 93*
Longto, Frank J. 1940- *St&PR 93*
Longuemard, Jean-Paul 1940- *WhoScE 91-2*
Longuet, Gregory Arthur 1945- *WhoSSW 93*
Longuet, Jean 1876-1938 *BioIn 17*
Longuet-Higgins, Hugh Christopher *WhoScE 91-1*
Longuet-Higgins, Michael Selwyn *WhoScE 91-1*
Longueville, Jacques Joseph 1935- *WhoWor 93*
Longus, Tiberius Sempronius d210BC *HarEnMi*
Longval, Gaston 1937- *St&PR 93*
Long Val, Nathalie *Law&B 92*
Longway, A. Hugh *ConAu 137, MajAI*
Longwell, Dennis Charles 1941- *St&PR 93*
Longwell, John Ploeger 1918- *WhoAm 92*
Longworth, David S. 1934- *St&PR 93*
Longworth, Nicholas 1869-1931 *PolPar*
Longworth, Richard Cole 1935- *WhoAm 92*
Longy, (Gustave-) Georges (-Leopold) 1868-1930 *Baker 92*
Longyear, Barry B. *BioIn 17*
Longyear, Barry B. 1942- *ScF&FL 92*
Longyear, Caroline Judkins *AmWomPl*
Longyear, John Paul 1949- *St&PR 93*
Longyear, Russell Hammond 1935- *St&PR 93, WhoAm 92*
Lonigan, Paul Raymond 1935- *WhoWrEP 92*
Lo Nigro, S. *WhoScE 91-3*
Lonkart, Georgia Faith 1947- *WhoAmW 93, WhoE 93, WhoEmL 93*
Lonker, Arthur 1917- *St&PR 93*
Lonnberg, K. Bruno 1940- *WhoScE 91-4*
Lonnebotn, Trygve 1937- *St&PR 93*
Lonneke, Michael Dean 1943- *WhoAm 92*
Lonner, Joseph 1928- *St&PR 93*
Lonngren, Karl Erik 1938- *WhoAm 92*
Lonning, Inge Johan 1938- *WhoWor 93*
Lon Nol 1913-1985 *DcTwHis*
Lonnquist, George Eric 1946- *WhoAm 92, WhoEmL 93*
Lonnqvist, Jouko K. 1943- *WhoScE 91-4*
Lono, John Mark 1942- *WhoSSW 93*
Lonque, Georges 1900-1967 *Baker 92*
Lonquist, Bert Arthur 1926- *WhoAm 92*
Lonsdale, Earl of 1857-1944 *BioIn 17*
Lonsdale, G.F. 1932- *St&PR 93*
Lonsdale, Helen Lea *AmWomPl*
Lonsdale, Jorge d1990 *BioIn 17*
Lonsdale, Judith A. *Law&B 92*
Lonsdale, Pamela *ScF&FL 92*
Lonsdale-Hands, Richard de Prilleux 1953- *WhoWor 93*
Lonsdorf, Joseph Charles 1937- *WhoSSW 93*
Lonsford, Florence Elizabeth Hutchinson 1914- *WhoE 93*
Lonson, Thomas J. 1937- *St&PR 93*
Lonsted, Knud 1942- *WhoWor 93*
Lontoc, Jorge Pacheco 1936- *WhoWor 93*
Loo, Beverly Jane *WhoAm 92*
Looby, Patrick A. *Law&B 92*
Looft, Walter Gene 1938- *St&PR 93*
Look, Alice 1952- *WhoAmW 93*
Look, Barbara *AmWomPl*
Look, Bradley Michael 1959- *WhoEmL 93*
Look, Donald M. *St&PR 93*
Look, Vivian Ann *WhoAmW 93*
Lookabill, Reid Davis 1949- *St&PR 93*
Looker, Terence *WhoScE 91-1*
Lookinland, Mike 1960- *BioIn 17*
Loomans, Leslie Louis 1943- *St&PR 93*
Loomes, Graham Christopher *WhoScE 91-1*
Loomes, Martin James *WhoScE 91-1*
Loomis, Alfred Lee, Jr. 1913- *St&PR 93*
Loomis, Bernard 1923- *St&PR 93*
Loomis, Carol J. 1929- *WhoAmW 93*
Loomis, Charles W. *Law&B 92*
Loomis, Christopher Knapp 1947- *WhoEmL 93, WhoWor 93*
Loomis, Christopher R. *Law&B 92*
Loomis, Clarence 1889-1965 *Baker 92*
Loomis, Craig Alan 1952- *St&PR 93*
Loomis, Dale Susan *Law&B 92*
Loomis, David Lawrence 1945- *WhoSSW 93*
Loomis, Frederick Pierson 1950- *WhoSSW 93*
Loomis, Gregg *ScF&FL 92*
Loomis, Harvey Worthington 1865-1930 *Baker 92*
Loomis, Henry 1919- *WhoAm 92*
Loomis, Howard Krey 1927- *WhoAm 92, WhoWor 93*
Loomis, Jacqueline Chalmers 1930- *WhoAmW 93*
Loomis, James Richard 1926- *St&PR 93*
Loomis, Jan 1944- *WhoWrEP 92*
Loomis, John Norman 1933- *WhoWor 93*
Loomis, L.C. *Law&B 92*
Loomis, L. Rodger 1951- *St&PR 93*
Loomis, Lee Rodger 1951- *WhoE 93*
Loomis, Mary Ellen 1929- *WhoAmW 93*
Loomis, Philip Clark 1926- *WhoAm 92*
Loomis, Priscilla Lockwood d1990 *BioIn 17*
Loomis, Ralph E. *Law&B 92*
Loomis, Robert Duane 1926- *WhoAm 92*
Loomis, Robert Strother 1955- *St&PR 93*
Loomis, Ronald Earl 1954- *WhoE 93*
Loomis, Sabra 1937- *WhoWrEP 92*
Loomis, Stephen P. 1960- *St&PR 93*
Loomis, Wesley Horace, III 1913- *WhoAm 92, WhoWor 93*
Loomis, Worth 1923- *St&PR 93, WhoAm 92*
Loonan, Joseph I. *Law&B 92*
Loonen, Anton Joseph Maria 1953- *WhoWor 93*
Looney, Anthony Glen 1949- *St&PR 93*
Looney, Arthur J. 1939- *St&PR 93*
Looney, Claudia Arlene 1946- *WhoEmL 93*
Looney, Dennis Joseph, Jr. 1934- *WhoIns 93*
Looney, Dennis Matthew 1954- *WhoAm 92*
Looney, H. Ray 1935- *St&PR 93*
Looney, J. Anna 1951- *WhoEmL 93*
Looney, Jack *ScF&FL 92*
Looney, John Joseph *St&PR 93*
Looney, Marlene J. 1959- *WhoEmL 93*
Looney, Norman Earl 1938- *WhoAm 92*
Looney, Patrick Steven *Law&B 92*
Looney, Patrick Steven 1950- *WhoEmL 93*
Looney, Ralph 1927- *St&PR 93*
Looney, Ralph Edwin 1924- *WhoAm 92, WhoWor 93*
Looney, Robert Joseph *Law&B 92*
Looney, Ronald Lee 1956- *WhoEmL 93, WhoSSW 93*
Looney, Terry J. 1954- *St&PR 93*
Looney, William Boyd 1922- *WhoSSW 93*
Looney, William D. 1951- *St&PR 93*
Looney, William Francis, Jr. 1931- *WhoAm 92, WhoE 93, WhoWor 93*
Loop, Floyd D. 1936- *WhoAm 92*
Loop, Gary Gordon 1950- *WhoSSW 93*
Looper, Charles B. 1931- *St&PR 93*
Looper, Loretta B. *Law&B 92*
Looper, Valerie E. *Law&B 92*
Looper-Fago, Annette Marie 1960- *WhoEmL 93*
Loori, Phillip E. *St&PR 93*
Loory, Stuart Hugh 1932- *WhoAm 92*
Loos, A.W. 1928- *St&PR 93*
Loos, A. William 1908-1992 *BioIn 17*
Loos, Adolf 1870-1933 *BioIn 17*
Loos, Anita 1888?-1981 *AmWomPl*
Loos, Anita 1894-1981 *BioIn 17*
Loos, Carole Marie 1946- *St&PR 93*
Loos, Jackie Jaynine 1960- *WhoEmL 93*
Loos, John Thompson 1947- *WhoSSW 93*
Loos, Karl D. 1950- *St&PR 93*
Loos, Robert Willis, III 1958- *WhoEmL 93*
Loose, Emmy 1914-1987 *Baker 92*
Loose, John W. 1942- *St&PR 93*
Loose, Thomas A. *Law&B 92*
Loose, Thomas Arthur 1932- *St&PR 93*
Loosemore, Craig Steven 1947- *St&PR 93*
Loosemore, Kevin Michael 1952- *St&PR 93*
Looser, Donald William 1939- *WhoSSW 93*
Looser, Rolf 1920- *Baker 92*
Loosley, Grace K. *AmWomPl*
Loosley, Janine Elisabeth 1962- *WhoEmL 93*
Loosley, William Robert *ScF&FL 92*
Loosli, Heinz Hugo *WhoScE 91-4*
Loosli, Stuart 1939- *St&PR 93*
Lootens, James B. *Law&B 92*
Loots, Barbara Kunz 1946- *WhoEmL 93*
Loots, James Mason 1958- *WhoEmL 93*
Looye, Johanna Wilhelmina 1956- *WhoAmW 93*
Lopach, Dennis R. *Law&B 92*
Lopach, James Joseph 1942- *WhoAm 92*
Lopaciuk, Stanislaw K. 1935- *WhoScE 91-4*
Lopacki, Edward Joseph, Jr. 1947- *WhoSSW 93*
Lopacki, Joan Marie 1957- *WhoAmW 93, WhoEmL 93*
Lopadiotes, Andrew fl. c. 1300-1330 *OxDcByz*
Lopardo, Donald Leonard 1947- *St&PR 93*
Lopat, Eddie d1992 *NewYTBS 92 [port]*
Lopat, Edmund Walter 1918- *BiDAMSp 1989*
Lopata, Edwin L. 1909- *St&PR 93*
Lopata, Helena Znaniecka *BioIn 17*
Lopata, Helena Znaniecka 1925- *WhoAm 92*
Lopata, James Randolph 1945- *St&PR 93*
Lopata, Martin Barry 1939- *WhoWor 93*
Lopata, Stanley L. 1914- *St&PR 93*
Lopate, Phillip 1943- *BioIn 17*
Lopategui, Eduardo M. 1949- *St&PR 93*
Lopatin, Judy 1954- *WhoWrEP 92*
Lopatnikoff, Nicolai 1903-1976 *Baker 92*
Lopato, Esther Wolf 1920- *WhoAmW 93*
Lopatynski, Edmund Walter *BiDAMSp 1989*
Lopdrup, Kjeld Emil 1927- *WhoSSW 93*
Lope Abdul Aziz, Ahmad Ali 1935- *WhoWor 93*
Lopeman, Janice *Law&B 92*
Loper, Candice Kay 1953- *WhoAmW 93*
Loper, Carl Richard, Jr. 1932- *WhoAm 92*
Loper, Charlene Marie 1958- *WhoAmW 93, WhoEmL 93*
Loper, James Leaders 1931- *WhoAm 92*
Loper, Janet Swanson 1934- *WhoAmW 93*
Loper, John Robert 1951- *WhoE 93*
Loper, Linda Sue 1945- *WhoSSW 93*
Loper, Mark Warren 1954- *St&PR 93*
Loper, Merle William 1940- *WhoAm 92*
Loper, Robert Bruce 1925- *WhoAm 92*
Loper, Stewart Collins 1948- *WhoEmL 93*
Loper, Warren Edward 1929- *WhoWor 93*
Lopes, David Earl 1945- *BiDAMSp 1989*
Lopes, Henri 1937- *WhoUN 92*
Lopes, Ignacio Brandao *ScF&FL 92*
Lopes, James Joseph 1952- *St&PR 93*
Lopes, Lola Lynn 1941- *WhoAm 92, WhoAmW 93*
Lopes, Maria Fernandina 1934- *WhoAmW 93*
Lopes, Martinho da Costa d1991 *BioIn 17*
Lopes, Myra Amelia 1931- *WhoAmW 93*
Lopes, Rafael M. 1966- *WhoEmL 93*
Lopes-Graca, Fernando 1906- *Baker 92*
Lopes Rato Rodrigues De Carvalho, Isabel Maria 1960- *WhoScE 91-3*
Lopes Xavier, Antonio Dos Santos 1940- *WhoScE 91-3*
Lopez, Aaron 1731-1782 *BioIn 17*
Lopez, Al 1908- *HispAmA*
Lopez, Al Ignatius G. 1962- *WhoAsAP 91*
Lopez, Alberto J. 1932- *WhoAsAP 91*
Lopez, Alfonso 1913- *DcTwHis*
Lopez, Alfred L. 1931- *St&PR 93*
Lopez, Alfred R. *WhoAm 92*
Lopez, Amando d1989 *BioIn 17*
Lopez, Antoinette Sedillo 1957- *WhoEmL 93*
Lopez, Antonio Vincent 1938- *WhoSSW 93*
Lopez, Aurelio d1992 *NewYTBS 92*
Lopez, Barry 1945- *Au&Arts 9 [port], ScF&FL 92*
Lopez, Barry Holstun 1945- *BioIn 17, WhoAm 92, WhoWrEP 92*
Lopez, Benito Moleiro, Jr. 1933- *WhoAm 92*
Lopez, Beverly R. *Law&B 92*
Lopez, Candido *BioIn 17*
Lopez, Carlos 1908-1953 *HispAmA*
Lopez, Carolyn Catherine 1951- *WhoEmL 93*
Lopez, David Barwis *Law&B 92*
Lopez, David Barwis 1938- *St&PR 93*
Lopez, David Tiburcio 1939- *WhoSSW 93, WhoWor 93*
Lopez, Diana 1948- *NotHsAW 93*
Lopez, Diana Montes de Oca 1937- *HispAmA*
Lopez, Dick *BioIn 17*
Lopez, Edward J. *Law&B 92*
Lopez, Enrique Angel 1940- *St&PR 93*
Lopez, Enrique Hank 1920-1985 *ScF&FL 92*
Lopez, Felix A. 1942- *HispAmA*
Lopez, Gabriel *Law&B 92*
Lopez, George 1925- *HispAmA*
Lopez, George Mario 1967- *WhoEmL 93*
Lopez, Gerald P. 1948- *HispAmA*
Lopez, Gerardo Daniel 1951- *WhoWor 93*
Lopez, German 1933- *St&PR 93*
Lopez, Hector *WhoSSW 93*
Lopez, Israel 1918?- *BioIn 17*
Lopez, Jack, Jr. 1953- *WhoEmL 93, WhoSSW 93, WhoWor 93*
Lopez, Jaime C. 1934- *WhoAsAP 91*
Lopez, Jo Willa Gramling *Law&B 92*
Lopez, Joaquin Lopez y d1989 *BioIn 17*
Lopez, John H. *Law&B 92*
Lopez, Jose Dolores 1868-1937 *HispAmA*
Lopez, Jose Manuel 1948- *WhoEmL 93*
Lopez, Jose Salazar 1910-1991 *BioIn 17*
Lopez, Josefina 1969?- *NotHsAW 93*
Lopez, Joseph Anthony 1951- *St&PR 93*
Lopez, Joseph B. 1931- *St&PR 93*
Lopez, Joseph Jack 1932- *WhoE 93*
Lopez, Judith Carroll *Law&B 92*
Lopez, Kay Strickland 1946- *WhoAmW 93*
Lopez, Laura 1957- *ConAu 136*
Lopez, Lourdes 1958- *NotHsAW 93, WhoAm 92*
Lopez, Manuel D. d1991 *BioIn 17*
Lopez, Manuel Dennis 1934- *WhoWrEP 92*
Lopez, Mara Awilda 1951- *NotHsAW 93*
Lopez, Maria Cristina 1944- *NotHsAW 93*
Lopez, Mauricio Antonio 1960- *St&PR 93*
Lopez, Maxine 1942- *WhoAmW 93*
Lopez, Nancy 1957- *BioIn 17, HispAmA [port], NotHsAW 93 [port], WhoAm 92, WhoAmW 93*
Lopez, Priscilla 1948- *NotHsAW 93 [port], WhoAm 92*
Lopez, Rafael 1873-1943 *DcMexL*
Lopez, Ralph Ivan 1942- *WhoE 93*

Lopez, Ramon 1933- St&PR 93
Lopez, Ramon Moleiro 1937- St&PR 93
Lopez, Raoul 1952- St&PR 93
Lopez, Raul Padilla 1954- WhoWor 93
Lopez, Raymond Michael 1959- WhoWrEP 92
Lopez, Remi 1939- WhoWor 93
Lopez, Robert 1961- BioIn 17
Lopez, Rubens 1938- WhoScE 91-3
Lopez, Sally Ann 1958- WhoAmW 93
Lopez, Tami Lynn Law&B 92
Lopez, Temistocles MiSFD 9
Lopez, Thomas Lee 1959- WhoSSW 93
Lopez, Thomas Samuel 1948- WhoSSW 93
Lopez, Tony 1950- WhoWor 93
Lopez, Vincent (Joseph) 1894-1975 Baker 92
Lopez, Vincent Joseph Michael 1953- St&PR 93
Lopez, Wilma I. 1938- St&PR 93
Lopez, Yolanda 1942- HispAmA
Lopez Albujar, Enrique 1872-1966 SpAmA
Lopez Arellano, Oswaldo 1921- DcCPCAm
Lopez Arroyo, Manuel WhoScE 91-3
Lopez Barreiro, Jose Benito 1959- WhoWor 93
Lopez-Bellido, Luis 1942- WhoWor 93
Lopez-Buchardo, Carlos 1881-1948 Baker 92
Lopez-Cacicedo, C.L. WhoScE 91-1
Lopez-Calo, Jose 1922- Baker 92
Lopez Chinas, Gabriel 1911- DcMexL
Lopez-Cobos, Jesus 1940- Baker 92, WhoAm 92
Lopez-Cotarelo, Villaamil Jesus 1933- WhoUN 92
Lopez del Castillo, Gerardo HispAmA
Lopez De Mantaras, Ramon 1952- WhoScE 91-3, WhoWor 93
Lopez De Vinaspre Urquiola, Teodoro 1939- WhoWor 93
Lopez Fuentes, Hector Mario DcCPCAm
Lopez Garcia, Antonio BioIn 17
Lopez-Garrido, A.C. 1943- WhoScE 91-3
Lopez Gonzalez, Gines A. 1950- WhoScE 91-3
Lopez-Gonzalez, Juan de Dios 1924- WhoWor 93
Lopez Gorge, Julio 1935- WhoScE 91-3
Lopez-Hernandez, Ivan Danilo 1943- WhoWor 93
Lopez Mateos, Adolfo 1910-1969 DcTwHis
Lopez Mateos, Adolfo 1911-1970 DcCPCAm
Lopez Morales, Gloria 1940- WhoUN 92
Lopez-Moratalla, Natalia 1946- WhoScE 91-3
Lopez-Morillas, Juan 1913- WhoAm 92
Lopez-Munoz, Maria Rosa P. 1938- WhoAmW 93
Lopez Nuila, Reynaldo DcCPCAm
Lopez-Oliver, Rosa Maria 1963- WhoWor 93
Lopez-Olvera, Josefina Law&B 92
Lopez Paez, Jorge 1922- DcMexL
Lopez-Penela, Juan Antonio 1932- WhoUN 92
Lopez Perez, Rigoberto DcCPCAm
Lopez-Pina, Antonio 1937- WhoWor 93
Lopez-Pineiro, Angel 1954- WhoWor 93
Lopez-Polo, Clemente 1934- WhoUN 92
Lopez Portillo, Jose 1920- DcTwHis
Lopez-Portillo, Jose Ramon 1954- WhoWor 93
Lopez Portillo y Pacheco, Jose 1920- DcCPCAm
Lopez Portillo y Rojas, Jose 1850-1923 DcMexL
Lopez Reyes, Walter DcCPCAm
Lopez-Rios, Tomas 1946- WhoWor 93
Lopez Rivera, Oscar DcCPCAm
Lopez Rodriguez, Nicolas de Jesus Cardinal 1936- WhoWor 93
Lopez-Romano, Sylvia Silva 1937- WhoAmW 93
Lopez-Romo, Daniel Francisco 1945- WhoAm 92
Lopez-Ruiz, Jose 1942- WhoScE 91-3
Lopez-Soler, Angel 1940- WhoScE 91-3
Lopez Trujillo, Alfonso DcCPCAm
Lopez Trujillo, Alfonso Cardinal 1935- WhoWor 93
Lopez Velarde, Ramon 1888-1921 DcMexL
Lopez-Vito, Rafael J. WhoAsAP 91
Lopez y Fuentes, Gregorio 1897-1966 DcMexL
Lopez y Lopez, Joaquin d1989 BioIn 17
Lopiano, Donna A. BioIn 17
Lo Piccolo, Charles Joseph 1954- WhoEmL 93
LoPiccolo, Frank A. 1943- St&PR 93
LoPiccolo, Joseph 1943- WhoAm 92
Lopienski, Jan 1838-1907 PolBiDi
Lopina, Lawrence Thomas 1930- St&PR 93, WhoAm 92
LoPinto, Joseph Michael 1958- WhoE 93
Lopker, Anita Mae 1955- WhoAmW 93, WhoE 93, WhoEmL 93
Lopmeier, F.-J. WhoScE 91-3
Lopokov, Fyodor Vasilievich 1887?-1973 BioIn 17
Lopokova, Lydia 1892-1981 BioIn 17
Lopp, Susan Jane 1944- WhoAmW 93
Lopp, Walter James d1990 BioIn 17
Loppnow, Harald 1954- WhoWor 93
Loppnow, Horst 1927- WhoScE 91-3
Loppnow, Milo Alvin 1914- WhoAm 92
Lopreato, Joseph 1928- WhoAm 92, WhoWor 93
Lopresti, Philip Vincent 1932- WhoAm 92
Lopresti, Robert 1954- ConAu 137
Lo Presti, Ronald 1933- Baker 92
LoPrete, James Hugh 1929- WhoAm 92
Lopukhov, Fyodor Vasilievich 1887?-1973 BioIn 17
Lopukhova, Ludmila A. WhoAm 92
Lopusanskij, Konstantin 1947- DrEEuF
Lopuski, Jan 1917- WhoWor 93
Lopuszanski, Jan Tadeusz 1923- WhoScE 91-4
Loquasto, Santo WhoAm 92, WhoE 93
Loquasto, Santo 1944- BioIn 17
Lorah, Clay L. 1935- St&PR 93
Loraine, Philip ScF&FL 92
Loran, Carlos Anthony 1945- WhoAm 92
Loran, Erle 1905- WhoAm 92
Loran, Haim 1932- St&PR 93
Loran, Jason D. WhoWrEP 92
Lorand, Laszlo 1923- WhoAm 92
Loranger, Francoise 1913- WhoCanL 92
Loranger, George Peter 1946- St&PR 93
Loranger, J. Albert 1943- St&PR 93
Loranger, Jean-Aubert 1896-1942 BioIn 17
Loranger, Leo Joseph 1949- St&PR 93
Loranger, Richard Leo 1936- St&PR 93
Loranger, Robert 1951- St&PR 93
Lorant, Stefan 1901- BioIn 17, WhoAm 92
Lorantas, Raymond Martin 1928- WhoE 93
Loras, Enrique 1947- WhoWor 93
Lorbacher, Peter 1936- WhoWor 93
Lorber, Charlotte Laura 1952- WhoEmL 93
Lorber, Curt Gerhard 1931- WhoScE 91-3, WhoWor 93
Lorber, Daniel Louis 1946- WhoE 93
Lorber, Mortimer 1926- WhoE 93
Lorber, Richard Jan BioIn 17
Lorber, Richard Jan 1946- WhoE 93
Lorber, Stephen Neil 1943- WhoE 93
Lorbeski, William Vincent 1955- St&PR 93
Lorca, Federico Garcia 1898-1936 BioIn 17
Lorcee, Peter WhoWrEP 92
Lorch, Edgar Raymond 1907-1990 BioIn 17
Lorch, Ernest Henry 1932- WhoAm 92
Lorch, George A. 1941- St&PR 93
Lorch, Irmgard Joan 1923- WhoAmW 93
Lorch, Maristella De Panizza 1919- WhoAm 92, WhoE 93
Lorch, Robert Frederick, Jr. 1952- WhoEmL 93
Lord, Albert Bates 1912-1991 BioIn 17
Lord, Anthony 1900- WhoAm 92
Lord, Anthony William Grattan 1942- WhoE 93
Lord, Athena V. DcAmChF 1960
Lord, Beman 1924-1991 BioIn 17, ScF&FL 92, SmATA 69
Lord, Bette Bao 1938- DcAmChF 1985, WhoAmW 93
Lord, Claude Franklin, Jr. 1921- WhoSSW 93
Lord, Dick 1941- WhoSSW 93
Lord, Evelyn Marlin 1926- WhoAm 92, WhoSSW 93
Lord, Farrell 1938- St&PR 93
Lord, Fonchen Usher 1926- WhoAm 92
Lord, Gabrielle 1946- ScF&FL 92
Lord, Geoffrey Craig 1946- WhoEmL 93
Lord, George D. St&PR 93
Lord, George deForest 1919- WhoAm 92, WhoE 93
Lord, Glenn 1920- ScF&FL 92
Lord, Graham 1943- ScF&FL 92
Lord, H.G.D. St&PR 93
Lord, Harold Wilbur 1905- WhoAm 92
Lord, Helen Tucker AmWomPl
Lord, Herbert Mathew 1917- WhoAm 92
Lord, Howard Blaine 1926- WhoSSW 93
Lord, J. Edward ScF&FL 92
Lord, Jack 1928- MiSFD 9
Lord, Jack 1930- WhoAm 92
Lord, Jacklynn Jean 1940- WhoWor 93
Lord, Jacqueline Ward 1936- WhoAmW 93
Lord, Jacques Passerat 1957- WhoSSW 93
Lord, Jane Anne 1932- WhoAmW 93
Lord, Jean-Claude 1943- MiSFD 9
Lord, Jeffrey ScF&FL 92
Lord, Jere Johns 1922- WhoAm 92
Lord, Jerome Edmund 1935- WhoAm 92, WhoWor 93
Lord, John Govan 1924- WhoE 93
Lord, John H. 1932- St&PR 93
Lord, John James, Jr. Law&B 92
Lord, John Keast 1818-1872 BioIn 17
Lord, John Michael WhoScE 91-1
Lord, John Wesley 1902-1989 BioIn 17
Lord, Jonathan Peter 1952- WhoEmL 93, WhoSSW 93
Lord, Joseph S. 1912-1991 BioIn 17
Lord, Katharine AmWomPl
Lord, M. G. 1955- WhoAm 92
Lord, Marion Manns 1914- WhoE 93
Lord, Marvin 1937- WhoAm 92
Lord, Mia W. 1920- WhoAmW 93, WhoWor 93
Lord, Milton Edward 1898-1985 BioIn 17
Lord, Morton A. 1938- St&PR 93
Lord, N. Philip 1925- St&PR 93
Lord, Peter WhoScE 91-1
Lord, Raymond Morrieson 1930- St&PR 93
Lord, Reginald Sidney 1936- WhoWor 93
Lord, Richard C. 1910-1989 BioIn 17
Lord, Richard J. 1925- WhoAm 92, WhoE 93
Lord, Robert Powers, Jr. Law&B 92
Lord, Robert Wilder 1917- WhoWrEP 92
Lord, Roy Alvin 1918- WhoAm 92
Lord, Sally Law&B 92
Lord, Susan Moses Law&B 92
Lord, Suzanne Mary 1962- WhoEmL 93
Lord, Todd Mitchell 1957- WhoEmL 93
Lord, Walter 1917- WhoAm 92
Lord, William Grogan 1914- WhoAm 92
Lord, William Jackson, Jr. 1926- WhoAm 92
Lord, Winston 1937- WhoAm 92
Lorde, Audre BioIn 17
Lorde, Audre d1992 NewYTBS 92 [port]
Lorde, Audre 1934- AmWomWr 92, ConLC 71 [port]
Lorde, Audre Geraldin 1934- WhoWrEP 92
Lorden, Jessica Essex Law&B 92
Lordi, Katherine Mary 1949- WhoEmL 93
Lordi, Peter 1943- St&PR 93
Lordinot, Guy 1944- DcCPCAm
Lords, Steven DeMar 1953- St&PR 93
Lords, Traci BioIn 17
LoRe, Barbara 1936- St&PR 93
Lore, Charles Eli 1934- WhoSSW 93
Lore, Elana ScF&FL 92
Lore, Martin Maxwell 1914- WhoAm 92
Lore, Mary J. 1956- St&PR 93
Loree, Paul James 1936- WhoE 93
Lorefice, Laurence Santo 1950- WhoEmL 93
Lorelli, Charles A. Law&B 92
Lorelli, Charles A. 1953- St&PR 93
Lorelli, Michael Kevin 1950- WhoAm 92, WhoE 93, WhoWor 93
Lorello, Benjamin David 1953- St&PR 93
Loren, Harold d1990 BioIn 17
Loren, John Walter 1949- WhoEmL 93
Loren, Pamela 1944- WhoAm 92
Loren, Sophia 1934- BioIn 17, IntDcF 2-3 [port], WhoAm 92, WhoWor 93
Lorenc, Jan 1954- WhoEmL 93
Lorenc, Stanislaw 1943- WhoScE 91-4
Lorence, John G. Law&B 92
Lorengar, Pilar 1928- Baker 92, IntDcOp, OxDcOp
Lorens, M. K. ConAu 138
Lorens, Michael Wojciech 1942- WhoWor 93
Lorenson, David A. Law&B 92
Lorenson, Harold Walfred 1928- St&PR 93
Lorente, Elena 1952- WhoAmW 93
Lorente, Roderick Dana 1949- WhoE 93
Lorente de No, Rafael 1902-1990 BioIn 17
Lorentson, Holly Jean 1956- WhoAmW 93, WhoEmL 93
Lorentz, Alfred 1872-1931 Baker 92
Lorentz, John A. Law&B 92
Lorentz, John A. 1927- St&PR 93
Lorentz, Klaus 1933- WhoScE 91-3
Lorentz, Pare BioIn 17
Lorentz, Pare d1992 NewYTBS 92 [port]
Lorentz, Pare 1905-1992 CurBio 92N
Lorentz, Stanislaw 1899- PolBiDi
Lorentz, William Beall 1937- WhoSSW 93
Lorentzen, Bent 1935- Baker 92
Lorentzen, Carl W. 1929- St&PR 93
Lorentzen, Gustav 1915- WhoWor 93
Lorentzen, James Clifford 1957- WhoSSW 93
Lorentzen, Lee A. Law&B 92
Lorentzen, Robert R. 1935- St&PR 93
Lorentzsen, Norman Martin 1916- St&PR 93, WhoAm 92
Lorenz, A.E. Law&B 92
Lorenz, Albert 1941- WhoE 93
Lorenz, Alfred (Ottokar) 1868-1939 Baker 92
Lorenz, Brian E. 1939- St&PR 93
Lorenz, Carol Elaine 1946- WhoEmL 93
Lorenz, Carrie AmWomPl
Lorenz, Charlotte Reinhold 1923- St&PR 93
Lorenz, Detlef Manfred 1929- WhoWor 93
Lorenz, Donald Henry 1936- WhoE 93
Lorenz, Donald Norman 1935- St&PR 93
Lorenz, Edward Norton 1917- WhoAm 92
Lorenz, Gary W. 1949- St&PR 93
Lorenz, Geoffrey R. 1943- St&PR 93
Lorenz, Hans Ernest 1940- WhoSSW 93
Lorenz, Hellmut 1942- WhoWor 93
Lorenz, Hugo A. Law&B 92
Lorenz, Hugo Albert 1926- WhoAm 92
Lorenz, John Douglas 1942- WhoAm 92
Lorenz, John George 1915- WhoAm 92
Lorenz, Jonathan Charles 1951- St&PR 93
Lorenz, Joseph F. Law&B 92
Lorenz, Katherine Mary 1946- WhoAmW 93, WhoEmL 93
Lorenz, Konrad BioIn 17
Lorenz, Konrad Zacharias 1903-1989 IntDcAn
Lorenz, Lee Sharp 1932- WhoAm 92
Lorenz, Linda Lee 1944- WhoAmW 93
Lorenz, Linda Lee 1957- WhoAmW 93
Lorenz, Max 1901-1975 Baker 92, IntDcOp, OxDcOp
Lorenz, Patricia Ann 1938- WhoAmW 93
Lorenz, Patrick William Law&B 92
Lorenz, Paul A. St&PR 93
Lorenz, Ralph Wesley 1957- WhoSSW 93
Lorenz, Richard Theodore, Jr. 1931- WhoAm 92
Lorenz, Ronald Theodore 1936- WhoWor 93
Lorenz, Ruediger 1932- WhoWor 93
Lorenz, Sarah E. WhoWrEP 92
Lorenz, Susan Jean 1954- WhoE 93
Lorenz, Walter J. 1932- WhoScE 91-3
Lorenzani, Paolo 1640-1713 Baker 92
Lorenze, George Doubleday 1925- St&PR 93
Lorenzelli, Vincenzo 1933- WhoScE 91-3
Lorenzen, John BioIn 17
Lorenzen, John M. Law&B 92
Lorenzen, Louis Otto 1935- WhoE 93
Lorenzen, Myron L. 1925- St&PR 93
Lorenzen, Philip A. 1942- St&PR 93
Lorenzen, Robert Frederick 1924- WhoAm 92
Lorenzen, Shelley A. Law&B 92
Lorenzetti, Franco 1928- WhoScE 91-3
Lorenzetti, Maureen Shields 1965- WhoEmL 93
Lorenzetti, Ole J. 1936- WhoAm 92
Lorenzi-Fabris, Ausonio de 1861-1935 Baker 92
Lorenzini, Carlo 1826-1890 MajAI [port]
Lorenzini, Enrico Carlo 1954- WhoE 93
Lorenzini, Kathryn Marie 1953- WhoEmL 93
Lorenzini, Luciano 1921- WhoScE 91-3
Lorenzo, Alfred Paul Law&B 92
Lorenzo, F. 1947- WhoIns 93
Lorenzo, Francisco A. BioIn 17
Lorenzo, Francisco A. 1940- St&PR 93
Lorenzo, Frank BioIn 17
Lorenzo, Frank 1940- EncABHB 8 [port]
Lorenzo, Frank A. 1940- HispAmA
Lorenzo, Leonardo de 1875-1962 Baker 92
Lorenzo, Michael 1920- WhoAm 92, WhoWor 93
Lorenzo de' Medici 1449-1492 BioIn 17
Loreto, Charles A. 1902-1990 BioIn 17
Loreto, Eriberto V. 1931- WhoAsAP 91
Lorette, Robert Charles 1952- WhoEmL 93
Loretto, Michael Henry WhoScE 91-1
Lorey, Frank William 1929- St&PR 93
Lorge, John Scott 1956- WhoAm 92
Lorge, Robert Gerald Augustine 1959- WhoEmL 93
Lorge, Timothy Sean 1969- WhoE 93
Lorhan, George Joseph 1949- WhoEmL 93
Lorho, B. WhoScE 91-2
Lori, Chris BioIn 17
Lori, John Martin 1951- WhoE 93
Loria, Lamberto 1855-1913 IntDcAn
Loria, Walter J. d1992 NewYTBS 92
Loria, Walter J. 1907-1992 BioIn 17
Loriaux, Maurice Lucien 1909- WhoAm 92
Lorick, Herbert C., III 1940- St&PR 93
Lorie, James Hirsch 1922- WhoAm 92
Loriferne, Bernard 1941- WhoScE 91-2
Lorigan, Michael Colm Law&B 92
Lorijn, Johannes Albertus 1925- WhoWor 93
Lorimer, Donald d1992 BioIn 17, NewYTBS 92
Lorimer, George Horace BioIn 17
Lorimer, Gordon Winston WhoScE 91-1
Lorimer, Janet 1941- BioIn 17

Lorimer, Linda Koch *BioIn 17, WhoAm 92, WhoAmW 93*
Lorimer, Maxwell George 1908-1990 *BioIn 17*
Lorimer, Robert Stodart 1864-1929 *BioIn 17*
Lorimer, Rodric Alan 1936- *St&PR 93*
Lorimer, Scat *WhoWrEP 92*
Lorimer, Susan Elaine 1957- *WhoSSW 93*
Lorimer, William 1861-1933 *PolPar*
Lorimier, Don L. 1951- *St&PR 93*
Lorincz, Albert Bela 1922- *WhoAm 92*
Lorincz, Allan Levente 1924- *WhoAm 92*
Lorinczi, George Gabriel 1929- *WhoAm 92*
Loring, Ann 1915- *ScF&FL 92*
Loring, Arthur *Law&B 92*
Loring, Arthur 1947- *WhoAm 92*
Loring, Arthur S. *Law&B 92*
Loring, Arthur Stanley 1947- *St&PR 93*
Loring, Caleb, Jr. 1921- *St&PR 93, WhoAm 92*
Loring, Charles, Jr. *BioIn 17*
Loring, David William 1956- *WhoSSW 93, WhoWor 93*
Loring, Emilie Baker *AmWomPl*
Loring, Gloria Jean 1946- *WhoAm 92*
Loring, H. Helmut *Law&B 92*
Loring, Jaime 1929- *WhoScE 91-3*
Loring, Janet Mason 1931- *WhoAmW 93*
Loring, John *BioIn 17*
Loring, John Robbins 1939- *St&PR 93, WhoAm 92*
Loring, Kimball A., Jr. 1918- *St&PR 93*
Loring, Lina *AmWomPl*
Loring, Murray 1917- *WhoWrEP 92*
Loring, Richard William 1928- *WhoE 93*
Loring, Rosemary C. 1950- *St&PR 93*
Loring, William Cushing 1879-1959 *BioIn 17*
Loring, William Wing 1818-1886 *HarEnMi*
Loriod, Yvonne 1924- *Baker 92*
Lorion, Raymond Paul 1946- *WhoE 93*
Loris-Teghem, Jacqueline 1943- *WhoScE 91-2*
Loritsch, K.B. 1949- *St&PR 93*
Loritsch, Kenneth Bruce 1949- *WhoSSW 93*
Lorius, Claude J. 1932- *WhoScE 91-2*
Lorman, Barbara K. 1932- *WhoAmW 93*
Lorman, William Rudolph 1910- *WhoAm 92, WhoWor 93*
Lorn, Ly *BioIn 17*
Lorne, David *WhoWrEP 92*
Lorne, David 1945- *ScF&FL 92*
Lorne, Simon Michael 1946- *WhoEmL 93*
Lornquest, Olaf 1921- *ScF&FL 92*
Loro, Laura Jean 1959- *WhoAmW 93*
Lorprayoon, Charussri 1940- *WhoWor 93*
Lorquet, Jean Claude 1935- *WhoScE 91-2*
Lorrah, Jean *WhoWrEP 92*
Lorrah, Jean 1938?- *ScF&FL 92*
Lorraine, Lilith 1894-1967 *BioIn 17, ScF&FL 92*
Lorraine, Louise 1901-1981 *SweetSg B [port]*
Lorrance, Arleen 1939- *WhoAmW 93, WhoWrEP 92*
Lorre, Peter 1904-1964 *BioIn 17, IntDcF 2-3 [port]*
Lorren, Loy Raymond 1938- *WhoSSW 93*
Lorsch, Susan E. 1950- *WhoAmW 93*
Lorscheider, Aloisio *DcCPCAm*
Lorscheider, Aloisio Cardinal 1924- *WhoWor 93*
Lortel, Lucille 1905- *WhoAm 92*
Lortie, Alain *ScF&FL 92*
Lortie, Gary A. 1959- *St&PR 93*
Lortie, John William 1920- *WhoWor 93*
Lorton, Donald Martin 1930- *WhoAm 92*
Lorton, Lewis 1939- *WhoAm 92*
Lorton, Mary Manning 1948- *WhoEmL 93*
Lorts, Jack E. 1940- *WhoWrEP 92*
Lortz, Charles William, Jr. 1941- *St&PR 93*
Lortz, Richard 1917-1980 *ScF&FL 92*
Lortzing, Albert 1801-1851 *OxDcOp*
Lortzing, (Gustav) Albert 1801-1851 *Baker 92*
Lortzing, Gustav Albert 1801-1851 *IntDcOp [port]*
LoRusso, Lawrence R. 1940- *St&PR 93*
LoRusso, Terri L. 1961- *WhoAmW 93*
Lorusso, Tina Marie Elena 1957- *WhoEmL 93*
Lory, Peter Korbinian 1947- *WhoWor 93*
Lory, Robert 1936- *ScF&FL 92*
Los, Cornelis Albertus 1951- *WhoEmL 93*
Losada-Paisey, Gloria 1957- *WhoAmW 93, WhoEmL 93*
Los Angeles, Victoria de *BioIn 17, IntDcOp*
Los Angeles, Victoria de 1923- *OxDcOp*
los Angeles Torres, Maria de *NotHsAW 93*
Losanno, Carmen 1938- *St&PR 93*
Losansky, Rolf 1931- *DrEEuF*
LoSapio, Kathleen 1955- *WhoAmW 93, WhoE 93, WhoEmL 93, WhoWor 93*
Loscalzo, Anthony Joseph 1946- *WhoEmL 93*
Loscalzo, Frank E. *St&PR 93*
Loscalzo, Joseph 1951- *WhoE 93*
Loscavio, Elizabeth *BioIn 17, WhoAm 92*
Losch, David Edward 1954- *WhoEmL 93*
Loscheider, Paul Henry 1954- *WhoEmL 93*
Loscher, Wolfgang 1949- *WhoScE 91-3*
Loschhorn, (Carl) Albert 1819-1905 *Baker 92*
Lo Schiavo, John Joseph 1925- *WhoAm 92*
Loschiavo, Linda Ann *WhoWrEP 92*
LoSchiavo, Robert W. *Law&B 92*
Loschiavo, Robert William 1957- *St&PR 93*
Losching, B.H. 1917- *St&PR 93*
Loschner, Hans F.E. 1945- *WhoWor 93*
Losco, Dennis Armando 1946- *St&PR 93*
Losco, John Joseph 1944- *St&PR 93*
Loscutoff, Lynn Leon 1934- *WhoE 93*
Losee, John Frederick, Jr. 1951- *WhoEmL 93*
Losee, Robert MacLean, Jr. 1952- *WhoSSW 93*
Losee, Thomas Penny, Jr. 1940- *WhoAm 92*
Loser, Ernest L. 1926- *St&PR 93*
Loser, Gary L. *Law&B 92*
Loser, Hermann 1940- *WhoScE 91-3*
Losey, Beverley Brown 1948- *WhoEmL 93*
Losey, Jeanne K. 1925- *WhoWrEP 92*
Losey, Joseph 1909-1984 *MiSFD 9N*
Losey, Michael Robert 1938- *WhoAm 92*
Losey, Ralph Colby 1951- *WhoEmL 93*
Loshinsky, James R. *Law&B 92*
Losi, Maxim John 1939- *WhoE 93, WhoWor 93*
Losice, Abraham S. 1960- *St&PR 93*
Losier, Gaetan 1934- *St&PR 93*
Loskywitz, Rochelle Ruth *Law&B 92*
Losowsky, Monty Seymour *WhoScE 91-1*
Loss, John C. 1931- *WhoAm 92, WhoWor 93*
Loss, Louis 1914- *WhoAm 92*
Loss, Margaret Ruth 1946- *WhoAm 92*
Loss, Stuart Harold *WhoAm 92*
Losse, Arlyle Mansfield 1917- *WhoAmW 93*
Losse, John W., Jr. 1916- *St&PR 93*
Losse, John William, Jr. 1916- *WhoAm 92*
Lossett, Ronald D. *St&PR 93*
Lossing, Frederick Pettit 1915- *WhoAm 92*
Losten, Basil Harry 1930- *WhoE 93*
Losty, Barbara Paul 1942- *WhoAmW 93*
Lo Surdo, Antonio 1943- *WhoAm 92*
Losure, Joyce Nelma 1928- *WhoWrEP 92*
Lotas, Judith Patton 1942- *WhoAm 92, WhoAmW 93*
Lotchin, Roger W. 1935- *ConAu 139*
Loteanu, Emil 1936- *MiSFD 9*
LoTempio, Julia Matild 1934- *WhoAmW 93, WhoE 93*
Lotfy, Refaat Labib 1936- *WhoUN 92*
Loth, Edward 1884-1944 *PolBiDi*
Loth, Gerald Lawrence 1936- *St&PR 93*
Loth, Helmut 1926- *WhoScE 91-3*
Loth, Stanislaw Jerzy 1929- *WhoWor 93*
Lothair 941-986 *HarEnMi*
Lothar, Ernst 1890-1974 *ScF&FL 92*
Lothe, Jens 1931- *WhoScE 91-4*
Lothian, Niall *WhoScE 91-1*
Lothringen, Otto von Habsburg- *BioIn 17*
Lothrop, Kristin Curtis 1930- *WhoAm 92, WhoE 93*
Lothrop, Samuel Kirkland 1892-1965 *IntDcAn*
Loti, Pierre 1850-1923 *DcLB 123 [port]*
Lotinga, Ernie 1876-1951 *QDrFCA 92 [port]*
Lotjanu, Emil' 1936- *DrEEuF*
Lotochinski, Eugene B. 1938- *St&PR 93*
Lotringer, Sylvere 1938- *WhoAm 92*
Lotspeich, George Oscar 1926- *St&PR 93*
Lotstein, James I. 1944- *WhoAm 92*
Lott, Albert Eduard Gunter 1936- *WhoScE 91-4*
Lott, Arnold S(amuel) 1912-1992 *ConAu 139*
Lott, Bret 1958- *WhoWrEP 92*
Lott, Charles H. 1950- *St&PR 93*
Lott, Clarinda Harriss 1939- *WhoWrEP 92*
Lott, Felicity 1947- *OxDcOp*
Lott, Felicity (Ann) 1947- *Baker 92*
Lott, George d1991 *BioIn 17*
Lott, Kench Lee 1920- *St&PR 93*
Lott, Kench Lee, Jr. 1920- *WhoAm 92*
Lott, Marianna 1954- *WhoSSW 93*
Lott, Peter DeForest 1933- *St&PR 93*
Lott, Ralph Phillips 1770-1845 *BioIn 17*
Lott, Rick 1950- *WhoWrEP 92*
Lott, Ronald Mandel 1959- *WhoAm 92*
Lott, Ronnie 1959- *BioIn 17*
Lott, Sandra Ward 1937- *WhoAmW 93*
Lott, Trent 1941- *CngDr 91, WhoAm 92, WhoSSW 93*
Lotta, Tom 1924- *WhoE 93*
Lotter, Charles R. *Law&B 92*
Lotter, Charles R. 1937- *WhoAm 92*
Lotter, Friedrich Johann 1924- *WhoWor 93*
Lotter, John George 1925- *St&PR 93*
Lotter, Lisa Ellen 1959- *WhoEmL 93*
Lotter, William H., Jr. 1934- *St&PR 93*
Lotterman, Hal 1920- *WhoAm 92*
Lottes, Patricia Joette Hicks 1955- *WhoAmW 93*
Lottes, Ronald L. 1945- *St&PR 93*
Lotti, Antonio c. 1667-1740 *Baker 92, OxDcOp*
Lotti, Victor Joseph 1938- *WhoE 93*
Lottinger, Morris Albert, Jr. 1937- *WhoSSW 93*
Lottman, Eileen 1927- *ScF&FL 92*
Lotto, Lorenzo c. 1480-1556 *BioIn 17*
Lotton, Donald R. 1940- *St&PR 93*
Lotts, Gordon R. 1923- *St&PR 93*
Lottspeich, Friedrich *WhoScE 91-3*
Lotwin, Stanford Gerald 1930- *WhoAm 92*
Lotz, Arthur William 1927- *St&PR 93, WhoAm 92*
Lotz, Benno Paul 1931- *St&PR 93*
Lotz, Denton 1939- *WhoAm 92*
Lotz, George Michael 1928- *WhoE 93*
Lotz, Joan Theresa 1948- *WhoAmW 93, WhoEmL 93*
Lotz, Wolfgang 1912-1981 *BioIn 17*
Lotzbire, Bruce John 1941- *WhoAm 92*
Lotze, Barbara 1924- *WhoAmW 93, WhoWor 93*
Lotze, Evie Daniel 1943- *WhoAmW 93*
Lotze, Rudolf Hermann 1817-1881 *Baker 92*
Lotze, Werner Heinz 1934- *WhoWor 93*
Lou, Peter Louis 1945- *WhoE 93*
Louallen, Sharon 1960- *WhoE 93*
Louati, Ezzeddine 1950- *WhoUN 92*
Loube, Samuel Dennis 1921- *WhoAm 92*
Loubet, Emile 1838-1929 *BioIn 17*
Loubet, Rene Pierre Emmanuel 1925- *WhoScE 91-2*
Loubriel, Tere 1952- *WhoAm 92*
Loucas, Nancy Held 1955- *WhoAmW 93*
Louch, Alfred Richard 1927- *WhoAm 92*
Loucheur, Louis 1872-1931 *BioIn 17*
Loucheur, Raymond 1899-1979 *Baker 92*
Loucheux, Claude 1931- *WhoScE 91-2*
Loucheux, Henriette *WhoScE 91-2*
Loucheux-Lefebvre, Marie-Henriette 1934- *WhoScE 91-2*
Louchheim, Donald Harry 1937- *WhoAm 92*
Louchheim, Frank Pfeifer 1923- *WhoAm 92*
Louchheim, Katie 1903-1991 *AnObit 1991, BioIn 17*
Louchheim, Mark S. *St&PR 93*
Louchheim, William S. 1904- *St&PR 93*
Louchheim, William Sandel, Jr. 1930- *St&PR 93*
Louckes, Theodore Nicholas 1930- *St&PR 93*
Loucks, A. Paul 1943- *WhoE 93*
Loucks, Daniel Peter 1932- *WhoAm 92*
Loucks, Nancy J. 1957- *WhoAmW 93, WhoEmL 93*
Loucks, Thomas Alexander 1949- *St&PR 93, WhoEmL 93*
Loucks, Timothy George *Law&B 92*
Loucks, Vernon R. 1934- *St&PR 93*
Loucks, Vernon R., Jr. 1934- *WhoAm 92, WhoWor 93*
Loucks, W. John 1931- *St&PR 93*
Loud, G(raham) A(nthony) 1953- *ConAu 136*
Loud, James John 1946- *WhoEmL 93, WhoSSW 93*
Loud, Lawrence John, Jr. 1947- *WhoSSW 93*
Loud, Nelson M. 1914- *St&PR 93*
Loud, Ruth McAneny d1990 *BioIn 17*
Loud, Warren Simms 1921- *WhoAm 92*
Loud, Yvonne *Law&B 92*
Louden, J. Keith 1905- *St&PR 93*
Louden, James A., Jr. 1937- *St&PR 93*
Louden, James Keith 1905- *WhoAm 92*
Louden, Nancy *Law&B 92*
Louden, Robert B. 1953- *ConAu 139*
Louden, Thomas A. 1919- *St&PR 93*
Louden, William G. 1921- *St&PR 93*
Louden, William Herbert 1946- *WhoE 93*
Loudenslager, Larry Neal 1949- *WhoEmL 93, WhoSSW 93*
Louderback, Lew *ScF&FL 92*
Loudermilk, Joey *Law&B 92*
Loudermilk, Joey M. 1953- *WhoAm 92*
Loudermilk, R. Charles 1927- *WhoAm 92*
Loudermilk, Robert Carlton 1954- *WhoEmL 93*
Loudermilk, Robert Charles, Sr. 1927- *St&PR 93*
Loudon, Aarnout A. *BioIn 17*
Loudon, Craig Michael 1950- *WhoWor 93*
Loudon, Dorothy 1933- *WhoAm 92*
Loudon, Douglas M. 1944- *St&PR 93*
Loudon, Rodney *WhoScE 91-1*
Loudoun, R.B. *WhoScE 91-1*
Loudova, Ivana 1941- *Baker 92*
Louel, Jean (Hippolyte Oscar) 1914- *Baker 92*
Louganis, Greg *BioIn 17*
Louganis, Greg E. 1960- *WhoAm 92*
Lougeay, Denruth Colleen 1943- *WhoAmW 93*
Lougee, Alan T. 1953- *St&PR 93*
Lougee, Robert Wayne, Jr. 1945- *St&PR 93, WhoAm 92, WhoE 93*
Lough, Charles Allen 1946- *WhoIns 93*
Lough, Rebecca M. *Law&B 92*
Lougheed, David P. *Law&B 92*
Lougheed, Peter 1928- *BioIn 17, WhoAm 92*
Lougheed, Robert 1910-1982 *BioIn 17*
Loughery, John 1953- *ConAu 138*
Loughery, Kevin Michael 1940- *WhoAm 92, WhoSSW 93*
Loughhead, J.N. *WhoScE 91-1*
Loughlin, Donald Alexander 1926- *WhoE 93*
Loughlin, Kathi Puglise 1958- *WhoEmL 93*
Loughlin, Lawrence Joseph, Jr. 1932- *St&PR 93*
Loughlin, Mary Anne Elizabeth 1956- *WhoAm 92*
Loughlin, Richard L(awrence) 1907- *WhoWrEP 92*
Loughman, Aleda P. 1932- *St&PR 93*
Loughman, B.C. *WhoScE 91-1*
Loughmiller, Bert Edward 1942- *St&PR 93*
Loughmiller, Robert Alden 1931- *St&PR 93*
Loughnane, Lee David 1946- *WhoAm 92*
Loughney, John Anthony 1947- *WhoE 93*
Loughran, F. Kevin *Law&B 92*
Loughran, Gerard Vincent *Law&B 92*
Loughran, James 1931- *Baker 92*
Loughran, James Newman 1940- *WhoAm 92*
Loughran, Matthew George 1962- *WhoE 93*
Loughran, Robert Hall 1916- *WhoAm 92*
Loughran, Roger Alan 1945- *WhoIns 93*
Loughran, Thomas Joseph 1929- *St&PR 93*
Loughrey, Jim *BioIn 17*
Loughrey, Kevin 1950- *WhoAm 92*
Loughridge, John Halsted, Jr. *Law&B 92*
Loughridge, Robert Foster, Sr. 1906- *St&PR 93*
Louhanapessy, Johannes Petrus 1929- *WhoUN 92*
Louie, Alexina Diane 1949- *WhoAmW 93*
Louie, David Wong 1954- *ConAu 139, ConLC 70 [port]*
Louie, Denise *Law&B 92*
Louie, Douglas 1928- *WhoSSW 93*
Louie, Edward d1990 *BioIn 17*
Louie, Judy *Law&B 92*
Louie, Karen P. *Law&B 92*
Louie, Karen Patricia *Law&B 92*
Louie, Kwok Ying 1953- *WhoE 93*
Louie, Raymond *Law&B 92*
Louie, Richard d1990 *BioIn 17*
Louie, Ron 1955- *BioIn 17*
Louie, Theodore Y. 1956- *St&PR 93*
Louis, Father 1915-1968 *BioIn 17*
Louis, I, Emperor 778-840 *BioIn 17*
Louis, II c. 822-875 *OxDcByz*
Louis, VII 1120?-1180 *OxDcByz*
Louis, XIII 1601-1643 *Baker 92*
Louis, XIV, King of France 1638-1715 *BioIn 17*
Louis, XV, King of France 1710-1774 *BioIn 17*
Louis, Brian P. 1958- *WhoE 93*
Louis, Conan Noel 1951- *WhoEmL 93*
Louis, Deborah Kiyo 1952- *WhoAmW 93*
Louis, Ernest G. 1923- *St&PR 93*
Louis, Henry 1927- *St&PR 93*
Louis, Joe 1914-1981 *EncAACR*
Louis, John Jeffry, Jr. 1925- *WhoAm 92*
Louis, Kenneth C. 1938- *St&PR 93, WhoIns 93*
Louis, Kenneth Clair 1938- *WhoAm 92*
Louis, Lester 1928- *WhoAm 92*
Louis, Louis F. 1955- *St&PR 93*
Louis, M. *WhoScE 91-2*
Louis, Martha *BioIn 17*
Louis, Murray 1926- *WhoAm 92*
Louis, Paul Adolph 1922- *WhoAm 92*
Louis, Rene Paul 1933- *WhoWor 93*
Louis, Roger W. *Law&B 92*
Louis, Rudolf 1870-1914 *Baker 92*
Louis, Tobi *WhoAmW 93*
Louis, Valerie *ConAu 139*

Louis, Victor 1928-1992 *NewYTBS 92 [port]*
Louis, William Charles, III 1951- *WhoEmL 93*
Louis, William Roger 1936- *WhoAm 92, WhoWor 93, WhoWrEP 92*
Louisakis, Anastassios 1936- *WhoScE 91-3*
Louis-Dreyfus, Robert *BioIn 17*
Louis-Dreyfus, Robert 1946- *WhoAm 92*
Louise, Mina *AmWomPl*
Louiselle, Roger William 1951- *WhoE 93*
Louis Ferdinand 1772-1806 *Baker 92*
Louis Francis, Prince of Battenberg 1900-1979 *BioIn 17*
Louis-Joseph-Dogue, Maurice 1927- *DcCPCAm*
Louis of Blois 1171-1205 *OxDcByz*
Louison, George 1951- *DcCPCAm*
Louisot, Pierre *WhoScE 91-2*
Louisot, Pierre Auguste Alphonse 1933- *WhoWor 93*
Louisy, Allan *DcCPCAm*
Loukaitis, N. *Law&B 92*
Loukas Chrysoberges *OxDcByz*
Loukas the Stylite 879?-979 *OxDcByz*
Loukas the Younger c. 900-953 *OxDcByz*
Loukopoulos, Dimitris 1935- *WhoWor 93*
Loulie, Etienne c. 1655-c. 1707 *Baker 92*
Lounamaa, Pertti 1956- *WhoScE 91-4*
Lounasmaa, Olli V. 1930- *WhoScE 91-4*
Lounberg, Katherine *AmWomPl*
Lounder, Arthur B., Jr. *Law&B 92*
Loundy, Mason A. 1906- *St&PR 93*
Loundy, Richard A. *St&PR 93*
Lounguine, Pavel *BioIn 17, MiSFD 9*
Lounsberry, Barbara 1946- *ConAu 138*
Lounsberry, Grace Constant *AmWomPl*
Lounsberry, Robert Horace 1918- *WhoAm 92*
Lounsbery, James A. 1946- *WhoEmL 93*
Lounsbury, Charles B. 1942- *St&PR 93, WhoAm 92*
Lounsbury, Jay Willard 1944- *WhoE 93*
Lounsbury, John Frederick 1918- *WhoAm 92*
Lounsbury, Richard *Law&B 92*
Loup, Francois Bernard 1940- *WhoAm 92*
Loup, Jacques Alain 1942- *WhoUN 92*
Loupis, Michalis 1962- *WhoWor 93*
Lourdeaux, Lee 1951- *ConAu 136*
Lourdusamy, Simon Cardinal 1924- *WhoWor 93*
Loureiro-Dias, Maria Da Conceicao 1947- *WhoWor 93*
Lourenco, Ruy Valentim 1929- *WhoAm 92*
Lourey, Joseph R. 1940- *St&PR 93*
Lourie, Alan D. 1935- *CngDr 91*
Lourie, Alan David 1935- *WhoAm 92, WhoE 93*
Lourie, Arthur (Vincent) 1892-1966 *Baker 92*
Lourie, Dick 1937- *WhoWrEP 92*
Lourie, Eugene 1905-1991 *BioIn 17*
Lourie, Eugene 1908-1991 *MiSFD 9N*
Lourie, Iven B. 1946- *WhoWrEP 92*
Lourie, Norman Victor 1912- *WhoAm 92*
Lourie, Peter (King) 1952- *ConAu 137*
Lourie, Richard 1940- *ScF&FL 92*
Lourie, Roger H. 1943- *St&PR 93*
Lousberg, Emmanuel J.P.F. 1930- *WhoScE 91-2*
Lousberg, Peter Herman 1931- *WhoAm 92*
Lousin, Ann Marie 1943- *WhoAmW 93*
Loustaunau-Lacau, Georges 1894-1955 *BioIn 17*
Loutfy, Aly 1935- *WhoWor 93*
Louth, William T. 1926- *St&PR 93*
Louthan, Thomas Alan 1947- *WhoEmL 93*
Loutrel, Agnes 1964- *St&PR 93*
Loutrel, Claude Yves 1930- *WhoAm 92*
Louttit, Gordon J. *Law&B 92*
Louttit, Gordon James 1947- *St&PR 93*
Louttit, James Russell 1924- *WhoAm 92*
Louttit, Richard Talcott 1932- *WhoAm 92*
Loutzenheiser, Edwin J., Jr. 1917- *St&PR 93*
Louvet, Jean E.R. 1928- *WhoScE 91-2*
Louvish, Simon 1947- *ScF&FL 92*
Louvois, Francois-Michel le Tellier, Marquis de 1639-1691 *HarEnMi*
Louwerenburg, Jan 1927- *WhoScE 91-3*
Loux, G. Ridgley *Law&B 92*
Loux, Gordon Dale 1938- *WhoWor 93*
Loux, Joseph Anthony, Jr. 1945- *WhoWor 93*
Loux, Michael Joseph 1942- *WhoAm 92*
Loux, Norman Landis 1919- *WhoAm 92*
Louys, Pierre 1870-1925 *DcLB 123 [port]*
Louza, Ramzi Shawki 1952- *WhoWor 93*
Louzil, Eric *MiSFD 9*
Louziotis, Demetrios, Sr. 1927- *WhoE 93*
Lovaas, M. John 1936- *St&PR 93*
Lovallo, Patricia Gaffney 1957- *WhoEmL 93*
Lovano, Joe *BioIn 17*
Lovas, Francis J. 1941- *WhoE 93*
Lovas, Istvan 1931- *WhoScE 91-4*
Love, Andrew *SoulM*
Love, Arthur Richard 1945- *St&PR 93*
Love, Barbara 1949- *WhoAmW 93*
Love, Ben F. 1924- *St&PR 93, WhoAm 92*
Love, Bessie 1898-1986 *IntDcF 2-3 [port]*
Love, Beverly Anne 1947- *WhoEmL 93*
Love, Bob *BioIn 17*
Love, Bob 1946- *WhoEmL 93*
Love, Bonnie 1948- *WhoEmL 93*
Love, C.A. *Law&B 92*
Love, Charles David 1952- *WhoSSW 93*
Love, Clara M. *AmWomPl*
Love, Clinton Kenneth 1952- *WhoAm 92*
Love, Cynthia Yvonne 1962- *WhoAmW 93*
Love, Daniel Joseph 1926- *WhoAm 92*
Love, Darlene 1938- *SoulM*
Love, Dennis A. *Law&B 92*
Love, Derrold Jon 1961- *WhoE 93*
Love, E.M. *ScF&FL 92*
Love, Ed *BioIn 17*
Love, Edith Holmes 1950- *WhoAmW 93, WhoSSW 93*
Love, Edmund G. *BioIn 17*
Love, Edmund G. 1912-1990 *ScF&FL 92*
Love, Edward M., Jr. d1991 *NewYTBS 92*
Love, Fount L., Jr. *Law&B 92*
Love, Frank, Jr. 1927- *WhoAm 92*
Love, Franklin Sadler 1915- *WhoAm 92*
Love, G.B. 1939- *ScF&FL 92*
Love, Gary H. *Law&B 92*
Love, Geoff 1917-1991 *AnObit 1991*
Love, George C. 1928- *St&PR 93*
Love, George Hutchinson 1900-1991 *BioIn 17*
Love, Harriet *AmWomPl*
Love, Howard McClintic 1930- *St&PR 93*
Love, James Edward 1948- *WhoEmL 93*
Love, Janet Anne *Law&B 92*
Love, Jennifer A. *Law&B 92*
Love, Joe R. 1938- *St&PR 93*
Love, John Edward 1932- *St&PR 93*
Love, John Wesley, Jr. 1932- *WhoSSW 93*
Love, Jon E. 1954- *St&PR 93*
Love, Joseph D. *Law&B 92*
Love, Kenneth E. 1932- *St&PR 93*
Love, Kenya *BioIn 17*
Love, Linda Jean 1948- *WhoAmW 93*
Love, Lynette *BioIn 17*
Love, Margaret C. 1942- *WhoAm 92*
Love, Mary Catherine *AmWomPl*
Love, Michael Harrison *Law&B 92*
Love, Michael Kenneth 1951- *WhoEmL 93*
Love, Mike 1941- *See* Wilson, Brian 1942- *Baker 92*
Love, Mildred Allison 1915- *WhoAmW 93*
Love, Mildred Lois 1928- *WhoAmW 93*
Love, Montagu 1877-1943 *BioIn 17*
Love, Nancy 1927- *WhoWrEP 92*
Love, Philip Noel 1939- *WhoWor 93*
Love, Phillip E., Jr. 1950- *WhoIns 93*
Love, Richard Emerson 1926- *WhoAm 92*
Love, Richard Gordon 1945- *WhoScE 91-1*
Love, Richard Harvey 1915- *WhoAm 92*
Love, Richard M. *Law&B 92*
Love, Richard M. 1946- *St&PR 93*
Love, Robert Lyman 1925- *WhoAm 92*
Love, Robert Merton 1909- *WhoAm 92*
Love, Robert William, Jr. 1929- *WhoAm 92*
Love, Robertus Donnell 1867-1930 *JrnUS*
Love, Rodney Marvin 1908- *WhoAm 92*
Love, Rosaleen 1940- *ScF&FL 92*
Love, Sandra Rae 1947- *WhoAmW 93*
Love, Shirley 1940- *Baker 92*
Love, Stanley 1926- *St&PR 93*
Love, Susan Denise 1954- *WhoAmW 93*
Love, Tom Jay, Jr. 1923- *WhoSSW 93*
Love, Walter Bennett, Jr. 1921- *WhoWor 93*
Love, William Edward 1926- *WhoAm 92*
Love, William Jeffrey 1958- *WhoE 93*
Loveberg, Aase 1923- *Baker 92*
Lovec, Rosita Borunda 1935- *WhoAmW 93*
Lovecraft, H.P. 1890-1937 *BioIn 17, ScF&FL 92*
Lovecraft, Howard Phillips 1890-1937 *BioIn 17*
Lovecraft, Linda *ScF&FL 92*
Lovecraft, Sonia *ScF&FL 92*
Loveday, Edna *BioIn 17*
Loveday, Leo John 1955- *WhoWor 93*
Loveday, Paul E. *Law&B 92*
Lovegren, Eleanor 1916-1991 *BioIn 17*
Lovegrove, James *ScF&FL 92*
Lovejoy, Allen Fraser 1919- *WhoAm 92*
Lovejoy, Ann Louise 1949- *WhoAmW 93*
Lovejoy, Barbara Campbell 1919- *WhoAm 92*
Lovejoy, David Ray 1948- *WhoAm 92*
Lovejoy, David William 1942- *St&PR 93*
Lovejoy, Donald Meston d1990 *BioIn 17*
Lovejoy, Donald Walker 1931- *WhoSSW 93*
Lovejoy, Elijah Parish 1802-1837 *JrnUS*
Lovejoy, Jack 1937- *ScF&FL 92*
Lovejoy, Jean Hastings 1913- *WhoAmW 93*
Lovejoy, Jerry L. *Law&B 92*
Lovejoy, Joseph Ensign 1940- *St&PR 93*
Lovejoy, Margot R. 1930- *WhoE 93*
Lovejoy, Owen 1811-1864 *PolPar*
Lovejoy, Patricia T. 1954- *St&PR 93*
Lovejoy, Paul R. *Law&B 92*
Lovejoy, Robert B. 1937- *St&PR 93*
Lovejoy, Robert M. 1943- *St&PR 93*
Lovejoy, Roya Lynn 1946- *WhoEmL 93*
Lovejoy, Stephen D. 1950- *St&PR 93*
Lovejoy, Thomas E. *BioIn 17*
Lovejoy, Thomas E. 1941- *St&PR 93*
Lovejoy, Thomas Eugene 1941- *WhoAm 92*
Lovejoy, William H. *ScF&FL 92*
Lovejoy, William Joseph 1940- *WhoAm 92*
Lovejoy, Winslow Meston 1927-1990 *BioIn 17*
Lovelace, Countess of 1815-1852 *BioIn 17*
Lovelace, Byron Keith 1935- *WhoSSW 93*
Lovelace, Carey 1952- *WhoWrEP 92*
Lovelace, Donna Landon 1947- *WhoEmL 93, WhoSSW 93*
Lovelace, Earl 1935- *BioIn 17, DcLB 125 [port], IntLitE*
Lovelace, Eldridge Hirst 1913- *WhoAm 92*
Lovelace, George David, Jr. 1952- *WhoEmL 93, WhoSSW 93*
Lovelace, Gloria E. *AfrAmBi*
Lovelace, Jon B. 1927- *WhoAm 92*
Lovelace, Jon B., Jr. 1927- *St&PR 93*
Lovelace, Maud Hart 1892-1980 *ConAu 39NR, MajAI [port]*
Lovelace, Richard 1618-1658 *BioIn 17*
Lovelace, Robert Frank 1950- *WhoAm 92*
Lovelace, Rose Marie Sniegon 1937- *WhoAmW 93*
Loveland, Charles E. 1916- *St&PR 93*
Loveland, Donald William 1934- *WhoAm 92*
Loveland, Eugene Franklin 1920- *WhoAm 92*
Loveland, George W. *Law&B 92*
Loveland, George Watson, II 1949- *WhoEmL 93*
Loveland, Joseph Albert, Jr. 1932- *WhoAm 92*
Loveland, Peter Graham 1926- *St&PR 93*
Loveland, Steven R. 1950- *St&PR 93*
Loveless, Edward Eugene 1919- *WhoAm 92*
Loveless, Homer Jackson, Jr. 1931- *St&PR 93*
Loveless, Howard William 1927- *St&PR 93*
Loveless, Keith *Law&B 92*
Loveless, Lea *WhoAmW 93*
Loveless, Mary Hewitt 1899-1991 *BioIn 17*
Loveless, Patty *BioIn 17*
Loveless, William Edward 1951- *WhoWrEP 92*
Loveless, William Michael 1949- *WhoSSW 93*
Lovell, A. Buffum *Law&B 92*
Lovell, A.L. *WhoScE 91-1*
Lovell, Alfred H. d1990 *BioIn 17*
Lovell, Arnold Buffum 1937- *WhoAm 92*
Lovell, Bernard 1913- *BioIn 17, WhoWor 93*
Lovell, Brenda Sue 1953- *WhoAmW 93*
Lovell, Carl Erwin, Jr. 1945- *WhoWor 93*
Lovell, Caroline C. *AmWomPl*
Lovell, Charles C. 1929- *WhoAm 92*
Lovell, Christopher Ward 1943- *WhoE 93*
Lovell, Edward George 1939- *WhoAm 92*
Lovell, Emily Kalled 1920- *WhoWor 93*
Lovell, Francis Joseph, III 1949- *WhoE 93*
Lovell, Gerald Donald *St&PR 93*
Lovell, James A., Jr. 1928- *WhoAm 92*
Lovell, James Arthur 1928- *St&PR 93*
Lovell, James C. 1926- *St&PR 93*
Lovell, James Frederick 1934- *WhoAm 92*
Lovell, Khalida *BioIn 17*
Lovell, Lucile *AmWomPl*
Lovell, Malcolm Read, Jr. 1921- *WhoAm 92*
Lovell, Mansfield 1822-1884 *HarEnMi*
Lovell, Marc 1930- *ScF&FL 92*
Lovell, Michael C. 1930- *WhoAm 92*
Lovell, Nancy Grace 1942- *WhoAmW 93*
Lovell, Peter H. *Law&B 92*
Lovell, Robert Eugene 1939- *WhoE 93*
Lovell, Robert Gibson 1920- *WhoAm 92*
Lovell, Robert Harold *Law&B 92*
Lovell, Robert Marlow, Jr. 1930- *St&PR 93, WhoAm 92, WhoE 93, WhoIns 93*
Lovell, Rose Mary 1961- *WhoAmW 93*
Lovell, Stephen S. 1941- *St&PR 93*
Lovell, Walter Carl 1934- *WhoE 93, WhoWor 93*
Lovell, William George 1939- *St&PR 93*
Lovelock, James 1919- *CurBio 92 [port], ScF&FL 92*
Lovely, Candace Whittemore 1953- *WhoEmL 93*
Lovely, Louise 1896-1980 *SweetSg A*
Lovely, Mary Ruth 1961- *WhoAmW 93, WhoEmL 93*
Lovely, Thomas Dixon 1930- *St&PR 93, WhoAm 92*
Loveman, David Bernard 1942- *St&PR 93*
Loveman, Gail J. 1949- *St&PR 93*
Loveman, Lucile *AmWomPl*
Loveman, Marc 1938- *St&PR 93*
Loveman, Samuel 1885-1976 *ScF&FL 92*
Loven, Andrew Witherspoon 1935- *WhoAm 92*
Lovenberg, Walter M. 1934- *St&PR 93, WhoAm 92*
Lovenskjold, Herman Severin 1815-1870 *Baker 92*
Loventhal, Charlie *MiSFD 9*
Loventhal, Milton 1923- *WhoWor 93*
Lover, Samuel 1797-1868 *Baker 92*
Loverd, William N. 1911- *St&PR 93*
Loveridge, Nigel *WhoScE 91-1*
Lovering, James Stanley 1951- *St&PR 93*
Lovero, Robert John 1955- *WhoEmL 93*
Loversky, Frank G. 1934- *St&PR 93*
Lovesey, Andrew 1941- *ScF&FL 92*
Lovesey, Peter *BioIn 17, ScF&FL 92*
Lovesey, Stephen William *WhoScE 91-1*
Lovestone, Jay 1898-1990 *BioIn 17*
LoVetere, Arthur J. 1939- *St&PR 93*
Lovetri, Jeannette Louise 1949- *WhoAmW 93*
Lovett, Carlus L. 1944- *St&PR 93*
Lovett, Clara Maria 1939- *WhoAm 92*
Lovett, David F.G. 1942- *St&PR 93*
Lovett, Ellis H. 1936- *St&PR 93*
Lovett, Eva Gruber 1940- *WhoAmW 93*
Lovett, Gail Ellison *Law&B 92*
Lovett, Henry Malcolm 1902- *WhoAm 92*
Lovett, James Everett 1930- *WhoSSW 93*
Lovett, John Carlton *Law&B 92*
Lovett, John Robert 1931- *St&PR 93, WhoAm 92, WhoE 93*
Lovett, Laurence Dow 1930- *WhoAm 92, WhoWor 93*
Lovett, Lisetta Marianne 1955- *WhoWor 93*
Lovett, Lyle *BioIn 17*
Lovett, Mary Deloache 1909- *St&PR 93*
Lovett, Michael A. *Law&B 92*
Lovett, Michael Francis 1946- *St&PR 93*
Lovett, Miller Currier 1923- *WhoE 93*
Lovett, Radford Dow 1933- *WhoAm 92*
Lovett, Robert A. 1895-1986 *ColdWar 1 [port]*
Lovett, Robert Morss 1870-1956 *GayN*
Lovett, Rosalee 1949- *St&PR 93*
Lovett, Ruth L. *Law&B 92*
Lovett, Wendell Harper 1922- *WhoAm 92*
Lovett, William Anthony 1934- *WhoSSW 93*
Lovette, Lillie Faye 1951- *WhoAmW 93*
Love Unlimited *SoulM*
Lovewell, Hubart Stonex, Jr. 1936- *WhoSSW 93*
Lovgren, Richard H. *Law&B 92*
Lovick, Norman 1942- *WhoE 93*
Lovig, Grant 1954- *St&PR 93*
Lovig, Lawrence, III 1942- *WhoE 93*
Lovill, John Randal 1946- *WhoSSW 93*
Lovin, Keith Harold 1943- *WhoAm 92*
Lovin, Roger 1941- *ScF&FL 92*
Loving, Dabney Carr 1929- *St&PR 93*
Loving, Frank 1854?-1882 *BioIn 17*
Loving, George Gilmer, Jr. 1923- *WhoAm 92*
Loving, Mabel F. *AmWomPl*
Loving, Susan B. *WhoAm 92, WhoAmW 93, WhoSSW 93*
Loving, William Lloyd 1931- *WhoSSW 93*
Loving, William Rush, Jr. 1934- *WhoSSW 93*
Lovinger, Joseph 1914-1991 *BioIn 17*
Lovinger, Richard Ralph 1927- *St&PR 93*
Lovinger, Sophie Lehner 1932- *WhoAmW 93*
Lovinger, Warren Conrad 1915- *WhoAm 92*
Lovingood, Rebecca Britten 1939- *WhoE 93*
Lovins, Amory B. 1947- *BioIn 17*
Lovins, Amory Bloch 1947- *WhoAm 92*
Lovins, L. Hunter 1950- *BioIn 17, WhoAmW 93*
Lovins, Sharron Joyce 1946- *WhoAmW 93, WhoEmL 93*
Lovinson, Martin 1859-1930 *BioIn 17*
Lovisi, Gary 1952- *ScF&FL 92*
Lovitt, Bert *MiSFD 9*
Lovitt, Chip *ScF&FL 92*
Lovitt, George Harold 1922- *WhoAm 92*
Lovitz, David D. 1920- *St&PR 93*
Lovitz, Jon *BioIn 17*
Lovoi, Paul Anthony 1947- *WhoEmL 93*
Lovric, Tomislav 1925- *WhoScE 91-4*

Lovrien, Phyllis Ann 1941- St&PR 93
Lovtrup-Rein, Huguette 1938- WhoScE 91-4
Lovvorn, Dixon Cannon 1925- St&PR 93
Lovvorn, Joella 1934- WhoAmW 93
Lovy, Andrew 1935- WhoWor 93
Lovy, Steve MiSFD 9
Low, Alice 1926- ScF&FL 92
Low, Anthony 1935- WhoAm 92, WhoWrEP 92
Low, Barbara Wharton 1920- WhoAm 92
Low, Chow-Eng 1938- WhoWor 93
Low, Dana E. 1932- St&PR 93
Low, David 1903-1987 BioIn 17
Low, David A. 1939- St&PR 93
Low, David B. 1942- St&PR 93
Low, Denise Lea 1949- WhoWrEP 92
Low, Donald Gottlob 1925- WhoAm 92
Low, Edmon 1902-1983 BioIn 17
Low, Emmet Francis, Jr. 1922- WhoAm 92, WhoSSW 93
Low, Esther Law&B 92
Low, Florence W. BioIn 17
Low, Francis Eugene 1921- WhoAm 92
Low, Frank James 1933- WhoAm 92
Low, Frank Norman 1911- WhoAm 92, WhoWor 93
Low, G. David BioIn 17
Low, H. Burton 1929- St&PR 93
Low, Harry William 1931- WhoAm 92
Low, Hock S. Jack 1959- WhoWor 93
Low, Jaclyn Faglie 1941- WhoSSW 93
Low, James A. 1925- WhoAm 92
Low, James Patterson 1927- WhoAm 92
Low, John W. St&PR 93
Low, John Wayland 1923- WhoAm 92
Low, Joseph 1834-1886 Baker 92
Low, Joseph 1911- MajAI [port], WhoAm 92
Low, Juliette Gordon 1860-1927 BioIn 17, WomChHR [port]
Low, K. Prescott BioIn 17
Low, Leone Yarborough 1935- WhoAmW 93
Low, Louise Anderson 1944- WhoAmW 93
Low, Marissa Eva 1960- WhoAmW 93
Low, Max M. 1901-1989 BioIn 17
Low, Merry Cook 1925- WhoAmW 93, WhoWor 93
Low, Morton David 1935- WhoAm 92
Low, Paul M. 1930- WhoAm 92
Low, Paul Revere 1933- WhoAm 92
Low, Peter James Burton 1939- WhoWor 93
Low, Philip Funk 1921- WhoAm 92
Low, Remington 1911- St&PR 93
Low, Richard H. 1927- WhoAm 92, WhoWor 93
Low, Seth 1850-1916 PolPar
Low, Stephen 1927- WhoAm 92
Low, Stuart M. 1917- St&PR 93
Low, Susan A. 1946- WhoAmW 93
Low, Virginia Barr 1921- WhoAmW 93
Low, Wanda K. Denson- BioIn 17
Low, Wye Ming 1960- WhoAmW 93, WhoE 93, WhoWor 93
Lowa, Patterson 1943- WhoAsAP 91
Lowd, Judson Dean 1918- WhoAm 92
Lowden, Francis V., III Law&B 92
Lowden, John L. 1921- WhoAm 92
Lowden, Kathleen Law&B 92
Lowden, Scott Richard Law&B 92
Lowden, Scott Richard 1940- WhoAm 92
Lowder, Chris ScF&FL 92
Lowder, James ScF&FL 92
Lowder, Rachael Della 1942- WhoAmW 93
Lowdin, Per-Olov 1916- WhoWor 93
Lowe, Adolph 1893- BioIn 17
Lowe, Alfred Mifflin, III 1948- WhoE 93
Lowe, Alvin Jenkins 1931- WhoSSW 93
Lowe, Barbara 1946- WhoAmW 93
Lowe, Betty Ann 1934- WhoAm 92
Lowe, Bill BioIn 17
Lowe, Brian 1935- St&PR 93
Lowe, Cameron Anderson 1932- WhoSSW 93
Lowe, (Johann) Carl Gottfried Baker 92
Lowe, Chad BioIn 17
Lowe, Christopher Robin 1945- WhoWor 93
Lowe, D. Nelson 1938- St&PR 93
Lowe, Daniel 1932- St&PR 93
Lowe, Dato Charles Jerome 1921- WhoWor 93
Lowe, David (Garrard) 1933- WhoWrEP 92
Lowe, David John WhoScE 91-1
Lowe, David Jon 1949- St&PR 93
Lowe, Donald C. 1932- St&PR 93
Lowe, Donald Cameron 1932- WhoAm 92
Lowe, Douglas Hayse 1952- WhoWrEP 92
Lowe, Douglas Howard 1952- WhoEmL 93, WhoSSW 93
Lowe, Douglas R. Law&B 92
Lowe, Eaph St&PR 93
Lowe, Edwin Nobles 1912- WhoAm 92, WhoWor 93
Lowe, Ethel Black 1904- WhoE 93
Lowe, Felix Caleb 1933- WhoAm 92
Lowe, Ferdinand 1865-1925 Baker 92
Lowe, Florence Segal WhoAmW 93, WhoE 93
Lowe, G. Nelson 1929- St&PR 93
Lowe, G. Ralph 1916- St&PR 93
Lowe, George Ralph, III 1941- St&PR 93
Lowe, Gordon WhoScE 91-1
Lowe, Gordon 1933- WhoWor 93
Lowe, Harold Gladstone, Jr. 1933- WhoSSW 93
Lowe, Harry 1922- WhoAm 92
Lowe, Holly Law&B 92
Lowe, Ida Brandwayn 1946- WhoE 93
Lowe, James Earl, Jr. Law&B 92
Lowe, James J. 1915- St&PR 93
Lowe, James Robert Law&B 92
Lowe, Jewell Parkerson WhoSSW 93
Lowe, Joan Clay 1931- WhoSSW 93
Lowe, Joe 1842-1899 BioIn 17
Lowe, John, III 1916- WhoAm 92
Lowe, Jonathan F. 1953- WhoWrEP 92
Lowe, Joseph, III 1943- WhoSSW 93
Lowe, Joseph John WhoScE 91-1
Lowe, Justus Frederick, Jr. 1927- WhoAm 92
Lowe, Kenneth Stephen 1921- WhoAm 92, WhoWrEP 92
Lowe, Larry Taylor 1936- WhoSSW 93
Lowe, Laura Susan Law&B 92
Lowe, Lester Vincent, Jr. 1936- St&PR 93
Lowe, Lucy AmWomPl
Lowe, Lynette-Machelle Cutchins 1967- WhoAmW 93
Lowe, Mark A. Law&B 92
Lowe, Marvin 1922- WhoAm 92
Lowe, Mary Frances 1952- WhoAm 92
Lowe, Mary Johnson 1924- WhoAm 92, WhoAmW 93, WhoE 93
Lowe, Mary P. ScF&FL 92
Lowe, Max Alan 1948- WhoSSW 93
Lowe, Michael D. Law&B 92
Lowe, Oariona 1948- WhoEmL 93
Lowe, Paul Edward 1936- BiDAMSp 1989
Lowe, Percival G. 1828-1908 BioIn 17
Lowe, Peter Stephen 1958- WhoSSW 93
Lowe, R. Stanley Law&B 92
Lowe, Ralph Edward 1931- WhoWor 93
Lowe, Richard E. 1941- St&PR 93
Lowe, Richard Gerald, Jr. 1960- WhoEmL 93
Lowe, Richard Grady 1942- WhoSSW 93
Lowe, Richard L. 1928- St&PR 93
Lowe, Rob BioIn 17
Lowe, Rob 1964- WhoAm 92
Lowe, Robert A. d1991 BioIn 17
Lowe, Robert A. 1938- St&PR 93
Lowe, Robert Anthony William 1937- WhoWor 93
Lowe, Robert Charles 1927- WhoAm 92
Lowe, Robert Charles 1949- WhoAm 92, WhoSSW 93, WhoWor 93
Lowe, Robert Lincoln 1868-1951 BiDAMSp 1989
Lowe, Robert Stanley 1923- WhoAm 92
Lowe, Sheldon 1926- WhoAm 92
Lowe, Stella Catherine 1943- WhoSSW 93
Lowe, Steve BioIn 17
Lowe, Steve 1946?- ScF&FL 92
Lowe, Steven Warren 1948- St&PR 93
Lowe, Sue Esther 1954- WhoEmL 93
Lowe, Susan M. Law&B 92
Lowe, Ted R. 1936- St&PR 93
Lowe, Teddy R. 1936- WhoIns 93
Lowe, William C. WhoAm 92
Lowe, Winston I. Law&B 92
Lowe, Winston I. 1951- St&PR 93
Lowell, Alan I. 1939- St&PR 93, WhoE 93
Lowell, Amy 1874-1925 BioIn 17
Lowell, Charles Russell 1835-1864 BioIn 17
Lowell, Edith AmWomPl
Lowell, Frank 1960- WhoE 93
Lowell, Howard Parsons 1945- WhoAm 92, WhoE 93
Lowell, Jacqueline Peters WhoAmW 93
Lowell, James Russell 1819-1891 BioIn 17
Lowell, John 1919- St&PR 93
Lowell, John H. BioIn 17
Lowell, Josephine Shaw 1843-1905 BioIn 17
Lowell, Juliet 1901- WhoAm 92
Lowell, Payson W. 1932- St&PR 93
Lowell, Percival 1855-1916 BioIn 17
Lowell, Richard William 1952- WhoSSW 93
Lowell, Robert 1917-1977 BioIn 17, MagSAmL [port], WorLitC [port]
Lowell, Stanley Edgar 1923- WhoE 93
Lowell, Stanley Herbert 1919- WhoE 93
Lowell, Stephen Craig 1953- WhoEmL 93, WhoSSW 93
Lowell, Wayne Brian 1955- St&PR 93
Lowen, Allen Wayne 1946- WhoEmL 93, WhoSSW 93
Lowen, Gerard Gunther 1921- WhoAm 92
Lowen, Irwin 1923- St&PR 93
Lowen, Lynne Marie 1960- St&PR 93
Lowen, Theodore Whitney, III 1955- WhoE 93
Lowen, Walter 1921- WhoAm 92
Lowenberg, Edward Law&B 92
Lowenberg, Georgina Grace 1944- WhoAmW 93
Lowenberg, John David 1942- St&PR 93
Lowenberg, Susan 1957- WhoAmW 93
Lowenbraun, Leslie 1953- St&PR 93
Lowenfeld, Andreas Frank 1930- WhoAm 92
Lowenfeld, Berthold BioIn 17
Lowenfeld, Philipp 1887-1963 BioIn 17
Lowenfels, Albert Brownold 1927- WhoE 93
Lowenfels, Fred M. Law&B 92
Lowenfels, Fred M. 1944- St&PR 93, WhoAm 92
Lowenhaupt, Charles Abraham 1947- WhoEmL 93
Lowenkamp, William Charles, Jr. 1941- WhoWrEP 92
Lowenkron, Michael 1943- St&PR 93
Lowenkron, Ruth 1960- WhoEmL 93
Lowens, Irving 1916-1983 Baker 92
Lowenstam, Susan Guggenheim Law&B 92
Lowenstam, Susan Guggenheim 1942- St&PR 93
Lowenstein, Alan Victor 1913- WhoAm 92
Lowenstein, Alfred Samuel 1931- WhoE 93
Lowenstein, Allard 1929-1980 PolPar
Lowenstein, Bedrich W. 1929- WhoWor 93
Lowenstein, David Carl 1945- St&PR 93
Lowenstein, Derek Irving 1943- WhoAm 92, WhoE 93
Lowenstein, Felicia Lynn 1962- WhoAmW 93
Lowenstein, Glenn Walker 1943- St&PR 93
Lowenstein, Irwin Lang 1935- WhoAm 92
Lowenstein, Jack Gert 1927- WhoAm 92
Lowenstein, James Gordon 1927- WhoAm 92
Lowenstein, Louis 1925- WhoAm 92
Lowenstein, Mark G. 1937- St&PR 93
Lowenstein, Paul Law&B 92
Lowenstein, Peter David 1935- WhoAm 92
Lowenstein, Ralph Lynn 1930- WhoAm 92
Lowenstein, Richard MiSFD 9
Lowenstein, Robert S. 1945- St&PR 93
Lowenstein-Lom, Walter 1919- WhoWor 93
Lowenstine, Maurice Richard, Jr. 1910- WhoAm 92
Lowenthal, Abraham Frederic 1941- WhoAm 92
Lowenthal, Alan J. Law&B 92
Lowenthal, Constance 1945- WhoAm 92
Lowenthal, Henry 1931- St&PR 93, WhoAm 92
Lowenthal, Jack St&PR 93, WhoIns 93
Lowenthal, Jerome BioIn 17
Lowenthal, Jerome (Nathaniel) 1932- Baker 92
Lowenthal, Malcolm Paul 1935- St&PR 93
Lowenthal, Mark M. ScF&FL 92
Lowenthal, Mort 1931- St&PR 93, WhoAm 92
Lowenthal, Nancy H. Law&B 92
Lowenthal, Richard 1908-1991 BioIn 17
Lowenthal, Richard L. 1952- St&PR 93
Lowenthal, Ronit Amir d1990 BioIn 17
Lowenthal, Ruth Kelman Law&B 92
Lowenthal, Susan 1946- WhoAmW 93, WhoEmL 93
Lowentrout, Christine ScF&FL 92
Lower, Angelica Yachnis 1960- WhoAmW 93
Lower, Frederick Joseph, Jr. 1935- WhoAm 92
Lower, James Brian 1949- WhoEmL 93
Lower, Johannes 1944- WhoScE 91-3
Lower, Joyce Q. 1943- WhoAm 92
Lower, Martin Avery 1938- St&PR 93
Lower, Milton Dale 1933- WhoSSW 93
Lower, Philip Edward 1949- WhoEmL 93
Lower, Richard Daniel Law&B 92
Lower, Richard Lawrence 1935- WhoAm 92
Lowerre, William G. Law&B 92
Lowers, Gina Cattani 1961- WhoAmW 93, WhoEmL 93
Lowery, Anne Barrow 1958- WhoAmW 93
Lowery, Bill 1924- WhoAm 92
Lowery, Bill 1947- CngDr 91
Lowery, Charles Douglas 1937- WhoAm 92
Lowery, Clinton Hershey 1929- WhoAm 92
Lowery, Dennis Joseph 1933- St&PR 93
Lowery, Elizabeth A. Law&B 92
Lowery, Floyd Lynn, Jr. 1940- WhoSSW 93
Lowery, Joseph BioIn 17
Lowery, Joseph E. WhoAm 92
Lowery, Joseph E. 1921- EncAACR [port]
Lowery, Joseph E. 1924- AfrAmBi
Lowery, Kermit Franklin Law&B 92
Lowery, Lee Leon, Jr. 1938- WhoAm 92
Lowery, Linda ScF&FL 92
Lowery, Marion Margaret 1934- WhoAmW 93
Lowery, Michael A. Law&B 92
Lowery, Patricia Ann 1941- WhoWor 93
Lowery, Sharon A. 1943- WhoAmW 93
Lowery, Willa Dean 1927- WhoAmW 93
Lowery, William David 1947- WhoAm 92
Lowery, William Herbert 1925- WhoAm 92
Lowery, Zeanta Law&B 92
Lowes, Gary H. 1951- St&PR 93
Lowey, Nita M. 1937- BioIn 17, CngDr 91, WhoAm 92, WhoAmW 93, WhoE 93
Lowey-Ball, Alfred Harry 1942- WhoWor 93
Lowi, Theodore Jay 1931- WhoAm 92, WhoE 93, WhoWor 93
Lowidski, Witt ConAu 38NR
Lowie, Robert H. 1883-1957 IntDcAn
Lowin, David A. Law&B 92
Lowinger, Margaret 1922- BioIn 17
Lowinsky, Edward E(lias) 1908-1985 Baker 92
Lowish, Michael David 1950- WhoEmL 93
Lowitt, Richard 1922- WhoAm 92
Lowitz, David Aaron 1928- WhoSSW 93
Lowitz, Glenn Howard 1952- WhoSSW 93
Lowke, George E. 1939- St&PR 93
Lowke, John James 1934- WhoWor 93
Lowman, George Frederick 1916- St&PR 93, WhoAm 92
Lowman, J.E. Law&B 92
Lowman, James 1947- St&PR 93
Lowman, Kenneth Kerwyn 1956- WhoSSW 93
Lowman, Mary Bethena Hemphill 1922- WhoAmW 93
Lowman, Meredith Ann 1950- WhoAmW 93
Lowman, Patricia J. 1941- WhoAmW 93
Lowman, Shirley Ann WhoSSW 93
Lowndes, David Alan 1947- WhoEmL 93
Lowney, Bruce Stark 1937- WhoAm 92
Lowney, Frank J. 1933- St&PR 93
Lowney, Karen Anne Law&B 92
Lownsbury, M.H., Jr. 1932- St&PR 93
Lowrance, Deborah Burgess 1962- WhoAmW 93
Lowrance, Martha Wray 1950- WhoSSW 93
Lowrance, Muriel Edwards 1922- WhoAmW 93
Lowrance, William Bailey 1932- WhoSSW 93
Lowrey, Christopher 1829-1864 BioIn 17
Lowrey, E. James 1928- WhoAm 92
Lowrey, Ernest James 1928- St&PR 93
Lowrey, John Patrick Auriol WhoScE 91-1
Lowrey, Joseph Patrick 1945- St&PR 93
Lowrey, Joyce Ann 1939- WhoE 93
Lowrey, Judith Gale 1939- WhoSSW 93
Lowrey, K.W. WhoScE 91-1
Lowrey, Michael A. 1942- St&PR 93
Lowrey, Richard William 1938- WhoE 93, WhoWor 93
Lowrey, William C. Law&B 92
Lowrie, Arthur Lewis 1930- WhoSSW 93
Lowrie, Douglas Bruce 1944- WhoWor 93
Lowrie, Gerald M. 1935- WhoAm 92
Lowrie, Gerald Marvin 1935- St&PR 93
Lowrie, Jean Elizabeth 1918- WhoAm 92
Lowrie, John M. 1940- St&PR 93
Lowrie, Kathryn Yanacek 1958- WhoAmW 93, WhoEmL 93
Lowrie, W.G. 1943- St&PR 93
Lowrie, Walter Olin 1924- WhoAm 92
Lowrie, William 1939- WhoScE 91-4
Lowrie, William G. 1943- WhoAm 92
Lowright, Richard Henry 1940- WhoE 93
Lowrimore, Mike 1961- St&PR 93
Lowry, A. Robert 1919- WhoAm 92
Lowry, Bates 1923- WhoAm 92
Lowry, Brian Robert Law&B 92
Lowry, Candace Elizabeth 1950- WhoEmL 93
Lowry, Charles Bryan 1942- WhoSSW 93
Lowry, Charles Wesley 1905- WhoAm 92
Lowry, Craig R. 1950- St&PR 93
Lowry, David Mahlon Law&B 92
Lowry, Dennis Martin 1953- WhoEmL 93, WhoWor 93
Lowry, Dick MiSFD 9
Lowry, Donald M. Law&B 92
Lowry, Donald Michael 1929- St&PR 93
Lowry, Edward Francis, Jr. 1930- WhoAm 92
Lowry, Edwin R. 1928- WhoAm 92
Lowry, Elizabeth Grace 1966- WhoAmW 93

Lowry, Ethel Joyce 1933- WhoAmW 93
Lowry, Gary William 1936- St&PR 93
Lowry, George W. 1913- St&PR 93
Lowry, Glenn David WhoAm 92
Lowry, James David 1942- WhoAm 92
Lowry, James H. 1923- St&PR 93
Lowry, James H. 1939- AfrAmBi
Lowry, John Christopher 1942- WhoWor 93
Lowry, Kirk William 1960- WhoEmL 93
Lowry, Larry L. 1947- St&PR 93
Lowry, Larry Lorn 1947- WhoAm 92
Lowry, Leo Elmo 1916- WhoSSW 93
Lowry, Lois BioIn 17
Lowry, Lois 1937- ChlFicS, MajAI [port], SmATA 70 [port]
Lowry, Lois (Hammbersberg) 1937- DcAmChF 1960
Lowry, Lois (Hammersberg) 1937- DcAmChF 1985, WhoAm 92, WhoAmW 93
Lowry, Malcolm 1909-1957 BioIn 17, IntLitE
Lowry, Meri Nan Law&B 92
Lowry, Oliver H. 1910- BioIn 17
Lowry, Philip John WhoScE 91-1
Lowry, Robert 1826-1899 Baker 92
Lowry, Sheldon Gaylon 1924- WhoAm 92
Lowry, Thomas C. Law&B 92
Lowry, Thomas Hastings 1938- WhoAm 92
Lowry, William Brian 1954- WhoEmL 93
Lowry, William K., Jr. 1951- WhoIns 93
Lowry, William Ketchin, Jr. 1951- WhoAm 92, WhoE 93, WhoEmL 93, WhoWor 93
Lowry, Wilson McNeil 1913- WhoAm 92
Lowson, Kathleen 1953- WhoAmW 93, WhoEmL 93
Lowson, Martin Vincent 1938- WhoWor 93
Lowther, Frank Eugene 1929- WhoSSW 93, WhoWor 93
Lowther, Gerald Halbert 1924- WhoAm 92
Lowther, Hugh Cecil 1857-1944 BioIn 17
Lowther, William (Anthony) 1942- ConAu 136
Lowtzky, Hermann 1871-1957 Baker 92
Lowum, David Donald 1932- St&PR 93
Lowy, Ernest d1990 BioIn 17
Lowy, Frederick Hans 1933- WhoAm 92
Lowy, Harvey David 1947- WhoE 93
Lowy, Jay Stanton 1935- WhoAm 92
Lowy, Steven R. 1946- St&PR 93
Lowy, Steven Rudolf 1946- WhoAm 92
Lowy, Susanna M. Law&B 92
Loxley, John 1942- WhoAm 92
Loxsmith, John ConAu 37NR
Loxton, George Robert Law&B 92
Loy, Frank Ernest 1928- WhoAm 92
Loy, Jessica Knight 1959- WhoAmW 93
Loy, Michael Warren 1949- St&PR 93
Loy, Mina 1882-1966 AmWomPl
Loy, Myrna BioIn 17
Loy, Myrna 1905- IntDcF 2-3 [port], WhoAm 92, WhoAmW 93
Loy, Nanni 1925- MiSFD 9
Loy, Richard Nelson 1945- St&PR 93
Loy, Rosetta 1931- ConAu 138, ScF&FL 92
Loyal, William Barry Law&B 92
Loyd, Joseph H. Law&B 92
Loyd, Randall M. 1957- St&PR 93
Loyd, Robert W. 1936- St&PR 93
Loyd, Ronald L. 1950- St&PR 93
Loye, Dieter zur 1928- St&PR 93
Loyen, Sylvain Law&B 92
Loyer, Raymond C. Law&B 92
Loyer-Carlson, Vicki Lee 1960- WhoAmW 93
Loyless, Bonnie Wainright 1954- WhoEmL 93
Loynaz, Dulce Maria 1903- SpAmA
Loynd, Richard B. 1927- St&PR 93
Loynd, Richard Birkett 1927- WhoAm 92
Loynes, John H. 1933- WhoIns 93
Loynes, John Hamilton 1933- St&PR 93, WhoAm 92
Loynes, Robert Michael WhoScE 91-1
Loyola, Andrea Angel 1952- WhoAmW 93
Loyttyniemi, Kari 1941- WhoScE 91-4
Lozano, Ignacio Eugenio, Jr. 1927- WhoAm 92
Lozano, Monica Cecilia 1956- NotHsAW 93 [port]
Lozano, Paul BioIn 17
Lozano, Ricardo 1941- WhoScE 91-3
Lozano, Roberto Daniel 1934- WhoWor 93
Lozano, Rudolpho 1942- HispAmA
Lozano, Rudy 1942- WhoAm 92
Lozano Diaz, Julio DcCPCAm
Lozano-Teruel, Jose A. 1939- WhoScE 91-3
Lozansky, Edward D. 1941- BioIn 17
Lozansky, Edward Dmitry 1941- WhoE 93
Lozeau, Albert 1878-1924 BioIn 17
Lozeau, Roland U. 1941- St&PR 93
Lozier, Allan G. 1933- St&PR 93, WhoAm 92
Lozier, Daniel William 1941- WhoE 93
Lozier, Gilmour Gregory 1945- WhoE 93
Lozinski, Janusz 1926- WhoScE 91-4
Lozinskiy, Valentin V. 1931- WhoUN 92
Lozito, Gilda Lelia WhoAmW 93
Lozito, Rosalie Marie 1950- WhoAmW 93
Lozner, Jerrold Stanley 1947- WhoE 93
Lozowick, Louis 1892-1973 BioIn 17
Lozowicki, Adam Tadeusz 1946- WhoWor 93
Lozowski, Thomas Edward 1963- WhoE 93
Lozsadi, L. Karoly 1935- WhoScE 91-4
Lozyniak, Andrew 1931- St&PR 93, WhoAm 92
LTD SoulM
Lu, Christopher Dah-Cheng 1951- WhoSSW 93
Lu, Chu-Ho 1954- WhoSSW 93
Lu, Chuanrong 1933- WhoWor 93
Lu, Da-Ren 1940- WhoWor 93
Lu, David John 1928- WhoAm 92, WhoWrEP 92
Lu, Frank Kerping 1954- WhoEmL 93, WhoSSW 93
Lu, Hongwen 1939- WhoWor 93
Lu, Hsun 1881-1936 BioIn 17
Lu, I-Li 1956- WhoE 93
Lu, Janny M. 1958- St&PR 93
Lu, Jian 1961- WhoWor 93
Lu, Keh-Ming 1949- WhoE 93, WhoEmL 93
Lu, Linyu Laura 1957- WhoE 93
Lu, Ming Gao 1943- WhoWor 93
Lu, Ning WhoSSW 93
Lu, Pang-Chia 1949- WhoE 93
Lu, Ponzy 1942- WhoAm 92
Lu, Shan Zhen 1939- WhoWor 93
Lu, Shaozeng 1932- WhoWor 93
Lu, Wudu 1947- WhoWor 93
Lu, Yimin 1935- WhoWor 93
Lu, Zhen-Qiu 1937- WhoWor 93
Lualdi, Adriano 1885-1971 Baker 92, OxDcOp
Luallen, Sally Carol Shank 1938- WhoAmW 93
Luandrew, Albert BioIn 17
Luan Enjie WhoAsAP 91
Luard, Evan 1926-1991 BioIn 17
Luard, Nicholas 1937- ScF&FL 92
Luba, R.W. 1942- St&PR 93
Lubac, Henri de 1896-1991 BioIn 17
Lubachivsky, Myroslav Ivan Cardinal 1914- WhoWor 93
Lubalin, Irwin 1918- St&PR 93
Luban, Norman Alan 1945- WhoE 93
Lubar, Jeffrey Stuart 1947- WhoAm 92
Lubar, Joel F. 1938- WhoSSW 93
Lubar, Robert 1920- WhoWrEP 92
Lubart, David 1915- St&PR 93
Lubart, David 1915-1991 BioIn 17
Lubasch, Richard J. 1946- St&PR 93
Lubatti, Henry Joseph 1937- WhoAm 92
Lubavitcher Rebbe 1902- JeAmHC
Lubbe, Wilhelm Frederick 1938- WhoWor 93
Lubben, Rick Ronald 1959- WhoEmL 93
Lubben, Vicki M. Law&B 92
Lubbers, Ruud Rudolphus Franciscus Marie 1939- WhoWor 93
Lubbock, Dan Grayson Law&B 92
Lubbock, Emma Rachel 1952- WhoWor 93
Lubbock, Fiona Constance 1957- WhoE 93
Lubbock, John 1834-1913 IntDcAn
Lubbock, S.G. ScF&FL 92
Lubbs, Russel Dean 1946- WhoEmL 93
Lubcker, Robert L. 1937- St&PR 93
Lube, Frank H 1938- WhoWor 93
Lubeck, Ernst 1829-1876 Baker 92
Lubeck, Johann Heinrich 1799-1865 Baker 92
Lubeck, L. WhoScE 91-4
Lubeck, Louis 1838-1904 Baker 92
Lubeck, Marvin Jay 1929- WhoAm 92, WhoWor 93
Lubeck, Vincent 1654-1740 Baker 92
Lubecke, Shelia Ann 1948- WhoEmL 93
Lubecker, Carolyn Kent 1964- WhoEmL 93
Lubega, Mathias K.L. 1933- WhoUN 92
Lubell, Ellen 1950- WhoEmL 93
Lubell, Harold 1925- WhoAm 92
Lubensky, Amy Ruth 1943- WhoE 93
Lubensky, Lloyd C. 1922- St&PR 93
Lubensky, Tom Carl 1943- WhoE 93
Luber, Elliot B. 1959- WhoWrEP 92
Luber, Frederick George 1925- St&PR 93
Luber, Thomas Julian 1949- WhoWor 93
Luberoff, Benjamin J. 1925- WhoWrEP 92
Lubespere, Andre 1926- WhoScE 91-2
Lubet, Pierre Edmond 1925- WhoScE 91-2
Lubetkin, Alvin Nat 1933- St&PR 93
Lubetkin, Berthold 1901-1990 BioIn 17
Lubetkin, Charles Schiller 1932- St&PR 93, WhoAm 92
Lubetsky, Elsie 1917- WhoWrEP 92
Lubey, Patricia J. Law&B 92
Lubic, Benita Joan Alk 1936- WhoE 93
Lubic, Ruth Watson 1927- WhoAm 92, WhoAmW 93
Lubick, Donald Cyril 1926- WhoAm 92
Lubienski, Henryk 1793-1883 PolBiDi
Lubin, Arthur 1901- MiSFD 9
Lubin, Benjamin L. 1934- St&PR 93
Lubin, Benjamin Livingston 1934- WhoAm 92
Lubin, Bernard 1923- WhoAm 92
Lubin, Bruce S. 1953- St&PR 93
Lubin, Donald d1991 BioIn 17
Lubin, Donald G. 1934- WhoAm 92
Lubin, Germaine 1890-1979 IntDcOp, OxDcOp
Lubin, Germaine (Leontine Angelique) 1890-1979 Baker 92
Lubin, Jack 1931- St&PR 93, WhoAm 92
Lubin, James Arnold 1936- WhoUN 92
Lubin, Joy Kathleen 1943- WhoAmW 93
Lubin, Leonard ConAu 38NR, MajAI
Lubin, Leonard B. 1943- ConAu 38NR, MajAI
Lubin, Martin 1923- WhoAm 92
Lubin, Michael Frederick 1947- WhoAm 92, WhoEmL 93, WhoSSW 93
Lubin, Ruth 1911- WhoAmW 93
Lubin, Seth Michael Law&B 92
Lubin, Steven 1942- Baker 92, WhoAm 92
Lubin, William Joseph 1952- St&PR 93
Lubiner, Judith Okoshkin 1950- WhoAmW 93
Lubinski, Arthur 1910- WhoAm 92
Lubinsky, Marian Solomon 1946- WhoEmL 93
Lubit, Roy Howard 1953- WhoE 93
Lubitsch, Ernst 1892-1947 BioIn 17, MiSFD 9N
Lubitz, Cecil Robert 1925- WhoE 93
Lubitz, Robin Lee 1948- WhoSSW 93
Lubitz, Wolfgang Walter Botho 1949- WhoWor 93
Lubker, John William, II 1943- WhoSSW 93
Lubker, Robert Alfred 1920- WhoSSW 93
Lubkin, Gloria Becker 1933- WhoAm 92, WhoAmW 93
Lubkin, Howard 1934- WhoE 93
Lubkin, Ilene Morof 1928- WhoAmW 93
Lubkin, Saul 1939- WhoE 93
Lubkin, Virginia Leila 1914- WhoE 93
Lublenski, Ida AmWomPl
Lublin, Irving St&PR 93
Lubling, Chanoch Law&B 92
Lublinski, Michael 1951- WhoEmL 93
Lubniewski, Angela B. Law&B 92
Luboff, Norman 1917-1987 Baker 92
Luborsky, Fred Everett 1923- WhoAm 92
Luboschik, Ulrich J. 1943- WhoScE 91-3
Luboshitz, Lea 1885-1965 Baker 92
Luboshitz, Pierre 1891-1971 Baker 92
Luboshutz, Lea 1885-1965 Baker 92
Luboshutz, Pierre 1891-1971 Baker 92
Lubot, Eugene Stephen 1942- WhoE 93
Lubotsky, Mark (Davidovich) 1931- Baker 92
Luboviski, Martin E. 1942- St&PR 93
Lubovitch, Lar BioIn 17, WhoAm 92
Lubovitch, Lar 1943?- CurBio 92 [port]
Lubow, Nathan Myron 1929- WhoE 93, WhoWor 93
Lubowsky, Jack 1940- WhoE 93
Lubowsky, Susan 1949- WhoE 93
Lubrano, Alfred BioIn 17
Lubrano, Mike 1961- WhoEmL 93
Lubrano, Vincent P. 1941- St&PR 93
Lubs, Herbert Augustus 1929- WhoAm 92
Lubs, James D. 1925- St&PR 93
Lubuska, Adam Zbigniew 1925- WhoScE 91-4
Luby, Dallas W. 1940- WhoIns 93
Luby, Elliot Donald 1924- WhoAm 92
Luby, Jay F. 1951- St&PR 93
Luby, Joe O., Jr. Law&B 92
Luby, Mary Ann Law&B 92
Luby, Patrick Joseph 1930- St&PR 93
Luby, Thomas Stewart 1952- WhoEmL 93
Luby, William P. Law&B 92
Luca, Raymond Joseph 1941- St&PR 93
Luca, Sergiu 1943- Baker 92
Lucadello, Tony 1913-1989 BioIn 17
Lucado, F. Greg, Jr. 1954- St&PR 93
Lucan 39-65 OxDcOp
Lucan, Arthur 1887-1954 & McShane, Kitty 1898-1964 QDrFCA 92 [port]
Lucan, Patrick Sarsfield, Earl of 1650-1693 BioIn 17, HarEnMi
Lucander, Nils 1924- WhoWrEP 92
Lucani, Paolo 1941- WhoUN 92
Lucanio, Patrick 1949- ScF&FL 92
Lucansky, Terry Wayne 1942- WhoSSW 93
Lucantoni, Giovanni 1825-1902 Baker 92
Lucarotti, John ScF&FL 92
Lucas, Adele Etoch Law&B 92
Lucas, Adetokunbo Olumide Oluwole 1931- WhoAm 92
Lucas, Alec 1913- WhoWrEP 92
Lucas, Alexander Ralph 1931- WhoAm 92
Lucas, Alfred Winslow, Jr. 1950- WhoE 93
Lucas, Allison Grace Law&B 92
Lucas, Anthony S. 1933- St&PR 93
Lucas, Arthur Clay 1931- St&PR 93
Lucas, Aubrey Keith 1934- WhoAm 92, WhoSSW 93
Lucas, Barbara B. 1945- St&PR 93, WhoAm 92, WhoAmW 93
Lucas, Beth Anne 1960- WhoAmW 93
Lucas, Bill L. 1940- St&PR 93
Lucas, Billy Joe 1942- WhoE 93, WhoWor 93
Lucas, Bonnie Lynn 1950- WhoEmL 93
Lucas, Brian C. Law&B 92
Lucas, Carol Lee 1940- WhoAm 92
Lucas, Carolyn E. Law&B 92
Lucas, Charles Fred 1902-1986 BiDAMSp 1989
Lucas, Charles M. 1938- St&PR 93
Lucas, Claude Paul 1945- St&PR 93
Lucas, Craig BioIn 17
Lucas, Craig 1951- ConAu 137, ConTFT 10, WhoAm 92
Lucas, Diana Dee 1952- WhoAmW 93
Lucas, Donald Brooks 1914- WhoAm 92
Lucas, Donald L. 1930- St&PR 93
Lucas, Donald Leo 1930- WhoAm 92
Lucas, E.V. 1868-1938 BioIn 17, ScF&FL 92
Lucas, Edward Verrall 1868-1938 BioIn 17
Lucas, Elizabeth Coughlin 1918- WhoAmW 93
Lucas, Elizabeth Mary 1954- WhoAmW 93
Lucas, F.L. 1894-1967 ScF&FL 92
Lucas, Frank Edward 1934- WhoAm 92
Lucas, Franz D. 1921- WhoWor 93
Lucas, Fred Vance 1922- WhoAm 92
Lucas, George BioIn 17
Lucas, George 1944- MiSFD 9, ScF&FL 92
Lucas, George B. d1991 BioIn 17
Lucas, George Gordon WhoScE 91-1
Lucas, George Ramsdell, Jr. 1949- WhoAm 92, WhoE 93, WhoEmL 93
Lucas, George W., Jr. 1944- WhoAm 92
Lucas, Georges 1915- WhoWor 93
Lucas, Georgetta Marie Snell 1920- WhoAmW 93, WhoWor 93
Lucas, Gregory Dean 1951- WhoEmL 93
Lucas, Helene Elise AmWomPl
Lucas, Henry Cameron, Jr. 1944- WhoAm 92
Lucas, Hinton J., Jr. Law&B 92
Lucas, Hugh H. 1937- St&PR 93
Lucas, Hugh Hampton 1937- WhoAm 92
Lucas, J.R., Jr. Law&B 92
Lucas, J. Richard 1929- WhoAm 92
Lucas, Jacklyn H. 1928- BioIn 17
Lucas, Jacqueline Marie 1962- WhoSSW 93
Lucas, Jacques 1927- WhoScE 91-2
Lucas, James A. Law&B 92
Lucas, James Dornan 1932- St&PR 93
Lucas, James Evans 1933- WhoAm 92
Lucas, James Howard 1927- WhoIns 93
Lucas, James Raymond 1950- WhoEmL 93
Lucas, James Walter 1940- WhoAm 92
Lucas, Jeffrey Tran BioIn 17
Lucas, John, Jr. 1930- St&PR 93
Lucas, John Allen 1943- WhoAm 92
Lucas, John Harding, Jr. 1953- BiDAMSp 1989
Lucas, John Kenneth 1946- WhoAm 92
Lucas, John M. Law&B 92
Lucas, John Porter 1890-1949 HarEnMi
Lucas, Joni Marlene 1962- WhoAmW 93
Lucas, Kenneth Alexander 1963- WhoSSW 93
Lucas, Klaus 1943- WhoScE 91-3
Lucas, Laura Roberts 1946- WhoEmL 93
Lucas, Lawrence Newton 1906- WhoAm 92
Lucas, Leighton 1903-1982 Baker 92
Lucas, Linda Lucille 1940- WhoAmW 93
Lucas, Luis BioIn 17
Lucas, Malcolm Millar 1927- WhoAm 92
Lucas, Mark Thornton 1953- WhoEmL 93
Lucas, Mary Anderson 1882-1952 Baker 92
Lucas, Melinda Ann 1953- WhoSSW 93
Lucas, Michel 1944- WhoScE 91-2
Lucas, Ouida La Forrest 1915- WhoWrEP 92
Lucas, Penelope ScF&FL 92
Lucas, Peter Charles 1934- WhoWor 93
Lucas, Prudence W. 1954- St&PR 93
Lucas, Raymond D. 1937- St&PR 93
Lucas, Robert Alan 1935- WhoE 93
Lucas, Robert Elmer 1916- WhoAm 92
Lucas, Robert J. 1946- St&PR 93
Lucas, Russell 1930- ConAu 137

Lucas, Ruth Frances 1929- *WhoAmW 93*
Lucas, S. Akridge 1949- *WhoAmW 93*
Lucas, Scott W. 1892-1968 *PolPar*
Lucas, Sharron Riessinger 1961- *WhoEmL 93*
Lucas, Shelley V. *Law&B 92*
Lucas, Shirley Agnes Hoyt 1921- *WhoAmW 93*
Lucas, Stacy A. *Law&B 92*
Lucas, Stanley Jerome 1929- *WhoAm 92*
Lucas, Steven Mitchell 1948- *WhoEmL 93*
Lucas, Steven Robert 1959- *WhoEmL 93, WhoSSW 93*
Lucas, Stuart Mitchell 1952- *St&PR 93*
Lucas, Thomas E. *Law&B 92*
Lucas, Tim *ScF&FL 92*
Lucas, Valerie Patricia 1951- *WhoEmL 93*
Lucas, William Charles *Law&B 92*
Lucas, William John 1940- *St&PR 93*
Lucas, William Max, Jr. 1934- *WhoAm 92*
Lucas, William Ray 1922- *WhoAm 92*
Lucas, William Ray, Jr. 1955- *WhoEmL 93*
Lucas, Wingate Hezekiah 1943- *WhoSSW 93*
Lucas Caballeros, Jorge *DcCPCAm*
Lucas Garcia, Fernando Romeo 1924- *DcCPCAm*
Lucas Garcia, Manuel Benedicto *DcCPCAm*
Lucasson, Pierre 1923- *WhoScE 91-2*
Lucas-Tauchar, Margaret Frances 1956- *WhoAmW 93*
Lucca, John James 1921- *WhoAm 92*
Lucca, Pauline 1841-1908 *Baker 92, OxDcOp*
Lucca, Thomas George 1938- *St&PR 93*
Luccarelli, Peter Anthony, Jr. *Law&B 92*
Lucchesi, Andrea 1741-1801 *Baker 92*
Lucchesi, Bruno 1926- *WhoAm 92*
Lucchesi, Donald Albert 1950- *WhoAm 92*
Lucchesi, Fernando 1954- *BioIn 17*
Lucchesi, John C. *WhoAm 92*
Lucchesi, Raymond John 1954- *WhoEmL 93*
Lucchesini, Andrea 1965- *Baker 92*
Lucchetti, Lynn L. 1939- *WhoAmW 93, WhoSSW 93*
Lucchetti, Vincent Anton 1954- *WhoEmL 93*
Lucchi, Leonard Louis 1958- *WhoEmL 93*
Lucchitta, Baerbel Koesters 1938- *WhoAmW 93*
Lucci, Guy Daniel, Jr. 1929- *St&PR 93*
Lucci, Susan *BioIn 17, WhoAm 92, WhoAmW 93*
Lucci, William Ralph, Jr. 1956- *WhoE 93*
Lucciani, Pierre 1935- *WhoScE 91-2*
Lucco, George Edward 1947- *St&PR 93*
Luce, Alethea *AmWomPl*
Luce, Bill J. 1946- *St&PR 93*
Luce, Carol Bringman 1951- *WhoAmW 93*
Luce, Carolyn Buck- *BioIn 17*
Luce, Charles Franklin 1917- *St&PR 93, WhoAm 92*
Luce, Clare Boothe 1903-1987 *BioIn 17, JrnUS*
Luce, Connie P. 1941- *WhoAmW 93*
Luce, Gordon Hannington 1889-1979 *IntDcAn*
Luce, Grace A. *AmWomPl*
Luce, Henry, III 1925- *St&PR 93, WhoAm 92*
Luce, Henry, III, Mrs. 1925- *WhoWor 93*
Luce, Henry R. 1898-1967 *ColdWar 1 [port]*
Luce, Henry Robinson 1898-1967 *BioIn 17, JrnUS*
Luce, James A. 1940- *WhoWrEP 92*
Luce, James Edward 1935- *WhoE 93*
Luce, James Jay Dudley 1959- *WhoE 93*
Luce, James W. 1947- *WhoIns 93*
Luce, Jon D. 1951- *St&PR 93*
Luce, Kenyon Eldridge *Law&B 92*
Luce, Robert Duncan 1925- *WhoAm 92*
Luce, Thomas A. 1956- *St&PR 93*
Luce, Thomas W., III *NewYTBS 92 [port]*
Luce, Thomas Warren, III 1940- *WhoAm 92, WhoWor 93*
Luce, Walter Arthur 1920- *WhoAm 92*
Luceno, Charles Edward 1958- *WhoEmL 93*
Luceno, James *ScF&FL 92*
Lucente, Edward E. 1939- *St&PR 93, WhoAm 92*
Lucente, Francesco *MiSFD 9*
Lucente, Rosemary Dolores 1935- *WhoAmW 93*
Lucero, Eric Andres Donayre 1964- *WhoWor 93*
Lucero, Frank Anthony 1935- *St&PR 93, WhoE 93*
Lucero-Schayes, Wendy 1963- *NotHsAW 93 [port]*
Lucertini, Mario *WhoScE 91-3*
Lucey, Charles Timothy 1905- *WhoAm 92*
Lucey, Donna M. 1951- *BioIn 17*
Lucey, Douglas Michael 1947- *St&PR 93*
Lucey, Jerold Francis 1926- *WhoAm 92*
Lucey, Thomas Joseph 1943- *St&PR 93*
Lucey, William F., Jr. 1935- *St&PR 93*
Lu Cheng-ts'ao 1904- *HarEnMi*
Luches, A. 1940- *WhoScE 91-3*
Luches, Armando 1940- *WhoWor 93*
Luchetti, Daniele 1960- *MiSFD 9*
Luchetti, Raymond 1944- *St&PR 93*
Luchetti, Robert James 1949- *WhoE 93*
Luchetti, Veriano 1939- *OxDcOp*
Luchnick, Lance J. *BioIn 17*
Luchs, David L. 1939- *St&PR 93*
Luchs, Fred Emil 1904- *WhoWor 93*
Luchsinger, Arlene Edith 1937- *WhoAmW 93*
Luchsinger, John F. 1920-1992 *BioIn 17*
Luchsinger, John F., Jr. *Law&B 92*
Lucht, Irmgard 1937- *BioIn 17*
Lucht, John Charles 1933- *St&PR 93, WhoAm 92*
Lucht, Lutz Gerhard 1943- *WhoWor 93*
Lucht, Sondra Moore 1942- *WhoAmW 93*
Luchte, Charles Eugene 1926- *St&PR 93*
Luchterhand, Ralph Edward 1952- *WhoEmL 93*
Luchtrath, Helmut Friedrich 1921- *WhoWor 93*
Luci, James S. 1937- *St&PR 93*
Lucia, Ellis (Joel) 1922- *WhoWrEP 92*
Lucia, Jose Maria 1935- *WhoWor 93*
Lucia, Marilyn Reed *WhoAmW 93*
Lucia, Philip John 1928- *WhoAm 92*
Lucian c. 120-c. 180 *OxDcByz*
Luciana, Eugene D. 1941- *St&PR 93*
Luciana, Joseph Leonard, III 1954- *WhoEmL 93*
Luciani, Sisto 1936- *WhoScE 91-3, WhoWor 93*
Luciano, Mark R. *WhoIns 93*
Luciano, Mark R. 1959- *St&PR 93*
Luciano, Robert Anthony 1934- *WhoE 93*
Luciano, Robert Peter 1933- *St&PR 93, WhoAm 92*
Lucian of Antioch d312 *OxDcByz*
Lucid, Robert Francis 1930- *WhoAm 92*
Lucid, Shannon *BioIn 17*
Lucid, Shannon W. 1943- *WhoAmW 93*
Lucidi, Marsha DeLuca 1943- *WhoAmW 93*
Lucido, Chester C., Jr. 1939- *St&PR 93*
Lucido, Frank Cesare 1937- *St&PR 93*
Lucido, John Anthony 1952- *St&PR 93*
Lucido, Louis Charles 1948- *WhoAm 92*
Lucie, Mitchell K. *Law&B 92*
Lucien, Jon *BioIn 17*
Lucientes, Francisco Jose de Goya y 1746-1828 *BioIn 17*
Lucier, Alvin (Augustus, Jr.) 1931- *Baker 92*
Lucier, David Bruce 1949- *WhoSSW 93*
Lucier, Francis Paul 1927- *WhoAm 92*
Lucier, James Alfred 1920- *WhoSSW 93*
Lucier, Mary *BioIn 17*
Lucier, P. Jeffrey 1941- *St&PR 93, WhoAm 92*
Lucillianus d383 *HarEnMi*
Lucio, Eduardo Andres, Jr. 1946- *WhoSSW 93*
Luciuk, Juliusz (Mieczyslaw) 1927- *Baker 92*
Lucius, Michel Claude 1942- *WhoScE 91-2*
Luck, Andrew Peter 1960- *WhoEmL 93, WhoWor 93*
Luck, Bruce Murray *Law&B 92*
Luck, David Jonathan Lewis 1929- *WhoAm 92*
Luck, Edward E. *St&PR 93*
Luck, Gary Edward 1937- *WhoAm 92*
Luck, Georg Hans Bhawani 1926- *WhoAm 92*
Luck, Gilbert Clayton 1935- *St&PR 93*
Luck, Heinz Otto 1934- *WhoScE 91-3*
Luck, James I. 1945- *WhoAm 92*
Luck, Sheila M. *Law&B 92*
Luck, Werner A.P. 1922- *WhoScE 91-3*
Luck, William Clifton 1943- *St&PR 93*
Lucke, James Thomas *Law&B 92*
Lucke, Kurt 1921- *WhoScE 91-3*
Lucke, Loren Ernest 1930- *St&PR 93*
Lucke, Madeleine Veronica 1950- *WhoEmL 93*
Luckel, Florence R. 1917- *St&PR 93*
Luckel, Lucien J. 1921- *St&PR 93*
Lucken, Edwin Anthony Charles 1931- *WhoScE 91-4*
Luckenbach, Alexander Heinrich 1956- *WhoWor 93*
Luckenbach, Helga 1935- *WhoWor 93*
Luckenbaugh, Richard Lee 1937- *St&PR 93*
Luckenbill-Edds, Louise 1936- *WhoAmW 93*
Luckens, Karl R. *Law&B 92*
Lucker, Howard P. *Law&B 92*
Lucker, Jay K. 1930- *WhoAm 92*
Lucker, Raymond 1927- *BioIn 17*
Lucker, Raymond Alphonse 1927- *WhoAm 92*
Luckett, Jack Cooper 1932- *St&PR 93*
Luckett, Karen Beth *WhoWrEP 92*
Luckett, Paul H., III 1935- *St&PR 93*
Luckett, Paul Herbert, III 1935- *WhoAm 92*
Luckey, Irene 1949- *WhoAmW 93, WhoEmL 93*
Luckey, Joseph Frank 1936- *St&PR 93*
Luckey, Laura Colby *WhoAm 92*
Luckey, Robert Reuel Raphael 1917- *WhoAm 92*
Luckey-Jordan, Ellen Jane 1951- *WhoSSW 93*
Luckhurst, Geoffrey Roger *WhoScE 91-1*
Luckie, Blanche Gomillion 1965- *WhoSSW 93*
Luckie, L.F. *ScF&FL 92*
Luckie, Robert Ervin, Jr. 1917- *WhoAm 92*
Luckinbill, Laurence George 1934- *WhoAm 92*
Lucking, John Terrence *Law&B 92*
Lucking, Peter Stephen 1945- *WhoWor 93*
Luckman, Charles 1909- *St&PR 93, WhoAm 92*
Luckman, James McElroy 1935- *St&PR 93*
Luckman, Sid 1916- *BioIn 17*
Luckmann, Kenneth Frederick 1945- *WhoSSW 93*
Luckmann, William Henry 1926- *WhoAm 92*
Luckner, Herman Richard, III 1933- *WhoWor 93*
Luckoff, Cheryl B. *Law&B 92*
Luckow, Elizabeth Ellen 1934- *WhoAmW 93*
Luckow, Lynn D.W. 1949- *St&PR 93*
Luckow, Sherry Louise 1963- *WhoE 93*
Lucks, Julius Jack 1928- *St&PR 93*
Lucksinger, Michael John 1952- *WhoSSW 93*
Lucktenberg, Kathryn 1958- *WhoAm 92*
Lucky, Robert Wendell 1936- *WhoAm 92*
Lucky, Stepan 1919- *Baker 92*
Luckyn-Malone, Laura Elizabeth 1952- *St&PR 93*
Lucow, Milton 1924- *WhoAm 92*
Lucrezi, Cathy Louise 1956- *WhoAmW 93*
Lucullus, Lucius Licinius c. 117BC-56BC *HarEnMi*
Lucus, William Roy 1953- *St&PR 93*
Lucy, Autherine Juanita 1929- *EncAACR*
Lucy, Dennis Durwood, Jr. 1934- *WhoAm 92*
Lucy, Jack Albert *WhoScE 91-1*
Lucy, Kavaler E. *St&PR 93*
Lucy, Paul Edward 1936- *St&PR 93*
Lucy, Robert Meredith 1926- *WhoAm 92*
Lucyshyn, Peter Stephen *Law&B 92*
Luczak, Holger 1943- *WhoScE 91-3*
Luczak, Holger Theodor 1943- *WhoWor 93*
Luczak, Janet Williams 1955- *WhoEmL 93*
Luczka, Jerzy 1952- *WhoWor 93*
Luczkowski, Barbara Jean 1958- *WhoEmL 93*
Luczun, Mary Ellen Teresa 1951- *WhoWrEP 92*
Ludden, George Clemens 1945- *WhoSSW 93*
Ludden, John Franklin 1930- *WhoE 93*
Ludden, Thomas Marcellus 1946- *WhoSSW 93*
Ludden, Timothy Wayne 1940- *St&PR 93*
Luddie, Walter Joseph 1917- *WhoWrEP 92*
Luddy, Marc Joseph *Law&B 92*
Ludeking, Judson Scott 1951- *WhoE 93*
Ludel, Jacqueline 1945- *BioIn 17*
Ludeman, Robert Ervin 1929- *St&PR 93*
Ludeman Family *BioIn 17*
Ludemann, Doreen A. *Law&B 92*
Ludemann, Heinz *WhoScE 91-3*
Ludemann, Roger Reo 1948- *WhoEmL 93*
Ludendorff, Erich 1865-1937 *DcTwHis, HarEnMi*
Luder, Owen Harold 1928- *WhoWor 93*
Luderer, Bernd 1949- *WhoWor 93*
Luders, Adam 1950- *WhoAm 92*
Ludes, J.E. 1938- *St&PR 93*
Ludford, Nicholas c. 1485-c. 1557 *Baker 92*
Ludgin, Chester (Hall) 1925- *Baker 92, WhoAm 92*
Ludgin, Donald Hugh 1929- *WhoE 93*
Ludgus, Nancy Lucke *Law&B 92*
Ludick, Paul *BioIn 17*
Ludikar, Pavel 1882-1970 *Baker 92*
Ludington, C. Townsend 1896-1968 *EncABHB 8 [port]*
Ludington, Charles Townsend, Jr. 1936- *WhoAm 92*
Ludington, Christopher P. 1953- *St&PR 93*
Ludington, Francis Henry, Jr. 1923- *St&PR 93*
Ludington, Helen Gilman *AmWomPl*
Ludington, John Samuel 1928- *St&PR 93*
Ludington, Thomas Lamson 1953- *WhoEmL 93*
Ludington, William F. 1935- *St&PR 93*
Ludington, William Fletcher 1935- *WhoAm 92*
Ludkewycz, Stanislaus 1879-1979 *Baker 92, PolBiDi*
Ludkiewicz, A. *Law&B 92*
Ludlam, Harry *ScF&FL 92*
Ludlam, James Edward, III 1943- *WhoAm 92*
Ludlam, Roger 1942- *St&PR 93*
Ludlam, Roger James 1942- *WhoAm 92*
Ludlow, Edmund 1898-1979 *ScF&FL 92*
Ludlow, Jean W. 1935- *WhoSSW 93*
Ludlow, John A. d1990 *BioIn 17*
Ludlow, Madeleine Weigel 1954- *WhoAmW 93*
Ludlow, Thomas Hibbard 1946- *WhoEmL 93*
Ludlow, Warren Jay *Law&B 92*
Ludlum, David Blodgett 1929- *WhoAm 92, WhoE 93*
Ludlum, John Charles 1913- *WhoSSW 93*
Ludlum, Robert 1927- *Au&Arts 10 [port], BioIn 17, WhoAm 92, WhoWrEP 92*
Ludmer, Alba 1940- *WhoE 93*
Ludmerer, Kenneth Marc 1947- *WhoAm 92*
Ludolph, Charles M. *BioIn 17*
Ludolph, Pamela Sears 1950- *WhoAmW 93*
Ludovici, Anthony 1927- *WhoAm 92*
Ludovico *DcAmChF 1960*
Ludsin, Steven Alan 1948- *WhoEmL 93*
Ludt, Rudolph E. 1914-1990 *BioIn 17*
Ludtke, Helmut Hermann Wilhelm 1926- *WhoWor 93*
Ludtke, James Buren 1924- *WhoAm 92*
Ludtke, John LeRoy 1950- *WhoE 93, WhoEmL 93*
Ludtke, Mary Alice 1950- *WhoEmL 93*
Ludvigsen, Frants Josef Bernhard Thoger 1923- *WhoSSW 93*
Ludvigson, David L. 1938- *St&PR 93*
Ludvigson, Neil A. 1935- *St&PR 93*
Ludvigson, Susan 1942- *DcLB 120 [port]*
Ludvigson, Susan Gayle 1942- *WhoWrEP 92*
Ludvigsson, Roger Sten Olof 1955- *WhoWor 93*
Ludviksson, Vilhjalmur 1940- *WhoScE 91-4*
Ludwick, Adriane Gurak 1941- *WhoAmW 93*
Ludwick, Andrew K. 1945- *St&PR 93*
Ludwick, John D. 1941- *St&PR 93*
Ludwig, I, King of Bavaria 1786-1868 *BioIn 17*
Ludwig, II 1845-1886 *Baker 92*
Ludwig, II, King of Bavaria 1845-1886 *OxDcOp*
Ludwig, Allan Ira 1933- *WhoAm 92*
Ludwig, Ann Mary 1953- *WhoAmW 93*
Ludwig, August 1865-1946 *Baker 92*
Ludwig, Charles F. *Law&B 92*
Ludwig, Charles Fine 1931- *St&PR 93*
Ludwig, Christa *IntDcOp, WhoAm 92, WhoWor 93*
Ludwig, Christa 1924- *Baker 92, OxDcOp*
Ludwig, Christopher J. 1945- *St&PR 93*
Ludwig, Daniel K. 1897-1992 *NewYTBS 92*
Ludwig, Daniel Keith *BioIn 17*
Ludwig, Daniel Keith 1897-1992 *CurBio 92N*
Ludwig, Donald Alfred 1933- *WhoAm 92*
Ludwig, Douglas Leroy 1953- *St&PR 93*
Ludwig, Edmund David 1940- *St&PR 93*
Ludwig, Edmund Vincent 1928- *WhoAm 92, WhoE 93*
Ludwig, Edward B., Jr. 1930- *St&PR 93*
Ludwig, Edward Lee 1948- *WhoE 93*
Ludwig, Edward W. 1920-1990 *ScF&FL 92*
Ludwig, Franz 1889-1955 *Baker 92*
Ludwig, Friedrich 1872-1930 *Baker 92*
Ludwig, George Harry 1927- *WhoAm 92*
Ludwig, Gunther 1918- *WhoScE 91-3*
Ludwig, Harry *Law&B 92*
Ludwig, Harvey Fred 1916- *WhoAm 92*
Ludwig, Hermann-Henry 1954- *WhoEmL 93, WhoSSW 93*
Ludwig, Horst 1931- *WhoWor 93*
Ludwig, Jack 1922- *WhoCanL 92*
Ludwig, Jay L. 1941- *St&PR 93*
Ludwig, Jeannette Marie 1949- *WhoE 93*
Ludwig, Jeffrey R. *Law&B 92*
Ludwig, Kenneth J. 1922- *St&PR 93*
Ludwig, Kristine Nicole 1969- *WhoEmL 93*
Ludwig, Leopold 1908-1979 *Baker 92*
Ludwig, Lloyd, Jr. 1944- *St&PR 93*
Ludwig, Lyndell 1923- *BioIn 17, ConAu 38NR*

Ludwig, Marek W. Law&B 92
Ludwig, Margaret G. WhoAmW 93
Ludwig, Mark Allen 1958- WhoEmL 93
Ludwig, Ora Lee J., Ms. 1919- St&PR 93
Ludwig, Ora Lee Kirk 1925- WhoAmW 93
Ludwig, Patricia A. 1949- WhoE 93, WhoEmL 93
Ludwig, Patricia Aileen 1951- WhoAmW 93
Ludwig, Patricia Aileen Hanwacker 1951- WhoEmL 93
Ludwig, Paul Lou 1934- St&PR 93
Ludwig, Peter K. 1931- WhoScE 91-3
Ludwig, Richard 1930- WhoAm 92
Ludwig, Richard Joseph 1937- WhoAm 92
Ludwig, Richard Marshall 1931- St&PR 93
Ludwig, Richard Milton 1920- WhoAm 92
Ludwig, Robert Cleo 1931- St&PR 93
Ludwig, Robert Paul 1953- WhoE 93
Ludwig, Vernell P. 1944- St&PR 93
Ludwig, Vernell Patrick 1944- WhoAm 92
Ludwig, Walther 1902-1981 Baker 92
Ludwig, Walther 1929- WhoWor 93
Ludwig, William 1912- WhoAm 92
Ludwig, William D. 1938- St&PR 93
Ludwig, William John 1955- WhoAm 92
Ludwig, William Orland 1931- WhoAm 92
Ludwig, Wolfgang E. 1929- WhoScE 91-3
Ludwigsen, Per Bo 1949- WhoScE 91-2
Ludwigson, Albert 1954- St&PR 93
Ludwigson, Curt 1943- St&PR 93
Ludwikowski, Rett R. 1943- ConAu 139
Ludwikowski, Rett Ryszard 1943- WhoAm 92
Ludwin, Richard M. Law&B 92
Ludwiszewski, Raymond Bernard 1958- WhoEmL 93
Ludy, Andrew William 1947- WhoWrEP 92
Ludy, Kenneth John 1945- St&PR 93
Luebke, Barbara Francine 1949- WhoE 93
Luebke, Curtis D. St&PR 93
Luebke, Neil Robert 1936- WhoAm 92
Lueck, Debra Ann Law&B 92
Lueck, Therese Louise 1956- WhoEmL 93
Luecke, Carl William 1943- St&PR 93
Luecke, Conrad John 1932- WhoSSW 93
Luecke, David A. 1948- St&PR 93
Luecke, Jerome E. Law&B 92
Luecke, John D. 1922- St&PR 93
Luecke, Richard Harry 1930- WhoAm 92
Luecke, Richard William 1917- WhoAm 92
Lueckel, Earl R. 1923- St&PR 93
Lueckel, William John, Jr. 1928- WhoE 93
Luecken, Peter Grant 1950- WhoE 93
Luedde, Charles Edwin Howell 1944- WhoAm 92
Luedde, Dona Speziale 1945- WhoAmW 93
Luedecker, Margaret Rague 1950- WhoEmL 93
Luedeman, John Keith 1941- WhoSSW 93
Luedemann, Hans-Dietrich 1934- WhoScE 91-3
Lueder, Ernst H. 1932- WhoScE 91-3
Lueder, Robert Gregg 1922- St&PR 93
Lueders, Edward George 1923- WhoAm 92, WhoWrEP 92
Lueders, Richard E. 1945- St&PR 93
Lueders, Thomas C. 1958- St&PR 93
Lueders, W.M. 1951- St&PR 93
Luedke, Frederick L. 1938- St&PR 93
Luedke, Frederick Lee 1938- WhoE 93
Luedke, Keith Alan 1949- St&PR 93
Luedtke, Karl Elroy 1930- St&PR 93
Luedtke, Norman D. 1928- WhoIns 93
Luedtke, Roland Alfred 1924- WhoAm 92
Luedy, Laurence Glenn 1940- St&PR 93
Luehrmann, Adele AmWomPl
Luehrmann, Paul Frank, Jr. 1960- WhoWor 93
Lueje, Anna Law&B 92
Lueke, Donna Mae 1946- WhoE 93
Lueking, Herman August, Jr. 1930- St&PR 93
Luellen, Charles J. 1929- St&PR 93, WhoAm 92, WhoSSW 93, WhoWor 93
Luellen, Diana Elizabeth 1940- WhoAmW 93
Luelmo, Fabio 1937- WhoUN 92
Luem, Walter Kurt 1923- WhoWor 93
Luenberger, David Gilbert 1937- WhoAm 92
Luening, Otto BioIn 17
Luening, Otto 1900- WhoAm 92
Luening, Otto (Clarence) 1900- Baker 92
Luening, Robert Adami 1924- WhoAm 92
Luenn, Nancy 1954- ConAu 39NR, ScF&FL 92
Luepke, Gretchen 1943- WhoAmW 93
Luepke, Henry Francis, Jr. 1935- WhoAm 92
Luepnitz, Roy Robert 1955- WhoSSW 93
Luera, Yolanda 1953- DcLB 122 [port]
Luers, William Henry 1929- WhoAm 92, WhoE 93, WhoWor 93
Luerssen, Frank Wonson 1927- St&PR 93, WhoAm 92
Lueschen, Guenther 1930- WhoWor 93
Lueschen, Sandra Lu 1959- WhoAmW 93
Luessenhop, Valerie J. Law&B 92
Luest, R. WhoScE 91-2
Lueth, Faith M. 1943- WhoAmW 93, WhoE 93
Lueth, Randy Carl 1956- St&PR 93
Lueth, Shirley 1930- WhoWrEP 92
Luetkemeyer, Mary Jane 1951- WhoEmL 93
Luetkenhaus, Anna May 1874- AmWomPl
Luettgen, Michael John 1960- WhoEmL 93
Luettgen, Robert A. Law&B 92
Luettgens, Floyd Roy 1935- WhoIns 93
Luetzelschwab, John William 1940- WhoE 93
Luetzow, William Kenneth 1952- WhoWor 93
Luey, A. Thomas BioIn 17
Luff, Carl Richard 1954- St&PR 93
Luff, Gerald Meredith, Jr. 1937- WhoE 93
Luff, Peter John Roussel 1946- WhoWor 93
Luffingham, John Kingsley WhoScE 91-1
Luffsey, Walter Stith 1934- WhoAm 92
Lufkin, Joseph Charles Francis 1955- WhoEmL 93
Lufkin, Kent C. 1952- St&PR 93
Luft, David G. BioIn 17
Luft, Harold S. 1947- WhoAm 92
Luft, Rene W. 1943- St&PR 93
Luftglass, Murray A. 1931- St&PR 93
Luftglass, Murray Arnold 1931- WhoAm 92, WhoWor 93
Luftig, David 1916- St&PR 93
Luftman, Michael Eric 1946- WhoE 93
Lugar, Richard G. BioIn 17
Lugar, Richard G. 1932- CngDr 91
Lugar, Richard Green 1932- WhoAm 92
Lugar, Todd Riley 1961- St&PR 93
Lugard, Frederick Dealtry 1858-1945 DcTwHis
Lugbill, Ann 1954- WhoEmL 93
Lugbill, Jon BioIn 17, NewYTBS 92 [port]
Lugenbeel, Edward Elmer 1932- WhoAm 92, WhoE 93
Luger, Anton 1918- WhoScE 91-4
Luger, Donald R. 1938- WhoAm 92
Luger, Donald Richard 1938- St&PR 93
Luger, Ellen G. Law&B 92
Luger, George P. 1932- St&PR 93
Lugert, Josef 1841-1936 Baker 92
Lugg, David Knox 1955- St&PR 93
Lughes, Joseph Albert 1928- St&PR 93
Lugiato, Luigi Alberto 1944- WhoWor 93
Luginbuhl, William Hossfeld 1929- WhoAm 92
Lugo, Gail Maxson 1943- WhoSSW 93
Lugo, Hector M. 1938- St&PR 93
Lugo, Jose Francisco 1938- WhoSSW 93
Lugo, Leslie Allan Law&B 92
Lugo, Yolanda BioIn 17
Lu Gongxun 1933- WhoAsAP 91
Lugosi, Bela 1882-1956 BioIn 17, IntDcF 2-3 [port]
Lugo-Somolinos, Aida Maria 1960- WhoAmW 93
Lugowski, Andrzej Mieczyslaw 1952- WhoWor 93
Lugt, Hans Josef 1930- WhoE 93
Luguet, Jacques 1940- WhoScE 91-2
Lu Gwei-Djen 1904-1991 AnObit 1991
Luh, Jiang 1932- WhoSSW 93
Luhan, Mabel Ganson Dodge 1879-1962 BioIn 17
Luhat Wan 1944- WhoAsAP 91
Luhman, Hope Elizabeth 1958- WhoAmW 93
Lu Houshan BioIn 17
Luhowy, Victor M. 1948- St&PR 93
Luhr, Gary Wayne 1948- WhoAm 92
Luhring, John William 1912- WhoAm 92
Luhring, R.A. 1947- St&PR 93
Luhrs, H. Ric 1931- St&PR 93, WhoAm 92, WhoE 93, WhoWor 93
Luhrs, James E. 1936- WhoAm 92
Luhrs, James Everett 1934- St&PR 93
Luhrs, Stephen F. 1952- St&PR 93
Luhta, Caroline Naumann 1930- WhoAmW 93
Lui, Chin Wing 1939- WhoWor 93
Lui, Eric Mun 1958- WhoE 93
Lui, James Harold 1965- WhoEmL 93
Luialamo, George 1945- WhoAsAP 91
Luick, Gary L. 1940- St&PR 93
Luick, Robert B. 1911- St&PR 93
Luick, Robert Burns 1911- WhoAm 92
Luigini, Alexandre (-Clement-Léon-Joseph) 1850-1906 Baker 92
Luigs, Charles Russell 1933- St&PR 93, WhoAm 92
Luikart, Fordyce Whitney 1910- WhoAm 92
Luikart, John F. 1949- St&PR 93
Luikart, John Ford 1949- WhoAm 92
Luing, Gary Alan 1937- WhoAm 92
Luipersbeck, Walter Frank 1949- St&PR 93
Lui Po-ch'eng 1892- HarEnMi
Luippold, Peter Henry 1960- WhoEmL 93
Luis, Ernesto Saguiguit 1946- WhoWor 93
Luis, Juan 1941- DcCPCAm
Luis, Juanita Bolland Law&B 92
Luis, Juanita Bolland 1950- St&PR 93, WhoAm 92, WhoEmL 93, WhoIns 93
Luis, Michael R. Law&B 92
Luis, Saldanha WhoScE 91-3
Luis, Sales WhoScE 91-3
Luisetti, Hank 1916- BioIn 17
Luisi, Kathi Anne 1962- WhoAmW 93
Luiso, Anthony 1944- St&PR 93, WhoAm 92
Lui Yu 356-422 HarEnMi
Luiz, Douglas Edmund 1934- St&PR 93
Luizzo, Anthony John 1942- WhoE 93
Lujan, Leonard 1948- WhoWor 93
Lujan, Manuel, Jr. 20th cent.- HispAmA [port]
Lujan, Manuel, Jr. 1928- CngDr 91, WhoAm 92, WhoE 93, WhoWor 93
Luk, John Wang Kwong 1944- WhoWor 93
Luk, King Sing WhoAm 92
Luka, Edward W. 1933-1991 BioIn 17
Luka, Lisbeth Sheppard 1947- WhoAmW 93
Luka, Thomas Phillip 1946- St&PR 93
Lukac, Carlos N. 1950- St&PR 93
Lukac, Pavel David 1935- WhoScE 91-4
Lukach, Arthur S., Jr. 1935- St&PR 93
Lukach, Teresa Ann 1948- WhoE 93
Lukacic, (Marko) Ivan 1587-1648 Baker 92
Lukacs, Andrew Z. Law&B 92
Lukacs, Bela Bernard 1915- St&PR 93
Lukacs, Gyorgy 1885-1971 BioIn 17, ColdWar 2 [port]
Lukacs, John 1924- BioIn 17
Lukacs, John Adalbert 1924- WhoAm 92, WhoWrEP 92
Lukacs, Michael Edward 1946- WhoE 93, WhoEmL 93
Lukacs, Miklos 1905-1986 Baker 92
Lukacs, Tibor 1928- WhoScE 91-4
Lukander, Tuula WhoScE 91-4
Lukas, D. Wayne BioIn 17
Lukas, Daniel A. 1959- WhoEmL 93
Lukas, Darrell Wayne 1935- BiDAMSp 1989
Lukas, Elsa Victoria 1927- WhoWor 93
Lukas, Gaze Elmer 1907- WhoSSW 93
Lukas, Harriet Virginia 1941- WhoAmW 93
Lukas, J. Anthony 1933- BioIn 17, WhoAm 92
Lukas, Jay Anthony 1933- JrnUS
Lukas, Joan Donaldson 1942- WhoE 93
Lukas, Johannes 1901-1980 IntDcAn
Lukas, Paul 1895-1971 IntDcF 2-3
Lukas, Seth M. St&PR 93
Lukas, Susan 1940- WhoWrEP 92
Lukas, Zdenek 1928- Baker 92
Lukaschek, Heinz 1943- WhoScE 91-4
Lukasiewicz, Ignacy 1822-1882 PolBiDi
Lukasiewicz, Jan 1878-1956 PolBiDi
Lukasiewicz, Szczepan Franciszek 1927- WhoWor 93
Lukasik, Jacques WhoScE 91-2
Lukasik, John Peter, Jr. 1947- WhoE 93
Lukasik, Seweryn J. 1919- WhoScE 91-4
Lukassen, Gerard H. 1946- St&PR 93
Lukaszewicz, Kazimierz 1927- WhoScE 91-4
Lukaszewski, James Edmund 1942- WhoE 93
Lukat, Robert Norton 1946- St&PR 93
Lukatch, Edward 1954- St&PR 93
Lukatch, Susan Vikstrom 1951- St&PR 93
Luke OxDcByz
Luke, Barry P. St&PR 93
Luke, David L., III 1923- St&PR 93
Luke, Dorothy Rawls 1907- WhoWrEP 92
Luke, Douglas Sigler 1941- WhoAm 92
Luke, H. Dieter 1935- WhoScE 91-3
Luke, Hans Dieter 1935- WhoWor 93
Luke, James Phillip 1942- St&PR 93, WhoAm 92
Luke, John A., Jr. 1948- St&PR 93
Luke, John Anderson 1925- St&PR 93, WhoAm 92
Luke, Kathleen A. Law&B 92
Luke, Keye 1904-1991 AnObit 1991, BioIn 17
Luke, Lance Lawton 1955- WhoWor 93
Luke, Mary 1919- ScF&FL 92
Luke, Randall Dan 1935- WhoAm 92
Luke, Ray 1926- Baker 92
Luke, Robert George 1935- WhoAm 92
Luke, Robert Phillips 1940- St&PR 93
Luke, Thomas ScF&FL 92
Luke, Victor Stirling 1927- St&PR 93
Lukehurst, Clare Therese WhoScE 91-1
Lukeman, Karen Calmon 1953- WhoEmL 93
Lukeman, Tim ScF&FL 92
Luken, Charles WhoAm 92
Luken, Charles 1951- CngDr 91
Luken, David A. Law&B 92
Lukenbill, Gregg WhoAm 92
Lukens, Alan Wood 1924- WhoAm 92
Lukens, Barbara 1930- St&PR 93
Lukens, Kenneth B. 1951- WhoEmL 93
Lukens, Paul Bourne 1934- WhoAm 92
Lukens, Walter Patrick 1924- St&PR 93, WhoAm 92
Luker, Jeffrey Paul 1954- WhoAm 92, WhoE 93
Luker, Kristin 1946- WhoAm 92
Luker, Ralph E(dlin) 1940- ConAu 139
Luker, Robert Charles 1927- St&PR 93
Luker, Sharon Lynne 1957- WhoAmW 93
Lukey, Joan A. 1949- WhoAm 92
Lukianuk, Richard A. Law&B 92
Lukin, Philip 1903-1990 BioIn 17
Lukins, Scott B. 1929- St&PR 93
Lukins, Sheila 1942- ConAu 139
Lukjan, Hieronim 1937- WhoScE 91-4
Lukka, Anita 1946- WhoScE 91-4
Lukman, John C. 1922- St&PR 93
Lukodianov, Isai 1913-1984 ScF&FL 92
Lukomski, Kazmierz 1920- PolBiDi
Lukomski, Stefan 1921- WhoScE 91-4
Lukomskii, Sergei Fedor 1949- WhoWor 93
Lukov, Leonid 1909-1963 DrEEuF
Lukowiak, Joan Ann 1946- WhoAmW 93, WhoEmL 93
Luks, Jerome M. Law&B 92
Luks, Jerome M. 1935- St&PR 93
Luks, Jonathan Cerf 1954- WhoE 93
Luksch, James A. 1930- St&PR 93
Lulay, Gail C. 1938- WhoAmW 93
Lull, Ramon 1235?-1315 BioIn 17
Lull, Robert Adelbert 1931- St&PR 93
Lull, William Paul 1954- WhoWor 93
Lulla, Jack 1929- St&PR 93
Lulla, Jack David 1929- WhoAm 92, WhoE 93
Lulli, Giovanni Battista 1632-1687 Baker 92
Lullo, Thomas A. Law&B 92
Lulloff, Charlene Louise 1943- WhoAmW 93
Lully, Jean-Baptiste 1632-1687 Baker 92, IntDcOp [port], OxDcOp
Lully, Raymond 1235?-1315 BioIn 17
Lulof, Fred W.Z. 1938- St&PR 93
Lulu, Donald James 1926- WhoAm 92
Luludis, Frederick Law&B 92
Lum, Dale Whitney 1957- WhoEmL 93
Lum, Darrell H.Y. 1950- WhoWrEP 92
Lum, Herman Tsui Fai 1926- WhoAm 92
Lum, Jean Loui Jin 1938- WhoAm 92, WhoAmW 93
Lum, Linda Li Ching 1957- WhoEmL 93
Luma, Yahya 1949- WhoScE 91-4
Lumadue, Donald Dean 1938- WhoE 93
Lu Maozeng 1928- WhoAsAP 91
Lumauig, Gualberto B. 1933- WhoAsAP 91
Lumb, J. Trevor Law&B 92
Lumbard, Eliot Howland 1925- WhoE 93, WhoWor 93
Lumbard, Joseph Edward, Jr. 1901- WhoAm 92
Lumbiganon, Pisake 1953- WhoWor 93
Lumbra, Reuben W. 1931- St&PR 93
Lumbye, Carl 1841-1911
See Lumbye, Hans Christian 1810-1874 Baker 92
Lumbye, Georg 1843-1922
See Lumbye, Hans Christian 1810-1874 Baker 92
Lumbye, Hans Christian 1810-1874 Baker 92
Lumenganeso, Kiobe 1943- WhoWor 93
Lumens, Armand Jean 1968- WhoWor 93
Lumer, Mark Joseph 1951- WhoE 93
Lumet, Sidney BioIn 17
Lumet, Sidney 1924- MiSFD 9, WhoAm 92
Luminet, Daniel 1929- WhoScE 91-2
Lumley, Benjamin 1811-1875 OxDcOp
Lumley, Brian 1937- ScF&FL 92
Lumley, John Leask 1930- WhoAm 92
Lumley, Robert Alan 1936- St&PR 93
Lumme, Kari A. WhoScE 91-4
Lumme, Paavo O. 1923- WhoScE 91-4
Lummis, Charles F. 1859-1928 GayN
Lummis, Charles F(letcher) 1859-1928 Baker 92
Lummis, Charles Fletcher 1859-1928 BioIn 17
Lummis, Eliza O'Brien AmWomPl
Lummis, Gordon H. 1937- St&PR 93
Lummis, John M. Law&B 92
Lummus, Marion Morris 1934- WhoWrEP 92
Lumpe, Adolf Ingo 1927- WhoWor 93
Lumpkin, Alva Moore, III 1948- WhoEmL 93, WhoSSW 93, WhoWor 93

Lumpkin, Anne Craig 1919- WhoSSW 93
Lumpkin, Bruce Keyser 1944- WhoE 93
Lumpkin, Houston ScF&FL 92
Lumpkin, JimmieLou Fisher 1941- WhoAm 92, WhoAmW 93, WhoSSW 93
Lumpkin, John Henderson 1916- WhoAm 92
Lumpkin, John Robert 1951- WhoAm 92
Lumpkin, Joseph Burton 1955- WhoSSW 93
Lumpkin, Kenneth Charles 1951- WhoWrEP 92
Lumpkin, Lee Roy 1925- WhoAm 92
Lumpp, Karen Eve 1951- WhoEmL 93
Lumpris, Roberto A. 1962- St&PR 93
Lumry, Rufus Worth, II 1920- WhoAm 92
Lumsdaine, Arthur A. 1913-1989 BioIn 17
Lumsdaine, Arthur Allen 1913- WhoWrEP 92
Lumsdaine, David (Newton) 1931- Baker 92
Lumsdaine, Edward 1937- WhoAm 92
Lumsden, D(an) Barry 1939- WhoWrEP 92
Lumsden, David (James) 1928- Baker 92
Lumsden, Ian Gordon 1945- WhoAm 92, WhoE 93
Lumsden, James Gerard 1940- WhoWor 93
Lumsden, Keith Grant 1935- WhoWor 93
Lumsden, Louisa Innes 1844-1935 BioIn 17
Lumsden, Lynne Ann 1947- WhoAm 92
Lumsden, Robert Douglas 1938- WhoE 93
Lumumba, Patrice 1925-1961 ColdWar 2 [port]
Lumumba, Patrice Emergy 1925-1961 DcTwHis
Luna, Alfonso DcCPCAm
Luna, Bigas MiSFD 9
Luna, Casey 1931- WhoAm 92
Luna, Charles Stephen Law&B 92
Luna, Cherry Martin WhoSSW 93
Luna, Donna Jeanne 1952- WhoAmW 93
Luna, Elizabeth Jean 1951- WhoEmL 93
Luna, Joseph Luis, III 1960- WhoE 93
Luna, Patricia Adele 1956- WhoAmW 93, WhoEmL 93, WhoSSW 93
Luna, Sonia 1960- St&PR 93
Luna, Wilson 1951- WhoE 93
Luna-Acosta, German Aurelio 1953- WhoWor 93
Lunan, Charles Burnett 1941- WhoWor 93
Lunan, Duncan 1945- ScF&FL 92
Luna Padilla, Nitza Enid 1959- WhoAmW 93, WhoEmL 93
Lunarski, Jerzy 1937- WhoScE 91-4
Luna Smith, Carla Marie 1960- WhoEmL 93
Lunceford, Jimmie 1902-1947 Baker 92
Lunceford, Laura 1954- WhoEmL 93
Lunch, Lydia 1959- ConAu 38NR
Lunchbox, Deacon d1992 BioIn 17, NewYTBS 92
Lund, Alan Howard 1949- St&PR 93
Lund, Anders O. 1938- WhoScE 91-4
Lund, Art 1915-1990 BioIn 17
Lund, Arthur K. 1933- St&PR 93
Lund, Barbara Mary WhoScE 91-1
Lund, Barrie Geddes 1927- WhoSSW 93
Lund, Bert O. 1920- St&PR 93
Lund, Bert Oscar, Jr. 1920- WhoAm 92
Lund, Bruce Donald 1951- WhoEmL 93
Lund, Candida WhoAm 92, WhoAmW 93
Lund, David H. Law&B 92
Lund, David H. 1927- St&PR 93
Lund, David H., Jr. Law&B 92
Lund, David Harrison 1927- WhoAm 92
Lund, David Nathan 1925- WhoAm 92
Lund, Doris Hibbs 1923- WhoAmW 93
Lund, Ebba WhoScE 91-2
Lund, Edwin Harrison 1954- WhoE 93
Lund, Flemming 1920- WhoScE 91-2
Lund, Francis Leroy 1913- BiDAMSp 1989
Lund, Frederick Henry 1929- WhoSSW 93
Lund, George Edward 1925- WhoAm 92, WhoE 93
Lund, Gunnar 1918- St&PR 93
Lund, Hal J. 1930- St&PR 93
Lund, Hans Bruno 1933- WhoWor 93
Lund, Harold Howard 1928- St&PR 93
Lund, Harry James 1931- St&PR 93
Lund, Henning 1929- WhoScE 91-2
Lund, Ivar 1882-1975 ScF&FL 92
Lund, Jessica S. 1950- WhoAmW 93
Lund, John d1992 NewYTBS 92 [port]
Lund, John 1913-1992 BioIn 17
Lund, Jon Paul 1964- WhoE 93
Lund, Joseph John 1937- St&PR 93
Lund, Kent J. Law&B 92
Lund, Lois Ann 1927- WhoAm 92, WhoAmW 93
Lund, Martin Allan 1936- WhoAm 92
Lund, Mogens 1933- WhoScE 91-2
Lund, Niels Anker Nissen 1945- WhoWor 93
Lund, Orval A., Jr. 1940- WhoWrEP 92
Lund, Paul A. 1938- St&PR 93
Lund, Pauline Kay 1955- WhoEmL 93
Lund, Peter Anthony 1941- WhoAm 92
Lund, Peter Buch WhoScE 91-4
Lund, Richard A. 1951- St&PR 93
Lund, Rita Pollard 1950- WhoWor 93
Lund, Ronald Eugene Law&B 92
Lund, Signe 1868-1950 Baker 92
Lund, Stephen D. St&PR 93
Lund, Steve 1923- WhoAm 92
Lund, Thore Birger 1945- WhoWor 93
Lund, Ulla Oxenboll 1950- WhoScE 91-2
Lund, Victor L. 1947- WhoAm 92
Lund, Victor Lynn 1947- St&PR 93
Lund, Virginia Llego 1939- WhoAmW 93
Lund, Wendell Luther 1905- WhoAm 92
Lund, William Boyce 1959- WhoEmL 93
Lunda, Donald L. 1923- St&PR 93
Lundahl, Harald I. 1944- WhoScE 91-4
Lundahl, Steven Mark 1955- WhoE 93, WhoEmL 93
Lundberg, Bengt A. 1943- WhoScE 91-4
Lundberg, Dag B.A. 1940- WhoScE 91-4
Lundberg, Erik F(ilip) 1907-1987 ConAu 38NR
Lundberg, Ferdinand Edgar 1902- WhoWrEP 92
Lundberg, George David, II 1933- WhoAm 92
Lundberg, Isabel Cary d1991 BioIn 17
Lundberg, Jon Clark 1961- WhoEmL 93
Lundberg, Lance B. 1956- St&PR 93
Lundberg, Larry Thomas 1938- St&PR 93
Lundberg, Lawrence Laska 1927- St&PR 93
Lundberg, Lois Ann 1928- WhoAmW 93
Lundberg, Martin 1938- WhoWor 93
Lundberg, Merrill C. Law&B 92
Lundberg, Per Christer Folke 1943- WhoWor 93
Lundberg, Per Olov 1931- WhoScE 91-4
Lundberg, Robert Dean 1928- WhoE 93
Lundberg, Uly R. Law&B 92
Lundbergh, Per 1938- WhoScE 91-4
Lundbom, Jack Russell 1939- WhoWor 93
Lundby, Arne 1923- WhoScE 91-4
Lundby, Julius Eric 1944- WhoIns 93
Lunde, Anders Steen 1914- WhoSSW 93
Lunde, Charles A. 1940- St&PR 93
Lunde, David Eric 1941- WhoWrEP 92
Lunde, Diane S. 1942- WhoWrEP 92
Lunde, Dolores Benitez 1929- WhoAmW 93, WhoWor 93
Lunde, Harold Irving 1929- WhoAm 92
Lunde, Harry 1947- St&PR 93
Lunde, Henry B. 1943- St&PR 93
Lunde, Katherine L. 1947- WhoAmW 93, WhoEmL 93
Lunde, Knut 1941- WhoScE 91-4
Lunde, Per Knut M. 1934- WhoScE 91-4
Lundeberg, Goran 1929- WhoScE 91-4
Lundeberg, Philip Karl 1923- WhoAm 92
Lundeberg, Roger Victor 1934- WhoE 93
Lundeen, Ardelle Anne 1929- WhoAmW 93
Lundeen, Barbara Berta 1922- WhoAmW 93
Lundeen, David E. 1928- St&PR 93
Lundeen, John Anton 1952- WhoE 93
Lundeen, Malvin 1901-1991 BioIn 17
Lundegard, John Thomas 1931- St&PR 93
Lundelius, Ernest Luther, Jr. 1927- WhoAm 92
Lunden, Arnold 1925- WhoScE 91-4
Lunden, Joan 1950- ConTFT 10, WhoAm 92, WhoAmW 93
Lunden, Samuel Eugene 1897- WhoAm 92
Lunder, Peter Harold 1933- St&PR 93
Lundergan, Barbara Keough 1938- WhoAm 92
Lundering, Scott Douglas Law&B 92
Lunderman, Mary Ann 1951- WhoEmL 93
Lunderstadt, Jorg 1935- WhoScE 91-3
Lundestad, Geir 1945- WhoWor 93
Lundgren, Clara Eloise 1951- WhoEmL 93, WhoSSW 93, WhoWor 93
Lundgren, Erik 1942- WhoScE 91-4
Lundgren, Jeffrey BioIn 17
Lundgren, Kenneth B. 1948- St&PR 93, WhoIns 93
Lundgren, Lennart Stig Ake 1944- WhoWor 93
Lundgren, R. Bjorn M. 1941- WhoScE 91-4
Lundgren, Robert B. 1944- St&PR 93
Lundgren, Robert Wayne 1917- WhoAm 92
Lundgren, Ruth Williamson Wood WhoAmW 93, WhoWor 93
Lundgren, Stig 1925- WhoScE 91-4
Lundgren, Susan Elaine 1949- WhoEmL 93
Lundh, Yngvar Gundro 1932- WhoWor 93
Lundhagen, Edwin Wayne 1937- St&PR 93
Lundholm, Nancy Tishkin 1959- WhoEmL 93
Lundin, Adolf Henrik 1932- WhoWor 93
Lundin, Bruce Theodore 1919- WhoAm 92
Lundin, David Erik 1949- WhoAm 92
Lundin, Marjorie Ellen 1936- WhoAmW 93
Lundin, Norman BioIn 17
Lundin, Robert Lee 1933- WhoUN 92
Lundin, Roger E. 1944- St&PR 93
Lundin, Sven Ragnar 1939- WhoWor 93
Lundine, Stanley Nelson 1939- WhoAm 92, WhoE 93, WhoWor 93
Lunding, Christopher Hanna 1946- WhoEmL 93
Lunding, Franklin J. d1992 NewYTBS 92 [port]
Lund-Johansen, Per 1931- WhoScE 91-4
Lundkvist, Artur 1906-1991 BioIn 17
Lundkvist, Resa Labbe 1960- St&PR 93
Lundkvist, Ulf G. 1938- WhoScE 91-4
Lundman, Richard J. 1944- ConAu 138
Lundman, Richard Jack 1944- WhoAm 92
Lundon, Ace 1936- WhoWrEP 92
Lundquist, Bruce G. 1956- St&PR 93
Lundquist, Carl 1913- WhoWrEP 92
Lundquist, Carl H. 1916-1991 BioIn 17
Lundquist, Charles Arthur 1928- WhoAm 92
Lundquist, Dana R. 1941- WhoAm 92, WhoE 93
Lundquist, David John 1942- St&PR 93
Lundquist, David Robert 1950- WhoEmL 93
Lundquist, Gene Alan 1943- St&PR 93, WhoAm 92
Lundquist, James 1941- ScF&FL 92
Lundquist, James Harold 1931- WhoAm 92
Lundquist, Kathleen Kappy 1953- WhoE 93
Lundquist, Linda Ann Johnson 1945- WhoAmW 93
Lundquist, Mary Elizabeth 1954- WhoAmW 93
Lundquist, Patricia 1941- WhoAmW 93
Lundquist, Per Birger 1945- WhoWor 93
Lundquist, Per-Gotthard 1937- WhoScE 91-4
Lundquist, Richard D. 1947- WhoWrEP 92
Lundquist, Torbjorn (Iwan) 1920- Baker 92
Lundquist, Violet Elvira 1912- WhoAmW 93, WhoWor 93
Lundquist, Weyman Ivan 1930- WhoAm 92
Lundqvist, Jan H. 1926- WhoScE 91-4
Lundqvist, Stig 1925- WhoScE 91-4
Lundregan, William Joseph 1940- WhoE 93
Lundren, K. Thor Law&B 92
Lundrigan, Lee Tarkington Law&B 92
Lundsgaard, J.S. 1945- WhoScE 91-2
Lundsgaarde, Henry Peder 1938- WhoAm 92
Lundstedt, Peter Sanford 1958- WhoE 93
Lundstedt, Sven Bertil 1926- WhoAm 92
Lundsten, Ralph 1936- Baker 92
Lundstrom, Frank E. 1930- St&PR 93
Lundstrom, K. Ingemar 1941- WhoScE 91-4
Lundstrom, Marjie WhoSSW 93
Lundstrom, Mary Meyer 1948- WhoAmW 93
Lundstrom, Sharon A. Law&B 92
Lundstrom, William John 1944- WhoSSW 93
Lundwall, Sam J. 1941- ScF&FL 92
Lundwall, Sam J(errie) 1941- ConAu 37NR
Lundy, Albro, Jr. BioIn 17
Lundy, Audie Lee, Jr. 1943- St&PR 93, WhoAm 92
Lundy, Barbara Carol 1935- WhoAmW 93
Lundy, Benjamin 1789-1839 BioIn 17
Lundy, Cynthia Ross 1955- WhoSSW 93
Lundy, Daniel F. Law&B 92
Lundy, Daniel F. 1930- St&PR 93
Lundy, Francis E. 1937- St&PR 93
Lundy, Gary David 1954- WhoSSW 93
Lundy, Harold W. WhoSSW 93
Lundy, J. Thomas BioIn 17
Lundy, Joseph Edward 1915- WhoAm 92, WhoWor 93
Lundy, Lisa Gail 1962- WhoEmL 93
Lundy, Phyllis 1950- WhoEmL 93
Lundy, Richard Alan 1934- WhoAm 92
Lundy, Richard Bruce 1941- St&PR 93
Lundy, Sadie Allen 1918- WhoAmW 93, WhoWor 93
Lundy, Victor Alfred 1923- WhoAm 92
Lundy, William R., Jr. Law&B 92
Luneburg, Thomas Richard Law&B 92
Lunec, Joseph WhoScE 91-1
Lunelli, Massimiliano 1933- WhoScE 91-3
Lunenfeld, Marilyn Jane 1952- St&PR 93
Lunetta, Vincent Norman 1937- WhoE 93
Luney, William Ross 1930- St&PR 93
Lung, Chang WhoWrEP 92
Lung, David D. 1947- St&PR 93
Lung, David Edward 1936- St&PR 93
Lung, Mervin Dean 1928- St&PR 93
Lung, William Dale 1941- St&PR 93
Lunger, Charles William 1927- WhoAm 92
Lunger, Gary Edward 1942- St&PR 93
Lunger, Irvin Eugene 1912- WhoAm 92
Lunghino, Donald Joseph 1921- WhoAm 92
Lungren, Daniel Edward 1946- WhoAm 92
Lungu, Malani Mordecai WhoWor 93
Luning, Fredrik N:son 1936- WhoWor 93
Luning, H.A. 1932- WhoScE 91-3
Luning, K.G. 1924- WhoScE 91-4
Luning, Klaus 1941- WhoScE 91-3
Luning, Ulrich Ernst 1956- WhoWor 93
Lunis, Arlene Alice 1935- WhoAmW 93
Lunn, Carolyn BioIn 17
Lunn, Carolyn Kowalczyk 1960- ConAu 136
Lunn, Deborah BioIn 17
Lunn, Gorm 1947- WhoScE 91-2
Lunn, Janet 1928- DcChlFi, ScF&FL 92, WhoCanL 92
Lunn, Janet Louise Swoboda 1928- BioIn 17, MajAI [port], WhoWrEP 92
Lunn, Jean 1933- WhoWrEP 92
Lunn, Joseph Scott 1931- WhoSSW 93
Lunn, Kitty Elizabeth 1950- WhoAmW 93
Lunn, Louise Kirkby Baker 92
Lunn, Louise Kirkby 1873-1930 OxDcOp
Lunn, Paul G. Law&B 92
Lunn, Richard 1926- ScF&FL 92
Lunne, Tom A. 1946- WhoScE 91-4
Lunney, Joan Katherine 1946- WhoE 93
Luns, Joseph Marie Antoine Hubert 1911- WhoWor 93
Lunsford, Cin Forshay- BioIn 17
Lunsford, Donald Wayne 1938- WhoSSW 93
Lunsford, Everett Pollard, Jr. 1949- WhoEmL 93
Lunsford, Julius R., Jr. 1915- WhoAm 92
Lunsford, M. Rosser 1922- WhoWrEP 92
Lunsford, Ray St&PR 93
Lunsford, Walter 1951- St&PR 93
Lunssens, Martin 1871-1944 Baker 92
Lunt, Carolyn Swanson 1936- WhoAmW 93
Lunt, Denham C., Jr. 1926- St&PR 93
Lunt, George Gordon WhoScE 91-1
Lunt, Horace Gray 1918- WhoAm 92
Lunt, Jack Law&B 92
Lunt, Jack 1944- St&PR 93, WhoAm 92
Luntey, Donald Rae 1945- WhoSSW 93
Luntz, Gregory William 1952- St&PR 93
Luntz, Perry 1927- WhoWrEP 92
Luntz, Susan 1942- WhoAmW 93
Luntz, Theodore M. 1926- St&PR 93
Luntz, Theodore Michael 1926- WhoAm 92
Luntz, William L. 1924- St&PR 93
Lunven, Paul 1930- WhoScE 91-3
Lunz, William Edward 1952- WhoEmL 93
Luo, Chenglin 1934- WhoUN 92
Luo, Dawei 1939- WhoWor 93
Luo, Dingjun 1936- WhoWor 93
Luo, Yang 1934- WhoWor 93
Luo, Yuanquan 1938- WhoWor 93
Luo, Zongqian 1934- WhoWor 93
Luo Gan 1935- WhoAsAP 91
Luoma, Eric V. Law&B 92
Luoma, Heikki 1926- WhoScE 91-4
Luomajoki, Alpo Jyrki 1940- WhoScE 91-4
Luong, Minh Phong 1937- WhoScE 91-2
Luong, Nguyen 1928- WhoUN 92
Luong, Uyen Ngoc 1941- WhoUN 92
Luongo, C. Paul 1930- WhoAm 92
Luongo, Giuseppe WhoScE 91-3
Luongo, Janet Duffy 1949- WhoE 93, WhoEmL 93
Luongo, Lucille Francesca 1948- WhoAmW 93, WhoE 93, WhoEmL 93
Luongo, Mario 1945- WhoWor 93
Luongo, Pino BioIn 17
Luongo, Stephen Earle 1947- WhoEmL 93
Luoni, Joelle Ann 1961- WhoAmW 93
Luo Ruiqing 1906-1978 BioIn 17
Luo Shangcai 1929- WhoAsAP 91
Lupberger, Edwin Adolph 1936- St&PR 93, WhoAm 92, WhoSSW 93
Lupe, John Edward, Jr. 1939- WhoAm 92
Lu Peijian 1928- WhoAsAP 91
Luper, Edna Lane 1942- WhoSSW 93
Luper, William Donald, Sr. 1933- St&PR 93
Lupert, Leslie Allan 1946- WhoE 93, WhoEmL 93, WhoWor 93
Lupertz, Markus 1941- BioIn 17
Lupi, Johannes c. 1506-1539 Baker 92
Lupi, Roberto 1908-1971 Baker 92
Lupia, Harry E. 1925- St&PR 93
Lupiani, Donald Anthony 1946- WhoE 93, WhoWor 93

Lupica, Mike BioIn 17
Lupicinus, Flavius dc. 366 HarEnMi
Lupien, John R. 1937- WhoScE 91-3
Lupien, John Reilly 1937- WhoUN 92
Lupin, Ellis Ralph 1931- WhoAm 92
Lupinacci, Arthur J. 1941- St&PR 93
Lupino, Ida 1916?- IntDcF 2-3 [port]
Lupino, Ida 1918- MiSFD 9, WhoAm 92
Lupino, Stanley 1893-1942 QDrFCA 92 [port]
Lupinski, Thomas Marion 1952- St&PR 93, WhoEmL 93
Lupo, Joseph Vincent St&PR 93
Lupo, Mary E. 1947- BioIn 17
Lupo, Robert Edward Smith 1953- WhoEmL 93, WhoSSW 93, WhoWor 93
Lupo, Thomas A. 1948- St&PR 93
Lupoff, Richard A. 1935- BioIn 17, ScF&FL 92
Lupold, Harry F. 1936- ConAu 139
Lupoletti, Claudia Ann 1961- WhoAmW 93
Lupone, E. Robert Law&B 92
LuPone, Patti 1949- ConMus 8 [port], WhoAm 92, WhoAmW 93
Luporini, Gaetano 1865-1948 Baker 92
Luporini, Pierangelo 1940- WhoScE 91-3
Lupot, Liberato Hurano, Jr. 1953- WhoWor 93
Lupovici, Marius 1931- WhoWor 93
Lupp, Joerg Stefan 1955- WhoEmL 93, WhoSSW 93
Luptak, David A. Law&B 92
Lupton, Debbie Ann 1962- WhoAmW 93
Lupton, Ellen 1963- WhoAm 92
Lupton, Mary Hosmer 1914- WhoAmW 93
Lupton, Whitney Blair 1965- WhoEmL 93, WhoSSW 93
Lupu, Radu 1945- Baker 92, WhoAm 92
Lupulescu, Aurel Peter 1923- WhoWor 93
Lupus, Eduardus Baker 92
Luqman, Al Hajj Anas Mahmoud BioIn 17
Luque, Adolfo 1890-1957 BiDAMSp 1989
Luque, Jose 1938- WhoScE 91-3
Luques, Emmie Antoinette 1854- AmWomPl
Luquin, Eduardo 1896- DcMexL
Luquire, Hans 1958- St&PR 93
Luraschi, Tony MiSFD 9
Lurensky, Harriet Claire 1962- WhoAmW 93
Lurey, Alfred Saul 1942- WhoAm 92
Luria, A.R. 1902-1977 BioIn 17
Luria, Aleksandr Romanovich 1902-1977 BioIn 17
Luria, Gloria 1925- St&PR 93
Luria, Leonard 1923- St&PR 93
Luria, Mary Mercer 1942- WhoAm 92
Luria, Peter P. 1952- St&PR 93
Luria, Remy 1953- WhoEmL 93
Luria, S.E. 1912-1991 BioIn 17
Luria, Salvador 1912-1991 AnObit 1991
Luria, Salvador Edward 1912-1991 BioIn 17
Luria, Sydney A. St&PR 93
Luria, Zella 1924- WhoAm 92
Lurie, Alison BioIn 17
Lurie, Alison 1926- MagSAmL [port], ScF&FL 92, WhoAm 92, WhoAmW 93, WhoWrEP 92
Lurie, Alvin David 1923- WhoAm 92
Lurie, Harold 1919- WhoAm 92
Lurie, John BioIn 17
Lurie, Jonathan Adam 1956- WhoEmL 93
Lurie, Michael Edward 1943- St&PR 93
Lurie, Morris 1938- DcChlFi, SmATA 72
Lurie, Robert A. WhoAm 92
Lurie, Robert H. d1990 BioIn 17
Lurie, Ruth B. Law&B 92
Lurie, Sol David 1928- WhoSSW 93
Lurie, Toby 1925- WhoWrEP 92
Lurie, William L. 1931- St&PR 93, WhoAm 92
Lurier, Peter Bruce 1961- WhoSSW 93
Lurin, Mitch 1941- St&PR 93
Lurix, Paul Leslie, Jr. 1949- WhoEmL 93, WhoSSW 93, WhoWor 93
Lurkis, Alexander 1908- WhoE 93
Luro, Horatio BioIn 17
Lu Rongjing 1934- WhoAsAP 91
Lurton, Ernest Lee 1944- WhoWor 93
Lurton, H. William BioIn 17
Lurton, H. William 1929- St&PR 93, WhoAm 92
Lurton, Horace Harmon 1844-1914 OxCSupC [port]
Lurton, Horace Van Deventer 1941- St&PR 93
Lurton, Horace VanDeventer 1941- WhoAm 92
Lury, Adam Thomas 1956- WhoWor 93
Luryi, Serge 1947- WhoAm 92
Lus, Pita 1935- WhoAsAP 91
Lusardi, Lawrence Mario 1952- WhoEmL 93
Lusby, Thomas Reed 1954- St&PR 93
Lusch, Charles Jack 1936- WhoE 93, WhoWor 93
Lusch, Frans Ernest 1925- St&PR 93
Luschan, Felix von 1854-1924 IntDcAn
Luscher, Edgar 1925- WhoScE 91-3
Luscher, Edgar 1925-1990 BioIn 17
Luscher, Thomas P. Law&B 92
Luscinski, Steven Michael 1951- St&PR 93, WhoAm 92, WhoEmL 93
Luscomb, Robert Charles, Jr. 1936- WhoWor 93
Luscombe, David Keith WhoScE 91-1
Luscombe, Herbert Alfred 1916- WhoAm 92
Luscombe, Wendy 1951- WhoAm 92
Luscu, Damian 1931- WhoUN 92
Lush, Jay Laurence 1896-1982 BioIn 17
Lush, Samuel Robert 1961- WhoE 93
Lushbough, Channing H. 1929- St&PR 93
Lushington, Brian Christopher 1952- WhoWor 93
Lushington, Laura Patricia 1963- WhoAmW 93
Lushington, Nolan 1929- WhoE 93
Lusht, Kenneth Michael 1942- WhoE 93
Lusignan, Donald A. St&PR 93
Lusignans OxDcByz
Lusinchi, Jaime 1924- WhoWor 93
Lusinchi, Xavier WhoScE 91-2
Lusk, Alice BioIn 17
Lusk, Charles Michael, III 1948- WhoSSW 93
Lusk, Georgia L. 1893-1971 PolPar
Lusk, Georgia Lee 1892-1971 BioIn 17
Lusk, Glenna Rae Knight 1935- WhoAmW 93, WhoSSW 93
Lusk, Harlan Gilbert 1943- WhoAm 92
Lusk, Jim BioIn 17
Lusk, Lisa Marie 1957- WhoSSW 93, WhoWor 93
Lusk, Martha Larche 1925- WhoWrEP 92
Lusk, Pearl AmWomPl
Lusk, William Edward 1916- WhoAm 92
Luskacova, Marketa 1944- BioIn 17
Luskey, Louis 1920- St&PR 93
Luskin, Bernard 1925- St&PR 93
Luskin, Bert L. 1911- WhoAm 92
Luskin, Jack 1928- St&PR 93, WhoAm 92
Luskin, Meyer 1925- St&PR 93
Luskin, Michael 1951- WhoEmL 93
Luskin, Robert David 1950- WhoEmL 93
Luskus, Paula Maria 1943- WhoAmW 93
Lusky, Larry E. 1949- St&PR 93
Lusky, Louis 1915- WhoAm 92
Lusky, Monnie I., Jr. 1921- St&PR 93
Luss, Dan 1938- WhoAm 92
Luss, Michael Alexander 1945- WhoSSW 93
Luss, Robert David Law&B 92
Lussan, Zelie de OxDcOp
Lussan, Zelie de 1862-1949 Baker 92
Lussen, John F. 1942- St&PR 93
Lussen, John Frederick 1942- WhoAm 92
Lussi, Caroline Frances Draper 1939- WhoWor 93
Lussier, Diane L. Law&B 92
Lussier, Gaetan 1941- WhoAm 92
Lussier, Jacques 1941- WhoAm 92
Lussier, Jean-Paul 1917- WhoAm 92
Lussier, John H. 1927- St&PR 93
Lussier, Marcel 1925- WhoAm 92
Lussky, Warren Alfred 1919- WhoSSW 93
Lusso, Del Patrick 1954- St&PR 93
Lussy, Mathis 1828-1910 Baker 92
Lust, Elenore WhoAmW 93, WhoE 93, WhoWor 93
Lust, Herbert Cohnfeldt, II 1926- WhoE 93, WhoWor 93
Lust, Johan Hugo 1937- WhoWor 93
Lust, Noel 1942- WhoScE 91-2
Lust, Reimar 1923- BioIn 17, WhoScE 91-3
Lustbader, Eric Van 1946- ScF&FL 92
Lustbader, Mark Adam Law&B 92
Lustbader, Philip L. Law&B 92
Lustbader, Philip Lawrence 1949- St&PR 93, WhoAm 92
Lustbader, Robert St&PR 93
Lustberg, Eugene Joseph 1923- St&PR 93
Luste, Joseph Francis, Jr. 1940- WhoE 93
Lusted, Lee Browning 1922- WhoAm 92
Lustenberger, Louis Charles, Jr. 1936- WhoAm 92
Luster, Deanna Mee Yee 1962- WhoEmL 93
Luster, Fred BioIn 17
Luster, George Orchard 1921- WhoAm 92
Lustgarden, Steven 1951- MiSFD 9
Lustgarten, Ira Howard 1929- WhoAm 92
Lustgarten, Stewart J. 1943- WhoE 93
Lustica, Katherine Grace 1958- WhoAmW 93
Lustick, Ian Steven 1949- ConAu 40NR
Lustig, Arnost 1926- WhoWor 93
Lustig, Barbara Ellen 1946- WhoE 93
Lustig, David Vernon 1947- WhoE 93
Lustig, Edith Perkins 1929- WhoAmW 93
Lustig, Gerald J. 1920-1991 BioIn 17
Lustig, Harry 1925- WhoAm 92
Lustig, Irvin Jay 1961- WhoE 93
Lustig, Joanne 1952- WhoE 93
Lustig, Nora Claudia 1951- WhoE 93
Lustig, Patrick Foran 1956- WhoEmL 93
Lustig, William 1955- MiSFD 9
Lustiger, Jean-Marie Cardinal 1926- WhoWor 93
Lusty, James Richard WhoScE 91-1
Lusty, Robert 1909-1991 AnObit 1991
Lusvardi, Anthony Amedeo 1958- WhoEmL 93
Luszczkiewicz, Andrzej 1945- WhoScE 91-4
Luszczkiewicz, Wladyslaw 1828-1900 PolBiDi
Luszki, Margaret Barron 1907- WhoAmW 93
Luszki, Walter Aloise WhoSSW 93
Lusztig, Peter Alfred 1930- WhoAm 92
Lutenski, Richard P. WhoIns 93
Luter, Carol E. St&PR 93
Luter, John 1919- WhoAm 92, WhoWor 93
Luter, Joseph W., III BioIn 17
Luter, Joseph Williamson, III 1939- St&PR 93
Luter, Joseph Williamson, III 1940- WhoSSW 93
Luter, Melvin A. 1944- WhoE 93
Luter, Yvonne d1991 BioIn 17
Luterman, Arnold 1946- WhoEmL 93, WhoSSW 93
Lutes, Benjamin Franklin, Jr. 1927- WhoSSW 93
Lutes, Donald Henry 1926- WhoAm 92
Lutes, Joseph W. 1950- St&PR 93
Lutes, Joseph Wycoff 1950- WhoAm 92, WhoE 93, WhoEmL 93
Lutes Family BioIn 17
Lutfalla, Michel William 1938- WhoWor 93
Lutfi, Sultan Najib 1941- WhoE 93
Lutgen, Grace Welsh 1888- AmWomPl
Lutgen, Mike 1951- WhoEmL 93
Lutgendorff, Willibald Leo 1856-1937 Baker 92
Lutgens, Harry Gerardus WhoAm 92
Lutgert, Willem Hendrik 1955- WhoWor 93
Luth, Hans 1940- WhoScE 91-3, WhoWor 93
Luth, James Curtis 1961- WhoEmL 93
Luth, Robert J. St&PR 93
Luther, Allen C. 1940- St&PR 93
Luther, Andrew C. 1942- St&PR 93
Luther, David B. 1936- St&PR 93
Luther, David Byron 1936- WhoAm 92
Luther, Florence Joan 1928- WhoAmW 93
Luther, George Albert 1926- WhoSSW 93
Luther, George Aubrey 1933- WhoAm 92
Luther, James E. 1940- St&PR 93
Luther, James H. 1929- St&PR 93
Luther, James Howard 1928- WhoAm 92
Luther, Karen Rae 1956- WhoAmW 93
Luther, Lois Margaret 1937- WhoAmW 93
Luther, Louise Ellen 1943- WhoAmW 93
Luther, Luana Mae 1939- WhoAmW 93
Luther, Martin 1483-1546 Baker 92, BioIn 17
Luther, Robert 1948- WhoUN 92
Luther, Robert Karl, Jr. 1954- St&PR 93
Luther, Robert W. 1948- St&PR 93
Luther, Ron B. 1932- St&PR 93
Luther, Susan Militzer 1946- WhoWrEP 92
Luther, Wallace John 1947- St&PR 93
Luther, William Lee 1952- WhoE 93, WhoEmL 93, WhoWor 93
Luther-Lemmon, Carol Len 1955- WhoAmW 93, WhoE 93, WhoEmL 93
Luthey, Graydon Dean Law&B 92
Luthey, Graydon Dean, Jr. 1955- WhoAm 92, WhoSSW 93
Luthi, Brenda M. 1963- St&PR 93
Luthi, Max 1909- ScF&FL 92
Luthi, Werner P. 1943- WhoWor 93
Luthin, Henry Conrad, IV 1952- WhoEmL 93
Luthje, Sven WhoScE 91-3
Luthra, Gurinder Kumar 1964- WhoSSW 93
Luthringshausen, Jacqueline R. Law&B 92
Luthringshauser, Daniel R. 1935- St&PR 93
Luthringshauser, Daniel Rene 1935- WhoAm 92
Luthro, John O. 1937- St&PR 93
Luthuli, Albert John 1898-1967 DcTwHis
Luthy, Richard Godfrey 1945- WhoAm 92, WhoE 93
Lutken, Donald C. 1924- St&PR 93
Lutkenhouse, Anne 1957- WhoAmW 93
Lutkestratkotter, H. WhoScE 91-3
Lutkin, Peter Christian 1858-1931 Baker 92
Lutkins, William Burgess 1926- St&PR 93
Lutkowski, Karol 1939- WhoWor 93
Lutkowski, Noel J. 1944- St&PR 93, WhoIns 93
Lutley, John H. 1935- WhoAm 92
Lutman, Mark Edward 1949- WhoWor 93
Lutman, Peter John Wilson WhoScE 91-1
Lutomski, Dorothy Odile 1920- WhoWrEP 92
Lutomski, Jerzy 1931- WhoScE 91-4
Luton, Jean-Marie WhoScE 91-2
Luton, Jean-Marie 1942- WhoScE 91-2
Luton, Mary Kathryn WhoSSW 93
Lutoslawski, Witold 1913- Baker 92, BioIn 17, PolBiDi, WhoWor 93
Lutowiecka-Wranicz, Anita 1933- WhoScE 91-4
Lutschg, Karl 1839-1899 Baker 92
Lutschg, Waldemar 1877-1948 See Lutschg, Karl 1839-1899 Baker 92
Lutter, Charles W., Jr. Law&B 92
Lutter, Judy Mahle BioIn 17
Lutter, Rudolph Victor, Jr. 1932- WhoE 93
Lutterbein, Richard 1924- St&PR 93
Luttermoser, Donald Louis 1941- St&PR 93
Luttgau, Hans-Christoph 1926- WhoScE 91-3
Luttig, Arthur William John 1957- WhoSSW 93
Luttig, Gerd Walter 1926- WhoScE 91-3
Luttig, J. Michael 1954- WhoAm 92
Luttinger, David A. Law&B 92
Luttinger, Joaquin Mazdak 1923- WhoAm 92
Luttjohann, John Robert 1956- WhoEmL 93
Lutton, Claude 1941- WhoScE 91-2
Lutton, Lewis Montfort 1945- WhoE 93
Luttrell, Everett Stanley 1916-1988 BioIn 17
Luttrell, Georgia Bena 1927- WhoAmW 93
Luttrell, Gregory Brent 1962- WhoE 93, WhoEmL 93
Luttrell, Janet Yvonne 1940- WhoAmW 93
Luttrell, John W. 1931- St&PR 93
Luttrell, Michael C. 1950- St&PR 93
Luttrell, Robert Grant 1937- St&PR 93
Luttrell, Robert Samuel 1944- St&PR 93
Luttrell, Robert Stephens 1933- WhoSSW 93
Lutts, John Albert 1932- WhoE 93
Luttwak, Edward Nicolae 1942- WhoAm 92
Lutvak, Mark Allen 1939- WhoWor 93
Lutwak, Leo 1928- WhoAm 92
Luty, Theodore St&PR 93
Lutyens, Elisabeth 1906-1983 BioIn 17, OxDcOp
Lutyens, (Agnes) Elisabeth 1906-1983 Baker 92
Lutyens, Emily 1874-1964 BioIn 17
Lutynski, Adam M. Law&B 92
Lutynski, Adam M. 1942- St&PR 93
Lutz, Adelle BioIn 17
Lutz, Andrew S. 1927- St&PR 93
Lutz, Carl Freiheit 1934- WhoAm 92
Lutz, Carlene 1946- WhoAmW 93
Lutz, Christopher Louis 1957- St&PR 93
Lutz, Connie Jean 1959- WhoAmW 93
Lutz, David S. 1945- St&PR 93
Lutz, Elizabeth May 1928- St&PR 93
Lutz, Francis Charles 1944- WhoAm 92
Lutz, Frank Wenzel 1928- WhoSSW 93
Lutz, Frederick Ray 1944- WhoSSW 93
Lutz, George D. 1941- St&PR 93
Lutz, Hans-Rudolf WhoScE 91-4
Lutz, Hartwell Borden 1932- WhoAm 92
Lutz, Heinz Dieter 1934- WhoScE 91-3
Lutz, Jeffrey Christian 1959- WhoEmL 93
Lutz, Jeffry R. 1946- St&PR 93
Lutz, John 1939- ScF&FL 92
Lutz, John N. 1926- St&PR 93
Lutz, Julie 1944- BioIn 17
Lutz, Julie Haynes 1944- WhoAmW 93
Lutz, Matthew Charles 1934- WhoAm 92
Lutz, (Wilhelm) Meyer 1822-1903 Baker 92
Lutz, Paul Eugene 1934- WhoSSW 93
Lutz, Raymond Price 1935- WhoAm 92, WhoSSW 93
Lutz, Robert A. BioIn 17
Lutz, Robert Anthony 1932- WhoAm 92
Lutz, Robert W. Law&B 92
Lutz, William Andrew 1944- WhoWor 93
Lutz, William Lan 1944- WhoAm 92
Lutze, Frederick Henry, Jr. 1937- WhoSSW 93
Lutze, P. Michael 1944- St&PR 93
Lutze, Ruth Louise 1917- WhoAmW 93, WhoE 93
Lutzeier, Elizabeth 1952- SmATA 72 [port]
Lutzenberger, Jose BioIn 17
Lutzer, David John 1943- WhoAm 92
Lutzke, Arthur Saul 1945- WhoAm 92
Lutzker, Edythe 1904-1991 BioIn 17

Lutzker, Elliot Howard 1953- WhoEmL 93
Lutzky, Frank Joseph, Jr. 1934- WhoE 93
Lutzky, Michael 1967- BioIn 17
Luu, Si-Nang 1930- WhoScE 91-2
Luvisi, Lee 1937- Baker 92, WhoAm 92
Lu Wenfu 1928- BioIn 17
Lux, C.L. 1914- St&PR 93
Lux, Florence T. BioIn 17
Lux, Frank J. Law&B 92
Lux, Friedrich 1820-1895 Baker 92
Lux, John H. 1918- St&PR 93, WhoAm 92, WhoE 93
Lux, Paul S. 1950- St&PR 93
Lux, Philip Gordon 1928- WhoAm 92
Lux, Samuel Edward, IV 1940- WhoE 93
Lux, Stefan 1888-1936 BioIn 17
Luxembourg, Francois Henri de Montmorency-Boutteville, Duke of 1628-1695 HarEnMi
Luxemburg, Harold L. 1912-1990 BioIn 17
Luxemburg, Jack Alan 1949- WhoE 93, WhoEmL 93, WhoWor 93
Luxemburg, Rosa 1871-1919 BioIn 17, DcTwHis, PolBiDi
Luxemburg, Wilhelmus Anthonius Josephus 1929- WhoAm 92
Luxenberg, Malcolm Neuwahl 1935- WhoAm 92, WhoSSW 93
Luxmoore, Robert John 1940- WhoAm 92
Luxner, Morton Bennett 1917- WhoWrEP 92
Luxon, Benjamin 1937- Baker 92, OxDcOp
Luxorius fl. 5th cent.-6th cent. OxDcByz
Luxton, John 1946- WhoAsAP 91
Luxton, Malcolm WhoScE 91-1
Luxton, Richard N. 1950- WhoE 93
Lu Xun 1881-1936 BioIn 17
Luyckx, Leon A. 1933- St&PR 93
Lu Yongxiang 1942- WhoAsAP 91
Lu You-Wen 1926- WhoAsAP 91
Luyten, James Reindert 1941- WhoE 93
Luython, Charles c. 1556-1620 Baker 92
Luz, Eberhard Ludwig 1933- WhoWor 93
Luz, Paul L. 1967- WhoSSW 93
Luz, Thomas J. Law&B 92
Luza, Radomir Vaclav 1922- WhoAm 92, WhoSSW 93
Luzader, S.D. WhoWrEP 92
Luzarraga, Alberto 1937- St&PR 93
Luzi, Mario 1914- DcLB 128 [port]
Luzinski, Gregory Michael 1950- BiDAMSp 1989
Luzum, James Aloysius 1940- St&PR 93
Luzum, William J. 1938- St&PR 93
Luzuriaga, Adel 1949- WhoEmL 93
Luz Villanueva, Alma NotHsAW 93
Luzzaschi, Luzzasco 1545?-1607 Baker 92
Luzzati, Emanuele 1921- OxDcOp
Luzzati, Victor 1923- WhoScE 91-2
Luzzati, Vittorio 1923- WhoWor 93
Luzzatto, Lucio WhoScE 91-1
Luzzi, Luigi 1828-1876 Baker 92
Lvov, Alexei Feodorovich 1798-1870 Baker 92
Lvov, Alexey 1798-1870 OxDcOp
L'Vov, Georgii Evgenievich 1861-1925 BioIn 17
Lvov, Nikolay 1751-1803 OxDcOp
Lvov, Victor Anatoliyevich 1954- WhoWor 93
L'Vov, Vladimir Nikolaevich 1872- BioIn 17
Lwin, Nanda L. St&PR 93
Lwin, U. 1912- WhoWor 93
Lwoff, Andre Michel 1902- WhoAm 92, WhoWor 93
Ly, Ahmadou Abdoul 1946- WhoUN 92
Ly, Raymond Hoa Binh 1943- WhoSSW 93, WhoWor 93
Ly, Sekou 1933- WhoAfr
Lyagoubi-Ouahchi, Souad 1938- WhoUN 92
Lyall, D.K. ScF&FL 92
Lyall, Gavin BioIn 17
Lyall, George Albert 1924- St&PR 93
Lyall, Katharine Culbert 1941- WhoAm 92, WhoAmW 93
Lyall, Tony Allen 1949- St&PR 93, WhoEmL 93, WhoIns 93
Lyamshev, Leonid Mikhailovich 1928- WhoWor 93
Lyatoshinsky, Boris 1895-1968 OxDcOp
Lyautey, Louis Hubert 1854-1934 DcTwHis
Lyautey, Louis Hubert Gonzalve 1854-1934 BioIn 17, HarEnMi
Lybarger, Adrienne Reynolds 1926- WhoAmW 93, WhoE 93
Lybarger, Jerry L. Law&B 92
Lybarger, Marjorie Kathryn 1956- WhoEmL 93
Lybbert, Donald 1923-1981 Baker 92
Lyberg, Mats Douglas 1942- WhoScE 91-4
Lycan, Kelly G. 1958- WhoWrEP 92
Lycan, Rebecca Tatum 1960- WhoAmW 93, WhoEmL 93, WhoSSW 93
Lycke, Erik Nils Oskar 1926- WhoScE 91-4
Lycke, Sally Ann 1948- WhoAmW 93
Lyckman, John Arch Law&B 92
Lyczko, Catherine M. Law&B 92
Lyczko, Judith Elizabeth 1947- WhoEmL 93
Lyday, David Paul ScF&FL 92
Lyddan, Jeffrey D. Law&B 92
Lydden, Phillip Schuyler 1932- St&PR 93
Lyddon, William John 1951- WhoEmL 93, WhoSSW 93
Lydecker, Howard 1911-1969 BioIn 17
Lydecker, John ScF&FL 92
Lydecker, Richard Ackerman 1944- St&PR 93
Lydecker, Theodore 1908-1990 BioIn 17
Lyden, Fremont James 1926- WhoAm 92
Lyden, William G., Jr. 1926- St&PR 93
Lydenberg, Robin 1947- ScF&FL 92
Lydens, Peter Franklin 1930- WhoSSW 93
Lyders, Richard A. 1934- BioIn 17
Lydick, Barbara C. 1944- WhoAmW 93
Lydick, J. Lee 1939- St&PR 93
Lydick, Lawrence Tupper 1916- WhoAm 92, WhoWor 93
Lydolph, Paul Edward 1924- WhoAm 92
Lydon, Antony F. 1936- WhoUN 92
Lydon, James M. 1928- St&PR 93
Lydon, James Patrick 1967- WhoSSW 93
Lydon, Michael Clery 1942- WhoE 93
Lydon, Patrick S. 1942- St&PR 93
Lydon, Philip F. 1931- St&PR 93
Lydon, Thomas J. 1927- CngDr 91, WhoAm 92
Lydon, Thomas Michael 1923- St&PR 93
Lydos, John OxDcByz
Lyduch, Leonard 1934- WhoScE 91-4
Lye, Michael WhoScE 91-1
Lyerly, Elaine Myrick 1951- WhoSSW 93
Lyerly, Melia Lynn 1956- WhoEmL 93
Lyerly, William Voigt 1928- St&PR 93
Lyford, Cabot 1925- WhoAm 92
Lyford, Carol Gray 1956- WhoEmL 93
Lyford, Fred S. 1928- St&PR 93
Lyford, Joseph P. d1992 NewYTBS 92 [port]
Lyford, Joseph Philip 1918- WhoWrEP 92
Lyford, Ralph 1882-1927 Baker 92
Lyght, John Richard 1927- AfrAmBi [port]
Lyke, James d1992 NewYTBS 92
Lyke, James P. BioIn 17
Lyke, James Patterson 1939- WhoAm 92, WhoSSW 93
Lyke, Kathleen Anne 1958- WhoAmW 93
Lyke, Ward N. 1951- St&PR 93
Lyken, Leslie C. Law&B 92
Lykes, Joseph T., III 1948- WhoAm 92
Lykes, M. Brinton 1949- WhoAmW 93
Lykins, Marshall Herbert 1944- St&PR 93, WhoAm 92
Lykken, David T. BioIn 17
Lyklema, J. 1930- WhoScE 91-3
Lykos, George J. Law&B 92
Lykos, Peter George 1927- WhoAm 92
Lykoudis, Paul S. 1926- WhoAm 92
Lyle, Aaron Kerr, III 1929- WhoSSW 93
Lyle, Charles Thomas 1946- WhoAm 92
Lyle, Christopher Branthwaite 1944- WhoUN 92
Lyle, Claude Weiss 1932- St&PR 93
Lyle, Henry Richard Philip 1954- WhoEmL 93
Lyle, Idalee Martin 1907- WhoWrEP 92
Lyle, James Arthur 1945- WhoSSW 93
Lyle, John Donald 1933- St&PR 93
Lyle, John Tillman 1934- WhoAm 92
Lyle, John William, Jr. 1950- WhoE 93
Lyle, Joseph M. 1912-1990 BioIn 17
Lyle, Kevin R. 1960- St&PR 93
Lyle, Linda Gayle 1952- WhoSSW 93
Lyle, Marguerite Richard 1929- WhoSSW 93
Lyle, Peter ScF&FL 92
Lyle, Quentin Ernest 1958- WhoE 93, WhoEmL 93
Lyle, Robert Edward 1926- WhoAm 92
Lyle, Robert G. 1929- St&PR 93
Lyle, S. Paul, III 1955- WhoSSW 93
Lyle, Sparky 1944- BioIn 17
Lyle, Virginia Reavis 1926- WhoAm 92, WhoSSW 93
Lyle, William David 1950- WhoWrEP 92
Lyles, Barbara Diggs 1930- WhoE 93
Lyles, Carol Yvette 1954- WhoAmW 93
Lyles, John Oliver 1945- St&PR 93
Lyles, Lawrence France Law&B 92
Lyles, William H. 1946- ScF&FL 92
Lyles, Yvonne Suzette 1956- WhoAmW 93
Lyles-Anderson, Barbara Dunbar 1954- WhoAmW 93, WhoEmL 93
Lyman, Arthur Joseph 1953- WhoAm 92, WhoEmL 93
Lyman, Cabot St&PR 93
Lyman, Charles Edson 1946- WhoWor 93
Lyman, Charles Peirson 1912- WhoAm 92
Lyman, Daniel Franklin Law&B 92
Lyman, David 1936- WhoAm 92, WhoWor 93
Lyman, Edward Wells, Jr. 1942- St&PR 93
Lyman, Elisabeth Reed 1912- WhoAmW 93
Lyman, Ellyn Elizabeth 1951- WhoEmL 93
Lyman, Frederic A. 1934- WhoAm 92
Lyman, Harold S. 1935- St&PR 93
Lyman, Henry 1915- WhoAm 92
Lyman, Howard Burbeck 1920- WhoWor 93
Lyman, John 1921- WhoAm 92
Lyman, John Root 1939- St&PR 93, WhoAm 92
Lyman, Link 1898-1972 BioIn 17
Lyman, Mabel AmWomPl
Lyman, Melville Henry 1942- WhoE 93
Lyman, Nicholas E. 1946- St&PR 93
Lyman, Peggy 1950- WhoAm 92, WhoAmW 93, WhoEmL 93
Lyman, Phillip Casey 1947- WhoEmL 93
Lyman, Phineas 1715-1774 HarEnMi
Lyman, Ransom Huffman, Jr. 1924- St&PR 93
Lyman, Richard Jeffrey 1963- WhoEmL 93
Lyman, Richard Wall 1923- WhoAm 92
Lyman, Robert Dennis 1947- WhoSSW 93
Lyman, William W., Jr. 1916- WhoAm 92
Lymington, John 1911-1983 ScF&FL 92
Lymon, Frankie BioIn 17
Lymon, Frankie 1942-1968
See Lymon, Frankie, & the Teenagers SoulM
Lymon, Frankie, & the Teenagers SoulM
Lympany, Moura 1916- Baker 92, WhoWor 93
Lynam, Jim 1941- WhoAm 92
Lynam, Terence Joseph 1953- WhoEmL 93
Lynam, William T. Law&B 92
Lynass, Jack 1933- St&PR 93
Lynch, Abrum John 1937- WhoSSW 93
Lynch, Alexander P. 1952- St&PR 93
Lynch, Aubrey, II BioIn 17
Lynch, B. Quinton 1941- WhoWor 93
Lynch, Barbara Deutsch 1940- WhoE 93
Lynch, Ben E. 1937- St&PR 93
Lynch, Benjamin Leo 1923- WhoAm 92
Lynch, Bernard Joseph 1935- St&PR 93
Lynch, Beverly Pfeifer 1935- WhoAm 92, WhoAmW 93
Lynch, Brian Francis 1950- WhoEmL 93
Lynch, Candace Lois 1952- WhoAmW 93
Lynch, Carlyle 1909-1989 BioIn 17
Lynch, Carol Lee 1943- WhoAmW 93
Lynch, Carole Yard 1951- WhoEmL 93, WhoSSW 93
Lynch, Catherine Gores 1943- WhoAmW 93, WhoSSW 93, WhoWor 93
Lynch, Charles Allen 1927- WhoAm 92
Lynch, Charles Andrew 1935- WhoE 93
Lynch, Charles B. Law&B 92
Lynch, Charles B. 1919- ConAu 137
Lynch, Charles F., Jr. 1953- St&PR 93
Lynch, Charles Stafford Law&B 92
Lynch, Charles Theodore, Sr. 1932- WhoWor 93
Lynch, Charles Thomas 1918- WhoAm 92
Lynch, Craig Taylor 1959- WhoEmL 93
Lynch, Daniel 1946- ConAu 139, WhoE 93
Lynch, Daniel J. 1930- St&PR 93
Lynch, David BioIn 17
Lynch, David 1946- MiSFD 9
Lynch, David A. Law&B 92
Lynch, David B. WhoAm 92
Lynch, David C. 1948- St&PR 93
Lynch, David E. St&PR 93
Lynch, David K. 1946- WhoAm 92
Lynch, David William 1932- WhoAm 92
Lynch, Dona McFaddin 1948- WhoAmW 93
Lynch, Donald Francis, Jr. 1946- WhoEmL 93, WhoSSW 93
Lynch, Donald Frederick 1950- WhoE 93
Lynch, Douglas 1927- WhoWor 93
Lynch, Edward J. Law&B 92
Lynch, Edward John 1933- WhoAm 92
Lynch, Edward M. 1920-1991 BioIn 17
Lynch, Edward Stephen 1911- WhoAm 92, WhoWor 93
Lynch, Etta Lee 1924- WhoWrEP 92
Lynch, Eugene F. 1931- WhoAm 92
Lynch, Fran Jackie 1948- WhoAmW 93, WhoE 93, WhoEmL 93, WhoWor 93
Lynch, Frances AmWomPl
Lynch, Francis Charles 1944- WhoAm 92
Lynch, Francis Xavier 1918- WhoE 93
Lynch, Frank J. St&PR 93
Lynch, Frank W. 1921- St&PR 93
Lynch, Frank William 1921- WhoAm 92
Lynch, Frederick C., Jr. 1944- St&PR 93
Lynch, Gearoid 1932- WhoScE 91-3
Lynch, George Michael 1943- WhoAm 92
Lynch, Gerald John 1906- WhoAm 92
Lynch, Gerald Weldon 1937- WhoAm 92, WhoE 93
Lynch, Gerard E. 1951- WhoAm 92
Lynch, Harry James 1929- WhoE 93
Lynch, Henry P. Law&B 92
Lynch, Howard William 1947- St&PR 93
Lynch, J. Michael 1952- WhoE 93
Lynch, J. Robert 1943- St&PR 93
Lynch, James 1936- ConAu 40NR
Lynch, James B., Jr. 1933- WhoIns 93
Lynch, James Bernard, Jr. 1933- St&PR 93
Lynch, James E. 1956- St&PR 93
Lynch, James Edward 1951- WhoEmL 93, WhoWor 93
Lynch, James Henry, Jr. 1931- WhoAm 92
Lynch, James J.D., Jr. Law&B 92
Lynch, James M. 1930- St&PR 93
Lynch, James Terry 1946- WhoEmL 93, WhoSSW 93
Lynch, Jane ScF&FL 92
Lynch, Janis Elizabeth 1948- WhoE 93
Lynch, Joan Driscoll 1935- WhoE 93
Lynch, John A. BioIn 17, St&PR 93
Lynch, John A. 1938- WhoE 93
Lynch, John Brown 1929- WhoAm 92, WhoSSW 93
Lynch, John D. 1926- St&PR 93
Lynch, John Edward, Jr. 1952- WhoAm 92
Lynch, John Henry 1938- St&PR 93
Lynch, John Howard Law&B 92
Lynch, John J. Law&B 92
Lynch, John Joseph 1947- St&PR 93
Lynch, John Patrick 1943- WhoAm 92
Lynch, John Peter 1942- WhoAm 92
Lynch, John R. BioIn 17
Lynch, John Roy 1825-1892 BioIn 17
Lynch, John Roy 1847-1939 EncAACR [port]
Lynch, John T. 1948- St&PR 93
Lynch, John Thomas 1923- St&PR 93
Lynch, Jonathan David 1930- WhoSSW 93
Lynch, Joseph John 1949- WhoE 93, WhoEmL 93
Lynch, Joseph Patrick 1926- St&PR 93
Lynch, Joseph Patrick 1950- WhoSSW 93
Lynch, Judy D. 1952- St&PR 93
Lynch, Karen Emery 1958- WhoEmL 93
Lynch, Karen Renzulli 1946- WhoEmL 93
Lynch, Kathleen Marie 1949- WhoEmL 93
Lynch, Kathryn Leona 1951- WhoE 93
Lynch, Kelly BioIn 17
Lynch, Kevin 1959- BioIn 17
Lynch, Lee 1945- ScF&FL 92
Lynch, Leslie O. 1946- St&PR 93
Lynch, Lorenzo 1932- BlkAuII 92
Lynch, Luba Holod 1947- WhoE 93
Lynch, Luke D. 1921- WhoIns 93
Lynch, M. Teri 1952- St&PR 93
Lynch, Mamie Ruth 1932- WhoAmW 93
Lynch, Margaret Murphy 1949- WhoAmW 93
Lynch, Maria Rosaria 1962- WhoEmL 93
Lynch, Mark Jeffrey 1954- WhoE 93
Lynch, Mark W. Law&B 92
Lynch, Marta 1925-1985 BioIn 17
Lynch, Marta 1930-1985 SpAmA
Lynch, Martin Andrew 1937- St&PR 93, WhoAm 92
Lynch, Mary Ann 1955- St&PR 93
Lynch, Mary Patricia 1932- WhoAmW 93
Lynch, Matthew James, Jr. Law&B 92
Lynch, Michael D. 1947- St&PR 93
Lynch, Michael Eugene 1962- WhoEmL 93
Lynch, Michael Felix WhoScE 91-1
Lynch, Michael H.T. 1944- St&PR 93
Lynch, Michael P. Law&B 92
Lynch, Mildred Virginia 1928- WhoSSW 93
Lynch, Milton Terrence 1931- WhoAm 92
Lynch, Miriam ScF&FL 92
Lynch, Molly Gretsch 1961- WhoAmW 93
Lynch, Nancy Ann 1948- WhoAm 92
Lynch, Nnenna NewYTBS 92 [port]
Lynch, Owen Martin 1931- WhoAm 92
Lynch, Patricia Ann Law&B 92
Lynch, Patricia Gates 1926- WhoAm 92, WhoAmW 93
Lynch, Patrick Cornelius 1960- WhoEmL 93
Lynch, Patrick David 1933- St&PR 93
Lynch, Patrick J. 1937- St&PR 93
Lynch, Paul 1946- MiSFD 9
Lynch, Paul Vincent 1932- WhoE 93, WhoWor 93
Lynch, Pauline Ann 1939- WhoAmW 93
Lynch, Peter BioIn 17
Lynch, Peter 1947- WhoScE 91-3
Lynch, Peter George 1932- WhoE 93
Lynch, Peter J. 1951- St&PR 93
Lynch, Peter John 1936- WhoAm 92

Lynch, Peter Michael 1925- *St&PR 93*
Lynch, Rececca 1956- *St&PR 93*
Lynch, Reinhardt *BioIn 17*
Lynch, Richard Harold 1935- *WhoSSW 93*
Lynch, Richard J. *Law&B 92*
Lynch, Rip *BioIn 17*
Lynch, Robert Bernard *Law&B 92*
Lynch, Robert Dennis 1951- *WhoSSW 93*
Lynch, Robert Emmett 1932- *WhoAm 92*
Lynch, Robert John 1937- *St&PR 93*
Lynch, Robert L. 1918- *St&PR 93*
Lynch, Robert M. *Law&B 92*
Lynch, Robert Martin 1950- *WhoAm 92*
Lynch, Ronald P. 1935- *St&PR 93, WhoAm 92*
Lynch, Rose Peabody 1949- *WhoAm 92, WhoE 93, WhoEmL 93*
Lynch, Sandra Lea 1946- *WhoEmL 93*
Lynch, Sean Dennis 1957- *WhoE 93, WhoEmL 93*
Lynch, Sherry Kay 1957- *WhoAmW 93*
Lynch, Sonia 1938- *WhoAmW 93, WhoE 93, WhoWor 93*
Lynch, Stephanie Nadine 1951- *WhoEmL 93*
Lynch, Stephen A., III *Law&B 92*
Lynch, T. Stephen *Law&B 92, St&PR 93*
Lynch, Ted 1947- *St&PR 93*
Lynch, Terence Joseph *Law&B 92*
Lynch, Teresa A. 1954- *WhoAmW 93*
Lynch, Thomas 1922- *WhoScE 91-3, WhoWor 93*
Lynch, Thomas Brendan 1937- *WhoWor 93*
Lynch, Thomas Francis 1938- *WhoAm 92*
Lynch, Thomas Gregory 1954- *WhoE 93*
Lynch, Thomas M. 1926- *St&PR 93*
Lynch, Thomas Peter 1924- *WhoAm 92*
Lynch, Thomas W. *Law&B 92*
Lynch, Thomas W. 1930- *St&PR 93*
Lynch, Timothy Bruce 1949- *WhoEmL 93*
Lynch, Timothy J. 1948- *WhoScE 91-3*
Lynch, Timothy Jeremiah-Mahoney *Law&B 92*
Lynch, Timothy Jeremiah-Mahoney 1952- *WhoWor 93*
Lynch, Timothy John 1941- *St&PR 93*
Lynch, Timothy Joseph 1954- *WhoEmL 93*
Lynch, Timothy P. 1952- *St&PR 93*
Lynch, Tom 1950- *BioIn 17*
Lynch, Vivian Elizabeth 1940- *WhoAmW 93, WhoWor 93*
Lynch, Wendell A. 1951- *St&PR 93*
Lynch, William Dennis, Jr. 1945- *WhoAm 92*
Lynch, William F. 1952- *St&PR 93*
Lynch, William J. *St&PR 93*
Lynch, William L. *Law&B 92*
Lynch, William L., Jr. 1932- *St&PR 93*
Lynch, William Redington 1928- *WhoAm 92*
Lynch, William Thomas, Jr. 1942- *WhoAm 92*
Lynch, William Walker 1926- *WhoAm 92*
Lynch, William Wright, Jr. 1936- *WhoSSW 93*
Lyncheski, Robert F. 1934- *WhoIns 93*
Lynd, Albert Bertram 1937- *WhoSSW 93*
Lynd, Grant Albert 1949- *WhoEmL 93*
Lynd, Helen Merrell 1896-1982 *BioIn 17*
Lynd, Jeffrey Lee 1952- *WhoEmL 93, WhoSSW 93*
Lynd, Priscilla Ann 1942- *WhoSSW 93*
Lynd, Robert 1879-1949 *BioIn 17*
Lynd, Robert D. *Law&B 92*
Lyndaker, Kermit L. 1931- *St&PR 93*
Lyndon, Amy *WhoWrEP 92*
Lyndon, J.L. *Law&B 92*
Lyndon, John 1956- *ConMus 9 [port]*
Lyndon, Maynard 1907- *WhoAm 92*
Lynds, Beverly Turner 1929- *WhoAm 92*
Lynds, Dennis 1924- *ScF&FL 92, WhoWrEP 92*
Lyndsay, David *BioIn 17*
Lyndsay, David 1490-1555 *LitC 20*
Lyne, Adrian *MiSFD 9, WhoAm 92*
Lyne, Austin Francis 1927- *WhoAm 92*
Lyne, Dorothy-Arden 1928- *WhoE 93*
Lyne, Felice 1887-1935 *Baker 92*
Lyne, James Coleman, Jr. 1944- *WhoSSW 93*
Lyne, Robert Chamberlayne, Jr. *Law&B 92*
Lyne, Simon John 1945- *WhoWor 93*
Lynen, Uli 1938- *WhoScE 91-3*
Lynes, Barbara Buhler 1942- *WhoAmW 93*
Lynes, Frank 1858-1913 *Baker 92*
Lynes, Joseph Russell 1910-1991 *BioIn 17*
Lynes, Russell 1910-1991 *AnObit 1991, BioIn 17*
Lynes, (Joseph) Russell, Jr. 1910- *WhoWrEP 92*
Lynett, Lawrence Wilson 1921- *WhoAm 92, WhoWor 93*
Lynett, Matthew Joseph 1948- *St&PR 93*
Lynett, William R. 1947- *St&PR 93*
Lynett, William Ruddy 1947- *WhoAm 92*
Lynford, Ruth K. 1924- *BioIn 17*
Lyng, Richard Edmund 1918- *WhoAm 92*
Lyng, Stig *WhoScE 91-4*
Lynga, Gosta 1930- *WhoScE 91-4*
Lyngaas, Michael E. 1951- *WhoIns 93*
Lyngseth, Joan 1934- *ScF&FL 92*
Lyngsie, Stig Kaare 1944- *WhoWor 93*
Lyngso, Soren T. 1921- *WhoScE 91-2*
Lyngstad, Sverre 1922- *ConAu 37NR*
Lyngved, Viggo R. 1945- *St&PR 93*
Lynham, C. Richard 1942- *St&PR 93*
Lynham, Charles Richard 1942- *WhoAm 92*
Lynk, M. Jane *Law&B 92*
Lynley, Carol Ann 1942- *WhoAm 92*
Lynn, Andrew S. *Law&B 92*
Lynn, Arthur B. 1947- *St&PR 93*
Lynn, Arthur Dellert, Jr. 1921- *WhoAm 92*
Lynn, Barbara 1942- *SoulM*
Lynn, Brian F. *Law&B 92*
Lynn, C. Stephen 1947- *St&PR 93*
Lynn, Charles Randal 1954- *WhoEmL 93*
Lynn, Charles Stephen 1947- *WhoAm 92*
Lynn, Clarence E. 1928- *St&PR 93*
Lynn, Cynthia Schumo 1951- *St&PR 93*
Lynn, Darrell L. *Law&B 92*
Lynn, David Ayers 1936- *St&PR 93*
Lynn, Dennis Brown 1946- *St&PR 93*
Lynn, Diann Karin 1953- *WhoAmW 93*
Lynn, Donna Maria 1945- *WhoAmW 93, WhoE 93*
Lynn, E.M. 1918- *St&PR 93*
Lynn, Elisabeth 1957- *WhoAmW 93*
Lynn, Elizabeth A. 1946- *ScF&FL 92*
Lynn, Eugene Matthew 1918- *WhoWor 93*
Lynn, Frederick Anson 1946- *WhoE 93*
Lynn, Fredric Michael 1952- *WhoAm 92*
Lynn, George 1915-1989 *Baker 92*
Lynn, Grey *ScF&FL 92*
Lynn, James A. *Law&B 92*
Lynn, James Dougal 1934- *WhoAm 92*
Lynn, James T. 1927- *WhoAm 92*
Lynn, James Thomas 1927- *St&PR 93*
Lynn, Janet 1953- *WhoAm 92, WhoEmL 93*
Lynn, Joe Joshua 1931- *St&PR 93*
Lynn, John A. 1946- *St&PR 93*
Lynn, John M. *Law&B 92*
Lynn, John P. 1916- *WhoAm 92*
Lynn, John Warren 1921- *St&PR 93*
Lynn, John William 1952- *WhoEmL 93*
Lynn, Jonathan 1943- *MiSFD 9*
Lynn, Katherine Lyn 1954- *WhoEmL 93*
Lynn, Kathryn Louise 1953- *WhoEmL 93*
Lynn, Laurence Edwin, Jr. 1937- *WhoAm 92*
Lynn, Lawrence Richard 1948- *WhoEmL 93*
Lynn, Loretta *BioIn 17*
Lynn, Loretta 1932- *Baker 92*
Lynn, Loretta Webb 1935- *WhoAm 92, WhoAmW 93*
Lynn, Merissa Sherrill 1942- *WhoE 93*
Lynn, Michael Edward, III 1936- *WhoAm 92*
Lynn, Michael Francis 1947- *St&PR 93*
Lynn, Michael Robert 1957- *WhoEmL 93*
Lynn, Milton M. 1918- *St&PR 93*
Lynn, Minnie L. 1902-1990 *BioIn 17*
Lynn, Mitchell Gordon 1948- *WhoAm 92*
Lynn, Nanne Joyce 1938- *WhoAmW 93*
Lynn, Naomi 1933- *NotHsAW 93*
Lynn, Naomi B. 1933- *WhoAm 92, WhoAmW 93*
Lynn, Otis Clyde 1927- *WhoAm 92*
Lynn, Pamela Ann 1961- *WhoAmW 93*
Lynn, Patricia Ann 1939- *WhoAmW 93*
Lynn, Pauline Judith Wardlow 1920- *WhoAmW 93*
Lynn, Phyllis Jean 1936- *WhoAmW 93*
Lynn, Ralph 1881-1962 & Walls, Tom 1883-1949 *QDrFCA 92 [port]*
Lynn, Richard B. 1934- *WhoUN 92*
Lynn, Richard Brian 1956- *WhoE 93*
Lynn, Richard C. *Law&B 92*
Lynn, Robert C. *Law&B 92*
Lynn, Robert G. 1950- *WhoAm 92, WhoWor 93*
Lynn, Robert Lilburn 1937- *St&PR 93*
Lynn, Robert R. 1926- *St&PR 93*
Lynn, Robert Wood 1925- *WhoAm 92*
Lynn, Ruth Nadelman 1948- *ScF&FL 92*
Lynn, Sandra Dykes 1944- *WhoWrEP 92*
Lynn, Sheilah Ann 1947- *WhoAmW 93, WhoEmL 93, WhoSSW 93*
Lynn, Stephen 1956- *WhoE 93*
Lynn, Theodore Stanley 1937- *WhoAm 92*
Lynn, Thomas Edward 1930- *WhoWrEP 92*
Lynn, Thomas Neil, Jr. 1930- *WhoAm 92*
Lynn, Thomas W. 1941- *St&PR 93*
Lynn, Tiffany Mary 1947- *WhoSSW 93*
Lynn, Tony Lee 1939- *WhoSSW 93*
Lynn, Vanessa S. d1992 *NewYTBS 92*
Lynn, Verne Lauriston 1930- *WhoE 93*
Lynn, Walter Royal 1928- *WhoAm 92*
Lynn, Willard E. 1943- *St&PR 93*
Lynn, William B. 1945- *St&PR 93*
Lynn, William Brian 1945- *WhoAm 92*
Lynn, William H. d1990 *BioIn 17*
Lynn, William Harcourt 1931- *WhoAm 92*
Lynn, Yen-Mow 1935- *WhoE 93*
Lynne, Gillian *BioIn 17*
Lynne, Gillian Barbara *WhoAm 92*
Lynne, Jeff *BioIn 17*
Lynne, Jeff 1942- *WhoAm 92*
Lynne, Seybourn Harris 1907- *WhoAm 92*
Lynnerup, Niels 1960- *WhoWor 93*
Lynnes, R. Milton 1934- *WhoAm 92*
Lynott, Brad C. *Law&B 92*
Lynskey, Edward Charles 1956- *WhoWrEP 92*
Lynskey, Martin J. 1951- *WhoIns 93*
Lynt, Richard King 1917- *WhoE 93*
Lynton, Ernest Albert 1926- *WhoAm 92*
Lynton, Harold Stephen 1909- *WhoAm 92*
Lynton, Harriet Ronken 1920- *WhoSSW 93*
Lynwander, Peter 1936- *St&PR 93*
Lynyak, Robert M. 1942- *St&PR 93*
Lynyrd Skynyrd *ConMus 9 [port]*
Lyon, Adriane Torrey 1945- *WhoAmW 93*
Lyon, Andrew Bennet 1958- *WhoE 93*
Lyon, Ann Patterson Durr 1927- *WhoE 93*
Lyon, Arthur S., Jr. 1951- *WhoIns 93*
Lyon, Ben *QDrFCA 92*
Lyon, Ben Harris *Law&B 92*
Lyon, Berenice Iola Clark 1920- *WhoAmW 93*
Lyon, Beulah *AmWomPl*
Lyon, Birgit Blatt 1933- *WhoWor 93*
Lyon, Bryce Dale 1920- *WhoAm 92*
Lyon, C. Dale 1923- *St&PR 93*
Lyon, C.H. Randolph 1943- *St&PR 93*
Lyon, Carl Francis, Jr. 1943- *WhoAm 92*
Lyon, Carol S. *Law&B 92*
Lyon, Carolyn Bartel 1908- *WhoAmW 93*
Lyon, Cecil Burton 1903- *WhoAm 92*
Lyon, Charles P. 1934- *St&PR 93*
Lyon, Clara O. *AmWomPl*
Lyon, Cynthia Rachel 1957- *WhoAmW 93*
Lyon, D.J. de B. *WhoScE 91-1*
Lyon, David Harry 1956- *WhoScE 91-1*
Lyon, David William 1941- *St&PR 93, WhoAm 92*
Lyon, David William 1949- *WhoWrEP 92*
Lyon, E. Barry *Law&B 92*
Lyon, Elisabeth *ScF&FL 92*
Lyon, Frank Emery, Jr. 1928- *St&PR 93*
Lyon, Gene F. 1932- *WhoIns 93*
Lyon, George Ella 1949- *BioIn 17, DcAmChF 1985, WhoWrEP 92*
Lyon, George Robert 1923-1990 *BioIn 17*
Lyon, George Washburn 1820- *Baker 92*
Lyon, Gordon Edward 1942- *WhoE 93*
Lyon, Harllee Wingate 1935- *St&PR 93*
Lyon, Harold Clifford, Jr. 1935- *WhoWrEP 92*
Lyon, Harvey T. 1927- *St&PR 93*
Lyon, Hugh C. 1931- *St&PR 93*
Lyon, James 1735-1794 *Baker 92*
Lyon, James Burroughs 1930- *WhoAm 92, WhoE 93, WhoWor 93*
Lyon, James Karl 1934- *WhoAm 92*
Lyon, James McDonald 1952- *WhoAm 92*
Lyon, James Travers 1922- *WhoAm 92*
Lyon, Jane Maureen Mahan 1931- *WhoAmW 93*
Lyon, Jeffrey 1943- *WhoAm 92*
Lyon, John *ScF&FL 92*
Lyon, Kate 1856- *GayN*
Lyon, Keith Anthony 1952- *St&PR 93*
Lyon, Keith Geoffrey 1951- *WhoSSW 93*
Lyon, Lawrence Bruce 1947- *WhoAm 92*
Lyon, Loren L. 1952- *St&PR 93*
Lyon, Margaret Currier *AmWomPl*
Lyon, Mark Andrew 1953- *WhoEmL 93*
Lyon, Martha Sue 1935- *WhoAmW 93*
Lyon, Mary F. *WhoScE 91-1*
Lyon, Matthew 1749-1822 *JrnUS*
Lyon, Maud Margaret 1954- *WhoAmW 93*
Lyon, Melvin 1930- *WhoSSW 93*
Lyon, Michael 1943- *St&PR 93*
Lyon, Nathaniel 1818-1861 *BioIn 17, HarEnMi*
Lyon, Philip Kirkland 1944- *WhoAm 92*
Lyon, Randolph Matthew 1955- *WhoEmL 93*
Lyon, Richard 1923- *WhoAm 92*
Lyon, Richard 1936- *St&PR 93*
Lyon, Richard Eugene, Jr. 1932- *WhoAm 92*
Lyon, Richard F. *Law&B 92*
Lyon, Richard Harold 1929- *WhoAm 92*
Lyon, Richard Jordan *Law&B 92*
Lyon, Richard K. 1933- *ScF&FL 92*
Lyon, Richard Kenneth 1933- *WhoE 93*
Lyon, Richard W. *Law&B 92*
Lyon, Robert Francis 1952- *WhoSSW 93*
Lyon, Robert Louis 1906- *WhoWor 93*
Lyon, Ronald Edward 1936- *WhoE 93*
Lyon, Russell Thomas 1940- *St&PR 93*
Lyon, S. Desiree 1946- *WhoSSW 93*
Lyon, Samuel C. 1932- *St&PR 93*
Lyon, Sherman Orwig 1939- *WhoAm 92*
Lyon, Stanley Winship *Law&B 92*
Lyon, Sterling Rufus 1927- *WhoAm 92*
Lyon, Ted 1939- *WhoWrEP 92*
Lyon, Waldo Kampmeier 1914- *WhoAm 92*
Lyon, Wayne Barton 1932- *St&PR 93*
Lyon, Wilford Charles, Jr. 1935- *St&PR 93, WhoAm 92, WhoIns 93, WhoSSW 93*
Lyon, William 1923- *WhoAm 92*
Lyon, William Carl 1938- *WhoAm 92*
Lyon, William S. 1951- *St&PR 93*
Lyon & Healy *Baker 92*
Lyon-Loftus, Gregory Thomas 1944- *WhoE 93*
Lyon Oram, Jane Elizabeth 1956- *WhoWor 93*
Lyons, Arlyne Marie 1960- *WhoAmW 93*
Lyons, Carol R. *St&PR 93*
Lyons, Cathy 1943- *WhoE 93*
Lyons, Champ, Jr. 1940- *WhoAm 92*
Lyons, Charles Henry 1941- *WhoE 93*
Lyons, Charles R. 1933- *WhoAm 92*
Lyons, Charles Richard 1960- *WhoEmL 93*
Lyons, Charlotte *BioIn 17*
Lyons, Cherie Ann 1948- *WhoEmL 93*
Lyons, Chopeta C. 1949- *WhoWrEP 92*
Lyons, Christine 1943- *ConAu 136*
Lyons, Christopher Garrett 1945- *WhoScE 91-3*
Lyons, Cornelius J. *Law&B 92*
Lyons, David Barry 1935- *WhoAm 92*
Lyons, Dennis G. 1931- *St&PR 93*
Lyons, Dennis Gerald 1931- *WhoAm 92*
Lyons, Dennis Patrick Aloysius 1866-1929 *BiDAMSp 1989*
Lyons, Donald Richard 1946- *St&PR 93*
Lyons, Dorothy A. 1953- *WhoEmL 93*
Lyons, Edward Timothy 1946- *WhoWrEP 92*
Lyons, Ellis 1915- *WhoAm 92*
Lyons, Francis Joseph 1921- *WhoAm 92*
Lyons, Frederick James 1950- *WhoUN 92*
Lyons, Gary F. *Law&B 92*
Lyons, Gary G. *Law&B 92*
Lyons, Gene Martin 1924- *WhoAm 92*
Lyons, George Harris 1947- *WhoEmL 93*
Lyons, George Sage 1936- *WhoAm 92*
Lyons, Harriet *AmWomPl*
Lyons, Heidi Held 1962- *WhoAmW 93, WhoEmL 93*
Lyons, Henry Earnest 1952- *WhoEmL 93*
Lyons, Henry Warren 1924- *St&PR 93*
Lyons, Ivan 1934- *WhoE 93*
Lyons, James 1925-1973 *Baker 92*
Lyons, James Dennis *Law&B 92*
Lyons, James E. *WhoSSW 93*
Lyons, James Edward 1952- *WhoAm 92, WhoEmL 93*
Lyons, James Francis 1934- *WhoSSW 93*
Lyons, James M. *Law&B 92*
Lyons, James Michael 1961- *WhoEmL 93*
Lyons, James R. *Law&B 92*
Lyons, James S. 1941- *St&PR 93*
Lyons, James Stephen 1941- *WhoAm 92*
Lyons, Jane Ellen 1958- *WhoSSW 93*
Lyons, Jerry Lee 1939- *WhoAm 92, WhoWor 93*
Lyons, John, Jr. 1951- *WhoSSW 93*
Lyons, John B. 1922- *WhoScE 91-3*
Lyons, John David 1946- *WhoAm 92*
Lyons, John E. 1932- *WhoAm 92*
Lyons, John Edward 1926- *St&PR 93*
Lyons, John Joseph 1939- *WhoWor 93*
Lyons, John Matthew 1948- *WhoE 93, WhoWor 93*
Lyons, John Ormsby 1927- *WhoAm 92*
Lyons, John Winship 1930- *WhoAm 92, WhoE 93*
Lyons, Joseph Aloysius 1879-1939 *DcTwHis*
Lyons, Joseph Chisholm 1927- *St&PR 93, WhoAm 92*
Lyons, Joseph Norman 1901- *WhoAm 92*
Lyons, Kenneth Lea 1938- *St&PR 93*
Lyons, Kevin *Law&B 92*
Lyons, Laurence 1911- *St&PR 93, WhoAm 92*
Lyons, Lawrence Michael 1919- *St&PR 93*
Lyons, Lloyd *St&PR 93*
Lyons, Lloyd Carson 1942- *St&PR 93*
Lyons, Lynda 1949- *ScF&FL 92*
Lyons, MacLeod *WhoCanL 92*
Lyons, Margaret J. 1964- *WhoEmL 93*
Lyons, Marilyn C. 1938- *WhoAmW 93*
Lyons, Martin Jesse 1952- *WhoEmL 93*
Lyons, Mary *WhoAmW 93*
Lyons, Mary Fulton *Law&B 92*
Lyons, Michael Henry, II 1936- *St&PR 93*
Lyons, Michael John 1952- *WhoEmL 93*
Lyons, Michael T. 1934- *St&PR 93*
Lyons, Nancy Irene 1946- *WhoSSW 93*
Lyons, Nick 1932- *WhoE 93*
Lyons, Orville Richard 1942- *St&PR 93*
Lyons, Patrick Joseph 1943- *WhoE 93*
Lyons, Paul Michael 1932- *WhoAm 92*
Lyons, Paul Vincent 1939- *WhoAm 92*

Lyons, Phillip Michael, Sr. 1941- *WhoSSW 93, WhoWor 93*
Lyons, Phyllis Ilona 1942- *WhoWrEP 92*
Lyons, Richard Chapman 1919- *WhoAm 92*
Lyons, Richard E. 1920- *WhoWrEP 92*
Lyons, Richard Gerald 1934- *WhoE 93*
Lyons, Richard Kent 1961- *WhoE 93, WhoEmL 93*
Lyons, Richard M. 1935- *WhoWrEP 92*
Lyons, Robert E. *St&PR 93*
Lyons, Robert John 1954- *St&PR 93, WhoAm 92, WhoEmL 93*
Lyons, Robert R. 1944- *St&PR 93*
Lyons, Ronald L. *Law&B 92*
Lyons, Stephen Michael, II 1931- *St&PR 93*
Lyons, Steve *BioIn 17*
Lyons, Terence John *WhoScE 91-1*
Lyons, Terrence Allan 1949- *WhoEmL 93*
Lyons, Terry A. 1949- *St&PR 93*
Lyons, Thomas Patrick 1953- *WhoE 93*
Lyons, Timothy F. *Law&B 92*
Lyons, Warren 1949- *WhoE 93*
Lyons, Warren R. 1945- *St&PR 93*
Lyons, William Drewry 1927- *St&PR 93*
Lyons, William Edward 1939- *WhoWor 93*
Lyons, William J. *Law&B 92*
Lyons, William M. *Law&B 92*
Lyons, William M. 1955- *St&PR 93*
Lyons, William P. 1941- *St&PR 93*
Lyons, William W. 1935- *St&PR 93*
Lyons-Gary, Deirdre Faye 1962- *WhoSSW 93*
Lyra, Justus Wilhelm 1822-1882 *Baker 92*
Lyrer-Gaugler, Philippe Alexander 1957- *WhoWor 93*
Lysaght, Elizabeth J. *ScF&FL 92*
Lysak, George Julian 1943- *St&PR 93*
Lysander d395BC *HarEnMi*
Lysaught, Thomas Francis 1936- *St&PR 93*
Lysberg, Charles-Samuel *Baker 92*
Lysek, Hynek 1929- *WhoScE 91-4*
Lysen, Edward John 1937- *St&PR 93*
Lysenko, Mykola 1842-1912 *OxDcOp*
Lysimachus c. 355BC-281BC *HarEnMi*
Lysinger, Rex Jackson 1937- *St&PR 93, WhoAm 92*
Lysionok, Igor Gerontevich 1963- *WhoWor 93*
Lyski, Wayne D. 1941- *St&PR 93*
Lysko, Lisa Ann *Law&B 92*
Lyskowski, Stan Albin 1947- *WhoE 93*
Lysle, Richard Scott 1947- *WhoEmL 93*
Lysne, Douglas L. 1944- *St&PR 93*
Lysohir, Marilyn 1950- *BioIn 17*
Lysons, Richard James *WhoScE 91-1*
Lyst, John Henry 1933- *WhoAm 92*
Lystad, Lars Petter 1943- *WhoScE 91-4*
Lystad, Mary Hanemann 1928- *WhoAm 92, WhoWrEP 92*
Lystad, Robert Arthur Lunde 1920- *WhoAm 92*
Lystra, Helen Percy 1939- *WhoWrEP 92*
Lysun, Gregory 1924- *WhoE 93, WhoWor 93*
Lysyk, Kenneth Martin 1934- *WhoAm 92*
Lythgoe, David John 1960- *WhoWor 93*
Lytle, Andrew Nelson 1902- *WhoAm 92*
Lytle, Charles Franklin 1932- *WhoSSW 93*
Lytle, Edward Lloyd *Law&B 92*
Lytle, Elliott Kent 1953- *WhoEmL 93*
Lytle, James C. *St&PR 93*
Lytle, Michael Allen 1946- *WhoEmL 93*
Lytle, Mike 1948- *St&PR 93*
Lytle, Richard 1935- *WhoE 93*
Lytle, Richard Harold 1937- *WhoAm 92*
Lytle, Shirley Ann *Law&B 92*
Lytle, Victoria Elizabeth 1951- *WhoAmW 93*
Lytras, C.S. *WhoScE 91-4*
Lytras, Panayiotis 1947- *WhoWor 93*
Lyttelton, Humphrey Richard Adeane 1921- *WhoWor 93*
Lyttkens, Sonja Marie-Louise 1919- *WhoWor 93*
Lyttle, Cosima Venet 1948- *WhoSSW 93*
Lyttle, Douglas Alfred 1919- *WhoAm 92*
Lyttle, John 1933-1991 *AnObit 1991*
Lyttle, Thomas Peyton 1947- *WhoEmL 93, WhoSSW 93*
Lytton, Edward Robert Bulwer 1831-1891 *BioIn 17*
Lytton, Linda Rountree 1951- *WhoAmW 93*
Lytton, Robert Leonard 1937- *WhoSSW 93*
Lytton, Rosina Bulwer- 1802-1882 *BioIn 17*
Lytton, William B. *Law&B 92*
Lyubimov Dmitry, Victorovitch 1949- *WhoWor 93*
Lyu-Volckhausen, Grace *BioIn 17*
Lyverse, Steven H. *Law&B 92*
Lyytinen, Asa-Matti 1950- *WhoWor 93*

M

M. Angeline Teresa, Mother 1893-1984 *BioIn 17*
M. C. Clever
See Digital Underground *ConMus 9*
Ma, Guru *BioIn 17*
Ma, Akana K.J. *Law&B 92*
Ma, Chuan Yu 1939- *WhoWor 93*
Ma, Fai 1954- *WhoEmL 93*
Ma, Fengchow Clarence 1919- *WhoWor 93*
Ma, Fuming 1957- *WhoWor 93*
Ma, Hiao-Tsiun 1911-1991 *BioIn 17*
Ma, Mark Tsu-han 1933- *WhoAm 92*
Ma, Patricia C. *Law&B 92*
Ma, Shau Ping Alice 1947- *WhoAmW 93*
Ma, Sheng-mei 1958- *WhoSSW 93*
Ma, Shui-Long 1939- *WhoWor 93*
Ma, Wai-sai 1943- *WhoAm 92*
Ma, Xin-Hua 1963- *WhoAm 92*
Ma, Yo Yo *WhoAm 92*
Ma, Yo-Yo 1955- *Baker 92, BioIn 17*
Ma, Yuan Yuan 1952- *WhoE 93, WhoEmL 93, WhoWor 93*
Ma, Yuzhen 1934- *WhoWor 93*
Ma, Zhi-Zhou 1924- *WhoWor 93*
Ma, Zuguang 1928- *WhoWor 93*
Maa, Dah-You 1915- *WhoWor 93*
Maack, Annegret 1944- *WhoWor 93*
Maag, Joan L. 1963- *WhoAmW 93*
Maag, John C. 1949- *St&PR 93*
Maag, Peter 1919- *OxDcOp, WhoWor 93*
Maag, (Ernst) Peter (Johannes) 1919- *Baker 92*
Maag, Urs Richard 1938- *WhoAm 92*
Maage, Finn 1941- *WhoScE 91-4*
Maahn, Ernst 1934- *WhoScE 91-2*
Maal, Baaba *BioIn 17*
Maaloe, Sven Baastrup 1943- *WhoScE 91-4*
Maalouf, Louis T. *St&PR 93*
Maalouf, Wajih D. 1928- *WhoScE 91-3, WhoUN 92*
Maar, Gyula 1934- *DrEEuF*
Maarbjerg, Mary Penzold 1943- *St&PR 93, WhoAm 92*
Maarse, Johannes A.M. 1948- *WhoScE 91-3*
Maartens, Maretha 1945- *SmATA 73 [port]*
Maas, Albert L. 1926- *St&PR 93*
Maas, Curtis N. 1955- *St&PR 93*
Maas, Dick *MiSFD 9*
Maas, Duane Harris 1927- *WhoAm 92*
Maas, Fredric Jon 1957- *WhoEmL 93*
Maas, G. *WhoScE 91-3*
Maas, James Beryl 1938- *WhoAm 92, WhoWor 93*
Maas, James Weldon 1929- *WhoAm 92, WhoSSW 93*
Maas, Jane Brown *WhoAm 92, WhoAmW 93*
Maas, Joan Louise 1961- *WhoAmW 93*
Maas, Joe *WhoAm 92*
Maas, Kevin 1965- *BioIn 17*
Maas, Leo Richardus Marie 1956- *WhoWor 93*
Maas, Louis (Philipp Otto) 1852-1889 *Baker 92*
Maas, Peter 1929- *WhoAm 92, WhoWrEP 92*
Maas, Peter 1939- *WhoWor 93*
Maas, Richard Theodore 1957- *WhoEmL 93, WhoSSW 93*
Maas, Ronald J. *Law&B 92*
Maas, Werner Karl 1921- *WhoAm 92*
Maasalo, Armas (Toivo Valdemar) 1885-1960 *Baker 92*
Maasik, Rein 1942- *St&PR 93*
Maasoumi, Esfandiar 1950- *WhoSSW 93*
Maass, Alfred Roland 1918- *WhoE 93*
Maass, Arthur 1917- *WhoAm 92*
Maass, Brenda Joyce 1939- *WhoAmW 93*
Maass, James Eric 1942- *St&PR 93*
Maass, R. Andrew 1946- *WhoAm 92, WhoSSW 93*
Maass, Sophia Hantzes 1952- *WhoEmL 93*
Maassen, Johannes Antonie 1945- *WhoWor 93*
Maassen, Johannes Hans Dominicus 1951- *WhoWor 93*
Maat, Benjamin 1947- *WhoWor 93*
Maathai, Wangari *BioIn 17*
Maatman, Gerald L. 1930- *WhoIns 93*
Maatman, Gerald Leonard 1930- *St&PR 93, WhoAm 92*
Maatsch, Deborah Joan 1950- *WhoAmW 93*
Maatta, John D. *Law&B 92*
Maattanen, Mauri P. 1943- *WhoScE 91-4*
Maavara, Gary A. *Law&B 92*
Ma'ayani, Ami 1936- *Baker 92*
Maazel, Lorin 1930- *IntDcOp, OxDcOp, WhoAm 92, WhoE 93*
Maazel, Lorin (Varencove) 1930- *Baker 92*
Mabbett, Alan John *WhoScE 91-1*
Mabbs, Edward Carl 1921- *St&PR 93, WhoAm 92, WhoSSW 93*
Mabe, Alan R. 1942- *WhoSSW 93*
Mabe, Chauncey 1955- *WhoWrEP 92*
Mabe, Julian Arthur 1956- *WhoSSW 93*
Mabe, Sam *BioIn 17*
Mabeck, Carl Erik 1938- *WhoScE 91-2*
Mabee, Carleton 1914- *WhoAm 92, WhoWrEP 92*
Mabee, Dave 1950- *St&PR 93*
Mabee, Keith Vance 1947- *St&PR 93, WhoIns 93*
Mabellini, Teodulo 1817-1897 *Baker 92, OxDcOp*
Maben, Burton Freeman 1961- *WhoEmL 93*
Maberg, Olle 1931- *WhoWor 93*
Mabie, Gifford M. 1940- *St&PR 93*
Mabie, Hamilton W. 1845-1916 *GayN*
Mabie, John Carl *Law&B 92*
Mabille, Jean-Pierre 1929- *WhoScE 91-2*
Mabinton, Loretta Inei *Law&B 92*
Mabley, Jack 1915- *WhoAm 92*
Mabli, Charles E. 1941- *WhoIns 93*
Mabomba, Rodrick Samson 1948- *WhoWor 93*
Mabon, Inez d1992 *BioIn 17*
Mabon, Inez Camprubi d1992 *NewYTBS 92*
Mabon, James M., Jr. *Law&B 92*
Mabrey, Harold Richard 1927- *St&PR 93*
Mabrey, Janet S. 1946- *St&PR 93*
Mabrouk, Sarah Lou 1962- *WhoEmL 93*
Mabry, Charles Ray 1931- *WhoSSW 93*
Mabry, Donald J(oseph) 1941- *ConAu 37NR*
Mabry, Donald Joseph 1941- *WhoSSW 93*
Mabry, Donald R. 1933- *St&PR 93*
Mabry, George L. 1917-1990 *BioIn 17*
Mabry, Guy O. 1926- *WhoAm 92*
Mabry, Katherine Hamm 1928- *WhoAmW 93*
Mabry, Marcus *BioIn 17*
Mabry, Nelloise Johnson 1921- *WhoSSW 93*
Mabry, Ronald D. 1951- *St&PR 93*
Mabry, Sam 1918- *St&PR 93*
Mabry, Sharon Cody 1945- *WhoSSW 93*
Mabus, Catherine Adam 1948- *WhoAmW 93*
Mabus, Cynthia Anne 1958- *WhoEmL 93*
Mabus, Raymond Edwin, Jr. 1948- *WhoAm 92, WhoWor 93*
Mabuse, Sipho *BioIn 17*
Maca, Allan Leigh 1934- *St&PR 93*
MacAdam, Walter Kavanagh 1913- *WhoAm 92*
MacAdam, William Foster, Jr. 1942- *St&PR 93*
Macado, Mary Stanley 1912- *WhoWrEP 92*
MacAfee, James T. *St&PR 93*
Mac Afee, Norman 1943- *WhoWrEP 92*
Macak, Ivan 1935- *Baker 92*
Macal, Zdenek 1936- *Baker 92, WhoAm 92*
Macaleer, Richard James 1934- *St&PR 93*
Macaleese, John Elmer 1932- *St&PR 93*
Macalister, Kim Porter 1954- *WhoAm 92*
MacAlister, Robert Lee 1956- *WhoE 93*
MacAllister, Robert M. *Law&B 92*
MacAllister, William H. *Law&B 92*
MacAlpine, Loretta 1960- *WhoEmL 93*
MacAlroy, Patricia *Law&B 92*
Macaluso, James 1943- *WhoSSW 93*
Macaluso, Joseph P. 1951- *St&PR 93*
Macaluso, Joseph Peter, Jr. *Law&B 92*
Macaluso, Mary Christelle 1931- *WhoAmW 93*
Macaluso, Vincent 1937- *St&PR 93*
Macan, William Alexander, IV 1942- *WhoAm 92*
Mac An Airchinnigh, Micheal 1950- *WhoWor 93*
MacAndrew, Elizabeth 1924-1983? *ScF&FL 92*
Macao, Marshall *ScF&FL 92*
MacApp, C.C. 1913-1971 *ScF&FL 92*
Macaraig, Catalino, Jr. 1927- *WhoAsAP 91*
MacArdle, Donald Wales 1897-1964 *Baker 92*
Macardle, Dorothy 1889-1958 *ScF&FL 92*
Macarell, John D. 1933- *WhoIns 93*
Macari, Mario D. *ScF&FL 92*
Macario, Alberto Juan Lorenzo 1935- *WhoAm 92, WhoE 93*
MacArthur, Arthur 1845-1912 *BioIn 17, HarEnMi*
MacArthur, Brian Henry 1949- *WhoE 93, WhoEmL 93*
MacArthur, Charles 1895-1956 *MiSFD 9N*
MacArthur, D.M. *ScF&FL 92*
MacArthur, Diana Taylor 1933- *WhoAmW 93, WhoWor 93*
MacArthur, Douglas 1880-1964 *BioIn 17, ColdWar 1 [port], CmdGen 1991 [port], DcTwHis, HarEnMi, PolPar*
Macarthur, Gloria 1924- *WhoWrEP 92*
MacArthur, James 1937- *WhoAm 92*
MacArthur, James Y. 1938- *St&PR 93*
MacArthur, Jeffrey H. 1941- *St&PR 93*
MacArthur, John Daniel 1930- *St&PR 93*
MacArthur, John Donald 1897-1978 *BioIn 17*
Macarthur, John Durno *WhoScE 91-1*
MacArthur, John R. 1956- *St&PR 93*
MacArthur, John Roderick C. G. 1956- *WhoAm 92, WhoE 93*
Mac Arthur, Loren 1935- *WhoWrEP 92*
MacArthur, Marjorie E. *Law&B 92*
MacArthur, Pauline Arnoux *AmWomPl*
MacArthur, Sandra Lea 1946- *WhoAmW 93, WhoEmL 93*
MacArthur, Stephen M. *Law&B 92*
Macartney, Frank P. 1931- *St&PR 93*
Macartney, Michelle Lynn 1963- *WhoEmL 93*
Macartney, Syd *MiSFD 9*
Macasek, Fedor 1937- *WhoScE 91-4*
Macaulay, Allen F. 1949- *WhoEmL 93*
Macaulay, Ann Saunders 1958- *WhoEmL 93*
Macaulay, Catherine Sawbridge 1731-1791 *BioIn 17*
Macaulay, Colin A. 1931- *St&PR 93*
Macaulay, Colin Alexander 1931- *WhoAm 92, WhoE 93, WhoWor 93*
Macaulay, David 1946- *BioIn 17, ScF&FL 92*
Macaulay, David (Alexander) 1946- *MajAI [port], SmATA 72 [port], WhoAm 92*
Macaulay, Donald A. *St&PR 93*
Macaulay, H.L. 1925- *St&PR 93*
Macaulay, Hugh L. *WhoAm 92*
MacAulay, J. Blair 1934- *St&PR 93*
Macaulay, Linda Ann *WhoScE 91-1*
Macaulay, Ronald Kerr Steven 1927- *WhoAm 92*
Macaulay, Rose 1881-1958 *ScF&FL 92*
Macaulay, Susan J. *Law&B 92*
Macaulay, William Edward 1945- *WhoAm 92*
Macauley, Arnold *BioIn 17*
Macauley, Robert Conover 1923- *St&PR 93*
Macauley, Robie 1919- *ScF&FL 92*
Macauley, Robie Mayhew 1919- *WhoAm 92, WhoWrEP 92*
MacAusland, Mary Ann 1959- *WhoE 93*
Macavinta-Tenazas, Gemorsita 1938- *WhoAmW 93*
MacAvoy, Paul Webster 1934- *WhoAm 92*
MacAvoy, R.A. 1949- *ScF&FL 92*
Mac Avoy, Thomas Coleman 1928- *WhoAm 92, WhoSSW 93*
MacBain, William Halley 1916- *WhoAm 92*
MacBean, Lawrence J. 1943- *St&PR 93*
Macbeth, King of Scotland d1057 *BioIn 17*
Macbeth, Allan 1856-1910 *Baker 92*
Macbeth, Florence 1891-1966 *Baker 92*
MacBeth, George *BioIn 17*
MacBeth, George 1932-1992 *ScF&FL 92*
MacBeth, George (Mann) 1932-1992 *ConAu 136, SmATA 70*
Macbeth, Hugh James 1947- *WhoSSW 93, WhoWor 93*
Macbeth, Madge Hamilton Lyons 1878-1965 *BioIn 17*
Macbeth, William *St&PR 93*

MacBrayne, Pamela Sue 1948- WhoE 93
MacBride, Maud Gonne 1866-1953 BioIn 17
MacBride, Sean BioIn 17
MacBride, Teri J. 1957- WhoAmW 93
MacBride, Thomas Jamison 1914- WhoAm 92
MacBurney, Edward Harding 1927- WhoAm 92
MacCabe, Bernard S., Jr. 1927- St&PR 93
Maccabees OxDcByz
Maccabeus, Judas d161BC BioIn 17
MacCallum, Iain Robert WhoScE 91-1
MacCallum, James Martin 1940- WhoSSW 93
MacCallum, James R. WhoScE 91-1
MacCallum, Kenneth John WhoScE 91-1
MacCallum, Lorene 1928- WhoAmW 93
MacCallum, Malcolm Angus Hugh WhoScE 91-1
MacCallum, Malcolm Angus Hugh 1944- WhoWor 93
Mac Cana, Proinsias 1926- WhoWor 93
Maccario, Maurice Malcolm 1942- WhoE 93
Maccaro, Peter Anthony 1948- St&PR 93
MacCarone, Gaetano Law&B 92
Maccarone, Joseph Thomas 1952- WhoEmL 93
Maccarrone, Harry Vincent 1947- St&PR 93
MacCarthy, John Peters 1933- St&PR 93, WhoAm 92
MacCarthy, Lillian Gayton AmWomPl
MacCarthy, Terence 1934- WhoAm 92
MacCartney, John William 1945- St&PR 93
MacCauley, Hugh Bournonville 1922- WhoWor 93
MacCausland, Janet 1947- WhoE 93
Maccecchini, Maria-Luisa 1951- WhoE 93
MacChesney, John Burnette 1929- WhoAm 92
Macchi, I. Alden 1922- WhoE 93
Macchi, Julio Augusto 1940- WhoWor 93
Macchi, Odile 1943- WhoScE 91-2
Macchia, Donald Dean 1948- WhoWrEP 92
Macchia, Joseph D. 1935- WhoIns 93
Macchia, Joseph Dominick 1935- St&PR 93
Macchia, Richard 1951- St&PR 93
Macchiarini, Paolo 1958- WhoWor 93
Macchiarola, Frank Joseph 1941- WhoAm 92
Macchio, Ralph BioIn 17
Macchio, Ralph 1962- ConTFT 10
Maccini, Margaret Agatha 1931- WhoAmW 93
Maccio, Guillermo A. 1934- WhoUN 92
Macclaren, Joel Daniel 1955- WhoE 93
MacClean, Walter Lee 1935- WhoWor 93
MacCleery, Russell Eldridge, Sr. 1913- WhoE 93
MacClintock, Anne U. Law&B 92
MacClintock, Stuart 1919-1990 BioIn 17
Maccloud, Malcolm DcAmChF 1960, ScF&FL 92
MacCluer, Jean Walters 1937- WhoSSW 93
Maccluggage, Reid 1938- St&PR 93, WhoAm 92
Maccoby, Eleanor E. 1917- BioIn 17
Maccoby, Eleanor Emmons 1917- WhoAm 92, WhoAmW 93
MacColl, Ewan 1915-1989 BioIn 17
Maccoll, John A. Law&B 92
MacColl, Ray BioIn 17
MacCombie, Bruce BioIn 17
MacCombie, Bruce Franklin 1943- WhoAm 92
MacConkey, Dorothy I. WhoAm 92, WhoAmW 93, WhoSSW 93
MacConnachie, Nancy 1957- WhoAmW 93
MacConnell, Brian David 1957- WhoEmL 93
MacConnell, Colum ScF&FL 92
MacConnell, Joseph T. WhoScE 91-1
MacConnell, Stephen Thomas 1947- WhoEmL 93
MacConnell-Davinroy, Irene J. H. 1936- WhoAmW 93
MacCormac, Deborah A.G. Law&B 92
MacCormac, Vincent Peter 1936- WhoIns 93
MacCormack, John Newton 1936- WhoSSW 93
MacCormack, Sylvia P. Law&B 92
MacCoull, Leslie Shaw Bailey 1945- WhoE 93
MacCoy, Clinton Viles 1905- WhoE 93
MacCracken, Mark Mitchell 1954- St&PR 93
MacCracken, Mary Jo 1943- WhoAmW 93, WhoWor 93
MacCracken, William P., Jr. 1888-1969 EncABHB 8 [port]
MacCrate, Robert 1921- WhoAm 92
MacCready, Paul B. BioIn 17
Mac Cready, Paul Beattie 1925- WhoAm 92
MacCrimmon, Kenneth Robert 1937- WhoAm 92
MacCubbin, Emmett C. 1909- St&PR 93
Mac Culloch, William Thomson 1929- WhoScE 91-3
MacCullough, Martha Elizabeth 1940- WhoE 93
MacCunn, Hamish 1868-1916 Baker 92, OxDcOp
MacCurdy, John A. 1947- WhoEmL 93, WhoSSW 93
MacCurdy, Raymond Ralph, Jr. 1916- WhoAm 92
MacCutcheon, Edward Mackie 1915- WhoE 93
MacCutcheon, James A. 1952- St&PR 93
Macdaid, Gerald Philip 1954- WhoSSW 93
MacDermot, John WhoScE 91-1
MacDermott, Donald B. Law&B 92
MacDew, Peggy Sue 1963- WhoAmW 93
MacDiarmid, Hugh 1892-1978 BioIn 17
Mac Diarmid, William Donald 1926- WhoAm 92
Macdissi, Thomas John 1960- WhoEmL 93
MacDomhnaill, Somhairle Bui c. 1505-1590 BioIn 17
Macdonald, A. Ewan 1941- St&PR 93
Mac Donald, Adelaide Florence Law&B 92
Macdonald, Alan D. Law&B 92
MacDonald, Alan Douglas 1939- St&PR 93, WhoAm 92
MacDonald, Alan Hugh 1943- WhoAm 92
Macdonald, Alastair 1920- WhoCanL 92
Macdonald, Alastair (A.) 1920- ConAu 136
MacDonald, Alison Elizabeth 1961- WhoAmW 93
Macdonald, Alphonse Leonie 1940- WhoUN 92
MacDonald, Andrew 1933- ScF&FL 92
Macdonald, Ann-Marie 1959- WhoCanL 92
MacDonald, Anne Elizabeth Campbell Bard ConAu 136
MacDonald, Anne Elizabeth Campbell Bard 1908-1958 MajAI [port]
Macdonald, Anne L. 1920- ConAu 136
MacDonald, Anson MajAI, SmATA 69
MacDonald, Bernard Callaghan 1927- St&PR 93
MacDonald, Betty MajAI
Macdonald, Betty 1908-1958 ConAu 136
MacDonald, Brian Scott 1939- WhoAm 92
MacDonald, Bruce Kenneth 1933- WhoAm 92
MacDonald, Bruce Raymond 1942- WhoE 93
Macdonald, Caroline DcChlFi, ScF&FL 92
MacDonald, Charles 1944- St&PR 93
MacDonald, Charles Brown 1922-1990 BioIn 17
Macdonald, Clifford Palmer 1919- WhoAm 92
Macdonald, Cynthia BioIn 17
Macdonald, Cynthia 1928- WhoWrEP 92
MacDonald, D.L. 1955- ScF&FL 92
MacDonald, David Elliot 1946- WhoScE 91-1
MacDonald, David Richard 1953- WhoWor 93
Macdonald, David Robert 1930- WhoAm 92, WhoWor 93
MacDonald, Deborah Law&B 92
Macdonald, Donald Ian 1931- WhoAm 92
Macdonald, Donald Stone 1919- WhoE 93
Macdonald, Donald Stovel 1932- WhoAm 92
MacDonald, Donald William 1935- WhoAm 92
MacDonald, Dora Mary AmWomPl
Macdonald, Douglas J. 1947- ConAu 138
MacDonald, Duncan WhoE 93
MacDonald, Duncan A. Law&B 92
Macdonald, Dwight 1906-1982 JrnUS
MacDonald, Edgar E. 1919- ScF&FL 92
MacDonald, Edward King 1929- St&PR 93
MacDonald, Elizabeth G. d1992 BioIn 17, NewYTBS 92
MacDonald, Erin St&PR 93
MacDonald, Frederick H. 1934- St&PR 93
MacDonald, Gary Bruce 1950- WhoE 93
MacDonald, George 1824-1905 ConAu 137, MajAI [port], ScF&FL 92
MacDonald, Gerald Glenn 1959- WhoEmL 93
MacDonald, Gerald V. 1938- St&PR 93
MacDonald, Geraldine 1949- WhoAmW 93
MacDonald, Golden ConAu 136, MajAI
MacDonald, Golden 1910-1952 BioIn 17
MacDonald, Gordon Chalmers 1928- WhoAm 92
MacDonald, Gordon James 1929- St&PR 93
Mac Donald, Gordon James Fraser 1929- WhoAm 92
MacDonald, Helen L. 1910- St&PR 93
Macdonald, Hugh Ian 1929- WhoAm 92
Macdonald, Hugh (John) 1940- Baker 92
MacDonald, Ian WhoScE 91-1
MacDonald, Ian Duncan 1944- WhoAm 92
MacDonald, Ian Grant WhoScE 91-1
MacDonald, J. Farrell 1875-1952 BioIn 17
MacDonald, J. Howard 1928- St&PR 93
Macdonald, Jacques Etienne Joseph Alexandre 1765-1840 HarEnMi
MacDonald, James d1991 BioIn 17
MacDonald, James Craig 1948- WhoWor 93
MacDonald, James D. 1954- ScF&FL 92
MacDonald, James Gordon 1925- St&PR 93
Macdonald, James Kennedy, Jr. 1956- WhoE 93
MacDonald, James Ramsay 1866-1937 BioIn 17, DcTwHis
Macdonald, James Ross 1923- WhoAm 92
MacDonald, Jeanette 1901-1965 IntDcF 2-3 [port]
MacDonald, Jeanette (Anna) 1903-1965 Baker 92
MacDonald, Jeffrey L. 1961- St&PR 93
MacDonald, Jeffrey R. BioIn 17
MacDonald, Jerome Edward 1925- WhoE 93, WhoWor 93
MacDonald, Jill N. Law&B 92
MacDonald, John 1930- St&PR 93
Macdonald, John A. 1815-1891 BioIn 17
MacDonald, John A. 1943- WhoE 93
MacDonald, John Alexander 1948- WhoEmL 93
Macdonald, John Barfoot 1918- WhoAm 92
Macdonald, John Coury 1966- WhoE 93
MacDonald, John D. 1916-1986 BioIn 17, ScF&FL 92
MacDonald, John Monahan 1949- WhoCanL 92
MacDonald, John Thomas 1932- WhoAm 92
Macdonald, Jonathan B. Law&B 92
MacDonald, Joseph St&PR 93
Macdonald, Joseph Albert Friel 1942- WhoAm 92
Macdonald, Karen Bjornson BioIn 17
Macdonald, Karen Crane 1955- WhoAmW 93, WhoE 93, WhoEmL 93, WhoWor 93
MacDonald, Karenlee 1956- WhoEmL 93
Macdonald, Katharine March 1949- WhoAmW 93
Macdonald, Kathryn Elizabeth 1948- WhoWrEP 92
MacDonald, Kenneth 1905- WhoAm 92
MacDonald, Kenneth D. 1946- St&PR 93
Macdonald, Leo T. St&PR 93
Mac Donald, Linda S. Law&B 92
MacDonald, Lindsay William 1950- WhoWor 93
MacDonald, M. Gail Law&B 92
Mac Donald, Malcolm Murdoch 1935- WhoAm 92, WhoWrEP 92
MacDonald, Marcella Anne 1963- WhoE 93
Macdonald, Margaret 1870-1911 BioIn 17
Mac Donald, Marian Louise 1947- WhoAmW 93
MacDonald, Maril Gagen 1956- WhoEmL 93
MacDonald, Mark Douglas 1955- WhoE 93
MacDonald, Mark Edward 1943- WhoAm 92
MacDonald, Maryann 1947- SmATA 72 [port]
Mac Donald, Matthew Anita 1938- WhoAm 92
MacDonald, Michael H. 1945- ScF&FL 92
MacDonald, Nestor Joseph 1895-1991 BioIn 17
MacDonald, Peter BioIn 17, MiSFD 9
MacDonald, Peter David 1946- WhoEmL 93
MacDonald, Philip ScF&FL 92
Macdonald, R. Fulton 1940- WhoE 93, WhoWor 93
MacDonald, R.W. Law&B 92
MacDonald, Ralph Lewis, Jr. 1942- St&PR 93, WhoAm 92
Macdonald, Ranald H., Jr. 1923- St&PR 93
MacDonald, Reby Edmund ScF&FL 92
MacDonald, Reynold C. 1918- St&PR 93
MacDonald, Richard Annis 1928- WhoAm 92, WhoWor 93
MacDonald, Robert Alan 1927- WhoSSW 93
MacDonald, Robert B. 1931- St&PR 93
MacDonald, Robert Bruce 1930- WhoE 93
Macdonald, Robert Rigg, Jr. 1942- WhoAm 92, WhoE 93
MacDonald, Robert Taylor 1930- WhoAm 92
MacDonald, Robert W. 1943- WhoIns 93
Mac Donald, Robert William 1922- WhoWrEP 92
MacDonald, Robert William 1943- St&PR 93, WhoAm 92
MacDonald, Rod 1948- WhoE 93
MacDonald, Roderick 1931- WhoAm 92
MacDonald, Ronald Angus Neil 1935- WhoAm 92
MacDonald, Ronald F. 1930- St&PR 93
MacDonald, Ronald Francis 1946- WhoE 93
MacDonald, Rosemary Anne 1930- WhoAmW 93
MacDonald, Ross 1915-1983 BioIn 17, MagSAmL [port]
Macdonald, Ross Alexander 1958- WhoWor 93
MacDonald, Ross W. 1946- St&PR 93
MacDonald, Sara Jean 1955- WhoAmW 93
MacDonald, Sharon Ethel 1952- WhoAmW 93, WhoE 93, WhoEmL 93, WhoWor 93
Macdonald, Sheila de Marillac 1952- WhoAmW 93, WhoSSW 93, WhoWor 93
MacDonald, Stephen Hugh 1962- WhoSSW 93
Macdonald, Stewart Robert 1925- WhoSSW 93
MacDonald, Suse & Oakes, Bill ChlBIID [port]
MacDonald, Thomas Cook, Jr. 1929- WhoAm 92
MacDonald, Thomas J. 1940- St&PR 93
MacDonald, Thomas S. 1952- St&PR 93
Macdonald, Timothy BioIn 17
MacDonald, Timothy Lee 1948- WhoSSW 93
Macdonald, Valerie L. Law&B 92
Macdonald, Victor Roderick 1930- WhoAm 92
Macdonald, Virginia B. 1920- WhoAmW 93
MacDonald, Wallace 1891-1978 BioIn 17
MacDonald, Wesley Angus Reginald 1932- WhoAm 92
MacDonald, William E. 1918- WhoAm 92
MacDonald, William Francis, Jr. 1944- St&PR 93
MacDonald, William Lloyd 1921- WhoAm 92, WhoWrEP 92
MacDonald, William Weir WhoScE 91-1
MacDonald, Wilson 1880-1967 BioIn 17
MacDonald, Zillah Katherine 1885- AmWomPl
MacDonald Glenn, Linda 1955- WhoAmW 93
MacDonall, James Sinclair 1946- WhoE 93
Macdonell, A.G. 1895-1941 ScF&FL 92
MacDonell, Cameron 1938- WhoE 93
MacDonnell, Amice AmWomPl
MacDonnell, James ScF&FL 92
MacDonnell, Joanne Capella 1937- WhoAmW 93
MacDonnell, Megan SmATA 70
Macdonough, John N. 1943- St&PR 93
MacDonough, Thomas 1783-1825 HarEnMi
MacDougal, Gary Edward 1936- WhoAm 92
Macdougald, James A. 1928- St&PR 93
MacDougall, Ann Louise Law&B 92
MacDougall, Donald Alastair 1912- WhoWor 93
MacDougall, Hugh Cooke 1932- WhoE 93
Macdougall, Iver Cameron 1926- WhoAm 92
MacDougall, John Douglas 1944- WhoAm 92
MacDougall, Joseph W., Jr. Law&B 92
MacDougall, Malcolm D. WhoAm 92
MacDougall, Mark Allen Law&B 92
Mac Dougall, Mary Katherine WhoWrEP 92
MacDougall, Peter 1937- WhoAm 92
MacDougall, Ranald 1915-1973 MiSFD 9N
MacDougall, William F. 1955- WhoWor 93
Mac Dougall, William Lowell 1931- WhoAm 92, WhoWrEP 92
Macdowall, Ian d1991 BioIn 17
MacDowell, Andie BioIn 17, WhoAm 92
MacDowell, Edward 1861-1908 BioIn 17, GayN
MacDowell, Edward (Alexander) 1860-1908 Baker 92
MacDowell, Edward Alexander 1861-1908 BioIn 17
MacDowell, Lawrence James 1951- St&PR 93
MacDowell, Marian Griswold AmWomPl

MacDowell, Robert Karl 1937- *WhoWor 93*
MacDowell, Roland H. 1929- *St&PR 93*
Mac Dowell, Samuel Wallace 1929- *WhoE 93*
MacDuff, William F. 1955- *St&PR 93*
MacDuffee, Robert Colton 1923- *WhoSSW 93*
Mace, David 1951- *ScF&FL 92*
Mace, David Jay 1957- *St&PR 93*
Mace, David R. 1907-1990 *BioIn 17*
Mace, Edgar G. 1929- *St&PR 93*
Mace, Elisabeth 1933- *ScF&FL 92*
Mace, Elizabeth Rhoda 1943- *ConAu 38NR*
Mace, Gabriel d1990 *BioIn 17*
Mace, Georgia M. 1949- *St&PR 93*
Mace, John Weldon 1938- *WhoAm 92*
Mace, Joni M. *St&PR 93*
Mace, Mary Alice 1949- *WhoAmW 93*
Mace, Richard L. 1929- *St&PR 93*
Mace, Robert Rhoton 1930- *St&PR 93*
Mace, Terence Richard 1956- *St&PR 93*
MacEachen, Allan Joseph *BioIn 17*
MacEachen, Allan Joseph 1921- *WhoAm 92*
MacEachen, Roberto D. 1938- *WhoUN 92*
MacEachern-Condon, Laura 1954- *WhoAmW 93*
MacEachron, Susan *Law&B 92*
Macebuh, Sandy *WhoWrEP 92*
Maceda, Ernesto Madarang 1935- *WhoAsAP 91*
Maceda, Jose 1917- *Baker 92*
Macedo, Cheryl Ann 1964- *WhoAmW 93*
Macedo, Fernando Wolfango 1931- *WhoWor 93*
Macedo, Richard Stanley 1941- *WhoAm 92*
Macedo, Stephen 1957- *ConAu 138*
Macek, Gary M. *Law&B 92*
Maceljski, Milan 1925- *WhoScE 91-4*
Macemon, Mark *BioIn 17*
Macemon, Sue *BioIn 17*
MacEoin, Denis *ScF&FL 92*
Macer, Dan Johnstone 1917- *WhoAm 92*
Macera, Salvatore 1931- *WhoAm 92*
Macero, Teo 1925- *WhoAm 92*
Macer-Story, Eugenia Ann 1945- *WhoAmW 93, WhoE 93, WhoWor 93*
Macesic, Nedeljko 1956- *WhoWor 93*
MacEwan, Craig Edward 1954- *WhoE 93*
Macewan, Nigel Savage 1933- *St&PR 93, WhoAm 92*
MacEwen, Bruce John *Law&B 92*
MacEwen, David Martin *WhoScE 91-1*
MacEwen, Edward C. 1938- *St&PR 93*
MacEwen, Edward Carter 1938- *WhoAm 92*
Mac Ewen, George Dean 1927- *WhoAm 92*
MacEwen, Gwendolyn 1941-1987 *BioIn 17, ScF&FL 92, WhoCanL 92*
MacEwen, Malcolm 1911- *BioIn 17*
Macey, Chester O. 1938- *St&PR 93*
Macey, Karen Elizabeth 1962- *WhoSSW 93*
Macey, Morris William 1922- *WhoAm 92*
Macey, Peter *ScF&FL 92*
Macey, Scott J. *Law&B 92*
Macey, William Blackmore 1920- *WhoAm 92*
Macfadden, Bernarr 1868-1955 *BioIn 17, JrnUS*
MacFadden, Clifford Herbert 1908- *WhoAm 92*
MacFadden, James P. 1957- *St&PR 93*
Macfadden, Johnnie Lee d1992 *BioIn 17, NewYTBS 92*
MacFadden, Karen Elizabeth 1959- *WhoAmW 93, WhoEmL 93*
MacFadden, Patricia Ann Laura 1936- *WhoE 93*
MacFadden, Patrick *ScF&FL 92*
MacFadden, William Semple, Jr. 1928- *St&PR 93*
MacFadyen, Alex G., Jr. 1941- *St&PR 93*
Mac Fadyen, Scott Douglas 1961- *WhoEmL 93*
MacFarland, Nancy Foley 1952- *WhoAmW 93*
Macfarland, Robert Fredrick 1931- *St&PR 93*
Macfarlane, Alastair Iain Robert 1940- *WhoAm 92, WhoSSW 93*
MacFarlane, Alistair George James *WhoScE 91-1*
MacFarlane, Andrew Walker 1928- *WhoAm 92*
Mac Farlane, Anne *AmWomPl*
MacFarlane, Bruce A. 1952- *St&PR 93*
MacFarlane, Charles N. *Law&B 92*
Macfarlane, David Gordon 1947- *WhoEmL 93*
Macfarlane, Elizabeth *ScF&FL 92*
Macfarlane, Ellen *BioIn 17*
MacFarlane, I.M. *WhoScE 91-1*
MacFarlane, J. *WhoScE 91-1*
Macfarlane, Jean Walker 1894-1989 *BioIn 17*
Macfarlane, John *BioIn 17, ScF&FL 92*
Macfarlane, John 1942- *St&PR 93*
MacFarlane, John Alexander 1916- *WhoAm 92*
MacFarlane, John Charles 1939- *St&PR 93, WhoAm 92*
MacFarlane, John Craig 1947- *St&PR 93*
MacFarlane, Kirk R. *Law&B 92*
MacFarlane, M. David 1940- *St&PR 93*
MacFarlane, Malcolm David 1940- *WhoAm 92*
Macfarlane, Robert Bruce 1896- *WhoSSW 93*
MacFarlane, Roderick Ross 1833-1920 *IntDcAn*
Macfarlane, W.A.S. *Law&B 92*
Macfarren, George 1813-1887 *OxDcOp*
Macfarren, George (Alexander) 1813-1887 *Baker 92*
Macfarren, Natalia 1826-1916 *See* Macfarren, George (Alexander) 1813-1887 *Baker 92*
Macfarren, Natalia 1828-1916 *OxDcOp*
Macfarren, Walter (Cecil) 1826-1905 *Baker 92*
Macfie, Halliday James 1948- *WhoWor 93*
MacGaffey, Wyatt 1932- *WhoAm 92*
MacGibbon, David John 1934- *WhoAsAP 91*
MacGill, Patrick 1890-1963 *BioIn 17*
MacGill, Richard Gambrill, Jr. 1932- *St&PR 93*
Mac Gillis, Robert Donald 1936- *WhoE 93*
MacGillivray, Lois Ann 1937- *WhoAm 92, WhoAmW 93*
MacGillivray, Lorna D. *Law&B 92*
MacGillivray, Lorna D. 1951- *St&PR 93*
MacGillivray, MaryAnn Leverone 1947- *WhoAmW 93*
Macgillivray, O.A. *WhoIns 93*
MacGillivray, William D. *Law&B 92*
MacGinitie, Walter Harold 1928- *WhoAm 92*
MacGiolla Bhrighde, Maud 1866-1953 *BioIn 17*
MacGowan, Charles Frederic 1918- *WhoAm 92*
MacGowan, Christopher John 1948- *WhoSSW 93*
Macgowan, Kenneth Owen 1921- *St&PR 93*
Mac Gowan, Mary Eugenia 1928- *WhoAm 92, WhoWor 93*
MacGowan, Sandra Firelli 1951- *WhoAmW 93*
Macgowan, W.A.L. 1925- *WhoScE 91-3*
MacGrady, Glenn J. *Law&B 92*
MacGrath, C. Richard 1921- *WhoAm 92*
MacGrath, Leueen 1914-1992 *BioIn 17, NewYTBS 92 [port]*
MacGraw, Ali *BioIn 17*
MacGraw, Ali 1939- *ConAu 139, WhoAm 92*
MacGregor, David Lee 1932- *WhoAm 92*
MacGregor, Donald Lane, Jr. 1930- *WhoAm 92*
MacGregor, Ellen 1906-1954 *ConAu 137, MajAI [port], ScF&FL 92*
MacGregor, Geddes 1909- *WhoAm 92*
MacGregor, George Lescher, Jr. 1936- *WhoAm 92*
MacGregor, Herbert C. *WhoScE 91-1*
MacGregor, Ian K. 1912- *St&PR 93*
MacGregor, J. Kelly *Law&B 92*
Macgregor, James *ScF&FL 92*
MacGregor, James Grierson 1934- *WhoAm 92*
MacGregor, James P. 1932- *St&PR 93*
MacGregor, Janet Elizabeth *WhoScE 91-1*
MacGregor, John 1937- *BioIn 17*
MacGregor, John Russell Roddick 1937- *WhoWor 93*
MacGregor, Keith Robert 1949- *St&PR 93*
MacGregor, Kenneth Robert 1906- *WhoAm 92, WhoIns 93*
MacGregor, Loren 1950- *ScF&FL 92*
MacGregor, Mary Esther Miller 1874?-1961 *BioIn 17*
MacGregor, Neil 1946- *BioIn 17*
MacGregor, Patricia *ScF&FL 92*
MacGregor, Richard *ScF&FL 92*
MacGregor, Rob *ScF&FL 92*
MacGregor, Robert W. d1992 *NewYTBS 92*
MacGregor, Roy 1948- *WhoCanL 92*
MacGregor, T.J. *ScF&FL 92*
Macgregor, Wallace 1917- *WhoAm 92, WhoWor 93*
Mac Gregor-Hastie, Roy Alasdhair Niall 1929- *WhoWor 93*
MacGrianna, Seosamh 1901-1990 *BioIn 17*
MacGuigan, Mark R. 1931- *WhoAm 92, WhoE 93*
MacGuinness, Rosemary Anne *Law&B 92*
MacGuire, James M. 1931- *St&PR 93*
MacGuire, Mary C. 1930- *St&PR 93*
MacGunnigle, Bruce Campbell 1947- *WhoE 93*
Mach, Bernard F. 1933- *WhoScE 91-4*
Mach, David 1956- *WhoAm 92*
Mach, Ernst 1838-1916 *Baker 92*
Mach, George D. 1944- *St&PR 93*
Mach, Josef 1909-1987 *DrEEuF*
Mach, Kenneth 1949- *St&PR 93*
Mach, Leta Marie 1947- *WhoE 93*
Mach, Rostislav 1943- *WhoScE 91-4*
Macha, Otmar 1922- *Baker 92*
Machabey, Armand 1886-1966 *Baker 92*
Machado, Alfredo C. 1922-1991 *BioIn 17*
Machado, Antonio 1875-1939 *BioIn 17*
Machado, Augusto (de Oliveira) 1845-1924 *Baker 92*
Machado, Bruno Paul 1945- *WhoUN 92*
Machado, Gerardo *DcCPCAm*
Machado, Jaime Ulises 1962- *WhoE 93*
Machado, Jeffrey D. 1953- *St&PR 93*
Machado, Manuel 1874-1947 *BioIn 17*
Machado, Rodolfo 1942- *BioIn 17*
Machado, Tito 1955- *St&PR 93*
Machado Caetano, Joaquim Antonio 1935- *WhoScE 91-3*
Machado de Sousa, Maria Leonor 1932- *WhoWor 93*
Machado y Alvarez, Antonio 1846-1893 *IntDcAn*
Machairas, Leontios c. 1380-c. 1432 *OxDcByz*
Machaj-Schutz, Janice Lynn 1953- *WhoAmW 93, WhoEmL 93*
MacHale, John 1791-1881 *BioIn 17*
MacHale, Joseph P. 1951- *WhoAm 92*
Machalinski, Richard 1955- *WhoIns 93*
MacHalski, Jerzy 1935- *WhoScE 91-4*
Machan, Gary R. 1944- *St&PR 93*
Machan, Katharyn Howd 1952- *WhoWrEP 92*
Machan, Myrle Bernice 1927- *WhoWrEP 92*
Machanic, Harmon Jack 1923- *WhoE 93*
Machanic, Roger *WhoSSW 93*
Machanidas fl. c. 208BC- *HarEnMi*
Ma Chan-shan 1885-1950 *HarEnMi*
Machar, Agnes Maule 1837-1927 *BioIn 17*
Macharski, Franciszek 1927- *PolBiDi*
Macharski, Franciszek Cardinal 1927- *WhoWor 93*
Machas, Richard Frank 1940- *St&PR 93*
Machatzke, Heinz Wilhelm 1932- *WhoAm 92*
Machau, Guillaume de c. 1300-1377 *Baker 92*
Machault, Guillaume de c. 1300-1377 *Baker 92*
Machaut, Guillaume de c. 1300-1377 *Baker 92*
Machavariani, Alexei 1913- *Baker 92*
Mache, Francois-Bernard 1935- *Baker 92*
Mache, Regis 1933- *WhoScE 91-2*
Macheinski, Victor *Law&B 92*
Machel, Samora Moises 1930-1986 *DcTwHis*
Machelak, Zygmunt *Law&B 92*
Machemer, Hans Georg 1934- *WhoScE 91-3*
Machemer, Robert 1933- *WhoAm 92*
Machen, Arthur 1863-1947 *BioIn 17, ScF&FL 92*
Machen, Arthur Webster, Jr. 1920- *WhoAm 92*
Ma Chen-Fang 1924- *WhoAsAP 91*
Machenschalk, Ruddolf A. 1928- *WhoWor 93*
Macheras, Panayotis 1947- *WhoWor 93*
Macherauch, Eckard 1926- *WhoWor 93*
Machesney, Lisa A. *Law&B 92*
Machgeels, Claude J.F.E. 1939- *WhoScE 91-2*
Machgeels, Claude Jacques 1939- *WhoWor 93*
Machiavelli, Niccolo 1469-1527 *HarEnMi*
Machiaverna, Frank Edward 1951- *WhoE 93*
Machida, Ken Jyoso 1955- *St&PR 93*
Machida, Minoru 1918- *WhoWor 93*
Machida, Noboru 1962- *WhoWor 93*
Machimura, Nobutaka 1944- *WhoAsAP 91*
Machin, Javier 1943- *WhoScE 91-3*
Machin, Peter J. 1950- *WhoScE 91-1*
Machinski, Michael Francis 1950- *WhoE 93, WhoEmL 93*
Machiz, Leon 1924- *St&PR 93*
Machl, Tadeusz 1922- *Baker 92*
Machlin, Claire Tajen 1925- *WhoAmW 93*
Machlin, Eugene Solomon 1920- *WhoAm 92*
Machlin, Lawrence J. 1927- *WhoAm 92*
Machlin, Milton Robert 1924- *WhoAm 92, WhoWrEP 92*
Machlin, Robert N. 1957- *St&PR 93*
Machlis, Joseph 1906- *Baker 92*
Machlis, Roger M. *Law&B 92*
Machlowitz, David S. *Law&B 92*
Machlowitz, David Steven 1954- *WhoEmL 93*
Machlowitz, Marilyn Marcia *WhoE 93*
Machner, Kurt Hartmut 1945- *WhoWor 93*
Macho, Heinz *WhoScE 91-4*
Machold, Roland Morris 1936- *WhoAm 92*
Machold, William F. 1906- *St&PR 93*
Machon, Jeannine Marie 1963- *WhoAmW 93*
Machov, Steven J. *Law&B 92*
Machov, Steven J. 1951- *St&PR 93*
Machova, Marie 1941- *WhoScE 91-4*
Machovec, Jaroslav 1926- *WhoScE 91-4*
Machover, Carl 1927- *WhoE 93, WhoWor 93*
Machover, Tod 1953- *Baker 92*
Machovich, Raymund 1936- *WhoScE 91-4*
MacHoy, Zygmunt 1924- *WhoScE 91-4*
Macht, Carol Malisoff *WhoAm 92*
Machtiger, Harriet Gordon 1927- *WhoAmW 93*
Machtinger, Steven N. *Law&B 92*
Machtley, Ronald K. 1948- *CngDr 91*
Machtley, Ronald Keith 1948- *WhoAm 92, WhoE 93*
Machuca, Pedro fl. 1520-1550 *BioIn 17*
Machulak, Edward A. 1951- *St&PR 93*
Machulak, Edward L. 1926- *St&PR 93*
Machulak, Edward Leon 1926- *WhoAm 92*
Machulski, Juliusz 1955- *DrEEuF*
Machungo, Mario da Graca *WhoWor 93*
Machungo, Mario Fernandes de Graca 1940- *WhoAfr*
Machura, Raymond Stephen 1946- *WhoEmL 93*
Macia, Lillian *Law&B 92*
Maciag, Gregory A. 1947- *WhoIns 93*
Maciag, John Andrew, Jr. 1953- *WhoEmL 93*
Maciakowski, Ryszard 1928- *WhoScE 91-4*
Macias, Carlos Fuentes *ScF&FL 92*
Macias, Edward S. 1944- *WhoAm 92*
Macias, Salvador, III 1953- *WhoSSW 93*
Macias, Thomas 1932- *St&PR 93*
Maciejewicz, Janusz *WhoScE 91-4*
Maciejewski, Roman 1910- *Baker 92, PolBiDi*
Maciel, Patricia Ann 1940- *WhoAmW 93*
Macielag, Michael 1949- *WhoE 93*
MacIlroy, John Whittington 1946- *WhoEmL 93, WhoSSW 93*
MacIlvaine, Chalmers Acheson 1921- *WhoAm 92*
Macina, Marianne Pasque 1951- *WhoAmW 93*
Macindoe, Francis Grey Smith 1958- *WhoWor 93*
MacInnes, Colin 1914-1976 *BioIn 17*
MacInnes, David Fenton, Jr. 1943- *WhoSSW 93*
MacInnes, Helen 1907-1985 *BioIn 17*
MacInnes, John *Law&B 92*
Mac Innis, Ronald 1943- *St&PR 93*
Mac Intire, Elizabeth Jelliffe *AmWomPl*
MacIntosh, Alexander John 1921- *WhoAm 92*
MacIntosh, Charles W. *Law&B 92*
MacIntosh, Craig 1959- *BioIn 17*
MacIntosh, David Alan 1940- *St&PR 93*
Macintosh, Dean *St&PR 93*
Macintosh, Keitha K. *WhoCanL 92*
MacIntosh, Monica Bernadette 1957- *WhoE 93, WhoEmL 93*
MacIntosh, Robert 1923- *ConAu 137*
MacIntosh, Robert Edward 1945- *WhoE 93*
MacIntosh, Robert Mallory 1923- *BioIn 17, St&PR 93, WhoAm 92*
MacIntyre, A.J. *WhoScE 91-1*
MacIntyre, Alasdair Chalmers 1929- *WhoAm 92*
MacIntyre, Alfonso Everette 1901- *WhoAm 92*
MacIntyre, Carlyle Ferren 1890-1967 *BioIn 17*
Mac Intyre, Donald John 1939- *WhoAm 92*
MacIntyre, F. Gwynplaine 1949- *ScF&FL 92*
Macintyre, George W. 1945- *St&PR 93*
MacIntyre, Giles T. d1992 *NewYTBS 92*
MacIntyre, John Alexander 1937- *WhoE 93*
MacIntyre, John Alexander 1939- *St&PR 93*
MacIntyre, Malcolm Ames d1992 *NewYTBS 92 [port]*
MacIntyre, Malcolm Ames 1908-1992 *BioIn 17*
MacIntyre, Pamela J. *St&PR 93*
MacIntyre, R. Douglas 1951- *WhoAm 92*
Mac Intyre, Regina *WhoWrEP 92*

Macintyre, Robert Charles 1926- St&PR 93
MacIntyre, Sally WhoScE 91-1
Macioce, Frank M., Jr. Law&B 92
Macioce, Thomas M. BioIn 17
Macioce, Thomas M. 1919- St&PR 93
Maciocia, Gabriel James 1948- WhoE 93
Maciolek, John L. 1936- St&PR 93
Maciolek, Kenneth J. Law&B 92
Maciorowski, Anthony Francis 1948- WhoSSW 93
Macip, Vecente c. 1475-c. 1550 BioIn 17
Macisco, John Joseph 1936- WhoE 93
Maciulis, Linda S. 1949- WhoAmW 93
Maciuszko, Kathleen Lynn 1947- WhoAm 92
MacIver, J. Robertson Law&B 92
MacIver, Loren 1909- BioIn 17
MacIvor, Hazel Judith Arnold 1921- WhoAmW 93, WhoSSW 93, WhoWor 93
MacIvor, Richard Edward 1947- WhoEmL 93
Mack, Alan Wayne 1947- WhoEmL 93
Mack, Anna E. Law&B 92
Mack, Anthony A. 1949- St&PR 93
Mack, Barbara M. 1952- WhoAmW 93
Mack, Barry V. 1943- St&PR 93
Mack, Betty d1980 SweetSg C [port]
Mack, Brenda Lee 1940- WhoAmW 93
Mack, Carol K. 1941- ScF&FL 92
Mack, Carolyn L. 1932- WhoAmW 93
Mack, Catherine R. Law&B 92
Mack, Clifford Glenn 1927- WhoAm 92
Mack, Connie 1862-1956 BioIn 17
Mack, Connie 1940- CngDr 91
Mack, Connie, III 1940- WhoAm 92, WhoSSW 93
Mack, Conrad John 1936- St&PR 93
Mack, Cressy AmWomPl
Mack, Cristina Iannone 1940- WhoAmW 93
Mack, Daniel Richard 1947- WhoE 93
Mack, David BioIn 17
Mack, David J. 1947- St&PR 93
Mack, Dennis Wayne 1943- St&PR 93, WhoAm 92
Mack, Donald Roy 1925- WhoE 93
Mack, Earle Irving 1939- WhoAm 92, WhoE 93, WhoWor 93
Mack, Edward Gibson 1917- WhoAm 92
Mack, Ellie Johnson 1944- WhoAmW 93
Mack, Eugene K. 1922- St&PR 93
Mack, Evelyn Walker 1930- St&PR 93
Mack, Francis Marion 1949- WhoEmL 93
Mack, George Francis 1944- WhoE 93
Mack, George M. 1929- WhoAm 92
Mack, Gregory John 1954- WhoE 93
Mack, H. Bert d1992 BioIn 17, NewYTBS 92 [port]
Mack, J. Alan Law&B 92
Mack, J. Curtis, II 1944- WhoAm 92
Mack, James Edgar 1934- St&PR 93
Mack, James Franklin 1924- St&PR 93
Mack, James R. Law&B 92
Mack, Jane Barnes 1942- WhoAmW 93
Mack, Jim St&PR 93
Mack, John BioIn 17
Mack, John Duncan 1924- St&PR 93
Mack, John Edward, III 1934- St&PR 93, WhoAm 92, WhoE 93
Mack, John Parker 1926- St&PR 93
Mack, Joseph P. 1939- WhoAm 92
Mack, Judith Cole Schrim 1938- WhoAmW 93
Mack, Julia Cooper 1920- WhoAm 92
Mack, Karol Page Law&B 92
Mack, Keith R. WhoScE 91-2
Mack, Kenneth D. 1955- St&PR 93
Mack, Kevin David Law&B 92
Mack, L.V. WhoWrEP 92
Mack, Lorraine Ann 1942- St&PR 93
Mack, Mark Philip 1950- WhoEmL 93, WhoSSW 93
Mack, Mary Margaret 1955- WhoWor 93
Mack, Maynard 1909- BioIn 17
Mack, Norman E. 1858-1932 PolPar
Mack, Pamela Etter 1955- WhoAmW 93
Mack, Paul Frederick 1932- St&PR 93
Mack, Raymond Francis 1912- WhoAm 92
Mack, Raymond Phillip 1940- St&PR 93
Mack, Raymond Wright 1927- WhoAm 92
Mack, Robert Emmet 1924- WhoAm 92
Mack, Robert N. 1952- St&PR 93
Mack, Robert William BioIn 17
Mack, Russell Ray, Jr. 1951- WhoSSW 93
Mack, Sharon Ellen 1953- WhoAmW 93
Mack, Stan 1936- WhoE 93
Mack, Stephen BioIn 17
Mack, Stephen W. 1954- WhoEmL 93
Mack, Steven Philp 1951- St&PR 93
Mack, Thomas H. 1942- St&PR 93
Mack, Vernon Lucian 1944- WhoUN 92
Mack, Walter BioIn 17, Law&B 92
Mack, Wayne WhoWrEP 92
Mack, William F. Law&B 92
Mackail, J.W. 1859-1945 ScF&FL 92
MacKaill, Dorothy 1903-1990 BioIn 17
Mackall, Henry Clinton 1927- WhoWor 93
Mackall, Laidler Bowie 1916- WhoAm 92
Mackall, Robert Wain 1942- WhoAm 92
Mackall, Virginia Woods AmWomPl
Mackaman, Donald Hayes 1912- St&PR 93
Mackaness, George Bellamy 1922- WhoAm 92
Mackasey, Michael P. 1954- St&PR 93
Mackavey, William Raymond 1932- WhoAm 92
Mackay, Lord 1927- WhoWor 93
Mackay, Alan L(indsay) 1926- ConAu 137
MacKay, Alan Lindsay WhoScE 91-1
Mackay, Alexander Russell 1911- WhoWor 93
MacKay, Andrew Dougal 1946- WhoEmL 93
Mackay, Calder Mead Law&B 92
Mackay, Claire 1930- DcChlFi, WhoCanL 92, WhoWrEP 92
Mackay, Colin 1951- ScF&FL 92
Mackay, Connie Lynn 1958- WhoAmW 93
Mackay, Constance D'Arcy AmWomPl
Mackay, Donald (Alexander) 1914- ConAu 136
Mac Kay, Donald MacGregor 1935- WhoE 93
Mackay, Edward 1936- WhoWor 93
Mackay, Edward F. 1942- St&PR 93
MacKay, Elmer MacIntosh 1936- WhoAm 92, WhoE 93
MacKay, George Murray WhoScE 91-1
Mackay, H.H. 1940- St&PR 93
MacKay, Harold Hugh 1940- WhoAm 92
Mackay, Harvey BioIn 17
Mackay, Hugh c. 1640-1692 HarEnMi
MacKay, Isabel Ecclestone 1875-1928 BioIn 17
Mackay, James G. 1934- St&PR 93
MacKay, John 1914- WhoSSW 93
Mackay, John 1920- WhoAm 92
MacKay, John Robert 1945- St&PR 93
MacKay, Jon Charles Law&B 92
Mackay, Katherine AmWomPl
Mackay, Kenneth Donald 1942- WhoAm 92
MacKay, Kenneth Hood 1933- WhoAm 92
Mackay, Kirk Allen 1946- WhoEmL 93
MacKay, Malcolm 1940- St&PR 93, WhoAm 92
MacKay, Malcolm S. d1991 BioIn 17
Mackay, Martha Elizabeth Law&B 92
Mackay, Maureen Florence 1927- WhoWor 93
MacKay, Neil Duncan 1931- WhoE 93
Mackay, Patricia McIntosh 1922- WhoAmW 93
MacKay, Paul 1932- St&PR 93
Mac Kay, Pierre Antony 1933- WhoAm 92
MacKay, R.S. WhoScE 91-1
MacKay, Victoria Lynn 1956- WhoAmW 93
MacKay, William Andrew 1929- WhoAm 92
Mackay-Cantell, Lilia AmWomPl
MacKaye, Dorothy D. 1904-1992 NewYTBS 92
Mackaye, Hazel 1880-1944 AmWomPl
MacKaye, Hazel 1888-1944 BioIn 17
Mackaye, Mary Keith Medbury AmWomPl
MacKaye, William Ross 1934- WhoAm 92
MacKay-Edell, Susanne Micheaux 1938- WhoWor 93
Mackay-Smith, Sandy Law&B 92
Mackay-Smith, Sandy 1941- WhoAm 92
Macke, August 1887-1914 BioIn 17
Macke, Donald L. 1937- St&PR 93
Macke, Donald LaVerne 1937- WhoAm 92
Macke, Kenneth A. BioIn 17
Macke, Kenneth A. 1938- St&PR 93, WhoAm 92
Macke, Richard Chester 1938- WhoAm 92
Mackechnie, Linda Allen 1950- WhoEmL 93
MacKeigan, Ian Malcolm 1915- WhoAm 92
Mackell, Thomas J. d1992 NewYTBS 92 [port]
Mackell, Thomas J. 1914-1992 BioIn 17
MacKellar, Michael John Randal 1938- WhoAsAP 91
Mackel-Rice, Gwendolyn Rosetta 1941- WhoAmW 93
Mackelworth, R.W. 1930- ScF&FL 92
Macken, Daniel Loos 1933- WhoE 93
Macken, Maria Luisa Medina WhoE 93
Mackendrick, Alexander 1912- MiSFD 9
Mac Kendrick, Madra AmWomPl
MacKendrick, Paul Lachlan 1914- WhoAm 92
Mackenna, Juan 1771-1814 BioIn 17
Mackenroth, D. Irwin, Jr. Law&B 92
Mackenroth, Nancy ScF&FL 92
Mackensen, August von 1849-1945 HarEnMi
MacKenzie, A. Ross 1934- St&PR 93
Mackenzie, Alexander 1755?-1820 BioIn 17
Mackenzie, Alexander 1764-1820 Expl 93 [port], IntDcAn
Mackenzie, Alexander 1847-1935 OxDcOp
Mackenzie, Alexander (Campbell) 1847-1935 Baker 92
MacKenzie, Andrew Ross 1934- WhoAm 92
Mackenzie, Blair Law&B 92
Mackenzie, Brian S. 1951- St&PR 93
MacKenzie, Carolyn Kay 1941- St&PR 93
Mackenzie, Charles Edward 1943- WhoAm 92
MacKenzie, Charles Sherrard 1924- WhoAm 92
Mackenzie, Charles Westlake, III 1946- WhoAm 92
Mackenzie, Clara Childs 1931- WhoWrEP 92
Mackenzie, Compton 1883-1972 BioIn 17
MacKenzie, D.J. WhoScE 91-1
Mackenzie, Dianne Veronica 1947- WhoAmW 93, WhoEmL 93
Mackenzie, Donald 1918- WhoWrEP 92
MacKenzie, Donald Murray 1947- WhoAm 92
MacKenzie, Donald W.R. 1929- WhoScE 91-1
MacKenzie, Douglas G. 1943- St&PR 93
Mackenzie, Douglas George 1947- WhoAm 92
MacKenzie, Edna I. AmWomPl
Mackenzie, Fred Hartsell 1950- St&PR 93
MacKenzie, G. Allan 1931- St& PR 93
Mackenzie, George 1949- St&PR 93, WhoAm 92
MacKenzie, George Allan 1931- WhoAm 92
Mackenzie, Ginny Lee 1945- WhoWrEP 92
MacKenzie, Gordon BioIn 17
MacKenzie, Hugh Sinclair 1911- St&PR 93
MacKenzie, Jake ScF&FL 92
Mackenzie, James 1933- WhoE 93
Mac Kenzie, James Donald 1924- WhoSSW 93
Mackenzie, James William, IV 1947- St&PR 93
MacKenzie, Jeanne 1922-1986 ScF&FL 92
Mackenzie, Joan WhoCanL 92
Mackenzie, John 1932- MiSFD 9
MacKenzie, John A. 1917- WhoAm 92
Mackenzie, John Anderson Ross 1927- WhoE 93
MacKenzie, John Douglas 1926- WhoAm 92
MacKenzie, John Edward 1934- St&PR 93
MacKenzie, John Pettibone 1930- WhoAm 92
Mackenzie, John W. Law&B 92
MacKenzie, John William 1947- WhoAm 92
MacKenzie, Joseph Wilkes 1924- St&PR 93
MacKenzie, K. Colin 1933- St&PR 93
MacKenzie, Kathleen K. 1957- WhoAmW 93
MacKenzie, Kenneth Allen 1934- St&PR 93
Mackenzie, Kenneth Donald 1937- WhoAm 92
Mackenzie, Kenneth Victor 1911- WhoAm 92
MacKenzie, Lewis Wharton 1940- WhoAm 92
Mackenzie, Linda Alice 1949- WhoAmW 93
MacKenzie, M.J. WhoScE 91-1
MacKenzie, Malcolm George 1938- St&PR 93
Mackenzie, Malcolm Lewis 1926- WhoAm 92
Mac Kenzie, Malcolm Robert 1924- WhoSSW 93
Mac Kenzie, Margaret AmWomPl
MacKenzie, Mark Scott 1959- WhoE 93, WhoEmL 93
MacKenzie, Mary Hawkins 1936- WhoAmW 93
MacKenzie, Norman 1921- ScF&FL 92
Mac Kenzie, Norman Hugh 1915- WhoAm 92, WhoWrEP 92
MacKenzie, Peter Sean 1954- WhoAm 92
MacKenzie, Ralph Sidney 1934- WhoAm 92
Mackenzie, Ranald Slidell 1840-1889 HarEnMi
MacKenzie, Richard A. Law&B 92
Mackenzie, Richard D. 1943- St&PR 93, WhoIns 93
MacKenzie, Steve ScF&FL 92
Mackenzie, Suzanne 1950- ConAu 136
MacKenzie, Thomas D. 1945- WhoIns 93
MacKenzie, Trix ScF&FL 92
MacKenzie, Warren 1924- BioIn 17
Mackenzie, Will MiSFD 9
Mackenzie, William 1849-1923 BioIn 17
Mackenzie, William Forbes, III 1959- WhoE 93
Mackenzie, William Lyon DcChlFi
Mackenzie, William Lyon 1795-1861 BioIn 17
MacKenzie-Childs, Richard L. BioIn 17
MacKenzie-Childs, Victoria BioIn 17
Mackerodt, Fred 1938- WhoAm 92
Mackerras, Charles 1925- IntDcOp, OxDcOp
Mackerras, (Alan) Charles (Maclaurin) 1925- Baker 92
Mackerras, Charles Mac Laurin 1925- WhoAm 92, WhoWor 93
Mackertich, Seroj 1942- WhoE 93
Mackesy, Jerome C. 1934- St&PR 93
Mackety, Carolyn J. 1932- WhoAmW 93
Mackevicius, Nijole Romualda 1944- WhoAm 92
Mackey, Clarence L. 1932- St&PR 93
Mackey, Curtis Thelbert 1927- WhoSSW 93
Mackey, Cynthia Hervey 1954- WhoSSW 93
Mackey, Dallas L. 1920- WhoWor 93
Mackey, Douglas A. 1947- ScF&FL 92
Mackey, Druzilla Ruth 1885- AmWomPl
Mackey, Elizabeth Jocelyn 1927- WhoAmW 93
Mackey, Howard Hamilton, Jr. 1926- WhoWrEP 92
Mackey, James Ethan 1947- St&PR 93
Mac Key, James Fredrik 1919- WhoScE 91-4
Mackey, Jeffrey Allen 1952- WhoE 93
Mackey, John St&PR 93
Mackey, John E. 1946- St&PR 93
Mackey, Katherine Helen Rice Law&B 92
Mackey, Leonard B. 1925- St&PR 93
Mackey, Leonard Bruce 1925- WhoAm 92
Mackey, Louis Henry 1926- WhoAm 92, WhoSSW 93
Mackey, Lynn Marie 1964- WhoE 93
Mackey, Marilyn Ruth 1953- WhoAmW 93
Mackey, Mary 1945- ScF&FL 92, WhoWrEP 92
Mackey, Maurice Cecil 1929- WhoAm 92, WhoWor 93
Mackey, Patrick Glenn 1946- WhoAm 92
Mackey, Richard James 1931- St&PR 93
Mackey, Rob R. Law&B 92
Mackey, Rob Roy Law&B 92
Mackey, Sally 1930- WhoAm 92
Mackey, Sandra 1951- St&PR 93
Mackey, Sheldon Elias 1913- WhoAm 92
Mackey, Steve R. Law&B 92
Mackey, Steve R. 1950- St&PR 93
Mackey, Vaino Ilmar 1911- WhoWrEP 92
Mackey, Warren Cornell 1950- WhoEmL 93
Mackey, William Arthur Godfrey 1946- WhoAm 92
Mackey, William Sturges, Jr. 1921- WhoAm 92
Macki, Ahmed A. Nabi 1939- WhoWor 93
MacKichan, Margaret Anna 1948- WhoAmW 93
Mackichan, Robin Kenneth 1935- WhoWor 93
Mackie, Anne Wolking 1937- WhoAmW 93
Mackie, Bob BioIn 17
Mackie, Carolyn Lee 1962- WhoAmW 93
Mackie, Charles Keith WhoScE 91-1
Mackie, David F. 1937- WhoAm 92
Mackie, David L. Law&B 92
Mackie, Dian Boyce 1950- WhoAmW 93, WhoEmL 93
Mackie, Diana Jane 1946- WhoEmL 93
Mackie, Donald John, Jr. 1944- WhoSSW 93, WhoWor 93
Mackie, Douglas Law&B 92
Mackie, Elizabeth Louise 1950- WhoEmL 93
Mackie, Frederick David 1910- WhoAm 92
Mackie, George Owen 1929- WhoAm 92
Mackie, James L. 1944- St&PR 93
Mackie, Mary ScF&FL 92
Mackie, Peter F. 1941- St&PR 93
Mackie, Peter Fearing 1941- WhoWor 93
Mackie, Robert Gordon 1940- WhoAm 92
Mackie, Rona McLeod WhoScE 91-1
Mackiewicz, Edward Robert 1951- WhoAm 92
Mackiewicz, Laura WhoAmW 93
Mackil, Joseph D. 1945- St&PR 93

MacKimm, James Bradley 1932- *WhoAm 92*
Mac Kimm, Margaret Pontius 1933- *WhoAm 92*
Mackin, Bernard John 1917- *St&PR 93*
Mackin, Cooper Richerson 1933- *WhoAm 92*
Mackin, Frank D. (Patrick), Jr. *Law&B 92*
Mackin, H. Carroll 1940- *St&PR 93*
Mackin, J. Stanley *WhoSSW 93*
MacKin, James Edward 1944- *WhoAm 92*
Mackin, James Stanley 1932- *St&PR 93*
Mackin, Jeanne A. 1948- *WhoWrEP 92*
Mackin, Joan Emma 1941- *WhoAmW 93*
Mackin, Lois Irene 1950- *WhoAmW 93*
Mackin, Rick *ScF&FL 92*
Mackin, Scott G. *Law&B 92*
Mackin, Scott George 1957- *WhoAm 92*
Mackin, Terrence Christian 1947- *WhoEmL 93*
Mackin, Thomas H. 1929- *St&PR 93*
Mackinder, Halford John 1861-1947 *BioIn 17*
Mac Kinney, Archie Allen, Jr. 1929- *WhoAm 92*
MacKinney, Arthur Clinton, Jr. 1928- *WhoAm 92*
MacKinnon, A. Donald 1895-1990 *BioIn 17*
MacKinnon, Aleck M. 1924- *St&PR 93*
MacKinnon, Bernard Leo 1957- *WhoAm 92*
MacKinnon, Bernie 1957- *ConAu 137, SmATA 69 [port]*
MacKinnon, Catharine A. *BioIn 17, WhoAmW 93*
MacKinnon, Catharine A. 1946- *News 93-2 [port]*
MacKinnon, Charles *ScF&FL 92*
MacKinnon, Charles Walter *Law&B 92*
MacKinnon, Cyrus Leland 1916- *WhoAm 92*
MacKinnon, Donald Sargent 1942- *St&PR 93*
Mac Kinnon, Elizabeth *AmWomPl*
MacKinnon, George E. 1906- *CngDr 91, WhoAm 92, WhoE 93*
Mackinnon, Giles *MiSFD 9*
MacKinnon, Joyce Leslie 1950- *WhoE 93*
MacKinnon, Kevin S. *Law&B 92*
MacKinnon, Larry D. 1949- *St&PR 93*
MacKinnon, M.C. 1934- *St&PR 93*
MacKinnon, Malcolm David 1931- *WhoAm 92*
MacKinnon, Mary Helen 1963- *WhoAmW 93*
MacKinnon, Paul Joseph 1949- *St&PR 93, WhoAm 92*
MacKinnon, R. Peter 1947- *WhoAm 92*
MacKinnon, Roderick C. *Law&B 92*
MacKinnon, Rodrick K. *Law&B 92*
MacKinnon, Rodrick Keith 1943- *WhoAm 92*
MacKinnon, Roger Alan 1927- *WhoAm 92, WhoE 93*
MacKinnon, Sally Anne 1938- *WhoAm 92*
Mackinnon, W.G. *St&PR 93*
MacKinnon, Walter Allan 1929- *WhoAm 92, WhoE 93*
Mackintosh, Allan R. 1936- *WhoScE 91-2*
Mackintosh, Allan Roy 1936- *WhoScE 91-2, WhoWor 93*
MacKintosh, Cameron *BioIn 17*
Mackintosh, Cameron 1946- *WhoAm 92*
Mackintosh, Charles Rennie 1868-1928 *BioIn 17*
Mackintosh, Graham *BioIn 17*
Mackintosh, Helen K. 1897-1980 *BioIn 17*
Mackintosh, James 1765-1832 *BioIn 17*
Mackintosh, James Euan *Law&B 92*
Mackintosh, Nicholas John *WhoScE 91-1*
Mackiw, Christine I. *Law&B 92*
Mackiw, Vladimir Nicholaus 1923- *WhoAm 92*
Mackle, Francis Elliott, Jr. 1916- *WhoAm 92*
Macklem, Francesca *ScF&FL 92*
Macklem, Michael Kirkpatrick 1928- *WhoAm 92*
Mackler, Tina *WhoAm 92*
Mackley, Jon 1970- *ScF&FL 92*
Macklin, Charles 1699-1797 *BioIn 17*
Macklin, George Kane *Law&B 92*
Macklin, Gordon S. 1928- *St&PR 93*
Macklin, John Edward 1936- *St&PR 93*
Macklin, Michael John 1943- *WhoAsAP 91*
Macklin, Philip Alan 1925- *WhoAm 92*
Macklin, Ruth *BioIn 17*
Macklin, Ruth 1938- *WhoAm 92, WhoAmW 93*
Macklin, Thomas Jack 1947- *WhoSSW 93*
Macklon, Alan E.S. 1936- *WhoScE 91-1*
Macklow-Smith, Stephen Peter Francis 1963- *WhoWor 93*
Mackness, John Robert *WhoScE 91-1*
Mackness, Michael D. *Law&B 92*
Mackney, Richard 1953- *St&PR 93*
MacKnight, Carol Bernier 1938- *WhoAmW 93*
MacKnight, David Laurence 1947- *WhoEmL 93*
MacKnight, William John 1936- *WhoAm 92, WhoWor 93*
Macknight, William L. *St&PR 93*
Macko, Helen Ann 1937- *WhoAmW 93*
Macko, John 1947- *WhoE 93, WhoEmL 93, WhoWor 93*
Mackorell, James Theodore, Jr. 1959- *WhoEmL 93, WhoSSW 93*
Mackoul, Sabry Joseph 1940- *St&PR 93*
Mackovic, John 1943- *WhoAm 92*
Mackowiak, Elaine DeCusatis 1940- *WhoE 93*
MacKown, Diana *BioIn 17*
Mackowski, J. Matthew 1954- *St&PR 93*
MacKowski, John Joseph 1926- *WhoAm 92*
Macks, Jonathan P. *Law&B 92*
Macksey, Kenneth 1923- *ScF&FL 92*
Mack Smith, Denis 1920- *BioIn 17, ConAu 39NR*
Mackta, Barnett 1935- *St&PR 93*
Mack Von Leiberich, Karl 1752-1828 *HarEnMi*
Mackworth, Alan Keith 1945- *WhoAm 92*
Maclachlan, Alexander 1933- *St&PR 93, WhoAm 92*
MacLachlan, Alistair Andrew Duncan 1946- *WhoWor 93*
Maclachlan, Colin 1939- *WhoWor 93*
MacLachlan, Douglas Lee 1940- *WhoAm 92*
Maclachlan, Gordon Alistair 1930- *WhoAm 92*
MacLachlan, James 1934-1991 *BioIn 17*
MacLachlan, Kyle *BioIn 17*
MacLachlan, Kyle 1960- *WhoAm 92*
MacLachlan, Patricia *BioIn 17, DcAmChF 1960*
MacLachlan, Patricia 1938- *ConAu 136, DcAmChF 1985, MajAI [port], WhoAmW 93*
Maclagan, John Lyall 1929- *WhoAm 92*
MacLaine, Allan Hugh 1924- *WhoAm 92*
MacLaine, Shirley *BioIn 17*
MacLaine, Shirley 1934- *IntDcF 2-3 [port], WhoAm 92, WhoAmW 93, WhoWrEP 92*
MacLane, Jack 1941- *ScF&FL 92*
MacLane, Saunders 1909- *WhoAm 92*
Maclaren, David S. 1941- *St&PR 93*
Mac Laren, David Sergeant 1941- *WhoAm 92*
Maclaren, Jeff 1951- *St&PR 93*
Mac Laren, Margaret *AmWomPl*
MacLaren, Robert Ian, II 1947- *WhoEmL 93*
MacLaren, Ronny K. 1939- *St&PR 93*
MacLaren, Roy 1934- *WhoAm 92*
MacLaughlan, Robert Elwood 1942- *St&PR 93*
MacLaughlin, Donald C. 1925- *St&PR 93*
MacLaughlin, Francis Joseph 1933- *WhoAm 92*
MacLaughlin, Harry Hunter 1927- *WhoAm 92*
Maclaurin, John d1992 *BioIn 17*
MacLaury, Bruce King 1931- *WhoAm 92*
Maclay, Donald Merle 1934- *WhoAm 92*
Maclay, John 1944- *ScF&FL 92*
Maclay, William Nevin 1924- *WhoAm 92*
MacLean, A. *WhoScE 91-1*
Maclean, Alick 1872-1936 *Baker 92*
Maclean, Alison *MiSFD 9*
MacLean, Alistair 1922-1987 *BioIn 17*
MacLean, Annie Marion 1870?-1934 *BioIn 17*
Maclean, Archibald 1938- *St&PR 93*
MacLean, Babcock 1946- *WhoEmL 93*
MacLean, Barbara Barondess *BioIn 17*
MacLean, Barry L. 1938- *St&PR 93*
MacLean, C. Ian *Law&B 92*
MacLean, Catherine Anne 1946- *WhoAmW 93*
Maclean, Charles 1945- *WhoAm 92*
Maclean, Charles (Donald) 1843-1916 *Baker 92*
Maclean, Charles Hector Fitzroy 1916-1990 *BioIn 17*
MacLean, Daniel C. *Law&B 92*
Maclean, Daniel Crawford, III 1942- *St&PR 93*
MacLean, David Bailey 1923- *WhoAm 92*
Maclean, Donald 1913-1983 *ColdWar 1 [port]*
Maclean, Donald Duart 1913-1983 *BioIn 17*
MacLean, Donald I. 1929-1989 *BioIn 17*
MacLean, Douglas *BioIn 17*
Maclean, Fitzroy 1911- *BioIn 17*
MacLean, George H. *Law&B 92*
MacLean, Guy Robertson 1929- *WhoAm 92*
Maclean, J.B. 1946- *St&PR 93*
MacLean, James A. *Law&B 92*
MacLean, Janet Rockwood 1917- *WhoAm 92*
MacLean, John Angus 1914- *WhoAm 92*
MacLean, John Ronald 1938- *WhoAm 92*
MacLean, Katherine 1925- *BioIn 17, ScF&FL 92*
MacLean, Kenneth H. *Law&B 92*
Mac Lean, Lloyd Douglas 1924- *WhoAm 92*
MacLean, Merrilee Ann 1952- *WhoEmL 93*
MacLean, Norman 1902-1990 *BioIn 17*
MacLean, Paul Donald 1913- *WhoAm 92*
Maclean, Quentin (Stuart Morvaren) 1896-1962 *Baker 92*
Maclean, Richard James *Law&B 92*
Maclean, Stephen *MiSFD 9*
Maclean, Suzan *Law&B 92*
Macleay, Donald 1908- *WhoAm 92*
MacLeay, Kathy Jean 1952- *WhoAmW 93*
MacLeay, Ronald Edward 1935- *WhoE 93*
MacLeay, Thomas H. 1949- *St&PR 93*
MacLeay, William Branson, III 1947- *WhoE 93*
MacLeish, Archibald 1892-1982 *BioIn 17*
MacLeish, Archibald Bruce 1947- *WhoAm 92*
MacLeish, Kenneth 1894-1918 *BioIn 17*
MacLeish, Martin 1955- *WhoWor 93*
MacLeish, Roderick 1926- *ScF&FL 92*
MacLellan, Hugh O. 1912- *St&PR 93*
MacLennan, Beryce W. 1920- *WhoAm 92, WhoAmW 93*
Mac Lennan, David Herman 1937- *WhoAm 92*
MacLennan, David N. 1940- *WhoScE 91-1*
MacLennan, David Neall 1940- *WhoWor 93*
Maclennan, Francis 1879-1935 *Baker 92*
MacLennan, Hugh *BioIn 17*
MacLennan, Hugh 1907-1990 *MagSWL [port], ScF&FL 92, WhoCanL 92*
MacLennan, Ian Calman Muir *WhoScE 91-1*
MacLennan, William Jardine *WhoScE 91-1*
MacLeod, Alexander Joseph James *WhoScE 91-1*
Macleod, Alistair 1936- *WhoCanL 92*
MacLeod, Ann 1940- *ConAu 138*
Macleod, Anthony Michael *Law&B 92*
Macleod, Anthony Michael 1947- *St&PR 93, WhoAm 92*
Macleod, Brian *Law&B 92*
MacLeod, Charlotte 1922- *ConAu 40NR, DcAmChF 1960, ScF&FL 92, WhoAmW 93*
MacLeod, Daniel Broyles 1941- *St&PR 93*
MacLeod, Denis Frederick 1954- *WhoEmL 93, WhoWor 93*
Macleod, Donald 1914- *WhoAm 92*
MacLeod, Donald G. 1930- *St&PR 93*
MacLeod, Donald Martin 1929- *WhoSSW 93*
MacLeod, Donald W. 1925- *St&PR 93*
MacLeod, Doug 1959- *BioIn 17*
MacLeod, Edward James Waring 1950- *WhoE 93*
Macleod, Finlay *BioIn 17*
MacLeod, Fred Lawrence 1926- *St&PR 93*
MacLeod, Gavin 1931- *ConTFT 10, WhoAm 92*
MacLeod, George 1895-1991 *BioIn 17*
MacLeod, Gordon Albert 1926- *WhoAm 92*
MacLeod, Gordon Kenneth 1929- *WhoAm 92*
MacLeod, Iain 1913-1970 *ColdWar 1 [port]*
MacLeod, Iain Alasdair *WhoScE 91-1*
MacLeod, Ian R. *Law&B 92*
MacLeod, Ian Roberts 1931- *St&PR 93, WhoAm 92*
MacLeod, J.M. *BioIn 17*
MacLeod, Jack 1931- *WhoAm 92*
MacLeod, Jack 1932- *WhoCanL 92*
MacLeod, John 1937- *WhoAm 92*
Macleod, John A., Jr. 1951- *St&PR 93*
Macleod, John Amend 1942- *WhoAm 92*
MacLeod, John Daniel, Jr. 1922- *WhoAm 92, WhoSSW 93*
Macleod, John Graeme 1930- *WhoSSW 93*
MacLeod, John Kenneth 1957- *WhoWor 93*
MacLeod, John Matthew 1937- *BiDAMSp 1989*
MacLeod, John Munroe 1937- *WhoAm 92*
MacLeod, Joseph Gordon 1903-1984? *ScF&FL 92*
MacLeod, Kathi Ann 1960- *St&PR 93*
MacLeod, Kenneth J. 1955- *St&PR 93*
Macleod, Kenneth James 1938- *WhoUN 92*
MacLeod, Malcolm W. *St&PR 93*
MacLeod, Margaret Jayne 1948- *WhoAmW 93*
MacLeod, Marylynn 1965- *WhoAmW 93*
MacLeod, Michael Christopher 1947- *WhoSSW 93*
MacLeod, Norman Cloud 1931- *WhoWor 93*
MacLeod, Norman Z. 1898-1964 *MiSFD 9N*
MacLeod, Robert Angus 1921- *WhoAm 92*
MacLeod, Robert Fredric 1917- *WhoAm 92*
MacLeod, Sheila 1939- *ScF&FL 92*
MacLeod, Tracy S. *Law&B 92*
MacLeod of Fuinary, Baron 1895-1991 *BioIn 17*
MacLeod of Fuinary, Lord 1895-1991 *AnObit 1991*
MacLeoid, Fionnlagh *BioIn 17*
MacLetchie, J. Graeme, III 1937- *St&PR 93*
MacLiammoir, Micheal 1899-1978 *BioIn 17*
Maclin, Ernest 1931- *St&PR 93, WhoAm 92*
Mac Low, Jackson 1922- *Baker 92*
MacLure, Laurens, Jr. *Law&B 92*
MacLure, Laurens, Jr. 1956- *WhoEmL 93*
MacMahon, Aline 1899-1991 *AnObit 1991, BioIn 17*
MacMahon, Brian 1923- *WhoAm 92*
MacMahon, Charles Hutchins, Jr. 1918- *WhoAm 92*
MacMahon, Heber 1600-1650 *BioIn 17*
MacMahon, Marie Edme Patrice Maurice de 1808-1893 *BioIn 17, HarEnMi*
MacMahon, Paul 1945- *WhoAm 92*
MacMahon, Thomas Desmond *WhoScE 91-1*
MacMannis, Russell Fraser 1958- *St&PR 93*
MacManus, Mary Simpson *AmWomPl*
MacManus, Quentin 1944- *WhoSSW 93*
MacManus, Seamus 1869-1960 *BioIn 17*
MacManus, Susan A(nn) 1947- *ConAu 40NR*
MacManus, Susan Ann 1947- *WhoAm 92, WhoAmW 93, WhoEmL 93, WhoSSW 93, WhoWor 93*
MacManus, Yvonne 1931- *ScF&FL 92*
MacManus, Yvonne Cristina 1931- *WhoAm 92, WhoWrEP 92*
MacMartin, Barry H. 1934- *St&PR 93*
MacMaster, Daniel Miller 1913- *WhoAm 92*
MacMaster, Douglas Joseph, Jr. 1930- *St&PR 93*
MacMaster, Harriett Schuyler 1916- *WhoAmW 93*
MacMaster, Robert Ellsworth 1919- *WhoAm 92*
Macmeans, C.R. 1954- *St&PR 93*
Macmeeken, John Peebles 1924- *WhoAm 92*
MacMieikan, William 1944- *WhoUN 92*
Macmillan, Andrew Allardice 1942- *WhoUN 92*
MacMillan, Bruce Edward *Law&B 92*
MacMillan, Catherine Cope 1947- *WhoAmW 93*
MacMillan, Chrystal 1872-1937 *BioIn 17*
MacMillan, Claire Elizabeth 1953- *WhoE 93*
MacMillan, Daniel James 1953- *WhoEmL 93*
MacMillan, David Wishart 1937- *WhoSSW 93*
MacMillan, Diane Frances 1938- *St&PR 93*
MacMillan, Douglas Clark 1912- *WhoAm 92*
MacMillan, Douglas Hathaway 1946- *St&PR 93, WhoAm 92*
MacMillan, Ernest (Alexander Campbell) 1893-1973 *Baker 92*
Macmillan, Harold 1894-1986 *ColdWar 1 [port]*
MacMillan, Ian *ScF&FL 92*
Macmillan, J. Graham 1941- *St&PR 93*
MacMillan, James *BioIn 17*
MacMillan, Jean Isabel Ross d1990 *BioIn 17*
MacMillan, Joann Lawler 1926- *WhoAmW 93*
MacMillan, John Hugh 1895-1960 *BioIn 17*
MacMillan, John Lavergne 1928- *WhoAm 92*
MacMillan, Judith Ruth 1943- *WhoAmW 93*
MacMillan, Kenneth *BioIn 17*
MacMillan, Kenneth 1929- *WhoAm 92, WhoWor 93*
MacMillan, Kenneth 1929-1992 *NewYTBS 92 [port], News 93-2*

MacMillan, Kip Van Metre 1937- WhoWor 93
MacMillan, Marie Violet 1955- WhoAmW 93
MacMillan, Mary Louise 1870- AmWomPl
Macmillan, Maurice Harold 1894-1987 DcTwHis
MacMillan, Peter Alan 1955- WhoEmL 93
MacMillan, Whitney BioIn 17
Macmillan, William Hooper 1923- WhoAm 92
MacMillan, William Leedom, Jr. 1913- WhoAm 92
Macmillen, Francis 1885-1973 Baker 92
MacMillen, Richard Edward 1932- WhoAm 92
MacMinn, Aleene Merle Barnes 1930- WhoAm 92
MacMinn, Pamela Lee 1951- WhoAmW 93
MacMinn, Strother 1918- ScF&FL 92
MacMorran, Henry G. 1942- St&PR 93
MacMullen, Jean Alexandria Stewart 1945- WhoSSW 93
MacMullen, Ramsay 1928- WhoAm 92
MacMurray, Fred 1908-1991 AnObit 1991, BioIn 17, ConTFT 10, CurBio 92N, IntDcF 2-3 [port], News 92
MacMurray, James A. 1925- St&PR 93
MacMurren, Harold Henry, Jr. 1942- WhoE 93, WhoWor 93
Macnabb, W.V. 1937- St&PR 93
MacNair, Irene Taylor AmWomPl
MacNamara, Brinsley BioIn 17
Mac Namara, Donal E. J. 1916- WhoWrEP 92
Mac Namara, Donal Eoin Joseph 1916- WhoAm 92
MacNamara, Margaret AmWomPl
Macnamara, Thomas Edward 1929- WhoAm 92
MacNaughton, Angus Athole 1931- WhoAm 92
Mac Naughton, Anne L. 1945- WhoWrEP 92
MacNaughton, Bruce A. 1930- St&PR 93
Macnaughton, D. Bruce St&PR 93
MacNaughton, Donald S. 1917- St&PR 93
MacNaughton, Donald Sinclair 1917- WhoAm 92
MacNaughton, John D. BioIn 17
MacNaughton, John David Francis 1932- WhoAm 92
MacNaughton, Malcolm, Jr. 1938- St&PR 93
MacNaughton, Ruth D. Law&B 92
MacNeal, Edward Arthur 1925- WhoE 93
Macnee, Alan Breck 1920- WhoAm 92
MacNee, James M., III Law&B 92
Macnee, Patrick 1922- ScF&FL 92, WhoAm 92
MacNeice, Louis 1907-1963 BioIn 17
MacNeil, Cornell 1922- Baker 92, IntDcOp, OxDcOp
Macneil, Ian Roderick 1929- WhoAm 92
MacNeil, John Raymond 1941- St&PR 93
Mac Neil, Joseph Neil 1924- WhoAm 92
MacNeil, Kathrine Jean 1943- WhoSSW 93
MacNeil, Madeline Reed 1940- WhoSSW 93
Mac Neil, Melinda Sopher 1957- WhoEmL 93, WhoSSW 93
MacNeil, Robert 1931- JrnUS
MacNeil, Robert Breckenridge Ware 1931- WhoAm 92
MacNeil, Walter 1949- OxDcOp
MacNeill, D. Gilmore 1931- St&PR 93
MacNeill, Eoin 1867-1945 BioIn 17
MacNeill, H.G. 1925- St&PR 93
Mac Neill, James William 1928- WhoAm 92
MacNeill, John 1867-1945 BioIn 17
MacNeill, Robert Charles 1946- St&PR 93
MacNeill, William E. 1941- St&PR 93
Macneill, William Eric 1941- WhoAm 92
MacNeill, William R. 1939- St&PR 93
Mac Neish, Richard Stockton 1918- WhoAm 92
MacNelly, Jeff BioIn 17
Mac Nelly, Jeffrey Kenneth 1947- WhoAm 92
MacNichol, Edward Ford, Jr. 1918- WhoAm 92
MacNider, Jack 1927- St&PR 93, WhoAm 92
Maco, Paul Stephen, Jr. 1952- WhoE 93, WhoEmL 93, WhoWor 93
Maco, Teri Regan 1953- WhoAmW 93, WhoEmL 93
Macom, John Morgan, III 1965- St&PR 93
Macomb, Alexander 1782-1841 CmdGen 1991 [port], HarEnMi
Macomber, Ada S. AmWomPl
Macomber, Gary Reed Law&B 92
Macomber, George 1927- St&PR 93
Macomber, J. Locke 1923- St&PR 93
Macomber, John D. 1928- WhoAm 92
Macomber, John D. 1955- St&PR 93
Macomber, Richard Wiltz 1932- WhoE 93
Macon, Carol Ann Gloeckler 1942- WhoAmW 93
Macon, Irene Elizabeth 1935- WhoWor 93
Macon, John Edward 1938- WhoIns 93
Macon, Jorge 1924- WhoWor 93
Macon, Mark BioIn 17
Macon, Myra Faye 1937- WhoAmW 93
Macon, Nathaniel 1758-1837 PolPar
Macon, Seth Craven 1919- WhoAm 92
Maconchy, Elizabeth 1907- Baker 92, BioIn 17
Maconi, Richard Curtis 1922- WhoWor 93
Maconie, Robin (John) 1942- Baker 92
Macosko, Paul John, II 1952- WhoE 93
Macoun, John 1832-1920 BioIn 17
Macovski, Albert 1929- WhoAm 92
Macoy, Elvie Kimball AmWomPl
Macphail, Agnes Campbell 1890-1954 BioIn 17
Macphail, Andrew 1864-1938 BioIn 17
MacPhail, Andy WhoAm 92
MacPhail, Daniel David 1948- WhoE 93
MacPhail, Douglas Francis Law&B 92
Macphail, Moray St. John 1912- WhoAm 92
MacPhail, Stephen Michael Law&B 92
MacPhaul, Charles H. Law&B 92
MacPhee, Craig Robert 1944- WhoAm 92
MacPhee, Donald Albert 1928- WhoAm 92
MacPhee, Ian Malcolm 1938- WhoAsAP 91
MacPherson, Alan MacKay 1943- WhoWor 93
Macpherson, Angus BioIn 17
Macpherson, Colin Robertson 1924- WhoAm 92
Macpherson, Craig 1944- St&PR 93
MacPherson, Dick 1930- WhoAm 92
MacPherson, Frank B., III 1948- St&PR 93
MacPherson, Frank Becker, III 1948- WhoAm 92
MacPherson, Herbert Grenfell 1911- WhoAm 92
Macpherson, James 1736-1796 BioIn 17
Macpherson, James (Campbell) 1942- ConAu 136
Macpherson, Jay 1931- WhoCanL 92
MacPherson, Mandana BioIn 17
MacPherson, Richard Frederick 1930- WhoAm 92, WhoE 93
MacPherson, Robert Duncan 1944- WhoAm 92, WhoE 93
MacPherson, Robert W. 1924- St&PR 93
Macquarre, John F., Sr. 1943- St&PR 93
Macquarrie, Heath Nelson 1919- WhoAm 92
Macque, Giovanni (Jean) de c. 1548-1614 Baker 92
MacQueen, Robert Mitchell 1939- St&PR 93
MacQueen, Robert Moffat 1938- WhoAm 92
MacQuiddy, Jean Elizabeth 1943- WhoE 93
MacQuitty, William 1905- BioIn 17
Macquown, David K. 1948- St&PR 93
MacQuown, Richard Sladden 1919- St&PR 93
Mac Rae, Alfred Urquhart 1932- WhoAm 92
MacRae, Cameron Farquhar, III 1942- WhoAm 92
MacRae, Donald Alexander 1916- WhoAm 92
MacRae, Duncan, Jr. 1921- WhoAm 92, WhoSSW 93
Macrae, Duncan A. 1943- St&PR 93
MacRae, Duncan Alexander 1943- WhoE 93
Macrae, G.V. ScF&FL 92
MacRae, Gordon 1921-1986 Baker 92, BioIn 17
Mac Rae, Herbert Farquhar 1926- WhoAm 92
MacRae, Mary Jenkins 1954- WhoAmW 93, WhoEmL 93
Macrae, Sheila Mary 1945- WhoUN 92
Macrakis, A. Lily WhoE 93
Mac Rane, Buick WhoWrEP 92
MacRaois, Cormac 1944- SmATA 72 [port]
Macri, Theodore William WhoAm 92
Macridis, Roy C. BioIn 17
Macridis, Roy C(onstantine) 1918-1991 ConAu 136
Macrinus, Marcus Opellius 164-218 HarEnMi
Macris, Constantin J. 1913- WhoScE 91-3
Macris, Richard George 1957- WhoE 93
Macro, Lucia Ann 1959- WhoAm 92
MacRobert, Ethelda Bliebtrey BiDAMSp 1989
MacRoberts, P.B. 1938- St&PR 93
Macrobius fl. 4th cent.-5th cent. OxDcByz
Macroe-Wiegand, Viola Lucille 1920- WhoWor 93
Macrone, John 1809-1837 BioIn 17
Macrory, Patrick Francis John 1941- WhoAm 92
MacRury, King 1915- WhoAm 92, WhoE 93, WhoWor 93
Macsai, John 1926- WhoAm 92
MacShane, Frank BioIn 17
MacSween, Roderick Norman McIver WhoScE 91-1
MacSwiney, Mary 1872-1942 BioIn 17
MacTaggart, Barry 1931- WhoAm 92
MacTaggart, Kenneth Dugald 1953- WhoWor 93
MacTaggart, Terrence Joseph 1946- WhoAm 92
Macuch, Rudolf 1919- WhoWor 93
Macumber, John Paul 1940- WhoWor 93
Macune, Mary Julia 1956- St&PR 93
Macura, Miroslav 1944- WhoUN 92
Macura, Stanislav 1946- WhoWor 93
Macurda, Donald Bradford, Jr. 1936- WhoSSW 93
Macurda, Hayden B. 1939- St&PR 93
Macurdy, John 1929- Baker 92
Macurdy, John Edward 1929- WhoAm 92
Macut, Sally L. 1950- St&PR 93
Macvey, John W. 1923- ScF&FL 92
Macvey, S. St&PR 93
MacVicar, John WhoScE 91-1
MacVicar, Margaret L.A. 1943-1991 BioIn 17
Mac Vicar, Robert William 1918- WhoAm 92
Mac Vittie, Robert William 1920- WhoAm 92
Mac Watters, Virginia Elizabeth WhoAm 92
Mac Whinnie, John Vincent 1945- WhoWor 93
MacWhorter, Robert Bruce 1930- WhoAm 92
MacWilliams, Kenneth Edward 1936- WhoAm 92, WhoWor 93
Macy, Anne Sullivan 1866-1936 ConHero 2 [port]
Macy, Bruce Wendell 1930- St&PR 93
Macy, Dayna Alison 1960- WhoEmL 93
Macy, John Patrick 1955- WhoEmL 93
Macy, Mark H. 1949- WhoWrEP 92
Macy, Patricia Ann 1955- WhoWor 93
Macy, Ruth Carol 1952- WhoEmL 93
Macy, Terrence William 1946- WhoE 93, WhoEmL 93
Macy, W. H. MiSFD 9
Macy, William H. BioIn 17
Maczulski, Margaret Louise 1949- WhoAmW 93, WhoEmL 93
Madaiah, Madappa 1936- WhoWor 93
Madakson, Peter Bitrus 1953- WhoWor 93
Madama, Patrick Stephen 1951- WhoE 93, WhoEmL 93
Madame Alexander d1990 BioIn 17
Madan, Paul S. Law&B 92
Madan, Stanley Krishen 1922- WhoE 93
Madanayake, Lalith Prasanna 1965- WhoWor 93
Madansky, Albert 1934- WhoAm 92
Madansky, Leon 1923- WhoAm 92
Madansky, Tracy L. Law&B 92
Madar, Alexander Paul Law&B 92
Madar, Jean 1961- St&PR 93
Madar, William P. BioIn 17
Madar, William P. 1939- St&PR 93
Madarasz, Laszlo 1947- WhoScE 91-4
Madariaga, Salvador 1886-1978 ScF&FL 92
Madatang, Henry WhoAsAP 91
Madavo, Callisto Enias 1942- WhoUN 92
Madda, Carl J. 1936- St&PR 93
Maddalena, James BioIn 17
Maddalena, Lucille Ann 1948- WhoAm 92, WhoAmW 93, WhoEmL 93
Madden, Antoinette Liadis 1957- WhoEmL 93
Madden, Arthur Allen 1960- WhoSSW 93
Madden, Bartley Joseph 1943- WhoWor 93
Madden, Bert Conger 1932- St&PR 93
Madden, Dann Michael 1932- St&PR 93
Madden, David 1933- BioIn 17, WhoAm 92, WhoSSW 93, WhoWrEP 92
Madden, David William 1950- WhoEmL 93
Madden, Dean E. 1921- St&PR 93
Madden, Debbie Siegal 1960- WhoAmW 93
Madden, Edward BioIn 17
Madden, Edward George, Jr. 1924- WhoE 93
Madden, Edward Harry 1925- WhoAm 92
Madden, Eva Annie 1863- AmWomPl
Madden, G. William 1925- St&PR 93
Madden, George Martin, (Mrs.) AmWomPl
Madden, Gerald Patrick 1942- WhoE 93
Madden, Ian Beresford 1931- WhoWor 93
Madden, James Desmond 1940- WhoWor 93
Madden, James Edward Law&B 92
Madden, Janice Fanning 1947- WhoEmL 93
Madden, Jerome Anthony 1948- WhoEmL 93
Madden, Joan Mayne 1932- St&PR 93
Madden, John BioIn 17, MiSFD 9
Madden, John 1936- WhoAm 92
Madden, John, Jr. 1929- St&PR 93
Madden, John Dale 1957- WhoEmL 93
Madden, John Kevin 1938- WhoAm 92
Madden, Joseph Daniel 1921- WhoAm 92
Madden, Joseph R. 1919- St&PR 93
Madden, Kenneth Cromwell, Jr. 1950- WhoE 93, WhoEmL 93
Madden, Lawrence J. St&PR 93
Madden, Lee MiSFD 9
Madden, Leo James 1932- St&PR 93
Madden, Lynne S. Law&B 92
Madden, Marie Frances 1928- WhoSSW 93, WhoWor 93
Madden, Michael Daniel 1949- WhoAm 92
Madden, Murdaugh Stuart 1922- WhoAm 92
Madden, Paul M. 1950- MiSFD 9
Madden, Paul Robert 1926- WhoAm 92
Madden, Penny Lynn 1949- WhoAmW 93
Madden, Peter 1939- WhoCanL 92
Madden, Peter Michael Law&B 92
Madden, Peter Robert 1939- WhoE 93
Madden, Rhonda Lois 1943- WhoAmW 93
Madden, Richard B. 1929- St&PR 93
Madden, Richard Blaine 1929- WhoAm 92
Madden, Richard Lewis 1951- WhoEmL 93, WhoSSW 93
Madden, Richard Othick 1948- St&PR 93
Madden, Robert T. 1922- St&PR 93
Madden, Susan ConAu 138
Madden, Teresa Darleen 1960- WhoSSW 93
Madden, Thomas J. 1947- St&PR 93
Madden, Thomas James 1941- WhoAm 92
Madden, Timothy A. ScF&FL 92
Madden, Wales Hendrix, Jr. 1927- St&PR 93, WhoAm 92
Madden, William Lee, Jr. 1948- WhoEmL 93
Maddern, Bruce Robert 1954- WhoEmL 93, WhoSSW 93
Maddern, Richard Kenneth 1922- WhoWor 93
Maddex, Myron Brown 1924- WhoAm 92
Maddicks, Nona Mihr 1942- WhoAmW 93
Maddie, John E. 1934- St&PR 93
Maddin, Guy MiSFD 9
Maddin, Robert 1918- WhoE 93
Maddirala, James Samuel 1945- WhoSSW 93
Maddix, Beverly Ann 1966- WhoAmW 93
Maddock, Ieuan WhoScE 91-1
Maddock, Jeffrey WhoScE 91-1
Maddock, Lawrence Hill 1923- WhoSSW 93
Maddock, Rosemary Schroer 1919- WhoAmW 93, WhoWor 93
Maddock, Thomas Michael 1946- WhoEmL 93
Maddocks, John H. St&PR 93
Maddocks, Robert Allen 1933- St&PR 93, WhoAm 92
Maddow, Ben d1992 NewYTBS 92
Maddow, Ben 1909- BioIn 17
Maddow, Jeffrey A. 1941- St&PR 93
Maddox, Alva Hugh 1930- WhoAm 92
Maddox, Beverly Bell 1948- WhoAmW 93, WhoSSW 93
Maddox, Dan W. 1909- St&PR 93
Maddox, Donald 1944- WhoE 93
Maddox, Edwin Thomas, Jr. 1941- WhoSSW 93
Maddox, Hugh 1930- WhoSSW 93
Maddox, Ivor John WhoScE 91-1
Maddox, Jay R. 1936- St&PR 93
Maddox, Lester 1915- PolPar
Maddox, Milton Roland 1937- St&PR 93
Maddox, Richard Lee 1952- WhoEmL 93
Maddox, Robert Alan 1944- WhoAm 92
Maddox, Robert Nott 1925- WhoAm 92, WhoSSW 93
Maddox, Roger Dean 1948- WhoSSW 93
Maddox, Russell Wayne 1947- WhoSSW 93
Maddox, Terry Ladd 1956- WhoEmL 93
Maddox, Thomas E. Law&B 92
Maddox, Tom ScF&FL 92

Maddox, Tom Smith, Jr. 1943- *WhoSSW 93*
Maddox-Miller, Annette 1947- *WhoAmW 93*
Maddrell, Simon Hugh Piper *WhoScE 91-1*
Maddrey, Willis Crocker 1939- *WhoAm 92*
Maddux, Benigna Susan Harris 1957- *WhoSSW 93*
Maddux, Bob *ScF&FL 92*
Maddux, Gregory Alan Greg 1966- *WhoAm 92*
Maddux, Lewis A. 1949- *WhoSSW 93*
Maddux, Parker Ahrens 1939- *WhoAm 92*
Maddux, Rachel 1912-1983 *ScF&FL 92*
Maddux, Rachel 1913-1983 *BioIn 17*
Maddy, Joe 1891-1966 *Baker 92*
Madeira, Edward Walter, Jr. 1928- *WhoAm 92*
Madeira, Francis 1917- *Baker 92*
Madeira, Francis King Carey 1917- *WhoAm 92*
Madeira, Jean 1918-1972 *Baker 92*
Madeira, Maria Amelia Filipe 1947- *WhoScE 91-3*
Madeira, Robert Lehman 1915- *WhoAm 92*
Madeira, Vitor Manuel Calado 1943- *WhoWor 93*
Madej, Eligiusz 1936- *WhoScE 91-4*
Madej, James Thomas *Law&B 92*
Madej, Jan Dominik 1926- *WhoScE 91-4*
Madej-McCoy, Michelle Marie 1963- *WhoAmW 93*
Madejski, Jan 1925- *WhoScE 91-4*
Madeley, Gerald Roland 1941- *WhoSSW 93*
Madeley, J. Douglas 1938- *WhoAm 92*
Madeley, John 1934- *WhoWor 93*
Madeley, Richard John *WhoScE 91-1*
Mademann, Barry E. 1939- *St&PR 93*
Maden, Barry Edward Howorth *WhoScE 91-1*
Madenwald, Almeda Florence 1961- *WhoSSW 93*
Mader, Gerlinde 1946- *BioIn 17*
Mader, Ken *BioIn 17*
Mader, Leanne Marie 1967- *WhoAmW 93*
Mader, Pamela Beile 1939- *WhoAmW 93*
Mader, Thomas Francis 1930- *WhoE 93*
Mader, William 1934- *WhoWor 93*
Mader, Wolfgang Konrad Wilhelm 1937- *WhoWor 93*
Madera, Joseph J. 1927- *WhoAm 92*
Madera, Marie Louise 1955- *WhoAmW 93, WhoEmL 93*
Madera, Neil *Law&B 92*
Maderazo, Eufronio Gala 1942- *WhoE 93*
Maderer, William F. 1947- *WhoEmL 93*
Maderia, Carole Mary 1939- *WhoAmW 93*
Maderna, Bruno 1920-1973 *Baker 92, OxDcOp*
Madero, Francisco *DcCPCAm*
Madero, Luis Octavio 1908-1964 *DcMexL*
Madero, Pablo Emilio *DcCPCAm*
Madetoja, Leevi (Antti) 1887-1947 *Baker 92*
Madey, Boguslaw 1932- *Baker 92*
Madey, John M. J. 1943- *WhoAm 92*
Madey, Ronald Eliot 1959- *WhoE 93, WhoEmL 93*
Madge, Bruce Eltham 1956- *WhoWor 93*
Madge, Geoffrey Douglas 1941- *Baker 92*
Madge, R.J. *Law&B 92*
Madgett, Naomi Long 1923- *WhoAm 92*
Madgett, Naomilong 1923- *WhoWrEP 92*
Madguerova, Andreana Stefanova 1940- *WhoWor 93*
Madhubuti, Haki R. *BioIn 17*
Madhubuti, Haki R. 1942- *ConLC 73 [port], PoeCrit 5 [port]*
Madhubuti, Safisha *BioIn 17*
Madhubuti, Safisha 1935- *BlkAuII 92*
Madia, Sandra 1943- *St&PR 93*
Madia, William Juul 1947- *St&PR 93, WhoAm 92*
Madigan, Amy 1957- *WhoAm 92, WhoAmW 93*
Madigan, Daniel Paul 1956- *St&PR 93*
Madigan, Dennis Eugene 1952- *WhoEmL 93*
Madigan, Doris Mary *St&PR 93*
Madigan, Doris Mary 1925- *WhoAmW 93*
Madigan, Edward R. 1936- *CngDr 91, CurBio 92 [port], WhoAm 92, WhoE 93*
Madigan, Grace Evelyn 1902- *WhoWrEP 92*
Madigan, James E. 1923- *St&PR 93*
Madigan, Janet Lee 1951- *WhoAmW 93*
Madigan, John Powers 1907-1990 *BioIn 17*
Madigan, John S. *Law&B 92*
Madigan, John William 1937- *St&PR 93, WhoAm 92*
Madigan, Joseph Edward 1932- *WhoAm 92*
Madigan, Mark Steven *Law&B 92*
Madigan, Michael Joseph *Law&B 92*
Madigan, Michael Joseph 1942- *WhoAm 92*
Madigan, Micheal Gerard 1957- *WhoE 93*
Madigan, Richard Allen 1937- *WhoAm 92, WhoSSW 93*
Madigan, Stephen Joseph *Law&B 92*
Madigan, Terrell Courtney 1958- *WhoSSW 93*
Madis, Voldemar 1941- *St&PR 93*
Madison, Arnold 1937- *DcAmChF 1960*
Madison, Bernard L. 1941- *WhoAm 92, WhoSSW 93*
Madison, D. Raymond 1910- *St&PR 93*
Madison, Dennis S. *St&PR 93*
Madison, Dolley 1768-1849 *BioIn 17*
Madison, Douglas H. 1950- *St&PR 93*
Madison, Eddie Lawrence, Jr. 1930- *WhoE 93*
Madison, James 1751-1836 *BioIn 17, OxCSupC, PolPar*
Madison, James H. 1944- *ConAu 138*
Madison, James Raymond 1931- *WhoAm 92*
Madison, Martha *AmWomPl*
Madison, Octavia Dianne 1960- *WhoSSW 93*
Madison, Robert Prince 1923- *WhoAm 92*
Madison, Roberta Eleanor 1932- *WhoAmW 93*
Madison, Thomas Frederick 1936- *St&PR 93*
Madison-Brotman, Marie *AmWomPl*
Madle, Robert Albert 1920- *WhoE 93, WhoWor 93*
Madlee, Dorothy 1917-1980 *ScF&FL 92*
Madlener, Elizabeth W. 1941- *WhoAmW 93*
Madler, Paul W. 1929- *St&PR 93*
Madley, Maurice Andrew 1936- *St&PR 93*
Madni, Asad Mohamed 1947- *WhoEmL 93*
Madni, Azad M. 1945- *St&PR 93*
Madni, Maulana Azad 1928- *WhoAsAP 91*
Madoff, Steven *Law&B 92*
Madole, Cynthia Joyce *Law&B 92*
Madonia, Tina 1955- *WhoE 93*
Madonia, Valerie *WhoAm 92*
Madonna *BioIn 17*
Madonna 1958- *Baker 92, HolBB [port], WhoAm 92, WhoAmW 93*
Mador, Joseph F. 1940- *St&PR 93*
Madore, Bernadette 1918- *WhoAmW 93*
Madorma, Marie Avona 1943- *WhoWrEP 92*
Madorsky, Harold A. *Law&B 92*
Madorsky, Harold A. 1950- *St&PR 93*
Madorsky, Marsha Gerre 1951- *WhoEmL 93*
Madory, James Richard 1940- *WhoSSW 93*
Madow, Leo 1915- *WhoAm 92*
Madow, Paul Brian 1956- *WhoEmL 93*
Madrazo, Carlos *DcCPCAm*
Madrazo, Jose *Law&B 92*
Madresehee, Mehrdad 1948- *WhoEmL 93*
Madrey, Francine Giles 1949- *WhoSSW 93*
Madri, Alberta Maria 1924- *WhoWrEP 92*
Madriaga, Fred 1950- *St&PR 93*
Madrigal-Segura, Enrique 1941- *WhoUN 92*
Madriguera, Enric 1904-1973 *Baker 92*
Madril, Lee Ann 1944- *WhoAmW 93*
Madris, Russell L. 1957- *St&PR 93*
Madsen, Adam M. 1936- *St&PR 93*
Madsen, Arch Leonard 1913- *WhoAm 92*
Madsen, Arnold James 1958- *WhoEmL 93*
Madsen, Axel 1932- *ScF&FL 92*
Madsen, Bjarne 1949- *WhoScE 91-2*
Madsen, Brigham Dwaine 1914- *WhoAm 92*
Madsen, Chris d1944 *BioIn 17*
Madsen, David 1929- *ScF&FL 92*
Madsen, David Burton 1946- *WhoEmL 93*
Madsen, Dennis G. 1943- *St&PR 93*
Madsen, Donald Howard 1922- *WhoAm 92*
Madsen, Dorothy Louise *WhoAmW 93*
Madsen, Douglas Fred 1942- *WhoAm 92*
Madsen, E. *WhoScE 91-4*
Madsen, Edwin L. 1942- *St&PR 93*
Madsen, Erik 1933- *WhoScE 91-2*
Madsen, Francis Armstrong, Jr. 1931- *WhoSSW 93*
Madsen, Harald 1890-1949 & Schenstrom, Carl 1881-1942 *IntDcF 2-3*
Madsen, Henry Stephen 1924- *WhoAm 92*
Madsen, Jakob Brochner 1955- *WhoWor 93*
Madsen, John W. 1950- *St&PR 93*
Madsen, Joop J.V. *WhoScE 91-2*
Madsen, K.B. 1939- *WhoScE 91-2*
Madsen, Kaj 1943- *WhoScE 91-2*
Madsen, Kenneth *MiSFD 9*
Madsen, Loren Wakefield 1943- *WhoAm 92*
Madsen, Mila Cordero 1930- *WhoWor 93*
Madsen, Neil Bernard 1928- *WhoAm 92*
Madsen, Peter Eric 1945- *WhoAm 92*
Madsen, Richard Wellington *Law&B 92*
Madsen, Robert Leon *Law&B 92*
Madsen, Rud F. 1930- *WhoScE 91-2*
Madsen, Rud Frik 1930- *WhoWor 93*
Madsen, Soren Fl. 1938- *WhoScE 91-2*
Madsen, Stephen Stewart 1951- *WhoAm 92*
Madsen, Stuart J. *Law&B 92*
Madsen, Terje 1950- *WhoWor 93*
Madsen, Ulf 1958- *WhoWor 93*
Madsen, Virginia *BioIn 17*
Madson, Jerry 1948- *WhoWrEP 92*
Madson, Paul 1944- *St&PR 93*
Madson, Philip Ward 1948- *WhoEmL 93*
Madtes, Nancy Louise 1936- *WhoAmW 93*
Madueme, Godswill C. 1943- *WhoWor 93*
Madueme, Godswill Chukwueloka 1943- *WhoUN 92*
Maduh, Edward Uzorezie 1957- *WhoWor 93*
Madurga, Gonzalo 1928- *WhoScE 91-3*
Maduro, Conrad *DcCPCAm*
Madyun, Audrey 1956- *WhoAmW 93*
Maebori, Stanley T. 1943- *St&PR 93*
Maecenas, Caius Cilnius d8BC *BioIn 17*
Maechler, Erwin 1925- *St&PR 93, WhoAm 92*
Maechling, Charles, Jr. 1920- *WhoAm 92*
Maeda, Gen'i 1539-1602 *HarEnMi*
Maeda, Hiroshi 1919- *WhoWor 93*
Maeda, Isao 1943- *WhoAsAP 91*
Maeda, J. A. 1940- *WhoAmW 93*
Maeda, Mitsuo 1942- *WhoWor 93*
Maeda, Tadashi 1946- *WhoAsAP 91*
Maeda, Takashi 1937- *WhoAsAP 91*
Maeda, Toshiie 1538-1599 *HarEnMi*
Maeda, Yukio 1922- *WhoWor 93*
Maeder, Andre 1942- *WhoScE 91-4, WhoWor 93*
Maeder, Anthony John 1958- *WhoWor 93*
Maeder, Gary William 1949- *WhoEmL 93*
Maeder, Paul Albert 1954- *WhoEmL 93*
Maefs, Fredric L. *Law&B 92*
Maegaard, Jan (Carl Christian) 1926- *Baker 92*
Maegawa, Hirotoshi 1956- *WhoWor 93*
Maehara, Gary A. *Law&B 92*
Maehata, Sachiko 1937- *WhoAsAP 91*
Maehl, William Harvey 1915- *WhoAm 92, WhoWor 93*
Maehl, William Henry 1930- *WhoAm 92*
Maehle, Leid *WhoScE 91-4*
Maehr, Martin Louis 1932- *WhoAm 92*
Maejima, Hideyuki 1941- *WhoAsAP 91*
Maejima, Noboru 1939- *St&PR 93*
Maekawa, Mamoru 1942- *WhoWor 93*
Mael, Rodney Ernest 1949- *WhoEmL 93*
Maelicke, Alfred 1938- *WhoScE 91-3*
Maelzel, Johannes Nepomuk 1772-1838 *Baker 92*
Maena, Michael 1954- *WhoAsAP 91*
Maene, Ludo J. 1954- *WhoScE 91-2*
Maeno, H. *Law&B 92*
Maeno, Norikazu 1940- *WhoWor 93*
Maenz, Paul 1939- *BioIn 17*
Maercker, Adalbert 1932- *WhoScE 91-3*
Maerker, Richard Erwin 1928- *WhoSSW 93*
Maerki, Max H. 1940- *St&PR 93*
Maeroff, Gene I. 1939- *WhoAm 92*
Maersch, Nancy Kay 1942- *WhoAmW 93*
Maes, Charles Joseph 1957- *WhoEmL 93*
Maes, Hugo M. A. 1948- *WhoWor 93*
Maes, Jef 1905- *Baker 92*
Maes, Petra Jimenez *WhoAm 92*
Maes, Petra Jimenez 1947- *NotHsAW 93*
Maes, Robert Adamson 1910-1991 *BioIn 17*
Maese, Carlos Octavio, Jr. 1946- *WhoEmL 93, WhoSSW 93*
Maesen, Albert A.L. 1915- *IntDcAn*
Maess, Gerhard S.W. 1937- *WhoWor 93*
Maestas, David *Law&B 92*
Maestro, Betsy C(rippen) 1944- *ConAu 37NR, MajAI [port]*
Maestro, Giulio 1942- *ConAu 37NR, MajAI [port]*
Maestrone, Frank Eusebio 1922- *WhoAm 92*
Maeterlinck, Maurice 1862-1949 *BioIn 17, ConAu 136, OxDcOp*
Maetia, Alfred 1939- *WhoAsAP 91*
Maetzig, Kurt 1911- *DrEEuF*
Maezawa, Eiichi 1947- *WhoWor 93*
Maffei, Dorothy Jean 1951- *WhoEmL 93*
Maffei, Fredric *ScF&FL 92*
Maffei, Lamberto *WhoScE 91-3*
Maffei, Paolo 1926- *WhoWor 93*
Maffei, Paul R. 1936- *St&PR 93*
Maffei, Rocco John 1949- *WhoEmL 93*
Maffei, Stephen R. 1939- *St&PR 93*
Maffei, Stephen Roger 1939- *WhoE 93*
Maffeo, Gilbert Joseph, Jr. 1947- *WhoE 93*
Maffeo, Sabino *WhoScE 91-3*
Maffeo, Vincent Anthony *Law&B 92*
Maffet, Meri West *Law&B 92*
Maffett, Dan Wesley 1929- *St&PR 93*
Maffett, Mack D. *Law&B 92*
Maffie, Michael Otis 1948- *St&PR 93*
Maffioli, Francesco 1941- *WhoScE 91-3*
Maffly, Roy Herrick 1927- *WhoAm 92*
Maffre, Muriel 1966- *WhoAm 92*
Mafico, Temba Levi Jackson 1943- *WhoSSW 93*
Mag, Morton 1903- *St&PR 93*
Maga, Joseph Andrew 1940- *WhoAm 92*
Magad, Samuel 1932- *WhoAm 92*
Magafan, Ethel 1916- *WhoAm 92, WhoAmW 93*
Magafas, Byron Otis *Law&B 92*
Magafas, Byron Otis 1956- *WhoEmL 93*
Magaldi, Donatello 1938- *WhoScE 91-3*
Magalhaes, Filipe c. 1571-1652 *Baker 92*
Magalhaes, Luis Torres 1951- *WhoWor 93*
Magalini, Sergio 1927- *WhoScE 91-3*
Magalnick, Barbara 1942- *WhoAmW 93*
Magaloff, Nikita 1912- *Baker 92*
Magalong, Romeo 1948- *WhoEmL 93*
Magaloni, Honorato Ignacio 1898- *DcMexL*
Magalska, James M. 1942- *St&PR 93, WhoIns 93*
Magana, Sergio 1924-1990 *DcMexL*
Magana Esquivel, Antonio 1909- *DcMexL*
Magana Martinez, Luis *WhoScE 91-3*
Maganini, Quinto 1897-1974 *Baker 92*
Magar, Guy *MiSFD 9*
Magargal, Larry Elliot 1941- *WhoE 93*
Magarian, Elizabeth Ann 1940- *WhoAmW 93, WhoSSW 93*
Magarian, Robert Armen 1930- *WhoAm 92*
Magarity, Russell Lynn 1946- *WhoAm 92*
Magarrell, Elaine 1928- *WhoWrEP 92*
Magary, Richard 1940- *St&PR 93*
Magassy, Daniel 1939- *WhoScE 91-4*
Magassy, Lajos 1929- *WhoScE 91-4*
Magatti, Anita Westcott *Law&B 92*
Magavern, Samuel D. 1905-1991 *BioIn 17*
Magavern, William J. 1934- *St&PR 93*
Magaw, Roger Wayne 1933- *WhoAm 92*
Magazine, Alan Harrison 1944- *WhoAm 92*
Magaziner, Elliot Albert 1921- *WhoE 93*
Magaziner, Henry Jonas 1911- *WhoAm 92*
Magdaleno, Mauricio 1906- *DcMexL*
Magdeleno, Vicente 1908- *DcMexL*
Magdi, Galal 1939- *WhoUN 92*
Magdol, Michael O. 1937- *St&PR 93*
Magdol, Michael Orin 1937- *WhoAm 92*
Magdovitz, Earl J. 1943- *St&PR 93*
Magdovitz, Lawrence Maynard 1937- *WhoSSW 93*
Magdziarz, David John 1958- *WhoEmL 93*
Magdzik, W. *WhoScE 91-4*
Magdzik, Wieslaw 1932- *WhoScE 91-4*
Mage, Rose Goldman 1935- *WhoAmW 93*
Magee, Charles L. *Law&B 92*
Magee, Charles Thomas 1932- *WhoE 93*
Magee, Dana Thomas 1949- *WhoE 93*
Magee, David B. 1925- *St&PR 93*
Magee, Debra Rahenkamp 1958- *WhoE 93*
Magee, Forrest Craig 1943- *WhoAm 92*
Magee, Frank Lynn 1896-1991 *BioIn 17*
Magee, Glenn A. *ScF&FL 92*
Magee, James, Jr. *Law&B 92*
Magee, John Douglas 1946- *WhoEmL 93*
Magee, John Francis 1926- *St&PR 93, WhoAm 92*
Magee, Kathy *BioIn 17*
Magee, M. Ann Sheen 1939- *WhoAmW 93*
Magee, Michelle Coyne 1950- *WhoAmW 93*
Magee, Paul Terry 1937- *WhoAm 92*
Magee, Richard Layne *Law&B 92*
Magee, Robert Lyle, Jr. *Law&B 92*
Magee, Robert Paul 1947- *WhoAm 92*
Magee, Sharon Lynn 1952- *WhoAmW 93, WhoEmL 93*
Magee, Stephen Pat 1943- *WhoAm 92*
Magee, Thomas H. *Law&B 92*
Magee, Wayland Wells 1881- *BioIn 17*
Magee, Wayne Edward 1929- *WhoAm 92, WhoE 93*
Magee, Wes *BioIn 17*
Magee, William P. *BioIn 17*
Magee-Egan, Paulien Cecilia 1934- *WhoE 93*
Magel, Mark Lawrence 1960- *WhoEmL 93*

Magellan, Ferdinand 1480?-1521 *BioIn 17, Expl 93 [port]*
Magelli, Paul John 1931- *WhoAm 92*
Magenes, Enrico *WhoScE 91-3*
Magenheim, Michael Joseph 1941- *WhoAm 92*
Magenheimer, Edward F. 1948- *St&PR 93*
Magenheimer, Fred E. 1939- *St&PR 93*
Magenheimer, Fred Edward 1939- *WhoE 93*
Mager, Artur 1919- *St&PR 93, WhoAm 92*
Mager, Donald Northrop 1942- *WhoSSW 93, WhoWrEP 92*
Mager, Ezra Pascal 1941- *St&PR 93, WhoAm 92*
Mager, Howard M. 1948- *St&PR 93, WhoAm 92, WhoE 93*
Mager, Jorg 1880-1939 *Baker 92*
Magera, John Michael 1955- *WhoEmL 93*
Magerfleisch, Sandra Lynn *Law&B 92*
Magers, David A. 1955- *St&PR 93*
Magers, Judy Ann 1951- *WhoAmW 93*
Magers, Lauralyn Jay 1944- *WhoSSW 93*
Maggard, Marjorie Louise 1939- *WhoE 93, WhoWor 93*
Maggard, Michael James 1937- *WhoE 93*
Maggin, Bruce 1943- *St&PR 93, WhoE 93*
Maggin, Elliot S. 1950- *ScF&FL 92*
Maggini, Gio(vanni) Paolo 1579-c. 1630 *Baker 92*
Maggio, Carmen J. 1925- *St&PR 93*
Maggio, Edward P. 1949- *St&PR 93*
Maggio, Karen Kay 1954- *WhoEmL 93*
Maggio, Loida Weber 1919- *WhoWrEP 92*
Maggio, Michael John 1951- *WhoAm 92*
Maggio, Robert A. *Law&B 92*
Maggio, Rosalie 1943- *SmATA 69 [port], WhoWrEP 92*
Maggio, Thomas Edward 1935- *St&PR 93*
Maggiolo, Allison Joseph 1943- *WhoWor 93*
Maggioni, Aurelio Antonio 1908- *Baker 92*
Maggiore, Francesco c. 1715-1782? *OxDcOp*
Maggiore, Quirino 1933- *WhoScE 91-3*
Maggiore, Susan 1957- *WhoAmW 93, WhoEmL 93*
Maggiotto, Louis J., Jr. *Law&B 92*
Maggipinto, V. Anthony 1943- *WhoE 93*
Maggs, D.T. *St&PR 93*
Maggs, Peter Blount 1936- *WhoAm 92*
Maggs, Robert W., Jr. *Law&B 92*
Maggs, Robert W., Jr. 1944- *St&PR 93*
Maggs, Robert William, Jr. 1944- *WhoAm 92*
Maggs, Roger John 1946- *St&PR 93*
Maghielse, Craig 1949- *St&PR 93*
Maghrak, Monica 1957- *WhoEmL 93*
Maghuin-Rogister, Guy C.A. 1942- *WhoScE 91-2*
Magid, Barbara Ruth 1937- *WhoAmW 93*
Magid, Gail Avrum 1934- *WhoAm 92*
Magid, Ken 1946- *BioIn 17*
Magid, Nora d1991 *BioIn 17*
Magid, Per 1943- *WhoWor 93*
Magid, Ron *ScF&FL 92*
Magid, Samuel E. *St&PR 93*
Magida, Arthur Jay 1945- *WhoAm 92*
Magida, Nathan H. 1928- *St&PR 93*
Magida, Phyllis 1936- *WhoWrEP 92*
Magida, Stephen A. 1943- *St&PR 93*
Magidin, Mario 1943- *WhoWor 93*
Magidson, Jay 1947- *WhoE 93*
Magidson, William Howard *Law&B 92*
Magie, William Ashley, Jr. 1931- *WhoAm 92*
Magill, Charlotte Jean 1933- *WhoAmW 93*
Magill, Frank C. *Law&B 92*
Magill, Frank John 1927- *WhoAm 92*
Magill, Frank N. 1907- *ScF&FL 92*
Magill, J. Marion 1921-1991 *BioIn 17*
Magill, J. Patrick 1953- *St&PR 93*
Magill, John 1949- *St&PR 93*
Magill, Joseph Henry 1928- *WhoE 93*
Magill, Kent B. *Law&B 92*
Magill, Lawrence J. 1954- *St&PR 93*
Magill, Michael James Ponsonby 1942- *WhoAm 92*
Magill, Samuel Hays 1928- *WhoAm 92*
Magill, Samuel Wallace 1919- *WhoWor 93*
Magill, Saraswathi Subbiah 1929- *WhoE 93*
Maginn, John L. 1940- *St&PR 93*
Maginn, John Leo 1940- *WhoAm 92*
Maginn, Raymond Graham 1925- *St&PR 93*
Maginn, William 1793-1842 *BioIn 17*
Maginness, Craig Richard *Law&B 92*
Maginnis, Corinne F. 1948- *St&PR 93*
Maginnis, John A. 1952- *St&PR 93*
Maginnis, Silvia P. 1945- *WhoUN 92*
Maginot, Andre 1877-1932 *BioIn 17*
Maginot, Paul James *Law&B 92*
Magis, Thomas H. *Law&B 92, WhoIns 93*
Magistrale, Anthony 1952- *ScF&FL 92*
Magistrale, Tony *ScF&FL 92*
Magistris, Aldo 1941- *WhoScE 91-3*
Magliano, John V. 1945- *St&PR 93*
Magliano, Mario 1923- *WhoWor 93*
Maglich, Bogdan C. 1934- *WhoAm 92*
Maglie, Sal 1917-1992 *NewYTBS 92 [port]*
Maglie, Salvatore Anthony 1917- *BiDAMSp 1989*
Maglio, Anthony E. d1991 *BioIn 17*
Maglio, Mitchell *ScF&FL 92*
Magliola, Gertrude Louise 1933- *WhoAmW 93, WhoE 93*
Maglione, Alejandro Francisco 1945- *WhoWor 93*
Maglione, Ferdinando 1943- *WhoUN 92*
Magnaga, Martin-Pidele *WhoWor 93*
Magnago Lampugnani, Vittorio 1951- *BioIn 17*
Magnan, Christian 1942- *WhoScE 91-2*
Magnani, Anna 1908-1973 *BioIn 17, IntDcF 2-3 [port]*
Magnani, Bruno 1926- *WhoScE 91-3*
Magnani, Giorgio 1921- *WhoScE 91-3*
Magnano, Louis A. *St&PR 93*
Magnano, Louis M. *St&PR 93*
Magnano, Salvatore Paul 1934- *St&PR 93*
Magnant, Lawrence C., Jr. 1949- *WhoIns 93*
Magnard, Alberic 1865-1914 *IntDcOp, OxDcOp*
Magnard, (Lucien-Denis-Gabriel-) Alberic 1865-1914 *Baker 92*
Magnarelli, Louis Anthony 1945- *WhoE 93*
Magnavaca, Ricardo 1943- *WhoWor 93*
Magne, Michel 1930-1984 *Baker 92*
Magnell, Steffen Ingvar 1945- *St&PR 93*
Magnelli, Andrea Dale 1959- *WhoEmL 93*
Magnentius c. 303-353 *OxDcByz*
Magnentius, Flavius Magnus d351 *HarEnMi*
Magner, Frederic 1950- *St&PR 93*
Magner, Fredric Michael 1950- *WhoAm 92*
Magner, James Edmund, Jr. 1928- *WhoWrEP 92*
Magner, Jerome Allen 1929- *WhoAm 92*
Magner, John Cruse 1921- *WhoAm 92*
Magner, Martin 1900- *WhoAm 92*
Magner, Rachel Harris *WhoAmW 93*
Magner, Steve 1949- *WhoAm 92*
Magness, B. Don *BioIn 17*
Magness, Bob John 1924- *St&PR 93*
Magness, Howard Albert 1945- *St&PR 93*
Magness, Rhonda Ann 1946- *WhoEmL 93*
Magness Seneschal, Jacquelyn 1957- *WhoE 93*
Magnhagen, Bengt Ake 1937- *WhoWor 93*
Magni, Debra Kay 1954- *WhoAmW 93*
Magnin, Jean-Jacques 1940- *WhoWor 93*
Magnin, Roland E. 1932- *St&PR 93*
Magnoli, Albert *MiSFD 9*
Magnon, Alberto H., Jr. 1934- *St&PR 93, WhoAm 92*
Magnor, William T. 1915- *St&PR 93*
Magnum, Wyatt D. 1961- *WhoSSW 93*
Magnus, III c. 1073-1103 *HarEnMi*
Magnus, Erikson, II 1316-1374 *HarEnMi*
Magnus, Frederick Samuel 1932- *St&PR 93, WhoAm 92*
Magnus, Wilhelm 1907-1990 *BioIn 17*
Magnusen, Donald Walter 1942- *St&PR 93*
Magnusen, Olga Cristina 1949- *WhoAmW 93, WhoSSW 93*
Magnus Olafsson, I 1024-1047 *HarEnMi*
Magnuson, Ann *BioIn 17*
Magnuson, Clyde R. 1928- *St&PR 93*
Magnuson, Donald Lee 1949- *WhoAm 92*
Magnuson, Donald Richard 1951- *WhoEmL 93, WhoWor 93*
Magnuson, Donald V. 1925- *St&PR 93*
Magnuson, Gerald E. 1930- *St&PR 93*
Magnuson, Gerald Edward 1930- *WhoAm 92*
Magnuson, Harold Joseph 1913- *WhoAm 92*
Magnuson, Jerry Ross 1943- *St&PR 93, WhoIns 93*
Magnuson, Kathy Ann 1959- *WhoAmW 93*
Magnuson, Keith B. 1942- *St&PR 93*
Magnuson, Kristen Louise 1956- *WhoAmW 93*
Magnuson, Marcus Richard *Law&B 92*
Magnuson, Mark G. *Law&B 92*
Magnuson, Nancy 1944- *WhoAm 92*
Magnuson, Nels Gustav *Law&B 92*
Magnuson, Robert John 1943- *St&PR 93*
Magnuson, Robert Martin 1927- *WhoAm 92*
Magnuson, Roger James 1945- *WhoAm 92*
Magnuson, Scott P. *Law&B 92*
Magnuson, Warren G. 1905-1989 *PolPar*
Magnussen, Daniel Osar 1919- *WhoWrEP 92*
Magnusson, Claes F. 1941- *WhoScE 91-4*
Magnusson, David 1925- *WhoScE 91-4*
Magnusson, Elva Cooper *AmWomPl*
Magnusson, Gudmar Eyjolfur 1941- *WhoWor 93*
Magnusson, Jakob 1926- *WhoScE 91-4*
Magnusson, Mogens *WhoScE 91-2*
Magnusson, Staffan M.E. 1933- *WhoScE 91-2*
Magnusson, Thordur Eydal 1931- *WhoScE 91-4*
Mago dc. 203BC *HarEnMi*
Magoffin, Carole Jean 1942- *WhoAmW 93*
Magoffin, Richard I. 1939- *St&PR 93*
Magoffin, Susan Shelby 1827-1855 *BioIn 17*
Magoma, Athmani Ramadhani 1934- *WhoUN 92*
Magomayev, (Abdul) Muslim 1885-1937 *Baker 92*
Magon, Jymn *ScF&FL 92*
Magon, Ricardo Flores 1873-1922 *BioIn 17*
Magon-Kleinworth, Marie Claire 1947- *WhoAmW 93*
Magoon, David L. 1933- *St&PR 93*
Magoon, Linda J. 1950- *St&PR 93*
Magor, Emily E. *AmWomPl*
Magor, Howard 1922- *St&PR 93*
Magor, Louis Roland 1945- *WhoAm 92*
Magorian, James 1942- *ConAu 40NR*
Magorian, James Irvin 1942- *WhoWrEP 92*
Magorian, Michelle 1947- *BioIn 17, MajAI [port]*
Magoteaux, Cheryl Ann 1955- *WhoWrEP 92*
Magouirk, Conrad W. 1931- *St&PR 93*
Magovern, Linda Lee 1957- *WhoE 93*
Magovern, Thomas J. 1942- *St&PR 93*
Magowan, Peter Alden 1942- *St&PR 93, WhoAm 92*
Magram, Saul H. *Law&B 92*
Magrans, Ralph 1947- *St&PR 93*
Magrans, Ramon 1947- *WhoSSW 93*
Magrath, C. Peter 1933- *WhoAm 92, WhoSSW 93*
Magrath, David I. 1932- *WhoUN 92*
Magrath, Geoffrey Thompson 1944- *St&PR 93*
Magri, Deborah Brennan *Law&B 92*
Magriel, Paul David 1906-1990 *BioIn 17*
Magrill, Rose Mary 1939- *WhoSSW 93*
Magrino, Michael J. 1922- *St&PR 93*
Magrino, Peter Frank 1952- *WhoSSW 93*
Magro, Anthony John 1954- *St&PR 93*
Magruder, Alexander Leonard C. 1934- *St&PR 93*
Magruder, John Bankhead 1810-1871 *HarEnMi*
Magruder, Kevin Michael 1949- *WhoSSW 93*
Magruder, Lloyd 1825-1863 *BioIn 17*
Magruder, Richard Allen 1924- *WhoSSW 93*
Magsaysay, Ramon 1907-1957 *HarEnMi*
Magubane, Peter 1932- *BlkAull 92*
Magugu, Arthur Kinyanjui 1935- *WhoAfr*
Maguire, Albert Leo 1916- *WhoAm 92*
Maguire, Bassett 1904-1991 *BioIn 17, WhoWor 93*
Maguire, Bryan V. *Law&B 92*
Maguire, Cary M. 1928- *St&PR 93*
Maguire, Cary McIlwaine 1928- *WhoWor 93*
Maguire, Charlotte Edwards 1918- *WhoAm 92, WhoWor 93*
Maguire, David Edward 1938- *WhoAm 92*
Maguire, Deborah 1955- *WhoAmW 93*
Maguire, Deborah Anne 1963- *WhoAmW 93*
Maguire, Eileen Marie 1952- *WhoAmW 93*
Maguire, Emma M. *AmWomPl*
Maguire, Francis Vesey *Law&B 92*
Maguire, Graham Ross 1945- *WhoAsAP 91*
Maguire, Gregory 1955- *ScF&FL 92*
Maguire, Henry Clinton, Jr. 1928- *WhoAm 92*
Maguire, John David 1932- *WhoAm 92*
Maguire, John K. *Law&B 92*
Maguire, John P. 1917- *St&PR 93*
Maguire, John Patrick 1917- *WhoAm 92*
Maguire, Joseph 1916- *St&PR 93*
Maguire, Joseph F. 1919- *WhoAm 92*
Maguire, Kevin 1951- *WhoEmL 93, WhoSSW 93*
Maguire, M.F. 1928- *WhoScE 91-3*
Maguire, Mildred May 1933- *WhoAmW 93, WhoE 93*
Maguire, Patrick 1838-1896 *PolPar*
Maguire, Robert Alan 1930- *WhoAm 92*
Maguire, Robert Edward 1928- *St&PR 93, WhoAm 92*
Maguire, Robert Francis, III 1935- *WhoAm 92*
Maguire, Robert Wyman, Jr. 1944- *WhoE 93*
Maguire, Thomas A. 1949- *WhoAm 92*
Maguire, William Francis, Jr. 1957- *WhoSSW 93*
Maguire-Krupp, Marjorie Anne 1955- *WhoAmW 93*
Maguire-Zinni, Deirdre 1954- *WhoAmW 93, WhoWor 93*
Magureanu, Emil 1928- *WhoScE 91-4*
Maguth, Frank Joseph 1916- *St&PR 93*
Magyar, Deborah Valela 1957- *WhoEmL 93*
Magyar, Dezso *MiSFD 9*
Magyar, Kalman 1933- *WhoScE 91-4*
Magyar, Mary Kay 1951- *St&PR 93*
Mah, Feng-hwa 1922- *WhoAm 92*
Mah, Paul 1932- *WhoSSW 93*
Mah, Richard Sze Hao 1934- *WhoAm 92*
Maha, George Edward 1924- *WhoAm 92, WhoSSW 93*
Maha, Richard Damian 1955- *St&PR 93*
Mahabir, Ramkhelawan Niranthan 1930- *WhoWor 93*
Mahabir Prasad 1939- *WhoAsAP 91*
Mahachi, Moven Enock 1948- *WhoWor 93*
Mahadeva, Manoranjan 1955- *WhoEmL 93, WhoSSW 93*
Mahadeva, Wijeyaraj Anandakumar 1952- *WhoE 93, WhoEmL 93*
Mahadevan, Kumar 1948- *WhoAm 92, WhoWor 93*
Mahadevan, Rajan *BioIn 17*
Mahadeva Rao, Koorapaty Venkata 1939- *WhoUN 92*
Mahadoo, C.S. *ScF&FL 92*
Mahaffey, Cynthia Ann 1957- *WhoSSW 93*
Mahaffey, John 1948- *WhoAm 92*
Mahaffey, Judith Miller 1942- *WhoAmW 93*
Mahaffey, Marcia Jeanne Hixson *WhoAmW 93, WhoWor 93*
Mahaffey, Martha Bernal 1959- *WhoEmL 93*
Mahaffey, Merrill 1937- *BioIn 17*
Mahaffey, Redge Allan 1949- *WhoAm 92*
Mahaffey, Robert L. 1934- *St&PR 93*
Mahaffey, Sherry Lynn *Law&B 92*
Mahaffey, Thomas Jasper *Law&B 92*
Mahaffey, Tuula M. 1944- *St&PR 93*
Mahaffey, Wilton Larron 1942- *St&PR 93*
Mahaffy, A. Paul *Law&B 92*
Mahaffy, Christopher Adams Lamont 1952- *WhoEmL 93, WhoSSW 93*
Mahaffy-Berman, Anne 1948- *St&PR 93*
Mahairas, Evelyn Phillipine 1933- *WhoAmW 93*
Mahajan, Pramod 1949- *WhoAsAP 91*
Mahal, Taj 1942- *BioIn 17, WhoAm 92*
Mahalingam, Padmanabhan 1954- *WhoWor 93*
Mahan, Alexis Armstrong, Jr. 1920- *WhoE 93*
Mahan, Alfred Thayer 1840-1914 *GayN, HarEnMi*
Mahan, Dennis Hart 1802-1871 *HarEnMi*
Mahan, Dulany, Jr. 1914- *WhoE 93*
Mahan, Gerald Dennis 1937- *WhoAm 92*
Mahan, Kieran Thomas 1953- *WhoE 93*
Mahan, Marsha Lee 1960- *WhoAmW 93*
Mahan, Randolph R. *Law&B 92*
Mahanaim, Anna *WhoWrEP 92*
Mahanes, David James, Jr. 1923- *WhoAm 92*
Mahanes, H. Patrick 1943- *St&PR 93*
Mahanes, Michael Wayne 1956- *WhoEmL 93, WhoSSW 93, WhoWor 93*
Mahaney, Calvin Merritt 1929- *WhoIns 93*
Mahaney, Elizabeth Florence 1962- *WhoEmL 93*
Mahanthappa, Kalyana Thipperudraiah 1934- *WhoAm 92*
Mahanty, Jagadishwar 1932- *WhoWor 93*
Mahapatra, Jayanta *BioIn 17*
Mahar, Harold W., Jr. 1943- *St&PR 93*
Mahar, Lawrence William 1928- *WhoE 93*
Maharaj, Anthony *MiSFD 9*
Maharaj Ji 1957- *BioIn 17*
Maharam, Lewis G. 1955- *WhoE 93*
Maharg, Meredith McClintock 1938- *WhoSSW 93*
Maharidge, Dale Dimitro 1956- *WhoAm 92*
Maharis, George 1938- *ConTFT 10*
Maharos, Sombat *WhoWor 93*
Mahata, Chitta 1937- *WhoAsAP 91*
Mahathir bin Mohamad *BioIn 17*
Mahathir Bin Mohamad 1925- *WhoWor 93*
Mah Bow Tan 1948- *WhoAsAP 91*
Mahdi, Sadiq El 1936- *BioIn 17, WhoAfr*
Mahel, Michal 1920- *WhoScE 91-4*

Mahendra Prasad 1940- *WhoAsAP 91*
Maher, Brendan Arnold 1924- *WhoAm 92*
Maher, Carolyn Alexander 1941- *WhoE 93*
Maher, Charles Andrew 1944- *WhoE 93*
Maher, Cornelius Creedon, III 1949- *WhoSSW 93*
Maher, Daniel J. 1946- *St&PR 93*
Maher, Daniel Jay 1950- *WhoE 93*
Maher, David L. 1939- *St&PR 93, WhoAm 92*
Maher, David Willard 1934- *WhoAm 92*
Maher, Dennis Patrick 1938- *WhoWor 93*
Maher, Fran 1938- *WhoAmW 93*
Maher, Francesca Marciniak 1957- *WhoAmW 93*
Maher, Francis Randolph *WhoWor 93*
Maher, Gerard A. *Law&B 92*
Maher, James *Law&B 92*
Maher, James, Jr. *BioIn 17*
Maher, James V. *Law&B 92*
Maher, James Vincent, Jr. 1942- *WhoE 93*
Maher, Jean Elizabeth 1953- *WhoAmW 93, WhoEmL 93*
Maher, John
See Buzzcocks, The *ConMus 9*
Maher, John Francis 1929- *WhoE 93*
Maher, John Francis 1943- *WhoAm 92*
Maher, John J. d1991 *BioIn 17*
Maher, John Joseph 1954- *WhoEmL 93, WhoSSW 93*
Maher, Joseph Patrick 1934- *WhoE 93*
Maher, Kevin Loyola 1934- *WhoSSW 93*
Maher, Kim Leverton 1946- *WhoAm 92, WhoSSW 93*
Maher, Leo *BioIn 17*
Maher, Louis J. 1922- *St&PR 93*
Maher, Louis James, Jr. 1933- *WhoAm 92*
Maher, Mary Ann 1949- *WhoAmW 93*
Maher, Michael J. 1945- *St&PR 93*
Maher, Patricia Marie 1954- *WhoAmW 93, WhoEmL 93*
Maher, Patrick J. 1936- *St&PR 93*
Maher, Patrick Joseph 1936- *WhoAm 92*
Maher, Peter Michael 1940- *WhoAm 92*
Maher, Peter Robert 1952- *St&PR 93*
Maher, Philip John 1945- *WhoWor 93*
Maher, Ramona 1934- *DcAmChF 1960*
Maher, Robert Leroy 1948- *WhoSSW 93*
Maher, Shannon M. 1960- *WhoAmW 93*
Maher, Sylvia Arlene 1946- *WhoAmW 93*
Maher, Terry Marina 1955- *WhoEmL 93*
Maher, Thomas Dunseath *Law&B 92*
Maher, Timothy Jerome *Law&B 92*
Maher, Timothy John 1953- *WhoE 93*
Maher, William James 1937- *WhoSSW 93, WhoWor 93*
Maher, William Lawrence 1928- *St&PR 93*
Maher, William Michael 1947- *WhoEmL 93*
Maher, William Patrick 1936- *WhoE 93*
Maher, William T., Jr. 1931- *St&PR 93*
Maher-Jada, Anna Elizabeth 1959- *WhoAmW 93*
Mahesh, Virendra Bhushan 1932- *WhoAm 92*
Maheshwari, Arun Kumar 1944- *St&PR 93*
Mahesh Yogi, Maharishi *BioIn 17*
Maheswaranathan, Ponn 1954- *WhoEmL 93, WhoSSW 93*
Maheswarappa, K.G. 1928- *WhoAsAP 91*
Maheu, Jean 1931- *WhoWor 93*
Maheu, Shirley 1931- *WhoAmW 93*
Maheux-Forcier, Louise 1929- *BioIn 17, WhoCanL 92*
Mahey, John Andrew 1932- *WhoAm 92*
Mahfood, Stephen Michael 1949- *WhoEmL 93, WhoWor 93*
Mahfouz, Naguib 1911- *WhoWor 93*
Mahfouz, Naguib 1912- *BioIn 17*
Mahfuz, Najib 1912- *BioIn 17*
Mahgoub, Rifaat al- 1926-1990 *BioIn 17*
Mahillon, Charles (-Borromee) 1814-1887 *Baker 92*
Mahillon, Fernand 1866-1948
See Mahillon, Charles (-Borromee) 1814-1887 *Baker 92*
Mahillon, Victor-Charles 1841-1924
See Mahillon, Charles (-Borromee) 1814-1887 *Baker 92*
Mahin, Charles D. 1940- *St&PR 93*
Mahin, Charles Douglas 1940- *WhoAm 92*
Mahindapala, Horawela Don 1931- *WhoWor 93*
Mahindra, Indira 1926- *ConAu 136*
Mahine Banou Qajar, Princess of Iran 1900-1990 *BioIn 17*
Mahinis, John Nicholas 1961- *WhoE 93*
Mahishi, Sarojini 1927- *WhoAsAP 91*
Mahjoub, Elisabeth Mueller 1937- *WhoAmW 93*
Mahl, George Franklin 1917- *WhoAm 92*
Mahland, Walter 1948- *St&PR 93*
Mahle, Christoph Erhard 1938- *WhoAm 92, WhoE 93*
Mahle, Walter Stephen 1938- *WhoE 93*
Mahler, Alan E. 1942- *St&PR 93*
Mahler, Alma 1879-1964 *BioIn 17*
Mahler, David 1911- *WhoWor 93*
Mahler, David A. 1956- *St&PR 93*
Mahler, Fritz 1901-1973 *Baker 92*
Mahler, Gustav 1860-1911 *Baker 92, BioIn 17, IntDcOp [port], OxDcOp*
Mahler, Halfdan T. 1923- *WhoScE 91-2*
Mahler, Halfdan Theodor 1923- *WhoUN 92*
Mahler, Harry Bez 1928- *WhoAm 92*
Mahler, Howard Samuel 1952- *WhoEmL 93*
Mahler, Jerry 1957- *WhoEmL 93*
Mahler, Joni Dolph 1955- *WhoAmW 93*
Mahler, Michael David 1936- *St&PR 93*
Mahler, Philippe Jean 1932- *WhoUN 92*
Mahler, Richard T. 1943- *WhoAm 92*
Mahler, Steven Wayne 1954- *WhoE 93*
Mahler, Theodore Wesley 1942- *WhoIns 93*
Mahler, Thomas Richard 1945- *St&PR 93*
Mahler, W. Keith 1942- *St&PR 93*
Mahler-Sussman, Leona Julia 1926- *WhoWrEP 92*
Mahlman, Harvey Arthur 1923- *WhoSSW 93*
Mahlman, Jerry David 1940- *WhoAm 92*
Mahlman, Kent Earl 1928- *St&PR 93*
Mahlman, Nancy Deering 1934- *St&PR 93*
Mahlmann, John James 1942- *WhoAm 92*
Mahlmeister, Joseph E. 1945- *St&PR 93*
Mahmood, Ash B. 1944- *St&PR 93*
Mahmood, Fazal 1956- *WhoWor 93*
Mahmoud, Adel A. F. 1941- *WhoAm 92*
Mahmoud, Aly Ahmed 1935- *WhoAm 92*
Mahmoud, Gharib Subhi 1955- *WhoWor 93*
Mahmoud, Wendy Ellen 1953- *WhoEmL 93*
Mahmoud, Youssef 1947- *WhoUN 92*
Mahmud, Anisul Islam 1947- *WhoAsAP 91*
Mahmud, Ibni Al-Marhum Tuanku Sultan Ismail Nasiruddin 1930- *WhoWor 93*
Mahmud, Meftah Uddin 1945- *WhoWor 93*
Mahmud, Rehan 1952- *WhoEmL 93*
Mahmud Al-Muktafi Billah Shan Ibni Al-M, His Royal Highness Sultan 1930- *WhoAsAP 91*
Mahn, Antony Leroy 1943- *WhoE 93*
Mahn, Klaus *ScF&FL 92*
Mahnau, Heinrich *WhoScE 91-3*
Mahni, Daniel Ezra 1945- *WhoE 93*
Mahnk, Karen 1956- *WhoEmL 93*
Mahnke, Kurt Luther 1945- *WhoWor 93*
Mahnken, Thomas Gilbert 1965- *WhoE 93*
Mahofski, Stephen Samuel 1961- *WhoWor 93*
Mahomet d632 *BioIn 17*
Mahon, Arthur Joseph 1934- *WhoAm 92, WhoE 93*
Mahon, Barry *MiSFD 9*
Mahon, Edward M. *Law&B 92*
Mahon, James F. *Law&B 92*
Mahon, John J. *Law&B 92*
Mahon, John M., Jr. *Law&B 92*
Mahon, Joseph Bond, Jr. 1965- *WhoEmL 93*
Mahon, Joseph J. 1935- *St&PR 93*
Mahon, Kenneth John 1951- *St&PR 93*
Mahon, Malachy Thomas, Sr. 1934- *WhoAm 92*
Mahon, Morgan B. *Law&B 92*
Mahon, Rita 1949- *WhoEmL 93*
Mahon, Robert Jerome 1946- *WhoEmL 93*
Mahon, Sal 1941- *St&PR 93*
Mahon, William Michael, III 1954- *WhoE 93*
Mahone, Barbara Jean 1946- *WhoAm 92*
Mahone, William 1826-1895 *HarEnMi*
Mahone, William L. 1951- *St&PR 93*
Mahoney, Bob *MiSFD 9*
Mahoney, Daniel B. *Law&B 92*
Mahoney, Daniel Dennis 1943- *St&PR 93*
Mahoney, David 1923- *WhoAm 92*
Mahoney, David J. *Law&B 92*
Mahoney, Donald Edwin *Law&B 92*
Mahoney, Edward Alexander 1919- *St&PR 93*
Mahoney, Edward M. 1930- *St&PR 93*
Mahoney, Edward Maurice 1930- *WhoAm 92*
Mahoney, Eugene Frederick 1923- *WhoWrEP 92*
Mahoney, George L. *Law&B 92*
Mahoney, George Robert, Jr. *Law&B 92*
Mahoney, George Robert, Jr. 1942- *St&PR 93*
Mahoney, Gerald F. 1943- *St&PR 93*
Mahoney, Gerald Francis 1943- *WhoAm 92*
Mahoney, Gerard M. 1933-1991 *BioIn 17*
Mahoney, Gregory *BioIn 17*
Mahoney, J. Daniel 1931- *WhoAm 92*
Mahoney, Jack John Aloysius 1931- *WhoWor 93*
Mahoney, James A., Jr. 1935- *WhoIns 93*
Mahoney, James Anthony, Jr. 1935- *St&PR 93*
Mahoney, James Joseph 1946- *WhoE 93*
Mahoney, James Vincent 1956- *WhoE 93*
Mahoney, Jane W. 1922- *St&PR 93*
Mahoney, Joelle Katherine 1948- *WhoE 93*
Mahoney, John *BioIn 17*
Mahoney, John 1940- *WhoAm 92*
Mahoney, John L. 1928- *WhoAm 92*
Mahoney, John M. *Law&B 92*
Mahoney, John Marquis 1935- *WhoWrEP 92*
Mahoney, John Shepherd *Law&B 92*
Mahoney, John Thomas Fitzsimmons 1941- *WhoWrEP 92*
Mahoney, John William 1942- *St&PR 93*
Mahoney, Katherine Hanora 1964- *WhoEmL 93*
Mahoney, Larry *BioIn 17*
Mahoney, Leonard P. d1990 *BioIn 17*
Mahoney, M. Ellen 1954- *WhoAmW 93*
Mahoney, Margaret Ann 1949- *WhoAmW 93*
Mahoney, Margaret Ellerbe 1924- *WhoAm 92, WhoAmW 93*
Mahoney, Margaret Ellis 1929- *WhoAmW 93*
Mahoney, Mary Denise 1953- *WhoEmL 93*
Mahoney, Mary Dzurko 1946- *WhoAmW 93, WhoEmL 93*
Mahoney, Mary Judith 1945- *WhoE 93*
Mahoney, Mary Kathryn Gibbons 1913- *WhoAmW 93*
Mahoney, Michael Robert Taylor 1935- *WhoAm 92*
Mahoney, Michael Sean 1939- *WhoAm 92*
Mahoney, Patricia L.C. *Law&B 92*
Mahoney, Patrick A. 1951- *St&PR 93*
Mahoney, Patrick B. 1930- *WhoIns 93*
Mahoney, Patrick Morgan 1929- *WhoE 93*
Mahoney, Paul George 1937- *St&PR 93*
Mahoney, Richard *WhoAm 92*
Mahoney, Richard John *BioIn 17*
Mahoney, Richard John 1934- *St&PR 93, WhoAm 92*
Mahoney, Robert C. 1926- *St&PR 93*
Mahoney, Robert Charles 1926- *WhoAm 92*
Mahoney, Robert W. 1936- *St&PR 93*
Mahoney, Robert William 1936- *WhoAm 92*
Mahoney, Scott McDonnell *Law&B 92*
Mahoney, Stephen Joseph 1934- *St&PR 93*
Mahoney, Thomas Arthur 1928- *WhoSSW 93*
Mahoney, Thomas Francis *Law&B 92*
Mahoney, Thomas Henry 1952- *WhoWor 93*
Mahoney, Thomas Henry Donald 1913- *WhoAm 92, WhoWor 93*
Mahoney, Thomas Wren 1928- *St&PR 93*
Mahoney, Timothy J. *St&PR 93*
Mahoney, William E. 1939- *St&PR 93*
Mahoney, William Francis 1935- *WhoE 93, WhoWor 93, WhoWrEP 92*
Mahoney, William Grattan 1925- *WhoAm 92*
Mahony, Christina Hunt 1949- *WhoE 93*
Mahony, Devin *BioIn 17*
Mahony, Elizabeth *ScF&FL 92*
Mahony, Elizabeth Alsop *WhoWrEP 92*
Mahony, Roger Cardinal 1936- *WhoWor 93*
Mahony, Roger Michael 1936- *WhoAm 92*
Mahony, Terence *St&PR 93*
Mahony, Walter Butler, Jr. d1992 *NewYTBS 92*
Mahood, James Edward 1948- *WhoEmL 93*
Ma Hood, James Herbert 1937- *WhoWrEP 92*
Mahood, Janice H. 1940- *WhoAmW 93*
Mahood, R. Wayne 1934- *WhoE 93*
Mahood, Ramona Madson 1933- *WhoSSW 93*
Mahood, Robert W. *Law&B 92*
Mahorn, Rick 1958- *BioIn 17*
Mahorney, William Richard 1930- *St&PR 93*
Mahowald, Anthony Peter 1932- *WhoAm 92*
Mahowald, Cynthia J. *Law&B 92*
Mahowald, Mark Edward 1931- *WhoAm 92*
Mahr, George Joseph 1947- *St&PR 93*
Mahr, George Joseph, Jr. 1947- *WhoAm 92*
Mahr, Kurt 1936- *ScF&FL 92*
Mahraun, Robert Wayne 1948- *WhoEmL 93*
Mahre, Phil 1957 *WhoAm 92*
Mahrenholz, Christhard 1900-1980 *Baker 92*
Mahto, Bandhu 1934- *WhoAsAP 91*
Mahunka, Imre 1938- *WhoScE 91-4*
Mahurin, Matt *MiSFD 9*
Mahuron, D. Jack 1926- *St&PR 93*
Mahy, Cristopher Carl 1958- *St&PR 93*
Mahy, Margaret 1936- *ChlFicS, ConAu 38NR, DcChlFi, MajAI [port], ScF&FL 92, SmATA 69 [port], WhoAm 92*
Mai, Amalia Isabel 1960- *WhoUN 92*
Mai, Chao C. 1936- *St&PR 93*
Mai, Christan Paul *Law&B 92*
Mai, Frieda Jean 1960- *WhoAmW 93*
Mai, Halalu 1947- *WhoAsAP 91*
Mai, Jurgen Konrad 1945- *WhoScE 91-3*
Mai, Kenton J. *Law&B 92*
Mai, Klaus L. 1930- *WhoAm 92, WhoSSW 93*
Mai, Mark F. *Law&B 92*
Mai, William Frederick 1916- *WhoAm 92*
Maia, Hernani L. Silva 1936- *WhoScE 91-3*
Maia, Ronaldo *BioIn 17*
Maianu, Alexandru 1931- *WhoWor 93*
Maibach, Ben C., Jr. 1920- *St&PR 93, WhoAm 92*
Maibach, Howard I. 1929- *WhoAm 92*
Maibaum, Richard 1909-1991 *AnObit 1991, BioIn 17*
Maibaum, Thomas Stephen Edward *WhoScE 91-1*
Maibawa, Castan Marbo 1956- *WhoAsAP 91*
Maibenco, Helen Craig 1917- *WhoAm 92*
Maiboroda, Georgi 1913- *Baker 92*
Maiboroda, Rostislav 1961- *WhoWor 93*
Maich, Robert Samuel 1941- *WhoAm 92*
Maich, Thomas W. *Law&B 92*
Maichel, Jeffrey R. 1955- *St&PR 93*
Maichel, Joseph Raymond 1934- *St&PR 93, WhoAm 92*
Maichelbeck, Franz Anton 1702-1750 *Baker 92*
Maicher, Gerd-Rudi 1952- *WhoWor 93*
Maickel, Roger Philip 1933- *WhoAm 92*
Maicki, G. Carol 1936- *WhoAmW 93*
Maico, R. Stephen 1951- *St&PR 93*
Maida, Adam J. 1930- *WhoAm 92*
Maidanik, Gideon 1925- *BioIn 17*
Maidenbaum, Aryeh Yehuda 1942- *WhoE 93*
Maides-Keane, Shirley Allen 1951- *WhoAmW 93*
Maidique, Mitch *BioIn 17*
Maidique, Modesto A. *BioIn 17*
Maidique, Modesto A. 1940- *HispAmA [port]*
Maidique, Modesto Alex 1940- *WhoSSW 93*
Maidl, Bernhard Robert 1938- *WhoScE 91-3*
Maidlow, Dolores Mary 1934- *WhoAmW 93, WhoWor 93*
Maidman, Richard Harvey Mortimer 1933- *WhoAm 92*
Maidman, Stephen Paul *Law&B 92*
Maidment, Frederick Herold 1947- *WhoE 93*
Maidom Pansai 1948- *WhoAsAP 91*
Maidon, Carolyn Howser 1946- *WhoAm 92, WhoEmL 93*
Maidt, Robert Louis 1923- *WhoSSW 93*
Maiello, Thomas Michael 1958- *WhoE 93*
Maienschein, Fred C. 1925- *WhoAm 92*
Maier, Alfred 1929- *WhoAm 92, WhoSSW 93*
Maier, Charles Steven 1939- *WhoAm 92, WhoE 93*
Maier, Craig F. 1949- *St&PR 93*
Maier, Craig Frisch 1949- *WhoAm 92*
Maier, Diana E. 1957- *WhoAmW 93*
Maier, Dietrich 1944- *WhoScE 91-3*
Maier, Donna Jane-Ellen 1948- *WhoAmW 93, WhoEmL 93*
Maier, Edward Handy 1944- *St&PR 93*
Maier, Edward Louis, Jr. 1955- *WhoE 93, WhoEmL 93*
Maier, Francis Xavier 1948- *WhoAm 92*
Maier, Frank d1990 *BioIn 17*
Maier, Franz Georg 1926- *WhoWor 93*
Maier, Gerald James 1928- *St&PR 93, WhoAm 92*
Maier, Gerald Robert *Law&B 92*
Maier, Gerhard 1960- *WhoWor 93*
Maier, Giulio 1931- *WhoWor 93*
Maier, Gunther 1932- *WhoScE 91-3*
Maier, Guy 1891-1956 *Baker 92*
Maier, Harold Geistweit 1937- *WhoAm 92*
Maier, Henry B. 1925- *WhoE 93, WhoWor 93*
Maier, Heribert 1932- *WhoUN 92*
Maier, Jack C. 1925- *St&PR 93*
Maier, John B. *Law&B 92*
Maier, Karl George 1937- *WhoSSW 93, WhoWor 93*
Maier, Paul Luther 1930- *WhoAm 92*

Maier, Paul Victor 1947- St&PR 93, WhoAm 92
Maier, Peter Klaus 1929- WhoAm 92
Maier, Raymond G. Law&B 92
Maier, Robert Andrew 1949- WhoEmL 93
Maier, Robert Hawthorne 1927- WhoAm 92
Maier, Robert Henry 1932- WhoSSW 93
Maier, Thomas James 1948- St&PR 93
Maier, Volker Albrecht 1941- WhoWor 93
Maier, Waldemar C. 1939- St&PR 93
Maier, Walter Arthur 1893-1950 BioIn 17
Maier-Katkin, Daniel 1945- WhoAm 92
Maier-Leibnitz, Heinz 1911- WhoWor 93
Maietta, Diane Marie 1957- WhoE 93
Maiette, Ralph Louis 1947- WhoE 93
Maignan, Georges 1932- WhoScE 91-2
Maihafer, Harry James 1924- WhoAm 92
Maihle, Nita Jane 1955- WhoAmW 93
Maijala, Kalle Jussi 1927- WhoScE 91-4
Maikarfi, Suzanne 1955- WhoUN 92
Maikowski, Michael F. ScF&FL 92
Mailander, Cat Margaret 1957- WhoAmW 93, WhoEmL 93
Maile, Ben ScF&FL 92
Mailer, Norman BioIn 17
Mailer, Norman 1923- ConLC 74 [port], MagSAmL [port], MiSFD 9, ScF&FL 92, WhoAm 92, WhoE 93, WhoWrEP 92
Mailhes, Corinne 1965- WhoWor 93
Mailhot, Louise 1940- WhoAmW 93
Mailhot, Michele 1932- WhoCanL 92
Maillard, Jean-Rene 1933- WhoWor 93
Maillard, Keith 1942- WhoCanL 92
Maillardet, Frederick James WhoScE 91-1
Maillart, Aime 1817-1871 Baker 92, OxDcOp
Maillart, Ella 1903- Expl 93
Maillart, Pierre 1551-1622 Baker 92
Maillefert, Alfredo 1889-1941 DcMexL
Mailler, William M. 1944- St&PR 93
Maillet, Andree 1921- WhoCanL 92
Maillet, Antonine 1929- BioIn 17, ScF&FL 92, WhoAmW 93, WhoCanL 92
Maillet, Lucienne 1934- WhoAm 92
Maillet, Martin Joseph, Sr. 1933- WhoE 93
Maillet, Michel 1932- WhoScE 91-2
Maillet, Pierre Paul 1923- WhoWor 93
Maillet, Robert 1947- WhoScE 91-2
Mailliard, John Ward, III 1914- St&PR 93
Maillol, Aristide 1861-1944 BioIn 17
Mailloux, Robert Joseph 1938- WhoAm 92
Mailly, Alphonse-Jean-Ernest 1833-1918 Baker 92
Mailman, Charles 1931- St&PR 93
Mailman, David Sherwin 1938- WhoSSW 93
Mailman, Harold Leigh 1926- WhoE 93
Mailman, Joseph L. d1990 BioIn 17
Mailman, Martin 1932- Baker 92
Maiman, George 1939- WhoE 93, WhoWor 93
Maiman, Julius David 1933- WhoE 93
Maiman, Theodore Harold 1927- WhoAm 92, WhoWor 93
Maimbourg, Odette McIntyre 1960- WhoEmL 93
Maimin, David Sidney, Jr. 1928- St&PR 93
Maimin, Joseph 1920- St&PR 93
Maimon, Elaine Plaskow 1944- WhoAmW 93, WhoE 93
Maimone, William G. Law&B 92
Maimonides, Moses 1135-1204 BioIn 17
Main, Bruce Lee 1939- St&PR 93
Main, Carol ScF&FL 92
Main, Charles Lloyd 1954- WhoE 93
Main, David M. Law&B 92
Main, David Michael 1949- WhoEmL 93
Main, Debra Kay 1956- WhoE 93
Main, Edna Dewey 1940- WhoAmW 93, WhoSSW 93, WhoWor 93
Main, Guy F. 1919- St&PR 93
Main, Jackson Turner 1917- WhoAm 92
Main, Janalyn Irene 1956- WhoWrEP 92
Main, Margaret Huntley 1921- WhoAmW 93
Main, Marjorie 1890-1975 QDrFCA 92 [port]
Main, Mary Rose 1931- WhoAm 92
Main, Michael R. Law&B 92
Main, Robert Gordon, Jr. 1951- WhoE 93
Main, Robert Peer 1930- St&PR 93
Maina, Charles Gatere 1931- WhoAfr
Mainardi, Cesare Roberto Giovanni 1962- WhoWor 93
Mainardi, Dominic 1914- St&PR 93
Mainardi, Enrico 1897-1976 Baker 92
Mainardi, James Albert 1939- WhoIns 93
Maine, Arthur Dale 1939- WhoAm 92
Maine, Basil (Stephen) 1894-1972 Baker 92
Maine, Charles Eric 1921-1981 ScF&FL 92
Maine, Henry Sumner 1822-1888 IntDcAn
Maine, Trevor ConAu 38NR, MajAI
Maine, Virginia Louise Mottorn 1937- WhoAmW 93
Mainelli, Michael R. 1935- St&PR 93
Mainer, Robert 1927- St&PR 93
Maines, C. Bruce 1926- WhoIns 93
Maines, Clifford Bruce 1926- St&PR 93, WhoAm 92
Maini, Philip Kumar 1959- WhoWor 93
Maini, Ravinder N. 1937- WhoScE 91-1
Mainka, Albert Pierre 1947- St&PR 93
Maino, Armando WhoScE 91-3
Maino, Juan Bautista 1578-1641 BioIn 17
Maino, Michael S. 1941- St&PR 93
Mainone, Robert Franklin 1929- WhoWrEP 92
Mainor, Gary Alan 1950- St&PR 93
Mainor, H. Earl 1940- St&PR 93
Mainor, Robert 1923- WhoSSW 93
Mainor, Robert Perez 1953- WhoEmL 93
Mainou, Athina 1943- WhoScE 91-3
Mainous, Arch G., Jr. 1933- St&PR 93
Mainous, Bruce Hale 1914- WhoAm 92
Mains, Donald Allen 1928- St&PR 93
Mainsant, Pascal WhoScE 91-2
Mainster, Donna Marie 1954- WhoWrEP 92
Mainwaring, A. Bruce 1927- St&PR 93
Mainwaring, Daniel d1978 BioIn 17
Mainwaring, John c. 1724-1807 Baker 92
Mainwaring, Thomas Lloyd 1928- WhoAm 92
Mainwaring, William Lewis 1935- WhoAm 92, WhoWrEP 92
Mainwaring, William R. 1943- St&PR 93
Mainwaring, William Robert 1943- WhoAm 92
Mainzer, Barry 1958- St&PR 93
Mainzer, Joseph 1801-1851 Baker 92
Mainzer, Ronald O. 1931- St&PR 93
Mainzer, Sari Patricia St&PR 93
Maio, Carl Anthony 1948- WhoEmL 93
Maio, Thomas Anthony 1936- St&PR 93
Maiocchi, Christine 1949- WhoAmW 93, WhoE 93, WhoEmL 93
Maiolo, Joseph 1938- WhoWrEP 92
Maiolo, Joseph Anthony 1935- WhoSSW 93
Maione, Theodore Edward 1956- WhoE 93
Maiorana, Charlie 1942- WhoE 93
Maiorana, Lucy F. Law&B 92
Maiorana, Ronald 1930- WhoWrEP 92
Maiorano, Gaetano OxDcOp
Maiorella, Marc Anthony 1957- St&PR 93
Maiorescu, Mircea 1926- WhoScE 91-4
Maioriello, Richard Patrick 1936- WhoWor 93
Mair, Barbara Yvonne 1954- WhoAmW 93
Mair, Bruce Logan 1951- WhoWor 93
Mair, Charles 1838-1927 BioIn 17
Mair, Franz 1821-1893 Baker 92
Mair, Joel St&PR 93
Mair, Joy AfrAmBi
Mair, Lucy Philip 1901-1986 IntDcAn
Maira, Arthur Francis 1943- St&PR 93
Maire, Barbara Jean 1932- WhoSSW 93
Maire, David G. Law&B 92
Maire, Edmond 1931- BioIn 17
Maire, Jacques 1925- WhoScE 91-2
Maire, Jean Claude 1934- WhoScE 91-2
Mairet, Jeanne AmWomPl
Mairose, Paul Timothy 1956- WhoEmL 93, WhoWor 93
Mairs, Nancy BioIn 17
Mairs, Nancy 1943- ConAu 136
Mairs, Nancy Pedrick 1943- WhoWrEP 92
Mais, Roger 1905-1955 BioIn 17, DcLB 125 [port]
Maisano, Daniel J. 1951- WhoE 93
Maisano, John Alexander 1957- WhoE 93
Maisano, Phillip Nicholas 1947- WhoAm 92, WhoE 93, WhoEmL 93
Maise, Ray E. 1933- St&PR 93
Maisel, Darrell Keith 1947- WhoEmL 93
Maisel, Eric Richard 1947- WhoWrEP 92
Maisel, Herbert 1930- WhoAm 92
Maisel, Jay 1931- BioIn 17
Maisel, Melvin L. 1924- WhoIns 93
Maisel, Michael 1947- WhoAm 92, WhoE 93, WhoEmL 93
Maisel, Sherman J. 1918- BioIn 17
Maisel, Sherman Joseph 1918- WhoAm 92
Maisel, Stuart 1955- St&PR 93
Maisey, Michael Norman WhoScE 91-1
Maish, James A. 1932- St&PR 93
Maisin, Jean R. 1928- WhoScE 91-2
Maisky, Mischa 1948- Baker 92
Maislin, Isidore 1919- WhoAm 92
Maisner, Irwin Gerald 1956- WhoE 93
Maison, Della ConAu 37NR
Maison, Rene 1895-1962 Baker 92
Maisonrouge, Jacques BioIn 17
Maisonrouge, Jacques Gaston 1924- St&PR 93
Maissa, Philipe 1949- WhoScE 91-2
Maissel, Leon Israel 1930- WhoAm 92
Maistre, Joseph de 1753-1821 NinCLC 37 [port]
Maistre, Joseph Marie, comte de 1753-1821 BioIn 17
Maistre, Paul Andre Marie 1858-1922 HarEnMi
Maitland, Alister Thirlestane 1941- WhoWor 93
Maitland, David J(ohnston) 1922- ConAu 38NR
Maitland, Derek 1943- ScF&FL 92
Maitland, Guy Edison Clay Law&B 92
Maitland, Guy Edison Clay 1942- WhoE 93
Maitland, J(ohn) A(lexander) Fuller Baker 92
Maitland, James Dean 1960- WhoWor 93
Maitland, Leo C. d1992 NewYTBS 92
Maitland, Leo C. 1928-1992 BioIn 17
Maitland, Lester J. 1899-1990 BioIn 17
Maitland, Margaret ScF&FL 92
Maitland, Robert Allan 1952- St&PR 93
Maitland, Sara 1950- ScF&FL 92
Maitland, William T. Law&B 92
Maitman, Jolyn Law&B 92
Maitner, John Joseph Law&B 92
Maitner, Robert Emil 1948- St&PR 93
Maitre, Doreen ScF&FL 92
Maitrot, Bernard 1937- WhoScE 91-2
Maitz, Don 1953- ScF&FL 92
Maivald, James John 1956- WhoWrEP 92
Maiwurm, James John 1948- WhoAm 92, WhoE 93, WhoEmL 93
Maize, John Christopher 1943- WhoSSW 93
Maizel, Boris 1907-1986 Baker 92
Maj, Jerzy Michal Jozef 1922- WhoScE 91-4
Maj, Leszek 1944- WhoScE 91-4
Maj, Stanislaw Josef 1932- WhoScE 91-4
Maja, Mario 1934- WhoScE 91-3
Majano, Adolfo DcCPCAm
Majcen, Marko 1924- WhoScE 91-4
Majchrowicz, Irena 1931- WhoScE 91-4
Majchrzak, David Joseph 1936- WhoE 93
Majdalawi, Fouad Farouk 1969- WhoWor 93
Majeed, Abdul 1937- WhoWor 93
Majek, Warren N. 1956- St&PR 93
Majer, Vladimir 1922- WhoScE 91-4
Majerich, Cynthia Ann 1959- WhoE 93
Majerle, Dan BioIn 17
Majerotto, Walter WhoScE 91-4
Majerowicz, Alfred 1925- WhoScE 91-4
Majerski, Zdenko 1937- WhoScE 91-4
Majerus, Philip Warren 1936- WhoAm 92
Majerus, Rick BioIn 17
Majeske, Daniel WhoAm 92
Majeske, Penelope Kantgias 1937- WhoAmW 93
Majeski, Anthony Chester 1931- St&PR 93
Majeski, Hank 1916-1991 BioIn 17
Majeski, Stephen L. Law&B 92
Majev, Howard Rudolph 1952- WhoEmL 93
Majewski, Frank Walter 1922- WhoIns 93
Majewski, Janusz 1931- DrEEuF
Majewski, Lech MiSFD 9
Majewski, Theodore Eugene 1925- WhoSSW 93
Majewski, Wojciech 1931- WhoScE 91-4
Majhi, Prithibi 1951- WhoAsAP 91
Majid, Ali Hassan 1940- BioIn 17
Majid, Shahnawaz Hasan 1960- WhoWor 93
Majidi-Mashhadi, Mahmoud 1953- WhoEmL 93
Majka, Joseph T. Law&B 92
Majka, Richard St&PR 93
Majkowski, Don BioIn 17
Majkowski, E. Jon 1942- St&PR 93
Majkowski, Jerzy 1928- WhoScE 91-4
Majkrzak, Charles Francis 1950- WhoE 93
Majle, Tadeusz 1929- WhoScE 91-4
Majluta, Jacobo 1934- DcCPCAm
Majnep, Saem BioIn 17
Majno, Guido 1922- WhoAm 92
Majo, Gian Francesco (de) 1732-1770 Baker 92
Majo, Gian Francesco di 1732-1770 OxDcOp
Majo, Giuseppe de 1697-1771 Baker 92
Majo, Giuseppe di 1697-1771 OxDcOp
Majone, Ascanio c. 1565-1627 Baker 92
Major, Andre 1942- WhoAm 92, WhoCanL 92
Major, Austin ScF&FL 92
Major, Charles 1856-1913 GayN
Major, Charles T., Jr. 1934- WhoAm 92
Major, Clare Tree AmWomPl
Major, Clarence Lee 1936- WhoAm 92, WhoWrEP 92
Major, Coleman Joseph 1915- WhoAm 92
Major, Deborah Riddle 1954- WhoAmW 93
Major, Ervin 1901-1967 Baker 92
Major, Gyorgyne 1931- WhoScE 91-4
Major, (Jakab) Gyula 1858-1925 Baker 92
Major, H.M. ScF&FL 92
Major, Henriette 1933- WhoCanL 92
Major, James Russell Richards 1921- WhoWrEP 92
Major, Janet G. Law&B 92
Major, Jean-Louis 1937- ConAu 40NR, WhoAm 92, WhoWrEP 92
Major, John 1943- BioIn 17, NewYTBS 92 [port], WhoWor 93
Major, John Keene 1924- WhoAm 92
Major, John R. 1944- St&PR 93
Major, Kevin 1949- DcChlFi, WhoCanL 92
Major, Kevin (Gerald) 1949- ConAu 38NR, MajAI [port], WhoAm 92, WhoWrEP 92
Major, Mark W. Law&B 92
Major, Nigel Paul 1966- WhoWor 93
Major, Roberta J. Law&B 92
Major, Warren R. 1947- St&PR 93
Major, William Alexander, Jr. 1942- WhoAm 92
Major, Winfield W. Law&B 92
Majorian d461 OxDcByz
Majorianus, Julius Valerius d461 HarEnMi
Majors, Clark Donald 1932- WhoSSW 93
Majors, John Terrill 1935- BiDAMSp 1989, WhoAm 92
Majors, Lee 1940- WhoAm 92
Majors, Nelda Faye 1938- WhoSSW 93
Majumdar, Amalendu Jyoti WhoScE 91-1
Majumdar, Dhirendra Nath 1903-1960 IntDcAn
Majumdar, Rabindra Nath 1932- WhoSSW 93
Majumdar, Sharmila 1961- WhoAmW 93
Majure, James T. 1924- St&PR 93
Majure, Michael K. 1957- St&PR 93
Majure, Wallace J. d1992 BioIn 17
Mak, George Edmond 1953- WhoWor 93
Mak, Gilbert Kwok Kwong 1963- WhoWor 93
Mak, Jimmy 1954- St&PR 93
Mak, Johnny 1949- MiSFD 9
Mak, Kai-Kwong 1948- WhoEmL 93, WhoSSW 93
Mak, Koon Hou 1961- WhoWor 93
Mak, Lai Wo 1946- WhoWor 93
Mak, Raymond T. Law&B 92
Mak, Reginald W. 1940- St&PR 93
Mak, Tak Wah 1946- WhoAm 92
Makabe, Osamu St&PR 93
Makadok, Stanley 1941- WhoWor 93
Makal, Kevin LeRoy 1956- WhoSSW 93
Makanoff, Lon David 1948- St&PR 93
Makant, Joseph Earle, Jr. 1929- WhoSSW 93
Makar, Arthur 1950- WhoE 93
Makar, Lindy Charlotte 1949- WhoAmW 93
Makar, Ralph 1960- WhoE 93
Makarem, Essam Faiz 1936- WhoWor 93
Makarem, Samir Said 1957- WhoWor 93
Makari, George Jack 1960- WhoE 93
Makarios, III 1913-1977 DcTwHis
Makarios of Philadelphia OxDcByz
Makarios of Rome OxDcByz
Makarios/Symeon fl. 4th cent.-5th cent. OxDcByz
Makarios the Great c. 300-c. 390 OxDcByz
Makarov, Nikolai 1810-1890 Baker 92
Makarov, Vladimir L. 1941- WhoWor 93
Makarova, Natalia 1940- BioIn 17, WhoAm 92, WhoWor 93
Makarova, Nina 1908-1976 Baker 92
Makarowski, William Stephen 1948- WhoE 93, WhoEmL 93, WhoWor 93
Makary, Archbishop 1938- WhoAm 92
Makauer, George A. 1944- St&PR 93
Makavejev, Dusan 1932- DrEEuF, MiSFD 9
Make, Isabel Rose 1947- WhoAmW 93
Makeba, Miriam 1932- Baker 92, BioIn 17, ConMus 8 [port]
Makedonios Consul fl. 6th cent.- OxDcByz
Makedonski, Kiril 1925-1984 Baker 92
Makeig, Duncan Law&B 92
Makela, Benjamin R. 1922- WhoAm 92
Makela, Klaus WhoScE 91-4
Makela, P. Helena 1930- WhoScE 91-4
Makelainen, Pentti Keijo 1944- WhoScE 91-4
Makepeace, Darryl Lee 1941- WhoWor 93
Makepeace, LeRoy d1990 BioIn 17
Maker, C. June BioIn 17
Maker, Edward, II Law&B 92
Maker, Janet Anne 1942- WhoAmW 93
Makeyev, Evgeny Nikolaevitch 1928- WhoUN 92, WhoWor 93
Makhalemele, Ratau Mike BioIn 17
Makhani, Madan P. 1937- St&PR 93

Makhija, Mohan 1941- WhoE 93
Makhnev, Alexander Alexeevich 1953- WhoWor 93
Makholm, Mark Henry 1915- WhoAm 92
Mak Hon Kam, Dato' 1939- WhoAsAP 91
Makhoul, John Ibrahim 1942- WhoAm 92
Maki, Allan Abel 1922- St&PR 93
Maki, Atsushi 1948- WhoWor 93
Maki, Charles E. 1928- St&PR 93
Maki, Dennis G. 1940- WhoAm 92
Maki, Eloise Joy Law&B 92
Maki, Fumihiko 1928- BioIn 17, WhoWor 93
Maki, John McGilvrey 1909- WhoE 93
Maki, Kazumi 1936- WhoAm 92
Maki, Yoshifumi 1930- WhoWor 93
Makiedonski, Alexander 1935- WhoWor 93
Makielski, Stanislaw John, Jr. 1935- WhoAm 92
Makigami, Yasuji 1936- WhoWor 93
Makihara, Minoru NewYTBS 92 [port], WhoAm 92
Makila, Eino 1929- WhoScE 91-4
Makiling, Mike Relon 1936- WhoWor 93
Makin, Al- 1205?-1273 OxDcByz
Makin, Bathsua fl. 1612-1673 BioIn 17
Makin, Brian WhoScE 91-1
Makin, Michael John 1938- WhoWor 93
Makinen, Juho Kaarlo 1945- WhoScE 91-4
Makinen, Marvin William 1939- WhoAm 92
Makinen, Raine WhoScE 91-4
Makinen, Veijo O.I. 1924- WhoScE 91-4
Makino, Keisuke 1945- WhoWor 93
Makino, Shiro 1893-1945 HarEnMi
Makino, Shojiro BioIn 17
Makino, Shojiro 1929- St&PR 93, WhoAm 92
Makino, Takamori 1926- WhoAsAP 91
Makins, James Edward 1923- WhoWor 93
Makinson, David Clement 1941- WhoWor 93
Makinson, Dwight Leland 1946- WhoEmL 93
Makinson, Gordon James WhoScE 91-1
Makios, Vassilios 1938- WhoScE 91-3
Makiya, Kanan BioIn 17
Makiya, Mohamed BioIn 17
Makk, Karoly 1925- DrEEuF, MiSFD 9
Makkawi, Khalil 1930- WhoUN 92
Makkay, Maureen Ann WhoAmW 93
Maklakiewicz, Jan Adam 1899-1954 Baker 92, PolBiDi
Makleit, Sandor 1930- WhoScE 91-4
Maklin, Mickey 1942- St&PR 93
Mako, William Lawrence 1958- WhoEmL 93
Makoetje, Ntai 1958- WhoUN 92
Makofske, Florence Louise 1939- WhoE 93
Makofski, Robert Anthony 1930- WhoE 93
Makohin, George M. Law&B 92
Makoski, Milton J. 1946- St&PR 93
Makoski, Milton John 1946- WhoEmL 93
Makosky, Thomas 1948- WhoEmL 93
Makosza, Mieczystaw 1934- WhoScE 91-4
Makoto, Asashima 1944- WhoWor 93
Makouke, Claude DcCPCAm
Makous, Walter Leon WhoAm 92
Makovsky, David 1960- WhoWor 93
Makovsky, Kenneth Dale 1940- WhoAm 92
Makower, Hermann 1830-1897 BioIn 17
Makower, Joel 1952- WhoEmL 93
Makowski, Andrzej 1931- WhoScE 91-4
Makowski, Edgar Leonard 1927- WhoAm 92
Makowski, Karen R. 1956- St&PR 93
Makowski, Karen Raechal 1956- WhoEmL 93
Makowski, M. Paul 1922- St&PR 93, WhoAm 92
Makowski, Tadeusz 1882-1932 PolBiDi
Makowski, Werner Max Michael 1929- WhoWor 93
Makowski, Zygmunt Stanislaw WhoScE 91-1
Makowsky, Veronica A(nn) 1954- ConAu 38NR
Makrembolites OxDcByz
Makrembolites, Alexios dc. 1349 OxDcByz
Makrembolites, Eustathios fl. 12th cent.- OxDcByz
Makres, Makarios c. 1383-1431 OxDcByz
Makrianes, James Konstantin, Jr. 1925- WhoAm 92
Makris, Andreas 1930- WhoAm 92, WhoWor 93
Makris, Constantine John 1927- WhoE 93
Maksic, Z.B. 1938- WhoScE 91-4
Maksimov, A.N. 1872-1941 IntDcAn
Maksimov, S.V. 1831-1901 IntDcAn
Maksimova, Larisa Lvovna 1943- WhoWor 93
Maksimovic, Cedo 1947- WhoScE 91-4
Maksimovic, Rajko 1935- Baker 92
Maksoud, Joao Gilberto 1937- WhoWor 93
Maksymiuk, Jerzy WhoWor 93
Maksymiuk, Jerzy 1936- Baker 92
Maksymowicz, John 1956- WhoWor 93
Maksymowych, Roman 1924- WhoE 93
Makuck, Peter 1940- WhoWrEP 92
Makupson, Amyre Porter 1947- WhoAmW 93
Makupson, Walter H. Law&B 92
Makuszynski, Kornel 1884-1953 PolBiDi
Makzimilijan, Jezernik 1922- WhoWor 93
Mala, Theodore Anthony 1946- WhoAm 92, WhoEmL 93, WhoWor 93
Malabanan, Ernesto Herella 1919- WhoWor 93
Malabre, Alfred Leopold, Jr. 1931- WhoAm 92
Malacarne, C. John Law&B 92
Malacarne, C. John 1941- St&PR 93, WhoAm 92
Malacavage, Robert D. 1944- St&PR 93
Malach, Herbert John 1922- WhoE 93, WhoWor 93
Malach, Monte 1926- WhoAm 92, WhoWor 93
Malachowski, Ernest S. 1946- St&PR 93
Malachowski, Jerome Alfred 1942- St&PR 93
Malachowski, Philip Alexander 1953- WhoE 93
Malachowski, Stanislaw c. 1630-1699 PolBiDi
Malachowsky, Martin Norman 1929- WhoE 93
Malachuk, Allan F. 1940- St&PR 93
Malachy, Saint 1094?-1148 BioIn 17
Maladina, Johnson Ephraim 1953- WhoAsAP 91
Malafeyev, Oleg Alexeyevich 1944- WhoWor 93
Malafronte, Donald 1931- WhoAm 92
Malafronte, Victor NewYTBS 92 [port]
Malaga, Hernan Alfredo 1943- WhoUN 92
Malagrino, Claudio 1964- WhoWor 93
Malaguti, Gino BioIn 17
Malahowski, Richard Anton Law&B 92
Malaise, Edmond P. 1930- WhoScE 91-2
Malak, Henry 1913-1987 PolBiDi
Malak, Stephen P. Law&B 92
Malakes, Euthymios c. 1115-c. 1204 OxDcByz
Malakoff, James Leonard 1933- St&PR 93
Malalas, John c. 490-57-? OxDcByz
Malamed, Sasha 1928- WhoE 93
Malamed, Seymour H. 1921- St&PR 93, WhoAm 92
Malamud, Barry Evan 1967- WhoE 93
Malamud, Bernard 1914-1986 BioIn 17, JeAmHC, MagSAmL [port], ScF&FL 92, WorLitC [port]
Malamud, Daniel 1939- WhoAm 92
Malamud, Mark Michaelovich 1950- WhoWor 93
Malamud, Phyllis Carole 1938- WhoAmW 93
Malamy, Michael Howard 1938- WhoAm 92
Malan, Daniel Francois 1874-1959 DcTwHis
Malan, Magnus Andre de Merindol 1930- WhoAfr, WhoWor 93
Malan, Rian BioIn 17
Malanaphy-Sorg, Marie Antoinette 1955- WhoEmL 93
Maland, Charles John 1949- WhoSSW 93
Malandra, Charles Robert, Jr. Law&B 92
Malanga, Gerard 1943- ConAu 17AS [port]
Malanga, Gerard Joseph 1943- WhoWrEP 92
Malanotte, Adelaide 1785-1832 OxDcOp
Malanotte (-Montresor), Adelaide 1785-1832 Baker 92
Malaparte, Curzio 1898-1957 BioIn 17
Malaquais, Elisabeth L. 1937- WhoUN 92
Malara, Anthony Carmelo 1936- WhoAm 92
Malara, Tony C. 1936- St&PR 93
Malarcher, David Julius 1894-1982 BiDAMSp 1989
Malarek, David Harby 1939- WhoE 93
Malarkey, Martin Francis, Jr. 1918- WhoAm 92
Malas, Spiro 1933- Baker 92
Malaschak, Dolores Boyer 1923- WhoWrEP 92
Malashevich, Bruce Peter 1952- WhoAm 92
Malashkin, Leonid 1842-1902 Baker 92
Malaska, Pentti Ensio 1934- WhoScE 91-4
Malaska, Stephen Lawrence Law&B 92
Malaspina, Alessandro 1754-1809 BioIn 17
Malaspina, Alex 1931- St&PR 93, WhoAm 92
Malaspina, Giovanni Battista Signorini See Caccini, Francesca 1587-c. 1626 OxDcOp
Malat, Alan 1944- St&PR 93
Malatesta, Enrico 1853-1932 DcTwHis
Malatesta, Mary T. 1946- St&PR 93
Malatesta, Peter d1990 BioIn 17
Malatestinic, Nicholas Patrick Law&B 92
Malatin, James A. 1942- St&PR 93
Malavasi, Fabio 1948- WhoWor 93
Malawer, Irving 1917- St&PR 93
Malawski, Artur 1904-1957 Baker 92, PolBiDi
Malawsky, Donald N. Law&B 92
Malaya, Ronald Penha 1951- WhoAm 92
Malba, Michael William 1946- WhoE 93
Malboeuf, John Alfred 1961- WhoEmL 93
Malbon, Craig Curtis 1950- WhoEmL 93
Malbon, Robert M. 1942- St&PR 93
Malbrain, Carl M. WhoScE 91-2
Malbrain, Carl Marie 1957- WhoWor 93
Malbrough, Ray Thomas 1952- WhoWrEP 92
Malby, Carsten 1950- WhoWor 93
Malby, Glenn St&PR 93
Malby, Heidi St&PR 93
Malcarne, Donald Leon 1933- WhoE 93
Malcarney, Arthur Edward 1942- St&PR 93
Mal'cev, Yuri Nikolaevich 1947- WhoWor 93
Malchaire, Jacques B.M. 1944- WhoScE 91-2
Malchodi, William B., Jr. Law&B 92
Malchos of Philadelphia fl. 5th cent.-6th cent. OxDcByz
Malchow, D.B. 1938- St&PR 93
Malcohn, Elissa WhoWrEP 92
Malcolm, Alan David McHarg 1948- WhoWor 93
Malcolm, Andrew Hogarth 1943- WhoAm 92, WhoE 93
Malcolm, Andrew I. 1927- ScF&FL 92
Malcolm, Beatrice Bowles BioIn 17
Malcolm, Bruce Gordon 1947- WhoAm 92
Malcolm, Dan MajAI
Malcolm, Donald 1930-1975 ScF&FL 92
Malcolm, Gail Baumgaertel 1954- WhoEmL 93
Malcolm, George (John) 1917- Baker 92
Malcolm, Ian Grenville 1938- WhoWor 93
Malcolm, J. Parke 1940- St&PR 93
Malcolm, Janet BioIn 17
Malcolm, Ronald Paul 1941- St&PR 93
Malcolm, Wesley R. 1934- St&PR 93
Malcolmson, Reginald d1992 NewYTBS 92
Malcolmson, Reginald 1912-1992 BioIn 17
Malcolm X 1925-1965 BioIn 17, DcTwHis, EncAACR [port]
Malcom, Grant ScF&FL 92
Malcomson, James Martin WhoScE 91-1
Malcomson, Scott L. 1961- ConAu 137
Malcor, Michael Joseph 1963- WhoEmL 93
Malcorps, H. WhoScE 91-2
Malcuzynski, Karol 1922-1984 PolBiDi
Malcuzynski, Witold 1914-1977 Baker 92, PolBiDi
Malczewski, Andrzej 1930- WhoScE 91-4
Malczewski, Antoni 1793-1826 PolBiDi
Malczewski, Jacek 1854-1929 PolBiDi
Maldeghem, Robert Julien van 1806-1893 Baker 92
Malden, Joan Williams 1931- WhoAmW 93
Malden, Karl BioIn 17
Malden, Karl 1914- IntDcF 2-3 [port]
Malden, Karl 1916- WhoAm 92
Maldere, Pierre van 1729-1768 Baker 92, OxDcOp
Malder Jamin, Francine Beverly 1946- WhoAmW 93
Maldini, Henry Carlos 1934- St&PR 93
Maldonado, Andres 1944- WhoScE 91-3
Maldonado, Betulio Leonidas 1946- WhoWor 93
Maldonado, Ellen Law&B 92
Maldonado, Gregory Matthew 1958- WhoWor 93
Maldonado, Irma 1946- NotHsAW 93
Maldonado, Jeffrey Arthur Law&B 92
Maldonado, Joseph G. Law&B 92
Maldonado, Otmara Lina 1944- WhoSSW 93
Maldonado Aguirre, Alejandro DcCPCAm
Maldonado-Bear, Rita Marinita 1938- WhoAmW 93
Maldonado-Moreno, Maria Delia 1946- WhoUN 92
Male, Donald Warren 1922- WhoSSW 93
Male, Mary Eileen 1949- WhoE 93
Male, Pete BioIn 17
Male, Roy Raymond 1919- WhoAm 92, WhoWrEP 92
Malea, Olga 1960- WhoWor 93
Malec, Alexander 1929- ScF&FL 92
Malec, Ivo 1925- Baker 92
Malec, John 1944- WhoAm 92
Malec, John William 1941- St&PR 93
Malec, Joseph, Jr. 1931- St&PR 93
Malec, Joseph, III St&PR 93
Malec, Michael Anthony 1940- WhoE 93
Malec, William Frank 1940- St&PR 93, WhoAm 92
Malec-DiGioia, Judith Mary 1955- WhoEmL 93
Malecela, John Samuel Cigwiyemisi 1934- WhoAfr
Malecela, John William Samuel 1934- WhoWor 93
Malecha, Marvin John 1949- WhoEmL 93
Malecki, Alfred 1921- WhoAm 92
Malecki, Cheryl Ann 1958- WhoEmL 93
Malecki, Edward Stanley, Jr. 1938- WhoAm 92
Malecki, Ignacy 1912- WhoWor 93
Malecki, Jean Marie 1953- WhoAmW 93, WhoEmL 93
Malecki, Jerzy Antoni 1933- WhoScE 91-4
Malecki, Madge Ann WhoAmW 93
Malecki, Richard Albert 1952- WhoSSW 93
Malecki, Wladyslaw Aleksander 1836-1900 PolBiDi
Maledon, Marilyn P. Law&B 92
Maledy, Linda Kay 1955- WhoEmL 93
Maleev, Atanas Hristov 1917- WhoScE 91-4
Maleev, Mihail WhoScE 91-4
Maleeva, Katerina BioIn 17
Maleeva, Magdalena 1975?- BioIn 17
Maleeva, Manuela BioIn 17
Maleeva, Yulia 1944?- BioIn 17
Malefakis, Edward E. 1932- WhoAm 92, WhoWrEP 92
Maleh, Edward B. 1951- St&PR 93
Maleh, Sam 1926- St&PR 93
Maleingreau, Paul (Eugene) de 1887-1956 Baker 92
Maleinos OxDcByz
Maleinos, Michael c. 894-961 OxDcByz
Malejan, Todd H. Law&B 92
Malej-Kveder, Sonja 1931- WhoScE 91-4
Malek, Ezzetta R. 1919- St&PR 93
Malek, Frank S., Jr. 1945- St&PR 93
Malek, Frederic Vincent 1936- WhoAm 92
Malek, James Stanley 1941- WhoAm 92
Malek, Marlene Anne 1939- WhoAmW 93, WhoWor 93
Malek, Zena Bella 1928- WhoAmW 93
Maleki, Nahid 1945- WhoE 93
Maleki, Parviz 1937- WhoUN 92
Malemud, Lee L. 1948- WhoAmW 93
Malenge, Jean-Pierre 1937- WhoScE 91-2
Malengreau, Paul (Eugene) de 1887-1956 Baker 92
Malenich, Linda Lou 1951- WhoWrEP 92
Malenka, Bertram Julian 1923- WhoAm 92
Malenkov, Georgi 1902-1988 ColdWar 2 [port]
Malenkov, Georgy Maksimilianovich 1902-1988 DcTwHis
Maler, Annie AmWomPl
Maler, Teobert 1842-1917 IntDcAn
Maler, Wilhelm 1902-1976 Baker 92
Malerba, Luigi 1927- WhoWor 93
Malerich, Edward P. ScF&FL 92
Malerich, Steven Floyd 1957- WhoIns 93
Malernee, James Kent, Jr. 1947- WhoWor 93
Males, Carolyn F. WhoAmW 93
Males, R.H. 1932- St&PR 93
Males, Rene Henri 1932- WhoAm 92
Males, William James WhoWor 93
Malesani, Gaetano WhoScE 91-3
Maleska, Eugene T. 1916- WhoAm 92
Maleska, Martin Edmund 1944- WhoAm 92
Maleski, Cynthia Maria 1951- WhoAmW 93, WhoEmL 93
Males-Madrid, Sandra Kay 1942- WhoAmW 93
Malesovas, Jerry L. Law&B 92
Malet, Arthur BioIn 17
Malet, Vincent Mills- ScF&FL 92
Maletsky, Evan Merle 1932- WhoE 93
Malettke, Klaus Ludwig Gustav 1936- WhoWor 93
Maletto, Silvano WhoScE 91-3
Maletz, Herbert N. 1913- CngDr 91
Maletz, Herbert Naaman 1913- WhoAm 92, WhoE 93
Malevich, Kazimir Severinovich 1878-1935 BioIn 17
Malewicki, Debra Suzanne 1954- WhoEmL 93
Malewitz, Bernard G. 1927- St&PR 93

Malewski, Jennifer Jean 1946- WhoAmW 93
Maley, Donald 1918- WhoAm 92
Maley, Louise Overstreet 1944- WhoAmW 93
Maley, Patricia Ann 1955- WhoAmW 93, WhoE 93
Maley, Patrick J. 1949- St&PR 93
Maley, Samuel Wayne 1928- WhoAm 92
Maley, Thomas Charles 1952- WhoEmL 93
Maley, William B. 1924- St&PR 93
Malfa, Horace M. 1933- St&PR 93
Malfas, Nicholas E., Jr. 1935- St&PR 93
Malfatti, Bartolomeo 1828-1892 IntDcAn
Malfitano, Catherine 1948- Baker 92, OxDcOp
Malfliet, R.A.R.L. WhoScE 91-3
Malgieri, Kathryn Driscoll 1951- WhoAmW 93
Malgoire, Jean-Claude 1940- Baker 92
Malgonkar, Manohar (Dattatray) 1913- ConAu 40NR
Malham, Nicholas Zachary 1937- St&PR 93
Malhame, Edmond C. d1992 BioIn 17
Malhammar, Goran 1938- WhoScE 91-4
Malherbe, Abraham Johannes, VI 1930- WhoAm 92
Malherbe, Charles 1853-1911 OxDcOp
Malherbe, Charles (-Theodore) 1853-1911 Baker 92
Malherbe, Dianne St&PR 93
Malherbe, Earl F. 1933- St&PR 93
Malherbe, Edmond Paul Henri 1870-1963 Baker 92
Malhi, Balwinder Singh 1944- WhoE 93
Malhotra, Naresh Kumar 1949- WhoSSW 93
Malhotra, Surin M. 1948- WhoAm 92
Malhotra, Tilak Raj 1932- WhoUN 92
Malhotra, Vijay Kumar 1931- WhoAsAP 91
Mali, Henry Allen Lord d1990 BioIn 17
Malia, Peter Justin 1951- WhoE 93
Malia, Thomas J. 1950- St&PR 93
Maliasenos OxDcByz
Malibran, Maria 1808-1836 OxDcOp
Malibran, Maria (Felicita) 1808-1836 Baker 92, IntDcOp [port]
Malicet, Alain Marcel 1947- WhoScE 91-2
Malick, Howard Morgan 1917- St&PR 93
Malick, Terrence 1943- BioIn 17, MiSFD 9
Malicki, Gregg Hillard 1947- WhoEmL 93
Malicky, Neal 1934- WhoAm 92
Malicoat, Jean Ann 1935- St&PR 93
Malietoa Tanumafili 1913- WhoWor 93
Maliff, John 1939- St&PR 93
Malik, Abdul St&PR 93
Malik, Abdul Hamid 1948- WhoWor 93
Malik, Adnan 1949- WhoUN 92
Malik, Arif H. 1968- St&PR 93
Malik, Chandra P. 1937- WhoUN 92
Malik, Gerald I. 1941- St&PR 93
Malik, Gerald Irvin 1941- WhoAm 92
Malik, Helen T. 1943- St&PR 93
Malik, Hussain Ghulam 1946- WhoE 93
Malik, Javed Zia 1958- WhoWor 93
Malik, Marek 1951- WhoWor 93
Malik, Muhammad Anwar 1940- WhoWor 93
Malik, Mukhtiar Singh 1912- WhoAsAP 91
Malik, Om Parkash 1932- WhoAm 92
Malik, Rabinder Nath 1934- WhoUN 92
Malik, Raymond Howard 1933- WhoAm 92
Malik, Rex 1928- ScF&FL 92
Malik, Shamim Ahmad 1958- WhoWor 93
Malik Saad Ullah Khan 1932- WhoAsAP 91
Malikshah 1055-1092 OxDcByz
Malin, David Frederick 1941- WhoWor 93
Malin, Howard Gerald 1941- WhoAm 92
Malin, Irving 1934- WhoAm 92, WhoWrEP 92
Malin, Kenneth William 1948- WhoE 93
Malin, Madonna M. Law&B 92
Malin, Michael Charles 1950- WhoAm 92
Malin, Nigel Anthony 1950- WhoWor 93
Malin, Patrick J. 1935- St&PR 93
Malin, Robert A. 1931- St&PR 93
Malin, Robert Abernethy 1931- WhoAm 92
Malin, Roni Sue 1939- WhoAmW 93
Malina, Judith 1926- WhoAm 92
Malina, Michael 1936- WhoAm 92
Malina, Witold 1937- WhoScE 91-4
Malinconico, S. Michael 1941- WhoSSW 93
Malindretos, John Nikolaou 1954- WhoE 93
Maling, Arthur (Gordon) 1923- WhoWrEP 92
Maling, George C., Jr. 1931- WhoWrEP 92
Maling, George Croswell, Jr. 1931- WhoAm 92, WhoE 93
Malingre, Th.M. 1929- WhoScE 91-3
Maliniak, Donald W. Law&B 92
Malinin, Mikhail Valentinovich 1955- WhoE 93
Malino, Jerome R. 1911- WhoAm 92
Malino, John G. 1939- St&PR 93
Malino, John Gray 1939- WhoAm 92
Malinoski, Frank Joseph 1954- WhoE 93, WhoEmL 93
Malinovskii, Aleksandr ScF&FL 92
Malinovskii, Roman Vatslavovich 1876-1918 BioIn 17
Malinovsky, Rodion 1898-1967 ColdWar 2 [port]
Malinowska, Lidia 1937- WhoScE 91-4
Malinowski, Andrea V. Law&B 92
Malinowski, Bronislaw 1884-1942 IntDcAn, PolBiDi
Malinowski, Bronislaw 1957-1981 PolBiDi
Malinowski, Bronislaw Kaspar 1884-1942 DcTwHis
Malinowski, Chester Joseph 1968- WhoSSW 93
Malinowski, Ernest 1818-1899 PolBiDi
Malinowski, Jordan 1923- WhoScE 91-4
Malinowski, Mike 1954- St&PR 93
Malinski, Mark A. 1955- St&PR 93
Malipiero, Francesco 1824-1887 Baker 92
Malipiero, Gian Francesco 1882-1973 Baker 92, IntDcOp, OxDcOp
Malipiero, Riccardo 1914- Baker 92, OxDcOp
Maliponte, Adriana 1938- Baker 92
Malis, David Herring 1957- WhoAm 92
Malis, Leonard Irving 1919- WhoAm 92
Malis, Louise 1921- WhoAm 92
Maliszewski, R.M. 1934- St&PR 93
Maliszewski, Witold 1873-1939 Baker 92, PolBiDi
Malitz, Sidney 1923- WhoAm 92
Malizia, Enrico G. 1926- WhoScE 91-3
Malizia, Samuel Joe 1954- WhoEmL 93
Maljan, Genrih 1925-1988 DrEEuF
Maljkovic, Darko 1935- WhoScE 91-4
Malkames, James Patterson, III 1950- St&PR 93
Malkasian, George Durand, Jr. 1927- WhoAm 92, WhoWor 93
Malkemes, Lois Constance 1940- WhoSSW 93
Malkerson, Elizabeth A. 1949- St&PR 93
Malkiel, Burton Gordon 1932- St&PR 93, WhoAm 92, WhoE 93
Malkiel, Nancy Weiss 1944- WhoAm 92
Malkiel, Yakov 1914- WhoAm 92
Malkiewicz, Michael Joseph 1948- WhoEmL 93
Malkin, Cary Jay 1949- WhoAm 92
Malkin, H. Louise Law&B 92
Malkin, Jacques 1875-1964 Baker 92
Malkin, Jerrold Allen 1959- WhoEmL 93
Malkin, Joseph 1879-1969 Baker 92
Malkin, Judd D. 1937- WhoAm 92
Malkin, Leonard E. 1946- St&PR 93
Malkin, Manfred 1884-1966 Baker 92
Malkin, Moses Montefiore 1919- WhoE 93, WhoWor 93
Malkin, Myron Samuel 1924- WhoAm 92
Malkin, Peter Laurence 1934- WhoAm 92
Malkin, Peter Z. BioIn 17
Malkin, Rachel Esther Law&B 92
Malkin, Roger David 1931- St&PR 93
Malkin, Stanley Lee 1942- WhoAm 92, WhoE 93
Malkinson, Carol E. Law&B 92
Malkinson, Frederick David 1924- WhoAm 92
Malkki, Pentti U. 1940- WhoScE 91-4
Malkki, Yrjo WhoScE 91-4
Malkmus, Lizbeth 1937- ConAu 139
Malko, Nicolai 1883-1961 Baker 92
Malko, Richard W. 1937- St&PR 93
Malkonen, Eino 1938- WhoScE 91-4
Malkonen, Pentti 1928- WhoScE 91-4
Malkov, Konstantin Viktorovich 1963- WhoWor 93
Malkovich, John BioIn 17
Malkovich, John 1953- HolBB [port], WhoAm 92
Malkovich, Mark Paul, III 1930- WhoAm 92, WhoWor 93
Malkovsky, Jeffrey M. 1956- WhoIns 93
Mall, James Richard 1952- WhoEmL 93
Mall, Kenneth George Law&B 92
Mall, Margaret Darphin 1943- WhoWrEP 92
Mall, Myron Merriell 1940- WhoSSW 93
Mall, William John, Jr. 1933- WhoAm 92
Malla, Krishana Bahadur 1941- WhoWor 93
Mallaby, Sebastian 1964- ConAu 138
Mallach, Aubrey 1905-1991 BioIn 17
Mallams, Rodney L. Law&B 92
Mallard, Carl Bruce 1947- WhoEmL 93
Mallard, Newton Joseph 1944- WhoE 93
Mallard, Stephen Anthony 1924- WhoAm 92
Mallardi, Joseph L. WhoAm 92
Mallardi, Michael Patrick 1934- St&PR 93, WhoAm 92
Mallarme, Stephane 1842-1898 BioIn 17
Mallary, Gertrude Robinson 1902- WhoAmW 93, WhoWor 93
Mallary, Raymond DeWitt 1898- WhoAm 92, WhoWor 93
Mallary, Robert 1917- WhoAm 92
Mallay, James Francis 1936- WhoE 93
Malle, Louis 1932- BioIn 17, MiSFD 9, WhoAm 92, WhoWor 93
Mallea, Eduardo 1903-1982 SpAmA
Malleck, Joseph William Law&B 92
Mallen, Ronald Edward 1942- WhoAm 92, WhoWrEP 92
Mallen, W. James St&PR 93
Mallenbaum, Allan Eliyahu 1931- WhoE 93
Mallender, Fred, II 1931- WhoAm 92
Mallender, William H. Law&B 92
Mallender, William Harry 1935- St&PR 93
Mallendick, Robert Jacob 1943- St&PR 93
Maller, Dennis Allen 1953- St&PR 93
Maller, Robert Russell 1928- WhoAm 92
Malleret, Louis 1901-1970 IntDcAn
Mallers, George Peter 1928- WhoAm 92
Mallery, Anne Louise 1934- WhoE 93
Mallery, Berrell WhoE 93
Mallery, Kathleen Joyce 1951- WhoAmW 93
Mallery, Richard 1937- WhoAm 92, WhoWor 93
Malleson, William Walter 1940- WhoE 93
Malless, Stanley 1914- St&PR 93
Mallet, Alexis, Jr. 1951- WhoEmL 93, WhoSSW 93
Mallet, Anthony Ivo WhoScE 91-1
Mallet, George DcCPCAm
Mallet, Jacques Robert 1945- WhoE 93, WhoWor 93
Mallet-Joris, Francoise 1930- BioIn 17, WhoWor 93
Mallett, A.W. 1917- St&PR 93
Mallett, Conrad LeRoy, Jr. 1953- WhoAm 92
Mallett, Daryl F. 1969- ScF&FL 92
Mallett, John W. 1831-1912 BioIn 17
Mallett, Norman St&PR 93
Mallette, Alfred John 1938- WhoAm 92
Mallette, Jacques 1957- St&PR 93
Mallette, Jennie A. AmWomPl
Mallette, Leo Albert 1953- WhoEmL 93
Mallette, Lila Gene Mohler 1931- WhoWor 93
Mallette, Malcolm Francis 1922- WhoAm 92
Malley, Eileen Law&B 92
Malley, Kenneth Cornelius 1934- WhoAm 92
Malley, Robert John Law&B 92
Malley, Robert Joseph 1923- WhoAm 92
Mallia, Joseph Carmelo 1945- WhoE 93
Mallick, Craig D. Law&B 92
Mallick, Kelley E. Law&B 92
Mallicoat, Frank H. 1925- St&PR 93
Mallie, Jean-Pierre 1937- WhoScE 91-2
Malliet, James W. St&PR 93
Mallin, Dea Adria 1942- WhoWrEP 92
Mallin, Jay 1927- WhoE 93
Mallin, Michael Curtis 1954- WhoE 93
Mallin, Sam 1923- St&PR 93
Mallinckrodt, George W. 1930- WhoAm 92
Malling, Heinrich Valdemar 1931- WhoSSW 93
Malling, Jorgen (Henrik) 1836-1905 Baker 92
Malling, Otto (Valdemar) 1848-1915 Baker 92
Mallinger, Burton Joel Law&B 92
Mallinger, Mathilde 1847-1920 Baker 92, OxDcOp
Mallinson, John Charles 1932- WhoAm 92
Mallinson, Naomi Ann 1945- WhoAmW 93
Mallinson, Nick BioIn 17
Mallinson, Sue ScF&FL 92
Mallion, Richard James 1940- WhoAm 92
Mallis, Barry A. 1946- WhoE 93
Mallison, Thomas C. 1941- St&PR 93
Mallius Maximus, Gnaeus fl. 105BC-103BC HarEnMi
Malloch, Theodore Roosevelt, Jr. 1952- WhoE 93
Mallo-Garrido, Josephine Ann 1955- WhoAm 92
Mallon, Barbara Anne 1958- WhoEmL 93
Mallon, David J. 1959- St&PR 93
Mallon, Edward John 1944- WhoIns 93
Mallon, Harry A. d1991 BioIn 17
Mallon, J.H. 1933- St&PR 93
Mallon, Jack 1925- St&PR 93
Mallon, John 1949- WhoScE 91-3
Mallon, John C. 1939- St&PR 93
Mallon, Mark 1951- St&PR 93
Mallon, Mary d1938 BioIn 17
Mallon, Maurus Edward 1932- WhoWrEP 92
Mallon, Meg WhoAmW 93
Mallon, Paul Frank 1925- WhoAm 92
Mallon, Robert James 1948- WhoEmL 93
Mallon, William George 1946- St&PR 93
Mallonee, Bruce Ervin 1918- St&PR 93
Mallory, Aileen Lucile 1917- WhoWrEP 92
Mallory, Alvin O. 1908- St&PR 93
Mallory, Arthur Lee 1932- WhoAm 92
Mallory, Charles King, III 1936- WhoAm 92
Mallory, Charles Shannon WhoAm 92
Mallory, Frank Bryant 1933- WhoAm 92
Mallory, Frank Linus 1920- WhoAm 92
Mallory, Harold D. Law&B 92
Mallory, J(ames) P(atrick) 1945- ConAu 136
Mallory, Jean Long 1962- WhoEmL 93
Mallory, Jeannine Marek 1958- WhoAmW 93, WhoWor 93
Mallory, John W. 1912- St&PR 93
Mallory, Joseph Samuel 1937- St&PR 93
Mallory, Lee W., III 1946- WhoWrEP 92
Mallory, Lewis ScF&FL 92
Mallory, Paul W. Law&B 92
Mallory, R. Mark 1950- St&PR 93
Mallory, Ray D. 1937- St&PR 93
Mallory, Robert Mark 1950- WhoAm 92, WhoEmL 93
Mallory, Stanley O. 1938- St&PR 93
Mallory, Troy L. 1923- WhoWor 93
Mallory, Veston H. 1933- St&PR 93
Mallory, Vincent Derek BioIn 17
Mallory, Virgil Standish 1919- WhoAm 92, WhoWor 93
Mallory, William Barton, III Law&B 92
Mallory, William Barton, III 1944- WhoAm 92
Mallory, William L. AfrAmBi [port]
Mallory, William Palmer 1925- St&PR 93
Mallott, Byron Ivar 1943- St&PR 93
Mallouk, Ann Marmon 1923- WhoAmW 93
Mallouk, Robert Salim 1926- WhoE 93
Mallove, Eugene Franklin 1947- WhoE 93
Mallowan, Agatha Christie ConAu 37NR
Malloy, Betsy Brownrigg 1952- WhoEmL 93
Malloy, Crystal Yvette 1964- WhoSSW 93
Malloy, Dale R. 1945- WhoAm 92
Malloy, Dennis Edward 1953- WhoEmL 93
Malloy, Edward Aloysius BioIn 17
Malloy, Edward Aloysius 1941- WhoAm 92, WhoWor 93
Malloy, Edwin Arthur 1926- St&PR 93
Malloy, Fred P. 1934- St&PR 93
Malloy, Gail Berkson 1932- WhoAmW 93
Malloy, Grace Louise 1959- WhoAmW 93, WhoEmL 93
Malloy, James B. 1927- St&PR 93
Malloy, James David 1955- WhoE 93
Malloy, James Matthew 1939- WhoAm 92, WhoSSW 93
Malloy, John Francis 1945- WhoAm 92, WhoE 93
Malloy, John R. 1932- St&PR 93
Malloy, John Richard 1932- WhoAm 92
Malloy, Joseph Thomas 1950- WhoEmL 93
Malloy, Kathleen S. Law&B 92
Malloy, Kathleen Sharon 1948- WhoAmW 93, WhoEmL 93, WhoIns 93
Malloy, Lillian Jenny 1901- WhoSSW 93
Malloy, Louise AmWomPl
Malloy, Michael Patrick 1951- WhoE 93
Malloy, Michael Terrence 1936- WhoAm 92
Malloy, Michele Law&B 92
Malloy, Pheobe Smalls 1954- WhoAmW 93, WhoSSW 93
Malloy, Ruth Lor 1932- WhoWrEP 92
Malloy, Suzanne Flint 1961- WhoAmW 93
Malloy, Tom 1950- WhoSSW 93
Malloy, William Manning 1922- St&PR 93
Malloy, William Michael 1960- WhoAm 92
Mallozzi, Edward J. 1945- WhoIns 93
Malluche, Hartmut Horst 1943- WhoWor 93
Mallum, Daniel William 1940- WhoAm 92
Malm, Daniel Joseph 1960- WhoSSW 93
Malm, David G. St&PR 93
Malm, James Royal 1925- WhoAm 92
Malm, Nancylee Wilson 1935- St&PR 93
Malm, Richard Lewis 1948- WhoEmL 93, WhoSSW 93
Malm, Rita P. 1932- WhoAmW 93
Malm, Roger Charles 1949- WhoEmL 93
Malm, Stephen M. Law&B 92
Malm, William P(aul) 1928- Baker 92

Malman, Bernard D. 1936- *St&PR 93*
Malmberg, David Curtis 1943- *St&PR 93*
Malmberg, James C. 1937- *St&PR 93, WhoSSW 93*
Malmberg, John Andrew 1944- *WhoAm 92*
Malmberg, John Holmes 1927- *WhoAm 92*
Malmberg, Torsten 1923- *WhoWor 93*
Malmborg, Anna-Stina 1929- *WhoScE 91-4*
Malmed, Leon *St&PR 93*
Malmed, Leon 1937- *WhoAm 92*
Malmen, Yngve 1955- *WhoScE 91-4*
Malmer, P. Nils J.A. 1928- *WhoScE 91-4*
Malmgren, Anders Helge Mikael 1945- *WhoWor 93*
Malmgren, Bjorn A. 1942- *WhoScE 91-4*
Malmgren, Carl D. 1948- *ScF&FL 92*
Malmgren, Dallin 1949- *BioIn 17*
Malmgren, Harald Bernard 1935- *WhoAm 92*
Malmgren, Rene Louise 1938- *WhoAmW 93*
Malmgren, Richard Clifford 1933- *St&PR 93*
Malmierca Peoli, Isidoro Octavio *WhoWor 93*
Malmin, Per Christian 1943- *WhoWor 93*
Malmio, Timo Jukka Antero 1946- *WhoWor 93*
Malmivuo, Jaakko A.V. 1944- *WhoScE 91-4*
Malmquist, Katherine Elizabeth 1958- *WhoEmL 93*
Malmqvist, Bjorn Edvard 1946- *WhoWor 93*
Malmqvist, Johan Lars 1964- *WhoWor 93*
Malmqvist, Magnus Waldemar 1947- *WhoWor 93*
Malmstrom, Ben Arne 1929- *WhoScE 91-4*
Malmstrom, Bo Gunnar 1927- *WhoScE 91-4*
Malmstrom, Lynn D. 1953- *St&PR 93*
Malmuth, Bruce 1934- *MiSFD 9*
Malnati, George Anthony 1946- *WhoEmL 93, WhoSSW 93*
Malo, Juan Alfredo 1932- *WhoUN 92*
Maloblocki, Gregory *Law&B 92*
Maloch, W.H., Jr. 1925- *St&PR 93*
Malock, Ronald Anthony 1944- *St&PR 93*
Maloff, Peter C. *Law&B 92*
Maloff, Saul 1922- *WhoWrEP 92*
Malofiejew, Michal 1934- *WhoScE 91-4*
Malojcic, Rajko 1944- *WhoScE 91-4*
Malone, Adrian *ScF&FL 92*
Malone, Alan Wayne 1951- *St&PR 93*
Malone, Annie M. 1869-1957 *BioIn 17*
Malone, Barbara E. 1930- *St&PR 93*
Malone, Bruce 1961- *BioIn 17*
Malone, Carol Cross 1941- *WhoSSW 93*
Malone, Charles Augustus *Law&B 92*
Malone, Dan F. 1955- *WhoAm 92*
Malone, Daniel Lee 1949- *WhoEmL 93*
Malone, Daniel Patrick 1953- *WhoEmL 93*
Malone, David Michael 1954- *WhoUN 92*
Malone, David Roy 1943- *WhoWor 93*
Malone, Dorothy 1925- *IntDcF 2-3, SweetSg D [port]*
Malone, Dorothy Ann 1931- *WhoAmW 93*
Malone, E. Maxwell 1937- *St&PR 93*
Malone, Edward Francis *Law&B 92*
Malone, Edward H. 1924- *WhoAm 92*
Malone, Edwin Scott, III 1938- *WhoAm 92*
Malone, Elmer Taylor, Jr. 1943- *WhoWrEP 92*
Malone, Francis Joseph 1937- *St&PR 93*
Malone, James Patrick 1942- *St&PR 93*
Malone, James Perry 1937- *WhoSSW 93*
Malone, James William 1920- *WhoAm 92*
Malone, Jan J. 1956- *St&PR 93*
Malone, Jean Hambidge 1954- *WhoAmW 93*
Malone, Jim 1947- *BioIn 17*
Malone, John *BioIn 17*
Malone, John C. 1941- *St&PR 93, WhoAm 92*
Malone, John E. 1943- *St&PR 93*
Malone, John F., Jr. 1958- *St&PR 93*
Malone, Joseph 1954- *WhoE 93*
Malone, Joseph James 1932- *WhoAm 92*
Malone, Joseph Lawrence 1937- *WhoAm 92*
Malone, Julia Louise 1947- *WhoAm 92*
Malone, Karl *BioIn 17*
Malone, Karl 1963- *WhoAm 92*
Malone, Keith Paul 1957- *St&PR 93*
Malone, Lloyd Alvin, Jr. 1964- *WhoEmL 93*
Malone, Marvin Herbert 1930- *WhoWrEP 92*
Malone, Mary Frances Alicia 1946- *WhoEmL 93*
Malone, Michael Christopher 1942- *WhoWrEP 92*
Malone, Michael G. *Law&B 92*
Malone, Michael Patrick 1951- *WhoWrEP 92*
Malone, Molly 1897- *SweetSg B [port]*
Malone, Monica 1953- *WhoE 93, WhoEmL 93*
Malone, Moses 1955- *WhoAm 92*
Malone, Nancy *MiSFD 9*
Malone, Pamela Altfeld 1943- *WhoWrEP 92*
Malone, Perrillah Atkinson 1922- *WhoAmW 93, WhoSSW 93, WhoWor 93*
Malone, Richard 1937- *WhoE 93*
Malone, Richard Frederick 1940- *WhoSSW 93*
Malone, Richard Wayne 1951- *WhoEmL 93, WhoSSW 93*
Malone, Robert *ScF&FL 92*
Malone, Robert J. 1945- *WhoAm 92*
Malone, Robert Roy 1933- *WhoAm 92*
Malone, Sue Anderson 1930- *WhoWor 93*
Malone, Terence S. *WhoAm 92*
Malone, Thomas Francis 1917- *WhoAm 92*
Malone, Thomas M. *Law&B 92*
Malone, Thomas P. 1956- *St&PR 93*
Malone, Tom 1947- *WhoEmL 93*
Malone, Wallace D., Jr. 1936- *St&PR 93, WhoSSW 93*
Malone, William *MiSFD 9*
Malone, William Curtis 1956- *St&PR 93*
Malone, William Grady 1915- *WhoAm 92*
Maloney, Andrew J. 1931- *BioIn 17*
Maloney, Carolyn Bosher 1948- *WhoAmW 93*
Maloney, Carolyn Scott 1950- *WhoAmW 93*
Maloney, Christopher W. 1958- *St&PR 93*
Maloney, Dennis Michael 1942- *St&PR 93*
Maloney, Dennis Michael 1951- *WhoWrEP 92*
Maloney, Edward Thomas 1943- *St&PR 93*
Maloney, George Thomas 1932- *St&PR 93, WhoAm 92*
Maloney, Gerald P. 1933- *St&PR 93, WhoAm 92*
Maloney, James Henry 1948- *WhoE 93*
Maloney, James Patrick 1940- *WhoSSW 93*
Maloney, James William 1940- *BiDAMSp 1989*
Maloney, John Alexander 1927- *WhoAm 92*
Maloney, John C. *Law&B 92*
Maloney, John C. 1943- *St&PR 93*
Maloney, John Frederick 1913- *WhoAm 92*
Maloney, John Timothy 1943- *St&PR 93*
Maloney, Joseph H. 1927- *St&PR 93*
Maloney, Joseph Henry 1927- *WhoAm 92*
Maloney, Kathleen R. *Law&B 92*
Maloney, Kristen W. 1957- *WhoEmL 93*
Maloney, Loran Dale *Law&B 92*
Maloney, Lucille Tinker 1920- *WhoAmW 93, WhoSSW 93*
Maloney, Mack *ScF&FL 92*
Maloney, Marilyn Clifford 1950- *WhoEmL 93*
Maloney, Mark A. 1957- *WhoIns 93*
Maloney, Mark James 1959- *WhoE 93*
Maloney, Marynell 1955- *WhoAmW 93, WhoSSW 93, WhoWor 93*
Maloney, Matthew C. *Law&B 92*
Maloney, Maureen Bertha 1967- *WhoAmW 93*
Maloney, Maurice Andrew, Jr. 1963- *St&PR 93*
Maloney, Michael B. *Law&B 92*
Maloney, Michael James 1942- *WhoAm 92*
Maloney, Michael Patrick *Law&B 92*
Maloney, Michael Patrick 1944- *St&PR 93, WhoAm 92*
Maloney, Miguel Guillermo 1938- *WhoWor 93*
Maloney, Milford Charles 1927- *WhoAm 92, WhoE 93, WhoWor 93*
Maloney, Neil J. *Law&B 92*
Maloney, Patricia M. 1950- *St&PR 93*
Maloney, Patrick John *Law&B 92*
Maloney, Paul 1942- *St&PR 93*
Maloney, Paul Joseph 1954- *WhoE 93*
Maloney, Robert B. 1933- *WhoAm 92, WhoSSW 93*
Maloney, Susan Yacher 1954- *WhoEmL 93*
Maloney, Therese A. 1929- *WhoIns 93*
Maloney, Therese Adele 1929- *St&PR 93, WhoAm 92, WhoAmW 93*
Maloney, William Gerard 1917- *WhoAm 92*
Maloney-Knauff, Patrice *Law&B 92*
Maloni, William R. 1944- *St&PR 93*
Maloof, Farahe 1921-1990 *BioIn 17*
Maloof, Richard C. 1945- *St&PR 93*
Malooly, William Joseph 1942- *St&PR 93*
Maloon, James Harold 1926- *WhoAm 92*
Maloon, Jeffrey Lee 1958- *WhoEmL 93*
Malory, Thomas 15th cent.- *BioIn 17*
Maloshevskii, Sergei Georgievich 1940- *WhoWor 93*
Malosky, S.S. 1923- *St&PR 93*
Malott, Adele Renee 1935- *WhoAm 92, WhoWrEP 92*
Malott, Alan Marc 1953- *WhoEmL 93*
Malott, B.N. 1913- *St&PR 93*
Malott, Dwight Ralph 1947- *WhoEmL 93*
Malott, James Raymond, Jr. 1917- *WhoAm 92*
Malott, Robert Harvey 1926- *St&PR 93, WhoAm 92*
Malotte, Albert Hay 1895-1964 *Baker 92*
Malouf, George S. 1942- *St&PR 93*
Malouf, Peter Joseph 1952- *St&PR 93*
Malouf-Cundy, Pamela Bonnie 1956- *WhoAmW 93, WhoEmL 93*
Malouff, Frank Joseph 1947- *WhoAm 92*
Malouin, Jean-Louis 1943- *WhoAm 92*
Malovany, Howard *Law&B 92*
Malovany, Howard 1950- *WhoEmL 93*
Malovec, Jozef 1933- *Baker 92*
Malowany, Moises Salomon 1934- *WhoE 93*
Maloy, Danita Loye 1946- *WhoEmL 93*
Maloy, Joseph T. 1939- *WhoE 93*
Maloy, Sean McAree 1958- *St&PR 93*
Maloy, Stephen A. *Law&B 92*
Malozemoff, Plato 1909- *St&PR 93, WhoAm 92*
Malpas, James Spencer 1931- *WhoScE 91-1*
Malpas, Robert 1927- *St&PR 93, WhoAm 92*
Malpass, Leslie Frederick 1922- *WhoAm 92*
Malphurs, Roger Edward 1933- *WhoWor 93*
Malquori, Alberto *WhoScE 91-3*
Malraux, Andre 1901-1976 *BioIn 17*
Malraux, Georges Andre 1901-1976 *BioIn 17*
Malriya, Radhakishan 1943- *WhoAsAP 91*
Malsack, James Thomas 1921- *WhoAm 92*
Malsbary, G. David 1941- *St&PR 93*
Malsch, Craig B. 1940- *St&PR 93*
Malshuk, Stephen K. *Law&B 92*
Malsky, Stanley Joseph 1925- *WhoAm 92, WhoWor 93*
Malson, Rex Richard 1931- *WhoAm 92*
Malson, Robert Allen 1944- *WhoAm 92*
Malson, Verna Lee 1937- *WhoAmW 93*
Malstrom, Robert Arthur 1950- *WhoSSW 93*
Malt, Carol Nora 1942- *WhoSSW 93*
Malt, Ronald Bradford 1954- *WhoEmL 93, WhoWor 93*
Malta, Demetrio Aguilera *ScF&FL 92*
Maltas, Michael *BioIn 17*
Maltby, Brant D. 1947- *St&PR 93*
Maltby, Frederick Lathrop 1917- *WhoE 93*
Maltby, Jack Allen *St&PR 93*
Maltby, John Newcombe 1928- *WhoWor 93*
Maltby, Lewis L. *Law&B 92*
Maltby, Per *WhoScE 91-4*
Maltby, Per Eugen 1933- *WhoScE 91-4, WhoWor 93*
Maltby, Peter Foote, Sr. 1942- *WhoE 93*
Maltby, Richard 1914-1991 *BioIn 17*
Maltby, Richard Eldridge, Jr. 1937- *WhoAm 92*
Malten, Therese 1855-1930 *Baker 92, OxDcOp*
Maltese, George John 1931- *WhoAm 92*
Maltese, John T. 1932- *WhoSSW 93*
Maltese, Louis d1990 *BioIn 17*
Malthus, T.R. 1766-1834 *BioIn 17*
Malthus, Thomas Robert 1766-1834 *BioIn 17*
Maltin, Larry 1941- *St&PR 93*
Maltlis, Peter Michael *WhoScE 91-1*
Maltman, Kim 1950- *WhoCanL 92*
Maltz, Albert 1908-1985 *BioIn 17*
Maltz, Andrew Hal 1960- *WhoEmL 93*
Maltz, Herschel 1929- *St&PR 93*
Maltz, J. Herbert 1920- *WhoAm 92*
Maltz, Margaret A. 1952- *St&PR 93*
Maltz, Michael David 1938- *WhoAm 92*
Maltz, Milton 1929- *St&PR 93*
Maltz, Milton Selwyn 1929- *WhoAm 92*
Maltzman, Irving Myron 1924- *WhoAm 92*
Maltzman, Marvin Stephen 1936- *St&PR 93*
Malueg, Sara Ellen 1932- *WhoAmW 93*
Maluf, Jeannette Yolanda 1961- *WhoAmW 93*
Maluf de Carvalho, Jose Antonio 1949- *WhoWor 93*
Malugen, Louise D. 1945- *WhoAmW 93*
Malura, Oswald 1906- *WhoWor 93*
Maluszynski, Miroslaw 1941- *WhoUN 92*
Malvache, Noel 1943- *WhoScE 91-2*
Malvasio, Paul John *St&PR 93*
Malvaux, Paul 1934- *WhoScE 91-2*
Malveaux, Julianne *BioIn 17*
Malveaux, Julianne Marie 1953- *WhoAmW 93*
Malvern, Donald 1921- *WhoAm 92*
Malvern, Lawrence Earl 1916- *WhoAm 92*
Malvestuto, Francesco Mario 1951- *WhoWor 93*
Malvezzi, Alberigo c. 1550-1615 *Baker 92*
Malvezzi, Cristofano 1547?-1599 *Baker 92*
Malvin, Frederick Bage 1932- *WhoSSW 93*
Malviya, Satya Prakash 1934- *WhoAsAP 91*
Malwitz, Donald Walter 1943- *St&PR 93*
Malwitz, James Edward 1940- *St&PR 93*
Maly, George J., Jr. *Law&B 92*
Maly, George Joseph, Jr. 1933- *St&PR 93, WhoAm 92*
Maly, Jiri 1899-1950 *IntDcAn*
Maly, Kurt John 1944- *WhoAm 92*
Maly, Radek 1964- *WhoEmL 93*
Maly, Vaclav *BioIn 17*
Malyan-Wilson, Peter John Edgar Malyan 1933- *WhoWor 93*
Malygin, Valery Vladimirovich 1939- *WhoWor 93*
Malyj, Laura Oresta 1951- *WhoEmL 93*
Malyon, Alan Kent 1941-1988 *BioIn 17*
Malysheff, G.A. 1951- *St&PR 93*
Malyshev, Vadim Alexandrovich 1938- *WhoWor 93*
Malyugin, Serguey Artem'jevitch 1951- *WhoWor 93*
Malzahn, Ray Andrew 1929- *WhoAm 92*
Malzberg, Barry N. *BioIn 17*
Malzberg, Barry N. 1939- *ScF&FL 92*
Mamada, Akira 1958- *WhoWor 93*
Mamalepot, Jean-Felix 1942- *WhoWor 93*
Mamaloni, Solomon 1943- *WhoAsAP 91, WhoWor 93*
Mamana, Joseph 1909- *WhoE 93, WhoWor 93*
Mamangakis, Nikos 1929- *Baker 92*
Mamantov, Gleb 1931- *WhoAm 92*
Mamas *OxDcByz*
Mamat, Frank Trustick 1949- *WhoEmL 93, WhoWor 93*
Mamatey, Victor Samuel 1917- *WhoAm 92*
Mamba, George Mbikwakhe 1932- *WhoAfr, WhoWor 93*
Mambon, Stephen B. 1945- *WhoAsAP 91*
Mambu-Ma-Disu, Dr. 1948- *WhoUN 92*
Mamdani, Ebrahim *WhoScE 91-1*
Mamdani, Iqbal Gulamhusein 1941- *WhoWor 93*
Mamelle, Nicole *WhoScE 91-2*
Mamelok, Alfred Edgar 1924- *WhoE 93*
Mamer, Stuart Mies 1921- *WhoAm 92*
Mamet, David *BioIn 17*
Mamet, David 1947- *MagSAmL [port], MiSFD 9*
Mamet, David Alan 1947- *WhoAm 92, WhoE 93, WhoWrEP 92*
Mamikonean *OxDcByz*
Mamiya, Michio 1929- *Baker 92*
Mamlet, Robin Gail 1960- *WhoE 93*
Mamlok, Ursula 1928- *Baker 92, WhoAm 92*
Mamluks *OxDcByz*
Mammel, Russell Norman 1926- *WhoAm 92, WhoWor 93*
Mammeri, Mouloud 1917-1989 *BioIn 17*
Mammi, Mario *WhoScE 91-3*
Mammi, Mario 1932- *WhoWor 93*
Mammitzsch, Volker 1938- *WhoWor 93*
Mammola, George C. 1940- *St&PR 93*
Mammone, Richard James 1953- *WhoEmL 93, WhoWor 93*
Mamo, George Elias 1935- *WhoE 93*
Mamon, Deborah Elaine 1966- *WhoEmL 93*
Mamon, Saleh *BioIn 17*
Mamoulian, Rouben 1897-1987 *Baker 92, MiSFD 9N*
Mampre, Virginia Elizabeth 1949- *WhoAmW 93, WhoEmL 93*
Mamrak, Sandra Ann 1944- *WhoAmW 93*
Ma'mun 786-833 *OxDcByz*
Mamut, Mary Catherine 1923- *WhoAmW 93*
Mamy, Jean 1935- *WhoScE 91-2*
Man, Cameron Robert James 1935- *WhoAm 92*
Man, Evelyn B. d1992 *NewYTBS 92 [port]*
Man, Piter *ScF&FL 92*
Manabe, Mitsuhiro 1926- *WhoAsAP 91*
Manabe, Shunji 1930- *WhoWor 93*
Manabe, Syukuro 1931- *WhoAm 92*
Manachini, Pier Luigi 1938- *WhoScE 91-3*
Manafort, Paul John 1949- *WhoSSW 93*
Manago, Joseph Nicholas 1954- *WhoE 93*
Manahon, Eugene *Law&B 92*

Manaker, Arnold Martin 1947- *WhoEmL 93, WhoSSW 93*
Manana, Ramon 1932- *WhoScE 91-3*
Manara, Luciano 1935- *WhoScE 91-3*
Manaras, John T. *Law&B 92*
Manard, Robert Lynn, III 1947- *WhoAm 92*
Manary, Richard Deane 1944- *WhoWor 93*
Manas, Oguz 1934- *WhoScE 91-4*
Manasarova, Aida 1925-1986 *DrEEuF*
Manasc, Vivian 1956- *WhoAmW 93, WhoEmL 93*
Manasrah, Mustafa Moh'd 1940- *WhoWor 93*
Manasse, Etan 1942-1991 *BioIn 17*
Manasse, Henri Richard, Jr. 1945- *WhoAm 92*
Manasse, Peter 1939- *St&PR 93*
Manassero, Henri J. P. 1932- *WhoAm 92*
Manasses, Constantine c. 1130-c. 1187 *OxDcByz*
Manaster, Melvyn Lee 1937- *St&PR 93*
Manatos, Andrew Emanuel 1944- *WhoAm 92*
Manatt, Charles T. 1936- *PolPar*
Manatt, Richard 1931- *WhoAm 92*
Manausa, Terry E. 1940- *St&PR 93*
Manay, R. Jayanth 1944- *St&PR 93*
Mana-Zucca 1887-1981 *Baker 92*
Manbeck, Harry Frederick, Jr. 1926- *WhoAm 92*
Manbeck, John Byron 1931- *WhoE 93*
Manberg, Richard I. 1938- *St&PR 93*
Manburg, Edwin 1924- *St&PR 93*
Manca, Gianni 1924- *WhoWor 93*
Manca, Vincenzo Giacomo 1949- *WhoWor 93*
Mancall, Elliott Lee 1927- *WhoAm 92*
Mancall, Jacqueline Cooper 1932- *WhoAmW 93*
Mancel, Claude P. 1942- *St&PR 93*
Mancel, Claude Paul 1942- *WhoAm 92, WhoWor 93*
Manchee, Katheryn Hait Dorflinger d1991 *BioIn 17*
Manchel, Frank 1935- *ScF&FL 92*
Mancher, Rhoda Ross 1935- *WhoAm 92*
Mancheski, Frederick J. 1926- *St&PR 93*
Mancheski, Frederick John 1926- *WhoAm 92, WhoE 93*
Manchester, Angela K. 1959- *WhoAmW 93*
Manchester, Carol Ann Freshwater 1942- *WhoAmW 93*
Manchester, David Fuller 1942- *St&PR 93*
Manchester, Edward Montagu, Earl of 1602-1671 *HarEnMi*
Manchester, Eli, Jr. *St&PR 93*
Manchester, Gilbert M. *Law&B 92*
Manchester, Gilbert Mott 1944- *St&PR 93*
Manchester, Glen P. 1952- *St&PR 93*
Manchester, H. E., Miss *AmWomPl*
Manchester, Kenneth Edward 1925- *WhoAm 92, WhoWor 93*
Manchester, Melissa 1951- *Baker 92*
Manchester, Robert D. 1942- *St&PR 93, WhoAm 92*
Manchester, Susan Jan 1945- *St&PR 93*
Manchester, William *BioIn 17*
Manchester, William 1922- *WhoAm 92, WhoWrEP 92*
Manchicourt, Pierre de c. 1510-1564 *Baker 92*
Manchisi, James 1957- *WhoEmL 93*
Mancia, Luigi 166-?-c. 1708 *OxDcOp*
Mancianti, Mario *WhoScE 91-3*
Manciaux, Michel *WhoScE 91-2*
Mancinelli, Bruce Regis 1946- *WhoSSW 93*
Mancinelli, Diane L. *Law&B 92*
Mancinelli, Luigi 1848-1921 *Baker 92, OxDcOp*
Mancinelli, Victor A. 1943- *St&PR 93*
Mancini, Alberto *BioIn 17*
Mancini, Anthony 1939- *ScF&FL 92*
Mancini, Brooks Thomas 1940- *St&PR 93*
Mancini, Elaine Carol 1953- *WhoE 93*
Mancini, Ernest Anthony 1947- *WhoSSW 93*
Mancini, Fiorenzo *WhoScE 91-3*
Mancini, Francesco 1672-1737 *Baker 92, OxDcOp*
Mancini, Henry 1924- *Baker 92, ConTFT 10, WhoAm 92*
Mancini, Jay August 1949- *WhoSSW 93*
Mancini, Louis Joseph 1950- *WhoWor 93*
Mancini, Mary Catherine 1953- *WhoAmW 93*
Mancini, Mary Elizabeth 1953- *WhoSSW 93*
Mancini, Michael J. *St&PR 93*
Mancini, Renato *WhoScE 91-3*
Mancini, Rose *Law&B 92*
Mancino, G. 1931- *WhoScE 91-3*
Mancino, John Gregory 1946- *WhoEmL 93, WhoWor 93*
Mancino, Peter Benedict *Law&B 92*
Mancinus, Aulus Hostilius fl. 180BC-169BC *HarEnMi*
Mancisidor, Jose 1894-1956 *DcMexL*
Mancke, Richard Bell 1943- *WhoAm 92*
Manclark, Charles Robert 1928- *WhoE 93*
Mancoff, Neal Alan 1939- *WhoAm 92*
Mancour, Stephen J. 1966- *WhoSSW 93*
Mancusi, Kathy Anne *Law&B 92*
Mancusi-Ungaro, Harold Raymond, Jr. 1947- *WhoSSW 93*
Mancuso, A.R. 1937- *St&PR 93*
Mancuso, Anthony J. 1941- *St&PR 93*
Mancuso, Dominick Joseph *Law&B 92*
Mancuso, Frank *BioIn 17*
Mancuso, Frank G. 1933- *WhoAm 92*
Mancuso, Gregory Jon *Law&B 92*
Mancuso, James Vincent 1918- *WhoWrEP 92*
Mancuso, Mary Katherine Teall 1964- *WhoAmW 93*
Mancuso, Richard A. 1939- *St&PR 93*
Mancuso, Ronald 1946- *St&PR 93*
Mancuso, Sam 1928- *St&PR 93*
Mancuso, Ted *ScF&FL 92*
Manczak, John Edward 1948- *WhoEmL 93*
Mand, Martin G. 1936- *St&PR 93, WhoAm 92*
Mand, Ranjit Singh 1956- *WhoWor 93*
Mandac, Evelyn (Lorenzana) 1945- *Baker 92*
Mandal, Sanat Kumar 1942- *WhoAsAP 91*
Mandanis, George P. 1927- *St&PR 93*
Mandart, Tracy Joseph, Jr. 1936- *St&PR 93*
Mandat, Eric Paul 1957- *WhoEmL 93*
Mandava, Nagejwara Rao 1955- *WhoE 93*
Mandel, Adley F. *Law&B 92*
Mandel, Alan M. 1942- *St&PR 93*
Mandel, Alan (Roger) 1935- *Baker 92*
Mandel, Alfred Jay 1952- *WhoEmL 93*
Mandel, Alice Solis *AmWomPl*
Mandel, Barry Irving 1943- *WhoE 93*
Mandel, Barry Jay 1946- *WhoEmL 93*
Mandel, Carola Panerai 1920- *WhoAmW 93, WhoWor 93*
Mandel, Charlotte *WhoWrEP 92*
Mandel, Eli 1922- *BioIn 17, WhoCanL 92*
Mandel, Ernest *BioIn 17*
Mandel, Francine Sharon *WhoE 93*
Mandel, Geoffrey 1959- *ScF&FL 92*
Mandel, Georges 1885-1944 *BioIn 17*
Mandel, Harold George 1924- *WhoAm 92, WhoE 93*
Mandel, Herbert Maurice 1924- *WhoAm 92, WhoE 93*
Mandel, Howard Marc 1950- *WhoWrEP 92*
Mandel, Irwin Daniel 1922- *WhoAm 92*
Mandel, Jack N. 1911- *St&PR 93, WhoAm 92*
Mandel, Jeff 1952- *WhoEmL 93, WhoWor 93*
Mandel, Jeffrey T. 1948- *St&PR 93*
Mandel, Jon 1944- *St&PR 93*
Mandel, Joseph C. 1913- *St&PR 93*
Mandel, Joseph David 1940- *WhoAm 92*
Mandel, K. Bates *BioIn 17*
Mandel, Karyl Lynn 1935- *WhoAmW 93, WhoWor 93*
Mandel, Leon, III 1928- *WhoAm 92*
Mandel, Leonard *WhoAm 92*
Mandel, Leslie Ann 1945- *WhoAmW 93, WhoWor 93, WhoWrEP 92*
Mandel, Lewis Richard 1936- *WhoE 93*
Mandel, Marcia Anne 1959- *WhoSSW 93*
Mandel, Maurice, II *WhoWor 93*
Mandel, Max A. 1914- *St&PR 93*
Mandel, Meyer 1913- *St&PR 93*
Mandel, Michel 1926- *WhoScE 91-3*
Mandel, Morton L. 1921- *St&PR 93*
Mandel, Morton Leon 1921- *WhoAm 92*
Mandel, Murray 1930- *St&PR 93*
Mandel, Norman Allan *Law&B 92*
Mandel, Oscar 1926- *WhoWrEP 92*
Mandel, Philip M. *Law&B 92*
Mandel, Richard E. 1958- *St&PR 93*
Mandel, Richard G. *Law&B 92*
Mandel, Richard Paul 1949- *WhoEmL 93*
Mandel, Robert *MiSFD 9*
Mandel, Robert C. 1926- *St&PR 93*
Mandel, Robert Jay 1926- *St&PR 93*
Mandel, Robert Livingstain 1957- *WhoEmL 93*
Mandel, Sally *BioIn 17*
Mandel, Siegfried 1922- *WhoAm 92, WhoWrEP 92*
Mandel, Stanley Wayne 1942- *St&PR 93*
Mandel, William E. 1953- *St&PR 93*
Mandel, William Kurt 1948- *WhoAm 92*
Mandela, Nelson *BioIn 17*
Mandela, Nelson Rolihlahia 1918- *WhoWor 93*
Mandela, Nelson Rolihlahla 1918- *DcTwHis, WhoAfr*
Mandela, Nomzamo Winnie 1934- *WhoWor 93*
Mandela, Winnie *BioIn 17*
Mandela-Amuah, Maki *BioIn 17*
Mandela Putra Hutomo *BioIn 17*
Mandelbaum, Bernard 1922- *WhoAm 92*
Mandelbaum, David Ben *Law&B 92*
Mandelbaum, David G. 1911-1987 *IntDcAn*
Mandelbaum, Dorothy Rosenthal 1935- *WhoAmW 93*
Mandelbaum, Frank 1934- *St&PR 93, WhoWor 93*
Mandelbaum, Gary 1949- *St&PR 93*
Mandelbaum, Harriet d1992 *BioIn 17, NewYTBS 92*
Mandelbaum, (Mayer) Joel 1932- *Baker 92*
Mandelbaum, Kathy Coons 1958- *WhoEmL 93*
Mandelbaum, Moshe Y. 1933- *WhoWor 93*
Mandelbaum, Paulette Ann 1947- *WhoAmW 93*
Mandelblatt, Michael *St&PR 93*
Mandelbrot, Benoit B. 1924- *WhoAm 92, WhoE 93*
Mandelert, Joseph C. 1925- *St&PR 93*
Mandelik, Nina 1933- *ScF&FL 92*
Mandelker, Daniel Robert 1926- *WhoAm 92*
Mandelker, Gershon *WhoE 93*
Mandelkern, Leo 1922- *WhoAm 92, WhoSSW 93*
Mandell, Allan Martin 1942- *St&PR 93*
Mandell, Arlene Linda 1941- *WhoAmW 93*
Mandell, Arnold Joseph 1934- *WhoAm 92*
Mandell, Barend Barnard 1927- *WhoWor 93*
Mandell, Betty Ellen 1936- *WhoSSW 93*
Mandell, Donald G. 1935- *St&PR 93*
Mandell, Edward Lewis *Law&B 92*
Mandell, Gary Lee 1957- *WhoEmL 93*
Mandell, Gerald Lee 1936- *WhoAm 92*
Mandell, Harry J. *St&PR 93*
Mandell, Mel 1926- *WhoWrEP 92*
Mandell, Muriel 1921- *BioIn 17*
Mandell, Patricia Athena 1952- *WhoWrEP 92*
Mandell, Peter H. *Law&B 92*
Mandell, Richard M. 1930- *St&PR 93*
Mandell, Richard S. 1953- *WhoWrEP 92*
Mandell, Samuel W. *Law&B 92*
Mandell, Samuel W. W. 1943- *WhoAm 92*
Mandella, Dennis George 1950- *WhoE 93*
Mandelli, Mariuccia *BioIn 17*
Mandel-Montello, George d1992 *BioIn 17, NewYTBS 92 [port]*
Mandelsberg-Weiss, Rose Gail 1956- *WhoAm 92*
Mandelstam, Charles Lawrence 1927- *WhoAm 92*
Mandelstam, Nadezhda 1899-1980 *BioIn 17*
Mandelstam, Stanley 1928- *WhoAm 92*
Mandelstamm, Jerome Robert 1932- *WhoAm 92*
Mandeltort, Stanley T. 1934- *St&PR 93*
Mander, Christine *ConAu 136*
Mander, Karel van 1548-1606 *BioIn 17*
Mander, Mary R. *ScF&FL 92*
Mander, Theodore Lionel d1990 *BioIn 17*
Mander, William Lewis 1947- *WhoEmL 93*
Manders, Karl Lee 1927- *WhoAm 92, WhoWor 93*
Manderscheid, Lester Vincent 1930- *WhoAm 92*
Manderson, Marge R. d1992 *NewYTBS 92*
Mandes, Ellen A. 1936- *WhoAmW 93*
Mandeville, Bernard 1670-1733 *BioIn 17*
Mandeville, Colin *ScF&FL 92*
Mandeville, Gilbert Harrison 1910- *WhoAm 92*
Mandeville, Mark David 1958- *WhoEmL 93*
Mandeville, Mary Delehanty 1941- *WhoE 93*
Mandeville, Robert Clark, Jr. 1927- *WhoAm 92*
Mandeville, Robert R. 1943- *St&PR 93*
Mandiargues, Andre Pieyre de 1909- *BioIn 17*
Mandic, Josip 1883-1959 *Baker 92*
Mandich, Donald Ralph 1925- *St&PR 93*
Mandicott, Grace Marie 1942- *WhoAmW 93*
Mandikian, Arda 1924- *OxDcOp*
Mandil, I. Harry 1919- *WhoAm 92*
Mandina, Michael Paul 1953- *St&PR 93*
Mandini, Maria fl. 178-?- *OxDcOp*
Mandini, Paolo 1757-1842 *OxDcOp*
Mandini, Stefano 1750-c. 1810 *OxDcOp*
Mandino, Og 1923- *ScF&FL 92, WhoAm 92, WhoWrEP 92*
Mandl, Alexander J. *BioIn 17*
Mandl, Bette 1940- *WhoE 93*
Mandl, David 1953- *WhoE 93, WhoEmL 93*
Mandl, Franz Joseph 1943- *WhoWor 93*
Mandl, Pierre-Emeric *WhoUN 92*
Mandl, Richard 1859-1918 *Baker 92*
Mandle, David Henry 1950- *St&PR 93*
Mandle, Earl Roger 1941- *WhoAm 92*
Mandler, George 1924- *WhoAm 92*
Mandler, Guy W. *Law&B 92*
Mandler, Jean Matter 1929- *WhoAm 92*
Mandler, Susan Ruth 1949- *WhoAm 92, WhoAmW 93, WhoE 93*
Mandlikova, Hana 1962- *WhoWor 93*
Mandly, Geoffrey Guy *Law&B 92*
Mando, Raymond A. 1935- *St&PR 93*
Mandoki, Luis *MiSFD 9*
Mandolia, Charles E. *Law&B 92*
Mandolini, Anthony Mario 1933- *WhoAm 92*
Mandolini, Luigi *WhoScE 91-3*
Mandour, Mohammed *BioIn 17*
Mandra, York T. 1922- *WhoAm 92*
Mandrake, Mark Wayne 1954- *WhoSSW 93, WhoWor 93*
Mandravelis, Patricia Jean 1938- *WhoAmW 93*
Mandrell, Barbara *BioIn 17*
Mandrell, Barbara (Ann) 1948- *Baker 92, ConAu 139, WhoAm 92, WhoAmW 93*
Mandri, Daniel Francisco 1950- *WhoWor 93*
Mandrioli, Dino Giusto 1949- *WhoWor 93*
Mandry, Paul William *Law&B 92*
Manduano, Joey Morgan 1947- *WhoSSW 93*
Mandujano, John Anthony 1955- *WhoE 93*
Manduke, Joseph *MiSFD 9*
Mandula, Jeffrey Ellis 1941- *WhoAm 92*
Mandula, Mark Stephen 1957- *WhoEmL 93*
Mandy, Ivan 1918- *BioIn 17*
Mandyczewski, Eusebius 1857-1929 *Baker 92*
Mandylor, Costas *BioIn 17*
Mandys, Vaclav 1951- *WhoScE 91-4*
Mandzia, William J. *Law&B 92*
Mane, Samba Lamine *WhoWor 93*
Maneatis, George A. 1926- *WhoAm 92*
Maneckji, Bhikhaji Maneck *Law&B 92*
Maneepairoj, Paitoon 1956- *WhoWor 93*
Mane Garzon, Fernando 1925- *WhoWor 93*
Manejias, Sergio 1909- *WhoWrEP 92*
Manejwala, Hameed 1953- *St&PR 93*
Maneker, Morton M. 1932- *WhoAm 92*
Manela, David 1955- *WhoE 93*
Manella, Daniel John 1925- *WhoAm 92*
Manelli, Donald Dean 1936- *WhoAm 92*
Manelli, Francesco 1594-1667 *Baker 92, OxDcOp*
Manen, Juan 1883-1971 *Baker 92*
Manenti, Thomas Joseph 1951- *WhoAm 92*
Maner, Charlotte Fawn 1951- *WhoEmL 93, WhoSSW 93*
Manera, Anthony S. 1940- *WhoAm 92*
Manera, Elizabeth Sturgis 1929- *WhoAmW 93*
Maneri, Remo R. 1928- *WhoAm 92*
Manes, Carl 1918- *St&PR 93*
Manes, Donald R. *BioIn 17*
Manes, Gina 1895-1989 *IntDcF 2-3 [port]*
Manes, Jack L., Jr. 1938- *St&PR 93*
Manes, John Dalton 1920- *WhoAm 92*
Manes, Michael Lewis 1946- *St&PR 93*
Manes, Nella Cellini 1920- *St&PR 93, WhoAm 92*
Manes, Rose Theresa 1923- *WhoAmW 93*
Manes, Stephen 1949- *ScF&FL 92*
Manes, Stephen Gabriel 1940- *WhoAm 92*
Manescu, Sergiu *WhoScE 91-4*
Manesh, Nancy L. Jacqueline *WhoSSW 93*
Maness, Alan Dean 1956- *WhoE 93*
Maness, Anthony Ray 1940- *WhoAm 92*
Maness, John D. 1920- *St&PR 93*
Maness, Sam A. 1907- *St&PR 93*
Manesse, Daniel Arthur 1921- *WhoWrEP 92*
Manet, Edouard 1832-1883 *BioIn 17*
Manetta, Richard Lawrence *Law&B 92*
Manetti, Mary Gorman *Law&B 92*
Maneval, Philip Aaron 1956- *WhoE 93*
Manewitz, Mark L. *Law&B 92*
Manewitz, Mark Lee 1946- *WhoEmL 93*
Manewitz, Sharon F. 1948- *WhoEmL 93*
Maney, Michael Mason 1936- *WhoAm 92*
Maney, Myra Annette Mintz 1962- *WhoAmW 93*
Maney, Thomas P. 1932- *St&PR 93*
Maney, William Jack 1949- *WhoIns 93*
Manfield, James J. 1940- *St&PR 93*
Manford, Barbara Ann 1929- *WhoAmW 93*
Manford, Morty d1992 *BioIn 17, NewYTBS 92*
Manfra, Jo Ann 1941- *WhoAmW 93*

Manfra-Marretta, Sandra 1949- *WhoEmL 93*
Manfre, Frank John 1957- *WhoE 93*
Manfred 1232-1266 *OxDcByz*
Manfred, Ernest *ScF&FL 92*
Manfred, Frederick Feikema 1912- *WhoAm 92, WhoWrEP 92*
Manfredi, Bartolomeo c. 1580-c. 1620 *BioIn 17*
Manfredi, John F. 1940- *WhoAm 92*
Manfredi, Joseph Francis 1935- *St&PR 93*
Manfredi, Mario Erminio 1934- *WhoWor 93*
Manfredini, Francesco 1688-1744 *OxDcOp*
Manfredini, Francesco Onofrio 1684?-1762 *Baker 92*
Manfredini, Giuseppe *OxDcOp*
Manfredini, Vincenzo 1737-1799 *Baker 92, OxDcOp*
Manfredini-Guarmani, Elisabetta 1786?- *OxDcOp*
Manfredonia, Catherine Carmela Bernitt 1946- *WhoAmW 93*
Manfro, Patrick James 1947- *WhoEmL 93*
Mang, Herbert Anton 1942- *WhoWor 93*
Mang, Warren George 1928- *St&PR 93*
Manga-Gonzalez, M. Yolanda 1949- *WhoScE 91-3*
Mangam, James Frederick 1946- *WhoEmL 93*
Mangan, Andrew Thomas 1955- *WhoSSW 93*
Mangan, Frank Thomas 1944- *WhoAm 92*
Mangan, James J. 1907- *ConAu 139*
Mangan, Jean 1934- *WhoWrEP 92*
Mangan, John Leo 1920- *WhoAm 92*
Mangan, Joseph Richard, Jr. *Law&B 92*
Mangan, Maureen Elizabeth 1955- *WhoAmW 93*
Mangan, Nancy Felix *Law&B 92*
Mangan, Patricia Ann Pritchett 1953- *WhoAmW 93, WhoEmL 93*
Mangan, Patrick Joseph 1958- *WhoE 93*
Mangan, Steve 1946- *St&PR 93*
Manganaris, Athanasios 1948- *WhoScE 91-3*
Manganaro, Francis Ferdinand 1925- *WhoAm 92*
Manganaro, James Lawrence 1939- *WhoE 93*
Manganello, Joseph James 1949- *WhoEmL 93, WhoSSW 93*
Manganello, Samuel John 1930- *WhoE 93*
Manganiello, Ronald James 1949- *St&PR 93*
Mangano, Joseph 1943- *WhoAm 92*
Mangano, Silvana *BioIn 17*
Mangano, Silvana 1930-1989 *IntDcF 2-3 [port]*
Mangapit, Conrado, Jr. 1946- *WhoEmL 93, WhoSSW 93*
Mangarella, James 1962- *WhoE 93*
Mangarelli, George E. 1943- *St&PR 93*
Mangas Coloradas d1863? *BioIn 17*
Mange, Franklin Edwin 1928- *St&PR 93*
Mangels, Arthur C. 1892-1966 *ScF&FL 92*
Mangels, John Donald 1926- *WhoAm 92*
Mangelsdorf, Harold G. 1907-1990 *BioIn 17*
Mangelsdorf, Jenny Lynn Moffitt 1957- *WhoEmL 93*
Mangelsdorf, Paul Christoph *BioIn 17*
Mangelsdorff, Arthur 1904-1990 *BioIn 17*
Mangelsen, William Paul 1943- *St&PR 93*
Manger, Warren Paul 1921- *WhoAm 92*
Manger, William Muir 1920- *WhoAm 92, WhoE 93*
Mangerud, Jan 1937- *WhoScE 91-4*
Manges, James H. 1927- *St&PR 93*
Manges, James Horace 1927- *WhoAm 92, WhoE 93, WhoWor 93*
Manghirmalani, Mona 1968- *WhoAmW 93*
Mangiafico, Josephine Mary 1916- *St&PR 93*
Mangiafico, Luciano 1938- *WhoE 93*
Mangiafico, Paul S. 1936- *St&PR 93*
Mangiagli, John Charles, Jr. 1954- *WhoE 93*
Mangiante, Gerard Andre 1946- *WhoWor 93*
Mangiaracina, Leonard 1939- *WhoE 93*
Mangiardi, Maureen Grace 1946- *WhoEmL 93*
Mangieri, John Nicholas 1946- *WhoAm 92, WhoSSW 93*
Mangieri, Robert Paul 1941- *WhoIns 93*
Mangieri, Samuel A. 1948- *WhoE 93*
Mangin, Charles Marie Emmanuel 1866-1925 *HarEnMi*
Mangin, P. *WhoScE 91-2*
Mangino, Angie Theresa 1949- *WhoEmL 93*
Mangino, Kristin Mikalson 1939- *WhoAmW 93*
Mangino, Matthew Thomas 1962- *WhoE 93, WhoWor 93*
Mangino, Robert Matthew 1936- *WhoIns 93*
Mangione, Barbara Ann 1958- *WhoAmW 93*
Mangione, "Chuck" 1940- *Baker 92, WhoAm 92*
Mangione, Jerre Gerlando 1909- *WhoAm 92, WhoWrEP 92*
Mangione, Patricia Anthony *WhoE 93*
Mangis, Donald E. 1937- *St&PR 93*
Manglapus, Raul S. 1918- *WhoAsAP 91, WhoWor 93*
Manglona, Benjamin T. 1938- *WhoWor 93*
Mango, Wilfred G., Jr. 1940- *St&PR 93*
Mangol, Leona Alvina 1942- *WhoE 93*
Mangold, Carl (Ludwig Amand) 1813-1889 *Baker 92*
Mangold, Charles Andre 1933- *WhoScE 91-2*
Mangold, Glenn E. 1942- *St&PR 93*
Mangold, H.K. *WhoScE 91-3*
Mangold, John Frederic 1927- *St&PR 93, WhoAm 92*
Mangold, Robert Peter 1937- *WhoAm 92*
Mangold, Sylvia Plimack 1938- *WhoAm 92*
Mangold, (Johann) Wilhelm 1796-1875 *Baker 92*
Mangon, Maureen Fielder 1951- *WhoAmW 93*
Mangone, Ann M. *Law&B 92*
Mangone, Dominic M. 1950- *St&PR 93*
Mangone, Gerard J. 1918- *WhoAm 92*
Mangoni, Alfonso 1929- *WhoScE 91-3*
Mangope, Lucas Manyane 1923- *WhoAfr*
Mangope, Lucas Manyane 1927- *WhoWor 93*
Mangor, Jorgen 1941- *WhoWor 93*
Mangouni, Norman 1932- *WhoAm 92*
Mangrum, Barbara Joy *Law&B 92*
Mangrum, Franklin Mayer 1925- *WhoSSW 93*
Mangrum, James Darrell 1966- *WhoSSW 93*
Mangrum, Richard Collin 1949- *WhoEmL 93*
Mangrum, Robert Glen 1948- *WhoSSW 93*
Manguel, Alberto 1948- *ScF&FL 92, WhoCanL 92*
Manguin, Henri Charles 1874-1949 *BioIn 17*
Mangum, Michelle Yvette 1964- *WhoSSW 93*
Mangum, T. Keith 1951- *WhoWor 93*
Mangum-Daniel, Elmira 1953- *WhoAmW 93*
Mangun, Turhan Karim 1938- *WhoUN 92*
Mangus, Carl William 1930- *WhoSSW 93*
Mangus, Larry Lee 1941- *WhoSSW 93*
Mangwende, Witness 1946- *WhoWor 93*
Mangwende, Witness Pasichigare Magunda 1946- *WhoAfr*
Manhar, Bhagatram 1938- *WhoAsAP 91*
Manhart, Marcia Yockey 1943- *WhoAm 92, WhoAmW 93, WhoSSW 93*
Manhattans *SoulM*
Manhattan Transfer, The *ConMus 8 [port]*
Manheim, Carl M. 1934- *St&PR 93*
Manheim, Carol Jean 1943- *WhoSSW 93*
Manheim, Jorol B(ruce) 1946- *WhoWrEP 92*
Manheim, Marvin Lee 1937- *WhoWor 93*
Manheim, Paul E. 1905- *St&PR 93*
Manheim, Ralph d1992 *NewYTBS 92 [port]*
Manheim, William V. *Law&B 92*
Manheimer, Alan Robert 1945- *St&PR 93*
Manheimer, Arnold L. 1945- *St&PR 93*
Manheimer, Bruce S. 1939- *St&PR 93*
Manheimer, Stephen R. 1941- *St&PR 93*
Manhertz, Huntley George 1938- *WhoWor 93*
Manhi, Daniel E. 1945- *St&PR 93*
Manhold, John Henry 1919- *WhoSSW 93*
Mani 216-c. 274 *OxDcByz*
Mani, Neel 1943- *WhoUN 92*
Mani, Raghunath Subra 1933- *WhoUN 92*
Maniaci, Elizabeth Hoffer 1955- *WhoAmW 93, WhoEmL 93*
Maniakes, George d1043 *OxDcByz*
Maniara, Dimis-Samuel 1949- *WhoWor 93*
Maniatis, George 1934- *WhoScE 91-3*
Maniatis, Thomas Peter 1943- *WhoAm 92*
Manibusan, Joaquin V. C. *WhoAm 92*
Manica, Victor Joseph *Law&B 92*
Manichello, Richard 1947- *WhoAm 92*
Manievich, Abraham 1883?-1942 *BioIn 17*
Maniewicz, Mario 1958- *WhoUN 92*
Manigat, Leslie 1930- *DcCPCAm*
Manigault, Earl *BioIn 17*
Manigault, Peter 1927- *WhoAm 92*
Manijak, Sandra A. 1948- *WhoAmW 93*
Manikas, Peter Michael 1946- *WhoEmL 93*
Manikowski, Jeanne Marie *Law&B 92*
Manilla, Jack 1941- *St&PR 93*
Maniloff, Jack 1938- *WhoAm 92, WhoE 93*
Manilow, Barry *BioIn 17*
Manilow, Barry 1946- *Baker 92, WhoAm 92*
Maninger, Ralph Carroll 1918- *WhoAm 92*
Manion, Daniel Anthony 1942- *WhoAm 92*
Manion, James R., III *Law&B 92*
Manion, James Robert, III *Law&B 92*
Manion, Jerry R. 1938- *WhoAm 92*
Manion, John E., III *Law&B 92*
Manion, John Richard 1933- *St&PR 93*
Manion, Michael Patrick *Law&B 92*
Manion, Sarah L. 1949- *St&PR 93*
Manion, Thomas A. 1934- *WhoAm 92*
Manion, William Joseph 1929- *St&PR 93*
Manire, George Philip 1919- *WhoAm 92*
Manire, James McDonnell 1918- *WhoAm 92, WhoWor 93*
Manire, Ross W. *St&PR 93*
Manis, Harriet Jo-Ann 1956- *WhoSSW 93*
Manis, Jimmy E. 1936- *St&PR 93*
Manis, Melvin 1931- *WhoAm 92*
Maniscalco, Joseph Stephen 1936- *St&PR 93, WhoAm 92, WhoIns 93*
Manischewitz, Bernard 1913- *WhoAm 92*
Manischewitz, David M. 1938- *St&PR 93*
Manisco, Joseph M. *Law&B 92*
Manishin, Glenn Brett *WhoE 93*
Manitius, Andrzej Zdzislaw 1938- *WhoAm 92*
Manitsas, Nikitas Constantin 1923- *St&PR 93*
Maniu, Iuliu 1873-1953 *DcTwHis*
Maniwa, Mitsuyuki 1934- *WhoWor 93*
Manix, John C. 1918- *St&PR 93*
Manji, Kurbanali Mohamed 1950- *WhoEmL 93*
Manjon, Maite *ConAu 38NR*
Manjon De Read, Maria Teresa 1931- *ConAu 38NR*
Manjos, Robert Michael 1944- *St&PR 93*
Manjura, Bonnie Doreen 1956- *WhoEmL 93, WhoSSW 93*
Mank, Gregory W. 1950- *ScF&FL 92*
Manka, Ronald Eugene 1944- *WhoAm 92*
Mankaba, David d1991 *BioIn 17*
Mankabady, Samir George *WhoScE 91-1*
Mankamyer, Jack L. 1931- *St&PR 93*
Mankaphas, Theodore fl. c. 1188-1205 *OxDcByz*
Manke, Dean Joseph 1949- *WhoE 93*
Manke, Dean V. 1949- *St&PR 93*
Mankell, (Ivar) Henning 1868-1930 *Baker 92*
Manker, Ernst M. 1893-1972 *IntDcAn*
Mankiewicz, Francis 1944- *MiSFD 9*
Mankiewicz, Frank F. 1924- *WhoAm 92*
Mankiewicz, Herman J. 1897-1953 *BioIn 17*
Mankiewicz, Joseph L. *BioIn 17*
Mankiewicz, Joseph L. 1909- *MiSFD 9*
Mankiewicz, Joseph Leo 1909- *WhoAm 92*
Mankiewicz, Tom 1942- *MiSFD 9*
Mankiller, Wilma *BioIn 17*
Mankiller, Wilma 1945- *ConHero 2 [port]*
Mankiller, Wilma Pearl 1945- *WhoAmW 93*
Mankin, Charles John 1932- *WhoAm 92*
Mankin, Hart Tiller 1933- *WhoAm 92*
Mankin, Helen Douglas *BioIn 17*
Mankin, Henry Jay 1928- *WhoAm 92*
Mankin, Jimmie Moore 1936- *WhoSSW 93*
Mankin, Robert Stephen 1939- *WhoAm 92, WhoE 93*
Mankiw, Deborah Roloff 1958- *WhoE 93*
Mankiw, Nicholas Gregory 1958- *WhoEmL 93*
Manko, Joseph Martin, Sr. 1939- *WhoAm 92*
Mankoff, Alan Howard 1933- *St&PR 93*
Mankoff, Ronald Morton 1931- *WhoAm 92*
Mankovska, Blanka 1942- *WhoScE 91-4*
Mankowitz, Wolf 1924- *ScF&FL 92*
Mankowski, Tomasz Piotr 1928- *WhoWor 93*
Manley, Albert Edward 1908- *WhoAm 92*
Manley, Albert Leslie 1945- *WhoUN 92*
Manley, Audrey Forbes 1934- *AfrAmBi [port], WhoAm 92, WhoAmW 93*
Manley, Barbara Lee Dean 1946- *WhoAmW 93*
Manley, Brenda Holsenbeck 1953- *WhoAmW 93*
Manley, Cathey Neracker 1951- *WhoAmW 93*
Manley, Charles G. 1944- *St&PR 93*
Manley, Charles Howland 1943- *WhoE 93*
Manley, David P. 1941- *St&PR 93*
Manley, Dexter *BioIn 17*
Manley, Donald Gene 1946- *WhoSSW 93*
Manley, Dorothy *AmWomPl*
Manley, Duncan John Russell 1938- *WhoWor 93*
Manley, Elizabeth *BioIn 17*
Manley, Frank 1930- *WhoAm 92, WhoSSW 93*
Manley, Geoffrey A. 1945- *WhoScE 91-3*
Manley, Geoffrey Allen 1945- *WhoWor 93*
Manley, Helen 1894-1987 *BioIn 17*
Manley, J.T. 1946- *St&PR 93*
Manley, Jo Ann Seagraves 1930- *WhoAmW 93*
Manley, Joan Adele Daniels 1932- *WhoAm 92*
Manley, Joey 1965- *ConAu 138*
Manley, John Frederick 1939- *WhoAm 92*
Manley, John H. 1907-1990 *BioIn 17*
Manley, John Hugo 1932- *WhoAm 92, WhoE 93*
Manley, Lance Filson 1945- *WhoSSW 93, WhoWor 93*
Manley, Larry Paul 1947- *WhoEmL 93*
Manley, Mark *ScF&FL 92*
Manley, Mark R. *Law&B 92*
Manley, Marshall 1940- *St&PR 93*
Manley, Michael 1924- *BioIn 17, DcCPCAm*
Manley, Michael A. *Law&B 92*
Manley, Michael Norman 1923- *DcTwHis*
Manley, Michael Norman 1924- *WhoWor 93*
Manley, Nancy Jane 1951- *WhoAmW 93, WhoEmL 93*
Manley, Norman *DcCPCAm*
Manley, Norman Washington 1893-1969 *BioIn 17, DcTwHis*
Manley, Richard Peter 1949- *WhoE 93*
Manley, Robert Edward 1935- *WhoAm 92*
Manley, Robert Merrill, Jr. 1947- *WhoWrEP 92*
Manley, Ruth *DcChlFi*
Manley, Seon 1921- *ScF&FL 92*
Manley, Walter Wilson, II 1947- *WhoSSW 93*
Manley, Will 1949- *BioIn 17*
Manley, William Tanner 1929- *WhoAm 92*
Manlich, Melchior 1513- *BioIn 17*
Manlius Vulso, Lucius dc. 216BC *HarEnMi*
Manlove, C.N. 1942- *ScF&FL 92*
Manlove, Robert Scott 1921- *St&PR 93*
Manly, David W. 1955- *St&PR 93*
Manly, Samuel 1945- *WhoSSW 93, WhoWor 93*
Manly, Sarah Letitia 1927- *WhoAmW 93*
Manly, William Donald 1923- *WhoAm 92*
Mann, A. Philo *ScF&FL 92*
Mann, Abby 1927- *MiSFD 9*
Mann, Alan Eugene 1939- *WhoE 93*
Mann, Alan Henry *WhoScE 91-1*
Mann, Alfred 1917- *Baker 92, WhoAm 92*
Mann, Alfred Kenneth 1920- *WhoE 93*
Mann, Andrew Hudson, Jr. 1947- *WhoEmL 93*
Mann, Anthony 1906-1967 *BioIn 17, MiSFD 9N*
Mann, Are 1925- *WhoScE 91-3*
Mann, Arline *Law&B 92*
Mann, Arthur 1922- *WhoAm 92, WhoWor 93, WhoWrEP 92*
Mann, Barry 1939- & Weil, Cynthia 1937- *SoulM*
Mann, Bartholomew Robin 1936- *WhoWor 93*
Mann, Benjamin Howard 1958- *WhoEmL 93, WhoWor 93*
Mann, Bernie *WhoAm 92*
Mann, Beth M. *Law&B 92*
Mann, Carol *BioIn 17*
Mann, Carroll Wesley 1927- *St&PR 93*
Mann, Carter Matthew *Law&B 92*
Mann, Catherine 1943- *ConAu 139*
Mann, Cecil 1923- *St&PR 93*
Mann, Cedric Robert 1926- *WhoAm 92*
Mann, Charles J. 1945- *St&PR 93*
Mann, Chelsea 1961- *WhoAmW 93, WhoEmL 93*
Mann, D. *WhoScE 91-1*
Mann, Daniel 1912-1991 *AnObit 1991, BioIn 17, MiSFD 9N*
Mann, David *WhoScE 91-1*
Mann, David George 1953- *WhoScE 91-1*
Mann, David Peter 1943- *WhoWor 93*
Mann, David Scott 1939- *WhoAm 92*
Mann, David Wayne 1950- *WhoEmL 93*
Mann, Del *ScF&FL 92*
Mann, Delbert 1920- *MiSFD 9, WhoAm 92*
Mann, Dennis Lee 1949- *St&PR 93*
Mann, Dick *WhoWrEP 92*

Mann, Edith Kerby 1946- *WhoEmL 93*
Mann, Edward Andrew 1932- *ScF&FL 92*
Mann, Emily Betsy 1952- *WhoAm 92*
Mann, F.W. 1856-1916 *BioIn 17*
Mann, Farhad *MiSFD 9*
Mann, Felice *BioIn 17*
Mann, Franklin Weston 1856-1916 *BioIn 17*
Mann, Frido 1940- *WhoScE 91-3*
Mann, Gail S. *Law&B 92*
Mann, Gary L. 1963- *WhoSSW 93*
Mann, Genevieve Coratti 1958- *WhoAmW 93*
Mann, George Stanley 1932- *St&PR 93, WhoAm 92*
Mann, Golo *BioIn 17*
Mann, Gordon Tyler 1936- *St&PR 93*
Mann, Hank 1888-1971 *QDrFCA 92 [port]*
Mann, Harold A. 1938- *St&PR 93*
Mann, Harvey Blount 1930- *WhoSSW 93*
Mann, Heinrich 1871-1950 *DcLB 118 [port]*
Mann, Herbie 1930- *Baker 92, WhoAm 92*
Mann, J.M. *St&PR 93*
Mann, J. Robert, Jr. 1930- *St&PR 93*
Mann, Jacinta 1925- *WhoAmW 93*
Mann, Jack Matthewson 1932- *WhoSSW 93*
Mann, James A. *ScF&FL 92*
Mann, James E. 1943- *WhoAm 92*
Mann, James Michael 1946- *WhoEmL 93*
Mann, James Michael 1949- *WhoSSW 93*
Mann, James Robert 1920- *WhoAm 92*
Mann, Jeff *WhoAm 92*
Mann, Jessica *Law&B 92*
Mann, Jim 1919- *WhoAm 92, WhoWrEP 92*
Mann, Jim 1955- *ScF&FL 92*
Mann, Joe E. 1922-1944 *BioIn 17*
Mann, Joel E. *Law&B 92*
Mann, Johannes F.E. 1949- *WhoWor 93*
Mann, John *WhoScE 91-1*
Mann, John 1928- *ScF&FL 92*
Mann, John Joseph 1951- *WhoEmL 93*
Mann, John M. *Law&B 92*
Mann, Jonathan Max 1947- *WhoAm 92*
Mann, Jonnie Yvonne 1939- *WhoAmW 93*
Mann, Karen 1942- *WhoAmW 93*
Mann, Katherine Kelly 1942- *WhoWrEP 92*
Mann, Kenneth Henry 1923- *WhoAm 92*
Mann, Kenneth Walker 1914- *WhoAm 92, WhoE 93*
Mann, Klaus 1906-1949 *BioIn 17*
Mann, Laura Susan 1958- *WhoAmW 93*
Mann, Laurie D.T. *ScF&FL 92*
Mann, Lawrence Duane 1935- *WhoSSW 93*
Mann, Lawrence Langston 1935- *St&PR 93*
Mann, Leslie (Douglas) 1923-1977 *Baker 92*
Mann, Lisa Beth *Law&B 92*
Mann, Lisa Gay 1962- *WhoAmW 93*
Mann, Lois 1950- *WhoAmW 93*
Mann, Lowell Kimsey 1917- *WhoAm 92*
Mann, Madeline *BioIn 17*
Mann, Marion 1920- *WhoAm 92*
Mann, Marvin L. 1933- *St&PR 93, WhoAm 92*
Mann, Maurice 1929- *WhoAm 92*
Mann, Maurice 1929-1990 *BioIn 17*
Mann, Michael *MiSFD 9*
Mann, Michael Martin 1939- *St&PR 93, WhoAm 92, WhoWor 93*
Mann, Milton 1922- *St&PR 93*
Mann, Mimi *BioIn 17*
Mann, N. David 1944- *St&PR 93*
Mann, Nathan Huguenor 1948- *WhoEmL 93*
Mann, Ned 1955- *WhoWrEP 92*
Mann, Norman 1930- *St&PR 93*
Mann, Oscar 1934- *WhoE 93*
Mann, P. Thomas 1947- *WhoSSW 93*
Mann, Paul *ScF&FL 92*
Mann, Peggy *BioIn 17, WhoAm 92*
Mann, Peter *ScF&FL 92*
Mann, Peter C. 1942- *St&PR 93*
Mann, Philip Roy 1948- *WhoEmL 93*
Mann, Phillip 1942- *ScF&FL 92*
Mann, Prem Singh 1947- *WhoE 93, WhoWor 93*
Mann, R. Bronson *Law&B 92*
Mann, Richard D. 1935- *St&PR 93*
Mann, Richard Dale 1931- *WhoWrEP 92*
Mann, Richard O'Brian 1946- *WhoEmL 93*
Mann, Richard Otto 1933- *WhoE 93*
Mann, Robert A. 1926- *St&PR 93*
Mann, Robert E. 1954- *St&PR 93*
Mann, Robert James 1951- *WhoEmL 93*
Mann, Robert M. *Law&B 92*
Mann, Robert (Nathaniel) 1920- *Baker 92, WhoAm 92*
Mann, Robert W., Jr. 1953- *St&PR 93*
Mann, Robert Wellesley 1924- *WhoAm 92*
Mann, Robert Wellesley, Jr. 1953- *WhoAm 92*
Mann, Roger Ellis 1948- *WhoE 93, WhoEmL 93*
Mann, Roger Leslie 1952- *WhoSSW 93*
Mann, Ron *BioIn 17*
Mann, Ron 1958- *MiSFD 9*
Mann, Sally *NewYTBS 92 [port]*
Mann, Seymour Zalmon 1921- *WhoAm 92*
Mann, Stephen Ashby 1947- *WhoEmL 93, WhoSSW 93*
Mann, Stephen L. 1938- *St&PR 93*
Mann, Stewart 1948- *WhoWor 93*
Mann, Susan 1941- *WhoAmW 93*
Mann, Susan M. *Law&B 92*
Mann, Susan S. *Law&B 92*
Mann, Ted *ScF&FL 92*
Mann, Theodore 1924- *WhoAm 92*
Mann, Theodore R. 1928- *WhoAm 92*
Mann, Thomas 1875-1955 *BioIn 17, MagSWL [port], OxDcOp, WorLitC [port]*
Mann, Thomas Edward 1944- *WhoAm 92*
Mann, Timothy 1942- *WhoAm 92*
Mann, Tom 1856-1941 *BioIn 17*
Mann, V. James *Law&B 92*
Mann, William Darrol 1949- *WhoSSW 93*
Mann, William E. 1929- *St&PR 93*
Mann, William F. 1917-1991 *BioIn 17*
Mann, William George 1934- *WhoE 93*
Mann, William Houston 1926- *St&PR 93*
Mann, William J.C. 1942- *St&PR 93*
Mann, William Jaggard 1942- *WhoAm 92*
Mann, William (Somervell) 1924-1989 *Baker 92*
Manna, Daniel Carl 1947- *St&PR 93*
Manna, Frank J. 1935- *St&PR 93*
Manna, Raffaele 1950- *WhoWor 93*
Manna, Ronald *St&PR 93*
Mannas, A.D.S. *WhoScE 91-1*
Manne, Alan S. 1925- *WhoAm 92*
Manne, Henry Girard 1928- *WhoAm 92, WhoSSW 93*
Manne, Rolf 1938- *WhoScE 91-4*
Manne, Shelly 1920-1984 *Baker 92*
Manneke, Daan 1939- *Baker 92*
Manner, Harold F. 1957- *St&PR 93*
Manner, Wendell A. 1924- *St&PR 93*
Mannerheim, Carl Gustav Emil, Baron von 1867-1951 *DcTwHis*
Mannerheim, Carl Gustav Emil von 1867-1951 *HarEnMi*
Mannering, Jerry Vincent 1929- *WhoAm 92*
Mannerkoski, Markku Berndt Veikko 1936- *WhoScE 91-4, WhoWor 93*
Manners, Charles 1857-1935 *Baker 92, OxDcOp*
Manners, George Emanuel 1910- *WhoAm 92*
Manners, Herbert Carl 1948- *WhoE 93*
Manners, Kim *MiSFD 9*
Manners, Paul E. 1918- *St&PR 93*
Manners, Robert Alan 1913- *WhoAm 92*
Manners, Sheila 1911- *SweetSg C [port]*
Manners, Timothy George 1957- *WhoE 93, WhoEmL 93*
Mannes, Barry Leonard 1939- *St&PR 93*
Mannes, Clara Damrosch 1869-1948 *Baker 92*
Mannes, David 1866-1959 *Baker 92*
Mannes, Elena Sabin 1943- *WhoAm 92, WhoAmW 93*
Mannes, Leopold (Damrosch) 1899-1964 *Baker 92*
Mannes, Londell Fredrick 1938- *St&PR 93*
Mannes, Marya 1904- *AmWomPl*
Mannes, Marya 1904-1990 *BioIn 17, ScF&FL 92*
Manney, Jimmy Darrell 1957- *WhoEmL 93*
Mannheim, L. Andrew 1925-1991 *BioIn 17*
Mannheimer, Isaak Noah 1793-1865 *BioIn 17*
Mannheimer, Lee R. 1943- *St&PR 93*
Mannheimer, Renato 1947- *WhoWor 93*
Mannherz, Hans G. 1943- *WhoScE 91-3*
Manni, Corrado 1923- *WhoScE 91-3*
Mannick, John Anthony 1928- *WhoAm 92, WhoWor 93*
Mannikainen, Osmo Tapio 1944- *WhoWor 93*
Mannin, Ethel 1900-1984 *ScF&FL 92*
Manning, Arthur Brewster 1913- *WhoAm 92*
Manning, Audrey Smoak *ScF&FL 92*
Manning, Bernadette Mary *Law&B 92*
Manning, Bernard *Law&B 92, St&PR 93*
Manning, Bertina Suida d1992 *NewYTBS 92*
Manning, Bonnie Lee 1958- *WhoEmL 93*
Manning, Brian *BioIn 17*
Manning, Burt *WhoAm 92, WhoE 93*
Manning, Burt 1931- *St&PR 93*
Manning, Catherine Marie 1938- *WhoAmW 93*
Manning, Charles Terrill 1925- *WhoAm 92*
Manning, Charles W. 1948- *WhoSSW 93*
Manning, Christopher Ashley 1945- *WhoWor 93*
Manning, Clarence B. *Law&B 92*
Manning, Cynthia Riette 1925- *WhoAmW 93*
Manning, Daniel Ricardo 1966- *BiDAMSp 1989*
Manning, Darrell V. 1932- *WhoAm 92*
Manning, David Lee 1950- *WhoSSW 93*
Manning, Dennis J. 1947- *St&PR 93*
Manning, Dick 1912-1991 *BioIn 17*
Manning, Donald O. *WhoAm 92*
Manning, Donald S. 1922- *St&PR 93*
Manning, Donald W. 1927- *St&PR 93*
Manning, Donald Waddington 1927- *WhoAm 92*
Manning, Dorothy *WhoAmW 93*
Manning, E. Baines 1940- *St&PR 93*
Manning, Ecton R. *Law&B 92*
Manning, Ellis E. 1933- *WhoAm 92, WhoIns 93*
Manning, Eric 1940- *WhoAm 92*
Manning, Eugene Baines 1940- *WhoAm 92*
Manning, Eugene Randolph 1942- *St&PR 93*
Manning, Farley 1909- *WhoAm 92, WhoWor 93*
Manning, Frank Arthur 1946- *WhoAm 92*
Manning, Frank E. 1919- *St&PR 93*
Manning, Frederic 1887?-1935 *BioIn 17*
Manning, Frederick J. 1947- *WhoIns 93*
Manning, Frederick William 1924- *WhoAm 92*
Manning, Guy *BioIn 17*
Manning, Henry Edward 1808-1892 *BioIn 17*
Manning, Henry Eugene 1935- *WhoAm 92*
Manning, Irwin 1929- *WhoE 93*
Manning, J. Frank, Jr. *Law&B 92*
Manning, Jack 1920- *WhoAm 92*
Manning, James Forrest 1929- *WhoAm 92*
Manning, James H., Jr. *Law&B 92*
Manning, James Matthew 1939- *WhoE 93*
Manning, James P. *Law&B 92*
Manning, James V. *St&PR 93*
Manning, Jane (Marian) 1938- *Baker 92*
Manning, Janet Mary 1952- *WhoAmW 93*
Manning, Jerome Alan 1929- *WhoAm 92*
Manning, Jim 1845?-1915 *BioIn 17*
Manning, Joan Elizabeth 1953- *WhoAmW 93*
Manning, John B., Jr. *Law&B 92*
Manning, John Patrick, V *Law&B 92*
Manning, Joseph A. 1946- *WhoAm 92*
Manning, Joseph A., III 1946- *St&PR 93*
Manning, Julia W. *Law&B 92*
Manning, Kathleen Lockhart 1890-1951 *Baker 92*
Manning, Kenneth P. 1942- *St&PR 93*
Manning, Kenneth Paul 1942- *WhoAm 92*
Manning, Laurance Rodney *Law&B 92*
Manning, Laurence 1899-1972 *ScF&FL 92*
Manning, Leah Perrett 1886-1977 *BioIn 17*
Manning, Lillian O'Neal 1956- *WhoWrEP 92*
Manning, Lisa Ellen *Law&B 92*
Manning, Lorita Gail 1946- *WhoSSW 93*
Manning, Lynn *BioIn 17*
Manning, Madeline *BlkAmWO [port]*
Manning, Marguerite *WhoAmW 93, WhoWor 93*
Manning, Marie 1873-1945 *AmWomPl, JrnUS*
Manning, Mary Kathleen 1963- *WhoSSW 93*
Manning, Michael P. 1943- *St&PR 93*
Manning, Michelle *MiSFD 9*
Manning, Myrtle Marion 1921- *St&PR 93*
Manning, Noel Thomas 1939- *WhoAm 92*
Manning, Olivia *BioIn 17*
Manning, Patricia Anne 1939- *WhoAmW 93*
Manning, Patricia Bryden *Law&B 92*
Manning, Patricia Kamaras 1953- *WhoAmW 93, WhoEmL 93, WhoWor 93*
Manning, Patrick 1946- *DcCPCAm*
Manning, Patrick Augustus Mervyn 1946- *WhoWor 93*
Manning, Peter Kirby 1940- *WhoAm 92, WhoWor 93*
Manning, Preston *BioIn 17*
Manning, Ralph Fabian 1945- *WhoAm 92*
Manning, Randolph H. 1947- *WhoE 93, WhoEmL 93*
Manning, Robert E. 1936- *St&PR 93*
Manning, Robert Edward 1946- *St&PR 93*
Manning, Robert Jeffrey *Law&B 92*
Manning, Robert John 1942- *St&PR 93*
Manning, Robert Joseph 1919- *WhoAm 92*
Manning, Robert Thomas 1927- *WhoAm 92*
Manning, Roger Warren 1944- *WhoSSW 93*
Manning, Ronald Lee 1951- *WhoEmL 93*
Manning, Rose Therese 1960- *WhoE 93*
Manning, Sandra Kay 1951- *WhoAmW 93, WhoEmL 93*
Manning, Sylvia 1943- *WhoAm 92*
Manning, Thomas 1772-1840 *Expl 93*
Manning, Thomas Joseph 1955- *WhoEmL 93*
Manning, Thomas Michael 1939- *St&PR 93*
Manning, Toni Ruth 1946- *WhoEmL 93*
Manning, Victor Patrick 1945- *St&PR 93*
Manning, Walter Scott 1933- *WhoSSW 93, WhoWor 93*
Manning, Walter Scott, Sr. 1912- *WhoSSW 93*
Manning, Warren J. 1957- *WhoE 93*
Manning, William Beckwith, III 1943- *WhoAm 92*
Manning, William Dudley, Jr. 1934- *WhoAm 92*
Manning, William Frank, Jr. 1965- *St&PR 93*
Manning, William Frederick 1920- *WhoAm 92*
Manning, William George 1923- *WhoE 93*
Manning, William Harry *WhoScE 91-1*
Manning, William Joseph 1926- *WhoAm 92*
Manning, William Raymond 1920- *WhoAm 92*
Manning, William Sinkler 1925- *St&PR 93*
Manning, Winton Howard 1930- *WhoAm 92, WhoE 93*
Manninger, Jeno 1918- *WhoScE 91-4*
Manning-Sanders, Ruth 1888-1988 *ScF&FL 92*
Manning-Sanders, Ruth 1895?-1988 *MajAI [port], SmATA 73 [port]*
Mannino, Anthony Colegero 1920- *WhoE 93*
Mannino, Edward Francis 1941- *WhoAm 92*
Mannino, Franco 1924- *Baker 92*
Mannion, Joan 1942- *WhoAmW 93*
Mannion, John F.X. 1932- *St&PR 93, WhoIns 93*
Mannion, John Francis Xavier 1932- *WhoAm 92*
Mannion, Michael *ScF&FL 92*
Mannion, Richard James *Law&B 92*
Mannis, Bob D. *Law&B 92*
Mannisto, Pekka T. 1976- *WhoScE 91-4*
Mannix, Bernadette Louise 1963- *WhoAmW 93*
Mannix, Daniel P. 1911-1984 *ScF&FL 92*
Mannix, Daniel Pratt 1842-1894 *BioIn 17*
Mannix, Frederick Phillip 1942- *St&PR 93*
Mannix, James G. 1941- *St&PR 93*
Mannix, James J. 1939- *St&PR 93*
Mannix, Mary Katherine 1960- *WhoE 93*
Mannix, Robert W. *Law&B 92*
Mannlein, Sally J. 1949- *WhoAmW 93*
Mannlein, William John 1935- *St&PR 93*
Manno, Bruno Victor 1947- *WhoE 93*
Manno, M.V. 1926- *St&PR 93*
Manno, Ned C. 1932- *St&PR 93*
Manno, Samuel F. 1940- *St&PR 93*
Manno, Theodore Paul *Law&B 92*
Mannon, Warwick 1914-1988 *ScF&FL 92*
Mannon, William H. 1921- *St&PR 93*
Mannonen, Matti 1954- *WhoScE 91-4*
Mannoni, Raymond 1921- *WhoAm 92*
Mannossos, Michael William 1930- *WhoWrEP 92*
Manns, August (Friedrich) 1825-1907 *Baker 92*
Manns, Carolyn Morrow *BioIn 17*
Manns, David G. 1945- *St&PR 93*
Mannschreck, Stephen L. 1945- *St&PR 93*
Mannsfeld, Sven Peter 1935- *St&PR 93*
Mannstrom, Bo *WhoScE 91-4*
Manny, Carter Hugh, Jr. 1918- *WhoAm 92*
Manny, Coto *MiSFD 9*
Mano, D. Keith *BioIn 17*
Mano, D. Keith 1942- *WhoWrEP 92*
Manocchi, James Charles 1953- *WhoE 93*
Manocchio, Vivienne Cinda 1949- *WhoSSW 93*
Manoff, Dinah *BioIn 17*
Manoff, Dinah Beth *WhoAm 92, WhoAmW 93*
Manoff, Lawrence M. *Law&B 92*
Manoff, Richard Kalman 1916- *WhoAm 92*
Manogue, Helen Smith 1931- *St&PR 93*
Manoharan, Thomas 1935- *WhoE 93*
Manojlovic, Kosta 1890-1949 *Baker 92*
Manolidis, Leonidas 1924- *WhoScE 91-3*
Manolis, James William 1960- *WhoEmL 93*
Manolo 1876-1945 *BioIn 17*

Manolov, Emanuil 1860-1902 OxDcOp
Manolov, Stephan 1925- WhoScE 91-4
Manoogian, Margaret Ann 1938- WhoAmW 93
Manoogian, Peter MiSFD 9
Manoogian, Richard 1936- St&PR 93
Manoogian, Richard Alexander 1936- WhoAm 92
Manoogian, Sion d1991 BioIn 17
Manor, Philip Craig 1944- WhoE 93
Manor, Thomas G. Law&B 92
Manos, Gregory 1927- WhoScE 91-3
Manos, John M. Law&B 92
Manos, John M. 1922- WhoAm 92
Manos, Mark MiSFD 9
Manos, Pete Lazaros 1936- St&PR 93, WhoAm 92
Manosevitz, Martin 1938- WhoAm 92
Manoukian, Noel Edwin 1938- WhoAm 92
Manousos, James William 1919- WhoAm 92, WhoWrEP 92
Manousos, Orestes Nicholas 1931- WhoWor 93
Manoussakis, George E. 1931- WhoScE 91-3
Manowarda, Josef von 1890-1942 Baker 92
Manowitz, J.G. 1932- St&PR 93
Manowitz, J. William 1925- St&PR 93
Manowitz, Paul 1940- WhoE 93
Man Ray 1890-1976 BioIn 17
Manring, Daniel Lee 1951- WhoEmL 93
Manrique (Ardila), Jaime 1949- ConAu 139
Manrique, Carlos D. 1945- St&PR 93
Manrique, Guillermo Daniel 1964- WhoWor 93
Manrique, Jaime 1949- WhoEmL 93
Manrique, Leonardo 1934- WhoWor 93
Manrique de Lara (y Berry), Manuel 1863-1929 Baker 92
Manrodt, W.H. 1948- St&PR 93
Manry, Larry Alan 1947- St&PR 93
Mans, Martha BioIn 17
Mansa, Bendt WhoScE 91-2
Mansbach, Robert A. Law&B 92
Mansberger, Arlie Roland, Jr. 1922- WhoAm 92
Mansbridge, Anne L. Law&B 92
Manschinger, Kurt 1902-1968 Baker 92
Manseau, Melissa Marie 1962- WhoAmW 93
Mansel, Robert Edward WhoScE 91-1
Mansel, Wendell Brian 1958- WhoEmL 93, WhoSSW 93
Manselian, Harold S. 1918- St&PR 93
Mansell, Darrel Lee, Jr. 1934- WhoAm 92
Mansell, Frank F. 1954- St&PR 93
Mansell, James R. 1929- WhoAm 92
Mansell, Nigel 1954- WhoWor 93
Mansell, Peter William Anson 1936- WhoSSW 93
Mansell, Thomas S. 1939- St&PR 93
Mansen, Steven Robert 1955- WhoEmL 93
Manser, Bruno BioIn 17
Manser, George Robert 1931- St&PR 93
Manser, Lyman A. 1926- WhoAm 92
Mansergh, Gordon Dwight 1962- WhoE 93
Mansfeld, Peter Ernst, Count of 1580-1626 HarEnMi
Mansfield, Arthur Rulon, Jr. 1926- St&PR 93
Mansfield, Beatrice Cameron 1868- AmWomPl
Mansfield, Bruce Alexander 1932- WhoE 93
Mansfield, Carl Major 1928- WhoAm 92
Mansfield, Charles Frank Law&B 92
Mansfield, Christopher C. Law&B 92
Mansfield, Christopher Charles 1950- St&PR 93, WhoAm 92
Mansfield, David Kay 1947- WhoSSW 93
Mansfield, Edward Patrick, Jr. 1947- WhoAm 92, WhoE 93
Mansfield, Edwin 1930- WhoAm 92
Mansfield, Fred W. 1928- St&PR 93
Mansfield, Guy Rhys John 1949- WhoWor 93
Mansfield, Harvey Claflin 1932- BioIn 17
Mansfield, Jayne 1933-1967 IntDcF 2-3 [port]
Mansfield, John T. Law&B 92
Mansfield, Joseph John 1938- WhoE 93
Mansfield, Joseph King Fenno 1803-1862 HarEnMi
Mansfield, Karla Jean 1950- St&PR 93, WhoEmL 93
Mansfield, Katherine 1888-1923 BioIn 17, IntLitE, MagSWL [port], WorLitC [port]
Mansfield, Kathleen Beauchamp 1888-1923 BioIn 17
Mansfield, Kathryn Law&B 92
Mansfield, Larry Alden 1934- St&PR 93
Mansfield, Lawrence Frederick 1922- WhoSSW 93
Mansfield, Lois Edna 1941- WhoAm 92, WhoSSW 93
Mansfield, M.P. WhoScE 91-1
Mansfield, Marc Lewis 1955- WhoAm 92
Mansfield, Margo 1947- WhoEmL 93
Mansfield, Maynard Joseph 1930- WhoAm 92
Mansfield, Michael J. 1903- PolPar
Mansfield, Michael Joseph 1903- WhoAm 92
Mansfield, Mike BioIn 17
Mansfield, Mike 1903- ColdWar 1 [port]
Mansfield, Norman Connie 1916- WhoSSW 93, WhoWor 93
Mansfield, Norman Jerome 1952- WhoSSW 93
Mansfield, Peter WhoScE 91-1
Mansfield, Roger WhoScE 91-1
Mansfield, Stephen Scott 1942- WhoSSW 93
Mansfield, Stephen W. Law&B 92
Mansfield, Terence A. WhoScE 91-1
Mansfield, Tobi Ellen 1949- WhoAmW 93
Mansfield, Victor Neil 1941- WhoE 93
Mansfield, William Herman, III 1932- WhoUN 92
Manshard, Walther 1923- WhoScE 91-3, WhoWor 93
Manshel, Warren D. 1924-1990 BioIn 17
Manshio, Calvin Katsumi 1947- WhoEmL 93
Manship, Charles P., Jr. 1908- St&PR 93
Manship, Charles Phelps, Jr. 1908- WhoAm 92
Manship, Douglas 1918- WhoAm 92
Manship, John Paul 1927- WhoE 93
Manship, Paul 1885-1966 BioIn 17
Mansi, Joseph Anneillo 1935- WhoAm 92
Manske, John St&PR 93
Manske, Paul Robert 1938- WhoAm 92
Mansker, Robert Thomas 1941- WhoE 93
Manski, Charles F. 1948- ConAu 138
Manski, Dorothee 1891-1967 Baker 92
Manski, Wladyslaw Julian 1915- WhoAm 92
Mansky, Terry Phillip Law&B 92
Mansmann, Carol Los 1942- WhoAm 92, WhoAmW 93, WhoE 93
Mansmann, Herbert C., Jr. 1924- WhoAm 92
Manso, Gilbert 1942- WhoWor 93
Manso, Luis Cortes 1962- WhoWor 93
Manson, Bruce Malcolm 1944- St&PR 93, WhoAm 92
Manson, Cynthia ScF&FL 92
Manson, David Joseph 1952- WhoEmL 93
Manson, Eddy Lawrence WhoAm 92
Manson, George P., Jr. Law&B 92
Manson, George Patterson, Jr. Law&B 92
Manson, Jeane Ann 1950- WhoWor 93
Manson, Karen Law&B 92
Manson, Lewis Auman 1918- WhoSSW 93
Manson, Numa Peter 1913- WhoWor 93
Manson, Paul David 1934- WhoAm 92
Manson, Robert Hunter 1941- St&PR 93
Manson, Steven Trent 1940- WhoSSW 93
Manson-Hing, Lincoln Roy 1927- WhoAm 92
Mansour, Awad Rasheed 1951- WhoWor 93
Mansour, George P. 1939- WhoAm 92
Mansour, Mohamed 1928- WhoScE 91-4
Mansour, N. Ned Law&B 92
Mansour, Nadia Omar 1950- WhoAmW 93
Mansour, Tag Eldin 1924- WhoAm 92
Mansouri, Ariane 1960- WhoWor 93
Mansouri, Lotfi BioIn 17
Mansouri, Lotfollah 1929- WhoAm 92
Mansourian, Pierre Boutros 1938- WhoWor 93
Mansson, Ake 1940- WhoScE 91-4
Mansson, Ingmar M. 1928- WhoScE 91-4
Manstein, Erich von 1887-1973 BioIn 17, HarEnMi
Mansueti, Albert E. 1924- St&PR 93
Mansueto Zecca, Graziella 1926- WhoScE 91-3
Mansur, Abby d1855 BioIn 17
Mansur, Ahsan Habib 1951- WhoUN 92
Mansur, Charles F. 1934- St&PR 93
Mansur, Ina 1910-1988 ConAu 38NR
Mansur, Paul Max 1926- WhoAm 92
Mansur-Brown, Patricia Marion Law&B 92
Mansurian, Tigran 1939- Baker 92
Mansur Ibn Sarjun dc. 636 OxDcByz
Mansuy, Buckey P. Law&B 92
Mansuy, Daniel 1945- WhoScE 91-2
Mansuy, Jane Webster 1951- WhoEmL 93
Mantalenakis, Serge J. 1932- WhoScE 91-3
Mantas, John 1954- WhoWor 93
Mantegazza, Giacomo BioIn 17
Mantegazza, Paolo 1831-1910 IntDcAn
Mantegna, Andrea 1431-1506 BioIn 17
Mantegna, Joe 1947- ConTFT 10, News 92 [port]
Mantegna, Joe 1948?- BioIn 17
Mantegna, Joe Anthony 1947- WhoAm 92
Mantel, Allan David 1951- WhoEmL 93
Mantel, Joan Licht Law&B 92
Mantel, Richard BioIn 17
Mantel, Samuel Joseph, Jr. 1921- WhoAm 92
Mantelet, Jean 1900-1991 AnObit 1991, BioIn 17
Mantell, Gideon Algernon 1790-1852 BioIn 17
Mantell, Lester J. 1937- WhoAm 92
Mantell, Suzanne 1944- WhoAm 92, WhoWrEP 92
Mantelli, Eugenia c. 1860-1926 Baker 92
Mantellini, Giuseppe WhoScE 91-3
Manter, Margaret Carpenter 1923- WhoE 93
Manterfield, Eric A. 1947- St&PR 93
Manteria, S. William Law&B 92
Mantero, Francisco Manuel 1968- WhoSSW 93
Manteuffel, Edwin von 1809-1885 HarEnMi
Manteuffel, Hasso von 1897-1978 BioIn 17, HarEnMi
Manteuffel, Henryk Michal 1944- WhoScE 91-4
Mantey, Elmer Martin 1926- WhoSSW 93
Mantey, James R. 1941- St&PR 93
Manthe, Cora De Munck 1928- WhoAmW 93, WhoWor 93
Manthe, Joanne L. Law&B 92
Manthei, Donald Frederick 1932- WhoWor 93
Manthei, Richard D. 1935- St&PR 93
Manthei, Richard Dale 1935- WhoAm 92
Manthey, Frank Anthony 1933- WhoSSW 93, WhoWor 93
Manthey, Mary Ellen N. 1950- St&PR 93
Manthey, Robert Wendelin 1935- WhoE 93
Manthey, Roberta Raye 1959- St&PR 93
Manthey, William Armand 1949- St&PR 93
Manthorne, Jackie Ann 1946- WhoAmW 93
Manthorpe, Rolf 1942- WhoWor 93
Manthy, Ray S. 1937- St&PR 93
Mantica, Francis Albert 1927- WhoE 93
Mantilla, Felix Anthony Law&B 92
Mantilla, Nectario Ruben 1940- WhoWor 93
Mantle, John Edward 1940- WhoAm 92
Mantle, Mickey 1931- BioIn 17
Mantle, Mickey Charles 1931- WhoAm 92
Mantle, Raymond Allan 1937- WhoWor 93
Mantler, Karen BioIn 17
Manton, Edwin A.G. 1909- St&PR 93
Manton, Edwin Alfred Grenville 1909- WhoAm 92, WhoIns 93
Manton, Linda Marie 1949- WhoEmL 93
Manton, Thomas J. 1932- CngDr 91
Manton, Thomas Joseph 1932- WhoAm 92, WhoE 93
Mantonya, John Butcher 1922- WhoAm 92
Mantooth, Frank BioIn 17
Mantooth, Margaret Larah 1909- WhoAmW 93
Mantor, Justine Claire 1943- WhoAmW 93
Mantor, Philip David 1936- WhoAm 92
Mantoura, Amira 1962- WhoE 93
Mantoura, R. Fauzi C. 1949- WhoScE 91-1
Mantovani, (Annunzio Paolo) 1905-1980 Baker 92
Mantovani, Elinora S. Law&B 92
Mantovani, Enzo 1945- WhoScE 91-3
Mantovani, G. WhoScE 91-2
Mantovani, Giorgio 1925- WhoScE 91-3
Mantovani, Giorgio Maria 1925- WhoWor 93
Mantravadi, Murty V. 1929- WhoWor 93
Mantsch, Henry Horst 1935- WhoAm 92
Mantua, Jose Amaral WhoScE 91-3
Mantuani, Josef 1860-1933 Baker 92
Manty, Jorma 1937- WhoScE 91-4
Mantyjarvi, Rauno A. 1936- WhoScE 91-4
Mantyla, Heikki WhoScE 91-4
Mantyla, Karen 1944- WhoAmW 93
Mantynen, Heimo 1937- WhoUN 92
Mantysalo, Esa E. 1934- WhoScE 91-4
Mantzell, Betty Lou 1938- WhoAmW 93
Mantzoros, Anne 1920- St&PR 93
Manuchar'iants, Shushanika Nikitichna BioIn 17
Manuel d838 OxDcByz
Manuel, Derrinita L. 1964- WhoEmL 93
Manuel, E. Arsenio 1909- IntDcAn
Manuel, Ellen Elizabeth 1958- WhoSSW 93
Manuel, Eric BioIn 17
Manuel, Frank Edward 1910- WhoWrEP 92
Manuel, G. Leonard Law&B 92
Manuel, Jenny Lynn 1964- WhoAmW 93
Manuel, Jimmy Lee 1934- St&PR 93
Manuel, Lau-Rene Anntwan 1964- WhoE 93
Manuel, Monte Morgan 1925- St&PR 93
Manuel, Ralph Nixon 1936- WhoAm 92
Manuel, Richard 1945-1986 See Band, The ConMus 9
Manuel, Robert 1916- WhoWor 93
Manuel, Roland Baker 92
Manuel, Teresa BlkAmWO
Manuel, Thomas Asbury 1936- WhoE 93
Manuel, Vivian 1941- WhoE 93, WhoWor 93
Manuel, Yves WhoScE 91-2
Manuela 1847-1933 BioIn 17
Manuel Angelos 1186?-c. 1241 OxDcByz
Manuelidis, Elias E. d1992 NewYTBS 92
Manuel Kantakouzenos c. 1326- OxDcByz
Manuel Komnenos, I OxDcByz
Manuel Komnenos, I 1118-1180 OxDcByz
Manuel Komnenos, III 1364-1417? OxDcByz
Manuell, Guy 1949- WhoWor 93
Manuell, Lynn Marie 1961- WhoEmL 93
Manuellan, G. WhoScE 91-2
Manuel Palaiologos, II 1350-1425 OxDcByz
Manulis, Martin 1915- WhoAm 92
Manulkin, Dena J. 1947- WhoWrEP 92
Manum, Svein B. 1926- WhoScE 91-4
Manus, Charles Ray 1946- WhoSSW 93
Manushkin, Fran 1942- ScF&FL 92
Manuszak, Ronald J. Law&B 92
Manuti, Annabelle Theresa 1928- WhoAmW 93
Manutius, Aldus Pius 1449?-1515 BioIn 17
Manuzio, Aldo Pio 1449?-1515 BioIn 17
Manvel, Allen Dailey 1912- WhoAm 92, WhoE 93
Manvell, Roger 1909-1987 ScF&FL 92
Manville, Richard W. 1926- St&PR 93
Manville, Stewart Roebling 1927- WhoE 93, WhoWor 93
Manwell, Edmund Ray 1942- St&PR 93
Manyak, Michael John 1951- WhoE 93
Manz, August Frederick 1929- WhoE 93
Manz, Betty Ann 1935- WhoAmW 93, WhoE 93
Manz, Friedrich Dieter 1941- WhoScE 91-3
Manz, Johannes 1938- WhoUN 92
Manz, Steven F. 1945- St&PR 93
Manzanares, Dennis 1950- WhoEmL 93
Manzano, Cesar 1942- WhoUN 92
Manzano, J. Mia 1952- WhoEmL 93
Manzano, Sonia 1950- NotHsAW 93
Manzari, Laura Lynn 1959- WhoEmL 93
Manzer, Virginia Lee 1951- St&PR 93
Manzetti, Roland Guido Christopher 1941- WhoWor 93
Manzi, Dante Anthony 1937- WhoE 93
Manzi, Jim P. 1951- St&PR 93
Manzi, Jim Paul 1951- WhoAm 92
Manzi, Joseph Edward 1945- WhoWor 93
Manzi, Vince BioIn 17
Manziarly, Marcelle de 1899-1989 Baker 92
Manzione, H.J. 1924- St&PR 93
Manzitti, Edward Thomas 1951- WhoE 93
Manzo, Edward David 1950- WhoEmL 93
Manzo, Peter Thomas 1947- WhoEmL 93
Manzo, Renata Law&B 92
Manzoli, Francesco WhoScE 91-3
Manzoni, Carlos 1960- WhoWor 93
Manzoni, Giacomo 1932- Baker 92
Manzu, Giacomo 1908-1991 AnObit 1991, BioIn 17
Manzuoli, Giovanni c. 1720-1782 OxDcOp
Mao, Madame 1914-1991 BioIn 17
Mao, Ho-kwang 1941- WhoAm 92
Mao, Jingzhong 1940- WhoWor 93
Mao, Tse-Tung 1893-1976 BioIn 17
Mao, Yu-shi 1929- WhoWor 93
Mao, Zhenhua 1958- WhoSSW 93
Mao Kao-Wen 1936- WhoAsAP 91
Maotani, Sakae 1939- WhoWor 93
Mao Tse-tung 1893-1976 HarEnMi
Mao Zedong 1893-1976 BioIn 17, ColdWar 2 [port], DcTwHis
Mao Zhiyong 1930- WhoAsAP 91
Map, Walter c. 1140-1209? OxDcByz
Mapel, William M.R. 1931- St&PR 93
Mapel, William Marlen Raines 1931- WhoAm 92
Mapelli, Enrique WhoScE 91-3
Mapelli, Roland L. 1922- St&PR 93
Mapelli, Roland Lawrence 1922- WhoAm 92
Mapes, Charles M. d1990 BioIn 17
Mapes, Ella Stryker 1870- AmWomPl
Mapes, Glynn Dempsey 1939- WhoAm 92
Mapes, Jane Stewart d1990 BioIn 17
Mapes, Lynn Calvin 1928- WhoAm 92

Mapes, Pierson *WhoAm 92*
Mapes, Pierson Godwin 1937- *St&PR 93*
Mapes, William E. 1934- *St&PR 93*
Mapham, Walter Russel 1947- *St&PR 93*
Maple, Carol Jean 1947- *WhoSSW 93*
Maple, Marilyn Jean 1931- *WhoAmW 93*
Maple, Opal Lucille 1935- *WhoAmW 93*
Maple, Timothy Michael 1936- *WhoSSW 93*
Maples, Marla *BioIn 17, NewYTBS 92 [port]*
Maples, Robert Carl 1957- *WhoEmL 93*
Maples, Stephen Russell 1961- *WhoSSW 93*
Maples, Sylvia Petit d1991 *BioIn 17*
Maples Arce, Manuel 1898-1981 *DcMexL*
Maplesden, Douglas Cecil 1919- *WhoSSW 93*
Maplesden, Joan 1943- *WhoSSW 93*
Mapleson, James Henry 1830-1901 *Baker 92, OxDcOp*
Mapleson, Lionel S. 1865-1937 *See* Mapleson, James Henry 1830-1901 *Baker 92*
Mapleson, William Wellesley *WhoScE 91-1*
Mapletoft, Lee 1940- *St&PR 93*
Mapother, Dillon Edward 1921- *WhoAm 92*
Mapou, Robert Lewis 1955- *WhoE 93*
Mapp, Alf Johnson, Jr. 1925- *WhoAm 92, WhoWor 93, WhoWrEP 92*
Mapp, Edward Charles 1929- *WhoE 93*
Mapp, Frederick Everett 1910- *WhoSSW 93*
Mappes, Richard Louis 1928- *St&PR 93*
Mapps, Desmond James *WhoScE 91-1*
Mapson, Charles Edwin *Law&B 92*
Ma Pu-fang 1903- *HarEnMi*
Mapula, Olga 1938- *HispAmA*
Maqdisi, Al- 946-c. 1000 *OxDcByz*
Maqrizi, Al- 1364-1442 *OxDcByz*
Maqtari, Ahmed Mohamed 1948- *WhoWor 93*
Maquart, Francois Xavier 1952- *WhoScE 91-2*
Maquestiau, Andre Henri Jules 1926- *WhoScE 91-2*
Maquet, Jacques Jerome 1919- *IntDcAn*
Maquet, Jacques Jerome Pierre 1919- *WhoAm 92*
Maquet, Paul G.J. 1928- *WhoScE 91-2*
Maquil, R. *WhoScE 91-3*
Mar, James Wah 1920- *WhoAm 92*
Mar, Maria del *DcMexL*
Mara, Adele 1923- *HispAmA, SweetSg D [port]*
Mara, Bernard *WhoCanL 92*
Mara, David Duncan *WhoScE 91-1*
Mara, Edward James, Jr. 1929- *St&PR 93*
Mara, Gertrud 1749-1833 *OxDcOp*
Mara, Gertrud (Elisabeth) 1749-1833 *Baker 92*
Mara, Gordon 1954- *WhoAsAP 91*
Mara, Janet 1948- *WhoAmW 93*
Mara, John Lawrence 1924- *WhoE 93*
Mara, Kamisese Kapaiwai Tuimacilai 1920- *WhoAsAP 91, WhoWor 93*
Mara, Timothy James 1887-1959 *BioIn 17*
Mara, Vincent Joseph 1930- *WhoAm 92*
Marabella, Anthony John, Jr. 1946- *WhoEmL 93*
Marabini, A.M. *WhoScE 91-3*
Marable, Simeon-David 1948- *WhoEmL 93, WhoWor 93*
Maracchi, G. *WhoScE 91-3*
Maracci, Carmelita 1911-1987 *BioIn 17*
Maracle, David Earl 1948- *WhoEmL 93*
Maradona, Diego *BioIn 17*
Marafino, Vincent Norman 1930- *St&PR 93, WhoAm 92*
Marafioti, Dominick 1926- *WhoE 93*
Marafioti, Robert D. *Law&B 92*
Maragno, Virtu 1928- *Baker 92*
Maragoudakis, Michael E. 1932- *WhoScE 91-3*
Marahiman, Ismail 1934- *ConAu 136*
Marai, Sandor 1900-1988 *BioIn 17*
Marais, Jean 1913- *IntDcF 2-3 [port]*
Marais, Josef 1905-1978 *Baker 92*
Marais, Marin 1656-1728 *Baker 92, OxDcOp*
Maraj, Ralph 1949- *WhoWor 93*
Marak, Otakar 1872-1939 *Baker 92, OxDcOp*
Marak, Randy Barton 1962- *WhoEmL 93, WhoSSW 93*
Marakas, John Lambros 1926- *WhoAm 92*
Maraman, Grady Vancil 1936- *WhoSSW 93*
Maramara, Alan Ocanada 1961- *WhoSSW 93*
Maramorosch, Karl 1915- *WhoAm 92, WhoE 93*
Maran, Arnold George Dominic *WhoScE 91-1*
Maran, Joe 1933- *WhoE 93*
Maran, Murasali 1939- *WhoAsAP 91*
Maran, Stephen Paul 1938- *WhoAm 92*
Marancik, Dorothy Irene 1922- *WhoAmW 93*
Marand, Herve 1960- *WhoSSW 93*
Maranda, Pierre Jean 1930- *WhoAm 92*
Maranda, Vincent *Law&B 92*
Marangell, Robert P. 1949- *St&PR 93*
Marangoni, Bruno A. 1907-1990 *BioIn 17*
Marangoni, Daniele 1947- *WhoWor 93*
Marangopoulos, Alice Yotopoulos 1917- *WhoUN 92*
Marangozis, John 1929- *WhoScE 91-3*
Maranha Das Neves, Emanuel J.L. 1938- *WhoScE 91-3*
Marani, Jean Victoria 1924- *WhoSSW 93*
Maraniss, James (Elliott) 1945- *ConAu 139*
Maraniss, Linda *BioIn 17*
Marano, Angeline Marie 1957- *WhoSSW 93*
Marano, Annamarie 1962- *WhoE 93*
Marano, Anthony Joseph 1934- *WhoAm 92, WhoE 93*
Marano, Frank Nicholus 1950- *WhoE 93*
Marano, Margo Margaret Carol 1961- *WhoSSW 93*
Marano, Philip Dennis 1932- *WhoSSW 93*
Marano, R.J. 1928- *St&PR 93*
Marano, Richard Michael 1960- *WhoE 93, WhoEmL 93*
Marano, Rocco Michael 1951- *WhoSSW 93*
Marano, Susan Elizabeth 1955- *WhoEmL 93*
Marans, J. Eugene 1940- *WhoAm 92*
Marantette, David Theodore, III 1941- *St&PR 93*
Maranto, Matthew Philip 1963- *WhoEmL 93*
Maranto, Paul A. 1938- *St&PR 93*
Marantz, Saul *BioIn 17*
Marasciullo, David Louis 1929- *WhoE 93*
Marasco, Amy L. 1954- *St&PR 93*
Marasco, Francis Anthony 1943- *WhoAm 92*
Marascuilo, Leonard A. *BioIn 17*
Marash, David 1942- *WhoAm 92*
Marash, Judith Ilene 1963- *WhoAmW 93*
Marash, Randy J. 1955- *WhoIns 93*
Marash, Stanley Albert 1938- *WhoE 93, WhoWor 93*
Marasinghe, Indra Tissa 1948- *WhoWor 93*
Maratea, James Michael 1946- *WhoE 93*
Maratea, Thomas R. 1947- *St&PR 93*
Maravel, Patricia 1949- *WhoEmL 93*
Maravelas, Paul 1956- *WhoWrEP 92*
Maravich, Mary Louise 1951- *WhoAmW 93*
Maravich, Pete 1948-1988 *BioIn 17*
Maraynes, Allan Lawrence 1950- *WhoAm 92, WhoE 93, WhoEmL 93*
Marazita, Eleanor Marie Harmon 1933- *WhoAmW 93*
Maraziti, Joseph J. 1912-1991 *BioIn 17*
Marazzoli, Marco 1602?-1662 *Baker 92, OxDcOp*
Marbach, Deborah *BioIn 17*
Marbach, Lois Betty 1946- *WhoAmW 93*
Marbaix, Gerard 1941- *WhoScE 91-2*
Marbe, Myriam 1931- *Baker 92*
Marbeck, John c. 1505-1585 *Baker 92*
Marbecke, John c. 1505-1585 *Baker 92*
Marberry, Fredrick 1899-1976 *BiDAMSp 1989*
Marbert, Larry David 1953- *WhoAm 92*
Marble, Alexander d1992 *NewYTBS 92 [port]*
Marble, Alice 1913-1990 *BioIn 17*
Marble, Annie Russell 1864-1936 *AmWomPl*
Marboutie, Georges *WhoScE 91-2*
Marburger, John Harmen, III 1941- *WhoAm 92, WhoE 93, WhoWor 93*
Marburger, Ronald Ross 1943- *St&PR 93*
Marburg-Goodman, Jeffrey Emil 1957- *WhoEmL 93*
Marbury, Anita Louise 1947- *WhoAmW 93*
Marbury, Benjamin Edward 1914- *WhoAm 92*
Marbury, Carl Harris 1935- *AfrAmBi [port]*
Marbury, Donald Lee *BioIn 17*
Marbury, Virginia Lomax 1918- *WhoAmW 93*
Marbury, William L. 1901-1988 *BioIn 17*
Marbut, Robert Gordon 1935- *St&PR 93, WhoAm 92*
Marc, Christian A. 1951- *WhoWor 93*
Marc, David 1951- *ConAu 138*
Marc, Franz 1880-1916 *BioIn 17*
Marca, Jerry 1951- *WhoEmL 93*
Marcacci, Donna A. 1954- *St&PR 93*
Marcaccio, Mario J., Jr. *Law&B 92*
Marcaccio Matthews, Tonia Michele 1948- *WhoAmW 93*
Marcal, Dawn *BioIn 17*
Marcali, Jean Gregory 1926- *WhoAmW 93, WhoWor 93*
Marcantel, Silva Cooper 1940- *WhoAmW 93*
Marcantonio, Vito 1902-1954 *PolPar*
Marca-Relli, Conrad 1913- *WhoAm 92*
Marcarelli, Dean Paul 1961- *WhoSSW 93*
Marcarelli, Louis G. 1942- *St&PR 93*
Marcarelli, Robert *MiSFD 9*
Marcasiano, Mary Jane 1955- *WhoAmW 93*
Marcatante, John Joseph 1930- *WhoE 93, WhoWor 93*
Marce, Denis 1932- *WhoScE 91-2*
Marceau, Jane C. 1948- *St&PR 93*
Marceau, Lawrence Edward 1954- *WhoSSW 93*
Marceau, Marcel 1923- *WhoAm 92, WhoWor 93*
Marcel, Gabriel 1889-1973 *BioIn 17*
Marcel, Georges Anthony 1940- *WhoWor 93*
Marcel, John H. 1947- *St&PR 93*
Marcel, Lucille 1885-1921 *Baker 92*
Marcel, Terry 1942- *MiSFD 9*
Marcela, Paul A. *Law&B 92*
Marcela, Paul A. 1956- *WhoEmL 93*
Marcela-Froideval, Francois *ScF&FL 92*
Marcell, David Wyburn 1937- *WhoAm 92*
Marcella, Gabriel 1942- *WhoE 93*
Marcella, Joseph 1948- *St&PR 93*
Marcellas, Thomas Wilson 1937- *WhoWor 93*
Marcelle, R.D.G. 1931- *WhoScE 91-2*
Marcelli, Emanuel *WhoScE 91-3*
Marcelli, Romolo 1958- *WhoWor 93*
Marcellin, Pierre 1923- *WhoScE 91-2*
Marcellin, Raymond 1914- *BioIn 17*
Marcellini, A. *WhoScE 91-3*
Marcellino, Fred 1939- *BioIn 17, WhoAm 92*
Marcellinus c. 420-468 *HarEnMi*
Marcellinus, Marcus Claudius d148BC *HarEnMi*
Marcellinus Comes fl. 6th cent.- *OxDcByz*
Marcello, Alessandro 1669-1747 *Baker 92*
Marcello, Benedetto 1686-1739 *Baker 92, OxDcOp*
Marcello, Carlotta *BioIn 17*
Marcello, Rosita Luisa 1935- *WhoE 93*
Marcello, Vettor *BioIn 17*
Marcellus, David Ward 1942- *St&PR 93*
Marcellus, John Robert, III 1939- *WhoAm 92*
Marcellus, Marcus Claudius c. 268BC-208BC *HarEnMi*
Marcellus, W.J. 1915- *St&PR 93*
Marcelo, Cynthia Luz 1945- *HispAmA*
Marcels *SoulM*
Marcey, M. Nicole *Law&B 92*
March, Ausias 1397?-1459 *BioIn 17*
March, Beryl Elizabeth 1920- *WhoAm 92, WhoAmW 93*
March, Brookman P. 1945- *St&PR 93*
March, C.N. *WhoScE 91-1*
March, Carl *ConAu 37NR, MajAI*
March, Carol 1955- *WhoWor 93*
March, Donald E. 1948- *St&PR 93*
March, Eugene A. 1919- *St&PR 93*
March, Fredric 1897-1975 *BioIn 17, IntDcF 2-3*
March, Gene *ScF&FL 92*
March, Helen Dorothy *AmWomPl*
March, Jacqueline Front *WhoAmW 93, WhoSSW 93*
March, James Gardner 1928- *WhoAm 92*
March, John P. 1941- *St&PR 93*
March, John William 1923- *WhoAm 92*
March, Kathleen Patricia 1949- *WhoAmW 93*
March, Louise 1900-1987 *BioIn 17*
March, Melisand 1927- *ScF&FL 92*
March, Michael Richard 1956- *WhoEmL 93*
March, N.H. *WhoScE 91-1*
March, Peyton Conway 1864-1955 *CmdGen 1991 [port], HarEnMi*
March, Philip Vincent *WhoScE 91-1*
March, Ralph Burton 1919- *WhoAm 92*
March, Richard S. 1941- *WhoIns 93*
March, Valerie *ConAu 137*
March, William Victor 1935- *St&PR 93*
Marchais, Georges 1920- *BioIn 17, WhoWor 93*
Marchak, Betty J. 1926- *St&PR 93*
Marchak, Frank James 1923- *St&PR 93*
Marchak, Maureen Patricia 1936- *WhoAmW 93*
Marchal, A.W. 1942- *St&PR 93*
Marchal, Andre (-Louis) 1894-1980 *Baker 92*
Marchal, Christian Leon 1939- *WhoWor 93*
Marchal, Jean 1938- *WhoScE 91-2*
Marchalonis, John Jacob 1940- *WhoAm 92, WhoWor 93*
Marcham, Frederick G. d1992 *NewYTBS 92*
Marcham, Timothy Victor 1943- *WhoE 93*
Marchan, Bobby *SoulM*
Marchand, A. Whitman 1936- *WhoAm 92*
Marchand, Cecelia Gloria 1933- *WhoWrEP 92*
Marchand, Douglas James 1947- *St&PR 93*
Marchand, Gerard Andre 1943- *WhoWor 93*
Marchand, J. C. de Montigny 1936- *WhoAm 92*
Marchand, Jacquelyn 1961- *WhoE 93*
Marchand, Jean-Baptiste 1863-1934 *Expl 93*
Marchand, John F. 1912-1990 *BioIn 17*
Marchand, Jorge E. 1953- *St&PR 93*
Marchand, Leslie Alexis 1900- *BioIn 17, WhoAm 92*
Marchand, Louis 1669-1732 *Baker 92*
Marchand, Nancy 1928- *WhoAm 92, WhoAmW 93*
Marchand, Nathan 1916- *WhoAm 92, WhoE 93*
Marchand, R. *Law&B 92*
Marchandise, Patrick 1947- *WhoScE 91-2*
Marchand-Tonel, Maurice J. 1944- *WhoWor 93*
Marchant, Eric Walter *WhoScE 91-1*
Marchant, G. Todd 1938- *St&PR 93*
Marchant, Maurice Peterson 1927- *WhoAm 92*
Marchant, Michelle Marie *Law&B 92*
Marchant, Murray Scott 1940- *St&PR 93*
Marchant, Philip Louis 1922- *St&PR 93*
Marchant, Roger *WhoScE 91-1*
Marchant, Stanley (Robert) 1883-1949 *Baker 92*
Marchant, Trelawney Eston 1920- *WhoAm 92, WhoSSW 93*
Marchau, Marcel Michel Bernhard 1939- *WhoWor 93*
Marchbank, Tammy Jo 1960- *WhoEmL 93*
Marche, Michel 1933- *WhoScE 91-2*
Marchek, Richard J. *Law&B 92*
Marchel, Peter M. *Law&B 92*
Marchelek, Krzysztof Stanislaw 1938- *WhoScE 91-4*
Marchello, Joseph Maurice 1933- *WhoAm 92, WhoSSW 93*
Marchelos, George Franklin 1937- *WhoE 93, WhoWor 93*
Marchena, Ana Isabel 1965- *WhoAmW 93*
Marchenko, Vladimir Matveyevich 1949- *WhoWor 93*
Marchese, Anthony Peter, Jr. *Law&B 92*
Marchese, Cristiana Alessandra 1953- *WhoWor 93*
Marchese, Diane S. *Law&B 92*
Marchese, John Lloyd 1931- *St&PR 93*
Marchese, Joseph Francis 1934- *WhoAm 92*
Marchese, Mel F. 1939- *St&PR 93*
Marchese, Paul J. 1955- *St&PR 93*
Marchese, Paul Stephan 1945- *WhoE 93, WhoWor 93*
Marchese, Ronald Thomas 1947- *WhoAm 92*
Marchesi, Blanche 1863-1940 *Baker 92, OxDcOp*
Marchesi, Gian Franco 1940- *WhoWor 93*
Marchesi, Guy Anthony 1950- *St&PR 93*
Marchesi, Luigi 1755-1829 *OxDcOp*
Marchesi, Luigi (Lodovico) 1754-1829 *Baker 92*
Marchesi, Mathilde 1821-1913 *OxDcOp*
Marchesi, Salvatore 1822-1908 *OxDcOp*
Marchesi, Stephanie Pauline Hauck 1963- *WhoAmW 93*
Marchesi de Castrone, Mathilde 1821-1913 *Baker 92*
Marchesi de Castrone, Salvatore 1822-1908 *Baker 92*
Marchessault, Gregg Arthur 1957- *WhoEmL 93*
Marchessault, Jovette 1938- *BioIn 17, WhoCanL 92*
Marchessault, Thomas Edward 1948- *WhoE 93, WhoEmL 93*
Marchetti, Cesare *BioIn 17*
Marchetti, Christopher *Law&B 92*
Marchetti, Emerino John 1929- *St&PR 93*
Marchetti, Filippo 1831-1902 *Baker 92, OxDcOp*
Marchetti, Gino 1927- *BioIn 17*
Marchetti, Joseph Peter, Jr. 1956- *WhoEmL 93, WhoSSW 93*
Marchetti, Kimberly 1958- *WhoEmL 93*
Marchetti, Richard J. 1930- *St&PR 93*
Marchetti, Ronald Andrew 1947- *WhoE 93*
Marchetto da Padua c. 1274-c. 1326 *Baker 92*
Marchettus de Padua c. 1274-c. 1326 *Baker 92*

Marchi, Enrico 1925- *WhoScE 91-3*
Marchi, Ezio 1940- *WhoWor 93*
Marchi, Jason J. 1960- *WhoWrEP 92*
Marchi, Lorraine June 1923- *WhoE 93*
Marchi, Rosemarie 1927- *WhoAmW 93*
Marchiafava, Pier Lorenzo 1935- *WhoScE 91-3*
Marchibroda, Theodore Joseph Ted 1931- *WhoAm 92*
Marchido, William Frank 1950- *St&PR 93*
Marchildon, Jean 1934- *St&PR 93*
Marchildon, Michael Bert 1940- *WhoE 93*
Marchington, Anthony David 1934- *St&PR 93*
Marchington, Michael Philip 1949- *WhoWor 93*
Marchini, Julio Sergio 1952- *WhoWor 93*
Marchio, Albert Nicholas, II 1952- *WhoE 93*
Marchione, Sharyn Lee 1947- *WhoAmW 93*
Marchioni, Allen *WhoAm 92*
Marchioni, Marco Alessandro 1957- *WhoWor 93*
Marchiori, D. *WhoScE 91-2*
Marchiori, Mario *WhoScE 91-3*
Marchisio, Barbara 1833-1919 *Baker 92*
Marchisio, Carlotta 1835-1872 See Marchisio, Barbara 1833-1919 *Baker 92*
Marchisotto, Alan 1949- *St&PR 93*
Marchisotto, Alan Lewes *Law&B 92*
Marchitti, Elizabeth Van Houten 1931- *WhoWrEP 92*
Marchitto, Alfred Joseph 1941- *St&PR 93*
Marchlen, Louis Thomas *Law&B 92*
Marchlewicz, Margaret Ann 1950- *WhoAmW 93, WhoEmL 93*
Marchlewski, Julian 1866-1925 *PolBiDi*
Marchman, Ray E., Jr. 1933- *St&PR 93*
Marchman, Robert L., III 1925- *St&PR 93, WhoAm 92*
Marchment, Alan Roy 1927- *St&PR 93*
Marchol, Paul Jerome 1948- *WhoEmL 93*
Marchosky, Leo 1956- *WhoWor 93*
Marchuk, Raymond 1951- *St&PR 93*
Marcian c. 392-457 *OxDcByz*
Marciani, Dante J. 1939- *St&PR 93*
Marciano, Richard Alfred 1934- *WhoAm 92*
Marciano, Rocky 1924-1969 *BioIn 17*
Marcianus 396-457 *HarEnMi*
Marcil, Benoit 1963- *St&PR 93*
Marcil, Denise *BioIn 17*
Marcil, Denise Mary 1952- *WhoWrEP 92*
Marcil, William Christ 1936- *St&PR 93*
Marcil, William Christ, Sr. 1936- *WhoAm 92*
Marcillac, Philippe 1959- *WhoEmL 93*
Marci-Mariani, Anita 1960- *WhoAmW 93*
Marcinek, Margaret Ann 1948- *WhoAmW 93*
Marcinek, Michael S. 1956- *St&PR 93*
Marciniak, W. *WhoScE 91-4*
Marcinko, Richard *BioIn 17*
Marcinkowski, Jacek 1946- *WhoScE 91-4*
Marcinkowski, Karol 1800-1846 *PolBiDi*
Marcinkowski, Marion John 1931- *WhoAm 92*
Marcinkowski, Witold *WhoScE 91-4*
Marcinowski-Rainbolt, Karen Eileen 1964- *WhoAmW 93*
Marcioch, Norm *St&PR 93*
Marciulionis, Inga *BioIn 17*
Marciulionis, Sarunas *BioIn 17, NewYTBS 92 [port]*
Marckoon, Stuart Ellsworth 1958- *WhoEmL 93*
Marcks, Gerhard 1889-1981 *BioIn 17*
Marclay, Christian *BioIn 17*
Marco, Carol Lenore 1960- *WhoWrEP 92*
Marco, David Duane 1951- *WhoEmL 93*
Marco, Guy Anthony 1927- *WhoAm 92, WhoWor 93*
Marco, Paul *BioIn 17*
Marco, Tomas 1942- *Baker 92*
Marcoccia, Louis Gary 1946- *WhoAm 92, WhoE 93*
Marcolini, Marietta c. 1780- *OxDcOp*
Marcon, Elio L. 1934- *St&PR 93*
Marcon, Fred R. 1937- *WhoIns 93*
Marcone, Jorge Tobias 1959- *WhoE 93*
Marconi, Alex B. *Law&B 92*
Marconi, David *MiSFD 9*
Marconi, David 1956- *ScF&FL 92*
Marconi, Enrico 1792-1863 *PolBiDi*
Marconi, Guglielmo 1874-1937 *BioIn 17*
Marconi, Guillermo Rafael 1959- *WhoWor 93*
Marconi, Joe d1992 *NewYTBS 92*
Marconis, Carolyn Mary 1957- *WhoE 93*
Marcontell, William A. *Law&B 92*
Marcos, Ferdinand E. 1917-1989 *BioIn 17*
Marcos, Ferdinand Edralin 1917-1989 *DcTwHis*
Marcos, Imelda *BioIn 17*
Marcosson, Thomas I. 1936- *WhoAm 92*
Marcotte, Brian Michael 1949- *WhoE 93, WhoEmL 93*
Marcotte, Frank Basil 1923- *WhoAm 92, WhoE 93*
Marcotte, Gilles 1925- *WhoCanL 92*
Marcotte, Joseph B., Jr. 1934- *St&PR 93*
Marcotte, Joseph Bernard, Jr. 1934- *WhoAm 92*
Marcotte, Michael Steven 1951- *WhoEmL 93, WhoSSW 93*
Marcotte, Michael T. *Law&B 92*
Marcotte, Robert S. 1932- *St&PR 93, WhoAm 92*
Marcotte, Ronald P. 1945- *St&PR 93*
Marcouiller, Sheryl A. *Law&B 92*
Marcoux, Carl Henry 1927- *WhoAm 92*
Marcoux, Craig 1949- *St&PR 93*
Marcoux, Jules Edouard 1924- *WhoAm 92*
Marcoux, Lee C. 1951- *St&PR 93*
Marcoux, Marie Celeste 1951- *WhoEmL 93*
Marcoux, Thomas A. *Law&B 92*
Marcoux, Vanni 1877-1962 *Baker 92, IntDcOp, OxDcOp*
Marcoux, William Joseph 1927- *WhoAm 92*
Marcoux, Yvon 1941- *WhoAm 92*
Marcovicci, Andrea *BioIn 17*
Marcovicci, Andrea 1949- *NewYTBS 92 [port]*
Marcovici, Silvia 1952- *Baker 92*
Marcovici, Sorin 1948- *St&PR 93*
Marcovitz, Leonard Edward 1934- *WhoAm 92, WhoWor 93*
Marcovsky, Gerald Bennett *Law&B 92*
Marcricostas, Constantine *St&PR 93*
Marcstrom, Vidar E.J. 1924- *WhoScE 91-4*
Marcu, Gheorghe 1926- *WhoScE 91-4*
Marcucci, Frank James 1940- *St&PR 93*
Marcucci, Louis Leo 1914- *St&PR 93*
Marcuccio, Phyllis Rose 1933- *WhoAm 92*
Marcucella, Henry 1942- *WhoE 93*
Marculescu, Nicolae N. 1921- *WhoScE 91-4*
Marculescu, Victoria-Lucia 1938- *WhoScE 91-4*
Marcum, Deanna Bowling 1946- *WhoAm 92, WhoAmW 93, WhoE 93*
Marcum, Gordon George, II 1942- *WhoSSW 93*
Marcum, Harold Anthony 1934- *St&PR 93*
Marcum, James Benton 1938- *WhoAm 92, WhoE 93*
Marcum, Jerry Dean 1931- *St&PR 93*
Marcum, Joseph L. 1923- *St&PR 93, WhoIns 93*
Marcum, Joseph LaRue 1923- *WhoAm 92*
Marcum, Kenneth William 1939- *St&PR 93*
Marcus, Aaron *BioIn 17*
Marcus, Adrianne Maris 1935- *WhoWrEP 92*
Marcus, Alexander 1913- *St&PR 93*
Marcus, Allan M. *Law&B 92*
Marcus, Arthur 1926- *St&PR 93*
Marcus, Barry *BioIn 17*
Marcus, Ben 1911- *St&PR 93, WhoAm 92*
Marcus, Bernard 1924- *WhoAm 92*
Marcus, Bernard 1929- *ConEn, St&PR 93, WhoAm 92, WhoSSW 93*
Marcus, Bernard P. 1922- *St&PR 93*
Marcus, Beverly 1944- *St&PR 93*
Marcus, C.A. *St&PR 93*
Marcus, Carl 1943- *St&PR 93*
Marcus, Claude 1924- *WhoAm 92*
Marcus, David *Law&B 92*
Marcus, David 1939- *WhoAm 92*
Marcus, David Donald 1943- *WhoSSW 93*
Marcus, David M. 1942- *St&PR 93*
Marcus, Donald Howard 1916- *WhoAm 92, WhoWor 93*
Marcus, Edward 1918- *WhoAm 92*
Marcus, Eileen 1946- *WhoAmW 93*
Marcus, Eric Colton 1957- *WhoE 93*
Marcus, Eric Robert 1944- *WhoE 93, WhoWor 93*
Marcus, Frank 1933- *WhoAm 92*
Marcus, Frank Isadore 1928- *WhoAm 92*
Marcus, Frank W. 1914- *St&PR 93*
Marcus, Franz R. 1928- *WhoScE 91-2*
Marcus, Fred 1933- *St&PR 93*
Marcus, Gail Boxer 1956- *WhoE 93*
Marcus, George Mathew 1941- *WhoAm 92*
Marcus, Gladys d1991 *BioIn 17*
Marcus, Greil *BioIn 17*
Marcus, Greil Gerstley 1945- *WhoAm 92*
Marcus, Guy Taylor 1938- *St&PR 93*
Marcus, H. Gwen *Law&B 92*
Marcus, Harold 1922-1991 *BioIn 17*
Marcus, Harriet 1917- *St&PR 93*
Marcus, Harris Leon 1931- *WhoAm 92, WhoSSW 93*
Marcus, Helen Mollie *WhoAmW 93*
Marcus, Hyman 1914- *WhoAm 92*
Marcus, Jacob Rader 1896- *JeAmHC, WhoAm 92*
Marcus, James S. 1929- *St&PR 93*
Marcus, James Stewart 1929- *WhoAm 92*
Marcus, Jay 1939- *St&PR 93*
Marcus, Jeffrey Arthur 1953- *WhoE 93, WhoEmL 93*
Marcus, Jeffrey H. *Law&B 92*
Marcus, Jeffrey Samuel 1957- *WhoEmL 93*
Marcus, Jodi Lynn *Law&B 92*
Marcus, Joseph 1928- *WhoAm 92*
Marcus, Joy John 1951- *WhoSSW 93*
Marcus, Junis Roberts 1935- *WhoAmW 93*
Marcus, Kenneth Jay *Law&B 92*
Marcus, Kenneth Neal 1941- *St&PR 93*
Marcus, Lee Evan 1953- *WhoSSW 93*
Marcus, Lyn *ConAu 138*
Marcus, Lynn *Law&B 92*
Marcus, Malcolm 1932- *St&PR 93*
Marcus, Manole 1928- *DrEEuF*
Marcus, Marie Eleanor 1914- *WhoE 93, WhoWor 93*
Marcus, Marshall M. *Law&B 92*
Marcus, Marshall Matthew 1933- *St&PR 93*
Marcus, Marvin 1927- *WhoAm 92*
Marcus, Matthew I. 1944- *St&PR 93*
Marcus, Michael Jay 1914- *WhoE 93*
Marcus, Mickey 1901-1949 *BioIn 17*
Marcus, Mordecai 1925- *ConAu 38NR*
Marcus, Morton Jay 1936- *WhoWrEP 92*
Marcus, Norman d1990 *BioIn 17*
Marcus, Norman 1932- *WhoAm 92*
Marcus, Palle 1937- *WhoWor 93*
Marcus, Paul 1946- *WhoAm 92*
Marcus, Percy d1991 *BioIn 17*
Marcus, Philip Irving 1927- *WhoAm 92*
Marcus, Philippe 1953- *WhoWor 93*
Marcus, Phillip Ronald 1947- *WhoEmL 93, WhoWor 93*
Marcus, Richard Alan 1933- *WhoAm 92*
Marcus, Richard C. 1938- *St&PR 93*
Marcus, Richard Cantrell 1938- *WhoAm 92*
Marcus, Richard Greenwald 1947- *St&PR 93, WhoAm 92*
Marcus, Richard S. 1932- *WhoAm 92*
Marcus, Richard Sheldon 1932- *St&PR 93*
Marcus, Richard Warren 1955- *WhoE 93*
Marcus, Robert 1925- *WhoAm 92*
Marcus, Robert B., Jr. 1947- *ScF&FL 92*
Marcus, Robert D. 1936- *WhoAm 92*
Marcus, Rudolph Arthur 1923- *WhoAm 92*
Marcus, Ruth Barcan *WhoAm 92*
Marcus, Samuel S. 1927- *St&PR 93*
Marcus, Seymour 1912- *St&PR 93*
Marcus, Sheldon 1937- *WhoAm 92*
Marcus, Stanley 1905- *BioIn 17, St&PR 93, WhoAm 92, WhoWrEP 92*
Marcus, Stanley 1946- *WhoAm 92*
Marcus, Stanley A. *Law&B 92*
Marcus, Stephen Cecil 1932- *St&PR 93*
Marcus, Stephen H. 1935- *St&PR 93*
Marcus, Stephen Howard 1935- *WhoAm 92*
Marcus, Steven 1928- *WhoAm 92, WhoWrEP 92*
Marcus, Steven Ezra 1946- *WhoSSW 93*
Marcus, Steven Irl 1949- *WhoAm 92*
Marcus, Thomas L. *Law&B 92*
Marcus, Walter F., Jr. 1927- *WhoAm 92, WhoSSW 93*
Marcus, Warren 1929- *St&PR 93*
Marcus, William M. 1938- *St&PR 93*
Marcus, William Michael 1938- *WhoAm 92*
Marcus Aurelius 121-180 *HarEnMi*
Marcus Aurelius, Emperor of Rome 121-180 *BioIn 17*
Marcus Aurelius Antoninus 121-180 *BioIn 17*
Marcuse, Dietrich 1929- *WhoAm 92*
Marcuse, Sibyl 1911- *Baker 92*
Marcuse, William 1924- *WhoE 93*
Marcuss, Stanley Joseph 1942- *WhoAm 92, WhoWor 93*
Marcuvitz, Nathan 1913- *WhoAm 92*
Marcuzzi, Giorgio 1919- *WhoScE 91-3*
Marcuzzo, Maria Cristina 1948- *WhoWor 93*
Marc-Vergnes, Jean-Pierre 1935- *WhoScE 91-2*
Marcy, Carl Milton 1913-1990 *BioIn 17*
Marcy, Jeannine Koonce 1935- *WhoAmW 93*
Marcy, John Allen 1952- *WhoEmL 93*
Marcy, Mary Edna 1877- *AmWomPl*
Marcy, William L. 1786-1857 *PolPar*
Marczak, Marian W. 1930- *WhoScE 91-4*
Marczenko, Zygmunt 1922- *WhoScE 91-4*
Marczewski, Wojciech 1944- *DrEEuF*
Marczynnska, Antonina Wanda 1927- *WhoScE 91-4*
Mard, Matti Pekka 1934- *WhoScE 91-4*
Mardar, Dianna 1948- *WhoAm 92*
Mardas, Dimitri Chrisovergis 1955- *WhoWor 93*
Mardell, Fred R. *Law&B 92*
Mardell, Fred Robert 1934- *St&PR 93, WhoAm 92*
Mardell-Czudnowski, Carol Dolores 1935- *WhoAmW 93*
Marden, Brice 1938- *BioIn 17*
Marden, Earle Rollins *Law&B 92*
Marden, John Newcomb 1935- *WhoAm 92*
Marden, Kenneth Allen 1928- *WhoAm 92*
Marden, Morris 1905- *BioIn 17*
Marden, Orison Swett 1848-1924 *GayN*
Marden, Philip Ayer 1911- *WhoAm 92*
Marden, Robert Allen 1927- *St&PR 93*
Marden, Steven Kenneth 1952- *WhoEmL 93*
Marder, Arnold Robert 1940- *WhoE 93*
Marder, Carol 1941- *WhoAmW 93*
Marder, Daniel 1923- *WhoWrEP 92*
Marder, John G. 1926- *WhoAm 92*
Marder, Michael Zachary 1938- *WhoAm 92*
Marder, Tod Allan 1947- *WhoE 93*
Marder, William Zev 1947- *WhoWor 93*
Marderosian, Ardash *BioIn 17*
Mardh, Per-Anders 1941- *WhoScE 91-4*
Mardia, Kantilal Vardichand *WhoScE 91-1*
Mardian, Samuel, Jr. 1919- *WhoAm 92*
Mardick, Max L. 1934- *St&PR 93*
Mardie 1933- *WhoAm 92*
Mardikes, Tom *BioIn 17*
Mardin, Arif 1932- *SoulM*
Mardinly, Ashe John 1949- *WhoEmL 93*
Mardirossian, Fabio 1947- *WhoScE 91-3*
Mardis, Hal Kennedy 1934- *WhoWor 93*
Mardis, Linda Keiser 1937- *WhoAmW 93*
Mardis, Richard Lyle 1963- *WhoWor 93*
Mardis, Terri *Law&B 92*
Mardrus, Lucie Delarue- d1945 *BioIn 17*
Mardus, Richard d1991 *BioIn 17*
Mardy, Michael J. 1949- *St&PR 93*
Mare, Robert V. 1928- *St&PR 93*
Mareachen, Josephine Ann 1953- *WhoEmL 93*
Maready, William Frank 1932- *WhoSSW 93, WhoWor 93*
Marechal, Adolphe 1867-1935 *Baker 92, OxDcOp*
Marechal, Andre 1916- *WhoWor 93*
Marechal, Ernest 1931- *WhoScE 91-2*
Marechal, Georges R.J.R. 1931- *WhoScE 91-2*
Marechal, (Charles-) Henri 1842-1924 *Baker 92*
Marechal, Leopoldo 1900-1970 *SpAmA*
Marechera, Dambudzo 1952-1987 *BioIn 17*
Marecki, Jacek 1930- *WhoScE 91-4*
Marecki, Michael Francis *Law&B 92*
Maree, Dominique 1932- *WhoScE 91-2*
Maree, Wendy 1938- *WhoWor 93*
Mareels, Iven Michiel Yvonne 1959- *WhoWor 93*
Marek, Alan J. *St&PR 93*
Marek, Celeste Jeanette 1964- *WhoAmW 93*
Marek, Charles Robert 1940- *WhoSSW 93*
Marek, Czeslaw (Josef) 1891-1985 *Baker 92*
Marek, Daniel Richard 1949- *WhoEmL 93*
Marek, Frank E., Jr. *Law&B 92*
Marek, Larry Ted 1955- *St&PR 93*
Marek, Richard *BioIn 17*
Marek, Richard William 1933- *St&PR 93*
Marek, Robert Thomas 1943- *St&PR 93*
Marek, Roxanne Ferraro 1958- *WhoEmL 93*
Marek, Stanislaw Jan 1925- *WhoScE 91-4*
Marek, Vladimir 1928- *WhoAm 92*
Marek, Zdzislaw K. 1924- *WhoScE 91-4*
Marella, Philip Daniel 1929- *WhoAm 92, WhoWor 93*
Marema, Lenore F. *Law&B 92*
Marencic, Richard John 1927- *St&PR 93*
Marenco, Romualdo 1841-1907 *Baker 92*
Marenich, Valery Borisovich 1955- *WhoWor 93*
Marentette, Navarre A. 1925- *St&PR 93*
Marenzio, Luca 1553?-1599 *Baker 92*
Marer, Jack W. *Law&B 92*
Mares, E. A. 1938- *DcLB 122 [port]*
Mares, Francis Hugh 1925- *WhoWor 93*
Mares, Frank James 1951- *WhoWor 93*
Mares, Johann Anton 1719-1794 *Baker 92*
Mares, Michael A. 1945- *ConAu 138*
Mares, Michael Allen 1945- *HispAmA, WhoAm 92*
Maresca, Christian A. 1939- *WhoScE 91-2*
Maresca, Daniel G. 1952- *WhoAm 92*
Maresca, Eugene Merrill 1944- *St&PR 93*
Maresca, Karen K. *Law&B 92*
Maresch, Johann Anton 1719-1794 *Baker 92*
Mareschall, Samuel 1554-1640? *Baker 92*

Mareschi, Jean Pierre 1937- *WhoWor 93*
Marescotti, Andre-Francois 1902- *Baker 92*
Mareth, Glenville *ConAu 37NR*
Mareth, Paul 1945- *WhoE 93*
Maretskaya, Vera 1906-1978 *IntDcF 2-3 [port]*
Marett, R.R. 1866-1943 *IntDcAn*
Maretta, Milan 1939- *WhoScE 91-4*
Marette, Gaston 1942- *WhoWor 93*
Maretzek, Max 1821-1897 *Baker 92*
Maretzo, Richard Joseph 1934- *WhoE 93*
Mareuse, Vania Yves 1954- *WhoWor 93*
Marevich, Michael M. 1949- *St&PR 93*
Marezio, Massimo *WhoScE 91-2*
Marez Oyens, Tera de 1932- *Baker 92*
Marfaing, Yves *WhoScE 91-2*
Marfey, Anne 1927- *WhoWrEP 92*
Marfi, Karoly 1947- *WhoScE 91-4*
Marg, Caroline Catherine 1962- *WhoWrEP 92*
Marg, Joseph 1924- *St&PR 93*
Margadonna, Daniele *WhoScE 91-3*
Margalef Lopez, Ramon 1919- *WhoScE 91-3*
Margall, Francisco Pi y 1824-1901 *BioIn 17*
Margaret, Duchess of Newcastle 1624?-1674 *BioIn 17*
Margaret, Princess 1930- *BioIn 17*
Margaretha 1480-1530 *BioIn 17*
Margaretha, Paul 1944- *WhoScE 91-3, WhoWor 93*
Margaret, of Austria, Regent of the Netherlands 1480-1530 *BioIn 17*
Margaret Rose 1930- *WhoWor 93*
Margaritis, John Paul 1949- *WhoAm 92, WhoE 93*
Margaritis, Nicholas 1944- *WhoWor 93*
Margaritoff, Dimitri Andrej 1947- *WhoEmL 93*
Margaritondo, Giorgio 1946- *WhoWor 93*
Margaroni, Gerasimina 1963- *WhoWor 93*
Marge, Michael 1928- *WhoAm 92*
Marged, Judith Michele 1954- *WhoAmW 93, WhoEmL 93, WhoSSW 93*
Margeot, Jean Cardinal 1916- *WhoWor 93*
Margerie, Emmanuel de 1924-1991 *BioIn 17*
Margerie, Jean-Claude 1928- *WhoScE 91-2*
Margerie, Roland de 1899-1990 *BioIn 17*
Margerison, Richard W. 1948- *St&PR 93*
Margerison, Richard Wayne 1948- *WhoAm 92*
Margerum, Anthony Jonas 1943- *St&PR 93*
Margerum, Dale William 1929- *WhoAm 92*
Margerum, Fred M. 1953- *St&PR 93*
Margerum, John David 1929- *WhoAm 92*
Margerum, Roger Williams, Jr. 1930- *WhoAm 92*
Margeson, Albert R. 1933- *St&PR 93*
Margeson, Hector 1924- *WhoWrEP 92*
Margetiak, Charlene Jean 1954- *WhoE 93*
Margeton, Stephen George 1945- *WhoAm 92*
Margetson, Stella 1912- *ConAu 40NR*
Margetts, Mark J. 1938- *St&PR 93*
Margetts, W. Thomas 1936- *St&PR 93, WhoAm 92*
Margheret, Janice M. *St&PR 93*
Margherio, Martin John 1945- *St&PR 93*
Margheriti, Antonio *MiSFD 9*
Margie, Joyce Daly 1940- *WhoWrEP 92*
Margileth, Andrew Menges 1920- *WhoAm 92*
Margino, Alphonso *St&PR 93*
Marginson, William R. 1947- *St&PR 93*
Margiotta, Daniel M. 1949- *St&PR 93*
Margiotta, Gary Steven *Law&B 92*
Margiotta, Joseph M. 1927- *PolPar*
Margiotta, Mary-Lou Ann 1956- *WhoAmW 93*
Margiotta, Umberto 1947- *WhoWor 93*
Margiotta, William Thomas, Jr. 1937- *St&PR 93*
Margitza, Rick *BioIn 17*
Margo 1917- *HispAmA*
Margo, Rod David 1950- *WhoEmL 93*
Margol, Irving 1930- *WhoAm 92*
Margola, Franco 1908- *Baker 92*
Margold, Nathan Ross 1899-1947 *EncAACR*
Margoliash, Emanuel 1920- *WhoAm 92*
Margolies, George Howard 1948- *WhoE 93*
Margolies, Joseph A. 1889-1982 *ScF&FL 92*
Margolies, Larry R. *Law&B 92*
Margolies, Luise 1947- *WhoWrEP 92*
Margolies, Matthew Eric 1948- *St&PR 93*
Margolies, Raymond 1920- *WhoAm 92*
Margolin, Arthur Stanley 1936- *St&PR 93*
Margolin, Carl M. 1939- *WhoE 93*
Margolin, Harold 1922- *WhoAm 92*
Margolin, Jean Maday 1937- *WhoE 93*
Margolin, Milton 1930- *WhoE 93*
Margolin, Olya d1990 *BioIn 17*
Margolin, Stuart *MiSFD 9*
Margolis, Aaron E. 1943- *St&PR 93*
Margolis, Bernard Allen 1948- *WhoAm 92*
Margolis, Daniel Herbert 1926- *WhoAm 92*
Margolis, David I. 1930- *St&PR 93*
Margolis, David Israel 1930- *WhoAm 92, WhoE 93*
Margolis, Diane Rothbard *WhoAmW 93*
Margolis, Esther Luterman 1939- *WhoAmW 93*
Margolis, Eugene 1935- *WhoAm 92*
Margolis, Gary Francis 1945- *WhoWrEP 92*
Margolis, George 1914- *WhoAm 92*
Margolis, Gerald Joseph 1935- *WhoAm 92, WhoE 93*
Margolis, Gwen Liedman 1934- *WhoAmW 93, WhoSSW 93*
Margolis, Harold Allen 1943- *St&PR 93*
Margolis, Harry W. 1943- *St&PR 93*
Margolis, Henry Melville 1909-1989 *BioIn 17*
Margolis, Howard 1943- *WhoE 93*
Margolis, Jack S. 1932- *ScF&FL 92*
Margolis, Jeff *MiSFD 9*
Margolis, Jonathan 1955- *ConAu 139*
Margolis, Joseph 1924- *WhoWrEP 92*
Margolis, Joseph D. *Law&B 92*
Margolis, Julius 1920- *WhoAm 92*
Margolis, Karl L. *WhoAm 92*
Margolis, Lawrence *Law&B 92*
Margolis, Lawrence Allen 1947- *St&PR 93, WhoAm 92*
Margolis, Lawrence S. 1935- *CngDr 91*
Margolis, Lawrence Stanley 1935- *WhoAm 92, WhoE 93*
Margolis, Leo 1927- *WhoAm 92*
Margolis, Leon *St&PR 93*
Margolis, Leonid Borisovich 1948- *WhoWor 93*
Margolis, Lisa *Law&B 92*
Margolis, Louis I. 1944- *WhoAm 92*
Margolis, Max Leopold 1866-1932 *BioIn 17*
Margolis, Maxine Luanna 1942- *WhoSSW 93*
Margolis, Michael C. 1951- *St&PR 93*
Margolis, Milton Joseph *St&PR 93*
Margolis, Milton Joseph 1925- *WhoAm 92*
Margolis, Naki B. *Law&B 92*
Margolis, Oscar *St&PR 93*
Margolis, Philip Marcus 1925- *WhoAm 92*
Margolis, Phyllis 1929- *WhoE 93*
Margolis, Richard D. 1938- *St&PR 93*
Margolis, Richard J. *BioIn 17*
Margolis, Richard Martin 1943- *WhoAm 92*
Margolis, Sidney O. 1925- *St&PR 93, WhoAm 92*
Margolis, Stanley V. d1992 *NewYTBS 92*
Margolis, Theodore 1941- *WhoAm 92*
Margolis, William Nathan 1960- *WhoEmL 93*
Margon, Bruce Henry 1948- *WhoAm 92*
Margoshes, Dave 1941- *WhoCanL 92*
Margosian, Lucille K. Manougian 1935- *WhoAmW 93*
Margot, Leslie *WhoWrEP 92*
Margot, Pierre 1950- *WhoScE 91-4*
Margot, Pierre Andre 1950- *WhoWor 93*
Margowski, Janusz 1929- *WhoScE 91-4*
Margowski, Marilyn Joyce 1949- *WhoAmW 93, WhoEmL 93*
Margrave, John Lee 1924- *WhoAm 92, WhoSSW 93*
Margrethe, II 1940- *WhoWor 93*
Margrethe, II, Queen of Denmark 1940- *BioIn 17*
Margroff, Robert 1930- *ScF&FL 92*
Marguard, Charles *St&PR 93*
Marguard, William A. *St&PR 93*
Marguerie, Gerard *WhoScE 91-2*
Marguerite, Queen 1492-1549 *BioIn 17*
Marguerite, Carl A. 1940- *St&PR 93*
Marguerite d'Angouleme, Queen of Navarre 1492-1549 *BioIn 17*
Marguerite de Navarre 1492-1549 *BioIn 17*
Margulan, A.Kh. 1904-1985 *IntDcAn*
Margulies, Alfred Salsbury 1948- *WhoEmL 93*
Margulies, Beth Zeldes 1954- *WhoEmL 93*
Margulies, David 1937- *ConTFT 10*
Margulies, Herman 1922- *WhoE 93*
Margulies, Irving 1934- *St&PR 93*
Margulies, James Howard 1951- *WhoAm 92, WhoE 93, WhoEmL 93*
Margulies, Jerome 1914- *St&PR 93*
Margulies, Joyce E. *Law&B 92*
Margulies, Martin B. 1940- *WhoAm 92*
Margulies, Newton *WhoAm 92*
Margulis, Alan D. 1937- *St&PR 93*
Margulis, Alexander Rafailo 1921- *WhoAm 92*
Margulis, Howard Lee 1961- *WhoEmL 93*
Margulis, Jerry 1929- *WhoWrEP 92*
Margulis, Lynn 1938- *BioIn 17, CurBio 92 [port], WhoAm 92, WhoAmW 93*
Margulis, Thomas N. 1937- *WhoE 93*
Margulois, David 1912- *WhoAm 92*
Margulus, Lisabeth Scharff 1947- *WhoAmW 93*
Margus, Edward A. 1920- *St&PR 93*
Margus, Paul E. 1948- *WhoIns 93*
Marguste, Anti 1931- *Baker 92*
Marhic, Michel Edmond 1945- *WhoAm 92*
Marhold, Aurel L.S. 1929- *WhoScE 91-4*
Marl, Joseph *St&PR 93*
Maria, Joseph Mario 1935- *St&PR 93*
Maria Antonia Walpurgis 1724-1780 *Baker 92*
Mariah, Paul *WhoWrEP 92*
Mariam, Thomas Fred 1957- *WhoEmL 93*
Mariani, Angelo 1821-1873 *IntDcOp, OxDcOp*
Mariani, Angelo 1963- *WhoE 93*
Mariani, Angelo (Maurizio Gaspare) 1821-1873 *Baker 92*
Mariani, David Frank 1942- *WhoE 93*
Mariani, Franco 1927- *WhoScE 91-3*
Mariani, Giuseppe 1948- *WhoWor 93*
Mariani, Joseph J. 1950- *WhoScE 91-2*
Mariani, Luciano 1801-1858 *OxDcOp*
Mariani, Luigi 1937- *WhoScE 91-3*
Mariani, Paul L. *BioIn 17*
Mariani, Paul Louis 1940- *WhoWrEP 92*
Mariani, Robert K. 1934- *St&PR 93*
Mariani, Rosa 1799- *OxDcOp*
Mariani, Veronica Joan 1960- *WhoEmL 93*
Mariani, Vincent Michael 1962- *WhoEmL 93*
Marianik, Charles Gabor 1946- *WhoEmL 93*
Mariani-Masi, Maddalena 1850-1916 *OxDcOp*
Marianne, of Molokai, Mother 1838-1918 *BioIn 17*
Mariano, Fernando 1946- *WhoWor 93*
Mariano, Michael A. *Law&B 92*
Marians, Kenneth Jay 1951- *WhoE 93*
Maria of Alania c. 1050-c. 1103 *OxDcByz*
Maria of Antioch 114-?-1182? *OxDcByz*
Mariaschin, Mark Arthur 1953- *WhoE 93*
Mariassy, Felix 1919-1975 *DrEEuF*
Mariau, Dominique 1936- *WhoScE 91-2*
Maria y Campos, Arnando de 1897- *DcMexL*
Mari Bras, Juan 1927- *DcCPCAm*
Maric, Ljubica 1909- *Baker 92*
Maric, Mileva Einstein- 1875-1948 *BioIn 17*
Maric, Vladimir 1939- *WhoScE 91-4*
Maricevic, Vince 1952- *St&PR 93*
Marich, Ronald R. *Law&B 92*
Marichal, Juan 1937- *HispAmA*
Maricich, Robert J. 1950- *St&PR 93*
Marie, Alain 1946- *WhoWor 93*
Marie, Andre 1897-1974 *BioIn 17*
Marie, Gabriel 1852-1928 *Baker 92*
Marie, Geraldine 1949- *BioIn 17*
Marie, Janet *WhoWrEP 92*
Marie Angeline Teresa 1893-1984 *BioIn 17*
Marie Antoinette, Queen 1755-1793 *BioIn 17*
Marie-Cardine, Michel 1935- *WhoScE 91-2*
Marie, de France 12th cent.- *BioIn 17*
Marie, de l'Incarnation, mere 1599-1672 *BioIn 17*
Marie Gabriella, soeur 1914-1939 *BioIn 17*
Mariella, Raymond P. 1919- *WhoAm 92*
Marien, Robert 1952- *WhoEmL 93*
Marienchild, Eva 1957- *WhoAmW 93, WhoEmL 93*
Marienthal, Elaine Wittert 1924- *WhoAmW 93*
Marienthal, George 1938- *WhoAm 92*
Marier, Raymond C. *Law&B 92*
Marier, Raymond C. 1945- *St&PR 93*
Marietta, Don Emmert, Jr. 1926- *WhoSSW 93*
Marietta, James R. *Law&B 92*
Marietta, Roger Bruce 1953- *WhoSSW 93*
Marie-Victorin 1885-1944 *BioIn 17*
Marihart, Donald Joseph 1926- *WhoAm 92*
Marik, Jan 1920- *WhoAm 92*
Marik, Raymond Lewis 1932- *WhoWrEP 92*
Marika, Mike John 1956- *St&PR 93*
Marikos, Kathryn Ann 1947- *WhoEmL 93*
Marilad, Rosella Querubin 1939- *WhoAmW 93*
Marill, Alvin H. 1934- *ScF&FL 92*
Marillaud, Albert 1934- *WhoScE 91-2*
Marilley, Jane E. d1976 *BioIn 17*
Marilley, Jill Margaret 1965- *WhoAmW 93*
Marimow, William Kalmon 1947- *WhoAm 92*
Marimuthu, Sinnathamby 1948- *WhoWor 93*
Marin, Biagio 1891-1985 *DcLB 128 [port]*
Marin, Cheech *BioIn 17*
Marin, Cheech 1946- *MiSFD 9*
Marin, Edwin L. 1899-1951 *MiSFD 9N*
Marin, John 1870-1953 *BioIn 17*
Marin, Juan 1900-1963 *SpAmA*
Marin, Juan A. 1954- *WhoScE 91-3*
Marin, Louis 1871-1960 *BioIn 17*
Marin, Pamela Ann 1947- *WhoAmW 93*
Marin, Patricia Woods 1939- *WhoAmW 93*
Marin, Richard 1946- *HispAmA*
See Also Cheech and Chong *QDrFCA 92*
Marin, Richard Anthony 1946- *WhoAm 92*
Marin, Robert S. *Law&B 92*
Marin, Robert S. 1945- *St&PR 93*
Marin, Sandra D. 1947- *St&PR 93*
Marin, Vincent Arul 1959- *WhoEmL 93, WhoWor 93*
Marina *OxDcByz*
Marina fl. 3rd cent.- *OxDcByz*
Marina c. 1505-c. 1530 *BioIn 17*
Marina, Princess of Savoy *BioIn 17*
Marinacci, Michael Anthony 1960- *WhoWrEP 92*
Marinaccio, Alexander Teresio 1912- *WhoSSW 93*
Marinaccio, Jim *BioIn 17*
Marinaccio, Marilyn *BioIn 17*
Marinaccio, Paul Joseph 1937- *WhoE 93*
Marinari, Anna 1928- *WhoScE 91-3*
Marinaro, Edward Francis 1950- *WhoAm 92*
Marinatos, Anthony 1946- *St&PR 93*
Marin-Bosch, Miguel 1942- *WhoUN 92*
Marincic, Nikola 1933- *St&PR 93*
Marincola, Dian Angela 1954- *WhoAmW 93*
Marindin, Deborah Sherin 1938- *WhoAmW 93*
Marine, Andrew Craig 1960- *WhoEmL 93*
Marine, Clyde Lockwood 1936- *St&PR 93, WhoAm 92*
Marine, Gene 1926- *WhoWrEP 92*
Marine, Jack J. 1955- *St&PR 93*
Marine, Michael Ray 1954- *WhoWrEP 92*
Marineau, Michele 1955- *WhoCanL 92*
Marinelli, Ada Santi 1942- *WhoAmW 93*
Marinelli, Donald 1953- *WhoEmL 93*
Marinelli, Jean *ScF&FL 92*
Marinelli, Joseph Marcello 1948- *WhoE 93*
Marinelli, Virgil *BioIn 17*
Marinello, Juan *DcCPCAm*
Marinello, Robert Maggio 1945- *WhoIns 93*
Mariner, Donna Marie 1934- *WhoAmW 93, WhoE 93*
Mariner, Elizabeth D. *St&PR 93*
Mariner, Scott *ConAu 37NR*
Mariner, William Martin 1949- *WhoEmL 93, WhoWor 93*
Marines, Louis Lawrence 1942- *WhoAm 92*
Marinescu, John 1940- *WhoWor 93*
Marinetti, Guido V. 1918- *WhoAm 92*
Marin Fernandez, Bernardo 1931- *WhoScE 91-3*
Maring, Norma Ann 1933- *WhoAmW 93*
Marinho, Rita Duarte 1942- *WhoE 93*
Marinho, Roberto 1904- *WhoWor 93*
Marini, Antonietta Rainer- *OxDcOp*
Marini, Biagio c. 1587-1665 *Baker 92*
Marini, Frank 1935- *WhoAm 92*
Marini, Gary J. *Law&B 92*
Marini, Giacomo 1951- *WhoEmL 93*
Marini, Guy L. 1956- *St&PR 93*
Marini, Ignazio 1811-1873 *Baker 92, OxDcOp*
Marini, Ingo Gerhard 1949- *WhoScE 91-3*
Marini, Marino 1901-1980 *BioIn 17*
Marini, Robert C. 1931- *St&PR 93*
Marini, Robert Charles 1931- *WhoAm 92*
Marini, Stephen Conrad 1949- *WhoE 93*
Marini-Abreu, Mario Manuel 1930- *WhoScE 91-3*
Marin Ibanez, Ricardo 1922- *WhoWor 93*
Marini Bettolo, Giovanni Battista 1915- *WhoScE 91-3, WhoWor 93*
Marinich, Vladimir George 1936- *WhoE 93*
Marinis, Rick de *ScF&FL 92*
Marinis, Thomas Paul, Jr. 1943- *WhoAm 92, WhoSSW 93*
Marini y Coppel, Alfredo *ScF&FL 92*
Marinko, Monica Marie 1948- *WhoEmL 93*
Marinkovi, Josef 1851-1931 *Baker 92*

Marinkovic, Dragoslav M. 1934- WhoScE 91-4
Marinkovic, Pribislav 1925- WhoScE 91-4
Marino, Amerigo 1925-1988 Baker 92
Marino, Dan BioIn 17
Marino, Daniel Constantine 1961- WhoAm 92, WhoSSW 93
Marino, Eugene A. BioIn 17
Marino, Eugene Louis 1929- WhoAm 92
Marino, Frank Anthony Law&B 92
Marino, Frank Anthony 1947- WhoEmL 93, WhoSSW 93
Marino, Frederick M. 1946- St&PR 93
Marino, Gary O. 1944- St&PR 93
Marino, Gianlorenzo 1928- WhoScE 91-3
Marino, Ignazio Roberto 1955- WhoWor 93
Marino, J.A. WhoScE 91-1
Marino, James F. WhoIns 93
Marino, James Francis 1943- St&PR 93
Marino, Joanne Marie 1951- WhoAmW 93
Marino, Joseph Anthony 1932- WhoAm 92
Marino, Joseph L. Law&B 92
Marino, Joseph L. 1940- St&PR 93
Marino, Joseph William 1939- St&PR 93
Marino, Lawrence de ScF&FL 92
Marino, Louis John 1949- WhoEmL 93, WhoSSW 93
Marino, Martin A. Law&B 92
Marino, Michael Joseph 1934- St&PR 93
Marino, Peter A. 1942- St&PR 93
Marino, Ralph J. 1928- WhoE 93
Marino, Richard John 1950- St&PR 93
Marino, Rick BioIn 17
Marino, Robert Anthony 1943- WhoE 93
Marino, Rocco Anthony 1952- WhoE 93
Marino, Sal F. 1920- St&PR 93
Marino, Sheila Burris 1947- WhoAmW 93, WhoEmL 93
Marino, Virgil John 1945- WhoAm 92
Marino, William Francis 1948- WhoWor 93
Marino, William J. 1949- WhoEmL 93
Marino-Acebal, Jose B. 1950- WhoScE 91-3
Marinos, Elia Peter 1941- WhoAm 92
Marinos, Paul 1944- WhoScE 91-3
Marinov, Ivan 1928- Baker 92
Marinov, Tenio Minkov 1927- WhoScE 91-4
Marinovich, Todd BioIn 17
Marinuzzi, Francesco WhoWor 93
Marinuzzi, Gino 1882-1945 Baker 92, OxDcOp
Marinuzzi, Gino 1920- Baker 92, OxDcOp
Mario 1810-1883 Baker 92
Mario, David A. Law&B 92
Mario, Ernest 1938- WhoAm 92
Mario, Giovanni 1810-1883 OxDcOp
Mario, Giovanni Matteo 1810-1883 Baker 92, IntDcOp [port]
Mario, Queena 1896-1951 Baker 92
Marion ScF&FL 92
Marion, Andre F. 1935- St&PR 93
Marion, Andrew Burnet 1919- WhoAm 92
Marion, Beth 1912- SweetSg C [port]
Marion, Bradford B. 1956- St&PR 93
Marion, Christopher James, III 1953- WhoEmL 93
Marion, Douglas Welch 1944- WhoAm 92, WhoWrEP 92
Marion, Frances d1973 BioIn 17
Marion, Frances 1888-1973 AmWomPl
Marion, Francis 1732-1795 HarEnMi
Marion, Georgette A. 1927- WhoAmW 93
Marion, Guy Elwood 1882-1969 BioIn 17
Marion, Jerome 1964- BioIn 17
Marion, John Francis 1922- WhoAm 92, WhoWrEP 92
Marion, John Louis 1933- St&PR 93, WhoAm 92
Marion, Kenneth Philip 1949- WhoE 93
Marion, Marjorie Anne 1935- WhoAm 92
Marion, Patrice Jules Jean 1949- WhoWor 93
Marion, Paul AmWomPl
Marion, Peller 1943- WhoAmW 93, WhoWor 93
Marion, Thomas D. 1946- St&PR 93
Mariotta, Alfredo 1939- WhoWor 93
Mariotte, Antoine 1875-1944 Baker 92
Mariotte, Michael Lee 1952- WhoE 93
Mariotti, John Louis 1941- St&PR 93, WhoAm 92
Mariotto, Paulo Antonio 1937- WhoWor 93
Maris, Anthony P. 1933- St&PR 93
Maris, Mona 1903- HispAmA
Maris, Peter MiSFD 9
Maris, Roger 1934-1985 BioIn 17
Maris, Ron SmATA 71
Mariscal, Richard North 1935- WhoSSW 93
Mariscalo, Rosemary Jean 1939- WhoE 93
Marisol WhoAm 92, WhoAmW 93
Marisol 1930- NotHsAW 93
Maris/Semel, Julie BioIn 17
Maritz, William E. WhoAm 92
Mariucci, Anne L. 1957- St&PR 93
Mariucci, John Ubaldo 1939- WhoAm 92
Marius, Gaius 157BC-86BC HarEnMi
Mariwalla, Gopal Chetanram 1944- WhoE 93, WhoWor 93
Mariz, Linda 1948- ConAu 139
Mariz, Vasco 1921- Baker 92
Marjal, Gyula 1930- WhoScE 91-4
Marjenhoff, Jana Lee 1959- WhoSSW 93
Marjolin, Robert E. 1911-1986 BioIn 17
Mark OxDcByz
Mark, Alan Samuel 1947- WhoAm 92
Mark, Andrew Peery 1950- WhoEmL 93
Mark, Andrew R. 1952- WhoEmL 93
Mark, Angela S. 1960- WhoWrEP 92
Mark, Bernard 1932- WhoE 93
Mark, Betsy Yvonne 1947- WhoEmL 93
Mark, Cecil James 1926- St&PR 93
Mark, Denis Hugh 1951- WhoEmL 93
Mark, Dennis John 1953- WhoEmL 93
Mark, Dewey 1927- St&PR 93
Mark, Enid Epstein 1932- WhoE 93
Mark, Evan 1964- WhoEmL 93
Mark, Grace Barrett Arons 1946- WhoAmW 93
Mark, Hans Michael 1929- WhoAm 92, WhoSSW 93, WhoWor 93
Mark, Harold Wayne 1949- WhoSSW 93
Mark, Herman F. 1895-1992 NewYTBS 92 [port]
Mark, Herman F(rancis) 1895-1992 CurBio 92N
Mark, Herman Francis 1895-1992 BioIn 17
Mark, James d1992 BioIn 17
Mark, James B. D. 1929- WhoAm 92
Mark, James Leland 1933- WhoAm 92
Mark, Jan 1943- ScF&FL 92, SmATA 69 [port]
Mark, Jan(et Marjorie) 1943- MajAI [port]
Mark, Jan (Marjorie) 1943- ChlFicS
Mark, Jannik 1957- WhoWor 93
Mark, John Peter Law&B 92
Mark, Jon Wei 1936- WhoAm 92
Mark, Jonathan Bruce 1952- WhoSSW 93
Mark, Jonathan Greenfield 1948- WhoEmL 93
Mark, Kathleen Mary 1951- WhoEmL 93
Mark, Kathleen Mary 1955- WhoAmW 93
Mark, Laurence Peter 1953- WhoE 93, WhoEmL 93
Mark, Leslie Dean 1961- WhoEmL 93
Mark, Lillian Gee 1932- WhoAmW 93
Mark, Margaret B. 1904-1990 BioIn 17
Mark, Mary Ellen 1940- BioIn 17, WhoAm 92
Mark, Mary L. St&PR 93
Mark, Melvin 1922- WhoAm 92
Mark, Michael Laurence 1936- WhoAm 92
Mark, Peter 1940- WhoAm 92, WhoSSW 93
Mark, Reuben 1939- St&PR 93, WhoAm 92
Mark, Richard Allen 1953- WhoAm 92
Mark, Robert E. 1948- St&PR 93
Mark, Robert M. Law&B 92
Mark, Robert Vincent 1942- WhoE 93
Mark, Ronald ScF&FL 92
Mark, Rose Law&B 92
Mark, Shelley Muin 1922- WhoAm 92
Mark, Shew-Kuey Tommy 1936- WhoAm 92
Markandaya, Kamala 1924- IntLitE
Markarian, Noubar 1922- WhoWor 93
Markatos, Nicolas-Chris Gregory 1944- WhoWor 93
Markbreiter, Stewart Daryl 1962- St&PR 93
Marke, Julius Jay 1913- WhoAm 92
Markee, Katherine Madigan 1931- WhoAmW 93, WhoWor 93
Markel, Anthony Foster 1942- WhoIns 93
Markel, Charles A. 1947- St&PR 93
Markel, Debby BioIn 17
Markel, Gregory Arthur 1945- WhoE 93, WhoWor 93
Markel, Helen d1990 BioIn 17
Markel, Howard BioIn 17
Markel, Janet L. 1937- St&PR 93
Markel, John Dundas 1943- WhoAm 92
Markel, Merwyn Robert 1942- WhoE 93
Markel, Steven A. 1948- St&PR 93
Markel, Steven Andrew 1948- WhoAm 92
Markell, Alan William 1933- WhoAm 92
Markellis, Anthony Steven 1952- WhoEmL 93
Markellos of Ankyra c. 280-c. 374 OxDcByz
Markellos the Akoimetos c. 400-c. 484 OxDcByz
Markels, Michael, Jr. 1926- St&PR 93, WhoAm 92
Marken, William Riley 1942- WhoAm 92
Marker, Chris 1921- MiSFD 9
Marker, David G. 1937- WhoAm 92
Marker, Frederick (Joseph, Jr.) 1936- ConAu 39NR
Marker, Jill Lorene 1966- WhoAmW 93
Marker, Leonard K. 1913- WhoE 93, WhoWor 93
Marker, Lise-Lone (Christensen) 1934- ConAu 39NR
Marker, Marc L. Law&B 92
Marker, Marc Linthacum 1941- WhoAm 92, WhoWor 93
Marker, Pat BioIn 17
Marker, Rhonda Joyce 1956- WhoAmW 93
Marker, Robert Sydney 1922- WhoAm 92
Markert, Clement Lawrence 1917- WhoAm 92
Markert, James Macdowell 1934- St&PR 93
Markert, John William 1947- St&PR 93
Markert, Leonard P., Jr. 1926- St&PR 93
Markert, Russell 1899-1990 Baker 92, BioIn 17
Markert, Wallace, Jr. 1924- WhoAm 92
Marker-White, Patricia Jean 1957- WhoAmW 93
Markes, Anthony MiSFD 9
Markesbery, William R. 1932- WhoAm 92
Markessini, Joan 1942- WhoAmW 93
Market, Gary Harold Law&B 92
Markevich, Fenton J. 1955- St&PR 93
Markevitch, Igor 1912-1983 Baker 92
Markey, Andrew J. 1931- St&PR 93
Markey, Arthur Andrew 1946- WhoE 93
Markey, Brian Michael 1956- WhoEmL 93
Markey, Constance Daryl 1945- WhoAmW 93
Markey, David John, III 1940- WhoAm 92
Markey, Edward J. 1946- CngDr 91
Markey, Edward John 1946- WhoAm 92, WhoE 93
Markey, Howard Thomas CngDr 91
Markey, Joanne Zink 1941- WhoAmW 93
Markey, John Brian 1951- WhoSSW 93
Markey, Joseph H., Jr. 1945- St&PR 93
Markey, Michael J. 1932- St&PR 93
Markey, Robert Guy 1939- St&PR 93, WhoAm 92
Markey, William Alan 1927- WhoAm 92
Markey, William C. 1906- St&PR 93
Markey, Winston Roscoe 1929- WhoAm 92
Markeys SoulM
Markferding, Gail Maureen 1947- WhoAmW 93
Markfort, Anne Marie 1950- WhoWrEP 92
Markgraf, John Hodge 1930- WhoAm 92
Markgraf, Karl F. 1956- WhoSSW 93
Markgraf, Rosemarie 1934- WhoAmW 93
Markham, Beryl 1902-1986 BioIn 17, Expl 93 [port]
Markham, Bradford M. Law&B 92
Markham, Catharine AmWomPl
Markham, Charles Buchanan 1926- WhoAm 92, WhoSSW 93
Markham, Charles Rinklin 1959- WhoE 93, WhoEmL 93
Markham, Charlotte AmWomPl
Markham, Clements R. 1830-1916 BioIn 17
Markham, Donna Jean 1947- WhoAmW 93
Markham, Edward D. St&PR 93
Markham, Edward Murphy, III 1930- St&PR 93
Markham, Edwin 1852-1940 GayN, TwCLC 47 [port]
Markham, Felix (Maurice Hippisley) 1908-1992 ConAu 139
Markham, Jerome David 1917- WhoSSW 93
Markham, Jesse William 1916- WhoAm 92
Markham, John Steven 1930- St&PR 93
Markham, Jordan J. 1916- WhoAm 92
Markham, Linda Gail 1951- WhoEmL 93
Markham, Marcella d1991 BioIn 17
Markham, Maria Clare 1919- WhoE 93
Markham, Marion M. 1929- BioIn 17, WhoWrEP 92
Markham, Monte 1938- MiSFD 9
Markham, Paul St&PR 93
Markham, Reed B. 1957- WhoWor 93
Markham, Rosemary 1946- WhoEmL 93
Markham, Sara Frances Norris 1947- WhoAmW 93
Markham, Susan 1946- WhoUN 92
Markham, Thomas N. 1934- St&PR 93
Markham, Walter Gray 1926- WhoE 93
Markianos of Herakleia OxDcByz
Markie, Peter Joseph 1950- WhoAm 92
Markievicz, Constance Georgina 1868-1927 BioIn 17
Markiewicz, James Edward 1932- St&PR 93
Markiewicz, Jan 1919- WhoScE 91-4
Markiewicz, Michael 1953- WhoEmL 93
Markiewicz, Steven Law&B 92
Markiewicz, Wladyslaw 1920- WhoWor 93
Markim, Alfred 1927- St&PR 93
Markin, David Robert 1931- WhoAm 92
Markin, Rom J. 1932- WhoAm 92
Markkula, Martti Antero 1926- WhoScE 91-4
Markl, Hubert 1938- WhoScE 91-3
Markland, Francis Swaby, Jr. 1936- WhoAm 92
Markland, Judith 1944- St&PR 93, WhoAmW 93
Markle, Ann Elizabeth 1952- WhoEmL 93
Markle, Cheri Virginia Cummins 1936- WhoWor 93
Markle, Fletcher 1921-1991 BioIn 17
Markle, Frank Harlan Law&B 92
Markle, George Bushar, IV 1921- WhoAm 92
Markle, John, Jr. 1931- WhoAm 92
Markle, Peter MiSFD 9
Markle, Roger Allan 1933- WhoAm 92
Markle, Sharon Lea 1945- WhoSSW 93
Markle, Susan Meyer 1928- WhoAmW 93
Markley, Brenda Eileen 1964- WhoAmW 93
Markley, Francis Landis 1939- WhoE 93
Markley, Lynn McMaster 1938- WhoWor 93
Markley, Theodore J. St&PR 93
Markley, Thomas R. 1940- St&PR 93
Markley, William C., III Law&B 92
Markman, Linda E. Law&B 92
Markman, Michael Law&B 92
Markman, Raymond Jerome 1927- WhoAm 92
Markman, Ronald 1931- WhoAm 92
Markman, Sherman 1920- WhoWor 93
Markman, Sherwin J. 1929- WhoAm 92
Marko, Debbie Rice- BioIn 17
Marko, Harold 1925- St&PR 93
Marko, Harold Meyron 1925- WhoAm 92
Marko, Laszlo 1928- WhoScE 91-4
Marko, Matthew P. 1958- St&PR 93
Markoe, Arnold Michael 1942- WhoSSW 93
Markoe, Frank, Jr. 1923- WhoAm 92, WhoWor 93
Markoe, Guy Leigh 1953- St&PR 93
Markoe, M.A. 1927- St&PR 93
Markoff, Elizabeth Kathryn 1968- WhoAmW 93
Markoff, Gary David 1956- WhoE 93, WhoEmL 93
Marko Kraljevic d1395 OxDcByz
Markopoulos, Gregory J. d1992 NewYTBS 92
Markoski, Joseph Peter 1948- WhoAm 92
Markou, Christos 1959- WhoSSW 93
Markou, Peter John 1940- WhoE 93
Markov, Georgii 1929-1978 ScF&FL 92
Markov, Pavel Kostadinov 1918- WhoScE 91-4
Markov, Todor 1918- WhoScE 91-4
Markov, Vladimir Vasilievich 1954- WhoWor 93
Markova, Alicia 1910- BioIn 17
Markova, Ivana WhoScE 91-1
Markova, Juliana 1945- Baker 92
Markovic, Aleksandar 1924- WhoScE 91-4
Markovic, Ante 1924- BioIn 17
Markovic, Goran 1946- DrEEuF
Markovic, Milan 1928- WhoScE 91-4
Markovich, Annie Marie 1947- WhoE 93
Markovich, Ched J. 1942- St&PR 93
Markovich, John M. 1956- St&PR 93
Markovich, Lois Ann Gimondo 1947- WhoEmL 93
Markovich, Nicholas Charles 1948- WhoSSW 93
Markovich, Stephen E. Law&B 92
Markovich-Treece, Patricia 1941- WhoAmW 93, WhoWor 93
Markovits, Andrei Steven 1948- WhoE 93, WhoEmL 93
Markovits, Ronald D. Law&B 92, WhoIns 93
Markovits, Ronald D. 1943- St&PR 93
Markovitz, Alvin 1929- WhoAm 92
Markovna, Nina BioIn 17
Markow, Leslie N. 1960- St&PR 93
Markow, Steven Alan 1952- WhoSSW 93
Markowich, Michael A. 1948- St&PR 93
Markowicz, Allen Lee 1947- WhoEmL 93
Markowicz, Victor 1944- St&PR 93
Markowitz, Alan Larry 1943- WhoSSW 93
Markowitz, Arthur Donald 1940- WhoAm 92
Markowitz, Barry St&PR 93
Markowitz, Bruce 1954- WhoEmL 93
Markowitz, David 1923- St&PR 93
Markowitz, Edwin R. 1930- St&PR 93
Markowitz, Harry M. 1927- BioIn 17, WhoAm 92, WhoE 93, WhoWor 93

Markowitz, John C. 1954- WhoEmL 93
Markowitz, Mark Joel 1951- St&PR 93
Markowitz, Mitch I. St&PR 93
Markowitz, Phyllis Frances 1931- WhoAmW 93, WhoE 93
Markowitz, Robert MiSFD 9
Markowitz, Steven H. Law&B 92
Markowski, Andrzej 1924-1986 Baker 92
Markowski, Benedict Stephen 1932- WhoWrEP 92
Markowski, Michael A. 1947- WhoWrEP 92
Markowsky, George WhoE 93
Markowsky, James J. 1945- St&PR 93
Marks, Abby Lynn 1961- WhoAmW 93
Marks, Ada Greiner 1896- WhoWrEP 92
Marks, Alan 1949- Baker 92
Marks, Alan 1957- ScF&FL 92
Marks, Alan D. 1955- St&PR 93
Marks, Arthur 1927- MiSFD 9
Marks, Barbara Hannah 1956- WhoAm 92, WhoAmW 93, WhoEmL 93
Marks, Bernard Bailin 1917- WhoAm 92
Marks, Brett L. Law&B 92
Marks, Bruce 1937- WhoAm 92, WhoE 93
Marks, C. Caldwell 1921- St&PR 93
Marks, Cara 1955- WhoAmW 93
Marks, Caroline F. Law&B 92
Marks, Charles Caldwell 1921- WhoAm 92
Marks, Charles L. Law&B 92
Marks, Charles L. 1936- WhoIns 93
Marks, Charles Preston 1941- WhoSSW 93
Marks, Claude 1915-1991 BioIn 17
Marks, Colin Herbert 1933- WhoE 93
Marks, Craig 1929- WhoAm 92
Marks, David Hunter 1939- WhoAm 92, WhoE 93
Marks, David Jackson 1951- WhoEmL 93
Marks, Dean S. Law&B 92
Marks, Dennis Howard BioIn 17
Marks, Dennis William 1944- WhoSSW 93
Marks, Dorothy K. Law&B 92
Marks, Dorothy Lind 1900- WhoAmW 93
Marks, Dorothy Louise Ames 1919- WhoAm 92
Marks, E. Matthew 1942- WhoIns 93
Marks, Edward 1934- WhoUN 92
Marks, Edward B. 1911- WhoAm 92
Marks, Edward B(ennett) 1865-1945 Baker 92
Marks, Edward D. Law&B 92
Marks, Edwin S. 1926- WhoAm 92
Marks, Elaine 1930- WhoAm 92
Marks, Emily Menlo 1938- WhoE 93
Marks, Erica Robin 1959- WhoAmW 93
Marks, Eugene Melvin 1921- WhoE 93
Marks, Frances 1956- WhoEmL 93
Marks, Frank Henry 1898- WhoWrEP 92
Marks, Friedrich R.R. 1936- WhoScE 91-3
Marks, Gary 1948- St&PR 93
Marks, Gary Lee Law&B 92
Marks, Geoffrey Charles 1932-1990 BioIn 17
Marks, Gordon William 1944- St&PR 93
Marks, Henry Thomas 1908- WhoAm 92
Marks, Henry Thomas 1908-1991 BioIn 17
Marks, Herbert Edward 1935- WhoAm 92
Marks, Howard Lee 1929- WhoAm 92
Marks, Ila Circle 1932- WhoSSW 93
Marks, Isaac M. WhoScE 91-1
Marks, J. BioIn 17, MajAI
Marks, Janice Elizabeth 1960- WhoEmL 93
Marks, Jay G. 1944- St&PR 93
Marks, Jeannette Augustus 1875-1964 AmWomPl
Marks, Jerome 1931- WhoAm 92
Marks, Joan 1932- St&PR 93
Marks, Joel E. 1956- St&PR 93
Marks, Joel Howard 1949- WhoE 93
Marks, John Barrett 1946- WhoEmL 93
Marks, John Henry 1923- WhoAm 92
Marks, Johnny 1909-1985 Baker 92
Marks, Jonathan Paul 1958- WhoWor 93
Marks, Josephine Preston Peabody AmWomPl
Marks, Keith Orin 1950- WhoEmL 93
Marks, Kenny BioIn 17
Marks, Laurie J. BioIn 17
Marks, Laurie J. 1957- ScF&FL 92
Marks, (Amelia) Lee 1948- ConAu 137
Marks, Leon Law&B 92
Marks, Leonard, Jr. 1921- WhoAm 92
Marks, Leonard Harold 1916- WhoAm 92
Marks, Leonard M. 1942- WhoWor 93
Marks, Lillian Shapiro 1907- WhoAmW 93
Marks, Lynn Wilson 1955- WhoEmL 93
Marks, Malvin 1931- St&PR 93
Marks, Marie Schulz 1957- WhoAmW 93
Marks, Marjorie d1990 BioIn 17
Marks, Martha Alford 1946- WhoAmW 93
Marks, Marvin Lee 1936- WhoE 93
Marks, Mary Whitten Law&B 92
Marks, Merton Eleazer 1932- WhoAm 92
Marks, Meyer Benjamin 1907-1991 WhoAm 92
Marks, Michael G. 1931- St&PR 93
Marks, Michael George 1931- WhoAm 92
Marks, Michael J. Law&B 92
Marks, Michael J. 1938- WhoAm 92
Marks, Mitchell 1940- St&PR 93
Marks, Monica Leigh 1965- WhoAmW 93
Marks, Patti H. Law&B 92
Marks, Paul Alan 1926- WhoAm 92, WhoWor 93
Marks, Pauline 1950- WhoE 93
Marks, Peter Amasa 1948- WhoEmL 93
Marks, Peter C. 1942- St&PR 93
Marks, R.J. WhoScE 91-1
Marks, Ramon Paul 1948- WhoEmL 93
Marks, Randolph Anthony 1935- St&PR 93
Marks, Raymond H. 1922- WhoAm 92
Marks, Richard 1943- ConTFT 10
Marks, Richard Berea WhoE 93
Marks, Richard C. 1937- St&PR 93
Marks, Richard Samuel 1937- St&PR 93
Marks, Robert 1955- WhoEmL 93
Marks, Robert Bosler 1953- WhoEmL 93
Marks, Robert E. 1950- WhoE 93
Marks, Robert Ernest 1946- WhoWor 93
Marks, Robert H. 1938- St&PR 93
Marks, Roberta Barbara WhoAmW 93
Marks, Roger Harris 1951- WhoEmL 93
Marks, Rosalind Law&B 92
Marks, Russell Edward, Jr. 1932- WhoAm 92
Marks, Ruth A. 1940- WhoIns 93
Marks, Ruth Antoinette 1920- WhoWrEP 92
Marks, Scott P., Jr. 1946- St&PR 93
Marks, Sherwin J. 1948- St&PR 93
Marks, Shula Eta 1936- WhoWor 93
Marks, Spencer Jonathon 1950- WhoE 93
Marks, Stan M. 1946- St&PR 93
Marks, Stephanie Lyn 1958- WhoEmL 93
Marks, Stephen Paul 1943- WhoE 93
Marks, Steven L. 1935- St&PR 93
Marks, Steven Walter 1953- WhoE 93, WhoWrEP 92
Marks, Tamara Elizabeth 1962- WhoAmW 93
Marks, Theodore Lee 1935- WhoE 93, WhoWor 93
Marks, Tobin Jay 1944- WhoAm 92
Marks, Tracy 1950- ScF&FL 92
Marks, Vincent WhoScE 91-1
Marks, Vincent 1930- WhoWor 93
Marks, William Louis 1933- St&PR 93
Marksheffel, Edward Everett 1949- WhoEmL 93
Marksheid, Jay Dennis 1946- WhoEmL 93
Marks-Highwater, J. MajAI
Markson, David BioIn 17
Markson, David 1927- ScF&FL 92
Markson, David M. 1927- WhoWrEP 92
Markson, Elizabeth Warren WhoAmW 93
Markson, Peter 1962- St&PR 93
Mark the Deacon fl. 5th cent.- OxDcByz
Mark the Hermit OxDcByz
Marktl, Wolfgang 1944- WhoScE 91-4
Markull, Friedrich Wilhelm 1816-1887 Baker 92
Markun, Frank O. 1947- WhoEmL 93, WhoSSW 93
Markun, Patricia Maloney 1924- WhoWrEP 92
Markun, Rachel 1957- WhoAmW 93
Markus, Andrew Joshua 1948- WhoEmL 93
Markus, David 1942- St&PR 93
Markus, Edward A., Jr. Law&B 92
Markus, Fred H. 1927- St&PR 93, WhoAm 92
Markus, James S. 1947- St&PR 93
Markus, Julia WhoWrEP 92
Markus, Lawrence 1922- WhoAm 92
Markus, N.W., Jr. 1925- St&PR 93
Markus, Norbert Williams, Jr. 1925- WhoAm 92
Markus, Richard M. 1930- WhoAm 92
Markus, Rixi d1992 BioIn 17
Markus, Rixi 1910-1992 NewYTBS 92
Markus, Robert Michael 1934- WhoAm 92
Markussen, Christine N. Law&B 92
Markuszka, Nancy Ann 1951- WhoAmW 93, WhoEmL 93
Markvoort, Jan Albert 1943- WhoWor 93
Mark Vs SoulM
Markwald, Roger R. 1943- WhoAm 92
Markwardt, Kenneth Marvin 1928- WhoAm 92
Markwart, Luther Allan 1954- WhoE 93
Markwell, Dick Robert 1925- WhoSSW 93
Markwell, Kenneth, Jr. 1923- St&PR 93
Markwick, Edward ScF&FL 92
Markwitz, Debra J. Law&B 92
Markwood, Sandra Reinsel 1955- WhoE 93
Markwort, Johann Christian 1778-1866 Baker 92
Marky Mark BioIn 17
Markytan, Manfred M.R. 1940- WhoScE 91-4
Marl, David ScF&FL 92
Marlan, Lori J. 1957- WhoEmL 93
Marland, Alkis Joseph 1943- WhoAm 92, WhoE 93, WhoWor 93
Marland, Christina ConAu 38NR
Marland, Michael 1934- ScF&FL 92
Marland, Sidney 1914-1992 BioIn 17
Marland, Sidney P., Jr. d1992 NewYTBS 92
Marland, Sidney P(ercy), Jr. 1914-1992 CurBio 92N
Marland, Sidney P(ercy, Jr.) 1914-1992 ConAu 137
Marlar, John Thomas 1939- WhoSSW 93
Marlas, James C. 1937- St&PR 93
Marlas, James Constantine 1937- WhoAm 92, WhoWor 93
Marlatt, Daphne 1942- WhoCanL 92
Marlatt, Daphne (Buckle) 1942- ConAu 39NR
Marlatt, Edward Thomas 1941- St&PR 93
Marlborough, Duchess of 1660-1744 BioIn 17
Marlborough, Duke of 1650-1722 BioIn 17
Marlborough, Donald John 1936- St&PR 93
Marlborough, John Churchill, Duke of 1650-1722 HarEnMi
Marleau, Diane 1943- WhoAmW 93
Marleau, Guy Georges 1951- St&PR 93
Marleau, Robert 1948- WhoAm 92
Marlek, Marilyn Law&B 92
Marlen, James S. St&PR 93
Marlen, James S. 1941- WhoAm 92
Marlenee, Ron 1935- CngDr 91
Marlenee, Ronald Charles 1935- WhoAm 92
Marler, Bob, Jr. 1942- St&PR 93
Marler, Linda Susan 1951- WhoAmW 93
Marler, Valerie Scalera 1944- WhoSSW 93
Marlett, Charles D. 1954- St&PR 93
Marlett, Charles David Law&B 92
Marlett, De Otis Loring 1911- WhoAm 92, WhoWor 93
Marlett, Eugene Byrns 1927- St&PR 93
Marlett, Judith Ann WhoAmW 93
Marlett, William Robert 1936- WhoSSW 93
Marlette, Doug 1949- BioIn 17
Marlette, Douglas Nigel 1949- WhoAm 92, WhoE 93
Marley, Bob BioIn 17
Marley, Bob 1945-1981 Baker 92
Marley, Elfriede 1943- WhoAmW 93
Marley, Everett Armistead, Jr. 1933- WhoAm 92, WhoSSW 93
Marley, Frank E., Jr. Law&B 92
Marley, James Earl 1935- St&PR 93
Marley, Kemper d1990 BioIn 17
Marley, Mary Louise 1923- WhoAmW 93, WhoE 93, WhoWor 93
Marley, Rita BioIn 17
Marley, Robert P. Law&B 92
Marley, Stephen 1946- ScF&FL 92
Marley, Toomas Law&B 92
Marley, Ziggy BioIn 17
Marliani, Marco Aurelio 1805-1849 Baker 92
Marliave, Joseph de 1873-1914 Baker 92
Marlier, John Thomas 1948- WhoEmL 93
Marlier, Michel Jean-Marie 1945- WhoScE 91-2
Marlin, Arthur David 1934- WhoE 93
Marlin, Davia Beth 1964- WhoAmW 93
Marlin, David John 1961- WhoScE 91-1
Marlin, Jeffrey 1940- ScF&FL 92
Marlin, Jeffrey Stuart 1948- WhoEmL 93
Marlin, John Tepper 1942- WhoE 93, WhoWor 93
Marlin, Kenneth Brian 1955- St&PR 93
Marlin, Richard 1933- WhoAm 92
Marlin, Robert Lewis 1937- WhoE 93
Marlin, Robert M. St&PR 93, WhoAm 92
Marlin, Therese Rose 1938- WhoAmW 93
Marlow, Ann 1946- WhoAmW 93
Marlow, Boone 1865-1889 BioIn 17
Marlow, Bruce Wendell 1949- WhoIns 93
Marlow, Herbert David, Jr. 1955- St&PR 93
Marlow, Max ScF&FL 92
Marlow, Michael F. 1947- St&PR 93
Marlow, Robert Allen 1948- WhoEmL 93
Marlow, Thomas A., II 1933- St&PR 93
Marlow, William WhoScE 91-1
Marlowe, Bob St&PR 93
Marlowe, Brad MiSFD 9
Marlowe, Charmaine Louise Law&B 92
Marlowe, Christopher 1564-1593 MagSWL [port], OxDcOp, WorLitC [port]
Marlowe, Derek 1938- ScF&FL 92
Marlowe, Edward 1935- St&PR 93, WhoAm 92
Marlowe, Fredrik Law&B 92
Marlowe, Howard David 1943- WhoAm 92
Marlowe, Hugh 1929- BioIn 17
Marlowe, James MiSFD 9
Marlowe, Jeanne 1942- WhoWrEP 92
Marlowe, Julia 1865?-1950 BioIn 17
Marlowe, Katherine WhoCanL 92
Marlowe, Mary Louise 1957- WhoEmL 93
Marlowe, Michael BioIn 17
Marlowe, Stephen 1928- ScF&FL 92
Marlowe, Sylvia 1908-1981 Baker 92
Marlyn, John 1912- WhoCanL 92
Marmaduke, John H. 1947- WhoEmL 93
Marmalstein, Morris H. 1934- St&PR 93
Marmaluk, Diana Wagner 1965- WhoEmL 93
Marmanillo, Nestor N. 1938- WhoUN 92
Marmann, Sigrid 1938- WhoWor 93
Marmaras, Vassilis 1938- WhoScE 91-3
Marmas, James Gust 1929- WhoAm 92
Marmash, B.V. 1937- St&PR 93
Marmelstein, Linda d1991 BioIn 17
Marmer, Ellen Lucille 1939- WhoAmW 93, WhoE 93
Marmet, Paul 1932- WhoAm 92
Marmion, Barrie Patrick 1920- WhoWor 93
Marmion, William Henry 1907- WhoAm 92
Marmion-Karnbach, William Francis 1938- St&PR 93
Marmitt, William E. St&PR 93
Marmo, Joseph 1931- St&PR 93
Marmolejo, Martin 1950- WhoWor 93
Marmon, Betty Lewis 1927- WhoAmW 93
Marmon, Owen H. 1923- St&PR 93
Marmon, Owen Holloway 1923- WhoAm 92
Marmont, Auguste Frederic Louis Viesse de 1774-1852 HarEnMi
Marmontel, Antoine-Francois 1816-1898 Baker 92
Marmontel, Antonin Emile Louis Corbaz 1850-1907 Baker 92
Marmontel, Jean Francois 1723-1799 OxDcOp
Marmor, Judd 1910- WhoAm 92, WhoWor 93
Marmor, Michael Franklin 1941- WhoAm 92
Marmor, Robert R. 1926- St&PR 93
Marmorstein, Harry John 1954- WhoE 93, WhoEmL 93
Marmorstein, Malcolm MiSFD 9
Marmosudjono, Sukarton 1937- WhoAsAP 91
Marn, Jeffrey 1979- BioIn 17
Marnell, Marjorie Ann 1954- WhoEmL 93
Marnelli, Kathleen Law&B 92
Marner, Eugene MiSFD 9
Marneros, Andreas 1946- WhoWor 93
Marnet, Chrysanth F.F. 1923- WhoScE 91-3
Marney, Dean 1952- ScF&FL 92
Marode, Emmanuel 1938- WhoScE 91-2
Marohn, Ann Elizabeth 1946- WhoAmW 93, WhoEmL 93
Marohn, Richard Charles 1934- WhoAm 92
Marohn, William D. 1940- St&PR 93
Marolakos, Laura BioIn 17
Marold, Allen D. 1940- St&PR 93
Marolda, Anthony Joseph 1939- St&PR 93, WhoE 93
Marolda, Robert L. 1950- St&PR 93
Maron, Alisa Jill 1963- WhoE 93
Maron, Barbara Clickenger 1949- St&PR 93
Maron, Bud BioIn 17
Maron, Mark S. 1955- St&PR 93
Maron, Melvin Earl 1924- WhoAm 92
Maron, Muriel BioIn 17
Maronde, Robert Francis 1920- WhoAm 92, WhoWor 93
Maronek, Dale Mark 1948- WhoSSW 93
Maroney, Barbara R. 1949- St&PR 93
Maroney, Jane 1923- WhoAmW 93
Maroney, Timothy Joseph, Jr. 1947- WhoAm 92
Maroni, Donna Farolino 1938- WhoAm 92, WhoAmW 93
Maroni, Paul L. 1947- St&PR 93, WhoAm 92
Marootian, George Alan Law&B 92
Maropis, Nicholas 1923- WhoE 93
Maros, Miklos 1943- Baker 92
Maros, Rudolf 1917-1982 Baker 92
Marosan, Gyorgy d1992 NewYTBS 92
Maroscher, Betty Jean 1934- WhoAmW 93
Maroscher, Janice Los 1963- WhoEmL 93

Marosi, Sandor 1929- WhoScE 91-4
Marosits, Robert J. 1942- St&PR 93
Marot, Lola 1939- WhoAmW 93
Maroteaux, Pierre WhoScE 91-2
Marotta, Carmine A. 1927- St&PR 93
Marotta, Charles Anthony 1945- WhoE 93
Marotta, Edward Anthony 1947- WhoE 93
Marotta, Joseph Thomas 1926- WhoAm 92
Marotta, Nicholas G. 1929-1991 BioIn 17
Marotta, Nicholas Gene 1929- WhoAm 92
Marotta, Richard Nathan 1941- WhoWor 93
Marotta, Robert Law&B 92
Marotta, Thomas S. 1943- St&PR 93
Marotti, Gastone 1935- WhoScE 91-3
Marotto, Leslie A. 1954- St&PR 93
Marouf, Taha Muhyiddin 1924- WhoWor 93
Maroules OxDcByz
Maroulis, George 1940- WhoScE 91-3
Marous, John Charles, Jr. 1925- WhoAm 92
Marovich, George M. 1931- WhoAm 92
Marovitz, James Lee 1939- WhoAm 92
Marovitz, William BioIn 17
Marozsan, John Robert 1941- WhoAm 92
Marpe, William J. Law&B 92
Marple, Dorothy Jane 1926- WhoAm 92
Marple, Elaine Noel 1951- WhoAmW 93
Marple, Gary Andre 1937- WhoAm 92, WhoE 93
Marple, Mary Lynn 1951- WhoEmL 93, WhoSSW 93
Marple, Raymond P. BioIn 17
Marple, Stanley Laurence, Jr. 1947- WhoAm 92
Marple, Waneta Ann 1966- WhoEmL 93
Marples, Richard Ransford WhoScE 91-1
Marples, Richard Ransford 1934- WhoWor 93
Marpurg, Friedrich 1825-1884 Baker 92
Marpurg, Friedrich Wilhelm 1718-1795 Baker 92
Marquand, Andre 1954- WhoWor 93
Marquand, John P. 1893-1960 BioIn 17
Marquand, Richard d1987 MiSFD 9N
Marquand, Robert 1957- ConAu 136
Marquard, Suzanne T. Law&B 92
Marquard, William Albert 1920- WhoAm 92, WhoSSW 93
Marquardt, Ann Marie 1964- WhoE 93
Marquardt, Christel Elisabeth 1935- WhoAm 92, WhoAmW 93
Marquardt, Deborah Lynn 1955- WhoAmW 93
Marquardt, Frederic Sylvester 1905- WhoAm 92
Marquardt, Hans Wilhelm Joe 1938- WhoScE 91-3
Marquardt, James Frederick 1925- WhoSSW 93
Marquardt, James Leonard 1957- WhoEmL 93
Marquardt, Kathleen Patricia 1944- WhoAmW 93, WhoWor 93
Marquardt, Meril E. 1926- WhoIns 93
Marquardt, Merritt R. Law&B 92
Marquardt, Niels 1940- WhoWor 93
Marquardt, Patricia Moore 1944- WhoAmW 93
Marquardt, Peter A. Law&B 92
Marquardt, Robert Richard Law&B 92
Marquardt, Terry Tyrone 1949- WhoWor 93
Marquardt, Thomas E. St&PR 93
Marquardt, Timothy A. 1955- St&PR 93
Marquart, Clifford L. 1938- St&PR 93
Marquart, Clifford Lynn 1938- WhoAm 92
Marquart, Dawn Rickey 1963- WhoAmW 93
Marquart, Robert Donald 1953- St&PR 93
Marques, Diane Marie 1958- WhoAmW 93, WhoE 93, WhoEmL 93
Marques, Luis G. 1932- WhoUN 92
Marques, Manuel N. WhoScE 91-3
Marques, Rene 1919-1979 HispAmA, SpAmA
Marques, Walter Waldemar Pego 1936- WhoWor 93
Marques Gomes, Jose Viana WhoScE 91-3
Marquess, Lawrence Wade 1950- WhoEmL 93
Marquess, William H. 1918- St&PR 93
Marquess, William Hoge 1918- WhoIns 93
Marques y Garcia, Pedro Miguel 1843-1918 Baker 92
Marquet, Adrien 1884-1955 BioIn 17
Marquet, Albert 1875-1947 BioIn 17
Marquet, Louis C. 1936- St&PR 93
Marquette, Jacques 1637-1675 Expl 93 [port]
Marquette, Robert, Jr. 1931- St&PR 93
Marquette-Reilly, N.E. Law&B 92
Marquez, Alfredo C. 1922- HispAmA, WhoAm 92
Marquez, Bienvenido O., Jr. 1947- WhoAsAP 91
Marquez, David W. Law&B 92
Marquez, Fidel 1959- WhoE 93
Marquez, Gabriel Garcia ScF&FL 92
Marquez, Gabriel Garcia 1928- BioIn 17
Marquez, Philip Anthony Law&B 92
Marquez, Rafael Benito 1938- WhoSSW 93
Marquez, Roberto 1942- HispAmA
Marquez, Synthia Laura 1963- WhoAmW 93, WhoEmL 93
Marquez Sterling, Carlos 1899-1991 BioIn 17
Marquie, Jean-Pierre 1938- WhoWor 93
Marquinez, Quirino Aquino 1931- WhoWor 93
Marquis, Albert Nelson 1855-1943 GayN
Marquis, Don 1878-1937 JrnUS
Marquis, Gail Annette 1954- WhoE 93
Marquis, Geraldine Mae Hildreth WhoWor 93
Marquis, Harold L. Law&B 92
Marquis, Jeanne Lorraine 1953- WhoAmW 93
Marquis, Julie J. AmWomPl
Marquis, Marjorie AmWomPl
Marquis, Max ConAu 136
Marquis, Oscar Law&B 92
Marquis, Robert B. 1927- WhoAm 92
Marquis, Robert William 1949- WhoEmL 93
Marquis, Rollin Park 1925- WhoAm 92
Marquis, Stephen B. Law&B 92
Marquis, William E. Law&B 92
Marr, Amelia P. Law&B 92
Marr, Carmel Carrington 1921- WhoAm 92
Marr, David Francis 1933- WhoAm 92
Marr, Donald W. 1948- St&PR 93
Marr, Geoffrey Vickers WhoScE 91-1
Marr, James R. 1952- St&PR 93
Marr, Joan Everett Emerson 1933- WhoAmW 93
Marr, John S. 1940- ScF&FL 92
Marr, Johnny BioIn 17
Marr, Leon 1948- MiSFD 9
Marr, Luther R. 1925- St&PR 93
Marr, Luther Reese 1925- WhoAm 92
Marr, Maurice Wayne, Jr. 1956- WhoSSW 93
Marr, Melissa ScF&FL 92
Marr, Phebe Ann 1931- WhoAmW 93
Marr, Richard Arnold 1936- St&PR 93
Marr, Robert Bruce 1932- WhoAm 92
Marr, Robert L. 1936- St&PR 93
Marra, Anthony F. 1941- St&PR 93
Marra, Anthony Francis Law&B 92
Marra, Donald Paul 1948- WhoE 93
Marra, Dorothea Catherine 1922- WhoAmW 93
Marra, Ersilia 1947- WhoScE 91-3
Marra, Michael A. Law&B 92
Marra, Michael Robert 1933- St&PR 93
Marra, Ralph Vincent 1937- St&PR 93
Marra, Thomas Anthony 1955- WhoEmL 93
Marra, Virginia Marie Law&B 92
Marra, William Anthony 1928- WhoE 93
Marraccini, Philip A. Law&B 92
Marraccini, Philip Anthony Law&B 92
Marrack, Philippa BioIn 17
Marrack, Philippa Charlotte 1945- WhoAmW 93
Marram, Ellen R. BioIn 17, St&PR 93
Marrano, Anthony B. 1947- St&PR 93
Marrazzo, William J. 1949- St&PR 93
Marre, E. BioIn 17
Marre, Erasmo BioIn 17
Marre, Ernst Karl 1932- WhoWor 93
Marren, Bernard T. 1935- St&PR 93
Marren, Howard Leslie 1946- WhoEmL 93
Marren, Joanne T. Law&B 92
Marren, Thomas Law&B 92
Marrero, Eliezer BioIn 17
Marrero, Georgina 1954- WhoAmW 93
Marrero, Linda BioIn 17
Marrero, Lucy G. 1954- WhoAmW 93
Marrero, Maria BioIn 17
Marrero, Martika NotHsAW 93
Marrero, Michael A. Law&B 92
Marrero, Robert ScF&FL 92
Marrero, Vicci Lee Haarhues 1954- WhoSSW 93
Marric, J.J. 1908-1973 BioIn 17
Marrichi, Glenn Thomas 1950- WhoAm 92
Marrie, Thomas Phillip 1938- St&PR 93, WhoAm 92
Marrin, Yvette 1937- WhoAmW 93, WhoE 93
Marrinan, Susan Law&B 92
Marrinan, Susan Faye 1948- WhoAm 92
Marriner, David Richard 1934- WhoAm 92
Marriner, Neville 1924- Baker 92, WhoAm 92, WhoWor 93
Marringa, Jacques Louis 1928- St&PR 93, WhoAm 92
Marriot, Salima Siler 1940- WhoAmW 93
Marriott, Alice Lee d1992 NewYTBS 92
Marriott, Alice Lee 1910-1992 BioIn 17, ConAu 137, CurBio 92N, SmATA 71
Marriott, Alice Sheets 1907- St&PR 93, WhoAm 92
Marriott, Anne 1913- WhoCanL 92
Marriott, B. Rodney d1990 BioIn 17
Marriott, Bubba 1938- St&PR 93
Marriott, Carmen A. Law&B 92
Marriott, Carol Ann WhoScE 91-1
Marriott, Christopher WhoScE 91-1
Marriott, J. Willard 1900-1985 BioIn 17
Marriott, J. Willard 1932- BioIn 17
Marriott, J. Willard, Jr. 1932- St&PR 93
Marriott, John W., Jr. 1932- WhoAm 92, WhoE 93
Marriott, Marcia Ann 1947- WhoAmW 93
Marriott, Michel BioIn 17
Marriott, Moore 1885-1949 & Moffatt, Graham 1919-1965 QDrFCA 92 [port]
Marriott, Richard Edwin 1939- St&PR 93, WhoAm 92
Marriott, Steve 1947-1991 AnObit 1991, BioIn 17
Marriott, Vincent J., III Law&B 92
Marro, Anthony James 1942- WhoAm 92, WhoE 93
Marro, Frank Law&B 92
Marro, Joaquin 1945- WhoWor 93
Marrocco, Victor G. Law&B 92
Marrocco, W(illiam) Thomas 1909- Baker 92
Marron, Darlene Lorraine 1946- WhoAmW 93
Marron, Donald B. 1934- St&PR 93
Marron, Donald Baird 1934- WhoAm 92
Marron, Edward Arthur Law&B 92
Marron, Joseph Francis 1888-1961 BioIn 17
Marron, Michael Thomas 1943- WhoSSW 93
Marrone, Daniel Scott 1950- WhoE 93, WhoEmL 93, WhoWor 93
Marrone, Michael John 1942- St&PR 93
Marrone-Puglia, Gaetana WhoE 93
Marroquin, Patricia 1957- WhoAmW 93
Marrou, Andre BioIn 17
Marrou, Jean Paul 1933- WhoScE 91-2
Marrow, Dorothy Combellack 1937- WhoE 93
Marrow, Tracy BioIn 17
Marrs, Barbara Jeanne 1943- WhoAmW 93
Marrs, Barry Lee 1942- WhoE 93
Marrs, Jim 1943- ConAu 139
Marrs, Leo Richard, Jr. 1949- WhoEmL 93
Marrs, Richard E. WhoAm 92
Marrs, Stuart Lynn 1948- WhoE 93
Marrs, Theodore C. d1990 BioIn 17
Marrs, Timothy Clive 1945- WhoWor 93
Marrucci, Giuseppe 1937- WhoWor 93
Marrus, Lauren Winer 1961- WhoE 93
Marryshow, T. Albert 1887-1958 DcCPCAm
Marryshow, Terry 1952- DcCPCAm
Mars, Alastair 1915-1988 ScF&FL 92
Mars, Forrest BioIn 17
Mars, Forrest, Jr. WhoAm 92
Mars, Michael S. Law&B 92
Mars, Philip WhoScE 91-1
Mars, Robert S., Jr. 1926- St&PR 93
Mars, Virginia Cretella WhoAmW 93
Marsac, Peter L. 1943- St&PR 93
Marsaglia, Stefano Eugenio 1955- WhoWor 93
Marsal, Frederic Francois- 1874-1958 BioIn 17
Marsala, Charles Eugene 1960- WhoEmL 93
Marsalek, Lawrence Fredrick 1938 St&PR 93
Marsalis, Branford BioIn 17, NewYTBS 92 [port]
Marsalis, Branford 1960- WhoAm 92
Marsalis, Wynton BioIn 17
Marsalis, Wynton 1961- Baker 92, WhoAm 92
Marsan, Jean-Claude 1938- WhoAm 92
Marsar, Joseph R., Jr. 1953- St&PR 93
Marschalk, Max 1863-1940 Baker 92
Marschalk, William J. 1944-1991 BioIn 17
Marschalk, William John 1944- St&PR 93
Marschall, Charles J. 1939- St&PR 93
Marschall, Phyllis AmWomPl
Marscheck, Larry 1956- WhoSSW 93
Marschel, C. Thomas 1945- St&PR 93
Marsching, Ronald Lionel 1927- WhoAm 92
Marschner, Franz 1855-1932 Baker 92
Marschner, Heinrich 1795-1861 IntDcOp, OxDcOp
Marschner, Heinrich (August) 1795-1861 Baker 92
Marscot, Ann WhoWrEP 92
Marsden, Brian G. BioIn 17
Marsden, Brian Geoffrey 1937- WhoAm 92
Marsden, Brian William H. 1932- St&PR 93
Marsden, Brian William Hugh 1932- WhoAm 92
Marsden, C.D. WhoScE 91-1
Marsden, Charles Alexander WhoScE 91-1
Marsden, Charles Joseph 1940- St&PR 93, WhoAm 92
Marsden, Dora 1882-1960 BioIn 17
Marsden, Herci Ivana 1937- WhoAmW 93, WhoE 93
Marsden, Jason BioIn 17
Marsden, John 1950- BioIn 17
Marsden, John Christopher WhoScE 91-1
Marsden, Lawrence Albert 1919- WhoAm 92
Marsden, Marilyn Weber 1944- WhoAmW 93
Marsden, Philip Law WhoScE 91-1
Marsden, Simon 1948- ScF&FL 92
Marsden, William 1940- WhoWor 93
Marsee, Stuart Earl 1917- WhoAm 92
Marsee, Susanne Irene 1941- WhoAm 92
Marsel, Joze 1931- WhoScE 91-4
Marselos, Marios A. 1948- WhoScE 91-3
Marsh, Adam d1259 BioIn 17
Marsh, Alan Christopher 1948- St&PR 93
Marsh, Alfred F. 1930- St&PR 93
Marsh, Alice Louise AmWomPl
Marsh, Amos d1811 BioIn 17
Marsh, Benjamin Franklin 1927- WhoAm 92
Marsh, Brian Richard 1948- WhoE 93
Marsh, Bryan Kenneth WhoScE 91-1
Marsh, Carole 1946- WhoAm 92, WhoAmW 93, WhoWrEP 92
Marsh, Caryl Amsterdam 1923- WhoAm 92, WhoAmW 93
Marsh, Caryl Glenn 1939- WhoAm 92
Marsh, Chares Russell, Jr. 1924- St&PR 93
Marsh, Charles Alan 1941- St&PR 93
Marsh, Cheryl Lynn Law&B 92
Marsh, Cheryl Lynn 1950- St&PR 93
Marsh, Clare Teitgen 1934- WhoAmW 93
Marsh, Colleen Beth Meylor 1957- WhoAmW 93, WhoEmL 93
Marsh, Corinna BioIn 17
Marsh, Daniel 1924- WhoE 93
Marsh, Dave BioIn 17
Marsh, Dave Rodney 1950- WhoAm 92
Marsh, David Barry Law&B 92
Marsh, David George 1940- WhoE 93
Marsh, David O. 1927- WhoAm 92
Marsh, Don E. 1938- St&PR 93, WhoAm 92
Marsh, Don Seagle 1927- WhoAm 92
Marsh, Donald B. 1950- St&PR 93
Marsh, Donald Jay 1934- WhoAm 92
Marsh, Dwight Chaney 1932- WhoWrEP 92
Marsh, Edward Marcus, Jr. Law&B 92
Marsh, Edward Neil Groethe 1963- WhoWor 93
Marsh, Elizabeth H. AmWomPl
Marsh, Florence Anne AmWomPl
Marsh, Florence Gertrude 1916- WhoWrEP 92
Marsh, Frank Irving 1924- WhoAm 92
Marsh, Gary W. 1948- WhoEmL 93
Marsh, Geoffrey ScF&FL 92
Marsh, George Perkins 1801-1882 BioIn 17
Marsh, Gilbert Reid 1946- St&PR 93
Marsh, Harriet Anne 1848-1933 AmWomPl
Marsh, Harry WhoScE 91-1
Marsh, Harry Dean 1928- WhoAm 92
Marsh, Herbert Rhea, Jr. 1957- WhoSSW 93
Marsh, Ian ScF&FL 92
Marsh, J.J., Jr. 1925- St&PR 93
Marsh, Jack 1949- St&PR 93
Marsh, James 1794-1842 BioIn 17
Marsh, James 1946- SmATA 73 [port]
Marsh, James W. 1947- St&PR 93
Marsh, Jayne Elizabeth 1954- WhoAmW 93, WhoEmL 93
Marsh, Jean Lyndsey Torren 1934- WhoAm 92
Marsh, Jeanne Cay 1948- WhoAm 92
Marsh, Jeri 1940- BioIn 17
Marsh, Joan Knight 1934- WhoAmW 93
Marsh, John 1932- WhoUN 92
Marsh, John David 1946- WhoScE 91-2
Marsh, John Frederick WhoScE 91-1
Marsh, John Howard 1959- WhoEmL 93
Marsh, John Lee 1916- WhoE 93
Marsh, John Otho, Jr. 1926- WhoAm 92
Marsh, John Richard 1935- St&PR 93, WhoIns 93

Marsh, Joseph Franklin, Jr. 1925- *WhoAm 92*
Marsh, Joseph Virgil 1952- *WhoEmL 93, WhoSSW 93*
Marsh, Judith Ann 1941- *WhoWrEP 92*
Marsh, Julia Alzada 1953- *WhoAmW 93*
Marsh, Kevin B. 1955- *St&PR 93*
Marsh, Leonard W. 1945- *St&PR 93*
Marsh, Mae 1895-1968 *IntDcF 2-3 [port]*
Marsh, Malcolm F. 1928- *WhoAm 92*
Marsh, Malcolm Roy, Jr. 1932- *WhoSSW 93*
Marsh, Marcia Barnes *Law&B 92*
Marsh, Marie Louise More *AmWomPl*
Marsh, Mark C.P. 1953- *WhoScE 91-1*
Marsh, Miles L. *WhoAm 92*
Marsh, Nelson Leroy 1937- *WhoSSW 93*
Marsh, Ngaio 1899-1982 *BioIn 17*
Marsh, Norman James 1936- *St&PR 93*
Marsh, Norman James, Jr. *Law&B 92*
Marsh, Ozan d1992 *BioIn 17, NewYTBS 92*
Marsh, Ozan James 1920- *WhoAm 92*
Marsh, Patricia McMurray *BioIn 17*
Marsh, Quinton Neely 1915- *WhoAm 92*
Marsh, Ralph 1928- *St&PR 93*
Marsh, Richard B. 1926- *St&PR 93*
Marsh, Richard Ken 1945- *WhoSSW 93*
Marsh, Richard Philip 1961- *WhoWrEP 92*
Marsh, Riley B. *Law&B 92*
Marsh, Robert C(harles) 1924- *Baker 92*
Marsh, Robert Charles 1924- *WhoAm 92, WhoWor 93*
Marsh, Robert Harry 1946- *WhoWor 93*
Marsh, Robert Mortimer 1931- *WhoAm 92*
Marsh, Robert Thomas 1925- *WhoAm 92*
Marsh, Robert William 1924- *WhoE 93*
Marsh, Roger 1949- *Baker 92*
Marsh, Rosalind J. 1950- *ScF&FL 92*
Marsh, Ruth Lorraine 1927- *WhoE 93*
Marsh, Sarah Taylor 1943- *WhoAmW 93*
Marsh, Sheila C. *Law&B 92*
Marsh, Shepherd R. 1946- *St&PR 93*
Marsh, Stanley *BioIn 17*
Marsh, Sue Ann 1949- *WhoAmW 93*
Marsh, Thomas R. 1946- *St&PR 93*
Marsh, Thompson G. d1992 *NewYTBS 92*
Marsh, Wayne C. 1936- *St&PR 93*
Marsh, William F. *Law&B 92*
Marsh, William L. 1944- *St&PR 93*
Marsh, William Laurence 1926- *WhoAm 92, WhoE 93*
Marsh, William T. *Law&B 92*
Marsh, William T. 1932- *St&PR 93*
Marshack, Megan *BioIn 17*
Marshak, Alan Howard 1938- *WhoAm 92*
Marshak, Bruce S. *Law&B 92*
Marshak, Hilary Wallach 1950- *WhoAmW 93*
Marshak, Marvin Lloyd 1946- *WhoAm 92*
Marshak, Robert E. d1992 *NewYTBS 92 [port]*
Marshak, Robert Eugene 1916- *WhoAm 92*
Marshak, Robert Reuben 1923- *WhoAm 92*
Marshak, Sondra 1940?- *ScF&FL 92*
Marshal, Kit *WhoWor 93*
Marshal, Peter C. 1942- *St&PR 93*
Marshal, William 1144?-1219 *BioIn 17*
Marshalek, Eugene Richard 1936- *WhoAm 92*
Marshalek, Jean Ray 1930- *WhoE 93*
Marshall, Abigail *AmWomPl*
Marshall, Adrian Gerald *WhoScE 91-1*
Marshall, Alan Peter 1938- *St&PR 93*
Marshall, Alexander Grieve 1942- *WhoUN 92*
Marshall, Alfred 1842-1924 *BioIn 17*
Marshall, Alison Buell 1959- *WhoEmL 93*
Marshall, Allen Wright, III 1941- *WhoSSW 93*
Marshall, Alton G. 1921- *St&PR 93*
Marshall, Alton Garwood 1921- *WhoAm 92*
Marshall, Anne Bradley 1952- *WhoEmL 93*
Marshall, Anne Carolyn 1932- *WhoAmW 93*
Marshall, Armina 1895-1991 *AnObit 1991*
Marshall, Armina 1900?-1991 *BioIn 17*
Marshall, Arthur Gregory George 1903- *WhoWor 93*
Marshall, Arthur K. 1911- *WhoAm 92*
Marshall, Brian Laurence 1941- *WhoWor 93*
Marshall, Bruce 1899-1987 *ScF&FL 92*
Marshall, Bryan Edward 1935- *WhoAm 92*
Marshall, Burke 1922- *EncAACR, St&PR 93, WhoAm 92*
Marshall, C. *WhoScE 91-1*
Marshall, C. Travis 1926- *WhoAm 92*
Marshall, Cak 1943- *WhoAmW 93*
Marshall, Carol Joyce 1967- *WhoAmW 93*
Marshall, Carol R. *Law&B 92*
Marshall, Carolyn Ann M. 1935- *WhoAm 92*
Marshall, Catherine 1880-1961 *BioIn 17*
Marshall, Catherine 1914-1983 *BioIn 17*
Marshall, Catherine S. 1933- *WhoAm 92*
Marshall, Cedric Russell 1936- *WhoAsAP 91*
Marshall, Charles 1929- *St&PR 93, WhoAm 92*
Marshall, Charles Burton 1908- *WhoAm 92, WhoWor 93*
Marshall, Charles J. *St&PR 93*
Marshall, Charles Louis 1912- *WhoAm 92*
Marshall, Charles Noble 1942- *St&PR 93*
Marshall, Charles R. d1990 *BioIn 17*
Marshall, Cheryl Lynn 1953- *St&PR 93*
Marshall, Chester R. 1952- *St&PR 93*
Marshall, Christopher John 1949- *WhoScE 91-1*
Marshall, Clifford Wallace 1928- *WhoAm 92*
Marshall, Consuelo B. *BioIn 17*
Marshall, Consuelo Bland 1936- *WhoAm 92, WhoAmW 93*
Marshall, Craig Robert *Law&B 92*
Marshall, Cynthia Louise 1956- *WhoAmW 93, WhoEmL 93*
Marshall, Dale Frederick 1953- *WhoE 93*
Marshall, Dallas Ray 1955- *WhoSSW 93*
Marshall, Dana X. 1939- *WhoAm 92*
Marshall, David 1914- *WhoE 93, WhoWor 93*
Marshall, David Antony Scott 1962- *WhoWor 93*
Marshall, David Frederick 1948- *WhoAm 92*
Marshall, David Lawrence 1939- *St&PR 93, WhoAm 92*
Marshall, Dawn Elaine 1958- *WhoAmW 93*
Marshall, Deborah 1956- *St&PR 93*
Marshall, Deborah A. *ScF&FL 92*
Marshall, Denis William Anson 1943- *WhoAsAP 91*
Marshall, Dennis R. *Law&B 92*
Marshall, Donald Glenn 1943- *WhoAm 92*
Marshall, Donald S. 1938- *St&PR 93*
Marshall, Donald Stewart 1938- *WhoAm 92*
Marshall, Donald Tompkins 1933- *WhoAm 92*
Marshall, Douglas A. 1948- *St&PR 93*
Marshall, Douglas C. *Law&B 92*
Marshall, Douglas H. *Law&B 92*
Marshall, Dwight A. *Law&B 92*
Marshall, E. G. 1910- *WhoAm 92*
Marshall, Edison 1894-1967 *BioIn 17*
Marshall, Edward *ConAu 139, -38NR, MajAI*
Marshall, Edward 1942- *BioIn 17*
Marshall, Ellen Ruth 1949- *WhoAmW 93*
Marshall, Eric C. *Law&B 92*
Marshall, Eric C. 1958- *WhoAm 92, WhoEmL 93*
Marshall, Eugene C. *Law&B 92*
Marshall, F. Ray *WhoAm 92*
Marshall, Francis Joseph 1923- *WhoAm 92*
Marshall, Frank *BioIn 17, MiSFD 9*
Marshall, Frank 1877-1944 *BioIn 17*
Marshall, Frank C., Jr. *Law&B 92*
Marshall, Frank W. *WhoAm 92*
Marshall, Franklin Nick 1933- *WhoAm 92*
Marshall, Fray Francis 1944- *WhoE 93*
Marshall, Garland Ross 1940- *WhoAm 92*
Marshall, Garry 1934- *BioIn 17, CurBio 92 [port], MiSFD 9, WhoAm 92*
Marshall, Gary Charles 1943- *WhoE 93*
Marshall, Gary D. 1955- *St&PR 93*
Marshall, Gary S. *Law&B 92*
Marshall, Gene *ScF&FL 92*
Marshall, Geoffrey 1938- *WhoAm 92*
Marshall, George *WhoScE 91-1*
Marshall, George 1891-1975 *MiSFD 9N*
Marshall, George C. 1880-1959 *BioIn 17, ColdWar 1 [port]*
Marshall, George Catlett 1880-1959 *CmdGen 1991 [port], DcTwHis, HarEnMi*
Marshall, George Dwire 1940- *St&PR 93, WhoAm 92*
Marshall, George Nichols 1920- *WhoAm 92*
Marshall, George Preston *BioIn 17*
Marshall, Gerald Francis 1929- *WhoAm 92*
Marshall, Gerald Robert 1934- *WhoAm 92*
Marshall, Gilly Anthony 1948- *WhoSSW 93*
Marshall, Gordon Bruce 1943- *St&PR 93, WhoAm 92*
Marshall, Gregory J. 1961- *WhoEmL 93*
Marshall, Harold D. 1936- *WhoAm 92*
Marshall, Herbert 1890-1966 *IntDcF 2-3*
Marshall, Herbert 1906-1991 *BioIn 17*
Marshall, Herbert A. 1917- *WhoAm 92*
Marshall, Howard Andrew 1931- *St&PR 93*
Marshall, Howard Lowen 1931- *WhoSSW 93*
Marshall, Ian G. *WhoScE 91-1*
Marshall, Ingram 1942- *BioIn 17*
Marshall, Ingram D(ouglass) 1942- *Baker 92*
Marshall, Innes 1924- *WhoWor 93*
Marshall, Irl H. 1929- *St&PR 93*
Marshall, J. Howard, II 1905- *WhoAm 92, WhoWor 93*
Marshall, J. Howard, III 1936- *St&PR 93*
Marshall, Jack *WhoScE 91-1*
Marshall, James *BioIn 17*
Marshall, James d1992 *NewYTBS 92 [port]*
Marshall, James 1829-1889 *BioIn 17*
Marshall, James 1942- *BioIn 17, ChlBIID [port]*
Marshall, James Brayant, Jr. *Law&B 92*
Marshall, James D. 1936- *St&PR 93*
Marshall, James E. 1936- *WhoIns 93*
Marshall, James (Edward) 1942- *ConAu 38NR, MajAI [port], WhoAm 92*
Marshall, James (Edward) 1942-1992 *ConAu 139*
Marshall, James Lawrence 1937- *BiDAMSp 1989*
Marshall, James Waller, Mrs. *AmWomPl*
Marshall, Jane *WhoScE 91-1*
Marshall, Janice 1946- *WhoIns 93*
Marshall, Jean McElroy 1922- *WhoAm 92*
Marshall, Jeanette 1952- *WhoAmW 93*
Marshall, Jeanie 1944- *WhoAmW 93*
Marshall, Jim Loyn 1948- *WhoSSW 93*
Marshall, Joan Holwell 1916- *WhoWrEP 92*
Marshall, John *BioIn 17, WhoAm 92, WhoSSW 93*
Marshall, John 1755-1835 *BioIn 17, OxCSupC [port]*
Marshall, John 1913- *WhoWrEP 92*
Marshall, John 1951- *WhoSSW 93*
Marshall, John Aloysius 1928- *WhoAm 92*
Marshall, John Carl *BioIn 17*
Marshall, John David 1940- *WhoAm 92*
Marshall, John E. 1945- *St&PR 93*
Marshall, John Elbert, III 1942- *WhoAm 92*
Marshall, John Francis 1939- *WhoE 93*
Marshall, John Franklin 1947- *WhoE 93*
Marshall, John H. 1941- *St&PR 93*
Marshall, John Harris, Jr. 1924- *WhoSSW 93, WhoWor 93*
Marshall, John Leslie 1947- *WhoEmL 93*
Marshall, John Maynard 1953- *WhoE 93*
Marshall, John Patrick 1950- *WhoAm 92, WhoE 93, WhoWor 93*
Marshall, John Paul 1941- *WhoWor 93*
Marshall, John S. 1919- *St&PR 93*
Marshall, John Treutlen 1934- *WhoAm 92, WhoSSW 93*
Marshall, John W. *BioIn 17*
Marshall, Joseph Hartwell, III 1936- *WhoSSW 93*
Marshall, Joseph Michael *WhoScE 91-1*
Marshall, Joseph W. 1936- *St&PR 93*
Marshall, Joseph W. 1938- *St&PR 93*
Marshall, Julian Howard, Jr. 1922- *WhoAm 92, WhoWor 93*
Marshall, Karyn *BioIn 17*
Marshall, Katharine Boehringer 1956- *WhoE 93*
Marshall, Kay Valerie 1960- *WhoE 93*
Marshall, Kelvin A. A. 1947- *WhoAm 92*
Marshall, Kenneth Allan 1938- *WhoE 93*
Marshall, L. B. 1928- *WhoWor 93*
Marshall, L. Jay *BioIn 17*
Marshall, Laura *AmWomPl*
Marshall, Laura 1950- *ScF&FL 92*
Marshall, Leonard 1961- *BioIn 17*
Marshall, Leonard Briggs, Jr. 1932- *St&PR 93*
Marshall, Linda Lee 1948- *WhoAmW 93*
Marshall, Linda Rae 1940- *WhoAmW 93*
Marshall, Lois (Catherine) 1924- *Baker 92*
Marshall, Loren Dean 1953- *WhoWrEP 92*
Marshall, Louis 1856-1929 *JeAmHC*
Marshall, Louise Owen 1941- *WhoAmW 93*
Marshall, Lowell Larry 1940- *St&PR 93*
Marshall, Margaret (Anne) 1949- *Baker 92*
Marshall, Margo 1934- *WhoAmW 93*
Marshall, Maria *BioIn 17*
Marshall, Marie Annette Fuschich 1958- *WhoAmW 93*
Marshall, Martha Seitz 1945- *WhoAmW 93*
Marshall, Martin Vivan 1922- *WhoAm 92*
Marshall, Marvin G. *St&PR 93*
Marshall, Marvin G. 1937- *WhoAm 92*
Marshall, Mary Aydelotte 1921- *WhoAmW 93*
Marshall, Mary Gladys 1939- *WhoSSW 93*
Marshall, Mary Jones *WhoAmW 93, WhoWor 93*
Marshall, Maryann Chorba 1952- *WhoAmW 93, WhoEmL 93*
Marshall, Maryann Radke 1955- *WhoEmL 93*
Marshall, Michael Borden 1957- *WhoE 93, WhoEmL 93, WhoWor 93*
Marshall, Michael Grant 1943- *BiDAMSp 1989*
Marshall, Michael J. 1938- *St&PR 93*
Marshall, Michael John 1932- *WhoWor 93*
Marshall, Michael Joseph 1949- *WhoSSW 93*
Marshall, Michele Janice 1940- *WhoAmW 93*
Marshall, Mike 1957- *Baker 92*
Marshall, Mortimer Mercer, Jr. 1929- *WhoAm 92*
Marshall, Muriel *WhoWrEP 92*
Marshall, Myrna Estey 1938- *WhoWrEP 92*
Marshall, Nancy Haig 1932- *WhoAm 92*
Marshall, Natalie Junemann 1929- *WhoAm 92, WhoAmW 93, WhoE 93*
Marshall, Navarre 1916- *WhoAmW 93*
Marshall, Pamela Goodrich 1951- *WhoAmW 93*
Marshall, Patricia J. *BioIn 17*
Marshall, Paul, Jr. 1927- *WhoE 93*
Marshall, Paula E. 1957- *WhoAmW 93*
Marshall, Paule 1929- *AmWomWr 92, BioIn 17, ConLC 72 [port]*
Marshall, Penny *BioIn 17, NewYTBS 92 [port]*
Marshall, Penny 1942- *CurBio 92 [port], MiSFD 9*
Marshall, Penny 1943- *Au&Arts 10 [port], WhoAm 92, WhoAmW 93*
Marshall, Peter 1902-1949 *BioIn 17*
Marshall, Peter W. *Law&B 92*
Marshall, Philips Williamson 1935- *WhoAm 92*
Marshall, Phyllis 1933- *WhoAmW 93*
Marshall, Phyllis Ellinwood 1929- *WhoAmW 93, WhoE 93, WhoWor 93*
Marshall, Prentice Henry 1926- *WhoAm 92*
Marshall, Rachael *AmWomPl*
Marshall, Richard 1947- *WhoAm 92*
Marshall, Richard E. 1946- *WhoAm 92*
Marshall, Richard Paul, Jr. 1949- *WhoEmL 93*
Marshall, Richard Treeger 1925- *WhoWor 93*
Marshall, Rob *BioIn 17*
Marshall, Robert Charles 1931- *St&PR 93, WhoAm 92*
Marshall, Robert Doris, Jr. 1949- *WhoEmL 93*
Marshall, Robert Gerald 1919- *WhoAm 92*
Marshall, Robert Herman 1929- *WhoAm 92*
Marshall, Robert J. 1928- *WhoE 93*
Marshall, Robert James 1918- *WhoAm 92*
Marshall, Robert L(ewis) 1939- *Baker 92*
Marshall, Robert Lewis 1939- *WhoAm 92*
Marshall, Robert P., Jr. *Law&B 92*
Marshall, Roby *BioIn 17*
Marshall, Roderick 1903-1975 *ScF&FL 92*
Marshall, Rodney Jeff 1965- *WhoSSW 93*
Marshall, Ronald Lester 1939- *WhoSSW 93*
Marshall, Sally Ann 1942- *WhoWrEP 92*
Marshall, Sally Jean 1949- *WhoAmW 93*
Marshall, Sandra P. 1947- *WhoAmW 93*
Marshall, Sarah Catherine Wood 1914-1983 *BioIn 17*
Marshall, Scott Mark 1958- *WhoEmL 93*
Marshall, Sheila Hermes 1934- *WhoAm 92, WhoAmW 93*
Marshall, Sherrie Patrice 1953- *WhoAm 92, WhoAmW 93*
Marshall, Simone Verniere *WhoAmW 93, WhoE 93*
Marshall, Siri Swenson *Law&B 92*
Marshall, Stanley 1923- *WhoAm 92*
Marshall, Stuart Alan 1946- *WhoE 93*
Marshall, Susan 1950- *WhoEmL 93*
Marshall, Susan Lockwood 1939- *WhoAmW 93*
Marshall, Sylvan Mitchell 1917- *WhoAm 92*
Marshall, Terrell 1908- *WhoAm 92*
Marshall, Terry Dean 1945- *St&PR 93*
Marshall, Theresa Hooper *WhoAm 92*

Marshall, Thomas 1929- *St&PR 93*
Marshall, Thomas Archibald 1938- *ConAu 38NR*
Marshall, Thomas Carlisle 1935- *WhoAm 92*
Marshall, Thomas Matthew 1950- *WhoEmL 93*
Marshall, Thomas Oliver, Jr. 1920- *WhoAm 92, WhoSSW 93*
Marshall, Thomas R. 1854-1925 *PolPar*
Marshall, Thurgood *BioIn 17*
Marshall, Thurgood 1908- *AfrAmBi, CngDr 91, ConHero 2 [port], EncAACR [port], OxCSupC [port], WhoAm 92, WhoE 93*
Marshall, Tom *ConAu 38NR*
Marshall, Tom 1938- *WhoCanL 92*
Marshall, Tully 1864-1970 *BioIn 17*
Marshall, Tyler 1941- *ConAu 136*
Marshall, Verne Monroe 1923- *WhoE 93*
Marshall, Victor Fray 1913- *WhoAm 92*
Marshall, Vincent de Paul 1943- *WhoAm 92*
Marshall, W.W. *BioIn 17*
Marshall, Wayne Edward 1944- *WhoSSW 93*
Marshall, Wayne Keith 1948- *WhoE 93, WhoEmL 93, WhoWor 93*
Marshall, William 1767-1815 *BioIn 17*
Marshall, William 1924- *BioIn 17*
Marshall, William 1944- *ScF&FL 92*
Marshall, William, Jr. 1925- *WhoAm 92*
Marshall, William Clifford 1929- *WhoWor 93*
Marshall, William Edward 1925- *WhoAm 92*
Marshall, William Edward 1948- *WhoSSW 93*
Marshall, William Emmett 1935- *WhoAm 92*
Marshall, William Gene, Jr. 1953- *WhoSSW 93*
Marshall, William Gilbert 1946- *St&PR 93, WhoAm 92*
Marshall, William Lawrence, III 1937- *St&PR 93*
Marshall, William Leitch 1925- *WhoWor 93*
Marshall, Willis Henry *WhoSSW 93, WhoWor 93*
Marshall-Goodell, Beverly Sue 1953- *WhoAmW 93*
Marshall-Nadel, Nathalie 1932- *WhoAmW 93, WhoWrEP 92*
Marshall-Reed, Diane 1950- *WhoAmW 93*
Marshand, La Mer 1926- *WhoWrEP 92*
Marshburn, Gary Howard 1952- *St&PR 93*
Marshella, Thomas Joseph 1957- *WhoE 93*
Marshman, Homer Henry, Jr. 1954- *WhoSSW 93*
Marsicano, Jon 1940- *St&PR 93*
Marsicano, Nicholas 1914-1991 *BioIn 17*
Marsick, Armand (Louis Joseph) 1877-1959 *Baker 92*
Marsick, Martin (-Pierre-Joseph) 1848-1924 *Baker 92*
Marsico, Beverley Brinkerhoff 1932- *WhoAmW 93*
Marsico, Theodore W. 1917- *St&PR 93*
Marsiglia, Anthony J. *BioIn 17*
Marsik, Frederic John 1943- *WhoE 93*
Marsilius, Newman M., III 1946- *St&PR 93*
Marsilius, Philip Roger 1921- *St&PR 93*
Marsilius, Richard Alan 1947- *St&PR 93*
Marsini, Nicholas Michael, Jr. 1955- *St&PR 93*
Marsipal, Arnold 1942- *WhoAsAP 91*
Marsland, David Wentworth *WhoScE 91-1*
Marsland-Shaw, Lionel John 1952- *St&PR 93*
Marsocci, Velio Arthur 1928- *WhoE 93*
Marsolais, Harold Raymond 1942- *WhoAm 92*
Marson, Charles Michael 1956- *WhoWor 93*
Marson, Jeanine Diana 1967- *WhoAmW 93*
Marson, Kenneth, Jr. 1954- *St&PR 93*
Marson, Kenneth Gordon, Sr. 1931- *St&PR 93*
Marson, Ralph 1935- *WhoWor 93*
Marson, Stephen Mark 1951- *WhoEmL 93, WhoSSW 93*
Marson, William Stuart *WhoScE 91-1*
Marson-McNulty, Deborah *Law&B 92*
Marsteller, Julie V. d1990 *BioIn 17*
Marsten, Richard *ConAu 38NR*
Marsten, Richard 1926- *BioIn 17*
Marsten, Richard Barry 1925- *WhoAm 92*
Marstiller, Phyllis 1947- *St&PR 93*
Marstiller, Phyllis C. 1947- *WhoAm 92*
Marston, Betsy *BioIn 17*
Marston, Charles *WhoAm 92*
Marston, Donald David 1960- *WhoEmL 93*
Marston, Ed *BioIn 17*
Marston, Edgar J., III *Law&B 92*
Marston, Edgar Jean, III 1939- *WhoAm 92*
Marston, Edward *ConAu 139*
Marston, Jeffrey P. *Law&B 92*
Marston, Michael 1936- *WhoAm 92*
Marston, Robert Andrew 1937- *WhoAm 92*
Marston, Robert Quarles 1923- *WhoAm 92*
Marston-Scott, Mary Vesta 1924- *WhoAm 92*
Marstrand, John Martin *WhoScE 91-1*
Marstrand-Jorgensen, Mads 1947- *WhoWor 93*
Marszalek, Georgia Ann 1946- *WhoEmL 93*
Marszalek, Jerzy 1936- *WhoScE 91-4*
Marszalek, John Francis 1939- *WhoSSW 93*
Marszalek, Wieslaw 1957- *WhoWor 93*
Marszowski, Bruno Anthony 1941- *St&PR 93*
Marta, Ferenc 1929- *WhoScE 91-4*
Marta, Robert John 1949- *St&PR 93*
Martarella, Franc David *WhoE 93*
Martaus, Cecilia M. *Law&B 92*
Marte, Kenneth James 1951- *St&PR 93*
Marteau, Henri 1874-1934 *Baker 92*
Marteeny, Jennifer Elaine 1961- *WhoAmW 93*
Martegani, Enzo 1950- *WhoWor 93*
Marteka, Vincent James, Jr. 1936- *WhoAm 92, WhoWrEP 92*
Martel, Emile 1941- *WhoCanL 92*
Martel, Eugene Harvey 1934- *St&PR 93*
Martel, Eva Leona 1945- *WhoAmW 93*
Martel, Jane Susan 1959- *WhoAmW 93*
Martel, Jeffrey A. *Law&B 92*
Martel, John Sheldon 1931- *WhoAm 92*
Martel, Suzanne 1924- *WhoCanL 92*
Martel, William 1927- *WhoAm 92*
Martela, Matti Tapio 1939- *WhoWor 93*
Martelet, Claude 1945- *WhoScE 91-2*
Martell, Arthur Earl 1916- *WhoAm 92, WhoSSW 93*
Martell, John Raymond, Jr. 1955- *WhoE 93*
Martell, Michael Joseph, Jr. 1932- *WhoE 93*
Martell, Saundra Adkins 1946- *WhoEmL 93*
Martell, Victoria Martell 1966- *WhoAmW 93*
Martella, Enzo 1922- *WhoScE 91-3*
Martella, Joseph Edward, Jr. 1957- *St&PR 93*
Martelli, Claudio 1943- *WhoWor 93*
Martelli, Francesco G. 1946- *WhoScE 91-3*
Martelli, Giovanni P. 1935- *WhoScE 91-3*
Martelli, Henri 1895-1980 *Baker 92*
Martelli, Marcos *Law&B 92*
Martelli, Susan A. 1958- *WhoAmW 93*
Martello, Antonio Guillermo 1943- *WhoWor 93*
Martello, Benjamin F. 1940- *St&PR 93*
Martellucci, Anthony 1930- *St&PR 93, WhoAm 92*
Marten, Gordon Cornelius 1935- *WhoAm 92*
Marten, Jacqueline *ScF&FL 92*
Marten, James F. 1931- *St&PR 93, WhoE 93*
Marteney, Larry G. 1943- *St&PR 93*
Martenot, Maurice (Louis Eugene) 1898-1980 *Baker 92*
Martens, Alexander Eugene 1923- *WhoE 93*
Martens, Barbara Lynne 1953- *WhoAmW 93*
Martens, David Baker 1942- *St&PR 93*
Martens, Donald G. 1932- *St&PR 93*
Martens, Ernesto *WhoSSW 93*
Martens, Harlan Craig *Law&B 92*
Martens, Harry 1928- *St&PR 93*
Martens, Henri J. 1945- *WhoScE 91-2*
Martens, John Dale 1943- *WhoE 93*
Martens, Jurgen 1948- *WhoScE 91-3*
Martens, Keith O. *St&PR 93*
Martens, Keith Otto 1939- *WhoAm 92*
Martens, Koenraad 1959- *WhoWor 93*
Martens, Laurent R.E. 1938- *WhoScE 91-2*
Martens, Lorna Cutts 1946- *WhoSSW 93*
Martens, Michel 1929- *WhoScE 91-2*
Martens, Patricia Margaret 1962- *WhoAmW 93*
Martens, Robert Edmund 1945- *St&PR 93*
Martens, Roy Michael 1950- *WhoEmL 93, WhoWor 93*
Martens, Ted William 1938- *St&PR 93*
Martens, Wilfried 1936- *WhoWor 93*
Martenson, Carroll Mooney 1921- *St&PR 93*
Martenson, Edward Allen 1949- *WhoAm 92*
Martenson, Jan Per Gosta 1933- *WhoUN 92*
Martensson, Heine G. 1930- *WhoWor 93*
Martensson, Kaj B. 1947- *WhoScE 91-4*
Martenstein, Thomas E. *Law&B 92*
Martenstein, Thomas E. 1949- *St&PR 93*
Martenstein, Thomas Ewing 1949- *WhoAm 92*
Marter, Allan J. 1947- *St&PR 93*
Marter, Ian *ScF&FL 92*
Marter, Joan 1946- *WhoEmL 93*
Marter, Sarah Savery 1950- *WhoAmW 93*
Marterer, Gerald Charles 1945- *St&PR 93*
Martersteck, K.E. 1934- *St&PR 93*
Marth, Dave S. 1929- *St&PR 93*
Marth, Elmer Herman 1927- *WhoAm 92, WhoWrEP 92*
Marth, Fritz Ludwig 1935- *WhoE 93*
Martha, Crown Princess of Norway 1901-1954 *BioIn 17*
Martha & the Vandellas *SoulM*
Marthaler, Thomas Martin 1929- *WhoScE 91-4*
Marti, Agustin Farabundo 1893-1932 *DcCPCAm*
Marti, Alfred Armin 1909- *WhoWor 93*
Marti, Gloria 1924- *St&PR 93*
Marti, Hans Rudolf 1922- *WhoScE 91-4*
Marti, Jose 1853-1895 *BioIn 17, DcCPCAm*
Marti, Kurt 1936- *WhoAm 92*
Marti, Othmar Josef 1958- *WhoWor 93*
Marti, Peter 1949- *WhoScE 91-4*
Marti, Todd Robert 1958- *WhoEmL 93*
Martia, Astron Del *ScF&FL 92*
Martial, Joseph A. 1945- *WhoScE 91-2*
Martian, Paul *Law&B 92*
Marticelli, Joseph John 1921- *WhoAm 92*
Marti-Colon, Noelia *Law&B 92*
Martienssen, Carl Adolf 1881-1955 *Baker 92*
Martignoni, Ronald W. 1955- *St&PR 93*
Marti-Huang, Duen 1948- *WhoWor 93*
Marti-Ibanez, Felix 1911-1972 *ScF&FL 92*
Martika 1969- *NotHsAW 93 [port]*
Martikainen, Aune Helen 1916- *WhoAmW 93*
Martikainen, Teppo Lasse 1965- *WhoWor 93*
Martimucci, Richard Anthony 1934- *WhoE 93*
Martin, I d655 *OxDcByz*
Martin, A. Damien d1991 *BioIn 17*
Martin, A.G. *WhoScE 91-1*
Martin, Abby L. *Law&B 92*
Martin, Alan Douglas *WhoScE 91-1*
Martin, Alan Douglas 1937- *WhoWor 93*
Martin, Alan Joseph 1959- *WhoEmL 93*
Martin, Albert C. 1913- *St&PR 93*
Martin, Albert Carey 1913- *WhoAm 92*
Martin, Albert Charles 1928- *WhoAm 92*
Martin, Alejandro *WhoWrEP 92*
Martin, Alex 1953- *ConAu 137*
Martin, Alex G. 1960- *WhoWor 93*
Martin, Alexander Stella 1929- *WhoWrEP 92*
Martin, Alfred 1919- *WhoAm 92*
Martin, Alfred DeLoach, Jr. 1929- *St&PR 93*
Martin, Allen 1937- *WhoAm 92*
Martin, Alvin Charles 1933- *WhoAm 92*
Martin, Andre Daniel 1930- *WhoScE 91-2*
Martin, Andrew 1952- *ConAu 137, ScF&FL 92*
Martin, Andrew N., III 1942- *St&PR 93*
Martin, Andy *ConAu 137*
Martin, Angela 1959- *WhoEmL 93*
Martin, Ann 1955- *NewYTBS 92 [port]*
Martin, Ann M. 1955- *ScF&FL 92, SmATA 70 [port]*
Martin, Ann M(atthews) 1955- *MajAI [port]*
Martin, Anne Judy 1960- *WhoAmW 93*
Martin, Anne Lauriston 1946- *WhoWor 93*
Martin, Anne Michelle 1963- *WhoAmW 93*
Martin, Anne Sorenson 1964- *WhoAmW 93*
Martin, Archer John Porter 1910- *WhoWor 93*
Martin, Art S. 1962- *WhoEmL 93, WhoSSW 93*
Martin, Arthur Raymond 1949- *WhoEmL 93*
Martin, Aubran Wayne d1991 *BioIn 17*
Martin, Barbara Jessica 1950- *WhoEmL 93*
Martin, Barbara Lee 1941- *WhoAmW 93*
Martin, Barney *ConTFT 10*
Martin, Barry *BioIn 17*
Martin, Becca Bacon 1957- *WhoSSW 93*
Martin, Benjamin David 1964- *WhoSSW 93*
Martin, Bernard Joseph 1925- *WhoAm 92*
Martin, Bernard Lee 1923- *WhoAm 92*
Martin, Bernice Adelle 1926- *WhoAmW 93*
Martin, Bertha 1926- *WhoAmW 93*
Martin, Betty Carolyn 1933- *WhoAmW 93*
Martin, Betty Clement 1938- *St&PR 93*
Martin, Bill *MajAI*
Martin, Bill 1916- *BioIn 17*
Martin, Bill 1943- *WhoAm 92*
Martin, Bill, Jr. *MajAI*
Martin, Billy *BioIn 17*
Martin, Billy 1928-1989 *BioIn 17*
Martin, Bob *ScF&FL 92*
Martin, Boe Willis 1940- *WhoAm 92*
Martin, Boyce Ficklen, Jr. 1935- *WhoAm 92, WhoSSW 93*
Martin, Boyd Archer 1911- *WhoAm 92, WhoWor 93*
Martin, Brett E. 1952- *St&PR 93*
Martin, Brian K. 1944- *St&PR 93*
Martin, Brian P(hilip) 1947- *ConAu 38NR*
Martin, Bruce A. 1931- *WhoSSW 93*
Martin, Bruce Douglas 1934- *WhoAm 92*
Martin, C.N. 1945- *WhoScE 91-1*
Martin, C. Robert 1925- *St&PR 93*
Martin, Cam J. 1942- *WhoAm 92*
Martin, Carl 1950- *ScF&FL 92*
Martin, Carol Ann 1959- *WhoWrEP 92*
Martin, Carol Jacquelyn 1943- *WhoAmW 93, WhoSSW 93, WhoWor 93*
Martin, Carolyn Stewart 1951- *WhoAmW 93, WhoEmL 93*
Martin, Carter Williams 1933- *WhoSSW 93*
Martin, Catherine *ScF&FL 92*
Martin, Catherine Maria 1948- *WhoE 93*
Martin, Cecile M. 1936- *St&PR 93*
Martin, Charles 1942- *DcLB 120 [port]*
Martin, Charles A., Jr. 1927- *St&PR 93*
Martin, Charles Blake *Law&B 92*
Martin, Charles E. 1910- *SmATA 70 [port]*
Martin, Charles E., Sr. *AfrAmBi*
Martin, Charles Gaines 1952- *WhoSSW 93*
Martin, Charles Howard *Law&B 92*
Martin, Charles John 1935- *WhoSSW 93*
Martin, Charles Neil, Jr. 1942- *WhoAm 92*
Martin, Charles R. *Law&B 92*
Martin, Charles Thomas 1940- *St&PR 93*
Martin, Charles Wade 1952- *WhoSSW 93*
Martin, Charles Wallace 1916- *WhoAm 92*
Martin, Cheri Christian 1956- *WhoAmW 93*
Martin, Chester Y. 1934- *WhoAm 92*
Martin, Chris-Pin 1893-1953 *HispAmA*
Martin, Christian F. 1955- *St&PR 93*
Martin, Christina Alice 1961- *WhoAmW 93*
Martin, Christine Marie 1942- *WhoAmW 93*
Martin, Christopher *BioIn 17, Law&B 92*
Martin, Christopher E. 1941- *St&PR 93*
Martin, Christopher John *WhoScE 91-1*
Martin, Christopher K. *St&PR 93*
Martin, Christopher Michael 1928- *WhoAm 92*
Martin, Claire *BioIn 17*
Martin, Claude G. 1946- *St&PR 93*
Martin, Claude Raymond, Jr. 1932- *WhoAm 92, WhoWor 93*
Martin, Clyde Verne 1933- *WhoAm 92, WhoWor 93*
Martin, Connie Ruth 1963- *WhoAmW 93, WhoEmL 93*
Martin, Craig Harold 1943- *St&PR 93*
Martin, Craig Mell 1951- *WhoEmL 93*
Martin, Cynthia Lea 1957- *WhoEmL 93*
Martin, Dale 1935- *WhoAmW 93*
Martin, Dale Alison 1941- *WhoSSW 93*
Martin, Dale Floyd 1942- *St&PR 93*
Martin, Dale Richard 1936- *St&PR 93*
Martin, Dana 1946- *WhoSSW 93*
Martin, Dana Ray 1952- *WhoSSW 93*
Martin, Daniel L. *Law&B 92*
Martin, Daniel Lee 1955- *St&PR 93*
Martin, Daniel R. 1937- *St&PR 93*
Martin, Daniel Richard 1937- *WhoAm 92, WhoE 93*
Martin, Daniel William 1918- *WhoAm 92*
Martin, Danielle *BioIn 17*
Martin, Dannie *BioIn 17*
Martin, Darlene Irene 1958- *WhoAmW 93*
Martin, Darnell *WhoAm 92*
Martin, Darris Lee 1950- *WhoE 93*
Martin, Darryl Wayne 1948- *WhoEmL 93*
Martin, Daryll Wendall *Law&B 92*
Martin, David 1915- *DcChlFi*
Martin, David 1935- *ScF&FL 92*
Martin, David 1939- *WhoE 93*
Martin, David 1945- *WhoAm 92*
Martin, David Allan 1939- *St&PR 93*
Martin, David B. 1947- *St&PR 93*
Martin, David D. 1939- *WhoSSW 93*

Martin, David E. Law&B 92
Martin, David Edward 1939- WhoAm 92
Martin, David H. 1947- WhoIns 93
Martin, David Hugh 1952- WhoSSW 93
Martin, David J. Law&B 92
Martin, David J. 1937- St&PR 93
Martin, David Kevin 1960- WhoEmL 93
Martin, David Lee 1938- St&PR 93
Martin, David Lee 1941- WhoE 93
Martin, David Leo 1945- WhoWor 93
Martin, David Luther 1947- WhoEmL 93
Martin, David O'B. 1944- CngDr 91
Martin, David O'Brien 1944- WhoAm 92, WhoE 93
Martin, David Porter 1943- WhoSSW 93
Martin, David R. 1931- WhoAm 92
Martin, David Stone BioIn 17
Martin, David Stone d1992 NewYTBS 92
Martin, David Wallace 1938- St&PR 93
Martin, David William, Jr. 1941- WhoAm 92
Martin, Dean 1917- IntDcF 2-3, WhoAm 92
Martin, Dean Frederick 1933- WhoWrEP 92
Martin, Deborah Jones 1956- WhoEmL 93
Martin, Deidre Mercer 1963- WhoSSW 93
Martin, Del ConAu 138
Martin, Denise Belisle 1940- WhoWrEP 92
Martin, Dennis Charles 1960- WhoWor 93
Martin, Derek 1923- WhoAm 92
Martin, Derek H. WhoScE 91-1
Martin, Dexter Law&B 92
Martin, Diane D. WhoWrEP 92
Martin, Dick 1923- ScF&FL 92
Martin, Donald Beckwith 1927- WhoE 93
Martin, Donald E. 1937- WhoIns 93
Martin, Donald L. Law&B 92
Martin, Donald Leon 1920- WhoE 93
Martin, Donald Ray 1915- WhoAm 92
Martin, Donald Timothy 1957- WhoEmL 93
Martin, Donald Victor 1929- St&PR 93
Martin, Donald Vincent 1952- WhoSSW 93
Martin, Donald William 1921- WhoAm 92
Martin, Donna Lee 1935- WhoAm 92, WhoAmW 93
Martin, Dorothy L. 1921- ConAu 138
Martin, Dorothy Regina 1943- WhoAmW 93
Martin, Douglas 1939- ScF&FL 92
Martin, E. WhoScE 91-4
Martin, Earl Francis 1941- WhoSSW 93
Martin, Earle Wilson 1952- WhoEmL 93
Martin, Edgar Bertram 1939- St&PR 93
Martin, Edgar Thomas 1918- WhoAm 92
Martin, Edgardo 1915- Baker 92
Martin, Edith 1945- BioIn 17
Martin, Edith Kingdon Gould 1920- WhoAmW 93
Martin, Edith Waisbrot 1945- WhoAmW 93
Martin, Edward 1879-1967 BioIn 17
Martin, Edward B. 1951- St&PR 93
Martin, Edward Curtis, Jr. 1928- WhoAm 92
Martin, Edward J., Jr. 1934- WhoIns 93
Martin, Edward Joseph 1932- WhoE 93
Martin, Edward L. 1954- St&PR 93
Martin, Edward Lee 1954- WhoEmL 93
Martin, Edwin Dennis 1920- WhoSSW 93
Martin, Edwin John 1934- WhoAm 92
Martin, Edwin McCammon, Jr. 1942- St&PR 93
Martin, Edwin W. 1917-1991 BioIn 17
Martin, Elaine Louise 1957- WhoAmW 93
Martin, Elaine M. Law&B 92
Martin, Elaine P. 1953- St&PR 93
Martin, Elizabeth Courtney 1953- WhoAmW 93
Martin, Elliot Edwards 1924- WhoAm 92, WhoWor 93
Martin, Eric Lewis 1953- WhoSSW 93
Martin, Ernest H. 1919- WhoAm 92
Martin, Eva BioIn 17
Martin, Everett Anthony 1935- St&PR 93
Martin, F. WhoScE 91-2
Martin, Fay Maureen 1935- WhoAmW 93
Martin, Florence J. AmWomPl
Martin, Frances BioIn 17
Martin, Francine L. 1937- WhoScE 91-2
Martin, Francis Paul 1924- WhoE 93
Martin, Francois 1727-1757 Baker 92
Martin, Francois 1934- WhoScE 91-2
Martin, Frank MiSFD 9
Martin, Frank 1890-1974 Baker 92, BioIn 17, OxDcOp
Martin, Frank Gene 1938- WhoSSW 93
Martin, Frank Kieffer 1938- WhoAm 92, WhoSSW 93
Martin, Fred 1925- WhoAm 92
Martin, Fred 1927- WhoAm 92
Martin, Fred Kenneth, Jr. 1942- WhoWor 93
Martin, Frederick 1908- St&PR 93
Martin, Frederick H. 1912- St&PR 93
Martin, Frederick Noel 1931- WhoAm 92
Martin, Frederick Warren 1948- WhoSSW 93
Martin, Frederick Wight 1936- WhoE 93
Martin, Fredric MajAI
Martin, G.M. St&PR 93
Martin, Gary C. 1935- St&PR 93
Martin, Gary Duncan 1954- WhoEmL 93
Martin, Gary L. 1946- St&PR 93
Martin, Gaven John 1958- WhoWor 93
Martin, Gaylon E. 1946- St&PR 93
Martin, Ged ConAu 38NR
Martin, Gene Allen 1965- St&PR 93
Martin, Geoffrey John 1934- WhoE 93
Martin, George Coleman 1910- WhoAm 92
Martin, George Conner 1933- WhoAm 92
Martin, George D. 1946- St&PR 93
Martin, George Maybee 1906- WhoAm 92, WhoWor 93
Martin, George R.R. BioIn 17
Martin, George R.R. 1948- ScF&FL 92
Martin, George Raymond Richard 1948- WhoAm 92, WhoWrEP 92
Martin, George Reilly 1933- WhoAm 92
Martin, George Whitney 1926- WhoAm 92, WhoWrEP 92
Martin, George Wilbur 1930- WhoAm 92
Martin, George William 1924- WhoAm 92
Martin, Gerald Warren 1945- ConAu 38NR
Martin, Gerard Jean 1932- WhoScE 91-2
Martin, Gerri Lynn 1952- WhoAmW 93
Martin, Glenn Michael 1950- WhoE 93, WhoEmL 93
Martin, Gordon Mather 1915- WhoAm 92
Martin, Grace Burkett 1939- WhoWor 93
Martin, Graham Anderson 1912-1990 BioIn 17
Martin, Graham Dunstan 1932- ScF&FL 92
Martin, Gregory Allan 1950- WhoE 93
Martin, Gregory Keith 1956- WhoEmL 93, WhoSSW 93
Martin, Guy BioIn 17
Martin, Guy 1911- WhoAm 92
Martin, Gwendolyn G. Law&B 92
Martin, H. Curtiss Law&B 92
Martin, H.T. WhoScE 91-1
Martin, Harold Clark 1917- WhoAm 92
Martin, Harold Eugene 1923- WhoAm 92
Martin, Harold Harber 1910- WhoWrEP 92
Martin, Harrold Bert 1916- WhoE 93
Martin, Harry Corpening 1920- WhoAm 92
Martin, Heather BioIn 17
Martin, Helen Elizabeth 1945- WhoAmW 93
Martin, Helen Reimensnyder 1868-1939 AmWomPl
Martin, Helene Getter 1940- WhoAmW 93
Martin, Henno 1910- WhoScE 91-3
Martin, Herbert Wayne 1929- St&PR 93
Martin, Herbert Woodward 1933- WhoWrEP 92
Martin, Howard B. St&PR 93
Martin, Ian A. 1935- St&PR 93
Martin, Ian Alexander 1935- WhoAm 92
Martin, Ian George 1927- WhoWor 93
Martin, Ivy B. Law&B 92
Martin, J. David BioIn 17
Martin, J. Landis 1945- WhoAm 92
Martin, J. Landis 1946- WhoSSW 93
Martin, J.P. WhoScE 91-1
Martin, J. Peter 1939- WhoSSW 93
Martin, J. Stephen Law&B 92
Martin, Jack ScF&FL 92
Martin, Jack Peter 1936- WhoUN 92
Martin, Jacqueline Byrd WhoAmW 93
Martin, Jacques d1992 NewYTBS 92
Martin, Jacques Cardinal 1908- WhoWor 93
Martin, James Alan 1954- WhoEmL 93
Martin, James Alfred, Jr. 1917- WhoAm 92
Martin, James Aloysius, III 1947- WhoSSW 93
Martin, James Cullen 1928- WhoAm 92, WhoSSW 93
Martin, James Edward 1926- St&PR 93
Martin, James Eugene 1953- WhoIns 93
Martin, James Francis 1945- WhoSSW 93
Martin, James Gilbert 1926- WhoAm 92
Martin, James Grubbs 1935- WhoAm 92, WhoSSW 93, WhoWor 93
Martin, James Harbert 1941- WhoSSW 93
Martin, James Hubert Augustus 1933- WhoUN 92
Martin, James Jay 1948- WhoEmL 93
Martin, James John, Jr. 1936- WhoAm 92
Martin, James Kirby 1943- WhoAm 92
Martin, James Landis 1945- St&PR 93
Martin, James Lloyd 1949- WhoSSW 93
Martin, James Patrick 1946- WhoEmL 93, WhoWor 93
Martin, James Robert 1943- WhoAm 92
Martin, James Royer 1946- WhoAm 92
Martin, James Russell 1947- WhoEmL 93
Martin, James S. BioIn 17
Martin, James S. 1936- WhoIns 93
Martin, James Scott Law&B 92
Martin, James Smith 1936- St&PR 93, WhoAm 92
Martin, James Victor, Jr. 1916- WhoE 93, WhoWor 93
Martin, James W. WhoSSW 93
Martin, James W. 1927- St&PR 93
Martin, James William 1949- WhoSSW 93
Martin, Jane Roland 1929- WhoE 93
Martin, Janella Sue BioIn 17
Martin, Janet M. Daddino 1954- WhoE 93
Martin, Janette Gould 1957- WhoWrEP 92
Martin, Janis 1939- Baker 92
Martin, Jay BioIn 17
Martin, Jay G. Law&B 92
Martin, Jay Herbert 1935- WhoAm 92, WhoWrEP 92
Martin, Jaye B. Law&B 92
Martin, Jean Ann 1942- WhoAmW 93, WhoSSW 93
Martin, Jean-Blaise 1768-1837 OxDcOp
Martin, (Nicolas-) Jean-Blaise 1768-1837 Baker 92
Martin, Jean Claude 1929- WhoAm 92
Martin, Jean-Hubert 1944- WhoWor 93
Martin, Jean-Jacques 1935- WhoScE 91-2
Martin, Jean-Luc 1938- WhoScE 91-4
Martin, Jean Mc Fall 1955- WhoWrEP 92
Martin, Jean-Pierre WhoScE 91-2
Martin, Jeffrey Lynn 1951- WhoE 93
Martin, Jeffrey Scott 1961- WhoEmL 93
Martin, Jeffrey W. 1961- WhoEmL 93
Martin, Jennifer Jae 1967- WhoAmW 93
Martin, Jerald L. 1948- WhoEmL 93
Martin, Jerald L. 1953- St&PR 93
Martin, Jerry C. 1932- WhoAm 92, WhoSSW 93
Martin, Jerry Calhoun 1932- St&PR 93
Martin, Jerry Harold 1945- WhoSSW 93
Martin, Jim 1939- WhoWrEP 92
Martin, Joan Callaham 1930- WhoAm 92
Martin, Joan M. Law&B 92
Martin, Joan Marie 1938- St&PR 93
Martin, Joann M. 1954- St&PR 93
Martin, Joanne 1946- WhoAmW 93
Martin, Joanne 1956- WhoAmW 93
Martin, Joe P. Law&B 92
Martin, Joel Jerome 1939- WhoSSW 93
Martin, John Law&B 92, ScF&FL 92
Martin, John Alexander 1839-1889 BioIn 17
Martin, John Bartlow 1915-1987 BioIn 17
Martin, John Bruce 1922- WhoAm 92
Martin, John C., III 1952- St&PR 93
Martin, John Cephas, Jr. 1958- WhoE 93
Martin, John E. BioIn 17
Martin, John E. 1947- St&PR 93
Martin, John Edward 1916- WhoAm 92
Martin, John Garvie, III 1945- WhoE 93
Martin, John Gustin 1928- St&PR 93, WhoAm 92
Martin, John Hugh 1918- WhoAm 92
Martin, John Hume WhoScE 91-1
Martin, John J. Law&B 92
Martin, John J. d1992 NewYTBS 92
Martin, John J. 1940- WhoIns 93
Martin, John Joseph 1931- St&PR 93, WhoAm 92
Martin, John Joseph 1938- WhoAm 92
Martin, John Joseph 1956- WhoAm 92
Martin, John L. d1992 BioIn 17, NewYTBS 92
Martin, John L. 1941- WhoAm 92, WhoE 93
Martin, John M. 1913-1990 BioIn 17
Martin, John P. 1939- St&PR 93
Martin, John Perry, Jr. 1924- WhoSSW 93
Martin, John R. Law&B 92
Martin, John Richard, Jr. 1941- WhoSSW 93
Martin, John Rupert 1916- WhoWrEP 92
Martin, John Russell 1950- WhoE 93
Martin, John S. 1900-1977 ScF&FL 92
Martin, John S. 1928- WhoIns 93
Martin, John Thomas 1924- WhoWor 93
Martin, John W., Jr. Law&B 92
Martin, John William 1946- WhoEmL 93, WhoWor 93
Martin, John William, Jr. 1936- WhoAm 92
Martin, Jose Ginoris 1941- WhoWor 93
Martin, Joseph, Jr. 1915- WhoAm 92, WhoWor 93
Martin, Joseph Boyd 1938- WhoAm 92, WhoWor 93
Martin, Joseph Ramsey 1930- WhoAm 92
Martin, Joseph Robert 1947- WhoEmL 93
Martin, Joseph W., Jr. 1884-1968 PolPar
Martin, Joseph William 1884-1968 BioIn 17
Martin, Josephine L. St&PR 93
Martin, Joshua W., III Law&B 92
Martin, Judith BioIn 17
Martin, Judith 1938- JrnUS, WhoWrEP 92
Martin, Judith Sylvia 1938- WhoAm 92
Martin, Judson Phillips 1921- WhoAm 92
Martin, Judy Brackin Hereford 1943- WhoSSW 93
Martin, Julia M. AmWomPl
Martin, Julian S. 1929- WhoAm 92
Martin, Julian S.S. 1929- WhoWrEP 92
Martin, Julie Warren 1943- WhoSSW 93
Martin, June Johnson Caldwell WhoAmW 93
Martin, Justus Carlile, Jr. 1925- St&PR 93
Martin, Karen Krausche 1947- WhoAmW 93, WhoE 93, WhoEmL 93
Martin, Karen Lucille Law&B 92
Martin, Katherine Broyles 1941- WhoAmW 93
Martin, Katherine Helen 1966- WhoAmW 93
Martin, Kathleen Anne 1942- WhoAmW 93
Martin, Kathleen M. Law&B 92
Martin, Kathryn Lee 1935- WhoAmW 93
Martin, Keith ScF&FL 92
Martin, Keith Lambert 1956- WhoE 93
Martin, Kellie Sue 1961- WhoAmW 93, WhoEmL 93
Martin, Ken BioIn 17
Martin, Kendra Leigh 1961- WhoEmL 93
Martin, Kenneth Albert 1940- WhoE 93
Martin, Kenneth D. Law&B 92
Martin, Kenneth Douglas 1940- WhoAm 92
Martin, Kenneth Frederick WhoScE 91-1
Martin, Kenneth R(obert) 1938- ConAu 38NR
Martin, Kenneth Ray 1953- WhoEmL 93
Martin, Kenneth Wayne 1939- WhoSSW 93
Martin, Kiel d1990 BioIn 17
Martin, Kim Irene 1952- WhoEmL 93, WhoSSW 93
Martin, LaBrena Law&B 92
Martin, Larry Woods Law&B 92
Martin, Laura Anne 1958- WhoAmW 93
Martin, Laura Belle 1915- WhoAmW 93
Martin, Laura K. 1906-1990 BioIn 17
Martin, LaVonna WhoAmW 93
Martin, Lee 1920- St&PR 93, WhoAm 92
Martin, (Margery) Lee WhoWrEP 92
Martin, Leila 1936- ConTFT 10
Martin, Leland Morris 1930- WhoSSW 93, WhoWor 93
Martin, Lena Prather AmWomPl
Martin, Leon Jean 1927- WhoWor 93
Martin, Leroy WhoAm 92
Martin, Les 1934- ScF&FL 92
Martin, Lincoln A. 1912- St&PR 93
Martin, Linda Gaye 1947- WhoE 93
Martin, Linda Lovering 1942- WhoAmW 93
Martin, Linda Rickson 1947- WhoEmL 93
Martin, Linda S. Law&B 92
Martin, Lisa Ann 1961- WhoAmW 93
Martin, Lisa C. Law&B 92
Martin, Lisa Diane 1957- WhoWor 93
Martin, Lisandra Lorraine 1958- WhoWor 93
Martin, Lori ScF&FL 92
Martin, Lorraine B. 1940- WhoAmW 93, WhoE 93
Martin, Louis Edward 1928- WhoAm 92
Martin, Louis Frank 1951- WhoE 93
Martin, Lucy Z. 1941- WhoAm 92, WhoAmW 93
Martin, Luther 1748-1826 OxCSupC
Martin, Lynn 1939- CngDr 91
Martin, Lynn Morley 1939- BioIn 17, WhoAm 92, WhoAmW 93, WhoE 93
Martin, M.C. WhoScE 91-1
Martin, Madeleine d1991 BioIn 17
Martin, Maggie Ann 1945- WhoAmW 93, WhoSSW 93
Martin, Malcolm Elliot 1935- WhoAm 92, WhoE 93
Martin, Malcolm Mencer 1920- WhoE 93
Martin, Malcolm Woods 1912- WhoAm 92
Martin, Marcia ScF&FL 92
Martin, Marcia Campbell 1934- WhoAmW 93
Martin, Margaret Gately 1928- WhoAmW 93
Martin, Margaret Shirley 1952- St&PR 93
Martin, Marilyn Herod Law&B 92
Martin, Marilynne 1959- WhoAmW 93
Martin, Marion E. 1900-1987 PolPar
Martin, Mark 1914- WhoAm 92
Martin, Marlene June Elmer 1934- WhoAmW 93
Martin, Martha Jo d1990 BioIn 17

Martin, Mary 1892-1975 BioIn 17
Martin, Mary 1913-1990 BioIn 17
Martin, Mary-Anne 1943- WhoAm 92
Martin, Mary Coates WhoSSW 93
Martin, Mary Evelyn WhoAmW 93, WhoEmL 93
Martin, Mary Kathleen Beatty 1946- WhoEmL 93
Martin, Mary Priest 1933- WhoAmW 93
Martin, Mary (Virginia) 1913-1990 Baker 92
Martin, Mary Wolf 1930- WhoAmW 93
Martin, Matthew Eric Law&B 92
Martin, Maurice John 1929- WhoAm 92
Martin, Melissa Diana 1967- WhoAmW 93
Martin, Michael 1932- WhoWor 93
Martin, Michael Alexander 1939- St&PR 93
Martin, Michael David 1927- St&PR 93
Martin, Michael Frederick 1957- WhoE 93
Martin, Michael L. 1949- St&PR 93
Martin, Michael Lawton 1948- WhoEmL 93
Martin, Michael Lee 1947- WhoE 93, WhoEmL 93
Martin, Michael S. 1946- St&PR 93
Martin, Michael Timothy 1960- WhoE 93
Martin, Michael Townsend 1941- WhoE 93, WhoWor 93
Martin, Michel 1933- WhoScE 91-4
Martin, Milton T., Jr. 1939- WhoAm 92
Martin, Murray Simpson 1928- WhoAm 92
Martin, Nancy BioIn 17, Law&B 92
Martin, Nancy Ann 1946- WhoAmW 93
Martin, Nancy Lee 1962- WhoEmL 93
Martin, Nathaniel Frizell Grafton 1928- WhoAm 92
Martin, Neal Anderson 1946- WhoSSW 93
Martin, Ned Harold 1945- WhoAm 92, WhoSSW 93
Martin, Neil Bertell Law&B 92
Martin, Nigel WhoScE 91-1
Martin, Nina AmWomPl
Martin, Noel 1922- WhoAm 92
Martin, Norman K. 1926- St&PR 93
Martin, Norman K. 1930- WhoIns 93
Martin, Norman Keith 1930- WhoAm 92
Martin, O.V. 1923- St&PR 93
Martin, Oscar Thaddeus 1908- WhoAm 92
Martin, Osvaldo Jose 1952- WhoWor 93
Martin, P.A. WhoScE 91-1
Martin, Paris Leveret 1944- WhoSSW 93
Martin, Patricia Ann Bryant 1950- WhoAmW 93
Martin, Patricia Ellen Law&B 92
Martin, Patricia J. 1954- WhoEmL 93
Martin, Patricia Miles 1899-1986 ConAu 37NR, MajAI [port]
Martin, Patricia Stone 1931- WhoWrEP 92
Martin, Patrick 1941- WhoAm 92
Martin, Patrick Albert 1950- WhoEmL 93
Martin, Patrick M. 1946- St&PR 93
Martin, Paul 1903-1992 NewYTBS 92 [port]
Martin, Paul 1920- St&PR 93
Martin, Paul 1938- BioIn 17, WhoAm 92
Martin, Paul A. Law&B 92
Martin, Paul Cecil 1931- WhoAm 92
Martin, Paul Edward 1914- WhoAm 92
Martin, Paul Edward 1928- WhoSSW 93
Martin, Paul Joseph 1936- WhoAm 92
Martin, Paul (Joseph James) 1903-1992 CurBio 92N
Martin, Paul S. 1899-1974 IntDcAn
Martin, Peter Edward WhoWor 93
Martin, Peter M. 1937- St&PR 93
Martin, Peter R. Law&B 92
Martin, Peter Robert 1949- WhoEmL 93, WhoSSW 93
Martin, Peter Ross 1940- WhoE 93
Martin, Peter Ruppert 1957- WhoEmL 93
Martin, Peter William 1939- WhoAm 92
Martin, Philip ScF&FL 92
Martin, Philip Dale 1958- WhoSSW 93
Martin, Philip James 1951- WhoWor 93
Martin, Preston BioIn 17
Martin, Preston 1923- WhoAm 92
Martin, Quinn William 1948- WhoEmL 93
Martin, R.B. 1934- St&PR 93
Martin, R. Keith 1933- WhoAm 92
Martin, R. William 1943- WhoWrEP 92
Martin, Ralph Arthur 1927- St&PR 93
Martin, Ralph Edward Law&B 92
Martin, Ralph Guy 1920- WhoAm 92, WhoWrEP 92
Martin, Raphael 1934- WhoSSW 93
Martin, Ray 1936- WhoAm 92
Martin, Ray D. 1927- St&PR 93
Martin, Raymond Edward 1957- WhoEmL 93
Martin, Rebecca Reist 1952- WhoAmW 93, WhoE 93
Martin, Reginald Gilbert, Jr. 1957- St&PR 93
Martin, Rene Alain Louis 1935- WhoScE 91-2
Martin, Renee M. Law&B 92
Martin, Ret 1961- St&PR 93
Martin, Retha Jane Law&B 92
Martin, Riccardo 1874-1952 Baker 92
Martin, Richard BioIn 17
Martin, Richard A. 1934- St&PR 93
Martin, Richard Cornish 1936- WhoE 93
Martin, Richard Douglas 1959- WhoWor 93
Martin, Richard Eugene 1947- WhoEmL 93
Martin, Richard Harrison 1946- WhoAm 92, WhoE 93, WhoWor 93
Martin, Richard Jay 1946- WhoAm 92
Martin, Richard L. 1932- WhoAm 92, WhoE 93
Martin, Richard L. 1933- St&PR 93
Martin, Richard Theodore 1925- WhoE 93
Martin, Richard W. Law&B 92
Martin, Rita A. Law&B 92
Martin, Robert Allan 1948- St&PR 93
Martin, Robert B. 1933- St&PR 93
Martin, Robert Bernard 1918- WhoWrEP 92
Martin, Robert Brooke Law&B 92
Martin, Robert Bruce 1929- WhoAm 92, WhoSSW 93
Martin, Robert C. 1926- WhoIns 93
Martin, Robert E. 1913- BioIn 17
Martin, Robert Edward 1928- WhoWor 93
Martin, Robert Edward, Jr. 1931- WhoAm 92
Martin, Robert F. 1923- St&PR 93
Martin, Robert Finlay, Jr. 1925- WhoAm 92
Martin, Robert Francis 1942- WhoE 93
Martin, Robert G. 1945- St&PR 93
Martin, Robert Gregory 1959- WhoEmL 93
Martin, Robert Huxley 1916- St&PR 93
Martin, Robert Richard 1910- WhoAm 92
Martin, Robert Roy 1927- St&PR 93, WhoAm 92
Martin, Robert T. Law&B 92
Martin, Robert V., Jr. 1915- St&PR 93
Martin, Robert W., Jr. Law&B 92
Martin, Robert William 1936- WhoAm 92
Martin, Roblee B. 1922- St&PR 93
Martin, Roblee Boettcher 1922- WhoAm 92
Martin, Rod 1928- ScF&FL 92
Martin, Rodney, Jr. 1952- WhoIns 93
Martin, Roger Bond 1936- WhoAm 92
Martin, Roger F. 1927- St&PR 93
Martin, Roger Harry 1943- WhoAm 92
Martin, Roger Lawrence 1958- WhoAm 92
Martin, Rogers William 1956- WhoSSW 93
Martin, Ronald Allen 1952- WhoEmL 93
Martin, Ronald Anthony 1963- WhoEmL 93
Martin, Ronald Joseph 1949- St&PR 93
Martin, Ronald Lavern 1922- WhoAm 92
Martin, Rose Kocsis 1928- WhoAmW 93
Martin, Roy Butler, Jr. 1921- WhoAm 92
Martin, Roy M. St&PR 93
Martin, Roy O., III 1960- St&PR 93
Martin, Ruby Julene Wheeler 1931- WhoSSW 93
Martin, Rudolf Ernst 1925- WhoScE 91-3
Martin, Russ ScF&FL 92
Martin, Russell W. 1933- ScF&FL 92
Martin, Ruth M. d1990 BioIn 17
Martin, Sallie 1896-1988 Baker 92
Martin, Sam 1920- WhoAm 92
Martin, Samuel Albert 1945- St&PR 93
Martin, Samuel John WhoScE 91-1
Martin, Samuel Preston, III 1916- WhoAm 92
Martin, Sandra Meisterhans 1953- WhoSSW 93
Martin, Scott E. Law&B 92
Martin, Scott J. BioIn 17
Martin, Serge G. Law&B 92
Martin, Shane 1973- BioIn 17
Martin, Shirley 1932- WhoAm 92, WhoAmW 93
Martin, Stacey Lynn 1951- WhoAmW 93, WhoSSW 93
Martin, Stephen David 1947- WhoEmL 93
Martin, Stephen Paul 1948- WhoAsAP 91
Martin, Stephen-Paul 1949- WhoWrEP 92
Martin, Steve NewYTBS 92 [port], WhoAm 92
Martin, Steve 1945?- BioIn 17, IntDcF 2-3 [port], News 92 [port], QDrFCA 92 [port]
Martin, Steve Jackson 1948- WhoSSW 93
Martin, Steven M. Law&B 92
Martin, Susan Fry 1952- WhoEmL 93
Martin, Susan J. Law&B 92
Martin, Susan Katherine 1942- WhoAm 92, WhoAmW 93
Martin, Susan Kaye 1954- WhoEmL 93
Martin, Susan Taylor 1949- WhoAm 92
Martin, Suzanne Gabrielle 1954- WhoAmW 93
Martin, Tamela Sheree 1962- WhoAmW 93
Martin, Teresa G. 1958- WhoEmL 93
Martin, Terrence E. 1951- WhoAm 92, WhoE 93
Martin, Theodore Krinn 1915- WhoAm 92
Martin, Theresa Marie 1965- WhoAmW 93
Martin, Thomas Brooks 1935- St&PR 93
Martin, Thomas E. 1942- WhoAm 92
Martin, Thomas H. ScF&FL 92
Martin, Thomas Howard Law&B 92
Martin, Thomas Jackson 1942- WhoSSW 93
Martin, Thomas L. Law&B 92
Martin, Thomas Lyle 1921- St&PR 93
Martin, Thomas Lyle, Jr. 1921- WhoAm 92
Martin, Thomas P. 1960- St&PR 93
Martin, Thomas Patrick 1936- WhoWor 93
Martin, Thomas S. 1849-1919 PolPar
Martin, Timothy Dale 1956- WhoEmL 93
Martin, Timothy (Peter) 1950- ConAu 138
Martin, Todd David 1955- WhoWor 93
Martin, Tom Francis 1951- WhoE 93
Martin, Ursula Hilda Mary WhoScE 91-1
Martin, Valentina Kuchynka 1925- WhoAmW 93
Martin, Valerie BioIn 17
Martin, Valerie 1948- ScF&FL 92
Martin, Valerie Metcalf 1948- WhoWrEP 92
Martin, Vicki Jean 1954- WhoEmL 93
Martin, Vincent George 1922- WhoAm 92
Martin, Vincent Lionel 1939- St&PR 93, WhoAm 92
Martin, Violet Florence 1862-1915 BioIn 17
Martin, Virginia L. Law&B 92
Martin, Virve Paul 1928- WhoAmW 93
Martin, Wade Omer 1911-1990 BioIn 17
Martin, Walter B. Law&B 92
Martin, Walter Edwin 1908- WhoAm 92
Martin, Walter John 1932- WhoE 93
Martin, Walter Lee 1921- WhoIns 93
Martin, Walter Patrick 1912- WhoAm 92
Martin, Walter Ralston 1928-1989 BioIn 17
Martin, Warren H. 1956- St&PR 93
Martin, Warren O. 1917- St&PR 93
Martin, Wayne Joseph 1939- St&PR 93
Martin, Webb Franklin 1944- St&PR 93
Martin, Webber MajAI
Martin, Wendy Lynn WhoE 93
Martin, Wesley George 1946- WhoEmL 93
Martin, William A. 1941- St&PR 93
Martin, William Bizzell 1926- WhoSSW 93
Martin, William F. Law&B 92
Martin, William F., Jr. Law&B 92
Martin, William Frederick 1917- St&PR 93
Martin, William Harry 1955- WhoEmL 93
Martin, William Henry 1947- WhoAm 92
Martin, William Ivan 1916- BioIn 17, MajAI
Martin, William John 1951- WhoE 93
Martin, William Joseph, III 1953- WhoE 93
Martin, William McChesney 1906- BioIn 17
Martin, William Oliver 1919- WhoIns 93
Martin, William Owen, III 1937- WhoSSW 93
Martin, William Robert 1921- WhoAm 92
Martin, William Royall, Jr. 1926- WhoAm 92, WhoSSW 93
Martin, William Russell, Jr. 1939- St&PR 93
Martin, William Stewart Law&B 92
Martin, William Thomas Law&B 92
Martin, William Vandever 1944- St&PR 93
Martin, William W. WhoScE 91-4
Martin, William Walker 1925- St&PR 93
Martin, Wyatt 1930- St&PR 93
Martina c. 598-c. 641 OxDcByz
Martina, Don 1935- DcCPCAm
Martinac, Paula 1954- ScF&FL 92
Martinak, Rosemary 1954- WhoEmL 93
Martin-Alonso, Olga 1959- WhoAmW 93, WhoWor 93
Martin-Anderson, Vicki Law&B 92
Martin-Aranda, Jose 1925- WhoScE 91-3
Martinaud, Cl. WhoScE 91-2
Martin-Baro, Ignacio BioIn 17
Martin-Bittman, Lawrence Michael 1931- WhoE 93
Martin-Bowen, Lindsey 1949- WhoWor 93
Martin-Cannici, Cynthia Elaine 1953- WhoSSW 93
Martincic, Joseph Anton 1941- St&PR 93
Martin-Cuccio, Roanne Law&B 92
Martindale, David L. Law&B 92
Martindale, Hilda 1875-1952 BioIn 17
Martindale, J. WhoScE 91-1
Martindale, Louisa 1873-1966 BioIn 17
Martindale, Louisa Spicer 1839-1914 BioIn 17
Martindale, Mary AmWomPl
Martindale, Robert H. 1919- St&PR 93
Martindale, T. Chris ScF&FL 92
Martin del Campo, Diego Ramiro 1929- WhoWor 93
Martin-Del-Campo, Enrique 1940- WhoUN 92
Martindell, Jackson 1900-1990 BioIn 17
Martine 1940- ScF&FL 92
Martineau, Elizabeth Ada Snyder 1954- WhoEmL 93
Martineau, Harriet 1802-1876 BioIn 17
Martineau, James Louis 1940- St&PR 93
Martineau, Michel Law&B 92
Martineau, Reed Lynn 1932- WhoAm 92
Martineau, Thomas Richard 1946- WhoWor 93
Martine-Barnes, Adrienne 1942- ScF&FL 92
Martinek, Karel WhoScE 91-4
Martinek, Michael Gerhard 1950- WhoWor 93
Martinell, Robert G. Law&B 92
Martinelli, A.W. 1928- St&PR 93
Martinelli, Alyse F. Law&B 92
Martinelli, Elsa 1933?- BioIn 17
Martinelli, Gary Robert 1950- WhoEmL 93
Martinelli, Giovanni 1885-1969 Baker 92, OxDcOp
Martinelli, Kenneth Dean 1946- WhoIns 93
Martinelli, Louis Adrio 1933- St&PR 93
Martinelli, Martin V. Law&B 92
Martinelli, Robert Angelo 1947- WhoSSW 93
Martinelli, Robert Owens 1924- St&PR 93
Martinelli, Rosemary 1957- WhoAmW 93, WhoE 93, WhoEmL 93
Martinello, Marty E. 1931- St&PR 93
Martinen, John A. 1938- WhoAm 92
Martines, Lauro 1927- WhoAm 92, WhoWrEP 92
Martinet, Jean d1672 HarEnMi
Martinet, Jean-Louis 1912- Baker 92
Martinet, Jean Marie Andre 1925- WhoScE 91-2
Martinet, Louis 1934- WhoScE 91-4
Martinetto, Thomas Peter 1939- WhoSSW 93
Martinez, A. BioIn 17
Martinez, Adrian R. Law&B 92
Martinez, Al 1929- WhoAm 92
Martinez, Alonso 1955- St&PR 93
Martinez, Andre Georges Joseph 1953- WhoWor 93
Martinez, Andres A. 1949- St&PR 93
Martinez, Arabella 1937- NotHsAW 93
Martinez, Augusto Julio 1930- WhoE 93
Martinez, Bert Jose Norberto Jose 1962- WhoSSW 93
Martinez, Bob 1934- BioIn 17, News 92 [port], WhoAm 92, WhoE 93, WhoWor 93
Martinez, Boris DcCPCAm
Martinez, Brian Michael 1957- WhoEmL 93
Martinez, Celestine E., Jr. 1942- WhoAsAP 91
Martinez, Cesar 1944- HispAmA
Martinez, Chuck MiSFD 9
Martinez, Cuenca Alejandro E. 1947- WhoWor 93
Martinez, Cynthia I. Law&B 92
Martinez, David Roger 1954- WhoEmL 93, WhoSSW 93
Martinez, Demetria 1960- NotHsAW 93
Martinez, Dennis 1955- BioIn 17
Martinez, Elena 1940- WhoAmW 93
Martinez, Eliana BioIn 17
Martinez, Elisa M. Law&B 92
Martinez, Eliud 1935- DcLB 122 [port]
Martinez, Elizabeth 1943- NotHsAW 93
Martinez, Elizabeth Ann 1958- WhoSSW 93
Martinez, Ernesto, III 1953- WhoSSW 93
Martinez, Felipe M. 1944- WhoScE 91-3
Martinez, Fidel DcCPCAm
Martinez, Gary Wayne 1950- St&PR 93
Martinez, George O. Law&B 92
Martinez, Gregorio 1942- SpAmA
Martinez, Gustave WhoAm 92
Martinez, Herminia S. WhoAmW 93
Martinez, Ifigenia DcCPCAm
Martinez, Irene Beatrice 1944- WhoAmW 93

Martinez, Jacinto Benavente y 1866-1954 *BioIn 17*
Martinez, Joanne Elaine 1945- *WhoAmW 93*
Martinez, Joaquin 1942- *WhoWor 93*
Martinez, John Stanley 1930- *WhoWor 93*
Martinez, Jorge Navarrete 1946- *WhoWor 93*
Martinez, Jose Daniel 1956- *Baker 92*
Martinez, Jose de Jesus 1929-1991 *BioIn 17*
Martinez, Jose Luis 1918- *DcMexL*
Martinez, Jose Luis 1962- *WhoSSW 93*
Martinez, Jose Mario 1948- *WhoWor 93*
Martinez, Juan J. 1908- *St&PR 93*
Martinez, Lissa Ann 1954- *NotHsAW 93*
Martinez, Lourdes E. *Law&B 92*
Martinez, Luis A. 1955- *WhoE 93*
Martinez, Luis Antonio Sanchez 1959- *WhoWor 93*
Martinez, Luis Osvaldo 1927- *WhoAm 92*
Martinez, Lynne 1948- *WhoAmW 93*
Martinez, Manuel Albert 1959- *WhoEmL 93*
Martinez, Maria-Ester 1939- *WhoWor 93*
Martinez, Maria Leonor 1948- *WhoAmW 93*
Martinez, Maria Montoya 1887-1980 *BioIn 17*
Martinez, Marianne 1744-1812 *Baker 92*
Martinez, Marianne von 1744-1812 *BioIn 17*
Martinez, Mario Jose 1954- *WhoSSW 93*
Martinez, Matthew G. 1929- *HispAmA [port]*
Martinez, Matthew G., Jr. 1929- *CngDr 91*
Martinez, Matthew Gilbert 1929- *WhoAm 92*
Martinez, Maximiliano Hernandez 1882-1966 *DcCPCAm*
Martinez, Melquiades R. 1946- *WhoEmL 93*
Martinez, Michael, Jr. 1951- *WhoSSW 93*
Martinez, Miguel Angel Gomez *Baker 92*
Martinez, Odaline de la 1949- *Baker 92*
Martinez, Orlando 1924- *ConAu 138*
Martinez, Oscar 1943- *HispAmA*
Martinez, Pedro M. 1936- *WhoScE 91-3*
Martinez, Ramon *BioIn 17*
Martinez, Richard Isaac 1944- *HispAmA*
Martinez, Rita L. *Law&B 92*
Martinez, Robert 1934- *HispAmA [port]*
Martinez, Robert Anthony d1992 *BioIn 17*
Martinez, Robert C. *Law&B 92*
Martinez, Roman, IV 1947- *WhoAm 92*
Martinez, Romeo 1912-1990 *BioIn 17*
Martinez, Ruben Martin 1948- *WhoEmL 93, WhoWor 93*
Martinez, Salvador 1942- *WhoWor 93*
Martinez, Salvador Nava d1992 *BioIn 17*
Martinez, Silvia Jacinta 1955- *WhoE 93, WhoEmL 93*
Martinez, Thomas *BioIn 17*
Martinez, Vilma *BioIn 17*
Martinez, Vilma 1943- *NotHsAW 93 [port]*
Martinez, Vilma S. 1943- *HispAmA*
Martinez, Vilma Socorro 1943- *WhoAm 92*
Martinez, Walter Baldomero 1937- *WhoAm 92*
Martinez, Y. *WhoScE 91-2*
Martinez, Yolanda R. 1936- *WhoAmW 93*
Martinez, Zarela *BioIn 17*
Martinez-Aragon, Antonio 1952- *WhoScE 91-3*
Martinez Arias, Cesar 1954- *WhoWor 93*
Martinez-Canas, Maria 1960- *NotHsAW 93*
Martinez-Carrasco, Rafael 1949- *WhoScE 91-3*
Martinez-Carrion, Marino 1936- *WhoAm 92*
Martinez-Cid, Ricardo 1950- *WhoEmL 93*
Martinez de Navarrete, Jose Manuel 1768-1809 *DcMexL*
Martinez Dominguez, Guillermo 1923- *WhoWor 93*
Martinez-Duart, Jose Manuel 1940- *WhoScE 91-3*
Martinez-Echevarria, Miguel A. 1943- *WhoWor 93*
Martinez Estrada, Ezequiel 1895-1964 *SpAmA*
Martinez Gomez, Francisco 1935- *WhoScE 91-3*
Martinez Hugue, Manuel 1876-1945 *BioIn 17*
Martinez Jaramillo, Cleofas *NotHsAW 93*
Martinez Jimeno, Adolfo *WhoScE 91-3*
Martinez-Lopez, Jorge Ignacio 1926- *WhoSSW 93*
Martinez-Maldonado, Manuel 1937- *WhoAm 92, WhoWor 93*
Martinez Martinez, Pedro M. 1936- *WhoScE 91-3*
Martinez Moreno, Carlos 1917-1986 *SpAmA*
Martinez-Ona, Rafael J. 1954- *WhoWor 93*
Martinez Ortega, Judith 1908- *DcMexL*
Martinez Penaloza, Porfirio 1916- *DcMexL*
Martinez Rivas, Carlos 1924- *SpAmA*
Martinez-Selva, Jose Maria 1955- *WhoWor 93*
Martinez Smith, Elizabeth *WhoAm 92*
Martinez Somalo, Eduardo Cardinal 1927- *WhoWor 93*
Martinez Sotomayor, Jose 1895-1980 *DcMexL*
Martinez Tagle, Tessa *NotHsAW 93*
Martinez Tatum, Grace *NotHsAW 93*
Martinez-Tejeda, Juan J. 1908- *WhoAm 92*
Martinez Verdugo, Arnaldo *DcCPCAm*
Martinez Y Ferrer, Marcelino Codilla, Jr. 1947- *WhoEmL 93*
Martin Fernandez, Miguel 1943- *WhoWor 93*
Marting, Diane E. 1952- *ConAu 138*
Marting, William Locke 1936- *St&PR 93*
Martin Gaite *BioIn 17*
Martin-Garcia, Maria Emilia 1951- *NotHsAW 93*
Martin-Gerhards, Rebecca Ann 1949- *WhoEmL 93*
Martin-Hall, Patricia Jean 1949- *WhoEmL 93*
Martinho, Eduardo J.C. 1936- *WhoScE 91-3*
Martini, Anita *BioIn 17*
Martini, Arthur Pete 1943- *WhoWor 93*
Martini, Arturo 1889-1947 *BioIn 17*
Martini, Carlo Maria Cardinal 1927- *WhoWor 93*
Martini, Charles C. 1940- *WhoIns 93*
Martini, Giovanni Battista 1706-1784 *Baker 92*
Martini, Jean Paul Egide 1741?-1816 *Baker 92*
Martini, Luciano 1927- *WhoScE 91-3*
Martini, Nicholas 1904-1991 *BioIn 17*
Martini, R.E. 1932- *St&PR 93*
Martini, Richard *MiSFD 9*
Martini, Richard K. 1952- *WhoE 93, WhoWor 93*
Martini, Robert Edward 1932- *WhoAm 92*
Martini, Ronald Anthony 1937- *St&PR 93*
Martinic, Leo Daniel 1958- *St&PR 93*
Martinich, Aloysius Patrick 1946- *WhoEmL 93, WhoSSW 93*
Martinie, Steven *Law&B 92*
Martinis, William J. 1941- *St&PR 93*
Martin-Jenkins, Timothy Dennis 1947- *WhoWor 93*
Martinko, Mark James 1949- *WhoEmL 93, WhoSSW 93*
Martinkus, Stanley J. 1947- *St&PR 93*
Martin-Mateo, M.P. 1935- *WhoScE 91-3*
Martin Mendiluce, Jose Maria 1925- *WhoScE 91-3*
Martin-Nagle, Renee *Law&B 92*
Martino, Amy Marie 1963- *WhoAmW 93*
Martino, Angel *WhoAmW 93*
Martino, Ann Louise *Law&B 92*
Martino, Anthony A. *BioIn 17*
Martino, Babette 1956- *WhoEmL 93*
Martino, Bruce F. *Law&B 92*
Martino, Donald 1931- *BioIn 17*
Martino, Donald (James) 1931- *Baker 92, WhoAm 92*
Martino, Frank N. 1929- *St&PR 93*
Martino, Gary James 1956- *WhoEmL 93*
Martino, Germain-Pierre 1940- *WhoScE 91-2*
Martino, James B. 1951- *St&PR 93*
Martino, James Boyd 1951- *WhoEmL 93*
Martino, John 1936- *St&PR 93*
Martino, Joseph Paul 1931- *WhoAm 92*
Martino, Maria Linda 1962- *WhoWrEP 92*
Martino, Marie G. *St&PR 93*
Martino, Marie L. *Law&B 92*
Martino, Michael Charles 1950- *WhoE 93*
Martino, Nina Florence 1952- *WhoEmL 93*
Martino, Peter Dominic 1963- *WhoE 93*
Martino, Robert Salvatore 1931- *WhoAm 92*
Martino, Rocco Leonard 1929- *WhoAm 92, WhoE 93, WhoWor 93*
Martino, Steve *WhoAm 92*
Martino, Tony *BioIn 17*
Martino, Victor 1929- *WhoScE 91-2*
Martino, Virginia Eileen 1944- *WhoAmW 93*
Martinon, Jean 1910-1976 *Baker 92*
Martinotti, Enrico 1931- *WhoWor 93*
Martinovich, Paula Jean Hill *Law&B 92*
Martin-Pascual, Carlos 1945- *WhoScE 91-3*
Martin-Piera, Fermin 1954- *WhoScE 91-3*
Martin-Pitman, Kari Lisa 1958- *WhoWrEP 92*
Martin Roldan, Rafael 1924- *WhoScE 91-3*
Martins, A. Gomes 1954- *WhoScE 91-3*
Martins, Ana Paula 1960- *WhoWor 93*
Martins, Heitor Miranda 1933- *WhoAm 92*
Martins, Joao Carlos 1940- *Baker 92*
Martins, Joao R. 1938- *St&PR 93*
Martins, Julio B. 1930- *WhoScE 91-3*
Martins, Manuel Goncalves 1936- *WhoWor 93*
Martins, Peter *BioIn 17*
Martins, Peter 1946- *WhoAm 92, WhoE 93*
Martin Sanchez, Alejandro 1958- *WhoWor 93*
Martin-Sanchez, J. Antonio 1940- *WhoScE 91-3*
Martin Sanchez, Juan Antonio 1940- *WhoScE 91-3*
Martinsen, Erik 1952- *WhoWor 93*
Martinsen, Keith Alan 1965- *WhoEmL 93*
Martinsen, Martin *ScF&FL 92*
Martins Ferreira, Jose A. 1953- *WhoScE 91-3*
Martinson, A. Denise 1947- *WhoWrEP 92*
Martinson, David John 1942- *St&PR 93*
Martinson, David Keith 1946- *WhoWrEP 92*
Martinson, Fred L. 1921- *St&PR 93*
Martinson, Ida Marie 1936- *WhoAm 92, WhoAmW 93*
Martinson, Jacob Christian, Jr. 1933- *WhoAm 92*
Martinson, Jodie Hawkins Hough 1936- *WhoAmW 93*
Martinson, Judith Ann 1951- *WhoEmL 93*
Martinson, Karin Ann 1961- *WhoAmW 93*
Martinson, Leslie H. *MiSFD 9*
Martinson, Melinda R. *Law&B 92*
Martinson, William Henry 1926- *St&PR 93*
Martinsson, Gunnar Folke 1934- *WhoUN 92*
Martinu, Bohuslav 1890-1959 *IntDcOp, OxDcOp*
Martinu, Bohuslav (Jan) 1890-1959 *Baker 92*
Martinucci, Nicola 1941- *OxDcOp*
Martinussen, John Emil 1947- *WhoWor 93*
Martinuzzi, Leo Sergio, Jr. 1928- *WhoAm 92*
Martinuzzi, Santo 1937- *WhoScE 91-2*
Martin-Vasquez, Manolo *BioIn 17*
Martin Vicente, Luis 1926- *WhoScE 91-3*
Martin y Soler, Vicente 1754-1806 *Baker 92, IntDcOp [port], OxDcOp*
Martio, Olli T. 1941- *WhoScE 91-4*
Martio, Olli Tapani 1941- *WhoWor 93*
Martirano, Salvatore 1927- *Baker 92*
Marti-Recober, Manuel 1940- *WhoScE 91-3*
Martland, Carl Douglas 1946- *WhoE 93*
Martocchio, Emilio F. 1927- *St&PR 93*
Martocci, Angeline Anne 1930- *St&PR 93*
Martoccia, Charles Thomson 1930- *WhoSSW 93*
Martoff, Charles Jeff 1954- *WhoEmL 93*
Marton, Andrew d1992 *NewYTBS 92*
Marton, Andrew 1904-1992 *BioIn 17, MiSFD 9N*
Marton, Denes 1943- *WhoScE 91-4*
Marton, Elisabeth d1992 *BioIn 17, NewYTBS 92 [port]*
Marton, Emery 1922- *WhoAm 92*
Marton, Eric M. *Law&B 92*
Marton, Eva 1943- *Baker 92, IntDcOp [port], OxDcOp, WhoAm 92, WhoAmW 93, WhoWor 93*
Marton, G.E. 1940- *St&PR 93*
Marton, Kati *BioIn 17*
Marton, Lajos Csaba 1954- *WhoScE 91-4*
Marton, Laurence Jay 1944- *WhoAm 92*
Martone, Michael 1955- *WhoWrEP 92*
Martone, Patricia Ann 1947- *WhoEmL 93*
Martoni, Charles J. 1936- *WhoE 93, WhoWor 93*
Marton-Lefevre, J. *WhoScE 91-2*
Marton-Lefevre, Julia *WhoScE 91-2*
Martonosi, Anthony Nicholas 1928- *WhoAm 92*
Martopangrawit, R.L. 1914-1986 *Baker 92*
Martorana, Sebastian Vincent 1919- *WhoAm 92, WhoWor 93*
Martore, Joseph A. 1953- *St&PR 93*
Martorell, Mario Francisco 1942- *WhoE 93*
Martorell Hundt, Guillermo Eduardo 1941- *WhoWor 93*
Martorelli, Louis, Jr. 1949- *St&PR 93*
Martos, Ferenc 1918- *WhoScE 91-4*
Martos, Rafael 1943?- *BioIn 17*
Martov, Julius 1873-1923 *DcTwHis*
Martre, Henri 1928- *WhoWor 93*
Martschink, Sherry Shealy 1949- *WhoAmW 93*
Marttala, Lassi Pekka 1957- *WhoWor 93*
Marttila, James Konstantin 1948- *WhoEmL 93*
Marttin, Paul *WhoWrEP 92*
Marttinen, Tauno 1912- *Baker 92*
Martucci, Giuseppe 1856-1909 *Baker 92*
Martucci, Paolo 1881-1980 *Baker 92*
Martucci, Vincent James 1954- *WhoE 93*
Martucci, William Christopher 1952- *WhoEmL 93*
Martuccio, Joseph 1953- *WhoEmL 93*
Marturana, Louis 1932- *St&PR 93*
Marturano, Janice L. *Law&B 92*
Martuscelli, Ezio *WhoScE 91-3*
Martuscello, Diane Mataraza 1952- *WhoE 93, WhoEmL 93*
Marty, Alvin Leonard 1927- *WhoE 93*
Marty, Andre 1886-1956 *BioIn 17*
Marty, C. *WhoScE 91-2*
Marty, Francois Cardinal 1904- *WhoWor 93*
Marty, Georges-Eugene 1860-1908 *Baker 92*
Marty, Hans Ulrich 1946- *WhoWor 93*
Marty, Jeanne Marie 1943- *WhoSSW 93*
Marty, M. *WhoScE 91-2*
Marty, M.E. 1946- *WhoScE 91-2*
Marty, Martin Emil 1928- *WhoAm 92*
Marty, Raymond 1929- *WhoWor 93*
Marty, Sid 1944- *WhoCanL 92*
Marty, Werner 1943- *WhoScE 91-4*
Martyak, Joseph J. *WhoAm 92*
Martyl 1918- *WhoAm 92*
Martyn, Dorothy *AmWomPl*
Martyn, Edith How- 1875-1953 *BioIn 17*
Martyn, Henry 1781-1812 *BioIn 17*
Martyn, Linda LaBonte 1961- *WhoEmL 93*
Martynov, Serguei Nikolaevich 1953- *WhoUN 92*
Martyr, Crista L. 1946- *St&PR 93*
Martz, Clyde Ollen 1920- *WhoAm 92*
Martz, Donna Kay 1959- *WhoAmW 93*
Martz, Jack W. 1945- *St&PR 93*
Martz, Louis Lohr 1913- *WhoAm 92*
Martz, Robert L. 1930- *St&PR 93*
Martz, Stephen 1942- *St&PR 93*
Martz, Willard Harry 1934- *WhoSSW 93*
Martzett, Carol Marie Preston 1948- *WhoAmW 93*
Martzial, Terrence Joseph, III 1960- *WhoEmL 93*
Martzke, Rudy *BioIn 17*
Martzy, Johanna 1924-1979 *Baker 92*
Maruani, Alain David 1946- *WhoWor 93*
Maruani, Jean 1937- *WhoScE 91-2*
Marubini, Ettore 1934- *WhoScE 91-3*
Marucheau, Louis Joseph *Law&B 92*
Maruhn, Joachim A. 1949- *WhoScE 91-3*
Marullo, Michael Anthony 1947- *WhoSSW 93*
Marum, Petter *WhoScE 91-4*
Marumoto, William Hideo 1934- *WhoAm 92*
Maruna, J.I. 1946- *St&PR 93*
Marushack, Andrew Joseph 1935- *St&PR 93*
Marut, Ret *BioIn 17*
Marutzky, R. *WhoScE 91-3*
Maruvada, Pereswara Sarma 1938- *WhoAm 92*
Maruyama, Henry Hatsuo 1923- *WhoWor 93*
Maruyama, Hiromi B. 1939- *WhoWor 93*
Maruyama, Hiroshi 1958- *WhoWor 93*
Maruyama, Hitoshi Mark 1929- *WhoWor 93*
Maruyama, Kazuhiro 1929- *WhoWor 93*
Maruyama, Koshi 1932- *WhoWor 93*
Maruyama, Masao 1889-1957 *HarEnMi*
Maruyama, Shoichi 1928- *WhoWor 93*
Maruyama, Yosh 1930- *WhoAm 92, WhoSSW 93*
Marvan, George Jivri Jan 1936- *WhoWor 93*
Marvel, Andrew Scott 1962- *WhoE 93, WhoEmL 93*
Marvel, Carl S. *BioIn 17*
Marvel, James Kenneth 1947- *WhoEmL 93*
Marvel, Kenneth Robert 1952- *WhoEmL 93*
Marvel, Thomas Stahl 1935- *WhoAm 92*
Marvel, Wanda Faye 1951- *WhoAmW 93*
Marvel, William 1909-1991 *BioIn 17*
Marvel, William 1949- *ConAu 139*
Marvelettes *SoulM*
Marvell, Andrew 1621-1678 *MagSWL [port], WorLitC [port]*
Marvell, Cindy *BioIn 17*
Marvelley, Brian 1947- *St&PR 93*
Marvenko-Smith, Patricia Ann 1947- *WhoEmL 93*
Marver, James D. 1950- *St&PR 93*
Marvil, Rebecca Elaine 1958- *WhoAmW 93*
Marvil, Richard A. 1938- *St&PR 93*

Marvin, Daniel E., Jr. 1938- St&PR 93
Marvin, David Keith 1921- WhoAm 92
Marvin, Douglas Raymond 1947- WhoAm 92
Marvin, Frederick 1923- Baker 92
Marvin, Guy, III Law&B 92
Marvin, Guy, III 1941- St&PR 93
Marvin, H.A. St&PR 93
Marvin, Helen Rhyne 1917- WhoAmW 93
Marvin, James Conway 1927- WhoAm 92
Marvin, John Bingham 1935- WhoE 93
Marvin, John George 1912- WhoE 93, WhoWor 93
Marvin, Kenneth St&PR 93
Marvin, Kurt St&PR 93
Marvin, Lee 1924-1987 IntDcF 2-3 [port]
Marvin, Michael B. Law&B 92
Marvin, Mike MiSFD 9
Marvin, Oscar McDowell 1924- WhoAm 92
Marvin, Robert Earle 1920- WhoAm 92
Marvin, Roy Mack 1931- St&PR 93, WhoAm 92
Marvin, Susan 1933- ScF&FL 92
Marvin, Ursula Bailey 1921- WhoAmW 93
Marvin, Wilbur 1921- WhoSSW 93
Marvin, William A. Law&B 92
Marvin, William Glenn, Jr. 1920- WhoAm 92
Marvinny, Charles Joseph 1915- WhoE 93
Marvit, Robert Charles 1938- WhoAm 92
Marwazi, Al- fl. 11th cent.-12th cent. OxDcByz
Marwedel, Peter 1949- WhoWor 93
Marwell, Edward M. 1922- St&PR 93
Marwell, Emily 1950- WhoEmL 93
Marx, Adolf Bernhard 1795-1866 Baker 92
Marx, Andrew C. 1931- St&PR 93
Marx, Anne WhoAm 92
Marx, Arthur 1921- WhoAm 92
Marx, Charles Henri 1920- WhoScE 91-2
Marx, Chico 1886-1961
See Marx Brothers, The QDrFCA 92
Marx, Chico 1887-1961
See Marx Brothers JeAmHC
Marx, Chico 1891?-1961
See Marx Brothers IntDcF 2-3
Marx, Claus 1931- WhoScE 91-3
Marx, David L. 1952- St&PR 93
Marx, Edward L. Law&B 92
Marx, Egon 1937- WhoE 93
Marx, Eleanor 1855-1898 BioIn 17
Marx, Frederick Henry 1942- St&PR 93
Marx, Gary Samuel 1948- WhoWor 93
Marx, Gertie Florentine 1912- WhoAm 92
Marx, Groucho 1890?-1977
See Marx Brothers IntDcF 2-3
See Also Marx Brothers JeAmHC
See Also Marx Brothers, The QDrFCA 92
Marx, Groucho 1891-1977 BioIn 17
Marx, Gummo
See Marx Brothers IntDcF 2-3
Marx, Gummo 1897-1977
See Marx Brothers JeAmHC
Marx, Harpo 1888-1964
See Marx Brothers JeAmHC
See Also Marx Brothers, The QDrFCA 92
Marx, Harpo 1893?-1964
See Marx Brothers IntDcF 2-3
Marx, Joe E., III 1947- St&PR 93
Marx, Josef 1913-1978 Baker 92
Marx, Joseph 1882-1964 Baker 92
Marx, Julius H. 1891-1977 BioIn 17
Marx, Karl 1818-1883 BioIn 17
Marx, Karl 1897-1985 Baker 92
Marx, Leo 1919- WhoAm 92
Marx, Leo A., Jr. Law&B 92
Marx, Leo A., Jr. 1946- St&PR 93
Marx, Michael H. St&PR 93
Marx, Michael Thomas 1948- WhoEmL 93
Marx, Morris Leon 1937- WhoSSW 93
Marx, Nanette Jean 1951- WhoEmL 93
Marx, Oscar Bruno, III 1939- WhoAm 92
Marx, Otto 1909-1991 BioIn 17
Marx, Patrick Keane 1947- WhoWor 93
Marx, Philip R. Law&B 92
Marx, Richard BioIn 17
Marx, Roberto Burle- BioIn 17
Marx, Samuel d1992 NewYTBS 92
Marx, Samuel 1902-1992 BioIn 17, ConAu 137
Marx, Thomas George 1943- WhoAm 92
Marx, Walter D. 1918- St&PR 93
Marx, Walter Herbert 1926- St&PR 93
Marx, William B., Jr. 1939- WhoAm 92
Marx, Zeppo 1901-1979
See Marx Brothers IntDcF 2-3
See Also Marx Brothers JeAmHC
See Also Marx Brothers, The QDrFCA 92
Marx Brothers BioIn 17, IntDcF 2-3 [port], JeAmHC
Marx Brothers, The QDrFCA 92 [port]
Marxer, Joseph Henry Law&B 92
Marxhausen, Reinhold Pieper BioIn 17
Marxsen, Eduard 1806-1887 Baker 92
Marxuacl, Rafael Law&B 92
Mary, Blessed Virgin, Saint BioIn 17
Mary, Queen 1867-1953 BioIn 17
Mary, Queen of Scots 1542-1587 BioIn 17
Mary, I, Queen of England 1516-1558 BioIn 17
Mary Jane Girls SoulM
Marylebone, Quintin Hogg Hailsham of St. 1907- BioIn 17
Mary Magdalene OxDcByz
Mary Magdalene, Saint BioIn 17
Mary of Egypt OxDcByz
Mary, of Egypt, Saint BioIn 17
Maryon (-d'Aulby), (John) Edward 1867-1954 Baker 92
Maryon Davis, A.R. WhoScE 91-1
Mary the Younger c. 866-c. 902 OxDcByz
Mary Tudor 1516-1558 BioIn 17
Marz, Martin Law&B 92
Marz, Wolf Gerhard 1929- WhoWor 93
Marzan, Julio 1946- BioIn 17
Marzano, A.M. 1929- St&PR 93
Marzano, Angelo Mario 1929- WhoAm 92
Marzano, Gilberto Maria 1948- WhoWor 93
Marzano, Janice 1949- St&PR 93
Marzec, Marcia Smith 1948- WhoAmW 93
Marzendorfer, Ernst 1921- Baker 92
Marziale, Antonio 1959- WhoSSW 93
Marziano, Fredric G. WhoAm 92
Marzio, Leonardo WhoScE 91-3
Marzio, Peter Cort 1943- WhoAm 92, WhoSSW 93
Marzluf, George Austin 1935- WhoAm 92
Marzman, Sidney S. St&PR 93
Marzo, Eduardo 1852-1929 Baker 92
Marzollo, Jean 1942- ScF&FL 92, SmATA 15AS [port]
Marzulli, Francis Nicholas 1917- WhoE 93
Mas, Jean-Bernard 1938- WhoWor 93
Masa, Antonin 1935- DrEEuF
Masahito, Nagasaka 1924- WhoWor 93
Masai, Mitsuo 1932- WhoWor 93
Masaitis, Ceslovas 1912- WhoE 93
Masaki, Akira 1925- WhoWor 93
Masaki, Yoshiki 1934- St&PR 93
Masaliyev, Absamat 1933- WhoWor 93
Masamori, Kotani 1930- WhoWor 93
Masamori, Seiji 1927- WhoAsAP 91
Masamune, Satoru 1928- WhoAm 92
Masani, Pesi Rustom 1919- WhoAm 92
Masaoka, Mike M. 1915-1991 BioIn 17
Masarik, Albert E. 1943- WhoWrEP 92
Masaryk, Alice 1879-1966 BioIn 17
Masaryk, Jan 1886-1948 DcTwHis
Masaryk, T.G. 1850-1937 BioIn 17
Masaryk, Tomas Garrigue 1850-1937 BioIn 17, DcTwHis
Masaschi, John E. 1933- St&PR 93
Masaschi, John Ellsworth 1933- WhoAm 92
Masayuki, Hamada 1922- WhoWor 93
Masbruch, Randal J. 1954- St&PR 93
Masbruch, Randal John 1954- WhoEmL 93
Mascagni, Pietro 1863-1945 Baker 92, BioIn 17, IntDcOp [port], OxDcOp
Mas Canosa, Jorge BioIn 17
Mascarenas, Alberto Lucero 1952- WhoEmL 93
Mascarenhas, Antonio Monteiro WhoWor 93
Mascari, J. Barry 1948- WhoE 93
Mascaro, Barbara J. 1948- St&PR 93
Mascart, Patrick 1949- WhoScE 91-2
Mascavage, Joseph Peter 1956- WhoEmL 93
Mascher, Alice St&PR 93
Maschera, Florentio c. 1540-c. 1584 Baker 92
Mascherin, Toni K. 1955- WhoAmW 93
Mascheroni, Aldo 1954- St&PR 93
Mascheroni, Angelo 1855-1895 OxDcOp
Mascheroni, Edoardo 1852-1941 Baker 92
Mascheroni, Edoardo 1892-1941 OxDcOp
Maschin, Douglas Raymond 1950- WhoE 93
Maschio, Giuseppe 1935- WhoWor 93
Maschmann, Michael Wayne 1949- St&PR 93
Mascho, George Leroy 1925- WhoAm 92
Masci, Carmela 1964- WhoAmW 93
Masciangelo, Bill ConAu 139
Masciangelo, William R., Jr. 1944- ConAu 139
Masciantonio, Philip Xavier 1929- St&PR 93
Mascio, Joyce Ann 1957- WhoEmL 93
Masciocchi, Norberto 1959- WhoWor 93
Masciola, Catherine Elizabeth 1962- WhoAmW 93
Masciole, Denis Michael 1941- St&PR 93
Mascioli, Mario V. 1921- St&PR 93
Mascioli-Charlton, Maria C. 1956- St&PR 93
Mascle, Georges H.M. 1937- WhoScE 91-2
Masco, Matt Schelb 1940- St&PR 93
Mascoll, Doris Walker 1936- WhoAmW 93
Mascolo, Giuseppe 1963- WhoWor 93
Mascolo, Nino J. Law&B 92
Mascotte, John P. St&PR 93
Mascotte, John Pierre 1939- WhoAm 92
Masdit, Supatra WhoAsAP 91
Mase, Hiromasa 1938- WhoWor 93
Mase, Raymond James 1951- WhoEmL 93
Masefield, John 1878-1967 BioIn 17
Masefield, John 1933- St&PR 93
Masek, Barry Michael 1955- WhoEmL 93
Masek, Edward J. Law&B 92
Masek, Elizabeth A. Law&B 92
Masek, Joseph Peter 1947- St&PR 93
Masek, Karel 1933- WhoScE 91-4
Masek, Vincenz 1755-1831 Baker 92
Masekela, Hugh BioIn 17
Masekela, Hugh 1939- WhoWor 93
Masel, William H. 1949- WhoE 93
Masella, Joseph 1950- St&PR 93, WhoIns 93
Maselli, John Anthony 1929- WhoAm 92
Masello, Robert ScF&FL 92
Masemola, Jafta d1990 BioIn 17
Masemore, Gerald L. 1938- St&PR 93
Masens, Liana Yvonne 1936- WhoWor 93
Maser, Frederick Ernest 1908- WhoAm 92, WhoWor 93
Maser, James Ellison 1938- St&PR 93
Maser, Karl A. 1937- St&PR 93, WhoIns 93
Maser, Mark Allen 1958- WhoEmL 93
Maser, Rebecca Jane 1957- WhoAmW 93
Maserati, Ettore d1990 BioIn 17
Maseth, William Everd, Jr. Law&B 92
Masetti, Enzo 1893-1961 Baker 92
Masetti, M. WhoScE 91-3
Masey, Jack 1924- WhoAm 92
Masey, Mary Lou 1932-1991 BioIn 17
Masgay, Thomas Michael 1962- WhoE 93
Mash, David Stefan 1952- WhoE 93
Mash, Donald J. 1942- WhoAm 92
Mash, Marlene Julia 1944- WhoAmW 93
Masha, F. Lwanyantika 1940- WhoUN 92
Mashaal, Victor 1938- St&PR 93
Mashack, Barbara Jean 1953- WhoAmW 93
Mashall, Michael J. Law&B 92
Masham, Baroness d1734 BioIn 17
Masham, Francis d1722 BioIn 17
Masham, Samuel 1679?-1758 BioIn 17
Masham, Samuel 1712-1776 BioIn 17
Ma Shaofang WhoAsAP 91
Mashariqa, Muhammad Zuhayr WhoWor 93
Mashat, Mohammed al- BioIn 17
Mashaw, Dawn Ella 1962- WhoAmW 93
Mashburn, C. N. Law&B 92
Mashburn, Guerry Leonard 1952- WhoEmL 93, WhoWor 93
Mashburn, Kimberly Joy Needham 1957- WhoAmW 93
Mashburn, Lillian Tauxe 1943- WhoAmW 93
Mashburn, R. Howard Law&B 92
Masheck, Joseph Daniel 1942- WhoAm 92
Mashelkar, Raghunath Anant 1943- WhoWor 93
Mashiko, Teruhiko 1947- WhoAsAP 91
Mashimo, Paul Akira 1926- WhoE 93
Mashin, Jacqueline Ann Cook 1941- WhoAmW 93, WhoE 93, WhoWor 93
Mashinini, Emma 1929- BioIn 17
Mashitz, Isaac 1952- WhoIns 93
Masho, Paul Nicholas Law&B 92
Masi, Dale A. WhoAm 92
Masi, J. Roger 1954- WhoE 93, WhoEmL 93
Masi, Jane Virginia 1947- WhoEmL 93, WhoWor 93
Masi, Pierluigi 1920- WhoScE 91-3
Masica, James Gerald 1943- St&PR 93
Masie, Elliott 1950- WhoE 93
Masiello, Alberta d1990 BioIn 17
Masiello, Richard James 1965- WhoEmL 93
Masiello, Rocco Joseph 1922- WhoAm 92
Masiero, Ronald J. 1942- WhoIns 93
Masilla, Thomas Anthony, Jr. 1946- St&PR 93
Masin, Leo 1916- St&PR 93
Masina, Giulietta 1921- BioIn 17, IntDcF 2-3 [port]
Masington, Nicholas J., Jr. Law&B 92
Masini, Angelo 1844-1926 Baker 92, OxDcOp
Masini, Donald Joseph 1935- St&PR 93
Masini, Gerardo 1920- WhoWor 93
Masinter, Edgar M. 1931- St&PR 93
Masinter, Edgar Martin 1931- WhoAm 92
Masip, Paulino 1899-1963 DcMexL
Masip, Vicente c. 1475-c. 1550 BioIn 17
Masip, Vicente Juan d1579 BioIn 17
Masire, Quett 1925- WhoWor 93
Masire, Quett Ketumile Joni 1925- WhoAfr
Masironi, Roberto 1931- WhoWor 93
Ma Sizhong 1930- WhoAsAP 91
Maskarino, Cornelio 1927- WhoAsAP 91
Masket, Edward Seymour 1923- WhoAm 92
Masket, Steven N. Law&B 92
Maskill, Mary Helen 1952- WhoSSW 93
Maskinen, Oskari ConAu 138
Maskovich, Linda K. St&PR 93
Maslach, Christina 1946- WhoAm 92, WhoAmW 93
Maslach, George James 1920- WhoAm 92
Maslak, Samuel H. 1948- ConEn, St&PR 93
Maslama dc. 733 OxDcByz
Maslamani, Ibrahim Mohammad 1937- WhoUN 92
Maslan, Neal L. 1940- St&PR 93
Masland, Frank E., III 1921- St&PR 93
Masland, Lynne S. 1940- WhoAmW 93
Masland, William S. 1921-1991 BioIn 17
Maslanka, Daniel Chester 1955- WhoEmL 93
Maslanka, Raymond A. 1932- St&PR 93
Maslansky, Paul 1933- MiSFD 9
Maslen, Neil Leonard 1933- St&PR 93
Maslen, Stephen Harold 1926- WhoAm 92
Maslennikov, Mikhail Valerianovitch 1931- WhoWor 93
Maslennikova, Leokadia 1918- OxDcOp
Masley, Michael 1952- Baker 92
Maslinkov, Dimiter 1929- WhoScE 91-4
Maslinski, Czeslaw 1921- WhoScE 91-4
Masloff, Sophie 1917- BioIn 17, NewYTBS 92 [port], WhoAm 92, WhoAmW 93, WhoE 93
Maslov, Edward I. Law&B 92
Maslova, Nina B. 1939- WhoWor 93
Maslow, Abraham Harold BioIn 17
Maslow, Will 1907- WhoAm 92
Maslowski, Jozef 1931- WhoScE 91-4
Maslowski, Piotr 1919- WhoScE 91-4
Maslowski, Stanislaw 1853-1926 PolBiDi
Maslowski, Stefan 1938- WhoScE 91-3
Maslyk, Cheri Ann 1949- WhoAmW 93, WhoEmL 93
Maslyn, Michael E. 1940- St&PR 93
Maslyn, Robert T. 1948- WhoSSW 93
Masman, Greggory Arthur 1953- WhoE 93
Masnari, Nino Antonio 1935- WhoAm 92, WhoSSW 93
Masnata, Francois 1934- WhoWor 93
Maso, Carole BioIn 17
Masodkar, Bhaskar Annaji 1927- WhoAsAP 91
Masoin, Michel-Henry 1946- WhoWor 93
Mason, A. George, Jr. Law&B 92
Mason, Aimee Hunnicutt Romberger 1918- WhoAmW 93, WhoSSW 93, WhoWor 93
Mason, Alpheus Thomas 1899-1989 BioIn 17
Mason, Anita 1942- ConAu 139, ScF&FL 92
Mason, Anne 1941- ScF&FL 92
Mason, Anthony Halstead 1938- WhoAm 92, WhoWor 93
Mason, Arthur Noel WhoScE 91-1
Mason, Audrey Garrison 1908- WhoAmW 93
Mason, Barbara 1947- SoulM
Mason, Barry Jean 1930- WhoAm 92
Mason, Belinda BioIn 17
Mason, Benjamin McMullan 1958- WhoEmL 93
Mason, Bobbie Ann BioIn 17
Mason, Bobbie Ann 1940- WhoAm 92, WhoAmW 93, WhoWrEP 92
Mason, Brian Harold 1917- WhoAm 92
Mason, Brick 1953- WhoE 93
Mason, Bruce BioIn 17
Mason, Bruce 1939- WhoAm 92
Mason, C. Richard 1942- St&PR 93
Mason, Caroline Atwater 1853-1939 AmWomPl
Mason, Carolyn B. ScF&FL 92
Mason, Charles Ellis, III 1938- WhoAm 92, WhoWrEP 92
Mason, Cheryl White 1952- WhoAmW 93
Mason, Christopher May 1957- WhoEmL 93
Mason, Craig Watson 1954- WhoE 93, WhoEmL 93
Mason, Cyn 1952- ScF&FL 92
Mason, Daniel Gregory 1873-1953 Baker 92
Mason, David 1924-1974 ScF&FL 92
Mason, David Aaron 1940- St&PR 93
Mason, David C., Jr. St&PR 93
Mason, David Dickenson 1917- WhoAm 92

Mason, David Edmund 1939- *St&PR 93*
Mason, David Ernest 1928- *WhoAm 92*
Mason, David Stewart 1947- *WhoWrEP 92*
Mason, Dean Towle 1932- *WhoAm 92, WhoWor 93*
Mason, Douglas R. 1918- *ScF&FL 92*
Mason, Earl Leonard 1947- *WhoAm 92*
Mason, Edith Huntington *AmWomPl*
Mason, Edward Allen 1926- *WhoAm 92*
Mason, Edward Archibald 1924- *St&PR 93, WhoAm 92*
Mason, Edward Eaton 1920- *WhoAm 92*
Mason, Edward S. d1992 *NewYTBS 92 [port]*
Mason, Edward S(agendorph) 1899-1992 *ConAu 137*
Mason, Edward Sagendorph 1899-1992 *BioIn 17*
Mason, Elizabeth Abruzese 1960- *WhoAmW 93*
Mason, Ellsworth Goodwin 1917- *WhoAm 92, WhoWor 93*
Mason, Emma Newby 1937- *St&PR 93*
Mason, Ernst *ConAu 37NR*
Mason, F. Eugenia 1947- *St&PR 93*
Mason, Frank H. 1936- *St&PR 93*
Mason, Frank Henry, III 1936- *WhoAm 92*
Mason, Franklin Rogers 1936- *WhoAm 92, WhoSSW 93*
Mason, Gail Diane 1948- *WhoEmL 93*
Mason, George 1725-1792 *BioIn 17, PolPar*
Mason, George L. 1946- *St&PR 93*
Mason, George Robert 1932- *WhoAm 92*
Mason, H. Griff 1944- *St&PR 93*
Mason, Harold J. 1926-1991 *BioIn 17*
Mason, Harry M. 1908- *ConAu 139*
Mason, Henry Lloyd 1921- *WhoAm 92*
Mason, Henry Lowell, III 1941- *WhoAm 92*
Mason, Herbert Warren, Jr. 1932- *ConAu 38NR, WhoAm 92*
Mason, Homer Livingston 1938- *WhoSSW 93*
Mason, Howard E., Jr. 1932- *St&PR 93*
Mason, Jack F. 1940- *St&PR 93*
Mason, Jackie *BioIn 17*
Mason, Jackie 1934- *WhoAm 92*
Mason, James 1909-1984 *BioIn 17, IntDcF 2-3 [port]*
Mason, James Albert 1929- *WhoAm 92*
Mason, James Boyd 1941- *WhoAm 92*
Mason, James F. 1942- *St&PR 93*
Mason, James Ostermann 1930- *WhoAm 92*
Mason, James Tate 1913- *WhoAm 92*
Mason, Jean Robbins 1932- *WhoAmW 93*
Mason, Jeff *ScF&FL 92*
Mason, Jeffrey Nelson *Law&B 92*
Mason, Jeffrey V. 1956- *St&PR 93*
Mason, Jerry 1913- *WhoWrEP 92*
Mason, Jerry 1913-1991 *BioIn 17*
Mason, John c. 1600-1672 *HarEnMi*
Mason, John 1927- *BioIn 17*
Mason, John 1935- *WhoSSW 93*
Mason, John Allen 1944- *St&PR 93*
Mason, John Beverly 1944- *WhoUN 92*
Mason, John Charles *WhoScE 91-1*
Mason, John Grouard 1946- *WhoE 93*
Mason, John H. *Law&B 92*
Mason, John H. 1936- *St&PR 93*
Mason, John Hayes 1950- *WhoE 93, WhoEmL 93*
Mason, John L. *BioIn 17*
Mason, John Latimer 1923- *WhoAm 92*
Mason, John Lemear 1921- *St&PR 93*
Mason, John Milton 1938- *WhoAm 92*
Mason, John Murwyn, Jr. 1940- *WhoAm 92*
Mason, Jonathan 1916- *St&PR 93*
Mason, Joseph 1932- *WhoAm 92*
Mason, Judith Ann 1945- *WhoAmW 93*
Mason, Julian Dewey, Jr. 1931- *WhoSSW 93*
Mason, Kenneth Robert 1933- *WhoAm 92*
Mason, Leo 1946- *BioIn 17*
Mason, Linda 1946- *WhoEmL 93*
Mason, Linda Ann 1947- *WhoAmW 93*
Mason, Linda C. *St&PR 93*
Mason, Lisa 1953- *ScF&FL 92*
Mason, Louis Boyd 1955- *WhoSSW 93*
Mason, Lowell 1792-1872 *Baker 92, BioIn 17*
Mason, Lowell B. 1893-1983 *ScF&FL 92*
Mason, Lucile Gertrude 1925- *WhoAmW 93, WhoE 93*
Mason, Lucy Randolph 1882-1959 *BioIn 17, EncAACR*
Mason, Luther Whiting 1828-1896 *Baker 92*
Mason, Marilyn Gell 1944- *WhoAm 92, WhoAmW 93*
Mason, Marilyn (May) 1925- *Baker 92*
Mason, Mark 1955- *ConAu 138*
Mason, Mark Evan 1955- *WhoE 93*
Mason, Marsha *WhoAm 92, WhoAmW 93*
Mason, Marshall W. 1940- *WhoAm 92*
Mason, Martha 1931- *WhoAmW 93, WhoWor 93*
Mason, Mary *ScF&FL 92*
Mason, Mary L. *AmWomPl*
Mason, Mary Margaret 1934- *WhoAmW 93*
Mason, Michael E. 1929- *WhoAm 92*
Mason, Miles Herbert, III 1947- *WhoSSW 93*
Mason, Morgan *BioIn 17*
Mason, Nancy Tolman 1933- *WhoAmW 93*
Mason, Nicholas Michael 1955- *WhoWor 93*
Mason, Otis Tufton 1838-1908 *IntDcAn*
Mason, Pamela Helen 1922- *WhoAm 92*
Mason, Pappy *BioIn 17*
Mason, Patricia Keane d1990 *BioIn 17*
Mason, Paul *ScF&FL 92*
Mason, Paul E. *Law&B 92*
Mason, Perry Carter 1939- *WhoAm 92*
Mason, Peter Ian 1952- *WhoEmL 93*
Mason, Philip (Parker) 1927- *ConAu 38NR*
Mason, Phillip Howard 1932- *WhoAm 92*
Mason, R.H. 1912-1991 *BioIn 17*
Mason, Ralph L. 1932- *St&PR 93*
Mason, Rausey Wood 1937- *St&PR 93*
Mason, Raymond A. 1936- *St&PR 93*
Mason, Raymond Adams 1936- *WhoAm 92, WhoE 93*
Mason, Raymond Edward, Jr. 1920- *St&PR 93*
Mason, Rebecca S. 1945- *WhoAmW 93*
Mason, Richard Gordon 1930- *St&PR 93*
Mason, Robert 1942- *ScF&FL 92*
Mason, Robert A. 1952- *WhoE 93*
Mason, Robert Allan 1943- *WhoAm 92*
Mason, Robert Edward 1934- *WhoSSW 93*
Mason, Robert F. 1927- *St&PR 93*
Mason, Robert Joseph 1918- *WhoAm 92*
Mason, Robert Lester 1945- *WhoSSW 93*
Mason, Robert Shephard 1943- *St&PR 93*
Mason, Roger *ScF&FL 92*
Mason, Roger 1941- *WhoWor 93*
Mason, Roger LeRoy 1952- *St&PR 93*
Mason, Roger Stanley *WhoScE 91-1*
Mason, Ronald Lee 1952- *WhoSSW 93*
Mason, Sally W. 1930- *WhoAmW 93*
Mason, Samuel *ScF&FL 92*
Mason, Sara Smith 1948- *WhoAmW 93*
Mason, Scott Aiken 1951- *WhoSSW 93*
Mason, Scott C. 1959- *WhoEmL 93*
Mason, Scott MacGregor 1923- *WhoE 93*
Mason, Sharon L. *Law&B 92*
Mason, Shipley Childs 1946- *St&PR 93*
Mason, Simone *ScF&FL 92*
Mason, Stephen Finney *WhoScE 91-1*
Mason, Stephen Finney 1923- *WhoWor 93*
Mason, Stephen Olin 1952- *WhoEmL 93, WhoWor 93*
Mason, Stephen Renard *St&PR 93*
Mason, Steven Charles 1936- *St&PR 93, WhoAm 92*
Mason, Steven Harold 1959- *WhoSSW 93*
Mason, Steven Jude 1944- *St&PR 93, WhoAm 92*
Mason, Susan E. *Law&B 92*
Mason, Susan Elizabeth 1952- *WhoE 93*
Mason, Theodore Toner 1935- *St&PR 93*
Mason, Thomas Albert 1936- *WhoAm 92*
Mason, Thomas C. *Law&B 92*
Mason, Thomas F. *BioIn 17*
Mason, Tim 1940-1990 *BioIn 17*
Mason, Timothy James *WhoScE 91-1*
Mason, Timothy Patrick 1940- *St&PR 93*
Mason, Tom 1958- *ScF&FL 92*
Mason, William 1829-1908 *Baker 92*
Mason, William Alvin 1926- *WhoAm 92*
Mason, William Cordell, III 1938- *WhoAm 92*
Mason, William Edward 1954- *WhoEmL 93*
Mason, William Ernest, IV 1949- *WhoEmL 93*
Mason, William Robert, III 1941- *WhoE 93*
Mason, William T. 1939- *St&PR 93*
Mason & Hamlin Co. *Baker 92*
Masone, Jino Lewis 1950- *WhoE 93*
Masoner, Paul Henry 1908- *WhoAm 92*
Mason-O'Neal, Beth Barwick 1939- *WhoSSW 93*
Masood, Rasheed 1947- *WhoAsAP 91*
Masoro, Edward Joseph, Jr. 1924- *WhoAm 92*
Masotti, Lewis Richard 1933- *St&PR 93*
Masotti, Louis Henry 1934- *WhoAm 92*
Masquelier, Adeline 1960- *WhoAmW 93*
Masquelier, John Roger 1947- *WhoEmL 93*
Masquelier, Sibyl W. 1946- *WhoEmL 93*
Masri, Sami Faiz 1939- *WhoAm 92*
Masri, Taher Nashat 1942- *WhoWor 93*
Mass, Allen R. *Law&B 92*
Mass, Donna Marie 1954- *WhoAmW 93, WhoEmL 93*
Mass, Edward R. 1926- *St&PR 93*
Mass, Edward Rudolph 1926- *WhoAm 92*
Mass, Karen Sueno 1964- *WhoE 93*
Mass, Robin D. *Law&B 92*
Massa, Conrad Harry 1927- *WhoAm 92*
Massa, Don Joseph 1923- *St&PR 93*
Massa, Donald Patrick 1946- *St&PR 93*
Massa, Enrico 1943- *WhoScE 91-3*
Massa, Frank B. *Law&B 92*
Massa, Harold A. 1938- *St&PR 93*
Massa, Jack 1953- *ScF&FL 92*
Massa, John A. *ScF&FL 92*
Massa, Juan Bautista 1885-1938 *Baker 92*
Massa, Miguel Souza, III 1950- *WhoE 93*
Massa, Nicolo 1854-1894 *Baker 92*
Massa, Paul Peter 1940- *WhoAm 92*
Massa, Peter 1926- *St&PR 93*
Massa, Robert A. 1937- *WhoE 93*
Massa, Robert P. 1947- *St&PR 93*
Massa, Salvatore Peter 1955- *WhoAm 92*
Massad, Carlos *WhoUN 92*
Massagee, Deanie Herman 1947- *WhoEmL 93, WhoSSW 93, WhoWor 93*
Massah, Cherilyn 1951- *WhoEmL 93*
Massaini, Tiburtio c. 1549-c. 1609 *Baker 92*
Massaino, Tiburtio c. 1549-c. 1609 *Baker 92*
Massalski, Thaddeus Bronislaw 1926- *WhoAm 92*
Massameno, John Mark 1952- *WhoEmL 93*
Massara, Aldo 1935- *St&PR 93*
Massarani, Renzo 1898-1975 *Baker 92*
Massarano, John R. 1933- *St&PR 93*
Massare, Carol Angela 1944- *WhoAmW 93*
Massarelli, Stanley Myron 1933- *St&PR 93*
Massari, Jeffrey T. *Law&B 92*
Massaro, Edward Joseph 1933- *WhoSSW 93*
Massaro, Louis L. 1946- *St&PR 93*
Massaro, Patti L. *Law&B 92*
Massarrat, Sadegh 1932- *WhoScE 91-3*
Massart, (Joseph) Lambert 1811-1892 *Baker 92*
Massart, Nestor-Henri-Joseph 1849-1899 *Baker 92*
Massarueh, Abdulsalam Yousef 1936- *WhoE 93*
Massaua, John Roger 1947- *WhoE 93, WhoEmL 93*
Masschelein, Willy J. 1936- *WhoScE 91-2*
Masse, Ernest J. 1944- *St&PR 93*
Masse, Laurel c. 1954- *See* Manhattan Transfer, The *ConMus 8*
Masse, Laurence Raymond 1926- *St&PR 93, WhoAm 92*
Masse, Marcel 1936- *WhoWor 93*
Masse, Marcel 1940- *WhoAm 92*
Masse, P.F. 1950- *St&PR 93*
Masse, Peggy Hart 1925- *WhoWrEP 92*
Masse, Victor 1822-1884 *Baker 92, OxDcOp*
Masse, Yvon H. 1935- *WhoAm 92*
Masse, Yvon Henri 1935- *St&PR 93*
Massee, David Lurton, Jr. 1936- *WhoAm 92*
Massee, Ned Walter 1950- *St&PR 93*
Massel, Stanislaw 1939- *WhoScE 91-4*
Masselli, Michael A. 1938- *St&PR 93*
Masselos, William 1920- *Baker 92*
Masselos, William 1920-1992 *NewYTBS 92 [port]*
Massena, Andre 1758-1817 *HarEnMi*
Massenet, I. *WhoScE 91-2*
Massenet, Jules 1842-1912 *IntDcOp [port], OxDcOp*
Massenet, Jules (-Emile-Frederic) 1842-1912 *Baker 92*
Massenet, Yves 1944- *WhoScE 91-2*
Massengale, Curt LeRoy 1959- *WhoSSW 93*
Massengale, Jimmy Edgar 1942- *WhoIns 93*
Massengale, Martin Andrew 1933- *WhoAm 92*
Massengale, Roger Lee 1953- *WhoEmL 93*
Massengale, Shari Louise 1958- *WhoEmL 93*
Massengill, Dennis Alan 1946- *St&PR 93*
Masser, Ian *WhoScE 91-1*
Masser, William J. 1937- *St&PR 93*
Masserman, Jules Homan 1905- *WhoAm 92*
Masseron, Jean Henri 1935- *WhoWor 93*
Masset, Claude 1925- *WhoWor 93*
Masset, Jean-Pierre 1936- *WhoWor 93*
Masseus, Jan 1913- *Baker 92*
Massey, Andrew John 1946- *WhoAm 92*
Massey, Brian Avery 1960- *WhoSSW 93*
Massey, C.T. *WhoScE 91-1*
Massey, Charles Knox, Jr. 1936- *WhoAm 92*
Massey, Charles L. 1922- *WhoAm 92*
Massey, Clinton Edward 1947- *WhoEmL 93, WhoSSW 93*
Massey, Connie 1949- *WhoAmW 93*
Massey, David Eugene 1938- *WhoSSW 93*
Massey, Dawn Michele *Law&B 92*
Massey, Donald Wayne 1938- *WhoSSW 93*
Massey, Donna Harris *Law&B 92*
Massey, Dorothea *AmWomPl*
Massey, E. Morgan 1926- *St&PR 93*
Massey, Ellen Gray 1921- *WhoWrEP 92*
Massey, Enid Adeline *WhoAmW 93*
Massey, Gaye Adams *Law&B 92*
Massey, Henrietta Floyd 1933- *WhoAmW 93*
Massey, Henry Heath, Jr. 1935- *St&PR 93*
Massey, Jack C. 1904-1990 *BioIn 17*
Massey, Jack T. 1927- *St&PR 93, WhoIns 93*
Massey, James 1943- *WhoWor 93*
Massey, James D. 1935- *St&PR 93*
Massey, James E. 1951- *St&PR 93*
Massey, James Earl 1930- *WhoWor 93*
Massey, James L. *St&PR 93*
Massey, James Lee 1934- *WhoAm 92*
Massey, Judith Elaine 1941- *WhoAmW 93*
Massey, Julia England 1942- *WhoSSW 93*
Massey, Karen B. 1948- *WhoIns 93*
Massey, Karen Michelle 1967- *WhoAmW 93*
Massey, Kathleen Marie Oates 1955- *WhoEmL 93*
Massey, Kathy Diane 1964- *WhoEmL 93*
Massey, Leon R. 1930- *WhoAm 92*
Massey, Marvin S., Jr. 1943- *St&PR 93*
Massey, Michael M. *Law&B 92*
Massey, Mitchell Vaughn 1949- *WhoE 93*
Massey, Morris R. 1931- *St&PR 93*
Massey, Patti Chryl 1952- *WhoEmL 93, WhoSSW 93*
Massey, R. Daniel 1942- *St&PR 93*
Massey, Raymond 1896-1983 *IntDcF 2-3*
Massey, Richard R. 1941- *St&PR 93*
Massey, Richard Walter, Jr. 1917- *WhoAm 92*
Massey, Robert L. 1934- *St&PR 93*
Massey, Robert Unruh 1922- *WhoAm 92*
Massey, Ronald Charles 1933- *WhoWor 93*
Massey, Shelby D. 1933- *St&PR 93*
Massey, Stephen Charles 1946- *WhoAm 92*
Massey, Stephen Walter 1956- *WhoEmL 93*
Massey, Thomas Benjamin 1926- *WhoAm 92, WhoE 93*
Massey, Tim R. 1940- *WhoSSW 93*
Massey, Veta Hamblen 1940- *WhoAmW 93*
Massey, Vincent 1887-1967 *DcTwHis*
Massey, Wallace W. 1924- *St&PR 93*
Massey, Walter E. *BioIn 17*
Massey, Walter Eugene 1938- *WhoAm 92*
Massey, William Ferguson 1856-1925 *DcTwHis*
Massey, William S. 1920- *WhoAm 92*
Masseyeff, Rene F. 1927- *WhoScE 91-2*
Masseyeff, Rene Francis 1927- *WhoWor 93*
Massialas, Byron George *WhoSSW 93*
Massiani, Francisco 1944- *SpAmA*
Massiano, Michael Francis 1934- *St&PR 93*
Massick, James William 1932- *WhoWor 93*
Massicott, Andre Jean 1937- *St&PR 93*
Massicotte, Guy-Paul *Law&B 92*
Massicotte, Guy-Paul 1940- *St&PR 93*
Massicotte, Jacques 1940- *St&PR 93*
Massicotte, Joseph H. 1923- *St&PR 93*
Massicotte, Normand D. 1935- *St&PR 93*
Massie, Chris 1880-1964 *ScF&FL 92*
Massie, Donald Gene 1941- *WhoSSW 93*
Massie, Edward 1910-1990 *BioIn 17*
Massie, Edward Lindsey 1929- *St&PR 93*
Massie, Edward Lindsey, Jr. 1929- *WhoAm 92*
Massie, James William, III *Law&B 92*
Massie, James William, III 1949- *St&PR 93*
Massie, John A. 1944- *St&PR 93*
Massie, Martha Dettner 1937- *WhoSSW 93*
Massie, Perry T. 1962- *St&PR 93*
Massie, Robert Joseph 1949- *WhoAm 92*
Massie, Robert K. 1929- *BioIn 17*
Massie, Robert K(inloch) 1929- *ConAu 40NR*
Massie, Robert Kinloch 1929- *WhoAm 92*
Massie, Wm. C. *St&PR 93*
Massien, Jeffrey Hal 1951- *St&PR 93*
Massignon, Daniel 1919- *WhoWor 93*
Massimilla, Leopoldo 1930- *WhoScE 91-3*
Massimino, Roland V. 1934- *WhoAm 92*

Massina, Vincent M. 1932- *St&PR 93*
Massing, Dale F. 1944- *St&PR 93*
Massion, Walter Herbert 1923- *WhoSSW 93*
Massler, Howard Arnold 1946- *WhoAm 92, WhoE 93, WhoEmL 93*
Massman, Virgil Frank *WhoAm 92*
Massoglia, Martin F. *ScF&FL 92*
Massoglia, Marty 1946- *ScF&FL 92*
Massol, Eugene 1802-1887 *OxDcOp*
Massolo, Arthur James 1942- *WhoAm 92*
Masson, Andre 1896-1987 *BioIn 17*
Masson, Claude *St&PR 93*
Masson, Claudine *WhoScE 91-2*
Masson, Gayl Angela 1951- *WhoAmW 93*
Masson, Gerard 1936- *Baker 92*
Masson, Henri 1940- *WhoScE 91-4*
Masson, Henri 1946- *WhoScE 91-2*
Masson, J. Moussaieff 1941- *BioIn 17*
Masson, Jean-Pierre 1945- *WhoScE 91-2*
Masson, Jeffrey Moussaieff 1941- *BioIn 17*
Masson, Louise Anglae 1827-1887 *See* Massart, (Joseph) Lambert 1811-1892 *Baker 92*
Masson, Paul-Marie 1882-1954 *Baker 92*
Masson, Pierre 1928- *St&PR 93*
Masson, Robert B. d1991 *BioIn 17*
Masson, Robert Henry 1935- *St&PR 93*
Massone, Raul Enrique 1944- *WhoWor 93*
Massonneau, Louis 1766-1848 *Baker 92*
Massot, Christian Thierry 1960- *WhoWor 93*
Massot, Federico 1949-1990 *BioIn 17*
Massot, Jean-Noel 1939- *WhoScE 91-2*
Massoulie, Jean 1938- *WhoScE 91-2*
Massu, Jacques 1908- *BioIn 17*
Massue, Henri de 1648-1720 *BioIn 17*
Massumi, Mehrdad Mike 1957- *WhoE 93*
Massung, Howard G. *Law&B 92*
Massura, Edward Anthony 1938- *WhoAm 92*
Massy, Patricia Graham Bibbs 1918- *WhoAmW 93*
Massy, William Francis 1934- *WhoAm 92*
Mast, Frederick William 1910- *WhoAm 92*
Mast, Gifford Morrison 1943- *St&PR 93*
Mast, Gregory Lewis 1954- *WhoEmL 93*
Mast, Jane *AmWomPl*
Mast, Jay K. 1937- *St&PR 93*
Mast, Katherine Byrne d1991 *BioIn 17*
Mast, Miriam Eileen 1955- *WhoEmL 93*
Mast, Richard Melvin 1934- *St&PR 93*
Mast, Stewart Dale 1924- *WhoAm 92, WhoSSW 93*
Mastai-Ferretti, Giovanni Maria 1792-1878 *BioIn 17*
Mastandrea, Salvatore J. *Law&B 92*
Masten, Ann Stringfellow 1951- *WhoEmL 93*
Masten, Elizabeth R. 1947- *St&PR 93*
Masten, Helen Adams d1989 *BioIn 17*
Masten, John S. *Law&B 92*
Master, Dave *BioIn 17*
Master, Geofrey L. *Law&B 92*
Master, Steven Bruce 1953- *WhoE 93*
Masterfield, Maxine Louise 1933- *WhoAmW 93*
Masteria, Marie Antoinette 1944- *WhoAmW 93*
Master Juba 1825?-1852 *BioIn 17*
Master-Karnik, Paul Joseph 1948- *WhoE 93*
Masterman, Jack Verner 1930- *St&PR 93, WhoAm 92*
Masterman, Vicki O'Meara 1957- *WhoAmW 93*
Masterman-Smith, Virginia 1937- *WhoWrEP 92*
Masters, Anthony 1940- *ScF&FL 92*
Masters, Beda Doris 1942- *WhoAmW 93*
Masters, Bettie Sue Siler 1937- *WhoAm 92*
Masters, Brian William 1954- *WhoE 93, WhoWor 93*
Masters, Bruce Allen 1936- *WhoSSW 93, WhoWor 93*
Masters, Carl *BioIn 17*
Masters, Carole Ann *Law&B 92*
Masters, Charles Day 1929- *WhoAm 92*
Masters, Claude Bivin 1930- *WhoSSW 93*
Masters, David Romey 1947- *WhoEmL 93*
Masters, Dexter 1908-1989 *ScF&FL 92*
Masters, Doug *ScF&FL 92*
Masters, Edgar Lee 1868-1950 *BioIn 17*
Masters, Edgar Lee 1869-1950 *MagSAmL [port]*
Masters, Edward E. 1924- *WhoAm 92, WhoE 93*
Masters, Gary *WhoAm 92*
Masters, Gary Everett 1941- *WhoE 93*
Masters, George Mallary 1936- *WhoSSW 93*
Masters, George William 1940- *St&PR 93*
Masters, Helen Geneva *AmWomPl*
Masters, Hilary Thomas 1928- *WhoWrEP 92*
Masters, J.D. *ScF&FL 92*
Masters, John *BioIn 17*
Masters, John 1914-1983 *ScF&FL 92*
Masters, John Christopher 1941- *WhoAm 92*
Masters, Jon Joseph 1937- *WhoAm 92*
Masters, Judith Mary 1956- *WhoAmW 93*
Masters, Kathy Marie 1954- *WhoAmW 93*
Masters, Laurance E. 1932- *WhoIns 93*
Masters, Lowell Forrest 1946- *WhoEmL 93*
Masters, Quentin 1946- *MiSFD 9*
Masters, Robert Edward Lee 1927- *WhoWrEP 92*
Masters, Roger Davis 1933- *WhoAm 92*
Masters, William Howell 1915- *WhoAm 92*
Masterson, Bat 1853-1921 *BioIn 17*
Masterson, Byron Jackson 1933- *WhoAm 92*
Masterson, Carlin 1940- *WhoAm 92*
Masterson, Charles Francis 1917- *WhoAm 92*
Masterson, Donald Earl, Jr. 1932- *St&PR 93*
Masterson, Ed 1852-1878 *BioIn 17*
Masterson, J. Bruce *Law&B 92*
Masterson, James Francis 1926- *WhoAm 92*
Masterson, James Joseph 1958- *WhoEmL 93*
Masterson, Jim 1855-1895 *BioIn 17*
Masterson, Joe A. 1943- *St&PR 93, WhoAm 92*
Masterson, John Patrick 1925- *WhoAm 92*
Masterson, Joseph G. 1930- *WhoScE 91-3*
Masterson, Kate 1870- *AmWomPl*
Masterson, Kenneth R. *Law&B 92*
Masterson, Kenneth Rhodes 1944- *St&PR 93, WhoAm 92*
Masterson, Kleber Sandlin 1908- *WhoAm 92, WhoWor 93*
Masterson, Kleber Sanlin, Jr. 1932- *WhoAm 92*
Masterson, Linda Histen 1951- *WhoAmW 93*
Masterson, Mary Stuart *BioIn 17*
Masterson, Michael Rue 1946- *WhoAm 92*
Masterson, Norton Edward 1902- *WhoIns 93*
Masterson, Patricia O'Malley 1952- *WhoAmW 93, WhoE 93, WhoEmL 93, WhoWrEP 92*
Masterson, Patrick 1936- *WhoWor 93*
Masterson, Peter 1934- *MiSFD 9, WhoAm 92*
Masterson, Richard Ramon 1966- *WhoSSW 93*
Masterson, Thomas Marshall 1959- *WhoE 93*
Masterson, Valerie 1937- *Baker 92, OxDcOp*
Masterson, Veronica Ann 1961- *WhoAmW 93*
Masterson, Wendy Lynn 1963- *WhoEmL 93*
Masterson, William A. 1931- *WhoAm 92*
Masterson, William N. *St&PR 93*
Master Therion 1875-1947 *BioIn 17*
Masterton, Graham 1946- *ScF&FL 92*
Mastick, Seabury Cone, Mrs. 1895- *WhoWor 93*
Mastilovic, Danica 1933- *Baker 92*
Mastin, Robert Eldon 1940- *WhoSSW 93*
Mastin, William Charles 1931- *WhoSSW 93*
Mastny, Catherine Louise 1939- *WhoAmW 93*
Mastny, Vojtech 1936- *WhoWor 93*
Mastorakis, Nico 1941- *MiSFD 9, ScF&FL 92*
Mastos, Louis T. 1921- *St&PR 93*
Mastos, Louis T., Jr. 1921- *WhoIns 93*
Mastrantonio, Mary Elizabeth *BioIn 17*
Mastrantonio, Mary Elizabeth 1958- *WhoAm 92*
Mastreta, Angeles (Maria de) 1949- *DcMexL*
Mastriani, John P. 1952- *St&PR 93*
Mastrianni, Alfred J. *St&PR 93*
Mastro, John M. 1950- *St&PR 93*
Mastrodonato, George Carl 1950- *WhoEmL 93*
Mastroianni, Armand *MiSFD 9*
Mastroianni, Luigi, Jr. 1925- *WhoAm 92*
Mastroianni, Marcello 1924- *BioIn 17, IntDcF 2-3 [port], WhoAm 92, WhoWor 93*
Mastrolia, Lilyan Spitzer 1934- *WhoAmW 93*
Mastromarco, Dan Ralph 1958- *WhoEmL 93*
Mastromonaco, Ellen G. *WhoAm 92*
Mastromonico, Arnold Michael 1933- *St&PR 93*
Mastronardi, Richard 1947- *St&PR 93*
Mastrosimone, Claude Anthony 1937- *WhoE 93*
Mastry, Nicholas Joseph, III 1947- *St&PR 93*
Mastura, Michael O. 1941- *WhoAsAP 91*
Masubuchi, Koichi 1924- *WhoAm 92, WhoE 93, WhoWor 93*
Masucci, Christina Marie 1958- *WhoE 93*
Masucci, Richard Paul 1947- *St&PR 93*
Masucci, Robert N. 1937- *St&PR 93*
Masuch, Michael F. 1949- *WhoWor 93*
Mas'ud, I d1155 *OxDcByz*
Masuda, Gohta 1940- *WhoWor 93*
Masuda, Shigeru *St&PR 93*
Masuda, Sumiko 1930- *WhoWor 93*
Masuda, Toshio 1929- *WhoAsAP 91*
Mas'udi, Al- 893?-956 *OxDcByz*
Mas'udi, Al- 895?-956? *Expl 93*
Masuhara, D.M. *Law&B 92*
Masuhara, Hiroshi 1944- *WhoWor 93*
Masumoto, David Mas 1954- *WhoWrEP 92*
Masunaga, Rei 1935- *WhoWor 93*
Masuo, Ryuichi 1928- *WhoWor 93*
Masuoka, Hiroyuki 1923- *WhoAsAP 91*
Masur, Corinne 1954- *WhoAmW 93*
Masur, Kurt 1927- *Baker 92, BioIn 17, WhoAm 92, WhoE 93, WhoWor 93*
Masure, Roger Louis 1922- *WhoWor 93*
Masurel, Jean-Louis Antoine Nicolas 1940- *WhoAm 92*
Masurok, Yuri (Antonovich) 1931- *Baker 92*
Masurovsky, Marc Jean 1956- *WhoE 93*
Masursky, Harold 1923-1990 *BioIn 17*
Masury, Julia Anne 1962- *WhoEmL 93*
Masuya, Yoshihiro 1933- *WhoWor 93*
Masyukov, Vadim Arseniy 1933- *WhoWor 93*
Mata, Eduardo 1942- *Baker 92, HispAmA [port], WhoAm 92, WhoSSW 93*
Mata, Elizabeth Adams 1946- *WhoAmW 93, WhoEmL 93, WhoWor 93*
Mata, George 1945- *St&PR 93*
Mata, Pedro F. 1944- *St&PR 93*
Mata, Pedro Francisco 1944- *WhoAm 92*
Mata, Zoila 1937- *WhoAmW 93, WhoSSW 93*
Matache, Savel 1936- *WhoScE 91-4*
Matacic, Lovro von 1899-1985 *Baker 92, OxDcOp*
Mataga, Noboru 1927- *WhoWor 93*
Mata Hari 1876-1917 *BioIn 17*
Matala, Heikki 1942- *WhoScE 91-4*
Matalam, Guimid P. 1937- *WhoAsAP 91*
Matalin, Mary *BioIn 17*
Matalon, Norma 1949- *WhoEmL 93, WhoWor 93*
Matalon, Vivian 1929- *ConTFT 10, MiSFD 9, WhoAm 92*
Mataraso, M.H. 1929- *St&PR 93*
Matarasso, Alan 1953- *WhoE 93*
Matarazzo, Franco 1955- *WhoWor 93*
Matarazzo, Harris Starr 1957- *WhoEmL 93*
Matarazzo, Joseph Dominic 1925- *WhoAm 92*
Matarazzo, Ruth Gadbois 1926- *WhoAm 92, WhoAmW 93*
Matare, Ewald 1887-1965 *BioIn 17*
Matarese, James M. 1930- *St&PR 93*
Matarese, Laura Ellen 1956- *WhoEmL 93*
Matas, Carol 1949- *DcChlFi*
Matas, Julio 1931- *HispAmA*
Matas, Myra Dorothea 1938- *WhoWor 93*
Matasar, Ann B. 1940- *WhoAm 92, WhoAmW 93*
Matasar, Robert Martin *Law&B 92*
Matasovic, Marilyn Estelle 1946- *WhoAmW 93, WhoEmL 93, WhoWor 93*
Matasuntha c. 518-c. 551 *OxDcByz*
Matathia, Ira *BioIn 17*
Matathia, Ira Leslie 1949- *WhoAm 92*
Mataxis, Theodore Christopher 1917- *WhoAm 92, WhoWor 93*
Matayoshi, Kathryn S. *Law&B 92*
Match, Robert Kreis 1926- *WhoAm 92*
Matcha, Jack 1919- *WhoWrEP 92*
Matchar, David Bruce 1955- *WhoEmL 93*
Matchett, William Hayes 1932- *WhoAm 92*
Matchett, William Henry 1923- *WhoAm 92*
Matchette, Phyllis Lee 1921- *WhoAmW 93*
Mate, Rudolph 1898-1964 *MiSFD 9N*
Matecki, Jerzy *WhoScE 91-4*
Mateen, Einola 1932- *St&PR 93*
Mateer, Don Metz 1945- *WhoWor 93*
Mateer, Donald D. 1927- *St&PR 93*
Matei, Gheorghe 1934- *WhoScE 91-4*
Matej, Henryk 1926- *WhoScE 91-4*
Matej, Josef 1922- *Baker 92*
Mateja, Michael E. 1938- *St&PR 93*
Matejic, Marie *BioIn 17*
Matejka, Vaclav 1937- *DrEEuF*
Matejko, Jan 1838-1893 *PolBiDi*
Mateju, Joseph Frank 1927- *WhoAm 92*
Mateker, Emil Joseph, Jr. 1931- *St&PR 93, WhoSSW 93*
Matel, Daniel F. 1959- *WhoAm 92*
Matela, Ireneusz 1936- *WhoUN 92*
Matelan, Mathew Nicholas 1945- *St&PR 93*
Mateles, Richard Isaac 1935- *WhoAm 92*
Maten, Mark James 1957- *St&PR 93*
Mateo, Fernando *BioIn 17*
Mateo, J.L. *WhoScE 91-3*
Mateo, Julio Cesar 1951- *WhoE 93*
Mateos, Juan 1831-1913 *DcMexL*
Mateo-Sagasta, Eloy 1932- *WhoScE 91-3*
Mater, Gene P. 1926- *WhoAm 92*
Mater, Jonathan W. 1949- *St&PR 93*
Mater, Maude E. *WhoAmW 93*
Matera, Jack John 1940- *St&PR 93*
Matera, Mark V. *Law&B 92*
Materas, Alfred Patrick, Jr. 1938- *St&PR 93*
Materassi, Riccardo *WhoScE 91-3*
Materazzo, Patrick R. 1934- *St&PR 93*
Materia, Kathleen Patricia Ayling 1954- *WhoAmW 93*
Materna, Amalie 1844-1918 *Baker 92, OxDcOp*
Materna, Linda Susan 1948- *WhoE 93*
Materna, Thomas Walter 1944- *WhoE 93*
Maternowski, Jo Lene A. *Law&B 92*
Maters, Bruce R. *Law&B 92*
Materson, Richard Stephen 1941- *WhoWor 93*
Mates, Lucille M. *Law&B 92*
Mates, Robert Edward 1935- *WhoE 93*
Mates, Sharon 1953- *St&PR 93*
Matesich, Mary Andrew 1939- *WhoAmW 93*
Matesky, Sondra Faye *WhoAmW 93*
Mateson, Patricia Hart 1941- *WhoE 93*
Mateu, Andreu 1962- *WhoE 93*
Mateus, Amilcar de Magalhaes 1911- *WhoScE 91-3*
Mateus, Lois *WhoAm 92, WhoAmW 93*
Matevich, Branislava 1949- *WhoEmL 93*
Matey, James Regis 1951- *WhoE 93*
Mateyka, James Allan 1942- *St&PR 93*
Mateyo, George R. 1942- *St&PR 93*
Matez, Jerome *St&PR 93*
Matfess, William 1928- *St&PR 93*
Mathabane, Mark *BioIn 17*
Mathai, Catherine Ann 1963- *WhoAmW 93*
Mathai, Chirathalakal Varughese 1945- *WhoWor 93*
Mathai, Joseph 1952- *WhoE 93*
Mathalon, Charles 1925- *St&PR 93*
Mathamel, Martin Steven 1949- *WhoE 93*
Mathaudhu, Sukhdev Singh 1946- *WhoEmL 93*
Mathavan, Sudershan Kumar 1945- *WhoWor 93*
Mathay, Ismael A., Jr. 1932- *WhoAsAP 91*
Mathe, Akos 1947- *WhoScE 91-4*
Mathe, George 1930- *WhoScE 91-4*
Mathe, Imre, Jr. 1942- *WhoScE 91-4*
Mathe, Lynda Anne Paloma 1948- *WhoAmW 93*
Matheiu, Raymond Maurice 1947- *St&PR 93*
Mathelot, Pierre *WhoScE 91-2*
Mathelot, Pierre 1929- *WhoScE 91-2*
Matheny, Adam Pence, Jr. 1932- *WhoSSW 93*
Matheny, Charles Woodburn, Jr. 1914- *WhoWor 93*
Matheny, Donald R. 1942- *St&PR 93*
Matheny, Edward Taylor, Jr. 1923- *WhoAm 92*
Matheny, Marc William 1956- *WhoEmL 93*
Matheny, Paul Edward, Jr. 1947- *WhoEmL 93, WhoSSW 93*
Matheny, Randall Floyd 1952- *WhoSSW 93*
Matheny, Robert Lavesco 1933- *WhoAm 92*
Matheny, Ruth Ann 1918- *WhoAm 92*
Matheny, Tom Harrell *WhoAm 92, WhoSSW 93*
Matheny-White, Patricia Lynn 1945- *WhoAmW 93*
Mather, Allen Frederick 1922- *WhoAm 92*
Mather, Arthur 1925- *ScF&FL 92*
Mather, Betty Bang 1927- *WhoAm 92, WhoWor 93*
Mather, Bruce 1939- *Baker 92*
Mather, Bryant 1916- *WhoAm 92*
Mather, Charles E., III 1934- *St&PR 93, WhoIns 93*
Mather, Cotton 1663-1728 *BioIn 17*
Mather, Dave H. 1845- *BioIn 17*

Mather, Elizabeth Vivian 1941- *WhoAmW 93*
Mather, Gary Douglas 1944- *St&PR 93*
Mather, Herbert 1934- *WhoSSW 93*
Mather, Increase 1639-1723 *BioIn 17*
Mather, Jennie Powell 1948- *WhoAmW 93*
Mather, John *WhoScE 91-1*
Mather, John David *WhoScE 91-1*
Mather, John Gordon 1946- *WhoEmL 93*
Mather, John Norman 1942- *WhoAm 92*
Mather, John Russell 1923- *WhoAm 92*
Mather, Kirtley F. 1888-1978 *BioIn 17*
Mather, Melissa 1917- *ScF&FL 92*
Mather, Mildred Eunice 1922- *WhoAm 92*
Mather, Norman Wells 1914-1990 *BioIn 17*
Mather, Patricia Lynn 1950- *WhoAmW 93*
Mather, Paul Michael *WhoScE 91-1*
Mather, Richard 1596-1669 *BioIn 17*
Mather, Richard Burroughs 1913- *WhoAm 92*
Mather, Roger Frederick 1917- *WhoWor 93*
Mather, Stephen John *WhoScE 91-1*
Mather, Ted *MiSFD 9*
Matherley, Steve Allen 1954- *WhoSSW 93*
Matherly, Teresa Carolyn 1955- *WhoAmW 93*
Mathern, Gary F. 1944- *St&PR 93*
Matherne, J. Marion 1924- *WhoSSW 93*
Matherne, Louis K. 1951- *St&PR 93*
Matheron, Marie *BioIn 17*
Mathers, C.W. 1868-1950 *BioIn 17*
Mathers, Charles Wesley 1868-1950 *BioIn 17*
Mathers, Margaret 1929- *WhoAmW 93*
Mathers, Petra *ChlBIID [port]*
Mathers, Richard E. 1946- *St&PR 93*
Mathers, Thomas Nesbit 1914- *WhoAm 92*
Mathers, William Harris 1914- *St&PR 93, WhoAm 92*
Mathes, Caryn G. 1955- *WhoAm 92*
Mathes, Charles Elliott 1949- *WhoE 93, WhoEmL 93*
Mathes, Daniel Benjamin 1958- *WhoE 93*
Mathes, Dorothy Jean Holden 1953- *WhoAmW 93*
Mathes, Edward Conrad 1943- *WhoSSW 93*
Mathes, John Charles 1931- *WhoAm 92*
Mathes, Kenneth Natt 1913- *WhoE 93*
Mathes, Mary Louise 1919- *WhoAmW 93*
Mathes, Patricia A. *Law&B 92*
Mathes, Sorrell Mark 1936- *WhoAm 92*
Mathes, Stephen Jon 1945- *WhoAm 92, WhoE 93, WhoWor 93*
Matheson, Alan Adams 1932- *WhoAm 92*
Matheson, Alastair Taylor 1929- *WhoAm 92*
Matheson, Alex 1951- *St&PR 93*
Matheson, Chris *MiSFD 9*
Matheson, David Stewart 1945- *WhoAm 92*
Matheson, G.D. *WhoScE 91-1*
Matheson, Hugh J. 1928- *St&PR 93*
Matheson, Ian M. 1944- *St&PR 93*
Matheson, Jane Gesell 1955- *WhoAmW 93*
Matheson, Karen *Law&B 92*
Matheson, Linda 1918- *WhoAmW 93, WhoWor 93*
Matheson, Norman Keith 1929- *WhoWor 93*
Matheson, Richard 1926- *BioIn 17, ScF&FL 92*
Matheson, Richard Christian 1953- *ScF&FL 92*
Matheson, Robert Stuart 1919- *St&PR 93*
Matheson, Scott *BioIn 17*
Matheson, Stephen H. 1946- *St&PR 93*
Matheson, Tim Lewis 1947- *St&PR 93*
Matheson, W.A., Jr. 1919- *St&PR 93*
Matheson, Wayne Malcolm, Jr. 1929- *WhoWrEP 92*
Matheson, William Lyon 1924- *WhoAm 92*
Matheu, Federico Manuel 1941- *WhoAm 92*
Mathew, Edward 1729-1805 *HarEnMi*
Mathew, Mathew Bobby 1958- *WhoE 93*
Mathew, Theobald 1790-1856 *BioIn 17*
Mathewes, J.C. Ogier 1943- *St&PR 93*
Mathewes, James *Law&B 92*
Mathews, Alice L. *AmWomPl*
Mathews, Alice McWhirter 1942- *WhoSSW 93*
Mathews, Arthur Frank 1860-1945 *BioIn 17*
Mathews, Barbara Edith 1946- *WhoAmW 93*
Mathews, Beverly 1928- *WhoWrEP 92*
Mathews, C. Richard *Law&B 92*
Mathews, Carmen Sylva 1918- *WhoAm 92*
Mathews, Carole 1920- *SweetSg D [port]*
Mathews, Cheri Rene 1958- *WhoEmL 93*
Mathews, Christopher King 1937- *WhoAm 92*
Mathews, Claudius Floyd *Law&B 92*
Mathews, David 1935- *WhoAm 92*
Mathews, David L. 1947- *St&PR 93*
Mathews, David Louis 1947- *WhoEmL 93*
Mathews, Donald G. 1932- *WhoAm 92*
Mathews, Eddie 1931- *BioIn 17*
Mathews, Emma June 1914- *WhoWrEP 92*
Mathews, Frances Aymar c. 1855-1923 *AmWomPl*
Mathews, Fred Leroy 1938- *WhoSSW 93*
Mathews, George Meprathu 1960- *WhoE 93*
Mathews, Harry *BioIn 17*
Mathews, Harry 1930- *ConAu 40NR*
Mathews, I. Charles *Law&B 92*
Mathews, Jack *ScF&FL 92*
Mathews, Jack Wayne 1939- *WhoAm 92*
Mathews, Jacqueline J. *Law&B 92*
Mathews, Jane Y.C. *Law&B 92*
Mathews, Jeanne M. *Law&B 92*
Mathews, Jeremy Fell 1941- *WhoAsAP 91*
Mathews, Jessica Tuchman *BioIn 17*
Mathews, Jessica Tuchman 1946- *WhoAm 92*
Mathews, John David 1947- *WhoAm 92*
Mathews, John R. *Law&B 92*
Mathews, Judith Ann 1947- *WhoAmW 93*
Mathews, Keith Rowland 1934- *WhoWrEP 92*
Mathews, Kenneth Pine 1921- *WhoAm 92*
Mathews, Linda McVeigh 1946- *WhoAm 92*
Mathews, Lucia Kleinhans 1870-1955 *BioIn 17*
Mathews, Lynda Jennings 1951- *WhoEmL 93*
Mathews, Marsha 1952- *WhoWrEP 92*
Mathews, Mary Kathryn 1948- *WhoAmW 93, WhoEmL 93*
Mathews, Mary Kuriyan 1944- *WhoAmW 93*
Mathews, Mary McNair fl. 1869-1879 *BioIn 17*
Mathews, Mary Painter 1932- *WhoAmW 93*
Mathews, Max (Vernon) 1926- *Baker 92*
Mathews, Michael S. *St&PR 93*
Mathews, O. Donna *St&PR 93*
Mathews, Richard 1944- *ScF&FL 92*
Mathews, Richard Barrett 1944- *WhoSSW 93*
Mathews, Richard John *Law&B 92*
Mathews, Richard Stewart M. 1946- *St&PR 93*
Mathews, Richard Stewart Monteague 1946- *WhoE 93*
Mathews, Robert Daniel 1928- *St&PR 93, WhoAm 92*
Mathews, Robert E. 1940- *St&PR 93*
Mathews, Robert Edward 1909- *WhoAm 92*
Mathews, Robin Daniel 1931- *WhoCanL 92*
Mathews, Roderick Bell 1941- *WhoAm 92, WhoSSW 93*
Mathews, Sarae Susan 1947- *WhoEmL 93*
Mathews, Sharon Walker 1947- *WhoAm 92*
Mathews, Susan McKiernan 1946- *WhoAmW 93, WhoEmL 93*
Mathews, Valerie Anderson 1960- *WhoAmW 93*
Mathews, W(illiam) S(mythe) B(abcock) 1837-1912 *Baker 92*
Mathews, William Alwood 1947- *WhoEmL 93*
Mathews, William Gregory 1946- *WhoSSW 93*
Mathews, William Henry 1919- *WhoAm 92*
Mathews, Wilma 1945- *WhoAmW 93*
Mathewson, Charles N. *St&PR 93*
Mathewson, Charles N. 1928- *WhoAm 92*
Mathewson, Christopher Colville 1941- *WhoAm 92, WhoSSW 93*
Mathewson, Christy 1880-1925 *BioIn 17*
Mathewson, Elizabeth Farley 1953- *WhoAmW 93*
Mathewson, Hugh Spalding 1921- *WhoAm 92, WhoWor 93*
Mathewson, Robert 1955- *St&PR 93*
Mathews-Roth, Micheline Mary 1934- *WhoE 93*
Mathey, Claire Kessinger 1950- *WhoE 93*
Mathey, Horst Karl 1935- *WhoE 93*
Mathias, Alice Irene 1949- *WhoAmW 93, WhoWor 93*
Mathias, Alyce Ann 1947- *WhoEmL 93, WhoSSW 93*
Mathias, Betty Jane 1923- *WhoAmW 93*
Mathias, Bob *BioIn 17*
Mathias, Carol Chapman 1945- *WhoAmW 93*
Mathias, Charles McCurdy, Jr. 1922- *WhoAm 92*
Mathias, Edward Joseph 1941- *WhoAm 92*
Mathias, Elizabeth Ann 1940- *WhoAmW 93*
Mathias, Franz Xaver 1871-1939 *Baker 92*
Mathias, Georges (-Amedee-Saint-Clair) 1826-1910 *Baker 92*
Mathias, Gerald Dodson 1930- *St&PR 93*
Mathias, James Herman 1913- *WhoAm 92*
Mathias, James P. 1950- *St&PR 93*
Mathias, John H. 1946- *St&PR 93*
Mathias, Joseph Simon 1925- *WhoAm 92*
Mathias, Margaret Grossman 1928- *St&PR 93, WhoAmW 93, WhoWor 93*
Mathias, Mildred Esther 1906- *BioIn 17, WhoAm 92*
Mathias, Reuben Victor 1926- *WhoAm 92*
Mathias, Richard Douglas 1940- *St&PR 93, WhoAm 92*
Mathias, Rob *St&PR 93*
Mathias, Timothy *BioIn 17*
Mathias, William J. 1934- *WhoWor 93*
Mathias, William (James) 1934- *Baker 92*
Mathiasen, Geneva 1899-1990 *BioIn 17*
Mathiason, John R. 1942- *WhoUN 92*
Mathies, Allen Wray, Jr. 1930- *WhoAm 92*
Mathies, Archibald 1918-1944 *BioIn 17*
Mathiesen, Pat Harmon 1934- *WhoAmW 93*
Mathieson, Andrew Wray 1928- *St&PR 93, WhoAm 92*
Mathieson, Carol Ann Fisher 1948- *WhoAmW 93*
Mathieson, Douglas George 1942- *St&PR 93*
Mathieson, Garrett A. 1952- *St&PR 93*
Mathieson, Garrett Alfred 1952- *WhoE 93*
Mathieson, Kelly Anne 1965- *WhoE 93*
Mathieson, Michael Raymond 1952- *WhoE 93, WhoEmL 93*
Mathieu, C.M. *WhoScE 91-2*
Mathieu, Emile (-Louis-Victor) 1844-1932 *Baker 92*
Mathieu, Georges Victor Adolphe 1921- *WhoWor 93*
Mathieu, Helen M. 1940- *WhoAmW 93*
Mathieu, Henri *WhoScE 91-2*
Mathieu, Henri Donat 1936- *WhoWor 93*
Mathieu, Michel 1943- *WhoScE 91-2*
Mathieu, Patrick 1953- *WhoWor 93*
Mathieu, Pierre 1933- *WhoCanL 92*
Mathieu, Rene 1943- *WhoScE 91-2*
Mathieu, Robert J. 1935- *St&PR 93*
Mathieu, Rodolphe 1890-1962 *Baker 92*
Mathieu-Harris, Michele Suzanne 1950- *WhoAmW 93*
Mathile, Clayton Lee 1941- *WhoAm 92, WhoWor 93*
Mathis, A. *WhoScE 91-3*
Mathis, Aaron L. 1933- *St&PR 93*
Mathis, Allen W., Jr. 1920- *St&PR 93*
Mathis, Allen Washington, Jr. 1920- *WhoSSW 93*
Mathis, Belinda Sharon *WhoAmW 93*
Mathis, Carolyn Ayers 1950- *WhoEmL 93*
Mathis, Claude 1930- *WhoScE 91-2*
Mathis, David B. *WhoAm 92*
Mathis, Deborah *BioIn 17*
Mathis, Earnest, Jr. *St&PR 93*
Mathis, Edith 1938- *Baker 92, IntDcOp, OxDcOp*
Mathis, George Russell 1926- *WhoSSW 93*
Mathis, Jack David 1931- *WhoWor 93*
Mathis, James Forrest 1925- *WhoAm 92*
Mathis, James O. 1929- *WhoSSW 93*
Mathis, Jeremy *Law&B 92*
Mathis, Joel H. 1939- *St&PR 93*
Mathis, John Bernard 1936- *WhoE 93*
Mathis, John Samuel 1931- *WhoAm 92*
Mathis, Johnny *BioIn 17*
Mathis, Johnny 1935- *Baker 92, WhoAm 92*
Mathis, Judy Moore 1951- *St&PR 93*
Mathis, June *AmWomPl*
Mathis, Larry Lee 1943- *WhoAm 92*
Mathis, Laura Anne 1948- *WhoAmW 93*
Mathis, Lois Reno 1915- *WhoAmW 93*
Mathis, Luster Doyle 1936- *WhoAm 92*
Mathis, Mark J. *Law&B 92*
Mathis, Mark Jay 1947- *WhoAm 92, WhoEmL 93*
Mathis, Marsha Debra 1953- *WhoAmW 93, WhoEmL 93, WhoSSW 93*
Mathis, Paul Carl, III 1948- *WhoEmL 93*
Mathis, Peyton S. 1949- *St&PR 93*
Mathis, Sharon Ann 1957- *WhoEmL 93*
Mathis, Sharon Bell 1937- *BlkAull 92, DcAmChF 1960, MajAI [port], WhoAm 92, WhoWrEP 92*
Mathis, Shawn *Law&B 92*
Mathis, T. Harvey d1991 *BioIn 17*
Mathis, Terry Don 1943- *WhoSSW 93*
Mathis, W. Hubert 1933- *St&PR 93*
Mathis, Warner Livingston 1926- *St&PR 93*
Mathis, William Hubert 1933- *St&PR 93*
Mathis, William Lowrey 1926- *WhoAm 92*
Mathis, William Walter 1939- *WhoAm 92*
Mathis-Eddy, Darlene Fern 1937- *WhoWrEP 92*
Mathisen, Irwin Wald, Jr. 1928- *St&PR 93*
Mathisen, Jan-Petter 1947- *WhoScE 91-4*
Mathisen-Reid, Rhoda Sharon 1942- *WhoAmW 93*
Mathison, Harry Lee 1952- *WhoEmL 93*
Mathison, Ian William 1938- *WhoAm 92*
Mathison, Lyle R. 1927- *St&PR 93*
Mathison-Bowie, Stephen Loch 1955- *WhoEmL 93*
Mathison-Bowie, Tiare Louise 1953- *WhoEmL 93*
Mathlouthi, Mohamed 1940- *WhoScE 91-2, WhoWor 93*
Mathog, Robert Henry 1939- *WhoAm 92*
Mathos dc. 237BC *HarEnMi*
Mathrani, Arjun K. *WhoAm 92*
Mathues, Jennifer L. 1960- *WhoSSW 93*
Mathues, Thomas Oliver 1923- *WhoAm 92*
Mathuny, Robert Stephen 1959- *St&PR 93*
Mathur, Ike 1943- *WhoWor 93*
Mathur, Manmohan 1946- *WhoAsAP 91*
Mathur, Pershottam Prasad 1938- *WhoE 93*
Mathur, Suresh Behari 1936- *WhoScE 91-2*
Mathur, Veerendra Kumar 1935- *WhoWor 93*
Mathurin, Trevor 1946- *St&PR 93*
Mathwich, Dale F. 1934- *St&PR 93*
Mathys, Gautier 1957- *WhoWor 93*
Mathys, Gertrud E. 1939- *St&PR 93*
Mathys, Gus 1919- *WhoScE 91-4*
Mathysen Gerst, F.E. *WhoScE 91-3*
Matiabe, Aruru 1955- *WhoAsAP 91*
Matic, Milan 1938- *WhoScE 91-4*
Matics, Kathleen Isabelle 1946- *WhoWor 93*
Matiegka, Jindrich 1862-1941 *IntDcAn*
Matienzo, Rafael Antonio 1956- *WhoWor 93*
Matier, William L. 1939- *St&PR 93*
Matijevic, Egon 1922- *WhoAm 92, WhoE 93*
Matikaien, Raimo Tapani 1938- *WhoScE 91-4*
Matikainen, Yrjo 1943- *WhoScE 91-4*
Matilainen, Riitta Marja 1948- *WhoWor 93*
Matile, Valerie *St&PR 93*
Matilla, Alfredo 1937- *HispAmA*
Matinale, Richard Joseph 1947- *St&PR 93*
Mating, Bela 1932- *WhoScE 91-4*
Matinsky, Mikhail 1750-c. 1820 *OxDcOp*
Matis, Bonnie Leah *WhoAmW 93*
Matis, Katina A. 1946- *WhoEmL 93*
Matise, Salvatore A. *Law&B 92*
Matise, Salvatore Anthony 1945- *St&PR 93*
Matisse, Henri *BioIn 17*
Matius, Cynthia Kay 1956- *St&PR 93*
Matkarimov, Bakhit 1965- *WhoWor 93*
Matkins, Robert Edwin 1934- *St&PR 93*
Matkovic, Boris 1927- *WhoScE 91-4*
Matkovich, Vlado I. 1924- *St&PR 93*
Matkovics, Bela 1927- *WhoScE 91-4*
Matkowski, Janusz Teofil 1942- *WhoWor 93*
Matkowski, Walter P. 1943- *St&PR 93*
Matkowski, Walter Paul 1943- *WhoSSW 93*
Matkowsky, Bernard Judah 1939- *WhoAm 92*
Matlac, Ioan 1937- *WhoScE 91-4*
Matlack, George Miller 1921- *WhoAm 92*
Matlack, Judith *AmWomPl*
Matlack, Rex William 1957- *St&PR 93*
Matlack, Terry Clyde 1956- *WhoEmL 93*
Matlaga, Joan 1942- *WhoWrEP 92*
Matlaga, Richard Allen 1944- *St&PR 93, WhoAm 92*
Matlaw, Ralph E. 1927-1990 *BioIn 17*
Matlengiewicz, Marek Aleksander 1951- *WhoWor 93*
Matles, Harold Bernard 1936- *St&PR 93*
Matlick, John P. *St&PR 93*
Matlin, Eric S. 1941- *St&PR 93*
Matlin, Marlee *BioIn 17, NewYTBS 92 [port]*
Matlin, Marlee 1965- *ConHero 2 [port], CurBio 92 [port], News 92 [port], WhoAm 92, WhoAmW 93*
Matlin, Marvin Lawrence 1924- *St&PR 93*

Matlin, Robert Law&B 92
Matlin, Stephen Alan WhoScE 91-1
Matlock, Clifford Charles 1909- WhoAm 92
Matlock, Hudson 1919- WhoAm 92
Matlock, Jack Foust, Jr. 1929- WhoAm 92, WhoWor 93
Matlock, John F., Jr. BioIn 17
Matlock, Kenneth Jerome 1928- St&PR 93, WhoAm 92
Matlock, Stephen J. St&PR 93
Matlof, Richard Alan 1955- St&PR 93
Matloff, Gregory 1945- SmATA 73
Matloff, Gregory Lee 1945- WhoE 93
Matloff, Mark Alexander 1950- WhoE 93
Matloff, Maurice 1915- WhoAm 92
Matlon, Chris J. WhoAm 92
Matlon, Chris John 1943- St&PR 93
Matlow, Linda Monique 1955- WhoAmW 93, WhoEmL 93
Matney, Angelique E. Law&B 92
Matney, Arthur St&PR 93
Matney, David Earl 1928- St&PR 93
Matney, Elizabeth Ann 1957- WhoAmW 93
Matney, Reed D. 1949- St&PR 93
Mato, Christine Yuriko 1950- WhoAmW 93
Mato, Jose Maria 1949- WhoWor 93
Mato, M.C. WhoScE 91-3
Mato, Mary-Cruz 1934- WhoScE 91-3
Matoesian, M. Jane Law&B 92
Matoff, Theodore Ronald WhoScE 91-1
Matolcsy, Gyorgy 1920- WhoScE 91-4
Matolyak, John 1939- WhoE 93
Maton, Andre 1928- WhoScE 91-2
Matonti, Frank R. 1944- St&PR 93
Matorin, N.M. 1898-1936 IntDcAn
Matos, Cruz Alfonso 1929- WhoWor 93
Matos, Huber 1918- DcCPCAm
Matos, Lajos 1935- WhoScE 91-4
Matos, Philip Waite 1936- WhoAm 92
Matos-Schultz, Frances Marie 1957- WhoSSW 93
Matous, Jiri 1930- WhoScE 91-4
Matousek, Vaclav WhoScE 91-4
Matovic, Anton 1930- WhoScE 91-4
Matovina, John Michael 1954- St&PR 93, WhoAm 92, WhoEmL 93
Matovu, Henry 1938- WhoUN 92
Mato Wanahtaka BioIn 17
Matoy, Elizabeth Anne 1946- WhoAm 92, WhoAmW 93
Matrai, Jozsef 1936- WhoScE 91-4
Matranga, Frances Carfi 1922- WhoWrEP 92
Matranga, Valeria 1954- WhoScE 91-3
Matras, Jean Pierre 1942- WhoUN 92
Matray, Gabor 1797-1875 Baker 92
Matrazzo, Donna J. 1948- WhoWrEP 92
Matre, Susan Jane 1952- WhoEmL 93
Matsa, Loula Zacharoula 1935- WhoAmW 93, WhoE 93
Matschat, Cecile 1895?-1976 ScF&FL 92
Matschinsky, Franz Maximilian 1931- WhoAm 92
Matschulat, Natel Kypriotou 1944- WhoAm 92
Matschullat, Dale Law&B 92
Matschullat, Dale L. 1945- St&PR 93
Matsen, John Morris 1936- WhoE 93
Matsen, Matthew James 1969- WhoE 93
Matsikoudis, Philip John Paul 1953- WhoEmL 93
Matsler, Edward Jay 1939- St&PR 93
Matsler, Franklin Giles 1922- WhoAm 92
Matson, A. James 1934- WhoAm 92
Matson, Amy Schram 1954- WhoAmW 93
Matson, Eric H. Law&B 92
Matson, Frances Shober 1921- WhoAmW 93
Matson, James Herbert 1940- St&PR 93
Matson, Jill Marie 1960- WhoAmW 93
Matson, John E. Law&B 92
Matson, John William, II 1944- WhoWrEP 92
Matson, Mariechen Anne 1957- WhoEmL 93, WhoWrEP 92
Matson, Molly 1921- ConAu 139
Matson, Ollie 1930- BioIn 17
Matson, Peggy Kepuraitis 1961- WhoEmL 93
Matson, Robert Edward 1930- WhoAm 92
Matson, Robert J. 1942- St&PR 93
Matson, Sheila Jackson 1946- WhoAmW 93
Matson, Shirley BioIn 17
Matson, Suzanne Marie 1959- WhoE 93
Matson, Wayne R. 1942- St&PR 93
Matson, Wesley Jennings 1924- WhoAm 92
Matsson, Lars Nils Reinhold Law&B 92
Matsubara, Kazuo 1933- WhoWor 93
Matsubara, Shuo 1945- WhoAsAP 91
Matsubara, Tomoo 1929- WhoWor 93
Matsuda, Fujio 1924- WhoAm 92
Matsuda, Iwao 1937- WhoAsAP 91
Matsuda, Masayuki Morris 1933- WhoWor 93
Matsuda, Minoru 1933- WhoWor 93
Matsuda, Yasuhiro 1947- WhoWor 93
Matsuda, Yusaku d1989 BioIn 17
Matsudaira, Hideyasu 1574-1607 HarEnMi
Matsudaira, Yoriaki 1931- Baker 92
Matsudaira, Yoritsune 1907- Baker 92
Matsueda, Rei 1941- WhoWor 93
Matsugo, Seiichi 1952- WhoWor 93
Matsui, Dorothy Nobuko 1954- WhoAmW 93, WhoEmL 93
Matsui, Iwane 1878-1948 HarEnMi
Matsui, Ken 1932- WhoWor 93
Matsui, Kineo 1939- WhoWor 93
Matsui, Robert T. 1941- CngDr 91
Matsui, Robert Takeo 1941- WhoAm 92
Matsui, Saburo 1944- WhoWor 93
Matsui, Wesley Tak 1950- WhoE 93
Matsui, Yoshihiko 1921- WhoWor 93
Matsui, Yoshihisa 1940- WhoWor 93
Matsui, Yoshito 1931- WhoWor 93
Matsuka, Mitsuo 1942- WhoWor 93
Matsukage, Fay Mariko 1955- WhoEmL 93
Matsukata, Masahiko 1960- WhoWor 93
Matsumae, Aogu 1935- WhoAsAP 91
Matsumae, Shigeyoshi 1901-1991 BioIn 17
Matsumae, Tatsuro 1927- WhoAsAP 91
Matsumota, Kentaro 1924- WhoWor 93
Matsumoto, Eiichi 1921- WhoAsAP 91
Matsumoto, George 1922- WhoAm 92
Matsumoto, Hiroshi 1948- WhoWor 93
Matsumoto, Juro 1918- WhoAsAP 91
Matsumoto, Kikuji 1931- WhoWor 93
Matsumoto, Mitsunori 1939- WhoWor 93
Matsumoto, Ryu 1951- WhoAsAP 91
Matsumoto, Shigeru 1933- WhoWor 93
Matsumoto, Teruo 1929- WhoAm 92
Matsumoto, Tsutomu Ben 1942- WhoE 93
Matsumoto, Yawara 1860-c. 1925 HarEnMi
Matsumoto, Yoshiji 1929- WhoWor 93
Matsumura, Akio 1942- WhoE 93
Matsumura, Akira 1880-1936 IntDcAn
Matsumura, Fumitake 1942- WhoWor 93
Matsumura, Masanobu 1939- WhoWor 93
Matsumura, Masataka 1945- St&PR 93
Matsumura, Seimei 1954- WhoWor 93
Matsumura, Sharon K. Law&B 92
Matsumura, Tatsuo 1868-1932 HarEnMi
Matsumura, Teizo 1929- Baker 92
Matsunaga, Hikaru 1928- WhoAsAP 91
Matsunaga, Len 1959- WhoEmL 93
Matsunaga, Shin BioIn 17
Matsunaga, Spark M. BioIn 17
Matsunaga, Yoshio 1933- WhoWor 93
Matsunami, Hiroyuki 1939- WhoWor 93
Matsuno, Koichiro 1940- WhoWor 93
Matsuo Basho 1644-1694 MagSWL [port]
Matsuoka, Toshikatsu 1945- WhoAsAP 91
Matsuoka, Toshio 1940- WhoWor 93
Matsushige, Yoshito 1912- BioIn 17
Matsushima, Akira Paul 1937- St&PR 93, WhoWor 93
Matsushima, David T. Law&B 92
Matsushima, Keiji 1938- WhoAm 92
Matsushima, Satoshi 1923- WhoAm 92
Matsushita, Keiichiro 1953- WhoWor 93
Matsushita, Shin-ichi 1922- Baker 92
Matsutani, Makoto 1903- HarEnMi
Matsuura, Akira 1929- WhoAsAP 91
Matsuura, George A. St&PR 93
Matsuura, Isao 1923- WhoAsAP 91
Matsuura, Kanjiro 1942- WhoWor 93
Matsuura, Koji WhoAsAP 91
Matsuura, Shuji 1945- WhoWor 93
Matsuura, Toshihisa 1925- WhoAsAP 91
Matsuyama, Brian St&PR 93
Matsuyama, W. Brian Law&B 92
Matsuzaka, Hirohuki 1959- WhoWor 93
Matsuzaki, Takao 1945- WhoWor 93
Matt, Francis X. 1933- St&PR 93
Matt, Linda Ann 1952- WhoWrEP 92
Matt, Michael Voorhies 1949- WhoEmL 93
Matt, Nicholas O. 1945- St&PR 93
Matt, Walter J., Jr. 1938- WhoE 93
Matta, Alberto 1933- WhoScE 91-3
Matta, John A. Law&B 92
Matta, Ram Kumar 1946- WhoAm 92
Mattacola Family BioIn 17
Mattar, Ahmad 1936- WhoWor 93
Mattar, Philip 1944- WhoE 93
Mattarolo, Fredolino 1920- WhoScE 91-3
Mattason, Donald J. St&PR 93
Mattathias d166?BC BioIn 17
Mattauch, Robert Joseph 1940- WhoAm 92
Mattausch, Thomas Edward 1944- WhoAm 92
Matte, James Allan 1931- WhoWrEP 92
Mattea, Kathy BioIn 17, WhoAm 92, WhoAmW 93
Matteau, Mark Joseph 1953- WhoSSW 93
Mattei, Loren Neal 1949- WhoWrEP 92
Mattei, Stanislao 1750-1825 OxDcOp
Mattei, Tito 1841-1914 Baker 92
Matteis, Nicola Baker 92
Mattelaer, Jean-Claude 1967- WhoWor 93
Mattelaer, Pierre Marcel Maria 1949- WhoWor 93
Matteman, J.L. 1935- WhoScE 91-3
Mattenson, Charles Ross Law&B 92
Mattenson, Laurie S. Law&B 92
Matteo da Perugia dc. 1418 Baker 92
Matteotti, Giacomo 1885-1924 DcTwHis
Matter, Bruce Edward Law&B 92
Matter, David 1925- St&PR 93
Matter, John P. 1952- St&PR 93
Mattera, Paul Law&B 92
Mattern, Bruce William 1943- St&PR 93
Mattern, Diane Romero 1959- WhoAmW 93
Mattern, Donald Eugene 1930- WhoAm 92
Mattern, Douglas James 1933- WhoWor 93
Mattern, Gerry A. 1935- WhoE 93
Mattern, Keith E. Law&B 92
Mattern, Robert Franklin 1921- St&PR 93
Matters, Arnold 1904-1990 OxDcOp
Matters, Clyde Burns 1924- WhoAm 92
Matterson, Joan McDevitt 1949- WhoAmW 93
Mattes, Arthur S. 1901-1972 ScF&FL 92
Mattes, Hans George 1943- WhoAm 92
Mattes, Max H. St&PR 93
Mattes, Rainer U. 1937- WhoScE 91-3
Matteson, Carolyn 1944- WhoSSW 93
Matteson, E. David 1939- St&PR 93
Matteson, Frederick Edgar 1956- WhoEmL 93
Matteson, Lawrence James 1939- St&PR 93
Matteson, Patricia E. 1945- St&PR 93
Matteson, Robert Eliot 1914- WhoAm 92
Matteson, Thomas Dickens 1920- WhoSSW 93
Matteson, Thomas T. WhoAm 92
Matteson, Vicky Lynn 1957- WhoE 93
Mattessich, Richard Victor Alvarus 1922- WhoAm 92
Matteucci, Pellegrino 1850-1881 IntDcAn
Mattey, John Joseph 1927- WhoAm 92, WhoE 93, WhoWor 93
Mattfeld, Jacquelyn 1925- See Mattfeld, Victor Henry 1917- Baker 92
Mattfeld, Julius 1893-1968 Baker 92
Mattfeld, Victor Henry 1917- Baker 92
Matthaei, Charles W.H. 1920- St&PR 93
Matthaei, Frederick C., Jr. 1925- St&PR 93
Matthaei, Gay Humphrey 1931- WhoE 93
Matthaei, Karl 1897-1960 Baker 92
Matthaeus, Renate G. 1942- WhoAmW 93
Matthan, Jacob 1943- WhoScE 91-4
Matthau, Carol 1932- ConAu 139
Matthau, Charles 1964- MiSFD 9
Matthau, Walter 1920- IntDcF 2-3 [port], MiSFD 9, WhoAm 92
Matthay, Tobias (Augustus) 1858-1945 Baker 92
Matthei, Edward Hodge 1927- WhoAm 92
Matthei, Warren Douglas 1951- WhoAm 92
Mattheou, Anthony Alexander 1945- WhoWor 93
Matthes, Karl J. 1931- WhoScE 91-3
Mattheson, Johann 1681-1764 Baker 92, IntDcOp, OxDcOp
Matthess, Georg 1932- WhoWor 93
Matthess, George 1932- WhoScE 91-3
Matthew OxDcByz
Matthew, I c. 1360- OxDcByz
Matthew, Eunice d1990 BioIn 17
Matthew, James Andrew Davidson WhoScE 91-1
Matthew, Kathryn Kahrs WhoAmW 93
Matthew, Lyn 1936- WhoAmW 93, WhoWor 93
Matthew, Millard E., Jr. Law&B 92
Matthew, Robert 1934- ScF&FL 92
Matthew Kantakouzenos, I c. 1325-c. 1383 OxDcByz
Matthew of Edessa fl. 12th cent.- OxDcByz
Matthew of Ephesus OxDcByz
Matthew of Khazaria fl. 14th cent.- OxDcByz
Matthews, Adelaide 1886- AmWomPl
Matthews, Agnes Cynthia 1924- WhoAmW 93
Matthews, Albert E., Jr. 1935- St&PR 93
Matthews, Alexander George 1935- St&PR 93
Matthews, Allan Freeman 1916- WhoWrEP 92
Matthews, Andrew A., Jr. Law&B 92
Matthews, Andrew Philip Law&B 92
Matthews, Ann ScF&FL 92
Matthews, Arthur Morris, Jr. 1946- WhoEmL 93
Matthews, Artie 1888-1958 Baker 92
Matthews, Becky ScF&FL 92
Matthews, Beverley, Mr. 1905- St&PR 93
Matthews, Beverly A.M. Law&B 92
Matthews, Billy 1847-1904 BioIn 17
Matthews, Brian W. 1938- WhoAm 92
Matthews, Bruce BioIn 17, WhoScE 91-1
Matthews, Caitlin 1952- ScF&FL 92
Matthews, Cari Pineiro 1942- WhoAm 92
Matthews, Carrie Leonda 1954- WhoAmW 93
Matthews, Cecilia M. AmWomPl
Matthews, Charles Donald 1923- WhoAm 92
Matthews, Charles Sedwick 1920- WhoAm 92, WhoWor 93
Matthews, Charles W., Jr. Law&B 92
Matthews, Charlotte WhoE 93
Matthews, Clark J., II 1936- St&PR 93
Matthews, Clark Jio, II 1936- WhoAm 92
Matthews, Clay BioIn 17
Matthews, Clayton 1918- ScF&FL 92
Matthews, Clifford William 1947- WhoE 93
Matthews, Clyde 1917- ScF&FL 92
Matthews, Colin 1946- Baker 92
Matthews, Craig G. 1943- St&PR 93
Matthews, Craig Gerard 1943- WhoAm 92
Matthews, Dan Gus 1939- WhoAm 92
Matthews, Daniel George 1932- WhoAm 92, WhoE 93, WhoWor 93
Matthews, Daniel Hobson 1961- WhoE 93
Matthews, Darlene Theresa 1953- WhoEmL 93
Matthews, Daryl Bruce 1947- WhoSSW 93
Matthews, Daud Robert 1938- WhoWor 93
Matthews, David 1920- WhoAm 92
Matthews, David 1943- Baker 92
Matthews, David Fort 1944- WhoSSW 93
Matthews, David J., III 1942- St&PR 93
Matthews, David W. Law&B 92
Matthews, Deborah Gail 1956- WhoE 93
Matthews, Denis (James) 1919-1988 Baker 92
Matthews, Domina Marvyl 1947- WhoAmW 93, WhoEmL 93
Matthews, Donald John 1933- WhoAm 92
Matthews, Donald Rowe 1925- WhoAm 92
Matthews, Downs 1925- SmATA 71 [port]
Matthews, Drexel Gene 1952- WhoEmL 93, WhoSSW 93, WhoWor 93
Matthews, Duane Ellison 1929- WhoAm 92
Matthews, Dwight Earl 1951- WhoEmL 93
Matthews, E. Vince, III Law&B 92
Matthews, Edith Virginia Brander AmWomPl
Matthews, Edward E. 1931- WhoAm 92
Matthews, Edward Easton 1931- St&PR 93, WhoIns 93
Matthews, Edwin Spencer, Jr. 1934- WhoAm 92
Matthews, Elizabeth Woodfin 1927- WhoAmW 93
Matthews, Ellen WhoWrEP 92
Matthews, Elva De Pue AmWomPl
Matthews, Esther Elizabeth 1918- WhoAmW 93
Matthews, Eugene Edward 1931- WhoAm 92
Matthews, F.P. 1921- St&PR 93
Matthews, Ford WhoWrEP 92
Matthews, Francis Richard 1920- St&PR 93, WhoAm 92
Matthews, Frank Lewis WhoScE 91-1
Matthews, Franklin 1858-1917 JrnUS
Matthews, G.M. WhoScE 91-1
Matthews, Gale F. Law&B 92
Matthews, Gary Nathaniel 1950- BiDAMSp 1989
Matthews, George A., Jr. 1934- St&PR 93
Matthews, George Tennyson 1917- WhoAm 92
Matthews, Gilbert Elliott 1930- St&PR 93, WhoAm 92
Matthews, Graham G. WhoScE 91-1
Matthews, Graham Peter WhoScE 91-1
Matthews, Gwenda J. 1941- WhoUN 92
Matthews, Harriett 1940- WhoE 93
Matthews, Herbert DcCPCAm
Matthews, Herbert L. 1900-1977 JrnUS
Matthews, J.B.L. WhoScE 91-1
Matthews, Jack 1917- WhoAm 92, WhoE 93
Matthews, Jack 1925- ScF&FL 92, WhoAm 92, WhoWrEP 92

Matthews, Jack Beverly, Jr. 1951- *WhoEmL 93*
Matthews, Jack Edward 1928- *WhoAm 92*
Matthews, James Bernard 1950- *WhoEmL 93, WhoSSW 93*
Matthews, James F. *Law&B 92*
Matthews, James Francis 1935- *WhoSSW 93*
Matthews, James Gordon, Jr. 1916- *WhoSSW 93*
Matthews, James H. *BioIn 17*
Matthews, James Shadley 1951- *St&PR 93*
Matthews, Jay Arlon, Jr. 1918- *WhoSSW 93*
Matthews, Jessie 1907-1981 *IntDcF 2-3 [port]*
Matthews, John *WhoScE 91-1*
Matthews, John 1930- *WhoScE 91-1*
Matthews, John Anthony 1947- *WhoWor 93*
Matthews, John B.L. 1935- *WhoScE 91-1*
Matthews, John Bowers *BioIn 17*
Matthews, John Clark *BioIn 17*
Matthews, John Floyd 1919- *WhoAm 92, WhoWrEP 92*
Matthews, John H., Jr. *ScF&FL 92*
Matthews, John K., Jr. 1929- *St&PR 93*
Matthews, John Louis 1932- *WhoAm 92*
Matthews, Joseph E. 1938- *St&PR 93*
Matthews, Kathryn Ann 1958- *WhoAmW 93*
Matthews, Kelly K. 1944- *St&PR 93*
Matthews, Kelly King 1944- *WhoAm 92*
Matthews, L. White, III 1945- *St&PR 93, WhoAm 92*
Matthews, Larryl Kent 1951- *WhoAm 92, WhoWor 93*
Matthews, Lawrence Millbourne 1920- *WhoE 93*
Matthews, Lee A. *Law&B 92*
Matthews, Leonard J. *ScF&FL 92*
Matthews, Leonard Sarver 1922- *WhoAm 92*
Matthews, Lorena McElroy Causey 1912- *WhoAmW 93*
Matthews, Margaret *BlkAmWO*
Matthews, Margaret 1935- *BioIn 17*
Matthews, Margaret Ellen 1951- *WhoEmL 93*
Matthews, Mart C. *Law&B 92*
Matthews, Mart C. 1945- *St&PR 93*
Matthews, Mary Ruth 1948- *WhoAmW 93*
Matthews, Michael Gough 1931- *Baker 92*
Matthews, Mike *WhoWrEP 92*
Matthews, Monte Lee 1958- *WhoSSW 93*
Matthews, Norman Stuart 1933- *WhoAm 92*
Matthews, Patricia 1927- *BioIn 17, ScF&FL 92*
Matthews, Patrick J. 1942- *St&PR 93*
Matthews, Patrick John 1942- *WhoAm 92*
Matthews, Paul 1940- *WhoUN 92*
Matthews, Paul Chandler 1926- *WhoE 93*
Matthews, Paul D. 1929- *St&PR 93*
Matthews, Paul Deacon 1929- *WhoAm 92*
Matthews, Pearl Parkerson 1941- *WhoWrEP 92*
Matthews, Peggy Jean 1945- *WhoAmW 93*
Matthews, Peter Ash *WhoScE 91-1*
Matthews, Peter B.C. *WhoScE 91-1*
Matthews, Peter John 1943- *WhoScE 91-1*
Matthews, Philip Richard 1952- *WhoEmL 93*
Matthews, Richard David *WhoScE 91-1*
Matthews, Richard Ellis Ford 1921- *WhoWor 93*
Matthews, Richard G. 1959- *St&PR 93*
Matthews, Richard Lee 1946- *WhoSSW 93*
Matthews, Robert C., Jr. 1947- *St&PR 93*
Matthews, Robert Charles Oliver 1927- *WhoWor 93*
Matthews, Robert D. *Law&B 92*
Matthews, Robert J. *Law&B 92*
Matthews, Rodney 1945- *ScF&FL 92*
Matthews, Roger Hardin 1948- *WhoEmL 93*
Matthews, Ronald Alan 1952- *WhoEmL 93*
Matthews, Ronald W. 1940- *St&PR 93*
Matthews, Rowena Green 1938- *WhoAmW 93*
Matthews, Roy S. 1945- *St&PR 93*
Matthews, Russell Edward 1950- *WhoWor 93*
Matthews, Ruth Ilene 1931- *WhoAmW 93*
Matthews, Sharon Lee Williams 1938- *WhoSSW 93*
Matthews, Sharron Debra 1950- *WhoAmW 93*
Matthews, Stanley *WhoScE 91-1*
Matthews, Stephen George 1932- *St&PR 93*
Matthews, Steve Allen 1955- *WhoAm 92*
Matthews, Steven Dee 1946- *WhoEmL 93*
Matthews, Steven Richard 1962- *WhoEmL 93*
Matthews, Stuart 1936- *WhoSSW 93*
Matthews, Sue Froman *AmWomPl*
Matthews, Susan Diane 1964- *WhoAmW 93*
Matthews, T.K., II 1926- *St&PR 93*
Matthews, T.S. 1901-1991 *AnObit 1991, BioIn 17*
Matthews, Temple Gregory, III 1940- *WhoSSW 93*
Matthews, Thomas Edward 1943- *WhoE 93*
Matthews, Thomas Stanley 1824-1889 *OxCSupC [port]*
Matthews, Thomas Stanley 1901-1991 *BioIn 17*
Matthews, Thomas W. 1934- *St&PR 93*
Matthews, Valerie Jo 1947- *WhoAmW 93, WhoEmL 93*
Matthews, Virginia L. *AfrAmBi*
Matthews, Wanda Miller 1930- *BioIn 17, WhoAm 92*
Matthews, Watt 1891- *BioIn 17*
Matthews, Wendy Schempp 1945- *WhoAmW 93*
Matthews, Westina L. *AfrAmBi*
Matthews, Westina L. 1948- *WhoAmW 93*
Matthews, Wilbur Lee 1903- *WhoAm 92, WhoWor 93*
Matthews, William *BioIn 17*
Matthews, William 1942- *BioIn 17, WhoWrEP 92*
Matthews, William Baxter, Jr. *Law&B 92*
Matthews, William Cary 1920-1991 *BioIn 17*
Matthews, William D. 1934- *St&PR 93*
Matthews, William Doty 1934- *WhoAm 92*
Matthews, William Procter 1942- *WhoAm 92*
Matthews, William R. *BioIn 17*
Matthewson, Clive Denby 1944- *WhoAsAP 91*
Matthias, C. David 1955- *St&PR 93*
Matthias, George Frank 1934- *WhoE 93*
Matthias, Rebecca *BioIn 17*
Matthias, Reinhard 1938- *WhoScE 91-3*
Matthias, Russell Howard, Jr. *Law&B 92*
Matthias, Russell Howard, Jr. 1934- *St&PR 93*
Matthias, Virginia Park *AmWomPl*
Matthias Corvinus, I 1440-1490 *HarEnMi*
Matthiasdottir, Louisa 1917- *BioIn 17*
Matthias Yao Chih 1956- *WhoAsAP 91*
Matthies, Duane Darwin 1960- *St&PR 93*
Matthies, Frederick John 1925- *WhoAm 92*
Matthies, Hans Jurgen 1921- *WhoScE 91-3*
Matthies, Hansjurgen 1925- *WhoScE 91-3*
Matthies, Hermann Georg 1951- *WhoWor 93*
Matthies, Joyce Muriel 1948- *WhoEmL 93*
Matthies, Mary Constance T. 1948- *WhoEmL 93*
Matthiesen, Leroy Theodore 1921- *WhoAm 92*
Matthiessen, Christian Wichmann 1945- *WhoScE 91-2*
Matthiessen, F.O. 1902-1950 *BioIn 17*
Matthiessen, Francis Otto 1902-1950 *BioIn 17*
Matthiessen, Martin Ebbe 1929- *WhoScE 91-2*
Matthiessen, P.C. *WhoScE 91-2*
Matthiessen, Peter *BioIn 17*
Matthiessen, Peter 1927- *MagSAmL [port], WhoAm 92, WhoWrEP 92*
Matthieu, Marcia Perreault 1946- *WhoAmW 93*
Matthis, Eva Mildred Boney 1927- *WhoAmW 93*
Matthison-Hansen, (Johan) Gottfred 1832-1909 *Baker 92*
Matthison-Hansen, Hans 1807-1890 *Baker 92*
Matthus, Siegfried 1934- *Baker 92, BioIn 17*
Matthy, Peter D. 1946- *St&PR 93*
Matthys, Heinrich 1935- *WhoScE 91-3*
Matti, Edward M. 1928- *WhoAsAP 91*
Mattice, Paul M. 1913- *WhoIns 93*
Mattice, Stanley E. 1945- *St&PR 93*
Mattics, Jeri Denise 1964- *WhoAmW 93*
Mattie, Herman 1933- *WhoWor 93*
Mattielli, Louis D. *Law&B 92*
Mattig, Wolfgang K. 1927- *WhoScE 91-3*
Mattila, Eero 1950- *WhoScE 91-4*
Mattila, Karita 1960- *Baker 92*
Mattila, Lasse *WhoScE 91-4*
Mattila, Markku Kalevi 1945- *WhoScE 91-4*
Mattila, Matti A.K. 1937- *WhoScE 91-4*
Mattila, Severi 1935- *WhoScE 91-4*
Mattila, Timo *WhoScE 91-4*
Mattimore, Bryan William 1954- *WhoEmL 93*
Mattingley, Christobel 1931- *DcChlFi*
Mattingley, Christobel (Rosemary) 1931- *MajAI [port]*
Mattingly, Charles M. *Law&B 92*
Mattingly, Don *BioIn 17*
Mattingly, Donald Arthur 1961- *WhoAm 92*
Mattingly, John H. 1950- *St&PR 93*
Mattingly, Lisa Price 1962- *WhoAmW 93*
Mattingly, Richard E. (Rick) 1950- *WhoWrEP 92*
Mattingly, Robert Kerker 1921- *WhoWor 93*
Mattingly, Robert Martin 1939- *WhoE 93, WhoWor 93*
Mattingly, Thomas K. 1936- *WhoAm 92*
Mattingly, William Earl 1948- *WhoEmL 93*
Mattingly, William J. 1938- *St&PR 93*
Mattinson, Burny *MiSFD 9*
Mattioli, Joseph Reginald 1925- *St&PR 93*
Mattioli, Joseph Reginald, Jr. 1925- *WhoE 93*
Mattioli, Rose C. 1927- *St&PR 93*
Mattis, Louis P. *St&PR 93*
Mattis, Louis Price 1941- *WhoAm 92*
Mattison, Catherine Mary 1965- *WhoAmW 93*
Mattison, Donald Roger 1944- *WhoE 93*
Mattison, George Chester, Jr. 1940- *WhoSSW 93*
Mattison, Harry D. 1936- *WhoAm 92*
Mattison, Joel 1931- *WhoSSW 93*
Mattison, Priscilla Jane 1960- *WhoAmW 93*
Mattison, Robert M. *Law&B 92*
Mattison, Robert Mayer 1948- *WhoEmL 93*
Mattison, Sally *MiSFD 9*
Mattison, Stanley Barron 1943- *St&PR 93, WhoAm 92*
Mattiussi, Andrea 1935- *St&PR 93*
Mattke, Dunnley L. 1953- *St&PR 93*
Mattmuller-Keller, Markus 1928- *WhoWor 93*
Matto, Ghulan Rassool 1925- *WhoAsAP 91*
Mattock, John Nicholas 1938- *WhoWor 93*
Mattock, Martin Benjamin *WhoScE 91-1*
Mattocks, N. Randolph, Jr. 1944- *St&PR 93*
Mattocks-Williams, Linda Foy 1949- *WhoAmW 93*
Matto de Turner, Clorinda 1852-1909 *BioIn 17*
Mattola, Guy A. *St&PR 93*
Matton, Guido Emile 1930- *WhoScE 91-2*
Matton, Roger 1929- *Baker 92*
Mattone, Joseph Michael 1931- *WhoE 93*
Mattone, Vincent J. *WhoAm 92*
Mattoon, Henry Amasa, Jr. 1914- *WhoAm 92*
Mattoon, Peter Mills 1931- *WhoAm 92*
Mattoon, Sara Halsey 1947- *WhoEmL 93*
Mattos, John F. 1924- *St&PR 93*
Mattos, Joseph Glenn 1953- *St&PR 93*
Mattos, Roberto de Carvalho 1936- *WhoWor 93*
Mattos, William Joseph 1949- *WhoEmL 93*
Mattox, Janis 1949- *Baker 92*
Mattox, Karen Sigrid 1952- *WhoAmW 93*
Mattox, Kenneth Leon 1938- *WhoAm 92*
Mattox, Richard Davis, Jr. *Law&B 92*
Mattox, Robert James 1957- *WhoSSW 93*
Mattox, Ronald Eugene 1948- *WhoSSW 93*
Mattox, William C. 1950- *St&PR 93*
Mattozzi, Richard A. *Law&B 92*
Mattran, Donald Albert 1934- *WhoAm 92*
Mattrella, Anne Laura 1954- *WhoE 93, WhoEmL 93*
Mattrella, Linda Anne *Law&B 92*
Mattrella, Linda Anne 1959- *WhoEmL 93*
Matts, Carrie E. 1962- *St&PR 93*
Mattson, Bradford C. 1952- *St&PR 93*
Mattson, Bradford Craig 1952- *WhoAm 92*
Mattson, Carol Linnette 1946- *WhoAmW 93*
Mattson, Carol Louise 1952- *WhoE 93*
Mattson, Catherine Cox 1961- *St&PR 93*
Mattson, Clarence Russell 1924- *WhoE 93*
Mattson, David Harold 1963- *WhoE 93*
Mattson, David Roald 1947- *WhoEmL 93*
Mattson, Eric Leonard 1951- *St&PR 93*
Mattson, Francis Oscar 1931- *WhoAm 92*
Mattson, Gail 1950- *WhoEmL 93*
Mattson, Guy Charles 1927- *WhoSSW 93*
Mattson, Harold Frazyer, Jr. 1930- *WhoE 93*
Mattson, Harry Auwae 1951- *WhoEmL 93*
Mattson, James Stewart 1945- *WhoSSW 93*
Mattson, Janet Marie 1947- *WhoEmL 93*
Mattson, Marcus 1904- *WhoAm 92*
Mattson, Mark Edward 1957- *WhoE 93*
Mattson, Peter Humphrey 1932- *WhoE 93*
Mattson, Roy Henry 1927- *WhoAm 92*
Mattson, Susan Cummings *Law&B 92*
Mattson, Ursula Ingrid 1953- *WhoWrEP 92*
Mattson, Victor F. 1925- *St&PR 93*
Mattson, Victor Frank 1925- *WhoSSW 93*
Mattson, Walter Edward 1932- *WhoAm 92, WhoWor 93*
Mattson, William Royce, Jr. 1946- *WhoEmL 93*
Mattsson, Ake 1929- *WhoAm 92*
Mattsson, Donald Marvin 1923- *St&PR 93*
Mattsson, Rolf 1933- *WhoScE 91-4*
Mattsson, Stein-Erik 1959- *WhoWor 93*
Mattu, Kashi *Law&B 92*
Mattuchio, Frank Edward 1934- *St&PR 93*
Matty, Allen John *WhoScE 91-1*
Matukaitis, Paul D. *Law&B 92*
Matula, Julius 1943- *DrEEuF*
Matula, Richard Allan 1939- *WhoAm 92, WhoSSW 93*
Matulich, Erika 1963- *WhoEmL 93*
Matune, Frank Joseph 1948- *WhoE 93*
Matune, Timothy Jude *Law&B 92*
Matunis, Frank X. 1941- *St&PR 93*
Matura, Robert J. 1933- *WhoAm 92*
Mature, Victor 1915- *IntDcF 2-3 [port]*
Maturi, Raymond R. 1938- *St&PR 93*
Maturi, Raymond Rockne 1938- *WhoAm 92*
Maturo, Jim V. 1943- *St&PR 93*
Matus, Marlene Wechsler 1934- *WhoAmW 93*
Matus, Wayne Charles 1950- *WhoE 93, WhoEmL 93*
Matusak, Larraine R. 1930- *WhoAmW 93*
Matusewicz, Alfred 1931- *WhoScE 91-4*
Matushek, Donald Gerhard 1953- *WhoEmL 93*
Matusiak, Thomas 1948- *St&PR 93*
Matusinec, Sharon Bergold 1947- *WhoAmW 93*
Matuson, Hanna *BioIn 17*
Matusow, Allen Joseph 1937- *WhoAm 92*
Matussek, Paul 1919- *WhoScE 91-3*
Matuszak, Alice Jean Boyer 1935- *WhoAmW 93*
Matuszeski, John *Law&B 92*
Matuszewski, Roman 1951- *WhoWor 93*
Matuszkiewicz, Wladyslaw Jozef 1921- *WhoScE 91-4*
Matuszkiewicz, Wojciech Zbigniew 1940- *WhoScE 91-4*
Matuszko, Anthony Joseph 1926- *WhoAm 92*
Matut, Deborah 1958- *WhoAmW 93*
Matute, Ana Maria 1925- *ScF&FL 92*
Matute, Ana Maria 1926- *BioIn 17*
Matutina, Donna Anne Luna 1962- *WhoWor 93*
Matuz, Janos 1947- *WhoScE 91-4*
Matuzak, Joseph Matthew 1955- *WhoWrEP 92*
Matveev, Alexsandr Fedorovich 1947- *WhoWor 93*
Matveev, Evgenij 1922- *DrEEuF*
Matveev, Oleg Vladimirovich 1969- *WhoWor 93*
Matveev, Sergej Vladimirovich 1947- *WhoWor 93*
Matviishyn, Yaroslav Oleksa 1941- *WhoWor 93*
Matyas, Csaba 1943- *WhoScE 91-4*
Matyas, Diane Catherine 1961- *WhoE 93*
Matyas, Robert Michael 1926- *WhoE 93*
Matys, Jiri 1927- *Baker 92*
Matysiak, Stanislaw Jan 1947- *WhoWor 93*
Matyszewski, Tomislaw Remigiusz 1911- *WhoScE 91-4*
Matz, Gilbert 1934- *WhoScE 91-2*
Matz, Glenn M. 1939- *St&PR 93*
Matz, Jerome Gershin 1927- *St&PR 93*
Matz, Kay Elaine 1946- *WhoAmW 93*
Matz, Leonard Marvin 1950- *WhoE 93*
Matz, Oliver *WhoWor 93*
Matz, Peter S. 1928- *WhoAm 92*
Matz, Robert 1931- *WhoAm 92*
Matz, Rudolf 1901- *Baker 92*
Matz, William R. *Law&B 92*
Matza, Bruce R. 1943- *St&PR 93*
Matzdorff, James Arthur 1956- *WhoEmL 93, WhoWor 93*
Matzeliger, Jan *BioIn 17*
Matzen, Lynn Robert 1938- *St&PR 93*
Matzen, Richard Norman, Jr. 1957- *WhoWrEP 92*
Matzen, Robert T. 1924- *WhoIns 93*
Matzenauer, Margaret 1881-1963 *IntDcOp [port]*
Matzenauer, Margarete 1881-1963 *Baker 92, OxDcOp*
Matzer, John W. 1945- *St&PR 93*

Matzlorinis, Kenneth N. 1954- *WhoE 93*
Matzka, John 1924- *St&PR 93*
Matzka, Michael Alan 1954- *WhoEmL 93*
Matzke, Bruce Carter 1951- *WhoEmL 93*
Matzke, Frank J. 1922- *WhoAm 92*
Matzke, Gary Roger 1950- *WhoAm 92, WhoEmL 93*
Matzke, Hansjoechim 1936- *WhoScE 91-3*
Matzke, Peter 1928- *WhoScE 91-3*
Matzkin, Donald Robert 1940- *WhoE 93*
Matzkin, M. *ScF&FL 92*
Matzko, Donna Jeanne 1963- *WhoAmW 93*
Matzner, Chester Michael *WhoE 93*
Matzner, Egon 1938- *WhoWor 93*
Matzner, Thomas Alexander 1953- *WhoWor 93*
Mau, Ernest Eugene 1945- *WhoWrEP 92*
Mau, George Fredric 1961- *WhoSSW 93*
Mau, Glenn S. 1946- *St&PR 93*
Mau, Hans 1921- *WhoWor 93*
Mau, James Anthony 1935- *WhoAm 92*
Mau, Jean B. 1920- *St&PR 93*
Mau, Ronald D. 1946- *St&PR 93*
Mau, William Koon-Hee 1913- *WhoAm 92*
Mauceri, Albert 1931- *WhoIns 93*
Mauceri, John 1945- *BioIn 17*
Mauceri, John (Francis) 1945- *Baker 92, WhoAm 92*
Mauceri, Valerie Frances *Law&B 92*
Mauch, C. Alan 1950- *WhoIns 93*
Mauch, Douglas Bruce 1944- *St&PR 93*
Mauch, Gene William 1925- *BiDAMSp 1989*
Mauch, Robert Carl 1939- *St&PR 93*
Mauch, Werner Oscar 1934- *WhoScE 91-3*
Mauchamp, Jean *WhoScE 91-2*
Mauchline, John 1933- *WhoScE 91-1*
Mauchly, Virginia Ellen 1954- *WhoE 93*
Mauck, Henry Page, Jr. 1926- *WhoAm 92*
Maucker, Earl Robert 1947- *WhoSSW 93*
Maud, Humphrey John Hamilton 1934- *WhoWor 93*
Maude, Edward Joseph 1924- *WhoAm 92*
Maude, Frederick Stanley 1864-1917 *HarEnMi*
Mauderli, Walter 1924- *WhoAm 92*
Mauderly, Joe Lloyd 1943- *WhoAm 92*
Maudgal, Dharam Pal 1943- *WhoWor 93*
Maudlin, Bradley W. *Law&B 92*
Maudlin, Robert V. 1927- *WhoE 93*
Maudslay, Alfred Percival 1850-1931 *IntDcAn*
Mauduit, Jacques 1557-1627 *Baker 92*
Mauer, Alvin Marx 1928- *WhoAm 92*
Mauer, Kenneth John *Law&B 92*
Mauer, Michael D. 1952- *St&PR 93*
Mauer, Michael Leonard 1940- *WhoAm 92*
Mauer, Steven G. 1955- *St&PR 93*
Mauersberger, Rudolf 1889-1971 *Baker 92*
Maugans, Edgar H. 1935- *St&PR 93*
Maugans, Edgar Hurley 1935- *WhoAm 92*
Mauger, Alain Jean 1949- *WhoScE 91-2*
Mauger, Leonard Albert 1923- *WhoWor 93*
Mauger, Patricia Ann 1937- *WhoAm 92*
Mauger, Stephen John 1949- *St&PR 93, WhoAm 92*
Maugeri, Sam J. 1933- *St&PR 93*
Maugham, Robert C. *ScF&FL 92*
Maugham, Robert Cecil Romer 1916-1981 *ConAu 40NR*
Maugham, Robin *ConAu 40NR*
Maugham, Robin 1916-1981 *ScF&FL 92*
Maugham, Somerset 1874-1965 *BioIn 17*
Maugham, W. S. *ConAu 40NR*
Maugham, W. Somerset 1874-1965 *BioIn 17, MagSWL [port], WorLitC [port]*
Maugham, W(illiam) Somerset 1874-1965 *ConAu 40NR*
Maugham, William Somerset *ConAu 40NR*
Maugham, William Somerset 1874-1965 *BioIn 17*
Maughan, Deryck *BioIn 17*
Maughan, Deryck C. *WhoAm 92*
Maughan, Deryck C. 1947- *St&PR 93*
Maughan, Matthew Michael 1938- *WhoWor 93*
Maughan, Sharon *BioIn 17*
Maughan, Willard Zinn 1944- *WhoWor 93*
Maughmer, Mark David 1950- *WhoEmL 93*
Maughn, James D. 1947- *St&PR 93*
Maughn, James David 1947- *WhoIns 93*
Maugue, Pierre 1940- *WhoUN 92*
Mauguiere, Benedicte Nicole 1958- *WhoSSW 93*
Mauhs, Frederic Myers *Law&B 92*
Mauk, Kenneth Leon 1945- *St&PR 93*
Mauke, Leah Rachel 1924- *WhoAmW 93*
Mauke, Otto Russell 1924- *WhoAm 92*
Mauke, Wilhelm 1867-1930 *Baker 92*
Maukonen, Timo Paavali 1944- *WhoUN 92*
Maul, Arthur Benjamin 1924- *WhoWor 93*
Maul, Carol Elaine 1953- *WhoAmW 93*
Maul, Stephen Bailey 1942- *WhoE 93*
Maul, Terry Lee 1946- *WhoEmL 93*
Maulbetsch, Stephen Robert 1957- *St&PR 93*
Maulden, Jerry L. 1936- *St&PR 93, WhoSSW 93*
Mauldin, Brenda Marie 1958- *WhoAmW 93*
Mauldin, Curtis Aaron 1947- *WhoSSW 93*
Mauldin, John Inglis 1947- *WhoEmL 93*
Mauldin, Karen Singley 1964- *WhoWrEP 92*
Mauldin, Robert Ray 1935- *WhoAm 92*
Mauldin, William H. 1921- *WhoAm 92*
Maulding, Barry Clifford 1945- *St&PR 93*
Maule, Cynthia Lea 1949- *WhoEmL 93*
Maule, Hamilton Bee 1915- *WhoWrEP 92*
Maule, James Edward 1951- *WhoE 93*
Maule, James Joseph, Jr. 1947- *WhoEmL 93*
Maulik, Dev 1942- *WhoAm 92*
Maulin, Jack Doolin 1934- *St&PR 93*
Maulion, Richard Peter 1949- *WhoSSW 93*
Maull, Flora Davis 1904- *WhoAm 92*
Maull, George Marriner 1947- *WhoE 93, WhoEmL 93, WhoWor 93*
Maulnier, Thierry 1909-1988 *BioIn 17*
Maulsby, Allen Farish 1922- *WhoAm 92*
Maulson, Tom *BioIn 17*
Maulson, Vernon C. *Law&B 92*
Maultsby, Thomas Edward 1945- *WhoSSW 93*
Maun, John F. d1991 *BioIn 17*
Maun, Mary Ellen 1951- *WhoAmW 93, WhoE 93, WhoEmL 93, WhoWor 93*
Maund, Joe B. *Law&B 92*
Maunder, Addison Bruce 1934- *WhoAm 92, WhoSSW 93*
Maunder, Allen *BioIn 17*
Maunder, John Henry 1858-1920 *Baker 92*
Maunder, John William *WhoScE 91-1*
Maunder, Leonard *WhoScE 91-1*
Maunder, Richard John 1949- *WhoEmL 93*
Mauney, Keith James 1948- *WhoAm 92, WhoE 93*
Mauney, William Kemp, Jr. 1917- *St&PR 93*
Mauney, William Kemp, III 1951- *St&PR 93*
Maung, Lay 1935- *WhoUN 92*
Maung, Mya 1933- *WhoE 93*
Maung-Mercurio, Alice Marie 1949- *WhoAmW 93*
Maunoury, Maurice Bourges- 1914- *BioIn 17*
Maunoury, Michel Joseph 1847-1923 *HarEnMi*
Maunsbach, Kay Benedicta 1933- *WhoE 93*
Maupain, Francis 1941- *WhoUN 92*
Maupassant, Guy de 1850-1893 *DcLB 123 [port], MagSWL [port], ScF&FL 92, WorLitC [port]*
Maupay, Walter R. 1939- *St&PR 93*
Maupin, Armistead *BioIn 17*
Maupin, Armistead 1944- *ConGAN*
Maupin, Armistead Jones 1914- *WhoAm 92*
Maupin, Armistead Jones, Jr. 1944- *WhoAm 92*
Maupin, Bob W. 1932- *St&PR 93*
Maupin, Levi Pleasant 1924- *St&PR 93*
Maupin, Robert Wade 1932- *St&PR 93*
Maura, Carmen *BioIn 17*
Maura, Carmen 1945- *IntDcF 2-3*
Maura, Carmen 1946?- *CurBio 92 [port], WhoWor 93*
Maura, Giancarlo 1925- *WhoScE 91-3*
Maura, Michael John, Jr. 1964- *WhoSSW 93*
Mauran, Duncan H. 1926- *St&PR 93*
Mauras, Marta 1947- *WhoUN 92*
Maurat, Jean-Pierre 1922- *WhoScE 91-2*
Maurel, Raymond *WhoScE 91-2*
Maurel, Victor 1848-1923 *Baker 92, IntDcOp [port], OxDcOp*
Maurer, Armand Augustine 1915- *WhoWrEP 92*
Maurer, Arthur Willshire 1940- *WhoE 93*
Maurer, Barbara V. *Law&B 92*
Maurer, Carter 1959- *WhoSSW 93*
Maurer, Charles Frederick William, III 1939- *WhoWor 93*
Maurer, Donald D. 1937- *St&PR 93*
Maurer, Eleanor Johnson 1914- *WhoSSW 93*
Maurer, Emilia Sherman d1992 *BioIn 17, NewYTBS 92 [port]*
Maurer, Evan Maclyn 1944- *WhoAm 92*
Maurer, Fred Dry 1909- *WhoAm 92*
Maurer, Frederic George, III 1952- *WhoEmL 93*
Maurer, Fredrick Richard 1945- *WhoSSW 93*
Maurer, Gernant E. 1949- *St&PR 93*
Maurer, Gernant Elmer 1949- *WhoAm 92*
Maurer, Gilbert Charles 1928- *WhoAm 92*
Maurer, H. *WhoScE 91-4*
Maurer, H. Rainer 1937- *WhoScE 91-3*
Maurer, Hans Hilarius 1950- *WhoWor 93*
Maurer, Harold Maurice 1936- *WhoAm 92*
Maurer, I. Gyula 1927- *WhoScE 91-4*
Maurer, Jakob 1929- *WhoScE 91-4*
Maurer, James R. 1939- *St&PR 93*
Maurer, Jeffrey S. 1947- *St&PR 93*
Maurer, Jeffrey Stuart 1947- *WhoAm 92*
Maurer, John A. 1954- *St&PR 93*
Maurer, John Sylvester 1938- *WhoAm 92*
Maurer, Joy Adelaide 1934- *St&PR 93*
Maurer, Lucille Darvin 1922- *WhoAm 92, WhoAmW 93, WhoE 93*
Maurer, Ludwig J. 1946- *WhoScE 91-4*
Maurer, Ludwig (Wilhelm) 1789-1878 *Baker 92*
Maurer, Marc Morgan 1951- *WhoAm 92*
Maurer, Morris Lee 1951- *WhoAm 92*
Maurer, Paul Herbert 1923- *WhoAm 92*
Maurer, Paul Reed 1937- *WhoWor 93*
Maurer, Philip A. *Law&B 92*
Maurer, Pierre 1924- *St&PR 93*
Maurer, Ralph A. 1931- *St&PR 93*
Maurer, Rene 1946- *WhoWor 93*
Maurer, Robert Distler 1924- *WhoAm 92*
Maurer, Robert G. *Law&B 92*
Maurer, Robert James 1943- *WhoWor 93*
Maurer, Robert Stanley 1933- *WhoWor 93*
Maurer, Robert W. *Law&B 92*
Maurer, Rosalie Grace 1945- *WhoAmW 93*
Maurer, Steven M. *Law&B 92*
Maurer, Tracey Lynn 1963- *WhoEmL 93*
Maurer, Virginia Gallaher 1946- *WhoSSW 93*
Maurer, Wesley Henry 1897- *WhoWor 93*
Maurer, Wolfgang 1944- *WhoScE 91-3*
Mauretti, Gerald Joseph 1943- *St&PR 93*
Maurex *OxDcByz*
Mauri, Robert L. 1935- *St&PR 93*
Mauriac, Claude 1914- *BioIn 17, WhoWor 93*
Mauriac, Francois 1885-1970 *BioIn 17*
Maurice 539-602 *HarEnMi, OxDcByz*
Maurice, Prince Palatine of the Rhine 1621-1652 *HarEnMi*
Maurice, Alphons 1862-1905 *Baker 92*
Maurice, Eleanore Ingersoll 1901- *WhoE 93*
Maurice, Emile 1910- *DcCPCAm*
Maurice, Gerald D. 1933- *St&PR 93*
Maurice, James Richard 1941- *WhoWor 93*
Maurice, Lois Jane 1953- *WhoEmL 93*
Maurice, Pierre, Baron de 1868-1936 *Baker 92*
Maurice, Samuel Joseph 1945- *St&PR 93*
Maurice, Thomas F. 1916- *St&PR 93*
Maurice & Mac *SoulM*
Maurice of Nassau, Prince 1567-1625 *HarEnMi*
Mauricio, Jose 1752-1815 *Baker 92*
Maurier, Daphne du *ScF&FL 92*
Maurin, Gayle Elizabeth 1950- *WhoEmL 93*
Maurin, Herre *WhoScE 91-2*
Maurin, Louis Felix Thomas 1869-1956 *BioIn 17*
Mauritz, Karl Heinz 1944- *WhoWor 93*
Maurizot, Jean Claude 1943- *WhoScE 91-2*
Mauro, A.V. *Law&B 92*
Mauro, Albert P. 1929- *St&PR 93*
Mauro, Alessandro fl. 1709-1748 *OxDcOp*
Mauro, Anthony R. 1934- *St&PR 93*
Mauro, Arthur Valentine 1927- *St&PR 93*
Mauro, Domenico fl. 1669-1707 *OxDcOp*
Mauro, Domenico fl. 1733-1780 *OxDcOp*
Mauro, Ermanno 1939- *Baker 92*
Mauro, Gary 1944- *BioIn 17*
Mauro, Gaspare fl. 1657-1719 *OxDcOp*
Mauro, Gerolamo 1725-1766 *OxDcOp*
Mauro, Jean B. *Law&B 92*
Mauro, John Baptist 1923- *WhoAm 92*
Mauro, Joseph Anthony 1951- *WhoE 93*
Mauro, Joseph William 1932- *St&PR 93*
Mauro, Mariann 1964- *WhoAmW 93*
Mauro, Pietro fl. 1669-1697 *OxDcOp*
Mauro, Raymond Vincent 1958- *WhoE 93*
Mauro, Richard Frank 1945- *WhoAm 92*
Mauro, Thomas Vincent 1939- *WhoAm 92*
Maurois, Andre 1885-1967 *BioIn 17, ScF&FL 92*
Maurokatakalon *OxDcByz*
Mauropous, John c. 1000-c. 1075 *OxDcByz*
Mauroy, Pierre 1928- *BioIn 17, WhoWor 93*
Maurozomes *OxDcByz*
Maurras, Charles 1868-1952 *BioIn 17*
Maurrasse, Maria Vidalina *Law&B 92*
Maurstad, Toralv 1926- *WhoWor 93*
Maury, Anne Fontaine *AmWomPl*
Maury, Lowndes 1911-1975 *Baker 92*
Maury, Marc A. 1938- *St&PR 93*
Maury, Mario A., Jr. 1936- *St&PR 93*
Maus, Daniel S. *Law&B 92*
Maus, Gerald J. 1955- *St&PR 93*
Maus, Gerard Peter 1951- *St&PR 93*
Maus, Katharine Eisaman 1955- *WhoSSW 93*
Maus, Octave 1856-1919 *Baker 92*
Maus, Robert Nikolaus 1958- *WhoEmL 93*
Mauschbaugh, Andrew John 1963- *WhoE 93*
Mausel, Paul Warner 1936- *WhoAm 92*
Mauser, Kevin Edward 1959- *WhoEmL 93*
Mauser, Particia A. 1951- *St&PR 93*
Mausert, William H. 1940- *St&PR 93*
Maushart, Brad *BioIn 17*
Mauskopf, Seymour Harold 1938- *WhoAm 92*
Mausner, Dorothy *St&PR 93*
Mausner, Leonard F. *St&PR 93*
Mausner, Seymour *St&PR 93*
Mauss, Marcel 1872-1950 *IntDcAn*
Maute, Robert Lewis 1924- *WhoSSW 93*
Mautner, Bradley Edward 1955- *St&PR 93*
Mautner, Henry George 1925- *WhoAm 92, WhoE 93*
Mautner, Irwin 1933- *St&PR 93*
Mautner, Kathie P. *Law&B 92*
Mautone, Louis Joseph 1945- *WhoSSW 93*
Mautz, Bernhard Frederick 1936- *St&PR 93*
Mautz, Robert Barbeau 1915- *WhoAm 92*
Mauvais-Jarvis, Pierre J.P. 1929- *WhoScE 91-2*
Mauz, Henry Herrward, Jr. 1936- *WhoAm 92*
Mauzerall, David Charles 1929- *WhoAm 92, WhoE 93*
Mauzy, Anne 1929- *WhoAmW 93*
Mauzy, Larry R. 1949- *St&PR 93*
Mauzy, Michael Philip 1928- *St&PR 93*
Mauzy, Oscar Holcombe 1926- *WhoAm 92, WhoSSW 93*
Mauzy, Robert Larry 1949- *WhoIns 93*
Mavel, Gerard 1935- *WhoScE 91-2*
Maver, Thomas Watt *WhoScE 91-1*
Maverick, Maury 1895-1954 *EncAACR, PolPar*
Maves, Paul Benjamin 1913- *WhoAm 92*
Maves, Susan Lyn 1967- *WhoAmW 93*
Mavia fl. 4th cent.- *OxDcByz*
Mavis, John Leahy *Law&B 92*
Mavor, John *WhoScE 91-1*
Mavor, Salley *BioIn 17*
Mavrides, Gregory 1955- *WhoEmL 93, WhoSSW 93*
Mavridis, Lyssimachos 1928- *WhoScE 91-3*
Mavrinac, Susan E. *Law&B 92*
Mavrogiannis, Dionysos G. 1931- *WhoUN 92*
Mavrommati, Lily 1945- *WhoScE 91-3*
Mavrommatis, Andreas V. 1932- *WhoUN 92*
Mavrommatis, Andrew St. 1920- *WhoScE 91-3*
Mavros, George S. 1957- *WhoEmL 93, WhoSSW 93, WhoWor 93*
Mavros, Paul Scott 1937- *WhoIns 93*
Mavroules, Nicholas 1929- *CngDr 91, WhoAm 92, WhoE 93*
Maw, Herbert B. 1893-1990 *BioIn 17*
Maw, J. Gordon 1936- *St&PR 93*
Maw, James Gordon 1936- *WhoAm 92*
Maw, Nicholas 1935- *IntDcOp, OxDcOp*
Maw, (John) Nicholas 1935- *Baker 92*
Maw, Sam H. 1933- *WhoAm 92*
Maw, Samuel H. 1933- *St&PR 93*
Mawani, Al W. 1951- *St&PR 93*
Mawardi, Osman Kamel 1917- *WhoAm 92*
Mawas, Claude E. 1940- *WhoScE 91-2*
Mawdsley, William H. 1951- *St&PR 93*
Mawe, Kevin F. *Law&B 92*
Mawhinney, Donald M., Jr. 1926- *St&PR 93*
Mawhinney, King 1947- *WhoEmL 93*
Mawhorter, Robert Lee 1939- *St&PR 93*
Mawlawi, Farouk 1933- *WhoUN 92*
Mawson, Douglas 1882-1958 *BioIn 17, Expl 93*
Mawyer, Stan R. 1948- *WhoE 93*
Max, Buddy *WhoSSW 93*
Max, Claire Ellen 1946- *WhoAmW 93, WhoEmL 93*
Max, Friedrich 1912- *WhoWor 93*
Max, Herbert B. 1931- *WhoAm 92*

Max, Peter 1937- *News 93-2 [port], WhoAm 92*
Maxa, John G. *Law&B 92*
Maxa, Rudolph Joseph, Jr. 1949- *WhoAm 92*
Maxam, Louella 1896-1970 *SweetSg A*
Maxcy, Edward Ellis 1944- *WhoE 93*
Maxeiner, Clarence William 1914- *WhoAm 92*
Maxeiner, James R. *Law&B 92*
Maxemchuk, Nicholas Frank 1946- *WhoAm 92*
Maxentius c. 286-312 *OxDcByz*
Maxentius, Marcus Aurelius Valerius d312 *HarEnMi*
Maxey, Catherine Annette 1938- *WhoSSW 93*
Maxey, Joy Ann 1958- *WhoSSW 93*
Maxey, Margaret Nan *WhoAm 92*
Maxey, Thomas F. 1937- *St&PR 93, WhoAm 92*
Maxfield, Anna Belle 1933- *WhoAmW 93*
Maxfield, Anne M. 1961- *WhoAmW 93*
Maxfield, John *WhoScE 91-1*
Maxfield, John Edward 1927- *WhoAm 92*
Maxfield, Lee Alan 1947- *WhoEmL 93*
Maxfield, Lori Rochelle 1959- *WhoEmL 93*
Maxfield, Maria Ursula 1932- *WhoWrEP 92*
Maxfield, Mary Constance 1949- *WhoAmW 93, WhoSSW 93*
Maxfield, Michael G. 1953- *St&PR 93*
Maxfield, Michael Gerald 1954- *WhoAm 92*
Maxfield, Mina Rosenthal *AmWomPl*
Maxfield, Richard (Vance) 1927-1969 *Baker 92*
Maxfield, Robert F. *Law&B 92*
Maxheim, John Howard 1934- *St&PR 93, WhoAm 92*
Maxi, Joseph *DcCPCAm*
Maxim, John R. 1937- *ScF&FL 92*
Maximay, Steve Vincent 1956- *WhoWor 93*
Maximian c. 245-310 *HarEnMi, OxDcByz*
Maximilian, Father 1894-1941 *BioIn 17*
Maximilian, Prince of Wied-Neuwied 1782-1867 *BioIn 17*
Maximilian, I, Duke and Elector of Bavaria 1573-1651 *HarEnMi*
Maximilian, I, Holy Roman Emperor 1459-1519 *BioIn 17*
Maximinus Daia c. 270-313 *OxDcByz*
Maximinus Daia, Gaius Galerius Valerius c. 270-313 *HarEnMi*
Maximinus Thrax, Gaius Julius Verus d238 *HarEnMi*
Maximo, Paulo Roberto Lemos 1966- *WhoWor 93*
Maximos, Bishop 1935- *WhoAm 92*
Maximos Kausokalybites c. 1270-c. 1365 *OxDcByz*
Maximos of Ephesus c. 300-371? *OxDcByz*
Maximos the Confessor 580-662 *OxDcByz*
Maximuk, Lynn Paul 1950- *WhoEmL 93*
Maximus d388 *OxDcByz*
Maximus, Magnus Clemens d388 *HarEnMi*
Maximus Allobrogicus, Quintus Fabius c. 164BC-c. 105BC *HarEnMi*
Maxman, Susan Abel 1938- *WhoAm 92*
Maxmin, James *BioIn 17*
Maxner, Joyce Karen 1929- *WhoAm 92*
Maxon, Don Carlton 1914- *WhoAm 92, WhoWor 93*
Maxon, Gene Harland 1932- *St&PR 93*
Maxon, J.G. *ScF&FL 92*
Maxon, Robert John 1927- *St&PR 93*
Maxson, Barbara Kinzie 1948- *WhoAmW 93*
Maxson, Linda Ellen 1943- *WhoAmW 93*
Maxson, Noel Tope 1926- *WhoWrEP 92*
Maxson-Ladage, Wanda Lee 1929- *WhoAmW 93*
Maxton, James 1885-1946 *DcTwHis*
Maxvill, Dal 1939- *WhoAm 92*
Maxwell, Alice S. *WhoWrEP 92*
Maxwell, Allen R. 1939- *St&PR 93*
Maxwell, Anders John 1946- *WhoAm 92, WhoE 93, WhoEmL 93*
Maxwell, Ann 1944- *ScF&FL 92*
Maxwell, Arthur Eugene 1925- *WhoAm 92*
Maxwell, Barbara Sue 1950- *WhoAmW 93, WhoE 93*
Maxwell, Brian Allen *Law&B 92*
Maxwell, Bruce David 1949- *WhoWrEP 92*
Maxwell, Bryce 1919- *WhoAm 92*
Maxwell, Carla *BioIn 17*
Maxwell, Carla Lena 1945- *WhoAm 92*
Maxwell, Charles Thoburn 1931- *St&PR 93*
Maxwell, Christine 1950- *WhoAm 92, WhoAmW 93*
Maxwell, Christine Tierney 1963- *St&PR 93*
Maxwell, D. Malcolm 1934- *WhoAm 92*
Maxwell, Daniel Louis 1960- *WhoSSW 93*
Maxwell, David E. 1944- *WhoAm 92*
Maxwell, David Ogden 1930- *WhoAm 92*
Maxwell, David R. 1938- *St&PR 93*
Maxwell, Donald Robert 1929- *WhoAm 92*
Maxwell, Donald S. 1930- *St&PR 93*
Maxwell, Donald Stanley 1930- *WhoAm 92*
Maxwell, Dorothea Bost Andrews 1911- *WhoAmW 93*
Maxwell, Douglas Richard *Law&B 92*
Maxwell, Earle W., Jr. 1939- *St&PR 93*
Maxwell, Edward 1918- *ScF&FL 92*
Maxwell, Elsa *AmWomPl*
Maxwell, Florence Hinshaw 1914- *WhoAmW 93*
Maxwell, Frank 1916- *WhoAm 92*
Maxwell, Gavin 1914-1969 *BioIn 17*
Maxwell, George M. *WhoScE 91-1*
Maxwell, H. D., Jr. 1931- *WhoAm 92*
Maxwell, Hamish 1926- *St&PR 93, WhoAm 92*
Maxwell, Holly 1945- *BioIn 17*
Maxwell, Ian *BioIn 17*
Maxwell, Isabel Sylvia 1950- *WhoAm 92, WhoAmW 93*
Maxwell, J. Douglas, Jr. 1941- *WhoAm 92*
Maxwell, Jack E. 1926- *St&PR 93*
Maxwell, Jack Erwin 1926- *WhoAm 92*
Maxwell, James Ashley, Jr. 1944- *WhoSSW 93*
Maxwell, James Leo *Law&B 92*
Maxwell, James Leroy 1951- *St&PR 93*
Maxwell, James M. *Law&B 92*
Maxwell, James S. *Law&B 92*
Maxwell, James Wehr 1950- *WhoE 93*
Maxwell, Jane *WhoWrEP 92*
Maxwell, Jerome E. 1944- *St&PR 93*
Maxwell, John d1895 *BioIn 17*
Maxwell, John A. *Law&B 92*
Maxwell, John C. *ScF&FL 92*
Maxwell, John Daniel 1950- *WhoEmL 93*
Maxwell, John Raymond 1909- *WhoAm 92*
Maxwell, John Thomas 1962- *St&PR 93*
Maxwell, Judith 1943- *WhoAm 92, WhoAmW 93*
Maxwell, Kevin *BioIn 17*
Maxwell, Larry A. *Law&B 92*
Maxwell, Leah R. 1954- *St&PR 93*
Maxwell, Leo Chambers 1941- *WhoSSW 93*
Maxwell, Lisa *BioIn 17*
Maxwell, Marcia Gail 1948- *WhoEmL 93*
Maxwell, Margaret Witmer 1918- *WhoAmW 93*
Maxwell, Mary Sutherland 1910- *WhoWor 93*
Maxwell, Melissa Faye 1939- *WhoAmW 93*
Maxwell, Otis Allen 1915- *WhoWrEP 92*
Maxwell, Patricia Anne 1942- *WhoAmW 93*
Maxwell, R.J. *BioIn 17, WhoScE 91-1*
Maxwell, Ralph Kerr 1934- *WhoAsAP 91*
Maxwell, Rebecca *Law&B 92*
Maxwell, Richard A. 1927- *St&PR 93*
Maxwell, Richard Callender 1919- *WhoAm 92*
Maxwell, Robert *BioIn 17*
Maxwell, Robert 1923-1991 *AnObit 1991, News 92*
Maxwell, Robert Allan, Jr. 1933- *WhoE 93*
Maxwell, Robert D. 1920- *BioIn 17*
Maxwell, Robert Earl 1924- *WhoAm 92, WhoSSW 93*
Maxwell, (Ian) Robert 1923-1991 *CurBio 92N*
Maxwell, Robert Lee 1933- *St&PR 93*
Maxwell, Robert Oliver 1940- *St&PR 93*
Maxwell, Robert Wallace, II 1943- *WhoAm 92*
Maxwell, Robert William 1950- *WhoSSW 93*
Maxwell, Robin Lee 1956- *WhoAmW 93*
Maxwell, Roger Francis Hamilton 1941- *WhoAsAP 91*
Maxwell, Ronald F. 1947- *MiSFD 9*
Maxwell, Ruby Hoots 1924- *WhoAmW 93*
Maxwell, Ruth Elaine 1934- *WhoAmW 93*
Maxwell, Sara Ann *Law&B 92*
Maxwell, Scott H. 1956- *St&PR 93*
Maxwell, Susan *BiDAMSp 1989*
Maxwell, Thomas Eugene 1945- *WhoAm 92*
Maxwell, Thomas Jefferson 1940- *WhoScE 91-1*
Maxwell, Vincent Oluoma 1926- *WhoWor 93*
Maxwell, Virginia *AmWomPl*
Maxwell, Wilbur Richard 1920- *WhoAm 92*
Maxwell, William 1908- *WhoAm 92, WhoWrEP 92*
Maxwell, William L. 1951- *St&PR 93, WhoSSW 93*
Maxwell, William Laughlin 1934- *WhoAm 92*
Maxwell, William Stirling 1922- *WhoAm 92*
Maxwell-Brogdon, Florence Morency 1929- *WhoAmW 93*
Maxwell Davies, Peter *Baker 92, OxDcOp*
Maxwell-Jones, J. *WhoScE 91-1*
Maxworthy, Tony 1933- *WhoAm 92*
Maxxe, Robert *ScF&FL 92*
May, A. John 1928- *St&PR 93*
May, Addison Cushman 1933- *WhoAm 92*
May, Adolf Darlington 1927- *WhoAm 92*
May, Alfred, Jr. 1914- *WhoSSW 93*
May, Amelia Ruth 1956- *WhoEmL 93*
May, Anne Catherine 1940- *WhoAmW 93*
May, Anthony Dormer *WhoScE 91-1*
May, Arthur W. 1937- *WhoAm 92*
May, Aviva Rabinowitz *WhoAmW 93*
May, Barbara L. 1937- *WhoWrEP 92*
May, Benjamin T. 1957- *St&PR 93*
May, Bernard Peter d1990 *BioIn 17*
May, Bernhard Felix 1952- *WhoWor 93*
May, Billy *BioIn 17*
May, Bradford *MiSFD 9*
May, Bridget Ann 1950- *WhoAmW 93*
May, Bruce Barnett 1948- *WhoEmL 93*
May, Bruce R. 1942- *St&PR 93*
May, Carolyn 1942- *WhoAmW 93*
May, Caryn R. *Law&B 92*
May, Catherine Dean 1914- *BioIn 17*
May, Charles D. d1992 *NewYTBS 92*
May, Charles Kent 1939- *WhoAm 92, WhoWor 93*
May, Charles Robert 1941- *St&PR 93*
May, Cheryl Elaine 1949- *WhoEmL 93*
May, Clifford 1908-1989 *BioIn 17*
May, Clifford D. 1951- *ConAu 136*
May, Clifford E. 1933- *St&PR 93*
May, Curry Julian 1933- *WhoAm 92*
May, Daniel F. 1930- *St&PR 93*
May, Daryl (Alden) 1936- *ConAu 139*
May, David 1934- *WhoE 93*
May, David P. *Law&B 92*
May, David Sterling *Law&B 92*
May, Dennis Gerard 1953- *WhoEmL 93*
May, Diane Elizabeth 1947- *WhoEmL 93*
May, Donald R. 1945- *WhoAm 92*
May, Douglas Heller 1956- *St&PR 93*
May, Edgar 1929- *WhoAm 92*
May, Edward Collett 1806-1887 *Baker 92*
May, Elaine 1932- *MiSFD 9, WhoAm 92, WhoAmW 93*
May, Elvira Margarite 1927- *WhoAmW 93*
May, Ernest Dewey 1942- *WhoE 93*
May, Ernest Max 1913- *WhoAm 92*
May, Ernest Richard 1928- *WhoWrEP 92*
May, Felton Edwin 1935- *WhoAm 92*
May, Florence 1845-1923 *Baker 92*
May, Francis Hart, Jr. 1917- *WhoAm 92*
May, Francis R. 1957- *St&PR 93*
May, Francisco W. 1928- *WhoWor 93*
May, G. Lynwood 1927- *WhoAm 92*
May, George W. d1990 *BioIn 17*
May, Georges Claude 1920- *WhoAm 92, WhoE 93*
May, Gerald William 1941- *WhoAm 92*
May, Gita 1929- *WhoE 93*
May, Harold Edward 1920- *WhoAm 92*
May, Henry Lloyd, IV 1941- *WhoE 93*
May, J. Michael *Law&B 92*
May, J. Peter 1939- *WhoAm 92*
May, James 1921- *WhoE 93*
May, James Colbry, Jr. 1954- *WhoSSW 93*
May, James L. 1947- *St&PR 93*
May, James Sturgis 1917- *WhoSSW 93*
May, Jean-Francois 1940- *WhoScE 91-2*
May, Jeffrey H. *Law&B 92*
May, Jerry Russell 1942- *WhoAm 92*
May, John *ScF&FL 92*
May, John Franklin 1929- *WhoE 93*
May, John Frederic 1950- *WhoE 93*
May, John Lawrence 1922- *BioIn 17, WhoAm 92*
May, John M. 1948- *WhoE 93, WhoEmL 93, WhoWor 93*
May, John M. 1952- *WhoE 93*
May, John S. *Law&B 92*
May, John Walter 1936- *WhoE 93*
May, Johnny Paul 1945- *WhoSSW 93*
May, Joseph A. 1927-1989 *BioIn 17*
May, Joseph Leserman 1929- *WhoSSW 93, WhoWor 93*
May, Joseph Patrick 1953- *WhoEmL 93*
May, Joseph W. 1945- *St&PR 93*
May, Julian 1931- *BioIn 17, ScF&FL 92*
May, Justin d1992 *BioIn 17*
May, Karl 1842-1912 *ScF&FL 92*
May, Keith M. 1927- *ScF&FL 92*
May, Kenneth Austin 1960- *WhoSSW 93*
May, Kenneth Nathaniel 1930- *St&PR 93, WhoAm 92, WhoSSW 93*
May, Klaus Jurgen Wolfgang 1957- *WhoWor 93*
May, Lawrence Edward 1947- *WhoEmL 93*
May, Leopold 1923- *WhoE 93*
May, Lewis Sylvester d1991 *BioIn 17*
May, M.J. 1948- *WhoScE 91-1*
May, Maben Floyd 1942- *St&PR 93*
May, Marion A. *Law&B 92*
May, Mary Diane 1930- *WhoAmW 93*
May, Mary Lil 1953- *St&PR 93*
May, Mary Louise 1946- *WhoAmW 93*
May, Mathilda *BioIn 17*
May, Melanie Ann 1955- *WhoAmW 93, WhoEmL 93*
May, Melvin Arthur 1940- *WhoAm 92*
May, Merrill 1935- *St&PR 93*
May, Michael Wayne 1949- *WhoWor 93*
May, Paula Joe 1947- *WhoAmW 93*
May, Peter William 1942- *WhoAm 92*
May, Philip Raymond 1942- *WhoAm 92*
May, Phyllis Jean 1932- *WhoAmW 93, WhoWor 93*
May, Rebecca F. 1956- *WhoSSW 93*
May, Richard Cameron 1939- *WhoE 93*
May, Richard Den 1952- *St&PR 93*
May, Richard Edward 1946- *WhoAm 92*
May, Richard L. 1956- *St&PR 93*
May, Richard Warren 1944- *WhoE 93, WhoWor 93*
May, Robert A. 1911- *WhoAm 92*
May, Robert George 1943- *WhoAm 92*
May, Robert McCredie 1936- *WhoAm 92*
May, Robert P. *Law&B 92*
May, Robert S. *ScF&FL 92*
May, Robert V. 1943- *St&PR 93*
May, Robin 1929- *ScF&FL 92*
May, Roger B. 1931- *St&PR 93*
May, Roger Lee *Law&B 92*
May, Rollo 1909- *WhoAm 92*
May, Ronald Alan 1928- *WhoAm 92, WhoSSW 93*
May, Samuel Joseph 1797-1871 *BioIn 17*
May, Scott Glenn 1954- *BiDAMSp 1989*
May, Stephen 1931- *WhoAm 92*
May, Sterling Randolph 1946- *WhoAm 92*
May, Steven E. 1956- *St&PR 93*
May, Steven William 1941- *WhoSSW 93*
May, Thomas Daniel 1950- *WhoEmL 93*
May, Thomas J. 1947- *St&PR 93*
May, Timothy James 1932- *WhoAm 92, WhoWor 93*
May, Tony *BioIn 17*
May, Vern Tempest 1940- *WhoAm 92*
May, Walter Grant 1918- *WhoAm 92*
May, Walter Herbert, Jr. 1936- *St&PR 93*
May, William Frederick 1915- *WhoAm 92*
May, William Hathaway *Law&B 92*
May, William Leopold, Jr. *Law&B 92*
May, William P. 1942- *St&PR 93*
Maya, Semisi *BioIn 17*
Maya, William 1948- *WhoEmL 93*
Maya, William E. 1949- *St&PR 93*
Mayall, John *BioIn 17*
Mayall, John 1933- *Baker 92*
Mayall, Loretta M. 1935- *WhoAmW 93*
Mayall, Rik 1958- *QDrFCA 92 [port]*
Mayanja, Abubakar Kaakyama 1929- *WhoAfr*
Mayanja-Nkangi, Joshua Sibakyalwayo 1931- *WhoAfr*
Mayaud, Noel 1899-1980 *BioIn 17*
Maybank, Joseph 1930- *WhoAm 92*
Mayben, Sara Beth 1963- *WhoAmW 93*
Mayberry, Evelyn Louise *AmWomPl*
Mayberry, John Claiborn 1949- *BiDAMSp 1989*
Mayberry, Julius Eugene 1935- *WhoSSW 93*
Mayberry, Lee *BioIn 17*
Mayberry, Rodney Scott 1947- *WhoSSW 93*
Mayberry, Russ *MiSFD 9*
Mayberry, Susan Neal 1951- *WhoAmW 93*
Mayberry, William Eugene 1929- *WhoAm 92*
Maybin, John Edwin 1925- *St&PR 93*
Mayborn, Frank Willis 1903-1987 *BioIn 17*
Maybrick, Michael 1844-1913 *Baker 92*
Maybruck, Patricia Pendergraft 1926- *WhoAmW 93*
Maybury, Edward A. 1939- *St&PR 93*
Maybury, Ged *ScF&FL 92*
Maybury, Paul Calvin 1924- *WhoAm 92, WhoSSW 93*
Maybury, Richard J. 1946- *SmATA 72 [port]*
Maybury, Robert Harris 1923- *WhoSSW 93*
Maycen, Dale F. 1938- *WhoAm 92*
Mayces, Adrian 1950- *St&PR 93*
Maycock, Ian David 1935- *St&PR 93, WhoAm 92*
Maycock, Joseph Farwell, Jr. 1930- *WhoAm 92*

Maycock, Lan L. 1939- *St&PR 93*
Maycock, William E. *Law&B 92*
Mayda, Jaro 1918- *WhoAm 92*
Maydan, Dan *St&PR 93*
Mayden, Barbara Mendel 1951- *WhoAm 92*
Mayden, James F. *Law&B 92*
Maydonik, N.A. *Law&B 92*
Maye, Michael *BioIn 17*
Mayeda, Edward Yoshio 1931- *St&PR 93*
Mayehoff, Eddie 1911- *QDrFCA 92 [port]*
Mayenne, Charles de Lorraine, Duke of 1554-1611 *HarEnMi*
Mayer, Alfons 1927- *St&PR 93*
Mayer, Anne Brestel 1935- *WhoAm 92*
Mayer, Audrey Doris 1943- *WhoSSW 93*
Mayer, Bena Frank 1898-1991 *BioIn 17*
Mayer, Bernard C. 1935- *St&PR 93*
Mayer, Bob 1959- *ConAu 137*
Mayer, Bruce Hillis 1945- *WhoSSW 93*
Mayer, Carl Joseph 1959- *WhoAm 92, WhoE 93*
Mayer, Charles 1799-1862 *Baker 92*
Mayer, Charles Arthur 1949- *WhoE 93*
Mayer, Charles H. 1947- *St&PR 93*
Mayer, Charles James 1936- *WhoAm 92, WhoE 93*
Mayer, Charles Theodore 1924- *WhoAm 92*
Mayer, Daniel 1909- *BioIn 17*
Mayer, David G. *Law&B 92*
Mayer, David Louis 1927- *St&PR 93*
Mayer, David Robert 1938- *WhoWor 93*
Mayer, Dennis M. *Law&B 92*
Mayer, Dennis Thomas 1901- *WhoAm 92*
Mayer, Diana K. *St&PR 93*
Mayer, Dieter H. 1936- *St&PR 93*
Mayer, Donald L. 1947- *St&PR 93*
Mayer, Donald Lawrence *Law&B 92*
Mayer, Elizabeth A. 1966- *WhoAmW 93*
Mayer, Elizabeth Emma 1960- *WhoAmW 93*
Mayer, Emmett J., Jr. 1943- *St&PR 93*
Mayer, Erich Anton 1930- *WhoWor 93*
Mayer, Erin Garrett 1961- *WhoAmW 93*
Mayer, Eugene Stephen 1938- *WhoAm 92*
Mayer, Ferdy *WhoScE 91-2*
Mayer, Foster Lee, Jr. 1942- *WhoAm 92*
Mayer, Frank H. 1850-1954 *BioIn 17*
Mayer, Frederick Miller 1898- *WhoAm 92, WhoSSW 93*
Mayer, Frederick Rickard 1928- *St&PR 93*
Mayer, Friedrich Reinhold 1915- *WhoWor 93*
Mayer, George W. d1991 *BioIn 17*
Mayer, Gregg Lindstrom 1958- *St&PR 93*
Mayer, H. Robert 1941- *CngDr 91*
Mayer, Haldane Robert 1941- *WhoAm 92, WhoE 93*
Mayer, Hannes 1922- *WhoScE 91-4*
Mayer, Henry L. 1918- *St&PR 93*
Mayer, Henry Michael 1922- *WhoAm 92*
Mayer, Ira 1952- *WhoWrEP 92*
Mayer, Irwin 1934- *St&PR 93*
Mayer, J. Gerald 1908- *WhoAm 92*
Mayer, James Herbert *Law&B 92*
Mayer, James J. *Law&B 92*
Mayer, James Joseph 1938- *St&PR 93, WhoAm 92*
Mayer, James Julian 1962- *WhoE 93*
Mayer, James Lamoine 1951- *WhoEmL 93*
Mayer, James Walter 1930- *WhoAm 92, WhoE 93*
Mayer, Jane *BioIn 17*
Mayer, Jane S. 1929- *WhoWrEP 92*
Mayer, Jean *NewYTBS 92*
Mayer, Jean 1920- *BioIn 17, WhoAm 92, WhoE 93, WhoWor 93*
Mayer, Jean Philippe 1931- *WhoUN 92*
Mayer, Joan Marilyn Weiss 1930- *WhoAmW 93*
Mayer, John 1948- *WhoAm 92*
Mayer, John A. 1940- *St&PR 93*
Mayer, John Anton, Jr. 1940- *WhoAm 92*
Mayer, John David 1953- *WhoE 93*
Mayer, Joseph Anton 1855-1936 *Baker 92*
Mayer, Joseph W. *Law&B 92*
Mayer, Kathleen K. 1954- *St&PR 93*
Mayer, Kay Magnor 1943- *WhoAmW 93*
Mayer, Lawrence Arnold 1918- *WhoE 93*
Mayer, Leo Vernon 1936- *WhoE 93*
Mayer, Leonard *St&PR 93*
Mayer, Lothar L. 1939- *St&PR 93*
Mayer, Louis B. 1885-1957 *BioIn 17*
Mayer, Lynne Supovitz 1946- *WhoAmW 93*
Mayer, M. *WhoScE 91-2*
Mayer, Marcel Jean 1921- *WhoScE 91-2*
Mayer, Marcia Kramer 1946- *St&PR 93*
Mayer, Margery Weil 1952- *WhoAm 92*
Mayer, Maria Goeppert- 1906-1972 *BioIn 17*
Mayer, Marianna 1945- *BioIn 17*
Mayer, Marilyn Gooder *WhoAmW 93*
Mayer, Martin 1928- *BioIn 17*
Mayer, Martin Prager 1928- *WhoAm 92, WhoWrEP 92*
Mayer, Mavis Margaret *WhoAmW 93*
Mayer, Meinrad *BioIn 17*
Mayer, Mercer 1943- *ConAu 38NR, MajAI [port], SmATA 73 [port]*
Mayer, Michael L. *Law&B 92*
Mayer, Morris Lehman 1925- *WhoAm 92*
Mayer, Myra Lou 1944- *St&PR 93, WhoSSW 93*
Mayer, Nancy I. *Law&B 92*
Mayer, Nancy S. *Law&B 92*
Mayer, Neil 1934- *St&PR 93*
Mayer, Nina Ann *WhoAmW 93*
Mayer, Patricia Jayne 1950- *WhoAmW 93, WhoEmL 93, WhoWor 93*
Mayer, Patricia Victoria *Law&B 92*
Mayer, Paul Augustin Cardinal 1911- *WhoWor 93*
Mayer, Paul Joseph 1932- *St&PR 93*
Mayer, Paul L. 1931- *St&PR 93*
Mayer, Peter 1936- *WhoAm 92*
Mayer, Peter Arno 1929- *St&PR 93*
Mayer, Peter Conrad 1938- *WhoWor 93*
Mayer, Peter Paul *WhoScE 91-1*
Mayer, Peter Paul 1943- *WhoWor 93*
Mayer, Ralph 1952- *St&PR 93*
Mayer, Randi C. *Law&B 92*
Mayer, Raymond Richard 1924- *WhoAm 92*
Mayer, Rene 1895-1972 *BioIn 17*
Mayer, Richard Dean 1930- *WhoAm 92*
Mayer, Richard Edwin 1947- *WhoAm 92*
Mayer, Richard Frederick 1929- *WhoE 93*
Mayer, Richard Henry 1930- *WhoAm 92*
Mayer, Richard L. 1913- *St&PR 93*
Mayer, Richard Thomas 1945- *WhoSSW 93*
Mayer, Rick A. *Law&B 92*
Mayer, Robert 1879-1985 *Baker 92*
Mayer, Robert 1939- *ConAu 136, ScF&FL 92*
Mayer, Robert Anthony 1933- *WhoAm 92*
Mayer, Robert E., Jr. 1947- *St&PR 93*
Mayer, Robert M. 1922- *St&PR 93*
Mayer, Robert Wallace 1909- *WhoAm 92*
Mayer, Roland John *WhoScE 91-1*
Mayer, Ronald C. *Law&B 92*
Mayer, Simon 1763-1845 *IntDcOp*
Mayer, Stanley 1945- *St&PR 93*
Mayer, Steven Charles 1953- *WhoEmL 93*
Mayer, Steven M. *Law&B 92*
Mayer, Steven M. 1946- *WhoE 93*
Mayer, Susan M. *WhoWrEP 92*
Mayer, Sydney L. 1937- *WhoE 93*
Mayer, Thomas C. *Law&B 92*
Mayer, Vera 1927- *WhoAmW 93*
Mayer, Victor 1913- *WhoE 93*
Mayer, Victor James 1933- *WhoAm 92*
Mayer, (Benjamin) Wilhelm 1831-1898 *Baker 92*
Mayer, William Dixon 1928- *WhoAm 92*
Mayer, William E. 1940- *St&PR 93*
Mayer, William Emilio 1940- *WhoAm 92*
Mayer, William L. *WhoSSW 93*
Mayer, William (Robert) 1925- *Baker 92*
Mayer, Wolfgang Ulrich 1937- *WhoE 93*
Mayerhofer, James T. 1944- *St&PR 93*
Mayerhofer, James Thomas 1944- *WhoAm 92*
Mayerhoff, David Isak 1958- *WhoEmL 93*
Mayerik, Theresa Ann 1954- *WhoAmW 93*
Mayer-Koenig, Wolfgang 1946- *WhoWor 93*
Mayer-Kuckuk, Theo 1927- *WhoScE 91-3, WhoWor 93*
Mayer-Reece, Abigail *BioIn 17*
Mayers, Al 1960- *St&PR 93*
Mayers, Barbara Susan 1943- *WhoAmW 93*
Mayers, David 1936- *WhoAm 92*
Mayers, David Wm. 1916- *St&PR 93*
Mayers, Eugene David 1915- *WhoAm 92*
Mayers, Howard Alex 1946- *St&PR 93*
Mayers, Jean 1920- *WhoAm 92*
Mayers, Lawrence Michael 1935- *St&PR 93*
Mayers, Leonard Warren 1950- *St&PR 93*
Mayers, Stanley Penrose, Jr. 1926- *WhoAm 92*
Mayersberg, Paul 1941- *MiSFD 9*
Mayer-Serra, Otto 1904-1968 *Baker 92*
Mayersohn, Arnold Linn, Jr. 1955- *WhoAm 92*
Mayersohn, Robert Alan 1958- *St&PR 93*
Mayerson, Philip 1918- *WhoAm 92, WhoWrEP 92*
Mayes, Cheryl Darlene 1948- *WhoAmW 93*
Mayes, Frances *BioIn 17*
Mayes, Frank G. 1930- *St&PR 93, WhoAm 92*
Mayes, Helen 1918- *WhoSSW 93*
Mayes, Herbert R. 1900-1987 *BioIn 17*
Mayes, Jonathan O'Herbert *Law&B 92*
Mayes, Kathleen 1931- *WhoWrEP 92*
Mayes, Kathryn J. 1949- *St&PR 93*
Mayes, Lorene Anderson 1939- *WhoSSW 93, WhoWor 93*
Mayes, Maureen Davidica 1945- *WhoAmW 93*
Mayes, Paul Eugene 1928- *WhoAm 92*
Mayes, Phyllis L. *Law&B 92*
Mayes, Ralph Thomas, Jr. 1966- *WhoSSW 93*
Mayes, Roy, Jr. 1934- *St&PR 93*
Mayes, Samuel Houston 1917-1990 *BioIn 17*
Mayes, Wayne K. 1935- *St&PR 93*
Mayes, Wendell d1992 *NewYTBS 92*
Mayes, Wendell 1919-1992 *BioIn 17, ConAu 137, ConTFT 10*
Mayes, Wendell Wise, Jr. 1924- *WhoAm 92*
Mayeux, Sally Brown 1947- *WhoEmL 93*
Mayfair, Bertha *WhoWrEP 92*
Mayfarth, Frances McClelland 1901- *BioIn 17*
Mayfield, Bill 1838-1863 *BioIn 17*
Mayfield, Curtis 1942- *Baker 92, BioIn 17, ConMus 8 [port], SoulM*
Mayfield, Curtis Lee 1942- *WhoAm 92*
Mayfield, David Allen 1960- *WhoAm 92*
Mayfield, David Merkley 1942- *WhoAm 92*
Mayfield, Frank Henderson 1908-1991 *BioIn 17*
Mayfield, J. W. 1937- *WhoSSW 93*
Mayfield, John Emory 1937- *WhoSSW 93*
Mayfield, Josephine 1956- *WhoAmW 93*
Mayfield, Les *MiSFD 9*
Mayfield, Lori Jayne 1955- *WhoAmW 93, WhoEmL 93*
Mayfield, Mark Alan 1954- *WhoSSW 93*
Mayfield, MaryLynn 1923- *WhoAmW 93*
Mayfield, Melvin 1919-1990 *BioIn 17*
Mayfield, Peggy Jordan 1934- *WhoSSW 93*
Mayfield, Percy 1920-1984 *SoulM*
Mayfield, Richard Dean 1944- *WhoIns 93*
Mayfield, Richard Heverin 1921- *WhoAm 92*
Mayfield, Rita *WhoWrEP 92*
Mayfield, Robert Charles 1928- *WhoAm 92*
Mayfield, Sue 1963- *SmATA 72 [port]*
Mayfield, T. Brient, IV 1947- *WhoAm 92*
Mayfield, William Cary 1958- *WhoSSW 93*
Mayfield, William Stephen 1919- *WhoAm 92*
Maygarden, Jerry Louis 1948- *WhoSSW 93*
Mayhall, David 1938- *St&PR 93*
Mayhall, Dorothy Ann 1925- *WhoE 93*
Mayhall, Jane Francis 1922- *WhoWrEP 92*
Mayhall-Andrews, Florence Ann 1945- *WhoSSW 93*
Mayhar, Ardath 1930- *ScF&FL 92*
Mayher, Arnold J. 1919- *St&PR 93*
Mayher, Matt R. 1923- *St&PR 93*
Mayhew, Anne 1936- *WhoAmW 93*
Mayhew, Aubrey 1927- *WhoWor 93*
Mayhew, Bridget Mergens *BioIn 17*
Mayhew, David L. 1951- *St&PR 93*
Mayhew, David Raymond 1937- *WhoAm 92*
Mayhew, Elizabeth Whitehouse 1951- *WhoEmL 93*
Mayhew, Eric George 1938- *WhoE 93*
Mayhew, Experience 1673-1758 *BioIn 17*
Mayhew, Gary George 1936- *St&PR 93*
Mayhew, Harry Eugene 1933- *WhoAm 92*
Mayhew, Jonathan 1720-1766 *BioIn 17*
Mayhew, Kenneth E., Jr. 1934- *St&PR 93*
Mayhew, Kenneth Edwin, Jr. 1934- *WhoAm 92, WhoSSW 93*
Mayhew, Lawrence Lee 1933- *St&PR 93, WhoAm 92*
Mayhew, Linda S. 1939- *St&PR 93*
Mayhew, Mabel *AmWomPl*
Mayhew, Michael John Edward *WhoScE 91-1*
Mayhew, Patrick Barnabas Burke 1929- *WhoWor 93*
Mayhew, Shannon Jane 1965- *WhoE 93*
Mayhew, Terence Michael *WhoScE 91-1*
Mayhew, Vic *ScF&FL 92*
Mayhew, William E. 1942- *St&PR 93*
Mayhugh, Joel Ogden, Jr. 1941- *WhoSSW 93*
Ma Ying-Jeou 1950- *WhoAsAP 91*
Ma Yixi *BioIn 17*
Maykapar, Samuil 1867-1938 *Baker 92*
Maykus, Janet Lee 1962- *WhoAmW 93*
Maylam, Tony 1943- *MiSFD 9*
Mayland, Bertrand Jesse 1916- *WhoSSW 93*
Mayland, Kenneth T. 1951- *St&PR 93*
Mayland, Kenneth Theodore 1951- *WhoAm 92*
Maylath, Heinrich 1827-1883 *Baker 92*
Maylath, Sharon R. *Law&B 92*
Mayle, David R. *Law&B 92*
Mayle, Peter *BioIn 17*
Mayle, Peter 1939?- *ConAu 139, CurBio 92 [port]*
Mayle, Robert Edward 1938- *WhoAm 92*
Mayleas, William *ScF&FL 92*
Maylon, Gary Joseph 1949- *WhoSSW 93*
Maylor, Alan Ford 1935- *St&PR 93*
Mayman, Martin 1924- *WhoWrEP 92*
Maymi, Carmen 1938- *NotHsAW 93*
Maymon, Gilbert William 1927- *WhoE 93*
Maynadier, Alain De 1929- *St&PR 93*
Maynard, Alan *WhoScE 91-1*
Maynard, Allegra 1897-1991 *BioIn 17*
Maynard, Anna Morse 1920- *WhoE 93*
Maynard, Charles Douglas 1934- *WhoAm 92*
Maynard, Charles N. 1936- *St&PR 93*
Maynard, Clement 1928- *DcCPCAm*
Maynard, Clement T. *WhoWor 93*
Maynard, Cora *AmWomPl*
Maynard, Curtis G. 1922- *St&PR 93*
Maynard, David Benton 1951- *WhoSSW 93*
Maynard, David L. *Law&B 92*
Maynard, David W. 1943- *St&PR 93*
Maynard, Don 1937- *BioIn 17*
Maynard, Donald Nelson 1932- *WhoAm 92*
Maynard, Fredelle Bruser *BioIn 17*
Maynard, George Fleming, III 1947- *WhoEmL 93, WhoSSW 93*
Maynard, Gertrude *AmWomPl*
Maynard, James G. 1926- *St&PR 93*
Maynard, Joan 1932- *WhoAmW 93, WhoWor 93*
Maynard, Joe 1942- *ScF&FL 92*
Maynard, John Irwin 1954- *St&PR 93*
Maynard, John (Rogers) 1941- *ConAu 40NR, WhoAm 92*
Maynard, Joyce 1953- *BioIn 17*
Maynard, Ken 1895-1973 *BioIn 17*
Maynard, Kenneth Alan 1948- *St&PR 93*
Maynard, Kenneth Douglas 1931- *WhoAm 92*
Maynard, L.H. *ScF&FL 92*
Maynard, Lawrence Eugene 1955- *WhoSSW 93*
Maynard, Libby 1948- *WhoEmL 93*
Maynard, Marilyn Joan 1930- *WhoAmW 93*
Maynard, Michael Anthony 1953- *WhoE 93, WhoEmL 93, WhoWor 93*
Maynard, Nancy Gray 1941- *WhoAmW 93*
Maynard, Nancy Hicks 1946- *St&PR 93*
Maynard, Peter David 1950- *WhoEmL 93*
Maynard, Rex Alderman 1947- *St&PR 93*
Maynard, Richard 1926- *ScF&FL 92*
Maynard, Robert *BioIn 17*
Maynard, Robert C. 1937- *JrnUS*
Maynard, Robert Clyve 1937- *WhoAm 92, WhoWrEP 92*
Maynard, Robert Edgerton *WhoIns 93*
Maynard, Robert Edward, Jr. 1941- *St&PR 93*
Maynard, Ronald C. 1944- *St&PR 93*
Maynard, Virginia Madden 1924- *WhoAmW 93*
Mayne, Alfred P., Jr. 1947- *WhoE 93*
Mayne, David Quinn *WhoScE 91-1*
Mayne, David Ray 1943- *WhoE 93*
Mayne, Jasper 1604-1672 *DcLB 126*
Mayne, Lucille Stringer 1924- *WhoAm 92*
Mayne, Seymour 1944- *WhoCanL 92*
Mayne, William 1928- *BioIn 17, ChlFicS, ScF&FL 92, WhoAm 92*
Mayne, William (James Carter) 1928- *ConAu 37NR, MajAI [port]*
Maynes, Charles William 1938- *WhoAm 92*
Maynes, John L. *Law&B 92*
Maynes, Judith A. *Law&B 92*
Maynes, Leo P. 1937- *St&PR 93*
Maynes, Robert *Law&B 92*
Maynihan, Daniel P. 1927- *BioIn 17*
Maynor, Beth Pockman 1951- *WhoSSW 93*
Maynor, Dorothy (Leigh) 1910- *Baker 92*
Maynor, Harry D. *Law&B 92*
Mayo, Archie 1891-1968 *MiSFD 9N*
Mayo, Aryan R. 1926- *St&PR 93, WhoAm 92*
Mayo, Barry *BioIn 17*
Mayo, Clara Alexandra Weiss 1931-1981 *BioIn 17*
Mayo, Clark 1938- *ScF&FL 92*
Mayo, Clyde Calvin 1940- *WhoSSW 93*
Mayo, Eddie 1910- *BioIn 17*
Mayo, Eli 1933- *WhoWor 93*
Mayo, Frank 1889-1963 *BioIn 17*
Mayo, Frank Joseph 1948- *WhoEmL 93*
Mayo, Gary Robert 1955- *WhoE 93*
Mayo, George Douglas 1917- *WhoSSW 93*
Mayo, Gerald Edgar 1932- *St&PR 93, WhoAm 92, WhoIns 93*
Mayo, Gerald M. *Law&B 92*
Mayo, Hope *ScF&FL 92*
Mayo, James Otis 1920- *St&PR 93*
Mayo, Janice *BioIn 17*
Mayo, Janice Lynne 1952- *St&PR 93*

Mayo, Jim *ConAu 40NR*
Mayo, Jim 1908-1988 *BioIn 17*
Mayo, Joan Bradley 1942- *WhoAmW 93*
Mayo, John Sullivan 1930- *St&PR 93, WhoAm 92, WhoE 93*
Mayo, Joseph Anthony 1957- *WhoSSW 93*
Mayo, Leonard W. 1899-1992 *NewYTBS 92 [port]*
Mayo, Linda Faye 1954- *WhoAmW 93*
Mayo, Louis Allen 1928- *WhoE 93, WhoWor 93*
Mayo, Margaret 1882-1951 *AmWomPl*
Mayo, Martin 1967- *WhoE 93*
Mayo, Ofelia Marina *Law&B 92*
Mayo, Oliver 1942- *WhoWor 93*
Mayo, Pamela Elizabeth 1959- *WhoEmL 93*
Mayo, Payton Colquit 1926- *St&PR 93*
Mayo, Phyllis Jean 1950- *WhoEmL 93*
Mayo, R. Michael 1957- *WhoE 93*
Mayo, Ralph E. *Law&B 92*
Mayo, Renate Weidner 1948- *WhoAmW 93*
Mayo, Richard C. 1947- *St&PR 93*
Mayo, Robert Porter 1916- *WhoAm 92*
Mayo, Stephen I. 1952- *St&PR 93*
Mayo, Steven Waddell 1960- *WhoSSW 93*
Mayo, Virginia 1920- *SweetSg D [port]*
Mayo, Walker Porter 1922- *WhoSSW 93*
Mayo, Walter Allen 1959- *WhoSSW 93*
Mayo, Wayne 1939- *St&PR 93*
Mayock, Robert Lee 1917- *WhoAm 92*
Mayol, Hector M., Jr. 1950- *St&PR 93*
Mayol, Richard Thomas 1949- *WhoEmL 93*
Mayol, Robert Francis 1941- *WhoE 93*
Mayor, F.M. 1872-1932 *ScF&FL 92*
Mayor, Federico *BioIn 17*
Mayor, Federico 1934- *WhoUN 92*
Mayor, Heather Donald 1930- *WhoAm 92, WhoSSW 93*
Mayor, Richard Blair 1934- *WhoAm 92*
Mayor, Zaragoza *BioIn 17*
Mayora Dawe, Hector *DcCPCAm*
Mayoral, Ernesto *Law&B 92*
Mayoral, Marina 1942- *BioIn 17*
Mayoras, Donald Eugene 1939- *WhoAm 92*
Mayorga, Jose Bernardo 1944- *WhoWor 93*
Mayorga, Oscar Danilo 1949- *WhoSSW 93*
Mayorga, Silvio *DcCPCAm*
Mayor Zaragoza, Federico 1934- *WhoWor 93*
Mayo-Smith, Michael Fox 1953- *WhoE 93*
Mayotte, Tim *BioIn 17*
Maypole, John Floyd 1939- *St&PR 93, WhoAm 92*
Mayr, Dallas *ScF&FL 92*
Mayr, Ernst 1904- *WhoAm 92*
Mayr, Fritz W. 1925- *WhoScE 91-3*
Mayr, Herbert 1947- *WhoWor 93*
Mayr, Johann Simon 1763-1845 *OxDcOp*
Mayr, Peter 1938- *WhoScE 91-3*
Mayr, Richard 1877-1935 *Baker 92, OxDcOp*
Mayr, Simon 1763-1845 *IntDcOp*
Mayr, (Johannes) Simon 1763-1845 *Baker 92*
Mayr, Walter 1940- *WhoScE 91-3*
Mayrhofer-Grunbuhel, Ferdinand 1945- *WhoUN 92*
Mayrhofer-Krammel, Otto 1920- *WhoScE 91-4*
Mayrides, James J. 1942- *WhoUN 92*
Mayron, Melanie *BioIn 17*
Mayron, Melanie 1952- *ConTFT 10, WhoAm 92, WhoAmW 93*
Mayrose, William C. 1942- *St&PR 93*
Mays, A. Earl *Law&B 92*
Mays, Benjamin Elijah 1894-1984 *EncAACR*
Mays, Bowdre P. 1927- *St&PR 93*
Mays, Carl 1891-1971 *BioIn 17*
Mays, Charles A. 1939- *St&PR 93*
Mays, David *BioIn 17*
Mays, Elizabeth Blake 1958- *WhoAmW 93*
Mays, G.D. *WhoScE 91-1*
Mays, Geoffrey Charles *WhoScE 91-1*
Mays, Gerald Anthony 1935- *St&PR 93*
Mays, Gerald Avery 1939- *BiDAMSp 1989, WhoAm 92*
Mays, Jan F. 1938- *St&PR 93*
Mays, Janice Ann 1951- *WhoEmL 93*
Mays, John Hearn 1947- *St&PR 93*
Mays, John Robert 1961- *St&PR 93*
Mays, Joy *AmWomPl*
Mays, Kimberly *BioIn 17*
Mays, L. Lowry 1935- *WhoAm 92, WhoSSW 93*
Mays, Landis Rudolph 1932- *WhoSSW 93*
Mays, Norman Gerald, Jr. 1954- *St&PR 93*
Mays, Penny Sandra 1940- *WhoAmW 93*
Mays, Phillip T. *ScF&FL 92*
Mays, R.T. *Law&B 92*
Mays, Robert W. *BioIn 17*
Mays, Roy Mark 1915- *WhoAm 92*
Mays, Scott P. 1941- *St&PR 93*
Mays, William C., IV 1959- *WhoSSW 93*
Mays, William Gay, II 1947- *WhoEmL 93*
Mays, Willie 1931- *BioIn 17, ConBlB 3 [port]*
Mays, Willie Howard, Jr. 1931- *WhoAm 92*
Mayse, Arthur 1912- *WhoCanL 92*
Mayseder, Joseph 1789-1863 *Baker 92*
Maysent, Harold Wayne 1923- *WhoAm 92*
Maysilles, Elizabeth *WhoAmW 93*
Maysles, Albert 1926- *MiSFD 9*
Maysles, David 1932-1987 *MiSFD 9N*
Maystadt, Philippe 1948- *WhoWor 93*
Maystead, Suzanne Rae 1955- *WhoAmW 93*
Mayston, David John *WhoScE 91-1*
Maystre, Lucien Yves 1933- *WhoScE 91-4*
Maytag, Lewis B. 1926-1990 *BioIn 17*
Mayton, James L., Jr. 1943- *St&PR 93*
Mayton, Terrell Allen 1956- *WhoSSW 93*
Ma Yuan 14BC-49AD *HarEnMi*
Ma Yuhai *WhoAsAP 91*
Mayuzumi, Toshiro 1929- *Baker 92*
Maza, Penelope Lee 1946- *WhoEmL 93*
Mazaika, Robert J. 1934- *St&PR 93*
Mazaki, Jinsaburo 1876-1956 *HarEnMi*
Mazalov, Vladimir Viktorovich 1954- *WhoWor 93*
Mazanek, Eugeniusz 1939- *WhoScE 91-4*
Mazankowski, Donald Frank 1935- *WhoAm 92, WhoE 93, WhoWor 93*
Mazanowski, Adam 1933- *WhoScE 91-4*
Mazar, Adrian Emil 1958- *WhoEmL 93*
Mazar, Debi *BioIn 17*
Mazaraki-Baltsavia, Phedon 1932- *WhoWor 93*
Mazarakis, Michael Gerassimos *WhoWor 93*
Mazarin, Jules 1602-1661 *OxDcOp*
Mazaris fl. c. 1414-1415 *OxDcByz*
Mazars, Jacky 1946- *WhoScE 91-2*
Mazas, Jacques-Fereol 1782-1849 *Baker 92*
Mazdak c. 450-528? *OxDcByz*
Maze *SoulM*
Maze, James Ray 1950- *WhoEmL 93*
Mazeiko, Peter John 1952- *WhoEmL 93*
Mazek, Warren Felix 1938- *WhoAm 92*
Mazel, Joseph Lucas 1939- *WhoE 93*
Mazepa, Ivan Stepanovich 1640-1709 *PolBiDi*
Mazeppa, Ivan c. 1644-1709 *HarEnMi*
Mazer, Anne *BioIn 17*
Mazer, Edward Howard *Law&B 92*
Mazer, Harry 1925- *BioIn 17, MajAI [port]*
Mazer, Helen Cohen d1990 *BioIn 17*
Mazer, Jeffrey A. *Law&B 92*
Mazer, Lawrence F. *Law&B 92*
Mazer, Norma Fox 1931- *BioIn 17, DcAmChF 1960, DcAmChF 1985, MajAI [port], ScF&FL 92, WhoAm 92*
Mazer, Richard Neal *Law&B 92*
Mazer, Sherry 1953- *WhoE 93*
Mazeroff, Paul 1946- *WhoSSW 93*
Mazeski, Edward J., Jr. *Law&B 92*
Mazeski, Edward James, Jr. 1929- *St&PR 93, WhoAm 92*
Mazess, Richard B. 1939- *St&PR 93*
Ma Zhongchen 1936- *WhoAsAP 91*
Maziar, Harry 1934- *St&PR 93*
Maziarka, Stefan 1929- *WhoScE 91-4*
Mazidah Binti Hj Zakaria *WhoAsAP 91*
Mazie, Marvin E. 1930- *St&PR 93*
Mazie, Marvin Edward 1930- *WhoAm 92*
Maziejka, Edward Michael, Jr. 1959- *St&PR 93*
Mazieres, Charles M. 1920- *WhoScE 91-2*
Mazille, Henri M.J. 1941- *WhoScE 91-2*
Mazin, Joseph 1946- *St&PR 93*
Mazique, Robert J. *Law&B 92*
Mazjanis, Heather Campbell 1964- *WhoAmW 93*
Mazlen, Roger Geoffrey 1937- *WhoAm 92, WhoWor 93*
Mazliak, Paul 1936- *WhoScE 91-2*
Mazlish, Bruce 1923- *WhoAm 92, WhoWrEP 92*
Mazo, Earl 1919- *WhoAm 92*
Mazo, Juan Bautista Martinez del c. 1612-1667 *BioIn 17*
Mazo, Mark Elliott 1950- *WhoE 93, WhoEmL 93, WhoWor 93*
Mazo, Michael *MiSFD 9*
Mazo, Robert Marc 1930- *WhoAm 92*
Mazoff, Stephen Michael *Law&B 92*
Mazoh, Judith Anne *WhoE 93*
Mazol, Thomas George 1947- *WhoE 93, WhoEmL 93*
Mazou, Moussibahou Liamidi 1936- *WhoUN 92*
Mazow, Benjamin A. *Law&B 92*
Mazowiecki, Tadeusz *BioIn 17*
Mazowiecki, Tadeusz 1927- *ColdWar 2 [port], PolBiDi*
Mazrui, Ali A(l'Amin) 1933- *DcLB 125 [port]*
Mazrui, Ali Al'Amin 1933- *WhoAm 92, WhoWor 93*
Mazujian, David Aram 1960- *WhoEmL 93*
Mazur, Alicia 1963- *WhoAmW 93*
Mazur, Allan Carl 1939- *WhoAm 92*
Mazur, Arnold S. 1942- *St&PR 93*
Mazur, Bernice C. *St&PR 93*
Mazur, Edward *BioIn 17*
Mazur, Edward John, Jr. 1948- *WhoE 93, WhoEmL 93*
Mazur, Gail Beckwith 1937- *WhoWrEP 92*
Mazur, Jay J. *WhoAm 92*
Mazur, Joseph A. 1938- *St&PR 93*
Mazur, Kazimierz 1931- *WhoScE 91-4*
Mazur, Marilyn *BioIn 17*
Mazur, Marjorie Akers 1927- *WhoSSW 93*
Mazur, Mark Steven 1955- *WhoE 93*
Mazur, Matthew E. 1943- *St&PR 93*
Mazur, Meredith Margie Handley 1941- *WhoWor 93*
Mazur, Michael 1935- *WhoAm 92*
Mazur, Peter 1922- *WhoScE 91-3*
Mazur, Peter 1928- *WhoWor 93*
Mazur, Robert Andrew 1949- *WhoE 93*
Mazur, Stanislaw 1921- *WhoScE 91-4*
Mazur, Stella Mary 1923- *WhoAmW 93*
Mazur, Teofil 1927- *WhoScE 91-4*
Mazur, Tomasz 1953- *WhoScE 91-4*
Mazura, Franz 1924- *Baker 92*
Mazur-Baker, Deborah Joan 1958- *WhoEmL 93*
Mazurek, Jan 1931- *WhoScE 91-4*
Mazurek, Stephen M. 1931- *St&PR 93*
Mazurki, Mike 1909-1990 *BioIn 17*
Mazurkiewicz, Boleslaw K. 1931- *WhoScE 91-4*
Mazurkiewicz, Carolyn 1948- *St&PR 93*
Mazurkiewicz, Jan 1871-1947 *PolBiDi*
Mazurkiewicz, Stanislaw B. 1937- *WhoScE 91-4*
Mazurok, Yury 1931- *OxDcOp*
Mazurov, Anatoly Afanasjevich 1955- *WhoWor 93*
Mazurov, Victor Danilovich 1943- *WhoWor 93*
Mazursky, Paul *BioIn 17*
Mazursky, Paul 1930- *MiSFD 9, WhoAm 92*
Mazutis, Juris 1940- *WhoWrEP 92*
Mazyck, Reaven Elaine 1954- *WhoE 93*
Mazza, Arlene Joan 1944- *WhoAmW 93*
Mazza, Barbara Boland 1955- *WhoSSW 93*
Mazza, Christine Elaine 1952- *WhoEmL 93*
Mazza, Cosmo 1966- *WhoE 93*
Mazza, Don 1949- *St&PR 93*
Mazza, John Gamble 1945- *St&PR 93*
Mazza, L. 1937- *WhoScE 91-3*
Mazza, Maurice 1935- *WhoScE 91-2*
Mazza, Michael J. *Law&B 92*
Mazza, Richard J. *Law&B 92*
Mazza, Terilyn McGovern 1952- *WhoEmL 93*
Mazzacane, John Royal 1940- *WhoE 93*
Mazzacurati, Carlo 1956- *MiSFD 9*
Mazzaferri, Ernest Louis 1936- *WhoAm 92*
Mazzaferri, Katherine Aquino 1947- *WhoAm 92*
Mazzaglia, Alfio Joseph 1932- *WhoE 93*
Mazzara, Marie Dorothy 1936- *WhoAmW 93*
Mazzarella, Andrew J. 1950- *St&PR 93*
Mazzarese, Joseph M. *Law&B 92*
Mazzarese, Michael Louis 1941- *WhoE 93*
Mazzaro, Jerome Louis 1934- *WhoWrEP 92*
Mazzaschi, Anthony Joseph 1955- *WhoE 93*
Mazze, Edward Mark 1941- *WhoAm 92*
Mazze, Roger Steven 1943- *WhoAm 92*
Mazzei, Augustine A., Jr. *Law&B 92*
Mazzei, Augustine Anthony, Jr. 1936- *St&PR 93, WhoAm 92*
Mazzei, Jo Ann 1963- *WhoAmW 93*
Mazzei, Lapo 1925- *WhoWor 93*
Mazzella, Lauren Weilburg *Law&B 92*
Mazzella, Mary Jo *BioIn 17*
Mazzeo, Henry 1909?-1980? *ScF&FL 92*
Mazzeo-Merkle, Linda L. 1947- *WhoAmW 93, WhoWor 93*
Mazzi, Fiorenzo 1924- *WhoScE 91-3*
Mazzia, Valentino Don Bosco 1922- *WhoAm 92*
Mazzie, Sandra Anne 1951- *WhoE 93, WhoEmL 93*
Mazzilli, Paul John 1948- *WhoAm 92*
Mazzinghi, Joseph 1765-1844 *Baker 92, OxDcOp*
Mazzini, Giuseppe 1805-1872 *BioIn 17*
Mazziotti, Richard 1941- *St&PR 93*
Mazziotti, Thomas *MiSFD 9*
Mazzo, Kay 1946- *WhoAm 92*
Mazzocchi, Domenico 1592?-1665 *Baker 92, OxDcOp*
Mazzocchi, Virgilio 1597?-1646 *Baker 92, OxDcOp*
Mazzocco, Angelo 1936- *WhoE 93*
Mazzocco, Reynold Anthony 1957- *St&PR 93*
Mazzola, Anthony Thomas 1923- *WhoAm 92, WhoE 93*
Mazzola, Christian Larsen 1939- *St&PR 93*
Mazzola, Claude Joseph 1936- *WhoE 93*
Mazzola, Domenica 1940- *WhoAmW 93*
Mazzola, Frank *MiSFD 9*
Mazzola, John William 1928- *WhoAm 92*
Mazzolal, Michael *St&PR 93*
Mazzolani, Antonio 1819-1900 *Baker 92*
Mazzoleni, Ettore 1905-1968 *Baker 92*
Mazzoli, Antoinette M. 1937- *St&PR 93*
Mazzoli, Romano L. 1932- *CngDr 91*
Mazzoli, Romano Louis 1932- *WhoAm 92, WhoSSW 93*
Mazzone, A. David 1928- *WhoE 93*
Mazzone, James Vincent 1938- *WhoE 93*
Mazzone, Mark Carl 1947- *St&PR 93*
Mazzoni, B.C. *St&PR 93*
Mazzoni, Michael James 1946- *WhoAm 92*
Mazzorana, Edward C. 1932- *St&PR 93*
Mazzotta, Dorothy 1935- *St&PR 93*
Mazzotta, Giuseppe 1942- *ConAu 37NR*
Mazzotta, Robert J. 1954- *St&PR 93*
Mazzotti, Joan C. *Law&B 92*
Mazzuca, Marc-Pierre *WhoScE 91-2*
Mazzuca, Robin Lynn 1958- *WhoAmW 93, WhoEmL 93*
Mazzucato, Alberto 1813-1877 *Baker 92*
Mazzucchelli, Louis Joseph, Jr. 1956- *WhoE 93*
Mazzucchetti, G. *WhoScE 91-3*
Mazzucelli, Colette Grace 1962- *WhoE 93*
Mazzuki, Michael Robert 1960- *WhoE 93*
Mba Allo, Emmanuel 1948- *WhoUN 92*
Mbanefo, Monica Nkechi 1948- *WhoUN 92*
Mbaya, Robert B. *WhoUN 92*
Mbaye, Marietou (Bileoma) 1948- *ConAu 139*
Mbayen, Rene 1943- *WhoWor 93*
Mbeki, Thabo Mvuyelwa 1942- *WhoAfr*
Mbele-Mbong, Samuel 1942- *WhoUN 92*
Mbella Mbappe, Robert 1937- *WhoAfr*
Mbodj, Samba 1948- *WhoUN 92*
Mbonimpa, Cyprien 1946- *WhoAfr, WhoWor 93*
Mbonu, Faith Janerette 1943- *WhoAmW 93*
Mboya, Benedict John 1949- *WhoUN 92*
Mboya, Tom 1926-1969 *DcTwHis*
M.C. Hammer *BioIn 17*
MC5, The *ConMus 9 [port]*
McAbee, Cheryl Rosilyn *Law&B 92*
McAbee, Dorothy Reading 1963- *WhoE 93*
McAbee, Jeffrey Deane 1957- *WhoEmL 93, WhoSSW 93*
McAbee, Myra Wilson *Law&B 92*
McAbee, Robin 1956- *WhoEmL 93*
McAbee, Thomas Allen 1949- *WhoEmL 93, WhoSSW 93*
McAbeer, Sara Carita 1906- *WhoAmW 93*
McAboy, Thomas Hatfield 1930- *WhoAm 92*
McAdam, Constance Rollison 1930- *WhoAmW 93*
McAdam, Robert Crandall 1935- *St&PR 93*
McAdam, Will 1921- *WhoAm 92, WhoE 93*
McAdams, Brian 1942- *WhoAm 92*
McAdams, David d1992 *NewYTBS 92*
McAdams, David 1931- *WhoUN 92*
McAdams, Donald Ray 1941- *WhoSSW 93*
McAdams, Herbert H., II 1915- *St&PR 93*
McAdams, Herbert Hall, II 1915- *WhoAm 92*
McAdams, John A. 1942- *WhoAm 92*
Mc Adams, John Michael 1952- *WhoSSW 93*
McAdams, Leonard I. 1943- *St&PR 93*
McAdams, M.A. 1944- *St&PR 93*
McAdams, Melinda Jeanne 1959- *WhoEmL 93*
McAdams, Richard S. 1945- *St&PR 93*
McAdams, Robert, Jr. 1939- *St&PR 93, WhoAm 92*
Mc Adams, Ronald Earl 1910- *WhoAm 92*
McAdoo, William G. 1863-1941 *PolPar*
McAdorey, Hugh Joseph *Law&B 92*
McAfee, Alexander 1927- *St&PR 93*
McAfee, Arthur J. *BioIn 17*
McAfee, Barbara Boyd 1957- *WhoSSW 93*
McAfee, Donald A. 1941- *St&PR 93*
McAfee, Donald R. *St&PR 93*
McAfee, George 1918?- *BioIn 17*
McAfee, Gerald Brent 1935- *WhoSSW 93*

McAfee, Horace J. 1905- *WhoAm 92*
McAfee, Ila 1897?- *BioIn 17*
McAfee, James T., Jr. 1939- *St&PR 93*
Mc Afee, Jerry 1916- *WhoAm 92*
McAfee, John Gilmour 1926- *WhoAm 92*
Mc Afee, Joyce Janine 1958- *WhoEmL 93*
McAfee, Larry *BioIn 17*
McAfee, Lawrance Wiley 1955- *WhoAm 92*
McAfee, Naomi Jones 1934- *WhoE 93*
McAfee, Paul 1948- *St&PR 93*
McAfee, Robert, Jr. 1937- *WhoAm 92*
McAfee, Rosa Thompson 1953- *WhoAmW 93*
Mc Afee, Virginia Thurston 1950- *WhoWrEP 92*
Mc Afee, William 1910- *WhoAm 92*
McAfee, William Gage 1943- *WhoWor 93*
McAhren, Robert Willard 1935- *WhoAm 92*
McAinsh, K.G. *WhoScE 91-1*
McAlary, Mike *BioIn 17*
Mcalduff, John D. 1930- *St&PR 93*
McAlduff, John Daniel 1930- *WhoAm 92*
McAlear, Robert T. 1942- *St&PR 93*
Mc Aleavey, David Willard 1946- *WhoWrEP 92*
McAleavey, Gerald P. 1935- *St&PR 93*
Mc Aleece, Donald John 1918- *WhoAm 92*
Mcaleer, Howard J. 1915- *St&PR 93*
McAleer, John Joseph 1923- *WhoE 93*
McAleer, Joseph Patrick 1929- *St&PR 93*
McAleer, Kevin William 1950- *St&PR 93, WhoAm 92*
McAleer, Neil 1942- *ScF&FL 92*
McAleer, Robert J. *St&PR 93*
McAleese, Desmond M. 1928- *WhoScE 91-3*
McAleese, Mary Patricia 1951- *WhoWor 93*
Mc Alester, Arcie Lee, Jr. 1933- *WhoAm 92, WhoSSW 93*
McAlester, Virginia Savage 1943- *WhoAm 92*
McAlevey, John Francis 1923- *WhoE 93*
McAlexander, Alvis Lemuel 1922- *WhoSSW 93*
McAlexander, Gary A. 1944- *St&PR 93*
McAlexander, Hubert Horton 1939- *WhoSSW 93*
McAlinden, Joseph J. 1943- *St&PR 93*
McAlindon, Mary Naomi 1935- *WhoAmW 93*
McAliskey, Bernadette Devlin 1947- *BioIn 17*
McAlister, Alexander 1920-1987 *WhoCanL 92*
McAlister, Daniel K. *Law&B 92*
McAlister, Daniel K. 1938- *St&PR 93*
McAlister, E. Elmo, Jr. 1939- *WhoAm 92*
McAlister, Harold Alister 1949- *WhoSSW 93*
McAlister, Kyle Ross 1967- *WhoSSW 93*
Mc Alister, Linda Lopez 1939- *WhoAmW 93*
McAlister, Mark Dean 1952- *WhoEmL 93*
McAlister, Robert Beaton 1932- *WhoAm 92*
McAlister, Sidney Stinson 1924- *St&PR 93*
Mc Alister, Thomas Allen 1948- *WhoWrEP 92*
McAll, Christopher 1948- *ConAu 137*
McAllan, Robert Edward 1946- *St&PR 93*
McAllaster, Claudia 1952- *WhoEmL 93*
McAllester, David (Park) 1916- *Baker 92*
McAllister, Angus *ScF&FL 92*
McAllister, Annie Laurie *ScF&FL 92*
McAllister, Bruce 1946- *ScF&FL 92*
McAllister, Chris *BioIn 17*
McAllister, Claude Huntley, Jr. 1930- *WhoSSW 93*
McAllister, Constance Smith *Law&B 92*
McAllister, Dale Eugene *Law&B 92*
McAllister, Don 1934- *ScF&FL 92*
McAllister, Donal G. 1930- *St&PR 93*
McAllister, Donald 1902- *St&PR 93*
McAllister, Francis R. 1942- *St&PR 93*
McAllister, Francis Ralph 1942- *WhoAm 92*
McAllister, Gene Robert 1930- *St&PR 93*
Mc Allister, Gerald Nicholas 1923- *WhoAm 92*
McAllister, Helen Lydia Seibold 1936- *WhoAmW 93*
McAllister, J. Garry 1947- *St&PR 93*
McAllister, J. Gilbert 1904- *IntDcAn*
McAllister, James Charles 1954- *WhoEmL 93*
McAllister, John David 1949- *WhoE 93*
McAllister, John H. 1927- *St&PR 93*
Mc Allister, Joseph Charles 1928- *WhoWor 93*
Mc Allister, Kenneth D. 1943- *WhoSSW 93*
McAllister, Kenneth W. *Law&B 92*
McAllister, Kenneth W. 1949- *St&PR 93*
McAllister, Maria Sheridan 1960- *WhoAmW 93*
McAllister, Marialuisa Nicosia 1933- *WhoAmW 93*
McAllister, Marie 1947- *WhoAmW 93*
McAllister, Michael Flynn *Law&B 92*
McAllister, Nancy Hardacre 1940- *WhoAmW 93*
McAllister, Neill d1991 *BioIn 17*
McAllister, Patricia B. 1939- *St&PR 93*
McAllister, Paul Robert 1952- *WhoE 93*
McAllister, Robert Cowden 1940- *St&PR 93, WhoAm 92*
McAllister, Robert H. *Law&B 92*
McAllister, Robert H. 1916- *St&PR 93*
McAllister, Russell Greenway, Jr. 1941- *WhoSSW 93*
McAllister, Terrence J. *Law&B 92*
McAllister, Thomas Grear 1937- *WhoSSW 93*
McAllister, Ward 1827-1895 *GayN*
McAllister, William Howard, III 1941- *WhoAm 92*
McAllister, William Middleton 1933- *WhoAm 92*
McAllister-Black, Randi Clay 1951- *WhoAmW 93*
McAlmon, Robert 1896-1956 *BioIn 17*
McAlonan, John Patrick *Law&B 92*
McAlpin, Kenneth *St&PR 93*
McAlpin, Kirk Martin 1923- *WhoAm 92*
McAlpine, Mark L. 1956- *WhoEmL 93*
McAlpine, Stephen A. 1949- *WhoWor 93*
McAlpine, William Ray 1931- *St&PR 93*
McAlpine of West Green, Baron 1942- *BioIn 17*
McAmis, Edwin Earl 1934- *WhoAm 92, WhoWor 93*
McAmis, Robert Wood 1962- *WhoSSW 93*
Mc Anally, Don 1913- *WhoWrEP 92*
Mcanally, Mary E(llen) 1939- *WhoWrEP 92*
McAnaney, Brian T. *Law&B 92*
McAnaney, Francis Aloysius, Jr. *Law&B 92*
McAnaney, Patrick 1954- *WhoEmL 93*
McAndrew, Michael Kenneth 1948- *WhoEmL 93*
McAndrew, Thomas Francis 1931- *WhoUN 92*
Mc Andrews, Anita Grosvenor 1924- *WhoWrEP 92*
McAndrews, James Patrick 1929- *WhoAm 92*
McAndrews, John P. 1925- *St&PR 93*
McAndrews, Phillip James 1950- *St&PR 93*
McAndrews, Thomas *BioIn 17*
McAnelly, Elaine Simpson *Law&B 92*
McAnelly, W. James, Jr. *Law&B 92*
McAneny, Eileen Susan *Law&B 92*
McAninch, Barbara A. *Law&B 92*
McAninch, Harold D. 1933- *WhoAm 92*
Mc Aninch, Robert Danford 1942- *WhoSSW 93*
McAnuff, Des 1952- *WhoAm 92*
Mc Anulty, Henry Joseph 1915- *WhoAm 92*
Mc Anulty, Mary Catherine Cramer 1908- *WhoAmW 93*
McAnulty, Thomas 1942- *WhoE 93*
McAra, Cam *BioIn 17*
McArdle, Allan B. 1917- *St&PR 93*
Mcardle, Francis T. *St&PR 93*
McArdle, Frank Brian 1946- *WhoE 93, WhoEmL 93*
McArdle, John Edward 1928- *St&PR 93*
McArdle, John J. 1928- *St&PR 93*
McArdle, John Walter 1946- *WhoWor 93*
McArdle, Joseph Withrow 1941- *St&PR 93*
McArdle, Maureen *Law&B 92*
McArdle, Paul Francis 1918- *WhoAm 92*
McArdle, Richard Joseph 1934- *WhoAm 92*
McAree, D.T. 1944- *WhoScE 91-3*
Mc Arthur, Barbara Jean *WhoWrEP 92*
McArthur, Charles 1895-1956 *JrnUS*
McArthur, Charlton Bryan 1937- *St&PR 93*
McArthur, Clovis W. *Law&B 92*
McArthur, Edwin 1907-1987 *Baker 92*
Mc Arthur, George 1924- *WhoAm 92*
McArthur, J. William *Law&B 92*
Mc Arthur, Janet Ward 1914- *WhoAm 92, WhoE 93*
McArthur, John Hector 1934- *WhoAm 92*
McArthur, John William, Jr. 1955- *WhoEmL 93, WhoSSW 93*
McArthur, Joseph B. 1928- *St&PR 93*
McArthur, Nancy *ScF&FL 92*
McArthur, Peter 1866-1924 *BioIn 17*
McArthur, Robert Paul 1944- *WhoE 93*
McArthur, Sara Dee 1948- *WhoEmL 93*
McArthur, Sara Reed 1944- *WhoAmW 93*
McArthur, Stewart 1937- *WhoAsAP 91*
McArthur, Victoria Holloway 1949- *WhoSSW 93*
McArthur, William 1809-1887 *BioIn 17*
McArthur, William Duncan, Jr. 1940- *WhoSSW 93*
McArtor, Allan 1942- *WhoAm 92*
McAtee, Charles Patrick 1955- *WhoE 93*
McAtee, James C. 1944- *St&PR 93*
McAtee, James Wayne 1945- *St&PR 93, WhoAm 92*
McAtee, Patricia Anne Rooney 1931- *WhoAm 92, WhoAmW 93*
McAteer, Bernie 1936-1990 *BioIn 17*
McAteer, Deborah Grace 1950- *WhoAmW 93*
McAteer, John Joseph 1920- *St&PR 93*
McAulay, George *ScF&FL 92*
McAulay, Jeffrey J. 1953- *St&PR 93*
McAulay, Jeffrey John 1953- *WhoEmL 93*
McAulay, Louise Salzman 1940- *WhoAmW 93*
Mc Aulay, Sara W. 1940- *WhoWrEP 92*
McAuley, Catherine 1786-1841 *BioIn 17*
Mcauley, Charles G. 1950- *St&PR 93*
McAuley, Joanne Elaine 1932- *WhoAmW 93, WhoSSW 93, WhoWor 93*
McAuley, John P. 1952- *WhoIns 93*
Mc Auley, John Thomas 1939- *St&PR 93*
McAuley, Kathleen Anne 1951- *WhoEmL 93*
Mc Auley, Milton Kenneth 1919- *WhoWrEP 92*
Mcauley, Patrick J. 1923- *St&PR 93*
McAuley, Paul J. 1955- *ScF&FL 92*
McAuley, Thomas Joseph 1949- *WhoEmL 93*
McAuliffe, C.A. *WhoScE 91-1*
McAuliffe, Charles Henry *Law&B 92*
McAuliffe, Christa *BioIn 17*
McAuliffe, Clayton Doyle 1918- *WhoAm 92*
McAuliffe, David John 1924- *St&PR 93*
McAuliffe, Dennis Philip 1922- *WhoAm 92*
McAuliffe, Eugene Vincent 1918- *WhoE 93*
Mc Auliffe, Frank Malachi 1926- *WhoWrEP 92*
McAuliffe, James R. 1944- *St&PR 93*
McAuliffe, James Robert 1944- *WhoIns 93*
Mc Auliffe, John 1943- *WhoAm 92*
McAuliffe, John F. 1932- *WhoAm 92*
McAuliffe, Joseph Shevlin *Law&B 92*
Mc Auliffe, Michael F. 1920- *WhoAm 92*
McAurther, John 1934- *St&PR 93*
McAuslan, John Patrick William Buchanan *WhoScE 91-1*
McAuslan, Mary Elizabeth Kane 1955- *WhoEmL 93*
McAusland, Randolph M. 1934- *WhoE 93*
McAvaddy, John Patrick 1966- *WhoE 93*
McAviney, Donald *Law&B 92*
McAvity, John Gillis 1950- *WhoAm 92*
McAvoy, Bruce Ronald 1933- *WhoAm 92*
McAvoy, David R. *Law&B 92*
McAvoy, Don L. 1942- *St&PR 93*
McAvoy, James Edward 1955- *WhoAm 92*
Mc Avoy, Katherine Turner 1925- *WhoWrEP 92*
McAvoy, Kenneth 1951- *WhoAm 92*
McAvoy, Thomas James *WhoAm 92, WhoE 93*
Mc Avoy, William Charles 1921- *WhoWrEP 92*
McAward, Patrick J., Jr. 1934- *St&PR 93*
McAward, Patrick Joseph, Jr. 1934- *WhoAm 92*
McBain, Ed *ConAu 38NR, ScF&FL 92, WhoWrEP 92*
McBain, Ed 1926- *BioIn 17*
McBain, Gordon 1946-1992 *ScF&FL 92*
McBain, Robert Mark 1946- *WhoEmL 93*
Mcbane, Alan R. 1938- *St&PR 93*
McBarnette, Bruce *Law&B 92*
McBath, Donald Linus 1935- *WhoSSW 93*
McBay, Arthur John 1919- *WhoAm 92, WhoSSW 93*
McBean, Angus 1904-1990 *BioIn 17*
McBeath, Andrew Alan 1936- *WhoAm 92*
Mc Beath, William Henninger 1931- *WhoAm 92*
McBee, Barbara Lynn 1954- *WhoAmW 93*
McBee, Barry Ross 1956- *WhoEmL 93*
Mc Bee, Denis 1952- *WhoWrEP 92*
McBee, Frank W., Jr. 1920- *St&PR 93*
McBee, Frank Wilkins, Jr. 1920- *WhoAm 92, WhoSSW 93*
McBee, Janice Beth 1959- *WhoSSW 93*
McBee, Lillian De Simone 1953- *WhoAmW 93*
McBee, Mary Louise 1924- *WhoAmW 93*
McBee, Susanna Barnes 1935- *WhoWor 93*
McBennett, Robert J. 1942- *St&PR 93*
McBennett, Robert Joseph 1942- *WhoAm 92*
McBeth, Robert D. 1940- *St&PR 93*
McBeth, W. Francis *BioIn 17*
McBirney, Martita 1951- *WhoAmW 93*
McBrady, William J. 1931- *St&PR 93*
Mc Brand, Quinten *WhoWrEP 92*
McBratney, Sam *ChlFicS, ScF&FL 92*
McBratnie, Wanda Teresa 1930- *WhoAmW 93*
McBrayer, James Franklin 1941- *WhoSSW 93*
McBrayer, Staley T. *BioIn 17*
Mc Brearty, Robert Garner 1954- *WhoWrEP 92*
McBrian, Andrew Kimbel 1954- *WhoE 93*
McBride, Angela Barron 1941- *WhoAmW 93*
McBride, Barry Clarke 1940- *WhoAm 92*
McBride, Beverly Jean *Law&B 92*
McBride, Cindy 1953- *St&PR 93*
McBride, Daniel A. 1922- *St&PR 93*
McBride, David J. *Law&B 92*
McBride, Dennis Raymond 1953- *WhoEmL 93*
McBride, Donald M. 1938- *St&PR 93*
McBride, Douglas J. *Law&B 92*
McBride, Edwin S. 1926- *St&PR 93*
McBride, Elissa *BioIn 17*
McBride, Elizabeth Anne 1933- *WhoAmW 93*
Mc Bride, Ella Andrepont 1919- *WhoWrEP 92*
Mc Bride, Guy Thornton, Jr. 1919- *WhoAm 92*
McBride, H. Colin *Law&B 92*
McBride, H. T. 1916- *WhoAm 92*
McBride, J.M. *WhoScE 91-3*
McBride, James Charles 1943- *St&PR 93, WhoAm 92*
McBride, James E. 1911- *St&PR 93*
McBride, Jim 1941- *MiSFD 9*
Mc Bride, John Alexander 1918- *WhoAm 92*
McBride, John Cormie, Jr. *Law&B 92*
McBride, John Hyatt 1938- *St&PR 93*
McBride, Jonathan Evans 1942- *WhoAm 92*
McBride, Joseph A. 1919- *St&PR 93*
McBride, Joyce Browning 1927- *WhoAmW 93*
McBride, Judith Bliss 1959- *WhoEmL 93*
McBride, Kenneth Eugene 1948- *WhoEmL 93, WhoWor 93*
McBride, Lori *Law&B 92*
McBride, Mary Fletcher 1927- *WhoSSW 93*
McBride, Michael F. *Law&B 92*
McBride, Michael R. 1955- *WhoEmL 93*
McBride, Milford L., Jr. 1923- *St&PR 93*
McBride, Milford Lawrence, Jr. 1923- *WhoWor 93*
McBride, Murray Brian 1948- *WhoAm 92*
McBride, Paul Wilbert 1940- *WhoE 93*
Mcbride, Peter David 1949- *St&PR 93*
Mc Bride, Raymond Andrew 1927- *WhoAm 92*
McBride, Richard A. 1958- *St&PR 93*
McBride, Robert Cooke *Law&B 92*
Mc Bride, Robert Dana 1927- *WhoAm 92*
McBride, Robert (Guyn) 1911- *Baker 92*
McBride, Robert John 1931- *St&PR 93*
McBride, Robert Terrence 1935- *WhoAm 92*
McBride, Rodney Lester 1941- *WhoAm 92, WhoE 93*
McBride, Stephen Paul 1957- *WhoAm 92*
McBride, Steven Randall 1954- *WhoWor 93*
McBride, Terry W. 1942- *St&PR 93*
McBride, Thomas Francis 1935- *St&PR 93*
Mc Bride, Thomas Frederick 1929- *WhoAm 92*
McBride, William Bernard 1931- *WhoAm 92*
Mc Bride, William Leon 1938- *WhoAm 92*
McBride, William T. 1938- *St&PR 93*
McBride-Jones, Jacqueline Rae 1950- *WhoAmW 93*
McBrien, John Robert 1944- *WhoE 93*
McBrien, Richard P. *BioIn 17*
McBrien, Richard Peter 1936- *WhoAm 92*
McBrierty, Vincent Joseph 1941- *WhoScE 91-3*
McBroom, Jeffrey Lynn Woodard 1957- *WhoSSW 93*
McBroom, John K. 1907- *St&PR 93*
Mc Broom, Mary Catherine 1923- *WhoWrEP 92*
Mcbroom, Mary J. 1913- *St&PR 93*
McBroom, Nancy Lee 1925- *WhoAmW 93*
McBroom, Thomas William 1963- *WhoSSW 93*
McBroom, Victoria Marie *Law&B 92*
McBryan, John Paul 1948- *St&PR 93*
McBryde, Carolyn Sue 1948- *WhoAmW 93*

Mc Bryde, Felix Webster 1908- *WhoAm 92, WhoE 93, WhoWor 93*
McBryde, John Henry 1931- *WhoAm 92, WhoSSW 93*
Mcbryde, Michael P. 1945- *St&PR 93*
McBryde, Neill Gregory 1944- *WhoAm 92*
McBryde, Sarah Elva 1942- *WhoE 93*
McBryde, Vincent 1941- *St&PR 93*
McBurney, Andrew M. 1913-1991 *BioIn 17*
McBurney, Andrew Marvell 1913- *St&PR 93, WhoAm 92*
McBurney, Elizabeth Innes 1944- *WhoSSW 93*
McBurney, George William 1926- *WhoAm 92*
McBurney, Linda Lee 1942- *WhoAmW 93*
McBurney, Margot B. *WhoAm 92, WhoAmW 93*
McBurney, Mark E. *Law&B 92*
McBurney, Mary Zaniewski 1952- *WhoAmW 93*
McBurney, Venita Rich *AmWomPl*
McCaa, M. D. 1965- *WhoAmW 93*
McCabe, Anderson L. 1955- *St&PR 93*
McCabe, Beverly Jean 1942- *WhoSSW 93*
McCabe, Brooks Fleming, Jr. 1949- *WhoSSW 93*
McCabe, Charles Henry, Jr. 1937- *WhoAm 92*
McCabe, Charles Law 1922- *WhoAm 92*
McCabe, Charles Thomas 1950- *WhoE 93*
McCabe, Dennis P. *WhoSSW 93*
McCabe, Donald G. 1933- *St&PR 93*
McCabe, Dorothy E. *Law&B 92*
McCabe, Edward Aeneas 1917- *WhoAm 92*
McCabe, Edward Arthur *BioIn 17*
McCabe, Edward Arthur 1938- *WhoAm 92*
McCabe, Edward Francis, III 1942- *WhoE 93*
McCabe, Esther B. *AmWomPl*
McCabe, Frank Lacey 1943- *WhoAm 92, WhoE 93*
McCabe, Fred *BioIn 17*
McCabe, Gary Franke 1945- *WhoWor 93*
Mc Cabe, Gerard Benedict 1930- *WhoAm 92*
McCabe, Gwendolyn Leola 1927- *WhoAmW 93*
McCabe, Harriet A. *AmWomPl*
McCabe, Hazel G. *AmWomPl*
McCabe, James E. 1937- *St&PR 93*
McCabe, James Edward *Law&B 92*
McCabe, James Freeland, Jr. 1950- *WhoE 93*
McCabe, James J. 1929- *WhoAm 92*
McCabe, James Patrick 1937- *WhoE 93*
McCabe, Jean Marie 1952- *WhoAmW 93*
McCabe, Joan Yanish 1955- *WhoAmW 93, WhoEmL 93*
McCabe, John 1939- *Baker 92, BioIn 17, OxDcOp*
Mc Cabe, John Charles, III 1920- *WhoWrEP 92*
McCabe, John F. *Law&B 92*
McCabe, John Henry 1947- *St&PR 93*
McCabe, Joseph P. 1948- *St&PR 93*
McCabe, Joseph V., Jr. *Law&B 92*
McCabe, Kevin Francis 1959- *WhoEmL 93*
McCabe, Lance C. 1949- *St&PR 93*
McCabe, Laurence Jerome 1930- *St&PR 93*
McCabe, Lawrence E. *St&PR 93*
McCabe, Lawrence J. *Law&B 92*
McCabe, Lawrence J. 1935- *St&PR 93*
McCabe, Lawrence James 1935- *WhoAm 92*
McCabe, Louise Marie 1957- *WhoEmL 93*
McCabe, Mary Beth 1957- *WhoAmW 93*
McCabe, Mary Otillia Sorg 1934- *WhoAmW 93*
McCabe, Mary Williamson 1934- *WhoAmW 93*
McCabe, Michael J. *Law&B 92*
McCabe, Michael J. 1945- *WhoAm 92*
McCabe, Michael James 1957- *WhoEmL 93*
McCabe, Regina Kay 1956- *WhoEmL 93*
McCabe, Robert *Law&B 92*
McCabe, Robert Albert 1914- *WhoAm 92*
McCabe, Robert F., Jr. 1936- *St&PR 93*
McCabe, Robert Howard 1929- *WhoSSW 93*
McCabe, Robert Owen 1952- *WhoEmL 93*
Mccabe, Roger J. 1944- *St&PR 93*
McCabe, St. Clair Landerkin 1915- *St&PR 93*
McCabe, Thomas A. *BioIn 17*
McCabe, Thomas Bayard 1893-1982 *BioIn 17*
McCabe, Thomas J., Jr. *Law&B 92*
Mccabe, Thomas R. 1945- *St&PR 93*
McCabe, Timothy Patrick 1957- *St&PR 93*
McCabe, Verne L. 1948- *St&PR 93*
Mc Cabe, Victoria 1948- *WhoWrEP 92*
McCabe, Vincent J. 1927- *WhoScE 91-3*
McCachran, Marshall Thomas 1948- *WhoEmL 93*
McCachren, Jo Renee 1955- *WhoAmW 93, WhoEmL 93*
McCadam, Paul Rutherford 1948- *WhoIns 93*
McCaffer, Ronald *WhoScE 91-1*
McCafferty, Barbara Jean 1940- *WhoAmW 93*
McCafferty, Barbara Taylor 1946- *WhoSSW 93, WhoWrEP 92*
McCafferty, Charles T. 1934- *St&PR 93*
McCafferty, James Arthur 1926- *WhoE 93, WhoWor 93*
McCafferty, John Martin 1956- *WhoEmL 93*
McCafferty, Michael Gilbert 1938- *WhoAm 92*
McCafferty, Sarah 1954- *WhoEmL 93*
McCafferty, William 1938- *St&PR 93, WhoAm 92*
McCaffery, Larry 1946- *ScF&FL 92*
McCaffery, Lawrence F. *ScF&FL 92*
McCaffery, Lloyd *BioIn 17*
McCaffery, Steve 1947- *WhoCanL 92*
McCaffery, Thomas F., III *Law&B 92*
McCaffree, Burnham Clough, Jr. 1931- *WhoAm 92*
McCaffree, Donald Robert 1943- *WhoSSW 93*
McCaffrey, Anne *BioIn 17*
McCaffrey, Anne 1926- *DcAmChF 1960, ScF&FL 92, SmATA 70 [port]*
McCaffrey, Anne (Inez) 1926- *MajAI [port], WhoAm 92*
McCaffrey, Barry *BioIn 17*
McCaffrey, Barry Richard 1942- *WhoAm 92*
McCaffrey, Brian 1953- *WhoEmL 93*
McCaffrey, Candace Sue 1954- *WhoAmW 93*
McCaffrey, Carlyn Sundberg 1942- *WhoAmW 93*
McCaffrey, Carol Suzanne 1936- *WhoAmW 93*
McCaffrey, Daniel Vincent 1946- *WhoSSW 93*
McCaffrey, Deborah 1941- *WhoE 93*
McCaffrey, Donna Therese 1949- *WhoAmW 93, WhoE 93*
McCaffrey, Edward Michael, Jr. 1958- *WhoE 93*
McCaffrey, James P. *St&PR 93*
McCaffrey, John Anthony 1944- *WhoE 93*
McCaffrey, John P. 1935- *St&PR 93*
McCaffrey, Judith Elizabeth 1944- *St&PR 93, WhoAm 92*
McCaffrey, Kevin J. *Law&B 92*
McCaffrey, Mark Robert 1953- *St&PR 93*
McCaffrey, Neil 1925- *WhoAm 92*
McCaffrey, Robert H. 1927- *St&PR 93*
McCaffrey, Robert Henry, Jr. 1927- *WhoAm 92*
McCaffrey, Shaun Matthew *Law&B 92*
McCaffrey, Shellyn Gae 1957- *WhoAm 92, WhoAmW 93*
McCaffrey, Stephen W. *Law&B 92*
McCaffrey, Thomas Joseph 1960- *WhoEmL 93*
McCaffrey, Thomas M. *Law&B 92*
McCaffrey, Thomas Michael 1933- *St&PR 93*
Mc Caffrey, Thomas R. *WhoAm 92*
McCaffrey, Timothy T. *Law&B 92*
McCaffrey, Timothy T. 1939- *WhoIns 93*
Mccaffrey, William T. 1936- *St&PR 93*
McCaffrey, William Thomas 1936- *WhoAm 92*
McCaghren, Marty Don 1953- *WhoEmL 93, WhoSSW 93*
McCaghy, Charles Henry 1934- *WhoAm 92*
McCague, William L., II *Law&B 92*
McCague, William Langan, II 1945- *St&PR 93*
McCahey, Jeanne *WhoWrEP 92*
McCahill, Barry Winslow 1947- *WhoE 93*
McCaig, Charles George 1943- *St&PR 93*
McCaig, Donald *ScF&FL 92*
McCaig, Jeffery James 1951- *WhoAm 92*
McCaig, John Robert 1929- *St&PR 93, WhoAm 92*
McCaig, Joseph John 1944- *St&PR 93*
McCaige, Daniel L. 1940- *St&PR 93*
McCain, Betty Landon Ray 1931- *WhoAmW 93*
McCain, Carter Braxton 1963- *WhoEmL 93, WhoSSW 93*
McCain, George Wallace F. 1930- *WhoAm 92*
McCain, Harrison *BioIn 17*
McCain, John 1936- *CngDr 91*
McCain, John Burns 1937- *St&PR 93*
McCain, John L. 1927- *St&PR 93*
McCain, John S. 1936- *BioIn 17*
McCain, John Sidney 1884-1945 *HarEnMi*
McCain, John Sidney, III 1936- *WhoAm 92*
McCain, Linn H., III *Law&B 92*
Mc Cain, Maurice Edward 1909- *WhoSSW 93*
Mccain, Richard *St&PR 93*
McCain, Robert G. *Law&B 92*
McCain, Russell P. 1927- *St&PR 93*
McCain, Steven E. *Law&B 92*
McCain, Taryn-Marie *Law&B 92*
McCain, Warren Earl 1925- *St&PR 93*
McCain, William B. 1931- *St&PR 93*
McCairns, Regina Carfagno 1951- *WhoAmW 93, WhoEmL 93*
McCaleb, Michael Lyle 1953- *WhoE 93*
Mccalendon, Zach 1937- *St&PR 93*
McCalister, Cheryl Kaye 1968- *WhoAmW 93*
Mc Call, Abner Vernon 1915- *WhoAm 92*
McCall, Albert Burr 1929- *St&PR 93*
McCall, Alvin A., Jr. 1927- *ConEn, St&PR 93*
McCall, Betty Ann 1948- *WhoAmW 93*
McCall, Billy Gene 1928- *WhoAm 92*
McCall, Bruce P. G. *WhoAm 92*
McCall, Candace Smith 1947- *WhoWor 93*
Mc Call, Charles Barnard 1928- *WhoAm 92*
McCall, Clyde Samuel, Jr. 1931- *WhoSSW 93*
McCall, Colleen Joy *Law&B 92*
McCall, Daniel Thompson, Jr. 1909- *WhoAm 92, WhoSSW 93*
McCall, David W. 1928- *WhoAm 92*
McCall, Debra Laurette Hansford 1958- *WhoEmL 93*
McCall, Donald Lee 1932- *St&PR 93*
McCall, Dorothy Kay 1948- *WhoAmW 93, WhoEmL 93, WhoWor 93*
McCall, Douglas Mark 1951- *WhoEmL 93*
McCall, Duke Kimbrough 1914- *WhoAm 92*
McCall, E.W. 1913- *St&PR 93*
McCall, Frederick C., Jr. *Law&B 92*
McCall, George Aloysius 1939- *WhoIns 93*
McCall, H. Carl *BioIn 17*
Mc Call, Hobby Halbert 1919- *WhoWor 93*
McCall, Howard W., Jr. 1907- *St&PR 93*
Mccall, J.A. 1947- *St&PR 93*
McCall, James Franklin 1934- *AfrAmBi [port]*
McCall, James Levonsky 1927- *WhoSSW 93*
Mc Call, Jerry Chalmers 1927- *WhoAm 92*
McCall, John 1850?-1877 *BioIn 17*
McCall, John Anthony 1940- *WhoAm 92*
McCall, John Patrick 1927- *WhoAm 92*
McCall, John Richard 1943- *WhoAm 92*
McCall, Judith Tate 1944- *WhoSSW 93*
McCall, Julien L. 1921- *St&PR 93*
Mc Call, Julien Lachicotte 1921- *WhoAm 92*
McCall, Kevin M. *Law&B 92*
McCall, Linda Combs *WhoAmW 93, WhoSSW 93*
McCall, Linda Rae 1947- *WhoAmW 93*
McCall, Louise Harrup 1925- *WhoAmW 93*
McCall, Loyd Henry, Jr. 1927- *WhoSSW 93*
Mccall, Mabel Bunny 1923- *WhoWrEP 92*
McCall, Michael John *WhoScE 91-1*
McCall, Raymond J. 1913-1990 *BioIn 17*
McCall, Rex C. *Law&B 92*
McCall, Robert 1919- *BioIn 17*
Mc Call, Robert R. 1926- *WhoAm 92*
McCall, Rod *MiSFD 9*
McCall, Ronald Leon 1941- *St&PR 93*
McCall, Russell Lowell 1945- *WhoSSW 93, WhoWor 93*
McCall, Stuart Allan 1946- *WhoEmL 93*
McCall, Thomas A. 1950- *WhoIns 93*
McCall, Thomas E. 1916-1965 *BioIn 17*
McCall, Virginia Nielsen 1909- *ConAu 39NR*
McCall, W. Calder 1906- *St&PR 93*
McCall, W. Kent 1940- *St&PR 93*
McCall, William Calder 1906- *WhoAm 92*
McCall, William Frank *BioIn 17*
McCalla, Alexander Frederick 1937- *WhoAm 92*
McCalla, Gary E. *BioIn 17*
McCalla, Gary Edward 1931- *WhoAm 92, WhoWrEP 92*
McCalla, James 1946- *Baker 92*
McCalla, Jan 1935- *WhoAmW 93*
McCalla, John F. 1941- *St&PR 93*
McCalla, Mary Elizabeth Hartson 1922- *WhoAmW 93*
McCalla, Sandra Ann 1939- *WhoAmW 93, WhoSSW 93*
McCalla, William James 1943- *WhoAm 92*
McCalley, Robert Bruce, Jr. 1922- *WhoE 93*
McCalley-Whitters, Mona Kay 1956- *WhoEmL 93*
McCallie, S. Wyatt *Law&B 92*
McCallin, John C. 1946- *WhoUN 92*
McCallion, Hazel *WhoAmW 93*
McCallion, James 1918-1991 *BioIn 17*
McCallion, John James 1932- *WhoAm 92*
McCallion, Michele 1964- *WhoAmW 93*
McCallion, R.J. *WhoScE 91-3*
McCallister, J. Wilson *Law&B 92*
McCallister, Larry Dwayne 1955- *WhoE 93*
McCallister, Mark Anthony *Law&B 92*
McCallon, John Louis 1965- *WhoSSW 93*
McCall-Simpson, Mary Muyelinda 1963- *WhoAmW 93, WhoEmL 93*
McCall Smith, Alexander 1948- *SmATA 73*
McCall-Torrence, Merry Lyn 1955- *WhoSSW 93*
McCallum, Bennett Tarlton 1935- *WhoAm 92*
Mc Callum, Charles Alexander 1925- *WhoAm 92, WhoSSW 93*
Mc Callum, Charles Edward 1939- *WhoAm 92*
Mc Callum, David 1933- *WhoAm 92*
McCallum, Dean Ames *Law&B 92*
McCallum, Francis A. 1917- *WhoAm 92*
Mccallum, Fred J., Jr. *Law&B 92*
McCallum, G.W. 1945- *St&PR 93*
McCallum, Ian A.C. 1936- *St&PR 93*
McCallum, Jack 1949- *BioIn 17*
McCallum, James Scott 1950- *WhoAm 92*
McCallum, Jason *BioIn 17*
McCallum, Kenneth James 1918- *WhoAm 92*
McCallum, Louise 1947- *St&PR 93*
Mccallum, Richard Dee 1936- *St&PR 93*
McCallum, Richard Warwick 1945- *WhoAm 92*
McCally, Charles Richard 1958- *WhoWor 93*
McCally, Russell Lee 1940- *WhoE 93*
McCalment, Maebelle *AmWomPl*
McCalmon, Jeffrey Alan 1955- *WhoEmL 93*
McCaman, Marilyn Wales 1928- *WhoAmW 93*
McCambridge, John James 1933- *WhoAm 92*
McCambridge, Mercedes 1918- *IntDcF 2-3 [port], WhoAm 92*
Mc Cameron, Fritz Allen 1929- *WhoAm 92*
McCamish, Larry O. *Law&B 92*
McCammon, Catherine Ann 1957- *WhoWor 93*
McCammon, David N. 1934- *St&PR 93*
Mc Cammon, David Noel 1934- *WhoAm 92*
McCammon, James Andrew 1947- *WhoAm 92*
McCammon, Phillip R. *Law&B 92*
McCammon, Robert R. *BioIn 17*
McCammon, Robert R. 1952- *ScF&FL 92*
McCammon, Robert R(ick) 1952- *ConAu 40NR*
McCampbell, David 1910- *BioIn 17*
McCamus, David R. *BioIn 17*
Mc Camy, James Lucian 1906- *WhoAm 92*
McCamy, Sam C. 1930- *St&PR 93*
Mccamy, W.R. 1930- *St&PR 93*
McCance, William 1894-1970 *BioIn 17*
McCandless, Alfred A. 1927- *CngDr 91, WhoAm 92*
Mc Candless, Anna Loomis 1897- *WhoAmW 93*
McCandless, Barbara J. 1931- *WhoAmW 93*
McCandless, Brian *BioIn 17*
Mc Candless, Bruce, II 1937- *WhoAm 92*
McCandless, Carolyn Keller 1945- *St&PR 93, WhoAm 92, WhoAmW 93*
McCandless, George T., Jr. 1947- *ConAu 139*
McCandless, Jane Bardarah 1925- *WhoE 93*
McCandless, Stephen Porter 1941- *WhoAm 92*
McCandless, William Howard, Jr. 1955- *WhoE 93*
McCane, Stephen Todd 1954- *WhoSSW 93*
McCanles, Michael Frederick 1936- *WhoAm 92*
McCanless, R. William *Law&B 92*
McCann, Anthony F. 1940- *St&PR 93*
McCann, Barbara Marie 1931- *WhoSSW 93*
McCann, Cecil Vincent, III 1962- *WhoEmL 93*

Mc Cann, Cecile Nelken *WhoAm 92, WhoWrEP 92*
McCann, Charles Paul 1954- *WhoE 93*
McCann, Christine Marie-Schmidt 1962- *WhoAmW 93*
McCann, Clarence David, Jr. 1948- *WhoAm 92*
McCann, Colleen Mary 1964- *WhoAmW 93*
McCann, D. Michael *Law&B 92*
Mccann, David A. 1929- *St&PR 93*
McCann, David DeWitt 1943- *WhoAm 92*
McCann, David M. 1939-1991 *BioIn 17*
McCann, David Stewart 1945- *WhoE 93*
McCann, Dean Merton 1927- *WhoAm 92*
McCann, Donald V. 1934- *St&PR 93*
McCann, Edson *ConAu 37NR*
McCann, Edward 1943- *WhoAm 92, WhoE 93*
McCann, Elizabeth Ireland 1931- *WhoAm 92*
Mc Cann, Frances Veronica 1927- *WhoAm 92, WhoAmW 93*
McCann, George McDonald *WhoScE 91-1*
McCann, Gerald R. 1950- *WhoAm 92, WhoE 93*
McCann, James P. 1930- *WhoAm 92*
McCann, Janet 1942- *WhoWrEP 92*
McCann, John Francis 1937- *WhoAm 92*
McCann, John Giles 1950- *WhoSSW 93*
Mc Cann, John Joseph 1937- *WhoAm 92*
Mccann, John Patrick 1944- *St&PR 93*
McCann, Joseph A. *Law&B 92*
McCann, Joseph J., Jr. *Law&B 92*
McCann, Joseph John, Jr. 1939- *WhoAm 92*
McCann, Kenneth R. *Law&B 92*
McCann, Louise Mary 1949- *WhoAmW 93*
McCann, Mark Thomas 1962- *WhoSSW 93*
McCann, Mary Cheri 1956- *WhoAmW 93*
McCann, Maurice Joseph 1950- *WhoEmL 93, WhoWor 93*
McCann, Michael F. 1943- *WhoE 93, WhoWrEP 92*
McCann, Owen Cardinal 1907- *WhoWor 93*
McCann, Philip Patrick *Law&B 92*
Mccann, R. Keith 1949- *St&PR 93*
McCann, Raymond C. *Law&B 92*
Mccann, Raymond Joseph 1934- *St&PR 93*
McCann, Robin April 1956- *WhoAmW 93*
Mc Cann, Samuel McDonald 1925- *WhoAm 92*
McCann, Taylor Lee 1943- *WhoIns 93*
McCann, Terence D. *Law&B 92*
Mccann, Thomas J. 1937- *St&PR 93*
McCann, Timothy C. *Law&B 92*
McCann, Walter Joseph 1937- *WhoWor 93*
McCann, William Vern, Jr. 1943- *WhoAm 92*
Mccanna, William Joseph 1940- *St&PR 93*
Mccanne, William G. 1939- *St&PR 93*
McCanney, James Michael 1948- *WhoEmL 93*
McCannon, Dindga 1947- *BlkAuII 92*
McCanny, John Vincent *WhoScE 91-1*
McCanse-Adkins, Anne Marie Adams 1954- *WhoAmW 93*
McCants, David Arnold 1937- *WhoAm 92*
McCants, Keith *BioIn 17*
McCants, Zauditu Esther 1944- *WhoAmW 93*
McCard, Harold Kenneth 1931- *WhoAm 92*
McCardell, James Elton 1931- *WhoAm 92*
McCardell, John Malcolm, Jr. 1949- *WhoAm 92*
McCardell, Robert A. d1992 *BioIn 17*
Mccardle, Thomas F. 1932- *St&PR 93*
McCarey, Leo 1898-1969 *MiSFD 9N*
McCarey, Peter 1956- *ConAu 138*
McCarey, Wilma R. *Law&B 92*
McCargar, James (Goodrich) 1920- *ConAu 137, WhoE 93, WhoWor 93*
McCargar, Susan Elaine 1945- *WhoAmW 93*
Mccarl, Foster James 1947- *St&PR 93*
McCarl, Henry N. 1941- *WhoSSW 93*
McCarl, Howard H., Jr. *Law&B 92*
McCarl, Howard Hinds, Jr. 1948- *WhoSSW 93*
Mccarley, Bobby Joe 1928- *St&PR 93*
Mccarley, Joe Bruce 1931- *St&PR 93*
Mccarley, Kenneth Wayne 1942- *St&PR 93*
Mccarley, Kyle Wade 1957- *St&PR 93*
McCarley, Robert William 1937- *WhoE 93*
McCarley, Thomas David 1942- *WhoSSW 93*
Mccarragher, Bernard John 1927- *St&PR 93, WhoAm 92*
McCarran, Patrick A. 1876-1954 *EncABHB 8 [port], PolPar*
McCarrel, Daniel J. *Law&B 92*
McCarrell, Vicki Lammers 1951- *WhoAmW 93*
McCarrey, Cordell *Law&B 92*
McCarrick, Martin *See* Siouxsie and the Banshees *ConMus 8*
Mc Carrick, Theodore Edgar 1930- *WhoAm 92, WhoE 93*
McCarrison, Robert 1878-1960 *BioIn 17*
Mc Carriston, Linda 1943- *WhoWrEP 92*
Mccarroll, John R. 1940- *St&PR 93*
McCarroll, John R., Jr. *Law&B 92*
McCarroll, Kathleen Ann 1948- *WhoAmW 93*
McCarroll, Michael Arthur 1938- *WhoWor 93*
Mccarroll, Michael Vincent 1952- *St&PR 93*
McCarroll, Patrick J. *Law&B 92*
McCarroll, William Henry 1930- *WhoE 93*
Mccarron, James *St&PR 93*
McCarron, John Francis 1949- *WhoAm 92*
Mccarron, John R. 1940- *St&PR 93*
McCarron, Paul J. 1933- *WhoE 93*
McCarron, Robert Andrew 1949- *WhoE 93*
McCarron, Robert Frederick, II 1952- *WhoSSW 93*
McCarron, Sandra Simon 1946- *WhoSSW 93*
McCarry, Charles *BioIn 17*
McCarry, Charles Eugene 1956- *WhoEmL 93*
Mccart, Harold Franklin, Jr. 1938- *St&PR 93*
McCart, Jack Frederick, Jr. 1956- *WhoSSW 93*
McCartan, Lucy 1942- *WhoAmW 93*
McCarten, William Weisel 1948- *WhoAm 92*
McCarter, Charles Chase 1926- *WhoAm 92*
Mccarter, Craig A. 1945- *St&PR 93*
Mccarter, Gary 1936- *St&PR 93*
Mc Carter, John Alexander 1918- *WhoAm 92*
Mccarter, John Walter 1950- *St&PR 93*
Mccarter, John Wilbur, Jr. 1938- *St&PR 93, WhoAm 92*
McCarter, Lloyd G. 1917-1956 *BioIn 17*
McCarter, Lowell Harold *Law&B 92*
McCarter, Pete Kyle, Jr. 1945- *WhoAm 92*
McCarter, Peter N. *Law&B 92*
McCarter, Rus Larry 1940- *WhoSSW 93*
Mc Carter, Thomas N., III 1929- *WhoAm 92, WhoE 93*
McCarter, William J., Jr. 1929- *WhoAm 92*
Mccarthey, Thomas Kearns 1950- *St&PR 93*
McCarthy, Albert Henry 1944- *WhoE 93*
McCarthy, Andrew C. *Law&B 92*
McCarthy, Anne Marie 1958- *WhoAmW 93*
McCarthy, Anne Sibille 1949- *WhoAmW 93*
McCarthy, Barry Wayne 1943- *WhoE 93*
McCarthy, Bea 1935- *WhoAmW 93*
McCarthy, Bill *BioIn 17*
Mccarthy, Burkley F. 1930- *St&PR 93*
McCarthy, Carol A. *Law&B 92*
McCarthy, Carol M. 1940- *WhoAm 92*
McCarthy, Catherine Frances 1921- *WhoAmW 93*
Mc Carthy, Charles Joseph 1907- *WhoAm 92*
McCarthy, Charles Justin 1937- *WhoAm 92*
Mccarthy, Charles R., Jr. 1938- *St&PR 93*
McCarthy, Christopher M. *Law&B 92*
McCarthy, Clement Daniel 1933- *WhoAm 92*
McCarthy, Colman *BioIn 17*
McCarthy, Cormac *NewYTBS 92*
McCarthy, Cormac 1933- *BioIn 17, MagSAmL [port]*
Mc Carthy, D. Justin *WhoAm 92*
Mccarthy, D.M. 1962- *St&PR 93*
Mccarthy, Daniel C. 1924- *St&PR 93*
Mc Carthy, Daniel Christopher, Jr. 1924- *WhoAm 92*
Mccarthy, Daniel F. 1944- *St&PR 93*
McCarthy, Daniel J. *Law&B 92*
McCarthy, Daniel William 1952- *WhoE 93*
Mc Carthy, David Jerome, Jr. 1935- *WhoAm 92*
Mc Carthy, Denis Michael 1942- *WhoAm 92*
McCarthy, Denise Eileen 1941- *WhoAmW 93*
McCarthy, Dennis Michael 1944- *WhoSSW 93*
Mc Carthy, Dennis Michael 1952- *WhoSSW 93*
McCarthy, Dianne Elizabeth 1957- *WhoEmL 93*
McCarthy, Donal F. *Law&B 92*
Mccarthy, Donald Wans 1922- *St&PR 93*
McCarthy, Ed d1990 *BioIn 17*
Mc Carthy, Edward, Jr. 1931- *WhoSSW 93*
McCarthy, Edward Anthony 1918- *WhoAm 92, WhoSSW 93*
McCarthy, Edward C. *Law&B 92*
McCarthy, Edward David, Jr. 1955- *WhoE 93, WhoEmL 93*
Mccarthy, Edwward Joseph 1942- *St&PR 93*
McCarthy, Eugene J. 1916- *BioIn 17, ColdWar 1 [port], PolPar*
Mccarthy, Eugene John 1938- *St&PR 93*
Mc Carthy, Eugene Joseph 1916- *WhoAm 92, WhoWrEP 92*
McCarthy, Francis Barry 1946- *WhoEmL 93*
Mccarthy, Francis Xavier 1952- *St&PR 93*
McCarthy, Frank A. *Law&B 92*
McCarthy, Frank A., Jr. 1953- *St&PR 93*
Mc Carthy, Frank Martin 1924- *WhoAm 92*
McCarthy, Frederick William 1941- *WhoE 93*
Mccarthy, G.D. *St&PR 93*
McCarthy, G. Daniel *Law&B 92*
McCarthy, G. Daniel 1949- *WhoAm 92*
McCarthy, G. Doane 1914-1991 *BioIn 17*
McCarthy, Gerald M. 1941- *St&PR 93*
McCarthy, Gerald Michael 1941- *WhoAm 92*
McCarthy, Gerald Patrick 1943- *WhoSSW 93*
McCarthy, Gerald T. 1909-1990 *BioIn 17*
McCarthy, Grace *BioIn 17*
McCarthy, Grace Dietrich *AmWomPl*
McCarthy, H. Vincent 1936- *WhoScE 91-3*
McCarthy, Harold C. 1926- *WhoIns 93*
Mc Carthy, Harold Charles 1926- *WhoAm 92*
McCarthy, Helen H. *WhoAmW 93*
McCarthy, Hugh T. *Law&B 92*
McCarthy, Ian Ellery 1930- *WhoWor 93*
McCarthy, Iris 1947- *WhoAmW 93*
McCarthy, J. Thomas 1937- *WhoAm 92*
McCarthy, J.V. *WhoScE 91-3*
Mccarthy, Jack D. 1943- *St&PR 93*
McCarthy, James A. 1927- *St&PR 93*
McCarthy, James Jadidi 1965- *WhoE 93*
McCarthy, James Joseph 1944- *WhoAm 92, WhoE 93*
McCarthy, James P. 1935- *WhoAm 92*
McCarthy, James S. 1941- *St&PR 93*
McCarthy, James W. *Law&B 92*
McCarthy, Jerome F. 1907- *St&PR 93*
McCarthy, John *BioIn 17*
McCarthy, John 1927- *WhoAm 92*
McCarthy, John Connell 1952- *WhoEmL 93*
McCarthy, John Donald 1935- *St&PR 93*
Mc Carthy, John Edward 1930- *WhoAm 92, WhoSSW 93*
McCarthy, John J. *BioIn 17*
Mc Carthy, John Michael 1927- *WhoAm 92*
McCarthy, John Michael 1946- *St&PR 93*
McCarthy, John Patrick 1921- *WhoE 93*
McCarthy, John R. *St&PR 93*
McCarthy, John Robert 1945- *WhoE 93*
McCarthy, John Thomas 1939- *WhoAm 92, WhoWor 93*
McCarthy, John Timothy 1945- *St&PR 93*
McCarthy, Joseph F. *Law&B 92*
McCarthy, Joseph Gerald 1938- *WhoAm 92*
McCarthy, Joseph Harold 1921- *St&PR 93, WhoAm 92*
McCarthy, Joseph Justin 1949- *WhoE 93*
Mc Carthy, Joseph Michael 1940- *WhoAm 92, WhoE 93*
McCarthy, Joseph R. 1908-1957 *PolPar*
McCarthy, Joseph R. 1909-1957 *ColdWar 1 [port]*
McCarthy, Joseph Raymond 1908-1957 *DcTwHis*
McCarthy, Justin Milton 1924- *WhoE 93*
McCarthy, Justin V. d1991 *BioIn 17*
McCarthy, Kathleen D. 1949- *WhoE 93*
Mc Carthy, Kathryn A. 1924- *WhoAm 92, WhoAmW 93*
McCarthy, Kathryn O'Laughlin 1894-1952 *BioIn 17*
McCarthy, Kevin *BioIn 17*
McCarthy, Kevin 1947- *WhoWor 93*
McCarthy, Kevin A. 1957- *St&PR 93*
Mc Carthy, Kevin Michael 1940- *WhoWrEP 92*
McCarthy, Kevin Patrick 1954- *WhoIns 93*
McCarthy, Kevin Paul 1957- *WhoE 93*
McCarthy, Leo Tarcisius 1930- *WhoAm 92*
McCarthy, Margaret William 1931- *WhoAmW 93, WhoE 93*
McCarthy, Marie d1992 *NewYTBS 92*
McCarthy, Marietta Dian *WhoAmW 93*
McCarthy, Marija Pavlovich *BioIn 17*
McCarthy, Marina Chukayeff 1950- *WhoEmL 93*
McCarthy, Martha May 1945- *WhoAmW 93*
McCarthy, Mary 1912-1989 *BioIn 17, MagSAmL [port]*
McCarthy, Mary Abigail d1990 *BioIn 17*
McCarthy, Mary Kay 1960- *WhoAmW 93*
McCarthy, Mary Lynn 1950- *WhoAm 92, WhoEmL 93*
McCarthy, Mary McCloskey 1923- *WhoAmW 93*
McCarthy, Mary Pat 1963- *WhoAmW 93*
McCarthy, Mary Viterbo 1920- *WhoAmW 93*
McCarthy, Matthew F. 1938- *WhoScE 91-3*
McCarthy, Matthew M. *WhoAm 92*
McCarthy, Matthew M. 1947- *St&PR 93*
McCarthy, Matthew Mills *Law&B 92*
McCarthy, Michael 1937- *St&PR 93*
McCarthy, Michael A. *Law&B 92*
McCarthy, Michael Anthony 1934- *WhoAm 92*
McCarthy, Michael Edward Smythe 1951- *WhoEmL 93*
McCarthy, Michael F. *Law&B 92*
McCarthy, Michael Gerard 1962- *WhoEmL 93*
McCarthy, Michael Joseph *Law&B 92*
Mccarthy, Michael Joseph 1944- *St&PR 93*
McCarthy, Michael P. *Law&B 92*
McCarthy, Michael W. 1941- *St&PR 93*
McCarthy, Mignon *ConAu 138*
McCarthy, Nancy *BioIn 17*
McCarthy, Nobu *WhoAm 92*
McCarthy, Patrice Ann 1957- *WhoEmL 93*
Mc Carthy, Patricia Margaret 1943- *WhoAmW 93*
McCarthy, Patrick A. 1945- *ScF&FL 92, WhoAm 92*
Mc Carthy, Patrick Edward 1930- *WhoAm 92*
McCarthy, Patrick Francis 1901- *WhoAm 92*
McCarthy, Patrick Michael 1936- *St&PR 93*
McCarthy, Paul 1956- *WhoEmL 93*
McCarthy, Paul Fenton 1934- *WhoAm 92*
McCarthy, Paul James 1924- *WhoE 93*
McCarthy, Paul V. *Law&B 92*
McCarthy, Paul W. 1951- *St&PR 93*
McCarthy, Peter John 1943- *St&PR 93*
McCarthy, Raymond Joseph, Jr. *Law&B 92*
McCarthy, Raymond Lawrence 1920- *WhoE 93*
McCarthy, Raymond M. 1927-1989 *BioIn 17*
McCarthy, Richard 1942- *WhoScE 91-3*
McCarthy, Richard, IV 1965- *WhoSSW 93*
McCarthy, Robert E. 1949- *WhoE 93*
McCarthy, Robert E., Jr. 1931- *St&PR 93*
McCarthy, Robert Emmett 1951- *WhoEmL 93*
McCarthy, Robert John *Law&B 92*
McCarthy, Robert John 1953- *WhoEmL 93*
McCarthy, Roger L. 1948- *St&PR 93*
Mccarthy, Ronald L. 1933- *St&PR 93*
Mc Carthy, Rosemary P. 1928- *WhoWrEP 92*
McCarthy, Sean A. *Law&B 92*
McCarthy, Shawna 1954- *ScF&FL 92*
McCarthy, Sherri Lynn 1958- *WhoSSW 93*
McCarthy, Stephen A. d1990 *BioIn 17*
McCarthy, Susan Mulcahy *Law&B 92*
McCarthy, Susan Stacy 1962- *WhoE 93*
McCarthy, Thomas J. *Law&B 92*
McCarthy, Thomas J., Jr. 1932- *WhoIns 93*
Mc Carthy, Thomas James 1941- *WhoAm 92*
Mc Carthy, Thomas Patrick 1928- *WhoAm 92*
McCarthy, Thomas Patrick 1954- *WhoEmL 93*
McCarthy, Timothy A. *Law&B 92*
McCarthy, Timothy F. *Law&B 92*
McCarthy, Timothy Francis 1951- *WhoE 93*
McCarthy, Vern I., Jr. 1927- *St&PR 93*
McCarthy, Vincent Paul 1940- *WhoAm 92*

McCarthy, Walter John, Jr. 1925- *St&PR 93, WhoAm 92*
McCarthy, Wil 1966- *ScF&FL 92*
McCarthy, William d1990 *BioIn 17*
McCarthy, William J. 1919- *WhoAm 92*
McCarthy, William J. 1938- *St&PR 93*
McCarthy, William Joseph *Law&B 92*
McCartin, William Robert 1928- *St&PR 93*
McCartney, Alison Caroline Elliott 1950- *WhoWor 93*
McCartney, Allen Papin 1940- *WhoAm 92*
McCartney, B.S. *WhoScE 91-1*
McCartney, Bill *BioIn 17*
McCartney, Carol A. *Law&B 92*
McCartney, Charles Price 1912- *WhoAm 92*
McCartney, Christine Maye 1949- *WhoEmL 93*
McCartney, Daniel Patrick 1951- *St&PR 93*
Mc Cartney, Dorothy Wilson 1914- *WhoWrEP 92*
McCartney, Douglas 1938- *St&PR 93*
McCartney, Frank Howard, III 1949- *WhoEmL 93*
McCartney, George F. 1946- *WhoIns 93*
McCartney, George Francis *Law&B 92*
McCartney, Gibson 1939- *St&PR 93*
McCartney, Helen Carole 1927- *WhoAmW 93*
McCartney, Hugh Alastair *WhoScE 91-1*
McCartney, J. A. G. S. *DcCPCAm*
McCartney, Jerry Thomas 1943- *St&PR 93*
McCartney, John *DcCPCAm, St&PR 93*
McCartney, John F. *Law&B 92*
McCartney, John Joseph 1943- *St&PR 93, WhoAm 92*
Mc Cartney, Kenneth Hall 1924- *WhoAm 92*
McCartney, Louis Neil 1943- *WhoWor 93*
McCartney, Nancy Mae 1956- *WhoAmW 93*
McCartney, O. Kenton, III 1943- *St&PR 93*
McCartney, P. *ScF&FL 92*
McCartney, Paul *BioIn 17*
McCartney, Paul 1942- *Baker 92, WhoAm 92, WhoWor 93*
McCartney, Robert Charles 1934- *St&PR 93, WhoAm 92, WhoE 93, WhoWor 93*
McCartney, Scott 1960- *ConAu 138*
McCartney, Sheila J. *Law&B 92*
McCartney, W.G. 1934- *St&PR 93*
McCarty, Billy d1991 *BioIn 17*
Mc Carty, Bruce 1920- *WhoAm 92*
McCarty, Chester Earl 1905- *WhoWor 93*
McCarty, Danny J. *Law&B 92*
McCarty, David Lewis 1950- *WhoSSW 93*
McCarty, Dennis 1950- *ScF&FL 92*
McCarty, Donald James 1921- *WhoAm 92*
McCarty, Douglass W. *Law&B 92*
McCarty, Gil 1934- *WhoIns 93*
McCarty, Harry Downman 1946- *WhoAm 92, WhoE 93*
McCarty, Henry *BioIn 17*
McCarty, James E. *Law&B 92*
McCarty, James Joseph 1930- *St&PR 93*
McCarty, James T. 1947- *WhoIns 93*
McCarty, Jesse Louis Henry 1941- *WhoWrEP 92*
McCarty, John 1944- *ScF&FL 92*
McCarty, John B. 1944- *St&PR 93*
McCarty, Joseph C. 1942- *St&PR 93*
McCarty, Joseph C., III *Law&B 92*
Mccarty, Joseph William, Jr. 1944- *St&PR 93*
McCarty, Kathryn Shane 1954- *WhoE 93*
McCarty, Kim *BioIn 17*
McCarty, L. Thomas 1940- *St&PR 93*
McCarty, Laura Smith 1967- *WhoEmL 93*
McCarty, LuAnn 1960- *WhoE 93*
McCarty, Maclyn 1911- *WhoAm 92*
McCarty, Michael *BioIn 17*
McCarty, Michiel C. 1951- *St&PR 93*
McCarty, Michiel Cleve 1951- *WhoAm 92*
McCarty, Patricia Ann 1947- *WhoAmW 93*
McCarty, Patti d1985 *SweetSg C [port]*
Mc Carty, Perry Lee 1931- *WhoAm 92*
McCarty, Philip N. 1938- *St&PR 93*
McCarty, Philip Norman 1938- *WhoAm 92*
Mc Carty, Raymond M. 1908- *WhoSSW 93*
McCarty, Richard Charles 1947- *WhoAm 92*
McCarty, Richard Earl 1938- *WhoAm 92, WhoE 93*
McCarty, Richard Gerard *Law&B 92*
McCarty, Robert *MiSFD 9*
Mc Carty, Robert Lee 1920- *WhoAm 92*
McCarty, Robert Lee 1934- *St&PR 93*
McCarty, Shirley Carolyn 1934- *WhoAmW 93*
McCarty, Stuart 1923- *St&PR 93*
McCarty, Theodore Frederick 1937- *St&PR 93, WhoAm 92*
McCarty, Theodore M. 1909- *St&PR 93*
Mc Carty, Theodore Milson 1909- *WhoAm 92*
McCarty, Thomas J. 1938- *St&PR 93*
McCarty, Thomas Joseph 1938- *WhoAm 92*
McCarty, Tom 1855?-1900? *BioIn 17*
McCarty, Vet R. 1940- *St&PR 93*
McCarty, Vida Finch 1945- *WhoE 93*
McCarty, William Bonner, Jr. 1921- *St&PR 93, WhoAm 92*
Mc Carty, William Michael, Jr. 1938- *WhoWor 93*
McCarty-Powell, Debra Lynn 1955- *WhoAmW 93*
McCarus, Ernest Nasseph 1922- *WhoAm 92*
Mccarver, Frank 1941- *St&PR 93*
McCarver, James Timothy 1941- *BiDAMSp 1989, WhoAm 92*
McCarville, Mark John 1946- *St&PR 93, WhoAm 92*
Mccary, Leon E. 1937- *St&PR 93*
McCaskey, Douglas William 1942- *WhoIns 93*
McCaskey, Edward *WhoAm 92*
McCaskey, Michael 1943- *WhoAm 92*
McCaskill, Austin, Sr. 1920- *St&PR 93*
McCaskill, Linda Ann Wellington 1959- *WhoAmW 93*
McCaskill, Patricia Lorenz 1948- *WhoAmW 93, WhoEmL 93*
McCaskill, R.W. *Law&B 92*
McCaskill, Richard E. 1936- *St&PR 93*
McCasland, Thomas H., Jr. 1933- *St&PR 93*
McCaslin, F. Catherine 1947- *WhoAmW 93, WhoEmL 93*
McCaslin, Teresa Eve 1949- *WhoAmW 93*
McCastlain, Hugh M. 1943- *St&PR 93*
McCathren, Randall R. *Law&B 92*
McCathren, Randall Ross 1949- *WhoEmL 93*
McCaughan, D.V. *WhoScE 91-1*
Mccaughan, James William 1950- *St&PR 93*
McCaughan, Janice E. *Law&B 92*
McCaughan, John F. 1935- *WhoAm 92*
McCaughan, John Forbes 1935- *St&PR 93*
McCaughan, R.E.M. 1908-1989 *BioIn 17*
McCaughey, Andrew G. 1922- *St&PR 93*
Mc Caughey, Andrew Gilmour 1922- *WhoAm 92, WhoE 93*
McCaughey, Davis 1914- *WhoAsAP 91*
McCaughey, John Willett 1936- *St&PR 93*
McCaughey, Lorraine B. 1950- *WhoAm 92, WhoAmW 93*
McCaughey, M. *St&PR 93*
McCaughrean, Geraldine 1951- *ChlFicS, ScF&FL 92*
McCaughren, Tom *ScF&FL 92*
McCaul, Bruce W. 1939- *St&PR 93*
McCauley, Ann *Law&B 92*
McCauley, Brenda Julia 1929- *WhoAmW 93*
McCauley, Brenda S. 1964- *WhoAmW 93*
McCauley, Bruce D. 1936- *St&PR 93*
McCauley, Bruce Gordon *WhoAm 92*
Mc Cauley, Carole Spearin 1939- *WhoWrEP 92*
McCauley, Clarice Vallette *AmWomPl*
McCauley, Cleyburn Lycurgus 1929- *WhoSSW 93*
McCauley, Daniel J. *Law&B 92*
McCauley, David F. 1925- *St&PR 93*
McCauley, David W. 1958- *WhoWor 93*
McCauley, Floyce Reid 1933- *WhoE 93, WhoWor 93*
McCauley, Henry Berton 1913- *WhoE 93*
McCauley, Herbert Nicholas 1933- *St&PR 93*
McCauley, James Ewan, Jr. 1958- *WhoSSW 93*
McCauley, James P. 1943- *St&PR 93*
McCauley, James Paul 1939- *WhoSSW 93*
McCauley, Janie Caves 1946- *WhoSSW 93*
McCauley, Joel Arthur 1938- *WhoSSW 93*
McCauley, John Edward 1946- *St&PR 93*
McCauley, John Francis 1932- *WhoAm 92*
McCauley, Kevin John *Law&B 92*
McCauley, Kirby 1941- *ScF&FL 92*
McCauley, Matthew P. *Law&B 92*
McCauley, Michael J. 1961- *ConAu 138*
McCauley, Norman A. 1953- *St&PR 93*
Mc Cauley, R. Paul 1943- *WhoAm 92*
McCauley, Richard G. *Law&B 92*
McCauley, Richard Gray 1940- *St&PR 93, WhoAm 92*
McCauley, Robert Joseph 1933- *St&PR 93*
McCauley, Robert Neil 1952- *WhoEmL 93, WhoSSW 93*
McCauley, Robert William 1926- *WhoAm 92*
McCauley, Rosemarie Garossino 1935- *WhoE 93*
Mc Cauley, Roy Barnard 1919- *WhoAm 92*
McCauley, William 1947- *WhoE 93*
McCauley, William (Alexander) 1917- *Baker 92*
McCauley-Griffin, Roseanne 1964- *WhoE 93*
Mc Caull, Julian Lincoln 1936- *WhoWrEP 92*
McCaulley, Glen L. 1942- *St&PR 93*
McCausland, George Jackson 1933- *St&PR 93*
McCausland, Susan Austin 1839- *AmWomPl*
McCausland, Thomas J., Jr. 1934- *St&PR 93*
McCausland, Thomas James, Jr. 1934- *WhoAm 92*
McCausland, Timothy S. *Law&B 92*
McCave, Ian Nicholas *WhoScE 91-1*
Mccaw, Craig O. 1949- *St&PR 93*
McCaw, John Wheeler 1956- *WhoEmL 93*
McCaw, Kenneth M., Jr. *Law&B 92*
McCaw, William Ralph 1927- *WhoE 93*
McCawley, Austin 1925- *WhoAm 92, WhoE 93*
McCay, Bill *ScF&FL 92*
McCay, R. Scott *Law&B 92*
McCay, Winsor 1871-1934 *BioIn 17*
McChesney, Marion *ScF&FL 92*
McChesney, Paul Townsend 1953- *WhoEmL 93*
McChesney, Robert Michael, Sr. 1942- *WhoAm 92, WhoSSW 93*
Mc Chesney, Robert Pearson 1913- *WhoAm 92*
McChesney, William S. 1909-1990 *BioIn 17*
McChristian, Joseph Alexander 1914- *WhoWor 93*
McChristy, Thomas A. *St&PR 93*
McClafferty, John Joseph 1906- *WhoAm 92, WhoWor 93*
McClafferty, Steven Joseph 1957- *WhoE 93*
McClain, Benjamin Richard 1931- *WhoSSW 93*
McClain, Charles James 1931- *WhoAm 92*
McClain, Charles William, Jr. 1940- *WhoAm 92*
McClain, Dennis *NewYTBS 92 [port]*
McClain, Ernest Glenn 1918- *Baker 92*
McClain, J. Kyle *Law&B 92*
McClain, Janet Treichel *Law&B 92*
McClain, John David 1944- *St&PR 93*
McClain, John R. 1952- *St&PR 93*
McClain, Larry French 1937- *St&PR 93*
McClain, Lee Bert 1943- *WhoAm 92*
McClain, Marlene Stella 1937- *WhoAmW 93*
McClain, Richard Stan 1951- *WhoEmL 93*
McClain, Ronald R. *Law&B 92*
McClain, Terry James 1948- *St&PR 93*
McClain, Thomas E. 1950- *WhoWor 93*
McClain, Tomey Van 1952- *WhoE 93*
McClain, Vickie S. 1959- *WhoSSW 93*
Mc Clain, William Harold 1917- *WhoAm 92*
McClain, William K. 1954- *St&PR 93*
McClain, William L. *Law&B 92*
McClain, William Thomas 1926- *WhoE 93*
McClam, Robert Warne 1954- *WhoSSW 93*
McClammy, Joseph C. 1934- *St&PR 93*
McClammy, Robert Karl 1942- *St&PR 93*
McClamroch, N. Harris 1942- *WhoAm 92*
McClanaghan, Mary Ellen 1944- *WhoAmW 93*
McClanahan, Harry Allen, III 1949- *WhoEmL 93*
McClanahan, Kerry P. 1948- *WhoSSW 93*
McClanahan, Lowell P. 1943- *St&PR 93*
McClanahan, Preston Moore, III 1933- *WhoE 93*
McClanahan, Rue *BioIn 17, WhoAm 92, WhoAmW 93*
McClane, A.J. 1922-1991 *BioIn 17*
McClane, A(lbert) J(ules) 1922-1991 *ConAu 136*
McClane, Albert Jules 1922-1991 *BioIn 17*
McClane, John William, III 1952- *WhoSSW 93*
McClane, Kenneth A. 1951- *BioIn 17*
Mc Clane, Kenneth Anderson, Jr. 1951- *WhoWrEP 92*
McClane, Robert S. 1939- *St&PR 93*
McClane, Robert Sanford 1939- *WhoAm 92, WhoSSW 93*
McClaran, George Joseph 1924- *St&PR 93*
McClard, Cynthia Ann 1951- *WhoAmW 93*
McClaren, Bob *Law&B 92*
Mcclaren, Fred 1947- *St&PR 93*
McClaren, Steven A. *Law&B 92*
McClarren, Robert Royce 1921- *BioIn 17, WhoAm 92*
McClary, James Daly 1917- *WhoAm 92, WhoWor 93*
McClary, Jane Stevenson 1919-1990 *BioIn 17*
McClary, Jim Marston 1949- *WhoEmL 93, WhoSSW 93*
McClary, Patricia Ann 1957- *WhoEmL 93*
McClary, Susan 1946- *Baker 92*
McClary, Thomas Calvert 1909?-1972 *ScF&FL 92*
McClaskey, James D. 1948- *St&PR 93*
McClaskey, Norman D. *Law&B 92*
McClatchey, Devereaux F. 1906- *St&PR 93*
Mc Clatchey, Devereaux Fore 1906- *WhoAm 92*
McClatchey, John Francis 1929- *WhoAm 92*
McClatchey, Maureen Wilhelmina 1952- *WhoAmW 93*
McClatchy, C. K. 1858-1936 *JrnUS*
McClatchy, James *St&PR 93*
McClatchy, James B. *WhoAm 92*
Mc Clatchy, Joseph Donald 1945- *WhoWrEP 92*
McClaugherty, Joe L. 1951- *WhoEmL 93*
McClave, Donald Silsbee 1941- *WhoAm 92*
McClave, Larry Wayne 1947- *WhoSSW 93*
McClave, Norman, III 1943- *WhoAm 92*
McClave, Wilkes, III *Law&B 92*
McClave, William H., Jr. 1943- *WhoAm 92*
McClay, Harvey Curtis 1939- *WhoSSW 93, WhoWor 93*
McClay, Roger Neville 1945- *WhoAsAP 91*
McClay, Wayne Dennis 1945- *St&PR 93*
McClean, Celeita A. 1956- *WhoAmW 93*
McClean, Graham J. *WhoAm 92*
McClean, Henry Joseph 1941- *St&PR 93*
McClean, S.P. *WhoScE 91-1*
McClear, Kevin Richard *Law&B 92*
Mccleary, Benjamin W. 1944- *St&PR 93*
McCleary, Benjamin Ward 1944- *WhoAm 92, WhoE 93*
McCleary, Beryl Nowlin 1929- *WhoAmW 93*
McCleary, Henry Glen 1922- *WhoAm 92*
Mccleary, Herbert Elwood 1931- *St&PR 93*
McCleary, James Kent 1941- *St&PR 93*
McCleary, Ken Ward 1947- *WhoEmL 93, WhoSSW 93*
McCleary, Lloyd Everald 1924- *WhoAm 92*
McCleary, Monica Jean 1952- *WhoEmL 93*
McCleary, Nancy Jane Cornish 1951- *WhoAmW 93*
McCleary, Robert D. *St&PR 93*
McCleary, Robert L. 1932- *St&PR 93*
Mc Cleery, William Thomas 1911- *WhoWrEP 92*
McClees, Charles J., Jr. *Law&B 92*
Mccleese, Dale 1938- *St&PR 93*
McCleland, Desmond Geoffrey 1924- *WhoWor 93*
McClellan, Barbara Vogl 1945- *WhoSSW 93*
McClellan, Bion Walton 1933- *WhoE 93*
McClellan, C. Scott *Law&B 92*
Mc Clellan, Catharine 1921- *WhoAm 92*
McClellan, Catherine R. *Law&B 92*
McClellan, Craig Rene 1947- *WhoWor 93*
McClellan, Donald William, Jr. 1960- *WhoEmL 93*
McClellan, Ezra Ernest 1925- *St&PR 93*
McClellan, George B. 1826-1885 *PolPar*
McClellan, George Brinton 1826-1885 *BioIn 17, CmdGen 1991 [port], HarEnMi*
McClellan, James E. 1948- *St&PR 93*
Mc Clellan, James Edward, Jr. 1922- *WhoAm 92*
McClellan, James Harold 1947- *WhoAm 92*
McClellan, Jason Eugene 1926- *WhoSSW 93*
McClellan, Joan C. Osmundson 1934- *WhoAmW 93*
McClellan, John James, Jr. 1931- *St&PR 93*
McClellan, Judith Ann 1950- *WhoAmW 93*
McClellan, Leo F. 1933- *St&PR 93*
McClellan, Lewis Reid 1930- *St&PR 93*
McClellan, Margaret N. 1936- *St&PR 93*

McClellan, Mildred Nolte 1922- WhoAmW 93
McClellan, Richard Augustus 1930- WhoSSW 93
Mcclellan, Roger O. 1937- St&PR 93
McClellan, Roger Orville 1937- WhoAm 92
McClellan, Ross BioIn 17
McClellan, Tara J. 1962- WhoEmL 93
McClellan, Thomas C. Law&B 92
Mc Clellan, William Monson 1934- WhoAm 92
McClelland, Bramlette 1920- WhoAm 92
Mc Clelland, Gene Mc Lain 1929- WhoWrEP 92
Mcclelland, George D. 1946- St&PR 93
McClelland, Harold Franklin 1918- WhoAm 92
Mc Clelland, James Craig 1901- WhoAm 92
Mcclelland, James E., III 1943- St&PR 93
McClelland, James L. 1948- WhoAm 92
McClelland, James Morris 1943- St&PR 93
McClelland, James Ray 1946- WhoSSW 93
McClelland, Jean Elizabeth 1949- WhoEmL 93
McClelland, Jeffrey Wilson 1942- St&PR 93
McClelland, John Fleming 1946- WhoSSW 93
McClelland, John P. 1933- St&PR 93
Mc Clelland, John Peter 1933- WhoAm 92
McClelland, K.S. Law&B 92
McClelland, Kerwin T. 1927- St&PR 93
McClelland, Patricia G. 1944- WhoAmW 93
McClelland, Peter Dean 1934- WhoAm 92
McClelland, Rex Arnold 1936- St&PR 93, WhoAm 92
McClelland, Richard Lee 1927- WhoE 93
McClelland, Richard W. 1948- St&PR 93
Mc Clelland, Robert Nelson 1929- WhoAm 92, WhoWor 93
McClelland, Robert William Law&B 92
McClelland, Roy J. WhoScE 91-1
McClelland, Sandra Lynn 1960- WhoAmW 93
McClelland, Shearwood, Jr. 1947- WhoWor 93
McClelland, Shearwood Junior 1947- WhoEmL 93
McClelland, T. Bramlette 1920- St&PR 93
McClelland, W. Clark 1939- St&PR 93
McClelland, W. Craig 1934- St&PR 93
McClements, Robert, Jr. 1928- St&PR 93, WhoAm 92, WhoE 93
McClenachan, George 1769-1833 BioIn 17
Mcclenathan, John Leroy 1944- St&PR 93
McClendon, Charles Youmans 1923- WhoAm 92, WhoSSW 93
McClendon, Edwin James 1921- WhoAm 92
McClendon, Ernestine d1991 BioIn 17
Mc Clendon, Fred Vernon WhoSSW 93, WhoWor 93
McClendon, Joe N. Law&B 92
McClendon, L.B. Law&B 92
McClendon, L. Philip Law&B 92
McClendon, L. Philip 1942- St&PR 93
McClendon, Mary Angie 1929- St&PR 93
McClendon, Mary Ellen 1936- WhoSSW 93
McClendon, Maxine 1931- WhoAmW 93
McClendon, Sarah 1910- JrnUS
Mc Clendon, Sarah Newcomb 1910- WhoAm 92
Mc Clendon, William Hutchinson, III 1933- WhoAm 92
McClendon, Zach, Jr. 1937- St&PR 93
McClennan, Mort C. 1945- St&PR 93
Mcclennen, George Michael 1943- St&PR 93
Mc Clennen, Louis 1912- WhoAm 92
McClennen, Miriam J. 1923- WhoAmW 93
McClennen, Samuel L. 1918- St&PR 93
McClennen, Sandra Elaine 1942- WhoAmW 93
Mc Clenney, Byron Nelson 1939- WhoAm 92
McClenon, John Raymond 1937- WhoAm 92
McClernand, John Alexander 1812-1900 HarEnMi
Mc Clernon, Crystal Dawn 1960- WhoWrEP 92
McCleskey, Warren BioIn 17
McCleverty, Jon Armistice WhoScE 91-1
McCleverty, Jon Armistice 1937- WhoWor 93
McClimon, Timothy John 1953- WhoEmL 93
McClintic, Howard Gresson 1951- WhoE 93, WhoEmL 93
McClintic, Madison P. 1928- St&PR 93
McClintick, Robert Roy 1924- St&PR 93
McClintock, Andrew 1942- WhoScE 91-1
Mc Clintock, Archie Glenn 1911- WhoAm 92
McClintock, Barbara BioIn 17
McClintock, Barbara 1902- WhoAm 92
McClintock, Barbara 1902-1992 CurBio 92N, NewYTBS 92 [port]
McClintock, Donald William, III 1954- WhoEmL 93
McClintock, Francis Leopold 1819-1907 Expl 93 [port]
McClintock, George Dunlap 1920- WhoAm 92
McClintock, Jessica 1930- WhoAm 92
McClintock, Keith E. Law&B 92
McClintock, Robert L. 1926- St&PR 93
McClintock, Sandra Janise 1938- WhoAmW 93
McClintock, Simms 1927- WhoSSW 93
Mcclintock, Theodore E. 1940- St&PR 93
McClintock, William Thomas 1934- WhoWor 93
McClinton, Delbert 1940- SoulM
Mc Clinton, Donald G. 1933- WhoAm 92
McClinton, Dorothy Hardaway 1925- WhoAmW 93
Mcclinton, Robert 1950- St&PR 93
Mcclister, Debra L. 1954- St&PR 93
McClister, Debra Lynn 1954- WhoAmW 93
McClockin, James P. St&PR 93
McCloskey, Candice Joy 1953- WhoEmL 93
Mccloskey, Daniel 1936- St&PR 93
McCloskey, Donald Nansen 1942- WhoAm 92
McCloskey, Francis Gerard 1939- WhoE 93
McCloskey, Frank 1939- CngDr 91, WhoAm 92
McCloskey, Jack WhoAm 92
McCloskey, James BioIn 17, NewYTBS 92 [port]
McCloskey, James c. 1944- News 93-1 [port]
McCloskey, James B. Law&B 92
McCloskey, James Boswell 1945- WhoSSW 93
McCloskey, James P. 1941- St&PR 93
Mccloskey, James W. 1931- St&PR 93
McCloskey, John L. 1920- WhoE 93
McCloskey, John Michael 1934- WhoAm 92
Mc Closkey, Mark 1938- WhoWrEP 92
McCloskey, Michael Joseph 1951- WhoEmL 93
McCloskey, Patrick 1948- ConAu 38NR
Mc Closkey, Paul N., Jr. 1927- WhoAm 92
McCloskey, Peter Francis 1935- WhoAm 92
McCloskey, Richard V. 1933- St&PR 93
Mc Closkey, Robert 1914- WhoAm 92
Mc Closkey, Robert James 1922- WhoAm 92
McCloskey, (John) Robert 1914- MajAI [port]
McCloskey, William Donald 1930- WhoE 93
McCloud, Colleen BioIn 17
McCloud, Raymond Ward 1955- St&PR 93
McCloud, Robert Olmsted, Jr. 1951- WhoEmL 93
McCloud, Ronald Bernard 1948- St&PR 93
McCloy, Clifford E., Jr. Law&B 92
McCloy, Helen ScF&FL 92
McCloy, John J. 1895-1989 ColdWar 1 [port]
McCloy, John J. 1937- St&PR 93
McCloy, John Jay 1895-1989 BioIn 17
McCloy, Marjorie BioIn 17
McCloy, Rodney Alan 1963- WhoSSW 93
McCluney, Gregory Day 1946- WhoSSW 93
McCluney, Joan Taylor 1929- WhoAmW 93
McClung, A. Keith, Jr. Law&B 92
McClung, A. Keith, Jr. 1934- St&PR 93
McClung, Barbara Gayle Law&B 92
McClung, Beverly R. 1952- St&PR 93
McClung, Christina J. 1948- WhoAmW 93
McClung, David W. 1927- St&PR 93
McClung, Frank Dixon 1946- WhoSSW 93
McClung, James A. 1937- St&PR 93
McClung, James Allen 1937- WhoAm 92
McClung, James David 1943- WhoAm 92
McClung, Jay C. 1948- St&PR 93
McClung, Jim Hill 1936- St&PR 93, WhoAm 92, WhoSSW 93
McClung, John Robinson, Jr. 1914- WhoAm 92
McClung, Kenneth Austin, Jr. 1947- WhoE 93, WhoEmL 93, WhoWor 93
Mc Clung, Leland Swint 1910- WhoAm 92
McClung, Leon Darrell, Jr. 1953- WhoWor 93
McClung, Linda Rose White 1948- WhoSSW 93
McClung, Nellie Letitia Mooney 1873-1951 BioIn 17
McClung, Richard Goehring 1913- WhoAm 92
McClung, Robert M. BioIn 17
McClung, Robert M. 1916- SmATA 15AS [port]
McClung, Robert M(arhall) 1916- WhoWrEP 92
McClung, Robert M(arshall) 1916- MajAI [port]
McClung, Robert Warren 1928- WhoSSW 93
McClung, Thomas Lee 1870-1914 BiDAMSp 1989
McClure, Alan Campbell 1923- WhoAm 92
McClure, Alvin Bruce 1953- WhoEmL 93
McClure, Betty Padgett 1929- St&PR 93
McClure, Bobby 1942- BioIn 17
McClure, Brian David WhoWor 93
McClure, Brooks 1919- WhoAm 92
McClure, Charles J. 1935- St&PR 93
McClure, Charles Robert 1949- WhoE 93
McClure, Chip BioIn 17
McClure, Christopher Ewart 1943- WhoSSW 93
McClure, Cissy BioIn 17
McClure, Connie Diane 1956- WhoEmL 93, WhoSSW 93
McClure, Cynthia Rowland BioIn 17
McClure, David 1748-1820 BioIn 17
McClure, David H. 1948- WhoEmL 93, WhoSSW 93
McClure, Donald G., Jr. 1943- St&PR 93
McClure, Donald J. 1940- St&PR 93
Mc Clure, Donald Stuart 1920- WhoAm 92
McClure, Doug 1935- WhoAm 92
McClure, Elaine 1949- WhoEmL 93
McClure, Frederick D. AfrAmBi [port]
McClure, Frederick Donald 1954- WhoAm 92
McClure, George R. 1921- St&PR 93
McClure, Gerald W. 1941- St&PR 93
McClure, Grover Benjamin 1918- WhoAm 92
McClure, Howard Gundry 1936- St&PR 93
McClure, James Focht, Jr. 1931- WhoAm 92, WhoE 93
Mc Clure, James J., Jr. 1920- WhoAm 92
McClure, Janice Lee 1941- WhoAmW 93
McClure, Jessica BioIn 17
McClure, Joe Daugherty 1950- WhoEmL 93
McClure, John Campbell Law&B 92
McClure, Joyce Kay 1942- WhoAmW 93
McClure, Kathy Blevins 1952- WhoAmW 93
McClure, Kenneth Allen 1947- WhoIns 93
McClure, Marcella Ann 1949- WhoAmW 93
McClure, Mark Stephen 1948- WhoE 93
McClure, Mary Anne 1939- WhoAm 92, WhoAmW 93
McClure, Michael BioIn 17
McClure, Michael DeStewart 1942- WhoSSW 93, WhoWor 93
Mc Clure, Michael Thomas 1932- WhoAm 92, WhoWrEP 92
McClure, Rebecca S. Law&B 92
McClure, Rex 1931- St&PR 93
McClure, Richard Fowler 1927- WhoAm 92
McClure, Robert 1807-1873 Expl 93
McClure, Robert H. d1991 BioIn 17
McClure, Robert Lynch 1953- WhoE 93
McClure, Robert W. Law&B 92
McClure, Ronnie Clyde 1941- WhoSSW 93
McClure, S.S. 1857-1949 GayN
McClure, Sam S. BioIn 17
McClure, Samuel Sidney 1857-1949 JrnUS
McClure, Thomas James 1955- WhoEmL 93
McClure, W. Donald 1906-1977 BioIn 17
McClure, Wilbert James 1938- WhoE 93
McClure, William F., Jr. Law&B 92
McClure, William Kyle 1922- WhoWor 93
McClure, William Owen 1937- WhoWor 93
Mc Clure, William Pendleton 1925- WhoAm 92
McClurg, E. Vane Law&B 92
McClurg, James Edward 1945- WhoAm 92
McClurg, Ned S. 1945- St&PR 93
McClurg, Patricia A. 1939- WhoAmW 93
McCluskey, Carolina P.S. 1949- WhoEmL 93
McCluskey, Edward Joseph 1929- WhoAm 92, WhoWor 93
McCluskey, Gayla Jacque 1955- WhoEmL 93, WhoWor 93
McCluskey, Jean Louise 1947- WhoAm 92
McCluskey, Joseph Paul 1911- BiDAMSp 1989
McCluskey, Kate Wisner AmWomPl
McCluskey, Lois Thornhill 1945- WhoAmW 93
McCluskey, Neil Gerard 1920- WhoE 93
McCluskey, Norman Dean 1952- WhoEmL 93, WhoSSW 93
McCluskey, Paul J. d1990 BioIn 17
McCluskey, Richard Thomas 1943- St&PR 93
McCluskey, Robert A. 1917- St&PR 93
McCluskey, Robert Timmons 1923- WhoAm 92
McCluskey, Stephen Christian 1942- St&PR 93
McCluskey, Walter H. 1939- St&PR 93
McCluskie, Arthur d1873 BioIn 17
McCluskie, Mike d1871 BioIn 17
McClusky, Thorp ScF&FL 92
McClymond, J.L., Jr. 1928- St&PR 93
McClymonds, Jean Ellen WhoAmW 93
McClymonds, Susan E. Law&B 92
McClymont, Eleanor Jean 1938- WhoE 93
Mc Clymont, Hamilton 1944- WhoAm 92
McClymont, Kenneth Ross 1924- WhoAm 92
Mccoach, Catherine M. 1957- St&PR 93
McCobb, John B., Jr. Law&B 92
Mc Coin, John Mack 1931- WhoWor 93
McCole, Robert Richard 1939- St&PR 93
McColgan, Liz BioIn 17
McColl, Hugh L., Jr. BioIn 17
McColl, Hugh L., Jr. 1935- St&PR 93
McColl, Hugh Leon, Jr. 1935- WhoSSW 93
McColl, James George 1938- St&PR 93
McColl, John Angus 1928- St&PR 93
McColl, Suzanne Bourns 1941- WhoAmW 93
McColl, William Frazer, Jr. 1930- BiDAMSp 1989
McCollam, William, Jr. 1925- St&PR 93, WhoAm 92
McColley, Robert McNair 1933- WhoAm 92
McCollin, Frances 1892-1960 BioIn 17
Mc Collister, John Charles 1935- WhoAm 92
McCollister, John S. St&PR 93
McCollister, Paul Wayne 1915- St&PR 93
McCollister, Scott A. Law&B 92
McColloch, John Kearney 1946- WhoAm 92
McColloch, Murray M. 1926- St&PR 93
McColloch, Murray Michael Law&B 92
McColloch, Murray Michael 1926- WhoIns 93
Mc Collom, Kenneth Allen 1922- WhoAm 92
McCollom, Walter Raymond, Jr. 1949- WhoEmL 93
McColloster, Lee Stephen 1948- WhoEmL 93
McCollough, Carol Keeney 1937- WhoAmW 93
McCollough, Carol Lee 1943- WhoAmW 93
Mccollough, Joseph R. 1943- St&PR 93
McCollough, Michael Leon 1953- WhoWor 93
Mc Collough, Newton Clark, III 1934- WhoAm 92
McCollough, W.H. 1928- St&PR 93
McCollough, Walter d1991 BioIn 17
McCollow, Thomas James 1925- St&PR 93, WhoAm 92
McCollum, Alice O. AfrAmBi
McCollum, Bill 1944- CngDr 91
McCollum, Clifford Glenn 1919- WhoAm 92
McCollum, Douglass J. Law&B 92
McCollum, Elsie Malone AmWomPl
McCollum, Eric Edward 1950- WhoEmL 93
McCollum, Gary Wayne 1939- WhoE 93
McCollum, Herbert W. WhoAm 92
Mc Collum, Ira William, Jr. 1944- WhoAm 92, WhoSSW 93
McCollum, James Fountain 1946- WhoEmL 93
McCollum, Jean Hubble 1934- WhoAmW 93
McCollum, John Morris 1922- WhoAm 92
McCollum, Julie M. 1946- St&PR 93
McCollum, Lisa Colleen 1955- WhoEmL 93
McCollum, Mack D. 1932- St&PR 93
McCollum, Michael 1946- ScF&FL 92
McCollum, Randall Hampton 1944- WhoE 93

McCollum, Robert Wayne 1925- *WhoAm 92*
McCollum, William Bruce 1951- *St&PR 93*
McCollum, William Henry 1930- *St&PR 93*
McCollum, William T. *Law&B 92*
McColm, Robert Bruce 1950- *WhoE 93*
McComas, Annette Peltz 1911- *ScF&FL 92*
McComas, Edith R. *AmWomPl*
McComas, Francis John 1874-1938 *BioIn 17*
McComas, James Douglas 1928- *WhoAm 92, WhoSSW 93*
McComas, Louis Gough, Jr. 1932- *St&PR 93*
McComas, Murray Knabb 1936- *St&PR 93, WhoAm 92*
McComas, R. Doss 1954- *St&PR 93*
McComb, Carolyn F. 1934- *St&PR 93*
McComb, Leann Marie 1956- *WhoAmW 93*
McComb, Mary Elizabeth 1949- *WhoAmW 93*
McCombe, Richard George Bramwell 1952- *WhoWor 93*
McCombie, Charles 1945- *WhoScE 91-4*
McCombie, Hamish M. 1938- *WhoUN 92*
McCombs, Bob 1956- *WhoEmL 93*
McCombs, Dorothy F. d1990 *BioIn 17*
Mc Combs, G. B. 1909- *WhoAm 92*
McCombs, J.B. 1955- *WhoEmL 93*
McCombs, Red *WhoAm 92*
McCombs, William F. 1875-1921 *PolPar*
McCombs, William Frank 1875-1921 *BioIn 17*
Mc Comic, Robert Barry 1939- *WhoAm 92*
Mc Comiskey, Bruce Thomas 1963- *WhoWrEP 92*
McCommon, Hubert 1929- *WhoAm 92*
McCommon, Robert L., Jr. 1925- *St&PR 93*
McComsey, Robert Ronald 1944- *WhoAm 92*
Mc Conagha, Glenn Lowery 1910- *WhoAm 92*
McConaghy, Elizabeth Ann *Law&B 92*
McConahay, John Bernard 1936- *WhoSSW 93*
McConahey, Stephen George 1943- *WhoAm 92*
McConaughy, David Francis 1932- *St&PR 93*
McConchie, John Lewis 1938- *St&PR 93*
McCone, John A. 1902-1991 *AnObit 1991, BioIn 17, ColdWar 1 [port]*
McCone, Susan *BioIn 17*
McConeghey, John Francis 1923- *St&PR 93*
McConkey, James *BioIn 17*
McConkey, James 1921- *ScF&FL 92*
McConkey, James R. 1921- *WhoAm 92, WhoWrEP 92*
Mc Conkie, George Wilson 1937- *WhoAm 92*
McConkle, Corinne Mildred 1954- *WhoAmW 93*
McConnaughey, George C., Jr. 1925- *St&PR 93*
Mc Connaughey, George Carlton, Jr. 1925- *WhoAm 92*
Mcconnaughey, Harlow 1911- *St&PR 93*
McConnaughey, James Walter 1951- *WhoE 93, WhoEmL 93*
McConnaughy, John E. 1929- *St&PR 93*
Mc Connaughy, John Edward, Jr. 1929- *WhoAm 92*
Mcconnel, W. Bruce, III 1943- *St&PR 93*
McConnell, Addison Mitchell, Jr. 1942- *WhoAm 92*
McConnell, Addison Mitchell Mitch, Jr. 1942- *WhoSSW 93*
McConnell, Albert Lynn 1946- *WhoEmL 93, WhoSSW 93*
McConnell, Andrew 1835?- *BioIn 17*
McConnell, Ashley *ScF&FL 92*
McConnell, Barbara *BioIn 17*
McConnell, Barbara 1943- *WhoAmW 93*
McConnell, Barbara Ann Rogers 1939- *WhoAmW 93, WhoSSW 93*
McConnell, Brenda Garfield 1963- *WhoSSW 93*
McConnell, Calvin Dale 1928- *WhoAm 92*
McConnell, Charles Goodloe 1943- *St&PR 93, WhoAm 92*
McConnell, Charles Warren 1939- *WhoAm 92*
McConnell, Daniel Edward *Law&B 92*
McConnell, David Graham 1926- *WhoAm 92*
McConnell, David H. d1990 *BioIn 17*
McConnell, David Moffatt 1912- *WhoAm 92*
McConnell, David Stuart 1935- *WhoAm 92*
McConnell, Donald Lee *Law&B 92*
McConnell, Donald Patrick 1950- *WhoAm 92*
McConnell, Dudley 1936-1991 *BioIn 17*
McConnell, E. Hoy, II 1941- *St&PR 93, WhoAm 92*
Mc Connell, Edward Bosworth 1920- *WhoAm 92*
McConnell, Elliott Bonnell, Jr. 1928- *WhoAm 92*
McConnell, Francis D. *ScF&FL 92*
McConnell, Frank 1942- *ScF&FL 92*
McConnell, Genevieve Knapp 1876- *AmWomPl*
McConnell, Gladys 1907-1979 *SweetSg B [port]*
McConnell, Harden Marsden 1927- *WhoAm 92*
McConnell, J.R. *BioIn 17*
McConnell, Jack Lewis *Law&B 92*
McConnell, Jack Lewis 1934- *St&PR 93, WhoAm 92*
McConnell, James Desmond Caldwell *WhoScE 91-1*
McConnell, James F. 1933- *St&PR 93*
McConnell, James Guy 1947- *WhoEmL 93, WhoWor 93*
McConnell, James Joseph 1946- *WhoSSW 93*
McConnell, James V. 1925-1990 *BioIn 17*
McConnell, Jean 1928- *ConAu 39NR*
McConnell, John Coulter *WhoScE 91-1*
Mc Connell, John Douglas 1932- *WhoAm 92*
McConnell, John Edward 1931- *WhoWor 93*
McConnell, John H. 1923- *St&PR 93*
McConnell, John Henderson 1923- *WhoAm 92*
McConnell, John Howard 1933- *WhoE 93*
McConnell, John James, Jr. 1958- *WhoEmL 93*
McConnell, John Paul 1908-1986 *HarEnMi*
McConnell, John Thomas 1945- *WhoAm 92*
McConnell, John W. *WhoAm 92*
McConnell, John W. 1941- *St&PR 93*
Mc Connell, John Wilkinson 1907- *WhoAm 92*
McConnell, John William, Jr. 1921- *WhoAm 92*
McConnell, Joseph H. 1906- *St&PR 93*
McConnell, Kenneth J. 1926- *St&PR 93*
McConnell, Kirk D. *Law&B 92*
McConnell, Lee Alan 1963- *WhoEmL 93*
McConnell, Marie Andrews 1938- *WhoSSW 93, WhoWor 93*
McConnell, Marilyn Anne Lee 1950- *WhoSSW 93*
McConnell, Melissa 1953- *WhoAmW 93*
McConnell, Michael 1954- *WhoAm 92*
McConnell, Michael Theodore 1954- *WhoEmL 93*
McConnell, Mitch 1942- *CngDr 91*
McConnell, Patricia Ann 1935- *WhoAmW 93*
McConnell, Patricia Lynn 1956- *WhoAmW 93*
McConnell, Richard Earl 1963- *WhoSSW 93*
McConnell, Richard Leon 1926- *WhoSSW 93*
McConnell, Richard Samuel, Jr. *Law&B 92*
Mc Connell, Robert Chalmers 1913- *WhoAm 92*
Mc Connell, Robert Eastwood 1930- *WhoAm 92*
McConnell, Shirley Russell 1934- *WhoSSW 93*
McConnell, Stephen A. 1952- *St&PR 93, WhoAm 92*
Mcconnell, Susan E. 1943- *St&PR 93*
McConnell, Theresa Dougherty 1938- *WhoAmW 93*
McConnell, Viola Carlberg 1903- *WhoAmW 93*
McConnell, William Ray 1943- *WhoSSW 93*
McConnell, William Thompson 1933- *St&PR 93, WhoAm 92*
McConner, Dorothy 1929- *St&PR 93*
McConner, Ora B. 1929- *WhoAmW 93, WhoWor 93*
McConnico, Hilton *NewYTBS 92 [port]*
McConnin, John E. *Law&B 92*
McConomy, James Herbert 1937- *WhoAm 92*
McConomy, John W. *Law&B 92*
McConomy, Thomas Arthur 1933- *St&PR 93, WhoAm 92, WhoE 93*
McConvey, D'Arcy F. 1918- *St&PR 93*
Mc Conville, Clarence Joseph 1925- *WhoAm 92*
McConville, John P. *Law&B 92*
McConville, Kristy *WhoAmW 93*
McConville, Paul David *Law&B 92*
McConville, Sean 1943- *ConAu 137*
McConville, William *WhoAm 92*
McCoo, Marilyn *BioIn 17*
McCoog, James H. 1931- *St&PR 93*
McCook, Alexander McDowell 1831-1903 *HarEnMi*
McCook, Allen W. 1947- *St&PR 93*
McCook, Daniel Gerow 1927- *WhoSSW 93*
McCook, James Marshall 1952- *WhoE 93*
McCook, Kathleen de la Pena *WhoAm 92*
McCook, Richard Paul 1953- *WhoAm 92*
McCool, Helen Bunting 1948- *WhoE 93*
McCool, Pamela Lynn Reed 1963- *WhoAmW 93*
McCool, Suzanne Florence 1949- *WhoAmW 93*
McCoole, Robert F. 1950- *St&PR 93*
McCoppin, Dorothy *Law&B 92*
McCoppin, Peter *WhoAm 92*
McCorcle, Marcus Duane 1951- *WhoEmL 93*
McCord, Alice Bird *WhoAm 92*
McCord, Arline Fujii 1935- *WhoE 93*
McCord, Betty J. 1940- *WhoSSW 93*
Mc Cord, Carole Ann 1948- *WhoWrEP 92*
Mc Cord, Catherine Gumm 1926- *WhoWrEP 92*
Mc Cord, Christian *WhoWrEP 92*
McCord, David (Thompson Watson) 1897- *ConAu 38NR, MajAI [port]*
Mc Cord, Guyte Pierce, Jr. 1914- *WhoSSW 93*
McCord, Howard 1932- *ConAu 40NR*
Mc Cord, Howard Lawrence 1932- *WhoWrEP 92*
McCord, James Iley 1919-1990 *BioIn 17*
McCord, Joan 1930- *WhoE 93*
Mc Cord, John Harrison 1934- *WhoAm 92*
Mc Cord, Kenneth Armstrong 1921- *WhoAm 92*
Mc Cord, Marshal 1917- *WhoAm 92*
McCord, Maxwell Laurent 1965- *WhoE 93*
McCord, Michael James 1961- *WhoE 93*
McCord, Patrick Joseph 1938- *St&PR 93*
McCord, Raymond V. *Law&B 92*
McCord, Ronald John 1938- *St&PR 93*
McCord, Samuel Ray 1933- *WhoSSW 93*
McCord, Steven Grant 1948- *St&PR 93*
McCord, Thomas Patrick 1954- *WhoEmL 93*
McCord, Vincent Abbott, Jr. 1946- *WhoEmL 93*
McCord, William Charles 1928- *St&PR 93, WhoAm 92, WhoSSW 93, WhoWor 93*
McCord, William Maxwell d1992 *NewYTBS 92*
McCord, William Maxwell 1930- *WhoAm 92*
McCord, William Maxwell 1930-1992 *ConAu 139*
Mc Corison, Marcus Allen 1926- *WhoAm 92, WhoE 93*
Mccorkell, Peter L. 1946- *St&PR 93*
McCorkindale, Douglas H. *Law&B 92*
McCorkindale, Douglas H. 1939- *St&PR 93*
McCorkindale, Douglas Hamilton 1939- *WhoAm 92*
McCorkindale, Laura Ann 1966- *WhoEmL 93*
McCorkle, Allan James 1931- *St&PR 93, WhoSSW 93, WhoWor 93*
McCorkle, Barbara Backus 1920- *WhoE 93*
McCorkle, Carter C. 1936- *St&PR 93*
McCorkle, Constance Marie 1948- *WhoEmL 93*
McCorkle, Donald M(acomber) 1929-1978 *Baker 92*
McCorkle, Horace Jackson 1905- *WhoAm 92*
McCorkle, Jill 1958- *BioIn 17*
McCorkle, Michael 1944- *St&PR 93*
McCorkle, Michael 1957- *WhoEmL 93, WhoSSW 93*
McCorkle, Pope, Jr. 1925- *St&PR 93*
McCorkle, Robert Ellsworth 1938- *WhoWor 93*
McCorkle, Ron *BioIn 17*
McCorkle, Susannah *BioIn 17*
McCormac, Billy Murray 1920- *WhoAm 92*
McCormac, John Simmen 1930- *St&PR 93*
Mc Cormac, John Waverly 1926- *WhoAm 92*
McCormack, Charles N. 1950- *St&PR 93*
McCormack, Donald Paul 1926- *WhoAm 92, WhoWor 93*
McCormack, Edward Joseph, Jr. 1923- *WhoWor 93*
McCormack, Ellen 1926- *PolPar*
McCormack, Eric 1938- *ScF&FL 92*
McCormack, Eric 1966- *WhoCanL 92*
McCormack, F.X. *Law&B 92*
McCormack, Francis Xavier 1929- *St&PR 93, WhoAm 92*
Mc Cormack, Fred Allen 1930- *WhoAm 92*
McCormack, Grace 1908- *WhoE 93*
McCormack, Grace Lynette 1928- *WhoAmW 93*
McCormack, John 1884-1945 *Baker 92, BioIn 17, IntDcOp, OxDcOp*
McCormack, John A. 1936- *St&PR 93*
McCormack, John J. *Law&B 92*
McCormack, John J., Jr. 1944- *WhoIns 93*
McCormack, John Joseph 1932- *WhoAm 92*
McCormack, John Joseph, Jr. 1944- *WhoAm 92*
McCormack, John T. 1947- *St&PR 93*
McCormack, John W. 1891-1980 *PolPar*
McCormack, Mark H. *BioIn 17*
McCormack, Mark Hume 1930- *WhoAm 92*
McCormack, Mary Beatrice 1925- *St&PR 93, WhoAmW 93*
McCormack, Mary Ellen 1864-1956 *BioIn 17*
McCormack, Mike 1930- *BioIn 17*
Mc Cormack, Olivia *WhoWrEP 92*
McCormack, Patricia Seger 1927- *WhoAm 92, WhoWor 93*
McCormack, Richard Austin *St&PR 93*
McCormack, Richard Thomas Fox 1941- *WhoAm 92*
McCormack, Robert Cornelius 1939- *WhoAm 92*
McCormack, Robert Emmett, Jr. 1923- *St&PR 93*
Mc Cormack, Sharon Renda 1961- *WhoWrEP 92*
McCormack, Thomas Joseph 1932- *St&PR 93*
McCormack, W.J. 1947- *ScF&FL 92*
McCormack, William Arthur 1951- *WhoEmL 93*
McCormack, William Orrin *Law&B 92*
McCormally, Kevin Jay 1950- *WhoE 93*
McCormick, Adele von Rust 1929- *WhoWor 93*
McCormick, Alma Heflin 1910- *WhoAmW 93*
McCormick, Anne 1889-1954 *JrnUS*
McCormick, Barnes Warnock 1926- *WhoAm 92*
McCormick, Barry 1949- *WhoWor 93*
McCormick, Betty Jean 1950- *WhoEmL 93*
McCormick, Charles Clair 1946- *WhoE 93*
McCormick, Charles Perry, Jr. 1928- *St&PR 93, WhoAm 92*
McCormick, Chris Weldon 1954- *WhoEmL 93*
McCormick, Clarence James 1925- *WhoAm 92*
McCormick, Clarence Okey 1925- *St&PR 93*
McCormick, Cyrus Hall 1809-1884 *BioIn 17*
McCormick, Dale 1947- *WhoAmW 93*
McCormick, David Arthur 1946- *WhoEmL 93*
McCormick, Deane E., Jr. *Law&B 92*
Mccormick, Dennis J. 1945- *St&PR 93*
McCormick, Dennis Ray 1942- *WhoAm 92*
McCormick, Don 1940- *St&PR 93*
McCormick, Donald 1898- *WhoAm 92*
Mc Cormick, Donald Bruce 1932- *WhoAm 92, WhoSSW 93*
McCormick, Donald E. 1941- *WhoAm 92*
McCormick, Donald P. *Law&B 92*
McCormick, Douglas Jess 1949- *WhoE 93*
McCormick, Edmund J. *St&PR 93*
Mc Cormick, Edward Allen 1925- *WhoAm 92*
McCormick, Edward James, Jr. 1921- *WhoAm 92*
McCormick, Edward Theodore 1911-1991 *BioIn 17*
McCormick, Edward Theodore, Jr. 1939- *WhoE 93*
McCormick, Elaine Alice 1943- *WhoAmW 93*
McCormick, Ernest James *BioIn 17*
McCormick, Eugene F., Jr. 1942- *WhoAm 92*
McCormick, Floyd Guy, Jr. 1927- *WhoAm 92*
McCormick, G. Roger 1940- *St&PR 93*
Mccormick, Gedney John 1936- *St&PR 93*
Mc Cormick, Hope Baldwin 1919- *WhoAm 92*
McCormick, Howard Charles 1951- *WhoWor 93*
McCormick, J. Philip 1942- *St&PR 93, WhoSSW 93*
McCormick, James C. 1938- *St&PR 93*
Mc Cormick, James Charles 1938- *WhoAm 92*

McCormick, James Clarence 1924- WhoAm 92
McCormick, James E. 1927- St&PR 93
McCormick, James Edward 1927- WhoAm 92
Mc Cormick, James Harold 1938- WhoAm 92, WhoE 93
McCormick, James Hillman 1921- WhoSSW 93
McCormick, James M. 1925- St&PR 93
McCormick, James S. 1926- WhoScE 91-3
McCormick, Joan A. 1938- St&PR 93
McCormick, John Crimmins 1935- WhoAm 92
McCormick, John Francis 1933- St&PR 93, WhoAm 92
McCormick, John Hoyle 1933- WhoSSW 93
McCormick, John J., Jr. 1931- St&PR 93
Mc Cormick, John Owen 1918- WhoAm 92
McCormick, John Patrick 1945- WhoE 93
McCormick, John R. 1942- St&PR 93
McCormick, Joseph Francis, Sr. 1933- WhoE 93
McCormick, Joseph Medill 1877-1925 JrnUS
McCormick, Karen Louise 1954- WhoAmW 93
Mc Cormick, Kenneth Dale 1906- WhoAm 92, WhoWrEP 92
McCormick, Kenneth James 1951- WhoE 93
McCormick, Leo, Jr. Law&B 92
McCormick, Leslie Sommer 1952- WhoWor 93
Mccormick, Leta Marie 1930- St&PR 93
McCormick, Lois Elizabeth ScF&FL 92
McCormick, Louise L. 1942- St&PR 93
McCormick, Mark St&PR 93
McCormick, Mary K. Law&B 92
McCormick, Maureen 1956- BioIn 17
McCormick, Maureen Olivea 1956- WhoAmW 93, WhoEmL 93
McCormick, Merle 1941- St&PR 93
McCormick, Michael D. 1948- St&PR 93, WhoAm 92
McCormick, Micheal Law&B 92
McCormick, N.C. Law&B 92
McCormick, Nancy Jane 1935- WhoSSW 93
McCormick, Neil Charles Law&B 92
McCormick, Pamela Ann 1948- WhoE 93, WhoEmL 93, WhoWor 93
McCormick, Patricia Keller 1930- BioIn 17
McCormick, Patrick Edward 1964- St&PR 93
McCormick, Richard Arthur 1922- WhoAm 92
McCormick, Richard C. 1832-1901 BioIn 17
McCormick, Richard D. 1940- St&PR 93
McCormick, Richard David 1940- WhoAm 92
Mccormick, Richard L. 1943- St&PR 93
Mc Cormick, Richard Patrick 1916- WhoAm 92
McCormick, Robert Gray Law&B 92
McCormick, Robert H. 1914- WhoE 93
McCormick, Robert Junior 1929- WhoAm 92
McCormick, Robert Lee 1928- St&PR 93
McCormick, Robert Matthew, III 1938- WhoAm 92
McCormick, Robert R. 1880-1955 JrnUS, PolPar
McCormick, Ruth Hanna 1880-1944 BioIn 17
McCormick, Scot M. 1953- St&PR 93
McCormick, Stephen Francis 1937- St&PR 93
McCormick, Steven Thomas 1955- WhoSSW 93
McCormick, Susan Konn 1953- St&PR 93
McCormick, Thomas Law&B 92
McCormick, Thomas Clark 1929- St&PR 93
McCormick, Thomas Emerick 1953- WhoEmL 93
Mccormick, Thomas H. 1940- St&PR 93
McCormick, Thomas Jay 1946- WhoE 93
Mc Cormick, Thomas Julian 1925- WhoAm 92
McCormick, Thomas Patrick 1953- St&PR 93
McCormick, Vance C. 1872-1946 PolPar
McCormick, Vance Criswell 1872-1946 BioIn 17
McCormick, William 1942- WhoE 93
McCormick, William Charles 1933- WhoAm 92
McCormick, William Edward 1912- WhoAm 92, WhoWor 93
Mc Cormick, William Frederick 1933- WhoAm 92
Mc Cormick, William Martin 1921- WhoAm 92
McCormick, William T., Jr. Law&B 92
McCormick, William T., Jr. 1944- St&PR 93
McCormick, William Thomas, Jr. 1944- WhoAm 92
Mc Cormick, Willie Mae Ward 1908- WhoWor 93
McCormick-Ray, Mary Geraldine 1943- WhoSSW 93
McCornock, J.M. 1938- St&PR 93
McCorquodale, Barbara ScF&FL 92
McCorquodale, Barbara Hamilton Cartland 1902- BioIn 17
McCorry, Mary Elenore 1925- WhoAmW 93
McCorry, Patrick George 1941- St&PR 93
McCorry, Vincent P. 1909-1990 BioIn 17
McCoskey, James John 1939- St&PR 93
McCosky, Barney 1918- BioIn 17
McCotter, Burney R. 1920- WhoIns 93
McCotter, James R. Law&B 92
McCotter, James R. 1943- St&PR 93
McCotter, James Rawson 1943- WhoAm 92
McCoubrey, J.D. WhoScE 91-1
McCoubrey, James BioIn 17
McCoubrey, R. James 1944- WhoAm 92
McCouch, Donald Grayson 1942- WhoAm 92
McCourt, Edna Wahlert AmWomPl
McCourt, Terence Peter Law&B 92
McCovey, Willie BioIn 17
Mc Covey, Willie Lee 1938- WhoAm 92
McCowan, George MiSFD 9
McCowen, Alec 1925- WhoWor 93
McCowen, Max Creager 1915- WhoAm 92
McCown, David Layton 1949- St&PR 93
McCown, Fred E. 1938- St&PR 93
McCown, George E. 1935- WhoAm 92
McCown, George Edwin 1935- St&PR 93
McCown, Hale 1914- WhoAm 92
McCown, Harrison J. Law&B 92
Mc Cown, John Clinton 1952- WhoWrEP 92
Mccown, John D. 1954- St&PR 93
McCown, Judith Porter 1904- WhoAmW 93
McCown, Laurie Rutherford 1954- WhoSSW 93
McCown, Shaun Michael Patrick 1949- WhoWor 93
McCown, Wayne Gordon 1942- WhoE 93
McCown, William L. Law&B 92
McCoy, Andrew 1945- ScF&FL 92
McCoy, Ann Brelsford 1940- WhoAmW 93
McCoy, Bob F. Law&B 92
McCoy, Bowen Hadley 1937- WhoAm 92
McCoy, Carol Ann Law&B 92
McCoy, Carol Louise 1947- WhoAmW 93
McCoy, Carol P. 1948- WhoAmW 93, WhoEmL 93
McCoy, Charles Wallace 1920- WhoAm 92, WhoSSW 93
Mc Coy, Clarence John, Jr. 1935- WhoAm 92
McCoy, Daniel Eugene 1937- St&PR 93
McCoy, Dean A. 1957- St&PR 93
McCoy, Debra J. 1958- St&PR 93
McCoy, Dennis R. Law&B 92
Mc Coy, Donald Richard 1928- WhoAm 92
McCoy, Dorothy Eloise 1916- WhoAmW 93
McCoy, Douglas Leon 1957- WhoEmL 93
McCoy, Dustan E. Law&B 92
Mc Coy, Easton Whitney 1918- WhoWrEP 92
McCoy, Edward Fitzgerald 1938- WhoAm 92
McCoy, Eileen Carey WhoE 93
McCoy, Elaine Jean 1946- WhoAmW 93
McCoy, Elijah BioIn 17
Mccoy, Elmer C. 1936- St&PR 93
McCoy, Esther 1904?-1989 BioIn 17
McCoy, Evelyn BioIn 17
Mc Coy, Frederick John 1916- WhoAm 92
McCoy, Gladys AfrAmBi [port], WhoAmW 93
McCoy, Glen ScF&FL 92
McCoy, Henry Banks, Jr. 1928- St&PR 93
McCoy, James Bertram 1926- WhoSSW 93
McCoy, James D. 1937- St&PR 93
McCoy, James Freeman 1926- St&PR 93
McCoy, James Henry 1947- WhoAm 92
McCoy, James M. 1946- ConEn, St&PR 93
McCoy, Janice Maxine 1945- WhoSSW 93
McCoy, Jason 1948- BioIn 17
McCoy, Jimmy Dean 1959- WhoSSW 93
McCoy, Joan Gail 1952- WhoAmW 93
McCoy, Joenne Rae 1941- WhoAmW 93
McCoy, John Bonnet BioIn 17
McCoy, John Bonnet 1943- St&PR 93, WhoAm 92
McCoy, John Gardner 1913- BioIn 17, St&PR 93, WhoAm 92
McCoy, John Greene 1946- WhoSSW 93
McCoy, John Joseph 1952- WhoEmL 93
McCoy, John O., Jr. 1951- St&PR 93
Mc Coy, Joseph Jerome, Jr. 1917- WhoWrEP 92
Mc Coy, Karen Kawamoto 1953- WhoWrEP 92
McCoy, Katherine Braden 1945- WhoAm 92
Mc Coy, Kathleen (Kathy) 1945- WhoWrEP 92
McCoy, Kathleen Lynne 1945- WhoAmW 93
McCoy, Kathryn L. Law&B 92
McCoy, Kevin 1942- St&PR 93
McCoy, Linda Jane 1951- WhoEmL 93
Mc Coy, Lois Clark 1920- WhoAmW 93
McCoy, Margaret Ann 1946- WhoAmW 93
McCoy, Marilyn 1948- WhoAmW 93, WhoEmL 93
McCoy, Martin Roger, Jr. 1947- St&PR 93
Mccoy, Maureen Ellen WhoWrEP 92
McCoy, Meredith 1949- WhoEmL 93
McCoy, Michael Dale 1944- WhoAm 92
McCoy, Michael James 1954- WhoEmL 93
McCoy, Michael Lawrence Law&B 92
Mc Coy, Miles Edward 1949- WhoWrEP 92
McCoy, Millington F. 1941- WhoAm 92
McCoy, Molly Anna 1948- WhoAmW 93
McCoy, Neal S. 1940- WhoAm 92
McCoy, Nicholas Francis Law&B 92
McCoy, Patricia Alice 1952- WhoAmW 93
McCoy, Patricia Ann 1954- WhoAmW 93
McCoy, Reagan Scott 1945- WhoSSW 93
McCoy, Richard Floyd 1942-1974 BioIn 17
Mc Coy, Robert Baker 1916- WhoAm 92
McCoy, Robert S., Jr. 1938- WhoAm 92, WhoSSW 93
McCoy, Robert Smith, Jr. 1938- St&PR 93
Mc Coy, Robin Renee 1957- WhoWrEP 92
McCoy, Seth 1928- Baker 92
McCoy, Stuart Sherman 1958- WhoEmL 93, WhoSSW 93
McCoy, Suzanne Donavant 1957- WhoEmL 93
McCoy, Thomas G. 1943- St&PR 93
McCoy, Thomas Raymond 1943- WhoAm 92
Mc Coy, Tidal Windham 1945- WhoAm 92
McCoy, Timothy Eugene Law&B 92
McCoy, Tom St&PR 93
McCoy, Van 1940-1979 SoulM
McCoy, Virginia Ruth 1941- WhoAmW 93
McCoy, Wanda Faye BioIn 17
McCoy, Wesley Lawrence 1935- WhoAm 92
McCoy, William AfrAmBi [port]
McCoy, William Carroll Law&B 92
Mc Coy, William Daniel 1929- WhoAm 92
McCoy, William J. 1848-1926 Baker 92
McCoy, William O. 1933- St&PR 93, WhoSSW 93
McCoy-Shay, Donna Carol 1952- WhoAmW 93, WhoEmL 93
Mccracken, Alan L. 1950- St&PR 93
McCracken, Alexander Walker 1931- WhoSSW 93
McCracken, Alistair R. 1951- WhoScE 91-1
McCracken, Caron Francis 1951- WhoAmW 93
Mc Cracken, Daniel Delbert 1930- WhoAm 92, WhoWrEP 92
McCracken, Donna Lee 1954- WhoEmL 93, WhoSSW 93
Mccracken, Edward R. 1943- St&PR 93
McCracken, Ellis W. Law&B 92
McCracken, Ellis W., Jr. WhoAm 92
McCracken, Ernest E. 1934- St&PR 93
Mc Cracken, George Herbert 1899- WhoAm 92
McCracken, Henry Joy 1767-1798 BioIn 17
McCracken, Ina 1939- WhoAmW 93
McCracken, Jack Jay Law&B 92
McCracken, James 1926-1988 OxDcOp
McCracken, James (John Eugene) 1926-1988 Baker 92
McCracken, Jarrell BioIn 17
McCracken, John Harvey 1934- WhoAm 92
McCracken, John Walter 1944- St&PR 93
McCracken, Linda 1948- WhoAmW 93
McCracken, Mary Ann 1770-1866 BioIn 17
Mc Cracken, Paul Winston 1915- WhoAm 92
Mc Cracken, Philip Trafton 1928- WhoAm 92
McCracken, R.M. WhoScE 91-1
McCracken, Robert C. Law&B 92
McCracken, Robert David 1934- St&PR 93
McCracken, Steven Carl 1950- WhoAm 92
McCracken, Thomas C. 1948- St&PR 93
McCracken, William Edward 1929- St&PR 93
McCrackin, Maurice F. 1905- BioIn 17
McCrackin, William K. 1933- WhoAm 92
McCrady, Barbara Sachs 1949- WhoAmW 93
McCrady, James David 1930- WhoAm 92
McCrady, Kenneth Allen 1930- St&PR 93
McCrae, David Anthony 1950- WhoEmL 93
McCrae, George 1944-1986 SoulM
McCrae, Gwen SoulM
McCrae, John 1872-1918 BioIn 17
McCrae, Robert Fletcher 1945- St&PR 93
Mc Crae, Sharon Elizabeth 1955- WhoWrEP 92
McCrae, Stewart A. Law&B 92
McCrae, William Law&B 92
McCrae, William 1934- WhoIns 93
McCranie, Ed 1948- St&PR 93
Mccranie, Stephen C. 1945- St&PR 93
McCrary, Dennie L. 1938- St&PR 93
McCrary, Douglas L. 1929- WhoAm 92
McCrary, Eugenia Lester 1929- WhoAmW 93, WhoE 93, WhoWor 93
McCrary, James Edward 1958- WhoSSW 93
McCrary, Larry Frank 1949- WhoEmL 93
McCrary, Sharon Kay 1952- WhoAmW 93
McCrary, William Anthony Law&B 92
McCraven, Carl Clarke 1926- WhoWor 93
McCraven, Marcus Rollins 1923- St&PR 93
McCraven, Stephen 1954- WhoE 93
McCraw, David Bruce 1942- WhoSSW 93
McCraw, Edward Lee 1951- WhoE 93
McCraw, Harris Lamar, III 1952- WhoEmL 93
McCraw, Les 1934- WhoAm 92
McCraw, Leslie G. 1934- St&PR 93
McCraw, Ronald Kent 1947- WhoWor 93
McCraw, Thomas Erwin 1948- St&PR 93
McCraw, Thomas Kincaid 1940- WhoAm 92
McCray, Bernard Winn, Jr. 1934- St&PR 93
Mc Cray, Evelina Williams 1932- WhoAmW 93
McCray, Harry Claxton, Jr. 1933- St&PR 93
Mc Cray, Katherine Lee 1961- WhoWrEP 92
McCray, Robert Cone 1926- St&PR 93
McCray, Ronald David Law&B 92
McCray, Ronald David 1957- WhoEmL 93
McCray, Yvonne 1950- WhoEmL 93
Mc Crea, Frank William 1942- WhoWrEP 92
McCrea, Joel 1905-1990 BioIn 17, IntDcF 2-3
McCrea, Joseph William 1946- St&PR 93
McCrea, Peter Frederick 1942- St&PR 93
McCrea, Terri Lyn 1967- WhoAmW 93
McCrea, William Sloan 1913- St&PR 93
McCready, K.F. 1939- St&PR 93
McCready, Kenneth Frank 1939- WhoAm 92
McCready, L. Stephen Law&B 92
McCready, Mary Elizabeth 1937- WhoAmW 93
McCready, Michael 1913- BioIn 17
McCready, Pamela Grigsby 1953- WhoAmW 93
McCready, Richard French 1905- St&PR 93
McCready, Sam 1936- WhoE 93
McCreary, Ann Margaret Law&B 92
McCreary, Dustin Campbell 1928- WhoAm 92
McCreary, Gail Ann 1951- WhoSSW 93
McCreary, Harry Clay 1926- St&PR 93
Mc Creary, James Franklin 1942- WhoAm 92
McCreary, Joseph BioIn 17
McCreary, Judy Marian 1946- WhoAmW 93, WhoEmL 93
McCreary, Marjorie AmWomPl
McCreary, Richard Temple 1955- WhoSSW 93
McCreary, Robert Grosvenor, Jr. 1918- WhoAm 92
McCreary, Sharron B. 1957- WhoAmW 93
McCredie, Kenneth B. 1935-1991 BioIn 17
McCree, Donald H., Jr. 1936- St&PR 93
McCree, Donald Hanna, Jr. 1936- WhoAm 92
McCree, Junie 1866-1918 AmWomPl
McCreery, Frank E. d1990 BioIn 17
McCreery, Harry K. 1946- St&PR 93

McCreery, James Allan 1933- *WhoSSW 93*
McCreery, Robert Atkeson 1917- *WhoSSW 93*
McCreery, Robert D. 1917- *St&PR 93*
McCreery, William 1931- *WhoAm 92*
McCreery, William 1932- *WhoWor 93*
McCreery, William G. *Law&B 92*
McCreigh, James *ConAu 37NR*
McCreight, Charles Edward 1913- *WhoSSW 93*
McCreight, Susan Buckley 1946- *WhoE 93*
McCrensky, Edward 1912- *WhoAm 92*
McCrery, James 1949- *WhoSSW 93*
McCrery, Jim 1949- *CngDr 91, WhoAm 92*
McCrevan, Rosemary Ann 1952- *WhoE 93*
Mc Crie, Robert Delbert 1938- *WhoAm 92, WhoWrEP 92*
McCright, John J. 1925- *St&PR 93*
McCrillis, Jennie Van Heyson *AmWomPl*
McCrimmon, Barbara Smith 1918- *WhoAmW 93*
McCrimmon, James McNab 1908- *WhoAm 92, WhoWrEP 92*
Mc Crone, Alistair William 1931- *WhoAm 92*
McCrone, John (Robert) 1957- *ConAu 139*
McCrone, Walter Cox 1916- *WhoAm 92*
McCrory, Bradley Lawrence 1953- *WhoSSW 93*
McCrory, Colleen *BioIn 17*
McCrory, Donald Brann 1946- *St&PR 93*
McCrory, Edwin Donald, III 1958- *WhoSSW 93*
McCrory, Ellann 1936- *WhoAmW 93, WhoWor 93*
McCrory, Heidi Hansen 1961- *WhoAmW 93*
McCrory, John Brooks 1925- *WhoAm 92*
McCrory, Martha *WhoSSW 93*
McCrory, Pamela Jean 1955- *WhoAmW 93*
McCrory, Robert Lee 1946- *WhoAm 92*
McCrory, Shirley Till 1935- *WhoAmW 93*
Mc Crory, Wallace Willard 1920- *WhoAm 92*
McCroskey, Cindy Price 1961- *WhoSSW 93*
McCroskey, Lenora Estelle 1943- *WhoSSW 93*
Mc Croskey, William James 1937- *WhoAm 92*
McCrossan, John Patrick 1943- *WhoE 93*
McCrossen, Melanie 1957- *St&PR 93*
McCrudden, Stephen Worth 1949- *WhoEmL 93*
McCrum, Blanche Prichard 1887-1969 *BioIn 17*
McCrum, Charles David 1946- *WhoEmL 93*
McCrum, Lindsay *BioIn 17*
McCrum, Michael William 1924- *WhoWor 93*
McCrumb, Sharyn *BioIn 17*
McCrumb, Sharyn 1948- *ScF&FL 92*
McCuan, William Patrick 1941- *WhoE 93, WhoWor 93*
McCubbin, Earline M. 1947- *WhoAmW 93*
McCubbin, Frederick 1855-1917 *BioIn 17*
McCubbin, Hamilton, II 1941- *WhoAm 92*
McCubbin, Horace W. *WhoIns 93*
McCubbin, Horace W. 1931- *St&PR 93*
McCubbin, Susan Brubeck 1948- *WhoAmW 93, WhoEmL 93*
McCudden, Bernard Joseph 1946- *St&PR 93*
McCue, Arthur Bernard 1926- *WhoE 93*
McCue, Arthur Harry 1944- *WhoE 93*
McCue, Bernice 1960- *WhoE 93*
Mc Cue, Carolyn Moore 1916- *WhoAm 92*
McCue, Edmund Bradley 1929- *WhoWor 93*
McCue, Florence Therese 1948- *WhoAmW 93*
McCue, Frances 1962- *ConAu 139*
McCue, Gerald Mallon 1928- *WhoAm 92*
McCue, Howard McDowell, III 1946- *WhoAm 92*
McCue, John Hollis 1945- *WhoAm 92*
McCue, Kenneth Russell 1946- *WhoE 93*
Mccue, Kevin 1959- *St&PR 93*
McCue, Lisa *BioIn 17*
McCue, Lisa (Emiline) 1959- *ConAu 136*
McCue, Mary E. *Law&B 92*
McCue, Mary Madeline 1947- *WhoAm 92*
McCue, Michael 1951- *WhoEmL 93*
McCue, Wolford Massie 1952- *WhoSSW 93*
McCuen, John Francis, Jr. 1944- *WhoAm 92*
McCuen, John Joachim 1926- *WhoWor 93*
McCuen, Peter Burton 1934- *WhoE 93*
McCuen, William James 1943- *WhoAm 92, WhoSSW 93*
McCuish, John Berridge 1906-1962 *BioIn 17*
McCuish, Michael J. 1957- *St&PR 93*
McCuistion, Jack Haywood 1934- *St&PR 93*
McCuistion, Robert Wiley 1927- *WhoAm 92*
McCullagh, Andrew M., Jr. 1948- *St&PR 93*
McCullagh, Clement George 1905-1952 *BioIn 17*
McCullagh, Grant Gibson 1951- *WhoEmL 93*
McCullagh, James Charles 1941- *WhoAm 92, WhoWrEP 92*
McCullagh, Joseph B. 1842-1896 *JrnUS*
McCullagh, Kevin Joseph 1945- *St&PR 93*
McCullar, Bruce Hayden 1953- *WhoEmL 93, WhoSSW 93, WhoWor 93*
McCullars, Denise Williams 1953- *St&PR 93*
McCullen, Michael John 1937- *WhoE 93*
McCullers, Carson 1917-1967 *AmWomWr 92, BioIn 17, MagSAmL [port], WorLitC [port]*
McCulley, Michael Bernard *Law&B 92*
McCulley, Michael Wilson 1953- *WhoEmL 93*
McCulley, Sandra Kay 1957- *WhoAmW 93, WhoEmL 93*
McCulley, Thomas Melvin 1947- *St&PR 93, WhoEmL 93, WhoSSW 93*
McCullin, Don 1935- *BioIn 17*
McCullins, John Thomas 1928- *WhoScE 91-1*
McCulloch, Anna Mary Knott 1964- *WhoE 93*
McCulloch, Ben 1811-1862 *HarEnMi*
McCulloch, Catharine Waugh *AmWomPl*
McCulloch, Cathy Marie 1954- *WhoAmW 93, WhoEmL 93*
McCulloch, Cedric Seymour 1938- *WhoUN 92*
McCulloch, David W. *Law&B 92*
Mc Culloch, Ernest Armstrong 1926- *WhoAm 92*
McCulloch, Frank 1930- *BioIn 17*
Mc Culloch, Frank W. 1905- *WhoAm 92*
McCulloch, Gail Corinne 1952- *WhoAmW 93*
McCulloch, J.S.G. *WhoScE 91-1*
McCulloch, James *WhoScE 91-1*
McCulloch, James Callahan 1947- *WhoAm 92, WhoEmL 93*
McCulloch, James L. *Law&B 92*
McCulloch, James L. 1952- *St&PR 93*
McCulloch, John Vincent 1927- *WhoIns 93*
McCulloch, Kathryn Valerie *Law&B 92*
McCulloch, Kenneth John 1943- *WhoAm 92*
McCulloch, Norman E., Jr. 1926- *St&PR 93*
McCulloch, Rachel 1942- *WhoAm 92*
Mc Culloch, Samuel Clyde 1916- *WhoAm 92*
McCulloch, Sarah *MajAI*
McCulloch, Terri 1957- *WhoAmW 93*
McCulloch, Thomas 1773-1843 *BioIn 17*
McCulloch, William Leonard 1921- *WhoAm 92*
McCulloh, Evelyn Butler 1910- *WhoSSW 93*
McCulloh, John R. *Law&B 92*
McCullom, Charles W. d1991 *BioIn 17*
McCullom, Cornell, Jr. 1932- *WhoE 93*
McCullouch, John M. *Law&B 92*
McCullough, Colin David 1929- *WhoAm 92*
McCullough, Colleen *WhoAm 92*
McCullough, Colleen 1937- *BioIn 17, ScF&FL 92*
McCullough, Dale H. 1937- *St&PR 93*
McCullough, David *NewYTBS 92 [port]*
Mc Cullough, David 1933- *WhoAm 92*
McCullough, David G. 1933- *BioIn 17*
McCullough, Edgar Joseph, Jr. 1931- *WhoAm 92*
Mc Cullough, Frances Monson 1938- *WhoWrEP 92*
McCullough, Frank V. 1920- *WhoIns 93*
McCullough, George Bierce 1925- *WhoAm 92*
McCullough, George R. 1929- *St&PR 93*
McCullough, George W., Jr. 1950- *AfrAmBi*
Mc Cullough, Helen Craig 1918- *WhoAm 92*
McCullough, Henry Glenn Luther 1939- *WhoWor 93*
McCullough, Hugh James 1950- *WhoSSW 93*
Mc Cullough, J. Lee 1945- *WhoWor 93*
McCullough, James Armstrong 1934- *St&PR 93*
McCullough, James Howard 1955- *WhoEmL 93*
McCullough, Jim, Sr. *MiSFD 9*
McCullough, John Jeffrey 1938- *WhoAm 92*
Mccullough, John Norcott 1932- *St&PR 93*
Mc Cullough, John Price 1925- *WhoAm 92*
McCullough, Joseph 1922- *WhoAm 92*
McCullough, Joseph E. 1942- *St&PR 93*
McCullough, Kathryn T. Baker 1925- *WhoAmW 93, WhoSSW 93*
Mc Cullough, Ken 1943- *WhoWrEP 92*
McCullough, Kimberly Anne 1956- *WhoEmL 93, WhoSSW 93*
McCullough, Michael Lloyd *Law&B 92*
McCullough, Pamela J. *Law&B 92*
McCullough, Paul 1883-1936 *See* Clark, Bobby 1888-1960 & McCullough, Paul 1883-1936 *QDrFCA 92*
McCullough, R. Michael 1938- *St&PR 93, WhoAm 92, WhoWor 93*
Mc Cullough, Ralph Clayton, II 1941- *WhoAm 92*
McCullough, Ray Daniel, Jr. 1938- *WhoAm 92*
McCullough, Richard Lawrence 1937- *WhoAm 92*
McCullough, Robert Dale, II 1937- *WhoSSW 93*
McCullough, Robert G. 1948- *WhoSSW 93*
McCullough, Robert Willis 1920- *WhoAm 92*
McCullough, Roy Lynn 1934- *WhoAm 92*
McCullough, Samuel Alexander 1938- *St&PR 93, WhoAm 92*
McCullough, Sandra Gail 1950- *WhoAmW 93*
McCullough, Scott Charles 1966- *WhoEmL 93*
McCullough, Susan Renee 1958- *WhoAmW 93*
McCullough, Timothy Joel 1945- *WhoWor 93*
McCullough, Todd Alan 1962- *WhoAm 92*
McCullough-Testa, Kathy Maria 1964- *WhoAmW 93*
McCullum, R. Gene 1934- *St&PR 93*
McCully, Emily Arnold *MajAI*
Mc Cully, Emily Arnold 1939- *WhoWrEP 92*
Mccully, L.D. 1929- *St&PR 93*
McCully, Murray S. 1953- *WhoAsAP 91*
McCully, Ruth Alida 1933- *WhoAmW 93*
McCumiskey, W. *WhoScE 91-3*
McCune, Amy Reed 1954- *WhoEmL 93*
McCune, Barbara Ann 1934- *WhoSSW 93*
Mc Cune, Barron Patterson 1915- *WhoAm 92*
McCune, Cecil Perry 1946- *WhoEmL 93*
McCune, David Franklin 1954- *WhoAm 92*
McCune, Diana R. *Law&B 92*
McCune, Ellis E. 1921- *WhoAm 92*
McCune, Francis Patrick *Law&B 92*
McCune, George D. 1924-1990 *BioIn 17*
McCune, James Augustus, III 1938- *St&PR 93*
Mc Cune, John Francis, III 1921- *WhoAm 92*
McCune, Mary Joan Huxley 1932- *WhoAmW 93*
McCune, R.G. *St&PR 93*
McCune, Samuel K. 1921- *St&PR 93*
McCune, Samuel Kirk 1921- *WhoAm 92*
McCune, Sara Miller 1941- *WhoAm 92*
McCune, William M. 1922- *St&PR 93*
McCune, William Minton 1922- *WhoAm 92*
McCuniff, Mara *ScF&FL 92*
McCunn, Ruthanne Lum *BioIn 17*
Mc Cunn, Ruthanne Lum 1946- *WhoWrEP 92*
Mccurdy, Daniel T. 1933- *St&PR 93*
McCurdy, Dave 1950- *CngDr 91*
McCurdy, Dave K. *BioIn 17*
McCurdy, David Keith 1950- *WhoAm 92*
McCurdy, David Keith Dave 1950- *WhoSSW 93*
McCurdy, Elmer d1911 *BioIn 17*
Mccurdy, Floyd A. *St&PR 93*
McCurdy, Gilbert Geier 1922- *St&PR 93, WhoAm 92*
Mc Curdy, Harold Grier 1909- *WhoAm 92*
McCurdy, Harry Ward 1918- *WhoAm 92*
McCurdy, Julius A. 1903- *St&PR 93*
McCurdy, Kurt Basquin 1952- *WhoEmL 93*
McCurdy, Larry Wayne 1935- *St&PR 93, WhoAm 92, WhoWor 93*
McCurdy, Mary Jacqueline 1933- *WhoAmW 93*
Mc Curdy, Patrick Pierre 1928- *WhoAm 92, WhoWor 93, WhoWrEP 92*
McCurdy, Richard Clark 1909- *WhoAm 92, WhoWor 93*
McCurdy, William A., Jr. *Law&B 92*
McCurley, Carl Michael 1946- *WhoEmL 93*
McCurley, F. C. 1934- *WhoAm 92*
Mc Curley, Robert Lee, Jr. 1941- *WhoAm 92*
McCurn, Neal Peters 1926- *WhoAm 92, WhoE 93*
McCurrach, James Crampton 1934- *WhoE 93*
McCurrich, L.H. *WhoScE 91-1*
McCurry, Edward Norris 1952- *WhoEmL 93*
McCurry, Margaret I. *BioIn 17*
McCurry, Margaret Irene 1942- *WhoAm 92*
McCurry, Margarethe Donhauser 1932- *WhoAmW 93*
McCurry, Rickey Neal 1959- *WhoSSW 93*
McCurry, Robert *BioIn 17*
McCurry, Robert O. *St&PR 93*
McCurry, Virginia Marie 1928- *WhoAmW 93*
McCurry, William Jeffery 1947- *St&PR 93*
McCurtain, Bradley Chris 1952- *WhoEmL 93*
McCusker, Alison 1933- *WhoScE 91-3*
McCusker, Diane Carol 1947- *WhoAmW 93*
McCusker, Harold 1940-1990 *BioIn 17*
McCusker, Jim A. 1939- *St&PR 93*
McCusker, Mary Lauretta 1919- *WhoAm 92*
McCusker, Thomas J. 1943- *St&PR 93*
McCusker, William LaValle 1918- *WhoWor 93*
McCutchan, Betty Ann 1931- *WhoSSW 93*
McCutchan, Gordon E. *Law&B 92*
McCutchan, Gordon E. 1935- *St&PR 93, WhoIns 93*
McCutchan, Gordon Eugene 1935- *WhoAm 92*
Mc Cutchan, Kenneth Peva 1913- *WhoWrEP 92*
McCutchan, Philip 1920- *ScF&FL 92*
McCutchan, Robert Guy 1877-1958 *Baker 92*
McCutchan, William M. 1954- *St&PR 93*
McCutchan, William Mark 1954- *WhoWor 93*
McCutchen, Ann *ScF&FL 92*
McCutchen, Audrey Jean 1942- *WhoAmW 93*
McCutchen, David Johnstone 1951- *WhoEmL 93*
McCutchen, John Robert 1950- *St&PR 93*
McCutchen, R. Terry 1947?- *ScF&FL 92*
McCutchen, Richard D. 1946- *St&PR 93*
McCutchen, William Walter, Jr. 1940- *WhoE 93*
McCutcheon, Allan Lee 1950- *WhoE 93*
McCutcheon, Clinton B. 1930- *St&PR 93*
McCutcheon, Douglas J. 1948- *St&PR 93*
McCutcheon, Elsie 1937- *BioIn 17*
McCutcheon, Floretta Doty 1888-1967 *BioIn 17*
McCutcheon, George Barr 1866-1928 *GayN*
McCutcheon, Irene 1940- *WhoE 93*
McCutcheon, John J. *WhoScE 91-1*
McCutcheon, John Oliver 1924- *St&PR 93*
Mc Cutcheon, John Tinney, Jr. 1917- *WhoAm 92*
McCutcheon, Stephen Christian 1939- *WhoSSW 93*
McDade, Herbert Hardinge, Jr. 1927- *St&PR 93*
McDade, James Russell 1925- *WhoWor 93*
McDade, Joseph M. 1931- *CngDr 91*
Mc Dade, Joseph Michael 1931- *WhoAm 92, WhoE 93*
McDade, Sandy D. *Law&B 92*
McDade, Sharon Ann 1952- *WhoEmL 93*
McDade, William Joseph 1937- *WhoAm 92*
McDade, William Robert 1936- *St&PR 93*
McDaid, Hugh d1992 *BioIn 17, NewYTBS 92*
McDaniel, Andrew Holmes *Law&B 92*
McDaniel, Barry 1930- *Baker 92*
McDaniel, Becky Bring 1953- *BioIn 17*
McDaniel, Benny Joe 1936- *WhoSSW 93*
McDaniel, Bobby L. 1939- *St&PR 93*
Mc Daniel, Bonny Elizabeth 1936- *WhoWrEP 92*
McDaniel, Boyce Dawkins 1917- *WhoAm 92*
McDaniel, C.J., III 1945- *WhoE 93*
McDaniel, Charles-Gene 1931- *WhoAm 92, WhoWrEP 92*

McDaniel, Claude Douglas 1952- *WhoEmL 93*
McDaniel, Curtis Lowell *Law&B 92*
McDaniel, D. Allen 1938- *St&PR 93*
McDaniel, David 1939-1977 *ScF&FL 92*
McDaniel, David J. 1942- *St&PR 93*
McDaniel, David Jamison 1913- *WhoAm 92*
McDaniel, Diane O. 1950- *St&PR 93*
McDaniel, Dolan Kenneth 1935- *WhoAm 92*
McDaniel, Elizabeth Logan *WhoAmW 93, WhoSSW 93*
McDaniel, F.E., Jr. 1955- *St&PR 93*
McDaniel, Felix C. 1939- *St&PR 93*
McDaniel, Gary Allan 1931- *WhoSSW 93*
Mcdaniel, George H. 1931- *St&PR 93*
McDaniel, Hattie 1895-1952 *IntDcF 2-3 [port]*
McDaniel, Henry 1867-1948 *BiDAMSp 1989*
Mcdaniel, James A. 1916- *St&PR 93*
Mc Daniel, James Edwin 1931- *WhoAm 92, WhoWor 93*
Mcdaniel, James R. 1944- *St&PR 93*
McDaniel, Jarrel Dave 1930- *WhoAm 92*
McDaniel, Jeffrey D. 1946- *St&PR 93*
McDaniel, John Perry 1942- *WhoAm 92*
McDaniel, John S., Jr. 1916- *WhoAm 92*
McDaniel, Kay Lynn 1960- *WhoAmW 93*
McDaniel, Lauralyn 1963- *WhoAmW 93*
McDaniel, Lisa Mae 1964- *WhoEmL 93*
McDaniel, Lurlene *BioIn 17*
McDaniel, Lurlene 1944- *SmATA 71 [port]*
McDaniel, Marianne Payne 1966- *WhoAmW 93*
McDaniel, Mary Grace Coen 1958- *WhoEmL 93*
McDaniel, Mary Jane 1946- *WhoEmL 93*
McDaniel, Maude Wheeler *AmWomPl*
McDaniel, Michael Conway Dixon 1929- *WhoAm 92, WhoSSW 93*
Mcdaniel, Michael L. 1947- *St&PR 93*
McDaniel, Mildred *BlkAmWO*
McDaniel, Mildred 1933- *BioIn 17*
McDaniel, Molly 1961- *WhoEmL 93*
McDaniel, Morey William *Law&B 92*
McDaniel, Myra Atwell 1932- *WhoAm 92, WhoAmW 93, WhoSSW 93*
McDaniel, Norwood Allan 1928- *WhoE 93*
McDaniel, Ollie Frank, Jr. 1945- *St&PR 93*
McDaniel, Raymond Deal, Jr. 1950- *WhoEmL 93*
Mc Daniel, Robbie Lee 1940- *WhoWrEP 92*
Mc Daniel, Roderick Rogers 1926- *WhoAm 92*
McDaniel, Ronald Lee 1939- *St&PR 93*
McDaniel, Sara Sherwood 1943- *WhoAmW 93, WhoSSW 93*
McDaniel, Stephen J. *Law&B 92*
McDaniel, Susan Holmes 1951- *WhoEmL 93*
McDaniel, Terry B. *Law&B 92*
McDaniel, Tom J. *Law&B 92*
McDaniel, William E. 1920- *WhoSSW 93*
McDaniel, William F., III 1951- *WhoSSW 93*
McDaniel, William J. 1943- *WhoAm 92*
McDaniel, William Jason, Jr. 1941- *WhoSSW 93*
McDaniel, William Patrick 1948- *St&PR 93*
McDaniel, William Windsor 1952- *WhoSSW 93*
McDaniel, Xavier *BioIn 17*
McDaniels, David Martin 1962- *WhoEmL 93, WhoSSW 93*
McDaniels, Gene 1935- *SoulM*
McDaniels, James *Law&B 92*
McDaniels, John Francis 1935- *WhoAm 92*
Mc Dannald, Clyde Elliott, Jr. 1923- *WhoWor 93*
McDannald, Werner Bagwell 1943- *St&PR 93*
Mcdargh-Elvins, Eileen 1948- *WhoWrEP 92*
McDarrah, Fred William 1926- *WhoAm 92, WhoWrEP 92*
McDarrah, Gloria Schoffel 1932- *WhoAm 92*
Mc David, George Eugene 1930- *WhoAm 92*
McDavid, J. Gary 1947- *WhoAm 92*
McDavid, Samuel L. 1946- *St&PR 93*
McDavid, William H. *Law&B 92*
McDavid, William H. 1946- *St&PR 93*
McDavid, William Henry 1946- *WhoAm 92*
McDede, James Bernard 1958- *WhoSSW 93*
McDermed, Marguerite E. *Law&B 92*
McDermid, Alice Marguerite Connell 1910- *WhoAmW 93*
McDermid, Edward J. 1908- *St&PR 93*
McDermid, John Alexander *WhoScE 91-1*
McDermid, John Alexander 1952- *WhoWor 93*
McDermott, Agnes Charlene Senape 1937- *WhoAm 92*
Mc Dermott, Albert Leo 1923- *WhoAm 92*
McDermott, Alice *BioIn 17*
McDermott, Alice 1953- *ConAu 40NR, CurBio 92 [port]*
McDermott, Arthur Dennis 1943- *St&PR 93*
McDermott, Cheryl Lynn 1953- *WhoEmL 93*
McDermott, Daniel John *Law&B 92*
McDermott, Daniel Joseph 1936- *St&PR 93*
McDermott, David *BioIn 17*
McDermott, Donna Crenshaw 1948- *WhoAmW 93*
McDermott, Drew Vincent 1949- *WhoAm 92*
McDermott, Edward Aloysious 1920- *WhoAm 92*
McDermott, Frances Gayle 1949- *WhoAmW 93*
McDermott, Francis Owen 1933- *WhoWor 93*
McDermott, Francis X. d1991 *BioIn 17*
McDermott, Gerald *ChlBIID [port]*
McDermott, Gerald (Edward) 1941- *MajAI [port]*
McDermott, Helen Crawford 1959- *WhoAmW 93*
McDermott, James A. 1936- *WhoAm 92*
McDermott, James Alexander 1938- *WhoAm 92*
McDermott, James Patrick *Law&B 92*
McDermott, James T. d1992 *NewYTBS 92*
McDermott, Jim 1936- *CngDr 91*
Mc Dermott, John Francis, Jr. 1929- *WhoAm 92*
McDermott, John Henry 1931- *WhoAm 92*
McDermott, John J. *Law&B 92*
McDermott, John James 1933- *WhoE 93*
Mc Dermott, John Joseph 1932- *WhoAm 92*
McDermott, John Joseph 1946- *WhoEmL 93*
McDermott, John Robert *Law&B 92*
McDermott, Joy Ann 1964- *WhoAmW 93*
McDermott, Julian A. d1990 *BioIn 17*
McDermott, Kay 1938- *WhoAmW 93*
McDermott, Kevin J. 1935- *WhoAm 92*
McDermott, Kevin L. 1954- *St&PR 93*
McDermott, Kevin M. 1950- *St&PR 93*
McDermott, L.T. 1948- *St&PR 93*
McDermott, Larry Arnold 1948- *WhoAm 92*
McDermott, Lucinda Mary 1947- *WhoAmW 93*
McDermott, Marianne *Law&B 92*
McDermott, Mary *Law&B 92*
McDermott, Mary 1943- *St&PR 93*
Mc Dermott, Michael James 1952- *WhoWrEP 92*
McDermott, Michael James 1956- *WhoEmL 93*
McDermott, Molly 1932- *WhoAmW 93*
McDermott, Norbert 1954- *St&PR 93*
McDermott, Patricia Ann 1943- *WhoAmW 93*
McDermott, Patricia Louise *WhoAmW 93*
McDermott, Patrick J. *Law&B 92*
McDermott, Peter P. 1950- *St&PR 93*
Mc Dermott, Philip Alan 1951- *WhoAm 92*
McDermott, Raymund Gerald 1927- *St&PR 93, WhoAm 92*
McDermott, Richard H. *Law&B 92*
McDermott, Robert B. 1927- *WhoAm 92*
McDermott, Robert F. 1920- *BioIn 17*
Mc Dermott, Robert Francis 1920- *WhoAm 92, WhoIns 93*
McDermott, Robert H. 1931- *WhoIns 93*
Mcdermott, Robert W. 1943- *St&PR 93, WhoIns 93*
McDermott, Susan Jean Cassi 1953- *WhoE 93*
McDermott, Thomas Albert 1932- *St&PR 93*
McDermott, Thomas Albert, Jr. 1959- *St&PR 93*
McDermott, Thomas C. 1936- *St&PR 93*
McDermott, Thomas C. 1946- *WhoUN 92*
McDermott, Thomas J. 1925-1990 *BioIn 17*
McDermott, Thomas Ward 1948- *St&PR 93*
McDermott, Vincent 1933- *Baker 92*
McDermott, William John *Law&B 92*
McDermott, William Thomas 1945- *WhoSSW 93, WhoWor 93*
Mc Dermott, William Vincent, Jr. 1917- *WhoAm 92*
McDevitt, Charles Francis 1932- *WhoAm 92*
McDevitt, Hugh O'Neill 1930- *WhoAm 92*
McDevitt, Jack 1935- *ScF&FL 92*
McDevitt, John C. *ScF&FL 92*
Mc Devitt, Joseph Bryan 1918- *WhoAm 92*
McDevitt, Joyce Ann 1957- *WhoEmL 93*
McDevitt, Richard E. 1919- *St&PR 93*
McDevitt, Richard H. 1936- *St&PR 93*
McDevitt, Sheila M. *Law&B 92*
McDevitt, Sheila Marie 1947- *WhoAmW 93*
McDew, Charles 1938- *EncAACR*
McDiarmid, Donald Lowson *WhoScE 91-1*
McDiarmid, Lucy 1947- *WhoAmW 93, WhoE 93*
McDilda, Wayne Allen 1960- *WhoEmL 93, WhoSSW 93*
McDill, Linda Abel 1964- *WhoSSW 93*
McDill, Thomas Allison 1926- *WhoAm 92*
Mcdivitt, James A. 1929- *St&PR 93*
McDivitt, James Alton 1929- *WhoAm 92*
McDonagh, David Bernard 1949- *WhoEmL 93*
Mc Donagh, Edward Charles 1915- *WhoAm 92*
McDonagh, Jan 1942- *WhoAmW 93*
McDonagh, Maitland *ScF&FL 92*
McDonagh, Michael J. 1959- *St&PR 93*
McDonagh, Michael James *Law&B 92*
McDonagh, Thomas Joseph 1932- *WhoAm 92*
McDonald, Adrian Thomas *WhoScE 91-1*
McDonald, Alan Angus 1927- *WhoAm 92*
McDonald, Alan James 1946- *WhoEmL 93*
McDonald, Alan Thomas *Law&B 92*
McDonald, Alice Coig 1940- *WhoAm 92*
McDonald, Allan James 1937- *WhoWor 93*
McDonald, Alonzo Lowry, Jr. 1928- *WhoAm 92*
Mc Donald, Andrew J. 1923- *WhoAm 92, WhoSSW 93*
McDonald, Andrew Jewett 1929- *St&PR 93, WhoAm 92*
McDonald, Andrew Melvin, Jr. 1941- *WhoAm 92*
McDonald, Angus Wheeler 1927- *WhoSSW 93, WhoWor 93*
McDonald, Anna Sprague *AmWomPl*
McDonald, Arlys M. Norcross 1943- *WhoAmW 93*
McDonald, Arthur Bruce 1943- *WhoAm 92*
Mc Donald, Barbara Ann 1932- *WhoAmW 93*
McDonald, Barbara Black Robertson 1951- *WhoEmL 93*
McDonald, Barbara Jean 1941- *WhoSSW 93*
McDonald, Barbara Louise 1947- *WhoAmW 93*
McDonald, Ben *BioIn 17*
McDonald, Bernard 1942-1991 *BioIn 17*
McDonald, Bonnie A. *Law&B 92*
McDonald, Bonnie Lynn Teresa 1951- *WhoE 93*
McDonald, Brendan John 1930- *WhoAm 92*
McDonald, Brian M. *Law&B 92*
McDonald, Brian M. 1947- *St&PR 93*
McDonald, Bruce *MiSFD 9*
McDonald, Bruce Edward 1939- *St&PR 93*
McDonald, Carol Anne 1960- *WhoAmW 93*
Mcdonald, Charles G. 1936- *St&PR 93*
McDonald, Charles H. 1938- *St&PR 93*
Mc Donald, Charles J. 1931- *WhoAm 92*
McDonald, Charles William 1950- *WhoEmL 93*
McDonald, Christopher J. *Law&B 92*
McDonald, Christopher John 1961- *WhoE 93*
McDonald, Christopher Joseph 1957- *WhoEmL 93*
McDonald, Collin 1943- *ScF&FL 92*
McDonald, Daniel William 1961- *WhoEmL 93*
McDonald, Daryl P. *Law&B 92*
McDonald, David J. 1936- *WhoIns 93*
McDonald, David John 1902-1979 *BioIn 17*
McDonald, David John 1928- *St&PR 93*
McDonald, David M. *Law&B 92*
Mc Donald, David William 1923- *WhoAm 92*
McDonald, Dennis Patrick 1954- *WhoE 93*
McDonald, Desmond P. 1927- *WhoAm 92*
McDonald, Donna Pflaumer 1962- *WhoSSW 93*
McDonald, Dorcas 1939- *WhoAmW 93*
McDonald, Dorothy Colette 1938- *WhoAmW 93*
McDonald, E. Ann *Law&B 92*
McDonald, Edward 1943- *WhoWor 93*
McDonald, Erroll *BioIn 17*
McDonald, Flash 1919- *BioIn 17*
McDonald, Forrest 1927- *WhoAm 92*
McDonald, Francis 1891-1968 *BioIn 17*
McDonald, Frank B. *Law&B 92*
Mc Donald, Frank Bethune 1925- *WhoAm 92*
McDonald, Frank Gracin *Law&B 92*
McDonald, Gail Clements 1944- *WhoAmW 93*
McDonald, Gail Margaret 1948- *WhoAm 92*
McDonald, Genny 1946- *WhoAmW 93*
McDonald, George Thomas 1944- *WhoE 93*
McDonald, Glena June 1947- *WhoWor 93*
Mcdonald, Gregory Christopher 1937- *WhoAm 92*
McDonald, Hamish G. 1945- *WhoScE 91-1*
McDonald, Harl 1899-1955 *Baker 92*
McDonald, Harley C. 1941- *St&PR 93*
McDonald, Harold Franklin 1923- *St&PR 93*
Mc Donald, Henry Stanton 1927- *WhoAm 92*
McDonald, Ian 1960- *ScF&FL 92*
McDonald, Ian MacLaren 1928- *WhoAm 92*
McDonald, Iverach 1908- *ConAu 138*
McDonald, J. David 1942- *WhoIns 93*
McDonald, Jack d1990 *BioIn 17*
McDonald, Jack K. *Law&B 92*
McDonald, Jack Russell 1920- *St&PR 93*
McDonald, James Charles 1955- *WhoEmL 93*
McDonald, James Clement, Jr. 1945- *WhoSSW 93*
McDonald, James D. *Law&B 92*
McDonald, James Dillard *Law&B 92*
McDonald, James F. 1940- *St&PR 93*
McDonald, James H., Jr. *Law&B 92*
McDonald, James H., Jr. 1953- *St&PR 93*
Mc Donald, James Michael, Jr. 1924- *WhoAm 92*
McDonald, Jamie *MajAI, WhoWrEP 92*
McDonald, Jeanne Harvey *Law&B 92*
McDonald, Jerry Nealon 1944- *WhoSSW 93*
McDonald, Joanne 1947- *WhoAmW 93*
McDonald, Joe 1952- *WhoE 93*
McDonald, John C. 1936- *WhoAm 92*
McDonald, John Cecil 1924- *WhoAm 92*
McDonald, John Charles 1936- *St&PR 93*
McDonald, John Clifton 1930- *WhoAm 92*
McDonald, John E., Jr. *Law&B 92*
McDonald, John Edwin 1943- *St&PR 93*
McDonald, John Francis Patrick 1942- *WhoAm 92, WhoE 93, WhoWor 93*
McDonald, John Gregory 1937- *WhoAm 92*
McDonald, John Harvey 1930- *St&PR 93*
McDonald, John J. *St&PR 93*
Mc Donald, John Joseph 1930- *WhoAm 92*
McDonald, John Patrick *Law&B 92*
Mc Donald, John Richard 1933- *WhoAm 92*
Mc Donald, John Warlick 1922- *WhoAm 92, WhoWor 93*
McDonald, Joseph J. *St&PR 93*
Mc Donald, Joseph Valentine 1925- *WhoAm 92*
McDonald, Judith Louise 1939- *WhoAmW 93*
Mc Donald, Julie J. 1929- *WhoWrEP 92*
McDonald, Kathleen Edna 1960- *WhoAmW 93*
McDonald, Kathleen Marie 1954- *WhoWor 93*
McDonald, Kay 1952- *WhoAmW 93, WhoEmL 93*
McDonald, Kenneth 1914- *ScF&FL 92*
McDonald, Kenneth J. *Law&B 92*
McDonald, Kim Suzanne 1965- *WhoAmW 93*
McDonald, Laetitia 1890- *AmWomPl*
McDonald, Larry Allen 1954- *WhoEmL 93*
McDonald, Laughlin *BioIn 17*
McDonald, Lisa Meyer 1957- *WhoSSW 93*
McDonald, Lucille *AmWomPl*
McDonald, M. C., Mrs. *AmWomPl*
McDonald, M. Robin *Law&B 92*
McDonald, Malcolm H.B. *WhoScE 91-1*
McDonald, Malcolm S. 1938- *WhoAm 92, WhoSSW 93*
McDonald, Marian Easton *Law&B 92*
McDonald, Marianne 1937- *WhoAmW 93, WhoWor 93*
McDonald, Mary Ann Melody 1944- *WhoAmW 93, WhoWor 93*
McDonald, Mary Anne 1955- *WhoAmW 93*
McDonald, Mary M. *Law&B 92*

McDonald, Marybeth 1955- *WhoEmL 93*
McDonald, Megan *BioIn 17*
McDonald, Michael *WhoScE 91-1*
McDonald, Michael D. *Law&B 92*
Mcdonald, Michael D. 1940- *St&PR 93*
McDonald, Michael Dennis 1955- *WhoEmL 93*
McDonald, Michael James 1948- *St&PR 93*
McDonald, Michael L. 1946- *St&PR 93*
McDonald, Miles F. 1905-1991 *BioIn 17*
McDonald, Miller Baird 1920- *WhoAm 92, WhoSSW 93*
McDonald, Miriam Gertrude *WhoAmW 93*
McDonald, Parker Lee 1924- *WhoAm 92, WhoSSW 93*
McDonald, Patricia Anne 1947- *WhoAmW 93*
McDonald, Patricia Hamilton 1952- *WhoAmW 93*
McDonald, Patrick 1956- *St&PR 93*
Mc Donald, Patrick Allen 1936- *WhoAm 92*
McDonald, Patrick Charles 1947- *St&PR 93*
McDonald, Paul J. 1943- *St&PR 93*
Mcdonald, Paul M. 1939- *St&PR 93*
McDonald, Peggy Ann Stimmel 1931- *WhoAmW 93*
McDonald, Peter Richard 1947- *WhoEmL 93*
McDonald, Ramona Robin 1955- *WhoAmW 93*
Mcdonald, Randal B. 1930- *St&PR 93*
Mcdonald, Raymond J. 1948- *St&PR 93*
McDonald, Rebecca A. 1952- *St&PR 93*
McDonald, Rebecca Ann 1952- *WhoAmW 93*
McDonald, Richard E. 1933- *St&PR 93*
McDonald, Richard Hugh *Law&B 92*
McDonald, Richard J. *Law&B 92*
McDonald, Robert *BioIn 17*
McDonald, Robert 1944- *St&PR 93*
Mcdonald, Robert B. 1936- *St&PR 93*
McDonald, Robert Bond 1936- *WhoAm 92*
McDonald, Robert D. 1931- *St&PR 93*
McDonald, Robert Delos 1931- *WhoAm 92*
McDonald, Robert Edward *Law&B 92*
Mc Donald, Robert Emmett 1915- *WhoAm 92, WhoWor 93*
McDonald, Robert L. d1990 *BioIn 17*
McDonald, Rod *MiSFD 9*
McDonald, Rosa Nell 1953- *WhoAmW 93*
McDonald, Roy Ketner 1901-1990 *BioIn 17*
McDonald, Sally Sanders *Law&B 92*
McDonald, Sandra Anne 1949- *WhoAmW 93*
McDonald, Scott Paul *Law&B 92*
McDonald, Sheila Jane 1963- *WhoAmW 93*
McDonald, Stephanie *BioIn 17*
Mc Donald, Stephen Lee 1924- *WhoAm 92*
Mcdonald, Sterling 1949- *St&PR 93*
McDonald, Steven E. 1956- *ScF&FL 92*
McDonald, Steven Ray 1965- *WhoSSW 93*
McDonald, Susan Marshall 1918- *WhoAm 92*
McDonald, Susan Schwartz 1949- *St&PR 93*
McDonald, Susann 1935- *Baker 92*
McDonald, Sylvia Camp 1952- *WhoAmW 93*
McDonald, T.J. 1949- *St&PR 93*
McDonald, Teresa Lewis 1957- *WhoAmW 93*
McDonald, Thomas Edwin, Jr. 1939- *WhoWor 93*
McDonald, Thomas James 1958- *WhoEmL 93*
McDonald, W. Wesley 1946- *WhoEmL 93*
McDonald, Walter *BioIn 17*
Mc Donald, Walter Robert 1934- *WhoWrEP 92*
McDonald, Warren George 1939- *WhoAm 92*
McDonald, William Andrew 1913- *WhoAm 92*
McDonald, William E. 1942- *St&PR 93*
McDonald, William Harrison 1944- *WhoSSW 93*
McDonald, William Henry 1924- *WhoAm 92*
McDonald, William Ian *WhoScE 91-1*
McDonald, William J. *Law&B 92*
McDonald, William J. 1927-1990 *BioIn 17*
McDonald, William Naylor, III 1913- *WhoE 93*
McDonald, William R. 1928- *St&PR 93*
McDonald, Wylene Booth 1956- *WhoAmW 93, WhoEmL 93*
McDonel, Michael Eugene 1946- *WhoE 93*
McDonell, Horace *BioIn 17*
McDonell, Horace George, Jr. 1928- *St&PR 93, WhoAm 92*
McDonell, Katheryn Davis 1945- *WhoSSW 93*
Mc Donell, Marcella Ann 1945- *WhoWrEP 92*
McDonell, Robert Terry 1944- *WhoAm 92, WhoE 93, WhoWrEP 92*
McDonell, Terry *BioIn 17*
McDonell, Terry 1944- *ScF&FL 92*
McDonie, Karen W. 1954- *St&PR 93*
McDonie, Karen Wynne 1954- *WhoEmL 93*
McDoniel, James William 1932- *WhoSSW 93*
McDonnell, Ann Alexander 1938- *WhoAmW 93*
McDonnell, David *ScF&FL 92*
Mc Donnell, Edward Francis 1935- *WhoAm 92*
McDonnell, Frank E. *Law&B 92*
McDonnell, J. Curtis *Law&B 92*
McDonnell, James Anthony Michael *WhoScE 91-1*
McDonnell, James Smith, III 1936- *St&PR 93*
McDonnell, John F. *BioIn 17*
Mcdonnell, John Finney 1938- *St&PR 93, WhoAm 92*
McDonnell, John P. *Law&B 92*
Mc Donnell, John Thomas 1926- *WhoAm 92*
McDonnell, Kathryn Ellen *Law&B 92*
Mc Donnell, Loretta Wade 1940- *WhoAmW 93*
McDonnell, Martin J. 1939- *St&PR 93*
McDonnell, Mary *BioIn 17*
McDonnell, Mary Theresa 1949- *WhoAmW 93*
McDonnell, MaryAnn Margaret 1947- *WhoAmW 93*
McDonnell, N.M. *WhoScE 91-1*
McDonnell, Pegeen Elizabeth 1966- *WhoAmW 93*
McDonnell, Robert Leroy 1951- *WhoSSW 93*
McDonnell, Robert Louis 1939- *WhoSSW 93*
McDonnell, Sanford Noyes 1922- *WhoAm 92*
McDonnell, T. Murray d1991 *BioIn 17*
McDonnell, Timothy David *Law&B 92*
McDonough, Alex *ScF&FL 92*
McDonough, Bridget Ann 1956- *WhoEmL 93*
McDonough, Colin 1944- *St&PR 93*
McDonough, Craig *ScF&FL 92*
McDonough, Douglas Spencer 1953- *WhoSSW 93*
McDonough, Eugene Francis, Jr. 1930- *WhoE 93*
Mc Donough, George Francis, Jr. 1928- *WhoAm 92*
McDonough, Gerald C. 1928- *St&PR 93*
McDonough, Greta Jo 1955- *WhoAmW 93*
McDonough, James Francis 1939- *WhoAm 92*
McDonough, James Michael 1945- *WhoSSW 93*
McDonough, John *Law&B 92*
McDonough, John L. *Law&B 92*
McDonough, John Michael 1944- *WhoAm 92*
Mc Donough, John Richard 1919- *WhoAm 92*
McDonough, Joseph Corbett 1924- *WhoAm 92*
McDonough, Joseph Edward 1937- *WhoAm 92*
McDonough, K.A. 1958- *St&PR 93*
McDonough, Kenneth E. *Law&B 92*
McDonough, Kenneth L. 1953- *St&PR 93*
McDonough, Mamie 1952- *WhoAmW 93, WhoEmL 93*
McDonough, Mark Raymond 1950- *St&PR 93*
Mcdonough, Michael Charles 1938- *St&PR 93*
McDonough, Michael Richard 1951- *WhoE 93, WhoEmL 93*
McDonough, Nancy Needham *Law&B 92*
McDonough, Patrick Dennis 1942- *WhoAm 92*
McDonough, Patrick J. *Law&B 92*
McDonough, Paul Diaz 1967- *WhoE 93*
McDonough, Paul Gerard 1930- *WhoAm 92*
McDonough, Paul S. *Law&B 92*
McDonough, Peter 1939- *ConAu 138*
McDonough, Raymond J. d1990 *BioIn 17*
McDonough, Reginald Milton 1936- *WhoAm 92*
McDonough, Richard A. *Law&B 92*
McDonough, Richard A. d1991 *BioIn 17*
McDonough, Richard A., III *Law&B 92*
Mc Donough, Richard Doyle 1931- *WhoAm 92*
McDonough, Russell Charles 1924- *WhoAm 92*
McDonough, Sean *BioIn 17*
McDonough, Susan Ellen 1949- *WhoSSW 93*
Mcdonough, Thomas Francis 1947- *St&PR 93*
McDonough, Thomas Patrick 1949- *WhoE 93*
McDonough, Thomas R. 1945- *ScF&FL 92*
McDonough, William *BioIn 17*
McDonough, William Eugene 1957- *WhoE 93*
McDonough, Yona Zeldis 1957- *SmATA 73 [port]*
McDorman, Barbara A. *Law&B 92*
McDorman, Joe
See Statler Brothers, The *ConMus 8*
McDougal, Alfred Leroy 1931- *WhoAm 92*
McDougal, Bruce Edward 1947- *St&PR 93*
McDougal, Bruce William 1941- *St&PR 93*
McDougal, Bryan L. 1953- *St&PR 93*
McDougal, Jerome R. 1928- *St&PR 93*
McDougal, Luther Love, III 1938- *WhoAm 92*
McDougal, Owen J., Jr. 1919- *St&PR 93*
Mcdougal, Richard John 1945- *St&PR 93*
McDougal, Stuart Yeatman 1942- *WhoAm 92*
McDougal, William Scott 1942- *WhoAm 92*
McDougald, Catherine Ann 1945- *WhoAmW 93*
McDougald, Cornelia E. *Law&B 92*
McDougald, Frank A. 1938- *St&PR 93*
McDougald, Worth *BioIn 17*
McDougall, Barbara Jean 1937- *WhoAm 92, WhoAmW 93, WhoE 93*
McDougall, Don *MiSFD 9*
McDougall, Douglas Christopher P. 1944- *WhoWor 93*
Mc Dougall, Dugald Stewart 1916- *WhoAm 92*
Mcdougall, Duncan C. 1943- *St&PR 93*
McDougall, I. Ross 1943- *WhoAm 92*
McDougall, Ian 1930- *St&PR 93*
Mcdougall, James T. 1942- *St&PR 93*
McDougall, Jo Garot 1935- *WhoWrEP 92*
Mc Dougall, John 1916- *WhoAm 92*
McDougall, John Roland 1945- *WhoAm 92*
McDougall, Kevin L. *Law&B 92*
McDougall, Michael Van d1991 *BioIn 17*
McDougall, Ronald A. 1942- *St&PR 93*
McDougall, Ronald Alexander 1942- *WhoAm 92*
McDougall, Sharon L. 1959- *WhoIns 93*
McDougall, Susan 1961- *WhoAmW 93, WhoEmL 93*
McDougall, William Alexander 1951- *WhoEmL 93*
McDougall, William Douglas *Law&B 92*
McDoulett, C.D., Jr. 1944- *St&PR 93*
Mc Dow, John Jett 1925- *WhoAm 92*
McDow, Patricia Diana 1953- *WhoE 93*
McDow, Russell Edward, Jr. 1950- *WhoSSW 93*
McDow, Thomas, III 1947- *St&PR 93*
McDowall, Robert Hugh 1956- *WhoE 93*
McDowall, Roddy 1928- *IntDcF 2-3, MiSFD 9, WhoAm 92, WhoWor 93*
McDowell, Betty Lawson 1930- *WhoAmW 93*
McDowell, Boyd, II 1926- *St&PR 93*
McDowell, Charleen *AmWomPl*
Mc Dowell, Charles Eager 1923- *WhoAm 92*
McDowell, Charles Patrick 1950- *WhoEmL 93*
McDowell, Charles Rice, Jr. 1926- *JrnUS*
McDowell, Charles Richard 1936- *St&PR 93*
McDowell, Charles S. 1942- *St&PR 93*
McDowell, David Andrews *WhoScE 91-1*
McDowell, David Jamison 1947- *WhoE 93, WhoEmL 93*
McDowell, Edward R. H. 1932- *WhoAm 92*
Mc Dowell, Edwin Stewart 1935- *WhoWrEP 92*
McDowell, Elizabeth Mary 1940- *WhoAm 92, WhoAmW 93*
McDowell, Fletcher Hughes 1923- *WhoAm 92*
McDowell, Frank Boone 1956- *WhoSSW 93*
McDowell, Fred 1904-1972 *BioIn 17*
McDowell, Frederick Glen 1929- *St&PR 93*
McDowell, George Edward 1944- *St&PR 93*
Mcdowell, Gloria A. 1936- *St&PR 93*
McDowell, Irvin 1818-1885 *HarEnMi*
McDowell, Jack *BioIn 17*
McDowell, Jack Burns 1966- *WhoAm 92*
Mc Dowell, Jack Sherman 1914- *WhoAm 92*
McDowell, James B. *Law&B 92*
McDowell, Janet Lee 1954- *WhoEmL 93*
McDowell, Jeffrey S. 1954- *St&PR 93*
McDowell, Jennifer 1936- *WhoAm 92, WhoAmW 93, WhoWor 93*
McDowell, Joe *St&PR 93*
Mc Dowell, John B. 1921- *WhoAm 92*
McDowell, John D. *Law&B 92*
McDowell, John Eugene 1927- *WhoAm 92*
McDowell, John Herbert 1926-1985 *Baker 92*
McDowell, John Moore 1943- *WhoWor 93*
McDowell, Josephine Sargent 1912- *WhoAmW 93*
McDowell, Karen Ann 1945- *WhoAmW 93*
McDowell, Leah Palki 1952- *WhoEmL 93*
McDowell, Lester 1951- *WhoEmL 93*
McDowell, Malcolm 1943- *IntDcF 2-3 [port], WhoAm 92*
Mc Dowell, Martha Shea 1925- *WhoWrEP 92*
McDowell, Mary Jane 1953- *WhoEmL 93*
McDowell, Michael 1950- *ScF&FL 92*
McDowell, Michael D. *Law&B 92*
McDowell, Michael David 1948- *WhoAm 92*
McDowell, Michael Hamilton Coulter 1952- *WhoE 93*
McDowell, Michael P. Kube- *ScF&FL 92*
McDowell, Nelson 1870-1947 *BioIn 17*
McDowell, Paul *Law&B 92*
McDowell, Peter William *WhoScE 91-1*
McDowell, Putnam B. 1924- *St&PR 93*
McDowell, Putnam Ballou 1924- *WhoAm 92*
McDowell, Ralph D. 1924- *St&PR 93*
Mcdowell, Renfrew Brighton *St&PR 93*
Mcdowell, Robert A. 1953- *WhoWrEP 92*
Mc Dowell, Robert Hull 1927- *WhoAm 92*
McDowell, Robert L. 1941- *WhoAm 92*
McDowell, Samuel Edward Thomas 1942- *BiDAMSp 1989*
McDowell, Stephen Geoffrey 1943- *St&PR 93*
McDowell, Stirling 1931- *WhoAm 92*
McDowell, Susan Graham 1952- *WhoAmW 93*
McDuff, Jack *BioIn 17*
McDuff, John Fred *Law&B 92*
McDuffie, David Wayne 1960- *WhoE 93, WhoWor 93*
McDuffie, Frederic Clement 1924- *WhoAm 92*
McDuffie, Harriet E. 1954- *WhoAmW 93*
McDuffie, Kenneth Phillips 1950- *WhoEmL 93*
Mc Duffie, Malcolm 1915- *WhoAm 92*
McDuffie, Malcolm Eugene 1942- *WhoSSW 93*
McDuffie, Michael Anthony 1954- *WhoE 93, WhoEmL 93*
McDugald, Barbara Hinske *Law&B 92*
McDugald, Richard C. *Law&B 92*
McDyer, James 1910-1987 *BioIn 17*
McEachen, Richard Edward 1933- *WhoAm 92*
McEachern, James Sterling, III 1960- *WhoEmL 93, WhoSSW 93*
McEachern, Patricia Rae 1943- *WhoAmW 93, WhoSSW 93*
McEachern, William Archibald 1945- *WhoE 93, WhoWor 93*
McEachnie, Robert Charles 1957- *WhoSSW 93*
McEachran, Angus 1939- *WhoAm 92*
McEachran, Bruce Allen 1947- *St&PR 93*
McEachran, Don 1906- *St&PR 93*
McEachron, Donald Lynn 1953- *WhoE 93, WhoEmL 93*
Mc Eathron, Margaret 1899- *WhoWrEP 92*
Mcelaney, Daniel W. 1932- *St&PR 93*
McElderry, Betty J. 1939- *WhoAmW 93*
McEldoon, Susan Ann 1952- *WhoEmL 93*
McEldowney, Henry Clay 1946- *WhoEmL 93*
McEleney, Brenda Jean 1956- *WhoEmL 93*
McElfresh, Newland S. 1934- *St&PR 93*
McElhaney, Jack Beattie 1940- *St&PR 93, WhoAm 92*
McElhaney, James Harry 1933- *WhoAm 92*
Mc Elhaney, James Willson 1937- *WhoAm 92*
Mc Elhaney, John Hess 1934- *WhoAm 92*
McElhaney, Ronald *St&PR 93*
McElhenny, Hugh 1928- *BioIn 17*
McElheny, Thomas J. 1947- *St&PR 93*
McElhiney, Gaile Churchill 1888-1978 *ScF&FL 92*
McElhinney, Susan Kay 1947- *WhoAmW 93*

McElhinny, Wilson D. 1929- *St&PR 93*
McElhinny, Wilson Dunbar 1929- *WhoAm 92*
McEliece, Robert James 1942- *WhoAm 92*
McElligott, Denise Nell 1963- *WhoAmW 93*
McElligott, James Patrick, Jr. 1948- *WhoAm 92*
Mcelligott, Paul J. 1953- *St&PR 93*
McElligott, Thomas James 1943- *WhoAm 92*
McElligott, Tom *BioIn 17*
McElliott, Janet V. *St&PR 93*
Mcelliott, Lawrence A. 1937- *St&PR 93*
McEllroy, W. Edward *Law&B 92*
McElnea, Jeffrey Kent 1948- *WhoAm 92*
McElrath, Joseph Richard, Jr. 1945- *WhoSSW 93*
McElrath, Richard Elsworth 1932- *St&PR 93, WhoAm 92*
McElrath, William N. 1932- *BioIn 17*
McElroy, Abby Lucille Wolman 1957- *WhoAmW 93, WhoEmL 93*
McElroy, Albert 1915-1975 *BioIn 17*
Mc Elroy, Benjamin Thomas 1922- *WhoAm 92*
McElroy, Bernard (Patrick, Jr.) 1938-1991 *ConAu 136*
McElroy, Blair *BioIn 17*
McElroy, Bridget Baird 1965- *WhoAmW 93*
McElroy, Charles Joseph 1954- *St&PR 93*
McElroy, Charlotte Ann 1939- *WhoAmW 93*
McElroy, Christopher John *Law&B 92*
McElroy, Clinton Eugene 1938- *St&PR 93*
McElroy, Colleen J(ohnson) 1935- *ConAu 38NR*
Mc Elroy, Colleen Johnson 1935- *WhoWrEP 92*
McElroy, Edmund G. 1941- *St&PR 93*
McElroy, Emilie Lin 1954- *WhoAmW 93*
McElroy, Frederick William 1939- *WhoE 93*
McElroy, Guy C. d1990 *BioIn 17*
McElroy, James A. 1932- *St&PR 93*
McElroy, Janice Helen 1937- *WhoAmW 93*
McElroy, Joan Christine 1952- *WhoAmW 93*
Mc Elroy, John Harley 1936- *WhoAm 92*
McElroy, Joseph 1930- *ScF&FL 92*
McElroy, Joseph 1950- *WhoSSW 93*
McElroy, Joseph L. *WhoAm 92*
McElroy, Joseph L. 1929- *St&PR 93*
McElroy, Joy Lynn 1963- *WhoAmW 93*
McElroy, June Patricia 1929- *WhoAmW 93*
McElroy, Kevin J. 1949- *St&PR 93*
McElroy, Linda Ann 1942- *WhoAmW 93*
McElroy, Lynne Carol 1949- *WhoAmW 93*
McElroy, Margaret Julia 1889- *AmWomPl*
McElroy, Michael 1939- *WhoAm 92*
McElroy, Michael Augustine 1944- *WhoAm 92*
McElroy, Paul E. 1952- *St&PR 93*
McElroy, Randolph Williams 1935- *St&PR 93*
McElroy, Richard Allen 1946- *WhoEmL 93*
McElroy, Richard Cavanagh, III 1951- *WhoEmL 93*
McElroy, Susan 1958- *WhoAmW 93*
McElroy, Terry L. *Law&B 92*
Mc Elroy, William David 1917- *WhoAm 92*
McElroy, William M., Jr. 1929- *St&PR 93*
Mc Elroy, William Theodore 1925- *WhoAm 92*
McElvain, David P. 1937- *St&PR 93*
McElvain, David Plowman 1937- *WhoAm 92*
McElvain, R.C. 1935- *St&PR 93*
McElvaine, Christopher H. 1936- *St&PR 93*
McElvane, Pamela Anne 1958- *WhoAmW 93*
McElveen, Dudley G. 1932- *St&PR 93*
McElveen, Faye Walker 1933- *WhoAmW 93*
McElveen, Joseph James, Jr. 1939- *WhoE 93, WhoWor 93*
McElveen, Junius Carlisle, Jr. 1947- *WhoAm 92*
McElveen-McKnight, Keran Elaine 1968- *WhoE 93*
McElvenny, Ralph Talbot 1906-1990 *BioIn 17*
McElwain, Charles F. d1991 *BioIn 17*
Mc Elwain, Joseph Arthur 1919- *WhoAm 92*
McElwain, Timothy John *WhoScE 91-1*
McElwaine, Robert Berentz 1912- *WhoSSW 93*
McElwee, Daniel *Law&B 92*
McElwee, Dennis John 1947- *WhoWor 93*
McElwee, John Gerard 1921- *St&PR 93, WhoAm 92*
McElwee, Joseph Monroe 1933- *St&PR 93*
McElwee, Paul E. *Law&B 92*
McElwee, Ross *MiSFD 9*
McElyea, James M. 1948- *St&PR 93*
McElynn, Philip J. 1931- *St&PR 93*
McEneaney, James F. 1938- *St&PR 93*
McEnerney, Michael Thomas 1948- *WhoEmL 93*
McEnerney, Thomas W. 1947- *St&PR 93*
McEnerny, Thomas W. *Law&B 92*
McEnery, Thomas 1945- *WhoAm 92*
McEniry, Robert Francis 1918- *WhoWor 93*
McEnroe, Christopher Padraic 1966- *WhoE 93*
McEnroe, Harry Damian 1960- *WhoE 93*
McEnroe, John *BioIn 17*
Mc Enroe, John Patrick, Jr. 1959- *WhoAm 92, WhoWor 93*
McEnroe, Megan Ellen *Law&B 92*
McEnroe, Patrick *BioIn 17*
McEnroe, Richard S. *ScF&FL 92*
Mc Entee, Grace Hall 1940- *WhoWrEP 92*
McEntee, Jervis 1828-1891 *BioIn 17*
McEntee, Martha E. *Law&B 92*
McEntee, Matthew A. *Law&B 92*
McEntee, R. Michael 1953- *St&PR 93*
McEntee, Richard J. 1935- *St&PR 93*
McEntee, Robert Edward 1932- *WhoAm 92*
McEntee, William Joseph, Jr. 1952- *WhoE 93, WhoEmL 93, WhoWor 93*
McEntire, B. Joseph 1962- *WhoSSW 93*
McEntire, James Edward 1944- *St&PR 93*
McEntire, Maleta Mae 1957- *WhoAmW 93, WhoEmL 93*
McEntire, Reba *BioIn 17*
McEntire, Reba N. 1955- *WhoAm 92, WhoAmW 93*
McEntyre, Joan Pauleen 1945- *WhoAmW 93*
McEntyre, Judith G. *Law&B 92*
McErlane, Joseph James 1948- *WhoAm 92, WhoEmL 93*
McErlean, Charles F., Jr. *Law&B 92*
McEveety, Bernard *MiSFD 9*
McEveety, Vincent *MiSFD 9*
McEver, Eugene T. 1908-1985 *BiDAMSp 1989*
Mc Evilly, Thomas Vincent 1934- *WhoAm 92*
McEvily, Ann C. *Law&B 92*
McEvily, John Vincent, Jr. 1949- *WhoEmL 93*
McEvily, Richard Patrick *Law&B 92*
McEvoy, A.H. 1947- *St&PR 93*
McEvoy, Charles Lucien 1917- *WhoAm 92*
McEvoy, Gerald William 1948- *St&PR 93*
Mcevoy, Gerard Peter 1928- *St&PR 93*
McEvoy, John Christie 1931- *St&PR 93*
McEvoy, Marjorie Harte *ConAu 40NR*
McEvoy, Mitzi Levi 1947- *WhoAmW 93*
McEvoy, Seth *ScF&FL 92*
McEvoy, Sharlene Ann 1950- *WhoAmW 93, WhoE 93*
McEvoy, Thomas 1942- *St&PR 93*
McEwan, Barbara 1926- *ConAu 139*
McEwan, Ian *BioIn 17*
McEwan, Ian 1948- *ScF&FL 92*
McEwan, John J. *Law&B 92*
McEwan, John James 1893-1970 *BiDAMSp 1989*
Mc Ewan, Leonard 1925- *WhoAm 92*
McEwan, William *WhoScE 91-1*
McEwen, Aila Erman 1941- *WhoAmW 93*
McEwen, Alexander Campbell 1926- *WhoAm 92*
McEwen, Alice *AmWomPl*
McEwen, Anne Williams 1965- *WhoAmW 93*
McEwen, Barry Allyn 1946- *WhoEmL 93*
McEwen, Bob 1950- *CngDr 91, WhoAm 92*
McEwen, James *WhoScE 91-1*
McEwen, Jane W. *St&PR 93*
McEwen, Jean 1923- *WhoAm 92*
McEwen, John (Blackwood) 1868-1948 *Baker 92*
McEwen, Keith Alistair *WhoScE 91-1*
McEwen, Mary Louise 1960- *WhoE 93*
McEwen, Robert Joseph 1916- *WhoE 93*
McEwen, Robert R. 1950- *St&PR 93*
McEwen, Thomas Ray 1931- *St&PR 93*
McEwing, John R. *Law&B 92*
McFadden, Barbara B. *Law&B 92*
McFadden, Bernard Joseph 1933- *St&PR 93*
McFadden, Bradford, Jr. 1940- *St&PR 93*
McFadden, Candace Renea 1961- *WhoEmL 93*
McFadden, Daniel Little 1937- *WhoAm 92*
McFadden, David 1940- *WhoCanL 92*
McFadden, David Revere 1947- *WhoAm 92*
McFadden, Dennis 1940- *WhoAm 92, WhoSSW 93*
McFadden, Dennis J. 1952- *St&PR 93*
McFadden, Denyse Irene 1953- *WhoEmL 93*
McFadden, Douglas J. *Law&B 92*
McFadden, Edward H. 1942- *St&PR 93*
McFadden, Elizabeth Apthorp 1875-1961 *AmWomPl*
McFadden, Frank Hampton *Law&B 92*
McFadden, Frank Hampton 1925- *St&PR 93, WhoAm 92*
Mc Fadden, G. Bruce 1934- *WhoAm 92*
Mc Fadden, George Linus 1927- *WhoAm 92*
McFadden, James Frederick, Jr. 1920- *WhoAm 92, WhoWor 93*
McFadden, James J. 1919- *WhoE 93*
Mc Fadden, James Patrick 1930- *WhoAm 92, WhoE 93*
McFadden, Jo Beth 1938- *St&PR 93*
McFadden, John J. 1937- *St&PR 93*
McFadden, John Lamont, Jr. 1927- *WhoSSW 93*
Mc Fadden, John Volney 1931- *WhoAm 92*
McFadden, Joseph B. 1935- *St&PR 93*
Mc Fadden, Joseph Michael 1932- *WhoAm 92, WhoSSW 93*
McFadden, Joseph Patrick 1939- *St&PR 93, WhoAm 92, WhoIns 93*
McFadden, Mary *BioIn 17*
McFadden, Mary 1950- *WhoAmW 93*
McFadden, Mary Josephine 1938- *St&PR 93, WhoAm 92, WhoAmW 93*
McFadden, Peter William 1932- *WhoAm 92, WhoE 93*
McFadden, Rosemary Theresa 1948- *WhoAm 92, WhoAmW 93, WhoEmL 93, WhoWor 93*
McFadden, Steven (S. H.) 1948- *ConAu 138*
McFadden, Thomas 1935- *WhoAm 92, WhoE 93*
McFadin, Robert L. 1921- *St&PR 93*
McFadin, Robert Lee 1921- *WhoAm 92*
McFadin, Vicki Lynn 1952- *WhoAmW 93*
McFadyen, Debra Sue 1959- *WhoAmW 93*
McFadyen, Ella *DcChlFi*
McFadzean, J.A. *WhoScE 91-1*
McFadzen, Ruth S. *St&PR 93*
McFall, Catherine Gardner 1952- *WhoAm 92*
McFall, Dan Frank 1945- *St&PR 93*
McFall, John *BioIn 17*
McFall, M. Louise *Law&B 92*
McFalls, Richard T. 1932- *WhoIns 93*
McFalls, Robert Alan 1945- *St&PR 93*
McFarlan, Franklin Warren 1937- *WhoAm 92*
McFarland, Alan Roberts 1942- *St&PR 93*
Mc Farland, Anne S. 1940- *WhoWrEP 92*
McFarland, David E. 1938- *WhoAm 92, WhoE 93*
McFarland, David Joseph 1916- *St&PR 93*
McFarland, Edward Paul, Jr. 1954- *WhoE 93*
McFarland, Ernest W. 1894-1984 *PolPar*
McFarland, Frances Wallack 1920- *WhoAmW 93*
McFarland, Francis Edmund 1947- *St&PR 93*
Mc Farland, Frank Eugene 1918- *WhoAm 92*
Mc Farland, H. Richard 1930- *WhoAm 92*
McFarland, Henry Bernard 1951- *WhoE 93*
McFarland, Howard Milton 1956- *WhoSSW 93*
McFarland, J.C. 1946- *St&PR 93*
McFarland, J.D. 1946- *St&PR 93*
McFarland, James Howard 1937- *WhoAm 92*
McFarland, James L. *Law&B 92*
McFarland, James P. 1912- *St&PR 93*
McFarland, James Thomas 1937- *St&PR 93*
McFarland, James W. *Law&B 92*
McFarland, James William 1948- *WhoEmL 93*
McFarland, Jane Elizabeth 1937- *WhoSSW 93*
McFarland, Jean Webb *WhoAmW 93, WhoSSW 93*
McFarland, John Anthony *Law&B 92*
Mc Farland, John Bernard 1943- *WhoWrEP 92*
McFarland, John T. 1941- *WhoIns 93*
McFarland, Kay Eleanor 1935- *WhoAm 92, WhoAmW 93*
McFarland, Kay Flowers 1942- *WhoAmW 93*
McFarland, Keith Donavon 1940- *WhoSSW 93*
Mc Farland, Keith Nielson 1921- *WhoAm 92*
McFarland, Kerri Ann 1961- *WhoSSW 93*
McFarland, Kevin John 1958- *WhoEmL 93, WhoWor 93*
McFarland, Lee Craig 1920- *St&PR 93*
McFarland, Lellan Lee 1937- *St&PR 93*
McFarland, Lynne Vernice 1953- *WhoAmW 93, WhoEmL 93*
McFarland, Maria J.E. 1943- *St&PR 93*
McFarland, Mary Ellen *BioIn 17*
McFarland, Molly Carol 1968- *WhoAmW 93*
Mc Farland, Norman Francis 1922- *WhoAm 92*
McFarland, Patrick E. 1937- *BioIn 17*
McFarland, Richard D. 1930- *St&PR 93*
McFarland, Richard M. 1923- *St&PR 93, WhoAm 92*
McFarland, Richard Macklin 1922- *WhoAm 92, WhoWor 93*
Mc Farland, Robert Harold 1918- *WhoAm 92*
McFarland, Stephen L. 1950- *ConAu 139*
McFarland, Susan Louise 1958- *WhoAmW 93, WhoEmL 93*
Mc Farland, Terry Lynn 1947- *WhoEmL 93, WhoSSW 93*
McFarland, Veda Dianne 1958- *WhoAmW 93, WhoEmL 93*
McFarland, Violet Sweet 1908- *WhoAmW 93*
McFarland, Waneta Joan 1936- *St&PR 93*
McFarland, William Joseph 1929- *WhoAm 92*
McFarland-Esposito, Carla Rae 1957- *WhoAmW 93*
McFarlane, Alexander W. *Law&B 92*
McFarlane, Beth Lucetta Troester 1918- *WhoAmW 93*
McFarlane, Bruce J. *BioIn 17*
McFarlane, Harry William 1929- *WhoWor 93*
Mc Farlane, Karen Elizabeth 1942- *WhoAm 92*
McFarlane, Leslie (Charles) 1902-1977 *ConAu 37NR, MajAI [port]*
McFarlane, Robert H.B. 1950- *St&PR 93*
McFarlane, Ross W. *Law&B 92*
McFarlane, Todd *BioIn 17*
McFarley, Kevin Michael 1951- *WhoEmL 93, WhoSSW 93*
McFarlin, Patricia A. *Law&B 92*
McFarlin, Robert Paul 1942- *WhoAm 92*
McFarling, Donald Partlow 1922- *St&PR 93*
McFarren, John C. *Law&B 92*
McFarthing, Kevin Gerard 1957- *WhoScE 91-1*
McFate, Joseph Robert, II 1935- *WhoSSW 93*
McFate, Linda Ann 1944- *WhoAmW 93*
Mc Fate, Patricia Ann 1936- *WhoAm 92*
McFatridge, Keith William, Jr. 1946- *St&PR 93*
McFaul, Patricia Louise 1947- *WhoAmW 93*
Mc Featters, Dale Stitt 1911- *WhoAm 92, WhoWor 93*
Mc Fedries, Robert, Jr. 1930- *WhoAm 92, WhoSSW 93*
McFee, Alfred Frank 1931- *WhoSSW 93*
Mc Fee, Arthur Storer 1932- *WhoAm 92*
McFee, Bruce C. 1957- *St&PR 93*
Mc Fee, Michael Alan 1954- *WhoWrEP 92*
McFee, Oonah *WhoCanL 92*
McFee, Richard 1925- *WhoAm 92*
McFee, Shirley Miller 1929- *WhoAmW 93*
Mc Fee, Thomas Stuart 1930- *WhoAm 92*
McFee, William Warren 1935- *WhoAm 92*
Mc Feeley, John Jay 1945- *WhoE 93*
McFeeley, Neil Douglas 1949- *WhoEmL 93*
McFeely, Clarence Edward 1929- *WhoAm 92*
McFeely, Ian R. *Law&B 92*
McFeely, John R. *Law&B 92*
Mc Feely, Laramie J. 1933- *WhoWrEP 92*
Mc Feely, William Shield 1930- *WhoAm 92, WhoWrEP 92*
McFeetors, R.L. 1944- *St&PR 93*
Mc Feron, Dean Earl 1923- *WhoAm 92*
McFerran, Douglass *ScF&FL 92*
McFerran, J.B. *WhoScE 91-1*
Mc Ferren, Martha Dean 1947- *WhoWrEP 92*
McFerrin, Bobby *WhoAm 92*
McFerrin, Bobby 1950- *Baker 92*
McFerrin, Daniel 1934- *WhoSSW 93*
McFerrin, Robert 1921- *Baker 92*
Mcferron, Kathryn L. 1951- *St&PR 93*
McFerron, Kathryn Lois 1951- *WhoAmW 93*
McFerson, D. Richard 1937- *St&PR 93, WhoIns 93*
McFerson, D. Richard 1952- *WhoAm 92*
McGaath, Peter E. 1931- *St&PR 93*
McGaffey, Frederick C. *Law&B 92*

Mc Gaffey, Jere D. 1935- WhoAm 92
McGagh, William Gilbert 1929- WhoAm 92, WhoWor 93
McGaghie, William Craig 1947- WhoSSW 93
McGah, Kathleen A. Law&B 92
McGaha, Charles L. 1914-1984 BioIn 17
McGahan, David Patrick 1960- WhoEmL 93
McGahen, Paul W. 1936- St&PR 93
McGahern, John 1934- BioIn 17, WhoWor 93
McGail, Neil 1956- St&PR 93
McGalliard, John D. 1943- WhoIns 93
McGann, Diane Mary Law&B 92
McGann, George J. 1941- St&PR 93
McGann, James Gerard 1955- WhoE 93
McGann, Jerome John 1937- WhoAm 92, WhoSSW 93
Mcgann, John M. 1948- St&PR 93
McGann, John P. Law&B 92
McGann, John Raymond 1924- WhoAm 92, WhoE 93
McGann, Michael ScF&FL 92
McGann, Michelle WhoAmW 93
McGann, Robert George 1947- St&PR 93
Mc Gara, Homer Joseph 1913- WhoAm 92
McGarity, Margaret Dee 1948- WhoAmW 93
McGarity, Mary Nell 1959- WhoAmW 93
McGarr, Charles Taylor 1956- WhoEmL 93, WhoSSW 93
McGarr, Evelyn Franz 1910- WhoAmW 93
McGarr, Frank J. 1921- WhoAm 92
Mc Garrah, Robert Eynon 1921- WhoAm 92
McGarrell, James 1930- WhoAm 92
McGarrigle, Philip L., Jr. Law&B 92
McGarrity, Gerard John 1940- WhoAm 92, WhoE 93
McGarrity, Mark 1943- ConAu 37NR, ScF&FL 92
McGarrity, Richard Allen 1948- WhoSSW 93
McGarry, Charles William 1957- WhoSSW 93
McGarry, Eugene L. 1930- WhoAm 92
McGarry, Frederick Jerome 1927- WhoAm 92
McGarry, John P., Jr. BioIn 17
McGarry, John Patrick, Jr. 1939- WhoAm 92, WhoE 93
McGarry, John Warren WhoAm 92
McGarry, Marcia Langston 1941- WhoAmW 93
McGarry, Mark J. 1958- ScF&FL 92
McGarry, Richard D. 1942- St&PR 93
McGarry, Robert Alan 1965- WhoE 93
McGarry, Susan Hallsten 1948- WhoEmL 93
McGarry, William Andrew, Jr. 1954- WhoAm 92
McGarry, William C. 1951- St&PR 93
McGarry, William G. 1926- St&PR 93
McGarry, William L., Jr. Law&B 92
McGarty, John Francis 1947- WhoEmL 93
McGarvey, Mary Hewitt WhoE 93
McGarvey, Ray 1932- St&PR 93
McGarvey, Robert Mattock 1929- St&PR 93
McGarvey, Virginia Claire Lancaster 1934- WhoAmW 93
McGarvey, Wayne Carlton 1939- St&PR 93
McGarvie, Mark D. Law&B 92
McGary, Betty Winstead 1936- WhoAmW 93, WhoWor 93
McGary, Johnny Sylvester 1948- WhoEmL 93, WhoSSW 93
Mc Gaugh, James Lafayette 1931- WhoAm 92
McGaugh, William Perry Law&B 92
Mc Gaughan, Alexander Stanley 1912- WhoAm 92
McGaughey, Edgar Howard, III 1947- WhoSSW 93
McGaughey, Emmett Connell 1911- WhoAm 92
McGaughey, Frank S. 1923- St&PR 93
McGaughey, John Cameron, Jr. 1963- WhoSSW 93, WhoWor 93
Mc Gaughey, Kathryn Elizabeth 1918- WhoWrEP 92
McGaughey, Lydia A. AmWomPl
McGaughey, Robert Howe, III 1943- WhoSSW 93
Mc Gaughy, John Bell 1914- WhoAm 92
McGauley, Jacquelyne Sue 1951- WhoAmW 93, WhoEmL 93, WhoWor 93
McGauley, James Charles 1947- WhoSSW 93
McGauran, Julian John 1957- WhoAsAP 91
Mcgauran, Peter John WhoAsAP 91
McGavin, Darren 1922- MiSFD 9, WhoAm 92
McGavin, Jock Campbell 1917- WhoWor 93
McGavran, Brenda Joyce 1946- WhoEmL 93
McGavran, Donald Anderson 1897-1990 BioIn 17
McGavran, Grace Winifred 1896- AmWomPl
McGaw, Kenneth Roy 1926- WhoAm 92
McGaw, Wayne T. Law&B 92
McGeady, Kathleen Birmingham 1949- WhoAmW 93, WhoEmL 93
McGeady, Marianne Palombo 1958- WhoAmW 93
McGeady, Mary Rose 1928- WhoAm 92, WhoE 93
McGeary, Duncan ScF&FL 92
Mcgeary, Karen J. St&PR 93
McGeary, Sidney Thomas 1928- WhoWor 93
McGechie, Alistair ScF&FL 92
McGee, A.G. WhoScE 91-1
McGee, Alan G. 1932- WhoScE 91-1
McGee, Barbara 1949- WhoAmW 93, WhoEmL 93
McGee, Becky Law&B 92
McGee, Betty Jean 1938- WhoSSW 93
McGee, Carol Yvette 1966- WhoAmW 93
McGee, Caroline Gilchrist 1945- WhoAmW 93
McGee, Carolyn M. 1947- St&PR 93
McGee, Charles E. 1935- St&PR 93
Mcgee, David 1957- St&PR 93
McGee, Dean A. 1904- BioIn 17
McGee, Donald Lorin Law&B 92
McGee, Donald Lorin 1941- St&PR 93
McGee, Dorothy Horton 1913- WhoAmW 93, WhoE 93, WhoWor 93
McGee, F. David Law&B 92
McGee, Francis David 1934- St&PR 93
McGee, Gale d1992 NewYTBS 92
McGee, Gale William 1915-1992 BioIn 17, CurBio 92N
McGee, Gary L. 1949- St&PR 93
McGee, Hall Thomas, Jr. 1913- WhoAm 92, WhoWor 93
McGee, Harold Johnston 1937- WhoAm 92, WhoSSW 93
McGee, Henry Alexander, Jr. 1929- WhoAm 92
McGee, Henry W., Jr. 1932- WhoAm 92
McGee, Humphrey Glenn 1937- WhoSSW 93
McGee, Jacqueline T. 1952- WhoAmW 93
McGee, James Edward 1958- WhoSSW 93
McGee, James Lee 1946- St&PR 93
McGee, James Leevert, Jr. 1965- WhoSSW 93
McGee, James O'Donnell 1939- WhoWor 93
McGee, James Patrick 1941- WhoE 93
McGee, James Sears 1942- WhoAm 92
McGee, Jan C. 1949- St&PR 93
McGee, Jane Marie 1926- WhoAmW 93
McGee, Janet 1958- WhoEmL 93
McGee, Jerry V. 1930- St&PR 93
McGee, John Frampton 1923- St&PR 93, WhoAm 92, WhoSSW 93
McGee, John Joseph 1946- WhoE 93
Mc Gee, Joseph John, Jr. 1919- WhoAm 92
McGee, Keith Isham 1950- WhoEmL 93
McGee, Lynne Kalavsky 1949- WhoAmW 93, WhoEmL 93
McGee, Marion Dewitt 1925- St&PR 93
McGee, Mark Thomas 1947- ScF&FL 92
McGee, Martha 1933- WhoSSW 93
McGee, Mary Alice 1950- WhoAmW 93
McGee, Mary Rye 1956- WhoSSW 93
McGee, Mary S. 1960- St&PR 93
McGee, Michael J. 1962- St&PR 93
McGee, Michael Jay 1952- WhoEmL 93, WhoWor 93
Mc Gee, Patrick Edgar 1944- WhoWrEP 92
McGee, Pattie Lee Biggers 1906- WhoAmW 93
McGee, Paula Maria WhoScE 91-1
McGee, Ralph E. 1937- St&PR 93
McGee, Rebecca S. Law&B 92
McGee, Reece Jerome 1929- WhoAm 92
McGee, Robert Walter 1922- St&PR 93
McGee, Sam 1943- WhoWor 93
McGee, Shirley Jean 1953- WhoAmW 93
McGee, Thomas D'Arcy 1825-1868 BioIn 17
McGee, Timothy Joseph 1954- WhoSSW 93
McGee, Vivienne Lydia 1959- WhoAmW 93
McGee, W.J. 1853-1912 IntDcAn
McGee, Willie 1958- WhoAm 92
McGeehan, Daniel P. 1929- St&PR 93
McGeehan, W. O. 1879-1933 JrnUS
McGeehee, Mary David AmWomPl
McGeeney, John Rudd Law&B 92
McGeer, Edith Graef 1923- WhoAm 92
McGeer, James Peter WhoAm 92
McGeever, Katherine Boothe WhoAmW 93
McGegan, Nicholas 1950- Baker 92
McGehee, C. Coleman 1924- St&PR 93
Mc Gehee, Carden Coleman 1924- WhoAm 92
McGehee, Frank S. 1928- St&PR 93
McGehee, Frank Sutton 1928- WhoAm 92
Mc Gehee, H. Coleman, Jr. 1923- WhoAm 92
McGehee, James Oliver, Jr. 1946- WhoE 93
McGehee, Kathe Anne 1946- WhoAmW 93
Mc Gehee, Larry Thomas 1936- WhoAm 92
McGehee, Richard Paul 1943- WhoAm 92
McGehee, Richard Vernon 1934- WhoSSW 93
McGehee, Thomas Rives 1924- St&PR 93, WhoAm 92, WhoSSW 93
McGeoch, Daisy AmWomPl
McGeorge, Ronald Kenneth 1944- WhoAm 92
McGeough, Joseph Anthony WhoScE 91-1
McGeough, Thomas J. Law&B 92
McGerity, Margaret Ann 1949- WhoAmW 93
McGervey, John Donald 1931- WhoAm 92
McGervey, Paul John, III 1947- WhoWor 93
McGettigan, Charles Carroll, Jr. 1945- WhoAm 92
McGettigan, Marianne 1950- WhoAm 92
McGettrick, Andrew David WhoScE 91-1
McGettrick, Andrew David 1944- WhoWor 93
McGhan, Barry 1939- ScF&FL 92
McGhan, Donald K. 1934- St&PR 93
McGhan, H.P. ScF&FL 92
Mc Ghan, William Frederick 1946- WhoE 93
McGhee, Brownie (Walter) 1915- Baker 92
McGhee, Charisse BioIn 17
McGhee, Doc BioIn 17
McGhee, Edward ScF&FL 92
McGhee, George Crews 1912- WhoAm 92
Mcghee, Harold Richard 1938- WhoWrEP 92
McGhee, Mary Elizabeth 1958- WhoAmW 93
McGhee, Samuel Timothy 1940- WhoE 93
McGhee, Terri Patricia 1960- WhoAmW 93
McGhee, Twyla Kawpel 1960- WhoAmW 93
McGhee, Victoria T. Law&B 92
McGhehey, John Howard 1943- St&PR 93
McGhie, John Bennie 1947- WhoUN 92
McGibbon, J. Ian 1927- St&PR 93
Mc Gibbon, Pauline Mills 1910- WhoAm 92
McGibbon, William c. 1690-1756 Baker 92
McGiff, John Charles 1927- WhoAm 92
McGiffen, Philo Norton 1860-1897 HarEnMi
McGiffert, Arthur Cushman 1861-1933 BioIn 17
Mc Giffert, David Eliot 1926- WhoAm 92
Mc Giffert, John Rutherford 1926- WhoAm 92
McGiffert, Michael 1928- WhoAm 92, WhoWrEP 92
McGihon, Anne Lee 1957- WhoEmL 93
McGill, Allyson Faith 1953- WhoE 93
Mc Gill, Archie Joseph 1931- WhoAm 92
McGill, Charles Beatty 1922- WhoIns 93
McGill, Charles Harry, III 1942- St&PR 93
McGill, Dan Mays 1919- WhoAm 92, WhoIns 93, WhoWor 93
Mc Gill, Esby Clifton 1914- WhoAm 92
McGill, Gerald Lee 1929- St&PR 93
McGill, Gordon 1943- ScF&FL 92
McGill, Grace Anita 1943- WhoAmW 93
McGill, James D. 1945- St&PR 93
McGill, James T. 1940- WhoIns 93
McGill, Jennifer Houser 1957- WhoAm 92
McGill, Joan Shaffer 1942- WhoSSW 93
McGill, John Barclay BioIn 17
McGill, John Gardner 1949- WhoEmL 93
McGill, John Knox 1956- WhoSSW 93
McGill, John Rudolph 1936- St&PR 93
McGill, Josephine 1877-1919 Baker 92
McGill, Kenneth James 1942- St&PR 93
McGill, Kenneth James, Jr. 1954- WhoEmL 93
McGill, Larry d1991 BioIn 17
McGill, Loy B. 1954- St&PR 93
McGill, Mary Theresa 1946- WhoAmW 93
McGill, Maurice Leon 1936- WhoAm 92
McGill, Pamela Jeanne 1947- WhoAmW 93
McGill, Ralph 1898-1969 EncAACR [port], JrnUS
McGill, Regina BioIn 17
McGill, Robert Ernest, III 1931- St&PR 93, WhoAm 92, WhoWor 93
McGill, Ross Kim 1955- WhoWor 93
McGill, Stephen Andrew 1957- WhoEmL 93, WhoSSW 93
McGill, Thomas Emerson 1930- WhoAm 92
McGill, Thomas Joseph 1937- WhoAm 92
McGill, Warren Everett 1923- WhoAm 92
McGill, William A. 1925- St&PR 93
McGill, William James, Jr. 1936- WhoAm 92
McGill, William W. 1947- St&PR 93
Mc Gillem, Clare Duane 1923- WhoAm 92
McGilley, Mary Janet 1924- WhoAm 92, WhoAmW 93
McGillicuddy, Cornelius 1862-1956 BioIn 17
McGillicuddy, John F. 1930- St&PR 93
Mc Gillicuddy, John Francis 1930- WhoAm 92, WhoE 93
McGilligan, Patrick 1889-1979 BioIn 17
McGillis, Eugene Guinane 1934- St&PR 93
McGillis, Kelly 1957- HolBB [port]
McGillivary, Christopher John 1947- St&PR 93
McGillivray, Donald Dean 1928- WhoAm 92
McGillivray, Warren Rodney 1941- WhoUN 92
McGillycuddy, Valentine T.O. 1849-1939 BioIn 17
McGilvray, James William WhoScE 91-1
McGimpsey, Ronald A. 1944- St&PR 93
Mc Gimpsey, Ronald Alan 1944- WhoAm 92
Mc Gimsey, Charles Robert, III 1925- WhoAm 92
McGimsey, Edward C. 1921- St&PR 93
McGimsey, Edward C., Jr. 1949- St&PR 93
McGinley, Dennis Gerard Law&B 92
McGinley, Edward Stillman, II 1939- WhoAm 92
McGinley, Joseph Patrick 1947- WhoAm 92, WhoE 93, WhoEmL 93
McGinley, Laurence J. d1992 NewYTBS 92 [port]
McGinley, Laurence J(oseph) 1905-1992 CurBio 92N
McGinley, Mark D. Law&B 92
McGinley, Michael James 1949- WhoIns 93
McGinley, Patrick 1937- BioIn 17
McGinley, Patrick John 1938- St&PR 93
McGinley, Paul Anthony, Jr. 1948- WhoEmL 93
McGinley, Ronald James 1950- WhoAm 92
McGinley, Stanley E. Law&B 92
McGinn, Bernard John 1937- WhoAm 92
McGinn, Charles Evans 1953- WhoEmL 93
McGinn, Connie 1947- WhoAmW 93
McGinn, Donald Joseph 1905- WhoE 93, WhoWor 93
McGinn, Eileen 1947- WhoEmL 93
McGinn, Frank L. 1929- St&PR 93
McGinn, Mary J. Law&B 92
McGinn, Mary Jovita 1947- WhoEmL 93
McGinn, Mary Lyn 1949- WhoAmW 93, WhoEmL 93
McGinn, Patricia Ferris 1938- WhoAmW 93
McGinn, Robert F. 1951- St&PR 93
McGinn, Susan Frances 1961- WhoAm 92
Mc Ginnes, Edgar Allen, Jr. 1926- WhoAm 92
McGinnes, Paul R. 1946- WhoAm 92
McGinness, James E. Law&B 92
Mc Ginness, William George, III 1948- WhoAm 92, WhoEmL 93, WhoSSW 93
McGinnies, Elliott Morse 1921- WhoAm 92
McGinnis, Arthur J. 1911- St&PR 93
Mc Ginnis, Arthur Joseph 1911- WhoAm 92
McGinnis, Arthur Joseph, Jr. 1952- St&PR 93, WhoAm 92, WhoEmL 93
McGinnis, Bernard C., III 1942- St&PR 93
McGinnis, Bryan T. Law&B 92
McGinnis, Charles I. Law&B 92
McGinnis, Charles Irving 1928- WhoAm 92
Mcginnis, Conrad D. 1938- St&PR 93
McGinnis, Daniel L. 1939- St&PR 93
McGinnis, Donald E. BioIn 17
Mcginnis, Elizabeth A. 1955- St&PR 93
McGinnis, Frank Thomas 1919- WhoAm 92
McGinnis, Homer BioIn 17

Mcginnis, James Arthur 1947- *St&PR 93, WhoEmL 93*
McGinnis, James Earl, Jr. 1928- *St&PR 93*
Mc Ginnis, James Michael 1944- *WhoAm 92*
McGinnis, John Oldham 1957- *WhoAm 92*
McGinnis, Marcy Ann 1950- *WhoAmW 93*
McGinnis, Mary-Jane 1964- *WhoAmW 93*
McGinnis, Michael J. *Law&B 92*
McGinnis, Patrick Michael 1954- *St&PR 93*
McGinnis, Robert Campbell 1918- *WhoAm 92*
McGinnis, Robert William 1930- *St&PR 93*
McGinnis, Terence A. *Law&B 92*
Mcginnis, Timothy 1940- *St&PR 93*
McGinnis, W. Patrick *WhoAm 92*
McGinnis, William John *Law&B 92*
Mcginnis, William W. 1935- *St&PR 93*
McGinniss, Edward J. 1929- *St&PR 93*
McGinniss, Joe *BioIn 17*
Mc Ginniss, Joe 1942- *WhoAm 92, WhoWrEP 92*
McGinnity, James M. 1942- *St&PR 93*
McGinnity, Maureen A. 1956- *WhoAmW 93*
Mcginnity, Ronald James 1940- *St&PR 93*
McGinty, John 1911- *WhoAm 92*
McGinty, John B. 1930- *WhoAm 92*
McGinty, John Edward 1946- *St&PR 93*
McGinty, John Joseph 1935- *WhoAm 92*
Mc Ginty, John Milton 1935- *WhoAm 92*
McGinty, Michael Dennis 1942- *WhoAm 92*
McGinty, Milton Bradford 1946- *WhoAm 92*
McGinty, Thomas Edward 1929- *WhoAm 92*
McGirk, Tim(othy Stephen) 1952- *ConAu 136*
McGirr, David William John 1954- *WhoAm 92*
McGirt, Aimee Despland Gibbons 1927- *WhoSSW 93*
McGirt, Dan 1967- *ScF&FL 92*
McGiverin, Arthur A. 1928- *WhoAm 92*
McGiverin, Donald Scott 1924- *St&PR 93*
McGivern, Arthur *Law&B 92*
McGivern, Arthur J. 1947- *St&PR 93*
McGivern, Mark J. *Law&B 92*
McGivern, Maureen 1921- *ScF&FL 92*
McGivern, Maureen Daly *ConAu 37NR, MajAI*
McGivern, Patrick *ScF&FL 92*
McGivern, William P. 1921-1982 *ScF&FL 92*
McGivern, William T. *WhoAm 92*
McGivney, William D. 1934- *St&PR 93*
McGivney, William David 1934- *WhoE 93*
McGlade, Edward Richard 1961- *St&PR 93*
Mc Glamery, Marshal Dean 1932- *WhoAm 92*
McGlamry, Beverly *ScF&FL 92*
McGlashan, James d1858 *BioIn 17*
McGlasson, William Barry 1929- *WhoWor 93*
McGlaston, Lisa S. *Law&B 92*
McGlaughlin, Daniel W. *WhoIns 93*
McGlaughlin, David Michael 1950- *WhoEmL 93*
McGlaughlin, William 1943- *Baker 92*
McGlennen, David Michael 1963- *WhoEmL 93*
McGlinchey, Dianne Watkins 1949- *WhoEmL 93*
McGlinchey, Joseph D. 1938- *St&PR 93*
McGlinchey, Joseph Dennis 1938- *WhoAm 92*
McGlinchy, Judith Marie 1960- *WhoAmW 93*
McGlinn, Bernard James, Jr. 1937- *St&PR 93*
McGlinn, Francis Michael 1945- *WhoIns 93*
McGlinn, Frank Cresson Potts 1914- *WhoAm 92*
McGlockton, Joan Rector *Law&B 92*
McGlohon, Margaret Ellen 1961- *WhoAmW 93*
McGloin, Joseph T(haddeus) 1917- *ConAu 39NR*
Mcglone, John Francis 1936- *St&PR 93*
McGlone, Michael Anthony 1951- *WhoEmL 93*
McGlone, Susie G. *AmWomPl*
McGlory, Willie Edward *Law&B 92*
McGlothen, Steven Raymond 1951- *WhoEmL 93*
McGlothlin, Charles H., Jr. *Law&B 92*
McGlothlin, David Edward 1950- *St&PR 93*
McGlothlin, James Edwin 1935- *St&PR 93*
Mc Glothlin, James Harrison 1910- *WhoAm 92*
McGlothlin, Stanley E. *Law&B 92*
McGlotten, Robert Miller 1938- *WhoAm 92*
McGlown, Kathlyn Joanne 1954- *WhoEmL 93, WhoSSW 93*
Mc Glynn, Brian James 1952- *WhoWrEP 92*
McGlynn, Don *MiSFD 9*
McGlynn, Elizabeth Joan 1930- *WhoAmW 93*
McGlynn, Frank Michael 1955- *WhoSSW 93*
McGlynn, John Francis 1941- *WhoE 93*
McGlynn, Joseph Leo, Jr. 1925- *WhoAm 92*
McGlynn, Martin Mary 1946- *St&PR 93*
McGlynn, Richard D. 1929- *St&PR 93*
Mc Glynn, Sean Patrick 1931- *WhoAm 92, WhoSSW 93*
McGoey, George William 1944- *St&PR 93*
Mc Goldrick, John Gardiner 1932- *WhoAm 92*
McGoldrick, Michael J. *Law&B 92*
McGoldrick, Paul Alexander *Law&B 92*
McGoldrick, Thomas John 1941- *St&PR 93*
McGoldrick, William Patrick 1946- *WhoE 93, WhoEmL 93*
McGonagall, William 1825?-1902 *BioIn 17*
McGonagle, Patrick Joseph *Law&B 92*
McGonigal, Pearl 1929- *WhoAm 92*
McGonigal, Shirley Joan O'Hey 1920- *WhoAmW 93*
McGonigal, Valarie Kay 1955- *WhoAmW 93*
McGonigal, W.L. *Law&B 92*
McGonigle, James Gregory 1945- *WhoE 93, WhoWor 93*
Mcgonigle, James R. *St&PR 93*
McGonigle, John William *Law&B 92*
McGonigle, John William 1938- *St&PR 93, WhoAm 92*
Mc Gonigle, Thomas *WhoWrEP 92*
McGonigle, Thomas 1944- *ConAu 137*
McGonigle, Thomas Patrick 1960- *WhoEmL 93*
McGoogan, Linda J. 1947- *WhoAmW 93*
McGoohan, Patrick 1928- *MiSFD 9*
McGoohan, Patrick Joseph 1928- *WhoAm 92*
McGookey, Donald Paul 1928- *WhoSSW 93*
Mc Goon, Clifford 1939- *WhoWrEP 92*
Mc Goon, Dwight Charles 1925- *WhoAm 92*
McGorrill, Bruce Courtney 1931- *WhoAm 92*
McGory, Michael P. *Law&B 92*
Mc Gouey, Robert 1928- *WhoWrEP 92*
McGough, Duane Theodore 1932- *WhoAm 92*
Mcgough, George Vincent 1940- *St&PR 93*
McGough, Hugh R. *Law&B 92*
McGough, James J. *Law&B 92*
McGough, John Paul 1935- *WhoAm 92, WhoE 93*
McGough, Kevin J. *Law&B 92*
McGough, Michael S. 1957- *St&PR 93*
McGough, Peter *BioIn 17*
McGough, Roger 1937- *ChlFicS*
McGough, W. Edward 1928-1991 *BioIn 17*
McGough, Walter Thomas 1919- *WhoAm 92*
McGourty, Stephen Lawrence 1954- *WhoEmL 93*
McGovern, Ann 1930- *MajAI [port], SmATA 70 [port]*
McGovern, Arthur F(rancis) 1929- *ConAu 40NR*
McGovern, Deirdre Joan 1963- *WhoE 93*
McGovern, Elizabeth *BioIn 17*
McGovern, Eugene J. 1932- *St&PR 93*
McGovern, George S. 1922- *BioIn 17, ColdWar 1 [port], PolPar*
Mc Govern, George Stanley 1922- *WhoAm 92*
McGovern, Hugh M. *Law&B 92*
McGovern, John Francis 1946- *St&PR 93, WhoAm 92*
McGovern, John Hugh 1924- *WhoAm 92, WhoE 93, WhoWor 93*
McGovern, John James 1932- *WhoIns 93*
McGovern, John Joseph 1920- *WhoAm 92*
McGovern, John Phillip 1921- *WhoAm 92*
Mc Govern, Joseph W. 1909- *WhoAm 92*
McGovern, Karen Burnis 1959- *St&PR 93*
McGovern, Maureen 1949- *BioIn 17*
Mc Govern, Maureen Therese 1949- *WhoAmW 93*
McGovern, Michael 1951- *St&PR 93*
McGovern, Michael M. *Law&B 92*
McGovern, Michael P. *WhoE 93*
McGovern, Michael Patrick 1955- *WhoEmL 93*
McGovern, Patricia A. *Law&B 92*
McGovern, Patrick *BioIn 17*
McGovern, Patrick W. *Law&B 92*
McGovern, Philip C. *Law&B 92*
McGovern, R. Gordon 1926- *St&PR 93*
McGovern, Raymond E. 1928- *St&PR 93*
McGovern, Raymond E., Jr. *Law&B 92*
McGovern, Richard Gordon 1926- *WhoAm 92*
McGovern, Thomas A. 1933- *St&PR 93*
McGovern, Thomas William 1957- *WhoEmL 93*
McGovern, Tim *WhoAm 92*
Mc Govern, Walter T. 1922- *WhoAm 92*
McGowan, Aileen Patricia 1963- *WhoSSW 93*
McGowan, Andrew John 1939- *WhoE 93*
McGowan, Carol Jean 1955- *WhoAmW 93*
McGowan, Christopher Thomas 1959- *St&PR 93*
McGowan, D.W. 1924- *St&PR 93*
McGowan, Daniel Leonard, Jr. 1957- *WhoEmL 93*
McGowan, David Alexander *WhoScE 91-1*
McGowan, David Allen 1952- *WhoEmL 93*
McGowan, Diane Lynne 1959- *WhoEmL 93*
McGowan, Donald William 1924- *WhoAm 92*
McGowan, Ed *Law&B 92*
McGowan, Edward J. *Law&B 92*
McGowan, George V. 1928- *St&PR 93*
McGowan, George Vincent 1928- *WhoAm 92, WhoE 93*
McGowan, Harold 1909- *WhoAm 92, WhoWrEP 92*
McGowan, Ian Duncan 1945- *WhoWor 93*
McGowan, J.C. 1937- *St&PR 93*
McGowan, J.P. 1880-1952 *BioIn 17*
Mc Gowan, James Atkinson 1914- *WhoAm 92*
McGowan, James J., Jr. *Law&B 92*
McGowan, Jeannette Adelaide 1930- *WhoAmW 93*
McGowan, Joan Yuhas 1955- *WhoE 93, WhoEmL 93*
McGowan, Joanne Suweyn 1955- *WhoEmL 93*
McGowan, John Edward, Jr. 1942- *WhoAm 92, WhoSSW 93*
McGowan, John P. 1926- *BioIn 17*
McGowan, John Patrick 1926- *WhoAm 92*
McGowan, Joseph Anthony, Jr. 1931- *WhoAm 92*
McGowan, Joseph Lamar, Jr. 1930- *St&PR 93*
Mc Gowan, Kathleen Keer 1918- *WhoWrEP 92*
McGowan, Margaret *BioIn 17*
McGowan, Marie C. *Law&B 92*
McGowan, Mark L. *Law&B 92*
McGowan, Mary *Law&B 92*
McGowan, Michael W. 1948- *St&PR 93*
McGowan, Patrick Francis 1940- *WhoAm 92*
McGowan, Patrick Jude 1939- *WhoAm 92*
McGowan, Stephen W. 1953- *St&PR 93*
McGowan, William Aloysius 1896-1954 *BiDAMSp 1989*
McGowan, William G. *BioIn 17*
McGowan, William G. 1927-1992 *NewYTBS 92 [port], News 93-1*
McGowen, Leon William 1929- *St&PR 93*
McGowen, Thomas *ScF&FL 92*
McGowen, Thomas N., Jr. 1926- *St&PR 93*
McGowen, Tom 1927- *ScF&FL 92*
McGowin, Nicholas Stallworth 1912- *WhoAm 92*
Mc Gowin, William Edward 1938- *WhoAm 92, WhoE 93*
McGown, Alan *WhoScE 91-1*
McGrady, Charles Worden 1953- *WhoEmL 93*
McGrady, Corinne Young 1938- *WhoAmW 93*
McGrady, James A. 1950- *St&PR 93*
McGrady, Sandra Lee 1951- *WhoSSW 93*
McGrail, Elizabeth E. *Law&B 92*
McGrail, Elizabeth Hutton 1962- *WhoAmW 93*
McGrail, Gail Suzanne 1961- *WhoSSW 93*
McGrail, Michael A. *Law&B 92*
McGrail, Susan King 1952- *WhoEmL 93*
McGranaghan, Joseph Thomas 1930- *St&PR 93*
McGrane, Michael C. *Law&B 92*
McGrath, Abigail Hubbell Rosen 1941- *WhoAmW 93*
McGrath, Barry *Law&B 92*
McGrath, Barry G. *BioIn 17*
McGrath, Bernard Dennin 1925- *St&PR 93*
McGrath, Brian 1941- *St&PR 93*
McGrath, Brian Edward 1959- *WhoSSW 93*
McGrath, Caroline C. 1952- *WhoE 93*
McGrath, Charles Arthur 1947- *WhoAm 92*
McGrath, Charles William, Jr. 1950- *WhoEmL 93*
McGrath, Claire Pavelka *Law&B 92*
McGrath, Deborah Field 1948- *WhoAmW 93*
McGrath, Dennis 1946- *ConAu 139*
McGrath, Dennis Britton 1937- *WhoAm 92*
McGrath, Don John 1948- *St&PR 93, WhoAm 92*
McGrath, Donald E. 1932- *St&PR 93*
McGrath, Dorn Charles, Jr. 1930- *WhoE 93, WhoWor 93*
McGrath, Eamonn 1929- *ConAu 139*
McGrath, Edward A. 1930- *WhoAm 92*
McGrath, Eugene R. 1942- *WhoAm 92*
Mc Grath, Francis Joseph 1908- *WhoAm 92*
McGrath, Gary Michael 1950- *WhoE 93*
McGrath, Gerald Thomas 1935- *St&PR 93*
McGrath, Geraldine *Law&B 92*
McGrath, J. Brian 1942- *WhoAm 92*
McGrath, J. David A. 1936- *St&PR 93*
McGrath, J. Dennis *Law&B 92*
McGrath, J. Howard 1903-1966 *PolPar*
McGrath, James Aloysius 1932- *WhoAm 92, WhoE 93*
McGrath, James Charles, III 1942- *WhoAm 92*
McGrath, James Edward 1951- *St&PR 93*
McGrath, James Howard 1903-1966 *BioIn 17*
McGrath, James Thomas 1942- *WhoAm 92*
McGrath, Joan M. 1936- *St&PR 93*
McGrath, John Christie *WhoScE 91-1*
McGrath, John Edward 1938- *St&PR 93*
McGrath, John F. 1954- *WhoIns 93*
McGrath, John Francis 1925- *WhoAm 92*
Mc Grath, John Joseph 1910- *WhoAm 92*
McGrath, Joseph *MiSFD 9*
McGrath, Joseph D. *Law&B 92*
McGrath, Joseph Edward 1927- *WhoAm 92*
McGrath, Kathleen Bernadette 1950- *WhoAmW 93*
McGrath, Kathryn Bradley 1944- *WhoAm 92, WhoAmW 93*
McGrath, Kenneth W. 1949- *St&PR 93*
McGrath, Kevin 1940- *WhoUN 92*
McGrath, Kevin John *Law&B 92*
McGrath, Lawrence A. 1943- *St&PR 93*
Mc Grath, Lee Parr *WhoAm 92, WhoWrEP 92*
McGrath, Margaret Mary 1950- *WhoAmW 93*
McGrath, Marian Hanly 1948- *WhoEmL 93*
McGrath, Mary F. 1954- *WhoEmL 93*
McGrath, Matthew T. *Law&B 92*
McGrath, Maureen *Law&B 92*
McGrath, Michael A. *Law&B 92*
McGrath, Michael Alan 1942- *WhoAm 92*
McGrath, Michael Anthony 1944- *WhoAm 92*
McGrath, Patrick 1950- *BioIn 17, ConAu 136, ScF&FL 92*
McGrath, Patrick J. 1934- *WhoAm 92*
McGrath, Peter E. 1931- *St&PR 93*
McGrath, Raymond J. 1942- *CngDr 91, WhoAm 92, WhoE 93*
McGrath, Steve Paul *WhoScE 91-1*
Mc Grath, Thomas 1916- *WhoAm 92*
McGrath, Thomas 1916-1990 *BioIn 17*
McGrath, Thomas A. 1919-1992 *BioIn 17*
McGrath, Thomas F., III 1947- *WhoIns 93*
McGrath, Thomas J. 1932- *WhoAm 92*
McGrath, Walter Joseph 1939- *WhoE 93*
Mc Grath, William Restore 1922- *WhoAm 92*
McGraw, Barbara *BioIn 17*
McGraw, Benjamin F. 1949- *St&PR 93*
McGraw, Beverly Anne 1936- *WhoSSW 93*
McGraw, Donald Jesse 1943- *WhoAm 92*
McGraw, Edward R. *Law&B 92*
McGraw, Eloise Jarvis *BioIn 17*
McGraw, Eloise Jarvis 1915- *DcAmChF 1960, MajAI [port], ScF&FL 92*
Mc Graw, Erin 1957- *WhoWrEP 92*
McGraw, Frank Edwin, Jr. 1944- *BiDAMSp 1989*
McGraw, Harold W., Jr. 1918- *St&PR 93*
Mc Graw, Harold Whittlesey, Jr. 1918- *WhoAm 92*
McGraw, Harold Whittlesey, III 1948- *St&PR 93*
McGraw, Jack Wilson 1943- *WhoAm 92*

McGraw, James 1945- *St&PR 93*
McGraw, James L. 1917- *WhoAm 92*
McGraw, James Michael 1945- *WhoAm 92*
McGraw, Janet Goller 1936- *WhoAmW 93*
McGraw, John 1873-1934 *BioIn 17*
McGraw, John J. *Law&B 92*
Mc Graw, Karen Kay 1938- *WhoWrEP 92*
McGraw, Lavinia Morgan 1924- *WhoAmW 93, WhoE 93, WhoWor 93*
McGraw, Lois Scheerer d1991 *BioIn 17*
McGraw, M.J. *Law&B 92*
McGraw, Myrtle B. 1899-1988 *BioIn 17*
McGraw, Phyllis Mae 1930- *WhoAmW 93*
McGraw, Robert James 1947- *St&PR 93*
McGraw, Robert P. 1954- *St&PR 93*
McGraw, Robert Pierce 1954- *WhoAm 92*
McGraw, Timothy J. *Law&B 92*
McGraw, Tug 1944- *BioIn 17*
McGraw, Walter J. 1928- *St&PR 93*
McGraw-Lewicki, Marjorie Lee 1957- *WhoE 93, WhoEmL 93*
McGray, Mary Jennifer 1966- *WhoE 93*
McGreal, Elizabeth Yates 1905- *BioIn 17*
McGreal, Eugene P. *Law&B 92*
McGreal, Joseph A., Jr. 1935- *WhoAm 92*
McGreal, Michael J. *Law&B 92*
McGreavy, Colin *WhoScE 91-1*
McGreevey, Mark F. *WhoIns 93*
McGreevey, Robert M. *Law&B 92*
McGreevy, Martin Kenneth 1931- *WhoIns 93*
McGreevy, Mary 1935- *WhoAmW 93*
McGreevy, Rebecca C. *St&PR 93*
McGreevy, Terrence Gerard 1932- *WhoAm 92*
McGreevy, Thomas James d1991 *BioIn 17*
McGreevy, Thomas James 1932- *St&PR 93*
McGregor, Brenda Whitlow 1953- *WhoSSW 93*
McGregor, Cecelia Jean 1952- *WhoEmL 93*
McGregor, Charles Thomas 1932- *WhoSSW 93*
McGregor, Don *ScF&FL 92*
Mc Gregor, Donald Thornton 1924- *WhoAm 92*
McGregor, Douglas J. 1941- *St&PR 93*
McGregor, Duncan Douglass 1930- *WhoE 93*
McGregor, G.I. 1934- *St&PR 93*
McGregor, G. Mark 1950- *St&PR 93*
McGregor, Gerald Lee 1935- *St&PR 93*
McGregor, Hamilton F. 1948- *St&PR 93*
McGregor, Howard Hill 1919- *St&PR 93*
McGregor, Ian 1947- *St&PR 93*
Mcgregor, Jack E. 1934- *St&PR 93*
McGregor, Jack Edwin 1934- *WhoAm 92*
McGregor, James Andrew 1948- *St&PR 93*
McGregor, James David 1924- *WhoAsAP 91*
McGregor, James H. 1946- *ConAu 138*
McGregor, Jane C. *Law&B 92*
McGregor, Loretta Neal 1964- *WhoAmW 93*
McGregor, M.H. 1936- *St&PR 93*
Mc Gregor, Maurice 1920- *WhoAm 92*
McGregor, Michael H. 1936- *WhoAm 92*
McGregor, Murray James *WhoScE 91-1*
McGregor, Patrick Vance 1946- *St&PR 93*
McGregor, Peter 1926- *WhoWor 93*
McGregor, Peter R. 1949- *St&PR 93*
McGregor, Phillip *ScF&FL 92*
McGregor, Robert G. 1947- *St&PR 93*
McGregor, Ruth Hill d1991 *BioIn 17*
McGregor, Scott Duncan 1952- *WhoEmL 93*
Mcgregor, Stewart D. 1945- *St&PR 93*
McGregor, Theodore Anthony 1944- *WhoWor 93*
Mcgregor, Wallace 1928- *St&PR 93*
McGregor, Walter 1937- *WhoE 93*
McGregor, Wheeler Kesey, Jr. 1929- *WhoSSW 93*
McGregor, William S. *St&PR 93*
McGrew, David Rollin 1936- *WhoWor 93*
McGrew, Kenneth Louis 1952- *St&PR 93*
McGrew, Raymond Daniel 1943- *St&PR 93*
McGrew, Wallace Raymond 1929- *St&PR 93*
McGriff, Deborah *WhoAm 92*
McGriff, Deborah M. 1949- *BioIn 17*
McGriff, Frederick Stanley 1963- *WhoAm 92*
McGriff, Jimmy 1936- *SoulM*
McGriff, Richard Bernard 1935- *WhoE 93*
Mc Groddy, James Cleary 1937- *WhoAm 92*
McGrory, John F. *Law&B 92*
McGrory, Josephine *BioIn 17*
McGrory, Larry James 1957- *WhoEmL 93*
McGrory, Mary Kathleen 1933- *WhoAmW 93, WhoWor 93*
McGrory, Nancy Ruth 1960- *WhoE 93*
McGruder, James P. *Law&B 92*
Mc Gruder, Stephen Jones 1943- *WhoAm 92*
McGuane, Emilie Ann 1938- *WhoAmW 93*
McGuane, Thomas *MiSFD 9*
McGuane, Thomas 1939- *BioIn 17, MagSAmL [port]*
Mc Guane, Thomas Francis, III 1939- *WhoAm 92, WhoWrEP 92*
McGuckin, James F. *St&PR 93*
Mc Guckin, James Frederick 1930- *WhoAm 92*
McGuckin, John H., Jr. *Law&B 92*
McGuckin, John Hugh, Jr. 1946- *St&PR 93*
McGuckin, Mildred Criss 1890- *AmWomPl*
McGuff, Joe *WhoAm 92*
McGuffey, Alexander Hamilton 1816-1896 *BioIn 17*
McGuffey, Carroll Wade, Sr. 1922- *WhoAm 92*
McGuffey, Carroll Wade, Jr. 1951- *WhoEmL 93*
McGuffey, William Holmes 1800-1873 *BioIn 17*
McGuffin, Peter *WhoScE 91-1*
McGuffog, Douglas Robert 1939- *WhoWor 93*
McGuigan, Donald Graham *Law&B 92*
Mc Guigan, Frank Joseph 1924- *WhoAm 92*
Mc Guigan, James Edward 1931- *WhoAm 92*
Mcguigan, Kathleen Bailey 1966- *WhoWrEP 92*
McGuigan, Thomas J. 1942- *St&PR 93, WhoAm 92, WhoE 93*
McGuigan, William Patrick 1948- *St&PR 93*
McGuinn, Martin G. *Law&B 92*
Mc Guinn, Martin Gregory 1942- *WhoAm 92*
McGuinn, Roger 1942- *BioIn 17*
  See Also Byrds, The *ConMus 8*
McGuinn, William David 1952- *WhoSSW 93*
McGuinness, Albert Leo 1926-1990 *BioIn 17*
McGuinness, Barbara Sue 1947- *WhoEmL 93*
McGuinness, Deborah Louise 1958- *WhoAmW 93, WhoEmL 93*
McGuinness, Edward J. 1931- *WhoE 93*
Mc Guinness, Frank Joseph 1928- *WhoAm 92, WhoE 93*
McGuinness, George J. 1950- *St&PR 93*
McGuinness, James Kevin 1894-1950 *BioIn 17*
McGuinness, John Seward 1922- *WhoE 93, WhoWor 93*
McGuinness, Lynette Ebeoglu 1963- *WhoSSW 93*
McGuinness, Margaret Elizabeth 1956- *WhoSSW 93*
McGuinness, Margaret Mary 1953- *WhoE 93*
McGuinness-Mukerjee, Joanne Helene 1942- *WhoAmW 93*
Mc Guire, Alfred James 1931- *WhoAm 92*
McGuire, Amos W. 1930- *St&PR 93*
McGuire, Arthur H. *Law&B 92*
McGuire, Arthur H. 1947- *St&PR 93*
McGuire, Brian Lyle 1959- *WhoEmL 93, WhoSSW 93*
McGuire, Carol Ann 1950- *WhoEmL 93*
McGuire, Carol Susann 1948- *WhoAmW 93*
McGuire, Catherine 1948- *ScF&FL 92*
McGuire, Charles Carroll 1932- *St&PR 93*
McGuire, Charles Carroll, Jr. 1932- *WhoAm 92*
McGuire, Charles Gerald 1954- *St&PR 93*
McGuire, Dianne Marie 1950- *WhoEmL 93*
McGuire, Donald Michael 1948- *WhoIns 93*
Mc Guire, Dorothy Hackett 1916- *WhoAm 92*
McGuire, Earl Eugene, Jr. 1934- *St&PR 93*
McGuire, Edith *BlkAmWO*
McGuire, Edith 1944- *BioIn 17*
McGuire, Edward 1932-1986 *BioIn 17*
McGuire, Edward David, Jr. 1948- *WhoSSW 93*
McGuire, Edward J., Jr. *Law&B 92*
McGuire, Edward Patrick 1932- *WhoE 93*
McGuire, Elinor *BioIn 17*
McGuire, Eugene Guenard *Law&B 92*
McGuire, Gregory M. *Law&B 92*
McGuire, J.M. *Law&B 92*
McGuire, James Charles 1934- *St&PR 93*
McGuire, James Edward 1931- *WhoE 93*
McGuire, James P. 1938- *St&PR 93*
McGuire, James Richard 1964- *WhoE 93*
McGuire, James Thomas 1863-1936 *BiDAMSp 1989*
McGuire, James Vincent 1944- *St&PR 93*
McGuire, Jean Flatley 1952- *WhoAmW 93*
McGuire, Jeanne Marie 1956- *WhoEmL 93*
McGuire, John *BioIn 17*
McGuire, John Albert 1950- *WhoSSW 93*
McGuire, John Francis, Jr. 1941- *WhoE 93*
McGuire, John J. 1917-1981 *ScF&FL 92*
McGuire, John J. 1948- *St&PR 93*
McGuire, John Lawrence 1942- *WhoAm 92*
McGuire, John Murray 1929- *WhoAm 92*
McGuire, John P. *Law&B 92*
McGuire, Joseph Edward 1926- *WhoE 93*
Mc Guire, Joseph William 1925- *WhoAm 92*
McGuire, Julie Elizabeth *Law&B 92*
McGuire, Kathleen H. *Law&B 92*
McGuire, Larry G. 1947- *St&PR 93*
McGuire, Marc C. *Law&B 92*
McGuire, Martin Cyril 1933- *WhoE 93*
McGuire, Mavis Louise 1948- *WhoE 93*
McGuire, Michael Francis 1946- *WhoAm 92*
McGuire, Michael George 1944- *St&PR 93*
Mc Guire, Michael John 1947- *WhoEmL 93*
McGuire, Michael T. *Law&B 92*
McGuire, Michael T. 1955- *St&PR 93*
McGuire, Michael William 1960- *WhoWor 93*
McGuire, Pamela C. *Law&B 92*
McGuire, Patricia A. 1952- *WhoAm 92, WhoAmW 93, WhoEmL 93*
McGuire, Patricia Jean 1928- *WhoAmW 93*
McGuire, Patrick L. 1949- *ScF&FL 92*
McGuire, Patrick Thomas 1944- *St&PR 93*
Mcguire, Paul R. 1936- *St&PR 93*
McGuire, Peter J. 1954- *St&PR 93*
McGuire, Peter Joseph 1943- *WhoSSW 93*
McGuire, Richard A. 1946- *WhoIns 93*
McGuire, Richard O. 1936- *St&PR 93*
McGuire, Richard Oliver 1936- *WhoAm 92*
McGuire, Richard P. *Law&B 92*
McGuire, Robert J. *Law&B 92*
McGuire, Robert J. 1936- *St&PR 93*
McGuire, Sandra Lynn 1947- *WhoAmW 93*
McGuire, Teresa 1943- *WhoAmW 93*
McGuire, Therese Benedict *WhoE 93*
Mcguire, Thomas A. 1932- *St&PR 93*
McGuire, Thomas J. *Law&B 92*
McGuire, Timothy John 1950- *WhoEmL 93*
McGuire, Timothy William 1938- *WhoAm 92*
McGuire, Virginia Marie 1955- *St&PR 93*
McGuire, Walter Gary 1943- *WhoE 93*
McGuire, Walter R. 1913- *St&PR 93*
Mc Guire, William 1917- *WhoWrEP 92*
McGuire, William 1950- *ScF&FL 92*
McGuire, William Dennis 1943- *WhoAm 92*
Mc Guire, William James 1925- *WhoAm 92*
McGuire, William L. d1992 *NewYTBS 92*
Mc Guire, William Lawrence 1926- *WhoAm 92*
McGuire, William W. 1948- *St&PR 93*
McGuire-Thompson, Marie C. *BioIn 17*
McGuirk, James Gerard 1955- *WhoE 93*
McGuirk, James Joseph *WhoScE 91-1*
McGuirk, Ronald Charles 1938- *St&PR 93, WhoAm 92, WhoE 93*
McGuirk, Terence F. 1951- *St&PR 93*
McGuirk, Terrence 1925- *WhoAm 92, WhoSSW 93*
McGuirl, Marlene Dana Callis 1938- *WhoAmW 93*
McGuirl, Robert Joseph 1952- *WhoEmL 93*
McGuirt, Ronald Theron 1953- *WhoSSW 93*
McGurk, Eugene David, Jr. 1951- *WhoEmL 93*
McGurk, Harry *WhoScE 91-1*
McGurk, L. Michael 1950- *St&PR 93*
McGurk, Laureen Ellen 1961- *WhoSSW 93*
McGurk, Nancy J. 1955- *St&PR 93*
McGurk, Tina 1951- *WhoAmW 93*
McGurk-Kremkow, Heather 1966- *WhoAmW 93, WhoEmL 93*
McGurl, Maureen Kathleen 1948- *St&PR 93, WhoE 93, WhoEmL 93*
Mc Gurn, Barrett 1914- *WhoAm 92*
McGurn, George William 1914- *WhoWor 93*
McGurn, James (Edward) 1953- *ConAu 136*
McGurn, William Barrett, III 1943- *WhoWor 93*
McGurty, Mark 1955- *Baker 92*
McGushin, Mary Eileen 1946- *St&PR 93*
McGwire, Mark *BioIn 17*
McGwire, Mark 1963- *WhoAm 92*
McHale, Anna Elizabeth 1953- *WhoAmW 93*
McHale, Brian 1952- *ScF&FL 92*
McHale, D. *WhoScE 91-1*
McHale, Edward Robertson 1921- *WhoAm 92*
McHale, Elaine R. *Law&B 92*
Mc Hale, Inez Pecore 1908- *WhoAm 92*
McHale, Jack F. *St&PR 93*
McHale, Kevin *BioIn 17*
McHale, Kevin 1957- *WhoAm 92*
McHale, Kevin Edward 1957- *BiDAMSp 1989*
McHale, Thomas Anthony 1914- *WhoAm 92*
McHale, Thomas J. 1938- *St&PR 93*
McHale, Thomas Joseph 1938- *WhoE 93*
McHale, Vincent Edward 1939- *WhoAm 92*
McHan, Eva Jane 1941- *WhoWor 93*
McHaney, Dennis *ScF&FL 92*
McHaney, Jane Sims 1956- *WhoSSW 93*
McHardy, Louis William 1930- *WhoAm 92*
McHardy, William James *WhoScE 91-1*
McHarg, Ian L. 1921- *BioIn 17*
McHarg, Ian Lennox 1920- *WhoAm 92*
McHargue, Charles E. 1952- *St&PR 93*
McHargue, Georgess 1941- *ScF&FL 92*
McHarris, William Charles 1937- *WhoAm 92*
McHenry, Barnabas 1929- *WhoAm 92*
Mc Henry, Dean Eugene 1910- *WhoAm 92*
McHenry, Donald F. 1936- *AfrAmBi, WhoAm 92*
McHenry, Doug *MiSFD 9*
McHenry, Eileen *BioIn 17*
McHenry, Gordon A., Jr. *Law&B 92*
McHenry, Henry Malcolm 1944- *WhoAm 92*
McHenry, Keith Welles, Jr. 1928- *WhoAm 92*
Mc Henry, Powell 1926- *WhoAm 92*
McHenry, Richard Lewis 1955- *WhoEmL 93*
McHenry, Robert Dale 1945- *WhoAm 92*
McHenry, Robert William 1953- *WhoEmL 93*
McHone, Elizabeth Anne 1964- *WhoSSW 93*
McHose, Allen Irvine 1902-1986 *Baker 92*
McHose, James Hayden 1937- *WhoAm 92*
McHugh, Brian Joseph 1959- *WhoE 93*
McHugh, Bryan 1930- *WhoScE 91-4*
McHugh, Charles T. *Law&B 92*
McHugh, Doreen Collins 1966- *WhoE 93*
McHugh, Earl Edward 1961- *WhoEmL 93*
McHugh, Edward Francis, Jr. 1932- *WhoAm 92*
McHugh, Edward Patrick 1936- *St&PR 93*
McHugh, Erin 1952- *WhoAmW 93*
McHugh, H. Bart, III 1933- *St&PR 93*
Mc Hugh, Heather 1948- *WhoWrEP 92*
McHugh, James B. *Law&B 92*
McHugh, James C. 1940- *St&PR 93*
McHugh, James Francis *Law&B 92*
McHugh, James J. 1929- *St&PR 93*
McHugh, James Joseph 1930- *WhoAm 92*
McHugh, James Lenahan, Jr. 1937- *WhoAm 92, WhoE 93*
McHugh, James T. *WhoAm 92*
McHugh, James T. 1932- *WhoE 93*
McHugh, Janet Ellen *Law&B 92*
Mchugh, Jeannette 1934- *WhoAsAP 91*
McHugh, Jimmy 1894-1969 *Baker 92*
McHugh, John James 1931- *St&PR 93, WhoAm 92*
Mc Hugh, John Laurence 1911- *WhoAm 92*
McHugh, John Michael 1948- *WhoE 93*
McHugh, Joseph W., Jr. 1955- *St&PR 93*
McHugh, Joseph William *St&PR 93*
McHugh, Josephine Flaherty 1947- *WhoEmL 93*
McHugh, June M. Hamvas 1958- *St&PR 93*
McHugh, Kevin James 1940- *St&PR 93*
McHugh, Kevin Joseph *Law&B 92*
McHugh, Larry F. 1949- *St&PR 93*
McHugh, Lyn Michelle *Law&B 92*
McHugh, Margaret Rose 1953- *WhoAmW 93*
McHugh, Matthew F. 1938- *CngDr 91, WhoAm 92, WhoE 93*
McHugh, Maureen F. *ConAu 139*
McHugh, Michael Joseph 1937- *St&PR 93*
Mchugh, Michael P. 1939- *St&PR 93*
Mc Hugh, Paul R. 1931- *WhoAm 92*
McHugh, Peter J. *Law&B 92*

Mc Hugh, Richard B. 1923- *WhoAm 92*
McHugh, Robert C. 1928- *St&PR 93*
Mc Hugh, Robert Clayton 1928- *WhoAm 92*
McHugh, Robert E. 1941- *St&PR 93*
McHugh, Robert Ernest 1946- *WhoE 93*
McHugh, Simon Francis, Jr. 1938- *WhoAm 92*
McHugh, Stuart Lawrence 1949- *WhoEmL 93*
McHugh, Thomas Edward 1936- *WhoAm 92, WhoSSW 93*
McHugh, Thomas J. 1931- *St&PR 93*
McHugh, Vincent 1904-1983 *ScF&FL 92*
McHugh, William Dennis 1929- *WhoAm 92*
McHugh-Turner, Karen Lynne 1960- *WhoAmW 93*
Mcilhaney, Sam Carl 1939- *WhoWrEP 92*
McIlhnenny, Edmund 1945- *St&PR 93*
McIlhone, John Thomas 1911- *WhoE 93*
McIlraith, Kathleen Ann 1948- *WhoSSW 93*
McIlraith, Mary Ann F. 1957- *WhoE 93*
McIlrath, Donald Christner 1929- *WhoAm 92*
McIlrath, Thomas James 1938- *WhoE 93*
Mcilreath, Fred J. 1929- *St&PR 93*
McIlroy, Gary T. 1940- *St&PR 93*
McIlroy, Harry Alexander 1940- *WhoWor 93*
McIlroy, James R. 1912- *St&PR 93*
McIlroy, William Dawson 1947- *St&PR 93*
McIlvain, Gordon *St&PR 93*
McIlvain, Helen Eugene 1942- *WhoAmW 93*
McIlvain, Jess Hall 1933- *WhoWor 93*
McIlvain, John Gibson, III 1948- *St&PR 93*
McIlvaine, Alice Nicolson 1924- *WhoE 93*
McIlvaine, Charles Pettit 1799-1873 *BioIn 17*
McIlvaine, Jane 1919-1990 *BioIn 17*
McIlvaine, John Harmon, Jr. 1936- *St&PR 93*
McIlvaine, Joseph Peter 1948- *WhoAm 92*
McIlveen, Edward E. 1911- *WhoAm 92*
Mc Ilveen, Walter 1927- *WhoE 93*
McIlvoy, Doug Graham 1939- *St&PR 93*
McIlwain, Carl Edwin 1931- *WhoAm 92*
McIlwain, Clara Evans 1919- *WhoAmW 93*
McIlwain, David *ScF&FL 92*
Mcilwain, Don Curtis 1938- *St&PR 93*
Mc Ilwain, John Frederick 1938- *WhoAm 92*
McIlwain, John Knox 1943- *WhoE 93, WhoWor 93*
McIlwain, Merrell S., II 1950- *St&PR 93*
McIlwain, Russell L. *Law&B 92*
McIlwain, Thomas David 1940- *WhoAm 92, WhoSSW 93*
McIlwain, William C., Jr. 1926- *St&PR 93*
McIlwain, William Clarence, Jr. 1926- *WhoIns 93*
Mc Ilwain, William Franklin 1925- *WhoAm 92, WhoWrEP 92*
McIlwan, Don Curtis 1938- *St&PR 93*
McIlwraith, Cyril Wayne 1947- *WhoAm 92, WhoWor 93*
McIlwraith, Jean Newton 1859-1938 *BioIn 17*
McIlwraith, Maureen *ScF&FL 92*
McIlwraith, Maureen Mollie Hunter *MajAI*
McIlwraith, T.F. 1899-1964 *IntDcAn*
McIndoe, Darrell Bruce, Sr. 1957- *WhoE 93*
Mc Indoe, Darrell Winfred 1930- *WhoAm 92*
McIndoe, George 1949- *MiSFD 9*
McInenly, Peter T. *Law&B 92*
McInerney, Barbara *Law&B 92*
McInerney, Christopher M. 1957- *St&PR 93*
McInerney, J. Barrett 1925- *St&PR 93*
McInerney, James 1942- *St&PR 93*
McInerney, James Eugene, Jr. 1930- *WhoAm 92*
McInerney, Jay 1955- *WhoAm 92*
McInerney, John *Law&B 92*
McInerney, Joseph Aloysius 1939- *WhoAm 92*
McInerney, Joseph John 1932- *WhoAm 92*
McInerney, Judith Whitelock 1945- *ScF&FL 92*
McInerney, Michael Joseph, III 1941- *St&PR 93*
McInerney, Michael Patrick 1941- *St&PR 93*
McInerney, P.T. *WhoScE 91-1*
McInerney, Robert J. 1945- *St&PR 93*
McInerney, Russell Arthur 1943- *WhoSSW 93*
McInerney, Thomas F. *Law&B 92*
McInerny, Ralph Matthew 1929- *WhoAm 92*
McInerny, Ray *BioIn 17*
Mc Ingvale, James Wesley 1954- *WhoWrEP 92*
Mc Ininch, Ralph Aubrey 1912- *WhoAm 92*
McInnes, David L. 1928- *St&PR 93*
McInnes, Edward 1935- *WhoWor 93*
McInnes, Graham 1912-1970 *ScF&FL 92*
McInnes, Harold A. 1927- *St&PR 93, WhoAm 92, WhoE 93*
McInnes, Robert Malcolm 1930- *St&PR 93, WhoAm 92*
Mc Innes, William Charles 1923- *WhoAm 92*
McInnes, William Wright 1948- *WhoAm 92*
McInnis, Donald J. 1946- *St&PR 93*
McInnis, Helen Louise *WhoAmW 93*
McInnis, James Milton 1934- *WhoAm 92, WhoE 93*
McInnis, Judy Bredeson 1943- *WhoAmW 93, WhoE 93*
McInnis, Lou Anne Dechen *Law&B 92*
McInnis, Susan Muse 1955- *WhoWor 93*
McInnis, Thomas Johnson 1945- *WhoAm 92*
McInnis, Thomas Michael 1937- *St&PR 93*
McInroe, Harold Alvis 1930- *St&PR 93*
McInroy, James William 1936- *St&PR 93*
McIntcer, Jack Scott 1947- *WhoEmL 93*
McIntire, Carl 1906- *BioIn 17*
McIntire, Dennis K(eith) 1944- *Baker 92*
McIntire, Fairy D. d1992 *NewYTBS 92*
McIntire, Jerald Gene 1938- *WhoAm 92, WhoWor 93*
McIntire, Jim 1846-c. 1910 *BioIn 17*
McIntire, John 1907-1991 *BioIn 17*
McIntire, Jon Williams 1944- *WhoSSW 93*
McIntire, Kenneth M. 1937- *St&PR 93*
McIntire, Larry Vern 1943- *WhoAm 92*
McIntire, Leanne 1957- *WhoEmL 93*
McIntire, Mary Beth 1943- *WhoSSW 93*
Mc Intire, Richard Lee 1934- *WhoAm 92*
McIntire, Samuel 1757-1811 *BioIn 17*
McIntire, Thomas J. 1943- *St&PR 93*
McIntosh, Alexander Ian 1941- *WhoWor 93*
McIntosh, Alice Marilyn 1950- *WhoSSW 93*
McIntosh, Daniel W. 1940- *St&PR 93*
McIntosh, David Angus 1944- *WhoWor 93*
McIntosh, David Kloss 1954- *WhoEmL 93*
McIntosh, David Martin 1958- *NewYTBS 92 [port]*
McIntosh, Donald Harry 1919- *WhoAm 92*
McIntosh, Edith Marie 1938- *WhoAmW 93*
McIntosh, Elaine Virginia 1924- *WhoAmW 93*
McIntosh, Gail H. *Law&B 92*
McIntosh, Graheme John 1956- *WhoWor 93*
McIntosh, Henry Deane 1921- *WhoSSW 93*
McIntosh, J.T. 1925- *ScF&FL 92*
McIntosh, James Boyd, Jr. 1950- *WhoE 93*
Mc Intosh, James Eugene, Jr. 1938- *WhoAm 92*
McIntosh, James O. *Law&B 92*
McIntosh, Jenny Clare 1948- *WhoEmL 93, WhoSSW 93*
Mc Intosh, John Richard 1939- *WhoAm 92*
McIntosh, John W. 1947- *St&PR 93*
McIntosh, Lawrence White 1934- *St&PR 93, WhoAm 92*
McIntosh, Lorne William 1945- *WhoAm 92*
McIntosh, Mark F. *Law&B 92*
McIntosh, Mildred 1958- *WhoAmW 93*
McIntosh, Neil *WhoScE 91-1*
McIntosh, Phillip Lee 1954- *WhoEmL 93*
McIntosh, Rhodina Covington 1947- *WhoAm 92, WhoAmW 93*
McIntosh, Robbie
See Pretenders, The *ConMus 8*
McIntosh, Robert Edward, Jr. 1940- *WhoAm 92*
Mc Intosh, Susan Jane 1943- *WhoWrEP 92*
McIntosh, Terrie Tuckett *Law&B 92*
McIntosh, Waldo Emerson d1991 *BioIn 17*
McIntosh, William Robert 1949- *WhoSSW 93*
McInturff, Don A. 1939- *WhoIns 93*
McIntyre, Alasdair Duncan 1926- *WhoWor 93*
McIntyre, Alister 1931- *DcCPCAm*
McIntyre, Bruce Herbert 1930- *WhoAm 92*
McIntyre, Carl Henry, Jr. 1958- *WhoE 93, WhoEmL 93, WhoWor 93*
McIntyre, Carlene V. *Law&B 92*
McIntyre, Christine 1911-1984 *SweetSg C [port]*
McIntyre, Clara Frances *ScF&FL 92*
McIntyre, Colin 1944- *WhoAm 92*
McIntyre, Daniel 1952- *WhoEmL 93*
McIntyre, Darel Dee 1939- *St&PR 93*
McIntyre, Deborah 1955- *WhoSSW 93*
McIntyre, Dennis d1990 *BioIn 17*
McIntyre, Donald 1934- *IntDcOp, OxDcOp*
McIntyre, Donald (Conroy) 1934- *Baker 92, WhoAm 92*
McIntyre, Donald G. *Law&B 92, St&PR 93*
McIntyre, Douglas Alexander 1955- *St&PR 93, WhoAm 92*
McIntyre, Edward A. *Law&B 92*
McIntyre, Edwina 1942- *WhoAmW 93*
McIntyre, George William, III 1949- *WhoEmL 93*
McIntyre, Glenn A. *St&PR 93*
McIntyre, Gordon 1937- *WhoWor 93*
McIntyre, Helen *AmWomPl*
Mc Intyre, Henry Langenberg 1912- *WhoAm 92*
McIntyre, Howard Lynn 1949- *WhoSSW 93*
McIntyre, Iain Matthew 1956- *WhoWor 93*
McIntyre, James 1827-1906 *BioIn 17*
McIntyre, James Eric *WhoScE 91-1*
McIntyre, James Philip 1934- *WhoE 93*
McIntyre, James Russel, Jr. 1941- *WhoE 93*
Mc Intyre, Jane O'Neill Mahady 1922- *WhoAm 92*
McIntyre, Janice A. 1933- *WhoAmW 93*
McIntyre, Joe 1972- *BioIn 17*
McIntyre, John Armin 1920- *WhoAm 92, WhoSSW 93*
McIntyre, John Finlay *Law&B 92*
McIntyre, John Finlay 1939- *St&PR 93*
McIntyre, John George Wallace 1920- *WhoAm 92*
McIntyre, John L. 1947- *St&PR 93*
McIntyre, John W. 1925- *St&PR 93*
McIntyre, John William 1930- *WhoSSW 93*
McIntyre, Joseph Charles 1926- *WhoAm 92*
McIntyre, Judith Watland 1930- *WhoAmW 93*
Mcintyre, Kathleen A. 1952- *St&PR 93*
McIntyre, Kathryn Joan 1952- *WhoAm 92*
McIntyre, Kaye 1950- *WhoAmW 93, WhoE 93, WhoEmL 93*
McIntyre, Kenneth E. 1926- *St&PR 93*
McIntyre, Lamar Calvert 1938- *St&PR 93*
McIntyre, Lee E. 1906- *St&PR 93*
Mc Intyre, Lee Emerson 1906- *WhoAm 92*
McIntyre, Loretta Miller 1944- *WhoAmW 93*
McIntyre, Louise S. 1924- *WhoAmW 93*
McIntyre, Mac Hugh 1947- *WhoSSW 93*
Mc Intyre, Maureen Anne 1949- *WhoWrEP 92*
McIntyre, Michael John 1946- *St&PR 93*
McIntyre, Nancy Sue *WhoAmW 93*
McIntyre, Neil *WhoScE 91-1*
McIntyre, O. O. 1884-1938 *JrnUS*
McIntyre, Oswald Ross 1932- *WhoAm 92*
McIntyre, Peter Martin 1958- *WhoWor 93*
Mcintyre, Richard A. 1943- *St&PR 93*
Mc Intyre, Robert Allen, Jr. 1940- *WhoAm 92*
McIntyre, Robert Donald 1932- *WhoAm 92*
McIntyre, Robert L. *Law&B 92*
McIntyre, Robert Lee 1946- *WhoEmL 93*
McIntyre, Robert Malcolm 1923- *St&PR 93, WhoAm 92*
Mc Intyre, Robert Walter 1922- *WhoAm 92*
McIntyre, Ronald Llewellyn 1934- *WhoAm 92*
McIntyre, Susan *BioIn 17*
McIntyre, Teresa Oglesby *Law&B 92*
McIntyre, Thomas J. d1992 *NewYTBS 92 [port]*
McIntyre, Thomas J(ames) 1915-1992 *CurBio 92N*
McIntyre, Valene Smith 1926- *WhoAmW 93*
McIntyre, Vonda N. *BioIn 17*
McIntyre, Vonda N. 1948- *ScF&FL 92*
Mc Intyre, Vonda Neel 1948- *WhoAm 92, WhoWrEP 92*
Mcintyre, William H. 1945- *St&PR 93*
McIntyre, Wilson Louis, Jr. 1948- *WhoSSW 93*
McIntyre-Ivy, Joan Carol 1939- *WhoAmW 93*
McIntyre Martin, Sherri 1950- *WhoSSW 93*
Mc Isaac, George Scott 1930- *WhoAm 92*
McIsaac, Kenneth James 1940- *St&PR 93*
McIsaac, Paul Rowley 1926- *WhoAm 92*
McIver, Angela 1955- *WhoWor 93*
McIver, G.A. *ScF&FL 92*
McIver, Jes David 1929- *St&PR 93*
McIver, John F., Jr. 1947- *St&PR 93*
McIver, Norman T. 1935- *St&PR 93*
McIvor, Donald Kenneth 1928- *WhoAm 92*
McIvor, Timothy James 1949- *WhoEmL 93*
McJilton, Diantha *Law&B 92*
McJoyner, Ernest McClauley, Jr. 1930- *WhoSSW 93*
McKague, Lee 1936- *WhoSSW 93*
McKaig, Calvin Newton 1936- *WhoSSW 93*
McKaig, Robert Lee 1950- *WhoEmL 93, WhoSSW 93*
Mc Kain, David W. 1937- *WhoWrEP 92*
McKane, David Bennett 1945- *WhoAm 92*
McKane, Terry John 1941- *WhoAm 92*
McKann, Michael Raysor 1941- *WhoSSW 93*
McKarns, John Charles 1934- *St&PR 93*
McKavitt, Thomas Patrick 1935- *WhoSSW 93*
Mc Kay, Alexander Gordon 1924- *WhoAm 92*
McKay, Alice Vitalich 1947- *WhoAmW 93, WhoEmL 93*
McKay, Cameron McDonald 1949- *WhoWor 93*
McKay, Carol Ruth 1948- *WhoAm 92*
McKay, Charles W. *Law&B 92*
McKay, Claude *BioIn 17*
McKay, Claude 1889-1948 *DcLB 117 [port], EncAACR, WorLitC [port]*
McKay, Claudia *ScF&FL 92*
McKay, Constance Gadow 1928- *WhoAmW 93*
McKay, D. Brian 1945- *WhoAm 92*
McKay, Dean R. 1921- *St&PR 93*
Mc Kay, Dean Raymond 1921- *WhoAm 92*
McKay, Dianne Adele Mills 1947- *WhoAmW 93*
McKay, Donald 1810-1880 *BioIn 17*
McKay, Donald 1942- *WhoCanL 92*
McKay, Donald A. 1945- *WhoAm 92*
McKay, Donald Arthur 1931- *St&PR 93, WhoE 93, WhoWor 93*
McKay, Douglas James *Law&B 92*
McKay, E. Monique *Law&B 92*
Mc Kay, Emily Gantz 1945- *WhoAm 92, WhoWor 93*
McKay, Esther S. 1941- *St&PR 93*
McKay, Eugene 1941- *WhoSSW 93*
Mc Kay, Evelyn Mc Daniel 1924- *WhoWrEP 92*
McKay, Gene 1934- *St&PR 93*
McKay, George Frederick 1899-1970 *Baker 92*
McKay, George L. d1990 *BioIn 17*
McKay, Gordon Thomas 1931- *WhoAm 92*
McKay, H. George 1944- *St&PR 93*
McKay, Jack Alexander 1942- *WhoAm 92, WhoE 93*
Mckay, James D. 1924- *St&PR 93*
McKay, James Edgar 1939- *St&PR 93*
McKay, James Robert 1955- *WhoE 93*
McKay, Janet Holmgren 1948- *WhoAmW 93*
McKay, Jean J. *Law&B 92*
McKay, Jerry Bruce 1935- *WhoAm 92*
Mc Kay, Jim 1921- *WhoAm 92*
McKay, John *BioIn 17*
McKay, John A. 1933- *St&PR 93*
McKay, John Patrick 1931- *WhoAm 92*
McKay, Joseph Gardiner, Sr. 1932- *St&PR 93*
McKay, Kathleen Ann *WhoAmW 93*
McKay, Kathryn C. *AmWomPl*
McKay, Kenneth *ScF&FL 92*
McKay, Kenneth Gardiner 1917- *WhoAm 92*
McKay, Laura L. 1947- *WhoAmW 93*
McKay, Linda Clair 1963- *WhoAmW 93*
McKay, Mabel *BioIn 17*
McKay, Margaret M. *Law&B 92*
McKay, Mary Ellen 1938- *WhoAmW 93*
McKay, Michael Dennis 1951- *WhoAm 92, WhoEmL 93*
McKay, Milton E. *Law&B 92*
McKay, Monroe Gunn 1928- *WhoAm 92*
McKay, Neil 1917- *St&PR 93, WhoAm 92*
McKay, Paula F. *Law&B 92*
McKay, Renee *WhoAmW 93*
McKay, Robert B. 1919-1990 *BioIn 17*
McKay, Robert G. 1936- *St&PR 93*
Mc Kay, Robert James, Jr. 1917- *WhoAm 92*
Mc Kay, Samuel Leroy 1913- *WhoSSW 93, WhoWor 93*
McKay, Steven Frank 1950- *WhoE 93*

McKay, Susan Ann R. 1942- *WhoAmW 93*
Mc Kay, Thomas, Jr. 1920- *WhoAm 92*
McKay, Verne Gordon 1942- *St&PR 93*
McKay, Wanda 1923- *SweetSg C [port]*
McKayle, Donald 1930- *BioIn 17*
Mc Kayle, Donald Cohen 1930- *WhoAm 92*
McKay-Rosa, Nancy 1958- *WhoSSW 93*
McKay-Shokoor, Judith Ann 1954- *WhoAmW 93*
Mc Keachie, Wilbert James 1921- *WhoAm 92*
McKeag, Ernest L. 1896-1976 *ScF&FL 92*
McKeague, David William 1946- *WhoEmL 93*
McKeague, Gordon C. 1926- *St&PR 93*
McKeague, Nancy Palmer 1955- *WhoEmL 93*
McKean, Catherine A. *Law&B 92*
McKean, Charles (Alexander) 1946- *ConAu 137*
McKean, Frank Newton 1940- *St&PR 93*
McKean, George Albert 1936- *St&PR 93*
Mc Kean, Hugh Ferguson 1908- *WhoAm 92*
McKean, John R. 1930- *St&PR 93*
Mc Kean, John Rosseel Overton 1928- *WhoAm 92*
McKean, Julie Johnson 1961- *WhoSSW 93*
Mc Kean, Keith Ferguson 1915- *WhoAm 92*
Mc Kean, Michael *WhoAm 92*
McKean, Paul A. *Law&B 92*
McKean, Paul A. 1941- *St&PR 93*
McKean, Quincy A. Shaw, Jr. 1924- *St&PR 93*
McKean, Robert d1991 *BioIn 17*
McKean, Robert Jackson, Jr. 1925- *WhoAm 92*
McKean, Scott H. 1940- *St&PR 93*
McKean, Thomas *ScF&FL 92*
McKean, Thomas 1734-1817 *BioIn 17*
McKean, Thomas Wayne 1928- *WhoAm 92*
McKean, William V. 1820-1903 *JrnUS*
McKearn, Thomas Joseph 1948- *WhoAm 92*
McKechnie, Donna *BioIn 17*
McKechnie, Ian D.G. 1937- *St&PR 93*
McKechnie, Paul (Richard) 1957- *ConAu 137*
McKedy, Janie Lea 1942- *WhoAmW 93*
McKee, Adele Dieckmann 1928- *WhoSSW 93*
McKee, Alexander d1992 *NewYTBS 92*
McKee, Charles Brian 1959- *WhoEmL 93*
McKee, Christopher Fulton 1935- *WhoAm 92*
McKee, Christopher Fulton 1942- *WhoAm 92*
McKee, Clark Watson 1940- *St&PR 93*
McKee, Clyde David, Jr. 1929- *WhoE 93*
McKee, Craig Lloyd 1960- *WhoE 93, WhoEmL 93*
McKee, Daniel J. 1950- *WhoE 93*
McKee, David 1935- *SmATA 70*
McKee, David C. *Law&B 92*
McKee, David (John) 1935- *ConAu 137, MajAI*
McKee, David John 1947- *WhoSSW 93*
McKee, Diane Claudia Gotta 1955- *WhoAmW 93*
McKee, E. Bates d1990 *BioIn 17*
McKee, Ed F. 1930- *St&PR 93*
McKee, Edith Merritt 1918- *WhoAmW 93*
McKee, Ellsworth 1932- *St&PR 93*
McKee, Erin *ScF&FL 92*
Mc Kee, Fran 1926- *WhoAm 92*
McKee, Francis John 1943- *WhoE 93, WhoWor 93*
McKee, Frederick J. 1934- *St&PR 93*
Mc Kee, George Moffitt, Jr. 1924- *WhoWor 93*
McKee, Georgina M. 1962- *WhoScE 91-1*
Mc Kee, Gerald 1930- *WhoWrEP 92*
McKee, Gregg L. 1943- *St&PR 93*
McKee, James 1931- *St&PR 93*
Mc Kee, James, Jr. 1918- *WhoAm 92*
McKee, James Clark St. Clair Sean *WhoScE 91-1*
McKee, James Clark St. Clair Sean 1945- *WhoWor 93*
McKee, James R. 1940- *WhoUN 92*
McKee, James W., Jr. 1922- *St&PR 93*
McKee, John Carothers 1912- *WhoWor 93*
Mc Kee, John De Witt 1919- *WhoWrEP 92*
McKee, John Keown 1891-1977 *BioIn 17*
McKee, John L. 1917- *St&PR 93*
McKee, Joseph Fulton 1921- *WhoAm 92*
McKee, Karen Lynette 1956- *WhoAmW 93*
McKee, Kathryn Dian 1937- *St&PR 93*
McKee, Kathryn Dian Grant 1937- *WhoAm 92*
McKee, Keith Earl 1928- *WhoAm 92*
McKee, Kent A. 1960- *St&PR 93*
Mc Kee, Kinnaird Rowe 1929- *WhoAm 92*
McKee, Laurel J. *Law&B 92*
McKee, Lauris Annette 1931- *WhoE 93*
McKee, Lewis K. 1921- *WhoAm 92*
Mc Kee, Louis 1951- *WhoWrEP 92*
McKee, Lynn Armistead *ScF&FL 92*
McKee, Margaret Crile 1945- *WhoAmW 93*
McKee, Margaret Jean 1929- *WhoAm 92, WhoAmW 93, WhoE 93, WhoWor 93*
McKee, Mary Elizabeth 1949- *WhoAmW 93*
McKee, Mike B. 1942- *St&PR 93*
McKee, Mitchell Edwin *Law&B 92*
McKee, Oather Dorris 1905- *St&PR 93, WhoAm 92*
McKee, Patricia Lynn 1964- *WhoEmL 93*
McKee, Penelope Melna 1938- *WhoAmW 93*
McKee, Phyllis *BioIn 17*
McKee, Ralph O. 1926- *St&PR 93*
Mc Kee, Raymond Walter 1899- *WhoWor 93*
McKee, Rhonda Denise 1960- *WhoAmW 93*
McKee, Robert J., Jr. *Law&B 92*
McKee, Ruth Louise 1946- *WhoAmW 93*
McKee, Susan Alice 1960- *WhoAmW 93*
McKee, Thomas Frederick 1948- *WhoEmL 93*
McKee, Thomas J. *Law&B 92*
McKee, Thomas J. 1930- *WhoAm 92*
McKee, Timothy Carlton 1944- *WhoSSW 93, WhoWor 93*
McKee, William Finley 1929- *WhoSSW 93*
McKee, William Paul 1946- *St&PR 93*
McKee-Hammad, Mary Ellen 1950- *WhoAmW 93*
McKeehen, Monte C. *Law&B 92*
Mc Keel, Sam Stewart 1926- *WhoAm 92*
Mc Keen, Chester M., Jr. 1923- *WhoAm 92*
McKeen, George B. 1924- *St&PR 93*
McKeen, P. Douglas *Law&B 92*
McKeever, Brian Evans 1949- *WhoAm 92, WhoE 93, WhoEmL 93*
McKeever, Edward D. *Law&B 92*
McKeever, Jeffrey D. 1942- *St&PR 93*
McKeever, John Eugene 1947- *WhoEmL 93*
McKeever, Porter *BioIn 17*
McKeever, Porter d1992 *NewYTBS 92 [port]*
McKeever, Thomas P. 1948- *St&PR 93*
McKegney, Tony 1958- *ConBlB 3 [port]*
McKeirnan, Agnes Cletus 1910- *WhoWor 93*
McKeithen, R.L. Smith *Law&B 92*
McKeithen, Walter Fox 1946- *WhoAm 92, WhoSSW 93*
McKeldin, William Evans 1927- *WhoE 93*
McKell, Cyrus M. 1926- *WhoAm 92*
McKell, Robert 1923- *St&PR 93*
McKell, Thomas 1935- *St&PR 93*
McKellar, Andrew Robert 1945- *WhoAm 92*
McKellar, Bruce Harold John *WhoWor 93*
McKellar, Kenneth 1927- *Baker 92*
McKellar, Kenneth D. 1869-1957 *PolPar*
McKellar, Neil Black 1942- *WhoScE 91-1*
McKellar, Robert Lewis *Law&B 92*
McKellar, Wayne Phelps 1934- *St&PR 93*
McKellen, Ian *BioIn 17, NewYTBS 92 [port]*
McKellen, Ian Murray 1939- *WhoWor 93*
McKellips, David Allan 1943- *WhoE 93*
McKelvey, Daniel Wayne *Law&B 92*
McKelvey, James Morgan 1925- *WhoAm 92*
Mc Kelvey, Jean Trepp 1908- *WhoAm 92*
McKelvey, Jeanne Wolford 1947- *WhoEmL 93*
McKelvey, John A. 1951- *St&PR 93*
McKelvey, John Clifford 1934- *St&PR 93, WhoAm 92*
Mc Kelvey, John Jay, Jr. 1917- *WhoAm 92*
McKelvey, John Philip 1926- *WhoE 93*
McKelvey, Judith Grant 1935- *WhoAm 92*
McKelvey, Randolph T. d1991 *BioIn 17*
McKelvey, Robert Kenneth 1922- *WhoWor 93*
McKelvey, Walter T. *St&PR 93*
McKelvie, James *WhoScE 91-1*
McKelvy, Charles Lockhart 1930- *St&PR 93*
McKelvy, Natalie 1950- *ConAu 138*
McKelvy, Natalie Ann 1950- *WhoAmW 93*
McKemie, George Ray 1954- *WhoSSW 93*
McKemy, Harold D. 1929- *St&PR 93*
Mc Kendrick, Joseph Edward, Jr. 1956- *WhoWrEP 92*
McKendrick, Melveena (Christine) 1941- *ConAu 37NR*
McKendry, Donald J. 1927- *St&PR 93*
McKendry, Erwin W. 1929- *St&PR 93*
McKendry, Francis James 1957- *St&PR 93*
McKenery, Deborah Lee 1952- *WhoEmL 93*
McKenna, Albert Bernard d1991 *BioIn 17*
Mc Kenna, Alex George 1914- *WhoAm 92*
McKenna, Andrew James 1929- *St&PR 93, WhoAm 92*
McKenna, Barbara Louise 1928- *WhoE 93*
McKenna, Brian 1950- *WhoWor 93*
McKenna, Bruce Alan 1943- *St&PR 93*
McKenna, David *Law&B 92*
Mc Kenna, David Loren 1929- *WhoAm 92, WhoSSW 93*
McKenna, Fay Ann 1944- *WhoAmW 93, WhoE 93*
McKenna, Francis Eugene 1921-1978 *BioIn 17*
McKenna, Frank *BioIn 17*
McKenna, Frank Joseph 1948- *WhoAm 92, WhoE 93*
McKenna, Frederick Gregory 1952- *WhoEmL 93*
McKenna, George LaVerne 1924- *WhoAm 92*
McKenna, Gerald Ward 1947- *WhoAm 92*
McKenna, Hugh Francis 1921- *WhoIns 93*
Mc Kenna, James A., III 1945- *WhoWrEP 92*
Mc Kenna, James Aloysius 1918- *WhoAm 92*
McKenna, James Michael 1945- *St&PR 93*
McKenna, John Dennis 1940- *WhoSSW 93*
McKenna, John Joseph 1940- *WhoE 93*
McKenna, John Thomas 1927- *St&PR 93*
McKenna, Joseph 1843-1926 *OxCSupC [port]*
McKenna, Mairead Maria *Law&B 92*
Mc Kenna, Malcolm Carnegie 1930- *WhoAm 92*
McKenna, Margaret Anne 1945- *WhoAm 92, WhoAmW 93*
Mc Kenna, Marian Cecilia 1926- *WhoAm 92, WhoWrEP 92*
McKenna, Mary Lucille 1950- *WhoSSW 93*
McKenna, Mary Patricia *WhoAmW 93*
McKenna, Maureen E. *Law&B 92*
McKenna, Michael J. 1935- *St&PR 93*
McKenna, Patrick James 1951- *WhoEmL 93*
McKenna, Quentin Carnegie 1926- *St&PR 93, WhoAm 92, WhoE 93*
McKenna, Richard *ScF&FL 92*
McKenna, Richard John *Law&B 92*
McKenna, Richard Milton 1913-1964 *ScF&FL 92*
McKenna, Robert *Law&B 92*
McKenna, Robert Patrick 1928- *St&PR 93*
McKenna, Rosalie Thorne *BioIn 17*
Mc Kenna, Sidney F. 1922- *WhoAm 92*
McKenna, Sidney Francis 1922- *St&PR 93*
McKenna, Stephen J. *Law&B 92*
McKenna, Stephen James 1940- *WhoAm 92*
McKenna, Terence Patrick 1928- *WhoAm 92*
Mc Kenna, Thomas Joseph 1929- *WhoAm 92*
McKenna, Thomas Morrison, Jr. 1937- *WhoAm 92*
Mc Kenna, William A., Jr. *WhoAm 92*
McKenna, William A., Jr. 1936- *St&PR 93*
McKenna, William E. 1919- *St&PR 93*
Mc Kenna, William Edward 1919- *WhoAm 92*
McKenna, William J. 1926- *St&PR 93*
McKenna, William John 1926- *WhoAm 92*
McKenney, Kenneth 1929- *ScF&FL 92*
McKenney, Michael Allen 1954- *WhoE 93*
McKenney, Samuel S., III *Law&B 92*
McKenney, Scott Alan 1955- *WhoEmL 93*
Mc Kenney, Walter Gibbs, Jr. 1913- *WhoAm 92, WhoWor 93*
McKennitt, H.L. *Law&B 92*
McKennon, Keith Robert 1933- *St&PR 93, WhoAm 92*
McKenny, Collin Grad 1944- *WhoAmW 93*
McKenny, Jere W. 1929- *St&PR 93*
McKenny, Jere Wesley 1929- *WhoAm 92, WhoSSW 93*
McKenny, John F. 1950- *St&PR 93*
McKenny, William D. 1940- *WhoIns 93*
McKenzie, Alexander P. 1850-1922 *PolPar*
McKenzie, Andre 1955- *WhoE 93*
Mckenzie, Charles Hayden 1953- *St&PR 93*
McKenzie, Claude *BioIn 17*
McKenzie, Clyde Ellis 1947- *St&PR 93*
McKenzie, Dan Peter *WhoScE 91-1*
McKenzie, Diana J.P. *Law&B 92*
McKenzie, Diana Jean Poznanski 1959- *WhoSSW 93*
Mckenzie, Donald J. 1938- *St&PR 93*
McKenzie, Donald Olafur 1948- *WhoScE 91-1*
McKenzie, Donald W. *Law&B 92*
McKenzie, Ellen Kindt *ScF&FL 92*
McKenzie, Fay 1920- *SweetSg C [port]*
McKenzie, Frank G. *Law&B 92*
McKenzie, Franklin Cooper, Jr. 1946- *WhoEmL 93*
McKenzie, Frederick Francis 1900-1986 *BioIn 17*
McKenzie, Gary Clifford 1939- *St&PR 93*
McKenzie, George Francis 1955- *WhoE 93*
McKenzie, Gwendolyn Veron *WhoE 93*
Mc Kenzie, Harold Cantrell, Jr. 1931- *WhoAm 92*
Mc Kenzie, Harold Jackson 1904- *WhoAm 92*
McKenzie, Herbert A. 1934- *St&PR 93*
McKenzie, Herbert Alonza 1934- *WhoAm 92*
McKenzie, Jack Harris 1930- *WhoAm 92*
McKenzie, James D. 1944- *St&PR 93*
McKenzie, James D., III *Law&B 92*
McKenzie, James Steven 1956- *WhoSSW 93*
McKenzie, Janet Stephens 1939- *WhoAmW 93*
Mc Kenzie, Jeremy Alec 1941- *WhoAm 92*
McKenzie, John L. 1910-1991 *BioIn 17*
Mc Kenzie, John Maxwell 1927- *WhoAm 92*
McKenzie, John Robertson 1936- *St&PR 93*
McKenzie, John Stuart 1922- *St&PR 93*
McKenzie, Kevin *BioIn 17, NewYTBS 92 [port]*
McKenzie, Kevin Patrick 1954- *WhoAm 92*
Mc Kenzie, Lionel Wilfred 1919- *WhoAm 92*
Mc Kenzie, Malroy Bernard 1951- *WhoWrEP 92*
McKenzie, Marcia *Law&B 92*
McKenzie, Melinda *ScF&FL 92*
McKenzie, Meredith Christine *WhoEmL 93*
McKenzie, Michael K. 1943- *St&PR 93*
McKenzie, Paula Tucker 1952- *WhoAmW 93*
Mc Kenzie, Ray 1927- *WhoAm 92*
McKenzie, Rita Lynn 1952- *WhoAmW 93*
McKenzie, Robert E. 1947- *WhoEmL 93*
McKenzie, Ruth Bates Harris *WhoAm 92*
McKenzie, Sandra K. 1952- *WhoAmW 93*
McKenzie, Sarah *Law&B 92*
McKenzie, Susan Beth *Law&B 92*
McKenzie, Susan Helen 1964- *WhoAmW 93, WhoEmL 93*
McKenzie, Vashti *BioIn 17*
McKenzie, Veanka Shelane *Law&B 92*
Mckeon, Barry J. 1954- *St&PR 93*
McKeon, David J. 1945- *St&PR 93*
McKeon, David Morey 1936- *WhoSSW 93*
McKeon, Edward T. 1947- *St&PR 93*
Mckeon, Elizabeth F. 1931- *St&PR 93*
McKeon, George A. *Law&B 92*
McKeon, George A. 1937- *St&PR 93, WhoAm 92, WhoIns 93*
McKeon, John Francis 1925- *St&PR 93*
McKeon, Kathleen Ann *Law&B 92*
McKeon, Maria F. *Law&B 92*
McKeon, Marie *St&PR 93*
McKeon, Michael Kearney 1955- *WhoE 93*
McKeon, Newton Felch 1904-1990 *BioIn 17*
McKeon, Robert B. 1954- *WhoAm 92*
McKeon, Warren Howard 1922- *WhoE 93*
McKeone, Lee *ScF&FL 92*
McKeough, Thomas R. *Law&B 92*
McKeough, William Darcy 1933- *WhoAm 92*
McKeown, Charles *ScF&FL 92*
McKeown, Craig W. *Law&B 92*
McKeown, Edmond F., Jr. *Law&B 92*
McKeown, Glenn Eliot *Law&B 92*
McKeown, James Charles 1945- *WhoAm 92*
McKeown, M. Margaret 1951- *St&PR 93*
McKeown, Martin 1943- *WhoE 93*
McKeown, Mary Elizabeth *WhoAmW 93*
McKeown, Mary Margaret 1951- *WhoAmW 93, WhoEmL 93*
McKeown, Mona Gail 1956- *WhoAmW 93*
McKeown, P.A. *WhoScE 91-1*
McKeown, Ronald Paul, Jr. 1951- *WhoE 93*
McKeown, Thomas W. *WhoAm 92*
McKeown, Thomas W. 1929- *St&PR 93*
Mc Keown, Tom 1937- *WhoWrEP 92*
Mc Keown, William Taylor 1921- *WhoAm 92, WhoWrEP 92*

McKernan, John Joseph 1942- *WhoSSW 93, WhoWrEP 92*
McKernan, John Rettie, Jr. 1948- *WhoAm 92, WhoE 93, WhoWor 93*
McKernan, Leo Joseph 1938- *St&PR 93, WhoAm 92*
Mc Kernan, Llewellyn Teresa 1941- *WhoWrEP 92*
McKernan, Regina Margaret *WhoAmW 93*
McKerns, Charles Joseph 1935- *WhoAm 92*
McKerrow, Amanda *WhoAm 92*
Mc Ketta, John J., Jr. 1915- *WhoAm 92*
McKetta, John J., III 1948- *WhoEmL 93*
McKew, Brigid Anne 1965- *WhoAmW 93*
McKey, N. Keith 1951- *St&PR 93*
McKhann, Emily Priest 1961- *WhoAmW 93*
McKhann, Guy Mead 1932- *WhoAm 92*
McKibben, Bernice Colleen 1926- *WhoAm 92*
McKibben, Gordon Charles 1930- *WhoAm 92*
McKibben, Howard D. 1940- *WhoAm 92*
McKibben, James Denis 1951- *WhoEmL 93*
McKibben, Ryan Timothy 1958- *WhoAm 92*
McKibbon-Turner, Bambi 1947- *WhoE 93*
McKie, David K. 1920- *St&PR 93*
Mc Kie, Todd Stoddard 1944- *WhoAm 92*
McKie, W. Gilmore 1927- *WhoE 93*
McKie, William C., Jr. 1949- *St&PR 93*
McKiernan, Dennis L. 1932- *ScF&FL 92*
McKiernan, James Philip 1944- *WhoAsAP 91*
McKiernan, John Francis 1933- *St&PR 93*
McKiernan, John William 1923- *WhoAm 92*
McKiernan, Michael J. *Law&B 92*
McKiernan, Thomas Joseph 1938- *St&PR 93*
McKiever, Kevin *BioIn 17*
McKillip, Donna LuAnn Gage 1953- *WhoAmW 93*
McKillip, Mable Elaine 1952- *WhoSSW 93*
McKillip, Patricia A. 1948- *BioIn 17, ScF&FL 92*
McKillip, Patricia Claire *WhoAmW 93, WhoE 93, WhoWor 93*
McKillip, T.F.W. *WhoScE 91-1*
McKillop, Alexander *WhoScE 91-1*
McKillop, Alexander Joseph *Law&B 92*
McKillop, James Hugh *WhoScE 91-1*
McKillop, M. Lucille 1924- *WhoAmW 93*
McKim, Audrey 1909- *WhoCanL 92*
McKim, Bradley S. *Law&B 92*
McKim, Paul Arthur 1923- *WhoAm 92*
McKim, Samuel John, III 1938- *WhoAm 92*
McKim, William J. *Law&B 92*
Mckimmey, James 1923- *WhoWrEP 92*
McKinlay, Donald Carl 1916- *WhoAm 92*
Mc Kinlay, Eleanor Grantham 1921- *WhoWrEP 92*
McKinlay, James Thomas, III *Law&B 92*
McKinlay, Scott D. *Law&B 92*
McKinless, Kathy Jean 1954- *WhoAm 92*
McKinley, Brunson 1943- *WhoAm 92*
McKinley, Carl 1895-1966 *Baker 92*
McKinley, Charles Hugh 1937- *WhoSSW 93*
McKinley, Charles Robert 1941-1986 *BiDAMSp 1989*
McKinley, Ellen Bacon 1929- *WhoAmW 93*
Mc Kinley, Gordon Wells 1915- *WhoAm 92*
McKinley, Ian G. 1954- *WhoScE 91-4*
McKinley, Ida Saxton 1847-1907 *BioIn 17*
McKinley, James Frank 1943- *St&PR 93*
McKinley, James T. 1947- *St&PR 93*
Mc Kinley, Jimmie Joe 1934- *WhoSSW 93, WhoWor 93*
McKinley, John 1780-1852 *OxCSupC [port]*
McKinley, John K. 1920- *St&PR 93*
Mc Kinley, John Key 1920- *WhoAm 92*
McKinley, Loren Dhue 1920- *WhoAm 92*
McKinley, Malcolm R. 1928- *St&PR 93*
McKinley, Martin John *Law&B 92*
McKinley, Marvin Dyal 1937- *WhoAm 92*
McKinley, Richard S. 1952- *St&PR 93*
McKinley, Robin 1952- *ScF&FL 92*
McKinley, (Jennifer Carolyn) Robin 1952- *DcAmChF 1960, DcAmChF 1985, MajAI [port]*
McKinley, Royce B. 1921- *St&PR 93*
McKinley, Terry L. *Law&B 92*
McKinley, William 1843-1901 *BioIn 17, GayN, PolPar*
McKinley, William A. 1917- *WhoAm 92*
McKinley, William Thomas 1938- *Baker 92, WhoAm 92*
McKinley-Haas, Mary *WhoE 93*
Mc Kinnell, Robert Gilmore 1926- *WhoAm 92*
McKinnell, Sue Ellen 1950- *St&PR 93*
Mc Kinney, Alexis 1907- *WhoAm 92*
McKinney, Baylus Benjamin 1886-1952 *Baker 92*
McKinney, Beverly S. *St&PR 93*
McKinney, Carol Ann 1950- *WhoE 93*
McKinney, Carolyn J. *Law&B 92*
McKinney, Carolyn Jean 1956- *WhoAmW 93*
McKinney, Charles Cecil 1931- *WhoAm 92*
McKinney, Chester Meek 1920- *WhoSSW 93*
McKinney, Cynthia Ann *WhoAmW 93*
McKinney, Cynthia Ward *WhoAmW 93*
McKinney, David Brooks 1952- *WhoE 93*
Mc Kinney, David Ewing 1934- *WhoAm 92*
McKinney, Dee Bruening *Law&B 92*
McKinney, Donald 1931- *WhoAm 92*
McKinney, Donald Eugene 1946- *St&PR 93*
McKinney, Donald Lee 1923- *WhoAm 92, WhoWrEP 92*
McKinney, E. Kirk, Jr. 1923- *St&PR 93, WhoAm 92*
McKinney, Frank E. 1904-1974 *PolPar*
McKinney, Frank E., Jr. d1992 *NewYTBS 92 [port]*
McKinney, Frank Edward 1904-1974 *BioIn 17*
McKinney, Frank Edward, Jr. 1938- *St&PR 93*
McKinney, Frank Kenneth 1943- *WhoSSW 93*
Mc Kinney, George Wesley, Jr. 1922- *WhoAm 92*
McKinney, Gerald Ray 1955- *WhoEmL 93*
McKinney, Harold Evans, Sr. 1929- *WhoSSW 93*
McKinney, Henry Daniel 1936- *WhoE 93*
McKinney, Hiram Yancey 1928- *St&PR 93*
McKinney, Ida Scott *AmWomPl*
Mc Kinney, Irene 1939- *WhoWrEP 92*
McKinney, Isabel *AmWomPl*
McKinney, Ivy Thomas *Law&B 92*
Mckinney, J. Bruce 1937- *St&PR 93*
McKinney, Jack *ScF&FL 92*
Mc Kinney, James Carroll 1921- *WhoAm 92*
McKinney, James Clayton 1940- *WhoAm 92*
McKinney, James D. 1947- *St&PR 93*
Mckinney, James I. 1933- *St&PR 93*
McKinney, Janet Kay 1959- *WhoAmW 93*
McKinney, Joe Clayton 1946- *St&PR 93*
McKinney, John Benjamin 1932- *WhoAm 92*
McKinney, John Edward 1925- *WhoE 93*
McKinney, Joseph E. 1945- *St&PR 93*
McKinney, Joseph F. 1931- *St&PR 93, WhoAm 92*
McKinney, Judson Thad 1941- *WhoAm 92*
McKinney, Julia C. *Law&B 92*
McKinney, Kathleen 1954- *ConAu 139*
McKinney, Larry J. 1944- *WhoAm 92*
McKinney, Leon Russell 1924-1990 *BioIn 17*
McKinney, Luther C. *Law&B 92*
McKinney, Luther C. 1931- *WhoAm 92*
McKinney, Margaret M. *Law&B 92*
McKinney, Margaret M. 1953- *St&PR 93*
McKinney, Martha Miller 1929- *WhoSSW 93*
McKinney, Meagan 1961- *ConAu 139*
Mc Kinney, Michael Whitney 1946- *WhoSSW 93*
Mc Kinney, Montgomery Nelson 1910- *WhoAm 92*
McKinney, Nina Mae 1913?-1967 *BioIn 17*
McKinney, Owen Dwight 1943- *St&PR 93*
McKinney, Pamela Anne 1947- *WhoAmW 93*
McKinney, Phyllis Louise Kellogg Henry 1932- *WhoAmW 93*
McKinney, Rebecca Meister 1954- *WhoSSW 93*
McKinney, Robert H. 1925- *St&PR 93*
Mc Kinney, Robert Moody 1910- *WhoAm 92*
McKinney, Robert Paterson *Law&B 92*
Mc Kinney, Ross Erwin 1926- *WhoAm 92*
McKinney, Rufus William 1930- *St&PR 93*
McKinney, Sally *St&PR 93*
McKinney, Sally Brown 1933- *WhoAmW 93*
McKinney, Sheila Jane *St&PR 93*
McKinney, Shirley Jean 1941- *WhoAmW 93*
McKinney, Stephanie Ann 1966- *WhoAmW 93*
McKinney, Stuart Bontecou 1919- *St&PR 93*
McKinney, Sue Ellen *Law&B 92*
McKinney, Susan Annette 1958- *WhoSSW 93*
McKinney, Thom *BioIn 17*
McKinney, Tip *BioIn 17*
McKinney, Venora Ware 1937- *WhoAm 92*
McKinney, William 1946- *WhoE 93*
McKinney, William Douthitt, Jr. 1955- *WhoEmL 93, WhoSSW 93, WhoWor 93*
McKinney, William J. 1932- *St&PR 93*
Mckinnies, Mark H. 1952- *St&PR 93*
McKinnis, Archie Price 1942- *St&PR 93*
McKinnis, Lee Vern 1948- *WhoEmL 93*
McKinnish, Richmond Dee 1949- *St&PR 93*
Mc Kinnon, Alan Leo 1928- *WhoAm 92*
Mckinnon, Alastair Thomson 1925- *WhoWrEP 92*
McKinnon, Alexander 1943- *St&PR 93*
McKinnon, Arnold Borden 1927- *St&PR 93, WhoAm 92, WhoSSW 93*
McKinnon, B.E. 1940- *St&PR 93*
McKinnon, Barry 1944- *WhoCanL 92*
McKinnon, Charles Walter 1960- *WhoEmL 93*
Mc Kinnon, Clinton D. 1906- *WhoAm 92*
Mc Kinnon, Clinton Dan 1934- *WhoAm 92*
McKinnon, Daniel Harold 1933- *St&PR 93*
McKinnon, Daniel Wayne, Jr. 1934- *WhoAm 92*
McKinnon, David C. 1916- *St&PR 93*
McKinnon, Donald Charles 1939- *WhoAsAP 91, WhoWor 93*
McKinnon, Floyd Wingfield 1942- *WhoAm 92, WhoE 93*
Mc Kinnon, Francis Arthur Richard 1933- *WhoAm 92*
McKinnon, James Buckner 1916- *WhoWor 93*
McKinnon, James Edwin *Law&B 92*
McKinnon, James William 1932- *WhoAm 92*
McKinnon, John Borden 1934- *St&PR 93*
McKinnon, John Q. 1944- *St&PR 93*
McKinnon, Linda Maney *Law&B 92*
McKinnon, Mary Ann *Law&B 92*
McKinnon, Roger Hugh 1950- *WhoE 93, WhoEmL 93*
McKinnon, Thomas E. 1944- *St&PR 93*
Mckinnon, Thomas K. 1945- *St&PR 93*
McKinsey, Brian Arthur *Law&B 92*
McKinsey, David Stephen 1955- *WhoEmL 93*
McKinsey, Elizabeth 1947- *ConAu 139, WhoAmW 93*
McKinstry, Arthur Raymond 1895-1991 *BioIn 17*
McKinstry, Elizabeth R. 1957- *WhoAmW 93*
McKinstry, Gregory John Duncan 1947- *WhoAm 92*
McKinstry, Lohr *ScF&FL 92*
McKinstry, Ronald Eugene 1926- *WhoAm 92*
McKinstry, William Earl *Law&B 92*
McKinzie, J. Mark *Law&B 92*
McKinzie, J. Mark 1953- *St&PR 93*
McKirahan, Richard Duncan, Jr. 1945- *WhoAm 92*
McKissack, Fredrick 1939- *BlkAuII 92*
McKissack, Fredrick L(emuel) 1939- *SmATA 73*
McKissack, Pat 1944- *BioIn 17*
McKissack, Patricia C. 1944- *BioIn 17, BlkAuII 92*
McKissack, Patricia (L'Ann) C(arwell) 1944- *ConAu 38NR, MajAI, SmATA 73 [port]*
McKissack, Perri *BioIn 17*
McKissick, A. Foster, III 1955- *St&PR 93*
McKissick, Floyd 1922-1991 *AnObit 1991*
McKissick, Floyd B. 1922-1991 *BioIn 17, ConBlB 3 [port], EncAACR [port]*
McKissick, Floyd Bixler, Sr. 1922-1991 *AfrAmBi*
McKissick, Michael Landon 1950- *WhoE 93*
Mckissick, Ronald L. 1948- *St&PR 93*
McKissock, Paul Kendrick 1925- *WhoAm 92*
Mckitrick, James T. 1945- *St&PR 93*
McKitrick, Ron Bruce 1932- *St&PR 93*
McKittrick, David Jay 1945- *St&PR 93*
McKittrick, Mary *AmWomPl*
McKittrick, Melanie *Law&B 92*
McKittrick, William Wood 1915- *WhoAm 92, WhoWor 93*
McKlveen, Joseph L. 1913- *St&PR 93*
McKlveen, Thomas Goodwin 1947- *St&PR 93*
McKneally, Martin B. d1992 *NewYTBS 92*
McKneally, Martin B(oswell) 1914-1992 *CurBio 92N*
McKnew, Thomas W. 1896-1990 *BioIn 17*
McKnight, Alan Samuel 1952- *WhoWor 93*
McKnight, Andrew Dennis 1936- *St&PR 93*
McKnight, Barbara Ann Ferrell 1938- *WhoAmW 93*
McKnight, Donald Emerson, Jr. 1961- *WhoEmL 93*
McKnight, Douglas G. *Law&B 92*
McKnight, Douglas Garth 1949- *St&PR 93*
McKnight, Edgar Vernon 1931- *WhoSSW 93*
McKnight, Elizabeth Conway 1945- *WhoAmW 93*
McKnight, Everett Astor, Jr. 1944- *WhoSSW 93*
McKnight, H. James *Law&B 92*
McKnight, Jeffery L. 1943- *St&PR 93*
McKnight, Joe Nip 1933- *WhoSSW 93*
McKnight, John James 1948- *WhoIns 93*
Mc Knight, John Lacy 1931- *WhoAm 92*
McKnight, Joseph Webb 1925- *WhoAm 92*
McKnight, Joyce Sheldon 1949- *WhoEmL 93*
McKnight, Karen Therese 1947- *WhoEmL 93*
McKnight, Kevin L. *Law&B 92*
McKnight, Lee Warren 1956- *WhoEmL 93*
McKnight, Louis Warren, Jr. 1947- *St&PR 93*
Mc Knight, Paul James, Jr. 1935- *WhoAm 92*
McKnight, Phillip Scott 1942- *WhoSSW 93*
McKnight, Reginald 1956- *BioIn 17*
McKnight, Robert A. 1937- *St&PR 93*
McKnight, Roy 1921- *St&PR 93*
McKnight, Ruth J. *Law&B 92*
McKnight, Steven Lanier 1949- *WhoAm 92*
McKnight, Susan Fleisher *Law&B 92*
McKnight, Thomas Felix *Law&B 92*
McKnight, William Baldwin 1923- *WhoAm 92*
McKnight, William Hunter 1940- *WhoAm 92, WhoWor 93*
McKnight, William J. 1939- *St&PR 93*
McKnight, William Lester 1887-1978 *BioIn 17*
Mc Knight, William Warren, Jr. 1913- *WhoAm 92*
McKone, Don T. 1921- *St&PR 93, WhoAm 92*
McKone, Francis L. 1934- *St&PR 93*
McKowen, Dorothy Keeton 1948- *WhoAmW 93, WhoEmL 93*
Mckowen, Gary R. 1945- *St&PR 93*
McKowen, Robert H. 1927- *St&PR 93*
McKown, Bobby Frank 1936- *WhoSSW 93*
McKown, Richard 1947- *St&PR 93*
McKown, Richard George 1947- *WhoE 93*
Mckown, Robin *DcAmChF 1960*
Mc Koy, Basil Vincent Charles 1938- *WhoAm 92*
Mc Kuen, Pamela Dittmer 1951- *WhoWrEP 92*
McKuen, Rod 1933- *ConAu 40NR, WhoAm 92, WhoWrEP 92*
McKuen, Rod (Marvin) 1933- *Baker 92*
McKune, Alison Jane *Law&B 92*
Mc Kusick, Victor Almon 1921- *WhoAm 92*
McKusick, Vincent Lee 1921- *WhoAm 92*
McLachlan, Alexander 1818-1896 *BioIn 17*
McLachlan, Amy N. *Law&B 92*
McLachlan, David J. *St&PR 93*
McLachlan, Iva Wolf 1956- *WhoEmL 93*
McLachlin, Beverley 1943- *WhoAm 92, WhoAmW 93*
McLafferty, Charles Lowry 1927- *WhoSSW 93*
McLafferty, Fred Warren 1923- *WhoAm 92*
McLaglen, Andrew V. 1920- *MiSFD 9*
McLaglen, Victor 1886-1959 *BioIn 17, IntDcF 2-3 [port]*
McLain, Christopher M. *Law&B 92*
McLain, Dennis Dale 1944- *BiDAMSp 1989*
McLain, Diane Louise 1946- *WhoAmW 93*
McLain, Douglas Walker 1962- *St&PR 93*
McLain, Eugene Milton 1931- *WhoSSW 93*
McLain, Gerald Grady 1953- *WhoEmL 93, WhoSSW 93*
McLain, H. Jack 1940- *St&PR 93*
McLain, Janice Darlene 1943- *WhoAmW 93*
McLain, Janice M. *Law&B 92*
McLain, Mason W. 1926- *St&PR 93*
McLain, Maurice Clayton 1929- *WhoAm 92*
McLain, Paul King 1960- *St&PR 93*

McLain, Paul King, III 1960- WhoEmL 93
McLain, Paul X. 1940- St&PR 93
McLain, Peter R. Law&B 92
McLain, Terri Lee 1953- WhoEmL 93
McLaine, Barbara Bishop 1954- WhoSSW 93
McLaine, James Murray 1938- St&PR 93
McLaine, Maureen Anne 1957- WhoAmW 93
McLaiw, Harvey Thomas Law&B 92
McLallen, John Addison 1905- St&PR 93
McLallen, Scott Jay 1948- St&PR 93
McLamb, F. Donald J. 1933- WhoSSW 93
Mclamb, Jerry S. St&PR 93
McLamb, Steven D. Law&B 92
McLanahan, Michael Ward 1938- St&PR 93
Mc Lanathan, Richard 1916- WhoAm 92, WhoWrEP 92
McLane, Bobbie Jones 1927- WhoAmW 93
McLane, Charles BioIn 17
McLane, Claudia Frances 1951- WhoAmW 93
McLane, David Glenn 1943- WhoAm 92
McLane, Donald Joseph 1943- St&PR 93
McLane, Fannie Moulton AmWomPl
McLane, Fanny B. AmWomPl
McLane, Henry Earl, Jr. 1932- WhoAm 92
McLane, James Woods 1939- WhoAm 92
Mc Lane, John Roy, Jr. 1916- WhoAm 92
McLane, Peter J. 1941- WhoAm 92
McLane, Robert Drayton, Jr. 1936- St&PR 93
McLane, Robert M. 1815-1898 PolPar
McLane, Robert Milligan 1815-1898 BioIn 17
Mclane, Stephen B. St&PR 93
McLane, Susan Neidlinger 1929- WhoAmW 93, WhoE 93
McLane, Thomas Lawrence 1932- WhoAm 92
McLane, Timothy E. 1955- St&PR 93
McLaren, Anne WhoScE 91-1
McLaren, Archie Campbell, Jr. 1942- WhoWor 93
McLaren, Charles Benjamin Bright 1850-1934 BioIn 17
McLaren, Colin 1940- ScF&FL 92
McLaren, Digby Johns 1919- WhoAm 92, WhoWor 93
McLaren, Donald Stewart WhoScE 91-1
McLaren, Felicia Iris Dible 1924- WhoE 93
McLaren, Jacques Law&B 92
McLaren, James Blackburn, Jr. 1955- WhoEmL 93
McLaren, James Clark 1925- WhoAm 92
McLaren, James Kevin 1960- WhoSSW 93
McLaren, Jane Minerva AmWomPl
Mc Laren, John Alexander 1919- WhoAm 92
McLaren, Karen Lynn 1955- WhoAmW 93, WhoEmL 93
McLaren, Laura Elizabeth 1855?-1933 BioIn 17
Mc Laren, Malcolm Grant, IV 1928- WhoAm 92
McLaren, Richard W., Jr. Law&B 92
McLaren, Roderic J. Law&B 92
McLaren, Ruth S. 1955- St&PR 93
McLaren, Thomas Myers 1931- WhoSSW 93
McLaren, Wayne d1992 NewYTBS 92
McLarey, Sandra Roberts 1940- WhoAmW 93
McLarnan, Donald Edward 1906- WhoAm 92
McLarnon, Gerard 1939- St&PR 93
McLarty, Thomas F., III NewYTBS 92 [port], St&PR 93
McLarty, Thomas F., III 1946- WhoSSW 93
McLary, Steve Michael Law&B 92
McLatchie, R.C.F. WhoScE 91-1
McLauchlin, D. L. WhoAm 92
McLauchlin, Robert Michael 1939- WhoSSW 93
McLaughin, John P. 1951- St&PR 93
McLaughlin, Albert Howard 1924- WhoE 93
McLaughlin, Alden McNee, Jr. 1961- WhoWor 93
McLaughlin, Alexander C. J. 1925- WhoSSW 93, WhoWor 93
McLaughlin, Ann 1941- WhoAm 92, WhoAmW 93
McLaughlin, Audrey BioIn 17
McLaughlin, Audrey 1936- WhoAm 92, WhoAmW 93
McLaughlin, Bette H. 1933- St&PR 93
McLaughlin, Brian D. 1942- St&PR 93
McLaughlin, Brian John 1946- WhoE 93
Mc Laughlin, Bruce 1921- WhoSSW 93
McLaughlin, Calvin Sturgis 1936- WhoAm 92
McLaughlin, Charles John 1950- WhoEmL 93
McLaughlin, Charles Michael 1938- St&PR 93
McLaughlin, Colette Beth 1960- WhoAmW 93
McLaughlin, David Jordan 1940- WhoAm 92
McLaughlin, David T. 1932- St&PR 93
Mc Laughlin, David Thomas 1932- WhoAm 92
McLaughlin, Dean 1931- ScF&FL 92
McLaughlin, Deborah Ann 1952- WhoAmW 93, WhoEmL 93
McLaughlin, Debra Lynn 1957- WhoAmW 93
McLaughlin, Denise K. 1947- St&PR 93
McLaughlin, Donald R. 1929- St&PR 93
McLaughlin, Edward 1928- WhoAm 92
McLaughlin, Edward David 1931- WhoWor 93
McLaughlin, Edward Manus 1934- WhoE 93
McLaughlin, Ellen Winnie 1937- WhoAmW 93
McLaughlin, Emily d1991 BioIn 17
McLaughlin, Emily 1928-1991 ConTFT 10
McLaughlin, Flora Shelia 1937- WhoAmW 93
McLaughlin, Frank 1934- SmATA 73
McLaughlin, Gayle A. 1949- St&PR 93
McLaughlin, George B. 1922- St&PR 93
McLaughlin, Glen 1934- WhoAm 92
Mc Laughlin, Harry Roll 1922- WhoAm 92
McLaughlin, Harry Y. 1934- St&PR 93
McLaughlin, Henry Elwood, Jr. 1946- WhoEmL 93, WhoSSW 93
McLaughlin, Ian M. Watson 1945- St&PR 93
Mc Laughlin, J. Richard 1939- WhoWrEP 92
McLaughlin, James Daniel Law&B 92
McLaughlin, James G. 1944- WhoScE 91-3
Mclaughlin, James Higgins 1946- St&PR 93, WhoAm 92
Mc Laughlin, Jerome Michael 1929- WhoAm 92
Mc Laughlin, Jerry Loren 1939- WhoAm 92
McLaughlin, John BioIn 17, WhoAm 92
McLaughlin, John 1942- Baker 92
McLaughlin, John A. Law&B 92
Mc Laughlin, John Francis 1927- WhoAm 92
McLaughlin, John Joseph 1927- WhoAm 92
McLaughlin, John Peter Law&B 92
McLaughlin, John Richardson 1929- St&PR 93
McLaughlin, John Sherman 1932- WhoAm 92
Mclaughlin, Jon A. 1955- St&PR 93
Mc Laughlin, Joseph Mailey 1928- WhoAm 92
McLaughlin, Joseph Michael 1933- WhoAm 92
McLaughlin, Joseph Michael 1943- WhoE 93
McLaughlin, Joseph W. 1940- St&PR 93
McLaughlin, Judith Block 1948- WhoE 93
Mc Laughlin, June WhoWrEP 92
McLaughlin, Kathleen 1898-1990 BioIn 17
McLaughlin, Larry W. 1950- WhoE 93
McLaughlin, Laura AmWomPl
Mc Laughlin, Leighton Bates, II 1930- WhoAm 92
McLaughlin, Lisa Dale 1956- WhoEmL 93
McLaughlin, Margaret Brown 1926- WhoAmW 93
McLaughlin, Marguerite P. WhoAmW 93
McLaughlin, Marie 1954- OxDcOp
McLaughlin, Marilyn BioIn 17
McLaughlin, Martin Michael 1918- WhoSSW 93
McLaughlin, Mary F. 1944- St&PR 93
McLaughlin, Mary Rittling WhoAm 92
McLaughlin, Matthew Aloysius 1936- St&PR 93
Mclaughlin, Michael A. 1946- St&PR 93
McLaughlin, Michael Angelo 1950- WhoEmL 93
McLaughlin, Michael John Law&B 92
McLaughlin, Michael John 1944- St&PR 93, WhoAm 92
McLaughlin, Michael John 1951- WhoAm 92
McLaughlin, Michael Joseph Law&B 92
McLaughlin, Michael Terry Law&B 92
McLaughlin, Michael Weston 1954- St&PR 93
McLaughlin, Miriam Westerman 1920- WhoAmW 93
McLaughlin, P. Michael WhoIns 93
McLaughlin, Patricia O'Leary Law&B 92
McLaughlin, Patrick Michael 1946- WhoAm 92
McLaughlin, Randolph William 1938- St&PR 93
McLaughlin, Renee L. 1963- WhoAmW 93
McLaughlin, Richard Warren 1930- WhoAm 92, WhoE 93
McLaughlin, Sean Patrick 1960- WhoWor 93
McLaughlin, Sharon Gail 1946- WhoAmW 93, WhoEmL 93
McLaughlin, Stephen P. Law&B 92
McLaughlin, Steve Dexter 1961- WhoEmL 93
McLaughlin, Steven J. Law&B 92
McLaughlin, Ted John 1921- WhoAm 92
McLaughlin, Thomas A., III 1941- St&PR 93
McLaughlin, Thomas Michael 1956- St&PR 93
McLaughlin, Thomas P. Law&B 92
McLaughlin, Walter Joseph 1931- WhoE 93
McLaughlin, Ward W. 1954- St&PR 93
McLaughlin, William Craig 1952- WhoEmL 93
Mc Laughlin, William De Witt 1918- WhoWrEP 92
McLaughlin, William Stephen 1937- WhoAm 92
McLaughlin, William Thomas, II 1937- St&PR 93
McLaughlin, Winston Alexander Law&B 92
McLaughlin-Smith, Nancy Esther 1947- WhoEmL 93
McLaughry, Richard G. Law&B 92
McLauglin, Richard D. Law&B 92
McLaurin, Eugene Bertram, II 1956- WhoSSW 93
McLaurin, Joyce Franklin 1944- WhoSSW 93
McLaurin, Kate L. 1885-1933 AmWomPl
McLaurin, Kathleen Ryan 1950- WhoEmL 93
McLaurin, Martha Regina 1948- WhoAmW 93
McLaurin, Monty Earl 1951- WhoEmL 93, WhoSSW 93
McLaurin, Robert Thornton 1930- St&PR 93
McLaurin, Ronald De 1944- WhoAm 92
McLaurin, William 1939- St&PR 93
McLaury, Frank 1851?-1881 BioIn 17
McLaury, Thomas 1852?-1881 BioIn 17
McLay, Kenneth Reid 1959- St&PR 93
McLean, A. Alexander, III St&PR 93
McLean, Andre E.M. WhoScE 91-1
McLean, Andrew Dewey 1963- WhoWor 93
McLean, Archie Henry 1955- WhoSSW 93
Mc Lean, Arthur Frederick 1929- WhoWor 93
McLean, Barton (Keith) 1938- Baker 92
McLean, Bonnie Shepherd 1945- WhoAmW 93
McLean, Bruce A.J. 1943- St&PR 93
McLean, Bruce C. Law&B 92
McLean, Christopher Anthony 1958- WhoEmL 93
McLean, Dan D. 1932- St&PR 93
McLean, David Colin 1940- WhoUN 92
McLean, David L. Law&B 92
McLean, Dennis Edgar 1954- WhoEmL 93
Mc Lean, Don 1945- WhoAm 92
McLean, Donald WhoScE 91-1
Mc Lean, Donald Millis 1926- WhoAm 92
McLean, Drake Allen Law&B 92
McLean, Edward Burns 1937- St&PR 93, WhoSSW 93
McLean, Edward Cochrane, Jr. 1935- WhoAm 92
McLean, Edward Peter 1941- WhoAm 92
McLean, Francis P. 1929- St&PR 93
McLean, George 1939- BioIn 17
Mc Lean, George Francis 1929- WhoAm 92
McLean, Helen Candis 1949- WhoAmW 93
McLean, Ian William 1943- WhoE 93
McLean, J.W. 1922- St&PR 93
McLean, Jackie BioIn 17
Mc Lean, Jackie 1932- WhoAm 92
McLean, James A. 1922- St&PR 93
McLean, James Edwin 1945- WhoSSW 93
McLean, James Frederick 1939- St&PR 93
McLean, James Ivan 1946- WhoEmL 93, WhoSSW 93
McLean, Janet Kathelaine 1953- WhoEmL 93
McLean, John 1785-1861 OxCSupC [port]
McLean, John R. 1849-1916 JrnUS
Mc Lean, John William 1922- WhoAm 92
McLean, Lauchlin Huiet 1921- St&PR 93
McLean, Lee, Jr. 1924- St&PR 93
Mclean, Leslie C. 1941- St&PR 93
Mc Lean, Malcolm 1927- WhoAm 92
McLean, Malcolm Dallas 1913- ConAu 39NR
McLean, Marci McCandless Law&B 92
McLean, Mark A. 1959- St&PR 93
McLean, Mary Ann Law&B 92
McLean, Max Edmund 1953- WhoEmL 93
McLean, Mendelssohn V. Law&B 92
McLean, Neil Bernard 1959- St&PR 93
McLean, Orvill Wade 1933- St&PR 93
McLean, Paul Alexander 1937- WhoAsAP 91
McLean, Philip R. 1957- St&PR 93
McLean, Porter 1946- St&PR 93
McLean, Priscilla 1942- Baker 92
McLean, Raymond A. 1923- St&PR 93
McLean, Richard 1953- St&PR 93
McLean, Robert Brennan 1935- WhoE 93
Mc Lean, Robert T. 1922- WhoAm 92
McLean, Robert William 1940- St&PR 93
McLean, Ronald C. Law&B 92
McLean, Ronald William 1927- WhoE 93
McLean, Sam Hays, Jr. 1951- WhoEmL 93
McLean, Sheila Ann Manson WhoScE 91-1
McLean, Sidney L., Jr. Law&B 92
McLean, Susan Amanda Law&B 92
McLean, T.P. WhoScE 91-1
Mc Lean, Thomas Edwin 1925- WhoAm 92
McLean, Thomas Irvin 1943- St&PR 93
McLean, Vincent Ronald 1931- St&PR 93, WhoAm 92
McLean, Walter Franklin 1936- WhoAm 92
McLean, Warner Hugh 1936- St&PR 93
McLean, William George 1910- WhoE 93
McLean, William L. 1852-1931 JrnUS
Mc Lean, William L., III 1927- WhoAm 92
McLean, William Ronald 1921- WhoE 93, WhoWor 93
McLean, William Youmans 1927- WhoSSW 93
McLean-Wainwright, Pamela Lynne 1948- WhoAmW 93
McLean Young, Victoria Ann 1951- WhoAmW 93
McLear, William Z. 1903- St&PR 93
McLearn, Michael B. Law&B 92
Mclearn, Michael B. 1936- St&PR 93
McLearn, Michael Baylis 1936- WhoAm 92
McLearn, R.M. Law&B 92
McLeavey, Dennis William 1946- WhoEmL 93
McLeay, Leo Boyce 1945- WhoAsAP 91
McLeer, Laureen Dorothy 1955- WhoAmW 93, WhoE 93, WhoEmL 93
McLees, Ainslie Armstrong 1947- WhoSSW 93
McLeish, David James Dow 1936- WhoAm 92
McLeish, Ernest D. 1939- St&PR 93
McLeland, Kim Allen 1949- WhoEmL 93, WhoSSW 93
McLellan, Connie Rae 1950- WhoEmL 93
McLellan, D. Daniel Law&B 92
McLellan, David Lindsay WhoScE 91-1
McLellan, Diana BioIn 17
McLellan, Harold Linden 1937- WhoAm 92
McLellan, Helen Christina 1947- WhoWor 93
McLellan, Joseph Duncan 1929- WhoAm 92
McLellan, Kenneth Hugh, Jr. 1931- St&PR 93
McLellan, Lawrence Phillip 1944- WhoE 93
McLellan, Richard Douglas 1942- WhoAm 92
McLellan, Robert 1933- WhoWor 93
McLellan, Scott W. Law&B 92
McLellan, Thomas Angus 1935- WhoAm 92
McLellan, William T. Law&B 92
McLelland, Douglas Charner 1946- St&PR 93
McLelland, Gwyneth Baach 1967- WhoAmW 93
McLelland, Joseph Cumming 1925- WhoAm 92
McLelland, Robert 1921- WhoSSW 93
McLelland, Stan L. Law&B 92
McLelland, Stan L. 1945- St&PR 93, WhoAm 92
McLemore, A. Keith St&PR 93
McLemore, Claiborne Kinnard, III 1955- WhoEmL 93
McLemore, Cleveland Leroy 1956- WhoSSW 93
Mc Lemore, Robert Henry 1910- WhoAm 92

McLenaghan, John Bernard 1935- *WhoUN 92*
McLendon, Christopher Martin 1961- *WhoEmL 93*
McLendon, Debra Lee 1957- *WhoAmW 93*
McLendon, George Leland 1952- *WhoAm 92*
McLendon, Gordon 1921-1986 *BioIn 17*
McLendon, Heath B. 1933- *St&PR 93*
Mc Lendon, Heath Brian 1933- *WhoAm 92*
McLendon, Jesse Lawrence 1950- *WhoEmL 93*
McLendon, Jesse Wilborn 1950- *WhoWor 93*
McLendon, Joan C. *Law&B 92*
McLendon, John B. *BioIn 17*
McLendon, Martin L. *Law&B 92*
McLendon, William 1951- *St&PR 93*
McLendon, William Woodard 1930- *WhoAm 92*
McLendon-McCullough, Beverly J. 1949- *WhoAmW 93*
McLenegan, Annie Susan *AmWomPl*
McLenithan, Gordon John 1940- *St&PR 93*
McLennan, Barbara Nancy 1940- *WhoAm 92*
McLennan, Bernice Claire 1936- *WhoE 93*
Mc Lennan, Bill 1944- *WhoWrEP 92*
McLennan, Don 1950- *MiSFD 9*
McLennan, John Ferguson 1827-1881 *IntDcAn*
Mc Lennan, Kenneth Alan 1936- *WhoAm 92*
Mclennan, Lawrence J. 1950- *St&PR 93*
McLennan, Rex J. 1952- *St&PR 93*
McLennan, Robert B. *Law&B 92*
McLennan, William 1856-1904 *BioIn 17*
McLennon, Daniel Frederick 1959- *WhoEmL 93*
McLeod, Alec J. *Law&B 92*
McLeod, Alexander Canaday 1935- *WhoSSW 93*
McLeod, Alexander Reeves 1941- *WhoSSW 93*
McLeod, Allan L., Jr. 1944- *St&PR 93*
McLeod, Angus M. 1910- *St&PR 93*
McLeod, Anthony John *WhoScE 91-1*
McLeod, Bruce 1941- *St&PR 93*
McLeod, Cameron William *WhoScE 91-1*
McLeod, Christopher Kevin 1955- *WhoAm 92*
McLeod, Christopher Neil *WhoScE 91-1*
McLeod, Daniel B. *Law&B 92*
McLeod, David 1946- *WhoWor 93*
McLeod, Deborah Jackson 1915- *WhoAm 92*
McLeod, Denny A. 1926- *St&PR 93*
McLeod, Donald J. *Law&B 92*
McLeod, Donald Neil 1934- *St&PR 93*
McLeod, E. Douglas 1941- *WhoSSW 93*
McLeod, Edwin A. 1927- *St&PR 93*
McLeod, Gerald Alan 1930- *WhoE 93*
McLeod, Glenda Kaye 1953- *WhoSSW 93*
McLeod, H.D. 1942- *St&PR 93*
McLeod, Harry O'Neal, Jr. 1932- *WhoSSW 93*
McLeod, Jack *WhoCanL 92*
McLeod, James Graham 1932- *WhoWor 93*
Mc Leod, James Richard 1942- *WhoWrEP 92*
McLeod, Jeffrey Scott 1961- *WhoSSW 93*
McLeod, Jody Marie *Law&B 92*
McLeod, John Bryce 1929- *WhoWor 93*
Mcleod, John G., Jr. *St&PR 93*
McLeod, John Wishart 1908- *WhoAm 92*
McLeod, Joseph 1929- *WhoCanL 92*
McLeod, Joyce Curry 1940- *WhoSSW 93*
McLeod, Michael John 1948- *WhoSSW 93*
McLeod, Neil A., Jr. 1938- *St&PR 93*
McLeod, Rima L. 1945- *WhoAmW 93*
McLeod, Robert I. *WhoScE 91-1*
McLeod, Robert Macfarlan 1925- *WhoAm 92*
McLeod, Robert Wesley 1949- *WhoSSW 93*
McLeod, Ross 1899-1991 *BioIn 17*
McLeod, Sharon Marie 1952 *WhoSSW 93*
McLeod, Skye 1954- *WhoEmL 93*
McLeod, Walton James, Jr. 1906- *WhoWor 93*
McLeod, William Lasater, Jr. 1931- *WhoSSW 93*
Mc Leran, James Herbert 1931- *WhoAm 92*
McLeroy, Barbre Stringfellow 1953- *WhoEmL 93*
McLeroy, Frederick Grayson 1951- *WhoEmL 93, WhoSSW 93*
McLeroy, Kenneth Riley 1946- *WhoSSW 93*
McLerran, Alice 1933- *BioIn 17, ConAu 136*
McLeskey, Sandra Soles 1948- *WhoSSW 93*
McLester, James Robert 1937- *St&PR 93*
McLester, Keith Price 1943- *St&PR 93*
Mclewee, Joseph Monroe 1933- *St&PR 93*
McLimans, Carol Ann 1936- *WhoAmW 93*
McLin, Elva Bell 1917- *WhoAmW 93*
McLin, Jon Blythe 1938- *WhoUN 92*
McLin, Nathaniel, Jr. 1928- *WhoWor 93*
McLin, Stephen T. 1946- *WhoAm 92*
McLin, William Merriman 1945- *WhoAm 92*
McLinden, Hugh Patrick 1928- *WhoSSW 93*
Mc Linden, Stephen Kerry 1955- *WhoWrEP 92*
McLindon, Gerald Joseph 1923- *WhoAm 92*
McLinn, Harry Marvin *WhoE 93*
McLintock, Gordon 1903-1990 *BioIn 17*
McLish, Rachel 1958- *NotHsAW 93*
McLish, Rachel Elizondo 1958- *HispAmA*
McLogan, Edward Austin 1920- *St&PR 93*
McLoone, J. Mark 1954- *WhoE 93*
McLoone, Michael E. 1945- *WhoIns 93*
McLoughlin, Donald Craig 1928- *St&PR 93*
McLoughlin, Donald J. 1956- *St&PR 93*
McLoughlin, Hollis Samuel 1950- *WhoAm 92*
McLoughlin, John C. 1949- *ScF&FL 92*
McLoughlin, John T. *Law&B 92*
McLoughlin, Kenneth Michael *Law&B 92*
McLoughlin, Maurice E., Jr. *Law&B 92*
McLoughlin, Michael 1947- *St&PR 93*
McLoughlin, Philip Robert 1946- *St&PR 93, WhoAm 92*
McLoughlin, Richard F. *BioIn 17*
McLoughlin, Therese Corinne 1931- *WhoAmW 93*
McLoughlin, Tom *MiSFD 9*
McLoughlin, William Gerald, Jr. 1922- *WhoAm 92*
McLowery, Frank 1851?-1881 *BioIn 17*
McLowery, Thomas 1852?-1881 *BioIn 17*
Mc Lucas, John Luther 1920- *WhoAm 92*
McLucas, William R. 1950- *WhoAm 92*
McLuckey, John Alexander, Jr. 1940- *WhoAm 92*
McLuhan, Marshall 1911-1980 *BioIn 17, DcTwHis*
Mc Lure, Charles E., Jr. 1940- *WhoAm 92*
McLurkin, Thomas Cornelius, Jr. 1954- *WhoEmL 93, WhoWor 93*
MC Lyte *BioIn 17*
MC Lyte c. 1971- *ConMus 8 [port]*
McMackin, John James 1925- *WhoAm 92*
McMackin, John William 1930- *WhoAm 92*
McMackin, Lorie Jean 1953- *St&PR 93*
McMackin, Thomas K. *Law&B 92*
McMahan, A. L., Mrs. *AmWomPl*
Mcmahan, Charles Brown 1946- *St&PR 93*
McMahan, Gary Lynn 1948- *WhoWor 93*
McMahan, Ian 1940- *ScF&FL 92*
McMahan, James M. *Law&B 92*
McMahan, Jeffrey N. *ScF&FL 92*
McMahan, Lynn Bryce 1946- *WhoSSW 93*
McMahan, Oliver B. 1928- *WhoIns 93*
McMahan, Richard A. 1926- *St&PR 93*
McMahan, Robert C. 1938- *WhoSSW 93*
McMahan, Robert Chandler 1940- *St&PR 93, WhoAm 92*
McMahan, Susan Evon 1962- *WhoAmW 93, WhoEmL 93*
McMahen, Charles E. 1939- *St&PR 93*
McMahon, Ann Marie 1950- *WhoAmW 93*
McMahon, Arlene Kay 1961- *WhoAmW 93*
McMahon, Brian Neil *Law&B 92*
McMahon, Carroll Francis 1923- *St&PR 93*
McMahon, Catherine Anne 1963- *WhoAmW 93*
McMahon, Catherine D. *Law&B 92*
McMahon, Charles James 1930- *St&PR 93*
McMahon, Colleen 1951- *WhoAmW 93*
McMahon, David Freyvogel 1949- *WhoEmL 93*
McMahon, David H. *Law&B 92*
McMahon, David H. 1943- *St&PR 93*
McMahon, Deborah Elizabeth 1953- *WhoAmW 93*
McMahon, Debra Brylawski 1956- *WhoAmW 93*
McMahon, Dennis A. *Law&B 92*
McMahon, Donald 1946- *St&PR 93*
McMahon, Donald Aylward 1931- *St&PR 93, WhoAm 92*
McMahon, Ed *BioIn 17*
Mc Mahon, Ed 1923- *WhoAm 92*
McMahon, Edward Francis 1930- *WhoSSW 93*
McMahon, Edward Joseph 1935- *St&PR 93*
McMahon, Edward Peter 1940- *WhoAm 92*
McMahon, Eileen Marie 1953- *WhoE 93, WhoEmL 93*
McMahon, Eleanor Marie 1929- *WhoAm 92*
McMahon, Elizabeth Mildred 1918- *WhoAmW 93*
McMahon, Elizabeth R. 1960- *St&PR 93*
McMahon, Ernest E. d1990 *BioIn 17*
Mc Mahon, George Joseph 1923- *WhoAm 92*
McMahon, Gregory D. *Law&B 92*
McMahon, Helen Marie 1956- *WhoAmW 93*
McMahon, Howard Olford 1914-1990 *BioIn 17*
McMahon, Ian 1959- *St&PR 93*
McMahon, J. Kevin *WhoAm 92*
McMahon, James Francis *Law&B 92*
McMahon, James P. 1948- *St&PR 93*
Mcmahon, Janice C. 1941- *St&PR 93*
McMahon, Jeremiah 1919- *ScF&FL 92*
McMahon, Jerome F. 1932- *St&PR 93*
McMahon, Jim *BioIn 17*
McMahon, Jim 1959- *WhoAm 92*
McMahon, John Alexander 1921- *WhoAm 92*
McMahon, John Barry *Law&B 92*
McMahon, John D. *Law&B 92*
McMahon, John E. *Law&B 92*
McMahon, John Francis 1910- *WhoAm 92, WhoWor 93*
McMahon, John J., Jr. *WhoAm 92*
McMahon, John Joseph 1960- *WhoWor 93*
McMahon, John Patrick 1919- *WhoAm 92*
McMahon, Joseph Einar 1940- *WhoAm 92*
McMahon, Judith Diane 1950- *WhoAmW 93*
McMahon, Kathleen Marie 1961- *WhoAmW 93*
McMahon, Kevin John 1956- *St&PR 93*
McMahon, Marghe May 1954- *WhoEmL 93*
McMahon, Maria O'Neil 1937- *WhoAmW 93*
McMahon, Maribeth Lovette 1949- *WhoAm 92*
McMahon, Mark Preston 1952- *WhoEmL 93*
McMahon, Michael Christopher 1947- *St&PR 93*
McMahon, Michael E. *Law&B 92*
McMahon, Michael Edward 1955- *WhoEmL 93*
McMahon, Neil *ScF&FL 92*
McMahon, Neil Michael 1953- *WhoE 93, WhoWor 93*
McMahon, Patrick E. *Law&B 92*
McMahon, Patrick Henry d1990 *BioIn 17*
McMahon, Patrick J. *Law&B 92*
McMahon, Patrick Vincent 1955- *St&PR 93*
McMahon, Paul Francis 1945- *WhoAm 92*
McMahon, Paul Joseph, III 1959- *WhoEmL 93*
McMahon, Paul M. 1954- *St&PR 93*
McMahon, Pierre Alain *Law&B 92*
McMahon, Robert Lee, Jr. 1944- *WhoSSW 93*
Mcmahon, Robert Tyler 1945- *St&PR 93*
McMahon, Ronald E. 1936- *St&PR 93*
Mcmahon, Russell E. 1946- *St&PR 93*
McMahon, S.E. *Law&B 92*
McMahon, Sara C. *AmWomPl*
McMahon, Seamus P. 1959- *St&PR 93*
McMahon, Stephen Thomas 1958- *WhoEmL 93*
McMahon, Thomas Arthur 1943- *WhoAm 92, WhoE 93, WhoWrEP 92*
McMahon, Thomas John 1954- *WhoSSW 93*
McMahon, Thomas Michael 1941- *WhoAm 92*
McMahon, Thomas W. 1921-1990 *BioIn 17*
McMahon, Vince, Jr. *BioIn 17*
McMains, Melvin L. 1941- *St&PR 93*
McMains, Melvin Lee 1941- *WhoAm 92*
McMaken, Lynda Hamilton *WhoAmW 93*
McMakin, Roy *BioIn 17*
McMamee, Arlene Arruda 1943- *St&PR 93*
McManama, Trudy E. 1945- *WhoAmW 93*
McManaman, Kenneth Charles 1950- *WhoEmL 93*
McManaman, William Robert 1947- *St&PR 93*
McManamon, Daniel Thomas 1952- *WhoE 93*
McManes, Alison Ann 1960- *WhoEmL 93, WhoSSW 93*
McManigal, Shirley Ann 1938- *WhoAmW 93*
McManis, Barbara M. *Law&B 92*
McManis, Bettye West 1943- *WhoAmW 93*
McManmon, John Joseph 1932- *WhoE 93*
McManmon, Thomas Arthur, Jr. 1943- *WhoE 93*
McMann, James P. *Law&B 92*
Mc Mann, Renville Hupfel, Jr. 1927- *WhoAm 92*
McManus, Arthur Terrence 1937- *St&PR 93*
McManus, Betty Reed 1943- *WhoAmW 93*
Mc Manus, Charles Anthony, Jr. 1927- *WhoAm 92*
McManus, Charles Kent 1942- *WhoAm 92*
McManus, Edward Hubbard 1939- *WhoAm 92*
McManus, Elizabeth Lee 1933- *WhoAmW 93*
McManus, Gregg *St&PR 93*
McManus, Hugh S. *Law&B 92*
McManus, Jacqueline K. 1952- *WhoEmL 93*
Mc Manus, James 1951- *WhoWrEP 92*
McManus, James E. 1942- *St&PR 93*
McManus, James F. 1930- *St&PR 93*
McManus, James P. 1937- *St&PR 93*
McManus, James William 1944- *WhoSSW 93*
McManus, Jason *BioIn 17*
McManus, Jason Donald 1934- *St&PR 93, WhoAm 92*
McManus, John *WhoScE 91-1*
McManus, John Francis, III 1919- *WhoAm 92*
McManus, John J. 1931- *WhoIns 93*
Mcmanus, John Stephen 1967- *WhoE 93*
McManus, Joseph Michael 1946- *WhoEmL 93*
McManus, Joseph Warn 1931- *WhoSSW 93*
McManus, Kevin Patrick 1953- *WhoE 93*
McManus, Leslie *ScF&FL 92*
McManus, Martin Joseph 1900-1966 *BiDAMSp 1989*
McManus, Martin Joseph 1919- *WhoAm 92, WhoWor 93*
McManus, Mary Monica 1962- *WhoAmW 93*
McManus, Michael A., Jr. 1943- *St&PR 93, WhoAm 92*
McManus, Michael John 1941- *WhoE 93*
McManus, Miriam Patrice 1957- *St&PR 93*
McManus, Philip E. 1941- *St&PR 93*
McManus, Rachel Elizabeth 1947- *WhoAmW 93*
McManus, Richard P. *Law&B 92*
McManus, Richard Philip 1929- *WhoAm 92*
McManus, Robert D. *Law&B 92*
Mc Manus, Samuel Plyler 1938- *WhoAm 92*
McManus, Steve *Law&B 92*
McManus, Timothy 1937- *St&PR 93*
McManus, Walter Leonard 1918- *WhoAm 92*
McManus, Walter Leonard, Jr. 1942- *WhoE 93*
McManus, William *BioIn 17*
McManus, William Jay 1900- *WhoAm 92*
McManus, William Raymond, Jr. 1967- *WhoE 93, WhoEmL 93, WhoWor 93*
McMartin, Ian W. *WhoIns 93*
Mc Martin, Paula J. 1955- *WhoWrEP 92*
McMartin, Peggy *BioIn 17*
McMaster, Beth 1935- *WhoCanL 92*
McMaster, Brian John 1943- *WhoAm 92*
McMaster, Harold Ashley 1916- *WhoAm 92*
McMaster, Juliet Sylvia 1937- *WhoAmW 93, WhoWrEP 92*
McMaster, Robert Raymond 1948- *WhoAm 92*
McMaster, Susan 1950- *WhoCanL 92*
McMasters, Sherman *BioIn 17*
McMath, Elizabeth Moore 1930- *WhoAmW 93*
Mc Math, Phillip H. 1945- *WhoWrEP 92*
McMeans, Shaun D. 1961- *St&PR 93*
McMeekin, Dorothy 1932- *WhoAm 92, WhoAmW 93*
McMeekin, Isabella 1895- *AmWomPl*
McMeel, John P. *BioIn 17*
Mc Meel, John Paul 1936- *WhoAm 92*
McMeen, Albert Ralph, III 1942- *WhoAm 92*
McMeen, Elmer Ellsworth, III 1947- *WhoAm 92*
McMeen, Michael Eugene 1955- *WhoEmL 93*

McMenamin, Joseph E. 1932- *St&PR 93*
McMenamin, Michael Terrence 1943- *WhoWor 93*
McMenamin, Peter David 1948- *WhoEmL 93*
McMenamy, Joseph P. *Law&B 92*
McMenamy, Kristen *BioIn 17*
Mc Mennamin, George Barry 1922- *WhoAm 92*
McMennamin, Michael J. 1945- *WhoAm 92*
McMennamin, Michael John 1945- *St&PR 93*
McMennamy, Roger Neal 1942- *St&PR 93, WhoSSW 93*
McMichael, Andrew James *WhoScE 91-1*
McMichael, Francis Clay 1937- *WhoAm 92*
McMichael, Jeane Casey 1938- *WhoWor 93*
McMichael, Jerry L. 1946- *St&PR 93*
McMichael, Lawrence Grover 1953- *WhoEmL 93*
McMichael, Nancy *BioIn 17*
McMickan, Walter Oliver 1937- *WhoScE 91-3*
McMickle, Robert Hawley 1924- *WhoE 93*
McMillan, Adell 1933- *WhoAmW 93*
McMillan, Allan W. d1991 *BioIn 17*
McMillan, Andrew Pickens, Jr. 1950- *WhoEmL 93*
Mc Millan, Brockway 1915- *WhoAm 92*
McMillan, Bruce *MajAI [port], SmATA 70 [port]*
McMillan, C. Steven 1945- *WhoAm 92*
McMillan, Campbell White 1927- *WhoAm 92*
McMillan, Charles H., Jr. 1927- *St&PR 93*
McMillan, Charles William 1926- *WhoAm 92*
McMillan, Clara Gooding 1894-1976 *BioIn 17*
McMillan, Colin Riley 1935- *WhoAm 92*
McMillan, David John *Law&B 92*
McMillan, Donald Edgar 1937- *WhoAm 92*
McMillan, Donald Ernest 1931- *WhoAm 92*
McMillan, Douglas Joseph 1931- *WhoSSW 93*
McMillan, Edward L. 1935- *St&PR 93*
McMillan, Edward Neil 1947- *St&PR 93*
McMillan, Edwin 1907-1991 *AnObit 1991*
McMillan, Edwin Mattison 1907-1991 *BioIn 17*
McMillan, Ellis Earl 1929- *St&PR 93*
Mc Millan, Elma Joyce 1934- *WhoWrEP 92*
McMillan, Francis Wetmore, II 1938- *WhoIns 93*
McMillan, G.H. Grant 1944- *WhoScE 91-1*
Mc Millan, George Duncan Hastie, Jr. 1943- *WhoAm 92*
McMillan, H. Wayne 1938- *St&PR 93*
McMillan, Harold Leslie 1952- *WhoAm 92*
McMillan, Howard Lamar, Jr. 1939- *WhoSSW 93*
McMillan, J. Alex 1932- *CngDr 91*
Mc Millan, James *WhoAm 92*
McMillan, James 1838-1902 *PolPar*
McMillan, James Bryan 1916- *WhoAm 92, WhoSSW 93*
McMillan, John 1951- *ConAu 138*
McMillan, John Alexander, III 1932- *WhoAm 92, WhoSSW 93*
Mc Millan, John Robertson 1909- *WhoAm 92*
Mc Millan, Karen Alice 1961- *WhoWrEP 92*
McMillan, Kevin *BioIn 17*
McMillan, Lee Richards, II 1947- *WhoSSW 93*
Mc Millan, Leona Pearl 1913- *WhoWrEP 92*
McMillan, Margaret 1860-1931 *BioIn 17*
McMillan, Martin Leslie 1955- *WhoWor 93*
McMillan, Mary 1912-1991 *BioIn 17*
McMillan, Mary Bigelow 1919- *WhoAm 92*
McMillan, Mary Lane *AmWomPl*
McMillan, Molly Colleen 1956- *WhoSSW 93*
Mc Millan, Patricia Ann 1946- *WhoWrEP 92*
McMillan, Peter *BioIn 17*
Mcmillan, Peter Aidan 1959- *WhoWrEP 92*
McMillan, Robert Allan 1942- *St&PR 93, WhoAm 92*
Mc Millan, Robert Bruce 1937- *WhoAm 92*
McMillan, Robert John 1952- *WhoIns 93*
McMillan, Robert Ralph 1932- *St&PR 93, WhoAm 92, WhoE 93, WhoWor 93*
McMillan, Robert Scott 1950- *WhoEmL 93*
McMillan, Roy 1937- *St&PR 93*
Mc Millan, Sally Hill 1949- *WhoWrEP 92*
McMillan, Samuel Sterling, III 1938- *St&PR 93, WhoAm 92*
McMillan, Sherry Lynn *Law&B 92*
McMillan, Terry *BioIn 17*
McMillan, Terry 1951- *ConBlB 4 [port], NewYTBS 92 [port], News 93-2 [port]*
McMillan, Virginia *AmWomPl*
McMillan, William 1929- *WhoWor 93*
McMillan, William Carl 1964- *WhoSSW 93*
McMillen, Abbie 1942- *WhoWor 93*
McMillen, Anne B. *Law&B 92*
McMillen, C. Thomas 1952- *CngDr 91*
McMillen, Harvey G. 1936- *St&PR 93*
McMillen, Howard Lawrence 1937- *WhoSSW 93*
McMillen, James E. 1941- *St&PR 93*
McMillen, John T. 1953- *St&PR 93*
McMillen, Larry *WhoAm 92*
McMillen, Loring 1906-1991 *BioIn 17*
McMillen, Louis Albert 1916- *WhoAm 92*
McMillen, Marvin Allan 1948- *WhoE 93*
McMillen, Mont Evans, Jr. 1936- *WhoAm 92*
McMillen, Patricia R. *Law&B 92*
McMillen, R. Scott *Law&B 92*
McMillen, Robert Doane 1916- *WhoSSW 93, WhoWor 93*
McMillen, Russell Gross 1918- *St&PR 93*
McMillen, Thomas 1952- *WhoAm 92, WhoE 93*
Mc Millen, Thomas Roberts 1916- *WhoAm 92*
McMillen, Wheeler d1992 *NewYTBS 92 [port]*
McMillen, Wheeler 1893-1992 *BioIn 17, WhoAm 92*
Mc Millen, William Earl 1947- *WhoWrEP 92*
McMiller, Anita Williams 1946- *WhoAmW 93, WhoE 93, WhoEmL 93, WhoWor 93*
McMillian, John G. *WhoAm 92*
McMillian, Sabrina Dodd 1955- *St&PR 93*
McMillian, Theodore 1919- *WhoAm 92*
McMillin, David Robert 1948- *WhoAm 92*
McMillin, Glenn Reinhard 1930- *WhoAm 92*
McMillin, Harvey Scott 1934- *WhoE 93*
McMillin, Jeanie Byrd 1939- *WhoAm 92*
McMillin, John P. 1936- *St&PR 93*
McMillin, Lawrence Eugene 1948- *St&PR 93*
McMillin, Timothy David 1943- *St&PR 93*
McMillion, Charles Wayne 1948- *WhoEmL 93*
Mc Million, John Macon 1929- *WhoAm 92*
McMillion, Margaret Kim 1951- *WhoAmW 93*
McMillion, S. Argyle 1936- *St&PR 93*
McMillon, R.L. 1921- *WhoIns 93*
McMindes, Lee P. 1931- *St&PR 93*
McMindes, Roy J. 1923- *St&PR 93*
McMindes, Roy James 1923- *WhoAm 92*
McMinn, B. C. 1921- *WhoSSW 93*
McMinn, James Stephen 1949- *WhoEmL 93*
McMinn, John Albert 1933- *St&PR 93*
McMinn, William Gene 1931- *WhoAm 92*
McMinn, William Scott 1956- *WhoE 93*
McMonagle, E.J. 1922- *St&PR 93*
McMonagle, Keith Duane 1947- *WhoEmL 93*
McMonagle, Mary C. *Law&B 92*
McMoran, George Andrew 1934- *St&PR 93*
McMorran, J. Burch 1899-1991 *BioIn 17*
McMorran, Sydney R. 1939- *St&PR 93*
McMorries, Melissa Eliot 1952- *WhoEmL 93*
McMorris, Charles Horatio 1890-1954 *HarEnMi*
McMorris, Howard S. 1910-1992 *BioIn 17*
McMorris, William *WhoAm 92*
McMorrow, John Patrick *Law&B 92*
McMorrow, Margaret Mary 1924- *WhoAmW 93*
McMorrow, Ralph J. 1921- *St&PR 93*
McMorrow, Rebecca Lynn 1951- *WhoAmW 93*
McMorrow, Richard M. 1941- *St&PR 93*
Mc Morrow, Richard Mark 1941- *WhoAm 92*
McMorrow, William J. 1931- *St&PR 93*
Mc Moy, John H. 1953- *WhoWrEP 92*
McMulkin, Francis John 1915- *WhoAm 92*
McMullan, Andrew 1923- *St&PR 93*
Mcmullan, Cornelius P. *St&PR 93*
Mc Mullan, Dorothy 1911- *WhoAm 92*
McMullan, James Franklin 1928- *WhoSSW 93*
McMullan, John T. *WhoScE 91-1*
McMullan, Kate 1947- *ScF&FL 92*
McMullan, Sarah Frances 1933- *WhoAmW 93*
McMullan, William Patrick, Jr. 1925- *WhoAm 92*
McMullan, William Patrick, III 1952- *WhoAm 92, WhoEmL 93*
McMullen, Barbara Elizabeth 1942- *WhoAmW 93*
Mc Mullen, Betty A. 1936- *WhoWrEP 92*
McMullen, Bruce R. 1945- *St&PR 93*
Mcmullen, Craig R. *St&PR 93*
Mc Mullen, Edwin Wallace, Jr. 1915- *WhoAm 92, WhoWrEP 92*
McMullen, Frederick E. *Law&B 92*
McMullen, George Andrew 1926- *St&PR 93*
McMullen, Jay L. 1921-1992 *ConAu 137*
McMullen, Jeanine *BioIn 17*
McMullen, John Henry, Jr. 1944- *WhoE 93*
McMullen, John J. *WhoAm 92, WhoSSW 93*
McMullen, John J. 1918- *St&PR 93*
Mcmullen, John Joseph 1933- *St&PR 93*
McMullen, John Michael *Law&B 92*
McMullen, Ken 1948- *MiSFD 9*
Mc Mullen, Leon F. 1930- *WhoWrEP 92*
McMullen, Lowell W. 1960- *St&PR 93*
McMullen, Melinda Kae 1957- *WhoAmW 93*
McMullen, Pamela R. Temples 1949- *WhoSSW 93*
McMullen, Sean 1948- *ScF&FL 92*
Mc Mullen, Thomas Henry 1929- *WhoAm 92*
McMullen, Virginia Elise 1943- *St&PR 93*
McMullian, Amos Ryals 1937- *St&PR 93, WhoAm 92, WhoSSW 93*
McMullin, Carleton Eugene 1932- *WhoAm 92*
McMullin, Diane M. 1947- *St&PR 93*
Mc Mullin, Ernan Vincent 1924- *WhoAm 92*
McMullin, Joyce Anne 1952- *WhoAmW 93*
McMullin, Ruth R. 1942- *St&PR 93*
McMullin, Ruth Roney 1942- *WhoAm 92, WhoAmW 93*
McMullin, Thomas Ryan *Law&B 92*
Mc Munn, Earl William 1910- *WhoAm 92*
McMunn, John Charles 1951- *WhoAm 92, WhoEmL 93*
McMunn, Richard Earl 1949- *WhoAm 92*
McMurdie, Annie Laurie *ScF&FL 92*
McMurdie, J. Neil *Law&B 92*
McMurphy, Michael Allen 1947- *WhoAm 92, WhoWor 93*
McMurray, Barbara Alisa 1953- *WhoEmL 93*
McMurray, C.H. *WhoScE 91-1*
McMurray, Georgia L. d1992 *NewYTBS 92 [port]*
McMurray, Joseph Patrick Brendan 1912- *WhoAm 92*
McMurray, Julia Lynne *Law&B 92*
McMurray, Mary 1949- *MiSFD 9*
McMurray, W.G. *Law&B 92*
McMurray, William 1929- *WhoAm 92*
Mc Murrin, Lee Ray 1930- *WhoAm 92*
Mc Murrin, Sterling Moss 1914- *WhoAm 92*
McMurry, Dorothy E. *AmWomPl*
Mc Murry, Idanelle Sam 1924- *WhoAm 92*
McMurry, Norman Edmund 1924- *WhoSSW 93*
McMurry, Patricia Margarite 1948- *WhoAmW 93*
McMurry, Preston V., Jr. *BioIn 17*
McMurry, Ralph L. *Law&B 92*
McMurry, Thomas Brian H. 1931- *WhoScE 91-3*
McMurry, Timothy D. 1948- *WhoEmL 93, WhoSSW 93*
McMurtrey, Irene Carman *AmWomPl*
McMurtrie, Edward C. *Law&B 92*
McMurtry, Arthur William 1910- *WhoE 93*
McMurtry, Carl Hewes 1931- *WhoE 93*
McMurtry, Florence Jean 1947- *WhoAmW 93*
McMurtry, George James 1932- *WhoAm 92*
Mc Murtry, James Gilmer, III 1932- *WhoAm 92*
McMurtry, Jane Gail 1948- *WhoAmW 93*
McMurtry, Larry *BioIn 17*
McMurtry, Larry 1936- *MagSAmL [port], WhoAm 92*
McMurtry, Larry (Jeff) 1936- *WhoWrEP 92*
McMurtry, R. Roy 1932- *WhoAm 92*
McMurtry, Stan 1936- *ScF&FL 92*
Mcnab, Clarissa O. *St&PR 93*
McNab, Frank d1878 *BioIn 17*
McNabb, Brenda A. *Law&B 92*
McNabb, Darcy LaFountain 1955- *WhoAmW 93*
McNabb, Frances Perle Cody 1913- *WhoSSW 93*
McNabb, Frank W. 1936- *St&PR 93*
McNabb, Frank William 1936- *WhoAm 92, WhoWor 93*
McNabb, James David 1940- *WhoSSW 93*
McNabb, Joseph William 1949- *WhoE 93*
McNabb, Julia Jane 1958- *WhoSSW 93*
McNabb, Mary *BlkAmWO*
McNabb, Steven Dennis 1949- *WhoEmL 93*
McNabb, Susan Lorene 1955- *WhoWor 93*
McNagny, William F. 1922- *St&PR 93*
McNair, Barbara 1939- *Baker 92*
McNair, Carl Herbert, Jr. 1933- *WhoAm 92*
McNair, Frances Ellen Firner 1950- *WhoAmW 93*
McNair, Frank Cornelious 1946- *WhoE 93*
McNair, Fred Louis 1945- *St&PR 93*
McNair, Harley R. 1939- *St&PR 93*
McNair, Harry E. 1924- *St&PR 93*
McNair, John Caldwell 1923- *WhoE 93*
McNair, John Franklin, III 1927- *St&PR 93, WhoAm 92, WhoSSW 93*
McNair, Kathy S. 1949- *WhoAmW 93*
McNair, Lesley James 1883-1944 *HarEnMi*
McNair, Loomis Lindberg 1929- *St&PR 93*
McNair, Nimrod, Jr. 1923- *WhoSSW 93, WhoWor 93*
Mc Nair, Rogers Mac Gowan *WhoWrEP 92*
McNair, Ronald 1950-1986 *AfrAmBi [port], ConBlB 3 [port]*
McNair, Ronald E. *BioIn 17*
McNair, Russell Arthur, Jr. 1934- *WhoAm 92*
Mc Nair, Sylvia *WhoAm 92*
McNair, Sylvia 1956- *Baker 92*
McNair, W(illiam) A(llen) *DcChlFi*
McNairy, Charles Banks, III 1928- *St&PR 93*
McNairy, Richard W. 1940- *St&PR 93*
McNall, Bruce *WhoAm 92*
McNall, Bruce P. *BioIn 17*
McNall, Scott Grant 1941- *WhoAm 92*
Mc Nallen, James Berl 1930- *WhoAm 92*
McNally, Andrew, III 1909- *St&PR 93, WhoAm 92*
McNally, Andrew, IV 1939- *St&PR 93, WhoAm 92*
McNally, Ann Claire Melone 1945- *WhoAmW 93*
McNally, Clare *ScF&FL 92*
McNally, D.J. 1961- *St&PR 93*
McNally, David Wendell 1956- *WhoEmL 93*
Mcnally, Derek *WhoScE 91-2*
McNally, Edward C. 1942- *St&PR 93*
McNally, Frank Thomas 1936- *WhoAm 92*
McNally, Frederick G. d1992 *NewYTBS 92*
McNally, Frederick G. 1916-1992 *BioIn 17*
McNally, Gerald, Jr. 1947- *WhoEmL 93*
McNally, James F. 1932- *St&PR 93*
McNally, James Henry 1936- *WhoWor 93*
McNally, John Joseph 1927- *WhoAm 92*
McNally, John Victor 1904-1985 *BioIn 17*
McNally, Judith 1950- *WhoAmW 93*
McNally, Margaret H. *Law&B 92*
McNally, Mariann *Law&B 92*
McNally, N.J. *WhoScE 91-1*
McNally, Pierce Aldrich 1949- *WhoEmL 93, WhoWor 93*
McNally, Raymond T. 1931- *ScF&FL 92*
McNally, Terrence 1939- *BioIn 17, WhoAm 92, WhoE 93*
McNally, Thomas Charles, III 1938- *WhoAm 92*
McNally, Thomas W. 1948- *St&PR 93*
McNally, Thomas William 1948- *WhoEmL 93, WhoSSW 93*
McNally, Timothy F. 1952- *St&PR 93*
McNally-Broscius, Regina 1965- *WhoEmL 93*
Mc Namar, Richard Timothy 1939- *WhoAm 92*
McNamara, A. J. 1936- *WhoAm 92, WhoSSW 93*
McNamara, Aida Shahid 1959- *WhoEmL 93*
McNamara, Ann Dowd 1924- *WhoAmW 93*
McNamara, Anne H. *Law&B 92, St&PR 93*

McNamara, Anne H. 1947- *WhoAm 92, WhoAmW 93*
McNamara, Brian F. *Law&B 92*
McNamara, Daniel L. *Law&B 92*
McNamara, David G. 1937- *St&PR 93*
McNamara, Dennis L. 1945- *ConAu 136*
McNamara, Dennis Louis 1945- *WhoE 93*
McNamara, Diane Louise 1949- *St&PR 93*
McNamara, Edward J. *Law&B 92*
McNamara, Elizabeth Taylor 1953- *WhoE 93*
McNamara, Eugene 1930- *WhoCanL 92*
McNamara, Francis J., III *Law&B 92*
McNamara, Francis John 1915- *WhoAm 92*
Mc Namara, Francis Joseph, Jr. 1927- *WhoAm 92*
McNamara, Francis T. 1927- *WhoAm 92, WhoWor 93*
McNamara, Glenn F. *Law&B 92*
McNamara, James M. 1954- *St&PR 93*
McNamara, John 1932- *WhoAm 92*
Mc Namara, John Donald 1924- *WhoAm 92, WhoWor 93*
McNamara, John J. 1934- *St&PR 93*
McNamara, John Jeffrey 1937- *WhoE 93*
Mc Namara, John Joseph 1934- *WhoAm 92*
McNamara, John Michael 1946- *St&PR 93, WhoAm 92*
McNamara, John Michael 1957- *WhoE 93*
McNamara, John Stephen 1950- *WhoE 93*
McNamara, Joseph D. *BioIn 17*
Mc Namara, Joseph Donald 1934- *WhoAm 92*
McNamara, Joseph G. *Law&B 92*
Mc Namara, Joseph Patrick 1906- *WhoWor 93*
McNamara, Joseph T. 1938- *St&PR 93*
McNamara, Julia Mary 1941- *WhoAmW 93*
McNamara, Julie Smith 1939- *St&PR 93*
McNamara, Kathleen Michele 1957- *WhoEmL 93*
McNamara, Kathryn M. *Law&B 92*
McNamara, Kevin J. *Law&B 92*
McNamara, Kevin J. 1953- *St&PR 93*
McNamara, Kevin John 1957- *WhoE 93*
McNamara, Kevin Michael 1956- *WhoAm 92*
Mc Namara, Lawrence J. 1928- *WhoAm 92*
McNamara, Marilyn Lally 1949- *WhoAmW 93*
McNamara, Martin Burr 1947- *St&PR 93, WhoAm 92*
McNamara, Martin D. 1949- *St&PR 93*
Mc Namara, Mary Ellen 1942- *WhoAmW 93*
McNamara, Michael John 1948- *WhoWor 93*
McNamara, Michael William 1945- *St&PR 93*
McNamara, Nancy Marie 1936- *WhoAmW 93*
McNamara, Patricia Rae 1936- *WhoSSW 93*
McNamara, Rieman, Jr. 1928- *St&PR 93, WhoAm 92*
McNamara, Robert 1916- *DcTwHis*
McNamara, Robert B. *WhoAm 92*
Mcnamara, Robert James 1950- *WhoWrEP 92*
McNamara, Robert S. 1916- *BioIn 17, ColdWar 1 [port]*
Mc Namara, Robert Strange 1916- *WhoAm 92, WhoWor 93, WhoWrEP 92*
McNamara, Susan Louise 1952- *WhoEmL 93*
McNamara, Susan RoseMary 1956- *WhoAmW 93*
McNamara, Thomas Neal 1930- *WhoAm 92*
McNamara, Timothy Connor 1946- *WhoEmL 93*
McNamara, Timothy James 1952- *WhoEmL 93*
McNamara, Tom 1944- *WhoWor 93*
McNamara, Valerie Lynn 1960- *WhoEmL 93*
McNamara, William A. 1909- *St&PR 93*
McNamara, William Albinus 1909- *WhoAm 92, WhoWor 93*
McNamee, Bernard J. *Law&B 92*
Mc Namee, Dardis 1948- *WhoWrEP 92*
McNamee, Dennis Patrick 1952- *WhoEmL 93*
McNamee, James M. 1945- *St&PR 93*
McNamee, John Stephen 1946- *St&PR 93*
McNamee, Joyce Marie 1934- *WhoE 93*
McNamee, Louise *WhoAm 92, WhoAmW 93*
McNamee, Louise R. *BioIn 17*
McNamee, Robert J. 1922- *St&PR 93*
McNamee, Roger *BioIn 17*
McNamer, Deirdre 1950- *ConLC 70 [port]*
McNaney, Robert T. *Law&B 92*
McNaney, Robert T. 1934- *St&PR 93*
McNany, Sarah Jane 1949- *WhoAmW 93*
McNarny, Patrick E. 1936- *St&PR 93*
McNaron, Toni (A. H.) 1937- *ConAu 139*
McNary, Charles L. 1874-1944 *PolPar*
McNary, Charles Linza 1874-1944 *BioIn 17*
McNary, Gene 1935- *WhoAm 92*
McNattin, Cynthia Alexandra Molenda *Law&B 92*
McNaught, John J. 1921- *WhoAm 92*
McNaught, Judith 1944- *ConAu 138, WhoAmW 93*
McNaught, William Gray 1849-1918 *Baker 92*
McNaughtan, David Pringle 1950- *WhoWor 93*
McNaughton, Brian *ScF&FL 92*
McNaughton, Gary Michael 1948- *St&PR 93*
McNaughton, John *BioIn 17, MiSFD 9*
McNaughton, John William 1950- *St&PR 93*
McNaughton, Robert Forbes, Jr. 1924- *WhoAm 92*
McNaughton, Robert L. 1935- *St&PR 93*
McNaughton, Samuel Joseph 1939- *WhoAm 92*
McNaughton, Stanley O. 1921- *WhoIns 93*
McNaughton, Thomas J. *Law&B 92*
McNaull, Thomas E. 1950- *St&PR 93*
McNay, Donald Joseph 1959- *WhoEmL 93, WhoSSW 93*
McNeal, Ann P. Woodhull 1942- *WhoAmW 93*
McNeal, Aquilla Osborne 1948- *WhoEmL 93*
McNeal, Brian Lester 1938- *WhoSSW 93*
McNeal, Dale William, Jr. 1939- *WhoAm 92*
McNeal, H.P. 1919- *St&PR 93*
McNeal, Karen Lynn 1947- *WhoEmL 93*
Mc Neal, Martha von Oesen 1952- *WhoEmL 93, WhoSSW 93*
McNeal, Robert Beattie *Law&B 92*
McNeal, Wayne 1939- *St&PR 93*
McNealy, Scott *BioIn 17*
McNealy, Scott 1954- *ConEn, WhoAm 92*
Mcnealy, Scott G. 1954- *St&PR 93*
McNear, Barbara Baxter 1939- *WhoAm 92*
McNear, Denman K. 1925- *St&PR 93*
Mc Near, Denman Kittredge 1925- *WhoAm 92*
McNear, Mark Mitchell 1960- *WhoWor 93*
McNeary, Joseph Allen 1948- *WhoAm 92*
McNee, Robert B. d1992 *NewYTBS 92 [port]*
McNee, Robert B. 1922-1992 *BioIn 17*
Mc Nee, Zeida *WhoWrEP 92*
McNeece, Richard A. *WhoAm 92*
McNeece, Richard A. 1939- *St&PR 93*
McNeel, Synott Lance 1923- *St&PR 93, WhoIns 93*
McNeeley, Donald Robert 1954- *WhoAm 92*
McNeely, Beverly Ann 1955- *WhoEmL 93*
McNeely, D. Dean 1944- *WhoAm 92*
McNeely, Donald Gregory 1914- *St&PR 93*
McNeely, E.L. 1918- *St&PR 93*
McNeely, E.L. 1919-1991 *BioIn 17*
McNeely, George H., III *Law&B 92*
McNeely, Harry Gregory, Jr. 1923- *St&PR 93*
McNeely, Jim Madison 1956- *WhoEmL 93*
McNeely, John J. 1931- *WhoAm 92*
McNeely, Kenneth Perry *Law&B 92*
McNeely, Marilyn DeLong 1940- *WhoSSW 93*
McNeely, Mark Hall 1950- *WhoAm 92*
McNeely, Michael Dale 1955- *WhoIns 93*
McNeely, Milinda L. *Law&B 92*
McNeely, Tori Leigh 1956- *WhoE 93*
McNeer, C.S. 1926- *St&PR 93*
Mc Neer, Charles Selden 1926- *WhoAm 92*
McNeer, John Daniel 1934- *St&PR 93*
Mc Nees, Patricia Ann 1940- *WhoWrEP 92*
McNees, Stephen Kent 1942- *St&PR 93*
McNees, William Scott *Law&B 92*
McNeff, John Charles 1926- *St&PR 93*
McNeice, John A., Jr. 1932- *St&PR 93*
Mc Neice, John Ambrose, Jr. 1932- *WhoAm 92*
McNeight, Michael T. 1944- *St&PR 93*
McNeil, Barbara Joyce 1941- *WhoAm 92*
McNeil, Bruce D. *BioIn 17*
McNeil, Bruce W. 1916- *St&PR 93*
McNeil, Charles K. *BioIn 17*
McNeil, Chris E., Jr. *Law&B 92*
Mc Neil, Donald Lewis 1926- *WhoAm 92*
McNeil, Edward Warren 1942- *WhoE 93*
McNeil, Florence *WhoCanL 92*
McNeil, George Joseph 1908- *WhoAm 92*
McNeil, Hoyle Graham, Jr. 1950- *WhoEmL 93, WhoSSW 93*
McNeil, Ian *BioIn 17*
McNeil, James D. *Law&B 92*
McNeil, James H., Jr. 1945- *WhoE 93*
McNeil, John 1939- *ScF&FL 92*
McNeil, John D. 1934- *St&PR 93, WhoIns 93*
McNeil, Joseph M. 1937- *St&PR 93*
McNeil, Joseph Malcolm 1937- *WhoAm 92*
McNeil, Kate *BioIn 17*
McNeil, Kenneth Martin 1941- *WhoE 93*
Mcneil, Lawrence Patrick 1933- *St&PR 93*
McNeil, Lori *BioIn 17*
McNeil, Lori Michelle 1963- *WhoAmW 93*
McNeil, Malcolm Stephen 1956- *WhoEmL 93*
McNeil, Manford Russell 1927- *St&PR 93*
McNeil, Mark Sanford 1950- *WhoEmL 93*
McNeil, Michael Brewer 1938- *WhoE 93*
McNeil, Mona Margaret 1947- *WhoEmL 93*
McNeil, Paul Joseph, Jr. 1941- *WhoWor 93*
McNeil, R. Gae 1965- *WhoSSW 93*
McNeil, Robert D. 1950- *St&PR 93*
McNeil, Ronald Dean 1952- *WhoEmL 93*
McNeil, Steven Arthur 1942- *WhoAm 92*
McNeil, Sue 1955- *WhoEmL 93*
McNeil, Susanna Markiewicz 1944- *WhoAmW 93*
McNeil, Vicki Laughter 1955- *WhoSSW 93*
McNeile, Herman *ScF&FL 92*
McNeill, Alfred Thomas, Jr. 1936- *WhoAm 92, WhoE 93*
McNeill, Andrea 1964- *WhoE 93*
McNeill, Blair E. 1944- *St&PR 93*
McNeill, Brandy Rachele 1956- *WhoEmL 93, WhoSSW 93*
McNeill, Carmen Mary *WhoIns 93*
Mc Neill, Charles James 1912- *WhoAm 92*
McNeill, Corbin Asahel, Jr. 1939- *St&PR 93, WhoAm 92, WhoE 93*
McNeill, Desmond James 1948- *WhoWor 93*
McNeill, Donald Woodrow *Law&B 92*
McNeill, Elisabeth *ScF&FL 92*
McNeill, Frederick Wallace 1932- *WhoSSW 93*
McNeill, G. David 1931- *WhoAm 92*
McNeill, Ian 1947- *St&PR 93, WhoIns 93*
McNeill, J. *WhoScE 91-1*
McNeill, James W. 1941- *St&PR 93*
McNeill, Janet 1907- *ScF&FL 92*
McNeill, Joan Reagin 1936- *WhoAmW 93, WhoSSW 93*
McNeill, John Henderson 1941- *WhoAm 92*
McNeill, John Hugh 1938- *WhoAm 92*
McNeill, John Ridgway 1947- *St&PR 93*
McNeill, Kenneth Gordon 1926- *WhoAm 92*
McNeill, Larry Richard 1941- *St&PR 93*
McNeill, Lloyd 1935- *Baker 92*
McNeill, Louise 1911- *ConAu 139*
McNeill, Maxine Currie 1934- *WhoAmW 93*
McNeill, Paul Deane 1954- *WhoEmL 93*
McNeill, Richard William 1945- *St&PR 93*
Mc Neill, Robert Eugene 1921- *WhoAm 92*
McNeill, Robert Patrick 1941- *WhoAm 92*
McNeill, Russell B., Jr. 1941- *St&PR 93*
McNeill, Thomas B. 1934- *WhoAm 92*
McNeill, Warren A. 1903- *ScF&FL 92*
McNeill, William Hardy 1917- *BioIn 17, WhoAm 92, WhoWor 93, WhoWrEP 92*
McNeilly, A.S. *WhoScE 91-1*
McNeilly, Edward R. *BioIn 17*
McNeilly, Jean Craig 1937- *WhoAm 92, WhoAmW 93*
McNeilly, Wilfred Glassford 1921-1983 *ScF&FL 92*
McNeily, Mary Zora 1952- *WhoAmW 93*
McNeish, Alexander S. *WhoScE 91-1*
McNeive, Gerald T., Jr. *Law&B 92*
McNelis, John 1957- *WhoE 93*
McNelley, Donald O. 1944- *St&PR 93*
McNellie, Elizabeth Anne 1964- *WhoAmW 93*
McNellis, G. Terry 1949- *St&PR 93*
McNelly, John Taylor 1923- *WhoAm 92*
McNelly, Leander H. 1843?-1877 *BioIn 17*
McNelly, Willis E. 1920- *ScF&FL 92*
McNemar, Donald William 1943- *WhoAm 92*
McNemee, A.J. 1848-1936 *BioIn 17*
McNerney, James Edward, Jr. 1946- *WhoE 93*
Mc Nerney, Joan 1945- *WhoWrEP 92*
McNerney, John Cornelius 1902- *WhoE 93*
McNerney, Patrick E. 1951- *St&PR 93*
McNerney, Walter J. 1925- *St&PR 93*
Mc Nerney, Walter James 1925- *WhoAm 92*
McNett, Jeanne Marie 1946- *WhoAmW 93*
McNett, John F. *Law&B 92*
McNeur, John Clarke 1950- *WhoEmL 93*
McNevin, Valerie Joan 1953- *WhoAmW 93*
Mc New, Bennie Banks 1931- *WhoAm 92*
McNew, Robert A. *Law&B 92*
McNichol, Kristy *BioIn 17*
Mc Nichol, Kristy 1962- *WhoAm 92*
McNichol, Michele Leneve 1965- *WhoAmW 93*
McNichol, Richard F. 1946- *St&PR 93*
McNicholas, David P. 1941- *St&PR 93*
McNicholas, David Paul 1941- *WhoAm 92*
McNicholas, Michael Joseph *Law&B 92*
McNichols, Eugene H. 1947- *St&PR 93*
McNichols, John P., Jr. 1936- *St&PR 93*
McNichols, Robert J. 1922- *WhoAm 92*
Mc Nichols, William Arthur 1951- *WhoWrEP 92*
McNickle, Michael M. *WhoAm 92*
McNicol, David Leon 1944- *WhoAm 92*
McNicol, Donald E. 1921- *St&PR 93*
Mc Nicol, Donald Edward 1921- *WhoAm 92*
McNicol, James William *WhoScE 91-1*
McNicol, John 1959- *St&PR 93*
McNicol, Paul Briggs 1918- *St&PR 93*
McNicol, Sharon-Ann Gopaul 1958- *WhoE 93*
McNicol, Ulric *Law&B 92*
McNicoll, William Joseph 1960- *WhoSSW 93*
McNiel, Kenneth Laurence 1955- *WhoE 93*
McNiell, William Donald 1918- *BiDAMSp 1989*
McNiesh, Lawrence Melvin 1949- *WhoEmL 93*
McNiff, Christine Marie 1946- *WhoE 93*
McNiff, John F. 1942- *WhoAm 92*
McNiff, Philip A. 1926- *St&PR 93*
Mc Niff, Thomas Alfred, Jr. 1940- *WhoWrEP 92*
McNinch, Emma *AmWomPl*
McNish, Jacqueline Elizabeth 1956- *WhoAmW 93*
McNish, Susan K. 1940- *St&PR 93*
McNitt, Joseph Edward 1929- *WhoAm 92*
Mc Nitt, Willard Charles 1920- *WhoAm 92*
McNitt, Willard Charles, III 1948- *WhoAm 92*
McNown, John Stephenson 1916- *WhoAm 92*
McNulty, C. Howard 1935- *St&PR 93*
McNulty, Carrell Stewart, Jr. 1924- *WhoAm 92*
McNulty, Chester Howard 1935- *WhoAm 92*
McNulty, Christopher Michael 1955- *WhoEmL 93*
McNulty, Daniel F. 1936- *St&PR 93*
McNulty, David P. 1935- *St&PR 93*
McNulty, Donald F. 1934- *St&PR 93*
McNulty, Earl Walker 1936- *St&PR 93*
McNulty, Francis A. *Law&B 92*
McNulty, Geraldine Myers 1939- *St&PR 93*
McNulty, Henry Bryant 1947- *WhoAm 92, WhoEmL 93*
McNulty, Jacquelyn *Law&B 92*
McNulty, James F.M. *WhoIns 93*
McNulty, Jeffrey Allen 1964- *WhoEmL 93*
McNulty, Jennifer Anne 1961- *WhoAmW 93*
Mc Nulty, John Bard 1916- *WhoWrEP 92*
McNulty, John Kent 1934- *WhoAm 92*
McNulty, John W. *Law&B 92*
McNulty, John William 1927- *WhoAm 92*
McNulty, Mark Daniel 1955- *St&PR 93*
McNulty, Mark Thomas 1949- *WhoEmL 93*
McNulty, Mary Florence 1953- *WhoAmW 93*
McNulty, Matthew Francis, Jr. 1914- *WhoAm 92, WhoSSW 93, WhoWor 93*
McNulty, Michael Joseph *Law&B 92*
McNulty, Michael R. 1947- *CngDr 91*
McNulty, Michael Robert 1947- *WhoAm 92, WhoE 93*
McNulty, Nancy Gillespie 1919- *WhoAmW 93, WhoE 93*
McNulty, Patricia Kathrine 1953- *WhoEmL 93*
McNulty, Paul B. 1940- *WhoScE 91-3*
McNulty, Raymond F. 1946- *St&PR 93*
McNulty, Robert Holmes 1940- *WhoAm 92*
Mcnulty, Roy W.R. 1937- *St&PR 93*

McNulty, Terence Patrick 1938- WhoAm 92
McNulty, Thomas A. 1933- St&PR 93
McNutt, Charles Harrison 1928- WhoSSW 93
McNutt, D. Gayle 1936- WhoSSW 93
McNutt, Dan J. 1938- ScF&FL 92
McNutt, Darrell L. 1945- St&PR 93
McNutt, Jack W. 1934- St&PR 93
McNutt, Jack Wray 1934- WhoSSW 93
McNutt, John Glenn 1951- WhoEmL 93
McNutt, John T. d1992 NewYTBS 92
McNutt, John W., Jr. 1952- WhoSSW 93
McNutt, Kristen Wallwork 1941- WhoAm 92
McNutt, Lee William, Jr. 1925- St&PR 93
McNutt, Merle Vernon 1928- St&PR 93
McNutt, Patrick Anthony 1957- WhoWor 93
McNutt, Richard Hunt 1943- WhoWor 93
McNutt, Robert P. St&PR 93
McNutt, Suzzanne Marie 1962- WhoAmW 93
McNutt, William James 1927- WhoAm 92
McOmber, G.E. 1933- St&PR 93
McOmber, Robert Alan Law&B 92
McOmber, Warren K. 1935- St&PR 93
McOwan, Rennie 1933- ConAu 37NR
McPartland, Jimmy 1907-1991 AnObit 1991, Baker 92, BioIn 17
McPartland, Marian 1918- Baker 92
McPartland, Patrick James Law&B 92
Mc Partlin, John 1918- WhoWrEP 92
McPartlon, James Peter, III 1959- WhoE 93
McPeak, Allan 1938- WhoSSW 93
McPeak, Bill 1926-1991 BioIn 17
McPeak, Merrill Anthony 1936- WhoAm 92
McPeak, Peggy Wright 1949- WhoSSW 93
McPeake, James Mason 1933- WhoSSW 93
Mc Phail, Andrew Tennent 1937- WhoAm 92
McPhail, David M(ichael) 1940- ConAu 38NR, MajAI [port]
McPhail, Graeme H. Law&B 92
McPhail, Irving Pressley AfrAmBi [port]
McPhail, John R. 1945- St&PR 93
McPhail, Neil 1928- St&PR 93
McPhail, Sharon BioIn 17
McPhail, W. Rex Law&B 92
McPharlin, Linda Hendrix BioIn 17
McPhatter, Clyde 1933- SoulM
McPhatter, Clyde 1933-1972 Baker 92
McPhedrain, Larry L. St&PR 93
McPhedran, Norman Tait 1924- WhoAm 92
McPhee, Alexander Hector 1911- WhoAm 92, WhoWor 93
McPhee, Bruce Gordon 1934- St&PR 93
McPhee, Colin 1901-1964 BioIn 17
McPhee, Colin (Carhart) 1900-1964 Baker 92
McPhee, Douglas Michael 1944- St&PR 93
Mc Phee, Henry Roemer 1925- WhoAm 92
McPhee, James ScF&FL 92
McPhee, John 1931- AmWrS3, JrnUS
McPhee, John A. BioIn 17
Mc Phee, John Angus 1931- WhoAm 92, WhoE 93
McPhee, Jonathan WhoAm 92
McPhee, Patricia Ann 1945- St&PR 93
McPhee, Ronald P. 1933- St&PR 93, WhoIns 93
McPhee, Ronald Paul 1933- WhoAm 92
Mc Pheeters, Edwin Keith 1924- WhoAm 92
McPherron, Thomas Ralph 1936- St&PR 93
Mc Pherson, A.J. WhoWrEP 92
McPherson, Aimee Semple 1890-1944 BioIn 17
Mc Pherson, Alice Ruth 1926- WhoAm 92
Mc Pherson, Bruce Rice 1951- WhoWrEP 92
McPherson, David E. 1942- WhoIns 93
McPherson, Deborah Ann Barnes 1957- WhoSSW 93
McPherson, Donald J. WhoAm 92
McPherson, Donald Paxton, III 1941- WhoAm 92
McPherson, Frank A. 1933- St&PR 93
Mc Pherson, Frank Alfred 1933- WhoAm 92, WhoSSW 93
McPherson, Gail WhoAmW 93
McPherson, George R. Law&B 92
McPherson, George Ray 1949- WhoSSW 93
Mc Pherson, Harry Cummings, Jr. 1929- WhoAm 92
Mc Pherson, Irene Wilson 1919- WhoWrEP 92
McPherson, James A. 1943- ConAu 17AS [port]
McPherson, James Alan 1943- BioIn 17, WhoAm 92
Mc Pherson, James Allen 1943- WhoWrEP 92
McPherson, James Birdseye 1828-1864 HarEnMi
McPherson, James M. BioIn 17
Mc Pherson, James Munro 1936- WhoAm 92
McPherson, James R. Law&B 92
McPherson, Janney AmWomPl
McPherson, Jessamyn West d1984 BioIn 17
McPherson, Johanna C. Law&B 92
McPherson, John MiSFD 9
Mc Pherson, John Barkley 1917- WhoAm 92
McPherson, Joseph Law&B 92
McPherson, Judy T. 1936- WhoUN 92
McPherson, Kenneth Francis 1956- WhoSSW 93
McPherson, Larry Eugene 1943- WhoAm 92
McPherson, Luz Maria 1938- WhoSSW 93
McPherson, Mary Patterson 1935- WhoAm 92, WhoAmW 93
McPherson, Melville Peter 1940- WhoAm 92
Mc Pherson, Michael C. 1949- WhoWrEP 92
McPherson, Michael James 1949- St&PR 93
Mc Pherson, Michael Mac Kenzie 1947- WhoWrEP 92
McPherson, Michael Steven 1947- WhoEmL 93
McPherson, Michelle Marie 1959- WhoEmL 93
McPherson, Paul Eugene 1953- WhoEmL 93
Mc Pherson, Paul Francis 1931- WhoAm 92
McPherson, Penny-Lynn Law&B 92
Mc Pherson, Robert Donald 1936- WhoAm 92
Mcpherson, Robert L. 1944- St&PR 93
McPherson, Robert Wesley 1947- WhoE 93
Mc Pherson, Rolf Kennedy WhoAm 92
McPherson, Sally Joan 1958- WhoAmW 93
McPherson, Samuel Dace, III 1957- WhoSSW 93
McPherson, Sandra Jean 1943- WhoAm 92, WhoWrEP 92
McPherson, Scott W. d1992 NewYTBS 92
Mcpherson, Stephen Mather 1937- St&PR 93
McPherson, Tracy Thompson 1961- WhoEmL 93
McPherson, Walter Scott 1884-1990 BioIn 17
McPhilliamy, Fred W. 1931- St&PR 93
McPhillips, George Franklin 1925- St&PR 93
McPhillips, Hugh d1990 BioIn 17
McPike, Frank R., Jr. 1949- St&PR 93
McPike, Richard Huizel Law&B 92
McQuade, Charles B. 1941- St&PR 93
McQuade, Charles Brian 1941- WhoAm 92
McQuade, Eugene M. WhoAm 92
McQuade, Francis X. d1992 BioIn 17, NewYTBS 92
Mc Quade, Henry Ford 1915- WhoAm 92
McQuade, Joseph J. 1952- St&PR 93
McQuade, Lawrence Carroll 1927- St&PR 93, WhoAm 92
Mc Quade, Walter 1922- WhoAm 92, WhoWrEP 92
McQuaid, Brian BioIn 17
Mcquaid, Brian P. 1954- St&PR 93
McQuaid, Frank J. 1929- St&PR 93
McQuaid, J. WhoScE 91-1
McQuaid, J.G. 1918- St&PR 93
McQuaid, J.W. 1949- St&PR 93
McQuaid, Joseph Woodbury 1949- WhoAm 92, WhoE 93
McQuaid, Sarah Linn Allen 1966- WhoE 93
McQuaide, Stan R. 1940- St&PR 93
McQuaide, William Frederick 1934- St&PR 93
McQuarrie, Bruce Cale 1929- WhoAm 92
McQuarrie, Claude Monroe, III 1950- WhoEmL 93
McQuarrie, Donald Gray 1931- WhoAm 92
McQuarrie, Gerald H. 1921- WhoAm 92
McQuarrie, Terry Scott 1942- WhoWor 93
McQuater, Patricia A. Law&B 92
McQuay, Michael D. ScF&FL 92
McQuay, Mike 1949- ScF&FL 92
McQuay, Mike J. 1949- St&PR 93
McQueen, Butterfly 1911- IntDcF 2-3
McQueen, David Randall 1961- WhoSSW 93
McQueen, George W. 1932- WhoIns 93
McQueen, Horace F. 1938- WhoSSW 93
McQueen, J.E. ScF&FL 92
McQueen, Jennifer Robertson 1930- WhoAm 92
McQueen, Jim BioIn 17
McQueen, Justice Ellis 1927- WhoAm 92
McQueen, Kenneth J. St&PR 93
Mc Queen, Marjorie 1927- WhoWrEP 92
McQueen, Patrick M. 1946- St&PR 93
McQueen, Paula F. 1946- St&PR 93
McQueen, Rebecca Hodges 1954- WhoAmW 93, WhoSSW 93
Mc Queen, Robert Charles 1921- WhoAm 92
McQueen, Ronald A. ScF&FL 92
McQueen, Sandra Marilyn 1948- WhoEmL 93
McQueen, Scott Robert 1946- WhoAm 92
McQueen, Steve 1930-1980 BioIn 17, IntDcF 2-3 [port]
McQueen, W.H. Law&B 92
McQueeney, Edward Law&B 92
Mc Queeney, Henry Martin, Sr. 1938- WhoAm 92
McQueeney, Thomas A. 1937- St&PR 93
McQuern, Marcia Alice 1942- St&PR 93, WhoAmW 93
McQuerry, Richard Wayne 1963- WhoSSW 93
McQueston, James K. Law&B 92
McQuiddy, David L., Jr. 1929- St&PR 93
McQuiddy, David Newton, Jr. 1938- WhoAm 92
McQuiddy, Marian Elizabeth 1952- WhoAmW 93
McQuien, Larry Jay Law&B 92
McQuigg, John Dolph 1931- WhoSSW 93
McQuiggan, Robert Francis 1938- St&PR 93
McQuilkin, John Robertson 1927- WhoAm 92
McQuilkin, Muriel BioIn 17
Mc Quilkin, Robert Rennie 1936- WhoWrEP 92
McQuilkin, Robertson 1927- BioIn 17
McQuilkin, William W. d1992 NewYTBS 92
McQuilkin, William W. 1907-1992 BioIn 17
McQuillan, Elizabeth Ann Law&B 92
McQuillan, Joseph Michael 1931- St&PR 93, WhoAm 92
McQuillan, Ray E. Law&B 92
McQuillan, Richard Carl Law&B 92
McQuillan, William Hugh 1935- St&PR 93, WhoAm 92
McQuillen, Albert Lawrence, Jr. 1925- WhoAm 92
McQuillen, Harry A. WhoAm 92
McQuillen, Jeremiah Joseph 1941- WhoE 93, WhoWor 93
McQuillen, Kristen Elizabeth WhoAmW 93
McQuillen, Michael John 1944- WhoE 93
Mc Quillen, Michael Paul 1932- WhoAm 92
McQuillen, Rebecca Ann 1949- WhoAmW 93
McQuillin, Christopher Alan 1960- WhoEmL 93
McQuillin, David L. 1957- St&PR 93
McQuin, Susan Coultrap ConAu 137
McQuinn, Alvin E. 1931- St&PR 93
McQuinn, Donald E. 1930- ScF&FL 92
McQuinn, George Hartley 1909-1978 BiDAMSp 1989
McQuinn, Michelle Renee 1968- WhoAmW 93
McQuinn, Peter BioIn 17
Mc Quinn, William P. 1936- WhoAm 92
McQuiston, Robert Earl 1936- WhoAm 92
McQuitty, David George 1944- WhoSSW 93
McQuivey, R.S. 1939- St&PR 93
McRae, Arnetta Law&B 92
McRae, Barbara Sears 1942- WhoAmW 93
McRae, Barry (Donald) 1935- ConAu 136
Mc Rae, Bettye Martin 1933- WhoWrEP 92
McRae, Branson Jackson 1920- St&PR 93
McRae, Brian 1967- BioIn 17
McRae, Carmen BioIn 17, WhoAm 92
McRae, Carmen 1922- Baker 92, ConMus 9 [port]
McRae, Carol Colin Law&B 92
McRae, Charles R. WhoSSW 93
McRae, Colin D. 1946- St&PR 93
McRae, Douglas C. 1935- WhoScE 91-1
McRae, Edna d1990 BioIn 17
Mc Rae, Garfield 1938- WhoWrEP 92
McRae, Hal 1945- BioIn 17
McRae, Hamilton Eugene, III 1937- WhoAm 92
McRae, Harold Abraham Hal 1945- WhoAm 92
McRae, John Leonidas 1917- WhoWor 93
McRae, John Malcolm 1942- WhoAm 92
Mc Rae, Kenneth Douglas 1925- WhoAm 92
McRae, Robert Malcolm, Jr. 1921- WhoAm 92, WhoSSW 93
Mcrae, Robin S. 1939- St&PR 93
McRae, Russell 1934- BioIn 17, DcChlFi
McRae, Thomas Alexander T. 1957- WhoEmL 93
McRae, Thomas Kenneth 1906- WhoAm 92
McRae, Thomas Watson WhoScE 91-1
McRaith, John Jeremiah 1934- WhoAm 92, WhoSSW 93
McRaney, Gerald BioIn 17, MiSFD 9, WhoAm 92
McRaney, Michael P. 1937- St&PR 93
McRea, Joseph 1946- St&PR 93
McRee, Celia WhoAmW 93, WhoSSW 93, WhoWor 93
McRee, John Browning, Jr. 1950- WhoEmL 93, WhoSSW 93, WhoWor 93
McRee, Sandra Kay 1956- WhoAmW 93
McReynolds, Charles Bertram 1916- WhoAm 92, WhoWor 93
McReynolds, David Hobert 1953- WhoEmL 93, WhoSSW 93
McReynolds, James Clark 1862-1946 OxCSupC [port]
McReynolds, James Evans 1942- WhoSSW 93
McReynolds, Mary Maureen 1940- WhoAmW 93
McReynolds, Michael Patrick 1951- WhoEmL 93
McReynolds, Neil Lawrence 1934- St&PR 93, WhoAm 92
McReynolds, Pamela Kay 1953- WhoAmW 93
McReynolds, Richard A. 1944- WhoSSW 93
McReynolds, W. Sam 1937- St&PR 93
McRight, Dan A. 1940- WhoSSW 93
McRitchie, Bruce D. 1938- St&PR 93
McRitchie, Bruce Dean 1938- WhoAm 92
McRitchie, Catherine Constance 1956- WhoAmW 93
McRobbie, Bonnie Jean Law&B 92
McRobbie, Kenneth 1929- WhoCanL 92
McRoberts, Joyce 1941- WhoAmW 93
McRoberts, Robert Arthur 1928- St&PR 93
McRobie, Fred S. Law&B 92
McRorie, Alice Rhyne 1946- WhoEmL 93
McRorie, William Edward Law&B 92
McRorie, William Edward 1940- St&PR 93, WhoAm 92, WhoIns 93
Mc Rostie, Clair Neil 1930- WhoAm 92
McShan, Clyde Griffin, II 1945- WhoSSW 93
McShan, John Tyler 1926- St&PR 93
Mc Shane, Claudette WhoWrEP 92
McShane, David R. 1941- St&PR 93
McShane, Edward Joseph, Jr. 1932- St&PR 93
McShane, Eugene Francis 1946- WhoEmL 93
McShane, John Francis 1928- St&PR 93
McShane, Julian J. d1992 BioIn 17
McShane, Julian J., Jr. d1992 NewYTBS 92
McShane, Kitty 1898-1964 See Lucan, Arthur 1887-1954 & McShane, Kitty 1898-1964 QDrFCA 92
McShane, Mark ScF&FL 92
McShane, Maureen M. Law&B 92
Mcshane, Michael 1952- St&PR 93
McShane, Michael Albert 1947- WhoE 93
McShane, Stephen J. 1943- St&PR 93
McShann, Jay 1909- Baker 92
McSharry, Nancy Ellen 1960- WhoAmW 93
McShea, Joseph 1907-1991 BioIn 17
McShea, Robert Joseph, Jr. 1940- WhoE 93
McShea, Sandra Wharton Law&B 92
McSheehy, Cornelia Marie 1947- WhoEmL 93
McSheehy, Trevor William 1933- WhoScE 91-3
McShefferty, John 1929- WhoAm 92
Mc Sheffrey, Gerald Rainey 1931- WhoAm 92
McSherry, Frank D., Jr. 1927- ScF&FL 92
McSherry, James Francis 1953- WhoEmL 93
McShirley, Susan Ruth 1945- WhoAmW 93
McShulkis, Joseph Jerome 1931- St&PR 93
McSorley, Arthur 1928- St&PR 93
McSorley, Danny Eugene 1960- WhoSSW 93
McSorley, Edward 1949- St&PR 93
McSorley, Marion Joseph 1933- St&PR 93
McSpadden, Bruce Lynn Law&B 92

Mc Spadden, Peter Ford 1930- WhoAm 92
McSpaden, Cheri Lynn 1953- WhoAmW 93
McSwain, Barbara Powell 1949- WhoAmW 93
McSwain, Donald D. 1936- St&PR 93
McSwain, Lon Arild 1953- WhoEmL 93
McSwain, Richard Horace 1949- WhoAm 92, WhoEmL 93, WhoSSW 93
McSwain, Shawn L. Law&B 92
McSweeney, Brenda Gael 1943- WhoUN 92
McSweeney, Edward F. d1991 BioIn 17
McSweeney, Frances Kaye 1948- WhoAm 92, WhoAmW 93, WhoEmL 93
McSweeney, Linda H. 1956- WhoE 93
McSweeney, Maurice J. 1938- WhoAm 92
McSweeney, Michael T. 1937- St&PR 93
McSweeney, Sean B. Law&B 92
McSweeney, William Lincoln, Jr. 1930- WhoAm 92
McSweeny, Austin John 1946- WhoEmL 93
McSweeny, John Edward 1936- WhoAm 92
McSweeny, William Francis 1929- WhoAm 92
McSwiggan, Jacqueline N. 1953- St&PR 93
McSwiney, C. Ronald 1943- St&PR 93
McSwiney, Charles Ronald 1943- WhoAm 92
Mc Swiney, James Wilmer 1915- WhoAm 92
McTaggart, David Fraser 1932- BioIn 17
McTaggart, Timothy Thomas 1949- WhoE 93
McTaggart-Cowan, Ian 1910- WhoAm 92
McTague, Jerome J. 1920- St&PR 93
McTague, John Paul 1938- St&PR 93, WhoAm 92
McTague, Shirley Fauber, Ms. 1924- St&PR 93
McTarnaghan, Roy E. WhoAm 92
Mc Tavish, John Elser 1926- WhoAm 92
McTeague, Bertrand L. 1935- St&PR 93
McTeague, Linda Bragdon WhoAmW 93, WhoE 93
McTeer, Everett 1942- St&PR 93
McTeer, Scott BioIn 17
McTernan, Maureen E. 1955- WhoIns 93
McTernan, Maureen Elizabeth Law&B 92
McTiernan, Charles E., Jr. Law&B 92
McTiernan, John 1951- MiSFD 9
McTighe, Robert Michael 1955- St&PR 93
McTighe, William J. 1949- St&PR 93
McTigue, Bernard Francis 1946- WhoAm 92
McTigue, James Joseph 1951- WhoEmL 93
Mc Tigue, John Francis 1960- WhoE 93
McTigue, Mary E. WhoAmW 93
McTigue, Maurice Patrick 1940- WhoAsAP 91
McTyeire, Holland Nimmons, IV 1930- St&PR 93
McTyeire, Rex Holland 1949- WhoEmL 93, WhoSSW 93
Mctyre, H. Edward 1944- St&PR 93
McVadon, Eric Alton, Jr. 1936- WhoAm 92
Mc Vay, Barry Lee 1951- WhoWrEP 92
McVay, Donald Wylie, Jr. 1953- WhoSSW 93
McVean, Duncan Edward 1936- St&PR 93
McVeigh, John Newburne, III 1947- St&PR 93
McVeigh, Karen Hendrika Geerte 1961- WhoE 93
McVeigh, Maureen ScF&FL 92
McVerry, Thomas Leo 1938- WhoAm 92, WhoSSW 93
McVetta, Roger Frank 1939- St&PR 93
McVety, James Robert 1941- St&PR 93
McVey, Devon Palmquist 1961- WhoEmL 93
McVey, Diane Elaine 1953- WhoAmW 93, WhoEmL 93
McVey, Eugene Steven 1927- WhoAm 92
McVey, Henry Hanna, III 1935- WhoAm 92
McVey, James Paul 1943- WhoE 93
McVey, James William 1931- WhoAm 92
McVey, Kenneth 1939- St&PR 93
McVey, Kenneth Kent 1923- St&PR 93
McVey, Samuel David 1955- WhoEmL 93
McVicar, Jamie Marshall Law&B 92
McVicar, Ronald C. 1946- St&PR 93
McVicar, Sherry Fisher 1952- WhoAmW 93
McVicker, H. Keith 1943- WhoIns 93
McVicker, J. William 1963- St&PR 93
McVicker, Jesse Jay 1911- WhoAm 92
McVicker, Mary Ellen Harshbarger 1951- WhoAmW 93
Mc Vie, Christine Perfect 1943- WhoAm 92
McVie, J. Gordon 1945- WhoScE 91-1
McVie, John 1942- See Fleetwood, Mick 1942- Baker 92
McVie, John Gordon 1945- WhoScE 91-3
McWade, Charles P. 1944- St&PR 93, WhoAm 92
McWain, Lyman Jay 1942- St&PR 93
McWard, Richard A. 1938- St&PR 93
McWeeny, Philip Law&B 92
McWethy, Patricia Joan 1946- WhoAm 92
Mc Wey, Michael 1953- WhoWrEP 92
McWha, J.A. WhoScE 91-1
McWhan, Denis Bayman 1935- WhoAm 92
McWherter, Ned Ray 1930- WhoAm 92, WhoSSW 93, WhoWor 93
McWhiney, Grady 1928- WhoAm 92
McWhinney, Henry G. WhoAm 92
McWhinney, Ian Renwick 1926- WhoAm 92
McWhinney, Madeline H. 1922- St&PR 93, WhoAm 92
McWhinney, Rodney O. 1933- St&PR 93
McWhinnie, David E. 1944- St&PR 93
McWhinnie, William Robin WhoScE 91-1
McWhinnie, William Robin 1937- WhoWor 93
McWhirter, Don Ray 1926- St&PR 93
McWhirter, George 1939- WhoCanL 92
McWhirter, Glenna Suzanne 1929- WhoAm 92
McWhirter, James Herman 1924- WhoAm 92
McWhirter, Joan Brighton 1954- WhoAmW 93
McWhirter, Norris Dewar 1925- WhoWor 93
McWhirter, Richard A. 1934- St&PR 93
McWhirter, William Buford 1918- WhoAm 92
McWhorter, Alan Louis 1930- WhoAm 92
McWhorter, Alexander Cumming 1771-1808 BioIn 17
McWhorter, Anthony L. 1949- St&PR 93
McWhorter, George T. 1931- ScF&FL 92
McWhorter, George Turberville, Jr. 1931- WhoSSW 93
Mc Whorter, Hezzie Boyd 1923- WhoAm 92
McWhorter, Kathleen 1953- WhoAmW 93, WhoSSW 93
McWhorter, Mildred BioIn 17
McWhorter, Ralph Clayton 1933- St&PR 93, WhoAm 92
McWhorter, Robert Dale, Jr. 1953- WhoEmL 93
McWilliam, Candia 1955- ConAu 136
McWilliam, James L. 1928- St&PR 93
McWilliams, Albert T., Jr. Law&B 92
McWilliams, Bayard Taylor WhoE 93
McWilliams, Betty Jane WhoAm 92, WhoAmW 93
McWilliams, Brent Nelson 1957- St&PR 93
McWilliams, Bruce Wayne 1932- WhoAm 92
McWilliams, Carey 1905-1980 ScF&FL 92
McWilliams, Edwin Joseph 1919- WhoAm 92
McWilliams, Elizabeth Ann 1950- WhoAmW 93
McWilliams, Harry Kenneth 1907- WhoE 93
McWilliams, John B. Law&B 92
McWilliams, John B. 1947- St&PR 93
McWilliams, John Michael 1939- WhoAm 92
McWilliams, Karen 1943- BioIn 17
McWilliams, Margaret Ann 1929- WhoAm 92, WhoAmW 93
McWilliams, Michael G. 1952- WhoAm 92
McWilliams, Mike C. 1948- WhoEmL 93
McWilliams, Robert Hugh 1916- WhoAm 92
McWilliams, Robert P. Law&B 92
McWilliams, Sara Pettes 1946- WhoAmW 93
McWilliams, Sonja Lee 1947- WhoEmL 93
McWilliams, Spencer Albert 1944- WhoSSW 93
McWilliams, Thomas F. 1957- WhoIns 93
McWilliams, Wilson Carey 1933- ConAu 40NR
MdZain Yang Berhormat Pehin Orang Kaya, Pehin Dato Haji 1936- WhoAsAP 91
Meacham, Andrew W. 1954- WhoSSW 93
Meacham, Arthur Paul 1946- WhoWrEP 92
Meacham, Beth 1951- ScF&FL 92
Meacham, Charles Harding 1925- WhoAm 92
Meacham, Ellis Kirby 1913- WhoWrEP 92
Meacham, John Allen 1944- WhoE 93
Meacham, Milo Louis, Jr. 1946- WhoEmL 93, WhoSSW 93
Meacham, Niles Corley 1932- St&PR 93
Meacham, Norma Grace 1952- WhoEmL 93
Meacham, Standish, Jr. 1932- WhoAm 92
Meacham, William Feland 1913- WhoAm 92
Meachin, David James Percy 1941- WhoAm 92, WhoE 93, WhoWor 93
Meachum, John W. Law&B 92
Meacock, Peter A. 1947- WhoScE 91-1
Meacock, Peter Anthony WhoScE 91-1
Mead, Adelaide B. AmWomPl
Mead, Andrea 1932- BioIn 17
Mead, Barbara Cheryl 1944- WhoSSW 93
Mead, Beverley Tupper 1923- WhoAm 92
Mead, Carver BioIn 17
Mead, Carver Andress 1934- WhoAm 92
Mead, Dana George 1936- St&PR 93, WhoAm 92
Mead, David Paul 1949- St&PR 93
Mead, Denys John WhoScE 91-1
Mead, Edward M. 1926- St&PR 93
Mead, Elwood 1858-1936 BioIn 17
Mead, Frank F. 1929- St&PR 93
Mead, Frank Waldreth 1922- WhoSSW 93
Mead, Gary Michael 1946- WhoSSW 93
Mead, George W., II 1927- St&PR 93
Mead, George Wilson, II 1927- WhoAm 92
Mead, Gilbert Dunbar 1930- WhoAm 92
Mead, Grace Hartley Jenkins d1991 BioIn 17
Mead, Harriet Council WhoAmW 93
Mead, Harriet Councill WhoWrEP 92
Mead, Hyrum Anderson 1947- St&PR 93
Mead, James M., Jr. 1918- St&PR 93
Mead, John BioIn 17
Mead, John Milton 1924- WhoAm 92
Mead, John R. 1942- St&PR 93
Mead, Jude 1919-1992 BioIn 17
Mead, Kevin William 1921- WhoWor 93
Mead, Lawrence Myers, Jr. 1918- WhoAm 92
Mead, Margaret 1901-1978 BioIn 17, IntDcAn
Mead, Mark Nathaniel 1961- WhoWrEP 92
Mead, Nathaniel BioIn 17
Mead, Philip Bartlett 1937- WhoAm 92
Mead, Robert E. 1938- WhoAm 92
Mead, Robert Norman 1948- WhoAm 92, WhoSSW 93
Mead, Roger WhoScE 91-1
Mead, States Morris d1991 BioIn 17
Mead, Susan W.A. 1950- St&PR 93
Mead, Syd BioIn 17, ScF&FL 92
Mead, Terry Eileen 1950- WhoWor 93
Mead, Theodore Charles 1931- WhoWor 93
Mead, Wayland M. 1931- St&PR 93
Mead, Wayland Mc Con Law&B 92
Mead, Wayland McCon 1931- WhoIns 93
Mead, William Allen 1943- St&PR 93
Mead, William J. 1927- St&PR 93
Meade, Adelaide B. AmWomPl
Meade, Carol Anne 1948- WhoAmW 93
Meade, Charles Richard 1826-1858 BioIn 17
Meade, David 1767-1799 BioIn 17
Meade, David Tolson 1961- St&PR 93
Meade, Donald F. Law&B 92
Meade, Donna BioIn 17
Meade, Donna Marie 1954- WhoSSW 93
Meade, Dorothy Winifred 1935- WhoAmW 93
Meade, E. Louise AmWomPl
Meade, Edward J., Jr. BioIn 17
Meade, Everard Kidder, Jr. 1919- WhoAm 92
Meade, Gary S. Law&B 92
Meade, Gary Scott 1946- St&PR 93
Meade, George Gordon 1815-1872 BioIn 17, HarEnMi
Meade, Henry William Matthew 1823-1865 BioIn 17
Meade, J.E. 1907- BioIn 17
Meade, James Edward 1907- BioIn 17, WhoAm 92, WhoWor 93
Meade, James F. 1942- St&PR 93
Meade, Joe Neal 1939- St&PR 93
Meade, Joseph F., Jr. 1921- St&PR 93
Meade, Joy 1959- WhoAmW 93
Meade, Norman SoulM
Meade, Patricia Sue 1960- WhoAmW 93, WhoEmL 93
Meade, Richard Alan 1952- St&PR 93
Meade, Richard E. Law&B 92
Meade, Richard Robert Law&B 92
Meade, Thomas B. 1915-1991 BioIn 17
Meade, Thomas F. 1934- St&PR 93
Meade, Thomas Wilson WhoScE 91-1
Meade, Walter Wathen 1930- WhoWrEP 92
Meaden, Charles Law&B 92
Meader, Cortland J. 1935- St&PR 93
Meader, Darrell Lee 1941- WhoSSW 93
Meader, George 1888-1963 Baker 92
Meader, Jean H. Law&B 92
Meader, John Daniel 1931- WhoE 93, WhoWor 93
Meader, Ralph Gibson 1904- WhoAm 92
Meaders, Paul Le Sourd 1930- WhoAm 92
Meades, Rob 1964- ScF&FL 92
Meade-Thayer, Nancy Jane 1959- WhoEmL 93
Meadley, Walter E. 1932- St&PR 93
Meadlock, James W. 1933- St&PR 93, WhoSSW 93
Meadnis, Constance AmWomPl
Meador, Alan R. 1943- St&PR 93
Meador, Charles Lawrence 1946- WhoE 93, WhoEmL 93
Meador, Daniel John 1926- WhoAm 92
Meador, Donald J. 1937- St&PR 93
Meador, H. David d1992 NewYTBS 92
Meador, Joe d1980 BioIn 17
Meador, John Milward, Jr. 1946- WhoAm 92
Meador, Prentice Avery, Jr. 1938- WhoSSW 93
Meadors, Allen Coats 1947- WhoEmL 93
Meadors, Emily Jeanette 1952- WhoAmW 93
Meadors, Howard Clarence, Jr. 1938- WhoAm 92
Meadors, Joe Richard 1931- St&PR 93
Meadow, Lynne 1946- WhoAm 92, WhoE 93
Meadow, Samuel Roy WhoScE 91-1
Meadowcraft, Lees 1899- BioIn 17
Meadowcroft, Robert Stanley 1937- WhoAm 92
Meadows, A(rthur) J(ack) 1934- ConAu 137
Meadows, Arthur Jack WhoScE 91-1
Meadows, Audrey WhoAm 92
Meadows, Barbara Mitchell 1937- WhoSSW 93
Meadows, Donald Frederick 1937- WhoAm 92
Meadows, Douglas Berry 1951- St&PR 93
Meadows, Earle Elmer 1913- BiDAMSp 1989
Meadows, George Lee 1938- WhoAm 92
Meadows, Glenn Hargus 1929- St&PR 93
Meadows, Gregory Paul 1962- WhoE 93
Meadows, Harry 1937- St&PR 93
Meadows, Jack ConAu 137
Meadows, James Dartlin 1957- WhoEmL 93, WhoSSW 93
Meadows, James R. 1953- St&PR 93
Meadows, Lynn W. 1943- St&PR 93
Meadows, Martha Elizabeth 1940- WhoAmW 93
Meadows, Millie 1946- WhoAmW 93
Meadows, Patricia BioIn 17
Meadows, Paul D. 1926- St&PR 93
Meadows, Peter Swithin 1936- WhoWor 93
Meadows, Robert E. 1961- St&PR 93
Meadows, Sharon M. 1950- St&PR 93
Meadows, Sharon Marie 1950- WhoAm 92, WhoAmW 93
Meadows, Steven F. Law&B 92
Meads, Donald Edward 1920- St&PR 93, WhoAm 92, WhoE 93
Meads, Walter Frederick 1923- WhoAm 92, WhoWor 93
Meadway, Jay Kenneth 1953- WhoEmL 93
Meager, A. Pier Law&B 92
Meagher, Diane Marie 1959- WhoAmW 93
Meagher, George E. 1895-1967 ScF&FL 92
Meagher, George Vincent 1919- WhoAm 92
Meagher, John B. 1936- St&PR 93
Meagher, Joseph B. 1945- St&PR 93
Meagher, Katherine AmWomPl
Meagher, Kevin Charles 1954- St&PR 93
Meagher, Mark Joseph 1932- St&PR 93, WhoAm 92
Meagher, Maude 1895?-1977? ScF&FL 92
Meagher, Michael 1843-1881 BioIn 17
Meagher, Michael J. 1942- St&PR 93
Meagher, Robert Stephen 1958- WhoE 93
Meagher, Thomas F. 1930- St&PR 93
Meagher, Thomas W. Law&B 92
Meagher, William H. Law&B 92
Meahan, Chip BioIn 17
Meahl, Jeffrey D. 1954- St&PR 93
Meaker, Isabelle Jackson 1874- AmWomPl
Meaker, M. J. ConAu 37NR, MajAI
Meaker, Marijane BioIn 17
Meaker, Marijane (Agnes) 1927- ConAu 37NR, MajAI [port], WhoAm 92
Meakin, John David 1934- WhoE 93
Meakin, Rob BioIn 17
Meakin, Viola ScF&FL 92

Meakins, Gene 1927- *St&PR 93*
Meal, Larie 1939- *WhoAmW 93, WhoWor 93*
Meale, Richard (Graham) 1932- *Baker 92*
Mealey, Brian Luke 1959- *WhoSSW 93*
Mealey, Linda Jeanne 1955- *WhoAmW 93*
Mealey, Michael Palmer 1940- *WhoE 93*
Mealing, Jerrie Jay *Law&B 92*
Meallier, Pierre 1938- *WhoScE 91-2*
Mealman, Glenn Edward 1934- *WhoAm 92, WhoSSW 93*
Mealor, William Theodore, Jr. 1940- *WhoAm 92*
Mealy, Dennis C. 1952- *St&PR 93, WhoIns 93*
Mealy, Mark Williams 1957- *WhoSSW 93*
Meaney, Daniel Joseph, Jr. 1936- *St&PR 93*
Meaney, Dee Morrison 1939- *ScF&FL 92*
Meaney, Kevin *BioIn 17*
Meaney, Lottie M. *AmWomPl*
Meaney, Michael Peter 1961- *WhoEmL 93*
Meaney, Patrick d1992 *NewYTBS 92*
Meaney, Patrick, Sir 1925- *St&PR 93*
Meaney, Patrick Michael 1925- *WhoAm 92*
Meaney, Richard Anthony 1942- *WhoScE 91-3*
Means, Cyril Chesnut, Jr. d1992 *NewYTBS 92*
Means, Cyril Chesnut, Jr. 1918- *WhoAm 92*
Means, David Hammond 1928- *WhoAm 92*
Means, Donald Bruce 1941- *WhoSSW 93*
Means, Elizabeth Rose Thayer 1960- *WhoE 93*
Means, Florence Crannell 1891-1980 *ConAu 37NR, MajAI [port]*
Means, Florence Crannell 1897- *AmWomPl*
Means, Fred Ernest *WhoE 93*
Means, Gardiner Coit 1896-1988 *BioIn 17*
Means, George Robert 1907- *WhoAm 92, WhoWor 93*
Means, Jack L. 1935- *St&PR 93*
Means, James Andrew 1943- *WhoSSW 93*
Means, John Barkley 1939- *WhoAm 92, WhoWor 93*
Means, Lane Lewis 1951- *WhoEmL 93*
Means, Marianne 1934- *WhoAm 92*
Means, Raymond B. 1930- *WhoAm 92*
Means, Richard K., Jr. 1945- *St&PR 93*
Meany, Daniel 1930- *St&PR 93*
Meany, Dennis M. *Law&B 92*
Meany, George *DcCPCAm*
Meany, George 1894-1980 *BioIn 17, ColdWar 1 [port]*
Meany, Helen d1991 *BioIn 17*
Meany, John Stewart, Jr. 1945- *St&PR 93*
Meany, William F. 1934- *St&PR 93*
Meany, William George 1894-1980 *BioIn 17*
Meara, Anne *WhoAm 92, WhoAmW 93*
Meares, Paula Gwendolyn *WhoAmW 93*
Mearns, David Chambers 1899-1981 *BioIn 17*
Mears, A.W. Downing, Jr. 1953- *St&PR 93*
Mears, Anna Maria 1954- *WhoSSW 93*
Mears, Cliff 1953- *WhoEmL 93*
Mears, Darlene Wanda 1946- *WhoEmL 93*
Mears, Ralph Marvin 1934- *St&PR 93*
Mears, Richard Walter 1940- *WhoSSW 93*
Mears, Rick *BioIn 17*
Mears, Rick Ravon 1951- *WhoAm 92*
Mears, Roger *BioIn 17*
Mears, Rona Robbins 1938- *WhoAmW 93*
Mears, Sandra A. 1954- *WhoAmW 93*
Mears, Walter Robert 1935- *St&PR 93, WhoAm 92*
Mearsheimer, John Joseph 1947- *WhoAm 92*
Mease, Cecil W. 1933- *St&PR 93*
Measer, George John 1925- *St&PR 93*
Measham, Anthony Ramond 1934- *WhoUN 92*
Meason, Robert D. 1947- *St&PR 93*
Meath, Brian Patrick *Law&B 92*
Meath, Michael *ConAu 136*
Meathe, Philip J. 1926- *St&PR 93*
Meats, Stephen 1944- *WhoWrEP 92*
Meatte, Luke L. 1923- *St&PR 93*
Meaux, Huey P. 1929- *SoulM*
Mebane, Alfred Holt 1932- *WhoSSW 93*
Mebane, Barbara Margot 1947- *WhoAmW 93, WhoEmL 93*
Mebane, David C. *Law&B 92*
Mebane, David Cummins 1933- *St&PR 93, WhoAm 92*
Mebane, George Allen 1929- *WhoSSW 93*
Mebane, Mary Virginia 1959- *WhoEmL 93*
Mebane, William Black 1927- *WhoAm 92*
Mebane, William deBerniere 1949- *WhoAm 92*
Mebiame, Leon 1934- *WhoAfr*
Mebkhout, Mohammed Lazhari 1936- *WhoScE 91-2*
Meblin, Rose Charlotte *AmWomPl*
Mebold, Ulrich 1939- *WhoScE 91-3*
Mebus, Charles Albert 1932- *WhoE 93*
Mebus, Robert Joseph 1943- *St&PR 93*
Mebust, Winston Keith 1933- *WhoAm 92*
Mecca, Donato Anthony 1904- *WhoWrEP 92*
Mecca, Joseph Nicholas 1947- *WhoAm 92, WhoE 93*
Mech, Terrence Francis 1953- *WhoE 93*
Mechai Viravaidhya *BioIn 17*
Mecham, Evan *BioIn 17*
Mecham, Kenneth Dale 1943- *St&PR 93*
Mechaneck, Ruth Sara 1941- *WhoAmW 93*
Mechanic, David 1936- *WhoAm 92, WhoE 93*
Mechel, F.P. 1930- *WhoScE 91-3*
Mechem, Charles S., Jr. 1930- *St&PR 93*
Mechem, Edwin Leard 1912- *WhoAm 92*
Mechem, James Harlan 1923- *WhoWrEP 92*
Mechem, John Edgar 1928- *St&PR 93*
Mechem, Kirke (Lewis) 1925- *Baker 92*
Mecherle, G. Robert 1930- *WhoAm 92*
Mechigian, Nancy Lee 1941- *WhoAmW 93*
Mechlem, Daphne Jo 1946- *WhoAmW 93*
Mechlin, George Francis 1923- *WhoAm 92*
Mechling, Ronald Eugene 1946- *St&PR 93*
Mechling, William C. *Law&B 92*
Mechlin-Levitt, Ellen Joan *Law&B 92*
Mechnikov, Ilya Ilich 1845-1916 *BioIn 17*
Mecholsky, John Joseph, Jr. 1944- *WhoSSW 93*
Mecia, Joseph Anthony *Law&B 92*
Meciar, Vladimir 1942- *WhoWor 93*
Mecimore, Charles Douglas 1934- *WhoAm 92*
Mecir, Jan 1925- *WhoScE 91-4*
Meck, Christopher R. 1944- *St&PR 93*
Meck, J.P. *Law&B 92*
Meck, Nadezhda von 1831-1894 *Baker 92*
Meck, Nancy Ellen 1954- *WhoAmW 93*
Meck, William L., II *Law&B 92*
Mecke, Theodore Hart McCalla, Jr. 1923- *WhoAm 92*
Meckel, David *BioIn 17*
Meckes, Waldemar 1920- *St&PR 93*
Meckl, Peter Heinrich 1958- *WhoEmL 93*
Mecklem, Todd 1965- *ScF&FL 92*
Mecklenburg, Daniel P. *Law&B 92*
Mecklenburg, Gary A. *WhoAm 92*
Mecklenburg, Karl Bernard 1960- *BiDAMSp 1989*
Meckler, Alan Marshall 1945- *WhoAm 92*
Meckler, Jerome 1941- *ScF&FL 92*
Meckler, Lawrence M. *Law&B 92*
Meckler, M. Jay d1991 *BioIn 17*
Meckler, Mark J. *Law&B 92*
Meckley, Daniel G., III 1923- *St&PR 93*
Meckley, David Grant 1951- *St&PR 93*
Meckley, Paul E. 1925- *St&PR 93*
Meckley, Thomas A. 1943- *St&PR 93*
Mecklosky, Morton Mathew 1932- *WhoE 93*
Meclewski, Ryszard S. 1926- *WhoScE 91-4*
Mecum, Barbara L. 1955- *WhoAmW 93*
Mecum, Jacqueline Ann 1938- *WhoAmW 93*
Mecz, Jane B. *Law&B 92*
Medaglia, Mary-Elizabeth 1947- *WhoEmL 93*
Medak, Peter *MiSFD 9*
Medalie, Gladys Vivian *BiDAMSp 1989*
Medalie, Richard James 1929- *WhoAm 92*
Medalie, Sherman George 1929- *St&PR 93*
Medani, Charles Richard 1949- *WhoAm 92*
Medanich, David K. 1956- *St&PR 93*
Medaris, John Bruce 1902- *BioIn 17*
Medary, Rhoda d1981 *BioIn 17*
Medary, Samuel 1801-1864 *BioIn 17*
Medavoy, Mike 1941- *ConTFT 10, St&PR 93, WhoAm 92*
Medawar, P.B. 1915-1987 *BioIn 17*
Medawar, Peter Brian 1915-1987 *BioIn 17*
Medbery, Arnold Bunker, Jr. 1955- *WhoEmL 93, WhoSSW 93*
Medcalf, Gordon Edward *WhoScE 91-1*
Medcalf, Robert Randolph, Jr. 1949- *WhoWrEP 92*
Meddaugh, R. Jay 1942- *St&PR 93*
Meddleton, Francis Charles 1942- *WhoSSW 93*
Meddock, Larry Joseph 1946- *St&PR 93*
Meddock, Wayne Douglas 1956- *WhoSSW 93*
Mede, Gary E. 1936- *St&PR 93*
Medearis, Angela Shelf 1956- *BlkAuII 92, SmATA 72 [port]*
Medearis, Donald Norman, Jr. 1927- *WhoAm 92*
Medearis, Kenneth Gordon 1930- *WhoWor 93*
Medearis, Roger Norman 1920- *WhoAm 92*
Medecin, Jacques *BioIn 17*
Medeiros, Aldo da Cunha 1948- *WhoWor 93*
Medeiros, Maria de *BioIn 17*
Medeiros, Peter William 1946- *WhoE 93, WhoEmL 93*
Medeiros, Prisca D. Bicoy 1928- *WhoWrEP 92*
Medeiros, Ronald C. 1942- *St&PR 93*
Medeiros, Thomas P. 1953- *St&PR 93*
Medek, Tilo 1940- *Baker 92*
Medel, Ariel Reynoso 1955- *St&PR 93*
Medel, Rebecca *BioIn 17*
Medellin, Octavio 1907- *HispAmA*
Medem, Wlodzimierz 1879-1923 *PolBiDi*
Medema, Ken *BioIn 17*
Meden, Harold S. 1928- *St&PR 93*
Meden, Robert Paul 1950- *WhoE 93*
Meder, Bennett J. 1949- *St&PR 93*
Meder, Cornel 1938- *WhoWor 93*
Meder, Janusz Andrzej 1947- *WhoScE 91-4*
Meder, Johann Valentin 1649?-1719 *Baker 92*
Medero, Joanne Trimble 1954- *WhoAmW 93*
Mederos, Carolina Luisa 1947- *WhoAm 92, WhoAmW 93*
Medford, Cecil L. *Law&B 92*
Medford, Dale L. 1950- *St&PR 93*
Medford, Dick 1939- *WhoSSW 93*
Medford, Don *MiSFD 9*
Medford, Donna Jean 1946- *WhoEmL 93*
Medford, Mark O. 1946- *St&PR 93*
Medford-Rosow, Traci J. *Law&B 92*
Medgyesi, Gyorgy A. 1936- *WhoScE 91-4*
Medgyesy, John P. 1932- *St&PR 93*
Mediate, Rocco *BioIn 17*
Medici, Franco 1956- *WhoWor 93*
Medici, Giovanni de' 1498-1526 *HarEnMi*
Medici, Lorenzo de' 1449-1492 *BioIn 17*
Medici, Stephen Francis 1952- *St&PR 93*
Medici family *OxDcOp*
Medicis, Catherine de, Queen 1519-1589 *BioIn 17*
Medicus, Heinrich Adolf 1918- *WhoAm 92*
Medicus, Hildegard Julie 1928- *WhoAmW 93*
Medill, Joseph 1823-1899 *JrnUS*
Medill, Mary 1936- *WhoWrEP 92*
Medill, Mary Lawson *WhoAmW 93*
Medin, A. Louis 1925- *WhoAm 92, WhoSSW 93*
Medin, Donna Mae 1932- *WhoWrEP 92*
Medin, Julia Adele 1929- *WhoSSW 93*
Medin, Lowell Ansgard 1932- *WhoWor 93*
Medin, Myron James, Jr. 1931- *WhoAm 92*
Medina, Augusto E.G. 1949- *WhoScE 91-3*
Medina, Benny *BioIn 17*
Medina, David 1948- *WhoE 93*
Medina, David Miguel *Law&B 92*
Medina, Everard Joseph 1930- *WhoWor 93*
Medina, Harold R. 1888-1990 *BioIn 17*
Medina, Harold R. 1912-1991 *BioIn 17*
Medina, Harold R., Sr. 1888-1991 *HispAmA*
Medina, Harold Raymond, III 1938- *WhoWor 93*
Medina, Jorge 1951- *WhoSSW 93*
Medina, Jose Collado 1952- *WhoWor 93*
Medina, Jose Enrique 1926- *WhoAm 92*
Medina, Kathryn Bach *WhoAm 92, WhoWrEP 92*
Medina, Leilani 1967- *WhoE 93*
Medina, Louis M. 1957- *St&PR 93*
Medina, Manuel 1952- *WhoScE 91-3*
Medina, Mary Helen *Law&B 92*
Medina, Pablo 1948- *BioIn 17*
Medina, Patricia 1919?- *SweetSg D [port]*
Medina, Pedro Andres 1960- *WhoWor 93*
Medina, Salvador 1950- *WhoWor 93*
Medina, Standish Forde, Jr. 1940- *WhoAm 92*
Medina Haro, Adolfo Facundo 1954- *WhoWor 93*
Medina Romero, Jesus 1921- *DcMexL*
Medina Sidonia, duque de 1550-1619 *BioIn 17*
Meding, Charles W. *WhoAm 92*
Meding, Charles W. 1944- *St&PR 93*
Medinger, Gregor W. 1943- *St&PR 93*
Medins *Baker 92*
Medins, Janis 1890-1966 *Baker 92*
Medins, Jazeps 1877-1947 *Baker 92*
Medins, Jekabs 1885-1971 *Baker 92*
Medio, Dolores 1914- *BioIn 17*
Medioni, Jean-Louis *Law&B 92*
Medis, Lynn Rebis 1961- *WhoSSW 93*
Meditch, James Stephen 1934- *WhoAm 92*
Meditz, Walter Joseph 1917- *WhoAm 92*
Mediz Bolio, Antonio 1884-1957 *DcMexL*
Medland, Anthony John *WhoScE 91-1*
Medland, John 1946-1990 *BioIn 17*
Medland, Mary Elizabeth 1952- *WhoE 93*
Medland, William James 1944- *WhoAm 92*
Medlen, Virginia Shaw 1949- *WhoEmL 93*
Medler, Albert 1913- *St&PR 93*
Medler, Rodney A. 1936- *St&PR 93*
Medley, Bill *SoulM*
Medley, Clayton Edward 1948- *WhoAm 92*
Medley, Donald Matthias 1917- *WhoAm 92, WhoSSW 93*
Medley, Gaines L. 1914- *St&PR 93*
Medley, Marc Allen 1962- *WhoE 93*
Medley, Mark J. 1953- *St&PR 93*
Medley, Mary Dee 1943- *WhoAmW 93*
Medley, Nancy May 1948- *WhoAmW 93*
Medley, Ronald D. 1934- *St&PR 93*
Medley, Sherrilyn 1946- *WhoAmW 93, WhoEmL 93*
Medley, William J. 1930- *St&PR 93*
Medlin, Dennis B. 1942- *WhoIns 93*
Medlin, Donna Jane 1955- *WhoAmW 93*
Medlin, John Grimes, Jr. 1933- *St&PR 93, WhoAm 92, WhoSSW 93*
Medlin, Kay Cowden *Law&B 92*
Medlin, Terry 1947- *WhoE 93*
Medlock, Ann 1933- *WhoAm 92*
Medlock, Donald Larson 1927- *WhoAm 92*
Medlock, Norman Dudley 1949- *WhoSSW 93*
Medlock, Randall Glenn 1946- *WhoSSW 93*
Medlock, Thomas Travis 1934- *WhoAm 92, WhoSSW 93*
Medman, Martha *AmWomPl*
Mednick, Lisa *Law&B 92*
Mednick, Murray 1939- *WhoAm 92*
Mednick, Robert 1940- *WhoAm 92*
Medof, Robert Gary 1953- *WhoEmL 93*
Medoff, James Lawrence 1947- *WhoAm 92*
Medoff, Mark Howard 1940- *WhoAm 92*
Medovar, Boris I. *BioIn 17*
Medowar, Debra Beth 1960- *WhoEmL 93*
Medoway, Cary 1949- *MiSFD 9*
Medrano, Jose Alberto *DcCPCAm*
Medsger, Betty 1942- *WhoAmW 93*
Medtner, Nicolai 1880-1951 *Baker 92*
Meduna, Russell P. 1954- *St&PR 93*
Medve, Richard John 1936- *WhoE 93*
Medvecky, Robert Stephen 1931- *WhoAm 92*
Medved, Albin *Law&B 92*
Medved, Alphonse Anthony 1910- *WhoWrEP 92*
Medved, Eva 1922- *WhoAmW 93*
Medved, Paul Stanley 1956- *WhoEmL 93*
Medvedev, Nikolai Yakovlevich 1951- *WhoWor 93*
Medvedev, Vladislav Sergeevich 1942- *WhoWor 93*
Medvedow, Phyllis Kronick 1931- *WhoAmW 93*
Medvescek, Chris *BioIn 17*
Medvey, Robert Emery 1946- *WhoEmL 93*
Medvin, Harvey N. 1936- *St&PR 93, WhoIns 93*
Medvin, Harvey Norman 1936- *WhoAm 92*
Medwadowski, Stefan J. 1924- *WhoAm 92*
Medway, Frederic Jeffrey 1947- *WhoSSW 93*
Medwecka-Kornas, Anna 1923- *WhoScE 91-4*
Medwedeff, Fred Marshall 1926- *WhoSSW 93, WhoWor 93*
Medwick, George M. *Law&B 92*
Medwick, Maury P. d1992 *NewYTBS 92*
Medwid, Stephen 1958- *WhoWrEP 92*
Medzerian, Barbara Lewis 1953- *WhoEmL 93*
Medzihradsky, Fedor 1932- *WhoAm 92, WhoWor 93*
Medzorian, Jack M. 1926- *St&PR 93*
Medzorian, Jack Marshall 1926- *WhoAm 92*
Mee, Charles L., Jr. 1938- *SmATA 72, WhoAm 92*
Mee, Herb, Jr. 1928- *St&PR 93, WhoAm 92*
Mee, Michael Francis 1942- *St&PR 93*
Meece, Volney 1925- *WhoSSW 93*
Meech, Mark Leon 1955- *WhoSSW 93*
Meech, Richard Campbell 1921- *WhoAm 92, WhoWor 93*
Meecham, William Coryell 1928- *WhoAm 92*

Meedel, Virgil Gene 1927- St&PR 93
Meegan, George Geoffrey 1952- WhoWor 93
Meehan, Andrew E. 1957- St&PR 93
Meehan, Anthony Edward 1943- WhoWor 93
Meehan, David Howard 1928- WhoAm 92
Meehan, David J. 1925- St&PR 93
Meehan, David Kevin 1947- St&PR 93
Meehan, David Ventura 1954- WhoSSW 93
Meehan, Dennis John 1944- WhoSSW 93
Meehan, Elizabeth Marian WhoScE 91-1
Meehan, Gerry WhoAm 92, WhoE 93
Meehan, Joan Barbara 1959- WhoEmL 93
Meehan, John WhoAm 92
Meehan, John E. 1927- St&PR 93
Meehan, John Joseph 1945- WhoAm 92
Meehan, John Joseph, Jr. 1946- WhoAm 92
Meehan, Joseph BioIn 17
Meehan, Joseph Gerard 1931- St&PR 93, WhoAm 92
Meehan, Kandy Lee 1951- WhoAmW 93, WhoEmL 93
Meehan, Mary BioIn 17
Meehan, Michael A. Law&B 92
Meehan, Paula Kent 1931- St&PR 93, WhoAm 92, WhoAmW 93
Meehan, Richard Thomas, Jr. 1949- WhoEmL 93
Meehan, Robert Henry 1946- WhoE 93, WhoEmL 93
Meehan, Sandra Gotham 1948- WhoAmW 93
Meehan, Susan Ilene 1943- WhoSSW 93
Meehan, Thomas C. 1931- ScF&FL 92
Meehan, Timothy S. Law&B 92
Meehan, Vincent E. 1949- WhoEmL 93
Meehan, William Austin 1946- St&PR 93
Meehl, James Robert 1926- St&PR 93
Meehl, Paul Everett 1920- BioIn 17, WhoAm 92
Meek, Amy Gertrude 1928- WhoAmW 93, WhoE 93
Meek, Brian Lawrence WhoScE 91-1
Meek, Carrie P. 1926- WhoAmW 93
Meek, Charles Kingsley 1885-1965 IntDcAn
Meek, Charles Richard 1941- WhoSSW 93
Meek, David WhoScE 91-1
Meek, Edward Stanley 1919- WhoAm 92
Meek, Jay 1937- WhoWrEP 92
Meek, Jethro C., Mrs. AmWomPl
Meek, Joe DcAmChF 1960
Meek, John 1956- St&PR 93
Meek, John B. 1951- St&PR 93
Meek, Leslie Applegate 1913- WhoWor 93
Meek, Louis G. 1950- St&PR 93
Meek, Mary Kay 1940- WhoAmW 93
Meek, Max A. 1944- St&PR 93
Meek, Patricia Susan 1958- WhoAmW 93
Meek, Paul Derald 1930- St&PR 93, WhoAm 92, WhoSSW 93
Meek, Peter Gray d1992 BioIn 17, NewYTBS 92 [port]
Meek, Phillip Joseph 1937- WhoAm 92, WhoE 93
Meek, Robert WhoScE 91-1
Meek, Robert M. Law&B 92
Meek, Ronald L. 1917-1978 BioIn 17
Meek, Shelba Diana 1949- WhoEmL 93
Meek, Stephen R. 1956- St&PR 93
Meek, Thomas J. Law&B 92
Meek, Violet Imhof 1939- WhoAmW 93
Meeke, Mary d1816? DcLB 116 [port]
Meeker, Alvin D. 1937- St&PR 93
Meeker, Arlene Dorothy 1935- St&PR 93
Meeker, Darcy Sue 1946- WhoWrEP 92
Meeker, Eloise ScF&FL 92
Meeker, Eunice Telfer Juckett 1914- WhoAmW 93
Meeker, Guy Bentley 1945- WhoAm 92, WhoE 93, WhoWor 93
Meeker, Isabelle AmWomPl
Meeker, Kenneth H. 1938- St&PR 93
Meeker, Lavern D., Mr. 1947- St&PR 93
Meeker, Merton L. 1929- St&PR 93
Meeker, Murray M. 1946- WhoE 93
Meeker, Robert Eldon 1930- WhoAm 92
Meeker, Robert L. Law&B 92
Meeker, Robert L. 1935- WhoIns 93
Meeker, Thomas Howard 1943- St&PR 93
Meeker, W. John ScF&FL 92
Meeker, William M. 1915- St&PR 93
Meekhof, Frances Eleanor 1925- St&PR 93
Meekins, Edward Joseph 1949- WhoEmL 93
Meekison, MaryFran 1919- WhoAmW 93, WhoWor 93
Meeks, Carol Jean 1946- WhoAmW 93
Meeks, D. Michael 1943- St&PR 93, WhoAm 92
Meeks, Donald Eugene 1930- WhoAm 92
Meeks, Frank BioIn 17
Meeks, Gary A. 1945- St&PR 93
Meeks, George Owen, Jr. 1950- WhoEmL 93
Meeks, Reginald BioIn 17
Meeks, Reginald Kline 1954- WhoEmL 93
Meeks, Warren Leonard 1926- St&PR 93
Meeks, William Herman, III 1939- WhoSSW 93
Meeks, Yvonne Joyce 1955- WhoEmL 93
Mee-Lee, David 1949- WhoE 93, WhoEmL 93
Meelheim, Helen Diane 1952- WhoAmW 93, WhoSSW 93
Meem, Deborah Townsend 1949- WhoAmW 93
Meem, James Lawrence, Jr. 1915- WhoAm 92
Meena, Dhuleshwar 1935- WhoAsAP 91
Meenaghan, James J. WhoAm 92
Meenan, Alan John 1946- WhoSSW 93, WhoWor 93
Meenan, James Ronald 1941- WhoE 93, WhoWor 93
Meenan, Patrick Henry 1927- WhoAm 92
Meenan, Peter 1942- St&PR 93
Meendsen, Fred Charles 1933- St&PR 93, WhoAm 92
Meengs, William Lloyd 1942- WhoWor 93
Meepagala, Gaminie 1955- WhoEmL 93
Meer, Ameena Bibi 1965- WhoE 93
Meer, E. Harvey 1942- St&PR 93
Meer, Richard H. 1941- St&PR 93
Meerdink, A. Glenn 1927- St&PR 93
Meerkamper, Meinrad 1936- St&PR 93
Meers, Henry W. 1908- St&PR 93, WhoAm 92
Meers, Patricia Margaret Boyd WhoScE 91-1
Meersman, John F. 1937- St&PR 93
Meert, Roland Julien 1933- WhoWor 93
Meerts, Lambert (-Joseph) 1800-1863 Baker 92
Meerwa, Thami BioIn 17
Mees, Barry J. 1947- St&PR 93
Meese, Ann Marie 1959- WhoEmL 93
Meese, Edwin DcCPCAm
Meese, Edwin, III 1931- WhoWor 93
Meese, George Clifford, Jr. 1932- WhoAm 92
Meese, Janice Kaye 1954- WhoAmW 93, WhoSSW 93
Meese, Robert Allen 1956- WhoEmL 93
Meester, Geert T. 1929- WhoScE 91-3
Meester, Louis de 1904-1987 Baker 92
Meetin, Ronald J. Law&B 92
Meetz, John Eugene 1944- WhoAm 92
Meeuwisse, Willy 1914-1952 Baker 92
Meezan, Elias 1942- WhoAm 92, WhoSSW 93
Mefano, Paul 1937- Baker 92
Mefferd, Roy B., Jr. 1920- WhoSSW 93
Meffert, Amelia A. 1938- St&PR 93
Meffert, H.F.Th. WhoScE 91-3
Meffert, John BioIn 17
Meffert-Stewart, Sarah 1962- WhoAmW 93
Mefford, Dean A. WhoAm 92
Megadeth ConMus 9 [port]
Megahy, Francis MiSFD 9
Megan, Thomas Ignatius 1913- WhoAm 92
Megargel, Burton Jonathan 1954- WhoAm 92
Megaro, Matthew A. St&PR 93
Megarry, A. Roy 1937- WhoAm 92, WhoWor 93
Megarry, Robert 1910- WhoWor 93
Megaw, Robert Neill Ellison 1920- WhoAm 92, WhoSSW 93
Megdal, Sharon Bernstein 1952- WhoEmL 93
Megee, Vernon E. d1992 NewYTBS 92 [port]
Megee, Vernon E. 1900-1992 BioIn 17
Megel, Carl J. d1992 NewYTBS 92 [port]
Megevand, Rene Pierre 1925- WhoScE 91-4
Meggers, Betty Jane 1921- WhoAm 92
Meggett, Joan 1909- BioIn 17
Megginson, David Frank WhoScE 91-1
Meghnot, Rupert Laurence Ali 1959- WhoSSW 93
Meghreblian, Robert Vartan 1922- WhoAm 92
Megill, David Wayne 1947- WhoEmL 93
Megilligan, John Paul, Jr. 1952- WhoEmL 93
Megivern, Kathleen 1950- WhoSSW 93
Megley, Richard B. Law&B 92
Megley, Sheila 1938- WhoAm 92, WhoE 93
Meglin, Linda Marie 1952- WhoEmL 93
Meglin, Nick 1935- WhoWrEP 92
Meglino, Don A. 1959- St&PR 93
Meglino, James V. 1957- St&PR 93
Meglino, Josephine 1928- St&PR 93
Meglio, Cheryl Ann 1957- WhoEmL 93
Megna, Jerome Francis 1939- WhoE 93
Megna, John Gregory 1965- WhoSSW 93
Megna, Michael S. 1935- St&PR 93
Megna, Ronald James Law&B 92
Megnin, Jean-Pierre WhoScE 91-2
Megnin, Jean Pierre 1940- WhoWor 93
Mego, Kathleen T. 1945- St&PR 93
Megown, John William 1931- WhoAm 92
Meguro, Kichinosuke 1934- WhoAsAP 91
Megy, Hector Carlos 1953- WhoSSW 93
Megzari, Abdelaziz 1944- WhoUN 92
Mehaffey, Blanche 1907-1968 SweetSg C [port]
Mehaffey, John Allen WhoWor 93
Mehaffey, Paul Wilson 1922- St&PR 93
Mehaffy, Thomas N. 1932- WhoAm 92
Mehaignerie, Pierre 1939- BioIn 17
Mehak, Michael K. 1955- St&PR 93
Mehal, Steven Robert 1964- WhoEmL 93, WhoSSW 93
Mehall, J. Robert 1942- St&PR 93
Mehall, Margaret Elizabeth 1940- WhoAmW 93
Mehan, John A. 1956- St&PR 93
Mehandru, Sushil Kumar 1947- WhoE 93, WhoEmL 93
Meharry, Ronald Lee 1950- WhoEmL 93
Mehboob, K. WhoUN 92
Mehearg, Clifford Wayne 1937- WhoSSW 93
Meher Baba 1894-1969 BioIn 17
Mehl, Lawrence R. Law&B 92
Mehl, Lawrence Richard 1946- St&PR 93
Mehl, Reidar 1937- WhoScE 91-4
Mehlenbacher, Dohn Harlow 1931- WhoWor 93
Mehler, David 1919- St&PR 93
Mehler, Gordon 1955- WhoEmL 93
Mehler, Marianne Dortea Szauer 1952- WhoEmL 93
Mehlhaff, Harvey WhoAm 92
Mehlhorn, Heinz 1944- WhoScE 91-3
Mehlhorn, Werner O. 1932- WhoScE 91-3
Mehlig, Donald Homer 1935- WhoIns 93
Mehlin, Bonnie Maxine 1932- WhoAmW 93
Mehling, Christopher John 1952- WhoEmL 93
Mehlinger, Howard Dean 1931- WhoAm 92
Mehlis, David L. 1943- St&PR 93
Mehlman, Edwin Stephen 1935- WhoE 93, WhoWor 93
Mehlman, Jerrold J. Law&B 92
Mehlman, Lon Douglas 1959- WhoEmL 93, WhoWor 93
Mehlman, Myron A. 1934- WhoE 93
Mehlman, Peter William Law&B 92
Mehlman, Samuel J. 1922- St&PR 93
Mehlman, Steven 1942- WhoE 93
Mehmed, I 1389?-1421 OxDcByz
Mehmed, II 1432-1481 OxDcByz
Mehn, W. Harrison 1918- WhoAm 92
Mehne, Paul Randolph 1948- WhoSSW 93
Mehnert, Hellmut 1928- WhoScE 91-3
Mehoffer, Jozef 1869-1946 PolBiDi
Mehr, Lara J. 1958- WhoEmL 93
Mehra, Brij Mohan 1937- St&PR 93
Mehra, Leila 1928- WhoUN 92
Mehra, Rajnish 1950- WhoAm 92, WhoWor 93
Mehra, Raman K. 1943- St&PR 93
Mehra, Raman Kumar 1943- WhoAm 92
Mehra, Ravinder C. 1942- St&PR 93
Mehrabian, Robert WhoAm 92, WhoE 93, WhoWor 93
Mehran, Farhad 1945- WhoUN 92
Mehren, George L. d1992 NewYTBS 92 [port]
Mehren, George Louis 1913- WhoAm 92
Mehrer, Helmut 1939- WhoScE 91-3
Mehrer-Tobin, Carolyn Monica 1959- WhoAmW 93
Mehreteab, Ghebre Selassie 1949- St&PR 93
Mehring, Clinton Warren 1924- WhoAm 92
Mehring, James Warren 1950- WhoSSW 93
Mehring, Michael W.H. 1937- WhoScE 91-3
Mehring, Vicky Lou 1965- WhoAmW 93
Mehringer, Barbara Crooks 1943- St&PR 93
Mehrkam, Q.D. 1921- St&PR 93
Mehrotra, Sunil 1950- WhoEmL 93
Mehrpore, Abdul Rauf 1948- WhoE 93
Mehrtens, Susan Emily 1945- WhoE 93
Mehta, A. S. 1943- WhoAm 92
Mehta, Chimanbhai 1925- WhoAsAP 91
Mehta, Darshan 1944- St&PR 93
Mehta, Deepa 1949- MiSFD 9
Mehta, Dhirendra 1953- WhoEmL 93
Mehta, Dwiref R. 1952- WhoE 93
Mehta, Ghanshyam 1943- WhoWor 93
Mehta, Harkishan 1934- WhoUN 92
Mehta, Homi K. 1938- St&PR 93
Mehta, Irene Kopp Law&B 92
Mehta, Jer K. 1956- St&PR 93
Mehta, Ketan 1952- MiSFD 9
Mehta, Kishor N. 1945- St&PR 93
Mehta, Madan Lal 1932- WhoWor 93
Mehta, Maharshi P. 1955- WhoE 93
Mehta, Mehli 1908- Baker 92
Mehta, Nancy BioIn 17
Mehta, Narinder Kumar 1938- St&PR 93, WhoAm 92, WhoE 93, WhoWor 93
Mehta, Pravin K. 1935- WhoE 93
Mehta, Rakesh Kumar 1952- WhoE 93
Mehta, Ramesh Pranlal 1945- WhoWor 93
Mehta, Sandeep 1966- WhoWor 93
Mehta, Shailesh J. 1949- St&PR 93, WhoAm 92
Mehta, Sunil St&PR 93
Mehta, Surjit 1948- St&PR 93
Mehta, Ved 1934- BioIn 17
Mehta, Ved Parkash 1934- WhoAm 92, WhoWrEP 92
Mehta, Zarin BioIn 17
Mehta, Zarin 1938- WhoAm 92
Mehta, Zubin 1936- Baker 92, OxDcOp, WhoAm 92, WhoWor 93
Mehta, Zulekha Saifuddin 1942- WhoE 93
Mehul, Etienne-Nicolas 1763-1817 Baker 92, IntDcOp, OxDcOp
Mehuron, William Otto 1937- WhoAm 92
Mei, Dolores Marie 1955- WhoAmW 93, WhoEmL 93
Mei, Giancarlo WhoScE 91-3
Mei, Girolamo 1519-1594 Baker 92, OxDcOp
Mei, Henry Long 1946- WhoE 93
Mei, Jia Liu 1941- WhoWor 93
Mei, Liang-mo 1935- WhoWor 93
Mei, Noel WhoScE 91-2
Mei, Ping 1943- WhoWor 93
Meibom, Marcus 1620?-1710 Baker 92
Meibomius, Marcus 1620?-1710 Baker 92
Meiboom, Marcus 1620?-1710 Baker 92
Meiburg, Charles Owen 1931- WhoAm 92
Meidan, Arthur WhoScE 91-1
Meidell, Sherry 1951- SmATA 73 [port]
Meider, Elmer Charles, Jr. 1946- St&PR 93, WhoAm 92
Meidner, Ludwig 1884-1966 BioIn 17
Meier, A. Jay, Jr. 1928- St&PR 93
Meier, August 1923- WhoAm 92, WhoWrEP 92
Meier, Carl C. Law&B 92
Meier, Charles Dietrich 1959- WhoEmL 93
Meier, David Wayne Law&B 92
Meier, Deborah BioIn 17
Meier, Donald M. 1941- St&PR 93
Meier, Enge WhoAmW 93
Meier, Everett 1934- St&PR 93
Meier, Frederick Richard 1934- St&PR 93, WhoAm 92
Meier, Fritz 1912- WhoWor 93
Meier, G.E.A. 1937- WhoScE 91-3
Meier, George Henry 1954- WhoE 93
Meier, George Karl, III 1944- WhoAm 92
Meier, Hans 1927- WhoScE 91-3
Meier, Hans-Ulrich 1938- WhoScE 91-3
Meier, Heinrich 1953- WhoWor 93
Meier, Henry George 1929- WhoAm 92
Meier, James F. 1928- St&PR 93
Meier, Jane Elizabeth 1951- WhoAmW 93
Meier, Jeannette 1947- St&PR 93
Meier, Jeannette P. Law&B 92
Meier, Johanna 1938- Baker 92
Meier, John Dale 1942- St&PR 93
Meier, John George 1943- WhoAm 92
Meier, Kay 1933- WhoWrEP 92
Meier, Louis Leonard, Jr. 1918- WhoAm 92
Meier, Manfred J. 1929- BioIn 17
Meier, Mark F. 1925- WhoAm 92
Meier, Matthias Sebastian 1917- WhoAm 92
Meier, Max 1948- WhoWor 93
Meier, Nancy Jo 1951- WhoAmW 93
Meier, Pamela Jean 1956- WhoAmW 93
Meier, Paul ScF&FL 92
Meier, Paul D. ConAu 136
Meier, Paul John 1936- WhoAm 92
Meier, Richard Alan 1934- WhoAm 92
Meier, Richard Louis 1920- WhoAm 92
Meier, Robert Henry, III 1940- WhoAm 92
Meier, Ronald Richard 1932- St&PR 93
Meier, Rudolf W. 1926- WhoScE 91-4
Meier, Shirley 1960- ScF&FL 92
Meier, Thomas Keith 1940- WhoAm 92
Meier, Timothy Eugene 1952- St&PR 93
Meier, Walter M. 1926- WhoScE 91-4
Meier, Waltraud 1956- Baker 92, OxDcOp
Meier, Werner Elard Carlos 1938- WhoSSW 93
Meier, Wilbur Leroy, Jr. 1939- WhoWor 93
Meier, William Walter 1929- WhoAm 92
Meierer, Robert E. 1943- St&PR 93
Meiergerd, Donald Clement 1941- St&PR 93

Meier-Hayoz, Arthur Hans 1922- *WhoWor 93*
Meierhenry, Roy A. 1938- *St&PR 93*
Meierjurgen, Betty A. 1935- *WhoAmW 93*
Meierkhol'd, V.E. 1874-1940 *BioIn 17*
Meierkhol'd, Vsevolod Emil'evich 1874-1940 *BioIn 17*
Mei-Figner, Medea *OxDcOp*
Mei-Figner, Medea 1859-1952 *IntDcOp [port]*
Meiggs, Russell *BioIn 17*
Meighan, Thomas 1879-1936 *BioIn 17*
Meigher, S. Christopher, III 1946- *St&PR 93, WhoAm 92*
Meigs, Cornelia Lynde 1884-1973 *AmWomPl, MajAI [port]*
Meigs, Walter R. *Law&B 92*
Meigs, Walter R. 1948- *St&PR 93*
Meihaus, James D. 1942- *St&PR 93*
Meihsner, Larry S. *Law&B 92*
Meijer, Albert Eduard Friedrich Hugo 1925- *WhoScE 91-3*
Meijer, B.J.M. 1952- *WhoScE 91-3*
Meijer, Barbara Elizabeth 1964- *WhoE 93*
Meijer, D.K.F. 1940- *WhoScE 91-3*
Meijer, Douglas 1954- *WhoAm 92*
Meijer, Paul Herman Ernst 1921- *WhoAm 92*
Meijering, M.P.D. 1933- *WhoScE 91-3*
Meijers, C.P. 1924- *WhoScE 91-3*
Meijler, Frits Louis 1925- *WhoWor 93*
Meikle, Fred C. 1931- *St&PR 93*
Meikle, James Robert 1941- *St&PR 93*
Meikle, Philip G. 1937- *WhoAm 92*
Meikle, R. James 1936- *St&PR 93*
Meikle, Steve M. 1923- *St&PR 93*
Meikle, Thomas Harry, Jr. 1929- *WhoAm 92, WhoWor 93*
Meikle, W. *WhoScE 91-1*
Meiklejohn, Donald 1909- *WhoAm 92*
Meiklejohn, Mindy June 1929- *WhoAmW 93*
Meiksin, Zvi H. 1926- *WhoAm 92, WhoE 93*
Meil, Kate 1925- *WhoAmW 93*
Meilach, Dona Z(weigoron) 1926- *WhoWrEP 92*
Meilan, Celia 1920- *St&PR 93, WhoAm 92*
Meiland, Jakob 1542-1577 *Baker 92*
Meilaq, Sammy 1949- *WhoWor 93*
Meilgaard, Morten Christian 1928- *St&PR 93, WhoAm 92*
Meilhac, Henri 1831-1897 *IntDcOp, OxDcOp*
Meili, Launi *WhoAmW 93*
Meiling, Dean S. 1948- *WhoIns 93*
Meiling, George Robert Lucas 1942- *St&PR 93, WhoAm 92*
Meiling, Gerald S. 1936- *St&PR 93*
Meiling, Gerald Stewart 1936- *WhoAm 92*
Meilke, Peter A. 1946- *WhoEmL 93*
Meiller, Morris 1931- *WhoE 93*
Meillier, Raymond A. 1934- *St&PR 93*
Meilman, Edward 1915- *WhoAm 92*
Meilman, Philip Warren 1951- *WhoSSW 93*
Meilman, Stephanie Kallet 1949- *WhoAmW 93*
Meima, Ralph Chester, Jr. 1927- *WhoAm 92*
Meinardi, Harry 1932- *WhoScE 91-3*
Meinardus, Ludwig (Siegfried) 1827-1896 *Baker 92*
Meindl, James Donald 1933- *WhoAm 92*
Meindl, James Richard 1952- *WhoE 93*
Meineke, Steven Eric 1949- *WhoEmL 93*
Meinel, Aden Baker 1922- *WhoAm 92*
Meinel, Carolyn *BioIn 17*
Meinel, Curt Robert 1949- *WhoE 93*
Meinelt, Ellen Marie 1956- *WhoAmW 93, WhoEmL 93*
Meiner, Sue Ellen Thompson 1943- *WhoAmW 93*
Meiners, Donald Edwin 1935- *St&PR 93*
Meiners, Hermann 1935- *WhoScE 91-3*
Meiners, Thomas Scott 1949- *WhoEmL 93*
Meinert, Denis J. 1960- *St&PR 93*
Meinert, Hasso 1929- *WhoWor 93*
Meinert, John Raymond 1927- *St&PR 93, WhoAm 92*
Meinert, Patricia Ann 1949- *WhoEmL 93*
Meinhard, David *Law&B 92*
Meinhardt, Carolyn Loris 1949- *WhoAmW 93, WhoEmL 93*
Meinhardt, William 1939- *St&PR 93*
Meinhart, Elaine Mary Knaub 1950- *WhoAmW 93, WhoEmL 93*
Meinhof, Carl 1857-1944 *IntDcAn*
Meinhold, Charles Boyd 1934- *WhoE 93*
Meinig, Donald William 1924- *WhoAm 92*
Meininger, Stephen Lee 1958- *WhoEmL 93*
Meinke, Alan Kurt 1952- *WhoE 93, WhoEmL 93*
Meinke, Peter 1932- *WhoAm 92, WhoSSW 93, WhoWrEP 92*
Meinke, Roy Walter 1929- *WhoAm 92*
Meinsen, Phyllis Arlene 1944- *WhoAmW 93*
Meinsen, Raymond J., Jr. 1906- *St&PR 93*
Meinstein, Crystal Ann 1955- *WhoWrEP 92*
Meinster, David R. 1941-1991 *BioIn 17*
Meintjes, Victor A. *WhoIns 93*
Meinwald, Jerrold 1927- *WhoAm 92*
Meinx, Robert *WhoScE 91-4*
Meinz, George E. *Law&B 92*
Meir, Golda 1898-1978 *BioIn 17, ColdWar 2 [port], DcTwHis*
Meira, Gregorio Raul 1945- *WhoWor 93*
Meira, Joao Carlos Alves *Law&B 92*
Meire, R.A.J. 1926- *WhoScE 91-2*
Meireles, A. Joaquim *WhoScE 91-3*
Meirik, Olav 1939- *WhoUN 92*
Meirion-Jones, Gwyn Idris *WhoScE 91-1*
Meirovitch, Leonard 1928- *WhoAm 92*
Meirowitz, Claire Cecile 1934- *WhoAm 92, WhoAmW 93, WhoE 93*
Meis, Charles H. 1946- *St&PR 93*
Meis, James *BioIn 17*
Meis, Nancy Ruth 1952- *WhoAmW 93, WhoEmL 93*
Meisch, Guy 1932- *WhoScE 91-3*
Meise, William H. *Law&B 92*
Meisel, Alan 1946- *WhoAm 92*
Meisel, Carl R. 1940- *St&PR 93*
Meisel, George Ira 1920- *WhoAm 92*
Meisel, George Vincent 1933- *WhoAm 92*
Meisel, Harald Wolfgang 1943- *St&PR 93*
Meisel, James Hans 1900-1991 *BioIn 17*
Meisel, Jerome 1934- *WhoAm 92*
Meisel, John 1923- *WhoAm 92*
Meisel, Louis Koenig 1942- *WhoAm 92*
Meisel, Martin 1931- *WhoAm 92, WhoE 93*
Meisel, Perry 1949- *WhoEmL 93*
Meisel, Philip L. 1928- *St&PR 93*
Meisel, Sidney 1917- *St&PR 93*
Meisel, Werner Paul Ernst 1933- *WhoWor 93*
Meiselas, Susan Clay 1948- *WhoAm 92*
Meisels, Dov Berush 1798-1870 *PolBiDi*
Meisels, Gerhard George 1931- *WhoAm 92*
Meisels, Saul d1990 *BioIn 17*
Meisen, Axel 1943- *WhoAm 92*
Meisen, Walter August 1934- *St&PR 93*
Meisenheimer, John Long 1933- *WhoSSW 93*
Meisenheimer, R.E. 1930- *St&PR 93*
Meisenhelder, Robert John, II *Law&B 92*
Meisenkothen, Walter Anton 1946- *WhoWor 93*
Meisenzahl, Roy Richard 1948- *WhoWor 93*
Meiser, Carroll Keith *Law&B 92*
Meisinger, Peter R. 1955- *St&PR 93*
Meiskey, Shirley Suzanne 1945- *WhoAmW 93*
Meislahn, Harry Post *Law&B 92*
Meislahn, Harry Post 1938- *WhoAm 92*
Meisler, Sharon Ruth 1959- *WhoEmL 93*
Meislich, Herbert 1920- *WhoAm 92*
Meislik, Stuart Robert *Law&B 92*
Meisner, Dee Dolores Annette 1936- *WhoWor 93*
Meisner, Gary Wayne 1949- *WhoAm 92*
Meisner, Joachim Cardinal 1933- *WhoWor 93*
Meisner, Lora Denise 1952- *WhoE 93*
Meisner, Roland D. 1957- *WhoEmL 93*
Meisner, Sanford 1905- *BioIn 17*
Meiss, Richard L. *Law&B 92*
Meiss, Thomas M. *Law&B 92*
Meissler-Daniels, Sandra Ruth 1946- *WhoAmW 93*
Meissner, Ann Loring 1924- *WhoAmW 93*
Meissner, Edwin Benjamin, Jr. 1918- *WhoAm 92*
Meissner, Franklin Newton 1933- *St&PR 93*
Meissner, Joachim 1929- *WhoScE 91-4*
Meissner, Mary Eileen 1950- *WhoAmW 93*
Meissner, Nicole *BioIn 17*
Meissner, Rudolf O. 1925- *WhoScE 91-3*
Meissner, Rudolf Otto 1925- *WhoWor 93*
Meissner, William Baynard 1944- *WhoWor 93*
Meissner, William Joseph 1948- *WhoWrEP 92*
Meissner, William Walter 1931- *WhoAm 92*
Meistad, Tore *WhoScE 91-4*
Meistas, Mary Therese 1949- *WhoAmW 93, WhoE 93, WhoEmL 93, WhoWor 93*
Meister, Alton 1922- *WhoAm 92*
Meister, Barbara 1926- *St&PR 93*
Meister, Bernard John 1941- *WhoAm 92*
Meister, Doris Powers 1954- *WhoAm 92*
Meister, Erhard 1948- *WhoScE 91-4*
Meister, Ernest M. 1923- *St&PR 93*
Meister, Frederick Anton, Jr. 1943- *WhoAm 92*
Meister, Karl H. 1935- *St&PR 93*
Meister, Lawrence Michael 1961- *WhoEmL 93*
Meister, Maria Joanne 1960- *WhoAmW 93*
Meister, Mark Jay 1953- *WhoAm 92*
Meister, Michael William 1942- *WhoE 93*
Meister, Peter William 1948- *WhoSSW 93*
Meister, Richard J. 1938- *WhoAm 92*
Meister, Robin *Law&B 92*
Meister, Ronald William 1947- *WhoEmL 93*
Meister, Shirley Vogler 1936- *WhoWrEP 92*
Meister, Steven Gerard 1937- *WhoAm 92*
Meister, Stuart G. *Law&B 92*
Meister, Thomas Francis 1954- *WhoEmL 93*
Meistermann, Georg 1911-1990 *BioIn 17*
Meistrich, Sydney 1927- *St&PR 93*
Meistrup, Per 1949- *WhoWor 93*
Meites, Louis 1926- *WhoAm 92*
Meitin, Deborah Dorsky 1951- *WhoAmW 93, WhoEmL 93*
Meitner, Pamela *Law&B 92*
Meitus, Vladimir Yulievich 1937- *WhoWor 93*
Meitus, Yuli (Sergievich) 1903- *Baker 92*
Meitzen, Manfred Otto 1930- *WhoAm 92*
Meitzler, Allen Henry 1928- *WhoAm 92*
Meitzler, Larry Clair 1946- *WhoAm 92*
Meixell, David Kevin 1955- *WhoEmL 93*
Meixner, Josef 1908- *WhoWor 93*
Meizell, Alvin 1932- *St&PR 93*
Mejeur, Gail 1946- *St&PR 93*
Mejeur, Sharon Kay 1947- *WhoAmW 93*
Mejia, Barbara Oviedo 1946- *WhoEmL 93*
Mejia, Carlos 1950- *St&PR 93*
Mejia, Gerardo *BioIn 17*
Mejia, Gilberto Castano 1956- *WhoWor 93*
Mejia, Jorge 1954- *WhoWor 93*
Mejia, Ricardo Anibal 1964- *WhoWor 93*
Mejia Arellano, Oscar *DcCPCAm*
Mejia Colindres, President *DcCPCAm*
Mejia Sanchez, Ernesto 1923- *DcMexL*
Mejia Valera, Manuel 1928- *DcMexL*
Mejia Vallejo, Manuel 1923- *SpAmA*
Mejia Victores, Oscar Humberto 1931- *DcCPCAm*
Mejia Xesspe, M. Toribio 1896-1983 *IntDcAn*
Mejta, Cheryl Lee 1952- *WhoAmW 93*
Mekeel, Joyce 1931- *Baker 92, BioIn 17*
Mekeel, Steven L. *Law&B 92*
Mekers, Omer P.B. 1950- *WhoScE 91-2*
Mekhtiyev, Tadzhaddin Ibragim ogly *WhoWor 93*
Mekler, Alexander 1944- *WhoWor 93*
Mekler, Arlen B. 1943- *WhoAm 92*
Meko, Andrew C. *Law&B 92*
Meksi, Aleksander 1939- *WhoWor 93*
Mel, Howard Charles *WhoAm 92*
Mel, Michael 1951- *WhoAsAP 91*
Mela, Martti 1933- *WhoScE 91-4*
Melachrino, George 1909-1965 *Baker 92*
Melada, Ivan 1931- *ScF&FL 92*
Melady, Thomas Patrick 1927- *WhoAm 92, WhoWor 93*
Melamed, Anna Sylwia 1946- *WhoAmW 93*
Melamed, Arthur Douglas 1945- *WhoAm 92, WhoWor 93*
Melamed, Carol D. *Law&B 92*
Melamed, David J. 1930-1990 *BioIn 17*
Melamed, Leo *BioIn 17*
Melamed, Leo 1932- *ScF&FL 92*
Melamed, Leo 1937- *WhoAm 92*
Melamed, Leonid *BioIn 17*
Melamede, Amos 1933- *St&PR 93*
Melampy, Donald Francis 1932- *St&PR 93*
Melancon, Andre 1942- *MiSFD 9*
Melancon, Vick J. 1948- *St&PR 93*
Meland, Bernard Eugene 1899- *WhoAm 92*
Melander, Arne 1948- *WhoScE 91-4*
Melander, Harlan Paul, Jr. 1956- *WhoEmL 93, WhoSSW 93*
Melandri, Pierre Christian 1946- *WhoWor 93*
Melani *Baker 92*
Melani, Alessandro 1639-1703 *Baker 92, OxDcOp*
Melani, Atto 1626-1714 *Baker 92, OxDcOp*
Melani, Bartolomeo 1634-1703 *OxDcOp*
Melani, Francesco Maria 1628-1663 *OxDcOp*
Melani, Jacopo 1623-1676 *Baker 92, OxDcOp*
Melani, Vincentio Paolo 1637-1667 *OxDcOp*
Melania the Younger 383-439 *OxDcByz*
Melanson, Anne M. *WhoAm 92, WhoAmW 93*
Melanson, James 1946- *WhoAm 92*
Melanson, Richard Stephen 1953- *St&PR 93*
Melanson, Sarah Gilian 1960- *WhoAmW 93*
Melara, Garrett Philip 1945- *St&PR 93*
Melartin, Erkki (Gustaf) 1875-1937 *Baker 92*
Melas, Anthony G. *Law&B 92*
Melba, Nellie 1861-1931 *Baker 92, IntDcOp [port], OxDcOp*
Melberg, Gordon Conrad 1926- *St&PR 93*
Melbin, Murray 1927- *WhoAm 92*
Melbo, Irving Robert 1908- *WhoAm 92, WhoWor 93*
Melbourne, Bertram Lloyd 1948- *WhoE 93*
Melbourne, Clive *WhoScE 91-1*
Melby, Claire Arlene 1931- *St&PR 93*
Melby, Edward Carlos, Jr. 1929- *WhoAm 92*
Melby, James Christian 1928- *WhoAm 92*
Melby, John F. d1992 *NewYTBS 92*
Melby, Orville Erling 1921- *WhoAm 92*
Melcer, David *Law&B 92*
Melcer, Henryk 1869-1928 *PolBiDi*
Melcer (-Szczawinski), Henryk 1869-1928 *Baker 92*
Melcher, Andrew Stephen 1949- *WhoWor 93*
Melcher, Carol F. *Law&B 92*
Melcher, Daniel 1912-1985 *BioIn 17*
Melcher, Jan Louise 1953- *WhoE 93*
Melcher, Jerry William 1948- *WhoSSW 93*
Melcher, John *BioIn 17*
Melcher, Katherine Jeannette 1946- *WhoEmL 93*
Melcher, Kirsten Jegsen 1934- *WhoAmW 93*
Melcher, Raymond H., Jr. 1952- *WhoAm 92*
Melcher, Stephen Alan 1943- *St&PR 93*
Melcher, Trini Urtuzuastegui 1931- *WhoAm 92*
Melchers, Henrik Melcher 1882-1961 *Baker 92*
Melchers, Robert Erich 1945- *WhoWor 93*
Melchert, Friedmund E.G. 1926- *WhoScE 91-3*
Melchert, James Frederick 1930- *WhoAm 92*
Melchin, Uwe Rudolf 1939- *WhoWor 93*
Melchione, Janet Burak *Law&B 92*
Melchione, Janet Burak 1950- *WhoIns 93*
Melchior, Ib 1917- *MiSFD 9*
Melchior, Ib (Jorgen) 1917- *WhoWrEP 92*
Melchior, Lauritz 1890-1973 *Baker 92, BioIn 17, IntDcOp [port], OxDcOp*
Melchior, Paul J.L. 1925- *WhoScE 91-2*
Melchior, Paul J.L.C. 1925- *WhoScE 91-2*
Melchior, Richard William 1947- *St&PR 93*
Melchiorre, Victor Andrew 1954- *WhoEmL 93*
Melchoir-Tellier, Siri 1946- *WhoUN 92*
Melconian, Linda Jean *WhoAmW 93, WhoE 93*
Melczek, Dale J. 1938- *WhoAm 92*
Meldahl, Edward Neill 1925- *WhoSSW 93*
Meldal-Johnson, Trevor 1944- *ScF&FL 92*
Meldau-Womack, Elke C. 1941- *WhoUN 92*
Meldeau, S. James 1949- *St&PR 93*
Meldman, Clifford Kay 1931- *WhoAm 92*
Meldman, Robert Edward *WhoAm 92, WhoWor 93*
Meldrum, Bob 1865- *BioIn 17*
Meldrum, Brian Stuart *WhoScE 91-1*
Meldrum, Don C. 1937- *St&PR 93*
Meldrum, Peter D. 1947- *St&PR 93*
Meldrum, Peter Durkee 1947- *WhoAm 92*
Mele, Alfred R. 1951- *ConAu 138*
Mele, Charles A. 1956- *St&PR 93*
Mele, Dennis Anthony 1950- *St&PR 93*
Mele, Gregg Charles 1965- *WhoE 93, WhoEmL 93*
Mele, Jim 1950- *ScF&FL 92*
Mele, John J. *St&PR 93*
Mele, Joseph C. *St&PR 93*
Mele, Robert D. *St&PR 93*
Mele, Sue A. *St&PR 93*
Melegari, Carl *BioIn 17*
Meleis, Afaf Ibrahim 1942- *WhoAm 92*
Melendez, Bill *MiSFD 9*
Melendez, Concha 1892- *NotHsAW 93*
Melendez, Francisco 1964- *SmATA 72 [port]*
Melendez, John *BioIn 17*
Melendez, Jorge *DcCPCAm*
Melendez, Manuel Gaspar 1935- *HispAmA*
Melendez, Tony *BioIn 17*
Melendez-Asensio, Enrique 1965- *WhoWor 93*
Melendez de Espinosa, Juana 1914- *DcMexL*

Melendez-Hevia, Enrique 1946- *WhoWor 93*
Melendy, Howard Brett 1924- *WhoAm 92*
Melendy, Peter S. 1950- *St&PR 93*
Meleras, Hermann Simon 1934- *WhoUN 92*
Meles Zenawi *BioIn 17, WhoWor 93*
Meles Zenawi 1955?- *ConBlB 3 [port]*
Meletio, Jack E. 1915- *St&PR 93*
Meletios the Monk *OxDcByz*
Meletios the Younger c. 1035-c. 1105 *OxDcByz*
Melezinek, Adolf 1932- *WhoWor 93*
Melfi, Frank C. 1936- *St&PR 93*
Melfi, James Joseph 1928- *St&PR 93*
Melfi, Mary 1951- *WhoCanL 92*
Melfi, William J. 1942- *St&PR 93*
Melford, D.A. *WhoScE 91-1*
Melford, Myra *BioIn 17*
Melgaard, Hans Leland 1940- *St&PR 93*
Melgaard, Leif 1898-1991 *BioIn 17*
Melgaard, Maureen Elizabeth 1944- *WhoAmW 93*
Melgar, Julio 1922- *WhoSSW 93*
Melgar Castro, Juan *DcCPCAm*
Melgarejo, Juan Arturo 1957- *WhoWor 93*
Melgarejo, Paloma 1956- *WhoWor 93*
Melges, David Louis 1943- *St&PR 93*
Melgosa Suarez, Julian 1934- *WhoScE 91-3*
Melhem, D(iana) H(elen) *WhoWrEP 92*
Melhorn, Wilton Newton 1921- *WhoAm 92*
Melhuish, G.S. *Law&B 92*
Meli, Anthony P. 1944- *St&PR 93*
Meli, Robert 1920- *St&PR 93*
Melia, Tamara Moser 1955- *WhoAmW 93*
Melian, Leo 1928- *WhoScE 91-3*
Melias d934 *OxDcByz*
Melican, James Patrick 1940- *St&PR 93*
Melican, James Patrick, Jr. 1940- *WhoAm 92*
Melich, Doris S. 1913- *WhoAmW 93, WhoWor 93*
Melich, Mitchell 1912- *WhoAm 92, WhoWor 93*
Melichar, Alois 1896-1976 *Baker 92*
Melicher, Ronald William 1941- *WhoAm 93*
Melick, Arden Davis 1940- *WhoWrEP 92*
Melick, Katherine 1924- *WhoAmW 93*
Melick, Virginia *AmWomPl*
Melickian, Gary Edward 1935- *WhoE 93, WhoWor 93*
Meliczek, Hans Alfred 1932- *WhoUN 92*
Melidosian, Mark Wm. 1947- *St&PR 93*
Melie, Michael D. *Law&B 92*
Melief, Cornelis J.M. 1943- *WhoScE 91-3*
Melies, Georges 1861-1938 *MiSFD 9N*
Melignano, Carmine 1936- *WhoE 93, WhoWor 93*
Melikian, Mary 1927- *WhoE 93*
Melikov, Arif (Djangirovich) 1933- *Baker 92*
Melik-Pashayev, Alexander (Shamilievich) 1905-1964 *Baker 92*
Melikyan, Arik Artavazdovich 1944- *WhoWor 93*
Melikyan, Romanos Hovakimi 1883-1935 *Baker 92*
Melillo, Joseph Vincent 1946- *WhoAm 92, WhoE 93*
Melin, David Ellis 1926- *St&PR 93*
Melin, Douglas R. *Law&B 92*
Meline, Jules 1838-1925 *BioIn 17*
Melino, James J. *Law&B 92*
Melinsky, Denise *BioIn 17*
Melis, Carmen 1885-1967 *Baker 92*
Melis, Patrick 1952- *WhoWor 93*
Melish, Diane Carol 1952- *WhoEmL 93*
Melissantos, Aris 1943- *St&PR 93*
Melissaropoulos, Nicos 1926- *WhoWor 93*
Melissenos *OxDcByz*
Melissenos, Makarios d1585 *OxDcByz*
Melissinos, Adrian Constantin 1929- *WhoAm 92, WhoE 93*
Meliteniotes, Theodore d1393 *OxDcByz*
Melius, Bradford C. *Law&B 92*
Melius, Nancy Lynn 1964- *WhoAmW 93*
Melius, Paul 1927- *WhoSSW 93*
Melkebeke, Guy R.M. 1955- *WhoScE 91-2*
Melkikh, Dmitri 1885-1943 *Baker 92*
Melkmann, Edwin *Law&B 92*
Melkus, Eduard 1928- *Baker 92*
Mell, Betty Lou 1935- *WhoWrEP 92*
Mell, Gertrud Maria 1947- *Baker 92*
Mell, John F., Jr. 1932- *St&PR 93*
Mell, Max 1882-1971 *DcLB 124 [port]*
Mella, Arthur J. 1937- *WhoIns 93*
Mella, Arthur John 1937- *WhoAm 92, WhoE 93*
Mella, John *ScF&FL 92*
Mellan, Olivia Julie 1946- *WhoE 93*
Mellander, Stefan John 1930- *WhoScE 91-4*
Mellard, Joan McGuire 1933- *WhoSSW 93*
Mellard, Kenneth Michel 1953- *WhoEmL 93*
Mellard, Nancy M. *Law&B 92*
Mellecker, John 1934- *WhoAm 92*
Mellem, Roger Calvin 1924- *WhoAm 92*
Melle Mel *SoulM*
Mellen, Charles S. 1929- *St&PR 93*
Mellen, Donald Boyd 1939- *St&PR 93*
Mellen, Evelyn A. 1932- *St&PR 93*
Mellen, Joan *WhoE 93*
Mellen, John Francis *Law&B 92*
Mellen, Kirk A. 1939- *St&PR 93, WhoIns 93*
Mellen, Mary B. 1817-1885 *BioIn 17*
Mellen, Timothy J. 1948- *St&PR 93*
Mellenbruch, Giles Johnny Edward 1911- *WhoWor 93*
Mellencamp, John *MiSFD 9*
Mellencamp, John 1951- *Baker 92, WhoAm 92*
Mellencamp, Tom Dickens *Law&B 92*
Meller, Anton 1932- *WhoScE 91-3*
Meller, Christopher Lawrence 1943- *WhoIns 93*
Meller, George Mieczyslaw Jerzy 1935- *WhoAm 92, WhoE 93*
Meller, Susan Jean 1952- *WhoAmW 93*
Mellers, Wilfred (Howard) 1914- *Baker 92*
Mellers, Wilfrid Howard 1914- *BioIn 17*
Mellert, Volker K. 1943- *WhoScE 91-3*
Mellerup, Erling Thyge 1939- *WhoWor 93*
Melles, Carl 1926- *Baker 92*
Melles, Warren H. 1935- *St&PR 93*
Mellett, Edwin R. 1939- *WhoAm 92*
Mellett, James Silvan 1936- *WhoE 93*
Mellette, M. Susan Jackson 1922- *WhoAm 92*
Melley, William P. 1931- *St&PR 93*
Mellgren, Svein Ivar 1943- *WhoScE 91-4*
Melli, Marygold Shire 1926- *WhoAmW 93*
Mellichamp, Leslie Ray, Jr. 1921- *WhoSSW 93*
Mellies, Charles B. *Law&B 92*
Mellin, Gilbert Myer 1915- *St&PR 93*
Mellin, Gilbert Wylie 1925- *WhoE 93*
Mellin, Norman 1953- *WhoE 93*
Mellin, Stephen David 1941- *St&PR 93*
Melling, O. R. *DcChlFi, ScF&FL 92*
Mellinger, Frederick d1990 *BioIn 17*
Mellinger, Jean 1935- *WhoScE 91-2*
Mellinger, Michael Vance 1945- *WhoE 93*
Mellinger, Peter T. 1957- *St&PR 93*
Mellink, Machteld J. 1917- *IntDcAn*
Mellinkoff, Abe d1992 *NewYTBS 92*
Mellinkoff, David 1914- *WhoAm 92*
Mellinkoff, Sherman Mussoff 1920- *WhoAm 92*
Mellins, Harry Zachary 1921- *WhoAm 92*
Mellins, Robert B. 1928- *WhoAm 92*
Mellis, Joel Paul 1934- *St&PR 93, WhoAm 92*
Mellis, Robert Scott 1940- *St&PR 93*
Mellish, Timothy Charles 1955- *St&PR 93*
Mellitt, Brian *WhoScE 91-1*
Mellman, Dennis *St&PR 93*
Mellman, Myer W. 1917- *St&PR 93*
Mellnas, Arne 1933- *Baker 92*
Mello, Custodio Jose de 1840-1902 *HarEnMi*
Mello, Dawn *BioIn 17*
Mello, Dawn c. 1938- *News 92 [port]*
Mello, Fernando Collor de *BioIn 17*
Mello, John J. *St&PR 93*
Mello, Milton Thiago de 1916- *WhoWor 93*
Mellon, Andrew W. 1855-1937 *PolPar*
Mellon, Andrew William 1855-1937 *DcTwHis*
Mellon, Edward Knox 1936- *WhoSSW 93*
Mellon, Evelyn Emig *AmWomPl*
Mellon, Francis Alfred *WhoScE 91-1*
Mellon, H.J. *St&PR 93*
Mellon, Howard Jay 1952- *WhoEmL 93*
Mellon, Jane Marie *Law&B 92*
Mellon, Joan Ann 1932- *WhoAmW 93*
Mellon, Margaret Gaydos 1945- *WhoAmW 93*
Mellon, Paul *BioIn 17*
Mellon, Paul 1907- *WhoAm 92*
Mellon, Richard Prosser 1939- *WhoAm 92*
Mellon, Seward Prosser 1942- *St&PR 93, WhoAm 92*
Mellon, W. Giles 1931- *WhoE 93*
Melloni, Giovanni 1938- *WhoWor 93*
Mellor, Anne K. 1941- *ScF&FL 92*
Mellor, Barbara Louise 1945- *WhoE 93*
Mellor, Gail McGowan 1942- *WhoAmW 93, WhoSSW 93*
Mellor, James Robb 1930- *WhoAm 92*
Mellor, John Anthony 1935- *St&PR 93*
Mellor, John Williams 1928- *WhoAm 92*
Mellor, Michael Lawton 1922- *WhoAm 92*
Mellor, Philip Scott *WhoScE 91-1*
Mellor, Rob C. 1934- *St&PR 93*
Mellor, Robert Carl 1934- *WhoAm 92*
Mellor, Robert Edward 1943- *St&PR 93*
Mellors, Robert Charles 1916- *WhoAm 92, WhoE 93*
Mellott, Cloyd Rowe 1923- *WhoAm 92, WhoE 93, WhoWor 93*
Mellott, John D. 1938- *St&PR 93*
Mellott, Paul C. 1926- *St&PR 93*
Mellott, Robert H. 1946- *St&PR 93*
Mellott, Robert Vernon 1928- *WhoAm 92, WhoWor 93*
Mellottee, Henry 1941- *WhoScE 91-2*
Mellow, James K. 1927- *St&PR 93*
Mellow, James R. *BioIn 17*
Mellow, James Robert 1926- *WhoWrEP 92*
Mellstedt, Hakan Soren Thure 1942- *WhoWor 93*
Mellups, Ivars V. *Law&B 92*
Melman, David A. 1942- *St&PR 93*
Melman, Israel J. 1920- *WhoAm 92, WhoE 93*
Melman, Jeffrey *MiSFD 9*
Melman, Joy 1927- *WhoAmW 93*
Melman, Rich *BioIn 17*
Melman, Seymour *WhoWrEP 92*
Melmed, Matthew Eliott 1954- *WhoE 93*
Melmon, Kenneth Lloyd 1934- *WhoAm 92*
Melner, Sinclair Lewis 1928- *WhoAm 92*
Melngailis, Ivars 1933- *WhoAm 92*
Melngailis, John 1939- *WhoE 93*
Melnick, Burton Alan 1940- *WhoWor 93*
Melnick, Daniel 1932- *WhoAm 92*
Melnick, Edward Lawrence 1938- *WhoE 93*
Melnick, Gilbert Stanley 1930- *WhoAm 92*
Melnick, Joseph L. 1914- *WhoAm 92, WhoSSW 93*
Melnick, Mark *Law&B 92*
Melnick, Norman 1931- *ConEn, St&PR 93*
Melnick, Robert Russell 1956- *WhoEmL 93*
Melnick, Sharon Kay 1956- *WhoAmW 93*
Melnik, Robert Edward 1933- *WhoAm 92*
Melnikoff, Sarah Ann 1936- *WhoAmW 93*
Melnikov, Ivan 1832-1906 *OxDcOp*
Melnikov, Ivan (Alexandrovich) 1832-1906 *Baker 92*
Melnikov, Vitaly Nicolai 1941- *WhoWor 93*
Melnikova, Irina Valerianovna 1944- *WhoWor 93*
Melnizky, Walter 1928- *WhoWor 93*
Melnuk, Paul D. 1954- *St&PR 93*
Melnyk, Blaine Gary *Law&B 92*
Melnyk, Michael *Law&B 92*
Melnykovych, Andrew O. 1952- *WhoAm 92*
Melo, James J. 1930- *St&PR 93*
Melo, Juan Vicente 1932- *DcMexL*
Melo, Skinner Chavez d1992 *BioIn 17*
Meloan, Taylor Wells 1919- *WhoAm 92*
Melody, Jay *St&PR 93*
Melody, Michael Edward 1943- *St&PR 93, WhoAm 92*
Melody, Michael Edward 1947- *WhoSSW 93*
Melody, W.A. *WhoWrEP 92*
Meloff, Eva 1948- *WhoAmW 93*
Melograna, Eleanor Burch Adams 1966- *WhoAmW 93*
Melon, Candy A. 1967- *WhoE 93*
Melonas, Jacqueline Marie *Law&B 92*
Melone, James T. *St&PR 93*
Melone, Joseph James 1931- *St&PR 93, WhoAm 92*
Melone, Victor Joseph 1933- *WhoAm 92*
Melo Neto, Joao Cabral de 1920- *BioIn 17*
Meloni, Christopher *BioIn 17*
Meloon, Daniel Thomas, Jr. 1935- *WhoE 93*
Meloon, Robert A. 1928- *WhoWor 93*
Meloon, Walter O. 1915- *St&PR 93*
Melore, Daniel G. 1939- *St&PR 93*
Meloy, Francis John 1946- *WhoEmL 93*
Melrose, Andrea LaSonde 1951- *ScF&FL 92*
Melrose, Barry James 1956- *WhoAm 92*
Melrose, Kendrick B. 1940- *St&PR 93*
Melrose, Ross McClellan *Law&B 92*
Melross, Alec Gurney *ScF&FL 92*
Melroy, Jane Ruth 1957- *WhoEmL 93*
Melroy, Theresa A. *Law&B 92*
Melsa, J.L. 1938- *St&PR 93*
Melsa, James Louis 1938- *WhoAm 92*
Melsen, Birte 1939- *WhoScE 91-2, WhoWor 93*
Melsheimer, Harold 1927- *WhoWor 93*
Melsheimer, Mel Powell 1939- *St&PR 93, WhoAm 92*
Melson, Charlene C. 1943- *St&PR 93*
Melson, Charlene Cox 1943- *WhoAmW 93*
Melsop, James William 1939- *St&PR 93, WhoAm 92*
Melter, Robert Alan 1935- *WhoE 93*
Melton, Andrew Joseph, Jr. 1920- *WhoAm 92*
Melton, Andrew T. 1946- *St&PR 93*
Melton, Arthur Ford 1954- *St&PR 93*
Melton, Augustus Allen, Jr. 1942- *WhoAm 92*
Melton, Charles Estel 1924- *WhoAm 92*
Melton, David Bruce 1952- *WhoSSW 93*
Melton, Doris M. *AmWomPl*
Melton, Edward Madison 1955- *WhoE 93*
Melton, Elaine Wallace 1948- *WhoAmW 93*
Melton, Gary Bentley 1952- *WhoAm 92, WhoEmL 93*
Melton, H. Burt 1942- *St&PR 93*
Melton, Helen Louise 1923- *WhoSSW 93*
Melton, Howard Eugene 1915- *St&PR 93*
Melton, Howell Webster 1923- *WhoAm 92, WhoSSW 93*
Melton, J. Scott *Law&B 92*
Melton, James 1904-1961 *Baker 92*
Melton, James Frederick, II 1946- *WhoEmL 93, WhoSSW 93*
Melton, James Howard 1942- *WhoSSW 93*
Melton, Jody Dean 1951- *WhoEmL 93*
Melton, Joseph Carl 1945- *St&PR 93*
Melton, Joy Regina 1960- *WhoSSW 93*
Melton, Karlyn Sue 1949- *WhoAmW 93*
Melton, Keith *WhoScE 91-1*
Melton, Laurie Alison 1964- *WhoWor 93*
Melton, Lynn Ayres 1944- *WhoSSW 93*
Melton, Martha A. 1934- *St&PR 93*
Melton, Michael Eric 1958- *WhoEmL 93, WhoSSW 93, WhoWor 93*
Melton, Owen B., Jr. 1946- *St&PR 93, WhoAm 92*
Melton, Richard H. 1935- *WhoAm 92, WhoWor 93*
Melton, Robert Graham 1954- *WhoEmL 93*
Melton, Ronald Benjamin 1955- *WhoEmL 93*
Melton, Ruby Helene *Law&B 92*
Melton, Saundra Lou 1939- *WhoAmW 93*
Melton, Stephen Reid 1949- *WhoEmL 93*
Melton, Thomas Ronald 1948- *WhoEmL 93, WhoSSW 93*
Melton, Timothy Merryl 1957- *WhoEmL 93*
Melton, Walter 1932- *St&PR 93*
Melton, Wayne Charles 1954- *WhoEmL 93, WhoWor 93*
Melton, William Couch 1947- *St&PR 93*
Meltz, Martin Lowell 1942- *WhoSSW 93*
Meltzer, Allan H. *BioIn 17*
Meltzer, Allan H. 1928- *ConAu 39NR, WhoAm 92, WhoE 93*
Meltzer, Bernard David 1914- *WhoAm 92, WhoWor 93*
Meltzer, Bernard Nathan 1916- *WhoAm 92*
Meltzer, Bonnie Rosenberg 1943- *WhoAmW 93*
Meltzer, Bruce G. 1948- *St&PR 93*
Meltzer, D.B. 1929- *St&PR 93*
Meltzer, David 1937- *WhoAm 92, WhoWrEP 92*
Meltzer, David Brian 1929- *WhoAm 92*
Meltzer, Debra Marie 1954- *St&PR 93*
Meltzer, Donald Richard 1932- *WhoAm 92*
Meltzer, E. Alyne 1934- *WhoAmW 93*
Meltzer, Evan Frederick 1946- *WhoE 93*
Meltzer, George J. 1921-1991 *BioIn 17*
Meltzer, Herbert Yale 1937- *WhoAm 92*
Meltzer, Ilese Sue 1961- *WhoEmL 93*
Meltzer, Irene Margaret 1953- *WhoAmW 93*
Meltzer, Jack 1921- *WhoAm 92, WhoE 93*
Meltzer, Jay H. *Law&B 92*
Meltzer, Jay H. 1944- *WhoAm 92*
Meltzer, Jay Howard 1944- *St&PR 93*
Meltzer, Jeff Matthew 1957- *WhoE 93*
Meltzer, Kim I. 1956- *St&PR 93*
Meltzer, Michael 1946- *St&PR 93*
Meltzer, Milton 1915- *BioIn 17, ConAu 38NR, MajAI [port], WhoAm 92, WhoWrEP 92*
Meltzer, Peter Claude 1949- *WhoE 93*
Meltzer, Zachary 1935- *St&PR 93*
Melucci, Alberto 1943- *WhoWor 93*
Melucci, Richard Charles 1946- *WhoE 93, WhoWor 93*
Meluch, R.M. 1956- *ScF&FL 92*
Meluch, Rebecca M. 1956- *WhoWrEP 92*
Melum, Mara Minerva 1951- *WhoAmW 93*
Meluzzi, Salvatore 1813-1897 *Baker 92*
Melville, A(lan) D(avid) 1912- *ConAu 137*
Melville, Charles (Peter) 1951- *ConAu 138*
Melville, Donald Robert 1926- *St&PR 93, WhoAm 92*
Melville, Herman 1819-1891 *BioIn 17, MagSAmL [port], WorLitC [port]*

Melville, James T. *Law&B 92*
Melville, James Thomas 1951- *St&PR 93*
Melville, Jean-Pierre 1917-1973 *MiSFD 9N*
Melville, Jennie 1922- *ScF&FL 92*
Melville, Margarita B. 1929- *NotHsAW 93 [port]*
Melville, Pauline *ScF&FL 92*
Melville, R. Jerrold 1953- *WhoE 93*
Melville, Robert Seaman 1913- *WhoAm 92, WhoE 93*
Melville, William Gordon 1928- *St&PR 93*
Melvill-Jones, Geoffrey 1923- *WhoAm 92*
Melvin, Ben Watson, Jr. 1926- *WhoAm 92*
Melvin, Billy Alfred 1929- *WhoAm 92*
Melvin, Carolyn S. *Law&B 92*
Melvin, Charles Edward, Jr. 1929- *WhoAm 92*
Melvin, Diane Irene 1946- *WhoEmL 93*
Melvin, Ella Herriman *AmWomPl*
Melvin, Harold, & the Blue Notes *SoulM*
Melvin, John A. 1944- *WhoIns 93*
Melvin, John Lewis 1935- *WhoAm 92*
Melvin, Joseph M. 1950- *WhoAm 92*
Melvin, Kenneth B. *ScF&FL 92*
Melvin, Margaret 1927- *WhoAmW 93, WhoSSW 93, WhoWor 93*
Melvin, Maxine Marie 1905- *WhoAmW 93*
Melvin, Norman Cecil 1916- *WhoAm 92*
Melvin, Peter Joseph 1944- *WhoE 93*
Melvin, Russell Johnston 1925- *St&PR 93, WhoAm 92*
Melvin, T. Stephen 1938- *WhoAm 92, WhoE 93, WhoWor 93*
Melvin, Thomas Robert 1932- *St&PR 93*
Melzack, Ronald 1929- *WhoAm 92*
Melzacka, Miroslawa 1933- *WhoScE 91-4*
Melzacki, Krzysztof 1932- *WhoWor 93*
Melzarek, Doris *BioIn 17*
Melzer, Andrew C. 1957- *St&PR 93*
Melzer, Dorothy Garrett *WhoWrEP 92*
Melzer, John T.S. 1938- *WhoWrEP 92*
Melzer, Klaus-Jurgen 1935- *WhoScE 91-3*
Melzer, Robert Max 1941- *St&PR 93*
Melzer, Thomas C. 1944- *St&PR 93*
Melzer, William C. *WhoAm 92*
Melzer, William George 1934- *St&PR 93*
Mematsu, Kunihiko *WhoScE 91-2*
Member of the Committee of Safety of 1908, A *ScF&FL 92*
Membree, Edmond 1820-1882 *Baker 92*
Membrino, Dennis Herman 1945- *St&PR 93*
Memmer, Russell M. 1931- *St&PR 93*
Memmert, Guenter 1944- *St&PR 93*
Memmert, Wolfgang 1933- *WhoWor 93*
Memnon *OxDcByz*
Memoli, Robert 1946- *St&PR 93*
Memon, Bashir Ahmed 1941- *WhoSSW 93*
Memon, Rajab A. 1944- *WhoWor 93*
Memory, Jasper Durham 1936- *WhoAm 92*
Memphis Horns *SoulM*
Mena, Danilo J. 1937- *WhoE 93*
Mena, Juan Pascual de *BioIn 17*
Menaboni, Athos 1895-1990 *BioIn 17*
Menachem, Arlene Meryl 1952- *WhoEmL 93*
Menachem, Marshall 1951- *St&PR 93*
Menager, Laurent 1835-1902 *Baker 92*
Menagh, Charles Molesworth 1920- *WhoE 93*
Menagh, Melanie Campbell 1959- *WhoAmW 93*
Menagh, Pamela Sue 1948- *WhoAmW 93*
Menaghan, Elizabeth Grace 1949- *WhoAmW 93*
Menagias, Elias Dennis 1949- *WhoE 93, WhoEmL 93*
Menaker, Frank H., Jr. *Law&B 92*
Menaker, Frank H., Jr. 1940- *St&PR 93, WhoAm 92*
Menaker, Howard Bruce 1936- *St&PR 93*
Menaker, Michael 1934- *WhoAm 92*
Menaker, Ronald Herbert 1944- *WhoE 93*
Menaker, Shirley Ann Lasch 1935- *WhoAm 92*
Menander c. 342BC-c. 292BC *ClMLC 9, DramC 3 [port], HarEnMi*
Menander of Laodikeia *OxDcByz*
Menander Protector fl. 6th cent.- *OxDcByz*
Menander Rhetor fl. 3rd cent.- *OxDcByz*
Menanteau, Bernard P. 1939- *WhoScE 91-2*
Menapace, John J. 1944- *St&PR 93*
Menard, Charles Walter 1929- *St&PR 93*
Menard, Edith 1919- *WhoE 93, WhoWor 93*
Menard, Jacques Edouard 1923- *WhoWor 93*
Menard, Jayne Bush 1946- *WhoEmL 93*
Menard, John Willis 1838-1893 *EncAACR*
Menard, M.R. 1949- *St&PR 93*
Menard, Michael Joseph 1948- *WhoEmL 93*
Menard, Stanley Clayton 1925- *St&PR 93*
Menas *OxDcByz*
Menasce, Jacques de 1905-1960 *Baker 92*
Menashe, Ari Ben- *BioIn 17*
Menashe, Samuel 1925- *WhoWrEP 92*
Menashe, Solomon D. 1925- *St&PR 93*
Menasveta, Deb 1930- *WhoUN 92*
Menaul, Christopher *MiSFD 9*
Mencarelli, Ronald Peter 1938- *St&PR 93*
Mencer, Charles David 1944- *St&PR 93, WhoIns 93*
Mencer, Glenn Everell 1925- *WhoAm 92, WhoE 93*
Mencey, Helen V. L. 1960- *WhoAmW 93, WhoEmL 93, WhoSSW 93*
Mench, John William 1943- *WhoAm 92*
Menchaca, Angel 1855-1924 *Baker 92*
Menchaca, Juan Roberto 1934- *WhoUN 92*
Menchaca, Peggy B. 1938- *St&PR 93*
Menchaca, Peggy Beard 1938- *WhoAm 92*
Menchel, Donald 1932- *WhoAm 92*
Menchen, Judith K. *Law&B 92*
Mencher, Bruce Stephan 1935- *WhoAm 92*
Mencher, Melvin 1927- *WhoAm 92*
Mencher, Peter Milton 1946- *WhoE 93, WhoEmL 93*
Mencher, Stuart Alan 1939- *WhoAm 92*
Menches, John David 1950- *St&PR 93*
Menchhofer, Donald L. 1937- *St&PR 93*
Menchin, Robert Stanley 1923- *WhoAm 92*
Menchinger, Steven R. 1959- *St&PR 93*
Menchini, Paul John 1954- *WhoSSW 93*
Menchions, C. William *Law&B 92*
Menchu, Rigoberta *DcCPCAm*
Menchu, Rigoberta c. 1960- *News 93-2 [port]*
Mencini, Jack E. 1943- *St&PR 93*
Mencken, H.L. 1880-1956 *BioIn 17*
Mencken, Henry Louis 1880-1956 *BioIn 17, DcTwHis, JrnUS*
Mencotti, Claude Decio *Law&B 92*
Mendana, Alvaro de 1541-1595 *Expl 93 [port]*
Mende, Robert Graham 1926- *WhoAm 92, WhoE 93*
Mende, Wolf Rudiger 1954- *WhoWor 93*
Mendel, Arthur 1905-1979 *Baker 92*
Mendel, Dennis D. *Law&B 92*
Mendel, Gregor 1822-1884 *BioIn 17*
Mendel, Hermann 1834-1876 *Baker 92*
Mendel, Jerry Marc 1938- *WhoAm 92*
Mendel, Johann Gregor 1822-1884 *BioIn 17*
Mendel, Paula *AmWomPl*
Mendel, Peter Paul 1949- *WhoEmL 93*
Mendel, Roberta Joan 1935- *WhoWrEP 92*
Mendel, Verne Edward 1923- *WhoAm 92*
Mendel-John, Elaine B. *Law&B 92*
Mendell, Oliver M. 1925- *WhoAm 92*
Mendell, Thomas G. 1946- *St&PR 93*
Mendeloff, Albert Irwin 1918- *WhoAm 92*
Mendelowitz, Allan Irwin 1943- *WhoE 93*
Mendels, Joseph 1937- *WhoAm 92*
Mendelsohn, Alfred 1910-1966 *Baker 92*
Mendelsohn, Everett Irwin 1931- *WhoAm 92*
Mendelsohn, Felix, Jr. 1906-1990 *ScF&FL 92*
Mendelsohn, Harold 1923- *WhoAm 92, WhoWrEP 92*
Mendelsohn, Hindley 1920- *St&PR 93*
Mendelsohn, Irwin 1928- *St&PR 93*
Mendelsohn, Jack 1918- *WhoWrEP 92*
Mendelsohn, John 1936- *WhoAm 92, WhoSSW 93*
Mendelsohn, Michael John 1931- *WhoSSW 93*
Mendelsohn, Naomi *WhoAmW 93*
Mendelsohn, Robert V. 1946- *St&PR 93*
Mendelsohn, Robert Victor 1946- *WhoAm 92*
Mendelsohn, Stuart 1952- *WhoEmL 93, WhoSSW 93*
Mendelsohn, Susan Lynn 1955- *WhoAmW 93*
Mendelsohn, Thomas Charles 1944- *St&PR 93*
Mendelsohn, Zehavah Whitney 1956- *WhoEmL 93*
Mendelson, Alan Michael 1947- *WhoEmL 93*
Mendelson, David Dale 1940- *WhoSSW 93*
Mendelson, Drew *ScF&FL 92*
Mendelson, Edward 1946- *ScF&FL 92*
Mendelson, Edward James 1946- *WhoAm 92*
Mendelson, Elliott 1931- *WhoAm 92*
Mendelson, George 1946- *WhoWor 93*
Mendelson, Haim 1923- *WhoAm 92, WhoE 93*
Mendelson, Ira 1952- *St&PR 93*
Mendelson, Irving 1920- *St&PR 93*
Mendelson, Kenneth Samuel 1933- *WhoAm 92*
Mendelson, Laurans A. 1938- *St&PR 93*
Mendelson, Lee M. 1933- *WhoAm 92*
Mendelson, Leonard M. 1923- *WhoE 93, WhoWor 93*
Mendelson, Richard Donald 1933- *WhoAm 92*
Mendelson, Robert 1933- *St&PR 93*
Mendelson, Robert Allen 1930- *WhoAm 92*
Mendelson, Samuel 1937- *St&PR 93*
Mendelson, Steven Earle 1948- *WhoEmL 93*
Mendelssohn, Arnold (Ludwig) 1855-1933 *Baker 92*
Mendelssohn (-Bartholdy), (Jacob Ludwig) Felix 1809-1847 *Baker 92*
Mendelssohn, Fanny *Baker 92*
Mendelssohn, Fanny Cecile 1805-1847 *BioIn 17*
Mendelssohn, Felix 1809-1847 *BioIn 17, OxDcOp*
Mendelssohn, Moses 1729-1786 *BioIn 17*
Mendelssohn-Bartholdy, Jacob Ludwig Felix 1809-1847 *BioIn 17*
Mendelsund, Benjamin d1991 *BioIn 17*
Mendeluk, George 1948- *MiSFD 9*
Menden, Erich K. 1924- *WhoScE 91-3*
Mendenhall, Corwin 1916- *BioIn 17*
Mendenhall, Geoffrey Norman 1947- *St&PR 93*
Mendenhall, Jeff Ralph 1955- *WhoEmL 93*
Mendenhall, John Ryan 1928- *St&PR 93, WhoAm 92*
Mendenhall, Oniel C. 1922- *St&PR 93*
Mendenhall, Robert Vernon 1920- *WhoAm 92*
Mendenhall, Robert W. 1954- *St&PR 93*
Mendenhall, Roberta K. *Law&B 92*
Mendenhall, Terril Ray 1948- *WhoAm 92*
Mender, Mona Siegler 1926- *WhoAmW 93, WhoE 93, WhoWor 93*
Mender, Per G. 1932- *WhoWor 93*
Mendera, Zbigniew 1933- *WhoScE 91-4*
Menderes, Adnan 1899-1961 *BioIn 17, DcTwHis*
Menders, Claude Emanuel 1944- *WhoE 93*
Mendes, Avelino 1935- *St&PR 93*
Mendes, Chico *BioIn 17*
Mendes, Chico 1944-1988 *ConHero 2 [port], DcTwHis*
Mendes, George Michael 1961- *WhoE 93*
Mendes, Henry Pereira 1852-1937 *JeAmHC*
Mendes, Maria de Fatima V.A. 1957- *WhoUN 92*
Mendes, Robert *Law&B 92*
Mendes, Robert Laurence 1947- *WhoIns 93*
Mendes, Robert Warner 1938- *WhoE 93*
Mendes, Ronald Terry *Law&B 92*
Mendes France, Michel 1936- *WhoWor 93*
Mendes-France, Pierre 1907-1982 *BioIn 17, ColdWar 1 [port], DcTwHis*
Mendes Gaspar, Abilio 1931- *WhoScE 91-3*
Mendes Mourao, Jose *WhoScE 91-3*
Mendes Neto, Arthur Teixeira 1952- *WhoWor 93*
Mendez, Albert Orlando 1935- *WhoAm 92, WhoE 93, WhoWor 93*
Mendez, Barbara Kay 1959- *WhoAmW 93*
Mendez, C. Beatriz 1952- *WhoAmW 93*
Mendez, Celestino Galo 1944- *WhoWor 93*
Mendez, Concha 1898- *DcMexL*
Mendez, Diana Teresa 1948- *WhoAmW 93*
Mendez, Gabriel Alejandro 1956- *WhoWor 93*
Mendez, Hector *Law&B 92*
Mendez, Hermann Armando 1949- *WhoWor 93*
Mendez, Ileana Maria 1952- *WhoAmW 93, WhoEmL 93*
Mendez, Jana Wells 1944- *WhoAmW 93*
Mendez, Jose 1888?-1928 *HispAmA*
Mendez, Jose 1921- *HispAmA*
Mendez, Jose de la Caridad 1888-1928 *BiDAMSp 1989*
Mendez, Julin *DcCPCAm*
Mendez, Larry Wayne 1956- *WhoEmL 93, WhoSSW 93*
Mendez, Monica Sue 1967- *WhoAmW 93*
Mendez, Olga A. *WhoAmW 93*
Mendez, Pedro d1990 *BioIn 17*
Mendez, Phil 1947- *BlkAull 92*
Mendez, Raymond A. *BioIn 17*
Mendez, Robert G. *Law&B 92*
Mendez, Ruben P. *WhoUN 92*
Mendez de Cuenca, Laura 1853-1928 *DcMexL*
Mendez-Longoria, Miguel Angel 1942- *HispAmA*
Mendez Montenegro, Julio Cesar *DcCPCAm*
Mendez Montenegro, Mario *DcCPCAm*
Mendez Plancarte, Alfonso 1909-1955 *DcMexL*
Mendez Plancarte, Gabriel 1905-1949 *DcMexL*
Mendez Quinones, Emma 1946- *WhoAmW 93*
Mendgen, Kurt Walter 1944- *WhoScE 91-3*
Mendham, Robert William, Jr. 1956- *WhoWor 93*
Mendia, Carlos F. 1941- *WhoSSW 93*
Mendicino, V. Frank 1939- *WhoAm 92*
Mendieta, Ana 1948-1985 *BioIn 17*
Mendieta, Carlos *DcCPCAm*
Mendik, Bernard H. 1929- *WhoE 93*
Mendini, Alessandro *BioIn 17*
Mendini, Douglas A. 1953- *WhoWrEP 92*
Mendini, Gaylen A. 1935- *St&PR 93*
Mendiola, Anna Maria G. 1948- *WhoAmW 93, WhoEmL 93*
Mendiola, Mario Gene J. *WhoAsAP 91*
Mendis, John Bertrand 1947- *WhoUN 92*
Mendis, Kamini Nirmala 1948- *WhoWor 93*
Mendius, Patricia Dodd Winter 1924- *WhoAmW 93, WhoWor 93*
Mendler, Allen Neil 1949- *WhoE 93*
Mendley, Laura Lichtenstein 1932- *WhoAmW 93*
Mendola, Joseph Vincent 1953- *WhoEmL 93*
Mendolia, Joseph C. 1949- *WhoE 93*
Mendoliera, Salvatore 1952- *WhoWor 93*
Mendonca, Susan *ScF&FL 92*
Mendonides, Diamond *Law&B 92*
Mendonsa, Arthur Adonel 1928- *WhoAm 92, WhoSSW 93, WhoWor 93*
Mendoza, Catherine Holmes *WhoAmW 93*
Mendoza, Corine 1952- *NotHsAW 93*
Mendoza, Genaro Tumamak 1943- *WhoWor 93*
Mendoza, George 1934- *WhoAm 92, WhoWor 93*
Mendoza, Hector 1932-1987 *DcMexL*
Mendoza, Joann Audilet 1943- *WhoAmW 93*
Mendoza, Juana Belen de Gutierrez 1880-1942 *BioIn 17*
Mendoza, Lydia 1916- *NotHsAW 93*
Mendoza, Manuel B. *Law&B 92*
Mendoza, Maria Luisa 1938- *BioIn 17*
Mendoza, Roberto G., Jr. 1945- *WhoAm 92*
Mendoza, Sally Patricia 1951- *WhoAmW 93*
Mendoza, Stanley Atran 1940- *WhoAm 92*
Mendoza, Vicente T. 1894-1964 *DcMexL*
Mendoza, Vince *BioIn 17*
Mendoza de Munoz, Ines d1990 *BioIn 17*
Mendoza Santoyo, Fernando 1956- *WhoWor 93*
Mendoza Schechter, Hope *NotHsAW 93*
Mendozo, Ranie G. *Law&B 92*
Mendrey, Kathleen Louise 1946- *WhoEmL 93*
Meneeley, Edward Sterling 1927- *WhoAm 92*
Meneely-Kyder, Sarah 1945- *Baker 92*
Menefee, Eileen *WhoSSW 93*
Menefee, Laura S. 1953- *WhoEmL 93*
Menefee, Samuel Pyeatt 1950- *WhoEmL 93, WhoSSW 93, WhoWor 93*
Menegas, Peter *ScF&FL 92*
Meneghetti, Alvise 1691-1768 *BioIn 17*
Menegon, Lucio 1962- *WhoE 93*
Menell, Norman J. 1931- *St&PR 93*
Menelly, Richard A. *Law&B 92*
Menem, Carlos Saul *BioIn 17*
Menem, Carlos Saul 1932- *WhoWor 93*
Menen, Aubrey 1912-1989 *ScF&FL 92*
Menendez, Carlos 1938- *St&PR 93, WhoAm 92*
Menendez, Catherine A. 1959- *WhoIns 93*
Menendez, Erik *BioIn 17*
Menendez, Jose d1989 *BioIn 17*
Menendez, Jose Luis Llovio- *BioIn 17*
Menendez, Kitty d1989 *BioIn 17*
Menendez, Lyle *BioIn 17*
Menendez, Manuel, Jr. 1947- *WhoSSW 93*
Menendez, Miguel Angel 1905- *DcMexL*
Menendez, Miguel Angel 1905-1982 *SpAmA*
Menendez, Ramon *MiSFD 9*
Menendez de Aviles, Pedro 1519-1574 *BioIn 17*
Menendez Park, Gonzalo *WhoWor 93*
Mener, Leon Z. *Law&B 92*
Menes, Paul Ira 1955- *WhoEmL 93*
Menes, Pauline H. 1924- *WhoAmW 93*
Meneses, Antonio 1957- *Baker 92*
Meneses, Guillermo 1911-1978 *SpAmA*
Menesini, Susan 1938- *WhoAmW 93*
Meney, George Harlow 1947- *WhoE 93*

Mercier, Jacques Louis 1933- *WhoWor 93*
Mercier, Jean Claude 1940- *WhoAm 92*
Mercier, Jean-Louis 1934- *WhoAm 92*
Mercier, Jean P. 1932- *WhoScE 91-2*
Mercier, Jean Pierre 1932- *WhoWor 93*
Mercier, Jean-Roger 1946- *WhoScE 91-2*
Mercier, Jonathan Lee *Law&B 92*
Mercier, Michel Jean 1935- *WhoUN 92*
Mercier, Monique *Law&B 92*
Mercier, Ronald H. 1947- *St&PR 93*
Mercier, Tyler *BioIn 17*
Mercier, Vivian 1919-1989 *BioIn 17*
Merck, Albert W. 1920- *St&PR 93*
Mercke, Charles D. 1907- *St&PR 93*
Mercorella, Anthony Joseph 1927- *WhoAm 92*
Mercorelli, Eugene 1947- *St&PR 93*
Mercoun, Dawn Denise 1950- *WhoAmW 93, WhoWor 93*
Mercouri, Melina *BioIn 17*
Mercouri, Melina 1925- *IntDcF 2-3 [port]*
Mercouri, Melina Maria Amalia 1925- *WhoWor 93*
Mercredi, Ovide *BioIn 17*
Mercredi, Ovide William *WhoWor 93*
Mercure, Gilbert Thomas 1934- *St&PR 93*
Mercure, Jean-Francois F. *Law&B 92*
Mercure, Pierre 1927-1966 *Baker 92*
Mercurio, Antonino Marco 1930- *WhoWor 93*
Mercurio, C.W. 1940- *St&PR 93*
Mercurio, Frank B. d1992 *NewYTBS 92*
Mercurio, Laura Deubler 1953- *WhoE 93, WhoEmL 93*
Mercurio, Peter 1968- *WhoE 93*
Mercurio, Renard Michael 1947- *WhoAm 92*
Mercurio, Roberto 1951- *WhoScE 91-3*
Mercurio, Sal L. *Law&B 92*
Mercuro, Tobia G. 1933- *St&PR 93*
Mercury, Freddie *BioIn 17*
Mercury, Freddie 1946-1991 *AnObit 1991, News 92*
Mercy, Franz von c. 1591-1645 *HarEnMi*
Mercz, Laszlo Imre 1940- *WhoUN 92*
Merdian, M. Jane *Law&B 92*
Merdinger, Charles John 1918- *WhoAm 92*
Merdinger, Emanuel 1906- *WhoSSW 93*
Merdinger, Susan 1943- *WhoAmW 93, WhoWor 93*
Mere, Manuel H. 1945- *St&PR 93*
Meredith, Anne LeBlanc 1968- *WhoE 93*
Meredith, Burgess 1908- *BioIn 17, IntDcF 2-3*
Meredith, Burgess 1909- *WhoAm 92*
Meredith, Dale Dean 1940- *WhoAm 92*
Meredith, David Robert 1940- *WhoAm 92*
Meredith, Edwin Thomas 1876-1928 *BioIn 17, JrnUS*
Meredith, Edwin Thomas, III 1933- *St&PR 93, WhoAm 92*
Meredith, Ellis Edson 1927- *WhoAm 92, WhoWor 93*
Meredith, Gary E. 1934- *St&PR 93*
Meredith, George Davis 1940- *WhoAm 92*
Meredith, George Marlor 1923- *WhoAm 92, WhoE 93*
Meredith, Gregory S. *Law&B 92*
Meredith, Iris d1980 *SweetSg C [port]*
Meredith, James Creed 1875-1942 *ScF&FL 92*
Meredith, James Howard 1933- *EncAACR, WhoAm 92*
Meredith, John Wylie 1943- *St&PR 93*
Meredith, Julia Alice 1943- *WhoAmW 93*
Meredith, Kevin Edward 1962- *WhoSSW 93*
Meredith, Lewis Douglas 1905- *WhoAm 92*
Meredith, Marilyn 1933- *WhoWrEP 92*
Meredith, Morris *WhoWrEP 92*
Meredith, Nevin W. 1935- *St&PR 93*
Meredith, Orsell Montgomery 1923- *WhoE 93*
Meredith, Owen Nichols 1924- *WhoSSW 93*
Meredith, Pamela Ann 1953- *WhoAmW 93*
Meredith, Pamela Louise 1956- *WhoE 93*
Meredith, Paul Wayne 1931- *WhoWor 93*
Meredith, Richard C. 1937-1979 *ScF&FL 92*
Meredith, Ronald Edward 1946- *WhoAm 92, WhoSSW 93*
Meredith, Roy Dickinson *Law&B 92*
Meredith, Scott 1923- *WhoWrEP 92*
Meredith, Sidney d1992 *NewYTBS 92*
Meredith, Spencer B., Jr. 1931- *St&PR 93*
Meredith, Stephen John 1956- *WhoWor 93*
Meredith, Ted Jordan 1950- *WhoWrEP 92*
Meredith, Thomas C. *WhoAm 92, WhoSSW 93*
Meredith, W. Douglas *St&PR 93*
Meredith, William 1919- *WhoE 93, WhoWrEP 92*
Meredith, William (Morris) 1919- *ConAu 40NR*
Merelli, Bartolomeo 1794-1879 *OxDcOp*
Merelli, Eugenio 1825-1882 *OxDcOp*
Meremba, Wagi 1953- *WhoAsAP 91*
Merenbloom, Elliot Y. *BioIn 17*
Merenbloom, Robert Barry 1947- *WhoE 93*
Merendino, K. Alvin 1914- *WhoAm 92*
Meretey, Katalin 1935- *WhoScE 91-4*
Meretta, James Leonard 1941- *St&PR 93*
Meretzky, S. Eric *ScF&FL 92*
Mergel, Stephanie Ann 1964- *WhoEmL 93*
Mergenhagen, Dieter 1939- *WhoScE 91-3*
Mergens, Bridget *BioIn 17*
Mergenthaler, Wolfgang Ludwig 1947- *WhoWor 93*
Mergentime, Charles E. 1931- *St&PR 93*
Mergler, H. Kent 1940- *WhoAm 92*
Mergler, Harry Winston 1924- *WhoAm 92*
Mergler, Neil R. 1948- *St&PR 93*
Mergner, Hans Konrad 1917- *WhoScE 91-3, WhoWor 93*
Merguerian, Anna 1955- *St&PR 93*
Merhige, Robert R., III *Law&B 92*
Merhige, Robert Reynold, Jr. 1919- *WhoAm 92, WhoSSW 93*
Meri, Lennart 1929- *WhoWor 93*
Merian, Harold Arthur 1959- *WhoEmL 93*
Merian, Wilhelm 1889-1952 *Baker 92*
Merians, Judith *Law&B 92*
Meriaux, J.B. Emile 1936- *WhoScE 91-2*
Meric, Rene Pierre, Jr. 1925- *St&PR 93*
Merickel, Michael Bruce 1947- *WhoSSW 93*
Meric-Lalande, Henriette 1798-1867 *OxDcOp*
Meric-Lalande, Henriette (Clementine) 1798-1867 *Baker 92*
Meridan, Paula M. 1955- *WhoAmW 93*
Meriel, Paul 1818-1897 *Baker 92*
Merigan, Thomas Charles, Jr. 1934- *WhoAm 92*
Merighi, Antonia fl. 1717-1740 *OxDcOp*
Merikanto, Aarre 1893-1958 *Baker 92, OxDcOp*
Merikanto, Oskar 1868-1924 *OxDcOp*
Merikanto, (Frans) Oskar 1868-1924 *Baker 92*
Merikoski, Jorma Kaarlo 1942- *WhoWor 93*
Meril, Alex Sylvere 1953- *WhoWor 93*
Merilainen, Usko 1930- *Baker 92*
Merilan, Charles Preston 1926- *WhoAm 92, WhoWor 93*
Merilan, Jean Elizabeth 1962- *WhoAmW 93*
Merilan, Michael Preston 1956- *WhoEmL 93*
Merilatt, Randall Lee 1951- *WhoEmL 93*
Merillat, Jeffery Stephen 1951- *St&PR 93*
Merimee, Jean-Bernard 1936- *WhoUN 92*
Merimee, Prosper 1803-1870 *DcLB 119 [port], OxDcOp*
Merimee, Thomas Joseph 1931- *WhoAm 92*
Merin, Andrew Jeffrey 1948- *St&PR 93*
Merin, Robert Lynn 1946- *WhoEmL 93*
Meringer, J.H. *Law&B 92*
Meringola, Paul Daniel 1958- *St&PR 93*
Merington, Marguerite 1860-1951 *AmWomPl*
Merino, Francisco *WhoWor 93*
Merino, Roberto Garreton *BioIn 17*
Merino Castro, Jose Toribio 1915- *WhoWor 93*
Merion, Richard Donald 1936- *WhoE 93*
Merisalo, Carl B. 1924- *WhoWor 93*
Meritt, Benjamin Dean 1899-1989 *BioIn 17*
Meritt, Lucy Taxis Shoe 1906- *WhoSSW 93*
Meritt, Paul Bruce 1945- *St&PR 93*
Merivale, John 1917-1990 *BioIn 17*
Merivale, John Herman 1779-1844 *BioIn 17*
Meriwether, Charles Minor 1911- *WhoAm 92*
Meriwether, Heath J. 1944- *St&PR 93, WhoAm 92*
Meriwether, J. Bruce 1938- *St&PR 93*
Meriwether, James Babcock 1928- *WhoAm 92, WhoWrEP 92*
Meriwether, John Robert 1937- *WhoSSW 93*
Meriwether, John Samuel, Jr. 1949- *St&PR 93*
Meriwether, John W. *St&PR 93*
Meriwether, Kathleen *Law&B 92*
Meriwether, Louise M. 1923- *BlkAull 92*
Meriwether, Nell W. 1931- *WhoWrEP 92*
Meriwether, Susan *AmWomPl*
Merk, Joseph 1795-1852 *Baker 92*
Merkel, Edward W., Jr. *Law&B 92*
Merkel, Edward Wagner, Jr. 1943- *WhoAm 92*
Merkel, Fred *BioIn 17*
Merkel, G. *WhoScE 91-3*
Merkel, Joelen Kilbas 1951- *St&PR 93*
Merkel, Judi Kay 1946- *WhoEmL 93*
Merkel, Patricia Mae 1935- *WhoAmW 93*
Merkel, Paul Barrett 1945- *WhoE 93*
Merkel, Pete 1933- *St&PR 93*
Merkel, Stephen M. *Law&B 92*
Merkel, Theresa Marano *WhoAmW 93*
Merkel, Una 1903-1986 *QDrFCA 92 [port]*
Merkel-Keller, Claudia Elisabeth 1948- *WhoE 93*
Merkelo, Henri 1939- *WhoAm 92*
Merkelson, Wayne P. *Law&B 92*
Merkens, Jacobus H.J. 1960- *WhoScE 91-3*
Merker, Edward 1940- *WhoE 93*
Merker, Frank Ferdinand 1909- *WhoAm 92*
Merker, Hans-Joachim 1929- *WhoScE 91-3*
Merkert, George *WhoAm 92*
Merkes, Rudolf 1940- *WhoScE 91-3*
Merkin, A. Barry 1935- *St&PR 93*
Merkin, Donald H. 1945- *WhoSSW 93*
Merkin, William Leslie 1929- *WhoAm 92*
Merkl, Neil Matthew 1931- *WhoAm 92*
Merkle, Alan Ray 1947- *WhoEmL 93*
Merkle, Dale Gordon 1933- *WhoE 93*
Merkle, Diana C. *Law&B 92*
Merkle, Fritz 1950- *WhoWor 93*
Merkle, Helen Louise 1950- *WhoAmW 93*
Merkle, Sharon Ann 1946- *WhoAmW 93*
Merkle, Walter John 1957- *WhoEmL 93*
Merklen, Hector Alfredo 1936- *WhoWor 93*
Merklin, David V. 1942- *St&PR 93*
Merklin, Joseph 1819-1905 *Baker 92*
Merkling, Frank 1924- *WhoWrEP 92*
Merkling, John R. *Law&B 92*
Merkourios *OxDcByz*
Merks, Nicolaas Antonius 1945- *St&PR 93*
Merkt, Hans 1923- *WhoScE 91-3*
Merkt, Richard Alan 1949- *WhoEmL 93*
Merla, Patrick *ScF&FL 92*
Merlack, William 1928- *St&PR 93*
Merle, H. Etienne 1944- *WhoE 93*
Merle, Robert 1908- *ScF&FL 92*
Merlevede, Wilfried Jozef 1937- *WhoScE 91-2*
Merley, Bruce Michael 1946- *WhoEmL 93*
Merli, Francesco 1887-1976 *Baker 92, OxDcOp*
Merli, John E. *Law&B 92*
Merli, Madeline *AmWomPl*
Merlin, Christina *ConAu 40NR*
Merlin, Joanna 1931- *ConTFT 10*
Merlini, Giovanni 1929- *WhoWor 93*
Merlini, Lucio 1934- *WhoScE 91-3, WhoWor 93*
Merlin-Jones, Sally Barbara 1946- *WhoEmL 93*
Merlino, Anthony Frank 1930- *WhoE 93*
Merlino, Gregory 1957- *WhoEmL 93*
Merlino, Maria B. *Law&B 92*
Merlin-Scholtes, Joana Soarez 1947- *WhoUN 92*
Merlis, George 1940- *WhoAm 92*
Merlis, Howard Sophian 1922- *WhoSSW 93*
Merliss, William Sidney 1922- *WhoSSW 93, WhoWor 93*
Merlo, D. *WhoScE 91-1*
Merlo, Harry A. 1925- *St&PR 93*
Merlo, Harry Angelo 1925- *WhoAm 92*
Merlo, Larry J. 1955- *St&PR 93*
Merlo, Marisa *OxDcOp*
Merlo, Pier Antonio 1935- *WhoWor 93*
Merlotti, Frank H. *BioIn 17*
Merlotti, Frank Henry 1926- *St&PR 93*
Merman, Ethel 1908-1984 *Baker 92*
Mermaz, Louis 1931- *BioIn 17*
Mermel, H. 1947- *St&PR 93*
Mermelstein, Isabel Mae Rosenberg 1934- *WhoAmW 93*
Mermelstein, Jules Joshua 1955- *WhoEmL 93*
Mermer, Ira 1924- *WhoE 93*
Mermin, Dorothy Milman 1936- *WhoAm 92*
Mermin, N. David 1935- *WhoAm 92*
Mermod, Ronald 1924- *WhoScE 91-4*
Mernagh, Terrence Patrick 1959- *WhoWor 93*
MernaLyn *WhoAmW 93, WhoWor 93*
Mernan, David W. 1928- *St&PR 93*
Merner, Peter W. 1935- *WhoE 93*
Mernit, Susan 1953- *WhoWrEP 92*
Mernoe, Erik *WhoScE 91-2*
Mero, Endre Gabor 1932- *WhoUN 92*
Merobaudes, Flavius fl. 5th cent.- *OxDcByz*
Merola, Fred T. 1934- *St&PR 93*
Merola, Gaetano 1881-1953 *Baker 92, OxDcOp*
Merola, John Joseph 1945- *St&PR 93*
Merold, Virginia Ann 1940- *WhoAmW 93*
Merolla, Michael John 1954- *St&PR 93*
Meron, Theodor 1930- *ConAu 138, WhoAm 92*
Meroney, James Perry 1938- *St&PR 93*
Meroney, Robert Nelson 1937- *WhoAm 92*
Meroni, Paul Damian 1956- *St&PR 93*
Merores, Leo 1943- *WhoUN 92*
Merow, James F. 1932- *CngDr 91*
Merrall, Anne Patricia Jane 1952- *WhoWor 93*
Merrell, Arnold B. 1937- *St&PR 93*
Merrell, James Bruce *Law&B 92*
Merrell, James Hart 1953- *BioIn 17*
Merrell, James Lee 1930- *WhoAm 92, WhoWrEP 92*
Merrell, Jesse Howard 1938- *WhoE 93*
Merrell, Pamela K. *Law&B 92*
Merrell, William John, Jr. 1943- *WhoAm 92*
Merrem, Gerd Dietrich 1938- *WhoUN 92*
Merrett, Michael John *WhoScE 91-1*
Merrett, N. Rhys *Law&B 92*
Merrey, Edward F. 1911-1990 *BioIn 17*
Merrheim, Alphonse Adolphe 1871-1925? *BioIn 17*
Merriam, Alan P(arkhurst) 1923-1980 *Baker 92*
Merriam, C. Hart 1855-1942 *IntDcAn*
Merriam, Esther Virginia 1940- *WhoAmW 93*
Merriam, Eve d1992 *NewYTBS 92 [port]*
Merriam, Eve 1916- *WhoWrEP 92*
Merriam, Eve 1916-1992 *BioIn 17, ConAu 137, MajAI [port], ScF&FL 92, SmATA 73 [port]*
Merriam, George Rennell, Jr. 1913- *WhoE 93*
Merriam, J. Alec 1935- *WhoAm 92*
Merriam, Layton Carl 1934- *St&PR 93*
Merriam, Lillie Fuller *AmWomPl*
Merriam, Mary-Linda Sorber 1943- *WhoAm 92, WhoAmW 93*
Merriam, Robert Loring 1924- *WhoWrEP 92*
Merrick, Andrea Thomas *Law&B 92*
Merrick, Craig Russell 1941- *WhoE 93*
Merrick, David 1912- *BioIn 17, WhoAm 92*
Merrick, Frank 1886-1981 *Baker 92*
Merrick, George Boesch 1928- *WhoAm 92*
Merrick, George Jeffrey 1949- *St&PR 93*
Merrick, Harold A. 1937- *St&PR 93*
Merrick, John 1859-1919 *EncAACR*
Merrick, Lew 1953- *WhoEmL 93*
Merrick, Lynn 1919- *SweetSg C [port]*
Merrick, Max Milton 1907- *St&PR 93*
Merrick, Michael John *WhoScE 91-1*
Merrick, R.S. 1914- *St&PR 93*
Merrick, Ronald Caswell 1951- *WhoEmL 93, WhoSSW 93*
Merrick, Roswell Davenport 1922- *WhoAm 92*
Merrick, Tag *Law&B 92*
Merrick, Thomas P. 1937- *St&PR 93*
Merrick, Thomas William 1939- *WhoAm 92*
Merrick, Williston 1886-1971 *ScF&FL 92*
Merrier, Helen 1932- *WhoWor 93*
Merrifield, Donald Paul 1928- *WhoAm 92*
Merrifield, Dudley Bruce 1921- *WhoAm 92*
Merrifield, Gladys d1992 *NewYTBS 92*
Merrifield, Lewis Biehl, III 1939- *St&PR 93*
Merrifield, Robert Bruce 1921- *WhoAm 92, WhoE 93, WhoWor 93*
Merrigan, Mary Ellen 1951- *WhoEmL 93*
Merril, Judith 1923- *BioIn 17, ScF&FL 92, WhoCanL 92*
Merrill, Aaron Stanton 1890-1961 *HarEnMi*
Merrill, Al d1990 *BioIn 17*
Merrill, Ambrose P. 1909-1991 *BioIn 17*
Merrill, Arthur Alexander 1906- *WhoAm 92*
Merrill, Aubrey James 1948- *WhoE 93*
Merrill, Augustus Lee 1946- *WhoWrEP 92*
Merrill, Bob *ConAu 136*
Merrill, Celia Dale 1951- *WhoEmL 93*
Merrill, Charles Edward 1885-1956 *BioIn 17*
Merrill, Charles Merton 1907- *WhoAm 92*
Merrill, Connie Rae 1947- *WhoEmL 93*
Merrill, Dale Marie 1954- *WhoAmW 93, WhoE 93, WhoEmL 93*
Merrill, Edward Clifton, Jr. 1920- *WhoAm 92*
Merrill, Edward Wilson 1923- *WhoE 93*
Merrill, Evan 1931- *St&PR 93*

Messemer, Glenn Matthew 1947- WhoAm 92
Messenger, Donald B. W. 1935- WhoE 93
Messenger, George Clement 1930- WhoAm 92, WhoWor 93
Messenger, George Louis 1932- St&PR 93
Messenger, James Robert 1948- WhoEmL 93
Messenger, John B. Law&B 92
Messenger, Rosemary Schaefer 1927- WhoAmW 93
Messenkopf, Eugene John 1928- WhoAm 92
Messens, Mark Richard 1952- WhoEmL 93
Messent, Peter B. ScF&FL 92
Messer, Ann Rutledge 1954- WhoAmW 93
Messer, Arnold W. St&PR 93
Messer, Bonnie Jeanne 1943- WhoAmW 93
Messer, Burton 1943- WhoAm 92
Messer, Carol Lynn Law&B 92
Messer, Donald E(dward) 1941- ConAu 138
Messer, Donald Edward 1941- WhoAm 92
Messer, Earl Kenneth 1954- WhoEmL 93
Messer, James 1934- St&PR 93
Messer, Kenny L. 1949- St&PR 93
Messer, Michael Adolf 1927- WhoWor 93
Messer, Neidy BioIn 17
Messer, Nellie Stearns AmWomPl
Messer, Norma Johnson 1939- WhoSSW 93
Messer, Phillip Lee 1927- St&PR 93
Messer, Richard E. 1938- WhoWrEP 92
Messer, Stanley Bernard 1941- WhoE 93
Messer, Thomas Maria 1920- WhoAm 92, WhoWor 93
Messerer, Asaf d1992 NewYTBS 92 [port]
Messerer, Asaf 1903-1992 BioIn 17
Messerer, Asaf Mikhailovich 1903-1992 ConAu 137
Messerle, Judith Rose 1943- WhoAm 92
Messerli, Douglas 1947- ConAu 39NR, WhoWrEP 92
Messerli, Franz Hannes 1942- WhoAm 92
Messerli, Jonathan Carl 1926- WhoAm 92
Messerotti, Mauro 1954- WhoWor 93
Messer-Rehak, Dabney Lee 1951- WhoAmW 93
Messerschmidt, Daniel Gottlieb 1685-1735 Expl 93
Messerschmitt, David Gavin 1945- WhoAm 92
Messersmith, Harry BioIn 17
Messersmith, John Alexander 1945- BiDAMSp 1989
Messersmith, Lanny Dee 1942- WhoWor 93
Messersmith, Robert E. 1939- St&PR 93
Messiaen, A.M. WhoScE 91-2
Messiaen, Olivier BioIn 17
Messiaen, Olivier 1908-1992 IntDcOp, NewYTBS 92 [port], OxDcOp
Messiaen, Olivier (Eugene Prosper Charles) 1908- Baker 92
Messiaen, Olivier (Eugene Prosper Charles) 1908-1992 CurBio 92N
Messick, Bill W. 1947- St&PR 93
Messick, Burton L. 1948- St&PR 93
Messick, Dale 1906- BioIn 17
Messick, Deborah L. 1956- WhoAmW 93
Messick, Joseph W., Jr. 1939- St&PR 93
Messick, Wiley Sanders 1929- WhoSSW 93
Messier, Donald Wilmore 1937- WhoE 93
Messier, Mark BioIn 17
Messier, Mark 1961- NewYTBS 92 [port], News 93-1 [port], WhoAm 92
Messier, Pierre Law&B 92
Messier, Pierre 1945- WhoAm 92
Messier, Thomas B. St&PR 93
Messin, Frank E. 1932- St&PR 93
Messin, Marlene Ann 1935- St&PR 93
Messina, Angelo J. Law&B 92
Messina, Baldassare 1926- WhoScE 91-3
Messina, Barbara Ann 1940- WhoE 93
Messina, Charles F. 1943- St&PR 93
Messina, Dana E. 1956- St&PR 93
Messina, Gaetano M. 1942- WhoScE 91-3
Messina, James Vincent 1957- St&PR 93
Messina, Joseph R., Jr. 1904- WhoE 93
Messina, Margaret Ann 1966- WhoAmW 93
Messina, Michael P. Law&B 92
Messina, Philip F. MiSFD 9
Messina, Raymond A. Law&B 92
Messing, Carol Sue WhoAmW 93
Messing, Frank J. 1929- WhoIns 93
Messing, Fred M. 1947- WhoEmL 93
Messing, Frederick Andrew, Jr. 1946- WhoAm 92
Messing, Gordon Myron 1917- WhoE 93
Messing, Janet Agnes Kapelsohn 1918- WhoAm 92
Messing, Joachim Wilhelm 1946- WhoAm 92
Messing, Mark P. 1948- WhoAm 92
Messing, Paul David 1949- WhoE 93
Messing, Paul R. St&PR 93
Messing, Richard David 1941- WhoE 93
Messing, Robin 1953- WhoWrEP 92
Messing, Simon David 1922- WhoE 93
Messinger, Charles G. 1933- St&PR 93
Messinger, Clifford F. d1990 BioIn 17
Messinger, Donald Hathaway 1943- St&PR 93, WhoAm 92
Messinger, Gertrude 1912- SweetSg C [port]
Messinger, James Peter 1953- WhoIns 93
Messinger, Joe BioIn 17
Messinger, Martin P. Law&B 92
Messinger, Richard C. 1930- WhoAm 92
Messino, Paul Anthony 1963- WhoSSW 93
Messler, Charles Lewis 1937- WhoSSW 93
Messler, Eunice Claire 1930- WhoAmW 93
Messman, Jack L. 1940- St&PR 93, WhoAm 92
Messmann, Jon ScF&FL 92
Messmann, Richard R. ScF&FL 92
Messmer, Donald Joseph 1936- WhoAm 92, WhoSSW 93
Messmer, Harold Maxmilian, Jr. 1946- St&PR 93
Messmer, Linda Sue 1949- WhoAmW 93
Messmer, Pierre 1916- BioIn 17
Messmore, S.L. Law&B 92
Messmore, Scott L. 1947- St&PR 93
Messmore, Scott Lindsey Law&B 92
Messmore, Scott Lindsey 1947- WhoEmL 93
Messmore, Thomas E. WhoIns 93
Messmore, Thomas E. 1945- St&PR 93
Messmore, Thomas Ellison 1945- WhoAm 92
Messner, Anthony John 1939- WhoAsAP 91
Messner, Ernest L. Law&B 92
Messner, Frederick Richard 1926- St&PR 93
Messner, Gary R. 1933- St&PR 93
Messner, Howard Myron 1937- WhoAm 92
Messner, Joseph 1893-1969 Baker 92
Messner, Kathryn Hertzog 1915- WhoAmW 93, WhoWor 93
Messner, Mary E. Law&B 92
Messner, Michael A. 1952- ConAu 138
Messner, Reinhold 1944- BioIn 17
Messner, Richard Stephen 1939- WhoE 93
Messner, Robert T. Law&B 92
Messner, Robert Thomas 1938- St&PR 93
Messner, Thomas G. 1944- WhoAm 92
Messtorff, J. WhoScE 91-3
Messud, Francois Michel 1931- St&PR 93
Messulam, Lewis Law&B 92
Mestad, Orville Laverne 1923- WhoWor 93
Mestel, Mark David 1951- WhoEmL 93
Mestepey, John Thomas 1943- WhoSSW 93
Mester, Jorge 1935- Baker 92
Mester, Robert Loyd 1948- WhoEmL 93
Mester, Ulrich 1944- WhoWor 93
Mesterhazy, Tom 1961- St&PR 93
Mesterton-Gibbons, Michael Patrick 1954- WhoEmL 93, WhoSSW 93
Mestha, Lingappa Keshav 1957- WhoSSW 93
Mestman, Steven A. 1946- WhoIns 93
Meston, Michael Charles WhoScE 91-1
Meston, Michael Charles 1932- WhoWor 93
Mestrallet, Gerard 1949- WhoWor 93
Mestre, Solana Daniel 1937- WhoWor 93
Mestres, Ricardo, III 1958- WhoAm 92
Mestres, Ricardo Angelo, Jr. 1933- WhoAm 92
Mestres-Quadreny, Josep (Maria) 1929- Baker 92
Mestrov, Milan 1929- WhoScE 91-4
Mesun, Kim Buechel 1957- WhoEmL 93
Mesyeux, Jean-Auguste DcCPCAm
Meszar, Frank 1915- WhoAm 92
Meszaros, Erno 1935- WhoScE 91-4
Meszaros, Jacqueline R. St&PR 93
Meszaros, Janos 1927- WhoScE 91-4
Meszaros, Lajos 1931- WhoScE 91-3
Meszaros, Magdalene H. Law&B 92
Meszaros, Marta 1931- DrEEuF, MiSFD 9
Meszaros, Terry D. Law&B 92
Meszaros, Zoltan 1936- WhoScE 91-4
Meszner-Eltrich, A. Suzanne Law&B 92
Mesznik, Joel R. 1945- WhoAm 92
Meszoely, Charles Aladar Maria 1933- WhoE 93
Metag, Volker 1942- WhoScE 91-3
Metalonis, Gary St&PR 93
Metalov, Vasili (Mikhailovich) 1862-1926 Baker 92
Metastasio, Pietro 1698-1782 Baker 92, IntDcOp [port], OxDcOp
Metaxas, Dionyssios 1927- WhoScE 91-3
Metaxas, Ioannis 1871-1941 DcTwHis
Metaxas, John C. 1958- WhoE 93
Metcalf, Arthur George Bradford 1908- WhoAm 92
Metcalf, Brian Walter 1945- WhoE 93
Metcalf, Charles David 1933- WhoAm 92
Metcalf, Christopher Peter 1943- WhoUN 92
Metcalf, David St&PR 93
Metcalf, David Harry WhoScE 91-1
Metcalf, Debra Ruppe 1962- WhoSSW 93
Metcalf, Frank J(ohnson) 1865-1945 Baker 92
Metcalf, Frederic Thomas 1935- WhoAm 92
Metcalf, Frederick Thomas 1921- St&PR 93, WhoAm 92
Metcalf, Harold R. 1947- WhoE 93
Metcalf, Helen Mary 1949- WhoAmW 93
Metcalf, James Michael 1954- WhoSSW 93
Metcalf, James Richard 1950- WhoE 93
Metcalf, John 1938- WhoCanL 92
Metcalf, Keyes DeWitt 1889-1983 BioIn 17
Metcalf, Lawrence E. 1915-1989 BioIn 17
Metcalf, Lynnette Carol 1955- WhoAmW 93, WhoEmL 93
Metcalf, Margaret Louise Faber 1943- WhoAmW 93
Metcalf, Marsha Linda 1947- WhoE 93
Metcalf, Michael Warren 1946- WhoE 93
Metcalf, Paul 1917- ConAu 39NR
Metcalf, Paul C. 1917- WhoWrEP 92
Metcalf, Robert Clarence 1923- WhoAm 92
Metcalf, Robert Lee 1916- WhoAm 92
Metcalf, Robert W. 1936-1991 BioIn 17
Metcalf, Sharon Law&B 92
Metcalf, Suesi 1951- WhoEmL 93
Metcalf, Susan Stimmel 1926- WhoAm 92
Metcalf, Suzanne MajAI
Metcalf, Timothy Clare 1951- WhoE 93
Metcalf, Virgil Alonzo 1936- WhoWor 93
Metcalf, William Edwards 1947- WhoAm 92
Metcalf, William Henry, Jr. 1928- WhoAm 92
Metcalfe, Charles WhoScE 91-1
Metcalfe, Christopher Douglas Toby 1936- WhoWor 93
Metcalfe, Clifford A., Jr. St&PR 93
Metcalfe, Darrel Seymour 1913- WhoAm 92
Metcalfe, David WhoScE 91-1
Metcalfe, David D. 1922- St&PR 93
Metcalfe, David Thomas 1958- WhoEmL 93
Metcalfe, Dean Darrel 1944- WhoE 93
Metcalfe, Dorothy Ann 1942- WhoAmW 93
Metcalfe, Edwin WhoScE 91-1
Metcalfe, Elizabeth Tyree AmWomPl
Metcalfe, Felicia Leigh 1889- AmWomPl
Metcalfe, Howard WhoScE 91-1
Metcalfe, Letha Mae 1929- AfrAmBi
Metcalfe, Murray Robert 1954- WhoE 93, WhoEmL 93
Metcalfe, Norman J. 1942- St&PR 93
Metcalfe, Ralph H. BioIn 17
Metcalfe, Ralph Harold 1910-1978 AfrAmBi
Metcalfe, Robert 1946- ConEn
Metcalfe, Tom Brooks 1920- WhoAm 92
Metcalfe, Walter Lee, Jr. 1938- WhoAm 92
Metchnikoff, Elie 1845-1916 BioIn 17
Metdepenninghen, Carlos Maurits W. 1935- WhoWor 93
Metellus, Lucius Caecilius c. 291BC-221BC HarEnMi
Metellus Macedonicus, Quintus Caecilius d115BC HarEnMi
Metellus Numidicus, Quintus Caecilius dc. 91BC HarEnMi
Metellus Pius, Quintus Caecilius dc. 63BC HarEnMi
Metellus Pius Scipio, Quintus Caecilius d46BC HarEnMi
Metens, Thierry Mi 1961- WhoWor 93
Meters SoulM
Meth, Joseph 1943- St&PR 93, WhoAm 92
Meth, Kim 1957- St&PR 93
Methe, Pierrette 1933- WhoWor 93
Metheney, Wesley William 1946- WhoEmL 93
Metheny, Pat(rick Bruce) 1954- Baker 92
Metheny, Patrick Bruce 1954- WhoAm 92
Metherell, Ian D. Law&B 92
Methfessel, Albert Gottlieb 1785-1869 Baker 92
Methfessel, Friedrich 1771-1807 See Methfessel, Albert Gottlieb 1785-1869 Baker 92
Methfessel, Siegfried I. 1922- WhoScE 91-3
Methlin, Gerard 1931- WhoScE 91-2
Methodios dc. 311 OxDcByz
Methodios c. 815-885 OxDcByz
Methodios, I 8th cent.- OxDcByz
Methodios of Boston, Bishop 1946- WhoAm 92
Methodios of Patara, Pseudo- OxDcByz
Methuen, Paul Sanford 1845-1932 HarEnMi
Methven, Stuart Eugene 1927- WhoWor 93
Metianu, Andrew Aurel 1942- WhoScE 91-1
Metianu, Lucian 1937- Baker 92
Metlitzki, Dorothee 1914- WhoWrEP 92
Metner, Nikolai Baker 92
Metochites OxDcByz
Metochites, Theodore 1270-1332 OxDcByz [port]
Metra, (Jules-Louis-) Olivier 1830-1889 Baker 92
Metrailer, A.C. Law&B 92
Metrailler, Gaston E. Law&B 92
Metras, Franck Leon Rene Claude 1936- WhoScE 91-2
Metras, Gary 1947- WhoWrEP 92
Metraux, Alfred 1905-1963 IntDcAn
Metraux, Rhoda Anna Elizabeth 1914- WhoAmW 93
Metress, Seamus P. 1933- WhoWrEP 92
Metrey, George David 1939- WhoAm 92
Metrick, Richard Lawrence 1941- St&PR 93
Metrophanes OxDcByz
Metropolis, Nicholas Constantine 1915- WhoAm 92
Metros, Mary Teresa 1951- WhoAmW 93
Metros, Nicholas C. 1931- St&PR 93
Metrot, Andre 1939- WhoScE 91-2
Mets, Lisa Ann 1954- WhoAmW 93, WhoEmL 93
Metselaar, Rudolf 1936- WhoScE 91-3, WhoWor 93
Metta, David Keith 1953- WhoEmL 93
Mette, Virgil Louis 1942- WhoAm 92
Mettee-McCutchon, Ila 1945- WhoAmW 93
Mettenleiter, Dominicus 1822-1868 Baker 92
Mettenleiter, Johann Georg 1812-1858 Baker 92
Metter, Alan MiSFD 9
Metter, Bertram Milton 1927- WhoAm 92
Metternich, Clemens Wenzel Lothar, Furst von 1773-1859 BioIn 17
Mettetal, Gwendolyn Wallace 1953- WhoAmW 93
Mettey, Joan E. 1931- St&PR 93
Mettica, Bonnie L. Law&B 92
Mettin, D. WhoScE 91-3
Metting, Patricia Jean 1954- WhoAmW 93
Mettler, Darlene Debault 1942- WhoSSW 93
Mettler, Robert L. WhoAm 92
Mettler, Ruben Frederick 1924- St&PR 93, WhoAm 92
Mettrick, David Francis 1932- WhoAm 92
Metts, Lewis L. 1942- St&PR 93
Metz, Arthur 1927- St&PR 93
Metz, Bernard G.M.C. 1920- WhoScE 91-2
Metz, Carl Edward 1946- St&PR 93
Metz, Cary Alan Law&B 92
Metz, Charles Edgar 1942- WhoAm 92
Metz, Charles Joseph Law&B 92
Metz, Clyde Raymond 1940- WhoSSW 93
Metz, Craig Huseman 1955- WhoAm 92, WhoE 93
Metz, David J. 1933- St&PR 93, WhoAm 92
Metz, Deborah Tiderman 1950- WhoAmW 93
Metz, Diana Lyn 1957- St&PR 93
Metz, Donald Edward 1962- WhoEmL 93
Metz, Donald Joseph 1924- WhoE 93
Metz, Douglas Wilber 1934- WhoAm 92
Metz, E. Michael BioIn 17
Metz, Emmanuel Michael 1928- WhoAm 92
Metz, Eric Bennett 1955- WhoEmL 93
Metz, Frank Andrew, Jr. 1934- WhoAm 92
Metz, Helen Chapin 1928- WhoE 93
Metz, Jerred 1943- WhoWrEP 92
Metz, Joan Lillian 1933- WhoAmW 93
Metz, Larry Edward 1955- WhoEmL 93
Metz, Lawrence A. Law&B 92
Metz, Lawrence Anthony 1941- WhoAm 92
Metz, Lora Ann 1936- WhoAmW 93
Metz, Margaret Elizabeth 1949- WhoE 93
Metz, Mark Kennedy Law&B 92
Metz, Mary Clare 1907- WhoAm 92
Metz, Mary Seawell 1937- WhoAm 92, WhoAmW 93

Metz, Michael Miller 1953- St&PR 93, WhoAm 92
Metz, Norbert 1941- WhoWor 93
Metz, Norman Carl 1948- St&PR 93
Metz, Patricia Anne 1936- WhoAmW 93
Metz, Patti Ellen Weston 1957- WhoAmW 93
Metz, Robert Edward 1945- WhoSSW 93
Metz, Robert Roy 1929- St&PR 93, WhoAm 92, WhoWrEP 92
Metz, Roger N. 1938-1991 BioIn 17
Metz, Ronald Irwin 1921- WhoE 93, WhoWor 93
Metz, Russ BioIn 17
Metz, Russell Louis 1919- WhoSSW 93
Metz, Theodore John 1932- WhoAm 92
Metz, Thomas Edward 1928- St&PR 93
Metz, Vernon Wahl 1917- WhoE 93
Metzbower, John Edgar, III 1949- St&PR 93
Metzbower, Michael Francis 1962- WhoE 93
Metzenbaum, Howard M. BioIn 17
Metzenbaum, Howard M. 1917- CngDr 91
Metzenbaum, Howard Morton 1917- WhoAm 92
Metzer, Patricia Ann 1941- WhoE 93, WhoWor 93
Metzer, Robert William Law&B 92
Metzgar, D. Robert 1943- St&PR 93
Metzgar, Patricia C. 1912- St&PR 93
Metzger, Alan MiSFD 9
Metzger, Alan W. 1936- St&PR 93
Metzger, Arthur ScF&FL 92
Metzger, Bernard A. 1954- WhoWor 93
Metzger, Bobbie A. 1948- WhoAm 92
Metzger, Bruce Manning 1914- WhoAm 92
Metzger, Burton F. 1940- St&PR 93
Metzger, Carolyn Dibble 1924- WhoAmW 93
Metzger, Darryl Eugene 1937- WhoAm 92
Metzger, Deena Posy 1936- WhoWrEP 92
Metzger, Diane Hamill 1949- WhoAmW 93, WhoE 93, WhoEmL 93, WhoWor 93, WhoWrEP 92
Metzger, Donald L. 1938- St&PR 93
Metzger, Edward J., Jr. 1935- St&PR 93
Metzger, Erica Louise 1968- WhoAmW 93
Metzger, Erich 1921- St&PR 93
Metzger, Ernest Hugh 1923- WhoAm 92
Metzger, Ernest Philip 1960- WhoEmL 93
Metzger, Frank 1929- St&PR 93, WhoAm 92
Metzger, Gerald W. 1936- St&PR 93
Metzger, Gerard 1940- WhoScE 91-2
Metzger, H.A. 1933- St&PR 93
Metzger, Heinz-Klaus 1932- Baker 92
Metzger, Henry 1932- WhoE 93
Metzger, Howell Peter 1931- WhoAm 92
Metzger, Imek R. 1925- St&PR 93
Metzger, J. Kirk 1947- WhoSSW 93
Metzger, Jeffrey P. Law&B 92
Metzger, Jill Leslie 1950- WhoAmW 93
Metzger, John Peter 1958- WhoEmL 93
Metzger, John U. 1935- St&PR 93, WhoIns 93
Metzger, John V. St&PR 93
Metzger, John V., Jr. 1952- St&PR 93
Metzger, Kathleen Ann 1949- WhoAmW 93
Metzger, Leigh Ann 1962- WhoAm 92
Metzger, Margaret AmWomPl
Metzger, Marian 1931- WhoAmW 93
Metzger, Michael Dennis 1947- St&PR 93
Metzger, Patricia Lacey 1946- WhoSSW 93
Metzger, Patricia Louise 1950- WhoEmL 93
Metzger, Paul S. 1925- WhoAm 92
Metzger, Paul Thomas 1950- WhoEmL 93
Metzger, Peter M. 1934- St&PR 93
Metzger, Pola P. 1928- St&PR 93
Metzger, Radley 1930- MiSFD 9
Metzger, Richard J. Law&B 92
Metzger, Robert BioIn 17
Metzger, Robert A. 1956- ScF&FL 92
Metzger, Sidney 1917- WhoAm 92
Metzger, Thom 1956- ScF&FL 92
Metzger, Thomas Andrew 1944- WhoE 93
Metzger, Thomas Michael 1952- St&PR 93, WhoAm 92
Metz-Goeckel, Sigrid Helene 1940- WhoWor 93
Metzheiser, Gerald F. 1932- St&PR 93
Metzinger, Bruce Law&B 92
Metzinger, Jean 1883-1956 BioIn 17
Metzker, Ray K. 1931- WhoAm 92
Metzler, Dwight Fox 1916- WhoAm 92
Metzler, Ken J. 1956- St&PR 93
Metzler, Kimberly Ann 1967- WhoE 93
Metzler, Lewis L. 1934- St&PR 93
Metzler, Michelle Renee 1958- WhoAmW 93
Metzler, Paul Raymond 1949- WhoEmL 93
Metzler, Philip Lowry, Jr. 1941- WhoAm 92
Metzler, Valentin d1833 Baker 92
Metzler, William Andrew 1942- WhoSSW 93
Metzner, Arthur Berthold 1927- WhoAm 92
Metzner, Barbara Stone 1940- WhoAmW 93, WhoWor 93
Metzner, Charles Miller 1912- WhoAm 92, WhoE 93
Metzner, George F. 1948- St&PR 93
Metzner, Helmut F. 1925- WhoScE 91-3
Metzner, Patricia Clark Law&B 92
Metzner, Richard Joel 1942- WhoAm 92
Meub, William Henry 1946- WhoEmL 93
Meudt, Edna Kritz 1906- WhoWrEP 92
Meulders, Jean-Pierre 1939- WhoScE 91-2
Meuleman, Ann Effinger Law&B 92
Meuleman, John A. 1943- St&PR 93
Meuleman, Robert Joseph 1939- St&PR 93
Meulemans, Arthur 1884-1966 Baker 92
Meulen, Daan van der 1894-1989 BioIn 17
Meuli, Judith K. 1938- WhoAm 92
Meunier, Bernard 1947- WhoScE 91-2
Meunier, Dominique J. 1956- WhoWor 93
Meunier, Jean-Claude 1940- WhoScE 91-2
Meunier, Jean-Pierre 1948- WhoScE 91-2
Meunier, Paul D. 1950- St&PR 93
Meunier, Paul Dennis 1950- WhoAm 92
Meunier, Pierre-Jean WhoScE 91-2
Meunier, Pierre Jean 1936- WhoWor 93
Meuninck, Tom BioIn 17
Meurant, A. Ross 1947- WhoAsAP 91
Meurend, Victorine 1844-1928 BioIn 17
Meurer, Bernd 1935- WhoWor 93
Meurin, Dawn Adele 1960- WhoE 93
Meurville, Francois X 1960- WhoE 93
Meusburger, Patricia Ann 1963- WhoAmW 93
Meuse, Kimberly Rae 1956- WhoE 93
Meusel, Ernst-Joachim 1932- WhoScE 91-3
Meusel, Thomas Hubert 1964- WhoE 93
Meuser, Fredrick William 1923- WhoAm 92
Meuser, Friedrich 1938- WhoScE 91-3
Meuter, Maria Coolman 1915- WhoAmW 93
Meuwissen, J.H.E.T. 1930- WhoScE 91-3
Meuwissen, Kenneth H. 1933- St&PR 93
Mevers, Frank Clement 1942- WhoE 93
Mew, Thomas Joseph, III 1942- WhoAm 92
Mewis, Jan WhoWor 93
Mewshaw, Franklin Lee d1991 BioIn 17
Mewshaw, Michael 1943- BioIn 17
Mewton-Wood, Noel 1922-1953 Baker 92
Mey BioIn 17
Meyaart, Paul Jan 1943- WhoAm 92
Meyappan, Govinda Raju 1953- WhoWor 93
Meyberg, Bernhard Ulrich 1917- WhoWor 93
Meybom, Marcus Baker 92
Meyburg, Arnim Hans 1939- WhoAm 92
Meydell, Stephan Barclay 1928- St&PR 93
Meye, Robert Paul 1929- WhoAm 92
Meyendorff, John d1992 NewYTBS 92 [port]
Meyendorff, John 1926-1992 ConAu 138
Meyer, Adolf 1866-1950 BioIn 17
Meyer, Agnes Elizabeth Ernst 1887-1970 JrnUS
Meyer, Alan E. 1950- St&PR 93
Meyer, Albert B. St&PR 93
Meyer, Albert H. 1935- St&PR 93
Meyer, Albert J. Law&B 92
Meyer, Alden Merrill 1952- WhoAm 92
Meyer, Alex Alfred 1931- WhoAm 92
Meyer, Alfred George 1920- WhoAm 92
Meyer, Alice K. 1928- WhoAm 92, WhoSSW 93
Meyer, Alice Virginia 1921- WhoAmW 93
Meyer, Allen A. Law&B 92
Meyer, Allen A. 1945- St&PR 93
Meyer, Andrea Peroutka 1963- WhoAmW 93, WhoEmL 93
Meyer, Andrew C., Jr. 1949- WhoAm 92, WhoE 93
Meyer, Andrew R. 1956- WhoE 93
Meyer, Angela 1933- WhoAmW 93
Meyer, Ann Jane 1942- WhoAmW 93
Meyer, Anne Elizabeth 1951- WhoAmW 93
Meyer, Annie Nathan 1867-1951 AmWomPl
Meyer, Anthony Edward 1961- WhoEmL 93, WhoSSW 93
Meyer, Armin Henry 1914- WhoAm 92
Meyer, August C. 1900-1991 BioIn 17
Meyer, August Christopher, Jr. 1937- St&PR 93, WhoAm 92
Meyer, B. Fred 1918- WhoSSW 93
Meyer, Barry A. Law&B 92
Meyer, Barry Joel 1942- WhoSSW 93
Meyer, Barry Michael 1943- WhoAm 92
Meyer, Bernard F. 1931- St&PR 93
Meyer, Bernard Mathew 1933- St&PR 93
Meyer, Bernard Stern 1916- WhoAm 92
Meyer, Bernd-Ulrich 1960- WhoWor 93
Meyer, Bernhard O. 1933- WhoIns 93
Meyer, Betty Jane 1918- WhoAmW 93
Meyer, Bill ScF&FL 92
Meyer, Brian Alan 1961- WhoEmL 93, WhoSSW 93
Meyer, Bruce E. Law&B 92
Meyer, Bruce R. 1941- St&PR 93
Meyer, Bruce Russell 1948- St&PR 93
Meyer, Bruce V. Law&B 92
Meyer, Brud Richard 1926- WhoAm 92
Meyer, Burnett Chandler 1921- WhoAm 92
Meyer, C. Victor 1934- St&PR 93
Meyer, Calvin H. 1944- St&PR 93
Meyer, Carl E. 1947- St&PR 93
Meyer, Carolyn 1935- ScF&FL 92
Meyer, Carolyn (Mae) 1935- MajAI [port], SmATA 70 [port]
Meyer, Charles Appleton 1918- WhoAm 92
Meyer, Charles Edward 1928- WhoAm 92
Meyer, Charles Howard 1952- WhoEmL 93
Meyer, Charles Stanton 1959- WhoEmL 93
Meyer, Clarence 1903- WhoWrEP 92
Meyer, Cord 1920- WhoE 93
Meyer, Cynthia Kay 1952- WhoAmW 93
Meyer, Cynthia Louise 1958- WhoAmW 93
Meyer, Dan Wesley 1956- WhoEmL 93
Meyer, Daniel Edward 1956- WhoEmL 93
Meyer, Daniel F. 1944- St&PR 93
Meyer, Daniel Joseph 1936- St&PR 93, WhoAm 92
Meyer, Daniel Patrick 1927- St&PR 93
Meyer, Daryl James 1949- St&PR 93
Meyer, David BioIn 17
Meyer, David Anthony 1953- WhoEmL 93
Meyer, David C. 1955- St&PR 93
Meyer, David N., II ScF&FL 92
Meyer, David Wainright 1956- WhoSSW 93
Meyer, Deborah Lynn 1948- WhoAmW 93, WhoEmL 93
Meyer, Dennis Irwin 1935- WhoAm 92
Meyer, Diane Crimmins 1945- WhoAmW 93
Meyer, Dominique 1939- WhoScE 91-2
Meyer, Don Allan 1929- St&PR 93
Meyer, Donald C. d1992 NewYTBS 92
Meyer, Donald Gordon 1934- WhoAm 92
Meyer, Donald R. Law&B 92
Meyer, Donald R. 1935- St&PR 93
Meyer, Donald Ray 1924- WhoAm 92
Meyer, Donald Robert 1942- WhoAm 92
Meyer, Donna Lea 1966- WhoAmW 93
Meyer, Doris 1942- WhoAmW 93
Meyer, Doris A. 1952- St&PR 93
Meyer, Dorothy Anna 1921- WhoWrEP 92
Meyer, Dorsey Ray, Sr. 1928- St&PR 93
Meyer, Douglas Robert Law&B 92
Meyer, Edith Patterson 1895- DcAmChF 1960
Meyer, Edmond Gerald 1919- WhoAm 92, WhoWor 93
Meyer, Edward Charles 1928- CmdGen 1991 [port]
Meyer, Edward H. 1927- St&PR 93
Meyer, Edward Henry 1927- WhoAm 92, WhoE 93
Meyer, Edwin A., Jr. 1927- St&PR 93
Meyer, Ernst Hermann 1905-1988 Baker 92
Meyer, Eugene 1875-1959 BioIn 17, JrnUS
Meyer, Eugene Carlton 1923- WhoAm 92
Meyer, F.R. 1927- St&PR 93
Meyer, F. Weller 1942- WhoAm 92
Meyer, Ferd. Charles, Jr. Law&B 92
Meyer, Frances Lee 1947- WhoEmL 93
Meyer, Francis G. 1952- St&PR 93
Meyer, Frank 1936- WhoE 93
Meyer, Frank Hildbridge 1923- WhoSSW 93
Meyer, Frank R., Jr. Law&B 92
Meyer, Fred J. 1931- St&PR 93
Meyer, Fred Josef 1931- WhoAm 92
Meyer, Fred Richard 1939- St&PR 93
Meyer, Frederick Robert Law&B 92
Meyer, Frederick William 1943- WhoIns 93
Meyer, G. Edward 1923- St&PR 93
Meyer, Geoffrey E. Law&B 92
Meyer, George Gotthold 1931- WhoAm 92
Meyer, George Herbert 1928- WhoAm 92
Meyer, George William 1941- St&PR 93
Meyer, Gerald J. 1940- St&PR 93
Meyer, Gerald Justin 1940- WhoAm 92
Meyer, Gerard Charles 1931- WhoAm 92
Meyer, Gregory K. 1959- St&PR 93
Meyer, Hans Bernhard 1924- WhoWor 93
Meyer, Hans Friedrich 1938- WhoUN 92
Meyer, Hans Paul 1928- WhoE 93
Meyer, Harold J. 1923- St&PR 93
Meyer, Harold Louis 1916- WhoWor 93
Meyer, Harry E. Law&B 92
Meyer, Harry Martin, Jr. 1928- WhoAm 92
Meyer, Harvey Kessler, II 1914- WhoWor 93
Meyer, Helen 1907- WhoAm 92
Meyer, Henry John 1927- WhoAm 92
Meyer, Hermann F. 1938- St&PR 93
Meyer, Horst 1926- WhoAm 92
Meyer, Howard Robert, Jr. 1955- WhoSSW 93
Meyer, Irwin Stephan 1941- WhoE 93, WhoWor 93
Meyer, Ivah Gene 1935- WhoAmW 93
Meyer, J. Theodore 1936- WhoWor 93
Meyer, Jack 1905-1991 AnObit 1991
Meyer, Jack 1947- WhoEmL 93
Meyer, Jack Reeder 1945- WhoAm 92
Meyer, Jackie Merri 1954- WhoAm 92
Meyer, James J. 1963- St&PR 93
Meyer, James M. 1957- St&PR 93
Meyer, James Maurice 1946- WhoAm 92
Meyer, Jane Littell Law&B 92
Meyer, Jane Stirling 1949- WhoSSW 93
Meyer, Janet Faye 1955- WhoEmL 93
Meyer, Jared H. Law&B 92
Meyer, Jarold Alan 1938- WhoAm 92
Meyer, Jean WhoScE 91-2
Meyer, Jean-Claude 1945- WhoWor 93
Meyer, Jean-Pierre 1949- WhoWor 93
Meyer, Jean-Pierre Gustave 1929- WhoAm 92
Meyer, Jeanette Marjorie 1961- WhoEmL 93
Meyer, Jeffery Wilson 1923- St&PR 93, WhoAm 92
Meyer, Jeffrey Scott Law&B 92
Meyer, Jerome J. 1938- WhoAm 92
Meyer, Joan Kathryn 1956- WhoEmL 93
Meyer, Joaquin E. d1990 BioIn 17
Meyer, Johannes 1929- St&PR 93, WhoIns 93
Meyer, John ScF&FL 92
Meyer, John Edward 1931- WhoAm 92
Meyer, John Frederick 1934- WhoAm 92
Meyer, John Matthew 1937- St&PR 93
Meyer, John Robert 1927- WhoAm 92
Meyer, John Robert 1946- St&PR 93
Meyer, Joseph B. 1941- WhoAm 92
Meyer, Joseph J., Jr. 1925- WhoIns 93
Meyer, Joseph Leo 1943- St&PR 93
Meyer, Josephine Amelia 1884- AmWomPl
Meyer, Judith Louise 1933- WhoAmW 93
Meyer, June MajAI
Meyer, Karen Arlene 1957- WhoAmW 93
Meyer, Karl Ernest 1928- WhoAm 92
Meyer, Karl L. 1937- St&PR 93
Meyer, Karl William 1925- WhoAm 92
Meyer, Kenneth 1942- St&PR 93
Meyer, Kenneth Marven 1932- WhoAm 92
Meyer, Kent L. 1943- St&PR 93
Meyer, Kerstin 1928- OxDcOp, WhoAm 92
Meyer, Kerstin (Margareta) 1928- Baker 92
Meyer, Kevin 1959- MiSFD 9
Meyer, Kristi J. 1956- St&PR 93
Meyer, Krzysztof 1943- Baker 92, PolBiDi
Meyer, Kuno 1858-1919 BioIn 17
Meyer, L. Donald 1933- WhoSSW 93
Meyer, Larry L. 1933- BioIn 17
Meyer, Lasker M. 1926- St&PR 93
Meyer, Lasker Marcel 1926- WhoAm 92
Meyer, Lawrence George 1940- WhoAm 92, WhoE 93, WhoWor 93
Meyer, Lawrence Walter Law&B 92
Meyer, Leonard A. 1925- St&PR 93
Meyer, Leonard B. 1918- WhoAm 92
Meyer, Leonard B(unce) 1918- Baker 92
Meyer, Leopold von 1816-1883 Baker 92
Meyer, Leroy W. 1936- St&PR 93
Meyer, Linda D(oreen) 1948- ConAu 37NR
Meyer, Linda Doreen 1948- WhoWrEP 92
Meyer, Louis B. 1933- WhoAm 92, WhoSSW 93
Meyer, Lyle E. 1945- St&PR 93
Meyer, Lynda Joyce 1955- WhoAmW 93
Meyer, Lynn Nix Law&B 92
Meyer, M.M. 1883- ScF&FL 92
Meyer, M. Yvonne WhoWrEP 92
Meyer, Mara Ellice 1952- WhoEmL 93
Meyer, Marc Gilbert 1959- WhoWor 93
Meyer, Marcel Andre 1944- WhoWor 93
Meyer, Margaret Eleanor 1923- WhoAm 92
Meyer, Margaret H. 1916- WhoWrEP 92
Meyer, Marilyn Clarita 1942- WhoAmW 93
Meyer, Marion M. 1923- WhoAmW 93, WhoE 93, WhoWor 93
Meyer, Mark Alan 1946- WhoEmL 93
Meyer, Mark Warren 1954- WhoEmL 93
Meyer, Marshall Theodore 1930- BioIn 17

Meyer, Mary-Beth 1950- WhoEmL 93
Meyer, Mary-Louise 1922- WhoAmW 93, WhoE 93, WhoWor 93
Meyer, Matthew d1992 NewYTBS 92
Meyer, Matthew 1904-1992 BioIn 17
Meyer, Maurice Wesley 1925- WhoAm 92
Meyer, Max Earl 1918- WhoAm 92
Meyer, Melanie Ann 1963- WhoAmW 93
Meyer, Michael 1881-1956 BioIn 17
Meyer, Michael 1958- WhoE 93, WhoEmL 93
Meyer, Michael A. Law&B 92
Meyer, Michael C. 1956- WhoEmL 93
Meyer, Michael Edwin 1942- WhoAm 92
Meyer, Michael Frank 1944- WhoSSW 93
Meyer, Michael J. 1956- ConAu 139
Meyer, Michael Leverson 1921- BioIn 17
Meyer, Michael Louis 1940- WhoAm 92
Meyer, Michael M. Law&B 92
Meyer, Michael W. Law&B 92, WhoAm 92
Meyer, Michele Jean 1949- WhoE 93
Meyer, Milton Edward, Jr. 1922- WhoAm 92, WhoWor 93
Meyer, Miriam Weiss ScF&FL 92
Meyer, Morton G. 1905- St&PR 93
Meyer, Nancy Reiter 1947- WhoAmW 93
Meyer, Natalie 1930- WhoAm 92, WhoAmW 93
Meyer, Nicholas 1945- MiSFD 9, ScF&FL 92
Meyer, Niels I. 1930- WhoScE 91-2
Meyer, Patricia Law&B 92
Meyer, Patricia Hanes 1947- WhoAmW 93
Meyer, Patricia Morgan 1934- WhoAm 92
Meyer, Paul J. 1947- St&PR 93
Meyer, Paul Joseph 1942- WhoAm 92
Meyer, Paul Norman 1940- WhoAm 92
Meyer, Paul Reims WhoAm 92, WhoWor 93
Meyer, Paul S. Law&B 92
Meyer, Paul William 1924- WhoAm 92
Meyer, Peter 1920- WhoAm 92
Meyer, Peter Arnold 1944- St&PR 93
Meyer, Philip Edward 1930- WhoAm 92
Meyer, Philippe WhoScE 91-2
Meyer, Pucci 1944- WhoAm 92, WhoWrEP 92
Meyer, Ralph Anthony, Jr. 1943- WhoSSW 93
Meyer, Ralph Henry 1933- WhoWor 93
Meyer, Ralph P. 1943- St&PR 93
Meyer, Randall 1923- WhoAm 92
Meyer, Ray BioIn 17
Meyer, Raymond George, II 1947- WhoEmL 93
Meyer, Raymond Joseph 1913- WhoAm 92
Meyer, Rich BioIn 17
Meyer, Richard Law&B 92
Meyer, Richard 1942- WhoWor 93
Meyer, Richard A. Law&B 92
Meyer, Richard Alan 1952- WhoE 93
Meyer, Richard Charles 1930- WhoAm 92
Meyer, Richard David 1943- WhoAm 92
Meyer, Richard Edward 1939- WhoAm 92
Meyer, Richard Jonah 1933- WhoAm 92, WhoSSW 93
Meyer, Richard Schlomer 1945- St&PR 93, WhoAm 92
Meyer, Richard Steven 1944- WhoAm 92
Meyer, Richard Townsend 1925- WhoAm 92
Meyer, Richard Tracy, Jr. 1947- WhoEmL 93
Meyer, Robert Alan 1946- WhoEmL 93
Meyer, Robert Dean 1934- WhoIns 93
Meyer, Robert F. 1935- WhoAm 92
Meyer, Robert L. 1949- St&PR 93
Meyer, Robert Norfleet 1957- WhoSSW 93
Meyer, Robert William 1939- St&PR 93
Meyer, Rockford G. Law&B 92
Meyer, Roelf WhoWor 93
Meyer, Roland Harry 1927- St&PR 93, WhoAm 92
Meyer, Ronald A. 1951- St&PR 93
Meyer, Ronald Frederick 1935- St&PR 93
Meyer, Ronald L. 1944- St&PR 93
Meyer, Ronald Shaw 1941- WhoAm 92
Meyer, Russ BioIn 17
Meyer, Russ 1922- MiSFD 9
Meyer, Russell William, Jr. 1932- St&PR 93, WhoAm 92
Meyer, Ruth Krueger 1940- WhoAm 92
Meyer, Sally Cave 1937- WhoAmW 93
Meyer, Sandra P. 1954- St&PR 93
Meyer, Sandra Wasserstein 1937- WhoAm 92, WhoAmW 93
Meyer, Scott John Law&B 92
Meyer, Sheldon 1926- WhoAm 92
Meyer, Sherman Wayne 1909- WhoAm 92
Meyer, Stephan Schutzmeister 1953- WhoEmL 93
Meyer, Stephen Alan 1949- St&PR 93, WhoE 93
Meyer, Stephen John 1946- St&PR 93
Meyer, Steve Law&B 92
Meyer, Susan E. BioIn 17
Meyer, Susan E. 1940- WhoAm 92
Meyer, Susan Maloney Law&B 92
Meyer, Susan Theresa 1950- WhoAmW 93, WhoEmL 93
Meyer, Susane E. 1940- WhoWrEP 92
Meyer, Sylvan Hugh 1921- WhoAm 92
Meyer, Theodore E. 1931- WhoWrEP 92
Meyer, Theresa T. 1944- St&PR 93
Meyer, Thomas Aloysius 1942- St&PR 93
Meyer, Thomas J. 1941- WhoAm 92
Meyer, Thomas J. 1949- WhoEmL 93
Meyer, Thomas James 1955- WhoAm 92
Meyer, Thomas John Law&B 92
Meyer, Thomas L. Law&B 92
Meyer, Thomas R. 1936- St&PR 93
Meyer, Thomas Robert 1936- WhoWor 93
Meyer, Timothy H. 1943- St&PR 93
Meyer, Ursula 1927- WhoAm 92
Meyer, Verena WhoScE 91-4
Meyer, Volkmar Albrecht 1933- WhoWor 93
Meyer, Walter F. 1931- St&PR 93
Meyer, Wilfred H. WhoIns 93
Meyer, Wilfried 1945- WhoScE 91-3
Meyer, William A. 1932- St&PR 93
Meyer, William Dale 1948- WhoEmL 93
Meyer, William Danielson 1923- WhoAm 92
Meyer, William Frederick 1933- St&PR 93
Meyer, William M. 1940- St&PR 93
Meyer, William S. 1946- St&PR 93
Meyer, William Steven 1959- WhoEmL 93
Meyer, Wolfgang Eberhard 1910- WhoE 93
Meyer, Zygmunt Jan 1944- WhoScE 91-4
Meyerand, Russell Gilbert, Jr. 1933- WhoAm 92
Meyer-Bahlburg, Heino F. L. 1940- WhoAm 92
Meyerbeer, Giacomo 1791-1864 Baker 92, BioIn 17, IntDcOp [port], OxDcOp
Meyer-Berkhout, Ulrich F.A. 1927- WhoScE 91-3
Meyerding, Eugene Villaume 1924- St&PR 93
Meyerer, Margaret Christine 1924- WhoWrEP 92
Meyer-Grass, Martin 1945- WhoScE 91-4
Meyerhardt, Marci Perlmutter 1960- WhoAmW 93
Meyer-Helmund, Erik 1861-1932 Baker 92
Meyerhoff, Erich 1919- WhoAm 92
Meyerhoff, Gunther 1919- WhoScE 91-3
Meyerhoff, Jack Fulton 1926- WhoAm 92, WhoSSW 93
Meyerhoff, William Lee 1940- WhoAm 92
Meyerhold, V.E. 1874-1940 BioIn 17
Meyerhold, Vsevolod 1874-1940 OxDcOp
Meyerhold, Vsevolod Emilyevich 1874-1940 IntDcOp
Meyerholz, John Philip 1941- St&PR 93, WhoAm 92
Meyering, Christopher P. Law&B 92
Meyering, Ralph, Jr. 1951- WhoEmL 93
Meyer-Kretschmer, Gustav 1939- WhoScE 91-3
Meyerman, Harold John 1938- St&PR 93
Meyer-Olbersleben, Max 1850-1927 Baker 92
Meyerowitz, Aaron David 1957- WhoEmL 93, WhoSSW 93
Meyerowitz, Jan 1913- Baker 92
Meyerowitz, Joel 1938- WhoWor 93
Meyerowitz, Steven A. 1955- WhoWrEP 92
Meyerowitz, William 1885-1981 BioIn 17
Meyer-Parpart, Wolfgang P. 1944- St&PR 93
Meyer-Piening, Hans-Reinhard 1937- WhoScE 91-4
Meyerrose, Sarah L. 1955- St&PR 93
Meyerrose, Sarah Louise 1955- WhoEmL 93
Meyers, Abbey Sue 1944- WhoE 93
Meyers, Albert Irving 1932- WhoAm 92
Meyers, Ann 1955- BioIn 17
Meyers, Ann Elizabeth 1955- WhoAmW 93, WhoEmL 93
Meyers, Ann Sipl 1943- WhoAmW 93
Meyers, Augie
See Texas Tornados, The ConMus 8
Meyers, Beatrice Nurmi 1929- WhoSSW 93
Meyers, Beverly Jean 1949- WhoAmW 93
Meyers, Bruce A. WhoAm 92
Meyers, C.J. St&PR 93
Meyers, Carl Gordon Law&B 92
Meyers, Carole Terwilliger 1945- WhoWrEP 92
Meyers, Carolyn Winstead 1946- WhoEmL 93, WhoSSW 93
Meyers, Christine Laine 1946- WhoAmW 93, WhoEmL 93, WhoWor 93
Meyers, Dale WhoAm 92
Meyers, Darlene Stetson 1939- WhoSSW 93
Meyers, David d1991 BioIn 17
Meyers, David P. St&PR 93
Meyers, David Victor 1949- St&PR 93
Meyers, Donald J. Law&B 92
Meyers, Dorothy 1927- WhoAmW 93, WhoWor 93
Meyers, Edna Ocko 1909- WhoAmW 93
Meyers, Edward 1934- WhoAm 92
Meyers, Edwin W. 1927- St&PR 93
Meyers, Eleanor Scott 1940- WhoAmW 93
Meyers, Eric Barton 1942-1990 BioIn 17
Meyers, Eric Mark 1940- WhoSSW 93
Meyers, Ernest S. 1910-1991 BioIn 17
Meyers, Eugene 1935- St&PR 93
Meyers, George Edward 1928- WhoE 93, WhoWor 93
Meyers, Gerald Carl 1928- WhoAm 92
Meyers, Glenn Scott 1961- WhoEmL 93
Meyers, Gregory Elliot Law&B 92
Meyers, Helen Renich 1916- WhoWrEP 92
Meyers, Howard Craig 1951- WhoEmL 93
Meyers, James Dwight 1948- St&PR 93
Meyers, James Edward 1953- WhoAm 92
Meyers, James Frank 1946- WhoSSW 93
Meyers, James M. 1946- St&PR 93
Meyers, Jan BioIn 17
Meyers, Jan 1928- CngDr 91, WhoAm 92, WhoAmW 93
Meyers, Jeffrey BioIn 17
Meyers, Jeffrey 1939- ScF&FL 92
Meyers, Jerry Ivan 1946- WhoEmL 93
Meyers, Joel D. d1991 BioIn 17
Meyers, John A. Law&B 92
Meyers, John Allen 1929- St&PR 93, WhoAm 92
Meyers, John Robert 1947- St&PR 93
Meyers, Karen Diane 1950- WhoAmW 93
Meyers, Karen Hopkins 1948- WhoEmL 93
Meyers, Ken BioIn 17
Meyers, Kenneth D. 1952- St&PR 93
Meyers, Kenneth R. 1954- St&PR 93
Meyers, Lisa Marie 1965- WhoAmW 93
Meyers, Lynn Betty 1952- WhoAmW 93
Meyers, Mark B. Law&B 92
Meyers, Mary Ann 1937- WhoAm 92
Meyers, May Lou 1930- WhoSSW 93
Meyers, Merrie Elyn 1957- WhoAmW 93
Meyers, Morton Allen 1933- WhoAm 92
Meyers, Nancy 1950- ConAu 138
Meyers, Nancy Jane 1949- WhoAm 92
Meyers, Norman O. 1929- St&PR 93
Meyers, Otto O., III Law&B 92
Meyers, Pamela S. Law&B 92
Meyers, Peter L. 1939- St&PR 93, WhoAm 92, WhoE 93
Meyers, Raymond N. 1938- St&PR 93
Meyers, Reid 1949- WhoIns 93
Meyers, Reid E. Law&B 92
Meyers, Ric ScF&FL 92
Meyers, Richard E. Law&B 92
Meyers, Richard James 1940- WhoAm 92
Meyers, Richard S. 1953- ScF&FL 92
Meyers, Richard Stuart 1938- WhoAm 92
Meyers, Robert Law&B 92
Meyers, Robert John 1950- WhoEmL 93
Meyers, Robert S. St&PR 93
Meyers, Roger Joseph 1955- WhoEmL 93
Meyers, Rosemary Casey 1946- WhoEmL 93
Meyers, Roy L. 1910-1974 ScF&FL 92
Meyers, Sharon May 1946- WhoEmL 93
Meyers, Sheldon 1929- WhoAm 92
Meyers, Stephen H. 1942- St&PR 93
Meyers, Steven J. Law&B 92
Meyers, Tedson Jay 1928- WhoAm 92
Meyers, Theda Maria WhoWor 93
Meyers, Thomas P. 1932- St&PR 93
Meyers, Valerie ScF&FL 92
Meyers, Victor Aloysius d1991 BioIn 17
Meyers, Walter E. 1939- ScF&FL 92
Meyers, Wayne Marvin 1924- WhoAm 92, WhoWor 93
Meyers, William Francis 1947- WhoE 93, WhoWor 93
Meyers, William John 1931- St&PR 93
Meyer-Siat, Pie 1913-1989 Baker 92
Meyerson, Charles 1955- WhoEmL 93
Meyerson, George O. 1940- St&PR 93
Meyerson, Ivan D. Law&B 92, WhoAm 92
Meyerson, Joelle A. St&PR 93
Meyerson, Linda Arlene 1954- WhoAmW 93
Meyerson, Martin 1922- St&PR 93
Meyerson, Martin 1927- WhoE 93
Meyerson, Martin Henry 1931- St&PR 93
Meyerson, Morton 1935- WhoE 93
Meyerson, Morton H. NewYTBS 92 [port]
Meyerson, Stan 1925- St&PR 93
Meyer-Tischler, Joerg Rudolf Erich 1944- WhoWor 93
Meylan, Charles Albert 1948- WhoWor 93
Meyler, Francis M. Law&B 92
Meyler, Ruth P. Law&B 92
Meyler, William Anthony 1944- WhoWor 93
Meymouth, Lawrence B., Jr. 1943- St&PR 93
Meyn, John H. 1920- St&PR 93
Meynardie, Jane Wallace 1960- WhoAmW 93
Meynell, Alice Christiana Thompson 1847-1922 BioIn 17
Meynell, Esther d1955 ScF&FL 92
Meynell, Laurence 1899-1989 BioIn 17, ScF&FL 92
Meyner, Helen Stevenson 1929- BioIn 17
Meyner, Robert Baumle 1908-1990 BioIn 17
Meyniel, G. WhoScE 91-2
Meyo, Raymond D. 1943- St&PR 93
Meyr, Shari Louise 1951- WhoAmW 93
Meyrich, Steven 1951- WhoEmL 93
Meyrick, Bette 1931- ScF&FL 92
Meyrink, Gustav 1868-1932 ScF&FL 92
Meyrowitz, Paul 1915- St&PR 93
Meyrowitz, Selmar 1875-1941 Baker 92
Meza, Pedro Thomas 1941- WhoE 93
Meza, Richard Albert 1957- St&PR 93
Mezack, Gary A. 1952- St&PR 93
Mezak, Daniel Stephen 1922- St&PR 93
Mezei, Ferenc 1942- WhoScE 91-4
Mezei, Gabor 1935- St&PR 93
Mezei, Mihaly 1944- WhoE 93
Mezera, James Allen 1930- WhoAm 92
Mezeray, Louis (-Charles-Lazare-Costard) de 1810-1887 Baker 92
Mezey, Peter Law&B 92
Mezey, Peter 1931- St&PR 93
Meziani, Jacqueline 1963- WhoAmW 93
Mezizios OxDcByz
Mezo, Francine ScF&FL 92
Mezvinsky, Marjorie Margolies WhoAmW 93
Mezzano, Sergio Agustin 1947- WhoWor 93
Mezzanotte, John Charles Law&B 92
Mezzapelle, Dominic M. Law&B 92
Mezzara, Jaime WhoUN 92
Mezzogiorno, Vincenzo 1926- WhoScE 91-3
MFSB SoulM
Mfume, Kweisi 1948- BioIn 17, CngDr 91, WhoAm 92, WhoE 93
Mgeni, Amani Yakobo 1939- WhoUN 92
Mhatre, Nagesh S. 1932- St&PR 93
Miachin, Konstantin 1886- BioIn 17
Mialaret, Bertrand Marie 1944- WhoWor 93
Miale, Joseph Nicolas 1919- WhoE 93
Miall, David Stephen 1947- WhoWor 93
Mian, Abdul Jamil 1933- WhoUN 92
Mian, Mary 1902- ScF&FL 92
Mianguo, Dong 1930- WhoWor 93
Miano, Louis Stephen 1934- St&PR 93, WhoAm 92
Miano, Rosemary Law&B 92
Miano, Rosemary Milton Law&B 92
Miars, Mark J. 1953- St&PR 93
Miars, Mark Jay 1953- WhoEmL 93
Miaskovsky, Nikolai (Yakovlevich) 1881-1950 Baker 92
Miaskowski, Deborah J. Law&B 92
Miatello, Roberto Jorge 1947- WhoWor 93
Miazga, Jean 1936- WhoScE 91-2
Mica, Dan BioIn 17
Mica, David Raymond 1955- WhoEmL 93
Mica, Frantisek Adam 1746-1811 Baker 92
Mica, Giovanni L. 1935- WhoScE 91-3
Micah BioIn 17
Micale, Anthony E. Law&B 92
Micale, Frances Ann 1954- WhoSSW 93
Micale, Frank Jude 1949- WhoEmL 93
Micale, Vincent Joseph 1943- St&PR 93
Micales, David E. 1953- St&PR 93
Micallef, Joseph C. 1947- St&PR 93
Mican, Stephen George Law&B 92
Micci, Eugene D. 1945- WhoAm 92
Micciche, Alphonse Salvatore 1942- WhoE 93
Micciche, Daniel John 1956- WhoAm 92
Micciche, Romano Joseph 1938- St&PR 93
Micciche, Salvatore A. St&PR 93
Micciche, Salvatore Joseph 1928- WhoAm 92
Miccio, Joseph V. 1915- WhoAm 92
Miceika, Gene 1947- WhoIns 93
Micek, Katherine Danley 1925- WhoE 93
Micek, Patricia G. Law&B 92
Miceli, Anthony J. 1962- St&PR 93
Miceli, Ignatius 1918- WhoAmW 93
Miceli, Jerome F. 1943- St&PR 93
Miceli, Vincent P. 1915-1991 BioIn 17
Mich, Alex, Jr. Law&B 92
Micha, Jean-Claude Michel Antoine 1941- WhoScE 91-2

Michael *Baker 92*
Michael 1962- *BioIn 17*
Michael, King 1921- *NewYTBS 92 [port]*
Michael, Princess of Kent *BioIn 17*
Michael, I, King of Romania 1921- *BioIn 17*
Michael, II d829 *OxDcByz*
Michael, III *OxDcByz*
Michael, III 840-867 *OxDcByz*
Michael, A. Steven 1950- *St&PR 93*
Michael, Alfred Frederick, Jr. 1928- *WhoAm 92*
Michael (Astrapas) and Eutychios fl. c. 1295-1317 *OxDcByz*
Michael, Barbara Ann 1942- *WhoAmW 93*
Michael, Caroline Marshall 1923- *WhoSSW 93*
Michael, Cecil 1909-1987 *ScF&FL 92*
Michael, Charles Louis, Jr. 1944- *St&PR 93*
Michael, Chester A., III 1947- *St&PR 93*
Michael, Christian c. 1593-1637 *Baker 92*
Michael, Christopher *WhoScE 91-1*
Michael, Christopher 1942- *WhoWor 93*
Michael, Colette V(erger) 1937- *ConAu 139*
Michael, Connie Elizabeth Trexler 1945- *WhoAmW 93*
Michael, David John 1959- *WhoSSW 93*
Michael, David Moritz 1751-1827 *Baker 92*
Michael, Dennis Mark 1951- *St&PR 93*
Michael, Donald Nelson 1923- *WhoAm 92*
Michael, Dorothy Ann 1950- *WhoAmW 93, WhoEmL 93*
Michael, Edward S. *BioIn 17*
Michael, Emily *WhoAmW 93*
Michael, Ernest Arthur 1925- *WhoAm 92*
Michael, Eugene Richard 1938- *WhoE 93*
Michael, Frederick William 1943- *WhoWor 93*
Michael, Gary G. 1940- *WhoAm 92*
Michael, Gary Glenn 1940- *St&PR 93*
Michael, Gary Linn 1934- *WhoAm 92*
Michael, George *BioIn 17, WhoAm 92*
Michael, George 1963- *ConMus 9 [port]*
Michael, Harold Louis 1920- *WhoAm 92*
Michael, Henry N. 1913- *WhoAm 92*
Michael, Ib 1945- *BioIn 17*
Michael, J. Christopher 1951- *St&PR 93*
Michael, James Eugene 1927- *St&PR 93*
Michael, James Harry, Jr. 1918- *WhoAm 92, WhoSSW 93*
Michael, Jeffrey J. 1956- *St&PR 93*
Michael, Jerrold Mark 1927- *WhoAm 92*
Michael, Jerry Dean *BioIn 17*
Michael, Jonathan Edward 1954- *St&PR 93*
Michael, Judith *ConAu 139*
Michael, Kurt David 1965- *WhoEmL 93*
Michael, Lanny H. 1951- *St&PR 93*
Michael, Larry Perry 1956- *WhoAm 92*
Michael, Margaret *AmWomPl*
Michael, Mark D. *Law&B 92*
Michael, Mark D. 1951- *St&PR 93*
Michael, Martin H. *Law&B 92*
Michael, Max, Jr. 1916- *WhoAm 92*
Michael, Miles Regan, II 1955- *WhoE 93*
Michael, Patricia Ann 1953- *WhoSSW 93*
Michael, Peter *ScF&FL 92*
Michael, Phyllis Callender 1908- *WhoAmW 93*
Michael, Robert Roy 1946- *WhoEmL 93*
Michael, Rogier c. 1552-c. 1619 *Baker 92*
Michael, Samuel c. 1597-1632 *Baker 92*
Michael, Sandra Dale 1945- *WhoAmW 93, WhoE 93*
Michael, Sandra Marie 1953- *WhoE 93*
Michael, Simon *ScF&FL 92*
Michael, Suzanne 1951- *WhoEmL 93*
Michael, Terrence Lynn 1958- *WhoEmL 93*
Michael, Tobias 1592-1657 *Baker 92*
Michael, William Burton 1922- *WhoAm 92*
Michael Alexandrovich, Grand Duke of Russia 1878-1918 *BioIn 17*
Michael Angelos, I *OxDcByz*
Michael Angelos, II *OxDcByz*
Michael Autoreianos, IV d1214 *OxDcByz*
Michaelcheck, William J. 1947- *WhoAm 92*
Michael Doukas, VII c. 1050-c. 1090 *OxDcByz*
Michael Grammatikos *OxDcByz*
Michaeli, Fred C. 1935- *St&PR 93*
Michaelides, Andreas Anastasiou 1937- *WhoWor 93*
Michaelides, Constantine Evangelos 1930- *WhoAm 92*
Michaelides, Doros Nikita 1936- *WhoWor 93*
Michaelides, Solon 1905-1979 *Baker 92*
Michaelis, Arthur F. 1941- *St&PR 93*
Michaelis, Arthur Frederick 1941- *WhoAm 92, WhoE 93, WhoWor 93*
Michaelis, Donald R. 1928- *St&PR 93*
Michaelis, George H. 1937- *St&PR 93*
Michaelis, Lynn Otto 1944- *WhoAm 92*
Michaelis, Michael 1919- *WhoAm 92*
Michaelis, Paul Charles 1935- *WhoAm 92*
Michaelis-Jena, Ruth 1905-1989 *BioIn 17*
Michael Italikos dc. 1157 *OxDcByz*
Michael Kalaphates, V *OxDcByz*
Michael-Kennedy, Joseph F. *Law&B 92*
Michael-Kenney, Shari A. 1957- *St&PR 93*
Michael Keroularios, I c. 1005-1059 *OxDcByz*
Michael Komnenos Doukas, I d1215 *OxDcByz*
Michael Komnenos Doukas, II c. 1206-c. 1266 *OxDcByz*
Michael of Ephesus *OxDcByz*
Michael Palaiologos, VIII 1224?-1282 *OxDcByz*
Michael Palaiologos, IX 1277-1320 *OxDcByz*
Michael Paphlagon, IV d1041 *OxDcByz*
Michael Rangabe, I d844 *OxDcByz*
Michael Rhetor fl. 12th cent.- *OxDcByz*
Michaels, Adlai Eldon 1913- *WhoE 93*
Michaels, Al *BioIn 17*
Michaels, Alan J. 1946- *WhoSSW 93*
Michaels, Alan Richard 1944- *BiDAMSp 1989*
Michaels, Alan Stuart 1954- *WhoEmL 93*
Michaels, Anne 1958- *WhoCanL 92*
Michaels, Barbara 1927- *ScF&FL 92*
Michaels, Carol Ann 1948- *WhoWrEP 92*
Michaels, Charles B. *St&PR 93*
Michaels, Charles Edward *Law&B 92*
Michaels, Claire F. 1948- *WhoWor 93*
Michaels, Courtland Rand 1937- *St&PR 93*
Michaels, Craig Adam 1954- *WhoE 93, WhoEmL 93*
Michaels, Deborah Downey 1959- *WhoEmL 93*
Michaels, Elise Marie 1958- *WhoAmW 93*
Michaels, Elizabeth *WhoWrEP 92*
Michaels, Eric Matthew *Law&B 92*
Michaels, Fern *ScF&FL 92*
Michaels, Gary 1950- *BioIn 17*
Michaels, George 1923?- *ScF&FL 92, St&PR 93*
Michaels, George M. d1992 *NewYTBS 92 [port]*
Michaels, Gordon Joseph 1930- *WhoWor 93*
Michaels, Henry H., Jr. 1909- *St&PR 93*
Michaels, Irene *WhoWrEP 92*
Michaels, J. Ramsey 1931- *ConAu 38NR*
Michaels, James Walker 1921- *WhoAm 92, WhoWrEP 92*
Michaels, Jennie P. *Law&B 92*
Michaels, Jeremy Daniel 1954- *WhoEmL 93*
Michaels, Joanne 1950- *BioIn 17, WhoAm 92, WhoWrEP 92*
Michaels, Leonard 1933- *BioIn 17, JeAmFiW, WhoAm 92, WhoWrEP 92*
Michaels, Loretta Ann 1950- *WhoAmW 93*
Michaels, Lorne *WhoAm 92*
Michaels, Louis Andrew 1935- *BiDAMSp 1989*
Michaels, Margaret *Law&B 92*
Michaels, Melisa C. *ScF&FL 92*
Michaels, Mickey 1940- *WhoSSW 93*
Michaels, Mike 1946- *MiSFD 9*
Michaels, Paul 1965- *WhoE 93*
Michaels, Pearl Dorothy 1936- *WhoAmW 93*
Michaels, Philip *ScF&FL 92*
Michaels, Rebecca 1955- *WhoAmW 93*
Michaels, Richard 1936- *ConTFT 10, MiSFD 9*
Michaels, Richard Edward 1952- *WhoEmL 93, WhoWor 93*
Michaels, Robert H. 1954- *St&PR 93*
Michaels, Sheldon S. *Law&B 92*
Michaels, Steve *ConAu 39NR*
Michaels, Steve 1955- *SmATA 71*
Michaels, Thomas Joseph 1957- *WhoE 93*
Michaels, Wayne H. *Law&B 92*
Michaels, Willard A. 1917- *WhoAm 92*
Michaelsen, Alfred L. *Law&B 92*
Michaelsen, Alfred L. 1940- *St&PR 93*
Michaelsen, Howard K. 1927- *St&PR 93*
Michaelsen, Terje E. 1942- *WhoScE 91-4*
Michael Sisman, III c. 1292-c. 1330 *OxDcByz*
Michaelson, Arthur M. 1927- *WhoAm 92*
Michaelson, Benjamin, Jr. 1936- *WhoE 93*
Michaelson, John Charles 1953- *WhoEmL 93*
Michaelson, Melvin 1928- *WhoAm 92*
Michaelson, Peter Lee 1952- *WhoWor 93*
Michaelson, Richard Aaron 1952- *St&PR 93*
Michael Stratiotikos, VI c. 1057- *OxDcByz*
Michael Synkellos c. 761-846 *OxDcByz*
Michael the Syrian, I 1126-1199 *OxDcByz*
Michael Visevic dc. 932 *OxDcByz*
Michak, Helen Barbara 1926- *WhoAmW 93*
Michalak, Bazyli Wieslaw 1932- *WhoWor 93*
Michalak, Charles Paul 1946- *St&PR 93*
Michalak, Edmund Charles *Law&B 92*
Michalak, Edward Francis 1937- *WhoAm 92*
Michalak, James L. *Law&B 92*
Michalak, Thomas 1940-1986 *Baker 92*
Michalak, Thomas J. 1940- *BioIn 17*
Michalczyk, Linda F. 1954- *St&PR 93*
Michalec, Stephen 1954- *St&PR 93*
Michalek, Bernard Joseph 1934- *WhoE 93*
Michalek, John S. 1954- *St&PR 93*
Michalek, Margaret M. 1926- *St&PR 93*
Michalek, Richard C. 1923- *St&PR 93*
Michalek, Rudolf 1941- *WhoScE 91-4*
Michalenko, Valerie Lou 1960- *WhoAmW 93*
Michalewicz, Marek Tadeusz 1957- *WhoWor 93*
Michalik, Christa 1942- *WhoScE 91-4*
Michalik, Edward Francis 1946- *WhoAm 92, WhoE 93, WhoEmL 93, WhoWor 93*
Michalik, Jerzy St. 1938- *WhoScE 91-4*
Michalik, John James 1945- *WhoAm 92*
Michalik, Krzysztof 1956- *WhoWor 93*
Michalik, Richard Edmund 1947- *WhoEmL 93*
Michalis, Clarence F. 1922- *St&PR 93*
Michalko, James Paul 1950- *WhoAm 92*
Michalle, Peter S. *Law&B 92*
Michalopoulos, Christos Demetrius 1931- *WhoWor 93*
Michalove, Sharon Deborah 1951- *WhoAmW 93*
Michalovsky, Paul M. 1965- *WhoE 93*
Michalowicz, Jan 1530-1583 *PolBiDi*
Michalowicz, Joseph Victor 1941- *WhoE 93*
Michalowski, Aleksander 1851-1938 *PolBiDi*
Michalowski, Daniel Richard 1938- *WhoE 93*
Michalowski, Kazimierz 1901-1981 *PolBiDi*
Michalowski, Piotr 1800-1855 *PolBiDi*
Michalowski, Zenon Eugene 1930- *WhoScE 91-4*
Michals, Duane 1932- *WhoAm 92*
Michals, George Francis 1935- *WhoAm 92, WhoE 93*
Michals, Lee Marie 1939- *WhoAmW 93*
Michalske, Mike 1903-1983 *BioIn 17*
Michalski, Celeste C. 1942- *WhoAmW 93*
Michalski, Donna Kaye 1946- *St&PR 93*
Michalski, Jan 1920- *WhoScE 91-4*
Michalski, Jeanne Ann 1958- *WhoAmW 93, WhoSSW 93*
Michalski, Joseph Walter 1943- *St&PR 93*
Michalski, Ludwik 1927- *WhoScE 91-4*
Michalski, Marek Andrzej 1930- *WhoScE 91-4*
Michalski, Miroslaw Mikolaj 1953- *WhoWor 93*
Michalski, Paul Peter 1961- *WhoEmL 93*
Michalski, Thomas Joseph 1933- *WhoAm 92*
Michalsky, Donal 1928-1976 *Baker 92*
Michalson, Karen *ScF&FL 92*
Micham, Nancy Sue 1956- *WhoAmW 93*
Michanowsky, George 1920- *WhoAm 92, WhoWor 93*
Michard, Gil 1937- *WhoScE 91-2*
Michard, R. *WhoScE 91-2*
Michard, Raymond 1925- *WhoScE 91-2*
Michas, George 1943- *St&PR 93*
Michaud, A.C. 1876-1975 *ScF&FL 92*
Michaud, Alphee Martial 1938- *WhoE 93*
Michaud, Ernest C. 1930- *St&PR 93*
Michaud, Hillary Jane *Law&B 92*
Michaud, Howard Henry 1902- *WhoAm 92*
Michaud, Jean Fernand 1932- *WhoWor 93*
Michaud, Marc A. *ScF&FL 92*
Michaud, Michael Alan George 1938- *WhoAm 92, WhoWrEP 92*
Michaud, Nancy A. *Law&B 92*
Michaud, Norma Alice Palmer 1946- *WhoAmW 93*
Michaud, Robert H. *Law&B 92*
Michaud, Steven J. *Law&B 92*
Michaudon, Andre F. 1929- *WhoScE 91-2*
Michaudon, Andre Francisque 1929- *WhoWor 93*
Michaux, C. *WhoScE 91-2*
Michaux, Christian Yvan 1960- *WhoWor 93*
Michaux, Donna Volney 1955- *WhoSSW 93*
Michaux, Henry Gaston 1934- *WhoSSW 93*
Michaux, Solomon Lightfoot 1884-1968 *EncAACR*
Michaux-Chevry, Lucette 1929- *DcCPCAm*
Michavila Pitarch, Francisco 1948- *WhoScE 91-3*
Micheau, Janine 1914-1976 *OxDcOp*
Micheaux, Oscar 1884-1951 *BioIn 17*
Micheelsen, Hans Friedrich 1902-1973 *Baker 92*
Michel, Aaron E. *Law&B 92*
Michel, Anthony Nikolaus 1935- *WhoAm 92*
Michel, Anthony R. *Law&B 92*
Michel, Barbara Rule 1957- *WhoAmW 93*
Michel, Benoit 1940- *St&PR 93, WhoAm 92*
Michel, Bernard 1930- *WhoAm 92*
Michel, C. Ray 1928- *St&PR 93*
Michel, Carol Loupe 1959- *WhoEmL 93*
Michel, D. Daniel, Jr. 1946- *WhoAm 92*
Michel, Daniel John 1949- *WhoEmL 93, WhoSSW 93, WhoWor 93*
Michel, Donald Charles 1935- *WhoAm 92*
Michel, Francois Claude 1928- *WhoWor 93*
Michel, George J., Jr. 1931- *St&PR 93*
Michel, Gilbert D. 1922- *WhoScE 91-2*
Michel, Gilles 1956- *WhoWor 93*
Michel, Harold Gustave 1926- *WhoE 93*
Michel, Hartmut *WhoScE 91-3*
Michel, Hartmut 1948- *WhoWor 93*
Michel, Henri Marie 1931- *WhoWor 93*
Michel, Henry Ludwig 1924- *St&PR 93, WhoAm 92, WhoWor 93*
Michel, James 1944- *WhoWor 93*
Michel, James H. 1939- *WhoAm 92*
Michel, Jean Christian 1951- *WhoWor 93*
Michel, Karon Rae 1946- *WhoAmW 93*
Michel, Louise 1830-1905 *BioIn 17*
Michel, Marianne H. *Law&B 92*
Michel, Marilyn Luella 1931- *WhoAmW 93*
Michel, Mary Ann Kedzuf 1939- *WhoAm 92*
Michel, Patricia Owen 1955- *WhoAmW 93*
Michel, Paul-Baudouin 1930- *Baker 92*
Michel, Paul R. 1941- *CngDr 91*
Michel, Paul Redmond 1941- *WhoAm 92, WhoE 93*
Michel, Peter Alexander 1943- *St&PR 93, WhoSSW 93*
Michel, Philip Martin 1939- *St&PR 93*
Michel, Pierre V. 1927- *WhoScE 91-2*
Michel, Richard C. 1953- *St&PR 93*
Michel, Richard Chris 1945- *WhoE 93*
Michel, Robert C. 1927- *St&PR 93*
Michel, Robert Charles 1927- *WhoAm 92*
Michel, Robert F. 1921- *St&PR 93*
Michel, Robert H. 1923- *BioIn 17, CngDr 91, PolPar*
Michel, Robert Henry 1923- *WhoAm 92*
Michel, Ronald Ralph 1941- *WhoSSW 93*
Michel, Sandy *Law&B 92*
Michel, Scott 1916- *WhoWrEP 92*
Michel, Scott D. 1955- *WhoEmL 93*
Michel, Sharon Lee 1946- *WhoAmW 93, WhoEmL 93*
Michelangeli, Arturo Benedetti 1920- *Baker 92*
Michelangelo Buonarroti 1475-1564 *BioIn 17*
Michelberger, Pal 1930- *WhoScE 91-4*
Michel-Briand, Yvon Roger 1934- *WhoScE 91-2*
Michele, Robert Charles 1959- *WhoE 93*
Michelena, Margarita 1917- *DcMexL*
Michelet, Edmond 1899-1970 *BioIn 17*
Michelet, Jules 1798-1874 *BioIn 17*
Michelet, Michel 1894- *Baker 92*
Micheletti, Carl Aldo 1936- *St&PR 93*
Micheletti, Gian Federico 1922- *WhoScE 91-3*
Micheletti, Raymond Earl 1926- *St&PR 93*
Micheletti, Thomas A. *Law&B 92*
Micheletti, Tony N. 1948- *St&PR 93*
Micheletto, Joe Raymond 1936- *St&PR 93, WhoAm 92*
Michelfelder, Ellen Haden 1945- *WhoAmW 93*
Michelfelder, William F. d1992 *NewYTBS 92*
Micheli, Frank James 1930- *WhoAm 92*
Micheli, Gene 1928- *WhoSSW 93*
Micheli, Romano c. 1575-c. 1659 *Baker 92*
Michelini, Alex J. 1937- *WhoE 93*
Michelini, Sylvia Hamilton 1946- *WhoAmW 93, WhoEmL 93, WhoSSW 93, WhoWor 93*
Michelinie, David *ScF&FL 92*
Michelis, Jurgen 1938- *WhoScE 91-3*
Michell, Robert Hall *WhoScE 91-1*
Michelle, Shelley *BioIn 17*
Michelman, Kate *BioIn 17*
Michelman, Peggy Crystal 1932- *WhoAmW 93*

Michelotti, Carla R. *Law&B 92*
Michels, Daniel Lester 1941- *WhoAm 92*
Michels, Doug 1943- *WhoE 93*
Michels, Eugene 1926- *WhoAm 92*
Michels, H.J.B.D. 1923- *WhoScE 91-2*
Michels, Kevin Howard 1960- *WhoEmL 93*
Michels, Michael E. 1951- *WhoWrEP 92*
Michels, Robert 1876-1936 *PolPar*
Michels, Robert 1936- *WhoAm 92*
Michels, Ronald G. 1943-1991 *BioIn 17*
Michels, Roy Samuel 1932- *WhoSSW 93*
Michels, Sharry *ScF&FL 92*
Michels, William Charles 1948- *St&PR 93*
Michelsen, Axel 1940- *WhoScE 91-2, WhoWor 93*
Michelsen, Christopher Bruce Hermann 1940- *WhoE 93*
Michelsen, John A. 1934- *St&PR 93*
Michelsen, Neil Raymond 1943- *WhoAm 92*
Michelsohn, Marie-Louise 1941- *WhoWor 93*
Michelson, Alan 1934- *St&PR 93*
Michelson, Bennett *ScF&FL 92*
Michelson, Bruce (N.) 1948- *ConAu 139*
Michelson, David Todd 1961- *WhoE 93*
Michelson, Edward J. 1915- *WhoAm 92*
Michelson, Gertrude Geraldine 1925- *St&PR 93, WhoAm 92*
Michelson, Harley M. 1949- *St&PR 93*
Michelson, Irving 1922- *WhoAm 92*
Michelson, James A. 1941- *St&PR 93*
Michelson, Lillian 1928- *WhoAm 92*
Michelson, Mark A. 1935- *WhoAm 92*
Michelson, Miriam 1870- *AmWomPl*
Michelson, Peter F. 1935- *WhoWrEP 92*
Michelson, Richard 1953- *WhoWrEP 92*
Michelstetter, Stanley Hubert 1946- *WhoEmL 93*
Michelucci, Giovanni 1891-1990 *BioIn 17*
Michener, Charles Duncan 1918- *WhoAm 92*
Michener, Daniel Roland 1900-1991 *BioIn 17*
Michener, Dave *MiSFD 9*
Michener, James A. 1907- *BioIn 17, MagSAmL [port]*
Michener, James Albert 1907- *WhoAm 92, WhoWrEP 92*
Michener, James Michael *Law&B 92*
Michener, John 1942- *St&PR 93*
Michener, John William 1924- *WhoSSW 93*
Michenfelder, John Donahue 1931- *WhoAm 92*
Michenfelder, Joseph Francis 1929- *WhoAm 92, WhoE 93*
Michero, William Henderson 1925- *WhoAm 92*
Micheron, Francois 1939- *WhoScE 91-2*
Michetti, Susan Jane 1948- *WhoAmW 93, WhoEmL 93, WhoWor 93*
Michi, Orazio c. 1595-1641 *Baker 92*
Michie, Clarence Richard 1937- *St&PR 93*
Michie, D. *WhoScE 91-1*
Michie, Robin Morris 1965- *WhoEmL 93*
Michie, Troy Willard 1923- *WhoSSW 93*
Michie, Walter *WhoScE 91-1*
Michielli, Donald Warren 1934- *WhoE 93*
Michigami, Wayne R. *Law&B 92*
Michinard, George S. 1935- *St&PR 93*
Michka, A. Richard 1947- *St&PR 93*
Michl, Heribert 1922- *WhoScE 91-4*
Michl, Lynn R. 1959- *St&PR 93*
Michler, Markwart Waldemar 1923- *WhoWor 93*
Michlin, Irving R. 1936- *St&PR 93*
Michlin, Norman 1922- *St&PR 93*
Michlink, Fred P. 1946- *St&PR 93*
Michniewicz, Marian 1922- *WhoScE 91-4*
Michnik, Adam *BioIn 17*
Michnik, Adam 1946- *ColdWar 2 [port]*
Michot, Jean 1930- *WhoScE 91-2*
Michulka, Robert F. 1947- *St&PR 93*
Micic, Miroslava 1948- *WhoScE 91-4*
Micic, Sava 1948- *WhoScE 91-4*
Micinski, Tadeusz 1873-1918 *PolBiDi*
Mick, Charles Lee 1946- *St&PR 93*
Mick, Colin Kennedy 1941- *WhoWrEP 92*
Mick, Diane Joan 1955- *WhoEmL 93*
Mick, Hettie Louise *AmWomPl*
Mick, Howard Harold 1934- *WhoAm 92*
Mick, Margaret Anne 1947- *WhoAmW 93*
Micka, Michelle M. 1959- *WhoAmW 93*
Mickal, Abe 1913- *WhoAm 92*
Mickel, Buck 1925- *St&PR 93*
Mickel, Ronald J. 1933- *St&PR 93*
Mickells, Edward F. 1952- *St&PR 93*
Mickelsen, Susan 1943- *St&PR 93*
Mickelson, Arnold Rust 1922- *WhoAm 92*
Mickelson, Daniel D. 1941- *St&PR 93*
Mickelson, George S. 1941- *WhoAm 92, WhoWor 93*
Mickelson, Hal M. *Law&B 92*
Mickelson, Nadine Rosena 1934- *WhoWrEP 92*
Mickelson, Phil *BioIn 17*
Mickelson, Sig 1913- *WhoAm 92*
Mickelson, Terry R. 1943- *St&PR 93*
Mickelwait, Lowell Pitzer 1905- *WhoAm 92*
Mickens, Ronald Elbert 1943- *WhoSSW 93, WhoWrEP 92*
Mickes, Carla Kay *Law&B 92*
Mickes, Thomas Aylward 1946- *WhoEmL 93*
Mickey, Paul Albert 1937- *WhoSSW 93*
Mickey, Paul Fogle, Jr. 1949- *WhoAm 92*
Mickey, Roger David 1945- *St&PR 93*
Mickey the Pope *BioIn 17*
Mickiewicz, Adam 1798-1855 *PolBiDi [port]*
Mickiewicz, Celina 1812-1854 *PolBiDi*
Mickiewicz, Ellen Propper 1938- *WhoAm 92*
Mickle, Anne Robinson 1967- *WhoAmW 93*
Mickle, Kathryn Alma 1946- *WhoAmW 93*
Micklewright, Jerrold J. 1934- *St&PR 93*
Mickley, G. Andrew 1948- *WhoSSW 93*
Micklos, John Joseph, Jr. 1956- *WhoWrEP 92*
Micklos-Maisey, Janet M. 1947- *WhoAmW 93, WhoEmL 93*
Micklow, Craig Woodward 1947- *WhoEmL 93, WhoSSW 93*
Micklow, James T. 1952- *St&PR 93*
Micko, Alexander S. 1947- *WhoAm 92, WhoEmL 93*
Micko, Hans Christoph 1931- *WhoWor 93*
Micks, Carl Matthew *Law&B 92*
Micks, Don Wilfred 1918- *WhoAm 92*
Mickum, Luke Anthony *Law&B 92*
Mickus, Christopher J. 1968- *WhoWor 93*
Mickus, Donald Vincent 1946- *St&PR 93*
Mickwitz, Gosta 1917- *WhoScE 91-4*
Micky & Sylvia *SoulM*
Miclaus, Victor *WhoScE 91-4*
Micoli, Richard Andrew 1949- *WhoEmL 93*
Micolo, Anthony Michael 1949- *WhoE 93*
Micou, William Chatfield 1806-1854 *OxCSupC*
Micovic, Ivan V. 1941- *WhoScE 91-4*
Micovic, Predrag Mico 1932- *WhoUN 92*
Micozzi, Donald P. 1934- *St&PR 93*
Micozzi, Marc Stephen 1953- *WhoAm 92, WhoEmL 93*
Micros *DcMexL*
Micsko, Rudolph J., Jr. 1946- *St&PR 93*
Micucci, Charles (Patrick, Jr.) 1959- *ConAu 137*
Miczek, Klaus Alexander 1944- *WhoAm 92, WhoE 93*
Miczuga, Mark N. 1962- *WhoWor 93*
Midanek, Deborah Hicks 1954- *WhoE 93*
Midby, John H. *BioIn 17*
Middaugh, Jack Kendall, II 1949- *WhoEmL 93, WhoSSW 93, WhoWor 93*
Middaugh, Robert Burton 1935- *WhoAm 92*
Middelkamp, John Neal 1925- *WhoAm 92*
Middelschulte, Wilhelm 1863-1943 *Baker 92*
Middelthon, Andreas *Law&B 92*
Midden, Mary Ann 1953- *WhoAmW 93*
Middendorf, Alice Carter 1940- *WhoAmW 93, WhoE 93*
Middendorf, Christina Marie 1958- *WhoEmL 93*
Middendorf, Helmut 1953- *BioIn 17*
Middendorf, J. William 1924- *WhoWor 93*
Middendorf, John Harlan 1922- *WhoAm 92, WhoWrEP 92*
Middendorf, William Henry 1921- *WhoAm 92*
Middlebrook, David *WhoWrEP 92*
Middlebrook, Diane Wood *BioIn 17*
Middlebrook, Diane Wood 1939- *WhoWrEP 92*
Middlebrook, Paul E. 1946- *St&PR 93*
Middlebrook, Stephen B., Sr. *Law&B 92*
Middlebrook, Stephen Beach 1937- *St&PR 93, WhoIns 93*
Middlebrooks, Eddie Joe 1932- *WhoAm 92, WhoSSW 93*
Middleditch, Alan E. *WhoScE 91-1*
Middleditch, Brian Stanley 1945- *WhoWor 93*
Middleditch, Leigh Benjamin, Jr. 1929- *WhoAm 92*
Middlekauff, Robert Lawrence 1929- *WhoAm 92, WhoWrEP 92*
Middleman, Raoul Fink 1935- *WhoE 93*
Middlemiss, John F. 1899-1990 *BioIn 17*
Middlesworth, Chester Paul 1929- *St&PR 93*
Middleton, Alan Charles 1946- *WhoAm 92*
Middleton, Anne 1949- *WhoAmW 93*
Middleton, Anthony Wayne, Jr. 1939- *WhoWor 93*
Middleton, Brian 1935- *WhoWor 93*
Middleton, Christopher 1926- *WhoAm 92*
Middleton, David 1920- *WhoAm 92, WhoWor 93*
Middleton, David Andrew 1966- *WhoEmL 93, WhoSSW 93*
Middleton, Dawn E. *WhoAmW 93, WhoE 93*
Middleton, Denise Marie 1954- *WhoAmW 93*
Middleton, Donald Earl 1930- *St&PR 93, WhoAm 92, WhoSSW 93*
Middleton, Drew 1913- *JrnUS*
Middleton, Drew 1913-1990 *BioIn 17*
Middleton, Elliott, Jr. 1925- *WhoAm 92, WhoE 93*
Middleton, Elwyn Linton 1914- *WhoAm 92*
Middleton, Finley Norman, II 1945- *WhoIns 93*
Middleton, Frank Walters, Jr. 1919- *WhoAm 92*
Middleton, Gerard Viner 1931- *WhoAm 92*
Middleton, Harry Joseph 1921- *WhoAm 92, WhoSSW 93*
Middleton, Haydn 1955- *ScF&FL 92*
Middleton, Herman David, Sr. 1925- *WhoAm 92*
Middleton, Hubert Stanley 1890-1959 *Baker 92*
Middleton, Jack Baer 1929- *WhoAm 92*
Middleton, James Franklin 1946- *WhoWrEP 92*
Middleton, John d1885 *BioIn 17*
Middleton, Lawrence W. *Law&B 92*
Middleton, Linda G. *Law&B 92*
Middleton, Linda Greathouse 1950- *St&PR 93*
Middleton, Linda Jean Greathouse 1950- *WhoAm 92*
Middleton, Lois Jean 1930- *WhoAmW 93*
Middleton, Lowell Glenn 1948- *St&PR 93*
Middleton, Marc S. 1950- *St&PR 93*
Middleton, Michael John 1953- *WhoWor 93*
Middleton, Mickey Edison 1953- *WhoSSW 93*
Middleton, Norman G. 1935- *WhoWrEP 92*
Middleton, Norman Graham 1935- *WhoSSW 93, WhoWor 93*
Middleton, P.E. *WhoScE 91-1*
Middleton, Paulette Bauer 1946- *WhoAmW 93*
Middleton, Peter J.H. 1947- *St&PR 93*
Middleton, Ray P., Jr. *Law&B 92*
Middleton, Silvia Gilbert 1953- *WhoEmL 93, WhoSSW 93*
Middleton, Stephanie A. *Law&B 92*
Middleton, Stephen 1954- *WhoEmL 93, WhoSSW 93*
Middleton, Steven Travis 1951- *WhoE 93*
Middleton, Troy H. 1889-1976 *HarEnMi*
Middleton, Vera Sue 1940- *WhoAmW 93*
Middleton, Vincent Francis 1951- *WhoEmL 93, WhoWor 93*
Middleton, Wallace Pierpont 1946- *St&PR 93*
Middour, Jay Wenger 1958- *WhoE 93*
Midei, Richard Allen 1947- *WhoEmL 93*
Midgett, John Thomas 1952- *WhoEmL 93, WhoSSW 93*
Midgley, Alvin Rees, Jr. 1933- *WhoAm 92*
Midgley, C. Edward 1937- *St&PR 93*
Midgley, John Morton *WhoScE 91-1*
Midili, Arthur R. 1931- *St&PR 93*
Midkiff, Robert R. 1920- *St&PR 93*
Midkiff, Robert Richards 1920- *WhoAm 92*
Midkiff, Stephen Jay 1952- *WhoEmL 93*
Midlarsky, Elizabeth Ruth Steckel *WhoAmW 93, WhoE 93*
Midlarsky, Manus Issachar 1937- *WhoAm 92*
Midler, Bette *BioIn 17*
Midler, Bette 1945- *Baker 92, ConMus 8 [port], IntDcF 2-3, WhoAm 92, WhoAmW 93*
Midnighters *SoulM*
Midori 1971- *Baker 92, BioIn 17*
Midoro, Vittorio 1948- *WhoScE 91-3*
Midrio, Menotti 1932- *WhoScE 91-3*
Midttun, Lars S. 1920- *WhoScE 91-4*
Midura, Edmund Michael 1935- *WhoE 93*
Midwinter, John Edwin *WhoScE 91-1*
Midwinter, Thomas Richard 1938- *WhoE 93*
Midyett, Charles L. 1939- *St&PR 93*
Midyett, Susan F. *Law&B 92*
Mieczkowski, Francis E., Jr. *Law&B 92*
Miedaner, Terrel *ScF&FL 92*
Miedel, Rainer 1937-1983 *Baker 92*
Miedema, Jack Arlon 1950- *WhoEmL 93*
Miedema, Sylvia Ann 1904- *St&PR 93*
Miederer, Siegfried-Ernst 1942- *WhoWor 93*
Miedzy Brocki, Edward Paul *Law&B 92*
Mieg, Peter 1906- *Baker 92*
Miehls, Donald E. *Law&B 92*
Miekisz, Stanislaw 1927- *WhoWor 93*
Miekka, Richard George 1933- *WhoE 93*
Miel, Alice *BioIn 17*
Miel, Ronald Joseph 1956- *WhoWor 93*
Miel, Vicky Ann 1951- *WhoAmW 93, WhoEmL 93*
Miela, Deborah L. *Law&B 92*
Miela, Deborah Lynn 1949- *WhoEmL 93*
Mielcarzewicz, E.Wl. 1924- *WhoScE 91-4*
Mielck, Ernst 1877-1899 *Baker 92*
Mielck, Jobst B. 1938- *WhoScE 91-3*
Mielcuszny, Albert John 1941- *WhoAm 92*
Mielczarek, Zbigniew 1931- *WhoScE 91-4*
Mielczewski, Marcin c. 1600-1651 *PolBiDi*
Miele, Alfonse Ralph 1922- *WhoAm 92*
Miele, Angelo 1922- *WhoAm 92, WhoSSW 93, WhoWrEP 92*
Miele, Anthony Michael *Law&B 92*
Miele, Anthony William 1926- *WhoAm 92*
Miele, Arthur R. *St&PR 93*
Miele, Arthur Robert 1941- *WhoAm 92*
Miele, David Thomas 1959- *WhoEmL 93*
Miele, Eileen Cecelia *WhoAm 92, WhoAmW 93*
Miele, Elizabeth 1900- *AmWomPl*
Miele, Joel Arthur, Sr. 1934- *WhoE 93*
Miele, Robert C. 1942- *St&PR 93*
Mielec, Kazimierz 1928- *WhoScE 91-4*
Mielecki, Max C. 1931- *St&PR 93*
Mielikainen, Kari Juhani 1950- *WhoScE 91-4*
Mieling, Terence Michael 1949- *WhoAm 92*
Mieliulis, Benjamin *Law&B 92*
Mielke, Antonia c. 1852-1907 *Baker 92*
Mielke, Clarence Harold, Jr. 1936- *WhoAm 92*
Mielke, Donald Craig 1943- *WhoAm 92*
Mielke, Erich *BioIn 17*
Mielke, Frederick William, Jr. 1921- *St&PR 93, WhoAm 92*
Mielke, Siegfried 1941- *WhoWor 93*
Mielke, Thomas J. *Law&B 92*
Mielke, Wayne Joseph 1954- *WhoWrEP 92*
Mien, John *DcCPCAm*
Mieno, Yasushi *BioIn 17*
Miercort, Clifford R. 1940- *St&PR 93*
Miercort, Clifford Roy 1940- *WhoAm 92*
Miereanu, Costin 1943- *Baker 92*
Mierkowicz, Ed 1924- *BioIn 17*
Mier Noriega y Guerra, Jose Servando Teresa de 1765-1827 *DcMexL*
Mierzecki, Roman 1921- *WhoScE 91-4*
Mierzwa, Zbigniew 1929- *WhoScE 91-4*
Mies, John Charles 1946- *WhoEmL 93*
Mies, Paul 1889-1976 *Baker 92*
Mies, Thomas Gerald 1953- *WhoEmL 93*
Miescher, Peter Anton 1923- *WhoScE 91-4*
Miesel, Sandra 1941- *ScF&FL 92*
Miesmer, Charlie *BioIn 17*
Miesnieks, Andre K. *Law&B 92*
Miesse, James Everett 1952- *WhoEmL 93*
Miesse, Mary Elizabeth *WhoAmW 93, WhoSSW 93*
Mies van der Rohe, Ludwig 1886-1969 *BioIn 17*
Mieszko, I 930-992 *PolBiDi*
Mieth, William S. 1944- *St&PR 93*
Mietzel, Dennis Oliver 1940- *St&PR 93*
Mifflin, James *BioIn 17*
Mifflin, Mark Jonathon 1957- *WhoEmL 93*
Mifflin, Theodore Edward 1946- *WhoE 93*
Mifflin, Thomas 1744-1800 *BioIn 17*
Mifsud, James Charles *Law&B 92*
Mifsud, Paul V. *Law&B 92*
Mifune, Toshiro 1920- *IntDcF 2-3 [port], WhoWor 93*
Migala, Joseph 1913- *PolBiDi*
Migala, Lucyna Jozefa 1944- *WhoAmW 93, WhoWor 93*
Migausky, Stephen Joseph *Law&B 92*
Migdal, A.B. 1911-1991 *BioIn 17*
Migdal, Sheldon Paul 1936- *WhoAm 92*
Migdalski, Janusz Wladyslaw 1935- *WhoScE 91-4*
Migden, Chester L. 1921- *WhoAm 92*
Migel, Christopher James 1951- *WhoIns 93*
Migell, Bruce Arthur 1933- *St&PR 93*
Migenes-Johnson, Julia 1945- *Baker 92, OxDcOp*
Migeon, Barbara Ruben 1931- *WhoE 93*
Migeon, Claude Jean 1923- *WhoAm 92, WhoE 93*
Mighell, Kenneth John 1931- *WhoAm 92, WhoSSW 93*
Mighels, Ella Sterling 1853-1934 *AmWomPl*

Mighty Sam 1941- SoulM
Migl, Donald Raymond 1947- WhoSSW 93
Migliacci, Steven 1959- St&PR 93
Migliaccio, John Nicholas 1949- WhoE 93
Migliaro, Marco William 1948- WhoAm 92
Miglietta, Angelo Louis 1928- St&PR 93
Miglietta, Francesco Giuseppe 1954- WhoWor 93
Miglio, Daniel J. 1940- St&PR 93
Miglio, Daniel Joseph 1940- WhoAm 92
Migliori, A. Tee 1936- St&PR 93
Migliozzi, Joseph J. 1950- St&PR 93
Miglis, John 1950- ScF&FL 92
Miglore, Joseph James 1945- WhoAm 92
Mignan, Edouard-Charles-Octave 1884-1969 Baker 92
Mignanelli, James R. 1932- St&PR 93
Mignanelli, Thomas D. BioIn 17, WhoAm 92
Mignanelli, Thomas E. 1948- St&PR 93
Mignani, Roberto 1946- WhoWor 93
Mignano, Richard Alan 1948- WhoEmL 93
Mignatti, Robert Anthony 1947- WhoSSW 93
Mignogna, Thomas S. 1933- St&PR 93
Mignon, Patrice 1946- WhoWor 93
Mignone, Francisco (Paulo) 1897-1986 Baker 92
Mignone, Mario B. 1940- WhoAm 92
Migot, Georges 1891-1976 Baker 92
Migue, Jean Luc 1933- WhoAm 92
Miguel, Antoli Guarch 1936- WhoWor 93
Miguel, Maria Thereza Law&B 92
Miguel, Mario Firmino 1938-1991 BioIn 17
Miguez, Leopoldo (Americo) 1850-1902 Baker 92
Mihaescu, A. Afion 1926- WhoScE 91-4
Mihaileanu, Andrei Calin 1923- WhoWor 93
Mihaileanu, Calin Andrei 1923- WhoScE 91-4
Mihailescu, Manuela 1950- WhoE 93, WhoEmL 93
Mihailescu, Mircea 1920- WhoScE 91-4
Mihailoff, Ivan d1990 BioIn 17
Mihailovic, Mihailo L. 1924- WhoScE 91-4
Mihailovic, Miodrag V. WhoScE 91-4
Mihailovich, Draggan NewYTBS 92 [port]
Mihailovich, Draggan 1962?- BioIn 17
Mihailovich, Draza 1893-1946 DcTwHis
Mihajlov, Marin WhoScE 91-4
Mihajlov, Mihajlo BioIn 17
Mihajlov, Mihajlo N. 1934- WhoWor 93
Mihajlovic, Bozidar 1925- WhoScE 91-4
Mihal, Charles Andrew 1939- St&PR 93
Mihal, Thomas Harlan 1949- WhoEmL 93
Mihalas, Dimitri Manuel 1939- WhoAm 92
Mihalchik, Larry L. 1947- St&PR 93
Mihalic, David Anthony 1946- WhoAm 92
Mihalic, Gary d1991 BioIn 17
Mihalik, Phyllis Ann 1952- WhoAmW 93, WhoEmL 93
Mihalka, George 1952- MiSFD 9
Mihalkov, Nikita 1945- DrEEuF
Mihalkov-Koncalovskij, Andrej 1937- DrEEuF
Mihalovich, Edmund von 1842-1929 Baker 92
Mihalovich, Odon 1842-1929 OxDcOp
Mihalovich, Tony L. 1948- St&PR 93
Mihalovici, Marcel 1898-1985 Baker 92
Mihalski, Timothy I. 1950- WhoE 93
Mihalszki, John Steven 1957- WhoE 93
Mihaly, Andras 1917- Baker 92, WhoWor 93
Mihaly, Eugene Bramer 1934- WhoAm 92, WhoWrEP 92
Mihaly, Orestes J. Law&B 92
Mihaly, Orestes J. 1932- St&PR 93
Mihaly, Stefan 1932- WhoScE 91-4
Mihaly, Szabolcs WhoScE 91-4
Mihalyi, Louis Leonard 1921- WhoWrEP 92
Mihara, Asahiko 1947- WhoAsAP 91
Mihaylo, Steven G. 1943- St&PR 93
Mihelic, Franjo 1919- WhoScE 91-4
Mihelich, Jan M. Law&B 92
Mihelich, Janet Adele 1948- WhoAmW 93
Mihelich, John L. 1937- WhoSSW 93
Mihich, Enrico 1928- WhoAm 92
Mihills, Joan L. 1929- St&PR 93
Mihlik, J. John 1942- St&PR 93
Mihm, Martin Charles, Jr. WhoAm 92, WhoE 93
Mihm, Michael Martin 1943- WhoAm 92
Mihm, Michael William Law&B 92
Mihopoulos, Effie H. 1952- WhoEmL 93
Mihov, B. WhoScE 91-4
Mihram, Danielle 1942- WhoAmW 93
Mihram, George Arthur 1939- WhoE 93
Mihran, Theodore Gregory 1924- WhoAm 92
Mihu, Iulian 1926- DrEEuF
Mii, Nobuo 1934- WhoAm 92
Miido, Endel 1922- St&PR 93
Miiller, Thomas O. Law&B 92
Mijnheer, Bernard J. 1941- WhoScE 91-3
Mika, Augustyn Ludwik 1935- WhoScE 91-4, WhoWor 93
Mika, John Joseph 1938- St&PR 93
Mika, Joseph John 1948- WhoAm 92
Mika, William J. 1931- St&PR 93
Mikaelian, Tamar, Ms. 1962- St&PR 93
Mikaeljan, Sergej 1923- DrEEuF
Mikaelsen, Ben(jamin John) 1952- ConAu 139, SmATA 73 [port]
Mikalow, Alfred Alexander, II 1921- WhoWor 93
Mikalson, Jon Dennis 1943- WhoAm 92
Mikami, Gregg K. Law&B 92
Mikami, Kazuhiko 1963- WhoWor 93
Mikami, Takao 1933- WhoAsAP 91
Mikan, Teresa Law&B 92
Mikawa, Gun'ichi 1890- HarEnMi
Mikdashi, Zuhayr 1933- ConAu 39NR
Mike, Deborah Denise 1959- WhoAmW 93, WhoEmL 93
Mikecz, Istvan 1924- WhoScE 91-4
Mikel, Mary Eberlein 1959- WhoEmL 93
Mikelberg, Arnold 1937- WhoAm 92
Mikelberg, Arnold S. 1937- St&PR 93
Mikelberg, Martin 1938- St&PR 93
Mikell, Alan Glen 1951- WhoSSW 93
Mikelonis, David A. Law&B 92
Mikelonis, David Alan 1948- WhoAm 92
Mikels, James Ronald 1937- WhoSSW 93
Mikels, Richard Eliot 1947- WhoE 93
Mikels, Ted V. MiSFD 9
Mikelson, Patricia Myers Wood 1946- WhoEmL 93, WhoSSW 93
Mike-Nard, Beverly Jean 1957- WhoAmW 93, WhoEmL 93
Mikes, George 1912-1987 ScF&FL 92
Mikes, Gyorgy ScF&FL 92
Mikes, Thomas Louis 1946- WhoAm 92
Mikesch, Raymond J. 1947- St&PR 93
Mikesell, Marvin Wray 1929- WhoAm 92
Mikesell, Mary 1943- WhoWor 93
Mikesell, Raymond Frech 1913- WhoAm 92
Mikesh, Josef 1952- WhoWor 93
Mikhail, Carmen 1957- WhoAmW 93
Mikhail, William Mesiha 1935- WhoWor 93
Mikhailov, A.I. 1905-1988 BioIn 17
Mikhailov, Aleksandr Ivanovich 1905-1988 BioIn 17
Mikhailov, Peter 1921- WhoScE 91-4
Mikhailova, Maria (Alexandrovna) 1866-1943 Baker 92
Mikhalev, Alexander Alexandrovich 1965- WhoWor 93
Mikhalkov, Nikita 1945- MiSFD 9
Mikhalkov, Sergey Vladimirovich 1913- WhoWor 93
Mikhalkov-Konchalovsky, Andrei MiSFD 9
Mikhaly, Magy WhoScE 91-4
Mikhashoff, Yvar (Emilian) 1941- Baker 92
Mikhaylov, Maxim 1893-1971 OxDcOp
Mikhaylova, Maria 1866-1943 OxDcOp
Mikheev, Mikhail Ivanovich 1936- WhoUN 92
Miki, Minoru 1930- Baker 92
Miki, Roy 1942- WhoCanL 92
Miki, Tadao 1935- WhoAsAP 91
Mikielewicz, Jaroslaw 1941- WhoScE 91-4
Mikiewicz, Anna Daniella 1960- WhoAmW 93
Mikill, Frederick Joseph, II 1945- St&PR 93
Mikita, Joseph Karl 1918- WhoAm 92
Miki Takeo 1907- DcTwHis
Mikitka, Gerald Peter 1943- WhoAm 92
Mikkanen, Arvo Quoetone 1961- WhoEmL 93
Mikkelsen, Poul Henrik 1949- WhoWor 93
Mikkelsen, Robert L. 1957- WhoEmL 93, WhoSSW 93
Mikkelsen, Soren Aggergaard 1952- WhoScE 91-2
Mikkelson, M.D. 1933- St&PR 93
Mikkola, Heimo Juhani 1945- WhoWor 93
Mikkola, Martti Juhani 1936- WhoScE 91-4, WhoWor 93
Miklas, Kestutis Kostas 1922- St&PR 93
Miklaucic, Michael James 1954- WhoE 93, WhoEmL 93
Miklave, Matthew Thaddeus 1959- WhoEmL 93
Miklich, Thomas Robert 1947- St&PR 93
Mikljukov, Vladimir Michaelovich 1944- WhoWor 93
Mikloshazy, Attila WhoWor 93
Miklowitz, Gloria D. 1927- BioIn 17, MajAI [port], ScF&FL 92
Miklukho-Maklai, N.N. 1846-1888 IntDcAn
Miko, Joseph 1934- WhoScE 91-4
Miko, William Joseph, Jr. Law&B 92
Mikol, Leslie Maria 1963- WhoEmL 93
Mikol, Paul ScF&FL 92
Mikolaitis, Sandra Mucowski Law&B 92
Mikolajczak, Boleslaw 1946- WhoE 93, WhoEmL 93
Mikolajczyk, Stanislaw 1901-1966 BioIn 17
Mikolajczyk, Stanislaw 1903-1966 PolBiDi
Mikolas, Miklos 1923- WhoScE 91-4
Mikolaycak, Charles 1937- ChlBIID [port], ConAu 38NR, MajAI [port]
Mikolji, Boris Hrvoje 1926- WhoAm 92
Mikols, Judith Estelle 1962- WhoAmW 93
Mikolyzk, Thomas A. 1953- ConAu 138
Mikorey, Franz 1873-1947 Baker 92
Mikoryak, David Wayne 1950- St&PR 93
Mikosz, Mark William 1948- St&PR 93
Mikoyan, Anastas 1895-1978 ColdWar 2 [port]
Mikoyan, Anastas Ivanovich 1895-1978 DcTwHis
Mikrut, Thomas John 1948- St&PR 93
Miksch, Johann Aloys 1765-1845 Baker 92
Miksch, John Hohl 1947- St&PR 93
Miksic, Boris Alexander 1948- WhoEmL 93
Miksich, William St&PR 93
Miksiewicz, Sally S. 1962- St&PR 93
Mikucki, Kathie Jo Law&B 92
Mikula, Bernard James 1936- St&PR 93
Mikula, Kenneth Richard 1950- WhoIns 93
Mikula, Pavel 1947- WhoScE 91-4
Mikulas, Joseph Frank 1926- WhoAm 92
Mikulas, Jozsef 1941- WhoScE 91-4
Mikuli, Karl 1819-1897 Baker 92
Mikuli, Karol 1819-1897 PolBiDi
Mikuliza, William Edward 1934- St&PR 93
Mikulka, Mark E. Law&B 92
Mikulski, Barbara 1936- News 92 [port]
Mikulski, Barbara A. BioIn 17
Mikulski, Barbara A. 1936- CngDr 91
Mikulski, Barbara A. 1939- PolPar
Mikulski, Barbara Ann 1936- WhoAm 92, WhoAmW 93, WhoE 93
Mikulski, James Joseph 1934- WhoAm 92
Mikulski, Jan Franciszek 1930- WhoScE 91-4
Mikulski, Piotr Witold 1925- WhoAm 92
Mikulski, Zdzislaw 1920- WhoScE 91-4
Mikuni, Rentaro MiSFD 9
Mikuriya, Hisao 1929- WhoWor 93
Mikuriya, Masahiro 1951- WhoWor 93
Mikus, Eleanore Ann 1927- WhoAm 92, WhoE 93
Mikusinski, Piotr 1956- WhoSSW 93
Mikutowicz, Michael Anthony 1958- WhoE 93
Mikva, Abner J. 1926- CngDr 91
Mikva, Abner Joseph 1926- WhoAm 92, WhoE 93
Mikva, Mary Lane 1953- WhoEmL 93
Mikva, Zoe Wise 1928- WhoE 93
Mila, Massimo 1910-1988 Baker 92
Milach, Peter Christian 1949- St&PR 93
Milad, Moheb Fawzy 1945- WhoWor 93
Milai, Kimberly Ivy 1958- WhoE 93
Milakovich, D.V. 1946- St&PR 93
Milakovich, F.S. 1937- St&PR 93
Milam, Cheryl Perilloux 1947- WhoEmL 93, WhoSSW 93
Milam, James H. 1911- St&PR 93
Milam, Joseph Walton, Jr. 1956- WhoEmL 93
Milam, Michael Foster 1955- WhoSSW 93
Milam, Michael Lee 1951- WhoSSW 93
Milam, Ruth Lining AmWomPl
Milam, William Bryant 1936- WhoAm 92, WhoWor 93
Milan, Edgar J. 1934- HispAmA [port], St&PR 93
Milan, Luis de c. 1500-c. 1561 Baker 92
Milan, Mark J. 1951- St&PR 93
Milan, Myrna 1954- NotHsAW 93
Milan, Richard Joseph, Jr. 1959- WhoSSW 93
Milan, Thomas Lawrence 1941- WhoAm 92
Milan, Victor 1954- ScF&FL 92
Milander, Henry Martin 1939- WhoAm 92
Milanes, Isabelle Maria 1959- St&PR 93
Milanesi, David Laurence 1947- St&PR 93, WhoEmL 93
Milanesio, Maurizio 1938- WhoWor 93
Milani, Diva 1958- WhoEmL 93
Milani, Ernest John 1929- WhoAm 92
Milani, James Anthony 1966- WhoSSW 93
Milani, Kathy 1963- MiSFD 9
Milani, Victor John 1945- WhoE 93
Milanich, Jerald Thomas 1945- WhoAm 92
Milani-Comparetti, Marco Severo 1926- WhoWor 93
Milano, Antonio 1931- WhoWor 93
Milano, Carol Ellen 1946- WhoEmL 93
Milano, Eugene John 1927- St&PR 93
Milano, Frank 1911- St&PR 93
Milano, Lynn Mary 1946- WhoEmL 93
Milanov, Zinka 1906-1989 Baker 92, BioIn 17, IntDcOp [port], OxDcOp
Milardo, Terrence John 1941- WhoE 93
Milart, Zbigniew Antoni 1926- WhoScE 91-4
Milas, Joseph St&PR 93
Milas, Lawrence William 1935- WhoE 93
Milaski, John Joseph 1959- WhoE 93, WhoEmL 93, WhoWor 93
Milaszewski, Bernice Marion 1954- WhoSSW 93
Milatovic, Ljubomir 1920- WhoScE 91-4
Milavsky, Harold Phillip 1931- St&PR 93
Mila y Fontanals, Manuel 1818-1884 BioIn 17
Milbank, Elizabeth Palmer AmWomPl
Milbank, Jeremiah 1920- St&PR 93, WhoAm 92
Milbank, Neil Oscar WhoScE 91-1
Milbank, Patricia Ann Law&B 92
Milberg, Susan Bodner 1949- WhoAmW 93, WhoEmL 93
Milberger, Patrick A. Law&B 92
Milbergs, Egils 1946- WhoE 93
Milbert, Roger P. 1940- WhoIns 93
Milbourn, Elizabeth Jean Law&B 92
Milbourn, G. WhoScE 91-1
Milbourne, Joseph C. 1951- St&PR 93
Milbourne, Robert J. 1941- St&PR 93
Milbourne, Thomas Elwood 1946- WhoEmL 93
Milbrath, Dennis Henry 1948- WhoEmL 93
Milbrath, Earlon L. 1941- WhoIns 93
Milbrath, Earlon Leroy 1941- WhoAm 92
Milbrath, Elizabeth R. Law&B 92
Milbrath, Mary Merrill Lemke 1940- WhoAmW 93
Milbrath, Robert Henry WhoAm 92
Milburn, A. WhoScE 91-1
Milburn, Anthony 1942- WhoScE 91-1
Milburn, Bryan L. 1896-1991 BioIn 17
Milburn, Ellsworth 1938- Baker 92
Milburn, George Henry William WhoScE 91-1
Milburn, Herbert Theodore 1931- WhoSSW 93
Milburn, Jeffrey Gerald 1935- St&PR 93
Milburn, Richard Allan 1933- St&PR 93, WhoSSW 93
Milburn, Richard Henry 1928- WhoAm 92
Milburn, Ruth Kurtzweil 1937- WhoAmW 93
Milbury, K. David 1939- St&PR 93
Milbury, Mike 1953- WhoAm 92
Milch, Neal Bruce 1958- St&PR 93
Milch, Pamela H. 1960- WhoAmW 93
Milch, Robert A. 1929-1991 BioIn 17
Milchan, Arnon BioIn 17
Milcic, Vuk 1921- WhoScE 91-4
Milcinski, Janez 1913- WhoScE 91-4
Milcinski, Janez Fran 1913- WhoWor 93
Milczarski, Thomas M. 1951- St&PR 93
Milde, Franz 1855-1929 OxDcOp
Milde, Hans Feodor von 1821-1899 Baker 92, OxDcOp
Milde, Helmut Ingo 1934- St&PR 93
Milde, Michael 1931- WhoUN 92
Milde, Rosa Agthe 1827-1906 See Milde, Hans Feodor von 1821-1899 Baker 92
Milde, Rudolf 1859-1927 OxDcOp
Mildenberg, Albert 1878-1918 Baker 92
Mildenberg, Anna von IntDcOp
Mildenburg, Anna 1872-1947 Baker 92
Mildenburg, Anna von OxDcOp
Mildenhall, Glen Thomas 1951- WhoEmL 93
Milder, Alvin Sherman 1932- St&PR 93
Milder, Jay 1934- WhoE 93
Milder, Theresa Tsai 1960- WhoEmL 93
Milder-Hauptmann, (Pauline) Anna 1785-1838 Baker 92
Milder-Hauptmann, Pauline Anna 1785-1838 OxDcOp
Mildmay, Audrey 1900-1953 OxDcOp
Mildner, Gerard C. S. 1959- ConAu 138
Mildner, Paul 1918- WhoScE 91-4
Mildon, James Lee 1936- WhoWor 93
Mildon, Marie Roberta 1935- WhoAmW 93, WhoWor 93
Mildren, Jack 1949- WhoAm 92, WhoSSW 93
Mildren, John Barry 1932- WhoAsAP 91
Mildren, Nan Langdon 1874- AmWomPl
Mildvan, Donna 1942- WhoAm 92, WhoAmW 93
Mileaf, Howard A. 1937- St&PR 93

Miledi, Ricardo 1927- *WhoAm 92*
Mileham, William Dunning 1946- *St&PR 93*
Milena 1896-1944 *BioIn 17*
Mileo, Janice *Law&B 92*
Miler, Miroslav 1935- *WhoScE 91-4*
Miles, Lord 1907-1991 *AnObit 1991*
Miles, Alan L. *Law&B 92*
Miles, Alexander Charles 1958- *WhoWor 93*
Miles, Alfred Lee 1913- *WhoWor 93*
Miles, Algene Stevens 1929- *St&PR 93*
Miles, Annie M. *AmWomPl*
Miles, Arthur J. 1920- *WhoAm 92*
Miles, Arthur X. 1947- *St&PR 93*
Miles, Barry 1943- *ScF&FL 92*
Miles, Bernard 1907-1991 *BioIn 17*
Miles, Betty *SweetSg C*
Miles, C.V. *WhoScE 91-1*
Miles, Candice St. Jacques 1951- *WhoWrEP 92*
Miles, Charlene 1928- *WhoAmW 93*
Miles, Charles Henry 1947- *WhoEmL 93*
Miles, Christine Marie 1951- *WhoAm 92, WhoAmW 93, WhoE 93*
Miles, Christopher 1939- *MiSFD 9*
Miles, Christopher 1947- *WhoAsAP 91*
Miles, Christopher Earl 1957- *WhoEmL 93*
Miles, Christopher Robin 1954- *WhoWor 93*
Miles, Dana E. *Law&B 92*
Miles, Donald Geoffrey 1952- *WhoWor 93*
Miles, Donald L. *BioIn 17*
Miles, Edward Harry 1936- *WhoE 93*
Miles, Ellen 1941- *ScF&FL 92*
Miles, Ellen Gross 1941- *WhoAm 92*
Miles, Frank Charles 1926- *WhoAm 92*
Miles, George *BioIn 17*
Miles, George Leroy, Jr. 1941- *WhoAm 92*
Miles, Gerard Francis 1954- *WhoEmL 93*
Miles, Gordon H. 1942- *WhoAm 92*
Miles, Helen *AmWomPl*
Miles, Herman Wilbur 1924- *WhoE 93*
Miles, Howard Douglass 1954- *St&PR 93*
Miles, Jack 1942- *WhoAm 92*
Miles, James Larry, Jr. 1958- *WhoSSW 93*
Miles, Janice Ann 1949- *WhoAmW 93*
Miles, Jeanne Patterson *WhoAm 92*
Miles, Jesse Mc Lane 1932- *WhoAm 92*
Miles, Jim *WhoAm 92, WhoSSW 93*
Miles, Joanna 1940- *WhoAm 92, WhoAmW 93*
Miles, John *WhoWrEP 92*
Miles, John A. d1992 *NewYTBS 92*
Miles, John C., II 1942- *St&PR 93*
Miles, John Frederick 1926- *WhoAm 92*
Miles, John Gerard 1938- *St&PR 93*
Miles, John J., III 1943- *St&PR 93*
Miles, John Karl 1937- *WhoAm 92*
Miles, John Morris 1960- *WhoSSW 93*
Miles, John R. 1941- *St&PR 93*
Miles, John Russiano 1942- *WhoWrEP 92*
Miles, Judith A. *Law&B 92*
Miles, Keith *ConAu 40NR*
Miles, Keith 1940- *ConAu 139, ScF&FL 92*
Miles, Laveda Ann 1945- *WhoAmW 93*
Miles, Lawrence E. 1938- *St&PR 93*
Miles, Lawrence Robert *Law&B 92*
Miles, Lawrence William, Jr. 1953- *WhoEmL 93*
Miles, Leland 1924- *St&PR 93*
Miles, Leland Weber 1924- *WhoAm 92, WhoWor 93*
Miles, Leo W. 1927- *St&PR 93*
Miles, Linda DeFina 1947- *WhoAmW 93*
Miles, Margaret 1963- *WhoAmW 93*
Miles, Margaret Ruth 1937- *WhoAm 92*
Miles, Maurice 1908-1985 *Baker 92*
Miles, Michael *BioIn 17*
Miles, Michael A. 1939- *BioIn 17*
Miles, Michael Alexander *WhoScE 91-1*
Miles, Michael Arnold 1939- *St&PR 93, WhoAm 92*
Miles, Michele Gae 1958- *WhoEmL 93*
Miles, Minnie Caddell 1910- *WhoWor 93*
Miles, Minnie Marianne 1941- *WhoWor 93*
Miles, Miska *ConAu 37NR, MajAI*
Miles, Mitchell Scott 1954- *WhoE 93*
Miles, Nelson A. 1839-1925 *GayN*
Miles, Nelson Appleton 1839-1925 *BioIn 17, CmdGen 1991 [port], HarEnMi*
Miles, Patricia 1930- *ScF&FL 92*
Miles, Patricia A. *ConAu 37NR, MajAI*
Miles, Philip Napier 1865-1935 *Baker 92*
Miles, Raymond Edward 1932- *WhoAm 92*
Miles, Raymond Kenneth *WhoScE 91-1*
Miles, Rebecca Stepek 1950- *WhoAmW 93, WhoE 93*
Miles, Rebecca Susan 1957- *WhoSSW 93*
Miles, Richard Bryant 1943- *WhoE 93*
Miles, Richard Donald 1942- *St&PR 93*
Miles, Richard Jones 1932- *St&PR 93*
Miles, Richard Lewis 1947- *WhoSSW 93*
Miles, Robert Henry 1944- *WhoAm 92, WhoSSW 93*
Miles, Ron *BioIn 17*
Miles, Ronald Alexander 1952- *WhoEmL 93*
Miles, Samuel Israel 1949- *WhoAm 92*
Miles, Stephen H. 1946- *St&PR 93*
Miles, T(homas) R(ichard) 1923- *ConAu 38NR*
Miles, Thomas Caswell 1952- *WhoSSW 93*
Miles, Thomas Richard *WhoScE 91-1*
Miles, Travis Anthony 1937- *WhoSSW 93*
Miles, Vera 1929?- *SweetSg D [port]*
Miles, Vera 1930- *WhoAm 92*
Miles, Virginia 1916- *WhoAm 92*
Miles, Wendell A. 1916- *WhoAm 92*
Miles-LaGrange, Vicki 1953- *WhoAmW 93*
Miles-Rosenfield, Marti Lynne 1959- *WhoSSW 93*
Milessi, Hanno *WhoScE 91-4*
Milestone, Dale Lynn *Law&B 92*
Milestone, Lewis 1895-1980 *MiSFD 9N*
Mileti, Robert John 1954- *St&PR 93*
Miletic, Miroslav 1925- *Baker 92*
Miletic, Pavao 1930- *WhoScE 91-4*
Miletti, Kathryn Louise 1951- *WhoAmW 93*
Milewczik, Hans 1954- *WhoWor 93*
Milewich, Daniel A. *Law&B 92*
Milewski, Andrzej 1939- *WhoScE 91-4*
Milewski, Frank R. 1932- *St&PR 93*
Milewski, Ronald L. 1951- *St&PR 93*
Milewski, Thomas J. *Law&B 92*
Miley, Deborah Karlene 1949- *WhoEmL 93*
Miley, George Hunter 1933- *WhoAm 92*
Miley, Robert William 1940- *WhoSSW 93*
Miley, Samuel A. *Law&B 92*
Miley, Samuel A. 1957- *St&PR 93, WhoAm 92*
Milford, Arthur Eugene d1991 *BioIn 17, NewYTBS 92*
Milford, Charles Pickens, Jr. *Law&B 92*
Milford, Frederick John 1926- *WhoAm 92*
Milford, Murray Hudson 1934- *WhoAm 92, WhoSSW 93*
Milford, Patricia Polino 1940- *WhoAmW 93*
Milford, Peggy R. 1945- *WhoAm 92*
Milford, Robin (Humphrey) 1903-1959 *Baker 92*
Milford Haven, Marquis of 1854-1921 *BioIn 17*
Milfred, Linda L. *Law&B 92*
Milgate, Murray 1950- *WhoAm 92, WhoEmL 93*
Milgram, Jerome H. 1938- *WhoAm 92*
Milgram, Morris 1916- *WhoE 93*
Milgrim, Franklin Marshall 1925- *WhoAm 92*
Milgrom, Edwin 1936- *WhoScE 91-2*
Milgrom, Elie 1944- *WhoScE 91-2*
Milgrom, Felix 1919- *WhoAm 92, WhoE 93*
Milhaud, Darius 1892-1974 *Baker 92, IntDcOp [port], OxDcOp*
Milhaud, Gerard *WhoScE 91-2*
Milhaud, Guy E. 1934- *WhoScE 91-2*
Milhaud, Guy Emile 1934- *WhoWor 93*
Milhaven, John Giles 1927- *WhoAm 92*
Milholland, Inez 1886-1916 *AmWomPl*
Milholland, John E. 1860-1925 *EncAACR*
Milholm, Dale Milton 1926- *St&PR 93*
Milhorat, Thomas Herrick 1936- *WhoAm 92*
Milhous, Robert E. 1937- *WhoAm 92*
Milhouse, Paul William 1910- *WhoAm 92*
Miliadis, George Emmanuel 1953- *WhoWor 93*
Milic, Bozidar Lj. 1935- *WhoScE 91-4*
Milic, Louis Tonko 1922- *WhoAm 92*
Milic, Nikola 1933- *WhoScE 91-4*
Milic-Emili, Joseph 1931- *WhoAm 92*
Milicevic, Jelena 1939- *WhoAmW 93, WhoE 93, WhoWor 93*
Milicevic, Milic 1934- *WhoScE 91-4*
Milich, S. Herb 1955- *St&PR 93*
Milici, Ray 1919- *WhoAm 92*
Milicic, Asja *WhoScE 91-4*
Milicic, Davor 1915- *WhoScE 91-4*
Milicic, Dusko 1934- *WhoScE 91-4*
Milillo, L. 1946- *St&PR 93*
Milione, Jeanette Margaret 1947- *WhoAmW 93*
Miliora, Maria Teresa 1938- *WhoAm 92*
Milios, Rita 1949- *WhoAmW 93*
Milioti, James J. 1945- *St&PR 93*
Miliotis, Demitrios 1930- *WhoWor 93*
Miliotis, Demitrios 1931- *WhoScE 91-3*
Milis, Robert J. *Law&B 92*
Milius, John 1944- *MiSFD 9*
Milius, John Frederick 1944- *WhoAm 92*
Milius, Richard A. 1950- *WhoAm 92*
Miljevic, Vujo Ilija 1931- *WhoWor 93*
Miljkovic, Ivo 1932- *WhoScE 91-4*
Milk, Harvey 1930-1978 *PolPar*
Milk, Robert William 1926- *St&PR 93*
Milkani, Piro 1939- *DrEEuF*
Milken, Michael R. *BioIn 17*
Milkiewicz, Franciszek 1929- *WhoScE 91-4*
Milkman, Marianne Friedenthal 1931- *WhoAmW 93*
Milkman, Roger Dawson 1930- *WhoAm 92, WhoWor 93*
Milkovic-Zulj, Karmela 1918- *WhoScE 91-4*
Milkowski, Forrest 1951- *St&PR 93*
Milks, Norman S. *Law&B 92*
Milks, Sally Ann 1949- *WhoAmW 93*
Milks, William Claude, III *Law&B 92*
Milks-Martin, Marte Elizabeth 1951- *WhoEmL 93*
Mill, Andy *BioIn 17*
Mill, James 1773-1836 *BioIn 17*
Mill, John Stuart 1806-1873 *BioIn 17*
Mill, Victor J., Jr. 1915- *St&PR 93*
Mill, Victor J., III 1943- *St&PR 93*
Milla, Roger *BioIn 17*
Milla Gravalos, Emilio 1944- *WhoWor 93*
Millan, Hector A. *WhoUN 92*
Millan, Hector Smitmans 1941- *WhoWor 93*
Millan, Jose-Luis 1931- *WhoScE 91-3*
Millan, Maria del Carmen 1914- *DcMexL*
Milland, Ray 1905-1986 *BioIn 17, MiSFD 9N*
Milland, Ray 1907-1986 *IntDcF 2-3 [port]*
Millan De La O, Juan Carlos 1960- *WhoWor 93*
Millane, Arthur Jerome 1925- *St&PR 93*
Millane, John A. *BioIn 17*
Millane, Lynn 1928- *WhoAm 92, WhoAmW 93*
Millan Ruiz, Mercedes 1948- *WhoWor 93*
Millar, Catherine *MiSFD 9*
Millar, Chester F. 1927- *St&PR 93*
Millar, Clarence 1925- *WhoAsAP 91*
Millar, Dorine Marie Agnes 1924- *WhoAmW 93*
Millar, Edwin N. 1937- *St&PR 93*
Millar, Gavin 1938- *MiSFD 9*
Millar, Gordon Halstead 1923- *WhoAm 92*
Millar, James Primrose Malcolm 1893-1989 *BioIn 17*
Millar, James Robert 1936- *WhoAm 92*
Millar, Jeffery Lynn 1942- *WhoAm 92, WhoSSW 93*
Millar, John Donald 1934- *WhoAm 92*
Millar, John F. 1936- *St&PR 93*
Millar, John Francis 1936- *WhoAm 92*
Millar, John Robert 1927- *WhoWor 93*
Millar, Keith *WhoScE 91-1*
Millar, Kenneth 1915-1983 *BioIn 17*
Millar, Kenneth Harvey, Jr. 1957- *WhoEmL 93, WhoSSW 93*
Millar, Kenneth Irwin 1947- *WhoAm 92*
Millar, Laurie Sue 1961- *WhoEmL 93*
Millar, Lowell James 1959- *St&PR 93*
Millar, Margaret 1915- *BioIn 17*
Millar, Margaret Ellis 1915- *WhoAm 92, WhoAmW 93*
Millar, Mildred *AmWomPl*
Millar, Richard W. 1899-1990 *BioIn 17*
Millar, Richard William, Jr. 1938- *WhoAm 92*
Millar, Robert James 1951- *WhoE 93, WhoEmL 93*
Millar, Sally Gray 1946- *WhoAm 92*
Millar, Stuart 1929- *MiSFD 9*
Millard, Andre 1947- *ConAu 136*
Millard, Charles Warren, III 1932- *WhoAm 92, WhoSSW 93*
Millard, David Ralph, Jr. 1919- *WhoAm 92*
Millard, Donald R. 1947- *St&PR 93*
Millard, Edward Howard 1933- *St&PR 93*
Millard, Erma Mary 1957- *WhoSSW 93*
Millard, Frank Whittemore 1931- *St&PR 93*
Millard, Harrison 1829-1895 *Baker 92*
Millard, James Kemper 1948- *WhoE 93*
Millard, Joseph 1908-1989 *ScF&FL 92*
Millard, Keith *BioIn 17*
Millard, Lavergne Harriet 1925- *WhoAmW 93, WhoWor 93*
Millard, Neal Steven 1947- *WhoAm 92, WhoEmL 93*
Millard, Patricia Barnett 1952- *WhoAmW 93*
Millard, Peter Henry *WhoScE 91-1*
Millard, Peter Tudor 1932- *WhoAm 92*
Millard, Richard M. *BioIn 17*
Millard, Richard M. d1992 *NewYTBS 92*
Millard, Robert Glenn 1931- *St&PR 93*
Millard, Suzanne T. 1936- *St&PR 93*
Millard, William *BioIn 17*
Millares, Joe M. 1953- *St&PR 93*
Millasich, Hazel Ashton 1902- *WhoWrEP 92*
Millay, Edna St. Vincent 1892-1950 *AmWomPl, BioIn 17, PoeCrit 6 [port]*
Millay, M.J. *WhoWrEP 92*
Millbank, N.O. *WhoScE 91-1*
Millbern, Mary Lou 1936- *WhoAmW 93*
Millbrooke, Anne 1952- *WhoAmW 93*
Millek, Donald F. 1941- *St&PR 93*
Millen, Robert G. 1947- *St&PR 93*
Millenbruch, Gary Lee 1937- *St&PR 93*
Millender, Dharathula 1920- *BlkAuII 92*
Millenson, Debra Ann 1947- *WhoAmW 93, WhoEmL 93*
Miller, A. Edward 1918-1991 *BioIn 17*
Miller, A. Ronald 1934- *St&PR 93*
Miller, Adele Engelbrecht 1946- *WhoAmW 93*
Miller, Adolph Caspar 1866-1953 *BioIn 17*
Miller, Adrienne Nyman 1954- *WhoEmL 93*
Miller, Agnes *AmWomPl*
Miller, Alan 1954- *WhoE 93*
Miller, Alan B. 1937- *St&PR 93, WhoAm 92, WhoWor 93*
Miller, Alan J. 1949- *St&PR 93*
Miller, Alan James *Law&B 92*
Miller, Alan Jay 1936- *WhoAm 92*
Miller, Alan M. 1934- *WhoE 93*
Miller, Alan Scott *Law&B 92*
Miller, Albert 1936- *WhoE 93*
Miller, Albert Jay 1927- *WhoAm 92*
Miller, Albert Leon 1953- *WhoWor 93*
Miller, Albert R. 1947- *St&PR 93*
Miller, Alice Duer 1874-1942 *AmWomPl*
Miller, Alice Ruth 1939- *WhoAmW 93*
Miller, Allan John 1921- *WhoAm 92*
Miller, Allan L. 1932- *St&PR 93*
Miller, Allen Blair 1953- *WhoAm 92*
Miller, Allen Irwin 1938- *St&PR 93*
Miller, Allen R. 1951- *WhoE 93*
Miller, Allen Terry, Jr. 1954- *WhoEmL 93*
Miller, Andrew *WhoScE 91-1*
Miller, Andrew D. 1930- *St&PR 93*
Miller, Andrew David 1963- *WhoWor 93*
Miller, Andrew Pickens 1932- *WhoAm 92*
Miller, Andrew Woodfin *St&PR 93*
Miller, Anita 1926- *WhoWrEP 92*
Miller, Ann *WhoAm 92*
Miller, Ann 1923- *BioIn 17, IntDcF 2-3 [port]*
Miller, Ann Kristine 1951- *WhoAmW 93, WhoEmL 93*
Miller, Anne Burke 1956- *WhoEmL 93*
Miller, Anne Small 1907- *WhoAmW 93, WhoE 93, WhoWor 93*
Miller, Anthony 1942- *WhoAm 92*
Miller, Anthony Bernard 1931- *WhoAm 92*
Miller, Anthony Eugene *Law&B 92*
Miller, Anthony G. 1958- *St&PR 93*
Miller, Anthony George 1951- *WhoScE 91-1*
Miller, Anthony T. *Law&B 92*
Miller, Arjay 1916- *WhoAm 92*
Miller, Arlene *WhoSSW 93*
Miller, Arline W. *WhoAmW 93*
Miller, Arlyn James 1940- *WhoAm 92*
Miller, Arne 1942- *WhoWor 93*
Miller, Arnold 1928- *WhoAm 92*
Miller, Arnold M. d1992 *NewYTBS 92*
Miller, Arthur 1915- *BioIn 17, JeAmHC, MagSAmL [port], WhoAm 92, WhoWor 93, WhoWrEP 92, WorLitC [port]*
Miller, Arthur 1930- *WhoE 93*
Miller, Arthur Leonard 1907- *WhoAm 92*
Miller, Arthur Maher 1934- *St&PR 93*
Miller, Arthur Raphael 1934- *WhoAm 92*
Miller, Arthur Robert 1950- *WhoEmL 93*
Miller, Arthur Rockwell 1915- *WhoE 93*
Miller, Asher H. 1952- *WhoEmL 93*
Miller, B. Dan 1955- *WhoSSW 93*
Miller, B.J. *WhoScE 91-1*
Miller, Barbara Ann 1955- *WhoWrEP 92*
Miller, Barbara E. *St&PR 93*
Miller, Barbara Jean 1933- *St&PR 93, WhoSSW 93*
Miller, Barbara Jean 1941- *WhoAmW 93*
Miller, Barbara Jean Washbish 1947- *WhoAmW 93*
Miller, Barbara Mathis *Law&B 92*
Miller, Barbara Stallcup 1919- *WhoAmW 93*
Miller, Barbara Stephenson 1950- *WhoEmL 93*
Miller, Barbara Stoler *WhoAm 92*
Miller, Bardell Dayle *Law&B 92*
Miller, Barry 1942- *WhoAm 92, WhoE 93*
Miller, Barry 1958- *ConTFT 10*
Miller, Barry Louis 1959- *WhoEmL 93*
Miller, Barry M. 1932- *St&PR 93*
Miller, Barry M. 1952- *WhoSSW 93*
Miller, Beatrice Ellen 1946- *WhoEmL 93*
Miller, Bebe 1950- *ConBlB 3 [port]*
Miller, Ben 1936- *WhoAm 92*
Miller, Ben Neely 1910- *WhoAm 92*
Miller, Benjamin Louis 1955- *WhoEmL 93*
Miller, Bennett 1938- *WhoAm 92*
Miller, Benton *BioIn 17*
Miller, Bernard d1990 *BioIn 17*
Miller, Bernard 1931- *WhoE 93*
Miller, Bernard J., Jr. 1925- *St&PR 93*

Miller, Bernard Joseph, Jr. 1925- *WhoAm 92*
Miller, Berton 1941- *St&PR 93*
Miller, Bertram Jack 1945- *WhoAm 92*
Miller, Beth 1941- *ConAu 136*
Miller, Betty Carol 1945- *WhoAmW 93*
Miller, Betty Louise 1926- *WhoAmW 93, WhoSSW 93*
Miller, Beverly B. 1933- *WhoAmW 93*
Miller, Beverly White *WhoAm 92, WhoAmW 93*
Miller, Bonnie K. 1938- *St&PR 93*
Miller, Bonnie Mary 1956- *WhoWrEP 92*
Miller, Bonnie Sewell 1932- *WhoAmW 93*
Miller, Bradley Adam 1959- *WhoE 93, WhoEmL 93*
Miller, Brenda 1941- *WhoE 93*
Miller, Brenda Joyce 1954- *WhoAmW 93*
Miller, Brian Keith 1957- *WhoSSW 93*
Miller, Brian Keith 1958- *St&PR 93, WhoSSW 93*
Miller, Brian LaVaughn 1964- *WhoSSW 93*
Miller, Bruce Kent 1951- *WhoSSW 93*
Miller, Bruce Louis 1942- *St&PR 93, WhoAm 92*
Miller, Bruce Richard 1944- *WhoWor 93*
Miller, Bruce W. *Law&B 92*
Miller, Bruce Winsterd, III 1951- *WhoWrEP 92*
Miller, Bryan C. 1927- *St&PR 93*
Miller, Buffy *BioIn 17*
Miller, C. Arden 1924- *WhoAm 92*
Miller, C. Joseph *Law&B 92*
Miller, Calvin 1936- *ScF&FL 92*
Miller, Calvin Pierce 1930- *St&PR 93*
Miller, Carl *ScF&FL 92*
Miller, Carl Edward *Law&B 92*
Miller, Carl Eugene 1942- *WhoAm 92*
Miller, Carl George 1942- *St&PR 93, WhoAm 92*
Miller, Carla Clark *Law&B 92*
Miller, Carlos Oakley 1923- *WhoAm 92*
Miller, Carol *St&PR 93*
Miller, Carol Motyka 1941- *WhoAmW 93*
Miller, Carole Ann 1941- *WhoE 93*
Miller, Carole Christine 1962- *WhoAmW 93*
Miller, Caroline Adams 1961- *BioIn 17*
Miller, Carolyn Olivia 1944- *WhoAmW 93*
Miller, Carroll Lee Liverpool 1909- *WhoAm 92*
Miller, Cate 1964- *WhoAmW 93*
Miller, Catharine Keyes 1905-1966 *BioIn 17*
Miller, Catherine Chee Jian 1954- *WhoWor 93*
Miller, Catherine Diane 1952- *WhoWrEP 92*
Miller, Chad Robert 1956- *St&PR 93*
Miller, Chapin Bemis, II 1946- *St&PR 93*
Miller, Charles A. 1935- *WhoAm 92*
Miller, Charles D. 1928- *St&PR 93*
Miller, Charles Daly 1928- *WhoAm 92*
Miller, Charles E. 1950- *St&PR 93*
Miller, Charles Edmond 1938- *WhoAm 92*
Miller, Charles Edward, Jr. 1950- *WhoAm 92*
Miller, Charles F. *Law&B 92, ScF&FL 92*
Miller, Charles Freeman 1948- *St&PR 93*
Miller, Charles Henry, Jr. 1933- *WhoSSW 93*
Miller, Charles Jay 1924- *WhoE 93, WhoWor 93*
Miller, Charles Leo, Jr. 1959- *WhoEmL 93*
Miller, Charles Leslie 1929- *WhoAm 92*
Miller, Charles Q. 1945- *St&PR 93*
Miller, Charles R. *Law&B 92*
Miller, Charles W. 1947- *St&PR 93*
Miller, Charles William 1922- *WhoAm 92*
Miller, Cheryl *BioIn 17*
Miller, Chester Robert 1936- *St&PR 93*
Miller, Christine Lee 1948- *WhoE 93*
Miller, Christine Marie 1950- *WhoAmW 93, WhoEmL 93*
Miller, Chuck 1952- *ScF&FL 92*
Miller, Claire Ellen 1936- *WhoSSW 93*
Miller, Clarence E. 1917- *CngDr 91*
Miller, Clarence Ellsworth 1917- *WhoAm 92*
Miller, Clark W. 1930- *St&PR 93*
Miller, Claude *MiSFD 9*
Miller, Clell d1876 *BioIn 17*
Miller, Cliff 1958- *WhoE 93*
Miller, Clifford Albert 1928- *WhoAm 92*
Miller, Clifford Joel 1947- *WhoWor 93*
Miller, Clyde *Law&B 92*
Miller, Connie *WhoWrEP 92*
Miller, Connie J. *Law&B 92*
Miller, Corbin R. 1948- *St&PR 93*
Miller, Corbin Russell 1948- *WhoE 93*
Miller, Craig Johnson 1950- *WhoAm 92*
Miller, Craig S. 1949- *St&PR 93*
Miller, Creig D. *Law&B 92*
Miller, Cynthia Lynne 1952- *WhoEmL 93*
Miller, D.A. *WhoScE 91-1*
Miller, D. Arlene 1930- *WhoE 93*
Miller, D. Byron *Law&B 92*
Miller, D. Eugene 1941- *St&PR 93, WhoIns 93*
Miller, Dale Merrily 1943- *WhoAmW 93, WhoE 93, WhoWor 93*
Miller, Dan S. 1943- *St&PR 93*
Miller, Dane A. *BioIn 17*
Miller, Dane Alan 1946- *ConEn, St&PR 93*
Miller, Daniel 1918- *WhoE 93*
Miller, Daniel E. *Law&B 92*
Miller, Daniel G. 1925- *St&PR 93*
Miller, Daniel H. *St&PR 93*
Miller, Daniel McLarren *Law&B 92*
Miller, Daniel Newton, Jr. 1924- *WhoAm 92*
Miller, David *Law&B 92*
Miller, David 1906- *WhoAm 92*
Miller, David 1909- *MiSFD 9*
Miller, David 1965- *WhoE 93*
Miller, David Allen 1954- *WhoEmL 93, WhoSSW 93*
Miller, David Andrew Barclay 1954- *WhoAm 92*
Miller, David Brian 1954- *WhoEmL 93*
Miller, David C. *ScF&FL 92*
Miller, David D. *Law&B 92*
Miller, David Danen 1949- *St&PR 93*
Miller, David Earl 1950- *WhoEmL 93, WhoSSW 93*
Miller, David Edmond 1930- *WhoWor 93*
Miller, David Emanuel 1943- *WhoE 93, WhoWor 93*
Miller, David Eugene 1926- *WhoAm 92*
Miller, David F., III 1948- *St&PR 93*
Miller, David Francis 1929- *St&PR 93*
Miller, David Fredrick 1959- *WhoE 93*
Miller, David Hewitt 1918- *WhoAm 92*
Miller, David Jergen 1933- *WhoE 93*
Miller, David John 1956- *WhoE 93*
Miller, David Julian 1952- *WhoEmL 93*
Miller, David L. 1947- *WhoIns 93*
Miller, David Lee 1951- *ScF&FL 92*
Miller, David Lyndel 1945- *WhoSSW 93*
Miller, David M. 1934- *ScF&FL 92*
Miller, David P. 1932- *St&PR 93*
Miller, David Powell 1942- *WhoAm 92*
Miller, David S. 1916- *St&PR 93*
Miller, David Samuel 1937- *WhoSSW 93*
Miller, David W. *Law&B 92*
Miller, David Walter 1957- *WhoEmL 93*
Miller, David Ward 1957- *WhoWor 93*
Miller, David William 1940- *WhoAm 92*
Miller, Dawn Marie 1963- *WhoAmW 93, WhoE 93, WhoEmL 93*
Miller, Dawn Marie 1964- *WhoEmL 93*
Miller, Dayton C(larence) 1866-1941 *Baker 92*
Miller, Dean Arthur 1931- *WhoAm 92*
Miller, Dean Jeffrey 1951- *WhoWor 93*
Miller, Deane Guynes 1927- *WhoAm 92*
Miller, Deborah *BioIn 17, Law&B 92*
Miller, Deborah Ann 1949- *WhoEmL 93*
Miller, Deborah Jean 1951- *WhoAmW 93, WhoEmL 93, WhoWor 93*
Miller, Decatur Howard 1932- *WhoAm 92*
Miller, Dennis 1953- *ConTFT 10, News 92 [port]*
Miller, Dennis David 1941- *WhoSSW 93*
Miller, Dennis Dixon 1950- *WhoWor 93*
Miller, Dennis Edward 1951- *WhoSSW 93*
Miller, Dennis Maurer 1941- *St&PR 93*
Miller, Diane B. 1944- *St&PR 93*
Miller, Diane Doris 1954- *WhoAmW 93*
Miller, Diane Serisa 1953- *WhoAmW 93*
Miller, Diane Wilmarth 1940- *WhoAmW 93*
Miller, Diantha *BioIn 17*
Miller, Dirk J. 1951- *St&PR 93*
Miller, Don 1923- *BlkAuII 92*
Miller, Don K. 1935- *WhoIns 93*
Miller, Don Robert 1925- *WhoAm 92*
Miller, Don W. 1952- *St&PR 93*
Miller, Don Wilson 1942- *WhoAm 92*
Miller, Donald B., Jr. 1942- *St&PR 93*
Miller, Donald Dale 1928- *St&PR 93*
Miller, Donald E. *Law&B 92*
Miller, Donald E. 1931- *St&PR 93*
Miller, Donald Errol 1938- *WhoUN 92*
Miller, Donald Eugene 1947- *WhoAm 92*
Miller, Donald Fletcher 1924- *WhoSSW 93*
Miller, Donald Frederick 1961- *WhoSSW 93*
Miller, Donald J. 1943- *St&PR 93*
Miller, Donald Jerome 1944- *St&PR 93*
Miller, Donald Keith 1932- *WhoE 93*
Miller, Donald Kenneth 1925- *WhoE 93*
Miller, Donald L. 1923- *WhoE 93*
Miller, Donald Lane 1918- *WhoWor 93*
Miller, Donald Larry 1964- *WhoWrEP 92*
Miller, Donald Lesessne 1932- *St&PR 93, WhoAm 92*
Miller, Donald Morton 1930- *WhoAm 92*
Miller, Donald Paul 1936- *St&PR 93*
Miller, Donald R. 1931- *St&PR 93*
Miller, Donald Ross 1927- *WhoE 93*
Miller, Donald Spencer 1932- *WhoAm 92, WhoE 93*
Miller, Donald V. 1937- *St&PR 93*
Miller, Donn Biddle 1929- *WhoAm 92*
Miller, Doris Mae *BioIn 17*
Miller, Dorothy Anne Smith 1931- *WhoAmW 93*
Miller, Dorothy Eloise 1944- *WhoAmW 93*
Miller, Douglas Andrew 1959- *WhoEmL 93*
Miller, Douglas Deane 1947- *WhoEmL 93*
Miller, Douglas Kenneth 1947- *WhoE 93*
Miller, Douglas L. *Law&B 92*
Miller, Duane Francis 1931- *St&PR 93*
Miller, Duane King 1931- *WhoAm 92, WhoE 93, WhoWor 93*
Miller, Duane L. 1937- *WhoIns 93*
Miller, Duane Leon 1937- *St&PR 93, WhoAm 92*
Miller, Dwight Richard 1943- *WhoWor 93*
Miller, Dwight W. *Law&B 92*
Miller, E. Willard 1915- *WhoAm 92*
Miller, E(ugene) Willard 1915- *ConAu 40NR*
Miller, Edmond Trowbridge 1933- *WhoAm 92*
Miller, Edmund Charles, III 1943- *WhoE 93*
Miller, Edmund Kenneth 1935- *WhoAm 92*
Miller, Edna Rae Atkins 1915- *WhoAmW 93*
Miller, Edward Albert 1931- *WhoAm 92*
Miller, Edward Andrew 1953- *WhoEmL 93*
Miller, Edward B. 1922- *WhoAm 92*
Miller, Edward C., Jr. *Law&B 92*
Miller, Edward Carl William 1952- *WhoEmL 93*
Miller, Edward D. 1940- *St&PR 93*
Miller, Edward Daniel 1940- *WhoAm 92*
Miller, Edward Doring, Jr. 1943- *WhoAm 92*
Miller, Edward F. 1942- *St&PR 93*
Miller, Edward Henry, Jr. 1925- *St&PR 93*
Miller, Edward J. 1933- *St&PR 93*
Miller, Edward Jeremy 1940- *WhoE 93*
Miller, Edward John 1922- *WhoAm 92*
Miller, Edward Joseph 1935- *WhoSSW 93*
Miller, Edward K. 1949- *St&PR 93*
Miller, Edward Percival 1924- *WhoAm 92*
Miller, Edwin Clarence 1939- *WhoSSW 93*
Miller, Edwin Haviland 1918- *WhoE 93*
Miller, Edwin O. 1920- *St&PR 93*
Miller, Eldon Earl 1919- *WhoAm 92*
Miller, Elijah Lewis, Jr. 1944- *WhoE 93*
Miller, Elizabeth Jane 1953- *WhoAm 92, WhoAmW 93, WhoE 93*
Miller, Elizabeth Markland *Law&B 92*
Miller, Elliott Cairns 1934- *WhoAm 92*
Miller, Emanuel 1917- *WhoAm 92, WhoSSW 93*
Miller, Emerson Waldo 1920- *WhoWor 93*
Miller, Emilie F. 1936- *WhoAmW 93, WhoSSW 93*
Miller, Emily Clark 1833-1913 *AmWomPl*
Miller, Eric J. 1953- *St&PR 93*
Miller, Eric N. *Law&B 92*
Miller, Eric Raymond 1943- *WhoAm 92*
Miller, Erica A. 1963- *WhoAmW 93*
Miller, Erica Tillinghast 1950- *WhoAmW 93*
Miller, Ernest Arthur 1925- *WhoE 93*
Miller, Ernest Charles 1925- *WhoAm 92, WhoE 93*
Miller, Ernest Joseph, Jr. 1928- *St&PR 93*
Miller, Ernest St. Clair, Jr. 1946- *WhoSSW 93*
Miller, Estelle *AmWomPl*
Miller, Esther Jean 1947- *WhoEmL 93*
Miller, Eugene 1925- *WhoAm 92*
Miller, Eugene Albert *WhoAm 92*
Miller, Eugene Albert 1937- *St&PR 93*
Miller, Eugene F. *Law&B 92*
Miller, Eugene H. 1927- *St&PR 93*
Miller, Evangeline Lynn 1949- *WhoE 93*
Miller, Ewing Harry 1923- *WhoAm 92*
Miller, F. Hudson 1957- *WhoEmL 93*
Miller, Faren 1950- *ScF&FL 92*
Miller, Fay A. 1945- *WhoE 93*
Miller, Fay Ann 1945- *WhoAmW 93*
Miller, Florence Maria 1872- *AmWomPl*
Miller, Frances Elizabeth 1939- *WhoAmW 93*
Miller, Francesca Falk 1888- *AmWomPl*
Miller, Francis G. 1946- *St&PR 93*
Miller, Francis Roy 1926- *St&PR 93*
Miller, Frank *BioIn 17*
Miller, Frank 1957- *ScF&FL 92*
Miller, Frank L., Jr. 1944- *WhoAm 92*
Miller, Frank William 1921- *WhoAm 92*
Miller, Franklin 1945- *BioIn 17*
Miller, Fred D. 1940- *St&PR 93*
Miller, Fred D., Jr. 1944- *ScF&FL 92*
Miller, Fred L. 1949- *WhoEmL 93*
Miller, Freddie R. 1927- *St&PR 93*
Miller, Frederick 1937- *WhoAm 92*
Miller, Frederick Powell 1936- *WhoAm 92*
Miller, Frederick Robeson 1927- *WhoAm 92*
Miller, Frederick Staten 1930- *WhoAm 92*
Miller, Frederick William 1912- *WhoAm 92*
Miller, Frederick William 1951- *WhoE 93*
Miller, G. Kent 1951- *WhoIns 93*
Miller, G. Wayne 1954- *ScF&FL 92*
Miller, G. William 1925- *BioIn 17, St&PR 93*
Miller, Gabriel Lorimer 1928- *WhoAm 92*
Miller, Garfield Lankard, III 1950- *WhoAm 92*
Miller, Gary Evan 1935- *WhoAm 92*
Miller, Gary George 1948- *WhoEmL 93*
Miller, Gary J. 1949- *WhoAm 92*
Miller, Gary W. 1940- *WhoIns 93*
Miller, Gary Wynn 1954- *WhoEmL 93*
Miller, Gavin 1926- *St&PR 93, WhoAm 92*
Miller, Gaylen D. *St&PR 93*
Miller, Gene Edward 1928- *WhoAm 92*
Miller, Genevieve 1914- *WhoAm 92, WhoAmW 93*
Miller, George *MiSFD 9, WhoAm 92*
Miller, George 1945- *CngDr 91, MiSFD 9, WhoAm 92*
Miller, George Allen 1936- *St&PR 93*
Miller, George Armitage 1920- *BioIn 17, WhoAm 92*
Miller, George David 1930- *WhoAm 92*
Miller, George Evelyn 1932- *WhoAm 92*
Miller, George F. 1945- *St&PR 93*
Miller, George H. 1919- *WhoAm 92*
Miller, George McCord, Jr. 1957- *WhoE 93*
Miller, George Noyes 1845-1904 *ScF&FL 92*
Miller, George Paul 1950- *WhoEmL 93*
Miller, George Thomas 1915- *St&PR 93*
Miller, George William 1925- *BioIn 17, WhoAm 92*
Miller, Gerald A. 1941- *St&PR 93*
Miller, Gerald F. *Law&B 92*
Miller, Gerald H. 1941- *WhoIns 93*
Miller, Gerald Ray 1936- *WhoE 93*
Miller, Gerald Raymond 1931- *WhoAm 92*
Miller, Gerard C. 1928- *St&PR 93*
Miller, Gerhard A. *Law&B 92*
Miller, Gilbert D. 1947- *WhoEmL 93*
Miller, Gilbert N. 1941- *St&PR 93*
Miller, Glenda M. *Law&B 92*
Miller, Glenn *BioIn 17*
Miller, Glenn 1937- *WhoAm 92*
Miller, (Alton) Glenn 1904-1944 *Baker 92*
Miller, Glenn M. *Law&B 92*
Miller, Gloria Jean 1943- *WhoAmW 93*
Miller, Gordon R. 1936- *St&PR 93*
Miller, Gordon William *Law&B 92*
Miller, Gregory James 1959- *WhoEmL 93*
Miller, Gregory Joseph *Law&B 92*
Miller, Gregory Keith 1957- *WhoEmL 93*
Miller, Gregory Paul 1953- *St&PR 93*
Miller, Guy 1917- *WhoE 93*
Miller, H. Orlo *ConAu 138*
Miller, Hack d1990 *BioIn 17*
Miller, Hanson Orlo 1911- *ConAu 138*
Miller, Harbaugh 1902- *WhoAm 92*
Miller, Harma *BioIn 17*
Miller, Harmon Baker, III 1935- *St&PR 93*
Miller, Harold B. d1992 *NewYTBS 92 [port]*
Miller, Harold Blaine *BioIn 17*
Miller, Harold E. 1926- *St&PR 93*
Miller, Harold Edward 1926- *WhoAm 92*
Miller, Harold Joseph 1923- *WhoAm 92*
Miller, Harold Taylor 1923- *St&PR 93*
Miller, Harriet M. 1831-1918 *AmWomPl*
Miller, Harriet Sanders 1926- *WhoAmW 93*
Miller, Harriett Puffer 1919- *WhoWrEP 92*
Miller, Harry Charles, Jr. 1928- *WhoAm 92*
Miller, Harry George 1941- *WhoAm 92*
Miller, Hartman Cyril, Jr. 1948- *WhoWor 93*
Miller, Harvey 1935- *MiSFD 9*
Miller, Harvey 1942- *WhoAm 92*
Miller, Harvey Alfred 1928- *WhoAm 92*
Miller, Harvey Allan 1946- *WhoEmL 93*
Miller, Harvey S. Shipley 1948- *St&PR 93, WhoAm 92, WhoE 93, WhoEmL 93*
Miller, Hasbrouck Bailey 1923- *WhoAm 92*
Miller, Heather Ross 1939- *DcLB 120 [port]*
Miller, Heinrich 1944- *WhoScE 91-3*

Miller, Helen *BioIn 17*
Miller, Helen Booth 1941- *WhoAmW 93*
Miller, Helen Louise *AmWomPl*
Miller, Helen Lovena 1896-1990 *BioIn 17*
Miller, Helen Marie Dillen *WhoAmW 93*
Miller, Helen P. 1936- *St&PR 93*
Miller, Helen S. 1920- *WhoAmW 93*
Miller, Helena *AmWomPl*
Miller, Henry 1891-1980 *BioIn 17, MagSAmL [port], WorLitC [port]*
Miller, Henry E. 1904- *St&PR 93*
Miller, Henry Eugene, Jr. 1937- *St&PR 93*
Miller, Henry Forster 1916- *WhoAm 92*
Miller, Henry Franklin 1938- *WhoE 93*
Miller, Henry George 1924- *WhoE 93*
Miller, Henry Ross *Law&B 92*
Miller, Henry Sam, Jr. 1914- *St&PR 93*
Miller, Herbert A., Jr. *Law&B 92*
Miller, Herbert Allan, Jr. 1951- *St&PR 93*
Miller, Herbert David 1930- *St&PR 93*
Miller, Herbert Dell 1919- *WhoSSW 93, WhoWor 93*
Miller, Herbert Elmer 1914- *WhoAm 92*
Miller, Herbert John, Jr. 1924- *WhoAm 92*
Miller, Herman 1919- *WhoAm 92*
Miller, Hilda I. 1929- *St&PR 93*
Miller, Hillard Craig 1932- *WhoSSW 93*
Miller, Hope *BioIn 17*
Miller, Hope Ridings *WhoAm 92, WhoWrEP 92*
Miller, Howard 1928- *WhoSSW 93*
Miller, Hoyle Haywood, III *Law&B 92*
Miller, Hoyle Haywood, III 1959- *St&PR 93*
Miller, Hubert 1936- *WhoScE 91-3*
Miller, Hubert John 1927- *WhoSSW 93*
Miller, Hugh *ScF&FL 92*
Miller, Hugh Edward 1935- *WhoAm 92*
Miller, I. Dale 1946- *WhoSSW 93*
Miller, I. George 1937- *WhoAm 92*
Miller, I.H. d1990 *BioIn 17*
Miller, Ian *ScF&FL 92*
Miller, Ingeborg Carsten 1933- *WhoAmW 93*
Miller, Ira 1955- *WhoWrEP 92*
Miller, Iris Ann 1938- *WhoAmW 93, WhoE 93, WhoWor 93*
Miller, Irma *St&PR 93*
Miller, Irving Franklin 1934- *WhoAm 92*
Miller, Isadore *WhoE 93*
Miller, Israel 1918- *WhoAm 92, WhoE 93*
Miller, Ivan Lawrence 1914- *WhoAm 92*
Miller, J. Allen 1942- *WhoSSW 93*
Miller, J.C. 1948- *WhoScE 91-3*
Miller, J. Hills 1928- *BioIn 17*
Miller, J. Irwin *BioIn 17*
Miller, J. J. 1947- *WhoAm 92, WhoIns 93*
Miller, J.P. 1919- *ScF&FL 92*
Miller, J. Philip 1937- *WhoAm 92*
Miller, J. Randolph *Law&B 92*
Miller, Jacek Stanislaw 1952- *WhoScE 91-4*
Miller, Jack David 1945- *WhoIns 93*
Miller, Jack David R. 1930- *WhoAm 92*
Miller, Jack R. 1916- *CngDr 91*
Miller, Jacob W. 1927- *St&PR 93*
Miller, Jacqueline Winslow 1935- *WhoAm 92, WhoAmW 93*
Miller, Jake Charles 1929- *WhoSSW 93*
Miller, James 1934- *WhoAm 92*
Miller, James 1947- *ConAu 137*
Miller, James A. 1934- *St&PR 93*
Miller, James Alexander 1915- *WhoAm 92*
Miller, James Bernard 1930- *St&PR 93*
Miller, James C. 1929- *St&PR 93*
Miller, James Clifford, III 1942- *WhoAm 92*
Miller, James Douglas *WhoScE 91-1*
Miller, James Douglas 1937- *WhoWor 93*
Miller, James Duane 1939- *St&PR 93*
Miller, James E. *WhoAm 92*
Miller, James E. 1936- *St&PR 93*
Miller, James Edward 1916-1991 *BioIn 17*
Miller, James Edwin *Law&B 92*
Miller, James Edwin, Jr. 1920- *WhoAm 92, WhoWrEP 92*
Miller, James G. 1948- *St&PR 93*
Miller, James Gegan 1942- *WhoAm 92*
Miller, James Gormly 1914- *WhoAm 92, WhoE 93*
Miller, James Grier 1916- *WhoAm 92*
Miller, James Hugh, Jr. 1922- *WhoAm 92*
Miller, James I. 1956- *St&PR 93*
Miller, James J. 1950- *St&PR 93*
Miller, James Kevin 1957- *St&PR 93*
Miller, James Monroe 1948- *WhoEmL 93*
Miller, James P. *Law&B 92*
Miller, James Patrick 1954- *WhoEmL 93*
Miller, James R. 1947- *St&PR 93*
Miller, James R., II 1946- *St&PR 93*
Miller, James Ralph 1938- *WhoAm 92*
Miller, James Rumrill, III 1937- *WhoAm 92*
Miller, James Vince 1920- *WhoAm 92*
Miller, James Woodell 1927- *WhoSSW 93*
Miller, Jane Andrews 1952- *WhoAmW 93, WhoEmL 93*
Miller, Jane Nelson 1926- *WhoAmW 93*
Miller, Jane Ruth 1949- *WhoWrEP 92*
Miller, Jane S. *Law&B 92*
Miller, Jane Taylor *AmWomPl*
Miller, Janel Howell 1947- *WhoAmW 93, WhoEmL 93, WhoSSW 93*
Miller, Janet 1954- *WhoE 93*
Miller, Janice 1925- *WhoAmW 93*
Miller, Jason 1939- *MiSFD 9, WhoAm 92*
Miller, Jay Earl *WhoWrEP 92*
Miller, Jay William *Law&B 92*
Miller, Jean H. 1923- *St&PR 93*
Miller, Jean Marie 1951- *WhoE 93*
Miller, Jeanne C. *Law&B 92*
Miller, Jeanne Marie 1956- *St&PR 93*
Miller, Jeanne-Marie Anderson 1937- *WhoAmW 93, WhoE 93, WhoWor 93*
Miller, Jeffrey J. 1947- *St&PR 93*
Miller, Jeffrey James *Law&B 92*
Miller, Jeffrey M. 1955- *St&PR 93*
Miller, Jeffrey N. 1952- *St&PR 93*
Miller, Jeffrey Robert 1941- *WhoAm 92*
Miller, Jennifer B. *Law&B 92*
Miller, Jennifer L. *Law&B 92*
Miller, Jennifer Warren 1968- *WhoAmW 93*
Miller, Jerome G. 1931- *ConAu 139*
Miller, Jerome M. 1917- *WhoSSW 93*
Miller, Jerrold T. 1929- *St&PR 93*
Miller, Jerry B. 1946- *St&PR 93*
Miller, Jerry Brian 1961- *WhoEmL 93*
Miller, Jerry Dwayne 1936- *St&PR 93*
Miller, Jerry Huber 1931- *WhoAm 92*
Miller, Jerry Louis 1943- *WhoSSW 93*
Miller, Jerry M., Jr. *Law&B 92*
Miller, Jerry T. 1951- *St&PR 93*
Miller, Jerry Watson 1949- *WhoEmL 93*
Miller, Jewel 1956- *SmATA 73 [port]*
Miller, Jim *ScF&FL 92*
Miller, Jim 1866-1909 *BioIn 17*
Miller, Jim Wayne 1936- *BioIn 17, WhoWrEP 92*
Miller, Jo Carolyn 1942- *WhoAmW 93*
Miller, Joan L. 1931- *St&PR 93*
Miller, Joaquin c. 1837-1913 *GayN*
Miller, Jocelyn Carter- *BioIn 17*
Miller, John *Law&B 92*
Miller, John 1930- *BioIn 17*
Miller, John 1938- *CngDr 91*
Miller, John A. 1927- *St&PR 93*
Miller, John Adalbert 1927- *WhoAm 92*
Miller, John Albert 1939- *WhoAm 92*
Miller, John Alfred *WhoScE 91-1*
Miller, John Andrew 1942- *WhoAm 92*
Miller, John Brian 1936- *WhoUN 92*
Miller, John Charles 1942- *St&PR 93*
Miller, John Chester 1907-1991 *BioIn 17, ConAu 136*
Miller, John Clifford, Jr. 1908- *St&PR 93*
Miller, John Clifford, II 1935- *St&PR 93*
Miller, John D. *Law&B 92*
Miller, John D. 1943- *St&PR 93*
Miller, John David 1923- *WhoAm 92*
Miller, John David 1945- *WhoAm 92*
Miller, John Davidson, III 1945- *WhoAm 92*
Miller, John Douglas *BioIn 17*
Miller, John Edward 1941- *WhoAm 92*
Miller, John F. 1927- *St&PR 93*
Miller, John Francis 1908- *WhoAm 92*
Miller, John Frederick 1928- *WhoE 93*
Miller, John H., Jr. *Law&B 92*
Miller, John Henry 1917- *WhoAm 92*
Miller, John J. 1954- *ScF&FL 92*
Miller, John Keith 1927- *WhoWrEP 92*
Miller, John Laurence 1947- *WhoAm 92*
Miller, John Lester 1959- *WhoEmL 93*
Miller, John M. *Law&B 92*
Miller, John Paul 1948- *WhoE 93*
Miller, John Pendleton 1931- *WhoSSW 93*
Miller, John Perry 1911- *BioIn 17*
Miller, John Peter 1928- *WhoE 93*
Miller, John R. 1938- *WhoAm 92*
Miller, John R. 1946- *WhoE 93*
Miller, John Richard 1927- *WhoAm 92*
Miller, John Richard, Jr. 1920- *St&PR 93*
Miller, John Robert 1937- *St&PR 93, WhoAm 92*
Miller, John Simon Gilbert *WhoScE 91-1*
Miller, John Stewart, III 1946- *WhoEmL 93*
Miller, John T., Jr. 1922- *WhoE 93, WhoWor 93*
Miller, John Ulman 1914- *WhoAm 92*
Miller, John Wesley, III 1941- *WhoE 93*
Miller, John William 1955- *WhoEmL 93*
Miller, John William, Jr. 1942- *WhoAm 92*
Miller, Jon Hamilton 1938- *St&PR 93*
Miller, Jonathan 1934- *BioIn 17, IntDcOp, MiSFD 9, OxDcOp*
Miller, Jonathan Wolfe 1934- *WhoAm 92, WhoWor 93*
Miller, Jory E. *Law&B 92*
Miller, Joseph Alfred 1907- *WhoSSW 93*
Miller, Joseph Arthur 1933- *WhoWor 93*
Miller, Joseph Calder 1939- *WhoAm 92*
Miller, Joseph Herman 1944- *WhoAm 92*
Miller, Joseph Hillis 1928- *BioIn 17, WhoAm 92, WhoWrEP 92*
Miller, Joseph Irwin 1909- *St&PR 93, WhoAm 92*
Miller, Joseph James 1912- *St&PR 93*
Miller, Joseph Keith 1957- *WhoEmL 93, WhoSSW 93*
Miller, Joseph W. *Law&B 92*
Miller, Joseph William 1956- *WhoEmL 93*
Miller, Josephine S. *Law&B 92*
Miller, Joy 1966- *WhoAmW 93*
Miller, JP 1919- *WhoWor 93*
Miller, Judith Ayoung 1965- *WhoAmW 93, WhoEmL 93*
Miller, Judith Duda 1941- *WhoAmW 93*
Miller, Judith K. 1947- *WhoAmW 93*
Miller, Judith Scannella 1952- *WhoE 93*
Miller, Judson Frederick 1924- *WhoAm 92*
Miller, Judy Anne 1957- *St&PR 93*
Miller, Judy Lynn 1952- *WhoE 93*
Miller, Judy Statman 1938- *WhoAm 92, WhoAmW 93*
Miller, Jules F. *Law&B 92*
Miller, Julie A. *Law&B 92*
Miller, Julie Ann 1955- *WhoEmL 93*
Miller, Julie Anna 1960- *WhoEmL 93*
Miller, June *BioIn 17*
Miller, Karen 1944- *WhoE 93*
Miller, Karen-Ann 1949- *WhoAmW 93*
Miller, Katherine Browning *AmWomPl*
Miller, Katherine C. Hill *ConAu 139*
Miller, Kathleen *BioIn 17*
Miller, Kathleen Ann 1957- *WhoEmL 93*
Miller, Kathleen Elizabeth 1942- *WhoAm 92*
Miller, Kathleen Shovan 1953- *WhoAmW 93*
Miller, Kathryn Ann 1948- *WhoAmW 93*
Miller, Kathryn Kinard 1954- *WhoEmL 93*
Miller, Kathryn Schultz 1954- *WhoWrEP 92*
Miller, Kathy Ann 1958- *WhoEmL 93*
Miller, Kathy Collard 1949- *WhoWrEP 92*
Miller, Keith John *WhoScE 91-1*
Miller, Keith Wyatt 1941- *WhoAm 92*
Miller, Kelly 1863-1939 *EncAACR*
Miller, Ken Leroy 1933- *WhoSSW 93*
Miller, Kenneth E. 1928- *St&PR 93*
Miller, Kenneth Edward 1929- *WhoAm 92*
Miller, Kenneth Edward 1951- *WhoEmL 93*
Miller, Kenneth Gregory 1944- *WhoAm 92*
Miller, Kenneth Hull 1946- *WhoE 93*
Miller, Kenneth I. 1956- *St&PR 93*
Miller, Kenneth Irvin 1956- *WhoE 93*
Miller, Kenneth James 1950- *WhoEmL 93*
Miller, Kenneth L. 1927- *St&PR 93*
Miller, Kenneth Lehr 1961- *WhoEmL 93*
Miller, Kenneth Merrill 1930- *WhoE 93*
Miller, Kenneth Michael 1921- *WhoAm 92*
Miller, Kenneth Mount 1947- *WhoAm 92*
Miller, Kenneth Roy 1902- *WhoAm 92*
Miller, Kenneth Ward 1927- *WhoSSW 93*
Miller, Kenneth William 1947- *WhoAm 92, WhoEmL 93, WhoSSW 93, WhoWor 93*
Miller, Kent S. 1939- *St&PR 93*
Miller, Kevin A. 1957- *WhoEmL 93*
Miller, Kevin John 1955- *WhoEmL 93*
Miller, Kevin Robert 1961- *WhoEmL 93*
Miller, Kirk *WhoAm 92*
Miller, Kristy Ranae 1962- *WhoAmW 93*
Miller, Kuby Susie 1954- *WhoAmW 93*
Miller, L.A. 1925- *St&PR 93*
Miller, L. Martin 1939- *WhoAm 92, WhoE 93*
Miller, Laird F. *Law&B 92*
Miller, Lamar Carl 1931- *WhoSSW 93*
Miller, Lance Richard 1954- *WhoEmL 93*
Miller, Larry *ScF&FL 92*
Miller, Larry 1944- *St&PR 93*
Miller, Larry F. 1938- *St&PR 93*
Miller, Larry H. *WhoAm 92*
Miller, Larry James 1939- *St&PR 93*
Miller, Larry Joseph 1932- *WhoAm 92*
Miller, Larry S. 1952- *St&PR 93*
Miller, Laura *AmWomPl*
Miller, Laura A. *AmWomPl*
Miller, Laura Ann 1953- *WhoAmW 93*
Miller, Laura Jane 1965- *WhoSSW 93*
Miller, Laura Westphal *Law&B 92*
Miller, Laurence Gerard *Law&B 92*
Miller, Lawrence 1948- *St&PR 93*
Miller, Lawrence Albert 1932- *St&PR 93*
Miller, Lawrence Edward 1944- *WhoAm 92*
Miller, Lawrence K. 1907-1991 *BioIn 17*
Miller, Lawrence Orndorff *Law&B 92*
Miller, Lawrence R. *Law&B 92*
Miller, Lawrence Richard 1943- *WhoIns 93*
Miller, Lee A. 1931- *St&PR 93*
Miller, Lee Anne *WhoAm 92*
Miller, Lee Denmar 1935- *WhoAm 92*
Miller, Lee E. *Law&B 92*
Miller, Lee E. 1951- *St&PR 93*
Miller, Lee Hanford 1926- *St&PR 93*
Miller, Leila W. *AmWomPl*
Miller, Leland Bishop, Jr. 1931- *WhoAm 92*
Miller, Lenard Jackson 1941- *St&PR 93*
Miller, Lenore 1932- *WhoAm 92, WhoAmW 93*
Miller, Leon Cahill, II 1954- *WhoEmL 93*
Miller, Leonard 1932- *St&PR 93*
Miller, Leonard 1933- *WhoSSW 93*
Miller, Leonard David 1930- *WhoAm 92*
Miller, Leonard Doy 1941- *WhoAm 92*
Miller, Leonard J. 1935- *St&PR 93*
Miller, Leonard Martin 1941- *WhoAm 92, WhoE 93*
Miller, Leonard P. *Law&B 92*
Miller, Leonard W. 1951- *St&PR 93*
Miller, Leroy Benjamin 1931- *WhoAm 92*
Miller, Leslie Adrienne 1956- *WhoWrEP 92*
Miller, Leslie Beth 1951- *WhoEmL 93*
Miller, Leslie Samuel *Law&B 92*
Miller, Lew *WhoWrEP 92*
Miller, Lewis E. *St&PR 93*
Miller, Lewis Nelson, Jr. 1944- *WhoSSW 93*
Miller, Linda 1952- *St&PR 93*
Miller, Linda B. 1937- *WhoAm 92*
Miller, Linda Dianne 1947- *WhoWrEP 92*
Miller, Linda Lou 1955- *WhoAmW 93, WhoEmL 93*
Miller, Linda Patterson 1946- *WhoE 93*
Miller, Linda S. *Law&B 92*
Miller, Linda Suzanne 1953- *WhoEmL 93*
Miller, Lisa 1963- *WhoAmW 93*
Miller, Lisa A. *Law&B 92*
Miller, Lisa Ann 1958- *WhoAmW 93*
Miller, Lisa Anne 1958- *WhoAmW 93*
Miller, Lloyd Daniel 1916- *WhoAm 92*
Miller, Lon Frank 1951- *WhoSSW 93*
Miller, Lora Elizabeth 1960- *WhoAmW 93*
Miller, Loren Solomon 1949- *WhoEmL 93*
Miller, Loring Erik 1951- *WhoE 93, WhoEmL 93*
Miller, Lorraine *SweetSg C*
Miller, Lorraine Marie 1941- *WhoE 93*
Miller, Louis Adam 1917- *WhoWrEP 92*
Miller, Louis Howard 1935- *WhoAm 92*
Miller, Louis Rice 1914- *WhoAm 92*
Miller, Louise Anne 1963- *WhoEmL 93*
Miller, Louise Dean 1921- *WhoAmW 93*
Miller, Louise Winifred *AmWomPl*
Miller, Lowell B. *Law&B 92*
Miller, Lowell Donald 1933- *WhoAm 92*
Miller, Loye Wheat, Jr. 1930- *WhoAm 92*
Miller, Luann Wiley 1959- *WhoAmW 93*
Miller, Lucia A. *Law&B 92*
Miller, Lunelle Young 1941- *WhoSSW 93*
Miller, Lynn 1932- *WhoE 93*
Miller, Lynn C. 1938- *WhoIns 93*
Miller, Lynn Marie 1958- *WhoAmW 93*
Miller, Lynn Ruth 1933- *WhoWrEP 92*
Miller, Lynne Ewing 1938- *WhoE 93*
Miller, Lynne Marie 1951- *WhoAmW 93, WhoWor 93*
Miller, M. Clinton *BioIn 17*
Miller, Mabry Batson *WhoSSW 93*
Miller, Madeleine Sweeny 1890- *AmWomPl*
Miller, Madelyn Sue 1947- *WhoAmW 93*
Miller, Madge 1918- *BioIn 17*
Miller, Malcolm K., Jr. 1927- *St&PR 93*
Miller, Malcolm Lee 1923- *WhoAm 92*
Miller, Mandy E. *Law&B 92*
Miller, Mara 1952- *WhoE 93*
Miller, Marc Gary 1955- *St&PR 93*
Miller, Margaret Cecilia 1950- *WhoAmW 93*
Miller, Margaret Jean 1943- *WhoAmW 93*
Miller, Margaret Josephine 1941- *WhoSSW 93*
Miller, Marge 1948- *WhoWrEP 92*
Miller, Margery Silberman 1951- *WhoAmW 93*
Miller, Margery Staman 1945- *WhoE 93*
Miller, Marguerite Elizabeth 1917- *WhoWrEP 92*
Miller, Maria B. 1931- *WhoSSW 93*
Miller, Marilee Lois 1937- *WhoWrEP 92*
Miller, Marilyn E. *BioIn 17*
Miller, Marilyn Lea *BioIn 17*
Miller, Marion Mills 1864- *AmWomPl*
Miller, Marjory *Law&B 92*
Miller, Mark *WhoAm 92*
Miller, Mark A. *Law&B 92*
Miller, Mark Charles 1949- *WhoEmL 93*
Miller, Mark David 1955- *WhoEmL 93*
Miller, Mark Dawson 1919- *WhoWrEP 92*
Miller, Mark Elliott 1960- *WhoWrEP 92*
Miller, Mark Fulton 1947- *WhoAm 92*

Miller, Mark Jonathan 1955- WhoEmL 93
Miller, Mark L. 1943- St&PR 93
Miller, Mark Leon 1932- WhoAm 92
Miller, Mark S. Law&B 92
Miller, Mark S. 1957- St&PR 93
Miller, Marlene Rose 1951- WhoEmL 93
Miller, Marlow L. 1930- St&PR 93
Miller, Marsden, Jr. 1941- St&PR 93
Miller, Marsha Ann 1950- WhoAmW 93
Miller, Martha 1947- WhoWrEP 92
Miller, Martha Anne 1940- WhoAmW 93
Miller, Martin E. 1935- St&PR 93
Miller, Martin Eugene 1945- WhoSSW 93
Miller, Martin Jessee 1950- WhoWrEP 92
Miller, Martin John 1943- WhoAm 92
Miller, Marvin BioIn 17, Law&B 92
Miller, Marvin Edward 1929- WhoAm 92, WhoE 93
Miller, Marvin M. 1916- St&PR 93
Miller, Mary Angela 1956- WhoAmW 93
Miller, Mary Elizabeth 1947- WhoAmW 93, WhoEmL 93
Miller, Mary Emily 1934- WhoAm 92, WhoAmW 93
Miller, Mary Helen 1936- WhoAmW 93
Miller, Mary J. Law&B 92
Miller, Mary Jeannette 1912- WhoE 93, WhoWor 93
Miller, Mary M. St&PR 93
Miller, Mary Stephanie 1940- WhoAmW 93
Miller, Maryann 1943- SmATA 73 [port]
Miller, Matthew Jeffrey 1940- St&PR 93
Miller, Maude Barnes AmWomPl
Miller, Maureen 1922- WhoWrEP 92
Miller, Maurice James 1926- WhoAm 92
Miller, Max d1992 NewYTBS 92
Miller, Max 1895-1963 QDrFCA 92 [port]
Miller, Max Dunham, Jr. 1946- WhoAm 92
Miller, Maxine Klink 1963- WhoAmW 93
Miller, May AmWomPl
Miller, May 1899- BioIn 17
Miller, Maynard Malcolm 1921- WhoAm 92
Miller, Megan ScF&FL 92
Miller, Meier 1947- St&PR 93
Miller, Melissa F. Law&B 92
Miller, Melvin Eugene 1949- WhoEmL 93
Miller, Melvin Howard 1939- WhoE 93
Miller, Melvin Orville, Jr. 1937- WhoE 93
Miller, Merrill Anthony, Jr. 1950- WhoEmL 93
Miller, Merton H. BioIn 17
Miller, Merton Howard 1923- WhoAm 92, WhoWor 93
Miller, Michael BioIn 17, MiSFD 9
Miller, Michael Barbree 1938- WhoAm 92, WhoE 93
Miller, Michael C. d'E. 1929- St&PR 93
Miller, Michael Chilcott d'Elboux 1929- WhoAm 92
Miller, Michael Darrell 1959- WhoEmL 93
Miller, Michael E. 1941- St&PR 93
Miller, Michael Eugene 1953- WhoSSW 93
Miller, Michael Everett 1941- WhoAm 92
Miller, Michael Francis 1948- WhoE 93
Miller, Michael L. 1941- St&PR 93
Miller, Michael Paul 1938- St&PR 93, WhoAm 92
Miller, Michael Robert 1954- WhoSSW 93
Miller, Michael Roby Law&B 92
Miller, Michael S. 1951- St&PR 93
Miller, Michael Thurman 1956- WhoEmL 93
Miller, Michele Diane 1964- WhoAmW 93
Miller, Michele Gaetan 1965- WhoAmW 93
Miller, Michelle M. 1961- WhoAmW 93
Miller, Mildred WhoAm 92
Miller, Mildred 1924- Baker 92
Miller, Milton 1921- St&PR 93
Miller, Milton H. 1931- St&PR 93
Miller, Milton Howard 1927- WhoAm 92
Miller, Miranda 1950- ScF&FL 92
Miller, Mitch 1911- Baker 92, BioIn 17
Miller, Moira ScF&FL 92
Miller, Mollie MiSFD 9
Miller, Montana BioIn 17
Miller, Monte Lee 1958- WhoEmL 93
Miller, Morgan L. 1924- St&PR 93
Miller, Morgan Lincoln 1924- WhoAm 92
Miller, Morris Folsom 1919- WhoAm 92
Miller, Morris Henry 1954- WhoEmL 93
Miller, Nairn L. 1922- St&PR 93
Miller, Nairn Lockwood 1922- WhoE 93
Miller, Nancy A. Law&B 92
Miller, Nancy Ellen 1947- WhoEmL 93
Miller, Nancy Janet 1954- WhoE 93, WhoEmL 93
Miller, Nancy Maria 1958- WhoAmW 93
Miller, Nancy Smith 1951- WhoEmL 93
Miller, Naomi 1928- WhoAm 92
Miller, Nathan 1927- WhoWrEP 92
Miller, Neal MiSFD 9
Miller, Neal Elgar 1909- WhoAm 92, WhoE 93
Miller, Neil Austin 1932- WhoAm 92, WhoSSW 93
Miller, Neil S. 1958- WhoAm 92, WhoE 93, WhoEmL 93
Miller, Nellie Burget 1875- AmWomPl
Miller, Newton Edd, Jr. 1920- WhoAm 92
Miller, Nicole BioIn 17
Miller, Nicole Gabrielle 1962- WhoAmW 93
Miller, Nona Lee 1958- WhoAmW 93
Miller, Norman 1932- St&PR 93
Miller, Norman 1933- WhoAm 92
Miller, Norman Charles, Jr. 1934- WhoAm 92
Miller, Norman Richard 1922- WhoAm 92
Miller, Orlando Jack 1927- WhoAm 92
Miller, Orlo ConAu 138
Miller, Oscar, Mrs. AmWomPl
Miller, Oscar Victor, Jr. 1942- WhoSSW 93
Miller, P. Schuyler 1912-1974 ScF&FL 92
Miller, Pamela 1958- WhoEmL 93
Miller, Pamela B. 1952- WhoWrEP 92
Miller, Pamela Elizabeth 1958- WhoEmL 93
Miller, Patricia Ann 1933- WhoAmW 93
Miller, Patricia Ann 1957- WhoE 93
Miller, Patricia Ann 1958- WhoSSW 93
Miller, Patricia Elizabeth Cleary 1939- WhoAmW 93
Miller, Patricia Frances 1943- WhoAmW 93
Miller, Patricia Hackney 1945- WhoAmW 93
Miller, Patricia Louise 1936- WhoAmW 93
Miller, Patricia Lynn 1938- WhoWor 93
Miller, Patrick Dwight, Jr. 1935- WhoAm 92
Miller, Patrick M. 1924-1990 BioIn 17
Miller, Patrick M. 1942- St&PR 93
Miller, Patsy Ruth 1905- ScF&FL 92
Miller, Paul 1906-1991 BioIn 17, DcLB 127 [port]
Miller, Paul A. 1924- St&PR 93
Miller, Paul A. 1941- WhoAm 92
Miller, Paul Aaron 1954- WhoEmL 93
Miller, Paul Albert 1924- WhoAm 92
Miller, Paul Ausborn 1917- WhoAm 92
Miller, Paul Charles 1914- St&PR 93
Miller, Paul Charles Harvey WhoScE 91-1
Miller, Paul D. 1932- BioIn 17
Miller, Paul Emmert 1888-1954 BioIn 17
Miller, Paul F., Jr. 1927- St&PR 93
Miller, Paul Fetterolf, Jr. 1927- WhoAm 92
Miller, Paul George 1922- WhoAm 92
Miller, Paul Henderson 1928- WhoWor 93
Miller, Paul J. 1929- WhoAm 92, WhoWor 93
Miller, Paul James 1939- WhoAm 92, WhoWor 93
Miller, Paul L. 1919- St&PR 93
Miller, Paul Lukens 1919- WhoAm 92
Miller, Paul M. 1946- St&PR 93
Miller, Paul R. d1991 BioIn 17
Miller, Paul S. 1939- St&PR 93
Miller, Paul Samuel Law&B 92
Miller, Paul Samuel 1939- WhoAm 92
Miller, Paula 1955- WhoSSW 93
Miller, Paula Ann 1958- WhoE 93
Miller, Paula Belinda 1957- WhoEmL 93
Miller, Peggy McLaren 1931- WhoAmW 93
Miller, Penelope ConTFT 10
Miller, Penelope Ann BioIn 17
Miller, Penelope Ann 1964- ConTFT 10
Miller, Penny May Mullens 1943- WhoAmW 93
Miller, Percy Thomas 1931- WhoSSW 93
Miller, Perry 1905-1963 ScF&FL 92
Miller, Peter D. Law&B 92
Miller, Peter D. 1946- St&PR 93
Miller, Peter L. Law&B 92
Miller, Peter Paul WhoScE 91-1
Miller, Peter Putnam Law&B 92
Miller, Phebe C. Law&B 92
Miller, Phebe Condict 1949- St&PR 93, WhoAm 92
Miller, Philip 1691-1771 BioIn 17
Miller, Philip Boyd 1938- WhoAm 92
Miller, Philip Francis 1927- St&PR 93
Miller, Philip Lieson 1906- Baker 92
Miller, Philip S. 1937- St&PR 93
Miller, Philip William 1948- WhoEmL 93
Miller, Phillip Edward 1935- WhoWor 93, WhoWrEP 92
Miller, Phoebe Amelia 1948- WhoAmW 93
Miller, Phyllis 1920- ScF&FL 92
Miller, Preston Joel 1944- St&PR 93
Miller, R.B. WhoScE 91-1
Miller, Ralph L. BioIn 17
Miller, Ramona Elaine 1948- WhoAmW 93
Miller, Randal Howard 1947- WhoEmL 93
Miller, Randall MiSFD 9
Miller, Raymond Edward 1928- WhoAm 92
Miller, Raymond Francis 1941- St&PR 93
Miller, Raymond Jarvis 1934- WhoAm 92
Miller, Raymond John 1951- St&PR 93
Miller, Raymond K. 1956- St&PR 93
Miller, Raymond L. 1934- St&PR 93
Miller, Raymond P. 1930- St&PR 93
Miller, Raymond Russell, Jr. 1944- WhoWrEP 92
Miller, Ream V. d1990 BioIn 17
Miller, Reed 1918- WhoAm 92
Miller, Reggie BioIn 17
Miller, Remy 1958- WhoEmL 93, WhoSSW 93
Miller, Rene Harcourt 1916- WhoAm 92, WhoE 93, WhoWor 93
Miller, Reuben George 1930- WhoAm 92
Miller, Rex 1929- ScF&FL 92
Miller, Rhonda Lori 1955- WhoE 93
Miller, Richard 1925- ScF&FL 92
Miller, Richard 1930- BioIn 17
Miller, Richard Alan 1931- WhoAm 92
Miller, Richard Alan 1939- WhoAm 92
Miller, Richard Archibald 1927- WhoAm 92
Miller, Richard Bruce 1947- WhoE 93, WhoEmL 93
Miller, Richard C. St&PR 93
Miller, Richard Clark 1955- WhoEmL 93
Miller, Richard Dwight 1929- WhoAm 92
Miller, Richard E. BioIn 17
Miller, Richard F. St&PR 93
Miller, Richard G., Jr. 1918- St&PR 93
Miller, Richard Glen 1949- WhoEmL 93
Miller, Richard Hamilton 1931- WhoAm 92
Miller, Richard Harris 1943- WhoIns 93
Miller, Richard Herman 1954- WhoEmL 93, WhoSSW 93
Miller, Richard I. Law&B 92
Miller, Richard Irwin 1924- WhoAm 92
Miller, Richard Jackson 1946- WhoEmL 93
Miller, Richard Jerome 1939- WhoAm 92, WhoE 93
Miller, Richard Joseph 1941- WhoSSW 93
Miller, Richard Kermit 1946- WhoE 93
Miller, Richard Kidwell 1930- WhoAm 92
Miller, Richard L. 1941- WhoSSW 93
Miller, Richard Lee 1925- St&PR 93
Miller, Richard Leroy, Jr. 1951- WhoE 93, WhoEmL 93
Miller, Richard M. Law&B 92
Miller, Richard M. 1931- St&PR 93
Miller, Richard Mark 1952- WhoEmL 93
Miller, Richard McDermott 1922- WhoE 93
Miller, Richard Michael 1958- WhoEmL 93
Miller, Richard Morgan 1931- WhoAm 92
Miller, Richard S. 1922-1990 BioIn 17
Miller, Richard Sherwin 1930- WhoAm 92
Miller, Richard W. St&PR 93
Miller, Richard Wesley 1940- WhoAm 92, WhoE 93
Miller, Richard William, Jr. Law&B 92
Miller, Richards Thorn 1918- WhoE 93
Miller, Rick Harry 1947- WhoEmL 93
Miller, Rita 1925- WhoE 93
Miller, Robert BioIn 17, Law&B 92
Miller, Robert 1923- WhoAm 92
Miller, Robert 1930-1981 Baker 92
Miller, Robert A. d1990 BioIn 17
Miller, Robert Allen 1931- St&PR 93
Miller, Robert Allen 1945- WhoAm 92
Miller, Robert Arthur 1939- WhoAm 92
Miller, Robert B. 1917-1991 BioIn 17
Miller, Robert Bernard 1956- WhoEmL 93
Miller, Robert Branson, Sr. 1906- WhoAm 92
Miller, Robert Branson, Jr. 1935- WhoAm 92
Miller, Robert C. Law&B 92
Miller, Robert C.J. 1941- St&PR 93
Miller, Robert Carl 1936- WhoAm 92
Miller, Robert Carmi, Jr. 1942- WhoAm 92
Miller, Robert Charles 1925- WhoAm 92
Miller, Robert Clemens 1943- WhoE 93
Miller, Robert Clinton 1954- WhoEmL 93
Miller, Robert Daniel 1960- WhoEmL 93, WhoSSW 93
Miller, Robert David 1932- St&PR 93, WhoIns 93
Miller, Robert Earl 1932- WhoAm 92
Miller, Robert Edvin 1935- WhoE 93
Miller, Robert Ellis 1932- MiSFD 9
Miller, Robert Emil 1930- WhoE 93
Miller, Robert F. 1929- St&PR 93
Miller, Robert Franklin 1935- WhoAm 92
Miller, Robert Gerry, II 1944- WhoSSW 93
Miller, Robert H. 1930- St&PR 93
Miller, Robert Harvey 1940- WhoAm 92
Miller, Robert Haskins 1919- WhoAm 92
Miller, Robert Henry 1938- WhoAm 92
Miller, Robert J. Law&B 92
Miller, Robert James 1923- WhoAm 92, WhoWrEP 92
Miller, Robert James 1926- WhoAm 92
Miller, Robert James 1933- WhoAm 92, WhoWrEP 92
Miller, Robert Jeffrey 1961- WhoEmL 93
Miller, Robert Joseph 1945- WhoAm 92
Miller, Robert K. 1958- St&PR 93
Miller, Robert Keith 1940- WhoE 93
Miller, Robert L. St&PR 93, WhoAm 92
Miller, Robert L., Jr. 1950- WhoAm 92
Miller, Robert Lang 1927- St&PR 93
Miller, Robert Leo 1932- WhoE 93
Miller, Robert Louis 1926- WhoAm 92
Miller, Robert M. Law&B 92, St&PR 93
Miller, Robert MacFarlane 1945- WhoSSW 93
Miller, Robert Nolen Law&B 92
Miller, Robert Nolen 1940- WhoAm 92
Miller, Robert R.C. 1925- St&PR 93
Miller, Robert S. 1941- St&PR 93
Miller, Robert Scott 1947- WhoEmL 93
Miller, Robert Sterling 1926- St&PR 93
Miller, Robert Steven 1963- WhoWor 93
Miller, Robert Stevens, Jr. 1941- WhoAm 92
Miller, Robert T. 1920- WhoAm 92
Miller, Robert Wayne 1941- WhoAm 92
Miller, Robert Wesley 1928- St&PR 93
Miller, Robert Wiley 1928- WhoAm 92
Miller, Robert William 1922- WhoSSW 93
Miller, Roberta Balstad 1940- WhoAm 92
Miller, Roberta Davis 1931- WhoAm 92, WhoWrEP 92
Miller, Roger d1992 NewYTBS 92 [port]
Miller, Roger 1936-1992 News 93-2
Miller, Roger (Dean) 1936- Baker 92, WhoAm 92
Miller, Roger William 1946- WhoAm 92
Miller, Ron 1947- ScF&FL 92
Miller, Ron M. 1944- St&PR 93
Miller, Ronald Alan 1947- WhoAm 92, WhoSSW 93
Miller, Ronald Alfred 1943- WhoAm 92
Miller, Ronald Anthony 1940- WhoAm 92
Miller, Ronald Baxter 1948- WhoSSW 93
Miller, Ronald Eugene 1933- WhoAm 92
Miller, Ronald G. 1928- St&PR 93
Miller, Ronald Irvine 1943- WhoSSW 93
Miller, Ronald M. 1944- St&PR 93, WhoAm 92
Miller, Ronald R. 1933- WhoWrEP 92
Miller, Rosemary Margaret 1935- WhoAmW 93, WhoE 93
Miller, Ross Douglas Law&B 92
Miller, Ross Hays 1923- WhoAm 92
Miller, Ross Lincoln 1946- WhoE 93
Miller, Roy Andrew 1924- ConAu 40NR
Miller, Rudolph Peter, Jr. 1926- WhoSSW 93
Miller, Rudy R. 1947- St&PR 93
Miller, Russell 1938- ScF&FL 92
Miller, Russell Bryan 1940- WhoAm 92
Miller, Russell Flynn 1921- WhoAm 92
Miller, Russell Loyd, Jr. 1939- WhoAm 92
Miller, Russell Ray 1928- St&PR 93
Miller, Russell Rowland 1937- WhoIns 93
Miller, Rusty 1970?- ScF&FL 92
Miller, S. R. Law&B 92
Miller, Sally 1925- WhoE 93
Miller, Sam M. 1954- St&PR 93
Miller, Sam Scott 1938- WhoAm 92
Miller, Samuel Aaron 1955- WhoEmL 93
Miller, Samuel Clifford 1930- WhoAm 92, WhoE 93
Miller, Samuel Freeman 1816-1890 OxCSupC [port]
Miller, Samuel H. 1921- St&PR 93
Miller, Samuel Martin 1938- WhoAm 92
Miller, Sandra Long 1955- St&PR 93
Miller, Sandra (Peden) 1948- ConAu 38NR
Miller, Sandy ConAu 38NR
Miller, Sanford Allen 1951- WhoIns 93
Miller, Sanford Arthur 1931- WhoAm 92
Miller, Sarabeth 1927- WhoWor 93
Miller, Scott 1956- WhoEmL 93
Miller, Scott Allan, III 1955- WhoSSW 93
Miller, Scott D. Law&B 92
Miller, Scott David Law&B 92
Miller, Scott Douglas 1959- WhoSSW 93
Miller, Scott Joseph 1958- WhoSSW 93
Miller, Seymour Michael 1922- WhoAm 92
Miller, Shannon 1977- WhoAmW 93
Miller, Sharon Charlotte 1949- WhoWrEP 92

Mills, Catherine Lotterhos 1958- *WhoEmL 93*
Mills, Celeste Louise 1952- *WhoAmW 93, WhoWor 93*
Mills, Charles *BioIn 17*
Mills, Charles (Borromeo) 1914-1982 *Baker 92*
Mills, Charles G. 1935- *WhoAm 92*
Mills, Charles Gardner 1940- *WhoE 93, WhoWor 93*
Mills, Charles Wright 1916-1962 *BioIn 17*
Mills, Christine Anne 1954- *WhoEmL 93*
Mills, Claudia Elise Elkema 1964- *WhoE 93*
Mills, Craig 1955- *ScF&FL 92*
Mills, Cyril 1902-1991 *AnObit 1991*
Mills, D.F. *ScF&FL 92*
Mills, Daniel C. *Law&B 92*
Mills, Daniel J. 1952- *St&PR 93*
Mills, Daniel Quinn 1941- *WhoAm 92*
Mills, Darryl Francis 1941- *St&PR 93*
Mills, David *BioIn 17*
Mills, David Harlow 1932- *WhoAm 92*
Mills, David Mackenzie Donald 1944- *WhoWor 93*
Mills, David N. 1918- *St&PR 93*
Mills, Don Harper 1927- *WhoAm 92*
Mills, Donald 1915- *BioIn 17*
Mills, Donn Laurence 1931-1990 *BioIn 17*
Mills, Donna *WhoAm 92*
Mills, Dorothy Allen 1920- *WhoAmW 93*
Mills, Earl B. 1928- *WhoAm 92*
Mills, Edgar Coy 1932- *St&PR 93*
Mills, Edward 1905- *St&PR 93*
Mills, Edward James 1954- *WhoEmL 93*
Mills, Edward Warren 1941- *WhoWor 93*
Mills, Elaine (Rosemary) 1941- *SmATA 72 [port]*
Mills, Eldon *BioIn 17*
Mills, Elizabeth *WhoScE 91-1*
Mills, Elizabeth Stilz 1925- *St&PR 93, WhoAm 92, WhoAmW 93, WhoSSW 93*
Mills, Erie 1953- *Baker 92*
Mills, Eugene Sumner 1924- *WhoAm 92*
Mills, Frances Debra 1954- *WhoEmL 93*
Mills, Frances Jones *WhoAmW 93*
Mills, G. Frank 1945- *St&PR 93*
Mills, Gary Ralph 1950- *WhoEmL 93*
Mills, Gary S. *Law&B 92*
Mills, George Alexander 1914- *WhoAm 92*
Mills, George Marshall 1923- *WhoE 93, WhoWor 93*
Mills, George R. 1953- *BioIn 17*
Mills, Gloria Adams 1940- *WhoAmW 93*
Mills, Gordon Lawrence 1933- *WhoAm 92*
Mills, Graham Andrew 1959- *WhoWor 93*
Mills, Gregory Douglas 1963- *WhoE 93*
Mills, Harlan Duncan 1919- *WhoAm 92*
Mills, Harley Douglas 1928- *St&PR 93*
Mills, Harry 1914-1982 *BioIn 17*
Mills, Hawthorne Quinn 1928- *WhoAm 92*
Mills, Henry C. d1992 *NewYTBS 92*
Mills, Henry Doyle 1948- *WhoEmL 93, WhoSSW 93*
Mills, Herbert 1912-1989 *BioIn 17*
Mills, Howard, Jr. 1929- *St&PR 93*
Mills, Howard C. 1933- *St&PR 93*
Mills, Ian Mark *WhoScE 91-1*
Mills, Ian Mark 1930- *WhoWor 93*
Mills, J. Fraser B. *Law&B 92*
Mills, James 1932- *ScF&FL 92*
Mills, James Carleton 1908- *WhoSSW 93*
Mills, James Niland 1937- *WhoAm 92*
Mills, James Spencer 1932- *WhoAm 92*
Mills, James Stephen 1936- *St&PR 93, WhoAm 92*
Mills, James Thoburn 1923- *WhoAm 92, WhoE 93*
Mills, James Thomas, Jr. 1930- *WhoAm 92*
Mills, Jane (Kathryn) 1948- *ConAu 139*
Mills, Jerry 1946- *St&PR 93*
Mills, John 1908- *IntDcF 2-3 [port], WhoAm 92*
Mills, John 1910-1936 *BioIn 17*
Mills, John 1930- *WhoCanL 92*
Mills, John A., III *St&PR 93*
Mills, John Gerald 1948- *WhoSSW 93*
Mills, John Grahame 1952- *St&PR 93*
Mills, John James 1939- *WhoSSW 93*
Mills, John T. *Law&B 92*
Mills, John Thomas 1938- *WhoSSW 93*
Mills, John W. *Law&B 92*
Mills, John Welch 1931- *WhoAm 92*
Mills, Jon K. *WhoAm 92*
Mills, Jonathan Clarke 1954- *WhoE 93*
Mills, Joshua Redmond 1936- *WhoE 93*
Mills, Karin Mahlberg 1949- *WhoE 93, WhoEmL 93*
Mills, Kathleen Claire 1948- *WhoAmW 93*
Mills, Kathleen Merry *Law&B 92*
Mills, Kenneth C. 1935- *WhoScE 91-1*
Mills, Kerry 1869-1948 *Baker 92*
Mills, Kevin 1962- *BioIn 17*
Mills, Larry K. 1948- *St&PR 93*
Mills, Lawrence 1932- *St&PR 93*
Mills, Letha Belknap 1939- *WhoSSW 93*
Mills, Lewis Craig 1923- *WhoAm 92*
Mills, Linda Fay 1950- *WhoSSW 93*
Mills, Linda S. 1951- *WhoAm 92, WhoAmW 93*
Mills, Liston Oury 1928- *WhoAm 92*
Mills, Lois R. 1946- *WhoAmW 93*
Mills, Lynne Maria 1954- *WhoAmW 93, WhoEmL 93*
Mills, Margret Ann 1949- *WhoWrEP 92*
Mills, Maria Jenkins 1949- *St&PR 93*
Mills, Marian M. 1948- *St&PR 93*
Mills, Marilyn *SweetSg B*
Mills, Martha Alice 1941- *WhoAmW 93*
Mills, Martin Gene 1948- *St&PR 93*
Mills, Mary K. *Law&B 92*
Mills, Michael Joseph 1968- *WhoSSW 93*
Mills, Michael R. *Law&B 92*
Mills, Miriam K. 1938- *WhoAmW 93*
Mills, Nancy Culp 1967- *WhoSSW 93*
Mills, Nancy Stewart 1950- *WhoAmW 93*
Mills, Nelda *BioIn 17*
Mills, Olan, II 1930- *WhoAm 92*
Mills, Paul Lance 1951- *WhoWrEP 92*
Mills, Paula H. *Law&B 92*
Mills, Pauline *AmWomPl*
Mills, Peter Richard 1955- *WhoScE 91-1*
Mills, Ralph J. d1990 *BioIn 17*
Mills, Ralph J(oseph), Jr. 1931- *ConAu 39NR*
Mills, Ralph Joseph, Jr. 1931- *WhoWrEP 92*
Mills, Reginald *MiSFD 9*
Mills, Richard *WhoAm 92*
Mills, Richard Gwyn *Law&B 92*
Mills, Richard Henry 1929- *WhoAm 92*
Mills, Robert A. 1934- *WhoAm 92*
Mills, Robert E. *ScF&FL 92*
Mills, Robert Gail 1924- *WhoAm 92*
Mills, Robert Laurence 1927- *WhoAm 92*
Mills, Robert Lee 1916- *WhoAm 92*
Mills, Robert N. *St&PR 93*
Mills, Robert P. 1920-1986 *ScF&FL 92*
Mills, Robert Stanley 1926- *St&PR 93*
Mills, Robin D. 1944- *St&PR 93*
Mills, Rowena Arthur *AmWomPl*
Mills, Russell Andrew 1944- *St&PR 93, WhoAm 92*
Mills, S(ebastian) B(ach) 1838-1898 *Baker 92*
Mills, Samuel John 1783-1818 *BioIn 17*
Mills, Saul d1988 *BioIn 17*
Mills, Sparling 1940- *WhoCanL 92*
Mills, Stanley R., Jr. *Law&B 92*
Mills, Stanley Robert, Jr. 1929- *St&PR 93*
Mills, Susan R. 1940- *WhoUN 92*
Mills, Theodore Mason 1920- *WhoAm 92*
Mills, Therman Arnold 1940- *St&PR 93*
Mills, Thomas Edward 1952- *WhoSSW 93*
Mills, W. David *Law&B 92*
Mills, Walter Garfield 1939- *St&PR 93*
Mills, Wilbur 1909- *PolPar*
Mills, Wilbur 1909-1992 *News 92*
Mills, Wilbur D. 1909-1992 *BioIn 17, NewYTBS 92 [port]*
Mills, Wilbur D(aigh) 1909-1992 *CurBio 92N*
Mills, William *St&PR 93*
Mills, William Harold, Jr. 1939- *WhoAm 92*
Mills, William Hayes 1931- *WhoAm 92*
Mills, William Raymond 1930- *WhoSSW 93*
Mills, William Steward 1920- *WhoE 93*
Mills, Willis Nathaniel 1907- *WhoAm 92*
Millsaps, Bryant 1947- *WhoAm 92, WhoSSW 93*
Millsaps, Ellen McNutt 1947- *WhoSSW 93*
Millsaps, Fred Ray 1929- *WhoAm 92*
Millsaps, John Howard, III 1954- *WhoEmL 93*
Mills-Cockell, John 1943- *Baker 92*
Mills James Spencer 1932- *WhoWrEP 92*
Mills-Malet, Vincent *ScF&FL 92*
Mills-Novoa, Beverly Ann 1954- *WhoEmL 93*
Millson, Jennifer E. *Law&B 92*
Millson, John Arthur 1952- *WhoAm 92*
Millspaugh, Daniel William 1945- *WhoSSW 93*
Millspaugh, Martin Laurence 1925- *WhoAm 92*
Millspaugh, Richard Paul 1958- *WhoEmL 93*
Millstead, Thomas *ScF&FL 92*
Millstein, David J. 1953- *WhoEmL 93*
Millstein, Herbert Sydney 1920- *WhoWor 93*
Millstein, Ira M. 1926- *WhoAm 92*
Millstein, Richard Allen 1945- *WhoAm 92*
Millward, Adrian 1939- *WhoWor 93*
Millward, Geoffrey Eric *WhoScE 91-1*
Millward, James Walter 1951- *WhoEmL 93*
Millward Robert *WhoScE 91-1*
Millwood, Pamela Evelyn 1958- *WhoWrEP 92*
Millwood, Sharron Lynn Clark 1956- *WhoAmW 93*
Milly, Raymond Anthony 1930- *WhoSSW 93*
Milman, Doris Hope 1917- *WhoAmW 93*
Milman, Douglas Scott 1953- *WhoE 93*
Milman, Henry Hart 1791-1868 *BioIn 17*
Milman, Patricia Ellen 1950- *WhoAmW 93, WhoE 93*
Milmoe, Cornelius J. *Law&B 92*
Milnamow, Richard B. *St&PR 93*
Milnar, Rosa Fay 1947- *WhoAmW 93, WhoEmL 93*
Milne, A.A. 1882-1956 *BioIn 17*
Milne, A(lan) A(lexander) 1882-1956 *MajAI [port]*
Milne, A.D. *WhoScE 91-1*
Milne, A.J. 1903-1991 *BioIn 17*
Milne, Alan Alexander 1882-1956 *BioIn 17*
Milne, Beverley Anne 1938- *WhoWor 93*
Milne, Cynthia J. 1950- *St&PR 93*
Milne, Douglas D., III 1951- *St&PR 93*
Milne, Eleanor *BioIn 17*
Milne, Garth LeRoy 1942- *WhoAm 92*
Milne, George *St&PR 93*
Milne, George M. *BioIn 17*
Milne, George McLean, Jr. 1943- *WhoE 93*
Milne, George R.A. 1936- *St&PR 93*
Milne, Howard David 1941- *St&PR 93*
Milne, J.R. *Law&B 92*
Milne, Janis *ScF&FL 92*
Milne, John Alexander *WhoScE 91-1*
Milne, Larry *ScF&FL 92*
Milne, Robert David 1930- *WhoAm 92*
Milne, Robert Duncan 1844-1899 *ScF&FL 92*
Milne, Robert Scott 1917- *WhoWrEP 92*
Milne, Robert William 1956- *WhoWor 93*
Milne, Ronald Douglas *WhoScE 91-1*
Milne, Teddy 1930- *WhoE 93*
Milne, Teddy (Margaret) 1930- *WhoWrEP 92*
Milne, William Ireland *WhoScE 91-1*
Milne, William M. 1943- *St&PR 93*
Milner, Alfred 1854-1925 *DcTwHis*
Milner, Anthony David *WhoScE 91-1*
Milner, Anthony (Francis Dominic) 1925- *Baker 92*
Milner, Arthur David *WhoScE 91-1*
Milner, Arthur John Robin Gorell *WhoScE 91-1*
Milner, Brenda Atkinson Langford 1918- *WhoAm 92*
Milner, C. *WhoScE 91-1*
Milner, Charles Fremont, Jr. 1942- *WhoE 93, WhoWor 93*
Milner, Clive 1936- *WhoUN 92*
Milner, Curtis Dean 1947- *St&PR 93*
Milner, David R. 1945- *St&PR 93*
Milner, Elizabeth Ann 1961- *WhoSSW 93*
Milner, Frances S. *Law&B 92*
Milner, Francy S. *Law&B 92*
Milner, Harold William 1934- *St&PR 93, WhoAm 92*
Milner, Howard M. 1937- *WhoAm 92, WhoWor 93*
Milner, Irvin Myron 1916- *WhoAm 92*
Milner, Jack Edward, Jr. 1937- *WhoSSW 93*
Milner, L.D. *Law&B 92*
Milner, Max 1914- *WhoAm 92*
Milner, Peter Marshall 1919- *WhoAm 92*
Milner, Richard Forbes 1930- *St&PR 93*
Milner, Ron 1938- *BioIn 17, ConTFT 10*
Milner, Stanley A. 1938- *St&PR 93*
Milner, William 1803-1850 *BioIn 17*
Milner-Brindley, Carol Sue 1952- *WhoAmW 93*
Milnes, Arthur George 1922- *WhoAm 92*
Milnes, Elizabeth Ellen 1957- *WhoAmW 93*
Milnes, Janet Florence Monckton 1946- *WhoWor 93*
Milnes, John Herbert 1912- *St&PR 93*
Milnes, Robert Antrim 1925- *St&PR 93*
Milnes, Sherrill *BioIn 17*
Milnes, Sherrill 1935- *IntDcOp, OxDcOp*
Milnes, Sherrill (Eustace) 1935- *Baker 92, WhoAm 92*
Milnes, William Robert, Jr. 1946- *St&PR 93*
Milnikel, Robert Saxon 1926- *WhoAm 92*
Milnor, George Sparks, II 1950- *St&PR 93*
Milnor, William Robert 1920- *WhoAm 92, WhoE 93*
Milo, Frank Anthony 1946- *WhoWor 93*
Milo, Gennaro Domenick 1946- *WhoE 93*
Milo, William P. 1947- *St&PR 93*
Milo, Wladyslaw 1943- *WhoWor 93*
Miloch, Theodore Charles *Law&B 92*
Milock, Richard Lee 1939- *St&PR 93*
Milofsky, Carl 1948- *ConAu 139*
Milofsky, David 1946- *WhoWrEP 92*
Milohnoja, Marjan 1927- *WhoScE 91-4*
Milojevic, Miloje 1884-1946 *Baker 92*
Milon, A. 1954- *WhoScE 91-2*
Milon, Ella Mae 1926- *WhoWrEP 92*
Milon, Marie Jeanne 1746-1818 *See* Trial, Antoine 1737-1795 *OxDcOp*
Milonas, Minos 1936- *WhoE 93*
Milone, Anthony M. 1932- *WhoAm 92*
Milongo, Andre *WhoWor 93*
Milosevic, M. 1955- *St&PR 93*
Milosevic, Slobodan *BioIn 17*
Milosevic, Slobodan 1941- *News 93-2 [port], WhoWor 93*
Milosevic, Zorka 1930- *WhoScE 91-4*
Milosevich, Natasha 1945- *WhoAmW 93*
Milosevich, Paul 1936- *BioIn 17*
Milosevich, Paul Roland 1959- *WhoEmL 93*
Miloslavskii, Nikolai Tolstoi- *ScF&FL 92*
Milosz, Czeslaw *BioIn 17*
Milosz, Czeslaw 1911- *MagSWL [port], PolBiDi, WhoAm 92, WhoWor 93, WhoWrEP 92*
Milot, H. *Law&B 92*
Milotte, Alfred George 1904-1989 *BioIn 17*
Milovanovic, Dejan 1937- *WhoScE 91-4*
Milovsky, Alexandr *BioIn 17*
Miloy, Leatha Faye 1936- *WhoAmW 93*
Milrod, Eve Meredith 1962- *WhoE 93*
Milroy, Robert Huston 1816-1890 *HarEnMi*
Milroy, Robert K. *Law&B 92*
Milsap, Rebecca Lynn 1952- *WhoEmL 93*
Milsap, Ronnie *WhoAm 92*
Milsap, Ronnie 1944- *Baker 92, BioIn 17*
Milshtein, Gregory Noah 1937- *WhoWor 93*
Mil'shtein, Samson 1940- *WhoE 93*
Milsom, Robert Cortlandt 1924- *WhoAm 92*
Milstam, Karl Osten 1928- *WhoWor 93*
Milstead, John W. 1924- *ScF&FL 92*
Milstead, Ken 1939- *WhoSSW 93*
Milstead, Neldon W. 1936- *St&PR 93*
Milstead, Wm. C. 1926- *St&PR 93*
Milsteen, Jeff L. 1959- *WhoEmL 93*
Milstein, C. *WhoScE 91-1*
Milstein, Cesar *WhoScE 91-1*
Milstein, Cesar 1927- *WhoAm 92, WhoWor 93*
Milstein, Harold Jeffrey *Law&B 92*
Milstein, Howard Roy 1944- *St&PR 93*
Milstein, Laurence Bennett 1942- *WhoAm 92*
Milstein, Nathan 1903-1992 *NewYTBS 92 [port]*
Milstein, Nathan 1904- *BioIn 17, WhoAm 92, WhoWor 93*
Milstein, Nathan (Mironovich) 1904- *Baker 92*
Milstein, Richard Craig 1946- *WhoWor 93*
Milstein, Richard Sherman 1926- *WhoAm 92*
Milstein, Ronald S. *Law&B 92*
Milstein, Stephen Eric 1956- *St&PR 93*
Milstein, Yakov (Isaakovich) 1911-1981 *Baker 92*
Milsten, David Randolph 1903- *WhoAm 92*
Milsten, Robert B. 1932- *WhoAm 92*
Milstien, Julie Block 1942- *WhoUN 92*
Miltenberger, Henry James, Jr. 1952- *WhoEmL 93*
Miltenberger, Steven Edward 1946- *St&PR 93*
Miltenberger, Thomas W. 1946- *WhoAm 92*
Miltenburg, Hans Van 1941- *WhoWor 93*
Miltenyi, Miklos 1924- *WhoScE 91-4*
Miltiades c. 550BC-c. 489BC *HarEnMi*
Miltner, Emily R. 1908- *WhoWrEP 92*
Miltner, John Robert 1946- *WhoAm 92, WhoEmL 93*
Miltner, Robert Francis 1949- *WhoWrEP 92*
Milton, Anthony Stuart *WhoScE 91-1*
Milton, Barbara 1947- *WhoWrEP 92*
Milton, Christian Michel 1947- *St&PR 93*
Milton, Edith 1931- *WhoWrEP 92*
Milton, Hilary 1920- *ScF&FL 92*
Milton, Hilary (Herbert) 1920- *WhoWrEP 92*
Milton, J. Russell *Law&B 92*
Milton, Jeff Davis 1861-1947 *BioIn 17*
Milton, John c. 1563-1647 *Baker 92*
Milton, John 1608-1674 *BioIn 17, MagSWL [port], OxDcOp, WorLitC [port]*
Milton, John Charles Douglas 1924- *WhoAm 92*
Milton, John F., Jr. *Law&B 92*
Milton, John Ronald 1924- *WhoAm 92, WhoWrEP 92*
Milton, Joyce 1946- *ScF&FL 92*
Milton, Patricia Ann 1948- *WhoAmW 93*
Milton, Peter 1928- *WhoAsAP 91*

Milton, Peter Winslow 1930- WhoAm 92
Milton, Philip Lafayette 1964- WhoE 93
Milton, Richard Henry 1938- WhoAm 92
Milton, Robert Mitchell 1920- WhoAm 92
Milton, Wilhelm WhoWrEP 92
Milton, William Hammond, III 1925- St&PR 93, WhoAm 92
Milunas, J. Robert 1947- WhoAm 92
Milutin OxDcByz
Milutinovic, Bora BioIn 17
Milveden, (Jan) Ingmar (Georg) 1920- Baker 92
Milveden, Olof Johannes 1953- WhoWor 93
Milvio, Arnaldo 1922- WhoScE 91-3
Milward, Jo AmWomPl
Milway, James Thomas 1935- WhoE 93
Milza, Cheryl Anne 1966- WhoE 93
Mimaroglu, Ilhan Kemaleddin 1926- Baker 92
Mimica, Milorad 1920- WhoScE 91-4
Mimica, Vatroslav 1923- DrEEuF
Mimms, Garnett 1935- SoulM
Mimms, Jacqueline Mix 1943- WhoAmW 93
Mimouni, Omar 1952- WhoWor 93
Mims, Albert 1924- WhoWor 93
Mims, Betty G. 1933- WhoAmW 93
Mims, David Abraham, Jr. Law&B 92
Mims, Dewey Jeffrey 1954- WhoSSW 93
Mims, Forrest M(arion), III 1944- ConAu 39NR
Mims, Frances Larkin Flynn 1921- WhoAmW 93
Mims, Hornsby 1926- WhoIns 93
Mims, Joseph Cleveland Law&B 92
Mims, Joyce Elaine 1942- WhoAm 92
Mims, Mary Charline 1921- WhoAmW 93
Mims, Ottis Eugene 1950- WhoSSW 93
Mims, Priscilla Ann Law&B 92
Mims, Stephen Michael 1949- WhoEmL 93
Mims, Thomas J. 1899- St&PR 93
Mims, Thomas Jerome 1899- WhoAm 92, WhoIns 93, WhoSSW 93, WhoWor 93
Min, Hokey 1954- WhoWor 93
Min, Kyaw 1932- WhoUN 92
Min, Kyung-Up 1952- WhoWor 93
Min, Tu-ki 1932- ConAu 138
Mina, George Louis 1940- WhoSSW 93
Minagawa, Hiroko WhoWor 93
Minaguchi, Hiroshi 1933- WhoWor 93
Minahan, Daniel F. 1929- St&PR 93, WhoAm 92, WhoWor 93
Minahan, John 1933- ScF&FL 92
Minahan, John English 1933- WhoAm 92, WhoWrEP 92
Minahan, Katharine AmWomPl
Minahan, Neal E. Law&B 92
Minahan, Roger C. 1910- St&PR 93
Minahan, Roger Copp 1910- WhoAm 92
Minaire, Yves 1935- WhoScE 91-2
Minaldi, Thad David 1957- St&PR 93
Minale, Luigi 1936- WhoScE 91-3
Minami, Jiro 1874-1957 HarEnMi
Minami, Ken R. Law&B 92
Minami, Ryoshin 1933- WhoWor 93
Minami, Satoshi 1955- Baker 92
Minami, Tsutomu 1941- WhoWor 93
Minami, Warren M. 1938- WhoUN 92
Minamoto, Noriyori 1156-1193 HarEnMi
Minamoto, Yoritomo 1147-1199 HarEnMi
Minamoto, Yoshiie 1041-1108 HarEnMi
Minamoto, Yoshinaka 1154-1184 HarEnMi
Minamoto, Yoshitomo 1123-1160 HarEnMi
Minamoto, Yoshitsune 1159-1189 HarEnMi
Minano, Dennis R. Law&B 92
Minano, Francisco Javier 1955- WhoWor 93
Minard, Everett Lawrence, III 1949- WhoAm 92
Minard, Frank Pell Lawrence 1945- WhoAm 92
Minard, Joanne Shalhoub 1950- WhoE 93
Minard, John D. 1951- St&PR 93
Minard, Maye C. AmWomPl
Minard, Rosemary 1939- BioIn 17
Minarich, Madonna 1949- St&PR 93
Minarik, Else Holmelund 1920- MajAI [port], WhoAmW 93
Minarik, Erich 1924- WhoScE 91-4
Minarik, James Edward 1953- St&PR 93
Minarik, Joseph John 1949- WhoAm 92
Minasi, Anthony 1948- WhoE 93
Minasy, Arthur John 1925- St&PR 93, WhoE 93
Minatelli, John A. 1948- St&PR 93
Minato, Nicolo c. 1630-1698 OxDcOp
Minc, Henryk 1919- WhoAm 92
Mince, Vernon Aubrey Law&B 92
Mincer, Jacob 1922- WhoAm 92
Minch, Jeffrey Leonard Stephen 1951- WhoEmL 93
Minch, Michael Jon 1941- St&PR 93
Minch, Virgil Adelbert 1924- WhoSSW 93, WhoWor 93
Minchen, Steven Lloyd 1961- WhoSSW 93
Minchev, Georgi 1939- Baker 92
Minchew, Harold R. 1932- St&PR 93
Minchew, John Randall 1957- WhoEmL 93
Minchew, Kaye Lanning 1958- WhoSSW 93
Minchin, Alice Ethel 1889-1966 BioIn 17
Minchin, Michael M., Jr. 1926- St&PR 93, WhoAm 92
Minchin, Nydia E. AmWomPl
Minchin, Peter Etheride Haviland 1947- WhoWor 93
Minchin, William J. 1937- St&PR 93
Minck, Richard V. 1932- WhoIns 93
Minco, Marga 1920- BioIn 17
Minczeski, John WhoWrEP 92
Minczeski, John 1947- ConAu 137
Minde, Abe Jude 1948- St&PR 93
Mindel, Samuel d1992 NewYTBS 92
Mindel, Seymour Stewart 1911- St&PR 93
Mindell, David A. St&PR 93
Mindell, Eugene Robert 1922- WhoAm 92
Mindell, Jodi Ann 1962- WhoE 93
Minden, Christina Gail 1967- WhoSSW 93
Mindes, Gayle Dean 1942- WhoAmW 93
Mindham, Richard Hugh Shiels WhoScE 91-1
Mindich, Stephen M. 1943- St&PR 93
Mindlin, Paula Rosalie 1944- WhoE 93
Mindlin, Richard Barnett 1926- WhoAm 92
Mindlin, Steven Todd 1958- WhoEmL 93
Mindszenty, Jozsef 1892-1975 DcTwHis
Mindszenty, Jozsef, Cardinal 1892-1975 ColdWar 2 [port]
Minear, Alana Wilfong 1947- WhoAmW 93, WhoSSW 93
Minehan, Cathy E. 1947- St&PR 93
Minehan, Cathy Elizabeth 1947- WhoAm 92, WhoAmW 93
Minehart, Jean Besse 1937- WhoAmW 93
Minehart, Ralph Conrad 1935- WhoSSW 93
Mineka, Susan 1948- WhoAmW 93
Minella, Raymond J. BioIn 17
Minenko, Mary Ellen Law&B 92
Mineo, Michael Joseph 1950- WhoEmL 93
Mineo, Sal 1939-1976 IntDcF 2-3
Miner, A. Bradford 1947- WhoAm 92
Miner, Bill 1847-1913 BioIn 17
Miner, Charles B. 1942- St&PR 93
Miner, Christopher M. 1951- St&PR 93
Miner, Debra Riggs 1953- WhoAmW 93
Miner, Earl Howard 1923- WhoAm 92
Miner, Earl Roy 1927- WhoAm 92
Miner, Harold BioIn 17
Miner, Henry C., III Law&B 92
Miner, Henry C., III 1936- St&PR 93
Miner, Horace Mitchell 1912- WhoAm 92
Miner, Jacqueline 1936- WhoAmW 93, WhoE 93
Miner, James Joshua 1928- St&PR 93
Miner, Jan 1917- WhoWor 93
Miner, John B. Law&B 92
Miner, John Burnham 1926- WhoAm 92, WhoE 93, WhoWor 93
Miner, John Ronald 1938- WhoAm 92
Miner, Karen Mills 1947- WhoE 93
Miner, Mark Alan 1961- WhoE 93
Miner, Michael MiSFD 9
Miner, Raynard 1946- BioIn 17
Miner, Robert Gordon 1923- WhoAm 92, WhoWrEP 92
Miner, Roger Jeffrey 1934- WhoAm 92
Miner, Steve 1951- MiSFD 9
Miner, Steven P. Law&B 92
Miner, Sydny Weinberg 1951- WhoAm 92
Miner, Thomas D. 1911-1991 BioIn 17
Miner, Thomas Hawley 1927- WhoAm 92
Miner, Valerie 1947- WhoWrEP 92
Miner, William A. 1847-1913 BioIn 17
Minerbrook, Scott BioIn 17
Mines, Jeanette 1948- BioIn 17
Mines, Jeanette Marie 1948- WhoWrEP 92
Mines, Richard Oliver, Jr. 1953- WhoWor 93
Minet, Guy Jean-Baptiste Joseph 1948- WhoSSW 93
Mineta, Norman Y. 1931- CngDr 91
Mineta, Norman Yoshio 1931- WhoAm 92
Minett, Steve Victor 1950- WhoWor 93
Minette, Dennis Jerome 1937- WhoSSW 93, WhoWor 93
Minetti, Luigi Eugenio 1924- WhoWor 93
Minev, Boris Radoslavov 1962- WhoWor 93
Mineyama, Akinori 1935- WhoAsAP 91
Minford, Anthony Patrick Leslie 1943- WhoWor 93
Ming, Kathleen 1939- WhoAmW 93
Ming, Si-Chun 1922- WhoAm 92, WhoE 93, WhoWor 93
Mingarro Martin, Francisco WhoScE 91-3
Mingay, David MiSFD 9
Mingay, F.R. WhoScE 91-1
Mingee, James C. Law&B 92
Minger, Terrell John 1942- WhoWor 93
Minghella, Anthony MiSFD 9
Minghella, Anthony 1954- ConTFT 10, ScF&FL 92
Minghine, Rocco Raymond 1938- WhoAm 92
Mingle, Charles Russell Law&B 92
Mingle, Charles Russell 1949- WhoEmL 93
Mingle, John Orville 1931- WhoAm 92
Mingledorff, Sarah McCarthy 1946- WhoAmW 93
Mingo, Frank BioIn 17
Mingo, James William Edgar 1926- WhoAm 92, WhoWor 93
Mingo-Castel, Angel M. 1944- WhoScE 91-3
Mingo Perez, Elvira 1930- WhoScE 91-3
Mingos, David Michael 1944- WhoWor 93
Mingotti, Angelo c. 1700-c. 1767 OxDcOp
Mingotti, Pietro c. 1702-1759 OxDcOp
Mingotti, Regina OxDcOp
Mings, William Thor 1956- WhoEmL 93
Min Guirong BioIn 17
Mingus, Charles 1922-1979 Baker 92, BioIn 17, ConMus 9 [port]
Mingus, Nancy Blumenstalk 1956- WhoE 93
Minh, Ho Quang MiSFD 9
Minhas, Faqir Ullah 1924- WhoWor 93
Mini, Louise Ann 1949- WhoE 93
Minice, Richard Lee 1937- St&PR 93
Minich, Mark A. Law&B 92
Minichiello, Steven Mark 1955- WhoEmL 93
Minick, Elaine Ingersoll AmWomPl
Minick, Michael 1945- WhoAm 92
Minick, Robert Dale 1946- WhoE 93
Miniclier, John Calvin, Jr. 1944- WhoSSW 93
Minicucci, Anthony John 1962- WhoE 93
Minicucci, Joseph A. d1991 BioIn 17
Minicucci, Raffaele WhoScE 91-3
Minicucci, Robert A. 1952- WhoAm 92
Minie, Claude E. 1804-1879 HarEnMi
Minier, Robert L. Law&B 92
Minigh, H.L. 1948- St&PR 93
Minihan, Patrick John 1942- WhoWor 93
Minikes, Michael 1943- WhoAm 92
Minikes, Stephan Michael 1938- WhoAm 92
Mininall, Jeanne Miller Law&B 92
Minini, Donald Joseph 1934- WhoE 93
Minio, Joseph C. 1943- St&PR 93
Minio, Peter Alan 1951- WhoE 93
Minion, Joseph MiSFD 9
Minirth, Frank B. ConAu 136
Minish, Robert Arthur 1938- St&PR 93, WhoAm 92
Minisi, Anthony S. 1926- WhoAm 92
Minister, Kristina 1934- WhoAmW 93
Minium, Faye E. 1935- St&PR 93
Minix, F. L. 1927- WhoSSW 93
Minix, Forrest Lee 1927- St&PR 93
Minix, James A. 1948- WhoEmL 93
Mink, Gary Stuart 1953- WhoE 93
Mink, Jeffrey A. 1955- St&PR 93
Mink, JoAnna Stephens 1947- ConAu 138
Mink, John Robert 1927- WhoAm 92
Mink, John W. 1940- St&PR 93
Mink, Maxine Mock 1938- WhoAmW 93
Mink, Patsy 1927- CngDr 91
Mink, Patsy T. 1927- BioIn 17
Mink, Patsy Takemoto 1927- WhoAm 92, WhoAmW 93
Mink, Robert L. Law&B 92
Mink, Robert Lee 1935- St&PR 93
Mink, Roberta 1941- St&PR 93
Minkel, Clarence W. 1928- WhoSSW 93
Minkel, Herbert Philip, Jr. 1947- WhoAm 92
Minker, Chuck d1992 BioIn 17
Minker, Emil 1929- WhoScE 91-4
Minker, Gary Alan 1955- WhoEmL 93
Minker, Jack 1927- WhoAm 92
Minker, Marion J., Jr. 1932- St&PR 93
Minkkinen, Pentti Olavi WhoScE 91-4
Minko, Philip Peter 1929- St&PR 93
Minkoff, Jack 1925- WhoAm 92, WhoE 93
Minkoff, Sandra Rita 1936- WhoAmW 93
Minkov, Minko WhoScE 91-4
Minkov, Svetoslav 1902-1966 ScF&FL 92
Minkow, Edward 1937- WhoE 93
Minkow, Gregg Ian Law&B 92
Minkowitz, Miriam WhoAmW 93
Minkowski, Jan 1916-1991 BioIn 17
Minkowycz, W. J. 1937- WhoAm 92
Minks, Albert K. 1934- WhoScE 91-3
Minkus, Leon 1826-1917 Baker 92
Minkus, Leslie Stanton 1944- St&PR 93
Minkus, Raymond David 1953- WhoAm 92
Minn, Sandra Kaye 1946- WhoAmW 93
Minne, Roland 1931- WhoScE 91-2
Minnelli, Liza BioIn 17
Minnelli, Liza 1946- Baker 92, IntDcF 2-3 [port], WhoAm 92, WhoAmW 93, WhoE 93
Minnelli, Vincente 1910-1986 BioIn 17, MiSFD 9N
Minnema, John Allen 1932- St&PR 93
Minneman, Steven Alan 1948- WhoEmL 93
Minner, Ruth Ann 1935- WhoAmW 93
Minner, Thomas Oliran 1956- WhoEmL 93
Minnet, Robert John, Jr. Law&B 92
Minnett, Constance A. Law&B 92
Minney, Martin William d1991 BioIn 17
Minnice, Karen Ann 1947- WhoEmL 93
Minnich, Edward Rolland 1961- WhoEmL 93
Minnich, Hans 1949- WhoE 93
Minnich, Virginia 1910- WhoAm 92
Minnick, Anna Jean WhoAmW 93
Minnick, Carlton Printess, Jr. 1927- WhoAm 92
Minnick, Daniel R. Law&B 92
Minnick, Molly BioIn 17
Minnick, Robert P. 1949- St&PR 93
Minnick, Stephen T. 1948- St&PR 93
Minnick, Terry J. 1951- St&PR 93
Minnick, Walter C. 1942- St&PR 93
Minnick, Walter Clifford 1942- WhoAm 92
Minnie, Mary Virginia 1922- WhoAmW 93
Minnie Memphis Baker 92
Minnig, Gary M. 1946- St&PR 93
Minnihan, John K. 1936- St&PR 93
Minning, David L. Law&B 92
Minnis, Jean Reynolds 1916- WhoAmW 93
Minnis, Stephen Douglas Law&B 92
Minnix, Bruce Milton 1923- WhoAm 92
Minno, Derek Frank 1959- WhoE 93
Minnotte, Linda Derr 1955- WhoAmW 93
Minns, Karen Marie Christa 1956- ScF&FL 92
Minns, Michael H. Law&B 92
Minns, Richard BioIn 17
Mino, Debbie W. St&PR 93
Mino, Joseph Sande 1941- St&PR 93
Mino, Michael George 1954- WhoE 93
Mino, Shigekazu 1923- St&PR 93
Mino, Yoshimi 1931- WhoAsAP 91
Minobe, Kyoko 1959- WhoWor 93
Minoff, Barry 1948- St&PR 93
Minogue, Jack 1934- St&PR 93
Minogue, John T. 1934- St&PR 93
Minogue, Robert Brophy 1928- WhoAm 92
Minoja, Ambrogio 1752-1825 Baker 92
Minoli, Becki Marie 1958- WhoEmL 93
Minor, Ann Lambert 1955- WhoE 93
Minor, Bob BioIn 17
Minor, Charles Daniel 1927- WhoAm 92
Minor, David L. 1943- St&PR 93
Minor, Edward Colquitt Law&B 92
Minor, Edward Colquitt 1942- WhoSSW 93
Minor, George Gilmer, Jr. 1912- St&PR 93, WhoAm 92
Minor, George Gilmer, III 1940- WhoAm 92
Minor, Henry H. 1921- St&PR 93
Minor, Jackson William 1927- St&PR 93
Minor, John T., IV 1957- WhoEmL 93
Minor, Joseph Edward 1938- WhoAm 92
Minor, Laird Law&B 92
Minor, Marian Thomas 1933- WhoAmW 93
Minor, Philip d1991 BioIn 17
Minor, Philip Morrison 1915- St&PR 93
Minor, Raleigh Colston 1936- WhoAm 92
Minor, Ray Charles 1953- WhoSSW 93
Minor, Robert Exum Law&B 92
Minor, Robert Lynn 1952- WhoEmL 93
Minor, Robert W. 1919- St&PR 93
Minor, Robert Walter 1919- WhoAm 92
Minor, Wendell ChlBIID [port]
Minor, Wilson F. BioIn 17
Minorikawa, Hide fumi 1936- WhoAsAP 91
Minoru, Isobe 1944- WhoWor 93
Minoru, Tsuneki 1913- WhoWor 93
Minoso, Orestes 1922- HispAmA
Minoso, Saturnino Orestes Armas Arrieta 1922- BiDAMSp 1989
Minot, Elizabeth AmWomPl
Minot, George Marshall 1933- St&PR 93
Minot, Jeffrey Robert Law&B 92
Minot, Stephen 1927- WhoWrEP 92
Minot, Susan BioIn 17
Minotis, Alexis 1900-1990 BioIn 17
Minott, Debra F. Law&B 92
Minotti, Americo M. Law&B 92
Minow, Josephine Baskin 1926- WhoAm 92

Minow, Martha 1954- ConAu 137
Minow, Newton N. 1926- PolPar, St&PR 93
Minow, Newton Norman 1926- WhoAm 92
Minowitz, Abraham A. 1920- St&PR 93, WhoAm 92
Minshall, Cheryl L. 1954- St&PR 93
Minshall, William E. 1911-1990 BioIn 17
Minshew, Hugh Franklin 1932- St&PR 93
Minshull, Ruth Ellen 1926- WhoWrEP 92
Minsker, Robert Stanley 1911- WhoWor 93
Minski, Margaret Jane WhoScE 91-1
Minsky, Bruce William Law&B 92
Minsky, Gerald L. 1945- St&PR 93
Minsky, Hyman P. BioIn 17
Minsky, Hyman Philip 1919- WhoE 93
Minsky, Marvin 1927- ScF&FL 92
Minsky, Merton D. 1928- St&PR 93
Minsky, Richard 1947- WhoEmL 93
Minsky, Stuart A. 1936- St&PR 93
Minster, Lawrence R. 1953- WhoE 93
Minster, Shirley Marion Rice 1953- WhoE 93
Minta, John H. 1940- St&PR 93
Minta, Zenon 1946- WhoScE 91-4
Mintchell, Gary Alan 1947- WhoEmL 93
Mintel, Judith K. Law&B 92
Minter, Albert H. Law&B 92
Minter, Alfred Leon 1951- WhoSSW 93
Minter, David Lee 1935- WhoAm 92, WhoSSW 93
Minter, James Franklin 1952- WhoE 93
Minter, Jerry B. 1913- St&PR 93
Minter, Jerry Burnett 1913- WhoAm 92
Minter, Jimmie Ruth 1941- WhoAmW 93
Minter, Kathy Mullins Law&B 92
Minter, Kendall Arthur 1952- WhoE 93, WhoEmL 93
Minter, Michael Kent 1950- WhoEmL 93
Minter, Philip Clayton 1928- WhoAm 92
Minter, R.O., Jr. 1926- St&PR 93
Minter, Steven Alan 1938- WhoAm 92
Minter, William Bethel 1932- St&PR 93
Minthorn, Tom 1948- St&PR 93
Minto, Barbara Lee WhoWor 93
Minto, Clive 1945- St&PR 93, WhoAm 92, WhoE 93
Minto, Karl Dean 1958- WhoE 93
Minto, William 1845-1893 ScF&FL 92
Minton, Carl 1928- St&PR 93
Minton, Dwight Church 1934- St&PR 93, WhoAm 92
Minton, Frank WhoIns 93
Minton, George Raymond 1953- WhoEmL 93
Minton, Gwendolyn Louise 1954- St&PR 93
Minton, Henry L. 1934- ConAu 138
Minton, Jerry Davis 1928- WhoAm 92
Minton, John Dean 1921- WhoAm 92, WhoWrEP 92
Minton, Joseph Paul 1924- WhoAm 92
Minton, Joseph Randel 1950- St&PR 93
Minton, Katie Barlow 1928- WhoAmW 93
Minton, Keith G. 1947- St&PR 93
Minton, Mark Allen 1950- WhoSSW 93
Minton, Paul Arthur Severin 1957- WhoEmL 93
Minton, Paula 1915-1987 ScF&FL 92
Minton, Pauline McKinney 1905- WhoAmW 93
Minton, Raymond L. 1937- St&PR 93
Minton, Sherman 1890-1965 OxCSupC [port]
Minton, Sylvia C. 1939- WhoAmW 93
Minton, T.M. ScF&FL 92
Minton, William C. 1950- St&PR 93
Minton, Yvonne 1938- IntDcOp, OxDcOp
Minton, Yvonne Fay WhoAm 92
Minton, Yvonne (Fay) 1938- Baker 92
Mints, Grigori Efroim 1939- WhoWor 93
Mints, Lloyd W. 1888-1989 BioIn 17
Mintun, James Harold, Jr. 1937- St&PR 93
Minturn, Robert Bowne, Jr. 1939- St&PR 93
Mintus, Jesse d1990 BioIn 17
Minty, Judith 1937- WhoWrEP 92
Mintz, A. Aaron 1922- WhoSSW 93
Mintz, Alan L. ConAu 139
Mintz, Albert 1929- WhoAm 92
Mintz, Benjamin Elliot d1991 BioIn 17
Mintz, Donald Edward 1932- WhoAm 92
Mintz, Ellis 1923- St&PR 93
Mintz, Florence Helen 1935- WhoAmW 93
Mintz, Fred 1918- WhoE 93
Mintz, Harry 1909- WhoAm 92
Mintz, Jack d1992 BioIn 17, NewYTBS 92
Mintz, Jeanne Shirley 1922- WhoAm 92
Mintz, Joel Alan 1949- WhoEmL 93
Mintz, Lenore Chaice 1925- WhoAmW 93
Mintz, M. J. 1940- WhoE 93
Mintz, Mitchell Lloyd 1951- St&PR 93
Mintz, Morton Abner 1922- WhoAm 92
Mintz, Norbett Lawrence 1931- WhoE 93
Mintz, Norman Nelson 1934- WhoAm 92
Mintz, Ronald Earl 1926- WhoSSW 93
Mintz, Ronald Steven 1947- WhoEmL 93
Mintz, Seymour Stanley 1912- WhoAm 92
Mintz, Shlomo 1957- Baker 92, WhoAm 92
Mintz, Sidney Wilfred 1922- WhoAm 92
Mintz, Stan 1940- St&PR 93
Mintz, Stephen Allan 1943- St&PR 93, WhoAm 92, WhoE 93
Mintz, Stuart A. Law&B 92
Mintz, Walter 1929- WhoAm 92
Mintz, Yale 1916-1991 BioIn 17
Mintzberg, Henry 1939- WhoAm 92
Mintzer, David 1926- WhoAm 92
Mintzer, Edward Carl, Jr. 1949- WhoWor 93
Mintzer, Harvey 1936- St&PR 93
Mintzer, Jonathan C. Law&B 92
Mintzer, Leo St&PR 93
Mintzes, David M. Law&B 92
Minucci, Dorothy Marie 1946- WhoAmW 93
Minucci, Rita Law&B 92
Minucci, Rita Romano Law&B 92
Minucci, William Robert Law&B 92
Minucius Rufus, Marcus d216BC HarEnMi
Minudri, Regina Ursula 1937- WhoAm 92
Minutillo, Patrick Michael 1949- WhoE 93
Minuto, Thomas Ralph 1958- St&PR 93
Minutoli, Armando BioIn 17
Minx, Lubomir 1931- WhoScE 91-4
Minyard, James Patrick, Jr. 1929- WhoAm 92, WhoSSW 93
Minyard, Robert J. Law&B 92
Minz, Alexander d1992 BioIn 17, NewYTBS 92
Minzer, Irwin K. Law&B 92
Miocque, Marcel Yves 1926- WhoScE 91-2
Miodonski, Adam Jan 1935- WhoScE 91-4
Miodownik, Alfred Peter WhoScE 91-1
Mioducki, John Frank 1954- WhoE 93
Miodus, Gerard Joseph 1956- St&PR 93
Mioduszewska, Olga T. 1927- WhoScE 91-4
Mioduszewski, James Francis 1954- WhoE 93
Mioduszewski, Waldemar 1938- WhoScE 91-4
Miolan, Marie Baker 92
Miolan-Carvalho, Marie 1827-1895 OxDcOp
Miolla, Raymond L., Jr. Law&B 92
Miolla, Raymond Louis 1934- St&PR 93
Mion, Barbara Louise 1929- WhoAmW 93
Mion, Henri-Marie 1931- WhoWor 93
Mion, Mario Romano 1937- WhoSSW 93
Mion, Nancy 1934- WhoAmW 93
Mione, N.A. St&PR 93
Mioni, Alberto M. 1942- WhoWor 93
Miotke, Thomas Oliver 1946- St&PR 93
Miquel, Bertrand Edouard 1940- WhoWor 93
Miquel, Jean-Pierre 1939- St&PR 93
Miquelon, Richard R. 1933- St&PR 93
Mir, M. Afzal 1936- WhoWor 93
Mir, Marilyn 1927- WhoAmW 93
Mir, Pedro 1913- SpAmA
Mirabaud, Pierre Georges 1948- WhoWor 93
Mirabeau, comte de 1749-1791 BioIn 17
Mirabella, Grace BioIn 17
Mirabella, Grace 1930- WhoAm 92, WhoAmW 93, WhoE 93, WhoWrEP 92
Mirabella, Stephen W. 1932- St&PR 93
Mirabelle, Alan P. 1943- St&PR 93
Mirabelle, Gary BioIn 17
Mirabelle, Gary John 1951- WhoE 93
Mirabile, Anthony T. St&PR 93
Mirabile, Mary Ann 1944- St&PR 93
Mirabile, Robert J. 1935- WhoIns 93
Mirabito, Paul S. 1915-1991 BioIn 17
Mirachi, Joseph d1991 BioIn 17
Miracle, Gabriel DcCPCAm
Miracle, Gordon Eldon 1930- WhoAm 92
Miracle, James Franklin 1938- WhoSSW 93
Miracle, Maria Rosa 1945- WhoScE 91-3
Miracle, Pamela Dadant 1950- WhoAmW 93
Miracle, Robert Warren WhoAm 92
Miracle, Robert Warren 1928- St&PR 93
Miracles SoulM
Mira Galiana, Jaime Jose Juan 1950- WhoWor 93
Miraglia, Joseph R. BioIn 17
Miraglio, Angela Maria 1944- WhoAmW 93
Miragliotta, Anthony 1954- WhoE 93
Miraldi, Leslee W. Law&B 92
Miralles, Leonardo 1955- WhoWor 93
Miralto, Antonio WhoScE 91-3
Miramond, M. WhoScE 91-2
Mira Monerris, Alejandro 1932- WhoScE 91-3
Miramontes, John S. 1955- WhoEmL 93
Miran, Benedicto G. 1924- WhoAsAP 91
Miran, Claudia Berry 1947- WhoEmL 93
Miran, Michael Law&B 92
Miranda, Anne 1954- SmATA 71 [port]
Miranda, Anthony Roy 1956- WhoEmL 93
Miranda, Ariel 1953- WhoSSW 93
Miranda, Astrid Janine 1961- WhoAmW 93
Miranda, Carlos Sa 1929- WhoWor 93
Miranda, Carmen 1909-1955 Baker 92, IntDcF 2-3 [port]
Miranda, Cesar 1941- St&PR 93
Miranda, Constancio Fernandes 1926- WhoAm 92
Miranda, George 1947- St&PR 93
Miranda, J.M. Dias WhoScE 91-3
Miranda, Juan Carreno de 1614-1685 BioIn 17
Miranda, Myra 1968- WhoE 93
Miranda, Nicholas J. d1992 NewYTBS 92
Miranda, Renee 1969- WhoAmW 93
Miranda, Robert N. 1934- St&PR 93
Miranda, Robert Nicholas 1934- WhoAm 92, WhoE 93
Miranda, Vincent d1992 ScF&FL 92
Miranda-Mazzucca, Isabel Law&B 92
Mirando, Louis 1932- St&PR 93
Mirando, Richard M. 1943- St&PR 93
Mirandola, Alberto 1942- WhoWor 93
Mirante, Linda Kay 1952- WhoAmW 93
Miranti, Joseph Peter, Jr. 1950- WhoEmL 93
Mirapaul, Walter Neil 1922- St&PR 93
Mirarchi, Saverio Law&B 92
Mirassou, Marlene Marie 1948- WhoAmW 93
Mirat, Olivier 1944- WhoWor 93
Miravet, Livia 1926- WhoScE 91-2
Miravitlles, Carlos 1942- WhoScE 91-3
Mirbach, Wilhelm, Graf von d1918 BioIn 17
Mirbeau, Octave 1848-1917 DcLB 123 [port]
Mircea the Elder d1418 OxDcByz
Mirchandaney, Arjan Sobhraj 1923- WhoWor 93
Mirchandani, Bhagwandas Naraindas 1920- WhoWor 93
Mirchev, S. WhoScE 91-4
Mirdha, Nathu Ram 1922- WhoAsAP 91
Mirecki, Franciszek Wincenty 1791-1862 PolBiDi
Mirecki, Franz 1791?-1862 Baker 92
Miree, Wimberly, Jr. 1941- St&PR 93, WhoSSW 93
Mirehouse, James H. 1935- St&PR 93
Mireles, Sandra 1964- WhoAmW 93
Mirelman, Victor A. 1943- ConAu 136
Mirels, Harold 1924- WhoAm 92
Mirenburg, Barry Leonard Steffan 1952- WhoEmL 93
Mires, Ronald E. 1930- St&PR 93
Miriam BioIn 17
Miriam, Henry, III Law&B 92
Miriani, Steven P. Law&B 92
Mirick, Henry Dustin 1905- WhoAm 92
Mirick, John O. 1946- WhoEmL 93
Miripol, Jerilyn Elise WhoAmW 93
Mirisch, Marvin Elliot 1918- WhoAm 92
Mirisch, Walter Mortimer 1921- WhoAm 92
Miriszlai, Ernest Vajai 1931- WhoScE 91-4
Mirk, Judy Ann 1944- WhoAmW 93
Mirka, Hans 1936- St&PR 93
Mirkil, Jay R. 1954- WhoIns 93
Mirkin, Abraham Jonathan 1910- WhoAm 92
Mirkin, Bernard Leo 1928- WhoAm 92
Mirkin, Ralph William 1932- St&PR 93
Mirkin, Wendy Law&B 92
Mirko, Rosemary Natalya 1958- WhoEmL 93
Mirkovic, Leo d1990 BioIn 17
Mirkowski, Jaroslaw 1966- WhoWor 93
Mirman, Irving R. 1915- WhoAm 92
Miro, Joan 1893-1983 BioIn 17
Miro, Ricardo 1883-1940 SpAmA
Miron, Avi N. Law&B 92
Miron, Gaston 1928- BioIn 17
Miron, Jerry 1936- St&PR 93
Miron, Robert J. BioIn 17
Mirones, Pedro Jacobo 1939- St&PR 93
Mironov, Nikolai Mikhailovich 1948- WhoUN 92
Miroshin, Nikolai Vasilievich 1948- WhoWor 93
Mirotin, Adolf 1952- WhoWor 93
Mirouze, Marcel 1906-1957 Baker 92
Mirovitch, Alfred 1884-1959 Baker 92
Mirow, Roland S. 1948- St&PR 93
Mirowitz, Leo I. 1923- St&PR 93
Mirowitz, Stuart Ray 1948- WhoEmL 93
Mirowski, Michel 1924-1990 BioIn 17
Mirowski, Philip Edward 1951- WhoAm 92
Mirozoyev, Akbar WhoWor 93
Mirren, Helen 1946- ConTFT 10, WhoWor 93
Mirrielees, James Fay, III 1939- WhoAm 92
Mirrlees, Hope 1887-1978 ScF&FL 92
Mirse, Ralph Thomas 1924- WhoAm 92
Mirsen, Thomas Robert 1957- WhoE 93
Mirski, Michael D. Sviatopolk 1904- WhoE 93
Mirskii, Peter Sviatopolk- BioIn 17
Mirsky, Arthur 1927- WhoAm 92
Mirsky, Ellis Richard Law&B 92
Mirsky, Jan S. 1941- St&PR 93
Mirsky, Mark Jay 1939- WhoWrEP 92
Mirsky, Sonya Wohl 1925- WhoAm 92
Mirsky, Susan 1939- WhoAm 92, WhoAmW 93
Mirsu, Ovidiu 1928- WhoScE 91-4
Mirth, Nancy Augustus 1946- WhoAmW 93
Mirtsopoulos, Christos 1947- WhoWrEP 92
Mirus, Thomas Ben 1953- WhoSSW 93
Mirvis, David Marc 1945- WhoSSW 93
Mirvish, Edwin BioIn 17
Miry, Karel 1823-1889 Baker 92
Mirza, David Brown 1936- WhoAm 92
Mirza, Humayun 1928- WhoE 93
Mirza, Leona Lousin 1944- WhoAmW 93
Mirza, Naseem 1932- WhoUN 92
Mirza, Tanveer Haroon 1942- WhoUN 92
Mirza, Taqi Ali ScF&FL 92
Mirza, Zaheer 1933- WhoWor 93
Mirza Asadullah Khan Ghalib 1797-1869 BioIn 17
Mirzai, Mohammed 1945- WhoWor 93
Mirzai, Pirooz 1953- WhoEmL 93
Mirza Irshadbaig 1949- WhoAsAP 91
Mirza Taqi Khan, Grand Vizier c. 1798-1852 BioIn 17
Mirzoyan, Edvard (Mikaeli) 1921- Baker 92
Misa, Kenneth Franklin 1939- WhoAm 92
Misaelides, Panagiotis 1949- WhoScE 91-3
Misaki, Akira 1930- WhoWor 93
Misaki, Katsumi St&PR 93
Misao, Setsu Murayama 1911- WhoWor 93
Misasi, Anthony P. 1943- St&PR 93
Misasi, Nicola 1927- WhoScE 91-3
Misawa, Giichi 1929- WhoWor 93
Misawa, Susumu 1951- WhoWor 93
Misbach, Grant Lemmon 1929- St&PR 93
Misch, Gisela Gertrud 1939- St&PR 93
Misch, Ludwig 1887-1967 Baker 92
Misch, Michael W. Law&B 92
Misch, Robert Jay 1905-1990 BioIn 17
Misch, William B. 1923- St&PR 93
Mischakoff, Mischa 1895-1981 Baker 92
Mische, Louis W. 1925- St&PR 93
Mischenko, G. 1946- St&PR 93
Mischer, Donald Leo 1940- WhoAm 92
Mischer, Walter M. BioIn 17
Mischer, Walter M. 1923- WhoAm 92
Mischgofsky, F.H.M. 1946- WhoScE 91-3
Mischka, James BioIn 17
Mischke, Carl Herbert 1922- WhoAm 92
Mischke, Frederick Charles 1930- St&PR 93, WhoAm 92
Mischler, Harland Louis WhoAm 92
Mischlich, Anne Marie 1959- WhoAmW 93
Mischner, Kenneth R. Law&B 92
Miscoll, James P. WhoAm 92
Miscovich, Timothy Joseph 1958- WhoEmL 93
Misek, Jan WhoScE 91-4
Misener, Austin Donald 1911- WhoAm 92
Misenheimer, Barry K. Law&B 92
Misenheimer, Barry K. 1953- St&PR 93
Misenheimer, Barry Kay 1953- WhoEmL 93
Misenheimer, Lester E. St&PR 93
Miser, Hugh Jordan 1917- WhoAm 92, WhoE 93
Miserandino, Marianne 1960- WhoE 93
Mises, Roger 1924- WhoScE 91-2
Misev, Tosko 1948- WhoScE 91-3
Misfeldt, Terry C. 1950- WhoWrEP 92
Mish, Frederick Crittenden 1938- WhoAm 92
Misha ScF&FL 92
Mishalanie, Phillip G., Jr. 1933- St&PR 93
Mishell, Daniel R., Jr. 1931- WhoAm 92
Misher, Allen 1933- WhoAm 92
Mishev, Kiril Ivanov 1918- WhoScE 91-4
Mishima, Yoshitsugu 1921- WhoWor 93
Mishima, Yukio 1925-1970 BioIn 17, MagSWL [port], MajAI [port]
Mishkin, Arthur I. 1935- St&PR 93

Mishkin, Mortimer 1926- WhoAm 92
Mishkin, Paul J. 1927- WhoAm 92
Mishkovsky, Zelda Schneerson- 1915?- BioIn 17
Mishky, Emery Joseph 1960- WhoEmL 93
Mishler, Clifford Leslie 1939- WhoAm 92, WhoWor 93, WhoWrEP 92
Mishler, John Milton 1946- WhoAm 92
Mishler, William, II 1947- WhoAm 92
Mishlove, Jeffrey 1946- WhoEmL 93
Mishnayevskiy, Peter A. 1948- WhoWor 93
Mishne, Jonathan Michael 1958- WhoE 93
Mishoe, Rainelle Dixon 1950- WhoEmL 93
Mishra, Arun Kumar 1945- WhoWor 93
Mishra, Chaturanan 1925- WhoAsAP 91
Mishra, Jagannath 1937- WhoAsAP 91
Mishra, Kailash Pati 1926- WhoAsAP 91
Mishra, Karen Elizabeth 1963- WhoEmL 93
Mishra, Sheo Kumar WhoAsAP 91
Mishra, Shiv Pratap WhoAsAP 91
Mishura, Yuliya Stepanovna 1952- WhoWor 93
Misiak, Jan Zdzislaw 1942- WhoScE 91-4
Misiano, Frank 1949- WhoE 93, WhoEmL 93
Misick, Ariel DcCPCAm
Misiek, Dale Joseph 1952- WhoEmL 93, WhoSSW 93
Misiolek, Zbigniew 1924- WhoScE 91-4
Misitigh, John 1948- St&PR 93
Miskawayh c. 942-1030 OxDcByz
Miskel, Cecil G. BioIn 17
Miskell, Cheryl J. 1946- WhoAmW 93
Miskell, William, II 1948- WhoEmL 93
Miskell, William Gene 1952- WhoEmL 93
Miskimen, George William 1930- WhoAm 92
Miskimin, Harry Alvin 1932- WhoAm 92
Miskinis, Peter Michael 1923- St&PR 93
Miskoe, William Isaac 1912- St&PR 93
Miskovic, M. WhoScE 91-4
Miskovits, Gusztav 1919- WhoScE 91-4
Miskovsky, George, Sr. 1910- WhoAm 92
Miskowski, Lee R. 1932- WhoAm 92
Miskus, Michael Anthony 1950- WhoEmL 93, WhoWor 93
Mislow, Kurt Martin 1923- WhoAm 92
Misner, Charles William 1932- WhoAm 92
Misner, Lorraine 1948- WhoAmW 93
Misner, Paul 1936- ConAu 138
Misner, Robert David 1920- WhoWor 93
Mison, Luis d1776 Baker 92
Misra, Jayadev 1947- WhoAm 92
Misra, Mahapurush 1933- Baker 92
Misra, Raghunath Prasad 1928- WhoAm 92, WhoSSW 93
Misra, Satyagopal 1939- WhoAsAP 91
Misra, Shekhar 1953- WhoWor 93
Misrach, Richard Laurence 1949- WhoAm 92
Miss, Mary 1944- BioIn 17, WhoAm 92
Missa, Edmond (Jean Louis) 1861-1910 Baker 92
Missala, Tadeusz 1926- WhoScE 91-4
Missall, Denise M. BioIn 17
Missan, Richard Sherman 1933- WhoAm 92
Missar, Charles Donald 1925- WhoAm 92
Missar, Richard R. 1930- WhoAm 92
Misselbrook, John WhoScE 91-1
Misseldine, Carol Kay 1959- WhoEmL 93
Misselhorn, Klaus 1934- WhoScE 91-3
Missell, Frank Patrick 1944- WhoWor 93
Missen, Lynne ScF&FL 92
Missey, James Lawrence 1935- WhoWrEP 92
Missick, Patricia Ann 1952- WhoEmL 93
Missimer, Thomas M. St&PR 93
Missimore, Maureen Margaret 1959- WhoAmW 93
Missinne, Leo E(miel) 1927- ConAu 39NR
Missler, Clinton E. 1931- St&PR 93
Missman, Jeffrey Stephan 1944- St&PR 93
Missol, Witold 1931- WhoScE 91-4
Missoni, Ottavio 1921- BioIn 17
Missonnier, Jacques 1924- WhoScE 91-2
Missotten, Luc 1931- WhoScE 91-2
Missry, Herb 1943- St&PR 93
Missulawn, Gideon St&PR 93
Mistarz, Barbara S. Law&B 92
Misteli, Jack M. Law&B 92
Mister, Coleen Warren 1934- WhoAmW 93
Mistichelli, Judith A. ScF&FL 92
Mistick, Barbara Knaus 1955- WhoAmW 93
Mistral, Bengo ScF&FL 92
Mistral, Gabriela 1889-1957 BioIn 17, SpAmA
Mistress Jacqueline 1951- BioIn 17
Mistretta, F. David Law&B 92
Mistretta, Nathan Joseph 1937- St&PR 93
Mistretta, Susan E. Law&B 92
Mistric, Mary Ann 1932- WhoWrEP 92
Mistry, Rohinton 1952- ConLC 71 [port], WhoCanL 92
Mistry, Sharad G. 1954- St&PR 93
Misu, Sotaro 1855-1921 HarEnMi
Misurelli, Joseph BioIn 17
Miswald, R. Scott 1955- St&PR 93
Misztal, Stanislaw H. 1927- WhoScE 91-4
Mita, Damiano Gustavo 1940- WhoScE 91-3
Mita, Itura 1929- WhoWor 93
Mita, Merata MiSFD 9
Mita, Munesuke 1937- WhoWor 93
Mita, Tomoyoshi 1943- WhoWor 93
Mitama, Masataka 1944- WhoWor 93
Mitani, Katsumi 1917- WhoWor 93
Mitarai, Osamu 1950- WhoWor 93
Mitby, Norman Peter 1916- WhoAm 92
Mitchal, Saundra BioIn 17
Mitcham, Carl 1941- ConAu 37NR, WhoE 93
Mitcham, Clinton A. d1989 BioIn 17
Mitcham, Julius Jerome 1941- WhoSSW 93, WhoWor 93
Mitcham, Patricia Ann Hamilton 1942- WhoSSW 93
Mitchamore, Patricia Ann 1934- WhoSSW 93
Mitchard, Shirley Anne 1953- WhoWor 93
Mitchel, Andrea K. Law&B 92
Mitchel, Frederick Kent 1927- WhoAm 92
Mitchel, Irene WhoE 93
Mitchel, Jane Verner 1821-1899 BioIn 17
Mitchel, John 1815-1875 BioIn 17
Mitchel, Lawrence T. 1933- WhoIns 93
Mitchel, Michael M. 1929- St&PR 93
Mitchelhill, James Moffat 1912- WhoSSW 93
Mitchell, A. Alan Law&B 92
Mitchell, Agnes E. AmWomPl
Mitchell, Alice Ann 1956- WhoE 93
Mitchell, Allison ConAu 40NR
Mitchell, Andrea 1946- WhoAm 92, WhoAmW 93, WhoE 93
Mitchell, Andrea L. 1946- WhoEmL 93
Mitchell, Anne M. AmWomPl
Mitchell, Arlene Harris 1940- WhoAmW 93
Mitchell, Arthur Law&B 92
Mitchell, Arthur 1934- BioIn 17, WhoAm 92
Mitchell, Arthur Harris 1916- WhoAm 92
Mitchell, Arthur P. Law&B 92
Mitchell, Arthur W. 1883-1968 EncAACR
Mitchell, Arthur Wergs 1883-1968 BioIn 17
Mitchell, Artie d1991 BioIn 17
Mitchell, Barbara Joanne 1940- WhoAmW 93, WhoWrEP 92
Mitchell, Bernice AmWomPl
Mitchell, Bert Breon 1942- WhoAm 92
Mitchell, Bert N. BioIn 17
Mitchell, Betsy ScF&FL 92
Mitchell, Betty Jo 1931- WhoAmW 93, WhoWrEP 92
Mitchell, Blair David 1950- WhoEmL 93
Mitchell, Bobby 1935- BioIn 17
Mitchell, Bradford W. 1927- WhoIns 93
Mitchell, Bradford William 1927- St&PR 93, WhoAm 92
Mitchell, Brenda K. WhoAmW 93, WhoE 93
Mitchell, Brent Olson 1949- St&PR 93
Mitchell, Bruce Logan 1947- WhoSSW 93
Mitchell, Bruce Tyson 1928- WhoAm 92
Mitchell, Bruce Walker 1950- WhoAm 92
Mitchell, Burley Bayard, Jr. 1940- WhoAm 92, WhoSSW 93
Mitchell, C.D. WhoScE 91-1
Mitchell, Cameron 1918- BioIn 17
Mitchell, Carol Ann 1942- WhoAmW 93
Mitchell, Carol Ann 1957- WhoE 93, WhoEmL 93
Mitchell, Carol L. Law&B 92
Mitchell, Carolyn Cochran 1943- WhoAmW 93
Mitchell, Cassandra Walton 1946- WhoAmW 93
Mitchell, Catherine Sue 1941- WhoSSW 93
Mitchell, Cathryn A. Law&B 92
Mitchell, Chad L. 1944- St&PR 93
Mitchell, Charles d1990 BioIn 17
Mitchell, Charles Archie 1926- WhoE 93
Mitchell, Charles E. Law&B 92
Mitchell, Charles Hill 1924- WhoE 93
Mitchell, Charles William 1928- St&PR 93
Mitchell, Cherie Jane 1934- WhoAmW 93
Mitchell, Cherry Anne 1950- WhoAmW 93
Mitchell, Cheryl Elaine 1951- WhoAmW 93, WhoEmL 93
Mitchell, Cheryl Lynn 1960- WhoEmL 93
Mitchell, Cheryl Ruth 1954- WhoEmL 93
Mitchell, Christopher John WhoScE 91-1
Mitchell, Clarence, Jr. BioIn 17
Mitchell, Claybourne, Jr. 1923- WhoAm 92
Mitchell, Clyde MajAI
Mitchell, Constance Ayer 1952- WhoAmW 93
Mitchell, Cynthia Mary 1946- St&PR 93
Mitchell, Damon Larry 1951- WhoSSW 93
Mitchell, Daniel R. Law&B 92
Mitchell, Daniel Wertz 1928- St&PR 93
Mitchell, David Frisch 1953- WhoE 93
Mitchell, David John 1939- WhoWor 93
Mitchell, David Milton 1954- WhoEmL 93
Mitchell, David Walker 1935- WhoAm 92
Mitchell, Dawn 1969- St&PR 93
Mitchell, Dean 1957- BioIn 17
Mitchell, Dean Lewis 1929- WhoSSW 93
Mitchell, Debra F. Law&B 92
Mitchell, Debra Joy 1949- WhoWrEP 92
Mitchell, Denise Delois 1964- WhoAmW 93
Mitchell, Derek 1922- WhoWor 93
Mitchell, Derek I. WhoScE 91-3
Mitchell, Diane B. 1947- WhoEmL 93
Mitchell, Don BioIn 17
Mitchell, Donald (Charles Peter) 1925- Baker 92
Mitchell, Donald J. 1923- WhoAm 92
Mitchell, Douglas Donnell 1948- St&PR 93
Mitchell, Douglas F. 1940- St&PR 93
Mitchell, Douglas Farrell 1940- WhoAm 92
Mitchell, Dwike 1930- Baker 92
Mitchell, E. Benjamin, Jr. Law&B 92
Mitchell, E.W.J. WhoScE 91-1
Mitchell, Earl Dean 1939- WhoWor 93
Mitchell, Earl Lamonte 1912- St&PR 93
Mitchell, Earl Nelson 1926- WhoAm 92
Mitchell, Earlene Dixon 1945- WhoSSW 93
Mitchell, Edward F. 1931- St&PR 93
Mitchell, Edward Franklin 1931- WhoAm 92
Mitchell, Edward John 1936- St&PR 93
Mitchell, Edward John 1937- WhoAm 92
Mitchell, Edward Lee 1932- WhoIns 93
Mitchell, Ehrman Burkman, Jr. 1924- WhoAm 92
Mitchell, Elaine King 1941- WhoAmW 93
Mitchell, Eleanor Early AmWomPl
Mitchell, Elizabeth 1954- ScF&FL 92
Mitchell, Elizabeth Irwin 1957- WhoAmW 93
Mitchell, Ellen Clabaugh 1942- WhoE 93
Mitchell, Ellison Capers, Jr. 1941- WhoSSW 93
Mitchell, Elyne 1913- ScF&FL 92
Mitchell, (Sibyl) Elyne (Keith Chauvel) 1913- DcChlFi
Mitchell, Enid 1919- WhoWrEP 92
Mitchell, Eric Ignatius 1948- WhoE 93
Mitchell, Fanny Todd AmWomPl
Mitchell, Faye L. AmWomPl
Mitchell, Flora Eva 1929- WhoAm 92
Mitchell, Francis Douglas 1913- St&PR 93
Mitchell, Gary Earl 1935- WhoAm 92
Mitchell, Gary G. 1956- St&PR 93
Mitchell, Geneva 1908- SweetSg C [port]
Mitchell, Geoffrey P. 1916- St&PR 93
Mitchell, Geoffrey Robert 1949- WhoWor 93
Mitchell, Geoffrey Sewell 1940- WhoAm 92
Mitchell, George, III 1940- St&PR 93
Mitchell, George B. 1940- WhoIns 93
Mitchell, George E. 1937- St&PR 93
Mitchell, George Ernest, Jr. 1930- WhoAm 92
Mitchell, George Frederick 1937- WhoE 93
Mitchell, George Hall 1939- WhoAm 92
Mitchell, George J. BioIn 17
Mitchell, George J. 1933- CngDr 91, PolPar
Mitchell, George John 1933- WhoAm 92, WhoE 93
Mitchell, George P. 1919- BioIn 17, St&PR 93, WhoSSW 93
Mitchell, George W. 1950- St&PR 93
Mitchell, George Washington, Jr. 1917- WhoAm 92
Mitchell, George Wilder 1904- BioIn 17
Mitchell, Gerald R. 1939- St&PR 93
Mitchell, Gregory Roderick 1960- WhoWor 93
Mitchell, Guy Patrick 1937- WhoSSW 93
Mitchell, H.L. 1906-1989 BioIn 17
Mitchell, H. Thomas 1957- St&PR 93
Mitchell, Hal 1916- BioIn 17
Mitchell, Hamilton Barnes 1916- WhoAm 92
Mitchell, Harold Hanson 1886-1966 BioIn 17
Mitchell, Harry E. 1940- WhoAm 92
Mitchell, Harry Leland 1906-1989 BioIn 17, EncAACR
Mitchell, Herbert Hall 1916- WhoAm 92
Mitchell, Howard 1911-1988 Baker 92
Mitchell, Howard Andrew 1949- WhoSSW 93
Mitchell, Howard Estill 1921- WhoAm 92
Mitchell, J. Murray 1928-1990 BioIn 17
Mitchell, Jacquelyn A. Law&B 92
Mitchell, Jacques August d1991 BioIn 17
Mitchell, James 1931- DcCPCAm
Mitchell, James Austin 1941- WhoAm 92, WhoIns 93
Mitchell, James B. 1954- St&PR 93
Mitchell, James E., Jr. 1950- St&PR 93
Mitchell, James Edwin 1942- WhoE 93
Mitchell, James Fabian WhoScE 91-1
Mitchell, James Fitzallen 1931- WhoWor 93
Mitchell, James G. 1917- St&PR 93
Mitchell, James Kenneth 1930- WhoAm 92
Mitchell, James L. Law&B 92
Mitchell, James Lowry 1937- WhoAm 92
Mitchell, James Nicola 1931- St&PR 93, WhoE 93
Mitchell, James P. 1900-1964 BioIn 17
Mitchell, James W. Law&B 92
Mitchell, James Walter 1921- WhoSSW 93
Mitchell, James Winfield 1943- WhoAm 92
Mitchell, Janet Aldrich 1928- WhoAmW 93
Mitchell, Jay SmATA 72
Mitchell, Jay E. 1950- WhoEmL 93
Mitchell, Jeffrey L. 1946- St&PR 93
Mitchell, Jeffrey Thomas 1946- WhoEmL 93
Mitchell, Jeffrey Thomas 1948- WhoE 93
Mitchell, Jere Holloway 1928- WhoWor 93
Mitchell, Jerrilavia Jefferson Law&B 92
Mitchell, Jerry Calvin 1938- WhoSSW 93
Mitchell, Jim BioIn 17
Mitchell, Jo Ann 1935- WhoAmW 93
Mitchell, Jo Kathryn 1934- WhoAmW 93
Mitchell, Joan BioIn 17
Mitchell, Joan 1926- WhoAm 92
Mitchell, Joan 1926-1992 NewYTBS 92 [port]
Mitchell, John Adam, III 1944- St&PR 93
Mitchell, John Cameron NewYTBS 92 [port]
Mitchell, John David 1924- WhoE 93
Mitchell, John Dietrich 1917- WhoE 93
Mitchell, John F. 1946- St&PR 93
Mitchell, John H. Law&B 92
Mitchell, John Hanson BioIn 17
Mitchell, John Henderson 1933- WhoAm 92
Mitchell, John Irby 1939- St&PR 93
Mitchell, John N. 1913-1988 PolPar
Mitchell, John R. 1930- St&PR 93
Mitchell, John R., Jr. 1863-1929 EncAACR
Mitchell, John Raymond 1868-1933 BioIn 17
Mitchell, John Richard 1945- WhoWor 93
Mitchell, John Wesley 1913- WhoAm 92
Mitchell, John William 1944- St&PR 93
Mitchell, Joni BioIn 17
Mitchell, Joni 1943- Baker 92, WhoAm 92, WhoAmW 93
Mitchell, Joseph Brady 1915- WhoAm 92, WhoSSW 93
Mitchell, Joseph Cheatham 1929- WhoSSW 93
Mitchell, Joseph David 1958- WhoEmL 93
Mitchell, Joseph Martin Law&B 92
Mitchell, Joseph Nathan 1922- WhoAm 92
Mitchell, Joseph Patrick 1939- WhoWor 93
Mitchell, Joseph Quincy 1908- WhoAm 92, WhoWor 93
Mitchell, Josephine Margaret 1912- WhoAmW 93
Mitchell, Juanita J. d1992 NewYTBS 92 [port]
Mitchell, Judith Ann 1941- WhoSSW 93
Mitchell, Judith Paige ConAu 40NR
Mitchell, Judy Overby 1939- WhoAmW 93
Mitchell, Julia D. AmWomPl
Mitchell, Julia L. 1933- St&PR 93, WhoAm 92, WhoAmW 93, WhoSSW 93
Mitchell, (Charles) Julian (Humphrey) 1935- ConAu 39NR
Mitchell, Katherine P. 1943- WhoAmW 93
Mitchell, Kathleen Ann 1948- WhoEmL 93
Mitchell, Keith d1992 NewYTBS 92

Mitchell, Keith 1946- *DcCPCAm*
Mitchell, Keith Phillip 1944- *WhoE 93*
Mitchell, Keith William *WhoScE 91-1*
Mitchell, Ken 1940- *WhoCanL 92*
Mitchell, Ken(neth Ronald) 1940- *ConAu 37NR*
Mitchell, Kenneth J. 1949- *St&PR 93*
Mitchell, Kenneth P. *St&PR 93*
Mitchell, Kevin Darrell 1962- *WhoAm 92*
Mitchell, Kim S. *Law&B 92*
Mitchell, Kim Warner 1950- *WhoEmL 93*
Mitchell, Kirk 1950- *ScF&FL 92*
Mitchell, Lansing Leroy 1914- *WhoAm 92*
Mitchell, Larry 1938- *ConGAN*
Mitchell, Larry Kenneth 1944- *St&PR 93*
Mitchell, Lawrence Alton 1941- *WhoAm 92*
Mitchell, Lee M. 1943- *St&PR 93*
Mitchell, Lee Mark 1943- *WhoAm 92, WhoWor 93*
Mitchell, Leona 1948- *Baker 92*
Mitchell, Leona Pearl 1949- *WhoAm 92*
Mitchell, Lewis E. 1924- *St&PR 93*
Mitchell, Louis Livingston 1930- *WhoE 93*
Mitchell, Malcolm Stuart 1937- *WhoAm 92*
Mitchell, Margaret 1900-1949 *BioIn 17, WomChHR [port]*
Mitchell, Margaret Anne 1925- *WhoAmW 93*
Mitchell, Margaret Howell 1901-1988 *BioIn 17*
Mitchell, Maria *WhoWrEP 92*
Mitchell, Maria 1818-1889 *BioIn 17*
Mitchell, Marilyn R. 1957- *St&PR 93*
Mitchell, Marilyn Sue 1942- *WhoAmW 93*
Mitchell, Mark Allan 1950- *WhoSSW 93*
Mitchell, Mark Thomson 1942- *WhoWor 93*
Mitchell, Martin Morgan, Jr. 1937- *WhoAm 92*
Mitchell, Mary Ellen 1955- *WhoAmW 93*
Mitchell, Mary M. *AmWomPl*
Mitchell, Matthew W. 1942- *St&PR 93*
Mitchell, Maurice B. 1915- *WhoAm 92, WhoWor 93*
Mitchell, Maurice McClellan, Jr. 1929- *WhoAm 92*
Mitchell, McKinley 1934-1986 *BioIn 17*
Mitchell, Melanie J. *Law&B 92*
Mitchell, Michael Allan 1951- *WhoSSW 93*
Mitchell, Michael James 1945- *WhoWor 93*
Mitchell, Michael Stuart 1948- *WhoEmL 93*
Mitchell, Michael W. 1939- *St&PR 93*
Mitchell, Milton 1916- *WhoAm 92*
Mitchell, Minnie Belle 1860- *AmWomPl*
Mitchell, Mitch 1946- *BioIn 17*
Mitchell, Mozella Gordon 1936- *WhoAmW 93, WhoSSW 93*
Mitchell, Myron James 1947- *WhoE 93*
Mitchell, Nancy H. *Law&B 92*
Mitchell, Nancy Sue 1955- *WhoWrEP 92*
Mitchell, Norma 189-?-1967 *AmWomPl*
Mitchell, O. Jack d1992 *NewYTBS 92*
Mitchell, O. Jack 1931-1992 *BioIn 17*
Mitchell, Orlan E. 1933- *WhoAm 92*
Mitchell, Oscar Elmer, Jr. 1948- *WhoEmL 93*
Mitchell, Otis Clinton, Jr. 1935- *WhoAm 92*
Mitchell, Paige *ConAu 40NR*
Mitchell, Pamela Holsclaw 1940- *WhoAmW 93*
Mitchell, Pamela J. 1952- *St&PR 93*
Mitchell, Parren J. *AfrAmBi [port], BioIn 17*
Mitchell, Patsy Malier 1948- *WhoSSW 93*
Mitchell, Paul David 1959- *WhoWrEP 92*
Mitchell, Paul Douglas 1953- *WhoUN 92*
Mitchell, Paul Lee 1940- *WhoSSW 93*
Mitchell, Paula Rae 1951- *WhoAmW 93, WhoEmL 93*
Mitchell, Peggy Carroll 1953- *WhoAmW 93*
Mitchell, Peter Edward Gordon 1929- *WhoWor 93*
Mitchell, Peter Kenneth, Jr. 1949- *WhoAm 92, WhoE 93*
Mitchell, Peter McQuilkin 1934- *WhoAm 92*
Mitchell, Peter R. *ScF&FL 92*
Mitchell, Philip Michael 1953- *WhoE 93*
Mitchell, Philip W. 1941- *WhoIns 93*
Mitchell, R. Clayton, Jr. 1936- *WhoAm 92*
Mitchell, R.F. *WhoScE 91-1*
Mitchell, Rava L. 1932- *St&PR 93*
Mitchell, Raymond Lewis 1915- *St&PR 93*
Mitchell, Rhea 1893-1957 *SweetSg A*
Mitchell, Richard A. 1939- *St&PR 93*
Mitchell, Richard Boyle 1947- *WhoAm 92, WhoE 93*
Mitchell, Richard Leigh 1941- *WhoWor 93*
Mitchell, Richard W. 1937- *St&PR 93*
Mitchell, Ricky Kent 1960- *WhoSSW 93*
Mitchell, Rita Gayle 1957- *WhoAmW 93*
Mitchell, Robert Alan 1953- *WhoEmL 93*
Mitchell, Robert Arthur 1926- *WhoAm 92*
Mitchell, Robert Brian *Law&B 92*
Mitchell, Robert Burdette 1953- *WhoEmL 93*
Mitchell, Robert C. *Law&B 92*
Mitchell, Robert Dale 1910- *WhoAm 92*
Mitchell, Robert deCalvin, III 1960- *WhoSSW 93*
Mitchell, Robert Edward 1930- *WhoAm 92*
Mitchell, Robert Everitt 1929- *WhoAm 92*
Mitchell, Robert Greene 1925- *WhoAm 92*
Mitchell, Robert Irvin 1950- *St&PR 93*
Mitchell, Robert Joseph 1947- *WhoEmL 93*
Mitchell, Robert L. 1923- *St&PR 93*
Mitchell, Robert Lee, III 1957- *WhoEmL 93*
Mitchell, Robert Lynn 1933- *St&PR 93*
Mitchell, Robert M. 1938- *St&PR 93*
Mitchell, Robert Watson 1910- *WhoAm 92*
Mitchell, Robert Wayne 1950- *WhoWrEP 92*
Mitchell, Roberta King 1951- *WhoAmW 93*
Mitchell, Roger 1935- *WhoWrEP 92*
Mitchell, Ronald Wayne 1933- *St&PR 93*
Mitchell, Ronald William 1953- *WhoSSW 93*
Mitchell, Ross Edouard 1952- *WhoE 93*
Mitchell, Ross Galbraith 1920- *WhoWor 93*
Mitchell, Roy Truslow 1945- *St&PR 93*
Mitchell, Russell Harry 1925- *WhoAm 92*
Mitchell, Ruth Comfort 1882- *AmWomPl*
Mitchell, Ruth Ellen 1940- *WhoAmW 93*
Mitchell, S. Weir 1829-1914 *GayN*
Mitchell, Sally Hayden 1937- *WhoAmW 93, WhoE 93*
Mitchell, Samuel P. 1932- *St&PR 93*
Mitchell, Samuel U. 1931- *St&PR 93*
Mitchell, Sharon Ann 1954- *WhoWrEP 92*
Mitchell, Shirley Marie 1953- *WhoEmL 93*
Mitchell, Sollace *MiSFD 9*
Mitchell, Stephanie J. 1957- *WhoEmL 93*
Mitchell, Stephen A. 1903-1974 *PolPar*
Mitchell, Stephen Arnold 1903-1974 *BioIn 17*
Mitchell, Stephen Connally 1943- *St&PR 93*
Mitchell, Stephen M. *Law&B 92*
Mitchell, Stephen Milton 1943- *WhoSSW 93*
Mitchell, Steven K. 1956- *St&PR 93*
Mitchell, Steven Thomas 1953- *WhoEmL 93*
Mitchell, Stewart L. *Law&B 92*
Mitchell, Stuart 1908- *St&PR 93*
Mitchell, Susan Baranowski 1955- *WhoAmW 93*
Mitchell, Suzanne E. Wagner 1958- *WhoAmW 93*
Mitchell, Terence Edward 1937- *WhoAm 92*
Mitchell, Terence Nigel 1942- *WhoScE 91-3*
Mitchell, Terrell Keith 1955- *St&PR 93*
Mitchell, Thomas Edward 1946- *WhoE 93*
Mitchell, Thomas Livingstone 1792-1855 *Expl 93*
Mitchell, Thomas Robert 1937- *St&PR 93*
Mitchell, Thomas Wayne 1945- *WhoSSW 93*
Mitchell, Tim *ScF&FL 92*
Mitchell, Timothy P. 1949- *WhoIns 93*
Mitchell, Timothy T. 1960- *WhoEmL 93*
Mitchell, Tom Herron 1924- *WhoSSW 93*
Mitchell, Tyrone 1944- *BioIn 17*
Mitchell, V.E. 1954- *ScF&FL 92*
Mitchell, Vernice Virginia 1921- *WhoAmW 93*
Mitchell, W. Garry 1938- *WhoE 93*
Mitchell, W. J. T. 1942- *WhoAm 92, WhoWrEP 92*
Mitchell, Walter Roy 1961- *WhoE 93*
Mitchell, Warren I. 1937- *St&PR 93, WhoAm 92*
Mitchell, Wayland J. 1926- *St&PR 93*
Mitchell, Wesley Clair 1874-1948 *BioIn 17*
Mitchell, Wiley Francis, Jr. *Law&B 92*
Mitchell, William 1879-1936 *HarEnMi*
Mitchell, William Alexander 1911- *WhoE 93*
Mitchell, William Avery, Jr. 1933- *WhoSSW 93, WhoWor 93*
Mitchell, William B. 1935- *WhoSSW 93*
Mitchell, William B. 1936- *WhoAm 92*
Mitchell, William C. *Law&B 92*
Mitchell, William D. *Law&B 92*
Mitchell, William E. 1944- *St&PR 93*
Mitchell, William Edmund 1944- *WhoAm 92*
Mitchell, William Edward Alexander 1929- *WhoWor 93*
Mitchell, William Frank 1925- *St&PR 93*
Mitchell, William George 1931- *St&PR 93*
Mitchell, William Graham Champion 1946- *WhoE 93, WhoWor 93*
Mitchell, William Grant 1921- *WhoAm 92*
Mitchell, William J(ohn) 1906-1971 *Baker 92*
Mitchell, William James Rae 1950- *WhoWor 93*
Mitchell, William M. *Law&B 92*
Mitchell, William Marvin 1935- *WhoSSW 93*
Mitchell, William Ormond 1914- *WhoCanL 92*
Mitchell, William Patrick 1937- *WhoE 93*
Mitchell, William Richard 1930- *WhoWrEP 92*
Mitchell, William S. 1931- *St&PR 93*
Mitchell, Willie 1928- *SoulM*
Mitchell, Winalee G. 1921- *St&PR 93*
Mitchell, Wylie Hopkins 1946- *St&PR 93*
Mitchelle, Richard L. 1934- *St&PR 93*
Mitchell-Innes, Lucy *BioIn 17*
Mitchell-Karega, Deborah Annette 1953- *WhoAmW 93, WhoEmL 93*
Mitchell-Rankin, Zinora *BioIn 17*
Mitchelson, Austin *ScF&FL 92*
Mitchelson, Fred *St&PR 93*
Mitchelson, Marvin Morris 1928- *WhoAm 92*
Mitchelson, William Harry 1942- *St&PR 93*
Mitchem, James E. 1949- *WhoEmL 93*
Mitchenson, Francis Joseph Blackett 1911-1992 *ConAu 139*
Mitchenson, Joe *ConAu 139*
Mitchinson, Malcolm James *WhoScE 91-1*
Mitchison, Denis Anthony *WhoScE 91-1*
Mitchison, Naomi 1897- *ScF&FL 92*
Mitchner, Gary L. 1946- *WhoWrEP 92*
Mitcho, Joseph Charles 1941- *St&PR 93, WhoSSW 93*
Mitchum, Donald Chaney 1937- *St&PR 93*
Mitchum, Johnny Burge 1947- *WhoSSW 93*
Mitchum, Margaret Elaine 1945- *WhoAmW 93*
Mitchum, Robert *BioIn 17*
Mitchum, Robert 1917- *IntDcF 2-3 [port]*
Mitchum, Robert Charles Duran 1917- *WhoAm 92*
Mitelman, Bonnie Cossman 1941- *WhoAmW 93*
Mitelman, Felix 1940- *WhoScE 91-4*
Mitev, I. *WhoScE 91-4*
Mitford, Clement Napier Bertram 1932-1991 *BioIn 17*
Mitford, Jessica 1917- *BioIn 17, ConAu 17AS [port], WhoAm 92, WhoWrEP 92*
Mitford, Mary Russell 1787-1855 *BioIn 17, DcLB 116 [port]*
Mitgang, Herbert 1920- *ScF&FL 92, WhoAm 92, WhoWrEP 92*
Mithers, Carol Lynn *BioIn 17*
Mithun, Raymond O. 1909- *St&PR 93, WhoAm 92*
Mitic, Zoran 1960- *WhoWor 93*
Mitidieri, Dario *BioIn 17*
Mitidieri, Emilio 1927- *WhoWor 93*
Mitiguy, Michael John 1944- *St&PR 93*
Mitilier, Terry John 1949- *WhoIns 93*
Mitin, Vladimir 1931- *WhoScE 91-4*
Mitio, John, III 1950- *WhoEmL 93*
Mitjana y Gordon, Rafael 1869-1921 *Baker 92*
Mitjavila, Salvador *WhoScE 91-2*
Mitjavile, Regis Louis 1946- *WhoWor 93*
Mitka, Boleslaw *WhoScE 91-4*
Mitlyng, Errol Paul 1936- *St&PR 93, WhoAm 92*
Mitman, Stewart Phipard 1925- *WhoE 93*
Mitnick, Carl T. d1992 *NewYTBS 92*
Mitnick, Harold 1923- *WhoE 93*
Mitnick, Harvey D. *Law&B 92*
Mitnick, J.G. 1917- *St&PR 93*
Mitnick, Mindy Faith 1950- *WhoEmL 93*
Mitnick, Sadie Rachel *Law&B 92*
Mitofsky, Warren Jay 1934- *WhoE 93*
Mitoraj, Suzanne Ogorzalek 1945- *WhoE 93*
Mitos, James Walter 1956- *St&PR 93*
Mitov, Kosto Valov 1954- *WhoWor 93*
Mitovich, John 1927- *WhoAm 92*
Mitra, Gautam *WhoScE 91-1*
Mitra, Keesha-Lu *Law&B 92*
Mitra, Nimai-Kumar 1939- *WhoWor 93*
Mitra, Ramon V., Jr. *WhoAsAP 91*
Mitra, Robin 1953- *WhoWor 93*
Mitra, Sanjit Kumar 1935- *WhoAm 92*
Mitra, Shashanka Shekhar 1933- *WhoE 93*
Mitrano, Daniel Francis 1940- *St&PR 93*
Mitrano, Michael 1956- *St&PR 93*
Mitrano, Peter Paul 1951- *WhoEmL 93*
Mitrany, Devora 1947- *WhoAmW 93, WhoEmL 93*
Mitrea-Celarianu, Mihai 1935- *Baker 92*
Mitreva, Mariya Ivanova 1951- *WhoWor 93*
Mitri, Salvatore C. *Law&B 92*
Mitrione, Michael Vincent 1951- *WhoEmL 93*
Mitrisin, Eldon J. *Law&B 92*
Mitropolsky, Yuri Alexeevich 1917- *WhoWor 93*
Mitropoulos, Dimitri 1896-1960 *Baker 92*
Mitropoulos, Dmitri 1896-1960 *OxDcOp*
Mitrov, Gerasim Georgiev 1923- *WhoScE 91-4*
Mitrovgenis, James William, Jr. 1950- *WhoSSW 93*
Mitrovic, Michael 1952- *St&PR 93*
Mitrovic, Zivorad 1921- *DrEEuF*
Mitsanyi, Attila 1933- *WhoScE 91-4*
Mitsch, Heinz 1944- *WhoWor 93*
Mitsch, Robert F. *Law&B 92*
Mitsch, Ronald Allen 1934- *WhoAm 92*
Mitschele, H.J. 1929- *St&PR 93*
Mitschele, Michael Douglas 1956- *WhoE 93, WhoEmL 93*
Mitscher, Lester Allen 1931- *WhoAm 92*
Mitscher, Marc Andrew 1887-1947 *BioIn 17, HarEnMi*
Mitschke, Manfred 1929- *WhoScE 91-3*
Mitschke-Collande, Constantine von 1884-1956 *BioIn 17*
Mitseff, Carl 1928- *WhoAm 92*
Mitskevich, Anatoly P. 1919-1975 *BioIn 17*
Mitsotakis, Constantin 1918- *WhoWor 93*
Mitsotakis, Constantine 1918- *BioIn 17*
Mitsubayashi, Yataro *WhoAsAP 91*
Mitsuhashi, Shinichiro 1948- *St&PR 93*
Mitsui, Patricia Teruko 1946- *WhoEmL 93*
Mitsuishi, Hisae 1927- *WhoAsAP 91*
Mitsuishi, Nobuo 1928- *WhoWor 93*
Mitsuke, Koichiro 1959- *WhoWor 93*
Mitsukuri, Shukichi 1895-1971 *Baker 92*
Mitsuma, Shingo 1916- *WhoWor 93*
Mitsuru, Sekioka 1930- *WhoWor 93*
Mitsutake, Akira 1931- *WhoAsAP 91*
Mitsuzawa, Shigeo 1939- *WhoWor 93*
Mitsuzuka, Hiroshi 1927- *WhoAsAP 91*
Mitta, Aleksandr 1933- *DrEEuF*
Mitta, Alexander *MiSFD 9*
Mittal, Banwari Lal 1936- *WhoWor 93*
Mittal, Piyush D. *Law&B 92*
Mittal, Sat Paul 1931- *WhoAsAP 91*
Mitteau, Martine 1943- *WhoScE 91-2*
Mittel, John J. *WhoSSW 93, WhoWor 93*
Mitteldorf, Klaus 1953- *BioIn 17*
Mittelholzer, Edgar Austin 1909-1965 *DcLB 117 [port]*
Mittelholzer, George E. *Law&B 92*
Mittell, Larry C. 1941- *St&PR 93*
Mittelman, Gary Lee 1960- *St&PR 93*
Mittelmark, Abraham 1926- *WhoWrEP 92*
Mittelmeier, Heinz 1927- *WhoScE 91-3*
Mittelstadt, Charles Anthony 1918- *WhoAm 92*
Mittelstadt, Miles Steven 1961- *WhoEmL 93*
Mittelstaedt, Horst 1923- *WhoScE 91-3*
Mitten, David Gordon 1935- *WhoAm 92*
Mitten, George Thomas 1952- *St&PR 93*
Mitten, L. Russell 1951- *St&PR 93*
Mitten, L. Russell, II *Law&B 92*
Mittendorf, Theodor Henry 1895- *WhoWor 93*
Mitter, Werner Sepp 1941- *WhoWor 93*
Mitterer, Felix 1948- *DcLB 124 [port]*
Mitterer, Ignaz Martin 1850-1924 *Baker 92*
Mitterlehner, Mark Edward 1961- *WhoEmL 93, WhoSSW 93*
Mittermaier, Armin Eugene 1932- *St&PR 93*
Mittermaier, Rosi 1950- *BioIn 17*
Mittermeier, Russell *BioIn 17*
Mittermeier, Russell A. 1949- *CurBio 92 [port]*
Mittermeier, Russell Alan 1949- *WhoE 93*
Mitterrand, Francois 1916- *BioIn 17, ColdWar 1 [port], DcTwHis*
Mitterrand, Francois Maurice 1916- *WhoAsAP 91*
Mitterrand, Francois Maurice Marie 1916- *WhoWor 93*
Mitterwurzer, Anton 1818-1876 *Baker 92*
Mittleman, Aaron N. 1925- *St&PR 93*
Mittlemann, David 1913- *St&PR 93*
Mittler, Diana 1941- *WhoAmW 93*
Mittler, Franz 1893-1970 *Baker 92*
Mittler, Herbert J. 1931- *St&PR 93*
Mittler, Joan Morgan 1941- *WhoE 93*
Mittler, Paul d1991 *BioIn 17*

Mittman, Betty 1932- St&PR 93
Mittmann, Hans-Ulrich 1942- WhoScE 91-3
Mitton, Jacqueline BioIn 17
Mitton, Michael Anthony 1947- WhoEmL 93
Mitton, Simon 1946- BioIn 17
Mitts, Bill BioIn 17
Mitty, Lizbeth 1952- WhoE 93
Mitura, Michael David 1946- WhoSSW 93
Mitvalsky, Cheryle Watts 1944- WhoAmW 93
Mitz, Vladimir 1943- WhoWor 93
Mitzner, Bonnie Mae 1958- WhoEmL 93
Mitzner, Donald BioIn 17
Mitzner, Donald H. 1940- WhoAm 92
Mitzner, Ethan BioIn 17
Mitzner, Judith BioIn 17
Mitzner, Kenneth Martin 1938- WhoAm 92
Mitzner, Miles Leemon 1957- WhoEmL 93
Miu, Patrick WhoE 93
Miullo, Nathaniel Jerome 1957- WhoWrEP 92
Miura, Goro 1846-1926 HarEnMi
Miura, Hisashi 1931- WhoAsAP 91
Miura, Makoto 1934- WhoUN 92
Miura, Robert Mitsuru 1938- WhoAm 92
Miura, Tamaki 1884-1946 OxDcOp
Miura, Tanetoshi 1920- WhoWor 93
Miura, Tokuhiro 1928- WhoWor 93
Miura, Yoshiaki 1915- WhoWor 93
Miwa, Makiko 1951- WhoWor 93
Mix, Ron 1938- BioIn 17
Mix, Ruth 1912-1977 BioIn 17, SweetSg C [port]
Mix, Tom 1880-1940 BioIn 17, IntDcF 2-3 [port]
Mixdorf, Glen R. Law&B 92
Mixer, Ronald Wayne 1954- WhoWor 93
Mixner, Mark Philip 1952- WhoSSW 93
Mixon, Aaron Malachi, III 1940- St&PR 93
Mixon, Ada AmWomPl
Mixon, Alan 1933- WhoAm 92
Mixon, E.P. 1926- St&PR 93
Mixon, Forest O. 1931- St&PR 93
Mixon, Harry Nelson Law&B 92
Mixon, Hayward E. 1928- St&PR 93
Mixon, John 1933- WhoAm 92
Mixon, John A. St&PR 93
Mixon, Joseph Edward Law&B 92
Mixon, Laura J. ScF&FL 92
Mixon, Myron Glenn 1950- St&PR 93
Mixon, Peggy Dorsey 1935- WhoSSW 93
Mixon, Susan Ann 1961- WhoSSW 93
Mixson, Riley Dewitt 1936- WhoAm 92
Mixson, William Tunno 1924- WhoSSW 93
Miya, Tom Saburo 1923- WhoAm 92, WhoSSW 93
Miyachi, Iwao 1916- WhoWor 93
Miyachi, Shosuke 1940- WhoAsAP 91
Miyagawa, Ichiro 1922- WhoAm 92, WhoWor 93
Miyagaya, Tokuzo 1935- WhoWor 93
Miyagi, Hiroo W. 1917- St&PR 93
Miyagi, Michio 1894-1956 Baker 92
Miyahara, Yoshihiko 1937- WhoAm 92
Miyahira, Harrison Y. 1935- St&PR 93
Miyahira, Keith Y. Law&B 92
Miyahira, Sarah Diane 1948- WhoEmL 93
Miyaji, Kazuaki 1940- WhoAsAP 91
Miyajima, Tatsuo BioIn 17
Miyakado, Masakazu 1947- WhoWor 93
Miyake, Akio 1931- WhoWor 93
Miyake, Akira 1925- WhoWor 93
Miyake, Issey BioIn 17
Miyake, Issey 1938- WhoAm 92
Miyake, Junji 1956- WhoWor 93
Miyakoda, Kikuro 1927- WhoAm 92
Miyamoto, Eishichi 1936- WhoWor 93
Miyamoto, Gabriella R. Law&B 92
Miyamoto, Misako 1928- WhoWor 93
Miyamoto, Richard Takashi 1944- WhoAm 92
Miyamoto, Sigenori 1931- WhoWor 93
Miyao, Stanley K. 1946- WhoIns 93
Miyao, Stanley Kenji 1946- St&PR 93
Miyares, Benjamin David 1940- WhoAm 92
Miyasaki, Gail Yotsue 1949- WhoE 93
Miyasaki, George Joji 1935- WhoAm 92
Miyasaki, Shuichi 1928- WhoWor 93
Miyasato, Matsusho 1927- WhoAsAP 91
Miyashiro, Yoshito 1931- St&PR 93
Miyashita, Sohei 1927- WhoAsAP 91, WhoWor 93
Miyata, Gen 1933- WhoWor 93
Miyata, Keijiro 1951- WhoEmL 93
Miyata, Teru 1921- WhoAsAP 91
Miyazaki, Eizo 1935- WhoWor 93
Miyazaki, Eliane 1962- WhoWor 93
Miyazaki, Hideki 1931- WhoAsAP 91
Miyazaki, Jim J. 1929- St&PR 93
Miyazaki, Moichi 1917- WhoAsAP 91
Miyazaki, Nagao 1931- WhoWor 93
Miyazaki, Tugio 1942- WhoWor 93
Miyazaki, Yukiji 1930- WhoWor 93
Miyazawa, Hiroshi 1921- WhoAsAP 91
Miyazawa, Kenji 1896-1933 BioIn 17
Miyazawa, Kiichi 1919- BioIn 17, CurBio 92 [port], News 92 [port], WhoAsAP 91, WhoWor 93
Miyoshi, Akira 1933- Baker 92
Miyoshi, David Masao 1944- WhoWor 93
Miyoshi, Kiyoshi Kawakami 1929- WhoWor 93
Miyoshi, Linda Ann Davis 1953- WhoAmW 93
Miyoshi, Masayoshi 1926- WhoWor 93
Mizanin, Michael O. 1948- St&PR 93
Mizdail, Barbara Estella Neff 1950- WhoEmL 93
Mize, Bryan Curtis 1963- WhoSSW 93
Mize, E. Jack, Jr. 1946- St&PR 93
Mize, Franklin H. 1929- St&PR 93
Mize, Franklin M. Law&B 92
Mize, Joe Henry 1934- WhoAm 92, WhoWrEP 92
Mize, Johnny 1913- BioIn 17
Mize, Johnny Edwin 1960- WhoSSW 93
Mize, Richard A. Law&B 92
Mize, Shirley J. WhoWrEP 92
Mizejewski, Gerald Jude 1939- WhoE 93
Mizel, Anne-Marie 1961- WhoEmL 93
Mizel, Ken 1951- St&PR 93
Mizell, Al Philip 1934- WhoWor 93
Mizell, Andrew Hooper, III 1926- St&PR 93
Mizell, Hubert Coleman 1939- WhoSSW 93
Mizell, Merle 1927- WhoAm 92
Mizell, William A. 1928- St&PR 93
Mizelle, Janice Labarre 1956- WhoAmW 93
Mizelle, John Dary 1903-1989 BioIn 17
Mizelle, (Dary) John 1940- Baker 92
Mizener, Arthur 1907-1988 BioIn 17
Mizer, Richard Anthony 1952- WhoEmL 93, WhoWor 93
Mizgala, Henry F. 1932- WhoAm 92
Miziolek, Andrzej Wladyslaw 1950- WhoEmL 93
Mizis, Marvin L. Law&B 92
Mizler, Lorenz Christoph 1711-1778 Baker 92
Mizner, Addison 1872-1933 BioIn 17
Mizner, Ann Joyce Law&B 92
Mizner, Elizabeth H. ScF&FL 92
Mizoguchi, Kenji 1898-1956 MiSFD 9N
Mizon, Grayham Ernest WhoScE 91-1
Mizrach, Larry Melvin 1932- St&PR 93
Mizrahi, Abraham Mordechay 1929- WhoAm 92
Mizrahi, David Toufic BioIn 17
Mizrahi, Isaac BioIn 17
Mizrahi, Jack David 1948- St&PR 93
Mizrahi, Moshe 1931- MiSFD 9
Mizroch, John F. 1948- WhoAm 92
Mizruchi, Susan Laura 1959- WhoE 93
Mizuguchi, Shigeo 1926- WhoWor 93
Mizuguchi, Yasuo 1935- WhoWor 93
Mizuma, Noriaki 1946- WhoWor 93
Mizuno, Genzo BioIn 17
Mizuno, Hajime 1930- WhoWor 93
Mizuno, Kiyoshi 1925- WhoAsAP 91
Mizuno, Nobuhiko 1933- WhoWor 93
Mizuno, Shinji 1956- WhoWor 93
Mizusawa, Bert Kameaaloha 1957- WhoE 93
Mizusawa, Joji 1937- WhoWor 93
Mizushima, Yoshihiko 1925- WhoWor 93
Mizuta, Minoru 1925- WhoAsAP 91
Mizuta Mary Ellen 1949- WhoWrEP 92
Mizutani, Junya 1932- WhoWor 93
Mizuuchi, Kiyoshi 1944- WhoAm 92
Mizzi, Maurice Frank 1936- WhoWor 93
Mjor, Ivar Andreas 1933- WhoScE 91-4
Mkapa, Benjamin William 1938- WhoAfr
Mkhatshwa, Smangaliso BioIn 17
Mladenka, Mark 1954- WhoSSW 93
Mladenov, Georgy 1941- WhoScE 91-4
Mladenov, Ivailo Milachkov 1951- WhoWor 93
Mladenov, Ivan 1927- WhoScE 91-4
Mladenov, Mileti Hristov 1943- WhoWor 93
Mladenov, Peter Toshev 1936- WhoWor 93
Mladenov, Zahari Mihajlov 1919- WhoScE 91-4
Mladenova, Clementina Dimitrova 1954- WhoWor 93
Mladenovic, Dragomir 1919- WhoScE 91-4
Mladin, Gheorghe I. 1946- WhoScE 91-4
Mladota, John 1917- St&PR 93
Mlakar, Anthony F. 1934- St&PR 93
Mlakar, Charles L., Jr. 1946- St&PR 93
Mlakar, France 1921- WhoScE 91-4
Mlakar, Roy A. 1953- WhoAm 92
Mlaki, Morrison Elifuraha 1943- WhoUN 92
Mlangeni, Bheki d1991 BioIn 17
Mlay, Marian 1935- WhoAm 92
Mlekush, Kenneth C. 1938- WhoIns 93
Mlochowski, Jacek W. 1937- WhoScE 91-4
Mlodozeniec, Wieslaw WhoScE 91-4
Mlodzinski, Boleslaw Z. 1919- WhoScE 91-4
Mlotek, Herman Victor 1922- WhoWor 93
Mlotkowski, Michael John Law&B 92
Mlsna, Kathryn Kimura Law&B 92
Mlsna, Kathryn Kimura 1952- WhoEmL 93
Mlsna, Timothy Martin 1947- WhoAm 92
Mlynarczyk, J. WhoScE 91-4
Mlynarski, Emil 1870-1935 PolBiDi
Mlynarski, Emil (Simon) 1870-1935 Baker 92
Mlynarski, Tadeusz 1929- WhoScE 91-4
Mmahat, Arlene Cecile 1943- WhoAmW 93
Mmusi, Peter Simako 1929- WhoAfr
Mnookin, Robert Harris 1942- WhoAm 92
Mnouchkine, Ariane BioIn 17
Mo, Jiaqi 1937- WhoWor 93
Mo, Luke Wei 1934- WhoAm 92
Mo, Timothy BioIn 17
Mo, Timothy 1950- IntLitE
Mo, Y. Joseph 1948- St&PR 93
Moak, E.H. 1904- St&PR 93
Moak, Richard John 1947- WhoEmL 93
Moak, Robert E. 1939- St&PR 93
Moake, Brenda Joy 1959- St&PR 93
Moakley, Joe 1927- CngDr 91
Moakley, John J. BioIn 17
Moakley, John Joseph 1927- WhoAm 92, WhoE 93
Moakley, Thomas J. 1938- St&PR 93
Moak Mazur, Connie J. 1947- WhoAm 92, WhoE 93, WhoEmL 93
Moal, Michelle WhoScE 91-2
Moan, Joseph Patrick Law&B 92
Moan, Torgeir 1944- WhoWor 93
Moar, Peter J. 1936- St&PR 93
Moat, Douglas Clarkson 1931- WhoIns 93
Moat, Mike 1961- BioIn 17
Moat, Stanley F. 1927- St&PR 93
Moates, G. Paul 1947- WhoAm 92
Moates, Kathleen Law&B 92
Moawad, Atef 1935- WhoAm 92
Moawad, Rene BioIn 17
Moazam, Farhat 1945- WhoWor 93
Moazzami, Sara 1960- WhoAmW 93
Mobarak, Habib 1932- WhoUN 92
Mobasseri, Bijan Gholamreza 1953- WhoE 93
Mobbs, Nigel 1937- WhoWor 93
Moberg, Carl Allan 1896-1978 Baker 92
Moberg, David Oscar 1922- WhoAm 92
Moberg, Jill Anne WhoAmW 93
Moberg, Leif C. 1945- WhoScE 91-4
Moberger, Barbara Montgomery 1931- St&PR 93
Moberly, Bonnie Lou 1930- WhoAmW 93
Moberly, Charlotte Anne 1846-1937 BioIn 17
Moberly, Linden Emery 1923- WhoWor 93
Moberly, Mary Ruth d1992 NewYTBS 92
Moberly, Robert Blakely 1941- WhoAm 92
Mobert, Helen L. AmWomPl
Mobilia, Louis 1932- St&PR 93
Mobilia, Pamela Ann Kristin 1956- WhoE 93
Mobley, Andrew Hundley 1953- WhoEmL 93
Mobley, Beverly Dewease 1953- WhoSSW 93
Mobley, Charles M(urray) 1954- ConAu 139
Mobley, Connie Chenevert 1944- WhoSSW 93
Mobley, Emily Davis BioIn 17
Mobley, Emily Ruth WhoAm 92, WhoAmW 93
Mobley, George Melton, Jr. 1948- WhoEmL 93
Mobley, Jane 1947- ScF&FL 92
Mobley, John A. St&PR 93
Mobley, John Homer, II 1930- WhoAm 92, WhoWor 93
Mobley, Karen Ruth 1961- WhoAmW 93
Mobley, Mamie BioIn 17
Mobley, Mamie Harris AmWomPl
Mobley, Michael Howard 1945- WhoAm 92
Mobley, Robert 1953- WhoE 93, WhoEmL 93
Mobley, Sandra Ann 1947- WhoAmW 93
Mobley, Stacey J. 1945- St&PR 93
Mobley, Steven Clark 1948- WhoEmL 93, WhoSSW 93, WhoWor 93
Mobley, Steven M. St&PR 93
Mobley, Thomas M. St&PR 93
Mobley, Tony Allen 1938- WhoAm 92
Mobley, William Frost BioIn 17
Mobley, William Hodges 1941- WhoAm 92, WhoSSW 93
Mobraaten, William Lawrence 1929- St&PR 93, WhoAm 92
Moburg, Mark Law&B 92
Mobutu, Sese Seko 1930- DcTwHis, WhoAfr
Mobutu Sese Seko NewYTBS 92 [port]
Mobutu Sese Seko 1930- BioIn 17, ColdWar 2 [port], WhoWor 93
Moca-Cioroiu, Monica 1948- WhoAmW 93
Mocarski, Cara Schmid 1958- WhoEmL 93
Mocarski, Laura Lada- 1902- BioIn 17
Moccio, John Raymond 1947- WhoE 93
Mocellin, Alain 1943- WhoScE 91-4
Moceri, Nicholas Anthony, Jr. 1950- WhoEmL 93
Moceri, William Thomas 1936- St&PR 93
Moch, Jules 1893-1985 BioIn 17
Moch, Kenneth Ian 1954- WhoEmL 93
Moch, Robert Gaston 1914- WhoAm 92
Mochar, Ernst 1909- BioIn 17
Mochar, Ingeborg 1945- BioIn 17
Mochary, Mary Veronica 1942- WhoAmW 93
Mochel, Myron George 1905- WhoE 93
Mochida, Yoshihiro 1931- WhoWor 93
Mochinaga, Kazumi 1927- WhoAsAP 91
Mochizuki, Shigeru 1931- WhoWor 93
Mochrie, Dottie BioIn 17, WhoAmW 93
Mochrie, Margaret AmWomPl
Mochrie, Richard D. 1928- WhoAm 92
Mochtar, Radinal 1930- WhoAsAP 91
Mocino, Jose Moriano 1757-1820 BioIn 17
Mock, Alois 1934- WhoWor 93
Mock, Bruno Paul 1937- WhoWor 93
Mock, Charles A. 1945- WhoE 93
Mock, Charles Newman 1927- St&PR 93
Mock, Clyde A. 1948- St&PR 93
Mock, David Clinton, Jr. 1922- WhoAm 92, WhoWor 93
Mock, David George 1925- St&PR 93
Mock, Douglas E. Law&B 92
Mock, Douglas F. 1955- St&PR 93
Mock, Henry Byron 1911- WhoAm 92
Mock, Jesse Alexander, Jr. 1920- WhoWrEP 92
Mock, Lawrence Edward 1917- WhoAm 92
Mock, Linda Colangelo 1948- WhoEmL 93
Mock, Robert Claude 1928- WhoAm 92, WhoE 93
Mock, Sandra Ford 1944- WhoAmW 93
Mock, Theodore Jaye 1941- WhoAm 92
Mockbee, William Clyde 1926- St&PR 93
Mockel, Andreas 1927- WhoWor 93
Mockel, Dennis Edward 1952- WhoEmL 93
Mockel, Gottfried 1926- WhoWor 93
Mockel, Jean 1941- WhoScE 91-2
Mockler, Colman Michael 1929-1991 BioIn 17
Mockler, Edward Joseph 1954- WhoEmL 93
Mockler, James Patrick 1928- WhoAm 92
Mocknick, David Lee 1958- WhoE 93
Mockoviak, John Wade 1944- WhoE 93
Mockridge, Norton 1915- WhoAm 92
Mockus, Jonas 1931- WhoWor 93
Mockus, Linas 1960- WhoWor 93
Mocniak, Michael Joseph Law&B 92
Mocny, R.C. 1929- St&PR 93
Mocquereau, Andre 1849-1930 Baker 92
Mocsary, Attila Laszlo 1931- St&PR 93
Mocumbi, Pascoal Manuel 1941- WhoWor 93
Moczarski, Kazimierz 1907-1975 PolBiDi
Moczygemba, Leopold 1825-1901 PolBiDi
Modahl, Mary Alden 1962- WhoAmW 93
Modak, Meena 1944- St&PR 93
Modansky, Aaron 1923- St&PR 93
Modarressi, Hossein 1942- WhoAm 92
Modderman, Melvin Earl 1940- WhoSSW 93
Mode, Charles J. 1927- WhoAm 92
Mode, Paul J., Jr. 1938- WhoAm 92
Modeen, Tore Gunnar Werner 1929- WhoWor 93
Modeer, Ulf Thomas 1945- WhoScE 91-4
Model, Ben MiSFD 9
Model, Elisabeth Dittman WhoAm 92
Model, Peter 1933- WhoAm 92
Model, Walter 1891-1945 BioIn 17
Model, Walther 1891-1945 HarEnMi
Modell, Arthur BioIn 17
Modell, Arthur B. 1925- WhoAm 92
Modell, Frank B. 1917- ConAu 39NR
Modell, Franklyn B. WhoAm 92
Modell, Jerome Herbert 1932- WhoAm 92
Modell, John 1941- WhoAm 92
Modell, Michael S. 1953- St&PR 93
Modell, Michael Steven Law&B 92
Modell, Michael Steven 1953- WhoAm 92
Modell, Mitchell B. 1954- WhoAm 92
Modell, Walter 1907-1990 BioIn 17

Modell, William 1921- St&PR 93
Modena, Giorgio 1924- WhoScE 91-3
Modena, Giulio 1940- WhoScE 91-3
Moder, John Joseph 1948- WhoAm 92
Moderacki, Edmund Anthony 1946- WhoE 93
Moderow, Joseph Robert Law&B 92
Moderow, Joseph Robert 1948- St&PR 93, WhoAm 92
Moderow, Richard Carl Law&B 92
Modersbach, Roger J. Law&B 92
Modersohn-Becker, Paula 1876-1907 BioIn 17
Modery, Richard Gillman 1941- WhoE 93
Modesitt, Jody M. 1952- St&PR 93
Modesitt, L.E., Jr. 1943- ScF&FL 92
Modest, Michael Fritz 1944- WhoE 93
Modestino, James William 1940- WhoAm 92
Modiano, Patrick 1945- BioIn 17
Modiano, Patrick (Jean) 1945- ConAu 40NR, WhoWor 93
Modic, Stanley John 1936- WhoAm 92, WhoWrEP 92
Modica, Frank A. 1928- St&PR 93
Modica, Roy H. St&PR 93
Modica, Terry Ann 1955- WhoWrEP 92
Modiga, Mircea 1939- WhoScE 91-4
Modigliani, Amedeo 1884-1920 BioIn 17
Modigliani, Elio 1860-1932 IntDcAn
Modigliani, Franco 1918- WhoAm 92, WhoE 93, WhoWor 93
Modigliani, Lazzaro 1932- St&PR 93
Modine, Matthew BioIn 17
Moding, Philip 1934- WhoScE 91-4
Modisane, Bloke 1923-1986 BioIn 17
Modise, Johannes 1929- WhoAfr
Modjeska, Gerald S. 1925- St&PR 93
Modjeska, Helena 1840-1909 BioIn 17, PolBiDi [port]
Modjeski, Ralph 1861-1940 PolBiDi
Modjeski, Richard Bruce 1946- WhoSSW 93
Modl, Martha 1912- Baker 92, IntDcOp [port], OxDcOp
Modlin, Beverly Cutter 1947- WhoAmW 93
Modlin, Elihu H. 1928- St&PR 93
Modlin, George Matthews 1903- WhoAm 92
Modlin, Howard S. 1931- St&PR 93, WhoAm 92, WhoE 93, WhoWor 93
Modlin, L. Ronald Law&B 92
Modlowski, Paul Barry 1948- St&PR 93
Modny, Michael T. 1916-1991 BioIn 17
Modolo, Maria Antonia 1929- WhoScE 91-3
Modot, Gaston 1887-1970 IntDcF 2-3 [port]
Modotti, Tina 1896-1942 BioIn 17
Modoux, Alain 1941- WhoUN 92
Modrall, James R. 1932- St&PR 93
Modrell, Dolores 1933- SmATA 72 [port]
Modrell, Jim B. 1935- St&PR 93
Modresky, Michael John 1946- WhoEmL 93
Modrow, Douglas Kevin 1958- WhoEmL 93
Modugno, Agatha M. Law&B 92
Modugno, Marco 1943- WhoWor 93
Modzelewska, Maria Irena 1921- WhoScE 91-4
Modzelewski, Stanley J. BiDAMSp 1989
Moe, Alden John 1939- WhoE 93
Moe, Carl R. 1936- St&PR 93
Moe, Chesney Rudolph 1908- WhoAm 92
Moe, Douglas Edwin 1938- BiDAMSp 1989, WhoAm 92
Moe, Frank Harrison 1941- St&PR 93
Moe, Geir 1938- WhoWor 93
Moe, Gordon K. 1915-1989 BioIn 17
Moe, Henrik 1940- St&PR 93
Moe, Henry Stanley Rawle 1935- WhoWor 93
Moe, James D. Law&B 92
Moe, Kare B. WhoScE 91-4
Moe, Marxianna M. 1953- St&PR 93
Moe, Maynard L. 1935- St&PR 93
Moe, Mildred Minasian 1929- WhoAmW 93
Moe, Palmer L. 1944- WhoSSW 93
Moe, Peter Johan 1923- WhoScE 91-4
Moe, Richard Palmer 1936- WhoAm 92
Moe, Roar 1939- WhoScE 91-4
Moe, Sharon Lynn 1948- WhoAmW 93
Moe, Vida Delores 1928- WhoAmW 93
Moebius, William 1941- WhoWrEP 92
Moeck, Hermann 1896-1982 Baker 92
Moeck, Hermann, Jr. 1922- See Moeck, Hermann 1896-1982 Baker 92
Moeckel, Bill Reid 1925- WhoAm 92
Moeckel, Henry Theodore 1918- WhoE 93
Moed, J.R. 1938- WhoScE 91-3
Moede, Walter M. 1940- St&PR 93
Moeder, Marsha Kay 1952- WhoAmW 93
Moe-Fishback, Barbara Ann 1955- WhoAmW 93
Moehlenpah, Henry A. 1867-1944 BioIn 17
Moehlman, Michael Scott 1938- WhoAm 92
Moehring, Karl-Heinz 1922- St&PR 93
Moelhman, Amy J. 1954- WhoAmW 93
Moeling, Walter Goos, IV 1943- WhoAm 92
Moelis, Herbert 1931- St&PR 93
Moelleken, Wolfgang Wilfried 1934- WhoAm 92
Moellenberg, Karen Nikki 1954- WhoEmL 93
Moeller, Achim Ferdinand Gerd 1942- WhoWor 93
Moeller, Audrey Carolyn 1935- St&PR 93, WhoAm 92
Moeller, Dade W. 1927- ConAu 138
Moeller, Dade William 1927- WhoAm 92
Moeller, Donald Joseph 1933- WhoAm 92
Moeller, Elnora Frances 1948- WhoAmW 93
Moeller, Erick Frederick, Jr. Law&B 92
Moeller, Floyd Douglas 1949- WhoEmL 93
Moeller, Francis Xavier, Jr. 1948- WhoE 93
Moeller, Guido K. Law&B 92
Moeller, Helen Hergenroder 1954- WhoAmW 93, WhoEmL 93
Moeller, Herman G. BioIn 17
Moeller, James 1933- WhoAm 92
Moeller, John Arnold 1936- WhoAm 92
Moeller, John E. Law&B 92
Moeller, Linda Kay 1945- WhoAmW 93
Moeller, M(athias) P(eter) Baker 92
Moeller, Mark Robert Law&B 92
Moeller, Mary Ella 1938- WhoAmW 93, WhoE 93
Moeller, Ordin 1943- WhoScE 91-4
Moeller, Peter H. 1939- WhoIns 93
Moeller, Raymond M. 1927- St&PR 93
Moeller, Richard 1939- St&PR 93
Moeller, Robert C. 1954- St&PR 93
Moeller, Robert Charles 1954- WhoEmL 93
Moeller, Robert Charles, III 1938- WhoAm 92
Moeller, Robert John 1938- WhoAm 92
Moeller, Warren Elbert 1926- WhoSSW 93
Moeller, Wayne Eldon 1926- WhoSSW 93
Moeller, William D. Law&B 92
Moeller, William E. 1942- WhoAm 92
Moellering, John H. 1938- St&PR 93
Moellering, John Henry 1938- WhoAm 92
Moellering, Richard Edwin 1929- St&PR 93
Moellering, Robert Charles, Jr. 1936- WhoAm 92, WhoWor 93
Moelling, Karin 1943- WhoScE 91-3
Moelo, Yves 1949- WhoScE 91-2
Moely, Barbara E. 1940- WhoAmW 93
Moen, Asbjorn 1944- WhoScE 91-4
Moen, C.H. 1942- WhoScE 91-3
Moen, Daniel J. 1951- St&PR 93
Moen, Donne P. WhoAm 92
Moen, Edward T., II Law&B 92
Moen, Hans-Olav 1939- WhoScE 91-4
Moen, Ronald S. BioIn 17
Moench, Francis J. d1991 BioIn 17
Moench, Mark C. Law&B 92
Moench, Priscilla Waters 1957- WhoEmL 93
Moench, Robert William 1927- WhoAm 92
Moens, Peter B. 1931- WhoAm 92
Moens, R. WhoScE 91-2
Moentmann, Melanie Ruth 1960- WhoEmL 93
Moeran, E(rnest) J(ohn) 1894-1950 Baker 92
Moerdani, Benny 1932- WhoAsAP 91
Moerdani, Leonardus Benny WhoWor 93
Moerdiono, Drs. 1934- WhoAsAP 91
Moerdler, Charles Gerard 1934- WhoAm 92, WhoE 93, WhoWor 93
Moerdler, Jeffrey Alan 1957- WhoEmL 93
Moerer, Gary 1938- St&PR 93
Moeri, Louise 1924- ScF&FL 92
Moeri, Louise (Healy) 1924- DcAmChF 1960
Moermans, R. WhoScE 91-2
Moermond, Jack Eugene Law&B 92
Moerner, William Esco 1953- WhoEmL 93
Moerpratomo, A. Sulasikin 1927- WhoAsAP 91
Moertel, Charles George 1927- WhoAm 92
Moertl, Margaret M. 1956- WhoEmL 93
Moes, Charles E., Jr. 1953- St&PR 93
Moeschinger, Albert 1897-1985 Baker 92
Moeschl, Deborah M. Law&B 92
Moeschler, Pierre 1930- WhoScE 91-4
Moesel, Peter A. Law&B 92
Moesgen, Karl John 1949- WhoWor 93
Moeslein, Frank A. 1943- St&PR 93
Moessinger, David MiSFD 9
Moessinger, David 1930- WhoAm 92, WhoWor 93
Moessner, Joerg Manfred 1941- WhoWor 93
Moest, Franz Welser- BioIn 17
Moeur, Benjamin Baker 1869-1937 BioIn 17
Moevs, Robert 1920- BioIn 17
Moevs, Robert W(alter) 1920- Baker 92
Mofenson, Lynne Meryl 1950- WhoEmL 93
Moffat, Alec W. 1947- St&PR 93
Moffat, David Halliday 1839-1911 BioIn 17
Moffat, Donald Law&B 92
Moffat, Donald 1930- WhoAm 92
Moffat, James N.C., III 1941- St&PR 93
Moffat, John L. 1941- WhoUN 92
Moffat, John William 1932- WhoAm 92
Moffat, Kenneth M. 1932- St&PR 93, WhoIns 93
Moffat, M.E.B. WhoScE 91-1
Moffat, MaryBeth 1951- WhoAmW 93
Moffat, Robert 1795-1883 Expl 93 [port]
Moffat, Robert John 1927- WhoAm 92
Moffat, Robin 1927- WhoWor 93
Moffat, Virginia AmWomPl
Moffat, W. Graham 1866- ScF&FL 92
Moffatt, B.R. 1934- St&PR 93
Moffatt, David John 1939- WhoAm 92
Moffatt, Derry ScF&FL 92
Moffatt, Donald ScF&FL 92
Moffatt, Graham 1919-1965 See Marriott, Moore 1885-1949 & Moffatt, Graham 1919-1965 QDrFCA 92
Moffatt, Henry Keith WhoScE 91-1
Moffatt, Hugh McCulloch, Jr. 1933- WhoWor 93
Moffatt, James 1922- ScF&FL 92
Moffatt, Joyce Anne 1936- WhoAm 92, WhoAmW 93
Moffatt, Katy 1950- WhoAm 92
Moffatt, Kevin L. 1956- WhoEmL 93
Moffatt, Mindy Ann 1951- WhoAmW 93
Moffet, Donald Pratt 1932- WhoAm 92
Moffet, Hugh Lamson 1932- WhoAm 92
Moffet, Margaret J. 1953- WhoAmW 93
Moffett, Becky May 1963- WhoE 93
Moffett, Charles Simonton 1945- WhoAm 92
Moffett, Charnett BioIn 17
Moffett, Dawn Schulten 1946- WhoAmW 93
Moffett, James H. Law&B 92
Moffett, James R. 1938- St&PR 93
Moffett, James Robert 1938- WhoAm 92, WhoSSW 93
Moffett, Jonathan Phillip 1954- WhoEmL 93
Moffett, Judith 1942- ScF&FL 92
Moffett, Laurie Golden Law&B 92
Moffett, Lawrence Rector 1927- St&PR 93
Moffett, Marian Scott 1949- WhoSSW 93
Moffett, Robert J. WhoScE 91-1
Moffett, Roy James 1947- WhoE 93
Moffett, Terrill Kay 1949- WhoSSW 93
Moffett, Todd Law&B 92
Moffett, William Andrew 1933- WhoAm 92
Moffit, George Seth 1947- WhoAm 92
Moffitt, Catherine Dyess 1908- WhoAmW 93
Moffitt, Charles William 1932- WhoAm 92
Moffitt, Daniel E. St&PR 93
Moffitt, Donald 1936- ScF&FL 92
Moffitt, Donald Eugene 1932- St&PR 93, WhoAm 92
Moffitt, George, Jr. 1918- WhoAm 92
Moffitt, Jane M. Law&B 92
Moffitt, John MiSFD 9
Moffitt, Peggy BioIn 17
Moffitt, Peggy 1937- ConAu 138
Moffitt, Peter M. 1926- St&PR 93
Moffitt, Phillip William 1946- WhoAm 92, WhoE 93
Moffitt, Virginia Lynn 1949- WhoE 93
Moffitt, William C. 1944- St&PR 93
Moffitt, William F. 1949- St&PR 93
Moffly, John Wesley, IV 1926- WhoE 93
Moffo, Anna BioIn 17
Moffo, Anna 1932- Baker 92, IntDcOp
Mofford, Rose 1922- WhoAmW 93
Mofield, William Ray 1921- WhoSSW 93, WhoWor 93
Mofran, John R. St&PR 93
Moftah, Mounir Amin 1922- WhoWor 93
Moga, Iuliu 1928- WhoScE 91-4
Moga, Thomas Traian 1957- WhoEmL 93
Mogabgab, William Joseph 1921- WhoAm 92, WhoSSW 93
Mogami, Takeo 1943- WhoWor 93
Mogan, Glen R. 1949- WhoE 93
Mogan, Michael F. Law&B 92
Mogel, Marcia G. 1950- St&PR 93
Mogelever, Bernard 1940- WhoAm 92, WhoE 93
Mogen, David 1945- ScF&FL 92
Mogen, James August, Sr. 1946- St&PR 93
Mogensen, Charles Ray, Jr. 1946- WhoE 93
Mogensen, Ejvind 1938- WhoUN 92
Mogensen, Finn 1934- WhoWor 93
Mogensen, Paul Robert 1941- WhoE 93
Mogerman, Veronica Linda 1954- WhoAmW 93, WhoEmL 93, WhoWor 93
Mogessie, Aberra 1950- WhoWor 93
Mogford, I.L. WhoScE 91-1
Mogg, Donald Whitehead 1924- WhoWor 93
Mogge, Harriet Morgan WhoAmW 93, WhoSSW 93
Moggie Anak Irok, Leo 1941- WhoAsAP 91
Moghadam, Ruth Anne 1945- WhoAmW 93
Moghissi, Kamran S. 1925- WhoWor 93
Mogil, Bernard Marc 1949- WhoEmL 93, WhoWor 93
Mogilner, Alan J. 1941- St&PR 93
Mogk, John Edward 1939- WhoAm 92
Moglia, Paul Louis 1954- WhoE 93
Mogol, Alan Jay 1946- WhoEmL 93
Mogren, William John 1948- St&PR 93
Mogro-Campero, Antonio Alberto 1940- WhoE 93
Mogstad, Rolf 1932- St&PR 93
Moguel, Kathleen Doris 1957- WhoEmL 93, WhoSSW 93
Mogul, Malcolm Daniel 1930- St&PR 93
Mogwe, Archibald Mooketa 1921- WhoAfr
Mogyorosy, Gyorgy WhoScE 91-4
Moh, Guenter H. 1929- WhoScE 91-3
Moh, Za Lee 1928- WhoWor 93
Mohacsi, Christina Vitez 1963- WhoAmW 93
Mohagatra, Basudeb 1932- WhoAsAP 91
Mohai, Bela 1927- WhoScE 91-4
Mohamad, Lucia 1941- WhoAmW 93
Mohamad Maidin Bin Packer Mohd 1957- WhoAsAP 91
Mohamad Said Keruak WhoWor 93
Mohamed, Ali Hamud WhoWor 93
Mohamed, Ali Mahdi WhoWor 93
Mohamed, Dato' Wan Abu Bakar Wan 1953- WhoAsAP 91
Mohamed, Harbi 1941- WhoUN 92
Mohamed Bin Khalifa Hamid Al-Khalifa, Sheikh 1937- WhoWor 93
Mohamed Najib bin Tun Haji Abdul Razak WhoWor 93
Mohamed Noah bin Omar 1894-1991 BioIn 17
Mohamed Said Keruak, Tuan Yang Terutama Tun Haji 1926- WhoAsAP 91
Mohamed Salleh bin Abas 1929- BioIn 17
Mohammad, Dato' Mustaffa Bin 1941- WhoAsAP 91
Mohammad, Golam 1955- WhoWor 93
Mohammad Reza Pahlevi 1919-1980 ColdWar 2 [port]
Mohammad Sunoh Bin Marso, Tan Sri Datuk 1927- WhoAsAP 91
Mohammed d632 BioIn 17
Mohammed, II 1432-1481 HarEnMi
Mohammed, Ali Mahdi 1940- WhoAfr
Mohammed, Didaoui 1947- WhoUN 92
Mohammed, Mervyn Mozam 1941- WhoWor 93
Mohammed, Zulkifli 1948- WhoAsAP 91
Mohammed Reza Pahlavi, Shah of Iran 1919-1980 BioIn 17
Mohammed Zahir Shah, King of Afghanistan 1914- BioIn 17
Mohan, Brij 1939- WhoSSW 93
Mohan, Daniel J. Law&B 92
Mohan, J. Patrick Law&B 92
Mohan, J. Patrick 1948- WhoAm 92
Mohan, John F. WhoScE 91-1
Mohan, John F., Jr., Mrs. 1944- WhoE 93
Mohan, Kim 1949- ScF&FL 92
Mohan, Pamela ScF&FL 92
Mohan, Robert P. Law&B 92
Mohan, Sal 1941- St&PR 93
Mohan, Tungesh Nath 1949- WhoEmL 93, WhoSSW 93, WhoWor 93
Mohan, Venkat Achari 1953- St&PR 93
Mohanan, Karuvannur Puthanveettil 1947- WhoWor 93
Mohan-Roberts, Veena 1939- WhoWor 93
Mohanty, Subas 1949- WhoAsAP 91
Mohaupt, Richard 1904-1957 Baker 92
Mohd Adam, Seri Mohd Adib Bin Haji 1941- WhoAsAP 91
Mohd Farid Bin Ariffin 1942- WhoAsAP 91
Mohd Kassim Bin Ahmad 1936- WhoAsAP 91
Mohd Noor Bin Mohd Mansoor, Haji 1943- WhoAsAP 91

Mohd Rashid, Mohd Yusof 1959- *WhoWor 93*
Mohel, Arnold D. 1925- *St&PR 93*
Moher, Frank 1955- *WhoCanL 92*
Moher, M. R. *Law&B 92*
Mohiuddin, Ahmed 1944- *WhoUN 92*
Mohiuddin, Syed Maqdoom 1934- *WhoAm 92*
Mohl, D. C. *Law&B 92*
Mohl, F. James 1948- *St&PR 93*
Mohl, Norman David 1931- *WhoE 93*
Mohleji, Satish Chandra 1940- *WhoSSW 93, WhoWor 93*
Mohlenbrock, Robert Herman, Jr. 1931- *WhoWrEP 92*
Mohlenbrok, Karen Marie 1963- *WhoEmL 93*
Mohler, Delmar Ray 1950- *WhoEmL 93*
Mohler, Mary Gail 1948- *WhoAm 92*
Mohler, Randall Lynn 1958- *WhoWrEP 92*
Mohler, Richard Edmond 1950- *St&PR 93*
Mohler, Richard Lee 1933- *WhoSSW 93*
Mohler, Ronald Rutt 1931- *WhoAm 92*
Mohler, Stanley Ross 1927- *WhoAm 92*
Mohler, Terence John *WhoWor 93*
Mohler, William Edward, III *Law&B 92*
Mohlie, Raymond Eugene 1928- *WhoAm 92*
Mohn, Blair B. 1959- *St&PR 93*
Mohn, David Prouty 1944- *WhoSSW 93*
Mohn, George William, Jr. 1935- *WhoE 93*
Mohn, J. Peter *Law&B 92*
Mohn, Melvin Paul 1926- *WhoAm 92*
Mohn, Reinhard 1921- *WhoWor 93*
Mohner, Carl Martin Rudolf 1921- *WhoSSW 93*
Mohner Langhamer, Wilma Maria 1942- *WhoAmW 93, WhoSSW 93*
Mohney, Franklin Walter 1927-1991 *BioIn 17*
Mohney, Ralph Wilson 1918- *WhoAm 92, WhoWor 93*
Mohnkern, Ann H. *Law&B 92*
Mohnkern, Ann Hubbell 1948- *WhoAmW 93*
Mohnkern, Lee P. *Law&B 92*
Mohorc, Daniel C. 1952- *St&PR 93*
Mohorovic, Jesse Roper 1942- *St&PR 93*
Mohorovicic, Andre 1913- *WhoScE 91-4*
Mohos, Ferenc 1942- *WhoScE 91-4*
Mohr, Anthony James 1947- *WhoEmL 93*
Mohr, Barbara Jean 1939- *WhoAmW 93*
Mohr, Barbara Jeanne 1953- *WhoAmW 93, WhoEmL 93*
Mohr, C. Donald *Law&B 92*
Mohr, Charles Donald 1930- *St&PR 93*
Mohr, Charles Jeffrey 1947- *St&PR 93*
Mohr, Charles T. *St&PR 93*
Mohr, Clarence L(ee) 1946- *ConAu 137*
Mohr, Cristina A. 1956- *WhoAm 92*
Mohr, Eric Simpson 1956- *WhoSSW 93*
Mohr, Frederick W., III 1927- *St&PR 93*
Mohr, Hans 1930- *WhoScE 91-3*
Mohr, J. Gary *Law&B 92*
Mohr, Jan Gunnar Faye 1921- *WhoScE 91-2*
Mohr, Jay Preston 1937- *WhoAm 92*
Mohr, Jeffrey Michael 1960- *WhoSSW 93*
Mohr, Jeffrey Thomas 1950- *WhoEmL 93*
Mohr, John Edward Springer *Law&B 92*
Mohr, John Luther 1911- *WhoAm 92, WhoWor 93*
Mohr, John R. *Law&B 92*
Mohr, Julian Boehm 1930- *WhoWor 93*
Mohr, Larry 1950- *St&PR 93*
Mohr, Lawrence Charles 1947- *WhoAm 92*
Mohr, Mary Hull 1934- *WhoAmW 93*
Mohr, Matthew D. 1960- *St&PR 93*
Mohr, Michael Arthur *Law&B 92*
Mohr, Milton Ernst 1915- *WhoAm 92*
Mohr, Myron George 1942- *WhoSSW 93*
Mohr, Nicholasa 1935- *BioIn 17, HispAmA [port], NotHsAW 93*
Mohr, Nicholasa (Golpe) 1935- *DcAmChF 1960*
Mohr, Paul 1931- *WhoScE 91-3*
Mohr, Robert Roy 1950- *WhoAm 92*
Mohr, Roger John 1931- *St&PR 93, WhoAm 92*
Mohr, Stephen F. *Law&B 92*
Mohr, Thomas Matthew 1951- *WhoEmL 93*
Mohr, William G. 1936- *St&PR 93*
Mohrfeld, Richard Gentel 1945- *WhoAm 92, WhoE 93*
Mohrhardt, Foster Edward 1907- *WhoAm 92, WhoWor 93*
Mohrhauser, James Edward 1922- *St&PR 93*
Mohri, Hideo 1930- *WhoWor 93*
Mohrle, Hans 1930- *WhoScE 91-3*
Mohrman, Kenneth A. 1932- *St&PR 93*
Mohrmann, J.C.J. *WhoScE 91-3*
Mohrmann, Johannes C.J. 1927- *WhoScE 91-3*
Mohs, Frederic Edward 1910- *WhoAm 92*
Mohsen, Amr 1947- *BioIn 17*
Mohsen, Mohamed Marwan 1933- *WhoUN 92*
Mohtadi, Shahruz 1955- *WhoEmL 93*
Mohtashemi, Ali Akbar *BioIn 17*
Mohwald, Helmuth 1946- *WhoScE 91-3*
Mohydin, Mohammed Abu Zafar 1928- *WhoWor 93*
Moi, arap Daniel 1924- *WhoAfr*
Moi, Daniel Arap *BioIn 17*
Moi, Daniel arap 1924- *DcTwHis, News 93-2 [port]*
Moily, Jaya Padubidri 1951- *WhoE 93*
Moinereau, Jacques Roger 1939- *WhoScE 91-2*
Moinet, Eric Emil 1952- *WhoEmL 93, WhoSSW 93*
Moir, Alfred Kummer 1924- *WhoAm 92, WhoWrEP 92*
Moir, Edward 1932- *WhoAm 92, WhoIns 93*
Moir, Graeme K. 1947- *WhoScE 91-1*
Moir, Margaret Ann 1958- *WhoAmW 93*
Moir, Monte *SoulM*
Moir, Robert J. *Law&B 92*
Moir, Robert Jesse 1942- *St&PR 93*
Moir, Ronald Brown, Jr. 1953- *WhoE 93*
Moir, Virgil Peter, III 1932- *St&PR 93*
Moiroux, Auguste F. 1928- *WhoScE 91-2*
Mois, Joseph *ScF&FL 92*
Moisan, Anne Sherman 1936- *WhoAmW 93*
Moisdon, Jean-Claude 1943- *WhoScE 91-2*
Moise, Edwin Evariste 1918- *WhoAm 92, WhoWrEP 92*
Moise, Rudolph 1954- *WhoSSW 93*
Moiseev, Alexei Alexeyevich 1932- *WhoUN 92*
Moiseev, Evgeny Ivanovich 1948- *WhoWor 93*
Moiseiwitsch, Benjamin Lawrence *WhoScE 91-1*
Moiseiwitsch, Benno 1890-1963 *Baker 92*
Moisen, Chandler Jon 1935- *St&PR 93*
Moishezon, Boris *BioIn 17*
Moisio, Tapani Jouko Ilmari 1934- *WhoScE 91-4*
Moisse, Gaston Jules 1928- *WhoWor 93*
Moita Dos Santos, C.J. 1926- *WhoScE 91-3*
Moix, Ana Maria 1947- *BioIn 17*
Moizer, Peter *WhoScE 91-1*
Mojadedi, Sibgatullah *NewYTBS 92 [port]*
Mojarro, Tomas 1932- *DcMexL*
Mojcher, J. Jeffrey *Law&B 92*
Mojden, Wallace William 1922- *St&PR 93*
Mojekwu, Victoria Ifeyinwa 1933- *WhoUN 92*
Mojica, Aurora 1939- *WhoAmW 93*
Mojovic, Bozidar Lj 1956- *WhoWor 93*
Mojsiewicz, Czestaw 1925- *WhoWor 93*
Mojsisovics, Roderich, Edler von 1877-1953 *Baker 92*
Mojsisovics-Mojsvar, Roderich, Elder von 1877-1953 *Baker 92*
Mojtabai, Ann Grace 1937- *WhoWrEP 92*
Mojzes, I. 1948- *WhoScE 91-4*
Mok, Carson Kwok-Chi 1932- *WhoE 93*
Mok, Mary Whun-Wa 1947- *WhoEmL 93*
Mok, Peter Pui Kwan 1938- *WhoE 93*
Mok, Soon Cheong 1946- *WhoWor 93*
Mok, William Shu-Lai 1959- *WhoEmL 93*
Moke, Anne Marie 1955- *WhoAmW 93*
Moke, Marilie 1941- *St&PR 93*
Moken, George L. *Law&B 92*
Mokhehle, Ntsu 1918- *WhoAfr*
Mokhiber, Albert *BioIn 17*
Mokhov, Oleg Ivanovich 1959- *WhoWor 93*
Mokios *OxDcByz*
Mokken, Robert Jan 1929- *WhoWor 93*
Mokodean, George David 1955- *St&PR 93*
Mokodean, Michael John 1923- *WhoAm 92*
Mokotoff, Michael 1939- *WhoE 93*
Mokranjac, Stevan 1856-1914 *Baker 92*
Mokranjac, Vasilije 1923-1984 *Baker 92*
Mokrasch, Lewis Carl 1930- *WhoAm 92*
Mokulis, Paula 1947- *WhoAmW 93, WhoEmL 93*
Mokyr, Joel 1946- *ConAu 136*
Molan, Herbert D. 1936- *St&PR 93*
Moland, Bruce U. *Law&B 92*
Molapo, Pius 1961- *WhoWor 93*
Molatto, Ronald H. 1948- *WhoIns 93*
Molay, Hilary S. *Law&B 92*
Molbak, Kare 1955- *WhoWor 93*
Molbeck, Rhonda Lynn 1967- *WhoAmW 93*
Molbegott, Mark Robert 1952- *WhoEmL 93*
Molchan, Thomas M. *Law&B 92*
Molchan, Thomas Michael 1955- *St&PR 93*
Molchanoff, Robert Michael 1932- *St&PR 93*
Molchanov, Igor Nikolaevich 1929- *WhoWor 93*
Molchanov, Il'ya Stepanovich 1962- *WhoWor 93*
Molchanov, Kirill (Vladimirovich) 1922-1982 *Baker 92*
Mold, Frederick, Jr. 1926- *WhoE 93*
Mold, Herman *WhoWrEP 92*
Moldave, Peter M. *Law&B 92*
Molden, Fredrik 1949- *WhoWor 93*
Molden, Herbert George 1912- *WhoAm 92*
Moldenhauer, Hans 1906-1987 *Baker 92*
Moldenhauer, Howard H. *Law&B 92*
Moldenhauer, Howard Herman 1929- *St&PR 93, WhoAm 92*
Moldenhauer, Joseph J. 1934- *ScF&FL 92*
Moldenhauer, Judith A. 1951- *WhoAm 92*
Moldenhauer, William Calvin 1923- *WhoAm 92*
Moldin, Richard Finley 1947- *St&PR 93*
Moldo, Byron Z. 1956- *WhoEmL 93*
Moldovan, Mihai 1937-1981 *Baker 92*
Moldovan, Virgil 1929- *WhoScE 91-4*
Moldover, Edward David 1926- *WhoE 93*
Moldover, Judith Ann *Law&B 92*
Moldover, Michael Robert 1940- *WhoE 93*
Moldow, Bruce J. *Law&B 92*
Moldvay, Lorand 1927- *WhoScE 91-4*
Mole, Harvey E. 1908- *St&PR 93*
Mole, Marie L. 1957- *WhoAmW 93*
Mole, Matthew C. *Law&B 92*
Mole, Mink *ScF&FL 92*
Molella, Arthur Philip 1944- *WhoAm 92*
Molen, George Marshall 1945- *WhoSSW 93*
Molen, Gerald Robert 1935- *WhoWor 93*
Molenaar, Martien 1949- *WhoScE 91-3*
Molendorp, Dayton H. 1947- *WhoIns 93*
Molenkamp, Rene John 1960- *WhoE 93*
Moler, Donald Lewis, Jr. 1955- *WhoEmL 93*
Moler, Edward Harold 1923- *WhoAm 92*
Moler, Elizabeth Anne 1949- *WhoAmW 93*
Moler, Spencer C. 1947- *St&PR 93*
Moler, William Cary 1937- *St&PR 93*
Molero, Wilson Joseph 1909- *WhoWrEP 92*
Moles, Douglas S. *Law&B 92*
Moles, Douglas Stewart *Law&B 92*
Moles, Nicholas *Law&B 92*
Moles, Robert L. 1941- *WhoAm 92*
Moles, Robert Leighton 1922- *WhoAm 92*
Molesworth, Mrs. 1839-1921 *ScF&FL 92*
Molesworth, Mary L. *ScF&FL 92*
Molesworth, Mary Louisa 1839-1921 *BioIn 17*
Molesworth, Thomas 1890-1977 *BioIn 17*
Molette, Carlton Woodard 1939- *WhoE 93*
Molev, Alexander Ivanovich 1961- *WhoWor 93*
Moley, Raymond C. 1886-1975 *PolPar*
Moley, Raymond Charles 1886-1975 *DcTwHis*
Molfino, Alessandra Mottola 1939- *WhoWor 93*
Molho, Anthony 1939- *WhoAm 92*
Molho, Emanuel 1936- *St&PR 93, WhoAm 92*
Molholm, Kurt Nelson 1937- *WhoAm 92, WhoSSW 93*
Molholt, Pat 1943- *WhoAm 92*
Molian, Samuel *WhoScE 91-1*
Moliere 1622?-1673 *MagSWL [port], WorLitC [port]*
Moliere, Gerard *WhoScE 91-2*
Moliere, Henriette Sylvie de d1683 *BioIn 17*
Molin, Charles *ConAu 37NR, MajAI*
Molin, Stanley 1941- *St&PR 93*
Molina, Antonio (Jesus) 1894-1980 *Baker 92*
Molina, Arturo *DcCPCAm*
Molina, Edwin *St&PR 93*
Molina, Gloria *BioIn 17*
Molina, Gloria 1948- *HispAmA [port], NotHsAW 93 [port], WhoAmW 93*
Molina, J. C. *Law&B 92*
Molina, Jacinto 1938- *BioIn 17*
Molina, John Francis 1950- *WhoE 93*
Molina, Maria Teresa 1932- *WhoAmW 93*
Molina, Marilyn Aguirre *NotHsAW 93*
Molina, Mario Jose 1943- *WhoAm 92*
Molina, R.S. *Law&B 92*
Molina, Rafael Leonidas Trujillo 1891-1961 *BioIn 17*
Molina, Richard, Jr. *Law&B 92*
Molina, Solomon Undag 1951- *WhoWor 93*
Molina, William Henry 1962- *WhoEmL 93*
Molinari, Bernardino 1880-1952 *Baker 92*
Molinari, Delmo Charles 1926- *St&PR 93*
Molinari, E. *WhoScE 91-3*
Molinari, Guy Victor 1928- *WhoE 93*
Molinari, Juan Alberto E. 1947- *WhoWor 93*
Molinari, Susan 1958- *BioIn 17, CngDr 91*
Molinari, Susan K. 1958- *WhoAm 92, WhoAmW 93, WhoE 93*
Molinari, William R. *WhoAm 92*
Molinari-Pradelli, Francesco 1911- *Baker 92, OxDcOp*
Molinaro, Albert Philip, Jr. 1928- *WhoAm 92*
Molinaro, Edouard 1928- *MiSFD 9*
Molinaro, Mario Andre 1952- *WhoE 93*
Molinaro, Robert 1949- *St&PR 93*
Molinaro, Thomas J. 1952- *St&PR 93*
Molinaro, Ursule *ScF&FL 92*
Molinaro, Valerie Ann 1956- *WhoAmW 93*
Molinder, John Irving 1941- *WhoAm 92*
Moline, Edwin Robert 1947- *WhoSSW 93*
Moline, Harold Emil 1939- *WhoE 93*
Moline, Jon Nelson 1937- *WhoAm 92*
Moline, Judith Ann 1941- *WhoWrEP 92*
Moline, Michael Edward 1953- *WhoEmL 93*
Moline, Michael S. *Law&B 92*
Molineaux, Charles Borromeo 1930- *WhoAm 92*
Molineaux, Louis 1932- *WhoUN 92*
Molinelli, Nimar Guillermo *Law&B 92*
Molinet, Joaquin S. *Law&B 92*
Molinier, Pierre 1900- *BioIn 17*
Molino, Jose A. *DcCPCAm*
Molino, Virginia Louise *Law&B 92*
Molino-Bonagura, Lory Jean 1964- *WhoE 93, WhoWor 93*
Molinski, Frank David 1944- *St&PR 93*
Molique, (Wilhelm) Bernhard 1802-1869 *Baker 92*
Molisa, Sela 1950- *WhoAsAP 91*
Moliteus, Magnus 1939- *St&PR 93*
Molitor, Donald J. 1948- *St&PR 93*
Molitor, Doris Jean 1957- *WhoAmW 93, WhoEmL 93, WhoWor 93*
Molitor, Gary William 1940- *WhoWor 93*
Molitor, Graham Thomas Tate 1934- *WhoAm 92, WhoWrEP 92*
Molitor, Margaret Anne 1920- *WhoAm 92*
Molitor, Paul *BioIn 17*
Molitor, Paul Leo 1956- *BiDAMSp 1989, WhoAm 92*
Molitor, Raphael 1873-1948 *Baker 92*
Molitor, Thomas Mark 1955- *St&PR 93*
Molitoris, Bruce Albert 1951- *WhoWor 93*
Molitoris, H. Peter 1935- *WhoScE 91-3*
Molitoris, Joseph John 1961- *WhoEmL 93*
Moliver, Morris *St&PR 93*
Molkenbuhr, M. Edward 1947- *St&PR 93*
Moll, Bertram Daniel 1926- *St&PR 93*
Moll, Clarence Russel 1913- *St&PR 93, WhoAm 92, WhoE 93, WhoWor 93*
Moll, Curtis E. 1933- *St&PR 93*
Moll, David Carter 1948- *WhoSSW 93, WhoWor 93*
Moll, Eberhard 1937- *WhoScE 91-4*
Moll, Edwin Allan 1934- *WhoWor 93*
Moll, Jack Auldin 1922- *St&PR 93*
Moll, John Edgar 1934- *St&PR 93, WhoAm 92, WhoWor 93*
Moll, John Lewis 1921- *WhoAm 92*
Moll, Kurt 1938- *Baker 92, IntDcOp, OxDcOp*
Moll, Lauretta Jane 1954- *WhoAmW 93*
Moll, Lloyd Henry 1925- *St&PR 93, WhoAm 92*
Moll, Manfred 1939- *WhoScE 91-2*
Moll, Otto E. 1929- *St&PR 93*
Moll, Richard L. 1938- *St&PR 93*
Moll, Robert C. 1933- *St&PR 93*
Moll, William Gene 1937- *St&PR 93*
Mollan, Raymond Alexander Boyce *WhoScE 91-1*
Mollard, Emile 1895-1991 *BioIn 17*
Mollard, John Douglas 1924- *WhoAm 92, WhoWor 93*
Mollberg, Rauni 1929- *MiSFD 9*
Molle, Kristian G. 1924- *WhoScE 91-2*
Molleda, Julio 1920- *WhoWor 93*
Mollegen, Albert Theodore, Jr. 1937- *St&PR 93, WhoAm 92*
Mollel, Tololwa 1952- *WhoCanL 92*
Mollel, Tololwa M. 1952- *ConAu 137*
Mollenauer, James F. *BioIn 17*
Mollendorff, Willi von 1872-1934 *Baker 92*
Mollenhauer, Eduard 1827-1914 *Baker 92*
Mollenhauer, Emil 1855-1927 *Baker 92*
Mollenhoff, Clark R. 1921-1991 *BioIn 17*
Mollenhoff, Clark Raymond 1921- *WhoWrEP 92*
Mollenkamp, James J. *Law&B 92*
Moller, Aage Richard 1932- *WhoWor 93*
Moller, Birgitte 1946- *WhoUN 92*
Moller, Claus Juan 1962- *WhoWor 93*
Moller, Detlev 1947- *WhoWor 93*
Moller, Dietrich 1927- *WhoScE 91-3*
Moller, Erik 1929- *WhoScE 91-2*
Moller, Eskil H. 1926- *WhoScE 91-4*
Moller, Goran 1931- *WhoScE 91-4*

Moller, Goran 1936- WhoScE 91-4, WhoWor 93
Moller, Hans 1905- WhoAm 92
Moller, Hans 1915- WhoWor 93
Moller, Hans Bjerrum 1932- WhoScE 91-2
Moller, Herbert W. St&PR 93
Moller, Ingolf J. 1928- WhoScE 91-2
Moller, Joachim Baker 92
Moller, John Christopher 1755-1803 Baker 92
Moller, Kjeld Rahbaek 1938- WhoWor 93
Moller, Louis C. 1943- WhoIns 93
Moller, M(athias) P(eter) 1855-1937 Baker 92
Moller, Morten 1942- WhoScE 91-2
Moller, Per 1955- WhoWor 93
Moller, Rolf WhoScE 91-3
Moller, William Richard, Jr. 1941- St&PR 93, WhoAm 92, WhoWor 93
Mollerick, Jeffrey D. 1958- St&PR 93
Moller-Larsen, Anne 1943- WhoScE 91-2
Mollerova, Jana 1948- WhoScE 91-4
Mollet, Chris John 1954- WhoEmL 93
Mollet, Guy 1905-1975 BioIn 17, DcTwHis
Molleur, Kermit Joseph 1936- St&PR 93
Molleur, Richard R. Law&B 92
Mollicone, Joe BioIn 17
Mollinet, Richard M. Law&B 92
Mollins, Herman 1926- St&PR 93
Mollison, Denis WhoScE 91-1
Mollison, Richard Devol 1916- WhoAm 92
Mollman, John Peter 1931- WhoAm 92
Mollo, Peter E. St&PR 93
Mollo-Christensen, Erik Leonard 1923- WhoAm 92, WhoE 93
Mollohan, Alan B. 1943- CngDr 91, WhoAm 92, WhoSSW 93
Mollohan, Helen Gail 1946- WhoWrEP 92
Mollohan, Jeannie Shirley 1959- WhoAmW 93
Mollon, Mark L. Law&B 92
Mollon, Roger Kevin 1952- WhoEmL 93
Mollov, Nikola 1926- WhoScE 91-4
Molloy, Donald Elliott Law&B 92
Molloy, Frances ConAu 138
Molloy, James Dennis 1943- WhoE 93
Molloy, James Lyman 1837-1909 Baker 92
Molloy, James T. 1936- CngDr 91
Molloy, Jim BioIn 17
Molloy, Jonathon Andrew 1958- St&PR 93
Molloy, Kenneth H. 1938- St&PR 93
Molloy, Lawrence T.P. 1956- WhoIns 93
Molloy, Richard J. Law&B 92
Molloy, Robert 1936- WhoWor 93
Molloy, Robert U. d1991 BioIn 17
Molloy, Spencer George 1927- St&PR 93
Molloy, Susanne Prattson 1952- St&PR 93
Molloy, William J. WhoScE 91-1
Molls, Vera Maria 1940- WhoAmW 93
Mollura, Carlos A. 1934- St&PR 93
Molmed, Stephen Jeffrey 1954- WhoE 93
Molnar, Alex BioIn 17
Molnar, Antal 1890-1983 Baker 92
Molnar, Anthony William 1938- WhoAm 92
Molnar, Bela 1934- WhoScE 91-4
Molnar, Bela 1951- WhoEmL 93
Molnar, Carrieann L. 1962- WhoAmW 93
Molnar, Charles Edwin 1935- WhoAm 92
Molnar, E.F. 1891-1986 ScF&FL 92
Molnar, Gary R. Law&B 92
Molnar, Janos 1934- WhoScE 91-4
Molnar, Jeno 1945- WhoScE 91-4
Molnar, Joseph 1936- WhoScE 91-4
Molnar, Kalman 1936- WhoScE 91-4
Molnar, Lawrence 1927- WhoE 93, WhoWor 93
Molnar, Michael R. 1945- St&PR 93
Molnar, Thomas 1921- WhoAm 92, WhoWrEP 92
Molnar, Thomas J. 1944- St&PR 93
Molne, Kare 1933- WhoScE 91-4
Moloff, Alan Lawrence 1954- WhoSSW 93
Moloney, Donal 1931- WhoScE 91-3
Moloney, Marianne Scanlon WhoAmW 93
Moloney, T.J. Law&B 92
Moloney, Terrence Patrick 1960- WhoWrEP 92
Moloney, Thomas E. 1943- St&PR 93
Moloney, Thomas Walter 1946- WhoAm 92
Molony, Douglas A. Law&B 92
Molony, Gretchen St&PR 93
Molony, Michael Janssens, Jr. 1922- WhoAm 92, WhoSSW 93, WhoWor 93
Molotov, Vyacheslav Michailovich 1890-1986 ColdWar 2 [port]
Molotov, Vyacheslav Mikhailovich 1890-1986 DcTwHis
Molpus, C. Manly 1941- WhoAm 92
Molpus, Dick 1949- WhoAm 92, WhoSSW 93
Molson, E.H. 1937- St&PR 93
Molson, Eric H. 1937- WhoAm 92, WhoWor 93
Molson, Francis J. 1932- ScF&FL 92
Molster, Charles B., Jr. 1928- St&PR 93
Molt, Angela 1913- DcMexL
Molt, Cynthia Marylee 1957- ConAu 138, WhoAmW 93, WhoEmL 93
Molter, Colleen Patricia 1957- WhoAmW 93
Molter, Johann Melchior 1696-1765 Baker 92
Molter, Lynne Ann 1957- WhoE 93
Molter, William 1910-1960 BiDAMSp 1989
Moltke, Freya von BioIn 17
Moltke, Helmuth James, Graf von 1907-1945 BioIn 17
Moltke, Helmuth Johannes Ludwig von 1848-1916 HarEnMi
Moltke, Helmuth Karl Bernhard von 1800-1891 HarEnMi
Moltmann, Jurgen Dankwart 1926- WhoWor 93
Moltz, James Edward 1932- St&PR 93, WhoAm 92
Moltzau, Hughitt Gregory 1914- WhoSSW 93
Molva, Engin Sevket 1954- WhoWor 93
Molyneaux, James Henry 1920- WhoWor 93
Molyneaux, Margaret Mary 1961- WhoE 93
Molyneax, Lyle Gordon 1934- St&PR 93
Molyneux, David Hurst WhoScE 91-1
Molyneux, Juan Pablo BioIn 17
Molyneux, Michael 1944- St&PR 93
Molz, Emmet George 1922- St&PR 93
Molz, Fred John, III 1943- WhoAm 92
Molz, Redmond Kathleen 1928- WhoAm 92
Molz, Robert Joseph 1937- WhoAm 92
Molzahn, Johannes 1892-1965 BioIn 17
Molzahn, S.W. WhoScE 91-1
Molzen, Dayton Frank 1926- WhoAm 92
Momaday, N. Scott BioIn 17
Momaday, N. Scott 1934- MagSAmL [port]
Momaday, Natachee Scott DcAmChF 1960
Momaday, Navarre Scott 1934- WhoAm 92, WhoWrEP 92
Momah, Reginald C. Law&B 92
Moman, Chips 1936- SoulM
Momayez, Fred 1952- St&PR 93
Momayez-Zadeh, Hamid R. 1955- St&PR 93
Momayez-Zadeh, Hamid Reza 1955- WhoEmL 93
Momayez-Zadeh, Majid R. 1963- St&PR 93
Mombelli, Alessandro OxDcOp
Mombelli, Anna 1795- OxDcOp
Mombelli, Domenico 1751-1835 OxDcOp
Mombelli, Ester 1794- OxDcOp
Mombelli, Luisa Laschi 176-?-c. 1790 OxDcOp
Momcilo d1345 OxDcByz
Momigliano, Arnaldo BioIn 17
Momigny, Jerome-Joseph de 1762-1842 Baker 92
Momirovic, Konstantin 1932- WhoScE 91-4
Momis, John 1942- WhoAsAP 91
Momjian, Set Charles 1930- WhoAm 92
Mommaerts, Barbara Gloria 1939- WhoAmW 93
Mommer, Kerri E. 1958- St&PR 93
Mommertz, Karl Heinz 1929- WhoScE 91-3
Mommsen, Katharina 1925- WhoAm 92
Mommsen, Theodor 1817-1903 BioIn 17
Mommsen, Wolfgang Justin 1930- WhoWor 93
Momoh, Joseph Saidu 1937- WhoAfr, WhoWor 93
Momoki, Kozo 1921- WhoWor 93
Mompean Rodriguez, Luis 1929- WhoScE 91-3
Momper, Arthur William 1950 WhoEmL 93
Mompou, Federico 1893-1987 Baker 92
Momsen, Wiliam Laurence 1932- WhoWrEP 92
Mona, David Luther 1943- St&PR 93
Mona, Stephen Francis 1957- WhoEmL 93, WhoSSW 93
Monacelli, Amleto Andres 1961- HispAmA [port]
Monacelli, Gianfranco 1939- WhoAm 92
Monachino, Francis Leonard WhoAm 92
Monack, Ronald Albert 1929- St&PR 93
Monaco, Anthony Peter 1932- WhoAm 92
Monaco, Daniel Joseph 1922- WhoWor 93
Monaco, David 1955- St&PR 93
Monaco, Eugene A. St&PR 93
Monaco, James 1942- WhoWrEP 92
Monaco, James Frederick 1942- WhoE 93
Monaco, Joseph R. 1945- WhoAm 92
Monaco, Mario A. Law&B 92
Monaco, Mario del Baker 92
Monaco, Michael P. WhoAm 92
Monaco, Richard 1940- ScF&FL 92
Monaco, Vincenzo WhoScE 91-3
Monaco, Vito Antonio 1932- WhoScE 91-3
Monaghan, Dennis Michael 1943- St&PR 93
Monaghan, Eileen 1911- WhoAm 92
Monaghan, J.J. WhoScE 91-1
Monaghan, James Edward, Jr. 1947- WhoEmL 93
Monaghan, James J. 1938- WhoScE 91-1
Monaghan, James Peter 1927- St&PR 93
Monaghan, John Michael 1944- WhoScE 91-3
Monaghan, John Patrick 1954- WhoSSW 93
Monaghan, John T. 1943- St&PR 93
Monaghan, Mary L. AmWomPl
Monaghan, Mary Patricia 1946- WhoWrEP 92
Monaghan, Nancy C. 1945- WhoAmW 93
Monaghan, Patricia 1946- WhoAmW 93
Monaghan, Paul 1950- WhoScE 91-1
Monaghan, Rinty 1920-1984 BioIn 17
Monaghan, Robert Emmet 1931- St&PR 93
Monaghan, Thomas BioIn 17
Monaghan, Thomas Stephen 1937- WhoAm 92
Monaghan, William Henry 1928- St&PR 93, WhoAm 92
Monaghan, William Patrick 1944- WhoE 93
Monagle, Daniel E. Law&B 92
Monago, Frank Anthony 1941- St&PR 93
Monahan, Bernard Patrick 1936- St&PR 93
Monahan, Brent 1948- ScF&FL 92
Monahan, Catherine E. 1949- WhoIns 93
Monahan, Edward Charles 1936- WhoE 93
Monahan, Edward F. 1928- St&PR 93
Monahan, Edward Francis 1928- WhoAm 92
Monahan, Gayle 1941- WhoE 93
Monahan, George Francis 1939- WhoSSW 93
Monahan, George Lennox, Jr. 1933- WhoAm 92
Monahan, Janice L. Law&B 92
Monahan, John 1946- BioIn 17
Monahan, John E. 1940- St&PR 93
Monahan, Kathleen Mary 1938- WhoAmW 93
Monahan, Leo 1933- BioIn 17
Monahan, Marie Terry 1927- WhoAmW 93
Monahan, Thomas Andrew, Jr. 1920- WhoE 93
Monahan, Thomas F., Jr. 1939- St&PR 93
Monahan, Thomas Paul 1951- WhoSSW 93
Monahan, William Louis 1940- St&PR 93
Monajem, Fred 1931- St&PR 93
Monan, James Donald 1924- WhoAm 92, WhoE 93
Monarch, G. Huston 1954- St&PR 93
Monares, Anibal 1938- WhoUN 92
Monarque, Steven BioIn 17
Monas, Steve S. 1946- St&PR 93
Monasee, Charles Arthur 1924- WhoAm 92
Monash, John 1865-1931 DcTwHis, HarEnMi
Monasta, Gregorio 1938- WhoUN 92
Monasterio, Jesus de 1836-1903 Baker 92
Monastra, Francesco 1939- WhoScE 91-3
Monat, William Robert 1924- WhoAm 92
Monat-Haller, Rosalyn Kramer 1945- WhoSSW 93
Monberg, Torben Axel 1929- WhoWor 93
Moncada, Eduardo Hernandez Baker 92
Moncada, Jose Maria DcCPCAm
Moncada, L. Patricia Law&B 92
Moncada Vigo, Gilberto Alejandro 1956- WhoWor 93
Moncarraz, Raul HispAmA [port]
Moncaster, Michael Edward 1937- WhoScE 91-1
Moncayo Garcia, Jose Pablo 1912-1958 Baker 92
Moncayo-Medina, Alvaro 1941- WhoUN 92
Moncey, Bon Adrien Jeannot de 1754-1842 HarEnMi
Monch, Winfried 1934- WhoScE 91-3
Moncharsh, Jane Kline 1943- WhoAmW 93
Monchick, Louis 1927- WhoE 93
Moncik, Bonnie Shnier St&PR 93
Monck, George 1608-1670 HarEnMi
Monck, Margaret 1911-1991 BioIn 17
Monck, Sarah Knight 1961- WhoAmW 93
Moncomble, Dominique WhoScE 91-2
Moncreiff, Robert P. 1930- St&PR 93, WhoAm 92
Moncrief, Kit Tennison 1952- WhoSSW 93
Moncrief, Lawrence E. Law&B 92
Moncrief, Mary Kathryn 1955- WhoAmW 93
Moncrief, Sidney BioIn 17
Moncrieff, Isabel AmWomPl
Moncur, Carolee 1940- WhoAmW 93
Moncure, Ashby Carter 1934- WhoWor 93
Moncure, James Ashby 1926- WhoAm 92
Moncure, John Lewis 1930- WhoAm 92
Mond, Bernhard Stanislaw 1887-1944 PolBiDi
Mond, Keith Law&B 92
Mond, Keith 1935- St&PR 93
Monda, Keith 1946- St&PR 93
Monda, Marilyn 1956- WhoAmW 93
Mondadori, Katherine BioIn 17
Mondadori, Laura d1991 BioIn 17
Mondadori, Leonardo BioIn 17
Mondal, Mohammad Abdul Kayum 1945- WhoWor 93
Mondale, Joan Adams 1930- WhoAm 92
Mondale, Walter F. 1928- BioIn 17, PolPar
Mondale, Walter Frederick 1928- WhoAm 92, WhoWor 93
Mondanaro, Philip J. 1950- WhoIns 93
Mondani, Thomas Patrick, Sr. 1934- WhoE 93
Mondavi, Robert BioIn 17
Mondavi Family BioIn 17
Monday, John C. 1925- St&PR 93
Monday, John Christian 1925- WhoAm 92
Monday, Jon Ellis 1947- WhoWor 93
Monday, Mitch Dow 1951- St&PR 93
Monday, Robert James 1945- BiDAMSp 1989
Mondecar, Mercedes Consuelo 1951- WhoEmL 93
Mondelli, Rosanna 1934- WhoScE 91-3
Mondello, John Paul 1948- WhoE 93, WhoWor 93
Mondello, Nuncio F. d1992 NewYTBS 92
Monder, Steven I. 1945- WhoAm 92
Monderer, Howard Law&B 92
Mondini, G. Franco Law&B 92
Mondino, Aldo 1938- BioIn 17
Mondino, Gian Paolo 1933- WhoScE 91-3
Mondino, Jean-Baptiste BioIn 17
Mondlin, Marvin 1927- WhoE 93, WhoWor 93
Mondolfo, Paolo 1943- WhoWor 93
Mondonville, Jean-Joseph Cassanea de 1711?-1772 Baker 92, OxDcOp
Mondor, Kenneth James 1949- WhoAm 92
Mondore, Patricia Anne 1956- WhoE 93
Mondovi, Bruno 1927- WhoScE 91-3
Mondragon, Carlos 1950- WhoSSW 93
Mondragon, Lawrence A. Law&B 92
Mondragon Aguirre, Magdalena 1913- DcMexL
Mondre, Erwin 1940- WhoScE 91-4
Mondrian, Piet 1872-1944 BioIn 17
Mondriguez, Amalia Mercedes 1953- WhoSSW 93
Mondry, Florence BioIn 17
Mondry, Ira 1953- St&PR 93
Mondschein, Susan Richardson 1943- WhoAmW 93
Mondt, Denise Law&B 92
Mondy, Nell Irene 1921- WhoAm 92
Mone, Bernard J. 1940- WhoIns 93
Mone, Robert Paul 1934- WhoAm 92
Monegal, Emir Rodriguez ScF&FL 92
Moneghetti, Steve BioIn 17
Monek, Donna Marie 1947- WhoAmW 93
Monek, Francis Herman 1913- WhoAm 92
Monell, Nathan Reed 1957- WhoSSW 93
Monelli, Raffaele 1782-1859 OxDcOp
Monelli, Savino 1784-1836 OxDcOp
Monello, Joseph D. 1945- St&PR 93
Monemar, Bo Anders Ingemar 1942- WhoScE 91-4
Moneo, Jose Rafael 1937- WhoAm 92
Moneret-Vautrin, Denise Anne 1939- WhoScE 91-2
Mones, Federico Quinagon 1934- WhoWor 93
Mones, Joan Michele 1952- WhoSSW 93
Mones, Paul ConAu 138, MiSFD 9
Monesson, Harry S. 1935- WhoE 93
Monestel, Alejandro 1865-1950 Baker 92
Monet, Claude 1840-1926 BioIn 17
Monet, Maria P. BioIn 17
Monet, Maria Pereira 1949- WhoAm 92, WhoAmW 93, WhoWor 93
Monet, Philippe Jacques Law&B 92
Monette, Donald J. 1934- St&PR 93
Monette, John Philip 1954- WhoEmL 93
Monette, Paul 1945?- ConAu 139, ConGAN

Monette, Paul 1946?- *ScF&FL 92*
Money, Charles Stewart 1941- *St&PR 93*
Money, Jack W. 1929- *St&PR 93*
Money, James E. 1942- *St&PR 93*
Money, John William 1921- *WhoAm 92*
Money, Margaret Sarah 1942- *WhoAmW 93*
Money-Coutts, P.A.C. 1932- *WhoScE 91-1*
Moneypenny, Edward William 1942- *St&PR 93, WhoAm 92*
Monferrato, Angela Maria 1948- *WhoAmW 93*
Monfils, Andre G.V.M. 1925- *WhoScE 91-2*
Monfort, Josep M. 1954- *WhoScE 91-3*
Monfort, Kenneth 1928- *St&PR 93*
Monfort, Narciso D. 1928- *WhoAsAP 91*
Monfort, Richard L. 1954- *WhoAm 92*
Monfred, Avenir de 1903-1974 *Baker 92*
Monfried, Thomas S. 1932- *St&PR 93*
Monfroglio, Angelo 1951- *WhoWor 93*
Mong, Robert William, Jr. 1939- *WhoSSW 93*
Mong, Ronald W. 1955- *St&PR 93*
Mongan, Agnes 1905- *WhoAm 92*
Mongan, James John 1942- *WhoAm 92*
Mongan, Marie Madeline 1933- *WhoE 93*
Mongan, Thomas R. *St&PR 93*
Mongan, Tod V. *Law&B 92*
Mongan, Tod Vernon 1950- *St&PR 93*
Mongardi, Gianfranco 1933- *WhoIns 93*
Mongbe, Rene Valery 1939- *WhoUN 92*
Monge, Antonio 1942- *WhoScE 91-3*
Monge, Carl Albert, Jr. 1930- *St&PR 93*
Monge Alvarez, Luis Alberto 1925- *DcCPCAm*
Mongeau, David C. *Law&B 92*
Mongeau, David C. 1956- *St&PR 93*
Mongella, Gertrude Ibengwe 1945- *WhoAfr*
Mongelli, Thomas Guy 1952- *WhoE 93, WhoEmL 93, WhoWor 93*
Monge Pacheco, Emilio 1944- *WhoScE 91-3*
Monger, Christopher 1950- *MiSFD 9*
Monger, James William Heron 1937- *WhoAm 92*
Mongereau, N. *WhoScE 91-2*
Monget, Jean-Marie 1944- *WhoScE 91-2*
Mongiardini, Vittorio 1923- *WhoScE 91-3*
Mongiardino, Renzo *BioIn 17*
Mongilardi, Erman Piero 1932- *WhoWor 93*
Mongillo, Romolo T. 1939- *St&PR 93*
Mongin, Pierre *WhoScE 91-2*
Mongini, Pietro 1828-1874 *OxDcOp*
Mongiovi, Gary Vincent 1957- *WhoE 93*
Mongkul Kanjanapas *BioIn 17*
Mongold, Sandra K. 1947- *WhoAmW 93*
Mongole, Larry 1949- *St&PR 93*
Monguno, Shettima Ali (Alhaji) 1926- *WhoAfr*
Monheit, Alan Goodman 1949- *WhoE 93*
Monheit, Barbara A. *Law&B 92*
Monhemius, Andrew John 1942- *WhoWor 93*
Monhollon, Jimmie R. 1933- *St&PR 93*
Monhollon, Leland 1925- *WhoSSW 93*
Monia, Joan 1938- *WhoAmW 93*
Monica, Saint 332-387 *BioIn 17*
Monica, Laura L. 1957- *St&PR 93*
Monical, Robert Duane 1925- *WhoAm 92*
Monicelli, Mario 1915- *MiSFD 9*
Monien, Burkhard 1943- *WhoScE 91-3*
Monier, R. *WhoScE 91-2*
Moniglia, Giovanni Andrea 1624-1700 *OxDcOp*
Monihan, Mary Elizabeth 1957- *WhoEmL 93*
Monin, Andre 1924- *WhoScE 91-2*
Monin, Lawrence Owen *Law&B 92*
Monin, Lawrence Owen 1942- *WhoIns 93*
Monin, Robert C. 1948- *WhoEmL 93*
Monis, Ernest 1846-1929 *BioIn 17*
Monismith, Carl Leroy 1926- *WhoAm 92*
Monita, Alfonso 1942- *St&PR 93*
Monitz, Jay L. *Law&B 92*
Monius, David Anthony 1956- *WhoE 93*
Moniuszko, Stanislaw 1819-1872 *Baker 92, IntDcOp, OxDcOp, PolBiDi*
Moniuszko-Jakoniuk, Janina 1943- *WhoScE 91-4*
Moniz, Antonio Brandao 1956- *WhoWor 93*
Monjo, F(erdinand) N(icholas, III) 1924-1978 *ConAu 37NR, MajAI*
Monjo, John Cameron 1931- *WhoAm 92, WhoWor 93*
Monjoie, Alberic 1937- *WhoScE 91-2*
Monjoy, Michael Anthony *Law&B 92*
Monk, Allan James 1942- *WhoAm 92*
Monk, Art 1957- *News 93-2 [port], WhoAm 92*
Monk, Charlene Faye 1951- *WhoSSW 93*
Monk, Christopher 1921-1991 *BioIn 17*
Monk, Darilyn Anita 1951- *WhoAmW 93, WhoEmL 93*
Monk, Douglas R. 1945- *St&PR 93*
Monk, Edwin George 1819-1900 *Baker 92*
Monk, Julius *BioIn 17*
Monk, Julius Withers 1920- *WhoAm 92*
Monk, Kathy Charlotte 1955- *WhoAmW 93*
Monk, Meredith *MiSFD 9*
Monk, Meredith 1942- *BioIn 17*
Monk, Meredith (Jane) 1942- *Baker 92, WhoAm 92*
Monk, Raymond 1925- *ConAu 136*
Monk, Robert Clarence 1930- *WhoSSW 93*
Monk, Sean Charles 1916- *WhoWrEP 92*
Monk, Thelonious 1917-1982 *Baker 92, BioIn 17*
Monk, William Henry 1823-1889 *Baker 92*
Monke, Edwin John 1925- *WhoAm 92*
Monkemeier, Edward Norbert 1926- *St&PR 93*
Monkhouse, Bob 1928- *QDrFCA 92 [port]*
Monkman, Forest C. 1929- *St&PR 93*
Monk-Reaves, Antonia Lucette 1965- *WhoAmW 93*
Monks, Donald Richard 1948- *WhoAm 92*
Monks, Robert Augustus Gardner 1933- *WhoAm 92*
Monleone, Domenico 1875-1942 *Baker 92*
Monleon-Pradas, Manuel 1959- *WhoWor 93*
Monluc, Blaise de Lasseran-Massencome, Seigneur of 1501?-1577 *HarEnMi*
Monmonier, Mark 1943- *WhoAm 92*
Monmouth, James Scott, Duke of 1649-1685 *HarEnMi*
Monn, Gordon R. *St&PR 93*
Monn, Johann Christoph 1726-1782 *Baker 92*
Monn, Matthias Georg 1717-1750 *Baker 92*
Monnerville, Gaston 1897-1991 *BioIn 17*
Monnet, Jacques 1946- *WhoScE 91-2*
Monnet, Jean 1703-1785 *OxDcOp*
Monnet, Jean 1888-1979 *BioIn 17, ColdWar 1 [port], DcTwHis*
Monnet, Raymond *WhoScE 91-2*
Monnett, John Hamilton 1944- *WhoWrEP 92*
Monnett, Kenneth Eugene 1936- *St&PR 93*
Monney, Paul-Andre 1961- *WhoWor 93*
Monni, Raimo *WhoScE 91-4*
Monnich, John Robert 1947- *WhoEmL 93*
Monnier, Philippe *MiSFD 9*
Monnig, John J. 1951- *St&PR 93*
Monnig, Oscar 1902- *BioIn 17*
Monnikendam, Marius 1896-1977 *Baker 92*
Monnin, Michael J. 1951- *St&PR 93*
Monning, Richard Frank 1946- *WhoE 93*
Monninger, Robert Harold George 1918- *WhoAm 92, WhoWor 93*
Monod, Hugues *WhoScE 91-2*
Monod, Jacques-Louis 1927- *Baker 92*
Monohan, K.C. *BioIn 17*
Mononen, Sakari (Tuomo) 1928- *Baker 92*
Monos, Emil 1935- *WhoScE 91-4*
Monosson, Adolf F. 1926- *St&PR 93*
Monoyios, Nikolaos D. 1949- *St&PR 93*
Monpere, Carol *MiSFD 9*
Monpou, Hippolyte 1804-1841 *OxDcOp*
Monpou, (Francois Louis) Hyppolite 1804-1841 *Baker 92*
Monrad, Elizabeth A. 1954- *WhoIns 93*
Monrad, Ernest E. 1930- *St&PR 93*
Monrad, Ernest Ejner 1930- *WhoAm 92*
Monrad, Ernest Scott 1953- *WhoE 93*
Monrad Johansen, David *Baker 92*
Monreal, Gerhard 1928- *WhoScE 91-3*
Monro, Alastair M. 1934- *WhoScE 91-2*
Monro, C. Bedell 1901-1972 *EncABHB 8 [port]*
Monro, Charles Carmichael 1860-1929 *HarEnMi*
Monro, Jean *BioIn 17*
Monroche, Andre Victor Jacques 1941- *WhoWor 93*
Monroe, Andromeda *Law&B 92*
Monroe, Arianne Hale *Law&B 92*
Monroe, Barbara 1913- *St&PR 93*
Monroe, Bill 1911- *Baker 92*
Monroe, Brooks 1925- *St&PR 93, WhoAm 92*
Monroe, Burt Leavelle, Jr. 1930- *WhoAm 92*
Monroe, Carl Dean, III 1960- *WhoE 93*
Monroe, Charles L., III 1943- *St&PR 93*
Monroe, Charles McCantlas, Jr. 1940- *WhoSSW 93*
Monroe, Christopher John 1951- *WhoEmL 93*
Monroe, Clarence A. d1990 *BioIn 17*
Monroe, Denise Angela Bakema 1961- *WhoAmW 93*
Monroe, Donald 1888-1972 *ScF&FL 92*
Monroe, Elizabeth Kortright 1768-1830 *BioIn 17*
Monroe, Eric George 1944- *WhoWor 93*
Monroe, Frederick Leroy 1942- *WhoWor 93*
Monroe, Gerald Morgan 1919- *WhoAm 92*
Monroe, Harriet 1860-1936 *AmWomPl, BioIn 17, JrnUS*
Monroe, Harriet Earhart 1842- *AmWomPl*
Monroe, Haskell M., Jr. 1931- *WhoAm 92, WhoWor 93*
Monroe, Helen Leola 1931- *WhoSSW 93*
Monroe, Herman Eugene, Jr. 1930- *St&PR 93*
Monroe, James 1758-1831 *BioIn 17, HarEnMi, PolPar*
Monroe, James 1821-1898 *BioIn 17*
Monroe, James C., Jr. 1948- *St&PR 93*
Monroe, James W. 1942- *AfrAmBi*
Monroe, James Walter 1936- *WhoAm 92*
Monroe, John B. *ScF&FL 92*
Monroe, Karen R. *Law&B 92*
Monroe, Keith 1917-1973 *ScF&FL 92*
Monroe, Kendyl Kurth 1936- *WhoAm 92*
Monroe, L. A. J. 1919- *WhoAm 92*
Monroe, Lee Alexander 1932- *WhoAm 92*
Monroe, Lyle *MajAI*
Monroe, Marilyn 1926-1962 *BioIn 17, IntDcF 2-3 [port]*
Monroe, Mark A. *Law&B 92*
Monroe, Mark Eden 1954- *St&PR 93*
Monroe, Mary *ScF&FL 92*
Monroe, Mary Beth 1947- *WhoEmL 93, WhoSSW 93*
Monroe, Max 1956- *WhoSSW 93*
Monroe, Melrose 1919- *WhoAmW 93, WhoSSW 93*
Monroe, Michael J. 1948- *St&PR 93*
Monroe, Michael James 1948- *WhoAm 92*
Monroe, Murray Shipley 1925- *WhoAm 92, WhoWor 93*
Monroe, N. Carl 1921- *St&PR 93*
Monroe, Patrick Wininger 1941- *WhoSSW 93*
Monroe, Paula Ruth 1951- *WhoAmW 93*
Monroe, Rita M. 1941- *WhoAmW 93*
Monroe, Robert A. *BioIn 17*
Monroe, Robert Rawson 1927- *WhoAm 92*
Monroe, Rose Maria Mask 1955- *WhoE 93*
Monroe, Russell Ronald 1920- *WhoAm 92*
Monroe, Sandra Lee 1955- *WhoEmL 93*
Monroe, Stanley Edwin 1902- *WhoWor 93*
Monroe, Stephen Noel 1957- *WhoEmL 93*
Monroe, Thomas Edward 1947- *WhoAm 92*
Monroe, Thomas Frank 1944- *WhoAm 92*
Monroe, Thomas O. 1948- *St&PR 93*
Monroe, Vernon Earl, Jr. 1944- *WhoAm 92*
Monroe, Virginia Marie 1933- *WhoAmW 93*
Monroe, Wayne K. 1954- *St&PR 93*
Monroe, William 1876?-1915? *BiDAMSp 1989*
Monroe, William Eugene 1930- *St&PR 93, WhoSSW 93*
Monroe, William Frank 1952- *WhoSSW 93*
Monroe, William John 1964- *WhoE 93*
Monroe, William Lewis 1941- *WhoAm 92*
Monroe, William R. 1921- *St&PR 93*
Monroe, William Smith 1911- *WhoAm 92*
Monroy, Gladys H. 1937- *WhoAmW 93*
Monroy Cabra, Jaime Enrique 1935- *WhoWor 93*
Monsalve, Martha Eugenia 1968- *WhoSSW 93*
Monsanto, Pablo *DcCPCAm*
Monsarrat, Nicholas 1910-1979 *ScF&FL 92*
Monsees, Gregg Peters, Sr. 1949- *St&PR 93*
Monsees, James Eugene 1937- *WhoAm 92*
Monsees, Warren R. 1922- *St&PR 93*
Monsell, Elizabeth G. 1955- *St&PR 93*
Monsell, Helen Albee 1895- *AmWomPl*
Monsell, Stephen *WhoScE 91-1*
Monsen, Elaine Ranker 1935- *WhoAm 92, WhoWor 93*
Monsen, Raymond Joseph, Jr. 1931- *WhoAm 92*
Monseur, Xavier Guillaume Antoine 1923- *WhoScE 91-2*
Monsigny, Michel L.P. 1941- *WhoScE 91-2*
Monsigny, Pierre-Alexandre 1729-1817 *Baker 92, OxDcOp*
Monsivais, Carlos 1938- *DcMexL*
Monsky, John Bertrand 1930- *WhoAm 92*
Monsky, Michael David Wolf Von Sommer 1947- *WhoEmL 93*
Monsma, Robbie E. *Law&B 92*
Monsma, Robbie E. 1952- *St&PR 93*
Monson, Ann Marie 1951- *WhoEmL 93*
Monson, Arch, Jr. 1913- *WhoAm 92*
Monson, Carol Lynn 1946- *WhoEmL 93, WhoWor 93*
Monson, David Smith 1945- *WhoAm 92*
Monson, Dianne Lynn 1934- *WhoAmW 93*
Monson, Forrest Truman 1915- *WhoAm 92*
Monson, James Edward 1932- *WhoAm 92*
Monson, John Rowat Telford 1956- *WhoWor 93*
Monson, Judith *BioIn 17*
Monson, Kevin Wayne 1951- *WhoEmL 93*
Monson, Nancy Peckel 1959- *WhoAmW 93*
Monson, Robert Joseph 1947- *WhoEmL 93*
Monson, Thomas A. *Law&B 92*
Monson, Thomas Spencer 1927- *St&PR 93, WhoAm 92*
Monster, Aart C. 1944- *WhoScE 91-3*
Montag, A. *WhoScE 91-3*
Montag, Anthony 1934- *St&PR 93*
Montag, David 1954- *St&PR 93*
Montag, Diane *BioIn 17*
Montag, Ulrich Johannes 1938- *WhoWor 93*
Montag, Volker *St&PR 93*
Montaggioni, Francois 1931- *St&PR 93*
Montagna, Richard A. 1948- *St&PR 93*
Montagna, William 1913- *WhoAm 92*
Montagnana, Antonio fl. 1730-1750 *OxDcOp*
Montagner, Hubert *WhoScE 91-2*
Montagnier, Luc *BioIn 17*
Montagnier, Luc Antoine 1932- *WhoWor 93*
Montagnino, James G. 1941- *St&PR 93*
Montagu, Lady 1689-1762 *BioIn 17*
Montagu, Ashley 1905- *IntDcAn, WhoAm 92*
Montagu, Edwin Samuel 1879-1924 *BioIn 17*
Montagu, Ewen 1901-1985 *BioIn 17*
Montagu, John 1718-1792 *BioIn 17*
Montagu, Lodovick *ScF&FL 92*
Montagu, Venetia Stanley 1887-1948 *BioIn 17*
Montague, Brian John 1951- *WhoAm 92*
Montague, Charles Howard *ScF&FL 92*
Montague, David Ririe 1944- *WhoWrEP 92*
Montague, Diana 1954- *OxDcOp*
Montague, Gary Leslie 1939- *WhoWor 93*
Montague, J. David *Law&B 92*
Montague, John *BioIn 17*
Montague, Kevin Frederick Francis 1956- *WhoEmL 93*
Montague, Owen Douglas 1962- *WhoAm 92*
Montague, Peter *WhoScE 91-1*
Montague, Sally 1944- *WhoAmW 93*
Montague, Stephen (Rowley) 1943- *Baker 92*
Montague, William Patrick 1946- *St&PR 93*
Montagu-Nathan, M(ontagu) 1877-1958 *Baker 92*
Montagut-Buscas, Miguel 1920- *WhoScE 91-3*
Montaigne, Michel de 1533-1592 *BioIn 17, MagSWL [port], WorLitC [port]*
Montalban, Carlos d1991 *BioIn 17*
Montalban, Ricardo 1920- *HispAmA [port], WhoAm 92*
Montalbano, Joseph Edward 1927- *WhoAm 92*
Montalbano, Salvatore Aurelio 1938- *WhoSSW 93*
Montalbine, Carl T. *St&PR 93*
Montalcini, Rita Levi- 1909- *BioIn 17*
Montaldo, Giuliano 1930- *MiSFD 9*
Montale, Eugenio 1896-1981 *BioIn 17*
Montalembert, comte de 1810-1870 *BioIn 17*
Montalto, Richard Michael 1951- *WhoSSW 93*
Montalvo, Jose Luis 1946- *WhoWrEP 92*
Montalvo, Walter A. 1950- *WhoWor 93*
Montambaux, Gilles Jean 1955- *WhoWor 93*
Montan, Cheryl A. *Law&B 92*
Montana, Arthur 1935- *WhoAm 92*
Montana, Claude *BioIn 17*
Montana, Claude 1949- *CurBio 92 [port]*
Montana, Joe *BioIn 17*
Montana, Jordi 1949- *WhoEmL 93, WhoWor 93*
Montana, Joseph C., Jr. 1956- *WhoAm 92*
Montana, Patrick Joseph *WhoAm 92*
Montana, Patsy *WhoAm 92*
Montana, Paul Bernard 1947- *WhoE 93*
Montana, Ron 1943- *ScF&FL 92*
Montana, Ruby *BioIn 17*
Montana, Vanni B. d1991 *BioIn 17*
Montanari, Fernando 1924- *WhoScE 91-3*
Montanaro, Felix *Law&B 92*
Montanaro, Linda 1945- *WhoAmW 93*

Montanaro, Robert Joseph 1961- *St&PR 93*
Montand, Yves *BioIn 17*
Montand, Yves 1921-1991 *AnObit 1991, ConTFT 10, CurBio 92N, IntDcF 2-3 [port], News 92*
Montandon, Pierre 1935- *WhoScE 91-4*
Montane, Paulino 1942- *WhoScE 91-3*
Montaner, Lluis Domenech i 1850-1923 *BioIn 17*
Montane Sangra, Paulino *WhoScE 91-3*
Montanes Garcia, Luis 1934- *WhoScE 91-3*
Montanez, Carmen L. 1944- *WhoSSW 93*
Montani, Anthony Albert 1939- *St&PR 93*
Montano, Daniel Joseph 1961- *WhoEmL 93*
Montano, Jorge 1945- *WhoUN 92, WhoWor 93*
Montano, Katherine Anne Szwedo 1958- *WhoAmW 93*
Montano, Kevin *Law&B 92*
Montant, Michel Jean Louis 1962- *WhoWor 93*
Montante, Claudia W. *Law&B 92*
Montanus, Lawrence W. 1945- *WhoSSW 93*
Montanye, George *Law&B 92*
Montanye, Larry L. *Law&B 92*
Montaquila, Madeline Ann 1933- *St&PR 93*
Montasser, Mohamed Salah El Din 1933- *WhoWor 93*
Montaudo, Giorgio 1934- *WhoScE 91-3*
Montaug, Haoui 1952-1991 *BioIn 17*
Montavon, Dennis R. 1948- *St&PR 93*
Montcalm, Louis-Joseph de Montcalm-Gozon, Marquis of 1712-1759 *HarEnMi*
Montcalm, Norman Joseph 1945- *WhoAm 92*
Monte, Bonnie J. 1954- *WhoAmW 93*
Monte, Bryan Robert 1957- *WhoWrEP 92*
Monte, Erika G. 1940- *St&PR 93*
Monte, Philippe de 1521-1603 *Baker 92*
Monte, Salvatore Joseph 1939- *St&PR 93*
Monte, Toti dal *Baker 92*
Montealegre, Anibal Francisco 1958- *WhoSSW 93*
Montebello, Mary A. *Law&B 92*
Montecino, Marcel 1945- *ConAu 137*
Monteclair, Michel Pignolet de 1667?-1737 *Baker 92, OxDcOp*
Montecuccoli, Raimondo 1609-1680 *HarEnMi*
Montefeltro, Federigo da 1422-1482 *HarEnMi*
Montefiore, Hugh *BioIn 17*
Montefiore, Simon Sebag *ConAu 136*
Monteforte Toledo, Mario 1911- *DcMexL, SpAmA*
Monteil, Henri 1940- *WhoScE 91-2*
Monteil, R.A. 1938- *WhoScE 91-2*
Monteiro, Antonio Manuel Mascarenhas Gomes 1944- *WhoAfr*
Monteiro, George 1932- *WhoE 93*
Monteiro, Jose H. 1939- *WhoScE 91-3*
Monteiro, Lois A. 1934- *WhoAm 92*
Monteiro, Luis Sieuve 1935- *WhoScE 91-3*
Monteiro Marques, M. 1929- *WhoScE 91-3*
Monteith, David Yates, III 1935- *WhoSSW 93*
Monteith, Dennis Paul *Law&B 92*
Monteith, Diana Lynne 1957- *St&PR 93*
Monteith, Dianne Souther 1935- *WhoAmW 93*
Monteith, Don 1942- *St&PR 93*
Monteith, Edward Everett, Jr. 1922- *St&PR 93*
Monteith, Katherine Simmons 1957- *WhoEmL 93*
Monteith, Larry King 1933- *WhoAm 92, WhoSSW 93*
Monteith, Randall Allison 1955- *WhoEmL 93*
Monteith, Walter H., Jr. 1930- *St&PR 93*
Monteith, Walter Henry, Jr. 1930- *WhoE 93*
Montejo, Cirilo Roy G. 1928- *WhoAsAP 91*
Montejo, Victor (D.) 1951- *ConAu 139*
Montel, Janet Marie 1954- *WhoEmL 93*
Monteleone, Iona *St&PR 93*
Monteleone, Maurizio 1930- *WhoScE 91-3*
Monteleone, Raymond R. 1947- *WhoAm 92, WhoSSW 93*
Monteleone, Thomas F. 1946- *ScF&FL 92*
Montelius, Susan Ann 1956- *WhoWrEP 92*
Montella, Giovanni Domenico c. 1570-1607 *Baker 92*
Montellaro, Lee R. 1945- *St&PR 93*
Montellaro, Randell 1960- *WhoEmL 93*
Montello, George Mandel- d1992 *BioIn 17*
Montemayor, Carlos 1947- *SpAmA*
Montemayor, Carlos R. 1945- *WhoSSW 93*
Montemayor, Fernando R. *St&PR 93*
Montemayor, Jesus Samson 1939- *WhoWor 93*
Montemayor, Linda F. *Law&B 92*
Montemezzi, Italo 1875-1952 *Baker 92, IntDcOp, OxDcOp*
Montemurro, G.A. 1933- *St&PR 93*
Montenay-Garestier, Therese 1941- *WhoScE 91-2*
Montenegro, A. Pena *WhoScE 91-3*
Montenegro, Carlos 1900-1981 *SpAmA*
Montenegro, Jean Baker *WhoAmW 93*
Montenegro de Garcia, Nineth *DcCPCAm*
Montenes, Francis A. 1930- *St&PR 93*
Montenes, Francis Anthony 1930- *St&PR 93*
Monteoliva-Hernandez, Miguel *WhoScE 91-3*
Monterde, Alberto 1923- *DcMexL*
Monterde, Francisco 1894- *DcMexL*
Monterey, Honey *WhoWrEP 92*
Montero, Darrel Martin 1946- *WhoEmL 93, WhoWor 93*
Montero, Edmundo 1945- *WhoWor 93*
Montero, Fernan Gonzalo 1948- *WhoE 93*
Montero, Kenneth Beverly Eduardo 1948- *WhoEmL 93*
Montero, Rosa 1951- *BioIn 17*
Monterroso, Augusto 1921- *DcMexL, ScF&FL 92, SpAmA*
Montes, Carlos 1939- *WhoScE 91-2*
Montes, Eduardo *MiSFD 9*
Montes, Felipe J. 1934- *WhoUN 92*
Montes, J.A. *Law&B 92*
Montes, Jose M. 1931- *WhoScE 91-3*
Montes, Raul R. *Law&B 92*
Montes, Segundo d1989 *BioIn 17*
Montesano, Aldo Maria 1939- *WhoWor 93*
Montesano, Gail Jean 1948- *WhoE 93, WhoEmL 93*
Montesano, Gian Marco 1955- *BioIn 17*
Montesano, Ruggero 1939- *WhoScE 91-2*
Montes Contreras, Celestino 1957- *WhoWor 93*
Montes Corripio, Ramon 1956- *WhoWor 93*
Montes de Oca, Marco Antonio 1932- *DcMexL*
Montes de Oca y Obregon, Ignacio 1840-1921 *DcMexL*
Montes Huidobro, Matias 1931- *HispAmA*
Montesi, John W. 1920- *St&PR 93, WhoAm 92*
Montesi, Jorge 1950- *MiSFD 9*
Montesino, Orlando C. 1950- *St&PR 93, WhoAm 92*
Montesino, Paul V. 1937- *St&PR 93*
Montessori, Maria 1870-1952 *BioIn 17, DcTwHis*
Monteux, Pierre 1875-1964 *Baker 92, IntDcOp*
Monteux, Pierre 1876-1964 *OxDcOp*
Monteverdi, Claudio 1567-1643 *BioIn 17, IntDcOp [port], OxDcOp*
Monteverdi, Claudio (Giovanni Antonio) 1567?-1643 *Baker 92*
Monteverdi, Giulio Cesare 1573?-1630? *Baker 92*
Montez, Lola 1818-1861 *BioIn 17*
Montez, Maria 1920-1951 *HispAmA*
Montezuma, II, Emperor of Mexico c. 1480-1520 *BioIn 17*
Montezuma, Carlos 1866-1923 *BioIn 17*
Montford, John Thomas 1943- *WhoSSW 93*
Montfort, Simon de 1208?-1265 *BioIn 17*
Montforts, Franz-Peter 1948- *WhoScE 91-3*
Montgomerie, Claire M. *Law&B 92*
Montgomerie, Lee *ScF&FL 92*
Montgomery, Alexandra E. 1957- *St&PR 93*
Montgomery, Alfred Eugene 1891-1961 *HarEnMi*
Montgomery, Andrew Stuart 1960- *WhoEmL 93, WhoWor 93*
Montgomery, Austin J. d1990 *BioIn 17*
Montgomery, Belinda J. *ConTFT 10*
Montgomery, Bernard Law 1887-1976 *DcTwHis, HarEnMi*
Montgomery, Betty D. *WhoAmW 93*
Montgomery, Brainerd S. *Law&B 92*
Montgomery, Carolyn Williams 1940- *WhoAmW 93*
Montgomery, Charles Howard 1930- *WhoAm 92*
Montgomery, Charles Rodney *Law&B 92*
Montgomery, Charlotte A. *WhoAmW 93*
Montgomery, Charlotte Ann 1949- *WhoAmW 93*
Montgomery, Chester Craig 1937- *St&PR 93*
Montgomery, Christopher 1959- *WhoEmL 93*
Montgomery, Clark Taylor 1941- *St&PR 93, WhoAm 92*
Montgomery, Constance Montague d1992 *BioIn 17, NewYTBS 92*
Montgomery, Dale Alan 1948- *WhoEmL 93*
Montgomery, David *WhoScE 91-1*
Montgomery, David Bruce 1938- *WhoAm 92, WhoWrEP 92*
Montgomery, David Campbell 1936- *WhoAm 92*
Montgomery, David Paul *WhoAm 92*
Montgomery, Deane d1992 *NewYTBS 92*
Montgomery, Deane 1909-1992 *BioIn 17, CurBio 92N*
Montgomery, Denise Karen 1951- *WhoAmW 93*
Montgomery, Don W. 1925- *St&PR 93, WhoIns 93*
Montgomery, Donald Joseph 1917- *WhoAm 92*
Montgomery, Donald Russell 1920- *WhoAm 92*
Montgomery, Edith *AmWomPl*
Montgomery, Edward A. d1990 *BioIn 17*
Montgomery, Edward Alembert, Jr. 1934- *WhoAm 92*
Montgomery, Edward Benjamin 1915- *WhoAm 92*
Montgomery, Edward Finley 1918- *WhoSSW 93*
Montgomery, Elinor White d1992 *BioIn 17*
Montgomery, Elisabeth Frederick *Law&B 92*
Montgomery, Elizabeth *AmWomPl*
Montgomery, Elizabeth Ann 1957- *WhoAmW 93*
Montgomery, G. V. *CngDr 91*
Montgomery, George 1938- *WhoWrEP 92*
Montgomery, George Cranwell 1944- *WhoAm 92, WhoE 93*
Montgomery, George Franklin 1921- *WhoAm 92*
Montgomery, Gillespie V. 1920- *WhoAm 92, WhoSSW 93*
Montgomery, Gladys *WhoAmW 93*
Montgomery, Glenn A. *WhoAm 92*
Montgomery, Gordon Homer 1922- *WhoSSW 93*
Montgomery, H. Dubose *St&PR 93*
Montgomery, Harold Hench 1959- *WhoEmL 93, WhoSSW 93*
Montgomery, Harry T. 1909-1991 *BioIn 17*
Montgomery, Helen 1861-1934 *BioIn 17*
Montgomery, Henry Irving 1924- *WhoWor 93*
Montgomery, Herbert D. 1942- *St&PR 93*
Montgomery, Herbert J. 1933- *ConAu 40NR*
Montgomery, Hubert Theron, Jr. 1935- *WhoSSW 93*
Montgomery, Hugh Everett, Jr. 1944- *WhoE 93*
Montgomery, Isaiah T. 1841-1924 *BioIn 17*
Montgomery, James 1771-1854 *BioIn 17*
Montgomery, James 1794-1880 *BioIn 17*
Montgomery, James D., Jr. *Law&B 92*
Montgomery, James E. 1929- *St&PR 93*
Montgomery, James F. 1934- *St&PR 93*
Montgomery, James Fischer 1934- *WhoAm 92*
Montgomery, James Loyd 1924- *St&PR 93*
Montgomery, James Morton 1931- *WhoAm 92, WhoSSW 93*
Montgomery, Janet Ann 1946- *WhoAmW 93*
Montgomery, Jeffrey A. *BioIn 17*
Montgomery, Jerry E. 1946- *WhoSSW 93*
Montgomery, John *WhoWrEP 92*
Montgomery, John Atterbury 1924- *WhoAm 92*
Montgomery, John Dickey 1920- *WhoAm 92, WhoWrEP 92*
Montgomery, John Franklin 1944- *WhoSSW 93*
Montgomery, John McVey 1919- *WhoWrEP 92*
Montgomery, John Warwick 1931- *WhoAm 92, WhoWor 93*
Montgomery, Johnny Lester 1934- *WhoAm 92*
Montgomery, Joseph William 1951- *WhoEmL 93*
Montgomery, Judy Glass 1945- *WhoAmW 93*
Montgomery, Kathryn Grace 1959- *WhoEmL 93*
Montgomery, Kathy Aleta *Law&B 92*
Montgomery, Kenneth (Mervyn) 1943- *Baker 92*
Montgomery, Kirby Vincent 1953- *WhoIns 93*
Montgomery, L.M. 1874-1942 *BioIn 17, ScF&FL 92*
Montgomery, L(ucy) M(aud) 1874-1942 *ConAu 137, DcChlFi, MajAI [port]*
Montgomery, Lane *BioIn 17*
Montgomery, Larry H. 1945- *St&PR 93*
Montgomery, Leslie David 1939- *WhoAm 92*
Montgomery, Lucy Maud 1874-1942 *AmWomPl, BioIn 17*
Montgomery, Marianne Beatty 1931- *WhoSSW 93*
Montgomery, Marion 1925- *WhoWrEP 92*
Montgomery, Marion H., Jr. 1925- *ScF&FL 92*
Montgomery, Mark A. *Law&B 92*
Montgomery, Martha Barber d1992 *BioIn 17, NewYTBS 92*
Montgomery, Merle 1904-1986 *Baker 92*
Montgomery, Michael Davis 1936- *St&PR 93*
Montgomery, Michael E. *St&PR 93*
Montgomery, Michael Edward 1948- *WhoAm 92*
Montgomery, Monty *MiSFD 9*
Montgomery, Ogden Knox *Law&B 92*
Montgomery, Parker G. *BioIn 17*
Montgomery, Parker G. 1928- *St&PR 93*
Montgomery, Parker Gilbert 1928- *WhoAm 92*
Montgomery, Patrick 1949- *MiSFD 9, St&PR 93*
Montgomery, Patrick E. 1949- *WhoEmL 93*
Montgomery, Patrick Matthew 1957- *WhoIns 93*
Montgomery, Peggy *SweetSg B [port]*
Montgomery, Philip O'Bryan, III 1954- *WhoSSW 93*
Montgomery, R.A. 1936- *ScF&FL 92*
Montgomery, R.L. 1922- *St&PR 93*
Montgomery, Ramsey *ScF&FL 92*
Montgomery, Rex *ScF&FL 92*
Montgomery, Rex 1923- *WhoAm 92*
Montgomery, Richard 1738-1775 *HarEnMi*
Montgomery, Robert 1904-1981 *BioIn 17, IntDcF 2-3, MiSFD 9N*
Montgomery, Robert Humphrey, Jr. 1923- *WhoAm 92*
Montgomery, Robert Morel, Jr. 1930- *WhoAm 92*
Montgomery, Robert Raynor 1943- *St&PR 93*
Montgomery, Roger 1925- *WhoAm 92*
Montgomery, Roy Delbert 1926- *WhoAm 92*
Montgomery, Roy Taylor *Law&B 92*
Montgomery, Royce W. *Law&B 92*
Montgomery, Ruth Shick *WhoAm 92, WhoWrEP 92*
Montgomery, Rutherford (George) 1894- *DcAmChF 1960*
Montgomery, Rutherford George 1894-1985 *ScF&FL 92*
Montgomery, Scott Kirk 1956- *WhoEmL 93*
Montgomery, Seth David 1937- *WhoAm 92*
Montgomery, Sharon Kate 1939- *WhoAmW 93*
Montgomery, Sonny 1920- *WhoSSW 93*
Montgomery, Steven J. 1946- *St&PR 93*
Montgomery, Susan Jane 1944- *St&PR 93*
Montgomery, Suzanne Howard 1949- *WhoEmL 93*
Montgomery, Theodore Ashton 1923- *WhoAm 92*
Montgomery, Thomas E. *Law&B 92*
Montgomery, Thomas G. *Law&B 92*
Montgomery, Thomas Wylie 1951- *WhoSSW 93*
Montgomery, Timothy L. 1957- *St&PR 93*
Montgomery, Tommie Sue 1942- *WhoSSW 93*
Montgomery, Toni-Marie 1956- *WhoAmW 93*
Montgomery, Velmanette *WhoAmW 93*
Montgomery, Victoria *AmWomPl*
Montgomery, Walter George 1945- *WhoAm 92*
Montgomery, Walter S. 1900- *St&PR 93*
Montgomery, Wayne *Law&B 92*
Montgomery, Wendy *ScF&FL 92*
Montgomery, Wes 1923-1968 *Baker 92*
Montgomery, Willard G. *Law&B 92*
Montgomery, William Adam 1933- *WhoAm 92*
Montgomery, William Adam, Jr. *Law&B 92*
Montgomery, William E. 1937- *St&PR 93*
Montgomery, William J. 1930- *WhoAm 92*
Montgomery, William Jester 1930- *St&PR 93*
Montgomery, William Layton 1934- *WhoE 93*
Montgomery, William Wayne 1923- *WhoAm 92*
Montgomery-Davis, Joseph 1940- *WhoSSW 93*

Montgoris, William J. St&PR 93, WhoAm 92
Montgrain, Noel 1933- WhoAm 92
Monthan, Doris Born 1924- ConAu 37NR
Montherlant, Henry de BioIn 17
Monti, Anna Maria 1704-c. 1727 OxDcOp
Monti, Eugenio 1928- BioIn 17
Monti, Gaetano c. 1750-1816? OxDcOp
Monti, Grazia OxDcOp
Monti, John Louis 1933- WhoSSW 93
Monti, Joseph, Jr. 1937- WhoSSW 93
Monti, Laura c. 1704-1760 OxDcOp
Monti, Laura Anne 1959- WhoAmW 93, WhoEmL 93, WhoWor 93
Monti, Luigi M. WhoScE 91-3
Monti, Marianna 1730-1814 OxDcOp
Monti, Stephen Arion 1939- WhoAm 92
Monticelli, Angelo Maria c. 1710-1764 OxDcOp
Monticelli, Gianluigi 1946- WhoWor 93
Monticone, Diane Therese 1941- WhoAmW 93
Monticue, Deborah Yvonne Law&B 92
Montidoro, Emy B. 1957- St&PR 93
Montiel, Eduardo Luis 1949- WhoWor 93
Monties, Jean-Raoul E. 1934- WhoScE 91-2
Montigny, Louvigny de 1876-1955 BioIn 17
Montijo, Ralph Elias, Jr. 1928- WhoAm 92, WhoSSW 93, WhoWor 93
Montilla, Cesar A., Jr. 1942- St&PR 93
Montini, Giovanni Battista 1897-1978 BioIn 17
Montjoy, John Law&B 92
Montjoy, William Wright 1950- WhoSSW 93
Montlack, Edith 1921- WhoE 93
Montle, Paul J. 1947- St&PR 93
Montle, Paul Joseph 1947- WhoAm 92
Montmerle, Bruno Didier 1949- St&PR 93
Montminy, Marc R. BioIn 17
Montmorency, Anne, Duke of 1493-1567 HarEnMi
Montmorency, Henri, duc de 1534-1614 BioIn 17
Montmorency, Henri, II, Duke of 1595-1632 HarEnMi
Montney, Wayne W. Law&B 92
Montoliu, Jesus 1949- WhoWor 93
Monton, Anthony Allen 1951- WhoEmL 93
Montone, Kenneth Alan 1938- WhoWor 93
Montonen, Michael Kari 1957- WhoEmL 93
Montoni, Mario Enrico 1962- WhoE 93
Montooth, Sheila Christine 1952- WhoAmW 93, WhoEmL 93
Montopoli, Duane Carmen 1948- St&PR 93
Montori, Rosa Tudela Bentin de 1941- WhoWor 93
Montoto, Manuel 1942- St&PR 93
Montour, Phyllis Jean 1947- WhoEmL 93
Montouri, Claudia B. 1951- St&PR 93
Montoya, Carlos 1903- Baker 92
Montoya, Carlos Garcia 1903- WhoAm 92
Montoya, Jorge P. 1946- St&PR 93
Montoya, Jorge Peregrino 1946- WhoAm 92
Montoya, Jose 1932- DcLB 122
Montoya, Joseph M. 1915-1978 HispAmA
Montoya, Juan BioIn 17
Montoya, Juan F. 1945- WhoAm 92
Montoya, Nestor 1862-1923 HispAmA
Montoya de Lopez, Julieta 1949- WhoWor 93
Montparker, Carol BioIn 17
Montpetit, Christopher Mark 1965- WhoE 93
Montpezat, Jean WhoWor 93
Montresor, Beni ChlBIID [port]
Montresor, Beni 1926- BioIn 17, MajAI [port]
Montresor, Louis D. Law&B 92
Montresor, Louis Dominick Law&B 92
Montret, Jean-Claude 1940- WhoScE 91-2
Montreuil, Charles Frederick Law&B 92
Montreuil, Claire WhoCanL 92
Montrone, Paul M. 1941- St&PR 93
Montrone, Thomas L. 1948- St&PR 93
Montrose, Catherine ScF&FL 92
Montrose, Donald W. 1923- WhoAm 92
Montrose, James Graham, Marquess of 1612-1650 HarEnMi
Montrose, Lester ScF&FL 92
Montrose, Stephen Foster 1958- WhoSSW 93
Montross, Albert Edward 1936- WhoAm 92
Montross, Franklin, IV 1956- St&PR 93, WhoIns 93
Montry, Gerald F. 1938- St&PR 93
Monts, Michael A. Law&B 92
Montsalvatge, Bassols Xavier 1911- Baker 92
Monts De Oca, Clinton H., Jr. 1946- St&PR 93
Montserrat I. Marti, J.M. 1955- WhoScE 91-3
Monturiol, Narciso 1819-1885 BioIn 17
Montvenoux WhoScE 91-2
Montville, Leigh BioIn 17
Montville, Thomas Joseph 1953- WhoE 93
Montwill, Alex 1935- WhoScE 91-3
Monty, Barbara Helen 1931- WhoSSW 93
Monty, Charles Embert 1927- WhoAm 92
Monty, Gloria WhoAm 92, WhoAmW 93
Monty, Gloria 1921?- ConTFT 10
Monty, Jean Claude 1947- St&PR 93
Monty, Kenneth James 1930- WhoSSW 93
Monty, Stephen Andrew Law&B 92
Montz, Linda Ann 1950- WhoAmW 93
Monza, Carlo c. 1735-1801 Baker 92
Monzel, Catherine Luise 1960- WhoAmW 93
Monzie, Anatole de 1876-1947 BioIn 17
Monzingo, Agnes Yvonne 1942- WhoAmW 93
Monzingo, Freida Haynes 1944- WhoSSW 93
Monzini, Andrea WhoScE 91-3
Monzino, Guido BioIn 17
Monzon, Robert d1991 BioIn 17
Moo, Paul Edward 1949- WhoEmL 93, WhoSSW 93
Mooar, Caroline H. AmWomPl
Moodee, Valaree Marcia Law&B 92
Moodey, James Collins 1941- St&PR 93
Moodhe, Joseph Patrick 1955- WhoE 93
Moodie, Alma 1900-1943 Baker 92
Moodie, Dahlia Maria 1959- WhoAmW 93
Moodie, Douglas Rome 1951- WhoE 93
Moodie, J.W.D. 1797-1869 BioIn 17
Moodie, John Wedderburn Dunbar 1797-1869 BioIn 17
Moodie, Susanna Strickland 1803-1885 BioIn 17
Moodie, Walter Taylor 1943- WhoE 93
Moody, Ann 1935- St&PR 93
Moody, Ann Berry 1935- WhoSSW 93
Moody, Anne 1940- EncAACR
Moody, Anne King AmWomPl
Moody, Barbara 1946- WhoE 93
Moody, Blair Edwin 1950- WhoEmL 93
Moody, Cheryle Anne 1959- WhoSSW 93
Moody, Christopher John WhoScE 91-1
Moody, Christopher John 1951- WhoWor 93
Moody, Dale 1915-1992 BioIn 17
Moody, Dale George 1944- St&PR 93
Moody, Dan T. 1950- St&PR 93
Moody, Daniel James 1947- St&PR 93
Moody, Denman, Jr. 1942- WhoWor 93
Moody, Fanny 1866-1945 Baker 92, OxDcOp
Moody, Florence Elizabeth 1932- WhoAm 92, WhoE 93
Moody, Frank M. 1915- St&PR 93
Moody, Frederick Jerome 1935- WhoAm 92
Moody, G. William 1928- WhoAm 92
Moody, Gene Byron 1933- WhoSSW 93
Moody, George Ernest 1938- WhoSSW 93
Moody, George Walter 1943- WhoSSW 93, WhoWor 93
Moody, George William WhoScE 91-1
Moody, Grace AmWomPl
Moody, Graham Blair 1925- WhoAm 92
Moody, Helen Wills 1905- BioIn 17
Moody, Hiram F., III 1961- ConAu 138
Moody, Hiram Frederick, Jr. 1935- WhoAm 92
Moody, James Carol 1937- St&PR 93
Moody, James L., Jr. 1931- WhoAm 92, WhoE 93
Moody, James Leander, Jr. 1931- St&PR 93
Moody, James Michael 1954- WhoWrEP 92
Moody, Jim 1935- CngDr 91, WhoAm 92
Moody, Jo Nita P. Law&B 92
Moody, Joanne Barker 1950- WhoSSW 93
Moody, John (Henry) 1953- ConAu 138
Moody, John W. 1949- St&PR 93
Moody, Lamon Lamar, Jr. 1924- WhoSSW 93, WhoWor 93
Moody, Laura Bettye 1944- WhoAmW 93, WhoE 93
Moody, Linda Ann 1954- WhoAmW 93
Moody, Lori Hanley WhoE 93
Moody, LoVeen J. Law&B 92
Moody, M. Bradford Law&B 92
Moody, Marilyn Dallas WhoAmW 93
Moody, Max Dale WhoSSW 93
Moody, Maxwell, Jr. 1921- WhoSSW 93
Moody, R. Bruce 1933- WhoWrEP 92
Moody, Rhea Phenon 1930- WhoAmW 93
Moody, Richard Steven 1948- St&PR 93, WhoSSW 93
Moody, Rick ConAu 138
Moody, Robert Adams 1934- WhoAm 92
Moody, Robert Elbridge 1897- WhoE 93
Moody, Robert L. 1936- WhoSSW 93
Moody, Rodger 1950- WhoWrEP 92
Moody, Roland Herbert 1916- WhoAm 92
Moody, Ron 1924- WhoWor 93
Moody, Ruth T. 1917- St&PR 93
Moody, Stephen Kreigh 1942- St&PR 93
Moody, Susan Anne 1956- St&PR 93
Moody, W.B., Sr. 1933- St&PR 93
Moody, William Henry 1853-1917 OxCSupC [port]
Moody, William Terry 1939- St&PR 93
Moody, William Vaughn 1869-1910 GayN
Mooers, Christopher Northrup Kennard 1935- WhoAm 92, WhoSSW 93
Mooers, Philip F. 1940- St&PR 93, WhoIns 93
Moog, Robert (Arthur) 1934- Baker 92
Mooibroek, Joseph 1942- St&PR 93
Mooij, Jan J. A. 1945- WhoWor 93
Mooij, Jan Johann Albinn 1929- WhoWor 93
Mook, James 1939- WhoWrEP 92
Mook, Sarah 1929- WhoAmW 93
Mook, Willem G. 1932- WhoScE 91-3
Moomaw, Donn Dement 1931- BiDAMSp 1989
Moomaw, Ronald Lee 1943- WhoAm 92, WhoSSW 93
Moomjian, Cary A., Jr. Law&B 92
Moomjian, Cary Avedis, Jr. 1947- St&PR 93
Moon, Alan ScF&FL 92
Moon, Alan C. 1945- St&PR 93
Moon, Alfred E. d1991 BioIn 17
Moon, Anna M. 1956- St&PR 93
Moon, Archie AfrAmBi [port]
Moon, Brenda Gayle 1944- WhoAmW 93
Moon, Carolyn Davis Law&B 92
Moon, Clarence Norman 1934- WhoE 93
Moon, Dale E. 1938- St&PR 93
Moon, David 1941- St&PR 93
Moon, David C. Law&B 92
Moon, Dudley George 1950- WhoE 93
Moon, Elizabeth 1945- ScF&FL 92
Moon, Eric 1923- JrnUS
Moon, Francis Richard 1965- WhoE 93
Moon, Franklin Boyd 1922- St&PR 93
Moon, Geraldine N. d1991 BioIn 17
Moon, Harley William 1936- WhoAm 92
Moon, Ilse 1932- WhoAm 92
Moon, James Clark 1938- WhoE 93
Moon, James Virgil 1950- WhoEmL 93
Moon, Jay ScF&FL 92
Moon, Jeffrey Hunter Law&B 92
Moon, John Henry, Sr. 1937- WhoSSW 93
Moon, Joseph F., Jr. 1946- St&PR 93
Moon, Lewis P. 1930- St&PR 93
Moon, Marcia A. 1945- WhoAmW 93
Moon, Marla Lynn 1956- WhoAmW 93
Moon, Mollie Lewis d1990 BioIn 17
Moon, Mona McTaggart 1934- WhoAmW 93
Moon, Pattie 1946- WhoAmW 93
Moon, Peter Stevenson 1953- WhoE 93
Moon, Randall James Law&B 92
Moon, Ronald T. Y. 1940- WhoAm 92
Moon, Sandra Elaine 1957- WhoAm 92
Moon, Sheila (Elizabeth) 1910- DcAmChF 1960
Moon, Spencer 1948- WhoEmL 93
Moon, Sun Myung DcCPCAm
Moon, Thomas Young-Jun 1934- St&PR 93
Moon, Warren BioIn 17
Moon, Warren 1956- AfrAmBi [port], WhoAm 92
Moon, Warren G. 1945- WhoAm 92, WhoWrEP 92
Moon, Willard Bailey 1938- St&PR 93
Moon, William Lawrence 1958- WhoEmL 93
Moon, Wilson L. 1916- St&PR 93
Moonan, Jeffrey P. Law&B 92
Moonan, Jeffrey Patrick 1956- St&PR 93
Moonan, Joan C. 1933- St&PR 93
Moonchild ScF&FL 92
Mooney, Bel 1946- ConAu 138, ScF&FL 92
Mooney, Brian ScF&FL 92
Mooney, Catherine Lee 1953- WhoAmW 93
Mooney, Charles P.J. 1938- St&PR 93
Mooney, Christopher Francis 1925- WhoE 93
Mooney, Clifford Eugene 1918- St&PR 93
Mooney, Donald J. 1926- St&PR 93
Mooney, Donald James 1926- WhoAm 92
Mooney, Edward ScF&FL 92
Mooney, James 1861-1921 IntDcAn
Mooney, James Hugh 1929- WhoAm 92, WhoSSW 93, WhoWrEP 92
Mooney, James Patrick 1931- St&PR 93
Mooney, James Pierce 1943- WhoAm 92, WhoWor 93
Mooney, John Allen 1918- WhoAm 92, WhoWor 93
Mooney, John Bradford, Jr. 1931- WhoAm 92, WhoSSW 93
Mooney, Joyce E. 1930- St&PR 93
Mooney, Kevin Xavier 1933- WhoIns 93
Mooney, Lori 1929- WhoE 93, WhoWor 93
Mooney, Lucia M. AmWomPl
Mooney, Martha Vaughan 1952- WhoAmW 93
Mooney, Marybeth A. 1961- St&PR 93
Mooney, Michael Edward 1945- WhoAm 92
Mooney, Michael Joseph 1942- WhoAm 92
Mooney, Michael Joseph 1950- WhoE 93
Mooney, Michael Mark 1950- St&PR 93
Mooney, Michael Morse 1939- WhoWrEP 92
Mooney, Nancy 1959- WhoAmW 93
Mooney, Patricia Anne 1948- WhoAmW 93, WhoEmL 93
Mooney, Peter J. 1944- St&PR 93
Mooney, Philip F. 1944- ScF&FL 92
Mooney, Raymond 1951- St&PR 93
Mooney, Richard E. 1927- WhoAm 92
Mooney, Richard J. 1942- St&PR 93
Mooney, Robbi Gail 1955- WhoSSW 93
Mooney, Robert J. Law&B 92
Mooney, Robert Michael 1945- WhoE 93
Mooney, Robert W. 1949- St&PR 93
Mooney, Stephen Eugene 1944- St&PR 93
Mooney, Ted 1951- ScF&FL 92, WhoAm 92
Mooney, William M. WhoAm 92
Mooney, William P. 1951- St&PR 93
Mooney, William Piatt 1936- WhoAm 92
Mooney-Getoff, Mary Josephine 1928- WhoAmW 93
Mooneyham, Bobby G. 1944- St&PR 93
Mooneyham, W. Stanley 1926-1991 BioIn 17
Mooneyham, Walter Stanley 1926-1991 BioIn 17
Mooneyhan, Esther Louise 1920- WhoAm 92, WhoWor 93
Moonglows SoulM
Moonie, Clyde Wickliffe 1918- WhoAm 92
Moon Jung Soo 1940- WhoAsAP 91
Moon Jun Sik 1924- WhoAsAP 91
Moon-Meier, Delia Ann 1965- WhoAmW 93, WhoEmL 93
Moons, Karla R. 1946- WhoAmW 93, WhoEmL 93
Moon Tong Hwan 1923- WhoAsAP 91
Moonves, Leslie BioIn 17
Moonves, Leslie 1949- WhoAm 92
Moopanar, G.K. 1931- WhoAsAP 91
Moor, Edgar Jacques 1912- WhoWor 93
Moor, Emanuel 1863-1931 Baker 92
Moor, Karel 1873-1945 Baker 92
Moor, Kristian P. 1959- St&PR 93
Moor, Manly Eugene, Jr. 1923- WhoAm 92
Moor, Roy Edward 1924- WhoAm 92
Moora, Kh.A. 1900-1968 IntDcAn
Moorachian, H. Harry 1944- St&PR 93
Mooradian, Ara John 1922- WhoAm 92
Moorcock, Michael 1939- BioIn 17, ScF&FL 92
Moorcock, Michael (John) 1939- ConAu 38NR
Moore, A.J. Law&B 92
Moore, A. Ronald 1937- St&PR 93
Moore, Acel 1940- WhoAm 92
Moore, Ada d1991 BioIn 17
Moore, Adam 1979- BioIn 17
Moore, Adrienne 1945- BioIn 17
Moore, Albert Cunningham 1931- WhoAm 92
Moore, Albert G., Jr. Law&B 92
Moore, Alderine Bernice Jennings 1915- WhoAmW 93
Moore, Alexander 1937- WhoAm 92
Moore, Alfred 1755-1810 OxCSupC [port]
Moore, Alfred Anson 1925- WhoAm 92
Moore, Alice Manns 1936- WhoAmW 93
Moore, Allan Baron 1964- WhoE 93
Moore, Allen Murdoch 1940- WhoSSW 93
Moore, Alma C. WhoAmW 93
Moore, Alvin Crawford BioIn 17
Moore, Amzie 1911-1982 EncAACR
Moore, Andrew Given Tobias, II 1935- WhoAm 92, WhoE 93
Moore, Andrew T., Jr. 1940- St&PR 93
Moore, Andrew Taylor, Jr. 1940- WhoAm 92
Moore, Ann BioIn 17
Moore, Ann Dombourian 1939- WhoAmW 93
Moore, Anne AmWomPl
Moore, Anthony Roger 1945- WhoWor 93
Moore, Archie 1913- BioIn 17
Moore, Armond William 1955- WhoEmL 93
Moore, Arthur 1939- St&PR 93
Moore, Arthur B. Law&B 92
Moore, Arthur Cotton 1935- WhoAm 92
Moore, Arthur James 1922- WhoAm 92
Moore, Arthur T. Law&B 92
Moore, B.H. Rutledge 1937- St&PR 93

Moore, Barbara A. *Law&B 92*
Moore, Barbara Ellen 1956- *WhoAmW 93*
Moore, Barbara Jean Gowans *WhoAmW 93*
Moore, Barbara Sloan 1948- *WhoAm 92*
Moore, Barney M., Jr. 1937- *St&PR 93*
Moore, Barry *BioIn 17*
Moore, Basil John 1933- *WhoAm 92*
Moore, Bealer Gwen 1944- *WhoAmW 93*
Moore, Bessie Boehm 1902- *BioIn 17*
Moore, Bessie Collins *AmWomPl*
Moore, Betty Jean 1927- *WhoAmW 93, WhoSSW 93*
Moore, Betty Jean 1930- *WhoAmW 93*
Moore, Betty Jo *WhoAmW 93*
Moore, Betty Westbrooks 1941- *WhoAmW 93*
Moore, Beverly Cooper 1909- *WhoAm 92*
Moore, Bill 1903-1984 *BioIn 17*
Moore, Billy Don 1956- *WhoEmL 93*
Moore, Bob Stahly 1936- *WhoAm 92, WhoWor 93*
Moore, Brenton B. *Law&B 92*
Moore, Brian 1921- *BioIn 17, ScF&FL 92, WhoAm 92, WhoCanL 92, WhoWor 93, WhoWrEP 92*
Moore, Brian C. 1945- *St&PR 93*
Moore, Brooke Noel 1943- *WhoAm 92*
Moore, Bruce Alan 1952- *WhoEmL 93*
Moore, Burton Eberle 1914- *St&PR 93*
Moore, Burton Ray 1941- *WhoAm 92*
Moore, C. Bradley 1939- *WhoAm 92*
Moore, C.L. 1911- *BioIn 17*
Moore, C.L. 1911-1987 *ScF&FL 92*
Moore, Calvin C. 1936- *WhoAm 92*
Moore, Candace Rae 1952- *WhoEmL 93*
Moore, Carla Sue Walker 1958- *WhoEmL 93*
Moore, Carman (Leroy) 1936- *Baker 92, BlkAull 92*
Moore, Carolyn Calista 1953- *WhoAmW 93*
Moore, Catherine Lucille 1911- *BioIn 17*
Moore, Cathleen Turner 1944- *WhoAmW 93, WhoE 93*
Moore, Chandra Turner *Law&B 92*
Moore, Charles A.B. *Law&B 92*
Moore, Charles Brown 1941- *WhoSSW 93*
Moore, Charles Dudley, Jr. 1946- *WhoEmL 93*
Moore, Charles Hewes, Jr. 1929- *St&PR 93, WhoAm 92*
Moore, Charles J. *Law&B 92*
Moore, Charles Julian 1931- *WhoAm 92*
Moore, Charles L., Jr. *Law&B 92*
Moore, Charles M. *Law&B 92*
Moore, Charles Phillip *MiSFD 9*
Moore, Charles Willard *BioIn 17*
Moore, Charles Willard 1925- *WhoAm 92*
Moore, Charles Willard 1930- *WhoSSW 93*
Moore, Charlotte Eleanor 1923- *WhoAmW 93*
Moore, Cheryl Hannert 1958- *WhoEmL 93*
Moore, Christine Alice 1956- *WhoSSW 93*
Moore, Clark D'Arcy 1932- *WhoSSW 93*
Moore, Claude N. 1929- *St&PR 93*
Moore, Clayton *ConAu 38NR*
Moore, Clement Clarke 1779-1863 *BioIn 17, MajAI [port]*
Moore, Cleon 1928- *St&PR 93*
Moore, Cleon Emerson 1928- *WhoSSW 93*
Moore, Clyde W. 1937- *St&PR 93*
Moore, Colleen 1902-1988 *IntDcF 2-3 [port]*
Moore, Conrad Lee 1937- *WhoAm 92*
Moore, Cornell Leverette *Law&B 92*
Moore, Cornell Leverette 1939- *St&PR 93*
Moore, Curtis R. 1956- *St&PR 93*
Moore, D.W. *WhoScE 91-1*
Moore, Daisy M. *AmWomPl*
Moore, Daisy Seale 1933- *WhoWrEP 92*
Moore, Dalton, Jr. 1918- *WhoSSW 93, WhoWor 93*
Moore, Dan Algernon, Sr. 1935- *WhoSSW 93*
Moore, Daniel A., Jr. 1934- *WhoAm 92*
Moore, Daniel Charles 1918- *WhoAm 92*
Moore, Daniel E. 1931- *St&PR 93*
Moore, Daniel Edmund 1926- *WhoE 93, WhoWor 93*
Moore, Daniel J. 1929-1992 *BioIn 17*
Moore, Daniel L. 1953 *WhoSSW 93*
Moore, Daniel Michael *Law&B 92*
Moore, Darcy Jean 1956- *WhoAmW 93, WhoEmL 93*
Moore, Darlene Sybil 1954- *WhoAmW 93*
Moore, Darrell *ScF&FL 92*
Moore, Daryl Duane 1957- *St&PR 93*
Moore, David A. *St&PR 93*
Moore, David Austin 1935- *WhoE 93, WhoWor 93*
Moore, David Bruce 1956- *WhoEmL 93, WhoSSW 93, WhoWor 93*
Moore, David C. 1941- *WhoIns 93*
Moore, David Graham 1918- *WhoAm 92*
Moore, David Gregory 1946- *WhoEmL 93*
Moore, David Lloyd 1948- *WhoWor 93*
Moore, David Lowell 1930- *WhoAm 92*
Moore, David Max 1949- *WhoEmL 93*
Moore, David Michael *Law&B 92*
Moore, Deborah Caulk 1959- *WhoAmW 93*
Moore, Deborah L. 1956- *St&PR 93*
Moore, Demi *BioIn 17*
Moore, Demi 1962- *ConTFT 10, WhoAm 92, WhoAmW 93*
Moore, Dennis Merrill *Law&B 92*
Moore, Diane Lynn 1953- *St&PR 93*
Moore, Dianne Lea 1949- *WhoEmL 93*
Moore, Donald Eugene 1928- *WhoAm 92*
Moore, Donald Francis 1937- *WhoAm 92*
Moore, Donald John 1959- *WhoWrEP 92*
Moore, Donald L. *ScF&FL 92*
Moore, Donald Lynn 1947- *WhoEmL 93*
Moore, Donna Jean 1955- *St&PR 93*
Moore, Donna Maria 1955- *WhoAmW 93*
Moore, Donnie 1954-1989 *BioIn 17*
Moore, Donnie M. 1948- *St&PR 93*
Moore, Dora Mavor 1888-1979 *BioIn 17*
Moore, Dorothy 1946- *SoulM*
Moore, Dorothy Marie 1928- *WhoAm 92*
Moore, Dorothy N(elson) 1915- *WhoWrEP 92*
Moore, Dorothy Rudd 1940- *Baker 92*
Moore, Dorsey Jerome 1935- *WhoAm 92*
Moore, Douglas 1893-1969 *OxDcOp*
Moore, Douglas E. *Law&B 92*
Moore, Douglas Matthew, Jr. 1939- *WhoAm 92*
Moore, Douglas Raymond 1957- *St&PR 93*
Moore, Douglas (Stuart) 1893-1969 *Baker 92, IntDcOp*
Moore, Dudley *BioIn 17*
Moore, Dudley 1935- *IntDcF 2-3, QDrFCA 92 [port]*
Moore, Dudley Donald 1928- *St&PR 93*
Moore, Dudley L., Jr. 1936- *WhoIns 93*
Moore, Dudley Lester, Jr. 1936- *WhoSSW 93*
Moore, Dudley Stuart John 1935- *WhoAm 92, WhoWor 93*
Moore, E. Joseph 1916- *St&PR 93*
Moore, E. Keith 1922- *St&PR 93*
Moore, Earl Dean 1955- *WhoSSW 93*
Moore, Earl Vincent 1890-1987 *Baker 92*
Moore, Earle Kennedy 1921- *WhoAm 92*
Moore, Eddie Christopher d1991 *BioIn 17*
Moore, Eddie N., Jr. *WhoSSW 93*
Moore, Edgar M. 1940- *St&PR 93*
Moore, Edith *BioIn 17*
Moore, Edith Louise 1957- *WhoAmW 93*
Moore, Edmund Wright 1938- *WhoWor 93*
Moore, Edna R. *BioIn 17*
Moore, Edward 1887-1959 *BioIn 17*
Moore, Edward B. 1922- *St&PR 93*
Moore, Edward F., Jr. 1920- *St&PR 93*
Moore, Edward Forrest 1925- *WhoAm 92*
Moore, Edward James 1935- *ConTFT 10*
Moore, Edward Lynn 1949- *WhoSSW 93*
Moore, Edward Raymond, Jr. 1943- *WhoSSW 93*
Moore, Edwina Vesta *WhoAmW 93*
Moore, Eileen Marie 1959- *WhoAmW 93*
Moore, Eleanor Marchman 1913- *WhoAmW 93*
Moore, Elizabeth Kimberly 1954- *WhoEmL 93*
Moore, Ellen Marie 1947- *WhoSSW 93*
Moore, Ellis Oglesby 1924- *WhoAm 92*
Moore, Emerson *BioIn 17*
Moore, Emily Allyn 1950- *WhoAmW 93*
Moore, Emily R. 1948- *BlkAull 92*
Moore, Emma Sims 1937- *WhoAmW 93*
Moore, Emmett Burris, Jr. 1929- *WhoAm 92*
Moore, Ernest Carroll, III 1944- *WhoWor 93*
Moore, Ernest Dowl 1934- *WhoSSW 93*
Moore, Ernest Eugene, Jr. 1946- *WhoAm 92*
Moore, Farney *AfrAmBi [port]*
Moore, Fay Linda 1942- *WhoAmW 93*
Moore, Faye Halford 1941- *WhoAmW 93*
Moore, Felicia Ann 1961- *WhoAmW 93*
Moore, Fletcher Brooks 1926- *WhoAm 92, WhoSSW 93*
Moore, Florence Bradley *AmWomPl*
Moore, Forrest Weatherford 1931- *WhoSSW 93*
Moore, Francis Daniels 1913- *BioIn 17, WhoAm 92*
Moore, Franklin Hall, Jr. 1937- *WhoAm 92*
Moore, Freddie d1992 *NewYTBS 92*
Moore, Freddie 1900- *BioIn 17*
Moore, Frederick C. 1933- *WhoAm 92*
Moore, Frederick Salling 1938- *St&PR 93*
Moore, Gary L. 1955- *St&PR 93*
Moore, Gary Vern 1951- *St&PR 93*
Moore, Geoffrey Hoyt 1914- *WhoAm 92, WhoWrEP 92*
Moore, George Campp 1935- *St&PR 93*
Moore, George Crawford Jackson *WhoAm 92*
Moore, George Elliott 1935- *WhoSSW 93*
Moore, George Emerson, Jr. 1914- *WhoAm 92*
Moore, George Eugene 1920- *WhoAm 92*
Moore, George K. *Law&B 92*
Moore, George Kenneth 1927- *St&PR 93*
Moore, George Milton 1931- *WhoSSW 93*
Moore, George S. 1905- *St&PR 93*
Moore, George Washington 1926-1991 *BioIn 17*
Moore, Gerald 1899-1987 *Baker 92*
Moore, Gerald Dowsland 1937- *WhoUN 92*
Moore, Gerald Keith Frederick 1939- *WhoUN 92*
Moore, Gerald Ray 1951- *WhoEmL 93*
Moore, Gerald Thomas 1932- *St&PR 93*
Moore, Glenn Ray 1937- *St&PR 93*
Moore, Gloria Ann 1955- *WhoAmW 93*
Moore, Gloria Gene 1951- *WhoSSW 93*
Moore, Gloria Jean *Law&B 92*
Moore, Gordon E. *BioIn 17*
Moore, Gordon E. 1929- *St&PR 93, WhoAm 92, WhoWor 93*
Moore, Grace 1898-1947 *Baker 92, IntDcOp, OxDcOp*
Moore, Gregory Clayton 1954- *St&PR 93*
Moore, Gwen *AfrAmBi [port]*
Moore, Gwendolynne S. *AfrAmBi [port]*
Moore, H. Brian 1948- *St&PR 93*
Moore, Hal G. 1929- *WhoAm 92*
Moore, Hank 1947- *WhoSSW 93*
Moore, Harold Joseph 1947- *St&PR 93*
Moore, Harrison Lyman 1946- *WhoWrEP 92*
Moore, Harry E., Jr. 1918- *WhoWrEP 92*
Moore, Harry Lowell 1956- *WhoEmL 93*
Moore, Harry Russell 1921- *WhoSSW 93, WhoWor 93*
Moore, Harry T. 1905-1951 *EncAACR*
Moore, Harvielee Ann Offutt 1948- *WhoWrEP 92*
Moore, Hayden Albert 1929- *WhoAm 92*
Moore, Hazel Stamps 1924- *WhoAmW 93*
Moore, Helen 1862-1954 *ScF&FL 92*
Moore, Helen Elizabeth 1920- *WhoAmW 93*
Moore, Henderson Alfred, Jr. 1912- *WhoWor 93*
Moore, Henry 1898-1986 *BioIn 17, DcTwHis*
Moore, Henry Rogers 1916- *WhoAm 92*
Moore, Herbert Bell 1926- *WhoAm 92, WhoE 93*
Moore, Herbert Howard 1928- *WhoSSW 93*
Moore, Herff Leo, Jr. 1937- *WhoSSW 93, WhoWor 93*
Moore, Honor 1945- *WhoWrEP 92*
Moore, Howard Ellison, Jr. 1936- *St&PR 93*
Moore, Howard James 1947- *WhoUN 92*
Moore, Howard R. *Law&B 92*
Moore, Howard W. *BioIn 17*
Moore, Hugh M., Jr. 1931- *St&PR 93*
Moore, Irving J. *MiSFD 9*
Moore, J. Dennis *Law&B 92*
Moore, J.F. 1936- *WhoScE 91-3*
Moore, J. Mavor 1919- *WhoCanL 92*
Moore, J. T. 1939- *WhoSSW 93*
Moore, Jack Zebulon 1933- *St&PR 93*
Moore, Jacqueline Shaleem 1937- *WhoAmW 93*
Moore, Jamel L., Jr. 1942- *St&PR 93*
Moore, James A. 1915- *St&PR 93*
Moore, James Alfred 1915- *WhoAm 92*
Moore, James Alfred 1939- *WhoE 93*
Moore, James Allan 1939- *WhoAm 92*
Moore, James B. d1991 *BioIn 17*
Moore, James E. 1936- *WhoSSW 93*
Moore, James E., III 1950- *St&PR 93*
Moore, James Everett, Jr. 1950- *WhoEmL 93*
Moore, James F. 1928- *WhoIns 93*
Moore, James Kelly 1950- *WhoEmL 93*
Moore, James L., Jr. 1942- *WhoAm 92*
Moore, James Mendon 1925- *WhoAm 92*
Moore, James Patrick *Law&B 92*
Moore, James Patrick, Jr. 1953- *WhoAm 92*
Moore, James R. 1948- *St&PR 93*
Moore, James Robert 1925- *WhoAm 92*
Moore, James T(almadge) 1936- *ConAu 139*
Moore, James Terrence, II 1948- *WhoAm 92*
Moore, James Warren 1942- *St&PR 93*
Moore, Jane Ann 1950- *WhoAmW 93*
Moore, Jane Ross 1929- *WhoAm 92*
Moore, Janet Marie 1947- *WhoAmW 93*
Moore, Janet P. *Law&B 92*
Moore, Janet Ruth 1949- *WhoAmW 93, WhoE 93*
Moore, Janice Rose 1938- *WhoAmW 93, WhoWor 93*
Moore, Janice Townley 1939- *WhoWrEP 92*
Moore, Jean Oliver 1925- *St&PR 93*
Moore, Jeffrey C. *Law&B 92*
Moore, Jeri 1953- *WhoAmW 93*
Moore, Jerrold Northrop 1934- *Baker 92*
Moore, Jesse A. 1951- *St&PR 93*
Moore, Jessica *AmWomPl*
Moore, Jill Ann 1956- *WhoAmW 93*
Moore, Jo Ella 1954- *WhoAmW 93*
Moore, Joan L. 1935- *WhoAmW 93*
Moore, Joanna Elizabeth 1937- *WhoSSW 93, WhoWor 93*
Moore, Joanna L. *Law&B 92*
Moore, Joanne Iweita 1928- *WhoAm 92, WhoAmW 93*
Moore, Jock d1990 *BioIn 17*
Moore, John 1761-1809 *HarEnMi*
Moore, John A. *Law&B 92*
Moore, John Allen 1912- *WhoWrEP 92*
Moore, John Arthur 1939- *WhoAm 92*
Moore, John Ashton 1940- *WhoAm 92*
Moore, John Atkin 1931- *St&PR 93, WhoAm 92*
Moore, John Colinton 1936- *WhoAsAP 91*
Moore, John Cordell 1912- *WhoAm 92, WhoWor 93*
Moore, John D. *St&PR 93*
Moore, John David *Law&B 92*
Moore, John David 1952- *WhoE 93*
Moore, John Dennis 1931- *WhoAm 92*
Moore, John Eddy 1943- *WhoAm 92*
Moore, John Edward 1920- *WhoWor 93*
Moore, John Edward, Jr. 1939- *St&PR 93*
Moore, John Edwin, Jr. 1942- *WhoAm 92*
Moore, John George, Jr. 1917- *WhoAm 92*
Moore, John H. 1926- *St&PR 93*
Moore, John Hampton 1935- *WhoAm 92*
Moore, John Hebron 1920- *WhoAm 92, WhoSSW 93*
Moore, John Henry, II 1929- *WhoAm 92*
Moore, John Ivan 1954- *St&PR 93*
Moore, John Joseph 1933- *WhoAm 92*
Moore, John L. *BioIn 17*
Moore, John Lee, III 1953- *WhoE 93*
Moore, John Lovell, Jr. 1929- *WhoAm 92*
Moore, John Morrison 1904- *WhoE 93*
Moore, John Newton 1920- *WhoAm 92*
Moore, John Norton 1937- *WhoAm 92, WhoWrEP 92*
Moore, John Porfilio 1934- *WhoAm 92*
Moore, John Rees 1918- *WhoWrEP 92*
Moore, John Robert 1947- *WhoEmL 93, WhoSSW 93, WhoWor 93*
Moore, John Ronald 1935- *WhoAm 92*
Moore, John Runyan 1929- *WhoE 93*
Moore, John Scott 1951- *St&PR 93*
Moore, John Spaeth, Jr. 1950- *WhoE 93*
Moore, John T. 1915- *St&PR 93*
Moore, John Travers 1908- *WhoAm 92*
Moore, John W(eeks) 1807-1889 *Baker 92*
Moore, John William 1928- *WhoE 93*
Moore, John William 1939- *WhoAm 92*
Moore, John Wilson 1920- *WhoAm 92*
Moore, Johnny 1940- *BioIn 17*
Moore, Jonathan 1932- *WhoAm 92*
Moore, Joseph Burton 1926- *WhoAm 92*
Moore, Joseph D. 1955- *St&PR 93*
Moore, Josephine Carroll 1925- *WhoAmW 93*
Moore, Joyce Kristina 1955- *WhoE 93, WhoEmL 93, WhoWor 93*
Moore, Judy I. 1940- *WhoAmW 93*
Moore, Judy King *Law&B 92*
Moore, Julia Alice 1950- *WhoE 93*
Moore, Junius T., Jr. 1922- *St&PR 93*
Moore, K.A. *Law&B 92*
Moore, Karen Lindsay 1946- *WhoAmW 93*
Moore, Kathleen Green 1934- *WhoAmW 93*
Moore, Kathleen Mary 1910- *WhoAmW 93*
Moore, Kay Wideman 1949- *WhoAmW 93*
Moore, Kenneth Cameron 1947- *WhoAm 92*
Moore, Kenneth Creyton 1932- *St&PR 93*
Moore, Kenneth Edwin 1933- *WhoAm 92*
Moore, Kenneth J. *Law&B 92*
Moore, Kenneth L. 1959- *St&PR 93*
Moore, Kevin Michael 1951- *WhoAm 92*
Moore, Kevin Wayne 1951- *WhoE 93*
Moore, Kim Alan 1951- *WhoEmL 93, WhoSSW 93*
Moore, Kurt Richard 1955- *WhoEmL 93*
Moore, L. Franklin, Jr. 1922- *St&PR 93*
Moore, Lahman D. 1946- *St&PR 93*
Moore, Larry *Law&B 92*
Moore, Laura Warren 1964- *WhoAmW 93*
Moore, Laurence John 1938- *WhoAm 92*
Moore, Lawrence Jack *Law&B 92*
Moore, Lee 1939- *DcCPCAm*
Moore, Lee Llewellyn 1939- *BioIn 17*
Moore, Lee Permenter 1923- *St&PR 93*
Moore, Lenard Duane 1958- *WhoWrEP 92*
Moore, Lenny 1933- *BioIn 17*

Moore, Leon *St&PR 93*
Moore, Leslie David 1931- *WhoAm 92*
Moore, Lewis Edward, Jr. 1932- *WhoSSW 93*
Moore, Libbie Ann 1960- *WhoAmW 93*
Moore, Lidian Ruth *AmWomPl*
Moore, Lilian 1909- *DcAmChF 1985, MajAI [port]*
Moore, Lillian 1909- *ConAu 38NR*
Moore, Linda B. *St&PR 93*
Moore, Linda Diane 1951- *WhoAmW 93*
Moore, Linda Kathleen 1944- *WhoAmW 93, WhoSSW 93*
Moore, Linda Marie Zajicek 1943- *WhoAmW 93*
Moore, Linda Perigo 1946- *WhoAmW 93, WhoWor 93*
Moore, Linda Picarelli 1943- *WhoAmW 93*
Moore, Linda Young 1942- *WhoAmW 93*
Moore, Lloyd Tolson, Jr. 1940- *St&PR 93*
Moore, Lois Jean *WhoAm 92, WhoAmW 93*
Moore, Loretta Westbrook 1938- *WhoAmW 93*
Moore, Lorrie *ConAu 39NR*
Moore, Lorrie (Marie L.) 1957- *WhoWrEP 92*
Moore, Loy Beene 1937- *WhoSSW 93*
Moore, Lucile 1910- *WhoAmW 93*
Moore, Luther T. *Law&B 92*
Moore, M. Thomas 1934- *St&PR 93*
Moore, Malcolm A. S. 1944- *WhoAm 92*
Moore, Malcolm Arthur 1937- *WhoAm 92*
Moore, Marc Anthony 1928- *WhoAm 92*
Moore, Margaret Anne Fort 1933- *WhoAmW 93*
Moore, Margaret Bear 1925- *WhoSSW 93*
Moore, Margaret D. 1948- *St&PR 93*
Moore, Margie Fay 1952- *WhoSSW 93*
Moore, Marianne 1887-1972 *BioIn 17, MagSAmL [port]*
Moore, Marie 1933- *WhoAm 92*
Moore, Marie Denise 1954- *WhoAmW 93*
Moore, Marie Lorena 1957- *ConAu 39NR*
Moore, Marilyn Adams 1933-1991 *BioIn 17*
Moore, Marilyn Bracey 1944- *WhoE 93*
Moore, Marilyn M. 1932- *WhoWrEP 92*
Moore, Marilyn Patricia 1950- *WhoEmL 93*
Moore, Marilyn R. 1935- *St&PR 93*
Moore, Mark Harrison 1947- *WhoAm 92, WhoWrEP 92*
Moore, Marlene 1957-1988 *BioIn 17*
Moore, Marsha Lynn 1946- *WhoE 93*
Moore, Mary *BioIn 17, WhoAm 92, WhoAmW 93*
Moore, Mary Ann 1953- *WhoAmW 93*
Moore, Mary (Louise) Carr 1873-1957 *Baker 92*
Moore, Mary Charlotte 1945- *WhoAm 92*
Moore, Mary Julia 1949- *WhoAmW 93, WhoE 93, WhoEmL 93*
Moore, Mary Louise 1928- *WhoAmW 93*
Moore, Mary Needham 1934- *WhoAmW 93*
Moore, Mary Tyler *BioIn 17*
Moore, Mary Tyler 1936- *WhoAm 92, WhoAmW 93*
Moore, Maurine 1932- *WhoWrEP 92*
Moore, Mavor 1919- *WhoAm 92*
Moore, Mechlin Dongan 1930- *St&PR 93, WhoAm 92*
Moore, Melanie Ethel 1952- *WhoAmW 93, WhoWor 93*
Moore, Melba *BioIn 17*
Moore, Melba 1945- *AfrAmBi, Baker 92*
Moore, Melba 1947- *WhoAm 92*
Moore, Melvin d1992 *NewYTBS 92*
Moore, Melvin 1924-1992 *BioIn 17*
Moore, Meryl Dale 1949- *WhoEmL 93*
Moore, Michael *BioIn 17, MiSFD 9*
Moore, Michael Arthur *WhoScE 91-1*
Moore, Michael D. 1939- *WhoAm 92*
Moore, Michael Edward 1948- *WhoEmL 93*
Moore, Michael Frederick *Law&B 92*
Moore, Michael Frederick 1957- *St&PR 93*
Moore, Michael Harve 1944- *St&PR 93*
Moore, Michael Henry 1943- *St&PR 93*
Moore, Michael Kenneth *WhoWor 93*
Moore, Michael Kenneth 1949- *WhoAsAP 91*
Moore, Michael Scott 1943- *WhoAm 92*
Moore, Michael T. 1948- *WhoAm 92*
Moore, Michael Thomas 1934- *WhoAm 92*
Moore, Michele Adrienne *Law&B 92*
Moore, Mike *WhoAm 92, WhoSSW 93*
Moore, Mildred *SweetSg A [port]*
Moore, Milo Anderson 1942- *WhoAm 92*
Moore, Minet Blackwell *AmWomPl*
Moore, Mona 1952- *WhoWrEP 92*
Moore, Morris Bill 1938- *WhoSSW 93*
Moore, Myron L., Jr. 1924- *St&PR 93*
Moore, Nancy Ann Gardner 1941- *WhoE 93*
Moore, Nancy Fischer 1937- *WhoAmW 93*
Moore, Nancy Lorene 1938- *WhoWrEP 92*
Moore, Nancy Newell 1939- *WhoAmW 93*
Moore, Nancy Quinn 1955- *WhoSSW 93*
Moore, Norman Slawson 1901- *WhoAm 92*
Moore, Oliver S., III 1942- *WhoAm 92*
Moore, Omar K. *BioIn 17*
Moore, P.S. *ScF&FL 92*
Moore, Pamela A. *Law&B 92*
Moore, Pamela Renee 1960- *WhoAmW 93, WhoSSW 93*
Moore, Pamela Rosewell *BioIn 17*
Moore, Pat Howard 1930- *St&PR 93, WhoAm 92*
Moore, Patricia Ann 1954- *WhoAmW 93, WhoEmL 93*
Moore, Patricia Anne *Law&B 92*
Moore, Patricia Anne 1956- *WhoE 93*
Moore, Patricia Kay 1947- *WhoAmW 93*
Moore, Patrick 1923- *ScF&FL 92*
Moore, Patrick Shawn 1956- *WhoEmL 93*
Moore, Paul *BioIn 17*
Moore, Paul, Jr. 1919- *WhoAm 92*
Moore, Paul Raymond 1913-1991 *BioIn 17*
Moore, Paula Jane 1960- *WhoEmL 93*
Moore, Paula Ruth 1953- *WhoSSW 93*
Moore, Pauline 1914- *SweetSg C [port]*
Moore, Pearl B. 1936- *WhoAm 92*
Moore, Peggy Sue 1942- *WhoAmW 93*
Moore, Perry *Law&B 92*
Moore, Peter Bartlett 1939- *WhoAm 92*
Moore, Peter O'Bannon 1961- *WhoSSW 93*
Moore, Philip Walsh 1920- *WhoAm 92*
Moore, Phyllis Lee 1953- *WhoWrEP 92*
Moore, Powell Allen 1938- *WhoAm 92, WhoE 93, WhoSSW 93*
Moore, Preston 1931- *St&PR 93*
Moore, Preston, Jr. *WhoAm 92*
Moore, R. Stuart 1924- *St&PR 93*
Moore, Randolph Graves 1939- *St&PR 93*
Moore, Rasheeda *BioIn 17*
Moore, Rayburn Sabatzky 1920- *ConAu 37NR, WhoAm 92*
Moore, Raylyn 1928- *ScF&FL 92*
Moore, Raymond S. 1915- *WhoWrEP 92*
Moore, Raymond Thomas 1926- *St&PR 93*
Moore, Richard *BioIn 17*
Moore, Richard 1925- *MiSFD 9*
Moore, Richard 1927- *BioIn 17, WhoWrEP 92*
Moore, Richard Alan 1930- *WhoAm 92*
Moore, Richard Alan 1948- *WhoEmL 93, WhoWor 93*
Moore, Richard Albert 1915- *WhoAm 92*
Moore, Richard Allan 1924- *WhoAm 92*
Moore, Richard Anthony 1914- *WhoAm 92, WhoWor 93*
Moore, Richard Carroll, Jr. 1946- *WhoSSW 93*
Moore, Richard Cone 1936- *St&PR 93*
Moore, Richard Earl 1940- *WhoAm 92*
Moore, Richard George *Law&B 92*
Moore, Richard George 1957- *WhoEmL 93*
Moore, Richard Glenn 1947- *WhoEmL 93*
Moore, Richard Harlan 1945- *WhoAm 92, WhoSSW 93*
Moore, Richard Horace 1950- *WhoE 93*
Moore, Richard Ilsley 1943- *St&PR 93*
Moore, Richard John 1954- *WhoEmL 93*
Moore, Richard Kerr 1923- *WhoAm 92*
Moore, Richard Lawrence 1934- *WhoE 93*
Moore, Richard Leroy, II 1948- *WhoE 93, WhoEmL 93*
Moore, Richard P. 1949- *St&PR 93*
Moore, Richard Thomas 1943- *WhoE 93*
Moore, Richard W. 1927- *St&PR 93*
Moore, Richard Wraxall 1949- *WhoEmL 93*
Moore, Robert 1927-1984 *MiSFD 9N*
Moore, Robert B. 1949- *St&PR 93*
Moore, Robert C. *Law&B 92*
Moore, Robert Charles *Law&B 92*
Moore, Robert Clay 1934- *St&PR 93*
Moore, Robert Clyde, Jr. 1947- *St&PR 93*
Moore, Robert Condit 1921- *WhoAm 92*
Moore, Robert E. 1925- *St&PR 93*
Moore, Robert Edward 1923- *WhoAm 92*
Moore, Robert Eric 1927- *WhoE 93*
Moore, Robert Francis 1952- *WhoE 93*
Moore, Robert Franklin 1945- *WhoSSW 93*
Moore, Robert Henry 1940- *WhoAm 92, WhoIns 93, WhoWor 93*
Moore, Robert Howard 1940- *St&PR 93*
Moore, Robert J. 1928- *St&PR 93*
Moore, Robert John, Jr. 1948- *WhoE 93*
Moore, Robert L. *ScF&FL 92*
Moore, Robert Laurence 1940- *WhoAm 92, WhoWrEP 92*
Moore, Robert Lowell, Jr. 1925- *WhoAm 92, WhoWrEP 92*
Moore, Robert Madison 1925- *WhoAm 92*
Moore, Robert Samuel *WhoScE 91-1*
Moore, Robert Stuart 1924- *WhoAm 92*
Moore, Robert William 1924- *WhoAm 92*
Moore, Robert Yates 1931- *WhoAm 92*
Moore, Roberta Lynn 1952- *WhoWrEP 92*
Moore, Robin 1925- *ScF&FL 92*
Moore, Rod Alan 1930- *St&PR 93*
Moore, Roger A. 1931-1990 *BioIn 17*
Moore, Roger E. 1955- *ScF&FL 92*
Moore, Roger George 1927- *WhoAm 92*
Moore, Roland Edward 1920- *WhoScE 91-3*
Moore, Ronald Lester 1924- *St&PR 93*
Moore, Ronald W. *Law&B 92, MiSFD 9*
Moore, Rosalie 1910- *WhoWrEP 92*
Moore, Rosemary A. *Law&B 92*
Moore, Roy Dean 1940- *WhoAm 92*
Moore, Roy Edward 1956- *St&PR 93*
Moore, Roy Leamon 1947- *WhoEmL 93*
Moore, Royal Norman, Jr. 1935- *WhoAm 92*
Moore, Rudin *ScF&FL 92*
Moore, S. Donald *St&PR 93*
Moore, Sally Falk 1924- *WhoAm 92*
Moore, Sally Joy Donohue 1943- *WhoAmW 93*
Moore, Sam 1935- *See* Sam & Dave *SoulM*
Moore, Samuel David 1935- *See* Sam and Dave *ConMus 8*
Moore, Sandra 1945- *WhoE 93*
Moore, Sandra Crockett 1945- *ConAu 139*
Moore, Sandra Kay 1957- *WhoAmW 93, WhoEmL 93*
Moore, Scott D. 1953- *WhoIns 93*
Moore, Sean 1926- *WhoAm 92*
Moore, Sheila A. *Law&B 92*
Moore, Sherry S. *St&PR 93*
Moore, Shirley Beaham 1934- *WhoAmW 93*
Moore, Shirley May *St&PR 93*
Moore, Shirley Throckmorton 1918- *WhoAmW 93*
Moore, Sidney *BioIn 17*
Moore, Simon *MiSFD 9*
Moore, Sonia 1902- *WhoAm 92, WhoE 93, WhoWor 93*
Moore, Stanley J. *Law&B 92*
Moore, Stanley R. *ScF&FL 92*
Moore, Stephen Edward 1946- *WhoEmL 93*
Moore, Stephen Gates 1923- *WhoAm 92*
Moore, Stephen Jefferson 1948- *St&PR 93*
Moore, Steve M. 1957- *St&PR 93*
Moore, Steven Eaton *Law&B 92*
Moore, Susan Evelyn 1954- *WhoAmW 93*
Moore, Susan Lynn 1944- *WhoAmW 93*
Moore, Suzan E. *Law&B 92*
Moore, T. Justin, Jr. 1925- *St&PR 93*
Moore, Tanna Lynn 1954- *WhoAmW 93*
Moore, Tara 1950- *BioIn 17, ConAu 38NR*
Moore, Teresa *WhoWrEP 92*
Moore, Terrill Mackenzie 1955- *St&PR 93*
Moore, Terris 1908- *WhoAm 92*
Moore, Terry Bluford 1912- *BiDAMSp 1989*
Moore, Theodore 1934- *St&PR 93*
Moore, Theresa A. *Law&B 92*
Moore, Thomas 1779-1852 *Baker 92, BioIn 17, OxDcOp*
Moore, Thomas 1946- *ScF&FL 92*
Moore, Thomas Aloysius *Law&B 92*
Moore, Thomas Carrol 1936- *WhoAm 92*
Moore, Thomas David 1933- *WhoSSW 93*
Moore, Thomas David 1937- *WhoAm 92*
Moore, Thomas Dickson 1930- *St&PR 93*
Moore, Thomas Evan 1942- *WhoSSW 93*
Moore, Thomas F., Jr. *Law&B 92*
Moore, Thomas Gale 1930- *WhoAm 92*
Moore, Thomas LeVal d1990 *BioIn 17*
Moore, Thomas Lloyd 1942- *WhoAm 92*
Moore, Thomas M. *Law&B 92*
Moore, Thomas Nash 1927- *WhoAm 92*
Moore, Thomas Paul 1928- *WhoAm 92*
Moore, Thomas R. 1932- *WhoAm 92, WhoWor 93*
Moore, Thomas W. *Law&B 92*
Moore, Thomas W. 1939- *St&PR 93*
Moore, Thomas William 1940- *WhoE 93*
Moore, Thurston c. 1959- *See* Sonic Youth *ConMus 9*
Moore, Timothy Glen 1950- *WhoSSW 93*
Moore, Todd Allen 1937- *WhoWrEP 92*
Moore, Tom *MiSFD 9*
Moore, Tom 1943- *WhoAm 92*
Moore, Toni E. *Law&B 92*
Moore, Tyrone Bradley 1949- *WhoE 93*
Moore, Undine Smith 1904-1989 *BioIn 17*
Moore, Vernon *BioIn 17*
Moore, Vernon Francis 1947- *WhoWor 93*
Moore, Vernon Lee 1928- *WhoAm 92*
Moore, Victor 1876-1962 *QDrFCA 92 [port]*
Moore, Virginia Blanck 1915- *WhoWrEP 92*
Moore, Virginia Bradley 1932- *WhoAmW 93, WhoE 93*
Moore, Virginia Lee Smith 1943- *WhoAmW 93*
Moore, W. Henson 1939- *BioIn 17*
Moore, W. James 1916- *St&PR 93*
Moore, Waddy William 1928- *WhoSSW 93*
Moore, Wallace *ScF&FL 92*
Moore, Walter Bruce 1940- *WhoAm 92*
Moore, Walter Calvin 1910- *WhoWor 93*
Moore, Walter D., Jr. 1924- *WhoSSW 93*
Moore, Ward 1903-1978 *ScF&FL 92*
Moore, Ward Wilfred 1924- *WhoAm 92*
Moore, Weldon Leslie 1957- *WhoEmL 93*
Moore, Wesley C. 1950- *St&PR 93*
Moore, Wesley Sanford 1935- *WhoAm 92*
Moore, Wildey J. 1937- *St&PR 93*
Moore, William d1992 *NewYTBS 92*
Moore, William A., Jr. *Law&B 92*
Moore, William B. *Law&B 92*
Moore, William B. 1942- *St&PR 93*
Moore, William B. 1952- *St&PR 93*
Moore, William Black, Jr. 1924- *WhoSSW 93*
Moore, William Edward 1949- *WhoIns 93*
Moore, William Evan, II 1925- *St&PR 93*
Moore, William Grover, Jr. *WhoAm 92*
Moore, William H. d1992 *NewYTBS 92 [port]*
Moore, William H., III 1940- *St&PR 93*
Moore, William J. 1934- *St&PR 93*
Moore, William Jason 1938- *WhoAm 92, WhoSSW 93*
Moore, William John Myles 1924- *WhoAm 92*
Moore, William L. 1927-1963 *EncAACR*
Moore, William Leroy, Jr. 1934- *WhoAm 92*
Moore, William P. *Law&B 92*
Moore, William Whitney 1918- *WhoWrEP 92*
Moore, Willis Henry Allphin 1940- *WhoWor 93*
Moore, Woodrow L. 1945- *St&PR 93*
Moore, Yvette 1958- *SmATA 70*
Moore, Yvonne Laughlin Howard R. 1943- *WhoAmW 93*
Moore, Zephyr B. *St&PR 93*
Moore-Carroll, Patricia Susan 1957- *WhoAmW 93*
Moore-Day, Bonnie Lou 1956- *WhoEmL 93*
Moorefield, James Lee 1922- *WhoAm 92*
Moorehead, Agnes 1906-1974 *IntDcF 2-3*
Moorehead, Alan 1910-1983 *BioIn 17*
Moorehead, Caroline 1944- *ConAu 39NR*
Moorehead, Edward A. 1932- *St&PR 93*
Moorehead, Robert S., Jr. *Law&B 92*
Moore-Jason, Linda J. *Law&B 92*
Moorer, Thomas Hinman 1912- *WhoAm 92*
Moores, Anita Jean Young 1944- *WhoAmW 93*
Moores, Brian *WhoScE 91-1*
Moores, John J. *BioIn 17*
Moorfoot, Mark V. 1945- *St&PR 93*
Moorhead, Carlos J. 1922- *CngDr 91, WhoAm 92*
Moorhead, David Farrell 1932- *St&PR 93*
Moorhead, Gerald Lee 1947- *WhoAm 92, WhoSSW 93*
Moorhead, Joanna L. *Law&B 92*
Moorhead, John *WhoScE 91-1*
Moorhead, John c. 1760-1804 *Baker 92*
Moorhead, Paul Sidney 1924- *WhoAm 92*
Moorhead, Robert G. 1921- *St&PR 93*
Moorhead, Robert James, II 1958- *WhoSSW 93*
Moorhead, Rolande Annette Reverdy 1937- *WhoAmW 93*
Moorhead, Ruth Anne 1948- *WhoEmL 93*
Moorhead, Sylvester Andrew 1920- *WhoAm 92*
Moorhead, Thomas B. 1934- *St&PR 93*
Moorhead, Thomas Burch 1934- *WhoAm 92, WhoE 93*
Moorhead, Thomas L. *Law&B 92*
Moorhead, Thomas Leib 1936- *St&PR 93*
Moorhouse, Ellen Catherine 1928- *WhoScE 91-3, WhoWor 93*
Moorhouse, Jocelyn *MiSFD 9*
Moorhouse, John *ScF&FL 92*
Moorhouse, Linda Virginia 1945- *WhoAmW 93*
Moorhouse, Robert E. 1943- *St&PR 93*
Moorhouse, Robert Gordon *WhoScE 91-1*
Mooring, Robert Franklin 1946- *St&PR 93*
Moorman, Charles 1925- *ScF&FL 92*
Moorman, Charlotte 1933-1991 *BioIn 17*
Moorman, Gilbert Wayne 1943- *St&PR 93*
Moorman, Margaret *BioIn 17*
Moorman, Michael F. 1942- *WhoAm 92*
Moorman, Michael Field 1942- *St&PR 93*

Moorman, Rosemary Lucille 1957- *WhoWrEP 92*
Moorman, Sally *BioIn 17*
Moorman, Theo 1907-1990 *BioIn 17*
Moormann, David Lawrence 1953- *WhoSSW 93*
Moorshead, John Earl 1939- *St&PR 93*
Moos, Edward A. 1937- *St&PR 93, WhoE 93*
Moos, Julian Clifford 1923- *St&PR 93*
Moos, Ludwig von 1910-1990 *BioIn 17*
Moos, Paul 1863-1952 *Baker 92*
Moosa, Ibrahim Rasheed 1951- *WhoWor 93*
Moosbrugger, Mary Coultrip 1947- *WhoEmL 93*
Moosbruker, Jane Barbara 1938- *WhoE 93*
Moose, George E. 1944- *WhoAm 92*
Moose, Joseph Stephen 1964- *WhoSSW 93*
Moose, Richard M. *WhoAm 92*
Moose, Ruth Morris 1938- *WhoWrEP 92*
Moose, Vicki Clark 1958- *WhoAmW 93*
Moose, William Whitaker, Jr. 1961- *WhoSSW 93*
Mooser, (Jean Pierre Joseph) Aloys 1770-1839 *Baker 92*
Mooser, R(obert) Aloys 1876-1969 *Baker 92*
Mooser, Stephen 1941- *ScF&FL 92*
Moosman, Elizabeth Darlene 1942- *WhoAmW 93*
Moosman, George L. 1941- *St&PR 93*
Moosmayer, Hans-Ulrich *WhoScE 91-3*
Moossa, A. R. 1939- *WhoAm 92*
Moossy, John 1925- *WhoAm 92*
Moote, A. Lloyd 1931- *WhoAm 92*
Mooty, John W. 1922- *St&PR 93*
Mooty, John William 1922- *WhoAm 92*
Mooz, Ralph Peter 1940- *WhoAm 92*
Moquist, Paul *St&PR 93*
Mor, Anthonis c. 1512-c. 1576 *BioIn 17*
Mora, David Saul 1956- *WhoSSW 93*
Mora, Enrique J. *Law&B 92*
Mora, Ernest J. *St&PR 93*
Mora, Eugene J. 1935- *St&PR 93*
Mora, Francisco 1922- *WhoAm 92*
Mora, Francisco Luis 1874-1940 *HispAmA*
Mora, James Ernest 1935- *BiDAMSp 1989, WhoAm 92, WhoSSW 93*
Mora, Jean Claude Pierre 1944- *WhoWor 93*
Mora, Jose Ferrater 1912-1991 *BioIn 17*
Mora, Jose Maria Luis 1794-1850 *DcMexL*
Mora, Judith Stevens 1946- *WhoEmL 93*
Mora, Kathleen Rita 1948- *WhoEmL 93*
Mora, Marcial Jose *Law&B 92*
Mora, Pat 1942- *NotHsAW 93 [port]*
Mora, Philippe *MiSFD 9*
Mora, Philippe 1949- *WhoEmL 93*
Moraal, Johannes 1934- *WhoScE 91-3*
Morabito, Bruno Paul 1922- *WhoAm 92*
Morabito, John R. 1924- *WhoAm 92*
Morace, Christine T. *Law&B 92*
Morack, Albert John, Jr. 1948- *St&PR 93*
Moraczewski, Robert Leo 1942- *WhoAm 92*
Moradas Ferreira, Pedro 1952- *WhoScE 91-3*
Moradi, Ahmad F. 1955- *WhoEmL 93, WhoSSW 93*
Moradzadeh, Michael D. *Law&B 92*
Moraff, Barbara 1939- *WhoWrEP 92*
Moraga, Cherrie 1952- *AmWomWr 92, HispAmA, NotHsAW 93 [port]*
Moraga, Gary A. Thompson- *ScF&FL 92*
Moragne E Silva, Michele Lowe 1955- *WhoEmL 93, WhoSSW 93*
Morahan, Christopher 1929- *MiSFD 9*
Morahan, Page S. 1940- *WhoAmW 93*
Morahan-Martin, Janet May 1944- *WhoAmW 93*
Morain, Lloyd L. 1917- *St&PR 93*
Morain, Mary Stone Dewing 1911- *WhoWor 93*
Morain, Stephen Michael 1945- *St&PR 93*
Morais, Carlos A.P. Campos 1939- *WhoScE 91-3*
Morais, Joao Luiz 1934- *WhoWor 93*
Morais, Joao M. Figueiredo 1953- *WhoScE 91-3*
Morais, Jose Mauro 1948- *WhoUN 92*
Moraitis, Karen Karl 1943- *WhoAmW 93, WhoSSW 93*
Morake, Kebathlamang Pitseyosi 1930- *WhoAfr*
Morakis, James Anthony 1934- *WhoE 93*
Moral, Alex N. 1956- *St&PR 93*
Morales *WhoWrEP 92*
Morales, Adelaida Garcia *BioIn 17*
Morales, Alberto J. 1952- *St&PR 93*
Morales, Alberto Jesus 1962- *WhoWor 93*
Morales, Alejandro 1944- *HispAmA [port]*
Morales, Andres, Jr. *Law&B 92*
Morales, Aurora Levins 1954- *BioIn 17*
Morales, Carl E. *WhoAm 92*
Morales, Carlos Alberto 1946- *WhoE 93*
Morales, Carlos M. *Law&B 92*
Morales, Carlos O. 1953- *Baker 92*
Morales, Carlota Eloisa 1946- *WhoAmW 93, WhoEmL 93, WhoSSW 93, WhoWor 93*
Morales, Catherine Phillips 1949- *WhoAmW 93*
Morales, Cristobal de c. 1500-1553 *Baker 92*
Morales, Cynthia Torres 1952- *WhoAmW 93*
Morales, Dan *WhoAm 92, WhoSSW 93*
Morales, David 1947- *WhoE 93*
Morales, Diane K. 1946- *WhoAmW 93*
Morales, Diane Kay 1946- *WhoAm 92*
Morales, Esai *ConTFT 10*
Morales, Jacobo *MiSFD 9*
Morales, Jaime E. 1947- *WhoIns 93*
Morales, Larry L. 1939- *St&PR 93*
Morales, Luis de c. 1509-1586 *BioIn 17*
Morales, Manuel Sebastian 1956- *WhoEmL 93*
Morales, Melesio 1838-1908 *Baker 92*
Morales, Miguel Angel 1962- *WhoSSW 93*
Morales, Olallo (Juan Magnus) 1874-1957 *Baker 92*
Morales, Pablo A. 1918- *WhoAm 92*
Morales, Pedro 1947- *WhoE 93*
Morales, Peter 1947- *St&PR 93*
Morales, Rafael 1919- *BioIn 17*
Morales, Rosario 1930- *BioIn 17*
Morales, Sylvia 20th cent.- *HispAmA [port]*
Morales, Sylvia 1953- *WhoAmW 93*
Morales, Yull Gary *BioIn 17*
Morales Carrion, Arturo *BioIn 17*
Morales Florez, Martin Carlos 1920- *WhoWor 93*
Morales-Rodriguez, Eduardo-Antonio 1936- *WhoUN 92*
Morales Troncoso, Carlos 1940- *DcCPCAm*
Morales Troncoso, Carlos A. 1940- *WhoWor 93*
Moralt *Baker 92*
Moralt, Georg 1781-1818 *Baker 92*
Moralt, Johann Baptist 1777-1825 *Baker 92*
Moralt, Joseph 1775-1855 *Baker 92*
Moralt, Philipp 1780-1830 *Baker 92*
Moralt, Rudolf 1902-1958 *Baker 92*
Moran, Allan V. 1948- *St&PR 93*
Moran, Barbara Burns 1944- *WhoAm 92, WhoAmW 93*
Moran, Charles A. 1943- *WhoAm 92, WhoWor 93*
Moran, Christa Ilse Merkel 1946- *WhoSSW 93*
Moran, D. *WhoScE 91-1*
Moran, Daniel *ScF&FL 92*
Moran, Daniel Austin 1936- *WhoAm 92*
Moran, Daniel Edward 1941- *St&PR 93*
Moran, Daniel Keys 1962- *ScF&FL 92*
Moran, David E. *Law&B 92*
Moran, Dorothy D. *Law&B 92*
Moran, Edward Joseph *Law&B 92*
Moran, Edward Martin 1956- *St&PR 93*
Moran, Emilio Federico 1946- *WhoEmL 93*
Moran, Gary M. 1941- *St&PR 93*
Moran, George William 1964- *WhoEmL 93*
Moran, Gerald Joseph 1939- *St&PR 93*
Moran, Glenn J. *Law&B 92*
Moran, Glenn J. 1947- *St&PR 93*
Moran, Gordon William 1938- *WhoAm 92*
Moran, Gregory J. 1954- *St&PR 93*
Moran, Harry J. 1932- *St&PR 93*
Moran, Hugh Alexander, Jr. 1947- *WhoSSW 93*
Moran, J.A. 1932- *St&PR 93*
Moran, Jackie d1990 *BioIn 17*
Moran, James Byron 1930- *WhoAm 92*
Moran, James D., III 1951- *WhoEmL 93, WhoSSW 93*
Moran, James J. 1940- *St&PR 93*
Moran, James Joseph 1925- *St&PR 93*
Moran, James P. 1945- *CngDr 91*
Moran, James Patrick 1945- *WhoAm 92, WhoSSW 93*
Moran, Jeffrey William 1954- *WhoE 93, WhoEmL 93*
Moran, John *BioIn 17*
Moran, John A. 1932- *WhoAm 92*
Moran, John Bernard 1936- *WhoAm 92*
Moran, John C. *Law&B 92*
Moran, John C. 1942- *ScF&FL 92*
Moran, John Charles 1942- *WhoWrEP 92*
Moran, John Charles, Jr. 1942- *WhoSSW 93*
Moran, John D. *Law&B 92*
Moran, John Douglas 1926- *WhoE 93*
Moran, John Henry, Jr. 1923- *WhoAm 92*
Moran, John J., Jr. *Law&B 92*
Moran, John Joseph 1916- *WhoAm 92*
Moran, John Patrick, Jr. 1943- *WhoE 93*
Moran, John W. 1914- *St&PR 93*
Moran, Joseph Milbert 1929- *WhoAm 92*
Moran, Joseph Richard 1942- *St&PR 93*
Moran, Joseph Sullivan *Law&B 92*
Moran, Joseph William 1927- *St&PR 93*
Moran, Joyce E. *Law&B 92*
Moran, Julie Lumpkin 1963- *WhoE 93*
Moran, Juliette M. 1917- *WhoAm 92, WhoAmW 93*
Moran, Kevin 1948- *WhoScE 91-1*
Moran, Kevin P. 1952- *St&PR 93*
Moran, Kyle *Law&B 92*
Moran, Kyle Anne 1960- *WhoEmL 93*
Moran, Lois 1909-1990 *BioIn 17*
Moran, M. Marcus, Jr. 1943- *St&PR 93*
Moran, Mabel M. *AmWomPl*
Moran, Marshall d1992 *BioIn 17*
Moran, Martin J. *Law&B 92*
Moran, Martin Joseph 1930- *WhoAm 92, WhoE 93*
Moran, Mary Anne 1947- *WhoEmL 93*
Moran, Mary Bernadette 1941- *WhoWor 93*
Moran, Mary Chapar *WhoAm 92*
Moran, Mary E. *Law&B 92*
Moran, Mary Hurley 1947- *WhoSSW 93*
Moran, Maura K. *Law&B 92*
Moran, Melvin Robert 1930- *St&PR 93*
Moran, Michael G. 1947- *ConAu 138*
Moran, Michael George 1947- *WhoSSW 93*
Moran, Michael Marcus, Jr. 1943- *WhoE 93*
Moran, Michael P. *Law&B 92*
Moran, Michael R. *Law&B 92*
Moran, Michael R. 1946- *St&PR 93*
Moran, Noel F. 1936- *St&PR 93*
Moran, Patrick Joseph 1876-1924 *BiDAMSp 1989*
Moran, Paul James 1947- *WhoAm 92*
Moran, Peter *WhoScE 91-1*
Moran, Philip David 1937- *WhoE 93, WhoWor 93*
Moran, Polly 1883-1952 *QDrFCA 92 [port]*
Moran, Rachel 1956- *WhoAm 92, WhoAmW 93*
Moran, Ria *BioIn 17*
Moran, Ricardo Julio 1939- *WhoE 93*
Moran, Richard 1942- *ScF&FL 92*
Moran, Richard Adrian 1931- *St&PR 93*
Moran, Robert Daniel 1929- *WhoAm 92*
Moran, Robert Earl 1936- *St&PR 93*
Moran, Robert J. 1941- *St&PR 93*
Moran, Robert (Leonard) 1937- *Baker 92*
Moran, Rolando *DcCPCAm*
Moran, Ronald P. *Law&B 92*
Moran, Sarah Judson 1956- *WhoAmW 93*
Moran, Sean T. 1958- *St&PR 93*
Moran, Susan Elaine 1964- *WhoAmW 93*
Moran, Teresa 1952- *WhoAmW 93*
Moran, Terrence R. 1941- *St&PR 93*
Moran, Thomas Francis 1936- *WhoAm 92, WhoSSW 93*
Moran, Thomas Joseph 1920- *WhoAm 92*
Moran, Thomas P. 1937- *WhoSSW 93*
Moran, Tom 1943- *BioIn 17*
Moran, Tom M. *Law&B 92*
Moran, Victor John, III 1951- *WhoIns 93*
Moran, W. Dennis 1940- *St&PR 93, WhoAm 92*
Moran, Wilfred F. 1928- *St&PR 93*
Moran, William Charles 1935- *WhoSSW 93*
Moran, William Edward 1932- *WhoAm 92, WhoSSW 93*
Moran, William Madison 1948- *WhoEmL 93, WhoSSW 93*
Moran Castaneda, Rafael *DcCPCAm*
Morand, Peter 1935- *WhoAm 92*
Morand, Robert F. *Law&B 92*
Morandi, Carlo 1947- *WhoWor 93*
Morandi, Giorgio 1890-1964 *BioIn 17*
Morandi, Riccardo 1902-1989 *BioIn 17*
Morandini, Riccardo 1925- *WhoScE 91-3*
Morando, Bruno L.J. 1931- *WhoScE 91-2*
Moranis, Rick *MiSFD 9*
Moranis, Rick 1954- *QDrFCA 92*
Morano, Carl John 1958- *WhoEmL 93*
Morano, Michael Robert 1918- *St&PR 93*
Moran-Olden, Fanny 1855-1905 *Baker 92*
Morant, Brenda White 1944- *WhoAmW 93*
Morant, Mack Bernard 1946- *WhoWrEP 92*
Morant, Ricardo Bernardino 1926- *WhoAm 92*
Morante, Elsa 1916-1985 *BioIn 17*
Morante, Laura *BioIn 17*
Moranz, Gary A. 1950- *St&PR 93*
Morar, Roman 1932- *WhoScE 91-4*
Morari, Manfred 1951- *WhoAm 92*
Moraru, Constantin 1933- *WhoScE 91-4*
Moraru, Ioan 1927- *WhoScE 91-4*
Moras, Dino 1944- *WhoScE 91-2*
Mora Salas, Manuel *DcCPCAm*
Morash, Frederick Douglas 1947- *St&PR 93*
Morash, Kenneth R. 1943- *St&PR 93*
Morat, Philippe L. 1937- *WhoScE 91-2*
Morath, Inge 1923- *WhoAm 92*
Morath, Max Edward 1926- *WhoAm 92*
Moratti, Gian Marco 1936- *WhoWor 93*
Moratz, Hermann 1921- *St&PR 93*
Morauski, Karen A. *Law&B 92*
Morava, Carol *Law&B 92*
Mora Valverde, Manuel 1908- *DcCPCAm*
Moravcik, Gary Joseph 1959- *St&PR 93*
Moravcsik, Michael J. *BioIn 17*
Moravec, Ivan 1930- *Baker 92*
Moravec, Lisa Kay 1962- *WhoAmW 93, WhoEmL 93, WhoWor 93*
Moravek, John P. *Law&B 92*
Moravia, Alberto 1907-1990 *BioIn 17, ScF&FL 92*
Moravia, Carmen Llera 1954- *BioIn 17*
Moravitz, Francis Edward 1933- *WhoAm 92*
Moravsik, R.J. 1942- *St&PR 93*
Moravsik, Robert J. *Law&B 92*
Moravy, L. Joe 1950- *WhoAm 92*
Morawetz, Cathleen Synge 1923- *WhoAm 92, WhoAmW 93, WhoE 93*
Morawetz, Herbert 1915- *WhoAm 92*
Morawetz, Oskar 1917- *Baker 92*
Morawiec, Alicja Swierzb 1946- *WhoEmL 93*
Morawiec, Henryk 1933- *WhoScE 91-4*
Morawiecki, Andrzej 1929- *WhoScE 91-4*
Morawski, Tadeusz 1940- *WhoScE 91-4*
Morayati, Shamil Jassim 1953- *WhoEmL 93, WhoWor 93*
Moray Williams, Ursula 1911- *MajAI [port], SmATA 73 [port]*
Moraz, Patrick 1948- See Yes *ConMus 8*
Morbach, John P. 1943- *St&PR 93*
Morbidi, Mario 1953- *WhoWor 93*
Morby, Jacqueline 1937- *WhoAm 92*
Morby, Jeffrey L. 1937- *St&PR 93*
Morby, Jeffrey Lewis 1937- *WhoAm 92*
Morcheles, Bernard 1939- *St&PR 93*
Morcillo Linares, Manuel 1948- *WhoScE 91-3*
Morco, John d1873 *BioIn 17*
Morcott, Southwood J. 1938- *St&PR 93*
Morcott, Southwood J. 1939- *WhoAm 92*
Mordane, Thomas *ScF&FL 92*
Mordarski, Marian 1927- *WhoScE 91-4*
Mordaunt, Walter d1991 *BioIn 17*
Mordchelles-Regnier, G. *WhoScE 91-2*
Mordden, Ethan 1949- *Baker 92, ConGAN*
Mordecai, Alfred 1804-1887 *BioIn 17*
Mordecai, Benjamin 1944- *WhoAm 92*
Mordecai, Jacob 1762-1838 *BioIn 17*
Mordek, Hubert Klaus Wolfgang 1939- *WhoWor 93*
Morden, John Reid 1941- *WhoAm 92*
Mordfin, Leonard 1929- *WhoE 93*
Mordhorst, Carl-Heinrich 1926- *WhoScE 91-2*
Mordike, Barry Leslie 1934- *WhoScE 91-3*
Mordini, Patrick 1949- *WhoScE 91-2*
Mordkin, Mikhail 1880-1944 *BioIn 17*
Mordler, John Michael 1938- *WhoWor 93*
Mordo, Jean Henri 1945- *St&PR 93*
Morduchow, Morris 1921- *WhoE 93*
Mordue, John Graham 1934- *WhoScE 91-1*
Mordwin, John Rickford 1947- *WhoEmL 93*
Mordy, C. Edward 1943- *St&PR 93*
Mordy, James Calvin 1927- *WhoAm 92*
More, Anthony c. 1512-c. 1576 *BioIn 17*
More, Caroline *ConAu 37NR*
More, Dominick D. 1942- *St&PR 93*
More, Douglas McLochlan 1926- *WhoAm 92*
More, Florence E. *AmWomPl*
More, Hannah 1745-1833 *BioIn 17, DcLB 116 [port]*
More, Henry 1614-1687 *BioIn 17, DcLB 126 [port]*
More, John R. *Law&B 92*
More, Kenneth 1914-1982 *IntDcF 2-3 [port]*
More, Meredith 1937- *ScF&FL 92*
More, Philip Harvey Birnbaum 1944- *WhoWor 93*
More, Philip Jerome 1911- *WhoAm 92, WhoSSW 93, WhoWor 93*
More, Ron J. 1950- *St&PR 93*
More, Syver Wakeman 1950- *WhoWor 93*
More, Thomas, Saint 1478-1535 *BioIn 17*
Morea, Douglas Michael *Law&B 92*
Moreau, Bernard Claude 1947- *WhoE 93*
Moreau, Claude 1924- *WhoScE 91-2*
Moreau, James William 1948- *WhoE 93, WhoWor 93*
Moreau, Jean-Baptiste 1656-1733 *Baker 92*
Moreau, Jean Victor Marie 1763-1813 *HarEnMi*
Moreau, Jeanne *BioIn 17*
Moreau, Jeanne 1928- *IntDcF 2-3 [port], MiSFD 9, WhoWor 93*

Moreau, Leon 1870-1946 Baker 92
Moreau, Marie Colette 1955- WhoWor 93
Moreau, Mireille 1925- WhoScE 91-2
Moreau, Robert 1939- St&PR 93
Moreau, Ronald A. 1947- St&PR 93
Moreau, Stephen John 1944- WhoE 93
Moreby, David H. WhoScE 91-1
Morecambe, Eric 1926-1984 ScF&FL 92
Morecambe, Eric 1926-1984 & Wise, Ernie 1925- QDrFCA 92 [port]
Morecki, Adam 1929- WhoScE 91-4
Morecroft, Michael John 1942- St&PR 93
Moredock, Gerald Michael 1948- WhoSSW 93
Moreels, A.A. 1928- WhoScE 91-2
Moreels, Guy 1943- WhoScE 91-2
Morehart, Donald Hadley 1938- St&PR 93, WhoAm 92
Morehead, Charles Richard 1947- St&PR 93, WhoAm 92, WhoIns 93
Morehead, James Bruce BioIn 17
Morehead, James Caddall, Jr. 1913- WhoAm 92
Morehead, John 1946- St&PR 93
Morehead, Martha Hines 1923- WhoSSW 93
Morehead, Russel R. 1947- St&PR 93
Morehead, Seth Marvin, Jr. 1934- WhoSSW 93
Morehead, Simon Eber 1941- St&PR 93
Morehous, Dean Allen, Jr. 1957- WhoEmL 93
Morehous, Lynn G. Law&B 92
Morehouse, Dale H. 1933- St&PR 93
Morehouse, David C. WhoAm 92
Morehouse, Edward John Law&B 92
Morehouse, James Ernest 1944- St&PR 93
Morehouse, John Farley 1964- WhoE 93
Morehouse, Sherri K. 1955- WhoEmL 93
Morehouse, Tom 1957- St&PR 93
Morehouse, Ward 1929- WhoE 93
Moreillon, Jacques Pierre 1939- WhoWor 93
Morein, Bror 1934- WhoScE 91-4
Morein, Joan Zaret 1942- WhoAmW 93
Morein, Joseph A. WhoAm 92
Morein, Joseph A. 1938- St&PR 93
Morein, Leeann 1954- St&PR 93
Morein, Mary fl. 1707- BioIn 17
Moreines, Susan Fern 1956- WhoAmW 93
Moreira, Antone F. 1938- St&PR 93
Moreira, Antonio Leal 1758-1819 Baker 92, OxDcOp
Moreira, Delio 1931- WhoWor 93
Moreira, Ilidio WhoScE 91-3
Moreira, Joaquim Manhaes Law&B 92
Moreira, Marcilio Marques 1931- WhoWor 93
Moreira, Marcio Martins 1947- St&PR 93, WhoAm 92, WhoEmL 93, WhoWor 93
Moreira, Tomaz WhoScE 91-3
Moreira Mesquita, Jose F. WhoScE 91-3
Morejon, Nancy 1944- BioIn 17, SpAmA
Morel, Auguste-Francois 1809-1881 Baker 92
Morel, (Joseph Raoul) Francois (d'Assise) 1926- Baker 92
Morel, Guy E. 1949- WhoWor 93
Morel, James C. Law&B 92
Morel, Jean 1903-1975 Baker 92
Morel, Justin Junior 1950- WhoWor 93
Morel, Marisa 1914- OxDcOp
Morel, Pierre 1933- WhoScE 91-4
Morelan, Paula Kay 1949- WhoAm 92, WhoSSW 93
Moreland, Alvin Franklin 1931- WhoAm 92
Moreland, Alvin LeRoy 1946- WhoSSW 93
Moreland, Brendan Francis 1933- St&PR 93
Moreland, Cheryl Jean Law&B 92
Moreland, Donald Carl 1923- WhoAm 92
Moreland, Donald Edwin 1919- WhoSSW 93
Moreland, Ferrin Bates 1909- WhoSSW 93
Moreland, Gus Turner 1911- WhoSSW 93
Moreland, Jeffrey R. Law&B 92
Moreland, Jeffrey R. 1944- St&PR 93
Moreland, Lois Baldwin 1933- WhoAmW 93
Moreland, Margaret Eyring d1991 BioIn 17
Moreland, Richard James 1947- St&PR 93, WhoAm 92
Morelewicz, R.H. 1943- St&PR 93
Moreley, Thomas S. 1935- St&PR 93
Morell, Barry 1927- Baker 92
Morell, William Nelson, Jr. 1920- WhoWor 93
Morella, Constance A. 1931- BioIn 17, CngDr 91
Morella, Constance Albanese 1931- WhoAm 92, WhoAmW 93, WhoE 93
Morelli, Anthony Frank 1956- WhoEmL 93, WhoWor 93
Morelli, Bruno M. WhoWor 93
Morelli, Carlo 1897-1970 Baker 92
See Also Zanelli, Renato 1892-1935 OxDcOp
Morelli, Carlo 1917- WhoScE 91-3
Morelli, Frank P. 1947- St&PR 93
Morelli, J.L. 1930- St&PR 93
Morelli, Joseph 1947- St&PR 93
Morelli, Luis M. Law&B 92
Morelli, Roger H. 1944- St&PR 93
Morelli, Ronald Joseph 1948- WhoEmL 93
Morelli, William Annibale, Sr. 1938- WhoAm 92
Morelli, William P. Law&B 92
Morello, Carol Jean 1957- WhoEmL 93
Morello, John Patrick 1952- St&PR 93
Morello, Joseph Albert 1928- WhoAm 92
Morelock, James Crutchfield 1920- WhoAm 92, WhoSSW 93, WhoWor 93
Morelock-Roy, Lynne Allyn 1959- WhoAmW 93
Morelot, Stephen 1820-1899 Baker 92
Moren, Nicholas Charles 1946- St&PR 93
Morena, Berta 1878-1952 Baker 92
Morena, Berthe 1878-1952 OxDcOp
Morency, Paula J. 1955- WhoAmW 93
Morency, Pierre 1942- WhoCanL 92
Moreno, Albert F. Law&B 92
Moreno (Andrade), Segundo Luis 1882-1972 Baker 92
Moreno, Anthony James 1960- WhoEmL 93
Moreno, Antonio 1887-1967 HispAmA
Moreno, Antonio 1887-1969 BioIn 17
Moreno, Arturo 1954- St&PR 93
Moreno, Carlos Americo 1951- WhoEmL 93, WhoSSW 93
Moreno, Carlos Sanchez 1964- WhoE 93
Moreno, Catherine Hartmus 1935- WhoWrEP 92
Moreno, Diego Alejandro 1959- WhoWor 93
Moreno, Dorinda 1939- DcLB 122 [port]
Moreno, Eusebio Carlos 1960- WhoWrEP 92
Moreno, Federico A., Sr. 1952- HispAmA [port]
Moreno, Federico Antonio 1952- WhoAm 92
Moreno, Gilbert St&PR 93
Moreno, Glen R. 1943- St&PR 93
Moreno, Glen Richard 1943- WhoAm 92
Moreno, J.L. 1892-1974 BioIn 17
Moreno, Jacob Levy 1892-1974 BioIn 17
Moreno, Jose Guillermo 1951- WhoE 93
Moreno, Joseph Florencio 1964- WhoEmL 93
Moreno, Juan Ramon d1989 BioIn 17
Moreno, Luisa 1907-1990? NotHsAW 93
Moreno, Luz Maria 1955- St&PR 93
Moreno, Manuel D. 1930- WhoAm 92
Moreno, Mary of the Cross 1922- WhoAmW 93
Moreno, Perez BioIn 17
Moreno, Rachel Sara 1947- WhoAmW 93
Moreno, Richard Julian Law&B 92
Moreno, Rita 1931- BioIn 17, HispAmA [port], NotHsAW 93 [port], SweetSg D, WhoAm 92
Moreno, Susan Ingalls 1959- WhoEmL 93
Moreno, Valerie Lucille 1939- WhoE 93
Moreno Barbera, Fernando 1913- WhoWor 93
Moreno de Angel, Pilar WhoWor 93
Moreno Gonzalez, Juan Pedro 1937- WhoScE 91-3
Moreno-Lopez, Jorge 1941- WhoWor 93
Morenon, Elise 1939- WhoE 93
Moreno Rojas, R. WhoScE 91-3
Moreno Rojas, Rafael 1936- WhoScE 91-3, WhoUN 92
Moreno Villa, Jose 1887-1955 DcMexL
Morens, David Michael 1948- WhoEmL 93
More O'Ferrall, Gerald J. 1935- WhoScE 91-3
Morer, Lana BioIn 17
Morera, Enrique 1865-1942 Baker 92
Morere, Jean 1836-1887 Baker 92
Moreschi, Alessandro 1858-1922 Baker 92
Moreschi, Roger P. 1938- St&PR 93, WhoIns 93
Moreshead, Joseph A. 1957- St&PR 93
Moresi, Remo P. 1952- WhoWor 93
Morest, Donald Kent 1934- WhoAm 92
Moret, Laura M. Law&B 92
Moret, Pamela J. Law&B 92
Moret, Vernon H. 1925- St&PR 93
Moreton, Brian B. WhoScE 91-1
Moreton, Charles P. 1927- St&PR 93
Moreton, Edward Burton 1932- St&PR 93
Moreton, Frederick A., Jr. 1939- St&PR 93
Moreton, Robert WhoScE 91-1
Moreton, Robert Dulaney 1913- WhoAm 92
Moreton, Roger Bernard WhoScE 91-1
Morett, Margaret 1938- WhoWrEP 92
Moretti, Giancarlo 1943- WhoScE 91-3
Moretti, James R. 1956- St&PR 93
Moretti, Nanni 1953- MiSFD 9
Moretti, Peter M. A. 1935- WhoSSW 93
Moretto, Jane Ann 1934- WhoAmW 93
Moretz, Cheryl Ann 1950- WhoEmL 93
Moretz, George A. 1942- St&PR 93
Moretz, Roger Clark 1942- WhoE 93
Moretzsohn, Dianne G. Law&B 92
Morey, Carl Reginald 1934- WhoAm 92
Morey, Christin Williams 1957- WhoAmW 93
Morey, David Edward 1956- WhoE 93
Morey, James Newman 1933- WhoAm 92
Morey, Jeri Lynn Snyder 1943- WhoSSW 93
Morey, John W. 1943- St&PR 93
Morey, Kathleen Johnson 1946- WhoWrEP 92
Morey, Larry Wayne 1949- WhoEmL 93
Morey, Lloyd William, Jr. 1930- WhoWor 93
Morey, Marion Louise 1926- WhoAmW 93
Morey, Philip Stockton, Jr. 1937- WhoSSW 93
Morey, Robert Hardy 1956- WhoEmL 93, WhoWor 93
Morey, Robert M. 1947- St&PR 93
Morey, Robert Thomas 1933- WhoE 93
Morey, Roy D. 1937- WhoUN 92
Morey, Ruth A. St&PR 93
Morey, Sharon Lynn 1948- WhoAmW 93
Morey, Walt d1992 NewYTBS 92
Morey, Walt 1907-1992 BioIn 17
Morey, Walt(er Nelson) 1907- DcAmChF 1960
Morey, Walt(er Nelson) 1907-1992 ConAu 136, MajAI [port], SmATA 70
Morey-Radach, Melinda Louise 1955- WhoEmL 93
Mor Faye 1948-1985 BioIn 17
Morfill, Gregor E. 1945- WhoScE 91-3
Morfin, Jesse BioIn 17
Morfopoulos, Vassilis C.P. 1937- St&PR 93
Morford, Richard Douglas 1953- WhoWor 93
Morford, Steven Douglas 1949- WhoEmL 93
Morford-Burg, JoAnn 1956- WhoAmW 93
Morga Bellizzi, Celeste 1921- WhoAmW 93
Morgado, Ernest F. 1917- St&PR 93
Morgado, Richard Joseph 1946- WhoEmL 93
Morgado, Robert WhoAm 92
Morgan, Agnes 1879-1976 AmWomPl
Morgan, Agnes Bangs AmWomPl
Morgan, Al 1920- ScF&FL 92
Morgan, Alan D. WhoAm 92
Morgan, Alan G. 1946- WhoScE 91-1
Morgan, Alan Vivian 1943- WhoAm 92
Morgan, Alfred Y., Jr. 1939- St&PR 93
Morgan, Alison 1959- ConAu 137
Morgan, Allen 1946- WhoCanL 92
Morgan, Allen Benners, Jr. 1942- St&PR 93
Morgan, Allen H. d1990 BioIn 17
Morgan, Andrew Gilbert, Jr. 1956- WhoSSW 93
Morgan, Andrew John 1952- WhoWor 93
Morgan, Andrew Wesley 1922- WhoAm 92
Morgan, Ann Marie 1949- WhoAmW 93
Morgan, Anna 1851-1936 AmWomPl
Morgan, Anna Jane 1953- WhoAmW 93
Morgan, Anne Margaret Barclay 1952- WhoAmW 93
Morgan, Anthony Ian 1938- WhoAm 92
Morgan, Ardys Nord 1946- WhoEmL 93
Morgan, Arlene Notoro 1945- WhoAm 92
Morgan, Armand Malcolm d1992 NewYTBS 92
Morgan, Armand Malcolm 1902-1992 BioIn 17
Morgan, Arthur Anthony 1938- St&PR 93
Morgan, Arthur Edward 1929- St&PR 93, WhoAm 92
Morgan, Arthur Ernest 1878-1975 BioIn 17
Morgan, Audrey 1931- WhoWor 93
Morgan, B. WhoScE 91-1
Morgan, Barbara d1992 NewYTBS 92 [port]
Morgan, Barbara Janette 1916- WhoAmW 93
Morgan, Barbara Joan 1940- WhoAmW 93
Morgan, Beverly Carver 1927- WhoAm 92, WhoAmW 93
Morgan, Brian Lealan WhoScE 91-1
Morgan, Brian S. 1942- St&PR 93
Morgan, Bronwyn Jordan 1949- WhoSSW 93
Morgan, Bruce Curtis 1939- WhoE 93
Morgan, Bruce Harry WhoE 93
Morgan, Bruce L. Law&B 92
Morgan, Bruce Ray 1932- WhoAm 92
Morgan, Burton D. 1916- St&PR 93
Morgan, Calvert A., Jr. 1948- St&PR 93
Morgan, Calvin d1992 BioIn 17, NewYTBS 92
Morgan, Camille Law&B 92
Morgan, Carl Robert 1929- WhoAm 92
Morgan, Carl Wayne Law&B 92
Morgan, Carol Ellis Law&B 92
Morgan, Carolyn F. Law&B 92
Morgan, Carolyn Y. Law&B 92
Morgan, Catherine Marie 1947- WhoSSW 93
Morgan, Cathy Lynn 1959- WhoEmL 93
Morgan, Cecilia Hufstedler 1952- WhoEmL 93
Morgan, Celia Ann 1932- WhoAmW 93, WhoSSW 93
Morgan, Charles 1894-1958 BioIn 17
Morgan, Charles, Jr. 1930- EncAACR
Morgan, Charles Donald, Jr. 1943- WhoAm 92
Morgan, Charles Edward Law&B 92
Morgan, Charles Hermann, Jr. 1949- WhoEmL 93, WhoSSW 93
Morgan, Charles Robert 1934- WhoE 93
Morgan, Charles Russell Law&B 92
Morgan, Charles Sumner 1915- WhoAm 92
Morgan, Charles Thomas 1933- St&PR 93
Morgan, Charles Wesley 1951- WhoEmL 93, WhoSSW 93
Morgan, Cheryle L. Law&B 92
Morgan, Chris 1946- ScF&FL 92
Morgan, Christopher B. 1964- WhoE 93
Morgan, Christopher H. Law&B 92
Morgan, Christy M. 1943- St&PR 93
Morgan, Claudia Law&B 92
Morgan, Clayton A. BioIn 17
Morgan, Clive Idris WhoScE 91-1
Morgan, Colin J. 1935- St&PR 93
Morgan, Constance Louise 1941- WhoAmW 93, WhoSSW 93
Morgan, Councilman 1920-1990 BioIn 17
Morgan, D. Russell, Jr. Law&B 92
Morgan, Dan 1925- ScF&FL 92
Morgan, Daniel 1736-1802 HarEnMi
Morgan, Daniel Joseph 1957- WhoEmL 93
Morgan, Daniel Louis 1952- WhoEmL 93
Morgan, Daniel Thomas 1957- WhoSSW 93
Morgan, Daryle Whitney 1929- WhoSSW 93
Morgan, Dave ScF&FL 92
Morgan, David BioIn 17
Morgan, David Allen 1962- WhoEmL 93, WhoWor 93
Morgan, David Eugene, II 1965- WhoSSW 93
Morgan, David Gethin 1929- WhoWor 93
Morgan, David Lewis 1936- St&PR 93
Morgan, David Page 1927- WhoWrEP 92
Morgan, David Vernon WhoScE 91-1
Morgan, Deloris Jackson 1947- WhoAmW 93
Morgan, Denise Lyn 1964- WhoAmW 93
Morgan, Denise Williams 1952- WhoE 93
Morgan, Dennis Alan 1947- WhoE 93
Morgan, Diane Pope 1949- WhoAmW 93, WhoEmL 93
Morgan, Dodge D. BioIn 17
Morgan, Donald Crane 1940- WhoWor 93
Morgan, Donald Farrell 1938- St&PR 93
Morgan, Donald Francis 1941- WhoWor 93
Morgan, Donald Stuart 1948- WhoAm 92
Morgan, Donna Evensen 1957- WhoEmL 93
Morgan, Donna Jean 1955- WhoAmW 93, WhoEmL 93
Morgan, E. Louise 1929- St&PR 93
Morgan, Eben Cornelius 1934- St&PR 93
Morgan, Edmund Sears 1916- WhoAm 92
Morgan, Edward WhoAm 92, WhoScE 91-1
Morgan, Edward Charles 1933- St&PR 93
Morgan, Edward L., Jr. 1943- WhoIns 93
Morgan, Edward Nash, Mrs. AmWomPl
Morgan, Edward Thomas 1954- WhoSSW 93
Morgan, Edwin D. 1811-1883 PolPar
Morgan, Elizabeth 1947- BioIn 17, WhoAm 92
Morgan, Elizabeth Anne 1947- WhoAmW 93
Morgan, Elizabeth N. Law&B 92
Morgan, Elmo Rich 1913- WhoAm 92
Morgan, Elyse 1954- WhoAmW 93
Morgan, Eric Lee 1940- WhoSSW 93
Morgan, Ernest 1905- WhoWrEP 92
Morgan, Evan 1930- WhoSSW 93
Morgan, Evelyn Buck 1931- WhoAmW 93, WhoSSW 93
Morgan, Frank BioIn 17
Morgan, Frank 1933- ConMus 9 [port]
Morgan, Frank Brown Webb, Jr. 1935- WhoAm 92

Morgan, Frank Edward, II 1952- St&PR 93, WhoAm 92
Morgan, Frank T. 1944- WhoSSW 93
Morgan, Frederick 1922- BioIn 17, WhoAm 92
Morgan, (George) Frederick 1922- WhoWrEP 92
Morgan, G. Kenneth 1947- WhoSSW 93
Morgan, Gareth Glyn WhoScE 91-1
Morgan, Garrett A. 1877-1963 BioIn 17
Morgan, Gary M. 1959- WhoSSW 93
Morgan, Gay Hattaway 1952- WhoEmL 93, WhoSSW 93
Morgan, George 1743-1810 BioIn 17
Morgan, George Beers 1929- WhoSSW 93
Morgan, George Carl 1931- WhoAm 92
Morgan, George Dennis 1935- St&PR 93
Morgan, George H. 1936- St&PR 93
Morgan, George Jefferson 1908- WhoAm 92
Morgan, George Tad 1933- St&PR 93, WhoAm 92
Morgan, George William 1935- WhoSSW 93
Morgan, Georgia Bazacos 1926- WhoAmW 93
Morgan, Gerthon Laird 1953- WhoSSW 93
Morgan, Gilda Fay 1963- WhoSSW 93
Morgan, Glenn R. 1947- St&PR 93
Morgan, Gordon Daniel 1931- WhoSSW 93
Morgan, Gordon K. 1939- St&PR 93
Morgan, Graham James 1917- St&PR 93
Morgan, Gretna Faye 1927- WhoAmW 93
Morgan, Gwen Cartee 1927- WhoSSW 93
Morgan, Gwyn 1945- St&PR 93
Morgan, Gwynne James WhoScE 91-1
Morgan, H.L. WhoScE 91-1
Morgan, H(oward) Wayne 1934- ConAu 40NR
Morgan, Hal B. Law&B 92
Morgan, Harry Casswallon 1928- St&PR 93
Morgan, Helen Fairley 1931- St&PR 93
Morgan, Henry 1915- WhoAm 92
Morgan, Hicks B. Law&B 92
Morgan, Hilda ScF&FL 92
Morgan, Hillary A. 1958- St&PR 93
Morgan, Howard Campbell 1935- WhoAm 92
Morgan, Howard Edwin 1927- WhoAm 92
Morgan, Howard K. 1917- St&PR 93
Morgan, Howard Paul WhoScE 91-1
Morgan, Hugh ScF&FL 92
Morgan, Hugh Jackson, Jr. 1928- St&PR 93, WhoAm 92
Morgan, J.M. 1946- ScF&FL 92
Morgan, J(ill) M(eredith) 1946- ConAu 137
Morgan, J. P. 1837-1913 PolPar
Morgan, Jack Collins 1937- WhoSSW 93
Morgan, Jacob Richard 1925- WhoWor 93
Morgan, Jacqui 1939- WhoAm 92, WhoWor 93
Morgan, James 1944- WhoWrEP 92
Morgan, James A. Law&B 92, WhoAm 92
Morgan, James Allen 1934- WhoAm 92
Morgan, James Alvin 1935- St&PR 93
Morgan, James Andrew 1948- WhoEmL 93, WhoSSW 93
Morgan, James Chandler BioIn 17
Morgan, James Chandler 1938- St&PR 93
Morgan, James Dayle WhoSSW 93
Morgan, James Durward 1936- WhoAm 92, WhoWor 93
Morgan, James Frederick 1954- WhoEmL 93
Morgan, James G. Law&B 92
Morgan, James Harvey 1947- WhoEmL 93
Morgan, James J. 1942- St&PR 93
Morgan, James Jay 1942- WhoAm 92
Morgan, James John 1932- WhoAm 92
Morgan, James Lloyd 1954- WhoEmL 93
Morgan, James Louis 1943- WhoSSW 93
Morgan, James Mcclay 1947- St&PR 93
Morgan, James Newton 1918- WhoAm 92
Morgan, James Orval 1933- WhoE 93
Morgan, James Thomas 1930- WhoSSW 93
Morgan, Jane Brennan 1955- WhoAmW 93, WhoEmL 93
Morgan, Jane Hale 1926- WhoAm 92
Morgan, Janet F. WhoWrEP 92
Morgan, Janet Marie Fain 1956- WhoWrEP 92
Morgan, Jasper William, Jr. 1936- St&PR 93
Morgan, Jay Law&B 92
Morgan, Jeanne ConAu 138
Morgan, Jeffrey David 1959- WhoEmL 93
Morgan, Jerry A. 1938- St&PR 93
Morgan, Joan L. BioIn 17
Morgan, Joe Leonard 1943- WhoAm 92
Morgan, Joe Michael 1959- WhoSSW 93
Morgan, John 1770-1819 BioIn 17
Morgan, John A. 1930- WhoAm 92
Morgan, John Adams, Jr. 1954- WhoEmL 93
Morgan, John Andrew, Jr. 1935- WhoE 93
Morgan, John Augustine 1934- WhoWor 93
Morgan, John Black 1938- WhoE 93
Morgan, John Bruce 1919- WhoAm 92
Morgan, John C. 1914-1991 BioIn 17
Morgan, John Davis 1921- WhoAm 92
Morgan, John Derald 1939- WhoAm 92
Morgan, John Edwin 1933- WhoUN 92
Morgan, John Hunt 1825-1864 HarEnMi
Morgan, John L. St&PR 93
Morgan, John Pierpont 1837-1913 GayN
Morgan, John Smith 1921- WhoE 93, WhoWrEP 92
Morgan, John Stephen 1963- WhoE 93
Morgan, John T. 1824-1907 PolPar
Morgan, John Thomas 1929- St&PR 93
Morgan, Jonathan G. 1954- St&PR 93
Morgan, Joseph L. 1927- St&PR 93
Morgan, Joseph V. 1932- WhoScE 91-3
Morgan, Josephine d1992 NewYTBS 92
Morgan, Julia BioIn 17
Morgan, Julian Earl, III 1950- WhoEmL 93
Morgan, Junius S. 1947- St&PR 93
Morgan, Karen Johnson 1945- WhoE 93
Morgan, Kathleen ScF&FL 92
Morgan, Kay Summersby 1908?-1975 BioIn 17
Morgan, Kelly A. Law&B 92
Morgan, Kenneth WhoScE 91-1
Morgan, Kenneth Bryan 1950- WhoSSW 93
Morgan, Kieran WhoScE 91-1
Morgan, Lanier Vernon WhoWrEP 92
Morgan, Larry Ronald 1936- WhoAm 92, WhoSSW 93
Morgan, Lawrence J. 1951- St&PR 93
Morgan, Lee 1938-1972 BioIn 17
Morgan, Lee Anne 1943- WhoAmW 93
Morgan, Lee L. 1920- BioIn 17, St&PR 93
Morgan, Leigh WhoWrEP 92
Morgan, Leon Alford 1934- St&PR 93, WhoAm 92
Morgan, Leonard Eugene 1946- WhoEmL 93
Morgan, Leslie Yarborough 1956- WhoWor 93
Morgan, Lewis B. 1934- WhoE 93
Morgan, Lewis Henry 1818-1881 BioIn 17, IntDcAn
Morgan, Lewis Render 1913- WhoSSW 93
Morgan, Linda C. 1958- WhoEmL 93
Morgan, Linda Rice 1949- WhoEmL 93, WhoSSW 93
Morgan, Linda Rogers 1950- WhoAmW 93
Morgan, Lorrie BioIn 17
Morgan, Louis J. 1936- St&PR 93
Morgan, Louise Frances 1954- WhoWor 93
Morgan, Lucy W. 1940- WhoAm 92
Morgan, Lynda Jane 1956- WhoAmW 93
Morgan, M. Jane 1945- WhoAmW 93, WhoSSW 93, WhoWor 93
Morgan, Madel Jacobs 1918- WhoAm 92, WhoAmW 93
Morgan, Malcolm Bruce 1938- WhoSSW 93
Morgan, Marabel 1937- WhoAm 92, WhoWrEP 92
Morgan, Marcia Ann 1966- WhoAmW 93
Morgan, Margaret Ward 1939- WhoAmW 93
Morgan, Marianne 1940- WhoSSW 93
Morgan, Marilyn 1947- WhoAmW 93
Morgan, Marilyn Kay 1955- WhoEmL 93
Morgan, Maritza Leskovar 1920- WhoAmW 93
Morgan, Mary Louise Fitzsimmons 1946- WhoAmW 93, WhoE 93
Morgan, Melanie Law&B 92
Morgan, Memo ConAu 39NR
Morgan, Meredith ConAu 137
Morgan, Michael BioIn 17
Morgan, Michael Brewster 1953- WhoEmL 93
Morgan, Michael Gavin 1946- WhoAm 92
Morgan, Michael James 1942- WhoWor 93
Morgan, Michael John WhoScE 91-1
Morgan, Michael Joseph 1953- WhoEmL 93, WhoSSW 93
Morgan, Michael R.A. WhoScE 91-1
Morgan, Michael Scott 1953- WhoE 93
Morgan, Michele 1920- IntDcF 2-3 [port]
Morgan, Millett Granger 1941- WhoAm 92
Morgan, Monroe 1921- WhoAm 92
Morgan, Murray Dean 1946- WhoSSW 93
Morgan, Myfanwy Irene 1951- WhoAmW 93
Morgan, Neil 1924- WhoAm 92, WhoWrEP 92
Morgan, Nicholas Heath 1953- WhoEmL 93, WhoWrEP 92
Morgan, Niel C. St&PR 93
Morgan, O. Forrest, Jr. Law&B 92
Morgan, Owen WhoScE 91-1
Morgan, P. J. WhoAm 92
Morgan, Pamela Antoinette 1947- WhoE 93
Morgan, Pamela Yvonne 1961- WhoE 93
Morgan, Patrick Joseph Law&B 92
Morgan, Paul Evan 1961- WhoEmL 93
Morgan, Paul F. Law&B 92
Morgan, Philip D. Law&B 92
Morgan, Phyliss Joan 1936- WhoAmW 93
Morgan, Raleigh, Jr. 1916- WhoAm 92
Morgan, Ralph BioIn 17
Morgan, Ralph Rexford 1944- WhoSSW 93
Morgan, Randall H. 1948- St&PR 93
Morgan, Ray Ellingwood, Jr. 1922- WhoWor 93
Morgan, Raymond F. 1948- WhoAm 92
Morgan, Raymond Scott 1949- WhoEmL 93
Morgan, Raymond Victor, Jr. 1942- WhoAm 92, WhoSSW 93
Morgan, Rebecca Quinn 1938- WhoAmW 93
Morgan, Rhea Volk 1952- WhoEmL 93
Morgan, Rhelda Elnola 1947- WhoWor 93
Morgan, Richard Ernest 1937- WhoAm 92
Morgan, Richard H. 1935- St&PR 93
Morgan, Richard T. WhoAm 92
Morgan, Richard Thomas 1937- WhoAm 92
Morgan, Robert BioIn 17
Morgan, Robert Arthur 1918- WhoAm 92
Morgan, Robert B. 1931- WhoWrEP 92
Morgan, Robert B. 1934- WhoAm 92
Morgan, Robert Bruce 1934- St&PR 93, WhoIns 93
Morgan, Robert Dale 1912- WhoAm 92
Morgan, Robert Earle 1935- WhoSSW 93
Morgan, Robert Edward 1924- WhoAm 92
Morgan, Robert H. 1944- St&PR 93
Morgan, Robert Marion 1930- WhoAm 92
Morgan, Robert P. 1934- WhoAm 92
Morgan, Robert Peter 1934- WhoAm 92
Morgan, Robert (R.) 1944- DcLB 120 [port]
Morgan, Robert Ray 1944- WhoWrEP 92
Morgan, Robert Steve 1945- WhoSSW 93
Morgan, Roberta Arlene Hansen 1944- WhoAmW 93
Morgan, Robin BioIn 17
Morgan, Robin Evonne 1941- WhoAm 92, WhoAmW 93, WhoE 93
Morgan, Rodger F. 1944- WhoE 93
Morgan, Russell E. 1956- St&PR 93
Morgan, Ruth 1938- WhoE 93
Morgan, Ruth Prouse 1934- WhoAm 92
Morgan, Samuel Pope 1923- WhoAm 92, WhoE 93
Morgan, Sarah 1959- BioIn 17
Morgan, Sarah (Nicola) 1959- ConAu 136
Morgan, Seth BioIn 17
Morgan, Sharon Denise 1964- WhoEmL 93
Morgan, Sheldon LeGrande 1929- St&PR 93
Morgan, Sherry Rita Guy 1949- WhoEmL 93, WhoSSW 93
Morgan, Shirley Ann 1940- WhoAmW 93
Morgan, Silver WhoWrEP 92
Morgan, Speer 1946- WhoWrEP 92
Morgan, Stanley ScF&FL 92
Morgan, Stanley Leins 1918- St&PR 93, WhoAm 92
Morgan, Stephen Barry WhoScE 91-1
Morgan, Stephen Charles 1946- WhoAm 92
Morgan, Steven R. 1948- St&PR 93
Morgan, Susan 1943- ConAu 137
Morgan, Sydney Owenson 1783?-1859 BioIn 17
Morgan, Sydney Owenson, Lady 1776?-1859 DcLB 116 [port]
Morgan, Ted 1932- ScF&FL 92
Morgan, Theodore N. 1940- St&PR 93
Morgan, Theresa Marie Law&B 92
Morgan, Thomas d1743 BioIn 17
Morgan, Thomas Bruce 1926- WhoAm 92, WhoE 93
Morgan, Thomas Geoffrey WhoScE 91-1
Morgan, Thomas Joseph 1943- WhoE 93
Morgan, Thomas Phelps 1952- WhoEmL 93
Morgan, Thomas Rowland 1930- WhoAm 92
Morgan, Timothy Ian 1955- WhoEmL 93
Morgan, Timothy Stewart 1947- WhoEmL 93
Morgan, Todd Byers 1956- WhoE 93, WhoEmL 93
Morgan, Todd Michael 1947- WhoAm 92
Morgan, Tommy Dean 1956- WhoWor 93
Morgan, Travis C. 1929- WhoIns 93
Morgan, Travis Crue 1929- St&PR 93
Morgan, Vicki BioIn 17
Morgan, Virginia Deapo 1934- WhoSSW 93
Morgan, W. Robert 1924- WhoWrEP 92
Morgan, W.T. MiSFD 9
Morgan, Walter WhoScE 91-1
Morgan, Wanda Busby 1930- WhoAmW 93, WhoE 93
Morgan, Wayne Philip 1942- WhoAm 92
Morgan, Wesley K. 1918- WhoAm 92
Morgan, William 1944- WhoSSW 93
Morgan, William Basil WhoScE 91-1
Morgan, William Bruce 1926- WhoAm 92
Morgan, William Douglass 1925- WhoAm 92
Morgan, William J. 1947- WhoAm 92
Morgan, William James 1910- WhoSSW 93, WhoWor 93
Morgan, William Lionel, Jr. 1927- WhoAm 92
Morgan, William Robert 1924- WhoAm 92
Morgan, William T. 1928- WhoAm 92
Morgan, William Travis 1928- St&PR 93
Morgan, William Wilson 1906- WhoAm 92
Morganfield, McKinley Baker 92
Morgano, Anthony Frank 1939- St&PR 93
Morgan Pantuck, Jodi Beth 1967- WhoAmW 93
Morganroth, Fred 1938- WhoWor 93
Morganroth, Joel 1945- WhoE 93
Morganroth, Mayer 1931- WhoWor 93
Morgans, David Bryan 1933- St&PR 93
Morgans, James Patrick 1946- WhoWrEP 92
Morganstern, Barry Frasier 1948- WhoE 93
Morganstern, Daniel Robert 1940- WhoAm 92
Morganstern, Kennard Harold 1924- St&PR 93
Morganstern, Monroe Jay 1931- St&PR 93
Morganstern, Priya S. Law&B 92
Morgante, Samuel 1953- WhoEmL 93
Morganteen, James Frederick Law&B 92
Morgan-Witts, Max 1931- ConAu 40NR
Morgart, Michele 1947- WhoAmW 93
Morgen, Per 1944- WhoWor 93
Morgenroth, Earl Eugene 1936- WhoWor 93
Morgenroth, Irving Law&B 92, St&PR 93
Morgenroth, Robert William 1957- WhoEmL 93
Morgens, Virginia Dare Davis 1934- WhoWrEP 92
Morgens, Warren Kendall 1940- WhoE 93
Morgensen, Jerry L. 1942- St&PR 93
Morgensen, Jerry Lynn 1942- WhoAm 92
Morgenstein, William 1933- WhoAm 92, WhoWor 93
Morgenstern, Arthur S. Law&B 92
Morgenstern, Barbara Weisman 1936- St&PR 93
Morgenstern, Bodo 1934- WhoScE 91-3
Morgenstern, Dan Michael 1929- WhoAm 92, WhoWrEP 92
Morgenstern, Daniel 1947- St&PR 93
Morgenstern, Dietrich Kurt 1924- WhoWor 93
Morgenstern, Frieda Homnick 1917- WhoWrEP 92
Morgenstern, Hans George 1936- WhoE 93
Morgenstern, Jacques 1939- WhoScE 91-2
Morgenstern, James C. Law&B 92
Morgenstern, Jane Ellen 1941- WhoAmW 93
Morgenstern, Janusz 1922- DrEEuF
Morgenstern, Joe BioIn 17
Morgenstern, Leon 1919- WhoAm 92
Morgenstern, Leslie N. 1953- St&PR 93
Morgenstern, Norbert Rubin 1935- WhoAm 92
Morgenstern, Reinhard 1942- WhoScE 91-3
Morgenstern, S. ScF&FL 92
Morgenstern, Saul Phillip 1953- WhoEmL 93
Morgenstern, Sheldon Jon 1938- WhoAm 92
Morgenstern, Stephen 1940- WhoE 93
Morgenstern, Walter J. 1948- St&PR 93
Morgenthal, Becky Holz 1947- WhoAmW 93, WhoE 93, WhoEmL 93
Morgenthaler, Alisa Marie 1960- WhoEmL 93
Morgenthaler, Frederic Richard 1933- WhoAm 92
Morgenthaler, George J. Law&B 92
Morgenthaler, George Jefferson 1949- St&PR 93
Morgenthaler, Larry C. 1944- WhoAm 92
Morgenthaler, Larry Carl 1944- St&PR 93

Morgenthau, Hans J. 1904-1980 *ColdWar 1 [port]*
Morgenthau, Henry 1856-1946 *BioIn 17*
Morgenthau, Henry 1891-1967 *BioIn 17*
Morgenthau, Henry, Jr. 1891-1967 *ColdWar 1 [port]*
Morgenthau, Lazarus 1815-1897 *BioIn 17*
Morgenthaus, Henry, Sr. 1856-1946 *See* Morgenthaus, Henry, Sr., Henry, Jr., and Robert *JeAmHC*
Morgenthaus, Henry, Jr. 1891-1967 *See* Morgenthaus, Henry, Sr., Henry, Jr., and Robert *JeAmHC*
Morgenthaus, Henry, Sr., Henry, Jr., and Robert *JeAmHC*
Morgenthaus, Robert 1919- *See* Morgenthaus, Henry, Sr., Henry, Jr., and Robert *JeAmHC*
Morgera, Salvatore Domenic 1946- *WhoAm 92*
Morgison, Daryl Lee 1950- *St&PR 93*
Morgner, Aurelius 1917- *WhoAm 92*
Morgner, Ronald H. 1943- *St&PR 93*
Morgon, Alain 1931- *WhoScE 91-2*
Morgridge, Howard Henry 1919- *WhoAm 92*
Morhaim, Joe *ScF&FL 92*
Mori, Arinori 1847-1889 *BioIn 17*
Mori, Eisuke 1948- *WhoAsAP 91*
Mori, Frank 1820-1873 *Baker 92*
Mori, Hanae 1926- *WhoAm 92, WhoAmW 93*
Mori, Ichio 1937- *WhoWor 93*
Mori, Masatake 1937- *WhoWor 93*
Mori, Masatomo 1947- *WhoWor 93*
Mori, Masayuki 1911-1973 *IntDcF 2-3*
Mori, Mitsuya 1937- *WhoWor 93*
Mori, Motonari 1497-1571 *HarEnMi*
Mori, Nicolas 1796-1839 *Baker 92*
Mori, Nobuko 1932- *WhoAsAP 91*
Mori, Nobuo 1932- *WhoWor 93*
Mori, Ogai 1862-1922 *BioIn 17*
Mori, Sadao 1935- *WhoWor 93*
Mori, Shigeya 1926- *WhoWor 93*
Mori, Taikichiro 1904- *WhoWor 93*
Mori, Takashi 1894-1945 *HarEnMi*
Mori, Takeo 1929- *WhoWor 93*
Mori, Terumoto 1553-1625 *HarEnMi*
Mori, Yoshiro 1937- *WhoAsAP 91*
Moriah, Sonja-Jacqueline 1944- *WhoWor 93*
Morial, Ernest N. 1929- *AfrAmBi*
Morial, Ernest N. 1929-1989 *EncAACR*
Morial, Ernest Nathan *BioIn 17*
Morial, Marc Haydel 1958- *WhoWor 93*
Moriani, Napoleone 1806-1878 *Baker 92, OxDcOp*
Moriarity, Judith K. 1942- *WhoAmW 93*
Moriarity, Patrick Kevin 1955- *WhoEmL 93*
Moriarty, Anna Marie 1945- *WhoAmW 93*
Moriarty, Brian David 1942- *St&PR 93*
Moriarty, Cathy 1961?- *ConTFT 10*
Moriarty, Cynthia Ann *BioIn 17*
Moriarty, Donald W. 1939- *St&PR 93*
Moriarty, Donald William, Jr. 1939- *WhoAm 92*
Moriarty, John 1930- *WhoAm 92*
Moriarty, John Alden 1938- *WhoAm 92*
Moriarty, John W. 1930- *St&PR 93*
Moriarty, Kevin 1943- *St&PR 93*
Moriarty, Kevin Joseph *Law&B 92*
Moriarty, Maureen C. 1946- *WhoAmW 93*
Moriarty, Michael *BioIn 17*
Moriarty, Michael 1941- *WhoAm 92*
Moriarty, Morgan Johanna 1955- *WhoWrEP 92*
Moriarty, Patricia J. 1953- *St&PR 93*
Moriarty, Philip S.J. 1940- *St&PR 93*
Moriarty, Richard Patrick 1933- *St&PR 93*
Moriarty, Richard William 1939- *WhoAm 92*
Moriarty, Thomas V., II 1943- *WhoAm 92*
Moriarty, Thomas Vincent, II 1943- *St&PR 93*
Moriarty, Timothy *ScF&FL 92*
Moriarty, William E., Jr. 1952- *WhoIns 93*
Moriarty, William Edward 1926- *St&PR 93*
Morice, David Jennings 1946- *WhoWrEP 92*
Morice, Jacques 1929- *WhoScE 91-2*
Morice, Joseph Richard 1923- *WhoAm 92*
Morice, Peter Beaumont *WhoScE 91-1*
Morice, Stella *DcChlFi*
Morich, Joyce Pigeon 1954- *WhoAmW 93*
Morici, Peter George, Jr. 1948- *WhoEmL 93*
Moric-Petrovic, Slavka 1919- *WhoScE 91-4*
Moricz, Ferenc 1939- *WhoScE 91-4*
Moridaira, Soichiro 1947- *WhoWor 93*
Morie, G. Glen *Law&B 92, WhoAm 92*
Morie, G. Glen 1942- *St&PR 93*
Morien, Lyle J. 1944- *WhoIns 93*
Morier, James Justinian 1782?-1849 *DcLB 116 [port]*
Morieri, Virgilio 1945- *WhoWor 93*
Moriguchi, Ikuo 1928- *WhoWor 93*
Moriguchi, Yoshiki 1935- *WhoWor 93*
Morii, Churyo 1929- *WhoAsAP 91*
Morii, Kiyoji *WhoAm 92*
Morikawa, Shoji 1939- *WhoUN 92*
Morikawa, Yoshinobu 1923- *WhoWor 93*
Morillo, Roberto Garcia 1911- *Baker 92*
Morimanno, Paul 1939- *St&PR 93*
Morimoto, Akiko Charlene 1948- *WhoAmW 93*
Morimoto, Carl Noboru 1942- *WhoAm 92*
Morimoto, Gary S. 1941- *St&PR 93*
Morimoto, Koji 1942- *WhoAsAP 91*
Morimoto, Masaki 1932- *WhoWor 93*
Morin, Andre 1935- *WhoScE 91-2*
Morin, Anita 1945- *WhoAmW 93*
Morin, Bernard George 1922- *WhoSSW 93*
Morin, Bruce Leo 1963- *WhoE 93*
Morin, Carlton Paul 1932- *WhoAm 92*
Morin, Catherine A. *AmWomPl*
Morin, Catherine Joselin 1950- *WhoSSW 93*
Morin, Curtis L. 1952- *St&PR 93*
Morin, Earl U. 1935- *St&PR 93*
Morin, Gary Michael 1952- *WhoEmL 93*
Morin, Gaston Jean Francois 1938- *WhoE 93*
Morin, Gilles *Law&B 92*
Morin, Jill Jarecki 1961- *WhoAmW 93*
Morin, Michael L. *Law&B 92*
Morin, Nancy Ruth 1948- *WhoAmW 93*
Morin, Patrick Joyce 1938- *WhoAm 92*
Morin, Paul 1889-1963 *BioIn 17*
Morin, Pierre Jean 1931- *WhoAm 92*
Morin, Real E. 1946- *St&PR 93*
Morin, Richard Lewis 1949- *WhoEmL 93*
Morin, Roland L. 1944- *WhoE 93*
Morin, Rudolph G. 1937- *St&PR 93*
Morin, Theodore J. 1931- *St&PR 93*
Morin, William J. 1939- *WhoAm 92*
Morin, Wm. J. 1940- *St&PR 93*
Morin, Wollaston G. 1936- *St&PR 93*
Morin, Wollaston Gerald 1936- *WhoAm 92*
Morin, Yves-Charles 1944- *WhoAm 92*
Morina, J. Thomas *Law&B 92*
Morinaga, Tomoaki 1930- *WhoWor 93*
Morine, Bruce Phillip 1947- *St&PR 93*
Moriner, Robert H. *Law&B 92*
Moring, Douglas T. *Law&B 92*
Moring, James D. 1936- *St&PR 93*
Moring, John Frederick 1935- *WhoAm 92, WhoE 93*
Moring, Rebecca Owen 1939- *WhoAmW 93*
Moring, Stuart Alan 1947- *WhoEmL 93*
Morini, Albert Edward 1945- *St&PR 93*
Morini, Augusto 1937- *WhoScE 91-3*
Morini, Christopher E. 1955- *St&PR 93*
Morini, Erica 1904- *Baker 92*
Morini, Ralph E. 1949- *St&PR 93*
Morinigo, Higinio 1897-1985 *DcTwHis*
Morin-Miller, Carmen Aline 1929- *WhoE 93*
Morioka, Kenji 1917- *WhoWor 93*
Moriondo, Francesco *WhoScE 91-3*
Moris, Donald J. 1938- *St&PR 93*
Morisato, Susan Cay 1955- *WhoAmW 93, WhoEmL 93*
Morishige, Fukumi 1925- *WhoWor 93*
Morishima, Akira 1930- *WhoE 93*
Morishima, Isao 1942- *WhoWor 93*
Morishita, Yasumichi *BioIn 17*
Morishita, Yoko *BioIn 17*
Morison, Elsie 1924- *See* Kubelik, Rafael 1914- *OxDcOp*
Morison, Elsie (Jean) 1924- *Baker 92*
Morison, Elting Elmore 1909- *WhoAm 92*
Morison, John H. 1913- *St&PR 93*
Morison, John Hopkins 1913- *WhoAm 92*
Morison, Stephen G. *Law&B 92*
Morison, Stephen G. 1943- *St&PR 93*
Morisot, Alain 1947- *WhoScE 91-2*
Morisot, Berthe 1841-1895 *BioIn 17*
Morissette, Carol Lynne 1941- *WhoAmW 93*
Morita, Akio *BioIn 17*
Morita, Akio 1921- *WhoAm 92*
Morita, Hajme 1934- *WhoAsAP 91*
Morita, James Masami 1913- *WhoAm 92*
Morita, Kazutoshi 1937- *WhoWor 93*
Morita, Makoto 1940- *WhoWor 93*
Morita, Masaaki *BioIn 17*
Morita, Masayoshi Teddy 1947- *WhoWor 93*
Morita, Richard Yukio 1923- *WhoAm 92*
Morita, Shigemitsu 1927- *WhoAm 92*
Morita, Shinano 1961- *St&PR 93*
Morita, Yoshimitsu *MiSFD 9*
Moritsugu, Kenneth Paul 1945- *WhoAm 92*
Moritz, Landgrave of Hessen-Kassel 1572-1632 *Baker 92*
Moritz, A.F. 1947- *WhoCanL 92*
Moritz, Charles Fredric 1917- *WhoAm 92, WhoWrEP 92*
Moritz, Charles Worthington 1936- *St&PR 93, WhoAm 92*
Moritz, Donald Brooks 1927- *WhoAm 92*
Moritz, Donald I. 1927- *St&PR 93*
Moritz, Donald Irwin 1927- *WhoAm 92*
Moritz, Edward 1920- *WhoAm 92*
Moritz, Helmut 1933- *WhoScE 91-4*
Moritz, James R. 1945- *WhoAm 92*
Moritz, John Reid 1951- *WhoEmL 93*
Moritz, Karl Philipp 1757-1793 *BioIn 17*
Moritz, Margaret E. *Law&B 92*
Moritz, Michael Everett 1933- *St&PR 93, WhoAm 92*
Moritz, Milton Edward 1931- *WhoAm 92, WhoE 93, WhoWor 93*
Moritz, Reiner *BioIn 17*
Moritz, Roger Homer 1937- *WhoE 93*
Moriyama, Hiroyoshi 1955- *WhoWor 93*
Moriyama, Mayumi 1927- *WhoAsAP 91*
Moriyama, Raymond 1929- *WhoAm 92*
Morizumi, Yushin 1924- *WhoAsAP 91*
Mork, Atle 1948- *WhoScE 91-4*
Mork, C.A. 1945- *St&PR 93*
Mork, Kim Jorgensen 1961- *WhoWor 93*
Mork, Philip W. 1939- *St&PR 93*
Mork, William John 1942- *St&PR 93*
Morkan, John Francis 1932- *St&PR 93*
Morkowski, Janusz A. 1932- *WhoScE 91-4*
Morkved, Karl 1924- *WhoScE 91-4*
Morkwed, Richard Arlan 1930- *St&PR 93*
Morla, Jennifer *BioIn 17*
Morlacchi, Francesco 1784-1841 *OxDcOp*
Morlacchi, Francesco (Giuseppe Baldassare) 1784-1841 *Baker 92*
Morlan, A.R. *ScF&FL 92*
Morland, Jessie Parrish 1924- *WhoSSW 93*
Morland, John Kenneth 1916- *WhoAm 92*
Morland, Leslie William *WhoScE 91-1*
Morland, Martin Robert 1933- *WhoUN 92*
Morland, Nigel 1905-1986 *ScF&FL 92*
Morland, Richard Boyd 1919- *WhoSSW 93*
Morley, Adam R. *ScF&FL 92*
Morley, Bradford C. 1946- *St&PR 93*
Morley, Christopher Darlington 1890-1957 *BioIn 17*
Morley, David *WhoScE 91-1*
Morley, Felix 1894-1982 *ScF&FL 92*
Morley, George William 1923- *WhoAm 92*
Morley, Harry Thomas, Jr. 1930- *WhoAm 92, WhoWor 93*
Morley, Jeffrey Joshua 1953- *WhoEmL 93*
Morley, John 1838-1923 *BioIn 17*
Morley, John C. 1931- *St&PR 93*
Morley, John P. *Law&B 92*
Morley, Lawrence Whitaker 1920- *WhoAm 92*
Morley, Lloyd Albert 1940- *WhoAm 92*
Morley, Malcolm A. 1931- *WhoAm 92*
Morley, Patricia 1929- *WhoCanL 92*
Morley, Patricia Brady 1957- *WhoAmW 93*
Morley, Paul Bernard 1936- *St&PR 93*
Morley, R. *ConAu 137*
Morley, Raymond Albert 1922- *St&PR 93*
Morley, Robert 1908-1992 *BioIn 17, CurBio 92N, NewYTBS 92 [port]*
Morley, Robert (Adolph Wilton) 1908-1992 *ConAu 137*
Morley, Ruth d1991 *BioIn 17*
Morley, Steven Allan 1956- *WhoEmL 93*
Morley, Sylvanus Griswold 1883-1948 *IntDcAn*
Morley, Thomas 1557?-1602 *Baker 92*
Morley, Thomas Summer 1935- *St&PR 93*
Morlock, Carl Grismore 1906- *WhoAm 92*
Morlock, Dieter Bruno 1938- *St&PR 93*
Morlock, Jill Elizabeth 1963- *WhoEmL 93*
Morlok, Edward Karl 1940- *WhoE 93*
Morman, Michael Tod 1945- *WhoSSW 93*
Morman, William Harold *Law&B 92*
Mormon, Darwin Leigh 1945- *WhoSSW 93*
Morneau, Louis *MiSFD 9*
Morneau, Thomas Michael *Law&B 92*
Morner, C. Johan T. 1951- *WhoScE 91-4*
Mornex, Rene 1927- *WhoScE 91-2*
Morning, John 1932- *WhoAm 92*
Morningstar, Mildred Whaley 1912- *BioIn 17*
Morningstar, Ramon Sender 1934- *ScF&FL 92*
Morningstar, Richard Louis 1945- *St&PR 93*
Morningstar, Robert David 1948- *WhoE 93*
Mornington, Garret Wesley, Earl of 1735-1781 *Baker 92*
Moro, Aldo 1916-1978 *DcTwHis*
Moro, Antonio c. 1512-c. 1576 *BioIn 17*
Moro, Cesar 1903-1956 *SpAmA*
Moro, Ferruccio 1920- *WhoScE 91-3*
Moro, Italo *BioIn 17*
Moro, Joseph Michael 1952- *WhoEmL 93*
Moroder, Giorgio 1941?- *ConTFT 10*
Moroi, Makoto 1930- *Baker 92*
Moroi, Saburo 1903-1977 *Baker 92*
Moroi, Yoshikiyo 1941- *WhoWor 93*
Morokuma, Keiji 1934- *WhoWor 93*
Moroles, Jesus Bautista 1950- *BioIn 17*
Morones, Bob *MiSFD 9*
Moroney, Francis Xavier 1949- *WhoEmL 93*
Moroney, Linda L. S. 1943- *WhoAmW 93, WhoSSW 93*
Moroney, M. Josephine *AmWomPl*
Moroney, Michael J. *Law&B 92*
Moroney, Robert Emmet 1903- *WhoWor 93*
Morong, C. Oscar, Jr. *WhoAm 92*
Morong, C. Oscar, Jr. 1935- *St&PR 93, WhoIns 93*
Moros, Nicholas P. 1947- *St&PR 93*
Morosani, George Warrington 1941- *WhoSSW 93, WhoWor 93*
Morosky, Robert Harry 1941- *WhoAm 92*
Morosky, Thomas 1925- *St&PR 93*
Moroso, Michael Joseph 1923- *WhoWor 93*
Moroso, Rob d1990 *BioIn 17*
Morosoli, Eugene Baptista, Jr. 1930- *St&PR 93*
Morosoli, Juan Jose 1899-1947 *SpAmA*
Moross, Jerome 1913-1983 *Baker 92*
Moross, M.D. 1930- *St&PR 93*
Morot-Sir, Edouard Barthelemy 1910- *WhoAm 92*
Moroux, Anthony Drexel, Sr. 1948- *WhoEmL 93, WhoSSW 93, WhoWor 93*
Morowitz, Harold Joseph 1927- *WhoAm 92*
Morowitz, Murray 1924- *St&PR 93*
Moroz, Anne 1953- *ScF&FL 92*
Moroz, K.J. *Law&B 92*
Moroz, Robin L. *Law&B 92*
Moroze, M. Brian *Law&B 92*
Morozov, Andrei Sergeevich 1959- *WhoWor 93*
Morozov, Konstantyn *WhoWor 93*
Morozov, Vladilen Mikhailovich 1939- *WhoUN 92*
Morozova, Irina Vasil'evna 1929- *BioIn 17*
Morpeau, William Antoine 1937- *WhoE 93*
Morphew, Dorothy Richards-Bassett 1918- *WhoAmW 93*
Morphonios, Ellen 1929- *BioIn 17*
Morphy, Guillermo, Conde de 1836-1899 *Baker 92*
Morphy, John 1947- *St&PR 93, WhoAm 92*
Morphy, Michael A. 1932- *St&PR 93*
Morphy, Paul 1837-1884 *BioIn 17*
Morpurgo, Giacomo 1927- *WhoWor 93*
Morpurgo, J.E. 1918- *BioIn 17*
Morpurgo, Michael *ScF&FL 92*
Morpurgo, Michael 1943- *ChlFicS*
Morpurgo Davies, Anna Elbina 1937- *WhoWor 93*
Morr, James Earl 1946- *WhoEmL 93*
Morr, Theresa Helen 1939- *WhoAmW 93*
Morra, Michael A. *Law&B 92*
Morra, Robert 1952- *WhoEmL 93*
Morra, Robert G. 1935- *St&PR 93*
Morrah, Dave 1914-1991 *BioIn 17*
Morral, William G. 1946- *St&PR 93*
Morre, D. James 1935- *WhoAm 92*
Morreale, Justin P. *St&PR 93*
Morreale, Leonard J., Jr. *Law&B 92*
Morreau, James Earl, Jr. 1955- *WhoEmL 93, WhoSSW 93*
Morrel, Judith Harper 1946- *WhoAmW 93*
Morrel, Ruth Yudenfriend *Law&B 92*
Morrel, William Griffin, Jr. 1933- *St&PR 93, WhoAm 92*
Morrell, Anne Christine Edith *WhoScE 91-1*
Morrell, Charles Raynor 1928- *St&PR 93*
Morrell, David 1943- *ScF&FL 92*
Morrell, David Cameron *WhoScE 91-1*
Morrell, Della *AmWomPl*
Morrell, Donald R. 1958- *St&PR 93*
Morrell, Gene Paul 1932- *St&PR 93, WhoAm 92*
Morrell, James Lloyd 1953- *St&PR 93*
Morrell, James Wilson 1931- *WhoAm 92*
Morrell, Laura L. *Law&B 92*
Morrell, Michael Preston 1948- *WhoAm 92*
Morrell, Robert Ellis 1930- *WhoAm 92*
Morrell, Roger 1946- *WhoWor 93*
Morrell, William Albert *WhoScE 91-1*
Morressy, John 1930- *ScF&FL 92, WhoE 93, WhoWrEP 92*
Morrice, Norman Alexander 1931- *WhoWor 93*

Morricone, Ennio *BioIn 17*
Morril, Mark C. *Law&B 92*
Morril, Mark C. 1947- *St&PR 93*
Morrill, Alice *AmWomPl*
Morrill, Belle Chapman *AmWomPl*
Morrill, Bernard 1910- *WhoE 93*
Morrill, Carolyn Kuklinski 1956- *WhoEmL 93*
Morrill, David Earl *Law&B 92*
Morrill, David Earl 1932- *WhoAm 92*
Morrill, Dexter George 1938- *WhoE 93*
Morrill, Edmund Needham 1834-1909 *BioIn 17*
Morrill, Geary Steven 1953- *WhoEmL 93*
Morrill, James Agrippa 1946- *WhoE 93*
Morrill, John Hugh 1960- *WhoE 93*
Morrill, Kevin Wilson 1955- *WhoSSW 93*
Morrill, Leslie H(olt) 1934- *MajAI [port]*
Morrill, Marilyn L. *Law&B 92*
Morrill, Richard Leland 1934- *WhoAm 92*
Morrill, Richard Leslie 1939- *WhoAm 92*
Morrill, Rowena 1944- *ScF&FL 92*
Morrill, Sibley S. *ScF&FL 92*
Morrill, Thomas Clyde 1909- *WhoAm 92*
Morrill, William Ashley 1930- *St&PR 93, WhoAm 92*
Morrin, Peter Patrick 1945- *WhoAm 92*
Morrin, Thomas Harvey 1914- *WhoAm 92*
Morrin, Virginia White 1913- *WhoAmW 93*
Morring, Oweni L. *Law&B 92*
Morris, A.W.L. *WhoScE 91-1*
Morris, Aaron Myles 1952- *WhoSSW 93*
Morris, Alan R. 1950- *St&PR 93*
Morris, Alan Steel *WhoScE 91-1*
Morris, Albert Jerome 1919- *WhoAm 92*
Morris, Allan Agapitos 1940- *WhoAsAP 91*
Morris, Alun O. *WhoScE 91-1*
Morris, Alvin Lee 1920- *WhoWor 93*
Morris, Alvin Leonard 1927- *WhoAm 92*
Morris, Angela *AmWomPl*
Morris, Anna Rochelle 1957- *WhoAmW 93*
Morris, Anthony P. 1849-1921 *ScF&FL 92*
Morris, Arlene Myers 1951- *WhoAmW 93, WhoE 93, WhoEmL 93*
Morris, Barbara Albers 1956- *WhoAmW 93, WhoEmL 93*
Morris, Barbara Louise 1947- *WhoAmW 93, WhoE 93*
Morris, Barbara Young 1945- *St&PR 93*
Morris, Barry A. 1954- *St&PR 93*
Morris, Barry Livingston 1947- *WhoEmL 93*
Morris, Barry Stephen 1948- *WhoE 93*
Morris, Ben Rankin 1922- *WhoAm 92*
Morris, Benjamin Franklin, Jr. 1948- *WhoEmL 93*
Morris, Berenice Robinson d1990 *BioIn 17*
Morris, Bernard Ross 1932- *WhoE 93*
Morris, Betty Jo 1938- *WhoAmW 93*
Morris, Bradley Thomas 1947- *WhoEmL 93*
Morris, Brenda Kay 1941- *WhoSSW 93*
Morris, Brewster H. 1909-1990 *BioIn 17*
Morris, C.E. 1938- *St&PR 93*
Morris, C.J. *WhoScE 91-1*
Morris, C. Timothy 1950- *WhoIns 93*
Morris, Calvin Curtis 1955- *WhoEmL 93*
Morris, Carl 1911- *WhoAm 92*
Morris, Carl 1943- *WhoWor 93*
Morris, Carloss 1915- *WhoAm 92*
Morris, Carol J. 1953- *WhoEmL 93*
Morris, Carol Lynn 1957- *WhoAmW 93*
Morris, Caroline Jane McMasters Stewart 1923- *WhoAmW 93, WhoWor 93*
Morris, Celia 1935- *ConAu 138*
Morris, Charles d1990 *BioIn 17*
Morris, Charles Elliot 1929- *WhoAm 92*
Morris, Charles Howard 1937- *WhoSSW 93*
Morris, Charles John 1966- *WhoSSW 93*
Morris, Charles Joseph, Jr. 1940- *WhoAm 92*
Morris, Charles Lester 1908-1991 *BioIn 17*
Morris, Chris 1946- *BioIn 17, ScF&FL 92*
Morris, Christopher Alan 1960- *WhoWor 93*
Morris, Christopher David 1957- *WhoEmL 93*
Morris, Clifton H. 1935- *St&PR 93*
Morris, Cooper H. 1953- *St&PR 93*
Morris, Cordell Yvonne 1944- *WhoAmW 93, WhoE 93*
Morris, Craig S. 1948- *St&PR 93*
Morris, Cynthia L. *St&PR 93*
Morris, Cynthia Taft 1928- *WhoAmW 93, WhoE 93*
Morris, Daniel Hyman 1948- *WhoE 93*
Morris, Daniel Joseph 1951- *WhoE 93*
Morris, Daniel Kearns 1954- *WhoAm 92*
Morris, Daniel Peter *Law&B 92*
Morris, Darvin *Law&B 92*
Morris, Dave 1957- *ScF&FL 92*
Morris, David Brown 1942- *WhoWrEP 92*
Morris, David Burton *MiSFD 9*
Morris, David H. 1941- *St&PR 93*
Morris, David Hargett 1920- *WhoAm 92*
Morris, David Hugh 1941- *WhoAm 92*
Morris, David Michael 1948- *WhoEmL 93*
Morris, David Woollard 1935- *WhoE 93*
Morris, Deborah H. *Law&B 92*
Morris, Deborah Regina 1955- *WhoAmW 93*
Morris, Denise Herrold 1950- *WhoAmW 93*
Morris, Desmond *BioIn 17, WhoAm 92*
Morris, Desmond (John) 1928- *ConAu 38NR*
Morris, Diane 1961- *WhoAmW 93*
Morris, Donal Franklin 1932- *St&PR 93*
Morris, Donald Arthur Adams 1934- *WhoAm 92*
Morris, Donald Charles 1925- *WhoAm 92*
Morris, Donald Charles 1951- *WhoEmL 93*
Morris, Donald E. 1946- *St&PR 93*
Morris, Donna *Law&B 92*
Morris, Dorothy Mathews 1918- *St&PR 93*
Morris, Dorothy Olga 1941- *WhoAmW 93*
Morris, Duncan Rowland Gordon 1938- *WhoUN 92*
Morris, Dwayne A. *Law&B 92*
Morris, Earl 1909-1992 *BioIn 17*
Morris, Earl F(ranklin) 1909-1992 *CurBio 92N*
Morris, Earl Franklin 1909- *WhoAm 92*
Morris, Earl Halstead 1889-1956 *IntDcAn*
Morris, Earl L. 1913- *St&PR 93*
Morris, Earle Elias, Jr. 1928- *WhoAm 92, WhoSSW 93*
Morris, Edmund 1940- *WhoWrEP 92*
Morris, Edward Austin 1951- *St&PR 93*
Morris, Edward L. 1942- *St&PR 93*
Morris, Edward Louis 1942- *WhoAm 92*
Morris, Edward Louis 1947- *WhoE 93*
Morris, Edward W. 1943- *St&PR 93*
Morris, Edwin Alexander 1903- *WhoAm 92*
Morris, Edwin Bateman, III 1939- *WhoAm 92*
Morris, Edwin Robert *WhoScE 91-1*
Morris, Edwin Robert 1944- *WhoWor 93*
Morris, Edwin Thaddeus 1912- *WhoAm 92*
Morris, Elizabeth J. 1934- *WhoWrEP 92*
Morris, Elizabeth Johnson 1937- *WhoE 93*
Morris, Elizabeth Treat 1936- *WhoAmW 93, WhoWor 93*
Morris, Elizabeth Woodbridge 1870-1964 *AmWomPl*
Morris, Elliot Michael 1956- *WhoEmL 93*
Morris, Elliott J. 1933- *St&PR 93*
Morris, Emma Ward 1952- *St&PR 93*
Morris, Ernest B. 1908-1991 *BioIn 17*
Morris, Errol *NewYTBS 92 [port]*
Morris, Errol 1948- *MiSFD 9*
Morris, Eugene Jerome 1910- *WhoAm 92*
Morris, Everett Lee 1928- *St&PR 93*
Morris, Frank Charles, Jr. 1948- *WhoEmL 93, WhoWor 93*
Morris, Frank Eugene 1923- *St&PR 93, WhoAm 92*
Morris, Frank Lee *BioIn 17*
Morris, Fred Jefferson, Jr. 1950- *WhoSSW 93*
Morris, G.L. 1941- *St&PR 93*
Morris, G. Ronald 1936- *WhoAm 92, WhoWor 93*
Morris, Garrett *WhoAm 92*
Morris, George Cooper, Jr. 1924- *WhoAm 92*
Morris, George Douglas *Law&B 92*
Morris, George N. 1930- *St&PR 93, WhoIns 93*
Morris, George Norton 1930- *WhoAm 92*
Morris, George Ronald 1943- *St&PR 93*
Morris, George Thomas Arnold 1934- *WhoSSW 93*
Morris, Gerald *St&PR 93*
Morris, Gerald F. 1943- *St&PR 93*
Morris, Gina Lee 1967- *WhoAmW 93*
Morris, Grace *AmWomPl*
Morris, Grant Harold 1940- *WhoAm 92*
Morris, Gregory L. 1950- *ScF&FL 92*
Morris, Gwladys Evan *ScF&FL 92*
Morris, Harold 1890-1964 *Baker 92*
Morris, Harold G. 1948- *St&PR 93*
Morris, Harold Mercer, Jr. 1929- *WhoSSW 93*
Morris, Harry C. 1921- *St&PR 93*
Morris, Harry Lyon d1992 *NewYTBS 92 [port]*
Morris, Helen Hussman 1910- *BioIn 17*
Morris, Henry A. 1928- *St&PR 93*
Morris, Henry Madison, Jr. 1918- *WhoAm 92, WhoWor 93*
Morris, Herman *Law&B 92*
Morris, Herman 1951- *St&PR 93*
Morris, Hilda *AmWomPl*
Morris, Hildred Ann 1955- *WhoEmL 93*
Morris, Howard 1919- *MiSFD 9*
Morris, Howard Eugene 1934- *WhoSSW 93*
Morris, Hugh C. 1932- *St&PR 93*
Morris, J. Malcolm *Law&B 92*
Morris, J. Roy 1938- *St&PR 93*
Morris, Jack *BioIn 17*
Morris, Jack 1923- *WhoE 93*
Morris, Jack 1955- *WhoAm 92*
Morris, Jack Cassius 1911-1954 *BioIn 17*
Morris, Jack Pershing 1918- *WhoAm 92*
Morris, James *Law&B 92*
Morris, James 1764?-1827 *BioIn 17*
Morris, James 1926- *BioIn 17*
Morris, James 1947- *BioIn 17, IntDcOp, OxDcOp*
Morris, James Allen 1929- *WhoSSW 93*
Morris, James Aloysius 1918- *WhoAm 92, WhoWor 93*
Morris, James Bruce 1943- *WhoSSW 93*
Morris, James E. 1937- *St&PR 93*
Morris, James Francis 1943- *WhoSSW 93*
Morris, James G. 1951- *St&PR 93*
Morris, James Graham 1928- *WhoSSW 93*
Morris, James J. *Law&B 92*
Morris, James Malachy 1952- *WhoE 93, WhoEmL 93, WhoWor 93*
Morris, James Matthew 1935- *WhoSSW 93*
Morris, James McGrath 1954- *WhoE 93*
Morris, James (Peppler) 1947- *Baker 92, WhoAm 92*
Morris, James Phillip 1942- *St&PR 93*
Morris, James Polk 1943- *WhoSSW 93*
Morris, James Robert 1951- *WhoSSW 93*
Morris, James Thomas 1943- *WhoAm 92*
Morris, James Thomas 1960- *WhoIns 93*
Morris, Jan 1926- *BioIn 17, ScF&FL 92, WhoWor 93*
Morris, Janet 1946- *BioIn 17, ScF&FL 92*
Morris, Janet Ellen 1946- *WhoE 93*
Morris, Jean 1924- *ScF&FL 92*
Morris, Jeffrey Joseph 1961- *WhoEmL 93*
Morris, Jeffrey L. *Law&B 92*
Morris, Jeffrey Lee 1959- *WhoEmL 93*
Morris, Jeffrey Philip *Law&B 92*
Morris, Jennifer Ann *Law&B 92*
Morris, Jerry Dean 1935- *WhoAm 92, WhoSSW 93*
Morris, Jerry O'S 1937- *St&PR 93*
Morris, Jim *NewYTBS 92 [port]*
Morris, Jim 1940- *ScF&FL 92*
Morris, Joe Alex 1904-1990 *ScF&FL 92*
Morris, John B. 1910- *St&PR 93*
Morris, John Churchill *WhoAm 92*
Morris, John E. 1916- *WhoE 93, WhoWor 93*
Morris, John Gareth *WhoScE 91-1*
Morris, John H. 1942- *St&PR 93*
Morris, John Hite 1942- *WhoAm 92*
Morris, John Joseph 1936- *WhoAsAP 91*
Morris, John Lunden 1943- *WhoE 93*
Morris, John McLean 1914- *WhoAm 92*
Morris, John Philip 1958- *WhoEmL 93*
Morris, John R. 1909- *St&PR 93*
Morris, John Scott 1955- *BiDAMSp 1989, WhoSSW 93*
Morris, John Selwyn 1925- *WhoAm 92*
Morris, John Steven 1947- *WhoEmL 93*
Morris, John Woodland 1921- *WhoAm 92*
Morris, Jonathan *Law&B 92*
Morris, Jonathan Edward 1956- *WhoEmL 93*
Morris, Joseph Allan 1951- *WhoEmL 93*
Morris, Joseph Anthony 1918- *WhoE 93*
Morris, Joseph Erwin, III 1959- *WhoEmL 93, WhoSSW 93*
Morris, Joseph V. *Law&B 92*
Morris, Judy *MiSFD 9*
Morris, Judy K. *BioIn 17*
Morris, Jules Jay *Law&B 92*
Morris, Julia Lisa 1961- *WhoAmW 93*
Morris, June E. 1934- *St&PR 93*
Morris, Karen Louise 1940- *WhoAmW 93*
Morris, Kathleen Beth 1948- *WhoAmW 93*
Morris, Kathleen Elizabeth 1949- *WhoEmL 93*
Morris, Keith D. *St&PR 93*
Morris, Kenneth 1879-1937 *ScF&FL 92*
Morris, Kenneth Baker 1922- *WhoAm 92*
Morris, Kenneth D. *Law&B 92*
Morris, Kenneth Donald 1946- *WhoAm 92, WhoE 93, WhoEmL 93*
Morris, Kenneth Wayne 1939- *WhoSSW 93*
Morris, L. Daniel, Jr. *Law&B 92*
Morris, Larry Garner 1938- *St&PR 93*
Morris, Laura Ann 1957- *WhoAmW 93*
Morris, Lee Butler 1944- *St&PR 93*
Morris, Leslie R. 1935- *WhoE 93*
Morris, Lester A. 1938- *St&PR 93*
Morris, Lester Joseph 1915- *St&PR 93*
Morris, Linda B. 1948- *WhoAmW 93*
Morris, Linda Marie 1950- *WhoEmL 93*
Morris, Lois Lawson 1914- *WhoAmW 93*
Morris, Loren J. *Law&B 92*
Morris, Louis Allen *Law&B 92*
Morris, Lynda Mitchum 1950- *WhoEmL 93, WhoSSW 93, WhoWor 93*
Morris, Lyndon H. 1945- *St&PR 93*
Morris, Lynn Keith *Law&B 92*
Morris, Lynne Louise 1946- *WhoAmW 93*
Morris, M. *WhoCanL 92*
Morris, M.E. 1926- *ScF&FL 92*
Morris, Mac Glenn 1922- *WhoAm 92*
Morris, Malcolm S. 1946- *St&PR 93*
Morris, Marcia C. *St&PR 93*
Morris, Margaret 1903-1968 *SweetSg B [port]*
Morris, Margaret Elizabeth 1962- *WhoAmW 93, WhoEmL 93*
Morris, Marilyn Phenecia 1960- *WhoSSW 93*
Morris, Marion *AmWomPl*
Morris, Marjorie Hale 1940- *WhoAm 92*
Morris, Mark *BioIn 17, ScF&FL 92, WhoAm 92, WhoE 93*
Morris, Mark Edwin 1956- *WhoSSW 93*
Morris, Mark Lewis 1958- *WhoEmL 93*
Morris, Mark Ronald 1941- *WhoAm 92*
Morris, Marna Jay 1949- *WhoWrEP 92*
Morris, Martin Azelle, Jr. 1941- *WhoSSW 93*
Morris, Mary 1947- *WhoWrEP 92*
Morris, Mary Ann 1946- *WhoAmW 93, WhoEmL 93*
Morris, Mary McGarry *BioIn 17*
Morris, Mary (Joan) McGarry 1943- *ConAu 139*
Morris, Mary Rosalind 1920- *WhoAmW 93*
Morris, Max King 1924- *WhoWor 93*
Morris, May 1862-1938 *ScF&FL 92*
Morris, Melanie Marie 1963- *WhoEmL 93*
Morris, Melanie T. *Law&B 92*
Morris, Melvin Lewis 1914- *WhoE 93*
Morris, Michael 1914- *WhoWor 93*
Morris, Michael Charles 1934- *WhoScE 91-1*
Morris, Michael Geoffrey 1947- *WhoWor 93*
Morris, Michael George *WhoScE 91-1*
Morris, Michael H. *Law&B 92*
Morris, Michael Lee 1948- *WhoWrEP 92*
Morris, Michelle T. *Law&B 92*
Morris, Nancy *Law&B 92*
Morris, Neil Eugene 1937- *St&PR 93*
Morris, Nila-Vae Lanier 1933- *St&PR 93*
Morris, Oswald 1915- *ConTFT 10*
Morris, Owen Glenn 1927- *WhoAm 92*
Morris, Pamela Anne *Law&B 92*
Morris, Patricia Anne 1931- *WhoE 93*
Morris, Paul F. *St&PR 93*
Morris, Penny Sandra 1960- *WhoAmW 93*
Morris, Peter *BioIn 17*
Morris, Peter Edwin *WhoScE 91-1*
Morris, Peter Fredrick 1932- *WhoAsAP 91*
Morris, Peter Gordon *WhoScE 91-1*
Morris, Peter R. *St&PR 93*
Morris, Philip Edward 1934- *St&PR 93*
Morris, Philip John 1946- *WhoAm 92, WhoE 93*
Morris, Phillip Ray 1960- *WhoSSW 93*
Morris, Phillip Spencer 1948- *WhoSSW 93*
Morris, R(eginald) O(wen) 1886-1948 *Baker 92*
Morris, Ralph William 1928- *WhoAm 92*
Morris, Raymond Philip 1904-1990 *BioIn 17*
Morris, Rebecca R. *Law&B 92*
Morris, Rebecca Robinson 1945- *St&PR 93, WhoAm 92*
Morris, Richard Alan 1944- *St&PR 93*
Morris, Richard Brandon 1904-1989 *BioIn 17*
Morris, Richard Herbert 1928- *WhoAm 92*
Morris, Richard Joel 1945- *St&PR 93*
Morris, Richard Randahl 1952- *WhoEmL 93*
Morris, Richard W. 1939- *WhoWrEP 92*
Morris, Richard (Ward) 1939- *ConAu 39NR*
Morris, Rita Louise *Law&B 92*
Morris, Robert *BioIn 17*
Morris, Robert 1910- *WhoE 93*
Morris, Robert 1915- *WhoAm 92*
Morris, Robert 1923- *WhoE 93, WhoIns 93*
Morris, Robert 1931- *WhoAm 92*
Morris, Robert Arthur 1942- *St&PR 93*
Morris, Robert Booton 1931- *St&PR 93*
Morris, Robert C. 1942- *WhoAm 92*
Morris, Robert Christian 1948- *WhoAm 92*

Morris, Robert Crawford 1916- *WhoAm 92*
Morris, Robert (Daniel) 1943- *Baker 92*
Morris, Robert Erwin 1945- *WhoE 93*
Morris, Robert Gemmill 1929- *WhoAm 92*
Morris, Robert John 1934- *WhoWor 93*
Morris, Robert Julian, Jr. 1932- *WhoAm 92*
Morris, Robert Lee 1948- *BioIn 17*
Morris, Robert Lester 1932- *WhoE 93*
Morris, Robert Louis 1932- *St&PR 93, WhoAm 92*
Morris, Robert McQuary 1933- *WhoWrEP 92*
Morris, Roland 1933- *WhoAm 92*
Morris, Ronald Anthony 1946- *WhoE 93*
Morris, Ronald Lee 1947- *St&PR 93*
Morris, Ronald Mark *Law&B 92*
Morris, Rosanna Maria Holbert 1953- *WhoAmW 93*
Morris, Ruth Andrews 1950- *WhoSSW 93*
Morris, Ruth Ann 1947- *WhoEmL 93*
Morris, Sara 1955- *WhoE 93*
Morris, Seth Irwin 1914- *WhoAm 92*
Morris, Sharon Louise Stewart 1956- *WhoAmW 93*
Morris, Stanley *Law&B 92*
Morris, Stanley E. 1942- *WhoAm 92*
Morris, Stanley M. 1942- *WhoAm 92*
Morris, Stephanie Anne 1950- *WhoEmL 93*
Morris, Stephen Alan 1950- *St&PR 93*
Morris, Stephen Brent 1950- *WhoE 93, WhoEmL 93*
Morris, Stephen Burritt 1943- *WhoAm 92*
Morris, Stephen James Michael 1934- *WhoAm 92*
Morris, Steveland *BioIn 17*
Morris, Steven C. 1949- *St&PR 93*
Morris, Stevland 1950- *WhoWor 93*
Morris, Stewart, Jr. 1948- *WhoAm 92*
Morris, Susan I. 1945- *WhoAmW 93*
Morris, Susan Marie 1955- *WhoEmL 93*
Morris, Sylvia Marie 1952- *WhoAmW 93*
Morris, Teresa Ann 1960- *WhoEmL 93*
Morris, Thad James, Jr. 1929- *St&PR 93*
Morris, Theodore Allan 1952- *WhoEmL 93*
Morris, Thomas, III *Law&B 92*
Morris, Thomas Bateman, Jr. 1936- *WhoAm 92*
Morris, Thomas E. 1946- *WhoAm 92*
Morris, Thomas F. 1932- *St&PR 93*
Morris, Thomas Quinlan 1933- *WhoAm 92*
Morris, Thomas Ross 1960- *WhoEmL 93*
Morris, Thomas V., Jr. 1950- *St&PR 93*
Morris, Thomas William 1944- *WhoAm 92*
Morris, Timothy Martin 1955- *WhoScE 91-1*
Morris, Trisha Ann 1941- *WhoE 93*
Morris, Victor Franklin, Jr. 1947- *WhoEmL 93, WhoSSW 93*
Morris, Virginia Lee 1948- *WhoAmW 93*
Morris, W. Richard *Law&B 92*
Morris, W.S., III 1934- *St&PR 93*
Morris, Walter Kenneth 1930- *St&PR 93*
Morris, Walter Scott 1912- *WhoAm 92*
Morris, Wayne E. 1940- *St&PR 93*
Morris, Wayne Robert 1945- *WhoSSW 93*
Morris, William 1834-1896 *BioIn 17, ScF&FL 92*
Morris, William 1913- *WhoAm 92, WhoWrEP 92*
Morris, William 1941- *WhoAm 92*
Morris, William Allan 1933- *WhoWor 93*
Morris, William Anthony *WhoScE 91-1*
Morris, William Charles 1938- *WhoAm 92*
Morris, William David 1936- *WhoWor 93*
Morris, William Harrell, Jr. 1929- *WhoAm 92*
Morris, William Joseph 1923- *WhoAm 92*
Morris, William L. 1908- *St&PR 93*
Morris, William Noel, Jr. 1932- *WhoAm 92*
Morris, William Otis, Jr. 1922- *WhoAm 92*
Morris, William T. 1937- *St&PR 93*
Morris, Willie *BioIn 17*
Morris, Willie 1934- *WhoAm 92*
Morris, Willie Herman, III 1953- *WhoEmL 93, WhoSSW 93*
Morris, Winifred *ScF&FL 92*
Morris, Wm. David 1947- *St&PR 93*
Morris, Wright 1910- *BioIn 17, MagSAmL [port], ScF&FL 92, WhoAm 92, WhoWrEP 92*
Morris, Wyn 1929- *Baker 92*
Morris Archinal, Gretchen Suzanne 1963- *WhoAmW 93, WhoEmL 93*
Morrisett, Lloyd N. 1929- *St&PR 93*
Morrisey, Donald C. 1931- *St&PR 93*
Morrisey, Michael A. 1952- *WhoEmL 93, WhoSSW 93*
Morrisey, P.D. 1939- *St&PR 93*
Morrisey, Thomas 1952- *WhoWrEP 92*
Morrish, Alan Richard 1944- *St&PR 93*
Morrish, Allan Henry 1924- *WhoAm 92*
Morrish, Kathleen Anne 1956- *WhoEmL 93*
Morrison, Alec P. 1943- *St&PR 93*
Morrison, Alexander Damien *WhoWrEP 92*
Morrison, Alvin Constantine 1928- *WhoE 93*
Morrison, Angus Curran 1919- *WhoAm 92, WhoWor 93*
Morrison, Anne 189-?- *AmWomPl*
Morrison, April Dawn 1971- *WhoWrEP 92*
Morrison, Ashton Byrom 1922- *WhoAm 92*
Morrison, Audrey A. Lesiak 1941- *St&PR 93*
Morrison, Barbara d1992 *NewYTBS 92*
Morrison, Barbara 1907-1992 *BioIn 17*
Morrison, Bart William 1951- *WhoE 93*
Morrison, Bill 1935- *BioIn 17*
Morrison, (Philip) Blake 1950- *ConAu 138*
Morrison, Bruce *MiSFD 9*
Morrison, Caroline Elizabeth *WhoScE 91-1*
Morrison, Carolyn Don 1966- *WhoAmW 93*
Morrison, Carroll Kelly 1956- *WhoSSW 93*
Morrison, Charles *WhoScE 91-1*
Morrison, Charles Clayton *BioIn 17*
Morrison, Charles M., Jr. *Law&B 92*
Morrison, Charles R. *BioIn 17*
Morrison, Cheryl Lynn 1953- *WhoEmL 93*
Morrison, Chloe *ScF&FL 92*
Morrison, Clinton 1915- *WhoAm 92*
Morrison, Connie Faith *WhoAmW 93*
Morrison, Craig Michael 1958- *WhoE 93*
Morrison, Curtis Angus *Law&B 92*
Morrison, Darrel Gene 1937- *WhoAm 92*
Morrison, Daryl 1931- *St&PR 93*
Morrison, David A. 1960- *St&PR 93*
Morrison, David Ashley 1967- *WhoSSW 93*
Morrison, David Campbell 1941- *WhoAm 92*
Morrison, David Fred 1953- *WhoAm 92*
Morrison, David Lee 1933- *St&PR 93, WhoAm 92*
Morrison, David R. *Law&B 92*
Morrison, David Scott 1953- *WhoEmL 93*
Morrison, De Lesseps S. 1912-1964 *PolPar*
Morrison, Deborah J. *Law&B 92*
Morrison, Delcy Schram 1935- *WhoAmW 93, WhoWor 93*
Morrison, Denise Annette *WhoWrEP 92*
Morrison, Dennis Brian 1946- *St&PR 93*
Morrison, Dolphus Compton 1934- *St&PR 93*
Morrison, Donald A. 1931- *St&PR 93*
Morrison, Donald Bruce 1929- *St&PR 93*
Morrison, Donald Franklin 1931- *WhoAm 92, WhoE 93*
Morrison, Donald Graham 1939- *WhoAm 92*
Morrison, Donald W. *Law&B 92*
Morrison, Donald William 1926- *WhoAm 92*
Morrison, Doris 1906- *WhoAmW 93*
Morrison, Dorothy Nafus *ScF&FL 92*
Morrison, Edward W., Jr. 1921- *St&PR 93*
Morrison, Edward Walter, Jr. 1921- *WhoSSW 93*
Morrison, Francis Secrest 1931- *WhoAm 92*
Morrison, Frank 1918- *WhoWrEP 92*
Morrison, Fred Beverly 1927- *WhoAm 92*
Morrison, Gayle V. 1921- *St&PR 93*
Morrison, George Chalmers *WhoScE 91-1*
Morrison, George Chalmers 1930- *WhoWor 93*
Morrison, George Harold 1921- *WhoAm 92*
Morrison, Gilbert Caffall 1931- *WhoAm 92*
Morrison, Gladys Mae 1928- *WhoAmW 93*
Morrison, Gordon Mackay, Jr. 1930- *WhoAm 92, WhoE 93*
Morrison, Grace *WhoWrEP 92*
Morrison, Grace Blanch Simpson 1933- *WhoAmW 93*
Morrison, Greg *ScF&FL 92*
Morrison, Gregg Scott 1964- *WhoEmL 93, WhoSSW 93*
Morrison, H. Robert 1938- *WhoE 93*
Morrison, H. Russell, Jr. 1929- *St&PR 93*
Morrison, Harriet Barbara 1934- *WhoAmW 93*
Morrison, Harry 1937- *WhoAm 92*
Morrison, Herbert Stanley 1888-1965 *DcTwHis*
Morrison, Ian Alastair 1924- *WhoE 93*
Morrison, J. Ken 1950- *WhoWrEP 92*
Morrison, J. Kent 1940- *WhoE 93*
Morrison, James Douglas 1943-1971 *ConAu 40NR*
Morrison, James Frederick 1933- *WhoE 93*
Morrison, James Harris 1918- *St&PR 93*
Morrison, James Ian 1952- *WhoAm 92*
Morrison, James R. 1924- *WhoAm 92*
Morrison, James S. 1929- *St&PR 93, WhoAm 92*
Morrison, Jeanette Helen 1927- *WhoAm 92*
Morrison, Jeffrey E. *Law&B 92*
Morrison, Jim *ConAu 40NR, St&PR 93*
Morrison, Jim 1943-1971 *Baker 92, BioIn 17*
Morrison, Joan 1922- *BioIn 17, WhoAmW 93*
Morrison, John 1949- *ConAu 137*
Morrison, John Bennett 1938- *WhoE 93*
Morrison, John Dittgen 1921- *WhoWor 93*
Morrison, John Egan 1950- *WhoSSW 93*
Morrison, John F.B. *WhoScE 91-1*
Morrison, John Gill 1914- *WhoAm 92*
Morrison, John Haddow, Jr. 1933- *St&PR 93*
Morrison, John Horton 1933- *WhoAm 92*
Morrison, John James 1949- *WhoEmL 93*
Morrison, John Michael 1957- *WhoEmL 93*
Morrison, John Peirce 1956- *WhoEmL 93*
Morrison, John R. 1928- *St&PR 93*
Morrison, John S. *Law&B 92*
Morrison, John Washburn 1922- *WhoAm 92*
Morrison, Joseph Francis, Jr. 1943- *WhoAm 92*
Morrison, Joseph Young 1951- *WhoEmL 93, WhoSSW 93, WhoWor 93*
Morrison, Joshua 1900- *St&PR 93*
Morrison, K. Jaydene 1933- *WhoSSW 93*
Morrison, Karl Frederick 1936- *WhoAm 92*
Morrison, Kathy Weaver *Law&B 92*
Morrison, Kay Ellen 1961- *WhoEmL 93*
Morrison, Kenneth Allen 1940- *WhoE 93*
Morrison, Kenneth Douglas 1918- *WhoAm 92*
Morrison, Kenneth Ray 1948- *St&PR 93*
Morrison, Laura Mary 1927- *WhoWrEP 92*
Morrison, Lillian 1917- *WhoWrEP 92*
Morrison, Louise D. *ScF&FL 92*
Morrison, Mabel Jean 1927- *WhoSSW 93*
Morrison, Madison 1940- *WhoWrEP 92*
Morrison, Manley Glenn 1915- *WhoAm 92*
Morrison, Marion Michael 1907-1979 *BioIn 17*
Morrison, Mark Dennis 1959- *WhoE 93*
Morrison, Mark S. *Law&B 92*
Morrison, Martin Earl 1947- *WhoAm 92*
Morrison, Marvin L. 1940- *WhoWrEP 92*
Morrison, Meredith 1921- *St&PR 93*
Morrison, Michael Anthony *Law&B 92*
Morrison, Michael Gordon 1937- *WhoAm 92*
Morrison, Michael Ian Donald 1929- *St&PR 93*
Morrison, Michelle Williams 1947- *WhoAmW 93, WhoWor 93*
Morrison, Murray Allan 1939- *WhoE 93*
Morrison, Nancy Anne 1953- *WhoEmL 93*
Morrison, Patricia K. *ScF&FL 92*
Morrison, Perry David 1919- *WhoAm 92*
Morrison, Perry Erwin 1929- *St&PR 93, WhoE 93*
Morrison, Pete 1890-1973 *BioIn 17*
Morrison, Peter Daniel 1943- *St&PR 93*
Morrison, Philip *BioIn 17*
Morrison, Preston A. *Law&B 92*
Morrison, Ralph W. 1878-1948 *BioIn 17*
Morrison, Ray Leon 1952- *WhoEmL 93*
Morrison, Richard J. *Law&B 92*
Morrison, Richard N. 1958- *St&PR 93*
Morrison, Richard Scott 1944- *St&PR 93*
Morrison, Robert 1952- *WhoEmL 93*
Morrison, Robert Irwin 1938- *St&PR 93*
Morrison, Robert Kariher 1931- *WhoAm 92*
Morrison, Robert R. 1935- *St&PR 93*
Morrison, Robert S. 1909- *St&PR 93*
Morrison, Robert Scheck 1942- *WhoAm 92*
Morrison, Robert William 1941- *WhoIns 93*
Morrison, Roger Barron 1914- *WhoWor 93*
Morrison, Roger F. 1937- *St&PR 93*
Morrison, Ronald *WhoScE 91-1*
Morrison, Roy Dennis, II 1926- *WhoE 93*
Morrison, Shelley 1936- *WhoAm 92*
Morrison, Sid 1933- *CngDr 91, WhoAm 92*
Morrison, Stephen D. *Law&B 92*
Morrison, Steve 1947- *ConTFT 10*
Morrison, Stuart Innes 1949- *WhoEmL 93*
Morrison, Susan *Law&B 92*
Morrison, Susan M. *WhoAmW 93*
Morrison, Thomas Keith 1944- *WhoUN 92*
Morrison, Thomas Truxton *WhoAm 92*
Morrison, Todd A. *Law&B 92*
Morrison, Tommy *BioIn 17*
Morrison, Toni 1931- *AmWomWr 92, AmWr S3, BioIn 17, ConHero 2 [port], MagSAmL [port], ScF&FL 92, WhoAm 92, WhoAmW 93, WhoWrEP 92, WorLitC [port]*
Morrison, Van *BioIn 17*
Morrison, Van 1945- *Baker 92, SoulM, WhoAm 92*
Morrison, Virden H. 1927- *St&PR 93*
Morrison, W. Rodney 1946- *WhoEmL 93, WhoSSW 93*
Morrison, Walton Stephen 1907- *WhoSSW 93*
Morrison, Wilbur H. 1915- *BioIn 17*
Morrison, Wilbur J. 1931- *St&PR 93*
Morrison, William Fowler, Jr. 1928- *WhoAm 92, WhoSSW 93*
Morrison, William Gamble Boyd, III 1952- *WhoE 93*
Morrison, William Russell *WhoScE 91-1*
Morrison, William Stanley Gordon 1928- *WhoUN 92*
Morrison, Winifred Elaine Haas 1925- *WhoAmW 93*
Morrison, Winsor Verdon 1925- *WhoAm 92*
Morrison-Givens, Theresa Renee 1960- *WhoAmW 93*
Morrisroe, Edward L. 1950- *St&PR 93*
Morrisroe, Susan Higgins *Law&B 92*
Morriss, Frank Howard, Jr. 1940- *WhoAm 92*
Morriss, George Wyman 1947- *St&PR 93*
Morriss, James A. 1930- *St&PR 93*
Morriss, Mary Rachel *WhoAmW 93, WhoWor 93*
Morrissette, Bruce Archer 1911- *WhoAm 92*
Morrissette, Jean Fernand 1942- *WhoWor 93*
Morrissette, Rosemary D. *WhoAm 92*
Morrissey, Alice 1967- *WhoE 93*
Morrissey, Bruce W. *Law&B 92*
Morrissey, Charles Thomas 1933- *WhoAm 92*
Morrissey, Dolores Josephine *WhoAm 92*
Morrissey, Edmond Joseph 1943- *WhoAm 92*
Morrissey, J.L. *ScF&FL 92*
Morrissey, Jean Grundman 1958- *WhoAmW 93*
Morrissey, Joanne 1947- *WhoAmW 93*
Morrissey, John Carroll 1914- *WhoAm 92*
Morrissey, John Daniel 1929- *St&PR 93, WhoAm 92*
Morrissey, John E. *Law&B 92*
Morrissey, John Edward 1930- *St&PR 93*
Morrissey, John J. *Law&B 92*
Morrissey, Kathleen Davis 1947- *WhoE 93*
Morrissey, Kim 1955- *WhoCanL 92*
Morrissey, Leo 1958- *WhoE 93*
Morrissey, Martin G. 1952- *St&PR 93*
Morrissey, Patrick T. 1950- *St&PR 93*
Morrissey, Paul *BioIn 17*
Morrissey, Paul 1939- *MiSFD 9*
Morrissey, Peter A. 1953- *WhoAm 92*
Morrissey, Robert John 1944- *WhoAm 92*
Morrissey, Stephen 1950- *WhoCanL 92*
Morrissey, Stuart *St&PR 93*
Morrissey, Stuart J. 1953- *St&PR 93*
Morrissey, Thomas Francis 1932- *St&PR 93*
Morrissey, Thomas J. 1936- *St&PR 93*
Morrissey, Walter Edward *Law&B 92*
Morrissey, William Paul 1927- *St&PR 93*
Morrissey, William Thomas 1950- *WhoEmL 93*
Morrissey Family *BioIn 17*
Morris Society *ScF&FL 92*
Morris-Sweetland, Gayle D. 1943- *St&PR 93*
Morrissy, Mary Jule 1952- *WhoEmL 93*
Morriston, Donald Robert 1941- *St&PR 93*
Morris-Yamba, Trish *WhoE 93*
Morritt, Graham Nathaniel 1942- *WhoWor 93*
Morritt, Hope *WhoCanL 92*
Morrone, Edward P. 1950- *WhoE 93*
Morros, Lucy Schmitz *WhoAmW 93*
Morrow, Allen Roy 1949- *St&PR 93*
Morrow, Andrew 1964- *St&PR 93*
Morrow, Andrew Nesbit 1929- *WhoAm 92*
Morrow, Ann Bolton 1952- *St&PR 93*
Morrow, Ann Marie *Law&B 92*
Morrow, Barry Nelson 1948- *WhoAm 92*
Morrow, Beth Ellen 1951- *St&PR 93*
Morrow, Bradford 1951- *BioIn 17, ScF&FL 92*

Morrow, Bruce W. 1946- *WhoEmL 93, WhoSSW 93*
Morrow, Carol *Law&B 92*
Morrow, Carolyn Clark *BioIn 17*
Morrow, Charlene Lynn 1959- *WhoAmW 93*
Morrow, Charles, III 1956- *AfrAmBi [port]*
Morrow, Charles Tabor 1917- *WhoAm 92*
Morrow, Charlie *BioIn 17*
Morrow, Cherylle Ann 1950- *WhoAmW 93*
Morrow, David Austin, III 1935- *WhoAm 92*
Morrow, Dennis Robert 1951- *WhoWor 93*
Morrow, Diane Mougey *Law&B 92*
Morrow, Douglas Morgan 1955- *WhoEmL 93*
Morrow, Dwight Whitney 1873-1931 *BioIn 17*
Morrow, E. Frederic 1909- *WhoAm 92*
Morrow, Elizabeth 1947- *WhoEmL 93, WhoWor 93*
Morrow, Everette Frederic 1909- *EncAACR*
Morrow, Fred C. 1926- *St&PR 93*
Morrow, George Lester 1922- *WhoAm 92*
Morrow, George Telford, II 1943- *WhoWrEP 92*
Morrow, Gregory William 1963- *WhoE 93*
Morrow, H.M. *ScF&FL 92*
Morrow, Hilda Howard 1942- *WhoSSW 93*
Morrow, Honore Willsie 1880?-1940 *AmWomPl*
Morrow, Hugh 1915-1991 *BioIn 17*
Morrow, Jacqueline R. *Law&B 92*
Morrow, James 1947- *ScF&FL 92*
Morrow, James B. 1926- *St&PR 93*
Morrow, James Benjamin 1926- *WhoAm 92*
Morrow, James Coles 1931- *St&PR 93*
Morrow, James E. *Law&B 92*
Morrow, James E. 1938- *St&PR 93*
Morrow, Jane Bates 1947- *WhoEmL 93, WhoSSW 93*
Morrow, Jeff 1913- *BioIn 17*
Morrow, Jeffrey *St&PR 93*
Morrow, Joan Schieferstein 1949- *WhoEmL 93*
Morrow, John A. 1942- *St&PR 93*
Morrow, John Ellsworth 1943- *WhoAm 92*
Morrow, John Howard 1910- *WhoAm 92*
Morrow, John Ottern, Jr. 1953- *WhoEmL 93*
Morrow, Jon Stanley *WhoE 93*
Morrow, Joseph T. 1930- *St&PR 93*
Morrow, Kathy 1938- *BioIn 17*
Morrow, Lance *BioIn 17*
Morrow, Lance 1939- *WhoAm 92*
Morrow, Laura Annette 1958- *WhoAmW 93, WhoEmL 93*
Morrow, Marilyn Sue 1943- *WhoSSW 93*
Morrow, Martina *AmWomPl*
Morrow, Mary Jane 1952- *St&PR 93*
Morrow, Melanie Marie 1968- *WhoAmW 93*
Morrow, Nancy Ann 1958- *WhoAmW 93*
Morrow, Patrick Bryan 1947- *WhoSSW 93*
Morrow, Paul Edward 1922- *WhoAm 92*
Morrow, Ralph Ernest 1920- *WhoAm 92*
Morrow, Randall R. *Law&B 92*
Morrow, Rebecca O'Connor *Law&B 92*
Morrow, Richard Forrest 1935- *St&PR 93*
Morrow, Richard Martin 1926- *St&PR 93, WhoAm 92*
Morrow, Richard Towson 1926- *WhoAm 92*
Morrow, Rob *BioIn 17, NewYTBS 92 [port]*
Morrow, Rob 1962- *WhoAm 92*
Morrow, Rob 1963?- *ConTFT 10*
Morrow, Robert 1930- *St&PR 93*
Morrow, Robert Maxwell 1946- *WhoAm 92*
Morrow, Robert Sproul 1928- *St&PR 93*
Morrow, Ronald B. 1945- *St&PR 93*
Morrow, Sam R. 1949- *St&PR 93*
Morrow, Samuel Roy, III 1949- *WhoAm 92*
Morrow, Scott Douglas 1954- *WhoE 93, WhoEmL 93, WhoWor 93*
Morrow, Sharon M. 1953- *WhoAmW 93*
Morrow, Sheila Ann 1936- *WhoWrEP 92*
Morrow, Susan Dagmar 1932- *WhoAmW 93*
Morrow, Susan H. 1943- *WhoAmW 93*
Morrow, Thomas H. *Law&B 92*
Morrow, Thomas H. 1941- *St&PR 93*
Morrow, Timothy Titus 1911- *WhoWor 93*
Morrow, Walter Edwin, Jr. 1928- *WhoAm 92, WhoE 93*
Morrow, William B. 1948- *St&PR 93*
Morrow, William Berryman 1948- *WhoWor 93*
Morrow, William Clarence 1935- *WhoAm 92*
Morrow, William Earl 1923- *WhoWor 93*
Morrow, William Owen 1927- *St&PR 93*
Morrow, William Penn, Jr. 1933- *St&PR 93, WhoAm 92*
Morrow, Winston Vaughan 1924- *St&PR 93, WhoAm 92*
Morrow-Jones, Hazel Ann 1952- *WhoEmL 93*
Morsbach, Charles Albert *Law&B 92*
Morsch, Thomas Harvey 1931- *WhoAm 92*
Morsching, Germaine Ann 1934- *WhoAmW 93*
Morse, A. Reynolds 1914- *ScF&FL 92*
Morse, Aaron *BioIn 17*
Morse, Alan R., Jr. 1938- *St&PR 93*
Morse, Alfred G. 1924- *St&PR 93*
Morse, Alfreda Theodora Strandberg 1890-1953 *See* Morse, Theodore 1873-1924 *Baker 92*
Morse, Anne Elizabeth 1947- *WhoWor 93*
Morse, Bradford 1921- *WhoAm 92*
Morse, Brian 1948- *ScF&FL 92*
Morse, Bruce Warren 1957- *WhoEmL 93*
Morse, Carl A. d1989 *BioIn 17*
Morse, Carlton E. 1901- *WhoAm 92*
Morse, Carmel Lei 1953- *WhoEmL 93, WhoWrEP 92*
Morse, Chalmers Ingersoll 1950- *WhoEmL 93*
Morse, Charles William, Jr. 1934- *WhoAm 92*
Morse, Daniel Warren, Jr. 1954- *WhoEmL 93*
Morse, David Abner 1907-1990 *BioIn 17*
Morse, David Bradford 1943- *St&PR 93*
Morse, David M. *Law&B 92*
Morse, David Rockwell 1954- *St&PR 93*
Morse, Donald E. 1936- *ScF&FL 92*
Morse, Donald R(oy) 1931- *WhoWrEP 92*
Morse, Edmond N. 1922- *St&PR 93*
Morse, Edmond Northrop 1922- *WhoAm 92*
Morse, Edward Sylvester 1838-1925 *BioIn 17*
Morse, F. D., Jr. 1928- *WhoWor 93*
Morse, Francis 1917- *WhoE 93*
Morse, Frank Alan 1938- *St&PR 93*
Morse, Gail *BioIn 17*
Morse, Garlan, Jr. 1947- *WhoAm 92*
Morse, George Wray, II 1942- *WhoSSW 93*
Morse, Harry N. 1835-1912 *BioIn 17*
Morse, Herbert E. *WhoAm 92*
Morse, Herbert R. 1929- *St&PR 93*
Morse, Jack Hatton 1923- *WhoAm 92*
Morse, James Buckner 1930- *WhoAm 92*
Morse, James Harold 1939- *WhoE 93*
Morse, James K. 1937- *St&PR 93*
Morse, James L. 1940- *WhoAm 92*
Morse, Jami *BioIn 17*
Morse, Jedidiah 1761-1826 *BioIn 17*
Morse, John H. 1910- *St&PR 93*
Morse, John Harleigh 1910- *WhoAm 92*
Morse, John L. 1932- *St&PR 93*
Morse, John Lougee 1932- *WhoAm 92*
Morse, John Moore 1911- *WhoAm 92*
Morse, John Walker 1940- *WhoWor 93*
Morse, Joseph 1920- *St&PR 93, WhoAm 92*
Morse, Josiah Mitchell 1912- *WhoE 93*
Morse, Karen Williams 1940- *WhoAm 92*
Morse, Katherine Duncan 1888- *AmWomPl*
Morse, Kathleen Ann 1952- *WhoEmL 93*
Morse, Kenneth Pratt 1905- *WhoAm 92*
Morse, Kerry L. *Law&B 92*
Morse, L.A. 1945- *WhoCanL 92*
Morse, Laura M. *AmWomPl*
Morse, Leon William 1912- *WhoWor 93*
Morse, Lucius B., III 1938- *St&PR 93*
Morse, M. Howard 1959- *WhoEmL 93*
Morse, Margaret Patricia 1912- *WhoWrEP 92*
Morse, Mark Russell 1959- *WhoEmL 93*
Morse, Marvin Henry 1929- *WhoAm 92*
Morse, Michele Block *BioIn 17*
Morse, Mildred S. *AfrAmBi [port]*
Morse, Mona Helen 1951- *WhoAmW 93*
Morse, Nancy Wood 1930- *St&PR 93*
Morse, Patrick Gary 1961- *WhoSSW 93*
Morse, Peggy Mansfield *WhoWrEP 92*
Morse, Peter Hodges 1935- *WhoAm 92*
Morse, Phillip H. *St&PR 93*
Morse, R.C. *Law&B 92*
Morse, Rebecca Lynne 1956- *WhoSSW 93*
Morse, Richard 1922- *WhoAm 92*
Morse, Richard Alan 1954- *WhoE 93*
Morse, Richard Jay 1933- *WhoWor 93*
Morse, Richard McGee 1922- *WhoAm 92*
Morse, Richard Stetson, Jr. 1941- *St&PR 93*
Morse, Robert *BioIn 17*
Morse, Robert 1931- *QDrFCA 92 [port]*
Morse, Robert Alan 1931- *WhoAm 92*
Morse, Robert E. *ScF&FL 92*
Morse, Robert Harry 1941- *WhoAm 92*
Morse, Robert Moreton 1937- *St&PR 93*
Morse, Robert Parker 1945- *St&PR 93*
Morse, Robert Warren 1921- *WhoAm 92*
Morse, Roy Earl 1916- *WhoSSW 93*
Morse, Samuel Finley Breese 1791-1872 *BioIn 17*
Morse, Saul Julian 1948- *WhoEmL 93*
Morse, Scott David 1950- *WhoWor 93*
Morse, Stephen Scott 1951- *WhoE 93*
Morse, Theodore 1873-1924 *Baker 92*
Morse, Thomas R. *Law&B 92*
Morse, Thomas Robeson 1927-1991 *BioIn 17*
Morse, True Delbert 1896- *WhoAm 92*
Morse, Vicki Paulson 1946- *WhoAmW 93*
Morse, Warner Alden d1991 *BioIn 17*
Morse, William Michael 1947- *WhoE 93*
Morselli, Adriano fl. 1679-1683 *OxDcOp*
Morselli, Enrico 1852-1929 *IntDcAn*
Morselli, Paolo Lucio 1937- *WhoWor 93*
Morse-Shamosh, Stephanie Lynn *Law&B 92*
Morshead, Richard Williams 1931- *WhoAm 92*
Morsiani, Mario 1926- *WhoWor 93*
Morsky, Jorma Niilo 1935- *WhoScE 91-4*
Morson, A.E. 1934- *St&PR 93*
Morss, Charles Anthony, Jr. 1931- *St&PR 93, WhoAm 92*
Morss, Esther Proctor 1964- *WhoAmW 93*
Morstain, Barry Rolan 1944- *WhoE 93*
Morstin, Jerzy 1938- *WhoScE 91-4*
Morstin, Ludwik H. 1886-1966 *PolBiDi*
Morstrom, Lois Cool *AmWomPl*
Morstyn, George 1950- *WhoWor 93*
Morsy, Samir Amin 1942- *WhoUN 92*
Mort, Anthony Gordon 1949- *WhoWor 93*
Mortarelli, Robert J. 1941- *St&PR 93*
Mortari, Virgilio 1902- *Baker 92*
Morte, Armand E. 1929- *St&PR 93*
Mortelmans, Fernand Karel 1926- *WhoScE 91-2*
Mortelmans, Ivo (Oscar) 1901-1984 *Baker 92*
Mortelmans, Jos M.H. 1924- *WhoScE 91-2*
Mortelmans, Lodewijk 1868-1952 *Baker 92*
Mortelmans, Luc A.A. 1947- *WhoScE 91-2*
Mortemore, Lenore Mary 1927- *WhoWrEP 92*
Morten, Larry *Law&B 92*
Morten, Spencer W., Jr. 1922- *St&PR 93*
Morten, Stanley W. 1943- *St&PR 93*
Morten, Stanley Wilbur 1943- *WhoAm 92*
Mortensen, Arvid LeGrande 1941- *WhoAm 92*
Mortensen, Ellen L. 1943- *WhoAmW 93*
Mortensen, Eugene Phillips 1941- *WhoE 93*
Mortensen, Finn (Einar) 1922-1983 *Baker 92*
Mortensen, Gordon Louis 1938- *WhoAm 92*
Mortensen, James E. 1925- *WhoAm 92*
Mortensen, James Michael 1937- *WhoIns 93*
Mortensen, Mary Ellen 1951- *WhoAmW 93*
Mortensen, Morris D. 1929- *St&PR 93*
Mortensen, Otto (Jacob Hubertz) 1907-1986 *Baker 92*
Mortensen, Peter 1935- *WhoAm 92*
Mortensen, Peter Vejby 1965- *WhoWor 93*
Mortensen, Robert Henry 1939- *WhoAm 92*
Mortensen, Roberta *WhoWrEP 92*
Mortensen, Stan 1921-1991 *AnObit 1991*
Mortensen, Stanley John 1949- *WhoEmL 93, WhoWor 93*
Mortensen, Walter G. *Law&B 92*
Mortensen, William H. 1903-1990 *BioIn 17*
Mortenson, Carl Norman 1919- *St&PR 93*
Mortenson, Leonard Earl 1928- *WhoSSW 93*
Mortenson, Philip D. *Law&B 92*
Mortenson, Thomas Theodore 1934- *St&PR 93*
Mortge, Barry Ira 1960- *WhoEmL 93*
Mortham, Sandra Barringer 1951- *WhoAmW 93*
Morthenson, Jan W(ilhelm) 1940- *Baker 92*
Morthland, Constance Amelia Grant 1915- *WhoAmW 93*
Morthland, William Grant 1956- *WhoSSW 93*
Morthorst, Thomas 1948- *St&PR 93*
Mortier, Edouard Adolphe Casimir Joseph 1768-1835 *HarEnMi*
Mortier, Gerard *BioIn 17*
Mortier, Gerard 1943- *WhoWor 93*
Mortier, Roland Fabien Jules 1920- *WhoWor 93*
Mortimer, Anita Louise 1950- *WhoAmW 93*
Mortimer, Edward Albert, Jr. 1922- *WhoAm 92*
Mortimer, Harold E. 1928- *St&PR 93*
Mortimer, Henry T. *BioIn 17*
Mortimer, Henry Tilford, Jr. 1942- *St&PR 93, WhoAm 92*
Mortimer, J. Thomas 1939- *WhoAm 92*
Mortimer, Joanne Stafford 1929- *WhoAmW 93*
Mortimer, John Clifford 1923- *BioIn 17*
Mortimer, Keith Vernon *WhoScE 91-1*
Mortimer, Lillian d1946 *AmWomPl*
Mortimer, Philip Paul *WhoScE 91-1*
Mortimer, Robert Thomas, Jr. 1954- *St&PR 93*
Mortimer, Susan *BioIn 17*
Mortimer, Terry J. 1945- *St&PR 93*
Mortimer, William James 1932- *WhoAm 92*
Mortimer, William John 1934- *WhoWrEP 92*
Mortimer, Wm. James 1932- *St&PR 93*
Mortimore, Peter John *WhoScE 91-1*
Mortinger, Stephen Ashley *Law&B 92*
Mortini, Raymond Rene 1958- *WhoWor 93*
Mortland, Donald Frank 1927- *WhoE 93*
Mortley, Raoul John 1944- *WhoWor 93*
Mortlock, Robert Paul 1931- *WhoAm 92, WhoE 93*
Mortola, Edward Joseph 1917- *WhoAm 92*
Morton, Alan Whitman 1938- *St&PR 93*
Morton, Alexander A., III *WhoAm 92*
Morton, Andrew *NewYTBS 92 [port]*
Morton, Anne Marie Judith 1965- *WhoWrEP 92*
Morton, Anthony 1908-1973 *BioIn 17*
Morton, Arthur Ray 1936- *WhoSSW 93*
Morton, Beecher Edward 1922- *WhoSSW 93*
Morton, Bernice Finley 1923- *WhoAmW 93*
Morton, Betty J. *Law&B 92*
Morton, Carlos 1942- *DcLB 122 [port]*
Morton, Carlos 1947- *HispAmA*
Morton, Caroline Julia *WhoAmW 93*
Morton, Carolyn K. 1951- *St&PR 93*
Morton, Catherine Anne *Law&B 92*
Morton, Charles Brinkley 1926- *WhoAm 92, WhoSSW 93*
Morton, Charles Edward, Jr. 1945- *WhoSSW 93*
Morton, Charles F. 1945- *St&PR 93*
Morton, Charles M. 1908- *St&PR 93*
Morton, Charlotte Ann 1958- *WhoWrEP 92*
Morton, Claude Cammack 1951- *WhoEmL 93*
Morton, Clifford A. 1936- *WhoAm 92*
Morton, Cynthia Ann 1950- *WhoAmW 93*
Morton, Daniel W. *Law&B 92*
Morton, David 1929- *WhoAm 92, WhoWor 93*
Morton, David Michael 1947- *WhoUN 92*
Morton, Dean O. 1932- *WhoAm 92*
Morton, Donald Charles 1933- *WhoAm 92*
Morton, Donald John 1931- *WhoAm 92*
Morton, Donald Lee 1934- *WhoAm 92, WhoWor 93*
Morton, Donald S. *Law&B 92*
Morton, Donna M. 1933- *WhoAmW 93*
Morton, Edward Francis 1951- *WhoEmL 93*
Morton, Edward James 1926- *WhoAm 92, WhoE 93*
Morton, Elaine Leslie 1937- *WhoE 93*
Morton, Eleanor 1890-1954 *BioIn 17*
Morton, Everett 1951- *See* English Beat, The *ConMus 9*
Morton, Florrinell 1905-1990 *BioIn 17*
Morton, Frances McKinnon *AmWomPl*
Morton, Frederic 1924- *WhoAm 92, WhoWrEP 92*
Morton, Gregg Harrison 1955- *WhoEmL 93*
Morton, Harold Sylvanus, Jr. 1924- *WhoSSW 93*
Morton, Henrietta Mann *BioIn 17*
Morton, Henrietta Olive 1937- *WhoAmW 93*
Morton, Henry C.V. 1892-1979 *ScF&FL 92*
Morton, Herbert Charles 1921- *WhoAm 92*
Morton, Herwald Hutchins 1931- *WhoAm 92*
Morton, Holmes *BioIn 17*
Morton, Ian Douglas *WhoScE 91-1*
Morton, J.B. 1893-1979 *ScF&FL 92*
Morton, James Irwin 1935- *WhoSSW 93*
Morton, Janice Kenefake 1951- *WhoSSW 93*
Morton, Jeffrey Bruce 1941- *WhoAm 92*

Morton, Jelly Roll *BioIn 17*
Morton, "Jelly Roll" 1890-1941 *Baker 92*
Morton, Jerome Holdren 1942- *WhoSSW 93*
Morton, Joanne McKean 1953- *WhoAmW 93*
Morton, Joe *BioIn 17*
Morton, John *WhoScE 91-1*
Morton, John C. *ScF&FL 92*
Morton, Judy d1991 *BioIn 17*
Morton, Keith William *WhoScE 91-1*
Morton, Larry Craig 1943- *BiDAMSp 1989*
Morton, Lawrence 1904-1987 *Baker 92*
Morton, Leah 1890-1954 *BioIn 17*
Morton, Leland Clure 1916- *WhoAm 92*
Morton, Leslie Hugh Glyn *WhoScE 91-1*
Morton, Linda 1944- *WhoAm 92*
Morton, Margaret E. *AfrAmBi*
Morton, Margaret E. 1924- *WhoAmW 93*
Morton, Marguerite W. *AmWomPl*
Morton, Marilyn Miller 1929- *WhoAmW 93, WhoWor 93*
Morton, Mark Edward 1956- *St&PR 93, WhoEmL 93, WhoSSW 93, WhoWor 93*
Morton, Marshall Nay 1945- *St&PR 93, WhoAm 92*
Morton, Martha 1865-1925 *AmWomPl*
Morton, Michael Dale 1957- *St&PR 93*
Morton, Michael Phillip 1955- *WhoEmL 93*
Morton, Michael Ray 1952- *WhoEmL 93, WhoSSW 93*
Morton, Miriam 1918?-1985 *ScF&FL 92*
Morton, Nelle 1905-1987 *BioIn 17*
Morton, Newton Ennis *WhoScE 91-1*
Morton, Oliver H. P. T. 1823-1877 *PolPar*
Morton, Perry Wilkes 1923- *WhoSSW 93*
Morton, Perry Williams 1939- *St&PR 93*
Morton, Ramon E. *Law&B 92*
Morton, Robert c. 1430-c. 1476 *Baker 92*
Morton, Robert Allen 1954- *WhoE 93*
Morton, Robert Dallas 1940- *St&PR 93*
Morton, Robert John 1949- *WhoE 93*
Morton, Rocky *MiSFD 9*
Morton, Rogers C. B. 1914-1979 *PolPar*
Morton, Samuel George 1799-1851 *IntDcAn*
Morton, Terry Wayne 1957- *WhoSSW 93*
Morton, Thomas C. 1937- *St&PR 93*
Morton, Thomas John 1958- *St&PR 93*
Morton, Thomas Judson 1949- *WhoEmL 93*
Morton, Thruston B. 1907-1982 *PolPar*
Morton, Thruston Ballard 1907-1982 *BioIn 17*
Morton, Victoria C. 1952- *St&PR 93*
Morton, William G. 1937- *St&PR 93*
Morton, William Gilbert 1906- *WhoAm 92*
Morton, William Gilbert, Jr. 1937- *WhoE 93*
Morton, William Hardy 1915-1988 *BioIn 17*
Morton, William S. *Law&B 92*
Morton, William T. *Law&B 92*
Morton-Fincham, Christopher *WhoScE 91-1*
Morton-Sale, John 1901-1990 *BioIn 17*
Morton-Smith, Stephen 1951- *WhoEmL 93*
Mortvedt, John Jacob 1932- *WhoAm 92, WhoSSW 93*
Mortyn, Mollie C. 1937- *St&PR 93*
Mortz, Betty Jane 1924- *WhoAmW 93*
Morua, Maria Elena 1963- *WhoAmW 93*
Morucci, Jean Pierre 1937- *WhoScE 91-2*
Morvan, Alain Yves 1939- *St&PR 93*
Morvan, Fabrice *BioIn 17*
Morwood, Peter 1956- *ScF&FL 92*
Mory, Douglas C. 1943- *St&PR 93*
Moryl, Walter John 1937- *WhoAm 92*
Morzak, Kimberly Sue 1960- *WhoEmL 93*
Mosack, Carl Lewis 1931- *St&PR 93*
Mosack, Glenn L. 1964- *St&PR 93*
Mosack, Marguerite Ann 1951- *WhoE 93*
Mosaddeq, Mohammad 1880-1967 *BioIn 17*
Mosak, Barbara Marcia 1950- *WhoAmW 93, WhoEmL 93, WhoWor 93*
Mosatche, Harriet Sandra 1949- *WhoAmW 93, WhoEmL 93*
Mosbach, Klaus 1932- *WhoScE 91-4*
Mosbacher, Emil, Jr. 1922- *WhoAm 92*
Mosbacher, Georgette *BioIn 17*
Mosbacher, Georgette Paulsin 1947- *WhoE 93*
Mosbacher, Martin Bruce 1951- *WhoAm 92, WhoWor 93*
Mosbacher, Robert *BioIn 17*
Mosbacher, Robert A. 1927- *CngDr 91*
Mosbacher, Robert Adam 1927- *WhoAm 92, WhoWor 93*
Mosby, David Gregory 1957- *WhoEmL 93*
Mosby, Dewey Franklin 1942- *WhoE 93*
Mosby, Dorothea Susan 1948- *WhoEmL 93*
Mosby, John Davenport, III 1956- *WhoAm 92*
Mosby, John Oliver 1917- *WhoSSW 93*
Mosby, Richard 1765-1808 *BioIn 17*
Mosca, Edoardo 1940- *WhoScE 91-3*
Mosca, Giuseppe 1772-1839 *Baker 92, OxDcOp*
Mosca, Leonardo 1922- *WhoScE 91-3*
Mosca, Luigi 1775-1824 *Baker 92, OxDcOp*
Mosca, William K., Jr. *Law&B 92*
Moscardi, Nino 1951- *St&PR 93*
Moscardini, Alfredo Osvaldo *WhoScE 91-1*
Moscatelli, John Joseph 1944- *WhoE 93*
Moscati, Anthony F. 1947- *St&PR 93*
Moscato, Anthony Charles 1945- *WhoAm 92*
Moscato, Nicholas, Jr. 1942- *WhoAm 92*
Moscato, Ugo Emanuele 1957- *WhoWor 93*
Mosch, Wolfgang Christian 1928- *WhoWor 93*
Moschabar, George fl. 13th cent.- *OxDcByz*
Moscheles, Charlotte 1805-1889 See Moscheles, Ignaz 1794-1870 *Baker 92*
Moscheles, Ignaz 1794-1870 *Baker 92, BioIn 17*
Moschella, Samuel L. 1921- *WhoAm 92*
Moschen, Michael *BioIn 17*
Moschetta, Anthony R. *Law&B 92*
Moschetto, Yves *WhoScE 91-2*
Moschopoulos, Manuel c. 1265- *OxDcByz*
Moschopoulos, Nikephoros dc. 1322 *OxDcByz*
Moschos, John 54-?-619? *OxDcByz*
Moschytz, George S. 1934- *WhoScE 91-4*
Moscicki, Ignacy 1867-1946 *PolBiDi*
Moscinski, David Joseph 1948- *WhoEmL 93*
Mosco, Marlene D. 1946- *St&PR 93*
Moscona, Aron Arthur 1922- *WhoAm 92*
Moscona, Nicola 1907-1975 *Baker 92*
Mosconi, Roger Paul 1945- *WhoAm 92*
Moscoso (Mora Rodriguez), (Jose) Teodoro 1910-1992 *CurBio 92N*
Moscoso, Teodoro *DcCPCAm*
Moscoso, Teodoro d1992 *NewYTBS 92 [port]*
Moscovit, Andrei *WhoWrEP 92*
Moscovit, Andrei 1937- *ScF&FL 92*
Moscovitch, Henry 1941- *WhoCanL 92*
Moscow, Warren 1908- *WhoAm 92*
Moscow, Warren 1908-1992 *NewYTBS 92 [port]*
Moscowitz, Albert Joseph 1929- *WhoAm 92, WhoWor 93*
Moscowitz, Jane Wollner 1946- *WhoEmL 93*
Moscozo, Flore Celestine Therese Henriette Tristan 1803-1844 *BioIn 17*
Mose, Jeffrey Lee 1953- *WhoE 93*
Mose, Josef Richard 1920- *WhoScE 91-4*
Moseka, Aminata *WhoAm 92*
Mosel, Edward Frank 1949- *St&PR 93*
Mosel, Ignaz Franz von 1772-1844 *Baker 92*
Mosel, Ulrich B. 1943- *WhoScE 91-3*
Mosel, Ulrich Bernd 1943- *WhoWor 93*
Mosele, Patricia Kyle 1957- *WhoSSW 93*
Moseley, Aubrey Howard 1936- *WhoSSW 93*
Moseley, B.E.B. *WhoScE 91-1*
Moseley, Carlos DuPre 1914- *WhoAm 92*
Moseley, Chris Rosser 1950- *WhoAm 92, WhoE 93, WhoEmL 93*
Moseley, Diane Hortensia 1958- *WhoWor 93*
Moseley, Frederick Strong, III 1928- *St&PR 93, WhoAm 92*
Moseley, Furman C. 1935- *WhoAm 92*
Moseley, George Edward *Law&B 92*
Moseley, George Edward 1939- *St&PR 93*
Moseley, Jack 1931- *St&PR 93, WhoAm 92*
Moseley, James Francis 1936- *WhoAm 92, WhoSSW 93, WhoWor 93*
Moseley, James G(wyn) 1946- *ConAu 38NR*
Moseley, John C. *St&PR 93*
Moseley, John Marshall 1911- *WhoSSW 93*
Moseley, Katharine Prescott *AmWomPl*
Moseley, M. Lewis 1937- *St&PR 93*
Moseley, Mark DeWayne 1948- *WhoAm 92*
Moseley, Michael E(dward) 1941- *ConAu 139*
Moseley, Norman Byron 1929- *St&PR 93*
Moseley, Roger Lester 1949- *WhoIns 93*
Moseley, Samuel G. 1952- *St&PR 93*
Moseley, Seth Hamilton, III 1933- *St&PR 93*
Moseley, Spencer Dumaresq 1919-1991 *BioIn 17*
Moseley, Thomas James 1913- *St&PR 93*
Moseley, William 1935- *WhoWrEP 92*
Moseley, William Latimer Tim 1936- *WhoSSW 93*
Moseley, William R. d1990 *BioIn 17*
Mosely, Linda Hays 1941- *WhoAm 92*
Moseman, Mildred Mae 1917- *WhoAmW 93*
Mosemann, Lloyd Kenneth, II 1936- *WhoAm 92*
Mosenfelder, Donn Merrill 1928- *St&PR 93*
Mosenthal, Peter Booth 1947- *WhoE 93*
Mosenthine, Amy Manuel 1963- *WhoEmL 93, WhoSSW 93*
Moser, Andreas 1859-1925 *Baker 92*
Moser, Ann Boody 1940- *WhoE 93*
Moser, Anton Alfred Richard 1939- *WhoWor 93*
Moser, Barry *ChlBIID [port]*
Moser, Barry 1940- *MajAI [port], SmATA 15AS [port]*
Moser, Bruno Chrysler 1940- *WhoAm 92*
Moser, Clarence John 1928- *St&PR 93*
Moser, Claus Adolf 1922- *WhoWor 93*
Moser, D.J. 1942- *St&PR 93*
Moser, Dietz-Rudiger 1939- *WhoWor 93*
Moser, Donald Bruce 1932- *WhoAm 92, WhoE 93, WhoWrEP 92*
Moser, Edda (Elisabeth) 1938- *Baker 92*
Moser, Elizabeth M. *Law&B 92*
Moser, George M. 1945- *St&PR 93*
Moser, Hans Joachim 1889-1967 *Baker 92*
Moser, Harold Dean 1938- *WhoAm 92, WhoWrEP 92*
Moser, Harry Crane 1944- *St&PR 93*
Moser, Heinz Ernst 1957- *WhoWor 93*
Moser, Hugo Wolfgang 1924- *WhoAm 92*
Moser, Jack L. 1943- *St&PR 93*
Moser, James Howard 1928- *WhoSSW 93*
Moser, Jean Hudgens 1934- *WhoSSW 93*
Moser, Joann Gail 1948- *WhoAm 92*
Moser, Justus 1720-1794 *BioIn 17*
Moser, Kenneth Miles 1929- *WhoAm 92*
Moser, Kurt George 1944- *St&PR 93*
Moser, Leo John 1929- *WhoWrEP 92*
Moser, Lois Anne Hunter 1935- *WhoAmW 93*
Moser, Martin Peter 1928- *WhoAm 92, WhoE 93*
Moser, Marvin 1924- *WhoAm 92*
Moser, Meinhard M. 1924- *WhoScE 91-4*
Moser, Michael Edward 1956- *WhoScE 91-1*
Moser, Michael Joseph 1950- *WhoWor 93*
Moser, Michael Matthew 1953- *WhoAm 92*
Moser, Miklos 1930- *WhoScE 91-4*
Moser, Norman Calvin 1931- *WhoWrEP 92*
Moser, Oskar 1914- *IntDcAn*
Moser, Peter 1962- *WhoWor 93*
Moser, Richard Goodwin d1992 *NewYTBS 92*
Moser, Richard Goodwin 1909-1992 *BioIn 17*
Moser, Robert Gary 1945- *WhoSSW 93*
Moser, Robert Harlan 1923- *WhoAm 92*
Moser, Robert W. 1938- *St&PR 93*
Moser, Roger Alden 1929- *St&PR 93, WhoAm 92*
Moser, Royce, Jr. 1935- *WhoAm 92, WhoWor 93*
Moser, Rudolf 1892-1960 *Baker 92*
Moser, Sandra Kay 1952- *WhoAmW 93*
Moser, Sarah Gunning 1953- *WhoAmW 93, WhoEmL 93*
Moser, Stephen V. *Law&B 92*
Moser, Thomas E. 1937- *St&PR 93*
Moser, Thomas Michael 1948- *WhoEmL 93*
Moser, Virginia Clayton 1954- *WhoAmW 93*
Moser, William Oscar Jules 1927- *WhoAm 92*
Moser Family *BioIn 17*
Moser-Proell, Annemarie 1953- *BioIn 17*
Moses *BioIn 17*
Moses fl. 4th cent.- *OxDcByz*
Moses, Abe Joseph 1931- *WhoAm 92*
Moses, Alfred 1914- *St&PR 93*
Moses, Alfred Henry 1929- *WhoAm 92, WhoE 93*
Moses, Andy 1962- *BioIn 17*
Moses, Anna Mary Robertson 1860-1961 *BioIn 17*
Moses, Anne Elaine *Law&B 92*
Moses, Ben *MiSFD 9*
Moses, Bradley Lynn 1947- *WhoEmL 93*
Moses, Carole Ann Horsburgh 1947- *WhoAmW 93*
Moses, Claire Goldberg 1941- *WhoWrEP 92*
Moses, Daniel 1952- *WhoCanL 92*
Moses, David H. 1903-1990 *BioIn 17*
Moses, Ed 1926- *BioIn 17*
Moses, Edward Crosby *WhoAm 92*
Moses, Edwin 1955- *WhoAm 92*
Moses, Elbert Raymond, Jr. 1908- *WhoWor 93, WhoWrEP 92*
Moses, Estelle M. *AmWomPl*
Moses, Franklin Maxwell 1918- *WhoAm 92*
Moses, Geraldine Gorman 1944- *WhoSSW 93*
Moses, Gilbert 1942- *MiSFD 9, WhoAm 92*
Moses, Grace Celeste *AmWomPl*
Moses, Grandma 1860-1961 *BioIn 17, ConHero 2 [port]*
Moses, Gregory Allen 1950- *WhoAm 92*
Moses, Gregory Hayes, Jr. 1933- *WhoAm 92*
Moses, Hamilton, III 1950- *WhoE 93, WhoWor 93*
Moses, Harry *MiSFD 9*
Moses, Irving Byron 1925- *WhoAm 92*
Moses, Irving M. 1939- *St&PR 93*
Moses, Janet Estelle 1946- *WhoEmL 93*
Moses, Jerome J. 1912- *St&PR 93*
Moses, Joel 1941- *WhoAm 92*
Moses, Johnnie, Jr. 1939- *WhoE 93*
Moses, Kathy Sue 1948- *WhoEmL 93*
Moses, Lincoln E. 1921- *WhoAm 92*
Moses, Louis Jeffrey 1943- *WhoE 93*
Moses, Lucina Lea *Law&B 92*
Moses, Lucy Goldschmidt d1990 *BioIn 17*
Moses, Marilyn Cecelia 1956- *WhoAmW 93*
Moses, Marvin C. 1944- *St&PR 93*
Moses, Marvin Charles 1944- *WhoAm 92*
Moses, Michael Howard 1940- *St&PR 93, WhoIns 93*
Moses, Michael W. 1945- *St&PR 93*
Moses, Nancy 1948- *WhoE 93*
Moses, Nancy Lee Heise 1947- *WhoEmL 93*
Moses, Paul Davis 1938- *WhoAm 92*
Moses, Raphael Jacob 1913- *WhoAm 92*
Moses, Robert 1888-1981 *PolPar*
Moses, Robert 1935- *EncAACR*
Moses, Robert Davis 1919- *WhoAm 92*
Moses, Robert Edward 1936- *WhoAm 92*
Moses, Robert K., Jr. 1940- *St&PR 93*
Moses, Robert Kenneth 1952- *WhoEmL 93*
Moses, Robert Wilkins 1945- *St&PR 93*
Moses, Ronald Elliot 1930- *St&PR 93, WhoAm 92*
Moses, Ryan O. *ScF&FL 92*
Moses, Stephen A. 1943- *WhoSSW 93*
Moses, Stephen Arthur 1943- *St&PR 93*
Moses, Vivian *WhoScE 91-1*
Moses, William Daniel 1936- *St&PR 93*
Moses, William John *Law&B 92*
Moses, William Robert 1911- *WhoWrEP 92*
Moses, Wilson Jeremiah 1942- *WhoE 93*
Moses Ben Maimon 1135-1204 *BioIn 17*
Moses Dasxuranc'i fl. 10th cent.?- *OxDcByz*
Moses of Bergamo dc. 1157 *OxDcByz*
Moseson, Richard S. 1955- *WhoEmL 93*
Moses Xorenac'i *OxDcByz*
Mosettig, Michael David 1942- *WhoAm 92*
Mosewius, Johann Theodor 1788-1858 *Baker 92*
Mosey, Caron Lee 1956- *WhoWrEP 92*
Mosha, Felix G.N. 1943- *WhoUN 92*
Mosher, Arthur A. 1942- *St&PR 93*
Mosher, Arthur T. d1992 *NewYTBS 92*
Mosher, Frederick C. *BioIn 17*
Mosher, Frederick Kenneth 1943- *WhoE 93, WhoWor 93*
Mosher, George Allan 1939- *WhoAm 92*
Mosher, Giles E., Jr. 1933- *St&PR 93*
Mosher, Gregory Dean 1949- *WhoAm 92, WhoE 93*
Mosher, Hattie Lount 1865-1945 *BioIn 17*
Mosher, Howard Frank *ScF&FL 92*
Mosher, Howard Frank 1943?- *ConAu 139*
Mosher, Howard Ira 1946- *WhoAm 92*
Mosher, Larey Laverne 1951- *WhoEmL 93*
Mosher, Loren Richard 1933- *WhoE 93*
Mosher, Michael *ScF&FL 92*
Mosher, Paul H. 1936- *WhoAm 92*
Mosher, Richard C. *Law&B 92*
Mosher, Ronald Francis 1943- *St&PR 93*
Mosher, Sally Ekenberg 1934- *WhoAmW 93, WhoWor 93*
Mosher, Sue Ann 1953- *WhoAmW 93*
Mosher, Thomas Bird 1852-1923 *BioIn 17*
Mosher, Walter W., Jr. 1934- *St&PR 93*
Mosher, Wendy Jean 1966- *WhoAmW 93*
Mosher, William Eugene 1950- *WhoEmL 93*
Mosher, William John *Law&B 92*
Moshier, Juanita Chavez 1955- *WhoAmW 93*
Moshinsky, Elijah *MiSFD 9*
Moshinsky, Elijah 1946- *IntDcOp*
Moshman, Jack 1924- *WhoAm 92*
Moshoeshoe, II 1938- *WhoAfr*

Moshoeshoe, Constantine Bereng Seeivo, III 1938- *WhoWor 93*
Mosich, Anelis Nick 1928- *WhoAm 92*
Mosier, Andrew P., Jr. *Law&B 92*
Mosier, Eugene Bruce 1939- *St&PR 93*
Mosier, Frank Eugene 1930- *St&PR 93*
Mosier, Harry David, Jr. 1925- *WhoAm 92*
Mosier, John 1944- *WhoWrEP 92*
Mosier, Kenneth Cope, II 1944- *St&PR 93*
Mosier, Mike L. 1951- *St&PR 93*
Mosier, Virginia Lou 1951- *WhoAmW 93*
Mosig, Dirk Walter 1943- *ScF&FL 92*
Mosimann, Anton 1947- *WhoWor 93*
Mosk, Richard Mitchell 1939- *WhoAm 92*
Mosk, Stanley 1912- *WhoAm 92, WhoWor 93*
Moskal, Anthony John 1946- *WhoE 93, WhoEmL 93*
Moskal, Harry Matthew 1937- *St&PR 93*
Moskal, Janina 1944- *WhoAmW 93*
Moskal, Robert M. 1937- *WhoAm 92*
Moskalenko, Aza Irmovna 1940- *WhoWor 93*
Moskalski, E.A. 1939- *St&PR 93*
Moski, Gregory Edward 1953- *WhoE 93*
Moskin, John Robert 1923- *WhoAm 92*
Moskin, Morton 1927- *St&PR 93, WhoAm 92*
Mosko, John Edward 1928- *St&PR 93*
Mosko, "Lucky" 1947- *Baker 92*
Moskoff, Stephane *Law&B 92*
Moskos, Charles C. 1934- *WhoAm 92*
Moskovic, Ernst 1922- *WhoWor 93*
Moskovitz, Carole Giges 1948- *WhoAmW 93*
Moskovitz, David *BioIn 17*
Moskovitz, I.L. 1904- *St&PR 93*
Moskovitz, Irving 1912- *WhoAm 92*
Moskow, Bernard 1937- *St&PR 93*
Moskow, Michael H. 1938- *St&PR 93, WhoAm 92*
Moskow, Shirley Blotnick 1935- *WhoWrEP 92*
Moskowa, Joseph Napoleon Ney, Prince de la 1803-1857 *Baker 92*
Moskowitz, Andre Joseph 1962- *WhoWor 93*
Moskowitz, Arnold X. 1944- *WhoAm 92*
Moskowitz, Belle 1877-1933 *PolPar*
Moskowitz, David J. *Law&B 92*
Moskowitz, Ellen S. 1955- *WhoE 93*
Moskowitz, Eugene 1912-1990 *BioIn 17*
Moskowitz, Faye *BioIn 17*
Moskowitz, Herbert 1935- *WhoAm 92*
Moskowitz, Jay 1943- *WhoAm 92*
Moskowitz, Joel P. 1939- *St&PR 93*
Moskowitz, Joel Steven 1947- *WhoEmL 93*
Moskowitz, Louis A. 1916-1990 *BioIn 17*
Moskowitz, Moses 1911-1990 *BioIn 17*
Moskowitz, Nancy Lanard *Law&B 92*
Moskowitz, Randi Zucker 1948- *WhoAmW 93*
Moskowitz, Robert S. 1935- *BioIn 17*
Moskowitz, Ronald 1939- *St&PR 93, WhoAm 92*
Moskowitz, Sam 1920- *ScF&FL 92, WhoAm 92*
Moskowitz, Shirley Edith 1920- *WhoE 93*
Moskowitz, Stanley Alan 1956- *WhoEmL 93, WhoWor 93*
Moskowitz, Stuart S. *Law&B 92*
Mosle, Huter-Georg 1924- *WhoScE 91-3, WhoWor 93*
Mosle, Jennifer Torbett *Law&B 92*
Mosle, Sara *BioIn 17*
Moslehi, Farid 1959- *WhoE 93*
Mosler, John 1922- *WhoAm 92, WhoWor 93*
Mosley, Cynthia 1898-1933 *BioIn 17*
Mosley, Diana 1910- *BioIn 17*
Mosley, Donald Crumpton 1932- *WhoAm 92*
Mosley, Elwood A. 1943- *St&PR 93*
Mosley, Gail *BioIn 17*
Mosley, Henrietta E. *Law&B 92*
Mosley, Ivan Sigmund, Jr. 1946- *St&PR 93*
Mosley, Jean Carol 1963- *WhoSSW 93*
Mosley, Jonetta Delaine 1955- *WhoAmW 93*
Mosley, Judi K. *Law&B 92*
Mosley, Leonard O(swald) 1913-1992 *ConAu 139*
Mosley, Mary Mac 1926- *WhoSSW 93*
Mosley, Michael Steven *Law&B 92*
Mosley, Nicholas 1923- *BioIn 17, ConLC 70 [port]*
Mosley, Oswald 1896-1980 *BioIn 17*
Mosley, Oswald Ernald 1896-1980 *DcTwHis*
Mosley, Paul *WhoScE 91-1*
Mosley, Phillip M. 1938- *St&PR 93*
Mosley, Samuel Adolphus 1923- *WhoSSW 93*
Mosley, Sandra Sherrill 1946- *WhoWrEP 92*
Mosley, Weldon V. 1924- *WhoIns 93*
Mosley, Wilbur Clanton, Jr. 1938- *WhoSSW 93*
Mosley, Zack Terrell 1906- *WhoAm 92*
Mosoeunyane, Khethang Aloysius 1942- *WhoAfr*
Mosoff, Serle Ian 1942- *St&PR 93*
Mosolov, Alexander (Vasilievich) 1900-1973 *Baker 92*
Mosonyi, Mihaly 1814-1870 *Baker 92*
Mosonyi, Mihaly 1815?-1870 *OxDcOp*
Moss, Adam *BioIn 17*
Moss, Alfred Alfonso, Jr. 1943- *WhoE 93*
Moss, Alfred Spellman d1991 *BioIn 17*
Moss, Ambler Holmes, Jr. 1937- *WhoAm 92*
Moss, Amy *Law&B 92*
Moss, Andrea 1943- *WhoAmW 93, WhoE 93*
Moss, Arnold 1910-1989 *ConTFT 10*
Moss, Arthur Henshey 1930- *WhoAm 92, WhoE 93*
Moss, Bernard 1937- *WhoAm 92*
Moss, Bill Ralph 1950- *WhoEmL 93, WhoSSW 93, WhoWor 93*
Moss, Brian *WhoScE 91-1*
Moss, Bridget M. *Law&B 92*
Moss, Carl Jack 1959- *WhoWor 93*
Moss, Charles 1938- *St&PR 93, WhoAm 92*
Moss, Charles Leland 1946- *St&PR 93*
Moss, Charles Norman 1914- *WhoWor 93*
Moss, Charlotte *BioIn 17*
Moss, Clement Murphy, Jr. 1926- *WhoAm 92*
Moss, Cruse Watson 1926- *St&PR 93, WhoAm 92*
Moss, Dan, Jr. 1948- *WhoEmL 93, WhoSSW 93*
Moss, David (Michael) 1949- *Baker 92*
Moss, Debra Ann 1953- *WhoEmL 93*
Moss, Donald William 1928- *WhoScE 91-1*
Moss, Donna Jeanne 1947- *WhoAmW 93*
Moss, Douglas Mabbett 1954- *WhoEmL 93*
Moss, Dubenion Joseph *BioIn 17*
Moss, Edward Charles 1948- *WhoEmL 93*
Moss, Elizabeth J. 1947- *WhoAmW 93*
Moss, Elizabeth Lucille 1939- *WhoAmW 93*
Moss, Francine Hope 1951- *WhoEmL 93*
Moss, Franklin Kass 1947- *WhoEmL 93*
Moss, George F. 1936- *St&PR 93*
Moss, Geraldine A. *Law&B 92*
Moss, Gerard Peter 1938- *WhoWor 93*
Moss, Gerry *BioIn 17*
Moss, Grave Yard 1946- *WhoWrEP 92*
Moss, Hal 1932- *St&PR 93*
Moss, Harold 1932- *St&PR 93*
Moss, Harriet Calhoun *AmWomPl*
Moss, J. *WhoScE 91-1*
Moss, Jack 1928- *WhoE 93*
Moss, James A. 1920-1990 *BioIn 17*
Moss, James H. 1953- *St&PR 93*
Moss, James Percy *WhoScE 91-1*
Moss, Jane Penelope 1963- *WhoAmW 93*
Moss, Jeff(rey) *SmATA 73 [port]*
Moss, Joe A. 1925- *St&PR 93*
Moss, Joe Albaugh 1925- *WhoAm 92, WhoSSW 93, WhoWor 93*
Moss, Joe Francis 1933- *WhoAm 92, WhoE 93*
Moss, Joel 1946- *WhoE 93*
Moss, John 1940- *WhoCanL 92*
Moss, John Barrie *WhoScE 91-1*
Moss, John Emerson 1915- *WhoAm 92*
Moss, Joseph H., Jr. *Law&B 92*
Moss, Joseph H., Jr. 1950- *St&PR 93*
Moss, Justin Leslie 1947- *WhoE 93*
Moss, Kirby Glenn 1954- *WhoEmL 93*
Moss, Lawrence Craig 1952- *WhoE 93, WhoEmL 93*
Moss, Lawrence (Kenneth) 1927- *Baker 92, WhoAm 92*
Moss, Leslie Otha 1952- *WhoAmW 93, WhoEmL 93, WhoWor 93*
Moss, Logan V. *Law&B 92*
Moss, Louis B. 1917- *St&PR 93*
Moss, Lynda Towle 1941- *WhoAmW 93*
Moss, Marissa 1959- *SmATA 71*
Moss, Marsha Kelman 1951- *WhoAmW 93*
Moss, Michael Eric 1947- *WhoAm 92*
Moss, Miriam Jackson 1948- *WhoAmW 93*
Moss, Monique Hope 1959- *WhoAmW 93*
Moss, Morrie Alfred 1907- *St&PR 93*
Moss, Myra E. 1937- *WhoAmW 93, WhoWor 93*
Moss, N. Henry 1925-1990 *BioIn 17*
Moss, Pat *St&PR 93*
Moss, Patricia Diane 1960- *WhoEmL 93*
Moss, Peter D. *ScF&FL 92*
Moss, Phillip Allen 1946- *WhoSSW 93*
Moss, Piotr 1949- *Baker 92*
Moss, Richard H. *Law&B 92*
Moss, Richard Spencer 1949- *WhoWor 93*
Moss, Robert 1946- *ScF&FL 92*
Moss, Robert Drexler 1909- *WhoAm 92*
Moss, Robert F. 1942- *ScF&FL 92*
Moss, Robert L. 1947- *WhoSSW 93*
Moss, Robert Williams 1942- *WhoSSW 93*
Moss, Roger 1951- *ScF&FL 92*
Moss, Roger William, Jr. 1940- *WhoE 93*
Moss, Ronald Eugene 1932- *St&PR 93*
Moss, Ronald Jay 1930- *WhoAm 92*
Moss, Rose 1937- *WhoWrEP 92*
Moss, Samuel J. d1990 *BioIn 17*
Moss, Sandra Hughes 1945- *WhoSSW 93*
Moss, Sidney P. 1917- *ScF&FL 92*
Moss, Stanley 1935- *WhoAm 92*
Moss, Stephen Edward 1940- *WhoE 93, WhoWor 93*
Moss, Steven David 1955- *WhoEmL 93*
Moss, Thomas Henry 1939- *WhoAm 92*
Moss, Thomas Warren, Jr. 1928- *WhoSSW 93*
Moss, Thylias 1954- *DcLB 120 [port]*
Moss, Timothy Roger *WhoScE 91-1*
Moss, Victoria Biedebach 1964- *WhoAmW 93*
Moss, William John 1921- *WhoAm 92*
Moss, William Stewart 1950- *WhoSSW 93*
Moss, William W. 1935- *St&PR 93*
Moss, William Wallace 1948- *WhoSSW 93*
Mossadegh, Mohammad 1882-1967 *BioIn 17, ColdWar 2 [port]*
Mossaides, Paula Xenis 1954- *WhoEmL 93*
Mossakowski, Miroslaw J. 1929- *WhoScE 91-4*
Mossavar-Rahmani, Bijan 1952- *WhoWor 93*
Mossbarger, John W. 1933- *St&PR 93*
Mossbauer, Rudolf L. 1929- *WhoScE 91-3*
Mossbauer, Rudolf Ludwig 1929- *WhoAm 92, WhoWor 93*
Mossbrooks, Scott Allen 1965- *WhoSSW 93*
Mossbrucker, Tom *WhoAm 92*
Mossburg, Richard, Jr. *Law&B 92*
Mosse, George L. 1918- *WhoAm 92, WhoWrEP 92*
Mosse, Peter John Charles 1947- *St&PR 93, WhoAm 92, WhoE 93, WhoEmL 93*
Mosselmans, Jean-Marc 1963- *WhoWor 93*
Mosser, Bart H. 1940- *St&PR 93*
Mosser, Frederick William 1945- *WhoAm 92*
Mosser, Hans Matthias 1955- *WhoWor 93*
Mosset, Olivier *BioIn 17*
Mossholder, Stephen B. 1942- *St&PR 93*
Mossinghoff, Gerald Joseph 1935- *WhoAm 92, WhoWor 93*
Mossman, Burton 1867-1956 *BioIn 17*
Mossman, Deborah Jean 1956- *WhoEmL 93*
Mossman, Donald P., III *Law&B 92*
Mossman, Harland Winfield 1898- *WhoAm 92*
Mossman, Hugh Vaughan 1946- *WhoAm 92*
Mossman, Jennifer 1944- *ConAu 38NR*
Mossman, Thomas Mellish, Jr. 1938- *WhoAm 92*
Mossner, Joachim 1950- *WhoWor 93*
Mosso, Claudia Gruenwald 1952- *WhoEmL 93*
Mosso, David 1926- *WhoAm 92*
Mossotto, Cesare *WhoScE 91-3*
Moss-Salentijn, Letty 1943- *WhoAmW 93*
Most, Charles Johannes 1952- *WhoE 93*
Most, Jack Lawrence 1935- *St&PR 93, WhoE 93*
Most, Joseph Morris 1943- *WhoE 93*
Most, Konrad *BioIn 17*
Most, Nathan 1914- *St&PR 93, WhoAm 92*
Mostafa, A.B.M. Ghulam 1934- *WhoAsAP 91*
Mostafa, Shawki M. 1940- *WhoUN 92*
Mostafa, Sobhy Morsy *WhoScE 91-1*
Mostarda, Mario Steven 1944- *St&PR 93*
Mostart, August Egbert Laurent Marie 1951- *WhoAm 92*
Mostbeck, Adolf *WhoScE 91-4*
Mostehy-Davis, Randa 1962- *WhoEmL 93*
Mostel, Zero 1915-1977 *QDrFCA 92 [port]*
Mosteller, Charles Frederick 1916- *BioIn 17*
Mosteller, David Elias 1944- *St&PR 93*
Mosteller, Frederick 1916- *BioIn 17, WhoAm 92*
Mosteller, James Scott 1961- *WhoSSW 93*
Mosteller, Jon N. 1940- *St&PR 93*
Mostert, Paul Stallings 1927- *WhoAm 92*
Mostillo, Ralph 1944- *WhoE 93, WhoWor 93*
Mostkoff, Samuel *Law&B 92*
Mostoff, Allan Samuel 1932- *WhoAm 92*
Mostofi, Khosrow 1921- *WhoAm 92, WhoWor 93*
Mostovoy, Marc Sanders 1942- *WhoAm 92*
Mostow, George Daniel 1923- *WhoAm 92*
Mostow, Jonathan *MiSFD 9*
Mostowich, Philip 1954- *St&PR 93*
Mostyn, William J., III *Law&B 92*
Mosunic, John Ignatius 1928- *St&PR 93*
Moszczynski, Wieslaw 1928- *WhoScE 91-4*
Moszczynski, Piotr 1934- *WhoScE 91-4*
Moszkowski, Benjamin Charles 1956- *WhoWor 93*
Moszkowski, Lena Iggers 1930- *WhoAmW 93*
Moszkowski, Moritz 1854-1925 *Baker 92*
Moszumanska-Nazar, Krystyna 1924- *Baker 92*
Moszynski, Kazimierz 1887-1959 *IntDcAn*
Mota, Ana Celia 1935- *WhoWor 93*
Mota, Miguel E.G.M. 1922- *WhoScE 91-3*
Mota, Ronaldo 1955- *WhoWor 93*
Mota, Rosa *BioIn 17*
Motchan, Dennis Glenn 1950- *WhoEmL 93*
Motchane, Jean-Loup 1933- *WhoScE 91-2*
Mote, Clayton Daniel, Jr. 1937- *WhoAm 92*
Mote, Karl William 1927- *St&PR 93*
Mote, Larry Roger 1937- *St&PR 93*
Mote, Nancy Stammelbach 1940- *WhoE 93*
Motegi, Makoto 1959- *WhoWor 93*
Motejunas, Gerald William 1950- *WhoEmL 93*
Moten, Bennie 1894-1935 *Baker 92*
Moten, Gary W. *Law&B 92*
Moten, Lane Howard *Law&B 92*
Motes, Joseph Mark 1948- *WhoSSW 93*
Moth, Brian C. 1920- *WhoSSW 93*
Motheo, Artur de Jesus 1952- *WhoWor 93*
Mother 1878-1973 *BioIn 17*
Motheral, M. Susan 1952- *WhoEmL 93*
Mothersdale, Sandra J. 1961- *WhoWor 93*
Mother Teresa 1910- *BioIn 17, News 93-1 [port]*
Motherway, Joseph Edward 1930- *WhoAm 92*
Motherwell, Robert *BioIn 17*
Motherwell, Robert 1915-1991 *AnObit 1991, News 92*
Mothes, Joan M. 1934- *St&PR 93*
Mothkur, Sridhar Rao 1950- *WhoEmL 93, WhoWor 93*
Mothner, Carol 1943- *BioIn 17*
Mothon, Philip 1949- *WhoEmL 93*
Mothopeng, Zephania Lakonane 1913-1990 *BioIn 17*
Motier, Donald 1943- *WhoWrEP 92*
Motion, Andrew 1952- *BioIn 17*
Motiwalla, Dadi Noshir 1954- *WhoWor 93*
Motko, Debbie 1952- *St&PR 93*
Motl, Daniel Francis 1946- *St&PR 93*
Motley, Constance Baker 1921- *BioIn 17, EncAACR [port], WhoAm 92, WhoE 93*
Motley, Denise 1963- *WhoAmW 93*
Motley, James A. 1928- *St&PR 93*
Motley, John Paul 1927- *WhoAm 92*
Motley, Lyle Carter, Jr. 1941- *St&PR 93*
Motley, Marion 1920- *BioIn 17*
Motley, Marvin Ray *Law&B 92*
Motloch, David L. *Law&B 92*
Moto, Shoji *Law&B 92*
Motoba, Toshio 1944- *WhoWor 93*
Motoki, Ken 1930- *WhoWor 93*
Motola, Ben *BioIn 17*
Motola, Nancy Carmen 1952- *WhoEmL 93*
Motolinia *DcMexL*
Motolo, Paul Leon 1964- *WhoE 93*
Motomura, Hiroshi 1953- *WhoEmL 93*
Motomura, Kazuki 1935- *WhoAsAP 91*
Moton, Robert Russa 1867-1940 *EncAACR [port]*
Motono, Moriyuki 1924- *WhoWor 93*
Motonobu, Takashi 1944- *WhoAsAP 91*
Motooka, Shoji 1931- *WhoAsAP 91*
Motroni, Hector John 1943- *WhoE 93*
Motsch, John Vincent 1928- *WhoSSW 93*
Motsch, Wolfgang 1934- *WhoWor 93*
Motschwiller, Kenneth W. 1956- *St&PR 93*
Motsett, Charles Bourke 1949- *WhoEmL 93, WhoSSW 93*
Motsinger, Kenneth L. 1953- *St&PR 93*
Motsinger, Linda Susan Baumgardner 1941- *WhoAmW 93*
Motsko, Donald Russell 1935- *St&PR 93*
Motson, Meredith *ScF&FL 92*
Mott, Alyce Evelyn 1946- *WhoEmL 93*
Mott, Anita *BioIn 17*
Mott, Darcy G. 1952- *St&PR 93*
Mott, Derek Braithwaite- *BioIn 17*
Mott, Edward Raymond 1928- *WhoE 93*
Mott, Eliza 1829-1909 *BioIn 17*
Mott, James C. 1928- *St&PR 93*
Mott, John Raleigh 1865-1955 *BioIn 17*

Mott, June Marjorie 1920- *WhoWor 93*
Mott, Kenneth E. 1939- *WhoUN 92*
Mott, Mary Elizabeth 1931- *WhoAmW 93*
Mott, Michael Charles Alston 1930- *WhoWrEP 92*
Mott, Nevill *WhoScE 91-1*
Mott, Nevill 1905- *WhoAm 92, WhoWor 93*
Mott, Norbert 1924- *WhoScE 91-3*
Mott, Ralph Oliver 1903- *WhoAm 92*
Mott, Samuel E., III *Law&B 92*
Mott, Stephen Charles 1940- *ConAu 38NR*
Mott, Stephen Craig 1949- *St&PR 93, WhoEmL 93*
Mott, Stewart R. 1937- *PolPar*
Mott, Stewart Rawlings 1937- *WhoAm 92*
Mott, Vincent Valmon 1916- *WhoAm 92*
Mott, William Chamberlain 1911- *WhoAm 92, WhoWor 93*
Mott, William P., Jr. d1992 *NewYTBS 92 [port]*
Motta, John J. 1949- *St&PR 93*
Motta, John Richard 1931- *WhoAm 92*
Motta, Jose Vianna da *Baker 92*
Motta, Marcella 1936- *WhoScE 91-3*
Motta, Maria *BioIn 17*
Motta, Pietro M. 1942- *WhoScE 91-3*
Motta, R. *WhoScE 91-2*
Motta, Richard Allen 1955- *WhoE 93*
Motta, Richard B. 1931- *St&PR 93*
Motta, Richard P. 1943- *St&PR 93*
Mottahedeh, Roy Parviz 1940- *WhoWrEP 92*
Mottalini, John A. *Law&B 92*
Mottana, Annibale 1940- *WhoScE 91-3*
Mottar, Jozef F.C. 1950- *WhoScE 91-2*
Mott-Dreizler, Gisela 1941- *BioIn 17*
Motte, Daryl 1922- *St&PR 93*
Motte, Roger *WhoScE 91-1*
Mottelson, Ben R. 1926- *WhoAm 92, WhoWor 93*
Motter, David Calvin 1926- *WhoAm 92*
Motter, Diane Allyn 1950- *St&PR 93*
Motter, Frank 1927- *St&PR 93*
Motter, Othmar 1927- *BioIn 17*
Motter, William D. 1957- *St&PR 93*
Mottet, Norman Karle 1924- *WhoAm 92*
Motteu, Henri 1931- *WhoScE 91-2*
Mottl, Felix 1856-1911 *IntDcOp, OxDcOp*
Mottl, Felix (Josef) 1856-1911 *Baker 92*
Mottley, Charles C. *ScF&FL 92*
Mottley, Charles M. *ScF&FL 92*
Motto, Anna Lydia *WhoAmW 93*
Motto, Jerome A. 1921- *WhoAm 92*
Mottola, Alexander R. d1992 *BioIn 17, NewYTBS 92*
Mottola, John T. 1945- *WhoIns 93*
Mottola, Joseph James 1928- *St&PR 93*
Mottram, David Ross *WhoScE 91-1*
Mottram, Eric *ScF&FL 92*
Mottram-Doss, Renee 1939- *WhoAm 92, WhoAmW 93*
Motts, David 1952- *St&PR 93*
Mottu, Alexandre 1883-1943 *Baker 92*
Motulsky, Arno Gunther 1923- *WhoAm 92*
Motush, James 1954- *St&PR 93*
Motyl, Alexander John 1953- *WhoE 93*
Motyl', Vladimir 1927- *DrEEuF*
Motylev, Leonid Yulievich 1955- *WhoWor 93*
Motz, John Frederick 1942- *WhoAm 92, WhoE 93*
Motz, Kenneth Lee 1922- *WhoAm 92*
Motz, Linda B. *Law&B 92*
Motz, Lloyd 1910- *WhoE 93*
Motzer, William Raymond 1947- *St&PR 93*
Motzkin, Evelyn Herszkorn 1933- *WhoAmW 93*
Mouat, Ricardo Gutierrez 1951- *WhoSSW 93*
Mouch, Frank Messman *WhoAm 92*
Moucha, Nancy Susan 1960- *WhoE 93*
Mouchly-Weiss, Harriet 1942- *WhoAm 92*
Mouchot, Jean-Francois 1944- *WhoWor 93*
Mouchy, Duchesse de 1935- *WhoAmW 93*
Mouchy, Duchesse de 1935- *WhoWor 93*
Moudiki, Jacques 1932- *WhoUN 92*
Moudon, Anne Vernez 1945- *WhoAmW 93*
Mouftah, Hussein Talaat 1947- *WhoAm 92*
Mougel, Francois Charles 1947- *WhoWor 93*
Mougeot, Robert F. 1943- *St&PR 93*
Mougey, Charles L. 1940- *St&PR 93*
Mouhamed Lemine, Ould Kettab 1950- *WhoWor 93*
Mouhot, Henri 1826-1861 *IntDcAn*
Mouiel, Jean 1936- *WhoScE 91-2*
Mouis, Marie-Christine *WhoAm 92*
Moul, Francis D. 1940- *St&PR 93*
Moul, Maxine *WhoAm 92, WhoAmW 93*
Moul, Maxine Burnett 1947- *St&PR 93*
Moul, R. Keith 1953- *WhoSSW 93*
Moul, William Charles 1940- *WhoAm 92*
Moulaert, Pierre 1907-1967 *Baker 92*
Moulaert, Raymond 1875-1962 *Baker 92*
Moulard, Henri 1938- *WhoWor 93*
Mould, Bob *BioIn 17*
Mould, Clifford Andrew Pointon 1942- *WhoWor 93*
Mould, F. Ethel *AmWomPl*
Mould, Ralph N. d1991 *BioIn 17*
Moulder, James Edwin 1926- *WhoAm 92*
Moulder, Peter Vincent 1921- *WhoSSW 93*
Moulding, Linton A. 1953- *St&PR 93*
Moulds, Elizabeth Ellen 1947- *WhoAmW 93*
Moulds, Ronald Gary 1940- *St&PR 93*
Moule, James C. 1936- *St&PR 93*
Moule, William R. 1912- *BioIn 17*
Mouledoux, Rene J. *Law&B 92*
Moulias, Robert 1932- *WhoScE 91-2*
Moulin, A. Edward *Law&B 92*
Moulin, Jacquelyn Bernadette 1947- *WhoAmW 93*
Moulin, Jean 1899-1943 *BioIn 17*
Moulinasse, Robert Jules Bernard 1935- *WhoWor 93*
Moulins, Maurice L. 1936- *WhoScE 91-2*
Moulonguet, Thierry 1951- *WhoWor 93*
Moulopoulos, Rena J. *Law&B 92*
Moulthrop, Edward Allen 1916- *WhoAm 92, WhoSSW 93*
Moulthrop, Robert Wallace *WhoE 93*
Moultine, Geraldine Ann 1945- *WhoAmW 93*
Moulton, Beth Christine 1946- *WhoAmW 93*
Moulton, Deborah *ScF&FL 92*
Moulton, E. Curtis, III 1959- *St&PR 93*
Moulton, Edward Quentin 1926- *WhoAm 92*
Moulton, Grace Charbonnet 1923- *WhoAmW 93*
Moulton, Herbert F. 1936- *WhoIns 93*
Moulton, Hope H. *AmWomPl*
Moulton, Horace P. 1907-1991 *BioIn 17*
Moulton, Hugh G. *Law&B 92*
Moulton, Hugh G. 1933- *St&PR 93*
Moulton, Hugh Geoffrey 1933- *WhoAm 92*
Moulton, James Roger 1950- *WhoEmL 93, WhoSSW 93*
Moulton, John Harmon 1956- *WhoEmL 93*
Moulton, Joy Wade 1928- *WhoAmW 93*
Moulton, Katherine Klauber 1956- *WhoAmW 93, WhoEmL 93*
Moulton, Lynda Warner 1946- *WhoAmW 93*
Moulton, Michael J. 1957- *St&PR 93*
Moulton, Patricia Jean 1948- *WhoEmL 93*
Moulton, Peter Franklin 1946- *WhoAm 92*
Moulton, Richard Way 1948- *WhoEmL 93*
Moulton, Robert Alan 1949- *St&PR 93*
Moulton, Sara Jonene 1958- *WhoEmL 93*
Moulton, Virginia Nodine 1925- *WhoWrEP 92*
Moulton, Wilbur Wright, Jr. 1935- *WhoAm 92*
Moulton, William A. *Law&B 92*
Moulton-Ely, Robert 1958- *St&PR 93*
Moultrie, Fred 1923- *WhoAm 92*
Moultrie, James B. *WhoWor 93*
Moultrie, James B. 1944- *WhoUN 92*
Moultrie, William 1730-1805 *HarEnMi*
Mouly, Eileen Louise 1955- *WhoEmL 93, WhoWor 93*
Moulyn, Adriaan Cornelis 1937- *WhoWor 93*
Moumin, Amini Ali 1944- *WhoWor 93*
Mouncer, Albert E. *Law&B 92*
Mound, Peggy Elaine 1947- *WhoWrEP 92*
Mounds, Leona Mae Reed 1945- *WhoAmW 93*
Mounds, Monica *ScF&FL 92*
Mounier, Emmanuel 1905-1950 *BioIn 17*
Mounier, Jean 1928- *WhoScE 91-2*
Mounla-Haydar, Nasrat 1930- *WhoWor 93*
Mounsey, Joseph Backhouse 1949- *St&PR 93*
Mount, Charles Morris 1942- *WhoE 93*
Mount, Donald Raymond 1946- *WhoE 93*
Mount, Ellis 1921- *ConAu 39NR*
Mount, John Meredith 1942- *St&PR 93*
Mount, Karen 1953- *WhoAmW 93*
Mount, Karl A. 1945- *St&PR 93, WhoAm 92*
Mount, Marsha Louise 1962- *WhoAmW 93*
Mount, Peggy 1916- *QDrFCA 92 [port]*
Mount, Richard Edward 1947- *WhoE 93*
Mount, Robert Hughes 1931- *WhoSSW 93*
Mount, Stephen Joseph John 1968- *WhoWrEP 92*
Mount, Thom 1948- *ConTFT 10*
Mount, Thomas Henderson 1948- *WhoAm 92*
Mount, Wendy Elizabeth 1954- *WhoAmW 93*
Mountain, Clifton Fletcher 1924- *WhoAm 92, WhoSSW 93, WhoWor 93*
Mountain, Dan *BioIn 17*
Mountain, Evelyn Marie 1917- *WhoAmW 93*
Mountain, Robert *ScF&FL 92*
Mountain, Thomas Raymond 1916- *St&PR 93*
Mountain, Worrall F. d1992 *NewYTBS 92*
Mountain, Worrall Frederick 1909- *WhoAm 92*
Mountbatten, Louis Alexander 1854-1921 *BioIn 17*
Mountbatten, Louis Francis Albert Victor Nicholas 1900-1979 *DcTwHis, HarEnMi*
Mountbatten of Burma, Countess 1901-1960 *BioIn 17*
Mountbatten of Burma, Earl 1900-1979 *BioIn 17*
Mountcastle, Katharine Babcock 1931- *WhoAm 92*
Mountcastle, Kenneth F. 1928- *St&PR 93*
Mountcastle, Kenneth Franklin, Jr. 1928- *WhoAm 92*
Mountcastle, Vernon B. *BioIn 17*
Mountcastle, Vernon Benjamin, Jr. 1918- *WhoAm 92*
Mount-Edgcumbe, Earl of 1764-1839 *OxDcOp*
Mount-Edgcumbe, Richard, Earl of 1764-1839 *Baker 92*
Mountford, Alexander G.C. 1941- *WhoUN 92*
Mountford, Charles Percy 1890-1976 *IntDcAn*
Mountford, John Graham 1933- *WhoAsAP 91*
Mountjoy, Christopher *ConAu 139*
Mountjoy, Donald A. *St&PR 93*
Mountjoy, Roberta Jean *WhoWrEP 92*
Mountjoy, William Blount d1534 *BioIn 17*
Mountz, Louise Carson Smith 1911- *WhoAmW 93, WhoWor 93*
Mountz, Wade 1924- *WhoAm 92, WhoSSW 93*
Mouquet, Jules 1867-1946 *Baker 92*
Moura, Jose Manuel Fonseca 1946- *WhoAm 92, WhoEmL 93*
Moura, Manuel de d1651 *BioIn 17*
Moura E Silva, Luis Filipe Tavares 1945- *WhoWor 93*
Mourao, Leopoldo *WhoScE 91-3*
Mouravieff-Apostol, Andrew 1913- *WhoWor 93*
Mouray, Henri Lionel 1934- *WhoScE 91-2*
Moure, Erin 1955- *WhoCanL 92*
Moureaux, Philippe 1939- *WhoWor 93*
Mourek, Joseph Edward 1910- *WhoAm 92*
Mourelatos, Alexander Phoebus Dionysiou 1936- *WhoAm 92*
Mouren, Herve 1948- *WhoWor 93*
Mouret, Jean-Joseph 1682-1738 *Baker 92, OxDcOp*
Mourfield, Joe D. 1943- *St&PR 93*
Mouris, Caroline Ahlfors *MiSFD 9*
Mouris, Frank *MiSFD 9*
Mouritsen, Ole Gunner 1950- *WhoWor 93*
Mourkides, George A. 1923- *WhoScE 91-3*
Mourning Dove 1888-1936 *BioIn 17*
Moursund, Albert Wadel, III 1919- *WhoSSW 93*
Moursund, Kenneth Carroll 1937- *WhoSSW 93*
Mousa, Alyaa Mohammed Ali 1964- *WhoWor 93*
Mousa, Fathi Salim 1941- *WhoUN 92*
Mousa, John J. 1948- *St&PR 93*
Mousaios fl. 5th cent.-6th cent. *OxDcByz*
Mousel, Craig Lawrence 1947- *WhoEmL 93*
Moushey, Nora E. 1949- *St&PR 93*
Mousky, Stafford King 1932- *WhoUN 92*
Mousourakis, Ioannis Nikolaos 1944- *WhoSSW 93*
Mousouris, Sotirios 1934- *WhoUN 92*
Moussa, Farid George *St&PR 93*
Moussa, Pierre Louis 1922- *St&PR 93*
Moussalli, Georges Fathi 1942- *WhoUN 92*
Moussavi-Rahpeyma, Abbas 1938- *WhoWor 93*
Mousseau, Doris Naomi Barton 1934- *WhoAmW 93*
Mousset, Joseph 1932- *WhoScE 91-2*
Moussorgsky, Modest (Petrovich) *Baker 92*
Moustafa, Karen Raye 1953- *WhoAmW 93*
Moutaery, Khalaf Reden 1949- *WhoWor 93*
Moutet, Marius 1876-1968 *BioIn 17*
Mouton, Jean c. 1459-1522 *Baker 92*
Mouton, John Olivier 1944- *WhoAm 92*
Mouton, Sylvia Craig 1951- *WhoEmL 93*
Moutoussamy, Ernest 1941- *DcCPCAm*
Moutoussamy, John Warren 1922- *WhoAm 92*
Moutoussamy-Ashe, Jeanne 1951- *BioIn 17*
Moutrie, Chester L. 1946- *St&PR 93*
Moutsopoulos, Haralampos M. 1944- *WhoScE 91-3*
Moutz, T.J. *Law&B 92*
Moutzouris, C.I. 1949- *WhoScE 91-3*
Mouw, Irma Marian 1928- *WhoAmW 93*
Mouzakes-Siler, Helen Harriet 1929- *WhoAmW 93*
Mouzalon *OxDcByz*
Mouzalon, George c. 1220-1258 *OxDcByz*
Mouzalon, Nicholas *OxDcByz*
Movassaghi, Mehrzard 1951- *St&PR 93*
Moverman, Judith Ellen *Law&B 92*
Movsesijan, Miodrag 1932- *WhoScE 91-4*
Movshon, Joseph Anthony 1950- *WhoEmL 93*
Mow, Douglas Farris 1928- *WhoAm 92*
Mow, Robert Henry, Jr. 1938- *WhoAm 92*
Mow, Van C. 1939- *WhoAm 92*
Mow, William C.W. *BioIn 17*
Mowad, Yolanda Carmen Perez 1947- *WhoAmW 93*
Mowat, Farley *BioIn 17*
Mowat, Farley 1921- *MagSWL [port], WhoCanL 92*
Mowat, Farley (McGill) 1921- *DcChlFi, MajAI [port], WhoAm 92, WhoWor 93, WhoWrEP 92*
Mowat, William Henry, Jr. 1940- *WhoE 93*
Mowatt, Paul *BioIn 17*
Mowbray, Caral Beatrice Thiessen 1948- *WhoAmW 93*
Mowbray, Elmer Eugene 1941- *WhoSSW 93*
Mowbray, John Code 1918- *WhoAm 92*
Mowbray, Malcolm *MiSFD 9*
Mowbray, Robert Norman 1935- *WhoE 93*
Mowchan, Patrick J. 1936- *St&PR 93*
Mowchanuk, Timothy 1939- *WhoWor 93*
Mowday, Richard Thomas 1947- *WhoAm 92*
Mowder, Gary Leroy 1940- *WhoAm 92*
Mowell, John 1934- *St&PR 93*
Mower, Eric Andrew 1944- *WhoAm 92*
Mower, Henry William 1943- *St&PR 93*
Mowers, Thomas John 1943- *St&PR 93*
Mowery, Anna Renshaw 1931- *WhoAmW 93*
Mowery, Bob Lee 1920- *WhoAm 92*
Mowery, Marlene Bonnie 1945- *WhoSSW 93*
Mowery, Michael W. *Law&B 92*
Mowery, Nathan R. *Law&B 92*
Mowett, J.D. *WhoScE 91-1*
Mowrer, Edgar Ansel 1892-1977 *JrnUS*
Mowrer, Lilian Thomson d1990 *BioIn 17*
Mowrer, Paul Scott 1887-1971 *JrnUS*
Mowrer, Tony Alan 1956- *WhoE 93*
Mowrey, David F. *Law&B 92*
Mowrey, John William 1940- *St&PR 93*
Mowrey, Timothy James 1958- *WhoEmL 93*
Mowry, Oliver Warren, Jr. 1956- *WhoEmL 93*
Mowry, Philip Stephen 1953- *WhoEmL 93, WhoSSW 93*
Mowry, Robert Dean 1945- *WhoAm 92*
Mowry, Robert Wilbur 1923- *WhoAm 92, WhoWor 93*
Mowry, Sylvester d1871 *BioIn 17*
Mowshowitz, Abbe 1939- *ScF&FL 92*
Mowshowitz, Israel 1914-1992 *NewYTBS 92 [port]*
Moxey, John Llewellyn 1920- *MiSFD 9*
Moxey, P.A. *WhoScE 91-1*
Moxley, John Howard, III 1935- *WhoAm 92*
Moxnes, Hans Petter 1929- *WhoWor 93*
Moxness, John Michael *Law&B 92*
Moxon, Edward 1801-1858 *BioIn 17*
Moxon, Gaylord E. 1922- *St&PR 93*
Moxon, George W. *Law&B 92*
Moy, Adrianus 1937- *WhoAsAP 91*
Moy, Audrey 1942- *WhoAmW 93*
Moy, Cara L. 1964- *WhoEmL 93*
Moy, Celeste M. *Law&B 92*
Moy, Curt Wayne 1961- *WhoWor 93*
Moy, Edward J. *Law&B 92*
Moy, James S. 1948- *WhoWrEP 92*
Moy, Richard Henry 1931- *WhoAm 92*
Moy, Robert Clifford 1938- *WhoSSW 93*
Moy, Robert Joseph 1960- *St&PR 93*
Moya, Hidalgo 1920- *WhoWor 93*
Moya, Jose Maria 1933- *WhoWor 93*
Moya, Margaret-Haley Soper 1946- *WhoAmW 93*

Moya, Sara Dreier 1945- *WhoAmW 93*
Moya de Guerra, Elvira 1947- *WhoWor 93*
Moya del Pino, Jose 1891-1969 *HispAmA*
Moyano, Daniel 1928- *SpAmA*
Moyano, Graciela Barcala *WhoWor 93*
Moya Sanchez, Dimas Eduardo 1962- *WhoWor 93*
Moya y Contreras, Pedro de *BioIn 17*
Moye, Catherine 1960- *ConAu 136*
Moye, Eric Vaughn 1954- *WhoEmL 93*
Moye, John Edward 1944- *WhoAm 92*
Moye, Judy Henley 1944- *WhoAmW 93*
Moyed, Ralph Sam 1930- *WhoE 93*
Moyer, Alan Dean 1928- *WhoAm 92*
Moyer, Charles Frederick 1930- *WhoE 93*
Moyer, Charles R. *Law&B 92*
Moyer, Craig Alan 1955- *WhoEmL 93, WhoWor 93*
Moyer, David Lee 1940- *WhoE 93*
Moyer, David M. *Law&B 92*
Moyer, F. Stanton 1929- *WhoAm 92*
Moyer, Geralyn Marie 1959- *WhoAmW 93*
Moyer, James Wallace 1919- *WhoE 93*
Moyer, Jay E. *Law&B 92*
Moyer, John Henry, IV 1950- *WhoEmL 93*
Moyer, Kenneth Evan 1919- *WhoAm 92*
Moyer, Kermit 1943- *ConAu 136*
Moyer, Kerri Salls 1954- *WhoAmW 93*
Moyer, Merrill S. 1934- *St&PR 93*
Moyer, Ralph Owen, Jr. 1936- *WhoE 93*
Moyer, Ray Allen 1946- *WhoEmL 93*
Moyer, Robert Howard 1928- *St&PR 93*
Moyer, Steven G. 1952- *St&PR 93*
Moyer, Terry T. *Law&B 92*
Moyer, Thomas J. 1939- *WhoAm 92*
Moyerman, Robert Max 1925- *WhoE 93*
Moyers, Bill *BioIn 17*
Moyers, Bill 1934- *ConLC 74 [port], PolPar*
Moyers, Bill D. 1934- *WhoAm 92*
Moyers, Billy Don 1934- *JrnUS*
Moyers, Diana Kim 1955- *WhoAmW 93*
Moyers, Ernest Everett S. 1933- *WhoSSW 93*
Moyers, Gary W. *St&PR 93*
Moyers, John 1958- *BioIn 17*
Moyers, K. Douglas *Law&B 92*
Moyers, K. Douglass *Law&B 92*
Moyers, Kevin Keith 1964- *WhoSSW 93*
Moyers, Robert Charles 1951- *WhoEmL 93, WhoSSW 93*
Moyers, Sylvia Dean 1936- *WhoSSW 93*
Moyers, Terri Kelly 1953- *BioIn 17*
Moyes, Patricia *BioIn 17*
Moylan, David John, III 1951- *WhoE 93, WhoEmL 93*
Moylan, James E., Jr. 1951- *WhoAm 92*
Moylan, James Emmett, Jr. 1951- *St&PR 93*
Moylan, Jay Richard 1950- *WhoE 93*
Moylan, Peter James 1948- *WhoWor 93*
Moylan, Richard John 1954- *WhoE 93*
Moylan, Thomas P. *ScF&FL 92*
Moylan, Tom 1943- *ScF&FL 92*
Moylan, William Alexander 1952- *WhoEmL 93*
Moylan-Torruella, Trish 1953- *NotHsAW 93*
Moyle, Allan *BioIn 17, MiSFD 9*
Moyle, Bennett Isaac 1946- *WhoEmL 93*
Moyle, Peter Briggs 1942- *WhoAm 92*
Moyles, William Philip 1930- *St&PR 93*
Moyna, John J. *Law&B 92*
Moynahan, John Daniel, Jr. 1935- *St&PR 93, WhoAm 92*
Moynahan, John F. 1957- *St&PR 93*
Moynahan, Julian Lane 1925- *WhoAm 92, WhoWrEP 92*
Moyne, John Abel 1920- *WhoAm 92, WhoE 93*
Moynihan, Antony Patrick Andrew Cairnes Berkeley 1936-1991 *BioIn 17*
Moynihan, Barbara Ann *WhoAmW 93*
Moynihan, Colleen Meade 1938- *WhoAmW 93*
Moynihan, Daniel Patrick 1927- *CngDr 91, WhoAm 92, WhoE 93*
Moynihan, Daniel Patrick 1948- *WhoEmL 93*
Moynihan, Daniel W. *Law&B 92*
Moynihan, David Stanton 1942- *WhoE 93*
Moynihan, James J. 1944- *St&PR 93*
Moynihan, Jeremiah d1991 *BioIn 17*
Moynihan, John F. *Law&B 92*
Moynihan, John T., Jr. *Law&B 92*
Moynihan, Jonathan Patrick 1948- *WhoEmL 93*
Moynihan, Kevin *Law&B 92*
Moynihan, Robert Duncan 1936- *WhoE 93*
Moynihan, Rodrigo 1910-1990 *BioIn 17*
Moynihan, Ruth Barnes 1933- *WhoAmW 93*
Moynihan, Walter R. 1923- *St&PR 93*
Moyo, Edward Maklobo 1935- *WhoUN 92*
Moyse, Hermann, Jr. 1921- *WhoAm 92*
Moyse, Hermann, III 1948- *St&PR 93*
Moyse, Louis 1912- *Baker 92*
Moyse, Marcel (Joseph) 1889-1984 *Baker 92*
Moyses, Carol Ann 1940- *WhoAmW 93*
Moysey, A. Warren 1939- *WhoAm 92*
Moyssiadis, James David 1948- *WhoEmL 93*
Moyzes, Alexander 1906-1984 *Baker 92*
Moyzes, Mikulas 1872-1944 *Baker 92*
Moz, Adriano 1946- *WhoSSW 93*
Mozaffari, Mojtaba 1952- *WhoWor 93*
Mozarsky, Peter *Law&B 92*
Mozart, Constanze 1763-1842 *BioIn 17*
Mozart, Franz Xaver Wolfgang 1791-1844 *Baker 92*
Mozart, Johann Chrysostom Wolfgang Amadeus 1756-1791 *BioIn 17*
Mozart, (Johann Georg) Leopold 1719-1787 *Baker 92*
Mozart, Maria Anna (Walburga Ignatia) 1751-1829 *Baker 92*
Mozart, Wolfgang Amadeus 1756-1791 *Baker 92, BioIn 17, IntDcOp [port], OxDcOp*
Mozeleski, Peter A. 1940- *WhoE 93*
Mozeley, Thomas Edwin 1944- *WhoSSW 93*
Mozena, John Daniel 1956- *WhoWor 93*
Mozer, Doris Ann 1929- *WhoWor 93*
Mozer, Paul W. 1955- *BioIn 17*
Mozes, Samuel R. 1923-1990 *BioIn 17*
Mozeson, Isaac Elchanan 1951- *WhoWrEP 92*
Mozheiko, Igor *ScF&FL 92*
Mozhukin, Ivan 1887?-1939 *IntDcF 2-3 [port]*
Mozian, Gerard P. 1945- *St&PR 93*
Mozian, Gerard Paul 1945- *WhoAm 92*
Mozifio, Jose Moriano 1757-1820 *BioIn 17*
Mozinski, Cathlee Rae 1940- *WhoWrEP 92*
Mozley, Paul David 1928- *WhoAm 92*
Mozo, Ann Elizabeth 1958- *WhoAmW 93, WhoEmL 93*
Mozo, Walter MacLeod, Jr. 1946- *WhoSSW 93*
Mozzer, Alanna Jean 1952- *WhoWrEP 92*
Mpelkas, Christos Charles 1920- *WhoWor 93*
Mphahlele, Es'kia 1919- *DcLB 125 [port]*
Mphahlele, Ezekiel *BioIn 17*
M'Pherson, Philip Keith *WhoScE 91-1*
Mpho, Motsamai Keyecwe 1921- *WhoWor 93*
Mpozagara, Gabriel 1941- *WhoUN 92*
Mrabet, Mohammed *ConAu 38NR*
Mrabet, Mohammed 1940- *ScF&FL 92*
Mracek, Joseph Gustav 1878-1944 *Baker 92*
Mrachek, William J. 1944- *St&PR 93*
Mraczek, Joseph Gustav 1878-1944 *Baker 92*
Mrak, Emil Marcel 1901-1987 *BioIn 17*
Mrak, Robert Emil 1948- *WhoEmL 93*
Mrass, Walter 1930- *WhoScE 91-3*
Mravina, Evgeniya 1864-1914 *OxDcOp*
Mravina, Evgeniya (Konstantinovna) 1864-1914 *Baker 92*
Mravinskaya, Evgeniya (Konstantinovna) 1864-1914 *Baker 92*
Mravinsky, Evgeni (Alexandrovich) 1903-1988 *Baker 92*
Mraz, Sharon Janeen Towner 1948- *WhoEmL 93*
Mrazek, David Allen 1947- *WhoAm 92, WhoEmL 93*
Mrazek, Robert J. 1945- *CngDr 91, WhoAm 92, WhoE 93*
Mrkonic, George Ralph, Jr. 1952- *WhoAm 92*
Mrna, Boris 1932- *WhoScE 91-4*
M-Roblin, John 1958- *WhoE 93, WhoWor 93*
Mroczka, Edward Joseph 1940- *WhoAm 92*
Mroczkowski, James V. 1945- *St&PR 93*
Mross, Charles Dennis 1948- *WhoAm 92*
Mroszczyk, Rose Victoria 1945- *WhoE 93*
Mrowca, Jerome *Law&B 92*
Mroz, John Edwin 1948- *WhoE 93*
Mroz, Mitchell D. 1944- *St&PR 93*
Mroz, Sue 1943- *WhoWrEP 92*
Mroz, Zenon 1930- *WhoScE 91-4, WhoWor 93*
Mrozek, Ron *Law&B 92*
Mrozek, Slawomir 1930- *BioIn 17, PolBiDi*
Mrozewski, Stefan 1894-1975 *PolBiDi*
Mroziewicz, Robert 1942- *WhoUN 92*
Mrozik, Helmut 1931- *WhoE 93*
Mrugalski, Zdzislaw 1930- *WhoScE 91-4*
Mruk, Charles Karzimer 1926- *WhoE 93*
Mruk, Eugene Robert 1927- *St&PR 93, WhoE 93, WhoWor 93*
Mruvka, Alan Scott 1957- *WhoEmL 93*
Mrykalo, Frank Michael 1943- *WhoE 93*
Mselle, C.S.M. 1938- *WhoUN 92*
Mshevelidze, Shalva 1904-1984 *OxDcOp*
Mshvelidze, Shalva (Mikhailovich) 1904-1984 *Baker 92*
Mshvenieradze, Vladimir V. 1926-1990 *BioIn 17*
Msuya, Cleopa David 1931- *WhoAfr*
Mswati, III 1968- *WhoWor 93*
Mswati, Makhosetive, III 1968- *WhoAfr*
Mtewa, Mekki 1946- *WhoAm 92, WhoE 93*
Mtshali, Oswald Mbuyiseni 1940- *DcLB 125 [port]*
Mu'awiya 60-?-680 *OxDcByz*
Mubarak, Hosni *BioIn 17*
Mubarak, Mohamed Hosni 1928- *DcTwHis*
Mubarak, Muhammad Hosni 1928- *WhoWor 93*
Mubin, Abulkasem Abdul 1943- *WhoWor 93*
Mucci, Carolyn Taylor 1953- *WhoAmW 93*
Mucci, Donald Robert 1942- *St&PR 93*
Mucci, Gary Louis 1946- *WhoE 93*
Mucci, Louie 1958- *WhoE 93*
Mucci, Patrick John 1947- *St&PR 93, WhoE 93*
Mucci, Paul Leonard 1952- *St&PR 93*
Muccia, Joseph William 1948- *WhoE 93*
Muccini, Mario *WhoScE 91-3*
Muccino, Richard Robert 1946- *WhoEmL 93*
Muccino, Robert D. 1930- *St&PR 93*
Muccione, Gary J. 1943- *St&PR 93*
Muccione, Irene T. *St&PR 93*
Muccione, Vincent J. 1937- *St&PR 93*
Muccitelli, John Anthony 1953- *WhoEmL 93*
Muce, Paul Maximilian 1940- *WhoWor 93*
Mucha, Frank A. 1927- *St&PR 93*
Mucha, John Frank 1950- *WhoE 93*
Mucha, Robert John 1939- *St&PR 93*
Muchanga, Albert Mudenda 1959- *WhoUN 92*
Muche, Georg 1895-1987 *BioIn 17*
Muchmore, Carolin M. 1944- *WhoAmW 93*
Muchmore, Don Moncrief 1922- *WhoAm 92, WhoWor 93*
Muchmore, Robert Boyer 1917- *WhoAm 92*
Muchmore, William Breuleux 1920- *WhoAm 92*
Muchnick, Alberto 1959- *St&PR 93*
Muchnick, Richard Stuart 1942- *WhoE 93, WhoWor 93*
Muchow, William Charles 1922- *WhoAm 92*
Muchowski, Patrice Maureen 1951- *WhoEmL 93*
Muck, Carl 1859-1940 *OxDcOp*
Muck, George Arthur 1937- *St&PR 93, WhoAm 92*
Muck, Karl 1859-1940 *Baker 92, IntDcOp*
Muck, Philip Francis 1938- *St&PR 93*
Muck, Terry Charles 1947- *WhoWrEP 92*
Muckenhoupt, Benjamin 1933- *WhoAm 92*
Muckerman, Norman James 1917- *WhoAm 92*
Mucklestone, Peter John 1955- *WhoEmL 93*
Muckley, Brian Stewart *WhoScE 91-1*
Mucklow, Neale Harmon 1929- *WhoSSW 93*
Mucklow, Nigel Biggles 1957- *WhoE 93*
Muczynski, Robert 1929- *Baker 92*
Muda Hassanal Bolkiah 1946- *BioIn 17*
Mudan, Krishna 1947- *St&PR 93*
Mudano, Frank Robert 1928- *WhoAm 92*
Mudar, Marian Jean *WhoE 93*
Mudarra, Alonso de c. 1508-1580 *Baker 92*
Mudbone, Butch R. *WhoWrEP 92*
Mudbone, Vivian Esmeralda *WhoWrEP 92*
Mudd, Anne Chestney 1944- *WhoAmW 93*
Mudd, Emily Hartshorne 1898- *WhoAm 92*
Mudd, Jodie *BioIn 17*
Mudd, John Philip 1932- *WhoAm 92*
Mudd, Joseph Delbert 1964- *WhoEmL 93*
Mudd, Kim Marie 1959- *WhoEmL 93*
Mudd, Reginald M. 1953- *St&PR 93*
Mudd, Richard Alan 1952- *St&PR 93*
Mudd, Roger 1928- *JrnUS*
Mudd, Roger Harrison 1928- *WhoAm 92*
Mudd, Samuel Alexander *BioIn 17*
Mudd, Sidney Peter 1917- *WhoAm 92*
Mudd, Stephen B. 1932- *St&PR 93*
Mudd, Steve *ScF&FL 92*
Mudd, Susan Elizabeth 1955- *WhoEmL 93*
Mudd, William R. 1943- *St&PR 93*
Muddiman, John 1947- *ConAu 136*
Muddy Waters *Baker 92*
Mudenda, Elijah Haatukali Kaiba 1927- *WhoAfr*
Muder, Robert Richard 1951- *WhoE 93*
Mudford, Anthony L. 1939- *St&PR 93*
Mudge, B.F. 1817-1879 *BioIn 17*
Mudge, Benjamin Franklin 1817-1879 *BioIn 17*
Mudge, Dirk Francis 1928- *WhoAfr*
Mudge, Lewis Seymour 1929- *WhoAm 92*
Mudge, Richard 1718-1763 *Baker 92*
Mudge, Richard Ragsdale 1945- *WhoE 93*
Mudge, Shaw, Jr. 1953- *St&PR 93*
Mudge, William O'Brien 1930- *St&PR 93*
Mudholkar, Shivdas Shivling Elias Rajas 1946- *WhoWor 93*
Mudick, Mitchell A. *Law&B 92*
Mudie, Thomas Molleson 1809-1876 *Baker 92*
Mudrick, David Phillip *Law&B 92*
Mudrick, Lucy J. 1928- *St&PR 93*
Mudry, Michael 1926- *WhoE 93*
Muecke, Charles Andrew 1918- *WhoAm 92*
Muecke, Manfred K. 1942- *St&PR 93*
Muedeking, George Herbert 1915- *WhoAm 92*
Muegel, Glenn Allen 1934- *WhoSSW 93*
Muehlbauer, James H. 1940- *St&PR 93*
Muehlbauer, James Herman 1940- *WhoAm 92*
Muehlbauer, William L. 1948- *WhoSSW 93*
Muehlberg, Robert Steven 1954- *St&PR 93*
Muehleib, William Henry 1922- *St&PR 93*
Muehleis, Mary Lou 1937- *St&PR 93*
Muehleis, Victor Emanuel 1926- *St&PR 93*
Muehleisen, Gene Sylvester 1915- *WhoAm 92*
Muehlemann, Kathy *BioIn 17*
Muehlhausen, Richard W. 1938- *St&PR 93*
Muehlstein, Sophia E. 1910- *St&PR 93*
Muehrcke, Juliana Obright 1945- *WhoAmW 93*
Muehrcke, Robert Carl 1921- *WhoAm 92*
Muelas, Ernesto 1943- *WhoScE 91-3*
Mueller, Anton Peter 1948- *WhoWor 93*
Mueller, Arno W. d1991 *BioIn 17*
Mueller, Barbara Ruth 1925- *WhoAm 92, WhoAmW 93*
Mueller, Barbara Stewart *WhoAmW 93*
Mueller, Betty Jeanne 1925- *WhoAm 92, WhoAmW 93*
Mueller, Carl Gustav, Jr. 1929- *WhoAm 92*
Mueller, Carl Richard 1931- *WhoAm 92*
Mueller, Carl Werner 1931- *WhoWor 93*
Mueller, Charles Barber 1917- *WhoAm 92*
Mueller, Charles William 1938- *St&PR 93, WhoAm 92*
Mueller, Claire 1944- *WhoAmW 93*
Mueller, Cookie d1989 *BioIn 17*
Mueller, Curt H. *Law&B 92*
Mueller, D.D. 1937- *St&PR 93*
Mueller, Daniel M. *Law&B 92*
Mueller, David John 1950- *St&PR 93*
Mueller, David R. 1952- *St&PR 93*
Mueller, Dennis C(ary) 1940- *ConAu 39NR*
Mueller, Dennis Cary 1940- *WhoE 93, WhoWor 93*
Mueller, Diane M. *Law&B 92*
Mueller, Dieter Heinrich 1942- *WhoWor 93*
Mueller, Donald Dean 1937- *WhoAm 92*
Mueller, Earl G. 1932- *St&PR 93*
Mueller, Edward Albert 1923- *WhoAm 92*
Mueller, Ernest 1925- *St&PR 93*
Mueller, Erwin Maria 1927- *WhoScE 91-3*
Mueller, Gail Delories 1957- *WhoAmW 93*
Mueller, Gerald Gustav 1924- *WhoAm 92*
Mueller, Gerd Dieter 1936- *WhoAm 92*
Mueller, Gerhard Gottlob 1930- *WhoAm 92*
Mueller, Gerhard Joseph 1936- *St&PR 93*
Mueller, Gerhard Otto 1930- *St&PR 93*
Mueller, Hans P. 1942- *St&PR 93*
Mueller, Helmut Andreas 1929- *WhoWor 93*
Mueller, Herbert 1931- *WhoScE 91-3*
Mueller, James Bernhard 1952- *WhoAm 92*
Mueller, James Edward 1931- *St&PR 93*
Mueller, James Paul 1956- *WhoE 93*
Mueller, James R. 1951- *ConAu 138*
Mueller, Jens Helmut 1956- *WhoEmL 93*
Mueller, Joachim W(ilhelm) 1953- *ConAu 139*
Mueller, Joerg 1942- *BioIn 17, ConAu 136*
Mueller, John Alfred 1906- *WhoAm 92*
Mueller, John D. 1934- *WhoAm 92*
Mueller, John David 1934- *St&PR 93*
Mueller, John David 1943- *WhoSSW 93*
Mueller, John E. 1937- *WhoAm 92*
Mueller, John R. *St&PR 93*

Mueller, John S. 1930- *St&PR 93*
Mueller, Kai Uwe 1957- *WhoWor 93*
Mueller, Kathy *MiSFD 9*
Mueller, Keith Richard 1957- *WhoEmL 93*
Mueller, Klaus 1958- *WhoWor 93*
Mueller, Lisel *BioIn 17*
Mueller, Loraine Dorothy 1920- *WhoWrEP 92*
Mueller, Margaret Reid 1929- *WhoAmW 93*
Mueller, Marilyn Jean 1946- *WhoAmW 93, WhoEmL 93, WhoWor 93*
Mueller, Mark Christopher 1945- *WhoSSW 93, WhoWor 93*
Mueller, Marnie Wagstaff 1937- *St&PR 93, WhoAm 92, WhoAmW 93, WhoIns 93*
Mueller, Michael J. 1948- *St&PR 93*
Mueller, Michael Lee 1959- *WhoSSW 93*
Mueller, Nancy Schneider 1933- *WhoAmW 93*
Mueller, Neal R. 1954- *St&PR 93*
Mueller, Norbert 1946- *WhoWor 93*
Mueller, Otto 1874-1930 *BioIn 17*
Mueller, Otto-Werner 1926- *Baker 92*
Mueller, Paul 1925- *WhoWor 93*
Mueller, Paul Henry 1917- *WhoAm 92, WhoWor 93*
Mueller, Paul John 1892-1964 *HarEnMi*
Mueller, Peggy Jean 1952- *WhoAmW 93, WhoSSW 93, WhoWor 93*
Mueller, Peter K. 1931- *WhoUN 92*
Mueller, Peter Sterling 1930- *WhoAm 92, WhoWor 93*
Mueller, Raymond A. 1922- *St&PR 93*
Mueller, Raymond Anthony *Law&B 92*
Mueller, Richard *ScF&FL 92*
Mueller, Richard Edward 1927- *WhoAm 92*
Mueller, Richard Walter 1944- *WhoAm 92*
Mueller, Robert Clemens 1923- *St&PR 93*
Mueller, Robert J. 1929- *St&PR 93*
Mueller, Robert Kirk 1913- *St&PR 93, WhoAm 92*
Mueller, Robert Swan, III 1944- *WhoAm 92*
Mueller, Ronald James 1935- *St&PR 93*
Mueller, Ronald John *Law&B 92*
Mueller, Ronald Raymond 1947- *WhoAm 92*
Mueller, Rudhard Klaus 1936- *WhoWor 93*
Mueller, Shannon Marie 1963- *WhoEmL 93*
Mueller, Siegfried 1940- *WhoWor 93*
Mueller, Stanley R. *Law&B 92*
Mueller, Stephan 1930- *WhoScE 91-4, WhoWor 93*
Mueller, Stephen Nations *Law&B 92*
Mueller, Sue Marie 1953- *WhoAmW 93*
Mueller, Walter L. 1930- *WhoIns 93*
Mueller, Warren Arthur 1932- *St&PR 93*
Mueller, Werner August 1947- *WhoWor 93*
Mueller, Willard Fritz 1925- *WhoAm 92*
Mueller, William Martin 1917- *WhoAm 92*
Mueller, William R. 1921- *St&PR 93*
Mueller, Wolfgang Siegfried 1937- *St&PR 93*
Mueller-Heubach, Eberhard August 1942- *WhoAm 92*
Mueller-Stahl, Armin *BioIn 17*
Mueller-Stahl, Armin 1930- *IntDcF 2-3*
Mueller von Asow, Erich Hermann 1892-1964 *Baker 92*
Muench, David *BioIn 17*
Muench, Donald Leo 1934- *WhoE 93*
Muench, Donald P. 1931- *St&PR 93*
Muench, Gerhart 1907-1988 *Baker 92*
Muenchinger, Nancy *Law&B 92*
Muenks, Sue Ann 1950- *WhoAmW 93*
Muenster, John Rolfing 1949- *WhoEmL 93*
Muensterman, David B. 1941- *St&PR 93*
Muenter, Annabel Adams 1944- *WhoAmW 93, WhoE 93*
Muenzen, Lee J. 1942- *St&PR 93*
Mues, Gregory R. *Law&B 92*
Mueshihange, Peter *WhoWor 93*
Muesing Ellwood, Edith Elizabeth 1947- *WhoAm 92, WhoE 93, WhoEmL 93, WhoWrEP 92*
Muessen, Henry J. d1991 *BioIn 17*
Muessig, Robert Andrew 1928- *WhoE 93*
Mueth, Dale 1947- *St&PR 93*
Mueth, Joseph Edward 1935- *WhoAm 92*
Muetterties, John Henry *Law&B 92*
Muetterties, John Henry 1953- *St&PR 93*
Muffat, Georg 1653?-1704 *Baker 92*
Muffat, Gottlieb (Theophil) 1690?-1770 *Baker 92*
Muffler, Howard Walter 1959- *WhoSSW 93*
Mufson, Maurice Albert 1932- *WhoAm 92*
Mufson, Michael J. 1954- *St&PR 93*
Mufti, Jean *BioIn 17*
Mufti, Navaid Ahmed 1967- *WhoWor 93*
Muftic, Sead 1948- *WhoWor 93*
Muftuoglu, Yucel 1947- *WhoScE 91-4*
Mugabe, Robert 1924- *ColdWar 2 [port]*
Mugabe, Robert Gabriel 1924- *BioIn 17, DcTwHis, WhoAfr, WhoWor 93*
Mugabe, Sally d1992 *BioIn 17, NewYTBS 92*
Mugan, Daniel Joseph 1933- *WhoE 93*
Mugavero, Francis J. 1914-1991 *BioIn 17*
Mugdan, Kate 1859-1942 *BioIn 17*
Mugellini, Bruno 1871-1912 *Baker 92*
Mugford, Alfred George 1928- *WhoAm 92*
Mugge, Andreas 1956- *WhoWor 93*
Muggeo, Michele 1938- *WhoWor 93*
Muggeridge, Malcolm 1903-1990 *BioIn 17, ScF&FL 92*
Muggeridge, Marie *AmWomPl*
Muggia, Judith Palmer 1938- *WhoAmW 93*
Mughal, Abdul-Quadir 1944- *WhoWor 93*
Mugica, Rafael 1911-1991 *BioIn 17*
Mugler, Thierry 1946- *BioIn 17*
Mugnone, Leopoldo 1858-1941 *Baker 92, IntDcOp, OxDcOp*
Mugot, Isabelo y Oco 1937- *WhoWor 93*
Mugur-Schachter, Mioara 1929- *WhoScE 91-2*
Muh, Jean-Pierre 1935- *WhoScE 91-2*
Muha, Andrew Thomas 1929- *St&PR 93*
Muha, Denise Boustead 1959- *WhoE 93*
Muhaimin, Wilhelmina Squires 1954- *WhoAmW 93*
Muhammad d632 *BioIn 17*
Muhammad 570?-632 *OxDcByz*
Muhammad, V, King of Morocco 1909-1961 *BioIn 17*
Muhammad, Alberta 1937- *WhoAmW 93*
Muhammad, Ali Nasser 1939- *BioIn 17*
Muhammad, Elijah *EncAACR*
Muhammad, Elijah 1897-1975 *BioIn 17, ConBlB 4 [port]*
Muhammad, Khalil Abdul 1962- *WhoE 93*
Muhammad, Talib-Karim 1936- *WhoSSW 93*
Muhammad, Wallace D. 1933- *EncAACR, WhoAm 92*
Muhammad Aslam Saleemi 1933- *WhoAsAP 91*
Muhammad Bin Mubarak Al-Khalifa, Sheikh 1935- *WhoWor 93*
Muhammad ibn'Abd Allah ibn Batutah 1304-1377 *BioIn 17*
Muhammad ibn Ishaq ibn al-Nadim fl. 987- *BioIn 17*
Muhammad ibn Rashid Al-Maktum, Sheikh 1946- *WhoWor 93*
Muhammed ibn-Ahmad al-Muqaddasi 945-1000 *Expl 93*
Muhe, Erich 1938- *WhoWor 93*
Muhl, Edward L. 1945- *St&PR 93*
Muhlanger, Erich 1941- *WhoWor 93*
Muhlanger, Gilda O. *Law&B 92*
Muhlbach, Robert Arthur 1946- *WhoEmL 93*
Muhlbacher, Jorg R. 1946- *WhoScE 91-4*
Muhlbauer, Alfred 1932- *WhoScE 91-3*
Muhlbauer, Rita 1941- *BioIn 17*
Muhlbeier, Barbara *Law&B 92*
Muhlberger, Richard Charles 1938- *WhoAm 92*
Muhlemann, Alan Paul *WhoScE 91-1*
Muhlenberg, Frederick A. C. 1756-1801 *PolPar*
Muhlenbruch, Carl W. 1915- *WhoAm 92, WhoWor 93*
Muhlenfeld, Eike 1938- *WhoScE 91-3*
Muhlenkamp, Bernard Joseph 1945- *St&PR 93*
Muhlert, Jan Keene 1942- *WhoAm 92, WhoAmW 93*
Muhlfeld, Fritz Burger- 1882-1969 *BioIn 17*
Muhlfeld, Richard (Bernhard Herrmann) 1856-1907 *Baker 92*
Muhling, August 1786-1847 *Baker 92*
Muhlitner, David R. *Law&B 92*
Muhlke, William E. 1941- *St&PR 93*
Muhlmann, Wilhelm Emil 1904-1988 *IntDcAn*
Muhlradt, Peter F. 1937- *WhoScE 91-3*
Muhmaad-Ali, Baggi *Law&B 92*
Muhn, Donna L. 1947- *St&PR 93*
Muhoho, George Kamau 1938- *WhoAfr*
Muhrcke, Gary *BioIn 17*
Muhren, Arnold Dominicus Alphonsu 1944- *WhoWor 93*
Muhsam, Paul 1876-1960 *BioIn 17*
Mui, Jimmy Kun 1958- *WhoE 93, WhoEmL 93*
Muijderman, E.A. 1931- *WhoScE 91-3*
Muilenburg, Robert Henry 1941- *WhoAm 92*
Muilenburg, Robert William 1933- *St&PR 93, WhoE 93*
Muir, Bonnie Ann 1959- *WhoEmL 93*
Muir, Brockett 1905- *WhoE 93*
Muir, C.S. *WhoScE 91-2*
Muir, D. Stephen 1951- *St&PR 93*
Muir, Douglas *ScF&FL 92*
Muir, Edwin 1887-1959 *BioIn 17*
Muir, Glenn Patrick 1959- *WhoEmL 93*
Muir, Gordon Russell 1956- *WhoEmL 93*
Muir, Helen *BioIn 17*
Muir, Helen 1911- *WhoAmW 93, WhoSSW 93*
Muir, Isabella Helen Mary *WhoScE 91-1*
Muir, J. Dapray 1936- *WhoAm 92*
Muir, James Dyer 1932- *St&PR 93*
Muir, Jeffrey Shepardd 1949- *St&PR 93*
Muir, John 1838-1914 *BioIn 17, GayN*
Muir, John Robert 1936- *WhoWor 93*
Muir, Malcolm 1914- *WhoAm 92, WhoE 93*
Muir, Michael Bill 1941- *St&PR 93*
Muir, Pauli *BioIn 17*
Muir, Richard 1955- *St&PR 93*
Muir, Robert Eugene *Law&B 92*
Muir, Ruth Brooks 1924- *WhoAmW 93*
Muir, Sandy 1931- *BioIn 17*
Muir, Warren R. 1945- *WhoAm 92*
Muir, William Ker 1931- *BioIn 17*
Muir, William Ker, Jr. 1931- *WhoAm 92*
Muir, William W., Jr. 1936- *St&PR 93*
Muir-Broaddus, Jacqueline Elizabeth 1961- *WhoEmL 93*
Muirhead, Vincent Uriel 1919- *WhoAm 92*
Muirhead, William, III 1932- *St&PR 93*
Muis, Patrice Raia 1953- *WhoWrEP 92*
Muittari, Antero 1933- *WhoWor 93*
Mujahed, Mary Elizabeth 1929- *WhoAmW 93*
Mujahida, Syeda 1966- *WhoWor 93*
Mujeriego, Rafael 1946- *WhoScE 91-3*
Mujezinovic, Dzevad 1934-1992 *NewYTBS 92*
Mujica, Barbara 1943- *ConAu 138*
Mujica, Barbara Louise 1943- *WhoWrEP 92*
Mujica Lainez, Manuel 1910-1984 *ScF&FL 92, SpAmA*
Mukai, Cromwell Daisaku 1917- *WhoE 93*
Mukai, Don *Law&B 92*
Mukai, Donald M. *Law&B 92*
Mukai, Francis K. *Law&B 92*
Mukai, Francis Ken 1956- *WhoEmL 93*
Mukaiyama, Kazuto 1914- *WhoAsAP 91*
Mukamal, David Samier 1944- *WhoWor 93*
Mukamal, Steven Sasoon 1940- *WhoE 93, WhoWor 93*
Mukando, Justin Jeremiah 1936- *WhoAfr*
Mukasey, Michael B. 1941- *WhoE 93*
Mukawa, Akio 1928- *WhoWor 93*
Mukerjee, Pasupati 1932- *WhoAm 92*
Mukerji, Dhan Gopal 1890-1936 *ConAu 136, MajAI [port]*
Mukharji, Sabyasachi d1990 *BioIn 17*
Mukhedkar, Dinkar 1936- *WhoAm 92*
Mukherjee, Bharati *BioIn 17, WhoCanL 92*
Mukherjee, Bharati 1940- *CurBio 92 [port], IntLitE, MagSAmL [port], WhoAmW 93*
Mukherjee, Geeta 1924- *WhoAsAP 91*
Mukherjee, Kalinath 1932- *WhoAm 92*
Mukherjee, Kanak 1921- *WhoAsAP 91*
Mukherjee, Kumar Deb 1938- *WhoScE 91-3*
Mukherjee, Margaret Reed 1934- *WhoE 93*
Mukherjee, Samar 1913- *WhoAsAP 91*
Mukherjee, Srimati 1959- *WhoSSW 93*
Mukhometov, Ravil Galatdinovich 1937- *WhoWor 93*
Mukhopadhyay, Nikhiles 1944- *WhoE 93*
Mukhopadhyay, Vivekananda 1947- *WhoSSW 93*
Mukhransky, Teymuraz Bagration- 1912-1992 *BioIn 17*
Mukoyama, Helen Kiyoko 1914- *WhoWor 93*
Mukula, Jaakko Antero 1923- *WhoScE 91-4*
Mukula, Pambi Mwape 1931- *WhoWor 93*
Mul, Jan 1911-1971 *Baker 92*
Mula, Frank M. 1955- *WhoE 93*
Mulach, J.F., Jr. 1907- *St&PR 93*
Mulaik, Stanley Allen 1935- *WhoAm 92*
Mulari, Mary Elizabeth 1947- *WhoEmL 93, WhoWrEP 92*
Mularz, Theodore Leonard 1933- *WhoAm 92*
Mulas, Pablo 1939- *WhoWor 93*
Mulase, Motohico 1954- *WhoWor 93*
Mulay, James J. *ScF&FL 92*
Mulberger, Charles d1992 *BioIn 17*
Mulcahy, Brian J. *Law&B 92*
Mulcahy, Daniel J. 1947- *WhoIns 93*
Mulcahy, Francis Joseph *Law&B 92*
Mulcahy, J. Patrick *WhoAm 92*
Mulcahy, John 1950- *WhoE 93*
Mulcahy, John J. 1947- *St&PR 93*
Mulcahy, Joseph L. 1938- *St&PR 93*
Mulcahy, Kathleen Ann 1950- *WhoEmL 93*
Mulcahy, Michael James *Law&B 92*
Mulcahy, Michael Joseph 1932- *WhoScE 91-3*
Mulcahy, Michael T. *Law&B 92*
Mulcahy, Noel 1930- *WhoScE 91-3*
Mulcahy, Paul N. 1930- *St&PR 93*
Mulcahy, Peter H. *Law&B 92*
Mulcahy, Richard T. 1938- *St&PR 93*
Mulcahy, Risteard 1922- *WhoScE 91-3*
Mulcahy, Robert Edward 1932- *WhoAm 92*
Mulcahy, Robert W. *Law&B 92*
Mulcahy, Russell 1953- *MiSFD 9*
Mulcahy, Thomas F. 1921- *St&PR 93*
Mulcay, Robert A. 1941- *St&PR 93*
Mulch, Barbara Elizabeth Gooden 1935- *WhoAmW 93*
Mulchey, Ronald Douglas 1937- *WhoAm 92*
Mulcihy, Dorothy Jean 1961- *WhoAmW 93*
Mulckhuyse, Jacob John 1922- *WhoE 93, WhoSSW 93*
Mulcock, James B., Jr. *WhoAm 92*
Muldaur, Diana Charlton 1938- *WhoAm 92, WhoAmW 93*
Mulder, C.J. *Law&B 92*
Mulder, David S. 1938- *WhoAm 92*
Mulder, Donald Gerrit 1924- *WhoAm 92*
Mulder, Donald William 1917- *WhoAm 92*
Mulder, Elizabeth A. 1936- *WhoE 93*
Mulder, Ernest Willem 1898-1959 *Baker 92*
Mulder, Herman 1894-1989 *Baker 92*
Mulder, Mary *BioIn 17*
Mulder, Patricia Marie 1944- *WhoAmW 93*
Mulder, R.W.A.W. *WhoScE 91-3*
Mulder, Tom Alan 1959- *WhoSSW 93*
Mulder, Willem Gerard 1921- *St&PR 93*
Mulder, William W. *Law&B 92*
Mulderig, Robert A. *St&PR 93*
Mulderig, Robert A. 1953- *WhoIns 93*
Mulders, Peter J. 1953- *WhoWor 93*
Muldoon, Brian 1947- *WhoEmL 93*
Muldoon, Francis Creighton 1930- *WhoE 93*
Muldoon, John P. 1940- *St&PR 93*
Muldoon, Leonie Maree 1959- *WhoWor 93*
Muldoon, Nancy Louise 1946- *St&PR 93*
Muldoon, Paul 1951- *ConLC 72 [port]*
Muldoon, Robert 1921- *DcTwHis, WhoAsAP 91*
Muldoon, Robert 1921-1992 *NewYTBS 92 [port]*
Muldoon, Robert D(avid) 1921-1992 *CurBio 92N*
Muldoon, Robert Joseph, Jr. 1936- *WhoAm 92*
Muldoon, William 1852-1933 *BioIn 17*
Muldowney, Dominic (John) 1952- *Baker 92*
Muldowney, Jerome Thomas 1945- *WhoIns 93*
Muldowney, Shirley *BioIn 17*
Muldowney, Terry Michael 1944- *St&PR 93*
Muldowney, Tyrone F. 1957- *St&PR 93*
Muldrow, Charles Norment 1930- *WhoE 93*
Muldrow, Jennifer Lee 1949- *WhoAmW 93*
Muldrow, Tressie Wright 1941- *WhoAmW 93*
Mule, Ann Christine *Law&B 92*
Mule, Anthony V. 1943- *St&PR 93*
Mule, Anthony Vincent 1943- *WhoAm 92*
Mule, Giuseppe 1885-1951 *Baker 92, OxDcOp*
Mule, Guy R. 1946- *St&PR 93*
Mule, Harris 1936- *BioIn 17*
Mule, Harris Mutio 1936- *WhoUN 92*
Mulee, Annette Marie 1953- *WhoEmL 93*
Mulemba, Humphrey 1932- *WhoAfr*
Mules, Norman A. 1930- *St&PR 93*
Mules, Vernon W. 1929- *St&PR 93*
Muleski, Kathleen Rubsam 1951- *St&PR 93*
Mulet, Oscar Mario 1937- *WhoWor 93*
Mulford, Arthur 1924- *St&PR 93*
Mulford, Clarence Edward 1883-1956 *BioIn 17*
Mulford, David Campbell 1937- *WhoAm 92*
Mulford, Philippa Greene 1948- *WhoEmL 93, WhoWrEP 92*
Mulford, Rand P. 1943- *St&PR 93*
Mulford, Robert D. 1942- *St&PR 93*
Mulford, Thomas James 1943- *WhoE 93*
Mulgrew, John 1936- *WhoSSW 93*
Mulgrew, John B. d1991 *BioIn 17*
Mulgrew, Kate 1955- *ConTFT 10*

Mulgrew, Katherine Kiernan 1955- WhoAm 92
Mulhall, Anne Bridget WhoScE 91-1
Mulhall, Jack 1887-1979 BioIn 17
Mulhall, Robert Lee 1920- WhoWrEP 92
Mulhare, Edward 1923- ConTFT 10
Mulhare, Eileen Margaret 1953- WhoE 93, WhoEmL 93
Mulhauser, Karen 1942- WhoE 93
Mulheren, John BioIn 17
Mulherin, Lori Gene M. 1956- WhoEmL 93
Mulhern, Eugene Edward Law&B 92
Mulhern, James Francis Law&B 92
Mulhern, John David 1928- WhoAm 92
Mulhern, Joseph Patrick 1921- WhoAm 92
Mulhern, Kathryn Andersen 1955- WhoAmW 93
Mulhern, Laurence F. 1954- St&PR 93
Mulhollan, Paige Elliott 1934- WhoAm 92
Mulholland, Allan E. 1949- WhoIns 93
Mulholland, Angela Broadway 1957- WhoAm 92
Mulholland, Jack Russell 1929- St&PR 93
Mulholland, John H. (Bert) Law&B 92
Mulholland, Karen 1942- WhoCanL 92
Mulholland, Kenneth Bruce 1937- WhoSSW 93
Mulholland, Kenneth D. 1946- St&PR 93
Mulholland, Kenneth Leo, Jr. 1943- WhoAm 92
Mulholland, Linda F. Law&B 92
Mulholland, Robert Edge 1933- WhoAm 92
Mulholland, S. Grant 1936- WhoAm 92
Mulholland, William D. BioIn 17
Mulholland, William David 1926- St&PR 93
Mulholland, William David, Jr. 1926- WhoAm 92, WhoWor 93
Mulic, Jusuf 1933- WhoScE 91-4
Mulier, Jozef-Cyriel 1922- WhoScE 91-2
Mulino-Betancourt, Freddy Antonio 1934- WhoWor 93
Muliro, Masinde d1992 NewYTBS 92
Mulitz, Lewis 1926- St&PR 93
Mulitz, Milton M. 1918- St&PR 93
Muljana, B.S. 1931- WhoAsAP 91
Muljono, Winar Hartono 1943- WhoWor 93
Mulkerin, John Patrick 1937- St&PR 93
Mulkey, Jack Clarendon 1939- WhoAm 92
Mull, Charles Leroy, II 1927- WhoE 93
Mull, Gary William 1947- St&PR 93
Mull, Martin BioIn 17
Mull, Martin 1943- WhoAm 92
Mull, Pamela Ann Law&B 92
Mull, Rolf 1938- WhoScE 91-3
Mull, Sandra Sue 1943- WhoAmW 93
Mullaley, Robert Charles 1926- WhoAm 92
Mullally, Frederic 1920- ScF&FL 92
Mullally, Robert E. 1933- St&PR 93
Mullan, David Stewart 1935- WhoWor 93
Mullan, James Boyd 1903- WhoAm 92
Mullan, James F. 1939- St&PR 93
Mullan, John Francis 1925- WhoAm 92
Mullan, John H. Law&B 92
Mullan, Lisa Fay 1966- WhoAmW 93
Mullane, Denis Francis 1930- St&PR 93, WhoAm 92, WhoIns 93
Mullane, Donald A. 1938- WhoAm 92
Mullane, John Francis 1937- WhoAm 92
Mullane, Maria Concetta 1953- WhoEmL 93
Mullane, Robert E. 1932- St&PR 93
Mullaney, Dora Aileen 1943- WhoAmW 93
Mullaney, Frank C. 1923- St&PR 93
Mullaney, Joseph E. Law&B 92
Mullaney, Joseph E. 1933- St&PR 93, WhoAm 92
Mullaney, Thomas Law&B 92
Mullaney, Thomas F., Jr. 1939- St&PR 93
Mullaney, Thomas H. 1932- St&PR 93
Mullani, Nizar Abdul 1942- WhoWor 93
Mullany, Brian Robert 1945- St&PR 93
Mullany, David John 1965- St&PR 93
Mullare, T. Kenwood, Jr. 1939- St&PR 93
Mullare, Thomas Kenwood, Jr. 1939- WhoAm 92
Mullarkey, Mary J. 1943- WhoAm 92, WhoAmW 93
Mulle, George Ernest 1919- WhoSSW 93
Mulle, Robert J. 1922- St&PR 93
Mulleedy, Joyce Elaine 1948- WhoAmW 93
Mullen, Andrew Judson 1923- WhoSSW 93, WhoWor 93
Mullen, Brian 1955- WhoE 93
Mullen, Brian Joseph 1959- WhoSSW 93
Mullen, Bruce Diedrich 1962- WhoSSW 93
Mullen, C. Richard 1937- St&PR 93
Mullen, Daniel J. Law&B 92
Mullen, Daniel Robert 1941- St&PR 93, WhoAm 92
Mullen, Danny Walter 1954- WhoE 93
Mullen, David Bruce 1950- St&PR 93
Mullen, Denise Cartier 1952- WhoAmW 93
Mullen, Douglas B. 1940- St&PR 93
Mullen, Douglas T. 1940- St&PR 93
Mullen, Edward John, Jr. 1942- WhoAm 92
Mullen, Eileen Anne 1943- WhoAmW 93, WhoWor 93
Mullen, Eileen Marie 1959- WhoSSW 93
Mullen, Gary L. 1947- WhoEmL 93
Mullen, Graham C. 1940- WhoSSW 93
Mullen, James Gentry 1933- WhoAm 92
Mullen, James J. Law&B 92
Mullen, James N. Law&B 92
Mullen, Jim BioIn 17
Mullen, John 1924-1991 BioIn 17
Mullen, John W. 1947- WhoIns 93
Mullen, Joseph T. NewYTBS 92 [port]
Mullen, Kevin Edward 1955- St&PR 93
Mullen, L. Michael Law&B 92
Mullen, Michael 1937- ConAu 39NR
Mullen, Nancy Lee 1940- WhoAmW 93
Mullen, R.D. 1915- ScF&FL 92
Mullen, Regina Marie 1948- WhoAmW 93, WhoEmL 93
Mullen, Regina Marie 1952- WhoEmL 93
Mullen, Richard Charles 1927- St&PR 93
Mullen, Robert Lee 1948- WhoE 93
Mullen, Robert Lynn 1949- WhoEmL 93
Mullen, Ron 1939- WhoAm 92
Mullen, Roy C. St&PR 93
Mullen, Sanford Allen 1925- WhoAm 92, WhoSSW 93, WhoWor 93
Mullen, Stanley 1911-1974 ScF&FL 92
Mullen, T. David 1927- St&PR 93
Mullen, Thomas W. St&PR 93
Mullen, Victor ScF&FL 92
Mullen, William 1940- St&PR 93
Mullen, William Joseph, III 1937- WhoAm 92
Mullendore, Edward Clinton 1927- St&PR 93
Mullendore, John W. 1934- St&PR 93
Mullendore, Patricia Ann Law&B 92
Mullendore, Richard Harvey 1948- WhoSSW 93
Mullendore, Walter Edward 1940- WhoAm 92, WhoSSW 93
Mullenger, Leonard WhoScE 91-1
Mullenheim-Rechberg, Burkard, Freiherr von 1910- BioIn 17
Mullenix, Kenneth Eugene 1947- WhoEmL 93, WhoSSW 93
Mullenix, Patsy Lorraine Law&B 92
Mullenix, Paul Douglas 1957- WhoEmL 93, WhoSSW 93
Mullenix, Travis H. 1931- WhoAm 92
Mullens, Jules 1944- WhoScE 91-2
Mullens, Priscilla BioIn 17
Mullens, William Reese 1921- WhoAm 92
Muller, Achim 1938- WhoScE 91-3
Muller, Adolf 1801-1886 OxDcOp
Muller, Adolf 1839-1901 OxDcOp
Muller, Adolf, Sr. 1801-1886 Baker 92
Muller, Adolf, Jr. 1839-1901 Baker 92
Muller, Adolphe 1936- WhoScE 91-3
Muller, Alex F. 1921- WhoScE 91-4
Muller, Alexandra Lida 1949- WhoAmW 93
Muller, Alfred 1940- WhoE 93
Muller, Anthony R. St&PR 93
Muller, August Eberhard 1767-1817 Baker 92
Muller, Bernd W. 1943- WhoScE 91-3
Muller, Berndt 1950- WhoScE 91-3
Muller, Bernhard 1825-1895 See Muller Quartet Baker 92
Muller, Bruce M. 1942- St&PR 93
Muller, Carl Anton 1938- St&PR 93
Muller, Carl Richard Law&B 92
Muller, Catherine Marie 1961- WhoEmL 93
Muller, Charles William 1930- WhoE 93
Muller, Charlotte Feldman 1921- WhoAm 92
Muller, Claudya Barbara 1946- WhoAm 92
Muller, Claus 1920- WhoWor 93
Muller, Courtenay David Law&B 92
Muller, Daniel Victor 1943- St&PR 93
Muller, David F. 1948- St&PR 93
Muller, Dietrich Alfred Helmut 1936- WhoAm 92
Muller, Eberhard 1934- WhoScE 91-3
Muller, Edward R. Law&B 92
Muller, Edward Robert 1952- St&PR 93, WhoAm 92, WhoEmL 93
Muller, Elsie Ferrar 1913- WhoAmW 93
Muller, Emil 1920- WhoScE 91-4
Muller, Emile 1915-1988 BioIn 17
Muller, Ernest H. 1923- WhoAm 92
Muller, Ernst-August 1925- WhoScE 91-3
Muller, Eugene William 1956- WhoE 93
Muller, Ferdinand 1942- WhoScE 91-4
Muller, Ferdinand A.H. 1923- WhoScE 91-3
Muller, Frank B. 1926- WhoAm 92
Muller, Franz 1932- WhoScE 91-3
Muller, Franz 1934- WhoWor 93
Muller, Fred Paul 1926- WhoWor 93
Muller, Frederick Arthur 1937- WhoE 93
Muller, Friedrich 1749-1825 BioIn 17
Muller, Friedrich 1786-1871 Baker 92
Muller, Fritz WhoScE 91-3
Muller, Georg 1808-1855 See Muller Quartet Baker 92
Muller, George Godfrey 1762-1821 Baker 92
Muller, George T. 1949- St&PR 93
Muller, Georgene K. 1950- WhoWrEP 92
Muller, Gottfried 1914- Baker 92
Muller, Gustav 1799-1855 See Muller Quartet Baker 92
Muller, Hans Rudolf 1941- WhoScE 91-4
Muller, Hansjakob 1941- WhoScE 91-4
Muller, Hansjorg WhoScE 91-4
Muller, Heidy Margrit 1952- WhoWor 93
Muller, Heiner 1929- BioIn 17, DcLB 124 [port]
Muller, Heinrich Fidelis 1827-1905 Baker 92
Muller, Heinz Jurgen 1957- WhoWor 93
Muller, Henry James 1947- WhoAm 92, WhoE 93
Muller, Henry John 1919- WhoAm 92
Muller, Henry Nicholas, III 1938- WhoAm 92
Muller, Herbert 1926- WhoScE 91-3
Muller, Horst 1929- WhoScE 91-3, WhoWor 93
Muller, Hugo 1832-1886 See Muller Quartet Baker 92
Muller, Iwan 1786-1854 Baker 92
Muller, Jans 1930- WhoAm 92
Muller, Jean 1929- WhoScE 91-4
Muller, Jean-Charles 1930- WhoScE 91-2
Muller, Jennifer 1944- WhoAm 92
Muller, Jerome Kenneth 1934- WhoWor 93
Muller, Joachim W. ConAu 139
Muller, Johann 1436-1476 BioIn 17
Muller, John ScF&FL 92
Muller, John Bartlett 1940- WhoAm 92
Muller, John Henry, Jr. 1924- St&PR 93
Muller, John P. 1940- ScF&FL 92
Muller, Jorg ConAu 136
Muller, Jorg 1942- BioIn 17
Muller, Jorge Ernesto 1943- WhoWor 93
Muller, Jorn 1936- WhoScE 91-3
Muller, Karen Law&B 92
Muller, Karl 1797-1873 See Muller Quartet Baker 92
Muller, Karl 1829-1907 See Muller Quartet Baker 92
Muller, Karl Alexander 1927- WhoAm 92, WhoWor 93
Muller, Kelli BioIn 17
Muller, Kimbley L. Law&B 92
Muller, Klaus Jurgen 1923- WhoScE 91-3
Muller, Kurt 1934- WhoScE 91-4
Muller, Kurt Alexander 1955- WhoEmL 93
Muller, Manfred Wolfgang 1936- WhoWor 93
Muller, Marcel Wettstein 1922- WhoAm 92
Muller, Marcia 1944- ScF&FL 92
Muller, Margie H. 1927- WhoAmW 93
Muller, Maria 1898-1958 Baker 92, OxDcOp
Muller, Mervin Edgar 1928- WhoAm 92
Muller, Michael M.S. 1951- WhoScE 91-4
Muller, Miklos 1930- WhoE 93
Muller, Nicholas Guthrie 1942- WhoAm 92
Muller, Otto 1874-1930 BioIn 17
Muller, Otto 1905- BioIn 17
Muller, Pal 1932- WhoScE 91-4
Muller, Patricia Ann 1943- WhoAmW 93, WhoSSW 93
Muller, Patricia Olga 1948- WhoSSW 93
Muller, Paul ScF&FL 92
Muller, Paul 1939- WhoScE 91-4, WhoWor 93
Muller, Paul F. 1915- St&PR 93
Muller, Peter 1791-1877 Baker 92
Muller, Peter 1920 St&PR 93
Muller, Peter 1947- St&PR 93, WhoAm 92
Muller, R.L.J. WhoScE 91-1
Muller, Ralph Louis WhoScE 91-1
Muller, Reid Thomas 1960- WhoE 93
Muller, Richard 1945- WhoScE 91-2
Muller, Richard August 1944- WhoAm 92
Muller, Richard Stephen 1933- WhoAm 92
Muller, Robert 1920- BioIn 17
Muller, Robert 1925- ScF&FL 92
Muller, Robert H. 1949- WhoAm 92
Muller, Robert J. 1946- St&PR 93
Muller, Robert Joseph 1946- WhoSSW 93
Muller, Robert K. 1925- WhoScE 91-3
Muller, Robin Lester 1953- WhoCanL 92
Muller, Ronald H. 1946- St&PR 93
Muller, Rudolf 1944- WhoScE 91-4
Muller, Sidney B., Jr. Law&B 92
Muller, Sigfrid Augustine 1930- WhoAm 92
Muller, Sigfrid Walther 1905-1946 Baker 92
Muller, Stephen Anthony 1933- St&PR 93
Muller, Steven 1927- WhoWor 93
Muller, Theodor 1802-1875 See Muller Quartet Baker 92
Muller, Ulrich 1940- WhoScE 91-3
Muller, Virginia A. St&PR 93
Muller, Virginia Lewis 1949- WhoAmW 93
Muller, Vlastimil WhoScE 91-4
Muller, W. WhoScE 91-2
Muller, Warren 1939- St&PR 93
Muller, Wenzel 1767-1835 Baker 92, OxDcOp
Muller, Werner E.G. 1942- WhoScE 91-3
Muller, Wilhelm 1794-1827 BioIn 17
Muller, Wilhelm 1834-1897 See Muller Quartet Baker 92
Muller, Willard Chester 1916- WhoAm 92
Muller, William Albert, III 1943- WhoSSW 93
Muller, William G. Law&B 92
Muller, William Henry, Jr. 1919- WhoAm 92
Muller, William S. Law&B 92
Muller, Wolfgang 1940- WhoScE 91-3
Muller-Berghaus, Gert 1937- WhoScE 91-3
Muller-Blattau, Joseph (Maria) 1895-1976 Baker 92
Muller-Broich, Adolf 1927- WhoScE 91-3
Muller-Buschbaum, Hanskarl 1931- WhoScE 91-3
Muller-Eberhard, Hans Joachim 1927- WhoAm 92, WhoWor 93
Muller-Graff, Peter Christian 1945- WhoWor 93
Muller-Hartmann, Erwin 1941- WhoScE 91-3
Muller-Hartmann, Robert 1884-1950 Baker 92
Muller-Haye, B. WhoScE 91-3
Muller-Haye, Berndt 1935- WhoUN 92
Muller-Hermann, Johanna 1878-1941 Baker 92
Muller-Hohenstein, Klaus 1936- WhoScE 91-3
Muller-Isberner, Joachim Rudiger 1952- WhoWor 93
Muller-Kray, Hans 1908-1969 Baker 92
Muller-Kunast, Hendrik BioIn 17
Muller-Merbach, Heiner 1936- WhoScE 91-3
Muller-Mohnssen, Helmuth K.E. 1928- WhoScE 91-3
Muller-Ortega, Paul Eduardo 1949- WhoEmL 93
Muller Quartet Baker 92
Muller-Reuter, Theodor 1858-1919 Baker 92
Muller-Ruchholtz, Wolfgang 1928- WhoScE 91-3
Muller von Kulm, Walter 1899-1967 Baker 92
Muller-Warmuth, Werner Rudolf 1929- WhoScE 91-3
Mullery, Robert Richard Law&B 92
Muller-Zurich, Paul 1898- Baker 92
Mullestein, William Ernest 1911- WhoAm 92
Mullett, Charles Samuel 1931- St&PR 93
Mullett, Heather M. Law&B 92
Mullett, Lisa BioIn 17
Mullett, Steve BioIn 17
Mullette, Julienne 1940- WhoWrEP 92
Mullette, Julienne Patricia 1940- WhoAmW 93, WhoE 93
Mullican, Carl Denver 1961- WhoSSW 93
Mullick, Mohammad Afzal 1934- WhoUN 92
Mulligan, Andrew Phillip 1927- WhoSSW 93
Mulligan, Deanna Marie 1963- WhoAmW 93
Mulligan, Dee A. 1946- WhoAmW 93
Mulligan, Edward W. 1925- St&PR 93
Mulligan, Elinor Patterson 1929- WhoWor 93
Mulligan, Gerald Joseph 1927- WhoAm 92
Mulligan, Gerald T. 1945- St&PR 93
Mulligan, Gerry BioIn 17
Mulligan, Gerry 1927- Baker 92
Mulligan, Gregory John Law&B 92
Mulligan, Hugh Augustine 1925- WhoAm 92
Mulligan, James Francis 1925- WhoAm 92
Mulligan, James J. 1921- St&PR 93
Mulligan, James Kenneth 1911- WhoAm 92
Mulligan, John L. WhoAm 92
Mulligan, John Mosher d1991 BioIn 17
Mulligan, Joseph Francis 1920- WhoAm 92

Mulligan, Martin Frederick 1940- *WhoAm 92*
Mulligan, Michael Dennis 1947- *WhoAm 92*
Mulligan, Mollie *BioIn 17*
Mulligan, Richard *BioIn 17*
Mulligan, Richard M. 1932- *WhoAm 92*
Mulligan, Robert 1925- *ConTFT 10, MiSFD 9*
Mulligan, Robert Francis, Jr. 1961- *WhoE 93*
Mulligan, Robert J. 1938- *St&PR 93, WhoAm 92*
Mulligan, Robert Patrick *WhoAm 92*
Mulligan, Robert Peter 1924- *St&PR 93*
Mulligan, Robert William 1916- *WhoAm 92*
Mulligan, Stephen Edward *Law&B 92*
Mulligan, Steven Thomas *Law&B 92*
Mulligan, Susan Amrhein 1943- *St&PR 93*
Mulligan, Thomas J. 1933- *St&PR 93*
Mulligan, William G. 1906-1991 *BioIn 17*
Mulligan, William G. 1930- *St&PR 93*
Mulligan, William Goeckel 1930- *WhoAm 92*
Mulligan, William Hughes 1918- *WhoAm 92*
Mulligan, William P. 1943- *St&PR 93*
Mulliken, William D. 1939- *St&PR 93*
Mullikin, Harry Copeland 1940- *WhoAm 92*
Mullikin, Thomas Wilson 1928- *WhoAm 92*
Mullikin, Vernon Eugene 1935- *WhoAm 92*
Mullin, Albert Edward, Jr. 1933- *St&PR 93, WhoAm 92*
Mullin, Chris 1947- *ScF&FL 92*
Mullin, Christopher Paul 1963- *BiDAMSp 1989, WhoAm 92*
Mullin, Constance Hammond 1939- *WhoAmW 93*
Mullin, Dennis Alan 1948- *WhoAm 92*
Mullin, J. *WhoScE 91-3*
Mullin, J. Shan 1934- *WhoAm 92*
Mullin, James A. 1946- *WhoAm 92*
Mullin, James P. *Law&B 92*
Mullin, Jeanne *BioIn 17*
Mullin, Jerome Patrick 1933- *WhoAm 92*
Mullin, John Frederick 1940- *St&PR 93*
Mullin, John Hatchman, III 1941- *St&PR 93*
Mullin, John Stanley 1907- *St&PR 93*
Mullin, John William *WhoScE 91-1*
Mullin, John William 1925- *WhoWor 93*
Mullin, Leo F. 1943- *St&PR 93*
Mullin, Leo Francis 1943- *WhoAm 92*
Mullin, Mark *MiSFD 9*
Mullin, Mary A. *Law&B 92*
Mullin, Mary Regina *Law&B 92*
Mullin, Patricia E. *WhoIns 93*
Mullin, Patricia Evelyn *Law&B 92, St&PR 93*
Mullin, Richard J. 1951- *St&PR 93*
Mullin, Sherman N. *BioIn 17*
Mullin, Sherman Neil 1935- *St&PR 93*
Mullin, Sue 1943- *WhoSSW 93*
Mullin, William Francis 1921- *WhoSSW 93*
Mullinax, Harvey Owen 1913- *St&PR 93*
Mullinax, Otto B. 1912- *WhoAm 92*
Mullinax-Jones, Anne Elise 1932- *WhoAmW 93*
Mullineaux, Donal Ray 1925- *WhoAm 92*
Mullineaux, Jewel E. 1917- *WhoAmW 93*
Mulliner, Roberta *BioIn 17*
Mullineux, Andrew William *WhoScE 91-1*
Mullinger, Ann Margaret *WhoScE 91-1*
Mullings, Frank 1881-1953 *OxDcOp*
Mullings, Frank (Coningsby) 1881-1953 *Baker 92*
Mullinix, Edward W., Jr. 1953- *St&PR 93*
Mullinix, Edward Wingate 1924- *WhoAm 92, WhoE 93*
Mullinix, Joseph Philip 1942- *WhoE 93*
Mullinix, Kathleen Patricia 1944- *WhoAmW 93*
Mullinix, Randy LeRoy 1956- *WhoSSW 93*
Mullins, Betty Johnson 1925- *WhoAmW 93*
Mullins, Betty Kaye 1942- *WhoE 93*
Mullins, Brian C. 1941- *St&PR 93*
Mullins, Carolyn Johns 1940- *WhoWrEP 92*
Mullins, Charles Brown 1934- *WhoAm 92*
Mullins, Chucky *BioIn 17*
Mullins, David R. *St&PR 93*
Mullins, David W. *BioIn 17*
Mullins, Donald Eugene 1944- *WhoSSW 93*
Mullins, Edward Wade, Jr. 1936- *WhoSSW 93, WhoWor 93*
Mullins, Helene 1898-1991 *BioIn 17*
Mullins, Helene 1899- *AmWomPl, WhoWrEP 92*
Mullins, James B. 1934- *WhoIns 93*
Mullins, Jeremiah Andrew 1936- *WhoAm 92*
Mullins, Jim Austin 1942- *St&PR 93*
Mullins, John Thomas 1932- *WhoSSW 93*
Mullins, Judith Nelson 1940- *WhoAmW 93*
Mullins, Kenneth Delbert 1957- *WhoEmL 93*
Mullins, Lorin John 1917- *WhoAm 92*
Mullins, Mary Sue 1954- *WhoSSW 93*
Mullins, N.D. *Law&B 92*
Mullins, Nancy Claire 1946- *WhoEmL 93*
Mullins, Obera 1927- *WhoAmW 93*
Mullins, Peggy *Law&B 92*
Mullins, Philip Aldon, III 1940- *St&PR 93*
Mullins, Richard Austin 1918- *WhoWor 93*
Mullins, Robin Hassler 1953- *WhoEmL 93*
Mullins, Ronald Gift 1938- *WhoWrEP 92*
Mullins, Theodore C. 1932- *St&PR 93*
Mullins, Wayman C. 1951- *WhoEmL 93, WhoSSW 93*
Mullins, Wayne E. *Law&B 92*
Mullins, William B. d1990 *BioIn 17*
Mullins-Gopp, Wendy Jo 1968- *WhoAmW 93*
Mullis, Brent Barker 1942- *St&PR 93*
Mullis, Kary B. *BioIn 17*
Mullis, Kary Banks 1944- *WhoAm 92*
Mullis, Perry E. 1933- *St&PR 93*
Mullis, Ronald Lynn 1942- *WhoSSW 93*
Mulloney, Peter Black 1932- *St&PR 93, WhoAm 92*
Mullova, Viktoria 1959- *Baker 92*
Mulloy, Eric Everett *Law&B 92*
Mulloy, Fergal 1933- *WhoScE 91-3*
Mulloy, Gardnar Putnam 1913- *BiDAMSp 1989*
Mulloy, Lawrence *BioIn 17*
Mulloy, Robert Emmett, Jr. *Law&B 92*
Mullrooney, Michael James *Law&B 92*
Mulock, Dinah Maria *MajAI*
Mulock, Edwin Thomas 1943- *WhoSSW 93*
Mulqueen, John 1935- *WhoScE 91-3*
Mulqueen, Michael Patrick 1938- *WhoAm 92*
Mulready, Thomas James, Jr. 1958- *WhoEmL 93*
Mulreany, Robert Henry 1915- *St&PR 93, WhoAm 92*
Mulreed, Ellen Marie 1963- *WhoE 93*
Mulroney, Brian *BioIn 17*
Mulroney, Brian 1939- *WhoAm 92, WhoE 93, WhoWor 93*
Mulroney, Dermot *BioIn 17*
Mulroney, John Patrick 1935- *St&PR 93, WhoE 93*
Mulroney, Martin Brian 1939- *DcTwHis*
Mulroney, Mila 1953- *WhoAm 92, WhoAmW 93*
Mulrow, Patrick Joseph *WhoAm 92*
Mulroy, Barry Michael 1946- *St&PR 93*
Mulroy, George Alan 1934- *St&PR 93*
Mulroy, James *Law&B 92*
Mulroy, Matthew Patrick *Law&B 92*
Mulroy, Richard Edward, Jr. *Law&B 92*
Mulry, Laura Jane 1958- *WhoAmW 93*
Mulryan, Henry Trist 1927- *WhoAm 92*
Mulryan, Lawrence E. 1937- *St&PR 93*
Mulryan, Patricia Trist 1953- *WhoEmL 93*
Mulryan, Thomas Stephen 1942- *St&PR 93*
Mulshine, Michael A. 1939- *St&PR 93*
Multach, Mark 1956- *WhoSSW 93*
Multack, Dennis G. 1947- *St&PR 93*
Multer, Gerald J. d1991 *BioIn 17*
Mulva, J.J. 1946- *St&PR 93*
Mulvaney, Donald Murphy 1947- *WhoEmL 93*
Mulvaney, James N. *Law&B 92*
Mulvaney, Liam J. 1946- *WhoSSW 93*
Mulvaney, Mary Frederica 1945- *WhoAmW 93, WhoE 93*
Mulvaney, Mary Jean 1927- *WhoAm 92*
Mulvaney, Maureen Gail 1950- *WhoAmW 93*
Mulvaney, Thomas Joseph 1937- *St&PR 93*
Mulvee, Robert D. *Law&B 92*
Mulvee, Robert Edward 1930- *WhoAm 92*
Mulvehill, Barbara Anne 1951- *WhoAmW 93*
Mulveney, William Harold 1936- *St&PR 93*
Mulvey, Christopher John 1946- *WhoWor 93*
Mulvey, Helen Frances 1913- *WhoAmW 93, WhoWor 93*
Mulvey, Margaret Ellen 1952- *WhoEmL 93*
Mulvey, Mary C. 1909- *WhoAmW 93*
Mulvey, Michael 1949- *St&PR 93*
Mulvey, Thomas *ScF&FL 92*
Mulvey, William W. 1916- *WhoE 93*
Mulvihill, David Brian 1956- *WhoEmL 93*
Mulvihill, Edward Robert 1917- *WhoAm 92*
Mulvihill, James E. 1940- *WhoIns 93*
Mulvihill, James Edward 1940- *WhoAm 92*
Mulvihill, John Francis *Law&B 92*
Mulvihill, John Gary 1933- *WhoAm 92*
Mulvihill, John Timothy 1931- *WhoAm 92*
Mulvihill, Peter James 1956- *WhoEmL 93, WhoWor 93*
Mulvihill, Robert *ScF&FL 92*
Mulvihill, Terence Joseph 1931- *WhoAm 92*
Mulvihill, Thomas C. 1946- *St&PR 93*
Mulvoy, Mark *BioIn 17*
Mulvoy, Mark 1942- *WhoAm 92*
Mulvoy, Thomas F., Jr. 1943- *WhoAm 92, WhoE 93*
Mumaw, James Webster 1920- *WhoAm 92*
Mumaw, Kathleen Elizabeth 1952- *WhoAmW 93*
Mumbengegwi, Simbarashe Simbanenduku 1945- *WhoUN 92*
Mumbengegwi, Simbarshe Simbanenduku 1945- *WhoWor 93*
Mumdzhiev, N. *WhoScE 91-4*
Mumert, Tommy Lee 1955- *WhoSSW 93*
Mumford, Carrie H. *Law&B 92*
Mumford, Charles Lee *Law&B 92*
Mumford, Christopher G. 1945- *St&PR 93*
Mumford, Christopher Greene 1945- *WhoAm 92*
Mumford, David Bryant 1937- *WhoAm 92*
Mumford, Enid *WhoScE 91-1*
Mumford, Ethel Watts *AmWomPl*
Mumford, George Saltonstall, Jr. 1928- *WhoAm 92*
Mumford, Lawrence Quincy 1903-1982 *BioIn 17*
Mumford, Lewis 1895-1990 *BioIn 17*
Mumford, Manly Whitman 1925- *WhoAm 92*
Mumford, Michael David 1957- *WhoSSW 93*
Mumford, Sherwood Dean 1952- *WhoEmL 93*
Mumford, Willard Royal 1933- *WhoE 93*
Mumford, William Porter, II 1920- *WhoAm 92*
Mu'min, Dawud *BioIn 17*
Mumma, Albert G. 1906- *WhoAm 92, WhoWor 93*
Mumma, Albert Girard, Jr. 1928- *WhoAm 92*
Mumma, Gordon 1935- *Baker 92, WhoAm 92*
Mumma, Michael Jon 1941- *WhoAm 92*
Mummendey, Amelie Dorothea 1944- *WhoWor 93*
Mummert, Catherine Charlotte 1959- *WhoEmL 93*
Mummert, Frederic H. *Law&B 92*
Mummert, Gregory J. 1950- *St&PR 93*
Mummert, John S. 1949- *St&PR 93*
Mummius Achaicus, Lucius dc. 141BC *HarEnMi*
Mumm Von Mallinckrodt, Friedrich W. 1939- *WhoUN 92*
Mumola, Peter Benedict 1944- *WhoAm 92*
Mumy, Bill *BioIn 17*
Mumy, Billy 1954- *WhoEmL 93*
Mun *MajAI*
Mun, Albert, comte de 1841-1914 *BioIn 17*
Munack, Axel 1949- *WhoScE 91-3*
Munaf, Edison 1958- *WhoWor 93*
Munakata, Megumu 1941- *WhoWor 93*
Munakata, Seiya 1908-1970 *BioIn 17*
Munangagwa, Emmerson Dambudzo 1946- *WhoAfr*
Munari, Bruno 1907- *ConAu 38NR, MajAI [port]*
Munasinghe, Mohan 1945- *WhoE 93*
Muncaster, J.D. 1933- *St&PR 93*
Muncey, Barbara Deane 1952- *WhoAmW 93, WhoEmL 93*
Muncey, James Arthur, Jr. 1933- *WhoSSW 93*
Munch, Charles 1891-1968 *Baker 92*
Munch, D. Jean 1932- *WhoAmW 93*
Munch, David Edward 1948- *WhoAm 92*
Munch, Douglas Francis 1947- *WhoAm 92*
Munch, Edvard 1863-1944 *BioIn 17*
Munch, Ernst 1859-1928 *Baker 92*
Munch, Guido 1921- *WhoScE 91-3*
Munch, Hans 1893-1983 *Baker 92*
Munch, Jennifer Clise 1947- *WhoEmL 93*
Munch, Roxanne Frances 1947- *WhoAmW 93*
Munchak, Theodore J. *St&PR 93*
Munchinger, Karl 1915-1990 *Baker 92*
Munck, Allan Ulf 1925- *WhoAm 92*
Munck, Lars *WhoScE 91-2*
Munclinger, Milan 1923-1986 *Baker 92*
Muncy, Chris *BioIn 17*
Muncy, Martha Elizabeth 1919- *WhoAmW 93*
Muncy, Raymond Lee 1928- *WhoAm 92*
Mund, Geraldine 1943- *WhoAmW 93*
Mund, Richard Gordon 1942- *WhoAm 92*
Mundadan, Anthony Mathias 1923- *WhoWor 93*
Munday, Howard E. 1946- *St&PR 93*
Mundel, Marvin Everett 1916- *WhoAm 92*
Mundell, D.E. 1931- *St&PR 93*
Mundell, David Edward 1931- *WhoAm 92*
Mundell, Douglas *Law&B 92*
Mundell, Robert David 1936- *WhoAm 92*
Mundell, W. Jed 1950- *St&PR 93*
Mundell, William Andrew 1960- *WhoAm 92*
Munder, Barbara Ann 1945- *St&PR 93*
Munderloh, Royce M. 1935- *St&PR 93*
Mundheim, Robert Harry 1933- *WhoAm 92*
Mundhir, Al- *OxDcByz*
Mundhra, Jag 1948- *MiSFD 9*
Mundici, Daniele 1946- *WhoWor 93*
Mundie, Craig J. 1949- *St&PR 93*
Mundinger, Donald Charles 1929- *WhoAm 92*
Mundinger, William David 1941- *St&PR 93*
Mundis, Jerrold J. 1941- *ScF&FL 92*
Mundlak, Yair 1927- *WhoAm 92*
Mundo, April Jean 1951- *WhoAmW 93*
Mundorf, Nancy Kay 1947- *WhoAmW 93*
Mundorff Shrestha, Sheila Ann 1945- *WhoAmW 93, WhoWor 93*
Mundra, Anand Damodardas 1946- *WhoEmL 93*
Mundschau, Michael Victor 1955- *WhoWor 93*
Mundschau, Walter 1935- *St&PR 93*
Mundt, Barry Maynard 1936- *WhoAm 92*
Mundt, Gerald D. 1936- *St&PR 93, WhoIns 93*
Mundt, Randolph P. 1950- *St&PR 93*
Mundt, Ray B. 1928- *St&PR 93, WhoAm 92*
Mundt, Robert John 1938- *WhoSSW 93*
Mundt, Wolfgang 1935- *WhoScE 91-3*
Mundus d536 *HarEnMi*
Mundy, Carl Epting, Jr. 1935- *WhoE 93*
Mundy, E.J. *WhoScE 91-1*
Mundy, Elmer F. 1933- *St&PR 93*
Mundy, Gardner M. *Law&B 92*
Mundy, Gardner M. 1941- *St&PR 93*
Mundy, Jean 1930- *WhoE 93*
Mundy, John Francis 1946- *St&PR 93*
Mundy, John Hine 1917- *WhoAm 92*
Mundy, Simon 1954- *BioIn 17*
Mundy, Talbot 1879-1940 *ScF&FL 92*
Mundy, William G. *Law&B 92*
Mundy, William G. 1950- *St&PR 93*
Mundy, William Greg 1950- *WhoAm 92*
Mune, Ian 1941- *MiSFD 9*
Munemori, Sadao S. d1945 *BioIn 17*
Munera, Gerard Emmanuel 1935- *WhoAm 92, WhoWor 93*
Munford, Dillard 1918- *WhoAm 92*
Munford, John Durburrow 1928- *St&PR 93, WhoAm 92*
Munford, William Arthur *BioIn 17*
Mungall, Thomas Gordon, III 1954- *WhoEmL 93*
Munger, Bryce L. 1933- *WhoAm 92*
Munger, Carabel Lewis *AmWomPl*
Munger, Charles T. 1924- *WhoAm 92*
Munger, Charles Thomas 1924- *St&PR 93*
Munger, Edwin Stanton 1921- *WhoAm 92, WhoWor 93*
Munger, Elmer Lewis 1915- *WhoAm 92, WhoWor 93*
Munger, Harold Charles 1929- *WhoAm 92, WhoWor 93*
Munger, Harold Hawley, II 1947- *WhoEmL 93*
Munger, James Guy 1951- *WhoEmL 93, WhoSSW 93*
Munger, Judy Powell 1943- *WhoSSW 93*
Munger, Kathy Dies 1947- *WhoSSW 93*
Munger, Mary Virginia 1918- *WhoAmW 93*
Munger, Nicholas E. 1949- *St&PR 93*
Munger, Sharon *WhoAmW 93*
Munger, Sharon M. *BioIn 17*
Munger, Sharon M. 1946- *St&PR 93*
Munger, Theodore Thornton 1830-1910 *BioIn 17*
Munger, Thomas J. *Law&B 92*
Mungia, Sal Alejo, Jr. 1959- *WhoEmL 93*
Mungin, Horace *BioIn 17*
Mungin, Horace L. 1941- *WhoWrEP 92*
Mungo, M. Stewart 1952- *WhoAm 92*
Mungo, Michael J. 1928- *WhoAm 92*
Mungo, Raymond 1946- *ConLC 72*
Munhall, Edgar 1933- *WhoAm 92*

Munhollon, Samuel Clifford 1948- *WhoEmL 93, WhoSSW 93*
Muni, Paul 1895-1967 *BioIn 17, IntDcF 2-3 [port]*
Munich, Adrienne Auslander 1939- *WhoE 93*
Munich, Maritza *Law&B 92*
Munier, Robert S.C. 1953- *St&PR 93*
Munier, Ronald Alan 1933- *St&PR 93*
Munier, William Boss 1942- *WhoE 93*
Muniruzzaman, Mohammed 1948- *WhoWor 93*
Munisteri, Joseph George 1930- *WhoAm 92*
Munitz, Albert R. 1929- *St&PR 93*
Munitz, Barry 1941- *WhoAm 92*
Munitz, Milton Karl 1913- *WhoE 93*
Munizzi, Pam 1954- *WhoAmW 93*
Munk, Andrzej 1921-1961 *DrEEuF, PolBiDi*
Munk, Klaus 1922- *WhoScE 91-3*
Munk, Max Nosson 1942- *St&PR 93*
Munk, Peter *BioIn 17*
Munk, Peter 1927- *St&PR 93, WhoAm 92, WhoWor 93*
Munk, Walter Heinrich 1917- *WhoAm 92*
Munk, Zev Moshe 1950- *WhoSSW 93*
Munkacsi, Bernat 1860-1937 *IntDcAn*
Mun Keong, Tang Peter 1954- *WhoWor 93*
Munker, Dona 1945- *ConAu 138*
Munkholm, Hans J. 1940- *WhoScE 91-2*
Munkirs, Michelle Ann 1963- *WhoAmW 93*
Munko, Andrzej Stanislaw 1943- *WhoWor 93*
Munn, Bruce W. 1911?-1991 *BioIn 17*
Munn, Cecil E. 1923- *St&PR 93*
Munn, Cecil Edwin 1923- *WhoAm 92*
Munn, David Alfred 1954- *WhoEmL 93*
Munn, Debra Dee 1953- *WhoWrEP 92*
Munn, Edward Thomas 1933- *St&PR 93*
Munn, George D. 1926- *St&PR 93*
Munn, H. Warner 1903-1981 *ScF&FL 92*
Munn, Jacob 1951- *St&PR 93, WhoE 93*
Munn, James T. *St&PR 93*
Munn, Katherine Tracy 1959- *WhoE 93*
Munn, Richard Thomas 1967- *WhoE 93*
Munn, Robert William *WhoScE 91-1*
Munn, Stephen P. 1942- *St&PR 93*
Munna, John Charles 1934- *WhoSSW 93*
Munna, Raymond Joseph *Law&B 92*
Munneke, Russell Edward 1946- *WhoEmL 93*
Munnell, Alicia Haydock 1942- *WhoAm 92, WhoAmW 93*
Munnich, Richard 1877-1970 *Baker 92*
Munnikhuis, Bert H. 1952- *St&PR 93*
Munnis, Joseph W. 1925- *St&PR 93*
Munns, E.D. 1952- *St&PR 93*
Munns, Earle D. *Law&B 92*
Muno, Jean 1924-1988 *ScF&FL 92*
Munonye, John 1929- *DcLB 117 [port]*
Munoz, Adolfo Homero 1945- *St&PR 93*
Munoz, Anthony *BioIn 17*
Munoz, Anthony 1958- *HispAmA [port]*
Munoz, Carlos, Jr. 1939- *WhoWrEP 92*
Munoz, Carlos Ramon 1935- *St&PR 93, WhoAm 92, WhoE 93*
Munoz, Deborah Lynn 1956- *WhoEmL 93*
Munoz, Eduardo Manuel 1943- *WhoWor 93*
Munoz, Hector Jose 1967- *WhoE 93*
Munoz, Ines Mendoza de d1990 *BioIn 17*
Munoz, John Joaquin 1918- *WhoAm 92*
Munoz, Jose E., Jr. 1946- *St&PR 93*
Munoz, Jose Gayondatu, Jr. 1938- *WhoWor 93*
Munoz, Kenneth W. *Law&B 92*
Munoz, Mario Alejandro 1928- *WhoWor 93*
Munoz, Michael Anthony 1958- *WhoAm 92*
Munoz, Nubia 1940- *WhoScE 91-2*
Munoz, Paul Anthony 1948- *WhoEmL 93*
Munoz, Rafael Felipe 1899-1972 *DcMexL*
Munoz, Steven Michael 1952- *WhoEmL 93, WhoSSW 93*
Munoz Ledo, Porfirio *DcCPCAm*
Munoz Marin, Luis 1898-1980 *DcCPCAm, DcTwHis*
Munoz-Rivera, Manuelita *Law&B 92*
Munoz Ruiz, Emilio 1937- *WhoScE 91-3*
Munoz-Silva, Carmen *Law&B 92*
Munoz-Sola, Haydee S. 1943- *WhoAmW 93*
Munro, Alex W. *Law&B 92*
Munro, Alice *BioIn 17*
Munro, Alice 1931- *IntLitE, MagSWL [port], WhoAm 92, WhoAmW 93, WhoCanL 92, WhoWrEP 92*
Munro, Brent William *Law&B 92*
Munro, C. Lynn 1949- *WhoEmL 93*
Munro, Caroline 1952?- *BioIn 17*
Munro, Cristina Stirling 1940- *WhoAmW 93*
Munro, D.N. *WhoScE 91-1*
Munro, Dana Gardner 1892-1990 *BioIn 17*
Munro, Donald Jacques 1931- *WhoAm 92*
Munro, Douglas A. 1919-1942 *BioIn 17*
Munro, Elizabeth Bennett 1919- *WhoE 93*
Munro, H.H. 1870-1916 *BioIn 17*
Munro, Hamish Nisbet 1915- *WhoAm 92, WhoE 93*
Munro, Hedi 1916- *WhoAmW 93*
Munro, Helen Waite *AmWomPl*
Munro, Ian H. *WhoScE 91-1*
Munro, J. Richard 1931- *WhoAm 92*
Munro, Jane 1943- *WhoCanL 92*
Munro, John 1849-1930 *ScF&FL 92*
Munro, John A. 1948- *St&PR 93*
Munro, John Henry Alexander 1938- *WhoAm 92*
Munro, Joseph Barnes, Jr. 1930- *WhoE 93, WhoWor 93*
Munro, K.D. *Law&B 92*
Munro, K. Douglas 1933- *St&PR 93*
Munro, Laura B. *Law&B 92*
Munro, Marianne Emig *Law&B 92*
Munro, Martha 1947- *WhoEmL 93*
Munro, Neil *WhoScE 91-1*
Munro, R.J. 1942- *St&PR 93*
Munro, Ralph Davies 1943- *WhoAm 92*
Munro, Rob J.S. 1946- *WhoAsAP 91*
Munro, Robert C. 1932- *St&PR 93*
Munro, Robert John Sutherland 1946- *WhoWor 93*
Munro, Rona 1959- *ScF&FL 92*
Munro, Roxie *ChlBIID [port]*
Munro, Sanford Sterling, Jr. 1932- *WhoAm 92*
Munro, William G. 1926- *St&PR 93*
Munroe, Donna Buxton 1954- *WhoAmW 93*
Munroe, Donna Scott 1945- *WhoAmW 93*
Munroe, George B. 1922- *St&PR 93*
Munroe, George Barber 1922- *WhoAm 92*
Munroe, John MacGregor 1931- *WhoSSW 93*
Munroe, Lorne *WhoAm 92*
Munroe, M. Keith d1991 *BioIn 17*
Munroe, Mary Lou Schwarz 1927- *WhoAmW 93*
Munroe, Pat 1916- *WhoAm 92*
Munroe, Shirley Ann 1924- *WhoAmW 93*
Munroe, Thomas E. 1937- *St&PR 93*
Munroe, Trevor 1944- *DcCPCAm*
Munrow, David (John) 1942-1976 *Baker 92*
Muns Albuixech, Joaquim 1935- *WhoWor 93*
Munsat, Stanley Morris 1939- *WhoAm 92, WhoWrEP 92*
Munsat, Theodore L. 1930- *WhoAm 92*
Munsch, John L. *Law&B 92*
Munsch, Kenneth Michael 1947- *WhoEmL 93*
Munsch, Richard J. *Law&B 92*
Munsch, Robert 1945- *WhoCanL 92*
Munsch, Robert (Norman) 1945- *ConAu 37NR, MajAI [port]*
Munschauer, Frederick E., Jr. 1920- *St&PR 93*
Munschauer, John Lathrop 1919- *WhoE 93*
Munse, Scott Robert 1951- *WhoEmL 93*
Munsel, Patrice (Beverly) 1925- *Baker 92*
Munsell, Elsie Louise 1939- *WhoAm 92*
Munsell, Everett William 1925- *St&PR 93*
Munsell, Lelia *AmWomPl*
Munsell, Monroe Wallwork 1925- *WhoE 93*
Munsey, Frank A. 1854-1925 *BioIn 17, GayN, JrnUS*
Munsey, Virdell Everard, Jr. 1933- *WhoAm 92*
Munshaw, Nancy Clare 1947- *WhoEmL 93*
Munshi, Sushil G. 1939- *WhoAm 92*
Munshi, Sushil Gajendrari 1939- *St&PR 93*
Munson, Arnold *Law&B 92*
Munson, Brad *ScF&FL 92*
Munson, Carl J., Jr. *Law&B 92*
Munson, Claudette *BioIn 17*
Munson, Dee *BioIn 17*
Munson, Edwin Palmer 1935- *St&PR 93*
Munson, H. Carl 1930- *St&PR 93*
Munson, Harold Lewis 1923- *WhoAm 92*
Munson, Henry Lee d1991 *BioIn 17*
Munson, Henry (Lee), Jr. 1946- *ConAu 40NR*
Munson, Howard G. 1924- *WhoAm 92, WhoE 93*
Munson, Jeanne Anne *WhoAmW 93*
Munson, John Backus 1933- *WhoAm 92, WhoWor 93*
Munson, John Christian 1926- *WhoAm 92*
Munson, Joseph S. *Law&B 92*
Munson, Lawrence Shipley 1920- *WhoAm 92*
Munson, Lucille Marguerite 1914- *WhoAmW 93*
Munson, Nancy Kay 1936- *WhoAmW 93, WhoE 93*
Munson, Paul Lewis 1910- *WhoAm 92*
Munson, Rich A. *Law&B 92*
Munson, Richard Howard 1948- *WhoEmL 93*
Munson, Ronald Duane 1943- *WhoE 93*
Munson, Thurman Lee 1947-1979 *BiDAMSp 1989*
Munson, Virginia Aldrich 1932- *WhoWor 93*
Munson, William Leslie 1941- *WhoAm 92*
Munster, Andrew Michael 1935- *WhoE 93*
Munster, Bill 1947- *ScF&FL 92*
Munster, Mary Catherine 1966- *WhoE 93*
Munsterberg, Hugo 1916- *WhoWrEP 92*
Munsterteiger, Kay Diane 1956- *WhoEmL 93*
Munt, Donna S. 1950- *WhoIns 93*
Munt, Jane Ann 1956- *WhoE 93*
Muntasser, Bashir 1932- *WhoUN 92*
Munteanu, Francisc 1924- *DrEEuF*
Munteanu, Ioan 1923- *WhoScE 91-4*
Munter, Gabriele 1877-1962 *BioIn 17*
Munthe, Gert Wilhelm 1957- *WhoWor 93*
Muntjewerf, Alexander K. 1940- *WhoScE 91-3*
Munton, Richard John Cyril *WhoScE 91-1*
Muntoni, Sergio 1925- *WhoWor 93*
Muntz, Eric Phillip 1934- *WhoAm 92*
Muntz, Ernest Gordon 1923- *WhoAm 92*
Muntzer, Thomas c. 1490-1525 *BioIn 17*
Muntzing, Lewis Manning 1934- *WhoAm 92*
Munube, Germano Mashorogoto Rwakakindo 1936- *WhoUN 92*
Munves, David W. 1955- *St&PR 93*
Munyon, Wendy N. *Law&B 92*
Munz, Ann Carol 1956- *WhoSSW 93*
Munz, Mieczyslaw 1900-1976 *Baker 92*
Munzenrider, Robert Emmett 1945- *St&PR 93*
Munzer, Cynthia Brown 1948- *WhoAm 92*
Munzer, Jean Gruen 1934- *WhoE 93*
Munzer, Robert A. 1942- *St&PR 93*
Munzer, Stephen R. 1944- *WhoAm 92*
Munzer, Thomas c. 1490-1525 *BioIn 17*
Munzner, Robert Frederick 1936- *WhoE 93*
Munzur, Mehmet 1946- *WhoScE 91-4*
Muorie, Ida Rosemary 1950- *WhoEmL 93*
Mupo, Angelo 1944- *St&PR 93*
Mu Qizhong *NewYTBS 92 [port]*
Mur, Raphael 1927- *WhoAm 92*
Mura, David *BioIn 17*
Mura, David (Alan) 1952- *ConAu 138*
Mura, Karen Elizabeth 1956- *WhoAmW 93*
Mura, Toshio 1925- *WhoAm 92*
Murabito, Stephen Joseph 1956- *WhoE 93*
Muracco, Louis J. 1939- *St&PR 93*
Murad, I 1326?-1389 *OxDcByz*
Murad, II 1404-1451 *OxDcByz*
Murad, Ferid 1936- *WhoAm 92*
Murad, John Louis 1932- *WhoAm 92*
Murad, Thierry Joseph Lee 1960- *WhoEmL 93*
Muradeli, Vano (Ilyich) 1908-1970 *Baker 92*
Muradian, Vazgen 1921- *WhoAm 92*
Murado, M. Anxel *WhoScE 91-3*
Murahashi, Shun-ichi 1937- *WhoWor 93*
Murai, Jin 1937- *WhoAsAP 91*
Murai, Norimoto 1944- *WhoSSW 93*
Murai, Seiji 1953- *WhoWor 93*
Murai, Shinji 1938- *WhoWor 93*
Murai, Toshiaki 1957- *WhoWor 93*
Murakami, Edahiko 1922- *WhoWor 93*
Murakami, Frank Hachiro 1937- *WhoAm 92*
Murakami, Glenn Nobuki 1953- *St&PR 93*
Murakami, Haruki 1949- *BioIn 17, ScF&FL 92*
Murakami, Jimmy T. *MiSFD 9*
Murakami, Masakuni 1932- *WhoAsAP 91*
Murakami, Seiichiro 1952- *WhoAsAP 91*
Murakami, Yasuoki 1937- *WhoWor 93*
Murakami, Yukito 1931- *WhoWor 93*
Murakami Kakuichi 1862-1927 *HarEnMi*
Murakawa, Fay *WhoAmW 93*
Muraki, Shigeru 1952- *WhoWor 93*
Murakumo, Ayako 1949- *Baker 92*
Muralt, Alex von 1903-1990 *BioIn 17*
Muramatsu, Hiroshi 1947- *WhoWor 93*
Muramatsu, Ichiro 1928- *WhoWor 93*
Muramatsu, Michio 1940- *WhoWor 93*
Muramatsu, Tsuyoshi 1937- *WhoWor 93*
Muranaka, Hideo 1946- *WhoWor 93*
Muranaka, Ken-ichiro 1958- *WhoWor 93*
Murane, William Edward 1933- *WhoAm 92*
Murano, Minoru 1930- *WhoWor 93*
Murany, Andrew J. 1944- *St&PR 93*
Murao, Kenji 1946- *WhoWor 93*
Muraoka, Kanezo 1931- *WhoAsAP 91*
Murari, Timeri 1941- *ScF&FL 92*
Murarka, Kamal 1946- *WhoAsAP 91*
Muraro, Michelangelo 1913-1991 *BioIn 17*
Muraro, Robert *Law&B 92*
Murasaki Shikibu c. 978-c. 1030 *MagSWL [port]*
Murasaki Shikibu 978?- *BioIn 17*
Murasawa, Maki 1924- *WhoAsAP 91*
Murase, Jiro 1928- *WhoAm 92, WhoWor 93*
Murase, Sachiko 1905- *BioIn 17, NewYTBS 92 [port]*
Murashige, Allen 1946- *WhoE 93*
Muraski, Anthony Augustus 1946- *WhoEmL 93*
Murasky, Thomas F. 1945- *St&PR 93*
Murasugi, Kunio 1929- *WhoAm 92*
Muraszkiewicz, Mieczyslaw 1948- *WhoWor 93*
Murat, Ercan Pertev 1943- *WhoUN 92*
Murat, Jean E. 1934- *WhoScE 91-2*
Murat, Joachim 1767-1815 *HarEnMi*
Murata, Alice Kishiye 1940- *WhoAmW 93*
Murata, Keijiro 1924- *WhoAsAP 91*
Murata, Makoto 1926- *WhoWor 93*
Murata, Mitsuhei 1938- *WhoWor 93*
Murata, Ryohei 1929- *WhoWor 93*
Murata, Seijun 1947- *WhoAsAP 91*
Murata, Tadao 1938- *WhoAm 92*
Murata, Yasuo 1931- *WhoWor 93*
Murata, Yoshitaka 1944- *WhoAsAP 91*
Muratore, Lucien 1876-1954 *Baker 92*
Muratore, Lucien 1878-1954 *OxDcOp*
Muratore, Peter Frederick 1932- *WhoAm 92*
Muratore, Robert 1957- *WhoE 93*
Muratori, Fred 1951- *WhoWrEP 92*
Muratori, Gilbert Raphael 1938- *WhoSSW 93*
Muratori, Raymond J. *Law&B 92*
Muratova, Kira 1934- *DrEEuF*
Muravchik, Joshua 1947- *ConAu 136*
Murav'ev, V.S. *ScF&FL 92*
Muravitsky, Alexei 1948- *WhoWor 93*
Murawinski, Daniel Jude 1949- *WhoE 93*
Murawski, Elisabeth Anna 1936- *WhoAmW 93*
Murawski, Roman 1949- *WhoWor 93*
Murawski, Thomas Frank 1945- *St&PR 93*
Murayama, Kiichi 1921- *WhoAsAP 91*
Murayama, Makio 1912- *WhoAm 92, WhoWor 93*
Murayama, Tatsuo 1915- *WhoAsAP 91*
Murayama, Tomiichi 1924- *WhoAsAP 91*
Muraz, Gilbert Louis 1945- *WhoWor 93*
Murazawa, Tadashi 1940- *WhoWor 93*
Murbach, David Paul 1952- *WhoE 93, WhoEmL 93*
Murcer, Bobby Ray 1946- *BiDAMSp 1989*
Murch, Gary L. *St&PR 93*
Murch, Karl D. 1954- *St&PR 93*
Murch, Luella Annette 1929- *WhoAmW 93*
Murch, Pamela J. *Law&B 92*
Murch, Walter *MiSFD 9*
Murch, Walter Scott 1943- *WhoAm 92*
Murchake, John 1922- *St&PR 93*
Murchie, Edward M. 1947- *St&PR 93*
Murchie, Edward Michael 1947- *WhoEmL 93*
Murchie, Guy 1907- *WhoAm 92*
Murchison, Bradley Duncan *Law&B 92*
Murchison, Bruce K. 1950- *St&PR 93*
Murchison, Clinton Williams 1895-1969 *BioIn 17*
Murchison, David Claudius 1923- *WhoAm 92, WhoE 93, WhoWor 93*
Murchison, David Roderick 1948- *WhoAm 92, WhoEmL 93, WhoWor 93*
Murchison, Laura Edwards 1954- *WhoAmW 93, WhoSSW 93*
Murchison, Loren C. 1898-1979 *BiDAMSp 1989*
Murchison, Myles 1942- *ScF&FL 92*
Murchison, Nola Faye 1929- *WhoAmW 93*
Murchison, Roderick Impey 1792-1871 *BioIn 17*
Murcia Vela, Juan 1947- *WhoScE 91-3*
Murcko, Donald Leroy 1953- *WhoEmL 93*
Murdin, Paul G. 1942- *WhoScE 91-1*
Murdoch, Bernard Constantine 1917- *WhoAm 92, WhoSSW 93*
Murdoch, Britton 1957- *St&PR 93*
Murdoch, Britton Hubbard 1957- *WhoAm 92*
Murdoch, Bruce Thomas 1940- *WhoSSW 93*
Murdoch, David Armor 1942- *WhoE 93, WhoWor 93*
Murdoch, Helen Hembree 1928- *St&PR 93*
Murdoch, Iris *BioIn 17*
Murdoch, Iris 1919- *MagSWL [port], WhoAm 92*

Murdoch, Lawrence Corlies, Jr. 1926- *WhoAm 92*
Murdoch, Martin H. 1946- *WhoE 93*
Murdoch, Mary Charlotte 1864-1916 *BioIn 17*
Murdoch, Richard 1907-1990 *QDrFCA 92 [port]*
Murdoch, Robert John 1946- *WhoAm 92*
Murdoch, Robert W. 1942- *St&PR 93*
Murdoch, Robert Waugh *WhoAm 92*
Murdoch, Robert Waugh 1943- *WhoSSW 93*
Murdoch, Robert Whitten 1937- *WhoE 93, WhoWor 93*
Murdoch, Rupert *BioIn 17*
Murdoch, Rupert 1931- *WhoAm 92, WhoWor 93*
Murdoch, (Keith) Rupert 1931- *DcLB 127 [port]*
Murdoch-Kitt, Norma Hood 1947- *WhoSSW 93*
Murdock, B. Glenn *Law&B 92*
Murdock, Barbara Head 1932- *WhoAmW 93*
Murdock, Charles William 1935- *WhoAm 92*
Murdock, David H. 1923- *St&PR 93, WhoAm 92, WhoWor 93*
Murdock, Douglas William 1950- *WhoEmL 93*
Murdock, Edson K. *St&PR 93*
Murdock, Eugene Converse 1921- *WhoAm 92*
Murdock, George Peter 1897-1985 *IntDcAn*
Murdock, Harold George, Jr. 1935- *St&PR 93*
Murdock, Jay Walter 1947- *WhoEmL 93*
Murdock, John Edgar, III 1947- *WhoEmL 93*
Murdock, John M. *Law&B 92*
Murdock, Keith Chadwick 1928- *WhoE 93*
Murdock, M.S. 1947- *ScF&FL 92*
Murdock, Mark Leigh *Law&B 92*
Murdock, Mary-Elizabeth 1930- *WhoAm 92*
Murdock, Michele 1942- *WhoAmW 93*
Murdock, Michelle Marie 1959- *WhoAmW 93, WhoEmL 93*
Murdock, Mickey L. 1942- *WhoIns 93*
Murdock, Mickey Lane 1942- *St&PR 93*
Murdock, Moni 1938- *WhoAmW 93*
Murdock, Pamela Ervilla 1940- *WhoAmW 93, WhoWor 93*
Murdock, R.B. 1932- *St&PR 93*
Murdock, Richard D. *St&PR 93*
Murdock, Robert B. *Law&B 92*
Murdock, Robert Mead 1941- *WhoAm 92*
Murdock, Robert Miller 1911- *St&PR 93*
Murdock, Stuart Laird 1926- *St&PR 93, WhoAm 92*
Murdock, Turalu Brady *Law&B 92*
Murdock, Valerie E. 1964- *WhoSSW 93*
Murdock, Wendy Jean 1952- *WhoEmL 93*
Murdock, William John 1942- *WhoE 93*
Murdy, Wayne W. 1944- *St&PR 93*
Murdy, Wayne William 1944- *WhoAm 92*
Murdza, Deanna Carol 1966- *WhoE 93*
Muren, Dennis E. 1946- *WhoAm 92*
Murena, Hector A. 1923-1975 *SpAmA*
Murena, Lucius Licinius fl. 83BC-62BC *HarEnMi*
Murer, Fredi M. *MiSFD 9*
Murer, Heini 1944- *WhoScE 91-4*
Murer, Heini Ullrich Paul 1944- *WhoWor 93*
Muresan, Mircea 1928- *DrEEuF*
Muret, Barbara Ann 1948- *WhoAmW 93, WhoSSW 93*
Murez, Melanie Goodman 1954- *WhoEmL 93*
Murfee, Donald Gilbert, Jr. 1944- *St&PR 93*
Murfet, Ian Campbell 1934- *WhoWor 93*
Murfin, Donald Leon 1943- *WhoAm 92*
Murfin, Jane *AmWomPl*
Murfin, Ross C. 1948- *WhoAm 92*
Murfree, Joshua William, Jr. 1956- *WhoSSW 93*
Murgatroyd, Eric Neal 1950- *WhoEmL 93*
Murger, Henry 1822-1861 *DcLB 119 [port]*
Murgia-Musilek, Grace M. *Law&B 92*
Muri, Anthony Frederick 1948- *WhoEmL 93*
Muriana, Joseph Paul 1953- *WhoE 93*
Murie, Adolph 1899- *BioIn 17*
Murie, James R. 1862-1921 *IntDcAn*
Murie, Margaret E. *BioIn 17*
Muriel, Amador Cruz 1939- *WhoE 93*
Muriel, Miguel Angel 1955- *WhoWor 93*
Muriithi, Ishmael 1929- *BioIn 17*
Murillo, Bartolome Esteban fl. 17th cent.- *DcAmChF 1960*
Murillo, Bartolome Esteban 1617?-1682 *BioIn 17*
Murillo, Gerardo 1875-1964 *DcMexL*
Murillo, Josefa 1860-1898 *DcMexL*
Murillo-Rohde, Ildaura Maria *WhoAm 92*
Murino, Pasquale 1939- *WhoWor 93*
Muris, Johannes de c. 1300-c. 1351 *Baker 92*
Muris, Timothy Joseph 1949- *WhoAm 92*
Murison, Gerald Leonard 1939- *WhoSSW 93*
Murkett, Philip Tillotson 1931- *WhoSSW 93, WhoWor 93*
Murko, Matija 1861-1951 *IntDcAn*
Murkowski, Frank H. 1933- *CngDr 91*
Murkowski, Frank Hughes 1933- *WhoAm 92*
Murley, F.S. 1934- *St&PR 93*
Murlowski, R.L. *St&PR 93*
Murman, Earll M. *WhoAm 92*
Murmann, Peter *WhoScE 91-3*
Murnaghan, Francis Dominic, Jr. 1920- *WhoAm 92, WhoE 93*
Murnane, Frank E. *St&PR 93*
Murnane, George, Jr. d1992 *NewYTBS 92*
Murnane, Gerald 1939- *ScF&FL 92*
Murnane, James A. 1933- *St&PR 93*
Murnane, Thomas George 1926- *WhoAm 92*
Murnau, F.W. 1888-1931 *MiSFD 9N*
Murnin, Bette F. 1918- *WhoAmW 93*
Muro, Bernardo de 1881-1955 *Baker 92*
Muro, Dolores Jimenez y 1848-1925 *BioIn 17*
Muro, James Joseph 1934- *WhoSSW 93*
Muro, Jim *MiSFD 9*
Muro, Michael John 1949- *WhoE 93*
Muro, Roy Alfred 1942- *St&PR 93, WhoAm 92*
Muroff, Gloria 1927- *WhoAmW 93*
Muroff, Lawrence Ross 1942- *WhoAm 92, WhoWor 93*
Murofushi, Takeshi 1925- *WhoWor 93*
Muroga, Saburo 1925- *WhoAm 92*
Murooka, Yoshihiro 1931- *WhoWor 93*
Murov, Kenneth B. 1950- *WhoSSW 93*
Murov, Lazar M. 1918- *St&PR 93*
Muroyama, Paul Michihisa 1950- *WhoE 93, WhoEmL 93*
Murphey, Arthur Gage, Jr. 1927- *WhoAm 92*
Murphey, Elwood 1909- *WhoAm 92*
Murphey, Michael Martin 1945- *ConMus 9 [port]*
Murphey, Murray Griffin 1928- *WhoAm 92*
Murphey, Rhoads 1919- *WhoAm 92*
Murphey, Robert J. 1934- *St&PR 93*
Murphey, Robert Stafford 1921- *St&PR 93, WhoAm 92*
Murphey, Will B. 1928- *WhoIns 93*
Murphey-Corb, Michael *BioIn 17*
Murphree, Gwendolyn Cribbs 1921- *WhoWor 93*
Murphree, Henry Bernard Scott 1927- *WhoAm 92*
Murphree, Jon Tal 1936- *WhoSSW 93*
Murphree, Sharon Ann 1949- *WhoAmW 93*
Murphrey, Andrew Linwood, Jr. 1949- *WhoSSW 93*
Murphy, A.D. *WhoScE 91-1*
Murphy, Alan Gregory, Jr. 1940- *St&PR 93*
Murphy, Albert Thomas 1924- *WhoAm 92*
Murphy, Alvin Leo 1934- *WhoSSW 93*
Murphy, Andrew Phillip, Jr. 1922- *WhoE 93, WhoWor 93*
Murphy, Ann Margaret 1964- *WhoAmW 93*
Murphy, Ann Pleshette *BioIn 17*
Murphy, Anne St. Germaine 1951- *WhoAmW 93*
Murphy, Arthur 1727-1805 *BioIn 17*
Murphy, Arthur Ellery 1948- *WhoSSW 93*
Murphy, Arthur Thomas 1929- *WhoAm 92*
Murphy, Arthur William 1922- *WhoAm 92*
Murphy, Audie *BioIn 17*
Murphy, Audie 1924-1971 *IntDcF 2-3 [port]*
Murphy, Austin de la Salle 1917- *WhoAm 92*
Murphy, Austin J. 1927- *CngDr 91*
Murphy, Austin John 1927- *WhoAm 92, WhoE 93*
Murphy, Austin S. 1917- *St&PR 93*
Murphy, Barbara MacDonald 1927- *WhoE 93*
Murphy, Barry Ames 1938- *WhoAm 92*
Murphy, Barry John 1940- *WhoAm 92*
Murphy, Beatrice M. 1908-1992 *ConAu 137*
Murphy, Benjamin Edward 1942- *WhoAm 92*
Murphy, Betty Jane Southard *WhoAm 92*
Murphy, Beverley Elaine Pearson 1929- *WhoAm 92*
Murphy, Brenda B. *St&PR 93*
Murphy, Brenda Fettig 1942- *WhoAm 92*
Murphy, Brian 1939- *ScF&FL 92*
Murphy, Brian Charles 1948- *WhoEmL 93*
Murphy, Brianne *BioIn 17*
Murphy, Carl L. 1922- *St&PR 93*
Murphy, Caroline Ann 1938- *WhoE 93*
Murphy, Carolyn Fawcett 1939- *WhoUN 92*
Murphy, Carolyn Louise 1944- *WhoIns 93*
Murphy, Caryle *BioIn 17*
Murphy, Caryle Marie 1946- *WhoAm 92, WhoAmW 93, WhoWor 93*
Murphy, Catherine 1946- *WhoAm 92, WhoEmL 93*
Murphy, Catherine C. *St&PR 93*
Murphy, Charles Arnold 1932- *WhoAm 92*
Murphy, Charles D., III 1944- *St&PR 93*
Murphy, Charles F. d1992 *NewYTBS 92*
Murphy, Charles F. 1858-1924 *PolPar*
Murphy, Charles Francis, Jr. 1928- *WhoAm 92*
Murphy, Charles H. 1945- *St&PR 93*
Murphy, Charles Haywood, Jr. 1920- *St&PR 93, WhoAm 92, WhoSSW 93*
Murphy, Charles Henry 1927- *WhoE 93*
Murphy, Charles Joseph 1947- *WhoAm 92*
Murphy, Charlotte *BioIn 17*
Murphy, Christopher J., III 1946- *St&PR 93*
Murphy, Clarence John 1934- *WhoE 93*
Murphy, Clark W. 1956- *St&PR 93*
Murphy, Colin T. 1949- *St&PR 93*
Murphy, Colleen Frances 1960- *WhoAmW 93, WhoEmL 93*
Murphy, Colleen Patricia 1943- *WhoAmW 93*
Murphy, Cynthia Ann 1959- *WhoAmW 93*
Murphy, Dale *BioIn 17*
Murphy, Dale Bryan 1956- *WhoAm 92*
Murphy, Daniel Hayes, II 1941- *WhoAm 92*
Murphy, Daniel Ignatius 1927- *WhoE 93*
Murphy, Daniel Joseph 1921-1991 *BioIn 17*
Murphy, Daniel T. 1939- *St&PR 93*
Murphy, David Frank 1946- *WhoEmL 93, WhoSSW 93*
Murphy, David G. 1950- *St&PR 93*
Murphy, David John *WhoScE 91-1*
Murphy, David L. *St&PR 93*
Murphy, David McGregor 1917- *St&PR 93*
Murphy, David Ridgeway 1945- *WhoAm 92*
Murphy, David Thomas 1929- *WhoAm 92*
Murphy, Deborah Cotton 1951- *WhoAmW 93*
Murphy, Deborah June 1955- *WhoAmW 93*
Murphy, Denis Joseph *WhoScE 91-1*
Murphy, Dennis F. 1937- *St&PR 93, WhoAm 92*
Murphy, Dennis Joseph 1946- *WhoEmL 93*
Murphy, Dennis Patrick 1958- *WhoEmL 93, WhoWor 93*
Murphy, Derek James Murtagh 1946- *WhoWor 93*
Murphy, Diana 1934- *WhoAm 92, WhoAmW 93*
Murphy, Donald B. 1940- *St&PR 93*
Murphy, Donald Gerald 1948- *St&PR 93*
Murphy, Donald James 1946- *WhoEmL 93*
Murphy, Donn Brian 1930- *WhoE 93*
Murphy, Donna Marie 1955- *WhoAmW 93*
Murphy, Douglas E. 1926- *St&PR 93*
Murphy, Douglas Edward 1964- *WhoE 93*
Murphy, Dwayne *BioIn 17*
Murphy, E.J. *WhoScE 91-3*
Murphy, Eddie *BioIn 17, NewYTBS 92 [port]*
Murphy, Eddie 1961- *AfrAmBi, ConBlB 4 [port], IntDcF 2-3, MiSFD 9, QDrFCA 92 [port], WhoAm 92*
Murphy, Edmund Michael 1936- *WhoAm 92*
Murphy, Edrie Lee 1953- *WhoAmW 93*
Murphy, Edward *MiSFD 9*
Murphy, Edward Arthur 1941- *St&PR 93*
Murphy, Edward D. *Law&B 92*
Murphy, Edward Joseph 1927- *WhoAm 92*
Murphy, Edward P. *WhoAm 92*
Murphy, Edward Patrick, Jr. 1943- *WhoAm 92*
Murphy, Edwin J. 1932- *St&PR 93*
Murphy, Eileen Bridget 1940- *WhoAmW 93*
Murphy, Elaine *WhoScE 91-1*
Murphy, Eleanor J. *AmWomPl*
Murphy, Elinor *AmWomPl*
Murphy, Ellis *WhoAm 92*
Murphy, Elva Glenn 1934- *WhoAmW 93*
Murphy, Emily *BioIn 17*
Murphy, Emmett P. 1949- *St&PR 93*
Murphy, Erin Elizabeth 1965- *WhoAmW 93*
Murphy, Ernest Walter 1930- *St&PR 93*
Murphy, Ethel Allen *AmWomPl*
Murphy, Eugene 1930- *St&PR 93*
Murphy, Eugene F. 1936- *WhoAm 92*
Murphy, Eugene Francis 1913- *WhoAm 92*
Murphy, Eva Thompson 1936- *WhoE 93*
Murphy, Evelyn F. *BioIn 17*
Murphy, Evelyn Frances 1940- *WhoAm 92, WhoAmW 93, WhoE 93, WhoWor 93*
Murphy, Ewell Edward, Jr. 1928- *WhoAm 92*
Murphy, Frances Louise, II *WhoAmW 93*
Murphy, Francis *Law&B 92*
Murphy, Francis 1932- *WhoAm 92*
Murphy, Francis H. 1938- *St&PR 93*
Murphy, Francis J. 1946- *St&PR 93*
Murphy, Francis Seward 1914- *WhoWor 93*
Murphy, Frank 1890-1949 *OxCSupC [port], PolPar*
Murphy, Frank John, Jr. *Law&B 92*
Murphy, Franklin David 1916- *WhoAm 92*
Murphy, Gardner 1895-1979 *BioIn 17*
Murphy, Gene 1930- *St&PR 93*
Murphy, Geoff 1938- *MiSFD 9*
Murphy, George 1902-1992 *BioIn 17, NewYTBS 92 [port]*
Murphy, George (Lloyd) 1902-1992 *CurBio 92N*
Murphy, George Michael *Law&B 92*
Murphy, George William 1935- *St&PR 93*
Murphy, George William 1941- *WhoAm 92, WhoIns 93*
Murphy, Gerald *BioIn 17*
Murphy, Gerald 1938- *WhoAm 92*
Murphy, Gerald D. 1928- *St&PR 93*
Murphy, Gerald J., Jr. *Law&B 92*
Murphy, Gerald Patrick 1934- *WhoAm 92*
Murphy, Gerard 1958- *WhoScE 91-3*
Murphy, Gerard Daniel 1949- *WhoE 93*
Murphy, Gerard Norris 1950- *WhoE 93*
Murphy, Gillian *WhoScE 91-1*
Murphy, Gloria *ScF&FL 92*
Murphy, Gloria Walter 1940- *WhoE 93*
Murphy, Gordon John 1927- *WhoAm 92*
Murphy, Gordon Laurence 1935- *St&PR 93*
Murphy, Grattan Patrick 1935- *WhoE 93*
Murphy, Gregory Gerard 1954- *WhoAm 92, WhoEmL 93*
Murphy, H. Gabriel 1903- *St&PR 93*
Murphy, Harold Loyd 1927- *WhoAm 92, WhoSSW 93*
Murphy, Harold Morgan 1925- *St&PR 93*
Murphy, Harry S. *BioIn 17*
Murphy, Helen Agnes *AmWomPl*
Murphy, Henry B. 1925- *St&PR 93*
Murphy, Hoyt Campbell 1911- *St&PR 93*
Murphy, Hugh Cornelius 1915- *WhoAm 92*
Murphy, Irene 1906- *WhoAmW 93*
Murphy, Irene Helen *WhoAmW 93*
Murphy, Irma Andrea 1959- *WhoAmW 93*
Murphy, J. Allen d1992 *NewYTBS 92 [port]*
Murphy, J. Kevin 1927- *WhoAm 92*
Murphy, J. Neil 1934- *WhoSSW 93, WhoWor 93*
Murphy, Jacquelyn Maria 1952- *WhoAmW 93, WhoEmL 93, WhoWor 93*
Murphy, James 1937- *St&PR 93, WhoAm 92*
Murphy, James Allen 1938- *WhoAm 92*
Murphy, James Bryson, Jr. 1932- *WhoAm 92*
Murphy, James F. 1933- *WhoAm 92*
Murphy, James F. 1934- *St&PR 93*
Murphy, James J. 1943- *St&PR 93*
Murphy, James J. 1944- *WhoAm 92*
Murphy, James J. 1954- *WhoSSW 93*
Murphy, James Joseph *Law&B 92*
Murphy, James Joseph 1938- *WhoE 93*
Murphy, James L. 1939- *WhoAm 92*
Murphy, James M. 1947- *St&PR 93*
Murphy, James Michael 1947- *WhoAm 92*
Murphy, James P. *Law&B 92*
Murphy, James Paul 1944- *WhoAm 92*
Murphy, James R. 1922- *St&PR 93*
Murphy, James Robert *Law&B 92*
Murphy, James W. 1936- *WhoIns 93*
Murphy, James Woodyard 1932- *WhoSSW 93*
Murphy, Jane Rebecca 1945- *WhoAmW 93*
Murphy, Janet Gorman 1937- *WhoAmW 93*
Murphy, Jay W. d1992 *NewYTBS 92*
Murphy, Jeanette Carol 1931- *WhoAmW 93*

Murphy, Jeanne Ann *Law&B 92*
Murphy, Jefferson 1947- *WhoE 93*
Murphy, Jeffrey John *Law&B 92*
Murphy, Jeffrey John 1946- *St&PR 93*
Murphy, Jerome F. 1951- *St&PR 93*
Murphy, Jill 1949- *MajAI [port], SmATA 70 [port]*
Murphy, Jill (Francis) 1949- *ChlFicS*
Murphy, Jill Lucille 1946- *WhoAmW 93*
Murphy, Jo Anne *Law&B 92, WhoAmW 93*
Murphy, Joan S. *Law&B 92*
Murphy, Joanne Becker *WhoAmW 93*
Murphy, Joanne M. 1957- *WhoAmW 93*
Murphy, John A. *BioIn 17, Law&B 92*
Murphy, John A. 1931- *St&PR 93*
Murphy, John Anthony 1939- *WhoE 93*
Murphy, John Arthur 1929- *St&PR 93, WhoAm 92, WhoWor 93*
Murphy, John Austin 1956- *WhoEmL 93*
Murphy, John Carter 1921- *WhoAm 92, WhoSSW 93, WhoWor 93*
Murphy, John Cornelius 1936- *WhoE 93*
Murphy, John Crowley *Law&B 92*
Murphy, John Cullen 1919- *WhoAm 92*
Murphy, John George d1990 *BioIn 17*
Murphy, John H., III 1916- *DcLB 127 [port]*
Murphy, John J. 1928- *WhoIns 93*
Murphy, John J., Jr. 1920- *St&PR 93*
Murphy, John J., Jr. 1946- *WhoIns 93*
Murphy, John Joseph 1908-1970 *BiDAMSp 1989*
Murphy, John Joseph 1920- *WhoE 93*
Murphy, John Joseph 1931- *St&PR 93, WhoAm 92, WhoSSW 93*
Murphy, John Joseph 1936- *WhoIns 93*
Murphy, John Leonard 1950- *WhoEmL 93*
Murphy, John Michael 1941- *WhoAm 92*
Murphy, John P. *Law&B 92*
Murphy, John Patrick 1945- *WhoIns 93*
Murphy, John Thomas 1928- *WhoSSW 93*
Murphy, John Vincent 1949- *St&PR 93*
Murphy, Joseph E. *BioIn 17, Law&B 92*
Murphy, Joseph Edward, Jr. 1930- *WhoAm 92*
Murphy, Joseph F. 1915- *WhoAm 92*
Murphy, Joseph J. 1939- *St&PR 93*
Murphy, Joseph James 1956- *WhoE 93*
Murphy, Joseph Kemp 1951- *WhoE 93*
Murphy, Joseph Leon 1946- *WhoEmL 93*
Murphy, Joseph S. *BioIn 17*
Murphy, Joseph S. 1933- *WhoAm 92*
Murphy, Joseph T. 1940- *St&PR 93*
Murphy, Joy Waldron 1942- *WhoWrEP 92*
Murphy, Judith Chisholm 1942- *WhoAmW 93*
Murphy, Juneann Wadsworth 1937- *WhoAmW 93*
Murphy, Justin D. 1964- *WhoSSW 93*
Murphy, Karen Mitchell 1950- *WhoEmL 93*
Murphy, Katherine C. *AmWomPl*
Murphy, Kathleen A. *Law&B 92*
Murphy, Kathleen Ann 1950- *St&PR 93*
Murphy, Kathleen Jane 1962- *WhoSSW 93*
Murphy, Kathleen Mary 1945- *WhoAmW 93, WhoWor 93*
Murphy, Kathryn Marguerite *WhoAmW 93*
Murphy, Kathy Lynn 1958- *WhoAmW 93, WhoSSW 93*
Murphy, Kay Ann 1942- *WhoWrEP 92*
Murphy, Kenneth T. 1937- *St&PR 93*
Murphy, Kenyon W. *Law&B 92*
Murphy, Kevin Edgar 1928- *WhoWor 93*
Murphy, Kevin George 1952- *WhoE 93, WhoEmL 93*
Murphy, Kevin J. *BioIn 17*
Murphy, Kevin Keith 1962- *WhoE 93*
Murphy, Kevin P. *Law&B 92*
Murphy, Kim B. *Law&B 92*
Murphy, Laura M. *Law&B 92*
Murphy, Lawrence Michael *Law&B 92*
Murphy, Lawrence Patrick *Law&B 92*
Murphy, Leanna Kay 1968- *WhoAmW 93*
Murphy, Lester Fuller 1936- *WhoAm 92*
Murphy, Lewis Curtis 1933- *WhoAm 92*
Murphy, Linda Sue 1948- *WhoAmW 93*
Murphy, Louise Boyce *AmWomPl*
Murphy, Margaret A. 1934- *WhoAmW 93*
Murphy, Margaret H. 1948- *WhoAmW 93*
Murphy, Margo Raiford 1944- *WhoAmW 93*
Murphy, Marguerite *AmWomPl*
Murphy, Marie Ann *WhoE 93*
Murphy, Mark *BioIn 17*
Murphy, Mark Joseph 1956- *St&PR 93*
Murphy, Mark Joseph 1960- *WhoE 93*
Murphy, Martha W(atson) 1951- *ConAu 136*
Murphy, Martin Charles 1952- *WhoEmL 93*
Murphy, Mary Ann Burnett 1954- *WhoAmW 93*
Murphy, Mary C. *WhoAmW 93*
Murphy, Mary Kathleen Connors 1938- *WhoAmW 93, WhoSSW 93*
Murphy, Mary Kathryn 1941- *WhoAmW 93*
Murphy, Mary Reynolds 1948- *WhoEmL 93*
Murphy, Mary Therese 1957- *WhoAmW 93*
Murphy, Matt 1935- *WhoScE 91-3*
Murphy, Matthew F. 1937- *WhoScE 91-3*
Murphy, Matthew M. 1956- *WhoWor 93*
Murphy, Michael *BioIn 17*
Murphy, Michael 1930- *ScF&FL 92, WhoWrEP 92*
Murphy, Michael Alan *Law&B 92*
Murphy, Michael Anthony 1939- *WhoE 93*
Murphy, Michael Cary 1951- *WhoEmL 93*
Murphy, Michael E. 1936- *St&PR 93*
Murphy, Michael Emmett 1936- *WhoAm 92*
Murphy, Michael George 1938- *WhoAm 92*
Murphy, Michael J. *ScF&FL 92*
Murphy, Michael John *Law&B 92*
Murphy, Michael John 1959- *WhoEmL 93*
Murphy, Michael McKay 1946- *WhoE 93*
Murphy, Michael Patrick 1949- *WhoEmL 93*
Murphy, Michael W. *Law&B 92*
Murphy, Michael William *Law&B 92*
Murphy, Michael William 1949- *St&PR 93*
Murphy, Michelle *Law&B 92*
Murphy, Miriam Brigitte 1954- *WhoWor 93*
Murphy, Monica 1963- *WhoAmW 93*
Murphy, Nancy Ann 1936- *WhoAmW 93*
Murphy, Nancy L. 1929- *WhoAmW 93*
Murphy, Nancy Lee 1933- *St&PR 93*
Murphy, Nora Sharkey 1940- *WhoAmW 93, WhoE 93*
Murphy, P(eter) J(ohn) 1946- *ConAu 136*
Murphy, P.M. *Law&B 92*
Murphy, P. Sean *Law&B 92*
Murphy, Pat 1955- *ConAu 137, ScF&FL 92*
Murphy, Patrice Ann 1955- *WhoWrEP 92*
Murphy, Patricia A *WhoE 93*
Murphy, Patricia Ann 1951- *WhoAmW 93*
Murphy, Patrick 1946- *WhoE 93*
Murphy, Patrick D. 1951- *ScF&FL 92*
Murphy, Patrick Dennis 1951- *WhoWrEP 92*
Murphy, Patrick F. 1951- *St&PR 93*
Murphy, Patrick Francis 1958- *WhoSSW 93*
Murphy, Patrick Joseph 1949- *WhoAm 92*
Murphy, Patrick M. 1938-1991 *BioIn 17*
Murphy, Patrick Neil 1946- *WhoEmL 93*
Murphy, Patrick T. 1956- *WhoAm 92*
Murphy, Patrick Vincent 1920- *WhoAm 92*
Murphy, Paul D. 1937- *St&PR 93*
Murphy, Paul Francis 1939- *WhoSSW 93*
Murphy, Paul Gayleard *WhoScE 91-1*
Murphy, Paul J. d1990 *BioIn 17*
Murphy, Peregine Leigh 1954- *WhoAmW 93*
Murphy, Peter 1963- *BioIn 17*
Murphy, Philip J. *Law&B 92*
Murphy, Rae 1935- *ScF&FL 92*
Murphy, Randall Kent 1943- *WhoSSW 93, WhoWor 93*
Murphy, Richard *Law&B 92*
Murphy, Richard Brian *Law&B 92*
Murphy, Richard Patrick 1954- *WhoEmL 93*
Murphy, Richard William 1929- *WhoAm 92*
Murphy, Robert Blair 1931- *WhoAm 92, WhoE 93, WhoWor 93*
Murphy, Robert Brady Lawrence 1905- *WhoAm 92*
Murphy, Robert Charles 1926- *WhoAm 92*
Murphy, Robert D. 1894-1978 *BioIn 17*
Murphy, Robert E. 1950- *St&PR 93*
Murphy, Robert Earl 1941- *WhoAm 92*
Murphy, Robert F. *Law&B 92*
Murphy, Robert Francis 1921- *WhoAm 92*
Murphy, Robert Francis 1924-1990 *BioIn 17*
Murphy, Robert Franklin *ScF&FL 92*
Murphy, Robert G. *WhoAm 92*
Murphy, Robert Harry 1938- *St&PR 93, WhoAm 92*
Murphy, Robert P. 1943- *WhoE 93*
Murphy, Rose 1913-1989 *BioIn 17*
Murphy, Rose M. *Law&B 92*
Murphy, Rosemary *WhoAm 92*
Murphy, Roy James 1927- *St&PR 93*
Murphy, S. Wayne *Law&B 92*
Murphy, Samuel Wilson, Jr. 1927- *St&PR 93, WhoAm 92*
Murphy, Sandra Jean 1950- *WhoEmL 93*
Murphy, Sandra Robison 1949- *WhoAmW 93*
Murphy, Sara 1883-1975 *BioIn 17*
Murphy, Sharon Margaret 1940- *WhoAm 92*
Murphy, Shaun Edward 1961- *WhoE 93, WhoWor 93*
Murphy, Sheila E. 1951- *WhoWrEP 92*
Murphy, Shirley Rousseau 1928- *MajAI [port], ScF&FL 92, SmATA 71 [port]*
Murphy, Spencer A. *St&PR 93*
Murphy, Stephen Edward 1944- *WhoAm 92*
Murphy, Stephen G. *BioIn 17*
Murphy, Stephen P. 1926- *WhoAm 92*
Murphy, Stephen Vincent 1945- *WhoE 93*
Murphy, Stephen Willson 1946- *WhoEmL 93*
Murphy, Steven *WhoAm 92*
Murphy, Steven John 1958- *St&PR 93*
Murphy, Susan 1950- *BioIn 17, WhoAmW 93*
Murphy, Susan Lynn Jaycox 1961- *WhoAmW 93*
Murphy, Suzanne Tibbetts 1958- *WhoAmW 93*
Murphy, Terence Martin 1942- *WhoAm 92*
Murphy, Terry M. 1948- *St&PR 93*
Murphy, Therrell 1942- *St&PR 93*
Murphy, Thomas Aquinas 1915- *WhoAm 92*
Murphy, Thomas Bailey 1924- *WhoAm 92, WhoSSW 93*
Murphy, Thomas Bernard 1927- *St&PR 93*
Murphy, Thomas Edward *Law&B 92*
Murphy, Thomas Edward Gerard *Law&B 92*
Murphy, Thomas Francis 1905- *WhoAm 92, WhoE 93*
Murphy, Thomas Francis 1942- *WhoE 93, WhoWor 93*
Murphy, Thomas G. 1952- *St&PR 93*
Murphy, Thomas H. 1946- *St&PR 93*
Murphy, Thomas J. *Law&B 92*
Murphy, Thomas J. 1944- *WhoIns 93*
Murphy, Thomas J., Jr. *Law&B 92*
Murphy, Thomas James 1931- *St&PR 93*
Murphy, Thomas James 1956- *WhoE 93*
Murphy, Thomas Jefferson *Law&B 92*
Murphy, Thomas John 1931- *WhoAm 92*
Murphy, Thomas Joseph 1932- *WhoAm 92*
Murphy, Thomas M. 1947- *WhoScE 91-3*
Murphy, Thomas S. 1925- *St&PR 93, WhoAm 92, WhoE 93, WhoWor 93*
Murphy, Thomas S. 1932- *WhoIns 93*
Murphy, Timothy Edward 1947- *St&PR 93, WhoAm 92*
Murphy, Timothy J. d1991 *BioIn 17*
Murphy, Timothy Patrick 1928- *St&PR 93*
Murphy, "Turk" 1915-1987 *Baker 92*
Murphy, Vincent J., Jr. *Law&B 92*
Murphy, Walter F. 1929- *ScF&FL 92*
Murphy, Walter Francis 1929- *WhoAm 92, WhoWrEP 92*
Murphy, Walter T. *BioIn 17*
Murphy, Walter Young 1930- *WhoAm 92*
Murphy, Warren 1933- *ScF&FL 92*
Murphy, Warren Burton 1933- *WhoAm 92*
Murphy, Wilfred James *WhoScE 91-1*
Murphy, William *Law&B 92*
Murphy, William Beverly 1907- *WhoAm 92*
Murphy, William C. d1989 *BioIn 17*
Murphy, William E. 1933- *WhoScE 91-3*
Murphy, William Holland 1931- *St&PR 93, WhoAm 92*
Murphy, William James 1927- *WhoAm 92*
Murphy, William Joseph *Law&B 92*
Murphy, William K. 1940- *St&PR 93*
Murphy, William Michael 1916- *WhoAm 92*
Murphy, Winifred Lee 1931- *WhoWrEP 92*
Murphy-Anderson, Margaret A. *Law&B 92*
Murphy DelBello, Patricia 1959- *WhoEmL 93*
Murr, Danny Lee 1930- *WhoWrEP 92*
Murr, Lawrence Eugene 1939- *WhoSSW 93*
Murr, Susan J. *Law&B 92*
Murra, John Victor 1916- *WhoAm 92*
Murrah, Judith Ann 1958- *WhoE 93, WhoEmL 93*
Murrah, M. Lee *Law&B 92*
Murrah, Peggy Ferguson 1963- *WhoSSW 93*
Murray, A. Brean 1937- *WhoAm 92*
Murray, Abby Darlington Boyd 1928- *WhoAmW 93*
Murray, Alan *WhoScE 91-1*
Murray, Alan Page 1934- *WhoAm 92*
Murray, Albert Ketcham 1906-1992 *BioIn 17, NewYTBS 92*
Murray, Albert L. 1916- *ConLC 73 [port], WhoAm 92*
Murray, Allen Edward 1929- *St&PR 93, WhoAm 92, WhoSSW 93*
Murray, Alvin Lee 1950- *WhoSSW 93*
Murray, Amani A.W. *BioIn 17*
Murray, Andrew 1942- *WhoE 93*
Murray, Angie Anna Alice 1949- *WhoAmW 93, WhoEmL 93, WhoSSW 93, WhoWor 93*
Murray, Anita Jean 1943- *WhoAm 92, WhoE 93*
Murray, Ann 1949- *Baker 92, OxDcOp*
Murray, Ann Dennison 1945- *WhoAmW 93*
Murray, Ann Pennington 1959- *WhoWrEP 92*
Murray, Anna Pauline 1910-1985 *EncAACR*
Murray, Anne *AmWomPl*
Murray, Anne 1945- *WhoAm 92, WhoAmW 93*
Murray, (Morna) Anne 1945- *Baker 92*
Murray, Archibald James 1860-1945 *HarEnMi*
Murray, Arthur 1895-1991 *AnObit 1991, BioIn 17*
Murray, Arthur Joseph 1954- *WhoSSW 93*
Murray, Arthur R. 1931- *St&PR 93*
Murray, B. *WhoScE 91-1*
Murray, Bain 1926- *Baker 92*
Murray, Barbara Olivia 1947- *WhoAmW 93*
Murray, Betty Jean Kafka 1935- *WhoAmW 93*
Murray, Bill *BioIn 17*
Murray, Bill 1950- *HolBB [port], MiSFD 9, QDrFCA 92 [port], WhoAm 92*
Murray, Bryan Clarence 1942- *WhoAm 92*
Murray, C.A., Jr. 1928- *St&PR 93*
Murray, C.H. *WhoScE 91-3*
Murray, Calvin J. 1924- *St&PR 93*
Murray, Caroline Fish 1920- *WhoAm 92*
Murray, Charles A. *BioIn 17*
Murray, Charles Alan 1943- *WhoE 93*
Murray, Charles Dwight 1912- *WhoWor 93*
Murray, Charles Mansfield 1932- *WhoAm 92*
Murray, Charlie 1872-1941 *See* Sidney, George 1876-1945 & Murray, Charlie 1872-1941 *QDrFCA 92*
Murray, Cherry Ann 1952- *WhoAmW 93*
Murray, Cherry Roberts 1921- *WhoAmW 93*
Murray, Christine Marie 1949- *WhoE 93*
Murray, Clare M. *BioIn 17*
Murray, Claude Hollis 1930- *WhoUN 92, WhoWor 93*
Murray, Claude Robert, Jr. 1947- *WhoEmL 93, WhoSSW 93*
Murray, Conal E. *Law&B 92*
Murray, Connie Cowart 1945- *WhoAmW 93*
Murray, Constance Ann 1929- *WhoAm 92*
Murray, Corrine F. *Law&B 92*
Murray, Dale Norris 1945- *WhoSSW 93, WhoWor 93*
Murray, Daniel Alexander Payne 1852-1925 *BioIn 17*
Murray, Daniel T. *WhoAm 92*
Murray, David 1925- *WhoAm 92*
Murray, David 1953- *WhoWor 93*
Murray, David 1955- *BioIn 17*
Murray, David Austin 1943- *WhoE 93*
Murray, David George 1919- *WhoAm 92*
Murray, David George 1930- *WhoAm 92*
Murray, David S. 1932- *St&PR 93*
Murray, David Stuart 1953- *St&PR 93*
Murray, Dee 1946-1992 *BioIn 17*
Murray, Delbert Milton 1941- *WhoWor 93*
Murray, Dennis Joseph 1946- *WhoAm 92*
Murray, Don 1929- *MiSFD 9*
Murray, Donald C. 1936- *St&PR 93*
Murray, Donald F. 1921- *St&PR 93*
Murray, Donald Patrick 1929- *WhoAm 92*
Murray, Doug 1947- *ScF&FL 92*
Murray, Douglas M. 1945- *St&PR 93*
Murray, Douglas R. *Law&B 92*
Murray, Douglas Timothy Gordon 1938- *WhoSSW 93*
Murray, Duncan 1946- *St&PR 93*
Murray, E.B. 1927- *ScF&FL 92*
Murray, E. Patrick *ScF&FL 92*
Murray, Eddie Clarence 1956- *WhoAm 92*
Murray, Edward Leo 1920- *WhoE 93*

Murray, Edward N. 1921- *St&PR 93*
Murray, Edward Rock 1947- *WhoE 93*
Murray, Edward W. *Law&B 92*
Murray, Edward W. d1991 *BioIn 17*
Murray, Eleanor F. 1916- *WhoAmW 93*
Murray, Elizabeth *BioIn 17*
Murray, Elizabeth 1940- *WhoAm 92*
Murray, Elizabeth Davis Reid 1925- *WhoAm 92*
Murray, Emmet V. 1926-1990 *BioIn 17*
Murray, Ernest Don 1930- *WhoAm 92*
Murray, Florence Kerins 1916- *WhoAm 92, WhoAmW 93*
Murray, Francis W., III 1928- *St&PR 93*
Murray, Frederick Franklin 1950- *WhoAm 92, WhoEmL 93, WhoSSW 93*
Murray, Frederick Whittelsey, Jr. 1939- *WhoAm 92, WhoSSW 93*
Murray, Frieda A. *ScF&FL 92*
Murray, G. *WhoScE 91-1*
Murray, George 1694-1760 *HarEnMi*
Murray, George H. 1946- *St&PR 93*
Murray, George Washington 1853-1926 *BioIn 17*
Murray, Gerald E. *Law&B 92*
Murray, Gerald Edward 1945- *WhoWrEP 92*
Murray, Glenn Edward 1955- *WhoEmL 93*
Murray, Glenn Richard, Jr. 1930- *WhoAm 92*
Murray, Glenn William 1957- *WhoWor 93*
Murray, Grover Elmer 1916- *WhoAm 92*
Murray, Gwyn Firth *Law&B 92*
Murray, Harlan W. *WhoAm 92*
Murray, Harlan W. 1933- *St&PR 93*
Murray, Harlan Wyatt *Law&B 92*
Murray, Harold Dixon 1931- *WhoSSW 93*
Murray, Harry Lawrason, III 1942- *WhoE 93*
Murray, Haydn Herbert 1924- *WhoAm 92*
Murray, Herbert Frazier 1923- *WhoAm 92*
Murray, Hugh T., Jr. 1938- *WhoWrEP 92*
Murray, Ian Stewart 1951- *WhoEmL 93*
Murray, J. Alec G. 1936- *WhoSSW 93*
Murray, J. Ralph 1916- *WhoAm 92*
Murray, J. Terrence *BioIn 17*
Murray, Jack B., Jr. *Law&B 92*
Murray, Jack Dale 1946- *St&PR 93*
Murray, Jacqueline d1991 *BioIn 17*
Murray, James Brady, Jr. 1946- *WhoEmL 93*
Murray, James C. 1939- *WhoSSW 93*
Murray, James Calhoun 1939- *St&PR 93*
Murray, James Dickson *WhoScE 91-1*
Murray, James Doyle 1938- *WhoAm 92, WhoE 93*
Murray, James E. *Law&B 92*
Murray, James Edward 1932- *WhoAm 92*
Murray, James F. *WhoAm 92*
Murray, James H. 1928- *St&PR 93*
Murray, James Herchel 1948- *WhoSSW 93*
Murray, James Joseph, III 1933- *WhoAm 92*
Murray, James Kirtis, Jr. 1935- *WhoAm 92*
Murray, James Lothian *WhoScE 91-1*
Murray, James Michael 1944- *WhoAm 92, WhoWor 93*
Murray, James P. 1922- *WhoScE 91-3*
Murray, James Patrick 1919- *WhoAm 92*
Murray, James Vincent, III 1942- *WhoE 93*
Murray, James W., III *Law&B 92*
Murray, Jan *WhoScE 91-1*
Murray, Janet Ann 1945- *WhoSSW 93*
Murray, Jean Carolyn 1927- *WhoAm 92, WhoAmW 93*
Murray, Jeanne *WhoAm 92, WhoAmW 93*
Murray, Jeanne Evelyn 1932- *WhoAmW 93*
Murray, Jeanne Morris 1925- *WhoAm 92*
Murray, Jeneane Fountaine *Law&B 92*
Murray, Jennifer Jayne 1963- *WhoE 93*
Murray, Jesse George 1909- *WhoSSW 93, WhoWor 93*
Murray, Jim *BioIn 17*
Murray, Joan Kathleen 1957- *WhoSSW 93*
Murray, Jody I. *St&PR 93*
Murray, Joel Anthony 1948- *WhoE 93*
Murray, Johann Peter Christian 1952- *WhoEmL 93*
Murray, John A. 1954- *ConAu 138*
Murray, John Arthur 1937- *St&PR 93*
Murray, John Clifford Cox 1951- *WhoScE 91-1*
Murray, John D. *WhoIns 93*
Murray, John Edward, Jr. 1932- *WhoAm 92*
Murray, John Einar 1918- *WhoAm 92*
Murray, John F. 1939- *St&PR 93*
Murray, John Frederic 1927- *WhoAm 92*
Murray, John Joseph *WhoScE 91-1*
Murray, John Joseph 1915- *WhoAm 92, WhoWrEP 92*
Murray, John L. 1927- *St&PR 93*
Murray, John Morton 1933- *St&PR 93*
Murray, John Patrick 1943- *WhoAm 92*
Murray, John Peter 1936- *WhoAm 92*
Murray, John T. *Law&B 92*
Murray, John William *WhoScE 91-1*
Murray, John William 1943- *WhoAm 92*
Murray, Joseph Edward *BioIn 17*
Murray, Joseph Edward 1919- *WhoAm 92, WhoE 93, WhoWor 93*
Murray, Joseph James, Jr. 1930- *WhoAm 92*
Murray, Joseph W. *Law&B 92*
Murray, Joseph William 1944- *WhoAm 92*
Murray, Josepha Marie *AmWomPl*
Murray, Judith Ann 1946- *WhoSSW 93*
Murray, Judy Flachsland 1946- *WhoAmW 93*
Murray, Julia Kaoru 1934- *WhoAmW 93*
Murray, Kathleen Ann 1952- *WhoIns 93*
Murray, Kathleen Mary 1961- *WhoAmW 93*
Murray, Kathryn Hazel 1906- *WhoAm 92*
Murray, Kathryn Kelly 1939- *WhoAmW 93*
Murray, Kelly M. *Law&B 92*
Murray, Kenneth Richard 1938- *St&PR 93, WhoAm 92*
Murray, Kevin *BioIn 17*
Murray, Lawrence 1939- *St&PR 93, WhoE 93*
Murray, Lawrence M. 1942- *St&PR 93*
Murray, Lee Winslow 1949- *WhoWrEP 92*
Murray, Lenda *NewYTBS 92 [port]*
Murray, Leonard Hugh 1913- *WhoAm 92*
Murray, Leota Ann 1933- *WhoAmW 93*
Murray, Les 1938- *IntLitE*
Murray, Les A. 1938- *BioIn 17*
Murray, Leslie Glenn *Law&B 92*
Murray, Lillian Anderson 1943- *WhoAmW 93*
Murray, Lowell *BioIn 17*
Murray, Lowell 1936- *WhoAm 92, WhoE 93*
Murray, Lucille M. 1911- *St&PR 93*
Murray, Lynda Beran 1944- *WhoAmW 93*
Murray, Malcolm Arthur 1925- *WhoSSW 93*
Murray, Margaret Alice 1863-1963 *IntDcAn*
Murray, Margaret Marie 1946- *WhoSSW 93*
Murray, Margaret Thorell 1946- *WhoAmW 93*
Murray, Marguerite *BioIn 17*
Murray, Marie Jeannine 1962- *WhoEmL 93*
Murray, Marilyn C. 1946- *WhoAmW 93, WhoEmL 93*
Murray, Marita Diane 1935- *WhoAmW 93*
Murray, Mark H. 1950- *St&PR 93*
Murray, Marsha E. *Law&B 92*
Murray, Mary Aileen 1914- *WhoAmW 93*
Murray, Maurice *WhoScE 91-1*
Murray, Maurice Avery 1938- *St&PR 93*
Murray, Michael 1943- *Baker 92*
Murray, Michael H. *Law&B 92*
Murray, Michael J. 1939- *St&PR 93*
Murray, Michael J. 1944- *St&PR 93*
Murray, Michael Peter 1946- *WhoAm 92, WhoEmL 93*
Murray, Mimi *BioIn 17*
Murray, N. Leight 1951- *St&PR 93*
Murray, Nancy Jeanne 1956- *St&PR 93*
Murray, Neal J. *Law&B 92*
Murray, Noreen Elizabeth *WhoScE 91-1*
Murray, Norman J. 1917- *St&PR 93*
Murray, Pamela Alison 1955- *WhoAmW 93*
Murray, Patrick M. 1942- *St&PR 93*
Murray, Patty 1950- *WhoAmW 93*
Murray, Paul Brady 1923- *St&PR 93, WhoAm 92*
Murray, Pauli 1910-1985 *BioIn 17*
Murray, Peter 1920- *WhoAm 92*
Murray, Peter Bryant 1927- *WhoAm 92*
Murray, Peter (John) 1920-1992 *ConAu 137*
Murray, Peter John 1951- *St&PR 93*
Murray, Peter Loos 1943- *WhoAm 92*
Murray, Peter Robert 1956- *St&PR 93*
Murray, R.M. *WhoScE 91-1*
Murray, Ralbern H. 1929- *St&PR 93*
Murray, Ralbern Hugh 1929- *WhoAm 92*
Murray, Ralph Day 1944- *St&PR 93*
Murray, Randolph Sutherland 1910- *St&PR 93*
Murray, Raymond Carl 1929- *WhoAm 92*
Murray, Raymond Harold 1925- *WhoAm 92*
Murray, Raymond Le Roy 1920- *WhoAm 92*
Murray, Raymond William, Jr. 1925- *WhoAm 92*
Murray, Regina A. *Law&B 92*
Murray, Richard *WhoScE 91-1*
Murray, Richard Bennett 1928- *WhoAm 92*
Murray, Richard Maximilian 1922- *WhoAm 92*
Murray, Richard Newton 1942- *WhoAm 92*
Murray, Robert Charles *Law&B 92*
Murray, Robert Cooper 1938- *WhoUN 92*
Murray, Robert Douglas Hutton *WhoScE 91-1*
Murray, Robert Fox 1952- *WhoEmL 93*
Murray, Robert Fulton, Jr. 1931- *WhoAm 92*
Murray, Robert G. 1937- *St&PR 93*
Murray, Robert G. 1945- *St&PR 93*
Murray, Robert Gerald 1937- *WhoAm 92*
Murray, Robert Gray 1936- *WhoAm 92, WhoE 93*
Murray, Robert Keith 1922- *WhoAm 92*
Murray, Robert Nelson 1937- *St&PR 93*
Murray, Robert Sands 1955- *WhoEmL 93*
Murray, Robert Wallace 1928- *WhoAm 92*
Murray, Robin M. 1944- *WhoScE 91-1*
Murray, Roger Franklin 1911- *WhoAm 92*
Murray, Rona 1924- *WhoCanL 92*
Murray, Ronald 1931- *WhoE 93*
Murray, Royce Wilton 1937- *WhoAm 92*
Murray, Russell, II 1925- *WhoAm 92*
Murray, Shawn Michael 1956- *WhoE 93*
Murray, Simon *BioIn 17*
Murray, Simon 1940- *WhoWor 93*
Murray, Sims L. 1943- *WhoSSW 93, WhoWor 93*
Murray, Stephen James *Law&B 92*
Murray, Stephen James 1943- *WhoE 93, WhoWor 93*
Murray, Steven T. 1943- *WhoWrEP 92*
Murray, Susan Allen 1961- *WhoAmW 93*
Murray, Terence Rodney Terry 1950- *WhoAm 92, WhoE 93*
Murray, Terrence 1939- *St&PR 93, WhoAm 92*
Murray, Thomas Dwight 1923- *WhoAm 92*
Murray, Thomas Francis 1910- *WhoAm 92*
Murray, Thomas John 1938- *WhoAm 92*
Murray, Thomas Joseph 1924- *WhoAm 92*
Murray, Thomas (Mantle) 1943- *Baker 92*
Murray, Thomas Michael 1944- *WhoAm 92*
Murray, Thomas Owen 1954- *St&PR 93*
Murray, Timothy M. 1952- *St&PR 93*
Murray, Tracy 1940- *WhoSSW 93*
Murray, Ty *BioIn 17*
Murray, Verna Hazard 1909- *WhoAmW 93*
Murray, Virginia Klute 1942- *WhoAmW 93*
Murray, Virginia R. 1914- *WhoWrEP 92*
Murray, W. Ralph *BioIn 17*
Murray, Wallace Shordon 1921- *WhoAm 92*
Murray, Warren James 1936- *WhoAm 92*
Murray, Will 1953- *ScF&FL 92*
Murray, William 1926- *ScF&FL 92*
Murray, William Clark *Law&B 92*
Murray, William David 1908-1986 *BiDAMSp 1989*
Murray, William Eric *Law&B 92*
Murray, William Franklin 1940- *St&PR 93*
Murray, William G. *Law&B 92*
Murray, William Henry 1869-1956 *BioIn 17*
Murray, William J. *Law&B 92*
Murray, William J. 1948- *WhoIns 93*
Murray, William James 1933- *WhoSSW 93*
Murray, William James 1948- *WhoAm 92*
Murray, William Michael *Law&B 92*
Murray, William Michael 1953- *WhoE 93, WhoEmL 93*
Murray, William P. *ScF&FL 92*
Murray, William Peter 1924- *WhoWor 93*
Murray-Shelley, Richard *WhoScE 91-1*
Murray-Smith, David James *WhoScE 91-1*
Murray-Ward, Mildred 1948- *WhoAmW 93*
Murrel, Betty Elaine 1937- *WhoAmW 93*
Murrell, Anita McCauley 1955- *St&PR 93*
Murrell, Arlene 1948- *WhoAmW 93*
Murrell, Audrey Lena 1956- *WhoEmL 93*
Murrell, Carlton Decourcey 1945- *WhoE 93*
Murrell, Irvin Henry, Jr. 1945- *WhoSSW 93*
Murrell, Jack O. *Law&B 92*
Murrell, John 1945- *WhoCanL 92*
Murrell, John Norman *WhoScE 91-1*
Murrell, John Thomas 1949- *WhoSSW 93*
Murrell, Judith A. 1940- *St&PR 93*
Murrell, Judith Ann 1940- *WhoAmW 93*
Murrell, Kenneth E. 1939- *St&PR 93*
Murrell, Kenneth Lynn 1945- *WhoSSW 93*
Murrell, Leslie A. 1950- *St&PR 93*
Murrell, Michael David 1951- *St&PR 93*
Murrell, Michael David 1955- *WhoEmL 93*
Murrell, Stratton Chadwick 1928- *WhoSSW 93*
Murren, Doug(las) 1951- *ConAu 136*
Murrer, Gregory John *Law&B 92*
Murri, Alfredo 1912- *WhoScE 91-3*
Murrie, Michael Howard 1951- *WhoWrEP 92*
Murrieta, Joaquin 1832?-1853 *BioIn 17*
Murrill, Herbert (Henry John) 1909-1952 *Baker 92*
Murrill, Molly Lee 1930- *WhoWrEP 92*
Murrill, Paul Whitfield 1934- *St&PR 93, WhoAm 92*
Murrin, Charles John 1931- *St&PR 93*
Murrin, Craig Martin *Law&B 92*
Murrin, Regis Doubet 1930- *WhoAm 92*
Murrin, T.J. 1929- *St&PR 93*
Murrin, Thomas Edward 1923- *WhoAm 92*
Murrin, Thomas Joseph 1929- *WhoAm 92*
Murrish, Charles Howard 1940- *WhoAm 92, WhoSSW 93*
Murrone, Pietro di 1215-1296 *BioIn 17*
Murrow, Edward R. *BioIn 17*
Murrow, Edward Roscoe 1908-1965 *JrnUS*
Murry, Albert Bard 1940- *St&PR 93*
Murry, Barbara R. 1950- *WhoAmW 93*
Murry, Charles Emerson 1924- *WhoAm 92*
Murry, Colin *ScF&FL 92*
Murry, Dan *WhoWrEP 92*
Murry, John Middleton 1889-1957 *BioIn 17*
Murschhauser, Franz Xaver Anton 1663?-1738 *Baker 92*
Murska, Ilma di *OxDcOp*
Murska, Ilma di 1836-1889 *Baker 92*
Mursten, Michael Richard 1964- *WhoEmL 93, WhoSSW 93*
Murswiek, Dietrich Robert Wilheim 1948- *WhoWor 93*
Mursyid, Saadillah 1937- *WhoAsAP 91*
Murtagh, Fionn Diarmuid 1954- *WhoWor 93*
Murtagh, Frederick, Jr. 1917- *WhoAm 92*
Murtagh, Hugh V. *Law&B 92*
Murtagh, John Edward 1936- *WhoWor 93*
Murtagh, John P. *Law&B 92*
Murtagh, Liane Renee 1962- *WhoE 93*
Murtagh, Martin J. *Law&B 92*
Murtaugh, Daniel Edward 1917-1976 *BiDAMSp 1989*
Murtaugh, Maureen Ann 1961- *WhoAmW 93*
Murtaugh, Rodger W. 1938- *St&PR 93*
Murtazov, Todor Georgiev 1919- *WhoScE 91-4*
Murtfeldt, Robert L. 1952- *St&PR 93*
Murtha, John Francis 1930- *WhoAm 92*
Murtha, John P. *CngDr 91*
Murtha, John Patrick 1932- *WhoAm 92, WhoE 93*
Murtha, John S. 1913- *St&PR 93*
Murtha, John Stephen 1913- *WhoAm 92*
Murtha, Maryann Kathryn 1966- *WhoE 93*
Murtha, Richard A. 1933- *St&PR 93*
Murtha, Selena *Law&B 92*
Murtha, Sharon C. *Law&B 92*
Murthy, Andiappan 1943- *WhoSSW 93*
Murthy, Chandrashekara 1941- *WhoAsAP 91*
Murthy, Srinivasa B. 1944- *St&PR 93*
Murthy, Srinivasa K. 1949- *WhoE 93, WhoEmL 93, WhoWor 93*
Murtland, Elizabeth Helen 1943- *WhoAmW 93*
Murtlow, Ann Dragoumis 1960- *WhoAmW 93*
Murto, Susan D. *Law&B 92*
Murto, T. Juhani 1935- *WhoScE 91-4*
Murton, Thomas O. 1928?-1990 *BioIn 17*
Murumbi, Joseph 1911-1990 *BioIn 17*
Muruzabal, Claudio Norberto 1960- *WhoWor 93*
Murville, Maurice Couve de 1907- *BioIn 17*
Murvin, Harry James 1944- *WhoE 93*
Murza-Mucha, Pawel 1921- *WhoScE 91-4*
Murzanski, Michael J. 1955- *St&PR 93*
Murzewski, Janusz W. 1928- *WhoScE 91-4*
Murzin, Sandra Greenberg 1962- *WhoAmW 93*
Murzinski, Edward John 1946- *St&PR 93*
Murzycki, John Vincent 1953- *WhoE 93*
Mus, Publius Decius the Elder c. 383BC-340BC *HarEnMi*

Mus, Publius Decius the Younger 362BC-295BC HarEnMi
Musa d1413 OxDcByz
Musa, John Davis 1933- WhoAm 92
Musa, Said DcCPCAm
Musa, Samuel Albert WhoAm 92
Musa Bin Hitam, Datuk 1934- WhoAsAP 91
Musacchia, Mary U. Law&B 92
Musacchia, Xavier Joseph 1923- WhoAm 92
Musacchio, George Louis 1938- WhoSSW 93
Musaddiq, Mohammed 1880-1967 DcTwHis
Musafia, Judith N. 1941- WhoWrEP 92
Musa Islam Farah WhoWor 93
Musal, Edward Alfred 1946- WhoEmL 93
Musanna, Syed Ahmad 1934- WhoUN 92
Musante, Gerard John 1943- WhoSSW 93
Musante, Tony WhoAm 92
Musaph, Hermann d1992 NewYTBS 92
Musard, Philippe 1792-1859 Baker 92
Musaus, Johann Karl August 1735-1787 BioIn 17
Musawi, Abbas BioIn 17
Musburger, Brent Woody 1939- BiDAMSp 1989, WhoAm 92
Musca, Gavril 1931- WhoScE 91-4
Muscarella, Connie 1955- St&PR 93
Muscarella, John J. 1941- St&PR 93
Muscarella, Joseph 1946- St&PR 93
Muscarella, Lawrence G. Law&B 92
Muscarella, Oscar White BioIn 17
Muscarelle, Joseph Louis, Jr. 1935- WhoAm 92
Muscarnera, S.A. Law&B 92
Muscarnera, Simone A. 1940- St&PR 93
Muscatello, Umberto 1932- WhoScE 91-3
Muscatine, Charles 1920- WhoAm 92
Muschal, Judith Ann 1948- WhoAmW 93
Muschamp, Joan Fagnani 1955- WhoAmW 93
Muschel, Louis Henry 1916- WhoAm 92
Muschenheim, William 1902-1990 BioIn 17
Muschg, Adolf 1934- BioIn 17
Muschio, Henry Michael, Jr. 1931- WhoE 93
Muschler, Werner Georg 1930- WhoWor 93
Muschlitz, Larry D. 1948- St&PR 93
Musco, John BioIn 17
Muscoby, Walter Francis Law&B 92
Muscosky, Robert A. 1946- St&PR 93
Muse, A.C. 1936- St&PR 93
Muse, Charles Howard, Jr. 1936- St&PR 93
Muse, Ewell Henderson, III 1938- St&PR 93, WhoAm 92
Muse, Helen Elizabeth 1917- WhoWrEP 92
Muse, Helen Rose 1937- WhoAmW 93
Muse, M. Jane WhoAmW 93
Muse, Marion Lamar 1920- EncABHB 8 [port]
Muse, Martha Twitchell 1926- WhoAm 92
Muse, McGillivray 1909- WhoAm 92
Muse, Raquel 1962- WhoAmW 93
Muse, William Van 1939- WhoAm 92, WhoSSW 93
Musegades, Wally W. 1940- St&PR 93
Musel, Robert J. 1925- St&PR 93
Museler, William J. 1941- St&PR 93
Museles, Melvin 1929- WhoAm 92
Musembi, Musila 1950- WhoWor 93
Musetto, Vincent Albert, Jr. 1941- WhoAm 92
Museveni, Yoweri BioIn 17
Museveni, Yoweri 1944?- ConBlB 4 [port]
Museveni, Yoweri Kaguta 1944- WhoAfr, WhoWor 93
Musgjerd, John G. 1954- St&PR 93
Musgrave, Anna Miriam 1939- WhoSSW 93
Musgrave, Gerald WhoScE 91-1
Musgrave, Kathryn Elliott 1943- WhoAmW 93
Musgrave, Marian 1923-1988 BioIn 17
Musgrave, Mary Elizabeth 1954- WhoEmL 93
Musgrave, R. Kenton 1927- CngDr 91, WhoAm 92, WhoE 93
Musgrave, Richard Abel 1910- BioIn 17, WhoAm 92
Musgrave, Robert Paul, II 1955- WhoEmL 93
Musgrave, Story 1935- WhoAm 92, WhoSSW 93
Musgrave, Susan 1951- WhoCanL 92
Musgrave, Thea BioIn 17, WhoAm 92, WhoAmW 93
Musgrave, Thea 1928- Baker 92, OxDcOp
Musgrave, Thomas 1737-1812 HarEnMi
Musgraves, Robert E. Law&B 92
Musgraves, Robert E. 1955- St&PR 93
Musgraves, Skip S. 1958- St&PR 93
Musgrove, David Gregory 1944- St&PR 93
Musgrove, Harold Leonard, Jr. 1960- WhoEmL 93
Musgrove, Jack V. Law&B 92
Musgrove, John Conner 1929- WhoSSW 93
Musgrove, Judy Autry 1946- WhoAmW 93
Musgrove, Margaret 1943- BlkAuII 92
Musha, Jacob Roman 1936- WhoAm 92
Musha, Toshimitsu 1931- WhoWor 93
Musham, William C. 1915- St&PR 93
Musham, William Charles 1915- WhoAm 92
Musharbash, Jalal Sami 1954- WhoWor 93
Mushel, Georgi 1909- Baker 92
Mushen, Robert Linton 1943- WhoWor 93
Musher, Sidney 1905-1990 BioIn 17
Mushik, Corliss WhoAmW 93
Mushinski, Mark Alan 1959- St&PR 93
Mushkat, Miron 1945- WhoWor 93
Mushkin, Albert S. 1935- St&PR 93
Mushobekwa, Kalimba wa Katana 1943- WhoWor 93
Musholt, Frank H. 1939- St&PR 93
Mushotzky, Richard Fred 1947- WhoEmL 93
Musi, Maria Maddalena 1669-1751 OxDcOp
Musial, Stan 1920- BioIn 17
Musial, Stanley 1920- WhoAm 92
Music, John Farris 1921- WhoE 93
Musicescu, Gavriil 1847-1903 Baker 92
Musick, Dan Richard 1958- WhoEmL 93
Musick, Stuart 1934- St&PR 93
Musidora 1889-1957 IntDcF 2-3 [port]
Musielak, Victor A. 1929- St&PR 93
Musihin, Konstantin K. 1927- WhoWor 93
Musikas, Claude 1937- WhoWor 93
Musil, Jan 1927- WhoScE 91-4
Musil, Robert 1880-1942 DcLB 124 [port]
Musilli, John d1991 BioIn 17
Musilli, Thomas Gordon 1944- St&PR 93
Musin, Ovide 1854-1929 Baker 92
Musinsky, Gerald 1954- WhoWrEP 92
Musk, Arthur William 1943- WhoWor 93
Muska, Nick 1942- WhoWrEP 92
Muska, Thomas Wayne 1957- WhoEmL 93
Muskardin, Virgilio 1947- WhoWor 93
Muskas, Robert 1938- St&PR 93
Muskat, Carl S. 1938- St&PR 93
Muske, Carol Anne 1945- WhoWrEP 92
Muskelly, Anna Marie 1947- WhoAmW 93
Musker, John MiSFD 9
Muskie, Edmund S. 1914- PolPar
Muskie, Edmund Sixtus 1914- WhoAm 92, WhoE 93
Musnik, Denise d1990 BioIn 17
Musokotwane, Kebby 1946- WhoAfr
Musolf, Lloyd Daryl 1919- WhoAm 92
Musolino, Gina Maria 1964- WhoEmL 93
Musolino-Alber, Ella Marie 1942- WhoAmW 93
Muson, Howard Henry 1935- WhoAm 92
Musorgsky, Modest 1839-1881 OxDcOp
Musorgsky, Modest Petrovich 1839-1881 BioIn 17, IntDcOp [port]
Muss, Charles J. d1991 BioIn 17
Mussat, Andre 1912-1989 BioIn 17
Mussehl, Robert Clarence 1936- WhoAm 92
Musselman, Bill BioIn 17
Musselman, Clifford Allen 1947- St&PR 93
Musselman, David T. Law&B 92
Musselman, Deborah Myers 1964- WhoAmW 93, WhoEmL 93
Musselman, Eric BioIn 17
Musselman, Francis C. Law&B 92
Musselman, Francis Haas 1925- WhoAm 92, WhoWor 93
Musselman, James Arthur 1939- WhoAm 92
Musselman, Jamie Boothe 1950- St&PR 93
Musselman, John J. 1926- WhoAm 92
Musselman, Larry L. 1947- WhoEmL 93
Musselman, Paul Ernest 1950- St&PR 93
Musselman, Robert Metcalfe 1914- WhoSSW 93
Mussenden, Gerald 1941- WhoSSW 93
Mussenden, Maria Elisabeth 1949- WhoSSW 93
Musser, Amelia E. 1935- St&PR 93
Musser, C. Walton 1909- WhoAm 92
Musser, Charles Henry 1943- WhoE 93
Musser, Ellyn Zunker 1937- WhoSSW 93
Musser, Harry Plaine, Jr. 1922- St&PR 93
Musser, Jim ScF&FL 92
Musser, John M. d1990 BioIn 17
Musser, Robert D. 1932- St&PR 93
Musser, Stanton Richard 1936- WhoAm 92
Musser, Tharon 1925- WhoAm 92
Musser, Warren V. 1926- St&PR 93
Musser, William Allen 1924- St&PR 93
Musser, William Wesley, Jr. 1918- WhoAm 92
Musserian, John R. 1961- WhoWor 93
Mussett, Richard Earl 1948- WhoEmL 93, WhoSSW 93
Mussey, Joseph Arthur 1948- WhoAm 92
Mussey, Mabel Hay Barrows 1873- AmWomPl
Musshoff, Karl Albert 1910- WhoWor 93
Mussman, Carol Lynne 1957- WhoEmL 93
Mussman, Steven 1961- St&PR 93
Mussman, William Edward 1919- WhoWor 93
Musso, George BioIn 17
Musso, J.A. 1952- St&PR 93
Musso, J. Ricardo 1917-1989 BioIn 17
Musso, Laurie Duston 1919- WhoWrEP 92
Mussolini, Benito 1883-1945 BioIn 17, DcTwHis
Mussolini, Cesare 1735- Baker 92
Mussolini, Gioconda 1913-1969 IntDcAn
Mussomeli, Marilyn BioIn 17
Mussorgsky, Modest (Petrovich) 1839-1881 Baker 92, BioIn 17
Mustacchi, Henry 1930- St&PR 93
Mustacchi, Piero 1920- WhoAm 92
Mustaf, Jerrod BioIn 17
Mustafa, Ozdinch 1942- WhoUN 92
Mustafa, Rayman St&PR 93
Mustafa, Safdar Abbas 1943- WhoWor 93
Mustafa Kemal 1881-1938 BioIn 17
Mustain, Anne BioIn 17
Mustain, Wendy Christiana 1958- WhoAmW 93
Mustain, William G. 1942- St&PR 93
Mustaine, Dave c. 1962- See Megadeth ConMus 9
Mustakallio, Kimmo K. 1931- WhoScE 91-4
Mustakallio, Kimmo Kalervo 1931- WhoWor 93
Mustard, James Fraser 1927- WhoAm 92
Mustard, James R., Jr. Law&B 92
Mustard, M. Elizabeth Law&B 92
Mustard, Mary Carolyn 1948- WhoAmW 93
Muste, Abraham John 1885-1967 EncAACR
Mustel, Victor 1815-1890 Baker 92
Musters, George Chaworth 1841-1879 Expl 93
Mustin, Lloyd Montague, II 1959- WhoE 93
Mustin, Michel 1951- WhoScE 91-2
Musto, David Franklin 1936- WhoAm 92
Musto, Ronald Gerald 1948- WhoE 93
Mustoe, David Winston 1930- WhoAm 92
Mustoe, Jack S. Law&B 92
Mustoe, Linda Law&B 92
Mustokoff, Susan B. Law&B 92
Mustone, Amelia P. 1928- WhoAmW 93, WhoE 93
Mustonen, Aki Kaarlo 1948- WhoWor 93
Mustonen, Seppo Erkki 1931- WhoScE 91-4
Musulin, Mike BioIn 17
Muszbek, Laszlo 1942- WhoScE 91-4
Muszynski, Larry Chester 1949- WhoSSW 93
Muszynski, Peter Charles 1928- St&PR 93
Muszynski, Roman 1956- WhoE 93
Muszynski, Wladyslaw Peter 1920- WhoScE 91-4
Mutaftschiev, B. WhoScE 91-2
Mutaguchi, Ren'ya 1888-1966 HarEnMi
Mutai, Mitsuo 1896-1991 BioIn 17
Mutal, Sylvio Semantov 1932- WhoUN 92
Mutalibov, Ayaz Niiazi ogly WhoWor 93
Mutalov, Abdulkhashim WhoWor 93
Mutanabbi, Al- 915-965 OxDcByz
Mutang, Anderson BioIn 17
Mutang Tagal 1954- WhoAsAP 91
Mutasa, Didymus 1935- WhoAfr
Mu'tasim c. 795-842 OxDcByz
Mutawe, Ahmad Abdullah 1942- WhoWor 93
Mutch, Patricia Black 1943- WhoAmW 93
Mutch, Robert Alexander WhoScE 91-1
Mutchler, Edward Michael 1935- WhoAm 92
Mutchler, Thomas Edward 1945- St&PR 93
Mutek, Michael Wendell Law&B 92
Mutek, Michael Wendell 1951- WhoEmL 93
Muten, Lief Ingemar 1928- WhoUN 92
Mutesa, Edward Frederick, II 1924-1969 DcTwHis
Muth, Douglas Cameron 1957- St&PR 93
Muth, George Edward 1906- WhoAm 92
Muth, John Francis 1918- WhoAm 92
Muth, John Fraser 1930- WhoAm 92
Muth, Michael Don 1943- St&PR 93
Muth, Richard Ferris 1927- WhoAm 92, WhoSSW 93
Muth, Robert James 1933- St&PR 93, WhoAm 92
Muthel, Johann Gottfried 1728-1788 Baker 92
Muther, Stephen C. Law&B 92
Muthoo, M.K. 1939- WhoScE 91-3
Muthoo, Maharaj Krishen 1939- WhoUN 92
Muthsam, Herbert Johann 1947- WhoWor 93
Muthspiel, Wolfgang BioIn 17
Muthuswami, Venkatarama Iyer 1937- WhoUN 92
Muthuswamy, Petham Padayatchi 1945- WhoWor 93
Muti, Riccardo BioIn 17
Muti, Riccardo 1941- Baker 92, IntDcOp [port], OxDcOp, WhoAm 92, WhoE 93, WhoWor 93
Mutimukulu, Walter WhoWor 93
Mutis, Alvaro 1923- SpAmA
Mutis, Jose Celestino 1732-1808 Expl 93
Muto, Anthony J. Law&B 92
Muto, Joseph Yosio 1912- WhoWor 93
Muto, Kabun 1926- WhoAsAP 91
Muto, Nobuyoshi 1866-1933 HarEnMi
Muto, Sanji 1925- WhoAsAP 91
Muto, Susan Annette 1942- WhoAm 92
Muto, Takasuke 1930- WhoWor 93
Muto Akiro 1892-1948 HarEnMi
Mutola, Maria de Lurdes BioIn 17, NewYTBS 92 [port]
Mutombo, Dikembe BioIn 17
Mutone, Edward 1940- St&PR 93
Mutrie, James 1851-1938 BiDAMSp 1989
Mutrux, Floyd MiSFD 9
Mutsch, Franz J.N. 1948- WhoScE 91-4
Mutschler, Ernst 1931- WhoScE 91-3
Mutschler, Herbert Frederick 1919- WhoAm 92
Mutschler, John Robert 1947- St&PR 93
Mutsuura, Kouichi 1950- WhoWor 93
Mutt, John 1950- St&PR 93
Mutter, Anne-Sophie 1963- Baker 92, BioIn 17
Mutter, Bill BioIn 17
Mutterperl, William C. Law&B 92
Mutters, David Ray 1949- WhoEmL 93, WhoSSW 93
Mutty, Paul Roland 1939- WhoWor 93
Mutumbuka, Dzingai Barnabas 1945- WhoAfr
Mutz, Michael Joseph 1948- WhoSSW 93
Mutz, Oscar Ulysses 1928- St&PR 93, WhoAm 92
Mutziger, John Charles 1949- WhoSSW 93
Mutziger, Judy Lynn 1947- WhoEmL 93, WhoWor 93
Muul, Illar 1938- WhoSSW 93
Muuse, Bart G. 1943- WhoScE 91-3
Muuss, Rolf Eduard 1924- WhoAm 92, WhoE 93
Muwanga, Paulo BioIn 17
Muxart, Roland 1926- WhoScE 91-2
Muybridge, Eadweard 1830-1904 GayN
Muyuela, Roberto 1955- St&PR 93
Muzenda, Simon Vengai 1922- WhoAfr, WhoWor 93
Muzet, Alain 1942- WhoScE 91-2
Muzikant, Jaroslav WhoScE 91-4
Muzingo, Gregory S. Law&B 92
Muzio, Claudia 1889-1936 Baker 92, IntDcOp, OxDcOp
Muzio, Costante 1944- WhoUN 92
Muzio, (Donnino) Emanuele 1821-1890 Baker 92
Muzljakovich, Harriet Sue 1956- WhoAmW 93
Muzondo, Timothy R. 1944- WhoUN 92
Muzorewa, Abel Tendekayi 1925- DcTwHis, WhoAfr, WhoWor 93
Muzyka, Donald Richard 1938- WhoAm 92, WhoE 93
Muzzall, David Cleveland 1924- St&PR 93
Muzzarelli, Lisa Mary 1961- WhoAmW 93
Muzzatti, Loris D. 1957- St&PR 93
Muzzatti, Luciano Domenico 1954- WhoWor 93
Muzzy, James F. 1939- WhoIns 93
Mvouama, Pierre 1934- WhoUN 92
Mwaanga, Vernon 1944- WhoAfr
Mwadilifu, Mwalima Imara WhoWrEP 92
Mwakawago, Daudi Ngelautwa 1939- WhoAfr
Mwambazi, Wedson Chisha 1943- WhoUN 92
Mwangale, Elijah Wasike 1939- WhoAfr
Mwangi, Meja 1948- DcLB 125 [port]
Mwauluka, K. WhoWor 93
Mwenye Hadithi BioIn 17
Mwinyi, Ali Hassan BioIn 17
Mwinyi, Ali Hassan 1925- WhoAfr, WhoWor 93

Myra, Harold Lawrence 1939- *WhoAm 92*
Myrand, Maurice 1928- *St&PR 93*
Myrberg, Arthur August, Jr. 1933- *WhoAm 92*
Myrberget, Svein 1930- *WhoScE 91-4*
Myrdal, Alva Reimer 1902-1986 *BioIn 17*
Myrdal, Gunnar 1898-1987 *BioIn 17*
Myrdal, Jan *BioIn 17*
Myrdal, Jan 1927- *WhoWor 93*
Myrdal, Rosemarie Caryle 1929- *WhoAmW 93*
Myre, Florence *BioIn 17*
Myren, David James 1960- *WhoEmL 93*
Myren, Richard Albert 1924- *WhoAm 92*
Myren, Richard Thomas 1936- *St&PR 93*
Myrepsos, Nicholas *OxDcByz*
Myrer, Anton Olmstead 1922- *WhoAm 92*
Myres, Karen W. 1944- *WhoE 93*
Myrianthousis, T.S. 1933- *WhoScE 91-4*
Myrick, Henry L. 1946- *St&PR 93*
Myrick, James J. *Law&B 92*
Myrick, John Carlton 1963- *WhoSSW 93*
Myrick, John Southall, II 1933- *WhoSSW 93*
Myrick, Judith Myrna 1942- *WhoSSW 93*
Myrick, Julian Southall 1880-1969 *BiDAMSp 1989*
Myrick, Ronald E. *Law&B 92*
Myrick, Sue 1941- *WhoAm 92, WhoAmW 93*
Myrmo, Emil A. 1917- *St&PR 93*
Myrmo, George Arthur 1946- *St&PR 93*
Myron, William Paul 1966- *WhoE 93*
Myrus, Don 1927- *ScF&FL 92*
Myrvang, Tor 1947- *WhoUN 92*
Mysak, Lawrence Alexander 1940- *WhoAm 92*
Mysen, Bjorn Olav 1947- *WhoE 93*
Myslinski, Alice Diane 1946- *WhoAmW 93*
Myslinski, Norbert Raymond 1947- *WhoE 93, WhoEmL 93*
Myslivecek, Josef 1737-1781 *Baker 92*
Myslivecek, Joseph 1737-1781 *OxDcOp*
Mysliweczek, Josef 1737-1781 *Baker 92*
Mysliwiec, Mieczyslaw 1926- *WhoScE 91-4*
Myster, Jay D. *Law&B 92*
Myster, Jay D. 1938- *St&PR 93*
Mystics *SoulM*
Myszewski, Jan M. 1953- *WhoScE 91-4*
Mysz-Gmeiner, Lula 1876-1948 *Baker 92*
Myszkowski, Jerzy 1932- *WhoScE 91-4*
Myszuga, Alexander 1853-1922 *Baker 92*
Mytelka, Arnold Krieger 1937- *WhoE 93*
Myttenaere, C.O.M.R. 1927- *WhoScE 91-2*
Myung, John Y. *Law&B 92*
Mzali, Mohamed 1925- *WhoWor 93*

N

Na, Chi-Liang *BioIn 17*
Na, Teng-Choon 1942- *WhoWor 93*
Na, Tsung Shun 1932- *WhoSSW 93*
Naaktgeboren, Nico 1948- *WhoScE 91-3*
Naaman, Shirley E. d1991 *BioIn 17*
Nabarro, Frank Reginald Nunes 1916- *WhoWor 93*
Nabatoff, Robert Allan 1918- *WhoE 93*
Nabb, Lowery H. 1941- *St&PR 93*
Naber, Steven John 1952- *St&PR 93*
Naber, Thomas Charles *Law&B 92*
Naber, Thomas W. 1951- *St&PR 93*
Nabers, Drayton, Jr. 1940- *St&PR 93, WhoAm 92, WhoIns 93*
Nabeshima, Tamotsu 1935- *WhoWor 93*
Nabeshima, Tatsuya 1955- *WhoWor 93*
Nabet, Pierre 1936- *WhoScE 91-2*
Nabeya, Seiji 1925- *WhoWor 93*
Nabhan, Lou Anne Jones 1955- *WhoSSW 93*
Nabhani, Mohammed Kamel 1951- *WhoWor 93*
Nabi, Nurun 1947- *WhoWor 93*
Nabi, Stanley A. 1930- *St&PR 93*
Nabi, Stanley Andrew 1930- *WhoAm 92*
Nabial, John Walter 1957- *St&PR 93*
Nabielak, Ludwik 1804-1883 *PolBiDi*
Nabili, Marva *MiSFD 9*
NabiRahni, Mohammad Ali 1956- *WhoE 93*
Nabis d192BC *HarEnMi*
Nabiyev, Rakhman Nabievich 1930- *WhoWor 93*
Nabney, J. *WhoScE 91-1*
Naboicheck, N. Aaron 1917- *St&PR 93*
Naboicheck, Peter Mark 1952- *St&PR 93*
Naboicheck, Robert Jon 1954- *St&PR 93*
Nabokov, Nicolas 1903-1978 *Baker 92*
Nabokov, Vera 1902-1991 *BioIn 17*
Nabokov, Vladimir 1899-1977 *MagSAmL [port], MagSWL [port], ScF&FL 92, ShSCr 11 [port], WorLitC [port]*
Nabokov, Vladimir Vladimirovich 1899-1977 *BioIn 17*
Nabors, Clair Alson 1912- *St&PR 93*
Nabors, James D. 1942- *WhoAm 92*
Nabors, James Douglas 1942- *St&PR 93*
Nabors, James Thurston 1930- *WhoAm 92*
Nabors, Michael 1944- *St&PR 93*
Nabrit, James M., Jr. 1919- *OxCSupC*
Nabuco, Joaquim 1849-1910 *BioIn 17*
Nabulsi, Basam E. *Law&B 92*
Nabulsi, Mohammad Said 1928- *WhoWor 93*
Nabwera, Burudi 1927- *WhoAfr*
Naccache, Claude *WhoScE 91-2*
Naccarato, Duane Gabriel 1945- *St&PR 93, WhoAm 92*
Naccarato, Remo 1933- *WhoScE 91-3*
Naccarato, Vincent A. 1938- *St&PR 93*
Naccarella, Anthony D. 1931- *St&PR 93*
Nace, Harold Russ 1921- *WhoAm 92*
Nace, Pierce *ScF&FL 92*
Nace, Thomas C. 1944- *St&PR 93*
Nacey, Michael 1930- *St&PR 93*
Nachbar, Kenneth Jon 1956- *WhoEmL 93*
Nachbar, Marshall J. *Law&B 92*
Nachbar, Randa Roen 1956- *WhoEmL 93*
Nachbar Hapai, Marlene Marie 1948- *WhoEmL 93*
Nachbaur, Edgar 1932- *WhoScE 91-4*
Nachbaur, Franz 1830-1902 *OxDcOp*
Nachbaur, Franz (Ignaz) 1830-1902 *Baker 92*
Nachbin, Leopoldo 1922- *WhoWor 93*
Nachemson, Alf L. 1931- *WhoScE 91-4*
Nachman, Elana *ScF&FL 92*
Nachman, Gerald 1930- *St&PR 93*
Nachman, Gerald 1938- *ConAu 37NR*
Nachman, Gerald Weil 1938- *WhoAm 92*
Nachman, Merton Roland, Jr. 1923- *WhoAm 92*
Nachman, Norman Harry *WhoAm 92, WhoWor 93*
Nachman, Ronald James 1954- *WhoEmL 93*
Nachman, Steven Mark 1958- *WhoEmL 93*
Nachmias, Carolyn Sharenow 1956- *WhoEmL 93*
Nacht, Daniel Joseph 1915- *WhoAm 92*
Nachtigal, Gustav 1834-1885 *Expl 93 [port]*
Nachtigal, Patricia *Law&B 92*
Nachtigal, Patricia 1946- *WhoAm 92*
Nachtigall, George A. *Law&B 92*
Nachtigall, Werner 1934- *WhoScE 91-3*
Nacht-Samborski, Artur 1898-1974 *PolBiDi*
Nachtway, Donna F. 1959- *St&PR 93*
Nachtway, Michael 1953- *St&PR 93*
Nachtwey, James 1948- *BioIn 17*
Nack, Donald Henry 1923- *WhoAm 92*
Nack, Susan Helene 1949- *WhoAmW 93*
Nacker, Wayne Earl *Law&B 92*
Nacknouck, James Dominic 1950- *WhoE 93*
Naclerio, Steven *Law&B 92*
Nacol, Habeeb Mattar 1947- *St&PR 93*
Nacol, Mae 1944- *WhoWor 93*
Nacola, Jo *WhoAsAP 91*
Nad, Leon 1927-1991 *BioIn 17*
Nadal, Ramon Antonio 1935- *St&PR 93*
Nadal de Santa Coloma, Juan *HispAmA*
Nadar, Thomas Raymond 1946- *WhoSSW 93*
Nadas, Alexander Sandor 1913- *WhoAm 92*
Naddafi, Nancy Lee 1947- *WhoAmW 93*
Nadeau, Allan J. 1935- *WhoAm 92*
Nadeau, Bertin F. 1940- *WhoAm 92*
Nadeau, Eleanor Saxe 1909- *WhoAm 92*
Nadeau, Paul Joseph 1953- *St&PR 93*
Nadeau, R. *Law&B 92*
Nadeau, Timothy 1940- *St&PR 93*
Nadeem, Aslam Malik 1956- *WhoWor 93*
Nadeem, Rahat 1965- *WhoWor 93*
Nadel, Alan B. *Law&B 92*
Nadel, Arno 1878-1943 *Baker 92*
Nadel, Bernard 1909-1990 *BioIn 17*
Nadel, Edwin 1928- *WhoIns 93*
Nadel, Elliott 1945- *WhoAm 92, WhoWor 93*
Nadel, Fred S. 1936- *WhoE 93*
Nadel, Ira Bruce 1943- *ConAu 39NR*
Nadel, Jay C. 1957- *St&PR 93*
Nadel, Kay Chaney 1945- *WhoE 93*
Nadel, Kenneth Lyn 1965- *St&PR 93*
Nadel, Marvin 1926- *WhoAm 92*
Nadel, Norman Allen 1927- *WhoAm 92*
Nadel, S.F. 1903-1956 *IntDcAn*
Nadelberg, Eric Paul 1947- *WhoE 93, WhoEmL 93*
Nadelhoffer, Hans (L.) 1940-1988 *ConAu 137*
Nadell, Andrew Thomas 1946- *WhoWor 93*
Nadell, Jeffrey Allen *Law&B 92*
Nadelman, Elie 1882-1946 *BioIn 17, PolBiDi*
Nadelmann, Ethan Avram 1957- *WhoE 93, WhoEmL 93*
Nadelson, Carol Cooperman 1936- *WhoAm 92*
Nadelson, Eileen Nora 1938- *WhoAmW 93*
Naden, Vernon Dewitt 1947- *WhoEmL 93*
Nader, Abraham Lee 1941- *St&PR 93*
Nader, Blair 1931- *St&PR 93*
Nader, Francois Emile 1956- *WhoWor 93*
Nader, Fred *BioIn 17*
Nader, George 1940- *ScF&FL 92*
Nader, Julianna Chapman 1935- *WhoAmW 93*
Nader, Nathra d1991 *BioIn 17*
Nader, Ralph *BioIn 17*
Nader, Ralph 1934- *PolPar, WhoAm 92, WhoWrEP 92*
Nader, Robert Alexander 1928- *WhoAm 92*
Nadermann, Francois Joseph 1781-1835 *Baker 92*
Nadich, Judah 1912- *WhoAm 92, WhoE 93*
Nadig, David G. *Law&B 92*
Nadig, Gerald G. 1945- *St&PR 93*
Nadig, Gerald George 1945- *WhoAm 92*
Nadile, Janet *Law&B 92*
Nadiri, M. Ishaq 1936- *WhoAm 92*
Nadjita, Beassoumal *WhoWor 93*
Nadjmi, Maschallah 1929- *WhoScE 91-3*
Nadkarni, Girish Vishwanath 1957- *WhoEmL 93*
Nadkarni, Govind Bhalchandra 1950- *St&PR 93*
Nadler, Dorothy Luria *WhoWrEP 92*
Nadler, Emanuel 1934- *St&PR 93*
Nadler, Gerald 1924- *WhoAm 92*
Nadler, Harry 1930-1990 *BioIn 17*
Nadler, Henry Louis 1936- *WhoAm 92*
Nadler, Maurice 1908- *WhoSSW 93*
Nadler, Myron Jay 1923- *WhoAm 92*
Nadler, Paul S. 1930- *St&PR 93*
Nadler, Paul Stephen 1930- *WhoE 93*
Nadler, Sheila June 1943- *WhoAm 92*
Nadler, Sigmond Harold 1932- *WhoAm 92*
Nadley, Harris Jerome 1926- *WhoAm 92, WhoE 93*
Nadlman, Jay Michael *Law&B 92*
Nadolink, Richard Hughes 1943- *WhoE 93*
Nadolny, John R. *Law&B 92*
Nadolski, Roman 1940- *WhoScE 91-4*
Nadolsky, Richard J. 1940- *St&PR 93*
Nadorff, N.J. *Law&B 92*
Nadzick, Judith Ann 1948- *St&PR 93, WhoAmW 93*
Naeem, Ahmad 1946- *WhoWor 93*
Naef, Weston John 1942- *WhoAm 92*
Naegele, Carl Joseph 1939- *WhoAm 92*
Naegele, Philipp Otto 1928- *WhoAm 92*
Naegelin, Roland 1931- *WhoScE 91-4*
Naegle, Dale W. 1928- *WhoAm 92*
Naegle, Madeline Anne 1942- *WhoE 93*
Naeser, Nancy Dearien 1944- *WhoAmW 93*
Naeve, Milo Merle 1931- *WhoAm 92*
Naeve, Nancy Jammer 1931- *WhoAmW 93*
Naeve, Stephen W. 1947- *St&PR 93*
Naeye, Richard L. 1929- *WhoAm 92*
Nafe, John Elliott 1914- *WhoAm 92*
Nafeh, Sobhy Mohamed 1937- *WhoWor 93*
Naff, Charles 1943- *St&PR 93*
Naff, Colleen B. *Law&B 92*
Nafie, Laurence Allen 1945- *WhoAm 92*
Nafilyan, Guy 1945- *St&PR 93*
Naftalis, Gary Philip 1941- *WhoAm 92*
Naftolin, Frederick 1936- *WhoAm 92*
Naftzger, Jay R. *Law&B 92*
Naftzger, John E. 1918- *St&PR 93*
Naftzinger, H. Robert 1928- *St&PR 93*
Nafzger, Carl *BioIn 17*
Nafziger, Estel Wayne 1938- *WhoAm 92*
Nafziger, Marvin J. 1933- *St&PR 93*
Nagae, Yoshio 1928- *WhoWor 93*
Nagahara, Keiji 1922- *WhoWor 93*
Nagai, Kanegi 1931- *St&PR 93*
Nagai, Mariko 1943- *WhoWor 93*
Nagai, Takanobu 1930- *WhoAsAP 91*
Nagai, Takashi 1908-1951 *BioIn 17*
Nagai, Toshikazu 1932- *WhoWor 93*
Nagai, Tsuneji 1933- *WhoWor 93*
Nagai, Yohei 1938- *WhoWor 93*
Nagamatsu, Henry Takeshi 1916- *WhoAm 92*
Nagamiya, Shoji 1944- *WhoE 93, WhoWor 93*
Nagan, Douglas A. 1941- *St&PR 93*
Nagan, Douglas Andrew 1941- *WhoAm 92*
Nagan, Peter Seymour 1920- *WhoAm 92*
Nagano, Hiroaki 1948- *St&PR 93*
Nagano, Kent 1951- *BioIn 17*
Nagano, Kent (George) 1951- *Baker 92*
Nagano, Paul Tatsumi 1938- *WhoE 93*
Nagano, Shigeto 1922- *WhoAsAP 91*
Nagano Osami 1880-1947 *HarEnMi*
Nagant De Deuxchaisnes, Charles 1932- *WhoScE 91-2*
Nagao, Makoto 1936- *WhoWor 93*
Nagao, Shigeo 1919- *WhoWor 93*
Nagao, Takaaki 1939- *WhoWor 93*
Nagarkatti, Jai P. 1947- *St&PR 93*
Nagarkatti, Jai Prakash 1947- *WhoAm 92*
Nagasaka, Francis Genichiro 1921- *WhoWor 93*
Nagasako, Lynn T. *Law&B 92*
Nagasawa, Mitsuru 1923- *WhoWor 93*
Nagase, Hiroshi 1947- *WhoWor 93*
Nagase, Jinen 1943- *WhoAsAP 91*
Nagasue, Eiichi 1918- *WhoAsAP 91*
Nagata, Hiroshi 1949- *WhoWor 93*
Nagata, Kiyoshi 1937- *WhoWor 93*
Nagata, Minoru 1933- *WhoWor 93*
Nagata, Yoshio 1931- *WhoAsAP 91*
Nagata Tetsuzan 1884-1935 *HarEnMi*
Nagatoshi, Konrad R. 1951- *WhoAm 92*
Nagaya, Yoshihiko 1941- *St&PR 93*
Nagayasu, Yukimasa 1941- *WhoWor 93*
Nagel, Bruce F. 1946- *St&PR 93*
Nagel, Charles d1992 *NewYTBS 92 [port]*
Nagel, Charles 1899-1992 *BioIn 17*
Nagel, Conrad 1897-1970 *BioIn 17*
Nagel, David S. *BioIn 17*
Nagel, Doris Katherine *Law&B 92*

Nagel, Edward M. 1926- *St&PR 93*
Nagel, Edward McCaul 1926- *WhoAm 92*
Nagel, Ferenc 1931- *WhoScE 91-4*
Nagel, H.H. *WhoScE 91-3*
Nagel, H. Peter 1913- *St&PR 93*
Nagel, John Richard 1939- *St&PR 93*
Nagel, Karen D. *Law&B 92*
Nagel, Madeline 1939- *WhoAmW 93*
Nagel, Max Richard 1909- *WhoWor 93*
Nagel, Patricia A. *WhoAmW 93*
Nagel, Paul Chester 1926- *WhoAm 92*
Nagel, Richard 1957- *WhoWrEP 92*
Nagel, Robert W. 1940- *St&PR 93*
Nagel, Sidney Robert 1948- *WhoAm 92*
Nagel, Spencer Carlyle 1927- *St&PR 93*
Nagel, Stanley Blair 1928- *WhoWor 93*
Nagel, Stephen R. 1950- *St&PR 93*
Nagel, Terry LeRoy, Jr. 1963- *WhoSSW 93*
Nagel, Tracy Lynn 1967- *WhoAmW 93*
Nagel, Walter 1957- *WhoEmL 93*
Nagel, Wilibald 1863-1929 *Baker 92*
Nagel, William Lee 1949- *WhoWor 93*
Nagel'-Arbatskil, Konstantin Solimanovich *BioIn 17*
Nagele, Rainer 1943- *WhoAm 92*
Nageli, Hans Georg 1773-1836 *Baker 92*
Nagell, Raymond H. 1927- *WhoE 93*
Nagelmann, Eric *BioIn 17*
Nagel Soepenberg, Everhardus 1933- *WhoWor 93*
Nager, Rob 1948- *St&PR 93*
Nager, Steve 1949- *WhoWor 93*
Nagera, Humberto 1927- *WhoAm 92*
Nagey, David Augustus 1950- *WhoEmL 93*
Naggs, Karle Frederick 1933- *St&PR 93*
Naghdi, Paul Mansour 1924- *WhoAm 92*
Naghi, Gheorghe 1932- *DrEEuF*
Nagi, Catherine Raseh 1940- *WhoAmW 93*
Nagi, Mostafa Helmey 1934- *WhoWor 93*
Nagiel, Esther-Marie 1956- *WhoWrEP 92*
Nagin, Lawrence M. *Law&B 92*
Nagin, Lawrence M. 1941- *St&PR 93, WhoAm 92*
Naginski, Charles 1909-1940 *Baker 92*
Nagl, Manfred 1944- *WhoScE 91-3, WhoWor 93*
Naglak, Jeanne Rand 1959- *WhoEmL 93*
Nagle, Arlington, Jr. 1943- *St&PR 93, WhoAm 92*
Nagle, Arthur Joseph 1938- *WhoAm 92*
Nagle, Brandy *BioIn 17*
Nagle, David Edward 1954- *WhoEmL 93*
Nagle, David R. 1943- *CngDr 91, WhoAm 92*
Nagle, Dennis Charles 1945- *WhoE 93*
Nagle, Friend Richard 1930- *St&PR 93*
Nagle, George, Jr. 1932- *WhoE 93*
Nagle, George Raymond 1947- *WhoEmL 93*
Nagle, Hubert Troy, Jr. 1942- *WhoAm 92*
Nagle, James M. 1946- *St&PR 93*
Nagle, Jean Sue 1936- *WhoAmW 93*
Nagle, Justine Teresa 1940- *WhoWor 93*
Nagle, Karen M. *Law&B 92*
Nagle, N. Lawrence *Law&B 92*
Nagle, Nano 1718-1784 *BioIn 17*
Nagle, Peggy Jo 1955- *WhoAmW 93*
Nagle, Raymond J. 1900-1991 *BioIn 17*
Nagle, Robert John 1958- *WhoEmL 93*
Nagle, William B. 1939- *St&PR 93*
Naglee, David Ingersoll 1930- *WhoWrEP 92*
Nagler, Alois Maria 1907- *WhoAm 92*
Nagler, Barney *BioIn 17*
Nagler, Barry *Law&B 92*
Nagler, Eric 1942- *ConMus 8 [port]*
Nagler, Leon Gregory 1932- *St&PR 93, WhoAm 92*
Nagler, Nathan I. d1991 *BioIn 17*
Nagler, Ronald Markland 1931- *St&PR 93*
Nagler, Stewart Gordon 1943- *St&PR 93, WhoAm 92, WhoIns 93*
Nagler, Yaacov 1947- *St&PR 93*
Naglieri, Thomas Joseph 1937- *WhoAm 92*
Nagoda, Ludvik 1932- *WhoScE 91-4*
Nagorniak, John Joseph 1944- *WhoAm 92, WhoE 93*
Nagorske, Lynn A. 1956- *St&PR 93*
Nagorski, Edwin Allan 1926- *St&PR 93*
Nagoshi, Douglas N. 1942- *St&PR 93*
Nagourney, Herbert 1926- *St&PR 93, WhoAm 92*
Nagrodski, Ronald *BioIn 17*
Nagtegaal, B. *WhoScE 91-3*
Naguib, Mohsen Sobhy 1949- *WhoWor 93*
Nagumo, Chuichi 1886-1944 *HarEnMi*
Nagurski, Bronko 1908-1990 *BioIn 17*
Nagy, Albert N. 1929- *WhoSSW 93*
Nagy, Andrew Francis 1932- *WhoAm 92*
Nagy, Arpad Zoltan 1931- *WhoScE 91-4*
Nagy, Balint *WhoScE 91-4*
Nagy, Bartholomew Stephen 1927- *WhoAm 92*
Nagy, Beverly C. 1942- *St&PR 93*
Nagy, Charles F. 1951- *St&PR 93*
Nagy, Christa Fiedler 1943- *WhoAmW 93*
Nagy, Clive Michael 1936- *St&PR 93*
Nagy, Denes Lajos 1944- *WhoScE 91-4*
Nagy, Elemer 1934- *WhoScE 91-4*
Nagy, Elemer 1940- *WhoScE 91-4*
Nagy, Endre 1923- *WhoScE 91-4*
Nagy, Frank 1938- *St&PR 93*
Nagy, Gail Tyson *WhoAmW 93*
Nagy, Gerald P. *St&PR 93*
Nagy, Imre 1896-1958 *ColdWar 2 [port], DcTwHis*
Nagy, Imre V. 1927- *WhoScE 91-4*
Nagy, Ivan 1938- *MiSFD 9*
Nagy, Ivonne L. *Law&B 92*
Nagy, Janos B. 1941- *WhoScE 91-2*
Nagy, Lajos 1934- *WhoScE 91-4*
Nagy, Lajos 1935- *WhoScE 91-4*
Nagy, Lajos Gyorgy 1930- *WhoScE 91-4*
Nagy, Louis *Law&B 92*
Nagy, Louis Leonard 1942- *WhoAm 92*
Nagy, Melinda McCorkle 1959- *WhoEmL 93*
Nagy, Miklos *WhoScE 91-4*
Nagy, Nandor 1926- *WhoScE 91-4*
Nagy, Peter *BioIn 17*
Nagy, Phyllis 1961- *WhoAmW 93*
Nagy, Robert David 1929- *WhoAm 92*
Nagy, Robert E. 1942- *St&PR 93*
Nagy, Roy Alan 1951- *WhoE 93*
Nagy, Sandor 1932- *WhoScE 91-4*
Nagy, Stephen William 1940- *St&PR 93*
Nagy, Steven 1936- *WhoAm 92, WhoSSW 93*
Nagys, Elizabeth Ann *WhoAmW 93*
Nagyvary, Joseph *BioIn 17*
Naha, Ed 1950- *ScF&FL 92*
Nahabedian, Charles Edward 1940- *WhoE 93*
Nahabedian, Diane Sonia 1957- *WhoAmW 93*
Nahai, Hamid 1952- *WhoAm 92*
Nahan, David E. 1960- *St&PR 93*
Nahapetian, Ara Toonnaz 1942- *WhoE 93*
Nahas, Gabriel Georges 1920- *WhoAm 92, WhoE 93*
Nahat, Dennis F. 1946- *WhoAm 92*
Nahavandi, Amir Nezameddin 1924- *WhoAm 92*
Nahhas Pasha, Mustafa al- 1876?-1965 *BioIn 17*
Nahhas Pasha, Mustafa al- 1879-1965 *DcTwHis*
Nahigian, Alma Louise 1936- *WhoAmW 93*
Nahigian, Robert John 1956- *WhoE 93, WhoEmL 93, WhoWor 93*
Nahikian, William O. *WhoAm 92*
Nahirny, Michael 1948- *St&PR 93*
Nahm, Milton Charles 1903-1991 *BioIn 17*
Nahman, Murray 1927- *St&PR 93*
Nahman, Norris Stanley 1925- *WhoAm 92*
Nahmias, Andre Joseph 1930- *WhoAm 92*
Nahmlos, John *ScF&FL 92*
Nahodil, Vladimir 1925- *WhoScE 91-4*
Nahorski, Stefan R. *WhoScE 91-1*
Nahorski, Zbigniew Tadeusz 1945- *WhoWor 93*
Nahoun, Martin Joel 1945- *St&PR 93*
Nahr, K. Wilhelm 1938- *WhoUN 92*
Nahra, Barbara Hall *Law&B 92*
Nahra, Nancy Ann 1947- *WhoWrEP 92*
Nahrgang, Delfina 1943- *WhoAmW 93*
Nahrwold, David Lange 1935- *WhoAm 92*
Nahrwold, James Lange 1939- *WhoIns 93*
Nahum, Henri *WhoScE 91-2*
Naider, Fred Robert 1945- *WhoE 93*
Naides, Philip 1930- *St&PR 93*
Naidoo, Beverley *BioIn 17, DcChlFi*
Naidoo, Beverly 1943- *ChlLR 29 [port]*
Naidorf, Louis Murray 1928- *WhoAm 92*
Naidorf, Victoria B. *Law&B 92*
Naidorff, Victoria B. *Law&B 92*
Naidu, Seetala Veeraswamy 1957- *WhoSSW 93*
Naidus, R.A. *Law&B 92*
Naifeh, James O. 1939- *WhoSSW 93*
Naifeh, John Thomas 1958- *WhoEmL 93*
Naifeh, Steven Woodward 1952- *ConAu 40NR*
Naigur, Marvin A. *Law&B 92*
Naik, Arun R. 1941- *WhoScE 91-3*
Naik, G. Swamy 1934- *WhoAsAP 91*
Naik, L. Narsingh 1938- *WhoAsAP 91*
Naik, R.S. 1933- *WhoAsAP 91*
Naikar, D.K. 1927- *WhoAsAP 91*
Naiker, Utkatu 1937- *WhoUN 92*
Nail, Dawson B. 1928- *WhoWrEP 92*
Nail, Elizabeth Joana 1937- *WhoAmW 93*
Nail, Jasper Monroe 1939- *WhoSSW 93*
Nail, Lester C. *Law&B 92*
Nail, Sonya Kaye 1962- *WhoEmL 93*
Nail, Sue Lee 1948- *WhoAmW 93*
Nailen, Robert Edward 1960- *WhoEmL 93*
Nailing, Geneva M. 1940- *WhoAmW 93*
Nailling, Robert Anderson *Law&B 92*
Nailor, Richard Anthony 1935- *WhoSSW 93*
Nails, Kenneth H. *Law&B 92*
Nails, Kenneth H. 1942- *WhoIns 93*
Naim, John O. 1954- *WhoE 93*
Naiman, Adeline Lubell 1925- *WhoE 93*
Naiman, Barnet 1900-1991 *BioIn 17*
Naimark, Arnold 1933- *WhoAm 92*
Naimark, George Modell 1925- *WhoE 93*
Naimi, Shapur 1928- *WhoAm 92, WhoE 93, WhoWor 93*
Naimoli, Raymond Anthony 1942- *WhoAm 92*
Naimoli, Vincent Joseph 1937- *St&PR 93, WhoAm 92*
Naimy, Raymond Philip 1947- *WhoUN 92*
Naini, Bhoopal Reddy 1944- *WhoSSW 93*
Naipaul, Shiva 1945-1985 *BioIn 17*
Naipaul, V.S. 1932- *BioIn 17, IntLitE, MagSWL [port]*
Naipaul, V(idiadhar) S(urajprasad) 1932- *DcLB 125 [port]*
Naipaul, Vidiadhar Surajprasad 1932- *BioIn 17, WhoAm 92, WhoWor 93*
Nair, Bala Radhakrishnan 1936- *WhoE 93*
Nair, K. Aiyappan 1936- *WhoE 93*
Nair, Mira *BioIn 17*
Nair, Mira 1957- *MiSFD 9*
Nair, Padmanabhan Padmanabhan 1931- *WhoE 93*
Nair, Raghavan D. 1951- *WhoAm 92*
Nair, Ramachandran P.K. 1942- *WhoSSW 93*
Nair, Velayudhan 1928- *WhoAm 92, WhoWor 93*
Nair, Velupillai Krishnan 1941- *WhoE 93*
Nairn, James Francis 1945- *St&PR 93*
Naisbitt, H.A. 1908- *St&PR 93*
Naisbitt, John *BioIn 17*
Naisbitt, John 1929- *WhoWrEP 92*
Naisby, Alan 1956- *WhoEmL 93*
Naiser, Rick James, Jr. 1957- *WhoEmL 93*
Naish, J. Carrol 1900-1973 *BioIn 17*
Naish, John Carrol *Law&B 92*
Naismith, James 1861-1939 *GayN*
Naito, Akira 1949- *WhoWor 93*
Naito, Hisashi 1961- *WhoWor 93*
Naito, Jushichiro 1906- *WhoWor 93*
Naito, Kenji 1933- *WhoWor 93*
Naito, Solange Emma 1937- *WhoWor 93*
Naito, Takeshi 1929- *WhoAm 92*
Naitoh, Yutaka 1931- *WhoWor 93*
Naitove, Matthew Henry 1949- *WhoAm 92*
Naj, Richard *Law&B 92*
Najar, Jean-Claude *Law&B 92*
Najar, Maryse *St&PR 93*
Najar, Paul J. *Law&B 92*
Najarian, Beverly Elizabeth 1935- *St&PR 93*
Najarian, John Sarkis 1927- *WhoAm 92*
Najarian, Melvin K. *Law&B 92*
Najarian, Melvin Kenneth 1939- *WhoAm 92*
Najdzin, Jean M. 1932- *St&PR 93*
Najean, Yves 1931- *WhoScE 91-2*
Najera, Maria Esther 1906- *DcMexL*
Najera, Rafael 1938- *WhoWor 93*
Najewicz, Michael F. *Law&B 92*
Najgrakowski, Michal 1927- *WhoScE 91-4*
Najibullah, Dr. 1947- *WhoAsAP 91*
Najid, Driss 1949- *WhoWor 93*
Najita, Tetsuo 1936- *WhoAm 92*
Najjar, Barbara Jean 1951- *WhoAmW 93*
Najjar, Edward George 1934- *St&PR 93*
Najm, Emile *BioIn 17*
Najman, Ronald 1948- *WhoE 93*
Najmuddin Kawyani, Najmuddin Kawyani 1947- *WhoAsAP 91*
Najolia, Jo Ann 1946- *WhoAmW 93*
Najzar-Fleger, Dora 1931- *WhoScE 91-4*
Najzer, Mitja 1935- *WhoScE 91-4*
Naka, Akira 1926- *WhoWor 93*
Naka, Allan H. 1946- *St&PR 93*
Nakache, Maurice Joseph 1950- *WhoScE 91-2*
Nakada, Frank Shozo 1931- *WhoUN 92*
Nakada, Yoshinao 1934- *WhoWor 93*
Nakadate, Neil Edward 1943- *WhoWrEP 92*
Nakagaki, Masayuki 1923- *WhoWor 93*
Nakagami, Kenji d1992 *NewYTBS 92*
Nakagawa, Atsuo 1927- *WhoWor 93*
Nakagawa, Jean H. 1943- *St&PR 93*
Nakagawa, Jean Harue 1943- *WhoAm 92*
Nakagawa, Kiyoshi 1945- *WhoWor 93*
Nakagawa, Roger T. 1947- *St&PR 93*
Nakagawa, Roger Tatsuro 1947- *WhoAm 92*
Nakagawa, Shinji 1954- *WhoWor 93*
Nakagawa, Shoichi 1953- *WhoAsAP 91*
Nakagawa, Yoshimi 1933- *WhoAsAP 91*
Nakagawa, Yukio 1916- *WhoAsAP 91*
Nakagawa, Yuzo 1932- *WhoWor 93*
Nakahara, Akiya 1928- *WhoWor 93*
Nakahara, Masayoshi 1927- *WhoWor 93*
Nakahara, Yuji 1944- *WhoWor 93*
Nakai, Hiroshi 1935- *WhoWor 93*
Nakai, Hiroshi 1942- *WhoAsAP 91*
Nakai, Hisao 1934- *WhoWor 93*
Nakai, Minoru 1941- *St&PR 93*
Nakai, Mitsuru 1933- *WhoWor 93*
Nakai, Yoshikazu 1954- *WhoWor 93*
Nakai, Yoshiro 1952- *WhoE 93*
Nakajima, Amane 1961- *WhoWor 93*
Nakajima, Etsuko 1947- *WhoEmL 93*
Nakajima, Gentaro 1929- *WhoAsAP 91*
Nakajima, Hiroshi *WhoScE 91-4*
Nakajima, Hiroshi 1928- *WhoUN 92, WhoWor 93*
Nakajima, Ko *BioIn 17*
Nakajima, Mamoru 1935- *WhoAsAP 91*
Nakajima, Riichiro 1943- *WhoWor 93*
Nakajima, Tsuyoshi 1943- *WhoWor 93*
Nakajima, Yasuko 1932- *WhoAmW 93*
Nakamine, Wendell Tadao 1948- *WhoAm 92*
Nakamoto, Kazuo 1922- *WhoAm 92*
Nakamura, Eiichi 1930- *WhoAsAP 91*
Nakamura, Eiko 1931- *WhoWor 93*
Nakamura, Gen 1948- *WhoWor 93*
Nakamura, Hideshi 1952- *WhoWor 93*
Nakamura, Hiromichi 1942- *WhoWor 93*
Nakamura, Hiroshi 1933- *WhoWor 93*
Nakamura, Hiroyuki 1931- *WhoWor 93*
Nakamura, Iwao 1934- *WhoAsAP 91*
Nakamura, James I. 1919- *WhoAm 92*
Nakamura, Kazuo 1926- *WhoAm 92*
Nakamura, Kazuya 1948- *WhoWor 93*
Nakamura, Kenzo 1924- *St&PR 93*
Nakamura, Kishiro 1949- *WhoAsAP 91*
Nakamura, Leonard Isamu 1948- *WhoEmL 93*
Nakamura, Masako 1930- *WhoWor 93*
Nakamura, Masao 1931- *WhoAsAP 91*
Nakamura, Melvin Masato 1936- *St&PR 93*
Nakamura, Mikio 1946- *WhoWor 93*
Nakamura, Mitsuru James 1926- *WhoAm 92*
Nakamura, Nori 1946- *WhoWor 93*
Nakamura, Robert Motoharu 1927- *WhoAm 92*
Nakamura, Ryo 1937- *WhoWor 93*
Nakamura, Shigeo 1934- *WhoWor 93*
Nakamura, Shoshiro 1929- *WhoWor 93*
Nakamura, Shozaburo 1934- *WhoAsAP 91*
Nakamura, Tadashi 1935- *WhoUN 92*
Nakamura, Takashi 1946- *WhoAm 92*
Nakamura, Taro 1918- *WhoAsAP 91*
Nakamura, Yasuo *St&PR 93*
Nakamura, Yoshio 1950- *WhoSSW 93*
Nakamuta, Kuranosuke 1837-1916 *HarEnMi*
Nakane, Keiichi 1918- *WhoWor 93*
Nakane, Yoshibumi 1938- *WhoWor 93*
Nakanishi, Don Toshiaki 1949- *WhoEmL 93*
Nakanishi, Hiroaki 1946- *WhoWor 93*
Nakanishi, Ichiro 1915- *WhoAsAP 91*
Nakanishi, Keisuke 1941- *WhoAsAP 91*
Nakanishi, Koji 1925- *WhoAm 92*
Nakanishi, Sekisuke 1926- *WhoAsAP 91*
Nakanishi, Tamako 1919- *WhoAsAP 91*
Nakanishi, Terumasa 1947- *WhoWor 93*
Nakanishi, Tsutomu 1939- *WhoWor 93*
Nakanishi, Waro 1949- *WhoWor 93*
Nakano, Eizo 1922- *WhoWor 93*
Nakano, Kansei 1940- *WhoAsAP 91*
Nakano, Kunio 1920- *WhoWor 93*
Nakano, Raymond T. 1945- *St&PR 93*
Nakano, Tetsuzo 1927- *WhoAsAP 91*
Nakano, Wayne K. 1960- *St&PR 93*
Nakano, Yoshiaki 1946- *WhoWor 93*
Nakao, Eiichi 1930- *WhoAsAP 91*
Nakao, Shirley *Law&B 92*
Nakaoka, John Tatsuya 1952- *WhoEmL 93, WhoWor 93*
Nakashian, Mary Rose 1947- *WhoAmW 93, WhoEmL 93*
Nakashima, George 1905-1990 *BioIn 17*
Nakashima, Hideaki 1939- *WhoWor 93*
Nakashima, Katrin *Law&B 92*
Nakasone, Hirofumi 1945- *WhoAsAP 91*
Nakasone, Robert C. 1947- *WhoAm 92, WhoE 93*
Nakasone, Yasuhiro 1918- *WhoAsAP 91, WhoWor 93*
Nakasone Yasuhiro 1918- *DcTwHis*
Nakata, Atsuo 1929- *WhoWor 93*
Nakata, Herbert Minoru 1930- *WhoAm 92*
Nakata, Ikuo 1935- *WhoWor 93*
Nakata, Masaki 1942- *WhoWor 93*
Nakata, Shuji 1937- *WhoWor 93*
Nakata, William Jiro 1950- *St&PR 93*
Nakatani, Gen. 1957- *WhoAsAP 91*
Nakatani, Hiroki 1952- *WhoUN 92*
Nakatani, Roy Eiji 1918- *WhoAm 92*
Nakatsuka, Lawrence Kaoru 1920- *WhoWrEP 92*
Nakatsuyama, Mikio 1932- *WhoWor 93*
Nakauchi, Mitsuaki 1930- *WhoWor 93*

Nakauchi, Tsuneo 1931- *WhoWor 93*
Nakayama, Akiyoshi 1930- *WhoWor 93*
Nakayama, Hiroaki 1935- *WhoWor 93*
Nakayama, Kenichi *Law&B 92*
Nakayama, Masaaki 1932- *WhoAsAP 91*
Nakayama, Nakayama 1943- *WhoAsAP 91*
Nakayama, Shinichi 1946- *WhoWor 93*
Nakayama, Tadashi 1932- *WhoE 93, WhoUN 92*
Nakayama, Taro 1924- *WhoAsAP 91*
Nakayama, Toshio 1925- *WhoAsAP 91*
Nakazato, Hiroshi 1941- *WhoWor 93*
Nakazawa, Cheryl S. *Law&B 92*
Nakazawa, Hiromu 1938- *WhoWor 93*
Nakazawa, Kenji 1934- *WhoAsAP 91*
Nakazawa, Mitsuru 1956- *WhoWor 93*
Nakazawa, Paul Wesley 1951- *WhoE 93*
Nakazawa, Tohru 1929- *WhoWor 93*
Nakazi, Takahiko 1944- *WhoWor 93*
Nakdimen, Kenneth Alan 1947- *WhoEmL 93*
Naker, Mary Leslie 1954- *WhoAmW 93, WhoEmL 93, WhoWor 93*
Nakhimovsky, Alice Stone 1950- *ConAu 139, WhoAmW 93*
Nakhla, Atif Mounir 1946- *WhoE 93*
Nakhla, Ehsan Tawfiq 1937- *WhoUN 92*
Nakhleh, Emile A. 1938- *WhoAm 92*
Nakhleh, Mary Bird 1939- *WhoAmW 93*
Nakhost, Zahra 1948- *WhoAmW 93*
Nakicenovic, Nebojsa 1949- *WhoWor 93*
Nakken, Odd 1937- *WhoScE 91-4*
Nakonek, Michael L. 1951- *St&PR 93*
Nakovich, Frank 1947- *WhoE 93*
Nakrosis, Stephen M. 1965- *WhoE 93*
Nalbandian, Albert Bagratovich 1941- *WhoUN 92*
Nalcioglu, Orhan 1944- *WhoAm 92*
Naldi, Caroline 1801-1876 *OxDcOp*
Naldi, Giuseppe 1770-1820 *OxDcOp*
Naldrett, Anthony James 1933- *WhoAm 92*
Nalebuff, Barry James 1958- *WhoEmL 93*
Nalecz, Maciej 1922- *WhoScE 91-4*
Nalen, Craig Anthony 1930- *WhoAm 92*
Nalepka, Timothy J. *Law&B 92*
Nale Roxlo, Conrado 1898-1971 *SpAmA*
Nalewaja, Donna *WhoAmW 93*
Nalewako, Mary A. 1934- *St&PR 93*
Nalewako, Mary Anne 1934- *WhoAm 92*
Nalkowska, Zofia 1884-1954 *PolBiDi*
Nall, Anita *NewYTBS 92 [port], WhoAmW 93*
Nall, J. Rodman 1937- *St&PR 93*
Nall, Katherine Ligon 1952- *WhoAmW 93*
Nall, LaWanda Carol 1964- *WhoEmL 93*
Nall, Sandra Lillian 1943- *WhoSSW 93*
Nall, William N. 1936- *St&PR 93*
Nalle, George S., Jr. 1919- *St&PR 93*
Nalle, Horace D., Jr. *Law&B 92*
Nalle, Peter Devereux 1947- *WhoAm 92, WhoEmL 93*
Nalley, Elizabeth Ann 1942- *WhoAmW 93*
Nalley, George Burdine, Jr. 1938- *St&PR 93*
Nally, Thomas John 1949- *WhoE 93, WhoEmL 93*
Nalupta, Mariano R., Jr. 1945- *WhoAsAP 91*
Nam, Charles Benjamin 1926- *WhoAm 92, WhoWor 93*
Nam, Jung Wan 1927- *WhoWor 93*
Nam, Ki-Shim 1936- *WhoWor 93*
Nam, Sang Boo 1936- *WhoAm 92*
Namaan *OxDcByz*
Namaliu, Rabbie Langani 1947- *WhoAsAP 91*
Namatame, Akira 1950- *WhoWor 93*
Namath, Joe *BioIn 17*
Namath, Joseph William 1943- *WhoAm 92*
Namba, Tatsuji 1927- *WhoAm 92, WhoE 93, WhoWor 93*
Nambara, Shigeru 1889-1974 *BioIn 17*
Namboodiri, Krishnan 1929- *WhoAm 92*
Nambu, Yoichiro 1921- *WhoAm 92*
Namdari, Bahram 1939- *WhoWor 93*
Namerow, David M. 1947- *WhoE 93*
Nametz, Michael A. *Law&B 92*
Namias, Jerome 1910- *WhoAm 92*
Namier, Lewis 1888-1960 *BioIn 17*
Namihira, Isao *WhoWor 93*
Namikawa, Yukihiko 1945- *WhoWor 93*
Namioka, Lensey (Chao) *DcAmChF 1960*
Namiot, Milton *St&PR 93*
Nam Jae Hee 1935- *WhoAsAP 91*
Namjoshi, Suniti 1941- *WhoCanL 92*
Namkhai, Norbu Chosgyal 1938- *WhoWor 93*
Namour, Michel Alexandre 1935- *WhoAm 92*
Namphy, Henri 1932- *DcCPCAm*
Namuth, Hans 1915-1990 *BioIn 17*
Namyslowski, Karol 1856-1925 *PolBiDi*
Nana Sahib c. 1821-1860 *HarEnMi*
Nanasi, Leslie 1920- *St&PR 93*
Nanasi, Pal 1923- *WhoScE 91-4*
Nanavati, Grace Luttrell 1951- *WhoAmW 93*
Nanavati, Shishir Romeshchandra 1943- *WhoWor 93*
Nanay, Julia 1951- *WhoEmL 93*
Nanberg, Leslie J. 1945- *St&PR 93*
Nancarrow, Conlon 1912- *Baker 92*
Nance, Allan Taylor *Law&B 92*
Nance, Allan Taylor 1933- *WhoAm 92*
Nance, Betty Love 1923- *WhoAm 92, WhoAmW 93, WhoWor 93*
Nance, Cecil Boone, Jr. 1925- *WhoAm 92*
Nance, Earl Charles 1939- *WhoSSW 93*
Nance, Francis Carter 1932- *WhoE 93*
Nance, Harold W. 1924- *St&PR 93*
Nance, Jeremiah Milton, III 1948- *WhoSSW 93*
Nance, Jim d1992 *NewYTBS 92*
Nance, John F. *Law&B 92*
Nance, John J. 1946- *ConAu 137*
Nance, Joseph Milton 1913- *WhoAm 92*
Nance, Marjorie Greenfield 1949- *WhoE 93*
Nance, Mary Joe 1921- *WhoAmW 93, WhoSSW 93, WhoWor 93*
Nance, Mary Judene 1961- *WhoEmL 93*
Nance, Nancy M. 1951- *WhoAmW 93*
Nance, Noleta 1908- *WhoSSW 93*
Nance, Peter M. 1944- *WhoIns 93*
Nance, Peter Maurice 1944- *St&PR 93*
Nance, Rhita Tillotson 1948- *WhoEmL 93*
Nance, Sandra June Taddie 1953- *WhoEmL 93*
Nance, Thomas Charles 1956- *WhoSSW 93*
Nance, Tony Max-Perry 1955- *WhoAm 92*
Nandan, Satya Nand 1936- *WhoUN 92*
Nandino, Elias 1903- *DcMexL*
Nandoe, Kriesnadath 1935- *WhoUN 92*
Nandy, D. *WhoScE 91-1*
Naney, Anita Hope 1947- *WhoAmW 93*
Nanfeldt, Richard E. *Law&B 92*
Nanfria, Linda Jean 1949- *WhoWrEP 92*
Nangle, John Francis 1922- *WhoAm 92*
Nangniot, Paul 1927- *WhoScE 91-2*
Nanian, Marjorie Kay 1953- *WhoEmL 93*
Nanini, Giovanni Bernardino c. 1560-1623 *Baker 92*
Nanini, Giovanni Maria 1543?-1607 *Baker 92*
Nanino, Giovanni Bernardino c. 1560-1623 *Baker 92*
Nanino, Giovanni Maria 1543?-1607 *Baker 92*
Nanjo, Funio d1949 *BioIn 17*
Nank, Lois Rae *WhoAmW 93, WhoWor 93*
Nankin, Michael 1955- *MiSFD 9*
Nanna, Elizabeth Ann Will 1932- *WhoAmW 93*
Nanne, Louis Vincent 1941- *WhoAm 92*
Nanney, Arthur Preston 1945- *WhoIns 93*
Nanney, David Ledbetter 1925- *WhoAm 92*
Nanney, David Powell, Jr. 1958- *WhoEmL 93*
Nanney, Herbert Boswell 1918- *WhoAm 92*
Nanney, J. Edward *Law&B 92*
Nanney, Sondra Tucker 1937- *WhoAmW 93*
Nannichi, Yasuo 1933- *WhoWor 93*
Nannos, Arthur 1927- *St&PR 93*
Nanogak, Agnes 1925- *BioIn 17*
Nanonen, Pertti *WhoScE 91-4*
Nanos, John Michael *Law&B 92*
Nanos, Mark David 1954- *WhoEmL 93*
Nanovic, John L. 1906- *ScF&FL 92*
Nanovsky, William T. 1948- *St&PR 93, WhoAm 92*
Nansen, Fridjof 1861-1930 *DcTwHis*
Nansen, Fridtjof 1861-1930 *Expl 93 [port]*
Nan Shan d1895 *BioIn 17*
Nanson, Alphonse U.J.G. 1936- *WhoScE 91-2*
Nantell, Timothy James 1945- *WhoAm 92*
Nanthanson, Julie *BioIn 17*
Nantier-Didiee, Constance 1831-1867 *OxDcOp*
Nants, Bruce Arlington 1953- *WhoSSW 93*
Nantz, William C. 1935- *WhoSSW 93*
Nanu, Aurel Carol 1921- *WhoScE 91-4*
Nanula, Richard D. *BioIn 17*
Nanula, Richard J. 1932- *St&PR 93*
Nanus, Susan *ScF&FL 92*
Nanut Ries, Lucia Neda 1938- *WhoWor 93*
Nanz, Claus Ernest 1934- *WhoWor 93*
Nanz, Robert Augustus 1915- *WhoSSW 93*
Nanz, Robert Hamilton 1923- *WhoAm 92*
Nao, Ryoko 1917- *WhoAsAP 91*
Naomi *BioIn 17*
Naoroji, Dadabhai 1825-1917 *DcTwHis*
Naoshima, Yoshinobu 1948- *WhoWor 93*
Napack, George d1990 *BioIn 17*
Napadensky, Hyla Sarane 1929- *WhoAm 92*
Napal, Frank S. d1992 *BioIn 17*
Napalkov, Nikolai P. *WhoUN 92*
Napalkov, Valentin 1941- *WhoWor 93*
Naparstek, Arthur J. 1938- *WhoAm 92*
Naparstek, Nathan 1956- *WhoE 93*
Napier, Austin 1947- *WhoE 93*
Napier, Bonnie Dee Gavey 1945- *WhoAmW 93*
Napier, Charles James 1782-1853 *HarEnMi*
Napier, Donald D., III 1953- *St&PR 93*
Napier, Douglas William 1951- *WhoSSW 93, WhoWor 93*
Napier, Elizabeth *Law&B 92*
Napier, Ernest D. 1954- *St&PR 93*
Napier, George C. 1945- *St&PR 93*
Napier, James Voss 1937- *St&PR 93*
Napier, John Hawkins, III 1925- *WhoSSW 93*
Napier, John Light 1947- *WhoAm 92*
Napier, Lois Christine 1942- *WhoAmW 93*
Napier, Richard Hanes 1951- *WhoIns 93*
Napier, Richard Stephen 1949- *WhoAm 92*
Napier, Robert Cornelis 1810-1890 *HarEnMi*
Napier, Robert Jon 1934- *WhoAm 92*
Napier-Winch, John 1947- *WhoWor 93*
Napisa, Rodolfo Reyes 1960- *WhoSSW 93*
Naplatanov, Nikolaj Delchev 1923- *WhoScE 91-4*
Naples, Caesar Joseph 1938- *WhoWor 93*
Naples, Richard Francis Joseph, Jr. 1957- *WhoE 93*
Naples, Ronald James 1945- *St&PR 93, WhoAm 92*
Naples, Sharon J. 1952- *WhoE 93, WhoEmL 93*
Napodano, Rudolph Joseph 1933- *WhoAm 92*
Napoleon, I 1769-1821 *HarEnMi*
Napoleon, I, Emperor of the French 1769-1821 *BioIn 17*
Napoleon, III, Emperor of the French 1808-1873 *BioIn 17*
Napoleon, Donald Paul 1954- *WhoE 93, WhoEmL 93*
Napoleon, Rosalie Mabel 1940- *WhoAmW 93*
Napoleon, Vincent J. *Law&B 92*
Napoleoni, Claudio 1924-1988 *BioIn 17*
Napoles, Veronica Kleeman 1951- *WhoAm 92, WhoEmL 93*
Napoli, Gennaro 1881-1943 *Baker 92*
Napoli, Jacopo 1911- *Baker 92, OxDcOp*
Napoli, Joseph A. *Law&B 92*
Napoli, Joseph A. 1946- *St&PR 93*
Napoli, Thomas A. 1941- *St&PR 93*
Napoliello, Louis R. 1949- *St&PR 93*
Napoliello, Michael John 1942- *WhoAm 92*
Napolitan, Gene J., Jr. 1935- *St&PR 93*
Napolitan, Gene Joseph, Jr. 1935- *WhoE 93*
Napolitan, Joseph 1929- *PolPar*
Napolitano, Gary M. 1956- *St&PR 93*
Napolitano, Janet Ann 1957- *WhoEmL 93*
Napolitano, Joe *MiSFD 9*
Napolitano, Joseph A. 1942- *St&PR 93*
Napolitano, Leonard Michael 1930- *WhoAm 92*
Napolitano, Luigi G. 1928- *WhoScE 91-3*
Napolitano, M. *WhoScE 91-3*
Napolitano, Michael Louis 1945- *St&PR 93*
Napolitano, Pat 1916- *WhoSSW 93, WhoWor 93*
Napombejr, Supachai 1936- *WhoUN 92*
Napompeth, Banpot 1941- *WhoWor 93*
Napor, F. Jack *St&PR 93*
Napper, Alver Woodward, Jr. 1943- *WhoE 93*
Napper, Steven Edward *Law&B 92*
Nappi, Anthony R. 1935- *St&PR 93*
Nappi, Maureen A. 1951- *WhoE 93*
Nappi, Robert A. 1949- *St&PR 93*
Nappo, Elizabeth Hubbell 1959- *WhoEmL 93*
Nappy, Nicholas J. 1946- *WhoE 93*
Napravnik, Eduard 1839-1916 *OxDcOp*
Napravnik, Eduard (Francevic) 1839-1916 *Baker 92*
Naprstek, Kaya M. 1939- *St&PR 93*
Napsiah Bte Omar, Dato' 1943- *WhoAsAP 91*
Napurano, Virginia 1939- *WhoE 93*
Naquet, Alfed Joseph 1834-1916 *BioIn 17*
Naquet, Robert *WhoScE 91-2*
Naquin, Linton Joseph, Jr. 1947- *St&PR 93*
Naquin, Maurice J., Jr. *Law&B 92*
Naquin, Oliver F. *BioIn 17*
Naqvi, Rehan Hasan 1933- *St&PR 93*
Nara, Bonnie Ann 1949- *WhoEmL 93*
Nara, Harry Raymond 1921- *WhoAm 92*
Narabayashi, Hirotaro 1922- *WhoWor 93*
Narad, Joan Stern 1943- *WhoE 93*
Narad, Richard M. 1935- *WhoE 93*
Narahashi, Keiko *ChlBIID [port]*
Narahashi, Toshio 1927- *WhoAm 92*
Narang, Saran Adhar 1930- *WhoAm 92*
Naranjo, Carmen 1928- *SpAmA*
Naranjo, Carmen 1931- *BioIn 17*
Narasaka, Koichi 1944- *WhoWor 93*
Narasaki, Hisatake 1933- *WhoWor 93*
Narasimha, Roddam 1933- *WhoWor 93*
Narasimhalu, Arcot Desai 1949- *WhoWor 93*
Narasimhan, Ram 1947- *WhoAm 92*
Narasimha Rao, P.V. *BioIn 17*
Narath, Albert 1933- *WhoAm 92*
Naratil, William Albert 1936- *WhoE 93*
Narayan, Irene Jai 1932- *WhoAsAP 91*
Narayan, Krishnamurthi Ananth 1930- *WhoE 93*
Narayan, R.K. 1906- *BioIn 17, IntLitE, ScF&FL 92, WhoAsAP 91*
Narayan, Viswanathan 1931- *WhoE 93*
Narayana Guru 1856-1928 *BioIn 17*
Narayanamurti, Venkatesh 1939- *WhoAm 92*
Narayanan, Kocheril Raman 1921- *WhoAsAP 91*
Narayanasamy, V. 1947- *WhoAsAP 91*
Narazaki, Yanosuke 1920- *WhoAsAP 91*
Narber, Gregg R. *Law&B 92*
Narber, Gregg R. 1946- *WhoIns 93*
Narber, Gregg Ross 1946- *St&PR 93*
Narbey, Leon 1947- *MiSFD 9*
Narbonne, Albert Joseph, Sr. 1929- *St&PR 93*
Narbutas, Peter *WhoAm 92*
Narcejac, Thomas 1908- *ScF&FL 92*
Narciso, Anthony J., Jr. 1947- *WhoIns 93*
Narciso, David *Law&B 92*
Narcisse, Robbie E.B. *Law&B 92*
Nardangele, Peter *St&PR 93*
Narde, Kelli Denise 1960- *WhoAmW 93*
Nardelli, Fred *ScF&FL 92*
Nardelli, Mario 1922- *WhoScE 91-3*
Nardi, Catherine *Law&B 92*
Nardi, Henry J. 1943- *WhoUN 92*
Nardi, James C. 1943- *St&PR 93*
Nardi, Joseph A. 1933- *WhoUN 92*
Nardi, Joseph B. 1944- *WhoIns 93*
Nardi, Ralph A., Sr. *St&PR 93*
Nardiello, Robert 1946- *St&PR 93*
Nardini, Franco 1952- *WhoScE 91-3*
Nardini, Pietro 1722-1793 *Baker 92*
Nardino, Gary 1935- *WhoAm 92*
Nardi Riddle, Clarine 1949- *WhoAm 92, WhoAmW 93, WhoE 93*
Nardo, David D. *Law&B 92*
Nardo, Sebastian Vincent 1917- *WhoAm 92*
Nardon, P. *WhoScE 91-2*
Nardon, Paul Georges Edmond 1937- *WhoScE 91-2*
Nardone, Colleen Burke 1940- *WhoAmW 93*
Nardone, Philip A. 1959- *St&PR 93*
Nardozzi, Kathleen S. 1949- *WhoAmW 93*
Nardozzi, Thomas Charles 1952- *WhoEmL 93*
Nardulli, Giuseppe 1948- *WhoWor 93*
Narebska, Anna 1926- *WhoScE 91-4*
Narebski, Juliusz 1926- *WhoScE 91-4*
Narell, Irena Penzik 1923- *WhoWrEP 92*
Narendra, Kumpati Subrahmanya 1933- *WhoAm 92*
Nares, James 1715?-1783 *Baker 92*
Nargi, Janice Mary 1951- *WhoWrEP 92*
Nargis 1929-1981 *IntDcF 2-3 [port]*
Nariboli, Gundo Annacharya 1925- *WhoAm 92*
Narigan, Harold W. 1925- *WhoAm 92*
Narin, Stephen B. 1929- *WhoAm 92*
Narins, Charles Seymour 1909- *WhoWor 93*
Narins, Douglas Matthew 1964- *St&PR 93*
Narins, Lyn Ross 1937- *St&PR 93*
Narins, Robert 1929- *St&PR 93*
Narisi, S. Maria *Law&B 92*
Narisi, Stella Maria 1950- *St&PR 93*
Narita, George M. 1928- *St&PR 93*
Narita, Hiro 1941- *WhoAm 92*
Narita, Jujiro 1933- *WhoWor 93*
Narita, Susan L. 1949- *WhoAmW 93*
Narizzano, Silvio 1928- *MiSFD 9*
Narjes, L.K.O.B. 1926- *WhoScE 91-3*
Narjot, Erneste Erneste de Francheville 1826?-1898 *BioIn 17*
Narkis, Robert Joseph 1934- *St&PR 93, WhoAm 92*
Narliev, Hodzakuli 1937- *DrEEuF*
Narlikar, Jayant Vishnu 1938- *WhoWor 93*
Narmour, Eugene 1939- *Baker 92*
Naro, Anthony Julius 1942- *WhoWor 93*
Narodick, Margaret E. *Law&B 92*
Narodick, Sally G. 1945- *St&PR 93, WhoAm 92, WhoAmW 93*

Narodny, Leo Henry 1909- *WhoWor 93*
Narogin, Mudrooroo 1938- *IntLitE*
Narokobi, Bernard Mullu 1945- *WhoAsAP 91*
Narolewski, Bernard J. 1933- *St&PR 93*
Narotzky, Norman David 1928- *WhoWor 93*
Narrache, Jean 1893-1970 *BioIn 17*
Narro-Gonzalez, Celeste L. 1962- *WhoSSW 93*
Narsai of Edessa c. 399-c. 502 *OxDcByz*
Narses *OxDcByz*
Narses dc. 606 *HarEnMi, OxDcByz*
Narses c. 478-c. 573 *HarEnMi, OxDcByz*
Naruhito Shinno 1960- *BioIn 17*
Narus, Harold *Law&B 92*
Naruse, Jinzo 1858-1919 *BioIn 17*
Naruse, Mikio 1905-1969 *MiSFD 9N*
Naruse, Morishige 1933- *WhoAsAP 91*
Naruse, Tomonori 1933- *WhoAm 92*
Narusis, Regina Gyte Firant 1936- *WhoWor 93*
Naruszewic-Lesiuk, Danuta 1931- *WhoScE 91-4*
Naruszewicz, Adam Stanislaw 1733-1796 *PolBiDi*
Narutowicz, Gabriel 1865-1922 *PolBiDi*
Narvaez, Luis de fl. 1530-1550 *Baker 92*
Narvaez, Ramon Maria 1800-1868 *HarEnMi*
Narvaja, Gerardo Luis 1959- *WhoWor 93*
Narvekar, Prabhakar Ramkrishna 1932- *WhoE 93, WhoUN 92*
Narver, John Colin 1935- *WhoAm 92*
Narveson, Alan Duane 1945- *St&PR 93*
Narveson, Jan Fredric 1936- *WhoWrEP 92*
Narwold, Karen G. *Law&B 92*
Narwold, Lewis Lammers 1921- *WhoAm 92*
Nary, Gilbert Roy *WhoAm 92*
Nary, Gilbert Roy 1922- *St&PR 93*
Nary, Gordon *BioIn 17*
Nasar *OxDcByz*
Nasar, Jack Leon 1947- *WhoWrEP 92*
Nasar, Syed Abu 1932- *WhoAm 92*
Nasatir, Abraham Phineas 1904-1991 *BioIn 17*
Nasby, David Asher 1939- *WhoWor 93*
Naschy, Paul 1938- *BioIn 17*
Nascimento, Aristoteles Filho 1952- *WhoWor 93*
Nascimento, Isaias Goncalves do *BioIn 17*
Nascimento, Jose 1931- *WhoScE 91-3*
Nascimento, Lopo Fortunato Ferreira do 1942- *WhoAfr*
Nascimento, Milton *BioIn 17*
Nascimento Filho, Geraldo Alves 1942- *WhoUN 92*
Nase, Jonathan Paul 1960- *WhoEmL 93*
Naseem, Syed Mohammed 1932- *WhoUN 92*
Naseman, David Milford 1948- *St&PR 93*
Naser, Joseph Albert, II 1947- *WhoEmL 93*
Nasfeter, Janusz 1920- *DrEEuF*
Nasgaard, Roald 1941- *WhoAm 92*
Nash, Abigail Jones 1950- *St&PR 93*
Nash, Alanna K. 1950- *WhoWrEP 92*
Nash, Alanna Kay 1950- *WhoAmW 93, WhoEmL 93*
Nash, Allison Leigh *Law&B 92*
Nash, Bernard Elbert 1922- *WhoAm 92*
Nash, Beth *Law&B 92*
Nash, Bill F. 1930- *WhoAm 92*
Nash, Bradley DeLamater 1900- *WhoAm 92*
Nash, Carol A. 1957- *St&PR 93*
Nash, Charles D. 1943- *WhoSSW 93*
Nash, Charles Edmund 1844-1913 *BioIn 17*
Nash, Charles Presley 1932- *WhoAm 92*
Nash, Colin E. 1937- *WhoScE 91-3*
Nash, David 1929- *WhoE 93*
Nash, David 1942- *BioIn 17*
Nash, David Bret 1955- *WhoE 93*
Nash, David J. 1942- *St&PR 93*
Nash, David M. 1945- *St&PR 93*
Nash, Donald Gene 1945- *WhoAm 92*
Nash, Donald Robert 1938- *WhoSSW 93*
Nash, Edward L. 1936- *WhoAm 92*
Nash, Edward Thomas 1943- *WhoAm 92*
Nash, Father Stephen *ConAu 38NR*
Nash, Frank Erwin 1916- *WhoAm 92*
Nash, Frederick Copp 1908- *WhoWor 93*
Nash, Gardon L. 1928- *St&PR 93*
Nash, Gary Baring 1933- *WhoAm 92*
Nash, George (E.) 1948- *ConAu 138*
Nash, Gerald David 1928- *WhoAm 92*
Nash, Gordon Bernard, Jr. 1944- *WhoAm 92*
Nash, Grace Chapman 1909- *WhoWrEP 92*
Nash, Graham *BioIn 17*
Nash, Graham William 1942- *WhoAm 92*
Nash, Harold Garth 1940- *St&PR 93*
Nash, Heddle 1894-1961 *OxDcOp*
Nash, Heddle 1896-1961 *Baker 92*
Nash, Henry Warren 1927- *WhoAm 92*
Nash, Howard Allen 1937- *WhoAm 92, WhoE 93*
Nash, James E. 1950- *St&PR 93*
Nash, Jay Robert, III 1937- *WhoAm 92, WhoWor 93*
Nash, John Arthur 1938- *St&PR 93, WhoAm 92*
Nash, John Francis, Jr. *Law&B 92*
Nash, John Heddle 1928- *OxDcOp*
See Also Nash, Heddle 1896-1961 *Baker 92*
Nash, John N. 1946- *WhoAm 92, WhoE 93*
Nash, Johnny 1940- *SoulM*
Nash, Johnny Collin 1949- *WhoEmL 93, WhoSSW 93*
Nash, Jonathan David 1955- *WhoE 93*
Nash, Jonathon Michael 1942- *WhoAm 92*
Nash, Julie Watts 1956- *WhoAmW 93*
Nash, June Caprice 1927- *WhoAmW 93*
Nash, Karen Marsteller 1943- *WhoE 93*
Nash, Karl S. 1908- *St&PR 93*
Nash, Karl Seymour d1992 *NewYTBS 92*
Nash, Kenneth M. 1931- *St&PR 93*
Nash, Lee J. 1939- *WhoAm 92*
Nash, Leonard Kollender 1918- *WhoAm 92*
Nash, Mary Sue 1960- *WhoAmW 93*
Nash, Maureen Cecilia 1963- *WhoAmW 93*
Nash, Michael A. *Law&B 92*
Nash, Michael P. 1951- *St&PR 93*
Nash, Michaux, Jr. 1933- *WhoAm 92*
Nash, Monroe 1912- *St&PR 93*
Nash, N. Frederick 1936- *WhoAm 92*
Nash, Nancy Ann *Law&B 92*
Nash, Nicholas David 1939- *WhoAm 92*
Nash, Ogden 1902-1971 *BioIn 17*
Nash, (Frederic) Ogden 1902-1971 *MajAI [port]*
Nash, Patrick E. 1929- *St&PR 93*
Nash, Paul *WhoAm 92*
Nash, Peter David 1951- *WhoEmL 93*
Nash, Peter Hugh John 1921- *WhoAm 92, WhoWor 93*
Nash, Philleo 1909-1987 *IntDcAn*
Nash, Randall Leigh 1954- *WhoEmL 93*
Nash, Ray 1905-1982 *BioIn 17*
Nash, Richard, Jr. 1929- *St&PR 93*
Nash, Richard Eugene 1954- *WhoEmL 93*
Nash, Richard O. 1943- *WhoWor 93*
Nash, Robert Fred 1933- *St&PR 93, WhoAm 92*
Nash, Robert Warren 1964- *WhoSSW 93*
Nash, Ronald Herman 1936- *WhoAm 92, WhoSSW 93*
Nash, Roy C. 1942- *St&PR 93*
Nash, Rufus Wilson 1917- *St&PR 93*
Nash, Ruth Cowan *WhoAmW 93*
Nash, Sharon Scott 1947- *WhoSSW 93*
Nash, Sonja Huddleston 1947- *WhoEmL 93*
Nash, Spencer James 1938- *WhoAm 92*
Nash, Stanton Harris 1915- *WhoSSW 93*
Nash, Stephen Michael 1947- *WhoEmL 93, WhoWor 93*
Nash, Suzanne Patterson 1944- *St&PR 93*
Nash, Thomas B. 1953- *St&PR 93*
Nash, Veronica *WhoAm 92*
Nash, Virginia O. 1922- *St&PR 93*
Nash, Walter 1882-1968 *DcTwHis*
Nash, Walter Birdsall, III 1946- *WhoEmL 93*
Nash, Warren Leslie 1955- *WhoEmL 93, WhoSSW 93*
Nash, William Arthur 1922- *WhoAm 92, WhoE 93*
Nash, William Mitchell 1865-1929 *BiDAMSp 1989*
Nashan, Joy Ortiz 1948- *WhoAmW 93, WhoEmL 93*
Nashashibi, Karim Anwar 1941- *WhoUN 92*
Nashe, Carol *WhoAm 92*
Nashiha, Tokicki 1850-1923 *HarEnMi*
Nashman, Alvin E. 1926- *St&PR 93*
Nashman, Alvin Eli 1926- *WhoAm 92*
Nash-Williams, Crispin St. John Alvah *WhoScE 91-1*
Nasi, Brian T. 1950- *St&PR 93*
Nasidze, Sulkhan 1927- *Baker 92*
Nasielski, Jacques 1929- *WhoScE 91-2*
Nasilowski, Wladyslaw 1925- *WhoScE 91-4*
Nasky, H. Gregory 1942- *St&PR 93*
Naslain, Roger R. 1936- *WhoScE 91-2*
Naslund, Alan Joseph 1941- *WhoWrEP 92*
Naslund, Howard Richard 1950- *WhoE 93*
Nasman, David F. 1935- *St&PR 93*
Nasmyth, Alexander 1758-1840 *BioIn 17*
Nasmyth, Spike *BioIn 17*
Nasolini, Sebastiano c. 1768-c. 1806 *OxDcOp*
Nasolini, Sebastiano c. 1768-c. 1816 *Baker 92*
Nason, Charles T. 1946- *St&PR 93, WhoIns 93*
Nason, Charles Tuckey 1946- *WhoAm 92*
Nason, Charles William 1944- *St&PR 93*
Nason, Dolores Irene 1934- *WhoAmW 93, WhoWor 93*
Nason, Doris Elnora 1913- *WhoAmW 93*
Nason, Fred, Jr. 1930- *St&PR 93*
Nason, Freda Lee 1944- *WhoE 93*
Nason, John William 1905- *WhoAm 92*
Nason, Leonard Yoshimoto 1954- *WhoEmL 93*
Nason, Marilyn E. *WhoSSW 93*
Nason, Nancy Anne 1935- *WhoAmW 93*
Nason, Susan *BioIn 17*
Nason, Tema *ConAu 138*
Nason, Thelma *ConAu 138*
Nason, Thelma Stein *WhoAmW 93*
Nason, Walton Hooker, Jr. 1922- *St&PR 93*
Nason-Cruz, Sally Aurelia 1946- *WhoE 93, WhoEmL 93*
Nasr, Lama M. 1947- *WhoUN 92*
Nasr, Nubugh Elias 1946- *WhoWor 93*
Nasr, Salah 1952- *WhoE 93*
Nasra, George Yousef 1947- *WhoE 93, WhoEmL 93*
Nasrallah, Peter Sfei *WhoWor 93*
Nass, Herbert Evan 1959- *WhoEmL 93*
Nass, Howard *BioIn 17*
Nass, Howard 1939- *St&PR 93*
Nass, Jack 1948- *WhoEmL 93*
Nass, Marcia T. *Law&B 92*
Nassar, George d1989 *BioIn 17*
Nassar, Nahoum Philip 1942- *WhoIns 93*
Nassau, Kurt 1927- *WhoE 93*
Nassau, Michael Jay 1935- *WhoAm 92*
Nassau, Robert Hamill 1941- *St&PR 93*
Nassau-Dietz, Louis of 1538-1574 *HarEnMi*
Nassauer, Bernice *ScF&FL 92*
Nassberg, Richard T. 1942- *WhoAm 92, WhoSSW 93*
Nasser, Essam 1931- *WhoWor 93*
Nasser, Gamal Abd al- 1918-1970 *DcTwHis, HarEnMi*
Nasser, Gamal Abdel 1918-1970 *BioIn 17*
Nasser, Gamal Abdul 1918-1970 *ColdWar 2 [port]*
Nasser, Joseph Yousef 1943- *WhoSSW 93*
Nasser, Moes Roshanali 1956- *WhoEmL 93, WhoSSW 93*
Nasser, William Edward 1939- *St&PR 93*
Nasser, William Kaleel 1933- *WhoWor 93*
Nasseri, Sirous 1955- *WhoUN 92*
Nassif, Rosemarie 1941- *WhoAmW 93*
Nassif, Thomas Anthony 1941- *WhoAm 92*
Nassiff, Tonius *WhoWrEP 92*
Nassikas, John Nicholas 1917- *WhoAm 92*
Nasson, Bill 1952- *ConAu 139*
Nast, Conde 1873-1942 *BioIn 17*
Nast, Dianne Martha 1944- *WhoAm 92*
Nast, Thomas 1840-1902 *JrnUS, PolPar*
Nast, V. Frederick, III 1941- *St&PR 93*
Nastase, Adrian *WhoWor 93*
Nastase, Adriana *WhoScE 91-3*
Nastase, Ilie *BioIn 17*
Nastase, Ilie 1946- *WhoAm 92*
Nastasia, Helen A. *Law&B 92*
Nastasijevic, Svetomir 1902-1979 *Baker 92*
Nastich, Milan M. 1926- *St&PR 93*
Nastiuk, Virginia 1923- *WhoWor 93*
Nastro, Charles P. 1942- *St&PR 93*
Nastro, Charles Paul 1942- *WhoAm 92*
Nasu, Masahiko 1928- *WhoWor 93*
Nasu, Noriyuki 1924- *WhoWor 93*
Nasu, Shoichi 1933- *WhoWor 93*
Nasuto, Romuald 1932- *WhoScE 91-4*
Nasypony, Raymond 1932- *St&PR 93*
Nasyrov, Samyon Raphailovich 1958- *WhoWor 93*
Nasz, Istvan 1927- *WhoScE 91-4*
Nat, Yves 1890-1956 *Baker 92*
Nata, Theophile *WhoWor 93*
Nataf, Helene Michele 1939- *WhoAmW 93*
Natale, A. Charles 1931- *St&PR 93*
Natale, Anthony Gilbert 1952- *St&PR 93*
Natale, Kathleen Rourke 1966- *WhoAmW 93*
Natale, Samuel Michael 1943- *WhoAm 92*
Nataletti, Giorgio 1907-1972 *Baker 92*
Natalicio, Diana S. 1939- *WhoAm 92, WhoAmW 93, WhoSSW 93*
Natalie, Andrea Leigh 1958- *WhoE 93*
Natan-Leod d508 *HarEnMi*
Natansohn, Samuel 1929- *WhoE 93*
Natanson, Jakub 1832-1884 *PolBiDi*
Natanson, Ludwik 1822-1896 *PolBiDi*
Natanson, Maurice Alexander 1924- *WhoAm 92, WhoWrEP 92*
Natanson, Tadeusz 1927-1990 *Baker 92*
Natanson, Wladyslaw 1864-1937 *PolBiDi*
Natarajan, Jayanthl 1954- *WhoAsAP 91*
Natarajan, Ramachandran Nat *WhoEmL 93*
Natarajan, Ramanathan 1934- *WhoUN 92*
Natarajan, T. Raj 1948- *WhoSSW 93*
Natcher, Stephen D. *St&PR 93*
Natcher, Stephen Darlington *Law&B 92*
Natcher, Stephen Darlington 1940- *WhoAm 92*
Natcher, William H. 1909- *CngDr 91*
Natcher, William Huston 1909- *WhoAm 92, WhoSSW 93*
Nate, Thomas Edward 1954- *WhoEmL 93*
Natelson, Stephen Ellis 1937- *WhoAm 92*
Natenberg, Steven R. *Law&B 92*
Nath, Florine N. *St&PR 93*
Nath, Joginder 1932- *WhoAm 92, WhoSSW 93*
Nath, Prem 1937- *WhoUN 92*
Nathan *BioIn 17*
Nathan, Adele *AmWomPl*
Nathan, Alan 1940- *St&PR 93*
Nathan, Bobby 1950- *WhoEmL 93*
Nathan, Carl Francis 1946- *WhoAm 92*
Nathan, Daniel *ConAu 39NR*
Nathan, David 1926- *ScF&FL 92*
Nathan, Ernest 1905-1991 *BioIn 17*
Nathan, Frederic Solis 1922- *WhoAm 92*
Nathan, Hans 1910-1989 *Baker 92*
Nathan, Harris *BioIn 17*
Nathan, Henry C. 1924-1991 *BioIn 17*
Nathan, Isaac 1790-1864 *Baker 92, OxDcOp*
Nathan, Keith Harold 1955- *WhoEmL 93, WhoSSW 93*
Nathan, Kurt 1920- *WhoE 93*
Nathan, Leonard Edward 1924- *WhoAm 92, WhoWrEP 92*
Nathan, Lois Betty 1944- *WhoWor 93*
Nathan, Marshall Ira 1933- *WhoAm 92*
Nathan, May Rose *AmWomPl*
Nathan, Montagu *Baker 92*
Nathan, Norman 1915- *WhoWrEP 92*
Nathan, Paul S. 1913- *WhoAm 92*
Nathan, Peter E. 1935- *WhoAm 92*
Nathan, Phil Ove 1926- *WhoWor 93*
Nathan, Phyllis Kleinfeld 1947- *WhoE 93, WhoEmL 93*
Nathan, Richard Arnold 1944- *St&PR 93, WhoAm 92*
Nathan, Richard Perle 1935- *WhoAm 92*
Nathan, Robert 1894-1985 *JeAmFiW, ScF&FL 92*
Nathan, Robert Clark 1924- *St&PR 93*
Nathan, Robert R. 1908- *St&PR 93*
Nathan, Robert Stuart 1948- *WhoEmL 93, WhoWrEP 92*
Nathan, Syd 1904-1968 *SoulM*
Nathan, Thomas R. *Law&B 92*
Nathaniel, His Grace Bishop 1940- *WhoAm 92*
Nathaniel, Inez 1911-1990 *BioIn 17*
Nathans, Daniel 1928- *WhoAm 92, WhoE 93, WhoWor 93*
Nathanson, Benjamin 1929- *WhoE 93*
Nathanson, Fred E. 1933- *WhoAm 92*
Nathanson, Harvey Charles 1936- *WhoAm 92*
Nathanson, Linda Sue 1946- *WhoAmW 93, WhoEmL 93*
Nathanson, Melvyn Bernard 1944- *WhoAm 92*
Nathanson, Michael *WhoAm 92*
Nathanson, Minnie Mazer d1992 *NewYTBS 92*
Nathanson, Neal 1927- *WhoAm 92*
Nathanson, Robert London *Law&B 92*
Nathanson, Wayne R. 1934- *St&PR 93*
Nathan-Turner, John *ScF&FL 92*
Nathe, Gerald A. 1941- *St&PR 93*
Nathenson, Joseph *ScF&FL 92*
Nathenson, Lucille 1952- *WhoAmW 93*
Nathenson, Stanley G. 1933- *WhoAm 92*
Nather, Johann *WhoScE 91-4*
Nation, Carry Amelia Moore 1846-1911 *BioIn 17*
Nation, Earl F. 1910- *WhoAm 92*
Nation, Edna Leona 1937- *WhoWrEP 92*
Nation, Harry J. 1926- *WhoScE 91-1*
Nation, James Edward 1933- *WhoAm 92*
Nation, John Arthur 1935- *WhoAm 92, WhoE 93*
Nation, Roger John 1941- *St&PR 93*
Nation, Terry 1930- *ScF&FL 92*
Nations, Andrew Hall 1949- *St&PR 93*
Nations, Chester Bradley, Jr. 1939- *St&PR 93*
Nations, James Dale 1947- *WhoWrEP 92*
Nations, John Drewry 1918- *St&PR 93*
Nations, Opal L. 1941- *WhoCanL 92*
Nations, Robert Lloyd 1960- *WhoEmL 93, WhoSSW 93*
Nations, Sarah Bell 1954- *WhoAmW 93*
Nativi, Tomas *DcCPCAm*
Natke, Hans Guenther 1933- *WhoWor 93*
Natke, Hans Gunther 1933- *WhoScE 91-3*
Natkin, Alvin Martin 1928- *WhoAm 92*
Natoli, Anne Marie 1950- *WhoAmW 93*
Natoli, Frank R. *Law&B 92*
Natoli, John F. *Law&B 92*
Natori, Josie *BioIn 17*

Natori, Josie Cruz 1947- *ConEn, WhoAmW 93*
Natori, Kenneth *BioIn 17*
Natorp, Bernhard Christoph Ludwig 1774-1846 *Baker 92*
Natow, Annette Baum 1933- *WhoAm 92*
Natr, Lubomir 1934- *WhoScE 91-4*
Natra, Sergiu 1924- *Baker 92*
Natsios, Nicholas Andrew 1920- *WhoAm 92, WhoWor 93*
Natte, Bonnie S. 1954- *St&PR 93*
Natter, Barry N. *Law&B 92*
Nattiel, Christine Henry 1939- *WhoAmW 93, WhoSSW 93, WhoWor 93*
Nattiez, Jean-Jacques 1945- *Baker 92*
Nattinger, Christopher Wallis 1942- *St&PR 93*
Naturman, Louis 1931- *St&PR 93*
Natvig, Bent 1946- *WhoScE 91-4*
Natwick, Grim 1890-1990 *BioIn 17*
Natwick, Myron 1890-1990 *BioIn 17*
Natzke, Paulette Ann 1943- *WhoAmW 93*
Natzler, Otto 1908- *WhoAm 92*
Nau, Charles John *Law&B 92*
Nau, H. Gene *WhoAm 92*
Nau, Henry Richard 1941- *WhoAm 92*
Nauciel, Charles 1933- *WhoScE 91-2*
Naudascher, Eduard 1929- *WhoScE 91-3*
Naude, Beyers *BioIn 17*
Naudin, Emilio 1823-1890 *Baker 92*
Naudts, M. *WhoScE 91-2*
Naudzius, Ruth Winters 1929- *WhoAmW 93*
Nauert, Peter W. 1943- *WhoIns 93*
Nauert, Peter William 1943- *WhoAm 92*
Nauert, Roger Charles 1943- *WhoAm 92, WhoWor 93*
Naughter, Patrick M. 1943- *WhoIns 93*
Naughton, Ann Elsie 1942- *WhoAmW 93, WhoE 93, WhoWor 93*
Naughton, Bill *BioIn 17, ConAu 136*
Naughton, Bill d1992 *NewYTBS 92*
Naughton, Charlie 1887-1976 See Crazy Gang, The *IntDcF 2-3*
Naughton, Eleanor F. *AmWomPl*
Naughton, Howard Francis *Law&B 92*
Naughton, James 1945- *WhoAm 92, WhoE 93*
Naughton, James Martin 1938- *WhoAm 92*
Naughton, John Alexander 1947- *WhoEmL 93*
Naughton, John M. 1936- *St&PR 93, WhoAm 92*
Naughton, John Patrick 1933- *WhoAm 92*
Naughton, Marie Ann 1954- *WhoAmW 93*
Naughton, Noreen Kale 1945- *WhoAmW 93*
Naughton, Thomas Noel 1929- *St&PR 93*
Naughton, William Aloysius 1930- *St&PR 93, WhoAm 92*
Naughton, William John (Francis) 1910-1992 *ConAu 136*
Naugle, Robert Paul 1951- *WhoEmL 93, WhoWor 93*
Naujalis, Juozas 1869-1934 *Baker 92*
Nauke, M.K. 1938- *WhoScE 91-1*
Nauke, Manfred Kurt 1938- *WhoUN 92*
Nault, Fernand 1921- *WhoAm 92*
Nault, J. Lloyd, II *Law&B 92*
Nault, Sharon Brewer *Law&B 92*
Nault, William Henry 1926- *WhoAm 92*
Nauman, Bruce 1941- *BioIn 17*
Nauman, Coleen Sue 1963- *WhoAmW 93*
Nauman, Frances Irma 1914- *WhoWrEP 92*
Nauman, Gerald Marston 1931- *WhoIns 93*
Naumann, Dieter J. 1942- *WhoScE 91-3*
Naumann, Emil 1827-1888 *Baker 92*
Naumann, (Karl) Ernst 1832-1910 *Baker 92*
Naumann, Gottfried Otto Helmut 1935- *WhoScE 91-3*
Naumann, Hans Juergen 1935- *St&PR 93, WhoAm 92, WhoE 93*
Naumann, Joerg K.H.D. 1941- *WhoWor 93*
Naumann, Johann Gottlieb 1741-1801 *Baker 92, OxDcOp*
Naumann, Robert Bruno Alexander 1929- *WhoAm 92*
Naumann, Siegfried 1919- *Baker 92*
Naumann, William Edward 1909- *St&PR 93*
Naumann Zu Konigsbruck, Clas M. 1939- *WhoScE 91-3*
Naumburg, Cecile L. d1992 *BioIn 17, NewYTBS 92*
Naumburg, Nancy *AmWomPl*
Naumer, Helmuth Jacob 1934- *WhoAm 92*
Naumer, Janet Noll 1933- *WhoAmW 93*
Naumienko, Bohdan Jozef 1946- *WhoWor 93*
Naumkin, Pavel Ivanovich 1961- *WhoWor 93*
Naumoff, Philip 1914- *WhoAm 92*
Naum of Ohrid c. 830-910 *OxDcByz*
Naumov, Vladimir 1927- *DrEEuF*
Naumov, Yuri *BioIn 17*
Naumovski, Mirce *WhoScE 91-4*
Naunin, Dietrich Hans 1937- *WhoWor 93*
Naunton, Ralph Frederick 1921- *WhoAm 92*
Nauser, Debbie Engmark 1952- *St&PR 93*
Nauss, Richard 1938- *St&PR 93*
Nauta, Ronald H. 1935- *St&PR 93*
Nauwach, Johann c. 1595-c. 1630 *Baker 92*
Nauwelaers, Frans Albert Maria 1948- *WhoWor 93*
Nauwerck, Arnold *WhoScE 91-4*
Nava, Eloy Luis 1942- *WhoAm 92, WhoE 93*
Nava, Gaetano 1802-1875 *Baker 92*
Nava, Gregory 1949- *MiSFD 9*
Nava, Julian 1927- *HispAmA [port]*
Nava, Michael 1954- *ConGAN*
Nava, Romer Angel 1932- *WhoWor 93*
Nava, Thelma 1931- *DcMexL*
Navab, Farhad 1938- *WhoAm 92*
Navajas-Mogro, Hugo 1923- *WhoWor 93*
Navalkar, Ramchandra Govindrao 1924- *WhoAm 92*
Nava Marinez, Salvador d1992 *BioIn 17*
Nava Martinez, Salvador d1992 *NewYTBS 92 [port]*
Navar, Luis Gabriel 1941- *WhoAm 92*
Navaratnam, Visvan *WhoScE 91-1*
Navard, Patrick *WhoScE 91-2*
Navarra, Andre (-Nicolas) 1911-1988 *Baker 92*
Navarre, Robert Ward 1933- *St&PR 93, WhoAm 92*
Navarre, Tommy R. 1960- *St&PR 93*
Navarre, Yves Henri Michel 1940- *WhoWor 93*
Navarrete, Juan Fernandez de c. 1526-1579 *BioIn 17*
Navarrete, Manuel de *DcMexL*
Navarrini, Francesco 1853-1923 *Baker 92*
Navarro, A. *WhoScE 91-2*
Navarro, Andrew Jesus 1946- *WhoEmL 93, WhoSSW 93*
Navarro, Antonio Luis 1922- *WhoAm 92*
Navarro, Armando Salovicz 1930- *WhoWor 93*
Navarro, Beltran 1945- *WhoE 93*
Navarro, Bruce Charles 1954- *WhoAm 92*
Navarro, Carlos Arias 1908-1989 *BioIn 17*
Navarro, Constantino C. 1914- *WhoAsAP 91*
Navarro, Ephraim Neo 1961- *WhoWor 93*
Navarro, "Fats" 1923-1950 *Baker 92*
Navarro, Gabriel *HispAmA*
Navarro, (Luis Antonio) Garcia 1941- *Baker 92*
Navarro, Imelda 1958- *St&PR 93*
Navarro, Janyte Janeen 1935- *WhoAmW 93*
Navarro, Joseph Anthony 1927- *WhoAm 92*
Navarro, Juan c. 1530-1580 *Baker 92*
Navarro, Karyl Kay 1956- *WhoWor 93*
Navarro, Pedro c. 1460-1528 *HarEnMi*
Navarro, Rafael A. 1935- *St&PR 93*
Navarro, Richard J. 1952- *St&PR 93*
Navarro, Samuel Enrique 1955- *WhoEmL 93*
Navarro Sanchez, Jose Adalberto 1918- *DcMexL*
Navas, Ana 1959- *WhoScE 91-3*
Navas, Juan (Francisco) de fl. 1659-1709 *Baker 92*
Navas, Stanley R. 1919- *St&PR 93*
Navas, William Antonio, Jr. 1942- *WhoAm 92, WhoE 93*
Navasky, Bernard Seymour 1908- *St&PR 93*
Navasky, Edward 1933- *St&PR 93*
Navasky, Victor 1932- *ScF&FL 92*
Navasky, Victor Saul 1932- *WhoAm 92, WhoE 93, WhoWrEP 92*
Navatsky, Victor 1932- *JrnUS*
Nava-Villarreal, Hector Rolando 1943- *HispAmA*
Nave, Jonathan P. *Law&B 92*
Naveira-de Rodon, Miriam *WhoAm 92, WhoAmW 93*
Naveke, Rolf J.F. 1928- *WhoScE 91-3*
Navia, Juan Marcelo 1927- *WhoAm 92, WhoSSW 93*
Naviaux, LaRee DeVee 1937- *WhoAmW 93*
Navin, Louis E. 1938- *St&PR 93*
Navin, MaryAnn Elizabeth 1951- *WhoAmW 93, WhoEmL 93*
Navin, Sandy Joseph *Law&B 92*
Navkal, Shree Hari 1946- *WhoE 93*
Navon, Ionel Michael 1940- *WhoAm 92, WhoSSW 93*
Navon, Robert 1954- *WhoWrEP 92*
Navratil, Allan John 1937- *WhoWor 93*
Navratil, Johann 1909- *WhoScE 91-4*
Navratil, Karel 1867-1936 *Baker 92*
Navratil, Liz 1960- *St&PR 93*
Navratil, Milan 1931- *WhoScE 91-4*
Navratilova, Martina 1956- *BioIn 17, WhoAm 92, WhoAmW 93, WhoWor 93*
Navrozov, Lev 1928- *WhoE 93*
Nawara, Bruce Gerard 1957- *WhoEmL 93*
Nawara, Leszek 1927- *WhoScE 91-4*
Nawawi Mat Awin, Dr. 1939- *WhoAsAP 91*
Nawaz, Sardar Shah 1917-1991 *BioIn 17*
Nawaz, Shuja 1949- *WhoUN 92*
Nawrocki, Gary 1948- *St&PR 93*
Nawrocki, Henry Franz 1931- *WhoSSW 93*
Nawrocki, Lillian Alexandra 1954- *WhoAmW 93*
Nawrocki, Stanislaw 1927- *WhoScE 91-4*
Nawrocki, Stanley J. 1939- *St&PR 93*
Nawrocki, Thomas Dennis 1942- *WhoSSW 93*
Nawrocki, Tom L. 1947- *WhoWrEP 92*
Nawrot, Jan 1943- *WhoScE 91-4*
Nawy, Edward George 1926- *WhoAm 92, WhoE 93*
Nay, Ernst Wilhelm 1902-1968 *BioIn 17*
Nay, James Allen 1934- *WhoSSW 93*
Nayak, P. Narayan 1940- *St&PR 93*
Nayak, Pangal Ranganath 1942- *WhoAm 92, WhoWor 93*
Nayar, Baldev Raj 1931- *WhoAm 92*
Nayar, Pichirikkat Bhaskaran 1939- *WhoWor 93*
Nayden, Denis J. 1954- *WhoAm 92*
Nayder, Linda Ann 1962- *WhoEmL 93*
Nayer, Louise Bedford 1949- *WhoWrEP 92*
Nayerahmadi, Habib 1949- *WhoE 93*
Nayfeh, Ali Hasan 1933- *WhoAm 92*
Naylon, Betsy Zimmermann 1934- *WhoE 93*
Naylor, Aubrey Willard 1915- *WhoAm 92, WhoSSW 93*
Naylor, Bernard (James) 1907-1986 *Baker 92*
Naylor, Brian Thomas *Law&B 92*
Naylor, Cal *MiSFD 9*
Naylor, Charles *ScF&FL 92*
Naylor, Doug *ScF&FL 92*
Naylor, Douglas F. 1918- *St&PR 93*
Naylor, Edward (Woodall) 1867-1934 *Baker 92*
Naylor, Eleanor R. 1928- *St&PR 93*
Naylor, Eric Woodfin 1936- *WhoSSW 93*
Naylor, Ernest *WhoScE 91-1*
Naylor, Frank Wesley, Jr. 1939- *WhoAm 92*
Naylor, George LeRoy 1915- *WhoWor 93*
Naylor, Gloria *BioIn 17*
Naylor, Gloria 1950- *MagSAmL [port]*
Naylor, Grant *ScF&FL 92*
Naylor, Harry Brooks 1914- *WhoAm 92*
Naylor, Henry Edward *Law&B 92*
Naylor, James Charles 1932- *WhoAm 92*
Naylor, Jeannette L. 1956- *WhoAm 92*
Naylor, John 1838-1897 *Baker 92*
Naylor, John Lewis, Jr. 1927- *St&PR 93, WhoAm 92*
Naylor, John Thomas 1913- *WhoAm 92*
Naylor, Joseph D. *Law&B 92*
Naylor, Kerry R.U. *Law&B 92*
Naylor, Lewis C. 1914-1990 *BioIn 17*
Naylor, Lois Anne Mc Crea 1948- *WhoWrEP 92*
Naylor, Malcolm Neville *WhoScE 91-1*
Naylor, Mary 1955- *WhoAmW 93*
Naylor, Phyllis *MajAI*
Naylor, Phyllis Reynolds 1933- *BioIn 17, DcAmChF 1960, DcAmChF 1985, MajAI [port], ScF&FL 92, WhoAm 92, WhoWrEP 92*
Naylor, Ralph A. 1923- *St&PR 93*
Naylor, Richard N. 1943- *St&PR 93*
Naylor, Robert Ernest 1932- *St&PR 93*
Naylor, Robert Ernest, Jr. 1932- *WhoAm 92*
Naylor, Robert L. 1934- *WhoWrEP 92*
Naylor, Ruth Eileen 1934- *WhoWrEP 92*
Naylor, Ruth Eileen Bundy 1934- *WhoAmW 93*
Naylor, Thomas Herbert 1936- *WhoAm 92*
Naymark, Sherman 1920- *WhoAm 92*
Naymik, Daniel Allan 1922- *WhoSSW 93*
Nayroles, Bernard 1937- *WhoScE 91-2*
Nazaire, Michel Harry 1939- *WhoWor 93*
Nazar, Mohammad 1948- *WhoAsAP 91*
Nazarbayev, Nursultan *BioIn 17*
Nazarbayev, Nursultan Abishevich 1940- *WhoWor 93*
Nazare, Ernesto Julio de 1863-1934 *Baker 92*
Nazare, M.H. 1949- *WhoScE 91-3*
Nazareth, Annette La Porte 1956- *St&PR 93*
Nazareth, Annette LaPorte 1956- *WhoAm 92, WhoEmL 93*
Nazareth, Ernesto Julio de 1863-1934 *Baker 92*
Nazareth, George R. 1930- *St&PR 93*
Nazarian, John 1932- *WhoAm 92, WhoE 93*
Nazarowski, James J. 1949- *St&PR 93*
Nazek, Patricia A. *Law&B 92*
Nazel, Joe *ScF&FL 92*
Nazel, Joseph *ScF&FL 92*
Nazem, Fereydoun F. 1940- *WhoAm 92*
Nazer, Hisham Mohyeddin 1932- *WhoWor 93*
Nazette, Richard Follett 1919- *WhoAm 92*
Nazimova, Alla 1879-1945 *BioIn 17, IntDcF 2-3 [port]*
Nazos, Demetri Eleftherios 1949- *WhoEmL 93, WhoWor 93*
Nazz, James 1951- *WhoE 93*
Nazzaro, A. John 1927- *WhoWor 93*
Nazzaro, James Russell 1931- *WhoE 93*
Nazzaro, Joseph James 1913-1990 *BioIn 17*
Nchinda, Thomas Choffor 1935- *WhoUN 92*
Ndahura, Richard Bukenya 1951- *WhoWor 93*
N'Daw, Robert Tiebile 1935- *WhoUN 92*
Ndayiziga, Jeremie 1960- *WhoUN 92*
Ndiaye, Babacar 1936- *WhoWor 93*
N'Diaye, Babacar 1937- *BioIn 17*
N'Diaye, Salif 1934- *WhoUN 92*
Ndjonkou, Djankou 1950- *WhoUN 92*
N'donazi, Bernard *BioIn 17*
Ndouba Gervais, Bernard 1956- *WhoWor 93*
N'Dour, Youssou *BioIn 17*
Ndow, Wally Salieu 1943- *WhoUN 92*
Ndukwu, Azuwuike H. *Law&B 92*
Neafsey, John Patrick 1939- *St&PR 93*
Neagle, Anna 1904-1986 *IntDcF 2-3*
Neagle, Rosanna *Law&B 92*
Neagli, Douglas Bernard *Law&B 92*
Neagu, Romulus 1930- *WhoUN 92*
Neaher, Edward Raymond 1912- *WhoAm 92*
Neal, A. Curtis 1922- *WhoSSW 93*
Neal, Angela Marie 1960- *WhoAmW 93*
Neal, Ann Parker 1934- *WhoAm 92*
Neal, Annetta Susan 1949- *WhoSSW 93*
Neal, Anthony 1955- *WhoEmL 93*
Neal, Archie Eugene 1934- *St&PR 93*
Neal, Avon 1922- *WhoAm 92, WhoWrEP 92*
Neal, Barbara G. 1944- *WhoAmW 93*
Neal, Betty Marie 1936- *WhoAmW 93*
Neal, Bill L. *St&PR 93*
Neal, Bonnie Jean 1930- *WhoAmW 93*
Neal, Claude d1934 *EncAACR*
Neal, Curly *BioIn 17*
Neal, Darwina Lee 1942- *WhoAm 92*
Neal, David Lynn 1948- *WhoEmL 93*
Neal, Douglas Paul 1942- *St&PR 93*
Neal, Earlene Traylor 1944- *WhoAmW 93*
Neal, Edmond A. 1934- *St&PR 93*
Neal, Eric 1924- *WhoWor 93*
Neal, Fred *BioIn 17*
Neal, Fred Warner 1915- *WhoAm 92*
Neal, George P. 1926- *St&PR 93*
Neal, Gerald Dale, Jr. 1958- *WhoSSW 93*
Neal, Homer Alfred 1942- *WhoAm 92*
Neal, James Edward, Jr. 1933- *WhoWrEP 92*
Neal, James Preston 1935- *WhoE 93*
Neal, Janet M. *Law&B 92*
Neal, Jasper Taylor, Jr. 1942- *St&PR 93*
Neal, Jerry Eugene 1941- *WhoAm 92*
Neal, Jerry Harold 1943- *WhoAm 92, WhoSSW 93*
Neal, Joyce Olivia 1943- *WhoAmW 93*
Neal, Judith Ann 1947- *WhoE 93*
Neal, Kenneth Alton 1953- *WhoEmL 93*
Neal, Kevin R. 1951- *St&PR 93*
Neal, Larry 1937-1981 *BioIn 17*
Neal, Larry L. 1939- *BioIn 17*
Neal, Leonard *St&PR 93*
Neal, Leora Louise Haskett 1943- *WhoAmW 93*
Neal, Leslie Robert *WhoScE 91-1*
Neal, Lewis Grant 1933- *St&PR 93*
Neal, Louise Kathleen 1951- *St&PR 93, WhoAm 92*
Neal, Mansfield C., Jr. *Law&B 92*
Neal, Margaret Ruth 1944- *WhoAmW 93*
Neal, Marie Augusta 1921- *WhoAmW 93*
Neal, Michael James *WhoScE 91-1*
Neal, Michael James 1956- *WhoEmL 93*
Neal, Nelson Douglas 1947- *WhoSSW 93*
Neal, Patricia *BioIn 17*
Neal, Patricia 1926- *IntDcF 2-3 [port], WhoAm 92, WhoWor 93*
Neal, Phil Hudson, Jr. 1926- *WhoAm 92*
Neal, Philip Mark 1940- *St&PR 93, WhoAm 92*
Neal, Ralph A. 1938- *St&PR 93*
Neal, Richard E. 1949- *CngDr 91*
Neal, Richard Edmund 1949- *WhoAm 92, WhoE 93*
Neal, Richard Edward 1925- *St&PR 93*
Neal, Robert Allan 1928- *WhoAm 92*
Neal, Robert B. 1938- *WhoIns 93*
Neal, Robert Bell 1938- *St&PR 93*

Neal, Roger Lee 1930- St&PR 93
Neal, Rufus 1954- WhoWor 93
Neal, Stephen L. 1934- CngDr 91
Neal, Stephen Lybrook 1934- WhoAm 92, WhoSSW 93
Neal, Teresa Schreibeis 1956- WhoAmW 93, WhoEmL 93
Neal, Thomas Frederick 1960- WhoEmL 93
Neal, Tom, Sr. BioIn 17
Neal, Tom, Jr. BioIn 17
Neal, Wallace T. 1940- St&PR 93
Neal, Wendell A. BioIn 17
Neal, William H., Jr. 1930- St&PR 93
Neal, William Weaver 1932- WhoAm 92
Neal, Wilmer Lewis 1934- WhoSSW 93, WhoWor 93
Neal-Beliveau, Bethany Sue 1957- WhoAmW 93
Neale, Allen R. 1951- St&PR 93
Neale, Charles A. Law&B 92
Neale, Diane BioIn 17
Neale, Earle 1891-1973 BioIn 17
Neale, Edward George, Jr. 1926- St&PR 93
Neale, Ernest Richard Ward 1923- WhoAm 92
Neale, Frank Leslie George 1950- WhoWor 93
Neale, Gail Lovejoy 1935- WhoAmW 93
Neale, Gary L. 1940- St&PR 93
Neale, Gary Lee 1940- WhoAm 92
Neale, John Hamilton, Jr. 1946- WhoE 93
Neale, John William WhoScE 91-1
Neale, Michael 1926- WhoScE 91-1
Neale, Timothy Arthur 1948- WhoE 93, WhoEmL 93
Neale, Vincent, Mrs. AmWomPl
Neale, Walter 1873-1933 ScF&FL 92
Neale, Walter C. BioIn 17
Neale, William R. Law&B 92
Nealeigh, Michael Ray 1950- WhoSSW 93
Nealer, James Keifer 1928- WhoSSW 93
Nealey, Sue C. 1949- WhoAmW 93
Nealon, John R. Law&B 92
Nealon, Kevin BioIn 17
Nealon, William Joseph, Jr. 1923- WhoAm 92, WhoE 93
Neal-Ricker, Norma Candace 1947- WhoEmL 93
Nealy, Frances 1918- BioIn 17
Nealy, Melissa A. Rathbun- BioIn 17
Neame, Ronald 1911- MiSFD 9, WhoAm 92
Neander, Eckhart 1934- WhoScE 91-3
Near, Earl Wayne 1943- St&PR 93
Near, Holly BioIn 17
Near, Holly 1949- Baker 92
Near, James W. 1938- St&PR 93, WhoAm 92
Near, Mary Jane Willis 1915- St&PR 93
Nearchus d312BC HarEnMi
Nearchus 360BC-312BC Expl 93
Nearing, Dudley Woodruff, Jr. 1925- WhoAm 92
Nearing, Helen BioIn 17
Nearing, Scott 1883-1983 BioIn 17, EncAACR
Neary, Brian Joseph 1951- WhoEmL 93
Neary, Colleen 1952- WhoAm 92
Neary, Dennis R. 1952- St&PR 93
Neary, Douglas Patrick 1955- St&PR 93
Neary, Ellen M. 1951- St&PR 93
Neary, J. Michael Law&B 92
Neary, Lynn Patricia 1950- WhoAm 92
Neary, Martin (Gerard James) 1940- Baker 92
Neary, Patricia BioIn 17
Neary, Patricia Elinor WhoAm 92
Neary, Robert D. WhoAm 92
Neary, William Thomas 1957- WhoEmL 93
Neas, Eileen M. 1946- St&PR 93
Neas, Ralph G. 1946- BioIn 17
Neas, Ralph Graham 1946- WhoAm 92
Nease, Carl M. 1932- St&PR 93
Nease, Judith Allgood 1930- WhoAmW 93, WhoWor 93
Nease, Stephen Wesley 1925- WhoAm 92
Neate, Charles 1784-1877 Baker 92
Neath, James John Law&B 92
Neath, Mary Ann Law&B 92
Neathery, Patricia Sue 1934- WhoSSW 93
Neaton, Robert A. Law&B 92
Neave, Henry Robert 1942- WhoWor 93
Neaveill, Darla P. Law&B 92
Neaves, William Barlow 1943- WhoAm 92
Neavins, Thomas Keith 1943- St&PR 93
Nebbs, E. Louise 1954- St&PR 93
Nebeker, Sidney Jay 1929- St&PR 93
Nebel, Bernard James 1934- WhoE 93
Nebel, Carl 1937- St&PR 93
Nebel, Henry Martin, Jr. 1921- WhoAm 92
Nebel, Reynold 1928- WhoAm 92
Nebel, Richard Forrist, Sr. 1953- WhoEmL 93
Nebel, William Arthur 1936- WhoSSW 93, WhoWor 93
Nebel, Wolfgang Heinz Andreas 1956- WhoWor 93
Neben, Michael E. Law&B 92
Nebenzahl, Kenneth 1927- WhoAm 92, WhoWor 93
Nebergall, Cynthia Anne Law&B 92
Nebergall, Robert William 1954- WhoSSW 93
Nebergall, Roger Ellis 1926- WhoAm 92
Neberle, John M. Law&B 92
Nebert, Daniel Walter 1938- WhoAm 92
Nebgen, Mary Kathryn 1946- WhoAmW 93
Nebiker, John Herbert 1936- WhoWor 93
Nebil, Corinne Elizabeth 1918- WhoAm 92
Neblett, Carol 1946- Baker 92, OxDcOp, WhoAm 92
Neblett, George R. 1943- St&PR 93
Neblo, Albert A. 1936- St&PR 93
Nebolsine, Rostislav 1900-1990 BioIn 17
Neboulos OxDcByz
Nebra (Blasco), Jose (Melchor de) 1702?-1768 Baker 92
Nebra, Jose 1672?-1748
See Nebra (Blasco), Jose (Melchor de) 1702?-1768 Baker 92
Nebra, Jose de 1702?-1768 OxDcOp
Nebrensky, Alex ScF&FL 92
Nebuchadnezzar, II, King of Babylon BioIn 17
Necarsulmer, Henry 1914- WhoAm 92
Necco, Gustavo Victor 1944- WhoUN 92
Nece, Teresa Ann 1952- WhoEmL 93
Necesario, Fe Sepulveda 1929- WhoWor 93
Nechayev, Vasily 1895-1956 Baker 92
Nechemias, Stephen Murray 1944- WhoAm 92
Neches, Philip M. 1952- St&PR 93
Neches, Richard Brooks 1955- WhoE 93
Nechtelberger, Erich 1937- WhoScE 91-4
Neck, Philip Arthur 1935- WhoUN 92
Neck, Reinhard 1951- WhoWor 93
Necker, David C. 1944- St&PR 93
Neckerman, Peter Josef 1935- St&PR 93
Neckermann, Peter J. 1935- WhoIns 93
Neckermann, Peter Josef 1935- WhoAm 92
Necoechea, W.M. 1930- St&PR 93
Necula, Nicholas 1940- WhoE 93
Nedbal, Oskar 1874-1930 Baker 92
Nedd, LaShon BlkAmWO
Nedder, Janet Marie 1943- WhoAmW 93
Nedderman, Carl William, Jr. 1938- WhoSSW 93
Nedderman, Norma Faye Sandberg 1954- WhoAmW 93
Nedd-Friendly, Priscilla Anne 1955- WhoEmL 93
Neddo, Leon M., Jr. Law&B 92
Nedeljkovic, Ljubomir 1933- WhoScE 91-4
Nedelkoff, Rebecca Rochelle Law&B 92
Neden, Michael W. BioIn 17
Nedergaard, Ove A. 1931- WhoScE 91-2
Nederkoorn, Erik BioIn 17
Nederlander, James Laurence 1960- WhoE 93
Nederlander, James Morton 1922- BioIn 17, WhoAm 92, WhoE 93
Nederlander, Marjorie Smith 1922- WhoAmW 93
Nederlander, Robert St&PR 93
Nederlander, Robert E. 1933- WhoAm 92, WhoE 93
Nederlander, Sarah d1991 BioIn 17
Nederveld, Ruth Elizabeth 1933- WhoAmW 93
Nedom, H. Arthur 1925- WhoAm 92
Nedved, Petr BioIn 17
Nedwek, Thomas Wayne 1933- WhoAm 92
Nedwick, James C. 1945- St&PR 93
Nedza, Sandra Louise 1951- WhoAmW 93
Nedzi, Lucien Norbert 1925- WhoAm 92
Nee, Dave 1953- ScF&FL 92
Nee, David C. ScF&FL 92
Nee, Frank W. 1936- St&PR 93
Nee, Frank Walter 1936- WhoAm 92
Nee, Kay Bonner WhoWrEP 92
Nee, Lawrence Joseph 1952- WhoSSW 93
Nee, Mary Coleman 1917- WhoAm 92
Nee, Owen Dawes 1912-1991 BioIn 17
Nee, Paul M. d1990 BioIn 17
Nee, William R. Law&B 92
Neeb, Judy Ann 1937- WhoAmW 93
Neeb, Louis P. 1939- St&PR 93
Neece, Olivia Helene Ernst 1948- WhoAmW 93, WhoEmL 93
Neece, Richard Dale 1945- St&PR 93
Need, James D. 1944- St&PR 93
Needell, Elise Louise Babcock 1957- WhoAmW 93, WhoEmL 93, WhoWor 93
Needham, Charles William 1936- WhoAm 92, WhoWor 93
Needham, Denise Lynn 1952- WhoAmW 93
Needham, George Austin 1943- St&PR 93, WhoAm 92
Needham, Hal 1931- MiSFD 9, WhoAm 92
Needham, J. Gary 1930- WhoWor 93
Needham, Jack L. 1931- St&PR 93
Needham, James Joseph 1926- St&PR 93, WhoAm 92
Needham, John 1909-1990 BioIn 17
Needham, Joseph 1900- WhoAm 92
Needham, Lucien Arthur 1929- WhoAm 92
Needham, P. WhoScE 91-1
Needham, Paul W., Jr. 1943- St&PR 93
Needham, Richard Lee 1939- WhoAm 92, WhoWrEP 92
Needham, Roger Michael WhoScE 91-1
Needham, Sheena Kaye 1960- WhoAmW 93
Needle, Jan 1943- ChlFicS
Needleman, Alan 1944- WhoAm 92
Needleman, Harry Law&B 92
Needleman, Harry 1949- St&PR 93, WhoAm 92
Needleman, Heather 1947- WhoAmW 93
Needleman, Herbert Leroy 1927- WhoAm 92
Needleman, Jacob 1934- ScF&FL 92
Needleman, Rafe ScF&FL 92
Needler, George Treglohan 1935- WhoAm 92
Neefe, Christian Gottlob 1748-1798 Baker 92, OxDcOp
Neefe, Douglas Charles 1944- St&PR 93, WhoAm 92
Neefe, Felice 1782-1826 OxDcOp
Neefe, Hermann 1790-1854 OxDcOp
Neefe, Louise 1779-1846 OxDcOp
Neefe, Margarethe 1787-1808 OxDcOp
Neel, Alexandra David- 1868-1969 BioIn 17
Neel, Alice 1900-1984 BioIn 17
Neel, (Louis) Boyd 1905-1981 Baker 92
Neel, Bradley Law&B 92
Neel, Curtis Dean, Jr. 1946- St&PR 93
Neel, David S., Jr. Law&B 92
Neel, Elmer R. St&PR 93
Neel, Eula Barneycastle 1928- WhoAmW 93
Neel, Harry Bryan, III 1939- WhoAm 92
Neel, James Van Gundia 1915- WhoAm 92
Neel, John D. 1923- St&PR 93
Neel, John Dodd 1923- WhoAm 92
Neel, Judy Murphy 1926- WhoAm 92
Neel, Louis Eugene Felix 1904- WhoWor 93
Neel, Rebecca Potts Law&B 92
Neel, Richard Eugene 1932- WhoAm 92
Neel, Samuel Ellison 1914- WhoAm 92
Neel, Spurgeon Hart, Jr. 1919- WhoAm 92
Neel, Thomas M. 1937- St&PR 93
Neel, Timothy Joseph 1952- WhoEmL 93
Neel, Warren 1938- WhoSSW 93
Neeld, Elizabeth Harper 1940- WhoSSW 93
Neeld, Jerele Don 1960- WhoEmL 93, WhoSSW 93
Neeld, Judith 1928- WhoWrEP 92
Neeld, Renee Riecke 1959- WhoEmL 93
Neeld, Vaughn DeLeath 1943- WhoAmW 93
Neeley, Wayne P. 1947- St&PR 93
Neelis, Joseph M. St&PR 93
Neelly, E.C., III 1939- St&PR 93
Neely, Brenda Delores 1944- WhoAmW 93
Neely, Bruce A. 1942- St&PR 93
Neely, Cam 1965- WhoAm 92
Neely, Charles Lea, Jr. 1927- WhoAm 92
Neely, Dawn Mae-ry Musgrove 1960- WhoEmL 93
Neely, E.C., III 1939- St&PR 93
Neely, Edgar Adams, Jr. 1910- WhoAm 92
Neely, Harry A. 1946- St&PR 93
Neely, James Dennis 1952- WhoEmL 93
Neely, Jerome Charles 1940- St&PR 93
Neely, John J. Law&B 92
Neely, Larry F. 1938- St&PR 93
Neely, Paul 1946- WhoEmL 93, WhoSSW 93
Neely, Paul A. 1920- St&PR 93
Neely, Richard 1941- WhoAm 92, WhoSSW 93
Neely, Robert Allen 1921- WhoSSW 93
Neely, Robert Craig 1953- St&PR 93
Neely, Sandra L. Law&B 92
Neely, Stuart M. Law&B 92
Neely, Walter E. Law&B 92
Neely, Willard Ross 1925- St&PR 93
Ne'eman, Yuval 1925- WhoAm 92
Neemar, Carol Lee 1941- WhoE 93
Neem Karoli Baba BioIn 17
Neems, Harold J. Law&B 92
Neenan, Michael 1925- WhoScE 91-3
Neeper, Carolyn A. ScF&FL 92
Neeper, Cary 1937- ScF&FL 92
Neeper, Leonard A. 1930- St&PR 93
Neer, Charles Sumner, II 1917- WhoAm 92, WhoWor 93
Neer, Howard Lester 1929- WhoSSW 93
Neerhout, John 1931- St&PR 93
Neerhout, John, Jr. 1931- WhoAm 92
Nees, David K. Law&B 92
Nees, Lawrence 1949- ConAu 139, WhoEmL 93
Nees, William Earl Law&B 92
Neese, Dwight Vincent 1950- WhoEmL 93, WhoSSW 93
Neese, Elbert Haven 1923- WhoAm 92
Neese, James Edwin 1938- St&PR 93
Neese, Robert Stuart 1938- St&PR 93
Neese, Ruby S. 1930- WhoWrEP 92
Neese, Ruby Shaw 1930- WhoSSW 93
Neeson, Christine M. Law&B 92
Neeson, Liam BioIn 17
Neet, Sharon Eileen 1954- WhoAmW 93
Neeteson, Jacques J. 1954- WhoScE 91-3
Neevel, Raymond Richard 1922- St&PR 93
Nef, Albert 1882-1966 Baker 92
Nef, Evelyn Stefansson 1913- WhoAm 92
Nef, John Ulric 1899-1988 BioIn 17
Nef, Karl 1873-1935 Baker 92
Neff, Arlene Merle 1946- WhoAmW 93
Neff, Carole Cukell 1951- WhoEmL 93
Neff, Charles Edward Law&B 92
Neff, Charles Y. 1913- St&PR 93
Neff, Craig BioIn 17
Neff, Daniel Alan 1955- WhoEmL 93
Neff, Danny Joel 1948- WhoWor 93
Neff, David E. 1953- St&PR 93
Neff, Diane Irene 1954- WhoSSW 93
Neff, Donald Lloyd 1930- WhoAm 92
Neff, Edward August 1947- WhoAm 92
Neff, Francine Irving 1925- WhoAm 92
Neff, Franz Helmut 1948- WhoWor 93
Neff, Fred Leonard 1948- WhoEmL 93, WhoWor 93
Neff, Jack Hillman 1938- St&PR 93
Neff, Jack Kenneth 1938- WhoAm 92
Neff, James D. 1937- St&PR 93
Neff, John 1951- WhoAm 92
Neff, Marilyn Lee 1942- WhoAmW 93
Neff, Mary Ellen Andre 1943- WhoE 93
Neff, May T. AmWomPl
Neff, Michael J. 1943- WhoScE 91-3
Neff, Michael P. 1963- St&PR 93
Neff, P. Sherrill 1951- WhoWor 93
Neff, Ray Quinn 1928- WhoSSW 93, WhoWor 93
Neff, Robert Arthur 1931- WhoAm 92
Neff, Robert Clark 1921- WhoWor 93
Neff, Robert Wilbur 1936- WhoAm 92, WhoE 93
Neff, Thomas Joseph 1937- WhoAm 92
Neff, W. Perry 1927- St&PR 93
Neff, Wallace 1895-1982 BioIn 17
Neff, Wheeler K. Law&B 92
Neff, William DuWayne 1912- WhoAm 92
Nefsky, William Frank 1947- WhoEmL 93
Neft, David Samuel 1937- WhoAm 92, WhoE 93
Neft, Rhoda Shear WhoAmW 93
Negas, Taki 1939- St&PR 93
Negele, John William 1944- WhoAm 92, WhoE 93
Negga, Blandina Francis 1933- WhoUN 92
Negi, Chandra Mohan Singh 1939- WhoAsAP 91
Negi, Sharad Singh 1957- WhoWor 93
Negints, Thomas 1954- WhoAsAP 91
Negley, Glenn 1907-1988 ScF&FL 92
Negoita, Constantin 1923- WhoScE 91-4
Negovetich, John A. 1945- St&PR 93
Negovetich, John Anthony 1945- WhoAm 92
Negre, Martin Andre 1946- WhoWor 93
Negrea, Martian 1893-1973 Baker 92
Negrelli, Gerald M. 1947- St&PR 93
Negrelli, Mark John, III 1953- St&PR 93
Negrepontis, Michael 1928- WhoAm 92
Negrete, Jose 1855-1883 DcMexL
Negri, Gerald Louis 1936- St&PR 93
Negri, Gino 1919- Baker 92
Negri, Maria Caterina fl. 1720-1744 OxDcOp
Negri, Maria Rosa c. 1715-1760 OxDcOp
Negri, Pola 1894?-1987 IntDcF 2-3 [port]
Negri, Pola 1897-1987 PolBiDi [port]
Negri, Robert Joseph 1926- WhoAm 92
Negri, Rocco Antonio 1932- WhoE 93
Negri, Steven Joseph 1952- WhoE 93
Negri, Vittorio 1923- Baker 92
Negrier, Francois Charles 1928- WhoIns 93
Negrin, Alberto MiSFD 9
Negrin, Howard Elias 1935- WhoE 93
Negrin, I. Allen 1934- St&PR 93
Negrini, Carlo 1826-1865 OxDcOp
Negron, Jaime 1939- WhoE 93
Negron, Taylor BioIn 17

Nelson, Dorothy Wright 1928- *WhoAm 92, WhoAmW 93*
Nelson, Dotson McGinnis, Jr. 1915- *WhoAm 92*
Nelson, Douglas A. 1927- *WhoAm 92*
Nelson, Douglas Raymond 1934- *WhoSSW 93*
Nelson, Duane Russell *Law&B 92*
Nelson, E. Benjamin 1941- *WhoAm 92, WhoIns 93*
Nelson, Edward Gage 1931- *St&PR 93, WhoAm 92*
Nelson, Edward Humphrey 1918- *WhoAm 92*
Nelson, Edward L., Jr. *WhoAm 92*
Nelson, Edward Sheffield 1941- *WhoAm 92*
Nelson, Edward W. 1855-1934 *IntDcAn*
Nelson, Edwin Clarence 1922- *WhoAm 92*
Nelson, Edwin L. 1940- *WhoAm 92*
Nelson, Edwin Stafford 1928- *WhoAm 92*
Nelson, Elaine *Law&B 92*
Nelson, Elaine Marie 1939- *WhoAmW 93*
Nelson, Elizabeth Alice 1948- *WhoEmL 93*
Nelson, Elizabeth Colette 1953- *WhoAmW 93*
Nelson, Elizabeth Ellen *Law&B 92*
Nelson, Elizabeth Starnes 1958- *WhoAmW 93*
Nelson, Elmer Kingsholm, Jr. 1922- *WhoAm 92*
Nelson, Ethelyn Barnett 1925- *WhoAmW 93*
Nelson, Evelyn *SweetSg B*
Nelson, Faunie Mullvain *AmWomPl*
Nelson, Frank Raphael 1948- *WhoE 93*
Nelson, Fred Robert 1935- *WhoAm 92*
Nelson, Freda Nell Hein 1929- *WhoAmW 93*
Nelson, Frederick Carl 1932- *WhoAm 92*
Nelson, Frederick Dickson 1958- *WhoAm 92, WhoWor 93*
Nelson, Frederick N. 1941- *St&PR 93*
Nelson, Gareth Jon 1937- *WhoAm 92*
Nelson, Garrett R. *WhoAm 92*
Nelson, Garrett R. 1940- *St&PR 93*
Nelson, Gary *MiSFD 9*
Nelson, Gary D. 1941- *St&PR 93*
Nelson, Gary K. 1946- *St&PR 93*
Nelson, Gary Rohde 1942- *WhoSSW 93*
Nelson, Gary Thomas 1949- *WhoEmL 93, WhoSSW 93*
Nelson, Gayle Vance 1946- *WhoAmW 93*
Nelson, Gaylord Anton 1916- *WhoAm 92*
Nelson, Gene 1920- *BioIn 17, MiSFD 9*
Nelson, George 1786-1859 *IntDcAn*
Nelson, George Leonard 1897- *WhoAm 92*
Nelson, Gerald Charles 1951- *WhoEmL 93*
Nelson, Gerald Kenneth 1922- *WhoAm 92*
Nelson, Ginger K. 1939- *WhoWrEP 92*
Nelson, Glen David 1937- *WhoAm 92*
Nelson, Glenn F. 1952- *St&PR 93*
Nelson, Gloria Joann 1934- *WhoSSW 93*
Nelson, Gordon D. *Law&B 92*
Nelson, Gordon E. *Law&B 92*
Nelson, Gordon Leigh 1943- *WhoAm 92, WhoSSW 93, WhoWor 93*
Nelson, Gordon Leon 1919- *WhoAm 92*
Nelson, Grant Steel 1939- *WhoAm 92*
Nelson, Gregory *St&PR 93*
Nelson, Gregory Victor 1943- *WhoE 93*
Nelson, Gunnar *BioIn 17*
Nelson, Gwendolyn Diane 1950- *WhoAmW 93, WhoEmL 93*
Nelson, H. Donald 1933- *St&PR 93*
Nelson, H.H. 1912- *WhoIns 93*
Nelson, Harold Frederick 1928- *WhoE 93*
Nelson, Harriet Hilliard 1914- *WhoAm 92*
Nelson, Harry 1923- *WhoAm 92*
Nelson, Harry Donald *Law&B 92*
Nelson, Harry Donald 1933- *WhoAm 92*
Nelson, Harvey Frans, Jr. 1924- *WhoAm 92*
Nelson, Hedwig Potok 1954- *WhoAmW 93, WhoEmL 93*
Nelson, Helaine Q. 1945- *St&PR 93*
Nelson, Helaine Queen *Law&B 92*
Nelson, Helaine Queen 1945- *WhoAmW 93*
Nelson, Herbert d1990 *BioIn 17*
Nelson, Herbert Leroy 1922- *WhoAm 92*
Nelson, Hope *AmWomPl*
Nelson, Horatio 1758-1805 *BioIn 17, HarEnMi*
Nelson, Howard 1947- *ConAu 136*
Nelson, Howard Joseph 1919- *WhoAm 92*
Nelson, Howard L. 1954- *St&PR 93*
Nelson, Howard Thomas *Law&B 92*
Nelson, J. Garnett 1939- *WhoIns 93*
Nelson, Jack H. 1930- *WhoIns 93*
Nelson, Jack Henry 1930- *St&PR 93*
Nelson, Jack Lee 1932- *WhoAm 92*
Nelson, Jack Russell 1929- *WhoAm 92*
Nelson, Jacquelyn S. 1950- *ConAu 137*
Nelson, James Alan 1946- *St&PR 93*
Nelson, James Albert 1941- *WhoAm 92, WhoSSW 93*
Nelson, James Byron *Law&B 92*
Nelson, James Carmer, Jr. 1921- *WhoAm 92*
Nelson, James Clifford 1930- *WhoAm 92*
Nelson, James Dean 1956- *WhoEmL 93*
Nelson, James Delbert 1944- *St&PR 93*
Nelson, James E. *Law&B 92*
Nelson, James Edgar *Law&B 92*
Nelson, James Harold 1936- *WhoE 93, WhoWor 93*
Nelson, James I. *Law&B 92*
Nelson, James J. 1944- *St&PR 93*
Nelson, James R. *Law&B 92*
Nelson, James Ralph, Jr. 1948- *WhoSSW 93*
Nelson, James Vincent 1950- *St&PR 93*
Nelson, Jamie *BioIn 17*
Nelson, Jane Armstrong 1927- *WhoAmW 93*
Nelson, Jane Byrne 1926- *St&PR 93*
Nelson, Janet *BioIn 17*
Nelson, Janet Kathryn 1954- *WhoAmW 93, WhoEmL 93*
Nelson, Janet Louise 1930- *WhoAmW 93*
Nelson, Janette Cecile 1965- *WhoAmW 93*
Nelson, Janice Eileen 1943- *WhoE 93*
Nelson, Janice Marian 1951- *WhoEmL 93*
Nelson, Jay Phillip 1950- *WhoEmL 93*
Nelson, Jean Davenport 1931- *St&PR 93*
Nelson, Jean Edward, II 1952- *WhoEmL 93*
Nelson, Jean Kyle 1950- *WhoAmW 93*
Nelson, Jeffrey Morcom 1960- *WhoSSW 93*
Nelson, Jeffrey William *Law&B 92*
Nelson, Jennifer Kay 1953- *WhoAmW 93*
Nelson, Jerry *BioIn 17*
Nelson, Jerry A. 1935- *St&PR 93*
Nelson, Jill 1958- *WhoAmW 93*
Nelson, Jill B. *Law&B 92*
Nelson, Jimmie Jack 1928- *WhoE 93*
Nelson, Jo Ann 1946- *WhoWrEP 92*
Nelson, Joan 1958- *BioIn 17*
Nelson, Joel L. 1946- *St&PR 93*
Nelson, Joel Peter 1939- *St&PR 93*
Nelson, John d1734 *BioIn 17*
Nelson, John 1922- *St&PR 93*
Nelson, John 1947- *ScF&FL 92*
Nelson, John A. *Law&B 92*
Nelson, John Allan 1952- *WhoWrEP 92*
Nelson, John H. 1930- *St&PR 93*
Nelson, John Harvey 1955- *WhoE 93*
Nelson, John Howard 1929- *WhoAm 92*
Nelson, John Howard 1930- *WhoAm 92*
Nelson, John Keith 1943- *WhoAm 92*
Nelson, John M. 1931- *St&PR 93*
Nelson, John Martin 1931- *WhoAm 92*
Nelson, John Marvin 1933- *WhoSSW 93*
Nelson, John Ray 1926- *St&PR 93*
Nelson, John Robert 1920- *WhoAm 92*
Nelson, John Robert 1939- *WhoAm 92*
Nelson, John Robert, Jr. 1952- *WhoAm 92*
Nelson, John Thilgen 1921- *WhoAm 92*
Nelson, John (Wilton) 1941- *Baker 92, WhoAm 92*
Nelson, John Woolard 1928- *WhoAm 92*
Nelson, Jonathan P. *Law&B 92*
Nelson, Joni Lysett 1938- *WhoAm 92, WhoWor 93*
Nelson, Joseph Conrad 1926- *WhoAm 92*
Nelson, Joseph H. 1931- *St&PR 93*
Nelson, Joseph J. 1941- *St&PR 93*
Nelson, Judd 1959- *WhoAm 92*
Nelson, Judith (Anne) 1939- *Baker 92*
Nelson, Judith R. *Law&B 92*
Nelson, Judy *BioIn 17*
Nelson, Judy 1954- *WhoEmL 93*
Nelson, Julie D. *Law&B 92*
Nelson, Karin Becker 1933- *WhoAmW 93*
Nelson, Kathy Ann 1954- *WhoAmW 93, WhoEmL 93*
Nelson, Keith Adam 1953- *WhoE 93*
Nelson, Keith L. 1943- *St&PR 93*
Nelson, Keithe Eugene 1935- *WhoAm 92*
Nelson, Kenneth Edward 1948- *WhoAm 92*
Nelson, Kenneth M. d1991 *BioIn 17*
Nelson, Kenneth V. 1918- *St&PR 93*
Nelson, Kent *WhoWrEP 92*
Nelson, Kent Charles 1937- *St&PR 93*
Nelson, Kenwyn Gordon 1926- *WhoAm 92*
Nelson, Kevin Austin 1963- *WhoE 93*
Nelson, Kristen Carol *Law&B 92*
Nelson, Kurt Herbert 1924- *WhoE 93*
Nelson, L. Clair 1918- *St&PR 93*
Nelson, L. Scott 1938- *St&PR 93*
Nelson, Lance Shaylor 1939- *St&PR 93*
Nelson, Larry 1939- *St&PR 93*
Nelson, Larry N. *Law&B 92*
Nelson, Lars-Erik 1941- *WhoAm 92*
Nelson, Laurence Clyde 1947- *WhoEmL 93, WhoSSW 93*
Nelson, Lawrence B. 1931- *St&PR 93*
Nelson, Lawrence Barclay 1931- *WhoAm 92*
Nelson, Lawrence Evan 1932- *WhoAm 92*
Nelson, Lawrence J. *Law&B 92*
Nelson, Lawrence Olaf 1926- *WhoAm 92*
Nelson, Lawrence W. *Law&B 92*
Nelson, LeAnn Lindbeck 1937- *WhoAmW 93*
Nelson, Lee N. 1957- *St&PR 93*
Nelson, Leigh A. 1949- *St&PR 93*
Nelson, Leland *BioIn 17*
Nelson, Leonard 1920- *WhoAm 92*
Nelson, Leonard Earl 1944- *WhoE 93, WhoWor 93*
Nelson, Leslie Bergen 1925- *St&PR 93*
Nelson, Lewis Clair 1918- *WhoAm 92*
Nelson, Linda Beatrice D'Andrea 1926- *WhoE 93*
Nelson, Linda Carol 1954- *WhoAmW 93*
Nelson, Linda Shearer 1944- *WhoAmW 93*
Nelson, Lindsey 1919- *WhoAm 92*
Nelson, Liza 1950- *WhoWrEP 92*
Nelson, Lloyd Steadman 1922- *St&PR 93, WhoAm 92*
Nelson, Louis 1902-1990 *BioIn 17*
Nelson, Lowry, Jr. 1926- *ConAu 39NR, WhoAm 92, WhoWor 93*
Nelson, Lucy H. *AmWomPl*
Nelson, Lyle Morgan 1918- *WhoAm 92*
Nelson, M. Conrad 1943- *St&PR 93*
Nelson, M.G. 1914- *St&PR 93*
Nelson, Magnus Charles 1938- *WhoAm 92*
Nelson, Marguerite Hansen 1947- *WhoAmW 93, WhoEmL 93, WhoWor 93*
Nelson, Marietta 1953- *WhoAmW 93*
Nelson, Marietta Lou 1928- *WhoE 93*
Nelson, Marion Lawrence *AmWomPl*
Nelson, Marita Lee 1934- *WhoAmW 93*
Nelson, Mark Bruce 1921- *WhoAm 92*
Nelson, Mark Cranford 1954- *WhoSSW 93*
Nelson, Mark H. 1950- *WhoE 93*
Nelson, Marsh 1929- *BioIn 17*
Nelson, Martha Jane 1952- *WhoAm 92*
Nelson, Martha Ruth 1949- *WhoAmW 93*
Nelson, Martin O. 1912- *St&PR 93*
Nelson, Martin Oliver, Jr. 1946- *St&PR 93*
Nelson, Marvin R. 1926- *St&PR 93*
Nelson, Marvin Ray 1926- *WhoAm 92*
Nelson, Mary Ann 1938- *WhoAmW 93*
Nelson, Mary Carolyn *Law&B 92*
Nelson, Mary Carroll 1929- *WhoAmW 93*
Nelson, Mary Pennell 1943- *WhoAmW 93*
Nelson, Mary Renee 1915- *WhoE 93*
Nelson, Mary S. 1943- *WhoAmW 93*
Nelson, Matthew *BioIn 17*
Nelson, Merle R. 1934- *St&PR 93*
Nelson, Merlin Edward 1922- *WhoAm 92*
Nelson, Mervyn d1991 *BioIn 17*
Nelson, Michael Bernard 1951- *WhoEmL 93*
Nelson, Michael Edward 1955- *WhoEmL 93*
Nelson, Michael James 1951- *WhoEmL 93, WhoSSW 93*
Nelson, Michael Underhill 1932- *WhoAm 92*
Nelson, Michelle Hoghland 1953- *WhoWrEP 92*
Nelson, Mildred 1915- *WhoWrEP 92*
Nelson, Milo Gabriel 1938- *JrnUS, WhoWrEP 92*
Nelson, Nancy *Law&B 92*
Nelson, Nancy Eleanor 1933- *WhoAm 92, WhoWor 93*
Nelson, Natalie Elaine *Law&B 92*
Nelson, Nathaniel 1932- *See* Flamingos *SoulM*
Nelson, Neill Davenport 1954- *St&PR 93*
Nelson, Nels Christian 1875-1964 *IntDcAn*
Nelson, Nels Robert 1923- *WhoAm 92*
Nelson, Nette Adaline 1939- *WhoAmW 93*
Nelson, Nevin Mary 1941- *WhoAmW 93*
Nelson, Norman Crooks 1929- *WhoAm 92, WhoSSW 93*
Nelson, Norman R. *Law&B 92*
Nelson, Norton 1910-1990 *BioIn 17*
Nelson, O.T. 1941- *ScF&FL 92*
Nelson, O. Terry 1941- *BioIn 17*
Nelson, O'Ferrell Valentine 1927- *WhoSSW 93*
Nelson, Oliver (Edward) 1932-1975 *Baker 92*
Nelson, Oliver Evans, Jr. 1920- *WhoAm 92*
Nelson, Orvis M. 1907-1976 *EncABHB 8 [port]*
Nelson, Otto Millard 1935- *WhoSSW 93*
Nelson, Pamela *WhoAmW 93*
Nelson, Patricia Ann 1931- *WhoAmW 93*
Nelson, Paul L. 1949- *WhoEmL 93*
Nelson, Paul Richard 1947- *WhoAm 92*
Nelson, Paul S. *Law&B 92*
Nelson, Paula Morrison Bronson 1944- *WhoAmW 93, WhoWor 93*
Nelson, Peter Christian 1945- *St&PR 93*
Nelson, Peter N. 1953- *SmATA 73 [port]*
Nelson, Philip Arthur 1952- *WhoWor 93*
Nelson, Philip Francis 1928- *WhoAm 92*
Nelson, Prince Roger *Baker 92*
Nelson, Prince Rogers *BioIn 17*
Nelson, R. Stephen, Jr. *Law&B 92*
Nelson, R. Stuart *WhoScE 91-1*
Nelson, Radell *ScF&FL 92*
Nelson, Ralph 1916-1987 *MiSFD 9N*
Nelson, Ralph Alfred 1927- *WhoAm 92*
Nelson, Ralph Daniel 1949- *WhoSSW 93*
Nelson, Ralph Erwin 1946- *WhoSSW 93*
Nelson, Ralph James 1925- *St&PR 93*
Nelson, Ralph Lowell 1926- *WhoAm 92*
Nelson, Randall *BioIn 17*
Nelson, Randall Erland 1948- *WhoEmL 93*
Nelson, Ray Faraday 1931- *ScF&FL 92, WhoWrEP 92*
Nelson, Raymond John 1917- *WhoAm 92*
Nelson, Raymond John 1938- *WhoAm 92*
Nelson, Raymond L., Jr. 1938- *ConEn, St&PR 93*
Nelson, Renwick T. *Law&B 92*
Nelson, Richard *BioIn 17*
Nelson, Richard Alan 1954- *WhoEmL 93*
Nelson, Richard Bruce 1952- *WhoEmL 93*
Nelson, Richard Burton 1911- *WhoAm 92*
Nelson, Richard Copeland 1930- *WhoAm 92*
Nelson, Richard D. 1940- *St&PR 93*
Nelson, Richard David 1940- *WhoAm 92*
Nelson, Richard E., Jr. 1905- *St&PR 93*
Nelson, Richard Henry 1939- *WhoAm 92, WhoE 93, WhoWor 93*
Nelson, Richard Henry 1949- *WhoEmL 93*
Nelson, Richard Henry 1952- *WhoEmL 93*
Nelson, Richard K. *BioIn 17*
Nelson, Richard Leedom, Jr. 1939- *WhoSSW 93*
Nelson, Rick 1940-1985 *BioIn 17*
Nelson, Robert A. *Law&B 92*
Nelson, Robert Bruce 1935- *WhoAm 92*
Nelson, Robert C. 1956- *St&PR 93*
Nelson, Robert Charles 1924- *WhoAm 92*
Nelson, Robert Dale 1934- *St&PR 93*
Nelson, Robert Earl, Jr. 1938- *WhoSSW 93, WhoWor 93*
Nelson, Robert Eddinger 1928- *WhoWor 93*
Nelson, Robert G. 1948- *St&PR 93*
Nelson, Robert Gerald 1942- *St&PR 93*
Nelson, Robert Hartley 1921- *WhoAm 92*
Nelson, Robert J. 1935- *St&PR 93*
Nelson, Robert James 1935- *WhoIns 93*
Nelson, Robert L. 1943- *St&PR 93*
Nelson, Robert Louis 1931- *WhoAm 92*
Nelson, Robert Norton 1941- *WhoSSW 93*
Nelson, Robert Thompson, Jr. 1958- *WhoSSW 93*
Nelson, Robert U(riel) 1902- *Baker 92*
Nelson, Rodney 1941- *WhoWrEP 92*
Nelson, Roger C. 1948- *WhoSSW 93*
Nelson, Roger Hugh 1931- *WhoAm 92*
Nelson, Roger K. 1947- *St&PR 93*
Nelson, Roger William 1947- *WhoEmL 93*
Nelson, Rolf John 1955- *St&PR 93*
Nelson, Ron 1929- *WhoAm 92*
Nelson, Ron(ald Jack) 1929- *Baker 92*
Nelson, Ronald Harvey 1918- *WhoAm 92*
Nelson, Ronald M. 1951- *St&PR 93*
Nelson, Ronald Roy 1941- *WhoE 93, WhoWor 93*
Nelson, Ronald William 1956- *WhoEmL 93*
Nelson, Rose Estelle 1943- *WhoAmW 93*
Nelson, Rosemary *Law&B 92*
Nelson, Rosetta Pearson 1948- *WhoAmW 93*
Nelson, Roy C. *St&PR 93*
Nelson, Roy Paul 1923- *WhoWrEP 92*
Nelson, Russell Marion 1924- *WhoAm 92*
Nelson, Ruth d1992 *NewYTBS 92 [port]*
Nelson, Ruth Basha 1939- *WhoE 93*
Nelson, Sabrina Anne 1969- *WhoAmW 93*
Nelson, Samuel 1792-1873 *OxCSupC [port]*
Nelson, Sandra Lee 1947- *WhoEmL 93*
Nelson, Sandy *BioIn 17*
Nelson, Sara *BioIn 17*
Nelson, Sarah Jane 1927- *WhoAm 92*
Nelson, Sarah Milledge 1931- *WhoAmW 93*
Nelson, Scott H. 1932- *St&PR 93*
Nelson, Shelley M. *Law&B 92*
Nelson, Shelley Marie 1956- *WhoEmL 93*
Nelson, Sherman A. 1934- *St&PR 93*
Nelson, Stanley 1933- *ConAu 39NR, WhoE 93*
Nelson, Stanley Leroy 1941- *WhoSSW 93*
Nelson, Stebbins *Law&B 92*

Nelson, Stephen M. 1948- St&PR 93
Nelson, Steven Dwayne 1950- WhoEmL 93
Nelson, Stuart Owen 1927- WhoAm 92
Nelson, Susan 1936- WhoAmW 93
Nelson, Suzanne M. 1949- WhoAmW 93
Nelson, Sydney B. 1935- WhoSSW 93
Nelson, Terry BioIn 17
Nelson, Terry L. 1945- St&PR 93
Nelson, Theresa 1948- DcAmChF 1985
Nelson, Theresa Decker 1926- WhoAmW 93
Nelson, Thomas C. Law&B 92
Nelson, Thomas Edward 1965- WhoEmL 93
Nelson, Thomas George 1949- WhoEmL 93
Nelson, Thomas Wilfred 1954- WhoSSW 93
Nelson, Thomas William 1921- WhoAm 92
Nelson, Tracy 1963- ConTFT 10
Nelson, Vera Joyce 1903- WhoWrEP 92
Nelson, Virginia L. 1918- WhoWrEP 92
Nelson, Vita Joy 1937- WhoE 93
Nelson, W. Blair Law&B 92
Nelson, Waldemar Stanley 1916- St&PR 93
Nelson, Waldo Emerson 1898- WhoAm 92
Nelson, Wallace Boyd 1923- WhoSSW 93
Nelson, Wallace W. 1928- WhoAm 92
Nelson, Walter G. Law&B 92
Nelson, Walter Gerald 1930- WhoAm 92
Nelson, Walter Henry 1928- WhoWor 93
Nelson, Wanda Lee 1952- WhoAmW 93
Nelson, Wayne A. 1930- St&PR 93
Nelson, Wayne P. 1941- St&PR 93
Nelson, Wayne W. Law&B 92
Nelson, Wendel Lane 1939- WhoAm 92
Nelson, Werner Lind 1914- WhoAm 92
Nelson, Wesley D. Law&B 92
Nelson, William 1824-1862 HarEnMi
Nelson, William 1908-1978 BioIn 17
Nelson, William A. 1930- St&PR 93
Nelson, William Bruce 1950- WhoAm 92
Nelson, William E. 1926- St&PR 93
Nelson, William Edward 1940- WhoAm 92
Nelson, William George, IV 1934- WhoAm 92
Nelson, William James, Jr. 1939- St&PR 93
Nelson, William M. Law&B 92
Nelson, William R. 1947- St&PR 93
Nelson, William Rankin 1921- WhoAm 92
Nelson, William Rockhill 1841-1915 JrnUS
Nelson, William W. Law&B 92
Nelson, William W. 1945- St&PR 93
Nelson, Willie BioIn 17
Nelson, Willie 1933- WhoAm 92
Nelson, Willie (Hugh) 1933- Baker 92
Nelson-Humphries, Tessa WhoAm 92, WhoWrEP 92
Nelson-Mayson, Linda Ruth 1954- WhoAm 92
Nelsova, Zara 1918- Baker 92
Nelsson, Woldemar 1938- Baker 92
Neman, David 1951- St&PR 93
Nemanjid Dynasty OxDcByz
Nemara, Vanessa Anne 1953- WhoAmW 93, WhoEmL 93
Nemazee, Reza 1949- WhoE 93
Nembach, Eckhard H. 1937- WhoScE 91-3
Nembro, Alfredo Carlo 1953- WhoWor 93
Nemcsok, Janos Gyorgy 1949- WhoScE 91-4
Neme, Jacques 1930- WhoWor 93
Nemec, Ales 1944- WhoScE 91-4
Nemec, Carl Joseph 1940- St&PR 93
Nemec, Corky BioIn 17
Nemec, Jan 1936- DrEEuF, MiSFD 9
Nemec, Michael Lee 1949- WhoEmL 93, WhoSSW 93
Nemec, Vernita Ellen McClish 1942- WhoE 93
Nemecek, Albert Duncan, Jr. 1936- WhoAm 92, WhoWor 93
Nemecek, Franz Xaver Baker 92
Nemecek, Jeffrey Alan 1948- WhoEmL 93
Nemecz, Erno 1920- WhoScE 91-4
Nemeiri, Gaafar Mohammed 1930- BioIn 17
Nemelka, Lawrence P. 1936- St&PR 93
Nemeroff, Charles Barnet 1949- WhoSSW 93
Nemeroff, Michael Alan 1946- WhoE 93, WhoEmL 93
Nemerov, Howard BioIn 17
Nemerov, Howard 1920-1991 AnObit 1991, News 92
Nemerov, Howard Stanley 1920-1991 ConLC 70
Nemes, Laszlo 1937- WhoScE 91-4
Nemes, Sandor 1940- WhoScE 91-4
Nemes, Sheila Keohane 1949- WhoAmW 93
Nemescu, Octavian 1940- Baker 92
Nemesios fl. 4th cent.- OxDcByz
Nemeskeri, Janos 1914-1989 BioIn 17
Nemeth, Alan Peter 1940- St&PR 93
Nemeth, Charlan Jeanne 1941- WhoAm 92
Nemeth, Charles Paul 1951- WhoEmL 93
Nemeth, Edward J. 1938- WhoAm 92
Nemeth, Gizella 1942- WhoScE 91-4
Nemeth, Janos 1931- WhoScE 91-4
Nemeth, Jozsef 1953- WhoScE 91-4
Nemeth, Karoly 1922- WhoWor 93
Nemeth, Kathleen Lucas Law&B 92
Nemeth, Lane BioIn 17
Nemeth, Lane 1947- ConEn
Nemeth, Marc 1951- St&PR 93
Nemeth, Maria 1897-1967 Baker 92, OxDcOp
Nemeth, Miklos 1948- WhoWor 93
Nemeth, Patricia Marie 1959- WhoEmL 93
Nemethy, George 1934- WhoE 93
Nemetz, Allen P. 1940- St&PR 93
Nemetz, Carol Anne Law&B 92
Nemetz, Carol Anne 1953- WhoEmL 93
Nemetz, Christine Arax 1961- WhoWrEP 92
Nemetz, Nathaniel Theodore 1913- WhoAm 92, WhoWor 93
Nemetz, Peter Newman 1944- WhoWor 93
Nemeyer, Frank L. 1927- St&PR 93
Nemhauser, George Lann 1937- WhoAm 92, WhoSSW 93
Nemhauser, Nancy Law&B 92
Nemia, Frank J. 1948- St&PR 93
Nemieri, Jaafar al- 1930- DcTwHis
Nemir, Rosa Lee d1992 NewYTBS 92
Nemir, Rosa Lee 1905-1992 BioIn 17
Nemiro, Beverly Mirium Anderson 1925- WhoAmW 93, WhoWor 93
Nemiroff, Isaac 1912-1977 Baker 92
Nemiroff, Maxine Celia 1935- WhoAmW 93, WhoWor 93
Nemiroff, Robert d1991 BioIn 17
Nemirovich-Danchenko, Vladimir 1858-1943 IntDcOp, OxDcOp
Nemirow, Arnold Myles 1943- St&PR 93, WhoAm 92
Nemirow, Bruce Irving 1948- WhoE 93
Nemirow, Jill Karin 1961- WhoWrEP 92
Nemitz, Eugene Harold, Jr. 1948- WhoEmL 93
Nemitz, Sanford C. 1932- St&PR 93
Nemli, Tanju 1944- WhoScE 91-4
Nemmers, Sherry J. 1954- WhoAm 92, WhoAmW 93
Nemo, Lawrence 1916- St&PR 93
Nemo, Thomas Edward Law&B 92
Nemoto, Takuma 1930- WhoE 93
Nemours, Louis d'Armagnac, Duke of 1472-1503 HarEnMi
Nemoy, Leon 1901- WhoE 93
Nemoz, Guy 1946- WhoScE 91-2
Nemr, Georgette 1963- WhoAmW 93
Nemser, Robert Solomon 1938- WhoAm 92
Nemtin, Alexander 1936- Baker 92
Nena, Jacob 1941- WhoAsAP 91
Nenashev, Alexander Yur'evich 1961- WhoWor 93
Nendick, Thomas Bernard 1929- St&PR 93
Nengo, Pengau MiSFD 9
Nenkov, Nikolai Dimitrov 1928- WhoScE 91-4
Nenna, Pomponio c. 1550-1613? Baker 92
Nenneman, Richard Arthur 1929- WhoAm 92, WhoE 93
Nenner, Rodney Andrew 1961- WhoE 93
Nenno, Robert Peter 1922- WhoSSW 93
Nenov, Dimitar Atanassov 1928- WhoScE 91-4
Nenov, Dimiter 1902-1953 Baker 92
Nenstiel, Susan Kisthart 1951- WhoAmW 93, WhoEmL 93
Nentwig, James Richard 1936- St&PR 93
Neophytos Enkleistos c. 1134-1214 OxDcByz
Neophytos, the Recluse, Saint c. 1134-c. 1214 BioIn 17
Neophytou, Michael 1937- WhoWor 93
Neoral, Lubomir 1927- WhoScE 91-4
Neos, Peri Fitch 1938- WhoAmW 93
Neparko, Mary Margaret 1945- WhoSSW 93
Nephew, Arthur Wallace 1953- WhoE 93
Nephew, Oliver Thomas 1929- St&PR 93
Nepo, Mark Evan 1951- WhoWrEP 92
Nepomnyachy, Sergei Genriyevich 1964- WhoWor 93
Nepomuceno, Alberto 1864-1920 Baker 92
Neppe, Vernon Michael 1951- WhoWor 93
Neppel, Ralph G. d1987 BioIn 17
Nepper-Christensen, Palle 1934- WhoScE 91-2
Neppl, Walter J. 1922- St&PR 93
Neppl, Walter Joseph 1922- WhoAm 92
Neptune, John Addison 1919- WhoAm 92
Nepveu, Gerard 1950- WhoScE 91-2
Nepveu, Pierre 1946- WhoCanL 92
Nequist, John Leonard 1929- WhoAm 92
Nerad, Jerry 1942- St&PR 93
Nerandzic, Dragan Vidosav 1964- WhoWor 93
Nerbas, Grant Howard Law&B 92
Nerdal, Willy 1954- WhoWor 93
Nerdrum, Odd 1944- BioIn 17, WhoE 93
Nereberg, Eliot Joel 1949- WhoEmL 93
Nerem, Robert M. 1937- WhoAm 92
Nerem, Tracy Linn 1963- WhoWrEP 92
Nerenberg, Aaron Law&B 92
Nerenberg, Aaron 1940- WhoAm 92
Nerenberg, Milton 1933- WhoSSW 93
Nerger, H. Peter St&PR 93
Nerger, Therese A. 1935- St&PR 93
Neri, Dennis 1950- St&PR 93
Neri, Filippo, Saint 1515-1595 Baker 92
Neri, Giulio 1909-1958 Baker 92, OxDcOp
Neri, Greg 1963- MiSFD 9
Neri, Manuel 1930- HispAmA
Neri, Penelope ScF&FL 92
Neri, Phillip A. 1956- St&PR 93
Nerida, Victor Aceron 1951- WhoWor 93
Nerini, Emile 1882-1967 Baker 92
Nerison, Jane P. Law&B 92
Nerken, Albert d1992 NewYTBS 92
Nerken, Albert 1912- St&PR 93
Nerlinger, John William 1920- WhoAm 92
Nerlove, Marc L. 1933- WhoAm 92
Nermuth, Manfred 1948- WhoWor 93
Nern, Christopher C. Law&B 92
Nero 37-68 OxDcOp
Nero, Emperor of Rome 37-68 BioIn 17
Nero, Anthony Vincent, Jr. 1942- WhoAm 92
Nero, Gaius Claudius fl. 214BC-199BC HarEnMi
Nero, Mark Jeffrey Law&B 92
Nero, Peter 1934- WhoAm 92, WhoE 93
Nero, Peter (Bernard) 1934- Baker 92
Nero, Shirley Mae 1936- WhoSSW 93
Nero, William Thomas, Sr. 1935- WhoAm 92, WhoE 93
Nerode, Anil 1932- WhoAm 92
Nerses OxDcByz
Nersesian, G.A. 1935- St&PR 93
Nersesian, Robert S. 1950- WhoWrEP 92
Nerses of Lambron 1153-1198 OxDcByz
Nerses Snorhali 1102-1173 OxDcByz
Nerses the Great, I OxDcByz
Neruda Baker 92
Neruda, Francis Donald 1939- St&PR 93
Neruda, Franz 1843-1915 Baker 92
Neruda, Josef 1807-1875 Baker 92
Neruda, Marie (Arlbergova) 1840-1922 Baker 92
Neruda, Pablo 1904-1973 BioIn 17, SpAmA, WorLitC [port]
Neruda, Viktor 1836?-1852 Baker 92
Neruda, Wilma Maria Francisca 1838?-1911 Baker 92
Nerudova, Amalie 1834-1890 Baker 92
Nervo, Amado 1870-1919 DcMexL
Nervo, Jimmy 1890-1975 See Crazy Gang, The IntDcF 2-3
Nerz, Alexander 1947- WhoWor 93
Nes, Arnfinn WhoScE 91-4
Nes, David Gulick 1917- WhoE 93
Nesbeda, Eugene P. 1954- St&PR 93
Nesbeda, Eugene Paul 1954- WhoAm 92
Nesbett, John G. d1991 BioIn 17
Nesbit, Douglas Charles 1926- WhoE 93, WhoWor 93
Nesbit, E. 1858-1924 ScF&FL 92
Nesbit, E(dith) 1858-1924 ConAu 137, MajAI [port]
Nesbit, Larry Leonard 1944- WhoE 93
Nesbit, Lynn 1938- BioIn 17
Nesbit, Robert Carrington 1917- WhoAm 92, WhoWor 93, WhoWrEP 92
Nesbit, Robert Grover 1932- WhoAm 92
Nesbit, Wm. J., Jr. 1935- St&PR 93
Nesbitt, Archie J. 1949- St&PR 93
Nesbitt, Arthur W. 1927- St&PR 93
Nesbitt, Arthur Wallace 1927- WhoAm 92
Nesbitt, Charles Rudolph 1921- WhoAm 92
Nesbitt, Christopher S. St&PR 93
Nesbitt, Daniel F. Law&B 92
Nesbitt, DeEtte DuPree 1941- WhoAmW 93, WhoSSW 93
Nesbitt, Elizabeth 1897-1977 BioIn 17
Nesbitt, Ernest Van 1929- WhoSSW 93
Nesbitt, Fred 1936- St&PR 93
Nesbitt, Gregory Leon 1938- St&PR 93, WhoAm 92
Nesbitt, Ilse Buchert 1932- WhoE 93
Nesbitt, John Arthur 1933- WhoAm 92
Nesbitt, John Dawson 1951- WhoEmL 93, WhoSSW 93
Nesbitt, Lenore Carrero WhoAm 92
Nesbitt, Lenore Carrero 1932- WhoAmW 93, WhoSSW 93
Nesbitt, Leroy Edward 1925- WhoWor 93
Nesbitt, Lloyd Ivan 1951- WhoE 93, WhoWor 93
Nesbitt, Lowell 1933- WhoAm 92
Nesbitt, R.W. WhoScE 91-1
Nesbitt, Radian Beth 1945- WhoAmW 93
Nesbitt, Robert Edward Lee, Jr. 1924- WhoAm 92
Nesbitt, Rosemary Sinnett 1924- WhoAm 92
Nesbitt, Stephen L. Law&B 92
Nesci, Vincent P. Law&B 92
Nesfeder, Amy Davis Law&B 92
Nesh, Karen Lee 1957- WhoAmW 93
Nesheim, John Lamson 1942- St&PR 93
Nesheim, Robert Olaf 1921- WhoAm 92
Nesher, Avi MiSFD 9
Nesher, Robert Allen 1946- St&PR 93
Neshyba, Victor Peter 1922- WhoSSW 93
Nesin, Asher 1918- St&PR 93
Nesin, Noah 1929- St&PR 93
Nesius, Leo Anthony 1917- St&PR 93
Neskovic, Nesko 1943- WhoScE 91-4
Neslage, James Tim 1958- WhoSSW 93
Nesland, Ronald Richard 1945- St&PR 93
Nesler, Dennis John 1943- St&PR 93
Nesmith, Bruce ScF&FL 92
Nesmith, Frances Jane 1926- WhoAmW 93
Nesmith, Michael 1942- WhoAm 92
Nesmith, Richard Duey 1929- WhoAm 92
Nesnick, Victoria Gilvary 1945- WhoE 93
Nesom, Barbara B. 1939- St&PR 93
Nesom, John H. 1936- St&PR 93
Nesom, Ruth Evelyn 1916- WhoWrEP 92
Nespole, Joseph James 1936- WhoAm 92
Nesri dc. 1512 OxDcByz
Ness, Albert Kenneth 1903- WhoAm 92, WhoSSW 93, WhoWor 93
Ness, David James 1949- WhoEmL 93
Ness, Elisa BioIn 17
Ness, Ellyn Katherine 1952- WhoAmW 93
Ness, Evaline (Michelow) 1911-1986 ConAu 37NR, MajAI [port]
Ness, Frederic William 1914- WhoAm 92
Ness, Gary Clifford 1940- WhoAm 92
Ness, Gary Gene 1948- WhoEmL 93
Ness, Lika ConAu 139
Ness, Norman Frederick 1933- WhoAm 92
Ness, Owen McGregor 1930- WhoAm 92
Ness, Philip W. 1936- St&PR 93
Ness, Philip Wahmann, Jr. 1936- WhoAm 92
Ness, Steven Allyn 1947- St&PR 93
Ness, Thomas Joseph 1940- St&PR 93
Nessel, Edward Harry 1945- WhoE 93
Nessel, Jack Howard 1938- WhoAm 92
Nesselhauf, Lois Lucille 1938- WhoWor 93
Nesselroade, John Richard 1936- WhoE 93
Nesselrotte, Toni Moyer Law&B 92
Nessen, Ronald Harold 1934- WhoAm 92
Nessen, Ward Henry 1909- WhoE 93, WhoWor 93
Nesser, Alfred 1893-1967 BiDAMSp 1989
Nessesson, Elsa Behaim 1877-1969 AmWomPl
Nessim, David Jacques 1925- WhoAm 92
Nessler, Victor 1841-1890 OxDcOp
Nessler, Victor E(rnst) 1841-1890 Baker 92
Nessmith, Herbert Alva 1935- WhoSSW 93
Nesson, H. Richard 1932- WhoAm 92
Nesson, Marlene 1956- WhoAmW 93
Nesson, Richard Bryce Law&B 92
Nester, Francis J. 1929- St&PR 93
Nester, Irene Kay 1958- WhoAmW 93
Nester, William Raymond, Jr. 1928- WhoAm 92
Nesterenko, Evgeni 1938- Baker 92
Nesterenko, Evgeny 1938- OxDcOp
Nesterenko, Evgeny Evgenievich 1938- IntDcOp
Nesterenko, Yevgeniy Yevgeniyevich 1938- WhoWor 93
Nesteruk, Julia Ann 1955- WhoE 93
Nestico, John J. Law&B 92
Nestle, Joan 1940- WhoWrEP 92
Nestler, Andrew Payton BioIn 17
Nestler, Lloyd L., Jr. 1941- St&PR 93
Nestongos OxDcByz
Nestor d12th cent. OxDcByz
Nestor, Donald Eugene 1962- St&PR 93
Nestor, Jack I. 1933- St&PR 93
Nestor, Lula B. 1935- WhoAmW 93
Nestor, Marilyn Ferguson 1932- WhoE 93
Nestor Castellano, Brenda Diana 1955- WhoAmW 93, WhoEmL 93
Nestorios c. 381-c. 451 OxDcByz
Nestor of Thessalonike OxDcByz
Nestorovski, Mirce Law&B 92
Nestrick, Dwight L. 1947- St&PR 93
Nestripke, Denny W. St&PR 93
Nestroy, Johann Nepomuk von 1801-1862 OxDcOp

Nestvold, Elwood Olaf 1932- WhoWor 93
Nestyev, Izrail (Vladimirovich) 1911- Baker 92
Nesva, Scott B. 1952- St&PR 93
Nesvan, Geraldine Root WhoAmW 93
Nesvig, Elliot M. 1920- St&PR 93
Nesvold, Betty Anne Krambuhl 1922- WhoAm 92
Neswald, Barbara Anne 1935- WhoE 93
Netam, Arvind 1942- WhoAsAP 91
Netanyahu, Benjamin BioIn 17
Netemeyer, Joseph E. 1952- St&PR 93
Netemeyer, Margaret 1950- WhoEmL 93
Netemeyer, Maurice E. 1954- St&PR 93
Neter, John 1923- WhoAm 92
Netherclift, Beryl 1911- ScF&FL 92
Nethercot, David Arthur WhoScE 91-1
Nethercott, J.W. 1927- St&PR 93
Nethercut, Philip Edwin 1921- WhoAm 92
Nethercut, William Robert 1936- WhoAm 92, WhoWor 93
Netherland, Sally N. 1951- St&PR 93
Nethers, Elena Soto Law&B 92
Nethers, Jerry Steven 1939- St&PR 93
Nethersole, Jacqueline E. Law&B 92
Netherton, Dana Eugene 1950- WhoSSW 93
Netherton, Derek Nigel Donald 1945- WhoWor 93
Netherton, J. Nick Law&B 92
Netherton, Orville A. 1925- St&PR 93
Nethery, John Jay 1941- WhoAm 92
Nethery, Tom O. St&PR 93
Nething, Melissa Ann 1965- WhoAmW 93
Neto, Antonio Agostinho 1922-1979 ColdWar 2 [port]
Neto, Joao Cabral de Melo 1920- BioIn 17
Netravali, Arun N. 1946- WhoAm 92
Netsch, Dawn Clark 1926- WhoAm 92, WhoAmW 93
Netsky, Hankus 1955- WhoAm 92
Nett, Ann T. WhoWrEP 92
Nett, Marvin R. 1959- St&PR 93
Nett, Robert B. BioIn 17
Netteberg, Eric Bradley Law&B 92
Nettelbeck, Fred Arthur 1950- WhoWrEP 92
Nettels, Elsa 1931- WhoAm 92
Nettels, George Edward, Jr. 1927- St&PR 93, WhoAm 92
Nettels, John Curtis Law&B 92
Netter, Alfred E. 1950- St&PR 93
Netter, Cornelia Ann 1933- WhoAmW 93, WhoE 93, WhoWor 93
Netter, Donald T. St&PR 93
Netter, Frank H. 1906-1991 BioIn 17
Netter, Jean-Patrice 1940- WhoWor 93
Netter, K. Fred 1919- St&PR 93
Netter, Karl Joachim 1929- WhoScE 91-3
Netter, Kurt Fred 1919- WhoAm 92, WhoE 93, WhoWor 93
Netter, Mildrette BlkAmWO
Netter, Patrick 1947- WhoScE 91-2
Netter, Robert 1927- WhoScE 91-2
Netter, Robert J. St&PR 93
Netter, Susan ScF&FL 92
Netter, Virginia Thompson 1931- WhoAmW 93
Netterfield, Patricia Ann 1946- WhoAmW 93
Netterville, George Bronson 1929- WhoSSW 93
Nettesheim, Christine Cook 1944- CngDr 91, WhoAm 92, WhoAmW 93, WhoE 93
Nettie, Roger Allen 1961- WhoEmL 93
Nettl, Bruno 1930- Baker 92, WhoAm 92
Nettl, Paul 1889-1972 Baker 92
Nettles, Bert S. 1936- WhoSSW 93
Nettles, Graig 1944- BiDAMSp 1989
Nettles, John Barnwell 1922- WhoAm 92
Nettles, Joseph Lee 1954- WhoSSW 93
Nettles, Larry N. Law&B 92
Nettles, William Carl, Jr. 1934- WhoSSW 93
Nettleton, Asahel 1783-1844 BioIn 17
Nettleton, Eva Thomas AmWomPl
Nettleton, Lois WhoAm 92
Nettleton, M. Bridget 1954- WhoAmW 93
Netto-Ferreira, Jose Carlos 1947- WhoWor 93
Nettrour, Lila Groff WhoAmW 93
Nettrour, Mimi 1950- WhoAmW 93
Netzahualcoyotl 1402-1472 DcMexL
Netzel, Mary Ellen 1953- WhoAmW 93
Netzer, Dick 1928- WhoAm 92
Netzer, Lanore Agnes 1916- WhoAm 92
Netzler, Jack 1940- WhoAsAP 91
Netzley, Terry E. 1936- St&PR 93
Netzloff, Michael Lawrence 1942- WhoAm 92
Netzly, Vernon Dale 1930- St&PR 93
Netzorg, Katherine S. AmWomPl
Neu, Carl Herbert, Jr. 1937- WhoAm 92
Neu, Charles Eric 1936- WhoAm 92
Neu, Gladys Inez 1908- WhoSSW 93
Neu, Harold Conrad 1934- WhoAm 92
Neu, Jerome 1947- ConAu 138
Neu, Kenneth G. 1955- St&PR 93
Neu, Richard W. 1956- St&PR 93
Neubarth, Sanford L. 1948- St&PR 93, WhoIns 93
Neubauer, Ann Lucas 1956- WhoAmW 93
Neubauer, Anthony Charles 1953- WhoE 93
Neubauer, Charles Frederick 1950- WhoAm 92
Neubauer, Florence Butler 1955- WhoEmL 93
Neubauer, Franz Christoph 1750-1795 Baker 92
Neubauer, Fritz M. 1940- WhoScE 91-3
Neubauer, Joseph 1941- St&PR 93, WhoAm 92, WhoE 93, WhoWor 93
Neubauer, Perry K. 1940- St&PR 93
Neubauer, Peter Bela 1913- WhoAm 92
Neuber, Dieter 1937- St&PR 93
Neuberg, Hans W. 1921- WhoE 93
Neuberg, William B. 1930- St&PR 93
Neuberg-Doulman, Susan Ellen Law&B 92
Neuberger, Claus Helmut 1961- WhoWor 93
Neuberger, Egon 1925- WhoAm 92
Neuberger, Marie S. 1908- St&PR 93
Neuberger, Maurine Brown 1907- BioIn 17
Neuberger, Roy R. 1903- St&PR 93, WhoAm 92
Neuberger, Sharon Eunice 1939- WhoAmW 93
Neubig, Herbert Frederick 1934- St&PR 93
Neubohn, Naneen Hunter 1939- WhoAm 92
Neuburger, Werner 1926- St&PR 93
Neuckermans, Herman 1943- WhoScE 91-2
Neudeck, Gerold Walter 1936- WhoAm 92
Neudecker, Heinz 1933- WhoWor 93
Neudecker, Thomas J.S. 1949- WhoScE 91-3
Neudek, Kurt F.W.A. 1935- WhoUN 92
Neudoerffer, Volkmar Caj 1941- WhoIns 93
Neuefeind, Wilhelm 1939- WhoAm 92
Neuendorff, Adolph (Heinrich Anton Magnus) 1843-1897 Baker 92
Neuenschwander, Frederick Phillip 1924- WhoWor 93
Neuenschwander, Gordon Earle 1927- St&PR 93
Neuenschwander, Stephanie 1949- WhoSSW 93
Neuer, Philip David 1946- WhoEmL 93
Neufeld, David Samuel 1957- WhoEmL 93
Neufeld, Donn Ernest 1956- St&PR 93
Neufeld, Edward Peter 1927- WhoAm 92
Neufeld, Elizabeth Fondal 1928- WhoAm 92, WhoAmW 93
Neufeld, Eva Law&B 92
Neufeld, Henry d1992 BioIn 17
Neufeld, John (Arthur) 1938- ConAu 37NR, DcAmChF 1960, MajAI [port]
Neufeld, Mace 1928- WhoAm 92, WhoWor 93
Neufeld, Peter WhoScE 91-1
Neufeld, Roger ScF&FL 92
Neufeld, Rona 1949- WhoE 93
Neufeld, Timothy Lee 1947- WhoEmL 93
Neugaard, Edward Joseph 1933- WhoSSW 93
Neugarten, Bernice Levin 1916- BioIn 17, WhoAm 92, WhoAmW 93, WhoWrEP 92
Neugarten, Jerrold Lee 1948- WhoEmL 93
Neugebauer, Gerry 1932- WhoAm 92
Neugebauer, Marcia 1932- WhoAm 92, WhoAmW 93
Neugebauer, O. 1899-1990 BioIn 17
Neugebauer, Otto 1899-1990 BioIn 17
Neugeboren, Jay 1938- BioIn 17, JeAmFiW, WhoWrEP 92
Neuger, Sanford 1925- WhoWor 93
Neugroschel, Arnost 1942- WhoAm 92
Neugroschel, Joachim ScF&FL 92
Neugroschl, Jill Paulette 1949- WhoE 93
Neuhard, Jan 1937- WhoScE 91-2
Neuharth, Allen BioIn 17
Neuharth, Allen H. 1924- JrnUS
Neuharth, Allen Harold 1924- WhoAm 92, WhoWrEP 92
Neuhaus, Gustav 1847-1938 See Neuhaus, Heinrich (Gustavovich) 1888-1964 Baker 92
Neuhaus, Heinrich 1926- WhoScE 91-3
Neuhaus, Heinrich (Gustavovich) 1888-1964 Baker 92
Neuhaus, Julius Victor, III 1926- St&PR 93
Neuhaus, Konstantin 1940- WhoWor 93
Neuhaus, Lacey BioIn 17
Neuhaus, Max BioIn 17
Neuhaus, Max 1939- WhoAm 92
Neuhaus, Otto Wilhelm 1922- WhoAm 92
Neuhaus, Paulo 1946- WhoUN 92
Neuhaus, Peter Charles 1939- WhoE 93
Neuhaus, Philip Ross 1919- WhoAm 92
Neuhaus, Ralph 1909-1990 BioIn 17
Neuhaus, Richard John BioIn 17
Neuhaus, Rudolf 1914-1990 Baker 92
Neuhausen, Benjamin Simon 1950- WhoAm 92
Neuhausen, Kay Cushing 1944- WhoAmW 93
Neuhauser, Duncan von Briesen 1939- WhoAm 92
Neuhauser, Gerhard 1936- WhoScE 91-3
Neuhauser, Mary Helen 1943- WhoE 93, WhoWor 93
Neuhausl, Robert 1930- WhoScE 91-4
Neuhof, Marc d1990 BioIn 17
Neuhoff, John Patrick 1957- WhoSSW 93
Neuhoff, Kathleen Toepp 1953- WhoAmW 93
Neuhoff, Robert M. St&PR 93
Neuhoff, Volker 1928- WhoScE 91-3
Neukam, Randall Maurice 1951- WhoE 93
Neukirch, Manfred WhoScE 91-3
Neukom, Hans 1921- WhoScE 91-4
Neukom, W.H. 1941- St&PR 93
Neukom, William H. Law&B 92
Neukomm, Elisabeth 1789-1816 See Neukomm, Sigismund, Ritter von 1778-1858 Baker 92
Neukomm, Sigismund, Ritter von 1778-1858 Baker 92
Neukranz, Patricia Louise 1930- WhoAmW 93
Neulinger, John 1924-1991 BioIn 17
Neumaier, Bettina 1963- WhoSSW 93
Neumaier, Gerhard John 1937- WhoAm 92
Neuman, Ann Cameron Law&B 92
Neuman, Arlene Ann 1949- WhoAmW 93
Neuman, Charles P. 1940- WhoAm 92, WhoE 93
Neuman, David BioIn 17
Neuman, Donald Bernard 1934- WhoWrEP 92
Neuman, Gail L. 1953- St&PR 93
Neuman, Gail O'Sullivan Law&B 92
Neuman, Irving J. St&PR 93
Neuman, K. Sidney 1936- WhoAm 92
Neuman, Linda Kinney WhoAmW 93
Neuman, Maxine Darcy 1948- WhoEmL 93, WhoWor 93
Neuman, Nancy Adams Mosshammer 1936- WhoAmW 93
Neuman, Norman R. 1940- St&PR 93
Neuman, Richard Stephen 1945- WhoWor 93
Neuman, Robert Ballin 1920- WhoE 93
Neuman, Robert Henry 1936- WhoAm 92
Neuman, Robert Sterling 1926- WhoAm 92
Neuman, Sandra Faye 1946- WhoE 93
Neuman, Shlomo P. 1938- WhoAm 92
Neuman, Stephanie Sellors 1945- WhoWrEP 92
Neuman, Thomas Herbert 1955- WhoEmL 93
Neumann, Andrew Conrad 1933- WhoAm 92
Neumann, Angelo 1838-1910 Baker 92, OxDcOp
Neumann, Bernhard Hermann 1909- WhoWor 93
Neumann, Bonnie Rayford 1942- ScF&FL 92
Neumann, Calvin Lee 1938- WhoSSW 93
Neumann, Camilla 1892-1955 BioIn 17
Neumann, Cecilia M. Law&B 92
Neumann, Christopher James Law&B 92
Neumann, Dietrich 1931- WhoScE 91-3
Neumann, Forrest Karl 1930- WhoAm 92
Neumann, Frantisek 1874-1929 OxDcOp
Neumann, Franz 1874-1929 Baker 92
Neumann, Frederick 1907- Baker 92
Neumann, Frederick Loomis 1930- WhoAm 92
Neumann, G.L. 1954- WhoScE 91-2
Neumann, Hans-Adolf 1938- WhoWor 93
Neumann, Hans Joachim 1930- WhoScE 91-3
Neumann, Harry 1930- WhoAm 92
Neumann, Herschel 1930- WhoAm 92
Neumann, J.B. 1887-1961 BioIn 17
Neumann, Jeffrey Jay 1948- WhoEmL 93, WhoWor 93
Neumann, Kurt 1906-1958 MiSFD 9N
Neumann, Lon Richard 1949- WhoEmL 93
Neumann, Mark Erwin 1959- WhoWrEP 92
Neumann, Nancy Ruth 1948- WhoAmW 93, WhoEmL 93, WhoWor 93
Neumann, Nicki Engler 1951- WhoSSW 93
Neumann, Otto C. 1936-1991 BioIn 17
Neumann, Paul A. 1954- St&PR 93
Neumann, Peter 1938- WhoUN 92
Neumann, Peter 1946- St&PR 93
Neumann, Peter Christian 1937- WhoWor 93
Neumann, Peter D. 1939- WhoScE 91-3
Neumann, Robert G. 1954- St&PR 93
Neumann, Robert Gerhard 1916- WhoAm 92, WhoWor 93, WhoWrEP 92
Neumann, Ronald M. Law&B 92
Neumann, Roy Covert 1921- WhoAm 92
Neumann, Sara AmWomPl
Neumann, Thomas Lee 1945- St&PR 93
Neumann, Ulrich 1945- WhoScE 91-3
Neumann, Vaclav 1920- Baker 92, OxDcOp, WhoWor 93
Neumann, Veroslav 1931- Baker 92
Neumann, Vivian Coralie 1946- WhoEmL 93, WhoSSW 93
Neumann, Wencel A., Jr. 1914- St&PR 93
Neumann, Werner 1905- Baker 92
Neumann, Wilhelm Paul 1926- WhoWor 93
Neumann, William 1943- St&PR 93
Neumann-Mahlkau, P. WhoScE 91-3
Neumark, Georg 1621-1681 Baker 92
Neumark, Gertrude Fanny 1927- WhoAmW 93
Neumark, Michael 1946- St&PR 93
Neumark, Michael Harry 1945- WhoAm 92
Neumayer, A. WhoScE 91-4
Neumeier, John BioIn 17
Neumeier, John 1942- WhoAm 92, WhoWor 93
Neumeier, Matthew Michael 1954- WhoEmL 93, WhoWor 93
Neumeister, Sebastian George 1938- WhoWor 93
Neumeister, Susan Mary 1958- WhoAmW 93
Neumeyer, Jeffrey D. Law&B 92
Neumeyer, John Leopold 1930- WhoE 93, WhoWor 93
Neumeyer, Vicky Gerl Law&B 92
Neumeyer, Wendell Dean 1946- St&PR 93
Neumiller, Catherine Anne 1964- WhoEmL 93
Neumiller, Gayle BioIn 17
Neumiller, Louis B. 1896-1989 BioIn 17
Neumuller, Otto-Albrecht 1930- WhoWor 93
Neumyer, Stephen Edward 1950- WhoSSW 93
Neumyer, Terry R. 1941- WhoE 93
Neun, Carl W. St&PR 93
Neunhoeffer, Hans 1936- WhoScE 91-3, WhoWor 93
Neupert, Edmund 1842-1888 Baker 92
Neurath, Hans 1909- WhoAm 92
Neuray, Georges 1926- WhoScE 91-2
Neuschel, Robert P. 1919- St&PR 93
Neuschel, Robert Percy 1919- WhoAm 92, WhoWor 93
Neusidler, Conrad 1541?-c. 1604 See Neusidler, Melchior 1531-1590 Baker 92
Neusidler, Hans c. 1508-1563 Baker 92
Neusidler, Melchior 1531-1590 Baker 92
Neusner, Jacob 1932- WhoAm 92
Neustadt, Barbara Mae 1922- WhoAm 92, WhoWor 93
Neustadt, David Harold 1925- WhoAm 92
Neustadt, David J. Law&B 92
Neustadt, Frederic Lawton 1954- WhoEmL 93
Neustadt, Karen Anderson 1942- WhoWrEP 92
Neustadt, Paul Law&B 92
Neustadt, Richard Elliott 1919- WhoAm 92
Neustadt, Walter, Jr. 1919- St&PR 93
Neustifter, Robert M. Law&B 92
Neuthaler, Paul D. BioIn 17
Neuthaler, Paul David 1942- WhoAm 92
Neutjens, Clement Louis 1928- WhoWor 93
Neutra, Dione 1901- BioIn 17
Neutra, Richard Joseph 1892-1970 BioIn 17
Neutzler, George Daniel 1945- St&PR 93
Neutzling, Virginia Ruth 1942- WhoAmW 93
Neuville, Charlotte BioIn 17
Neuvo, Yrjo A. 1943- WhoScE 91-4
Neuvo, Yrjo Aunus Olavi 1943- WhoWor 93
Neuvonen, Ari Vilho Juhani 1950- WhoWor 93
Neuwalder, Cynthia Michiko 1960- WhoAmW 93
Neuweiler, Gerhard 1935- WhoScE 91-3
Neuwied, Maximilian Alexander Philipp, Prinz von Wied- 1782-1867 BioIn 17
Neuwirth, Allan Charles 1956- WhoE 93
Neuwirth, Bebe BioIn 17, ConTFT 10, WhoAm 92, WhoAmW 93
Neuwirth, Frank J. 1932- St&PR 93
Neuwirth, Fritz WhoScE 91-4

Neuwirth, Peyton Sidney WhoWor 93
Neuwirth, Robert Samuel 1933- WhoAm 92
Neuwirth, Sherri 1953- St&PR 93
Neuwirth, Sherri Gay 1953- WhoEmL 93
Neuwoehner, Robert F. 1918- St&PR 93
Neuzil, Eugene 1921- WhoScE 91-2
Neva, Franklin Allen 1922- WhoAm 92
Nevada, Emma 1859-1940 Baker 92, OxDcOp
Nevada, Mignon 1886-1971 OxDcOp
Nevada, Mignon (Mathilde Marie) 1886-1971 Baker 92
Nevalainen, Timo J. 1939- WhoScE 91-4
Nevalainen, Timo Olavi 1945- WhoScE 91-4
Nevans, Roy Norman 1931- St&PR 93, WhoE 93
Nevans-Palmer, Laurel Suzanne 1964- WhoE 93
Nevaquaya, Doc Tate BioIn 17
Nevarez, Miguel A. WhoSSW 93
Nevarez, Miguel A. 1937- HispAmA [port]
Nevas, Alan Harris 1928- WhoAm 92
Neveil, William F. 1951- St&PR 93
Nevejans, Mark Brian 1951- St&PR 93
Nevel, Avishai 1953- St&PR 93
Neveloff, Jay A. 1950- WhoAm 92, WhoWor 93
Nevelskoy, Gennady Ivanovich 1814-1876 Expl 93
Nevelson, Louise 1900-1988 BioIn 17
Nevelson, Mike BioIn 17
Nevelson, Mike 1922- WhoE 93
Nevelson, Myron BioIn 17
Neven-DuMont, Alfred 1927- BioIn 17
Neverett, Daniel Joseph 1949- WhoE 93
Nevers, Ernie 1903-1976 BioIn 17
Neves, Janette Wilhelmina 1958- WhoSSW 93
Neves, Janis Y. St&PR 93
Neves, Maria Apparecida Mamede 1936- WhoWor 93
Neves, Newton Jose Oliveira Law&B 92
Nevett, Brian Anthony WhoScE 91-1
Nevett, Robert Edmund 1929- St&PR 93
Neveu, Ginette 1919-1949 Baker 92
Neveux, Michael BioIn 17
Neviaser, Robert Jon 1936- WhoAm 92
Nevill, Amanda 1957- BioIn 17
Nevill, William Albert 1929- WhoAm 92
Neville, A. Munro 1935- WhoScE 91-4
Neville, Aaron BioIn 17, WhoAm 92
Neville, Aaron 1941- See Neville Brothers SoulM
Neville, Alan B. 1947- St&PR 93
Neville, Alexander Munro 1935- WhoWor 93
Neville, Art BioIn 17, WhoAm 92
Neville, Art 1938- See Neville Brothers SoulM
Neville, Charles BioIn 17, WhoAm 92
Neville, Charles 1939- See Neville Brothers SoulM
Neville, Charles William 1941- WhoE 93
Neville, Cyril BioIn 17, WhoAm 92
Neville, Cyril 1950- See Neville Brothers SoulM
Neville, Emily Cheney 1919- ConAu 37NR, DcAmChF 1960, MajAI [port], WhoWrEP 92
Neville, Gerald Worley 1943- St&PR 93
Neville, Gwen Kennedy 1938- WhoAm 92, WhoSSW 93
Neville, J.E. WhoScE 91-1
Neville, James Brian 1955- WhoE 93
Neville, James J. St&PR 93
Neville, James M. Law&B 92
Neville, James Morton 1939- St&PR 93, WhoAm 92
Neville, Janice Nelson 1930- WhoAmW 93
Neville, John Law&B 92
Neville, John 1925- WhoAm 92, WhoWor 93
Neville, Joseph B. Law&B 92
Neville, Joseph P. 1934- WhoIns 93
Neville, Joseph Patrick 1934- St&PR 93
Neville, Katherine 1945- ScF&FL 92
Neville, Kris 1925-1980 ScF&FL 92
Neville, Lloyd L. 1929- St&PR 93, WhoAm 92
Neville, Margaret Cobb 1934- WhoAm 92, WhoAmW 93
Neville, Monica Mary 1949- WhoAmW 93
Neville, Patrick Lyn 1946- St&PR 93
Neville, Phoebe 1941- WhoAm 92
Neville, R. Geoffrey 1932- St&PR 93
Neville, Robert ScF&FL 92
Neville, Robert Cummings 1939- WhoAm 92
Neville, Roy Gerald 1926- WhoAm 92
Neville, Susan Diane 1960- WhoAmW 93, WhoEmL 93
Neville, Thomas Lee 1947- WhoSSW 93
Neville Brothers SoulM
Nevils, Gertrude AmWomPl
Nevin, Arthur (Finley) 1871-1943 Baker 92
Nevin, Crocker 1923- St&PR 93, WhoAm 92
Nevin, David Wright 1947- WhoWor 93
Nevin, Ethelbert 1862-1901 GayN
Nevin, Ethelbert (Woodbridge) 1862-1901 Baker 92
Nevin, Ira 1909- St&PR 93
Nevin, Jean Shaw 1934- WhoAmW 93
Nevin, John J. 1927- St&PR 93
Nevin, John Robert 1943- WhoAm 92
Nevin, John S. 1937- St&PR 93
Nevin, Laura Louise 1958- WhoAmW 93
Nevin, Robert Charles 1940- St&PR 93, WhoAm 92
Nevin, Robert Peebles 1820-1908 JrnUS
Nevins, Albert J. 1915- WhoAm 92
Nevins, Barbara BioIn 17
Nevins, David Howard 1954- WhoEmL 93
Nevins, Donald L., Jr. 1938- St&PR 93
Nevins, Francis M., Jr. 1943- ScF&FL 92
Nevins, James Lawrence 1934- St&PR 93
Nevins, John E. Law&B 92
Nevins, John Edward 1940- St&PR 93
Nevins, John J. 1932- WhoAm 92, WhoSSW 93
Nevins, Joseph W. Law&B 92
Nevins, Joseph William 1928- St&PR 93
Nevins, Louis H. 1938- WhoAm 92
Nevins, Robert Charles 1933- St&PR 93
Nevins, Sheila 1939- WhoAmW 93
Nevision, John Metcalfe 1943- WhoE 93
Nevitt, George Allen 1940- WhoIns 93
Nevitt, Mary Ross AmWomPl
Nevitt, Neal 1946- St&PR 93
Nevius, Blake Reynolds 1916- WhoAm 92, WhoWrEP 92
Nevius, John Livingston 1829-1893 BioIn 17
Nevling, Harry Reed 1946- WhoEmL 93
Nevriva, Pavel 1941- WhoScE 91-4
Nevyjel, Alexander 1949- WhoWor 93
New, Anne Latrobe 1910- WhoAmW 93
New, Cheryl Carter 1946- WhoSSW 93
New, Geoffrey Herbert Charles WhoScE 91-1
New, Harry S. 1858-1937 PolPar
New, Harry Stewart 1858-1937 BioIn 17
New, Maria Iandolo WhoAm 92
New, Rosetta Holbrock 1921- WhoAmW 93
New, Samuel 1921- St&PR 93
New, Timothy D. Law&B 92
New, William 1938- WhoCanL 92
New, William L. 1943- St&PR 93
New, William Neil 1908- WhoAm 92, WhoSSW 93
Newall, Alan John WhoScE 91-1
Newall, James Edward Malcolm 1935- St&PR 93
Newandee, Kimberly Ann 1963- WhoEmL 93
Newark, T.P. 1961- ScF&FL 92
Neway, Patricia 1919- Baker 92, OxDcOp
Newbauer, John Arthur 1928- WhoAm 92, WhoWrEP 92
Newbegin, Robert 1905-1991 BioIn 17
Newberg, Dorothy Beck 1919- WhoAmW 93
Newberg, Herbert Barkan 1937- WhoAm 92
Newberger, Seth A. 1937- St&PR 93
Newbern, Gloria J. 1925- St&PR 93
Newbern, Laura Lynn 1954- WhoSSW 93
Newbern, William David 1937- WhoAm 92, WhoSSW 93
Newberry, Arthur Frederick 1935- St&PR 93
Newberry, Bertha AmWomPl
Newberry, Carol Yvonne 1952- WhoSSW 93
Newberry, Conrad Floyde 1931- WhoAm 92
Newberry, Dennis Lee, II 1928- WhoSSW 93
Newberry, Elizabeth Carter 1921- WhoAmW 93
Newberry, Tom 1946- St&PR 93
Newberry, William Marcus 1938- WhoAm 92
Newbery, Ilse Sofie Magdalene 1928- WhoAmW 93
Newbery, John 1713-1767 MajAI
Newbill, Sallie Puller 1940- WhoAmW 93
Newblatt, Stewart Albert 1927- WhoAm 92
Newbold, Herbert Leon, Jr. 1921- WhoAm 92, WhoE 93, WhoWor 93
Newbold, Jennifer 1960- WhoE 93
Newbold, John L. 1935- St&PR 93
Newbold, John Lowe 1935- WhoWor 93
Newbold, Joseph William WhoScE 91-1
Newbold, Philip A. BioIn 17
Newborn, Alan David 1926- St&PR 93
Newborn, Andrea R. Law&B 92
Newborn, Jud 1952- WhoAm 92
Newborn, Monroe Merrell 1938- WhoWor 93
Newbould, Brian 1936- Baker 92
Newbould, Peter WhoScE 91-1
Newbould, R.B. WhoScE 91-1
Newbound, Betty J. 1928- WhoWrEP 92
Newbrand, Charles Michael 1944- WhoAm 92
Newbrough, Celeste Etaire 1939- WhoAmW 93
Newbrough, Edgar Truett 1917- WhoAm 92, WhoWor 93
Newburg, Andre W. G. 1928- WhoAm 92
Newburg, Betty Ann 1931- WhoAmW 93
Newburg, Charlene O. 1927- WhoE 93
Newburge, Idelle Block WhoAmW 93
Newburger, Beth Weinstein 1937- WhoAm 92
Newburger, Cary 1959- WhoEmL 93
Newburger, Frank L., Jr. 1908- WhoAm 92
Newburger, Frank Lieberman, Jr. 1908- St&PR 93
Newburger, Howard Martin 1924- WhoAm 92
Newbury, Maud Christine 1883- AmWomPl
Newby, Brian Dale 1962- WhoEmL 93
Newby, Donald O. d1992 BioIn 17
Newby, Eric BioIn 17
Newby, Idus Atwell 1931- WhoWrEP 92
Newby, Leroy W. 1921- BioIn 17
Newby, P.H. 1918- BioIn 17, ScF&FL 92
Newby, Percy Howard 1918- BioIn 17, WhoWor 93
Newby, Richard Lorenzo WhoSSW 93
Newby, Thomas Cautley 1798-1882 BioIn 17
Newcastle, Margaret Cavendish, Duchess of 1624?-1674 BioIn 17
Newcomb, Clara AmWomPl
Newcomb, Danforth 1943- WhoAm 92
Newcomb, David Royal 1923- St&PR 93
Newcomb, Eldon Henry 1919- WhoAm 92
Newcomb, Elizabeth Wormwood 1944- WhoE 93
Newcomb, Ethel 1875-1959 Baker 92
Newcomb, George 1866-1895 BioIn 17
Newcomb, James M. 1948- St&PR 93
Newcomb, James Q. 1961- St&PR 93
Newcomb, Jim BioIn 17
Newcomb, John C. 1938- St&PR 93
Newcomb, Jonathan 1946- St&PR 93
Newcomb, Lawrence Howard 1947- WhoAm 92
Newcomb, Lindy BioIn 17
Newcomb, Nancy S. St&PR 93
Newcomb, Robert Carl 1926- WhoSSW 93, WhoWor 93
Newcomb, Robert Wayne 1933- WhoAm 92
Newcomb, Sylvia Weinberg 1942- WhoAmW 93
Newcomb, Thomas Finley 1927- WhoSSW 93
Newcomb, Virginia Lynn 1948- WhoEmL 93
Newcomb, Wilburn Wendell 1935- WhoWrEP 92
Newcomb, William Andrew, Jr. 1959- WhoSSW 93
Newcomb, William Edgar 1931- WhoSSW 93
Newcomb-Doty, Yvonne 1950- WhoAmW 93
Newcombe, Arthur Rowell, III 1932- St&PR 93
Newcombe, David Sugden WhoE 93
Newcombe, Gordon I. d1991 BioIn 17
Newcombe, Howard Borden 1914- WhoAm 92
Newcombe, Jack BioIn 17
Newcombe, Park Judson 1930- WhoSSW 93
Newcombe, Patricia Mary 1934- WhoAmW 93
Newcombe, Richard Sumner 1950- WhoAm 92
Newcome, Claire L. 1924- St&PR 93
Newcomer, Alan Bard 1946- ScF&FL 92
Newcomer, Clarence Charles 1923- WhoAm 92
Newcomer, Darrell Ray 1948- WhoSSW 93
New Edition SoulM
Newell, Alan Francis WhoScE 91-1
Newell, Allen d1992 NewYTBS 92
Newell, Allen 1927- WhoAm 92
Newell, Alma 1936- WhoAmW 93, WhoWor 93
Newell, Arlo F. 1926- St&PR 93
Newell, Barbara Warne 1929- WhoAm 92
Newell, Beverly Pringle 1959- WhoAmW 93
Newell, Byron Bruce, Jr. 1932- WhoAm 92
Newell, Cam McGillicuddy 1947- WhoE 93, WhoEmL 93
Newell, Charldean 1939- WhoAmW 93
Newell, Deborah Kelly Law&B 92
Newell, Dix A. Law&B 92
Newell, Donald Clifford, Jr. 1947- WhoSSW 93
Newell, E. Owen 1929- St&PR 93
Newell, Eric James 1930- WhoAm 92
Newell, Frank William 1916- WhoAm 92
Newell, Gladys Elizabeth 1908- WhoAmW 93
Newell, Henry H. 1907- St&PR 93
Newell, J. Louis 1936- St&PR 93
Newell, Jack C. 1938- St&PR 93
Newell, James David 1933- St&PR 93
Newell, James R. 1957- St&PR 93
Newell, James Robert 1941- WhoSSW 93
Newell, Jeanne Ann 1947- WhoAmW 93
Newell, John Wallace 1940- WhoSSW 93
Newell, Katherine Ann 1947- WhoAmW 93, WhoEmL 93
Newell, Martin L. 1939- WhoScE 91-3
Newell, Mary Etna 1944- WhoAmW 93
Newell, Meg Law&B 92
Newell, Melody Ann 1947- WhoAmW 93
Newell, Mike 1942- MiSFD 9
Newell, Neil K. 1953- ScF&FL 92, WhoWrEP 92
Newell, Norman Dennis 1909- WhoAm 92
Newell, Oswald, Jr. 1925- St&PR 93
Newell, Paul Haynes, Jr. 1933- WhoAm 92
Newell, Peter Carroll 1933- St&PR 93
Newell, Philip Stanley WhoScE 91-1
Newell, Rebecca Gail 1953- WhoAmW 93, WhoEmL 93
Newell, Reginald Edward 1931- WhoAm 92
Newell, Richard N. 1932- St&PR 93
Newell, Robert Lincoln 1922- WhoAm 92
Newell, Roger D. 1913- St&PR 93
Newell, Ronald Allin 1948- WhoEmL 93
Newell, Silvia Anna 1953- WhoEmL 93, WhoSSW 93
Newell, Sterling, Jr. 1921- WhoAm 92
Newell, William Edward 1936- St&PR 93
Newell, William Talman, Jr. 1932- WhoAm 92
Newell, William Templeton 1938- WhoAm 92
Newey, Paul Davis 1914- WhoAm 92, WhoWor 93
Newfarmer, Gerald Earl 1940- WhoAm 92
Newfeld, Mark Lawrence Law&B 92
Newfield, Jill Elayne Law&B 92
Newfield, Mayer Ullman 1905- WhoAm 92
Newgaard, Patricia Ann 1944- WhoWrEP 92
Newgard, Mark Gordon 1944- WhoAm 92
Newhall, Beaumont 1908- WhoAm 92
Newhall, Charles Crosby 1928- St&PR 93
Newhall, Charles Watson, III 1944- WhoAm 92
Newhall, David, III 1937- WhoAm 92
Newhall, David Sowle 1929- WhoSSW 93
Newhall, John Breed 1932- St&PR 93
Newhall, John Harrison 1933- WhoAm 92
Newhall, Lisa Marie 1965- WhoAmW 93
Newhall, Mark Alan 1954- WhoAm 92
Newhall, Patricia 1927- WhoE 93
Newhall, Scott d1992 NewYTBS 92 [port]
Newham, John WhoScE 91-1
Newhard, Ronald Arthur 1944- St&PR 93
Newhard, Steven B. 1949- St&PR 93
Newhart, Bob 1929- WhoAm 92
Newhart, Lawrence E., Jr. 1942- St&PR 93
Newhoff, Stanley Neal 1944- WhoWor 93
Newhouse, Albert 1914- WhoSSW 93
Newhouse, Eileen J. Law&B 92
Newhouse, Herbert A. 1945- St&PR 93
Newhouse, J.A. WhoScE 91-1
Newhouse, Joseph Paul 1942- WhoAm 92
Newhouse, Marilyn Cheryl 1951- WhoEmL 93
Newhouse, Patricia A. WhoAmW 93
Newhouse, Peter Malcolm 1944- WhoUN 92
Newhouse, Quentin, Jr. 1949- WhoE 93
Newhouse, Robert J., Jr. WhoAm 92
Newhouse, Samuel I., Jr. 1928- WhoAm 92
Newhouse, Samuel I(rving) 1895-1979 DcLB 127 [port]
Newhouse, Stanley d1991 BioIn 17
Newhouse, Stephen Robert 1958- WhoEmL 93
Newhouse, Vernon Leopold 1928- WhoAm 92
Newhouser, Hal 1921- BioIn 17
Newi, George Henry BioIn 17
Newick, Craig David 1960- WhoE 93
Ne Win 1911- DcTwHis, HarEnMi
Ne Win, U. 1911- WhoAsAP 91
Newitt, Ben J. 1924- St&PR 93, WhoAm 92
Newitt, John Garwood, Jr. 1941- WhoSSW 93, WhoWor 93
Newitter, Ralph S., Jr. 1943- St&PR 93

Newnham, Yve ScF&FL 92
Newport, Carol Wimmler 1946- WhoSSW 93
Newport, John Paul 1917- WhoAm 92
Newport, Michael Wilder Law&B 92
Newport, Walter 1917- St&PR 93
Newquist, Donald Stewart 1953- WhoEmL 93
Newquist, Lester J. d1989 BioIn 17
Newquist, Scott Crawford 1948- WhoAm 92
News, Kathryn Anne 1934- WhoAm 92
Newsham, John W. 1932- St&PR 93
Newsom, Barry Douglas 1953- WhoEmL 93, WhoSSW 93
Newsom, Carolyn Cardall 1941- WhoAm 92, WhoE 93
Newsom, Carroll Vincent 1904-1990 BioIn 17
Newsom, David Dunlop 1918- WhoAm 92
Newsom, Douglas Ann Johnson 1934- WhoAm 92, WhoAmW 93, WhoSSW 93, WhoWor 93
Newsom, Emma Lou 1928- WhoAmW 93
Newsom, Gene A. 1936- St&PR 93
Newsom, Gerald Higley 1939- WhoAm 92
Newsom, Hugh Raymond 1891-1978 Baker 92
Newsom, Jan Reimann Law&B 92
Newsom, Jan Reimann 1947- St&PR 93
Newsom, Lionel BioIn 17
Newsom, Louis Norman 1907-1962 BiDAMSp 1989
Newsom, Melvin Max 1931- WhoAm 92
Newsom, Ray 1926- St&PR 93
Newsom, Vida AmWomPl
Newsom, Will Roy 1912- WhoAm 92
Newsome, Alvin C. 1930- St&PR 93
Newsome, Beatrice Collins 1932- WhoAmW 93
Newsome, Clenon L. 1929- WhoSSW 93
Newsome, Frederick Vass 1946- WhoE 93
Newsome, George Lane, Jr. 1923- WhoAm 92
Newsome, Imani-Sheila Diane 1953- WhoAmW 93
Newsome, Jonathan Kent 1960- WhoEmL 93
Newsome, Larry James, Sr. 1948- WhoSSW 93
Newsome, Lisa Sellars 1956- WhoAmW 93
Newsome, Paula Renee 1955- WhoSSW 93
Newsome, William Roy, Jr. 1934- WhoAm 92
Newson, Elizabeth Ann WhoScE 91-1
Newson, Eula Mae 1931- WhoWrEP 92
Newson, Malcolm David WhoScE 91-1
Newson, Roger L. 1941- WhoUN 92
Newstead, Ronald Arthur 1925- WhoWor 93
Newstead, Stephen Edward 1946- WhoWor 93
Newton, Alexander Worthy 1930- WhoAm 92
Newton, Alice Faye 1937- WhoAm 92
Newton, Anthony WhoWor 93
Newton, Beth Ann 1964- WhoAmW 93
Newton, Bryan ScF&FL 92
Newton, C.M., Jr. 1915- St&PR 93
Newton, Candelas 1948- WhoSSW 93
Newton, Catherine Lynne 1948- WhoAmW 93
Newton, Charles 1870-1932 BioIn 17
Newton, Charles Chartier 1933- WhoAm 92
Newton, Christopher WhoAm 92
Newton, David 1941- WhoScE 91-1
Newton, David E. BioIn 17
Newton, Derek Arnold 1930- WhoAm 92
Newton, Don Allen 1934- WhoSSW 93
Newton, Douglas 1920- WhoAm 92
Newton, Earle Williams 1917- WhoAm 92, WhoSSW 93
Newton, Edythe Crout 1940- WhoAmW 93
Newton, Fletcher T. Law&B 92
Newton, Francis Lanneau 1928- WhoAm 92
Newton, Frank H. 1940- St&PR 93
Newton, Fred Julian 1937- WhoSSW 93
Newton, Frederick Carter 1924- St&PR 93
Newton, Gale JoAnn 1954- WhoAmW 93
Newton, George Addison 1911- WhoAm 92, WhoWor 93
Newton, George Durfee, Jr. 1931- WhoAm 92
Newton, George W. 1947- St&PR 93
Newton, George Washington 1947- WhoIns 93
Newton, Harold Gene 1937- WhoSSW 93
Newton, Harvey R. Law&B 92
Newton, Hector Carlton, III 1936- St&PR 93
Newton, Helen Pfeiffer 1942- WhoAmW 93
Newton, Helmut BioIn 17
Newton, Hilary Paul 1959- WhoWor 93
Newton, Huey BioIn 17
Newton, Huey P. 1942-1989 EncAACR
Newton, Isaac 1642-1727 BioIn 17
Newton, Ivor 1892-1981 Baker 92
Newton, Jack 1942- BioIn 17
Newton, James BioIn 17
Newton, James John 1949- WhoEmL 93, WhoSSW 93, WhoWrEP 92
Newton, James Quigg, Jr. 1911- WhoAm 92
Newton, James William 1948- WhoSSW 93
Newton, John 1725-1807 BioIn 17
Newton, John Edward, Jr. 1954- WhoE 93
Newton, John Michael WhoScE 91-1
Newton, John Milton 1929- WhoAm 92
Newton, John Oswald 1924- WhoWor 93
Newton, John Thomas 1930- St&PR 93
Newton, Judith Ann 1941- WhoAmW 93
Newton, Julius P. ScF&FL 92
Newton, June BioIn 17
Newton, Kellie L. Law&B 92
Newton, Kenneth WhoScE 91-1
Newton, Larry K. 1939- St&PR 93
Newton, Leonard Frank 1925- St&PR 93
Newton, Linda Elizabeth Law&B 92
Newton, Lisa Haenlein 1939- WhoAm 92
Newton, Marjorie Ann Law&B 92
Newton, Maxwell BioIn 17
Newton, Michael 1934- St&PR 93
Newton, Michael 1951- ScF&FL 92
Newton, Michael John WhoScE 91-1
Newton, Michael W. 1950- St&PR 93
Newton, Natalie Hope 1958- WhoAmW 93
Newton, Nate BioIn 17
Newton, Niles Rumely 1923- WhoAm 92
Newton, Norman 1898-1992 NewYTBS 92
Newton, Norman Thomas King 1898- WhoAm 92
Newton, Oscar Lee, Jr. 1927- WhoIns 93
Newton, Otto A. Law&B 92
Newton, Paul Robert Law&B 92
Newton, Philip BioIn 17
Newton, Randolph Harrison 1947- St&PR 93
Newton, Ray 1953- WhoEmL 93
Newton, Rhonwen Leonard 1940- WhoAmW 93, WhoSSW 93
Newton, Richard Matthew 1952- WhoIns 93
Newton, Robert 1905-1956 IntDcF 2-3 [port]
Newton, Robert Eugene 1917- WhoAm 92
Newton, Robert George 1948- WhoEmL 93
Newton, Robert R. 1939- St&PR 93
Newton, Robert Ryan 1935- WhoE 93
Newton, Rose Marie 1938- WhoAmW 93
Newton, Sarah Elizabeth 1960- WhoAmW 93
Newton, Saul BioIn 17
Newton, Sherrell Shelton 1950- WhoAmW 93
Newton, Stella Mary 1901- BioIn 17
Newton, Suzanne 1936- WhoAm 92
Newton, T. Eugene 1935- St&PR 93
Newton, V. Miller 1938- WhoE 93
Newton, Victor Joseph 1937- WhoE 93
Newton, Virginia 1938- WhoAmW 93
Newton, Wallace Berkeley 1949- St&PR 93, WhoEmL 93
Newton, Walter Logan 1956- St&PR 93
Newton, Warren S., Jr. 1938- WhoIns 93
Newton, Wayne BioIn 17
Newton, Wayne 1942- Baker 92, WhoAm 92
Newton, William A. Law&B 92
Newton, William Allen, Jr. 1923- WhoAm 92
Newton, William C. 1930- St&PR 93
Newton, William H., III 1947- St&PR 93
Newton, Willis H., Jr. 1949- St&PR 93
Newton-John, Olivia BioIn 17
Newton-John, Olivia 1948- Baker 92, ConMus 8 [port], WhoAm 92
Newton-Skelley, Martha Louise 1949- WhoEmL 93
Newton-Smith, William Herbert 1943- WhoWor 93
New York City Players SoulM
Nexsen, Julian J., Jr. Law&B 92
Nexsen, Julian Jacobs 1924- WhoAm 92
Nexsen, Julian Jacobs, Jr. 1954- WhoEmL 93
Ney, Bogdan 1935- WhoScE 91-4
Ney, Carol Jean Law&B 92
Ney, Charles 1912- WhoE 93
Ney, Edward Noonan 1925- WhoAm 92, WhoWor 93
Ney, Edward Purdy 1920- WhoAm 92
Ney, Elisabet 1833-1907 BioIn 17
Ney, Elly 1882-1968 Baker 92
Ney, James Walter Edward Colby 1932- WhoAm 92, WhoWrEP 92
Ney, Joanna Maria 1936- WhoE 93
Ney, John 1923- DcAmChF 1960
Ney, Judy Larson 1951- WhoEmL 93
Ney, Michael Vincent 1947- WhoEmL 93
Ney, Michel 1769-1815 HarEnMi
Neyhart, Amos E. 1898-1990 BioIn 17
Neylan, John Francis, III 1953- WhoSSW 93
Neyland, James 1939- ScF&FL 92
Neyland, Randolph Archer 1945- WhoSSW 93
Neylon, Martin Joseph 1920- WhoAm 92
Neylon, Terrance Bernard 1945- WhoE 93
Neyra, Pilar 1941- WhoAmW 93
Nezadal, Maria 1897- See Franckenstein, Clemens von und zu 1875-1942 OxDcOp
Nezer, Steven S. 1947- St&PR 93
Nezhdanova, Antonina 1873-1950 OxDcOp
Nezhdanova, Antonina (Vasilievna) 1873-1950 Baker 92
Neziroglu, Fugen 1953- WhoE 93
Nezu, Christine Maguth 1952- WhoAmW 93
Nezzar, Khaled WhoWor 93
Ng, Alan Wai-Sang Law&B 92
Ng, Amy Law&B 92
Ng, Chin Fai Stephen 1962- WhoWor 93
Ng, Chu-meng BioIn 17
Ng, Dennis Law&B 92
Ng, James See Hua 1965- WhoWor 93
Ng, Kheng Siang 1960- WhoWor 93
Ng, Lawrence Ming-Loy 1940- WhoWor 93
Ng, Maria St&PR 93
Ng, May-May Donna Lee 1952- St&PR 93
Ng, Ming Tak WhoE 93
Ng, Mun Hon 1938- WhoWor 93
Ng, Nicholas Sheung Choi 1934- WhoWor 93
Ng, Siu-Ah 1959- WhoWor 93
Ng, Sze Kui 1948- WhoWor 93
Ng, Wing Chiu 1947- WhoWor 93
Ng, Wing-fai 1956- WhoSSW 93
Ngai, Shih Hsun 1920- WhoAm 92
Ngai Shiu-Kit, Hon 1924- WhoAsAP 91
Ngan, Betty H.G. Law&B 92
Ngan, Stephen T. 1938- St&PR 93
Ngango, Georges 1932- WhoAfr
Ngata, Apirana Turupa 1874-1950 DcTwHis
Ng Cheng Kiat 1941- WhoAsAP 91
Ngei, Paul 1923- WhoAfr
Ngele, Victor 1953- WhoAsAP 91
Ngernmuen, Suthas WhoAsAP 91
Ngo, Khai Doan The 1957- WhoEmL 93, WhoSSW 93
Ngongo, Mundari Ernest 1954- WhoWor 93
Ngor, Haing S. BioIn 17
Ngoubeyou, Francois-Xavier WhoUN 92
Ng Sharp, Nancy 1960- WhoAmW 93
Ngu, Niba John 1932- WhoAfr
Nguesso, Edith Lucie Sassou- BioIn 17
Ngugi, James 1938- BioIn 17
Ngugi, James Thiong'o 1938- DcTwHis
Ngugi, Wa Thiong'o James 1938- WhoWor 93
Ngugi wa Thiong'o 1938- BioIn 17, DcLB 125 [port], IntLitE, IntvWPC 92 [port]
Ngulinzira, Boniface 1950- WhoWor 93
N'guti, Tallam I. Law&B 92
Nguy, Jootian Law&B 92
Nguyen, Ann Cac Khue WhoAmW 93
Nguyen, Bao Thai 1963- WhoEmL 93
Nguyen, Cao Lieu 1944- WhoWor 93
Nguyen, Charles Cuong 1956- WhoEmL 93
Nguyen, D.C. 1936- WhoScE 91-2
Nguyen, Dustin BioIn 17
Nguyen, Dzung Thai 1945- WhoWor 93
Nguyen, Henry Thien 1954- WhoSSW 93
Nguyen, Hoi-Chan Law&B 92
Nguyen, Hong Thai 1963- WhoWor 93
Nguyen, Kim Loan Thi 1953- WhoE 93
Nguyen, Lan Tuyet 1960- WhoEmL 93
Nguyen, Mike BioIn 17
Nguyen, Nghi Van 1939- WhoE 93
Nguyen, Nhien Duc 1947- WhoEmL 93
Nguyen, Quoc Son 1944- WhoScE 91-2
Nguyen, Quy Dao 1937- WhoScE 91-2
Nguyen, Thanh Van 1947- WhoSSW 93
Nguyen, Tien Manh 1957- WhoWor 93
Nguyen, Trong Anh 1935- WhoScE 91-2
Nguyen, Truc Chinh 1960- WhoSSW 93
Nguyen, Trung Duc 1951- WhoEmL 93
Nguyen, Tuan Quoc 1949- WhoWor 93
Nguyen, Van Hieu 1922-1991 BioIn 17
Nguyen, Van Tam d1990 BioIn 17
Nguyen, Van Thieu 1923- BioIn 17
Nguyen Co Thach WhoAsAP 91, WhoWor 93
Nguyen-Dinh, Thanh 1950- WhoE 93
Nguyen Huu Tho 1910- WhoAsAP 91, WhoWor 93
Nguyen Khanh 1927- WhoAsAP 91
Nguyen-Tang, Canh 1941- WhoUN 92
Nguyen Tat Thanh 1890-1969 BioIn 17
Nguyen Thi Binh 1927- WhoAsAP 91
Nguyen-Trong, Hoang 1936- WhoWor 93
Nguyen Van Linh 1913- WhoAsAP 91
Nguyen Van Thieu 1923- ColdWar 2 [port]
Nguza, Karl I. Bond 1938- WhoAfr
Nguza Karl I Bond 1938- WhoWor 93
Ngyuen, Ta 1940- WhoUN 92
Nha, Il-Seong 1932- WhoWor 93
Nhiwatiwa, Naomi Pasiharisutwi 1941- WhoUN 92
Nhouyvanisvong, Khamliene 1934- WhoUN 92
Ni, Yangchou Michael 1949- WhoEmL 93
Ni, Zhengyu 1906- WhoUN 92
Niad-Hannah, Cindy Law&B 92
Nianouris, Emmanuel 1930- St&PR 93
Niarchos, Michael Chris Law&B 92
Nias, Anthony Hugh Wade WhoScE 91-1
Niasse, Cheikh Moustapha 1939- WhoAfr
Niatum, Duane 1938- WhoWrEP 92
Niazi, Inayet-Ullah-Khan 1944- WhoWor 93
Nibbelink, Phil MiSFD 9
Nibbering, J.J.W. 1927- WhoScE 91-2
Nibbering, Nicolaas Martinus Maria 1938- WhoWor 93
Nibbi, Filippo 1935- WhoWor 93
Nibbs, Arthur DcCPCAm
Nibelle, Adolphe-Andre 1825-1895 Baker 92
Nibert, Gregory James 1958- WhoEmL 93
Niblack, Nancy Lee Parham 1941- WhoSSW 93
Nibley, Andrew Mathews 1951- WhoAm 92
Nibley, Robert Ricks 1913- WhoAm 92
Niblo, Fred 1874-1948 MiSFD 9N
Niblock, Phill 1933- WhoE 93
Niblock, W. Robert 1928- St&PR 93
Niblock, Walter Raymond 1927- WhoAm 92
Nibuya, Ryu 1928- WhoWor 93
Nicaise, Ghislain 1941- WhoScE 91-2
Nicander OxDcByz
Nicander, Lennart V. 1923- WhoScE 91-4
Nicandros, Constantine Stavros 1933- St&PR 93, WhoAm 92, WhoSSW 93
Nicarico, Jeanine BioIn 17
Nicas, James R. Law&B 92
Nicascio, Marcos BioIn 17
Nicastri, Monica 1958- St&PR 93
Nicastro, Francesco Vito Mario 1953- WhoWor 93
Nicastro, Francis Efisio 1942- WhoAm 92
Nicastro, Neil D. 1956- St&PR 93
Nicastro-Doherty, Cynthia Marie 1958- WhoE 93
Niccoli, Niccolo c. 1364-1437 BioIn 17
Niccolini, Dianora 1936- WhoAmW 93, WhoE 93
Niccolini, Drew George 1945- WhoE 93
Niccolo Da Martoni OxDcByz
Niccum, Leonard Maines 1928- St&PR 93
Niccum, Ronald J. 1932- St&PR 93
Nice, Carter 1940- WhoAm 92
Nice, Charles Monroe, Jr. 1919- WhoAm 92, WhoSSW 93
Nice, Jill 1940- ConAu 138
Nice, Lawrence William 1950- WhoE 93
Nice, Linda Lenore 1958- WhoAmW 93
Niceley, Harvey Tarver, Jr. 1935- WhoSSW 93
Nicely, C.M. 1911- St&PR 93
Nicely, William Abbott 1930- St&PR 93
Nicephorus Phocas, II 912-969 HarEnMi
Nicharot, Louis Frank Law&B 92
Nichetti, Maurizio BioIn 17
Nichetti, Maurizio 1948- MiSFD 9
Nicho, Raul A. 1954- St&PR 93
Nichol, B.P. 1944-1988 BioIn 17
Nichol, bp 1944-1988 WhoCanL 92
Nichol, Douglas 1947- WhoWor 93
Nichol, Fred Joseph 1912- WhoAm 92
Nichol, Henry Ferris 1911- WhoAm 92
Nichol, Norman J. 1944- WhoAm 92
Nichol, William H. 1951- St&PR 93
Nicholas, Grand Duke 1856-1929 HarEnMi
Nicholas, I c. 819-867 OxDcByz
Nicholas, I, Emperor of Russia 1796-1855 BioIn 17
Nicholas, II 1868-1918 DcTwHis
Nicholas, II, Emperor of Russia 1868-1918 BioIn 17
Nicholas, III c. 1216-1280 OxDcByz
Nicholas, V 1397-1455 OxDcByz
Nicholas, Albert O. 1931- St&PR 93
Nicholas, Andrew James, Jr. 1949- WhoEmL 93
Nicholas, Anna 1917- ScF&FL 92
Nicholas, Arthur Soterios 1930- WhoAm 92
Nicholas, Cecile Teresa 1958- WhoEmL 93
Nicholas, Christopher Paul Law&B 92
Nicholas, Christopher Paul 1949- WhoEmL 93
Nicholas, Denise BioIn 17
Nicholas, Dimitri 1914- St&PR 93

Nicholas, Donald Y. 1915- St&PR 93
Nicholas, Fayard BioIn 17
Nicholas, Fayard Antonio 1914- WhoAm 92
Nicholas, Francine E. Law&B 92
Nicholas, Gary A. 1946- St&PR 93
Nicholas, Georgette Cecelia 1964- WhoAmW 93
Nicholas, H.D. 1947- St&PR 93
Nicholas, Harold BioIn 17
Nicholas, James G. 1934- St&PR 93
Nicholas, Jonathan M.C. 1960- WhoScE 91-1
Nicholas, Lawrence Bruce 1945- WhoSSW 93, WhoWor 93
Nicholas, Martha Ann 1936- WhoSSW 93
Nicholas, Michael WhoWrEP 92
Nicholas, Michael Patrick 1947- St&PR 93
Nicholas, Michele M. Law&B 92
Nicholas, Millicent Belle 1938- WhoE 93
Nicholas, Nicholas J., Jr. BioIn 17
Nicholas, Nicholas J., Jr. 1939- St&PR 93
Nicholas, Nicholas John, Jr. 1939- WhoAm 92
Nicholas, Nicholas Soterios 1917- WhoAm 92
Nicholas, Nickie Lee 1938- WhoAmW 93
Nicholas, Paul MiSFD 9
Nicholas, Ralph Wallace 1934- WhoAm 92
Nicholas, Richard A. 1938- St&PR 93
Nicholas, Robert H., Jr. Law&B 92
Nicholas, Rosemary Theresa 1943- WhoAmW 93
Nicholas, Samuel John, Jr. 1937- WhoWor 93
Nicholas, Thomas Andrew 1934- WhoAm 92
Nicholas, Thomas Peter 1948- WhoAm 92
Nicholas, Wendy Priscilla 1953- WhoE 93
Nicholas, William Richard 1934- WhoAm 92
Nicholas, Wilson Cary 1761-1820 BioIn 17
Nicholas Brothers BioIn 17
Nicholas Grammatikos, III OxDcByz
Nicholas Mouzalon, IV c. 1070-1152 OxDcByz
Nicholas Mystikos, I 852-925 OxDcByz
Nicholas of Andida fl. 11th cent.- OxDcByz
Nicholas of Kerkyra fl. c. 1100- OxDcByz
Nicholas of Methone dc. 1160 OxDcByz
Nicholas of Myra OxDcByz [port]
Nicholas of Myra c. 430-c. 491 OxDcByz
Nicholas of Otranto c. 1155-1235 OxDcByz
Nicholas of Sion d564 OxDcByz
Nicholas of Stoudios 793-868 OxDcByz
Nicholas-Whitney, Linda 1940- St&PR 93
Nicholaw, George 1927- WhoAm 92
Nicholds, David Leonard Law&B 92
Nicholls, Agnes 1877-1959 Baker 92, OxDcOp
Nicholls, Allan 1945- MiSFD 9
Nicholls, Bernie BioIn 17
Nicholls, Christopher ScF&FL 92
Nicholls, David George WhoScE 91-1
Nicholls, Grant T. 1946- WhoIns 93
Nicholls, Grant Telfer 1946- WhoAm 92
Nicholls, H.A. WhoScE 91-1
Nicholls, Jeffrey Michael 1953- WhoEmL 93
Nicholls, John Anthony 1946- WhoWor 93
Nicholls, John G. 1929- WhoScE 91-4
Nicholls, Judith 1941- BioIn 17
Nicholls, Kenneth Wayne 1948- WhoAm 92
Nicholls, Peter 1939- ScF&FL 92
Nicholls, Philip Hazlewood WhoScE 91-1
Nicholls, Ralph William 1926- WhoAm 92
Nicholls, Richard Aurelius 1941- WhoSSW 93, WhoWor 93
Nicholls, Richard H. 1938- WhoAm 92
Nicholls, Robert Lee 1929- WhoE 93
Nicholls, S. Scott, Jr. 1934- St&PR 93
Nicholls, Sidney Oliver 1947- St&PR 93
Nicholls, Tatiana 1963- WhoAmW 93
Nicholos, Alex BioIn 17
Nichols, Adelaide AmWomPl
Nichols, Alan Hammond 1930- WhoWrEP 92
Nichols, Alan Hammond 1940- WhoWor 93
Nichols, Albert L. 1951- WhoEmL 93
Nichols, Alice Marshall 1947- WhoAmW 93
Nichols, Andrew L. 1936- St&PR 93
Nichols, Andrew Livingston 1936- WhoAm 92
Nichols, Anne 1891?-1966 AmWomPl
Nichols, Anne C. 1938- WhoE 93
Nichols, Audrey Violet Antoinnette 1915- WhoAmW 93
Nichols, Barbara Ann 1921- WhoAmW 93
Nichols, Barbara Ann 1947- WhoEmL 93
Nichols, Basil Bernard 1927- WhoSSW 93
Nichols, Beverley 1898-1983 ScF&FL 92
Nichols, Brenda Sue 1950- WhoAmW 93
Nichols, C. Walter, III 1937- WhoAm 92, WhoE 93
Nichols, Caleb Leroy 1947- WhoE 93
Nichols, Carl W. 1923- St&PR 93
Nichols, Carl Wheeler 1923- WhoAm 92
Nichols, Carol D. WhoAm 92, WhoAmW 93
Nichols, Carol D. 1943- St&PR 93
Nichols, Charles P. St&PR 93
Nichols, Charles Warren 1939- WhoAm 92
Nichols, Content S. AmWomPl
Nichols, Daisy D. AmWomPl
Nichols, Dale Kenneth Law&B 92
Nichols, Daniel A. 1940- St&PR 93
Nichols, David Anthony 1940- WhoE 93
Nichols, David Arthur 1917- WhoAm 92, WhoE 93
Nichols, David E. 1952- WhoEmL 93
Nichols, David Harry 1925- WhoAm 92
Nichols, David R. 1958- St&PR 93
Nichols, Dick 1926- CngDr 91
Nichols, Donald Arthur 1940- WhoAm 92
Nichols, Donald Clyde 1939- St&PR 93
Nichols, Donald Richardson 1911- WhoAm 92
Nichols, Dorothy E. AmWomPl
Nichols, Douglas R. Law&B 92
Nichols, Douglas Richard 1946- WhoE 93
Nichols, Dudley 1895- BioIn 17
Nichols, Edie Diane 1939- WhoAmW 93
Nichols, Edna Phyllis AmWomPl
Nichols, Elizabeth Christie 1963- WhoEmL 93
Nichols, Elizabeth Grace 1943- WhoAm 92
Nichols, Elizabeth L. 1922- WhoWrEP 92
Nichols, Eugene Douglas 1923- WhoAm 92
Nichols, Fenwick Tattnall, III 1950- WhoEmL 93, WhoSSW 93
Nichols, Frank St&PR 93
Nichols, Frank Andrew 1948- WhoEmL 93
Nichols, Frank J. 1929- St&PR 93
Nichols, Frederick Doveton 1911- WhoAm 92
Nichols, Frederick Ralph, Jr. 1936- St&PR 93
Nichols, George d1990 BioIn 17
Nichols, George Calloway 1943- WhoE 93, WhoWor 93
Nichols, George Quincy 1929- St&PR 93
Nichols, George Starr 1918- WhoSSW 93
Nichols, Georgia L. Law&B 92
Nichols, Gerald Lee 1935- St&PR 93
Nichols, Guy W. 1925- St&PR 93, WhoAm 92
Nichols, H. Gilman 1927- St&PR 93
Nichols, Harold Neil 1937- WhoAm 92
Nichols, Henry Eliot 1924- WhoAm 92
Nichols, Henry H. d1992 NewYTBS 92
Nichols, Henry Louis 1916- WhoAm 92
Nichols, Horace Elmo 1912- WhoAm 92
Nichols, Irby Coghill, Jr. 1926- WhoAm 92
Nichols, Irene Delores 1938- WhoAmW 93
Nichols, J. Hugh 1930- WhoSSW 93
Nichols, J. Larry 1942- St&PR 93
Nichols, Jack Britt 1936- WhoSSW 93
Nichols, Jackie Jordan 1947- WhoEmL 93
Nichols, James Hastings 1915-1991 BioIn 17
Nichols, James Henry 1962- WhoE 93
Nichols, James Monroe 1943- St&PR 93
Nichols, James Phillip 1944- WhoE 93, WhoWor 93
Nichols, James Richard 1923- WhoAm 92, WhoSSW 93
Nichols, James Richard 1938- WhoSSW 93, WhoWrEP 92
Nichols, James Robbs 1926- WhoAm 92
Nichols, Jane BioIn 17
Nichols, Janet 1952- BioIn 17
Nichols, Jerry ScF&FL 92
Nichols, Jesse Clyde 1880-1950 BioIn 17
Nichols, John D. 1930- WhoAm 92
Nichols, John David 1947- WhoSSW 93
Nichols, John David 1948- WhoE 93, WhoEmL 93
Nichols, John Doane 1930- St&PR 93
Nichols, John Treadwell 1940- BioIn 17
Nichols, John W. 1914- St&PR 93
Nichols, Joseph 1917- St&PR 93
Nichols, Joseph A. 1940- St&PR 93
Nichols, Karen Wentz Lynn 1942- WhoAmW 93, WhoSSW 93
Nichols, Kathryn L. 1960- WhoAmW 93
Nichols, Kathryn Marion 1946- WhoAmW 93
Nichols, Kenneth David 1907- WhoAm 92
Nichols, Kenneth Graham WhoScE 91-1
Nichols, Kyra 1959- WhoAm 92, WhoE 93
Nichols, Larry Sears 1948- WhoWrEP 92
Nichols, Leigh BioIn 17, ScF&FL 92
Nichols, Leo Thomas 1935- St&PR 93
Nichols, Lois Rowell 1916- WhoSSW 93
Nichols, Lorenzo BioIn 17
Nichols, Mack G. 1938- St&PR 93
Nichols, Margaret Landau 1936- WhoAmW 93
Nichols, Marian Theresa 1947- WhoEmL 93
Nichols, Mary Elizabeth 1955- WhoAmW 93
Nichols, Mary Eudora 1901- AmWomPl
Nichols, Mary Ivancevic 1951- WhoEmL 93
Nichols, Matthew Scott Law&B 92
Nichols, Michael C. 1952- WhoAm 92
Nichols, Michael Cooper 1952- St&PR 93
Nichols, Michael K. 1953- BioIn 17
Nichols, Mike BioIn 17
Nichols, Mike 1931- CurBio 92 [port], MiSFD 9, WhoAm 92
Nichols, Mike Thomas 1949- WhoSSW 93
Nichols, Nancy 1939- WhoAmW 93
Nichols, Nancy Ann 1946- WhoWrEP 92
Nichols, Norman J. 1928- WhoIns 93
Nichols, Pamela Amber 1956- WhoWrEP 92
Nichols, Paul d1990 BioIn 17
Nichols, Peter ConAu 37NR, MajAI
Nichols, Peter 1927- BioIn 17
Nichols, Ralph Arthur 1919- WhoAm 92
Nichols, Raymond Stanley 1946- WhoE 93
Nichols, "Red" (Ernest Loring) 1905-1965 Baker 92
Nichols, Richard Dale 1926- WhoAm 92
Nichols, Richard Maurice 1905- St&PR 93, WhoAm 92
Nichols, Robert 1919- ScF&FL 92
Nichols, Robert C. Law&B 92
Nichols, Robert Edmund 1925- WhoAm 92
Nichols, Robert Lee 1924- WhoAm 92
Nichols, Robert Leighton 1926- WhoAm 92
Nichols, Robert Sherman, Jr. 1945- WhoE 93
Nichols, Robert W. 1934- St&PR 93
Nichols, Roberta J. BioIn 17
Nichols, Rodney Wayson 1937- WhoAm 92
Nichols, Ronald Lee 1941- WhoAm 92, WhoWor 93
Nichols, Roy J. 1938- St&PR 93
Nichols, Ruth 1948- ScF&FL 92, WhoCanL 92
Nichols, (Joanna) Ruth 1948- ConAu 37NR, DcChlFi
Nichols, Sandi Lynn 1956- WhoEmL 93
Nichols, Sarah How-Ree 1933- WhoWrEP 92
Nichols, Scott B. Law&B 92
Nichols, Sharon D. 1936- WhoWrEP 92
Nichols, Stephen BioIn 17
Nichols, Stephen George 1936- WhoAm 92
Nichols, Stephen George, Jr. 1936- WhoWrEP 92
Nichols, Stuart J. Law&B 92
Nichols, Ted L. 1930- St&PR 93
Nichols, Terri Dawn Morris 1958- WhoEmL 93
Nichols, Todd BioIn 17
Nichols, Vicki Anne 1949- WhoAmW 93
Nichols, Virginia Violet 1928- WhoAmW 93
Nichols, Wade Hampton, III 1942- WhoAm 92
Nichols, Wallace Joseph, Jr. 1939- St&PR 93
Nichols, Wanda Marie 1955- WhoAmW 93
Nichols, Willard R. 1947- St&PR 93
Nichols, William Curtis, Jr. 1929- WhoAm 92, WhoSSW 93
Nichols, William Deming 1924- WhoAm 92
Nichols, William Ford, Jr. 1934- WhoAm 92
Nicholsen, James Therman 1950- WhoEmL 93, WhoWor 93
Nicholson, Anne AmWomPl
Nicholson, Arthur Raymond 1935- St&PR 93
Nicholson, Ben 1894-1982 BioIn 17
Nicholson, Bernice Loughran 1919- WhoAmW 93
Nicholson, Bruce WhoAm 92
Nicholson, Bryan BioIn 17
Nicholson, Cathy Ann 1947- WhoEmL 93, WhoSSW 93
Nicholson, Charles A. 1927- St&PR 93
Nicholson, Charles (Edward) 1946- ConAu 136
Nicholson, Charles Graham 1933- WhoIns 93
Nicholson, Charles Preston 1934- WhoSSW 93
Nicholson, Charles William 1929- WhoAm 92
Nicholson, Christopher Edgar 1940- WhoScE 91-1
Nicholson, Connie Jean 1953- WhoAmW 93
Nicholson, Donna Jean 1935- WhoAmW 93
Nicholson, Douglas Robert 1921- WhoAm 92
Nicholson, Dwight R. BioIn 17
Nicholson, Edna Elizabeth 1907- WhoAmW 93, WhoWor 93
Nicholson, Ellen Ellis 1940- WhoAmW 93
Nicholson, Freda Hyams 1934- WhoAm 92, WhoSSW 93
Nicholson, George Albert, Jr. 1908- WhoAm 92
Nicholson, George (Thomas Frederick) 1949- Baker 92
Nicholson, Glen Ira 1925- WhoAm 92
Nicholson, Godfrey 1901-1991 AnObit 1991
Nicholson, Harry B., Jr. 1938- St&PR 93
Nicholson, Homer Kittrell 1922- WhoSSW 93
Nicholson, J.F. 1919- St&PR 93
Nicholson, Jack BioIn 17
Nicholson, Jack 1937- IntDcF 2-3 [port], MiSFD 9, WhoAm 92
Nicholson, James Allen 1948- WhoSSW 93
Nicholson, James Evans, III 1952- WhoSSW 93
Nicholson, James Lloyd, Jr. 1928- St&PR 93
Nicholson, James Sidney 1948- WhoSSW 93
Nicholson, John D. Law&B 92
Nicholson, John L. 1945- St&PR 93
Nicholson, Joseph Bruce 1940- WhoAm 92
Nicholson, Leland Ross 1924- WhoAm 92
Nicholson, Lillie May 1884-1964 BioIn 17
Nicholson, Linda Barton 1949- WhoEmL 93
Nicholson, Lisa Loechler 1963- WhoAmW 93
Nicholson, Luther Beal 1921- WhoWor 93
Nicholson, M.G. WhoScE 91-1
Nicholson, Malcolm Paul WhoScE 91-1
Nicholson, Malcolm Wheeler- ScF&FL 92
Nicholson, Mark W. Law&B 92
Nicholson, Meredith 1866-1947 AmWomPl
Nicholson, Michelle Renee 1960- WhoAmW 93, WhoEmL 93
Nicholson, Morris Emmons, Jr. 1916- WhoAm 92
Nicholson, Morris G. Law&B 92
Nicholson, Myreen Moore 1940- WhoAmW 93, WhoWor 93
Nicholson, Nigel WhoScE 91-1
Nicholson, Norman 1914-1987 ScF&FL 92
Nicholson, Patrick James 1920- WhoAm 92
Nicholson, Paul Douglas 1938- WhoWor 93
Nicholson, Paul E. 1947- St&PR 93
Nicholson, Paul M. 1949- St&PR 93
Nicholson, R. Stephen 1926- WhoAm 92
Nicholson, Richard Joseph 1932- WhoAm 92
Nicholson, Richard S. 1938- St&PR 93
Nicholson, Richard Selindh 1938- WhoAm 92
Nicholson, Robert Arthur 1923- WhoAm 92
Nicholson, Robert David 1937- WhoWor 93
Nicholson, Robert Ian WhoScE 91-1
Nicholson, Robert J. 1939- St&PR 93
Nicholson, Roger L. Law&B 92
Nicholson, Roy S. 1903- WhoAm 92
Nicholson, Sam ScF&FL 92
Nicholson, Shelia Elaine 1963- WhoAmW 93, WhoEmL 93
Nicholson, Sheryl 1948- WhoAmW 93
Nicholson, Susan Jane Brown 1942- WhoWrEP 92
Nicholson, Susan Marie Law&B 92
Nicholson, Susan Orebaugh 1941- WhoSSW 93
Nicholson, Thomas A., Jr. 1945- St&PR 93
Nicholson, Thomas D. 1922-1991 BioIn 17
Nicholson, Thomas Laurence 1923- WhoAm 92
Nicholson, Thomas N., Jr. 1953- St&PR 93
Nicholson, Walter 1942- WhoAm 92
Nicholson, Will F., Jr. 1929- St&PR 93
Nicholson, Will Faust, Jr. 1929- WhoAm 92
Nicholson, William Beck 1914- BiDAMSp 1989
Nicholson, William Garrett Law&B 92

Nicholson, William George 1935- *WhoE 93*
Nicholson, William H. *Law&B 92*
Nicholson-Guthrie, Catherine S. *WhoAm 92*
Nicht, Sandra K. 1957- *WhoAmW 93*
Nichter, Mark S. 1951- *St&PR 93*
Nichtern, Claire Joseph *WhoAm 92*
Nici, Richard James 1955- *WhoE 93*
Nicias d413BC *HarEnMi*
Nick, Eugene Anthony 1951- *WhoEmL 93*
Nick, Fred Joseph 1951- *WhoEmL 93*
Nick, Jeffrey J. 1953- *St&PR 93*
Nick, Jeffrey Joseph 1953- *WhoAm 92*
Nick, Richard J. 1943- *St&PR 93*
Nickalls, Paul C. 1933- *St&PR 93*
Nickard, Gary Laurence 1954- *WhoE 93*
Nickel, Albert George 1943- *WhoAm 92, WhoE 93, WhoWor 93*
Nickel, Dieter Heinz 1936- *St&PR 93*
Nickel, Donald Lloyd 1933- *WhoAm 92*
Nickel, Erwin J.K. 1921- *WhoScE 91-4*
Nickel, Hans E. 1928- *St&PR 93*
Nickel, Hans Erich 1928- *WhoAm 92*
Nickel, Hubertus 1930- *WhoScE 91-3*
Nickel, Peter 1933- *WhoScE 91-3*
Nickel, Phyllis Fritchey 1932- *WhoAmW 93*
Nickel, Rosalie Jean 1939- *WhoAmW 93*
Nickel, Ruth Arnold *AmWomPl*
Nickel-Creusere, Karen Louise 1939- *WhoAmW 93*
Nickell, Beth Moore 1945- *WhoAmW 93*
Nickell, Bruce *BioIn 17*
Nickell, Christopher Shea 1959- *WhoEmL 93*
Nickell, Grason Templeton 1923- *St&PR 93*
Nickell, Joe 1944- *SmATA 73 [port]*
Nickell, Katherine Mary 1960- *WhoEmL 93*
Nickell, Laurel Kay 1943- *St&PR 93*
Nickell, Lou *BioIn 17*
Nickell, Sherri Marcia 1960- *WhoEmL 93*
Nickell, Stella *BioIn 17*
Nickel-Milstone, Sherri J. 1961- *WhoE 93*
Nickels, Beth Barnard 1918- *WhoSSW 93*
Nickels, Carl E., Jr. 1931- *St&PR 93*
Nickels, Jeffrey Lynn 1963- *WhoSSW 93*
Nickels, Patricia A. 1950- *St&PR 93*
Nickels, Terry Lee 1944- *WhoSSW 93*
Nickels, Thom *ScF&FL 92*
Nickels, William Carl 1920- *St&PR 93*
Nickelson, Donald Eugene 1932- *St&PR 93*
Nickelson, James Edward 1932- *St&PR 93*
Nickelson, Kim Rene 1956- *WhoAmW 93*
Nickelson, Richard Laman 1937- *WhoUN 92*
Nickelson, Vicki Ann 1963- *WhoAmW 93*
Nickens, Carl R. *Law&B 92*
Nickens, Dan Alan 1954- *WhoEmL 93*
Nickerson, Albert Lindsay 1911- *WhoAm 92*
Nickerson, Arthur Lee 1947- *WhoSSW 93*
Nickerson, Clarke Casey 1951- *St&PR 93*
Nickerson, David Charles 1959- *St&PR 93*
Nickerson, Eileen Tressler 1927- *WhoAm 92*
Nickerson, Eugene H. 1918- *WhoAm 92, WhoE 93*
Nickerson, Gary Allan 1951- *WhoE 93*
Nickerson, Gary Thomas 1943- *WhoAm 92*
Nickerson, Guy Robert 1956- *St&PR 93*
Nickerson, James Arnold 1931- *St&PR 93*
Nickerson, James Findley 1910- *WhoAm 92*
Nickerson, Jerry Edgar Alan 1936- *WhoAm 92*
Nickerson, John Mitchell 1937- *WhoAm 92*
Nickerson, Leroy C. 1950- *St&PR 93*
Nickerson, Louisa Talcott 1961- *WhoAmW 93*
Nickerson, Lucille M. *Law&B 92*
Nickerson, Lucille M. 1947- *St&PR 93*
Nickerson, Norman F. *St&PR 93*
Nickerson, Peter Ayers 1941- *WhoE 93*
Nickerson, Raymond Stephen 1931- *St&PR 93*
Nickerson, Richard Gorham 1927- *WhoE 93*
Nickerson, Ruth 1905- *WhoAm 92*
Nickerson, Sheila B. 1942- *WhoWrEP 92*
Nickerson, William d1945 *BioIn 17*
Nickerson, William Milnor 1933- *WhoAm 92, WhoE 93*
Nickey, Donald O. *Law&B 92*
Nickford, Juan 1925- *WhoAm 92*
Nickisch, Willard Wayne 1939- *WhoWor 93*
Nickl, Barbara 1939- *BioIn 17*
Nicklas, Elizabeth Ann *Law&B 92*
Nicklas, James B. 1949- *St&PR 93*
Nicklas, Robert Bruce 1932- *WhoAm 92*
Nicklaus, Barbara *BioIn 17*
Nicklaus, Carol *BioIn 17*
Nicklaus, (Charles) Frederick 1936- *WhoWrEP 92*
Nicklaus, Jack *BioIn 17*
Nicklaus, Jack 1940- *NewYTBS 92 [port]*
Nicklaus, Jack (William) 1940- *ConAu 39NR, WhoAm 92*
Nickle, Dennis Edwin 1936- *WhoSSW 93, WhoWor 93*
Nickleberry, Henry H. 1927- *AfrAmBi [port]*
Nickles, Don 1948- *CngDr 91, WhoAm 92*
Nickles, Donald Don 1948- *WhoSSW 93*
Nickles, Ernest A. *St&PR 93*
Nickless, Will 1902- *BioIn 17*
Nicklin, George Leslie, Jr. 1925- *WhoAm 92*
Nicklin, Walter Shirley, III 1945- *WhoSSW 93*
Nickodem, Robert J. 1929- *St&PR 93*
Nickolas, George Tom 1933- *WhoWrEP 92*
Nickolaus, Nicholas 1925- *St&PR 93*
Nickolayevsky, Yury Arkadyevich 1965- *WhoWor 93*
Nickolich, Barbara Ellen 1937- *WhoAmW 93*
Nickoloff, John Elia 1925- *St&PR 93*
Nickols, Sharon Yvonne 1942- *WhoAmW 93*
Nickolson, Victor J. 1945- *WhoScE 91-3*
Nickon, Alex 1927- *WhoAm 92*
Nickow, Martin Allen 1928- *St&PR 93*
Nicks, Baudouin 1950- *WhoScE 91-2*
Nicks, Larry 1942- *St&PR 93*
Nicks, Roy Sullivan 1933- *WhoSSW 93*
Nicks, Stephanie 1948-
See Fleetwood, Mick 1942- *Baker 92*
Nicks, Stevie 1948- *WhoAm 92*
Nicksa, Gary William 1957- *WhoE 93*
Nickse, Ruth Speirs 1931- *WhoE 93*
Nickson, Goldie Darlene 1922- *WhoAmW 93*
Nickson, M. Scott, Jr. *Law&B 92*
Nickson, M. Scott, Jr. 1934- *St&PR 93*
Nickson, Richard 1917- *WhoWrEP 92*
Nic Leodhas, Sorche *MajAI*
Nicoara, Laurentiu 1923- *WhoScE 91-4*
Nicod, Xavier *BioIn 17*
Nicode, Jean-Louis 1853-1919 *Baker 92*
Nicodemus, William Byron 1943- *WhoWor 93*
Nicol, Arthur Rory *WhoScE 91-1*
Nicol, Dan F. *Law&B 92*
Nicol, David John 1945- *St&PR 93*
Nicol, Davidson Sylvester Hector Willoughby 1924- *WhoWor 93*
Nicol, Dominik 1930- *WhoE 93*
Nicol, Eric P. 1919- *WhoCanL 92*
Nicol, Ian John 1953- *WhoWor 93*
Nicol, James *Law&B 92*
Nicol, Jessie Thompson 1931- *WhoSSW 93*
Nicol, Klaus 1939- *WhoWor 93*
Nicol, Leslie McKenzie *WhoScE 91-1*
Nicol, Marjorie Carmichael 1929- *WhoAmW 93, WhoE 93, WhoWor 93*
Nicol, Robert Ransom, Jr. 1932- *WhoE 93*
Nicol, William James 1943- *WhoAm 92*
Nicola, Ben A. 1945- *St&PR 93*
Nicola, James B. 1958- *WhoEmL 93*
Nicola, Robert 1924- *St&PR 93*
Nicoladis, Michael Frank 1960- *WhoSSW 93*
Nicolae, Bataga 1935- *WhoScE 91-4*
Nicolaescu, Sergiu 1930- *DrEEuF*
Nicolaev, Simion 1948- *WhoScE 91-4*
Nicola-Grossmiller, Kenneth N. 1955- *WhoE 93*
Nicolai, Frank A. 1941- *WhoAm 92*
Nicolai, Frank Al 1941- *St&PR 93*
Nicolai, Friedrich 1733-1811 *BioIn 17*
Nicolai, Judithe 1945- *WhoAmW 93, WhoWor 93*
Nicolai, Jurgen H.P.H. 1925- *WhoScE 91-3*
Nicolai, Otto 1810-1849 *IntDcOp, OxDcOp*
Nicolai, (Carl) Otto (Ehrenfried) 1810-1849 *Baker 92*
Nicolai, Paul Peter 1953- *WhoEmL 93*
Nicolai, Robert Louis 1940- *St&PR 93*
Nicolai, Van Olin 1924- *WhoSSW 93*
Nicolaide, Andrei 1933- *WhoScE 91-4*
Nicolaides, Cleanthes A. 1946- *WhoScE 91-3*
Nicolaides, George K. 1957- *WhoWor 93*
Nicolaidis, Nicholas Anthony C. 1943- *St&PR 93*
Nicolais, Luigi 1942- *WhoScE 91-3, WhoWor 93*
Nicolais, Michael A. 1925- *St&PR 93*
Nicolaisen, Bjarne 1943- *St&PR 93*
Nicolaisen, Bjorn 1952- *WhoWor 93*
Nicolaou, Ted *MiSFD 9*
Nicolardi, Donald Marc 1954- *WhoE 93*
Nicolarsen, David Jack 1948- *St&PR 93*
Nicolas, Adolphe 1936- *WhoScE 91-2*
Nicolas, Anne Eveline 1957- *WhoAmW 93*
Nicolas, Georges Spiridon 1952- *WhoEmL 93, WhoWor 93*
Nicolas, Jacques 1945- *WhoScE 91-2*
Nicolas, Jean 1931- *WhoScE 91-2*
Nicolas, Jean-Louis 1942- *WhoWor 93*
Nicolas, Jean-Marie 1945- *WhoScE 91-3*
Nicolatus, Stephen Jon 1950- *WhoEmL 93*
Nicolau, Antonio 1858-1933 *Baker 92*
Nicolau, Claude 1936- *WhoScE 91-2*
Nicolau, Edmond-Victor 1922- *WhoScE 91-4*
Nicolaus, A.R. 1931- *WhoScE 91-2*
Nicolay, Harry Joseph 1935- *WhoAm 92*
Nicolay, Jean Honore 1920- *WhoWor 93*
Nicole, Christopher 1930- *ScF&FL 92*
Nicole, Claudette *ScF&FL 92*
Nicolella, John *MiSFD 9*
Nicolella, Michael Bernard 1947- *WhoEmL 93*
Nicolescu, Basarab 1942- *WhoWor 93*
Nicolescu, Valeriu-Norocel 1961- *WhoScE 91-4*
Nicolet, Aurele 1926- *Baker 92*
Nicoletis, Claude *WhoScE 91-2*
Nicolette, Thomas Albert 1950- *St&PR 93*
Nicoletti, Francois-Xavier 1936- *WhoWor 93*
Nicoletti, Paul Lee 1932- *WhoAm 92*
Nicolich, John G. 1952- *WhoEmL 93*
Nicolin, A. *WhoScE 91-3*
Nicolini 1673?-1732 *Baker 92, OxDcOp*
Nicolini 1834-1898 *Baker 92*
Nicolini, Ernest *OxDcOp*
Nicolini, Marco 1962- *WhoWor 93*
Nicolis, F.B. 1928- *WhoScE 91-3*
Nicolis, G. *WhoScE 91-2*
Nicolis, Gregoire 1939- *WhoScE 91-2*
Nicolitz, Ernst 1947- *WhoAm 92*
Nicoll, Abimael Youngs *BioIn 17*
Nicoll, Charles Samuel 1937- *WhoAm 92*
Nicoll, David J.H. 1937- *St&PR 93*
Nicoll, Jeffrey Fancher 1948- *WhoSSW 93*
Nicoll, John *Law&B 92*
Nicoll, John 1931- *WhoAm 92*
Nicoll, Maurice *BioIn 17*
Nicolle, Hilary *BioIn 17*
Nicolle, Robert Arthur Bethune 1934- *WhoWor 93*
Nicollet, Jean 1598-1642 *Expl 93*
Nicollet, Michel Jean 1940- *WhoWor 93*
Nicolli, Renaldo R. 1923- *St&PR 93*
Nicolo *OxDcOp*
Nicolo, Fernando 1939- *WhoScE 91-3*
Nicolopoulos, Panayotis G. 1931- *WhoWor 93*
Nicolosi, Vincent *BioIn 17*
Nicolova-Christova, Nedjalka Panova 1930- *WhoScE 91-4*
Nicols, Henry *BioIn 17*
Nicolson, Charles White 1931- *St&PR 93, WhoAm 92*
Nicolson, Harold George 1886-1968 *BioIn 17*
Nicolson, Marjorie 1894-1981 *ScF&FL 92*
Nicolucci, Giustiniano 1819-1904 *IntDcAn*
Nicorata, Steven John 1959- *WhoEmL 93*
Nicosia, Hildebrando *DcCPCAm*
Nicosia, Roberto F. 1952- *WhoEmL 93*
Nicosia, Salvatore 1934- *WhoScE 91-3*
Nicoson, Patricia McLaughlin 1942- *WhoSSW 93*
Nicotera, Frank R. *Law&B 92*
Nicotera, Pasquale 1922- *WhoScE 91-3*
Nicotra, Antonino 1938- *WhoScE 91-3*
Nicotra, Joseph Charles 1931- *WhoE 93*
Nicpon, Norbert F. 1943- *St&PR 93*
Nicu, D. Mihail 1937- *WhoScE 91-4*
Niculescu, Debbie Eide 1956- *WhoEmL 93*
Niculescu, Stefan 1927- *Baker 92*
Nicusanti, Albert R., Jr. *St&PR 93*
Nida, Eugene Albert 1914- *WhoAm 92*
Nida, Jane Bolster 1918- *WhoAm 92*
Nida, Robert H. *Law&B 92*
Nidal, Abu *BioIn 17*
Nidiffer, Jana 1957- *WhoEmL 93*
Nie, Norman H. 1943- *WhoWrEP 92*
Nie, Shuming 1962- *WhoWor 93*
Nie, William L. *Law&B 92*
Nie, Yi-Yong 1940- *WhoWor 93*
Nie, Zenon S. 1950- *St&PR 93*
Nieb, Cynthia Dell 1958- *WhoE 93*
Niebelschutz, Wolf von 1913-1960 *ScF&FL 92*
Nieberding, James R. *St&PR 93*
Nieberg, Samuel I. *Law&B 92*
Niebergall, A. Thomas *Law&B 92*
Nieberlein, Vernon Adolph 1918- *WhoSSW 93*
Nie Bichu 1928- *WhoAsAP 91*
Niebisch, Dieter Eric 1937- *St&PR 93*
Niebling, Walter W. d1990 *BioIn 17*
Nieboer, James M. 1944- *St&PR 93*
Nieboer, W. 1937- *St&PR 93*
Niebroj, Tadeus Carl 1930- *WhoWor 93*
Niebroj-Dobosz, Irena Maria 1932- *WhoScE 91-4*
Niebuhr, Carsten 1733-1815 *Expl 93 [port]*
Niebuhr, Fred John 1926- *WhoE 93*
Niebuhr, Hulda 1888?-1959 *BioIn 17*
Niebuhr, Reinhold 1892-1971 *BioIn 17, ColdWar 1 [port], PolPar*
Niebuhr, Richard Reinhold 1926- *WhoAm 92*
Niebur, Marvin H. *St&PR 93*
Niebylski, Julian 1930- *WhoScE 91-4*
Niece, Julie Cole 1945- *WhoAmW 93*
Niecks, Frederick 1845-1924 *Baker 92*
Nied, Harriet Therese 1923- *WhoAmW 93*
Nied, Thomas H. 1942- *WhoAm 92*
Niedecker, Charles William 1913- *WhoIns 93*
Niedecker, Lorine 1903-1970 *BioIn 17*
Niedel, James E. 1944- *WhoAm 92*
Niedenthal, William Jeffrey 1947- *WhoSSW 93*
Nieder, William Henry 1933- *BiDAMSp 1989*
Niederdrenk, Klaus 1950- *WhoWor 93*
Niederfringer, Stephen C. 1939- *St&PR 93*
Niedergeses, James D. 1917- *WhoAm 92, WhoSSW 93*
Niederhauser, Hans Rudolf 1934- *WhoWor 93*
Niederhauser, Hans-Ulrich Walter 1945- *WhoWor 93*
Niederhauser, John S. *BioIn 17*
Niederhauser, Tom D. 1945- *St&PR 93*
Niederhofer, Laurence John 1932- *St&PR 93*
Niederhuber, John Edward 1938- *WhoAm 92*
Niederitter, Edward R. *Law&B 92*
Niederjohn, Russell James 1944- *WhoAm 92*
Niederland, William Guglielmo 1904- *WhoAm 92*
Niederlehner, Leonard 1914- *WhoAm 92*
Niederman, James Corson 1924- *WhoAm 92*
Niedermayer, Virginie Soubiran *Law&B 92*
Niedermeier, Christine Marie 1951- *WhoE 93*
Niedermeier, Lynn R. 1953- *St&PR 93*
Niedermeier, Mary B. 1914- *WhoAmW 93*
Niedermeyer, James P. *Law&B 92*
Niedermeyer, (Abraham) Louis 1802-1861 *Baker 92*
Niedermeyer, Maude *AmWomPl*
Niedermeyer, Terrence Patrick 1956- *St&PR 93*
Niederreiter, Harald 1944- *WhoScE 91-4*
Niederreiter, Harald Guenther 1944- *WhoWor 93*
Niederriter, Edward Raymond 1952- *WhoEmL 93*
Niedetzky, Antal 1933- *WhoScE 91-4*
Niedner, Kathryn Ellen 1946- *WhoAmW 93, WhoEmL 93*
Niedrig, Heinz 1935- *WhoScE 91-3*
Niedziela, Ronald L. 1940- *St&PR 93*
Niedzielska, Marie-Suzanne 1947- *WhoAmW 93, WhoE 93*
Niedzielski, Andrzej 1929- *WhoScE 91-4*
Niedzielski, Henri Zygmunt 1931- *WhoAm 92*
Niedzwiecki, Edward 1938- *WhoScE 91-4*
Niefeld, Jaye Sutter 1924- *WhoAm 92*
Nieforth, Karl Allen 1936- *WhoAm 92*
Niegelsky, Leon S. 1957- *St&PR 93*
Niegsch, William Charles 1952- *St&PR 93*
Nieh, Edward Chung-Yit 1939- *WhoSSW 93*
Niehaus, Merle H. 1933- *WhoAm 92*
Niehaus, Robert Henry 1955- *WhoE 93*
Niehaus, Robert James 1930- *WhoAm 92*
Niehaus-Hostetter, Mary E. 1961- *St&PR 93*
Niehaus Quesada, Bernd 1941- *WhoWor 93*
Nieh Jung-chen 1899- *HarEnMi*
Niehm, Bernard Frank 1923- *WhoAm 92*
Niehoff, Edward E. *Law&B 92*
Niehoff, K. Richard B. 1943- *WhoAm 92, WhoE 93*
Niehoff, Leonard Marvin 1957- *WhoEmL 93*
Niehoff, Marilee Schultz *WhoSSW 93, WhoWrEP 92*
Niehoff, Philip John 1959- *WhoEmL 93*
Niehouse, Oliver Leslie 1920- *WhoE 93, WhoWor 93*
Nieh Shih-ch'eng d1900 *HarEnMi*
Niekamp, Patricia *BioIn 17*
Niekamp, Ronald Edward 1942- *St&PR 93*
Niekerk, Hendrik Albertus van 1759-1833 *BioIn 17*
Niekrasz, Andrezej 1934- *WhoWor 93*
Niekro, Joe 1944- *BioIn 17*
Niekro, Phil *BioIn 17*
Nie Kuiju 1929- *WhoAsAP 91*

Nikkola, Antti Salomoni 1934- *WhoWor 93*
Nikodem, Kazimierz 1953- *WhoWor 93*
Nikodym, Otto 1887-1974 *BioIn 17*
Nikokavouras, John 1938- *WhoScE 91-3*
Nikolaev, Igor Georgievich 1953- *WhoWor 93*
Nikolaev, Yuri Alexandrovich 1941- *WhoWor 93*
Nikolai, Loren Alfred 1943- *WhoAm 92*
Nikolai, Norma Cloyd 1936- *WhoAmW 93*
Nikolaidis, A. *WhoScE 91-3*
Nikolaidis, Efstratios 1956- *WhoSSW 93*
Nikolaidis, Michael 1937- *WhoScE 91-3*
Nikolais, Alwin *BioIn 17*
Nikolais, Alwin Theodore 1910- *WhoAm 92*
Nikolais, Alwin (Theodore) 1912- *Baker 92*
Nikolaisen, Shirley *ScF&FL 92*
Nikolajeva, Maria *ScF&FL 92*
Nikola-lisa, W. 1951- *SmATA 71 [port]*
Nikolayev, Leonid (Vladimirovich) 1878-1942 *Baker 92*
Nikolayeva, Tatiana (Petrovna) 1924- *Baker 92*
Nikolchev, Julian Nikolov 1954- *WhoEmL 93*
Nikolic, Bozidar 1941- *WhoScE 91-4*
Nikolic, George 1945- *WhoWor 93*
Nikolic, Mihailo 1929- *WhoScE 91-4*
Nikolic, Predrag 1928- *WhoScE 91-4*
Nikolic, Vasilije 1933- *WhoScE 91-4*
Nikolic, Zivko 1941- *DrEEuF*
Nikolin, Ana 1932- *WhoScE 91-4*
Nikolin, Branko 1932- *WhoScE 91-4*
Nikolis, Theodore Peter *Law&B 92*
Nikoloff, John Andon 1950- *WhoEmL 93*
Nikolov, I. *WhoScE 91-4*
Nikolov, Lazar 1922- *Baker 92*
Nikolov, Milen 1938- *DrEEuF*
Nikolov, Nikola 1930- *WhoScE 91-4*
Nikolov, Stephan Emilov 1952- *WhoWor 93*
Nikolov, T.K. 1923- *WhoScE 91-4*
Nikolov, Todor G. 1931- *WhoScE 91-4*
Nikolova, Lyudmila Yordanova 1948- *WhoWor 93*
Nikolova, Mima 1943- *WhoScE 91-4*
Nikolovski, Vlastimir 1925- *Baker 92*
Nikolozis dze, Salia Revaz 1933- *WhoWor 93*
Nikolskii, Serguei Michailovich 1905- *WhoWor 93*
Nikonenko, Sergej 1941- *DrEEuF*
Nikon Ho Metanoeite c. 930-c. 1000 *OxDcByz*
Nikon of the Black Mountain c. 1025-c. 110-? *OxDcByz*
Nikonov, Oleg Igorevich 1951- *WhoWor 93*
Nikoui, Hossein Reza 1949- *WhoWor 93*
Niland, Deborah *BioIn 17*
Niland, Edward John 1916- *WhoAm 92*
Niland, Patricia E. *Law&B 92*
Niland, Rosina R. *ScF&FL 92*
Nile, Dorothea *ConAu 39NR, ScF&FL 92*
Niles, Barbara Elliott 1939- *WhoAmW 93*
Niles, Charles Kenneth 1945- *St&PR 93*
Niles, Charles Lannon, Jr. 1924- *WhoIns 93*
Niles, Darryl W. *Law&B 92*
Niles, David *BioIn 17*
Niles, Douglas *ScF&FL 92*
Niles, Franklin Elvie 1934- *WhoAm 92*
Niles, Hezekiah 1777-1839 *JrnUS*
Niles, John Gilbert 1943- *WhoAm 92*
Niles, John Jacob 1892-1980 *Baker 92*
Niles, John Lowell 1930- *St&PR 93*
Niles, Lawson R. *Law&B 92*
Niles, Nicholas Hemelright 1938- *St&PR 93, WhoAm 92*
Niles, P.H. *ScF&FL 92*
Niles, Robert O. 1935- *St&PR 93*
Niles, Russell D. d1992 *NewYTBS 92 [port]*
Niles, Steve *ScF&FL 92*
Niles, Thomas Michael Tolliver 1939- *WhoAm 92*
Nilges, Edward George 1949- *WhoE 93*
Nill, C. John 1938- *St&PR 93*
Nill, Kimball Roy 1958- *WhoEmL 93*
Nill, William C. 1938- *St&PR 93*
Nilles, Andrew J. 1960- *WhoEmL 93*
Nilles, John M. 1930- *St&PR 93*
Nilles, John Michael *Law&B 92*
Nilles, Paul E. 1934- *WhoScE 91-2*
Nilon, Laura Ann 1960- *WhoEmL 93*
Nilsen, Anders Mallabar 1946- *WhoSSW 93*
Nilsen, Andrew 1936- *WhoE 93*
Nilsen, Barbara Yvonne 1941- *St&PR 93*
Nilsen, Clifford T. 1932- *St&PR 93*
Nilsen, Kenneth Louis 1966- *WhoE 93*
Nilsen, Lloyd Raymond 1932- *WhoAm 92*
Nilsen, Nicholas 1937- *St&PR 93*
Nilsen, Odd Georg 1946- *WhoScE 91-4*
Nilsen, Richard Haldor 1948- *WhoWrEP 92*
Nilson, Arne Einar 1920- *WhoWor 93*
Nilson, Christian C. *Law&B 92*
Nilson, David Albert 1947- *St&PR 93*
Nilson, Donald E. 1944- *St&PR 93*
Nilson, Larry A. 1946- *St&PR 93*
Nilson, Richard Edwin 1948- *WhoEmL 93*
Nilssen, Arne Claus 1943- *WhoScE 91-4*
Nilssen, Bjorn Klerck 1939- *WhoUN 92*
Nilsson, A. Kenneth 1933- *St&PR 93*
Nilsson, Anders 1950- *WhoScE 91-4*
Nilsson, Bengt 1937- *St&PR 93*
Nilsson, Bengt 1942- *WhoScE 91-4*
Nilsson, Birgit 1918- *Baker 92, IntDcOp [port], OxDcOp, WhoAm 92, WhoWor 93*
Nilsson, Bjorn O. 1937- *WhoScE 91-4*
Nilsson, Bo 1937- *Baker 92*
Nilsson, Bo Bertil 1942- *WhoWor 93*
Nilsson, Christine 1843-1921 *Baker 92, IntDcOp, OxDcOp*
Nilsson, Edward Olof 1947- *WhoEmL 93*
Nilsson, Erik *WhoScE 91-2*
Nilsson, Goran 1935- *WhoScE 91-4*
Nilsson, Harry 1941- *WhoAm 92*
Nilsson, Jan S. 1932- *WhoScE 91-4*
Nilsson, Jeffrey A. 1945- *St&PR 93*
Nilsson, Jytte R. 1932- *WhoScE 91-2*
Nilsson, Kenneth N. 1942- *WhoScE 91-4*
Nilsson, Lars Erik 1937- *WhoScE 91-4*
Nilsson, Larsgunnar 1947- *WhoScE 91-4*
Nilsson, Lennart 1922- *BioIn 17*
Nilsson, Lennart Gustav 1950- *WhoWor 93*
Nilsson, Leo 1939- *Baker 92*
Nilsson, Martin J. 1929- *WhoScE 91-4*
Nilsson, Martin John 1929- *WhoWor 93*
Nilsson, Nic 1933- *WhoWor 93*
Nilsson, Olof Robert 1949- *WhoWor 93*
Nilsson, Per Olov 1936- *WhoScE 91-4*
Nilsson, Rob *MiSFD 9*
Nilsson, Sam Olof *WhoWor 93*
Nilsson, Stefan 1946- *WhoScE 91-4*
Nilsson, Sten Ake 1936- *WhoWor 93*
Nilsson, Suzanne Janet 1951- *WhoAmW 93*
Nilsson, Sven Erik G. 1931- *WhoScE 91-4*
Nilsson, Tage Oskar Erling 1945- *WhoWor 93*
Nilsson, Thomas 1941- *WhoScE 91-4*
Nilsson, Torsten 1920- *Baker 92*
Nilva, Sheila Cole 1930- *WhoE 93*
Nim, P.S. *ScF&FL 92*
Niman, John 1938- *WhoE 93*
Nimas 1907- *Baker 92*
Nimboonchaj, Voraratana 1951- *WhoWor 93*
Nimeiri, Gaafar Mohammed 1930- *BioIn 17, WhoAfr*
Nimer, Daniel A. 1921- *St&PR 93*
Nimetz, Matthew 1939- *WhoAm 92*
Ni Mhaille, Grainne c. 1530-1600 *BioIn 17*
Nimityongskul, Prajuab 1940- *WhoWor 93*
Nimitz, Chester W. 1885-1966 *BioIn 17*
Nimitz, Chester W., Jr. 1915- *St&PR 93*
Nimitz, Chester William 1885-1966 *DcTwHis, HarEnMi*
Nimitz, Chester William, Jr. 1915- *WhoAm 92*
Nimkin, Bernard William 1923- *WhoAm 92*
Nimkin, Margaret Lee 1955- *WhoAmW 93*
Nimmo, Dan 1933- *ScF&FL 92*
Nimmo, Jenny 1942- *ScF&FL 92*
Nimmo, Jenny 1944- *ChlFicS*
Nimmo, Nancy Ann 1959- *WhoSSW 93*
Nimmo, Robert Allen 1936- *St&PR 93*
Nimmo, Thomas Dewey 1938- *WhoIns 93*
Nimmo, Thomas Dewey 1939- *St&PR 93*
Nimmo, Walter S. 1947- *WhoScE 91-1*
Nimmo, William S. *St&PR 93*
Nimmons, Major Stuart, III 1940- *WhoSSW 93*
Nimmons, Phillip Rista 1923- *WhoAm 92*
Nimmons, William Ted 1955- *WhoSSW 93*
Nimni, Marcel Ephraim 1931- *WhoAm 92*
Nimnicht, Billie Nugent, Jr. 1941- *St&PR 93*
Nimnicht, Edward Aaron, II 1943- *St&PR 93*
Nimnicht, Nona Vonne 1930- *WhoWrEP 92*
Nimoityn, Philip 1951- *WhoE 93*
Nimons, John M. 1939- *St&PR 93*
Nimoy, Leonard 1931- *MiSFD 9, ScF&FL 92, WhoAm 92*
Nims, Arthur L., III 1923- *CngDr 91*
Nims, Arthur Lee, III 1923- *WhoAm 92*
Nims, John Frederick 1913- *ConAu 17AS [port], WhoWrEP 92*
Nims, Leslie Irving 1940- *WhoWor 93*
Nimsgern, Siegmund 1940- *Baker 92*
Nimuendaju, Curt 1883-1945 *IntDcAn*
Nimura, Yasuharu 1923- *WhoWor 93*
Nimz, Horst 1930- *WhoScE 91-3*
Nimz, Nancy M. *Law&B 92*
Nimzowitsch, Aron 1886-1935 *BioIn 17*
Nin, Anais 1903-1977 *BioIn 17, MagSAmL [port], ShSCr 10 [port]*
Nin (y Castellanos), Joaquin 1879-1949 *Baker 92*
Ninagawa, Yuzuru 1925- *WhoWor 93*
Nina Rodrigues, Raimundo 1862-1906 *IntDcAn*
Nin-Culmell, Joaquin (Maria) 1908- *Baker 92*
Niness, Samuel Francis, Jr. 1935- *St&PR 93*
Ning, Cun-Zheng 1958- *WhoWor 93*
Ning, Tak Hung 1943- *WhoAm 92*
Ning, Xue-Han Hsueh-Han 1936- *WhoWor 93*
Nini, Alessandro 1805-1880 *Baker 92*
Nininger, Alexander R. 1918-1942 *BioIn 17*
Ninkama, Bill 1954- *WhoAsAP 91*
Ninkovich, Thomas 1943- *ConAu 137, WhoWrEP 92*
Ninkovich, Tom *ConAu 137*
Nino, Alex *ScF&FL 92*
Nino, Noel M. *Law&B 92*
Ninos, Nicholas Peter 1936- *WhoAm 92, WhoWor 93*
Niordson, Frithiof I.N. 1922- *WhoScE 91-2*
Niordson, Frithiof Igor 1922- *WhoWor 93*
Niosi, James Peter 1935- *St&PR 93*
Nip, Kam-fan 1932- *WhoAsAP 91*
Nipe, Chris Alan 1956- *WhoEmL 93*
Nipert, Donna Ann 1952- *WhoAmW 93, WhoEmL 93*
Niphon d1328 *OxDcByz*
Niphon 1315-1411 *OxDcByz*
Nipitella, Alfio 1913- *WhoWor 93*
Nipkow, Karl-Ernst Heinrich 1928- *WhoWor 93*
Nipon, Albert 1927- *WhoAm 92*
Nipp, Francis Stuart 1914- *WhoWrEP 92*
Nippa, David A. 1946- *St&PR 93*
Nipper, Walter R., Jr. 1919- *St&PR 93*
Nippert, Russell A. 1937- *St&PR 93*
Nippes, Ernest Frederick 1918- *WhoE 93*
Nippo, Murn Marcus 1944- *WhoE 93*
Nipps, Randall Cramer 1955- *WhoEmL 93*
Nips, Nick L. *WhoWrEP 92*
Nique Agreda, Felix Nelson 1957- *WhoWor 93*
Nirdlinger, Cathy Jenkins 1949- *WhoAmW 93*
Nirenberg, Louis 1925- *WhoAm 92*
Nirenberg, Marshall Warren 1927- *WhoAm 92, WhoWor 93*
Nirenska, Pola d1992 *NewYTBS 92*
Nirenstein, Lawrence 1931-1991 *BioIn 17*
Nirvana *ConMus 8 [port], News 92 [port]*
Nisard, Theodore 1812-1888 *Baker 92*
Nisbet, Alex Richard 1938- *WhoSSW 93*
Nisbet, David B. 1934- *WhoScE 91-1*
Nisbet, Eileen 1929-1990 *BioIn 17*
Nisbet, Helen C. *ScF&FL 92*
Nisbet, Hugh A. *ScF&FL 92*
Nisbet, Joanne 1931- *WhoAm 92*
Nisbet, John Stirling 1927- *WhoAm 92*
Nisbet, Pauline Randow 1946- *WhoEmL 93, WhoSSW 93*
Nisbet, Robert A. *BioIn 17*
Nisbet, Robert A. 1913- *WhoAm 92, WhoWrEP 92*
Nisbet, Robert Stevenson 1946- *WhoWor 93*
Nisbet, Roger MacDonald *WhoScE 91-1*
Nisbet, Shirley J. 1935- *St&PR 93*
Nisbet, Sidney M. 1940- *St&PR 93*
Nisbet, W. Robb 1924- *St&PR 93*
Nisbett, Edward George 1929- *WhoE 93*
Nisbett, Richard Eugene 1941- *WhoAm 92*
Nischan, Gerda M. 1940- *WhoWrEP 92*
Nisen, Andre R.M. 1929- *WhoScE 91-2*
Nisenholtz, Frederick 1929- *WhoE 93*
Nisenholtz, Martin Abram 1955- *WhoAm 92*
Nisenson, David E. 1957- *WhoSSW 93*
Nishi, Kanjiro 1846-1912 *HarEnMi*
Nishi, Kazuhiko *BioIn 17*
Nishi, Kazunobu 1962- *WhoWor 93*
Nishi, Kenji 1949- *WhoWor 93*
Nishi, Kenyu 1930- *WhoWor 93*
Nishi, Masaru 1928- *WhoWor 93*
Nishida, Kazuhiko 1934- *WhoWor 93*
Nishida, Mamoru 1928- *WhoAsAP 91*
Nishida, Yoshihiro 1934- *WhoAsAP 91*
Nishikawa, Kiyoshi 1946- *WhoAsAP 91*
Nishikawa, Kyoji 1934- *WhoWor 93*
Nishikawa, Tetsuji 1926- *WhoWor 93*
Nishimoto, Kichisuke 1932- *WhoWor 93*
Nishimoto, Nobushige 1929- *WhoWor 93*
Nishimura, Chiaki 1928- *WhoWor 93*
Nishimura, Hirokazu 1953- *WhoWor 93*
Nishimura, Hisashi 1930- *WhoWor 93*
Nishimura, Joseph Yo 1933- *WhoAm 92*
Nishimura, Jun 1943- *WhoWor 93*
Nishimura, Manabu 1950- *WhoWor 93*
Nishimura, Masaru 1922- *WhoWor 93*
Nishimura, Mitsuo 1931- *WhoWor 93*
Nishimura, Pete Hideo 1922- *WhoAm 92*
Nishimura, Shoji 1889-1944 *HarEnMi*
Nishimura, Susumu 1931- *WhoWor 93*
Nishinaka, Kiyoshi 1932- *WhoAsAP 91*
Nishino, Fumio 1936- *WhoWor 93*
Nishino, Toshio 1932- *WhoWor 93*
Nishino, Yasuo 1949- *WhoAsAP 91*
Nishioka, Kiyoshi 1939- *WhoWor 93*
Nishioka, Ruriko 1934- *WhoAsAP 91*
Nishioka, Takeo 1936- *WhoAsAP 91*
Nishioka, Wayne S. *Law&B 92*
Nishita, Eiji 1936- *WhoWor 93*
Nishitani, Martha 1920- *WhoAm 92*
Nishiyama, Chiaki 1924- *WhoWor 93*
Nishiyama, Ken'Ichi *WhoWor 93*
Nishizato, Yusaku 1914- *WhoSSW 93*
Nishizawa, Teiji 1949- *WhoWor 93*
Nishizeki, Takao 1947- *WhoWor 93*
Nisi, Rudolph H. 1931- *St&PR 93*
Niska, Laurel Ann 1958- *WhoAmW 93*
Niskanen, William Arthur, Jr. 1933- *WhoAm 92*
Niskanen, Yrjo Hermanni 1932- *WhoWor 93*
Nisolle, Etienne 1964- *WhoWor 93*
Nisonoff, Alfred 1923- *WhoAm 92*
Nisperos, Arturo Galvez 1941- *WhoWor 93*
Nisselbaum, Jerome S. 1925- *WhoE 93*
Nissema, Aulis Kalervo 1930- *WhoScE 91-4*
Nissen, Clyde Theodore 1912- *WhoAm 92*
Nissen, Dorte Krestine Rhode 1956- *WhoWor 93*
Nissen, Elaine Mary 1942- *WhoAmW 93*
Nissen, Elise 1954- *St&PR 93*
Nissen, Georg Nikolaus 1761-1826 *Baker 92*
Nissen, Gerhardt 1923- *WhoScE 91-3*
Nissen, Greta 1905-1988 *BioIn 17*
Nissen, Gunther *WhoScE 91-2*
Nissen, Hans Hermann 1893-1980 *Baker 92, OxDcOp*
Nissen, William John 1947- *WhoAm 92*
Nissenfeld, Robert H. 1944- *St&PR 93*
Nissenson, Hugh 1933- *BioIn 17, JeAmFiW, WhoWrEP 92*
Nisseus, Eva Birgitta 1942- *WhoUN 92*
Nissila, Martti H.T. 1938- *WhoScE 91-4*
Nissinen, Mikko Pekka 1962- *WhoAm 92, WhoEmL 93*
Nissl, Colleen Kaye *Law&B 92*
Nissly, Nedric Lee 1956- *WhoEmL 93*
Nissman, Barbara 1944- *Baker 92*
Nissman, Kenneth I. d1992 *NewYTBS 92*
Nist, Charles William 1942- *St&PR 93*
Nistler, James Charles 1931- *WhoAm 92*
Nistri, Andrea 1947- *WhoWor 93*
Niswonger, Jeanne Du Chateau *WhoAm 92, WhoWor 93*
Nitcher, Eric Leslie *Law&B 92*
Nitchie, Elizabeth 1889- *ScF&FL 92*
Nitchie, George Wilson 1921- *WhoE 93*
Nitchke, Howard Dean 1949- *WhoAm 92*
Nitecki, Joseph Zbigniew 1922- *WhoAm 92*
Nithman, Charles Joseph 1937- *WhoSSW 93*
Nitido, Vincent, Jr. *Law&B 92*
Nitka, Hermann Guillermo 1926- *WhoWor 93*
Nitko, Anthony Joseph 1941- *WhoE 93*
Nitkowski, James Walter 1940- *St&PR 93*
Nitobe, Inazo 1862-1933 *BioIn 17*
Nitoburg, Eduard Lvovich 1919- *WhoWor 93*
Nitsch, Patrick Andrew *Law&B 92*
Nitsch, Robert A. 1928- *St&PR 93*
Nitsche, Johannes Carl Christian 1925- *WhoAm 92*
Nitsche, Richard A. 1931- *St&PR 93*
Nitschke, David F. *Law&B 92*
Nitschke, Ray 1936- *BioIn 17*
Nitso, Evelyn Agnes 1934- *WhoWrEP 92*
Nitta, Yoshisada 1301-1338 *HarEnMi*
Nitteberg, Jan 1936- *WhoScE 91-4*
Nitterhouse, Craig J. 1956- *St&PR 93*
Nitterhouse, William K. 1932- *St&PR 93*
Nittiskie, Leslie Collin 1957- *WhoEmL 93*
Nittoli, Thomas 1963- *WhoWor 93*
Nittolo, Albert P. 1928- *St&PR 93*
Nittuch, Nestor E. 1947- *St&PR 93*
Nitz, P. Kenneth, Jr. 1940- *WhoIns 93*
Nitzche, Oscar 1900-1991 *BioIn 17*
Nitze, Paul H. *BioIn 17*
Nitze, Paul H. 1907- *ColdWar 1 [port]*
Nitze, Paul Henry 1907- *WhoAm 92*
Nitze, William Albert 1942- *WhoE 93*
Nitzsche, Jane Chance *WhoWrEP 92*
Nitzsche, Jane Chance 1945- *ScF&FL 92*
Nitzschke, Dale Frederick 1937- *WhoAm 92, WhoE 93*
Niu, David *Law&B 92*
Niu, Keishiro 1929- *WhoWor 93*
Niu Manchiang 1914- *BioIn 17*

Nivat, Georges Michel 1935- *WhoWor 93*
Nivelle, Robert Georges 1856-1924 *HarEnMi*
Niven, David 1910-1983 *IntDcF 2-3*
Niven, Fernanda *BioIn 17*
Niven, Frederick John 1878-1944 *BioIn 17*
Niven, Ivan Morton 1915- *BioIn 17*
Niven, James *BioIn 17*
Niven, Kenneth W. *Law&B 92*
Niven, Kip *BioIn 17*
Niven, Larry *BioIn 17*
Niven, Larry 1938- *ScF&FL 92*
Niven, Laurence V.C. *ScF&FL 92*
Niven, Laurence Van Cott 1938- *WhoAm 92, WhoWrEP 92*
Nivens, Robert Glenn 1940- *WhoSSW 93*
Niver, Garry 1938- *ConAu 138*
Nivers, Guillaume Gabriel c. 1632-1714 *Baker 92*
Nivert, Judith A. 1949- *WhoIns 93*
Nivison, David Shepherd 1923- *WhoAm 92*
Niwa, Hyosuke 1911- *WhoAsAP 91*
Niwa, Hyosuke 1911-1990 *BioIn 17*
Niwa, Toshiyuki 1939- *WhoUN 92*
Niwa, Yuya 1944- *WhoAsAP 91*
Niwinski, Damian Tadeusz 1957- *WhoWor 93*
Nix, Barbara Lois 1929- *WhoAmW 93, WhoWor 93*
Nix, Dennis W. 1945- *St&PR 93*
Nix, Edmund Alfred 1929- *WhoAm 92*
Nix, Edward J. 1930- *St&PR 93*
Nix, Howard W., Jr. 1929- *St&PR 93*
Nix, Joseph Hanson, Jr. 1930- *WhoSSW 93*
Nix, Lesa Ann 1963- *WhoAmW 93*
Nix, Paul Berlin, Jr. *Law&B 92*
Nix, Robert N.C. d1987 *BioIn 17*
Nix, Stephan Jack 1952- *WhoEmL 93*
Nix, William Dale 1936- *WhoAm 92*
Nix, William J. 1940- *St&PR 93*
Nix-Early, Vivian 1949- *WhoAmW 93*
Nixey, Clifford 1939- *WhoWor 93*
Nixon, Agnes Eckhardt *WhoAm 92*
Nixon, Alfred J. 1927- *St&PR 93*
Nixon, Allen 1921- *St&PR 93*
Nixon, Ann Karen 1944- *St&PR 93*
Nixon, Barbara Elizabeth 1954- *WhoEmL 93*
Nixon, Brenda Harris 1949- *WhoAmW 93*
Nixon, Charles R. *Law&B 92*
Nixon, Charlotte Macdonald 1929- *St&PR 93*
Nixon, David *WhoAm 92*
Nixon, David Allen 1921- *St&PR 93*
Nixon, David Hall *WhoSSW 93*
Nixon, David Michael 1945- *WhoWrEP 92*
Nixon, E.J., Jr. 1931- *St&PR 93*
Nixon, Edgar Daniel 1899-1987 *EncAACR*
Nixon, Eugene Ray 1919- *WhoAm 92*
Nixon, Hollowell Cox 1920- *St&PR 93*
Nixon, Jack Lowell 1926- *WhoAm 92*
Nixon, James Alexander 1932- *St&PR 93*
Nixon, James Frederick 1947- *WhoEmL 93*
Nixon, Joan Lowery 1927- *ConAu 38NR, DcAmChF 1960, DcAmChF 1985, MajAI [port], ScF&FL 92, WhoAm 92*
Nixon, John E. *BioIn 17*
Nixon, John Forster *WhoScE 91-1*
Nixon, John Harold 1956- *WhoWor 93*
Nixon, John Howard *WhoScE 91-1*
Nixon, John Richard 1941- *WhoWor 93*
Nixon, John Trice 1933- *WhoSSW 93*
Nixon, John W. 1926- *St&PR 93*
Nixon, Joyce Elaine 1925- *WhoAmW 93, WhoE 93*
Nixon, Kenneth J. *Law&B 92*
Nixon, Kenneth Long 1960- *WhoEmL 93*
Nixon, L. Kathleen *St&PR 93*
Nixon, Lillian Edith *AmWomPl*
Nixon, Marian 1904-1983 *SweetSg B [port]*
Nixon, Marni 1930- *Baker 92, WhoAm 92, WhoAmW 93*
Nixon, Norman Arthur *Law&B 92*
Nixon, Norman Ellard 1955- *BiDAMSp 1989*
Nixon, P. Andrews 1938- *St&PR 93*
Nixon, Patricia *BioIn 17*
Nixon, Patricia Ryan 1912- *WhoAm 92, WhoAmW 93, WhoE 93*
Nixon, Philip John *WhoScE 91-1*
Nixon, Raymond Blalock 1903- *WhoAm 92*
Nixon, Richard 1913- *OxCSupC*
Nixon, Richard M. 1913- *BioIn 17, ColdWar 1 [port], PolPar*
Nixon, Richard Milhous 1913- *DcTwHis, WhoAm 92, WhoWor 93*
Nixon, Richard Neal 1942- *WhoAm 92*
Nixon, Robert James 1930- *WhoAm 92*
Nixon, Robert Pleasants 1913- *WhoAm 92, WhoWor 93*
Nixon, Roger 1921- *Baker 92*
Nixon, Ronald Gene 1942- *WhoSSW 93*
Nixon, Sallie White 1914- *WhoWrEP 92*
Nixon, Scott West 1943- *WhoAm 92*
Nixon, Shirnette Marilyn 1947- *WhoAmW 93*
Nixon, Tamara Friedman 1938- *WhoAmW 93*
Nixon, Terry L. *St&PR 93*
Nixon, William Penn 1833-1912 *JrnUS*
Niyazi 1912-1984 *Baker 92*
Niyazov, Saparmurad Atayevich 1940- *WhoWor 93*
Niyekawa, Agnes Mitsue 1924- *WhoAmW 93*
Niyibigira, Gerard 1946- *WhoAfr*
Niyibizi, Michel 1956- *WhoWor 93*
Ni Yixin 1946- *BioIn 17*
Ni Yuxian *BioIn 17*
Nizalowski, Edward Michael 1947- *WhoWrEP 92*
Nizalowski, John Anthony 1956- *WhoWrEP 92*
Nizam, Ihsan J. 1939- *St&PR 93*
Nizam, Javed 1948- *WhoWor 93*
Nizam Al-Mulk 1018-1092 *OxDcByz*
Nizan, Paul 1905-1940 *BioIn 17*
Nizer, Louis 1902- *St&PR 93*
Ni Zhifu 1933- *WhoAsAP 91*
Niziol, Jozef 1938- *WhoScE 91-4*
Niznik, Monica Lynne 1953- *WhoEmL 93*
Nizzi, Guido 1900-1983 *ScF&FL 92*
Njastad, Olav 1933- *WhoWor 93*
Njeri, Itabari *BioIn 17*
Njeri, Itabari (Lord) *ConAu 139*
N'jie, Abdul Bun Hatib 1938- *WhoUN 92*
N'jie, Baboucar Ebrima 1937- *WhoUN 92*
Njinga 1582-1663 *BioIn 17*
Njonjo, Charles 1920- *WhoAfr*
Njos, Arnor 1930- *WhoScE 91-4*
Nketia, J(oseph) H(ansen) Kwabena 1921- *Baker 92*
Nkobi, Thomas 1922- *WhoAfr*
Nkoli, Tseko Simon *BioIn 17*
Nkomo, Joshua 1917- *ConBlB 4 [port], WhoWor 93*
Nkomo, Joshua Mqabuko Nyongolo 1917- *DcTwHis, WhoAfr*
Nkosi, Lewis *BioIn 17*
Nkowane, Benjamin Mphamba 1954- *WhoUN 92*
Nkowani, Windsor Kapalakonje 1936- *WhoUN 92*
Nkrumah, Kwame 1909-1972 *BioIn 17, ColdWar 2 [port], ConBlB 3 [port]*
Nkrumah, Kwame Francis Nwia Kofi 1909-1972 *DcTwHis*
Nkurlu, Jackson Immanuel 1943- *WhoUN 92*
N'Namdi, Carmen *BioIn 17*
No, Jose E. 1946- *WhoScE 91-3*
No, Rafael Lorente de 1902-1990 *BioIn 17*
Noack, Charles *Law&B 92*
Noack, Cornelius C. 1935- *WhoScE 91-3*
Noack, Ken Everett 1948- *WhoEmL 93*
Noack, Klaus 1934- *WhoScE 91-3*
Noack, Linda Elin 1959- *WhoWor 93*
Noack, Thomas Joseph *Law&B 92*
Noad, Charles E. *ScF&FL 92*
Noah *BioIn 17*
Noah, Hope E. 1943- *WhoWrEP 92*
Noah, Hope Ellen 1943- *WhoAmW 93*
Noah, Julia Jeanine 1932- *WhoAmW 93*
Noah, Mordecai Manuel 1785-1851 *BioIn 17, JeAmHC, JrnUS*
Noah, Yannick 1960- *ConBlB 4 [port]*
Noailles, comtesse de 1876-1933 *BioIn 17*
Noaio, Aron 1951- *WhoAsAP 91*
Noakes, David Ernest *WhoScE 91-1*
Noakes, G.R. 1906-1990 *BioIn 17*
Noakes, William S. *Law&B 92*
Noall, Nancy Ann 1957- *WhoAmW 93*
Noall, Roger 1935- *St&PR 93*
Noaman, Qais Ghanem 1942- *WhoUN 92*
Noar, Mark David 1953- *WhoE 93*
Noback, Charles Robert 1916- *WhoAm 92*
Noback, Richardson Kilbourne 1923- *WhoAm 92*
Nobbs, David 1935- *ConAu 138*
Nobbs, Robert Gerrard *Law&B 92*
Nobe, Ken 1925- *WhoAm 92*
Nobel, Alfred Bernhard 1833-1896 *BioIn 17*
Nobel, Felix de 1907-1981 *Baker 92*
Nobel, Fred I. 1917- *St&PR 93*
Nobel, Joel J. 1934- *WhoAm 92, WhoE 93*
Nobel, Peter 1931- *WhoWor 93*
Nobes, Christopher William *WhoScE 91-1*
Nobes, Patrick 1933- *ScF&FL 92*
Nobetsu, Takatoshi 1927- *WhoAsAP 91*
Nobil, James Howard 1930- *St&PR 93*
Nobil, James Howard, Jr. 1955- *WhoEmL 93, WhoWor 93*
Nobile, John Frank 1940- *WhoE 93*
Nobile, Umberto 1885-1978 *Expl 93 [port]*
Noble, Aaron *BioIn 17*
Noble, Amanda Stevens 1960- *WhoE 93*
Noble, Bernard 1928- *WhoUN 92*
Noble, Brien H. *Law&B 92*
Noble, Chelsea *BioIn 17*
Noble, Chester Lehner 1912- *St&PR 93, WhoAm 92*
Noble, Christopher 1966- *BioIn 17*
Noble, Craig 1945- *St&PR 93*
Noble, David J. 1931- *St&PR 93, WhoIns 93*
Noble, David Thomas *Law&B 92*
Noble, David Watson 1925- *WhoWrEP 92*
Noble, Deborah J. *Law&B 92*
Noble, Dee 1942- *WhoAmW 93*
Noble, Denis *WhoScE 91-1*
Noble, Dennis 1899-1966 *OxDcOp*
Noble, Ernest Pascal 1929- *WhoAm 92*
Noble, F. Pierce 1943- *St&PR 93*
Noble, James Kendrick, Jr. 1928- *WhoAm 92, WhoE 93, WhoWor 93*
Noble, James Wilkes 1922- *WhoAm 92*
Noble, John R. 1921- *St&PR 93*
Noble, John Robert 1953- *WhoEmL 93*
Noble, Joseph Veach 1920- *WhoAm 92*
Noble, Kate Woodward *AmWomPl*
Noble, Laura Jo 1964- *WhoAmW 93*
Noble, Marion Ellen 1914- *WhoAmW 93*
Noble, Mark *ScF&FL 92*
Noble, Martin 1947- *ScF&FL 92*
Noble, Mary Bailey 1939- *WhoSSW 93*
Noble, Merrill Emmett 1923- *WhoAm 92*
Noble, Michael Thomas *Law&B 92*
Noble, Michele *MiSFD 9*
Noble, Nicholas R. *WhoWrEP 92*
Noble, Nigel *MiSFD 9*
Noble, Ray(mond Stanley) 1903-1978 *Baker 92*
Noble, Raymond Clifford *WhoScE 91-1*
Noble, Regina Catherine 1963- *WhoAmW 93*
Noble, Richard Lloyd 1939- *WhoAm 92, WhoWor 93*
Noble, Richard William 1952- *St&PR 93*
Noble, Robert Cutler 1938- *WhoSSW 93*
Noble, Robert Henry 1937- *St&PR 93*
Noble, Robert Warren 1937- *WhoE 93*
Noble, Scott *BioIn 17*
Noble, Scott Alan 1951- *WhoAm 92*
Noble, Sherwood d1991 *BioIn 17*
Noble, Stuart H. 1941- *St&PR 93*
Noble, Stuart Harris 1941- *WhoAm 92*
Noble, Sunny A. 1940- *WhoAmW 93*
Noble, Sybille Scott *Law&B 92*
Noble, (Thomas) Tertius 1867-1953 *Baker 92*
Noble, Thomas Paul 1958- *WhoEmL 93*
Noble, Ward S. 1930- *St&PR 93*
Noble, William Charles *WhoScE 91-1*
Noble, William John *Law&B 92*
Noble, William P(arker) 1932- *ConAu 39NR*
Nobleman, Roberta *BioIn 17*
Nobles, Charles Norman 1929- *St&PR 93*
Nobles, John E. *St&PR 93*
Nobles, Laurence Hewit 1927- *WhoAm 92*
Nobles, Lewis 1925- *WhoAm 92, WhoSSW 93*
Nobles, Lorraine Biddle 1926- *WhoSSW 93*
Nobles, Marilyn Gayle 1949- *WhoAmW 93*
Nobles, Patricia J. *Law&B 92*
Nobles, Robert Eugene 1964- *WhoSSW 93*
Noblin, Charles Donald 1933- *WhoSSW 93*
Noblit, Betty Jean 1948- *WhoEmL 93, WhoWor 93*
Noblitt, Harding Coolidge 1920- *WhoAm 92, WhoWor 93*
Noblitt, James Paul 1934- *St&PR 93*
Noblitt, James Randall 1948- *WhoSSW 93*
Noblitt, John R. 1936- *St&PR 93*
Noblitt, Nancy Anne 1959- *WhoAmW 93*
Noblitt, Niles Leonard 1951- *St&PR 93*
Noboa-Stanton, Patricia Lynn 1947- *WhoAmW 93*
Nobre, Marlos 1939- *Baker 92, WhoWor 93*
Nobutoki, Kiyoshi 1887-1965 *Baker 92*
Noce, Robert Henry 1914- *WhoAm 92*
Noce, Walter William, Jr. 1945- *WhoAm 92*
Nocera, Bruce *St&PR 93*
Nocerino, Kathryn M. 1947- *WhoWrEP 92*
Nochimson, David 1943- *WhoAm 92*
Nochman, Lois Wood Kivi 1924- *WhoAmW 93*
Nochur, Kumar Subramaniam 1955- *WhoEmL 93*
Nocilla, Renato 1939- *WhoWor 93*
Nocilla, Silvio 1925- *WhoScE 91-3*
Nocita, Gerard Ralph 1936- *St&PR 93*
Nocito, Judith Lytle *Law&B 92*
Nock, Marie Stone 1943- *WhoAmW 93, WhoSSW 93*
Nock, Robert Wayne 1949- *WhoE 93*
Nocke, Henry Herman 1916- *WhoSSW 93*
Nocket, Michael Keith *Law&B 92*
Nocks, James Jay 1943- *WhoAm 92, WhoE 93*
Noda, Ken 1962- *Baker 92*
Noda, Koichiro Masahiro 1933- *WhoWor 93*
Noda, Masaki 1952- *WhoWor 93*
Noda, Minoru 1937- *WhoAsAP 91*
Noda, Takeshi 1941- *WhoAsAP 91*
Noda, Teruyuki 1940- *Baker 92*
Noda, Tetsu 1926- *WhoAsAP 91*
Noda, Yutaka 1937- *WhoWor 93*
Nodar, Jose Luis 1934- *St&PR 93*
Noddegaard, E. *WhoScE 91-2*
Noddin, Kevin L. 1955- *St&PR 93*
Noddings, Nel 1929- *WhoAmW 93*
Noddings, Sarah *Law&B 92*
Noddings, Thomas Clayton 1933- *WhoWor 93*
Nodelman, Jared Robert 1937- *St&PR 93, WhoWor 93*
Noden, Alexandra B. *Law&B 92*
Nodermann, Preben (Magnus Christian) 1867-1930 *Baker 92*
Nodier, (Jean) Charles (Emmanuel) 1780-1844 *DcLB 119 [port]*
Nodine, Thomas Hamilton 1961- *WhoEmL 93*
Nodine, William Edward 1929- *WhoAm 92*
Nodot, Claude 1950- *WhoScE 91-2*
Nodtvedt, Magnus 1924- *St&PR 93*
Noe, Alphonse R. *Law&B 92*
Noe, Dorothy Cole 1943- *ConEn*
Noe, Elnora 1928- *WhoAmW 93*
Noe, George T. *Law&B 92*
Noe, Guy 1934- *WhoAm 92*
Noe, Jerre Donald 1923- *WhoAm 92*
Noe, Margaret Murray-Scholz 1953- *WhoEmL 93*
Noe, Randolph 1939- *WhoSSW 93*
Noe, Roger Clark 1949- *WhoSSW 93*
Noe, Stephen Lynn *Law&B 92*
Noecker, Rebecca H. *Law&B 92, St&PR 93*
Noecker, Rebecca Hitchcock 1951- *WhoAm 92*
Noehren, Robert 1910- *Baker 92, WhoAm 92*
Noel, Andre M.V.Ch. 1927- *WhoScE 91-2*
Noel, Artis M. *Law&B 92*
Noel, Atanielle Annyn 1947- *ScF&FL 92*
Noel, Barbara Hughes McMurtry 1929- *WhoAmW 93*
Noel, Charmian Edlund 1949- *St&PR 93*
Noel, Earl F. 1912- *St&PR 93*
Noel, Earl F., Jr. 1946- *St&PR 93*
Noel, Emile 1922- *WhoWor 93*
Noel, James B. *Law&B 92*
Noel, James Sheridan 1930- *WhoSSW 93*
Noel, Jean Claude 1947- *St&PR 93*
Noel, Jeanne Kay 1946- *WhoEmL 93*
Noel, Jena M. *Law&B 92*
Noel, John Baptist Lucius 1890-1989 *BioIn 17*
Noel, John E. *Law&B 92*
Noel, Kenneth Duane 1932- *St&PR 93*
Noel, Laurent 1920- *WhoAm 92*
Noel, Leon 1888-1987 *BioIn 17*
Noel, Lloyd T., Jr. 1935- *WhoSSW 93*
Noel, Lou Boone 1953- *WhoSSW 93*
Noel, Michael Lee 1941- *St&PR 93*
Noel, Patrick 1935- *WhoScE 91-2*
Noel, Randall Deane 1953- *WhoAm 92, WhoSSW 93*
Noel, Robert E. 1931- *St&PR 93*
Noel, Rose *AmWomPl*
Noel, Ruth S. *ScF&FL 92*
Noel, Stephen D. 1953- *St&PR 93*
Noel, Sterling 1903-1984 *ScF&FL 92*
Noel, Sybil Florine 1934- *St&PR 93*
Noel, T. Howard 1938- *St&PR 93*
Noel, Tallulah Ann 1945- *WhoAmW 93*
Noel, Thomas E. 1930- *St&PR 93*
Noel, Vanessa *BioIn 17*
Noel, Virginia Steel 1957- *WhoSSW 93*
Noel-Baker, Philip John 1889-1982 *BioIn 17*
Noel Hume, Ivor 1927- *BioIn 17, WhoAm 92*
Noelke, Paul 1915- *WhoAm 92*
Noelker, Joseph Michael *Law&B 92*
Noell, Mary Elizabeth 1956- *WhoAmW 93*
Noell, Nick John 1946- *St&PR 93*
Noell, William A., Jr. *Law&B 92*
Noelle, Horst Carl 1924- *WhoWor 93*
Noels, Alfred F. 1940- *WhoScE 91-2*
Noelte, A. Albert 1885-1946 *Baker 92*
Noennig, Alan H. 1938- *St&PR 93*
Noer, Carol Ann 1955- *WhoEmL 93*
Noer, Richard J. 1937- *WhoAm 92*
Noesberger, Josef *WhoScE 91-4*
Noeske, Nancy R. 1937- *St&PR 93*
Noestlinger, Christine *ScF&FL 92*
Noestlinger, Christine 1936- *BioIn 17, ConAu 38NR, MajAI*
Noeth, Carolyn Frances 1924- *WhoAmW 93, WhoWor 93*
Noeth, Louise Ann 1954- *WhoEmL 93*
Noether, Emiliana Pasca *WhoAm 92*
Noether, Gottfried E. 1915-1991 *BioIn 17*

Noetzel, Grover Archibald Joseph 1908- WhoAm 92
Noever, Janet Hubly 1937- WhoSSW 93
Noever, Nancy Kay 1961- WhoEmL 93
Nofal, Mohamed Magd Eldin 1929- WhoUN 92
Nofal, Mohammad Nabil 1937- WhoUN 92
Nofer, George Hancock 1926- WhoAm 92
Noffs, David Sharrard 1957- WhoEmL 93
Nofi, Susan Polla Law&B 92
Nofsinger, William M. 1932- St&PR 93
Nofziger, Lyn 1924- JrnUS
Nofziger, Sally A. 1936- St&PR 93
Nofziger, Sally Alene WhoAm 92, WhoAmW 93
Noga, Joseph Peter 1941- St&PR 93
Noga, Marian 1939- WhoWor 93
Noga, Milan 1939- WhoScE 91-4
Nogaki, Ken Rodger 1940- WhoE 93
Nogal, Joseph P. 1955- St&PR 93
Nogales, Luis Guerrero 1943- WhoAm 92
Nogay d1299 OxDcByz
Nogee, Jeffrey Laurence 1952- WhoE 93, WhoWor 93
Nogelo, A. Miles 1943- St&PR 93
Nogelo, Anthony Miles 1943- WhoAm 92
Nogene, Endel Jaan 1950- WhoWor 93
Noggle, Dennis Allen 1936- WhoSSW 93
Noggle, Lawrence Wesley 1935- WhoWor 93
Noggle-Doncaster, Steve Law&B 92
Nogi, Maresuke 1843-1912 HarEnMi
Nogi, Tiaki 1937- WhoWor 93
Nogradi, Peter G. 1927- St&PR 93
Nograles, Prospero C., Jr. 1947- WhoAsAP 91
Noguchi, Hiroshi 1946- WhoWor 93
Noguchi, Isamu 1904-1988 BioIn 17
Noguchi, Satoshi Francisco X 1943- WhoWor 93
Noguchi, Seiichiro 1927- WhoWor 93
Noguchi, Shun 1930- WhoWor 93
Noguchi, Teruhisa 1924- WhoWor 93
Noguchi, Thomas Tsunetomi 1927- WhoAm 92
Nogueira, Joaquim Fernando 1950- WhoWor 93
Nogueira, Jose Luis 1944- WhoWor 93
Nogueira e Silva, Jose Afonso 1946- WhoWor 93
Noguera, Carlos 1943- SpAmA
Noguerol de Ulloa, Francisco 16th cent.- BioIn 17
Noguiera, Maria Elisa Law&B 92
Noha, Edward J. 1927- St&PR 93
Nohalty, John P. 1952- St&PR 93
Noh Hung Jun 1946- WhoAsAP 91
Nohl, Hans 1949- WhoScE 91-4
Nohl, Jeffrey Joseph 1951- St&PR 93
Nohl, (Karl Friedrich) Ludwig 1831-1885 Baker 92
Noh Noo Hwun 1947- WhoAsAP 91
Nohowel, Stephen Rehm 1949- WhoEmL 93
Nohren, Joseph H. 1959- St&PR 93
Nohrnberg, James Carson 1941- WhoSSW 93
Noia, Alan James 1947- St&PR 93, WhoAm 92
Noid, Donald William 1949- WhoSSW 93
Noikov, Peter 1868-1921 BioIn 17
Noir, Michel 1944- BioIn 17
Noir, Stephard ScF&FL 92
Noiret, Philippe 1930- IntDcF 2-3 [port]
Nojd, Lars-Ake WhoScE 91-4
Nojek, Carlos Alberto 1948- WhoWor 93
Nokes, John Richard 1915- WhoAm 92
Nokes, Mary Triplett 1920- WhoSSW 93
Nola, Giovanni Domenico del Giovane da c. 1515-1592 Baker 92
Nolan, Agnes Peters 1908- WhoWrEP 92
Nolan, Alan Tucker 1923- WhoAm 92
Nolan, Arthur E. 1919- WhoIns 93
Nolan, B. 1911-1966 BioIn 17
Nolan, Barry Hance 1942- WhoAm 92
Nolan, Betty 1916- WhoAmW 93
Nolan, Betty Allen 1952- WhoSSW 93
Nolan, Christopher Aloysius, III 1950- WhoEmL 93
Nolan, Daniel Paul 1952- WhoEmL 93
Nolan, David Brian 1951- WhoEmL 93
Nolan, Denise Susan 1952- WhoEmL 93
Nolan, Dennis C. Law&B 92, St&PR 93
Nolan, Dennis M. St&PR 93
Nolan, Diane Agnes 1939- WhoAm 92
Nolan, Diane Sharp 1949- WhoAmW 93
Nolan, Elizabeth Joan 1946- WhoAmW 93
Nolan, Florence D. Law&B 92
Nolan, Florence Dorothy 1955- St&PR 93
Nolan, Francis Xavier, III 1949- WhoEmL 93
Nolan, Gerald 1947- WhoEmL 93, WhoSSW 93
Nolan, Howard Charles, Jr. 1932- WhoE 93
Nolan, James Francis, Jr. 1950- WhoEmL 93
Nolan, James Robert 1935- St&PR 93
Nolan, Jeanette 1911- SweetSg D
Nolan, Jenelle W. Law&B 92
Nolan, Joan S. 1930- St&PR 93
Nolan, John Blanchard 1943- WhoAm 92
Nolan, John D. 1946- WhoIns 93
Nolan, John Dean 1957- WhoSSW 93
Nolan, John E. Law&B 92
Nolan, John Edward 1925- WhoAm 92
Nolan, John Edward 1927- WhoAm 92
Nolan, John Francis 1940- St&PR 93
Nolan, John Mathias Law&B 92
Nolan, John Michael 1948- WhoEmL 93
Nolan, John Patrick 1954- WhoEmL 93
Nolan, John Thomas, Jr. 1930- WhoE 93
Nolan, Joseph Thomas 1920- WhoAm 92
Nolan, Karen Lynn 1963- WhoE 93
Nolan, Kathleen 1933- WhoAm 92
Nolan, Kevin Barry 1952- St&PR 93
Nolan, Lewis Earle 1943- WhoSSW 93
Nolan, Linda Caroline 1958- WhoAmW 93
Nolan, Louise Mary 1947- WhoAmW 93, WhoE 93, WhoEmL 93, WhoWor 93
Nolan, Madeena Spray 1943- ScF&FL 92
Nolan, Mae Ella Hunt 1886-1973 BioIn 17
Nolan, Marci Ann 1951- WhoAmW 93
Nolan, Michael Mary BioIn 17
Nolan, Michael William 1948- WhoEmL 93
Nolan, Miriam 1955- St&PR 93
Nolan, Patrick Joseph 1933- WhoAm 92
Nolan, Patrick Joseph 1938- St&PR 93
Nolan, Paul Thomas 1919- WhoAm 92, WhoWrEP 92
Nolan, Peter F. Law&B 92
Nolan, Peter F. 1943- St&PR 93
Nolan, Philip Frederick WhoScE 91-1
Nolan, Ralph H. 1912- St&PR 93
Nolan, Rathel Linwood 1956- WhoSSW 93
Nolan, Richard B. 1921-1991 BioIn 17
Nolan, Richard Edward 1928- WhoAm 92
Nolan, Richard Thomas 1937- WhoE 93, WhoWor 93
Nolan, Robert C. Law&B 92
Nolan, Robert Dan 1938- WhoSSW 93
Nolan, Robert F. 1927- St&PR 93
Nolan, Robert J. 1927- St&PR 93
Nolan, Robert W. 1943- St&PR 93
Nolan, Sandra M. Law&B 92
Nolan, Sarah M. BioIn 17
Nolan, Sidney 1917-1992 NewYTBS 92 [port]
Nolan, Stanton Peelle 1933- WhoAm 92, WhoWor 93
Nolan, Terence WhoScE 91-1
Nolan, Terence Magie 1941- WhoAm 92
Nolan, Terrance Joseph, Jr. 1950- WhoAm 92
Nolan, Thomas B. d1992 NewYTBS 92
Nolan, Thomas J. 1954- St&PR 93
Nolan, Thomas Patrick 1933- St&PR 93
Nolan, Val, Jr. 1920- WhoAm 92
Nolan, Victoria Holmes 1952- WhoAmW 93
Nolan, Walter Joseph 1924- St&PR 93
Nolan, William F. 1928- ConAu 16AS [port], ScF&FL 92
Nolan, William J., III St&PR 93
Nolan, William Joseph, III 1947- WhoAm 92
Noland, Anngiinette Roberts 1930- WhoAmW 93, WhoSSW 93
Noland, Cara Holly 1958- WhoAmW 93
Noland, Charles Eugene 1930- WhoWrEP 92
Noland, Donald F. Law&B 92
Noland, James E. 1920-1992 NewYTBS 92
Noland, James Ellsworth 1920- WhoAm 92
Noland, John W. 1949- St&PR 93
Noland, Jon D. Law&B 92
Noland, Jon David 1938- St&PR 93
Noland, Kenneth 1924- BioIn 17
Noland, Kenneth Clifton 1924- WhoAm 92
Noland, Lloyd U., Jr. 1917- St&PR 93
Noland, Lloyd U., III 1943- St&PR 93
Noland, Mariam Charl 1947- WhoAmW 93, WhoEmL 93
Noland, Robert Edgar 1930- WhoSSW 93
Noland, Robert LeRoy 1918- WhoAm 92
Noland, Royce Paul 1928- WhoAm 92
Noland, Thomas Turley 1918- St&PR 93
Noland, Thomas Turley, Jr. 1953- WhoEmL 93, WhoSSW 93
Nolane, Richard D. ScF&FL 92
Nolasco, Margarita 1948- WhoAmW 93
Nolasco, Ruben Rene/Encarnacion 1955- WhoWor 93
Nold, Carl Richard 1955- WhoAm 92
Nold, John 1951- WhoCanL 92
Nold, Michael F. 1938- St&PR 93
Nolde, Emil 1867-1956 BioIn 17
Nolde, Virgil George, Jr. Law&B 92
Nolder, Ann ScF&FL 92
Nolder, Sharlene Jan 1949- WhoAmW 93
Noldus, Erik J.L. 1940- WhoScE 91-2
Nole, Robert James 1933- St&PR 93
Nolen, Catherine Wilson AmWomPl
Nolen, Jerry Aften, Jr. 1940- WhoAm 92
Nolen, Samuel Augustus 1954- WhoEmL 93
Nolen, William A. 1928-1986 BioIn 17
Nolen, William Giles 1931- WhoAm 92
Nolen, William Lawrence, Jr. 1922- WhoSSW 93
Noles, Jackie Lewis 1938- WhoSSW 93
Noles, Martha Jean 1946- WhoSSW 93
Noles, Tammy Gaye 1965- WhoAmW 93
Nolf, David Manstan 1942- St&PR 93, WhoAm 92
Nolfe, Dana Jill Alexander 1964- WhoEmL 93
Nolfi, Frank Vincent, Jr. 1941- WhoAm 92
Nolin, Christine Lea 1952- WhoE 93
Nolin, Lillian Renee 1923- WhoWrEP 92
Noling, Lawrence J. 1930- St&PR 93
Noll, Andrew F., III 1930- St&PR 93
Noll, Anna Cecilia 1950- WhoAm 92
Noll, Charles Gordon 1948- WhoE 93
Noll, Charles Henry 1931- WhoAm 92
Noll, Cheryl Kirk 1950- WhoE 93
Noll, Chris Alan 1952- St&PR 93
Noll, Clair W. 1933- St&PR 93
Noll, Dorothy Lee 1936- WhoAmW 93
Noll, Francis Charles, Jr. 1952- WhoE 93
Noll, Irwin 1938- St&PR 93
Noll, Jonathan Boyd 1944- WhoAm 92
Noll, Kenneth Eugene 1936- WhoAm 92
Noll, Mark A. 1946- BioIn 17
Noll, Mark A(llan) 1946- ConAu 38NR
Noll, Mary Lou 1954- WhoAmW 93, WhoEmL 93
Noll, Michael William 1944- WhoE 93
Noll, Phyllis I. St&PR 93
Noll, Phyllis Jean 1947- WhoAmW 93
Noll, Rhona Susan 1947- WhoEmL 93
Noll, Roger Gordon 1940- WhoAm 92
Noll, S. Darwin 1920- St&PR 93
Noll, Warren Philip 1938- St&PR 93
Nollau, Lee Gordon 1950- WhoE 93, WhoEmL 93, WhoWor 93
Nollen, Margaret Roach 1963- WhoAmW 93
Nollen, Scott Allen ScF&FL 92
Nollen, Stanley Dale 1940- WhoE 93
Noller, Barry Neil 1946- WhoWor 93
Noller, Harry Francis, Jr. 1939- WhoAm 92
Noller, Ruth Brendel 1922- WhoAmW 93
Nollet, A.J.H. WhoScE 91-3
Nollet, Jerome Patrick 1960- WhoWor 93
Nollet, Lois Sophia 1921- WhoWrEP 92
Nollette, Dennis Robert Law&B 92
Nolley, J. Robert, Jr. 1929- WhoIns 93
Nollsch, William E. 1941- St&PR 93
Nolt, Joseph P. 1936- St&PR 93
Nolte, Anne BioIn 17
Nolte, Charles Winfield 1945- WhoWrEP 92
Nolte, Ewald V(alentin) 1909- Baker 92
Nolte, Harold Eugene, Jr. 1954- WhoSSW 93
Nolte, Henry R., Jr. 1924- WhoAm 92
Nolte, John Michael 1941- WhoWor 93
Nolte, Judith Ann 1938- WhoAm 92
Nolte, Katy BioIn 17
Nolte, Melvin, Jr. 1947- WhoEmL 93
Nolte, Nick BioIn 17
Nolte, Nick 1941- IntDcF 2-3, News 92 [port]
Nolte, Nick 1942- WhoAm 92
Nolte, Richard Henry 1920- WhoAm 92
Nolte, Ronald A. Law&B 92
Nolte, Walter Eduard 1911- WhoAm 92
Nolte, William Henry 1928- WhoAm 92
Nolte, Wolfram 1949- WhoWor 93
Noltes, Jan G. 1931- WhoScE 91-3
Noltie, David Mayo 1924- WhoE 93
Nolting, Paul 1939- St&PR 93
Nolting, Paul Edmund Law&B 92
Nolting, Ronald William 1937- WhoIns 93
Nolting-Morrissey, Caroline G. Law&B 92
Nome, William Andreas 1951- WhoEmL 93
Nomeland, Leslie C. 1936- St&PR 93
Nomellini, Leo 1924- BioIn 17
Nomen, Rosa 1956- WhoScE 91-3
Nomine, Gerard 1924- WhoScE 91-2
Nomine, Michel 1942- WhoScE 91-2
Nommensen, David 1957- St&PR 93
Nomoto, Otohiko 1912- WhoWor 93
Nomura, Itsuo 1941- WhoAsAP 91
Nomura, Masakatsu 1940- WhoWor 93
Nomura, Masayasu 1927- WhoAm 92
Nomura, Shunji 1940- WhoWor 93
Nomura, Tetsuzo St&PR 93
Nonaka, Hiromu WhoAsAP 91
Nonas, Constantine James 1934- WhoSSW 93
Nones Sucre, Carlos Enrique 1936- WhoUN 92
Nonet, Philippe 1939- WhoAm 92
Nong 1930- WhoAm 92
Noni, Alda 1916- Baker 92, OxDcOp
Nonn, James C. 1953- St&PR 93
Nonnon, Patricia BioIn 17
Nonnos, Theophanes OxDcByz
Nonnos of Panopolis fl. 5th cent.- OxDcByz
Nonnosos fl. 6th cent.- OxDcByz
Nono, Luigi BioIn 17
Nono, Luigi 1924-1990 Baker 92, IntDcOp, OxDcOp
Noodt, Wolfram 1927- WhoScE 91-3
Nooij, Michiel T. Law&B 92
Noon, David 1946- WhoEmL 93
Noon, David Warren 1956- St&PR 93
Noon, Dennis James 1947- St&PR 93
Noon, James H., Jr. 1946- St&PR 93
Noon, Patrick 1951- WhoAm 92
Noon, Walter D. 1930- St&PR 93
Noonan, Alison 1962- WhoAmW 93
Noonan, Daniel John Law&B 92
Noonan, Deborah Smith 1950- WhoSSW 93
Noonan, Frank R. 1942- WhoAm 92
Noonan, Jacqueline Anne 1928- WhoAmW 93
Noonan, James Rothwell 1931- WhoSSW 93
Noonan, John Michael 1933- St&PR 93
Noonan, John T., Jr. 1926- WhoAm 92
Noonan, Mary M. 1950- WhoIns 93
Noonan, Melinda Dunham 1954- WhoAmW 93
Noonan, Michael Dennis 1941- St&PR 93, WhoE 93
Noonan, Norine Elizabeth 1948- WhoAm 92, WhoAmW 93, WhoE 93
Noonan, Patrick Francis 1942- WhoAm 92
Noonan, Peggy BioIn 17
Noonan, Ray John 1914- WhoAm 92
Noonan, Ronald P. 1931- St&PR 93
Noonan, Thomas F. 1939- St&PR 93
Noonan, Thomas Schaub 1938- WhoAm 92
Noonan, William Donald 1955- WhoEmL 93
Noonan, William Francis 1932- WhoAm 92, WhoE 93
Noonan, William Moss 1942- WhoAm 92
Noonberg, Lewis Allan 1938- WhoAm 92
Noonburg, Joseph Nellis 1935- St&PR 93
Noone, Brian W. 1948- WhoE 93
Noone, David George 1953- St&PR 93
Noone, Edwina ConAu 39NR
Noone, Frank W. 1945- WhoIns 93
Noone, Jimmy 1895-1944 Baker 92
Noone, John T. Law&B 92
Noone, Joseph M. Law&B 92
Noone, Kathleen BioIn 17
Noone, Lana Mae 1946- WhoEmL 93
Noone, Robert Barrett 1939- WhoE 93, WhoWor 93
Noone, Thomas Mark 1927- WhoE 93
Noone, William Francis 1948- St&PR 93
Nooney, John J. 1929- St&PR 93
Nooney, John J. 1939- St&PR 93
Noonkester, James Ralph 1924- WhoAm 92
Noor, Ahmed Khairy 1938- WhoAm 92
Noor, Faiz A. WhoScE 91-1
Noor Ahmad Noor, Comrade 1937- WhoAsAP 91
Noor al-Hussein BioIn 17
Noorda, Raymond J. WhoAm 92
Noorda, Raymond J. 1924- St&PR 93
Noordeen, Shaik Khader 1933- WhoUN 92
Noordergraaf, Abraham 1929- WhoAm 92, WhoE 93
Noordzij, Leendert 1942- WhoScE 91-3
Noordzy, Karel Jacques 1946- WhoWor 93
Noorigian, Antonetta Letizia Law&B 92
Nooruddins, Veerjee S. 1958- St&PR 93
Noot, Donald Scott 1933- St&PR 93
Nootbaar, H.V. 1908- St&PR 93
Nooteboom, Adriaan 1928- WhoWor 93
Nooteboom, Cees 1933- ScF&FL 92
Nopar, Alan Scott 1951- WhoEmL 93
Noppenberger, Louis John 1963- WhoE 93
Nor, Mohamad Yusof 1941- WhoAsAP 91
Nora, Hope 1949- WhoEmL 93
Nora, James Jackson 1928- WhoAm 92
Nora, Mark Joseph Law&B 92
Nora, Wendy Alison 1951- WhoEmL 93
Norair, Jill S. 1956- St&PR 93
Norair, Richard H. 1929- St&PR 93
Norako, Vincent Walter, Sr. 1921- WhoSSW 93
Noramly, Bin Muslim 1941- WhoUN 92
Noran, Paul F. 1943- St&PR 93
Norback, Craig Thomas 1943- WhoAm 92, WhoE 93, WhoWor 93
Norbanus, Gaius dc. 82BC HarEnMi
Norbeck, Edward 1915- WhoWrEP 92
Norbeck, Timothy Burns 1938- WhoE 93

Norberg, Charles Robert 1912- *WhoAm 92, WhoWor 93*
Norberg, Hans S. *WhoScE 91-4*
Norberg, Per 1940- *WhoScE 91-4*
Norberg, Per Arild 1918- *WhoWor 93*
Norberg-Schulz, Christian 1926- *WhoScE 91-4*
Norbitz, Harold 1921- *St&PR 93*
Norbitz, Wayne *St&PR 93*
Norblin, Jean Pierre 1745-1830 *PolBiDi*
Norbury, Donna Lou 1963- *WhoAmW 93*
Norby, Barbara H. 1936- *St&PR 93*
Norby, Christopher 1949- *WhoAm 92*
Norby, Erik 1936- *Baker 92*
Norby, John K. 1931- *St&PR 93*
Norby, Rockford Douglas *WhoAm 92*
Norby, William Charles 1915- *WhoAm 92*
Norcel, Jacqueline Joyce Casale 1940- *WhoAmW 93*
Norcia, Stephen W. 1941- *St&PR 93*
Norcia, Stephen William 1941- *WhoAm 92*
Norcini, John J., Jr. 1952- *WhoE 93*
Norcini, Joyce M. *Law&B 92*
Norcross, David Frank Armstrong 1937- *WhoAm 92*
Norcross, John Conner 1957- *WhoE 93*
Norcross, Marvin Augustus 1931- *WhoAm 92*
Nord, Charles 1946- *WhoSSW 93*
Nord, Daniel A. 1953- *St&PR 93*
Nord, Eric T. 1917- *St&PR 93*
Nord, Eric Thomas 1917- *WhoAm 92*
Nord, Evan Walter 1919- *St&PR 93*
Nord, Henry J. 1917- *WhoAm 92*
Nord, Lasse *WhoScE 91-4*
Nord, Martha Andrews 1942- *WhoAmW 93*
Nord, Paul Elliott 1936- *WhoAm 92*
Nord, Roger Hans 1959- *WhoUN 92*
Nord, Thomas C. *Law&B 92*
Nord, Thomas C. 1940- *St&PR 93*
Nord, Walter Robert 1939- *WhoAm 92*
Nordahl, Norris George 1918- *WhoWor 93*
Nordal, Johannes 1924- *WhoWor 93*
Nordal, Jon 1926- *Baker 92*
Nordan, Lewis 1939- *ConAu 40NR*
Nordan, Lewis Alonzo 1939- *WhoWrEP 92*
Nordan, Robert *ScF&FL 92*
Nordberg, Gunnar F. 1941- *WhoScE 91-4*
Nordberg, Hans F. 1939- *WhoScE 91-4*
Nordberg, John Albert 1926- *WhoAm 92*
Nordberg, Rauli Matti Juhana 1949- *WhoWor 93*
Nordberg, Richard B. *St&PR 93*
Nordberg, Sten D. 1932- *WhoScE 91-4*
Nordbring, Folke E.S. 1921- *WhoScE 91-4*
Nordby, Alf Thorvald 1920- *WhoScE 91-4*
Nordby, Eugene Jorgen 1918- *WhoAm 92, WhoWor 93*
Nordby, Gene Milo 1926- *WhoAm 92*
Nordby, Roger A. 1945- *St&PR 93*
Nordbye, Richard Arthur 1919- *WhoAm 92*
Nordbye, Rodger Lincoln 1918- *WhoAm 92*
Norddahl, Birgir Valson 1947- *WhoEmL 93*
Nordell, Hans Roderick 1925- *WhoAm 92*
Norden, Bengt J.F. 1945- *WhoScE 91-4*
Norden, Charles *ConAu 40NR*
Norden, Eric *ScF&FL 92*
Norden, Ernest Elwood 1938- *WhoSSW 93*
Norden, F.A. 1930- *St&PR 93*
Norden, Harry V. 1933- *WhoScE 91-4*
Norden, Janet Burke 1940- *WhoSSW 93*
Norden, K. Elis 1921- *WhoWor 93*
Norden, Martin Frank 1951- *WhoWrEP 92*
Norden, Peter Christopher 1949- *WhoE 93*
Norden, Roger Craig 1950- *St&PR 93*
Nordenberg, Mark Alan 1948- *WhoAm 92, WhoE 93*
Nordenfelt, Johan 1939- *WhoUN 92*
Nordenshield, Jeanette *AmWomPl*
Nordenskiold, Erland 1877-1932 *IntDcAn*
Nordenskiold, Gustaf 1868-1895 *IntDcAn*
Nordenskjold, (Nils) Adolf Erik 1832-1901 *Expl 93 [port]*
Nordenskjold, Bo Axel 1940- *WhoScE 91-4*
Nordenson, Guy Jerome Pierre 1955- *WhoE 93*
Nordenstrom, Bjorn E.W. 1920- *WhoScE 91-4*
Nordenstrom, Hans J.N. 1927- *WhoScE 91-4*
Nordestgaard, Anton 1923- *WhoScE 91-2*
Nordet, Porfirio 1942- *WhoUN 92*
Nordgren, Pehr Henrik 1944- *Baker 92*
Nordgren, Peter David 1952- *WhoEmL 93*
Nordgren, Ronald Paul 1936- *WhoAm 92, WhoSSW 93*
Nordgren, Stanford Robert 1928- *St&PR 93*
Nordhagen, Hallie Huerth 1914- *WhoAmW 93*
Nordhagen, Rannveig 1933- *WhoScE 91-4*
Nordhaus, Jean 1939- *WhoWrEP 92*
Nordhaus, John P. 1920- *St&PR 93*
Nordhaus, William Dawbney 1941- *WhoAm 92*
Nordheim, Alfred Ernst 1951- *WhoWor 93*
Nordheim, Arne 1931- *Baker 92*
Nordheimer, Isaac 1809-1842 *BioIn 17*
Nordhoff, Charles 1830-1901 *JrnUS*
Nordhoff, Lynne Clark 1947- *WhoEmL 93*
Nordhougen, Curtis A. *Law&B 92*
Nordica, Lillian 1857-1914 *Baker 92, IntDcOp [port], OxDcOp*
Nordin, Bertil Donald 1934- *St&PR 93*
Nordin, Egil 1933- *WhoScE 91-4*
Nordin, Larry F. 1950- *St&PR 93*
Nordin, Phyllis Eck *WhoAmW 93*
Nordin, Vidar John 1924- *WhoAm 92*
Nordin Selat, Dr. *WhoAsAP 91*
Nordland, Gerald John *WhoAm 92*
Nordlie, Robert Conrad 1930- *WhoAm 92*
Nordling, Bernard Erick 1921- *WhoAm 92, WhoWor 93*
Nordling, Carl 1931- *WhoScE 91-4*
Nordling, Carl Leif Arne 1931- *WhoScE 91-4*
Nordlinger, Eric Allen 1939- *WhoAm 92*
Nordlinger, Richard E. 1919- *St&PR 93*
Nordloh, David J(oseph) 1942- *ConAu 137*
Nordlund, Donald Craig *Law&B 92*
Nordlund, Donald Craig 1949- *WhoAm 92*
Nordlund, Donald Elmer 1922- *WhoAm 92*
Nordlund, James John 1939- *WhoAm 92*
Nordlund, Sarah J. *Law&B 92*
Nordlund, William *Law&B 92*
Nordlund, William Chalmers 1954- *WhoAm 92, WhoEmL 93*
Nordly, Carl 1901-1990 *BioIn 17*
Nordman, Christer Eric 1925- *WhoAm 92*
Nordman, Eeva Mirjami 1931- *WhoScE 91-4*
Nordman, Lars S. 1919- *WhoScE 91-4*
Nordman, Richard D. 1946- *St&PR 93, WhoAm 92*
Nordmann, Joseph 1922- *WhoScE 91-2*
Nordmann, Roger 1926- *WhoScE 91-2*
Nordmeyer, George 1912-1990 *BioIn 17*
Nordmeyer, Mary Betsy 1939- *WhoAmW 93*
Nordoff, Paul 1909-1977 *Baker 92*
Nordquist, Myron Harry 1940- *WhoE 93*
Nordquist, Stephen Glos 1936- *WhoE 93*
Nordqvist, (Johan) Conrad 1840-1920 *Baker 92*
Nordqvist, Erik Askbo 1943- *WhoWor 93*
Nordraak, Rikard 1842-1866 *Baker 92*
Nordsieck, Graham *ScF&FL 92*
Nordsieck, Karen Ann 1955- *WhoAmW 93*
Nordsjo, Claes Torbjorn 1945- *WhoUN 92*
Nordskog, Bob *BioIn 17*
Nordskog, Robert d1992 *NewYTBS 92*
Nordstoga, Knut 1927- *WhoScE 91-4*
Nordstrand, Dennis L. 1935- *St&PR 93*
Nordstrand, Raymond William 1932- *WhoAm 92*
Nordstrom, Anders Jan-Olof 1941- *WhoWor 93*
Nordstrom, Bruce A. 1933- *St&PR 93, WhoAm 92*
Nordstrom, Frances 188-?- *AmWomPl*
Nordstrom, Harold 1946- *St&PR 93*
Nordstrom, James F. 1940- *WhoAm 92*
Nordstrom, Janis Lynn 1952- *WhoEmL 93*
Nordstrom, John N. 1937- *WhoAm 92*
Nordstrom, John W. 1937- *St&PR 93*
Nordstrom, Kurt 1935- *WhoScE 91-4, WhoWor 93*
Nordstrom, Mark *Law&B 92*
Nordstrom, Olle 1935- *WhoWor 93*
Nordstrom, Ursula (Litchfield) *DcAmChF 1960*
Nordstrom, Wilber C. 1918- *St&PR 93*
Nordt, Lawrence H. 1947- *St&PR 93*
Nordt, Paul W., Jr. 1914- *St&PR 93*
Nordt, Paul W., 3rd 1941- *St&PR 93*
Nordtvedt, Matilda *BioIn 17*
Nordyke, Eleanor Cole 1927- *WhoAmW 93, WhoWor 93*
Nordyke, James Walter 1930- *WhoAm 92*
Nordyke, Robert *BioIn 17*
Noreika, Joseph Casimir 1950- *WhoEmL 93*
Noreika, Sofia 1945- *WhoE 93, WhoWor 93*
Norek, Bernard Jean Marie 1938- *WhoWor 93*
Norek, Frances Therese 1947- *WhoAmW 93*
Norelli, Nancy Black 1949- *WhoEmL 93*
Norem, Richard Frederick, Sr. 1931- *WhoAm 92*
Noren, Andrew *BioIn 17*
Noren, Heinrich 1861-1928 *Baker 92*
Noren, Paul Harold Andreas 1910- *WhoWor 93*
Noren, Rees E. 1932- *St&PR 93*
Noren, Vern Michael 1948- *WhoEmL 93, WhoSSW 93*
Norena, Eide 1884-1968 *Baker 92, OxDcOp*
Norenberg, Wolfgang 1938- *WhoScE 91-3*
Norfleet, Bruce Gerard 1959- *WhoE 93*
Norfleet, George S., III 1947- *St&PR 93*
Norfleet, Robert F., Jr. 1940- *WhoAm 92*
Norfleet, Robert Fillmore 1940- *St&PR 93*
Norfolk, William Ray 1941- *WhoAm 92*
Norgaard, Lowell James 1936- *St&PR 93*
Norgard, John A. *Law&B 92*
Norgard, Per 1932- *Baker 92, OxDcOp*
Norgay, Tenzing 1914-1986 *BioIn 17*
Norgren, C. Neil 1923- *WhoAm 92*
Norhammar, S. Ulf 1937- *WhoScE 91-4*
Norholm, Axel 1932- *WhoScE 91-2*
Norholm, Ib 1931- *Baker 92, OxDcOp*
Nori, Andrew 1953- *WhoAsAP 91*
Nori, Franco Mauro 1959- *WhoWor 93*
Nori, Giuseppe 1958- *WhoWor 93*
Norian, Roger W. 1943- *St&PR 93*
Norick, Ronald 1941- *WhoAm 92, WhoSSW 93*
Noriega, Lamar Jernigan 1943- *WhoSSW 93*
Noriega, Manuel *HispAmA*
Noriega, Manuel Antonio *BioIn 17*
Noriega, Rudy Jorge 1937- *WhoSSW 93*
Noriega Hope, Carlos 1896-1934 *DcMexL*
Noriega Morena, Manuel Antonio 1938- *DcCPCAm*
Noriega Moreno, Manuel Antonio 1936- *ColdWar 2 [port]*
Noriel, Carmelo Cuevas 1939- *WhoUN 92*
Norikumo, Shunyu 1948- *WhoWor 93*
Norin, Allen J. 1944- *WhoE 93*
Norin, C. Torbjorn 1933- *WhoScE 91-4*
Norinelli, Armando 1919- *WhoScE 91-3*
Norins, Arthur Leonard 1928- *WhoAm 92*
Norio, Niikawa 1942- *WhoWor 93*
Norkin, Cynthia Clair 1932- *WhoAmW 93, WhoWor 93*
Norkin, Mark Mitchell 1955- *WhoEmL 93*
Norko, Michael Albert 1957- *WhoE 93, WhoEmL 93*
Norkunas, John Joseph 1947- *WhoEmL 93*
Norland, Cheryl M. 1950- *WhoEmL 93*
Norland, Cynthia J. *Law&B 92*
Norland, Donald Richard 1924- *WhoAm 92*
Norlander, John *BioIn 17*
Norlander, John A. 1930- *St&PR 93*
Norlander, John Allen 1930- *WhoAm 92*
Norlander, Lyle E. 1937- *St&PR 93*
Norlin, Eric C. 1940- *St&PR 93*
Norlind, (Johan Henrik) Tobias 1879-1947 *Baker 92*
Norling, Dennis *Law&B 92*
Norling, Erik E. 1931- *WhoScE 91-4*
Norlist *WhoAmW 93, WhoE 93, WhoWor 93*
Norman, Albert George, Jr. 1929- *WhoAm 92, WhoSSW 93, WhoWor 93*
Norman, Anthony Westcott 1938- *WhoAm 92*
Norman, Barry 1933- *ScF&FL 92*
Norman, Bo G. 1938- *WhoScE 91-4*
Norman, Charles 1904- *BioIn 17*
Norman, Colin Arthur 1948- *WhoAm 92, WhoEmL 93*
Norman, Cornelia Catherine *Law&B 92*
Norman, David A. 1935- *St&PR 93*
Norman, David Mark 1941- *WhoAm 92*
Norman, David Taylor 1947- *WhoEmL 93, WhoSSW 93*
Norman, Deborah L. *Law&B 92*
Norman, Diana *ScF&FL 92*
Norman, Donald Arthur 1935- *WhoAm 92*
Norman, Donald N. *ScF&FL 92*
Norman, Douglas K. *Law&B 92*
Norman, Dudley Kent 1949- *WhoAm 92*
Norman, Elizabeth 1924- *ScF&FL 92*
Norman, Frederick C. 1909- *St&PR 93*
Norman, Geoffrey R. 1944- *St&PR 93*
Norman, Geoffrey Robert 1944- *WhoAm 92*
Norman, George *WhoScE 91-1*
Norman, George, Mrs. *AmWomPl*
Norman, George Buford, Jr. 1945- *WhoAm 92, WhoSSW 93*
Norman, George C. 1943- *St&PR 93*
Norman, Gerald L. d1990 *BioIn 17*
Norman, Greg 1955- *BioIn 17, WhoAm 92*
Norman, Howard *ConAu 137*
Norman, Howard A. 1949- *ConAu 137*
Norman, J. Gregg *Law&B 92*
Norman, Jackie Delois 1941- *WhoWrEP 92*
Norman, James Addems *Law&B 92*
Norman, James Addems 1946- *WhoEmL 93*
Norman, Jennie Morris 1960- *WhoAmW 93*
Norman, Jessye 1945- *Baker 92, IntDcOp, OxDcOp, WhoAm 92, WhoAmW 93, WhoWor 93*
Norman, Joe G., Jr. 1947- *WhoAm 92*
Norman, John 1931- *ScF&FL 92*
Norman, John Barstow, Jr. 1940- *WhoAm 92*
Norman, John Malcolm *WhoScE 91-1*
Norman, John Nelson *WhoScE 91-1*
Norman, Justo Federico 1944- *WhoWor 93*
Norman, Kathryn Kite 1945- *WhoSSW 93*
Norman, L. Bruce *Law&B 92*
Norman, LaLander Stadig 1912- *WhoAm 92*
Norman, Lilith 1927- *DcChlFi*
Norman, Ludvig 1831-1885 *Baker 92*
Norman, Marsha *BioIn 17*
Norman, Marsha 1947- *ConTFT 10, ScF&FL 92, WhoAm 92, WhoAmW 93, WhoE 93*
Norman, Mary Marshall 1937- *WhoAmW 93*
Norman, Michael *BioIn 17*
Norman, Michael 1947- *WhoWrEP 92*
Norman, Nicolai 1919- *WhoScE 91-4*
Norman, Norma Allen 1934- *WhoSSW 93*
Norman, Norman B. 1914-1991 *BioIn 17*
Norman, Paralee Frances 1932- *WhoSSW 93*
Norman, Philip Sidney 1924- *WhoAm 92*
Norman, Ralph David 1915- *WhoAm 92*
Norman, Ralph Louis 1933- *WhoAm 92*
Norman, Reeve E. 1931- *St&PR 93*
Norman, Richard Arthur 1915- *WhoAm 92*
Norman, Rick (J.) 1954- *ConAu 137*
Norman, Roger *ScF&FL 92*
Norman, Ron 1953- *MiSFD 9*
Norman, Ronald Michael 1952- *WhoEmL 93*
Norman, Russell Lee 1947- *WhoWrEP 92*
Norman, Sharon Anne 1939- *WhoAmW 93*
Norman, Stephen Craig 1961- *WhoEmL 93*
Norman, Stephen Peckham 1942- *WhoAm 92*
Norman, Susan N. *Law&B 92*
Norman, Teoman Nuriddin 1934- *WhoScE 91-4*
Norman, Thomas J. *Law&B 92*
Norman, Torquil *BioIn 17*
Norman, William E. 1914- *St&PR 93*
Norman, William Stanley 1938- *St&PR 93, WhoAm 92*
Norman, Zack *MiSFD 9*
Normand, Jacques Marie 1936- *WhoWor 93*
Normand, Mabel 1892-1930 *IntDcF 2-3 [port], QDrFCA 92 [port]*
Normand, Robert 1940- *St&PR 93, WhoAm 92*
Normandeau, Andre Gabriel 1942- *WhoAm 92*
Normandin, Mary Anne 1928- *WhoWor 93*
Normandin, Robert A. 1945- *St&PR 93*
Normann, Louise *AmWomPl*
Normano, Bertha A. d1991 *BioIn 17*
Normant, Jean F. 1936- *WhoWor 93*
Normark, Staffan 1945- *WhoScE 91-4*
Normile, Michael T. 1949- *WhoAm 92*
Normile, Michael Timothy 1949- *St&PR 93*
Normington, Dale A. *Law&B 92*
Noro, Akihiko 1946- *WhoAsAP 91*
Norodom Sihanouk, His Royal Highness Prince 1922- *WhoWor 93*
Norodom Sihanouk, Prince 1922- *BioIn 17*
Norodom Sihanouk, Samdech Preah 1922- *WhoAsAP 91*
Norokorpi, Yrjo Eljas 1946- *WhoScE 91-4*
Noronha, Moema Para 1962- *WhoWor 93*
Noronha, Sirikit *Law&B 92*
Norota, Hosei *WhoAsAP 91*
Norquist, Galen R. 1926- *St&PR 93*
Norquist, Grover Glenn 1956- *WhoE 93*
Norquist, John Olof 1949- *WhoAm 92*
Norrback, Johan Ole 1941- *WhoWor 93*
Norrby, Erling Carl Jacob 1937- *WhoScE 91-4, WhoWor 93*
Norrby, S. Ragnar 1943- *WhoScE 91-4*
Norrell, Catherine Dorris 1901-1981 *BioIn 17*
Norrell, J. Elizabeth 1958- *WhoEmL 93*
Norrell, Robert J(efferson) 1952- *ConAu 139*
Norrgard, Kristin Ann 1957- *WhoAm 92*
Norrgard, Lee Edward 1945- *WhoE 93*
Norrie, Douglas Hector 1929- *WhoWor 93*
Norrie, K. Peter 1939- *St&PR 93*

Norrington, Roger 1934- BioIn 17, OxDcOp
Norrington, Roger (Arthur Carver) 1934- Baker 92
Norris, Aaron MiSFD 9
Norris, Alan Eugene 1935- WhoAm 92
Norris, Albert Stanley 1926- WhoAm 92
Norris, Andrea Spaulding 1945- WhoAm 92, WhoAmW 93
Norris, Anne E. Law&B 92
Norris, Arlene Robicheaux 1939- WhoAmW 93, WhoSSW 93
Norris, Berry E. 1927- St&PR 93
Norris, Blanche Lee 1958- WhoEmL 93
Norris, Carol Brooks 1943- WhoSSW 93
Norris, Carole Veronica 1948- WhoWrEP 92
Norris, Charles Head, Jr. 1940- WhoAm 92, WhoE 93, WhoWor 93
Norris, Chester Edward 1927- WhoAm 92
Norris, Christine Rossell 1960- WhoAmW 93
Norris, Christopher 1947- ScF&FL 92
Norris, Chuck BioIn 17, WhoAm 92
Norris, Curtis ScF&FL 92
Norris, Curtis Bird 1927- WhoE 93, WhoWor 93
Norris, Cynthia A. Law&B 92
Norris, Darell Forest 1928- WhoAm 92
Norris, David M. Law&B 92
Norris, David S. 1938- St&PR 93
Norris, David Stuart 1938- WhoAm 92
Norris, Debbie Carmichael 1959- WhoSSW 93
Norris, Diane Lee 1941- WhoWrEP 92
Norris, Edward P. 1940- St&PR 93
Norris, Edward Patrick 1940- WhoAm 92
Norris, Eileen C. 1953- WhoWrEP 92
Norris, Floyd Hamilton 1947- WhoE 93
Norris, Frances McMurtray 1946- WhoAm 92
Norris, Francis J. 1951- St&PR 93
Norris, Frank 1870-1902 GayN, MagSAmL [port]
Norris, Frank William 1920- St&PR 93, WhoSSW 93
Norris, Franklin Gray 1923- WhoAm 92
Norris, Fred Vincent 1958- WhoEmL 93
Norris, Geoffrey 1937- WhoAm 92
Norris, George W. 1861-1944 PolPar
Norris, George William 1933- St&PR 93
Norris, Guy Williams 1962- WhoSSW 93
Norris, H. Coleman 1931- St&PR 93
Norris, H. Jones, Jr. 1943- St&PR 93
Norris, H. Thomas 1934- WhoAm 92, WhoSSW 93
Norris, Hunt T., Jr. St&PR 93
Norris, J. Earle Law&B 92
Norris, J. Frank 1877-1952 BioIn 17
Norris, J.R. WhoScE 91-1
Norris, James Alexander 1938- WhoIns 93
Norris, James Goodrum 1964- WhoSSW 93
Norris, Joan Clafette Hagood 1951- WhoAmW 93
Norris, Joan Louise 1958- WhoEmL 93
Norris, John A. St&PR 93
Norris, John Anthony 1946- WhoAm 92, WhoE 93
Norris, John Hart 1942- WhoAm 92
Norris, John L. 1943- St&PR 93
Norris, John L., Jr. 1914- St&PR 93
Norris, John Windsor, Jr. 1936- WhoSSW 93
Norris, Kathleen 1947- WhoWrEP 92
Norris, Kathleen Thompson 1880-1966 AmWomPl
Norris, Ken 1951- WhoCanL 92
Norris, Kenneth Edward 1948- St&PR 93
Norris, Kenneth Michael 1952- WhoEmL 93, WhoSSW 93
Norris, Kevin A. Law&B 92
Norris, Lawrence Geoffrey Law&B 92
Norris, Linda Burney Law&B 92
Norris, Martin Joseph 1907- WhoAm 92
Norris, Melvin 1931- WhoAm 92
Norris, Michelle Celeste 1958- WhoAmW 93
Norris, P.E. 1942- St&PR 93
Norris, Pamela 1946- WhoAmW 93
Norris, Patrick BioIn 17
Norris, Peter Justin 1954- WhoEmL 93
Norris, Phillip Eric 1948- WhoSSW 93
Norris, Ralph C. Law&B 92
Norris, Rebecca 1955- WhoAmW 93
Norris, Richard Anthony 1943- WhoAm 92
Norris, Richard Paul 1948- St&PR 93
Norris, Richard S. 1930- St&PR 93
Norris, Robert F. 1922- WhoAm 92
Norris, Robert Fogg 1905- WhoAm 92
Norris, Robert Matheson 1921- WhoAm 92
Norris, Robert Wheeler 1932- WhoAm 92
Norris, Roland W. Law&B 92
Norris, S.D. ScF&FL 92
Norris, Steven James 1951- WhoSSW 93
Norris, Susan Beatrice Priess 1943- WhoE 93
Norris, Susan Elizabeth 1952- WhoAmW 93
Norris, Susan Fetner 1949- WhoEmL 93
Norris, Terry BioIn 17, NewYTBS 92 [port]
Norris, Thomas Clayton 1938- St&PR 93
Norris, Valerie Jo 1957- WhoAmW 93
Norris, Verle William Law&B 92
Norris, Virginia Oakley 1928- WhoAmW 93
Norris, Wayne Bruce 1947- WhoEmL 93, WhoWrEP 92
Norris, William A. 1953- St&PR 93
Norris, William Albert 1927- WhoAm 92
Norris, William Benny 1943- St&PR 93
Norris, William C. BioIn 17
Norris, William C. 1911- WhoAm 92
Norris, William Patrick, Jr. 1944- St&PR 93
Norris, William Randal 1961- WhoSSW 93
Norris, William Tobias WhoScE 91-1
Norrod, James Douglas 1948- WhoE 93
Norse, David 1939- WhoUN 92
Norse, Edwin Michael 1945- St&PR 93
Norse, Harold 1916- BioIn 17
Norseth, Tor 1936- WhoScE 91-4
Norstad, Lauris 1907-1988 HarEnMi
Norstrom, Eugene N. 1943- St&PR 93
Norstrom, Lars-Ake 1945- WhoScE 91-4
Norsworthy, Jeanne BioIn 17
Norsworthy, John Randolph 1939- WhoAm 92
Norsworthy, Lamar 1946- WhoAm 92
Norsworthy, Robert Joseph 1938- WhoAm 92
North, Alex 1910- Baker 92
North, Alex 1910-1991 AnObit 1991, BioIn 17
North, Andrew MajAI
North, Anthony Charles Thomas WhoScE 91-1
North, Captain George MajAI
North, Carol Sue 1954- WhoAmW 93, WhoEmL 93
North, Cecil J., III Law&B 92
North, Charles A. 1941- WhoIns 93
North, Charles Laurence 1941- WhoWrEP 92
North, David ScF&FL 92
North, Douglass Cecil 1920- WhoAm 92
North, Edmund H. 1911-1990 ScF&FL 92
North, Edmund Hall 1911-1990 BioIn 17
North, Edwin M. Law&B 92
North, Edwin M. 1945- St&PR 93
North, Eric 1884-1968 ScF&FL 92
North, Gary 1942- ConAu 38NR
North, Gerald David William 1951- WhoWor 93
North, Halsey M. 1947- WhoE 93
North, Helen Florence WhoAm 92, WhoWrEP 92
North, Henry Ringling 1909- St&PR 93
North, James R. 1963- St&PR 93
North, Kathryn E. Keesey 1916- WhoAmW 93
North, Kevin A. 1952- WhoIns 93
North, Kory Gray 1959- St&PR 93
North, Lex 1931- WhoE 93
North, Marianne 1830-1890 BioIn 17
North, Oliver DcCPCAm
North, Oliver 1943- CurBio 92 [port]
North, Oliver L., Jr. BioIn 17
North, Phil Record 1918- WhoAm 92
North, Philip Michael WhoScE 91-1
North, Richard Ralph 1934- WhoSSW 93
North, Rick ConAu 40NR, ScF&FL 92
North, Robert Carver 1914- WhoAm 92
North, Robert J. Law&B 92
North, Robert John 1935- WhoAm 92
North, Roger c. 1651-1734 Baker 92
North, Sterling 1906-1974 ConAu 40NR, DcAmChF 1960, MajAI [port]
North, Virginia Ann 1951- WhoAmW 93
North, Warren James 1922- WhoAm 92
North, Wheeler James 1922- WhoAm 92
North, William A. 1940- WhoAm 92
North, William Charles 1925- WhoAm 92
North, William Haven 1926- WhoAm 92
Northacker, Alfred Austin 1915- WhoWrEP 92
Northam, Robert E. 1930- St&PR 93
Northampton, William de Bohun, Earl of c. 1312-1360 HarEnMi
Northard, J.H. WhoScE 91-1
Northart, Leo Joseph 1929- WhoWrEP 92
Northcott, Nancy T. BioIn 17
Northcott, Nancy Tucker 1945- NewYTBS 92 [port]
Northcut, John D. 1941- WhoUN 92
Northcutt, Clarence Dewey 1916- WhoAm 92, WhoWor 93
Northcutt, Ernest O. 1929- St&PR 93
Northcutt, Marie Rose 1950- WhoAmW 93, WhoEmL 93
Northcutt, Robert Hull 1934- St&PR 93
Northcutt, Robert Hull, Jr. 1934- WhoAm 92
Northcutt, Wayne 1944- ConAu 138
Northen, Cathryn Mary 1966- WhoAmW 93
Northen, Charles Swift, III 1937- St&PR 93, WhoAm 92
Northen, Helen WhoWrEP 92
Northenor, Doris Jean 1932- WhoAmW 93
Northern, Chauncey Scott d1992 NewYTBS 92
Northey, Lorrie Dee Law&B 92
Northey, Margot ScF&FL 92
Northey, Randall B. Law&B 92
Northey, Richard John 1945- WhoAsAP 91
Northfield, Timothy Clive WhoScE 91-1
Northington, Ted Law&B 92
Northover, Basil John WhoScE 91-1
Northover, Robert R. 1930- St&PR 93
Northrop, Allen C. ScF&FL 92
Northrop, Cheri Elisabeth 1966- WhoSSW 93
Northrop, Cynthia E. d1989 BioIn 17
Northrop, Edward Skottowe 1911- WhoAm 92, WhoE 93
Northrop, F. S. C. 1893-1992 NewYTBS 92 [port]
Northrop, Filmer S(tuart) C(uckow) 1893-1992 ConAu 139
Northrop, Gaylord Marvin 1928- WhoSSW 93
Northrop, James A. 1947- St&PR 93
Northrop, James Allen 1947- WhoAm 92
Northrop, John H. 1891-1987 BioIn 17
Northrop, John Knudsen 1895-1981 BioIn 17
Northrop, John L.S. 1930- St&PR 93
Northrop, Monroe 1931- WhoAm 92
Northrop, Sam, Jr. 1931- St&PR 93
Northrop, Stuart Johnston 1925- St&PR 93, WhoAm 92, WhoWor 93
Northrup, Doyle d1991 NewYTBS 92
Northrup, Doyle Langdon 1906-1991 BioIn 17
Northrup, Herbert Roof 1918- WhoAm 92, WhoE 93
Northrup, Joan Cooke 1953- WhoAmW 93
Northrup, Steven Paul 1949- WhoEmL 93
Northup, Anne Meagher 1948- WhoAmW 93
Northup, George 1941- BioIn 17
Northup, John David 1910- WhoAm 92
Northway, Martin 1947- WhoWrEP 92
Northway, Wanda I. 1942- WhoAmW 93
Northwood, David Weston 1909- St&PR 93
Nortia, Teuvo A.O. 1922- WhoScE 91-4
Nortic, Max ScF&FL 92
Nortje, Arthur 1942-1970 DcLB 125 [port]
Norton, Alden H. 1903-1987 ScF&FL 92
Norton, Alexander Vernon 1951- St&PR 93
Norton, Alice M. ScF&FL 92
Norton, Alice Mary 1912- BioIn 17
Norton, Alice Whitson 1897- AmWomPl
Norton, Andre 1912- BioIn 17, MajAI [port], ScF&FL 92
Norton, Andre Alice WhoAm 92, WhoAmW 93
Norton, Augustus Richard 1946- WhoAm 92
Norton, Barry 1905-1956 HispAmA
Norton, Bill L. 1943- MiSFD 9
Norton, Brian WhoScE 91-1
Norton, Charles Eliot 1827-1908 GayN
Norton, Charles McKim 1907-1991 BioIn 17
Norton, Charles William, Jr. 1921- St&PR 93
Norton, Chester L. 1911- St&PR 93
Norton, Chris W. 1941- St&PR 93
Norton, Cliff 1919- BioIn 17
Norton, Clifford Charles 1918- WhoAm 92
Norton, Clinton Edward 1923- WhoAm 92
Norton, D.J. WhoScE 91-1
Norton, Dale Bentsen 1925- St&PR 93
Norton, David Ashley 1941- WhoE 93
Norton, David C. 1946- WhoAm 92, WhoSSW 93
Norton, David L. Law&B 92
Norton, David L. 1945- St&PR 93
Norton, Delmar Lynn 1944- WhoAm 92
Norton, Dennis H. Law&B 92
Norton, Desmond Anthony 1942- WhoWor 93
Norton, Diana Mae 1945- WhoAmW 93
Norton, Donn H. 1942- WhoAm 92
Norton, Edgar Albert, Jr. 1957- WhoE 93, WhoEmL 93
Norton, Edward Lee 1892-1966 BioIn 17
Norton, Edward Leon 1942- St&PR 93
Norton, Eleanor AmWomPl
Norton, Eleanor Holmes BioIn 17
Norton, Eleanor Holmes 1937- AfrAmBi, CngDr 91, EncAACR, WhoAm 92, WhoAmW 93, WhoE 93
Norton, Elizabeth Wychgel 1933- WhoAmW 93
Norton, Eric 1925- WhoSSW 93
Norton, Eunice 1908- WhoAm 92
Norton, Fay-Tyler Murray 1925- WhoAmW 93, WhoSSW 93
Norton, Gale 1954- WhoAm 92, WhoAmW 93
Norton, Geoffrey Andrew WhoScE 91-1
Norton, George Dawson 1930- WhoAm 92
Norton, Gerald Patrick 1940- WhoAm 92
Norton, Gregory Armstrong 1948- St&PR 93
Norton, H. Don 1945- WhoAm 92
Norton, H. Steve 1934- St&PR 93
Norton, Hamish William Mazur 1959- WhoEmL 93
Norton, Herbert Steven 1934- WhoAm 92
Norton, Howard Melvin 1911- WhoAm 92
Norton, Hugh Stanton 1921- WhoAm 92
Norton, Ida G. AmWomPl
Norton, J. William Law&B 92
Norton, Jack 1889-1958 QDrFCA 92 [port]
Norton, Jacki Lyn 1958- WhoAmW 93
Norton, James Adolphus 1922- WhoAm 92
Norton, James Edward 1939- St&PR 93
Norton, James Gerald 1933- St&PR 93
Norton, James J. 1930- WhoAm 92
Norton, James Lonnie, Jr. WhoWrEP 92
Norton, Jan Auburn 1946- WhoAm 92
Norton, Jeanna 1952- WhoEmL 93
Norton, Jeffrey 1925- WhoE 93
Norton, Jeffrey A. Law&B 92
Norton, Jeffrey A. 1942- St&PR 93
Norton, John Croft 1948- WhoEmL 93, WhoSSW 93
Norton, John F. St&PR 93
Norton, John Harry 1929- WhoSSW 93
Norton, John William 1941- St&PR 93
Norton, John William 1954- WhoEmL 93
Norton, Judy WhoAm 92
Norton, Julian Brook 1936- WhoSSW 93
Norton, Karen Ann 1950- WhoAmW 93
Norton, Kelly E. 1938- St&PR 93
Norton, Ken David 1957- WhoSSW 93
Norton, Larry Allan 1947- WhoEmL 93, WhoSSW 93
Norton, Laura Jean 1953- WhoSSW 93
Norton, Leslie Forth 1953- WhoEmL 93, WhoSSW 93
Norton, Lewis Franklin 1930- St&PR 93, WhoIns 93
Norton, Lisa Law&B 92
Norton, Louis Arthur 1937- WhoE 93
Norton, Louise AmWomPl
Norton, Mary AmWomPl
Norton, Mary 1903- MajAI [port]
Norton, Mary 1903-1992 BioIn 17, ConAu 139, NewYTBS 92, ScF&FL 92, SmATA 72
Norton, Mary Beth 1943- WhoAm 92
Norton, Mary Teresa Hopkins 1875-1959 BioIn 17
Norton, Maxwell Van Konynenburg 1954- WhoEmL 93
Norton, Melanie Jean 1959- WhoAmW 93
Norton, Michael C. 1947- ScF&FL 92
Norton, Michael Jeffrey 1938- WhoAm 92
Norton, Michael Peter 1951- WhoWor 93
Norton, Nancy Jeanne 1947- WhoAmW 93
Norton, Nancy Sherry 1961- WhoE 93
Norton, Nick WhoWrEP 92
Norton, Norman James 1933- WhoAm 92
Norton, P. Kay Law&B 92
Norton, P. Kay 1951- St&PR 93
Norton, Patrick J. St&PR 93
Norton, Paul Allen 1913- WhoAm 92
Norton, Peter Bowes 1929- St&PR 93, WhoAm 92
Norton, Ralph Gage 1932- St&PR 93
Norton, Randell Hunt 1948- WhoAm 92
Norton, Randolph Harrison 1939- St&PR 93
Norton, Rita Faye WhoSSW 93
Norton, Robert 1946- St&PR 93
Norton, Robert D. 1941- St&PR 93
Norton, Robert Dillard, Jr. 1964- WhoSSW 93
Norton, Robert E., Jr. Law&B 92
Norton, Robert H. 1929- WhoE 93
Norton, Robert Howard 1946- WhoSSW 93
Norton, Robert Leo, Sr. 1939- WhoWor 93
Norton, Robyn Lynn 1963- WhoEmL 93
Norton, Roger L. 1937- St&PR 93
Norton, Stephen Allen 1940- WhoAm 92
Norton, Thomas Edward 1934- WhoE 93
Norton, Trevor Alan WhoScE 91-1
Norton, Virginia Skeen 1907- WhoAmW 93
Norton, William R. 1948- St&PR 93
Norton, William Richard Law&B 92
Norton, William T. 1929- WhoE 93

Norton, William W. 1934- *St&PR 93*
Nortsov, Panteleymon 1900- *OxDcOp*
Norum, Kaare R. 1932- *WhoScE 91-4*
Norup, Kim Stefan 1945- *WhoWor 93*
Norvell, G. Todd 1942- *WhoAm 92*
Norvell, Nancy Kathleen 1957- *WhoEmL 93*
Norvell, Sam S. *Law&B 92*
Norvil, Manning *ScF&FL 92*
Norville, Craig H. *Law&B 92*
Norville, Craig Hubert 1944- *St&PR 93, WhoAm 92*
Norville, Deborah *BioIn 17*
Norville, Kenneth 1908- *Baker 92*
Norville, Russel Manley 1938- *St&PR 93*
Norvo, Red 1908- *Baker 92*
Norwalk, Kelli Curran 1949- *WhoAmW 93*
Norway, Nevil *ScF&FL 92*
Norwid, Cyprian Kamil 1821-1883 *PolBiDi*
Norwine, George F. 1948- *St&PR 93*
Norwitz, Steven Barry 1941- *WhoE 93*
Norwood, Barbara Ann Mann 1946- *WhoAmW 93*
Norwood, Bernard 1922- *WhoAm 92*
Norwood, Carol Ruth 1949- *WhoAmW 93*
Norwood, Cecilia Stubbs 1953- *St&PR 93*
Norwood, David *Law&B 92*
Norwood, Donald Mason 1952- *St&PR 93*
Norwood, George Joseph 1938- *WhoAm 92, WhoSSW 93*
Norwood, Janet L. *BioIn 17*
Norwood, Janet Lippe 1923- *WhoAm 92, WhoAmW 93*
Norwood, Joy Janell 1936- *WhoAmW 93*
Norwood, Lori *BioIn 17*
Norwood, Mark Edward 1961- *WhoSSW 93*
Norwood, P.E. 1949- *St&PR 93*
Norwood, Paula King 1946- *WhoE 93*
Norwood, Pete *BioIn 17*
Norwood, Ralph M. 1943- *St&PR 93*
Norwood, Robert Winkworth 1874-1932 *BioIn 17*
Norwood, Samuel Wilkins, III 1941- *St&PR 93*
Norwood, Victor 1920-1983 *ScF&FL 92*
Norwood, Warren 1945- *ScF&FL 92*
Norwood, William Thomas, Jr. 1948- *WhoSSW 93*
Nosacek, Gary John 1955- *WhoEmL 93*
Nosaka, Koken 1924- *WhoAsAP 91*
Nosal, John P. 1949- *St&PR 93*
Nosanow, Barbara Shissler *WhoAm 92, WhoAmW 93, WhoE 93*
Nosari, Raymond John 1931- *St&PR 93*
Noseda, Giorgio 1938- *WhoWor 93*
Nosek, Margaret Ann 1952- *WhoEmL 93, WhoSSW 93*
Noshpitz, Joseph Dove 1922- *WhoAm 92*
Noske, Frits (Rudolf) 1920- *Baker 92*
Noske, Hans-Dieter 1938- *WhoScE 91-3*
Noskowski, Zygmunt 1846-1909 *Baker 92, PolBiDi*
Nosler, Robert Amos 1946- *WhoEmL 93*
Noss, Stanley 1925- *St&PR 93, WhoAm 92*
Nosseck, Noel *MiSFD 9*
Nossen, Robert Joseph 1920- *WhoAm 92*
Nossett, Paula Marie 1937- *WhoAmW 93*
Nossig, Alfred 1864-1943 *PolBiDi*
Nossiter, Bernard D. d1992 *NewYTBS 92*
Nossiter, Bernard D(aniel) 1926-1992 *ConAu 138*
Nossiter, Bernard Daniel 1926- *WhoAm 92*
Nossiter, Jonathan *MiSFD 9*
Nossiter, Thomas Johnson *WhoScE 91-1*
Nostin, John M. 1947- *WhoE 93*
Nostlinger, Christine 1936- *ScF&FL 92*
Nostradamus 1503-1566 *BioIn 17*
Nostrand, Stephen Dudley, Jr. 1945- *WhoSSW 93*
Nosworthy, Darlene Marie 1948- *WhoEmL 93*
Notaras, Loukas d1453 *OxDcByz*
Notarbartolo, Albert 1934- *WhoAm 92*
Notari, Paul Celestin 1926- *WhoAm 92*
Notario, Vicente 1952- *WhoWor 93*
Notaro, Michael R. 1914- *WhoAm 92*
Notaro, Michael R. 1918- *St&PR 93*
Notas, Bernard M. 1950- *St&PR 93*
Notch, James Stephen 1950- *WhoEmL 93, WhoSSW 93, WhoWor 93*
Note, Jean 1859-1922 *Baker 92*
Notebaert, Richard J. 1943- *St&PR 93*
Notenboom, Jacob T.M. 1945- *St&PR 93*
Notestein, David Albert 1953- *St&PR 93, WhoIns 93*
Notestein, Garrett *Law&B 92*
Notestine, Wilbur Edmund 1931- *WhoAm 92*
Noth, Heinrich 1928- *WhoScE 91-3*
Noth, Mary-Jo Cone 1943- *WhoAmW 93*
Noth, Nancy Claire 1950- *WhoAmW 93*
Noth, Winfried Maximilian 1944- *WhoWor 93*
Nothdurft, Hans Jakob 1911- *WhoWor 93*
Nothem, James M. 1942- *WhoIns 93*
Nothmann, Gerhard Adolf 1921- *WhoAm 92*
Nothmann, Rudolf S. 1907- *WhoWor 93*
Nothstine, S. Ellsworth 1907- *WhoWrEP 92*
Nothwang, William L. 1937- *St&PR 93*
Notis-Mcconarty, Edward *St&PR 93*
Notker c. 840-912 *Baker 92*
Notkin, David 1955- *WhoEmL 93*
Notkin, Jerome Johannes 1926- *WhoE 93*
Notkin, Leonard Sheldon 1931- *WhoAm 92*
Notko, Terry Joseph 1951- *St&PR 93*
Noto, Don Joseph 1932- *St&PR 93*
Noto, Frank A. 1934- *St&PR 93*
Noto, Patricia Hoffman 1954- *WhoE 93*
Notowidigdo, Musinggih Hartoko 1938- *St&PR 93, WhoWor 93*
Nott, C.S. *BioIn 17*
Nott, Hugh William, III 1941- *St&PR 93*
Nott, K.C. 1909?- *ScF&FL 92*
Nott, Michael R. 1955- *St&PR 93*
Nottage, Daniel Bruce 1948- *St&PR 93*
Nottage, Geoffrey *MiSFD 9*
Nottage, Renae Clarice 1956- *WhoAmW 93*
Nottberg, Henry, III 1949- *St&PR 93*
Nottebohm, (Martin) Gustav 1817-1882 *Baker 92*
Notter, Randall P. 1957- *St&PR 93*
Nottidge, Oliver Richard 1932- *WhoUN 92*
Nottingham, Edward Willis, Jr. 1948- *WhoAm 92*
Nottingham, Joanne Eleanora 1949- *WhoSSW 93*
Nottingham, R. Kendall 1938- *WhoIns 93*
Nottingham, Robinson Kendall 1938- *WhoAm 92*
Nottle, Diane 1955- *WhoWrEP 92*
Notton, Brian Arthur 1929- *WhoScE 91-1*
Notz, John Kranz, Jr. 1932- *WhoAm 92*
Notz, Thierry *MiSFD 9*
Notzen, Randall Arthur *Law&B 92*
Notzon, Francis C. 1948- *WhoE 93*
Nouchi, Franck Charles 1956- *WhoWor 93*
Nougues, Jean 1875-1932 *Baker 92, OxDcOp*
Noumair, George J. 1930- *WhoAm 92*
Nour, Mohamed Abdalla 1925- *WhoUN 92*
Nouri, Abdul Motey Mohammed 1941- *WhoWor 93*
Nouri, Michael *BioIn 17*
Nourie, Alan (Raymond) 1942- *ConAu 138*
Nourie, Barbara (Livingston) 1947- *ConAu 138*
Nouri-Moghadam, Mohamad Reza 1949- *WhoE 93, WhoEmL 93*
Nourrit, Adolphe 1802-1839 *Baker 92, IntDcOp [port], OxDcOp*
Nourrit, Louis 1780-1831 *OxDcOp*
Nourse, Alan E. 1928-1992 *ScF&FL 92*
Nourse, Alan E(dward) 1928- *WhoWrEP 92*
Nourse, Hugh Oliver 1933- *WhoSSW 93*
Nourse, Jennifer Jon Williams 1953- *WhoAmW 93*
Nourse, Robert Eric Martin 1938- *St&PR 93*
Nourse, Robert Richard 1963- *WhoAm 92*
Noutsopoulos, George *WhoScE 91-3*
Nouveau-Ne', Roger Elliott 1948- *WhoSSW 93*
Nouvel, Jean 1945- *BioIn 17*
Noux, O'Neil De *ScF&FL 92*
Nova, Craig 1945- *WhoAm 92*
Nova, Lou 1915-1991 *BioIn 17*
Novacek, Ottokar (Eugen) 1866-1900 *Baker 92*
Novacek, Rudolf 1860-1929 *Baker 92*
Novack, Alvin John 1925- *WhoAm 92*
Novack, Catherine G. *Law&B 92*
Novack, Catherine Gail *Law&B 92*
Novack, Edith M. *Law&B 92*
Novack, George (Edward) 1905-1992 *ConAu 139*
Novack, Gianella Marie 1957- *WhoEmL 93, WhoSSW 93*
Novack, Irwin Mark 1947- *St&PR 93*
Novack, Joseph 1928- *WhoE 93*
Novack, Kenneth Joseph 1941- *WhoAm 92*
Novack, Paul Joseph *Law&B 92*
Novack, Sheldon 1938- *WhoE 93, WhoWor 93*
Novaes, Ana Dolores 1962- *WhoWor 93*
Novaes, Guiomar 1895-1979 *Baker 92, BioIn 17*
Novaes, Humberto M. 1936- *WhoUN 92*
Novaes, Sergio Ferraz 1956- *WhoWor 93*
Novak, Alan Lee 1928- *WhoSSW 93*
Novak, Alfred 1915- *WhoAm 92*
Novak, Alfred J. 1948- *St&PR 93*
Novak, Barbara *WhoAm 92*
Novak, Barbara Ellen 1949- *WhoEmL 93*
Novak, Blaine *MiSFD 9*
Novak, C. Michael *Law&B 92*
Novak, Carla T. *Law&B 92*
Novak, Daria Irene 1957- *WhoEmL 93*
Novak, David C. *BioIn 17*
Novak, Dennis Wayne 1941- *St&PR 93*
Novak, Donna Burnett 1947- *WhoAmW 93*
Novak, Erich 1953- *WhoWor 93*
Novak, Eugene Andrew 1950- *St&PR 93*
Novak, Eugene Francis 1925- *WhoAm 92*
Novak, Eva 1899-1988 *SweetSg B*
Novak, Gabrijela Jelka 1942- *WhoScE 91-4*
Novak, George 1948- *WhoEmL 93*
Novak, Gregory 1949- *WhoE 93, WhoEmL 93*
Novak, James Michael 1944- *WhoAm 92*
Novak, Jan 1921-1984 *Baker 92*
Novak, Jane 1896-1990 *SweetSg B [port]*
Novak, Jeannie *BioIn 17*
Novak, Jo-Ann Stout 1956- *WhoAmW 93*
Novak, Joan Tross 1927- *WhoE 93*
Novak, Johann Baptist c. 1756-1833 *Baker 92*
Novak, John Robert 1944- *St&PR 93, WhoAm 92*
Novak, John William, Jr. 1953- *WhoEmL 93*
Novak, Joseph 1956- *St&PR 93*
Novak, Joseph Donald 1930- *WhoAm 92, WhoE 93*
Novak, Kate *ScF&FL 92*
Novak, Katherine Bush 1948- *WhoAmW 93*
Novak, Kim 1933- *IntDcF 2-3 [port], WhoAm 92*
Novak, Linda Joyce 1954- *WhoAmW 93*
Novak, Lubos 1931- *WhoWor 93*
Novak, Marian Faye *BioIn 17*
Novak, Matt 1962- *BioIn 17*
Novak, Michael *BioIn 17*
Novak, Michael Andrew 1951- *WhoEmL 93*
Novak, Michael D. *Law&B 92*
Novak, Michael John 1933- *WhoAm 92, WhoWor 93*
Novak, Michael (John), Jr. 1933- *WhoWrEP 92*
Novak, Michael Paul 1935- *WhoWrEP 92*
Novak, Milan 1927- *Baker 92*
Novak, Miroslav *ScF&FL 92*
Novak, Nancy Ellen 1957- *WhoAmW 93*
Novak, Norman George 1946- *St&PR 93*
Novak, Paul 1946- *WhoAm 92*
Novak, Pavel 1936- *WhoScE 91-4*
Novak, Peter J. 1939- *St&PR 93*
Novak, Peter John *Law&B 92*
Novak, Peter John 1939- *WhoAm 92*
Novak, Raymond A. 1930- *St&PR 93*
Novak, Raymond Francis 1946- *WhoAm 92*
Novak, Richard E. 1944- *WhoWor 93*
Novak, Richard Joseph 1954- *WhoE 93*
Novak, Richey Asbury 1927- *WhoSSW 93*
Novak, Robert 1931- *See* Evans, Rowland 1921- & Novak, Robert 1931- *JrnUS*
Novak, Robert D. *BioIn 17*
Novak, Robert David Sanders 1931- *WhoAm 92*
Novak, Robert Lee 1933- *WhoWrEP 92*
Novak, Rose 1940- *WhoWrEP 92*
Novak, Rynell Stiff 1929- *WhoSSW 93*
Novak, Sandra Bernadean 1953- *WhoAmW 93, WhoEmL 93*
Novak, Scott H. *Law&B 92*
Novak, Sheri M. *Law&B 92*
Novak, Sigrid Scholtz 1931- *WhoSSW 93*
Novak, Terry Lee 1940- *WhoAm 92*
Novak, Vitezslav 1870-1949 *OxDcOp*
Novak, Vitezslav (Augustin Rudolf) 1870-1949 *Baker 92*
Novak, William Arnold 1948- *WhoAm 92*
Novak, Yvette 1946- *WhoEmL 93*
Novakov, Daniel P. *Law&B 92*
Novakovic, Branko Mane 1940- *WhoWor 93*
Noval, William F. *Law&B 92*
Novales, Ronald Richards 1928- *WhoAm 92*
Novalis 1772-1801 *BioIn 17*
Novander, Kenneth L. *Law&B 92*
Novario, Raffaele 1956- *WhoWor 93*
Novaro, Maria *MiSFD 9*
Novaro, Octavio 1910- *DcMexL*
Novarro, Ramon 1899-1968 *HispAmA, IntDcF 2-3 [port]*
Novas, Joseph, Jr. 1921- *WhoAm 92*
Novas Calvo, Lino 1905-1983 *SpAmA*
Nove, Alec *BioIn 17*
Novel, Georges 1935- *WhoScE 91-2*
Novell, Philip M. 1938- *St&PR 93*
Novell, Richard S. 1949- *St&PR 93*
Novelli, Florence *WhoCanL 92*
Novelli, Luca 1947- *BioIn 17*
Novelli, Thomas Charles 1942- *St&PR 93*
Novellino, Anthony Ronald 1949- *WhoAm 92*
Novello, (Joseph) Alfred 1810-1896 *Baker 92*
Novello, Antonia *BioIn 17*
Novello, Antonia 1944- *CurBio 92 [port], NotHsAW 93 [port]*
Novello, Antonia C. 1944- *HispAmA [port]*
Novello, Antonia Coello 1944- *HispAmA, WhoAm 92, WhoAmW 93*
Novello, Clara 1818-1908 *OxDcOp*
Novello, Clara (Anastasia) 1818-1908 *Baker 92*
Novello, Don 1943- *WhoAm 92, WhoWrEP 92*
Novello, Ivor 1893-1951 *IntDcF 2-3 [port]* *See Also* Novello-Davies, Clara 1861-1943 *Baker 92*
Novello, Leonard P. *Law&B 92*
Novello, Vincent 1781-1861 *Baker 92*
Novello & Co. *Baker 92*
Novello-Davies, Clara 1861-1943 *Baker 92*
Novelo, Jose Ines 1868-1956 *DcMexL*
November, Abigail Alma 1944- *WhoSSW 93*
November, Robert 1936- *St&PR 93*
November, Robert Stephen 1936- *WhoAm 92*
Novenstern, Samuel 1926- *WhoAm 92*
Nover, Fred Stuart 1937- *St&PR 93*
Nover, Naomi *WhoAm 92, WhoWor 93*
Noverre, Jean-Georges 1727-1810 *Baker 92, OxDcOp*
Novetzke, Sally J. 1932- *WhoAm 92*
Novetzke, Sally Johnson 1932- *WhoAmW 93, WhoWor 93*
Novey, Linda S. 1940- *WhoAmW 93*
Novgrod, Nancy *WhoAmW 93*
Novich, Bruce E. *St&PR 93*
Novich, Max M. 1914- *BioIn 17*
Novick, Andrew Carl 1948- *WhoAm 92*
Novick, David 1906-1991 *BioIn 17*
Novick, David 1926- *WhoAm 92*
Novick, David S. 1949- *St&PR 93*
Novick, Harold 1922- *WhoE 93*
Novick, Ivan J. 1927- *St&PR 93*
Novick, Julius Lerner 1939- *WhoAm 92*
Novick, Martin 1936- *St&PR 93*
Novick, Marvin 1931- *WhoAm 92*
Novick, Mary 1959- *St&PR 93*
Novick, Mindy S. *Law&B 92*
Novick, Nelson Lee 1949- *WhoAm 92, WhoE 93*
Novick, Peter 1934- *WhoAm 92*
Novick, Robert 1923- *WhoAm 92*
Novick, Sheldon M. 1941- *WhoAm 92*
Novicki, William Alan 1950- *St&PR 93*
Novicky, Genevieve 1919- *WhoSSW 93*
Novicoff, Melvyn Burt 1939- *St&PR 93*
Novik, Jay A. 1944- *WhoIns 93*
Novik, Sheffield 1918- *St&PR 93*
Novikoff, Laurent 1888-1956 *BioIn 17*
Novikov, Anatoly (Grigorievich) 1896-1984 *Baker 92*
Novikov, Igor Yakovlevich 1958- *WhoWor 93*
Novin, Donald 1936- *WhoAm 92*
Novinc, Judith Kaye 1947- *WhoAmW 93*
Novinski, Sybil Marie 1936- *WhoAmW 93*
Novinskie, Gary John 1950- *St&PR 93*
Novis, Derrick A. 1950- *WhoAm 92*
Novitch, Mark 1932- *St&PR 93, WhoAm 92*
Novitskii, G.I. d170-? *IntDcAn*
Novitt, Rita Amelia *WhoAmW 93*
Novitz, Charles Richard 1934- *WhoAm 92*
Novitz, David 1945- *ConAu 139*
Novkov, David A. 1931- *St&PR 93*
Novo, Guy P. *Law&B 92*
Novo, Salvador 1904-1974 *DcMexL, SpAmA*
Novo, Salvatore 1948- *WhoWor 93*
Novogrod, Nancy Ellen 1949- *WhoAm 92, WhoE 93*
Novokshenov, Viktor Yurievich 1951- *WhoWor 93*
Novoselic, Chris *See* Nirvana *ConMus 8* *See Also* Nirvana *News 92*
Novotna, Jana *BioIn 17*
Novotna, Jarmila 1907- *Baker 92, IntDcOp, OxDcOp*
Novotny, Anton 1904-1975 *DcTwHis*
Novotny, Antonin 1904-1975 *ColdWar 2 [port]*
Novotny, David Joseph 1953- *WhoWor 93*
Novotny, Deborah Ann 1964- *WhoAmW 93, WhoEmL 93*
Novotny, Donald Wayne 1934- *WhoAm 92*
Novotny, Ivo 1935- *WhoScE 91-4*
Novotny, Jiri 1943- *WhoE 93, WhoWor 93*
Novotny, Lois M. *Law&B 92*
Novotny, Norman E. *Law&B 92*
Novotny, Tibor *WhoScE 91-4*
Novovesky, Michael Paul 1938- *St&PR 93*
Novovich, Serge *Law&B 92, St&PR 93*
Novovich, Serge 1932- *WhoAm 92*
Nowack, George Paul 1948- *WhoE 93, WhoEmL 93*

Nowack, Wayne Kenyon 1923- *WhoE 93*
Nowacki, Melanie Joy 1963- *WhoAmW 93*
Nowaczek, Frank Huxley 1930- *WhoE 93*
Nowak, Amram *MiSFD 9*
Nowak, Andrzej 1945- *WhoScE 91-4*
Nowak, Carol A. 1950- *WhoAmW 93, WhoEmL 93*
Nowak, Dariusz 1961- *WhoWor 93*
Nowak, Edward, Jr. 1920- *WhoWrEP 92*
Nowak, Edward John *Law&B 92*
Nowak, Emmy 1923- *St&PR 93*
Nowak, Gerald L. 1930- *St&PR 93*
Nowak, Henry J. 1935- *CngDr 91*
Nowak, Henry James 1935- *WhoAm 92, WhoE 93*
Nowak, Henry Peter *Law&B 92*
Nowak, Henryk Zygmunt 1939- *WhoWor 93*
Nowak, Horst 1943- *WhoWor 93*
Nowak, Jacek Lech 1944- *WhoWor 93*
Nowak, Jacquelyn Louise 1937- *WhoAm 92, WhoAmW 93*
Nowak, James E. 1947- *St&PR 93*
Nowak, Jan Zdzislaw 1913- *WhoAm 92*
Nowak, Jeremy Lee *Law&B 92*
Nowak, Jerzy Maria 1937- *WhoUN 92*
Nowak, Jerzy S. 1946- *WhoScE 91-4*
Nowak, Joanna 1945- *WhoScE 91-4*
Nowak, John A. 1940- *St&PR 93*
Nowak, John E. 1947- *WhoEmL 93, WhoWor 93*
Nowak, John Michael 1941- *WhoAm 92*
Nowak, John W. 1941- *St&PR 93*
Nowak, Joseph J. 1931- *WhoAm 92*
Nowak, Judith 1944- *WhoScE 91-3*
Nowak, Judith Ann 1948- *WhoEmL 93*
Nowak, Karil *Law&B 92*
Nowak, Kenneth Edward 1945- *St&PR 93*
Nowak, Laura Stone *WhoE 93*
Nowak, Leopold 1904-1991 *Baker 92*
Nowak, Lionel (Henry) 1911- *Baker 92*
Nowak, Milton 1914- *WhoE 93*
Nowak, Patricia Plakut 1954- *WhoAmW 93*
Nowak, Patricia Rose 1946- *WhoEmL 93*
Nowak, Paul 1914- *BiDAMSp 1989*
Nowak, Raymond M. 1952- *St&PR 93*
Nowak, Robert Michael 1930- *WhoAm 92*
Nowak, Ronald A. 1953- *St&PR 93*
Nowak, Siegfried 1930- *WhoScE 91-3*
Nowak, Siegfried Erich 1930- *WhoWor 93*
Nowak, Terry F. 1961- *WhoSSW 93*
Nowak, Zygfryd Antoni 1933- *WhoScE 91-4*
Nowakowski, James Anthony 1947- *St&PR 93*
Nowakowski, Janusz 1937- *WhoScE 91-4*
Nowakowski, Patty *BioIn 17*
Nowakowski, Stanley Francis 1931- *St&PR 93*
Nowak-Vanderhoef, Deborah K. *Law&B 92*
Nowe, Kevin Gerard *Law&B 92*
Nowell, Amelia Ruth 1937- *WhoAmW 93*
Nowell, Eddie L. 1943- *St&PR 93*
Nowell, Elizabeth Cameron Clemons *WhoAmW 93*
Nowell, Glenna Greely 1937- *WhoAmW 93*
Nowell, Hugh Oliver 1943- *St&PR 93*
Nowell, Kathryn McCulloch 1944- *WhoAmW 93*
Nowell, Linda Gail 1949- *WhoEmL 93*
Nowell, Peter Carey 1928- *WhoAm 92*
Nowell, Ralph P. 1941- *St&PR 93*
Nowell-Smith, Simon Harcourt 1909- *BioIn 17*
Nowetner, Patricia Mary 1952- *WhoE 93*
Nowick, Arthur Stanley 1923- *WhoAm 92*
Nowicki, Andrzej 1945- *WhoScE 91-4*
Nowicki, Andrzej Wladyslaw 1949- *WhoWor 93*
Nowicki, George Lucian 1926- *WhoAm 92*
Nowicki, Jan 1939- *IntDcF 2-3*
Nowicki, Paul Anthony 1959- *WhoEmL 93*
Nowik, Dorothy Adam 1944- *WhoAmW 93*
Nowinski, Frank Lawrence 1955- *WhoEmL 93*
Nowinski, Richard Walter 1948- *WhoSSW 93*
Nowinski, Robert C. *St&PR 93*
Nowinski, Stuart Alan 1953- *WhoEmL 93*
Nowlan, George Joseph 1925- *WhoAm 92*
Nowlan, John Edward, Jr. 1949- *WhoEmL 93*
Nowlan, Michael O. 1937- *WhoCanL 92*
Nowlan, N.V. *WhoScE 91-3*
Nowlan, Philip Francis 1888-1944 *ScF&FL 92*
Nowlan, Raymond J. 1927- *St&PR 93*
Nowland, Rodney A. *Law&B 92*
Nowlin, Duane Dale 1937- *St&PR 93*
Nowlin, James Robertson 1937- *WhoAm 92, WhoSSW 93*
Nowlin, Jerry L. *St&PR 93*
Nowoslawski, Adam 1925- *WhoScE 91-4*
Nowotny, Ewald *WhoScE 91-4*
Nowotny, Janusz 1936- *WhoWor 93*
Nowowiejski, Feliks 1877-1946 *PolBiDi*
Nowowiejski, Felix 1877-1946 *Baker 92*
Nowrasteh, Cyrus 1956- *MiSFD 9*
Noxon, Deborah Homzak 1950- *WhoEmL 93, WhoSSW 93*
Noxon, George Bayard 1955- *WhoEmL 93*
Noxon, Margaret Walters 1903- *WhoAmW 93, WhoE 93*
Noy, R.J. *WhoScE 91-1*
Noyce, James William 1955- *WhoEmL 93, WhoIns 93*
Noyce, Phillip 1950- *MiSFD 9*
Noyce, Robert 1927-1990 *BioIn 17*
Noyce, Robert N. 1927- *St&PR 93*
Noye, Fred C. 1946- *WhoE 93, WhoEmL 93*
Noye, Georg 1943- *WhoScE 91-2*
Noyes, Androus Duane 1936- *WhoE 93*
Noyes, Anne L. *Law&B 92*
Noyes, Barbara Moore 1953- *St&PR 93*
Noyes, Charles Robert, Jr. 1953- *WhoE 93*
Noyes, Crosby S. 1825-1908 *JrnUS*
Noyes, Elisabeth J. 1940- *WhoAmW 93, WhoE 93*
Noyes, Elise Ripley *AmWomPl*
Noyes, Henry 1910- *BioIn 17*
Noyes, Henry Pierre 1923- *WhoAm 92*
Noyes, J.G. *WhoScE 91-1*
Noyes, James Elliot 1946- *St&PR 93, WhoAm 92*
Noyes, Jansen, Jr. 1917- *St&PR 93*
Noyes, Judith Gibson 1941- *WhoAmW 93, WhoE 93*
Noyes, Marion Ingalls Osgood 1859- *AmWomPl*
Noyes, Michael Lance 1946- *WhoEmL 93*
Noyes, Pierrepont Trowbridge d1992 *NewYTBS 92*
Noyes, Pierrepont Trowbridge 1914-1992 *BioIn 17*
Noyes, Ralph *ScF&FL 92*
Noyes, Ralph Richard 1947- *St&PR 93*
Noyes, Richard Hall 1930- *WhoAm 92*
Noyes, Richard Macy 1919- *WhoAm 92*
Noyes, Robert E. 1925- *St&PR 93*
Noyes, Robert Edwin 1925- *WhoAm 92*
Noyes, Robert Slater 1955- *WhoEmL 93*
Noyes, Stanley (Tinning) 1924- *WhoWrEP 92*
Noyes, Steven 1960- *WhoCanL 92*
Noyes, Theodore W. 1858-1946 *JrnUS*
Noyes, Walter Omar 1929- *WhoE 93*
Noyes-Stevens, Yvonne Leslie 1958- *WhoAmW 93*
Noymer, Bernard 1927- *St&PR 93*
Noymer, David S. 1953- *St&PR 93*
Nozato, Ryoichi 1926- *WhoWor 93*
Nozawa, Daizo 1933- *WhoAsAP 91*
Nozawa, Ryushi 1942- *WhoWor 93*
Nozemack, Richard J. 1945- *St&PR 93*
Nozero, Elizabeth Catherine *Law&B 92*
Nozick, Robert 1938- *WhoAm 92*
Nozieres, Philippe Pierre 1932- *WhoScE 91-2*
Noziglia, Carla Miller 1941- *WhoAmW 93*
Noziska, Charles Brant 1953- *WhoEmL 93*
Nozko, Henry W., Sr. 1920- *St&PR 93*
Nozko, Henry Walter, Jr. 1947- *St&PR 93*
Nozu, Michitsura 1841-1907 *HarEnMi*
Nozue, Chinpei 1932- *WhoAsAP 91*
Nozzari, Andrea 1775-1832 *Baker 92, OxDcOp*
Nsengiyaremye, Dismas 1945- *WhoWor 93*
Nsubuga, Emmanuel 1914-1991 *BioIn 17*
Ntahobari, Maurice 1939- *WhoWor 93*
Ntegeye, Bernard Robert 1948- *WhoUN 92*
Ntube, Dominic Kwang 1950- *WhoWrEP 92*
Nu, U 1907- *DcTwHis*
Nu'aymi, Rashid bin Abdallah al- *WhoWor 93*
Nuber, John Arthur 1943- *St&PR 93*
Nuber, Philip William 1939- *WhoAm 92*
Nuber, Richard Howard 1943- *WhoAm 92*
Nucci, Annamaria 1945- *WhoE 93*
Nucci, Leo 1942- *Baker 92, OxDcOp, WhoAm 92*
Nuccitelli, Michael Robert 1962- *St&PR 93*
Nuccitelli, Saul Arnold 1928- *WhoAm 92, WhoWor 93*
Nuchtern, Simon *MiSFD 9*
Nucis, Johannes c. 1556-1620 *Baker 92*
Nucius, Johannes c. 1556-1620 *Baker 92*
Nuckels, Jim C. 1938- *St&PR 93*
Nuckles, Elizabeth *BioIn 17*
Nuckles, Timothy J. *Law&B 92*
Nucklos, Shirley 1949- *WhoAmW 93, WhoWor 93*
Nuckolls, John Hopkins 1930- *WhoAm 92*
Nuckolls, Leonard Arnold 1917- *WhoAm 92*
Nuckolls, Robert Theodore 1933- *WhoAm 92*
Nuckols, Frank Joseph 1926- *WhoSSW 93*
Nuckols, Robert M. 1937- *St&PR 93*
Nudd, Graham Raymond *WhoScE 91-1*
Nudel, Ida *BioIn 17*
Nudelman, Arthur Edmund 1937- *WhoSSW 93*
Nudelman, Walter 1924-1991 *BioIn 17*
Nudo, Alan Frank 1948- *St&PR 93*
Nudo, Patrick Roman 1964- *St&PR 93*
Nudo, Samuel 1956- *St&PR 93*
Nudo, Thomas 1951- *St&PR 93*
Nudo, Wanda M. *St&PR 93*
Nuechterlein, Carole L. *Law&B 92*
Nuechterlein, Gerald F. 1930- *St&PR 93*
Nuehring, Stanley Paul 1952- *St&PR 93, WhoSSW 93*
Nuernberg, Robert Alan 1940- *St&PR 93*
Nuernberg, William Richard 1946- *WhoEmL 93*
Nuesch, Frederick Charles 1938- *WhoSSW 93*
Nuesse, Celestine Joseph 1913- *WhoAm 92*
Nuevo Kerr, Louise Ano *NotHsAW 93*
Nufer, Julia Louise 1951- *WhoAmW 93*
Nuffer, William G. 1931- *St&PR 93*
Nuffield, William Richard Morris 1877-1963 *DcTwHis*
Nugent, Ara Littell 1927- *WhoAmW 93*
Nugent, Barbara Ann 1941- *WhoAmW 93*
Nugent, Charles Arter 1924- *WhoAm 92*
Nugent, Charles Michael 1938- *St&PR 93*
Nugent, (Donald) Christopher 1930- *ConAu 139*
Nugent, D. Eugene 1927- *St&PR 93*
Nugent, Daniel Eugene 1927- *WhoAm 92*
Nugent, Edgar H., Jr. 1932- *St&PR 93*
Nugent, Edward James 1921- *St&PR 93*
Nugent, Edward Sharratt 1925- *WhoSSW 93*
Nugent, Elliott 1899-1980 *MiSFD 9N*
Nugent, G. Eugene 1927- *WhoAm 92*
Nugent, Gregory 1911- *WhoAm 92*
Nugent, Gregory W. d1992 *NewYTBS 92 [port]*
Nugent, James *ScF&FL 92*
Nugent, James R., Jr. *Law&B 92*
Nugent, Jane Kay 1925- *WhoAmW 93*
Nugent, Jean *ScF&FL 92*
Nugent, John O'Connell 1942- *St&PR 93*
Nugent, John W. *St&PR 93*
Nugent, Maynard Charles 1934- *WhoE 93*
Nugent, Michael *Law&B 92*
Nugent, Nelle 1939- *WhoAm 92*
Nugent, Nicholas 1949- *SmATA 73 [port]*
Nugent, P. Michael *Law&B 92*
Nugent, Patrick J. *Law&B 92*
Nugent, Peter E. 1942- *St&PR 93*
Nugent, Richard L. 1951- *St&PR 93*
Nugent, Robert M. *St&PR 93*
Nugent, Shane Vincent 1962- *WhoWor 93*
Nugent, Thomas D. 1943- *St&PR 93, WhoAm 92*
Nugent, Walter Terry King 1935- *WhoAm 92, WhoWrEP 92*
Nugent-Crocitto, Margaret Mary 1966- *WhoEmL 93*
Nugkuag, Evaristo *BioIn 17*
Nugnis, Alan W. 1942- *St&PR 93*
Nugteren, Cornelius 1928- *WhoAm 92*
Nuhn, Charles Kelsey 1925- *WhoE 93*
Nuitter, Charles Louis Etienne 1828-1899 *Baker 92*
Nujoma, Sam *BioIn 17*
Nujoma, Sam Daniel 1929- *DcTwHis, WhoWor 93*
Nujoma, Sam Saffishuna 1929- *WhoAfr*
Nukaga, Fukushiro 1944- *WhoAsAP 91*
Nuki, Klaus 1931- *WhoE 93*
Nukk, Mibs Wagner *WhoAmW 93*
Nuland, Harvey J. d1990 *BioIn 17*
Null, Douglas Peter 1926- *St&PR 93*
Null, Earl Eugene 1936- *WhoAm 92*
Null, Gregory Bruce 1953- *WhoEmL 93*
Null, Kathleen 1949- *WhoWrEP 92*
Null, Miriam Pincus 1926- *WhoAmW 93*
Nulman, Philip Roy 1951- *WhoE 93*
Nulman, Robert Alan 1942- *WhoE 93*
Nulman, Seymour Shlomo 1921- *WhoAm 92*
Nulton, John David 1945- *WhoE 93*
Nultsch, Wilhelm 1927- *WhoScE 91-3, WhoWor 93*
Nulty, George Patrick 1942- *St&PR 93*
Nulty, William H(arry) 1932- *ConAu 136*
Numa, Shosaku 1929- *WhoWor 93*
Numa, Shosaku 1929-1992 *BioIn 17*
Numai, Takahiro 1961- *WhoWor 93*
Nu'man, Al- *OxDcByz*
Numan, Eppo *BioIn 17*
Numann, Guy William 1932- *St&PR 93*
Numanoglu, Alilhsan 1923- *WhoScE 91-4*
Numata, Nobuo 1954- *WhoE 93, WhoEmL 93, WhoWor 93*
Numeriano, Ciudad Javier 1934- *St&PR 93*
Numerianus Marcus Aurelius Numerius d284 *HarEnMi*
Numero, Joseph A. d1991 *BioIn 17*
Numi, John 1952- *WhoAsAP 91*
Nummela, Eric Carl 1941- *WhoWor 93*
Nummi, Seppo (Antero Yrjonpoika) 1932-1981 *Baker 92*
Numminen, Kalevi 1932- *WhoWor 93*
Nunan, Francis A. 1932- *WhoE 93*
Nunan, Thomas R. d1990 *BioIn 17*
Nunemaker, Barbara Ann 1956- *St&PR 93*
Nunemaker, Richard A. 1948- *St&PR 93, WhoEmL 93*
Nunes, Alan Anthony 1957- *St&PR 93*
Nunes, Anthony A. 1928- *St&PR 93*
Nunes, Anthony Charles 1942- *WhoE 93*
Nunes, Claude 1924- *ScF&FL 92*
Nunes, Emmanuel 1941- *Baker 92*
Nunes, Geoffrey *Law&B 92*
Nunes, Geoffrey 1930- *St&PR 93*
Nunes, M. Adelaide *St&PR 93*
Nunes, Mark 1965- *WhoSSW 93*
Nunes, Morris A. 1949- *WhoEmL 93*
Nunez, Antonio 1922- *St&PR 93*
Nunez, Benjamin 1912- *WhoSSW 93*
Nunez, Emmanuel Adrien 1934- *WhoScE 91-2*
Nunez, Evian *BioIn 17*
Nunez, Jacques 1927- *WhoScE 91-2*
Nunez, Jorge A. 1941- *WhoAsAP 91*
Nunez, Patricia 1959- *WhoE 93*
Nunez, Peter K. *WhoAm 92*
Nunez, Richard Joseph W. 1958- *WhoEmL 93*
Nunez, Stephen Christopher 1961- *WhoSSW 93*
Nunez, Victor *MiSFD 9*
Nunez, William *MiSFD 9*
Nunez-Centella, Ramon Antonio 1946- *WhoWor 93*
Nunez Del Prado, Arturo 1939- *WhoUN 92*
Nunez-Harrell, Elizabeth *BioIn 17*
Nunez-Lagos Rogla, Rafael 1936- *WhoScE 91-3*
Nunez-Lawton, Miguel G. 1949- *WhoE 93, WhoEmL 93*
Nunez-Portuondo, Ricardo 1933- *WhoAm 92, WhoWor 93*
Nunez Tellez, Carlos d1990 *BioIn 17*
Nunez-Villaveiran, Ramiro 1950- *WhoWor 93*
Nungesser, Martha Kate 1953- *WhoEmL 93*
Nunis, Doyce Blackman, Jr. 1924- *WhoAm 92*
Nunis, Herman N. 1929- *St&PR 93*
Nunis, Richard Arlen 1932- *WhoAm 92, WhoSSW 93*
Nunley, Patricia A.L. *Law&B 92*
Nunley, Richard L. 1927- *St&PR 93*
Nunn, Bill *BioIn 17*
Nunn, Douglas E. 1928- *WhoScE 91-1*
Nunn, Dwight E. 1942- *St&PR 93*
Nunn, Grady Harrison 1918- *WhoAm 92*
Nunn, Jenny Wren 1944- *WhoSSW 93*
Nunn, John Francis 1925- *WhoScE 91-1*
Nunn, Julius Meyer 1951- *WhoSSW 93*
Nunn, Kent G. *Law&B 92*
Nunn, Leslie Edgar 1941- *WhoWor 93*
Nunn, Oscar Edmund, Jr. 1930- *WhoSSW 93*
Nunn, Randall Harrison *Law&B 92*
Nunn, Robert Eric 1947- *WhoE 93*
Nunn, Robert T. 1954- *St&PR 93*
Nunn, Robert Warne 1950- *WhoEmL 93*
Nunn, Sam *BioIn 17*
Nunn, Sam 1938- *CngDr 91, WhoAm 92*
Nunn, Samuel 1938- *WhoSSW 93*
Nunn, Trevor 1940- *MiSFD 9*
Nunn, Trevor Robert 1940- *WhoAm 92, WhoWor 93*
Nunn, Wallace H. 1943- *St&PR 93*
Nunn, Wilfred (Bill) 1926- *WhoWrEP 92*
Nunn, William Curtis 1908- *WhoWrEP 92*
Nunnallee, Karolyn *BioIn 17*
Nunnally, Elaine Wehle 1949- *WhoAmW 93*
Nunnally, Knox Dillon 1943- *WhoAm 92*
Nunnally, Marney Thomas 1942- *St&PR 93*
Nunnally, Sue Ann 1959- *WhoEmL 93*
Nunnari, Beverlee *BioIn 17*
Nunnelley, Douglas Buchanan 1942- *St&PR 93, WhoAm 92*
Nunnelley, Robert Berry 1929- *WhoE 93*
Nunnerley, Sandra *BioIn 17*
Nunnerley, Sandra T. 1953- *WhoAmW 93, WhoEmL 93*
Nunney, May Gertrude Gaffney 1877- *AmWomPl*
Nunns, Roger 1948- *St&PR 93*
Nuno, Jaime 1824-1908 *Baker 92*
Nunz, Gregory Joseph 1934- *WhoWor 93*
Nunz, William Robert, Sr. 1932- *St&PR 93*
Nunziato, Carl A. 1938- *St&PR 93*

Nunziato, Carl Anthony 1938- *WhoAm 92*
Nuorteva, Matti Kalevi 1928- *WhoScE 91-4*
Nuorteva, Pekka Olavi 1926- *WhoScE 91-4*
Nuotio, Kyosti Heikki 1934- *WhoWor 93*
Nuotio-Antar, Vappu Sinikka 1940- *WhoAmW 93, WhoWor 93*
Nupponen, Jarmo Tapio 1949- *WhoScE 91-4*
Nur Al-Din 1118-1174 *OxDcByz*
Nur el Hussein, Queen *BioIn 17*
Nuremberg, Michael Robert 1944- *St&PR 93*
Nurenberg, David 1939- *WhoAm 92*
Nureyev, Rudolf 1938- *BioIn 17*
Nureyev, Rudolf 1938-1993 *News 93-2*
Nureyev, Rudolf Hametovich 1938- *WhoAm 92, WhoWor 93*
Nurhachi 1559-1626 *HarEnMi*
Nuri al-Sa'id 1888-1958 *BioIn 17, DcTwHis*
Nuri As-Said 1888-1958 *HarEnMi*
Nurick, Gilbert 1906- *WhoAm 92*
Nuriev, Rinat Misbakchovich 1949- *WhoWor 93*
Nurimba, Frankie 1945- *WhoWor 93*
Nurimov, Chari 1941- *Baker 92*
Nurkin, Harry Abraham 1944- *WhoAm 92, WhoSSW 93*
Nurkse, Alan D. 1949- *WhoWrEP 92*
Nurmagambetov, Sagadat Kozhakhmet ogly *WhoWor 93*
Nurmi, Esko Viljo 1931- *WhoScE 91-4*
Nurmi, Juha 1956- *WhoScE 91-4*
Nurmi, Paavo 1897-1973 *BioIn 17*
Nurmi, Pekka A. 1953- *WhoScE 91-4*
Nurmio, Pekka A. 1930- *WhoScE 91-4*
Nurnberg, Eberhard Klaus Max 1928- *WhoScE 91-3*
Nurnberg, Walter 1907-1991 *AnObit 1991, BioIn 17*
Nurnberger, Gunther 1948- *WhoWor 93*
Nurnberger, Thomas S. 1918- *St&PR 93*
Nurnikman Abdullah 1953- *WhoAsAP 91*
Nurock, Kirk 1948- *Baker 92*
Nurock, Robert Jay 1937- *WhoAm 92*
Nurse, Paul 1949- *BioIn 17*
Nursey, W.C. *Law&B 92*
Nursey, William Charles 1943- *St&PR 93*
Nursten, H.E. *WhoScE 91-1*
Nuru, Zabra Mwana-Shariff 1945- *WhoUN 92*
Nusbaum, Daniel Michael 1946- *WhoEmL 93*
Nusbaum, Jack H. 1940- *St&PR 93*
Nusbaum, Julia K. *AmWomPl*
Nusbaum, Marlene Ackerman 1949- *WhoAmW 93, WhoE 93, WhoEmL 93*
Nusbaum-Hilarowicz, Josef 1859-1917 *PolBiDi*
Nusekabel, Mark Richard 1968- *WhoSSW 93*
Nusich, Lee Charles *Law&B 92*
Nusim, Roberta 1943- *WhoAmW 93*
Nusim, Stanley Herbert 1935- *WhoE 93*
Nusko, Bernard Newton, Sr. 1918- *WhoSSW 93*
Nuss, Barbara Gough 1939- *WhoAmW 93*
Nuss, Eldon Paul 1933- *WhoAm 92*
Nussbaum, Adolf Edward 1925- *WhoAm 92*
Nussbaum, Bernard J. 1931- *WhoAm 92*
Nussbaum, Hilary 1820-1895 *PolBiDi*
Nussbaum, Jan L. *Law&B 92*
Nussbaum, Janet Adelle *Law&B 92*
Nussbaum, Joel Herbert 1940- *St&PR 93*
Nussbaum, John Michael *Law&B 92*
Nussbaum, Joseph William 1931- *St&PR 93*
Nussbaum, Leo Lester 1918- *WhoAm 92, WhoWor 93*
Nussbaum, Martha Craven 1947- *WhoAm 92, WhoAmW 93*
Nussbaum, Paul Eugene 1952- *WhoAm 92*
Nussbaum, Raphael *MiSFD 9*
Nussbaum, Richard Anton, II 1952- *WhoEmL 93*
Nussbaum, V. M., Jr. 1919- *WhoAm 92, WhoSSW 93*
Nussbaumer, H. *WhoScE 91-4*
Nussbaumer, John George, II 1937- *St&PR 93*
Nussbaumer, Roger 1944- *St&PR 93*
Nussdorfer, Gastone 1943- *WhoScE 91-3*
Nussenbaum, Siegfried Fred 1919- *WhoWor 93*
Nussenzveig, Israel 1923- *WhoWor 93*
Nusser, Hans-Gustav 1936- *WhoScE 91-3*
Nusser, Peter R.C. 1936- *WhoWor 93*
Nussey, Clive 1943- *WhoScE 91-1*
Nussio, Otmar 1902- *Baker 92*
Nussle, James Allen 1960- *CngDr 91, WhoAm 92*
Nusslein-Volhard, Christiane *WhoScE 91-3*
Nussman, Donna Sue 1957- *WhoSSW 93*
Nusz, Debra Jane 1957- *WhoAmW 93*
Nusz, Phyllis Jane 1941- *WhoAmW 93*
Nutaitis, Charles Frank 1958- *WhoE 93*
Nutant, John Albert 1935- *St&PR 93*
Nute, Grace Lee 1895-1990 *BioIn 17*
Nute, James Boyce 1935- *St&PR 93*
Nuti, Domenico Mario 1937- *BioIn 17*
Nuti, Francesco 1955- *MiSFD 9*
Nutley, Peter *WhoScE 91-1*
Nutt, Barbara Jean 1944- *WhoAmW 93*
Nutt, Cecil Wilfred *WhoScE 91-1*
Nutt, Charles L. *ScF&FL 92*
Nutt, David 1810-1863 *BioIn 17*
Nutt, David John 1951- *WhoWor 93*
Nutt, Donald Arthur 1932- *St&PR 93*
Nutt, Niven Robert, Jr. 1929- *WhoSSW 93, WhoWor 93*
Nutt, Paul Charles 1939- *WhoAm 92*
Nutt, Roy d1990 *BioIn 17*
Nutt, Vinton Snyder 1924- *St&PR 93*
Nutt, William James 1945- *WhoAm 92*
Nuttall, Grant 1932- *WhoAm 92*
Nuttall, Zelia 1857-1933 *IntDcAn*
Nutter, David *MiSFD 9*
Nutter, Edward H. 1926- *St&PR 93*
Nutter, Franklin Winston 1946- *WhoAm 92*
Nutter, June Ann Knight 1947- *WhoEmL 93*
Nutter, Tommy d1992 *NewYTBS 92*
Nutter, Wallace Lee 1944- *WhoAm 92*
Nutter, Zoe Dell 1915- *WhoAmW 93*
Nutting, Betty Woods *BioIn 17*
Nutting, Cary James 1961- *WhoEmL 93, WhoSSW 93*
Nutting, Charles Bernard 1906- *WhoAm 92*
Nutting, George Ogden 1935- *St&PR 93, WhoAm 92*
Nutting, Jack *WhoScE 91-1*
Nutting, Robert M. 1962- *St&PR 93*
Nutting, Wallace Hall 1928- *WhoAm 92*
Nuttle, Thomas Oliver 1929- *WhoAm 92*
Nutzle, Futzie 1942- *WhoAm 92*
Nuvolari, Tazio 1892-1953 *BioIn 17*
Nuyts, Hans Theo 1962- *WhoWor 93*
Nuyts, Jean 1936- *WhoScE 91-2*
Nuytten, Bruno 1945- *MiSFD 9*
Nuzio, Alfred Anthony 1933- *St&PR 93*
Nuzum, John M. 1939- *St&PR 93*
Nuzum, John M., Jr. 1939- *WhoAm 92*
Nuzum, Robert Weston 1952- *WhoEmL 93*
Nuzzo, Paul L. 1944- *St&PR 93*
Nuzzo, Salvatore Joseph 1931- *St&PR 93, WhoAm 92*
Nwachukwu, Ike *WhoWor 93*
Nwagwu, Emmanuel Chijioke 1951- *WhoSSW 93*
Nwako, Moatlagola P.K. 1932- *WhoAfr*
Nwaneri, Angela Ngozi *Law&B 92*
Nwankwo, Victor Uzoma 1944- *WhoWor 93*
Nwapa, Flora 1931- *DcLB 125 [port]*
Nyachae, Simeon 1932- *BioIn 17*
Nyad, Diana *BioIn 17*
Nyad, Diana 1949- *ConAu 136*
Nyagah, Jeremiah Joseph Mwaniki 1920- *WhoAfr*
Nyakyi, Anthony Balthazar 1936- *WhoUN 92*
Nyarady, Elemer 1923- *St&PR 93*
Nyari, Linda Jean *Law&B 92*
Nyberg, Bjorn 1929- *ScF&FL 92*
Nyberg, David Alan 1943- *WhoE 93*
Nyberg, Donald A. 1951- *St&PR 93*
Nyberg, Jorn 1952- *WhoWor 93*
Nyberg, Lyle F. *Law&B 92*
Nyberg, (Everett Wayne) Morgan 1944- *DcChlFi*
Nyberg, Richard Lawrence 1940- *St&PR 93*
Nyberg, Ronald Andrew *Law&B 92*
Nyberg, William Arthur 1947- *WhoWor 93*
Nybo, Dennis O. 1944- *St&PR 93*
Nybolm, Erik Sten 1929- *WhoScE 91-4*
Nyborg, Wesley Le Mars 1917- *BioIn 17*
Nybro, Cheryl Lyn 1955- *WhoSSW 93*
Nyby, Christian I., II 1941- *MiSFD 9*
Nycander, Svante 1933- *WhoWor 93*
Nyce, David Scott 1952- *WhoSSW 93*
Nyce, Kinsley Frampton 1952- *WhoEmL 93*
Nyce-Campsey, Novella Fizzano 1946- *WhoAmW 93*
Nycum, Daryl Gordon 1954- *WhoSSW 93*
Nycum, Susan Hubbell *WhoAm 92*
Nydal, Reidar 1925- *WhoScE 91-4*
Nydam, Darlene 1961- *WhoAmW 93*
Nydam, David Alan 1936- *WhoAm 92*
Nydes, Lawrence B. *Law&B 92*
Nydick, David 1929- *WhoAm 92, WhoE 93*
Nydrle, Peter 1954- *MiSFD 9*
Nye, Barbara F. *Law&B 92*
Nye, Edgar (Bill) Wilson 1850-1896 *JrnUS*
Nye, Edwin Packard 1920- *WhoAm 92*
Nye, Erle 1937- *St&PR 93*
Nye, Erle Allen 1937- *WhoSSW 93*
Nye, F(rancis) Ivan 1918- *WhoWrEP 92*
Nye, Jody Lynn 1957- *ScF&FL 92*
Nye, John Frederick 1923- *WhoWor 93*
Nye, John Robert 1947- *WhoEmL 93*
Nye, Joseph Samuel, Jr. 1937- *WhoAm 92*
Nye, Judith Lin 1958- *WhoE 93*
Nye, Martin Nicholas 1944- *St&PR 93*
Nye, Miriam Maurine Baker 1918- *WhoAmW 93*
Nye, Naomi Shihab 1952- *DcLB 120 [port], WhoWrEP 92*
Nye, Nicholas *ScF&FL 92*
Nye, R. Randall *Law&B 92*
Nye, Robert 1939- *BioIn 17, ScF&FL 92*
Nye, Robert E. 1931- *St&PR 93*
Nye, Robert W. 1959- *St&PR 93*
Nye, Rollie Clayton, Jr. 1945- *WhoSSW 93*
Nye, Thomas Russell 1928- *WhoAm 92*
Nye, W. Marcus W. 1945- *WhoAm 92, WhoWor 93*
Nye, Warren Kirkeby 1914- *St&PR 93*
Nye, William Roger 1940- *WhoE 93*
Nyemaster, Ray 1914- *WhoAm 92*
Nyembo, Shabani 1937- *WhoAfr*
Nyenhuis, Jacob Eugene 1935- *WhoAm 92*
Nyer, Samuel 1925- *St&PR 93*
Nyere, Robert Alan 1917- *WhoAm 92*
Nyerere, Julius 1922- *ColdWar 2 [port]*
Nyerere, Julius Kambarage 1922- *DcTwHis, WhoAfr*
Nyerges, Alexander Lee 1957- *WhoAm 92, WhoSSW 93*
Nyerges, Christopher John 1955- *WhoWrEP 92*
Nyerges, John Elek 1958- *WhoE 93*
Nyers, Rezso 1923- *WhoWor 93*
Nyfenger, Thomas 1936-1990 *BioIn 17*
Nygaard, Henry Sigurd 1929- *WhoAm 92*
Nygaard, Jon O. *Law&B 92*
Nygaard, K.H. 1957- *WhoScE 91-2*
Nygaard, Marvin Richard 1929- *St&PR 93*
Nygaard, Richard Lowell 1940- *WhoAm 92, WhoE 93*
Nygard, Dewayne Dennis 1949- *St&PR 93*
Nygard, Holger Olof 1921- *WhoAm 92*
Nygren, Karl Francis 1927- *WhoAm 92, WhoWor 93*
Nygren, Lars Johan 1940- *WhoWor 93*
Nygren, Michael *St&PR 93*
Nygren, T. *WhoScE 91-4*
Nygren, W.D. 1926- *St&PR 93*
Nygylev, Maksim c. 1770- *IntDcAn*
Nyhan, William Leo 1926- *WhoAm 92*
Nyhart, Eldon Howard 1927- *WhoAm 92, WhoWor 93*
Nyhart, Peter G. *Law&B 92*
Nyhlen, Karen Elizabeth 1960- *WhoEmL 93*
Nyholm, Erik *WhoScE 91-4*
Nyhuis, Wayne A. 1934- *St&PR 93*
Nyhus, Lloyd Milton 1923- *WhoAm 92*
Nyilas, Istvan 1956- *WhoScE 91-4*
Nyiregyhazi, Erwin 1903-1987 *Baker 92*
Nyiri, Andras 1931- *WhoScE 91-4*
Nyiri, Balazs 1958- *WhoScE 91-4*
Nyiri, Joseph Anton 1937- *WhoWor 93*
Nyiri, Laszlo 1932- *WhoScE 91-4*
Nyirjesy, Istvan 1929- *WhoAm 92*
Nykanen, Markku 1948- *WhoWor 93*
Nykanen, Matti *BioIn 17*
Nykerk, K.M. 1940- *St&PR 93*
Nykiel, Frank Peter 1917- *WhoAm 92*
Nykiel, Ronald Alan 1945- *St&PR 93, WhoAm 92*
Nykrog, Per 1925- *WhoAm 92*
Nykvist, Sven 1922- *MiSFD 9*
Nykvist, Sven Vilhem 1922- *WhoAm 92*
Nylander, Richard Conrad 1944- *WhoE 93*
Nylander, Ulf Magnus Yngve 1931- *WhoWor 93*
Nymadawa, Pagbajabyn 1947- *WhoAsAP 91*
Nyman, Carl John, Jr. 1924- *WhoAm 92*
Nyman, Dave *BioIn 17*
Nyman, Donald Hilding 1934- *St&PR 93*
Nyman, Georgianna Beatrice 1930- *WhoE 93, WhoWor 93*
Nyman, Karen E. 1959- *St&PR 93*
Nyman, Lennart O. 1940- *WhoScE 91-4*
Nyman, Mary Mallon 1935- *WhoWrEP 92*
Nyman, Maud Ingalill 1932- *WhoWor 93*
Nyman, Nina Wachs 1942- *WhoAmW 93*
Nyman, Robert Jay 1948- *WhoE 93, WhoEmL 93*
Nyman, Svante *WhoScE 91-4*
Nyman, Sven 1925- *WhoWor 93*
Nymberg, Susan L. *Law&B 92*
Nyns, Edmond-Jacques 1933- *WhoWor 93*
Nynych, Stephanie *WhoCanL 92*
Nyondo, Andrew Chola 1956- *WhoWor 93*
Nyquist, John Davis 1918- *WhoAm 92*
Nyquist, Laura Kay *Law&B 92*
Nyquist, Thomas Eugene 1931- *WhoAm 92, WhoE 93*
Nyren, Neil Sebastian 1948- *WhoAm 92*
Nyro, Laura 1947- *SoulM*
Nyrop, Donald W. 1912- *EncABHB 8 [port]*
Nyrop, Donald William 1912- *WhoAm 92*
Nyrop, Kathryn C. *St&PR 93*
Nyros, Judith Lynne 1942- *WhoAmW 93*
Nys, John Nikki 1948- *WhoEmL 93*
Nys, Robert L. *Law&B 92*
Nysether, Mark A. 1955- *St&PR 93*
Nysmith, Charles Robert 1935- *WhoAm 92*
Nyssen, Hubert G. E. 1925- *WhoWor 93*
Nyssen, Michel Paul 1935- *St&PR 93*
Nystad, Arild N. 1948- *WhoScE 91-4*
Nystedt, Knut 1915- *Baker 92*
Nystrand, Daniel I. 1936- *St&PR 93*
Nystrand, Raphael Owens 1937- *WhoAm 92, WhoSSW 93*
Nystroem, Gosta 1890-1966 *Baker 92*
Nystrom, Carolyn *BioIn 17*
Nystrom, Carolyn 1940- *ConAu 37NR*
Nystrom, Clair Karl 1947- *WhoEmL 93, WhoWor 93*
Nystrom, Harold Charles 1906- *WhoAm 92*
Nystrom, Harry 1936- *WhoScE 91-4*
Nystrom, Harry Gustav 1936- *WhoWor 93*
Nystrom, John Warren 1913- *WhoAm 92*
Nystrom, Lars Henrik Edvard 1942- *WhoScE 91-4*
Nystrom, Lowell D. 1935- *St&PR 93*
Nystrom, Robert I. 1929- *St&PR 93*
Nystrom, Steven George 1941- *St&PR 93*
Nyswaner, Ron *MiSFD 9*
Nytko, Edward C. 1943- *WhoAm 92*
Nytko, Edward Charles 1943- *St&PR 93*
Nyunt, U. Han 1942- *WhoWor 93*
Nyy, Linda Kathleen 1950- *WhoEmL 93*
Nyyssonen, Aarne O. 1921- *WhoScE 91-4*
Nyz, Myra Anne 1967- *WhoAmW 93*
Nzegwu, Louis Ifeanyi 1953- *WhoEmL 93*
Nzekio, Ernest Pouemi 1944- *WhoUN 92*
Nzinga, Queen of Matamba 1582-1663 *BioIn 17*
Nzo, Alfred 1925- *WhoAfr*

O

Oak, Pauline Eaton *AmWomPl*
Oakar, Mary Rose 1940- *BioIn 17, CngDr 91, WhoAm 92, WhoAmW 93*
Oakden, David 1947- *ScF&FL 92*
Oakeley, Herbert (Stanley) 1830-1903 *Baker 92*
Oakes, Bill
See MacDonald, Suse & Oakes, Bill *ChlBIID*
Oakes, Calvin Hawley 1904-1991 *BioIn 17*
Oakes, Derek W. 1930- *St&PR 93*
Oakes, Donald R. 1940- *WhoIns 93*
Oakes, Ellen Ruth 1919- *WhoAmW 93*
Oakes, Georgia Hall 1954- *WhoSSW 93*
Oakes, Gordon Norman, Jr. 1941- *St&PR 93*
Oakes, Harry 1874-1943 *BioIn 17*
Oakes, Helen Miller 1932- *WhoSSW 93, WhoWor 93*
Oakes, Jack C. 1931- *St&PR 93*
Oakes, James L. 1924- *WhoAm 92, WhoE 93*
Oakes, John Bertram 1913- *WhoAm 92, WhoWor 93*
Oakes, John George Hartman 1961- *WhoE 93*
Oakes, Lester Cornelius 1923- *WhoAm 92*
Oakes, Marvin Gordon 1945- *St&PR 93*
Oakes, Maud 1903-1990 *BioIn 17*
Oakes, Melvin Ervin Louis 1936- *WhoAm 92*
Oakes, R.L. 1929- *St&PR 93*
Oakes, Robert James 1936- *WhoAm 92*
Oakes, Stephen B. 1955- *WhoAm 92*
Oakes, Terry Louis 1953- *WhoEmL 93*
Oakes, Timothy Wayne 1938- *St&PR 93*
Oakes, Walter Jerry 1946- *WhoAm 92*
Oakes, William Woodside 1947- *WhoEmL 93*
Oakeshott, Gordon Blaisdell 1904- *WhoAm 92*
Oakeshott, Michael Joseph 1901-1990 *BioIn 17*
Oakey, John Martin, Jr. 1935- *WhoAm 92*
Oakey, Samuel Goode 1960- *WhoSSW 93*
Oakey, Stephen *WhoScE 91-1*
OakGrove, Artemis 1952- *ScF&FL 92*
Oakhill, Jane Vivienne 1953- *WhoWor 93*
Oakie, Jack 1903-1978 *QDrFCA 92 [port]*
Oakland, John Stephen *WhoScE 91-1*
Oakland, Velma LeAne 1939- *WhoAmW 93*
Oakley, Annie 1860-1926 *BioIn 17*
Oakley, Carolyn Cobb 1946- *WhoEmL 93, WhoSSW 93*
Oakley, Carolyn Le 1942- *WhoAmW 93*
Oakley, Claron Louis 1924- *St&PR 93*
Oakley, Cletus Odia 1899-1990 *BioIn 17*
Oakley, Dawn Elliott *Law&B 92*
Oakley, Deborah Jane 1937- *WhoAmW 93*
Oakley, Donald Lilly 1939- *WhoE 93*
Oakley, Eve Jones 1937- *WhoAmW 93*
Oakley, Francis Christopher 1931- *WhoAm 92*
Oakley, Graham *BioIn 17*
Oakley, Graham 1929- *ConAu 38NR, MajAI [port]*
Oakley, James Franklin, III 1947- *WhoE 93*
Oakley, Jerrold *St&PR 93*
Oakley, Leah Fitzgerald 1932- *WhoWrEP 92*
Oakley, Mary Ann Bryant 1940- *WhoAmW 93*
Oakley, Robert Alan 1946- *St&PR 93, WhoAm 92*
Oakley, Violet 1874- *AmWomPl*
Oakley, W. Flake 1953- *St&PR 93*
Oakley, Wanda Faye 1950- *WhoAmW 93, WhoEmL 93*
Oakley, William Edwin 1939- *St&PR 93*
Oaks, B. Ann 1929- *WhoAm 92, WhoAmW 93*
Oaks, Dallin Harris 1932- *WhoAm 92*
Oaks, Emily Caywood Jordan 1939- *WhoAmW 93*
Oaks, James Allan 1928- *St&PR 93*
Oaks, Jimmie Ralph *Law&B 92*
Oaks, Margaret Marlene 1940- *WhoAmW 93, WhoWor 93*
Oaks, Maurice David 1934- *St&PR 93, WhoE 93, WhoWor 93*
Oaks, Robert C. 1936- *WhoAm 92*
Oaks, Roger D. *BioIn 17*
Oaksey, Geoffrey Lawrence 1880-1971 *BioIn 17*
Oandasan, William 1947- *WhoWrEP 92*
Oates, Carl Everette 1931- *WhoAm 92*
Oates, Dennis Matthew 1952- *St&PR 93*
Oates, James Maclay 1946- *St&PR 93, WhoAm 92*
Oates, John 1949-
See Hall, Daryl 1949- & Oates, John 1949- *SoulM*
Oates, John Alexander, III 1932- *WhoAm 92*
Oates, John Francis 1934- *WhoAm 92*
Oates, Johnny 1946- *WhoAm 92, WhoE 93*
Oates, Joyce Carol *ScF&FL 92*
Oates, Joyce Carol 1938- *BioIn 17, MagSAmL [port], WhoAm 92, WhoAmW 93, WhoWrEP 92, WorLitC [port]*
Oates, Kathleen Courtney 1934- *WhoAmW 93*
Oates, Peter Joseph 1947- *WhoE 93*
Oates, Richard Patrick 1937- *WhoE 93*
Oates, Stephen Baery 1936- *WhoAm 92*
Oates, Warren 1928-1982 *IntDcF 2-3 [port]*
Oates, William Armstrong, Jr. 1942- *WhoAm 92*
Oates, William Wilfred d1876 *BioIn 17*
Oates Domenick, Kathryn 1959- *WhoE 93*
Oathout, James M. *Law&B 92*
Oatis, Peter H. 1944-1990 *BioIn 17*
Oatman, Eric Furber 1939- *WhoWrEP 92*
Oatman, James Edward 1949- *St&PR 93*
Oatman, Olive Ann c. 1838-1903 *BioIn 17*
Oatman, Richard P. *Law&B 92*
Oatney, Cecilia Kay 1956- *WhoAmW 93, WhoEmL 93*
Oatway, Francis Carlyle 1936- *WhoAm 92*
Oba, Minako 1930- *BioIn 17*
Oba, Roger Myron 1960- *WhoSSW 93*
Obadia, Andre Isaac 1927- *WhoWor 93*
Obadiah, Victor 1942- *St&PR 93*
Obando y Bravo, Miguel 1926- *DcCPCAm*
O'Bannion, Margaret Jean 1954- *St&PR 93*
O'Bannion, Mindy Martha Martin 1953- *WhoAmW 93*
O'Bannon, Dan 1946- *MiSFD 9*
O'Bannon, Dan(iel Thomas) 1946- *ConAu 138*
O'Bannon, Don Tella, Jr. 1957- *WhoSSW 93*
O'Bannon, Frank Lewis 1930- *WhoAm 92*
O'Bannon, Rockne S. *MiSFD 9*
Obanya, Pius Augustine Ike 1939- *WhoUN 92*
Obara, Patricia E. *Law&B 92*
Obara, Patricia E. 1952- *St&PR 93*
O'Barr, Jean Fox 1942- *WhoWrEP 92*
O'Barr, William McAlston 1942- *WhoAm 92*
Obasanjo, Olusegun 1937- *WhoAfr*
Obaseki, Lovette I. 1953- *WhoAmW 93, WhoWor 93*
Obasi, G.O.P. *WhoScE 91-4*
Obasi, Godwin Olu Patrick 1933- *WhoUN 92*
Obata, Hideyoshi 1880-1944 *HarEnMi*
Obbie, Mark Joseph 1959- *WhoSSW 93*
Obdyke, Louis K. *Law&B 92*
Obear, Frederick Woods 1935- *WhoAm 92, WhoSSW 93*
Obedencio, Santiago Uyguangco 1940- *St&PR 93*
Obee, Jane E. *Law&B 92*
O'Beirne, Andrew Jon 1944- *WhoE 93*
O'Beirne, John W. d1990 *BioIn 17*
Obenauf, Henry C. 1930- *St&PR 93*
Obendorf, Sharon Kay 1939- *WhoAmW 93*
Obeng, Paul Victor 1947- *WhoAfr*
Obenhaus, Victor 1903- *WhoAm 92*
Obenschain, Eunice M. *AmWomPl*
Obenson, Philip 1948- *WhoWor 93*
Ober, A. Clinton 1944- *St&PR 93*
Ober, Douglas Gary 1946- *St&PR 93, WhoAm 92*
Ober, Eric W. *WhoAm 92, WhoE 93*
Ober, Ken *BioIn 17*
Ober, Richard Francis, Jr. *Law&B 92*
Ober, Richard Francis, Jr. 1943- *St&PR 93, WhoAm 92*
Ober, Russell John, Jr. 1948- *WhoAm 92, WhoE 93, WhoWor 93*
Ober, Stuart A. 1946- *WhoWrEP 92*
Ober, Stuart Alan 1946- *WhoAm 92*
Ober, Thomas M. *Law&B 92*
Oberbeck, Paul A. 1934- *St&PR 93*
Oberdick, John Ernest 1956- *WhoEmL 93*
Oberdier, Ronald Ray 1945- *WhoSSW 93*
Oberdorfer, Eugene, II 1932- *WhoIns 93*
Oberdorfer, Franz 1951- *WhoWor 93*
Oberdorfer, Louis F. 1919- *WhoAm 92, WhoE 93*
Oberdorfer, Louis Falk 1919- *CngDr 91*
Oberdorfer, Paul Ellsworth, III 1950- *WhoEmL 93*
Oberender, Frederick Garrett 1933- *WhoAm 92*
Oberg, Bo F. 1939- *WhoScE 91-4*
Oberg, Charlotte H. 1936- *ScF&FL 92*
Oberg, Charlotte Henley 1936- *WhoSSW 93*
Oberg, Debra A. 1965- *St&PR 93*
Oberg, Debra Ann 1964- *WhoEmL 93*
Oberg, Donald E. d1992 *NewYTBS 92*
Oberg, James Edward 1944- *WhoSSW 93*
Oberg, Jeffrey A. 1954- *St&PR 93*
Oberg, John 1951- *St&PR 93*
Oberg, Kalervo 1901-1973 *IntDcAn*
Oberg, Kjell Erik 1946- *WhoWor 93*
Oberg, P. Ake 1937- *WhoScE 91-4*
Oberg, Roger Winston 1919- *WhoAm 92*
Oberg, Sven Erik 1939- *St&PR 93*
Oberg, Wally *Law&B 92*
Obergfell, Richard R. 1934- *St&PR 93*
Oberhammer, Heinz Karl 1939- *WhoWor 93*
Oberhausen, Joyce Ann Wynn 1941- *WhoAmW 93, WhoSSW 93, WhoWor 93*
Oberhellman, Theodore Arnold, Jr. 1934- *St&PR 93*
Oberhoffer, Emil (Johann) 1867-1933 *Baker 92*
Oberholtzer, Craig S. 1952- *St&PR 93*
Oberholtzer, Steven Lee 1954- *WhoEmL 93*
Oberhuber, Konrad Johannes 1935- *WhoAm 92*
Oberlander, Cornelia Hahn *BioIn 17*
Oberlander, Hans-Erich 1925- *WhoScE 91-4*
Oberlander, Marjorie *BioIn 17*
Oberlander, Michael 1931- *St&PR 93*
Oberle, Edwin Francis 1941- *St&PR 93*
Oberle, Frank 1932- *WhoAm 92, WhoE 93*
Oberle, Gerard Charles Joseph 1956- *WhoE 93*
Oberle, Joseph 1958- *ConAu 136, SmATA 69 [port]*
Oberle, Mark S. 1956- *St&PR 93*
Oberleas, Donald 1933- *WhoSSW 93*
Oberlies, John W. 1939- *St&PR 93*
Oberlies, John William 1939- *WhoAm 92*
Oberlin, Earl Clifford, III 1956- *WhoEmL 93*
Oberlin, Guy 1940- *WhoScE 91-2*
Oberlin, Reba Ruth 1931- *WhoAmW 93*
Oberlin, Russell 1928- *OxDcOp*
Oberlin, Russell (Keys) 1928- *Baker 92*
Oberly, Charles Monroe, III 1946- *WhoAm 92, WhoE 93*
Oberly, Kathryn A. *Law&B 92*
Obermaier, Oldrich 1948- *WhoScE 91-4*
Obermaier, Otto George 1936- *WhoAm 92*
Oberman, Helena 1925- *WhoScE 91-4*
Oberman, Joy *Law&B 92*
Oberman, Kenneth J. d1992 *NewYTBS 92 [port]*
Oberman, Lawrence H. 1940- *St&PR 93*
Oberman, Paul E. 1945- *St&PR 93*
Obermann, C. Esco 1904- *WhoAm 92*
Obermann, George 1935- *WhoWor 93*
Obermann, Richard Michael 1949- *WhoE 93, WhoEmL 93, WhoWor 93*
Obermayer, Herman Joseph 1924- *WhoSSW 93, WhoWor 93*
Obermeier, Otto Robert 1928- *St&PR 93*
Obermeit, Theodore C. 1939- *St&PR 93*
Obermeyer, Isabella
See Rossi, Lauro 1812-1885 *OxDcOp*
Obermeyer, Klaus *BioIn 17*
Obermeyer, Nancy Joan 1955- *WhoAmW 93*
Obermeyer, Theresa Nangle 1945- *WhoAmW 93*
Obernauer, Marne 1919- *St&PR 93, WhoAm 92*
Obernauer, Marne, Jr. 1943- *St&PR 93, WhoAm 92*

Oberndorf, Meyera E. WhoAm 92, WhoAmW 93, WhoSSW 93
Obernier, Robert Bradley 1937- St&PR 93, WhoAm 92
Oberon, Merle 1911-1979 BioIn 17, IntDcF 2-3 [port]
Oberrecht, Wolfgang S. Law&B 92
Oberrieder, John L. 1924- St&PR 93
O'Berry, Carl Gerald 1936- WhoAm 92
O'Berry, Phillip Aaron 1933- WhoAm 92
Oberschlake, Dwight 1925- St&PR 93
Oberst, Paul 1914- WhoAm 92
Oberst, Robert Bruce 1931- St&PR 93
Oberst, Robert C. 1952- St&PR 93
Oberst, Robert John 1929- WhoE 93
Oberstar, Helen Elizabeth WhoAmW 93
Oberstar, James L. 1934- CngDr 91, WhoAm 92
Oberstein, Leonard Harold 1946- WhoE 93
Oberstein, Marydale 1942- WhoAmW 93, WhoWor 93
Obert, Charles Frank 1937- WhoAm 92
Obert, Edward Fredric 1910- WhoAm 92
Obert, Paul R. Law&B 92
Obert, Paul R. 1928- St&PR 93
Obert, Paul Richard 1928- WhoAm 92
Oberth, Hermann 1894-1989 BioIn 17
Oberthur, Charles 1819-1895 Baker 92
Oberwortmann, C. D. 1910- WhoAm 92
Obey, David R. 1938- CngDr 91, PolPar
Obey, David Ross 1938- WhoAm 92
Obey, Richard Arthur 1945- WhoSSW 93
Obi, James E. AfrAmBi
Obi, Keiichiro 1927- WhoWor 93
Obiang, Teodoro Nguema Mbasogo 1942- WhoAfr
Obiang Nguema Mbasogo, Teodoro 1942- WhoWor 93
Obimpeh, Steve G. 1941- WhoAfr
Obinata, Masuo 1943- WhoWor 93
Obis, Paul Barrett Luty, Jr. 1951- WhoAm 92
Oblad, Alexander Golden 1909- WhoAm 92
Oblak, John Byron 1942- WhoAm 92
Oblak, Robert O. 1941- St&PR 93
Oblath, Steven Bartley 1954- WhoE 93
Obledo, Mario G. 1932- HispAmA [port]
Obler, Kathryn E. Law&B 92
Obligado, Lilian 1931- BioIn 17
O'Block, Robert Paul 1943- WhoAm 92
Obloy, Gregory J. 1943- St&PR 93
Obloy, Leo A. 1913- St&PR 93
Obolensky, Ivan 1925- WhoAm 92, WhoE 93
Obolensky, Marilyn Wall 1929- WhoAm 92
Oboler, Arch 1907-1987 ScF&FL 92
Oboler, Arch 1909-1987 MiSFD 9N
Oboler, Eli M. 1915-1983 BioIn 17
Obomsawin, Alanis 1932- WhoAmW 93
Obone, Aloysius Edeke 1930- WhoWor 93
Obookiah, Henry 1792?-1818 BioIn 17
Oborin, Lev (Nikolaievich) 1907-1974 Baker 92
Obote, Milton 1924- DcTwHis
Obouhov, Nicolas 1892-1954 Baker 92
Oboussier, Robert 1900-1957 Baker 92
O'Boyle, James Bernard 1928- WhoAm 92
O'Boyle, Maureen BioIn 17
O'Boyle, Robert L. 1935- WhoAm 92
O'Boyle, Thomas Patrick 1920- St&PR 93
Oboyski-Battelene, Joanne Marie 1956- WhoEmL 93
Oboz, Kim M. Law&B 92
Obradovic, Aleksandar 1927- Baker 92
O'Branagan, Devin ScF&FL 92
Obrand, Barry S. 1948- St&PR 93
Obray, Colin Dudley WhoScE 91-1
Obraztova, Elena 1937- WhoWor 93
Obraztsova, Elena 1937- OxDcOp
Obraztsova, Elena (Vasilievna) 1937- Baker 92
Obrebski, Jozef 1905-1967 IntDcAn
Obrecht, Fred ScF&FL 92
Obrecht, Jacob 1450?-1505 Baker 92
Obrecht, Kenneth W. 1933- St&PR 93
O'Bree, Michael Peter 1949- St&PR 93
Obregon, Alvaro DcCPCAm
Obregon, Alvaro 1880-1928 DcTwHis
Obreht, Jacob 1450?-1505 Baker 92
Obremski, Charles Peter 1946- WhoEmL 93
Obretenov, Apostol 1930- WhoWor 93
Obretenov, Svetoslav 1909-1955 Baker 92
Obretenov, Tzvetan 1941- WhoScE 91-4
O'Briain, Niall P. WhoAm 92, WhoE 93
O'Brian, Frank WhoWrEP 92
O'Brian, Hugh 1930- WhoAm 92
O'Brian, Jack 1921- WhoAm 92
O'Briant, Charles Donald 1943- WhoSSW 93
O'Briant, Jannis Lynn 1950- WhoEmL 93
O'Briant, Pat Wayne 1960- WhoEmL 93
O'Brien, Albert J. 1914- St&PR 93
O'Brien, Albert James 1914- WhoAm 92
O'Brien, Ana Colomar NotHsAW 93
O'Brien, Andrew M. 1952- WhoIns 93
O'Brien, Anita M. Law&B 92
O'Brien, Anna Belle Clement WhoAmW 93
O'Brien, Annemarie 1963- WhoAmW 93
O'Brien, Anthony Francis 1938- WhoSSW 93
O'Brien, Beatrice Marie 1920- WhoWrEP 92
O'Brien, Carol Jean 1939- WhoAmW 93, WhoWor 93
O'Brien, Catherine Louise 1930- WhoAmW 93
O'Brien, Charles Francis 1939- WhoE 93
O'Brien, Charles G. 1931- St&PR 93, WhoAm 92
O'Brien, Charles H. 1920- WhoAm 92, WhoSSW 93
O'Brien, Charles James 1935- St&PR 93
O'Brien, Charles Loren, III 1951- WhoEmL 93
O'Brien, Charles P. 1936- St&PR 93
O'Brien, Charles Patrick 1936- WhoIns 93
O'Brien, Cheryl Lynn 1958- WhoE 93
O'Brien, Christopher J. d1991 BioIn 17
O'Brien, Clarence J. 1942- St&PR 93
O'Brien, Colleen Ann 1967- WhoE 93, WhoEmL 93
O'Brien, Colleen Ann Domitilla 1947- WhoAmW 93
O'Brien, Conor Cruise 1917- WhoWor 93
O'Brien, Cornelius Francis Law&B 92
O'Brien, D.J. WhoScE 91-3
O'Brien, Dan BioIn 17
O'Brien, Daniel R. 1946- St&PR 93
O'Brien, Daniel William 1926- St&PR 93, WhoAm 92
O'Brien, Danny H. 1950- St&PR 93
O'Brien, Darcy 1939- WhoAm 92, WhoWrEP 92
O'Brien, Darlene Anne 1955- WhoEmL 93
O'Brien, David George Law&B 92
O'Brien, David H. 1941- St&PR 93
O'Brien, David Martin 1949- WhoSSW 93
O'Brien, David P. 1941- St&PR 93
O'Brien, David Peter 1941- WhoAm 92
O'Brien, David W. 1923- WhoAm 92
O'Brien, Dawn Patterson 1961- WhoSSW 93
O'Brien, Denis Patrick WhoScE 91-1
O'Brien, Denis Patrick 1939- WhoWor 93
O'Brien, Dennis H. 1951- St&PR 93
O'Brien, Dennis Joseph 1955- WhoSSW 93
O'Brien, Donald Eugene 1923- WhoAm 92
O'Brien, Donald Gerard 1922- St&PR 93
O'Brien, E. G. MajAI, SmATA 70
O'Brien, Edmond 1915-1985 IntDcF 2-3
O'Brien, Edna BioIn 17
O'Brien, Edna 1930- MagSWL [port], WhoWor 93
O'Brien, Edna 1932- ShSCr 10 [port]
O'Brien, Edward BioIn 17
O'Brien, Edward Ignatius 1928- WhoAm 92
O'Brien, Edward W., Jr. ScF&FL 92
O'Brien, Ellen T. Law&B 92
O'Brien, Elmer John 1932- WhoAm 92
O'Brien, Erin Kathleen 1952- WhoEmL 93
O'Brien, Eugene 1927- WhoAm 92
O'Brien, Eugene 1945- Baker 92
O'Brien, Eugene James 1926- WhoE 93
O'Brien, Fitz-James 1828-1862 ScF&FL 92
O'Brien, Flann 1911-1966 BioIn 17, BritWr S2
O'Brien, Frances d1990 BioIn 17
O'Brien, Francis Anthony 1936- WhoAm 92
O'Brien, Frank B. 1926- WhoAm 92
O'Brien, Frank B. 1946- WhoAm 92, WhoEmL 93
O'Brien, G. Robert 1936- St&PR 93, WhoAm 92
O'Brien, Gail Lynne 1946- WhoAmW 93
O'Brien, Gail Maureen Law&B 92
O'Brien, George 1945- BioIn 17
O'Brien, George Aloysius 1944- WhoAm 92
O'Brien, George Aloysius, Jr. 1948- WhoE 93
O'Brien, George Dennis 1931- WhoAm 92, WhoE 93, WhoWor 93
O'Brien, Gerald A. Law&B 92
O'Brien, Gerald James 1923- WhoAm 92
O'Brien, Gregory Francis 1950- WhoE 93, WhoEmL 93, WhoWor 93
O'Brien, Gregory Michael St. Lawrence 1944- WhoSSW 93
O'Brien, Helene Jeannette 1946- WhoEmL 93
O'Brien, Hubert J., Jr. 1952- St&PR 93
O'Brien, J. Willard 1930- WhoAm 92
O'Brien, James Aloysius 1936- WhoAm 92
O'Brien, James B. 1949- St&PR 93
O'Brien, James Charles 1949- WhoE 93
O'Brien, James Edward 1912- WhoAm 92
O'Brien, James Henry, Jr. 1946- WhoEmL 93
O'Brien, James Jerome 1929- WhoAm 92
O'Brien, James Joseph 1935- WhoAm 92
O'Brien, James Kevin 1959- WhoSSW 93
O'Brien, James Leo 1924- St&PR 93
O'Brien, James W. 1935- St&PR 93
O'Brien, Jane M. 1953- WhoAmW 93
O'Brien, Jim 1947- MiSFD 9
O'Brien, Joanne Katherine 1955- WhoWor 93
O'Brien, John Law&B 92, MiSFD 9
O'Brien, John Conway WhoAm 92, WhoWor 93
O'Brien, John Donald 1938- WhoSSW 93
O'Brien, John F. 1943- WhoIns 93
O'Brien, John F., Jr. WhoAm 92
O'Brien, John Feighan 1936- WhoAm 92
O'Brien, John Francis 1943- St&PR 93
O'Brien, John Graham 1948- WhoEmL 93
O'Brien, John J. Law&B 92
O'Brien, John Kevin 1958- WhoEmL 93
O'Brien, John Kieran WhoScE 91-1
O'Brien, John M. 1942- St&PR 93
O'Brien, John Patrick Law&B 92
O'Brien, John Patrick 1959- WhoWor 93
O'Brien, John Steininger 1936- WhoE 93
O'Brien, John Thomas 1945- WhoWrEP 92
O'Brien, John Wilfrid 1931- WhoAm 92
O'Brien, John William, Jr. 1937- WhoWor 93
O'Brien, Joseph E. 1933- St&PR 93
O'Brien, Joseph E. 1940- WhoIns 93
O'Brien, Joseph P. 1940- St&PR 93
O'Brien, Joseph Patrick 1950- St&PR 93
O'Brien, Joseph Patrick, Jr. 1940- WhoAm 92
O'Brien, Kate 1897-1974 BioIn 17
O'Brien, Katharine WhoWrEP 92
O'Brien, Katherine DcChlFi
O'Brien, Katherine Akillian 1946- WhoAmW 93
O'Brien, Keith Thomas 1949- WhoE 93
O'Brien, Kenneth Robert 1937- WhoAm 92
O'Brien, Kevin J. 1934- WhoAm 92
O'Brien, Kevin James 1954- WhoAm 92
O'Brien, Kevin Patrick 1944- St&PR 93
O'Brien, Lawrence Alan 1956- WhoSSW 93
O'Brien, Lawrence F. BioIn 17
O'Brien, Lawrence F. 1917-1990 PolPar
O'Brien, Linda Grant Law&B 92
O'Brien, Lori L. Law&B 92
O'Brien, Louise BioIn 17
O'Brien, Lynn Denise Law&B 92
O'Brien, Margaret 1937- IntDcF 2-3 [port], WhoAm 92
O'Brien, Margaret Hoffman 1947- WhoAmW 93
O'Brien, Marge Ett 1938- WhoAmW 93
O'Brien, Mark Stephen 1933- WhoAm 92
O'Brien, Martin James, Jr. 1940- St&PR 93
O'Brien, Mary Devon 1944- WhoAmW 93, WhoE 93, WhoWor 93
O'Brien, Mary Kaye 1960- WhoAmW 93
O'Brien, Maurice James 1925- WhoAm 92
O'Brien, Michael J. WhoIns 93
O'Brien, Michael John 1930- WhoAm 92
O'Brien, Michael John 1960- WhoE 93
O'Brien, Michael Joseph 1962- St&PR 93
O'Brien, Michael Wilfrid 1944- St&PR 93
O'Brien, Moira 1933- WhoScE 91-3
O'Brien, Murrough Hall 1945- WhoE 93
O'Brien, Neal Ray 1937- WhoAm 92
O'Brien, Neil J. Law&B 92
O'Brien, Neil Justin 1932- St&PR 93
O'Brien, Niall BioIn 17
O'Brien, Patricia Mary 1951- WhoAmW 93, WhoEmL 93
O'Brien, Patricia Nevin 1957- WhoAmW 93
O'Brien, Patrick Anthony, III 1963- WhoSSW 93
O'Brien, Patrick J. 1947- WhoIns 93
O'Brien, Patrick Michael 1943- WhoAm 92, WhoSSW 93
O'Brien, Patrick W. d1990 BioIn 17
O'Brien, Patrick W. 1946- St&PR 93
O'Brien, Paul A. 1956- St&PR 93
O'Brien, Paul Charles 1939- St&PR 93
O'Brien, Paul Herbert 1930- WhoAm 92
O'Brien, Paul J. 1927- WhoAm 92
O'Brien, Paul Jerry 1925- St&PR 93
O'Brien, Paul T. Law&B 92
O'Brien, Penny 1928- WhoWrEP 92
O'Brien, Ralph H. 1929- St&PR 93
O'Brien, Raymond F. 1922- St&PR 93
O'Brien, Raymond Francis 1922- WhoAm 92
O'Brien, Raymond V., Jr. 1927- St&PR 93
O'Brien, Raymond Vincent, Jr. 1927- WhoAm 92
O'Brien, Richard ScF&FL 92
O'Brien, Richard Desmond 1929- WhoAm 92, WhoE 93, WhoWor 93
O'Brien, Richard Francis 1942- St&PR 93, WhoAm 92
O'Brien, Richard Lee 1934- WhoAm 92
O'Brien, Richard Rhys 1950- WhoWor 93
O'Brien, Richard Stephen 1936- St&PR 93
O'Brien, Richard Stephen 1949- WhoAm 92
O'Brien, Robert B. 1936- St&PR 93
O'Brien, Robert B., Jr. 1934- St&PR 93
O'Brien, Robert Brownell, Jr. 1934- WhoAm 92, WhoE 93
O'Brien, Robert C. MajAI
O'Brien, Robert C. 1918-1973 ChlFicS, DcAmChF 1960, ScF&FL 92
O'Brien, Robert E. WhoE 93
O'Brien, Robert Emmet 1923- WhoE 93
O'Brien, Robert Francis 1942- WhoE 93
O'Brien, Robert G. Law&B 92
O'Brien, Robert J. 1938- St&PR 93
O'Brien, Robert John, Jr. 1935- WhoAm 92
O'Brien, Robert K. 1934- St&PR 93
O'Brien, Robert Kenneth 1934- WhoAm 92
O'Brien, Robert Leonard 1936- WhoE 93
O'Brien, Robert Lewis 1942- St&PR 93
O'Brien, Robert S. 1918- WhoAm 92
O'Brien, Robert Thomas 1941- WhoE 93, WhoWor 93
O'Brien, Robert William 1935- St&PR 93
O'Brien, Roger Joseph 1947- WhoE 93
O'Brien, Romaine M. 1936- WhoAmW 93
O'Brien, Rosanne P. 1943- St&PR 93
O'Brien, Scott Timothy 1954- St&PR 93
O'Brien, Stephen Rothwell 1957- WhoWor 93
O'Brien, Sue 1939- WhoAmW 93
O'Brien, Susan Barbara 1954- WhoWrEP 92
O'Brien, Susan Theresa 1965- WhoEmL 93
O'Brien, T.D. Law&B 92
O'Brien, Terence 1915- BioIn 17
O'Brien, Thomas C. Law&B 92
O'Brien, Thomas C. d1991 BioIn 17
O'Brien, Thomas E. 1938- St&PR 93
O'Brien, Thomas F. 1938- St&PR 93
O'Brien, Thomas Francis 1938- WhoAm 92
O'Brien, Thomas George, III 1942- WhoAm 92, WhoSSW 93
O'Brien, Thomas Henry 1937- St&PR 93
O'Brien, Thomas Henry, Jr. 1943- WhoAm 92
O'Brien, Thomas Herbert 1921- WhoE 93
O'Brien, Thomas Ignatius 1925- WhoE 93
O'Brien, Thomas Joseph 1935- WhoAm 92
O'Brien, Thomas M. 1926- St&PR 93
O'Brien, Thomas Michael, Jr. Law&B 92
O'Brien, Thomas P., Jr. Law&B 92
O'Brien, Tim 1946- BioIn 17, ConAu 40NR, ScF&FL 92, WhoAm 92
O'Brien, Timothy 1926- OxDcOp
O'Brien, Timothy Andrew 1943- WhoAm 92
O'Brien, Timothy Charles 1948- St&PR 93
O'Brien, Timothy John Law&B 92
O'Brien, Timothy William 1960- WhoWor 93
O'Brien, Turlogh 1942- WhoScE 91-1
O'Brien, Walter John 1951- WhoEmL 93
O'Brien, Walter Joseph 1935- WhoAm 92
O'Brien, Wayne Joseph 1943- WhoSSW 93
O'Brien, Wendy Grahn 1961- WhoAmW 93
O'Brien, William 1852-1928 BioIn 17
O'Brien, William 1928- St&PR 93
O'Brien, William Daniel Law&B 92
O'Brien, William Daniel 1930- WhoAm 92
O'Brien, William Edward 1936- WhoE 93
O'Brien, William J. Law&B 92, WhoAm 92
O'Brien, William James 1954- WhoEmL 93, WhoSSW 93
O'Brien, William Jerome, II 1954- WhoAm 92
O'Brien-Bell, John 1929- WhoAm 92
O'Brien Smith, Valerie Elizabeth 1954- WhoEmL 93
O'Brient, David Warren 1927- WhoSSW 93
Obringer, Daniel J. 1948- St&PR 93
Obrinski, Virginia Wallin 1915- WhoE 93
Obrist, Theo J. 1936- St&PR 93
Obront, Curt David 1958- WhoEmL 93
Obrow, D. Irving St&PR 93
Obrow, Jeffrey MiSFD 9

O'Bryan, Leonel Campbell 1857-1938 *BioIn 17*
O'Bryan, Morlan *BioIn 17*
O'Bryan, Thomas W. 1947- *St&PR 93*
O'Bryan, William Hall 1919- *WhoAm 92, WhoIns 93*
O'Bryan, William Monteith 1912- *WhoAm 92*
O'Bryant, John D. d1992 *NewYTBS 92*
O'Bryant, Micheal Alfred 1939- *St&PR 93*
Obrycki, Gail Zuchniewicz 1956- *WhoAmW 93*
O'Bryon, Linda Elizabeth 1949- *WhoAmW 93*
Obrzut, Jan M. 1951- *WhoE 93*
Obsieger, Josip 1923- *WhoScE 91-4*
Obst, Lynda Rosen 1950- *WhoAm 92*
Obst, Richard C., Sr. 1936- *St&PR 93*
Obstbaum, Merilee *Law&B 92*
Obstfeld, Raymond *WhoWrEP 92*
Obstfeld, Raymond 1952- *ScF&FL 92*
Obstler, Harold 1925- *St&PR 93, WhoAm 92*
Obuchi, Keizo 1937- *WhoAsAP 91*
Obuchowski, Janice *BioIn 17*
Obuchowski, Raymond Joseph 1955- *WhoEmL 93*
Obukhova, Lydia 1924- *ScF&FL 92*
Obukhova, Nadezhda (Andreievna) 1886-1961 *Baker 92*
Obukhovskii, Valerii Vladimirovich 1947- *WhoWor 93*
Obwegeser, Hugo L. 1920- *WhoScE 91-4*
O'Byrne, Brian John 1948- *St&PR 93*
O'Byrne, Elizabeth Milikin 1944- *WhoE 93*
O'Byrne, Robert d1991 *BioIn 17*
Ocadlik, Josef *WhoScE 91-4*
O'Callaghan, Anthony Joseph 1948- *WhoSSW 93*
O'Callaghan, James Patrick 1949- *WhoEmL 93*
O'Callaghan, James Regis *WhoScE 91-1*
O'Callaghan, Jerry Alexander 1922- *WhoAm 92*
O'Callaghan, Joseph Edward 1938- *St&PR 93*
O'Callaghan, Kevin M. 1960- *St&PR 93*
O'Callaghan, Maxine 1937- *ScF&FL 92*
O'Callaghan, Pat 1905-1991 *AnObit 1991*
O'Callaghan, R.A. 1935- *St&PR 93*
O'Callaghan, Roger E. 1944- *St&PR 93*
Ocampo, Adriana C. 1955- *NotHsAW 93*
Ocampo, Angela Patricia 1946- *WhoEmL 93, WhoSSW 93*
Ocampo, Maria Luisa 1905-1974 *DcMexL*
Ocampo, Pablo V. 1925- *WhoAsAP 91*
Ocampo, Raymond L., Jr. *Law&B 92*
Ocampo, Silvina *BioIn 17*
Ocampo, Silvina 1906- *ScF&FL 92*
Ocampo, Silvinia 1906- *SpAmA*
Ocampo, Teresito P. 1942- *WhoWor 93*
Ocampo, Victoria 1891-1979 *BioIn 17*
Ocana, M. *WhoScE 91-3*
Ocana-Galvan, Oscar Rafael 1960- *WhoWor 93*
O'Canainn, Tomas 1930- *WhoScE 91-3*
Ocasek, Ric *WhoAm 92*
O'Casey, Ronan *BioIn 17*
O'Casey, Sean 1880-1964 *BioIn 17, MagSWL [port]*
Ocasio, Maureen Ann 1957- *WhoAmW 93*
Ocasio, Rafael 1960- *WhoSSW 93*
O'Cathasaigh, Donal *WhoWrEP 92*
Occelli de Salinas de Gortari, Yolanda C. *WhoAmW 93*
Occhetto, Achille 1936- *WhoWor 93*
Occhialini, David 1965- *St&PR 93*
Occhialini, Robert R. 1944- *St&PR 93*
Occhiato, Michael Anthony *WhoAm 92*
Occhicone, Michael J. 1953- *St&PR 93*
Occhiogrosso, Marilyn 1937- *WhoE 93*
Occhipinti, John *Law&B 92*
Occhiuzzo, Lucia Rajszel 1951- *WhoAmW 93, WhoEmL 93*
Occom, Samson 1723-1792 *BioIn 17*
Occomy, Marita Odette Bonner 1899-1971 *BioIn 17*
Ocean, Billy 1950- *SoulM*
O'Ceidigh, Padraig 1933- *WhoScE 91-3*
Ocenas, Andrej 1911- *Baker 92*
Och, Mohamad Rachid 1956- *WhoE 93, WhoEmL 93*
O'Chap, Dale A. 1949- *St&PR 93*
Ochberg, Frank Martin 1940- *WhoAm 92*
Ocheltree, Richard Lawrence 1931- *WhoAm 92*
Ochenkowski, Janice 1948- *WhoAmW 93, WhoEmL 93*
Ochester, Ed 1939- *WhoWrEP 92*
Ochi, Ihei 1920- *WhoAsAP 91*
Ochi, Michio 1929- *WhoAsAP 91*
Ochiai, Ei-Ichiro 1936- *WhoE 93*
Ochiai, Shinya 1935- *WhoSSW 93*
Ochiltree, Jamie 1952- *WhoIns 93*
Ochiltree, Ned A., Jr. 1919- *WhoAm 92*
Ochiltree, Stuart A. 1941- *WhoAm 92*
Ochiltree, Stuart Anderson 1941- *St&PR 93*
Ochirbat, Gombojavyn *WhoAsAP 91*
Ochirbat, Punsalmaagiyn 1942- *WhoWor 93*
Ochlis, Samuel 1923- *St&PR 93*
Ochman, Wieslaw 1937- *Baker 92*
Ochoa, Elizabeth Suzanne *WhoE 93*
Ochoa, Ellen 1958- *HispAmA, NotHsAW 93 [port], WhoAmW 93*
Ochoa, Enriqueta 1928- *DcMexL*
Ochoa, Severo 1905- *WhoAm 92, WhoWor 93*
Ochoa, Victor 1948- *HispAmA*
Ochoa Antich, Fernando *WhoWor 93*
Ochoa Barrios, Guillermina 1937- *WhoWor 93*
Ochoa-Piccardo, Victor Jose 1955- *WhoWor 93*
Ochoa Sanchez, Arnaldo *DcCPCAm*
Ochoa y Acuna, Anastasio Maria de 1783-1833 *DcMexL*
Ochs, Adolph Simon 1858-1935 *GayN, JrnUS*
Ochs, Ann W. 1955- *St&PR 93*
Ochs, Donald Elias 1936- *St&PR 93*
Ochs, Michael 1937- *WhoAm 92*
Ochs, Phil 1940-1976 *BioIn 17*
Ochs, Robert David 1915- *WhoAm 92*
Ochs, Robert F. *Law&B 92*
Ochs, Robert Hanson 1926- *WhoE 93*
Ochs, Sidney 1924- *WhoAm 92*
Ochs, Siegfried 1858-1929 *Baker 92*
Ochs, Stanley Gilbert 1931- *WhoSSW 93*
Ochsenbein, Elizabeth Jane 1951- *WhoAmW 93*
Ochsenwald, William Leo 1943- *WhoSSW 93*
Ochshorn, Susan 1953- *WhoAm 92*
Ochsner, Othon Henry, II 1934- *WhoWor 93*
Ochsner, Robert C. 1940- *St&PR 93*
Ochudlo, Stanislaw Grzegorz 1957- *WhoWor 93*
O'Cinneide, Sean 1922- *WhoScE 91-3*
Ockeghem, Johannes c. 1410-1497 *Baker 92*
Ockels, Theodore S. 1926- *St&PR 93*
Ockels, Wubbo Johannes 1946- *WhoScE 91-3, WhoWor 93*
Ockenden, John Michael 1933- *WhoWor 93*
Ockenheim, Johannes c. 1410-1497 *Baker 92*
Ocker, H.-D. *WhoScE 91-3*
Ocker, Ralph F. 1933- *St&PR 93*
Ockerbloom, Richard C. 1929- *St&PR 93, WhoAm 92*
Ockerse, Thomas 1940- *WhoAm 92*
Ockert, Roy Anthony, Jr. 1945- *WhoSSW 93*
Ockhuizen, Theodore 1948- *WhoScE 91-3*
Ockman, Nathan 1926- *WhoE 93*
Ock Man-Ho 1926- *WhoAsAP 91*
Ockrent, Mike *MiSFD 9*
O'Clair, David Francis 1941- *WhoIns 93*
O Cleirigh, Micheal c. 1590-1643 *BioIn 17*
O'Clock, Joy 1930- *WhoAmW 93*
Ocock, Raymond Henry 1928- *WhoE 93*
O Conaire, Padraic 1883-1928 *BioIn 17*
O'Connell, Angela Fullmer 1951- *WhoEmL 93*
O'Connell, Anthony J. 1938- *WhoAm 92, WhoSSW 93*
O'Connell, Antoinette Kathleen 1944- *WhoE 93*
O'Connell, Barbara Eustace 1926- *WhoAmW 93*
O'Connell, Brendan J. *WhoIns 93*
O'Connell, Brian 1930- *WhoAm 92*
O'Connell, Brian Charles 1958- *WhoEmL 93*
O'Connell, Brian James 1940- *WhoAm 92, WhoE 93*
O'Connell, Carmela Digristina 1925- *WhoE 93*
O'Connell, Caroline 1953- *ConAu 139*
O'Connell, Catherine Ann 1946- *WhoE 93, WhoEmL 93*
O'Connell, Charles 1900-1962 *Baker 92*
O'Connell, Charles Francis 1955- *WhoE 93*
O'Connell, Colman *WhoAm 92*
O'Connell, Daniel *BioIn 17*
O'Connell, Daniel Craig 1928- *WhoAm 92, WhoE 93*
O'Connell, Daniel H. *Law&B 92*
O'Connell, Daniel Moylan 1949- *WhoE 93*
O'Connell, Daniel P. 1885-1977 *PolPar*
O'Connell, Daniel Walter 1946- *WhoEmL 93*
O'Connell, David *BioIn 17*
O'Connell, David d1991 *BioIn 17*
O'Connell, Desmond H., Jr. *St&PR 93*
O'Connell, Desmond Henry, Jr. 1936- *WhoAm 92*
O'Connell, Edward *Law&B 92*
O'Connell, Edward J. 1952- *St&PR 93*
O'Connell, Edward James, Jr. 1932- *WhoAm 92*
O'Connell, Edward Joseph, III 1952- *WhoAm 92*
O'Connell, Edward William 1943- *WhoE 93*
O'Connell, Francis Joseph 1913- *WhoE 93, WhoWor 93*
O'Connell, Gary B. *BioIn 17*
O'Connell, George C. 1917- *St&PR 93*
O'Connell, George Danthine 1926- *WhoE 93*
O'Connell, H.E. 1916- *St&PR 93*
O'Connell, Harold P. 1933- *St&PR 93*
O'Connell, Harold Patrick, Jr. 1933- *WhoAm 92*
O'Connell, Helen 1920- *BioIn 17*
O'Connell, Henry Francis 1922- *WhoE 93, WhoWor 93*
O'Connell, Howard Vincent 1930- *St&PR 93*
O'Connell, Hugh Mellen, Jr. 1929- *WhoAm 92*
O'Connell, Jack *MiSFD 9*
O'Connell, Jack 1959- *ConAu 137*
O'Connell, James M. 1947- *St&PR 93*
O'Connell, James Michael *WhoScE 91-1*
O'Connell, James Stapleton, Jr. 1950- *WhoEmL 93*
O'Connell, James Thomas 1963- *WhoE 93*
O'Connell, Jeanne 1951- *WhoE 93, WhoEmL 93*
O'Connell, Jeffrey 1928- *WhoAm 92, WhoSSW 93, WhoWrEP 92*
O'Connell, John E. 1931- *St&PR 93*
O'Connell, John Edward 1943- *WhoIns 93*
O'Connell, John Joseph 1938- *St&PR 93*
O'Connell, Joseph F., III *Law&B 92*
O'Connell, Joseph P., Jr. 1944- *St&PR 93, WhoSSW 93*
O'Connell, Kathleen *Law&B 92*
O'Connell, Kathleen Ann 1956- *WhoEmL 93*
O'Connell, Kathleen M. *WhoAmW 93*
O'Connell, Kenneth John 1909- *WhoAm 92*
O'Connell, Kenneth Mark 1938- *St&PR 93*
O'Connell, Kevin 1933- *WhoAm 92*
O'Connell, Kevin George 1938- *WhoAm 92, WhoE 93*
O'Connell, Laurie *BioIn 17*
O'Connell, Lawrence B. 1947- *WhoEmL 93*
O'Connell, Lawrence J. *Law&B 92*
O'Connell, Lynne Christine 1957- *WhoAmW 93*
O'Connell, Margareta Bergelin 1945- *WhoAmW 93*
O'Connell, Martin P. d1991 *BioIn 17*
O'Connell, Mary Ann 1934- *WhoAmW 93*
O'Connell, Mary Ita 1929- *WhoAmW 93*
O'Connell, Matthew M. *Law&B 92*
O'Connell, Matthew M. 1952- *St&PR 93*
O'Connell, Matthew McGowan 1952- *WhoEmL 93*
O'Connell, Maura *BioIn 17*
O'Connell, Maurice Daniel 1929- *WhoAm 92*
O'Connell, Michael Leonard 1935- *WhoE 93*
O'Connell, Michael William 1943- *WhoAm 92*
O'Connell, Neil James 1937- *WhoAm 92, WhoE 93*
O'Connell, Patricia Mary 1924- *WhoWrEP 92*
O'Connell, Patrick *BioIn 17*
O'Connell, Paul Edmund 1924- *WhoAm 92*
O'Connell, Peter Kinney 1964- *WhoE 93*
O'Connell, Philip Raymond 1928- *WhoAm 92, WhoWor 93*
O'Connell, Quinn 1924- *WhoAm 92*
O'Connell, Richard 1928- *WhoWrEP 92*
O'Connell, Richard James 1928- *WhoE 93, WhoWor 93*
O'Connell, Richard Lawrence 1929- *St&PR 93*
O'Connell, Robert *Law&B 92*
O'Connell, Robert Francis 1933- *WhoAm 92*
O'Connell, Robert J. 1943- *WhoIns 93*
O'Connell, Robert John 1943- *WhoAm 92*
O'Connell, Robert M. *Law&B 92*
O'Connell, Robert Thomas 1938- *WhoAm 92*
O'Connell, Robert West 1943- *WhoAm 92*
O'Connell, Ronald Vincent 1944- *St&PR 93*
O'Connell, Rosann Joy 1946- *WhoAmW 93*
O'Connell, Susan Ann 1957- *WhoEmL 93*
O'Connell, Suzanne 1938- *St&PR 93*
O'Connell, Suzanne Bridget 1951- *WhoAmW 93*
O'Connell, Thomas Joseph *Law&B 92*
O'Connell, W.A. *St&PR 93*
O'Connell, Walter F. 1913-1991 *BioIn 17*
O'Connell, William Edward, Jr. 1937- *WhoAm 92, WhoSSW 93*
O'Connell, William Henry 1859-1944 *BioIn 17*
O'Connell, William J. *Law&B 92*
O'Connell, William James *Law&B 92*
O'Connell, William Parnell 1939- *St&PR 93*
O'Connell, William Raymond, Jr. 1933- *WhoAm 92*
O'Connell-Cooper, Sheila *Law&B 92*
O'Connolly, James *MiSFD 9*
O'Connor, Agnes *AmWomPl*
O'Connor, Anna Ray *Law&B 92*
O'Connor, Anthony M., Jr. *Law&B 92*
O'Connor, Arthur W., Jr. *Law&B 92*
O'Connor, Barbara Anne 1962- *WhoAmW 93*
O'Connor, Barbara B. *St&PR 93*
O'Connor, Bernadette Eileen 1943- *WhoSSW 93*
O'Connor, Betty Lou 1927- *WhoAmW 93*
O'Connor, Brenda M. *Law&B 92*
O'Connor, Brendan Michael 1945- *St&PR 93, WhoAm 92*
O'Connor, Brian Arthur *WhoScE 91-1*
O'Connor, Brian P. *Law&B 92*
O'Connor, Brian T. *Law&B 92*
O'Connor, Bridget Marie 1948- *WhoEmL 93*
O'Connor, C. Kelly 1944- *WhoAmW 93*
O'Connor, Carolyn Riester 1952- *WhoEmL 93*
O'Connor, Carroll *BioIn 17*
O'Connor, Carroll 1924- *WhoAm 92*
O'Connor, Charles W. *Law&B 92*
O'Connor, Christopher Bryan 1969- *WhoE 93*
O'Connor, Clarence D. d1990 *BioIn 17*
O'Connor, Colleen Mary 1956- *WhoEmL 93*
O'Connor, Daniel William 1925- *WhoAm 92*
O'Connor, Daryl John 1952- *WhoWor 93*
O'Connor, Denise Lynn 1958- *WhoAmW 93, WhoEmL 93*
O'Connor, Dennis Patrick 1955- *WhoWrEP 92*
O'Connor, Donald 1925- *BioIn 17, IntDcF 2-3, QDrFCA 92 [port]*
O'Connor, Donald John 1932- *WhoAm 92*
O'Connor, Donald Thomas 1935- *WhoAm 92*
O'Connor, Duane Lawrence *Law&B 92*
O'Connor, Duane Lawrence 1940- *St&PR 93*
O'Connor, Earl Eugene 1922- *WhoAm 92*
O'Connor, Edward Cornelius 1931- *WhoAm 92*
O'Connor, Edward Gearing 1940- *WhoAm 92*
O'Connor, Edward Gerard 1952- *WhoEmL 93*
O'Connor, Edward J. *St&PR 93*
O'Connor, Edward S. 1916- *St&PR 93*
O'Connor, Edward Thomas, Jr. 1942- *WhoE 93*
O'Connor, Edward Vincent, Jr. 1952- *WhoE 93, WhoEmL 93*
O'Connor, Eileen Mae 1944- *WhoE 93*
O'Connor, Flannery *BioIn 17*
O'Connor, Flannery 1925-1964 *AmWomWr 92, MagSAmL [port], WorLitC [port]*
O'Connor, Francine Marie 1930- *WhoAm 92, WhoAmW 93, WhoWrEP 92*
O'Connor, Francis Edward 1935- *WhoSSW 93*
O'Connor, Francis Martin 1926- *St&PR 93*
O'Connor, Francis X. 1929- *WhoAm 92*
O'Connor, Frank 1903-1966 *BioIn 17*
O'Connor, Frank D. 1909-1992 *NewYTBS 92 [port]*
O'Connor, Geoffrey J. 1947- *WhoE 93*
O'Connor, George Aquin 1921- *WhoAm 92, WhoAmW 93*
O'Connor, George Richard 1928- *WhoAm 92*
O'Connor, George Rufus 1951- *WhoSSW 93*
O'Connor, Gerald D. 1924- *St&PR 93*
O'Connor, Gerald J. 1933- *St&PR 93*
O'Connor, Ginger Hobba 1951- *WhoAmW 93*
O'Connor, Gregory Warren *Law&B 92*
O'Connor, Harold C. 1929- *St&PR 93*
O'Connor, Jack 1902-1978 *BioIn 17*
O'Connor, James *WhoAm 92*
O'Connor, James E. *Law&B 92*
O'Connor, James G. 1936- *St&PR 93*
O'Connor, James J. 1937- *St&PR 93*
O'Connor, James J. 1942- *St&PR 93*
O'Connor, James John 1937- *WhoAm 92, WhoWor 93*
O'Connor, James Joseph *Law&B 92*
O'Connor, James Joseph 1930- *WhoAm 92*

O'Connor, James P. Law&B 92
O'Connor, Jane 1947- ScF&FL 92
O'Connor, Jeremiah F. 1948- St&PR 93
O'Connor, Jim BioIn 17, ScF&FL 92
O'Connor, Joan Marie 1951- WhoAmW 93
O'Connor, John WhoScE 91-1
O'Connor, John A., Jr. 1931- St&PR 93
O'Connor, John Arthur 1940- WhoSSW 93
O'Connor, John Dennis 1942- WhoAm 92
O'Connor, John Francis 1926- WhoAm 92
O'Connor, John Ignatius 1954- WhoEmL 93
O'Connor, John J. Law&B 92
O'Connor, John J. 1948- St&PR 93
O'Connor, John J., III Law&B 92
O'Connor, John Jay, III 1930- WhoAm 92
O'Connor, John Joseph 1920- BioIn 17, WhoE 93
O'Connor, John Joseph 1959- WhoWor 93
O'Connor, John Joseph, Jr. 1913- WhoAm 92
O'Connor, John Joseph, Jr. 1954- WhoE 93
O'Connor, John Joseph Cardinal 1920- WhoAm 92, WhoWor 93
O'Connor, John Morris, III 1937- WhoAm 92
O'Connor, John P. 1925- WhoScE 91-3
O'Connor, John P., Jr. 1943- St&PR 93
O'Connor, Jon Joseph 1931- WhoAm 92
O'Connor, Joseph A., Jr. 1937- WhoAm 92
O'Connor, Joseph Daniel, III 1953- WhoEmL 93
O'Connor, Joseph Michael 1914- St&PR 93
O'Connor, Joseph W. 1942- WhoIns 93
O'Connor, Joseph William 1942- WhoAm 92
O'Connor, Julia Elizabeth 1962- WhoAmW 93
O'Connor, June Elizabeth 1941- WhoAm 92
O'Connor, Karl William 1931- WhoAm 92
O'Connor, Kathleen 1894-1957 SweetSg B [port]
O'Connor, Kathleen Green Law&B 92
O'Connor, Kathleen Maureen 1946- WhoAmW 93
O'Connor, Kevin d1991 BioIn 17
O'Connor, Kevin 1938-1991 ConTFT 10
O'Connor, Kevin Washburn 1955- WhoE 93, WhoEmL 93
O'Connor, Kim Claire 1960- WhoWor 93
O'Connor, Laurence P. WhoIns 93
O'Connor, Laurence P. 1941- St&PR 93
O'Connor, Lawrence Joseph, Jr. 1914- WhoAm 92, WhoSSW 93
O'Connor, Leonard A. 1926- St&PR 93
O'Connor, Leonard Albert 1926- WhoAm 92
O'Connor, Marge Law&B 92
O'Connor, Marianne R. 1954- St&PR 93
O'Connor, Mark G. Law&B 92
O'Connor, Martha Susan 1941- WhoE 93
O'Connor, Martin M. St&PR 93
O'Connor, Mary Ann Law&B 92
O'Connor, Mary C. d1991 BioIn 17
O'Connor, Mary Flannery BioIn 17
O'Connor, Mary Kay 1945- WhoAmW 93
O'Connor, Mary Scranton 1942- WhoAm 92
O'Connor, Maureen 1946- WhoAm 92, WhoAmW 93
O'Connor, Michael 1950- WhoEmL 93
O'Connor, Michael A. Law&B 92
O'Connor, Michael Arthur 1953- WhoEmL 93
O'Connor, Michael D. Law&B 92
O'Connor, Nancy Morrison 1951- WhoAm 92, WhoAmW 93
O'Connor, Neal William 1925- WhoAm 92
O'Connor, Neil WhoScE 91-1
O'Connor, Noreen Carr 1939- WhoE 93
O'Connor, Pat 1943- MiSFD 9
O'Connor, Patrica Walker 1931- ConAu 38NR
O'Connor, Patricia Eryl 1945- WhoAmW 93
O'Connor, Patricia Jo 1955- WhoAmW 93
O'Connor, Patricia M. Law&B 92
O'Connor, Patricia Weeks 1961- WhoAmW 93, WhoEmL 93
O'Connor, Patrick 1925- BioIn 17
O'Connor, Patrick Joseph WhoScE 91-3
O'Connor, Paul Daniel 1936- WhoAm 92
O'Connor, Paul Joseph 1944- WhoE 93
O'Connor, Paul Simon Rory 1966- WhoE 93
O'Connor, Peggy Lee 1953- WhoAmW 93
O'Connor, Peter Joseph 1932- WhoAm 92, WhoE 93
O'Connor, Philip F. WhoWrEP 92
O'Connor, R. Dennis WhoAm 92
O'Connor, Ralph Sturges 1926- WhoAm 92
O'Connor, Raymond St&PR 93
O'Connor, Richard 1962- WhoE 93
O'Connor, Richard D. 1931- St&PR 93
O'Connor, Richard Donald 1931- WhoAm 92
O'Connor, Richard E. 1932- St&PR 93
O'Connor, Richard Nugent 1889-1981 BioIn 17
O'Connor, Robert Barnard 1895- WhoAm 92
O'Connor, Robert Benson 1941- WhoSSW 93
O'Connor, Robert Edward 1931- St&PR 93
O'Connor, Robert Emmet 1919- WhoAm 92
O'Connor, Robert Emmett 1935- WhoSSW 93
O'Connor, Robert Emmett 1945- WhoE 93
O'Connor, Robert Francis 1928- St&PR 93
O'Connor, Rod 1934- WhoAm 92, WhoSSW 93
O'Connor, Sandra Day BioIn 17
O'Connor, Sandra Day 1930- CngDr 91, OxCSupC [port], WhoAm 92, WhoAmW 93, WhoE 93
O'Connor, Sinead BioIn 17
O'Connor, Sinead 1967- Baker 92
O'Connor, Stanley James 1926- WhoE 93
O'Connor, Stephen ScF&FL 92
O'Connor, Steven James 1958- WhoEmL 93
O'Connor, Terrence Law&B 92
O'Connor, Terrence John 1936- St&PR 93
O'Connor, Terrence Patrick 1958- WhoEmL 93
O'Connor, Thomas C. 1931- WhoScE 91-3
O'Connor, Thomas P. 1944- WhoIns 93
O'Connor, Thomas Patrick 1941- WhoE 93
O'Connor, Thomas Patrick 1944- St&PR 93, WhoAm 92
O'Connor, Thomas V., Jr. 1930- St&PR 93
O'Connor, Timothy G. Law&B 92
O'Connor, Tom 1942- WhoE 93, WhoWor 93
O'Connor, William Charles 1927- St&PR 93
O'Connor, William F. WhoAm 92
O'Connor, William Francis 1939- St&PR 93
O'Connor, William James 1921- WhoWor 93
O'Connor, William Matthew 1955- WhoE 93
O'Connor, William Michael 1947- WhoEmL 93, WhoWor 93
O'Connor Fraser, Susan Lee 1954- WhoEmL 93
O'Connor-Petrie, Catherine 1947- St&PR 93
O'Conor, Paul Ford 1947- St&PR 93
O'Con-Solorzano, Thelma 1942- WhoUN 92
O Criomhthain, Tomas 1856-1937 BioIn 17
O'Croix, Carl N. 1942- St&PR 93
O'Crowley, James Francis, Jr. 1923- WhoAm 92
Octavian 63BC-14AD BioIn 17
October, John 1923- ScF&FL 92
Ocvirk, Otto George 1922- WhoAm 92
Ocytko, Adam 1948- PolBiDi
Oczos, Kazimierz Emil 1931- WhoScE 91-4
Oda, Chikashi 1921- WhoWor 93
Oda, George T. 1930- St&PR 93
Oda, Hideo 1933- WhoWor 93
Oda, Nobunaga 1534-1582 HarEnMi
Oda, Randy Keith 1953- WhoEmL 93
Oda, Sennosuke 1930- WhoWor 93
Oda, Shigeru 1924- WhoWor 93
Oda, Takuzo 1923- WhoWor 93
Odaenathus, Septimius d267 HarEnMi
Odaga, Asenath 1938- BioIn 17
Odaga, Asenath (Bole) 1938- MajAI [port]
Odak, Krsto 1888-1965 Baker 92
Odaka, Hisatada Baker 92
O'Daly, Fergus 1943- St&PR 93
O'Daly, Fergus F., Jr. 1943- WhoAm 92
O'Daly, William 1951- ConAu 137
Oda Makoto 1932- ConAu 139
Odani, Tsutomu 1947- WhoWor 93
O'Daniel, Carolyn 1947- WhoAmW 93
O'Daniel, Gregory Richard 1948- WhoE 93
O'Daniel, John Alexander 1942- WhoSSW 93
Odar, Thomas John Law&B 92
Odasz, Ann Marie 1954- WhoScE 91-4
Odavic, Ranko 1931- WhoWor 93
Odawara, Ken'ichi 1933- WhoWor 93
O'Day, Anderson 1928- St&PR 93
O'Day, Anita 1919- Baker 92, BioIn 17
O'Day, Anita Belle Colton 1919- WhoAm 92
O'Day, Caroline Love Goodwin 1875-1943 BioIn 17
O'Day, Henry Francis 1862-1935 BiDAMSp 1989
O'Day, Nell d1989 SweetSg C [port]
O'Day, Paul Thomas 1935- WhoAm 92, WhoE 93
O'Day, Peggy 1900-1964 SweetSg B [port]
O'Day, Royal Lewis 1913- St&PR 93, WhoAm 92
O'Day, Sharon 1948- WhoAmW 93, WhoEmL 93, WhoSSW 93
O'Day-Flannery, Constance ScF&FL 92
Odberg, Lars G. 1941- WhoScE 91-4
Odden, Anne Seymour 1957- WhoAmW 93
Oddershede, Jens Norgaard 1945- WhoWor 93
Oddi, Frank F. 1923- St&PR 93
Oddi, Silvio Cardinal 1910- WhoWor 93
Oddi, Vincent J. 1943- St&PR 93
Oddis, Joseph Anthony 1928- WhoAm 92
Oddis, Ronald Michael, Sr. 1938- St&PR 93
Oddleifson, Peter 1932- St&PR 93
Oddo, Ross Vincent 1939- St&PR 93
Oddone, Piermaria Jorge 1944- WhoAm 92
Oddone Sulli-Rao, Elisabetta 1878-1972 Baker 92
Oddoye, David Emmanuel Michael 1930- WhoWor 93
Oddsson, David 1948- WhoWor 93
Oddy, John George 1934- WhoE 93
Ode, Kim 1955- BioIn 17
Ode, Paul Hicks, Jr. 1956- WhoEmL 93
Ode, Richard Herman 1941- WhoSSW 93
O'Dea, Constance Louise 1946- WhoAmW 93
O'Dea, Dennis Michael 1946- WhoEmL 93
O'Dea, G. Kelly 1948- WhoAm 92
O'Dea, Gregory Sean 1962- WhoSSW 93
O'Dea, Jimmy 1899-1965 BioIn 17
O'Dea, Marjory (Rachel) 1928- DcChlFi
O'Dea, Victoria Miller 1966- WhoAmW 93
O'Dea, William P. 1947- St&PR 93
Odean, Kathleen 1953- WhoWrEP 92
Odeen, Kai 1936- WhoScE 91-4
Odegaard, Charles Edwin 1911- WhoAm 92
Odegard, Margaret Bond 1925- WhoAmW 93
Odegard, Richard E. 1940- St&PR 93
Odegard, Richard Erwin 1940- WhoAm 92
Odeh, Aziz Salim 1925- WhoAm 92
Odeljan, Peter OxDcByz
O'Dell, Alan WhoScE 91-1
O'Dell, Charlene Anne Audrey 1963- WhoAmW 93
O'Dell, Charles Robert 1937- WhoAm 92
Odell, Clinton Brice 1933- St&PR 93
Odell, David MiSFD 9
O'Dell, Dennis C. Law&B 92
Odell, Donald Austin 1925- WhoAm 92
O'Dell, Edward Thomas, Jr. 1935- WhoAm 92
O'Dell, Elizabeth Ann 1960- WhoE 93
Odell, Frank Harold 1922- WhoAm 92
Odell, George Hamley 1942- WhoSSW 93
Odell, Herbert 1937- WhoAm 92, WhoWor 93
O'Dell, Irene Hamblin 1928- WhoAmW 93
Odell, Jerry A. 1926- St&PR 93
Odell, John Edward 1934- St&PR 93
Odell, John H. 1955- WhoEmL 93
Odell, Jonathan 1737-1818 BioIn 17
O'Dell, Karol Joanne 1936- WhoAmW 93
Odell, Kenneth A. Law&B 92
O'Dell, Len WhoWrEP 92
Odell, Leonard C. d1991 BioIn 17
Odell, Leonard E. 1945- WhoIns 93
Odell, Leonard Eugene 1945- St&PR 93
Odell, Lois Dorothea 1915- WhoAmW 93
O'Dell, Lynn Marie Luegge 1938- WhoAmW 93
O'Dell, Mary Ernestine 1935- WhoWrEP 92
Odell, Mary Jane 1923- WhoAmW 93
O'Dell, Michael James 1949- WhoE 93, WhoEmL 93
O'Dell, Michael Ray 1951- St&PR 93
Odell, Patrick Lowry 1930- WhoAm 92
Odell, Robert B., Jr. Law&B 92
O'Dell, Robert Benjamin Law&B 92
O'Dell, Roy William 1928- St&PR 93
O'Dell, Scott 1898-1989 BioIn 17, MajAI [port]
O'Dell, Scott 1903- DcAmChF 1960
O'Dell, Scott 1903-1989 DcAmChF 1985
Odell, Stuart Irwin 1940- WhoAm 92
Odell, William Douglas 1929- WhoAm 92, WhoWor 93
O'Dell, William Francis 1909- WhoAm 92
Oden, Chandra Renee 1968- WhoEmL 93
Oden, Gloria Catherine WhoWrEP 92
Oden, Jack David 1950- WhoSSW 93
Oden, Lon BioIn 17
Oden, Thomas C. BioIn 17
Oden, William Bryant 1935- WhoAm 92, WhoWor 93
Oden, William Eugene 1923- WhoSSW 93
Odenath, David R. 1957- St&PR 93
Odenkirchen, Carl Josef 1921- WhoAm 92
Odenwald, Sylvia Lavergne 1928- WhoAmW 93
Odenweller, John A. 1946- St&PR 93
Odenweller, Robert Paul 1938- WhoAm 92
Oder, Frederic Carl Emil 1919- WhoAm 92
Odermatt, Bruno George 1956- WhoE 93, WhoIns 93
Odermatt, Robert Allen 1938- WhoAm 92
Odersky, Walter 1931- WhoWor 93
Odescalchi, Edmond Pery 1928- WhoWor 93
O'Dess, Mary Abigail 1954- WhoEmL 93
Odets, Clifford 1906-1963 BioIn 17, JeAmHC
Odetta 1930- Baker 92
Odette, Caroline Kathryn 1961- WhoSSW 93
Odeyar, Channaiah 1921- WhoAsAP 91
Odgers, Richard W. Law&B 92
Odgers, Sally Farrell 1957- SmATA 72 [port]
Odhiambo, Thomas Risley WhoWor 93
Odhner, Carroll Gay 1945- WhoE 93
Odier, Daniel 1945- ScF&FL 92
Odin, Kyle Abram 1962- St&PR 93
Odington, Walter fl. 1298-1316 Baker 92
Odins, Williams G. 1935- St&PR 93
Odio, Eunice 1922-1974 BioIn 17, SpAmA
Odiorne, George S. BioIn 17
Odiorne, George S. d1992 NewYTBS 92 [port]
Odiorne, George Stanley 1920-1992 ConAu 136
Odioso, Raymond C. 1923- St&PR 93
Odland, George Fisher 1922- WhoAm 92
Odland, Gerald Clark 1946- WhoAm 92
Odland, Marcia Ann 1965- WhoAmW 93
Odle, E.V. 1890-1942 ScF&FL 92
Odle, Robert Charles, Jr. 1944- WhoAm 92
Odle, S. Gene 1926-1990 BioIn 17
Odle, Wesley Paul, Jr. 1933- WhoSSW 93, WhoWor 93
Odler, Ivan 1930- WhoScE 91-3
Odlevak, Robert John 1933- St&PR 93
Odlin, Richard Bingham 1934- WhoAm 92
Odling-Smee, John Charles 1943- WhoUN 92
Odlum, George 1934- DcCPCAm
Odlum, Jacqueline Cochran 1910?-1980 BioIn 17
Odlum, Jon DcCPCAm
Odlum, Karen Laubach 1949- WhoEmL 93
Odmann, Jan-Christer 1920- WhoWor 93
Odnoha, Andrew A. 1930- St&PR 93
Odnoposoff, Adolfo d1992 NewYTBS 92
Odnoposoff, Adolfo 1917- Baker 92
Odnoposoff, Adolfo 1917-1992 BioIn 17
Odnoposoff, Ricardo 1914- Baker 92
Odoacer c. 433-493 HarEnMi, OxDcByz
Odo de Cluny 878?-942 Baker 92
O'Doherty, Brian WhoAm 92
O'Doherty, Eva 1826-1910 BioIn 17
O'Doherty, Kevin 1823-1905 BioIn 17
O'Doherty, Kieran 1926-1991 BioIn 17
O Doirnin, Peadar 1704?-1769 BioIn 17
Odojewski, Stephen Stanley 1945- WhoE 93
Odom, Barbara Lin 1946- WhoAmW 93
Odom, Beth Helen 1960- WhoEmL 93
Odom, Bob 1935- WhoSSW 93
Odom, Bob 1946- St&PR 93
Odom, Carolyn 1944- St&PR 93
Odom, David Hakim 1951- WhoEmL 93
Odom, Edwin Dale 1929- WhoSSW 93
Odom, Guy Leary 1911- WhoAm 92
Odom, Ira Edgar 1932- St&PR 93
Odom, Jan Waltman Law&B 92
Odom, Joan H. BioIn 17
Odom, Joanna Beth 1949- WhoEmL 93
Odom, Karen D. WhoWrEP 92
Odom, Keith Conrad 1931- WhoSSW 93
Odom, Lorrie Furman 1943- WhoAmW 93
Odom, Mary Ann BioIn 17
Odom, Mel 1957- ScF&FL 92
Odom, Melissa Kay WhoSSW 93
Odom, Oris Leon, II 1946- WhoEmL 93, WhoSSW 93
Odom, Pat Reynolds 1935- WhoSSW 93
Odom, Robert William 1946- St&PR 93
Odom, Susan Ann 1957- WhoE 93, WhoWor 93
Odom, William Eldridge 1932- WhoAm 92

O'Donald, Burton T. St&PR 93
Odone, Augusto BioIn 17
Odone, Lorenzo BioIn 17
Odone, Michaela BioIn 17
Odoni, Robert Winston Keith WhoScE 91-1
O'Donnell, Adrian W. 1932- St&PR 93
O'Donnell, Alice Louise WhoAm 92
O'Donnell, Arthur Burgess 1924- St&PR 93
O'Donnell, Bryant 1925- St&PR 93
O'Donnell, Charles Patrick 1920- WhoAm 92
O'Donnell, Ciaran Gerard 1957- WhoWor 93
O'Donnell, Cletus Francis 1917- WhoAm 92
O'Donnell, Daniel E. Law&B 92
O'Donnell, Diane 1938- WhoAmW 93
O'Donnell, Dianne E. Law&B 92
O'Donnell, Edward 1938- WhoE 93
O'Donnell, Edward Anthony 1946- WhoAm 92
O'Donnell, Edward Francis, Jr. 1950- WhoEmL 93
O'Donnell, Edward J. 1907-1991 BioIn 17
O'Donnell, Edward Joseph 1931- WhoAm 92
O'Donnell, Edward Thomas 1939- WhoAm 92
O'Donnell, Elizabeth Martin 1944- WhoAmW 93
O'Donnell, Eugene J. 1946- WhoAm 92
O'Donnell, F. Scott 1940- St&PR 93, WhoAm 92
O'Donnell, George Fall Law&B 92
O'Donnell, Geraldine Law&B 92
O'Donnell, Hugh Christopher Law&B 92
O'Donnell, Hugh Roe 1571-1603 HarEnMi
O'Donnell, J. J. 1925- EncABHB 8 [port]
O'Donnell, James F. 1947- St&PR 93
O'Donnell, James Francis 1928- WhoAm 92
O'Donnell, James Preston 1917-1990 BioIn 17
O'Donnell, James Robert Law&B 92
O'Donnell, James Vincent 1941- WhoAm 92
O'Donnell, Jayne Patricia 1950- WhoSSW 93
O'Donnell, Jeffrey T. Law&B 92
O'Donnell, John George 1936- St&PR 93
O'Donnell, John Logan 1914- WhoAm 92
O'Donnell, Kathleen Marie 1955- WhoEmL 93
O'Donnell, Kevin 1925- St&PR 93, WhoAm 92
O'Donnell, Kevin, Jr. 1950- ScF&FL 92
O'Donnell, Kevin Patrick 1951- WhoEmL 93, WhoSSW 93
O'Donnell, Laurence Gerard 1935- WhoAm 92, WhoWrEP 92
O'Donnell, Lawrence, III Law&B 92
O'Donnell, Lisa Law&B 92
O'Donnell, Margaret 1899- ScF&FL 92
O'Donnell, Mark 1954- WhoWrEP 92
O'Donnell, Mark Joseph 1954- WhoWor 93
O'Donnell, Mark Patrick 1954- WhoEmL 93
O'Donnell, Mary Law&B 92
O'Donnell, Mary Murphy 1918- WhoSSW 93
O'Donnell, Maureen BioIn 17
O'Donnell, Michael James 1952- WhoEmL 93
O'Donnell, Michael Patrick 1936- WhoE 93
O'Donnell, Michael Paul 1956- WhoAm 92
O'Donnell, Michael R. 1957- St&PR 93
O'Donnell, Patrick E. 1937- WhoE 93
O'Donnell, Peadar 1893-1986 BioIn 17
O'Donnell, Peter 1920- ScF&FL 92
O'Donnell, Richard Michael 1951- WhoWrEP 92
O'Donnell, Richard Paul 1935- St&PR 93
O'Donnell, Richard W. 1945- St&PR 93
O'Donnell, Robert J. Law&B 92
O'Donnell, Robert John 1943- WhoE 93
O'Donnell, Robert Michael 1941- WhoAm 92
O'Donnell, Rosie BioIn 17
O'Donnell, Sandra Stehno 1950- WhoAmW 93
O'Donnell, Teresa Hohol 1963- WhoAmW 93
O'Donnell, Terrence 1944- WhoAm 92
O'Donnell, Thomas Alexander 1947- WhoEmL 93
O'Donnell, Thomas F. 1942- St&PR 93
O'Donnell, Thomas G. 1946- St&PR 93
O'Donnell, Thomas Lawrence Patrick 1926- WhoAm 92
O'Donnell, Thomas M. 1936- St&PR 93
O'Donnell, Thomas Mitchell 1936- WhoAm 92
O'Donnell, William David 1926- WhoAm 92, WhoWor 93
O'Donnell, William Hugh 1940- WhoAm 92, WhoSSW 93
O'Donnell, William J. Law&B 92
O'Donnell, William J. 1935- St&PR 93
O'Donnell, William James 1935- WhoAm 92, WhoWor 93
O'Donnell, William James 1944- WhoSSW 93
O'Donnell, William Robert 1960- WhoSSW 93
O'Donnell Simpson, Diane Louise 1955- WhoAmW 93
O'Donoghue, Bernard 1945- ConAu 137
O'Donoghue, Brian Michael 1956- WhoWor 93
O'Donoghue, Brigid 1931- WhoWrEP 92
O'Donoghue, John J. 1929- St&PR 93
O'Donoghue, John Lipomi 1947- WhoE 93
O'Donoghue, Michael MiSFD 9
O'Donoghue, Paul H. 1931- St&PR 93
O'Donohoe, John F. 1926- St&PR 93
O'Donohoe, Nicholas B. ScF&FL 92
O'Donohoe, Nicholas Benjamin 1952- WhoWrEP 92
O'Donohoe, Nick 1952- ScF&FL 92
O'Donohue, John A. Law&B 92
O'Donohue, Kathleen Meehan Law&B 92
O'Donohue, Walter John, Jr. 1934- WhoAm 92
O'Donovan, Daniel Joseph 1931- WhoScE 91-3
O'Donovan, Martin BioIn 17
O'Donovan, Michael 1903-1966 BioIn 17
O'Donovan, Thomas Raphael 1931- WhoAm 92
O'Donovan, Timothy James 1945- St&PR 93
Odo of Deuil c. 1100-1162 OxDcByz
Odor, Edwin Merle 1940- WhoE 93
Odoric of Pordenone 1286?-1331? Expl 93
O'Dorisio, Thomas Michael 1943- WhoAm 92
O'Doul, Frank Joseph 1897-1969 BiDAMSp 1989
O'Dowd, George Alan Baker 92
O'Dowd-Jana, Patricia Margaret 1949- WhoEmL 93
Odre, Steven M. Law&B 92
O'Driscoll, Anne Elizabeth 1964- WhoAmW 93
O'Driscoll, Gerald P. d1992 NewYTBS 92
O'Driscoll, Gerald P. 1947- St&PR 93
O'Driscoll, Jeremiah Joseph, Jr. 1925- WhoSSW 93
O'Driscoll, John 1936- WhoScE 91-3
O'Driscoll, Karen M. St&PR 93
O'Driscoll, Michael G. 1954- St&PR 93
O'Driscoll, William Law&B 92
Odrobinski, Wieslaw Kazimierz 1931- WhoScE 91-4
Odron, Edward Andrew 1938- WhoAm 92
Oduber, Nelson 1947- DcCPCAm, WhoWor 93
Oduber Quiros, Daniel 1921- DcCPCAm
O'Duffy, Eoin 1892-1944 BioIn 17
Odum, Eugene Pleasants 1913- WhoAm 92
Odum, Howard Washington 1884-1954 EncAACR
Odum, Jeffery Neal 1956- WhoEmL 93, WhoSSW 93
O'Dwyer, Brian 1945- WhoE 93
O'Dwyer, Eamon 1924- WhoScE 91-3
O'Dwyer, Eamonn 1923- St&PR 93
O'Dwyer, Robert 1862-1949 Baker 92
O'Dwyer, Thomas Stephen 1949- WhoEmL 93
Odzagov, Rasim 1933- DrEEuF
Odzinski, Christopher S. 1948- St&PR 93
Oe, Emily Norene 1942- WhoSSW 93
Oe, Kenzaburo BioIn 17
Oebser, Robert Charles 1939- St&PR 93
Oechsli, Kelly 1918- WhoE 93
Oechslin, Jean-Jacques Albert 1933- WhoUN 92
Oechsner, Allen G. 1945- St&PR 93
Oechsner, Frederick C(able) 1902-1992 CurBio 92N
Oechsner, Frederick Cable d1992 NewYTBS 92
Oechsner, Frederick Cable 1902-1992 BioIn 17
Oechsner, Hans 1934- WhoScE 91-3
Oeding, Lawrence Ignatius 1948- WhoEmL 93
Oeffinger, Jack Law&B 92
Oehl, Kurt (Helmut) 1923- Baker 92
OehLer, Cole 1915- WhoAm 92
Oehler, Dietrich 1915- WhoWor 93
Oehler, Jane Moody 1942- WhoSSW 93
Oehler, Jerri Moser 1943- WhoAmW 93
Oehler, Richard Dale 1925- WhoSSW 93, WhoWor 93
Oehlers, Kathleen Cecilia Robinson 1961- WhoAmW 93
Oehlert, Charles F. 1948- St&PR 93
Oehlert, Mary Esther 1954- WhoAmW 93
Oehlert, William Herbert, Jr. 1942- WhoSSW 93
Oehmann, Carl Martin 1887-1967 OxDcOp
Oehme, F. WhoScE 91-3
Oehme, Frederick Wolfgang 1933- WhoAm 92
Oehme, Michael 1950- WhoScE 91-4
Oehme, Peter K. 1937- WhoScE 91-3
Oehme, Reinhard 1928- WhoAm 92
Oehmke, Hans-Joachim 1934- WhoScE 91-3
Oehmler, George Courtland 1926- WhoAm 92
Oehrig, Robert J. 1921- St&PR 93
Oehrlein, Mary Lou 1950- WhoAm 92
Oehser, Paul Henry 1904- WhoWrEP 92
Oei, Tat Hway 1923- WhoWor 93
Oelbaum, Harold 1931- St&PR 93, WhoAm 92
Oelberg, David George 1952- WhoSSW 93, WhoWor 93
Oelert, Walter 1942- WhoWor 93
Oelgeschlager, Guenther Karl 1934- WhoAm 92
Oelkers, Kenneth Henry 1928- St&PR 93
Oellerich, David E. 1955- St&PR 93
Oellerich, Michael 1944- WhoWor 93
Oelman, Bradford C. 1938- St&PR 93
Oelman, Robert Schantz 1909- WhoAm 92
Oelofse, Jan Harm 1934- WhoWor 93
Oelrich, Paul Raymond 1950- WhoSSW 93
Oelschlaeger, Renee Louise 1948- WhoWrEP 92
Oelschlagel, Dieter 1935- WhoWor 93
Oelsner, Edward C. d1990 BioIn 17
Oelsner, Edward Carl, III 1942- St&PR 93
Oelsner, Lesley Law&B 92
Oenema, Oene 1953- WhoScE 91-3
Oepen, Irmgard 1929- WhoScE 91-3
Oeripan, Soegiharto 1963- WhoWor 93
Oermann, Marilyn Haag 1950- WhoAmW 93
Oertel, Goetz K. H. 1934- WhoAm 92, WhoE 93
Oertel, Herbert 1944- WhoScE 91-3
Oertel, John N. 1943- St&PR 93
Oerter, Al BioIn 17
Oerthel, Irmgard von 1934- BioIn 17
Oertley, Karen Oberlaender 1952- WhoEmL 93, WhoSSW 93
Oertli, Charles William 1930- St&PR 93
Oertli, J. Jakob 1927- WhoScE 91-4
Oertli, Philip A. 1927- St&PR 93
Oertli-Cajacob, Peter 1941- WhoWor 93
Oesch, Max Paul 1942- WhoWor 93
Oeslander, Rochelle Mona Law&B 92
Oess, George Peter 1936- St&PR 93
Oest, Janice Lynn 1953- WhoAmW 93
Oesterhelt, Dieter 1940- WhoScE 91-3
Oesterle, Dale Arthur 1950- WhoAm 92
Oesterlin, Peter Michael 1949- WhoWor 93
Oesterling, Thomas Ovid 1938- WhoAm 92
Oesterling, Wendy Lee 1949- WhoAmW 93
Oesterreich, Gerald W. 1946- St&PR 93
Oesterreicher, James E. 1941- St&PR 93, WhoAm 92
Oestreich, Charles Henry 1932- WhoAm 92
Oestreich, David Arthur 1933- St&PR 93
Oestreich, Linda Louise Garland 1948- WhoAmW 93
Oestreich, Martin Roy 1946- St&PR 93
Oestricher, Joy ScF&FL 92
Oestvig, Karl 1889-1968 OxDcOp
Oestvig, Karl (Aagaard) 1889-1968 Baker 92
Oeters, Fred A. 1945- WhoSSW 93
Oetken, Stanley Gene 1948- WhoSSW 93
Oetter, Bruce Christian 1949- WhoEmL 93
Oettgen, Herbert Friedrich 1923- WhoAm 92
Oetting, Mildred Katherine WhoAmW 93, WhoE 93
Oettinger, Anthony Gervin 1929- WhoAm 92
Oettinger, Julian Alan Law&B 92
O'Fallon, Peter MiSFD 9
O'Faolain, Julia 1932- BioIn 17
O'Faolain, Sean 1900-1991 AnObit 1991, BioIn 17, ConLC 70 [port], ScF&FL 92
O'Farrell, David Johnston 1948- WhoEmL 93
O'Farrell, Lisa Helme 1958- WhoAmW 93
O'Farrell, Patrick Neil WhoScE 91-1
O'Farrill, Alberto 1899- HispAmA
Ofcharsky, Edward Joseph 1947- St&PR 93
Ofek, Uriel 1926- ChlLR 28 [port]
Ofengand, Edward James 1932- WhoE 93
O'Ferrall, P.C.K. 1934- St&PR 93
Offa, King of the Mercians d796 BioIn 17
Offei, Daniel Nelson 1935- WhoWor 93
Offen, Brian Roger 1948- WhoWor 93
Offen, Mark D. 1946-1991 BioIn 17
Offen, Matt D. 1921- St&PR 93
Offenbach, Jacques 1819-1880 Baker 92, IntDcOp, OxDcOp
Offenbacker, Beth Sue 1965- WhoAmW 93
Offenberg, Sharon Lynne Law&B 92
Offenberger, Allan Anthony 1938- WhoAm 92
Offenborn, Hans P. 1936- St&PR 93
Offenhartz, Colin O'Donnell 1943- St&PR 93
Offenhartz, Edward 1928- WhoE 93
Offensend, David Glenn 1953- WhoAm 92
Offer, Daniel 1930- WhoAm 92
Offer, Francis T. d1990 BioIn 17
Offer, Mary Ellen Law&B 92
Offerdahl, John Arnold 1964- WhoAm 92
Offerman, Max 1931- St&PR 93
Offerman, Michael 1941- St&PR 93
Offerman, Muriel Kramer 1935- St&PR 93
Offermanns, Heribert WhoScE 91-3
Offet, Betty Vie 1934- WhoAmW 93
Offholter, Jean Mary 1932- WhoAmW 93
Office, Gerald Simms, Jr. 1941- WhoAm 92
Officer, Katherine AmWomPl
Officina, Stanley 1944- St&PR 93
Offield, Wrigley 1917- St&PR 93
Offit, Morris Wolf 1937- WhoAm 92, WhoE 93
Offit, Saul B. St&PR 93
Offit, Sidney 1928- WhoAm 92, WhoWrEP 92
Offner, Carl David 1943- WhoE 93
Offner, Clark Benjamin 1927- WhoWor 93
Offner, Eric Delmonte 1928- WhoAm 92
Offner, Franklin Faller 1911- WhoAm 92
Offodile, Onyebuchi Felix 1949- WhoWor 93
Offord, Robin Ewart 1940- WhoScE 91-4
Offredi, Paul St&PR 93
Offsey, Sol 1922- WhoWrEP 92
Offutt, Andrew J. 1934- ScF&FL 92
Offutt, Denver Clyde, Jr. 1949- WhoEmL 93
Offutt, James A. 1934- St&PR 93
Offutt, Nancy Jeannine 1967- WhoAmW 93
Offutt, Richard Ames 1948- WhoSSW 93
Offutt, Susan Denise 1953- WhoAmW 93, WhoEmL 93
Offutt, Warren Bernard 1928- St&PR 93
Ofhand, Jack WhoWrEP 92
O Fiaich, Tomas BioIn 17
O'Finn, Thaddeus ConAu 39NR
O'Flaherty, John F. Law&B 92
O'Flaherty, John Francis 1944- St&PR 93
O'Flaherty, Liam 1896-1984 BioIn 17, ScF&FL 92
O'Flaherty, Paul Benedict 1925- WhoAm 92
O'Flaherty, Sharon L. Law&B 92
O'Flaherty, T.H. Law&B 92
O'Flaherty, Terrence 1917- WhoAm 92, WhoWor 93
O'Flaherty, Thomas P. 1947- St&PR 93
O'Flarity, James P. 1923- WhoAm 92
Oflock, Jerry D. 1940- St&PR 93
Ofman, Jose O. 1943- St&PR 93
Ofner, James Alan 1922- WhoAm 92
Ofner, William Bernard 1929- WhoWor 93
O'Folliard, Tom 1858-1880 BioIn 17
Ofosu-Amaah, Samuel 1931- WhoUN 92
O'Friel, Daniel John 1935- St&PR 93
O'Friel, Michael F. Law&B 92
Ofshe, Richard 1941- ScF&FL 92
Ofte, Donald 1929- WhoAm 92
Ofte-Gibson, Nancy Carolyn 1957- WhoEmL 93
Ofuchi, Kinuko 1944 WhoAsAP 91
Ofverholm, Ivan WhoScE 91-4
Ofverholm, Stefan 1936- WhoWor 93
Ogada, Thomas Ariba 1936- WhoUN 92
Ogadai Khan c. 1185-1241 HarEnMi
Ogaki, Kishiro 1943- WhoWor 93
Ogaki, Masao 1958- WhoE 93
Ogan, Gerald Stanley 1925- St&PR 93
Ogan, Paula S. Law&B 92
Ogan, Russell Griffith 1923- WhoAm 92
O'Gara, Barbara Ann 1953- WhoAmW 93
O'Gara, Elaine Janet 1944- WhoWrEP 92
Ogarkov, Nikolai 1917- ColdWar 2 [port]
Ogasanovic, Dobrivoje 1938- WhoScE 91-4
Ogasawara, Isamu 1943- St&PR 93
Ogasawara, Sadako 1920- WhoAsAP 91
Ogata, Hiromaru 1931- WhoWor 93
Ogata, Katsuhiko 1925- WhoAm 92, WhoWor 93
Ogata, Katsuyo 1938- WhoAsAP 91
Ogata, Keith K. 1954- St&PR 93

Ogata, Sadako 1927- WhoUN 92
Ogata, Shijuro 1927- WhoWor 93
Ogawa, Eiji 1957- WhoWor 93
Ogawa, Hisashi 1951- WhoUN 92
Ogawa, Jinichi 1918- WhoAsAP 91
Ogawa, Kazuo 1954- WhoWor 93
Ogawa, Kunihiko 1933- WhoAsAP 91
Ogawa, Makio 1940- WhoAm 92
Ogawa, Makoto 1932- WhoAsAP 91
Ogawa, Mataji 1848-1909 HarEnMi
Ogawa, Shinichi 1948- WhoWor 93
Ogawa, Teiichiro 1936- WhoWor 93
Ogawa, Tomoya 1939- WhoWor 93
Ogawa, Toshio 1940- WhoWor 93
Ogbaa, Kalu 1945- WhoSSW 93
Ogbonnaya, Chuks Alfred 1953- WhoEmL 93, WhoWor 93
Ogborn, Martha Jo 1950- WhoAmW 93
Ogburn, Charlton 1911- WhoAm 92, WhoWrEP 92
Ogburn, David W., Jr. Law&B 92
Ogburn, David Wells, Jr. 1955- WhoEmL 93
Ogburn, Hugh B. 1923- St&PR 93
Ogburn, Hugh Bell 1923- WhoAm 92
Ogburn, Raymond R. 1922- St&PR 93
Ogburn, William F. 1886-1959 IntDcAn
Ogden, Adele 1902-1990 BioIn 17
Ogden, Alfred 1909- WhoAm 92
Ogden, Ann WhoAmW 93
Ogden, Bryan C. Law&B 92
Ogden, C.K. 1889-1957 BioIn 17
Ogden, C. Robert Law&B 92
Ogden, C. Robert 1923- WhoIns 93
Ogden, Charles Kay 1889-1957 BioIn 17
Ogden, Chester Robert 1923- St&PR 93
Ogden, Christopher Bennett 1945- WhoE 93
Ogden, Dale Francis 1951- WhoEmL 93
Ogden, David William 1953- WhoEmL 93
Ogden, Helen Gay 1945- WhoSSW 93
Ogden, Isaac 1764-1829 BioIn 17
Ogden, James Russell 1954- WhoEmL 93
Ogden, Janet AmWomPl
Ogden, Jean Lucille 1950- WhoEmL 93
Ogden, Joanne 1941- WhoAmW 93, WhoSSW 93
Ogden, John Hamilton Law&B 92
Ogden, John V. Law&B 92
Ogden, Kyle W. 1955- St&PR 93
Ogden, Maureen Black 1928- WhoAmW 93
Ogden, Megan ScF&FL 92
Ogden, P.J. WhoScE 91-1
Ogden, Peggy A. 1932- WhoAmW 93
Ogden, Peter James 1947- WhoAm 92, WhoEmL 93
Ogden, Peter Skene 1790-1854 Expl 93
Ogden, Ralph Lindsey 1941- WhoAm 92
Ogden, Raymond William WhoScE 91-1
Ogden, Robert Schuyler, Jr. Law&B 92
Ogden, Schubert Miles 1928- WhoAm 92
Ogden, Scott 1957- ConAu 138
Ogden, Stanley Lee BioIn 17
Ogden, Stephen 1951- St&PR 93
Ogden, Sylvester O. 1935- WhoSSW 93
Ogden, Tina Louise 1959- WhoEmL 93
Ogden, Valeria Juan 1924- WhoAmW 93
Ogden, Wendy Everett Law&B 92
Ogden, Will 1921- Baker 92
Ogden, William B., IV 1945- St&PR 93
Ogden, Wm. B., III 1920- St&PR 93
Ogdon, Colin WhoScE 91-1
Ogdon, John (Andrew Howard) 1937-1989 Baker 92
Ogdon, Thomas Hammer 1935- WhoAm 92
Ogdon, Wilbur 1921- WhoAm 92
Ogdon, William Duley d1991 BioIn 17
O'Geary, Dennis Traylor 1925- WhoSSW 93, WhoWor 93
Oger, Francis Raymond Emilien 1958- WhoWor 93
Oger, Robert 1947- WhoScE 91-2
Ogg, George Wesley 1932- WhoAm 92
Ogg, James Elvis 1924- WhoAm 92
Ogg, Robert D. 1918- St&PR 93
Ogg, Robert Danforth 1918- WhoWor 93
Ogg, Ronald Robert 1938- St&PR 93
Ogg, Thomas Charles 1947- St&PR 93
Ogg, Wilson Reid 1928- WhoWor 93
Oggenfuss, Robert Walter 1933- St&PR 93
Oggiano, Maria S. WhoScE 91-3
Oghigian, Haig Baptiste 1953- WhoWor 93
Ogier, James Michael 1952- WhoSSW 93
Ogier, Walter Thomas 1925- WhoAm 92, WhoWor 93
Ogihara, Toshitsugu 1910- Baker 92
Ogilby, Lyman Cunningham 1922-1990 BioIn 17
Ogilvie, Alan S. Law&B 92
Ogilvie, Christine Gay 1963- WhoAmW 93
Ogilvie, Denise M. Law&B 92
Ogilvie, Dian D. Law&B 92
Ogilvie, Donald Gordon 1943- WhoAm 92
Ogilvie, Elisabeth 1917- BioIn 17
Ogilvie, Fan S. 1944- WhoWrEP 92
Ogilvie, George MiSFD 9
Ogilvie, John Franklin 1938- WhoWor 93
Ogilvie, Kelvin Kenneth 1942- WhoAm 92
Ogilvie, Lloyd John 1930- WhoWrEP 92
Ogilvie, Margaret Pruett 1922- WhoAmW 93
Ogilvie, Marilyn Bailey 1936- WhoAmW 93
Ogilvie, Mary Hoffman 1955- WhoAmW 93
Ogilvie, Richard Ian 1936- WhoAm 92
Ogilvie, Robert Murray 1945- St&PR 93
Ogilvie, Thomas Francis 1929- WhoAm 92
Ogilvie, Victor Nicholas 1942- WhoSSW 93
Ogilvy, Colin F. 1952- St&PR 93
Ogilvy, David 1911- BioIn 17
Ogilvy, David Mackenzie 1911- WhoAm 92
Ogilvy, David Wallace 1945- St&PR 93
Ogilvy, Gavin ConAu 136, MajAI
Ogilvy, Marina BioIn 17
Ogino, Fumimaru 1941- WhoWor 93
Oginski, Franciszek Krawery 1801-1837 See Oginski, Michal Kleofas 1765-1833 Baker 92
Oginski, Michael Cleophas 1765-1833 PolBiDi
Oginski, Michal Kazimierz 1728-1800 See Oginski, Michal Kleofas 1765-1833 Baker 92
Oginski, Michal Kleofas 1765-1833 Baker 92
Ogio, Michael 1942- WhoAsAP 91
Ogle, Jerry M. Law&B 92
Ogle, Olive AmWomPl
Ogle, Sharon Ruth 1950- WhoSSW 93
Oglesbee, Della Houghton AmWomPl
Oglesby, Carole A. BioIn 17
Oglesby, Charles M. 1953- WhoAm 92
Oglesby, Clarkson Hill 1908- WhoAm 92
Oglesby, Daniel Kirkland, Jr. 1930- WhoAm 92
Oglesby, Donald Thomas 1947- WhoSSW 93
Oglesby, Douglas A. Law&B 92
Oglesby, Dwight Hadley 1941- St&PR 93
Oglesby, John Norman 1948- WhoEmL 93
Oglesby, Michael 1954- St&PR 93
Oglesby, R.H. WhoScE 91-1
Oglesby, Ray Thurmond 1932- WhoAm 92
Oglesby, Roger D. Law&B 92
Oglesby, Sabert, Jr. 1921- WhoAm 92
Oglesby, Samuel Crockett 1939- WhoUN 92
Oglesby, Sarah Ann 1950- WhoSSW 93
Oglesby, Theodore Nathaniel 1932- WhoSSW 93
Oglesby, Theodore Nathaniel, Jr. 1932- WhoWrEP 92
Ogletree, Thomas Vincent 1944- WhoAm 92
Oglevee, Jeffrey M. 1941- St&PR 93
Ogliaruso, Michael Anthony 1938- WhoAm 92
Ognibene, Andre John 1931- WhoAm 92
Ognibene, Frederick Peter 1953- WhoE 93
Ogogo, Tony Ojo BioIn 17
Ogolnik, Richard 1930- WhoScE 91-2
Ogorelec, Zvonimir 1930- WhoScE 91-4
O'Gorman, Carmella A. Law&B 92
O'Gorman, Eugene R. 1939- St&PR 93
O'Gorman, Jack 1960- WhoEmL 93
O'Gorman, James Vivian 1938- WhoScE 91-3
O'Gorman, Michael WhoScE 91-1
O'Gorman, Ned 1931- WhoWrEP 92
O'Gorman, Peter Joseph 1938- St&PR 93, WhoAm 92
O'Gorman, Shelagh F. Law&B 92
O'Gorman, Thomas J. BioIn 17
Ogorzalek, Lisa Lattal 1956- WhoAmW 93, WhoE 93
Ogorzaly, Kenneth Louis 1953- WhoEmL 93
Ogot, Grace 1930- DcLB 125 [port]
Ogra, Pearay L. 1939- WhoAm 92
O'Grady, Colleen M. Law&B 92
O'Grady, Desmond (James Bernard) 1935- ConAu 38NR
O'Grady, Desmond Patrick 1945- St&PR 93
O'Grady, Henry WhoWrEP 92
O'Grady, James Francis 1935- WhoScE 91-3
O'Grady, John Joseph, III 1933- WhoAm 92
O'Grady, Joseph G. 1927- WhoAm 92
O'Grady, Laurence Joseph 1943- St&PR 93
O'Grady, Mary J. 1951- WhoAmW 93, WhoE 93
O'Grady, Thomas Bernard 1926- St&PR 93
O'Grady, Thomas Joseph 1943- WhoWrEP 92
O'Grady, Thomas R. Law&B 92
O'Grady, Timothy 1951- ConAu 138
O'Grady, Timothy Patrick Law&B 92
O'Grady, William M. 1939- St&PR 93
O'Green, Frederick Wilbert 1921- St&PR 93
O'Green, Jennifer ScF&FL 92, SmATA 72
O'Green, Mark 1953- ScF&FL 92
Ogren, Carroll Woodrow 1927- WhoAm 92
Ogren, David Carl 1938- St&PR 93
Ogren, G.C. 1935- St&PR 93
Ogren, Jennifer Marie 1957- St&PR 93
Ogren, Robert Edward 1922- WhoAm 92
Ogren, William Lewis 1938- WhoAm 92
Ogrizovich, Dorothy Ann 1928- WhoWrEP 92
Ogrodnik, Eugene C. 1948- WhoE 93
Ogron, Y. 1925- St&PR 93
Ogston, Derek WhoScE 91-1
Oguchi, Tomohiro 1932- WhoWor 93
O'Guinn, Jimmie Wayne 1948- WhoSSW 93
Ogul, Morris Samuel 1931- WhoAm 92
Oguma, Koichi 1943- WhoWor 93
Oguni, Nobuki 1936- WhoWor 93
Oguntoye, Ferdinand Abayomi 1949- WhoWor 93
Ogura, Haruo 1928- WhoWor 93
Ogura, Kotaro 1943- WhoWor 93
Ogura, Kyozo 1933- WhoWor 93
Ogura, Roh 1916- Baker 92
Ogura, Tadao 1929- WhoWor 93
Ogura, Yasuhiro 1945- WhoWor 93
Oguri, Kohei 1945- MiSFD 9
Oguri, Kozaburo 1868-1944 HarEnMi
Oguz, Orhan 1923- WhoScE 91-4
Ogwyn, John Hardy 1949- WhoSSW 93
Oh, Jai Keun 1930- WhoUN 92
Oh, John Kie-Chiang 1930- WhoAm 92
Oh, May Buong Yu Lau 1940- WhoWor 93
Oh, Richard C. Law&B 92
Oh, Sang Hun 1961- WhoWor 93
Oh, Seog-Hong 1936- WhoWor 93
Oh, Stephen BioIn 17
Oh, Steve Kah-Weng 1964- WhoWor 93
Oh, Taeho 1958- WhoEmL 93, WhoSSW 93
Oh, Tai Keun 1934- WhoWor 93
Oh, William 1931- WhoAm 92
Oh, Yoon Kyung 1944- WhoUN 92
O'Hagan, A. WhoScE 91-1
O'Hagan, John M. d1992 NewYTBS 92
O'Hagan, John T. 1925-1991 BioIn 17
O'Hagan, Malcolm Edward 1940- WhoAm 92
O'Hagan, William D. 1942- St&PR 93
O'Hagen, Patricia WhoE 93
Ohain, Hans von BioIn 17
Ohala, John Jerome 1941- WhoAm 92
O'Halloran, Judy MacKenzie 1946- WhoWrEP 92
O'Halloran, Maura-san BioIn 17
O'Halloran, Michael Law&B 92
O'Halloran, Michael 1947- WhoIns 93
O'Halloran, Michael J. 1924- WhoScE 91-3
O'Halloran, Shawn Patrick 1958- St&PR 93
O'Halloran, Thomas Alphonsus, Jr. 1931- WhoAm 92
O'Halloran, Trish 1961- WhoAmW 93
O'Halloran, William John 1927- WhoE 93
Ohama, Hirobumi 1937- WhoWor 93
Ohama, Hoei 1927- WhoAsAP 91
Ohama, Yoshihiko 1937- WhoWor 93
Ohana, Maurice 1914- Baker 92
O'Handley, Douglas Alexander 1937- WhoE 93
Ohanesian, George Vaughn 1949- WhoE 93
Ohanesian, Susan Marie 1949- WhoAmW 93, WhoEmL 93
Ohanian, Krekor 1925- WhoAm 92
Ohanian, Lee Edward 1957- WhoE 93
O'Hanlon, Alvin Merle 1932- WhoWrEP 92
O'Hanlon, Daniel J. d1992 NewYTBS 92
O'Hanlon, Daniel John 1919-1992 ConAu 139
O'Hanlon, George 1912-1989 QDrFCA 92 [port]
O'Hanlon, George B. Law&B 92
O'Hanlon, James Barry 1927- WhoAm 92
O'Hanlon, James Patrick 1943- St&PR 93
O'Hanlon, John More 1963- WhoE 93
O'Hanlon, John R. Law&B 92
O'Hanlon, John R. 1932- St&PR 93
O'Hanlon, John Reed 1946- WhoEmL 93
O'Hanlon, Richard Thomas 1956- WhoE 93
O'Hanlon, Ruth AmWomPl
O'Hanrahan, Ellenore Law&B 92
O'Har, George M. ScF&FL 92
O'Hara, Alfred Peck 1919- WhoAm 92
O'Hara, Bradley BioIn 17
O'Hara, Brian M. St&PR 93
O'Hara, Catherine 1954- WhoAm 92
O'Hara, Charles G. Law&B 92
O'Hara, Constance Marie AmWomPl
O'Hara, David Oakes 1950- WhoE 93
O'Hara, David Patrick Law&B 92
O'Hara, Elizabeth Mary Law&B 92
O'Hara, Eugene Michael 1937- WhoAm 92
O'Hara, Frank 1926-1966 BioIn 17
O'Hara, Geoffrey 1882-1967 Baker 92
O'Hara, Gerald John ScF&FL 92
O'Hara, Gerry 1924- MiSFD 9
O'Hara, Henry Clive BioIn 17
Ohara, Hirotada 1930- WhoWor 93
Ohara, Ichizo 1924- WhoAsAP 91
O'Hara, James Edward 1844-1905 BioIn 17
O'Hara, James G. 1925- PolPar
O'Hara, James Thomas 1936- WhoAm 92
O'Hara, John 1905-1970 BioIn 17, MagSAmL [port]
O'Hara, John J. d1990 BioIn 17
O'Hara, John Montross 1929- St&PR 93
O'Hara, John Patrick 1930- WhoAm 92, WhoE 93
O'Hara, Laura Law&B 92
O'Hara, Margaret 1951- WhoEmL 93
O'Hara, Marion Malone 1932- WhoIns 93
O'Hara, Mary MajAI
O'Hara, Mary Margaret BioIn 17
O'Hara, Maureen WhoAm 92
O'Hara, Maureen 1920- BioIn 17, SweetSg D [port]
O'Hara, Maureen 1921- IntDcF 2-3
O'Hara, Maureen 1953- WhoAmW 93
O'Hara, Michael John WhoScE 91-1
O'Hara, Michael K. 1942- St&PR 93
O'Hara, Pamela M. Law&B 92
O'Hara, Paul M. 1946- WhoAm 92
O'Hara, Ralph L. 1944- St&PR 93
O'Hara, Robert Melvin 1926- St&PR 93
O'Hara, Terrence MiSFD 9
O'Hara, Thomas Edwin 1915- WhoAm 92
O'Hara, Thomas J. 1926- St&PR 93
O'Hara, Thomas Patrick 1947- WhoSSW 93
O'Hara, Timothy Michael 1958- WhoSSW 93
O'Hara, William F., Jr. 1953- WhoWrEP 92
O'Hara, William James 1930- WhoAm 92
O'Hare, Carrie Jane 1959- WhoAmW 93, WhoE 93
O'Hare, Dean Raymond 1942- St&PR 93, WhoAm 92, WhoE 93, WhoIns 93
O'Hare, Don R. 1922- St&PR 93
O'Hare, Edward H. 1914-1943 BioIn 17
O'Hare, James Raymond 1938- WhoAm 92
O'Hare, Jean Ann Law&B 92
O'Hare, Joseph Aloysius 1931- WhoAm 92, WhoE 93
O'Hare, Kate Richards 1877-1948 AmWomPl
O'Hare, Kathleen 1948- WhoAmW 93
O'Hare, Linda Parsons 1947- WhoAm 92, WhoEmL 93
O'Hare, Marianne Margaret 1945- WhoAmW 93
O'Hare, Mary V. Law&B 92
O'Hare, Patrick J. 1922- WhoScE 91-3
O'Hare, Robert E. Law&B 92
O'Hare, Robert J.M., Jr. Law&B 92
O'Hare, Robert Joseph Michael, Jr. 1943- St&PR 93, WhoIns 93
O'Hare, Stephen T. 1928- St&PR 93, WhoIns 93
O'Hare, Stephen Thomas 1928- WhoAm 92
O'Hare, Terrence Dean 1946- WhoEmL 93
O'Hare, Thomas James, Jr. 1937- WhoAm 92
O'Haren, Thomas Joseph 1934- WhoSSW 93, WhoWor 93
Oharenko, Maria T. 1950- WhoEmL 93
O'Hare-VanMeerbeke, Anne Marie 1960- WhoE 93
O'Harra, Catherine 1956- WhoAmW 93
Ohashi, Kenzaburo 1919- WhoWor 93
Ohashi, Kiyohide 1924- WhoWor 93
Ohashi, Kosuke 1943- WhoAm 92
Ohashi, Shoichi 1932- WhoWor 93
Ohata, Akihiro 1947- WhoAsAP 91
Ohaus, James G. 1950- St&PR 93
O'Haver, Thomas J. 1941- WhoIns 93
O'Hayer, Matthew 1955- WhoSSW 93
Ohayon, Charles BioIn 17
Ohayon, Elie 1935- WhoScE 91-2
Ohayon, Roger Jean 1942- WhoWor 93
Ohe, Shuzo 1938- WhoWor 93
O'Hea, Timothy E. 1945- St&PR 93
O'Heaney, Sheilah Maura 1959- WhoEmL 93, WhoSSW 93
O'Hearn, Barbara Ann 1950- WhoEmL 93

O'Hearn, John Howard 1937- St&PR 93, WhoAm 92
O'Hearn, Michael John 1952- WhoWor 93
O'Hearn, Robert Raymond 1921- WhoAm 92
O'Hearne, Brian D. Law&B 92
O'Hearne, John Joseph 1922- WhoAm 92
O Hehir, Brendan 1927-1991 BioIn 17
O'Hehir, Joseph M. St&PR 93
O'Hehir, Trisha E. 1947- WhoAmW 93
O hEithir, Breandan 1930-1990 BioIn 17
O'Henly, W.M. 1954- St&PR 93
O'Heocha, Colm 1926- WhoScE 91-3
O'Herin, Timothy Patrick 1955- WhoWrEP 92
O'Herlihy, Colm 1949- WhoScE 91-3
O'Herlihy, Michael 1928- MiSFD 9
O'Hern, Daniel Joseph 1930- WhoAm 92
O'Hern, Elizabeth Moot 1913- WhoAm 92
O'Hern, Jane Susan 1933- WhoAm 92, WhoAmW 93, WhoE 93
O'Hern, John L. Law&B 92
O'Herron, Jonathan 1929- St&PR 93, WhoAm 92
Ohga, Norio BioIn 17
Ohga, Norio 1930- WhoAm 92
Oh Han Koo 1935- WhoAsAP 91
O'Higgins, Anna G. Williams AmWomPl
O'Higgins, Bernardo 1776-1842 HarEnMi
O'Higgins, Bernardo 1778-1842 BioIn 17
O'Higgins, Niall J. 1942- WhoScE 91-3
Ohio Players SoulM
Ohiorhenuan, John Folorunsho Enahoro 1948- WhoUN 92
Ohira, Goro 1916- WhoWor 93
Ohira, Kazuto 1933- WhoWor 93
Ohira, Masayoshi 1910-1980 DcTwHis
Ohkawa, Hironori 1936- WhoWor 93
Ohkawa, Tihiro 1928- WhoAm 92
Ohki, Yoshimichi 1950- WhoWor 93
Ohkita, Shuichi 1940- St&PR 93
Oh Kyung Ui 1941- WhoAsAP 91
Ohl, Donald Charles 1924- WhoAm 92
Ohl, Ronald Edward 1936- WhoAm 92
Ohlemacher, Bradley R. 1963- St&PR 93
Ohlin, Goran 1925- WhoUN 92
Ohlke, Clarence Carl 1916- WhoAm 92
Ohlman, Charles Edward 1926- WhoAm 92
Ohlman, Douglas Ronald 1949- WhoWor 93
Ohlmann, G. WhoScE 91-3
Ohlmann, John Philip 1935- St&PR 93
Ohlmeier, Dieter 1936- WhoScE 91-3
Ohlmuller, Raymond P. Law&B 92
Ohlmuller, Raymond P. 1939- St&PR 93
Ohlon, Rolf Roland 1927- WhoScE 91-4
Ohlrogge, Anne ScF&FL 92
Ohlson, Kristin A. Law&B 92
Ohlson, Robert N. 1946- St&PR 93
Ohlson, Sara Faye 1944- WhoAmW 93
Ohlsson, Garrick (Olof) 1948- Baker 92
Ohlsson, Oscar Olof, Jr. 1926- WhoWor 93
Ohlsson, Thomas 1945- WhoScE 91-4
Ohly, D. Christopher 1950- WhoEmL 93
Ohly, Frederick C. Law&B 92
Ohly, John Hallowell d1990 BioIn 17
Ohm, Herbert Willis 1945- WhoAm 92
Ohm, Jack Elton 1932- WhoSSW 93
Ohm, Peter H. d1991 BioIn 17
Ohman, Diana J. 1950- WhoAm 92
Ohman, John Michael 1948- WhoEmL 93
Ohman, Paul F. 1932- WhoAm 92
Ohman, Ulf Karl Gustaf 1931- WhoWor 93
Ohmann, Carol Burke 1938-1989 BioIn 17
Ohmann, Richard Malin 1931- WhoWrEP 92
Ohmori, Keiji 1953- WhoWor 93
Ohmori, Shinji 1934- WhoWor 93
Ohmori, Yutaka 1949- WhoWor 93
Ohms, Elisabeth 1888-1974 Baker 92
Ohmstede, John Robert 1957- St&PR 93
Ohmstede, Robert Lee 1916- St&PR 93
Ohnaka, Kohzaburo 1947- WhoWor 93
Ohnami, Masateru 1931- WhoWor 93
Ohnesorge, Friedrich Karl 1925- WhoScE 91-3
Ohnishi, Stanley Tsuyoshi 1931- WhoE 93
Ohnmacht, Mark Walter 1956- WhoEmL 93
Ohno, Heikichi 1929- WhoWor 93
Ohno, Susumu 1928- WhoAm 92
Ohno, Taiichi 1912-1990 BioIn 17
Ohnsman, David Robert 1943- WhoSSW 93
Ohnsorge, Jochen 1937- WhoScE 91-3
O'Hollaren, Paul Joseph 1927- WhoAm 92, WhoWor 93
O'Horgan, Thomas Foster 1926- WhoAm 92
O'Horgan, Tom MiSFD 9
O'Horo, Kris Michael 1962- WhoSSW 93
O'Hoski, John J. Law&B 92
Ohotnicky, Stephen Thaddeus 1943- WhoSSW 93
Ohr, George E. 1857-1918 BioIn 17
Ohr, Leslie A. Law&B 92
Ohrbach, Carol Jean WhoAmW 93
Ohrbach, Jerome K. 1907-1990 BioIn 17
Ohrel, Alain Robert 1935- WhoWor 93
Ohrenstein, Roman Abraham 1920- WhoAm 92
Ohrn, James B. 1951- St&PR 93
Ohrn, Nils Yngve 1934- WhoAm 92
Ohrnberger, John M. Law&B 92
Ohrt, Pamela Jeanne 1952- WhoAmW 93
Ohrwashel, Norman A. Law&B 92
Ohs, Larry Dwight 1954- WhoEmL 93
Ohschlager, Edward J. WhoAm 92
Ohsol, Ernest Osborne 1916- WhoAm 92
Ohta, Hideaki 1955- WhoWor 93
Ohta, Hiroshi 1940- WhoWor 93
Ohta, Masatsugu 1953- WhoWor 93
Ohtaka, Naomasa 1941- WhoAm 92
Ohtake, Reizo 1934- WhoWor 93
Ohtaki, Hitoshi 1932- WhoWor 93
Oh Tan 1940- WhoAsAP 91
Ohtsu, Masakazu 1937- St&PR 93, WhoAm 92
Ohtsuka, Eiko 1936- WhoWor 93
Ohtsuka, Yoshihiro 1934- WhoWor 93
Ohtsuki, Yoshihiko 1936- WhoWor 93
Ohtsuru, Masaru 1943- WhoWor 93
O Huigin, Sean 1942- WhoCanL 92
Ohyama, Heiichiro 1947- WhoAm 92
Oh Yong Woon 1928- WhoAsAP 91
Oh You-Bang 1941- WhoAsAP 91
Oi, Noboro 1935- WhoUN 92
Oi, Shigemoto 1863-1951 HarEnMi
Oide, Kyoji 1940- WhoWor 93
Oide, Shun 1922- WhoAsAP 91
Oien, Harold A., Jr. Law&B 92
Oihus, Arthur L. 1925- St&PR 93
Oikari, Aimo O.J. 1947- WhoScE 91-4
Oikarinen, Valle Juhani 1927- WhoScE 91-4
Oikawa, Atsushi 1929- WhoWor 93
Oikawa, Hiroshi 1933- WhoWor 93
Oikawa, Junro 1937- WhoAsAP 91
Oikawa, Kazuo 1929- WhoAsAP 91
Oikawa, Shin 1924- WhoWor 93
Oikonomides, Nicholas Constantine 1934- WhoWrEP 92
Oikoumenios fl. 6th cent.- OxDcByz
Oimoen, Roger E. 1931- St&PR 93
Oinaiotes, George fl. 14th cent.- OxDcByz
Oinas, Felix Johannes 1911- WhoAm 92
Oinuma, Tokuji Law&B 92
Oishi, Gene BioIn 17
Oishi, Masamitsu 1945- WhoAsAP 91
Oishi, Satoshi 1927- St&PR 93, WhoAm 92
Oishi, Senpachi 1935- WhoAsAP 91
Oiso, Toshio 1908- WhoWor 93
Oiso, Yukio 1928- WhoWor 93
Oisteanu, Valery 1943- WhoWrEP 92
Oistrach Stabenau, Gunther 1925- WhoScE 91-3
Oistrakh, David (Fyodorovich) 1908-1974 Baker 92
Oiwa, Keibo ConAu 138
Oizumi, Hiroshi St&PR 93
Oja, Aarne Simo Juhani 1960- WhoWor 93
Oja, Erkki 1948- WhoScE 91-4
Oja, Hannes 1919- WhoCanL 92
Oja, Simo S. 1939- WhoScE 91-4
Ojakli, Sumya 1961- WhoAmW 93
Ojalvo, Maurice 1939- St&PR 93
Ojalvo, Morris 1924- WhoAm 92
Ojalvo, Morris Solomon 1923- WhoE 93
Ojard, Bruce Allen 1951- WhoEmL 93, WhoWor 93
O'Jays SoulM
Ojeda, Alonso de 1468?-1515? Expl 93
Ojeda, Dionisio S. 1911- WhoAsAP 91
Ojeda, Jo Ellen Law&B 92
Ojeda, Manuel R. Law&B 92
Ojeda, Virginia F. 1945- NotHsAW 93
Ojeda-Castaneda, Jorge 1949- WhoWor 93
Ojeda Rios, Filiberto DcCPCAm
Ojemann, Robert Gerdes 1931- WhoAm 92
Ojiaku, Alamezie Enwereaku 1947- WhoE 93, WhoWor 93
Ojiambo, Hillary Peter 1933- WhoUN 92
Ojiji d1983 BioIn 17
Ojile, Williams M., Jr. Law&B 92
Ojukwu, Chukwuemeka Odumegwu 1933- DcTwHis, WhoAfr
Oka, Kunio 1945- WhoWor 93
Oka, Takeshi 1932- WhoAm 92
Oka, Tetsuo 1938- WhoWor 93
Okabe, Mitsuaki 1943- WhoWor 93
Okabe, Saburo 1926- WhoAsAP 91
Okada, Eiji 1920- IntDcF 2-3 [port]
Okada, Fumiaki 1927- WhoWor 93
Okada, Fumihiko 1940- WhoWor 93
Okada, Hiroshi 1909- WhoAsAP 91
Okada, Hiroyuki 1928- WhoWor 93
Okada, Katsuya 1953- WhoAsAP 91
Okada, Keiji 1951- WhoWor 93
Okada, Keisuke 1868-1952 HarEnMi
Okada, Masaya 1938- ScF&FL 92
Okada, Mutsumi 1931- WhoWor 93
Okada, Robert Dean 1947- WhoSSW 93
Okada, Ryozo 1931- WhoWor 93
Okada, Shigeru 1940- WhoWor 93
Okada, Tetsuo 1957- WhoWor 93
Okada, Toshiharu 1925- WhoAsAP 91
Okada Keisuke 1868-1952 DcTwHis
Okagawa, Akio 1940- WhoWor 93
Okahashi, Sumio 1917- WhoWor 93
Okahata, Yoshio 1947- WhoWor 93
Okajima, Masayuki 1930- WhoAsAP 91
Okajima, Mitsuharu 1929- WhoWor 93
Okajima, Sadaichiro 1941- WhoUN 92
Okakura, Kakuzo 1862-1913 BioIn 17
Okamoto, Atsuki 1948- WhoWor 93
Okamoto, D.I. 1943- St&PR 93
Okamoto, Hiroshi 1939- WhoWor 93
Okamoto, Jeffrey Akira 1954- WhoEmL 93
Okamoto, Kihachi MiSFD 9
Okamoto, Masahiro 1952- WhoWor 93
Okamoto, Naomichi 1942- WhoWor 93
Okamoto, Nobuyuki 1941- WhoWor 93
Okamoto, Yasuo 1948- St&PR 93
Okamoto, Yoshio 1941- WhoWor 93
Okamura, Arthur 1932- WhoAm 92
Okamura, Kazumi 1957- WhoWor 93
Okamura, Kazumi N. Law&B 92
Okamura, Yasuji 1884-1966 HarEnMi
O'Kane, Francis Aloysius 1953- WhoE 93
O'Kane, Maureen Therese 1957- St&PR 93
O'Kane, Patrick Alan 1947- WhoEmL 93
O'Kane, R. Casey Law&B 92
Okano, Masayoshi 1936- WhoWor 93
Okano, Robert 1949- St&PR 93
Okano, Yutaka 1927- WhoAsAP 91
Okara, Gabriel Imomotimi Gbaingbain 1921- DcLB 125 [port]
Okarma, Jerome D. Law&B 92
Okawa, Yoshikuni 1934- WhoWor 93
Okawara, Merle Aiko 1941- WhoWor 93
Okawara, Taichiro 1922- WhoAsAP 91
Okawara, Yoshio 1919- WhoWor 93
Okazaki, Hiromi 1951- WhoAsAP 91
Okazaki, Steven BioIn 17
Okazaki, Steven 1952- MiSFD 9
Okazaki, Tomiko 1944- WhoAsAP 91
Okazaki, Tsuneko 1933- WhoWor 93
Okazawa-Rey, Margo 1949- WhoAmW 93
Okcu, Ibrahim 1942- WhoScE 91-4
Oke, John Beverley 1928- WhoAm 92
Oke, Keith Harrison WhoScE 91-1
Oke, Tommy Olawuyi 1939- WhoSSW 93
O'Keane, Eugene T. 1958- St&PR 93
Okebukola, Peter Akinsola 1948- WhoWor 93
O'Keefe, Beverly Disbrow 1946- WhoAmW 93, WhoEmL 93
O'Keefe, Claudia 1958- ScF&FL 92
O'Keefe, Constance 1948- WhoEmL 93
O'Keefe, Daniel J. 1942- St&PR 93
O'Keefe, Donald E. Law&B 92
O'Keefe, Edward Franklin 1937- WhoAm 92
O'Keefe, Edward P. Law&B 92
O'Keefe, Esther Kathleen AmWomPl
O'Keefe, Frank Robert, Jr. 1929- St&PR 93
O'Keefe, George W. 1924- St&PR 93
O'Keefe, Gerald Francis 1918- WhoAm 92
O'Keefe, J.M. 1944- St&PR 93
O'Keefe, James William, Jr. 1948- WhoAm 92
O'Keefe, John David 1941- WhoAm 92
O'Keefe, John J., Jr. Law&B 92
O'Keefe, John William Law&B 92
O'Keefe, Joseph Ross 1954- St&PR 93
O'Keefe, Joseph Thomas 1919- WhoAm 92
O'Keefe, Kathleen Mary 1933- WhoAmW 93
O'Keefe, Kenneth J. d1991 BioIn 17
O'Keefe, Kevin Charles 1958- WhoEmL 93
O'Keefe, Lynn Marie 1955- WhoEmL 93, WhoSSW 93
O'Keefe, M. Rush Law&B 92
O'Keefe, Marion R. AmWomPl
O'Keefe, Matthew John 1957- WhoEmL 93
O'Keefe, Mellen Patricia 1954- WhoE 93
O'Keefe, Michael BioIn 17
O'Keefe, Michael J. 1952- St&PR 93
O'Keefe, Nancy Jean 1926- WhoAmW 93
O'Keefe, Neil Patrick 1947- WhoAsAP 91
O'Keefe, Patricia Rigg 1926- WhoAmW 93
O'Keefe, Patrick F. Law&B 92
O'Keefe, Raymond Michael 1925- St&PR 93
O'Keefe, Robert James 1926- WhoAm 92
O'Keefe, Ronald W. Law&B 92
O'Keefe, Ruth Ann 1935- WhoAmW 93
O'Keefe, Sean NewYTBS 92 [port]
O'Keefe, Terence Michael 1959- WhoEmL 93
O'Keefe, Thomas Joseph 1935- WhoAm 92
O'Keefe, Thomas Michael 1940- WhoAm 92
O'Keefe, Tyler R. 1940- St&PR 93
O'Keefe, Vincent Thomas 1920- WhoAm 92
O'Keefe, William Francis 1938- WhoAm 92
O'Keeffe, Andrew WhoScE 91-1
O'Keeffe, Claire Sullivan d1991 BioIn 17
O'Keeffe, Daniel John 1923- St&PR 93
O'Keeffe, Gabhan BioIn 17
O'Keeffe, Georgia 1887-1986 BioIn 17
O'Keeffe, Hugh Williams 1905- WhoSSW 93
O'Keeffe, John 1747-1833 BioIn 17
O'Keeffe, Kevin Francis 1952- WhoSSW 93
O'Keeffe, Margaret 1940- WhoUN 92
O'Keeffe, Shan 1945- St&PR 93
O'Keeffe, Thomas J. St&PR 93
O'Keeffe, William 1939- St&PR 93
O'Keeffe, William B. 1939- St&PR 93
Okeev, Tolomus 1935- DrEEuF
Okeghem, Johannes Baker 92
O'Kehie, Collins Emeka 1952- WhoAm 92
Okel, Kenneth K. Law&B 92
O'Kelley, James Ligon 1950- WhoEmL 93
O'Kelley, Michael L. 1953- St&PR 93
O'Kelley, Timothy Guy 1958- WhoSSW 93
O'Kelley, William Clark 1930- WhoAm 92, WhoSSW 93
O'Kelly, Bernard 1926- WhoAm 92
O'Kelly, Conal M. 1933- WhoAsAP 91
O'Kelly, Denis WhoScE 91-1
O'Kelly, John 1955- WhoScE 91-3
O'Kelly, Michael E.J. 1937- WhoScE 91-3
O'Kelly, Michael Edmund James 1937- WhoWor 93
Oken, Donald Edward 1928- WhoAm 92
Okenfuss, Betty Jane Law&B 92
Okenson, Lois Wiley 1919- WhoWrEP 92
Oker, Michael R. Law&B 92
Oker-Blom, Nils Christian Edgar 1919- WhoScE 91-4
Okerlund, Arlene Naylor 1938- WhoAm 92, WhoAmW 93
Okes, Duke Wayne 1949- WhoWor 93
Okeson, Thomas L. 1946- WhoEmL 93
Oketcho, Frederick c. 1940- WhoAfr
Okezie, B. Onuma 1936- WhoSSW 93
Okhezin, Vladimir Pavlovich 1961- WhoWor 93
Oki, Hiroshi 1927- WhoAsAP 91
Oki, John Law&B 92
Oki, Masao 1901-1971 Baker 92
Oki, Shogo 1922- WhoAsAP 91
Okie, Frederick W., Jr. 1937- St&PR 93
O'Kiely, Padraig WhoScE 91-3
Okigbo, Christopher 1932-1967 BioIn 17
Okigbo, Christopher (Ifenayichukwu) 1932-1967 DcLB 125 [port]
Okiishi, Theodore Hisao 1939- WhoAm 92
Okimoto, Jean Davies 1942- ConAu 37NR
Okin, Michael Allen 1953- WhoSSW 93
Okino, Betty BioIn 17
Okins, Elliott Eugene 1915- WhoWrEP 92
Okishio, Nobuo 1926- BioIn 17
Okita, George T. 1922- WhoAm 92
Okita, Masato 1929- WhoAsAP 91
Okitani, Akihiro 1940- WhoWor 93
Okiyama, Yasuhiko 1932- St&PR 93, WhoAm 92
Okkema, Matthew 1931- St&PR 93
Okkonen, Ari Erkki 1951- WhoScE 91-4
Okladnikov, A.P. 1908-1981 IntDcAn
Oko, Andrew Jan 1946- WhoAm 92
Okola, Michael Joseph 1938- St&PR 93
O'Kon, James Alexander 1937- WhoSSW 93, WhoWor 93
Okondo, Peter Habenga 1925- WhoAfr
Okonogi, Hikosaburo 1928- WhoAsAP 91
Okonow, Dale Law&B 92
Okonska-Kozlowska, Irena 1934- WhoScE 91-4
O'Konski, Chester Thomas 1921- WhoAm 92
O'Konski, Paul Francis Law&B 92
Okorafor, James O. Law&B 92
Okoshi, Sumiye WhoAmW 93
Okoshi, Takanori 1932- WhoWor 93
Okot p'Bitek 1931-1982 DcLB 125 [port]
Okoye, Christian 1961- WhoAm 92
Okoye, George Ikechukwu 1964- WhoWor 93
Okrand, Marc 1948- ScF&FL 92
Okrasinski, Mary Ann Law&B 92
Okrasinski, Wojciech Kazimierz 1950- WhoWor 93
Okray, Albert P. 1917- St&PR 93
O'Kray, P. Dan Law&B 92
Okrent, Daniel BioIn 17
Okrent, Daniel 1948- WhoWrEP 92
Okrent, David 1922- WhoAm 92
Okrent, Rita BioIn 17

Okri, Ben 1959- ConAu 138, ScF&FL 92
Okrusch, Martin 1934- WhoScE 91-3
Okruszko, Henryk 1925- WhoScE 91-4
Okrutny, Jeffrey Joseph 1955- WhoEmL 93
Oksala, Erkki Jaakko 1930- WhoScE 91-4
Oksanen, Erkki H. 1926- WhoScE 91-4
Oksanen, Hans G. Erik 1925- WhoScE 91-4
Oksas, Joan K. 1927- WhoAm 92
Okscin, Allan 1951- St&PR 93
Oksenberg, Michel Charles 1938- WhoAm 92
Oksman, Jacques Maurice 1948- WhoScE 91-2
Oksman, Leevi Otto Juhani 1931- WhoScE 91-4
Oksuz, Muharrem 1949- WhoScE 91-4
Oktay, Julianne Shaberman 1943- WhoAmW 93
Oktem, Erol 1935- WhoScE 91-4
Oku, Tatsuo 1934- WhoWor 93
Oku, Yasukata 1846-1930 HarEnMi
Okubo, Edward T. Law&B 92
Okubo, Haruno 1846-1915 HarEnMi
Okuda, Jun 1957- WhoWor 93
Okuda, Keiwa 1927- WhoAsAP 91
Okuda, Kunio 1921- WhoWor 93
Okuda, Michael 1955- ScF&FL 92
Okuda, Mikio 1928- WhoAsAP 91
Okuda, Shigeo 1931- WhoWor 93
Okui, Kazumitsu 1933- WhoWor 93
O'Kulich, Nicholas Alexander 1943- St&PR 93
Okulicz, William Charles 1946- WhoE 93
Okulitch, Vladimir Joseph 1906- WhoAm 92
Okulo-Epak, Yefusa 1940- WhoWor 93
Okulski, John Allen 1944- WhoE 93
Okumura, Haruhiko 1951- WhoWor 93
Okumura, Randolph T. 1942- St&PR 93
Okumura, Shigetsugu 1925- WhoWor 93
Okumura, Winifred Elsa 1947- WhoEmL 93
Okun, Barbara Frank 1936- WhoAm 92
Okun, Charles 1942- St&PR 93
Okun, Daniel Alexander 1917- WhoAm 92
Okun, Erwin Donald 1934- St&PR 93
Okun, Herbert Stuart 1930- WhoAm 92
Okun, Lawrence 1929- ScF&FL 92
Okun, Richard Allen 1952- WhoEmL 93
Okuniewski, Jozef WhoScE 91-4
Okuno, Hiroaki Yohmei 1943- WhoWor 93
Okuno, Hiroshi Gitchang 1950- WhoWor 93
Okuno, Kenji 1954- WhoWor 93
Okuno, Seisuke 1913- WhoAsAP 91
Okusa, Shigeyasu 1935-1989 BioIn 17
Okutani, Rieko BioIn 17
Okutsu, Fumio 1935- WhoWor 93
Okuyama, Fumio 1938- WhoWor 93
Okuyama, Masanori 1946- WhoWor 93
Okuyama, Tadashi 1940- WhoWor 93
Okwumabua, Constance Lee 1947- St&PR 93
Oladipupo, Adebisi Oladimeji 1956- WhoSSW 93
Olaf Haraldsson, II c. 995-1030 HarEnMi
Olafson, Donald G. 1936- St&PR 93
Olafson, Frederick Arlan 1924- WhoAm 92
Olafson, Harlan Nestor 1928- WhoWrEP 92
Olafson, Robert M. 1949- St&PR 93
Olafsson, Johann Johannsson 1935- WhoWor 93
Olafsson, Olaf BioIn 17, WhoAm 92
Olafsson, Sigurjon 1943- WhoScE 91-4
Olafsson, William Craig Law&B 92
Olaf Tryggvesson, I c. 964-1000 HarEnMi
Olafur, Gunnarsson 1948- ScF&FL 92
Olague De Ros, Guillermo 1948- WhoWor 93
Olaguibel, Francisco M. de 1874-1924 DcMexL
Olah, George Andrew 1927- WhoAm 92
Olah, George John 1954- WhoEmL 93
Olah, Laszlo 1937- WhoScE 91-4
Olah, Nancy Lynne 1955- WhoIns 93
Olah, Tiberiu 1928- Baker 92
Olajos, Dezso 1941- WhoScE 91-4
Olajuwon, Akeem BioIn 17
Olajuwon, Hakeem BioIn 17
Olajuwon, Hakeem Abdul 1963- WhoAm 92
Olan, Carmen Lily 1960- WhoAmW 93
Olan, Irving d1992 BioIn 17
Olan, Sherry 1939- St&PR 93
Olan, Susan Torian ScF&FL 92
Oland, Mark 1947- WhoE 93
Oland, S. M. WhoAm 92
Oland, Warner 1880-1938 BioIn 17
Olander, Bradley Ward 1964- WhoEmL 93
Olander, Donald Edgar 1929- WhoWor 93
Olander, Joseph D. BioIn 17
Olander, Joseph D. 1939- ScF&FL 92
Olander, Ray G. Law&B 92
Olander, Ray Gunnar 1926- St&PR 93, WhoAm 92, WhoWor 93
Olander-Quamme, Glenn Joel Law&B 92
Olanich, Catherine Cecilia 1959- WhoAmW 93, WhoEmL 93
Olaniyan, Ebenezer Adesanya 1937- WhoUN 92
Olano, Agustin 1945- WhoWor 93
Olar, Terry Thomas 1947- WhoEmL 93, WhoSSW 93
Olariu, Virgil 1925- WhoScE 91-4
Olarsch, Eleanor Richter Law&B 92
Olasky, Marvin 1950- ConAu 139
Olason, Vesteinn 1939- WhoWor 93
Olason, Victor Bjorgvin 1930- WhoAm 92
Olaso-Yohn, Mariano 1958- WhoWor 93
O'Laughlin, Frederick J. 1954- WhoEmL 93
O'Laughlin, Jeanne 1929- WhoAm 92, WhoAmW 93, WhoSSW 93
O'Laughlin, Marjorie Hartley WhoAm 92, WhoAmW 93
O'Laughlin, Michael 1840-1867 BioIn 17
Olaus, Magnus 1490-1557 BioIn 17
Olaussen, David B. Law&B 92
Olausson, Hans-Lennart 1945- WhoScE 91-4
Olav, V, King of Norway 1903-1991 BioIn 17
Olavarria, Andres German 1947- WhoWor 93
Olavarria y Ferrari, Enrique de 1844-1918 DcMexL
Olav of Norway, V 1903-1991 AnObit 1991
Olayan, Suliman Saleh 1918- WhoAm 92, WhoWor 93
Olberding, Elaine Johnson 1955- WhoAmW 93, WhoEmL 93
Olberg, F. Forbes 1923- St&PR 93
Olbinski, Rafal 1943- BioIn 17
Olbrechts, Frans M. 1899-1958 IntDcAn
Olbrychski, Daniel 1945- IntDcF 2-3 [port]
Olbrycht, Alfred A. Law&B 92
Olbrysh, C. Ronald Law&B 92
Olcer, Nuri Yelman 1932- St&PR 93
Olcese, Edward Lewis 1940- St&PR 93
Olcott, Emery G. 1938- St&PR 93
Olcott, John W. 1936- St&PR 93
Olcott, John Whiting 1936- WhoE 93
Olcott, Rita AmWomPl
Olcott, Sidney 1873-1949 MiSFD 9N
Olcott, Virginia AmWomPl
Olcott, William Alfred 1931- WhoAm 92, WhoE 93
Olcott, William Tyler BioIn 17
Olczak, Paul Vincent 1943- WhoE 93
Olczewska, Maria 1892-1969 Baker 92, OxDcOp
Old, Bruce S. 1913- St&PR 93
Old, Bruce Scott 1913- WhoAm 92
Old, C.F. WhoScE 91-1
Old, Hughes Oliphant 1933- WhoE 93
Old, Jean Curtis 1925- WhoAmW 93
Old, John Michael 1949- WhoWor 93
Old, Lloyd John 1933- WhoAm 92
Oldaker, Bradley Russell 1962- WhoEmL 93
Oldaker, Richard B. 1927- St&PR 93
Oldale, Robert Nicholas 1929- WhoE 93
Oldam, Paul Bernard 1934- St&PR 93
Oldani, Norbert Louis 1936- WhoE 93
Oldberg, Arne 1874-1962 Baker 92
Oldekop, Werner E. 1927- WhoScE 91-3
Oldeman, G.J.W. WhoScE 91-3
Oldeman, L.R. 1942- WhoScE 91-3
Olden, Marc ScF&FL 92
Oldenburg, Christopher, Count of 1504-1566 HarEnMi
Oldenburg, Claes 1929- BioIn 17
Oldenburg, Claes Thure 1929- WhoAm 92, WhoWor 93
Oldenburg, Gosta 1898-1992 BioIn 17
Oldenburg, Kimberle Marie 1957- WhoAmW 93, WhoEmL 93
Oldenburg, Peter d1990 BioIn 17
Oldenburg, Reinhard Robert 1959- WhoWor 93
Oldenburg, Richard Erik 1933- WhoAm 92, WhoE 93, WhoWor 93
Oldenburg, William R. 1946- St&PR 93
Oldendorf, Jesse Bartlett 1887-1974 HarEnMi
Oldendorf, William Henry 1925- WhoAm 92
Oldenkamp, Leffert 1938- WhoScE 91-3
Oldenquist, Andrew G. 1932- WhoAm 92
Older, Effin 1942- WhoWrEP 92
Older, Fremont 1856-1935 JrnUS
Older, Jack Stanley 1934- WhoAm 92
Older, Julia D. 1941- WhoWrEP 92
Older, Mark A. Law&B 92
Olderog, Ernst-Rudiger 1955- WhoWor 93
Ol'derogge, D.A. 1903-1987 IntDcAn
Oldershaw, Louis Frederick 1917- WhoAm 92
Oldfather, Charles Eugene 1927- WhoAm 92
Oldfather, Grayson W. 1956- St&PR 93
Oldfield, Barney 1878-1946 BioIn 17
Oldfield, Edward Charles, Jr. 1919- WhoAm 92
Oldfield, Frank WhoScE 91-1
Oldfield, J. WhoScE 91-1
Oldfield, James Edmund 1921- WhoAm 92
Oldfield, Joe St&PR 93
Oldfield, Margery Lee 1950- WhoAmW 93
Oldfield, Maurice Herbert 1930- WhoWor 93
Oldfield, P.A. 1930- St&PR 93
Oldfield, Pamela 1931- ScF&FL 92
Oldfield, Pearl Peden 1876-1962 BioIn 17
Oldfield, Russell Miller 1946- St&PR 93
Oldham, Alice M. Law&B 92
Oldham, Anne Marie Law&B 92
Oldham, Arthur (William) 1926- Baker 92
Oldham, Betty J. 1927- St&PR 93
Oldham, Dale R. 1943- St&PR 93
Oldham, Dale Ralph 1943- WhoAm 92
Oldham, Darius Dudley 1941- WhoAm 92, WhoSSW 93
Oldham, David Joseph WhoScE 91-1
Oldham, Debbie Carol 1963- WhoSSW 93
Oldham, Edward H. Law&B 92
Oldham, Geoffrey WhoScE 91-1
Oldham, J. Thomas 1948- WhoEmL 93
Oldham, Joe 1943- WhoWrEP 92
Oldham, John David 1949- WhoScE 91-1
Oldham, John (M.) 1940- ConAu 138
Oldham, John Philip 1943- WhoE 93
Oldham, June ConAu 138, SmATA 70 [port]
Oldham, Lea Leever 1931- WhoWor 93
Oldham, Mary 1944- BioIn 17
Oldham, Maxine Jernigan 1923- WhoAmW 93, WhoWor 93
Oldham, Pamela Kay 1960- WhoAmW 93
Oldham, Spooner SoulM
Oldham, Steve A. Law&B 92
Oldham, Steve A. 1951- St&PR 93
Oldham, Steven Carstensen 1950- St&PR 93
Oldham, Susan Lorain 1954- WhoEmL 93
Oldham, Todd BioIn 17
Oldham, William George 1938- WhoAm 92
Oldiges, Hubert A. 1923- WhoScE 91-3
Oldin, Arthur K. 1931- St&PR 93
Oldknow, Antony 1939- WhoWrEP 92
Oldknow, Gerald T. 1936- St&PR 93
Oldknow, William Henry 1924- St&PR 93
Oldman, C(ecil) B(ernard) 1894-1969 Baker 92
Oldman, Gary BioIn 17, NewYTBS 92 [port]
Oldman, Marilyn 1936- WhoAmW 93
Oldman, Oliver 1920- WhoAm 92
Oldow, Lynda Lee 1952- WhoAmW 93
Oldroyd, George 1886-1951 Baker 92
Olds, Edson B. 1939- St&PR 93
Olds, Elizabeth 1896-1991 BioIn 17
Olds, George R. Law&B 92
Olds, Glenn Alvero 1921- WhoAm 92
Olds, Jacqueline 1947- WhoEmL 93
Olds, John T. 1943- St&PR 93
Olds, John Theodore 1943- WhoAm 92
Olds, Sally Wendkos 1933- ConAu 39NR
Olds, Sharon BioIn 17
Olds, Sharon 1942- DcLB 120 [port], WhoAmW 93, WhoWrEP 92
Olds, Sharron Lee 1939- WhoAmW 93
Oldsey, Bernard S. 1923- ScF&FL 92
Oldshue, James Y. 1925- St&PR 93, WhoAm 92, WhoWor 93
Oldshue, Mary Holl 1951- WhoEmL 93
Oldson, William Orville 1940- WhoSSW 93
Oldweiler, Thomas Patrick 1961- WhoEmL 93
Olearchyk, Andrew S. 1935- WhoAm 92, WhoWor 93
O'Leary, Alice 1932- WhoAmW 93
O'Leary, Arthur Francis 1924- WhoAm 92
O'Leary, Arthur J., Jr. Law&B 92
O'Leary, Arthur M. Law&B 92
O'Leary, Brian 1940- ScF&FL 92
O'Leary, Brian Michael 1960- WhoEmL 93
O'Leary, Colleen Enwright 1953- WhoE 93
O'Leary, Daniel Francis 1923- WhoE 93
O'Leary, Daniel J. 1939- WhoE 93
O'Leary, Daniel J. 1946- WhoAm 92
O'Leary, Daniel Vincent, Jr. 1942- WhoAm 92
O'Leary, Denis Joseph 1924- WhoAm 92
O'Leary, Dennis Sophian 1938- WhoAm 92
O'Leary, E.M. 1946- St&PR 93
O'Leary, Edward Cornelius 1920- WhoAm 92
O'Leary, Edward T. 1938- St&PR 93
O'Leary, George Dennis 1938- St&PR 93
O'Leary, Hazel R. 1937- St&PR 93, WhoAm 92, WhoAmW 93
O'Leary, James John 1914- St&PR 93, WhoAm 92
O'Leary, James Patrick 1951- WhoE 93, WhoEmL 93
O'Leary, John P., Jr. 1946- WhoAm 92
O'Leary, Joseph Evans 1945- WhoAm 92
O'Leary, Kathleen A. 1946- WhoE 93
O'Leary, Liam 1921- ScF&FL 92
O'Leary, Marion Hugh 1941- WhoAm 92
O'Leary, Mary BioIn 17
O'Leary, Maureen Teresa 1967- WhoAmW 93
O'Leary, Neil Joseph 1925- St&PR 93
O'Leary, P. WhoScE 91-3
O'Leary, Patrick F. 1937- St&PR 93
O'Leary, Patrick William 1955- St&PR 93
O'Leary, Paul A. 1927- St&PR 93
O'Leary, Paul Alistair 1942- WhoWor 93
O'Leary, Paul Gerard 1935- WhoAm 92
O'Leary, Paul Martin 1901- WhoE 93
O'Leary, R. Donald 1942- St&PR 93
O'Leary, Robert L. 1931- St&PR 93
O'Leary, Robert T. Law&B 92
O'Leary, Robert W. 1943- St&PR 93
O'Leary, Sharon A. Law&B 92
O'Leary, T.J. WhoScE 91-1
O'Leary, Thomas Law&B 92
O'Leary, Thomas Howard 1934- St&PR 93, WhoAm 92
O'Leary, Thomas Michael 1944- WhoAm 92
O'Leary, Thomas Michael 1948- WhoAm 92
O'Leary, Timothy H. 1933- St&PR 93
O'Leary, Wilfred Leo 1906- WhoAm 92
Olechny, Steven Law&B 92
Olechowski, Andrzej 1947- WhoWor 93
Oleck, Howard L. 1911- WhoAm 92
Oleck, Jack 1914-1981 ScF&FL 92
Oledzki, Andrzej Aleksander 1928- WhoScE 91-4
Oleen, Lana 1949- WhoAmW 93
Oleen-Burkey, MerriKay Adelle 1949- WhoAmW 93
Oleg dc. 911 OxDcByz
Oleinik, Olga Arsenievna 1925- WhoWor 93
Olejar, Paul Duncan 1906- WhoSSW 93
Olejer, Andrew Joseph 1925- WhoSSW 93
Olejko, Terry David 1950- WhoEmL 93
Olejniczak, Dominic 1908- WhoAm 92
Oleksa, D.J. 1946- St&PR 93
Oleksey, Vicky Joyce 1952- WhoAmW 93, WhoEmL 93
Oleksik, Mark Edward 1952- St&PR 93
Oleksiw, Daniel Philip 1921- WhoAm 92
Oleksy, Henryk 1930- WhoWor 93
Oleksy, Lester Stanley 1960- WhoEmL 93
Oleksy, Stephen A., II 1951- WhoIns 93
Olembo, Reuben James 1937- WhoUN 92
Olen, Arthur Joseph, Jr. 1953- St&PR 93
Olen, Gary 1942- St&PR 93
Olen, Stephanie Rose 1955- WhoE 93
Olena, Kenneth Arnold 1954- WhoEmL 93
Olenchak, Frank Richard 1950- WhoEmL 93, WhoSSW 93
Olender, Jack H. BioIn 17
Olender, Jeffrey Steven 1954- St&PR 93
Olender, Marvin 1928- St&PR 93
Olender, Robert Allan 1955- St&PR 93
Olendorf, William Carr, Jr. 1945- WhoSSW 93, WhoWor 93
O'Lenick, Anthony John, Jr. 1953- WhoEmL 93, WhoSSW 93
Olenin, Aleksei Nikolaevich 1763-1843 BioIn 17
Olenin, Alexander 1865-1944 Baker 92
Olenine d'Alheim, Marie (Alexeievna) 1869-1970 Baker 92
Oler, Douglas Blair Law&B 92
Oler, Douglas Blair 1940- St&PR 93
Oler, Howard Warren 1929- WhoE 93
Oler, Jacqueline 1932- WhoAmW 93
Oler, Wesley Marion, III 1918- WhoAm 92, WhoWor 93
Olerud, John BioIn 17
Oles, Andrzej 1923- WhoScE 91-4
Oles, Andrzej Michal 1951- WhoWor 93
Oles, Paul Joseph 1945- WhoAm 92
Oles, Paul Stevenson 1936- WhoAm 92
Olesen, Donald Louis 1952- WhoE 93, WhoEmL 93
Olesen, Dorte 1948- WhoScE 91-2
Olesen, Douglas Eugene 1939- St&PR 93, WhoAm 92
Olesen, Hans Jacob Esmann 1927- WhoWor 93
Olesen, Henrik 1945- WhoUN 92
Olesen, Jorgen E. 1958- WhoScE 91-2
Olesen, Marie 1952- WhoWor 93
Olesen, Mogens Norgaard 1948- WhoWor 93
Olesen, Poul 1939- WhoScE 91-2
Olesen, Svend Oivind 1938- WhoScE 91-2
Olesen, Virginia L. 1925- BioIn 17

Oleshko, Tatayana Anatolyevna 1962- WhoWor 93
Olesiak, Zbigniew Stanislaw 1927- WhoScE 91-4
Olesiuk, W.W.J. 1950- St&PR 93
Olesker, J. Bradford 1949- ScF&FL 92
Olesker, Jack ScF&FL 92
Oleskiewicz, Francis S. 1928- WhoIns 93
Oleskiewicz, Francis Stanley 1928- WhoAm 92
Oleskowicz, Jeanette 1956- WhoAmW 93
Olesnicki, Zbigniew 1389-1455 PolBiDi
Oleson, George T. Law&B 92
Oleson, Kenneth A. 1943- St&PR 93
Oleson, Ray Jerome 1944- St&PR 93
Oleson, Stan D. Law&B 92
Oleszczynski, Wladyslaw 1807-1866 PolBiDi
Oleszkiewicz, Jozef 1777-1830 PolBiDi
Oleszko, Pat BioIn 17
Oletta, Kelly St&PR 93
Olevskii, Alexander Moiseevich 1939- WhoWor 93
Olevskii, Victor Marcovich 1925- WhoWor 93
Olevsky, Julian 1926-1985 Baker 92
Olevson, Ken L.R. 1946- St&PR 93
Olexa, Jozef 1929- WhoWor 93
Olfers, Betty A. 1932- St&PR 93
Olfers, Rudy A. 1928- St&PR 93
Olfson, James Oliver 1927- St&PR 93
Olfson, Lewy 1937- ScF&FL 92
Ol'ga d969 OxDcByz
Olgaard, Anders 1926- WhoWor 93
Olgaard, Povl Lebeck 1928- WhoScE 91-2, WhoWor 93
Olgun, Tevfik 1931- WhoScE 91-4
Olgyay, Francis BioIn 17
Olheim, Helen d1992 NewYTBS 92
Olian, Jeffrey H. Law&B 92
Olian, JoAnne Constance WhoAmW 93
Oliansky, Joel 1935- MiSFD 9, WhoAm 92
Oliboni, Mark Louis 1957- WhoSSW 93
Olick, Arthur Seymour 1931- WhoAm 92
Olick, Philip Stewart 1936- WhoAm 92
Olien, Neil Arnold 1935- WhoAm 92
Oliensis, Sheldon 1922- WhoAm 92
Oligher, Robert Leo 1929- St&PR 93
Oliker, Vladimir 1945- WhoAm 92
Olimpo, Giorgio WhoScE 91-3
Olin, Bernie Ralph, III 1951- WhoEmL 93
Olin, Burton Howard 1925- St&PR 93
Olin, Gary BioIn 17
Olin, James R. 1920- WhoAm 92, WhoSSW 93
Olin, Jim 1920- CngDr 91
Olin, John George 1939- St&PR 93
Olin, Ken BioIn 17
Olin, Ken c. 1955- News 92 [port], -92-3 [port], WhoAm 92
Olin, Kent Oliver 1930- WhoAm 92
Olin, Lena BioIn 17
Olin, Lena Maria Jonna 1955- WhoAm 92
Olin, R. Brendan Law&B 92
Olin, Robert Floyd 1948- WhoEmL 93, WhoSSW 93
Olin, William Harold 1924- WhoAm 92
Olinde, Lancelot P. Law&B 92
Oline, Gary J. 1940- St&PR 93
Oliner, Arthur Aaron 1921- WhoAm 92
Olinger, Bob 1841?-1881 BioIn 17
Olinger, Brenda Sue 1958- WhoAmW 93
Olinger, Glenn S. 1929- St&PR 93
Olinger, Glenn Slocum 1929- WhoAm 92, WhoWor 93
Olinger, Haydee Law&B 92
Olinger, John Peter 1947- WhoE 93
Olinger, John Wallace BioIn 17
Olinger, Leon 1908-1990 BioIn 17
Olinger, Leon J. 1940- St&PR 93
Olinger, Thomas R. 1958- St&PR 93
Olins, Robert Abbot 1942- WhoAm 92
Oliounine, Iouri Veniamin 1939- WhoUN 92
Oliphant, Mrs. 1828-1897 ScF&FL 92
Oliphant, B. J. ConAu 137
Oliphant, Betty 1918- WhoAm 92, WhoAmW 93
Oliphant, Charles Romig 1917- WhoWor 93
Oliphant, Dave 1939- WhoWrEP 92
Oliphant, David E. 1939- St&PR 93
Oliphant, David J. Law&B 92
Oliphant, Eleana ScF&FL 92
Oliphant, Ernie L. 1934- WhoAmW 93
Oliphant, Hugh B. 1937- St&PR 93
Oliphant, Jodie Jenkins 1945- WhoSSW 93
Oliphant, John Hoyt 1943- St&PR 93
Oliphant, Margaret ScF&FL 92
Oliphant, Margaret 1828-1897 BioIn 17
Oliphant, Patrick BioIn 17
Oliphant, Patrick 1935- WhoAm 92
Oliphant, Robert D. 1949- St&PR 93
Oliphant, Thalia Elizabeth 1935- WhoAmW 93
Oliphant, Thomas 1799-1873 Baker 92
Olitski, Jules 1922- BioIn 17, WhoAm 92, WhoE 93
Olitsky, Gwen Miller 1942- WhoWrEP 92
Olitzka, Rosa 1873-1949 Baker 92
Olitzki, Walter 1903-1949 Baker 92
Olitzky, Kerry Marc 1954- WhoEmL 93
Oliv, Marvin d1991 BioIn 17
Oliva, Anne Sherrill 1965- WhoAmW 93
Oliva, Deborah A. 1952- WhoWor 93
Oliva, Lawrence Jay 1933- WhoAm 92, WhoE 93
Oliva, Neil d1990 BioIn 17
Oliva, Oscar 1937- DcMexL
Oliva, Pedro Lopez 1940- BiDAMSp 1989
Oliva, Ralph Angelo 1946- WhoEmL 93
Oliva, Stan 1952- WhoE 93
Oliva, Suzanne Dapra 1965- WhoEmL 93, WhoSSW 93
Oliva, Tony 1940- HispAmA
Olivar, Jordan 1915-1990 BioIn 17
Olivares, conde-duque de 1587-1645 BioIn 17
Olivares, Jose 1935- WhoScE 91-3
Olivares, Julian 1940- HispAmA [port]
Olivares, Oliver Del Fierro 1965- WhoWor 93
Olivares, Rene Eugenio 1941- WhoE 93
Olivares Carrillo, Armando 1910-1962 DcMexL
Olivarez, Graciela 1928- HispAmA
Olivarez, Graciela 1928-1987 NotHsAW 93
Olivarius-Imlah, MaryPat 1957- WhoAmW 93, WhoEmL 93
Olivarri, Leah Pagan 1951- WhoEmL 93
Olivas, J. Alfredo 1955- WhoSSW 93
Olivas, Michael A. 1951- HispAmA
Oliva Virgili, Rafael 1958- WhoWor 93
Olive, David Law&B 92
Olive, David Ian WhoScE 91-1
Olive, Georges 1931- WhoScE 91-2, WhoWor 93
Olive, John 1949- WhoAm 92
Oliveira, Cesar Cavalcanti 1941- WhoWor 93
Oliveira, Deodata Azevedo 1924- WhoWor 93
Oliveira, Elmar 1950- Baker 92, WhoAm 92
Oliveira, Eugenio da Costa 1948- WhoWor 93
Oliveira, Jaime Costa WhoScE 91-3
Oliveira, Jocy de 1936- Baker 92
Oliveira, Luiz Nunes 1951- WhoWor 93
Oliveira, M. Manuela 1947- WhoScE 91-3
Oliveira, Manuel J. 1936- St&PR 93
Oliveira, Nathan 1928- BioIn 17, WhoAm 92
Oliveira, Roberto Cardoso de BioIn 17
Oliveira-Filho, Ricardo Martins 1946- WhoWor 93
Oliveira Salazar, Antonio de 1889-1970 BioIn 17
Oliveira Santos, J.F. WhoScE 91-3
Olivella, Barry James 1947- St&PR 93, WhoAm 92
Olivelle, Patrick 1942- ConAu 138
Oliver, Allen Mennell 1939- St&PR 93
Oliver, Amy AmWomPl
Oliver, Ann Elizabeth 1953- St&PR 93
Oliver, Archibald Robert 1920- WhoWor 93
Oliver, Arnold Robert 1945- WhoSSW 93
Oliver, Bernard More 1916- BioIn 17, WhoAm 92
Oliver, Bonnie Bondurant 1933- WhoWor 93
Oliver, Bruce Lawrence 1951- WhoE 93, WhoEmL 93
Oliver, Byron D. 1942- St&PR 93
Oliver, Chad 1928- BioIn 17, ScF&FL 92
Oliver, Charles WhoScE 91-2
Oliver, Charles R. 1943- St&PR 93
Oliver, Christi Ruth 1949- WhoAmW 93
Oliver, Clifton, Jr. 1915- WhoSSW 93
Oliver, Dale Hugh 1947- WhoEmL 93
Oliver, Dan David 1952- WhoEmL 93
Oliver, Daniel 1939- WhoAm 92
Oliver, David MiSFD 9
Oliver, David 1958- St&PR 93
Oliver, David J. Law&B 92
Oliver, Don L. 1943- St&PR 93
Oliver, Douglas L. 1913- IntDcAn
Oliver, Eddy Glenn 1957- WhoSSW 93
Oliver, Edna May 1883-1942 QDrFCA 92 [port]
Oliver, Edward Carl 1930- St&PR 93
Oliver, Elizabeth Kimball 1918- WhoAmW 93, WhoWor 93
Oliver, Frank Sommars 1948- WhoEmL 93
Oliver, Gene Leech 1929- WhoE 93
Oliver, George ScF&FL 92
Oliver, George Benjamin 1938- WhoAm 92
Oliver, George L. 1929- St&PR 93
Oliver, Harry Maynard, Jr. 1921- WhoAm 92
Oliver, Hazel Simon 1905- WhoAmW 93
Oliver, Heath 1930- St&PR 93
Oliver, Helen Theresa 1949- WhoAmW 93, WhoEmL 93
Oliver, Henry Kemble 1800-1885 Baker 92
Oliver, Jack Ertle 1923- WhoAm 92
Oliver, Jacqueline Laha Law&B 92
Oliver, James BioIn 17
Oliver, James Michael Yorrick 1940- WhoWor 93
Oliver, James Reginald, Jr. 1954- WhoSSW 93
Oliver, James William 1947- WhoIns 93
Oliver, Jane 1903-1970 ScF&FL 92
Oliver, Jennifer Ball 1962- WhoAmW 93
Oliver, Jerry Joseph 1947- WhoEmL 93
Oliver, John WhoScE 91-1
Oliver, John 1939- Baker 92
Oliver, John Edward 1951- WhoEmL 93, WhoWor 93
Oliver, John Jacob, Jr. 1945- St&PR 93
Oliver, John Parker 1939- WhoSSW 93
Oliver, John Preston 1934- WhoAm 92
Oliver, John T., Jr. St&PR 93
Oliver, John Thomason, Jr. 1929- WhoAm 92
Oliver, Joseph McDonald, Jr. 1946- WhoEmL 93
Oliver, Jovan dc. 1355 OxDcByz
Oliver, Joyce Anne 1958- WhoAmW 93, WhoEmL 93, WhoWor 93
Oliver, "King" (Joseph) 1885-1938 Baker 92
Oliver, Laetitia Selwyn ScF&FL 92
Oliver, Larry Kenneth 1939- St&PR 93
Oliver, Leonard Paul 1933- WhoE 93
Oliver, Lynn d1992 NewYTBS 92
Oliver, M. Leon 1943- St&PR 93
Oliver, Margaret Scott AmWomPl
Oliver, Mark A. 1958- St&PR 93, WhoIns 93
Oliver, Mary 1935- BioIn 17, WhoAm 92, WhoWrEP 92
Oliver, Mary Wilhelmina 1919- WhoAm 92
Oliver, Maurice Leon Law&B 92
Oliver, Michael BioIn 17
Oliver, Orson Law&B 92
Oliver, Orson 1943- St&PR 93
Oliver, Paul Winthrop, Jr. 1941- WhoAm 92
Oliver, Pere 1950- WhoScE 91-3
Oliver, Philip Dudley 1947- WhoEmL 93
Oliver, Philip Manus 1920- WhoE 93
Oliver, Ralph David 1958- St&PR 93
Oliver, Raymond 1909-1990 BioIn 17
Oliver, Raymond Davies 1936- WhoAm 92
Oliver, Remedios Diaz NotHsAW 93
Oliver, Rich BioIn 17
Oliver, Robert Bruce 1931- WhoAm 92
Oliver, Robert Warner 1922- WhoAm 92
Oliver, Rodney John 1937- WhoWor 93
Oliver, Roger Meredith 1948- WhoEmL 93
Oliver, Ron MiSFD 9
Oliver, Rose Warshaw 1910- WhoWor 93
Oliver, Sandra 1941- WhoE 93
Oliver, Sharlyn Chyrel 1948- WhoEmL 93
Oliver, Stephen 1950-1992 BioIn 17, NewYTBS 92, OxDcOp
Oliver, Stephen (Michael Harding) 1950- Baker 92
Oliver, Steven W. 1947- St&PR 93
Oliver, Steven Wiles 1947- WhoAm 92, WhoWor 93
Oliver, Susan d1990 BioIn 17
Oliver, Symmes Chadwick 1928- BioIn 17
Oliver, Temple AmWomPl
Oliver, Terry James 1949- WhoEmL 93, WhoSSW 93
Oliver, Thomas Anthony 1937- St&PR 93
Oliver, Thomas D. Law&B 92
Oliver, Thomas R. 1941- St&PR 93
Oliver, Timothy Allen 1950- WhoEmL 93
Oliver, W. Thomas 1942- St&PR 93
Oliver, Wallace Lee Law&B 92
Oliver, Walter Maurice 1945- St&PR 93
Oliver, William Albert, Jr. 1926- WhoAm 92
Oliver, William John 1925- WhoAm 92
Olivera, Armando Juan 1949- St&PR 93
Olivera, Carlos Gabriel 1951- WhoWor 93
Olivera, Hector 1931- MiSFD 9
Olivera, Miguel Virgilio 1933- WhoUN 92
Oliver-Hoffmann, Camile BioIn 17
Oliver-Hoffmann, Paul BioIn 17
Oliveri, Ann Lenore 1951- WhoE 93
Oliveri, Mary Jane 1953- WhoAmW 93
Oliveri, Robert Peter 1942- WhoE 93
Oliverio, Alberto 1938- WhoScE 91-3, WhoWor 93
Oliverio, Antoinette Frances 1948- WhoEmL 93
Oliverio, William J. 1938- St&PR 93
Olivero, Magda 1910- OxDcOp
Olivero, Magda 1912- Baker 92
Olivero, Magda 1914- IntDcOp
Oliveros, Gilda 1949- NotHsAW 93
Oliveros, Nestor Panimdim 1954- WhoWor 93
Oliveros, Pauline BioIn 17
Oliveros, Pauline 1932- Baker 92
Oliver-Pickett, Cheryl Kay 1949- WhoWrEP 92
Oliver-Smith, Martha ScF&FL 92
Oliver-Warren, Mary Elizabeth 1924- WhoAmW 93
Olives Chavez, Marcia L. Law&B 92
Oliveto, Eugene Paul 1924- WhoE 93
Oliveto, Frank Louis 1956- WhoAm 92, WhoEmL 93, WhoSSW 93
Olivetti, Armand Edward, Jr. 1952- WhoEmL 93
Olivetti, Marco Maria 1943- WhoWor 93
Olivi, Oliviero 1917- WhoScE 91-3
Olivia, William Brian 1960- WhoEmL 93, WhoSSW 93
Olivier, Daniele 1942- WhoScE 91-2
Olivier, Donald Andrew 1931- St&PR 93
Olivier, Jason Thomas 1961- WhoEmL 93, WhoSSW 93
Olivier, John D. Law&B 92
Olivier, Jon Paul 1962- WhoEmL 93
Olivier, Joyce Elizabeth 1959- WhoSSW 93
Olivier, Laurence 1907-1989 BioIn 17, IntDcF 2-3 [port], MiSFD 9N
Olivier, Louis John 1913-1990 BioIn 17
Olivier, Nancy 1954- WhoAmW 93, WhoEmL 93
Olivieri, Anthony G. 1934- St&PR 93
Olivo, Anthony J. Law&B 92
Olivo, Margaret Ellen Anderson 1941- WhoAm 92
Olivo, Nancy Norman 1959- WhoAmW 93, WhoSSW 93
Olivos, Alejandro 1941- WhoWor 93
Olkhovsky, Paul George 1960- WhoEmL 93
Olkhovsky, Vladislav Sergeyevitch 1938- WhoWor 93
Olkinetzky, Sam 1919- WhoAm 92
Olkinuora, Pekka K. 1945- WhoScE 91-4
Olkkonen, Tauno Toivo 1925- WhoScE 91-4
Olkowska, Krystyna Maria Nardelli 1939- WhoAm 92
Olkowski, William F. 1957- WhoSSW 93
Ollari, Frank Joseph 1946- St&PR 93
Olle, Laura Newman 1952- WhoAmW 93
Olleman, Roger Dean 1923- WhoAm 92
Ollen, Richard Albin 1932- St&PR 93
Ollen-Bittle, Linda Elise 1950- WhoAmW 93
Ollendorff, S.A. St&PR 93
Oller, Donald Ray 1948- WhoEmL 93
Oller, Marie AmWomPl
Oller, William Maxwell 1924- WhoAm 92
Ollerenshaw, John Herbert WhoScE 91-1
Ollerenshaw, Kathleen 1912- WhoWor 93
Ollestad, Melvin E. 1942- St&PR 93
Ollevier, F.P. 1942- WhoScE 91-2
Olley, Randy Isabelle 1946- WhoEmL 93
Olley, Robert Edward 1933- WhoAm 92
Ollhoff, Elizabeth Anne 1953- WhoAmW 93
Ollie, Pearl Lynn 1953- WhoAmW 93
Ollier, Claude BioIn 17
Ollila, Leo W. 1916- St&PR 93
Ollis, Johnny R. 1942- St&PR 93
Ollis, Linda Neu 1952- WhoEmL 93
Olliver, Denis G. 1940- WhoAm 92
Ollivier, Louis 1934- WhoScE 91-2
Ollmann, Robert Raymond 1931- St&PR 93
Ollongren, Alexander Alexandrovich 1928- WhoWor 93
Ollstein, Marty MiSFD 9
Olman, Abe 1888-1984 Baker 92
Olman, Victor 1946- WhoWor 93
Olmeda de San Jose, Federico 1865-1909 Baker 92
Olmedo, Mario Ernesto 1955- St&PR 93
Olmedo de Olvera, Dolores BioIn 17
Olmer, Vit 1942- DrEEuF
Olmes, Donald Marinus 1950- WhoE 93, WhoEmL 93
Olmi, Ermanno 1931- MiSFD 9
Olmi, Urban A. 1952- St&PR 93
Olmo, Jaime Alberto 1930- WhoSSW 93, WhoWor 93
Olmos, Edward James BioIn 17, WhoAm 92
Olmos, Edward James 1947- CurBio 92 [port], HispAmA [port], MiSFD 9
Olms, Klaus 1939- WhoUN 92
Olmstead, Alan Mark 1948- WhoEmL 93
Olmstead, Cecil Jay 1920- WhoAm 92
Olmstead, David 1943- WhoAm 92
Olmstead, Earl P. 1920- ConAu 137
Olmstead, Francis Henry, Jr. 1938- WhoAm 92
Olmstead, Gary Eugene 1956- St&PR 93
Olmstead, Gertrude 1904-1975 SweetSg B [port]

Olmstead, Joan Parmelie 1939- *WhoAmW 93*
Olmstead, Laurence Daniel 1957- *WhoAm 92*
Olmstead, Nancy A. 1949- *St&PR 93*
Olmstead, Paul Smith 1897- *WhoSSW 93*
Olmstead, Steven W. 1951- *St&PR 93*
Olmstead, William Edward 1936- *WhoAm 92*
Olmstead, Williard G. 1944- *St&PR 93*
Olmsted, Frederick L. 1822-1903 *GayN*
Olmsted, Frederick Law 1822-1903 *BioIn 17*
Olmsted, George Hamden 1901- *WhoAm 92*
Olmsted, Jerauld Lockwood 1938- *WhoAm 92*
Olmsted, Joanna Belle 1947- *WhoAmW 93, WhoEmL 93*
Olmsted, Malcolm Ray 1944- *WhoSSW 93*
Olmsted, Mildred Scott d1990 *BioIn 17*
Olmsted, Robert Walsh 1936- *WhoE 93, WhoWrEP 92*
Olmsted, Theresa Lorraine 1964- *WhoAmW 93*
Olneck, Donald *Law&B 92*
Olness, John William 1929- *WhoE 93*
Olney, James 1933- *WhoAm 92, WhoWrEP 92*
Olney, Martha Louise 1956- *WhoEmL 93*
Olney, Michael E. *Law&B 92*
Olney, Robert C. 1926- *WhoAm 92*
Olofson, Tom William 1941- *WhoAm 92*
Olofsson, Klas Tuve 1943- *WhoWor 93*
O'Looney, Patricia Anne 1954- *WhoAmW 93, WhoEmL 93*
O'Loughlin, David Michael *Law&B 92*
O'Loughlin, Earl T. 1930- *WhoAm 92*
O'Loughlin, James Leo *Law&B 92*
O'Loughlin, John Kirby 1929- *WhoAm 92*
O'Loughlin, Kathryn 1894-1952 *BioIn 17*
O'Loughlin, Maurice Edwin James 1922- *WhoAm 92*
O'Loughlin, Theresa *Law&B 92*
Olovsson, Ivar Olov Gote 1928- *WhoWor 93*
Olovsson, Olov Ivar Gote 1928- *WhoScE 91-4*
Olowude, Samuel Adebisi 1939- *WhoUN 92*
Olpin, Owen 1934- *WhoAm 92*
Olschwang, Alan P. *Law&B 92*
Olschwang, Alan Paul 1942- *WhoAm 92, WhoE 93, WhoWor 93*
Olsem, Jean-Pierre 1942- *WhoWor 93*
Olsen, Alfred Jon 1940- *WhoAm 92*
Olsen, Allen Richard 1940- *St&PR 93*
Olsen, Alvin Gordon 1927- *WhoAm 92*
Olsen, Amy Eileen *WhoAmW 93*
Olsen, Arthur Martin 1909- *WhoAm 92*
Olsen, Ashley *BioIn 17*
Olsen, Bobby Gene 1951- *WhoEmL 93, WhoSSW 93*
Olsen, Brian W. 1952- *St&PR 93*
Olsen, Byron Donn 1934- *St&PR 93*
Olsen, Cande Joan 1950- *WhoAmW 93*
Olsen, Carl Christian 1930- *WhoScE 91-2*
Olsen, Carol M. 1946- *WhoIns 93*
Olsen, Charles J. 1951- *St&PR 93*
Olsen, David A. 1937- *WhoAm 92*
Olsen, David Alexander 1937- *St&PR 93*
Olsen, David George 1941- *WhoE 93*
Olsen, David P. *Law&B 92*
Olsen, Donald Bert 1930- *WhoAm 92*
Olsen, Donald D. 1931- *WhoWrEP 92*
Olsen, Donald Emmanuel 1919- *WhoAm 92, WhoWor 93*
Olsen, Douglas Marc 1957- *WhoE 93, WhoEmL 93*
Olsen, Edward Gustave 1908- *WhoAm 92*
Olsen, Edward John 1927- *WhoAm 92*
Olsen, Edward L. *Law&B 92*
Olsen, Elmer *BioIn 17*
Olsen, Erling 1933- *WhoScE 91-4*
Olsen, Florence Johanna 1924- *WhoAmW 93*
Olsen, Frances Elisabeth 1945- *WhoAm 92*
Olsen, Frederick Milton 1930- *St&PR 93*
Olsen, Gary 1953- *WhoEmL 93*
Olsen, Geoffrey G. *Law&B 92*
Olsen, George Allen 1928- *St&PR 93*
Olsen, George David 1940- *St&PR 93*
Olsen, George L. *Law&B 92*
Olsen, Gregory W. 1954- *St&PR 93*
Olsen, Haakon A. 1923- *WhoScE 91-4*
Olsen, Hans L. 1944- *St&PR 93*
Olsen, Hans Peter 1940- *WhoAm 92*
Olsen, Harold Fremont 1920- *WhoAm 92*
Olsen, Harris Leland 1947- *WhoEmL 93, WhoWor 93*
Olsen, Howard 1947- *BioIn 17*
Olsen, Humphrey Adoniram 1909- *WhoWrEP 92*
Olsen, Ib Spang 1921- *ConAu 37NR, MajAI [port]*
Olsen, Ib Steen 1938- *WhoScE 91-2*
Olsen, Inger Anna 1926- *WhoAmW 93*
Olsen, Irwin 1941- *WhoScE 91-1*
Olsen, Jack 1925- *WhoAm 92*
Olsen, Janus Staun 1937- *WhoScE 91-2*
Olsen, John Alvin 1938- *St&PR 93*
Olsen, John R. *Law&B 92*
Olsen, John R. 1949- *WhoEmL 93*
Olsen, John Richard 1930- *WhoSSW 93*
Olsen, John Robert 1928- *St&PR 93*
Olsen, John William 1950- *WhoE 93*
Olsen, Jorgen Lykke 1923- *WhoScE 91-4*
Olsen, Jorn 1946- *WhoScE 91-2*
Olsen, Jorn C. 1949- *St&PR 93*
Olsen, Kai 1933- *WhoWor 93*
Olsen, Kay Dannevig 1960- *WhoAmW 93*
Olsen, Kenneth H. *BioIn 17, NewYTBS 92 [port]*
Olsen, Kenneth H. 1926- *St&PR 93*
Olsen, Kenneth Harry 1926- *WhoAm 92, WhoE 93*
Olsen, Kevin Harry 1956- *WhoE 93*
Olsen, Kurt 1924- *WhoAm 92*
Olsen, Kurt Channell *Law&B 92*
Olsen, Lance *ScF&FL 92*
Olsen, Lance 1956- *ScF&FL 92*
Olsen, Leif H. 1926- *St&PR 93*
Olsen, Leif Ole 1921- *WhoE 93*
Olsen, Marian Claire 1954- *WhoAmW 93*
Olsen, Marvin Elliott 1936- *WhoAm 92*
Olsen, Mary Kate *BioIn 17*
Olsen, Melvin E. 1943- *St&PR 93*
Olsen, Merlin *BioIn 17*
Olsen, Merlin Jay 1940- *WhoAm 92*
Olsen, Miriam Gladys 1923- *WhoAmW 93*
Olsen, Murray R. 1953- *WhoEmL 93*
Olsen, Nels 1924- *St&PR 93*
Olsen, Odd Arvid 1947- *WhoScE 91-4*
Olsen, Olaf 1928- *WhoWor 93*
Olsen, Ole 1850-1927 *Baker 92*
Olsen, Ole 1892-1965 & Johnson, Chic 1891-1962 *QDrFCA 92 [port]*
Olsen, Ole Bernt 1928- *WhoScE 91-4*
Olsen, Ole Vestenskov 1939- *WhoUN 92*
Olsen, Patricia Graciela 1951- *WhoEmL 93*
Olsen, Poul Rovsing 1922-1982 *Baker 92*
Olsen, Ray 1937- *St&PR 93*
Olsen, Rex E. 1935- *WhoSSW 93*
Olsen, Rex Norman 1925- *WhoAm 92*
Olsen, Richard Ellison 1941- *WhoWrEP 92*
Olsen, Richard Galen 1945- *WhoSSW 93, WhoWor 93*
Olsen, Richard George 1937- *WhoAm 92*
Olsen, Richard James 1938- *St&PR 93*
Olsen, Robert John 1928- *WhoAm 92, WhoE 93, WhoWor 93*
Olsen, Robert Joseph *Law&B 92*
Olsen, Roger Milton 1942- *WhoAm 92*
Olsen, Rolf Arthur, Jr. 1956- *WhoE 93*
Olsen, Samuel Dagfinn 1950- *WhoWor 93*
Olsen, (Carl Gustav) Sparre 1903-1984 *Baker 92*
Olsen, Susan 1961- *BioIn 17*
Olsen, Susan Elaine 1948- *WhoWor 93*
Olsen, Sverre M., Jr. *Law&B 92*
Olsen, T(heodore) V(ictor) 1932- *ConAu 39NR*
Olsen, Thomas Richard, Sr. 1934- *WhoAm 92*
Olsen, Tillie *BioIn 17*
Olsen, Tillie 1912- *WhoAm 92, WhoWrEP 92*
Olsen, Tillie 1913- *AmWomWr 92, JeAmFiW, MagSAmL [port], ShSCr 11 [port]*
Olsen, Tore 1930- *WhoScE 91-4*
Olsen, Velma Lea 1938- *WhoAmW 93*
Olsen, Werner 1927- *WhoWor 93*
Olsen, William 1950- *MiSFD 9*
Olsen, William E. 1928- *St&PR 93*
Olseth, Dale R. 1930- *St&PR 93*
Olshaker, Mark 1951- *ScF&FL 92*
Olshan, Joseph R. *Law&B 92*
Olshan, Karen *WhoAm 92, WhoAmW 93*
Olshan, Kenneth S. 1932- *BioIn 17, St&PR 93, WhoAm 92*
Olshan, Regina *Law&B 92*
Olshanskii, Grigori Iosiphovich 1949- *WhoWor 93*
Olshansky, David Robert 1940- *WhoSSW 93*
Olshansky, Phyllis Macklin 1929- *WhoE 93*
Olshen, Abraham Charles 1913- *St&PR 93, WhoWor 93*
Olshen, Paul Robert 1938- *WhoE 93*
Olshin, Arnold S. 1940- *St&PR 93*
Olsinski, Peter Kevin 1942- *WhoAm 92, WhoE 93*
Olsman, Robert C. 1945- *St&PR 93*
Olson, Alfred E. 1939- *St&PR 93*
Olson, Arielle North *BioIn 17*
Olson, Arthur Dean *Law&B 92*
Olson, Barbara Ann *Law&B 92*
Olson, Barbara Jeannette Sloan 1950- *WhoAmW 93, WhoSSW 93*
Olson, Barbara Martha 1943- *WhoAmW 93*
Olson, Bob Moody 1934- *WhoAm 92*
Olson, Bonnie Waggoner-Breternitz *WhoAmW 93, WhoE 93*
Olson, Bruce *BioIn 17*
Olson, Bruce Joseph 1949- *St&PR 93*
Olson, Carl Eric 1914- *WhoE 93*
Olson, Carl L. 1941- *WhoE 93*
Olson, Carol Lea 1929- *WhoAmW 93*
Olson, Charles 1910-1970 *BioIn 17, MagSAmL [port]*
Olson, Charles Eric 1942- *WhoAm 92, WhoE 93*
Olson, Charles Lindbergh 1928- *St&PR 93, WhoAm 92*
Olson, Clarence Elmer, Jr. 1927- *WhoAm 92, WhoWrEP 92*
Olson, Clayton Leo 1947- *WhoWrEP 92*
Olson, Clifford Larry 1946- *WhoAm 92*
Olson, Clinton Louis 1916- *WhoAm 92*
Olson, D. Joseph *Law&B 92*
Olson, D. Joseph 1941- *St&PR 93*
Olson, Dale C. 1934- *WhoAm 92*
Olson, Daniel P. *Law&B 92*
Olson, David C. *Law&B 92*
Olson, David Chalmers 1952- *WhoE 93*
Olson, David H. *Law&B 92*
Olson, David Henry 1933- *WhoAm 92*
Olson, David Herman 1940- *WhoAm 92*
Olson, David John 1941- *WhoAm 92*
Olson, David P. *Law&B 92*
Olson, Dennis Alan 1959- *WhoEmL 93*
Olson, Diana Craft 1941- *WhoAmW 93*
Olson, Diane 1954- *WhoAmW 93*
Olson, Donald A. *St&PR 93*
Olson, Donald Ernest 1921- *WhoAm 92*
Olson, Donald Eugene 1934- *St&PR 93*
Olson, Donald Richard 1917- *WhoAm 92*
Olson, Donald W. 1934- *St&PR 93*
Olson, Edmund E. 1945- *St&PR 93*
Olson, Elder J. d1992 *NewYTBS 92*
Olson, Elder (James) 1909-1992 *ConAu 139*
Olson, Eldon *Law&B 92*
Olson, Elizabeth Fielder 1959- *WhoAmW 93*
Olson, Elizabeth Jeanette 1951- *WhoAmW 93*
Olson, Eric J. 1952- *WhoUN 92*
Olson, Esther E. 1901- *AmWomPl*
Olson, Eugene E. *ScF&FL 92*
Olson, Eugene Rudolph 1926- *WhoAm 92*
Olson, Everett C. 1910- *BioIn 17*
Olson, Everett Claire 1910- *WhoAm 92*
Olson, Floyd B. 1891-1936 *PolPar*
Olson, Frank Albert 1932- *St&PR 93, WhoAm 92, WhoE 93*
Olson, Frederick Irving 1916- *WhoAm 92*
Olson, Gail Diane 1954- *WhoAmW 93*
Olson, Gayle Augustine 1945- *WhoSSW 93*
Olson, Gen 1938- *WhoAmW 93*
Olson, George E. 1937- *St&PR 93*
Olson, Gordon Bennie 1924- *WhoAm 92*
Olson, Gordon D. 1927- *St&PR 93*
Olson, H. K. *Law&B 92*
Olson, Harold Dean 1946- *WhoEmL 93*
Olson, Harold Roy 1928- *WhoE 93*
Olson, Harry Andrew, Jr. 1923- *WhoAm 92*
Olson, Hilding Harold 1916- *WhoAm 92*
Olson, Howard Charles 1918- *WhoSSW 93*
Olson, Jack Francis 1925- *WhoAm 92*
Olson, James *BioIn 17*
Olson, James C. 1907-1992 *BioIn 17*
Olson, James Clifton 1917- *WhoAm 92*
Olson, James Duane, II 1943- *WhoAm 92*
Olson, James Richard 1941- *WhoAm 92*
Olson, James Robert 1940- *WhoAm 92*
Olson, James W. *Law&B 92*
Olson, James Wallace 1947- *WhoAm 92*
Olson, James Warren 1949- *WhoEmL 93*
Olson, James William Park 1940- *WhoAm 92*
Olson, Jane Virginia 1916- *WhoWrEP 92*
Olson, Janice Lynn 1946- *WhoAmW 93*
Olson, Jeffrey William 1958- *WhoE 93*
Olson, Jeffry Olav 1942- *St&PR 93*
Olson, Jerald W. 1931- *WhoAm 92*
Olson, Jerrald B. 1938- *St&PR 93*
Olson, Jerry Stephen 1951- *WhoEmL 93*
Olson, John Frederic 1951- *WhoEmL 93*
Olson, John Joseph 1960- *St&PR 93*
Olson, John Karl 1949- *WhoEmL 93*
Olson, John Melvin 1929- *WhoScE 91-2*
Olson, John R. 1952- *St&PR 93*
Olson, John Richard 1938- *WhoSSW 93*
Olson, John Victor 1913- *WhoAm 92*
Olson, Judith Mary Reedy 1939- *WhoAmW 93*
Olson, Julie Ann 1957- *WhoAmW 93*
Olson, K. Richard *Law&B 92*
Olson, Kathy Rae 1950- *WhoAmW 93*
Olson, Kay Melchisedech 1948- *WhoAm 92, WhoAmW 93, WhoWrEP 92*
Olson, Keith Waldemar 1931- *WhoAm 92*
Olson, Kenneth A. 1955- *St&PR 93*
Olson, Kenneth Paul 1935- *WhoWor 93*
Olson, Kent R. *Law&B 92*
Olson, Kirby 1956- *WhoWrEP 92*
Olson, Kristen Anne 1949- *WhoAmW 93, WhoEmL 93*
Olson, Larry Arlen 1942- *St&PR 93*
Olson, Lars 1942- *WhoScE 91-4*
Olson, Lawrence 1918- *WhoWrEP 92*
Olson, Lawrence 1918-1992 *BioIn 17*
Olson, Lawrence Alexander 1918-1992 *ConAu 137*
Olson, Leroy Calvin 1926- *WhoAm 92, WhoE 93*
Olson, Lisa *BioIn 17*
Olson, Lynn *WhoWrEP 92*
Olson, Lynn (Freeman) 1938-1987 *Baker 92*
Olson, Lynne Rae 1943- *WhoAmW 93*
Olson, Lynnette Gail 1945- *WhoAmW 93*
Olson, Madeline Mae 1944- *WhoAmW 93*
Olson, Mancur *BioIn 17*
Olson, Mancur Lloyd 1932- *WhoAm 92*
Olson, Marian Edna 1923- *WhoAmW 93*
Olson, Marian Katherine 1933- *WhoAmW 93*
Olson, Mark William 1946- *WhoE 93, WhoWrEP 92*
Olson, Mary E. *St&PR 93*
Olson, Mary Therese 1953- *WhoEmL 93*
Olson, Maxine Estelle 1948- *WhoUN 92*
Olson, Melvin E. 1917- *St&PR 93*
Olson, Michael J. 1953- *St&PR 93*
Olson, Michael Joseph 1953- *WhoEmL 93*
Olson, Milton Joseph 1910- *St&PR 93*
Olson, Nadine Faye 1948- *WhoSSW 93*
Olson, Norman Fredrick 1931- *WhoAm 92*
Olson, Oscar Julius 1933- *WhoE 93*
Olson, Pamela Faith 1954- *WhoAmW 93*
Olson, Paul F. *ScF&FL 92*
Olson, Paul Richard 1925- *WhoAm 92*
Olson, Peter Lowell *Law&B 92*
Olson, Peter M. *Law&B 92*
Olson, Peter Wesley 1950- *WhoE 93, WhoEmL 93*
Olson, R. Brent *Law&B 92*
Olson, Ramon L. 1926- *St&PR 93*
Olson, Randall J. 1947- *WhoAm 92*
Olson, Rebekah Ruth 1965- *WhoAmW 93*
Olson, Rex Melton 1940- *WhoSSW 93*
Olson, Richard David 1944- *WhoAm 92, WhoSSW 93*
Olson, Richard Dean 1949- *WhoAm 92, WhoEmL 93, WhoWor 93*
Olson, Richard F. 1927- *St&PR 93*
Olson, Richard George 1940- *WhoAm 92, WhoWrEP 92*
Olson, Richard Gustave 1959- *WhoEmL 93*
Olson, Richard H. 1925- *St&PR 93*
Olson, Robert A. 1933- *St&PR 93*
Olson, Robert E. 1940- *St&PR 93*
Olson, Robert Edward 1927- *WhoAm 92*
Olson, Robert Eugene 1919- *WhoAm 92*
Olson, Robert Goodwin 1924- *WhoAm 92*
Olson, Robert Grant 1952- *WhoEmL 93*
Olson, Robert H. 1934- *WhoIns 93*
Olson, Robert Leonard 1930- *WhoAm 92*
Olson, Robert Louis 1933- *St&PR 93*
Olson, Robert Luther 1934- *BiDAMSp 1989*
Olson, Robert Stanley 1925- *St&PR 93*
Olson, Robert W. *Law&B 92*
Olson, Robert W(illiam) 1940- *ConAu 136*
Olson, Robert Wyrick 1945- *St&PR 93, WhoAm 92*
Olson, Roberta Dawn 1960- *WhoAmW 93, WhoEmL 93*
Olson, Roberta Jeanne Marie 1947- *WhoEmL 93*
Olson, Roger D. 1967- *WhoAm 92*
Olson, Roger Grove 1935- *St&PR 93*
Olson, Ronald Dale 1947- *WhoAm 92*
Olson, Ronald Kenneth 1943- *WhoE 93*
Olson, Ronald Leroy 1895-1979 *IntDcAn*
Olson, Ronald Leroy 1941- *WhoAm 92*
Olson, Ronald Wayne 1931- *WhoAm 92*
Olson, Rue Eileen 1928- *WhoAmW 93, WhoWor 93*
Olson, Russel Einar 1931- *WhoAm 92*
Olson, Russell L. 1933- *WhoAm 92*
Olson, Sandra Dittman 1953- *WhoAmW 93*
Olson, Sandra L. 1963- *WhoEmL 93*
Olson, Sandra Lee 1948- *WhoAmW 93*
Olson, Scott Robert 1958- *WhoEmL 93*
Olson, Sharon 1942- *WhoAmW 93*
Olson, Shelley Lavonne 1951- *WhoSSW 93*
Olson, Sigmund Lars 1935- *WhoAm 92*
Olson, Sigurd F. 1899- *BioIn 17*
Olson, Stanley William 1914- *WhoAm 92*
Olson, Steven Stanley 1950- *WhoEmL 93*
Olson, Susan A. *Law&B 92*
Olson, Susan Diane 1958- *WhoAmW 93*
Olson, Susan Jane 1958- *WhoAmW 93*
Olson, Susan Kay 1959- *WhoAmW 93*
Olson, Sylvester Irwin 1907- *WhoAm 92*
Olson, Teresa Anne 1948- *WhoAmW 93*

Olson, Theodore Alexander 1904- *WhoAm 92*
Olson, Thomas Charles 1949- *WhoEmL 93*
Olson, Thomas Francis, II 1948- *WhoAm 92*
Olson, Thomas M. *Law&B 92*
Olson, Thomas Michael 1946- *St&PR 93, WhoIns 93*
Olson, Thorman *BioIn 17*
Olson, Timothy Allan 1952- *WhoEmL 93*
Olson, Toby 1937- *WhoWrEP 92*
Olson, Val 1933- *St&PR 93*
Olson, Walter G. 1924- *St&PR 93*
Olson, Walter Gilbert 1924- *WhoAm 92*
Olson, Walter Justus, Jr. 1941- *WhoAm 92*
Olson, Walter Theodore 1917- *WhoAm 92*
Olson, Wanda Jean 1957- *WhoAmW 93*
Olson, Wayne Charles 1949- *WhoEmL 93*
Olson, William Clinton 1920- *WhoAm 92*
Olson, William F. 1928- *St&PR 93*
Olson, William Furman 1928- *WhoAm 92*
Olson, William Henry 1936- *WhoAm 92, WhoSSW 93*
Olson, William Michael 1959- *WhoEmL 93*
Olson-Hagan, Arlene 1926- *WhoSSW 93*
Olsrud, Lois Christine 1930- *WhoAmW 93*
Olsson, A. Kerstin *WhoScE 91-4*
Olsson, Alexis Bruno 1960- *WhoEmL 93*
Olsson, Anders G. 1940- *WhoScE 91-4*
Olsson, Carl Alfred 1938- *WhoAm 92*
Olsson, Curt Gunnar 1927- *WhoWor 93*
Olsson, Eskil A.E. 1926- *WhoScE 91-4*
Olsson, George C.P. 1903-1991 *BioIn 17*
Olsson, Henry A. 1932- *WhoUN 92*
Olsson, Jan E. 1944- *WhoScE 91-4*
Olsson, Lars Erik 1937- *WhoUN 92*
Olsson, Lennart 1949- *WhoScE 91-2*
Olsson, Nils William 1909- *WhoAm 92*
Olsson, Otto (Emanuel) 1879-1964 *Baker 92*
Olsson, Ronald Arthur 1955- *WhoWor 93*
Olsson, Rune 1931- *WhoScE 91-4*
Olsson, Sture G. 1920- *St&PR 93*
Olsson, Sture Gordon 1920- *WhoAm 92*
Olstad, Roger Gale 1934- *WhoAm 92*
Olstein, Stephen Jeffrey 1952- *WhoE 93*
Olsten, Stuart 1952- *St&PR 93*
Olsten, William *BioIn 17*
Olston, Mary Kay 1949- *WhoAmW 93*
Olstowski, Franciszek 1927- *WhoSSW 93, WhoWor 93*
Olszak, Zbigniew 1946- *WhoWor 93*
Olszewska, Maria Joanna 1929- *WhoScE 91-4*
Olszewski, Edward John 1937- *WhoAm 92*
Olszewski, Edward Paul 1930- *St&PR 93*
Olszewski, Jan 1930- *WhoWor 93*
Olszewski, Karol 1846-1915 *PolBiDi*
Olszewski, Olgierd 1937- *WhoScE 91-4*
Olszewski, Richard Allen 1948- *St&PR 93*
Olszewski, Rick Allen 1948- *St&PR 93*
Olszowski, Krzysztof 1958- *WhoWor 93*
Olszta, Wenanty 1938- *WhoScE 91-4*
Olsztynski, James C. 1947- *WhoWrEP 92*
Olt, Schuyler John 1956- *WhoSSW 93*
Olthof, Henk 1944- *WhoWor 93*
Olti, Ferenc 1949- *WhoScE 91-4*
Oltion, Jerry 1957- *ScF&FL 92*
Oltman, C. Dwight 1936- *WhoAm 92*
Oltman, Henry George, Jr. 1927- *WhoAm 92*
Oltman, James H. 1930- *St&PR 93*
Oltman, James Harvey 1930- *WhoAm 92*
Olton, Roy 1922- *WhoAm 92*
Oltrogge, Cal G. 1945- *WhoE 93*
Olubadewo, Joseph Olanrewaju 1945- *WhoSSW 93*
Oludimu, Olufemi Ladipo 1951- *WhoWor 93*
Olum, Paul 1918- *WhoAm 92, WhoWor 93*
Oluwek, Arthur 1926- *St&PR 93*
Olver, A. David *WhoScE 91-1*
Olver, Graham Dudley *Law&B 92*
Olver, John 1936- *BioIn 17*
Olver, John Walter 1936- *WhoAm 92, WhoE 93*
Olver, Michael Lynn 1950- *WhoEmL 93*
Olver, Richard Boyce 1947- *WhoUN 92*
Olver, Richard Edmund *WhoScE 91-1*
Olvera, Dolores Olmedo de *BioIn 17*
Olvera, Joe 1944- *WhoWrEP 92*
Olvera Stotzer, Beatriz *NotHsAW 93*
Olvey, Daniel Richard 1948- *St&PR 93*
Olving, Sven 1928- *WhoScE 91-4*
Olwin, John Hurst 1907- *WhoAm 92*
Olyanova, Nayda d1991 *BioIn 17*
Olympias 361?-408 *OxDcByz*
Olympiodoros of Alexandria c. 500-c. 564 *OxDcByz*
Olympiodoros of Thebes fl. 5th cent.- *OxDcByz*
Olympios *OxDcByz*
Olyphant, David 1936- *WhoAm 92*
Olyschlaeger, Helmut 1950- *St&PR 93*
Olzacki, James Joseph 1949- *WhoIns 93*
Olzi, Emilio 1937- *WhoScE 91-3*
Olzman, Saul 1920- *St&PR 93, WhoAm 92*
Om *SmATA 70*
Om, Wendy 1956- *WhoEmL 93*
Oma, Kei 1937- *WhoAsAP 91*
O'Mahoney, Brian *WhoScE 91-1*
O'Mahoney, Elizabeth 1947- *WhoAmW 93*
O'Mahoney, James Mackey 1931- *St&PR 93*
O'Mahoney, Robert M. 1925- *WhoAm 92*
O'Mahony, Audrey Madeline 1938- *WhoAmW 93*
O'Mahony, E. *WhoScE 91-3*
O'Mahony, Kieran Timothy 1953- *WhoWrEP 92*
O'Maley, David Boyers 1946- *WhoAm 92*
O'Malley, Brian Richard 1937- *St&PR 93*
O'Malley, Carlon Martin 1929- *WhoAm 92*
O'Malley, Comerford J. 1902-1991 *BioIn 17*
O'Malley, Cormac K.H. *Law&B 92*
O'Malley, David 1944- *MiSFD 9*
O'Malley, Denis Michael 1943- *St&PR 93*
O'Malley, Edward 1926- *WhoAm 92*
O'Malley, Edward Patrick 1947- *WhoE 93*
O'Malley, Eugene Francis 1950- *WhoE 93, WhoEmL 93, WhoWor 93*
O'Malley, Frank *BioIn 17, ScF&FL 92*
O'Malley, Honor *WhoE 93*
O'Malley, James, Jr. 1910- *WhoAm 92*
O'Malley, James Patrick, III 1951- *WhoEmL 93*
O'Malley, John Daniel 1926- *WhoAm 92*
O'Malley, John Edward 1942- *WhoAm 92, WhoE 93, WhoWor 93*
O'Malley, Joseph Michael *Law&B 92*
O'Malley, Kathleen 1955- *ScF&FL 92*
O'Malley, Kevin T. *Law&B 92*
O'Malley, Marjorie Glaubach 1950- *WhoAmW 93, WhoEmL 93*
O'Malley, Michael John 1923- *WhoE 93*
O'Malley, Michael Joseph 1941- *St&PR 93*
O'Malley, Michael P. *Law&B 92*
O'Malley, Padraig *ConAu 139*
O'Malley, Patrick L. 1911- *St&PR 93*
O'Malley, Patrick Lawrence 1911- *WhoAm 92*
O'Malley, Peter 1937- *WhoAm 92*
O'Malley, Robert C. 1925- *St&PR 93*
O'Malley, Robert Edmund, Jr. 1939- *WhoAm 92*
O'Malley, Shaun F. *WhoE 93*
O'Malley, Suzanne Marie *WhoE 93*
O'Malley, Thomas D. 1941- *St&PR 93, WhoAm 92, WhoE 93*
O'Malley, Thomas Patrick 1930- *WhoAm 92*
O'Malley, Timothy John 1951- *WhoEmL 93*
O'Malley, W. Gresham, III 1933- *St&PR 93*
O'Malley, William Charles 1937- *St&PR 93, WhoAm 92, WhoSSW 93*
O'Malley, William J. *BioIn 17*
O'Malley-Harpel, Nancy *Law&B 92*
Oman, Charles McMaster 1944- *WhoE 93*
Oman, Deborah Sue 1948- *WhoAmW 93, WhoEmL 93*
Oman, Don *BioIn 17*
Oman, Elizabeth Ann 1940- *WhoWrEP 92*
Oman, Jack Allen 1939- *St&PR 93*
Oman, Julia Trevelyan 1930- *WhoWor 93*
Oman, LaFel Earl 1912- *WhoAm 92*
Oman, Richard Heer 1926- *WhoAm 92*
Omang, Myrna Louise 1934- *St&PR 93*
Omansky, Michael Laurence 1952- *WhoEmL 93*
Omar *OxDcByz*
Omar, I c. 586-644 *HarEnMi*
Omar, Alim 1944- *WhoUN 92*
Omar, Dato' Abu Hassan Bin Haji 1940- *WhoAsAP 91*
Omar, Jamshed 1934- *WhoWor 93*
Omar, Margaret Frances Rowe 1965- *WhoAmW 93*
O'Mara, Deborah Lynn 1957- *WhoWrEP 92*
O'Mara, Ethel Rose 1920- *WhoE 93*
O'Mara, Frank *BioIn 17*
O'Mara, John Aloysius 1924- *WhoAm 92*
O'Mara, Joseph 1864-1927 *OxDcOp*
O'Mara, Joseph James 1938- *WhoE 93*
O'Mara, Peggy Noreen 1947- *WhoAmW 93, WhoWrEP 92*
O'Mara, Robert Edmund George 1933- *WhoAm 92*
O'Mara, Stephen Paul 1951- *WhoAm 92*
O'Mara, Thomas George 1929- *St&PR 93*
O'Mara, Thomas Patrick 1937- *St&PR 93, WhoAm 92, WhoWor 93*
O'Marie, Carol Anne 1933- *ConAu 136*
Omatu, Sigeru 1946- *WhoWor 93*
Omawale 1940- *WhoUN 92*
O'May, John Gavin 1947- *WhoWor 93*
Omazur, Nicolas c. 1630-1698 *BioIn 17*
Omberg, Arthur Chalmers, Jr. 1939- *WhoE 93*
Ombu, Claudio *WhoWrEP 92*
Omdah, Lloyd B. 1931- *WhoAm 92*
Omdahl, Becky Lynn 1958- *WhoAmW 93*
Omdra 6 *ScF&FL 92*
O'Meallie, Kitty 1916- *WhoAm 92, WhoSSW 93*
O'Meally, Serge A. 1939- *St&PR 93*
O'Meara, Anna M. 1947- *WhoAmW 93*
O'Meara, David Collow 1929- *WhoAm 92*
O'Meara, Edward Francis, Jr. 1942- *WhoSSW 93*
O'Meara, Edward T. 1921-1992 *BioIn 17, NewYTBS 92*
O'Meara, Eva Judd 1884-1979 *BioIn 17*
O'Meara, Gary David 1955- *WhoWor 93*
O'Meara, James Joseph 1946- *St&PR 93*
O'Meara, John Corbett 1933- *WhoAm 92*
O'Meara, John M. 1946- *WhoAm 92*
O'Meara, Mary Joy *Law&B 92*
O'Meara, Onorato Timothy 1928- *WhoAm 92*
O'Meara, Patrick O. 1938- *WhoAm 92*
O'Meara, Robert P. 1938- *WhoAm 92*
O'Meara, Thomas Franklin 1935- *WhoAm 92*
O'Meara, Walter 1897-1989 *BioIn 17, ScF&FL 92*
O'Melia, Charles Richard 1934- *WhoAm 92*
O'Melia, Kevin M. 1944- *St&PR 93*
Omeljanovsky, Erazm M. 1937- *WhoUN 92*
O'Mell, Herbert Sidney 1935- *WhoSSW 93*
Omenn, Gilbert Stanley 1941- *WhoAm 92*
Omer, George Elbert, Jr. 1922- *WhoAm 92, WhoWor 93*
Omer, Guy C. *BioIn 17*
Omer, Laura Diane 1946- *WhoAmW 93*
Omholt, Bruce Donald 1943- *WhoWor 93*
Omi, Koji 1932- *WhoAsAP 91*
Omi, Mikio 1935- *WhoAsAP 91*
Ominsky, Harris 1932- *WhoAm 92*
Omiros, George James 1956- *WhoE 93*
Omland, Tov 1923- *WhoWor 93*
Omlor, John Joseph 1935- *WhoAm 92*
Ommaya, Ayub Khan 1930- *WhoAm 92, WhoWor 93*
Ommodt, Donald Henry 1931- *St&PR 93, WhoAm 92*
Omohundro, Joseph Roger 1910- *WhoE 93*
Omole, Gabriel Gbolabo 1940- *WhoWor 93*
Omoniyi, Bandele 1884-1913 *BioIn 17*
O'Morain, Sean *WhoWrEP 92*
O'Morchoe, Charles Christopher Creagh 1931- *WhoAm 92*
O'Morchoe, Patricia Jean 1930- *WhoAmW 93*
Omori, Akira 1927- *WhoAsAP 91*
Omori, Emiko *MiSFD 9*
Omori, Sentaro 1894- *HarEnMi*
O'Morrow, Gerald Stephen 1929- *WhoSSW 93*
Omoth, Wayne E. *Law&B 92*
Omotoso, Edward 1941- *WhoUN 92*
Omotoso, Kole 1943- *DcLB 125 [port]*
Omre, Henning 1951- *WhoScE 91-4*
Oms, Alejandro 1895-1946 *HispAmA*
Omsberg, Philip H. *Law&B 92*
Omura, George Adolf 1938- *WhoAm 92*
Omura, James Matsumoto 1912- *WhoWrEP 92*
Omura, Jimmy Kazuhiro 1940- *WhoAm 92*
Omura, Kenneth I. *Law&B 92*
Omura, Masujiro 1824-1869 *HarEnMi*
Omura, Tsuneo 1930- *WhoWor 93*
Omura, Yukiko 1955- *WhoWor 93*
Omurtag *OxDcByz*
Omurtag, Yildirim 1939- *WhoAm 92*
Omwake, H. Geiger 1907-1967 *IntDcAn*
Onadipe, Kola *DcChlFi*
Onaga, Corinne Yurie 1952- *WhoAmW 93*
Onak, Thomas Philip 1932- *WhoAm 92*
Onal, Mehmet Rifat 1948- *WhoScE 91-4*
O'Nan, Martha 1921- *WhoAm 92, WhoWor 93*
O'Nan, Regina Powell 1965- *WhoSSW 93*
Onaral, Banu Kum 1949- *WhoWor 93*
Onaran, Kasif 1928- *WhoScE 91-4*
Onarheim, Leif Frode 1934- *WhoWor 93*
Ona-Sarino, Milagros Felix 1940- *WhoSSW 93, WhoWor 93*
Onasch, Donald Carl 1927- *WhoAm 92*
Onassis, Christina *BioIn 17*
Onassis, Jacqueline Bouvier Kennedy 1929- *WhoAm 92, WhoAmW 93*
Onassis, Jacqueline Kennedy *BioIn 17*
Onat, Altan 1929- *WhoScE 91-4*
Onate, Eugenio 1953- *WhoScE 91-3*
Onate, Juan de fl. 1595-1622 *BioIn 17*
Onate, Santiago 1949- *WhoWor 93*
Onaya, Toshimasa 1935- *WhoWor 93*
Oncidi, Anthony Joseph 1959- *WhoEmL 93*
Oncina, Juan 1925- *Baker 92, OxDcOp*
Oncken, Henry Kuck 1938- *WhoAm 92*
Oncley, John Lawrence 1910- *WhoAm 92*
Ondaatje, Michael 1943- *BioIn 17, WhoCanL 92*
Ondaatje, (Philip) Michael 1943- *WhoWrEP 92*
Ondako, Michele *BioIn 17*
Ondeck, Thomas P. 1946- *WhoAm 92*
Onderdonk, Stephen Richter 1944- *St&PR 93*
Onders, Edward A. *Law&B 92*
Ondersma, David M. *WhoAm 92*
Ondersma, David M. 1942- *St&PR 93*
Ondetti, Miguel A. *BioIn 17*
Ondetti, Miguel Angel 1930- *WhoAm 92*
Ondobo Ndzana, Claude 1946- *WhoUN 92*
Ondra, Anny 1903-1987 *IntDcF 2-3 [port]*
Ondracek, Emanuel 1931- *WhoScE 91-4*
Ondrack, Esther Signe 1940- *St&PR 93*
Ondrejcek, Peter *WhoScE 91-4*
Ondrejka, Ronald 1932- *WhoAm 92*
Ondricek *Baker 92*
Ondricek, Emanuel 1882-1958 *Baker 92*
Ondricek, Frantisek 1857-1922 *Baker 92*
Ondricek, Ignac 1807-1871 *Baker 92*
Ondricek, Jan 1832-1900 *Baker 92*
Ondrick, Charles William 1942- *St&PR 93*
Ondrovich, Peggy Ann Chnupa 1952- *WhoAmW 93*
Ondrusek, David Francis 1955- *WhoSSW 93*
One, Ernest 1929- *St&PR 93*
One, Ernest G. 1929- *WhoIns 93*
One, Keith Jun 1953- *WhoEmL 93*
O'Neal, Ahtena Starr 1959- *WhoAmW 93*
O'Neal, Alexander 1954- *SoulM*
Oneal, Billie *AmWomPl*
O'Neal, Bob H. 1934- *WhoAm 92, WhoSSW 93*
O'Neal, Carole Kelley 1933- *WhoAmW 93*
O'Neal, Cathy Lynn 1955- *WhoEmL 93, WhoSSW 93, WhoWrEP 92*
O'Neal, Charles E. 1950- *St&PR 93*
O'Neal, Edgar Carl 1939- *WhoAm 92*
O'Neal, Edward A. 1944- *St&PR 93*
Oneal, Elizabeth 1934- *MajAI [port]*
O'Neal, Emmet 1921- *St&PR 93*
O'Neal, F. Hodge 1917-1991 *BioIn 17*
O'Neal, Forest Hodge 1917-1991 *BioIn 17*
O'Neal, Frederick 1905- *WhoAm 92*
O'Neal, Frederick 1905-1992 *NewYTBS 92 [port]*
O'Neal, Frederick (Douglas) 1905-1992 *CurBio 92N*
O'Neal, Gary R. 1951- *St&PR 93*
Oneal, Glen, Jr. 1917- *WhoE 93, WhoWor 93*
O'Neal, Harriet Roberts 1952- *WhoAmW 93, WhoEmL 93, WhoWor 93*
O'Neal, Henry L. 1942- *St&PR 93*
Oneal, James 1875-1962 *PolPar*
O'Neal, Kathleen Len 1953- *WhoEmL 93*
O'Neal, Kathleen M. *ScF&FL 92*
O'Neal, Kelle Snyder 1948- *WhoAmW 93*
O'Neal, Leslie K. *Law&B 92*
O'Neal, Linda Nichols 1958- *WhoSSW 93*
O'Neal, Michael Ralph 1951- *WhoEmL 93*
O'Neal, Michael Robert 1948- *St&PR 93*
O'Neal, Michael Scott, Sr. 1948- *WhoAm 92, WhoSSW 93*
O'Neal, Moncure Camper, Jr. 1947- *WhoEmL 93, WhoSSW 93*
O'Neal, Nell Self 1925- *WhoAmW 93*
O'Neal, Patricia Jane 1937- *WhoAmW 93*
O'Neal, Ralph *DcCPCAm*
O'Neal, Reagan *WhoWrEP 92*
O'Neal, Ron 1937- *MiSFD 9*
O'Neal, Russell E. 1925- *St&PR 93*
O'Neal, Ryan *BioIn 17*
O'Neal, Ryan 1941- *WhoAm 92*
O'Neal, Shaquille *BioIn 17, NewYTBS 92 [port]*
O'Neal, Shaquille 1972- *News 92 [port]*
O'Neal, Stephen Michael 1955- *WhoSSW 93*
O'Neal, Steve J. 1951- *St&PR 93*
O'Neal, William B. *ScF&FL 92*
O'Neal, William B. 1907- *WhoAm 92*
O'Neal, William K. 1939- *St&PR 93*
O'Neal, Winston James, Jr. 1948- *WhoSSW 93, WhoWrEP 92*
Oneal, Zibby *MajAI*
Oneal, Zibby 1934- *DcAmChF 1960, DcAmChF 1985*
O'Neale, Rosalyn Taylor 1950- *WhoAmW 93, WhoEmL 93*
Onegin, Eugene 1883-1919

See Onegin, (Elisabeth Elfriede Emilie) Sigrid 1889-1943 *Baker 92*
Onegin, Sigrid 1889-1943 *IntDcOp, OxDcOp*
Onegin, (Elisabeth Elfriede Emilie) Sigrid 1889-1943 *Baker 92*
Oneglia, Raymond Robert 1948- *WhoAm 92*
O'Neil, Amy Kessing 1954- *WhoSSW 93*
O'Neil, Brian Edward 1935- *St&PR 93*
O'Neil, C. Roderick 1931- *WhoAm 92*
O'Neil, Cleora Tanner 1946- *WhoE 93*
O'Neil, Daniel Joseph 1942- *WhoAm 92*
O'Neil, Edward Joseph, Jr. 1930- *St&PR 93*
O'Neil, Edward T. 1935- *St&PR 93*
O'Neil, James E. 1929- *WhoAm 92*
O'Neil, James Edward 1939- *WhoAm 92, WhoE 93*
O'Neil, James Joseph *Law&B 92*
O'Neil, James Joseph 1936- *St&PR 93*
O'Neil, James Peter 1944- *St&PR 93, WhoAm 92*
O'Neil, Janice Ann 1960- *WhoAmW 93*
O'Neil, John 1915- *WhoAm 92*
O'Neil, John G. A. d1992 *NewYTBS 92*
O'Neil, John Patrick 1921- *WhoAm 92*
O'Neil, Joseph C. *Law&B 92*
O'Neil, Joseph C. 1933- *St&PR 93*
O'Neil, Joseph Francis 1934- *WhoAm 92*
O'Neil, Kathleen Kay 1947- *WhoAmW 93*
O'Neil, Leo E. 1928- *WhoAm 92, WhoE 93*
O'Neil, Lloyd 1928-1992 *BioIn 17*
O'Neil, Lloyd Reginald Terrance 1937- *WhoAsAP 91*
O'Neil, Michael H. *WhoScE 91-1*
O'Neil, Patrick Arthur 1946- *St&PR 93*
O'Neil, Patrick Thomas 1947- *WhoEmL 93*
O'Neil, Richard J. 1929- *St&PR 93*
O'Neil, Robert Marchant 1934- *WhoAm 92, WhoWor 93*
O'Neil, Robert Vincent *MiSFD 9*
O'Neil, Rose Meller *AmWomPl*
O'Neil, Russell 1927-1991 *BioIn 17*
O'Neil, Shane 1947- *WhoAm 92*
O'Neil, Sharon Lund 1942- *WhoSSW 93*
O'Neil, Stephen Edward 1932- *WhoAm 92*
Oneil, Susan Jean 1952- *WhoAmW 93, WhoEmL 93*
O'Neil, Wayne 1931- *WhoAm 92, WhoWrEP 92*
O'Neil, William Andrew 1927- *WhoUN 92*
O'Neil, William Charles, Jr. 1934- *St&PR 93*
O'Neil, William Francis 1929- *WhoAm 92*
O'Neil, William Francis 1936- *WhoAm 92*
O'Neil, William Joseph 1951- *WhoEmL 93*
O'Neill, Albert Clarence, Jr. 1939- *WhoAm 92*
O'Neill, Anita Renee 1964- *WhoAmW 93*
O'Neill, Ann Renee 1959- *WhoAmW 93*
O'Neill, Anne *AmWomPl*
O'Neill, Arthur J. 1917- *WhoAm 92*
O'Neill, Barry William 1939- *WhoWor 93*
O'Neill, Beverly Lewis 1930- *WhoAmW 93*
O'Neill, Bonnie 1942- *WhoSSW 93*
O'Neill, Brian 1940- *WhoAm 92, WhoIns 93, WhoSSW 93*
O'Neill, Brian Collins 1934- *WhoE 93*
O'Neill, Brian Dennis 1946- *WhoAm 92*
O'Neill, Brian Donald *Law&B 92*
O'Neill, Brian Francis 1929- *WhoAm 92*
O'Neill, Brian M. *Law&B 92*
O'Neill, Buckey 1860-1898 *BioIn 17*
O'Neill, Charles Kelly 1933- *WhoAm 92, WhoWor 93*
O'Neill, Christopher W. *Law&B 92*
O'Neill, Cornelius Thomas 1935- *WhoSSW 93*
O'Neill, David Hugh 1949- *WhoScE 91-1*
O'Neill, David S. *Law&B 92*
O'Neill, Donald E. 1926- *St&PR 93*
O'Neill, Donald Edmund 1926- *WhoAm 92*
O'Neill, Donald Francis 1939- *St&PR 93*
O'Neill, Donald J. *St&PR 93*
O'Neill, Ed *BioIn 17*
O'Neill, Eoghan Rua c. 1590-1649 *BioIn 17*
O'Neill, Eugene 1888-1953 *BioIn 17, MagSAmL [port], WorLitC [port]*
O'Neill, Eugene Francis 1918- *WhoAm 92*
O'Neill, Eugene Milton 1925- *WhoAm 92*
O'Neill, Finbarr J. *Law&B 92*
O'Neill, Francis A., Jr. d1992 *NewYTBS 92*
O'Neill, Francis A(loysius), Jr. 1908-1992 *CurBio 92N*
O'Neill, Francis Aloysius 1908-1992 *BioIn 17*
O'Neill, Francis Xavier, III 1953- *WhoAm 92*
O'Neill, Frank G. d1990 *BioIn 17*
O'Neill, Gerard K. *BioIn 17*
O'Neill, Gerard K. d1992 *NewYTBS 92 [port]*
O'Neill, Gerard K(itchen) 1927-1992 *ConAu 137, CurBio 92N*
O'Neill, Gerard Kitchen 1927- *WhoWrEP 92*
O'Neill, Goerge D. 1926- *St&PR 93*
O'Neill, Gonzalo *HispAmA*
O'Neill, Grace O'Brien d1990 *BioIn 17*
O'Neill, Grover, Jr. 1922- *St&PR 93*
O'Neill, Harry J.J. *Law&B 92*
O'Neill, Harry William 1929- *WhoAm 92, WhoE 93*
O'Neill, Hugh *BioIn 17*
O'Neill, Hugh 1540?-1616 *BioIn 17*
O'Neill, J. Norman, Jr. *Law&B 92*
O'Neill, James *Law&B 92*
O'Neill, James Andrew, Jr. 1946- *St&PR 93*
O'Neill, James Edward 1923- *St&PR 93*
O'Neill, James J. 1934- *St&PR 93, WhoAm 92*
O'Neill, James Paul 1958- *WhoE 93, WhoWor 93*
O'Neill, Jennifer Lee 1948- *WhoAm 92*
O'Neill, Jimmy *BioIn 17*
O'Neill, John Francis 1947- *WhoE 93*
O'Neill, John J. 1920- *St&PR 93*
O'Neill, John Joseph 1920- *WhoAm 92*
O'Neill, John Joseph, Jr. 1919- *WhoAm 92*
O'Neill, John P. 1949- *St&PR 93*
O'Neill, John Robert 1937- *St&PR 93, WhoAm 92*
O'Neill, John T. 1944- *St&PR 93, WhoAm 92, WhoE 93*
O'Neill, John Thomas 1928- *St&PR 93*
O'Neill, Joseph 1878-1952 *ScF&FL 92*
O'Neill, June Ellenoff 1934- *WhoAmW 93*
O'Neill, Karen Krug *Law&B 92*
O'Neill, Katherine Templeton 1949- *WhoEmL 93*
O'Neill, Kathleen *Law&B 92*
O'Neill, Kathryn J. 1942- *WhoAmW 93*
O'Neill, Kevin *WhoAm 92*
O'Neill, Kevin 1958- *WhoWor 93*
O'Neill, Kevin B. 1957- *St&PR 93*
O'Neill, Lawrence Daniel 1946- *WhoAm 92, WhoWor 93*
O'Neill, Leo C. 1940- *St&PR 93*
O'Neill, M. Agatha *AmWomPl*
O'Neill, Marcia Taggart 1947- *WhoE 93*
O'Neill, Margaret E. 1935- *WhoAmW 93*
O'Neill, Marion W. *Law&B 92*
O'Neill, Mary Boniface 1916- *WhoAmW 93*
O'Neill, Mary Edwin 1867- *AmWomPl*
O'Neill, Mary Jane 1923- *WhoE 93*
O'Neill, Mary Le Duc 1908-1990 *BioIn 17*
O'Neill, Michael Francis *Law&B 92*
O'Neill, Michael G. *Law&B 92*
O'Neill, Michael J. *Law&B 92*
O'Neill, Michael J., Jr. *Law&B 92*
O'Neill, Michael James 1922- *WhoAm 92*
O'Neill, Michael Phillip 1947- *WhoWor 93*
O'Neill, Norman (Houstoun) 1875-1934 *Baker 92*
O'Neill, Owen Roe c. 1590-1649 *HarEnMi*
O'Neill, Pamela 1950- *ScF&FL 92*
O'Neill, Patricia Ann 1964- *WhoE 93*
O'Neill, Patrick F. *St&PR 93*
O'Neill, Patrick Henry 1915- *St&PR 93, WhoAm 92*
O'Neill, Patrick J. *WhoIns 93*
O'Neill, Patrick Joseph 1953- *WhoEmL 93*
O'Neill, Paul 1928- *WhoCanL 92*
O'Neill, Paul 1963- *BioIn 17*
O'Neill, Paul Henry 1935- *St&PR 93, WhoAm 92, WhoWor 93*
O'Neill, Peter J. *WhoWrEP 92*
O'Neill, Peter J. 1947- *St&PR 93*
O'Neill, Peter Michael 1946- *WhoEmL 93*
O'Neill, Peter X. *St&PR 93*
O'Neill, Philip Daniel, Jr. 1951- *WhoEmL 93*
O'Neill, Ralph A. 1896-1980 *EncABHB 8 [port]*
O'Neill, Randal Bruce 1956- *St&PR 93*
O'Neill, Robert B. *Law&B 92*
O'Neill, Robert Brendan 1938- *St&PR 93*
O'Neill, Robert Charles 1923- *WhoAm 92*
O'Neill, Robert Edward 1925- *WhoAm 92*
O'Neill, Robert F. 1923- *St&PR 93*
O'Neill, Robert Hugh 1928- *St&PR 93*
O'Neill, Robert John 1936- *WhoWor 93*
O'Neill, Robert W. *Law&B 92*
O'Neill, Russell Richard 1916- *WhoAm 92*
O'Neill, Stephen Francis 1891-1962 *BiDAMSp 1989*
O'Neill, Sylvia P. *Law&B 92*
O'Neill, Terence Marne 1914-1990 *BioIn 17*
O'Neill, Thomas E. *Law&B 92*
O'Neill, Thomas J. *Law&B 92*
O'Neill, Thomas Newman, Jr. 1928- *WhoAm 92, WhoE 93*
O'Neill, Thomas P. 1912- *PolPar*
O'Neill, Thomas P., Jr. 1912- *WhoAm 92*
O'Neill, Thomas P., Jr. 1953- *St&PR 93*
O'Neill, Timothy R. 1943- *ScF&FL 92*
O'Neill, W. Paul 1938- *WhoAm 92*
O'Neill, William Edward 1960- *WhoE 93*
O'Neill, William George 1943- *WhoE 93*
O'Neill, William J., Jr. 1933- *St&PR 93*
O'Neill, William James, Jr. 1933- *WhoAm 92*
O'Neill, William Lawrence 1935- *WhoAm 92, WhoWrEP 92*
O'Neill, William M. 1933- *St&PR 93*
O'Neill, William Owen 1860-1898 *BioIn 17*
O'Neill, William Patrick 1950- *St&PR 93*
O'Neill, William Robert 1950- *WhoEmL 93*
O'Neill Bidwell, Katharine Thomas 1937- *WhoAm 92*
O'Neill of the Maine, Baron 1914-1990 *BioIn 17*
Onengut, Gulsen 1944- *WhoScE 91-4*
Onesti, Silvio Joseph 1926- *WhoAm 92*
Onet, Traian 1937- *WhoScE 91-4*
Onet, Virginia 1939- *WhoAmW 93*
Oneto, Tom Laurence 1943- *St&PR 93*
Onetti, Juan Carlos 1909- *BioIn 17, SpAmA*
Oney, Joan M. *Law&B 92*
Ong, Boon Kheng 1935- *WhoWor 93*
Ong, Chee-Mun 1944- *WhoAm 92*
Ong, Colin Ghee Hock 1963- *WhoWor 93*
Ong, Fen Ching 1927- *St&PR 93*
Ong, Fook Sin 1958- *WhoWor 93*
Ong, John Doyle 1933- *St&PR 93, WhoAm 92*
Ong, Jose L., Jr. 1948- *WhoAsAP 91*
Ong, Michael Hock Guan 1955- *WhoWor 93*
Ong, Michael R. 1950- *St&PR 93*
Ong, Nancy d1991 *BioIn 17*
Ong, Patrick Kian-Seng 1951- *WhoWor 93*
Ong, Vincent 1961- *WhoWor 93*
Ong, Walter Jackson 1912- *WhoWrEP 92*
Ongpin, Jaime Velayo 1938-1987 *BioIn 17*
Ong Tee Kiat 1956- *WhoAsAP 91*
Ong Teng Cheong, Hon 1936- *WhoAsAP 91*
Ongyert, Werner 1938- *St&PR 93*
Onida, Fabrizio 1940- *WhoWor 93*
O'Niell, Herbert Edwin *Law&B 92*
Onillon, Marc 1937- *WhoScE 91-2*
Onions, David Edward *WhoScE 91-1*
Onions, Oliver 1873-1961 *ScF&FL 92*
O'Nions, R.K. *WhoScE 91-1*
Onischenko, Michael *Law&B 92*
Onishi, Akira 1929- *WhoWor 93*
Onishi, Hiroshi 1929- *WhoWor 93*
Onishi, Shoju 1935- *WhoWor 93*
Onishi, Takijiro 1891-1945 *HarEnMi*
Onizuka, Ellison S. 1946-1986 *BioIn 17*
Onken, George Marcellus 1914- *WhoAm 92, WhoWor 93*
Onken, Richard R. 1951- *St&PR 93*
Onken, Ulfert 1925- *WhoScE 91-3*
Onkotz, Dennis Henry 1948- *BiDAMSp 1989*
Onley, David C. 1950- *ScF&FL 92*
Onley, M. Francesca 1933- *WhoAmW 93*
Onn, Carrie *ScF&FL 92*
Onn, Hussein bin 1922-1990 *BioIn 17*
Onnen, Robert E. *Law&B 92*
Ono, Akira *WhoAsAP 91*
Ono, Hiroshi 1934- *WhoWor 93*
Ono, Kiyoko 1936- *WhoAsAP 91*
Ono, Richard Dana 1953- *WhoE 93*
Ono, Shinichi 1932- *WhoAsAP 91*
Ono, Takahiko 1951- *WhoWor 93*
Ono, Yoko *BioIn 17*
Ono, Yoko 1933- *Baker 92, WhoAmW 93*
Ono, Yoshinori 1935- *WhoAsAP 91*
Ono, Yuriko 1942- *WhoAsAP 91*
Onodera, Ryoji 1937- *WhoWor 93*
Onofrey, Debra Anne Catherine 1956- *WhoEmL 93*
Onofrey, John Francis 1935- *St&PR 93*
Onofri, Alessandro 1874-1932 *Baker 92*
Onokpise, Oghenekome Ukrakpo 1951- *WhoWor 93*
Onomarchus d352BC *HarEnMi*
Onopa, Robert 1943- *ScF&FL 92*
Onorato, Joseph A. 1949- *St&PR 93*
Onorato, Nicholas Louis 1925- *WhoAm 92*
Onorofski, Mark Alan 1950- *WhoEmL 93*
Onouphrios fl. c. 400- *OxDcByz*
Onozuka, Akira *BioIn 17*
Onslow, (Andre) Georges (Louis) 1784-1853 *Baker 92*
Onslow Ford, Gordon Max 1912- *WhoAm 92*
Onsrud, Mathias 1940- *WhoScE 91-4*
Onstott, Edward Irvin 1922- *WhoAm 92, WhoWor 93*
Onstott, Joseph E. 1949- *WhoEmL 93*
Onstott, Larry L. 1947- *St&PR 93*
Onsuwan, Visavarunee 1947- *WhoWor 93*
Ontiveros, Lupe 1942- *NotHsAW 93*
Ontjes, David Ainsworth 1937- *WhoAm 92*
Ontkean, Michael 1946?- *ConTFT 10*
Ontkean, Michael 1950- *WhoAm 92*
Ontko, Gary M. 1954- *St&PR 93*
Ontko, Joseph Andrew 1932- *WhoAm 92*
Onufrock, Richard Shade 1934- *WhoE 93*
Onufryk, Zenon B. 1953- *St&PR 93*
Onuki, Hideo 1943- *WhoWor 93*
Onukwuli, Francis Osita 1955- *WhoEmL 93, WhoSSW 93*
Onuoha, Everest 1953- *WhoE 93*
Onuscheck, David *Law&B 92*
Onusic, Helcio 1944- *WhoWor 93*
Onyonka, Zachary Theodore 1939- *WhoAfr*
Onyshko, Gary Joseph *Law&B 92*
Onyszchuk, Mario 1930- *WhoAm 92*
Onyszkiewicz, Janusz *BioIn 17*
Onyszkiewicz, Janusz 1937- *WhoWor 93*
Oo Gin Sun, Dato' 1933- *WhoAsAP 91*
Ooi, Boon S. 1957- *WhoE 93*
Oold, Tseveenjavyn 1942- *WhoAsAP 91*
Oolie, Sam 1936- *WhoE 93*
Oomen, A.J.A. *WhoScE 91-3*
Oommen, George 1942- *WhoAm 92*
Ooms, Gerritt *WhoScE 91-1*
Ooms, Van Doorn 1934- *WhoAm 92*
Oort, Frans 1935- *WhoWor 93*
Oort, Jan H. 1900-1992 *NewYTBS 92*
Oost, Wiebe A. 1938- *WhoScE 91-3*
Oostdam, Bernard Lodewijk 1932- *WhoE 93*
Oostdyk, Arlene Rosa 1926- *WhoE 93*
Oosten, Roger Lester 1937- *WhoSSW 93*
Oosterbaan, Bennie 1906-1990 *BioIn 17*
Oosterbaan, Gerhard Auke 1933- *WhoScE 91-3*
Oosterlinck, Andre 1946- *WhoScE 91-2*
Oosterlinck, Andre Jules Joseph 1946- *WhoWor 93*
Oostermeyer, Jan Stuart 1930- *WhoAm 92*
Oosterveld, M.W.C. 1933- *WhoScE 91-3*
Oosterzee, Cornelie van 1863-1943 *Baker 92*
Ooyama, Clara Michiko *Law&B 92*
Opacki, Bronislaw 1929- *WhoWor 93*
Opacki, Dennis George *Law&B 92*
O'Pake, Michael A. 1940- *WhoE 93*
Opal, Chet Brian 1942-1991 *BioIn 17*
Opal, Kenneth Edward 1940- *St&PR 93*
Opal, Robert T. *Law&B 92*
Opal, Robert Thad 1948- *WhoEmL 93*
Opala, Marian Peter 1921- *WhoAm 92, WhoSSW 93*
Opalek, Marvin 1939- *St&PR 93*
Opalenik, Stanley J. *Law&B 92*
Opalinski, Fred Stanley 1948- *WhoEmL 93*
Opalski, Douglas Victor 1942- *WhoE 93*
Oparil, Suzanne 1941- *WhoAm 92*
Opaschowski, Horst Werner 1941- *WhoWor 93*
Opat, Matthew John 1952- *WhoEmL 93*
Opatoshu, Joseph 1886-1954 *PolBiDi*
Opatrny, Donald C. 1952- *St&PR 93*
Opdam, Paul F.M. 1949- *WhoScE 91-3*
Opderbecke, H.W. 1922- *WhoScE 91-3*
Opdycke, Emerson 1830-1884 *HarEnMi*
Opeka, John Frank 1940- *St&PR 93, WhoAm 92*
Opel, Arthur William, Jr. 1943- *WhoAm 92*
Opel, John R. 1925- *St&PR 93, WhoAm 92*
Opelt, Vivian Lee *Law&B 92*
Opelz, Merle Sebrean 1942- *WhoUN 92*
Openden, Lori *WhoAmW 93*
Openhym, Evelyn Tennyson d1992 *BioIn 17, NewYTBS 92*
Openshaw, David Byron *Law&B 92*
Openshaw, Stan *WhoScE 91-1*
Opfel, Gregory L. *Law&B 92*
Opfer, Neil David 1954- *WhoWor 93*
Opgrande, Jarl L. 1938- *St&PR 93*
Opheim, Roberta Claire 1948- *WhoAmW 93*
Ophuls, Marcel 1927- *MiSFD 9, WhoAm 92*
Ophuls, Max 1902-1957 *MiSFD 9N*
Opich, Martha Evensen *Law&B 92*
Opie, Amelia 1769-1853 *DcLB 116 [port]*
Opie, Evarts W., Jr. 1934- *St&PR 93*
Opie, Iona Archibald *BioIn 17*
Opie, Peter d1982 *BioIn 17*
Opie, William Robert 1920- *WhoAm 92*
Opienski, Henryk 1870-1942 *Baker 92, PolBiDi*
Opihory, Kathleen Ann 1946- *WhoAmW 93*

Opitz, Bernard Francis, Jr. 1947- *WhoE 93, WhoEmL 93, WhoWor 93*
Opitz, John Marius 1935- *WhoAm 92*
Opitz, May *ConAu 139*
Opitz Von Boberfeld, Wilhelm 1941- *WhoScE 91-3*
Opland, Eve Victoria 1944- *St&PR 93*
Opland, Sam 1938- *St&PR 93*
O'Planick, Richard B. *Law&B 92*
Opler, Lewis Alan 1948- *WhoEmL 93*
Opler, Morris E. 1907- *IntDcAn*
Oplinger, Kathryn Ruth 1951- *WhoAmW 93*
Opoczky, Ludmilla 1933- *WhoScE 91-4*
Opolon, Pierre 1935- *WhoScE 91-2*
Opotowsky, Barbara Berger 1945- *St&PR 93*
Opotowsky, Maurice Leon 1931- *WhoAm 92*
Opotowsky, Mel 1931- *St&PR 93*
Opotowsky, Stuart B. 1935- *St&PR 93*
Opotowsky, Stuart Berger 1935- *WhoAm 92*
Opotzner, Paul Michael 1953- *WhoE 93*
Opp, Eric Neufville 1962- *WhoSSW 93*
Opp, W.R. 1939- *St&PR 93*
Oppe, Simon 1937- *WhoScE 91-3*
Oppedahl, John Fredrick 1944- *WhoAm 92*
Oppegaard, Grant E. 1943- *WhoAm 92*
Oppel, Richard Alfred 1943- *WhoAm 92*
Oppelt, Norman T. 1930- *ConAu 139*
Oppen, George 1908-1984 *BioIn 17*
Oppen, Steven Bernard 1946- *WhoEmL 93*
Oppenheim, Alan Victor 1937- *WhoAm 92*
Oppenheim, Antoni Kazimierz 1915- *WhoAm 92*
Oppenheim, Austin E. 1925- *St&PR 93*
Oppenheim, David Jerome 1922- *WhoAm 92*
Oppenheim, Dennis Allen 1938- *WhoAm 92*
Oppenheim, E. Phillips 1866-1946 *TwCLC 45 [port]*
Oppenheim, Ed *BioIn 17*
Oppenheim, Elliot 1915-1991 *BioIn 17*
Oppenheim, Henry 1926- *WhoE 93*
Oppenheim, Irwin 1929- *WhoE 93*
Oppenheim, Judith R. 1946- *WhoEmL 93*
Oppenheim, Lucy Linda 1959- *WhoWrEP 92*
Oppenheim, Michael 1940- *ConAu 138*
Oppenheim, Philip 1956- *ConAu 138*
Oppenheim, Robert 1925- *WhoE 93*
Oppenheim, Ruth 1927- *St&PR 93*
Oppenheim, Shulamith 1930- *ScF&FL 92*
Oppenheimer, Bertram Jay 1922- *WhoE 93*
Oppenheimer, Charles H. *Law&B 92*
Oppenheimer, Franz Martin 1919- *WhoAm 92*
Oppenheimer, Hamilton G. 1948- *St&PR 93*
Oppenheimer, Harry Frederick 1908- *WhoWor 93*
Oppenheimer, Heather Leigh 1949- *WhoEmL 93*
Oppenheimer, Hirsch 1805-1885 *BioIn 17*
Oppenheimer, J. Robert 1904-1967 *BioIn 17, ColdWar 1 [port], ConHero 2 [port]*
Oppenheimer, James Richard 1921- *WhoAm 92*
Oppenheimer, James Walter, Jr. 1955- *WhoE 93*
Oppenheimer, Jane Marion 1911- *WhoAm 92, WhoAmW 93*
Oppenheimer, Jerry L. 1937- *WhoAm 92*
Oppenheimer, Jesse Halff 1919- *WhoSSW 93*
Oppenheimer, Joan L(etson) 1925- *ConAu 37NR*
Oppenheimer, Joel K. 1957- *St&PR 93*
Oppenheimer, Joseph 1927- *WhoAm 92*
Oppenheimer, Judy 1942- *ScF&FL 92*
Oppenheimer, Lillian V. d1992 *NewYTBS 92 [port]*
Oppenheimer, Marc J. 1957- *St&PR 93*
Oppenheimer, Martin Foote 1948- *WhoE 93*
Oppenheimer, Max, Jr. 1917- *WhoAm 92*
Oppenheimer, Michael 1946- *WhoAm 92*
Oppenheimer, Monroe 1904-1990 *BioIn 17*
Oppenheimer, Peer J. *MiSFD 9*
Oppenheimer, Randolph Carl 1954- *WhoEmL 93*
Oppenheimer, Suzi 1934- *WhoAmW 93, WhoE 93*
Oppenheimer, Tamar Mariamne 1925- *WhoWor 93*
Oppenheimer, Valerie Kincade 1932- *WhoAm 92*
Oppenlander, Ann 1942- *St&PR 93*
Oppenlander, Robert 1923- *WhoAm 92*
Oppens, Ursula 1944- *Baker 92*
Opper, Loren M. *Law&B 92*
Opperdoes, Frederik R. 1945- *WhoScE 91-2*
Opperman, Dwight Darwin 1923- *WhoAm 92*
Opperman, Erik Carlton 1958- *WhoEmL 93*
Opperman, John R. 1953- *WhoEmL 93*
Oppermann, Andre 1924- *WhoScE 91-2*
Oppermann, B. *WhoScE 91-3*
Oppersdorff, Tony 1945- *ConAu 137*
Oppi, Ubaldo 1889-1942 *BioIn 17*
Oppian fl. 2nd cent.- *OxDcByz*
Oppido, Piero Andrea 1959- *WhoWor 93*
Oppizzi, Michael *BioIn 17*
Oppliger, Pearl Laviolette 1942- *WhoAmW 93*
Oppo, Gian-Luca 1958- *WhoWor 93*
Oppolzer, Wolfgang 1937- *WhoScE 91-4, WhoWor 93*
Opre, Thomas Edward 1943- *WhoAm 92, WhoWrEP 92*
Oprzedkiewicz, Janusz 1938- *WhoScE 91-4*
Opsahl, Richard Bernhard 1932- *WhoE 93*
Opsata, James Ball 1908- *WhoE 93*
Opsata, Margaret Ann 1944- *WhoAmW 93*
Opstvedt, Johannes 1933- *WhoScE 91-4*
Optic, Oliver *MajAI*
Opuchowski, Jerzy 1930- *WhoScE 91-4*
Opuko, Kwame Tua 1940- *WhoUN 92*
Oquendo, Antonio de 1577-1640 *HarEnMi*
O'Quin, Brenda Gail 1947- *WhoSSW 93*
O'Quinn, April Gale 1936- *WhoSSW 93*
O'Quinn, Kerry 1938- *WhoE 93*
O'Quinn, Michael Darren 1958- *WhoEmL 93*
Oquist, Gunnar 1941- *WhoScE 91-4*
O.R. *ScF&FL 92*
Ora, Sergio S., Jr. 1946- *St&PR 93*
Orabi, Ismail Ibrahim 1950- *WhoEmL 93*
Oracion, Timoteo S. 1911- *IntDcAn*
Orage, A.R. 1873-1934 *BioIn 17*
Orage, Alfred Richard 1873-1934 *BioIn 17*
Orahood, Jane R. *Law&B 92*
O'Raifeartaigh, Lochlainn 1933- *WhoScE 91-3*
Oral, Huseyin Ozay 1940- *WhoScE 91-4*
Oram, George A., Jr. *St&PR 93*
Oram, George Arthur, Jr. 1947- *WhoEmL 93*
Oram, Harold L. d1990 *BioIn 17*
Oram, John L. 1944- *WhoAm 92*
Oram, Neil 1938- *ScF&FL 92*
Oram, P.S.W. *Law&B 92*
Oram, Robert W. 1922- *WhoAm 92*
Oran, Elaine Surick 1946- *WhoAmW 93*
Oran, Frederic M. 1932- *St&PR 93*
Oran, Geraldine Ann 1938- *WhoAmW 93*
Oran, Yuksel Kazim 1934- *WhoScE 91-4*
Orander, Robert Lee 1961- *WhoSSW 93*
Orange, Charles William 1942- *WhoWor 93*
Orange, John W. 1949- *St&PR 93*
Orange, Larry Jay 1942- *WhoAm 92*
Oransky, John Joseph 1953- *WhoEmL 93*
Oraon, Smt Sumati 1935- *WhoAsAP 91*
Oras, Christine Marie 1965- *WhoAmW 93*
O Rathaille, Aodhagan 1670-1736 *BioIn 17*
Orav, Helle Reissar 1925- *WhoAmW 93*
Orava, Risto O. 1951- *WhoScE 91-4*
Oravitz, Joseph Vincent 1937- *WhoE 93*
Orazio, Paul Vincent 1957- *WhoEmL 93*
Orbach, Jerry 1935- *WhoAm 92*
Orbach, Raymond Lee 1934- *WhoAm 92*
Orban, Alex J. *Law&B 92*
Orban, Edmond Henry 1925- *WhoAm 92*
Orban, Frank A., III *Law&B 92*
Orban, Guy A. 1945- *WhoScE 91-2*
Orban, Gyorgy 1947- *Baker 92*
Orban, Joseph S. *Law&B 92*
Orban, Kurt 1916- *WhoAm 92*
Orbanyi, Ivan 1931- *WhoScE 91-4*
Orbe, Mercy Jeanette 1966- *WhoAmW 93*
Orbe, Octavius Anthony 1927- *WhoAm 92*
Orben, Jack R. 1938- *St&PR 93*
Orben, Jack Richard 1938- *WhoAm 92*
Orben, Robert 1927- *WhoAm 92, WhoE 93, WhoWrEP 92*
Orben, Robert A. 1936- *St&PR 93*
Orben, Robert Allen 1936- *WhoAm 92*
Orbik, James Allen 1954- *WhoEmL 93*
Orbison, David Vaillant 1952- *WhoE 93*
Orbison, James Graham 1953- *WhoEmL 93*
Orbison, Roy 1936-1988 *Baker 92, BioIn 17*
Orbon (de Soto), Julian 1925-1991 *Baker 92*
Orbon, Julian 1925-1991 *BioIn 17*
Orbos, Oscar *BioIn 17*
Orbos, Oscar M. 1951- *WhoAsAP 91*
Orbuch, Allen Harold 1928- *WhoAm 92*
Orchard, Cecil Clifford 1932- *WhoSSW 93*
Orchard, Donna Lee 1931- *WhoAmW 93*
Orchard, Henry John 1922- *WhoAm 92*
Orchard, Jack Louis 1947- *WhoEmL 93*
Orchard, Robert John 1946- *WhoAm 92*
Orchard, William (Arundel) 1867-1961 *Baker 92*
Orchard-Hays, William *BioIn 17*
Orci, Lelio 1937- *WhoScE 91-4*
Orcutt, Guy Henderson *BioIn 17*
Orcutt, James Douglas 1943- *WhoSSW 93*
Orcutt, Kevin *BioIn 17*
Orcutt, Robert Nicholas 1949- *WhoSSW 93*
Orcutt, Timothy Parkhurst 1939- *St&PR 93*
Orcutt, William P. 1928- *St&PR 93*
Orczyk, S.R. 1930- *St&PR 93*
Ord, Angustias de la Guerra *NotHsAW 93*
Ord, Duncan E. *WhoScE 91-1*
Ord, Edward Otho Cresap 1818-1883 *HarEnMi*
Ord, John Robert 1950- *St&PR 93*
Ord, Kenneth Stephen 1946- *St&PR 93*
Orda, Napoleon 1807-1883 *PolBiDi*
Ordal, Caspar Reuben 1922- *WhoAm 92*
Ordas, Amando 1945- *WhoScE 91-3*
Ordaz, Diego de 1480?-1532 *Expl 93*
Ordaz, Steven P. *Law&B 92*
Orde, A. J. *ConAu 137, ScF&FL 92*
Ordemann, Carl W. 1951- *St&PR 93*
Ordemann, Marshall F., Jr. *Law&B 92*
Orden, Charles Van *Law&B 92*
Orden, Ted 1920- *WhoAm 92*
Ordentlich, Ivan 1934- *WhoWor 93*
Order, Stanley Elias 1934- *WhoAm 92*
Orderic Vitalis 1075-1142? *OxDcByz*
Ordin, Andrea S. 1940- *HispAmA*
Ordin, Andrea Sheridan *WhoAm 92*
Ording, Burchard 1936- *WhoScE 91-3*
Ordjanian, Nikit 1918- *St&PR 93*
Ordman, Edward Thorne 1944- *WhoSSW 93*
Ordman, Jeannette *WhoWor 93*
Ordonez, Carlos d' 1734-1786 *Baker 92*
Ordonez, Nelson Gonzalo 1944- *WhoSSW 93*
Ordonez, Sedfrey A. 1921- *WhoUN 92*
Ordonez, Victor M. 1944- *WhoUN 92*
Ordonez Salazar, Hugo 1945- *WhoWor 93*
Ordonowna, Hanka 1904-1950 *PolBiDi*
Ordorica, Steven Anthony 1957- *WhoWor 93*
Ordowski, James E. *Law&B 92*
Ordoyne, John Philip 1952- *WhoSSW 93*
Ordroneaux, John *BioIn 17*
Ord-Smith, Richard Albert James *WhoScE 91-1*
Ordung, Philip Franklin 1919- *WhoAm 92*
Orduno, Robert 1933- *BioIn 17*
Orduno, Robert Daniel 1933- *WhoWor 93*
Ordway, Ellen 1927- *WhoAmW 93*
Ordway, Frederick Ira, III 1927- *WhoAm 92*
Ordway, Ronald D. 1941- *St&PR 93*
Ordynskij, Vasilij 1923-1985 *DrEEuF*
Ordynsky, George 1944- *WhoWor 93*
Ordzhonikidze, Sergei Alexander 1946- *WhoUN 92*
Ore, Rebecca 1948- *ScF&FL 92*
O'Reagan, Kevin Patrick 1960- *WhoE 93, WhoWor 93*
Oreamuno, Yolanda 1916-1956 *BioIn 17, SpAmA*
O'Rear, Edgar Allen, III 1953- *WhoSSW 93*
Orear, Jay 1925- *WhoAm 92, WhoWrEP 92*
Orechio, Frank Anthony 1917- *WhoWor 93*
Oredsson, Sverker 1937- *WhoScE 91-4*
Oreffice, Paul Fausto 1927- *St&PR 93, WhoAm 92, WhoWor 93*
Orefice, Antonio fl. 1708-1734 *OxDcOp*
Orefice, Giacomo 1865-1922 *Baker 92, OxDcOp*
O'Regan, Bartholomew Martin 1933 *WhoWor 93*
O'regan, Katherine Victoria 1946- *WhoAsAP 91*
O'Regan, P.G. 1934- *WhoScE 91-3*
O'Regan, Richard Arthur 1919- *WhoAm 92*
O'Regan, Ronan G. 1937- *WhoScE 91-3*
Orehek, Jean 1945- *WhoScE 91-2*
Orehosky, James George 1929- *St&PR 93*
O'Reilly, Anthony J.F. *BioIn 17*
O'Reilly, Anthony J.F. 1936- *St&PR 93*
O'Reilly, Anthony John Francis 1936- *WhoAm 92, WhoE 93*
O'Reilly, Bernard *DcChlFi*
O'Reilly, Charles Henry 1913- *St&PR 93*
O'Reilly, Charles Terrance 1921- *WhoAm 92*
O'Reilly, Denis 1950- *WhoE 93*
O'Reilly, Eugene F. 1931- *St&PR 93*
O'Reilly, George Robert 1930- *St&PR 93*
O'Reilly, Jackson *WhoWrEP 92*
O'Reilly, James Christopher 1943- *WhoWor 93*
O'Reilly, James J. 1962- *St&PR 93*
O'Reilly, James Michael 1934- *WhoE 93*
O'Reilly, James T. *Law&B 92*
O'Reilly, James Thomas 1947- *WhoEmL 93*
O'Reilly, James Timothy 1939- *St&PR 93*
O'Reilly, John F. 1945- *WhoAm 92*
O'Reilly, John James *WhoScE 91-1*
O'Reilly, John Joseph 1959- *WhoSSW 93*
O'Reilly, Kevin J. *Law&B 92*
O'Reilly, Knowlton J. 1939- *WhoAm 92*
O'Reilly, Larry P. 1946- *St&PR 93*
O'Reilly, Louis M. 1936- *WhoScE 91-3*
O'Reilly, Louise 1948- *WhoEmL 93*
O'Reilly, Mary *AmWomPl*
O'Reilly, Mary E. *Law&B 92*
O'Reilly, Michael J. *Law&B 92*
O'Reilly, Patricia H. 1939- *St&PR 93*
O'Reilly, Patrick J. 1939- *WhoScE 91-3*
O'Reilly, Richard Brooks 1941- *WhoAm 92*
O'Reilly, Richard John 1943- *WhoAm 92*
O'Reilly, Robert F. 1934- *St&PR 93*
O'Reilly, Rosann Tagliaferro 1948- *WhoEmL 93*
O'Reilly, Sue Ann 1950- *WhoWrEP 92*
O'Reilly, T. Mark *Law&B 92*
O'Reilly, Terrence M. *Law&B 92*
O'Reilly, Terrence M. 1945- *St&PR 93*
O'Reilly, Terrence Michael *Law&B 92*
O'Reilly, Terry *BioIn 17*
O'Reilly, Thomas Eugene 1932- *WhoAm 92*
O'Reilly, Timothy 1954- *ScF&FL 92*
O'Reilly, Timothy P. 1948- *St&PR 93*
O'Reilly, Trudy Orlaine 1946- *WhoSSW 93*
Orejuela, Gilberto Rodriguez *BioIn 17*
Orel, Alfred 1889-1967 *Baker 92*
Orel, Boris 1903-1952 *IntDcAn*
Orel, Dobroslav 1870-1942 *Baker 92*
Orel, Harold 1926- *WhoAm 92, WhoWrEP 92*
Orellana, Francisco de dc. 1546 *BioIn 17*
Orellana, Francisco de 1511?-1546 *Expl 93*
Orelove, Alex E. 1917- *St&PR 93*
Orem, Charles Annistone 1929- *St&PR 93*
Orem, John Marshall 1944- *WhoSSW 93*
Orem, Margaret G. 1948- *St&PR 93*
Orem, Nicholas Radcliffe 1945- *WhoE 93*
Oremland, S.L. 1942- *St&PR 93*
Oren, Bruce Clifford 1952- *WhoAm 92*
Oren, Dan A. 1958- *ConAu 138*
Oren, John Birdsell 1909- *WhoAm 92*
Oren, Ole 1947- *WhoWor 93*
Oren, Tuncer I. 1935- *WhoWor 93*
Orenbach, Kenneth Barry *Law&B 92*
Orenduff, J. Michael 1944- *WhoE 93*
Orenshein, Herbert 1931- *St&PR 93, WhoIns 93*
Orenstein, Harry C. *Law&B 92*
Orenstein, Jacqueline Sue 1962- *St&PR 93*
Orenstein, Michael 1939- *WhoWor 93*
Orenstein, Myra Goldstein 1952- *WhoEmL 93*
Orenstein-Bellia, Jessica 1959- *WhoE 93*
Orent, Clifford *St&PR 93*
Orent, Gerard M. 1931- *WhoAm 92*
Orentzel, Jack 1918- *St&PR 93*
Oresick, Peter Michael 1955- *WhoE 93, WhoWrEP 92*
Oreskes, Irwin 1926- *WhoAm 92*
Oresman, Donald *Law&B 92*
Oresman, Donald 1925- *St&PR 93, WhoAm 92*
Orestes d476 *HarEnMi*
Oretsky, Barry *BioIn 17*
Orezzoli, Hector d1991 *BioIn 17*
Orezzoli, Hector Alejandro 1953- *WhoAm 92*
Orf, John W. 1950- *St&PR 93*
Orf, Ted 1945- *St&PR 93*
Orfalea, Gregory Michael 1949- *WhoWrEP 92*
Orff, Carl 1895-1982 *Baker 92, IntDcOp, OxDcOp*
Orff, James Robert 1947- *WhoEmL 93, WhoSSW 93*
Orfield, Olivia Fuller 1922- *WhoWrEP 92*
Orford, Earl of 1676-1745 *BioIn 17*
Orfus, M. *WhoScE 91-2*
Orfuss, Mitchell Alan 1949- *WhoAm 92*
Orgad, Ben-Zion 1926- *Baker 92, WhoWor 93*
Orgain, Benjamin Darby 1909- *WhoAm 92*
Organ, Arnold Thomas 1938- *St&PR 93*
Organ, Debbie Jarie 1954- *WhoEmL 93*
Organek, Nancy Strickland 1937- *WhoAmW 93*
Organisak, Paul John 1962- *WhoE 93*
Organski, Abramo Fimo Kenneth 1923- *WhoAm 92*
Orgebin-Crist, Marie-Claire 1936- *WhoAm 92*

Orgel, Doris 1929- *DcAmChF 1960*
Orgel, Stephen (Kitay) 1933- *WhoWrEP 92*
Orgen, Andy G. 1931- *St&PR 93*
Orgeni, Aglaja 1841-1926 *Baker 92, OxDcOp*
Orgill, Douglas 1922-1984 *ScF&FL 92*
Orgill, John L. 1931- *St&PR 93*
Orhan 1281?-1362 *OxDcByz*
Ori, Kan 1933- *WhoWor 93*
Oriani, Ana Gloria 1953- *WhoAmW 93*
Oriani, Richard Anthony 1920- *WhoAm 92*
Orianne, Paul Alphonse 1925- *WhoWor 93*
Orians, Gordon Howell 1932- *WhoAm 92*
Orias Herrera, Jorge Eduardo 1951- *WhoWor 93*
Oribasios c. 325-c. 395 *OxDcByz*
Oribe *BioIn 17*
Orie, Ronald Thomas 1937- *St&PR 93*
Oriethyia 1951- *WhoEmL 93*
Origen c. 185-254? *OxDcByz*
Origliosso, James H. 1952- *St&PR 93*
Origo, Iris 1902-1988 *BioIn 17*
Orihel, Thomas Charles 1929- *WhoAm 92*
O'Riley, Carole Brown 1946- *WhoAmW 93*
O'Riley, Christopher 1956- *Baker 92*
O'Riley, Patrick Adelbert 1941- *WhoWrEP 92*
Oring, Michael Sanford 1957- *St&PR 93*
Oring, Stuart August 1932- *WhoE 93*
Oringdulph, Robert E. 1932- *WhoAm 92*
Oringer, Howard 1942- *St&PR 93*
Oringer, Kenneth W. 1931- *St&PR 93*
Oringer, Maurice Jules 1905- *WhoE 93*
Orio, Angelo A. 1938- *WhoScE 91-3*
Oriol-Bosch, Albert 1934- *WhoScE 91-3*
O'Riordain, Fionnbharr *WhoScE 91-3*
O'Riordan, Kaye L. *Law&B 92*
O'Riordan, Kaye L. 1949- *St&PR 93*
O'Riordan, Robert 1943- *ScF&FL 92*
O'Riordan, Timothy *WhoScE 91-1*
Oriordan, Timothy 1942- *WhoWor 93*
Orisek, Ivan 1945- *WhoE 93*
O'Risky, Dorothy Sandra 1939- *WhoAmW 93*
Oristano, Kerry M. *Law&B 92*
Orizondo, Jill Metcalf *Law&B 92*
Orkand, Donald Saul 1936- *WhoAm 92*
Orkin, Lazarus A. 1910-1991 *BioIn 17*
Orkin, Louis Richard 1915- *WhoAm 92*
Orkin, Michael *ScF&FL 92*
Orkow, Ben 1896-1988 *ScF&FL 92*
Orland, Frank Jay 1917- *WhoAm 92*
Orland, Rees M. 1944- *St&PR 93*
Orland, Richard A. 1952- *St&PR 93*
Orlander, Michael 1933- *St&PR 93*
Orlandic, Ratko 1959- *WhoWor 93*
Orlandin, Leo E. 1961- *St&PR 93*
Orlandini, Giuseppe Maria 1675-1760 *Baker 92, OxDcOp*
Orlando, Adolph Alfred 1943- *St&PR 93*
Orlando, Anthony Carl 1935- *St&PR 93*
Orlando, Danielle *WhoAm 92, WhoAmW 93, WhoE 93*
Orlando, Dominic *MiSFD 9*
Orlando, Donna Morrison 1941- *St&PR 93*
Orlando, George Joseph 1944- *WhoAm 92*
Orlando, Jacqueline Marie 1955- *WhoEmL 93*
Orlando, Jean M. *St&PR 93*
Orlando, Joe 1927- *ScF&FL 92*
Orlando, Joseph A. *St&PR 93*
Orlando, Joseph Francis 1953- *WhoEmL 93*
Orlando, Kathy R. 1942- *St&PR 93*
Orlando, Kathy Reber 1942- *WhoAmW 93*
Orlando, Louis Lynn 1931- *WhoSSW 93*
Orlando, Margaret Ann 1939- *WhoAmW 93*
Orlando, Vittorio Emanuele 1860-1952 *DcTwHis*
Orlans, Flora Barbara 1928- *WhoE 93*
Orlansky, Jesse 1914- *WhoSSW 93*
Orlean, Susan *BioIn 17*
Orleans, Henri 1908- *BioIn 17*
Orleans, Henri d' 1822-1897 *BioIn 17*
Orleans, Louis-Philippe-Albert d' 1838-1894 *BioIn 17*
Orleans, Philippe, Duke of 1674-1723 *HarEnMi*
Orleans-Borbon, Gerarda 1939- *WhoWor 93*
Orledge, Robert Nicholas 1948- *WhoWor 93*
Orlemanski, Stanislaw 1889-1960 *BioIn 17*
Orlen, Joel 1924- *WhoAm 92*
Orlen, Steve 1942- *WhoWrEP 92*
Orlesh, J. Michael, Jr. *Law&B 92*
Orlewicz, Stanislaw 1928- *WhoScE 91-4*
Orley, Catherine Ida Rosa 1921- *WhoWor 93*
Orlich, Donald C(harles) 1931- *WhoWrEP 92*
Orlick, Alan *BioIn 17*
Orlidge, Leslie Arthur 1953- *WhoE 93*
Orlikowski, Leszek B. 1944- *WhoScE 91-4*
Orlin, Karen J. *Law&B 92*
Orlin, Karen J. 1948- *St&PR 93, WhoSSW 93*
Orlinov, Victor Iliev 1927- *WhoScE 91-4*
Orlins, Stephen A. 1950- *St&PR 93*
Orlinsky, Harry M. d1992 *NewYTBS 92*
Orlinsky, Harry M(eyer) 1908-1992 *ConAu 137*
Orlinsky, Harry Meyer 1908-1992 *BioIn 17*
Orliss, Theodore Eugene 1936- *WhoAm 92*
Orlob, Gerald T. 1924- *WhoAm 92*
Orlock, Carol E. 1947- *WhoWrEP 92*
Orloff, Gary William 1946- *WhoAm 92*
Orloff, Gordon Matthew 1958- *WhoEmL 93*
Orloff, Karen Miriam 1952- *WhoAmW 93*
Orloff, Malcolm K. 1939- *St&PR 93*
Orloff, Neil 1943- *WhoAm 92*
Orloff, Roger Barton 1940- *St&PR 93, WhoSSW 93*
Orlov, Darlene 1949- *WhoE 93*
Orlov, Nikolai (Andreievich) 1892-1964 *Baker 92*
Orlov, Peter Andrew 1948- *WhoEmL 93*
Orlov, Vladimir 1936- *ScF&FL 92*
Orlov, Yuri *BioIn 17*
Orlowe, James 1933- *St&PR 93*
Orlowski, Aleksander 1777-1832 *PolBiDi*
Orlowski, Henry 1944- *St&PR 93*
Orlowski, Karel Ann 1949- *WhoE 93, WhoEmL 93*
Orlowski, Kenneth James *Law&B 92*
Orlowski, Ronald Joseph 1936- *St&PR 93*
Orlowski, Ryszard 1927- *WhoWor 93*
Orlowski, Stanislaw Tadeusz 1920- *WhoWor 93*
Orlowski, Steven 1933- *St&PR 93*
Orlowsky, Martin L. 1941- *WhoAm 92*
Orly, Elvira Jolan 1948- *WhoAmW 93*
Orman, John Leo 1949- *WhoEmL 93*
Orman, Leonard Arnold 1930- *WhoAm 92*
Ormand, Jarrell D. 1919- *St&PR 93*
Ormandy, Eugene 1899-1985 *Baker 92*
Ormasa, John 1925- *WhoWor 93*
Orme, Antony Ronald 1936- *WhoAm 92*
Orme, Cheryl L. 1953- *WhoEmL 93*
Orme, Denis Arthur 1946- *WhoEmL 93*
Orme, Jed *Law&B 92*
Orme, Michael Christopher L'Estrange *WhoScE 91-1*
Orme, Stuart *MiSFD 9*
Orme, William Aloysius 1924- *WhoAm 92*
Orme-Johnson, Nanette Roberts 1937- *WhoE 93*
Orme-Johnson, Rhoda Frances 1940- *WhoAmW 93*
Orme-Johnson, William Henry, III 1938- *WhoE 93*
Ormeling, Ferdinand Jan 1942- *WhoWor 93*
Ormerod, Charles Warren 1936- *St&PR 93*
Ormerod, Jan *BioIn 17*
Ormerod, Jan 1946- *ChlBIID [port]*
Ormerod, Jan(ette Louise) 1946- *MajAI [port], SmATA 70 [port]*
Ormerod, Paul Andrew 1950- *WhoWor 93*
Ormes, Jonathan Fairfield 1939- *WhoE 93*
Ormesson, Jean d' 1925- *WhoWor 93*
Ormond, Neal, III 1941- *St&PR 93*
Ormond, Wendy E. *Law&B 92*
Ormonde, Duke of 1610-1688 *BioIn 17*
Ormondroyd, Edward 1925- *DcAmChF 1960, ScF&FL 92*
Ormos, Jeno 1922- *WhoScE 91-4*
Ormos, Zoltan 1940- *WhoScE 91-4*
Ormrod, Peter *MiSFD 9*
Ormsbee, Allen Ives 1926- *WhoAm 92*
Ormsby, Alan *ScF&FL 92*
Ormsby, David G. 1933- *WhoAm 92*
Ormsby, Eric Linn 1941- *WhoAm 92*
Ormsby, Robert Benzein, Jr. 1924- *WhoAm 92*
Ormseth, Milo E. 1932- *WhoAm 92*
Orna, Mary Virginia 1934- *WhoE 93*
Ornano, Michel d' 1924-1991 *BioIn 17*
Ornati, Oscar A. 1922-1991 *BioIn 17*
Ornati, Oscar A(braham) 1922-1991 *ConAu 136*
Ornatski, Igor Alexandrovich 1931- *WhoUN 92*
Ornauer, Richard Lewis 1922- *WhoAm 92*
Ornburn, Kristee Jean 1956- *WhoEmL 93*
Orndoff, Eva Elizabeth Carlson 1918- *WhoAmW 93*
Orndoroff, Gary Joseph 1957- *St&PR 93*
Ornduff, Robert 1932- *WhoAm 92*
Orne, Martin T. *BioIn 17*
Ornelas, Victor F. 1948- *WhoAm 92*
Orner, Robert T. *Law&B 92*
Ornish, Dean *BioIn 17*
Ornithoparchus, Andreas c. 1485-c. 1535 *Baker 92*
Ornst, Robert A. 1930- *St&PR 93*
Ornsteen, Alan C. 1929- *St&PR 93*
Ornstein, Donald Samuel 1934- *WhoAm 92*
Ornstein, Ethel Rae Cohodas 1915- *WhoAmW 93, WhoSSW 93, WhoWor 93*
Ornstein, L.T.M. 1931- *WhoScE 91-3*
Ornstein, Leo 1892- *Baker 92*
Ornstein, Norman Jay 1948- *WhoAm 92*
Ornstein, R. Jeffrey 1942- *St&PR 93*
Ornstein, Robert 1925- *WhoAm 92, WhoWrEP 92*
Ornstein, Warren K. *Law&B 92*
Ornstein-Galicia, Jacob Leonard 1915- *WhoAm 92*
Oro, L.A. 1945- *WhoScE 91-3*
Orol, Elliot Scott *Law&B 92*
Orologas, Gus Nicholas 1953- *WhoEmL 93*
Oromaner, Mark 1941- *WhoE 93*
Oronsky, Arnold Lewis 1940- *WhoAm 92*
Oropeza, Vicente *HispAmA*
Oropeza Martinez, Roberto 1927- *DcMexL*
O'Rorke, James Francis, Jr. 1936- *WhoAm 92, WhoWor 93*
O'Rorke, Kenneth Eugene 1959- *WhoSSW 93*
Oros, John J. 1946- *St&PR 93*
Orosel, Gerhard Oskar 1946- *WhoWor 93*
Orosius, Paul dc. 418 *OxDcByz*
Oross, Emmerich 1940- *MiSFD 9*
Orosz, Janet E. Foley 1956- *WhoAmW 93*
O'Rourke, Andrew Patrick 1933- *WhoE 93*
O'Rourke, Charles Christopher 1917- *BiDAMSp 1989*
O'Rourke, Charles J. 1944- *WhoAm 92*
O'Rourke, Charles Philip, Jr. 1926- *St&PR 93*
O'Rourke, Denise Lynn *Law&B 92*
O'Rourke, Dennis *MiSFD 9*
O'Rourke, Dennis 1914- *St&PR 93, WhoAm 92*
O'Rourke, Edward Francis 1935- *St&PR 93*
O'Rourke, Frank 1916-1989 *ScF&FL 92*
O'Rourke, J. Tracy *BioIn 17*
O'Rourke, J. Tracy 1935- *St&PR 93, WhoAm 92*
O'Rourke, Jack 1937- *WhoSSW 93, WhoWor 93*
O'Rourke, James 1925- *WhoE 93*
O'Rourke, Jane Ellen 1955- *WhoAmW 93*
O'Rourke, Joan B. Doty Werthman 1933- *WhoWor 93*
O'Rourke, John 1861-1882 *BioIn 17*
O'Rourke, Kevin *Law&B 92*
O'Rourke, Laura Larben *Law&B 92*
O'Rourke, Lawrence Michael 1938- *WhoWrEP 92*
O'Rourke, Marguerite Patricia 1950- *WhoAmW 93*
O'Rourke, Michael Geoffrey Eric 1935- *WhoWor 93*
O'Rourke, Michael James *Law&B 92*
O'Rourke, Michael James 1944- *WhoAm 92*
O'Rourke, Michael P. *Law&B 92*
O'Rourke, P.J. *BioIn 17*
O'Rourke, P. J. 1947- *WhoAm 92*
O'Rourke, Patrick Gorman 1949- *WhoEmL 93*
O'Rourke, Patrick Jake *BioIn 17*
O'Rourke, Paul Gregory 1939- *St&PR 93*
O'Rourke, Ronald Eugene 1957- *WhoWor 93*
O'Rourke, Seamus *WhoWrEP 92*
O'Rourke, Sheila Anne 1941- *WhoWrEP 92*
O'Rourke, Terrence James 1932-1992 *ConAu 136*
O'Rourke, Thomas Walter 1937- *St&PR 93*
O'Rourke, Tracy *BioIn 17*
O'Rourke, William Andrew 1945- *WhoAm 92, WhoWrEP 92*
O'Rourke, William J., Jr. *Law&B 92*
Orozco, Esther 1945- *WhoWor 93*
Orozco, Juan Manuel 1938- *WhoWor 93*
Orozco, LuzMaria 1933- *WhoAmW 93*
Orozco, Olga 1920- *BioIn 17, SpAmA*
Orozco, Pascual *DcCPCAm*
Orozco, Rafael 1946- *Baker 92*
Orozco, Raymond E. 1933- *HispAmA, WhoAm 92*
Orozco Munoz, Francisco 1884-1950 *DcMexL*
Orozco y Berra, Fernando 1822-1851 *DcMexL*
Orozco y Berra, Manuel 1816-1881 *DcMexL*
Orpana, Veikko H.I. 1929- *WhoScE 91-4*
Orpana, Veikko Heikki 1929- *WhoWor 93*
Orpen, Anthony Guy 1955- *WhoWor 93*
Orphanides, G.M. *WhoScE 91-4*
Orphanides, George M. 1943- *WhoScE 91-4*
Orphanides, Gus George 1947- *WhoE 93*
Orphanides, Nora Charlotte 1951- *WhoAmW 93, WhoE 93, WhoEmL 93*
Orphanos, P.I. 1938- *WhoScE 91-4*
Orphee, Elvira 1929- *SpAmA*
Orr, A. 1950- *ScF&FL 92*
Orr, Andrew A. 1934- *St&PR 93*
Orr, Beverly Ann 1947- *WhoAmW 93*
Orr, Bobby 1948- *BioIn 17, WhoAm 92*
Orr, Bryan Ronald 1949- *St&PR 93*
Orr, C(harles) W(ilfred) 1893-1976 *Baker 92*
Orr, Carol Wallace 1933- *WhoAm 92*
Orr, Charles Lee 1943- *St&PR 93*
Orr, Clyde 1921- *St&PR 93*
Orr, Clyde, Jr. 1921- *WhoSSW 93*
Orr, David E. 1951- *WhoSSW 93*
Orr, David J. 1952- *St&PR 93*
Orr, David M.F. 1935- *WhoScE 91-3*
Orr, Dinah Tottenham 1930- *WhoE 93*
Orr, Donald E. *Law&B 92*
Orr, Donald Fraser 1943- *St&PR 93*
Orr, Donald James 1939- *St&PR 93*
Orr, Edward Carl 1943- *WhoWrEP 92*
Orr, Elaine L. 1951- *WhoWrEP 92*
Orr, Emma Jane 1956- *WhoEmL 93, WhoSSW 93*
Orr, Frank Howard, III 1932- *WhoSSW 93*
Orr, Gregory 1947- *WhoWrEP 92*
Orr, Gregory Simpson 1947- *WhoAm 92*
Orr, Harold E. 1923- *St&PR 93*
Orr, J. Meredith 1926- *St&PR 93*
Orr, J. Ritchie 1933- *WhoAm 92*
Orr, James *MiSFD 9*
Orr, James F., III 1943- *St&PR 93, WhoAm 92*
Orr, James L. 1822-1873 *PolPar*
Orr, James Robert 1952- *WhoAm 92*
Orr, Jennie Marie Thomas 1952- *WhoEmL 93*
Orr, Jerry 1936- *St&PR 93*
Orr, Joel Nathaniel 1947- *WhoAm 92*
Orr, John *BioIn 17*
Orr, John Brian 1966- *WhoSSW 93*
Orr, John Hunter 1951- *WhoEmL 93*
Orr, John P., Jr. 1951- *St&PR 93*
Orr, John Traylor, Jr. 1946- *WhoEmL 93*
Orr, Katherine S(helley) 1950- *SmATA 72 [port]*
Orr, Kay *BioIn 17*
Orr, Kay A. 1939- *WhoAmW 93, WhoWor 93*
Orr, Kenneth Bradley 1933- *WhoSSW 93*
Orr, Kenneth Dew 1913- *WhoAm 92*
Orr, Kenneth W. 1924- *St&PR 93*
Orr, L. Glenn, Jr. 1940- *WhoAm 92*
Orr, Laney Glenn, Jr. 1940- *St&PR 93*
Orr, Leighton E. 1907- *WhoE 93*
Orr, Linda 1943- *WhoWrEP 92*
Orr, Linda J. *WhoAmW 93*
Orr, Marcia 1949- *WhoAmW 93, WhoEmL 93*
Orr, Maxine Cortright 1915- *WhoAmW 93*
Orr, Michael P. 1947- *WhoAm 92*
Orr, Michael W. *St&PR 93*
Orr, Orville Dean 1930- *St&PR 93*
Orr, Parker Murray 1927- *WhoAm 92*
Orr, Quinn Lindsay 1957- *WhoEmL 93*
Orr, Randall L. *Law&B 92*
Orr, Richard Byron 1930- *WhoSSW 93*
Orr, Richard James 1921- *St&PR 93*
Orr, Richard Tuttle 1915- *WhoAm 92*
Orr, Richard W. *Law&B 92*
Orr, Robert Dunkerson 1917- *WhoAm 92, WhoWor 93*
Orr, Robert Gordon 1948- *BioIn 17*
Orr, Robin *BioIn 17*
Orr, Robin 1909- *Baker 92*
Orr, Rosemary B. *Law&B 92*
Orr, Roy Joseph 1952- *WhoEmL 93, WhoSSW 93*
Orr, San Watterson, Jr. 1941- *St&PR 93, WhoAm 92*
Orr, Sandra Jane 1930- *WhoAmW 93*
Orr, Shirley Ann 1935- *WhoE 93*
Orr, Teri Regina 1951- *WhoAmW 93*
Orr, Terrence S. 1943- *WhoAm 92*
Orr, Vance Womack 1916- *St&PR 93*
Orr, Violet 1904-1989 *ScF&FL 92*
Orr, Wayne L. 1926- *St&PR 93*
Orr, William Dayton 1935- *St&PR 93*
Orr, William Lyman 1956- *St&PR 93, WhoEmL 93*
Orrall, John H. 1925- *St&PR 93*
Orrall, Roy E. 1927- *St&PR 93*
Orr-Cahall, Christina 1947- *WhoAmW 93*
Orrego-Salas, Juan (Antonio) 1919- *Baker 92, WhoAm 92*
Orrego Vicuna, Francisco 1942- *WhoWor 93*
Orrell, Marthavan 1963- *WhoEmL 93*
Orren, Lowell H. *Law&B 92*
Orren, Michael John 1940- *WhoScE 91-3*
Orrenius, Sten 1937- *WhoScE 91-4*

Orrente, Pedro 1580?-1645? *BioIn 17*
Orrick, David Neil 1955- *WhoSSW 93*
Orrick, William Horsley, Jr. 1915- *WhoAm 92*
Orrico, Brent Anthony 1949- *St&PR 93*
Orringer, Mark Burton 1943- *WhoAm 92*
Orringer, Nelson Robert 1940- *WhoE 93*
Orris, Donald C. 1941- *St&PR 93*
Orris, Gary Dean 1955- *WhoEmL 93*
Orris, Michele Marie 1958- *WhoAmW 93*
Orrison, Brenda Krebs 1954- *WhoEmL 93*
Orrmont, Arthur 1922- *WhoWrEP 92*
Orrock, Jim *BioIn 17*
Orrock, Judy *BioIn 17*
Orrum, Eilley 1826-1903 *BioIn 17*
Orsak, Charlie George 1945- *WhoSSW 93*
Orsatti, Alfred Kendall 1932- *WhoAm 92*
Orsatti, Ernest Benjamin 1949- *WhoE 93, WhoEmL 93, WhoWor 93*
Orsbon, Richard Anthony 1947- *WhoAm 92, WhoSSW 93*
Orser, Brian *BioIn 17*
Orser, Earl H. *BioIn 17*
Orser, Earl Herbert 1928- *WhoAm 92, WhoWor 93*
Orsi, Henry James 1923- *St&PR 93*
Orsi, Romeo 1843-1918 *Baker 92*
Orsi, Vittorio 1917- *WhoWor 93*
Orsillo, James Steven 1943- *St&PR 93*
Orsini, Jean-Claude 1941- *WhoScE 91-2*
Orsini, Mary Elizabeth 1963- *WhoAmW 93*
Orsini, Theresa Maria 1937- *St&PR 93*
Orsini, Thomas 1953- *St&PR 93*
Orsino, Philip S. *St&PR 93*
Orski, C. Kenneth 1932- *WhoE 93*
Orskov, Egil Robert *WhoScE 91-1*
Orskov, Frits *WhoScE 91-2*
Orskov, Ida *WhoScE 91-2*
Orsler, Reginald James *WhoScE 91-1*
Orsola, Maria *BioIn 17*
Orsomarso, Don Frank 1925- *WhoE 93*
Orson, Marshall David 1960- *WhoEmL 93*
Orsos, Sandor 1927- *WhoScE 91-4*
Orsterwa, Juliusz 1885-1947 *PolBiDi*
Orszag, Steven Alan 1943- *WhoAm 92*
Ort, Charles G. 1911- *St&PR 93*
Ort, Edward A. 1929- *St&PR 93*
Ort, Peter E. 1944- *St&PR 93*
Ort, Peter Joel 1959- *St&PR 93*
Ort, Thomas William 1945- *WhoE 93*
Orta, O. 1944- *St&PR 93*
Ortalda, Robert Anselm, Jr. 1951- *WhoEmL 93*
Ortega, A. *Law&B 92*
Ortega, Cynthia Marie Altillero 1963- *WhoWor 93*
Ortega, Dimas 1954- *St&PR 93*
Ortega, Francisco de *BioIn 17*
Ortega, Isabel *WhoWrEP 92*
Ortega, James McDonough 1932- *WhoAm 92*
Ortega, Jose *BioIn 17*
Ortega, Jose Benito 1858-1941 *HispAmA*
Ortega, Katherine D. 20th cent.- *HispAmA [port]*
Ortega, Katherine D. 1934- *HispAmA, NotHsAW 93 [port]*
Ortega, Kenny *MiSFD 9*
Ortega, Pascua *BioIn 17*
Ortega, Robert, Jr. 1947- *HispAmA*
Ortega, Ruben Baptista 1939- *WhoAm 92*
Ortega, Victor F. 1934- *WhoAsAP 91*
Ortega-Rubio, Alfredo 1956- *WhoWor 93*
Ortega Saavedra, Daniel *BioIn 17*
Ortega Saavedra, Daniel 1945- *ColdWar 2 [port], DcCPCAm, DcTwHis, WhoWor 93*
Ortega y Gasset, Jose 1883-1955 *BioIn 17*
Ortego, Gilda Baeza 1952- *WhoAmW 93*
Ortegren, Roberta Jean 1946- *WhoAmW 93*
Ortel, Charles Kampmann 1956- *St&PR 93*
Ortel, Thomas Lee 1957- *WhoSSW 93*
Ortenberg, Arthur *BioIn 17*
Ortenberg, Arthur 1926- *WhoAm 92*
Ortenberg, Elisabeth Claiborne 1929- *WhoAm 92, WhoAmW 93, WhoE 93*
Ortenberg, Neil David 1951- *WhoE 93*
Ortenberg, Veronica 1961- *ConAu 139*
Ortengren, Roland E.F. 1942- *WhoScE 91-4*
Ortenstone, Lori L. *Law&B 92*
Ortenzi, Regina 1949- *WhoE 93*
Ortenzio, Rocco A. 1932- *St&PR 93*
Ortenzio, Rocco Anthony 1932- *WhoAm 92*
Ortez Sequeira, Enrique 1959- *WhoWor 93*
Orth, Daniel Adam, III *Law&B 92*
Orth, Daniel Adam, III 1937- *WhoIns 93*
Orth, David Morgan 1934- *St&PR 93*
Orth, David Nelson 1933- *WhoAm 92*
Orth, G. *WhoScE 91-2*
Orth, John 1850-1932 *Baker 92*
Orth, Kevin Robert 1961- *WhoWrEP 92*
Orth, L.E. d1913
See Orth, John 1850-1932 *Baker 92*
Orth, Richard *ScF&FL 92*
Orth, William Albert 1931- *WhoE 93*
Orthel, Leon 1905-1985 *Baker 92*
Orthman, Thomas F. 1934- *St&PR 93*
Orthwein, James Busch 1924- *St&PR 93*
Orthwein, William Coe 1924- *WhoAm 92, WhoWor 93*
Orticelli, Samuel A. *Law&B 92*
Orticke, Leslie Ann 1960- *WhoAmW 93*
Ortigosa-Perochena, Jose M. *Law&B 92*
Ortigue, Joseph(-Louis) d' 1802-1866 *Baker 92*
Ortinau, David Joseph 1948- *WhoEmL 93, WhoSSW 93, WhoWor 93*
Ortino, Hector Ruben 1942- *St&PR 93, WhoAm 92*
Ortino, Leonard James 1919- *St&PR 93*
Ortique, Revius Oliver, Jr. 1924- *WhoAm 92*
Ortiz, Adalberto 1914- *SpAmA*
Ortiz, Alfonso *BioIn 17*
Ortiz, Alfred Carl 1950- *WhoSSW 93*
Ortiz, Carlos 1936- *HispAmA*
Ortiz, Carlos G. *Law&B 92*
Ortiz, Carmen 1948- *NotHsAW 93*
Ortiz, Cristina 1950- *Baker 92*
Ortiz, Daisy 1951- *WhoEmL 93*
Ortiz, Diego c. 1510-c. 1570 *Baker 92*
Ortiz, Eduardo Leopoldo 1931- *WhoWor 93*
Ortiz, Eugene Denis 1956- *WhoWrEP 92*
Ortiz, Francis V., Jr. 1926- *HispAmA*
Ortiz, Francis Vincent, Jr. 1926- *WhoAm 92*
Ortiz, Frank Holguin 1946- *WhoSSW 93*
Ortiz, Ivan 1949- *WhoEmL 93*
Ortiz, Jay R. Gentry *Law&B 92*
Ortiz, Jose M. 1944- *WhoScE 91-3*
Ortiz, Judith Cofer *NotHsAW 93*
Ortiz, Lourdes *BioIn 17*
Ortiz, Luis Gonzaga 1825-1894 *DcMexL*
Ortiz, M.N. *WhoScE 91-3*
Ortiz, Manuel 1916-1970 *HispAmA*
Ortiz, Maria-Esther 1936- *WhoWor 93*
Ortiz, Pete *BioIn 17*
Ortiz, R. 1945- *WhoScE 91-3*
Ortiz, Rafael Montanez 1934- *WhoAm 92, WhoE 93*
Ortiz, Ralph 1934- *HispAmA [port]*
Ortiz, Raymond Zachary 1953- *WhoEmL 93*
Ortiz, Reynaldo U. 1946- *St&PR 93*
Ortiz, Roxanne Dunbar 1938- *WhoWrEP 92*
Ortiz, Sandra M. *Law&B 92*
Ortiz, Simon J(oseph) 1941- *DcLB 120 [port]*
Ortiz, Solomon P. 1937- *HispAmA [port], WhoAm 92, WhoSSW 93*
Ortiz, Solomon P. 1938- *CngDr 91*
Ortiz, Vilma *HispAmA*
Ortiz-Canavate, Jaime 1941- *WhoScE 91-3*
Ortiz Cofer, Judith 1952- *BioIn 17*
Ortiz-Del Valle, Sandra 1951- *NotHsAW 93*
Ortiz de Montellano, Bernardo 1899-1949 *DcMexL*
Ortiz de Torres, Georgina 1931- *WhoAmW 93*
Ortiz Mena, Antonio 1912- *WhoAm 92, WhoWor 93*
Ortiz Rubio, Pascual *DcCPCAm*
Ortiz Ruiz, Aida M. 1940- *WhoE 93*
Ortiz Tinoco, Cesar 1915-1991 *BioIn 17*
Ortiz-Truscott, Margarita 1942- *WhoAmW 93*
Ortleb, Rainer *BioIn 17*
Ortli, Patricia Gravatt 1938- *WhoAmW 93*
Ortlieb, Claus Peter 1947- *WhoWor 93*
Ortlieb, Mark R. *Law&B 92*
Ortlieb, Robert Eugene 1925- *WhoAm 92*
Ortlip, Mary Krueger *WhoAmW 93, WhoSSW 93, WhoWor 93*
Ortlip, Paul Daniel 1926- *WhoAm 92, WhoWor 93*
Ortloff, George Christian, Sr. 1947- *WhoE 93*
Ortman, Deborah S. *Law&B 92*
Ortman, Eldon E. 1934- *WhoAm 92*
Ortman, George Earl 1926- *WhoAm 92*
Ortman, Laurice W. 1908- *St&PR 93*
Ortmann, Dorothea 1912- *WhoAmW 93, WhoE 93, WhoWor 93*
Ortmann, Otto Rudolph 1889-1979 *Baker 92*
Ortmayer, Louis Lohman 1945- *WhoSSW 93*
Ortner, Donald Richard 1922- *WhoSSW 93*
Ortner, Everett Howard 1919- *WhoAm 92*
Ortner, Johannes 1933- *WhoScE 91-4*
Ortner, Karl Michael 1948- *WhoScE 91-4*
Ortner, Reinhold 1930- *WhoWor 93*
Ortner, Samuel 1912- *St&PR 93*
Orto, Marbrianus de c. 1460-c. 1529 *Baker 92*
Ortolani, Benito 1928- *WhoAm 92*
Ortolani, Minot Henry 1929- *WhoAm 92, WhoE 93*
Ortolani, Sergio 1947- *WhoScE 91-3*
Ortolani, Vincent 1941- *WhoE 93*
Ortolano, Joan S. *Law&B 92*
Ortolano, Leonard 1941- *WhoAm 92*
Ortoli, Sven Charles 1953- *WhoWor 93*
Orton, Bill 1949- *CngDr 91, WhoAm 92*
Orton, David 1956- *BioIn 17*
Orton, Don A. 1918- *BioIn 17*
Orton, Geraldine Leitl 1939- *WhoE 93*
Orton, Joe *BioIn 17*
Orton, Joe 1933-1967 *DramC 3 [port], ScF&FL 92*
Orton, John K. *ScF&FL 92*
Orton, Katharine Wilson 1953- *St&PR 93*
Orton, Robert C. *St&PR 93*
Orton, Robert Clayton 1934- *WhoAm 92*
Orton, Stewart 1915- *WhoAm 92, WhoWor 93*
Ortonne, Jean-Paul 1943- *WhoScE 91-2*
Orttung, William Herbert 1934- *WhoAm 92*
Ortuno, Manuel Joseph 1942- *WhoSSW 93*
Ortutay, M. 1942- *WhoScE 91-4*
Ortuzar, Juan de Dios 1949- *WhoWor 93*
Ortyl, Nicholas Edward, III 1961- *WhoEmL 93*
Orullian, B. LaRae 1933- *WhoAmW 93*
Orullian, LaRae 1933- *St&PR 93*
Orum, Terrell Beth 1961- *WhoEmL 93*
Orville, Harold Duvall 1932- *WhoAm 92*
Orville, Richard Edmonds 1936- *WhoAm 92*
Orvilliers, Louis Guillouet, Count of 1708-1792 *HarEnMi*
Orvin, George H. 1922- *St&PR 93*
Orvin, Jay S. 1949- *St&PR 93*
Orvini, Edoardo *WhoScE 91-3*
Orvis, Harold Heacock 1924- *WhoE 93*
Orvis, Robert Frank 1949- *WhoEmL 93*
Orwasky, Michael Craig 1959- *WhoSSW 93*
Orwell, George 1903-1950 *BioIn 17, DcTwHis, MagSWL [port], ScF&FL 92, WorLitC [port]*
Orwig, Cherie Lee 1948- *WhoEmL 93*
Orwig, Clara Beatrice *AmWomPl*
Orwin, Joanna *DcChlFi*
Orwin, John Micheal 1938- *WhoScE 91-2*
Orwoll, Edward Francis 1919- *WhoE 93*
Orwoll, Gregg S. K. 1926- *WhoAm 92, WhoWor 93*
Orwoll, Robert Arvid 1940- *WhoAm 92, WhoSSW 93*
Ory, Edward Butler 1926- *WhoAm 92*
Ory, "Kid" (Edward) 1886-1973 *Baker 92*
Ory, Marcia Gail 1950- *WhoAmW 93, WhoEmL 93*
Ory, Robert Louis 1925- *WhoSSW 93*
O'Ryan, Anne Wynne *AmWomPl*
O'Ryan, Connie Jean 1957- *WhoAmW 93*
Oryschuk, Roman 1953- *St&PR 93*
Oryshkevich, Roman Sviatoslav 1928- *WhoAm 92*
Orza, J.M. *WhoScE 91-3*
Orza, Vincent Frank 1950- *WhoEmL 93*
Orze, Walter J. *Law&B 92*
Orzech, Ann Dorothy 1950- *WhoEmL 93*
Orzech, Paul M. 1942- *St&PR 93*
Orzechowska-Juzwenko, Krystyna 1933- *WhoScE 91-4*
Orzechowski, R.J. 1943- *St&PR 93*
Orzechowski, Robert David 1949- *WhoE 93*
Orzeck, Eric A. 1940- *St&PR 93*
Orzel, Ronald F. 1934- *WhoWor 93*
Orzeszkowa, Eliza 1841-1910 *PolBiDi*
Orzeszyna, Stanislaw Andrzej 1941- *WhoUN 92*
Orzolek, Walter P. 1933- *St&PR 93*
Orzylowski, Marek 1943- *WhoWor 93*
Osacar, Jesus 1921- *WhoScE 91-3*
Osada, Takeshi 1931- *WhoAsAP 91*
Osada, Yoshihito 1943- *WhoWor 93*
Osada, Yuji 1917- *WhoAsAP 91*
Osadjan, Marie Frances *Law&B 92*
Osage, Frank John 1955- *WhoSSW 93*
O'Saile, Charles Murray 1944- *WhoSSW 93*
Osak, Frank, Jr. 1928- *St&PR 93*
Osaka, Richard *BioIn 17*
Osakada, Kohtaro 1955- *WhoWor 93*
Osako, Naotoshi 1844-1927 *HarEnMi*
Osakoda, Ronald Toshio 1956- *WhoEmL 93*
Osakwe, Christopher 1942- *WhoAm 92*
Osam, Harold Duane 1927- *St&PR 93*
Osami, Ishida 1948- *WhoWor 93*
Osato, Ruth Ludlow 1927- *WhoAmW 93*
Osawa, Eiji 1935- *WhoWor 93*
Osawa, Yoshio 1930- *WhoE 93*
Osbaldestin, Andrew Harold 1959- *WhoWor 93*
Osbaldeston, Gordon Francis 1930- *WhoAm 92*
Osberg, Allan F. 1924- *St&PR 93*
Osberg, Gregory John 1957- *WhoE 93*
Osberg, Timothy M. 1955- *WhoE 93*
Osbey, Brenda Marie 1957- *DcLB 120 [port]*
Osbon, Bradley Sillick 1827-1912 *JrnUS*
Osbon, Sue Brunning 1942- *WhoAmW 93*
Osborn, Carolyn Culbert 1934- *WhoWrEP 92*
Osborn, Cary Goodrich 1945- *WhoWrEP 92*
Osborn, Clifford J. 1917- *St&PR 93*
Osborn, Clifton Earl 1937- *WhoSSW 93*
Osborn, David 1923- *ScF&FL 92*
Osborn, David Chilcoat 1921- *WhoE 93*
Osborn, David Dudley 1958- *WhoE 93*
Osborn, Donald Herbert 1936- *St&PR 93*
Osborn, Donald Robert 1929- *WhoAm 92*
Osborn, Donald W. 1931- *St&PR 93*
Osborn, E.M. 1902- *ScF&FL 92*
Osborn, Elburt Franklin 1911- *WhoAm 92*
Osborn, Elodie Courter 1911- *WhoE 93*
Osborn, Fairfield 1887-1969 *BioIn 17*
Osborn, Frank D. *BioIn 17*
Osborn, Frank D. 1947- *St&PR 93*
Osborn, Guy A. 1936- *St&PR 93*
Osborn, Heidi S. *Law&B 92*
Osborn, Henry Fairfield 1887-1969 *BioIn 17*
Osborn, Holly Ann 1959- *WhoEmL 93*
Osborn, Innis Gardner *AmWomPl*
Osborn, J. D., Jr. 1945- *WhoSSW 93*
Osborn, Jacqueline Elizabeth 1951- *WhoAmW 93, WhoEmL 93, WhoSSW 93*
Osborn, James E., II 1925- *St&PR 93*
Osborn, John David 1948- *WhoEmL 93, WhoWor 93*
Osborn, John Edward 1957- *WhoEmL 93*
Osborn, John S., Jr. 1926- *St&PR 93*
Osborn, John Simcoe, Jr. 1926- *WhoAm 92*
Osborn, June Elaine 1937- *WhoAm 92, WhoAmW 93*
Osborn, Kent 1940- *St&PR 93*
Osborn, L.N. 1952- *St&PR 93*
Osborn, La Donna Carol 1947- *WhoEmL 93, WhoSSW 93*
Osborn, Leslie Andrewartha 1906- *WhoAm 92*
Osborn, Lois 1915- *BioIn 17*
Osborn, Lynn *AmWomPl*
Osborn, Mark Eliot 1950- *WhoEmL 93*
Osborn, Marvin Griffing, Jr. 1922- *WhoAm 92*
Osborn, Mary Jane Merten 1927- *WhoAm 92, WhoAmW 93*
Osborn, Nancy Jo 1950- *WhoAmW 93*
Osborn, Paul *BioIn 17*
Osborn, Rita Ann 1951- *WhoAmW 93*
Osborn, Robert Chesley 1904- *WhoAm 92, WhoE 93*
Osborn, Ron 1938- *St&PR 93*
Osborn, Ronald Edwin 1917- *WhoAm 92*
Osborn, Susan (E.) 1954- *ConAu 139*
Osborn, Terry Wayne 1943- *WhoAm 92*
Osborn, Theodore L., Jr. 1910- *WhoIns 93*
Osborn, Thomas Andrew 1836-1898 *BioIn 17*
Osborn, William George 1925- *WhoAm 92*
Osborne, Adrienne 1873-1951 *Baker 92*
Osborne, Bartley P., Jr. 1934- *WhoSSW 93*
Osborne, Bertrand 1935- *DcCPCAm*
Osborne, Bob 1931-
See Osborne Brothers, The *ConMus 8*
Osborne, Bobby 1931- *Baker 92*
Osborne, Brian George 1948- *WhoScE 91-1*
Osborne, Bruce F. 1942- *St&PR 93*
Osborne, Burl 1937- *St&PR 93, WhoAm 92, WhoSSW 93*
Osborne, Cynthia Monteiro 1951- *WhoAmW 93*
Osborne, Darrell W. *BioIn 17*
Osborne, David *BioIn 17, MajAI*
Osborne, Deborah Marie 1955- *WhoAmW 93*
Osborne, Dee S. 1930- *WhoAm 92*
Osborne, E.T. *WhoScE 91-1*
Osborne, Edward A. 1939- *St&PR 93*
Osborne, Elizabeth 1936- *WhoE 93*
Osborne, Frederick Spring, Jr. 1940- *WhoAm 92*
Osborne, Gayla Marlene 1956- *WhoAmW 93, WhoWor 93*
Osborne, Gayle Ann 1951- *WhoAmW 93, WhoEmL 93, WhoWor 93*
Osborne, Geoffrey James *WhoScE 91-1*
Osborne, George *MajAI*
Osborne, George Delano 1938- *WhoAm 92, WhoE 93*
Osborne, Gordon 1906- *St&PR 93*
Osborne, Gregory *WhoAm 92*

Osborne, Guy Laurence 1949- *WhoSSW 93*
Osborne, Harold Wayne 1930- *WhoAm 92*
Osborne, James Alfred 1927- *WhoAm 92*
Osborne, James L. 1928- *WhoIns 93*
Osborne, James Lee Edward 1953- *WhoEmL 93*
Osborne, James William 1928- *WhoAm 92*
Osborne, Jeffrey 1948- *SoulM*
Osborne, Jerry Paul 1944- *WhoWrEP 92*
Osborne, Joe C. 1948- *St&PR 93*
Osborne, John 1929- *BioIn 17, MagSWL [port], WorLitC [port]*
Osborne, John 1936- *DcCPCAm*
Osborne, John James 1929- *WhoWor 93*
Osborne, John Walter 1927- *WhoAm 92, WhoWrEP 92*
Osborne, Kenneth Ray 1936- *St&PR 93*
Osborne, LaRaye Marie *Law&B 92*
Osborne, Louise *ScF&FL 92*
Osborne, Maggie *ConAu 40NR*
Osborne, Maggie Ellen 1941- *WhoWrEP 92*
Osborne, Margaret Ellen 1941- *ConAu 40NR*
Osborne, Mark Lewis 1952- *WhoEmL 93, WhoWor 93*
Osborne, Mary d1992 *NewYTBS 92 [port]*
Osborne, Mary 1921-1992 *BioIn 17*
Osborne, Mary Pope 1949- *ScF&FL 92*
Osborne, MaryHelen 1936- *WhoAmW 93*
Osborne, Morris Floyd 1931- *WhoSSW 93*
Osborne, Nigel 1948- *Baker 92, OxDcOp*
Osborne, Paul R. 1963- *St&PR 93*
Osborne, Peter 1957- *WhoE 93*
Osborne, Quinton Albert 1951- *WhoEmL 93*
Osborne, Raymond Lester, Jr. 1939- *WhoE 93*
Osborne, Richard Cogswell 1944- *St&PR 93*
Osborne, Richard De Jongh 1934- *St&PR 93, WhoAm 92, WhoE 93*
Osborne, Richard E. 1932- *St&PR 93*
Osborne, Richard Hazelet 1920- *WhoAm 92*
Osborne, Richard Hugh *WhoScE 91-1*
Osborne, Richard Jay 1951- *WhoAm 92*
Osborne, Richard L. 1942- *St&PR 93*
Osborne, Robert V., Sr. 1916- *St&PR 93*
Osborne, Ronald Walter 1946- *WhoAm 92*
Osborne, Seward Russell 1946- *WhoE 93, WhoWor 93*
Osborne, Sonny 1937- *See* Osborne, Bobby 1931- *Baker 92* *See Also* Osborne Brothers, The *ConMus 8*
Osborne, Stanley de Jongh 1905- *WhoAm 92*
Osborne, Stanley J. 1905- *St&PR 93*
Osborne, Thomas Cramer 1927- *St&PR 93, WhoAm 92*
Osborne, Tom 1937- *WhoAm 92*
Osborne, Victor *ScF&FL 92*
Osborne, Walter Daryl 1954- *St&PR 93*
Osborne, Will 1949- *ScF&FL 92*
Osborne, William 1960- *ScF&FL 92*
Osborne, William Larry *WhoSSW 93*
Osborne, William Robert 1923- *WhoSSW 93*
Osborne, Willis Williams 1935- *St&PR 93*
Osborne, Zeb *BioIn 17*
Osborne, Zebulon L. 1946- *WhoSSW 93*
Osborne Brothers, The *ConMus 8 [port]*
Osborne Burke, Gerard Anthony 1951- *WhoWor 93*
Osborne-Popp, Glenna Jean 1945- *WhoAmW 93, WhoE 93*
Osborn-Hannah, Jane 1873-1943 *Baker 92*
Osbourne, John 1948- *See* Black Sabbath *ConMus 9*
Osbourne, Ozzy *NewYTBS 92 [port]*
Osbun, William N. 1914- *St&PR 93*
Osburn, Alice M. *Law&B 92*
Osburn, Charles Benjamin 1939- *WhoAm 92, WhoSSW 93*
Osburn, Donald Ray 1941- *WhoSSW 93*
Osburn, Jeffrey Brown 1947- *WhoEmL 93*
Osburne, Timothy Donald *Law&B 92*
Osby, Larissa Geiss 1928- *WhoAm 93*
O'Scannlain, Diarmuid Fionntain 1937- *WhoAm 92*
Oscar, Joyce Annette 1956- *WhoAmW 93*
Oscarsson, Bo *WhoScE 91-4*
Osceola 1804-1838 *BioIn 17, HarEnMi*
Oscherwitz, Mark 1931- *St&PR 93*
Oscherwitz, Millard Samuel 1921- *St&PR 93*
Oscura *ScF&FL 92*
Osdene, T.S. *WhoScE 91-2*
Osdene, Thomas Stefan 1927- *WhoAm 92, WhoWor 93*
Osei, Edward Kofi 1959- *WhoE 93*
O'Sell, Mark E. *Law&B 92*
Osella, James R. *Law&B 92*
Osella, Wayne Alexander 1945- *St&PR 93*
Osenar, Peter R. 1940- *St&PR 93, WhoAm 92*
Osenton, Thomas G. 1953- *St&PR 93*
Osenton, Thomas George 1953- *WhoAm 92*
Osepchuk, John Moses 1927- *WhoAm 92*
Oser, Bernard Levussove 1899- *WhoAm 92, WhoE 93*
Oser, Hans Joerg 1929- *WhoE 93*
Osero, Gloria Jean 1950- *WhoEmL 93*
Oseroff, Stephen L. 1941- *St&PR 93*
Osers, Ewald 1917- *ConAu 139*
Osfield, Kenneth James 1952- *WhoSSW 93*
Osghian, Petar 1932- *Baker 92*
Osgood, Barbara Travis 1934- *WhoAmW 93*
Osgood, Charles *BioIn 17*
Osgood, Charles 1933- *WhoAm 92*
Osgood, Charles Egerton 1916- *WhoWrEP 92*
Osgood, Christopher Sewall 1954- *WhoEmL 93*
Osgood, David Aldrich 1944- *WhoE 93*
Osgood, Edward H. 1916- *St&PR 93*
Osgood, Helen *AmWomPl*
Osgood, Judy Kay 1952- *WhoAmW 93*
Osgood, Peter Greer 1940- *WhoWor 93*
Osgood, Richard M., Jr. 1943- *WhoAm 92*
Osgood, Russell King 1947- *WhoAm 92*
Osguthorpe, David John *WhoScE 91-1*
Osguthorpe, Russell Trent 1946- *WhoEmL 93*
O'Shan, Philip H. 1921- *St&PR 93*
O'Shaughnessy, Eileen *BioIn 17*
O'Shaughnessy, Gary William 1939- *WhoAm 92*
O'Shaughnessy, James Patrick 1960- *WhoEmL 93*
O'Shaughnessy, James Shaw *Law&B 92*
O'Shaughnessy, John C. *Law&B 92*
O'Shaughnessy, John Patrick 1930- *St&PR 93*
O'Shaughnessy, Kathleen Kolbe 1951- *WhoWrEP 92*
O'Shaughnessy, Mark P. 1959- *WhoE 93*
O'Shaughnessy, Michael 1965- *ScF&FL 92*
O'Shaughnessy, Patricia Mary 1949- *WhoAmW 93*
O'Shaughnessy, Robert F. 1933- *St&PR 93*
O'Shaughnessy, Rosemarie Isabelle 1940- *WhoAmW 93, WhoWor 93*
O'Shaughnessy, Rowena Karsh 1942- *WhoAmW 93*
O'Shea, Arthur Joseph 1928- *WhoE 93*
O'Shea, Bart F. 1930- *St&PR 93*
O'Shea, Catherine Large 1944- *WhoAmW 93, WhoWrEP 92*
O'Shea, Daniel J. *Law&B 92*
O'Shea, Jim *St&PR 93*
O'Shea, John 1876-1956 *BioIn 17*
O'Shea, John Anthony 1939- *WhoWor 93*
O'Shea, John D. 1918- *St&PR 93*
O'Shea, John Edward 1932- *WhoIns 93*
O'Shea, John Joseph 1943- *St&PR 93*
O'Shea, John P. 1930- *WhoAm 92*
O'Shea, K.W. *Law&B 92*
O'Shea, Kathleen Ann 1962- *WhoEmL 93, WhoSSW 93*
O'Shea, Lynne Edeen 1945- *WhoAm 92*
O'Shea, Michael Edward *Law&B 92*
O'Shea, Monica Barrie *AmWomPl*
O'Shea, Pat 1931- *ScF&FL 92*
O'Shea, Patrick James *Law&B 92*
O'Shea, Patrick Joseph 1950- *WhoEmL 93*
O'Shea, Peter J., Jr. *Law&B 92*
O'Shea, Peter Joseph, Jr. 1937- *WhoAm 92*
O'Shea, Sean *ConAu 40NR*
O'Shea, Thomas Robert 1954- *St&PR 93*
Oshefsky, Robert Alan 1965- *WhoSSW 93*
O'Shello, Wanda Faye 1954- *WhoAmW 93*
Osheowitz, Michael William 1937- *WhoE 93*
Osher, Harold Louis 1924- *WhoE 93*
Osher, Robert M. *Law&B 92*
Osheroff, Douglas Dean 1945- *WhoAm 92*
Osheroff, Marjorie Helen 1948- *WhoE 93, WhoEmL 93*
Osherow, Jacqueline 1956- *ConAu 137*
O'Shields, Richard L. 1926- *St&PR 93*
O'Shields, Richard Lee 1926- *WhoAm 92*
O'Shields, Rose Anne 1966- *WhoAmW 93*
Oshima, Hiroshi 1885- *HarEnMi*
Oshima, Hisanao 1848-1928 *HarEnMi*
Oshima, Michael W. 1957- *WhoE 93, WhoEmL 93*
Oshima, Nagisa 1932- *MiSFD 9, WhoWor 93*
Oshima, Tadamori 1946- *WhoAsAP 91*
Oshima, Tairo 1935- *WhoWor 93*
Oshima, Tomoji 1916- *WhoAsAP 91*
Oshima, Tomoo 1925- *WhoWor 93*
Oshima, Yoshimasa 1850-1926 *HarEnMi*
Oshin, Sheldon Burton 1927- *St&PR 93*
Oshins, Harvey B. *Law&B 92*
Oshinsky, James Steven 1951- *WhoE 93*
Oshiro, Kathleen F. 1951- *St&PR 93*
Oshiro, Sharleen H. *St&PR 93*
Oshiro, Shinjun 1927- *WhoAsAP 91*
Oshita, Hosen 1926- *St&PR 93*
Oshita, Koji 1928- *WhoAm 92, WhoWor 93*
Oshiyoye, Adekunle Emmanuel 1951- *WhoEmL 93, WhoWor 93*
Oshlo, Eric Lee 1947- *WhoEmL 93, WhoSSW 93*
Oshman, Malin Kenneth 1940- *WhoAm 92*
Oshop, Robert Wm. 1946- *St&PR 93*
Oshry, Dee Jay 1939- *St&PR 93*
Oshry, George H. 1916- *St&PR 93*
Oshry, Harold L. 1918- *St&PR 93*
Oshtrakh, Michael Iosifovich 1956- *WhoWor 93*
Osias, Richard Allen 1938- *WhoAm 92, WhoSSW 93, WhoWor 93*
Osiecki, Andrzej 1929- *WhoScE 91-4*
Osier, John 1938- *ScF&FL 92*
Osigweh, Chimezie Anthony Baylon-Pascal 1955- *WhoSSW 93, WhoWor 93*
Osilenker, Boris Petrovich 1939- *WhoWor 93*
Osina, Leila Smith 1947- *WhoSSW 93*
Osing, Gordon T. 1937- *ConAu 136*
Osinga, Awke 1938- *WhoScE 91-3*
Osinski, Margaret Jean 1939- *WhoE 93*
Osinski, Martin Henry 1954- *WhoSSW 93*
Osinski, Patrick J. *Law&B 92*
Osipenko, Georgii Sergeevich 1945- *WhoWor 93*
Osipov, Edward Peter 1948- *WhoWor 93*
Osipov, Yurii 1937- *WhoWor 93*
Osipow, Samuel Herman 1934- *WhoAm 92*
Osius, Victoria M. *Law&B 92*
Osiyoye, Adekunle 1951- *WhoWor 93*
Oskandy, James Michael 1948- *St&PR 93*
Oskey, D. Beth 1921- *WhoAmW 93*
Oski, Frank Aram 1932- *WhoAm 92*
Oskin, David W. 1942- *St&PR 93*
Oskin, David William 1942- *WhoAm 92*
Oskolkov, Vladimir Alexandrovich 1946- *WhoWor 93*
Oslage, Hans Joachim 1923- *WhoScE 91-3*
Osler, Dorothy K. 1923- *WhoAmW 93*
Osler, Gordon Peter 1922- *WhoAm 92*
Osler, Howard Lloyd 1927- *WhoAm 92*
Osler, Julie 1947- *WhoAmW 93*
Osler, Mogens 1926- *WhoScE 91-2*
Osler, William 1849-1919 *BioIn 17*
Oslin, Kay Toinette *WhoAm 92, WhoAmW 93*
Osman d1326 *OxDcByz*
Osman, I d1326 *HarEnMi*
Osman, Dewaine Lowell 1934- *St&PR 93*
Osman, Edith Gabriella 1949- *WhoAmW 93, WhoEmL 93, WhoSSW 93*
Osman, Karen *ScF&FL 92*
Osman, Mahomed Hussen 1947- *WhoWor 93*
Osman, Mary Ella Williams *WhoAmW 93*
Osman, Mohamed Yousif 1944- *WhoWor 93*
Osman, Mohammed 1944- *WhoE 93*
Osman, Salih Mohamed 1939- *WhoUN 92*
Osman, Yusuf B. 1942- *WhoUN 92*
Osman Nuri Pasha 1832-1900 *HarEnMi*
Osmanov, Saladin 1951- *WhoUN 92*
Osmanski, William 1915- *BiDAMSp 1989*
Osmany, Mufleh R. 1940- *WhoUN 92*
Osmena, John Henry 1935- *WhoAsAP 91*
Osmer, Margaret *WhoAm 92*
Osmer, Patrick Stewart 1943- *WhoAm 92*
Osmer, Robert Henry 1952- *WhoEmL 93, WhoSSW 93*
Osmolska, Halszka M. 1930- *WhoScE 91-4*
Osmon, Bonita Cole 1947- *WhoSSW 93*
Osmon, Herbert E. 1936- *St&PR 93*
Osmond, Cliff 1937- *MiSFD 9*
Osmond, Dennis Gordon 1930- *WhoAm 92*
Osmond, Donald Clark 1957- *WhoAm 92*
Osmond, Donny *BioIn 17*
Osmond, Gordon Condie 1934- *WhoAm 92, WhoE 93*
Osmond, Marie 1959- *BioIn 17, WhoAm 92, WhoAmW 93*
Osmundson, Theodore Ole 1921- *WhoAm 92*
Osmycki, Daniel A. 1931- *WhoWor 93*
Osnos, David M. 1932- *St&PR 93*
Osnos, David Marvin 1932- *WhoAm 92, WhoWor 93*
Osnos, Marta d1990 *BioIn 17*
Osnos, Peter Lionel Winston 1943- *WhoAm 92*
Osoff, Jeffrey Arlin 1936- *WhoE 93*
Osofisan, Femi 1946- *DcLB 125 [port]*
Osofsky, Joy Doniger 1944- *WhoAmW 93, WhoSSW 93*
Osofsky, Robert Harris 1945- *WhoE 93*
Osorgin, Mikhail Andreevich 1878-1942 *BioIn 17*
Osorio, J.J.S. Pereira 1938- *WhoScE 91-3*
Osorio, Jorge Luis 1953- *WhoWor 93*
Osorio, Rosa 1946- *WhoEmL 93*
Osowiec, Darlene Ann 1951- *WhoAmW 93, WhoEmL 93, WhoWor 93*
Ospital, Judith Anne 1950- *WhoAmW 93*
Osrin, Raymond Harold 1928- *WhoAm 92*
Ossa, Cristian 1935- *WhoUN 92*
Osse, Jan W.M. 1935- *WhoScE 91-3*
Osseiran-Hanna, Khatmeh Aziz 1961- *WhoE 93*
Ossenberg, Friedrich-Wilhelm 1940- *WhoWor 93*
Osser, David Neal 1946- *WhoEmL 93*
Osserman, Richard A. 1930- *WhoE 93*
Osserman, Robert 1926- *WhoAm 92*
Ossewaarde, Anne Winkler 1957- *WhoAmW 93, WhoEmL 93*
Ossias, A. Lawrence 1940- *WhoE 93*
Ossicini, Luigia 1933- *WhoScE 91-3*
Ossip, Bobbi Ann 1938- *WhoAmW 93*
Ossipoff, Vladimir Nicholas 1907- *WhoAm 92*
Ossman, Albert John, Jr. 1927- *WhoSSW 93*
Ossmann, Robert E. 1944- *St&PR 93*
Ossoff, Robert Henry 1947- *WhoAm 92, WhoEmL 93, WhoWor 93*
Ossofsky, Jack d1992 *NewYTBS 92*
Ossola, Rinaldo 1913-1990 *BioIn 17*
Ossoli, marchesa d' 1810-1850 *BioIn 17*
Ossolinski, Jerzy 1595-1650 *PolBiDi*
Ossolinski, Jozef Maksymilian 1748-1826 *PolBiDi*
Ossont, Margaret Rebecca 1948- *WhoAmW 93*
Ossorio, Alfonso 1916-1990 *BioIn 17*
Ossorio, Gualberto 1949- *WhoWor 93*
Ost, Walter 1934- *WhoScE 91-3*
Ost, Warren William 1926- *WhoE 93*
Ostacher, Maureen Patrica 1952- *WhoAmW 93*
Ostachowicz, Wieslaw 1947- *WhoScE 91-4*
Ostachowicz, Wieslaw Mieczyslaw 1947- *WhoScE 91-4*
Ostan, William S. 1950- *St&PR 93*
Ostap, Martine Elizabeth 1959- *WhoAmW 93*
Ostapenko, Vladimir Victorovich 1956- *WhoWor 93*
Ostapowicz, Phillip Gary 1956- *St&PR 93*
Ostapuk, David Ray 1948- *WhoEmL 93, WhoWor 93*
Ostar, Allan W. *BioIn 17*
Ostar, Allan William 1924- *WhoAm 92, WhoE 93, WhoWor 93*
Ostaszewski, Dolores J. *Law&B 92*
Ostaszewski, Krzysztof Maciej 1957- *WhoEmL 93, WhoSSW 93*
Ostberg, Brita Elisabet 1934- *WhoUN 92*
Ostberg, Gustaf 1926- *WhoScE 91-4*
Ostberg, Henry D. 1928- *St&PR 93*
Ostby, Bryn Roe *Law&B 92*
Ostby, Kevin Charles 1956- *St&PR 93*
Ostby, Ronald 1937- *WhoAm 92*
Ostby, Sandra Josephine 1951- *WhoEmL 93, WhoSSW 93*
Ostdiek, Glen Richard 1930- *St&PR 93*
Osteen, Claude Wilson 1939- *BiDAMSp 1989*
Osteen, Hubert Duvall, Jr. 1936- *St&PR 93*
O'Steen, Jacqueline Janda 1953- *WhoEmL 93*
O'Steen, John A. 1944- *St&PR 93*
O'Steen, Judi K. 1947- *St&PR 93*
Osteen, Paul Allen 1960- *WhoSSW 93*
O'Steen, Sam 1923- *MiSFD 9*
O'Steen, Van 1946- *WhoEmL 93*
O'Steen, Wendall Keith 1928- *WhoAm 92*
Osteen, William Lawson, Jr. *Law&B 92*
Osten, Albert M. 1940- *St&PR 93*
Osten, Eva von der 1881-1936 *Baker 92, OxDcOp*
Osten, Judd F. *Law&B 92*
Osten, Leonard L. d1992 *BioIn 17*
Osten, Renee Fersen- *BioIn 17*
Ostendorf, Carole Glorine 1948- *WhoAmW 93*
Ostendorf, Joan Donahue 1933- *WhoAmW 93, WhoWor 93*
Ostendorf, JoEllen 1951- *WhoAmW 93*
Ostendorf, Lloyd 1921- *BioIn 17*
Ostendorf, Virginia Angelita 1942- *WhoAmW 93*
Ostendorff, William Charles 1954- *WhoE 93*

Ostendorp, Gary Lee 1941- *St&PR 93*
Ostenso, Brian T. 1951- *St&PR 93*
Ostenso, Martha 1900-1963 *BioIn 17*
Ostenso, Ned Allen 1930- *WhoE 93*
Oster, Avi Robert 1959- *St&PR 93*
Oster, Clinton Victor, Jr. 1947- *ConAu 139*
Oster, Frederick W. 1952- *WhoE 93*
Oster, Gerald 1918- *WhoAm 92*
Oster, Heidi Joy 1958- *St&PR 93*
Oster, Jeffrey Wayne 1941- *WhoAm 92*
Oster, Jerry 1929- *WhoWor 93*
Oster, Kim 1951- *WhoE 93*
Oster, Lewis Henry 1923- *St&PR 93*
Oster, Ludwig Friedrich 1931- *WhoAm 92*
Oster, Martin William 1947- *WhoE 93, WhoEmL 93*
Oster, Merrill James 1940- *WhoAm 92*
Oster, Michael L. 1952- *St&PR 93*
Oster, Pamela Ann 1951- *WhoSSW 93*
Oster, Patrick Ralph 1944- *WhoAm 92*
Oster, Peter 1946- *WhoWor 93*
Oster, Robert Alan 1944- *St&PR 93*
Oster, Rose Marie Gunhild 1934- *WhoAm 92, WhoE 93*
Osterback, Vernon L. 1932- *St&PR 93*
Osterberg, Becky 1946- *WhoAmW 93*
Osterberg, Charles Lamar 1920- *WhoAm 92*
Osterberg, Thomas Karl 1953- *WhoEmL 93, WhoWor 93*
Osterbrock, Donald E. *BioIn 17*
Osterbrock, Donald Edward *WhoAm 92*
Osterc, Slavko 1895-1941 *Baker 92*
Osterer, M.F. *St&PR 93*
Ostergaard, Geoffrey 1912-1990 *BioIn 17*
Ostergaard, Joni Hammersla 1950- *WhoEmL 93*
Ostergard, Holly Acklie 1957- *St&PR 93*
Ostergard, Paul Michael 1939- *WhoAm 92*
Ostergren, Gregory V. 1955- *WhoIns 93*
Osterhaus, Elizabeth Jean 1951- *WhoAmW 93*
Osterhaus, John *Law&B 92*
Osterhaus, William Eric 1935- *WhoAm 92*
Osterheld, Robert Keith 1925- *WhoAm 92*
Osterhoff, James M. 1936- *St&PR 93*
Osterhoff, James Marvin 1936- *WhoAm 92*
Osterhoudt, Hans Walter 1936- *WhoE 93*
Osterhout, Dan R. 1950- *St&PR 93*
Osterhout, Dan Roderick 1950- *WhoAm 92*
Osterhout, Michael Dennis 1948- *WhoAm 92*
Osterhout, Raymond L. 1931- *WhoIns 93*
Osterhout, Richard A. 1929- *St&PR 93*
Osterhout, Suydam 1925- *WhoAm 92*
Osterhus, Herman 1932- *St&PR 93*
Osterling, Allen W. 1926- *St&PR 93*
Osterloh, Douglas Dean 1956- *WhoEmL 93*
Osterloh, Wellington Frederick 1936- *St&PR 93*
Osterman, Constantine E. 1936- *WhoAmW 93*
Osterman, John C. *St&PR 93*
Osterman, Judith Diane *Law&B 92*
Osterman, Kenneth George 1947- *WhoE 93*
Osterman, Susan 1949- *WhoWrEP 92*
Ostermann, Arthur Christopher 1956- *WhoE 93*
Ostermeier, Wilmer John 1929- *St&PR 93*
Ostermiller, Wayne Harold 1943- *St&PR 93*
Ostern, Wilhelm Curt 1923- *WhoAm 92*
Osterndorf, Logan Carl 1917- *WhoE 93, WhoWor 93*
Osterneck, Guy-Kenneth 1934- *St&PR 93*
Osterrieth, Bernard Frederic 1931- *WhoWor 93*
Ostertag, Eric 1939- *WhoScE 91-2*
Ostertag, Robert Louis 1931- *WhoAm 92*
Ostertag, Thomas J. *Law&B 92*
Ostertag-Holtkamp, Barbara Jean 1962- *WhoAmW 93*
Ostervas, Magne 1931- *WhoUN 92*
Ostervemb, Frank Michael 1958- *WhoWor 93*
Osterwalder, Konrad 1942- *WhoWor 93*
Osterweil, Terry Gary 1955- *St&PR 93*
Osterweil, Wendy 1953- *WhoWrEP 92*
Osterweis, Steven L. 1912- *St&PR 93*
Osterweis, Steven Levy 1912- *WhoAm 92*
Osteryoung, Janet Gretchen 1939- *WhoAm 92, WhoAmW 93*
Ostfeld, Adrian Michael 1926- *WhoAm 92*
Ostfeld, Alexander Marion 1932- *WhoE 93*
Ostfeld, Leonard S. 1942- *St&PR 93, WhoAm 92*
Ostfield, Michael L. *Law&B 92*
Ostgulen, R.E. 1951- *St&PR 93*
Osthoff, Helmuth 1896-1983 *Baker 92*
Osthoff, Wolfgang 1927- *Baker 92*
Ostholm, Lars E.A. 1933- *WhoScE 91-4*
Ostiguy, Jean P.W. 1922- *St&PR 93*
Ostler, Clyde W. 1947- *WhoAm 92*
Ostler, James B. 1931- *St&PR 93*
Ostlie, Steven Dean *Law&B 92*
Ostling, Joan K. *ScF&FL 92*
Ostling, Paul James 1948- *WhoAm 92, WhoE 93*
Ostling, Richard Neil 1940- *WhoAm 92*
Ostlund, H. Gote 1923- *WhoAm 92*
Ostman, Arnold 1939- *Baker 92*
Ostmann, Barbara Gibbs 1948- *WhoAmW 93*
Ostmo, David Charles 1959- *WhoSSW 93, WhoWor 93*
Ostoich, Vladimir E. *St&PR 93*
Ostojic, Dejan Radov 1959- *WhoWor 93*
Ostrach, Michael Sherwood 1951- *St&PR 93*
Ostrach, Simon 1923- *WhoAm 92*
Ostrand, Don R. 1923- *St&PR 93*
Ostrander, (Willis) Frederick 1926- *WhoWrEP 92*
Ostrander, Gregg Alan 1953- *St&PR 93*
Ostrander, Patricia *BioIn 17*
Ostrander, Robert Edwin 1931- *WhoE 93, WhoWor 93*
Ostrander, Thomas William 1950- *WhoAm 92*
Ostrcil, Otakar 1879-1935 *Baker 92, OxDcOp*
Ostrea, Antonio Mapua 1938- *WhoWor 93*
Ostrem, Gunnar 1922- *WhoScE 91-4*
Ostrem, Gunnar Muldrup 1922- *WhoWor 93*
Ostriker, Alicia 1937- *WhoWrEP 92*
Ostriker, Alicia (Suskin) 1937- *DcLB 120 [port]*
Ostriker, Jeremiah Paul 1937- *WhoAm 92*
Ostroff, Alan M. 1952- *St&PR 93*
Ostroff, Arthur J. 1955- *St&PR 93*
Ostroff, Joel Harris 1943- *WhoSSW 93*
Ostroff, Jonathan Bruce 1956- *WhoE 93*
Ostrofsky, Benjamin 1925- *WhoAm 92, WhoSSW 93*
Ostrogorski, Moisei Y. 1854-1919 *PolPar*
Ostrogorsky, Michael 1951- *WhoEmL 93, WhoWor 93*
Ostrom, Anne Dietrich 1944- *WhoAmW 93*
Ostrom, Carol Marie 1947- *WhoAmW 93*
Ostrom, Elinor 1933- *WhoAm 92*
Ostrom, Grant J. 1941- *St&PR 93*
Ostrom, Hans 1954- *ConAu 139*
Ostrom, John H. 1928- *WhoAm 92*
Ostrom, Meredith Eggers 1930- *WhoAm 92*
Ostrom, Vincent Alfred 1919- *WhoAm 92*
Ostrorog, Jan 1436-1501 *PolBiDi*
Ostroski, Gerald Basil 1941- *St&PR 93*
Ostroski, Raymond B. *Law&B 92*
Ostroski, Raymond B. 1954- *St&PR 93*
Ostroski, Richard J. 1938- *St&PR 93*
Ostrov, Jerome 1942- *WhoE 93, WhoWor 93*
Ostrove, Paul Stuart 1931- *St&PR 93*
Ostrovski, Grisa 1918- *DrEEuF*
Ostrovskii, Mikhail Iosifovich 1960- *WhoWor 93*
Ostrovsky, Alexander 1823-1886 *OxDcOp*
Ostrovsky, Lev Aronovich 1934- *WhoWor 93*
Ostrovsky, Victor *BioIn 17*
Ostrow, Eric H. 1944- *St&PR 93*
Ostrow, Joseph W. 1933- *St&PR 93, WhoAm 92*
Ostrow, Robert W. 1926- *St&PR 93*
Ostrow, Rona Lynn 1948- *WhoAmW 93, WhoEmL 93*
Ostrow, Ronald F. 1944- *St&PR 93*
Ostrow, Samuel David 1945- *WhoAm 92*
Ostrow, Stephen Edward 1932- *WhoE 93*
Ostrow, Stuart 1932- *WhoAm 92*
Ostrowska, Wanda A. 1930- *WhoScE 91-4*
Ostrowska, Jerzy Sewerym 1924- *WhoScE 91-4*
Ostrowski, John S. 1933- *St&PR 93*
Ostrowski, Kazimierz L. 1921- *WhoScE 91-4*
Ostrowski, Paul S. 1936- *St&PR 93*
Ostrowski, Stanislaw K. 1878-1947 *PolBiDi*
Ostrowski, Waldemar 1928- *WhoScE 91-4*
Ostrowsky, Abbo 1889-1975 *BioIn 17*
Ostrowsky, D.B. 1939- *WhoScE 91-2*
Ostrum, Dean Gardner 1922- *WhoAm 92*
Ostruszka, Wayne DeVere 1947- *WhoEmL 93*
Ostry, Bernard 1927- *WhoAm 92*
Ostry, Jonathan David 1962- *WhoE 93*
Ostry, Sylvia *WhoAm 92, WhoAmW 93*
Ostrye, Thomas F. 1952- *St&PR 93*
Ostvedt, Ole Johan 1923- *WhoScE 91-4*
Ostwald, David Hugh 1955- *WhoEmL 93*
Ostwald, Martin 1922- *WhoAm 92*
O'Such, Frederick Michael 1937- *St&PR 93*
Osuka, Akira 1934- *WhoWor 93*
O'Sullivan, Daniel E. 1929-1990 *BioIn 17*
O'Sullivan, Daniel F. 1941- *St&PR 93*
O'Sullivan, Daniel John 1954- *WhoEmL 93*
O'Sullivan, Denis *BioIn 17*
O'Sullivan, Eileen Ann 1956- *WhoAmW 93, WhoEmL 93*
O'Sullivan, Emmet Patrick 1936- *St&PR 93*
O'Sullivan, Eugene Henry 1942- *WhoAm 92*
O'Sullivan, Eugene Joseph 1949- *St&PR 93*
O'Sullivan, Gerard 1959- *WhoE 93*
O'Sullivan, Heather Colleen 1968- *WhoAmW 93*
O'Sullivan, Hedley Patrick *WhoScE 91-1*
O'Sullivan, James *BioIn 17*
O'Sullivan, James Paul, Sr. *Law&B 92*
O'Sullivan, Joan D'Arcy 1930- *WhoAmW 93*
O'Sullivan, John 1878-1955 *OxDcOp*
O'Sullivan, John 1942- *WhoAm 92*
O'Sullivan, John Francis 1938- *St&PR 93*
O'Sullivan, John Patrick, Jr. 1942- *St&PR 93*
O'Sullivan, Judith Roberta 1942- *WhoAm 92, WhoAmW 93, WhoE 93*
O'Sullivan, Karl 1941- *WhoScE 91-3*
O'Sullivan, Mary G. 1927- *WhoScE 91-3*
O'Sullivan, Maureen 1911- *IntDcF 2-3, WhoAm 92*
O'Sullivan, Maurice J. d1992 *BioIn 17*
O'Sullivan, Maurice J., Sr. d1992 *NewYTBS 92*
O'Sullivan, Michael 1922- *WhoScE 91-3*
O'Sullivan, Paul Kevin 1938- *WhoAm 92*
O'Sullivan, Richard Guilford 1942- *WhoWor 93*
O'Sullivan, Sonia *BioIn 17*
O'Sullivan, Stephen D. *Law&B 92*
O'Sullivan, Thaddeus *MiSFD 9*
O'Sullivan, Thompson 1947- *WhoEmL 93*
O'Sullivan, Vincent 1872-1940 *ScF&FL 92*
Osunsade, Festus Lola 1940- *WhoUN 92*
Osvald, Per Hakan 1928- *WhoWor 93*
Osver, Arthur 1912- *WhoAm 92*
Oswald, Charles Wallace 1928- *St&PR 93*
Oswald, Delmont Richard 1940- *WhoWor 93*
Oswald, Eleazer 1755-1795 *JrnUS*
Oswald, Ernest John 1943- *WhoWrEP 92*
Oswald, George C. 1914- *St&PR 93*
Oswald, George Charles 1914- *WhoAm 92*
Oswald, Gerd 1916-1989 *MiSFD 9N*
Oswald, Gretchen 1945- *St&PR 93*
Oswald, John 1953- *Baker 92*
Oswald, John Henry 1949- *WhoAm 92*
Oswald, Lee Harvey *BioIn 17*
Oswald, Robert Bernard 1932- *WhoAm 92*
Oswald, Rudolph A. 1932- *WhoAm 92*
Oswald, Russell George 1909-1991 *BioIn 17*
Oswald, Stanton S. 1927- *WhoAm 92*
Oswald, Therese Anne 1960- *WhoEmL 93*
Oswald, Vincent E. 1912- *St&PR 93*
Oswald, Walter Paul 1919- *St&PR 93*
Oswald, William Jack 1927- *WhoWor 93*
Oswalt, Aria Lucinda 1953- *WhoAmW 93*
Oswalt, Bill G. 1933- *St&PR 93, WhoIns 93*
Oswalt, Nelda Langston 1949- *WhoAmW 93*
Oswalt, Robert McNeill 1938- *WhoE 93*
Oswell, William Cotton 1818-1893 *BioIn 17*
Oswold, Thomas J. 1952- *St&PR 93*
Osyka, Leonid 1940- *DrEEuF*
Osza, Debra Evans 1954- *WhoEmL 93*
Oszczapowicz, Janusz Michal 1932- *WhoScE 91-4*
Ota, Atsuo 1934- *WhoAsAP 91*
Ota, Ed K. *Law&B 92*
Ota, Isaac I. 1943- *St&PR 93*
Ota, Seiichi 1945- *WhoAsAP 91*
Ota, Tatsuyuki 1939- *WhoWor 93*
Otafire, Kahinde 1950- *WhoAfr*
Otaka, Hisatada 1911-1951 *Baker 92*
Otaka, Tadaaki 1947- *Baker 92*
Otaka, Yoshiko 1920- *WhoAsAP 91*
Otala, Matti N.T. 1939- *WhoScE 91-4*
Otani, Kikuro 1855-1923 *HarEnMi*
Otani, Mike 1945- *WhoE 93, WhoWor 93*
Otani, Shiro 1936- *BioIn 17*
Otano (y Eugenio), (Jose Maria) Nemesio 1880-1956 *Baker 92*
Otash, Fred *BioIn 17*
Otchet, Michael I. *Law&B 92*
Otchis, Jerald A. 1939- *St&PR 93*
Otchy, Thomas G. 1943- *St&PR 93*
Otelbaev, Muchtarbai 1942- *WhoWor 93*
Oteo, Carlos S. 1947- *WhoScE 91-3*
Otera, Junzo 1943- *WhoWor 93*
Otero, Carmen 1933- *NotHsAW 93*
Otero, Mariano S. 1844-1904 *HispAmA*
Otero, Miguel A., Sr. 1829-1882 *HispAmA*
Otero, Philip V. *Law&B 92*
Otero, Sandra B. *Law&B 92*
Otero Silva, Miguel 1908-1985 *SpAmA*
Otero-Smart, Ingrid Amarillys 1959- *WhoAmW 93*
Otero-Warren, Nina 1882-1965 *NotHsAW 93*
Otescu, Ion (Nonna) 1888-1940 *Baker 92*
Otey, Joyce Ann *BioIn 17*
Otey, Orlando 1925- *WhoAm 92*
Otfinoski, Steven 1949- *ScF&FL 92*
Otgon, Monkhdorjin 1939- *WhoUN 92*
Othegraven, August von 1864-1946 *Baker 92*
Othello, Maryann Cecilia 1946- *WhoAmW 93*
Othenin-Girard, Dominique *MiSFD 9*
Othersen, Cheryl Lee 1948- *WhoAmW 93*
Othersen, Henry Biemann, Jr. 1930- *WhoAm 92*
Othman, Iekhsan Bin 1956- *WhoWor 93*
Othman Bin Abdul 1951- *WhoAsAP 91*
Othmayr, Caspar 1515-1553 *Baker 92*
Othmer, David Artman 1941- *WhoE 93*
Othmer, Donald Frederick 1904- *WhoAm 92, WhoE 93*
Otho, Marcus Salvius 32-69 *HarEnMi*
Othon, Manuel Jose 1858-1906 *DcMexL*
Oths, Richard Philip 1935- *WhoAm 92*
Otis, Arthur Brooks 1913- *WhoAm 92*
Otis, Carre *BioIn 17*
Otis, Courtlandt d1991 *BioIn 17*
Otis, George Demont 1879-1962 *BioIn 17*
Otis, Glenn Kay 1929- *WhoAm 92*
Otis, Jack 1923- *WhoAm 92*
Otis, James, Jr. 1931- *WhoAm 92*
Otis, James D. 1939- *St&PR 93*
Otis, John James 1922- *WhoSSW 93, WhoWor 93*
Otis, Johnny 1921- *SoulM*
Otis, Katherine Marie 1958- *WhoEmL 93*
Otis, Richard Dickinson 1924- *WhoE 93*
Otis, Thomas *Law&B 92*
Otis, Thomas 1931- *St&PR 93*
Otlet, Paul 1868-1944 *BioIn 17*
Otley, David Templeton *WhoScE 91-1*
Otokpa, Augustine Emmanuel Ogaba, Jr. 1945- *WhoWor 93*
Otolorin, Michael Price 1914- *WhoWor 93*
Otomo, Katsuhiro *MiSFD 9*
Otomo, Sorin 1532-1587 *HarEnMi*
O'Toole, Allan Thomas 1925- *WhoAm 92*
O'Toole, Austin Martin *Law&B 92*
O'Toole, Austin Martin 1935- *St&PR 93, WhoAm 92*
O'Toole, Dennis John 1950- *St&PR 93*
O'Toole, Jack Francis 1946- *St&PR 93*
O'Toole, James Joseph 1945- *WhoAm 92*
O'Toole, John A. *Law&B 92*
O'Toole, John Dudley 1921- *WhoAm 92*
O'Toole, John E. 1929- *St&PR 93, WhoAm 92*
O'Toole, John James *Law&B 92*
O'Toole, Joseph W. *Law&B 92*
O'Toole, Joseph W. 1938- *WhoAm 92*
O'Toole, Joseph William 1938- *St&PR 93*
O'Toole, Kelly Ann 1962- *WhoEmL 93*
O'Toole, Laurence, Saint 1132-1180 *BioIn 17*
O'Toole, Margot *BioIn 17*
O'Toole, Marianne Therese 1963- *WhoAmW 93*
O'Toole, Michael Bradford 1934- *St&PR 93*
O'Toole, Niall L. *Law&B 92*
O'Toole, Peter *BioIn 17*
O'Toole, Peter 1932- *IntDcF 2-3 [port], WhoAm 92, WhoWor 93*
O'Toole, Rex *ConAu 40NR*
O'Toole, Robert J. 1941- *St&PR 93*
O'Toole, Robert Joseph 1941- *WhoAm 92*
O'Toole, Thomas 1941- *SmATA 71 [port]*
O'Toole, Thomas F. 1934- *St&PR 93*
O'Toole, Timothy S. 1955- *St&PR 93*
O'Toole, Timothy T. 1955- *St&PR 93*
O'Toole, Timothy Terrence *Law&B 92*
O'Toole, William P. 1942- *St&PR 93*
Otoshi, Tom Yasuo 1931- *WhoWor 93*
Otremba, Bernard Otto 1944- *WhoE 93*
Otruba, Emery 1934- *St&PR 93*
Otrzan, Durda 1953- *WhoWor 93*
Ots, Lennart 1933- *WhoWor 93*
Ots, Tony 1942- *St&PR 93*
Otstott, Charles Paddock 1937- *WhoAm 92*
Otsuji, Hidehisa 1940- *WhoAsAP 91*
Otsuka, Eizo 1929- *WhoWor 93*
Otsuka, Hideaki 1947- *WhoWor 93*
Otsuka, Kanji 1935- *WhoWor 93*
Otsuka, Masanori 1929- *WhoWor 93*
Otsuka, Seijiro 1935- *WhoAsAP 91*
Otsuka, Yuji 1929- *WhoAsAP 91*
Otsuki, Akira 1936- *WhoWor 93*
Otsuki, Jerro M. 1959- *St&PR 93*

Ott, Alan Wayne 1931- *St&PR 93*
Ott, Clyde E. 1930- *St&PR 93*
Ott, David 1947- *Baker 92*
Ott, David Michael 1952- *WhoAm 92*
Ott, Dennis McKay 1946- *St&PR 93*
Ott, Donald W. 1918- *St&PR 93*
Ott, George William, Jr. 1932- *WhoAm 92*
Ott, Geri L. 1950- *WhoEmL 93*
Ott, Gil 1950- *WhoWrEP 92*
Ott, Gilbert R., Jr. *Law&B 92*
Ott, Gilbert Russell, Jr. 1943- *St&PR 93, WhoAm 92, WhoE 93*
Ott, Holly-Brooks 1956- *WhoAmW 93*
Ott, Jack M. 1931- *WhoAm 92*
Ott, James F. *St&PR 93*
Ott, James Forgan 1935- *WhoAm 92*
Ott, John Harlow 1944- *WhoAm 92*
Ott, Joni K. *Law&B 92*
Ott, Karl Otto 1925- *WhoAm 92*
Ott, Kevin D. 1954- *St&PR 93*
Ott, Kevin Dowd 1953- *WhoE 93*
Ott, Linda Cheryl 1949- *WhoAmW 93*
Ott, Mel 1909-1958 *BioIn 17*
Ott, Millard Jeffrey 1946- *WhoEmL 93*
Ott, Paula Nisbet 1944- *WhoAmW 93*
Ott, Richard E. 1942- *St&PR 93*
Ott, Robert A. 1923- *WhoScE 91-4*
Ott, Robert B. 1923- *St&PR 93*
Ott, Robert John 1942- *WhoScE 91-1*
Ott, Robert Louis 1954- *WhoE 93*
Ott, Roy John *Law&B 92*
Ott, Stanley Joseph 1927- *WhoAm 92, WhoSSW 93*
Ott, Susana Clayton 1877- *AmWomPl*
Ott, Walter Richard 1943- *WhoAm 92*
Ott, Wayne Robert 1940- *WhoAm 92*
Ott, Wendell Lorenz 1942- *WhoAm 92*
Ottavino, A. George 1918- *St&PR 93*
Ottavino, Gerald A. 1921- *St&PR 93*
Ottaway, James 1911- *DcLB 127 [port]*
Ottaway, James H., Jr. 1938- *St&PR 93*
Ottaway, James Haller, Jr. 1938- *WhoAm 92*
Otte, A. Ray 1929- *WhoIns 93*
Otte, Daniel 1939- *WhoE 93*
Otte, Fred Lewis 1934- *WhoSSW 93*
Otte, Hans 1926- *Baker 92*
Otte, Monica A. *Law&B 92*
Otte, Paul John 1943- *WhoAm 92*
Otte, Ruth 1949- *News 92 [port]*
Otte, Ruth L. *WhoAm 92, WhoAmW 93*
Otte, Stephen 1943- *St&PR 93*
Otte, Stephen B. 1943- *WhoIns 93*
Ottemberg, Amalia 1926- *St&PR 93*
Otten, Adrian Timothy 1950- *WhoUN 92*
Otten, Arthur Edward, Jr. 1930- *WhoWor 93*
Otten, Douglas B. *St&PR 93*
Otten, Ernst W. 1934- *WhoScE 91-3*
Otten, Gerald Joseph 1932- *St&PR 93*
Otten, Leslie B. *BioIn 17*
Otten, Susan Kay 1956- *WhoAmW 93*
Ottenberg, James Simon 1918- *WhoAm 92*
Ottenberg, Simon 1923- *WhoAm 92*
Ottendorfer, Oswald 1826-1900 *JrnUS*
Ottenheijm, Harry C.J. 1943- *WhoScE 91-3*
Ottenheijm, Harry Carl 1943- *WhoWor 93*
Ottenhoff, Robert George 1948- *WhoE 93*
Ottenlips, Victor *Law&B 92*
Ottensmeyer, David Joseph 1930- *WhoAm 92*
Ottensmeyer, Peter 1939- *WhoAm 92*
Ottenweller, Albert Henry 1916- *WhoAm 92*
Otter, Anne Sofie von 1955- *Baker 92, OxDcOp*
Otter, Clement Leroy 1942- *WhoAm 92*
Otter, John M. 1930- *St&PR 93*
Otter, John Martin, III 1930- *WhoAm 92*
Otter, Mark William 1959- *WhoE 93*
Otter, N.R. *WhoScE 91-1*
Otterbourg, Robert Kenneth 1930- *WhoAm 92*
Otterloo, (Jan) Willem van 1907-1978 *Baker 92*
Otterman, Kenneth James 1949- *WhoE 93*
Otterman, Lloyd O. *BioIn 17*
Otterson, Jack Leroy 1950- *WhoWor 93*
Otterstedt, Jan-Erik A. 1933- *WhoScE 91-4*
Otterstetter, Joseph Henry *Law&B 92*
Ottesen, Otto Didrik 1816-1892 *BioIn 17*
Otteson, Schuyler Franklin 1917- *WhoAm 92*
Ottewill, R.H. *WhoScE 91-1*
Otth, Edward John, Jr. 1925- *WhoAm 92*
Otti, Fritz 1944- *WhoWor 93*
Ottie, Timothy Westerfield 1955- *St&PR 93*
Otting, Frederick P. 1916- *St&PR 93*
Ottinger, Andrew E., Jr. *Law&B 92*
Ottinger, August F. *Law&B 92*
Ottinger, Christoph 1933- *WhoWor 93*
Ottinger, Gregg Dillon 1950- *WhoEmL 93*
Ottinger, Mary Louise 1956- *WhoEmL 93*
Ottinger, Michael Bruce 1943- *St&PR 93*
Ottino, Julio Mario 1951- *WhoAm 92*
Ottley, Jerold Don 1934- *WhoAm 92*
Ottley, John King, Jr. 1931- *WhoSSW 93*
Ottley, Norman Franklin 1928- *St&PR 93*
Ottley, Peter J. *BioIn 17*
Ottley, Reginald (Leslie) *DcChlFi*
Ottley, Reginald (Leslie) 1909-1985 *MajAI [port]*
Ottlik, Geza 1912-1990 *ConAu 39NR*
Ottman, Jim 1945- *WhoWrEP 92*
Ottman, Josephine Kennedy 1955- *WhoAmW 93*
Ottman, Robert W(illiam) 1914- *Baker 92*
Ottmann, Judi 1959- *WhoAmW 93*
Ottmann, Thomas Alfons 1943- *WhoWor 93*
Ottmar, James H. 1946- *St&PR 93*
Ottmar, Peter H. 1947- *St&PR 93*
Otto, III 980-1002 *OxDcByz*
Otto, III, Holy Roman Emperor 980-1002 *BioIn 17*
Otto, Andreas 1936- *WhoScE 91-3*
Otto, Bruce M. 1936- *St&PR 93*
Otto, Calvin Peter 1930- *WhoSSW 93*
Otto, Catherine Nan 1953- *WhoEmL 93*
Otto, Charles Edward 1946- *WhoAm 92, WhoE 93*
Otto, Donald R. 1943- *WhoAm 92*
Otto, Edward D. 1926- *St&PR 93*
Otto, G.L. *Law&B 92*
Otto, George John 1904- *St&PR 93, WhoAm 92*
Otto, Gilbert Fred 1901- *WhoE 93, WhoWor 93*
Otto, Gunter B. *WhoAm 92*
Otto, Ingolf Helgi Elfried 1920- *WhoSSW 93, WhoWor 93*
Otto, Jean Hammond 1925- *WhoAm 92*
Otto, Jeffrey W. *Law&B 92*
Otto, Jim 1938- *BioIn 17*
Otto, John Francis 1919- *WhoE 93*
Otto, (Ernst) Julius 1804-1877 *Baker 92*
Otto, Kenneth Lee 1930- *WhoAm 92*
Otto, Klaus 1926- *WhoScE 91-3*
Otto, Lawrence James 1941- *WhoIns 93*
Otto, Leonard 1929- *WhoScE 91-3*
Otto, Linda *MiSFD 9*
Otto, Linda McHenry 1941- *WhoAmW 93*
Otto, Lisa 1919- *Baker 92*
Otto, Ludwig 1934- *WhoSSW 93*
Otto, Luther Benedict 1937- *WhoSSW 93*
Otto, Margaret Amelia 1937- *WhoAm 92, WhoAmW 93*
Otto, Marie 1930- *WhoAmW 93, WhoWor 93*
Otto, Myron L. 1942- *St&PR 93*
Otto, Peter 1938- *St&PR 93*
Otto, Richard 1935- *St&PR 93*
Otto, Richard E. 1928- *WhoIns 93*
Otto, Stanley Arnold 1949- *WhoWor 93*
Otto, Svend 1916- *BioIn 17*
Otto, Tammy 1960- *WhoE 93*
Otto, Teo 1904-1968 *OxDcOp*
Otto, Tony 1948- *WhoAsAP 91*
Otto, Wayne Raymond 1931- *WhoAm 92, WhoWrEP 92*
Otto, Whitney 1955- *ConLC 70 [port]*
Otto, William Tod 1816-1905 *OxCSupC*
Ottoboni, Pietro 1667-1740 *OxDcOp*
Ottoni, Filippo *MiSFD 9*
Otto of Freising c. 1111-1158 *OxDcByz*
Ottosen, P. Chr. *WhoScE 91-2*
Ottoson, David G.R. 1918- *WhoScE 91-2*
Ottoson, Howard Warren 1920- *WhoAm 92*
Ottoson, Lars B. 1931- *WhoScE 91-4*
Ottoson, Mary R. *Law&B 92*
Ottosson, Jan-Otto 1925- *WhoScE 91-4*
Ottosson, Mats Ola 1941- *WhoScE 91-4*
Otto the Great, I 912-973 *HarEnMi, OxDcByz*
Ottow, J.C.G. 1935- *WhoScE 91-3*
Otts, Mark G. *Law&B 92*
Otts, Mark Grafton 1956- *WhoEmL 93, WhoSSW 93*
Ottum, Bob 1925-1986 *ScF&FL 92*
Ottum, Robert *ScF&FL 92*
Ottun, Ella L. *AmWomPl*
Otugen, Mehmet Volkan 1956- *WhoE 93*
Otunga, Maurice Cardinal 1923- *WhoWor 93*
Otvos, Ervin George 1935- *WhoSSW 93*
Otvos, Gabor 1935- *Baker 92*
Otvos, Laszlo 1929- *WhoScE 91-4*
Otwell, Ralph Maurice 1926- *WhoAm 92*
Ou, Jonathan Tsien-hsiong 1934- *WhoWor 93*
Ou, Lo-Chang 1930- *WhoE 93*
Oualline, Viola Jackson 1927- *WhoSSW 93*
Ouattara 1957- *BioIn 17*
Ouattara, Alassane D. 1942- *WhoWor 93*
Ouattara, Alassane Dramane 1943- *WhoAfr*
Ouattara, Dramane 1937- *WhoUN 92*
Oubbi, Lahbib 1960- *WhoWor 93*
Ouborg, Peter *Law&B 92*
Oubre, Tanya E. *Law&B 92*
Ouchi, Keigo 1930- *WhoAsAP 91*
Ouchi, William George 1943- *WhoAm 92*
Ouchi, Yoshihiro 1355-1399 *HarEnMi*
Ouchterlony, Finn T. 1943- *WhoScE 91-4*
Ouchterlony, Finn Thomas 1943- *WhoWor 93*
Oudadess, Mohamed 1947- *WhoWor 93*
Oudaii, Hashmi el *ConAu 136*
Oudelaar, Hendrik G.J. 1938- *WhoScE 91-3*
Oudin, Eugene (Esperance) 1858-1894 *Baker 92*
Oudin, Jerome 1943- *WhoScE 91-2*
Oudinot, Nicolas Charles 1767-1847 *HarEnMi*
Oudjehane, Azzeddine 1965- *WhoWor 93*
Oudrid (y Segura), Cristobal 1825-1877 *Baker 92*
Oudshoorn, Michael John 1963- *WhoWor 93*
Oueddi, Goukouni 1944- *WhoAfr*
Ouedraogo, Idrissa *BioIn 17*
Ouedraogo, Idrissa 1954- *MiSFD 9*
Ouellet, Lyne *Law&B 92*
Ouellette, Bernard Charles 1936- *WhoAm 92*
Ouellette, Elizabeth Evone 1959- *WhoAmW 93*
Ouellette, Fernand 1930- *WhoCanL 92*
Ouellette, Gerard L. *Law&B 92*
Ouellette, Jane Lee Young 1929- *WhoSSW 93, WhoWor 93*
Ouellette, Reno Roland 1931- *St&PR 93*
Ouellette, Robert Paul 1938- *St&PR 93*
Ouellette-Michalska, Madeleine 1934- *WhoCanL 92*
Oughton, James Henry, Jr. 1913- *WhoWor 93*
Oughton, John 1942- *St&PR 93*
Oughton, Thomas Victor 1951- *WhoEmL 93*
Oughtred, Angus Winn 1942- *St&PR 93*
Oughtred, John W. 1949- *St&PR 93*
Ouimet, Guy 1954- *St&PR 93*
Ouimet, James M. 1947- *St&PR 93*
Ouimet, James Michael 1947- *WhoSSW 93*
Oujesky, Helen M. 1930- *WhoAmW 93*
Ouk, Chanrithy *BioIn 17*
Ouknine, Youssef 1958- *WhoWor 93*
Ouko, Robert John 1932-1990 *BioIn 17*
Ould, Chris 1959?- *ScF&FL 92*
Ould Abdel Kader, Ahmedou 1941- *WhoWor 93*
Ould Mohamed Mahmoud, Mohamedou 1944- *WhoUN 92, WhoWor 93*
Oulibicheff, Alexander Dmitrievich 1794-1858 *Baker 92*
Oulpios fl. 828-993 *OxDcByz*
Oulundsen, Donald C. *Law&B 92*
Ouma, Henry L. 1943- *WhoUN 92*
Oumarou, Ide 1937- *WhoAfr*
Oumarou, Mamane 1945- *WhoAfr*
Ounjian, Marilyn J. 1947- *WhoE 93*
Ounsley, Simon 1953- *ScF&FL 92*
Ounsworth, James A. *Law&B 92*
Ounsworth, James A. 1942- *St&PR 93*
Oura, Ichiro 1934- *WhoWor 93*
Ouranos, Nikephoros dc. 1007 *OxDcByz*
Ourant, Edwin L. 1933- *WhoAm 92*
Ourisman, Betty Lou Haydnet d1992 *BioIn 17*
Ourisson, Guy 1926- *WhoScE 91-2*
Ourivio, Jose Carlos Mello 1933- *WhoWor 93*
Ours, Robert Maurice 1936- *WhoWrEP 92*
Oursler, Fulton 1893-1952 *BioIn 17*
Oursler, Fulton, Jr. 1932- *WhoAm 92*
Ourso, J. Clifford 1937- *St&PR 93*
Ourso, Priscilla 1951- *WhoAmW 93*
Oury, Anna Caroline 1808-1880 *Baker 92*
Oury, Antonio James 1800-1883 *Baker 92*
Oury, Gerard 1919- *MiSFD 9*
Oury, William Sanders 1817-1887 *BioIn 17*
Ouseley, Frederick (Arthur) Gore 1825-1889 *Baker 92*
Ouseph, Florence 1949- *WhoAmW 93*
Oushalkas, Rose *Law&B 92*
Ousky, Lawrence 1942- *St&PR 93*
Ousley, David Alan 1951- *WhoE 93*
Ousley, James E. 1946- *St&PR 93*
Oussani, James John 1920- *WhoAm 92, WhoE 93, WhoWor 93*
Oussedik, Omar d1992 *NewYTBS 92*
Ousset, Cecile 1936- *Baker 92*
Oustrin, Jean 1931- *WhoScE 91-2*
Out, T.A. 1946- *WhoScE 91-3*
Outcalt, David Lewis 1935- *WhoAm 92*
Outcalt, Stephanie Lee 1964- *WhoAmW 93*
Outcault, Richard Felton 1863-1928 *JrnUS*
Outerbridge, Cheryl *Law&B 92*
Outerbridge, David E(ugene) 1933- *ConAu 38NR*
Outerbridge, Mary Ewing 1852-1886 *BiDAMSp 1989*
Outerbridge, William Fulwood 1930- *WhoSSW 93*
Outhwaite, Lucille Conrad 1909- *WhoAmW 93*
Outhwaite, Stephen J. 1943- *St&PR 93*
Outka, Gene Harold 1937- *WhoAm 92*
Outland, Charles (Faulkner) 1910-1988 *ConAu 40NR*
Outland, Max Lynn 1937- *WhoSSW 93*
Outland, Robert Frank 1943- *WhoSSW 93*
Outlaw, Arthur Robert 1926- *St&PR 93, WhoAm 92*
Outlaw, Baz 1855-1894 *BioIn 17*
Outlaw, Linda N. 1948- *St&PR 93*
Outler, Donald Wayne 1940- *WhoSSW 93*
Outram, J. *WhoScE 91-1*
Outram, James 1803-1863 *HarEnMi*
Outram, Richard Daley 1930- *WhoCanL 92*
Outterbridge, John 1933- *BioIn 17*
Ouvrard, Helene 1938- *WhoCanL 92*
Ouyang, Lin Min 1921- *WhoE 93*
Ouyang, Qian 1955- *WhoWor 93*
Ouziel, Chaim 1941- *WhoUN 92*
Ouziel, Jacky 1948- *WhoWor 93*
Ouzounian, Armenuhi 1942- *WhoAmW 93*
Ouzts, Daniel Rhett 1946- *St&PR 93*
Ouzts, James Wesley, Sr. 1937- *WhoSSW 93*
Ouzts, Steven Wayne 1954- *WhoEmL 93*
Ovalle, Pilar de *ScF&FL 92*
Ovalle, Ralph K. 1950- *St&PR 93*
Ovalles, Cesar Francisco 1957- *WhoWor 93*
Ovan, Mil *BioIn 17*
Ovando Hernandez, Francisco Xavier *DcCPCAm*
Ovcarov, Sergej 1955- *DrEEuF*
Ovchinnikov, Viacheslav 1936- *Baker 92*
Ove, Horace *MiSFD 9*
Ove, Peter 1930- *WhoAm 92*
Ovel, John A. 1947- *St&PR 93*
Ovenden, J.A. 1963- *St&PR 93*
Ovens, Richard Edmund 1942- *WhoE 93*
Over, J. Robert 1937- *WhoE 93*
Over, Jan 1949- *WhoScE 91-3*
Over, John F. 1940- *St&PR 93*
Over, Joost A. 1940- *WhoScE 91-3*
Over, Raymond van *ScF&FL 92*
Overall, Christine (Dorothy) 1949- *ConAu 138*
Overall, James Carney, Jr. 1937- *WhoAm 92*
Overall, John E. 1929- *WhoAm 92*
Overall, Orval 1881-1947 *BiDAMSp 1989*
Overall, Park *BioIn 17*
Overath, Peter *WhoScE 91-3*
Overbeck, Gene Edward 1929- *WhoAm 92*
Overbeck, Hans Jurgen *WhoScE 91-3*
Overbeck, Lois More 1945- *WhoSSW 93*
Overbeek, Garry L. 1945- *St&PR 93*
Overbeeke, Aernout *BioIn 17*
Overberg, Paul J. 1926- *St&PR 93*
Overberg, Paul Joseph 1926- *WhoAm 92*
Overbey, Terry L. *Law&B 92*
Overby, Charles Frederick 1959- *WhoEmL 93*
Overby, Charlotte Murphy 1965- *WhoAmW 93*
Overby, Donald Wesley 1938- *WhoE 93*
Overby, George Robert 1923-1992 *WhoAm 92*
Overby, Jon Jefferson 1953- *WhoEmL 93*
Overby, Lacy Rasco 1920- *WhoAm 92*
Overby, Osmund Rudolf 1931- *WhoAm 92*
Overcash, Michael Ray 1944- *WhoSSW 93*
Overcash, Reece A., Jr. 1926- *WhoAm 92*
Overcash, Reece Alexander, Jr. 1926- *St&PR 93*
Overend, James Scott 1958- *WhoE 93*
Overend, Jennifer M.C. 1953- *St&PR 93*
Overend, John J. 1928- *WhoIns 93*
Overend, John James 1928- *St&PR 93*
Overend, Robert Benjamin, Jr. 1943- *WhoWrEP 92*
Overeynder, Bernard *BioIn 17*
Overfelt, Eugene 1922- *St&PR 93*
Overfield, Ronald Edwin 1938- *WhoSSW 93*
Overgaag, A.J.M. *WhoScE 91-3*
Overgaard, Cordell Jersild 1934- *WhoAm 92*
Overgaard, Mitchell Jersild 1931- *WhoAm 92*
Overgaard, Willard Michele 1925- *WhoAm 92*
Overgard, R. Gail 1941- *St&PR 93*
Overgard, William 1926-1990 *ScF&FL 92*
Overgard, William (Thomas, Jr.) 1926-1990 *ConAu 138*
Overhauser, Albert Warner 1925- *WhoAm 92*
Overhiser, George R. 1921- *St&PR 93*
Overhof, Harald 1942- *WhoScE 91-3*
Overholser, Geneva *BioIn 17*

Overholser, Stephen 1944- *ScF&FL 92*
Overholser, Wayne D. 1906- *DcAmChF 1960*
Overholt, Hugh Robert 1933- *WhoAm 92*
Overholt, Mary Ann 1935- *St&PR 93*
Overholt, Mary Elizabeth *AmWomPl*
Overholt, Richard M. 1901-1990 *BioIn 17*
Overlander, Craig M. 1960- *St&PR 93*
Overlau, Pierre G. 1936- *WhoScE 91-2*
Overlock, Willard J., Jr. 1946- *St&PR 93*
Overlock, Willard Joseph, Jr. 1946- *WhoAm 92*
Overly, Helen Irene 1931- *WhoE 93*
Overly, Steven D. *Law&B 92*
Overly, Steven Duane 1958- *WhoEmL 93*
Overman, Dean Lee 1943- *WhoAm 92*
Overman, Edwin Scott 1922- *WhoIns 93*
Overman, Eric Mario 1969- *WhoE 93*
Overman, Glenn Delbert 1916- *WhoAm 92*
Overman, James Braden *Law&B 92*
Overman, Jerry Grey 1949- *WhoAm 92*
Overman, Marjorie Moore 1919- *WhoWrEP 92*
Overman, Timothy Lloyd 1943- *WhoSSW 93*
Overmeer, R.H.J.M. *WhoScE 91-3*
Overmeyer, Steven R. 1950- *St&PR 93*
Overmyer, Daniel Lee 1935- *WhoAm 92*
Overmyer, John Eugene 1933- *St&PR 93, WhoAm 92*
Overmyer, Randy Jay 1956- *WhoEmL 93*
Overseth, Oliver Enoch 1928- *WhoAm 92*
Overstreet, Carole 1948- *St&PR 93*
Overstreet, Joe William, Jr. 1954- *St&PR 93*
Overstreet, John Tyler 1958- *WhoSSW 93*
Overstreet, Kenneth E. *St&PR 93*
Overstreet, Sarah Gayle 1951- *WhoEmL 93*
Overstrom, Gunnar S., Jr. 1942- *St&PR 93*
Overton, Anthony 1865-1946 *BioIn 17*
Overton, Benjamin Frederick 1926- *WhoAm 92, WhoSSW 93*
Overton, Betty Jean 1949- *WhoAmW 93, WhoEmL 93*
Overton, Bruce 1941- *WhoAm 92*
Overton, Carl E. 1917- *St&PR 93*
Overton, David Ayward, Jr. 1950- *WhoSSW 93*
Overton, Donald Albert 1935- *WhoE 93*
Overton, Frank William 1938- *St&PR 93*
Overton, George Washington 1918- *WhoAm 92*
Overton, Grace Sloan *AmWomPl*
Overton, Gwendolen *AmWomPl*
Overton, Hall (Franklin) 1920-1972 *Baker 92*
Overton, Jane Taylor 1935- *WhoWrEP 92*
Overton, Jane Vincent Harper 1919- *WhoAm 92*
Overton, Joseph Allen, Jr. 1921- *WhoAm 92*
Overton, Karl Howard *WhoScE 91-1*
Overton, Lewis M. 1937- *St&PR 93*
Overton, Marcus Lee 1943- *WhoAm 92, WhoWor 93*
Overton, Michele Marie 1968- *WhoE 93*
Overton, Richard A. 1942- *St&PR 93*
Overton, Richard Albert 1942- *WhoAm 92*
Overton, Robert Anthony 1966- *WhoSSW 93*
Overton, Ronald Ernest 1943- *WhoWrEP 92*
Overton, Rosilyn Gay Hoffman 1942- *WhoAmW 93*
Overton, Shana L. *Law&B 92*
Overtree, Edward L. 1945- *St&PR 93*
Overturf, Elaine Vivian 1937- *St&PR 93*
Overweg, Norbert Ido Albert *WhoE 93*
Ovesen, Ellis *WhoWrEP 92*
Ovesen, Niels Krebs 1934- *WhoScE 91-2*
Oves Fernandez, Francisco d1990 *BioIn 17*
Oveson, W. Val 1952- *WhoAm 92*
Oveson, Wilford Val 1952- *WhoWor 93*
Ovid 43BC-17AD *MagSWL [port], OxDcByz*
Oving, R.K. *WhoScE 91-3*
Ovington, Mary White 1865-1951 *AmWomPl, EncAACR*
Ovitsky, Steven Alan 1947- *WhoAm 92*
Ovitz, Michael *BioIn 17, WhoAm 92*
Ovitz, Michael 1946- *ConTFT 10*
Ovlisen, Mads 1940- *WhoAm 92*
Ovrut, Barnett D. *Law&B 92*
Ovsenik, Edward Charles *Law&B 92*
Ovshinsky, Iris M. 1927- *St&PR 93*
Ovshinsky, Stanford R. 1922- *St&PR 93*
Ovshinsky, Stanford Robert 1922- *WhoAm 92*
Ovsievich, Boris Lvovitch 1936- *WhoWor 93*
Ovstedal, Barbara *ScF&FL 92*
Owaisi, Salahuddin 1936- *WhoAsAP 91*
Owczarek, Jerzy 1926- *WhoScE 91-4*
Oweiss, Ibrahim Mohamed 1931- *WhoAm 92*
Owen, Allan Jacobs 1952- *WhoEmL 93*
Owen, Amy *BioIn 17*
Owen, Amy 1944- *WhoAm 92, WhoAmW 93*
Owen, Arlene G. *Law&B 92*
Owen, B. David 1941- *St&PR 93*
Owen, Betty M. *ScF&FL 92*
Owen, Beverly Yvonne 1929- *WhoAmW 93*
Owen, Brian Dennis 1955- *WhoE 93*
Owen, Carol Elaine 1957- *WhoAmW 93*
Owen, Carol Thompson 1944- *WhoAmW 93*
Owen, Cindy Ann *St&PR 93*
Owen, Claude Bernard, Jr. 1945- *St&PR 93, WhoAm 92, WhoSSW 93*
Owen, Claudia 1965- *WhoAmW 93*
Owen, Cliff 1919- *MiSFD 9*
Owen, Curtis L. *Law&B 92*
Owen, Curtis L. 1930- *St&PR 93*
Owen, Cynthia Carol 1943- *WhoAmW 93*
Owen, Dan D. 1948- *St&PR 93*
Owen, Daniel B. 1950- *St&PR 93*
Owen, Daniel Bruce 1950- *WhoEmL 93, WhoSSW 93, WhoWor 93*
Owen, Daniel Thomas 1947- *WhoWor 93*
Owen, David 1938- *BioIn 17, ColdWar 1 [port]*
Owen, David 1939- *ScF&FL 92*
Owen, David 1955- *BioIn 17*
Owen, David Anthony Llewellyn 1938- *WhoWor 93*
Owen, David Dalrymple 1942- *WhoSSW 93*
Owen, David Gareth *WhoScE 91-1*
Owen, David I. 1940- *WhoE 93*
Owen, David Nicholas 1944- *WhoWor 93*
Owen, David P. 1954- *St&PR 93*
Owen, David Roger Jones *WhoScE 91-1*
Owen, David Rogers 1914- *WhoAm 92*
Owen, Deborah K. *WhoAm 92, WhoAmW 93*
Owen, Don 1935- *MiSFD 9*
Owen, Duncan Shaw, Jr. 1935- *WhoAm 92*
Owen, Eileen Edmunds 1949- *WhoWrEP 92*
Owen, Ellen Gray *Law&B 92*
Owen, Eugene H. 1929- *St&PR 93*
Owen, Fred Wynne 1928- *WhoAm 92*
Owen, Gareth *BioIn 17*
Owen, Gary E. 1945- *St&PR 93*
Owen, George, Jr. 1901-1986 *BiDAMSp 1989*
Owen, George Earle 1908- *WhoAm 92, WhoWor 93*
Owen, Gilberto 1905-1952 *DcMexL, SpAmA*
Owen, Grace Arlington *AmWomPl*
Owen, H. Martyn 1929- *WhoE 93*
Owen, Harvey W. 1949- *St&PR 93*
Owen, Helen Hammett d1990 *BioIn 17*
Owen, Henry 1920- *WhoAm 92*
Owen, Hugh R. 1930- *St&PR 93*
Owen, Ida May *AmWomPl*
Owen, Ivor *WhoScE 91-1*
Owen, J. Bradley *ScF&FL 92*
Owen, J.P. 1954- *St&PR 93*
Owen, Jack 1929- *ConAu 37NR*
Owen, Janet Kay 1946- *WhoAmW 93*
Owen, Jeffrey Lynn 1951- *WhoEmL 93*
Owen, Jennifer 1936- *ConAu 38NR*
Owen, John 1564-1622 *DcLB 121 [port]*
Owen, John 1929- *WhoAm 92*
Owen, John Atkinson, Jr. 1924- *WhoAm 92*
Owen, John Bryn *WhoScE 91-1*
Owen, John Douglas 1956- *St&PR 93*
Owen, John H., Jr. 1932- *St&PR 93*
Owen, John Joseph Thomas *WhoScE 91-1*
Owen, John Laverty 1923- *WhoE 93*
Owen, John Michael *WhoScE 91-1*
Owen, John Philip *WhoScE 91-1*
Owen, John R. 1929- *St&PR 93*
Owen, Karen Michelle 1952- *WhoAmW 93, WhoEmL 93*
Owen, Kenneth Dale 1938- *WhoSSW 93*
Owen, Kimberly B. *Law&B 92*
Owen, Kirby Campbell 1957- *WhoWor 93*
Owen, Langdon Talbot, Jr. 1951- *WhoEmL 93*
Owen, Larry Gene 1932- *WhoSSW 93*
Owen, Larry Lesley 1945- *WhoSSW 93*
Owen, Linda Kay 1958- *WhoAmW 93*
Owen, Lynn Rasmussen *WhoAm 92*
Owen, Maribel Vinson 1911-1961 *BioIn 17*
Owen, Marie Bankhead 1869-1958 *AmWomPl*
Owen, Mary 1906-1991 *BioIn 17*
Owen, Mary Jane 1936- *WhoWrEP 92*
Owen, May 1891-1988 *BioIn 17*
Owen, Melvin Lee 1951- *St&PR 93*
Owen, Michael *WhoAm 92*
Owen, Michael John *WhoScE 91-1*
Owen, Morfydd Llywn 1891-1918 *Baker 92*
Owen, Muriel 1929- *WhoAmW 93*
Owen, Nathan R. 1919- *St&PR 93*
Owen, Nathan Richard 1919- *WhoAm 92*
Owen, Norma Ann Marie 1963- *WhoAmW 93*
Owen, R. Neely 1951- *WhoEmL 93*
Owen, Randa M. *Law&B 92*
Owen, Ray David 1915- *WhoAm 92*
Owen, Richard *Law&B 92*
Owen, Richard 1922- *Baker 92, WhoAm 92, WhoE 93*
Owen, Richard 1942- *ScF&FL 92*
Owen, Robert 1771-1858 *BioIn 17*
Owen, Robert Dewit 1948- *WhoE 93*
Owen, Robert E. 1943- *St&PR 93*
Owen, Robert Hubert 1928- *WhoAm 92*
Owen, Robert John *WhoScE 91-1*
Owen, Robert Joseph, Jr. *Law&B 92*
Owen, Robert Roy 1921- *WhoAm 92*
Owen, Robert Vaughan 1920- *WhoAm 92*
Owen, Roberts Bishop 1926- *WhoAm 92*
Owen, Roger C(orey) 1928- *ConAu 37NR*
Owen, Ruth A. 1950- *St&PR 93*
Owen, Ruth Bryan *AmWomPl*
Owen, Ruth Bryan 1885-1954 *BioIn 17*
Owen, Sarah *BioIn 17*
Owen, Steve 1898-1964 *BioIn 17*
Owen, Sue Ann 1942- *WhoWrEP 92*
Owen, Suzanne 1926- *WhoAmW 93*
Owen, T.G. 1945- *St&PR 93*
Owen, Thomas 1910- *ScF&FL 92*
Owen, Thomas Barron 1920- *WhoAm 92*
Owen, Thomas Gold 1941- *WhoSSW 93*
Owen, Thomas H., Jr. *Law&B 92*
Owen, Thomas J. 1934- *St&PR 93*
Owen, Thomas Llewellyn 1928- *WhoAm 92, WhoE 93*
Owen, Thomas P. 1931- *St&PR 93*
Owen, Thomas R. *Law&B 92*
Owen, Thomas Walker 1925- *WhoAm 92*
Owen, Timothy C. 1953- *St&PR 93*
Owen, Timothy Charles 1956- *WhoEmL 93*
Owen, Virginia Lee 1941- *WhoAmW 93*
Owen, W. David *Law&B 92*
Owen, Warren Herbert 1927- *St&PR 93*
Owen, Wilfred 1893-1918 *MagSWL [port], WorLitC [port]*
Owen, William *ScF&FL 92*
Owen, William Frederick 1947- *WhoEmL 93*
Owen, William H., III 1948- *St&PR 93*
Owen, William Marshall *Law&B 92*
Owen, William Parker 1950- *WhoEmL 93*
Owens, A. *WhoScE 91-1*
Owens, Alice Watson *WhoSSW 93*
Owens, Ann Holderness *Law&B 92*
Owens, Anne Sherman 1933- *WhoSSW 93*
Owens, Bobbie Deane 1935- *WhoAm 92*
Owens, Bruce W. *Law&B 92*
Owens, "Buck" 1929- *Baker 92, WhoAm 92*
Owens, C. Richard 1930- *St&PR 93*
Owens, Carole Ehrlich 1942- *WhoE 93*
Owens, Caroline Mulford 1932- *WhoAmW 93, WhoE 93*
Owens, Charles Michael 1949- *St&PR 93*
Owens, Charles V., Jr. 1927- *St&PR 93*
Owens, Charles Vincent, Jr. 1927- *WhoAm 92*
Owens, Christopher G. 1961- *WhoWrEP 92*
Owens, Claude, Jr. *Law&B 92*
Owens, Commodore Perry 1852-1918 *BioIn 17*
Owens, Craig *BioIn 17*
Owens, Dana *BioIn 17*
Owens, Darryl T. *AfrAmBi*
Owens, David J. *Law&B 92*
Owens, David Whit 1950- *WhoEmL 93*
Owens, Delia *BioIn 17*
Owens, Don Ray 1949- *WhoSSW 93*
Owens, E(dwin) J(ohn) 1950- *ConAu 139*
Owens, Edwin Chandler 1935- *WhoIns 93*
Owens, Ethelrose James 1908-1991 *BioIn 17*
Owens, Frank S., Jr. 1931- *St&PR 93*
Owens, Fredric Newell 1941- *WhoAm 92*
Owens, G. Kay 1942- *WhoSSW 93*
Owens, G.L. 1936- *St&PR 93*
Owens, Garland Chester 1922- *WhoAm 92*
Owens, Gary *WhoAm 92*
Owens, Gary Mitchell 1949- *WhoE 93*
Owens, Gary Standifer 1949- *St&PR 93*
Owens, George Ray 1948- *WhoEmL 93*
Owens, Glynn I. 1949- *St&PR 93*
Owens, Gregory Randolph 1948- *WhoE 93*
Owens, Harold B. 1926- *WhoSSW 93*
Owens, Hettie Catherine 1930- *St&PR 93*
Owens, Hilda Faye 1939- *WhoAmW 93*
Owens, Hubert F. *Law&B 92*
Owens, Hugh F. 1909-1990 *BioIn 17*
Owens, J. Howell 1940- *St&PR 93*
Owens, Jack B. *Law&B 92*
Owens, Jack Byron 1944- *WhoAm 92*
Owens, James Cleveland 1913-1980 *AfrAmBi*
Owens, James Cuthbert 1916- *WhoAm 92, WhoWor 93*
Owens, James Donald 1927- *BiDAMSp 1989*
Owens, James Hilliard 1920- *St&PR 93*
Owens, James J. *Law&B 92*
Owens, James Jacob 1942- *St&PR 93*
Owens, James Samuel 1908- *WhoSSW 93*
Owens, James Wadsworth 1936- *WhoSSW 93*
Owens, James William 1950- *St&PR 93*
Owens, Jana Jae 1943- *WhoAmW 93, WhoSSW 93, WhoWor 93*
Owens, Jane E. *Law&B 92*
Owens, Janie Layne 1946- *WhoAmW 93*
Owens, Jesse 1913-1980 *BioIn 17, ConHero 2 [port], EncAACR*
Owens, John Franklin 1935- *WhoSSW 93*
Owens, John Michael 1951- *WhoEmL 93*
Owens, Joseph 1908- *WhoAm 92*
Owens, Joseph 1925- *St&PR 93*
Owens, Joseph Herron 1937- *WhoE 93*
Owens, Judith Myoli 1940- *WhoAmW 93*
Owens, Lindsay Meggs 1952- *WhoSSW 93*
Owens, Louis (D.) 1948- *ConAu 137*
Owens, Luvie Moore 1933- *WhoAm 92*
Owens, Major *BioIn 17*
Owens, Major 1936- *AfrAmBi*
Owens, Major R. 1936- *CngDr 91*
Owens, Major Robert Odell 1936- *WhoAm 92, WhoE 93*
Owens, Mark *BioIn 17*
Owens, Marvin Franklin, Jr. 1916- *WhoAm 92*
Owens, Michael *WhoAm 92*
Owens, Millard Fillmore, III 1952- *WhoEmL 93, WhoSSW 93*
Owens, Morlais *WhoScE 91-1*
Owens, Myles A. *Law&B 92*
Owens, Nancy Kay 1966- *WhoSSW 93*
Owens, Nicholas Russell 1940- *WhoAm 92*
Owens, Patrice Nan 1949- *WhoSSW 93*
Owens, Patrick H. 1947- *St&PR 93*
Owens, Paul Edwin 1953- *WhoSSW 93*
Owens, Paul Theodore 1952- *St&PR 93*
Owens, Perry 1852-1919 *BioIn 17*
Owens, Priscilla Jane-Kerr Smith 1952- *WhoAmW 93, WhoSSW 93*
Owens, Raymond Lambert *Law&B 92*
Owens, Richard George 1946- *WhoEmL 93*
Owens, Richard Hutchens 1932- *WhoSSW 93*
Owens, Richard J. 1946- *St&PR 93*
Owens, Richard Meredith 1944- *ConAu 37NR*
Owens, Richard Patrick *Law&B 92*
Owens, Richard Wilson 1941- *WhoSSW 93*
Owens, Rita *BioIn 17*
Owens, Robert Julian 1942- *St&PR 93*
Owens, Robert Owen *WhoScE 91-1*
Owens, Robert Patrick 1954- *WhoEmL 93*
Owens, Robert W. 1948- *St&PR 93*
Owens, Robin Maria 1956- *WhoAmW 93, WhoEmL 93, WhoSSW 93*
Owens, Rochelle 1936- *ConAu 39NR, WhoAm 92, WhoWrEP 92*
Owens, Sarah Eileen *Law&B 92*
Owens, Scott Andrew 1958- *WhoWor 93*
Owens, Shelby Jean 1936- *WhoAmW 93*
Owens, Susan Weir 1949- *WhoAmW 93*
Owens, Thomas R. *St&PR 93*
Owens, Tyler Benjamin 1944- *WhoSSW 93*
Owens, Vanassa Lynn 1953- *WhoEmL 93*
Owens, Vivian Ann 1948- *WhoSSW 93*
Owens, Wayne 1937- *CngDr 91, WhoAm 92*
Owens, Wesley A. 1958- *St&PR 93*
Owens, Wilbur Dawson, Jr. 1930- *WhoAm 92, WhoSSW 93*
Owens, William A. 1905-1990 *BioIn 17*
Owens, William Abbott, Jr. 1914- *WhoSSW 93*
Owens, William Arthur 1940- *WhoAm 92*
Owens, William Don 1939- *WhoAm 92*
Owens, William Hughes 1930- *WhoAm 92*
Owens, William Richard 1941- *WhoSSW 93*
Owens, Williams Lawrence 1936- *St&PR 93*
Owensby, Brenda Gail Earl 1950- *WhoEmL 93*
Owens-Wilson, Gwendolyn Ann 1938- *WhoAmW 93*
Owen-Towle, Carolyn Sheets 1935- *WhoAmW 93*
Owers, Brian Charles 1934- *St&PR 93, WhoAm 92*
Owings, Donald Henry 1943- *WhoAm 92*
Owings, Francis Barre 1941- *WhoAm 92*
Owings, Grant *Law&B 92*
Owings, Malcolm William 1925- *St&PR 93, WhoAm 92*
Owings, Margaret Wentworth 1913- *WhoAm 92*

Owings, Mark 1945- *ScF&FL 92*
Owings, Phillip Jeffrey 1944- *St&PR 93*
Owings, Robert Mason 1932- *WhoWrEP 92*
Ownby, Charlotte Ledbetter 1947- *WhoAmW 93, WhoEmL 93, WhoSSW 93*
Ownby, J. Steve 1939- *WhoAm 92*
Ownes, Owen Ernest 1925- *St&PR 93*
Owoseni, Biodun 1949- *WhoUN 92*
Owre, Oscar T. 1917-1990 *BioIn 17*
Owsley, Alvin 1926- *WhoAm 92*
Owsley, David Thomas 1929- *WhoAm 92*
Owsley, Frank Lawrence 1928- *BioIn 17*
Owsley, Norman Lee 1941- *WhoAm 92*
Owsley, Robert Warner 1940- *St&PR 93*
Owsley, Thomas L. *Law&B 92*
Owsley, William Clinton, Jr. 1923- *WhoAm 92*
Owston, C.E. *ScF&FL 92*
Owusu, Victor 1923- *WhoAfr*
Owusu-Ansah, Twum 1935- *WhoWor 93*
Owyang, King 1945- *St&PR 93*
Owyoung, Steven David 1947- *WhoAm 92*
Oxburgh, E.R. *WhoScE 91-1*
Oxby, Clement Bernard *WhoScE 91-1*
Oxelfelt, Per E. 1931- *WhoScE 91-4*
Oxenberg-Elwes, Christina *BioIn 17*
Oxenbould, Moffatt Benjamin 1943- *WhoWor 93*
Oxenburg, Allen Sven 1927- *WhoAm 92*
Oxenburg, Allen Sven 1927-1992 *NewYTBS 92 [port]*
Oxenbury, Helen 1938- *BioIn 17, MajAI [port]*
Oxendine, Glenda Holt 1956- *St&PR 93*
Oxendine, John Edward *BioIn 17*
Oxenham, J. Preston *Law&B 92*
Oxenhandler, Neal 1926- *WhoAm 92*
Oxenhorn, Harvey *BioIn 17*
Oxenreiter, Maurice Frank 1924- *WhoAm 92*
Oxenreiter, Robert A. 1936- *St&PR 93*
Oxenreiter, William F., Jr. *St&PR 93*
Oxer, John Paul Daniell 1950- *WhoSSW 93*
Oxford, Charles William 1921- *WhoAm 92*
Oxford, Hubert, III 1938- *WhoSSW 93*
Oxford, John Sidney *WhoScE 91-1*
Oxford, Michael Edward 1947- *WhoEmL 93*
Oxford, Rebecca Louise 1946- *WhoSSW 93*
Oxford, Sharon M. 1939- *WhoAmW 93*
Oxford Sf Group *ScF&FL 92*
Oxley, Ann 1924- *WhoAmW 93*
Oxley, B.T. *ScF&FL 92*
Oxley, David Anthony *ScF&FL 92*
Oxley, Dorothy 1948- *ScF&FL 92*
Oxley, Geraldine Motta 1930- *St&PR 93, WhoAm 92*
Oxley, Greg 1948- *St&PR 93*
Oxley, John 1785?-1828 *Expl 93*
Oxley, John Thurman 1909- *WhoAm 92*
Oxley, Lawrence Augustus 1887-1973 *EncAACR*
Oxley, Michael G. 1944- *CngDr 91*
Oxley, Michael Garver 1944- *WhoAm 92*
Oxley, Philip 1922- *St&PR 93, WhoAm 92*
Oxley, Philip Royston *WhoScE 91-1*
Oxman, Bruce 1930- *WhoAm 92*
Oxman, David Craig 1941- *WhoAm 92*
Oxman, Michael Adam *Law&B 92*
Oxman, Michael Allan 1935- *WhoE 93*
Oxman, Thomas Elliot 1949- *WhoEmL 93*
Oxnam, G. Bromley 1891-1963 *BioIn 17*
Oxnam, Garfield Bromley 1891-1963 *BioIn 17*
Oxnam, Robert Bromley 1942- *WhoAm 92*
Oxnard, Charles Ernest 1933- *WhoAm 92*
Oxsen, Jo Ann 1946- *WhoEmL 93*
Oxtoby, David William 1951- *WhoAm 92*
Oxtoby, John C. 1910-1991 *BioIn 17*
Oxtoby, Robert Boynton 1921- *WhoAm 92*
Oxtoby, Willard Gurdon 1933- *ConAu 37NR*
Oyaide, Omoefe James 1942- *WhoUN 92*
Oyake, Tsuneo 1932- *WhoWor 93*
Oyama, Iwao 1842-1916 *HarEnMi*
Oyama, Oliver Neal 1959- *WhoSSW 93*
Oye, Harald Arnljot 1935- *WhoScE 91-4*
Oye-Mba, Casimir 1942- *WhoAfr, WhoWor 93*
Oyen, Forulf *WhoScE 91-4*
Oyen, Gerald J. 1940- *St&PR 93*
Oyer, Herbert Joseph 1921- *WhoAm 92*
Oyer, Roselee M. *Law&B 92*
Oyjord, Egil 1928- *WhoScE 91-4*
Oyler, James R. 1946- *St&PR 93*
Oyler, James Russell, Jr. 1946- *WhoAm 92, WhoSSW 93, WhoWor 93*
Oyler, William Kennett, III 1958- *WhoEmL 93*
Oyler, William Kent 1958- *St&PR 93*
Oyster, Carol Kathleen 1948- *WhoAmW 93*
Oyster, Robert E. *St&PR 93*
Oz, Amos *BioIn 17*
Oz, Amos 1939- *WhoWor 93*
Oz, Frank *BioIn 17*
Oz, Frank 1944- *MiSFD 9*
Oz, Frank Richard 1944- *WhoAm 92*
Oz, Halis 1950- *WhoScE 91-4*
Oza, Dipak Harshadrai 1954- *WhoEmL 93*
Ozadovski, Andrii A. 1932- *WhoUN 92*
Ozag, David 1962- *WhoE 93, WhoEmL 93*
Ozaki, Hotsumi 1901-1944 *BioIn 17*
Ozaki, Luiz Shozo 1949- *WhoWor 93*
Ozaki, Toshio 1946- *WhoWor 93*
Ozal, Turgut *BioIn 17*
Ozal, Turgut 1927- *WhoWor 93*
Ozamiz, Julio H. 1933- *WhoAsAP 91*
Ozan, Paul H. *Law&B 92*
Ozanne, James Herbert 1943- *St&PR 93, WhoAm 92*
Ozari, Yehuda 1944- *St&PR 93*
Ozark, Chilly *WhoWrEP 92*
Ozark, Edward L. 1944- *St&PR 93*
Ozaroff, Gary R. 1933- *St&PR 93, WhoAm 92*
Ozato, Sadatoshi 1930- *WhoAsAP 91*
Ozawa, Fumiyuki 1954- *WhoWor 93*
Ozawa, Ichiro *BioIn 17, NewYTBS 92 [port]*
Ozawa, Ichiro 1942- *WhoAsAP 91, WhoWor 93*
Ozawa, Jisaburo 1886-1966 *HarEnMi*
Ozawa, Katsusuke 1944- *WhoAsAP 91*
Ozawa, Kazuaki 1931- *WhoAsAP 91*
Ozawa, Kazumasa 1942- *WhoWor 93*
Ozawa, Keiya 1953- *WhoWor 93*
Ozawa, Kiyoshi 1927- *WhoAsAP 91*
Ozawa, Martha Naoko 1933- *WhoAm 92, WhoAmW 93*
Ozawa, Paul M. 1929- *St&PR 93*
Ozawa, Seiji 1935- *Baker 92, OxDcOp, WhoAm 92, WhoE 93, WhoWor 93*
Ozawa, Steve H. *Law&B 92*
Ozawa, Takayuki 1932- *WhoWor 93*
Ozawa, Tatsuo 1916- *WhoAsAP 91*
Ozbal, Hadi 1943- *WhoScE 91-4*
Ozbay, Orhan 1944- *WhoScE 91-4*
Ozbek, Rifat *BioIn 17*
Ozbirn, Willie Paul 1944- *St&PR 93*
Ozbolt, Anthony *Law&B 92*
Ozbolt, Jesse Q. 1941- *St&PR 93*
Ozbun, Jim L. *WhoAm 92*
Ozcan, Lutfi 1933- *WhoScE 91-4*
Ozdemir, Nurettin 1939- *WhoScE 91-4*
Ozeki, Sumio 1952- *WhoWor 93*
Ozeler, Ahmet 1945- *WhoScE 91-4*
Ozelkok, I. Sozer 1940- *WhoScE 91-4*
Ozelli, Tunch 1938- *WhoE 93*
Ozemir, M. Yasar 1931- *WhoScE 91-4*
Ozenbaugh, Robert B. 1952- *St&PR 93*
Ozenberger, Laura L. *Law&B 92*
Ozenda, Paul G. 1920- *WhoScE 91-2*
Ozenda, Paul Gabriel 1920- *WhoWor 93*
Ozendo, Pierre L. 1950- *St&PR 93, WhoIns 93*
Ozenfant, Amedee 1886-1966 *BioIn 17*
Ozer, Bernard *BioIn 17*
Ozer, Harvey Leon 1938- *WhoE 93*
Ozer, Jerome Stanley 1927- *WhoE 93*
Ozeri, J. Wendy 1955- *St&PR 93*
Ozernoy, Leonid Moissey 1939- *WhoAm 92, WhoWor 93*
Ozero, Brian John 1932- *WhoAm 92, WhoE 93*
Ozerov, Jurij 1921- *DrEEuF*
Ozga-Zielinska, Maria 1930- *WhoScE 91-4*
Ozguc, Atilia 1943- *WhoScE 91-4*
Ozgumus, Ahmet 1947- *WhoScE 91-4*
Ozgunen, Tuncay 1942- *WhoScE 91-4*
Ozhan, Erdal 1948- *WhoScE 91-4*
Ozick, Cynthia *BioIn 17*
Ozick, Cynthia 1928- *AmWomWr 92, JeAmFiW, JeAmHC, MagSAmL [port], ScF&FL 92, WhoAm 92, WhoAmW 93, WhoWrEP 92*
Oziel, Jerome *BioIn 17*
Oziemblewski, Felix Walter 1934- *St&PR 93*
Ozier, Irving 1938- *WhoAm 92*
Ozier, Wanda Marie Chicola 1951- *WhoSSW 93*
Ozim, Igor 1931- *Baker 92*
Ozimek, Lewis Frank 1922- *St&PR 93*
Ozinga, James Richard 1932- *ConAu 37NR*
Ozisik, Seyfi *WhoScE 91-4*
Ozkan, Suha *WhoWor 93*
Ozkan, Umit Sivrioglu 1954- *WhoWor 93*
Ozley, Marvin W. 1934- *St&PR 93*
Ozmen, Atilla 1941- *WhoWor 93*
Ozment, Steven 1939- *WhoAm 92, WhoWrEP 92*
Ozmon, Kenneth Lawrence 1931- *WhoAm 92*
Ozocak, Ramiz 1939- *WhoScE 91-4*
Ozolins, Janis Alfreds 1919- *WhoWor 93*
Ozolins, Ruth D. *Law&B 92*
Ozone, Jun 1951- *WhoWor 93*
Ozorak, Elizabeth Weiss 1957- *WhoAmW 93, WhoE 93*
Ozorowski, Edward 1941- *WhoWor 93*
Ozpeker, Isik 1937- *WhoScE 91-4*
Ozsahinoglu, Can 1939- *WhoScE 91-4*
Ozsoylu, Sinasi N. 1927- *WhoScE 91-4*
Oztunali, Onder 1935- *WhoScE 91-4*
Ozturk, Erdal 1950- *WhoScE 91-4*
Ozu, Yasujiro 1903-1963 *MiSFD 9N*
Ozvath, Rose Mary Hornik 1951- *WhoAmW 93, WhoEmL 93*

P

Paak, Carl E. 1922-1991 *BioIn 17*
Paakkala, Timo Antero 1941- *WhoWor 93*
Paakki, Jukka Pekka 1955- *WhoWor 93*
Paal, Tamas L. 1943- *WhoScE 91-4*
Paalborg, Andrew M. *Law&B 92*
Paalman, Maria Elisabeth Monica 1951- *WhoWor 93*
Paalz, Anthony L. 1924- *WhoAm 92*
Paalzow, Lennart K. 1934- *WhoScE 91-4*
Paananen, Eloise Katherine 1923- *WhoWrEP 92*
Paananen, Victor Niles 1938- *WhoAm 92*
Paap, Wouter 1908-1981 *Baker 92*
Paar, Vladimir 1942- *WhoScE 91-4*
Paardekooper, Ernst J.C. 1931- *WhoScE 91-3*
Paas, Martha White 1946- *WhoAmW 93*
Paasche, Eystein 1932- *WhoScE 91-4*
Paasio, Pertti Kullervo 1939- *WhoWor 93*
Paasivirta, Jaakko 1931- *WhoScE 91-4*
Paasonen, Pauli 1925- *WhoScE 91-4*
Paaswell, Robert Emil 1937- *WhoAm 92, WhoWor 93*
Paavilainen, Eero S.S. 1936- *WhoScE 91-4*
Paavola, Cheryl Ann 1958- *WhoAmW 93*
Paaymans, Linda K. 1961- *WhoEmL 93*
Pabellon, Josefina Llarena 1944- *WhoWor 93*
Pabian, Michael S. *Law&B 92*
Pabis, Stanislaw 1925- *WhoScE 91-4*
Pablo (Costales), Luis (Alfonso) de 1930- *Baker 92*
Pablo, de San Leocadio 1447-1520 *BioIn 17*
Pabon-Perez, Heidi 1939- *WhoAmW 93*
Pabsch, Wiegand 1932- *WhoWor 93*
Pabst, Alan Joseph 1939- *St&PR 93*
Pabst, Edmund G. 1916- *WhoAm 92*
Pabst, G.W. 1885-1967 *MiSFD 9N*
Pabst, Louis 1846-1903 *Baker 92*
Pabst, Mark L. 1946- *St&PR 93, WhoAm 92*
Pabst, Paul 1854-1897 *Baker 92*
Pabst, Richard Stuart *Law&B 92*
Pabst, Robert D. 1936- *St&PR 93*
Pabst, Thomas Edward 1958- *WhoEmL 93*
Pacala, Leon 1926- *WhoAm 92*
Pacana, Edward J. *Law&B 92*
Pacault, Adolphe 1918- *WhoScE 91-2*
Paccaud, Fred 1951- *WhoScE 91-4*
Pacchiarotti, Gasparo 1740?-1821 *Baker 92*
Pacchierotti, Gaspare 1740?-1821 *OxDcOp*
Pacchierotti, Ubaldo 1875-1916 *Baker 92*
Pacchioni, Fabio *WhoUN 92*
Pacciardi, Randolfo 1899-1991 *BioIn 17*
Paccio, Claudine Anne 1967- *WhoAmW 93*
Paccione, Christina Marie 1964- *WhoAmW 93, WhoEmL 93*
Pace, Ann L. *WhoAmW 93*
Pace, Anthony M. 1938- *St&PR 93*
Pace, Barry *BioIn 17*
Pace, Carolina Jolliff 1938- *WhoAmW 93, WhoSSW 93*
Pace, Caroline Sanderson 1942- *WhoSSW 93*
Pace, Cecile Owens 1941- *WhoAmW 93*
Pace, Charles D. 1935- *St&PR 93*
Pace, Charles Robert 1912- *WhoAm 92*
Pace, Clint W. 1943- *St&PR 93*
Pace, Craig Joseph *Law&B 92*
Pace, De Wanna Williams 1954- *WhoWrEP 92*
Pace, Denise Ann 1955- *WhoSSW 93*
Pace, E. Anne *Law&B 92*
Pace, Eric Dwight 1936- *WhoAm 92*
Pace, Giuseppe 1941- *WhoUN 92*
Pace, Harry 1884-1943 *BioIn 17*
Pace, Jan Soderman 1951- *WhoSSW 93*
Pace, John H. 1930- *St&PR 93*
Pace, John Michael 1959- *WhoEmL 93*
Pace, Jonathan 1964- *WhoWor 93*
Pace, L. Vernon 1931- *St&PR 93*
Pace, Larry Leon 1950- *WhoSSW 93*
Pace, Laura Diane 1946- *WhoAmW 93*
Pace, Leonard 1924- *WhoAm 92*
Pace, M. Ray *Law&B 92*
Pace, Norma T. *St&PR 93*
Pace, Ralph Wayne 1931- *WhoAm 92*
Pace, Richard Alan 1945- *WhoAm 92*
Pace, Robert d1989 *BioIn 17*
Pace, Robert T. *Law&B 92*
Pace, Ronald Anthony 1947- *WhoE 93*
Pace, Salvatore P. *Law&B 92*
Pace, Simone J. 1941- *WhoAmW 93*
Pace, Stanley Carter 1921- *WhoAm 92*
Pace, Stephen Shell 1918- *WhoAm 92*
Pace, Vincent Terino 1949- *WhoEmL 93*
Pace, W.A., Jr. 1932- *St&PR 93*
Pace, William Fleming 1945- *St&PR 93*
Pace, William Roy 1951- *WhoEmL 93*
Pacejka, Hans B. 1934- *WhoScE 91-3*
Pacella, John 1924- *St&PR 93*
Pacella, Patrick Paul *Law&B 92*
Paces, Tomas 1937- *WhoScE 91-4*
Pach, Walter 1883-1958 *BioIn 17*
Pach, Zsigmond Pal 1919- *WhoWor 93*
Pachan, Mary Jude Kathryn Dorothy 1933- *WhoAmW 93*
Pachciarz, Judith *BioIn 17*
Pache, Bernard 1934- *WhoWor 93*
Pache, George Roger 1948- *St&PR 93*
Pacheco, Cristina 1941- *DcMexL*
Pacheco, Eduardo Rosendo 1964- *WhoWor 93*
Pacheco, Francisco 1564-1654 *BioIn 17*
Pacheco, Glen Joseph *Law&B 92*
Pacheco, Harry Adrian 1955- *St&PR 93*
Pacheco, Jose Emilio 1939- *DcMexL, SpAmA*
Pacheco, Linda 1957- *WhoAmW 93*
Pacheco, Manuel Trinidad 1941- *HispAmA [port], WhoAm 92*
Pacheco, Margaret Mary 1962- *WhoAmW 93*
Pacheco, Patricia Linda 1953- *WhoAmW 93*
Pacheco, Rachel A. 1945- *St&PR 93*
Pacheco, Robert Joseph 1953- *St&PR 93*
Pacheco, Romualdo 1831-1899 *BioIn 17, HispAmA*
Pacheco-Ransanz, Arsenio 1932- *WhoAm 92*
Pachelbel, Charles Theodore 1690?-1750? *Baker 92*
Pachelbel, Johann 1653?-1706? *Baker 92*
Pachelbel, Wilhelm Hieronymus 1686?-1764 *Baker 92*
Pacheleque, Calisto 1957- *WhoWor 93*
Pachence, Donald M. 1936- *St&PR 93*
Pacher, Eugen E. *Law&B 92*
Pachino, Barton P. *Law&B 92*
Pachios, Harold Christy 1936- *WhoAm 92*
Pachl, Jan 1949- *WhoWor 93*
Pachler-Koschak, Marie Leopoldine 1792-1855 *Baker 92*
Pachlewski, Roman 1923- *WhoScE 91-4*
Pachman, Daniel J. 1911- *WhoAm 92*
Pachman, Louis J. 1955- *St&PR 93*
Pachmann, Vladimir de 1848-1933 *Baker 92*
Pachner, William 1915- *WhoE 93*
Pachniak, Char Kay 1953- *WhoAmW 93, WhoEmL 93*
Pacholewski, Robert Thomas 1951- *St&PR 93*
Pacholick, John Roger 1938- *St&PR 93*
Pacholski, Leszek Maciej 1944- *WhoScE 91-4*
Pacholski, Richard Francis 1947- *WhoAm 92*
Pachomij Logofet c. 1405-1484? *OxDcByz*
Pachomios c. 290-346 *OxDcByz*
Pachon, Harry 1945- *HispAmA*
Pachouri, Suresh 1952- *WhoAsAP 91*
Pachter, Hedwig d1988 *BioIn 17*
Pachter, Irwin Jacob 1925- *WhoAm 92*
Pachter, Josh 1951- *ScF&FL 92*
Pachter, Milton H. *Law&B 92*
Pachter, Wendy Susan 1954- *WhoAmW 93*
Pachtman, Norman 1939- *St&PR 93*
Pachulski, Henryk 1859-1921 *PolBiDi*
Pachulski, James G. *Law&B 92*
Pachymeres, George 1242-c. 1310 *OxDcByz*
Paci, F.G. 1948- *WhoCanL 92*
Paci, Gabriel 1944- *St&PR 93*
Pacie, Ron 1952- *WhoE 93*
Pacifico, Albert Dominick 1940- *WhoAm 92*
Pacini, Franco 1939- *WhoScE 91-3*
Pacini, Giovanni 1796-1867 *Baker 92, IntDcOp, OxDcOp*
Pacini, Leonardo 1885-1937 *Baker 92*
Pacino, Al *BioIn 17*
Pacino, Al 1940- *IntDcF 2-3 [port], WhoAm 92*
Pacio, Janet Ann 1953- *WhoAmW 93*
Paciocco, P.J. 1938- *St&PR 93*
Pacioli, Luca 1445-1523 *BioIn 17*
Pacione, Michael *WhoScE 91-1*
Paciorkiewicz, Tadeusz 1916- *Baker 92*
Pacious, Shaun F. *Law&B 92*
Paciulan, Richard Joseph *Law&B 92*
Pacius, Fredrik 1809-1891 *Baker 92*
Pack, Allen S. 1930- *St&PR 93, WhoAm 92, WhoSSW 93*
Pack, Amy Thorpe 1910-1963 *BioIn 17*
Pack, Donald Cecil 1920- *WhoWor 93*
Pack, Gary V. *Law&B 92*
Pack, Han Woung 1931- *WhoUN 92*
Pack, Howard Meade 1918- *St&PR 93*
Pack, Janet Elaine 1952- *WhoWrEP 92*
Pack, Leonard Brecher 1944- *WhoAm 92*
Pack, Lola Kathryn Lee 1924- *WhoWrEP 92*
Pack, Phoebe Katherine Finley 1907- *WhoAmW 93, WhoWor 93*
Pack, Richard Morris 1915- *WhoAm 92*
Pack, Robert M. 1929- *WhoWrEP 92*
Pack, Roy Sanghun 1964- *WhoE 93*
Pack, Spencer J. 1953- *WhoEmL 93*
Pack, Stuart Harris 1950- *WhoEmL 93*
Pack, Susan Joan 1951- *WhoAmW 93, WhoEmL 93*
Pack, Walter Frank 1916- *WhoAm 92*
Packalen, Matti Heikki Juhani 1947- *WhoWor 93*
Packard, Andrea *ScF&FL 92*
Packard, Barbara Baugh 1938- *WhoAm 92*
Packard, Daniel Mark 1955- *St&PR 93*
Packard, David *BioIn 17*
Packard, David 1912- *St&PR 93, WhoAm 92*
Packard, David L. 1958- *St&PR 93*
Packard, Edward 1931- *ScF&FL 92*
Packard, Elizabeth Parsons Ware 1816-1897 *BioIn 17*
Packard, Fanny Hance *AmWomPl*
Packard, George Quincy 1933- *St&PR 93*
Packard, George Randolph 1932- *WhoAm 92*
Packard, Harry 1914-1991 *BioIn 17*
Packard, J.W. 1926- *St&PR 93*
Packard, John B. 1945- *St&PR 93*
Packard, John Mallory 1920- *WhoAm 92*
Packard, Julie *WhoAm 92*
Packard, Marc David 1960- *WhoEmL 93*
Packard, Martin Everett 1921- *St&PR 93*
Packard, Peter Kim 1938- *WhoAm 92*
Packard, Phyllis Whitcomb 1945- *WhoAmW 93*
Packard, Ralph Kempton 1945- *St&PR 93*
Packard, Robert Charles 1919- *WhoAm 92*
Packard, Ron 1931- *CngDr 91*
Packard, Ronald 1931- *WhoAm 92*
Packard, Sandra Podolin 1942- *WhoAm 92, WhoAmW 93*
Packard, Stephen Michael 1953- *WhoEmL 93*
Packard, Thomas Norris 1943- *St&PR 93*
Packard, Vance Oakley 1914- *WhoAm 92, WhoWor 93, WhoWrEP 92*
Packard, Warren C. 1934- *St&PR 93*
Packenham, Richard Daniel 1953- *WhoEmL 93*
Packer, Al 1923- *St&PR 93*
Packer, Alferd 1842-1907 *BioIn 17*
Packer, Brad H. 1953- *St&PR 93*
Packer, J(ames) I(nnell) 1926- *ConAu 37NR*
Packer, Joan Garrett 1947- *ConAu 139, WhoAmW 93*
Packer, K.J. 1938- *WhoScE 91-1*
Packer, Katherine Helen 1918- *WhoAm 92*
Packer, Kenneth John 1938- *WhoWor 93*
Packer, Kerry Francis Bullmore 1937- *WhoWor 93*
Packer, Mark Barry 1944- *WhoAm 92*
Packer, Mary A. 1952- *WhoAmW 93, WhoWor 93*
Packer, Milton Isaac 1919- *St&PR 93*
Packer, Rekha Desai 1955- *WhoAm 92*
Packer, Richard A. 1957- *St&PR 93*
Packer, Richard James 1965- *WhoWor 93*
Packer, Robert R. 1934- *St&PR 93*
Packer, Vin *BioIn 17, ConAu 37NR, MajAI*
Packer, William Fisher 1807-1870 *BioIn 17*
Packer, William Joseph 1939- *St&PR 93*
Packert, Gayla Beth 1953- *WhoEmL 93*

Packham, Marrian Aitchison 1927- *WhoAmW 93*
Packham, Ronald Frederick 1929- *WhoScE 91-1*
Packie, Susan 1946- *WhoWrEP 92*
Packman, Leonard Clive *WhoScE 91-1*
Packwood, Bob 1932- *CngDr 91, WhoAm 92*
Packwood, Richard B. 1944- *St&PR 93*
Pacovic, Nikola 1927- *WhoScE 91-4*
Pacovska, Kveta *BioIn 17*
Pacs, Istvan 1946- *WhoScE 91-4*
Pacter, Paul Allan 1943- *WhoAm 92*
Pacula, Carol S. *Law&B 92*
Pacun, Norman 1932- *WhoAm 92*
Pacurar, Ion 1928- *WhoScE 91-4*
Pacynski, Rick Alan *Law&B 92*
Paczelt, Istvan 1939- *WhoScE 91-4*
Paczynski, Bohdan 1940- *WhoAm 92*
Pad, Peter *MajAI*
Padavick, David William 1940- *St&PR 93*
Padberg, Daniel Ivan 1931- *WhoAm 92*
Padberg, Harriet Ann 1922- *WhoAmW 93*
Padbury, E. Helen 1957- *WhoScE 91-4*
Paddack, Ronald Lloyd 1938- *WhoSSW 93*
Paddack, Stephen Joseph 1934- *WhoE 93*
Paddack, Susan Craig 1961- *WhoSSW 93*
Padden, Anthony Aloysius, Jr. 1949- *WhoEmL 93*
Padden, Kathleen Griffin 1951- *WhoAmW 93*
Padden, Sarah 1881-1967 *SweetSg C [port]*
Padden, Thomas C. 1951- *St&PR 93*
Paddick, Garry E. 1937- *St&PR 93*
Paddison, Patricia Louise 1951- *WhoEmL 93*
Paddock, Austin Joseph 1908- *WhoAm 92*
Paddock, James Stephen 1941- *St&PR 93*
Paddock, John *WhoAm 92*
Paddock, M. David 1933- *St&PR 93*
Paddock, Paul Bradley 1942- *WhoSSW 93*
Paddock, Robert Young 1917- *St&PR 93*
Paddock, Stuart R., Jr. *WhoAm 92*
Paddock, Susan Blair 1957- *WhoAmW 93*
Paddock, Susan Mary 1946- *WhoAmW 93*
Paddon, Michael Emmett *Law&B 92*
Paddon, R. Stephen *Law&B 92*
Paddrik, Peter Endel 1947- *WhoEmL 93*
Padegs, Juris *Law&B 92*
Paden, Carter N., Jr. 1927- *St&PR 93*
Paden, Jack 1931- *WhoSSW 93*
Paden, John Wilburn 1933-1990 *BioIn 17*
Paden, Roberta L. 1938- *WhoE 93*
Paderewska, Helena 1856-1934 *PolBiDi*
Paderewski, Clarence Joseph 1908- *WhoAm 92*
Paderewski, Ignace Jan 1860-1941 *BioIn 17*
Paderewski, Ignacy (Jan) 1860-1941 *Baker 92, DcTwHis, PolBiDi [port]*
Padet, Jacques 1941- *WhoScE 91-2*
Padget, Pamela Estes 1947- *WhoSSW 93*
Padgett, Charles *Law&B 92*
Padgett, David Lee 1950- *WhoSSW 93*
Padgett, Don K. 1949- *WhoAm 92*
Padgett, Frank David 1923- *WhoAm 92*
Padgett, George A. *Law&B 92*
Padgett, George A. 1932- *St&PR 93*
Padgett, George Arthur 1932- *WhoAm 92*
Padgett, John David 1958- *WhoEmL 93*
Padgett, John David 1968- *WhoSSW 93*
Padgett, Kenneth M. 1944- *St&PR 93*
Padgett, Lawrence Joe 1945- *WhoSSW 93*
Padgett, Ron 1942- *WhoWrEP 92*
Padgett, Shirley Perry 1934- *WhoAmW 93*
Padgett, Stephen 1951- *ConAu 139*
Padgett, W.D. 1927- *St&PR 93*
Padgett, William R. 1932- *St&PR 93*
Padgitt, Willie Day, Mrs. *AmWomPl*
Padhy, Sisir Kumar 1966- *WhoSSW 93*
Padia, Alyssa 1959- *WhoAmW 93*
Padikal, Thomas N. 1947- *WhoE 93*
Padilla, Amado Manuel 1942- *HispAmA*
Padilla, Carlos M. 1944- *WhoAsAP 91*
Padilla, D. Laurence *Law&B 92*
Padilla, Donald G. 1921- *WhoAm 92*
Padilla, Elaine S. *WhoAmW 93*
Padilla, Ernesto Chavez 1944- *DcLB 122 [port]*
Padilla, Heberto 1932- *BioIn 17, SpAmA*
Padilla, Hernan *DcCPCAm*
Padilla, Irma Madrid 1957- *WhoAmW 93*
Padilla, James Earl 1953- *WhoAm 92, WhoE 93, WhoEmL 93*
Padilla, Joe *BioIn 17*
Padilla, Laureano 1942- *WhoWor 93*
Padilla, Lola Artot de 1876-1933 *Baker 92* *See Also* Artot, Desiree 1835-1907 *OxDcOp*
Padilla, Lorraine Marie 1952- *WhoEmL 93, WhoWor 93*
Padilla, Luiz Roberto Nunes 1958- *WhoWor 93*
Padilla, Mario Alfonso 1936- *WhoE 93*
Padilla, Mary Louise 1943- *WhoSSW 93*
Padilla, Raymond O. 1951- *St&PR 93*
Padilla, Steven Michael 1949- *St&PR 93*
Padilla Rush, Rigoberto *DcCPCAm*
Padilla y Ramos, Mariano *OxDcOp*
Padilla y Ramos, Mariano 1842-1906 *Baker 92*
Padiyara, Anthony Cardinal 1921- *WhoWor 93*
Padjen, Ann E. *Law&B 92*
Padleschat, Joyce A. *Law&B 92*
Padley, G. Barry *St&PR 93*
Padmini, R. 1933- *WhoUN 92*
Padnes, David R. *Law&B 92*
Padnos, Jeffrey Stephen 1948- *St&PR 93*
Padnos, Norman 1937- *WhoE 93*
Padnos, Seymour K. 1920- *St&PR 93*
Padoan, Giorgio 1933- *WhoWor 93*
Padon, Ella Florence *AmWomPl*
Pados, Frank John, Jr. 1944- *WhoAm 92*
Padovano, Anthony Thomas 1934- *WhoAm 92, WhoWor 93*
Padovano, Rose Marie 1937- *WhoE 93*
Padrick, Comer Woodward, Jr. 1926- *WhoAm 92*
Padron, Armando 1959- *WhoSSW 93*
Padua, Eric 1954- *WhoEmL 93*
Paduano, James A. 1942- *St&PR 93*
Padula, Cynthia Anne 1951- *WhoAmW 93*
Padula, Fred David 1937- *WhoAm 92*
Padulo, Louis 1936- *WhoAm 92*
Paeffgen, Manfred Johannes 1942- *WhoUN 92*
Paek Nam Chi 1945- *WhoAsAP 91*
Paeniu, Bikenibeu *WhoWor 93*
Paepe, Roland 1934- *WhoScE 91-2*
Paeper, Veronica 1944- *WhoWor 93*
Paer, Ferdinando 1771-1839 *Baker 92, IntDcOp, OxDcOp*
Paer, Herbert *St&PR 93*
Paes, Leander *BioIn 17*
Paese, Augie 1931- *St&PR 93*
Paes-Leme, Paulo Jorge Serpa 1948- *WhoWor 93*
Paetsch, Roland 1946- *WhoScE 91-2*
Paetus, Lucius Caesennius fl. 61-73 *HarEnMi*
Paetz Gen. Schieck, Hans Georg 1938- *WhoWor 93*
Paetzold, Horst 1926- *WhoScE 91-3*
Paetzold, Peter 1935- *WhoScE 91-3*
Paez, Manuel Jose 1944- *WhoWor 93*
Paez, Pedro d1622 *Expl 93*
Paez, Rafael Roberto 1931- *WhoWor 93*
Paffenbarger, Ralph *BioIn 17*
Paffenbarger, Ralph Seal, Jr. 1922- *WhoAm 92*
Paffenberger, Edith M. *AmWomPl*
Paffett, Pamela Elaine 1952- *WhoAmW 93*
Pafford, Leon Keith *Law&B 92*
Paffrath, Stephen Gerard 1953- *WhoE 93*
Pafko, Andrew 1921- *BiDAMSp 1989*
Pagan, John Ruston 1951- *WhoSSW 93*
Paganelli, Giuseppe Antonio 1710-c. 1762 *Baker 92*
Paganelli, Leonardo 1954- *WhoWor 93*
Paganes, R.M. 1956- *St&PR 93*
Paganini, Niccolo 1782-1840 *Baker 92*
Paganis, K. George 1937- *WhoIns 93*
Paganis, Karen Tillett *Law&B 92*
Pagano, Anthony Frank 1948- *WhoEmL 93*
Pagano, Carmela Victoria 1942- *WhoAmW 93*
Pagano, Filippo Frank 1939- *WhoSSW 93*
Pagano, Frank M. 1956- *St&PR 93*
Pagano, George Anthony 1952- *WhoE 93*
Pagano, Jo Anne 1946- *WhoAmW 93, WhoE 93*
Pagano, Joseph Stephen 1931- *WhoAm 92*
Pagano, Marco 1956- *WhoWor 93*
Pagano, Mary 1958- *St&PR 93*
Pagano, Michael J. 1939- *St&PR 93*
Pagano, Michael Pro 1946- *WhoSSW 93*
Pagano, Paul J. 1943- *St&PR 93*
Pagano, Richard C. *Law&B 92*
Pagano, Robert English 1948- *St&PR 93*
Pagano, Ross Joseph 1942- *WhoSSW 93*
Pagano, Sal J. *St&PR 93*
Pagan-Saez, Heriberto 1933- *WhoAm 92*
Paganucci, Paul D. 1931- *St&PR 93*
Paganucci, Paul Donnelly 1931- *WhoAm 92*
Pagaza, Arcadio 1839-1918 *DcMexL*
Page, Alan C. 1945- *BioIn 17*
Page, Alan G. 1949- *St&PR 93*
Page, Albert Lee 1927- *WhoAm 92*
Page, Allan R. 1947- *St&PR 93*
Page, Ann 1958- *WhoAmW 93, WhoEmL 93, WhoWor 93*
Page, Anne Ruth 1949- *WhoAmW 93, WhoWor 93*
Page, Armand Ernest 1955- *WhoSSW 93*
Page, Arthur Anthony 1922- *WhoWor 93*
Page, Arthur Hallett, IV 1955- *WhoE 93*
Page, Austin P. 1936- *St&PR 93, WhoAm 92*
Page, Barbara B. 1939- *St&PR 93*
Page, Benjamin Bakewell 1939- *WhoE 93*
Page, Benjamin Ingrim 1940- *WhoAm 92*
Page, Bettie *BioIn 17*
Page, Bill 1953- *ScF&FL 92*
Page, Billy d1866 *BioIn 17*
Page, Calvin A. 1922- *St&PR 93*
Page, Caroline Jane 1950- *WhoAmW 93*
Page, Charles H. d1992 *NewYTBS 92*
Page, Charles H(unt) 1909-1992 *ConAu 136*
Page, Charles Hunt 1909-1992 *BioIn 17*
Page, Christopher H. 1952- *ConAu 137*
Page, Christopher Kenneth 1966- *WhoE 93*
Page, Christopher Lyndon *WhoScE 91-1*
Page, Christopher N. 1942- *WhoScE 91-1*
Page, Clarence 1947- *ConBlB 4 [port]*
Page, Clarence E. 1947- *WhoAm 92*
Page, D. Edgar 1935- *WhoScE 91-3*
Page, David A. *St&PR 93*
Page, David K. 1933- *St&PR 93, WhoAm 92*
Page, David L. 1934- *St&PR 93*
Page, Dorothy *SweetSg C*
Page, Dozzie Lyons 1921- *WhoAmW 93*
Page, Earl Michael 1950- *WhoEmL 93*
Page, Earle Christmas Grafton 1880-1961 *DcTwHis*
Page, Edith Bennett 1937- *WhoAmW 93*
Page, Eleanor *MajAI*
Page, Ellis Batten 1924- *WhoAm 92, WhoSSW 93*
Page, Ernest 1927- *WhoAm 92*
Page, Francis Hilton 1905-1989 *BioIn 17*
Page, Francis Michael *WhoScE 91-1*
Page, Frederick West 1932- *WhoAm 92*
Page, Gale Charles 1943- *WhoSSW 93*
Page, Garilou *Law&B 92*
Page, Garrett David 1955- *WhoEmL 93*
Page, Gene *SoulM*
Page, Genevieve 1927- *WhoWor 93*
Page, George Keith 1917- *WhoAm 92*
Page, George W. 1956- *St&PR 93*
Page, Gerald W. 1939- *ScF&FL 92*
Page, Geraldine 1924-1987 *IntDcF 2-3*
Page, Gordon W. *St&PR 93*
Page, Harry Robert 1915- *WhoAm 92*
Page, "Hot Lips" (Oran Thaddeus) 1908-1954 *Baker 92*
Page, Ian 1960- *ScF&FL 92*
Page, Irvine H. 1901-1991 *BioIn 17*
Page, James Benjamin 1952- *WhoE 93*
Page, James W. 1944- *St&PR 93*
Page, Janice Ellen 1948- *WhoAmW 93*
Page, Jimmy *BioIn 17*
Page, Jimmy 1945- *Baker 92*
Page, Joel R., Jr. *Law&B 92*
Page, John c. 1760-1812 *Baker 92*
Page, John David 1950- *WhoEmL 93*
Page, John Hall d1990 *BioIn 17*
Page, John Henry, Jr. 1923- *WhoAm 92*
Page, John Upshur Dennis *BioIn 17*
Page, Jonathan R. 1946- *St&PR 93*
Page, Kate Stearns 1873- *AmWomPl*
Page, Katherine Hall 1947- *ConAu 136*
Page, Kathleen Barden 1946- *WhoAmW 93*
Page, Kathleen R.S. *Law&B 92*
Page, Kathy 1958- *ScF&FL 92*
Page, Ken *WhoScE 91-1*
Page, Larry Keith 1933- *WhoAm 92*
Page, Linda Kay 1943- *WhoAm 92, WhoAmW 93*
Page, Lorne Albert 1921- *WhoAm 92*
Page, Lot B. 1923-1990 *BioIn 17*
Page, Louis 1914-1990 *BioIn 17*
Page, Magdalen Elizabeth 1952- *WhoWor 93*
Page, Marcus William 1937- *WhoAm 92*
Page, Martin Robert 1944- *St&PR 93*
Page, Mary Shaw *AmWomPl*
Page, Mary Stancill 1958- *WhoAmW 93*
Page, Melvin Eugene 1944- *WhoSSW 93*
Page, Michael F. 1922- *ScF&FL 92*
Page, Michael I. *WhoScE 91-1*
Page, Michael William 1953- *St&PR 93*
Page, Michel 1940- *WhoAm 92*
Page, Morry *Law&B 92*
Page, Norvell W. 1906-1961 *ScF&FL 92*
Page, Oscar C. 1939- *WhoAm 92, WhoSSW 93*
Page, P.K. 1916- *BioIn 17, ScF&FL 92, WhoCanL 92*
Page, P(atricia) K(athleen) 1916- *WhoWrEP 92*
Page, Pamela *BlkAmWO, MiSFD 9*
Page, Patricia Ann 1941- *WhoAmW 93*
Page, Patricia Kathleen 1916- *BioIn 17*
Page, Patti 1927- *Baker 92*
Page, Paul Collins 1945- *WhoAm 92*
Page, Philip Charles 1955- *WhoWor 93*
Page, Philip Ronald 1951- *WhoWor 93*
Page, Phillip Edward 1949- *WhoEmL 93*
Page, Pierre *WhoAm 92, WhoE 93*
Page, Ralph E. d1991 *BioIn 17*
Page, Reba Neukom 1942- *ConAu 139*
Page, Rebecca Lee 1950- *St&PR 93*
Page, Richard Morton 1932- *WhoAm 92*
Page, Richard S. 1937- *WhoAm 92*
Page, Richard W. 1947- *St&PR 93*
Page, Robert 1927- *Baker 92*
Page, Robert Henry 1927- *WhoAm 92, WhoSSW 93, WhoWor 93*
Page, Robert Lee 1945- *WhoSSW 93*
Page, Robert Morris 1903-1992 *BioIn 17, CurBio 92N, NewYTBS 92 [port]*
Page, Robert Wesley 1927- *WhoAm 92*
Page, Roy Christopher 1932- *WhoAm 92*
Page, Roy William 1947- *St&PR 93*
Page, Ruth *BioIn 17*
Page, Ruth 1899-1991 *AnObit 1991*
Page, Ruth Hornby d1991 *BioIn 17*
Page, Ruth W. 1921- *WhoWrEP 92*
Page, Sally Jacquelyn 1943- *WhoWor 93*
Page, Sara E.R. *Law&B 92*
Page, Stephen Franklin 1940- *St&PR 93, WhoAm 92*
Page, Stephen Jeffrey Lawrence 1955- *WhoWor 93*
Page, Steven Lynn *Law&B 92*
Page, Susan *WhoWrEP 92*
Page, Theda W. *Law&B 92*
Page, Thomas 1942- *ScF&FL 92*
Page, Thomas A. 1933- *St&PR 93*
Page, Thomas Alexander 1933- *WhoAm 92*
Page, Thomas Nelson 1853-1922 *GayN*
Page, Thornton Leigh 1913- *WhoAm 92, WhoSSW 93*
Page, Tommy *BioIn 17*
Page, Trevor F. *WhoScE 91-1*
Page, Valda Denise 1958- *WhoAmW 93*
Page, Vicki *ConAu 39NR*
Page, Walter Hines 1855-1918 *BioIn 17, GayN*
Page, William 1811-1885 *BioIn 17*
Page, William C., Jr. 1939- *WhoAm 92*
Page, William Howard 1929- *WhoWrEP 92*
Page, William Marion 1917- *WhoAm 92*
Page, William Noble 1928- *St&PR 93*
Page, William R. *ScF&FL 92*
Page, Willis *WhoAm 92*
Pagel, Beverly Jean 1953- *WhoAmW 93*
Pagel, William Rush 1901- *WhoAm 92*
Pagelow, Stephen W. 1950- *St&PR 93*
Pagels, Elaine Hiesey *WhoAm 92*
Pagels, Elaine Hiesey 1943- *WhoWrEP 92*
Pagen, William Roland 1921- *St&PR 93*
Pagendarm, William F. 1949- *St&PR 93*
Pagenkopf, Andrea L. 1942- *WhoAmW 93*
Pagenkopf, Robert C. 1929- *St&PR 93*
Pagenstert, Gottfried 1928- *WhoWor 93*
Pages, M. *WhoScE 91-2*
Pages, Robert Charles Henri 1931- *WhoWor 93*
Paget, Allen Maxwell 1919-1992 *WhoAm 92*
Paget, Clarence 1909-1991 *BioIn 17, ScF&FL 92*
Paget, Debra *SweetSg D [port]*
Paget, Henry William 1768-1854 *HarEnMi*
Paget, James Robert 1942- *St&PR 93*
Paget, Richard M. 1913-1991 *BioIn 17*
Paget, Violet *ScF&FL 92*
Page-Wright, Josephine *AmWomPl*
Paglia, Camille 1947- *BioIn 17, CurBio 92 [port], News 92 [port], -92-3 [port], WhoAmW 93*
Pagliarani, Elio 1927- *DcLB 128 [port]*
Pagliardi, Giovanni Maria 1637-1702 *OxDcOp*
Pagliaro, Harold Emil 1925- *WhoAm 92, WhoE 93*
Pagliaro, James Domenic 1951- *WhoEmL 93*
Paglio, Lydia Elizabeth *WhoAm 92, WhoWrEP 92*
Paglio, Trish Anne 1945- *WhoAmW 93*
Pagliughi, Lina 1907-1980 *Baker 92, IntDcOp, OxDcOp*
Pagni, Albert Frank 1935- *WhoWor 93*
Pagni, Patrick John 1942- *WhoAm 92*
Pagnol, Marcel 1895-1974 *BioIn 17, MiSFD 9N*
Pagnozzi, Richard Douglas 1947- *St&PR 93, WhoIns 93*
Pagomenos *OxDcByz*
Pagonis, Gus *BioIn 17*
Pagonis, William G. 1941- *ConAu 139*
Pagonis, William Gust 1941- *WhoAm 92*
Pagony, Hubert 1925- *WhoScE 91-4*
Pagos, George Christopher *Law&B 92*
Pagsibigan, Abelardo y Balallo, Jr. 1956- *WhoWor 93*
Pagter, Carl Richard *Law&B 92*
Pagter, Carl Richard 1934- *St&PR 93, WhoAm 92*
Pahadia, Shanti 1936- *WhoAsAP 91*
Pahissa, Jaime 1880-1969 *Baker 92*
Pahl, Charles E. 1927- *St&PR 93*
Pahl, David R. *Law&B 92*
Pahl, Dennis *ScF&FL 92*
Pahl, Gerhard 1925- *WhoScE 91-3*
Pahl, Joy L. 1930- *St&PR 93*
Pahl, Kurt Gardner 1940- *St&PR 93*
Pahl, Manfred H. 1940- *WhoScE 91-3*

Pahl, Teresa Louise 1955- *WhoAmW 93*
Pahlavi, Mohammed Reza, Shah of Iran 1919-1980 *BioIn 17*
Pahlavi, Muhammad Reza Shah 1918-1980 *DcTwHis*
Pahlavi, Reza Shah 1878-1944 *DcTwHis*
Pahlow, Mark *BioIn 17*
Pahlsson, Birgit Monica 1936- *WhoWor 93*
Pahule, Edward Joseph 1957- *WhoWrEP 92*
Pai, Anantha M. 1931- *WhoAm 92*
Pai, Mohan 1941- *St&PR 93*
Pai, Shih I. 1913- *WhoE 93*
Paic, Guy 1937- *WhoScE 91-4*
Pai Ch'ung-hsi 1893-1966 *HarEnMi*
Paicopolos, Ernest Michael 1951- *WhoE 93, WhoEmL 93*
Paidas, George Peter 1946- *St&PR 93*
Paidoussis, Michael Pandeli 1935- *WhoAm 92*
Paiement, Andre L. *Law&B 92*
Paier, Adolf A., Jr. 1938- *St&PR 93*
Paier, Adolf Arthur 1938- *WhoAm 92*
Paiewonsky, Michael 1939- *ConAu 137*
Paiewonsky, Ralph 1907-1991 *BioIn 17*
Paige, Alvin 1934- *WhoE 93, WhoWor 93*
Paige, Anita Parker 1908- *WhoAmW 93, WhoE 93, WhoWor 93*
Paige, Cheryl Lee 1953- *WhoAmW 93*
Paige, Edward George Sydney *WhoScE 91-1*
Paige, Emmett, Jr. 1931- *AfrAmBi*
Paige, Glenn Durland 1929- *WhoAm 92, WhoWor 93*
Paige, H.H. *Law&B 92*
Paige, Hilliard Wegner 1919- *WhoAm 92*
Paige, Janis 1923- *BioIn 17*
Paige, Joseph Dale 1962- *BioIn 17*
Paige, Kevin *BioIn 17*
Paige, L. Stanley *Law&B 92*
Paige, Leroy Robert 1906-1982 *AfrAmBi*
Paige, Lisa Chaney 1954- *WhoAmW 93*
Paige, Norma 1922- *St&PR 93, WhoAm 92, WhoAmW 93*
Paige, Randolph Eugene 1952- *WhoE 93*
Paige, Richard *ScF&FL 92*
Paige, Richard Bruce 1949- *WhoAm 92*
Paige, Richard D. 1949- *St&PR 93*
Paige, Satchel *BioIn 17*
Paige, Susanne Ruiz 1952- *WhoAmW 93*
Paige, Vivian Jo-Ann 1960- *WhoAmW 93, WhoEmL 93*
Paigeer, Sayed Ekram 1946- *WhoAsAP 91*
Paigen, Beverly *BioIn 17*
Paigen, Kenneth 1927- *WhoAm 92, WhoE 93*
Paik, Byung-Dong 1936- *Baker 92*
Paik, Florence Paik 1922- *WhoAmW 93*
Paik, James S. 1950- *WhoE 93*
Paik, John Kee 1934- *WhoWor 93*
Paik, Kun-Woo 1946- *Baker 92*
Paik, Nam June *BioIn 17*
Paik, Nam June 1932- *Baker 92*
Paik, Young-Ki 1953- *WhoWor 93*
Paikeday, Thomas M. 1926- *WhoWor 93*
Paikert, Geza Charles 1902-1990 *BioIn 17*
Paikin, Lawrence S. 1933- *St&PR 93*
Paikowsky, Sandra Roslyn 1945- *WhoAm 92, WhoE 93*
Paillard, Jacques 1920- *WhoScE 91-2*
Paille, Antoine *BioIn 17*
Paillet, Frederick Lawrence 1946- *WhoEmL 93*
Paillet, Romain 1925- *WhoScE 91-2*
Pailliard, Jean-Francois 1928- *Baker 92*
Pailloz, Valerie Kennedy 1955- *WhoAmW 93*
Pain, Barry 1864-1928 *ScF&FL 92*
Pain, Charles Leslie 1913- *WhoAm 92*
Pain, Geoffrey Norman 1954- *WhoWor 93*
Pain, George H. *Law&B 92*
Pain, Larry *Law&B 92*
Pain, Roger H. *WhoScE 91-1*
Paine, Alan John *WhoScE 91-1*
Paine, Andrew J., Jr. 1937- *St&PR 93, WhoAm 92*
Paine, Bruce Edwin 1933- *WhoE 93*
Paine, C.W. Eliot 1936- *St&PR 93*
Paine, Charles William Eliot 1936- *WhoAm 92*
Paine, Dwight Milton 1931- *WhoE 93*
Paine, Frederick Camp *Law&B 92*
Paine, James Carriger 1924- *WhoSSW 93*
Paine, Jennie E. *AmWomPl*
Paine, John Knowles 1839-1906 *Baker 92*
Paine, Lauran 1916- *ScF&FL 92*
Paine, Lawrence *Law&B 92*
Paine, Michael *ScF&FL 92*
Paine, Natalie deWolf d1992 *NewYTBS 92*
Paine, R.M. 1914- *St&PR 93*
Paine, Ralph Delahaye 1906-1991 *BioIn 17*
Paine, Robert Treat 1933- *WhoAm 92*
Paine, Susan Douglas *Law&B 92*
Paine, Thomas 1737-1809 *BioIn 17, JrnUS*
Paine, Thomas O. 1921-1992 *NewYTBS 92 [port]*
Paine, Thomas Otten 1921- *St&PR 93*
Paine, Thomas Otten 1921-1992 *BioIn 17, CurBio 92N*
Painleve, Jean 1902-1989 *BioIn 17*
Painleve, Paul 1863-1933 *BioIn 17*
Paino, Felix A. 1939- *St&PR 93*
Painter, Allen Hall 1907- *St&PR 93*
Painter, Benjamin David 1924- *St&PR 93*
Painter, Charlotte *WhoWrEP 92*
Painter, Charlotte 1926- *ScF&FL 92*
Painter, David L. 1949- *St&PR 93*
Painter, Dewey Earl, Sr. 1941- *WhoSSW 93*
Painter, Gayle Stanford 1941- *WhoSSW 93*
Painter, Jack 1944- *St&PR 93*
Painter, Jack Timberlake 1930- *WhoAm 92*
Painter, Jack W. *Law&B 92*
Painter, John Hoyt 1934- *WhoAm 92*
Painter, John William 1929- *WhoAm 92*
Painter, Linda Robinson 1940- *WhoAmW 93*
Painter, Mary E. 1920- *WhoWor 93*
Painter, Mary S. d1991 *BioIn 17*
Painter, Michael Joseph 1957- *WhoEmL 93*
Painter, Michael Robert 1935- *WhoAm 92*
Painter, Pamela 1941- *WhoAmW 93*
Painter, Richard M. 1945- *St&PR 93*
Painter, Susan Ellen 1957- *WhoEmL 93*
Painter, Thomas Jay 1944- *St&PR 93*
Painter, Trina *BioIn 17*
Painter, William 1838-1906 *GayN*
Painter, William Hall 1927- *WhoAm 92*
Painting, Rodger T. 1938- *St&PR 93, WhoIns 93*
Painton, Edith F.A.U. Palmer 1878- *AmWomPl*
Painton, Ira Wayne 1917- *WhoAm 92*
Painton, Russell E. *Law&B 92*
Painton, Russell Elliott 1940- *St&PR 93, WhoAm 92*
Painvin, Jean-Marie 1951- *St&PR 93*
Painvin, Pierre Marie 1925- *WhoWor 93*
Pair, Joyce Morrow 1931- *WhoSSW 93*
Pair, Paul Milton 1898- *WhoAm 92*
Pairin Kitingan, Yab Datuk Seri Joseph 1940- *WhoAsAP 91*
Pairo, Jane M. d1991 *BioIn 17*
Pais, Abraham 1918- *WhoAm 92*
Pais, Istvan 1923- *WhoScE 91-4*
Pais, Josh *BioIn 17*
Pais, Randall M. *Law&B 92*
Pais, Tom 1945- *WhoAsAP 91*
Paisible, Louis Henri 1748-1782 *Baker 92*
Paisiello, Giovanni 1740-1816 *Baker 92, IntDcOp [port], OxDcOp*
Paisley, Ian R.K. 1926- *BioIn 17*
Paisley, Ian Richard Kyle 1926- *DcTwHis, WhoWor 93*
Paisley, J. Scott *Law&B 92*
Paisley, Melvyn 1924- *ConAu 139*
Paisley, T. E., III 1947- *WhoAm 92*
Paisley, Vicki *ConAu 139*
Paisner, Anna d1991 *BioIn 17*
Paisner, Bruce L. 1942- *St&PR 93*
Paisner, Bruce Lawrence 1942- *WhoAm 92*
Paisner, Claire Vivian 1933- *WhoAmW 93, WhoE 93*
Paisner, Martin Jay 1956- *WhoE 93*
Paiss, Doris Bell 1929- *WhoAmW 93, WhoE 93, WhoWor 93*
Pait, Gloria Ann 1948- *WhoAmW 93*
Pait, Larry Richard 1954- *WhoEmL 93*
Paita, Carlos 1932- *Baker 92*
Paiva, Jean 1944-1989 *ScF&FL 92*
Paiva, Joseph Moura 1955- *WhoE 93, WhoEmL 93, WhoWor 93*
Paiva, Manuel 1943- *WhoScE 91-2, WhoWor 93*
Paiva, Ronaldo Fonseca de 1955- *WhoWor 93*
Paivanen, Juhani *WhoScE 91-4*
Paiva Weed, Marie Teresa 1959- *WhoAmW 93*
Paivinen, Risto T.M. 1952- *WhoScE 91-4*
Paivio, Allan Urho 1925- *WhoAm 92*
Paiz, Catherine Jean 1957- *WhoAmW 93*
Pajak, David Joseph 1956- *WhoE 93, WhoWor 93*
Pajak, John J. *WhoAm 92*
Pajak, John Joseph 1935- *St&PR 93*
Pajakkala, Pekka *WhoScE 91-4*
Pajda, Thomas A. *Law&B 92*
Pajetta, Giancarlo 1911-1990 *BioIn 17*
Pajor, Robert E. 1937- *WhoAm 92*
Pajot, Gilles-Etienne 1958- *WhoWor 93*
Pajszczyk-Kieszkiewicz, Teresa 1930- *WhoScE 91-4*
Pajunen, Aarne Veikko 1939- *WhoScE 91-4*
Pajunen, Esko 1945- *WhoScE 91-4*
Pajunen, Esko Juhani 1945- *WhoScE 91-4*
Pajunen, Grazyna Anna 1951- *WhoAmW 93, WhoEmL 93*
Pajunen, V. Ilmari 1936- *WhoScE 91-4*
Pak, Chung K. *Law&B 92*
Pak, Eulyong 1925- *WhoWor 93*
Pak, Hyung Woong 1932- *WhoAm 92, WhoWrEP 92*
Pakalla, Paul A. 1922- *St&PR 93*
Pakalns, Gail Parshall 1945- *WhoE 93*
Pakan, Patricia Marie 1931- *WhoE 93*
Pakarinen, Maikki 1871-1929 *See* Jarnefelt, (Edvard) Armas 1869-1958 *Baker 92*
Pakasinski, James *St&PR 93*
Pake, George Edward 1924- *WhoAm 92*
Pakeer Mohamed, E.S.M. 1937- *WhoAsAP 91*
Pakel, Stanley Scott 1950- *St&PR 93*
Pakenham, Edward Michael 1778-1815 *HarEnMi*
Pakenham, Elizabeth Harman 1906- *BioIn 17*
Pakenham, Kevin John 1947- *WhoWor 93*
Paker, Yakup *WhoScE 91-1*
Pakhmutova, Alexandra (Nikolaievna) 1929- *Baker 92*
Pakiser, Louis Charles, Jr. 1919- *WhoAm 92*
Pakman, Leonard Marvin 1933- *WhoE 93*
Pakosta, Anthony 1941- *St&PR 93*
Pakou, Athena 1953- *WhoWor 93*
Pakourianos *OxDcByz*
Pak Song-chol 1913- *WhoWor 93*
Paksoy, H. B. 1948- *WhoE 93*
Pakula, Alan J. 1928- *MiSFD 9, WhoAm 92*
Pakula, Hannah (Cohn) 1933- *ConAu 139*
Pakula, Randall H. 1924- *St&PR 93*
Pal, Charlene *Law&B 92*
Pal, George 1908-1980 *MiSFD 9N, ScF&FL 92*
Pal, Lenard 1925- *WhoScE 91-4, WhoWor 93*
Pal, P.K. *Law&B 92*
Pal, P.K. 1936- *St&PR 93*
Pal, Prabir Kumar 1936- *WhoAm 92*
Pal, Pratapaditya 1935- *WhoAm 92*
Pala, Ted *Law&B 92*
Palabrica, Theresa Marie 1957- *WhoAmW 93*
Palacino, Richard A. *Law&B 92*
Palacio, June Rose Payne 1940- *WhoAmW 93*
Palacio, Pablo 1906-1947 *SpAmA*
Palacios, Adela 1908- *DcMexL*
Palacios, Emmanuel 1906- *DcMexL*
Palacios, Juan Antonio 1941- *WhoWor 93*
Palacios, Lucila 1902- *SpAmA*
Palacios, May Husni 1926- *WhoAmW 93*
Palacios, Pedro Pablo 1953- *WhoEmL 93*
Palacol, Magdaleno M. 1918- *WhoAsAP 91*
Palade, George Emil 1912- *WhoAm 92, WhoWor 93*
Paladilhe, Emile 1844-1926 *Baker 92*
Paladino, Daniel R. *Law&B 92, WhoAm 92*
Paladino, Daniel Ralph 1943- *St&PR 93*
Paladino, Francis E. 1935- *St&PR 93*
Paladino, Hugo Robert 1929- *St&PR 93*
Paladino, Jeanette M. *Law&B 92*
Paladino, Mimmo *BioIn 17*
Paladino, Raymond Anthony 1949- *WhoE 93*
Palagaino, Vincent F. 1940- *St&PR 93*
Palagonia, Chris *St&PR 93*
Palagonia, Joseph Peter 1957- *St&PR 93*
Palagonia, Peter Walter 1961- *WhoE 93*
Palagyi, Andras 1946- *WhoScE 91-4*
Palahnuk, Donald Walter, Jr. 1965- *WhoSSW 93*
Palaia, Franc Dominic 1949- *WhoEmL 93*
Palaima, Thomas Gerard 1951- *WhoAm 92*
Palaiologos *OxDcByz*
Palamar, Dave 1953- *WhoE 93*
Palamar, Mary Coyle 1940- *WhoE 93*
Palamara, Francis J. 1925- *St&PR 93*
Palamara, J. Francis 1950- *St&PR 93*
Palamarcuik, Nancy Ferris 1952- *WhoAmW 93*
Palamas, Gregory c. 1296-1359 *OxDcByz*
Palan, Robert V. 1944- *St&PR 93*
Palanca, Terilyn 1957- *WhoEmL 93*
Palance, Jack *WhoAm 92*
Palance, Jack 1920- *BioIn 17, IntDcF 2-3 [port]*
Palance, Jack 1921- *CurBio 92 [port]*
Palange, Louis S(alvador) 1917-1979 *Baker 92*
Palaniyandy, M. 1918- *WhoAsAP 91*
Palank, Mary A. *Law&B 92*
Palano, Christopher J. *Law&B 92*
Palans, Lloyd Alex 1946- *WhoEmL 93*
Palas, Miroslav 1936- *WhoScE 91-4*
Palasinski, Mieczyslaw 1924- *WhoScE 91-4*
Palasthy, Gyorgy 1931- *DrEEuF*
Palasz, Lech Zbigniew 1937- *WhoScE 91-4, WhoWor 93*
Palau, Luis, Jr. 1934- *ConAu 39NR*
Palau Boix, Manuel 1893-1967 *Baker 92*
Palay, Sanford Louis 1918- *WhoAm 92, WhoWrEP 92*
Palazzesi, Matilde 1802-1842 *Baker 92, OxDcOp*
Palazzetti, Richard R. 1941- *WhoWor 93*
Palazzi, Francis Andrew 1962- *WhoEmL 93*
Palazzi, Joseph Lazarro 1947- *WhoAm 92, WhoEmL 93*
Palazzi, Thomas 1916- *St&PR 93*
Palazzini, Pietro Cardinal 1912- *WhoWor 93*
Palazzo, Benjamin M. 1962- *St&PR 93*
Palazzo, Eugene Onofrio *Law&B 92*
Palazzo, Paul *BioIn 17*
Palazzolo, Andrea *Law&B 92*
Palazzolo, Carl *BioIn 17*
Palazzolo, Daniel J. *ConAu 139*
Palazzolo, Joseph A. *St&PR 93*
Palazzolo, Tom 1937- *WhoAm 92*
Palcanis, Gregory F. *Law&B 92*
Palcy, Euzhan 1957- *MiSFD 9*
Palczewski, Andrzej Czeslaw 1945- *WhoWor 93*
Palczewski, Roger L. 1946- *St&PR 93*
Palczynski, Richard W. 1947- *WhoIns 93*
Paldi, Emil 1936- *WhoScE 91-4*
Paldus, Josef 1935- *WhoAm 92*
Paleczny, Raymond John 1940- *St&PR 93*
Palek, Jiri 1934- *WhoE 93*
Palella, Antonio 1692-1761 *OxDcOp*
Palen, Thomas Eugene *Law&B 92*
Palenicek, Josef 1914-1991 *Baker 92*
Palenzona, Peter James 1952- *St&PR 93*
Paleo, Lyn *ScF&FL 92*
Paler, Irving H. 1933- *St&PR 93*
Palerm, Angel 1917-1980 *IntDcAn*
Palerme, Patrick 1957- *St&PR 93*
Palermo, Anthony Robert 1929- *WhoAm 92*
Palermo, David Stuart *WhoE 93*
Palermo, Gregory Sebastian 1946- *WhoAm 92, WhoEmL 93*
Palermo, Joseph 1917- *WhoAm 92, WhoWor 93*
Palermo, Joseph Leo 1958- *WhoEmL 93*
Palermo, Judy Hancock 1938- *WhoAmW 93, WhoSSW 93, WhoWor 93*
Palermo, Louis P. 1944- *St&PR 93*
Palermo, Nicholas J. 1937- *St&PR 93*
Palermo, Nicholas Joseph 1946- *WhoE 93*
Palermo, Peter M. 1941- *St&PR 93*
Palermo, Peter M., Jr. 1941- *WhoAm 92*
Palermo, Robert F. *Law&B 92*
Palermo, Robert James 1949- *WhoE 93*
Palermo, Steve *BioIn 17*
Pales, George Patrick 1950- *WhoEmL 93*
Paleschuck, Rita Frank 1928- *St&PR 93*
Pales Matos, Luis 1898-1959 *SpAmA*
Palester, Roman 1907-1989 *Baker 92*
Palestine, Eileen *ScF&FL 92*
Palestrina, Giovanni Pierluigi da 1525?-1594 *Baker 92*
Paletz, Leonard 1935- *St&PR 93*
Palevsky, Harry 1919-1990 *BioIn 17*
Palevsky, Max 1924- *BioIn 17, WhoAm 92*
Palewski, Gaston 1901-1984 *BioIn 17*
Palewski, Tomasz 1941- *WhoScE 91-4*
Paley, Alan L. 1943- *ScF&FL 92*
Paley, Albert Raymond 1944- *WhoAm 92*
Paley, Alfred Irving 1927- *WhoAm 92*
Paley, Babe Mortimer *BioIn 17*
Paley, Dianne Marie 1956- *WhoWrEP 92*
Paley, Gerald Larry 1939- *WhoAm 92*
Paley, Grace *BioIn 17*
Paley, Grace 1922- *AmWomWr 92, JeAmFiW, MagSAmL [port], WhoAm 92, WhoAmW 93, WhoWrEP 92*
Paley, James Alan 1946- *WhoEmL 93*
Paley, Richard Thomas 1936- *WhoWor 93*
Paley, Stanley R. 1940- *WhoE 93*
Paley, William 1743-1805 *BioIn 17*
Paley, William S. 1901-1990 *BioIn 17*
Palguta, Larry J. *Law&B 92*
Palgutt, William 1941- *St&PR 93*
Pali, Robert G. 1946- *St&PR 93*
Pali, Robert George 1946- *WhoE 93*
Paliashvili, Zakhari (Petrovich) 1871-1933 *Baker 92*
Palihnich, Nicholas Joseph, Jr. 1939- *WhoAm 92*
Palikao, Charles Guillaume Marie Apollinaire Antoine Cous, Count of 1796-1878 *HarEnMi*
Palileo, Hazel Valencia 1951- *WhoEmL 93*
Palin, Francis Terence 1939- *WhoScE 91-1*
Palin, Michael *BioIn 17*
Palin, Michael 1943- *QDrFCA 92 [port], ScF&FL 92*

Palincsar, John Ernest *Law&B 92*
Palinkas, James Thomas 1945- *St&PR 93*
Palinsky, Constance Genevieve 1927- *WhoAmW 93, WhoWor 93*
Palis, Michael Abueg 1957- *WhoE 93*
Palisca, Claude V(ictor) 1921- *Baker 92*
Palisca, Claude Victor 1921- *WhoAm 92*
Palisi, Anthony Thomas 1930- *WhoAm 92*
Palisin, Edward F. 1937- *St&PR 93*
Palitz, Bernard G. 1924- *St&PR 93, WhoAm 92*
Palitz, Clarence Y., Jr. 1931- *St&PR 93*
Palitz, Clarence Yale, Jr. 1931- *WhoAm 92*
Palitz, Irvin L. 1924- *St&PR 93*
Palitzsch, Johann Georg 1723-1788 *BioIn 17*
Paliwoda, Aleksander 1929- *WhoScE 91-4*
Paliwoda, Stanley Joseph 1948- *WhoWor 93*
Paliyenko, Adrianna Maria 1956- *WhoE 93*
Palizza, John Maurice *Law&B 92*
Palizzi, Anthony N. *Law&B 92*
Palizzi, Anthony N. 1942- *St&PR 93*
Palka, Krystyna 1949- *WhoWor 93*
Palkama, Arto 1934- *WhoScE 91-4*
Palker, Marc Paul 1952- *St&PR 93*
Palkivala, John K. 1933- *St&PR 93*
Palko, Michael James 1936- *St&PR 93, WhoAm 92*
Palkovic, Mark 1954- *ConAu 137*
Palkovitz, Jeffrey C. *Law&B 92*
Palkovitz, Robin Joseph 1954- *WhoE 93*
Palkovsky, Oldrich 1907-1983 *Baker 92*
Palkovsky, Pavel 1939- *Baker 92*
Pall, David B. 1914- *WhoAm 92*
Pall, Ellen Jane 1952- *WhoE 93*
Palla, M. Siddique 1952- *St&PR 93*
Palla, Sandro F. 1943- *WhoScE 91-4*
Palladas 319?- *OxDcByz*
Palladini, David (Mario) 1946- *MajAI*
Palladino, Barbara A. 1955- *WhoAmW 93*
Palladino, Grace 1953- *WhoE 93*
Palladino, Joseph J. *BioIn 17*
Palladino, Nunzio Joseph 1916- *WhoAm 92*
Palladino-Craig, Allys 1947- *WhoAm 92, WhoAmW 93, WhoSSW 93*
Palladio, Andrea 1508-1580 *BioIn 17*
Palladios c. 363-c. 431 *OxDcByz*
Pallai, David Francis 1950- *WhoE 93, WhoEmL 93, WhoWor 93*
Pallakoff, Owen E. 1930- *St&PR 93, WhoAm 92*
Pallam, John J. *Law&B 92*
Pallan, Richard Nelson 1943- *St&PR 93*
Pallandios, M. *WhoScE 91-3*
Pallandios, Menelaos 1914- *Baker 92*
Pallas, Christopher William 1956- *WhoSSW 93*
Pallasch, B. Michael 1933- *WhoAm 92, WhoWor 93*
Pallasch, Magdalena Helena 1908- *WhoWor 93*
Pallat, Daniel Jon 1938- *St&PR 93*
Pallauf, Josef 1939- *WhoScE 91-3*
Pallavicini, Federico von Berzeviczy- 1909-1989 *BioIn 17*
Pallavicino, Benedetto 1551-1601 *Baker 92*
Pallavicino, Carlo d1688 *Baker 92*
Pallavicino, Carlo c. 1630-1688 *OxDcOp*
Pallavicino, Stefano Benedetto 1672-1742 *OxDcOp*
Pallemaerts, Edmundo 1867-1945 *Baker 92*
Pallenberg, Barbara *ScF&FL 92*
Pallenberg, Rospo *MiSFD 9*
Pallenik, Christine Marie *Law&B 92*
Paller, Jack 1928- *St&PR 93*
Palles, Allen P. *Law&B 92*
Palleschi, John A. *Law&B 92*
Pallesen, Lars Christian 1947- *WhoScE 91-2*
Pallette, Eugene 1889-1954 *BioIn 17*
Palley, Marian Lief 1939- *WhoE 93*
Palley, Stephen W. *Law&B 92*
Palley, Stephen W. 1945- *St&PR 93*
Pallin, Irving M. 1910- *WhoAm 92*
Pallis, Mark T. *Law&B 92*
Palliser, Charles 1947- *ConAu 136*
Palliser, John 1817-1887 *Expl 93*
Pallister, Janis Louise 1926- *WhoWrEP 92*
Pallmann, Ronald Lee 1947- *WhoEmL 93*
Pallo, Imre 1941- *Baker 92*
Pallone, Adrian Joseph 1928- *WhoAm 92*
Pallone, Dave *BioIn 17*
Pallone, Frank, Jr. 1951- *CngDr 91, WhoAm 92, WhoE 93*
Pallone, Joseph Charles 1943- *St&PR 93*
Pallone, Julius Louis 1930- *St&PR 93, WhoAm 92*
Pallot, E. Albert 1908- *WhoAm 92*
Pallot, William L. 1912- *St&PR 93*
Pallotta, Gail Cassady 1942- *WhoWrEP 92*
Pallotta, Michael Vincent 1955- *St&PR 93*
Pallotti, Giovanni 1934- *WhoScE 91-3*
Pallotti, Marianne Marguerite 1937- *WhoAmW 93*
Pallozzi, Dennis Peter 1947- *WhoE 93*
Palluzi, Richard Peter 1952- *WhoEmL 93*
Palm, Carla L. *AmWomPl*
Palm, Christine Alice 1956- *WhoAmW 93*
Palm, Enok J. 1924- *WhoScE 91-4*
Palm, Frank Raymond 1937- *WhoE 93*
Palm, Gary Howard 1942- *WhoAm 92*
Palm, Gene 1912-1988 *ScF&FL 92*
Palm, Gerd 1951- *WhoScE 91-3*
Palm, Hans Dieter 1924- *WhoScE 91-3*
Palm, Irvin Davey, Jr. *Law&B 92*
Palm, Siegfried 1927- *Baker 92*
Palm, T. Arthur 1954- *WhoSSW 93*
Palm, William John 1944- *WhoE 93*
Palm, William Nixon 1938- *St&PR 93*
Palma, Athos 1891-1951 *Baker 92*
Palma, Christine A. 1950- *WhoAmW 93*
Palma, Clemente 1872-1946 *SpAmA*
Palma, Dolores Patricia 1951- *WhoAm 92*
Palma, Maria Damascus *Law&B 92*
Palma, Massimo Ugo 1927- *WhoScE 91-3*
Palma, Ruben *DcCPCAm*
Palma Carlos, Adelino da 1905-1992 *NewYTBS 92*
Palma-Gil, Benjamin *St&PR 93*
Palmas, Angelo 1914- *WhoE 93*
Palmatier, Rex V. 1955- *St&PR 93*
Palmatier, Robert Allen 1926- *WhoWrEP 92*
Palmatier, William Edwin 1943- *St&PR 93*
Palmberg-Lerche, Christel M. 1946- *WhoScE 91-3*
Palme, Olof 1927-1986 *BioIn 17*
Palme, Olof Joachim 1927-1986 *DcTwHis*
Palmer, A.B. 1924- *St&PR 93*
Palmer, A. Mitchell 1872-1936 *PolPar*
Palmer, Adrian B. 1910- *WhoAm 92*
Palmer, Agnes 1953- *WhoAmW 93*
Palmer, Alice Eugenia 1910- *WhoAm 92, WhoWor 93*
Palmer, Alice J. 1939- *WhoAmW 93*
Palmer, Anne *AmWomPl*
Palmer, Anne Buzby *AmWomPl*
Palmer, Anne Caldwell 1956- *WhoSSW 93*
Palmer, Anne M. *AmWomPl*
Palmer, Annie D. *AmWomPl*
Palmer, Arnold 1929- *BioIn 17*
Palmer, Arnold Daniel 1929- *WhoAm 92, WhoE 93*
Palmer, Ashley Joanne 1951- *WhoAmW 93, WhoEmL 93*
Palmer, Barbara Heslan 1945- *WhoAmW 93, WhoE 93*
Palmer, Bell Elliott 1873- *AmWomPl*
Palmer, Bert 1924- *St&PR 93*
Palmer, Beverly Blazey 1945- *WhoAmW 93*
Palmer, Brent David 1959- *WhoWor 93*
Palmer, Bruce *ScF&FL 92*
Palmer, Bruce, Jr. 1913- *CmdGen 1991 [port]*
Palmer, Bruce Harrison 1955- *WhoSSW 93*
Palmer, C. Everard 1930- *BlkAuII 92*
Palmer, Carol Ann 1949- *WhoEmL 93*
Palmer, Carolyn G. d1990 *BioIn 17*
Palmer, Cathy *BioIn 17*
Palmer, Charlene Noel 1930- *WhoWrEP 92*
Palmer, Charles L. 1942- *St&PR 93*
Palmer, Charles Ray 1940- *WhoWor 93*
Palmer, Charles Robert 1934- *St&PR 93, WhoAm 92*
Palmer, Chester I., Jr. 1947- *WhoEmL 93*
Palmer, Cruise 1917- *WhoAm 92*
Palmer, Curtis Dwayne 1947- *WhoSSW 93*
Palmer, Curtis Howard 1908- *St&PR 93, WhoAm 92*
Palmer, Curtis Ray *WhoWor 93*
Palmer, Darwin L. 1930- *WhoAm 92*
Palmer, Dave Richard 1934- *WhoAm 92*
Palmer, David Hamblin, Sr. 1920- *WhoAm 92*
Palmer, David R. 1941- *ScF&FL 92*
Palmer, David Randolph 1961- *WhoE 93*
Palmer, David Walter 1928- *WhoWrEP 92*
Palmer, Deborah Kay 1953- *WhoSSW 93*
Palmer, Don *MajAI*
Palmer, Douglas H. 1951- *WhoE 93*
Palmer, Earl *SoulM*
Palmer, Edward 1830?-1911 *IntDcAn*
Palmer, Edward Emery 1945- *WhoWor 93*
Palmer, Edward Kent 1960- *WhoSSW 93*
Palmer, Edward Lewis 1917- *WhoAm 92*
Palmer, Elaine Rivette 1956- *WhoAmW 93*
Palmer, Elizabeth Armstrong 1954- *St&PR 93*
Palmer, Fanny Purdy 1839-1923 *AmWomPl*
Palmer, Felicity 1944- *OxDcOp*
Palmer, Felicity (Joan) 1944- *Baker 92*
Palmer, Forrest Charles 1924- *WhoAm 92*
Palmer, Frank 1933- *ConAu 139*
Palmer, Frank K. 1955- *St&PR 93*
Palmer, Frank William 1940- *WhoAm 92*
Palmer, Gary Andrew 1953- *WhoAm 92*
Palmer, Gary James 1954- *WhoEmL 93, WhoSSW 93*
Palmer, Geoffrey 1912- *ScF&FL 92*
Palmer, Geoffrey 1942- *WhoAsAP 91*
Palmer, Georgia 1945- *WhoAmW 93*
Palmer, Glenn Dean 1933- *WhoSSW 93*
Palmer, Gregg 1927- *BioIn 17*
Palmer, Gregory Reginal 1953- *WhoSSW 93*
Palmer, Hall 1940- *St&PR 93*
Palmer, Hans Christian 1933- *WhoAm 92*
Palmer, Hap 1942- *BioIn 17, ConAu 136*
Palmer, Harvey John 1946- *WhoAm 92*
Palmer, Hazel *WhoAm 92*
Palmer, Helen M. *AmWomPl*
Palmer, Horatio R(ichmond) 1834-1907 *Baker 92*
Palmer, Howell M., III 1951- *WhoIns 93*
Palmer, Hubert Bernard 1912- *WhoSSW 93*
Palmer, Ian Robert 1940- *WhoWor 93*
Palmer, Innis Newton 1824-1900 *HarEnMi*
Palmer, Irene Sabelberg 1923- *WhoAm 92*
Palmer, Isaac *Law&B 92*
Palmer, Jaclyn C. *Law&B 92*
Palmer, James A. 1937- *St&PR 93*
Palmer, James Alvin 1945- *WhoAm 92*
Palmer, James Daniel 1930- *WhoAm 92*
Palmer, James Edward 1935- *WhoAm 92*
Palmer, James M. 1949- *St&PR 93*
Palmer, Jane 1946- *ScF&FL 92*
Palmer, Janet Fischer *WhoAmW 93*
Palmer, Janice Marie 1949- *WhoEmL 93*
Palmer, Jared *BioIn 17*
Palmer, Jean Tilford d1992 *BioIn 17*
Palmer, Jeffress Gary 1921- *WhoAm 92, WhoSSW 93*
Palmer, Jeffrey H. 1957- *St&PR 93*
Palmer, Jerry L. 1933- *St&PR 93*
Palmer, Jessica *ScF&FL 92*
Palmer, Jim 1945- *BioIn 17*
Palmer, Joanne Melton 1927- *WhoSSW 93*
Palmer, Jocelyn Beth 1927- *WhoAmW 93*
Palmer, Joel 1810-1881 *BioIn 17*
Palmer, John 1943- *WhoCanL 92*
Palmer, John Anthony, III 1955- *WhoE 93, WhoEmL 93*
Palmer, John J. 1939- *WhoIns 93*
Palmer, John Jacob 1939- *St&PR 93, WhoAm 92*
Palmer, John James Ellis 1913- *WhoAm 92*
Palmer, John L. 1943- *WhoAm 92*
Palmer, John Marshall 1906- *WhoAm 92*
Palmer, John McAuley 1870-1955 *HarEnMi*
Palmer, John Michael *WhoScE 91-1*
Palmer, John N. 1934- *St&PR 93*
Palmer, John Robert 1939- *WhoSSW 93*
Palmer, Josephine Ludlow *AmWomPl*
Palmer, Judith Grace 1948- *WhoEmL 93*
Palmer, Karen Feder 1946- *WhoE 93*
Palmer, Karen Louise 1955- *WhoAmW 93*
Palmer, Kate B. *AmWomPl*
Palmer, Kenneth A. 1939- *WhoIns 93*
Palmer, Kenneth Arthur 1939- *St&PR 93*
Palmer, Kristine Margaret 1963- *WhoE 93*
Palmer, Langdon 1928- *WhoAm 92*
Palmer, Laurence Clive 1932- *WhoE 93*
Palmer, Linda Conner 1949- *WhoAmW 93*
Palmer, Lucie Mackay 1913- *WhoE 93*
Palmer, Margaret Allene 1955- *WhoSSW 93*
Palmer, Marianne Eleanor 1945- *WhoSSW 93*
Palmer, Martha Jane 1947- *WhoAmW 93*
Palmer, Martha Royle *AmWomPl*
Palmer, Martin B. 1957- *St&PR 93*
Palmer, Mary Leslie 1959- *WhoEmL 93*
Palmer, Maude G. *AmWomPl*
Palmer, May McKinney 1865- *AmWomPl*
Palmer, Melville Louis 1924- *WhoAm 92*
Palmer, Michael 1942- *BioIn 17, ScF&FL 92*
Palmer, Michael Charles 1931- *WhoAm 92*
Palmer, Michael E. 1942- *St&PR 93*
Palmer, Michael Z. 1939- *St&PR 93*
Palmer, Mildred Eunice 1911- *WhoSSW 93*
Palmer, Milton Meade 1916- *WhoAm 92*
Palmer, Nancy Anne 1947- *WhoWor 93*
Palmer, Nathan Hunt 1936- *St&PR 93*
Palmer, Norman 1922- *St&PR 93*
Palmer, Norman Dunbar 1909- *WhoAm 92*
Palmer, Parker J. *BioIn 17*
Palmer, Parker J. 1939- *ConAu 38NR*
Palmer, Patricia Ann Texter 1932- *WhoAmW 93, WhoWor 93*
Palmer, Patrick Edward 1940- *WhoAm 92*
Palmer, Paul Richard 1917- *WhoE 93*
Palmer, Peter J. *Law&B 92*
Palmer, Peter Joseph 1941- *St&PR 93*
Palmer, Philip Edward Stephen 1921- *WhoAm 92*
Palmer, Philip Isham, Jr. 1929- *WhoWor 93*
Palmer, Potter 1826-1902 *GayN*
Palmer, Randall B. *Law&B 92*
Palmer, Randolph G. 1957- *St&PR 93*
Palmer, Raymond A. 1939- *WhoAm 92*
Palmer, Regina Kay 1961- *WhoAmW 93*
Palmer, Rex M. 1954- *St&PR 93*
Palmer, Richard Alan 1935- *WhoAm 92*
Palmer, Richard Eugene 1920- *WhoSSW 93*
Palmer, Richard N. 1948- *St&PR 93*
Palmer, Richard Ware 1919- *WhoAm 92, WhoWor 93*
Palmer, Richelle 1958- *WhoEmL 93*
Palmer, Robert *BioIn 17*
Palmer, Robert 1949- *SoulM*
Palmer, Robert A. *Law&B 92*
Palmer, Robert Alan 1948- *WhoEmL 93*
Palmer, Robert Baylis 1938- *WhoAm 92*
Palmer, Robert Bitts 1940- *St&PR 93, WhoAm 92*
Palmer, Robert Conrad, Jr. 1929- *WhoSSW 93*
Palmer, Robert D. 1915- *St&PR 93*
Palmer, Robert Erwin 1934- *WhoAm 92*
Palmer, Robert Franklin, Jr. 1945- *WhoWrEP 92*
Palmer, Robert Joseph 1934- *WhoAm 92*
Palmer, Robert K. 1946- *St&PR 93*
Palmer, Robert Leslie 1957- *WhoEmL 93*
Palmer, Robert (Moffat) 1915- *Baker 92*
Palmer, Robert Roswell 1909- *WhoAm 92*
Palmer, Robert Towne 1947- *WhoEmL 93, WhoWor 93*
Palmer, Robie Marcus Hooker Mark 1941- *WhoAm 92, WhoWor 93*
Palmer, Roger Farley 1931- *WhoAm 92*
Palmer, Roger P. 1937- *St&PR 93*
Palmer, Roger Raymond 1926- *WhoAm 92*
Palmer, Ronald DeWayne Faisal 1932- *WhoAm 92*
Palmer, Ronald Eugene 1952- *WhoE 93*
Palmer, Ronald J. *Law&B 92*
Palmer, Rose Amelia *AmWomPl*
Palmer, Russell Eugene 1934- *WhoAm 92, WhoWor 93*
Palmer, Ruth Nina 1934- *WhoSSW 93*
Palmer, Samuel Copeland, III 1934- *WhoAm 92, WhoWor 93*
Palmer, Sandra Kay 1950- *WhoAmW 93*
Palmer, Sarah Elizabeth *AmWomPl*
Palmer, Sidney M. *St&PR 93*
Palmer, Stephen 1954- *WhoAm 92*
Palmer, Stephen B. 1927- *St&PR 93*
Palmer, Stephen Eugene 1896- *WhoAm 92*
Palmer, Stephen Eugene, Jr. 1923- *WhoAm 92*
Palmer, Steven W. 1950- *St&PR 93*
Palmer, Steven William 1950- *WhoAm 92, WhoE 93*
Palmer, Stuart B. *WhoScE 91-1*
Palmer, Stuart Hunter 1924- *WhoAm 92, WhoE 93, WhoWor 93*
Palmer, Tekla Fredsall 1918- *WhoSSW 93*
Palmer, Thomas *ScF&FL 92*
Palmer, Thomas (Coryell) 1955- *ConAu 39NR*
Palmer, Thomas E. *Law&B 92*
Palmer, Thomas Howard, Jr. 1924- *WhoE 93*
Palmer, Thomas Ralph 1947- *WhoSSW 93*
Palmer, Tom 1955- *ScF&FL 92*
Palmer, Tom, Jr. *MiSFD 9*
Palmer, Tony *MiSFD 9*
Palmer, Trevor *WhoScE 91-1*
Palmer, Venrice R. *Law&B 92*
Palmer, Vickie Anne 1953- *WhoAmW 93*
Palmer, Waldron 1951- *St&PR 93*
Palmer, Walter B. 1954- *St&PR 93*
Palmer, Wayne Lewis 1949- *WhoE 93, WhoEmL 93, WhoWor 93*
Palmer, William A. 1916- *St&PR 93*
Palmer, William Fisher 1934- *WhoSSW 93*
Palmer, William J. 1890-1982 *ScF&FL 92*
Palmer, William W. d1991 *BioIn 17*
Palmer-Beard, Donna 1948- *WhoAmW 93*
Palmer-Carfora, Linda Louise 1950- *WhoAmW 93*
Palmer-Hass, Lisa Michelle 1953- *WhoAmW 93, WhoEmL 93*
Palmerston, Henry John 1784-1865 *BioIn 17*
Palmerton, Patricia Ruby 1949- *WhoAmW 93*

Palmese, Richard Dominick 1947- *St&PR 93, WhoAm 92*
Palmeter, N. David 1938- *WhoAm 92*
Palmgren, Selim 1878-1951 *Baker 92*
Palmieri, Alain John Verron 1941- *WhoE 93*
Palmieri, Eddie 1936- *BioIn 17, CurBio 92 [port]*
Palmieri, Guy Joseph 1936- *St&PR 93*
Palmieri, Joanne 1956- *WhoAmW 93*
Palmieri, Nicola W. 1935- *St&PR 93*
Palmieri, Peter C. 1934- *St&PR 93*
Palmieri, Ralph J. 1947- *WhoIns 93*
Palmieri, Robert Jeffrey 1952- *St&PR 93*
Palmieri, Sandro 1942- *WhoScE 91-3*
Palmieri, Victor H. *BioIn 17*
Palmieri, Victor Henry 1930- *WhoAm 92*
Palmiero, Joseph *St&PR 93*
Palminteri, Chazz *BioIn 17*
Palmisano, Conrad E. *MiSFD 9*
Palmisano, Gene S. *Law&B 92*
Palmisano, Louis 1930- *BioIn 17*
Palmisano, Luigi *ScF&FL 92*
Palmisano, Paul Anthony 1929- *WhoWor 93*
Palmiter, Richard DeForest 1942- *WhoAm 92*
Palmitier, Steven C. 1956- *St&PR 93*
Palmore, Jasmine *BioIn 17*
Palmore, John Stanley, Jr. 1917- *WhoAm 92*
Palmore, William Elbert 1946- *WhoEmL 93*
Palmosina, Michael Francis, II 1957- *WhoE 93*
Palmquist, James P. *Law&B 92*
Palmroth, John William 1939- *St&PR 93, WhoAm 92*
Palms, John Michael 1935- *WhoAm 92, WhoSSW 93*
Palms, Roger C(urtis) 1936- *ConAu 38NR*
Palms, Roger Curtis 1936- *WhoAm 92*
Palmunen, Arthur A. *Law&B 92*
Palo, Jorma H.I. 1936- *WhoScE 91-4*
Palo, Matti S. 1938- *WhoScE 91-4*
Palo, Nicholas Edwin 1945- *WhoAm 92, WhoWor 93*
Palo, Ralph *Law&B 92*
Palochak, John B. *Law&B 92*
Palochko, Eleanor LaRivere 1924- *WhoAmW 93*
Paloian, Ab 1929- *St&PR 93*
Palomaki, Mauri Juho 1931- *WhoWor 93*
Palomba, Giuseppe fl. 1765-1825 *OxDcOp*
Palomba, Susan Kay 1955- *WhoAmW 93*
Palombi, Barbara Jean 1949- *WhoEmL 93, WhoWor 93*
Palombo, Arthur James 1923- *St&PR 93*
Palombo, Paul (Martin) 1937- *Baker 92*
Palombo, Tony 1959- *St&PR 93*
Palomino, Ernesto 1933- *HispAmA*
Palomino de Castro y Velasco, Antonio 1655-1726 *BioIn 17*
Palosaari, Seppo Matti 1936- *WhoScE 91-4, WhoWor 93*
Palosuo, Timo Juhana 1939- *WhoScE 91-4*
Paloumpis, Andreas Athanasios 1925- *WhoSSW 93*
Palous, Radim 1924- *WhoWor 93*
Palovcik, Reinhard Anton 1950- *WhoSSW 93*
Palowicz, Efram O. *St&PR 93*
Paloyan, Edward 1932- *WhoAm 92*
Pals, Daphne L. *Law&B 92*
Pals, Dean Clifford 1938- *WhoSSW 93*
Palser, Barbara F. 1916- *WhoAm 92*
Palsho, Dorothea Coccoli 1947- *WhoAm 92, WhoAmW 93*
Palsis, Peter Paul 1937- *St&PR 93*
Palson, Patricia *BioIn 17*
Palsson, Pall (Pampichler) 1928- *Baker 92*
Palsson, Thorsteinn 1947- *WhoWor 93*
Pålsson, Tryggvi 1949- *WhoWor 93*
Palsulich, Ronda Marie 1965- *WhoAmW 93*
Paltauf, Fritz 1936- *WhoScE 91-4*
Palter, Alan D. *Law&B 92*
Palter, Robert Monroe 1924- *WhoAm 92*
Paltiel, Rae G. *Law&B 92*
Paltiel, Rae G. 1946- *St&PR 93*
Paltos, Robert N. *WhoE 93*
Paltrow, Bruce 1943- *MiSFD 9*
Paltrowitz, Donna 1950- *BioIn 17, ScF&FL 92*
Paltrowitz, Stuart 1946- *BioIn 17, ScF&FL 92*
Paltrowitz, Stuart Marshall 1946- *WhoE 93*
Palubiak, Richard Craig 1954- *WhoEmL 93*
Paluch, Andrzej Kazimierz 1944- *WhoWor 93*
Paluch, Edward Peter 1952- *WhoSSW 93*
Paluck, Robert J. 1947- *St&PR 93*
Paluck, Robert John 1947- *WhoAm 92*
Palumbo, Benjamin Lewis 1937- *WhoE 93*
Palumbo, Dennis 1929- *ScF&FL 92*
Palumbo, Dominic Joseph 1945- *WhoE 93*
Palumbo, Donald 1949- *ScF&FL 92*
Palumbo, Donald Emanuel 1949- *WhoE 93*
Palumbo, James F. 1950- *St&PR 93*
Palumbo, James Fredrick 1950- *WhoE 93, WhoEmL 93*
Palumbo, John P. *Law&B 92*
Palumbo, Lisa Marie *Law&B 92*
Palumbo, Mario Joseph 1933- *WhoAm 92, WhoSSW 93*
Palumbo, Mary Vincente *Law&B 92*
Palumbo, Michael Nicholas 1960- *WhoWrEP 92*
Palumbo, Robert Anthony 1951- *St&PR 93*
Palumbo, Ruth Ann 1949- *WhoAmW 93*
Palumbo, Vincent A. 1947- *St&PR 93*
Paluskiewicz, Anne Frances 1956- *WhoAmW 93*
Paluszak, Naoko 1957- *WhoEmL 93, WhoSSW 93*
Palva, L. Antti J. 1933- *WhoScE 91-4*
Palva, Tauno K. 1925- *WhoScE 91-4*
Palvino, Jack Anthony 1934- *WhoAm 92*
Palys, Peter George *Law&B 92*
Pamadi, Bandu Narasinha 1945- *WhoSSW 93*
Pamerleau, William Charles 1933- *St&PR 93*
Pamfilova, Ella *WhoWor 93*
Pamir, M. Hilmi 1924- *WhoScE 91-4*
Pampanini, Andrea Henry A. 1940- *St&PR 93*
Pampanini, Rosetta 1896-1973 *Baker 92, OxDcOp*
Pampel, George 1904-1991 *BioIn 17*
Pampel, Joseph Philip Stevenson 1932- *WhoAm 92, WhoE 93, WhoWor 93*
Pampel, Roland D. 1934- *St&PR 93*
Pampena, Ralph 1937- *St&PR 93*
Pamplin, Peter 1954- *St&PR 93*
Pamplin, Robert B. 1911- *St&PR 93*
Pamplin, Robert Boisseau, Sr. 1911- *WhoAm 92*
Pamplin, Robert Boisseau, Jr. 1941- *WhoAm 92, WhoWor 93*
Pampols, T. *WhoScE 91-3*
Pamprepios 440-484 *OxDcByz*
Pampusch, Anita Marie 1938- *WhoAm 92, WhoAmW 93*
Pampy, Edna Theresa 1948- *WhoEmL 93*
Pamuk, H. Onder 1940- *WhoScE 91-4*
P'an, Albert Yuan 1941- *WhoAm 92*
Pan, C. Jeff 1957- *WhoSSW 93*
Pan, Coda H. T. 1929- *WhoAm 92*
Pan, Elizabeth Lim 1941- *WhoAm 92*
Pan, Henry Yue-Ming 1946- *WhoAm 92, WhoE 93, WhoEmL 93*
Pan, Hermes d1990 *BioIn 17*
Pan, Huo-Ping 1921- *WhoWor 93*
Pan, Jie 1957- *WhoWor 93*
Pan, Joshua Jih 1942- *WhoWor 93*
Pan, Leonie S. *Law&B 92*
Pan, Loretta Ren-Qiu 1917- *WhoWor 93*
Pan, Maria Weiyei 1943- *WhoAmW 93, WhoE 93*
Pan, Mary Agnes 1951- *WhoAmW 93*
Pan, Qiyuan 1937- *WhoWor 93*
P'an, Shih Yi 1911-1990 *BioIn 17*
Pan, Shizhong 1943- *WhoWor 93*
Panagariya, Arvind 1952- *WhoE 93*
Panagiotakopoulos, Demetrios 1945- *WhoScE 91-3*
Panagiotakopoulos, Demetrios Christos 1945- *WhoWor 93*
Panagiotis, Merikas 1929- *WhoWor 93*
Panagiotopoulos, Panagiotis D. 1950- *WhoScE 91-3*
Panagiotopoulos, Vasos-Peter John, II 1961- *WhoEmL 93*
Panagiotou, Apostolos Dimitriou 1943- *WhoWor 93*
Panagopulos, Pericles Stavros 1935- *WhoWor 93*
Panagos, Athanasios 1926- *WhoScE 91-3*
Panagoulis, Elizabeth Dorothy 1948- *WhoE 93*
Panait, Constantin *BioIn 17*
Panama, Norman 1914- *MiSFD 9*
Panangala, Victor Sepala 1939- *WhoSSW 93*
Panarale, Joseph Anthony 1936- *St&PR 93*
Panarese, William C. 1929- *WhoAm 92*
Panaretos, John 1948- *WhoEmL 93, WhoScE 91-3, WhoWor 93*
Panaretos, Michael c. 1320-c. 1390 *OxDcByz*
Panarites, John P. 1939- *St&PR 93*
Panaro, Victor Anthony 1928- *WhoAm 92*
Panasci, Henry A., Jr. 1928- *St&PR 93*
Panasci, Nancy Ervin 1954- *WhoEmL 93*
Panasenko, Grigorij Petrovich 1954- *WhoWor 93*
Panassie, Hugues 1912-1974 *Baker 92*
Panati, Charles 1943- *BioIn 17, ScF&FL 92*
Panattoni, Marcia J. 1959- *St&PR 93*
Panayi, Gabriel Stavros *WhoScE 91-1, WhoWor 93*
Panayiotou, Andreas 1940- *WhoScE 91-4*
Panayiotou, Constantinos 1951- *WhoWor 93*
Panayirci, Erdal 1941- *WhoScE 91-4*
Panayirci, Sharon Lorraine 1957- *WhoAmW 93*
Pan Ch'ao 32-102 *HarEnMi*
Panchev, Stoycho 1933- *WhoScE 91-4*
Panciera, Frederick Lee 1937- *WhoIns 93*
Panciera, Richard Conner 1947- *WhoEmL 93*
Pancoast, David W. *Law&B 92*
Pancoast, Edwin C. 1925- *WhoAm 92*
Pancoast, Howard Roger, Jr. *Law&B 92*
Pancoast, Scott Rutledge 1958- *St&PR 93*
Pancoast, Terrence Russell 1942- *WhoAm 92*
Pancost, Karen B. *Law&B 92*
Pandak, Sharon Elizabeth 1953- *WhoAmW 93*
Pandaleon, A. George 1930- *St&PR 93*
Pandaleon, Alec A. *Law&B 92*
Panday, Basdeo 1932- *DcCPCAm*
Panday, Devendra Raj 1939- *WhoWor 93*
Pande, Badri Raj 1936- *WhoUN 92*
Pande, Krishna Prasad 1946- *WhoAm 92*
Pande, Rajmangal 1920- *WhoAsAP 91*
Pandey, Dhirendra Kumar 1951- *WhoAm 92, WhoEmL 93, WhoSSW 93*
Pandey, Manorama 1932- *WhoAsAP 91*
Pandey, Ramendra Narayan 1951- *WhoEmL 93*
Pandey, Ratnakar *WhoAsAP 91*
Pandey, Shyammanohar 1936- *WhoWor 93*
Pandeya, Nirmalendu Kumar 1940- *WhoWor 93*
Pandick, Thomas O'Donnell 1947- *WhoE 93*
Pandini, Davide 1961- *WhoWor 93*
Pandit, Vijaya Lakshmi 1900-1990 *BioIn 17*
Pandit, Vinay Yeshwant 1943- *WhoE 93*
Pando, Alan Oscar 1931- *WhoAm 92*
Pando, Robert Terry 1938- *WhoSSW 93*
Pandolfe, William David 1945- *WhoE 93*
Pandolfi, Maurizio 1932- *WhoScE 91-4*
Pandolfini, Angelica 1871-1959 *Baker 92, OxDcOp*
Pandolfini, Canzio 1939- *St&PR 93*
Pandolfini, Francesco 1833-1916 *OxDcOp*
Pandolfini, Francesco 1836-1916 *Baker 92*
Pandolfini, Thomas Joseph, Jr. 1961- *WhoE 93*
Pandolfo, Michael A. 1945- *St&PR 93*
Pandolfo, Sebastian L. *Law&B 92*
Pane, Joseph Francis 1921- *St&PR 93*
Pane, Michael Anthony 1942- *WhoWor 93*
Pane, Remigio Ugo 1912- *WhoAm 92, WhoWor 93*
Panecasio, Eugene L. 1936- *St&PR 93*
Panek, Carl Francis 1946- *WhoEmL 93*
Panek, Donald A. *Law&B 92*
Panek, Jan 1930- *WhoAm 92*
Panella, Pam *BioIn 17*
Panem, Sandra 1946- *BioIn 17*
Panerai, Rolando 1924- *Baker 92, OxDcOp*
Paneras, Evangelos Demetrios 1929- *WhoScE 91-3*
Panero, Leopoldo 1909-1962 *BioIn 17*
Panes, Jack Samuel 1925- *WhoAm 92*
Panes, Paul Benjamin 1928- *WhoE 93*
Panes, Pearl Shaine 1929- *WhoAmW 93*
Panet, Marc 1938- *WhoScE 91-2*
Panet, Margot E. *Law&B 92*
Paneth, Donald J. 1927- *WhoAm 92, WhoE 93, WhoWor 93*
Paneth, Thomas 1926- *WhoWor 93*
Panetsos, Konstantinos 1930- *WhoScE 91-3*
Panetta, Leon E. 1938- *CngDr 91*
Panetta, Leon Edward 1938- *NewYTBS 92 [port], WhoAm 92*
Panettiere, John Michael 1937- *WhoAm 92*
Paney, Harry Edmond 1926- *St&PR 93*
Paneyko, Stephen Hobbs 1942- *St&PR 93, WhoAm 92*
Panfile, Orlando Ernest 1928- *St&PR 93*
Panfile, Patricia McCloskey 1952- *WhoE 93*
Panfilov, Gleb 1934- *DrEEuF*
Panfilov, Gleb 1937- *MiSFD 9*
Pang, Dawn Bobbie 1955- *WhoAmW 93*
Pang, Herbert George 1922- *WhoAm 92, WhoWor 93*
Pang, Peter C. *Law&B 92*
Pang, Teck Wai 1955- *WhoWor 93*
Pangborn, Edgar 1909-1976 *BioIn 17, ScF&FL 92*
Pangborn, Franklin 1893-1958 *IntDcF 2-3, QDrFCA 92 [port]*
Pangborn, Joel W. *Law&B 92*
Pangburn, Arthur Dewitt 1942- *St&PR 93*
Pangburn, T. Michael *Law&B 92*
Pang Chun-Hoi, Hon 1921- *WhoAsAP 91*
Pangerapan, Bob George 1938- *WhoWor 93*
Pangia, Robert Anthony 1952- *WhoEmL 93*
Pangle, Laurie S. *Law&B 92*
Panholzer, Adam Paul 1964- *St&PR 93*
Panholzer, J. Robert 1958- *St&PR 93*
Panhorst, Donald Lee 1932- *WhoE 93*
Pani, Paolo 1940- *WhoWor 93*
Paniagua, John Charles 1962- *WhoE 93*
Panian, Michael G. *Law&B 92*
Panic, Milan 1929- *St&PR 93, WhoAm 92, WhoWor 93*
Panicali, Dennis 1949- *St&PR 93*
Paniccia, Mario Domenic 1948- *WhoE 93, WhoEmL 93*
Panich, Danuta Bembenista 1954- *WhoAmW 93*
Panich, Paula Marie 1947- *WhoWrEP 92*
Panichas, Edwin John *Law&B 92*
Panichas, George Andrew 1930- *WhoAm 92, WhoWrEP 92*
Panichi, Michele Ann 1959- *WhoAmW 93, WhoEmL 93*
Panico, Alison Mary 1967- *WhoAmW 93, WhoEmL 93*
Panico, C. Richard 1941- *St&PR 93*
Panico, Elaine Hartman 1924- *WhoAmW 93*
Panico, Frank S. 1958- *St&PR 93*
Panidis, Demetrios 1942- *WhoScE 91-3*
Panikar, Mathew John P. 1939- *WhoWor 93*
Panikar, Suresh Krishnakutty 1951- *WhoEmL 93*
Panish, Morton B. 1929- *WhoAm 92*
Panitch, Michael B. 1939- *WhoAm 92*
Panitt, Merrill 1917- *WhoAm 92, WhoWrEP 92*
Panitz, David Hirsh d1991 *BioIn 17*
Panitz, Esther L(eah) *ConAu 40NR*
Panitz, Lawrence 1928- *WhoE 93*
Panitz, Lawrence Herbert 1941- *WhoAm 92, WhoWor 93*
Panitz, Linda L. *Law&B 92*
Panizza, Ettore 1875-1967 *Baker 92, OxDcOp*
Panizza, John Horace 1931- *WhoAsAP 91*
Panizza, Mario 1935- *WhoScE 91-3*
Panizza, Michael 1946- *WhoWor 93*
Panizza, Sergio Archimede 1946- *WhoWor 93*
Panja, Ajit Kumar 1936- *WhoAsAP 91*
Pan Jifang 1896- *WhoWor 93*
Pankau, Anne F. *Law&B 92*
Pankau, Edmund J. *BioIn 17*
Panken, Irwin 1908-1990 *BioIn 17*
Panken, Peter Michael 1936- *WhoAm 92*
Pankey, Edgar Edward 1916- *WhoAm 92*
Pankey, Gail *BioIn 17*
Pankey, George Atkinson 1933- *WhoAm 92*
Pankey, George Edward 1903- *WhoWor 93*
Pankey, George Stephen 1922- *WhoSSW 93, WhoWor 93*
Pankey, Homer Richwell 1936- *WhoE 93*
Pankhurst, Christabel Harriette 1880-1958 *DcTwHis*
Pankhurst, Emmeline 1858-1928 *DcTwHis*
Pankhurst, Louise *WhoScE 91-1*
Pankiewicz, Eugeniusz 1857-1898 *Baker 92, PolBiDi*
Pankiewicz, Jozef 1866-1940 *PolBiDi*
Pankin, Boris Dmitrievich *BioIn 17*
Pankin, Boris Dmitrievich 1931- *WhoWor 93*
Pankin, Jayson Darryl 1957- *St&PR 93, WhoEmL 93*
Pankok, Otto 1893-1966 *BioIn 17*
Pankonien, Dean Austin *Law&B 92*
Pankopf, Arthur, Jr. 1931- *WhoAm 92*
Pankov, Alexander 1949- *WhoWor 93*
Pankov, Pavel Sergeevich 1950- *WhoWor 93*
Pankove, Jacques Isaac 1922- *WhoAm 92*
Pankow, Charles *BioIn 17*
Pankowski, Elsie Marie 1933- *WhoWrEP 92*
Pankratios of Taormina *OxDcByz*
Pankratov, Aleksandr 1946- *DrEEuF*
Pankratz, Henry J. 1939- *WhoAm 92*
Pankratz, Laura Jo 1957- *WhoAmW 93*
Pankratz, Paul Martin 1932- *WhoAm 92*
Pannabecker, James H. *Law&B 92*
Pannain, Guido 1891-1977 *Baker 92*
Pannarielo, Anthony Louis 1935- *St&PR 93*
Pannekoek, Hans 1944- *WhoScE 91-3*
Pannell, Berry Coleman 1933- *St&PR 93*
Pannell, William Robert 1936- *St&PR 93*
Pannenberg, Wolfhart 1928- *WhoWor 93*
Panner, Bernard J. 1928- *WhoAm 92*
Panner, Owen M. 1924- *WhoAm 92*
Pannese, Ennio Lucio Romano 1928- *WhoScE 91-3*
Panneton, Jacques 1943- *WhoAm 92*

Panneton, Philippe 1895-1960 BioIn 17
Pannier, Alan 1959- St&PR 93
Pannier, Clyde Robert 1930- St&PR 93
Pannier, Loren C. 1942- St&PR 93
Pannier, Robert P. 1957- St&PR 93
Panning, Anne 1966- ConAu 138
Panning, Bryce Bernard Law&B 92
Pannone, Richard R. 1942- St&PR 93, WhoAm 92
Pannone, Walter Anthony 1947- WhoEmL 93
Pannullo, Deborah Paolino 1953- WhoAmW 93, WhoEmL 93
Panoff, Robert C. 1947- St&PR 93
Panofka, Heinrich 1807-1887 Baker 92
Panofsky, Wolfgang Kurt Hermann 1919- WhoAm 92
Panong, Redulla Everjesto 1950- WhoWor 93
Panos, George 1911- St&PR 93
Panos, Louis G. 1925- ConAu 136
Panos, Peter 1933- St&PR 93
Panou, Georges 1934- WhoWor 93
Panouse, Jacques 1921- WhoScE 91-2
Panov, Alexander Nikolaevich 1944- WhoWor 93
Panova, Vera Fedorovna 1905-1973 BioIn 17
Panozzo, G. WhoScE 91-3
Panozzo, Michael Edward 1958- WhoWrEP 92
Pansa, Thomas Paul 1946- St&PR 93
Pansa Caetronianus, Gaius Vibius d43BC HarEnMi
Panschar, Ruth Mary 1964- WhoE 93
Panselinos, Manuel OxDcByz
Panseron, Auguste-Mathieu 1795-1859 Baker 92
Panshin, Alexei 1940- BioIn 17, ScF&FL 92, WhoWrEP 92
Panshin, Cory 1947- ScF&FL 92
Pansini, Michael Samuel 1928- WhoAm 92
Panson, Gilbert Stephen 1920- WhoAm 92, WhoE 93
Pansu Esclangon, Danielle F. 1932- WhoScE 91-2
Pant, Pushkar Nath 1932- WhoUN 92
Pantages, Louis James 1916- WhoAm 92
Pantaleano, Michael Joseph 1941- St&PR 93
Pantaleoni, Adriano 1837-1908 Baker 92, OxDcOp
Pantaleoni, Romilda 1847-1917 Baker 92, OxDcOp
Pantano, Bryant Frank 1960- St&PR 93
Pantazelos, Peter G. 1930- St&PR 93
Pantazelos, Peter George 1930- WhoAm 92
Pantazis, John A. 1941- St&PR 93
Pantechnes, Constantine fl. c. 1191- OxDcByz
Pantel, Glenn Steven 1953- WhoE 93
Pantel, Stan Ray 1950- St&PR 93
Pantel-Bakst, Sharon S. 1953- WhoAmW 93, WhoWor 93
Pantele, William James Law&B 92
Panteleemon OxDcByz
Panteleemon dc. 305 OxDcByz
Pantelic, Todor L. 1923- WhoScE 91-4
Pantelidis, Veronica Sexauer 1935- WhoSSW 93
Pantell, Dora ScF&FL 92
Pantenberg, Michel 1926- WhoAm 92
Panter, Terry Eve 1957- WhoAmW 93
Panteugenos, Soterichos fl. 12th cent.- OxDcByz
Pantili, Linda Dykes 1947- WhoSSW 93
Pantina, Donald M. 1933- St&PR 93
Pantina, Gloria Ann 1939- St&PR 93
Pantle, William David 1936- WhoAm 92
Panto, Gyorgy 1936- WhoScE 91-4
Pantoja, Antonia 1922- NotHsAW 93 [port]
Pantoleon OxDcByz
Pantoleon fl. 1001-1016 OxDcByz
Pantoliano, Joe BioIn 17
Panton, Ronald Lee 1933- WhoSSW 93
Pantovrc, Mihailo 1944- WhoScE 91-4
Pantozzi, Paul M. 1944- St&PR 93
Pantschak, Vera WhoAmW 93
Pantuliano, Michael J. Law&B 92
Pantuso, Vincent Joseph 1940- WhoAm 92
Pantzer, Kurt Friedrich, Jr. 1928- WhoAm 92, WhoWor 93
Panufnik, Andrzej 1914- Baker 92, PolBiDi
Panufnik, Andrzej 1914-1991 AnObit 1991, BioIn 17
Panula, Jorma 1930- Baker 92
Panum, Hortense 1856-1933 Baker 92
Panuska, Joseph Allan 1927- WhoAm 92
Panutich, Michael F. 1948- St&PR 93
Panwar, B.L. 1933- WhoAsAP 91
Panyarachun, Anand BioIn 17
Panyarachun, Anand 1932- WhoAsAP 91, WhoWor 93
Panyushev, Dmitri Ivanovich 1957- WhoWor 93
Panza, Georgene Sfraga 1950- St&PR 93
Panza, Giuliano Francesco 1945- WhoWor 93
Panza, Nicholas F. 1926- St&PR 93
Panza, Raymond H. 1950- St&PR 93
Panzarella, Angela J. Law&B 92
Panzarella, Catherine St&PR 93
Panzarella, T.A. 1947- St&PR 93
Panzer, Arnold N. 1932- St&PR 93
Panzer, Curtis C. Law&B 92
Panzer, Hans Peter 1922- WhoE 93
Panzer, Mary Ellen 1951- WhoAmW 93
Panzer, Mitchell Emanuel 1917- WhoAm 92
Panzer, Thomas P. 1939- St&PR 93
Panzera, Charles (Auguste Louis) 1896-1976 Baker 92
Panzone, Rafael 1932- WhoWor 93
Pao, Henry C. 1937- St&PR 93
Pao, Y.K. 1918-1991 AnObit 1991
Pao, Yih-Hsing 1930- WhoAm 92
Pao, Yoh-Han WhoAm 92
Pao, Yue-Kong BioIn 17
Paolano, Mary 1918- WhoWrEP 92
Paoletta, Mark R. A. 1962- WhoAm 92
Paoletta, Michael L. 1952- St&PR 93
Paoletti, Antonio 1930- WhoScE 91-3
Paoletti, Jo Barraclough 1949- WhoAmW 93
Paoletti, Pietro 1934- WhoScE 91-3
Paoletti, Rodolfo 1931- WhoScE 91-3
Paoli, Bob 1937- St&PR 93
Paoli, Pasquale 1725-1807 HarEnMi
Paolicelli, Lucia Marie 1961- WhoE 93
Paolillo, William P. 1937- St&PR 93
Paolinelli, Monika 1957- WhoAmW 93
Paolini, Albert, Jr. 1931- St&PR 93
Paolini, Angelo 1947- St&PR 93
Paolini, Bruce Paul Law&B 92
Paolini, Gilbert WhoAm 92
Paolini, Shirley Joan WhoSSW 93
Paolino, Joseph R., Jr. 1955- St&PR 93
Paolino, Joseph Robert, Jr. 1955- WhoAm 92
Paolino, Michael Anthony 1939- WhoE 93
Paolino, Richard Francis 1945- St&PR 93, WhoAm 92
Paolino, Ronald Mario 1938- WhoE 93
Paolino, Vincent A. 1943- St&PR 93
Paoloni, Virginia Ann 1961- WhoAmW 93
Paolozzi, Anthony C. 1945- St&PR 93
Paolozzi, Christina BioIn 17
Paolozzi, Eduardo Luigi 1924- WhoWor 93
Paolucci, Anne Attura WhoAm 92, WhoWrEP 92
Paolucci, Henry WhoAm 92
Paolucci, Ronald Vincent 1927- St&PR 93
Paone, John P., Jr. Law&B 92
Paone, Peter 1936- WhoAm 92
Paonessa, Philip John 1951- WhoE 93
Pap OxDcByz
Papa, Anthony Emil 1914- WhoAm 92, WhoWor 93
Papa, Frank Anthony 1950- St&PR 93
Papa, Joseph Ralph 1943- St&PR 93
Papa, Luigi 1942- WhoScE 91-3
Papa, Mark G. 1946- St&PR 93
Papa, Sergio 1935- WhoScE 91-3
Papa, Vincent T. 1946- WhoAm 92
Papa, Vincent Thomas 1946- St&PR 93
Papachatzi, Marietta 1948- WhoScE 91-3
Papachelas, Eugen 1933- WhoWor 93
Papachristodoulou, Stelios 1940- WhoScE 91-4
Papadakis, Constantine N. 1946- WhoAm 92, WhoEmL 93
Papadakis, Emmanuel Philippos 1934- WhoAm 92
Papadakos, Dimitri P. 1945- St&PR 93
Papadakos, Nicholas Peter 1925- WhoAm 92
Papadatos, Constantin 1920- WhoScE 91-3
Papadeas, Timothy George 1959- WhoSSW 93
Papadias, Basil C. 1932- WhoScE 91-3
Papadimitriou, Constantine 1939- WhoScE 91-3
Papadimitriou, D. Jane Law&B 92
Papadimitriou, Dimitri Basil 1946- WhoE 93, WhoEmL 93, WhoWor 93
Papadinis, James 1929- St&PR 93
"Papa Doc" DcCPCAm
Papadopoulo, Emile Nicholas 1929- WhoWor 93
Papadopoulo, Nicolas 1962- WhoIns 93
Papadopoulos, Athanase 1957- WhoWor 93
Papadopoulos, Athanasios 1955- WhoWor 93
Papadopoulos, Demetrios Panagiotou 1942- WhoWor 93
Papadopoulos, Konstantinos 1937- WhoE 93
Papadopoulos, Panos 1943- St&PR 93
Papadopoulos, Stelios B. 1941- St&PR 93
Papadopoulos, Thomas Constantinos 1957- WhoWor 93
Papadopoyloy, Kiriakoyla 1958- WhoWor 93
Papageorge, Deno D. 1938- St&PR 93
Papageorge, Deno Dennis 1938- WhoAm 92
Papageorge, Evangeline Thomas 1906- WhoAmW 93
Papageorge, Tod 1940- WhoAm 92
Papageorgiou, George C. WhoScE 91-3
Papageorgiou, John Constantine 1935- WhoAm 92, WhoE 93
Papageorgiou, Nicolaos 1941- WhoScE 91-3
Papageorgiou, Stathis BioIn 17
Papagiannis, Michael Dimitrios 1932- WhoAm 92
Papagos, Alexander 1883-1955 DcTwHis
Papagos, Alexandros 1883-1955 HarEnMi
Papaioannou, Evangelia-Lilly 1963- WhoE 93, WhoWor 93
Papaioannou, Yannis (Andreou) 1911-1989 Baker 92
Papaioannou-Souliotis, Pagona 1947- WhoScE 91-3
Papajcik, Dale E. Law&B 92
Papal, Laszlo 1927- WhoScE 91-4
Papaleo, Anthony 1928- WhoAm 92
Papaleo, Joseph 1927- WhoWrEP 92
Papalia, Diane Ellen 1947- WhoAm 92
Papalia, Frank Dominic Law&B 92
Papalian, George Kevork 1922- WhoE 93
Papaliolios, Costas Demetrios 1931- WhoAm 92
Papaloucas, Aristophanes 1930- WhoScE 91-3
Papamichael, Petros 1922- WhoScE 91-3
Papamichael, Thedon MiSFD 9
Papan, Helen WhoAmW 93
Papanastasis, Vasilios P. 1942- WhoScE 91-3
Papanayotou, Panayotis 1936- WhoScE 91-3
Papandopulo, Boris 1906- Baker 92
Papandreou, Andreas BioIn 17
Papandreou, Andreas George 1919- WhoWor 93
Papandreou, Constantine 1939- WhoWor 93
Papandreou, George 1888-1968 DcTwHis
Papanek, Andrew Phillip 1927- St&PR 93
Papanek, Gustav Fritz 1926- WhoAm 92
Papanek, Jan 1896-1991 BioIn 17
Papanek, John BioIn 17
Papanek, Victor 1926- WhoAm 92
Papanicolaou, Nicolas 1947- WhoWor 93
Papanicolaou, Nikos A. 1926- WhoScE 91-3
Papapanagiotou, John 1921- WhoScE 91-3
Papapetropoulos, Thodoros 1937- WhoScE 91-3
Paparazzo, Ernesto 1950- WhoWor 93
Paparella, William F. 1949- St&PR 93
Paparone, Salvatore A. Law&B 92
Papas, Irene 1926- BioIn 17, IntDcF 2-3 [port], WhoAm 92
Papas, Irene Kalandros 1931- WhoE 93
Papasan, Larry W. 1940- WhoAm 92
Papasolomontos, Andreas 1932- WhoUN 92
Papastergiou, Georgios Apostolos 1965- WhoWor 93
Papastrat, Helen Panayota 1958- WhoE 93
Papastrat, Louis A. 1950- St&PR 93
Papastratakos, Nick Law&B 92
Papathanassopoulos, Constantinos 1934- WhoScE 91-3
Papatheodorou, George N. 1939- WhoScE 91-3
Papathomas, Thomas Virgil 1949- WhoE 93, WhoWor 93
Papatzacos, Paul George 1941- WhoWor 93
Papavasiliou, Stathis Spyro 1950- WhoWor 93
Papavassiliou, Athanasios George 1961- WhoWor 93
Papavassiliov, C.T. 1950- WhoScE 91-3
Papay, Lawrence T. 1936- WhoAm 92
Papayanis, Nicholas 1940- WhoE 93
Papazachos, Basilis C. 1930- WhoScE 91-3
Papazian, Dennis Richard 1931- WhoAm 92
Papazian, Edmund Ray Law&B 92
Papazian, Mary Arshagouni 1959- WhoAmW 93
Papazickos, Chris George 1930- St&PR 93
Papazicos, George Law&B 92
Papazissis, Michael George 1935- WhoWor 93
Pape, Arthur Edward 1939- WhoAm 92
Pape, Dennis M. Law&B 92
Pape, E.C. 1937- St&PR 93
Pape, Eugene Thomas 1947- WhoE 93
Pape, Eva Janina WhoWor 93
Pape, Gordon 1936- ScF&FL 92, WhoCanL 92
Pape, Jerry Lee 1934- WhoWor 93
Pape, Kathy L. 1953- St&PR 93
Pape, Patricia Ann 1940- WhoAmW 93
Pape, Sharon B. 1947- ScF&FL 92
Pape, Sharon Barbara 1947- WhoWrEP 92
Pape, William J., II 1931- St&PR 93, WhoAm 92
Pape, William James, II 1931- WhoE 93
Papelian, Joseph E. Law&B 92
Papelino, Jeannine Marie 1968- WhoE 93
Papen, Frank O'Brien 1909- WhoAm 92
Papen, Franz von 1879-1969 DcTwHis
Papenfus, Robert George 1932- St&PR 93
Paper, Lewis 1928- St&PR 93, WhoAm 92
Papera, Gabriel L. 1905- St&PR 93
Paperin, Stewart J. 1948- St&PR 93
Paperin, Stewart Jules 1948- WhoAm 92
Papermaker, Peter ScF&FL 92
Papermaster, Barry A. 1954- St&PR 93
Papernik, Joel Ira 1944- WhoAm 92
Paperny, Myra 1932- DcChlFi
Paperny, Vladimir 1944- WhoWor 93
Papert, Seymour BioIn 17
Papes, Lawrence J. 1940- St&PR 93
Papesh, William G. 1943- St&PR 93
Papi, Gennaro 1886-1941 Baker 92
Papi, Vincent J. 1947- St&PR 93
Papianni, James John 1953- St&PR 93
Papiano, Neil Leo 1933- WhoAm 92
Papic, Krsto 1933- DrEEuF
Papier, Rosa 1858-1932 Baker 92
Papiernik, Donald 1937- St&PR 93
Papiernik, E. WhoScE 91-2
Papiernik, Serge 1958- WhoSSW 93
Papike, James Joseph 1937- WhoAm 92
Papilian-Todorutiu, Cornelia WhoScE 91-4
Papineau, Sarah Jane 1955- WhoUN 92
Papineau-Couture, Jean 1916- Baker 92, WhoAm 92
Papirer, Eugene J.L. 1935- WhoScE 91-2
Papirius Cursor, Lucius fl. 340BC-313BC HarEnMi
Papitto, Ralph Raymond 1926- St&PR 93, WhoAm 92
Papkin, Robert David 1933- WhoAm 92, WhoE 93
Paplauskas, Leonard Paul 1949- WhoE 93
Papock, Herbert 1917- St&PR 93
Papoff, Paolo 1921- WhoScE 91-3
Papoian, Aram Vardgesi 1959- WhoWor 93
Papon, Pierre WhoScE 91-2
Papon, Pierre 1939- WhoScE 91-2, WhoWor 93
Papone, Aldo 1932- St&PR 93
Papoulas, Anastasios 1859-1935 HarEnMi
Papoulias, Sotiri Aris 1953- WhoE 93
Papoulis, Athanasios 1921- WhoAm 92
Papousek, Jaroslav 1929- DrEEuF
Papoutsoglou, Sofronios E. 1943- WhoScE 91-3
Papows, Jeffery Peter 1954- WhoAm 92
Papp, James Michael 1953- WhoE 93
Papp, Janos 1938- WhoScE 91-4
Papp, Jerry 1951- BioIn 17
Papp, Joe 1921-1991 AnObit 1991
Papp, Joseph BioIn 17
Papp, Joseph 1921-1991 CurBio 92N, News 92
Papp, Laszlo George 1929- WhoAm 92, WhoE 93, WhoWor 93
Papp, Miklos 1929- WhoScE 91-4
Papp, Sandor 1936- WhoScE 91-4
Papp, Tony 1961-1991 BioIn 17
Papp, Zoltan Law&B 92
Papp, Zoltan 1942- WhoScE 91-4
Pappa, Michael Joseph 1936- St&PR 93
Pappachristou, Joyce Flores 1932- WhoSSW 93
Pappafava, Lorraine Beddick 1929- St&PR 93
Pappafava, Mona Lynn 1963- St&PR 93, WhoAmW 93
Pappafava, Premo John 1926- St&PR 93
Pappagianis, Demosthenes 1928- WhoAm 92
Pappajohn, John G. 1928- WhoIns 93
Pappalardo, G. WhoScE 91-3
Pappalardo, Rosa Gloria 1932- WhoE 93
Pappalardo, Salvatore Cardinal 1918- WhoWor 93
Pappanikou, Lisa Maria 1962- WhoAmW 93
Pappano, Robert Daniel 1942- St&PR 93, WhoAm 92
Papparis, Michael 1948- WhoWor 93
Pappas, Alceste Thetis 1945- WhoAm 92
Pappas, Alex L. 1932- St&PR 93
Pappas, Angelos ScF&FL 92
Pappas, Anthony John 1940- WhoSSW 93
Pappas, Athanassios Christos 1946- WhoScE 91-3
Pappas, Barbara S. 1931- St&PR 93
Pappas, Charles Engelos 1946- WhoE 93
Pappas, Charles W. 1931- St&PR 93

Pappas, Costas Ernest 1910- WhoAm 92, WhoWor 93
Pappas, Daniel 1947- St&PR 93
Pappas, Dean C. 1939- St&PR 93
Pappas, Edward Harvey 1947- WhoEmL 93
Pappas, Effie Vamis 1924- WhoAmW 93, WhoWor 93
Pappas, George Demetrios 1926- WhoAm 92
Pappas, George Frank 1950- WhoAm 92
Pappas, Greg WhoAm 92
Pappas, Hercules Chris 1928- WhoAm 92
Pappas, Kathryn Dorianne 1958- WhoSSW 93
Pappas, Leah Aglaia 1936- WhoAmW 93
Pappas, Michael 1940- WhoE 93
Pappas, Milton J. 1928- St&PR 93
Pappas, Nicholas 1930- WhoAm 92
Pappas, Nina Kalfas WhoSSW 93
Pappas, Peter A. 1937- St&PR 93
Pappas, Peter C. St&PR 93
Pappas, Phillip M., Jr. 1943- St&PR 93
Pappas, Sandra L. 1949- WhoAmW 93
Pappas, Stephanie Ann 1960- WhoAmW 93
Pappas, Susan Alicia 1952- WhoAmW 93
Pappas, Ted Phillip 1934- WhoAm 92
Pappas, Virginia C. Law&B 92
Pappas, William G. Law&B 92
Pappas, William John 1934- St&PR 93
Pappayliou, George S. Law&B 92
Pappazisis, Evangelos 1882-1974 ScF&FL 92
Pappenheim, Bertha 1859-1936 BioIn 17
Pappenheim, Gottfried Heinrich 1594-1632 HarEnMi
Pappenheimer, Alwin Max, Jr. 1908- WhoAm 92
Pappenheimer, Paul A. 1927- St&PR 93
Papper, Emanuel Martin 1915- WhoAm 92
Papper, Richard N. Law&B 92
Pappert, E. Thomas BioIn 17
Papponi, Paula 1943- WhoAmW 93
Pappos of Alexandria fl. c. 320- OxDcByz
Pappous, Periklis A. Law&B 92
Papp-Vary, Arpad 1938- WhoScE 91-4
Papsidero, Joseph Anthony 1929- WhoAm 92
Papulov, Yuri Grigoryevich 1935- WhoWor 93
Papunen, Heikki T. 1936- WhoScE 91-4
Papus, Lucius Aemilius fl. 225BC-216BC HarEnMi
Paquay, Raymond 1940- WhoScE 91-2
Paque, (Marie Joseph Leon) Desire 1867-1939 Baker 92
Paque, Ronald Edward 1948- WhoSSW 93
Paquet, Florent 1943- St&PR 93
Paquet, Gilles 1936- WhoAm 92
Paquet, Jean Guy 1938- WhoAm 92
Paquet, Karl-Joseph 1937- WhoScE 91-3
Paquet, Marie Louise Law&B 92
Paquet, P. 1937- WhoScE 91-2
Paquette, Andrew 1966- BioIn 17
Paquette, Jack Kenneth 1925- WhoAm 92
Paquette, Joseph F., Jr. 1934- WhoAm 92
Paquette, Rebecca Kvam 1948- WhoAmW 93
Paquette, Robert Hector 1933- St&PR 93
Paquin, Earle Francis 1945- WhoWor 93
Paquin, Madeleine 1962- St&PR 93
Paquin, Paul Peter 1943- WhoAm 92
Para, Elizabeth Marie 1956- WhoAmW 93
Paracchini, Alberto M. 1932- WhoAm 92
Paracka, Daniel Joseph 1949- St&PR 93
Paracsi, Alex Joseph 1939- WhoSSW 93
Paradeise, Catherine 1946- ConAu 138
Paradice, Sammy Irwin 1952- WhoEmL 93, WhoSSW 93
Paradies, (Pietro) Domenico 1707-1791 Baker 92
Paradies, Hasko Henrich 1940- WhoWor 93
Paradis, Adrian A. BioIn 17
Paradis, Adrian A(lexis) 1912- ConAu 40NR
Paradis, Andre 1938- WhoAm 92
Paradis, James Gardiner 1942- WhoE 93
Paradis, Jean Pierre 1940- St&PR 93
Paradis, John Ronald 1934- St&PR 93
Paradis, Marc BioIn 17
Paradis, Margaret R.A. Law&B 92
Paradis, Maria Theresia von 1759-1824 Baker 92, BioIn 17
Paradis, Marjorie Bartholomew AmWomPl
Paradis, Philip M. 1951- WhoWrEP 92
Paradis, Steven 1940- St&PR 93
Paradis, Suzanne 1936- WhoCanL 92
Paradise, David T. Law&B 92
Paradise, Louis Vincent 1946- WhoSSW 93
Paradise, Paul R. 1950- ConAu 137
Paradise, Philip Herschel 1905- WhoAm 92
Paradise, Robert Dennis 1956- St&PR 93
Paradise, Robert R. 1934- St&PR 93
Paradise, Robert Richard 1934- WhoAm 92, WhoE 93
Paradisi, (Pietro) Domenico 1707-1791 Baker 92
Paradissis, Pantelis Pete 1938- St&PR 93
Paradjanov, Sergei BioIn 17
Paradjanov, Sergei 1924-1990 MiSFD 9N
Parady, John Edward 1939- St&PR 93
Paradzanov, Sergo 1924-1990 DrEEuF
Paragon, John MiSFD 9
Paraiso, Moucharaf Justin 1949- WhoUN 92
Parak, Fritz Gunther 1940- WhoScE 91-3, WhoWor 93
Paralez, Linda Lee 1955- WhoAmW 93
Paramo Fabeiro, Ramon 1947- WhoWor 93
Paramore, Gwen AfrAmBi
Paramounts SoulM
Paran, Mark Lloyd 1953- WhoAm 92, WhoE 93
Parandowski, Jan 1895-1978 PolBiDi
Paranicas, Dean J. Law&B 92
Paranov, Moshe 1895- Baker 92
Parapia, Liakat Ali WhoScE 91-1
Paras, Jerome V. 1945- WhoAsAP 91
Paras, Lino S. 1946- St&PR 93
Paras, Nicholas A. 1942- St&PR 93
Paras, Nicholas Andrew 1942- WhoE 93, WhoWor 93
Paras, Richard Stanley Law&B 92
Paras, Sofia Dimitria 1943- WhoAmW 93, WhoE 93, WhoWor 93
Parascan, I. Darif 1927- WhoScE 91-4
Parascos, Edward Themistocles 1931- WhoE 93, WhoWor 93
Paraskakis, Michael Emanuel 1930- WhoWor 93
Paraskevas, Nancy Ann 1946- WhoAmW 93
Paraskeve of Epibatai OxDcByz
Paraskeve of Ikonion OxDcByz
Paraskeve the Elder OxDcByz
Paraskevopoulos, Notis 1953- WhoWor 93
Paraskos, Peter G. 1928- St&PR 93
Parasnis, D.S. 1927- WhoScE 91-4
Parasnis, Ila 1950- WhoAmW 93
Paraspondylos, Leo dc. 1057 OxDcByz
Paratore, Anthony 1944- Baker 92
Paratore, Jean 1949- WhoAmW 93
Paratore, Joseph 1948- See Paratore, Anthony 1944- Baker 92
Paravi, Anna Marie 1961- St&PR 93
Paravisini-Gebert, Lizabeth 1953- ConAu 139
Paray, Paul 1886-1979 Baker 92
Parbery, Betty Lou 1936- WhoAmW 93, WhoSSW 93
Parbhoo, Santilal Parag 1937- WhoWor 93
Parcells, Bill BioIn 17
Parcells, Bill 1941- WhoE 93
Parcells, Charles A., Jr. 1920- St&PR 93
Parch, Grace Dolores WhoAm 92
Parcher, Emily Seaber AmWomPl
Parcher, James Vernon 1920- WhoAm 92
Parchman, R.W. 1944- St&PR 93
Parco, Paul MiSFD 9
Pard, James Le 1930- St&PR 93
Pard, William Le St&PR 93
Pardavi-Horvath, Martha Maria 1940- WhoAmW 93
Pardee, Arthur Beck 1921- WhoAm 92
Pardee, Jack 1936- WhoAm 92, WhoSSW 93
Pardee, Otway O'Meara 1920- WhoAm 92
Pardee, Scott E. 1936- St&PR 93
Pardee, Scott Edward 1936- WhoAm 92
Parden, Robert James 1922- WhoAm 92
Pardes, Herbert 1934- BioIn 17, WhoAm 92
Pardey, William S. 1930- St&PR 93
Pardi, Leo WhoScE 91-3
Pardini, John Paul 1937- St&PR 93
Pardo, Dominick George 1918- WhoAm 92
Pardo, Joseph Frank, Jr. 1952- WhoSSW 93
Pardoc, Blaine ScF&FL 92
Pardoe, Rosemary 1951- ScF&FL 92
Pardoe-Russ, Susan Meredith 1948- WhoEmL 93
Pardo Garcia, German 1902- DcMexL
Pardon, Barry James 1951- St&PR 93
Pardon, Earl 1926-1991 BioIn 17
Pardo Rueda, Rafael WhoWor 93
Pardos, Francoise 1932- WhoWor 93
Pardos, Gregory c. 1070-1156 OxDcByz
Pardoux, Francois Pierre 1950- WhoWor 93
Pardue, Dwight Edward 1928- WhoAm 92
Pardue, James Peter d1991 BioIn 17
Pardue, Larry G. 1944- WhoSSW 93
Pardue, Mark David 1954- WhoSSW 93
Pardue, Mary Lou 1933- WhoAm 92, WhoAmW 93
Pardue, Michael Edward 1949- St&PR 93, WhoAm 92, WhoSSW 93
Pardus, Donald G. 1940- St&PR 93
Pardus, Donald Gene 1940- WhoAm 92
Parduski, Frank N. 1954- WhoE 93
Pare, Anne M. Law&B 92
Pare, Bernard 1944- St&PR 93
Pare, Jean-Claude Law&B 92
Pare, Jean-Jacques 1929- WhoAm 92
Paredes, Alfonso 1926- WhoAm 92
Paredes, Americo 1915- HispAmA, WhoAm 92
Paredes, James Anthony 1939- WhoAm 92
Paredes, Rachel Law&B 92
Paredes, Ruben Dario DcCPCAm
Paredes-Barros, Carlos Humberto 1939- WhoWor 93
Pareigat, Thomas G. Law&B 92
Pareira, Alan S. 1938- St&PR 93
Pareja Diez-Canseco, Alfredo 1908- SpAmA
Pareja-Heredia, Diego 1939- WhoWor 93
Parekh, Bhupendra Kumar 1940- WhoSSW 93
Parekh, Kishor Manubhai 1964- WhoSSW 93
Parell, Mary Law&B 92
Parelli, Attilio 1874-1944 Baker 92
Parello, Raymond Robert 1955- St&PR 93
Parello, Thomas R. 1931- St&PR 93
Parent, Andrew Dennis 1944- WhoAm 92
Parent, Annette Richards 1924- WhoAmW 93
Parent, Armand 1863-1934 Baker 92
Parent, Brian A. 1944- St&PR 93
Parent, Calvin L. 1935- St&PR 93
Parent, Edward E. 1946- St&PR 93
Parent, Jacques 1926- WhoScE 91-2
Parent, James E. 1939- St&PR 93, WhoAm 92
Parent, Louis N. 1927- St&PR 93
Parent, Louise M. Law&B 92
Parent, Mark L. 1948- St&PR 93
Parent, Michael J. 1950- St&PR 93
Parent, Ray R. 1952- St&PR 93
Parent, Rodolphe Jean 1937- WhoAm 92
Parente, Audrey 1948- ScF&FL 92, WhoWrEP 92
Parente, Connie BioIn 17
Parente, Emie J. 1930- St&PR 93
Parente, Emil J. 1930- WhoAm 92
Parente, Michael 1941- WhoAm 92
Parente, Michael A. 1956- St&PR 93
Parente, Michael D. 1955- St&PR 93
Parente, William Joseph 1937- WhoAm 92, WhoWor 93
Parenteau, Shirley 1935- ScF&FL 92
Parenteau, Zoe 1914-1990 BioIn 17
Parentela, Emelinda Maano 1959- WhoWor 93
Parenti, Francesco 1940- WhoScE 91-3
Parepa, Euphrosyne 1836-1874 See Rosa, Carl 1842-1889 OxDcOp
Parepa-Rosa, Euphrosyne OxDcOp
Parepa-Rosa, Euphrosyne 1836-1874 Baker 92
Parer, Warwick Raymond 1936- WhoAsAP 91
Pares, Marion ScF&FL 92
Paret, Peter 1924- WhoAm 92
Pareto, Graziella 1888-1973 Baker 92, OxDcOp
Paretsky, David 1918- WhoAm 92
Paretsky, Sara BioIn 17
Paretsky, Sara 1947- CurBio 92 [port]
Paretsky, Sara N. 1947- WhoAmW 93
Paretzky, Philip 1917-1992 NewYTBS 92
Paretzky, Yvonne Rucker 1949- WhoEmL 93
Parfait, Raymond Gilbert 1946- WhoWor 93
Parfet, William U. 1946- WhoAm 92
Parfet, William Upjohn 1946- St&PR 93
Parfomak, Andrew Nicefor Law&B 92
Pargeter, Edith 1913- BioIn 17, ScF&FL 92
Pargoff, Robert Michael 1961- WhoEmL 93, WhoWor 93
Parham, Betty Ely 1928- WhoAmW 93
Parham, Charles 1938- St&PR 93
Parham, Donald Albert 1930- WhoSSW 93
Parham, Ellen Speiden 1938- WhoAmW 93
Parham, Frederick 1901-1991 AnObit 1991
Parham, Iris Ann 1948- WhoSSW 93
Parham, James C. 1916- St&PR 93
Parham, Lloyd L. 1928- WhoIns 93
Parham, Robert Randall 1943- WhoWrEP 92
Parham, William Howard 1929- St&PR 93
Pariati, Pietro 1665-1733 OxDcOp
Paribeni, Giulio Cesare 1881-1960 Baker 92
Parichy, John B. 1935- St&PR 93
Paridaens, Robert J.H. 1948- WhoScE 91-2
Pariente, Rene 1929- WhoScE 91-2
Pariente, Rene Guillaume 1929- WhoScE 91-2, WhoWor 93
Parietti, Ronald B. 1936- St&PR 93
Parigi-Bini, Roberto 1929- WhoScE 91-3
Parik, Ivan 1936- Baker 92
Parikh, Nitin 1939- St&PR 93
Parikh, Shrikant Navnitlal 1956- WhoSSW 93, WhoWor 93
Parikh, Yogesh L. 1948- St&PR 93
Parikka, Pekka 1939- MiSFD 9
Parillaud, Anne BioIn 17
Parilli, Vito 1930- BiDAMSp 1989
Parillo, Anita C. 1963- WhoAmW 93
Parini, Gregory John 1947- St&PR 93
Parini, Jay BioIn 17, WhoE 93
Parini, Jay 1948- ConAu 16AS [port]
Parini, Joseph A. 1931- St&PR 93
Parins, James William 1939- WhoSSW 93
Parins, Robert James 1918- WhoAm 92
Paris BioIn 17
Paris, comte de 1838-1894 BioIn 17
Paris, Bernard Jay 1931- WhoSSW 93
Paris, Bubba BioIn 17
Paris, Demetrius Theodore 1928- WhoAm 92
Paris, Domonic 1950- MiSFD 9
Paris, Donna Francine 1951- WhoAmW 93
Paris, F. Donald Law&B 92
Paris, Frank Martin 1938- St&PR 93, WhoAm 92
Paris, Hailu Moshe 1933?- BioIn 17
Paris, Henri, comte de 1908- BioIn 17
Paris, Henry MiSFD 9
Paris, Jackie 1926- BioIn 17
Paris, Jane Helen 1953- WhoAmW 93
Paris, Jean d1990 BioIn 17
Paris, Jeffrey Bruce WhoScE 91-1
Paris, Jerry 1925-1986 MiSFD 9N
Paris, Margaret Lucy 1937- WhoE 93
Paris, Mark Frazer 1942- WhoSSW 93
Paris, Matthew Lionel 1938- WhoWrEP 92
Paris, Mica SoulM
Paris, Michel R.R. 1933- WhoScE 91-2
Paris, Michel Rene 1938- WhoScE 91-2
Paris, Nicole 1927- WhoScE 91-2
Paris, Paolo 1936- WhoScE 91-3
Paris, Paul Croce 1930- WhoAm 92
Paris, Peter Junior 1933- WhoAm 92
Paris, Pierre 1957- WhoWor 93
Paris, Raymond William 1937- St&PR 93
Paris, Ronnie d1992 BioIn 17, NewYTBS 92
Paris, Steven Mark 1956- WhoE 93, WhoWor 93
Paris, Tania de Faria Gellert 1951- WhoWor 93
Paris, William C. 1947- St&PR 93
Paris, Wyoming Benjamin BioIn 17
Paris, Yvette BioIn 17
Parise, F.S., Jr. 1951- St&PR 93
Parise, Frank D. ScF&FL 92
Parise, Stephen P. Law&B 92
Pariseau, Patricia 1936- WhoAmW 93
Pariseleti, Thomas William 1938- St&PR 93
Pariser, Andrew R. St&PR 93
Pariser, David Michael 1946- WhoSSW 93
Pariser, M. Charles 1911- St&PR 93
Pariser, Selma R. 1918- St&PR 93
Parish, Amy Mincher AmWomPl
Parish, Barbara Shirk 1942- WhoWrEP 92
Parish, Daniel J. Law&B 92
Parish, Harriet Mary 1930- WhoScE 91-3
Parish, James R. 1946- St&PR 93
Parish, James Robert 1944- ConAu 37NR, WhoAm 92
Parish, James Robert 1946- ScF&FL 92
Parish, John Cook 1910- WhoAm 92
Parish, Lawrence Charles 1938- WhoAm 92
Parish, Lee Anthony Law&B 92
Parish, Louis Leon 1925- WhoAm 92
Parish, Margaret Cecile 1927-1988 ConAu 38NR, MajAI [port], SmATA 73 [port]
Parish, Peggy ConAu 38NR, MajAI, SmATA 73
Parish, Rebecca M. AmWomPl
Parish, Rhonda J. Law&B 92
Parish, Robert 1953- BioIn 17
Parish, Robert L. 1953- WhoAm 92
Parish, Sister BioIn 17
Parish-Alvars, Elias 1808-1849 Baker 92
Parisi, Anthony J. d1991 BioIn 17
Parisi, Eugenio 1949- WhoWor 93
Parisi, Francis 1954- St&PR 93
Parisi, Franklin J. 1945- St&PR 93
Parisi, Franklin Joseph 1945- WhoAm 92
Parisi, Joseph 1944- WhoAm 92
Parisi, Joseph, Jr. 1952- St&PR 93
Parisi, Joseph (Anthony) 1944- WhoWrEP 92
Parisi, Michael Salvatore 1930- St&PR 93

Parisi, Ronald Frederick 1945- *St&PR 93*
Parisian, Edward Franklin 1949- *WhoAm 92*
Parisier, Carlos 1930- *WhoWor 93*
Pariso, Jean Brunner 1925- *WhoE 93*
Parisot, Dean *MiSFD 9*
Parisotto, Gloria 1938- *WhoAmW 93*
Parithivel, Vellore Sundararajan 1951- *WhoE 93*
Pariwa, Samuel 1948- *WhoAsAP 91*
Parizeau, Jacques 1930- *BioIn 17*
Parizek, Eldon Joseph 1920- *WhoAm 92*
Parizo, Victor Bruce 1931- *St&PR 93*
Park, Aloma Hyang Sue *Law&B 92*
Park, Bae Hun 1944- *WhoWor 93*
Park, Barbara 1947- *DcAmChF 1985*
Park, Betty 1938-1990 *BioIn 17*
Park, Bill *ConAu 39NR*
Park, Byeong-Jeon 1934- *WhoWor 93*
Park, Byiung Jun 1934- *WhoWor 93*
Park, Byung-Soo 1930- *WhoWor 93*
Park, Chang *BioIn 17*
Park, Charles D. 1945- *St&PR 93*
Park, Choi-Su *MiSFD 9*
Park, Chung Hee 1917-1979 *DcTwHis*
Park, Chung I. 1938- *WhoWrEP 92*
Park, Clara Claiborne 1923- *ConAu 39NR*
Park, Dabney Glenn, Jr. 1941- *WhoSSW 93*
Park, David Allen 1919- *WhoAm 92*
Park, Denise Cortis 1951- *WhoSSW 93*
Park, Donald L. 1935- *St&PR 93*
Park, Dong-hwan 1936- *WhoWor 93*
Park, Dorothy R. 1925- *St&PR 93*
Park, Dorothy Stagg 1945- *WhoAmW 93*
Park, Ellen *Law&B 92*
Park, Gerald M. *St&PR 93*
Park, Gilbert R. *WhoScE 91-1*
Park, Han Shick 1926- *WhoWor 93*
Park, James Charles 1937- *St&PR 93*
Park, James G. 1930- *St&PR 93*
Park, James Theodore 1922- *WhoAm 92*
Park, Jane Harting 1925- *WhoSSW 93*
Park, Jerry Dee 1936- *St&PR 93*
Park, John J. 1964- *St&PR 93*
Park, Jon Keith 1938- *WhoE 93*
Park, Jordan *ConAu 37NR*
Park, Julia E. *AmWomPl*
Park, Ki-Seong 1958- *WhoWor 93*
Park, Lawrence Kisong *WhoE 93*
Park, Lee Crandall 1926- *WhoE 93, WhoWor 93*
Park, Leland Madison 1941- *WhoAm 92, WhoSSW 93*
Park, Marian Ford 1918- *WhoWrEP 92*
Park, Marian Patricia Ford 1918- *WhoE 93*
Park, Mary Cathryne 1918- *WhoSSW 93*
Park, Mary Woodfill 1944- *WhoAmW 93, WhoE 93*
Park, Merle Florence 1937- *WhoWor 93*
Park, Min-Yong 1955- *WhoE 93*
Park, Mungo 1771-1806 *Expl 93 [port]*
Park, Myung Soo 1937- *WhoWor 93*
Park, Myungkark 1950- *WhoWor 93*
Park, P. Kilho 1931- *BioIn 17*
Park, Paul 1954- *ScF&FL 92*
Park, Paul Kilho 1931- *BioIn 17*
Park, Phocion Samuel, Jr. 1944- *WhoSSW 93*
Park, Rae-Hong 1954- *WhoWor 93*
Park, Robert Ezra 1864-1944 *BioIn 17*
Park, Robert Graham *WhoScE 91-1*
Park, Robert J. *Law&B 92*
Park, Robert S. *St&PR 93*
Park, Roderic Bruce 1932- *WhoAm 92*
Park, Rosemary Cutri 1945- *WhoAmW 93*
Park, Roy H. 1910- *St&PR 93*
Park, Roy Hampton 1910- *WhoAm 92*
Park, Roy Hampton, Jr. 1938- *WhoAm 92*
Park, Ruth *WhoAm 92*
Park, Ruth 1923- *ScF&FL 92*
Park, Ruth Ellen 1933- *WhoAmW 93*
Park, (Rosina) Ruth 1922?- *DcChlFi*
Park, (Rosina) Ruth (Lucia) *ChlFicS*
Park, Sang-Chul 1949- *WhoWor 93*
Park, Seong Yawng *BioIn 17*
Park, Soondal 1939- *WhoWor 93*
Park, Steven John 1957- *WhoWor 93*
Park, Stewart Pearce, Jr. 1936- *St&PR 93*
Park, Sun *BioIn 17*
Park, Sung Ho 1952- *WhoWor 93*
Park, Sungho 1942- *St&PR 93*
Park, Sungkwon 1959- *WhoSSW 93*
Park, Tae-Wi 1936- *WhoWor 93*
Park, Thomas d1992 *NewYTBS 92 [port]*
Park, Thomas 1908-1992 *BioIn 17, CurBio 92N*
Park, Tong-Jin 1922- *WhoWor 93*
Park, Tong Soo 1926- *WhoWor 93*
Park, W(illiam) B(ryan) 1936- *ConAu 39NR*
Park, William Herron 1947- *WhoWor 93*
Park, William John 1925- *St&PR 93*
Park, William Wynnewood 1947- *WhoE 93, WhoWor 93*
Parkany, John 1921- *WhoAm 92*
Parkanyi, Cyril 1933- *WhoSSW 93*
Parkas, Iva Richey 1907- *WhoAmW 93*
Park Chan Jong 1940- *WhoAsAP 91*
Park Chin Gu 1935- *WhoAsAP 91*
Park Chul On 1943- *WhoAsAP 91*
Park Chung-Soo 1933- *WhoAsAP 91*
Park Chung Soon 1935- *WhoAsAP 91*
Parke, Carol Santel 1965- *WhoE 93*
Parke, Dennis Vernon William *WhoScE 91-1*
Parke, Isobel 1926- *WhoE 93*
Parke, Jo Anne Mark 1941- *WhoAm 92, WhoE 93*
Parke, John Shepard 1933- *WhoE 93*
Parke, Margaret Jean 1920- *WhoAmW 93*
Parke, Robert Leon 1940- *WhoWor 93*
Parke, Robert Neal 1944- *St&PR 93*
Parke, Ross D(uke) 1938- *ConAu 38NR*
Parke, Wesley Wilkin 1926- *WhoAm 92*
Parkening, Christopher (William) 1947- *Baker 92*
Parkening, Terry Arthur 1943- *WhoSSW 93*
Parker, Aaron B. *Law&B 92*
Parker, Agnes Miller- 1895-1980 *BioIn 17*
Parker, Alan 1944- *BioIn 17, MiSFD 9*
Parker, Alan John 1944- *WhoAm 92*
Parker, Alan William 1944- *WhoAm 92*
Parker, Alfred Browning 1916- *WhoAm 92*
Parker, Alice 1925- *WhoAmW 93*
Parker, Alice Cline 1948- *WhoAmW 93*
Parker, Alice Constance *WhoE 93*
Parker, Allison *WhoWrEP 92*
Parker, Alton B. 1852-1926 *PolPar*
Parker, Amy Elizabeth 1951- *WhoAmW 93*
Parker, Amy Elizabeth 1956- *WhoAmW 93*
Parker, Andrew *WhoScE 91-1*
Parker, Ann 1934- *WhoAm 92*
Parker, Anne Elizabeth *Law&B 92*
Parker, Arri Sendzimir 1948- *WhoWrEP 92*
Parker, Barbara Jean 1937- *WhoAmW 93*
Parker, Barbara L. 1933- *WhoE 93*
Parker, Barrington Daniels 1915- *WhoAm 92*
Parker, Barry John 1938- *WhoWor 93*
Parker, Barry Richard 1935- *WhoWrEP 92*
Parker, Benjamin M. d1992 *NewYTBS 92*
Parker, Benjamin M. 1899-1992 *BioIn 17*
Parker, Benson *ScF&FL 92*
Parker, Betty June 1929- *WhoWrEP 92*
Parker, Bettye Jean 1931- *WhoAmW 93*
Parker, Beulah Mae 1943- *WhoSSW 93*
Parker, Bobby Eugene, Sr. 1925- *WhoAm 92*
Parker, Brent Mershon 1927- *WhoAm 92*
Parker, C.W. *St&PR 93*
Parker, Camille Killian 1918- *WhoAm 92, WhoWor 93*
Parker, Carol Taylor 1959- *WhoAmW 93*
Parker, Cary *MiSFD 9*
Parker, Cecilia *SweetSg C [port]*
Parker, Celia Ann 1956- *WhoAmW 93*
Parker, Chandler 1949- *St&PR 93*
Parker, Charles Brand 1936- *WhoSSW 93*
Parker, Charles Edward 1927- *WhoWor 93*
Parker, Charles Owen, II 1931- *St&PR 93*
Parker, Charles Walter, Jr. 1922- *WhoAm 92*
Parker, Charlie 1920-1955 *Baker 92, BioIn 17*
Parker, Charlotte Blair *AmWomPl*
Parker, Chris *BioIn 17, ScF&FL 92*
Parker, Christine Wright 1957- *WhoSSW 93*
Parker, Clara d1991 *BioIn 17*
Parker, Clarence 1913- *BioIn 17*
Parker, Clea Edward 1927- *WhoAm 92*
Parker, Clyde H. 1943- *WhoE 93*
Parker, Corey *BioIn 17*
Parker, Cortlandt 1921- *St&PR 93*
Parker, Craig 1957- *St&PR 93*
Parker, Curtis M. 1949- *St&PR 93*
Parker, Cynthia Ann 1827?-1864 *BioIn 17*
Parker, Cynthia Lee 1960- *WhoAmW 93*
Parker, D.F. *WhoScE 91-1*
Parker, D.M. *WhoScE 91-1*
Parker, Dale I. 1945- *St&PR 93*
Parker, Dallas Robert 1947- *WhoEmL 93*
Parker, Daniel d1992 *NewYTBS 92*
Parker, Daniel 1925-1992 *BioIn 17*
Parker, Daniel, Jr. *Law&B 92*
Parker, Daniel Fitzgeorge- *ScF&FL 92*
Parker, Dave 1951- *BioIn 17*
Parker, David 1956- *WhoWor 93*
Parker, David Forster 1934- *WhoSSW 93*
Parker, David Harrison 1949- *WhoWor 93*
Parker, David Joel 1944- *St&PR 93*
Parker, David P. *Law&B 92*
Parker, David R. 1957- *WhoAm 92*
Parker, David Raymond 1943- *WhoSSW 93*
Parker, David Robert 1939- *St&PR 93*
Parker, David S. 1919-1990 *BioIn 17*
Parker, David Shannon 1953- *WhoAm 92*
Parker, Deborah Wynne 1954- *WhoSSW 93*
Parker, Dehra 1882-1963 *BioIn 17*
Parker, Dennis John *WhoScE 91-1*
Parker, Diane Marie 1962- *WhoAmW 93*
Parker, Diane Michelle 1964- *WhoAmW 93*
Parker, Dianna Lynn 1960- *WhoAmW 93, WhoEmL 93*
Parker, Donald Emory 1933- *WhoIns 93*
Parker, Donald Fred 1934- *WhoAm 92*
Parker, Donald Henry 1912- *WhoAm 92*
Parker, Donald Howard 1922- *WhoAm 92*
Parker, Donald LaRue 1935- *WhoAm 92*
Parker, Donald Lester 1944- *St&PR 93*
Parker, Donald S. *Law&B 92*
Parker, Dorothy 1893-1967 *BioIn 17*
Parker, Dorothy Rothschild 1893-1967 *AmWomPl*
Parker, Douglas G. 1955- *St&PR 93*
Parker, Douglas Martin 1935- *WhoAm 92*
Parker, Ed d1990 *BioIn 17*
Parker, Edmond J. 1915- *St&PR 93*
Parker, Edna G. 1930- *CngDr 91, WhoAmW 93*
Parker, Edna Mae 1910- *WhoWrEP 92*
Parker, Edward Andrew *WhoScE 91-1*
Parker, Edward Leroy 1941- *St&PR 93*
Parker, Edwin Burke 1932- *WhoAm 92*
Parker, Edwin Chamberlin 1933- *St&PR 93*
Parker, Edwin Wiley, II *Law&B 92*
Parker, Ellen F. *Law&B 92*
Parker, Ellis Jackson, III 1932- *WhoAm 92, WhoE 93, WhoWor 93*
Parker, Eric William *WhoScE 91-1*
Parker, Ethel Max 1901- *WhoAmW 93*
Parker, Eugene Newman 1927- *WhoAm 92*
Parker, Evan H.C. *WhoScE 91-1*
Parker, Everett Carlton 1913- *WhoAm 92*
Parker, Everett Hoitt 1930- *WhoAm 92*
Parker, Flora L. 1941- *WhoE 93*
Parker, Frances Carr 1925- *WhoWrEP 92*
Parker, Francine *MiSFD 9*
Parker, Frank 1932- *WhoAm 92*
Parker, Frank H. 1941- *WhoAm 92*
Parker, Frank Joseph 1940- *WhoE 93*
Parker, Frank Leon 1926- *WhoAm 92*
Parker, Frank R. 1940- *ConAu 136*
Parker, Frank Solomon 1921- *WhoE 93*
Parker, Franklin 1921- *WhoAm 92, WhoSSW 93, WhoWrEP 92*
Parker, Fred N. 1954- *St&PR 93*
Parker, G.E. *Law&B 92*
Parker, Garth Rockwood 1933- *St&PR 93*
Parker, Gary Dean 1945- *WhoAm 92*
Parker, Gary Wayne 1945- *WhoIns 93*
Parker, Gene 1923- *WhoE 93*
Parker, Geoffrey Alan 1945- *WhoSSW 93*
Parker, George 1929- *WhoAm 92*
Parker, George 1940- *WhoUN 92*
Parker, George Edward, III 1934- *WhoAm 92*
Parker, George Marshall 1889-1968 *HarEnMi*
Parker, Gerald M. 1943- *WhoSSW 93, WhoWor 93*
Parker, Gerald William 1929- *WhoAm 92*
Parker, Gilbert 1862-1932 *BioIn 17*
Parker, Gloria Jean 1947- *WhoSSW 93*
Parker, Gordon Rae 1935- *St&PR 93*
Parker, Graham *St&PR 93*
Parker, Graham Alexander *WhoScE 91-1*
Parker, Gregory Francis 1966- *WhoWor 93*
Parker, Gwendolyn Hall 1946- *WhoEmL 93*
Parker, H. Lawrence 1926- *WhoAm 92*
Parker, Harold Talbot 1907- *WhoAm 92, WhoWor 93*
Parker, Harry John 1923- *WhoAm 92*
Parker, Harry Lambert 1935- *WhoAm 92*
Parker, Harry Lee 1944- *WhoSSW 93*
Parker, Harry S. *BioIn 17*
Parker, Helen N. 1947- *ScF&FL 92*
Parker, Helen Nethercutt 1947- *WhoAmW 93*
Parker, Henry Griffith, III 1926- *St&PR 93, WhoAm 92, WhoIns 93, WhoWor 93*
Parker, Henry Taylor 1867-1934 *Baker 92*
Parker, Horatio W. 1863-1919 *BioIn 17*
Parker, Horatio (William) 1863-1919 *Baker 92*
Parker, Howard E. 1939- *St&PR 93*
Parker, Hyde, Jr. 1739-1807 *HarEnMi*
Parker, Iola B. 1905- *WhoWrEP 92*
Parker, Israel Frank 1917- *WhoAm 92*
Parker, J(ames) C(utler) D(unn) 1828-1916 *Baker 92*
Parker, J. Dean *St&PR 93*
Parker, Jack Royal 1919- *WhoAm 92, WhoWor 93*
Parker, Jack Steele 1918- *WhoAm 92*
Parker, Jacob J. *St&PR 93*
Parker, James *Law&B 92*
Parker, James 1714-1770 *JrnUS*
Parker, James 1924- *WhoAm 92, WhoWor 93*
Parker, James Aubrey 1937- *WhoAm 92*
Parker, James Finklea, Jr. 1959- *WhoAm 92*
Parker, James Francis 1947- *WhoAm 92*
Parker, James L. 1938- *St&PR 93*
Parker, James Lee *Law&B 92*
Parker, James Terry 1958- *WhoEmL 93*
Parker, James W. *Law&B 92*
Parker, James Wilson 1952- *WhoSSW 93*
Parker, Janice H. *Law&B 92*
Parker, Jean *SweetSg C [port], WhoWrEP 92*
Parker, Jeanette Ann 1949- *WhoAmW 93*
Parker, Jeffrey Alan 1957- *WhoSSW 93*
Parker, Jeffrey M. *Law&B 92*
Parker, Jeffrey M. 1949- *St&PR 93*
Parker, Jennifer *ScF&FL 92*
Parker, Jennifer Ware 1959- *WhoAm 92*
Parker, Jerry Cowan 1944- *St&PR 93*
Parker, Jill Eileen 1955- *WhoAmW 93*
Parker, Jim 1934- *BioIn 17*
Parker, Jimmy Byron 1951- *WhoEmL 93*
Parker, Joan 1935- *WhoAm 92*
Parker, John Clarence 1935- *WhoAm 92*
Parker, John E. 1928- *St&PR 93*
Parker, John Eger 1928- *WhoAm 92*
Parker, John F. *Law&B 92*
Parker, John Havelock 1929- *WhoAm 92*
Parker, John Henry 1806-1884 *BioIn 17*
Parker, John Johnston 1885-1958 *OxCSupC*
Parker, John L. *Law&B 92*
Parker, John Malcolm 1920- *WhoSSW 93*
Parker, John Osmyn 1919- *WhoE 93*
Parker, John R., Jr. *Law&B 92*
Parker, John Sheldon 1928- *WhoE 93*
Parker, John Victor 1928- *WhoAm 92, WhoSSW 93*
Parker, John W. 1946- *St&PR 93*
Parker, John William 1792-1870 *BioIn 17*
Parker, John William 1931- *WhoAm 92*
Parker, Jonathan Edward 1936- *WhoAm 92*
Parker, Joseph B., Jr. 1916- *WhoAm 92*
Parker, Joseph Mayon 1931- *WhoAm 92, WhoSSW 93*
Parker, Joseph O. d1992 *NewYTBS 92*
Parker, Joseph O. 1908-1992 *BioIn 17*
Parker, Joseph Raymond 1950- *St&PR 93*
Parker, Joseph Roy, Jr. 1930- *WhoSSW 93*
Parker, Josephine Ann 1952- *WhoAmW 93*
Parker, Josephus Derward 1906- *WhoSSW 93, WhoWor 93*
Parker, Joyce Cave 1948- *WhoWrEP 92*
Parker, Judith Allen 1951- *WhoAmW 93*
Parker, Judith Patricia 1947- *WhoAmW 93*
Parker, Kathleen 1948- *WhoAmW 93, WhoWor 93*
Parker, Kenneth Alan 1945- *St&PR 93*
Parker, Kenneth Francis, Jr. 1964- *WhoE 93*
Parker, Kris *BioIn 17*
Parker, Larry L. 1938- *St&PR 93*
Parker, Laura 1948- *ScF&FL 92*
Parker, Lee Merkel 1939- *WhoSSW 93*
Parker, Lee William *Law&B 92*
Parker, Leonard Sam 1923- *WhoAm 92*
Parker, Leroy Albert, Jr. 1930- *WhoE 93*
Parker, Lewis E.S. 1941- *St&PR 93*
Parker, Linda Margaret 1958- *WhoWor 93*
Parker, Lois M(ay) 1912- *ConAu 39NR*
Parker, Lottie Blair 1858-1937 *AmWomPl*
Parker, Louise N. *AmWomPl*
Parker, M. *Law&B 92*
Parker, M. Linda 1942- *St&PR 93*
Parker, Maceo *BioIn 17, WhoAm 92*
Parker, Malcolm Spencer *WhoScE 91-1*
Parker, Marsha 1952- *ScF&FL 92*
Parker, Martha Ann 1948- *WhoAmW 93, WhoEmL 93*
Parker, Mary Elizabeth Hart 1931- *WhoAmW 93*
Parker, Mary Evelyn 1920- *WhoAm 92*
Parker, Mary Jessie 1948- *SmATA 71 [port]*
Parker, Mary-Louise *BioIn 17*
Parker, Mary Moncure Paynter *AmWomPl*
Parker, Maud May *AmWomPl*
Parker, Maynard Michael 1940- *WhoAm 92, WhoE 93, WhoWrEP 92*
Parker, Mel 1949- *WhoAm 92*
Parker, Michael A. 1950- *St&PR 93*
Parker, Michael L. *Law&B 92*
Parker, Michael Mike 1949- *WhoSSW 93*
Parker, Mike 1949- *CngDr 91, WhoAm 92*
Parker, Nancy Culbertson 1951- *WhoSSW 93*

Parker, Nancy Knowles 1929- *WhoE 93*
Parker, Nancy Snowden Deupree 1934- *WhoWor 93*
Parker, Nancy Winslow *BioIn 17, ChlBIID [port]*
Parker, Nancy Winslow 1930- *MajAI, SmATA 69, WhoAm 92, WhoWrEP 92*
Parker, Noel *ConAu 138*
Parker, Olivia 1941- *WhoAm 92*
Parker, Pamela Ann 1962- *WhoAmW 93*
Parker, Pat 1944- *WhoWrEP 92*
Parker, Pat 1944-1989 *BioIn 17*
Parker, Patricia Holmes 1936- *WhoE 93*
Parker, Patricia L. *ScF&FL 92*
Parker, Patrick Johnston 1931- *WhoWor 93*
Parker, Patrick S. 1929- *St&PR 93*
Parker, Patrick Streeter 1929- *WhoAm 92*
Parker, Paul A. *Law&B 92*
Parker, Paul Edmund, Jr. 1960- *WhoE 93*
Parker, Paula Louise Mason 1940- *WhoAmW 93*
Parker, Peter *BioIn 17*
Parker, Peter 1721-1811 *HarEnMi*
Parker, Peter (Robert Nevill) 1954- *ConAu 136*
Parker, Phillip A. 1935- *St&PR 93*
Parker, Pierson 1905- *WhoAm 92*
Parker, Quanah 1854?-1911 *BioIn 17*
Parker, R. Burton 1914- *St&PR 93*
Parker, R. Joseph 1944- *WhoAm 92*
Parker, Ralph *WhoScE 91-1*
Parker, Ralph H. 1909-1990 *BioIn 17*
Parker, Ray, Jr. 1954- *SoulM*
Parker, Raymond 1922-1990 *BioIn 17*
Parker, Reba Kidder *AmWomPl*
Parker, Ree 1929- *WhoAmW 93*
Parker, Richard Anthony 1905- *WhoAm 92*
Parker, Richard Bennett 1925- *WhoAm 92*
Parker, Richard Eugene, Jr. 1957- *WhoAm 92*
Parker, Richard G. 1926- *St&PR 93*
Parker, Richard Jonathan 1954- *WhoWor 93*
Parker, Richard Leroy 1941- *St&PR 93*
Parker, Richard S. 1943- *St&PR 93*
Parker, Richard W. *Law&B 92*
Parker, Robert *BioIn 17, SoulM*
Parker, Robert A. *Law&B 92*
Parker, Robert Allan Ridley 1936- *WhoAm 92*
Parker, Robert Andrew *ChlBIID [port]*
Parker, Robert Andrew 1927- *WhoAm 92*
Parker, Robert Andrew 1946- *WhoE 93*
Parker, Robert B. 1932- *BioIn 17*
Parker, Robert Brown 1932- *WhoAm 92*
Parker, Robert Chauncey Humphrey 1941- *WhoWor 93*
Parker, Robert Frank *Law&B 92*
Parker, Robert Frederic 1907- *WhoAm 92*
Parker, Robert George 1925- *WhoAm 92*
Parker, Robert Hallett 1922- *WhoAm 92, WhoSSW 93*
Parker, Robert Lee, Sr. 1923- *WhoAm 92*
Parker, Robert Lee, Jr. 1948- *St&PR 93, WhoAm 92*
Parker, Robert LeRoy 1866?- *BioIn 17*
Parker, Robert Louis 1929- *WhoE 93*
Parker, Robert M. 1937- *WhoAm 92, WhoSSW 93*
Parker, Robert M., Jr. *BioIn 17*
Parker, Robert Michael 1946- *WhoSSW 93*
Parker, Robert Orion 1915- *WhoE 93*
Parker, Robert R. 1933- *St&PR 93*
Parker, Robert William 1941- *WhoAm 92*
Parker, Roger Hill 1934- *WhoWor 93*
Parker, Ronn *ScF&FL 92*
Parker, Rosalie S.B. 1936- *St&PR 93*
Parker, Roy Havelock 1948- *WhoWrEP 92*
Parker, Roy Turnage 1920- *WhoAm 92*
Parker, Ruth Anne 1959- *WhoAmW 93*
Parker, S. Gilbert 1933- *St&PR 93*
Parker, Sandra G. *Law&B 92*
Parker, Sara Ann 1939- *WhoAm 92, WhoAmW 93*
Parker, Sarah Jessica *BioIn 17*
Parker, Scott Lane 1946- *WhoAm 92*
Parker, Selwyn James 1941- *WhoWor 93*
Parker, Sheryl Dawn 1948- *WhoSSW 93*
Parker, Stephen C. *Law&B 92*
Parker, Steve H. 1950- *St&PR 93*
Parker, Steven Petway 1951- *St&PR 93*
Parker, Susan Beauchamp 1961- *WhoE 93*
Parker, Susan Brooks 1945- *WhoAm 92*
Parker, Susan Huggard 1939- *WhoAmW 93*
Parker, Ted C., Jr. 1955- *St&PR 93*
Parker, Theodore Clifford 1929- *WhoWor 93*
Parker, Thomas Francis 1949- *WhoE 93*
Parker, Thomas Jason 1945- *St&PR 93*
Parker, Thomas L. 1949- *St&PR 93*
Parker, Thomas Lee 1921- *WhoAm 92*
Parker, Thomas Loyd 1948- *WhoSSW 93*
Parker, Thomas R. *Law&B 92*
Parker, Timothy H. 1946- *St&PR 93*
Parker, Tracey Korherr 1968- *WhoE 93*
Parker, Victor 1925- *St&PR 93*
Parker, Victoria *BioIn 17*
Parker, Virginia Anne 1918- *WhoAmW 93*
Parker, Virginia Lee 1935- *WhoAmW 93*
Parker, Walter Burr 1909- *WhoAm 92*
Parker, Walter K. 1948- *St&PR 93*
Parker, Whilden S. *Law&B 92*
Parker, Wilfred John *WhoScE 91-1*
Parker, William B. *Law&B 92*
Parker, William C. 1927- *St&PR 93*
Parker, William Covington 1927- *WhoE 93*
Parker, William Dale 1925- *WhoSSW 93*
Parker, William H., III 1937- *WhoAm 92*
Parker, William James 1926- *WhoE 93*
Parker, William L. *Law&B 92*
Parker, William Nelson 1919- *WhoAm 92*
Parker, William Riley 1906-1968 *BioIn 17*
Parker, William Skinker 1942- *WhoSSW 93*
Parker, William Stanley 1946- *WhoSSW 93*
Parker, Willis Lamont 1904- *WhoAm 92*
Parker, Woodrow W. 1913- *St&PR 93*
Parker Bowles, Camilla *BioIn 17*
Parker-Griffin, Alice L. *Law&B 92*
Parkerson, George Robert, Jr. 1927- *WhoAm 92*
Parkes, D.A. *WhoScE 91-1*
Parkes, John David *WhoScE 91-1*
Parkes, Karen Elizabeth 1942- *WhoAmW 93*
Parkes, Kenneth Carroll 1922- *WhoAm 92*
Parkes, Margaret Smith 1943- *WhoAmW 93*
Parkes, Nancy Hughes 1960- *St&PR 93*
Parkes, Walter F. *MiSFD 9*
Parkey, Robert Wayne 1938- *WhoWor 93*
Park Hee Tae 1939- *WhoAsAP 91*
Parkhill, Harold Loyal 1928- *WhoWor 93*
Parkhill, Miriam May 1913- *WhoAmW 93*
Parkhouse, Gerald Clive 1931- *WhoE 93*
Parkhurst, Beverly Susler 1944- *WhoAm 92*
Parkhurst, Charles 1913- *WhoAm 92*
Parkhurst, Charles Lloyd 1943- *WhoWor 93*
Parkhurst, Charlotte 1812-1879 *BioIn 17*
Parkhurst, Louis Gifford, Jr. 1946- *WhoWrEP 92*
Parkhurst, Philip A. 1947- *St&PR 93*
Parkhurst, Ted A. 1947- *WhoSSW 93*
Parkhurst, Todd Sheldon 1941- *WhoAm 92*
Park Hyung Oh 1933- *WhoAsAP 91*
Parkin, Andrew *WhoScE 91-1*
Parkin, Andrew Terence Leonard 1937- *WhoWor 93*
Parkin, Christopher John F. 1940- *WhoWor 93*
Parkin, Evelyn Hope 1910- *WhoAmW 93*
Parkin, James Lamar 1939- *WhoAm 92*
Parkin, James W. 1938- *St&PR 93*
Parkin, John Michael *WhoScE 91-1*
Parkin, Patricia *ScF&FL 92*
Parkin, Robert A. 1938- *St&PR 93*
Parkin, T.S.R. *WhoScE 91-1*
Parkins, Frederick Milton 1935- *WhoAm 92*
Parkins, Redvers Nicholson *WhoScE 91-1*
Parkins, Roger L. 1940- *St&PR 93*
Parkinson, Alexander Gordon *WhoScE 91-1*
Parkinson, Arthur David 1935- *WhoUN 92*
Parkinson, Bob d1991 *BioIn 17*
Parkinson, Bradford W. *WhoAm 92*
Parkinson, Cecil *BioIn 17*
Parkinson, Claire Lucille 1948- *WhoEmL 93*
Parkinson, Dale Alwyn George 1941- *St&PR 93*
Parkinson, Dan 1935- *ScF&FL 92, WhoWrEP 92*
Parkinson, David d1991 *BioIn 17*
Parkinson, David Stuart 1938- *St&PR 93*
Parkinson, Dennis *WhoScE 91-1*
Parkinson, Dennis 1927- *WhoAm 92*
Parkinson, Don 1943- *WhoAm 92*
Parkinson, Edythe A. 1948- *St&PR 93*
Parkinson, Ethelyn Minerva 1906- *WhoAm 92*
Parkinson, Georgina *WhoAm 92*
Parkinson, Greg Thomas 1950- *WhoAm 92*
Parkinson, J. David 1929- *St&PR 93*
Parkinson, John David 1929- *WhoAm 92*
Parkinson, John Michael *WhoScE 91-1*
Parkinson, John T. *Law&B 92*
Parkinson, Joseph L. 1945- *St&PR 93*
Parkinson, Kathy 1954- *SmATA 71 [port]*
Parkinson, Leonard Filson 1937- *St&PR 93*
Parkinson, Norman 1913-1990 *BioIn 17*
Parkinson, Richard D. 1949- *St&PR 93*
Parkinson, Roger P. 1941- *WhoAm 92*
Parkinson, T.L. *ScF&FL 92*
Parkinson, Thomas Francis 1920- *WhoWrEP 92*
Parkinson, Thomas Francis 1920-1992 *BioIn 17, ConAu 136*
Parkinson, Thomas Ignatius, Jr. 1914- *WhoAm 92, WhoE 93, WhoWor 93*
Parkinson, Ward D. 1945- *ConEn*
Parkinson, William Charles 1918- *WhoAm 92*
Parkinson, William Walker, Jr. 1919- *WhoSSW 93*
Parkitny, Ryszard 1941- *WhoScE 91-4*
Park Jae Hong 1942- *WhoAsAP 91*
Park Jae Kyu 1947- *WhoAsAP 91*
Park Ji Weon 1935- *WhoAsAP 91*
Park Jong Tae 1921- *WhoAsAP 91*
Park Jong Yul 1932- *WhoAsAP 91*
Park Jun Byung 1935- *WhoAsAP 91*
Park Jyun Kyu 1927- *WhoAsAP 91*
Park Kwan Yong 1939- *WhoAsAP 91*
Park Kyung Soo 1939- *WhoAsAP 91*
Parkman, Ebenezer 1703-1782 *BioIn 17*
Parkman, Elmerina *BioIn 17*
Parkman, Francis d1990 *BioIn 17*
Parkman, Francis 1823-1893 *BioIn 17*
Parkman, George 1790-1849 *BioIn 17*
Parkman, Paul D. *BioIn 17*
Parkman, Paul Douglas 1932- *WhoAm 92*
Parkman, Russell *BioIn 17*
Parkoff, I. David *Law&B 92*
Parkos, Gregory T. 1930- *WhoAm 92*
Parkos, Gregory Theodore 1930- *St&PR 93*
Parks, Arva Moore 1939- *WhoAmW 93*
Parks, Benjamin *Law&B 92*
Parks, Bert *BioIn 17*
Parks, Bert d1992 *NewYTBS 92 [port]*
Parks, Bert 1914-1992 *ConTFT 10, CurBio 92N, News 92, -92-3*
Parks, Betty Louise 1936- *WhoAmW 93*
Parks, Bruce Edward 1951- *WhoE 93*
Parks, Carl McDonald *Law&B 92*
Parks, Charles C. 1945- *St&PR 93*
Parks, Charles Cropper 1922- *BioIn 17, WhoAm 92*
Parks, Charles G., Jr. *Law&B 92*
Parks, Cynthia Agnes 1947- *WhoAmW 93*
Parks, David Jonathan 1955- *St&PR 93*
Parks, Donald Lee 1931- *WhoWor 93*
Parks, Edd Winfield 1906-1968 *ScF&FL 92*
Parks, Edgar E. 1929- *St&PR 93*
Parks, Elizabeth Koplar *Law&B 92*
Parks, Frank Bernard, Jr. 1930- *St&PR 93*
Parks, George M. d1990 *BioIn 17*
Parks, George Richard 1935- *WhoAm 92*
Parks, Gordon *BioIn 17*
Parks, Gordon 1912- *ConHero 2 [port], CurBio 92 [port], MiSFD 9*
Parks, Gordon Roger Alexander Buchanan 1912- *WhoAm 92*
Parks, Grace Susan 1948- *WhoE 93*
Parks, Harold Francis 1920- *WhoAm 92*
Parks, Harold Raymond 1949- *WhoWor 93*
Parks, Henry G., Jr. 1916- *St&PR 93*
Parks, Herbert L. 1925- *St&PR 93*
Parks, Herbert Louis 1925- *WhoIns 93*
Parks, J. Michael 1950- *WhoAm 92*
Parks, James Grant 1946- *WhoSSW 93*
Parks, James Henry, III 1956- *WhoEmL 93, WhoSSW 93, WhoWor 93*
Parks, James Thomas 1947- *St&PR 93, WhoAm 92*
Parks, Janet Elaine 1946- *WhoAmW 93*
Parks, Joe Benjamin 1915- *WhoE 93*
Parks, John Lindsay 1929- *WhoIns 93*
Parks, Karyn Ann 1955- *WhoEmL 93*
Parks, Keith E. *Law&B 92*
Parks, Kent E. 1957- *St&PR 93*
Parks, Leo W. 1930- *WhoSSW 93*
Parks, Leonard Cranford 1936- *WhoSSW 93*
Parks, Leonard Cranford, Jr. 1959- *WhoSSW 93*
Parks, Lloyd Lee 1929- *St&PR 93, WhoAm 92*
Parks, Louis 1955- *WhoE 93*
Parks, Madelyn N. *WhoAm 92*
Parks, Mama Lu d1990 *BioIn 17*
Parks, Marshall Miller 1918- *WhoAm 92*
Parks, Mary Irene 1919- *WhoAmW 93, WhoSSW 93, WhoWor 93*
Parks, Mary June 1926- *WhoIns 93*
Parks, Mary Lu 1928- *WhoWrEP 92*
Parks, Matthew William 1925- *WhoE 93*
Parks, Maurice D. 1935- *St&PR 93*
Parks, Michael 1938- *MiSFD 9*
Parks, Michael Christopher 1943- *WhoAm 92, WhoWor 93*
Parks, Nancy Ann 1955- *WhoAmW 93*
Parks, Patrick Christopher *WhoScE 91-1*
Parks, Patrick Christopher 1930- *WhoWor 93*
Parks, Paul 1923- *WhoWor 93*
Parks, Raymond E. *Law&B 92*
Parks, Richard Dee 1938- *WhoWor 93*
Parks, Richard Howard 1951- *WhoSSW 93*
Parks, Richard L. 1948- *St&PR 93*
Parks, Richard William 1938- *WhoAm 92*
Parks, Robert A. 1946- *St&PR 93*
Parks, Robert Allan 1946- *WhoE 93*
Parks, Robert Emmett, Jr. 1921- *WhoAm 92*
Parks, Robert Hall 1924- *WhoSSW 93*
Parks, Robert Henry 1924- *WhoAm 92*
Parks, Robert Myers 1927- *WhoAm 92*
Parks, Robin 1957- *WhoAmW 93, WhoEmL 93*
Parks, Robyn Leroy d1992 *BioIn 17*
Parks, Rosa 1913- *BioIn 17, EncAACR [port]*
Parks, Rosa Louise 1913- *AfrAmBi*
Parks, Susan Johnson 1951- *WhoE 93*
Parks, Sydney Jo 1950- *St&PR 93*
Parks, Thomas Jefferson 1903-1991 *BioIn 17*
Parks, Thomas Keith 1951- *WhoE 93*
Parks, Thomas W. 1939- *WhoAm 92*
Parks, Tom Gilliam, Jr. 1959- *WhoSSW 93*
Parks, Van Dyke *BioIn 17*
Parks, Vincent Joseph 1928- *WhoE 93*
Parks, Wilda Alice 1940- *WhoAmW 93*
Parks, William c. 1698-1750 *JrnUS*
Parks, William A. 1939- *St&PR 93*
Park Sang Cheon 1940- *WhoAsAP 91*
Park Seok Moo 1944- *WhoAsAP 91*
Park Seung-Jae 1934- *WhoAsAP 91*
Park Sil 1941- *WhoAsAP 91*
Parks-Karam, Deborah Lu 1954- *WhoAmW 93*
Parks McKay, Jane Raye 1952- *WhoAmW 93*
Parks-Veal, Phyllis Marcus 1947- *WhoSSW 93*
Park Tae Kwon 1947- *WhoAsAP 91*
Park Woo-Byong 1934- *WhoAsAP 91*
Parkyn, John William 1931- *WhoSSW 93*
Park Yong Man 1925- *WhoAsAP 91*
Park Young Sook 1933- *WhoAsAP 91*
Parl, Steen Allan 1945- *WhoAm 92*
Parlakian, Nishan 1925- *WhoE 93*
Parlamagni, Antonio 1759-1838 *OxDcOp*
Parlamis, Michael Frank 1940- *WhoE 93*
Parlato, Anthony Charles 1962- *WhoE 93*
Parlatore, Anselm 1943- *WhoWrEP 92*
Parler, William Carlos 1929- *WhoAm 92*
Parlett, Reg 1904-1991 *AnObit 1991*
Parlevliet, Jan E. 1932- *WhoScE 91-3*
Parley, Peter 1793-1860 *BioIn 17*
Parliament *SoulM*
Parlin, Charles C., Jr. 1928- *WhoAm 92*
Parlin, Gary Victor 1941- *St&PR 93*
Parlow, Kathleen 1890-1963 *Baker 92*
Parm, Teuvo V.J. 1937- *WhoScE 91-4*
Parma, Alessandro Farnese, Duke of 1545-1592 *HarEnMi*
Parma, Sikko 1931- *WhoScE 91-3*
Parmacek, Robert K. 1931- *St&PR 93*
Parmalee, Juliette B. *AmWomPl*
Parmalee, Paul Woodburn *BioIn 17*
Parman, Donald F. *Law&B 92*
Parman, Frank *WhoWrEP 92*
Parman, James Frank 1938- *WhoWrEP 92*
Parmar, Rajubhai A. 1950- *WhoAsAP 91*
Parmelee, Arthur Hawley, Jr. 1917- *WhoAm 92*
Parmelee, David Freeland 1924- *WhoAm 92*
Parmelee, Harold J. 1937- *WhoAm 92*
Parmelee, Harold Joseph 1937- *St&PR 93*
Parmelee, William Douglas 1957- *WhoSSW 93*
Parmely, Laurine Symula *Law&B 92*
Parmenion c. 400BC-330BC *HarEnMi*
Parmenter, Charles Stedman 1933- *WhoAm 92*
Parmenter, L. Richard 1949- *St&PR 93*
Parmenter, Mary Jane 1930- *WhoAmW 93*
Parmenter, Robert Haley 1925- *WhoAm 92*
Parmer, Edgar Alan 1928- *WhoE 93*
Parmerlee, Mark S. 1955- *WhoSSW 93, WhoWor 93*
Parmet, Herbert Samuel 1929- *WhoE 93*
Parmeter, J. Thomas *St&PR 93*
Parmiani, Giorgio 1938- *WhoScE 91-3*
Parmiter, Ian Myles 1957- *WhoSSW 93*
Parmiter, James Darlin 1934- *WhoAm 92*
Parmley, Loren Francis, Jr. 1921- *WhoAm 92, WhoWor 93*
Parmley, Robert Dunning *Law&B 92*
Parmley, Robert James 1950- *WhoSSW 93*
Parnall, Peter 1936- *MajAI [port], SmATA 69 [port]*
Parnas, David Lorge 1941- *WhoAm 92*
Parnas, Leslie 1931- *Baker 92*
Parnell, Andrea Hudson 1944- *WhoWrEP 92*

Parnell, Charles Stewart 1846-1891 BioIn 17
Parnell, Covert E., III Law&B 92
Parnell, Dale BioIn 17
Parnell, Dale Paul 1928- WhoAm 92
Parnell, Francis William, Jr. 1940- WhoAm 92
Parnell, Frank H. 1916- ScF&FL 92
Parnell, Jack Callihan 1935- WhoAm 92
Parnell, Jeffrey C. Law&B 92
Parnell, Lawrence J. 1953- St&PR 93
Parnell, Mel 1922- BioIn 17
Parnell, Melvin Lloyd 1922- BiDAMSp 1989
Parnell, Michael WhoWrEP 92
Parnell, Thomas 1679-1718 BioIn 17
Parnell, Thomas Alfred 1931- WhoAm 92
Parnes, Andrew H. 1958- St&PR 93
Parnes, Edmund Ira 1936- WhoSSW 93
Parnes, H. Elliot Law&B 92
Parnes, Robert Mark 1946- WhoE 93
Parness, Andrea Michelle 1956- WhoEmL 93
Parness, Howard Arthur 1942- WhoSSW 93
Parnham, Gary Peter 1950- WhoE 93
Parnia, Pirvan 1932- WhoScE 91-4
Parniak, M.F. St&PR 93
Parniczky, Gabor 1925- WhoScE 91-4
Parnis, Mollie 1905?-1992 CurBio 92N, NewYTBS 92 [port]
Parnov, Eremei 1935- ScF&FL 92
Paro, Robert T. 1964- St&PR 93
Paro, Tom Edward 1923- WhoAm 92
Parochetti, James Victor 1940- WhoE 93
Parode, Ann Law&B 92
Parode, Ann 1947- St&PR 93
Parodi, Alexandre 1901-1979 BioIn 17
Parodi, Lorenzo 1856-1926 Baker 92
Parodneck, Lloyd Law&B 92
Paroff, Harvey Michael Law&B 92
Paroissien, David Harry 1939- WhoE 93
Parola, John Joseph 1948- WhoAm 92
Parolari, Fred Foley 1929- St&PR 93
Parone, Edward MiSFD 9
Paronen, J. WhoScE 91-4
Paronen, Timo Petteri 1955- WhoScE 91-4
Paront, George John 1953- WhoE 93, WhoWor 93
Paroski, Paul d1990 BioIn 17
Parotti, Phillip Elliott 1941- WhoSSW 93
Parpola, Asko Heikki Siegfried 1941- WhoWor 93
Parque, Richard Anthony 1935- WhoWrEP 92
Parr, Albert Eide 1900-1991 BioIn 17
Parr, Ann Leslie Law&B 92
Parr, Carol Cunningham 1941- WhoAm 92
Parr, Carolyn Miller CngDr 91
Parr, Carolyn Miller 1937- WhoAm 92, WhoAmW 93
Parr, Cynthia Ohanian Law&B 92
Parr, David W. Law&B 92
Parr, Eugene Quincy 1925- WhoWor 93
Parr, Ferdinand Van Siclen, Jr. 1908- WhoAm 92
Parr, Grant Van Siclen 1942- WhoAm 92
Parr, James Gordon 1927- WhoAm 92
Parr, John 1928- WhoCanL 92
Parr, Larry MiSFD 9
Parr, Larry Michael 1946- St&PR 93
Parr, Lloyd Byron 1931- WhoAm 92
Parr, Mary Yohannan 1927- WhoAmW 93, WhoE 93
Parr, Richard A., II Law&B 92
Parr, Richard S. Law&B 92
Parr, Robert Ghormley 1921- WhoAm 92
Parr, Royse M. Law&B 92
Parr, Royse Milton 1935- WhoAm 92
Parr, Samuel E. 1921- St&PR 93
Parr, Sandra Hardy 1952- WhoAmW 93, WhoEmL 93
Parr, Susan Resneck 1943- WhoAm 92, WhoAmW 93
Parra, Consuelo BioIn 17
Parra, Nicanor 1914- BioIn 17, SpAmA
Parra, Porfirio 1856-1912 DcMexL
Parra, Robert Joseph 1940- WhoE 93
Parra, Teresa de la 1890-1936 BioIn 17, SpAmA
Parra, Violeta 1917-1967 BioIn 17
Parrado, Peter Joseph 1953- WhoSSW 93
Parraguirre, Ronald David 1959- WhoEmL 93
Parramore, Barbara Mitchell 1932- WhoAmW 93
Parratt, Walter 1841-1924 Baker 92
Parratto, Nanette Pamela 1956- WhoAmW 93, WhoEmL 93
Parravano, Amelia Elizabeth 1951- WhoE 93
Parrenas, Cecilia Salazar 1945- WhoAmW 93
Parrenas, Julius Caesar Fornes 1959- WhoWor 93
Parrent, Joanne 1948- BioIn 17
Parrent, Joanne Elizabeth 1948- WhoAmW 93, WhoEmL 93
Parrett, Brent F. 1955- St&PR 93
Parretti, Giancarlo BioIn 17
Parretti, Giancarlo 1942- WhoAm 92
Parriaud, Jean-Claude 1926- WhoScE 91-2
Parrick, Gerald Hathaway 1924- WhoWor 93
Parrilla Sanchez, Roberto 1941- WhoScE 91-3
Parrin, Robert L. 1950- St&PR 93
Parrinder, Patrick 1944- ScF&FL 92
Parrinello, Michele 1945- WhoWor 93
Parrini, Paolo 1933- WhoScE 91-3
Parriott, James D. MiSFD 9
Parriott, James Deforis, Jr. 1923- WhoAm 92
Parris, Cheryl Ann Elizabeth 1968- WhoE 93
Parris, Gail A. 1951- St&PR 93
Parris, Guichard BioIn 17
Parris, Herman 1903-1973 Baker 92
Parris, P.A. WhoScE 91-1
Parris, Prudence Langworthy Murphy 1934- WhoAmW 93
Parris, Robert 1924- Baker 92, WhoAm 92
Parris, Robert B. 1935- St&PR 93
Parris, Samuel 1653-1720 BioIn 17
Parris Family BioIn 17
Parrish, Alvin Edward 1922- WhoAm 92
Parrish, Barney ScF&FL 92
Parrish, Barry Jay 1946- WhoAm 92
Parrish, Benjamin F., Jr. Law&B 92
Parrish, Carl 1904-1965 Baker 92
Parrish, Charles M. 1947- St&PR 93
Parrish, Charles W. BioIn 17
Parrish, Danny Burke 1947- St&PR 93
Parrish, David Joe 1943- WhoSSW 93
Parrish, David Walker, Jr. 1923- WhoAm 92
Parrish, Delores M. 1935- St&PR 93
Parrish, Douglas D. 1945- St&PR 93
Parrish, E. Al 1945- St&PR 93
Parrish, Edgar Lee 1948- WhoAm 92, WhoE 93
Parrish, Edward Alton, Jr. 1937- WhoWor 93
Parrish, Edward L. 1939- St&PR 93
Parrish, Florence Tucker WhoSSW 93
Parrish, Frank Jennings 1923- St&PR 93, WhoAm 92, WhoWor 93
Parrish, Gilliam Young Law&B 92
Parrish, Harry Jacob 1922- St&PR 93
Parrish, Harry Jacob, II 1950- St&PR 93
Parrish, Helen d1959 SweetSg C [port]
Parrish, James L. Law&B 92
Parrish, James Nathaniel 1939- St&PR 93, WhoSSW 93
Parrish, James Ogden 1940- St&PR 93
Parrish, Jay 1921- WhoAm 92
Parrish, Jere Paul 1941- St&PR 93
Parrish, John A. Law&B 92
Parrish, John Bishop 1911- WhoAm 92
Parrish, John Brett 1934- WhoAm 92
Parrish, John Wayne 1916- St&PR 93
Parrish, John Wesley, Jr. 1941- WhoAm 92
Parrish, Joseph Cree 1964- WhoWor 93
Parrish, Kathleen BioIn 17
Parrish, Lawrence Wolcott 1936- St&PR 93
Parrish, Margaret Ann 1941- WhoAmW 93
Parrish, Marie McAdams 1916- WhoSSW 93
Parrish, Mary Frances ConAu 138
Parrish, Mattie C. 1921- St&PR 93
Parrish, Michael A. 1953- St&PR 93
Parrish, Michael Frederick Law&B 92
Parrish, Nancy Elaine Buchele 1948- WhoAmW 93
Parrish, Ophelia 1850-1915 BioIn 17
Parrish, Overton Burgin, Jr. 1933- WhoAm 92, WhoWor 93
Parrish, Pam D. Law&B 92
Parrish, R. Alan 1949- St&PR 93
Parrish, Richard B. 1938- WhoAm 92
Parrish, Richard Brooks 1938- St&PR 93
Parrish, Richard Thomas 1946- St&PR 93
Parrish, Robert 1916- MiSFD 9
Parrish, Robert Alton 1930- WhoAm 92
Parrish, Ronald L. 1942- St&PR 93
Parrish, Stephen Bennett 1952- St&PR 93
Parrish, Stephen L. 1951- St&PR 93
Parrish, Steven C. 1950- St&PR 93
Parrish, Steven Clay Law&B 92
Parrish, T.R. 1954- St&PR 93
Parrish, Thomas Douglas WhoSSW 93
Parrish, Thomas Evert Law&B 92
Parrish, Thomas Kirkpatrick, III 1930- WhoAm 92
Parrish, William Earl 1931- WhoAm 92, WhoSSW 93
Parrish-Porter, Vallerie 1951- WhoAmW 93
Parr-Johnston, Elizabeth BioIn 17
Parr-Johnston, Elizabeth 1939- WhoAmW 93
Parronchi, Alessandro 1914- DcLB 128 [port]
Parrondo, Tomas 1857-1900 BioIn 17
Parrot, Kenneth D. 1947- St&PR 93
Parrot, Kent Kane 1911- WhoE 93
Parrott, Andrew 1947- Baker 92
Parrott, B.J. 1951- St&PR 93
Parrott, Charles N. 1950- St&PR 93
Parrott, Charles Stephen 1952- WhoSSW 93
Parrott, Christopher A. 1949- St&PR 93
Parrott, Christopher Allen Law&B 92
Parrott, David Wesley 1950- WhoSSW 93
Parrott, (Horace) Ian 1916- Baker 92
Parrott, Jeffrey Michael Law&B 92
Parrott, John Edwin WhoScE 91-1
Parrott, John William 1948- St&PR 93
Parrott, Leslie 1922- WhoAm 92
Parrott, Robert Harold 1923- WhoAm 92
Parrott, Roy E. 1941- St&PR 93
Parrott, Wanda Sue 1935- WhoWrEP 92
Parrs, Walter, Jr. Law&B 92
Parry, Albert d1992 NewYTBS 92
Parry, Albert 1901-1992 BioIn 17, CurBio 92N
Parry, Andrea L. Law&B 92
Parry, Arthur Edward WhoIns 93
Parry, Brian James 1939- WhoScE 91-1
Parry, Carol Jacqueline 1941- WhoAm 92
Parry, Charles G. 1936- St&PR 93
Parry, Christine M. 1964- WhoE 93
Parry, (William) Edward 1790-1855 Expl 93 [port]
Parry, (Charles) Hubert (Hastings) 1848-1918 Baker 92
Parry, Hugh Jones 1916- WhoAm 92
Parry, John c. 1710-1782 Baker 92
Parry, John 1776-1851 Baker 92
Parry, John R. 1941- St&PR 93
Parry, John Robert 1941- WhoAm 92
Parry, Joseph 1841-1903 Baker 92
Parry, Katharine AmWomPl
Parry, Lance Aaron 1947- WhoAm 92
Parry, Linda English 1949- WhoAmW 93
Parry, Malcolm 1949- WhoScE 91-1
Parry, Michael David 1951- St&PR 93
Parry, Michel 1947- ScF&FL 92
Parry, Pamela Jeffcott 1948- BioIn 17, WhoAm 92
Parry, R.H.G. WhoScE 91-1
Parry, Rawdon Moira Crozier 1949- St&PR 93, WhoAm 92
Parry, Richard David 1939- WhoSSW 93
Parry, Richard Owen Law&B 92
Parry, Robert T. 1939- St&PR 93
Parry, Robert Templeton WhoScE 91-1
Parry, Robert Troutt 1939- WhoAm 92
Parry, Robert Walter 1917- WhoAm 92
Parry, Ruth Elaine 1952- WhoAmW 93
Parry, Thomas C. 1928- St&PR 93, WhoAm 92, WhoSSW 93
Parry, Thomas Herbert, Jr. 1928- WhoSSW 93
Parry, William WhoScE 91-1
Parsch, Arnost 1936- Baker 92
Parsche, Dorrie WhoScE 91-1
Parseghian, Ara Raoul 1923- WhoAm 92
Parshall, Donald Richard, Jr. Law&B 92
Parshall, George William 1929- WhoAm 92, WhoE 93
Parshall, Gerald 1941- WhoAm 92
Parshall, Joanne M. 1963- WhoAmW 93
Parshall, Walter Raymond 1905- WhoAm 92
Parshalle, Gerald S. 1924- St&PR 93
Parshley, Floyd Atwood 1935- St&PR 93
Parsky, Gerald Lawrence 1942- WhoAm 92
Parsky, Robert M. 1937- St&PR 93
Parsley, Brantley Hamilton 1927- WhoWor 93
Parsley, Jo Ann Foust 1931- WhoSSW 93
Parsley, Osbert 1511-1585 Baker 92
Parsley, Robert Horace 1923- WhoAm 92
Parsley, Steven Dwayne 1959- WhoEmL 93
Parslow, Philip Leo 1938- WhoAm 92
Parson, Christine Jennifer N. 1943- WhoE 93
Parson, Sheryl A. 1961- WhoAmW 93
Parsonage, John Roberts WhoScE 91-1
Parsons, A.H. WhoScE 91-1
Parsons, Albert Ross 1847-1933 Baker 92
Parsons, Alvin L. 1949- WhoIns 93
Parsons, Alvin Lewis 1949- WhoE 93
Parsons, Andrew John 1943- WhoAm 92
Parsons, Betty 1900-1982 BioIn 17
Parsons, Brian WhoScE 91-1
Parsons, Catherine B. WhoWrEP 92
Parsons, Coleman 1905-1991 BioIn 17
Parsons, Daniel Lankester 1953- WhoSSW 93, WhoWor 93
Parsons, David William Law&B 92
Parsons, Donald Gladwin 1927- St&PR 93
Parsons, Donald H. 1930- St&PR 93
Parsons, Donald James 1922- WhoAm 92
Parsons, Donna Jean 1951- WhoAmW 93
Parsons, Earl B., Jr. 1938- St&PR 93
Parsons, Edmund Morris 1936- WhoE 93, WhoSSW 93, WhoWor 93
Parsons, Edwin Spencer 1919- WhoAm 92
Parsons, Elizabeth W. 1910- St&PR 93
Parsons, Ellen MajAI
Parsons, Elmer Earl 1919- WhoAm 92
Parsons, Elsie Clews 1874-1941 IntDcAn
Parsons, Elsie Worthington Clews 1875-1941 BioIn 17
Parsons, Estelle 1927- WhoAm 92, WhoE 93
Parsons, Fletcher Ralph 1926- St&PR 93
Parsons, Frederick Ambrose 1916- WhoWor 93
Parsons, Gary M. 1950- St&PR 93
Parsons, Gene 1944- See Byrds, The ConMus 8
Parsons, Geoffrey (Penwill) 1929- Baker 92
Parsons, George H. Law&B 92
Parsons, George Raymond, Jr. 1938- WhoAm 92
Parsons, George Williams 1918- WhoAm 92
Parsons, Gerald Joseph 1952- St&PR 93
Parsons, Gram 1946-1973 Baker 92, BioIn 17
See Also Byrds, The ConMus 8
Parsons, Helga Lund 1906- WhoAmW 93
Parsons, Henry McIlvaine 1911- WhoAm 92
Parsons, Irene WhoAm 92
Parsons, J. A. 1935- WhoAm 92
Parsons, J. Graham 1907-1991 BioIn 17
Parsons, James B. 1921- ScF&FL 92
Parsons, James Benton 1913- WhoAm 92
Parsons, James Earl Law&B 92
Parsons, James Jerome 1915- WhoAm 92
Parsons, Jan BioIn 17
Parsons, Jeffrey Robinson 1939- WhoAm 92
Parsons, John David WhoScE 91-1
Parsons, John Morford 1938- WhoE 93
Parsons, John Sanford 1940- WhoUN 92
Parsons, John T. 1913- St&PR 93
Parsons, John William WhoScE 91-1
Parsons, John William 1943- WhoWor 93
Parsons, Joseph Edward 1957- WhoSSW 93
Parsons, Judson Aspinwall, Jr. 1929- WhoAm 92
Parsons, Kate AmWomPl
Parsons, Keith I. 1912- WhoAm 92
Parsons, Kermit Carlyle 1927- WhoAm 92
Parsons, Kitty AmWomPl
Parsons, Laura Matilda Stephenson 1855- AmWomPl
Parsons, Leonard Jon 1942- WhoAm 92
Parsons, Linda Lee 1947- WhoAmW 93
Parsons, Louella 1881-1972 BioIn 17, JrnUS
Parsons, Malcolm Barningham 1919- WhoAm 92
Parsons, Margaret Colby Getchell 1891- AmWomPl
Parsons, Maxwell S. 1959- St&PR 93
Parsons, Merribell Maddux WhoAm 92, WhoAmW 93
Parsons, Michael John 1935- WhoAm 92
Parsons, Mira Clark AmWomPl
Parsons, Peter Harold 1938- St&PR 93, WhoE 93
Parsons, Radford Royce 1965- WhoWrEP 92
Parsons, Richard Curtis 1942- St&PR 93
Parsons, Richard Dean 1948- WhoAm 92
Parsons, Robert M. Law&B 92
Parsons, Robert William, Jr. 1957- WhoSSW 93
Parsons, Roger WhoScE 91-1
Parsons, Roger G. 1943- St&PR 93
Parsons, Rosemarie Ann 1939- WhoAmW 93
Parsons, Stanley B., Jr. 1927- WhoWrEP 92
Parsons, Stuart N. 1942- St&PR 93
Parsons, Talcott 1902-1979 BioIn 17
Parsons, Timothy Richard 1932- WhoAm 92
Parsons, Victor WhoScE 91-1
Parsons, Vinson Adair 1932- WhoAm 92
Parsons, Virginia Mae 1942- WhoAmW 93
Parsons, Warren F. 1939- St&PR 93
Parsons, William 1922-1991 BioIn 17
Parsons, William A. 1910- St&PR 93
Parsons, William Flournoy 1930- WhoSSW 93
Parsons-Salem, Diane Lora Law&B 92
Parsons-Salem, Diane Lora 1945- WhoAmW 93
Parsont, Meg BioIn 17
Parsont, Robert E. 1936- St&PR 93
Parsont, Robert Edward 1936- WhoAm 92
Part, Antony 1916-1990 BioIn 17

Part, Arvo 1935- *BakerA 92, BioIn 17*
Part, Michael 1949- *MiSFD 9*
Partain, Clarence Leon 1940- *WhoAm 92*
Partain, Claude Raymond 1940- *St&PR 93*
Partain, Eugene Gartly 1930- *WhoAm 92*
Partain, Larry Dean 1942- *WhoAm 92*
Partain, Michael M. *Law&B 92*
Partain, Thomas A. 1955- *St&PR 93*
Partain, William A. *Law&B 92*
Partan, Daniel Gordon 1933- *WhoAm 92*
Partanen, Carl Richard 1921- *WhoAm 92*
Partanen, Juhani V.S. 1945- *WhoScE 91-4*
Partch, Harry 1901-1974 *Baker 92, BioIn 17*
Partch, Kenneth Paul 1925- *WhoAm 92, WhoWrEP 92*
Partee, Barbara Hall 1940- *WhoAm 92, WhoAmW 93, WhoWrEP 92*
Partee, John Charles 1927- *BioIn 17*
Partello-Hollingsworth, Helen *BioIn 17*
Parten, Joe W. 1927- *St&PR 93*
Parten, Jubal R. d1992 *NewYTBS 92 [port]*
Parthe, Erwin 1928- *WhoScE 91-4*
Parthemore, Jacqueline G. 1940- *WhoAmW 93*
Parthey, Lili 1800-1829 *BioIn 17*
Parthier, Benno *BioIn 17*
Parthier, Benno 1932- *WhoScE 91-3*
Parthum, Charles Albert 1929- *WhoAm 92*
Particelli, Marc C. 1945- *St&PR 93*
Partin, Kenneth August 1933- *St&PR 93*
Partinen, Markku Mikael 1948- *WhoWor 93*
Partington, Donald Eugene *Law&B 92*
Partington, James Wood 1939- *WhoAm 92*
Partington, John Edwin 1907- *WhoSSW 93*
Partington, Thomas Martin *WhoScE 91-1*
Partis, J.P. *WhoScE 91-1*
Partnoy, Ronald Allen *Law&B 92*
Partnoy, Ronald Allen 1933- *WhoAm 92*
Partoll, Alfred Carl 1934- *St&PR 93, WhoAm 92*
Parton, Dolly *BioIn 17*
Parton, Dolly 1946- *Baker 92*
Parton, Dolly Rebecca 1946- *WhoAm 92, WhoAmW 93*
Parton, James 1912- *WhoAm 92*
Parton, Raymond 1930- *St&PR 93*
Parton, Sara Payson Willis 1811-1872 *JrnUS*
Parton, W. Jeff 1925- *WhoIns 93*
Parton, William C. 1930- *St&PR 93*
Partos, Oedoen 1907-1977 *Baker 92*
Partosoedarso, Moeljono 1933- *WhoUN 92*
Partridge, Bruce James 1926- *St&PR 93, WhoAm 92*
Partridge, Cecily Janet *WhoScE 91-1*
Partridge, Connie R. 1941- *WhoAmW 93*
Partridge, Craig 1961- *WhoWor 93*
Partridge, Derek *WhoScE 91-1*
Partridge, Derek 1945- *WhoWor 93*
Partridge, Dixie Lee 1943- *WhoWrEP 92*
Partridge, Gerald Latimer 1949- *WhoWor 93*
Partridge, Ian 1938- *Baker 92*
Partridge, J.R. 1935- *St&PR 93*
Partridge, John Albert 1924- *WhoWor 93*
Partridge, John William 1929- *St&PR 93*
Partridge, Katie Ann 1958- *WhoEmL 93*
Partridge, Robert Bruce 1940- *WhoAm 92*
Partridge, Roi 1888-1984 *BioIn 17*
Partridge, William Schaubel 1922- *WhoAm 92*
Partusch, Mary Ellen 1952- *WhoAmW 93*
Partyka, Paul Peter 1949- *WhoSSW 93*
Paru, Marden David 1941- *WhoE 93*
Parviainen, Jari Vainamo 1950- *WhoScE 91-4*
Parvin, Brian *ScF&FL 92*
Parvin, Landon 1948- *BioIn 17*
Parvin, Rose A. 1950- *WhoEmL 93*
Parvin, RuthAnn 1948- *WhoAmW 93*
Parvizi, Nahid 1949- *WhoScE 91-3*
Paryjczak, Tadeusz 1932- *WhoScE 91-4*
Parzen, Emanuel 1929- *WhoAm 92*
Parzinger, Thomas Michael 1950- *WhoSSW 93*
Parzniewski, Zbigniew Juliusz 1929- *WhoScE 91-4, WhoWor 93*
Parzybok, William G. 1942- *St&PR 93*
Pas, Eric Ivan 1948- *WhoSSW 93*
Pas, Guido Edward Guy 1951- *WhoWor 93*
Pasachoff, Jay M(yron) 1943- *ConAu 40NR*
Pasachoff, Jay Myron 1943- *WhoAm 92*
Pasadis, Athan S. 1948- *St&PR 93*
Pasakarnis, Pamela Ann 1949- *WhoEmL 93*
Pasanella, Giovanni 1931- *WhoAm 92*
Pasarow, Reinee Elizabeth 1950- *WhoWor 93*
Pasatieri, Thomas 1945- *Baker 92*
Pasbrig, Dave 1944- *St&PR 93*
Pascal, Blaise 1623-1662 *BioIn 17*
Pascal, Cecil Bennett 1926- *WhoAm 92*
Pascal, David 1918- *WhoAm 92, WhoWor 93*
Pascal, Donald T. *St&PR 93*
Pascal, Francine 1938- *ConAu 39NR, MajAI [port], ScF&FL 92*
Pascal, Gabriel 1894-1954 *MiSFD 9N*
Pascal, Jacques *ScF&FL 92*
Pascal, Jamie *ScF&FL 92*
Pascal, Laurie *ScF&FL 92*
Pascal, Robert Joseph 1932- *St&PR 93*
Pascal, Roger 1941- *WhoAm 92*
Pascale, Daniel Richard 1940- *WhoAm 92*
Pascale, Michael Mauro 1952- *St&PR 93*
Pascale, Richard Tanner *BioIn 17*
Pascalis, Jacques Gerard 1929- *WhoScE 91-2*
Pascall, David *BioIn 17*
Pascall, Jeremy 1946- *ScF&FL 92*
Pascal-Trouillot, Ertha *BioIn 17*
Pascal-Trouillot, Ertha 1943- *ConBlB 3 [port], DcCPCAm*
Pascarella, Perry James 1934- *WhoAm 92, WhoWrEP 92*
Pascarella-Cantu, Tina-Marie 1956- *WhoE 93*
Pascasio, Lorraine *BioIn 17*
Pascat, B. *WhoScE 91-2*
Pascault, J.P. *WhoScE 91-2*
Pasch, Alan 1925- *WhoAm 92*
Pasch, Herbert A. 1906- *St&PR 93*
Pasch, Maurice Bernard 1910- *WhoAm 92*
Pasch, Steven Julian 1952- *WhoE 93*
Pasch, Thomas 1941- *WhoScE 91-4*
Paschal, II d1118 *OxDcByz*
Paschal, Beverly Jo 1955- *WhoEmL 93*
Paschal, Verlinda 1949- *WhoAmW 93*
Paschall, Edna *AmWomPl*
Paschall, Helen *AmWomPl*
Paschall, James Robert *Law&B 92*
Paschall, Jeanette 1921- *WhoE 93*
Paschall, Lee McQuerter 1922- *WhoAm 92*
Paschall, Pamela Genelle 1949- *WhoAmW 93*
Paschall, Samuel James 1929- *WhoE 93*
Paschang, John Linus 1895- *WhoAm 92*
Paschburg, Donald Bruce *Law&B 92*
Paschen, Henry Daniel 1927- *WhoAm 92*
Paschen, Kai 1939- *WhoWor 93*
Paschke, Edward F. 1939- *WhoAm 92*
Paschke, Fritz 1929- *WhoScE 91-4*
Paschkis, Victor 1898-1991 *BioIn 17*
Paschos, Emmanuel Anthony 1940- *WhoScE 91-3*
Paschyn, Lisa Jasewytsch 1954- *WhoEmL 93*
Pasco, H. Merrill 1915- *St&PR 93*
Pasco, Hansell Merrill 1915- *WhoAm 92*
Pasco, Richard Edward 1926- *WhoWor 93*
Pascoe, Blair Carl 1932- *St&PR 93*
Pascoe, Christopher J. *Law&B 92*
Pascoe, Christopher J.C. 1934- *St&PR 93*
Pascoe, Edmund Normoyle 1948- *WhoIns 93*
Pascoe, Patricia Hill 1935- *WhoAmW 93, WhoWrEP 92*
Pascoe, Peggy 1954- *ConAu 136*
Pascoe, Valentine *WhoWrEP 92*
Pascoli, Giovanni 1855-1912 *TwCLC 45 [port]*
Pascrell, William J., Jr. 1937- *WhoAm 92, WhoE 93*
Pascual, C. Martin *WhoScE 91-3*
Pascual, Miguel Andres 1953- *St&PR 93*
Pascual, Pedro 1934- *WhoScE 91-3*
Pascual, Reinaldo 1963- *WhoSSW 93*
Pascual, Virginia 1951- *St&PR 93*
Pascual Acosta, Antonio 1951- *WhoScE 91-3*
Pascual Buxo, Jose 1931- *DcMexL*
Pascucci, Silvana B. *Law&B 92*
Pasculano, Richard J. 1940- *WhoAm 92*
Pasculli, Leonard P. *Law&B 92*
Pasdar, Adrian *BioIn 17*
Pasdeloup, Jules-Etienne 1819-1887 *Baker 92*
Paseiro, Abelardo d1990 *BioIn 17*
Pasek, Gary B. *Law&B 92*
Pasek, Jan Chryzostom 1630-1701 *PolBiDi*
Pasek, Mary A. *WhoAmW 93*
Pasekoff, Marilyn 1949- *WhoAmW 93*
Pasemko, Larry *Law&B 92*
Pasen, Jerry K. 1949- *St&PR 93*
Paserman, Hyman Judah-Maier 1949- *WhoE 93*
Pasero, Tancredi 1893-1983 *Baker 92, IntDcOp, OxDcOp*
Pasetti, Louis Oscar 1916- *WhoSSW 93*
Paseur, C. Herbert 1925- *St&PR 93*
Pasewark, William Robert 1924- *WhoAm 92*
Pasfield, Charles James 1954- *WhoE 93*
Pash, George Kinnear 1938- *St&PR 93*
Pash, Hazel Rochelle 1941- *WhoAmW 93*
Pasha, Mustafa Al-Nahhas 1876?-1965 *BioIn 17*
Pashchenko, Andrei (Filippovich) 1883-1972 *Baker 92*
Pashchenko, Andrey 1885-1972 *OxDcOp*
Pashek, Robert Donald 1921- *WhoAm 92*
Pashelka, Richard A. *Law&B 92*
Pashina, LeAnn Marie 1961- *WhoAmW 93*
Pashkevich, Vasily c. 1742-1797 *OxDcOp*
Pashkevich, Vasily (Alexeievich) c. 1740-1797 *Baker 92*
Pashley, Donald William *WhoScE 91-1*
Pashley, Hattie *AmWomPl*
Pashley, Mary Martha 1956- *WhoSSW 93*
Pasho, Philip B. 1941- *WhoE 93*
Pashos, Kay E. *Law&B 92*
Pashos, Michael L. *Law&B 92*
Pashov, Ivan Zhelev 1952- *WhoWor 93*
Pasic, Nikola 1845-1926 *DcTwHis*
Pasierb, Janusz Stanislaus 1929- *WhoWor 93*
Pasik, Donald J. 1957- *St&PR 93*
Pasikov, Ian David 1948- *WhoE 93*
Pasinetti, Luigi L. *BioIn 17*
Pasinetti, Pier Maria 1913- *WhoAm 92*
Pasini, Lina 1872-1959 *See* Vitale, Edoardo 1872-1937 *OxDcOp*
Pasini, Roy 1927- *WhoIns 93*
Pasini (-Vitale), Lina 1872-1959 *Baker 92*
Pasinski, Edmond 1955- *WhoE 93*
Pasinski, Elena Maria 1967- *WhoAmW 93*
Pas-Itaya, Lan 1959- *WhoWor 93*
Pask, James Bruce 1943- *St&PR 93*
Pask, Joseph Adam 1913- *WhoAm 92*
Paskach, David Michael *Law&B 92*
Paskalis, Kostas 1929- *Baker 92, OxDcOp*
Paskaljevic, Goran *MiSFD 9*
Paskaljevic, Goran 1947- *DrEEuF*
Paskausky, David Frank 1938- *WhoE 93*
Paskell, Thad Joseph 1964- *St&PR 93*
Pasker, Debbie Ann 1960- *WhoAmW 93*
Pasker-De Jong, Pieternel Cornelia Maria 1966- *WhoWor 93*
Paskerian, Wayne H. 1940- *St&PR 93*
Paskin, Deborah Corthier *Law&B 92*
Paskins-Hurlburt, Andrea Jeanne 1943- *WhoAmW 93*
Pasko, Arlene E. *Law&B 92*
Pasko, Thomas Joseph, Jr. 1937- *WhoSSW 93*
Paskoff, Martin *Law&B 92*
Paskova, Magdalena Maria 1942- *WhoWor 93*
Paskowitz, Howard 1932- *WhoE 93*
Paskuly, Carol Anne 1943- *WhoAmW 93*
Paskvan, Kristie P. 1958- *WhoAmW 93*
Paslawsky, Jean Marie 1957- *WhoEmL 93*
Paslay, Le Roy Clay 1907- *WhoWor 93*
Pasler, Friedrich Anton 1924- *WhoScE 91-4*
Pasley, James Michael 1953- *WhoWor 93*
Pasley, Nancy L. *Law&B 92*
Pasley, Raymond Scott *Law&B 92*
Paslov, Eugene *WhoAm 92*
Pasman, Hans J. 1938- *WhoScE 91-3*
Pasman, James S., Jr. 1930- *St&PR 93*
Pasmanick, Kenneth 1924- *WhoAm 92*
Pasmanik, Guerman Aronovich 1945- *WhoWor 93*
Pasmatzis, Ioannis 1961- *WhoWor 93*
Pasmore, Henry Bickford 1857-1944 *Baker 92*
Pasnak, William 1949- *ScF&FL 92*
Pasnick, Raymond Wallace 1916- *WhoAm 92*
Paso, Fernando del 1935- *DcMexL, SpAmA*
Pasolini, Pier Paolo 1922-1975 *BioIn 17, DcLB 128 [port], MiSFD 9N*
Paspatis, E.A. *WhoScE 91-3*
Pasqua, Charles 1927- *BioIn 17*
Pasqua, Lauri M. 1963- *WhoAmW 93*
Pasquale, Douglas M. 1954- *St&PR 93*
Pasquale, Frank Anthony 1954- *WhoE 93, WhoWor 93*
Pasquale, Joanne Eileen 1940- *WhoAmW 93*
Pasquale, Michael Feaster 1947- *St&PR 93*
Pasquale, Rosemarie Diane 1958- *WhoAmW 93*
Pasquale, Vincent J. 1939- *St&PR 93*
Pasquali, Francesco c. 1590-1635? *Baker 92*
Pasquali, Niccolo c. 1718-1757 *Baker 92*
Pasquarelli, Joseph J. 1927- *WhoAm 92, WhoE 93, WhoWor 93*
Pasquarelli, Robert James 1946- *WhoAm 92*
Pasquarello, Alfredo 1963- *WhoWor 93*
Pasquariello, John Ray 1929- *St&PR 93*
Pasquerilla, Frank James 1926- *St&PR 93*
Pasquerilla, Mark E. 1959- *St&PR 93*
Pasquevich, Daniel Miguel 1958- *WhoWor 93*
Pasquier, Edme Armand Gaston Audiffret- 1823-1905 *BioIn 17*
Pasquier, Joel 1943- *WhoAm 92*
Pasquier, P. Michel 1939- *St&PR 93*
Pasquin, John *MiSFD 9*
Pasquini, Bernardo 1637-1710 *Baker 92*
Pasquini, Dan E. 1942- *St&PR 93*
Pasquini, Ercole c. 1550-1608? *Baker 92*
Pasquino, Ralph D. 1936- *St&PR 93*
Pasquotti, Corrado 1954- *Baker 92*
Pass, Bobby Clifton 1931- *WhoAm 92, WhoSSW 93*
Pass, Carolyn Joan 1941- *WhoE 93*
Pass, Henry Ian *Law&B 92*
Pass, Herman W. 1937- *St&PR 93*
Pass, Joe 1929- *Baker 92, WhoAm 92*
Pass, Ralph P., Jr. 1924- *St&PR 93*
Pass, W. Tauscher *WhoScE 91-4*
Pass, William F. 1946- *St&PR 93*
Passage, David 1942- *WhoAm 92, WhoWor 93*
Passailaigue, Tomas *ScF&FL 92*
Passalacqua, Kristine Gay 1955- *WhoEmL 93*
Passalacqua, S.A. 1949- *St&PR 93*
Passalaqua, Joseph Anthony Jacobi 1929- *Baker 92*
Passanisi, Pamela Elizabeth 1957- *WhoAmW 93*
Passano, Edward M. 1904- *St&PR 93*
Passano, Edward Magruder 1904- *WhoAm 92*
Passano, William M. 1929- *St&PR 93*
Passante, John A. 1940- *St&PR 93*
Passantino, George Christopher *WhoE 93*
Passarelli-Stamper, Phyllis 1944- *WhoAmW 93*
Passaro, Aurora *St&PR 93*
Passaro, Louis *St&PR 93*
Passeau, Claude William 1909- *BiDAMSp 1989*
Passendorfer, Jerzy 1923- *DrEEuF*
Passer, Ivan 1933- *MiSFD 9*
Passer, Morris Harry 1929- *St&PR 93, WhoAm 92*
Passereau, Pierre *Baker 92*
Passero, Donna L. *Law&B 92*
Passero, Michael Anthony 1945- *WhoE 93*
Passes, Alan 1943- *ScF&FL 92*
Passet, Michael Steven 1951- *WhoAm 92*
Passey, George Edward 1920- *WhoAm 92*
Passey, Helen K. *ScF&FL 92*
Passiak, Karen Marie 1958- *WhoSSW 93*
Passino, Roberto *WhoScE 91-3*
Pass Kesler, Delores Mercer 1940- *WhoAmW 93*
Passley, Paul L. *Law&B 92*
Passman, Irving 1910- *WhoSSW 93*
Passmore, George *BioIn 17*
Passmore, Howard Clinton, Jr. 1942- *WhoAm 92*
Passmore, Jan William 1940- *WhoAm 92*
Passmore, L. Ray 1942- *St&PR 93*
Passmore, Marsha Ann 1951- *WhoSSW 93*
Passon, Richard Henry 1939- *WhoAm 92*
Passons, Donna Janelle 1951- *WhoAmW 93*
Passow, A. Harry *BioIn 17*
Passow, Aaron Harry 1920- *WhoAm 92, WhoE 93*
Passow, Hermann 1925- *WhoScE 91-3*
Passty, Jeanette Nyda 1947- *WhoSSW 93*
Passwater, Barbara Gayhart 1945- *WhoAmW 93*
Passwater, Richard Albert 1937- *WhoAm 92, WhoE 93, WhoWor 93*
Passy, (Ludvig Anton) Edvard 1789-1870 *Baker 92*
Pasta, Giuditta 1797-1865 *IntDcOp [port], OxDcOp*
Pasta, Giuditta (Maria Costanza) 1797-1865 *Baker 92*
Pastan, Harvey Lewis 1927- *St&PR 93*
Pastan, Ira Harry 1931- *WhoAm 92*
Pastan, Linda 1932- *BioIn 17, WhoWrEP 92*
Pastan, Linda (Olenik) 1932- *ConAu 40NR*
Pasteels, J.L. 1934- *WhoScE 91-2*
Pastell, Mathew J. 1928- *St&PR 93*
Paster, Barry Nathan 1949- *St&PR 93*
Paster, Janice D. 1942- *WhoAmW 93*
Paster, Joseph Phillip 1945- *St&PR 93*
Pasternac, Andre 1937- *WhoE 93*
Pasternack, Amos Isak 1936- *WhoScE 91-4, WhoWor 93*
Pasternack, Beth I. *Law&B 92*
Pasternack, Bruce Arthur 1947- *St&PR 93*
Pasternack, Douglas Allan 1954- *St&PR 93*
Pasternack, Robert Francis 1936- *WhoAm 92*
Pasternak, Alvin *Law&B 92*
Pasternak, Boris 1890-1960 *PoeCrit 6 [port], WorLitC [port]*

Pasternak, Boris Leonidovich 1890-1960 *BioIn 17*
Pasternak, Charles A. *WhoScE 91-1*
Pasternak, Derick Peter 1941- *WhoAm 92*
Pasternak, Gunter 1932- *WhoScE 91-3*
Pasternak, Joe 1901-1991 *AnObit 1991, BioIn 17*
Pasternak, Stanley William 1949- *St&PR 93*
Pasterwitz, Georg von 1730-1803 *Baker 92*
Pasteur, Louis 1822-1895 *BioIn 17*
Pastidis, Stylianos Spyros 1948- *WhoWor 93*
Pastin, Mark Joseph 1949- *WhoEmL 93, WhoWor 93*
Pastirko-Kreins, Claudia Teresa *Law&B 92*
Pastizzi-Ferencic, Dunja 1936- *WhoUN 92*
Pastolove, Nadine L. *Law&B 92*
Paston, Alan Jay 1937- *St&PR 93*
Pastor, Ed 1943- *BioIn 17, WhoAm 92*
Pastor, Josette Celia 1950- *WhoWor 93*
Pastor, Robert Allen 1947- *WhoSSW 93*
Pastor, Stephen Daniel 1947- *WhoWor 93*
Pastora Gomez, Eden 1937- *DcCPCAm*
Pastore, John Orlando 1907- *BioIn 17*
Pastore, Joseph A. *Law&B 92*
Pastore, Joseph Dominic 1938- *St&PR 93*
Pastore, Joseph Michael, Jr. 1941- *WhoAm 92*
Pastore, Michael M. *Law&B 92*
Pastore, Michele *WhoScE 91-3*
Pastore, Nicholas 1938?- *BioIn 17*
Pastore, Peter Nicholas, Jr. 1950- *WhoSSW 93*
Pastore, Steven Louis 1948- *WhoE 93*
Pastorek, Norman Joseph 1939- *WhoE 93, WhoWor 93*
Pastorelle, Peter John 1933- *WhoAm 92*
Pastorelli, Robert *BioIn 17, WhoAm 92*
Pastorello, Thomas J. 1957- *St&PR 93*
Pastoret, Paul-Pierre 1946- *WhoScE 91-2*
Pastorino, Giovanni Battista 1952- *WhoWor 93*
Pastrav, Ioan 1929- *WhoScE 91-4*
Pastre, Ghislain M. *Law&B 92*
Pastreich, Peter 1938- *WhoAm 92*
Pastryk, John R. *Law&B 92*
Pastuch, Boris Max *WhoSSW 93*
Pastuszewska, B. *WhoScE 91-4*
Pasvol, Geoffrey *WhoScE 91-1*
Paswan, Ram Vilas *WhoAsAP 91*
Pasynkiewicz, Stanislaw 1930- *WhoScE 91-4*
Paszamant, Roger Bruce *Law&B 92*
Pasztor, Emil 1926- *WhoScE 91-4*
Pasztor, Jano 1955- *WhoUN 92*
Pasztor, Karoly 1924- *WhoScE 91-4*
Pasztor, Laszlo *BioIn 17*
Paszynski, Marian 1931- *WhoWor 93*
Patachich, Ivan 1922- *Baker 92*
Patacsil, Gregorio Banez, Jr. 1934- *WhoWor 93*
Patadopoulos, Stelios B. *WhoAm 92*
Patafio, Donald J. 1928- *St&PR 93*
Patafio, John J. 1926- *St&PR 93*
Patafio, Robert J. 1924- *St&PR 93*
Patai, Daphne 1943- *ScF&FL 92*
Patai, Raphael 1910- *IntDcAn, WhoAm 92*
Pataki, Balazs 1952- *WhoScE 91-4*
Pataki, Monica A. 1966- *WhoAmW 93*
Pataki-Schweizer, Kerry Josef 1935- *WhoWor 93*
Patala, Jarno Manu Kristian 1955- *WhoWor 93*
Patalano, Robert Michael 1944- *St&PR 93*
Patalas, Zygmunt *WhoScE 91-4*
Patane, Giuseppe 1932-1989 *Baker 92*
Patane, I. Edward 1935- *WhoIns 93*
Patanelli, Dolores Jean 1932- *WhoE 93*
Patarino, Vincent V. 1938- *St&PR 93*
Patarlageanu, Radu Contantin 1925- *WhoWor 93*
Patashnik, Ethan 1954- *St&PR 93*
Patau Rubis, Dr. 1946- *WhoAsAP 91*
Patava, M.J. 1953- *St&PR 93*
Patch, Alexander McCarrell, Jr. 1889-1945 *HarEnMi*
Patch, David A. 1943- *St&PR 93*
Patch, David Ellsworth 1936- *St&PR 93*
Patch, Don I. *BioIn 17*
Patch, Lauren Nelson 1951- *St&PR 93, WhoAm 92, WhoIns 93*
Patch, Merrie Christmas 1938- *WhoAmW 93*
Patch, Sam *BioIn 17*
Patchan, Joseph 1922- *WhoAm 92*
Patchell, Thomas A. 1928- *St&PR 93*
Patchen, Kenneth 1911-1972 *BioIn 17*
Patchett, Ann 1963- *ConAu 139*
Patchett, Mary Elwyn (Osborne) 1897- *DcChlFi*
Patchin, Stephen Ross 1958- *St&PR 93*
Patching, Barbara E. *Law&B 92*
Patchis, Pauline 1940- *WhoE 93, WhoWor 93*
Pate, Donald Wayne 1939- *WhoSSW 93*
Pate, Jacqueline Hail 1930- *WhoAmW 93, WhoSSW 93*
Pate, James Leonard 1935- *St&PR 93, WhoAm 92, WhoSSW 93*
Pate, James Littleton 1932- *WhoE 93*
Pate, James Wynford 1928- *WhoAm 92*
Pate, J'Nell L(aVerne) 1938- *ConAu 139*
Pate, J'Nell Laverne 1938- *WhoSSW 93*
Pate, Joan Seitz *WhoAm 92, WhoAmW 93*
Pate, Johnny 1923- *BioIn 17*
Pate, Mavis Orisca 1925-1972 *BioIn 17*
Pate, Michael 1920- *MiSFD 9*
Pate, Michael Laurence *Law&B 92*
Pate, Randolph McCall 1898-1961 *HarEnMi*
Pate, Robert Hewitt, Jr. 1938- *WhoAm 92*
Pate, Robert Lynn 1936- *St&PR 93*
Pate, Samuel Ralph 1937- *WhoAm 92*
Pate, Sharon Shamburger 1954- *WhoAmW 93*
Pate, Stephen Patrick 1958- *WhoSSW 93*
Pate, Vicki Miller 1943- *WhoAmW 93*
Pate, William Earl 1953- *WhoSSW 93*
Pate, Zack Taylor, Jr. 1936- *WhoAm 92*
Patee, Susan 1944- *WhoAmW 93*
Patek, Carl R. 1938- *St&PR 93*
Patel, A.K. 1931- *WhoAsAP 91*
Patel, Arvind Motibhai 1937- *WhoAm 92*
Patel, Atul Chimanlal 1943- *WhoE 93*
Patel, Bhaichand Dalpat 1937- *WhoUN 92*
Patel, Carol 1951- *WhoAmW 93*
Patel, Chandra Kumar Naranbhai 1938- *WhoAm 92, WhoWor 93*
Patel, Chandrakant 1941- *WhoUN 92*
Patel, Chhotubhai 1939- *WhoAsAP 91*
Patel, Dinesh C. 1950- *WhoWor 93*
Patel, Ghanshyam Ashabhai 1936- *St&PR 93*
Patel, Homi Burjor 1949- *WhoAm 92*
Patel, Jean-Claude 1931- *WhoScE 91-2*
Patel, Jeram 1930- *WhoWor 93*
Patel, Kirit V. 1951- *WhoSSW 93*
Patel, Lina D. *WhoAmW 93*
Patel, Magan 1937- *WhoWor 93*
Patel, Magan C. 1937- *St&PR 93*
Patel, Mahendra Rambhai 1939- *WhoE 93*
Patel, Marilyn Hall 1938- *WhoAm 92, WhoAmW 93*
Patel, Minoo Homi *WhoScE 91-1*
Patel, Mukund Ranchhodlal 1942- *WhoWor 93*
Patel, Neil *BioIn 17*
Patel, Rafiq Kassamali 1938- *WhoE 93*
Patel, Raju *MiSFD 9*
Patel, Ramesh 1951- *St&PR 93*
Patel, Ronald Anthony 1947- *WhoAm 92, WhoWor 93*
Patel, Sardar Vallabhbhai 1875-1950 *DcTwHis*
Patel, Sharad *MiSFD 9*
Patel, Shiris Ranchhodbhai 1957- *WhoE 93*
Patel, Vinod Motibhai 1944- *WhoSSW 93*
Patel, Virendra Chaturbhai 1938- *WhoAm 92*
Patel, Vithalbhai M. 1927- *WhoAsAP 91*
Patello, Joseph D. *Law&B 92*
Patelson, Joseph d1992 *BioIn 17*
Patenaude, Jean D. *Law&B 92*
Patenaude, John William 1946- *St&PR 93*
Patenotre, Raymond 1900-1951 *BioIn 17*
Patent, Dorothy Hinshaw 1940- *MajAI [port], SmATA 69 [port]*
Patent, Gregory 1939- *BioIn 17*
Pater, James V. 1927- *St&PR 93*
Paterek, Tina Marie 1922- *WhoE 93*
Paterna, Salvatore A. 1941- *St&PR 93*
Paterno, Joseph Vincent 1926- *WhoAm 92*
Paterno, Tomas Tirona 1932- *WhoWor 93*
Paterno, Vicente 1925- *WhoAsAP 91*
Paternosto, Cesar Pedro 1931- *WhoAm 92*
Paternostro, Patrick Joseph 1967- *WhoE 93*
Paterson, Alan Alexander *WhoScE 91-1*
Paterson, Alan C. 1950- *St&PR 93*
Paterson, Alan Gerard 1956- *WhoSSW 93*
Paterson, Allen Peter 1933- *WhoAm 92*
Paterson, Basil Alexander 1926- *WhoAm 92*
Paterson, Carol D. 1955- *WhoScE 91-1*
Paterson, Chat d1992 *NewYTBS 92*
Paterson, Chat 1920-1992 *BioIn 17, CurBio 92N*
Paterson, Clayton Holm *Law&B 92*
Paterson, D.C. *Law&B 92*
Paterson, D.S. 1918- *St&PR 93*
Paterson, Eileen 1939- *WhoAmW 93*
Paterson, Erik Thomas 1941- *WhoWrEP 92*
Paterson, James Hamilton- *BioIn 17*
Paterson, James Hunter 1947- *WhoAm 92*
Paterson, James Joseph 1937- *WhoE 93*
Paterson, Jeff Robert 1947- *St&PR 93*
Paterson, John Alan 1958- *WhoE 93*
Paterson, Katherine *BioIn 17*
Paterson, Katherine 1932- *ChlFicS*
Paterson, Katherine (Womeldorf) 1932- *DcAmChF 1960, DcAmChF 1985, MajAI [port], WhoAm 92*
Paterson, Lin Richter 1936- *WhoAmW 93, WhoWrEP 92*
Paterson, Linda 1951- *WhoAmW 93*
Paterson, Michael Stewart *WhoScE 91-1*
Paterson, Paul Charles 1927- *WhoSSW 93, WhoWor 93*
Paterson, R.C. 1950- *St&PR 93*
Paterson, Richard D. 1942- *St&PR 93*
Paterson, Richard Denis 1942- *WhoAm 92*
Paterson, Robert Cowans 1928- *St&PR 93, WhoAm 92*
Paterson, Robert Craig *WhoScE 91-1*
Paterson, Robert Douglas 1920- *St&PR 93*
Paterson, Robert E. 1926- *WhoAm 92*
Paterson, Robert William 1939- *WhoE 93*
Paterson, Sheila 1940- *WhoAm 92*
Paterson, W.S. *WhoScE 91-1*
Paterson, William 1745-1806 *OxCSupC [port]*
Paterson, William Guthrie Wilson *WhoScE 91-1*
Patey, Janet (Monach) 1842-1894 *Baker 92*
Pathak, Pinakin Y. 1945- *St&PR 93*
Pathak, Raghunandan Swarup 1924- *WhoWor 93*
Pathak, Sunit Rawly 1953- *WhoEmL 93, WhoSSW 93*
Pathiaux, Genevieve 1941- *WhoWor 93*
Pati, Patricia Ann 1949- *WhoAmW 93*
Patil, Balasaheb Vikhe 1932- *WhoAsAP 91*
Patil, Pratibha Devisingh 1934- *WhoAsAP 91*
Patil, Shivraj Vishwanathrao 1926- *WhoAsAP 91*
Patil, Smita 1954-1986 *IntDcF 2-3*
Patil, Suryakanta Jayawantrao 1948- *WhoAsAP 91*
Patil, Uttamrao 1944- *WhoAsAP 91*
Patil, Vishwasrao Ramrao 1934- *WhoAsAP 91*
Patil, Yashwantrao Gadakh 1943- *WhoAsAP 91*
Patin, Charles 1633-1693 *BioIn 17*
Patin, Gabriel J. 1929- *St&PR 93*
Patin, Jude W. P. 1940- *WhoAm 92*
Patin, Jude Wilmot Paul 1940- *AfrAmBi*
Patin, Robert W. 1942- *WhoIns 93*
Patin, Robert White 1942- *St&PR 93, WhoAm 92*
Patinkin, Don 1922- *WhoWor 93*
Patinkin, Mandy 1952- *Baker 92, ConTFT 10, HolBB [port], WhoAm 92, WhoE 93*
Patinkin, Mandy 1953?- *BioIn 17*
Patinkin, Mark Alan 1953- *WhoE 93*
Patinkin, Sheldon 1935- *WhoAm 92*
Patino, Carlos d1675 *Baker 92*
Patino, Douglas Xavier 1939- *WhoAm 92*
Patino, Maria Jose Martinez *BioIn 17*
Patino, Simon Iture 1860-1947 *DcTwHis*
Patino Duque, Gustavo 1928- *WhoWor 93*
Patitucci, John *BioIn 17*
Patitz, Dolores Rose *WhoWrEP 92*
Patitz, Tatjana *BioIn 17*
Patkar, Medha *BioIn 17*
Patkos, Istvan 1932- *WhoScE 91-4*
Patler, Louis 1943- *WhoWrEP 92*
Patlow, William J. 1929-1991 *BioIn 17*
Patlyek, James D. 1956- *St&PR 93*
Patman, Harold C. 1935- *WhoIns 93*
Patmore, Coventry Kersey Dighton 1823-1896 *BioIn 17*
Patmore, Lester Claudius, III 1946- *WhoE 93*
Patmore, Thomas Eugene 1928- *St&PR 93*
Patmos, Adrian Edward 1914- *WhoAm 92*
Patnaude, William E. 1937- *WhoAm 92*
Patokallio, Pasi 1949- *WhoUN 92*
Patomaki, Lauri Kalevi 1934- *WhoWor 93*
Paton, A.G. 1947- *St&PR 93*
Paton, Alan *BioIn 17*
Paton, Alan 1903-1988 *BritWr S2, IntLitE, MagSWL [port], WorLitC [port]*
Paton, Alexander Ray 1929- *WhoAm 92*
Paton, Allen Glenn 1947- *WhoAm 92*
Paton, David Macdonald 1913-1992 *ConAu 139*
Paton, George Edmiston Charles 1932- *WhoWor 93*
Paton, Jock Esmond 1952- *St&PR 93*
Paton, John 1921- *ScF&FL 92*
Paton, Joseph Noel 1821-1901 *BioIn 17*
Paton, Leland B. 1943- *WhoAm 92*
Paton, Mary Ann 1802-1864 *Baker 92, OxDcOp*
Paton, Mary Margaret 1918- *WhoAmW 93*
Paton, W. *WhoScE 91-1*
Paton, William 1941- *WhoScE 91-1*
Paton, William Andrew 1889-1991 *BioIn 17*
Paton, William Drummond Macdonald 1917- *WhoWor 93*
Paton Walsh, Gillian 1937- *ConAu 38NR, MajAI [port]*
Paton Walsh, Gillian 1939- *SmATA 72 [port]*
Paton Walsh, Jill *ConAu 38NR, MajAI, SmATA 72*
Paton Walsh, Jill 1937- *ScF&FL 92, WhoAm 92*
Patouhas, Marian Topping *BioIn 17*
Patrell, Oliver L. 1927- *St&PR 93*
Patriaco, Andrew Domenick 1927- *St&PR 93*
Patric, Jason *BioIn 17, ConTFT 10*
Patric, Lowell Craig 1945- *WhoAm 92*
Patric, Sharon K. 1957- *St&PR 93*
Patricelli, Robert E. 1939- *WhoAm 92*
Patrich, Barry A. *Law&B 92*
Patrichi, Mihai Dimitrie 1911- *St&PR 93*
Patricio, Luciana *WhoScE 91-3*
Patricio, Manuel F. *WhoScE 91-3*
Patricio, Odete Maria Alves Da Silva 1955- *WhoWor 93*
Patrick, Saint 373?-463? *BioIn 17*
Patrick, Allan 1946- *WhoAm 92*
Patrick, Allen Lee 1938- *WhoAm 92*
Patrick, Angela Arlene 1957- *WhoEmL 93*
Patrick, Bernard Sutherland 1927- *WhoSSW 93*
Patrick, Bruce Douglas *Law&B 92*
Patrick, Carl Lloyd 1918- *WhoAm 92*
Patrick, Charles Roger 1942- *St&PR 93*
Patrick, Christie A. *Law&B 92*
Patrick, Craig 1946- *WhoAm 92, WhoE 93*
Patrick, D.J. 1946- *St&PR 93*
Patrick, David Wayne 1947- *WhoSSW 93*
Patrick, DeAnn *ScF&FL 92*
Patrick, Debra Ann 1965- *WhoEmL 93*
Patrick, Dennis 1918- *WhoAm 92*
Patrick, Eileen 1950- *WhoWrEP 92*
Patrick, Eleanor Murray 1904- *WhoAmW 93*
Patrick, Freddie Benjamin 1953- *WhoSSW 93*
Patrick, Gary *BioIn 17*
Patrick, James Duvall, Jr. 1947- *WhoWor 93*
Patrick, James Gus 1946- *WhoEmL 93*
Patrick, James Nicholas, Sr. 1950- *WhoSSW 93*
Patrick, Jane Austin 1930- *WhoWor 93*
Patrick, Janet Cline 1934- *WhoAmW 93*
Patrick, Jennie R. 1949- *AfrAmBi, WhoSSW 93*
Patrick, John 1903- *WhoWor 93*
Patrick, John Franklin 1933- *WhoE 93*
Patrick, John Joseph 1935- *WhoAm 92*
Patrick, John William *WhoScE 91-1*
Patrick, Joseph A. 1910- *St&PR 93*
Patrick, Katherine *AmWomPl*
Patrick, Kit *WhoWrEP 92*
Patrick, Lynn *ScF&FL 92*
Patrick, Lynn Allen *Law&B 92*
Patrick, Lynn Allen 1935- *WhoAm 92*
Patrick, Marty 1949- *WhoSSW 93*
Patrick, Mason Mathews 1863-1942 *HarEnMi*
Patrick, Matthew *MiSFD 9*
Patrick, Michael James 1960- *WhoE 93*
Patrick, Michael Wynn 1950- *St&PR 93, WhoAm 92*
Patrick, Michele Mary 1963- *WhoE 93*
Patrick, Pamela Ann 1963- *WhoAmW 93*
Patrick, Patrick F. 1942- *St&PR 93*
Patrick, Paul A. 1942- *St&PR 93*
Patrick, Philip Howard *Law&B 92*
Patrick, Rayford Powell 1939- *WhoSSW 93*
Patrick, Rebecca Ratcliff 1958- *WhoAmW 93*
Patrick, Richard M. 1946- *WhoAm 92*
Patrick, Robert *BioIn 17*
Patrick, Robert M. 1934- *St&PR 93*
Patrick, Ronald Lee 1937- *St&PR 93*
Patrick, Sam J. 1937- *WhoWrEP 92*
Patrick, Shari L. *Law&B 92*
Patrick, Sharon L. *BioIn 17*
Patrick, Steven Dennis *Law&B 92*
Patrick, Stuart G. 1943- *WhoScE 91-1*
Patrick, Stuart Kavanaugh 1939- *St&PR 93, WhoE 93*
Patrick, Sue Ford 1946- *WhoAmW 93*
Patrick, Susan Nancy *Law&B 92*
Patrick, Thomas Donald 1942- *WhoE 93*
Patrick, Thomas H. 1944- *WhoAm 92*
Patrick, Ueal Eugene 1929- *St&PR 93, WhoAm 92*
Patrick, Vincent 1935- *WhoWrEP 92*
Patrick, Warren R. 1955- *St&PR 93*
Patrick, William Hardy, Jr. 1925- *WhoAm 92*
Patrick, William Samuel 1927- *WhoAm 92, WhoSSW 93*

Patrick Morales, Vita Jo 1953- *WhoEmL 93*
Patricof, Alan J. 1934- *St&PR 93*
Patrie, Cheryl Christine 1947- *WhoAmW 93*
Patrik, Gary Steven 1944- *WhoIns 93*
Patrikis, Ernest T. 1943- *St&PR 93, WhoAm 92*
Patriquin, David Ashley 1927- *WhoAm 92*
Patriquin, Edward Leroy, Jr. 1958- *WhoWor 93*
Patriquin, Redmond L. 1938- *St&PR 93*
Patrizio, Mark David *Law&B 92*
Patron, Ronald H. *St&PR 93*
Patrone, Edward N. 1935- *WhoAm 92*
Patrone, John D. *Law&B 92*
Patronik, Richard Stephen 1956- *WhoIns 93*
Patross, Lloyd Walter *Law&B 92*
Patry, Marcel Joseph 1923- *WhoAm 92*
Patsakos, P.G. *WhoScE 91-3*
Patscot, Michelle Patrice 1966- *WhoAmW 93*
Patsel, E. Ralph, Jr. 1935- *WhoSSW 93*
Patsey, Kevin Dean 1961- *WhoSSW 93*
Patsey, Shannon Florence 1961- *WhoWor 93*
Patsolic, Janice Lynn 1957- *WhoAmW 93*
Patt, Hans-Josef 1937- *WhoScE 91-3, WhoWor 93*
Pattanaik, Prasanta Kumar *WhoScE 91-1*
Pattarathammas, Vibul 1932- *WhoWor 93*
Patte, Dominique 1931- *WhoScE 91-2*
Patte, Jean-Claude 1932- *WhoScE 91-2*
Pattee, Eric 1930- *WhoScE 91-2*
Pattee, Gordon Burleigh 1948- *WhoAm 92, WhoE 93, WhoWor 93*
Patten, Anthony Robert 1940- *WhoUN 92*
Patten, Barbara Sue Brummett 1943- *WhoSSW 93*
Patten, Bebe Harrison 1913- *WhoAm 92, WhoAmW 93, WhoWor 93*
Patten, Brian 1946- *ScF&FL 92*
Patten, Charles Anthony 1920- *WhoAm 92*
Patten, Charles Robertson, Jr. 1941- *St&PR 93*
Patten, Chris 1944- *BioIn 17*
Patten, Christopher 1944- *WhoWor 93*
Patten, Clyde G. *Law&B 92*
Patten, Clyde Gowell 1930- *St&PR 93*
Patten, Cora Mel 1869- *AmWomPl*
Patten, Eileen Dunlevy *WhoE 93*
Patten, Gary N. 1947- *St&PR 93*
Patten, Gerland Paul 1907- *WhoAm 92*
Patten, John Haggitt Charles 1945- *WhoWor 93*
Patten, John W. 1930- *St&PR 93, WhoAm 92*
Patten, Joseph Michael *WhoSSW 93*
Patten, Keith *St&PR 93*
Patten, Lanny Ray 1934- *WhoAm 92*
Patten, Lewis B(yford) 1915-1981 *DcAmChF 1960*
Patten, Maurine Diane 1940- *WhoAmW 93*
Patten, Patricia A. *Law&B 92*
Patten, Richard E. 1953- *WhoEmL 93*
Patten, Robert Lowry 1939- *WhoSSW 93*
Patten, Ronald James 1935- *WhoAm 92*
Patten, Thomas Henry, Jr. 1929- *WhoAm 92*
Patten, William Russell 1954- *WhoSSW 93*
Patten, William W. *Law&B 92*
Pattenaude, Richard Louis 1946- *WhoE 93*
Pattenden, Gerald *WhoScE 91-1*
Patterson, Ada *AmWomPl*
Patterson, Alan Bruce 1953- *WhoAm 92, WhoEmL 93*
Patterson, Alicia 1906-1963 *JrnUS*
Patterson, Alicia Brooks 1906-1963 *DcLB 127 [port]*
Patterson, Anne Virginia Sharpe 1841- *AmWomPl*
Patterson, Annie Wilson 1868-1934 *Baker 92*
Patterson, Antoinette Decoursey *AmWomPl*
Patterson, Arthur Kenneth 1933- *St&PR 93*
Patterson, Aubrey B. 1942- *St&PR 93*
Patterson, Aubrey Burns, Jr. 1942- *WhoAm 92*
Patterson, Audrey Mickey *BlkAmWO*
Patterson, Barry S. 1951- *St&PR 93*
Patterson, Becky *WhoWrEP 92*
Patterson, Beverley Pamela Grace 1956- *WhoEmL 93*
Patterson, Beverly Ann Gross 1938- *WhoAmW 93*
Patterson, Blair 1947- *St&PR 93*
Patterson, Bobby Wayne 1954- *WhoSSW 93*
Patterson, Bradley H., Jr. 1921- *ConAu 136*
Patterson, Brenda Ann 1941- *WhoAmW 93*
Patterson, Burton Roe 1949- *WhoSSW 93*
Patterson, C.H. *BioIn 17*
Patterson, Carl D. 1938- *St&PR 93*
Patterson, Carol Anne 1944- *WhoAmW 93*
Patterson, Carrick Heiskell 1945- *St&PR 93*
Patterson, Catharine Yevonne 1964- *WhoAmW 93*
Patterson, Cathleen Erin 1958- *WhoAmW 93*
Patterson, Cecil Holden *BioIn 17*
Patterson, Charles D. 1928- *BioIn 17*
Patterson, Charles Darold 1928- *WhoAm 92*
Patterson, Charles K. 1933- *St&PR 93*
Patterson, Charles Wilson 1935- *WhoWrEP 92*
Patterson, Cindy Lee 1956- *WhoEmL 93*
Patterson, Daniel Watkins *WhoAm 92*
Patterson, David Alan 1948- *WhoSSW 93*
Patterson, David Andrew 1947- *WhoAm 92*
Patterson, David E. 1938- *St&PR 93*
Patterson, David Eric 1933- *WhoScE 91-1*
Patterson, David M. 1945- *St&PR 93*
Patterson, Dawn Marie *WhoAmW 93*
Patterson, Day L. *Law&B 92*
Patterson, Deborah G. 1953- *St&PR 93*
Patterson, Dennis Glen 1948- *WhoAm 92*
Patterson, Dirk Campbell 1954- *St&PR 93*
Patterson, Donis Dean 1930- *WhoAm 92*
Patterson, Doyle 1918- *St&PR 93, WhoAm 92*
Patterson, Duane Allen 1931- *St&PR 93*
Patterson, Dwight Fleming, Jr. 1939- *WhoSSW 93*
Patterson, Edward 1920- *WhoAm 92, WhoE 93, WhoWor 93*
Patterson, Eleanor Medill 1881-1948 *JrnUS*
Patterson, Elizabeth B. *Law&B 92*
Patterson, Elizabeth J. 1939- *BioIn 17, CngDr 91*
Patterson, Elizabeth Johnston 1939- *WhoAm 92, WhoAmW 93, WhoSSW 93*
Patterson, Elizabeth Knight 1909- *WhoE 93*
Patterson, Ellen Anne 1960- *St&PR 93*
Patterson, Ellmore Clark 1913- *WhoAm 92*
Patterson, Emma *AmWomPl*
Patterson, Eugene 1923- *DcLB 127 [port]*
Patterson, Eugene Corbett 1923- *JrnUS, WhoAm 92, WhoSSW 93*
Patterson, Florence Ghoram 1936- *WhoAmW 93, WhoWor 93*
Patterson, Floyd 1935- *WhoAm 92*
Patterson, Forrest T. *Law&B 92*
Patterson, Frank 1928- *St&PR 93*
Patterson, Franklin Peale 1871-1966 *Baker 92*
Patterson, Frederick D. *BioIn 17*
Patterson, G.S. 1909- *St&PR 93*
Patterson, G. Wesley 1947- *St&PR 93*
Patterson, Gary Wayne 1947- *WhoEmL 93, WhoSSW 93*
Patterson, George N(eilson) 1920- *ConAu 137*
Patterson, Glenn Wayne 1938- *WhoAm 92*
Patterson, Grady Leslie, Jr. 1924- *WhoAm 92, WhoSSW 93*
Patterson, Grady Siler, Jr. 1928- *WhoSSW 93*
Patterson, Grove Hiram 1881-1956 *JrnUS*
Patterson, Guy K. 1922- *St&PR 93*
Patterson, H.D. *WhoScE 91-1*
Patterson, Harlan Ray 1931- *WhoAm 92*
Patterson, Harry 1929- *BioIn 17, WhoAm 92*
Patterson, Henry 1929- *BioIn 17*
Patterson, Henry S., II 1922- *St&PR 93*
Patterson, Herbert M. 1919- *St&PR 93*
Patterson, Herman Fitch 1928- *WhoSSW 93*
Patterson, J.B. 1927- *St&PR 93*
Patterson, J.O. 1912-1989 *BioIn 17*
Patterson, James 1947- *ScF&FL 92*
Patterson, James A. 1942- *WhoIns 93*
Patterson, James Brendan 1947- *WhoE 93*
Patterson, James G. 1943- *St&PR 93*
Patterson, James Hardy 1935- *WhoSSW 93, WhoWor 93*
Patterson, James Milton 1927- *WhoAm 92*
Patterson, James Oglethorpe 1912-1989 *BioIn 17*
Patterson, James R. 1927- *St&PR 93*
Patterson, James Thurston 1944- *WhoSSW 93*
Patterson, James William 1940- *WhoAm 92*
Patterson, James Willis 1946- *WhoAm 92, WhoSSW 93, WhoWor 93*
Patterson, Jan D. 1936- *St&PR 93*
Patterson, Janice Lavelle 1938- *WhoAmW 93*
Patterson, Jeanne Boland 1947- *WhoSSW 93*
Patterson, Jerry Eugene 1931- *WhoAm 92*
Patterson, John *MiSFD 9, WhoScE 91-1*
Patterson, John Andrew 1966- *WhoSSW 93*
Patterson, John de la Roche, Jr. 1941- *WhoAm 92*
Patterson, John Malcolm 1921- *WhoAm 92*
Patterson, John Pershing 1933- *WhoAm 92*
Patterson, John R. 1950- *St&PR 93*
Patterson, John Richard 1932- *WhoSSW 93*
Patterson, Johnny 1926- *BioIn 17*
Patterson, Joseph H. 1939- *WhoAm 92*
Patterson, Joseph Medill 1879-1946 *JrnUS*
Patterson, Joseph Redwine 1927- *WhoAm 92*
Patterson, Joyce L. *Law&B 92*
Patterson, Karen Oakley 1942- *WhoAmW 93, WhoSSW 93*
Patterson, Kay Christine Lesley 1944- *WhoAsAP 91*
Patterson, Laird Dean *Law&B 92*
Patterson, Leland Francis 1937- *WhoE 93, WhoWor 93*
Patterson, Leon *BioIn 17*
Patterson, Leonard M., Jr. *Law&B 92*
Patterson, Lillie G. *BlkAuII 92*
Patterson, Lois B. *AmWomPl*
Patterson, Louise Thompson *BioIn 17*
Patterson, Lydia Ross 1936- *WhoAmW 93*
Patterson, Mabel Sue 1957- *WhoAmW 93*
Patterson, Marcella Mendoza 1956- *WhoAmW 93*
Patterson, Maria Jevitz 1944- *WhoAmW 93*
Patterson, Maria Monica *Law&B 92*
Patterson, Marjorie *AmWomPl*
Patterson, Mark Stribling 1952- *WhoAm 92*
Patterson, Marla Katherine 1950- *WhoEmL 93*
Patterson, Mary-Margaret Sharp 1944- *WhoAm 92*
Patterson, Mary Marvin Breckinridge 1905- *WhoAm 92*
Patterson, Matthew Allen 1959- *WhoSSW 93*
Patterson, Matthew Thomas *Law&B 92*
Patterson, Maurice Lee 1910- *WhoE 93*
Patterson, Michael E. *Law&B 92, St&PR 93*
Patterson, Michael Ellmore 1942- *WhoAm 92*
Patterson, Nancy-Lou 1929- *ScF&FL 92*
Patterson, Nancy Ruth 1944- *SmATA 72 [port]*
Patterson, Norman William 1917-1990 *BioIn 17*
Patterson, Orlando 1940- *BioIn 17, ConBlB 4 [port], WhoAm 92*
Patterson, Oscar, III 1945- *WhoSSW 93*
Patterson, P. J. *WhoWor 93*
Patterson, P.J. (Percival) 1935- *DcCPCAm*
Patterson, Pamela Jane 1951- *WhoAmW 93*
Patterson, Patricia *BioIn 17*
Patterson, Patricia Lynn 1946- *WhoSSW 93*
Patterson, Patricia Sue 1944- *WhoWrEP 92*
Patterson, Paul H. 1943- *WhoAm 92*
Patterson, Paul (Leslie) 1947- *Baker 92*
Patterson, Paula M. 1952- *WhoAmW 93*
Patterson, Polly Reilly 1906- *WhoAmW 93, WhoE 93, WhoWor 93*
Patterson, Randy *BioIn 17*
Patterson, Ray *MiSFD 9*
Patterson, Raymond Richard 1929- *WhoWrEP 92*
Patterson, Richard Brown 1937- *St&PR 93, WhoAm 92*
Patterson, Richard John 1945- *WhoWor 93*
Patterson, Richard Sheldon 1932- *WhoSSW 93*
Patterson, Rickey Lee 1952- *WhoEmL 93, WhoSSW 93*
Patterson, Rita Marie 1962- *WhoAmW 93*
Patterson, Robert 1792-1881 *HarEnMi*
Patterson, Robert Arthur 1915- *WhoAm 92*
Patterson, Robert Eugene 1932- *St&PR 93*
Patterson, Robert G. 1937- *St&PR 93*
Patterson, Robert H. *Law&B 92*
Patterson, Robert Hobson, Jr. 1927- *St&PR 93, WhoAm 92*
Patterson, Robert Hudson 1936- *WhoAm 92*
Patterson, Robert Logan 1940- *WhoAm 92*
Patterson, Robert Lynn 1939- *WhoSSW 93*
Patterson, Robert Porter, Jr. 1923- *WhoAm 92, WhoE 93*
Patterson, Robert S. 1941- *St&PR 93*
Patterson, Robert Youngman, Jr. 1921- *WhoAm 92*
Patterson, Roger 1950- *St&PR 93*
Patterson, Ronald J. 1951- *St&PR 93*
Patterson, Ronald Paul 1941- *WhoAm 92*
Patterson, Ronald Roy 1942- *WhoAm 92, WhoSSW 93*
Patterson, Roy 1926- *WhoAm 92*
Patterson, Roy 1942- *St&PR 93*
Patterson, Russel Hugo, Jr. 1929- *WhoAm 92*
Patterson, Russell 1930- *WhoAm 92*
Patterson, S. James *Law&B 92*
Patterson, S.R. *St&PR 93*
Patterson, Saidie 1906-1985 *BioIn 17*
Patterson, Scot G. 1953- *WhoWrEP 92*
Patterson, Seth Lynn 1953- *WhoAm 92*
Patterson, Shirley 1922-1990? *SweetSg C [port]*
Patterson, Solon P. 1935- *St&PR 93*
Patterson, Stephen F. 1939- *WhoIns 93*
Patterson, Steve 1957- *WhoAm 92, WhoSSW 93*
Patterson, Suzanne House 1955- *WhoAmW 93*
Patterson, Thomas C., Jr. 1949- *WhoE 93*
Patterson, Thomas Donald 1961- *WhoSSW 93*
Patterson, Thomas H. 1941- *St&PR 93*
Patterson, Thomas N.L. *WhoScE 91-1*
Patterson, Timothy Dale 1949- *WhoWrEP 92*
Patterson, Trudy Jenkins 1951- *WhoEmL 93*
Patterson, Veronica Shantz 1945- *WhoWrEP 92*
Patterson, Vivian Jane 1937- *WhoSSW 93*
Patterson, W. Bruce *Law&B 92*
Patterson, W. Linn *Law&B 92*
Patterson, W. Morgan 1925- *WhoAm 92*
Patterson, Willi *MiSFD 9*
Patterson, William Allan 1899-1980 *EncABHB 8 [port]*
Patterson, William Bradford 1921- *WhoAm 92*
Patterson, William Remington, Jr. 1948- *WhoE 93*
Patterson, William Robert 1924- *WhoAm 92*
Patterson, William Wayne 1943- *St&PR 93, WhoAm 92*
Patterson, Willie 1926- *BioIn 17*
Patteson, Charles Lynn 1923- *WhoSSW 93*
Patteson, Roy Kinneer, Jr. 1928- *WhoAm 92*
Patti *Baker 92*
Patti, Adelina 1843-1919 *Baker 92, IntDcOp [port], NotHsAW 93, OxDcOp*
Patti, Amalia 1831-1915 *Baker 92, OxDcOp*
Patti, Carlotta 1835-1889 *Baker 92*
Patti, Carlotta 1836-1889 *OxDcOp*
Patti, Carmen B. *Law&B 92*
Patti, Caterina Chiesa Barilli- d1870 *OxDcOp*
Patti, Frances Marie 1934- *WhoAmW 93*
Patti, Lisa Marie 1967- *WhoE 93*
Patti, Paul 1956- *ConAu 136*
Patti, Salvatore 1800-1869 *Baker 92, OxDcOp*
Patti, Sandi *WhoAmW 93*
Pattie, Kenton Harman 1939- *WhoSSW 93*
Pattie, Preston Stuart 1944- *WhoE 93*
Pattiera, Tino 1890-1966 *Baker 92*
Pattillo, David B. 1928- *St&PR 93*
Pattillo, M. Mason *Law&B 92*
Pattillo, Manning Mason, Jr. 1919- *WhoAm 92*
Pattillo, Nickles Keat 1947- *WhoSSW 93*
Pattinson, Michael *MiSFD 9*
Pattis, S. William 1925- *WhoAm 92*
Pattishall, Beverly Wyckliffe 1916- *WhoAm 92, WhoWor 93*
Pattison, Abbott Lawrence 1916- *WhoAm 92*
Pattison, Barrie 1940- *ScF&FL 92*
Pattison, Darcy (S.) 1954- *SmATA 72 [port]*
Pattison, David Harry 1939- *WhoWor 93*
Pattison, Edward W. 1932-1990 *BioIn 17*
Pattison, Graham Anthony 1944- *WhoWor 93*
Pattison, James A. *BioIn 17*
Pattison, James Allen 1928- *St&PR 93*
Pattison, Jim *BioIn 17*
Pattison, John R. *WhoScE 91-1*
Pattison, John Thurman *Law&B 92*

Pattison, Joseph E. *Law&B 92*
Pattison, Lee 1890-1966 *Baker 92*
Pattison, Mabel Katherine 1936- *WhoAmW 93*
Pattison, Patrick *ScF&FL 92*
Pattison, Robert Emory 1850-1904 *BioIn 17*
Pattison, Thomas Roy 1943- *WhoAm 92*
Pattiz, Norman J. 1943- *St&PR 93*
Pattnaik, Sunil Kumar 1924- *WhoAsAP 91*
Patto A/L Perumal 1946- *WhoAsAP 91*
Patton, A.M. *WhoScE 91-1*
Patton, Aaron L. *Law&B 92*
Patton, Alton DeWitt 1935- *WhoAm 92*
Patton, Audley Everett 1898- *WhoWor 93*
Patton, Bob J. 1925- *WhoSSW 93*
Patton, Carl Elliott 1941- *WhoAm 92*
Patton, Carl Vernon 1944- *WhoAm 92, WhoSSW 93*
Patton, Carlton Clement 1936- *WhoAm 92*
Patton, Charlie 1887-1934 *BioIn 17*
Patton, Chris *BioIn 17*
Patton, Cliff *ScF&FL 92*
Patton, Cynthia Maria *Law&B 92*
Patton, Darla June Eaton 1948- *WhoAmW 93*
Patton, Deanna Kay 1953- *WhoEmL 93*
Patton, Denise Jean 1946- *WhoAmW 93*
Patton, Diana Lee Wilkoc 1940- *WhoAm 92, WhoWor 93*
Patton, G. Thomas, Jr. 1929- *St&PR 93*
Patton, Gail Ann 1950- *WhoAmW 93*
Patton, Gary N. *Law&B 92*
Patton, George E. 1920-1991 *BioIn 17*
Patton, George S. 1885-1945 *BioIn 17*
Patton, George Smith 1885-1945 *DcTwHis, HarEnMi*
Patton, George Smith 1923- *WhoAm 92*
Patton, Harold R. *Law&B 92*
Patton, Henry H. 1913- *St&PR 93*
Patton, James Lewis 1928- *St&PR 93*
Patton, James McCurdy, Jr. 1927- *WhoSSW 93*
Patton, James Richard, Jr. 1928- *WhoAm 92, WhoE 93, WhoWor 93*
Patton, Janet Clara 1945- *WhoAmW 93*
Patton, Jean *BlkAmWO*
Patton, Joelle Delbourgo 1953- *WhoAm 92*
Patton, John J. *Law&B 92*
Patton, John Michael 1947- *WhoE 93*
Patton, Kate Holland *AmWomPl*
Patton, Kevin Joel 1967- *WhoSSW 93*
Patton, Kirk Michael 1959- *WhoE 93*
Patton, Lauren Leslie 1958- *WhoSSW 93*
Patton, Leah *ScF&FL 92*
Patton, Marvin Lee 1935- *WhoSSW 93*
Patton, Matthew Henry 1936- *WhoAm 92*
Patton, Melvin Emery 1924- *BiDAMSp 1989*
Patton, Michael Quinn (Halcolm) 1945- *WhoWrEP 92*
Patton, Mitchell 1931- *St&PR 93*
Patton, Nancy Matthews 1942- *WhoAmW 93*
Patton, Paul E. *WhoAm 92, WhoSSW 93*
Patton, Peter Clyde 1935- *WhoE 93*
Patton, Richard Bolling 1929- *St&PR 93*
Patton, Richard G. 1928- *St&PR 93*
Patton, Robert Frederick 1927- *WhoAm 92, WhoWor 93*
Patton, Robert J. *Law&B 92*
Patton, Robert Lee 1949- *WhoSSW 93*
Patton, Ronald C. 1947- *St&PR 93*
Patton, Ronald F. 1935- *St&PR 93*
Patton, Stephen Currie 1963- *WhoE 93*
Patton, Stuart 1920- *WhoAm 92*
Patton, Susan Kane 1950- *WhoAmW 93*
Patton, Thomas Earl 1940- *WhoAm 92*
Patton, Thomas F. 1903- *St&PR 93*
Patton, Thomas James 1948- *WhoEmL 93*
Patton, Walter *Law&B 92*
Patton, Wendell Melton, Jr. 1922- *WhoAm 92*
Patton, William *Law&B 92*
Patton, William A. 1937- *St&PR 93*
Pattou, Edith *ScF&FL 92*
Pattrick, William *ScF&FL 92*
Pattullo, Andrew 1917- *WhoAm 92*
Pattullo, Thomas Dufferin 1873-1956 *BioIn 17*
Patty, Ann Elizabeth 1951- *WhoWrEP 92*
Patty, Claibourne Watkins, Jr. 1934- *WhoAm 92*
Patty, Frank L. 1908- *St&PR 93*
Patty, James Singleton 1925- *WhoSSW 93*
Patty, R. Bruce 1935- *WhoAm 92*
Pattyn, Remi C. 1922- *St&PR 93*
Pattyn, Remi Ceasar 1922- *WhoAm 92*
Pattyn, Roland Louis 1937- *St&PR 93*
Pattyn, Stefaan Rogier 1927- *WhoScE 91-2*
Patulot, Jun J. R. 1947- *WhoEmL 93*
Paturel, Robert Paul 1947- *WhoWor 93*
Paturis, Emmanuel Michael 1933- *WhoSSW 93, WhoWor 93*
Patvaros, Jozsef 1934- *WhoScE 91-4*
Paty, Donald Winston 1936- *WhoAm 92*
Paty, Michel H.L.G. 1938- *WhoScE 91-2*
Patz, Arnall 1920- *WhoAm 92*
Patz, Edward Frank 1932- *WhoAm 92*
Patz, Etan *BioIn 17*
Patz, Lawrence Charles 1932- *WhoIns 93*
Patzak, Julius 1898-1974 *Baker 92, IntDcOp, OxDcOp*
Patzelt, Anthony Charles 1955- *WhoE 93*
Patzelt, Paul 1932- *WhoScE 91-3, WhoWor 93*
Patzelt, Vivienne Linda 1953- *WhoAmW 93*
Patzer, Emmons Michael 1954- *WhoEmL 93*
Patzke, Pamela McKenna *Law&B 92*
Patzke, Richard J. 1941- *St&PR 93*
Patzke, Richard Joseph 1941- *WhoAm 92*
Patzman, Stephen Narr 1942- *WhoIns 93*
Patzold, Gunter 1944- *WhoWor 93*
Pau, Hans 1918- *WhoWor 93*
Paua, Joel 1949- *WhoAsAP 91*
Pauer, Erich 1943- *WhoWor 93*
Pauer, Ernst 1826-1905 *Baker 92*
Pauer, Jiri 1919- *Baker 92, OxDcOp*
Pauer, Max von 1866-1945 *Baker 92*
Paugh, James Joseph, Jr. 1934- *St&PR 93*
Paugh, Patricia Lou 1948- *WhoAmW 93, WhoE 93*
Paugh, Thomas Francis 1929- *WhoAm 92, WhoWrEP 92*
Pauk, Gyorgy 1936- *Baker 92*
Pauk, Janos 1951- *WhoScE 91-4*
Pauk, Walter 1914- *ConAu 39NR*
Pauken, Patrick J. *Law&B 92*
Pauken, Thomas Weir 1944- *WhoSSW 93*
Pauker, John 1920-1991 *BioIn 17*
Paukstelis, Vytautas 1931- *St&PR 93*
Paukstis, Charles A. 1935- *St&PR 93*
Paul *OxDcByz*
Paul, I *OxDcByz*
Paul, I c. 300-351? *OxDcByz*
Paul, II *OxDcByz*
Paul, VI 1897-1978 *DcTwHis*
Paul, VI, Pope 1897-1978 *BioIn 17*
Paul, Aileen *WhoWrEP 92*
Paul, Alan c. 1950- *See* Manhattan Transfer, The *ConMus 8*
Paul, Alice 1885-1977 *PolPar*
Paul, Alida Ruth 1953- *WhoSSW 93*
Paul, Allen 1946- *WhoAsAP 91*
Paul, Andrew Robert 1938- *WhoSSW 93*
Paul, Ara Garo 1929- *WhoAm 92*
Paul, Arthur 1925- *WhoAm 92*
Paul, Axel 1942- *WhoScE 91-3*
Paul, Barbara 1925- *ScF&FL 92*
Paul, Barbara 1931- *ScF&FL 92*
Paul, Barbara Ann 1952- *WhoAmW 93*
Paul, Barbara H. *Law&B 92*
Paul, Benjamin David 1911- *WhoAm 92*
Paul, Billy 1934- *SoulM*
Paul, Biraja Bilash 1933- *WhoWor 93*
Paul, C. Robert *Law&B 92*
Paul, Carol Ann 1936- *WhoAmW 93, WhoE 93*
Paul, Celia Ann 1944- *WhoAmW 93*
Paul, Charles S. 1949- *WhoAm 92*
Paul, Charlotte P. 1941- *WhoAmW 93*
Paul, Chris A. *Law&B 92*
Paul, Christian Thomas 1926- *WhoAm 92*
Paul, Clarence 1928- *SoulM*
Paul, Connie Sue 1944- *WhoAmW 93*
Paul, Courtland Price 1927- *WhoAm 92*
Paul, Daniel J. *Law&B 92*
Paul, David L. 1942- *St&PR 93*
Paul, Debra *BioIn 17*
Paul, Dennis L. *Law&B 92*
Paul, Denny K. 1941- *WhoAm 92*
Paul, Don de *ScF&FL 92*
Paul, Donald J. 1932- *St&PR 93*
Paul, Donald Ross 1939- *WhoAm 92*
Paul, Doris Jessie 1903- *WhoWrEP 92*
Paul, Douglas Allan 1949- *St&PR 93, WhoAm 92*
Paul, Douglas Allen *Law&B 92*
Paul, Edith de *ScF&FL 92*
Paul, Edward Lee, Jr. 1961- *WhoSSW 93*
Paul, Elaine P. *WhoAmW 93*
Paul, Eldor Alvin 1931- *WhoAm 92*
Paul, Elias 1919- *WhoAm 92*
Paul, Ellen Louise 1948- *WhoAmW 93, WhoEmL 93*
Paul, Eric S. *WhoAm 92*
Paul, Eve W. 1930- *WhoAm 92*
Paul, Frank 1924- *WhoAm 92*
Paul, Frank R. *BioIn 17*
Paul, Frank Waters 1938- *WhoAm 92*
Paul, Fred 1938- *WhoScE 91-3*
Paul, Gabriel 1910- *WhoAm 92, WhoWor 93*
Paul, George James 1927- *St&PR 93*
Paul, Gerald 1924- *St&PR 93, WhoAm 92*
Paul, Gerald 1945- *WhoE 93*
Paul, Gordon Lee 1935- *WhoAm 92, WhoSSW 93*
Paul, Gordon Wilbur 1933- *WhoSSW 93*
Paul, H.L. *WhoScE 91-3*
Paul, Hap *BioIn 17*
Paul, Helmut 1929- *WhoScE 91-4*
Paul, Helmut 1940- *St&PR 93*
Paul, Herbert Morton *WhoAm 92, WhoE 93, WhoWor 93*
Paul, Igor 1936- *WhoE 93*
Paul, Jack 1928- *St&PR 93*
Paul, James Anthony 1946- *St&PR 93*
Paul, James Caverly Newlin 1926- *WhoAm 92*
Paul, James Donald 1956- *WhoE 93*
Paul, James Robert 1934- *St&PR 93, WhoSSW 93*
Paul, James T. 1918- *St&PR 93*
Paul, James William 1945- *WhoAm 92*
Paul, Jan Anders Karl 1955- *WhoWor 93*
Paul, Janis M. 1947- *WhoSSW 93*
Paul, Jay Snyder 1945- *WhoWrEP 92*
Paul, Jean 1763-1825 *BioIn 17*
Paul, Jeffery John Cameron 1954- *WhoSSW 93*
Paul, Jerome Edward 1942- *St&PR 93*
Paul, John Joseph 1918- *WhoAm 92*
Paul, John P. *WhoScE 91-1*
Paul, John Stephen 1944- *WhoSSW 93*
Paul, John Stuart 1937- *WhoWor 93*
Paul, John W. *Law&B 92*
Paul, Jon F. 1953- *St&PR 93*
Paul, Julian 1917- *St&PR 93*
Paul, Justus Fredrick 1938- *WhoAm 92*
Paul, Karen 1944- *WhoSSW 93*
Paul, Karen B. 1961- *WhoAmW 93*
Paul, Keith Thomas 1941- *WhoScE 91-1*
Paul, Lee Gilmour 1907- *WhoAm 92*
Paul, Les 1915- *Baker 92, WhoAm 92*
Paul, Louise 1950- *St&PR 93*
Paul, Lynne Marie 1958- *WhoAmW 93*
Paul, Margaret Beryl 1939- *WhoAmW 93*
Paul, Margo *Law&B 92*
Paul, Mark P. *Law&B 92*
Paul, Martin Ambrose 1910- *WhoAm 92*
Paul, Martin Gregory 1959- *WhoE 93*
Paul, Mary Melchior 1952- *WhoAmW 93*
Paul, Maurice M. 1932- *WhoAm 92*
Paul, Nanette Baker 1866-1928? *AmWomPl*
Paul, Ogden 1937- *WhoScE 91-1*
Paul, Oglesby 1916- *WhoAm 92*
Paul, Oscar 1836-1898 *Baker 92*
Paul, Patricia Christine 1954- *WhoWrEP 92*
Paul, Patricia Lynn 1946- *WhoAmW 93*
Paul, Pauline C. 1912-1989 *BioIn 17*
Paul, Philip F. 1941- *St&PR 93*
Paul, Philip Franklin, Jr. 1941- *WhoWor 93*
Paul, R.A. 1938- *St&PR 93*
Paul, Richard A. *Law&B 92*
Paul, Richard A. 1946- *St&PR 93*
Paul, Richard Dorsel 1927- *WhoAm 92*
Paul, Richard S. *Law&B 92*
Paul, Richard Stanley 1941- *WhoAm 92*
Paul, Robert 1931- *WhoSSW 93*
Paul, Robert Arthur 1937- *St&PR 93, WhoAm 92, WhoE 93*
Paul, Robert Carey 1950- *WhoAm 92, WhoWor 93*
Paul, Robert D. 1928- *St&PR 93*
Paul, Robert David 1928- *WhoAm 92*
Paul, Robert Dennis 1941- *WhoAm 92*
Paul, Robert G. 1942- *St&PR 93*
Paul, Robert Milton 1942- *WhoAm 92*
Paul, Robert T. 1928- *St&PR 93*
Paul, Roland A. *Law&B 92*
Paul, Roland Arthur *Law&B 92*
Paul, Roland Arthur 1937- *St&PR 93, WhoAm 92*
Paul, Ronald N. 1934- *St&PR 93*
Paul, Ronald Neale 1934- *WhoAm 92*
Paul, Ronald Stanley 1923- *WhoAm 92*
Paul, Russell Kent 1952- *WhoAm 92*
Paul, Sandra K. 1938- *WhoWrEP 92*
Paul, Sandra Koodin 1938- *WhoAmW 93, WhoE 93*
Paul, Sandra Lynne Joy 1962- *WhoAmW 93*
Paul, Sherman 1920- *WhoAm 92*
Paul, Sherrill Duncan 1948- *WhoAmW 93*
Paul, Sherry *WhoAmW 93*
Paul, Sol J. d1992 *NewYTBS 92*
Paul, Steven 1958- *MiSFD 9*
Paul, Stuart *MiSFD 9*
Paul, Susan L. 1944- *WhoAmW 93*
Paul, Swraj *BioIn 17*
Paul, T.R. 1932- *St&PR 93*
Paul, Thomas A. *WhoAm 92*
Paul, Thomas Daniel 1948- *WhoSSW 93*
Paul, Thomas (Warburton) 1934- *Baker 92*
Paul, Thomas Wayne 1950- *WhoE 93, WhoEmL 93, WhoWor 93*
Paul, Tommy 1907-1991 *BioIn 17*
Paul, William 1926- *WhoAm 92, WhoE 93*
Paul, William Bruce 1943- *WhoWrEP 92*
Paul, William Erwin 1936- *WhoAm 92*
Paul, William G., Sr. *Law&B 92*
Paul, William George 1930- *St&PR 93, WhoAm 92*
Paul, William Gerald 1948- *WhoE 93*
Paul, William Patrick 1950- *WhoE 93*
Paul, Wolfgang 1913- *WhoWor 93*
Paulan, Alverna M. *Law&B 92*
Paulapuro, Hannu Viljami 1947- *WhoScE 91-4*
Paulauskas, Edmund Walter 1937- *WhoSSW 93, WhoWor 93*
Paulauskas, Vygantas 1944- *WhoWor 93*
Paul-Boncour, Joseph 1873-1972 *BioIn 17*
Paul-David, Madeleine 1908-1989 *BioIn 17*
Paulding, James Y. 1927- *St&PR 93*
Paulding, Joseph DeBose 1956- *WhoSSW 93*
Paule, Jeffrey N. *Law&B 92*
Paulen, Ben Sanford 1869-1961 *BioIn 17*
Paulen, Jacques Roderick 1925- *WhoSSW 93*
Paulen, Judith Ann 1947- *WhoE 93*
Paulet, Claude Jean 1942- *WhoUN 92*
Pauley, Frances Freeborn 1905- *BioIn 17*
Pauley, Gary *Law&B 92*
Pauley, Jane *BioIn 17*
Pauley, Jane 1950- *JrnUS, WhoAm 92, WhoAmW 93*
Pauley, Karen L. *Law&B 92*
Pauley, Mary Sue 1958- *WhoSSW 93*
Pauley, Robert Reinhold 1923- *WhoAm 92*
Pauley, Stanley Frank 1927- *St&PR 93, WhoAm 92*
Paulhamus, Ronald F. 1952- *St&PR 93*
Paulhus, Joseph L.H. *BioIn 17*
Paulhus, Norman Gerard, Jr. 1950- *WhoE 93, WhoEmL 93, WhoWor 93*
Paulie 1947- *WhoWrEP 92*
Paulik, Mary Theresa 1939- *WhoAmW 93*
Paulikas, George Algis 1936- *WhoAm 92*
Paulin, Andre 1926- *WhoScE 91-2*
Paulin, Arthur *St&PR 93*
Paulin, Edward J. 1947- *St&PR 93*
Paulin, Guy d1990 *BioIn 17*
Paulin, Henry Sylvester 1927- *WhoAm 92*
Paulin, Stanley F. 1926- *St&PR 93*
Pauline-Pappas, Roseann Judith 1957- *WhoEmL 93*
Pauling, G.E. *Law&B 92*
Pauling, Linus C. 1901- *BioIn 17*
Pauling, Linus Carl 1901- *WhoAm 92, WhoWor 93*
Paulinus 353?-431 *OxDcByz*
Paulinus of Pella 376?-c. 460 *OxDcByz*
Paulitsch, David 1940- *St&PR 93*
Paulitsch, Peter 1922- *WhoScE 91-3*
Paulk, Michael W. 1945- *St&PR 93*
Paulk, William Eston 1929- *WhoSSW 93, WhoWrEP 92*
Paull, Barberi 1946- *Baker 92*
Paull, Irwin Leff 1946- *WhoSSW 93*
Paull, J. Will 1922- *St&PR 93*
Paull, James Bartlett 1945- *St&PR 93*
Paull, Richard Allen 1930- *WhoAm 92*
Paull, Theodore 1920- *St&PR 93*
Paulli, Holger Simon 1810-1891 *Baker 92*
Paulling, John Randolph, Jr. 1930- *WhoAm 92*
Paulmann, Gerhard 1926- *WhoScE 91-3*
Paulme, Denise 1909- *IntDcAn*
Paul of Aegina dc. 642 *OxDcByz*
Paul of Alexandria fl. 378- *OxDcByz*
Paul of Kallinikos fl. 6th cent.- *OxDcByz*
Paul of Latros d955 *OxDcByz*
Paul of Monemvasia fl. 10th cent.- *OxDcByz*
Paulos, John Allen 1945- *ConAu 136*
Paulouro das Neves, Jose Cesar 1937- *WhoWor 93*
Pauls, Charles W. 1946- *St&PR 93*
Pauls, John P. 1937- *St&PR 93*
Pauls, Theodore D. 1951- *St&PR 93*
Paulsen, Darlyne Evelyn 1936- *WhoSSW 93*
Paulsen, Darrell R. 1937- *St&PR 93*
Paulsen, David *MiSFD 9*
Paulsen, Douglas Frank 1952- *WhoSSW 93*
Paulsen, Eric Lynn 1951- *St&PR 93*
Paulsen, Frank Robert 1922- *WhoAm 92*
Paulsen, Frederic Charles 1943- *WhoSSW 93*
Paulsen, Gary *BioIn 17*
Paulsen, Gary 1939- *DcAmChF 1985, MajAI [port], ScF&FL 92*
Paulsen, Gary Melvin 1939- *WhoAm 92*
Paulsen, James Walter 1954- *WhoSSW 93*
Paulsen, John Andrew 1960- *St&PR 93*
Paulsen, John Quincy 1928- *St&PR 93*
Paulsen, Norman Deitrich 1929- *WhoWrEP 92*
Paulsen, Pat *BioIn 17*
Paulsen, Robert A. 1917- *St&PR 93*
Paulsen, Ruth Ann 1940- *WhoAmW 93*
Paulsen, Serenus Glen 1917- *WhoAm 92*
Paulsen, Stanley K. 1935- *St&PR 93*
Paulsen, Stephen W. 1948- *St&PR 93*
Paulsen, Thomas Dean 1936- *WhoAm 92*
Paulsen, Vivian 1942- *WhoAm 92*
Paulsen, William C. *St&PR 93*
Paul Silentiarios fl. 6th cent.- *OxDcByz*

Paulson, Alan Charles 1947- *WhoWrEP 92*
Paulson, Allen Eugene 1922- *WhoAm 92, WhoSSW 93*
Paulson, Belden Henry 1927- *WhoAm 92*
Paulson, Bernard Arthur 1928- *WhoAm 92*
Paulson, Cindy Patrice 1949- *WhoEmL 93*
Paulson, Donald Erwin 1934- *St&PR 93*
Paulson, Donald Robert 1943- *WhoAm 92*
Paulson, Gary L. *Law&B 92*
Paulson, George Melvin, Jr. *Law&B 92*
Paulson, Gerald C. 1935- *St&PR 93*
Paulson, Glenn 1941- *WhoAm 92*
Paulson, Gustaf 1898-1966 *Baker 92*
Paulson, Henry Merritt, Jr. 1946- *WhoAm 92*
Paulson, James Marvin 1923- *WhoAm 92*
Paulson, Jerome S. 1945- *St&PR 93*
Paulson, John D. 1915- *St&PR 93*
Paulson, John Doran 1915- *WhoAm 92*
Paulson, Lawrence C. *Law&B 92*
Paulson, Lawrence Charles *WhoScE 91-1*
Paulson, Leroy Arthur 1942- *St&PR 93*
Paulson, Loretta Nancy 1943- *WhoE 93*
Paulson, Marvel P. 1920- *St&PR 93*
Paulson, Mary Alice 1962- *WhoAmW 93*
Paulson, Michael G. 1945- *ConAu 139*
Paulson, Michael I. *Law&B 92*
Paulson, Paul Joseph 1932- *WhoAm 92*
Paulson, Peter John 1928- *WhoAm 92*
Paulson, Robert C. 1944- *St&PR 93*
Paulson, Ronald Howard 1930- *WhoAm 92*
Paulson, Sally Louise 1953- *WhoAmW 93*
Paulson, Stanley Fay 1920- *WhoAm 92*
Paulson, Terry L. 1945- *ConAu 136*
Paulson, Thomas L. 1949- *St&PR 93*
Paulson-Ellis, Jeremy David 1943- *WhoWor 93*
Paulsson, G. Valfrid V. 1925- *WhoScE 91-4*
Paulsson, Lars-Erik 1943- *WhoScE 91-4*
Paulston, Christina Bratt 1932- *WhoAm 92*
Paul, the Apostle, Saint *BioIn 17*
Paulu, Nancy Jean 1949- *WhoAmW 93*
Paulucci, Jeno F. *BioIn 17*
Paulucci, Jeno F. 1918- *St&PR 93*
Paulus, Friedrich von 1890-1957 *BioIn 17, DcTwHis, HarEnMi*
Paulus, Harold Edward 1929- *WhoAm 92*
Paulus, J.M. *WhoScE 91-2*
Paulus, John Douglas 1917- *St&PR 93*
Paulus, John Joseph 1907- *St&PR 93*
Paulus, John R. 1935- *St&PR 93*
Paulus, K. *WhoScE 91-3*
Paulus, Lucius Aemilius d216BC *HarEnMi*
Paulus, Olaf 1859-1912 *Baker 92*
Paulus, Stephen (Harrison) 1949- *Baker 92, WhoAm 92*
Paulus, Susan L. *Law&B 92*
Paulus, Wilma Florence 1930- *WhoAmW 93*
Paulus Macedonicus, Lucius Aemilius c. 229BC-160BC *HarEnMi*
Pauly, Bruce Henry 1920- *WhoAm 92*
Pauly, D. Tod 1954- *St&PR 93*
Pauly, David F. 1952- *WhoIns 93*
Pauly, Gregory E. 1926- *St&PR 93*
Pauly, Gregory N. 1951- *St&PR 93*
Pauly, John Edward 1927- *WhoAm 92*
Pauly, Nelson Anthony 1914- *St&PR 93*
Pauly, Rosa 1894-1975 *Baker 92, OxDcOp*
Paul Yee 1956- *WhoCanL 92*
Paumann, Conrad 1410?-1473 *Baker 92*
Paumet, J. Louis *WhoScE 91-2*
Paumgarten, Nicholas B. 1945- *St&PR 93*
Paumgartner, Bernhard 1887-1971 *Baker 92*
Paumier, Kay Ellen 1944- *WhoAmW 93*
Paunier, Jean-Pierre 1929- *WhoScE 91-4*
Paunier, Luc 1931- *WhoScE 91-4*
Paunio, Ilkka K. 1931- *WhoScE 91-4*
Paunovic, Milenko 1889-1924 *Baker 92*
Paur, Emil 1855-1932 *Baker 92*
Paus, Povel Nicolay 1939- *WhoWor 93*
Pausa, Carol L. 1951- *St&PR 93*
Pausa, Clements Edward 1930- *St&PR 93, WhoAm 92*
Pausacker, Jennifer *ScF&FL 92*
Pausacker, Jenny 1948- *ScF&FL 92, SmATA 72 [port]*
Pausanias dc. 470BC *HarEnMi*
Pausanias fl. 2nd cent.- *OxDcByz*
Pausch, Josef *St&PR 93*
Pausewang, Gudrun 1928- *ScF&FL 92*
Pausig, Ralph W. 1934- *St&PR 93*
Pauson, Peter Ludwig *WhoScE 91-1*
Paustian, Jodie Lee 1957- *WhoAmW 93, WhoEmL 93*
Paustian, John Earle 1928- *WhoE 93*
Pautsch, Bruce L. 1951- *St&PR 93*
Pautsch, Fryderyk 1877-1950 *PolBiDi*
Pautsch, Richard J. *Law&B 92*
Pautz, Peter D. 1952- *ScF&FL 92*
Pauw, Jan S. *Law&B 92*
Pauwels, Frans M.M.C. 1927- *WhoScE 91-2*
Pauwels, Louis Francois 1920- *BioIn 17*
Pava, Calvin H. P. d1992 *NewYTBS 92*
Pavalon, Eugene Irving 1933- *WhoAm 92, WhoWor 93*
Pavan, Pietro Cardinal 1903- *WhoAm 92, WhoWor 93*
Pavao, Leonel Maia 1934- *WhoAm 92, WhoSSW 93*
Pavarotti, Luciano *BioIn 17*
Pavarotti, Luciano 1935- *Baker 92, IntDcOp [port], OxDcOp, WhoAm 92, WhoWor 93*
Pavek, Bryn Carpenter 1955- *WhoAmW 93*
Pavel, Elmer Lewis 1918- *WhoSSW 93*
Pavel, Paul G. d1992 *NewYTBS 92 [port]*
Pavel, Richard A. *Law&B 92*
Pavelic, Ante 1889-1959 *DcTwHis*
Pavelic, Kresimir 1952- *WhoScE 91-4*
Pavelka, Ed *BioIn 17*
Pavelka, Leonard R. 1924- *St&PR 93*
Pavelka, Martha C. 1927- *St&PR 93*
Pavelka, Robert F. 1953- *St&PR 93*
Pavella, M. 1934- *WhoScE 91-2*
Pavels, Victor 1919- *St&PR 93*
Pavelski, Patrick M. 1942- *St&PR 93*
Paven, Ruth M. *Law&B 92*
Pavese, Alfonso 1939- *St&PR 93*
Pavese, Cesare 1908-1950 *DcLB 128 [port]*
Pavesi, Lorenzo Augusto Maria 1961- *WhoWor 93*
Pavesi, Stefano 1779-1850 *OxDcOp*
Pavia, Andre A. 1937- *WhoScE 91-2*
Pavia, Demetri *WhoScE 91-1*
Pavia, Mario J. 1950- *St&PR 93*
Pavic, Milorad 1929- *ConAu 136, ScF&FL 92*
Pavicich, Nicolas 1933- *WhoWor 93*
Pavik, Malvin A. 1932- *WhoAm 92*
Pavilanis, Vytautas 1920- *WhoAm 92*
Pavitt, Keith Leslie Richard *WhoScE 91-1*
Pavkovic, Aleksandar 1950- *WhoWor 93*
Pavlasek, Ivan *WhoScE 91-4*
Pavlat, Robert 1926-1983 *ScF&FL 92*
Pavlic, John T. 1944- *St&PR 93*
Pavlic, Zdravko 1923- *WhoScE 91-4*
Pavlica, Susan Regina 1957- *WhoAmW 93*
Pavlich, Walter David 1955- *WhoWrEP 92*
Pavlick, Harvey Naylor 1942- *WhoWor 93*
Pavlick, Pamela Kay 1944- *WhoAmW 93, WhoSSW 93*
Pavlick, W.E. *Law&B 92*
Pavlick, Walter E. 1934- *St&PR 93*
Pavlick, Walter Eugene 1934- *WhoAm 92*
Pavlides, George 1935- *St&PR 93*
Pavlidis, Theodosios 1934- *WhoAm 92*
Pavlik, Alan Edward *WhoWrEP 92*
Pavlik, James William 1937- *WhoAm 92*
Pavlik, Mary Althea 1959- *WhoAmW 93*
Pavlik, Raymond K. 1940- *St&PR 93*
Pavlik, William Bruce 1932- *WhoAm 92*
Pavlioglou, John 1930- *WhoWor 93*
Pavliv, Mark Alexander 1951- *WhoE 93, WhoWor 93*
Pavloff, Jonathan T. 1949- *St&PR 93*
Pavlopoulos, Andreas Christos 1943- *WhoWor 93*
Pavlos, Andrew John 1937- *WhoSSW 93*
Pavlou, George 1953- *MiSFD 9*
Pavlou, Maria K. *Law&B 92*
Pavlov, Boris Sergeevich 1936- *WhoWor 93*
Pavlov, Roberta Fritsche 1951- *WhoSSW 93*
Pavlov, Valentin *BioIn 17, WhoWor 93*
Pavlova, Elena Michailovna 1941- *WhoUN 92*
Pavlovic, Bosko V. 1928- *WhoScE 91-4*
Pavlovic, Dusko 1957- *WhoWor 93*
Pavlovic, Milija N. 1950- *WhoWor 93*
Pavlovic, Miodrag 1928- *BioIn 17*
Pavlovic, Zivojin 1933- *DrEEuF*
Pavlow, Paul *Law&B 92*
Pavlow, Shara Toursh 1950- *WhoEmL 93*
Pavlus, Craig S. 1946- *St&PR 93*
Pavone, Marco 1959- *WhoWor 93*
Pavony, William H. 1940- *WhoAm 92*
Pavord, Anna 1940- *ConAu 37NR*
Pavsek, Daniel Allan 1945- *WhoAm 92*
Pavuk, Daniel David 1946- *St&PR 93*
Pavuna, Davor 1952- *WhoWor 93*
Pawar, Sharadchandra Govindrao 1940- *WhoWor 93*
Pawel, Richard E. 1932- *WhoSSW 93*
Pawelec, Graham Peter 1951- *WhoWor 93*
Pawelec, William John 1917- *WhoE 93*
Pawelek, Catherine Eva 1955- *WhoAmW 93*
Pawelkiewicz, Jane Aileen 1947- *WhoAmW 93*
Pawelski, Slawomir 1922- *WhoScE 91-4*
Pawkowski, Marek 1929- *WhoScE 91-4*
Pawl, Debra Lynn *Law&B 92*
Pawl, Marc C. *Law&B 92*
Pawl, Ronald Phillip 1935- *WhoWor 93*
Pawlak, Andrzej Leon 1939- *WhoScE 91-4*
Pawlak, Mark Joseph 1948- *WhoE 93, WhoWrEP 92*
Pawlak, Michael A. 1954- *St&PR 93*
Pawlak, Ryszard Jerzy 1952- *WhoWor 93*
Pawletko, Joann Marie 1960- *WhoAmW 93*
Pawley, G. Stuart *WhoScE 91-1*
Pawley, Keenan L. *Law&B 92*
Pawlick, Joseph Lawrence 1942- *St&PR 93*
Pawlick, Thomas 1941- *WhoWor 93*
Pawlicka, Lilia *WhoScE 91-4*
Pawlicki, Marek 1934- *WhoScE 91-4*
Pawliczko, George Ihor 1950- *WhoE 93, WhoWor 93*
Pawlik, James David 1958- *WhoEmL 93*
Pawlik, Kurt F. 1934- *WhoScE 91-3*
Pawlik, Maciej 1940- *WhoScE 91-4*
Pawlik, Robert Altenloh 1940- *WhoAm 92*
Pawlik-Dobrowolski, Jacek 1937- *WhoScE 91-4*
Pawlikowska-Jasnorzewska, Maria 1891-1945 *PolBiDi*
Pawlikowski, Marek 1933- *WhoScE 91-4*
Pawlowski, Diane R. 1944- *WhoWrEP 92*
Pawlowski, Helen Katherine 1930- *WhoAmW 93*
Pawlowski, John J. 1925- *St&PR 93*
Pawlowski, Joseph P. 1941- *St&PR 93*
Pawlowski, Lucjan 1946- *WhoScE 91-4, WhoWor 93*
Pawlowski, Walter Chester 1947- *WhoE 93*
Pawlowski, Zdzislaw 1923- *WhoScE 91-4*
Pawlson, Leonard Gregory 1943- *WhoAm 92*
Pawol, Grace Lakota 1936- *WhoAmW 93*
Pawson, David Leo 1938- *WhoE 93*
Pawson, John 1949- *BioIn 17*
Pawson, Kenneth Vernon Frank 1923- *WhoWor 93*
P'awstos Buzand, Pseudo- *OxDcByz*
Pawula, Kenneth John 1935- *WhoAm 92*
Paxinos, Esther F. 1935- *St&PR 93*
Paxinos, Odysseas 1963- *WhoWor 93*
Paxman, Gale Freeman 1957- *WhoEmL 93*
Paxon, Bill 1954- *CngDr 91, WhoAm 92, WhoE 93*
Paxson, Diana L. 1943- *ScF&FL 92*
Paxson, James Malone 1912- *St&PR 93*
Paxson, Lowell White 1935- *WhoAm 92, WhoSSW 93*
Paxson, Susan *AmWomPl*
Paxson, Wesley C. 1923- *St&PR 93*
Paxton, Alice Adams 1914- *WhoAmW 93, WhoE 93, WhoWor 93*
Paxton, Anna *Law&B 92*
Paxton, Carolyn Marie 1960- *WhoAmW 93*
Paxton, Dan R. 1947- *St&PR 93*
Paxton, Harold William 1927- *WhoAm 92*
Paxton, J. Willene 1930- *WhoAmW 93, WhoSSW 93*
Paxton, James Fred 1932- *St&PR 93*
Paxton, Jeffrey C. *Law&B 92*
Paxton, Joan Susan 1963- *WhoAmW 93*
Paxton, John Van Middlesworth 1938- *WhoAm 92*
Paxton, John W. 1937- *St&PR 93*
Paxton, Joseph Samuel 1956- *WhoSSW 93*
Paxton, Laura Belle-Kent 1942- *WhoAmW 93*
Paxton, Marie d1992 *NewYTBS 92*
Paxton, Mary *AmWomPl*
Paxton, R. Robert 1920- *St&PR 93*
Paxton, Ralph 1950- *WhoSSW 93*
Paxton, Ralph Robert 1920- *WhoE 93*
Paxton, Robert Owen 1932- *WhoAm 92*
Paxton, Tom 1937- *SmATA 70 [port], WhoAm 92*
Paxton, W.L. 1931- *St&PR 93*
Paxton, Walter Blake 1944- *St&PR 93*
Paxton, William G. 1939- *St&PR 93*
Paxton, William Perce, II 1941- *St&PR 93*
Payatakes, Alkiviades C. 1945- *WhoScE 91-3*
Paydos, Charles J. 1940- *St&PR 93*
Payer, Hans *WhoScE 91-3*
Payer, Hans 1938- *WhoScE 91-3*
Payer, Stephen C. 1935- *St&PR 93*
Payer, Sue *ScF&FL 92*
Payes, Wm. J. 1906- *St&PR 93*
Payes-Mestres, Javier 1954- *WhoWor 93*
Payette, M.W. 1947- *St&PR 93*
Payette, Thomas M. 1932- *St&PR 93*
Payette, Thomas Martin 1932- *WhoAm 92*
Paykel, Eugene Stern *WhoScE 91-1*
Paylor, Larry E. 1943- *St&PR 93*
Payment, Robert C. 1934- *St&PR 93, WhoAm 92*
Payn, James 1830-1898 *ScF&FL 92*
Payne, Alan Lafayette 1929- *St&PR 93*
Payne, Ancil Horace 1921- *WhoAm 92*
Payne, Anita Hart 1926- *WhoAmW 93*
Payne, Anthony (Edward) 1936- *Baker 92*
Payne, Barbara Jeanette 1947- *WhoAmW 93*
Payne, Bernal C. 1941- *BioIn 17*
Payne, Bernal C., Jr. 1941- *ScF&FL 92*
Payne, Bruce 1911- *St&PR 93, WhoAm 92, WhoE 93*
Payne, Burnice Darwin 1937- *WhoSSW 93*
Payne, C.F. *BioIn 17*
Payne, Charles 1909- *ScF&FL 92*
Payne, Charles E. 1944- *St&PR 93*
Payne, Connie Sue 1946- *WhoAmW 93*
Payne, D.C. *WhoScE 91-1*
Payne, Daniel G. 1958- *WhoE 93*
Payne, David L. *BioIn 17*
Payne, David Neil *WhoScE 91-1*
Payne, Deborah Anne 1952- *WhoAmW 93, WhoE 93*
Payne, Donald 1934- *WhoAm 92, WhoE 93*
Payne, Donald Gordon *ScF&FL 92*
Payne, Donald M. 1934- *BioIn 17, CngDr 91*
Payne, Douglas Wilton 1951- *WhoE 93*
Payne, Duncan Macrae 1941- *St&PR 93*
Payne, E. Keith *Law&B 92*
Payne, Edgar Alwin 1882-1947 *BioIn 17*
Payne, Edward Carlton 1928- *WhoAm 92*
Payne, Edward Raymond 1906-1991 *BioIn 17*
Payne, Elizabeth Eleanore 1945- *WhoAmW 93*
Payne, Elizabeth Stancy *AmWomPl*
Payne, Emarie Stock *Law&B 92*
Payne, Ethel 1912-1991 *AnObit 1991*
Payne, Ethel L. 1911-1991 *BioIn 17*
Payne, Ethel L. 1912-1991 *EncAACR*
Payne, Eugene Edgar 1942- *WhoAm 92*
Payne, Fanny Ursula 1875- *AmWomPl*
Payne, Frances Anne 1932- *WhoAm 92*
Payne, Frank Valentino 1950- *WhoEmL 93*
Payne, Fred J. 1922- *WhoSSW 93, WhoWor 93*
Payne, Fred Ray 1931- *WhoAm 92, WhoSSW 93*
Payne, Gareld Gene 1931- *WhoWor 93*
Payne, Garfield M. *Law&B 92*
Payne, George Frederick 1941- *WhoAm 92*
Payne, Gerald Oliver 1930- *WhoAm 92*
Payne, Graham Stuart 1945- *St&PR 93*
Payne, Harry Charles 1947- *WhoAm 92*
Payne, Harry Morse, Jr. 1922- *WhoAm 92*
Payne, Henry C. 1843-1904 *PolPar*
Payne, Henry Clay 1843-1904 *BioIn 17*
Payne, Herb H. 1948- *St&PR 93*
Payne, Horace Preston, Jr. *Law&B 92*
Payne, James L. *WhoAm 92*
Payne, James L. 1937- *St&PR 93*
Payne, James Leroy 1936- *St&PR 93, WhoAm 92*
Payne, James R., Jr. 1916- *St&PR 93*
Payne, Janette O. *Law&B 92*
Payne, Jennifer Lynn 1965- *WhoEmL 93*
Payne, Jerry L., Sr. 1945- *WhoSSW 93*
Payne, John 1912-1989 *BioIn 17*
Payne, John B. *BioIn 17*
Payne, John H. d1991 *BioIn 17*
Payne, John Howard 1791-1852 *ScF&FL 92*
Payne, John Philip 1942- *WhoWor 93*
Payne, John Ross 1941- *WhoAm 92*
Payne, John W. 1940- *St&PR 93*
Payne, John Weston *WhoScE 91-1*
Payne, Judith Eleanor 1950- *WhoAmW 93*
Payne, Julie Thomas *Law&B 92*
Payne, Katherine Howell 1963- *WhoSSW 93*
Payne, L.N. *WhoScE 91-1*
Payne, Ladell 1933- *WhoAm 92*
Payne, Lawrence Edward 1923- *WhoAm 92*
Payne, Leanne 1932- *ConAu 37NR*
Payne, Lewis F., Jr. 1945- *CngDr 91*
Payne, Lewis Franklin 1945- *WhoAm 92*
Payne, Lewis Franklin L.F. 1945- *WhoSSW 93*
Payne, Lilian Harris *AmWomPl*
Payne, Linda Cohen 1953- *WhoAmW 93, WhoEmL 93*
Payne, Linda Elaine 1943- *WhoAmW 93*
Payne, Lionel Fitzgerald d1991 *BioIn 17*
Payne, Lisa R. 1962- *WhoAmW 93*
Payne, Mabel Louise 1949- *WhoEmL 93*
Payne, Margaret Anne 1947- *WhoAmW 93*
Payne, Martha G. *St&PR 93*
Payne, Mary *WhoWrEP 92*
Payne, Mary Ann 1936- *WhoSSW 93*

Payne, Maxwell Carr, Jr. 1927- *WhoAm 92*
Payne, Melanie 1938- *WhoAmW 93*
Payne, Melissa Anne 1964- *WhoAmW 93*
Payne, Melvin M. 1911-1990 *BioIn 17*
Payne, Michael David 1941- *WhoAm 92, WhoWrEP 92*
Payne, Michael Wilkinson 1963- *WhoSSW 93*
Payne, Mitchell W. 1956- *St&PR 93*
Payne, Norbert William 1930- *WhoWrEP 92*
Payne, Norvel Leon 1925- *WhoSSW 93*
Payne, Paula 1943- *St&PR 93*
Payne, Paula Gail *Law&B 92*
Payne, Peggy 1949- *WhoWrEP 92*
Payne, Peter Alfred *WhoScE 91-1*
Payne, Peter Lester *WhoScE 91-1*
Payne, Phil Stephensen- *ScF&FL 92*
Payne, R. Thomas *Law&B 92*
Payne, Rhoda 1934- *WhoE 93*
Payne, Richard L. 1940- *St&PR 93*
Payne, Richard S. *Law&B 92*
Payne, Richelle Denise 1967- *WhoAmW 93*
Payne, Robert 1911-1983 *ScF&FL 92*
Payne, Robert Bryan 1914- *WhoSSW 93*
Payne, Robert M. 1935- *WhoAm 92*
Payne, Robert Somers *WhoIns 93*
Payne, Robert Somers 1938- *St&PR 93*
Payne, Robert Walter 1925- *WhoAm 92*
Payne, Roger Lee 1946- *WhoAm 92, WhoSSW 93*
Payne, Roger William *WhoScE 91-1*
Payne, Ronald *ScF&FL 92*
Payne, Ronald D. *Law&B 92*
Payne, Roy Leonard *WhoScE 91-1*
Payne, Rufus Floyd 1909- *WhoSSW 93, WhoWor 93*
Payne, Sally *SweetSg C [port]*
Payne, Samuel Burton 1906-1991 *BioIn 17*
Payne, Sidney Stewart 1932- *WhoAm 92*
Payne, T. Michael *Law&B 92*
Payne, Terence L. 1946- *St&PR 93*
Payne, Theresa Mae 1955- *WhoEmL 93*
Payne, Thomas J. 1922- *WhoAm 92*
Payne, Tyson Elliott, Jr. 1927- *WhoAm 92*
Payne, Walter Fitch 1936- *St&PR 93*
Payne, William Bruce 1943- *St&PR 93*
Payne, William C. 1932- *St&PR 93*
Payne, William Clark, Sr. 1929- *WhoSSW 93*
Payne, William Haydon 1939- *WhoAm 92*
Payne, William J. *Law&B 92*
Payne, William Jackson 1925- *WhoAm 92*
Payne, William Joseph 1932- *St&PR 93*
Payne, William Spencer 1926- *WhoAm 92*
Payne, Winfield Scott 1917- *WhoWor 93*
Payne-Zajac, Patricia Laurene 1958- *WhoAmW 93*
Payno y Flores, Manuel 1810-1894 *DcMexL*
Paynter, Alan H. 1938- *St&PR 93*
Paynter, Harry Alvin 1923- *WhoAm 92*
Paynter, John Philip 1928- *WhoAm 92*
Paynter, MaryAnn 1937- *WhoAmW 93*
Paynter, Walter Raymond *Law&B 92*
Payntor, Carl S. *Law&B 92*
Pays, Amanda *BioIn 17*
Paysinger, Sherri *BioIn 17*
Payson, Darrell Erlon 1932- *WhoE 93*
Payson, Frances M. *AmWomPl*
Payson, Henry Edwards 1925- *WhoAm 92*
Payson, Henry S. 1921- *WhoIns 93*
Payson, John Whitney 1940- *WhoSSW 93*
Payson, Martin D. *Law&B 92*
Payson, Martin David 1936- *WhoAm 92*
Payson, Martin Fred 1940- *WhoAm 92*
Payson, Parker Laurence 1965- *WhoE 93*
Payson, Patricia *ScF&FL 92*
Payson, Stella T. *AmWomPl*
Paysour, Robert 1957- *St&PR 93*
Payte, Joseph Michael 1946- *St&PR 93*
Payton, Antoinette Shields 1926- *WhoAmW 93*
Payton, Benjamin Franklin 1932- *WhoAm 92*
Payton, Carolyn R. 1925- *BioIn 17*
Payton, Christopher Charles 1957- *WhoWor 93*
Payton, Crystal *ScF&FL 92*
Payton, Gary *BioIn 17*
Payton, Harry Francis 1936- *St&PR 93*
Payton, Jeffrey Lewis *Law&B 92*
Payton, Leland *ScF&FL 92*
Payton, Mitch *BioIn 17*
Payton, Philip A. 1876- *BioIn 17*
Payton, Randolph Randi 1954- *WhoWrEP 92*
Payton, Roger E. 1956- *St&PR 93*
Payton, Roger Edward 1956- *WhoAm 92*
Payton, Thomas W. 1946- *St&PR 93*
Payton, Thomas William 1946- *WhoAm 92*
Payton, Walter 1954- *WhoAm 92*
Payton, Walter Jerry 1954- *AfrAmBi*
Payumo, Felicito C. 1939- *WhoAsAP 91*
Paz, Denis George 1945- *WhoSSW 93*
Paz, Ezequiel Zavalia 1935- *WhoUN 92*
Paz, Francisco 1954- *WhoWor 93*
Paz, Horacio Jorge *Law&B 92*
Paz, Ireneo 1836-1924 *DcMexL*
Paz, Juan Carlos 1901-1972 *Baker 92*
Paz, Octavio 1914- *BioIn 17, DcMexL, MagSWL [port], SpAmA, WhoAm 92, WhoSSW 93, WhoWor 93, WorLitC [port]*
Pazandak, Carol Hendrickson *WhoAmW 93*
Pazden, Kathy Christine 1964- *WhoAmW 93*
Pazdera, John Paul 1948- *WhoE 93*
Pazdro, Przemyslaw J. 1932- *WhoScE 91-4*
Pazdur, M.F. 1946- *WhoScE 91-4*
Pazen, Thea M. *Law&B 92*
Pazera, D. Danielle 1963- *WhoE 93*
Paz Estenssoro, Victor 1907- *DcTwHis, WhoWor 93*
Pazgan, Kazimierz *BioIn 17*
Pazhwak, Niamatollah 1928- *WhoAsAP 91*
Pazicky, Edward P. 1946- *St&PR 93*
Pazik, George James 1921- *WhoAm 92*
Pazirandeh, Mahmood 1932- *WhoWor 93*
Pazolski, Alan Passes- *ScF&FL 92*
Pazos, Carlos Agustin 1956- *WhoSSW 93*
Paz Paredes, Margarita 1922- *DcMexL*
Paz-Pujalt, Gustavo Roberto 1954- *WhoE 93*
Pazur, John Howard 1922- *WhoAm 92*
Pazurek, John Andrew 1949- *St&PR 93*
Pazzaglini, Mario Peter, Jr. 1940- *WhoE 93*
Paz Zamora, Jaime 1939- *WhoWor 93*
Pazzi, Roberto 1946- *ScF&FL 92*
p'Bitek, Okot 1931-1982 *BioIn 17*
Pea, Barry G. *Law&B 92*
Peabody, Andrew Learned 1928- *WhoSSW 93*
Peabody, Charles W. 1941- *St&PR 93*
Peabody, David Caldwell 1962- *WhoE 93*
Peabody, Eleanor Lane *AmWomPl*
Peabody, Elizabeth Palmer 1804-1894 *BioIn 17*
Peabody, George 1795-1869 *Baker 92, BioIn 17*
Peabody, Grace Eddy 1924-1990 *BioIn 17*
Peabody, James Hamilton 1852-1917 *BioIn 17*
Peabody, Josephine Preston 1874-1922 *AmWomPl*
Peabody, Judith Dunnington 1930- *WhoAmW 93*
Peabody, Lucy Whitehead McGill 1861-1949 *BioIn 17*
Peabody, Maryanne 1946- *WhoAmW 93, WhoEmL 93*
Peabody, Myra Agnes 1912- *WhoWrEP 92*
Peabody, Richard Myers 1951- *WhoWrEP 92*
Peabody, Robert Henry 1941- *St&PR 93*
Peabody, Samuel S., III 1953- *WhoE 93*
Peabody, Susan Grace 1957- *WhoAmW 93*
Peabody, William Tyler, Jr. 1921- *WhoAm 92*
Peace, Barbara Lou Jean 1939- *WhoAmW 93*
Peace, D.M.S. 1944- *WhoScE 91-1*
Peace, H.W., II 1935- *St&PR 93, WhoAm 92, WhoSSW 93*
Peace, John Buck 1951- *WhoSSW 93*
Peace, Marshall S. *Law&B 92*
Peace, Roger Craft 1899-1968 *DcLB 127 [port]*
Peaceman, Donald William 1926- *WhoSSW 93*
Peach, Paul E. 1943- *WhoSSW 93*
Peach, Robert E. 1920-1971 *EncABHB 8 [port]*
Peaches & Herb *SoulM*
Peachey, Cathy Jean 1949- *WhoAmW 93, WhoEmL 93*
Peachey, Dennis William 1943- *WhoE 93*
Peachey, Douglas M. *Law&B 92*
Peachey, Lee DeBorde 1932- *WhoAm 92*
Peachey, Sidney R. 1922- *St&PR 93*
Peacock, Alvin Ward 1929- *WhoAm 92*
Peacock, Andrew Sharp 1939- *WhoAsAP 91, WhoWor 93*
Peacock, David Philip Spencer *WhoScE 91-1*
Peacock, Don 1919- *BioIn 17*
Peacock, Doug *BioIn 17*
Peacock, Douglas W. 1938- *WhoAm 92*
Peacock, Erle Ewart, Jr. 1926- *WhoAm 92*
Peacock, George Rowatt 1923- *St&PR 93, WhoAm 92*
Peacock, Graham Rex 1938- *WhoWor 93*
Peacock, James Daniel 1930- *WhoAm 92*
Peacock, James Harry 1928- *St&PR 93*
Peacock, John Edward Dean 1919- *WhoAm 92*
Peacock, John William 1939- *WhoUN 92*
Peacock, Judith Ann 1939- *WhoAm 92, WhoAmW 93*
Peacock, Karen L. *Law&B 92*
Peacock, Lamar Batts 1920- *WhoAm 92*
Peacock, Lelon James 1928- *WhoAm 92*
Peacock, Lewis d1871 *BioIn 17*
Peacock, Lowell L. 1926- *St&PR 93*
Peacock, Markham Lovick, Jr. 1903- *WhoAm 92*
Peacock, Mary Willa 1942- *WhoAm 92*
Peacock, Molly 1947- *DcLB 120 [port], WhoWor 93, WhoWrEP 92*
Peacock, Nancy Lyman 1954- *WhoAmW 93*
Peacock, Paul Frederick 1962- *WhoE 93*
Peacock, Peter Bligh 1921- *WhoAm 92*
Peacock, Robert Edward 1957- *WhoE 93*
Peacock, Robert Richard 1928- *WhoAm 92*
Peacock, Robert S. 1925- *St&PR 93*
Peacock, Shawn Brian 1960- *WhoE 93*
Peacock, Susan Rubenstein 1957- *WhoAmW 93*
Peacock, Thomas Love 1785-1866 *BioIn 17, DcLB 116 [port]*
Peacock, Valerie Lynn 1962- *WhoAmW 93, WhoEmL 93*
Peacock, William James 1937- *WhoWor 93*
Peacocke, Christopher Arthur Bruce 1950- *WhoWor 93*
Peairs, David N. *St&PR 93*
Peairs, Richard Hope 1929- *WhoAm 92*
Peak, David 1941- *WhoE 93*
Peak, James Matthew 1936- *WhoSSW 93*
Peak, Kenneth Raymond 1945- *St&PR 93*
Peak, Michael *ScF&FL 92*
Peak, Myra Lee 1954- *WhoEmL 93*
Peak, Robert d1992 *NewYTBS 92 [port]*
Peake, Albert Louis 1927- *St&PR 93*
Peake, Allen M. 1961- *St&PR 93*
Peake, Clifford M. 1927- *WhoAm 92*
Peake, Darryl L. *Law&B 92*
Peake, David J. 1938- *St&PR 93*
Peake, Ernest R. 1935- *St&PR 93*
Peake, Kirby 1915-1991 *BioIn 17*
Peake, Lorraine Elizabeth Fowler 1954- *WhoSSW 93*
Peake, Luise Eitel 1925- *WhoSSW 93*
Peake, Mervyn 1911-1968 *ScF&FL 92*
Peake, Mervyn Laurence 1911-1968 *BioIn 17*
Peake, Richard Henry, Jr. 1934- *WhoAm 92*
Peake, Thomas Rhea 1939- *WhoWrEP 92*
Peaker, Malcolm 1943- *WhoScE 91-1*
Peaks, Cheryl Lynn 1966- *WhoAmW 93*
Peal, S. Edward *BioIn 17*
Peal, Samuel Audiway *Law&B 92*
Peal, Stanley 1913- *WhoE 93*
Peale, Charles Willson 1741-1827 *BioIn 17*
Peale, Norman Vincent *BioIn 17*
Peale, Norman Vincent 1898- *St&PR 93, WhoAm 92, WhoE 93, WhoWor 93*
Peale, Rembrandt 1778-1860 *BioIn 17*
Peale, Ruth Stafford 1906- *WhoAm 92, WhoAmW 93*
Peale, Stanton Jerrold 1937- *WhoAm 92*
Pealor, Dennis L. 1952- *St&PR 93*
Peanasky, Robert Joseph 1927- *WhoAm 92*
Pear, Edwin *Law&B 92*
Pearce, Alice 1913-1966 *QDrFCA 92 [port]*
Pearce, Ann Philippa *MajAI*
Pearce, Beth J. *Law&B 92*
Pearce, Beth Jeanne 1949- *WhoAmW 93*
Pearce, Betty McMurray 1926- *WhoAmW 93, WhoSSW 93, WhoWor 93*
Pearce, Brenda 1935- *ScF&FL 92*
Pearce, Carol Ann *WhoWrEP 92*
Pearce, Charles A. 1923- *St&PR 93*
Pearce, David Frank *WhoScE 91-1*
Pearce, David R. *Law&B 92*
Pearce, David William *WhoScE 91-1*
Pearce, Doris Parsons 1929- *WhoSSW 93*
Pearce, Drue 1951- *WhoAmW 93*
Pearce, E.L. 1945- *St&PR 93*
Pearce, Edward Holroyd 1901-1990 *BioIn 17*
Pearce, Floyd Earl *WhoWrEP 92*
Pearce, Frances *DcChlFi*
Pearce, G. Martin 1942- *St&PR 93*
Pearce, Garrett E. *St&PR 93*
Pearce, George Hamilton 1921- *WhoAm 92*
Pearce, Harry J. *Law&B 92*
Pearce, Harry Jonathan 1942- *WhoAm 92*
Pearce, Howard D. 1931- *ScF&FL 92*
Pearce, Jack 1942- *WhoScE 91-1*
Pearce, James Walker 1951- *WhoSSW 93*
Pearce, James Wishart 1916- *WhoAm 92*
Pearce, Jennifer Sue 1954- *WhoSSW 93*
Pearce, Joan DeLap 1930- *WhoAmW 93*
Pearce, Karola K. *Law&B 92*
Pearce, Kevin 1949- *St&PR 93*
Pearce, Kevin E. *WhoIns 93*
Pearce, Michael *MiSFD 9*
Pearce, Michael L. 1933- *St&PR 93*
Pearce, Oralee *Law&B 92*
Pearce, Paul Francis 1928- *WhoAm 92*
Pearce, Perry Elizabeth *Law&B 92*
Pearce, Philippa 1920- *BioIn 17, MajAI [port], ScF&FL 92*
Pearce, (Ann) Philippa *ChlFicS*
Pearce, Ray *Law&B 92*
Pearce, Richard *MiSFD 9*
Pearce, Richard William, Jr. 1941- *St&PR 93, WhoIns 93*
Pearce, Robert Penrose *WhoScE 91-1*
Pearce, Ronald 1920- *WhoAm 92*
Pearce, Rosemary E. *Law&B 92*
Pearce, Roy Harvey 1919- *WhoWrEP 92*
Pearce, S(tephen) Austen 1836-1900 *Baker 92*
Pearce, Stanley Clifford *WhoScE 91-1*
Pearce, Stephen *BioIn 17*
Pearce, Stephen Lamar 1950- *WhoSSW 93*
Pearce, Susan Elizabeth 1949- *WhoWor 93*
Pearce, Susan M. 1937- *WhoAm 92, WhoAmW 93*
Pearce, Ted P. *Law&B 92*
Pearce, Tom B., III 1946- *St&PR 93*
Pearce, William Joseph 1925- *WhoAm 92, WhoE 93*
Pearce, William Martin 1913- *WhoAm 92*
Pearce, William Martin, III *Law&B 92*
Pearce-Percy, Henry Thomas 1947- *WhoWor 93*
Pearce-Smith, David Wayne *Law&B 92*
Pearcy, Robert D. 1943- *St&PR 93*
Pearcy, Robert Woodwell 1941- *WhoAm 92*
Pearen, Allan Edward 1939- *St&PR 93*
Pearincott, Joseph Verghese 1929- *WhoE 93, WhoWor 93*
Pearl, Allen B. *Law&B 92*
Pearl, Carleton Day 1943- *St&PR 93*
Pearl, David Eugene 1960- *WhoE 93*
Pearl, Eric *WhoWrEP 92*
Pearl, Erwin *St&PR 93*
Pearl, Esther Elizabeth *ConAu 40NR*
Pearl, George Clayton 1923- *WhoAm 92*
Pearl, Helen Zalkan 1938- *WhoAmW 93*
Pearl, Jack 1923- *ScF&FL 92*
Pearl, Jacques B. *ScF&FL 92*
Pearl, James G. 1941- *WhoIns 93*
Pearl, Laurence *WhoScE 91-1*
Pearl, Minnie 1912- *CurBio 92 [port], WhoAm 92*
Pearl, Natasha 1960- *WhoAmW 93*
Pearl, Raymond 1879-1940 *BioIn 17*
Pearl, Richard Alan 1943- *WhoE 93*
Pearl, Sara L. *Law&B 92*
Pearl, Stephen Barry 1934- *WhoUN 92*
Pearlman, Allan J. *St&PR 93*
Pearlman, David *Law&B 92*
Pearlman, David Samuel 1934- *WhoAm 92*
Pearlman, Elliot Stuart 1941- *St&PR 93*
Pearlman, Jerry K. 1939- *St&PR 93*
Pearlman, Jerry Kent 1939- *WhoAm 92*
Pearlman, Jordan Arthur 1937- *St&PR 93*
Pearlman, Louis Jay 1954- *WhoE 93, WhoEmL 93, WhoWor 93*
Pearlman, Martin N. 1938- *WhoE 93*
Pearlman, Melvin 1933- *St&PR 93*
Pearlman, Meyer 1917- *St&PR 93*
Pearlman, Michael A. *Law&B 92*
Pearlman, P.A. 1911- *St&PR 93*
Pearlman, Peter Steven 1946- *WhoE 93*
Pearlman, Richard *Law&B 92*
Pearlman, Robert Ira *Law&B 92*
Pearlman, Ronald Alan 1940- *WhoAm 92*
Pearlman, Sidney Burton 1940- *St&PR 93*
Pearlman, Sidney Simon 1932- *WhoAm 92*
Pearlman, William D. 1943- *WhoWrEP 92*
Pearlmutter, Anne Frances 1940- *WhoAmW 93*
Pearlmutter, Florence Nichols 1914- *WhoAmW 93*
Pearlson, Fredda S. 1949- *WhoWrEP 92*
Pearlstein, Joel P. 1936- *St&PR 93*
Pearlstein, Leonard *WhoAm 92*
Pearlstein, Philip 1924- *WhoAm 92*
Pearlstein, Seymour 1923- *WhoAm 92*
Pearlstine, Norman 1942- *St&PR 93, WhoAm 92, WhoE 93*
Pearman, Reginald James 1923- *WhoAm 92, WhoE 93*
Pearn, Victor 1950- *WhoWrEP 92*
Pearne, George Reginald 1948- *WhoEmL 93, WhoWor 93*
Pears, Arnold Neville 1964- *WhoWor 93*
Pears, Gary C. *Law&B 92*
Pears, Peter 1910-1986 *IntDcOp [port], OxDcOp*
Pears, Peter (Neville Luard) 1910-1986 *Baker 92*
Pearsall, George Wilbur 1933- *WhoAm 92*

Pearsall, Henry Batterman 1934- St&PR 93, WhoAm 92
Pearsall, Margaret R. 1930- St&PR 93
Pearsall, Mary Helen 1948- WhoAmW 93
Pearsall, Otis Pratt 1932- WhoAm 92
Pearsall, Paul BioIn 17
Pearsall, Phyllis BioIn 17
Pearsall, Robert Lucas 1795-1856 Baker 92
Pearsall, Willard H., Jr. 1923- St&PR 93
Pearsall, William Wright 1929- St&PR 93, WhoE 93
Pearse, John Melville 1939- WhoE 93
Pearse, Padraic 1879-1916 BioIn 17
Pearse, Patrick Henry 1879-1916 BioIn 17
Pearse, Peter H(ector) 1932- ConAu 138
Pearse, Robert Francis 1916- WhoE 93, WhoWor 93
Pearse, Thomas Jerome BioIn 17
Pearse, Warren Harland 1927- WhoAm 92
Pearson, Alan A. 1945- St&PR 93
Pearson, Alan W. WhoScE 91-1
Pearson, Albert Marchant 1916- WhoAm 92
Pearson, Alec 1924-1990 BioIn 17
Pearson, Allen Day 1925- WhoAm 92
Pearson, Anna Belle 1934- WhoSSW 93
Pearson, Anthony Alan 1954- WhoSSW 93
Pearson, Anthony John 1944- WhoAm 92
Pearson, April V. Law&B 92
Pearson, Becky Durham 1963- WhoSSW 93
Pearson, Belinda K. 1931- St&PR 93
Pearson, Belinda Kemp 1931- WhoAm 92
Pearson, Carolyn Swayne Law&B 92
Pearson, Charles Thomas, Jr. 1929- WhoAm 92
Pearson, Clarence Edward 1925- WhoAm 92
Pearson, Daniel Lynn 1950- WhoSSW 93
Pearson, Daniel S. 1930- WhoAm 92
Pearson, David Petri 1926- WhoAm 92
Pearson, Deborah Ann 1957- WhoEmL 93, WhoSSW 93
Pearson, Donald Edwin WhoScE 91-1
Pearson, Donald Emanual 1914- WhoAm 92, WhoSSW 93
Pearson, Drew 1897-1969 BioIn 17, JrnUS
Pearson, Durk BioIn 17
Pearson, Edward A. 1941- St&PR 93
Pearson, Edward O. Law&B 92
Pearson, Frederich C. St&PR 93
Pearson, Frederick Young 1941- St&PR 93
Pearson, Gary Dean 1952- WhoEmL 93
Pearson, George Burton, Jr. 1905- WhoE 93
Pearson, George D. 1919- St&PR 93
Pearson, Gerald Leon 1925- WhoAm 92
Pearson, H.J.S. 1921- St&PR 93
Pearson, Heather BioIn 17
Pearson, Henry Charles 1914- WhoAm 92
Pearson, Henry Clyde 1925- WhoAm 92
Pearson, Hugh John Sanders 1921- WhoAm 92
Pearson, J. Edward, Jr. St&PR 93
Pearson, J.R.A. WhoScE 91-1
Pearson, James M. 1947- St&PR 93
Pearson, Janaan K. 1920- St&PR 93
Pearson, Jean Elizabeth 1945- WhoWrEP 92
Pearson, Jerry Allen 1936- St&PR 93
Pearson, Jim Berry, Jr. 1948- WhoEmL 93, WhoSSW 93
Pearson, John 1923- WhoAm 92
Pearson, John Davis 1939- WhoAm 92
Pearson, John Edgar 1927- St&PR 93
Pearson, John F. Law&B 92
Pearson, John S., III 1950- St&PR 93
Pearson, John Trevor WhoScE 91-1
Pearson, Judy Cornelia 1946- WhoAmW 93
Pearson, Jules Michael 1908- WhoWrEP 92
Pearson, Keith M. 1921- St&PR 93
Pearson, Kit 1947- ScF&FL 92, WhoCanL 92
Pearson, Kit (Kathleen) 1947- DcChlFi
Pearson, Kristine Law&B 92
Pearson, Kristine Ann 1956- WhoEmL 93
Pearson, Larry Lester 1942- WhoAm 92
Pearson, Laura BioIn 17
Pearson, Lawrence D. Law&B 92
Pearson, Lester Bowles 1897-1972 DcTwHis
Pearson, Lilian J. AmWomPl
Pearson, Linley E. 1946- WhoAm 92
Pearson, Margit 1950- St&PR 93
Pearson, Margit Linnea 1950- WhoAm 92
Pearson, Michael 1941- ScF&FL 92
Pearson, Nathan W. 1911- St&PR 93
Pearson, Nathan Williams 1911- WhoAm 92
Pearson, Nathan Williams 1951- WhoE 93
Pearson, Norman 1928- WhoAm 92, WhoE 93, WhoWor 93
Pearson, Oscar Harris 1902- WhoAm 92
Pearson, P. A. 1939- WhoSSW 93
Pearson, Paul Brown 1905- WhoAm 92
Pearson, Paul David 1940- WhoAm 92
Pearson, Paul Guy 1926- WhoAm 92
Pearson, Paul Hammond WhoAm 92
Pearson, Paul Holding 1940- St&PR 93, WhoAm 92
Pearson, Peter ScF&FL 92
Pearson, Phillip Theodore 1932- WhoAm 92
Pearson, R.G. WhoScE 91-1
Pearson, Ralph E. d1991 BioIn 17
Pearson, Ralph Gottfrid 1919- WhoAm 92
Pearson, Ralph Jones, Jr. Law&B 92
Pearson, Richard 1731-1806 HarEnMi
Pearson, Richard J. 1925- St&PR 93
Pearson, Richard Jarvis 1925- WhoAm 92
Pearson, Richard Joseph 1938- WhoAm 92
Pearson, Ridley BioIn 17
Pearson, Robert 1937- WhoAm 92
Pearson, Robert Edwin 1923- WhoSSW 93
Pearson, Robert G. 1957- St&PR 93
Pearson, Robert Greenlees 1917- WhoAm 92
Pearson, Roger 1927- WhoAm 92, WhoWor 93
Pearson, Roger Lee 1940- WhoAm 92
Pearson, Ronald Dale 1940- WhoAm 92
Pearson, Ronald Earl 1944- WhoSSW 93
Pearson, Ronald Hayes 1924- WhoE 93
Pearson, Ronald Lee 1949- St&PR 93
Pearson, Ronald W. 1946- WhoE 93
Pearson, Roy Laing 1939- WhoSSW 93, WhoWor 93
Pearson, Roy Messer, Jr. 1914- WhoAm 92
Pearson, Steven V. 1935- St&PR 93
Pearson, Susan Winifred 1941- WhoSSW 93, WhoWor 93
Pearson, Thomas L. Law&B 92
Pearson, Tracey Campbell BioIn 17
Pearson, Walter Donald 1916- WhoAm 92
Pearson, Walter Howard 1946- WhoEmL 93
Pearson, Walter Leonard, Jr. 1945- WhoSSW 93
Pearson, Willard 1915- WhoAm 92
Pearson, William James 1938- WhoAm 92
Pearson, William Rowland 1923- WhoE 93
Pearson, William Whildey 1925- St&PR 93
Peart, Boyd 1952- St&PR 93
Peart, Neil 1952- See Rush ConMus 8
Peart, Sherry H. Law&B 92
Pearton, Stephen John 1957- WhoE 93, WhoWor 93
Peary, Dannis ScF&FL 92
Peary, Danny 1949- ScF&FL 92
Peary, Josephine BioIn 17
Peary, Kali 1906- BioIn 17
Peary, Robert E. 1856-1920 ConHero 2 [port]
Peary, Robert Edward 1856-1920 Expl 93 [port]
Peary, Robert Edwin 1856-1920 BioIn 17, GayN
Peary, Stephen Kenneth 1939- St&PR 93
Peary, Stephen Pochos 1948- St&PR 93
Peasback, David R. WhoAm 92
Pease, Barbara S.F. 1956- St&PR 93
Pease, Damaris BioIn 17
Pease, David Gordon 1932- WhoAm 92
Pease, Denise Louise 1953- WhoAmW 93, WhoEmL 93
Pease, Don J. 1931- CngDr 91
Pease, Donald E. 1936- WhoAm 92
Pease, Donald James 1931- WhoAm 92
Pease, Douglas Edward 1942- St&PR 93
Pease, Edward Charles 1960- WhoSSW 93
Pease, Howard 1894-1974 MajAI [port]
Pease, James Norman, Jr. 1921- WhoAm 92
Pease, John H. 1943- St&PR 93
Pease, Louise ConAu 139
Pease, Norma Maxine Feltz 1925- WhoAmW 93
Pease, Rendel Sebastian 1922- WhoWor 93
Pease, Robert A. 1940- St&PR 93
Pease, Roger Fabian Wedgwood 1936- WhoAm 92
Pease, Steven L. 1943- St&PR 93
Pease, Warren Stewart 1915- St&PR 93
Pease, Willard H. 1960- St&PR 93
Peaslee, Margaret Mae Hermanek 1935- WhoAm 92, WhoAmW 93
Peaslee, Richard Cutts 1930- WhoE 93
Peaslee, Robert L. 1917- St&PR 93
Peaston, David SoulM
Peat, David J. Law&B 92
Peat, Randall Dean 1935- WhoAm 92
Peatman, John Gray 1904- WhoE 93
Peattie, Elia Wilkinson, Mrs. 1862-1935 AmWomPl
Peattie, Lisa Redfield 1924- WhoAm 92
Peattie, Noel Roderick 1932- WhoWrEP 92
Peaudecerf, Pierre F.R. 1938- WhoScE 91-2
Peaud-Lenoel, Claude L. 1918- WhoScE 91-2
Peavey, Hartley Davis 1941- WhoAm 92
Peavler, Nancy Jean 1951- WhoAm 92, WhoAmW 93
Peavy, Dan Cornelius 1939- WhoSSW 93
Peavy, J.H. 1917- St&PR 93
Peavy, Lanny 1938- St&PR 93
Peavy, Linda 1943- WhoWrEP 92
Peavy, S. Lanny 1938- WhoIns 93
Peay, Francis AfrAmBi
Pebay-Peyroula, J.C. 1930- WhoScE 91-2
Pebbles BioIn 17
Peberdy, John F. WhoScE 91-1
Pebly, Harry Eugene 1923- WhoE 93
Pebly, Robert Roth 1929- St&PR 93
Pecanha, Claudio Araujo 1949- WhoWor 93
Pecani, Spartak 1952- DrEEuF
Pecano, Donald Carl 1948- WhoAm 92
Pecant, Pierre WhoScE 91-2
Peccia, Stephanie Norton 1951- WhoAmW 93
Pech, Lawrence Marion 1959- WhoAm 92
Pech, Leslie Dana Law&B 92
Pechacek, Mel Law&B 92
Pechauer, John Naeve 1937- St&PR 93
Pechaver, Ann BioIn 17
Pechilis, William John 1924- WhoAm 92
Pechillo, Jerome A. 1919-1991 BioIn 17
Pechkovsky, Nikolay 1896-1966 OxDcOp
Pechman, Joseph A. 1918-1989 BioIn 17
Pechner, Gerhard 1903-1969 Baker 92
Pechstein, Max 1881-1955 BioIn 17
Pecht, Joli B. Law&B 92
Pecht, Michael Gerard 1952- WhoE 93
Pechter, Gary E. Law&B 92
Pechter, Richard S. WhoAm 92
Pechter, Richard Scott 1945- St&PR 93
Pechukas, Philip 1942- WhoAm 92
Pechulis, Ann 1948- WhoAmW 93, WhoEmL 93
Pecile, Antonio M. 1929- WhoScE 91-3
Peck, A. John, Jr. Law&B 92
Peck, A. John, Jr. 1940- St&PR 93, WhoAm 92
Peck, Abraham 1945- WhoAm 92
Peck, Annie Smith 1850-1935 Expl 93 [port]
Peck, Austin H., Jr. 1913- WhoAm 92
Peck, Bernard Sidney 1915- WhoAm 92
Peck, Brian MiSFD 9
Peck, Charles Edward 1925- WhoAm 92, WhoE 93, WhoWor 93
Peck, Claudia A. ScF&FL 92
Peck, Curtiss Steven 1947- WhoWor 93
Peck, Dallas Lynn 1929- WhoAm 92
Peck, Daniel Farnum 1927- WhoAm 92
Peck, David W. 1902-1990 BioIn 17
Peck, David Warner, Jr. 1932- St&PR 93
Peck, Delbert E. 1924- St&PR 93
Peck, Dianne Kawecki 1945- WhoAmW 93, WhoSSW 93
Peck, Donald Vincent 1930- WhoAm 92
Peck, Edward Lionel 1929- WhoAm 92
Peck, Edwin Russell 1931- WhoAm 92
Peck, Ellie Enriquez 1934- WhoAmW 93
Peck, Fred Neil 1945- WhoAm 92, WhoE 93, WhoWor 93
Peck, Garnet Edward 1930- WhoAm 92
Peck, George Wilbur 1840-1916 JrnUS
Peck, George Williams, IV 1932- St&PR 93
Peck, Gregory 1916- BioIn 17, CurBio 92 [port], IntDcF 2-3 [port], NewYTBS 92 [port], WhoAm 92, WhoWor 93
Peck, H. Daniel 1940- WhoE 93
Peck, Harry Dowd, Jr. 1927- WhoSSW 93
Peck, Harry Thurston 1856-1914 BioIn 17
Peck, Ira 1922- ScF&FL 92
Peck, James Calvin Law&B 92
Peck, James Landis 1920- St&PR 93
Peck, James Stevenson 1923- WhoAm 92
Peck, Jane Cary d1990 BioIn 17
Peck, Jerry D. 1935- St&PR 93
Peck, John W. 1913- WhoAm 92
Peck, John W. 1944- St&PR 93
Peck, John Weld 1944- St&PR 93
Peck, Joseph Richard 1947- St&PR 93
Peck, Kathryn Chandler 1954- WhoWrEP 92
Peck, Keenen BioIn 17
Peck, Kevin T. Law&B 92
Peck, Larry A. Law&B 92
Peck, Louis F. 1904- ScF&FL 92
Peck, M. Scott BioIn 17
Peck, M(organ) Scott 1936- WhoWrEP 92
Peck, Marie Johnston 1932- WhoWrEP 92
Peck, Mary Gray AmWomPl
Peck, Maryly VanLeer 1930- WhoAm 92
Peck, Morgan Scott BioIn 17
Peck, Morgan Scott 1936- WhoAm 92
Peck, Paul Arthur 1926- WhoAm 92
Peck, Paul Lachlan 1928- WhoWor 93
Peck, R. Nicholas 1939- WhoE 93
Peck, Ralph Brazelton 1912- WhoAm 92
Peck, Richard BioIn 17
Peck, Richard 1934- DcAmChF 1960, DcAmChF 1985, ScF&FL 92
Peck, Richard E. 1936- ScF&FL 92
Peck, Richard Earl 1936- WhoAm 92
Peck, Richard (Wayne) 1934- ConAu 38NR, MajAI [port], WhoAm 92, WhoWrEP 92
Peck, Robert David 1929- WhoAm 92
Peck, Robert Newton 1928- BioIn 17, MajAI [port]
Peck, Robert Newton, III 1928- DcAmChF 1960
Peck, Rochelle L. WhoAmW 93
Peck, Ron MiSFD 9
Peck, Rosamond Reifsnyder 1934- WhoAmW 93
Peck, Russell A. 1933- WhoAm 92
Peck, Samuel M. d1991 NewYTBS 92
Peck, Samuel Mortimer 1900-1991 BioIn 17
Peck, Stephen J. MiSFD 9
Peck, Susan E. Law&B 92
Peck, Susanne Carter Law&B 92
Peck, Suzanne J. 1943- WhoAmW 93
Peck, Sylvia ScF&FL 92
Peck, Templeton 1908- WhoAm 92
Peck, Thomas A. 1917- St&PR 93
Peck, Tony BioIn 17
Peck, William Arno 1933- WhoAm 92
Peck, William Henry 1932- WhoAm 92
Peck, William Jay 1927- WhoSSW 93
Peckel, Stevan E. Law&B 92
Peckenpaugh, Angela J. 1942- WhoWrEP 92
Peckenpaugh, Patsy Bowen 1961- WhoSSW 93
Peckenpaugh, Robert E. 1926- St&PR 93
Peckenpaugh, Robert Earl 1926- WhoAm 92
Pecker, Daniel 1950- WhoWor 93
Pecker, David J. 1951- WhoAm 92, WhoE 93, WhoWor 93
Pecker, Jean-Claude 1923- WhoWor 93
Peckham, Catherine Stevenson WhoScE 91-1
Peckham, Donald Eugene 1922- WhoAm 92
Peckham, Gardner Greene 1953- WhoAm 92
Peckham, Gary R. 1947- St&PR 93
Peckham, Howard Henry 1910- WhoAm 92
Peckham, John Munroe, III 1933- WhoAm 92
Peckham, M.J. WhoScE 91-1
Peckham, Robert Francis 1920- WhoAm 92
Peckham, Rufus Wheeler 1838-1909 OxCSupC [port]
Peckham, Virginia 1925- ScF&FL 92
Peckham, Wheeler Hazard 1833-1905 OxCSupC
Peckinpah, Sam 1925-1984 BioIn 17, MiSFD 9N
Peckinpaugh, Jack WhoIns 93
Peckinpaugh, Roger Thorpe 1891-1977 BiDAMSp 1989
Peckolick, Alan 1940- WhoAm 92
Peckosh, Paul Joseph 1945- St&PR 93
Peconi, Maurice V. 1949- WhoSSW 93
Pecora, James Joseph, Jr. 1950- WhoSSW 93
Pecora, Maria Antonia 1956- WhoE 93
Pecora, Robert 1938- WhoAm 92
Pecorari, Domenico 1934- WhoScE 91-3
Pecoraro, Frank J. 1934- St&PR 93
Pecore, Jeffrey M. Law&B 92
Pecorin, Paul C. 1939- St&PR 93
Pecos, Bill WhoWrEP 92
Pecot, Charles Matthew 1934- St&PR 93, WhoIns 93
Pecot, David Edward 1939- St&PR 93
Pecoux, Pierre H.G. 1923- WhoScE 91-2
Pecseli, Hans Laszlo 1947- WhoWor 93
Pecsi, Marton 1923- WhoScE 91-4
Pecsi-Donath, Eva 1927- WhoScE 91-4
Pecsok, Robert Louis 1918- WhoAm 92
Pector, Elizabeth Ann 1958- WhoEmL 93
Pecukonis, Joseph 1948- St&PR 93
Peczarski, Feliks 1804-1862 PolBiDi
Pedalino, Michael Donald 1931- WhoE 93
Pedder, Douglas Michael 1948- WhoE 93
Peddicord, Roland Dale 1936- WhoAm 92, WhoWor 93
Peddie, Peter Charles 1932- WhoWor 93
Peddinghaus, Carl U. 1938- St&PR 93
Peden, Edith Sweetser 1934- WhoAmW 93

Peden, George Cameron 1943- WhoWor 93
Peden, Irene Carswell 1925- WhoAm 92
Peden, James McKenzie WhoScE 91-1
Peden, John Carl 1944- St&PR 93
Peden, Katherine Graham 1926- WhoAm 92
Peden, Keith S. Law&B 92
Peden, Robert F., Jr. 1911- WhoSSW 93
Peden, William Creighton 1935- WhoSSW 93
Pedersen, Are 1952- WhoScE 91-4
Pedersen, Barrie C. 1939- St&PR 93
Pedersen, Bent 1942- WhoWor 93
Pedersen, Bent C.C. 1933- WhoScE 91-2
Pedersen, Bent Carl Christian 1933- WhoWor 93
Pedersen, Bent Norgaard WhoScE 91-2
Pedersen, Berit Fjaertoft 1933- WhoWor 93
Pedersen, Bjarne Martin 1937- WhoE 93
Pedersen, Carl C. 1940- WhoUN 92
Pedersen, Carl R. 1930- St&PR 93
Pedersen, Carolyn Hanford 1942- WhoAmW 93, WhoE 93
Pedersen, Christine Frances 1947- WhoE 93
Pedersen, Ellis Hans 1948- WhoWor 93
Pedersen, Erik 1941- St&PR 93
Pedersen, Gary L. 1951- St&PR 93
Pedersen, Gaylen 1934- WhoWor 93
Pedersen, Gert Kjaergaard 1940- WhoWor 93
Pedersen, Hanne Juul 1961- WhoScE 91-2
Pedersen, (Thelma) Jean J(orgenson) 1934- WhoWrEP 92
Pedersen, John Richard 1926- St&PR 93
Pedersen, Jorgen A. 1927- WhoScE 91-4
Pedersen, K.B. 1942- WhoScE 91-2
Pedersen, Karen Sue 1942- WhoE 93
Pedersen, Keld Fuhr 1940- WhoWor 93
Pedersen, Knud George 1931- WhoAm 92
Pedersen, Laura BioIn 17
Pedersen, Nils Strandberg WhoScE 91-2
Pedersen, Norman BioIn 17
Pedersen, Paul Richard 1935- WhoAm 92
Pedersen, Peer 1925- St&PR 93, WhoIns 93
Pedersen, Peter Andreas 1952- WhoWor 93
Pedersen, Poul Axel 1931- WhoScE 91-2
Pedersen, Richard Foote 1925- WhoAm 92
Pedersen, Robert K. 1919- St&PR 93
Pedersen, Rolf Ingvar 1942- WhoScE 91-4
Pedersen, Ronald P. 1941- St&PR 93
Pedersen, Thelma Jean Jorgenson WhoAmW 93
Pedersen, Theresa Ann 1953- WhoAmW 93
Pedersen, Thor 1945- WhoWor 93
Pedersen, Tor Arve 1929- WhoScE 91-4
Pedersen, Torben Holm 1949- WhoScE 91-2
Pedersen, Walton Eric Law&B 92
Pedersen, Wesley Niels 1922- WhoAm 92, WhoE 93, WhoWor 93
Pedersen, William BioIn 17
Pedersen, William F. 1908-1990 BioIn 17
Pederson, Arnold S. 1927- St&PR 93
Pederson, Carrie Ann 1957- WhoAmW 93, WhoEmL 93
Pederson, Con WhoAm 92
Pederson, Cynthia Sue 1956- WhoWrEP 92
Pederson, David G. 1943- St&PR 93
Pederson, David J. Law&B 92
Pederson, Donald Oscar 1925- WhoAm 92
Pederson, Frank C. 1944- St&PR 93
Pederson, Kathryn Marie 1958- WhoAmW 93
Pederson, Mai 1960- WhoAmW 93, WhoEmL 93
Pederson, Mogens c. 1583-1623 Baker 92
Pederson, Robert Eugene Law&B 92
Pederson, Thoru Judd 1941- WhoAm 92
Pederson, Tony Weldon 1950- WhoAm 92, WhoSSW 93
Pederson, Vernon R. 1919- WhoAm 92
Pederson, William David 1946- WhoAm 92, WhoSSW 93, WhoWor 93
Pederson, Wm. G. 1955- St&PR 93
Pederzini, Gianna 1903-1988 Baker 92, OxDcOp
Pediadites, Basil dc. 1219 OxDcByz
Pedian, Ara 1931- St&PR 93
Pedian, Haig 1924- St&PR 93
Pediasimos OxDcByz
Pediasimos, John d14th cent. OxDcByz
Pediasimos, Theodore fl. 14th cent.- OxDcByz
Pedich, Wojciech Krystyn 1926- WhoWor 93
Pedicini, Louis J. 1926- St&PR 93
Pedicini, Louis James 1926- WhoAm 92
Pedigo, Anita AmWomPl
Pedigo, Leon 1932- St&PR 93
Pedigo, Tom B. 1945- St&PR 93
Pedisich, Anton J. Law&B 92
Peditto, Stephanie M. 1950- WhoE 93
Pedler, Christopher ScF&FL 92
Pedler, Kit 1927-1981 ScF&FL 92
Pedleton, Don ConAu 137
Pedley, John Griffiths 1931- WhoAm 92
Pedley, Timothy John WhoScE 91-1
Pedlosky, Joseph 1938- WhoAm 92
Pedlow, Robert Ian 1962- WhoWor 93
Pedneau, Dave 1947-1990 ScF&FL 92
Pedoe, Daniel 1910- WhoAm 92, WhoWrEP 92
Pedolsky, Andrea 1951- ConAu 38NR
Pedone, Denis Elie 1935- WhoWor 93
Pedone, Joseph Lawrence 1947- St&PR 93, WhoAm 92
Pedowicz, Lee Richard 1952- WhoE 93
Pedowitz, James M. 1915- WhoAm 92
Pedrals, Juan Gili 1924- WhoWor 93
Pedram, Marilyn Beth 1937- WhoAmW 93
Pedraza, Francisco Law&B 92
Pedregal, Pablo 1963- WhoWor 93
Pedreira, Carlos Eduardo 1956- WhoWor 93
Pedrell, Carlos 1878-1941 Baker 92
Pedrell, Felipe 1841-1922 Baker 92, OxDcOp
Pedri, Marilyn Doris 1936- WhoAmW 93
Pedro, I, Emperor of Brazil 1798-1834 BioIn 17
Pedro, II, Emperor of Brazil 1825-1891 BioIn 17
Pedrocchi, Ernesto 1936- WhoScE 91-3
Pedrocchi, Ernesto Leopoldo 1936- WhoWor 93
Pedrollo, Arrigo 1878-1964 Baker 92
Pedrosa, Carlos WhoScE 91-3
Pedrosa, Mary Jarvis 1944- WhoAmW 93
Pedrosa De Jesus, J.D. 1945- WhoScE 91-3
Pedrotti, Carlo 1817-1893 Baker 92, OxDcOp
Pedrotti, Leno Stephano 1927- WhoAm 92
Pedrotti, Paolo WhoScE 91-3
Pedry, Steven 1923- St&PR 93
Peduto, Robert Michael 1954- WhoIns 93
Pedzich, Joan 1948- WhoAmW 93
Peebles, Allene Kay 1938- WhoAmW 93
Peebles, Ann 1947- SoulM
Peebles, Carter David 1934- WhoAm 92
Peebles, Constance Grace 1939- WhoAmW 93
Peebles, Donald L. 1938- St&PR 93
Peebles, E. B., III 1943- WhoSSW 93
Peebles, James David 1949- WhoSSW 93
Peebles, John Leonard 1949- WhoE 93
Peebles, Linda Mae 1950- WhoAmW 93
Peebles, Lucretia Neal Drane 1950- WhoAmW 93, WhoWor 93
Peebles, Marvin L. 1944- WhoWrEP 92
Peebles, Peyton Zimmerman, Jr. 1934- WhoAm 92, WhoSSW 93
Peebles, Richard W. 1952- WhoSSW 93
Peebles, Robert Alvin 1947- WhoAm 92
Peebles, Ruth Addelle 1929- WhoAmW 93
Peebles, Samuel Warmuth 1948- WhoSSW 93
Peebles, William 1836-1862 BioIn 17
Peebles Kleiger, Mary Josephine 1950- WhoAmW 93
Peechatka, Walter Norman 1939- WhoAm 92
Peecher, John Phillip ScF&FL 92
Peed, Mary Jo Law&B 92
Peeden, Paula Zarbock 1958- WhoAmW 93
Peek, Donald Herbert 1954- WhoSSW 93
Peek, Gail L. Law&B 92
Peek, Margaret Frances 1948- WhoAmW 93
Peek, Samuel Millard 1956- WhoSSW 93
Peek, Walter Alva 1927- St&PR 93
Peek, Walter D., II 1958- St&PR 93
Peekner, Ray ScF&FL 92
Peel, Ms. AmWomPl
Peel, Colin D. 1936- ScF&FL 92
Peel, David Alan WhoScE 91-1
Peel, Edward B. Law&B 92
Peel, Edwin A(rthur) 1911-1992 ConAu 139
Peel, Henry A. 1957- WhoSSW 93
Peel, John 1954- ScF&FL 92
Peel, Kenneth Ronald Law&B 92
Peel, Mark BioIn 17
Peel, Robert 1788-1850 BioIn 17
Peel, Robert 1909-1992 BioIn 17, ConAu 136
Peel, Traci BioIn 17
Peel, William Laurie, Jr. 1952- WhoSSW 93
Peele, Beverly BioIn 17
Peele, Jon R. Law&B 92
Peele, Jon R. 1943- St&PR 93
Peele, Roger 1930- WhoAm 92, WhoWrEP 92
Peeler, Donald D. Law&B 92
Peeler, Marie Dona 1960- WhoE 93
Peeler, Ray Doss, Jr. 1929- WhoSSW 93
Peeler, Stuart Thorne 1929- St&PR 93, WhoAm 92
Peeling, William Brian 1930- WhoWor 93
Peelish, Michael R. Law&B 92
Peellaert, Augustin-Philippe (-Marie-Ghislain) 1793-1876 Baker 92
Peelor, Betsy BioIn 17
Peeney, James Doyle 1933- WhoAm 92, WhoE 93
Peeples, Edwin A., Jr. 1915- ScF&FL 92
Peeples, Edwin Augustus 1915- WhoE 93
Peeples, Fanniedell BioIn 17
Peeples, Minor, Jr. 1921- St&PR 93
Peeples, Nia BioIn 17
Peeples, Rebecca Gamblin 1940- WhoSSW 93
Peeples, Susan Whitlow 1963- WhoSSW 93
Peeples, William Dewey, Jr. 1928- WhoAm 92, WhoSSW 93
Peer, George J. 1925- St&PR 93
Peer, George Joseph 1925- WhoAm 92
Peer, Larry H. 1942- WhoAm 92
Peerce, Jan 1904-1984 Baker 92, IntDcOp, OxDcOp
Peerce, Larry MiSFD 9, WhoAm 92
Peerce, Stuart Bernard 1931- WhoAm 92
Peerman, Dean Gordon 1931- WhoAm 92
Peers, Michael Geoffrey 1934- WhoAm 92, WhoE 93
Peerschke, Ellinor Irmgard Barbara 1954- WhoEmL 93
Peerthum, Satteeanund 1941- WhoUN 92, WhoWor 93
Peery, Annette Rasbury 1938- WhoAmW 93
Peery, Benjamin BioIn 17
Peery, Troy A., Jr. 1946- St&PR 93
Peery, Troy Alfred, Jr. 1946- WhoAm 92
Peery, W.W. 1931- St&PR 93
Peeslake, Gaffer ConAu 40NR
Peet, Bill ConAu 38NR, MajAI
Peet, Charles D., Jr. 1935- WhoAm 92
Peet, Creighton Houck 1938- St&PR 93
Peet, Greg J. 1953- St&PR 93
Peet, J. Carlisle, III Law&B 92
Peet, Jack BioIn 17
Peet, John Carlisle, Jr. Law&B 92
Peet, John Carlisle, Jr. 1928- St&PR 93
Peet, Rex Leroy 1949- WhoSSW 93
Peet, William Bartlett 1915- ConAu 38NR, MajAI [port]
Peete, Calvin BioIn 17
Peete, William Pettway Jones 1921- WhoAm 92
Peeters, Emile-Gaston 1932- WhoScE 91-2
Peeters, Flor 1903-1986 Baker 92
Peeters, Francois M. 1955- WhoWor 93
Peeters, Johan E. 1951- WhoScE 91-2
Peeters, Jos 1948- WhoScE 91-2
Peeters, Marc D.V.F. 1946- WhoScE 91-2
Peeters, Theo 1943- WhoScE 91-2
Peeters, Theo Louis 1943- WhoWor 93
Peetoom, Frans 1913- WhoWor 93
Peets, Randolph D., Jr. 1925- St&PR 93
Peetz, Robert William 1947- WhoSSW 93
Peetz-Larsen, Hans 1940- WhoAm 92
Peev, G.A. 1935- WhoScE 91-4
Peevers, Barbara Hollands 1930- WhoAmW 93
Peevey, Michael R. 1938- St&PR 93
Peevey, Michael Robert 1938- WhoAm 92
Pefanis, Harry N. 1957- St&PR 93
Peffekoven, Rolf 1938- WhoWor 93
Peffer, Craig Dion 1934- St&PR 93
Peffer, James Michael Law&B 92
Peffer, William 1831-1914 PolPar
Pefley, Charles Saunders 1943- WhoSSW 93
Pegasios
See Akindynos & Pegasios OxDcByz
Pege, Deborah Ann Law&B 92
Pegels, C. Carl 1933- WhoAm 92
Pegg, David C. 1938- St&PR 93
Pegg, David Edward WhoScE 91-1
Pegg, Jerry Allen 1943- St&PR 93
Pegis, Anton George 1920- WhoAm 92
Pegler, Westbrook 1894-1969 JrnUS
Pegolotti, Francesco Balducci c. 1290-c. 1347 OxDcByz
Pegonites OxDcByz
Pegram, Charles Cuthbert, Jr. 1947- WhoSSW 93
Pegram, John Braxton 1938- WhoAm 92
Pegram, Patricia Isley Law&B 92
Pegram, William Ransom Johnson 1841-1865 BioIn 17
Pegrum, Colin Malcolm 1950- WhoWor 93
Peguy, Charles Pierre 1873-1914 BioIn 17
Pehar, Jakov 1928- WhoScE 91-4
Pehkonen, Olli-Pekka 1951- WhoWor 93
Pehl, Erich Ludwig 1939- WhoWor 93
Pehlke, Robert Donald 1933- WhoAm 92
Pehlke, Robert E. Law&B 92
Pehrson, Arthur G. 1929- St&PR 93
Pehrson, Barbara J. 1928- WhoWrEP 92
Pehrson, Douglas K. Law&B 92
Pehrson, Gordon Oscar, Jr. 1943- WhoAm 92
Pehrson, Peter Alvin 1939- St&PR 93
Pehrsson, Ebbe Bertil Lennart 1939- WhoWor 93
Pehu, Eija Paivi 1955- WhoWor 93
Pei, Dingyi 1941- WhoWor 93
Pei, I.M. 1917- BioIn 17
Pei, Ieoh Ming 1917- WhoAm 92, WhoWor 93
Pei, Ming L. 1923- WhoAm 92
Peifer, Charles L. 1950- St&PR 93
Peifer, Kathleen Hamel ScF&FL 92
Peiffer, Gerald M. 1948- St&PR 93
Peiffer, William F. d1990 BioIn 17
Peignaud WhoScE 91-2
Peignelin, Guy 1942- WhoScE 91-2
Peigny, Martine 1958- WhoWor 93
Peiker, Edwin W., Jr. 1931- St&PR 93
Peiko, Nikolai 1916- Baker 92
Peillon, Francoise WhoScE 91-2
Peimbert, Manuel 1941- WhoAm 92
Peinado, Arnold Benicio, Jr. 1931- WhoSSW 93
Peinado Lucena, Eduardo WhoScE 91-3
Peinemann, Edith 1937- Baker 92
Peins, Rudolph M., Jr. 1929- St&PR 93
Peiper, Hans-Jurgen 1925- WhoScE 91-3
Peiperl, Adam 1935- WhoAm 92, WhoWor 93
Peipert, James Raymond 1942- WhoSSW 93
Peirce, Brooke 1922- WhoAm 92
Peirce, Carol Marshall 1922- WhoAm 92
Peirce, George Leighton 1933- WhoAm 92
Peirce, Georgia Wilson 1960- WhoAmW 93, WhoE 93, WhoWor 93
Peirce, Hayford 1942- ScF&FL 92
Peirce, John Wentworth 1912- WhoAm 92
Peirce, Katharine V. AmWomPl
Peirce, Kenneth B. 1943- St&PR 93
Peirce, Neal R. 1932- WhoAm 92
Peirce, Roger D. 1937- St&PR 93
Peirce, William R. 1934- St&PR 93
Peiro, Jose Maria 1950- WhoWor 93
Peirson, George Ewell 1957- WhoWor 93
Peisen, Deborah Jean 1947- WhoAmW 93
Peiser, Herbert Steffen 1917- WhoE 93
Peiser, Robert A. 1948- St&PR 93
Peiser, Robert Alan 1948- WhoAm 92
Peisinger, Jon R. 1947- St&PR 93
Peisinger, Jon Robert 1947- WhoAm 92
Peisl, Johann S. 1933- WhoScE 91-3
Peisner, Arthur M. 1941- St&PR 93
Peisner, Arthur Mann 1941- WhoAm 92
Peiss, Clarence Norman 1922- WhoAm 92
Peist, William J. BioIn 17, NewYTBS 92 [port]
Peitersen, Erik 1931- WhoWor 93
Peitso, Martti Samuli 1924- WhoWor 93
Peitz, Earl F. 1930- WhoIns 93
Peitz, Earl Francis 1930- St&PR 93
Pei Wenzhong 1904-1982 IntDcAn
Peix, J.L. 1947- WhoScE 91-2
Peix, Jean-Louis 1947- WhoWor 93
Peixinho, Jorge (Manuel Rosada Marques) 1940- Baker 92
Peixoto, Renato Rodrigues 1930- WhoWor 93
Peixotto, Helen Esther 1913- WhoE 93
Peizer, Maurice Samuel 1912- WhoE 93
Pejovic, Stanislav 1933- WhoScE 91-4
Pekalski, Leonard 1896-1944 PolBiDi
Pekarsky, Melvin Hirsch 1934- WhoAm 92
Pekic, Borislav 1930-1992 ConAu 139
Pekich, Elizabeth Krams 1948- WhoE 93, WhoEmL 93
Pekich, Stephen 1941- St&PR 93
Pekin, D. James Law&B 92
Pekkanen, Timo Juhani 1933- WhoScE 91-4
Peknay, David P. 1962- St&PR 93
Pekor, Allan J. St&PR 93
Pekow, Eugene 1930- St&PR 93, WhoAm 92
Pekruhn, John Edward 1915- WhoAm 92
Pekrul, Kimberly Ann 1960- WhoWrEP 92
Pela, Nilza Teresa Rotter 1941- WhoWor 93
Peladeau, Marius Beaudoin 1935- WhoAm 92
Peladeau, Pierre 1925- St&PR 93, WhoAm 92, WhoE 93, WhoWor 93
Pelaez, Emanuel N. 1915- WhoAsAP 91
Pelaez, Emmanuel N. 1915- WhoWor 93
Pelaez, Francisco 1911- DcMexL
Pelaez, Isacio A. 1939- WhoAsAP 91
Pelaez-Hudlet, Jose 1946- WhoWor 93
Pelagia of Tarsos OxDcByz
Pelagia the Harlot OxDcByz
Pelagia the Virgin OxDcByz
Pelagius of Albano d1230 OxDcByz
Pelaia, Joseph C. Law&B 92

Pendergast, James F. *BioIn 17*
Pendergast, John Joseph, III 1936- *WhoAm 92*
Pendergast, Marcia A. *St&PR 93*
Pendergast, Mary Carita *BioIn 17*
Pendergast, Michael C. *Law&B 92*
Pendergast, Teresa A. 1958- *WhoSSW 93*
Pendergast, Thomas J. 1872-1945 *PolPar*
Pendergast, Thomas Patrick *Law&B 92*
Pendergast, William Ross 1931- *WhoAm 92*
Pendergraft, Jeffery R. *Law&B 92*
Pendergraft, Jeffrey R. 1948- *St&PR 93*
Pendergraft, Norman Elveis 1934- *WhoSSW 93*
Pendergrass, Ewell Dean 1945- *WhoSSW 93*
Pendergrass, Henry Pancoast 1925- *WhoAm 92*
Pendergrass, Jan Noble 1951- *WhoSSW 93*
Pendergrass, John R. 1935- *St&PR 93*
Pendergrass, Teddy 1950- *SoulM, WhoAm 92*
Pendergrast, James Edward *Law&B 92*
Pendergrast, William Jefferson, Jr. 1946- *WhoSSW 93*
Penders, James Robert 1927- *St&PR 93*
Pendexter, Harold E., Jr. 1934- *St&PR 93*
Pendlebury, Ralph 1929- *St&PR 93*
Pendleton, Barbara 1924- *St&PR 93*
Pendleton, Barbara Jean 1924- *WhoAm 92*
Pendleton, Carolyn Madge 1941- *St&PR 93*
Pendleton, Don *ScF&FL 92, WhoWrEP 92*
Pendleton, Don 1927- *ScF&FL 92*
Pendleton, Elmer Dean, Jr. 1927- *WhoAm 92, WhoWor 93*
Pendleton, Eugene Barbour, Jr. 1913- *WhoAm 92*
Pendleton, Gail Ruth 1937- *WhoAmW 93, WhoE 93*
Pendleton, Gary Herman 1947- *WhoSSW 93*
Pendleton, George H. 1825-1889 *PolPar*
Pendleton, Hugh Nelson 1935- *WhoE 93*
Pendleton, James Dudley 1930- *WhoWrEP 92*
Pendleton, James K. *Law&B 92*
Pendleton, Joan Marie 1954- *WhoAmW 93*
Pendleton, Julia Elizabeth 1954- *WhoAmW 93*
Pendleton, Moses Robert Andrew 1949- *WhoAm 92*
Pendleton, Shaun Wayne 1958- *WhoSSW 93*
Pendleton, Sumner Alden 1918- *WhoAm 92*
Pendleton, Susie B. *AmWomPl*
Pendleton, Terry Lee 1960- *WhoAm 92*
Pendleton, Thelma Brown 1911- *WhoAmW 93, WhoWor 93*
Pendleton, Thomas Hale 1936- *WhoSSW 93*
Pendleton, William B. 1949- *St&PR 93*
Pendleton, William Gion 1943- *WhoSSW 93*
Pendleton, William J. 1939- *St&PR 93*
Pendleton, William Joseph 1939- *WhoE 93*
Pendleton, William M. 1931- *St&PR 93*
Pendleton-Parker, Billiee Geraldine 1952- *WhoSSW 93*
Pendley, David Harold 1942- *St&PR 93*
Pendley, Donald Lee 1950- *WhoE 93*
Pendley, Elisabeth Y. *Law&B 92*
Pendley, Steve S. 1937- *St&PR 93*
Pendley, William Tyler 1936- *WhoAm 92*
Pendragon, Eric *ScF&FL 92*
Pendrak, Joseph John 1929- *St&PR 93*
Pendray, George *ScF&FL 92*
Pendrell, Ernest d1992 *BioIn 17, NewYTBS 92*
Pendry, Eric D. *ScF&FL 92*
Pendry, John Brian *WhoScE 91-1*
Pene, Pierre J. Marie 1924- *WhoScE 91-2*
Penecilla, Gerard Ledesma 1956- *WhoWor 93*
Penedo, Luis Filipe do Cruzeiro Goncalves 1941- *WhoWor 93*
Pene du Bois, William 1916- *BioIn 17*
Pene du Bois, William (Sherman) 1916- *MajAI [port]*
Penegar, Kenneth Lawing 1932- *WhoAm 92*
Penelle, G. *WhoScE 91-2*
Penev, Zlatko Yordanov 1933- *WhoScE 91-4*
Peneycad, W.A.N. *Law&B 92*
Penfield, Elizabeth Few 1939- *WhoAmW 93, WhoSSW 93*
Penfield, Marjorie Porter 1942- *WhoAmW 93*
Penfield, Paul Livingstone, Jr. 1933- *WhoAm 92*
Penfold, Marge 1942- *St&PR 93*
Peng, Hansheng 1937- *WhoWor 93*
Peng, Liang-Chuan 1936- *WhoSSW 93, WhoWor 93*
Peng, Mingdao 1935- *WhoUN 92*
Peng, Yun-O 1931- *WhoWor 93*
Peng Chong 1915- *WhoAsAP 91*
Peng Dehuai 1898-1974 *ColdWar 2 [port], DcTwHis*
Peng Deyin *BioIn 17*
Pengelly, John Henry 1935- *St&PR 93*
Peng Gongge *WhoAsAP 91*
Pengilly, Brian William 1930- *WhoAm 92*
Peng Khoon, Dato' Tan 1924- *WhoAsAP 91*
Penglase, Frank Dennis 1940- *St&PR 93, WhoAm 92*
Peng Pai 1896-1929 *DcTwHis*
Peng Peiyun 1929- *WhoAsAP 91*
P'eng Teh-huai 1898-1974 *HarEnMi*
Penhale, John 1944- *St&PR 93*
Penherski, Zbigniew 1935- *Baker 92*
Penhoet, Edward E. 1940- *St&PR 93*
Penhorwood, Herbert Frederick 1937- *St&PR 93*
Penhune, John Paul 1936- *St&PR 93, WhoAm 92, WhoWor 93*
Penick, George Dial, Jr. 1948- *WhoAm 92*
Penick, J. Edward *Law&B 92*
Penick, James Lal, Jr. 1932- *WhoSSW 93*
Penick, Joe Edward 1920- *WhoAm 92*
Penick, John Edgar 1944- *WhoWrEP 92*
Penie, Daniel R. *Law&B 92*
Penikett, Antony David John 1945- *WhoAm 92*
Penisten, Gary Dean 1931- *St&PR 93, WhoAm 92*
Penix, Vicki 1960- *WhoSSW 93*
Penka, Eloise Marie 1960- *WhoEmL 93*
Penkava, Robert Ray 1942- *WhoAm 92*
Penketh, David 1943- *St&PR 93*
Penkwitz, Martin William *Law&B 92*
Penland, Anna *AmWomPl*
Penland, Arnold Clifford, Jr. 1933- *WhoAm 92, WhoSSW 93*
Penland, John Thomas 1930- *WhoAm 92*
Penland, K.V. *St&PR 93*
Penley, Constance 1948- *ScF&FL 92*
Penley, Deborah Williamson 1949- *WhoAmW 93*
Penley, Stephen S. 1949- *St&PR 93*
Penman, Eugene John 1943- *St&PR 93*
Penman, Jack Lanier 1922- *WhoSSW 93*
Penman, Paul Duane 1937- *WhoE 93*
Penman, Sheldon 1930- *WhoAm 92*
Penn, A. Samuel 1935- *WhoAm 92*
Penn, Anthony A. 1945- *St&PR 93*
Penn, Arthur 1922- *MiSFD 9*
Penn, Arthur Hiller 1922- *WhoAm 92*
Penn, Charles Ehrig 1922- *St&PR 93*
Penn, Dan 1941- *SoulM*
Penn, Dawn Tamara 1965- *WhoAmW 93*
Penn, E.W. *St&PR 93*
Penn, Edwin Allen 1939- *WhoAm 92*
Penn, Elaine d1990 *BioIn 17*
Penn, Harold 1928- *St&PR 93*
Penn, Hugh Franklin 1917- *WhoSSW 93*
Penn, Irving *BioIn 17*
Penn, Irving 1917- *WhoAm 92*
Penn, Jean Cox 1944- *WhoWrEP 92*
Penn, John Garrett 1932- *CngDr 91, WhoE 93*
Penn, Jonathan Brian *Law&B 92*
Penn, Joni Leigh *BioIn 17*
Penn, Leo *MiSFD 9*
Penn, Lisa, Fonssagrives- *BioIn 17*
Penn, Lynn Sharon 1945- *WhoAmW 93*
Penn, Marc J.L. *BioIn 17*
Penn, Michael *BioIn 17*
Penn, Patricia Whitley 1953- *WhoEmL 93*
Penn, Pennetta *WhoWrEP 92*
Penn, Robert W. *AfrAmBi*
Penn, Robyn Carol 1949- *WhoAmW 93*
Penn, Sean *BioIn 17*
Penn, Sean 1960- *ConTFT 10, HolBB [port], MiSFD 9, WhoAm 92*
Penn, Stanley William 1928- *WhoAm 92*
Penn, Tom *BioIn 17*
Penn, William 1621-1670 *HarEnMi*
Penna, Angel d1992 *BioIn 17*
Penna, Angel, Sr. d1992 *NewYTBS 92*
Penna, Lorenzo 1613-1693 *Baker 92*
Penna, Nancy Sue 1956- *WhoAmW 93*
Penn & Teller *News 92 [port]*
Pennanen, Seppo Ilmari 1942- *WhoScE 91-4*
Pennario, Leonard 1924- *Baker 92, WhoAm 92*
Pennebaker, D. A. 1930- *MiSFD 9*
Pennebaker, James Whiting 1950- *WhoSSW 93*
Pennekamp, Frederick H. 1948- *St&PR 93*
Pennell, D. 1952- *WhoScE 91-1*
Pennell, Eagle *MiSFD 9*
Pennell, Jack 1934- *St&PR 93*
Pennell, Joseph 1857-1926 *GayN*
Pennell, Richard H. 1926- *St&PR 93*
Pennell, William Brooke 1935- *WhoAm 92*
Penneman, Robert Allen 1919- *WhoAm 92*
Penner, Alice Braeker 1934- *WhoAmW 93*
Penner, Eunice B. 1925- *WhoE 93*
Penner, Fred *BioIn 17*
Penner, Fred (Ralph Cornelius) 1946- *ConAu 136*
Penner, Hans Henry 1934- *WhoAm 92*
Penner, Harry Harold Hamilton, Jr. 1945- *WhoAm 92*
Penner, Helen 1937- *WhoWrEP 92*
Penner, Joe 1904-1941 *QDrFCA 92 [port]*
Penner, Jonathan 1940- *ConAu 39NR*
Penner, Jonathan David 1940- *WhoWrEP 92*
Penner, Roland 1924- *WhoAm 92*
Penner, Rudolph Gerhard 1936- *WhoAm 92, WhoE 93*
Penner, Stanford Solomon 1921- *WhoAm 92*
Penner, Uwe 1941- *WhoWor 93*
Penner, William A. 1933- *WhoAm 92*
Penney, Lord 1909-1991 *AnObit 1991*
Penney, Alexandra *WhoAmW 93*
Penney, Alphonsus Liguori 1924- *WhoAm 92*
Penney, Caroline A. d1992 *BioIn 17, NewYTBS 92*
Penney, Charles Rand 1923- *WhoAm 92, WhoE 93, WhoWor 93*
Penney, Christopher Freeland Dickson 1908- *WhoWor 93*
Penney, David Paul 1933- *WhoE 93*
Penney, Edward Thomas 1935- *WhoAm 92*
Penney, James Cash 1875-1971 *BioIn 17*
Penney, Jerre Franklin 1951- *St&PR 93*
Penney, Margaret *AmWomPl*
Penney, Robert Andrew 1955- *WhoE 93*
Penney, Sherry Hood 1937- *WhoAm 92, WhoAmW 93, WhoE 93*
Penney, Sheryl Ann 1945- *WhoAmW 93*
Penney, William George 1909-1991 *BioIn 17*
Penney, William H. *Law&B 92*
Pennie, Daniel R. *WhoAm 92*
Penniman, Caroline de F. *AmWomPl*
Penniman, Clara 1914- *WhoAm 92*
Penniman, Howard Rae 1916- *WhoAm 92*
Penniman, Nicholas Griffith, IV 1938- *St&PR 93, WhoAm 92*
Penniman, Richard *BioIn 17*
Penniman, Richard Wayne 1932- *Baker 92, WhoAm 92*
Penniman, W. David 1937- *WhoAm 92*
Penning, John Arthur, Jr. *Law&B 92*
Penning, Lourens 1922- *WhoScE 91-3*
Penning, Trevor Martin 1951- *WhoE 93*
Penninger, Frieda Elaine 1927- *WhoAmW 93, WhoSSW 93*
Penninger, William Holt, Jr. 1954- *WhoEmL 93*
Penning-Rowsell, Edmund Charles *WhoScE 91-1*
Pennings, Erik 1960- *WhoWor 93*
Pennington, Beverly Melcher 1931- *WhoAmW 93*
Pennington, Bruce 1944- *ScF&FL 92*
Pennington, Clarence 1925- *St&PR 93*
Pennington, David A. *ScF&FL 92*
Pennington, Dolores Catherine *WhoE 93*
Pennington, Dorothy Agnes 1944- *WhoSSW 93*
Pennington, Eliberto Escamilla 1958- *WhoE 93*
Pennington, Gary J. 1960- *St&PR 93*
Pennington, Huey B., Jr. 1947- *St&PR 93*
Pennington, Jean Ann Thompson 1946- *WhoE 93*
Pennington, Jean Zimmer *Law&B 92*
Pennington, Jeanne Rose 1955- *WhoEmL 93*
Pennington, Joseph G. *Law&B 92*
Pennington, Laurie A. *Law&B 92*
Pennington, Loyd Donald 1928- *St&PR 93*
Pennington, M. (Robert John) Basil 1931- *ConAu 37NR*
Pennington, Mary Anne 1943- *WhoAm 92, WhoSSW 93*
Pennington, Mary Engle 1872-1952 *BioIn 17*
Pennington, Richard M. 1926- *St&PR 93*
Pennington, Richard Maier 1926- *WhoAm 92*
Pennington, Rita Dolores 1928- *WhoAmW 93*
Pennington, Rodney Lee 1946- *WhoE 93*
Pennington, Theresa Sue 1948- *WhoEmL 93*
Pennington, Thomas Hugh *WhoScE 91-1*
Pennington, Thomas K. 1936- *WhoIns 93*
Pennington, William 1796-1862 *PolPar*
Pennisten, John William 1939- *WhoE 93, WhoWor 93*
Pennock, Carol Jean *Law&B 92*
Pennock, Donald William 1915- *WhoE 93, WhoWor 93*
Pennock, George T. 1912- *St&PR 93*
Pennock, George Tennant 1912- *WhoAm 92*
Pennock, James Roland 1906- *WhoAm 92*
Pennock, Peggy Ann 1947- *WhoEmL 93*
Pennoyer, Paul Geddes, Jr. 1920- *WhoAm 92*
Pennoyer, Robert M. 1925- *WhoAm 92*
Pennoyer, Russel P. *Law&B 92*
Pennoyer, Russell Parsons 1951- *St&PR 93*
Penny, Charles Richard 1934- *St&PR 93, WhoAm 92*
Penny, David G. 1950- *ScF&FL 92*
Penny, Donald Gordon 1955- *WhoE 93*
Penny, Joe *BioIn 17*
Penny, Josephine B. 1925- *WhoAmW 93*
Penny, Michael J. 1937- *St&PR 93*
Penny, Roger Pratt 1936- *St&PR 93, WhoAm 92*
Penny, Ronald 1936- *WhoWor 93*
Penny, Timothy J. 1951- *CngDr 91*
Penny, Timothy Joseph 1951- *WhoAm 92*
Pennypacker, Henry Sutton 1937- *St&PR 93*
Pennypacker, Samuel Whitaker 1843-1916 *BioIn 17*
Penot, Michel 1930- *WhoScE 91-2*
Penrod, Jack Ray *Law&B 92*
Penrod, James Wilford 1934- *WhoAm 92*
Penrod, Kenneth Earl 1916- *WhoAm 92*
Penrod, Sandra Lynne 1947- *WhoAmW 93*
Penrose, Anthea Dagmar 1949- *WhoSSW 93*
Penrose, Antony 1947- *ConAu 137*
Penrose, Boies 1860-1921 *PolPar*
Penrose, Charles, Jr. 1921- *WhoAm 92*
Penrose, Gilbert Quay 1938- *WhoWor 93*
Penrose, Gordon 1925- *BioIn 17*
Penrose, Oliver *WhoScE 91-1*
Penrose, R. *WhoScE 91-1*
Penrose, Roger 1931- *ConAu 139*
Penry, James Kiffin 1929- *WhoAm 92*
Penry, Walter P. 1933- *St&PR 93*
Pensar, K. Goran 1930- *WhoScE 91-4*
Pense, Alan Wiggins 1934- *WhoAm 92*
Pense, Jurgen K.E. 1931- *WhoScE 91-3*
Pense, Kevin M.E. 1951- *St&PR 93*
Penselin, Siegfried 1927- *WhoScE 91-3*
Penshorn, Mark A. 1957- *WhoSSW 93*
Penslar, Derek J(onathan) 1958- *ConAu 136*
Pensler, Sanford Nolan 1956- *St&PR 93*
Penson, Edward Martin 1927- *WhoAm 92*
Pensyl, William Edward 1913- *WhoSSW 93*
Penta, Lily Kim 1960- *WhoEmL 93*
Pentcheff, Nicolas 1911- *WhoE 93*
Pentek, Marion Stanton 1931- *WhoAmW 93, WhoSSW 93, WhoWor 93*
Pentelovitch, Robert Alan 1955- *WhoE 93*
Pentenrieder, Franz Xaver 1813-1867 *Baker 92*
Pentis, Charles J. *Law&B 92*
Pentland, Barbara 1912- *BioIn 17*
Pentland, Barbara (Lally) 1912- *Baker 92, WhoAm 92*
Pentler, Glenn Irving 1953- *St&PR 93*
Pentler, Irving Edward 1923- *St&PR 93*
Pentler, Marcelene Marion 1928- *St&PR 93*
Pentleton, Carol June 1952- *WhoAmW 93, WhoE 93*
Pentney, Roberta Jean 1936- *WhoAmW 93*
Penton, Cherri Daughdrill 1939- *WhoAmW 93*
Penton, David Noel 1941- *WhoSSW 93*
Penton, Jeffrey Todd 1966- *WhoSSW 93*
Penton, Nancy Purpura 1952- *WhoSSW 93*
Pentony, Alfred B. 1926- *St&PR 93*
Pentony, Carole Gentry *WhoSSW 93*
Penttala, Vesa Eljas 1945- *WhoScE 91-4*
Pentti, Anne Kyllikki 1960- *WhoWor 93*
Penttila, Ilkka Martti 1936- *WhoScE 91-4*
Pentz, Sara 1937- *WhoAmW 93*
Pentz, William H. *Law&B 92*
Penuel, Arnold McCoy 1936- *WhoSSW 93*
Penuel, Stephen G. *Law&B 92*
Penuelas, Josep *WhoWor 93*
Penuelas, Marcelino Company 1916- *WhoAm 92*
Penugoda, Haragopal Kusuma 1940- *WhoE 93*
Penwell, Richard Carlton 1942- *WhoE 93*
Penwell, William Frank 1932- *WhoAm 92*
Penz, Anton Jacob 1906- *WhoAm 92*
Penza, Patricia German 1957- *WhoEmL 93*
Penzel, Carl Gene 1934- *WhoWor 93*
Penzell, Andrew Wade 1945- *WhoSSW 93*
Penzer, Mark 1932- *WhoAm 92, WhoWrEP 92*
Penzes, Bethen 1934- *WhoScE 91-4*
Penzias, Arno Allan 1933- *St&PR 93, WhoAm 92, WhoE 93, WhoWor 93*
Penzien, Charles Henry 1945- *St&PR 93*
Penzien, Donald Baird 1957- *WhoSSW 93*
Penzien, Joseph 1924- *WhoAm 92*

Penzkofer, Alfons 1942- WhoScE 91-3, WhoWor 93
Penzl, Herbert 1910- WhoAm 92
Peo, Marc S. 1959- St&PR 93
Peon y Contreras, Jose 1843-1907 DcMexL
Peoples, David Alexander 1930- WhoSSW 93
Peoples, David Webb MiSFD 9
Peoples, John Arthur, Jr. 1926- WhoAm 92
Peoples, John Clifford Alexander 1942- WhoE 93
Peoples, Thomas Edward 1915- WhoAm 92
Peoples, William R. Law&B 92
Peopples, Jo Ann 1949- WhoAmW 93
Peover, M.E. WhoScE 91-1
Pep, Melchior 1951- WhoAsAP 91
Pepagomenos OxDcByz
Pepagomenos, Demetrios fl. 15th cent.- OxDcByz
Pepe, Dominick 1955- St&PR 93
Pepe, Frank A. 1931- WhoAm 92
Pepe, Fred 1957- St&PR 93
Pepe, John Michael 1939- St&PR 93
Pepe, Pamela Slane 1958- WhoAmW 93
Pepe, Philip S. d1991 BioIn 17
Pepe, Raymomd A. 1942- St&PR 93
Pepe, Teri-Anne 1967- WhoWor 93
Peper, Christian B. 1910- St&PR 93
Peper, Christian Baird 1910- WhoAm 92, WhoWor 93
Peper, George Frederick 1950- WhoAm 92, WhoWrEP 92
Pepera, John A. 1945- St&PR 93
Pepi, Lora C. Law&B 92
Pepi, Ugo 1932- WhoScE 91-3
Pepich, Bruce Walter 1952- WhoAm 92
Pepin, Carolan WhoAm 92
Pepin, (Jean-Josephat) Clermont 1926- Baker 92
Pepin, David Anthony 1963- WhoSSW 93
Pepin, E. Lyle 1941- St&PR 93
Pepin, Francois J. Law&B 92
Pepin, Jean-Luc 1924- WhoAm 92
Pepin, John Nelson 1946- WhoE 93
Pepin, Marcel 1941- WhoAm 92
Pepin, Yvonne Mary 1956- WhoAmW 93, WhoEmL 93
Pepin de Bonnerive, Jacques Fontaine 1927- WhoWor 93
Pepine, Carl John 1941- WhoAm 92
Pepitone, Byron Vincent 1918- WhoAm 92
Pepitone, Natal M. 1944- WhoE 93
Pepitone Arreola Rockwell, Frances Marie 1941- WhoAmW 93
Peplau, Hildegard Elizabeth 1909- WhoAm 92
Peplin, Van C. 1960- St&PR 93
Peplinski, James L. 1921- St&PR 93
Peploe, Clare MiSFD 9
Peploe, Mark MiSFD 9
Peplow, Michael W. 1940- ScF&FL 92
Peplow, William Edward 1934- St&PR 93
Peplowski, Celia Ceslawa 1918- WhoAmW 93
Pepock, August 1887-1967 Baker 92
Peppard, George 1928- MiSFD 9, WhoAm 92
Peppas, Nikolaos Athanassiou 1948- WhoAm 92
Peppe, M. John 1941- WhoIns 93
Peppe, Rodney (Darrell) 1934- MajAI [port]
Peppe, Ronald Law&B 92
Pepper, Allan Michael 1943- WhoAm 92
Pepper, Art 1925-1982 Baker 92
Pepper, Beverly 1924- BioIn 17, WhoAm 92
Pepper, Claude BioIn 17
Pepper, Claude 1900-1989 PolPar
Pepper, Claude Denson 1900-1989 EncAACR
Pepper, David M. 1949- WhoAm 92, WhoEmL 93
Pepper, Dorothy Mae 1932- WhoAmW 93, WhoWor 93
Pepper, Frank S. 1910-1988 BioIn 17, ScF&FL 92
Pepper, George Bonaventure 1926- WhoE 93
Pepper, George Wharton 1867-1961 OxCSupC
Pepper, Gordon Terry WhoScE 91-1
Pepper, Jack C. Law&B 92
Pepper, Jim d1992 BioIn 17, NewYTBS 92
Pepper, John Ennis 1938- St&PR 93
Pepper, Joyce M. Law&B 92
Pepper, Louis Henry 1924- St&PR 93
Pepper, Louis Thomas 1954- WhoSSW 93
Pepper, Mary Janice 1942- WhoAmW 93, WhoWor 93
Pepper, Michael WhoScE 91-1
Pepper, Robert BioIn 17
Pepper, Sam James 1949- St&PR 93
Pepper, Sheila F. Law&B 92
Peppercorn, Bert Leonard 1923- WhoSSW 93
Peppercorn, John Edward 1937- WhoAm 92
Peppercorn, Lisa M(argot) 1913- ConAu 138
Peppercorn, Wayne M. 1949- St&PR 93
Pepperdene, Margaret Williams 1919- WhoAm 92
Pepperell, William 1696-1759 HarEnMi
Pepperl, Joanne Margaret 1952- WhoAmW 93
Pepperman, Joy Law&B 92
Pepperney, Kenneth R. Law&B 92
Peppers, Donald Alan 1950- WhoAm 92
Peppers-Johnson, Mary Lynne 1960- WhoWrEP 92
Peppet, Russell Frederick 1939- WhoAm 92
Peppin, Brigid 1941- ScF&FL 92
Peppin, Gene Francis 1943- St&PR 93
Peppin, Richard Joseph 1943- WhoE 93
Pepping, Ernst 1901-1981 Baker 92
Pepple, David Ralph 1943- St&PR 93, WhoAm 92
Pepple, Otis Darrell 1921- St&PR 93
Peppler, Lonnie L. St&PR 93
Peppler, William Norman 1925- WhoAm 92
Pepples, Ernest 1935- WhoAm 92
Pepples, Ernest C. Law&B 92
Pepples, Ernest C. 1935- St&PR 93
Pepski, Kathleen Patrice 1955- St&PR 93
Pepus, Susan Retta 1935- WhoAmW 93
Pepusch, Johann Christoph 1667-1752 IntDcOp [port]
Pepusch, John Christopher 1667-1752 Baker 92, OxDcOp
Pepy, G. 1944- WhoScE 91-2
Pepyne, Edward Walter 1925- WhoAm 92
Pepys, Mark Brian WhoScE 91-1
Pepys, Samuel 1633-1703 BioIn 17, MagSWL [port], OxDcOp, WorLitC [port]
Pequignot, Henri 1914- WhoScE 91-2
Pera, Jean 1932- WhoScE 91-2
Perabo, (Johann) Ernst 1845-1920 Baker 92
Peracchia, Alberto 1931- WhoWor 93
Perachon, G. WhoScE 91-2
Perachon, Guy 1937- WhoScE 91-2
Peradejordi, Federico 1920- WhoScE 91-2
Peradotto, John Joseph 1933- WhoAm 92
Peragallo, Mario 1910- Baker 92
Perahia, Murray 1947- Baker 92, BioIn 17, WhoAm 92, WhoWor 93
Peraino, Roy T. 1928- St&PR 93
Perakis, James A. St&PR 93
Peraldo Bicelli, Luisa 1927- WhoScE 91-3
Peral Fernandez, Jose Luis 1942- WhoWor 93
Peralta, Angela 1845-1883 Baker 92
Peralta, Bertalicia 1939- SpAmA
Peralta, Genandrialine Laquian 1955- WhoWor 93
Peralta, Josefina 1966- WhoAmW 93
Peralta, Philip Charles 1958- WhoSSW 93
Peralta, Ralph D. 1954- St&PR 93
Peralta Azurdia, Enrique DcCPCAm
Peranda, Marco Gioseppe c. 1625-1675 Baker 92
Peranio, Doreen Ann 1948- WhoAmW 93
Peranio, Vince BioIn 17
Peranski, Robert Zigmunt 1935- WhoIns 93
Perbohner, Robert M. Law&B 92
Percas de Ponseti, Helena 1921- WhoAm 92
Percebois, Gilbert 1930- WhoScE 91-2
Percefull, Stephanie Butler 1964- WhoSSW 93
Percello, Louis John Law&B 92
Perceval, Julio 1903-1963 Baker 92
Perche, Alain 1945- WhoScE 91-2
Percheron, Francois Marcel 1926- WhoScE 91-2
Perchick, Morton Kenneth 1937- St&PR 93
Perchik, Benjamin Ivan 1941- WhoSSW 93
Percio, David R. Law&B 92
Percious, Jacquelin Marilyn 1934- WhoAmW 93
Percival, Dean Lee 1935- St&PR 93
Percival, Ian Colin WhoScE 91-1
Percival, Julie Helene AmWomPl
Percival, Roger B. 1926- St&PR 93
Percival, S. Piers Bassnett 1937- WhoWor 93
Percoco, Thelma Ann 1935- WhoSSW 93
Percus, Jerome Kenneth 1926- WhoAm 92
Percy, Ann Buchanan 1940- WhoAm 92
Percy, Charles Harting 1919- WhoAm 92
Percy, Charles Henry ConAu 37NR, MajAI
Percy, Constance 1914- WhoAmW 93
Percy, Henry 1342-1408 HarEnMi
Percy, Herbert Roland 1920- WhoCanL 92
Percy, Hugh 1742-1817 HarEnMi
Percy, James G. BioIn 17
Percy, Judith Seifried 1959- WhoAmW 93
Percy, Rachel 1930- BioIn 17
Percy, Thomas 1729-1811 BioIn 17
Percy, Walker 1916-1990 AmWrS3, BioIn 17, MagSAmL [port], ScF&FL 92
Percy-Robb, Iain W. WhoScE 91-1
Perczynska-Partyka, Wieslawa 1924- WhoScE 91-4
Perdang, Jean Marcel 1940- WhoWor 93
Perdiccas c. 365BC-321BC HarEnMi
Perdijon, Jean 1937- WhoWor 93
Perdikatsis, Vassilis 1942- WhoScE 91-3
Perdok, W.D. WhoScE 91-3
Perdreau, Michel S. BioIn 17
Perdrizet, Simone M. 1922- WhoScE 91-2
Perdue, Beth A. Law&B 92
Perdue, Beverly M. 1948- WhoAmW 93
Perdue, Dale Carl Law&B 92
Perdue, Donna Olivia 1959- WhoAmW 93
Perdue, Frank BioIn 17
Perdue, Franklin P. WhoAm 92, WhoE 93
Perdue, Garland Day 1926- WhoAm 92
Perdue, Georgia Persinos 1938- WhoE 93
Perdue, James Everett 1916- WhoAm 92
Perdue, Judy Clark WhoSSW 93
Perdue, Lewis 1949- ScF&FL 92
Perdue, T. Ramon 1932- St&PR 93
Perdue, Theda 1949- WhoAmW 93, WhoEmL 93
Perdunn, Richard Francis 1915- WhoAm 92
Perduto, James Vincent 1928- St&PR 93
Perduyn, John P. 1939- St&PR 93
Perduyn, John Price 1939- WhoAm 92
Perdziola, Kathleen Stecewycz 1958- WhoEmL 93
Perea, Francisco 1830-1913 HispAmA
Perea, Pedro 1852-1906 HispAmA
Perec, Ann Marie 1964- WhoAmW 93
Perec, Georges 1936-1982 BioIn 17
Pereda, Antonio de c. 1599-c. 1678 BioIn 17
Peredo, Manuel 1830-1890 DcMexL
Peregoff, Lee Steven 1959- WhoSSW 93, WhoWor 93
Peregoy, Richard Pierce 1934- WhoSSW 93
Peregrine, David BioIn 17
Peregrine, Dennis Howell WhoScE 91-1
Peregrine, Dennis Howell 1938- WhoWor 93
Pereira, A. Sardinha WhoScE 91-3
Pereira, Albert J. 1950- St&PR 93
Pereira, Alcides Rodrigues WhoScE 91-3
Pereira, Anibal de Lima 1956- WhoWor 93
Pereira, Antonio Maria 1924- WhoWor 93
Pereira, Aristides Maria 1923- WhoWor 93
Pereira, Aristides Maria 1924- WhoAfr
Pereira, Carl W. 1939- St&PR 93
Pereira, Carol Merrick Turner 1963- WhoAmW 93
Pereira, David Jose Fonseca 1956- WhoWor 93
Pereira, Fernando J.M.A. 1942- WhoScE 91-3
Pereira, Francesca Jeanne 1961- WhoAmW 93
Pereira, John 1950- St&PR 93
Pereira, Jose Francisco 1935- WhoWor 93
Pereira, Kenneth John 1957- WhoE 93
Pereira, Licinio Chainho 1939- WhoScE 91-3
Pereira, Linda Christine 1966- WhoEmL 93
Pereira, M. WhoScE 91-3
Pereira, Maryann Hanley 1959- WhoAmW 93
Pereira, Paul J. 1946- St&PR 93
Pereira, Rodrigues WhoScE 91-3
Pereira, Teresinha Alves 1934- WhoWrEP 92
Pereira, Vasco 1535-1609 BioIn 17
Pereira, W.D. 1921- ScF&FL 92
Pereira da Silva 1937- WhoWor 93
Pereira-Leite, Margarida Maria Alvim 1960- WhoWor 93
Pereira Leite, Sergio 1946- WhoUN 92
Pereira-Salas, Eugenio 1904-1979 Baker 92
Perejon Rincon, Antonio WhoScE 91-3
Perel, James Maurice 1933- WhoE 93
Perella, Joseph Robert 1941- St&PR 93, WhoAm 92
Perella, Susanne Brennan 1936- WhoAm 92
Perelle, Ira B. 1925- WhoAm 92
Perellis, Florie Shertzer Law&B 92
Perello, Hope MiSFD 9
Perelman, David H. 1950- St&PR 93
Perelman, Jeffrey St&PR 93
Perelman, Leon Joseph 1911- St&PR 93, WhoAm 92, WhoE 93, WhoWor 93
Perelman, Lewis Law&B 92
Perelman, Melvin 1930- St&PR 93, WhoAm 92
Perelman, Ronald O. St&PR 93
Perelman, Ronald Owen 1943- BioIn 17, WhoAm 92
Perelman, S.J. 1904-1979 BioIn 17
Perelman, Sidney Joseph 1904-1979 BioIn 17
Perenchio, Andrew Jerrold 1930- WhoAm 92
Perepichka, Igor Fodorovich 1959- WhoWor 93
Perera, Chrisantha Priyange Richard 1944- WhoWor 93
Perera, George A. 1911- WhoAm 92
Perera, Kahawalage Cyril Walter 1946- WhoWor 93
Perera, Lawrence Thacher 1935- WhoAm 92, WhoWor 93
Perera, M. Anandana Lahiru 1956- WhoWor 93
Perera, Mudalige Ariyapala 1945- WhoWor 93
Perera, Phillips d1992 NewYTBS 92
Perera, Phillips 1933-1992 BioIn 17
Perera, Ronald (Christopher) 1941- Baker 92
Perera, Thomas B. 1938- WhoE 93
Perera, Thomas Biddle 1938- WhoWrEP 92
Perera, Uduwanage Dayaratna 1945- WhoWor 93
Peres, Gabriel 1920- WhoScE 91-2
Peres, Shimon 1923- BioIn 17, WhoWor 93
Peress, Gilles 1946- WhoAm 92
Peress, Maurice 1930- Baker 92, WhoAm 92
Peress, Mwafak S. 1937- St&PR 93
Peressini, Richard 1928- St&PR 93
Peressini, William E. 1956- St&PR 93
Peressini, William Edward 1956- WhoAm 92
Peresson, Sergio d1991 BioIn 17
Peret, Jean 1925- WhoScE 91-2
Peretti, E.A. James 1943- St&PR 93
Peretti, Elsa 1940- WhoAmW 93
Peretti, Frank E. BioIn 17
Peretti, Frank E. 1951- ConAu 136, ScF&FL 92
Peretti, Hugo 1918-1986 SoulM
Peretti, Linda Franzoni 1958- WhoSSW 93
Peretto, Pierre Louis 1938- WhoWor 93
Peretyatkin, Mikhail Georgievich 1949- WhoWor 93
Peretz, Isaac Leib 1851?-1915 BioIn 17, PolBiDi
Peretz, Martin BioIn 17
Perey, Bernard Jean Francois 1930- WhoAm 92
Perez, Alina 1957- WhoAmW 93
Perez, Anna BioIn 17, WhoAm 92, WhoAmW 93
Perez, Anna 1951- AfrAmBi
Perez, Atanasio Rigal 1942- BiDAMSp 1989
Perez, Atilano V. 1937- WhoSSW 93
Perez, Carlos BioIn 17
Perez, Carlos A. 1934- WhoAm 92
Perez, Carlos Andres 1922- WhoWor 93
Perez, David 1711-1778 Baker 92, OxDcOp
Perez, David Harry Law&B 92
Perez, David W. Law&B 92
Perez, Donald G. Law&B 92
Perez, Edith Denise 1967- WhoAmW 93
Perez, Eduardo BioIn 17
Perez, Enrique David 1934- St&PR 93
Perez, Ernest 1957- St&PR 93
Perez, Galo Rene 1923- WhoWor 93
Perez, George BioIn 17
Perez, Gerard A. d1991 BioIn 17
Perez, Ginger Sprinkle 1962- WhoEmL 93
Perez, Hector 1951- WhoSSW 93
Perez, Hernando B. 1939- WhoAsAP 91
Perez, J.M. 1937- WhoScE 91-2
Perez, Jeffrey Joseph 1952- WhoSSW 93
Perez, Jorge Luis 1945- WhoSSW 93
Perez, Jose Luis 1951- WhoWor 93
Perez, Jose Miguel 1928- WhoWor 93
Perez, Judith Ann 1961- WhoAmW 93
Perez, Julie Anna 1961- WhoAmW 93, WhoEmL 93
Perez, Kenneth A. 1946- St&PR 93
Perez, Kenneth Anthony Law&B 92
Perez, Leander H. 1891-1969 PolPar
Perez, Lester Moreno BioIn 17
Perez, Lillian 1957- WhoAmW 93
Perez, Louis Anthony 1939- WhoE 93
Perez, Louis Michael 1946- WhoSSW 93
Perez, Luz Lillian 1946- WhoAmW 93
Perez, Marie Antoinette 1950- WhoAm 92
Perez, Melido 1966- BioIn 17
Perez, Michael J. St&PR 93
Perez, Minerva 1955- HispAmA

Perez, Pascual *BioIn 17*
Perez, Paul Bonada 1946- *WhoE 93*
Perez, Peter Manuel 1940- *WhoAm 92*
Perez, Plinio *Law&B 92*
Perez, R. *WhoScE 91-2*
Perez, Ralph *Law&B 92*
Perez, Ramon *BioIn 17*
Perez, Raymundo 1946- *DcLB 122*
Perez, Reinaldo 1957- *WhoWor 93*
Perez, Rosalinda R. 1953- *WhoAmW 93*
Perez, Rose Helen *Law&B 92*
Perez, Rosie *BioIn 17, NotHsAW 93*
Perez, Ruben Dario *BioIn 17*
Perez, Rudy, Jr. 1929- *WhoSSW 93*
Perez, Valerio *BioIn 17*
Perez, Vladimir *BioIn 17*
Perez-Arriaga, Ignacio J. 1948- *WhoScE 91-3*
Perez Casas, Bartolomeo 1873-1956 *Baker 92*
Perez Castillo, Susan Parsons 1948- *WhoWor 93*
Perez-Castro, Enrique 1934- *WhoUN 92*
Perez-Comas, Adolfo 1941- *WhoSSW 93, WhoWor 93*
Perez-Cuadrado, Salomon 1932- *WhoScE 91-3*
Perez de Arce, Hermogenes 1936- *WhoWor 93*
Perez de Cuellar, Javier *BioIn 17*
Perez de Cuellar, Javier 1920- *DcTwHis, WhoUN 92, WhoWor 93*
Perez de Vega, Javier 1941- *WhoUN 92*
Perez Esquivel, Adolfo 1931- *WhoWor 93*
Perez-Estevez, Antonio 1933- *WhoWor 93*
Perez-Farfante, Isabel Cristina 1916- *HispAmA [port], WhoAmW 93*
Perez Ferreira, Emma Victoria 1925- *WhoWor 93*
Perez-Firmat, Gustavo 1949- *HispAmA*
Perez-Firmat, Gustavo Francisco 1950- *WhoAm 92*
Perez Gil Salazar, Eugenio 1923- *St&PR 93*
Perez-Gimenez, Juan M. 1941- *HispAmA*
Perez-Gimenez, Juan Manuel 1941- *WhoSSW 93*
Perez Magallon, Jesus 1952- *WhoWor 93*
Perez-Mendez, Victor 1923- *HispAmA, WhoAm 92*
Perez Moreno, Jose 1900- *DcMexL*
Perez-Ortin, Jose Enrique 1959- *WhoWor 93*
Perez Pujalte, Aureliano *WhoScE 91-3*
Perez Sanchez, Alfonso Emilio 1935- *WhoWor 93*
Perez Schael, Irene *WhoWor 93*
Perez-Spencer, Eloisa 1935- *WhoAmW 93*
Perez-Stable, Maria Adelaida 1954- *WhoAmW 93*
Perez-Taiman, Jorge A. *Law&B 92*
Perez-Valtier, Marco Antonio 1952- *WhoWor 93*
Perez Velasco, Jorge Francisco 1957- *WhoSSW 93*
Perez y Jorba, Jean 1930- *WhoScE 91-2*
Perez Zavala, Carlos Eduardo 1931- *WhoWor 93*
Perfall, Karl, Freiherr von 1824-1907 *Baker 92*
Perfect, Christine 1943- See Fleetwood, Mick 1942- *Baker 92*
Perfect, T.J. *WhoScE 91-1*
Perfetti, Charles A. 1940- *ConAu 139*
Perfetti, P. *WhoScE 91-3*
Perfetti, Peter James 1950- *St&PR 93*
Perfiliev, Vadim Paulovich 1940- *WhoUN 92*
Pergam, Albert Steven 1938- *WhoAm 92*
Pergamenshchikov, Sergei Markovich 1958- *WhoWor 93*
Pergament, Louis d1991 *BioIn 17*
Pergament, Moses 1893-1977 *Baker 92*
Pergander, Mary Sue 1955- *WhoAmW 93, WhoEmL 93*
Pergen, Johann Anton 1725-1814 *BioIn 17*
Perger, Richard von 1854-1911 *Baker 92*
Pergola, Carl V. 1942- *St&PR 93*
Pergola, Charles A. 1933- *St&PR 93*
Pergolesi, Giovanni Battista 1710-1736 *Baker 92, BioIn 17, IntDcOp [port], OxDcOp*
Pergolizzi, Nancy Connolly *Law&B 92*
Pergolizzi, Robert George 1950- *WhoE 93*
Perhach, James Lawrence 1943- *WhoAm 92, WhoE 93*
Perhacs, Leslie 1940- *BioIn 17*
Perhacs, Marylouise Helen 1944- *WhoAmW 93, WhoE 93, WhoWor 93*
Perham, R.N. *WhoScE 91-1*
Perham, Roy Gates 1916- *WhoE 93, WhoWor 93*
Perheentupa, Jaakko P. 1934- *WhoScE 91-4*
Perheentupa, Jaakko Pentti 1934- *WhoWor 93*
Peri, Claudio 1938- *WhoScE 91-3*
Peri, Gabriel 1902-1941 *BioIn 17*
Peri, Jacopo 1561-1633 *Baker 92, IntDcOp, OxDcOp*
Peri, John Bayard 1923- *WhoE 93*
Peric, Ilija 1942- *WhoScE 91-4*
Perich, Wesley Raymond 1951- *WhoE 93*
Pericic, Danka 1943- *WhoScE 91-4*
Pericic, Vlastimir 1927- *Baker 92*
Perick, Christof 1946- *Baker 92*
Pericles c. 495BC-429BC *HarEnMi*
Pericles 499BC-429BC *BioIn 17*
Perico, Angelo *WhoScE 91-3*
Pericola, Julius Louis 1929- *St&PR 93*
Perie, Jacques 1939- *WhoScE 91-2*
Perience, Lotta X. *AmWomPl*
Perier, Etienne *MiSFD 9*
Perier, Francois 1919- *WhoWor 93*
Perier, Jean 1869-1954 *OxDcOp*
Perier, Jean (Alexis) 1869-1954 *Baker 92*
Perier, Jean Paul Pierre Casimir- 1847-1907 *BioIn 17*
Peries, Jorge 1928- *WhoScE 91-2*
Perigard, A.W. d1990 *BioIn 17*
Perignon, Dominique Catherine, Marquis of 1754-1818 *HarEnMi*
Perigyi, Jo-Ann Katherine 1953- *WhoEmL 93*
Perikly, Michael P. 1951- *St&PR 93*
Perillo, Frank Robert *Law&B 92*
Perilman, Nathan A. 1905-1991 *BioIn 17*
Perilstein, William 1933- *St&PR 93*
Periman, Larry E. 1939- *St&PR 93*
Perin, Antonio 1930- *WhoScE 91-3*
Perin, Donald Wise, Jr. 1915- *WhoAm 92*
Perin, Jacques 1932- *WhoScE 91-2*
Perin, Reuben L., Jr. 1938- *St&PR 93*
Perin, Robert Jean 1947- *WhoE 93*
Perine, Donna Lee 1955- *WhoAmW 93*
Perine, Martha L. 1948- *St&PR 93*
Perine, Martha Levingston 1948- *WhoAmW 93*
Perine, Maxine Harriet 1918- *WhoWor 93*
Peringer, Paul 1941- *WhoScE 91-4*
Perini, David B. 1937- *St&PR 93, WhoE 93*
Perini, Joseph R. 1930- *WhoAm 92*
Perini, Kimberly S. *Law&B 92*
Periolat, John Redmond *Law&B 92*
Periquet, Georges 1945- *WhoScE 91-2*
Peri Rossi, Cristina 1941- *BioIn 17, SpAmA*
Peris, Salvador V. 1922- *WhoScE 91-3*
Perisic, Vera 1923- *WhoScE 91-4*
Perisic, Zoran 1940- *MiSFD 9*
Perissin, Aldo Arrigo 1938- *WhoWor 93*
Peristiany, Jean George 1911-1987 *IntDcAn*
Perisutti, Stephen Joseph *Law&B 92*
Peritsky, Martin Michael 1946- *St&PR 93*
Peritz, Abraham D. 1940- *St&PR 93*
Peritz, Abraham Daniel 1940- *WhoAm 92*
Peritz, Richard Curt 1947- *WhoSSW 93*
Perivier, Jean-Claude 1946- *WhoWor 93*
Perju, Dan 1935- *WhoScE 91-4*
Perkampus, Heinz-Helmut 1925- *WhoScE 91-3*
Perkel, Robert Simon 1925- *WhoSSW 93*
Perkin, Frank S. *Law&B 92*
Perkins, A. William 1925- *WhoAm 92*
Perkins, Annie Stetson *AmWomPl*
Perkins, Anthony *BioIn 17*
Perkins, Anthony 1932- *IntDcF 2-3 [port], MiSFD 9, WhoAm 92*
Perkins, Anthony 1932-1992 *CurBio 92N, NewYTBS 92 [port], News 93-2*
Perkins, Arthur Burke 1954- *WhoE 93*
Perkins, B. Webster 1933- *St&PR 93*
Perkins, Benjamin Paul, Sr. 1934- *WhoSSW 93*
Perkins, Beverly 1937- *WhoAmW 93*
Perkins, Bill J. 1943- *WhoE 93*
Perkins, Bobby Frank 1929- *WhoAm 92*
Perkins, Bradford 1925- *WhoAm 92*
Perkins, Brenda Peters 1955- *WhoAmW 93*
Perkins, Carl 1932- *Baker 92, BioIn 17, ConMus 9 [port]*
Perkins, Carl C. 1954- *CngDr 91*
Perkins, Carl Christopher 1954- *WhoAm 92*
Perkins, Carl Christopher Chris 1954- *WhoSSW 93*
Perkins, Carroll M. 1929- *St&PR 93*
Perkins, Carroll Mason 1929- *WhoAm 92*
Perkins, David Dexter 1919- *WhoAm 92*
Perkins, David Layne, Sr. 1925- *WhoAm 92*
Perkins, David Mark 1958- *WhoSSW 93*
Perkins, David Miles 1949- *St&PR 93*
Perkins, Deborah Anne 1954- *WhoAmW 93, WhoEmL 93*
Perkins, Dennis Edward 1944- *St&PR 93*
Perkins, Donald A. 1929- *St&PR 93*
Perkins, Donald H. *WhoScE 91-1*
Perkins, Donald S. 1927- *St&PR 93*
Perkins, Donald Young 1923- *WhoSSW 93*
Perkins, Dorothy A. 1926- *WhoAm 92, WhoAmW 93*
Perkins, Douglas Merrill 1962- *WhoSSW 93*
Perkins, Dwight Heald 1934- *WhoAm 92*
Perkins, E. Lawrence 1927- *St&PR 93*
Perkins, Edward A. 1928- *WhoAm 92*
Perkins, Edward J. 1928- *WhoAm 92*
Perkins, Edwin Arend 1953- *WhoAm 92*
Perkins, Eleanor Ellis 1893- *AmWomPl*
Perkins, Elizabeth *BioIn 17*
Perkins, Elizabeth A. *AmWomPl*
Perkins, Elizabeth Ann 1960- *WhoAm 92*
Perkins, Elizabeth Chaffee *Law&B 92*
Perkins, Evelyn M. *AmWomPl*
Perkins, Faelton C., Jr. 1920- *St&PR 93*
Perkins, Frances 1882-1965 *BioIn 17, DcTwHis, PolPar*
Perkins, Frank Overton 1938- *WhoAm 92*
Perkins, Frederick Myers 1928- *WhoAm 92*
Perkins, G. Frederick 1936- *St&PR 93*
Perkins, George Frederick, Jr. 1936- *WhoAm 92*
Perkins, George Holmes 1904- *WhoAm 92*
Perkins, George William, II 1926- *WhoAm 92*
Perkins, Gordon P. 1937- *St&PR 93*
Perkins, Happy R. *Law&B 92*
Perkins, Henry S(outhwick) 1833-1914 *Baker 92*
Perkins, Herbert Asa 1918- *WhoAm 92*
Perkins, Homer G. 1916- *St&PR 93*
Perkins, Homer Guy 1916- *WhoAm 92*
Perkins, J.D. *WhoScE 91-1*
Perkins, Jack Edwin 1943- *WhoAm 92*
Perkins, James Alfred 1911- *WhoAm 92*
Perkins, James Ashbrook 1941- *WhoWrEP 92*
Perkins, James Eliab 1905-1990 *BioIn 17*
Perkins, James Francis 1924- *WhoSSW 93, WhoWor 93*
Perkins, James Lewis 1942- *St&PR 93*
Perkins, James O. 1940- *WhoIns 93*
Perkins, James Patrick 1939- *WhoAm 92*
Perkins, James Winslow 1955- *WhoE 93*
Perkins, James Wood 1924- *WhoAm 92*
Perkins, Jennifer Elizabeth *Law&B 92*
Perkins, John Allen 1919- *WhoAm 92*
Perkins, John MacIvor 1935- *Baker 92*
Perkins, John P. 1948- *St&PR 93*
Perkins, Judith L. *Law&B 92*
Perkins, Julie Anne Rate 1935- *WhoAmW 93*
Perkins, Karon Elaine 1959- *WhoEmL 93*
Perkins, Ken 1926- *ConAu 137*
Perkins, Kimora *BioIn 17*
Perkins, Laures T. *St&PR 93*
Perkins, Lawrence Leonard 1918- *St&PR 93*
Perkins, Leigh H. *NewYTBS 92 [port]*
Perkins, Leonard F. *Law&B 92*
Perkins, Louise Saunders *AmWomPl*
Perkins, Lucy Fitch 1865-1937 *ConAu 137, MajAI, SmATA 72 [port]*
Perkins, Malcolm Donald 1914- *WhoAm 92*
Perkins, Marvin Earl 1920- *WhoAm 92, WhoWor 93*
Perkins, Matthew R. d1990 *BioIn 17*
Perkins, Max, Mrs. *AmWomPl*
Perkins, Maxwell E. 1884-1947 *BioIn 17*
Perkins, Merle Lester 1919- *WhoAm 92, WhoWrEP 92*
Perkins, Michael 1942- *WhoWrEP 92*
Perkins, Michael John *WhoScE 91-1*
Perkins, Nancy Jane 1949- *WhoAmW 93, WhoEmL 93, WhoWor 93*
Perkins, Osgood 1892-1937 *BioIn 17*
Perkins, Paul Bouthillier 1961- *WhoWor 93*
Perkins, Paul Thomas 1939- *St&PR 93*
Perkins, Paula Michelle 1955- *WhoEmL 93*
Perkins, Peter 1930- *St&PR 93*
Perkins, Ralph Barron *Law&B 92*
Perkins, Ralph Linwood 1914- *WhoAm 92*
Perkins, Ray 1941- *WhoAm 92*
Perkins, Richard John 1936- *WhoUN 92*
Perkins, Robert Arthur, Jr. 1952- *WhoSSW 93*
Perkins, Robert Louis 1931- *WhoAm 92*
Perkins, Roger Allan 1943- *WhoE 93*
Perkins, Ronald Dee 1935- *WhoAm 92*
Perkins, Roswell Burchard 1926- *WhoAm 92*
Perkins, Sam *BioIn 17*
Perkins, Sam G. 1931- *St&PR 93*
Perkins, Sheldon *ScF&FL 92*
Perkins, Sophie Huth *AmWomPl*
Perkins, Stephanie S. *Law&B 92*
Perkins, Thomas Cole 1933- *WhoE 93, WhoIns 93*
Perkins, Thomas E. 1925- *St&PR 93*
Perkins, Thomas Keeble 1932- *WhoAm 92*
Perkins, Van L. 1930- *WhoAm 92*
Perkins, Victoria Marie 1942- *WhoAmW 93*
Perkins, (David) Walton 1847-1929 *Baker 92*
Perkins, Whitney Trow 1921- *WhoAm 92*
Perkins, William Allan, Jr. 1925- *WhoAm 92*
Perkins, William Frederick 1939- *WhoSSW 93*
Perkins, William H., Jr. 1921- *WhoAm 92*
Perkins, William Horace, Jr. 1931- *St&PR 93*
Perkins, William Hughes 1923- *WhoAm 92*
Perkins, William (Oscar) 1831-1902 *Baker 92*
Perkins, William Randolph 1934- *WhoAm 92*
Perkins, Winston E. 1935- *WhoIns 93*
Perkinson, Diana Agnes Zouzelka 1943- *WhoAm 92*
Perkinson, Henry 1930- *WhoE 93*
Perkinson, James Edward 1956- *St&PR 93*
Perkiss, Lewis *Law&B 92*
Perko, Bostjan G. 1956- *WhoScE 91-4*
Perko, Kenneth A., Jr. *Law&B 92*
Perko, Kenneth Albert, Jr. 1943- *WhoE 93*
Perko, Margaret Ruth 1915- *WhoWrEP 92*
Perkoff, Gerald Thomas 1926- *WhoAm 92*
Perkovic, Robert Branko 1925- *WhoAm 92*
Perkowitz, Robert M. 1954- *St&PR 93*
Perkowitz, Sidney 1939- *WhoAm 92, WhoSSW 93*
Perkowska, Malgorzata 1944- *WhoScE 91-4*
Perkowski, Jan 1946- *WhoScE 91-4*
Perkowski, Piotr 1901-1990 *Baker 92*
Perkowski, Ronald K. *Law&B 92*
Perks, D.A. *WhoScE 91-1*
Perks, Marcia Kay 1949- *St&PR 93*
Perks, Mary Edna Wilkins 1940- *WhoSSW 93*
Perl, Emily Jane 1965- *WhoAmW 93*
Perl, Jeffrey M(ichael) 1952- *ConAu 138*
Perl, Jeffrey Michael 1952- *WhoSSW 93*
Perl, Lila *ScF&FL 92, SmATA 72 [port]*
Perl, Martin Lewis 1927- *WhoAm 92*
Perlasca, Giorgio d1992 *NewYTBS 92*
Perlberg, Fred d1991 *BioIn 17*
Perlberg, Jules Martin 1931- *WhoAm 92*
Perlberg, William 1933- *St&PR 93*
Perle, Elizabeth *BioIn 17*
Perle, Eugene Gabriel 1922- *WhoAm 92*
Perle, George 1915- *Baker 92, BioIn 17, WhoAm 92*
Perle, Richard 1941- *ColdWar 1 [port]*
Perle, Richard Norman 1941- *WhoAm 92*
Perlea, Jonel 1900-1970 *Baker 92, OxDcOp*
Perleman, Leslie Cooper 1948- *WhoE 93*
Perlemuter, Vlado 1904- *Baker 92*
Perlen, Arthur Harold 1959- *WhoSSW 93*
Perler, Dennis Scott 1946- *WhoAm 92*
Perles, Julia 1914- *WhoAmW 93*
Perless, Ellen 1941- *WhoAm 92*
Perless, Robert L. 1938- *WhoAm 92, WhoE 93*
Perley, John Stephen 1937- *St&PR 93*
Perley, Moses Henry 1804-1862 *BioIn 17*
Perlik, William R. 1925- *WhoAm 92*
Perlin, Arthur Saul 1923- *WhoAm 92*
Perlin, Gary Laurence 1951- *St&PR 93*
Perlin, Marc *Law&B 92*
Perlin, Michael Louis 1946- *WhoE 93*
Perlin, Ruth Rudolph 1936- *WhoE 93*
Perlin, Seymour 1925- *WhoAm 92*
Perlis, Alan J. 1922-1990 *BioIn 17*
Perlis, Donald M. 1941- *WhoAm 92*
Perlis, Michael *NewYTBS 92 [port]*
Perlis, Michael Fredrick 1947- *WhoAm 92, WhoWor 93*
Perlis, Michael S. 1953- *St&PR 93*
Perlis, Michael Steven 1953- *WhoAm 92*
Perlish, Harvey Neil 1921- *WhoE 93*
Perlman, Barry Stuart 1939- *WhoAm 92*
Perlman, Bruce Michael *Law&B 92*
Perlman, Daniel Hessel 1935- *WhoAm 92*
Perlman, David 1918- *WhoAm 92*
Perlman, David 1920- *WhoAm 92*
Perlman, David B. *Law&B 92*
Perlman, David B. 1954- *St&PR 93*
Perlman, David Mitchell *Law&B 92*
Perlman, Dory *ScF&FL 92*
Perlman, Eric *BioIn 17*
Perlman, Henry B. 1901-1991 *BioIn 17*
Perlman, I. Lee 1930- *St&PR 93*
Perlman, Isador 1915-1991 *BioIn 17*
Perlman, Itzhak 1945- *Baker 92, WhoAm 92, WhoE 93, WhoWor 93*
Perlman, Janet *WhoAmW 93*
Perlman, Jerald Lee 1947- *WhoEmL 93*
Perlman, John Niels 1946- *WhoWrEP 92*
Perlman, John Richard 1956- *WhoSSW 93*
Perlman, Laura Saskin *Law&B 92*
Perlman, Lawrence 1938- *St&PR 93, WhoAm 92*

Perlman, Leonard G. 1932- *WhoAm 92*
Perlman, Mark *BioIn 17*
Perlman, Mark 1923- *WhoAm 92, WhoE 93, WhoWrEP 92*
Perlman, Matthew Saul 1936- *WhoAm 92*
Perlman, Michael Ellis 1954- *WhoSSW 93*
Perlman, Phil *BioIn 17*
Perlman, Philip 1927- *St&PR 93*
Perlman, Rhea *BioIn 17, WhoAm 92, WhoAmW 93*
Perlman, Richard Wilfred 1923- *WhoAm 92*
Perlman, Robert S. *Law&B 92*
Perlman, Sandra Lee 1944- *WhoAmW 93*
Perlman, Scott David 1957- *St&PR 93*
Perlman, Selig 1888-1959 *BioIn 17*
Perlman, Stephen Earl 1943- *WhoSSW 93*
Perlman, Steven Mark 1953- *St&PR 93*
Perlman, Susan Gail 1950- *WhoWrEP 92*
Perlmeter, Rosemary C. *Law&B 92*
Perlmuter, Ernest A. 1914- *St&PR 93*
Perlmuth, William Alan 1929- *WhoAm 92*
Perlmutter, Alvin Howard 1928- *WhoAm 92*
Perlmutter, Arnold 1928- *WhoSSW 93*
Perlmutter, Arthur 1930- *WhoE 93*
Perlmutter, Barbara 1936- *WhoAmW 93*
Perlmutter, Barbara S. 1941- *St&PR 93, WhoAmW 93, WhoE 93*
Perlmutter, Barry Arthur 1954- *WhoSSW 93*
Perlmutter, Diane F. 1945- *WhoAm 92, WhoAmW 93, WhoE 93, WhoWor 93*
Perlmutter, Donna *WhoAm 92, WhoAmW 93*
Perlmutter, Jack 1920- *WhoAm 92, WhoE 93*
Perlmutter, Jerome A. *Law&B 92*
Perlmutter, Jerome Herbert 1924- *WhoAm 92, WhoWrEP 92*
Perlmutter, Louis 1934- *WhoAm 92*
Perlmutter, Marion 1948- *WhoEmL 93*
Perlmutter, Martin Lee 1947- *WhoWor 93*
Perlmutter, Nathan Martin 1947- *WhoE 93*
Perlmutter, Nina *Law&B 92*
Perlmutter, Philip 1925- *WhoWrEP 92*
Perlmutter, William 1920-1975 *ScF&FL 92*
Perloff, Joseph Kayle 1924- *WhoAm 92*
Perloff, Marjorie Gabrielle 1931- *WhoAm 92*
Perloff, Robert 1921- *WhoAm 92, WhoWor 93*
Perlongo, Daniel 1942- *Baker 92*
Perlongo, Daniel James 1942- *WhoAm 92*
Perlov, Alexander Keever 1933- *WhoE 93*
Perlov, Dadie 1929- *WhoAm 92*
Perlow, Ari 1951- *St&PR 93*
Perlow, Paul *Law&B 92*
Perlowitz, Valerie Wienslaw 1962- *WhoAmW 93, WhoEmL 93*
Perls, Klaus Gunther 1912- *WhoAm 92*
Perls, Laura 1905-1990 *BioIn 17*
Perlstadt, Sidney Morris 1907- *WhoAm 92*
Perman, Norman Wilford 1928- *WhoAm 92*
Permanand, Rabindranath J. 1935- *WhoUN 92*
Permison, William Stephen *WhoE 93*
Permut, Susan I. *Law&B 92*
Permutt, Solbert 1925- *WhoAm 92*
Perna, Lance E. *Law&B 92*
Perna, Nicholas S. 1942- *St&PR 93*
Perna, Thomas Joseph 1950- *St&PR 93*
Pernai, Cheryl Kozerski 1959- *WhoAmW 93*
Pernal, Michael Edward 1943- *WhoE 93*
Perne, Francois Louis 1772-1832 *Baker 92*
Pernes, Jean *WhoScE 91-2*
Pernet, Andre 1894-1966 *Baker 92, OxDcOp*
Pernetta, John Christopher 1947- *WhoScE 91-1*
Pernetti, Robyn Marie 1964- *WhoE 93*
Pernick, Alan S. 1936- *St&PR 93*
Pernick, Leonard Jacob 1929- *St&PR 93*
Pernicone, Nicola 1935- *WhoWor 93*
Pernier, Jacques *WhoScE 91-2*
Pernkopf, Josef 1940- *WhoScE 91-4*
Pernoll, Martin Lester 1939- *WhoWrEP 92*
Pernollet, Jean-Claude 1946- *WhoScE 91-2*
Pernotto, Stephen John 1947- *St&PR 93*
Pernow, Bengt 1924- *WhoScE 91-4*
Pernyeszi, Jozsef *WhoScE 91-4*
Pero, Joseph John 1939- *St&PR 93, WhoAm 92, WhoIns 93*
Pero, Michael Andrew 1941- *WhoIns 93*
Perombelon, Michel Marie Clement 1934- *WhoWor 93*
Peron, Eva 1919-1952 *BioIn 17, DcTwHis*
Peron, Juan 1895-1974 *DcTwHis*
Peron, Juan Domingo 1895-1974 *BioIn 17*
Peronard, Guy 1942- *St&PR 93*
Perone, Al Charles 1933- *St&PR 93*
Peronneau, P. *WhoScE 91-2*
Peros, Vasilios 1961- *WhoE 93*
Perosch, Tony Anthony George 1930- *WhoWor 93*
Perosi, Lorenzo 1872-1956 *Baker 92*
Perot, H. Ross 1930- *NewYTBS 92 [port], News 92 [port], WhoAm 92, WhoSSW 93*
Perot, H. Ross, Jr. *WhoSSW 93*
Perot, Margot *BioIn 17*
Perot, Ross 1930- *BioIn 17*
Perotin fl. 12th cent.- *Baker 92*
Perotinus Magnus fl. 12th cent.- *Baker 92*
Perotti, Rose Norma *Law&B 92*
Perotto, Richard 1941- *St&PR 93*
Perovic, Bozidar 1923- *WhoScE 91-4*
Perovic, Jovan 1931- *WhoScE 91-4*
Perper, Karen Eileen *Law&B 92*
Perperna Veiento, Marcus d72BC *HarEnMi*
Perpich, Joseph George 1941- *WhoE 93*
Perpich, William M. 1937- *St&PR 93*
Perquel, Jean-Jacques 1931- *WhoWor 93*
Perr, Irwin 1928- *WhoAm 92*
Perr, Julius P. 1931- *St&PR 93*
Perram, John W. 1945- *WhoScE 91-2*
Perranoski, Ronald Peter 1936- *BiDAMSp 1989*
Perrault, Charles 1628-1703 *MajAI [port], OxDcOp*
Perrault, Georges Gabriel 1934- *WhoWor 93*
Perrault, Guy 1927- *WhoAm 92*
Perrault, Jacques Champlain 1903-1988 *BioIn 17*
Perrault, Michel (Brunet) 1925- *Baker 92*
Perrault, Paul A. 1951- *St&PR 93*
Perrault, Paul T. 1939- *WhoWor 93*
Perrault, Raymond 1926- *WhoAm 92*
Perreault, Jeanne 1929- *WhoAm 92, WhoAmW 93*
Perreault, Laura Cecile 1925- *WhoAmW 93*
Perreault, Mark D. *Law&B 92*
Perreault, Paul Frederick 1929- *St&PR 93*
Perreault, William Daniel, Jr. 1948- *WhoAm 92*
Perreiah, Alan Richard 1937- *WhoAm 92*
Perrell, Helen 1904- *BioIn 17*
Perrella, Donald J. *Law&B 92*
Perrella, James Elbert 1935- *St&PR 93, WhoAm 92*
Perrenoud, Barbara M. 1933- *St&PR 93*
Perrenoud, Jean Jacques 1947- *WhoWor 93*
Perret, Francois P. *Law&B 92*
Perret, Gerard Anthony, Jr. 1959- *WhoSSW 93*
Perret, Joseph A. 1929- *St&PR 93*
Perret, Joseph Aloysius 1929- *WhoAm 92*
Perret, Patti 1955- *ScF&FL 92*
Perret, Peter James 1941- *WhoAm 92*
Perret, Remi 1944- *WhoScE 91-2*
Perreten, Frank Arnold 1927- *WhoWor 93*
Perrett, Donna Sharon Bridges 1952- *WhoSSW 93*
Perrett, Keith W. *Law&B 92*
Perri, Carol Sue 1946- *WhoWrEP 92*
Perri, Dan *MiSFD 9*
Perri, Flavio Miragaia 1940- *WhoUN 92*
Perri, Joseph 1949- *St&PR 93*
Perriam, Wendy 1940- *ConAu 136*
Perriaux, Jacques 1925- *WhoScE 91-2*
Perrich, Jerry Robert 1947- *WhoAm 92*
Perricone, Bernard 1929-1990 *BioIn 17*
Perriello, David G. 1939- *St&PR 93*
Perrier, Xavier 1952- *WhoScE 91-2*
Perrin, Carl Richard 1930- *WhoE 93*
Perrin, Charles Robert 1915- *WhoE 93*
Perrin, Donald William 1947- *St&PR 93*
Perrin, Edward Burton 1931- *WhoAm 92*
Perrin, Emile-Cesar-Victor 1814-1885 *OxDcOp*
Perrin, Gail 1938- *ConAu 136, WhoAm 92*
Perrin, George M. *St&PR 93*
Perrin, Jack 1896-1967 *BioIn 17*
Perrin, James 1930- *WhoAm 92*
Perrin, Jane Frances 1940- *WhoAmW 93, WhoE 93*
Perrin, Jean Edmond 1921- *WhoScE 91-2*
Perrin, John Paul 1943- *WhoAm 92*
Perrin, John Robin 1930- *WhoAm 92*
Perrin, Kenneth Lynn 1937- *WhoE 93*
Perrin, Mark Nicholas *Law&B 92*
Perrin, Michel 1941- *WhoScE 91-2*
Perrin, Noel 1927- *WhoAm 92*
Perrin, Pat *ScF&FL 92*
Perrin, Pierre c. 1620-1675 *Baker 92, OxDcOp*
Perrin, Robert 1925- *WhoAm 92*
Perrin, Robert Maitland *Law&B 92*
Perrin, Robert Maitland 1950- *St&PR 93, WhoAm 92*
Perrin, Roy Albert, Jr. 1940- *WhoSSW 93*
Perrin, Sarah Ann 1904- *WhoAmW 93, WhoSSW 93, WhoWor 93*
Perrin, Steve *ScF&FL 92*
Perrine, Amos William *Law&B 92*
Perrine, Laurence 1915- *WhoWrEP 92*
Perrine, Richard Leroy 1924- *WhoAm 92*
Perrine, Serge 1959- *WhoWor 93*
Perrine, Valerie 1943- *WhoAm 92*
Perrine, William Chadwick *Law&B 92*
Perrine, William Everett 1933- *St&PR 93, WhoAm 92*
Perrine, William W. *St&PR 93*
Perrino, Albert Carl 1934- *St&PR 93*
Perrino, P. *WhoScE 91-3*
Perrins, C.M. *WhoScE 91-1*
Perris, Carlo 1928- *WhoScE 91-4*
Perris, Elizabeth L. 1951- *WhoAmW 93*
Perris, Terrence George 1947- *WhoAm 92*
Perriton, Alan G. *BioIn 17*
Perrochet, Jean-F. 1942- *WhoScE 91-4*
Perron, Bill *BioIn 17*
Perron, Claude 1959- *St&PR 93*
Perron, Eric 1950- *St&PR 93*
Perron, Gail Diane *WhoAmW 93*
Perron, Jacques R. *Law&B 92*
Perron, Jean 1946- *WhoAm 92*
Perron, Karl 1858-1928 *Baker 92, OxDcOp*
Perron, Marshall Bruce 1942- *WhoAsAP 91*
Perron, Michael 1932- *St&PR 93*
Perron, Pierre O. 1939- *WhoAm 92*
Perron, Roger 1926- *WhoScE 91-2*
Perrone, Frank Anthony *Law&B 92*
Perrone, Hector 1913-1991 *BioIn 17*
Perrone, Jerome Frank 1938- *St&PR 93*
Perrone, Joanne Frances 1943- *WhoAmW 93*
Perrone, Nicholas 1930- *WhoAm 92*
Perrone, Paul E. 1942- *St&PR 93*
Perrone, Robert W. 1929- *St&PR 93*
Perrone, Ronald David 1949- *WhoE 93*
Perros, Theodore Peter 1921- *WhoAm 92*
Perrot, Raoul Jean-Louis 1937- *WhoScE 91-2*
Perrott, John (R.) 1932- *ConAu 139*
Perrott, Ronald Henry *WhoScE 91-1*
Perrotta, Fioravante Gerald 1931- *WhoAm 92, WhoE 93*
Perrotta, Janna Marie 1965- *WhoAmW 93*
Perrotta, Robert John 1947- *St&PR 93*
Perrottet, Charles Michael 1944- *WhoE 93*
Perrotti, Joseph 1913- *St&PR 93*
Perrotti, Miguel Fernando Ribeiro 1964- *WhoWor 93*
Perroux, Francois 1903-1987 *BioIn 17*
Perrucci, Robert 1931- *WhoAm 92*
Perry, Alan Stoddard 1923- *St&PR 93*
Perry, Alexa Marie *Law&B 92*
Perry, Amy 1965- *WhoE 93*
Perry, Andre 1937- *WhoWor 93*
Perry, Ann *Law&B 92*
Perry, Ann Cristina 1952- *WhoSSW 93*
Perry, Anthony John 1919- *WhoAm 92*
Perry, Beth 1928- *WhoWrEP 92*
Perry, Betty Cotten 1950- *WhoSSW 93*
Perry, Billy Dwight 1933- *WhoAm 92*
Perry, Bradford Kent 1942- *WhoE 93*
Perry, Bradley Wilbur 1938- *WhoAm 92*
Perry, Brenda L. 1948- *WhoAmW 93*
Perry, Brian M. 1959- *St&PR 93*
Perry, Carlita Mia 1968- *WhoSSW 93*
Perry, Carrie Saxon *AfrAmBi, WhoAmW 93*
Perry, Catherine Eason 1946- *WhoAmW 93*
Perry, Charles E. 1932- *WhoWrEP 92*
Perry, Charles E. 1937- *WhoAm 92*
Perry, Charles Lynam 1937- *WhoUN 92*
Perry, Charles Norvin 1928- *WhoE 93*
Perry, Charles Owen 1929- *WhoAm 92, WhoE 93*
Perry, Chris Nicholas 1945- *WhoAm 92*
Perry, Christopher Richard 1932- *WhoWor 93*
Perry, Craig Crane 1948- *WhoAm 92*
Perry, Cynthia Norton Shepard 1928- *WhoAmW 93*
Perry, Dale Lynn 1947- *WhoAm 92, WhoEmL 93*
Perry, Dale M. 1946- *St&PR 93*
Perry, Daniel R. 1947- *St&PR 93*
Perry, David d1991 *BioIn 17*
Perry, David A. *St&PR 93*
Perry, David Lewis *Law&B 92*
Perry, David Lewis 1940- *St&PR 93, WhoAm 92*
Perry, Donald A. 1938- *WhoAm 92*
Perry, Dorothy Ann 1957- *WhoAmW 93*
Perry, Douglas *WhoAm 92*
Perry, Douglas S. *Law&B 92*
Perry, Dunman, Jr. 1926- *St&PR 93*
Perry, Edmund Payne *Law&B 92*
Perry, Edward Baxter 1855-1924 *Baker 92*
Perry, Edward Samuel 1937- *WhoE 93*
Perry, Edward Stanley 1942- *WhoE 93*
Perry, Edward T. *Law&B 92*
Perry, Elaine 1959- *BioIn 17*
Perry, Erma Jackson McNeil *WhoAm 92*
Perry, Ernie Wayne 1957- *WhoSSW 93*
Perry, Eston Lee 1936- *WhoAm 92*
Perry, Frances *AmWomPl*
Perry, Frank 1930- *MiSFD 9, WhoAm 92*
Perry, Fred *BioIn 17*
Perry, Frederick V. *Law&B 92*
Perry, Gaylord Jackson 1938- *WhoAm 92*
Perry, George Edward, Jr. 1936- *WhoAm 92*
Perry, George Frederick 1793-1862 *Baker 92*
Perry, George Lewis 1934- *WhoAm 92*
Perry, George Wilson 1929- *WhoSSW 93*
Perry, Glen Howard 1942- *St&PR 93*
Perry, Guy LaVerde 1905- *St&PR 93*
Perry, Harold *BioIn 17*
Perry, Harold A. c. 1917-1991 *News 92*
Perry, Harold Otto 1921- *WhoAm 92*
Perry, Harold Treston 1924- *WhoSSW 93*
Perry, Harold Tyner 1926- *WhoWor 93*
Perry, Harry Montford 1943- *WhoSSW 93*
Perry, Hart 1918-1991 *BioIn 17*
Perry, Harvey *Law&B 92*
Perry, Harvey Chace 1949- *St&PR 93*
Perry, Harvey Parnell *Law&B 92*
Perry, Harvey Parnell 1944- *St&PR 93*
Perry, Helen 1927- *WhoSSW 93*
Perry, Helen Frances *St&PR 93*
Perry, Helen Sage 1954- *WhoAmW 93*
Perry, Heman Edward 1873-1929 *BioIn 17*
Perry, J. Warren 1921- *WhoAm 92, WhoE 93*
Perry, Jack Richard 1945- *St&PR 93*
Perry, Jacquelin 1918- *WhoAm 92, WhoAmW 93*
Perry, James A. 1932- *St&PR 93*
Perry, James Benn 1950- *WhoAm 92*
Perry, James DeWolf 1941- *WhoE 93*
Perry, James F. *Law&B 92*
Perry, James Frederic 1936- *WhoSSW 93*
Perry, James Lee 1935- *WhoSSW 93*
Perry, James Martin 1953- *St&PR 93*
Perry, James Michael 1960- *WhoE 93*
Perry, James Nelson 1932- *St&PR 93*
Perry, Janet 1944- *Baker 92*
Perry, Janet Estelle 1953- *WhoAmW 93, WhoE 93*
Perry, Jean Louise 1950- *WhoAmW 93*
Perry, Joe 1927- *BioIn 17*
Perry, John Baldwin 1961- *WhoE 93*
Perry, John Curtis 1930- *WhoE 93*
Perry, John Grenville *WhoScE 91-1*
Perry, John Richard 1943- *WhoAm 92*
Perry, John Van Buren 1928- *WhoWor 93*
Perry, Joseph Nelson *WhoScE 91-1*
Perry, Joseph Quenton, Jr. 1942- *WhoE 93*
Perry, Joy Ann *Law&B 92*
Perry, Joy Sutton 1941- *WhoE 93*
Perry, Julia (Amanda) 1924-1979 *Baker 92*
Perry, Julia Kay 1960- *WhoEmL 93*
Perry, Karen J. *Law&B 92*
Perry, Kathryn Ann Harvey 1953- *WhoE 93*
Perry, Kathryn M. 1927- *St&PR 93*
Perry, Kathy R. *Law&B 92*
Perry, Kenneth E. 1920- *St&PR 93*
Perry, Kenneth Moore 1932- *St&PR 93, WhoSSW 93*
Perry, Kenneth Walter 1932- *WhoAm 92*
Perry, Kenneth Wilbur 1919- *WhoAm 92*
Perry, Kimberly Jean 1955- *WhoEmL 93*
Perry, L. Tom *WhoAm 92*
Perry, Landsford Wilder 1955- *St&PR 93*
Perry, Lee Rowan 1933- *WhoAm 92, WhoWor 93*
Perry, Leslie Blair 1942- *WhoE 93*
Perry, Lewis Charles 1931- *WhoSSW 93*
Perry, Lewis Curtis 1938- *WhoAm 92*
Perry, Lincoln *BioIn 17*
Perry, Lincoln Frederick 1949- *WhoE 93*
Perry, Linda Sternaman 1950- *WhoAmW 93*
Perry, Lois Wanda 1937- *WhoAmW 93*
Perry, Lon *BioIn 17*
Perry, Louis B. 1918- *St&PR 93*
Perry, Louis Barnes 1918- *WhoAm 92*
Perry, Louise Sublette 1901- *AmWomPl*
Perry, Lucia *AmWomPl*
Perry, Luke *BioIn 17*
Perry, Luke c. 1966- *News 92 [port], -92-3 [port]*
Perry, M. Sheryl 1931- *WhoSSW 93*
Perry, Malcolm Blythe 1930- *WhoAm 92*
Perry, Malcolm Oliver 1929- *WhoAm 92*
Perry, Margaret 1933- *WhoAm 92*
Perry, Margaret Hepburn 1920- *St&PR 93*
Perry, Margaret Liston 1930- *WhoAmW 93*
Perry, Margaret N. 1940- *WhoAmW 93, WhoSSW 93*
Perry, Marilyn Marie Ayers 1949- *WhoAmW 93*
Perry, Marion J.H. 1943- *WhoWrEP 92*
Perry, Mark C. 1960- *ScF&FL 92*
Perry, Marsha Gratz 1936- *WhoAmW 93*
Perry, Marvin Banks, Jr. 1918- *WhoAm 92*
Perry, Mary Loretta 1940- *WhoAmW 93*

Perry, Matthew Calbraith 1794-1858 *BioIn 17, HarEnMi*
Perry, Matthew J., Jr. 1921- *WhoAm 92, WhoSSW 93*
Perry, Matthew Richard 1962- *WhoSSW 93*
Perry, Megahn 1977- *ScF&FL 92*
Perry, Mervyn Francis 1923- *WhoAm 92*
Perry, Michael *WhoScE 91-1*
Perry, Michael Clinton 1945- *WhoAm 92*
Perry, Michael D. 1946- *St&PR 93*
Perry, Michael Dean *BioIn 17*
Perry, Michael Sydney 1934- *WhoAm 92, WhoWor 93*
Perry, Milton 1926-1991 *BioIn 17*
Perry, Nancy Estelle 1934- *WhoAmW 93*
Perry, Nancy Trotter 1935- *WhoAmW 93, WhoE 93*
Perry, Nina Diamond 1956- *WhoWrEP 92*
Perry, Norman 1941- *St&PR 93*
Perry, Norman L. 1928- *St&PR 93*
Perry, Norman Robert 1929- *WhoAm 92*
Perry, Oliver Hazard 1785-1819 *BioIn 17, HarEnMi*
Perry, Osgood Endecott 1930- *St&PR 93*
Perry, Osgood Endecott 1930-1990 *BioIn 17*
Perry, Patsy Brewington 1933- *WhoSSW 93*
Perry, Paul Alverson 1929- *WhoAm 92*
Perry, Pauline *BioIn 17*
Perry, Percival 1916- *WhoAm 92*
Perry, Phyllis J. 1933- *BioIn 17*
Perry, Ralph Barton, III 1936- *St&PR 93, WhoAm 92*
Perry, Raymond N. *Law&B 92*
Perry, Rhoda E. *WhoAmW 93*
Perry, Richard Alan 1953- *St&PR 93*
Perry, Richard Allan 1948- *WhoE 93*
Perry, Richard E. 1929- *St&PR 93*
Perry, Ritchie 1942- *ChlFicS, ScF&FL 92*
Perry, Robert A. *Law&B 92*
Perry, Robert Haynes, Sr. 1933- *WhoSSW 93*
Perry, Robert Joseph 1932- *WhoAm 92*
Perry, Robert Joseph 1934- *WhoAm 92*
Perry, Robert L. 1937- *St&PR 93*
Perry, Robert M. 1931- *St&PR 93*
Perry, Robert Palese 1931- *WhoAm 92*
Perry, Robert S. 1942- *St&PR 93*
Perry, Robin L. 1917- *WhoWrEP 92*
Perry, Roger *WhoScE 91-1*
Perry, Roger 1928- *ScF&FL 92*
Perry, Roger Lawrence 1923- *St&PR 93, WhoAm 92*
Perry, Roland 1946- *ScF&FL 92*
Perry, Roland Neil *WhoScE 91-1*
Perry, Ronald *WhoAm 92*
Perry, Ruth Anna 1937- *WhoSSW 93*
Perry, S.H. 1940- *WhoScE 91-3*
Perry, Samuel Cassius 1937- *WhoE 93*
Perry, Seymour Monroe 1921- *WhoAm 92*
Perry, Shirley Hendricks 1929- *WhoAmW 93*
Perry, Simon H. *WhoScE 91-1*
Perry, Stephen H. *Law&B 92*
Perry, Steve *MiSFD 9*
Perry, Steve 1947- *ScF&FL 92*
Perry, Susan 1946- *WhoWrEP 92*
Perry, Thomas Kennedy 1952- *WhoWrEP 92*
Perry, Val M. *WhoIns 93*
Perry, Veronica d1991 *BioIn 17*
Perry, Vincent Aloysius *WhoAm 92*
Perry, William Anthony *WhoE 93*
Perry, William H. 1918- *St&PR 93*
Perry, William J. 1927- *St&PR 93*
Perry, William James 1927- *WhoAm 92*
Perry, William Leon 1945- *WhoSSW 93*
Perry, Wilson David *Law&B 92*
Perry-Daniel, Annie Vee 1940- *WhoAmW 93*
Perry Hildebrand, Mary Elizabeth 1918- *WhoAmW 93*
Perryman, Thomas Ruben 1952- *WhoSSW 93*
Perry-Whitmore, Barbara Alida 1952- *WhoAmW 93*
Persac, Marie Adrien 1823-1873 *BioIn 17*
Persad, Toolsie 1960- *St&PR 93*
Persaud, Bishnodat 1933- *WhoWor 93*
Persaud, Nowrang 1937- *WhoUN 92*
Persaud, Trivedi Vidhya Nandan 1940- *WhoAm 92*
Persavich, Warren Dale 1952- *WhoAm 92*
Persch, William Joseph, Jr. 1944- *WhoE 93*
Perschbacher, Debra Bassett 1956- *WhoAmW 93*
Perschetz, Arthur D. 1943- *St&PR 93*
Perschetz, Arthur Driban 1943- *WhoIns 93*
Perschmann, Lutz Ingo 1940- *WhoSSW 93*
Perse, Elizabeth Moyer 1949- *WhoAmW 93*
Perse, Saint-John 1887-1975 *BioIn 17*
Persek, Stephen Charles 1945- *WhoE 93*
Persell, Caroline Hodges 1941- *WhoAm 92*
Persellin, Robert Harold 1930- *WhoAm 92*
Persen, John 1941- *Baker 92*
Perseus c. 213BC-165BC *HarEnMi*
Pershall, Mary K. 1951- *ConAu 138, SmATA 70 [port]*
Pershan, Peter Silas 1934- *WhoE 93*
Pershan, Richard H., Jr. *Law&B 92*
Pershan, Richard Henry 1930- *WhoAm 92*
Pershing, David Walter 1948- *WhoAm 92*
Pershing, John Joseph 1860-1948 *CmdGen 1991 [port], DcTwHis, HarEnMi*
Pershing, Marcella *SweetSg B [port]*
Pershing, Richard Wilson 1927- *St&PR 93*
Pershing, Robert George 1941- *WhoAm 92*
Persia, Margaret Anne 1951- *WhoAmW 93*
Persiani, Fanny 1812-1867 *Baker 92, OxDcOp*
Persiani, Giuseppe 1799-1869 *Baker 92*
Persiani, Giuseppe 1804-1869 *OxDcOp*
Persiani, Orazio fl. c. 1640- *OxDcOp*
Persichetti, Vincent (Ludwig) 1915-1987 *Baker 92*
Persichini, Venceslao 1827-1897 *OxDcOp*
Persico, Francesco Saverio 1938- *WhoWor 93*
Persico, Joseph Edward 1930- *WhoAm 92, WhoWrEP 92*
Persides, C. 1940- *WhoScE 91-3*
Persijn, Guido Gabriel 1945- *WhoScE 91-3*
Persing, Joel Howard 1953- *St&PR 93*
Persinger, Louis 1887-1966 *Baker 92*
Perske, Betty Joan 1924- *WhoAm 92*
Persky, Bill 1931- *MiSFD 9*
Persky, Lester 1927- *WhoAm 92*
Persky, Marla Susan *Law&B 92*
Persky, Mordecai (Mort) 1931- *WhoWrEP 92*
Persky, Robert Samuel 1930- *WhoWrEP 92*
Persky, Stan 1941- *ConAu 39NR*
Persky, Victoria Weyler 1945- *WhoAmW 93*
Persley, Sidney *Law&B 92*
Person, Abraham 1924- *WhoSSW 93*
Person, Clayton O. 1922-1990 *BioIn 17*
Person, Curtis S., Jr. 1934- *WhoSSW 93*
Person, Donald Ames, Sr. 1938- *WhoAm 92*
Person, Evert Bertil 1914- *WhoAm 92*
Person, Houston *BioIn 17*
Person, Robert John 1927- *WhoAm 92*
Person, Willis Bagley 1928- *WhoAm 92*
Personick, Stewart David 1947- *WhoAm 92*
Persons, Oscar N. 1939- *WhoAm 92*
Persons, Stow Spaulding 1913- *WhoAm 92*
Persons, Wallace R. 1909- *St&PR 93*
Persow, Meyer Joseph 1958- *WhoE 93*
Persoz, Francis 1935- *WhoScE 91-4*
Persson, Anders 1938- *WhoScE 91-4*
Persson, Bertil R.R. 1938- *WhoScE 91-4*
Persson, Carol Vona 1951- *WhoE 93*
Persson, Emil Lennart 1939- *WhoScE 91-4*
Persson, Gelorma Elizabeth 1931- *WhoE 93*
Persson, Goran Andre 1935- *WhoScE 91-4*
Persson, Helge *WhoScE 91-4*
Persson, Ingmar 1953- *WhoScE 91-4*
Persson, K. Maurits 1939- *WhoScE 91-4*
Persson, Lars B. 1934- *WhoScE 91-4*
Persson, Nills O.S.A. 1936- *WhoScE 91-4*
Persson, Olle Verner 1935- *WhoWor 93*
Persson, Sten Erik Bertil 1937- *WhoWor 93*
Persson, Stig Y. 1941- *St&PR 93*
Persson, Stig Yngve 1941- *WhoWor 93*
Persson, Sture Valter 1940- *WhoWor 93*
Persson, Sune G.B. 1931- *WhoScE 91-4*
Persyn, Gilbert Alphonse 1938- *WhoSSW 93*
Pert, Candace 1946- *BioIn 17*
Perthame, Benoit Lucien 1959- *WhoWor 93*
Perthou, Alison Chandler 1945- *WhoAmW 93, WhoWor 93*
Perti, Giacomo Antonio 1661-1756 *Baker 92, OxDcOp*
Perti, Rajesh Kumar 1935- *WhoWor 93*
Pertile, Aureliano 1885-1952 *Baker 92, IntDcOp, OxDcOp*
Pertillar, Lisa Ann 1968- *WhoAmW 93*
Pertinax, Publius Helvetius 126-193 *HarEnMi*
Pertini, Sandro 1896-1990 *BioIn 17*
Pertl, David E. 1952- *St&PR 93*
Pertschuk, Louis Philip 1925- *WhoWor 93*
Pertschuk, Michael 1933- *WhoWrEP 92*
Perttila, Matti V. 1946- *WhoScE 91-4*
Perttula, Norman K. 1927- *St&PR 93*
Pertuzon, Emile 1938- *WhoScE 91-2*
Pertwee, Jon 1917- *QDrFCA 92 [port]*
Pertz, Stuart K. 1936- *St&PR 93*
Peru, Mariantonietta *BioIn 17*
Peru, Rosita *WhoAmW 93*
Perucca, Giovanni 1937- *WhoScE 91-3*
Perucho, Joan 1920- *ScF&FL 92*
Perucic, Jasna 1947- *WhoWor 93*
Peruggi, Regina S. *WhoAmW 93*
Perugini, John N. 1959- *WhoE 93*
Perullo, Ralph F. 1941- *St&PR 93*
Perun, Jeanne Lou 1964- *WhoAmW 93*
Perun, John Joseph, Jr. 1963- *WhoE 93*
Peruo, Marsha Hope 1951- *WhoE 93*
Perusse, Carol Brush 1950- *WhoAmW 93*
Perusse, Roland Irving 1921- *WhoAm 92*
Perutz, Gerald E.A. 1929- *St&PR 93*
Perutz, Leo 1882-1957 *ScF&FL 92*
Perutz, Max Ferdinand 1914- *WhoAm 92, WhoWor 93*
Peruzzo, Albert Louis 1951- *WhoEmL 93, WhoWor 93*
Pervelis, George H. 1934- *St&PR 93*
Pervikov, Yuri 1943- *WhoUN 92*
Pervin, Lawrence Aaron 1936- *WhoE 93*
Pervin, William Joseph 1930- *WhoAm 92*
Pervozvanskii, Anatolii Arkadievich 1932- *WhoWor 93*
Perweiler, Elyse Ann 1945- *WhoAmW 93*
Perycz, Stefan Mieczyslaw 1918- *WhoScE 91-4*
Perzan, Jeffrey *Law&B 92*
Pesado, Jose Joaquin 1801-1861 *DcMexL*
Pesaresi, Beverly Joy 1961- *WhoE 93*
Pesaresi, Daniel J. 1939- *St&PR 93*
Pesaresi, Massimo Mandolini 1950- *WhoE 93*
Pesavento, Joseph Amedeo 1936- *WhoE 93*
Pescara, Ferdinando Francesco d'Avalos, Marquis of 1490-1525 *HarEnMi*
Pescatore, Vincent *BioIn 17*
Pescatrice, Michelle Elizabeth 1953- *WhoAmW 93*
Pesce, Cheryl J. 1952- *St&PR 93*
Pesce, Gaetano 1939- *WhoWor 93*
Pesce, P.J. *MiSFD 9*
Pescetti, Giovanni Battista c. 1704-1766 *OxDcOp*
Pescetto, Giuseppe 1919- *WhoScE 91-3*
Pesch, Alan James 1941- *St&PR 93*
Pesch, Leroy Allen 1931- *WhoAm 92*
Peschcke-Koedt, Lisa Du Val *Law&B 92*
Peschek, Johann 1947- *WhoScE 91-3*
Peschel, Stephen Stanley 1955- *St&PR 93*
Peschka, T. Alan *Law&B 92*
Peschka, Thomas Alan 1931- *St&PR 93*
Peschke, Richard A. 1943- *St&PR 93*
Peschken, Chris *MiSFD 9*
Peschle, Cesare 1940- *WhoScE 91-3*
Peschle, Cesare Alessandro 1940- *WhoWor 93*
Peschmann, Kristian R. 1940- *St&PR 93*
Pesci, Joe *BioIn 17*
Pesci, Joe 1943- *News 92 [port], WhoAm 92*
Pesci, Thomas Albert 1949- *WhoE 93*
Pesciotta, Barbara Phyllis 1936- *WhoAmW 93*
Pescod, Mainwaring Bainbridge *WhoScE 91-1*
Pescosolido, Carl A., Jr. d1992 *NewYTBS 92*
Pescosolido, William Bulkeley 1932- *WhoWor 93*
Pesek, Cyril Paul, Jr. 1932- *St&PR 93*
Pesek, Libor 1933- *Baker 92*
Pesek, Ludek 1919- *ScF&FL 92*
Pesek, Thomas L. 1952- *WhoSSW 93*
Peshev, Ognyan 1936- *WhoScE 91-4*
Peshev, Tsolo Hristov 1922- *WhoScE 91-4*
Peshkin, Alan 1931- *WhoAm 92*
Peshkin, Murray 1925- *WhoAm 92*
Peshkin, Samuel David 1925- *WhoAm 92, WhoWor 93*
Pesin, Harry 1919-1984 *ScF&FL 92*
Pesin, Meyer 1902-1989 *BioIn 17*
Pesin, Morris d1992 *NewYTBS 92 [port]*
Peskanov, Mark 1956- *Baker 92*
Peskin, Charlotte L. d1991 *BioIn 17*
Peskin, Kenneth *WhoAm 92*
Peskin, Martin Rudolph 1949- *St&PR 93*
Peskin, Sheila Harriet 1935- *WhoAmW 93*
Peskin, Sidney F. 1914- *St&PR 93*
Peskin-Jacobs, Marjorie Ruth 1952- *WhoAmW 93*
Pesko, Zoltan 1937- *Baker 92, WhoWor 93*
Peskoe, Michael P. *Law&B 92*
Peskoe, Sondra Helane 1955- *WhoAmW 93, WhoEmL 93, WhoWor 93*
Peslin, Rene *WhoScE 91-2*
Pesmen, Sandra 1931- *WhoAm 92*
Pesner, Carole Manishin 1937- *WhoAm 92, WhoE 93*
Pesola, Robert 1949- *WhoE 93, WhoWor 93*
Pesonen, Jori *WhoScE 91-4*
Pesonen, Jukka 1937- *WhoScE 91-4*
Pesonen, Lauri J. 1944- *WhoScE 91-4*
Pesonen, Olavi 1909- *Baker 92*
Pess, Daniel M. 1952- *St&PR 93*
Pess, Gary Martin 1956- *WhoE 93*
Pessa, Markus Viljo 1941- *WhoScE 91-4*
Pessard, Emile (-Louis-Fortune) 1843-1917 *Baker 92*
Pessemier, Robert Campbell 1956- *WhoWrEP 92*
Pessen, Edward d1992 *NewYTBS 92*
Pessen, Edward 1920- *WhoAm 92, WhoWrEP 92*
Pessen, Helmut 1921- *WhoE 93*
Pessia, Michael W. *Law&B 92*
Pessin, Karol M. *Law&B 92*
Pessina, Gian Paolo 1943- *WhoWor 93*
Pessl, Yella d1991 *BioIn 17*
Pessoa, Fernando 1888-1935 *BioIn 17*
Pessoa, Michelle Marie 1966- *WhoE 93*
Pessolano, Linda 1946- *WhoWrEP 92*
Pesson, Bernard 1947- *WhoScE 91-2*
Pessoni, Douglas Herbert 1941- *St&PR 93*
Pessoni, Philip Andrew 1938- *WhoE 93*
Pestaina, Karen Helena 1963- *WhoEmL 93*
Pestalozzi, Heinrich 1878-1940 *Baker 92*
Pestalozzi, Johann Heinrich 1746-1827 *BioIn 17*
Pestana, Angel 1938- *WhoScE 91-3*
Pestana, Carlos 1936- *WhoAm 92*
Pestana, Joseph Peter 1951- *St&PR 93*
Pestel, Michael Christian 1950- *WhoE 93*
Pestemer, Wilfried 1941- *WhoScE 91-3*
Pester, Jack C. 1935- *St&PR 93*
Pesti, Laszlo 1927- *WhoScE 91-4*
Pestillo, Peter J. *BioIn 17*
Pestillo, Peter John 1938- *St&PR 93, WhoAm 92*
Pestka, Sidney 1936- *WhoE 93*
Pestle, Ruth Ellen 1932- *WhoAmW 93, WhoSSW 93*
Pestolesi, Robert A. *BioIn 17*
Peston, The Right Honourable the Lord *WhoScE 91-1*
Pestritto, Anthony Charles 1926- *St&PR 93*
Pesty, Laszlo 1930- *WhoScE 91-4*
Pesut, Robert Nicholas 1938- *WhoSSW 93*
Pesut, Timothy Scott 1956- *WhoSSW 93*
Peszka, Jozef 1767-1831 *PolBiDi*
Peszke, Michael Alfred 1932- *WhoAm 92, WhoE 93*
Peta, James Joseph 1942- *St&PR 93*
Petacque, Art 1924- *ConAu 136, WhoAm 92, WhoWor 93*
Petain, Henri Philippe 1856-1951 *BioIn 17, DcTwHis, HarEnMi*
Petaja, Emil 1915- *ScF&FL 92*
Petaja, Timo Olavi 1945- *WhoScE 91-4*
Petajaniemi, Anne 1956- *WhoWor 93*
Petchclai, Bencha 1937- *WhoWor 93*
Pete, Jean Pierre 1937- *WhoScE 91-2*
Pet-Edwards, Julia Johanna Agricola 1955- *WhoSSW 93*
Petek, William Louis 1942- *St&PR 93*
Petelle, James F. *Law&B 92*
Petelska, Ewa 1920- *DrEEuF*
Petelski, Czeslaw 1922- *DrEEuF*
Peter *MajAI, OxDcByz*
Peter 1908-1980 *IntDcAn*
Peter, Archbishop 1926- *WhoAm 92*
Peter, II 1923- *DcTwHis*
Peter, III *OxDcByz*
Peter, IV 1319-1387 *HarEnMi*
Peter, Arnold Philimon 1957- *WhoEmL 93, WhoWor 93*
Peter, Bonnie Jean *Law&B 92*
Peter, Carl J. 1932-1991 *BioIn 17*
Peter, Davis E. *Law&B 92*
Peter, Frances Marchbank *WhoAm 92*
Peter, Harry W. 1939- *St&PR 93*
Peter, Helmut W. 1932- *WhoAm 92*
Peter, James P. *Law&B 92*
Peter, John Frederick 1746-1813 *Baker 92*
Peter, Laurence J. *BioIn 17*
Peter, Martin 1928- *WhoScE 91-4*
Peter, Phillips Smith 1932- *St&PR 93, WhoAm 92, WhoE 93, WhoWor 93*
Peter, Richard Ector 1943- *WhoAm 92*
Peter, Simon 1743-1819 *Baker 92*
Peter Capuano d1214 *OxDcByz*
Peter Damian, Saint c. 1007-1072 *BioIn 17*
Peterfreund, Emanuel 1924-1990 *BioIn 17*
Peterfreund, Norman 1920- *St&PR 93*
Peterfreund, Sheldon Paul 1917- *WhoAm 92*
Peterfreund, Stuart Samuel 1945- *WhoWrEP 92*
Petering, Janice Faye 1950- *WhoAmW 93*

Peterka, Cynthia JoAnne 1950- *WhoE 93*
Peterka, Richard A. 1927- *St&PR 93*
Peterkin, DeWitt, Jr. 1913- *WhoAm 92*
Peterkin, George A., Jr. 1927- *St&PR 93*
Peterkin, George Alexander, Jr. 1927- *WhoAm 92*
Peterkin, Julia Mood 1880-1961 *AmWomPl*
Peterle, Tony John 1925- *WhoAm 92*
Peterlik, Meinrad 1938- *WhoScE 91-4*
Peterman, Bruce E. 1931- *St&PR 93*
Peterman, Bruce Edgar 1931- *WhoAm 92*
Peterman, Debianne 1955- *WhoEmL 93*
Peterman, Jack Maurice 1931- *St&PR 93*
Peterman, John *BioIn 17*
Peterman, Michael 1942- *ScF&FL 92*
Petermann, Gotz Eike 1941- *WhoWor 93*
Petermann, Hartwig 1919- *WhoScE 91-3*
Petermann, Thomas J. *Law&B 92*
Petermeier, Norman Bruce 1941- *St&PR 93*
Peter Mongos *OxDcByz*
Peternell, Ben C. 1945- *St&PR 93*
Peternell, Ben Clayton 1945- *WhoAm 92*
Peter of Alexandria fl. 10th cent.- *OxDcByz*
Peter of Amiens *OxDcByz*
Peter of Argos *OxDcByz*
Peter of Atroa *OxDcByz*
Peter of Bracieux dc. 1210 *OxDcByz*
Peter of Bulgaria d1197 *OxDcByz*
Peter of Bulgaria c. 903-969 *OxDcByz*
Peter of Courtenay c. 1165-1219? *OxDcByz*
Peter of Damascus *OxDcByz*
Peter of Eboli d1220 *OxDcByz*
Peter of Sicily *OxDcByz*
Peter Patrikios c. 500-565 *OxDcByz*
Peter Porcupine 1763-1835 *BioIn 17*
Peters, A. Winniett 1927- *WhoAm 92*
Peters, Alan 1929- *WhoAm 92, WhoE 93*
Peters, Albert Alain 1940- *WhoUN 92*
Peters, Alec 1934- *St&PR 93*
Peters, Alice 1915- *WhoE 93*
Peters, Allen C. *Law&B 92*
Peters, Alma Dorothy 1953- *WhoAmW 93*
Peters, Alton Emil 1935- *WhoAm 92*
Peters, Arnold Thornton *WhoScE 91-1*
Peters, Arthur King 1919- *WhoAm 92*
Peters, Arthur W. 1942- *St&PR 93*
Peters, Augustus Winniett 1927- *St&PR 93*
Peters, Barbara *MiSFD 9*
Peters, Barbara Himmelfarb 1944- *WhoAmW 93*
Peters, Barbara Humbird 1948- *WhoEmL 93*
Peters, Barry W. *Law&B 92*
Peters, Bernadette *BioIn 17*
Peters, Bernadette 1948- *ConTFT 10, WhoAm 92, WhoAmW 93*
Peters, Beth Shepherd 1949- *WhoAmW 93*
Peters, Bobbie Jo 1947- *WhoSSW 93*
Peters, Bonnie Sigmon 1952- *WhoSSW 93*
Peters, Boyd Leon 1951- *WhoWor 93*
Peters, Brian Francis 1951- *St&PR 93*
Peters, Brock *BioIn 17*
Peters, Brock 1927- *WhoAm 92*
Peters, Bryan Paul 1954- *WhoE 93*
Peters, Calvin Ronald 1940- *WhoSSW 93*
Peters, Carl Friedrich 1779-1827 *Baker 92*
Peters, Carol Ann Dudycha 1938- *WhoAmW 93, WhoWor 93*
Peters, Carol Beattie Taylor 1932- *WhoAmW 93*
Peters, Carol Sparkman *Law&B 92*
Peters, Carolyn Valerie *Law&B 92*
Peters, Cathy J. 1951- *WhoAmW 93*
Peters, Charles 1926- *BioIn 17*
Peters, Charles Given, Jr. 1926- *WhoAm 92*
Peters, Charles L. 1933- *St&PR 93*
Peters, Charles Martin 1955- *WhoWor 93*
Peters, Charles Merrell 1953- *WhoAm 92*
Peters, Charles William 1927- *WhoAm 92*
Peters, Charlie *MiSFD 9*
Peters, Cheryl Curcio 1949- *WhoAmW 93*
Peters, Cheryl Olga 1951- *WhoIns 93*
Peters, Christine Marie 1949- *WhoAmW 93*
Peters, Clarice *WhoWrEP 92*
Peters, Colette *BioIn 17*
Peters, Daniel A. *St&PR 93*
Peters, Daniel (James) 1948- *ConAu 39NR*
Peters, Daniel L. 1952- *St&PR 93*
Peters, David *ScF&FL 92, St&PR 93*
Peters, David 1954- *SmATA 72 [port]*
Peters, David Allen 1947- *WhoAm 92*
Peters, David C. 1950- *St&PR 93*
Peters, David Keith *WhoScE 91-1*
Peters, David Michael 1940- *St&PR 93*
Peters, David Thomas 1926- *St&PR 93*
Peters, Deborah Lynn 1954- *WhoAmW 93*
Peters, Denis J. 1953- *St&PR 93*
Peters, Dennis Gail 1937- *WhoAm 92*
Peters, Donald Cameron 1915- *WhoAm 92*
Peters, Donald Delbert 1940- *WhoSSW 93*
Peters, Donald H. 1940- *St&PR 93*
Peters, Donald Joseph 1959- *WhoE 93*
Peters, Donna J. 1929- *St&PR 93*
Peters, Dorothy Marie 1913- *WhoWor 93*
Peters, Douglas Cameron 1955- *WhoEmL 93*
Peters, Douglas D. 1936- *St&PR 93*
Peters, Edward Michael, Jr. 1954- *WhoE 93*
Peters, Edward (Murray) 1936- *ConAu 40NR, WhoAm 92*
Peters, Elizabeth *Law&B 92, ScF&FL 92*
Peters, Ellen Ash 1930- *WhoAm 92, WhoAmW 93*
Peters, Ellis 1913- *BioIn 17*
Peters, Ernest 1926- *WhoAm 92*
Peters, Farnsley Lewellyn 1929- *WhoAm 92*
Peters, Frances Elizabeth 1915- *WhoAmW 93*
Peters, Frank Albert 1931- *WhoE 93*
Peters, Frank Lewis, Jr. 1930- *WhoAm 92*
Peters, Fransiscus Johannes 1945- *WhoWor 93*
Peters, Frederick P. d1990 *BioIn 17*
Peters, Garry Lowell 1952- *WhoAm 92*
Peters, Gary 1937- *BioIn 17*
Peters, George Thomas *Law&B 92*
Peters, Georges 1920- *WhoScE 91-4*
Peters, Gerald Joseph 1941- *WhoE 93*
Peters, Geraldine Joan *WhoAmW 93*
Peters, Glenn W. 1948- *St&PR 93*
Peters, Gordon Benes 1931- *WhoAm 92*
Peters, Grace Thomas 1929- *WhoAmW 93*
Peters, H. Fay *Law&B 92*
Peters, Hans-Rudolf Albert 1932- *WhoWor 93*
Peters, Heinz Norbert 1942- *WhoScE 91-3*
Peters, Henry Augustus 1920- *WhoAm 92*
Peters, Henry Buckland 1916- *WhoAm 92, WhoSSW 93*
Peters, House 1880-1967 *BioIn 17*
Peters, Howard Nevin 1938- *WhoAm 92*
Peters, Hugh M. 1943- *St&PR 93*
Peters, J. Michael *Law&B 92*
Peters, Jacques M. 1923- *WhoScE 91-2*
Peters, James M. 1935- *St&PR 93*
Peters, James Robert 1950- *St&PR 93*
Peters, James Ross 1938- *WhoSSW 93*
Peters, James Seaton 1925-1990 *BioIn 17*
Peters, James W. *Law&B 92*
Peters, James William *Law&B 92*
Peters, Jane Kastl 1954- *WhoEmL 93*
Peters, Janet J. 1930- *WhoAmW 93*
Peters, Jay *ScF&FL 92*
Peters, Jean Theresa 1944- *WhoAmW 93*
Peters, Joan Karen 1945- *WhoWrEP 92*
Peters, JoAnna *Law&B 92*
Peters, John 1917-1989 *BioIn 17*
Peters, John E. *Law&B 92*
Peters, John E. 1947- *St&PR 93*
Peters, John Edward 1931- *WhoAm 92*
Peters, John Leland 1907- *WhoSSW 93*
Peters, John Otto, III 1956- *WhoE 93*
Peters, John R. *Law&B 92*
Peters, John S. *St&PR 93*
Peters, Jon *BioIn 17*
Peters, Jon 1947- *WhoAm 92*
Peters, Joseph Edwin 1938- *St&PR 93*
Peters, Karen C. 1947- *St&PR 93*
Peters, Karen Elaine 1954- *WhoAmW 93*
Peters, Karen Ronell 1944- *WhoAmW 93*
Peters, Kelly Boyte 1958- *WhoEmL 93*
Peters, Kurt J. 1944- *WhoScE 91-3*
Peters, Lana *WhoWrEP 92*
Peters, Lauralee Milberg 1943- *WhoAmW 93*
Peters, Lawrence H. 1945- *WhoSSW 93*
Peters, Lenrie (Wilfred Leopold) 1932- *DcLB 117 [port]*
Peters, Leon, Jr. 1923- *WhoAm 92*
Peters, Leroy R. 1933- *St&PR 93*
Peters, Linda *ConAu 38NR, MajAI*
Peters, Lorraine A. *St&PR 93*
Peters, Louise *WhoWrEP 92*
Peters, Ludovic 1931-1984 *ScF&FL 92*
Peters, M.T. *WhoScE 91-1*
Peters, Marcel *DcCPCAm*
Peters, Margaret H. *Law&B 92*
Peters, Mark Thomas *Law&B 92*
Peters, Mark William *Law&B 92*
Peters, Mary E. 1911-1989 *BioIn 17*
Peters, Maureen *ScF&FL 92*
Peters, Maurice W. 1924- *St&PR 93*
Peters, Mercedes *WhoE 93, WhoWor 93*
Peters, Merle A. 1936- *St&PR 93*
Peters, Michael *BioIn 17*
Peters, Michael Arthur 1943- *WhoAm 92*
Peters, Michael Bartley 1943- *WhoAm 92*
Peters, Michael P. *St&PR 93*
Peters, Michele Ann 1952- *WhoAmW 93*
Peters, Othello *ScF&FL 92*
Peters, Paul 1931- *WhoUN 92*
Peters, Paul R. 1920- *St&PR 93*
Peters, Paula Anne 1962- *WhoAmW 93*
Peters, Philip C. *BioIn 17*
Peters, R.Y. *Law&B 92*
Peters, Ralph 1952- *ScF&FL 92*
Peters, Ralph Edgar 1923- *WhoE 93*
Peters, Ralph Frew 1929- *St&PR 93, WhoAm 92*
Peters, Ralph Irwin, Jr. 1947- *WhoSSW 93*
Peters, Ralph Martin 1926- *WhoAm 92*
Peters, Randolph William 1954- *WhoSSW 93*
Peters, Raymond Eugene 1933- *WhoWor 93*
Peters, Raymond Robert 1942- *WhoAm 92, WhoWor 93*
Peters, Reiner *WhoScE 91-3*
Peters, Richard, Jr. 1780-1848 *OxCSupC*
Peters, Richard H. 1920- *St&PR 93*
Peters, Richard Joseph 1937- *WhoE 93*
Peters, Richard Morse 1922- *WhoAm 92*
Peters, Robert 1924- *BioIn 17, WhoWrEP 92*
Peters, Robert J. 1940- *St&PR 93*
Peters, Robert Lee 1920- *WhoAm 92*
Peters, Robert Lynn, Jr. 1919- *St&PR 93*
Peters, Robert Nisley 1923- *St&PR 93*
Peters, Robert Wayne 1950- *WhoEmL 93*
Peters, Roberta 1930- *Baker 92, IntDcOp, WhoAm 92, WhoAmW 93*
Peters, Roger J. *Law&B 92*
Peters, Roger James *Law&B 92*
Peters, Ronald George 1944- *WhoE 93*
Peters, Ronald L. 1956- *St&PR 93*
Peters, Saul *ScF&FL 92*
Peters, Stanley Thomas 1934- *WhoAm 92*
Peters, Stephen 1946- *St&PR 93*
Peters, Tamara Susan 1959- *WhoEmL 93*
Peters, Theodore, Jr. 1922- *WhoE 93*
Peters, Thomas Guy 1945- *WhoSSW 93*
Peters, Thomas Joseph *WhoE 93*
Peters, Timothy John *WhoScE 91-1*
Peters, Tom P. d1991 *BioIn 17*
Peters, Uwe Henrik 1930- *WhoWor 93*
Peters, Vickie Jann 1951- *WhoWrEP 92*
Peters, Virginia 1924- *WhoAm 92*
Peters, Walter J. *Law&B 92*
Peters, Werner 1929- *WhoScE 91-3*
Peters, William 1921- *WhoAm 92, WhoWrEP 92*
Peters, William Frank 1934- *WhoWor 93*
Peters, William Henry 1928- *WhoAm 92*
Peters, William P. 1950- *WhoAm 92*
Peters, William R. *Law&B 92*
Peters, William Wesley 1912-1991 *AnObit 1991, BioIn 17*
Peters, Winston Raymond 1946- *WhoAsAP 91*
Peters, Yvonne *BioIn 17*
Petersdorf, Robert George 1926- *WhoAm 92*
Petersen, Aevar 1948- *WhoScE 91-4*
Petersen, Allen R. 1954- *St&PR 93*
Petersen, Ann Christine 1950- *WhoAmW 93*
Petersen, Anne Cheryl 1944- *WhoAm 92*
Petersen, Arne B. 1948- *WhoUN 92*
Petersen, Barry Rex 1949- *WhoE 93*
Petersen, Bruce Lawrence 1941- *WhoE 93*
Petersen, C. Neil *Law&B 92*
Petersen, Cindy 1945- *St&PR 93*
Petersen, Daniel Lee 1948- *St&PR 93*
Petersen, Daniel Ronald 1933- *St&PR 93*
Petersen, David *BioIn 17*
Petersen, David C. *Law&B 92*
Petersen, David John 1958- *WhoE 93*
Petersen, David L. *WhoAm 92*
Petersen, Dean Mitchell 1950- *WhoE 93*
Petersen, Donald E. *BioIn 17*
Petersen, Edgar N. 1938- *St&PR 93*
Petersen, Einar C. *Law&B 92*
Petersen, Erik Lundtang 1942- *WhoScE 91-2*
Petersen, Forrest S. 1922-1990 *BioIn 17*
Petersen, Frank E., Jr. *AfrAmBi*
Petersen, Frank Gerhard 1933- *WhoWor 93*
Petersen, G. Hopner 1930- *WhoScE 91-2*
Petersen, Georg 1947- *WhoUN 92*
Petersen, Glenn Thomas 1947- *WhoE 93*
Petersen, Gregory L. *Law&B 92*
Petersen, Gwenn Boardman 1924- *BioIn 17*
Petersen, Helge B. 1945- *WhoWor 93*
Petersen, Henry Edward 1921-1991 *BioIn 17*
Petersen, Inger *WhoScE 91-2*
Petersen, Ivar 1929- *WhoWor 93*
Petersen, Joan Marie 1942- *WhoAmW 93*
Petersen, Johannes 1934- *WhoScE 91-3*
Petersen, Johannes Bjelke- 1911- *BioIn 17*
Petersen, John Holger 1942- *WhoSSW 93*
Petersen, John James 1944- *St&PR 93*
Petersen, John Mark 1950- *St&PR 93*
Petersen, John William 1921- *St&PR 93*
Petersen, Jon Q. 1950- *St&PR 93*
Petersen, Keith John 1963- *St&PR 93*
Petersen, Kenneth C. 1936- *St&PR 93*
Petersen, Kenneth Clarence 1936- *WhoAm 92*
Petersen, Kim Eberhard 1956- *WhoWor 93*
Petersen, Lawrence Alfred 1928- *St&PR 93*
Petersen, Lee Bennett, Jr. 1951- *St&PR 93*
Petersen, Marie C. 1923- *St&PR 93*
Petersen, Marshall Arthur 1938- *WhoAm 92*
Petersen, Martin Eugene 1931- *WhoAm 92*
Petersen, Mary Lorraine 1944- *WhoAmW 93*
Petersen, Maureen Jeanette Miller 1956- *WhoAmW 93, WhoWor 93*
Petersen, Michael Frederic 1955- *St&PR 93*
Petersen, Michael J. *Law&B 92*
Petersen, Michael J. 1945- *St&PR 93*
Petersen, Michael Mack 1952- *WhoSSW 93*
Petersen, Norman Richard, Jr. 1933- *WhoAm 92, WhoE 93*
Petersen, P(eter) J(ames) 1941- *MajAI [port]*
Petersen, Patricia Ann 1935- *WhoAmW 93*
Petersen, Ralph A. 1923- *St&PR 93*
Petersen, Raymond J. 1919- *St&PR 93*
Petersen, Raymond Joseph 1919- *WhoAm 92*
Petersen, Richard Herman 1934- *WhoAm 92*
Petersen, Richard J. 1941- *St&PR 93*
Petersen, Robert Louis, Jr. *Law&B 92*
Petersen, Robert M. *Law&B 92*
Petersen, Rodney Lawrence 1949- *WhoE 93*
Petersen, Roger A. *Law&B 92*
Petersen, Roland 1926- *WhoAm 92*
Petersen, Russell J. 1937- *WhoAm 92*
Petersen, Sandy *ScF&FL 92*
Petersen, Scott P. *Law&B 92*
Petersen, Sheila *BioIn 17*
Petersen, Sidney R. 1930- *St&PR 93*
Petersen, Susan Jane 1944- *WhoAm 92*
Petersen, Toni 1933- *WhoAm 92*
Petersen, Ulrich 1927- *WhoAm 92*
Petersen, Virginia *AmWomPl*
Petersen, W. Harold 1928- *WhoIns 93*
Petersen, Warren R. 1946- *St&PR 93*
Petersen, Wilhelm 1890-1957 *Baker 92*
Petersen, William L. *BioIn 17*
Petersen, William Otto 1926- *WhoAm 92*
Petersen, Wolfgang 1941- *MiSFD 9*
Petersen-Frey, Roland 1937- *WhoWor 93*
Petersham, Maud (Fuller) 1890-1971 *MajAI [port]*
Petersham, Miska 1888-1960 *MajAI*
Petersmann, Hubert 1940- *WhoWor 93*
Petersmeyer, Charles Wrede 1919- *WhoAm 92*
Petersmeyer, John Clinton 1945- *WhoWor 93*
Peterson, Adaire *WhoIns 93*
Peterson, Agnes Emelie *AmWomPl*
Peterson, Alan C. 1938- *St&PR 93*
Peterson, Alan Lee 1958- *WhoSSW 93*
Peterson, Alfred H. 1938- *St&PR 93*
Peterson, Alfred H., III 1946- *St&PR 93*
Peterson, Alice Ann *Law&B 92*
Peterson, Andrew F. 1958- *St&PR 93*
Peterson, Andrew Norman 1952- *St&PR 93*
Peterson, Ann C. *WhoAm 92*
Peterson, Ann Mary 1943- *WhoAmW 93*
Peterson, Ann Sullivan 1928- *WhoAm 92, WhoAmW 93*
Peterson, Annamarie Jane 1936- *WhoAmW 93*
Peterson, Anne Virginia 1948- *WhoAmW 93, WhoEmL 93*
Peterson, Arthur Laverne 1926- *WhoAm 92, WhoWor 93*
Peterson, Barbara Ann Bennett 1942- *WhoAmW 93, WhoWor 93*
Peterson, Bernard V. *Law&B 92*
Peterson, Bess Catherine 1924- *WhoAmW 93*
Peterson, Betty Dugas 1913- *WhoAmW 93*
Peterson, Beverly d1991 *BioIn 17*
Peterson, Boyd F., Jr. *ScF&FL 92*
Peterson, Brian Lynn 1962- *WhoSSW 93*
Peterson, Brooke Alan 1949- *WhoEmL 93*
Peterson, Bruce *WhoIns 93*
Peterson, Bruce Edward 1943- *St&PR 93*
Peterson, Bryan S. 1949- *St&PR 93*
Peterson, Carl Eric 1944- *WhoAm 92*
Peterson, Carl J. 1937- *St&PR 93*
Peterson, Carl L. 1933- *St&PR 93, WhoAm 92*
Peterson, Carolyn Sue 1938- *WhoSSW 93*
Peterson, Carwin Y. *St&PR 93*
Peterson, Cathryn J. 1952- *WhoIns 93*
Peterson, Cathy Harasty 1957- *WhoE 93*
Peterson, Charles E. 1936- *St&PR 93*
Peterson, Charles Emil 1906- *WhoAm 92*

Peterson, Charles Gordon 1926- *WhoAm 92*
Peterson, Charles Hayes 1938- *WhoAm 92*
Peterson, Charles John 1933- *WhoAm 92*
Peterson, Charles Lee 1941- *St&PR 93*
Peterson, Charles Loren 1938- *WhoAm 92*
Peterson, Charles T. 1932- *St&PR 93*
Peterson, Charles T. 1937- *St&PR 93*
Peterson, Charles William, Jr. *Law&B 92*
Peterson, Chase N. 1929- *WhoAm 92*
Peterson, Chester, Jr. 1937- *WhoWrEP 92*
Peterson, Chester Gibe 1922- *WhoE 93*
Peterson, Clara Belle *AmWomPl*
Peterson, Clarence Wilford 1924- *St&PR 93*
Peterson, Claudia *BioIn 17*
Peterson, Collin C. 1944- *CngDr 91, WhoAm 92*
Peterson, Cordell Quentin 1941- *St&PR 93*
Peterson, Courtland Harry 1930- *WhoAm 92*
Peterson, Craig D. *Law&B 92*
Peterson, D. Wayne 1936- *WhoAm 92*
Peterson, Dale L. *BioIn 17*
Peterson, Dan W. 1930- *St&PR 93*
Peterson, Darwin Wilson 1938- *WhoSSW 93*
Peterson, David *St&PR 93*
Peterson, David A. *Law&B 92*
Peterson, David Allen *Law&B 92*
Peterson, David Andreas 1939- *WhoAm 92*
Peterson, David D. *Law&B 92*
Peterson, David Dalvey 1931- *St&PR 93*
Peterson, David Frederick 1937- *WhoAm 92*
Peterson, David Robert *BioIn 17*
Peterson, David Robert 1943- *WhoAm 92*
Peterson, David S. 1958- *St&PR 93*
Peterson, Dean E. *Law&B 92*
Peterson, Delaine C. 1936- *St&PR 93*
Peterson, Delaine Charles 1936- *WhoWor 93*
Peterson, Delmont Russell 1918- *St&PR 93*
Peterson, Denis J. *WhoE 93*
Peterson, Dennis Edwin 1938- *St&PR 93*
Peterson, Diane *BioIn 17*
Peterson, Diane Lynn 1955- *WhoEmL 93*
Peterson, Diane M. *Law&B 92*
Peterson, Donald Franklin 1925- *WhoIns 93*
Peterson, Donald Kent 1949- *WhoAm 92*
Peterson, Donald M. 1936- *WhoIns 93*
Peterson, Donald R. *BioIn 17*
Peterson, Donald Robert 1923- *WhoAm 92*
Peterson, Donald Robert 1929- *WhoAm 92, WhoWrEP 92*
Peterson, Donald V. 1938- *St&PR 93*
Peterson, Donald Walter 1925- *St&PR 93*
Peterson, Donna *BioIn 17*
Peterson, Douglas *Law&B 92*
Peterson, Douglas 1935- *WhoSSW 93*
Peterson, Douglas W. *Law&B 92*
Peterson, Duwayne J. 1932- *St&PR 93*
Peterson, Dwight A. 1933- *St&PR 93*
Peterson, Edith R. d1992 *NewYTBS 92*
Peterson, Edward Adrian 1941- *WhoAm 92*
Peterson, Edward Alfred 1928- *WhoAm 92*
Peterson, Edward Dale 1929- *WhoAm 92*
Peterson, Edward Nohl 1930- *WhoAm 92*
Peterson, Edwin J. 1930- *WhoAm 92*
Peterson, Elisabeth Thomas *Law&B 92*
Peterson, Ellsworth Lorin 1924- *St&PR 93*
Peterson, Elmor Lee 1938- *WhoAm 92, WhoSSW 93*
Peterson, Eric Christian 1950- *WhoAm 92*
Peterson, Eric Clinton 1944- *WhoWrEP 92*
Peterson, Eric Robert 1944- *WhoE 93*
Peterson, Esther 1906- *PolPar, WhoAm 92*
Peterson, Eugene H. 1932- *BioIn 17*
Peterson, Florence Marisa *Law&B 92*
Peterson, Frank K. *Law&B 92*
Peterson, Franklynn 1938- *ConAu 37NR*
Peterson, Franklynn Don 1938- *WhoWrEP 92*
Peterson, Fred McCrae 1936- *WhoAm 92*
Peterson, Frederick Morrison 1942- *WhoSSW 93*
Peterson, Fritz 1942- *BioIn 17*
Peterson, Gale Eugene 1944- *WhoAm 92*
Peterson, Gary Andrew 1940- *WhoAm 92*
Peterson, Gary E. *Law&B 92*
Peterson, Gary Jon 1939- *WhoAm 92*
Peterson, Gary William 1946- *WhoE 93*
Peterson, George Emanuel, Jr. 1931- *WhoAm 92*
Peterson, George P. 1930- *WhoAm 92*
Peterson, Gerald Alvin 1931- *WhoAm 92*
Peterson, Greg J. 1956- *St&PR 93*
Peterson, Gregg Lee 1943- *WhoAm 92*
Peterson, Gregor G. 1932- *St&PR 93*
Peterson, H. Geoffrey *Law&B 92*
Peterson, H. William 1922- *WhoE 93, WhoWor 93*
Peterson, Harold Albert 1908- *WhoAm 92*
Peterson, Harold Albert, III 1946- *St&PR 93*
Peterson, Harold Oscar 1909- *WhoAm 92*
Peterson, Harries-Clichy 1924- *WhoAm 92*
Peterson, Harry E. 1921- *St&PR 93*
Peterson, Helmer William 1936- *WhoSSW 93*
Peterson, Holger Martin 1912- *WhoSSW 93*
Peterson, Horthon L. 1924- *St&PR 93*
Peterson, Howard Cooper 1939- *WhoWor 93*
Peterson, Howard John 1951- *WhoAm 92*
Peterson, Hubert H. 1913- *St&PR 93*
Peterson, Irvin Leslie 1926- *WhoE 93*
Peterson, James A. d1992 *NewYTBS 92*
Peterson, James Alfred 1913-1992 *BioIn 17, ConAu 137*
Peterson, James Algert 1915- *WhoAm 92, WhoWor 93*
Peterson, James Allan 1932- *WhoE 93*
Peterson, James Craig *Law&B 92*
Peterson, James Gary 1937- *St&PR 93*
Peterson, James Kenneth 1934- *WhoAm 92*
Peterson, James Lincoln 1942- *WhoAm 92*
Peterson, James R. *Law&B 92*
Peterson, James Richard *Law&B 92*
Peterson, James Robert 1927- *WhoAm 92*
Peterson, James Robert 1932- *WhoSSW 93*
Peterson, Jan *BioIn 17*
Peterson, Jane White 1941- *WhoAmW 93*
Peterson, Janine Rogers 1954- *WhoAmW 93*
Peterson, Jean Margaret 1916- *WhoE 93*
Peterson, Jerry B. *Law&B 92*
Peterson, Jim L. 1935- *WhoAm 92*
Peterson, Jimmy Lee 1947- *WhoSSW 93*
Peterson, JoAnne Elizabeth 1947- *WhoAmW 93*
Peterson, John A. 1934- *St&PR 93*
Peterson, John C. *Law&B 92*
Peterson, John D. 1933- *St&PR 93*
Peterson, John Edgar, Jr. 1916- *WhoSSW 93*
Peterson, John Edward 1944- *St&PR 93*
Peterson, John Eric 1914- *WhoAm 92*
Peterson, John Frederick 1953- *St&PR 93*
Peterson, Karl Folke 1935- *WhoScE 91-4, WhoWor 93*
Peterson, Kathleen Flynn *BioIn 17*
Peterson, Kathryn Jean 1947- *WhoAmW 93*
Peterson, Kathy Marie 1951- *WhoEmL 93*
Peterson, Keith A. *Law&B 92*
Peterson, Keith E. 1933- *St&PR 93*
Peterson, Kenneth Allen, Sr. 1939- *WhoWor 93*
Peterson, Kenneth B. *Law&B 92*
Peterson, Kenneth J. 1935- *WhoIns 93*
Peterson, Kenneth James 1935- *St&PR 93*
Peterson, Kent Wright 1943- *WhoAm 92, WhoSSW 93*
Peterson, Kevin Bruce 1948- *WhoAm 92*
Peterson, Kirk Charles 1949- *WhoAm 92*
Peterson, Kristina *WhoAm 92*
Peterson, Kristine *MiSFD 9*
Peterson, Larry R. 1950- *St&PR 93*
Peterson, Larry Wayne 1941- *WhoE 93*
Peterson, Leona Mae 1929- *WhoAmW 93*
Peterson, Leroy 1930- *WhoWor 93*
Peterson, Leslie Raymond 1923- *WhoAm 92, WhoWor 93*
Peterson, Lester G. 1941- *St&PR 93*
Peterson, Linda S. *Law&B 92*
Peterson, Lisa Lee 1959- *WhoAmW 93*
Peterson, Lois Sirry 1934- *St&PR 93*
Peterson, Lorna Ingrid 1956- *WhoEmL 93*
Peterson, Louis Robert 1923- *WhoAm 92*
Peterson, Lowell 1950- *WhoEmL 93*
Peterson, Lynn Marie 1953- *WhoEmL 93*
Peterson, M. Roger 1929- *WhoAm 92*
Peterson, Maria Caroline 1950- *WhoAmW 93, WhoEmL 93*
Peterson, Marilyn Ethel 1926- *WhoWrEP 92*
Peterson, Mark *BioIn 17*
Peterson, Mary Anne 1950- *WhoAmW 93*
Peterson, Mary Kay 1955- *WhoE 93*
Peterson, Melvin Norman Adolph 1929- *WhoAm 92*
Peterson, Merrill Daniel 1921- *WhoAm 92*
Peterson, Mildred Othmer 1902- *WhoAm 92*
Peterson, Millie M. 1944- *WhoAmW 93*
Peterson, Milton M. *Law&B 92*
Peterson, Miriam Mears 1942- *WhoSSW 93*
Peterson, N. Curtis, Jr. 1922- *WhoAm 92*
Peterson, Nad A. 1926- *St&PR 93, WhoAm 92*
Peterson, Nadeen 1934- *WhoAmW 93*
Peterson, Nancy Jane 1955- *WhoAmW 93*
Peterson, Norma Jo 1938- *WhoAmW 93*
Peterson, Norman L. 1940- *St&PR 93*
Peterson, O. James, III 1935- *St&PR 93*
Peterson, Oscar 1925- *BioIn 17*
Peterson, Oscar (Emmanuel) 1925- *Baker 92, WhoAm 92, WhoWor 93*
Peterson, Oscar James, III 1935- *WhoAm 92*
Peterson, P.J. *WhoScE 91-1*
Peterson, Patricia Ann 1963- *WhoAmW 93*
Peterson, Patti McGill 1943- *WhoAm 92, WhoAmW 93*
Peterson, Paul Elliott 1940- *WhoAm 92*
Peterson, Paul M. *Law&B 92*
Peterson, Paul Quayle 1912- *WhoAm 92*
Peterson, Paul Richard *Law&B 92*
Peterson, Paul T. 1947- *St&PR 93*
Peterson, Pete 1935- *CngDr 91, WhoSSW 93*
Peterson, Peter A. 1925- *WhoAm 92*
Peterson, Peter G. 1926- *WhoAm 92*
Peterson, Philip Everett 1922- *WhoAm 92*
Peterson, Quintin 1956- *WhoE 93*
Peterson, Ralph 1924- *St&PR 93, WhoAm 92*
Peterson, Ralph, Jr. *BioIn 17*
Peterson, Ralph Edward 1932- *WhoAm 92*
Peterson, Ralph Randall 1944- *St&PR 93*
Peterson, Randolph Lee 1920-1989 *BioIn 17*
Peterson, Raymond Louis 1931- *St&PR 93*
Peterson, Richard Allan 1938- *St&PR 93*
Peterson, Richard Burnett 1949- *WhoE 93*
Peterson, Richard Carson 1953- *WhoAm 92*
Peterson, Richard Elton 1941- *WhoAm 92*
Peterson, Richard H(ermann) 1942- *ConAu 137*
Peterson, Richard Hamlin 1914- *WhoAm 92*
Peterson, Richard Lee 1945- *WhoSSW 93*
Peterson, Richard Lewis 1939- *WhoSSW 93*
Peterson, Richard S. 1930- *St&PR 93*
Peterson, Richard Scot 1938- *WhoE 93*
Peterson, Robert 1924- *WhoWrEP 92*
Peterson, Robert A. 1925- *St&PR 93*
Peterson, Robert Allen 1944- *WhoAm 92*
Peterson, Robert Austin 1925- *WhoAm 92*
Peterson, Robert Byron *St&PR 93, WhoAm 92, WhoWor 93*
Peterson, Robert L. 1931- *St&PR 93*
Peterson, Robert L. 1932- *WhoAm 92*
Peterson, Robert Lawrence 1939- *WhoAm 92*
Peterson, Robert Stephen 1947- *WhoSSW 93*
Peterson, Robert Thomas 1950- *St&PR 93*
Peterson, Robin Tucker 1937- *WhoAm 92*
Peterson, Roderick William 1921- *WhoAm 92*
Peterson, Rodney Delos 1932- *WhoAm 92*
Peterson, Roger E. 1937- *St&PR 93*
Peterson, Roger Tory 1908- *WhoAm 92*
Peterson, Roger William 1936- *St&PR 93*
Peterson, Roland Oscar 1932- *WhoAm 92, WhoWor 93*
Peterson, Ronald A. 1949- *St&PR 93*
Peterson, Ronald Arthur 1938- *WhoE 93, WhoWor 93*
Peterson, Ronald D. *Law&B 92*
Peterson, Ronald H. 1944- *St&PR 93*
Peterson, Ronald R. 1952- *St&PR 93*
Peterson, Rudolph A. 1904- *St&PR 93, WhoAm 92*
Peterson, Russell Wilbur 1916- *WhoAm 92*
Peterson, Sally Lu 1942- *WhoAmW 93*
Peterson, Scott K. *Law&B 92*
Peterson, Scott Lee 1959- *WhoE 93*
Peterson, Sharon Lee 1946- *WhoAmW 93*
Peterson, Shirley 1936- *WhoAmW 93*
Peterson, Shirley D. 1941- *WhoAmW 93*
Peterson, Shirley V. 1936- *St&PR 93*
Peterson, Sophia 1929- *WhoAmW 93*
Peterson, Spiro 1922- *WhoAm 92*
Peterson, Stanley Lee 1949- *WhoEmL 93, WhoWor 93*
Peterson, Stephen L. *Law&B 92*
Peterson, Steven A. 1947- *ConAu 138*
Peterson, Susan *BioIn 17*
Peterson, Susan Kathleen 1961- *WhoAmW 93*
Peterson, Susan Vietzke 1960- *WhoEmL 93*
Peterson, Sushila Jane 1952- *WhoEmL 93*
Peterson, Thage G. 1933- *WhoWor 93*
Peterson, Theodore Bernard 1918- *WhoAm 92*
Peterson, Thomas Lee *Law&B 92*
Peterson, Thomas Robert *Law&B 92*
Peterson, Thomas W. 1952- *St&PR 93*
Peterson, Tom L. *Law&B 92*
Peterson, Tom L. 1932- *St&PR 93*
Peterson, Vincent Michael, Sr. 1932- *WhoE 93*
Peterson, Virginia Beth 1946- *WhoAmW 93*
Peterson, Wallace Carroll, Sr. 1921- *WhoAm 92*
Peterson, Walter Fritiof 1920- *WhoAm 92, WhoWor 93*
Peterson, Walter Rutherford 1922- *WhoAm 92*
Peterson, Walter Scott 1944- *WhoE 93*
Peterson, Warren Randolph *Law&B 92*
Peterson, Wayne 1927- *Baker 92*
Peterson, Willard James 1938- *WhoAm 92*
Peterson, William B. *Law&B 92*
Peterson, William Canova 1945- *WhoSSW 93*
Peterson, William Dwight 1954- *WhoE 93*
Peterson, William Frank 1922- *WhoE 93, WhoWor 93*
Peterson, William Herbert 1921- *WhoAm 92*
Peterson, William Michael 1942- *St&PR 93*
Peterson, William Paul 1957- *WhoE 93*
Peterson, William R. d1992 *NewYTBS 92*
Peterson, Willis Lester 1932- *WhoAm 92*
Peterson-Berger, (Olof) Wilhelm 1867-1942 *Baker 92*
Peterson-More, Diana Lewis 1950- *WhoAm 92, WhoAmW 93*
Peterson-Nedry, Judith A. 1947- *WhoWrEP 92*
Peterson-Vita, Elizabeth Ann 1955- *WhoEmL 93*
Peters-Pike, Damaris Porter 1933- *WhoAmW 93*
Petersson, S. Birger 1932- *WhoScE 91-4*
Peter, the Apostle, Saint *BioIn 17*
Peter the Deacon fl. 12th cent.- *OxDcByz*
Peter the Fuller d488 *OxDcByz*
Peter the Great, I 1672-1725 *HarEnMi*
Peter, the Great, I, Emperor of Russia 1672-1725 *BioIn 17*
Peter, the Great, III 1239-1285 *HarEnMi*
Peter the Hermit c. 1050-1115 *OxDcByz*
Peter the Iberian 409?-488? *OxDcByz*
Petesch, Natalie L(evin) M(aines) *WhoWrEP 92*
Petetin, Bernard *WhoScE 91-2*
Pethahiah of Regensburg fl. 12th cent.- *Expl 93*
Pether, Donald A. 1948- *St&PR 93*
Petherick, Simon 1960- *ScF&FL 92*
Pethes, George 1926- *WhoScE 91-4*
Pethick, Christopher John 1942- *WhoAm 92, WhoScE 91-2*
Pethig, Ronald *WhoScE 91-1*
Petho, Arpad Gyorgy 1928- *WhoWor 93*
Petho, Szilveszter 1923- *WhoScE 91-4*
Pethon, Per 1939- *WhoScE 91-4*
Pethrick, Richard Arthur *WhoScE 91-1*
Pethrick, Richard Arthur 1942- *WhoWor 93*
Peticolas, Warner Leland 1929- *WhoAm 92*
Petiet, Carole Anne 1952- *WhoEmL 93*
Petika, David M. 1945- *WhoAm 92*
Petillo, James Thomas 1944- *WhoAm 92*
Petillo, John Joseph, Jr. 1949- *WhoIns 93*
Petillo-Megofna, Christine Gail 1949- *WhoAmW 93*
Petinga, Charles Michael 1946- *WhoWor 93*
Petiot, Marcel *BioIn 17*
Petiot, Michael L. 1936- *St&PR 93*
Petit, Brenda Joyce 1939- *WhoSSW 93*
Petit, Chris 1949- *MiSFD 9*
Petit, Claudine Andree 1920- *WhoScE 91-2*
Petit, E.M.A. 1927- *WhoScE 91-2*
Petit, Jacques Alain *WhoScE 91-2*
Petit, Janine Ann *Law&B 92*
Petit, Jean-Christophe 1930- *WhoScE 91-2*
Petit, Michael W. 1943- *St&PR 93*
Petit, Michel 1936- *WhoScE 91-2*
Petit, Michel Jean 1936- *WhoUN 92*
Petit, Parker H. 1939- *St&PR 93*
Petit, Parker Holmes 1939- *WhoAm 92, WhoWor 93*
Petit, Pierre 1922- *WhoWor 93*
Petit, Raymond 1893-1976 *Baker 92*
Petit, Roland 1924- *WhoWor 93*
Petitclair, Pierre 1813-1860 *BioIn 17*
Petitfils, Pierre (Robert) 1908- *ConAu 137*
Petitjean, Jean *WhoWrEP 92*
Petit-Maire, Nicole 1928- *WhoScE 91-2*
Petito, Anthony Paul 1950- *WhoWor 93*
Petito, Victor Thomas, Jr. 1936- *WhoSSW 93*
Petitt, Gerald William 1945- *St&PR 93, WhoAm 92*
Petitt, Richard G. 1948- *St&PR 93*
Petizon, Alice T. *Law&B 92*
Petkov, Dimiter 1919- *Baker 92*
Petkov, Krum 1937- *WhoScE 91-4*
Petkov, Vesselin D. 1916- *WhoScE 91-4*

Pettus, Sally Lockhart 1937- *WhoAmW 93*
Pettway, Doris Marie 1953- *WhoAmW 93*
Petty, Anne C. *WhoWrEP 92*
Petty, Anne C. 1945- *ScF&FL 92*
Petty, Bruce 1930- *St&PR 93*
Petty, Charles Sutherland 1920- *WhoAm 92*
Petty, David Herbert 1917- *St&PR 93*
Petty, Emma *AmWomPl*
Petty, Evan R. 1933- *WhoScE 91-3*
Petty, George G. 1940- *St&PR 93*
Petty, George Oliver *Law&B 92*
Petty, George Oliver 1939- *WhoAm 92*
Petty, Guy James 1951- *WhoWor 93*
Petty, John Robert 1930- *WhoAm 92*
Petty, Keith 1920- *St&PR 93*
Petty, Kenneth H. 1928- *St&PR 93*
Petty, Lori *ConTFT 10*
Petty, Marcia Lou 1957- *WhoAmW 93*
Petty, Marge 1946- *WhoAmW 93*
Petty, Mark E. 1955- *St&PR 93*
Petty, Marty 1952- *St&PR 93*
Petty, Mary Diane 1953- *WhoAmW 93*
Petty, Michael C. *WhoScE 91-1*
Petty, Michael D. *Law&B 92*
Petty, Milana Mc Lead 1954- *WhoWrEP 92*
Petty, Olive Scott 1895- *WhoSSW 93, WhoWor 93*
Petty, Richard *NewYTBS 92 [port], WhoAm 92*
Petty, Ronald Franklin 1947- *WhoE 93, WhoEmL 93*
Petty, Roy Kevin *Law&B 92*
Petty, Scott, Jr. 1937- *St&PR 93, WhoSSW 93*
Petty, Steven Patrick 1959- *WhoSSW 93*
Petty, Terry D. 1935- *St&PR 93*
Petty, Thomas Lee 1932- *WhoAm 92*
Petty, Tom *BioIn 17*
Petty, Tom 1950- *ConMus 9 [port]*
Petty, Tom 1952- *WhoAm 92*
Petty, Travis Hubert 1928- *WhoAm 92*
Petty, William Calvin, III 1940- *WhoE 93*
Petty-Fitzmaurice, Henry 1845-1927 *BioIn 17*
Petuchowski, Jakob Josef 1925-1991 *BioIn 17, ConAu 136*
Petuely, Friedrich *WhoScE 91-4*
Petunin, Jurij Ivanovich 1937- *WhoWor 93*
Petunina, Martha Yurijvna 1965- *WhoWor 93*
Petuskey, Thomas James 1941- *WhoE 93*
Petway, Bruce 1883-1941 *BiDAMSp 1989*
Petyo, Robert *ScF&FL 92*
Petyrek, Felix 1892-1951 *Baker 92*
Petz, Edwin V. 1935- *WhoAm 92*
Petz, Edwin Virgil 1935- *St&PR 93*
Petz, Joan Marie 1932- *WhoAmW 93*
Petz, Johann Christoph 1664-1716 *Baker 92*
Petzal, David Elias 1941- *WhoAm 92, WhoWor 93, WhoWrEP 92*
Petzall, Stanley Bert 1945- *WhoWor 93*
Petzel, Florence Eloise 1911- *WhoAmW 93, WhoWor 93*
Petzel, Johann Christoph *Baker 92*
Petzel, Thomas 1934- *WhoScE 91-3*
Petzet, Walter 1866-1941 *Baker 92*
Petzinger, Ernst 1950- *WhoScE 91-3*
Petzinger, Thomas, Jr. 1955- *ConAu 136*
Petzinger, William Charles 1960- *WhoWrEP 92*
Petzinger, William Charles, III 1960- *WhoE 93*
Petznick, Jerry Walter 1945- *St&PR 93*
Petzny, Wilfried Johann 1940- *WhoWor 93*
Petzold, Carol Stoker *WhoAmW 93*
Petzold, Konrad 1930- *DrEEuF*
Petzold, Robert W. 1940- *St&PR 93*
Petzold, Rudolf 1908- *Baker 92*
Petzoldt, David A. 1959- *St&PR 93*
Petzoldt, Detlef G. 1936- *WhoScE 91-3*
Petzoldt, Richard (Johannes) 1907-1974 *Baker 92*
Petzow, Gunter 1926- *WhoScE 91-3*
Peuerl, Paul 1570?-1625? *Baker 92*
Peugeot, Patrick 1937- *WhoE 93, WhoIns 93, WhoWor 93*
Peugh, Sarah Louise Pearson 1924- *WhoAmW 93*
Peukert, Stanislaw 1932- *WhoScE 91-4*
Peurl, Paul 1570?-1625? *Baker 92*
Peutz, R.J.M.G. 1935- *WhoScE 91-3*
Pevec, Anthony Edward 1925- *WhoAm 92*
Peveler, James J. 1936- *St&PR 93*
Pevenage, Gerard L.M. 1934- *WhoScE 91-2*
Peverelli, Gerard Joseph 1954- *St&PR 93*
Peverly, Francis William 1963- *WhoE 93*
Peverly, Linda Pauline Vaughan 1941- *WhoAmW 93, WhoSSW 93*
Pevernage, Andries 1543-1591 *Baker 92*
Pevetz, Werner 1937- *WhoScE 91-4*
Pevney, Joseph 1920- *MiSFD 9*
Pevovar, Eddy Howard 1953- *WhoE 93*
Pevsner, Nikolaus 1902-1983 *BioIn 17*
Pew, Douglas *Law&B 92*
Pew, John G., Jr. *St&PR 93*
Pew, Robert Anderson 1936- *WhoAm 92*
Pew, Robert Cunningham, II 1923- *WhoAm 92*
Pew, Thomas Richard 1959- *St&PR 93*
Pew, Thomas W., Jr. 1938- *WhoAm 92*
Pewe, Troy Lewis 1918- *WhoAm 92*
Pewitt, Edward Gale 1932- *WhoAm 92*
Pewitt, James Dudley 1930- *WhoAm 92*
Pexa, E. Joseph *Law&B 92*
Peyer, Karl 1934- *WhoScE 91-4*
Peyerimhoff, Sigrid D. 1937- *WhoScE 91-3*
Peyerl, Walter 1939- *WhoUN 92*
Peyman, Douglas Alastair Ralph 1920- *WhoSSW 93*
Peyrard, Jean-Marc *WhoScE 91-2*
Peyrefitte, Alain 1925- *BioIn 17*
Peyrelevade, Jean 1939- *WhoWor 93*
Peyrin, J.O. 1930- *WhoScE 91-2*
Peyron, Jacques Philippe 1945- *WhoWor 93*
Peyron, Jean-Luc 1957- *WhoScE 91-2*
Peyron, Marie R. *Law&B 92*
Peyrone, Paolo *BioIn 17*
Peyronel, Anthony Christopher 1961- *WhoE 93*
Peyronnin, Joseph Felix, III 1947- *WhoAm 92*
Peyser, Joan 1931- *Baker 92*
Peyser, John 1916- *MiSFD 9*
Peyser, Joseph Leonard 1925- *WhoAm 92*
Peyser, Nina Peskoe 1952- *WhoAmW 93*
Peyser, Peter A. 1921- *WhoAm 92*
Peyser, Robert F. 1932- *St&PR 93*
Peyton, Audrey *ScF&FL 92*
Peyton, Charles Randolph 1958- *WhoSSW 93*
Peyton, David A. 1943- *WhoSSW 93*
Peyton, Donald Leon 1925- *WhoAm 92*
Peyton, Helen E. 1921- *WhoWrEP 92*
Peyton, James William Rodney 1949- *WhoWor 93*
Peyton, K. M. *MajAI, ScF&FL 92*
Peyton, K.M. 1929- *BioIn 17, ChlFicS*
Peyton, Kathleen Wendy 1929- *BioIn 17, MajAI [port], ScF&FL 92*
Peyton, Marilyn Stephens 1931- *WhoAmW 93*
Peyton, Michael *ScF&FL 92*
Peyton, Patricia Rose 1947- *WhoAmW 93*
Peyton, Patrick d1992 *NewYTBS 92 [port]*
Peyton, Patrick 1908-1992 *BioIn 17*
Peyton, Patrick J(oseph) 1909-1992 *ConAu 137*
Peyton, Richard *ScF&FL 92*
Peyton, Robert Glen 1940- *St&PR 93*
Peyton, William Maupin 1932- *St&PR 93, WhoAm 92*
Peyton Jones, Simon Loftus *WhoScE 91-1*
Peza, Juan de Dios 1852-1910 *DcMexL*
Pezdek, John Victor *Law&B 92*
Pezel, Johann Christoph 1639-1694 *Baker 92*
Pezelius, Johann Christoph 1639-1694 *Baker 92*
Pezet, A. Washington 1889-1978 *ScF&FL 92*
Pezim, Murray *BioIn 17*
Pezold, Steven R. 1951- *St&PR 93*
Pezzack, Douglas E. *Law&B 92*
Pezzella, Jerry James, Jr. 1937- *WhoAm 92*
Pfab, Josef *WhoScE 91-1*
Pfaelzer, Jean *ScF&FL 92*
Pfaelzer, Mariana R. 1926- *WhoAm 92, WhoAmW 93*
Pfaender, Jay A. 1942- *St&PR 93*
Pfaff, Alan Rae 1935- *WhoAm 92*
Pfaff, Daniel W. 1940- *ConAu 136*
Pfaff, Donald W. 1939- *WhoAm 92*
Pfaff, Frederick A. 1962- *St&PR 93*
Pfaff, George Otto 1926- *WhoAm 92*
Pfaff, Gerhard 1932- *WhoScE 91-3*
Pfaff, Judy *BioIn 17*
Pfaff, Michelle D. 1953- *WhoAmW 93*
Pfaff, Richard William 1936- *ScF&FL 92*
Pfaff, Tom Martin 1924- *St&PR 93*
Pfaff, William Wallace 1930- *WhoAm 92*
Pfaffelberger, Sven 1950- *WhoWor 93*
Pfaffenroth, Peter Albert 1941- *WhoE 93*
Pfaffenroth, Sara Beekey 1941- *WhoWor 93*
Pfafflin, Sheila Murphy 1934- *WhoAmW 93*
Pfaffman, William Scott 1954- *WhoE 93*
Pfaffmann, Carl 1913- *WhoAm 92*
Pfaltz, Andreas Peter 1948- *WhoWor 93*
Pfaltzgraff, Robert Louis, Jr. 1934- *WhoAm 92*
Pfalzer, Frank A. 1923- *WhoSSW 93*
Pfalzer, Gerald Martin 1945- *WhoSSW 93*
Pfander, Wilhelm 1937- *St&PR 93*
Pfannenstiel, Hans-Dieter 1944- *WhoScE 91-3*
Pfanner, Helmut Franz 1933- *WhoSSW 93*
Pfanner, Louise 1955- *BioIn 17*
Pfanner, (Anne) Louise 1955- *ConAu 136*
Pfannhauser, Werner 1940- *WhoScE 91-4*
Pfannkuch, Robert Blaine 1935- *WhoAm 92*
Pfannstiehl, Bernhard 1861-1940 *Baker 92*
Pfatteicher, Carl F(riedrichs) 1882-1957 *Baker 92*
Pfau, Charles Julius 1935- *WhoAm 92*
Pfau, George Harold, Jr. 1924- *WhoAm 92*
Pfau, Michel Alexandre 1931- *WhoWor 93*
Pfau, Nancy Ann 1942- *WhoSSW 93*
Pfau, Richard Anthony 1942- *WhoAm 92*
Pfautsch, George E. 1935- *St&PR 93*
Pfautz, John Jay 1949- *WhoIns 93*
Pfeffer, Cynthia Roberta 1943- *WhoE 93, WhoWor 93*
Pfeffer, David H. 1935- *WhoAm 92*
Pfeffer, Edward Israel 1914- *WhoAm 92*
Pfeffer, James *Law&B 92*
Pfeffer, James Lawrence 1951- *St&PR 93*
Pfeffer, Jeffrey 1946- *WhoAm 92*
Pfeffer, Leo 1910- *WhoAm 92*
Pfeffer, Marian Alice 1936- *WhoAmW 93*
Pfeffer, Mary Graves 1951- *WhoAmW 93*
Pfeffer, Michael A. 1945- *St&PR 93*
Pfeffer, Murray B. 1926- *St&PR 93*
Pfeffer, Nathaniel Frederick 1860-1932 *BiDAMSp 1989*
Pfeffer, Philip Maurice 1945- *St&PR 93, WhoAm 92*
Pfeffer, Richard Lawrence 1930- *WhoAm 92*
Pfeffer, Robert 1935- *WhoAm 92, WhoE 93*
Pfeffer, Rubin H. 1951- *St&PR 93*
Pfeffer, Rubin Harry 1951- *WhoAm 92*
Pfeffer, Susan 1948- *ScF&FL 92*
Pfeffer, Susan Beth 1948- *DcAmChF 1985*
Pfeffer, Wendy E. 1951- *WhoSSW 93*
Pfefferle, Seth 1955- *ScF&FL 92*
Pfeifer, Alistair Robin 1948- *WhoScE 91-3*
Pfeifer, Elizabeth Rose 1947- *WhoAmW 93*
Pfeifer, Harry 1929- *WhoScE 91-3*
Pfeifer, James E. 1938- *WhoIns 93*
Pfeifer, Janine Sue 1962- *WhoAmW 93*
Pfeifer, Jim 1948- *St&PR 93*
Pfeifer, Joan Barbara 1948- *WhoAmW 93*
Pfeifer, John W. 1941- *St&PR 93*
Pfeifer, Keith Machold 1949- *WhoE 93*
Pfeifer, Kenneth Arthur 1948- *WhoSSW 93*
Pfeifer, Lee A. *St&PR 93*
Pfeifer, Marcuse Lucile 1936- *WhoE 93*
Pfeifer, Martin S. 1932- *St&PR 93*
Pfeifer, Michael David 1937- *WhoAm 92, WhoSSW 93*
Pfeifer, Norman F. 1942- *St&PR 93*
Pfeifer, Ruth N. 1932- *WhoE 93*
Pfeifer, Walter C. 1926- *St&PR 93*
Pfeiffer, Albert 1935- *St&PR 93*
Pfeiffer, Astrid Elizabeth 1934- *WhoAm 92*
Pfeiffer, Burkhard Robert Kurt 1934- *WhoScE 91-3*
Pfeiffer, C. Richard *Law&B 92*
Pfeiffer, Carl E. 1930- *WhoAm 92, WhoSSW 93*
Pfeiffer, Christine Janet 1951- *WhoAmW 93*
Pfeiffer, Christine Marie *Law&B 92*
Pfeiffer, David Graham 1934- *WhoE 93*
Pfeiffer, Eckhard *WhoAm 92, WhoSSW 93*
Pfeiffer, Edward Weston 1939- *WhoE 93*
Pfeiffer, Eric Armin 1935- *WhoAm 92*
Pfeiffer, Georges-Jean 1835-1908 *Baker 92*
Pfeiffer, Heinrich 1927- *WhoScE 91-3*
Pfeiffer, Hesna Johnson *Law&B 92*
Pfeiffer, Ida 1797-1858 *Expl 93*
Pfeiffer, J(ohn) Douglas 1927- *WhoWrEP 92*
Pfeiffer, James Thomas 1945- *WhoE 93*
Pfeiffer, Jan 1928- *WhoScE 91-4*
Pfeiffer, Jane Cahill 1932- *WhoAm 92, WhoAmW 93, WhoWor 93*
Pfeiffer, John David 1931- *WhoAm 92*
Pfeiffer, John Edward 1914- *WhoAm 92*
Pfeiffer, John Howard 1923- *St&PR 93*
Pfeiffer, John William 1937- *WhoAm 92, WhoWrEP 92*
Pfeiffer, Leonard, IV *WhoAm 92, WhoE 93*
Pfeiffer, Michelle *BioIn 17*
Pfeiffer, Michelle 1957- *HolBB [port], IntDcF 2-3 [port]*
Pfeiffer, Michelle 1958- *WhoAm 92*
Pfeiffer, Ralph Aloysius, Jr. 1927- *WhoAm 92*
Pfeiffer, Robert J. 1920- *St&PR 93*
Pfeiffer, Robert John 1920- *WhoAm 92*
Pfeiffer, Steven Eugene 1940- *WhoE 93*
Pfeiffer, Steven Ira 1950- *WhoE 93*
Pfeiffer, Theodor 1853-1929 *Baker 92*
Pfeiffer, Werner Bernhard 1937- *WhoAm 92, WhoE 93*
Pfeiffer, Wilhelm 1932- *WhoWor 93*
Pfeiffer, Wolfgang 1943- *WhoScE 91-3*
Pfeifle, William George 1944- *WhoSSW 93*
Pfeil, Don *ScF&FL 92*
Pfeil, Donald J. *ScF&FL 92*
Pfeil, Fred 1949- *ScF&FL 92*
Pfeil, Helena A. *AmWomPl*
Pfeil, Horst W. 1928- *WhoScE 91-3*
Pfeil, John Frederick 1949- *WhoWrEP 92*
Pfeil, Kenneth Carl 1948- *St&PR 93*
Pfeil, Richard J. 1932- *St&PR 93*
Pfeil, Richard John 1932- *WhoAm 92*
Pfeil, Robert L. 1924- *St&PR 93*
Pfeil, Ronald Harmon 1949- *WhoE 93*
Pfeilsticker, Jack L. *Law&B 92*
Pfellsticker, Konrad 1929- *WhoScE 91-3*
Pfeister, James L. 1951- *St&PR 93*
Pfeister, Suzanne E. *St&PR 93*
Pfender, Emil 1925- *WhoAm 92*
Pfender, Rochelle LaRue 1960- *WhoAmW 93*
Pfening, Fred D., III 1949- *St&PR 93*
Pfening, Frederic Denver, III 1949- *WhoAm 92*
Pfennig, Norbert 1925- *WhoScE 91-3*
Pfenniger, Richard C., Jr. 1955- *St&PR 93*
Pfennigstorf, Werner 1934- *WhoWor 93*
Pfenninger, Karl H. 1944- *WhoAm 92*
Pfeuffer, Robert John 1925- *WhoAm 92*
Pfiester, Charles E. *Law&B 92*
Pfingstl, Hans 1938- *St&PR 93*
Pfingston, Roger Carl 1940- *WhoWrEP 92*
Pfirrman, Drew J. *Law&B 92*
Pfirrman, Melvin T. 1931- *St&PR 93*
Pfirsch, Dieter Erwin 1927- *WhoScE 91-3*
Pfirter, H.P. *WhoScE 91-4*
Pfischner, Fred L. 1908- *St&PR 93*
Pfischner, Robert D. 1922- *St&PR 93*
Pfister, Charles 1940-1990 *BioIn 17*
Pfister, Cloyd Harry 1936- *WhoAm 92*
Pfister, Dean William 1932- *St&PR 93, WhoAm 92*
Pfister, Dennis Francis 1926- *St&PR 93*
Pfister, Donald Henry 1945- *WhoAm 92, WhoE 93*
Pfister, Herbert 1950- *WhoScE 91-3*
Pfister, James Joseph 1946- *WhoWor 93*
Pfister, Robert K. 1919-1991 *BioIn 17*
Pfister, Roswell Robert 1938- *WhoAm 92*
Pfister, Walter John, Jr. 1929- *WhoE 93*
Pfisterer, David L. 1952- *St&PR 93*
Pfisterer, Hermann R. 1934- *St&PR 93*
Pfister-Guillouzo, Genevieve A.M. 1936- *WhoScE 91-2*
Pfitzenmaier, Denise Diane 1958- *St&PR 93*
Pfitzmann, Andreas 1958- *WhoWor 93*
Pfitzner, Hans 1869-1949 *OxDcOp*
Pfitzner, Hans (Erich) 1869-1949 *Baker 92, IntDcOp*
Pfizenmaier, Klaus *WhoScE 91-3*
Pfizenmaier, Richard d1989 *BioIn 17*
Pfizenmayer, Frank J. *Law&B 92*
Pfizenmayer, Richard F. *Law&B 92*
Pflanze, Otto Paul 1918- *WhoAm 92, WhoE 93*
Pflaum, Susanna Whitney 1937- *WhoAm 92*
Pfleeger, Shari Lawrence 1950- *WhoAmW 93*
Pfleghar, David W. 1947- *St&PR 93*
Pfleider, James Kenneth 1940- *WhoAm 92*
Pfleider, Shirley Jean 1952- *WhoAmW 93*
Pfleiderer, Jorg 1931- *WhoScE 91-4, WhoWor 93*
Pfleiderer, Kurt 1931- *WhoScE 91-3*
Pflieger, Kenneth John 1952- *WhoSSW 93*
Pflieger, Larry Leonard 1923- *St&PR 93*
Pflieger, Pat *ScF&FL 92*
Pflimlin, Pierre 1907- *BioIn 17*
Pflueger, Edward Maximilian 1905- *WhoAm 92*
Pflueger, Melba Lee 1942- *WhoAmW 93*
Pflug, Christiane 1936-1972 *BioIn 17*
Pflug, Irving John 1923- *WhoAm 92*
Pflug, Reinhard 1932- *WhoScE 91-3*
Pflughaupt, Robert 1833-1871 *Baker 92*
Pflugradt, William d1991 *BioIn 17*
Pflum, William John 1924- *WhoE 93, WhoWor 93*
Pfnister, Allan Orel 1925- *WhoAm 92*
Pfohl, Dawn Gertrude 1944- *WhoAmW 93*
Pfohl, Ferdinand 1862-1949 *Baker 92*
Pfordresher, John 1943- *ScF&FL 92*
Pfordresher, John Charles 1943- *WhoE 93*
Pfordten, Hermann Ludwig von der 1857-1933 *Baker 92*
Pforr, Mary Martha 1948- *WhoE 93, WhoEmL 93*

Pforr, William John 1947- *WhoE 93, WhoEmL 93*
Pforzheimer, Carl H., Jr. 1907- *St&PR 93*
Pforzheimer, Carl Howard, Jr. 1907- *WhoAm 92, WhoWor 93*
Pfost, Dale Robert 1957- *WhoWor 93*
Pfost, Gracie Bowers 1906-1965 *BioIn 17*
Pfost, Heiner 1934- *WhoScE 91-3*
Pfountz, Harold J. 1943- *St&PR 93*
Pfountz, Harold John *Law&B 92*
Pfouts, John Christopher 1951- *WhoE 93*
Pfouts, Ralph William 1920- *WhoAm 92, WhoSSW 93, WhoWor 93*
Pfretzschner, Jaime *WhoScE 91-3*
Pfriem, Bernard Aldine 1914- *WhoAm 92*
Pfriender, Robert C. 1954- *St&PR 93*
Pfrommer, W. *WhoScE 91-3*
Pfrunder, Beat Victor Ernst Rudolf 1939- *WhoWor 93*
Pfund, Edward Theodore, Jr. 1923- *WhoWor 93*
Pfund, Peter Harry 1932- *WhoE 93*
Pfund, Randy *WhoAm 92*
Pfunder, Malcolm Gilkey 1919- *WhoAm 92*
Pfundt, Ernst (Gotthold Benjamin) 1806-1871 *Baker 92*
Pfundt, William N. *St&PR 93*
Pfurtscheller *WhoScE 91-4*
Phadke, Arun G. 1938- *WhoAm 92*
Phair, David 1921- *St&PR 93*
Phair, George A. *Law&B 92*
Phair, James Joseph 1939- *WhoIns 93*
Phair, Joseph B. *Law&B 92*
Phakrases *OxDcByz*
Phalan, James M. 1936- *St&PR 93*
Phalese, Pierre c. 1510-c. 1575 *Baker 92*
Phalon, Philip Anthony 1929- *St&PR 93*
Pham, Amy Ha 1968- *WhoSSW 93*
Pham, Chi Do 1948- *WhoUN 92*
Pham, Hung Gia 1960- *WhoE 93*
Pham-Jackel, Christine *Law&B 92*
Pham Xuan An *BioIn 17*
Phan, Kieu-Duong 1930- *WhoScE 91-2*
Phan, Thuy 1948- *WhoUN 92*
Phan Boi Chau 1867-1940 *DcTwHis*
Phaneendranath, Vellanky Venkata 1950- *WhoWor 93*
Phaneuf, Robert N. 1961- *WhoIns 93*
Phang, Alan Soy 1958- *St&PR 93*
Phan-Tan, Tai 1939- *WhoWor 93*
Phan-Thien, Nhan 1952- *WhoWor 93*
Phantinos the Younger 9th cent.-10th cent. *OxDcByz*
Phantom, D.S. *WhoWrEP 92*
Phan Van Loc 1923- *WhoScE 91-2*
Pharamond, Jean-Claude 1947- *St&PR 93*
Pharand, G. *Law&B 92*
Pharaon, Ghaith R. *BioIn 17*
Phares, Alain Joseph 1942- *WhoAm 92*
Phares, Donald M. 1931- *St&PR 93*
Phares, E. Jerry 1928- *WhoAm 92*
Phares, Elwood Willis, II 1930- *St&PR 93*
Phares, Lynn Levisay 1947- *WhoAm 92, WhoAmW 93*
Phares, Rebecca *BioIn 17*
Pharis, Carolyn Faye 1955- *WhoAmW 93, WhoSSW 93*
Pharis, Mary Evans 1938- *WhoAmW 93*
Pharis, Ruth McCalister 1934- *WhoAmW 93*
Pharis, William Leonard 1928- *WhoAm 92*
Pharo, James *Law&B 92*
Pharoah, Peter Oswald Derrick *WhoScE 91-1*
Pharoah, Peter Oswald Derrick 1934- *WhoWor 93*
Pharoux, Pierre *BioIn 17*
Pharr, Ann E. 1946- *WhoE 93*
Pharr, Ann L. *Law&B 92*
Pharr, Cynthia Ivy 1948- *WhoAmW 93*
Pharr, Michael M. 1940- *St&PR 93*
Pharr, Michael Milton 1940- *WhoAm 92*
Pharr, Naomi Henrietta *WhoAmW 93*
Pharr, Robert Deane d1992 *NewYTBS 92*
Pharr, Robert Deane 1916-1992 *BioIn 17, ConAu 137*
Pharris, Doris Jean 1931- *St&PR 93*
Pharriss, Bruce B. *St&PR 93*
Phaup, Jimmye Richard 1953- *WhoSSW 93*
Pheasant, Merle E., Jr. 1945- *St&PR 93*
Pheatt, David William 1947- *St&PR 93*
Pheidas, Athanasios C. 1958- *WhoWor 93*
Phelan, Anne Susan 1960- *WhoWrEP 92*
Phelan, Arthur Joseph 1915- *WhoAm 92*
Phelan, Charlotte Robertson 1917- *WhoAm 92*
Phelan, Ellen 1943- *WhoAm 92*
Phelan, Francis J. 1925- *WhoWrEP 92*
Phelan, Francis Joseph 1925- *WhoE 93*
Phelan, Jack P. 1941- *St&PR 93*
Phelan, James Francis 1950- *St&PR 93*
Phelan, John Densmore 1914- *WhoAm 92, WhoWor 93*
Phelan, John J. 1931- *St&PR 93*
Phelan, John J., Jr. *BioIn 17*
Phelan, John Martin 1932- *WhoE 93*
Phelan, Joseph Anthony 1937- *WhoUN 92*
Phelan, Martin DuPont 1913- *WhoAm 92*
Phelan, Patrick Joseph 1950- *WhoE 93*
Phelan, Paul J. *WhoAm 92*
Phelan, Paul James Aquinas 1961- *WhoWor 93*
Phelan, Richard John 1937- *WhoAm 92*
Phelan, Richard Magruder 1921- *WhoAm 92*
Phelan, Richard Paul 1939- *WhoAm 92*
Phelan, Robert J. 1947- *St&PR 93*
Phelan, Shane 1956- *ConAu 137*
Phelan, Thomas 1925- *WhoAm 92, WhoE 93, WhoWor 93*
Phelan, Thomas Anthony 1928- *WhoWrEP 92*
Phelan, Thomas Joseph, Jr. 1933- *St&PR 93*
Phelan, William Thomas 1941- *WhoE 93*
Phelip, Xavier 1936- *WhoScE 91-2*
Phelix, Bernard Robert 1942- *WhoSSW 93*
Phelizon, Jean Francois 1946- *WhoWor 93*
Phelps, Ashton, Jr. 1945- *BioIn 17, WhoAm 92*
Phelps, Carrie Lynn 1964- *WhoAmW 93*
Phelps, Charles E. 1943- *WhoAm 92*
Phelps, Charlotte DeMonte 1933- *WhoE 93*
Phelps, Christine Elizabeth 1959- *WhoAmW 93*
Phelps, Dean, Jr. 1944- *St&PR 93*
Phelps, Deanne Elayne 1949- *WhoAmW 93, WhoEmL 93, WhoSSW 93*
Phelps, Donald Eugene 1931- *WhoSSW 93*
Phelps, Edmund Strother 1933- *WhoAm 92*
Phelps, Elizabeth Stuart *AmWomPl*
Phelps, Elizabeth Stuart 1844-1911 *BioIn 17*
Phelps, Flora Louise Lewis 1917- *WhoAm 92, WhoE 93*
Phelps, George E. 1943- *St&PR 93*
Phelps, Gregory Kenneth 1958- *St&PR 93*
Phelps, Harriette Longacre 1936- *WhoAmW 93*
Phelps, James E. 1922- *St&PR 93*
Phelps, John Ray 1946- *WhoSSW 93*
Phelps, Joseph William 1927- *St&PR 93, WhoAm 92*
Phelps, Judson Hewett 1942- *WhoAm 92*
Phelps, Lee Barry 1938- *WhoE 93*
Phelps, Lewis McKinnie 1943- *St&PR 93*
Phelps, Malcolm E. 1905-1991 *BioIn 17*
Phelps, Margaret Simrell 1943- *WhoSSW 93*
Phelps, Michael Edward 1939- *WhoAm 92*
Phelps, Michael Joseph 1948- *St&PR 93*
Phelps, Nan 1904-1990 *BioIn 17*
Phelps, Norman Thomas 1913- *WhoE 93*
Phelps, Orme Wheelock 1906- *WhoAm 92*
Phelps, P. Michael *Law&B 92*
Phelps, Paul Michael 1933- *St&PR 93, WhoAm 92*
Phelps, Paulding 1933- *WhoAm 92*
Phelps, Pauline *AmWomPl*
Phelps, Peter Whittenhall d1990 *BioIn 17*
Phelps, Richard Frederick 1941- *BiDAMSp 1989*
Phelps, Richard J. 1928- *St&PR 93*
Phelps, Richard Stevens 1938- *WhoE 93*
Phelps, Richard William 1946- *WhoWor 93*
Phelps, Sandra Kaye 1966- *WhoSSW 93*
Phelps, Stanford N. *BioIn 17*
Phelps, Stanford N. 1934- *St&PR 93*
Phelps, Stephen Ferrel 1944- *WhoE 93*
Phelps, Steve Lynn 1958- *WhoSSW 93*
Phelps, Stewart J. 1933- *St&PR 93*
Phelps, Susan Van Buren 1951- *WhoAmW 93*
Phelps, Timothy Hunt 1953- *WhoE 93*
Phelps, Wade Lynn 1954- *WhoSSW 93*
Phelps, Walter Winslow 1918- *WhoSSW 93*
Phelps, William *MiSFD 9*
Phelps, William Cunningham 1934- *WhoIns 93*
Phelps, William H. *Law&B 92*
Phelps, William H. 1902-1988 *BioIn 17*
Phelps, William L. 1955- *St&PR 93*
Phelps, Win *MiSFD 9*
Phemister, Robert David 1936- *WhoAm 92*
Phemister, Sharon Kay 1946- *WhoAmW 93*
Phemister, Thomas Alexander 1940- *WhoAm 92*
Pheney, Dennis J. 1938- *St&PR 93*
Phenicie, Mark Elihu 1954- *WhoE 93*
Phenis, Nancy Sue 1943- *WhoAmW 93*
Pherigo, William L. 1941- *St&PR 93*
Phibbs, Clifford Matthew 1930- *WhoAm 92*
Phibbs, Harry Albert 1933- *WhoAm 92*
Phibbs, Philip Monford 1931- *WhoAm 92*
Phibbs, Roderic Henry 1930- *WhoAm 92*
Phifer, Forrest Keith 1956- *WhoSSW 93*
Phifer, J. Reese 1916- *St&PR 93*
Phifer, John Thomas 1956- *WhoSSW 93*
Phifer, Ross S. 1941- *WhoIns 93*
Phifer, Scott Craig *Law&B 92*
Philagathos 11th cent.-12th cent. *OxDcByz*
Philaniotis, Kleanthis *WhoScE 91-4*
Philanthropenos *OxDcByz*
Philanthropenos, Alexios c. 1270-c. 1323 *OxDcByz*
Philaretos Brachamios *OxDcByz*
Philaretos the Merciful 702-792 *OxDcByz*
Philbert, Georges Marie Victor 1922- *WhoScE 91-2*
Philbin, Ann Margaret 1941- *WhoE 93*
Philbin, Daniel Michael 1935- *WhoE 93*
Philbin, David A. *St&PR 93*
Philbin, Edward J. *BioIn 17*
Philbin, Edward James 1932- *WhoAm 92*
Philbin, John Arthur 1934- *WhoAm 92*
Philbin, Regis *BioIn 17*
Philbrick, Donald Lockey 1923- *WhoAm 92*
Philbrick, Julian W. *St&PR 93*
Philbrick, Lawrence Emery 1947- *St&PR 93*
Philbrick, Loretta J. 1934- *St&PR 93*
Philbrick, Margaret Elder 1914- *WhoAm 92, WhoE 93*
Philbrick, Ralph 1934- *WhoAm 92*
Philbrick, William R. *ScF&FL 92*
Philbrook, Brian P. *Law&B 92*
Philby, H. St. J.B. 1885-1960 *BioIn 17*
Philby, Harry St. John 1885-1960 *Expl 93*
Philby, Harry St. John Bridger 1885-1960 *BioIn 17*
Philby, Kim 1912-1988 *BioIn 17, ColdWar 1 [port]*
Philduis, Peter P. *St&PR 93*
Phile, Philip c. 1734-1793 *Baker 92*
Philen, James Gilbert, Jr. 1904- *St&PR 93*
Philes *OxDcByz*
Philes, Manuel c. 1275-c. 1345 *OxDcByz*
Philianos, Skevos 1923- *WhoScE 91-3*
Philidor *Baker 92*
Philidor, Andre Danican c. 1647-1730 *Baker 92*
Philidor, Anne 1681-1728 *OxDcOp*
Philidor, Anne Danican 1681-1728 *Baker 92*
Philidor, Francois-Andre Danican 1726-1795 *Baker 92, OxDcOp*
Philidor, Jacques Danican 1657-1708 *Baker 92*
Philidor, Jean Danican c. 1620-1679 *Baker 92*
Philidor, Pierre Danican 1681-1731 *Baker 92*
Philion, James Robert 1944- *St&PR 93*
Philip *OxDcByz*
Philip c. 1639-1676 *HarEnMi*
Philip, Prince 1921- *BioIn 17*
Philip, Sachem of the Wampanoags d1676 *BioIn 17*
Philip, II 383BC-336BC *HarEnMi*
Philip, II c. 1177-1208 *HarEnMi*
Philip, II, King of Spain 1527-1598 *BioIn 17*
Philip, IV 1268-1314 *HarEnMi*
Philip, IV, King of Spain 1605-1665 *BioIn 17*
Philip, V 238BC-179BC *HarEnMi*
Philip, A. G. Davis 1929- *WhoAm 92, WhoE 93, WhoWor 93, WhoWrEP 92*
Philip, Achille 1878-1959 *Baker 92*
Philip, Andre 1902-1970 *BioIn 17*
Philip, Craig E. 1953- *St&PR 93*
Philip, John 1930- *WhoScE 91-2*
Philip, Leila 1961- *ConAu 137*
Philip, Neil 1955- *ScF&FL 92*
Philip, Peter Van Ness 1925- *WhoAm 92*
Philip, Peter W. *St&PR 93*
Philip, T. Peter 1933- *St&PR 93*
Philip, William Warren 1926- *St&PR 93, WhoAm 92*
Philip Augustus, II 1165-1223 *HarEnMi*
Philipbar, William Bernard 1925- *St&PR 93*
Philipbar, William Bernard, Jr. 1925- *WhoAm 92*
Philipe, Gerard 1922-1959 *IntDcF 2-3 [port]*
Philip Monotropos fl. c. 1100- *OxDcByz*
Philip of Side fl. 5th cent.- *OxDcByz*
Philip of Spain, IV fl. 17th cent.- *DcAmChF 1960*
Philip of Swabia 1178-1208 *OxDcByz*
Philip of Taranto, I d1331 *OxDcByz*
Philipp, Anita Marie 1948- *WhoSSW 93*
Philipp, Burkart 1925- *WhoScE 91-3*
Philipp, Elizabeth R. *Law&B 92, St&PR 93*
Philipp, Isidor 1863-1958 *Baker 92*
Philipp, Ronald Emerson 1932- *WhoE 93*
Philipp, Walter Viktor 1936- *WhoAm 92*
Philipp, William A. 1955- *St&PR 93*
Philippaerts, Herman 1937- *WhoScE 91-2*
Philippakis, Ioannis Nicolas 1960- *WhoWor 93*
Philippe, Emile C. 1929- *WhoScE 91-2*
Philippe, Pierre 1560?-1628 *Baker 92*
Philippe, Scott Louis 1963- *WhoSSW 93*
Philippe-Auguste, Gerard *DcCPCAm*
Philippe de Vitry *Baker 92*
Philippi, Dieter Rudolph 1929- *WhoE 93*
Philippi, Edmond Jean 1936- *WhoWor 93*
Philippi, Pietro 1560?-1628 *Baker 92*
Philippides, Stylianos Andreas 1952- *St&PR 93*
Philippikos d714? *OxDcByz*
Philippon, Jean 1934- *WhoScE 91-2*
Philippot, Michel 1925- *Baker 92*
Philippou, John 1948- *WhoScE 91-3*
Philipps, Alice Evelyn *AmWomPl*
Philipps, Edward William 1938- *St&PR 93, WhoAm 92*
Philipps, Louis Edward 1906- *WhoAm 92*
Philippsen, John Newman 1952- *St&PR 93*
Philippu, Athineos 1931- *WhoScE 91-4*
Philippus, Petrus 1560?-1628 *Baker 92*
Philippus Arabus, Marcus Julius Verus d249 *HarEnMi*
Philips, B. Calvin 1941- *St&PR 93*
Philips, Constantinos L. 1934- *St&PR 93*
Philips, Danny 1951- *WhoAsAP 91*
Philips, David Evan 1926- *WhoAm 92, WhoWor 93*
Philips, Dixon Coale d1992 *BioIn 17*
Philips, Donald 1935- *St&PR 93*
Philips, Dorothy M. *St&PR 93*
Philips, F.C. 1849-1921 *ScF&FL 92*
Philips, George 1931- *St&PR 93*
Philips, Irving d1992 *NewYTBS 92*
Philips, Jesse 1914- *WhoAm 92*
Philips, John 1676-1709 *BioIn 17*
Philips, John Edward 1952- *WhoWor 93*
Philips, Judson P. 1903-1989 *ScF&FL 92*
Philips, Julia Therese 1953- *WhoAmW 93*
Philips, Lee *MiSFD 9*
Philips, Marjorie Rosenbluth 1958- *WhoAmW 93*
Philips, Michael 1942- *ScF&FL 92*
Philips, Peter 1560?-1628 *Baker 92*
Philips, R.J. *WhoScE 91-1*
Philipsborn, John David 1919- *WhoAm 92*
Philipsborn, John Timothy 1949- *WhoEmL 93*
Philipsborn, Thomas D. 1926- *St&PR 93*
Philipsen, Dirk 1959- *ConAu 139*
Philipson, C. Lennart 1929- *WhoScE 91-3*
Philipson, Herman Louis, Jr. 1924- *WhoAm 92*
Philipson, Julie 1963- *WhoSSW 93*
Philipson, Lennart *WhoScE 91-3*
Philipson, Morris 1926- *WhoAm 92, WhoWrEP 92*
Philipson, Willard Dale 1930- *WhoAm 92*
Philis, John 1936- *WhoScE 91-4*
Phillabaum, Leslie Ervin 1936- *WhoAm 92, WhoWrEP 92*
Phillabaum, Roberta Swarr 1937- *WhoAmW 93, WhoSSW 93*
Phillip, Cheryl T. *Law&B 92*
Phillip, Claude 1947- *WhoAsAP 91*
Phillipes, Debra Lynne *Law&B 92*
Phillipes, Peter Michael *Law&B 92*
Phillippe, Timothy Franklin 1952- *WhoSSW 93*
Phillippi, James Paul 1949- *WhoE 93*
Phillippi, Wendell Crane 1918- *ConAu 136, WhoAm 92*
Phillipps, Adelaide 1833-1882 *Baker 92*
Phillipps, Ian Hugh 1924- *WhoWor 93*
Phillippy, Patricia Anne 1960- *WhoSSW 93*
Phillips, Adran Abner 1924- *St&PR 93, WhoAm 92, WhoWor 93*
Phillips, Adrian d1990 *BioIn 17*
Phillips, Adrian 1936- *WhoScE 91-3*
Phillips, Aileen Paul 1917- *WhoWrEP 92*
Phillips, Al 1935- *St&PR 93*
Phillips, Alan *ConAu 39NR*
Phillips, Alexander M. 1907-1970 *ScF&FL 92*
Phillips, Alfred Carlton *Law&B 92*
Phillips, Almarin 1925- *WhoAm 92*
Phillips, Andre'e P. 1939- *St&PR 93*
Phillips, Anita Joyce 1958- *St&PR 93*
Phillips, Ann 1930- *ScF&FL 92*
Phillips, Anna 1936- *WhoWor 93*
Phillips, Anthony F. 1937- *St&PR 93*
Phillips, Anthony Francis 1937- *WhoAm 92*
Phillips, Anthony George 1943- *WhoAm 92*
Phillips, Anthony Mark 1945- *WhoAm 92*
Phillips, Arthur 1948- *St&PR 93, WhoIns 93*
Phillips, Arthur William, Jr. 1915- *WhoAm 92, WhoWor 93*

Phillips, Asa R., Jr. 1932- *St&PR 93*
Phillips, Barry 1929- *WhoAm 92*
Phillips, Berry W. 1943- *St&PR 93*
Phillips, Bessie Gertrude Wright *WhoE 93*
Phillips, Bettine K. *AmWomPl*
Phillips, Betty Jean Nanney 1935- *WhoSSW 93*
Phillips, Betty Lou *WhoAmW 93, WhoWor 93*
Phillips, Beverly Ann Blersch 1928- *WhoAmW 93*
Phillips, Bill *MiSFD 9*
Phillips, Brent *WhoAm 92*
Phillips, Brian Roger 1939- *St&PR 93*
Phillips, Bryan David Arthur *WhoScE 91-1*
Phillips, Bum 1923- *BioIn 17*
Phillips, Burrill 1907-1988 *Baker 92*
Phillips, Carlton V. 1924- *St&PR 93*
Phillips, Carlton Vernon 1924- *WhoWor 93*
Phillips, Carole Cherry 1938- *WhoE 93*
Phillips, Carolyn Ann 1952- *St&PR 93*
Phillips, Carroll D. *St&PR 93*
Phillips, Cecil B. 1924- *St&PR 93*
Phillips, Cecil Barton 1924- *WhoAm 92*
Phillips, Charles A. Speas 1922- *WhoAm 92*
Phillips, Charles Alan 1939- *WhoAm 92*
Phillips, Charles Albert *St&PR 93*
Phillips, Charles Franklin 1910- *WhoAm 92*
Phillips, Charles Franklin, Jr. 1934- *WhoAm 92*
Phillips, Charles Gorham 1921- *WhoAm 92*
Phillips, Charles Victor 1942- *WhoScE 91-1*
Phillips, Christopher Hallowell 1920- *WhoWor 93*
Phillips, Chynna *BioIn 17*
Phillips, Clifton J. 1919- *WhoAm 92*
Phillips, Craig 1922- *WhoAm 92*
Phillips, D.E. *Law&B 92*
Phillips, Dan L. 1948- *St&PR 93*
Phillips, Daniel Anthony 1938- *St&PR 93, WhoAm 92*
Phillips, Daniel Miller 1933- *WhoAm 92*
Phillips, David *ScF&FL 92, WhoScE 91-1*
Phillips, David 1939- *WhoWor 93*
Phillips, David Beltran 1946- *St&PR 93*
Phillips, David Chilton, Sir *WhoScE 91-1*
Phillips, David Colin 1940- *WhoWor 93*
Phillips, David George 1931- *WhoE 93*
Phillips, David Graham 1867-1911 *GayN*
Phillips, David John 1937- *St&PR 93*
Phillips, David Lowell 1952- *WhoE 93*
Phillips, David Meredith *WhoScE 91-1*
Phillips, David P. *Law&B 92*
Phillips, Dean Mark *Law&B 92*
Phillips, Delbert D. 1943- *ScF&FL 92*
Phillips, Dennis *ScF&FL 92*
Phillips, Dennis P. 1955- *BioIn 17*
Phillips, Derwyn Fraser 1930- *St&PR 93*
Phillips, Dewi Zephaniah 1934- *WhoWor 93*
Phillips, Diana Marie 1942- *WhoSSW 93*
Phillips, Don H. *Law&B 92*
Phillips, Donald Arthur 1945- *WhoAm 92*
Phillips, Donald E. 1932- *St&PR 93*
Phillips, Donald John 1930- *WhoAm 92*
Phillips, Donald Smith 1949- *WhoE 93*
Phillips, Dorothy Dean 1925- *WhoAmW 93*
Phillips, Dorothy Kay 1945- *WhoAmW 93*
Phillips, Dorothy Reid 1924- *WhoAmW 93, WhoWor 93*
Phillips, Douglas Edward 1943- *St&PR 93*
Phillips, Douglass Martin 1929- *St&PR 93*
Phillips, E(ugene) Lee 1941- *ConAu 40NR*
Phillips, E. Vaughn *Law&B 92*
Phillips, Earl Norfleet, Jr. 1940- *St&PR 93, WhoAm 92*
Phillips, Edith Schaffer d1990 *BioIn 17*
Phillips, Edward Everett 1927- *WhoAm 92*
Phillips, Edward H. 1920- *St&PR 93*
Phillips, Edward O. 1931- *WhoCanL 92*
Phillips, Edwin Allen 1915- *WhoWrEP 92*
Phillips, Edwin Charles 1917- *St&PR 93, WhoAm 92*
Phillips, Edwin L. 1948- *St&PR 93*
Phillips, Elizabeth 1919- *ScF&FL 92*
Phillips, Elizabeth Jason 1936- *WhoAmW 93*
Phillips, Elizabeth Joan 1938- *WhoAm 92, WhoAmW 93*
Phillips, Ellen Agnes 1950- *WhoAmW 93*
Phillips, Elliott H. 1919- *St&PR 93*
Phillips, Elliott Hunter 1919- *WhoAm 92*
Phillips, Ellis Laurimore, Jr. 1921- *WhoAm 92*
Phillips, Esther 1935-1984 *SoulM*
Phillips, Ethel C. 1908- *WhoAm 92*
Phillips, Euan Hywel 1928- *WhoAm 92*
Phillips, Frances Marie 1918- *WhoAm 92*
Phillips, Fred Ronald 1940- *St&PR 93, WhoE 93*
Phillips, Frederick Clayton 1915- *St&PR 93*
Phillips, Frederick Falley 1946- *WhoEmL 93*
Phillips, Gabriel 1933- *WhoAm 92*
Phillips, Gary Lee 1954- *St&PR 93*
Phillips, Gary Lynn 1947- *WhoAm 92*
Phillips, Gary Wilson 1940- *WhoE 93*
Phillips, Gene D(aniel) 1935- *ConAu 38NR*
Phillips, Gene E. 1937- *WhoAm 92*
Phillips, Geneva Ficker 1920- *WhoAmW 93, WhoWor 93*
Phillips, Geoffrey F. 1931- *WhoScE 91-1*
Phillips, George E. 1938- *St&PR 93*
Phillips, George L. 1949- *WhoAm 92*
Phillips, George Michael 1947- *WhoAm 92*
Phillips, George Richard 1930- *WhoSSW 93*
Phillips, George Wygant 1929- *WhoE 93*
Phillips, Gerald Baer 1925- *WhoAm 92*
Phillips, Gerald C. 1922- *St&PR 93*
Phillips, Gerald Cleveland 1922- *WhoAm 92*
Phillips, Gerald O. 1945- *St&PR 93*
Phillips, Gil 1929- *St&PR 93*
Phillips, Glenn A. 1934- *St&PR 93*
Phillips, Glynda Ann *WhoAmW 93*
Phillips, Graham Holmes 1939- *WhoAm 92, WhoE 93*
Phillips, Harold Leon 1935- *WhoSSW 93*
Phillips, Harriet Elizabeth 1930- *WhoE 93*
Phillips, Harry A., Jr. *Law&B 92*
Phillips, Harry J., Jr. 1950- *WhoAm 92*
Phillips, Harry Johnson, Sr. 1930- *WhoAm 92*
Phillips, Harvey 1929- *BioIn 17, WhoAm 92*
Phillips, Harvey (Gene) 1929- *Baker 92*
Phillips, Herbert Alvin, Jr. 1928- *WhoAm 92*
Phillips, Howard W. 1930- *St&PR 93*
Phillips, Howard William 1930- *WhoAm 92*
Phillips, Hugh D. 1952- *ConAu 139*
Phillips, Ian *WhoScE 91-1*
Phillips, Ivory Paul 1942- *WhoSSW 93*
Phillips, J. Gordon 1927- *St&PR 93*
Phillips, Jack *MajAI*
Phillips, Jack Carter 1935- *WhoSSW 93*
Phillips, Jack Ewart *Law&B 92*
Phillips, Jacqueline Marie *Law&B 92*
Phillips, James A. 1928- *St&PR 93*
Phillips, James Atlee 1915-1991 *BioIn 17*
Phillips, James Charles 1933- *WhoAm 92*
Phillips, James D. 1933- *WhoAm 92, WhoWor 93*
Phillips, James Dickson, Jr. 1922- *WhoAm 92, WhoSSW 93*
Phillips, James E., Jr. *Law&B 92*
Phillips, James Edward 1928- *St&PR 93, WhoSSW 93*
Phillips, James H., III 1939- *St&PR 93*
Phillips, James Henley, Jr. 1911- *WhoSSW 93*
Phillips, James Kenneth 1929- *St&PR 93*
Phillips, James Lee 1942- *WhoSSW 93*
Phillips, James Linford 1943- *WhoAm 92*
Phillips, James M. 1916- *St&PR 93*
Phillips, James Macilduff 1916- *WhoAm 92, WhoE 93, WhoWor 93*
Phillips, James Sylvester 1930- *St&PR 93*
Phillips, James W. 1930- *St&PR 93*
Phillips, Janet Colleen 1933- *WhoAm 92*
Phillips, Jayne Anne 1952- *BioIn 17, MagSAmL [port]*
Phillips, Jeannette Veronica 1940- *WhoAmW 93*
Phillips, Jerry Juan 1935- *WhoAm 92*
Phillips, Jerry Wayne 1935- *WhoSSW 93*
Phillips, Jill M. 1952- *ScF&FL 92*
Phillips, Jill (Meta) 1952- *ConAu 39NR, WhoAm 92*
Phillips, Jimmy E. 1939- *St&PR 93, WhoIns 93*
Phillips, Joe *BioIn 17*
Phillips, John 1920- *St&PR 93*
Phillips, John 1935- *Baker 92*
Phillips, John Benbow, Jr. 1933- *St&PR 93*
Phillips, John Benton 1959- *WhoWor 93*
Phillips, John C. 1948- *WhoWor 93*
Phillips, John David 1920- *WhoAm 92*
Phillips, John David 1942- *WhoSSW 93, WhoWor 93*
Phillips, John Davisson 1906- *WhoAm 92*
Phillips, John F. d1991 *BioIn 17*
Phillips, John F. 1938- *St&PR 93*
Phillips, John F. 1942- *AfrAmBi, WhoAm 92*
Phillips, John G. 1922- *St&PR 93*
Phillips, John Goldsmith d1992 *NewYTBS 92 [port]*
Phillips, John Goldsmith 1907-1992 *BioIn 17*
Phillips, John Hartley *WhoScE 91-1*
Phillips, John Michael 1935- *WhoE 93*
Phillips, John Paul 1932- *WhoWor 93*
Phillips, John Pierson 1925- *WhoAm 92*
Phillips, John Reed *Law&B 92*
Phillips, John Richard 1934- *WhoAm 92*
Phillips, John Wendell 1929- *St&PR 93*
Phillips, John William d1992 *NewYTBS 92*
Phillips, Jonathan *BioIn 17*
Phillips, Josef Clayton 1908- *WhoAm 92*
Phillips, Joseph *BioIn 17*
Phillips, Joseph G. *ScF&FL 92*
Phillips, Joseph L. 1928- *St&PR 93*
Phillips, Joy Lambert 1955- *WhoAmW 93*
Phillips, Joyce Martha 1952- *WhoAmW 93*
Phillips, Julia *BioIn 17, NewYTBS 92 [port]*
Phillips, Julia 1944- *News 92 [port]*
Phillips, Julia Mae 1954- *WhoAmW 93*
Phillips, Julia Miller 1944- *WhoAm 92*
Phillips, Karen 1942- *Baker 92*
Phillips, Karen Borlaug 1956- *WhoAm 92*
Phillips, Karen Elizabeth 1943- *WhoAmW 93*
Phillips, Kathleen A. *Law&B 92*
Phillips, Kathleen C(oleman) 1920- *ConAu 39NR*
Phillips, Kathy Conlan 1946- *WhoWrEP 92*
Phillips, Keith Charles *WhoScE 91-1*
Phillips, Kenneth E. 1944- *St&PR 93*
Phillips, Kenneth Higbie 1940- *WhoAm 92*
Phillips, Kenneth Wayne 1941- *St&PR 93*
Phillips, Kevin G. 1960- *WhoE 93*
Phillips, Kevin (Price) 1940- *ConAu 40NR, WhoAm 92, WhoWrEP 92*
Phillips, Kurt 1956- *St&PR 93*
Phillips, Larry Duane 1948- *WhoWor 93*
Phillips, Larry Edward 1942- *WhoAm 92*
Phillips, Laughlin 1924- *WhoAm 92, WhoE 93, WhoWor 93*
Phillips, Lawrence Disel 1943- *St&PR 93*
Phillips, Lawrence S. 1927- *St&PR 93, WhoAm 92, WhoE 93*
Phillips, Layn R. 1952- *WhoAm 92*
Phillips, Leo H., Jr. *Law&B 92*
Phillips, Leo Harold, Jr. 1945- *WhoE 93, WhoWor 93*
Phillips, Leonard Ellis, Jr. 1943- *WhoE 93*
Phillips, Leslie 1924- *QDrFCA 92 [port]*
Phillips, Lewis Allen 1933- *WhoSSW 93*
Phillips, Linda Darnell Elaine Fredricks 1940- *WhoAmW 93, WhoWor 93*
Phillips, Linda Thomas 1940- *St&PR 93*
Phillips, Lisa 1956- *ConAu 139*
Phillips, Logan B. 1923- *St&PR 93*
Phillips, Lou Diamond *BioIn 17*
Phillips, Louis James 1942- *WhoWrEP 92*
Phillips, Loyal 1905- *WhoAm 92*
Phillips, Lyman C. 1939- *St&PR 93, WhoAm 92*
Phillips, Lyn 1942- *ScF&FL 92*
Phillips, Margaret Imogene 1926- *WhoWrEP 92*
Phillips, Marguerita 1958- *WhoAmW 93*
Phillips, Marguerite Kreger *AmWomPl*
Phillips, Marilyn Chenault 1949- *WhoAmW 93*
Phillips, Marion Grumman 1922- *WhoAmW 93, WhoE 93*
Phillips, Mark 1948- *BioIn 17*
Phillips, Mark Anthony Peter 1948- *WhoWor 93*
Phillips, Mark Douglas 1953- *WhoE 93*
Phillips, Marlene Helen 1955- *WhoAmW 93*
Phillips, Martha Huggins 1950- *WhoAmW 93*
Phillips, Mary C. 1911- *St&PR 93*
Phillips, Mary McDonough d1991 *BioIn 17*
Phillips, Maureen A. *Law&B 92*
Phillips, Maureen Kay 1944- *WhoAmW 93*
Phillips, Maureen M. 1950- *St&PR 93*
Phillips, Maurice *MiSFD 9*
Phillips, Meredith Bowen 1943- *WhoWrEP 92*
Phillips, Michael Canavan 1940- *WhoE 93*
Phillips, Michael John 1948- *WhoAm 92*
Phillips, Michael Joseph 1937- *WhoWrEP 92*
Phillips, Michael Keith 1943- *WhoAm 92*
Phillips, Michael Lynn 1952- *WhoEmL 93, WhoSSW 93, WhoWor 93*
Phillips, Michael R. 1946- *ScF&FL 92*
Phillips, Michael S. 1943- *St&PR 93*
Phillips, Michael W. 1941- *St&PR 93*
Phillips, Michelle *BioIn 17*
Phillips, (Holly) Michelle 1944- *ConAu 137*
Phillips, Montague (Fawcett) 1885-1969 *Baker 92*
Phillips, Myra Lynn 1966- *WhoAmW 93*
Phillips, Neil Ramsey 1935- *WhoSSW 93*
Phillips, O.A. 1923- *BioIn 17*
Phillips, Oliver Clyde, Jr. 1929- *WhoAm 92*
Phillips, Owen Martin 1930- *WhoAm 92*
Phillips, Pamela Kim 1958- *WhoAmW 93, WhoE 93, WhoEmL 93, WhoWor 93*
Phillips, Patrick J. 1947- *St&PR 93*
Phillips, Paul T(homas) 1942- *ConAu 138*
Phillips, Pearl Raphelita 1941- *WhoAmW 93, WhoE 93*
Phillips, Ped Wesley 1943- *St&PR 93*
Phillips, Peggy Nell 1941- *WhoSSW 93*
Phillips, Peter Charles Bonest 1948- *WhoAm 92*
Phillips, Peter Lawrence 1942- *WhoWor 93*
Phillips, Philip 1834-1895 *Baker 92*
Phillips, Priscilla Nell 1960- *WhoAmW 93*
Phillips, Ralph Saul 1913- *WhoAm 92*
Phillips, Randall Clinger 1924- *WhoAm 92*
Phillips, Reginald Francis 1954- *St&PR 93*
Phillips, Richard A. *Law&B 92*
Phillips, Richard B. 1944- *St&PR 93*
Phillips, Richard E. *Law&B 92*
Phillips, Richard F., Jr. *Law&B 92*
Phillips, Richard Hart 1922- *WhoAm 92*
Phillips, Richard Helsden 1906-1991 *BioIn 17*
Phillips, Richard James 1960- *WhoSSW 93*
Phillips, Richard Loveridge 1939- *WhoAm 92, WhoWor 93*
Phillips, Richard Raymond 1950- *WhoE 93, WhoEmL 93, WhoWor 93*
Phillips, Richard Wendell, Jr. 1929- *WhoAm 92*
Phillips, Robert d1991 *BioIn 17*
Phillips, Robert 1926-1990 *BioIn 17*
Phillips, Robert 1938- *ScF&FL 92*
Phillips, Robert A. 1944- *St&PR 93*
Phillips, Robert Charles, Jr. 1962- *WhoE 93*
Phillips, Robert Glenn 1954- *WhoAm 92*
Phillips, Robert Haskell 1942- *WhoSSW 93*
Phillips, Robert James, Jr. 1955- *WhoSSW 93, WhoWor 93*
Phillips, Robert M. 1938- *St&PR 93*
Phillips, Robert Osborn *Law&B 92*
Phillips, Robert S. *BioIn 17*
Phillips, Robert Schaeffer 1938- *WhoWrEP 92*
Phillips, Robert Stephen *WhoScE 91-1*
Phillips, Robert Thomas 1940- *St&PR 93*
Phillips, Robin *Law&B 92*
Phillips, Roger 1939- *St&PR 93, WhoAm 92*
Phillips, Roger J.N. 1930- *WhoScE 91-1*
Phillips, Ronald 1942- *St&PR 93*
Phillips, Ronald Frank 1934- *WhoAm 92*
Phillips, Ronald Lewis 1940- *WhoAm 92*
Phillips, Rosalind Ann *Law&B 92*
Phillips, Rosalind Ann 1941- *St&PR 93*
Phillips, Roscoe Wendell, Jr. 1927- *WhoAm 92*
Phillips, Rufus Colfax, III 1929- *WhoAm 92*
Phillips, Russell Alexander, Jr. 1937- *WhoAm 92*
Phillips, S. Dave 1942- *St&PR 93*
Phillips, Sally R. *Law&B 92*
Phillips, Samuel C. 1921-1990 *BioIn 17*
Phillips, Sarah Anne 1965- *WhoE 93*
Phillips, Shelley 1934- *WhoWor 93*
Phillips, Sian *WhoWor 93*
Phillips, Sidney Frederick 1933- *WhoAm 92*
Phillips, Sierra Nevada d1921 *BioIn 17*
Phillips, Spencer Kleckner 1914- *WhoWor 93*
Phillips, Stanley F. 1925- *St&PR 93*
Phillips, Stephen J. *Law&B 92*
Phillips, Susan Elizabeth 1947- *WhoWrEP 92*
Phillips, Susan M. 1944- *WhoAm 92, WhoAmW 93*
Phillips, T. Stephen 1941- *WhoAm 92*
Phillips, Ted Ray 1948- *WhoAm 92*
Phillips, Terence Martyn 1946- *WhoAm 92*
Phillips, Teresa Gail 1948- *WhoAmW 93, WhoSSW 93*
Phillips, Terry *ScF&FL 92*
Phillips, Theodore Locke 1933- *WhoAm 92*
Phillips, Theresa Marie 1947- *WhoE 93*
Phillips, Thomas B. *Law&B 92*
Phillips, Thomas C. 1935- *St&PR 93*
Phillips, Thomas Edworth, Jr. 1944- *WhoSSW 93*
Phillips, Thomas Gerrard 1954- *WhoWor 93*
Phillips, Thomas L. 1924- *BioIn 17, St&PR 93, WhoAm 92*

Pickard, Myrna Rae 1935- *WhoAm 92, WhoSSW 93*
Pickard, Richard Vernon 1943- *St&PR 93*
Pickard, Robert Marshall 1954- *WhoSSW 93*
Pickard, Robert Stewart *WhoScE 91-1*
Pickard, Roy 1937- *ScF&FL 92*
Pick de Weiss, Susan Emily 1952- *WhoEmL 93*
Pickel, Grover Lee 1950- *WhoSSW 93*
Pickel, Robert G. *Law&B 92*
Pickell, John Leroy 1934- *WhoWrEP 92*
Pickell, Lloyd C. 1946- *St&PR 93*
Picken, David James *WhoScE 91-1*
Picken, Harry Belfrage 1916- *WhoWor 93*
Picken, Joseph Clarke 1943- *St&PR 93*
Picken, Joseph Clarke, III 1943- *WhoWor 93*
Picken, Laurence (Ernest Rowland) 1909- *Baker 92*
Picken, Mary E. *Law&B 92*
Picken, Robert F. 1910- *St&PR 93*
Pickens, Alexander Legrand 1921- *WhoAm 92, WhoWor 93*
Pickens, Boone 1928- *St&PR 93*
Pickens, Buford Lindsay 1906- *WhoAm 92*
Pickens, Carl *BioIn 17*
Pickens, David Richard, Jr. 1920- *WhoAm 92*
Pickens, Earl Franklin 1934- *St&PR 93*
Pickens, Ezekiel 1768-1813 *BioIn 17*
Pickens, Harry Richard 1947- *St&PR 93*
Pickens, Jack G. 1921- *St&PR 93*
Pickens, Jane d1992 *BioIn 17*
Pickens, Jane 1908?-1992 *CurBio 92N*
Pickens, Jimmy Burton 1935- *WhoSSW 93*
Pickens, John Paul, Jr. 1950- *WhoSSW 93*
Pickens, Kel Norris 1949- *WhoWrEP 92*
Pickens, Robert Bruce 1926- *WhoAm 92*
Pickens, Robert Fulton 1931- *St&PR 93*
Pickens, Robert J. *Law&B 92*
Pickens, T. Boone, Jr. *BioIn 17*
Pickens, Thomas Boone, Jr. 1928- *WhoAm 92*
Pickens, Thomas H., Jr. *Law&B 92*
Pickens, Willard E. 1940- *St&PR 93*
Pickens, William 1881-1954 *BioIn 17*
Pickens, William Stewart 1940- *WhoSSW 93, WhoWor 93*
Picker, Harvey *BioIn 17*
Picker, Harvey 1915- *WhoAm 92*
Picker, Jean Sovatkin 1921-1990 *BioIn 17*
Picker, Lester Alan 1947- *WhoE 93*
Picker, Tobias 1954- *Baker 92*
Pickerell, James Howard 1936- *WhoAm 92*
Pickerell, Rodney R. 1938- *WhoWrEP 92*
Pickering, Allen A. 1954- *St&PR 93*
Pickering, AvaJane 1951- *WhoEmL 93*
Pickering, Barbara Ann 1949- *WhoAmW 93*
Pickering, Betty Sue 1939- *WhoAmW 93*
Pickering, Brian Thomas *WhoScE 91-1*
Pickering, Charles W. 1937- *WhoSSW 93*
Pickering, David (Hugh) 1958- *ConAu 139*
Pickering, David Sidney 1937- *WhoAsAP 91*
Pickering, E.N. *WhoScE 91-1*
Pickering, Edward Charles 1846-1919 *BioIn 17*
Pickering, George W. 1937- *ConAu 136*
Pickering, Harold K. *Law&B 92*
Pickering, Howard William 1935- *WhoAm 92*
Pickering, J.F. *WhoScE 91-1*
Pickering, James Henry, III 1937- *WhoAm 92, WhoSSW 93*
Pickering, John Harold 1916- *WhoAm 92*
Pickering, Judith M. *Law&B 92*
Pickering, Judith M. 1942- *St&PR 93*
Pickering, Miles 1943-1991 *BioIn 17*
Pickering, Paul 1952- *ConAu 138, ScF&FL 92*
Pickering, Pollyanna 1942- *WhoWor 93*
Pickering, Robert E. 1952- *St&PR 93*
Pickering, Ron 1930-1991 *AnObit 1991*
Pickering, Samuel F. 1941- *BioIn 17*
Pickering, Thomas Reeve *BioIn 17*
Pickering, Thomas Reeve 1931- *WhoAm 92, WhoUN 92, WhoWor 93*
Pickering, Victoria L. 1951- *WhoIns 93*
Pickering, William 1796-1854 *BioIn 17*
Pickering, William H. 1910- *BioIn 17*
Pickering, William Hayward 1910- *WhoAm 92*
Pickert, Richard W. *St&PR 93*
Pickett, Betty Horenstein 1926- *WhoAm 92*
Pickett, Calder Marcus 1921- *WhoAm 92*
Pickett, Christopher *WhoScE 91-1*
Pickett, Debbie Sue 1961- *WhoAmW 93*
Pickett, Doyle Clay 1930- *WhoAm 92*
Pickett, Earnest S. *BioIn 17*
Pickett, Edwin G. 1946- *St&PR 93*
Pickett, Edwin Gerald 1946- *WhoAm 92*
Pickett, Elizabeth *AmWomPl*
Pickett, George Bibb, Jr. 1918- *WhoSSW 93, WhoWor 93*
Pickett, George E. 1953- *St&PR 93*
Pickett, George Edward 1825-1875 *HarEnMi*
Pickett, Hugh D. d1992 *BioIn 17*
Pickett, Jackson Brittain 1943- *WhoSSW 93*
Pickett, James D. *Law&B 92*
Pickett, Joan Frances 1955- *St&PR 93*
Pickett, John O., Jr. *WhoAm 92*
Pickett, Lawrence Kimball 1919- *WhoAm 92*
Pickett, Marcia Gayle 1963- *WhoAmW 93*
Pickett, Michael D. 1947- *WhoAm 92*
Pickett, Nancy Elizabeth 1948- *WhoSSW 93*
Pickett, Owen B. 1930- *CngDr 91, WhoAm 92, WhoSSW 93*
Pickett, Rex *MiSFD 9*
Pickett, Robert C. 1928- *St&PR 93, WhoIns 93*
Pickett, Robert Clement 1928- *WhoAm 92*
Pickett, Russell Stout 1951- *WhoE 93*
Pickett, Stephen E. *Law&B 92*
Pickett, Steward T. A. 1950- *WhoE 93*
Pickett, Susan H. 1949- *WhoAmW 93*
Pickett, Thomas W. 1957- *St&PR 93*
Pickett, Tidye *BlkAmWO*
Pickett, Tom 1858-1934 *BioIn 17*
Pickett, William Lee 1941- *WhoAm 92*
Pickett, William S. 1935- *St&PR 93*
Pickett, Wilson 1941- *BioIn 17, SoulM*
Pickford, James Herbert 1925- *WhoSSW 93*
Pickford, Mary 1893-1979 *BioIn 17, IntDcF 2-3 [port]*
Pickhardt, Carl Emile, Jr. 1908- *WhoAm 92, WhoE 93*
Pickhardt, Charles F., Jr. 1953- *St&PR 93*
Pickholtz, Raymond Lee 1932- *WhoAm 92*
Pickholz, Jerome W. 1932- *St&PR 93*
Pickholz, Jerome Walter 1932- *WhoAm 92*
Picking, Steven C. 1952- *St&PR 93*
Pickitt, John Leonard 1933- *WhoAm 92*
Pickle, G. Edward *Law&B 92*
Pickle, Hal B(rittain) 1929- *WhoWrEP 92*
Pickle, Herbert E. 1922- *St&PR 93*
Pickle, J. J. 1913- *CngDr 91*
Pickle, James C. 1943- *WhoAm 92*
Pickle, James Jarrell 1913- *WhoSSW 93*
Pickle, James Jarrell Jake 1913- *WhoAm 92*
Pickle, Jerry Richard 1947- *WhoSSW 93*
Pickle, Robert Douglas *Law&B 92*
Pickle, Robert Douglas 1937- *St&PR 93, WhoAm 92*
Pickler, James Joseph 1949- *WhoSSW 93*
Pick-Mangiagalli, Riccardo 1882-1949 *Baker 92*
Picknett, Lynn *ScF&FL 92*
Pickney, Barbara *BioIn 17*
Pickover, Gerald 1931- *St&PR 93*
Pickrel, Debra J. 1958- *WhoAmW 93*
Pickrel, Paul 1917- *WhoAm 92*
Pickrell, Thomas Richard 1926- *WhoAm 92, WhoWor 93*
Pickron, Carlton 1957- *WhoE 93*
Pickslay, Peter H. *Law&B 92*
Pickthall, Marjorie Lowry Christie 1883-1922 *BioIn 17*
Pickup, Roger William *WhoScE 91-1*
Pickus, Albert Pierre 1931- *WhoAm 92*
Pickus, Martin A. 1942- *St&PR 93*
Pickus, Russell T. 1956- *St&PR 93*
Pickwell, David *WhoScE 91-1*
Pico, Rafael 1912- *WhoAm 92*
Picon, Luc 1925- *WhoScE 91-2*
Picon, Molly 1898-1992 *BioIn 17, CurBio 92N, NewYTBS 92 [port]*
Picone, Anthony Joseph 1944- *WhoE 93*
Picone, Frances Jean 1940- *WhoE 93*
Picone, Joe Al 1942- *St&PR 93*
Picon-Salas, Mariano 1901-1965 *SpAmA*
Picorel 1950- *WhoScE 91-3*
Picornell, Jose 1927- *St&PR 93*
Picot, Auguste Henri Marie 1756-1793 *HarEnMi*
Picot, Derek Alexander 1952- *WhoWor 93*
Picot, Grissel Concepcion *Law&B 92*
Picotte, J. Charles 1941- *St&PR 93*
Picotte, Leonard Francis 1939- *WhoAm 92*
Picotte, Michael Bernard 1947- *WhoAm 92*
Picotte, Susan LaFlesche 1865-1915 *BioIn 17*
Picoult, Jodi 1966- *ConAu 138*
Picoux, P. *WhoScE 91-2*
Picower, Warren Michael 1934- *WhoAm 92*
Picozzi, Anthony 1917- *WhoAm 92*
Picquet, Pierre C. 1941- *WhoScE 91-2*
Picton, Denis Charles Alec *WhoScE 91-1*
Picton, Kenneth C. *Law&B 92*
Picton, Thomas 1758-1815 *HarEnMi*
Picton-Turbervill, Edith 1872-1960 *BioIn 17*
Piczak, Barbara Julianne 1964- *WhoAmW 93*
Pidany, John 1929- *St&PR 93*
Pidcock, Michael Kenneth *WhoScE 91-1*
Piddington, Andrew *MiSFD 9*
Pidgeon, Carl R. *WhoScE 91-1*
Pidgeon, Colin Ross 1939- *WhoWor 93*
Pidgeon, John Anderson 1924- *WhoAm 92, WhoE 93, WhoWor 93*
Pidgeon, Walter 1897-1984 *IntDcF 2-3*
Pidgeon, Walter Paul, Jr. 1942- *WhoE 93*
Pidoux, Jean Marie 1945- *WhoWor 93*
Pie, James L.J. 1922-1991 *BioIn 17*
Pie, Susan Schmidt *Law&B 92*
Piech, Kathleen A. *Law&B 92*
Piech, Margaret Ann 1942- *WhoAmW 93*
Piech, Marian 1929- *WhoWor 93*
Piech, Mary Lou Rohling 1927- *WhoAmW 93*
Piecha, Jan Pawel 1942- *WhoScE 91-4*
Piechnik, Stefan Sebastian 1930- *WhoScE 91-4*
Piechowski, Wojciech 1849-1911 *PolBiDi*
Pieck, R. 1925- *WhoScE 91-2*
Pieck, Robert 1925- *WhoScE 91-2*
Piecuch, John M. 1943- *WhoAm 92*
Piecuch, Robert Michael 1943- *St&PR 93*
Pieczarka, Marian Ignacy 1925- *WhoScE 91-4*
Pieczenik, Steve R. *ScF&FL 92*
Pieczynski, Joseph William 1934- *St&PR 93*
Piedade-Guerreiro, J. 1933- *WhoScE 91-3*
Piedmo, Doris R. 1929- *St&PR 93*
Piedmo, George Thomas 1928- *St&PR 93*
Piedmont, Richard Stuart 1948- *WhoWor 93*
Piefke, Gerhard 1920- *WhoScE 91-3*
Piehl, Donald Herbert 1939- *WhoAm 92*
Piehl, Fred 1946- *St&PR 93*
Piehler, Henry Ralph 1938- *WhoAm 92*
Piehler, Wendell Howard 1936- *WhoE 93*
Piekaar, D. *WhoScE 91-3*
Piekarowicz, Andrzej 1940- *WhoScE 91-4*
Piekarski, Henry 1939- *St&PR 93*
Piekarski, Kevin 1954- *WhoE 93*
Piekarski, Lois Jean 1959- *WhoAmW 93*
Piekarski, Salomon 1928- *WhoScE 91-2*
Piekos, Zofia 1906- *PolBiDi*
Piekut, Theresa Laura 1947- *WhoAmW 93*
Piel, Anthony L. 1936- *WhoUN 92*
Piel, Carolyn Forman 1918- *WhoAm 92, WhoAmW 93*
Piel, Eric Victor 1948- *St&PR 93*
Piel, Gerard 1915- *WhoAm 92, WhoWrEP 92*
Piel, H. Ronald 1940- *St&PR 93*
Piel, Jonathan B. 1938- *St&PR 93*
Piel, Kenneth Martin 1936- *WhoWor 93*
Piel, William, Jr. 1909- *WhoAm 92*
Piela, Lucjan 1943- *WhoScE 91-4*
Piele, Philip Kern 1935- *WhoAm 92*
Pieler, Tomas 1954- *WhoScE 91-3*
Pielichowski, Jan 1983- *WhoScE 91-4*
Pielou, Evelyn C. *WhoAm 92*
Piemont, Joseph Gregory *Law&B 92*
Piemont, Joseph Thomas 1923- *St&PR 93*
Pienaar, Louis Alexander 1926- *WhoWor 93*
Pienciak, Anne *ScF&FL 92*
Piene, Otto 1928- *WhoAm 92*
Piening, Robert O. 1937- *St&PR 93*
Pienkowski, Jan 1936- *ScF&FL 92*
Pienkowski, Jan (Michal) 1936- *ConAu 38NR, MajAI [port]*
Piepenburg, Donald R. 1933- *St&PR 93*
Pieper, George Francis, Jr. 1926- *WhoE 93*
Pieper, Heinz Paul 1920- *WhoAm 92*
Pieper, John W. 1935- *St&PR 93*
Pieper, John William 1935- *WhoAm 92*
Pieper, Oscar Robert 1935- *St&PR 93*
Pieper, Patricia Rita 1923- *WhoAm 92*
Pieper, Raymond F. 1926- *St&PR 93*
Pieper, Steven W. 1942- *St&PR 93*
Pieper, Wylie Bernard 1932- *St&PR 93, WhoAm 92*
Piepho, Lee 1942- *WhoSSW 93*
Piepho, Robert Walter 1942- *WhoAm 92*
Pier, Mary Lou 1954- *WhoAmW 93*
Piera-Gomez, Fernando 1939- *WhoWor 93*
Pierannunzi, Christine Ann 1963- *WhoAmW 93*
Pierard, Richard Victor 1934- *ConAu 38NR*
Pieras, Jaime, Jr. 1924- *HispAmA*
Pieratt, Alice *AmWomPl*
Pieratt, Asa B., Jr. 1938- *ScF&FL 92*
Pierce, Abby Nies 1913- *WhoAmW 93*
Pierce, Alan Kraft 1931- *WhoAm 92, WhoSSW 93*
Pierce, Allan D. 1936- *BioIn 17*
Pierce, Allan Dale 1936- *WhoAm 92, WhoE 93*
Pierce, Bruce John 1938- *WhoAm 92*
Pierce, Carol Jean 1946- *WhoAmW 93*
Pierce, Catherine Maynard 1918- *WhoAmW 93*
Pierce, Catherine Shevlin *WhoUN 92*
Pierce, Charles B. *MiSFD 9*
Pierce, Charles C. 1930- *St&PR 93*
Pierce, Charles Eliot, Jr. 1941- *WhoAm 92, WhoE 93*
Pierce, Charles R. 1922- *WhoAm 92*
Pierce, Charley d1895 *BioIn 17*
Pierce, Chester Middlebrook 1927- *WhoAm 92, WhoWor 93*
Pierce, Cleo *AmWomPl*
Pierce, Crystal Denise 1953- *WhoE 93*
Pierce, Daniel 1934- *St&PR 93, WhoAm 92*
Pierce, Daniel Marshall 1928- *WhoAm 92*
Pierce, David *BioIn 17*
Pierce, Deborah Mary *WhoAmW 93, WhoWor 93*
Pierce, Donald Fay 1930- *WhoWor 93*
Pierce, Edgar Harris, Jr. 1948- *WhoSSW 93*
Pierce, Edward Allen 1947- *WhoSSW 93*
Pierce, Edward Franklin 1927- *WhoAm 92*
Pierce, Elaine Conley 1953- *St&PR 93*
Pierce, Elizabeth Gay 1907- *WhoAmW 93, WhoE 93, WhoWor 93*
Pierce, Elliot Stearns 1922- *WhoAm 92*
Pierce, Frances R. 1941- *St&PR 93*
Pierce, Francis d1986 *BioIn 17*
Pierce, Francis Casimir 1924- *WhoAm 92, WhoE 93, WhoWor 93*
Pierce, Franklin 1804-1869 *BioIn 17, PolPar*
Pierce, Fred E. 1935- *St&PR 93*
Pierce, Frederick G., II 1955- *St&PR 93*
Pierce, Garrett E. 1944- *St&PR 93*
Pierce, Gary Lynn 1942- *St&PR 93*
Pierce, George Foster, Jr. 1919- *WhoAm 92, WhoSSW 93, WhoWor 93*
Pierce, George Washington 1872-1956 *BioIn 17*
Pierce, Grace Adele *AmWomPl*
Pierce, Gretchen Natalie 1945- *WhoAmW 93*
Pierce, Harvey R. *St&PR 93*
Pierce, Hazel Beasley 1918- *ScF&FL 92*
Pierce, Hilda *WhoAmW 93*
Pierce, Hinton Rainer 1927- *WhoAm 92*
Pierce, Ilona Lambson 1941- *WhoAmW 93*
Pierce, Irwin A. *Law&B 92*
Pierce, Irwin A. 1929- *St&PR 93*
Pierce, J. Paula *Law&B 92*
Pierce, Jack 1924-1991 *BioIn 17*
Pierce, James Clarence 1929- *WhoAm 92*
Pierce, James G. 1925- *St&PR 93*
Pierce, James Lee 1936- *WhoAm 92*
Pierce, James R. 1933- *St&PR 93*
Pierce, James Robert 1933- *WhoAm 92*
Pierce, Jane M. 1806-1863 *BioIn 17*
Pierce, Janis Vaughn 1934- *WhoSSW 93*
Pierce, Jessie Palmer *AmWomPl*
Pierce, Jim *BioIn 17*
Pierce, Jim 1932- *WhoSSW 93*
Pierce, John Hewett 1912- *WhoE 93, WhoWor 93*
Pierce, John J. 1941- *ScF&FL 92*
Pierce, John M. 1924-1991 *BioIn 17*
Pierce, John Peter 1944- *WhoE 93*
Pierce, John Robinson 1910- *BioIn 17, WhoAm 92*
Pierce, John Stephen 1922- *WhoScE 91-3*
Pierce, Josep William, Jr. 1960- *WhoSSW 93*
Pierce, Joseph *BioIn 17*
Pierce, Kay *Law&B 92*
Pierce, Keith Robert 1942- *WhoAm 92*
Pierce, Kenneth B. 1943- *St&PR 93*
Pierce, Kenneth H. 1924- *St&PR 93*
Pierce, Kenneth Ray 1934- *WhoAm 92*
Pierce, Kenney J. *St&PR 93*
Pierce, Lambert Reid 1930- *WhoSSW 93*
Pierce, Lawrence W. *AfrAmBi [port]*
Pierce, Lawrence Warren 1924- *WhoAm 92, WhoE 93*
Pierce, Linda Louise 1949- *St&PR 93*
Pierce, Linda May 1948- *WhoAmW 93*
Pierce, Lisa Margaret 1957- *WhoE 93*
Pierce, Lois M. *St&PR 93*
Pierce, Lyn S. *Law&B 92*
Pierce, Madelene Evans 1904- *WhoAmW 93*
Pierce, Margaret Hunter 1910- *WhoAm 92*
Pierce, Marianne Louise 1949- *WhoEmL 93*
Pierce, Mark Montgomery *Law&B 92*
Pierce, Martin 1925- *St&PR 93*
Pierce, Mary *BioIn 17*
Pierce, Mary 1975- *WhoAmW 93*
Pierce, Meredith Ann 1958- *BioIn 17, MajAI [port], ScF&FL 92*
Pierce, Meredith Ann 1959- *DcAmChF 1960*
Pierce, Milton 1928- *St&PR 93*

Pierce, Naomi Ellen 1954- *WhoAm 92*
Pierce, Naomi Louise 1963- *WhoE 93*
Pierce, Nathaniel d1992 *NewYTBS 92*
Pierce, Nathaniel Field 1934- *WhoUN 92*
Pierce, Norman Brayton 1940- *WhoE 93*
Pierce, Phyllis Harward 1947- *WhoAmW 93*
Pierce, Ponchitta Anne 1942- *WhoAm 92, WhoWor 93*
Pierce, Preston Eugene 1946- *WhoE 93*
Pierce, Ralph 1926- *WhoAm 92*
Pierce, Richard Craig 1946- *WhoSSW 93*
Pierce, Richard Hilton 1935- *WhoAm 92*
Pierce, Ricky *BioIn 17*
Pierce, Ricky Charles 1959- *WhoAm 92*
Pierce, Robert *BioIn 17*
Pierce, Robert E. 1947- *St&PR 93*
Pierce, Robert J. *Law&B 92*
Pierce, Robert Lorne *WhoAm 92*
Pierce, Robert Nash 1931- *WhoAm 92, WhoSSW 93*
Pierce, Robert Neal, Jr. *Law&B 92*
Pierce, Robert Raymond 1914- *WhoWor 93*
Pierce, Roy 1923- *WhoAm 92*
Pierce, Russell Dale 1938- *WhoE 93*
Pierce, Samuel Davis 1961- *WhoSSW 93*
Pierce, Samuel Riley, Jr. 1922- *WhoAm 92, WhoE 93, WhoWor 93*
Pierce, Scott 1930- *WhoAm 92*
Pierce, Shelby Crawford 1932- *WhoWor 93*
Pierce, Susan Marie Schmitz 1950- *WhoSSW 93*
Pierce, T.B. *WhoScE 91-1*
Pierce, Tamora 1954- *ScF&FL 92*
Pierce, Thomas A., Jr. *Law&B 92*
Pierce, Timothy E. 1941- *St&PR 93*
Pierce, Verlon Lane 1949- *WhoSSW 93*
Pierce, Walter Smith 1920- *WhoAm 92*
Pierce, Warren Wood, II *Law&B 92*
Pierce, Webb 1926-1991 *Baker 92, BioIn 17*
Pierce, Willard G. 1918- *St&PR 93*
Pierce, William C. 1940- *St&PR 93*
Pierce, William Cobb 1940- *WhoAm 92*
Pierce, William James 1921- *WhoAm 92*
Pierce, William Luther *ScF&FL 92*
Pierce, William Luther 1933- *WhoSSW 93*
Pierce, William Michael, Jr. 1953- *St&PR 93*
Pierce, William Schuler 1937- *WhoAm 92*
Pierce Buckelew, Carolyn Rose 1946- *WhoAmW 93*
Pierceson, D. Kraig 1948- *St&PR 93*
Pierch, Peter M., Jr. 1950- *St&PR 93*
Piercy, Alan Richard *WhoScE 91-1*
Piercy, Marge *BioIn 17*
Piercy, Marge 1936- *DcLB 120 [port], ScF&FL 92, WhoAm 92, WhoAmW 93, WhoE 93, WhoWrEP 92*
Piercy, Nigel Francis *WhoScE 91-1*
Piercy, Valerie Jo 1963- *WhoAmW 93*
Pierenkemper, Antonius 1944- *WhoWor 93*
Piereson, James Eugene 1946- *WhoAm 92, WhoE 93*
Pierfelice, Robert A. *St&PR 93*
Pierfelice, Robert Allen 1934- *WhoAm 92*
Piergallini, Alfred A. 1946- *St&PR 93, WhoAm 92*
Pierick, Jerry Devoe 1935- *WhoAm 92*
Pierik, Marilyn Anne 1939- *WhoAmW 93*
Pierik, R.L.M. 1935- *WhoScE 91-3*
Pierloot, Roland Alphonse 1924- *WhoScE 91-2*
Pierman, Carol J. 1947- *WhoWrEP 92*
Piermatteo, Joseph J. 1932- *St&PR 93*
Pierne, Gabriel 1863-1937 *OxDcOp*
Pierne, (Henri-Constant-) Gabriel 1863-1937 *Baker 92*
Pierne, Paul 1874-1952 *Baker 92*
Pierno, Anthony R. *Law&B 92*
Pierno, Anthony Robert 1932- *WhoAm 92*
Pierno, Michael *BioIn 17*
Piero, Elda M. *AmWomPl*
Pieron, Maurice 1937- *WhoScE 91-2*
Pieroni, Leonard J. 1939- *St&PR 93, WhoAm 92*
Pieroni, Mark C. *Law&B 92*
Pieroni, Nestor Baltasar 1940- *WhoUN 92*
Pieroni, Robert Edward 1937- *WhoSSW 93*
Pierotti, Daniel J.A. 1940- *WhoUN 92*
Pierotti, James Joseph 1932- *St&PR 93*
Pierotti, Robert Amedeo 1931- *WhoAm 92*
Pierotti, Thomas Monroe 1947- *WhoE 93*
Pierpan, Thomas E. *Law&B 92*
Pierpoint, Karen Ann 1944- *WhoAmW 93*
Pierpoint, Robert Charles 1925- *WhoAm 92*
Pierpoint, William Stanley *WhoScE 91-1*
Pierpont, Carleton Langley 1926- *St&PR 93*
Pierpont, James 1822-1893 *Baker 92*
Pierpont, Robert 1932- *WhoAm 92, WhoWor 93*
Pierpont, Wilbur K. 1914- *WhoAm 92*
Pierre *BioIn 17*
Pierre, Andrew J. 1934- *WhoE 93*
Pierre, Constant (-Victor-Desire) 1855-1918 *Baker 92*
Pierre, Jean-Louis 1939- *WhoScE 91-2, WhoWor 93*
Pierre, Kristine May 1957- *WhoAmW 93*
Pierre, Michael James, Sr. 1940- *WhoE 93*
Pierre, Walter R. 1922- *WhoSSW 93*
Pierre-Benoist, Jean 1947- *WhoWor 93*
Pierrepoint, Albert d1992 *NewYTBS 92*
Pierret, Alain Marie 1930- *WhoWor 93*
Pierro, Albino 1916- *DcLB 128 [port]*
Pierrot, Debbie Ewing 1959- *WhoAmW 93*
Pierrot, E.R. *Law&B 92*
Pierrot, Edward Roland *Law&B 92*
Pierrot, I. Laura 1949- *St&PR 93*
Pierskalla, William Peter 1934- *WhoAm 92*
Piersma, Peter M. 1923- *St&PR 93*
Pierson, Albert Chadwick 1914- *WhoAm 92*
Pierson, Anne Bingham 1929- *WhoAmW 93, WhoE 93*
Pierson, Carol Anne 1945- *WhoAmW 93*
Pierson, Curt Allan 1930- *St&PR 93*
Pierson, David R. 1923- *St&PR 93*
Pierson, Delbert J. 1947- *St&PR 93*
Pierson, Donald 1900- *IntDcAn, WhoSSW 93*
Pierson, Dorothy Fiske *AmWomPl*
Pierson, Edward P. *Law&B 92*
Pierson, Edward Samuel 1937- *WhoAm 92*
Pierson, Ellery Merwin 1935- *WhoE 93*
Pierson, Felix 1926- *St&PR 93*
Pierson, Frank 1925- *MiSFD 9*
Pierson, Frank Dwyer 1956- *WhoWor 93*
Pierson, George Wilson 1904- *WhoAm 92*
Pierson, Harriet H. *AmWomPl*
Pierson, Helen Hale 1941- *WhoAmW 93*
Pierson, Henry Hugo 1815-1873 *Baker 92*
Pierson, Henry L. 1908- *St&PR 93*
Pierson, Isaac 1770-1833 *BioIn 17*
Pierson, Jerry D. 1933- *St&PR 93*
Pierson, John Herman Groesbeck 1906- *WhoAm 92*
Pierson, John Theodore, Jr. 1931- *WhoAm 92*
Pierson, Kenneth Lantz 1932- *WhoE 93*
Pierson, Margaret Rosalind 1941- *WhoAmW 93*
Pierson, Marsha Sanderson 1961- *WhoAmW 93*
Pierson, Michael D. *Law&B 92*
Pierson, Michel L.A. 1925- *WhoScE 91-2*
Pierson, R. Earl 1920- *St&PR 93*
Pierson, Richard Allen 1944- *WhoAm 92*
Pierson, Richard Norris, Jr. 1929- *WhoAm 92, WhoE 93*
Pierson, Rita Tidd Anger 1939- *WhoSSW 93*
Pierson, Robert *St&PR 93*
Pierson, Robert C. 1930- *St&PR 93*
Pierson, Robert David 1935- *St&PR 93, WhoAm 92*
Pierson, Samuel D. 1924- *St&PR 93*
Pierson, Susan Judith 1959- *St&PR 93*
Pierson, Victor R. 1958- *St&PR 93*
Pierson, William C. *Law&B 92*
Pierson-Stein, Marjorie Maxine Gordon 1925- *WhoAmW 93*
Pieruzzi, Piero Romano 1938- *WhoWor 93*
Pies, David W. *Law&B 92*
Pies, Ronald William 1952- *WhoE 93*
Pieschel, G.M. 1927- *St&PR 93*
Pieschel, Sharon Gunda 1957- *St&PR 93*
Piessens, Jan 1941- *WhoScE 91-2*
Piet, Lawrence Frank 1940- *St&PR 93*
Piet, William M. 1943- *St&PR 93*
Pietarinen, Esko U. 1943- *WhoScE 91-4*
Pietarinen, Juhani Veli 1938- *WhoWor 93*
Pietch, Richard S. *Law&B 92*
Pieters, Robert B. 1944- *St&PR 93*
Pieterse, Johan D. 1944- *WhoUN 92*
Pieterse, Zola *BioIn 17*
Pietersen, Alex Alfonse 1946- *WhoE 93*
Pietersen, William Gerard 1937- *WhoAm 92*
Pieterson, Willem Adriaan 1944- *WhoWor 93*
Pietikainen, Juha 1925- *WhoScE 91-4*
Pietila, Jukka Pekka 1960- *WhoScE 91-4*
Pietila, Reima Frans Ilmari 1923- *WhoWor 93*
Pietila, Vernon Wesley 1945- *WhoAm 92*
Pietinen, Pirjo 1947- *WhoScE 91-4*
Pietkiewicz, J. *WhoScE 91-4*
Pietkiewicz, Jerzy Boleslaw 1943- *WhoScE 91-4*
Pietra, Italo 1911-1991 *BioIn 17*
Pietrafitta, Clifford E. 1962- *St&PR 93*
Pietrala, Robert Dale *Law&B 92*
Pietrangeli, Carlo 1912- *WhoWor 93*
Pietrangelo, Michael A. 1942- *St&PR 93*
Pietras, Philip R. 1949- *St&PR 93*
Pietras, Slawomir 1943- *WhoWor 93*
Pietrasik, Longin *WhoScE 91-4*
Pietraszkiewicz, Wojciech Piotr 1939- *WhoWor 93*
Pietri, Giuseppe 1886-1946 *Baker 92*
Pietri, Pedro 1943- *HispAmA [port]*
Pietri, Pedro 1944- *BioIn 17*
Pietrini, Andrew G. 1937- *St&PR 93*
Pietrini, Andrew Gabriel 1937- *WhoAm 92*
Pietro, Mary Therese 1961- *WhoAmW 93*
Pietro Damiani, Saint c. 1007-1072 *BioIn 17*
Pietrosanti, Roberto 1966- *BioIn 17*
Pietroski, Joseph J. 1938- *St&PR 93*
Pietrovito, James Anthony 1949- *WhoE 93*
Pietrucha, Martin Thomas 1955- *WhoE 93*
Pietruniak, Ed Stephen 1956- *WhoE 93*
Pietrus, Carol Lynn 1948- *WhoAmW 93*
Pietruski, John Michael 1933- *St&PR 93*
Pietruski, John Michael, Jr. 1933- *WhoAm 92*
Pietruszko, Stanislaw Marian 1948- *WhoWor 93*
Pietrzak, Alfred Robert 1949- *WhoE 93, WhoWor 93*
Pietrzak, Daniel M. 1939- *WhoE 93*
Pietrzak, Leonard Walter 1939- *St&PR 93*
Pietrzyk, Donald John 1934- *WhoAm 92*
Pietrzyk, Zbigniew Tadeusz 1929- *WhoScE 91-4*
Pietsch, Richard A. 1925- *St&PR 93*
Pietschmann, Herbert 1936- *WhoScE 91-4*
Piette, Barbara Ann 1955- *WhoAmW 93*
Piette, Lawrence Hector 1932- *WhoAm 92*
Pietz, Victoria Lynn 1962- *WhoAmW 93*
Pieyre de Mandiargues, Andre 1909- *BioIn 17*
Pieyre de Mandiargues, Andre 1909-1991 *ConAu 136*
Piez, William 1932- *WhoAm 92*
Pifer, Alan 1921- *St&PR 93, WhoAm 92*
Pifer, Ann Cecilia 1965- *WhoAmW 93*
Pifer, Glenn A. 1953- *St&PR 93*
Pifer, Kevin D. 1959- *St&PR 93*
Pifer, Robert Edwin 1925- *St&PR 93*
Piff, Frank Stephen 1940- *St&PR 93*
Pig, Edward *MajAI, SmATA 70*
Piga, Franco d1990 *BioIn 17*
Piga, Stephen Mulry 1929- *WhoAm 92*
Pigage, Leo Charles 1913- *WhoAm 92*
Pigaty, John B. 1922- *St&PR 93*
Pigeon, Jacques 1940- *WhoScE 91-2*
Pigford, Robert L. 1917-1988 *BioIn 17*
Pigford, Thomas Harrington 1922- *WhoAm 92*
Pigg, Kenneth E. 1945- *ConAu 139*
Pigg, Willie Howard 1948- *WhoE 93*
Piggford, Roland Rayburn 1926- *WhoAm 92*
Piggins, D.J. *WhoScE 91-3*
Piggott, (Alan) Derek 1923- *ConAu 37NR*
Piglia, Ricardo 1941- *SpAmA*
Pigliucci, Riccardo 1947- *St&PR 93*
Pigman, Harry Tschopik 1952- *WhoSSW 93*
Pignal, Pierre Ivan 1961- *WhoWor 93*
Pignataro, Louis James 1923- *WhoAm 92, WhoE 93*
Pignatelli, Debora Becker 1947- *WhoAmW 93*
Pignatelli, Samuel A. 1951- *St&PR 93*
Pignatiello, Constance C. *St&PR 93*
Pignato, Damiano J. 1941- *St&PR 93*
Pignone, Charles Joseph, III 1966- *WhoE 93*
Pignotti, Lamberto 1926- *DcLB 128 [port]*
Pigorini, Luigi 1842-1925 *IntDcAn*
Pigot, Robert 1720-1796 *HarEnMi*
Pigott, Brian Berkeley *WhoScE 91-1*
Pigott, Carole *BioIn 17*
Pigott, Charles McGee 1929- *St&PR 93, WhoAm 92*
Pigott, David Nevil 1949- *St&PR 93*
Pigott, H. Dale 1947- *WhoSSW 93*
Pigott, James Calvin 1936- *St&PR 93*
Pigott, John A. 1932- *St&PR 93, WhoAm 92*
Pigott, Melissa Ann 1958- *WhoSSW 93*
Pigott, Richard Edward *Law&B 92*
Pigott, Richard Lacy 1955- *St&PR 93*
Pigoury, Lucien *WhoScE 91-2*
Pigozzi, Jean *BioIn 17*
Pigozzi, Raymond Anthony 1928- *WhoAm 92*
Piguer, H. *WhoScE 91-2*
Piha, Jorma 1947- *WhoScE 91-4*
Piha, Tapani 1955- *WhoUN 92*
Pihlaja, Maxine Muriel Mead 1935- *WhoAmW 93*
Pihlstrom, Bruce 1943- *WhoAm 92*
Pihlstrom, Gary Dale *Law&B 92*
Pihos, Pete 1923- *BioIn 17*
Piiper, Johannes 1924- *WhoScE 91-3*
Piirma, Irja 1920- *WhoAmW 93*
Piirto-Navarre, Jane Marie 1941- *WhoWrEP 92*
Pijanowski, Eugene *BioIn 17*
Pijanowski, Hiroko Sato *BioIn 17*
Pijck, Jacques 1930- *WhoScE 91-2*
Pijor, Stanley G. *St&PR 93*
Pijper, Willem 1894-1947 *Baker 92*
Pijpers, Frank Peter 1964- *WhoWor 93*
Pikas, Bruce *St&PR 93*
Pike, Albert 1809-1891 *BioIn 17*
Pike, Albert R. 1916- *St&PR 93*
Pike, Albert Raymond 1916- *WhoAm 92*
Pike, Allen W. *WhoAm 92*
Pike, Billy W. 1940- *St&PR 93*
Pike, Bruce Parker 1933- *St&PR 93*
Pike, Carl Stephen 1945- *WhoE 93*
Pike, Charles P. 1941- *WhoE 93*
Pike, Christopher *BioIn 17, ChlLR 29, ConAu 136, ScF&FL 92*
Pike, David Hankins 1943- *WhoSSW 93*
Pike, Eileen Halsey 1918-1992 *BioIn 17*
Pike, Gayle Kemp 1949- *WhoSSW 93*
Pike, George Harold, Jr. 1933- *WhoAm 92*
Pike, James Albert *BioIn 17*
Pike, John J. 1912- *St&PR 93*
Pike, John Nazarian 1929- *WhoE 93*
Pike, John S. *WhoAm 92*
Pike, John Stack *BioIn 17*
Pike, Joseph *BioIn 17*
Pike, Kathy 1942- *WhoAmW 93*
Pike, Kenneth Lee 1912- *WhoAm 92*
Pike, Kermit Jerome 1941- *WhoAm 92*
Pike, Larry Ross 1935- *St&PR 93*
Pike, Larry Samuel 1939- *WhoAm 92, WhoSSW 93*
Pike, Laurence Bruce 1927- *WhoAm 92*
Pike, Lawrence 1932- *WhoWrEP 92*
Pike, Lip 1845-1893 *BioIn 17*
Pike, Milton 1921- *St&PR 93*
Pike, Nan Shelley 1937- *WhoAmW 93*
Pike, Patricia Louise 1951- *WhoAmW 93*
Pike, Ralph Webster 1935- *WhoSSW 93*
Pike, Richard Harry *WhoScE 91-1*
Pike, Robert William *Law&B 92*
Pike, Robert William 1941- *WhoAm 92, WhoIns 93*
Pike, Ronald Marston 1925- *WhoE 93*
Pike, William Edward 1929- *WhoAm 92*
Pike, William Edward Cathcart 1952- *WhoWor 93*
Pike, Zebulon 1779-1813 *Expl 93 [port]*
Pike, Zebulon Montgomery 1779-1813 *BioIn 17, HarEnMi*
Piket, Frederick 1903-1974 *Baker 92*
Pikhard, A. *WhoScE 91-4*
Pikkarainen, Jarmo A.J. 1933- *WhoScE 91-4*
Pikler, Charles *WhoAm 92*
Pikovsky, Arkady Samuilovich 1956- *WhoWor 93*
Pikovsky, Eugene 1920- *St&PR 93*
Pikrallidas, Mary Eugenia 1954- *WhoAmW 93*
Pikul, Diane d1987 *BioIn 17*
Pikul, Frank John 1951- *WhoSSW 93*
Pikul, Joseph *BioIn 17*
Pikul', Valentin Savvich 1928-1990 *BioIn 17*
Pikus, Joseph D. d1991 *BioIn 17*
Pikus, Stanton M. 1940- *St&PR 93*
Pilac, Pamela Ann 1954- *WhoWrEP 92*
Piland, David Thomas 1961- *WhoSSW 93*
Pilapil, Eduardo P. 1941- *WhoAsAP 91*
Pilarczyk, Adam 1924- *WhoScE 91-4*
Pilarczyk, Daniel Edward 1934- *WhoAm 92*
Pilarczyk, Helga 1925- *IntDcOp, OxDcOp*
Pilarczyk, Helga (Kathe) 1925- *Baker 92*
Pilarczyk, Jan *WhoScE 91-4*
Pilarczyk, Jan Pawel 1940- *WhoScE 91-4*
Pilarczyk, Richard Robert 1932- *St&PR 93*
Pilar Navarro, Maria del *WhoScE 91-3*
Pilaro, Joseph F. 1933- *St&PR 93*
Pilati, Mario 1903-1938 *Baker 92*
Pilatus, Rob *BioIn 17*
Pilawa, Dennis *Law&B 92*
Pilawski, Andrezj 1910- *WhoWor 93*
Pilbeam, David Roger 1940- *WhoAm 92, WhoE 93, WhoWor 93*
Pilbrow, Richard 1933- *WhoAm 92*
Pilcer, Sonia Hanna 1949- *WhoWrEP 92*
Pilch, Frederic Robert 1927- *St&PR 93*
Pilcher, Alan Rodney 1954- *WhoWor 93*
Pilcher, Benjamin Lee 1938- *WhoSSW 93*
Pilcher, Catherine Anne 1960- *WhoAmW 93*
Pilcher, James Brownie 1929- *WhoSSW 93*
Pilcher, Richard Paul 1946- *WhoE 93*
Pilcher, Rosamunde 1924- *BioIn 17*
Pilchik, Ely Emanuel 1913- *WhoAm 92, WhoWor 93*
Pile, Frederick Alfred 1884-1976 *BioIn 17*
Pile, Larry F. *Law&B 92*
Pile, Robert Bennett 1918- *WhoAm 92*
Pilecki, Alexander B. 1937- *St&PR 93*
Pilecki, Szymon 1925- *WhoScE 91-4*
Pileggi, Dominic J. 1951- *St&PR 93*
Pileggi, Vincent *St&PR 93*
Pilenzo, Ronald C. *BioIn 17*

Pilet, Charles 1931- *WhoScE 91-2*
Pilet, Paul Emile 1927- *WhoScE 91-4*
Pilger, John *BioIn 17*
Pilgreen, Annette James 1953- *WhoAmW 93*
Pilgreen, Norman Thomas, Sr. 1939- *WhoSSW 93*
Pilgrim, Anne *MajAI*
Pilgrim, D. *WhoScE 91-1*
Pilgrim, Deborah Annice 1956- *WhoAmW 93*
Pilgrim, Dianne Hauserman 1941- *WhoAm 92, WhoAmW 93, WhoE 93*
Pilgrim, Gail Louise *Law&B 92*
Pilgrim, James Rollins 1947- *WhoSSW 93*
Pilgrim, Lonnie 1928- *WhoAm 92*
Pilgrim, Michael *DcCPCAm*
Pilgrim-Guracar, Genevieve 1936- *WhoWrEP 92*
Pilibosian, Helene Rose 1933- *WhoWrEP 92*
Pilichowski, Leopold 1869-1933 *PolBiDi*
Pilidi, Vladimir Stavrovic 1946- *WhoWor 93*
Piliero, Catherine Anne 1962- *WhoE 93*
Piliponis, John A. *Law&B 92*
Pilisek, Vladimir 1927- *WhoScE 91-4*
Pilisuk, Marc 1934- *WhoAm 92*
Pilitsis, Stergios 1959- *WhoWor 93*
Pilitt, Patricia Ann 1942- *WhoAmW 93*
Piljac, Ivan 1934- *WhoScE 91-4*
Pilke, Ansa O. 1950- *WhoScE 91-4*
Pilkenton, Janice L. Morgan *Law&B 92*
Pilkenton, Jill I. *Law&B 92*
Pilkey, Dav 1966- *BioIn 17, ConAu 136*
Pilkey, Orrin H. 1934- *ConAu 40NR, WhoAm 92*
Pilkington, Alan Ralph 1943- *WhoAm 92*
Pilkington, Alastair 1920- *WhoWor 93*
Pilkington, Antony 1935- *BioIn 17*
Pilkington, Francis c. 1570-1638 *Baker 92*
Pilkington, John W. 1944- *St&PR 93*
Pilkington, Paul *BioIn 17*
Pilkington, Regina Marie 1951- *WhoAmW 93*
Pilko, Robert Michael 1952- *WhoSSW 93*
Pilkuhn, Manfred H. 1934- *WhoScE 91-3*
Pill, David M. *Law&B 92*
Pill, Stephen Michael 1945- *St&PR 93*
Pilla, Anthony Michael 1932- *WhoAm 92*
Pilla, Felix Mario 1932- *WhoAm 92*
Pilla, Mary Lee *Law&B 92*
Pillaert, Edna Elizabeth 1931- *WhoAm 92*
Pillagalli, Michael Anthony 1949- *WhoE 93*
Pillai, Arrackal Kesava Balakrishna 1930- *WhoE 93*
Pillai, Gopal 1937- *WhoE 93*
Pillar, Arlene M. d1990 *BioIn 17*
Pillar, Charles Littlefield 1911- *WhoWor 93*
Pillar, David Gene 1942- *St&PR 93*
Pillar, Tim M. 1951- *WhoScE 91-1*
Pillay, M. *WhoScE 91-3*
Piller, Emanuel 1907-1985 *ScF&FL 92*
Piller, G.J. *WhoScE 91-1*
Pillers, Robert Harvey 1932- *St&PR 93*
Pilleteri, Anthony 1917-1991 *BioIn 17*
Pilley, Lois Valliere 1961- *WhoAmW 93*
Pilling, Ann 1944- *ChlFicS*
Pilling, Charles Ashworth, Jr. 1932- *St&PR 93*
Pilling, Janet Kavanaugh 1951- *WhoAmW 93, WhoE 93*
Pilling, Michael John *WhoScE 91-1*
Pilling, Patricia Leslie 1926- *WhoAmW 93, WhoWrEP 92*
Pilling, Scott T. 1963- *St&PR 93*
Pillinger, James J. 1918- *WhoE 93*
Pilliod, Peter Patrick 1947- *WhoAm 92*
Pillion, Kieran E., Jr. *Law&B 92*
Pillips, William John *WhoWrEP 92*
Pilliter, Charles J. 1948- *WhoAm 92*
Pilliter, Chas J. *St&PR 93*
Pillman, M. Lynn *Law&B 92*
Pillois, Jacques 1877-1935 *Baker 92*
Pillorge, George John 1937- *WhoAm 92*
Pillot, Jacques 1927- *WhoScE 91-2*
Pillot, Patricia Lu 1954- *WhoWrEP 92*
Pillow, Gideon Johnson 1806-1878 *HarEnMi*
Pillow, Michael F. *Law&B 92*
Pillow, Raymond Eugene 1922- *St&PR 93*
Pillow, William Keith, Jr. 1946- *WhoSSW 93*
Pillsburg, Lawrence *St&PR 93*
Pillsbury, Earl Lyman 1928- *St&PR 93*
Pillsbury, Edmund Pennington 1943- *WhoAm 92, WhoSSW 93*
Pillsbury, Edward G. *Law&B 92*
Pillsbury, George S. 1921- *St&PR 93*
Pillsbury, George Sturgis 1921- *WhoAm 92*
Pillsbury, Gordon E. 1933- *St&PR 93*
Pillsbury, Leland Clark 1947- *WhoEmL 93*
Pillsbury, Sam *MiSFD 9*
Pillu, Francois 1919- *WhoWor 93*
Pilnick, Allen Edward 1929- *St&PR 93*
Pilo, Marvin R. *Law&B 92*
Pilon, A. Barbara *WhoE 93*
Pilon, Jean-Guy 1930- *WhoCanL 92*
Pilon, John E. 1925- *St&PR 93*
Pilon, Lawrence James 1948- *St&PR 93*
Pilot, Georges *WhoScE 91-2*
Pilotti, Francisco Javier 1947- *WhoWor 93*
Pilou, Jeannette 1931- *OxDcOp*
Pilpel, Harriet Fleischl *WhoWrEP 92*
Pilpel, Harriet Fleischl d1991 *BioIn 17*
Pilpel, Robert H. 1943- *WhoWrEP 92*
Pilskaln, Harold 1931- *St&PR 93*
Pilson, Neal H. *BioIn 17*
Pilson, Neal Howard 1940- *St&PR 93*
Pilson, Roger Lloyd 1950- *WhoSSW 93*
Pilsudski, Bronislaw Piotr 1866-1918 *IntDcAn*
Pilsudski, Joseph Klemens 1867-1935 *DcTwHis*
Pilsudski, Jozef 1867-1935 *PolBiDi [port]*
Piltzin, Norman Meyer 1929- *WhoE 93, WhoWor 93*
Pilvin, Barbara Jeanne 1951- *WhoE 93*
Pilyugin, Sergei Yuzievitch 1947- *WhoWor 93*
Pilz, Alfred Norman 1931- *WhoAm 92*
Pilz, Gunter 1945- *WhoScE 91-4*
Pilz, Gunter Franz 1945- *WhoWor 93*
Pilz, James William 1928- *St&PR 93*
Pilzer, Geraldine Fogel *Law&B 92*
Pim, Kendall Allan 1940- *St&PR 93*
Pimen, Patriarch of Moscow and All Russia 1910-1990 *BioIn 17*
Pimenta, Fernando 1950- *BioIn 17*
Pimenta, Simon Ignatius Cardinal 1920- *WhoWor 93*
Pimenta de Miranda, Thierry Louis Antoine 1947- *WhoWor 93*
Pimental, Frank J. *St&PR 93*
Pimental, Joseph Richard 1931- *St&PR 93*
Pimental, Patricia Ann 1956- *WhoAmW 93, WhoWor 93*
Pimentel, Albert A. 1955- *St&PR 93*
Pimentel, Aquilino Q. 1933- *WhoAsAP 91*
Pimentel, David 1925- *HispAmA, WhoAm 92*
Pimentel, Francisco 1832-1893 *DcMexL*
Pimentel, George C. *BioIn 17*
Pimentel, Luz Aurora 1946- *WhoWor 93*
Pimpinella, Ronald Joseph 1935- *WhoE 93, WhoWor 93*
Pimsler, Alvin J. 1918- *WhoAm 92*
Pimsleur, Solomon 1900-1962 *Baker 92*
Pimsner, Victor 1920- *WhoScE 91-4*
Pin, Paul J.J. 1920- *WhoScE 91-2*
Pina, Alberto Buffington 1957- *WhoSSW 93*
Pina, H.L. 1941- *WhoScE 91-3*
Pina, Leslie A. 1947- *ConAu 138*
Pina, Teresita Olga 1964- *WhoAmW 93*
Pinac, Andre Louis, III 1955- *WhoWor 93*
Pina-Cabral, Joao de 1954- *ConAu 136*
Pina-Cabral, Jose Manuel Goncalves 1929- *WhoWor 93*
Pina Mendes, Fernando 1936- *WhoScE 91-3*
Pinard, Gilbert Daniel 1940- *WhoAm 92*
Pinard, P. *WhoScE 91-2*
Pinard, Raymond R. 1930- *WhoAm 92*
Pinard, Steven C. 1944- *St&PR 93*
Pina-Rosales, Gerardo 1948- *WhoE 93*
Pinart, Robert 1927- *BioIn 17*
Pinasco, Carrie Lynn 1960- *WhoAmW 93*
Pinay, Antoine 1891- *BioIn 17*
Pincay, Laffit, Jr. 1946- *WhoAm 92*
Pincelli, Frank *Law&B 92*
Pinch, Patricia Ann 1947- *WhoAmW 93*
Pinch, Richard Gilmour Eric 1954- *WhoWor 93*
Pinchback, Pinckney Benton Stewart 1837-1921 *EncAACR*
Pinchbeck, Colin 1926-1991 *BioIn 17*
Pincherle, Alberto *ScF&FL 92*
Pincherle, Alberto 1907-1990 *BioIn 17*
Pincherle, Marc 1888-1974 *Baker 92*
Pinchin, Frank J. 1925-1990 *ScF&FL 92*
Pinchin, Wilfred James 1945- *WhoWor 93*
Pinchinat, Antonio Michael 1934- *WhoWor 93*
Pinchot, Ann *WhoWrEP 92*
Pinchot, Bronson 1959- *WhoAm 92*
Pinchot, Gifford 1865-1946 *BioIn 17, GayN, PolPar*
Pinchuck, Curt Paul 1960- *WhoE 93*
Pinchuk, Nicholas Thomas 1946- *St&PR 93*
Pinciaro, Dominick A. 1938- *St&PR 93*
Pinck, Joan Braverman 1929- *WhoE 93*
Pinckert, Warren Emmett, II 1943- *St&PR 93*
Pincket, Brian G. *Law&B 92*
Pinckley, Paul Edward, Sr. 1957- *WhoSSW 93*
Pinckney, Callan 1939- *WhoAmW 93*
Pinckney, Charles Cotesworth 1745-1825 *PolPar*
Pinckney, Neal Theodore 1935- *WhoAm 92*
Pinckney, Theodore Gaillard, Jr. 1955- *WhoSSW 93*
Pincock, Richard Earl 1935- *WhoAm 92*
Pincoffs, Edmund Lloyd 1919- *WhoAm 92*
Pincofski, Richard R. 1956- *St&PR 93*
Pincus, Florence Volkman *WhoAmW 93, WhoE 93*
Pincus, George 1935- *WhoAm 92*
Pincus, Gregory 1903-1967 *BioIn 17*
Pincus, Howard Jonah 1922- *WhoAm 92*
Pincus, Jacqueline Kron 1936- *WhoAmW 93*
Pincus, Joan T. *Law&B 92*
Pincus, Joseph 1919- *WhoAm 92*
Pincus, Laura R. 1923- *WhoSSW 93*
Pincus, Lionel I. 1931- *St&PR 93, WhoAm 92*
Pincus, Michael Stern 1931- *WhoSSW 93*
Pincus, Michael Stern 1936- *WhoAm 92*
Pincus, Patricia Hogan 1945- *WhoAmW 93*
Pincus, Steven R. *Law&B 92*
Pincus, Theodore Henry 1933- *WhoAm 92*
Pincus, Walter Haskell 1932- *WhoAm 92*
Pindar c. 520BC-c. 445BC *OxDcByz*
Pindar, Peter 1738-1819 *BioIn 17*
Pindborg, Jens Jorgen 1921- *WhoWor 93*
Pindell, Evangeline Covert 1938- *WhoAmW 93*
Pindell, Howardena Doreen 1943- *WhoAm 92*
Pinder, Albert William Joseph, II 1951- *WhoE 93*
Pinder, George Francis 1942- *WhoAm 92*
Pinder, John E. 1947- *St&PR 93*
Pinder, John H(umphrey) M(urray) *ConAu 39NR*
Pinder, Roger Martin 1941- *WhoScE 91-3*
Pinder, T.D. 1952- *St&PR 93*
Pinder, Wilma J. *Law&B 92*
Pindera, Jerzy Tadeusz 1914- *WhoAm 92*
Pinderhughes, Elaine *BioIn 17*
Pinderhughes, John 1946- *BioIn 17*
Pindling, Lynden 1930- *DcCPCAm*
Pindling, Lynden Oscar 1930- *WhoWor 93*
Pindyck, Bruce Eben 1945- *St&PR 93, WhoAm 92, WhoWor 93*
Pindyck, Mary E. 1946- *St&PR 93*
Pindyck, Mary Ellen *Law&B 92*
Pine, Bob *BioIn 17*
Pine, Charles 1943- *WhoSSW 93*
Pine, Charles Joseph 1951- *WhoAm 92*
Pine, Granville Martin 1915- *WhoAm 92*
Pine, Jack R. *Law&B 92*
Pine, John Christopher 1922- *WhoWrEP 92*
Pine, M. S. *AmWomPl*
Pine, Patricia Palmer 1940- *WhoAmW 93*
Pine, Robert John 1948- *WhoScE 91-1*
Pine, Thomas Allen 1940- *WhoE 93*
Pineas, Hermann 1892- *BioIn 17*
Pineau, Andre 1941- *WhoScE 91-2*
Pineau, Christian 1904- *BioIn 17*
Pineau, James B. 1957- *St&PR 93*
Pineau, Jean Philippe 1942- *WhoScE 91-2*
Pineda, Danilo Pestanas 1960- *WhoWor 93*
Pineda, Marciano M. 1938- *WhoAsAP 91*
Pineda, Marianna 1925- *WhoAm 92*
Pineda, Patricia Salas *Law&B 92*
Pinedo, Herbert M. 1943- *WhoScE 91-3*
Pinegar, Elizabeth Ann 1958- *WhoAmW 93*
Pineiro, Eduard Efraly 1952- *WhoSSW 93*
Pineiro, Melisa M. *Law&B 92*
Pinel, Philippe 1745-1826 *BioIn 17*
Pineles, Cipe 1910-1991 *BioIn 17*
Pinell, Patrice *WhoScE 91-2*
Pinelli, Paolo 1921- *WhoScE 91-3*
Pinelli, Tazio Sergio 1934- *WhoScE 91-3*
Pinelli, Thomas Edward 1947- *WhoSSW 93*
Pineno, Francis A. 1943- *St&PR 93*
Pineo, Patricia Prather 1946- *WhoAmW 93*
Piner, Dick Henley, Jr. 1929- *St&PR 93*
Pinera, Virgilio 1912-1979 *ScF&FL 92, SpAmA*
Pinero, Arthur Wing 1855-1934 *BioIn 17*
Pinero, Carlos 1937- *WhoWor 93*
Pinero, Gerald Joseph 1943- *WhoSSW 93*
Pinero, Miguel *BioIn 17*
Pinero, Miguel 1946-1988 *HispAmA*
Pinero, Sally B. Hernandez *NotHsAW 93*
Pineros Pardo, Rodrigo 1958- *WhoWor 93*
Pines, Alexander 1945- *WhoAm 92, WhoWor 93*
Pines, Burton Yale 1940- *WhoAm 92, WhoE 93*
Pines, David 1924- *WhoAm 92*
Pines, Dennis S. *Law&B 92*
Pines, Herman 1902- *WhoAm 92*
Pines, Isidore 1937- *St&PR 93*
Pines, Jack 1925- *St&PR 93*
Pines, Judith Aiello *WhoAm 92*
Pines, Lois G. 1940- *WhoAmW 93*
Pines, Robert H. 1924- *WhoAm 92*
Pines, T. *ScF&FL 92*
Pines, Wayne Lloyd 1943- *WhoE 93, WhoWor 93*
Pinet, Frank Samuel 1920- *WhoAm 92*
Pinfold, Wilfred Robert 1956- *WhoSSW 93*
Ping, Charles Jackson 1930- *WhoAm 92*
Ping, Douglas Edward 1960- *WhoE 93*
Pingatore, Joseph John *Law&B 92*
Pingel, Carl Raymond 1935- *WhoIns 93*
Pingel, John S. 1916- *St&PR 93*
Pingel, John Spencer 1916- *WhoAm 92*
Pinget, Robert *BioIn 17*
Pingitore, Linda *Law&B 92*
Pingitore, Raffaele 1945- *WhoScE 91-3*
Pingoud, Ernest 1888-1942 *Baker 92*
Pingree, Dale Scott 1957- *St&PR 93*
Pingree, Dianne *WhoAmW 93*
Pingree, Hazen S. 1840-1901 *PolPar*
Pingry, Julie 1957- *WhoE 93, WhoEmL 93*
Pings, Anthony Claude 1951- *WhoWor 93*
Pings, Cornelius John 1929- *WhoAm 92, WhoWor 93*
Pinheiro, Aileen Folson 1921- *WhoAmW 93*
Pinheiro, Francisco P. 1934- *WhoUN 92*
Pinheiro, JoseLuis Palma Almeida 1950- *WhoWor 93*
Pinheiro, M. *WhoScE 91-3*
Pinheiro Farinha, Joao De Deus 1919- *WhoWor 93*
Pinhorn, W.W. 1942- *St&PR 93*
Pini, Giorgio *WhoScE 91-3*
Pini, Richard 1950- *ScF&FL 92*
Pini, Wendy 1951- *ScF&FL 92*
Piniak, Stanislaw *WhoScE 91-4*
Pinianski, Patricia *ScF&FL 92*
Pinick, Byron Dan 1928- *St&PR 93*
Pini-Corsi, Antonio 1858-1918 *Baker 92, OxDcOp*
Pini-Corsi, Gaetano 1860-c. 1923 *OxDcOp*
Piniella, Lou 1943- *BioIn 17*
Piniella, Louis Victor 1943- *BiDAMSp 1989, WhoAm 92*
Pinigis, Florence J. *Law&B 92*
Pinilla, Jose Maria *DcCPCAm*
Pininska, Joanna 1939- *WhoScE 91-4*
Pinion, Robert A. 1943- *St&PR 93*
Pink *BioIn 17*
Pink, E.G. 1947- *WhoScE 91-1*
Pink, Fred G. 1934- *St&PR 93*
Pinka, Patricia Garland 1935- *WhoAmW 93*
Pinkau, Klaus 1931- *WhoScE 91-3*
Pinkayan, Subin 1934- *WhoAsAP 91*
Pinkel, Donald Paul 1926- *WhoAm 92*
Pinkenburg, Ronald Joseph 1940- *WhoSSW 93*
Pinkert, Daniel B. *Law&B 92*
Pinkert, Dorothy Minna 1921- *WhoE 93, WhoWor 93*
Pinkerton, Allan 1819-1884 *BioIn 17*
Pinkerton, Barbara P. *Law&B 92*
Pinkerton, Clayton David 1931- *WhoAm 92*
Pinkerton, Frank Merrill 1942- *St&PR 93*
Pinkerton, Guy Calvin 1934- *St&PR 93, WhoAm 92*
Pinkerton, Harlan S., Jr. *Law&B 92*
Pinkerton, James P. 1958- *BioIn 17*
Pinkerton, James Pearson 1958- *WhoAm 92*
Pinkerton, Jane E. 1940- *St&PR 93*
Pinkerton, Paul W. d1990 *BioIn 17*
Pinkerton, Richard LaDoyt 1933- *WhoAm 92*
Pinkerton, Robert Bruce 1941- *WhoAm 92, WhoE 93*
Pinkerton, Shelton 1926- *WhoAm 92*
Pinkerton, Wilbert Alvin, Jr. 1942- *St&PR 93*
Pinkes, Andrew J. *Law&B 92*
Pinkethman, William d1725 *BioIn 17*
Pinkham, Daniel 1923- *Baker 92, WhoAm 92*
Pinkham, Eleanor Humphrey 1926- *WhoAmW 93*
Pinkham, Frederick Oliver 1920- *WhoAm 92*
Pinkham, James Ronald 1960- *WhoSSW 93*
Pinkham, Janet Carol Mielke 1961- *WhoAmW 93*
Pinkham, Stephen William 1945- *St&PR 93*
Pinkin, James Edward 1947- *WhoAm 92*
Pinkney, Alphonso 1928- *WhoE 93*
Pinkney, Betty R. *Law&B 92*
Pinkney, Bill *BioIn 17*
Pinkney, Brian *ChlBIID [port]*
Pinkney, Brian 1961- *BlkAull 92*
Pinkney, David Henry 1914- *WhoAm 92*
Pinkney, Jerry 1939- *BioIn 17, BlkAull 92, ChlBIID [port], MajAI [port], SmATA 71 [port]*

Pinkney, William 1764-1822 *OxCSupC*
Pinkney, Yvonne Theresa 1947- *WhoAmW 93*
Pinkola, Clarissa Estes *NotHsAW 93*
Pinkstaff, Carlin Adam 1934- *WhoSSW 93*
Pinkston, Arnold Anthony *Law&B 92*
Pinkston, Edwin Stewart 1943- *WhoSSW 93*
Pinkston, Keli 1940- *WhoWrEP 92*
Pinkston, Larry Dean 1954- *St&PR 93*
Pinkwater, Daniel M. 1941- *ScF&FL 92*
Pinkwater, Daniel Manus 1941- *BioIn 17, ConAu 38NR, MajAI [port], WhoAm 92*
Pinkwater, Manus *ConAu 38NR, MajAI*
Pinkwater, Manus 1941- *BioIn 17*
Pin-Mei, Ignatius Kung Gong Cardinal 1901- *WhoWor 93*
Pinn, Vivian W. 1941- *WhoAmW 93*
Pinna, Lorenzo A. 1939- *WhoScE 91-3*
Pinnaduwage, Lal Ariyaritna *WhoSSW 93*
Pinnagoda, Chandradasa 1936- *WhoUN 92*
Pinnell, Brian C. 1932- *St&PR 93*
Pinnell, Gary Robert 1952- *WhoSSW 93*
Pinnell, Sherri L. *Law&B 92*
Pinnell, William Eugene 1956- *WhoSSW 93*
Pinneo, Jeffrey D. 1956- *St&PR 93*
Pinner, James Francis 1930- *WhoSSW 93*
Pinner, Jay Martin 1953- *WhoSSW 93*
Pinner, Mick *BioIn 17*
Pinney, David Gordon 1939- *St&PR 93*
Pinney, Delia Delight Dorrance *AmWomPl*
Pinney, E. Gilbert 1951- *WhoSSW 93*
Pinney, Lucy (Catherine) 1952- *ConAu 136*
Pinney, Rodger *St&PR 93*
Pinney, Sidney Dillingham, Jr. 1924- *WhoAm 92*
Pinney, Thomas Clive 1932- *WhoAm 92*
Pinnick, Larry V. 1947- *St&PR 93*
Pinnock, Trevor (David) 1946- *Baker 92*
Pinnow, Arno Lee 1941- *WhoWor 93*
Pinn-Wiggins, Vivian *BioIn 17*
Pino, Anthony John 1948- *WhoEmL 93*
Pino, Christopher Joseph 1942- *WhoE 93*
Pino, H. Eduardo 1949- *WhoE 93*
Pino, John Anthony 1923- *WhoAm 92*
Pino, Piero 1921- *WhoScE 91-4*
Pino, Vincent S. 1948- *St&PR 93*
Pinochet, Augusto 1915- *DcTwHis*
Pinochet Ugarte, Augusto 1915- *ColdWar 2 [port], WhoWor 93*
Pinoit, R. *WhoScE 91-2*
Pinola, Joseph J. 1925- *BioIn 17, St&PR 93*
Pinola, Joseph John 1925- *WhoAm 92*
Pinon, Evangelina Vigil *NotHsAW 93*
Pinon, Jean 1946- *WhoScE 91-2*
Pinon, Jean-Michel 1930- *WhoScE 91-2*
Pinos, Alois Simandl 1925- *Baker 92*
Pinover, Martin D. 1938- *St&PR 93*
Pinowski, Jan Krystyn 1930- *WhoScE 91-4*
Pinsent, Gordon 1930- *WhoCanL 92*
Pinsent, Richard Alan 1931- *WhoWor 93*
Pinske, Roy O. 1933- *St&PR 93*
Pinsker, Essie Levine *WhoAmW 93*
Pinsker, Penny Collias 1942- *WhoAmW 93*
Pinsker, Sanford 1941- *WhoE 93*
Pinsker, Sanford Sigmund 1941- *WhoWrEP 92*
Pinsker, Walter 1933- *WhoE 93*
Pinsky, Elizabeth Lear 1940- *WhoAmW 93*
Pinsky, Gerald A. 1938- *St&PR 93*
Pinsky, Marilyn Levin 1939- *WhoAmW 93*
Pinsky, Robert Neal 1940- *WhoAm 92, WhoWrEP 92*
Pinsof, Nathan 1926- *WhoAm 92*
Pinsof, Philip 1911- *St&PR 93*
Pinson, Ellis Rex, Jr. 1925- *WhoAm 92*
Pinson, Harley Frederick *Law&B 92*
Pinson, John Michael 1963- *WhoSSW 93*
Pinson, Kathleen Susan 1952- *St&PR 93*
Pinson, Martha Sibyl 1948- *WhoAmW 93*
Pinson, William Meredith 1934- *WhoSSW 93*
Pinsonneault, Alan A. 1946- *St&PR 93*
Pinstrup-Andersen, Per 1939- *WhoE 93*
Pinsuti, Ciro 1829-1888 *Baker 92*
Pintar, Robert George 1927- *St&PR 93*
Pintaric, Nedjeljko 1930- *WhoScE 91-4*
Pintat Solans, Josep 1925- *WhoWor 93*
Pintauro, Peter Nicholas 1951- *WhoSSW 93*
Pintea, Valeriu V. 1920- *WhoScE 91-4*
Pinter, Gabriel George 1925- *WhoE 93*
Pinter, Harold 1930- *BioIn 17, ConLC 73 [port], MagSWL [port], MiSFD 9, WhoAm 92, WhoWor 93, WorLitC [port]*
Pinter, J. James 1945- *St&PR 93*
Pinter, Joseph Kalman 1953- *WhoWor 93*
Pinter, Michael Robert 1948- *St&PR 93*
Pinter, Reinhard 1943- *WhoScE 91-4*
Pintero, John 1947- *ScF&FL 92*
Pinther, Miklos 1940- *WhoAm 92*
Pinti, John 1944- *St&PR 93*
Pinti, Mario 1920- *WhoWor 93*
Pintilie, Lucian 1933- *DrEEuF*
Pintner, James Charles *Law&B 92*
Pinto, Alfredo 1891-1968 *Baker 92*
Pinto, Carlos Gouveia 1949- *WhoWor 93*
Pinto, Charles J. *Law&B 92*
Pinto, Edgar Roquette- *IntDcAn*
Pinto, Emanuel 1952- *WhoE 93*
Pinto, Fernao Mendes 1509-1583 *Expl 93*
Pinto, Francesco *Law&B 92*
Pinto, George Frederick 1785-1806 *Baker 92*
Pinto, James Joseph 1937- *St&PR 93*
Pinto, James T. *Law&B 92*
Pinto, Janice Marie 1948- *WhoAmW 93*
Pinto, Joseph C. 1946- *St&PR 93*
Pinto, Luigi *WhoScE 91-3*
Pinto, Michael 1938- *St&PR 93*
Pinto, Octavio 1890-1950 *Baker 92*
Pinto, R.A. 1927- *St&PR 93*
Pinto, Rebecca Mary 1952- *WhoAmW 93*
Pinto, Ronald Joseph 1931- *St&PR 93*
Pinto, Rosalind *WhoE 93*
Pintoff, Ernest 1931- *MiSFD 9*
Pinto Lopes, Eduardo Manuel 1957- *WhoWor 93*
Pinto Ricardo, Rui 1925- *WhoScE 91-3*
Pintsov, Leon Aron 1948- *WhoE 93*
Pintzuk, Marcia D. *Law&B 92*
Pinyan, Hollis Fitzhugh 1931- *St&PR 93*
Pinyuh, Sam P. *St&PR 93*
Pinza, Ezio 1892-1957 *Baker 92, IntDcOp, OxDcOp*
Pinzino, Gerald J. *Law&B 92*
Pinzka, Barbara *BioIn 17*
Pinzon, Alonso *DcCPCAm*
Pinzon, Vicente Yanez 1463?-1514 *Expl 93*
Pinzone, Alison Lyons 1957- *WhoAmW 93*
Pinzone, Charles R. *Law&B 92*
Pinzotti, Peter J. 1911- *St&PR 93*
Pio, Antonio 1933- *WhoUN 92*
Pio, Casimiro Adriao 1951- *WhoScE 91-3*
Pio, Padre 1887-1968 *BioIn 17*
Pioli, Janet A. *Law&B 92*
Piombino, Alfred Ernest 1962- *WhoE 93*
Piombo, Bruno 1944- *WhoScE 91-3*
Pione, Frances Elaine 1952- *WhoE 93*
Pionk, Richard Cletus 1936- *WhoE 93*
Piontek, Heinz Robert 1925- *WhoWor 93*
Piontkowski, Chester Leonard 1934- *St&PR 93*
Piontkowsky, Andrei Andreevich 1940- *WhoWor 93*
Piontnica, Joseph 1929- *St&PR 93*
Piore, Emanuel Ruben 1908- *WhoAm 92*
Piore, Michael Joseph 1940- *WhoAm 92*
Pioske, Brian R. *Law&B 92*
Piot, J.Cl. *WhoScE 91-4*
Piot, Peter 1949- *WhoScE 91-2, WhoWor 93*
Piotr, Rafalski 1954- *WhoWor 93*
Piotrovskii, B.B. 1908-1990 *BioIn 17*
Piotrovskii, Boris Borisovich 1908-1990 *BioIn 17*
Piotrowski, Barbra *BioIn 17*
Piotrowski, Chester Joseph 1938- *St&PR 93*
Piotrowski, J. *WhoScE 91-3*
Piotrowski, Jerzy K. 1926- *WhoScE 91-4*
Piotrowski, John Henry 1949- *WhoE 93*
Piotrowski, John Louis 1934- *WhoAm 92*
Piotrowski, Linda Susan *WhoE 93*
Piotrowski, Richard Francis 1945- *WhoAm 92*
Pious, James Ethan 1957- *St&PR 93*
Piovene, Agostino fl. 1709-1726 *OxDcOp*
Piozzi, Hester Lynch 1741-1821 *BioIn 17*
Pipal, Faustin A. 1921- *St&PR 93*
Pipal, Faustin Anthony 1921- *WhoAm 92*
Pipal, George Henry 1916- *WhoAm 92*
Pipelare, Matthaeus c. 1450-c. 1512 *Baker 92*
Piper, Addison Lewis 1946- *WhoAm 92*
Piper, Carol Adeline 1924- *WhoAmW 93*
Piper, David 1918-1990 *BioIn 17*
Piper, Don Courtney 1932- *WhoAm 92*
Piper, Ernst Reinhard 1952- *WhoWor 93*
Piper, Frank Ivan 1933- *St&PR 93*
Piper, Frederick Charles *WhoScE 91-1*
Piper, George Earle 1932- *WhoAm 92*
Piper, H. Beam 1904-1964 *BioIn 17, ScF&FL 92*
Piper, Hans Michael 1952- *WhoWor 93*
Piper, Harry C. d1990 *BioIn 17*
Piper, Henry George 1922- *St&PR 93, WhoAm 92*
Piper, Jane *BioIn 17*
Piper, John 1903- *OxDcOp*
Piper, John 1903-1992 *BioIn 17, CurBio 92N, NewYTBS 92 [port]*
Piper, John Richard 1946- *WhoSSW 93*
Piper, Jon L. 1950- *St&PR 93*
Piper, Joyce Eileen 1946- *WhoE 93*
Piper, Linda Ammann 1949- *WhoEmL 93*
Piper, Lloyd Llewellyn, II 1944- *WhoSSW 93*
Piper, Mark Harry 1931- *WhoAm 92*
Piper, Mary A. *Law&B 92*
Piper, Myfanwy 1911- *OxDcOp*
Piper, Pat Kathryn 1934- *WhoAmW 93*
Piper, Priscilla J. *WhoScE 91-1*
Piper, Robert Johnston 1926- *WhoAm 92*
Piper, Samuel O'Dell 1951- *WhoSSW 93*
Piper, Stephanie Beaudouin 1947- *WhoSSW 93*
Piper, Stephen M. *Law&B 92*
Piper, Terry A. 1945- *St&PR 93*
Piper, Thomas L., III 1941- *St&PR 93*
Piper, Thomas Laurence, III 1941- *WhoAm 92*
Piper, W. Stephen 1945- *WhoE 93*
Piper, Watty *ConAu 137, MajAI*
Piper, William Howard 1933- *WhoAm 92*
Pipes, Daniel 1949- *WhoAm 92, WhoWor 93*
Pipes, Mai *AmWomPl*
Pipes, Richard Edgar 1923- *WhoAm 92, WhoWrEP 92*
Pipes, Robert Byron 1941- *WhoAm 92*
Pipes, Stanley Howard 1934- *St&PR 93*
Pipes, Wesley O'Feral 1932- *WhoAm 92*
Pipim, Joshua Kwaku 1955- *WhoWor 93*
Pipkin, Allen Compere, II 1931- *WhoAm 92*
Pipkin, Alva Claude 1931- *St&PR 93*
Pipkin, Francis M. d1992 *NewYTBS 92*
Pipkin, Francis M. 1925-1992 *BioIn 17*
Pipkin, James Harold, Jr. 1939- *WhoAm 92*
Pipkin, John B., II 1935- *St&PR 93*
Pipkin, Julian Thomas, Jr. 1944- *St&PR 93*
Pipkin, Wade Lemual, Jr. 1945- *WhoSSW 93*
Pipkov, Lubomir 1904-1974 *Baker 92*
Pipkowa, Malgorzata 1886-1963 *PolBiDi*
Pi Portales, Maria Victoria 1955- *WhoAmW 93*
Pippard, Alfred Brian *WhoScE 91-1*
Pippard, Brian 1920- *WhoWor 93*
Pippel, Winfried 1929- *WhoWor 93*
Pippen, Scottie 1965- *News 92 [port], WhoAm 92*
Pippenger, David L. *Law&B 92*
Pippenger, Lynn 1938- *St&PR 93*
Pippenger, Philip M. *Law&B 92*
Pippenger, Wilma Jean 1940- *WhoAmW 93*
Pippig, Uta *BioIn 17*
Pippin, John Eldon 1927- *WhoAm 92*
Pippin, Kenneth Andrew 1949- *St&PR 93*
Pippin, Lynda Lee Lanning 1960- *WhoAmW 93*
Pippin, Nick d1990 *BioIn 17*
Pique, Andrea *Law&B 92*
Piquer, Jose S. 1931- *WhoScE 91-3*
Piquette, Marice Ann 1954- *WhoWrEP 92*
Pira, Amin R. 1949- *St&PR 93*
Piracha, M. Akram 1936- *WhoUN 92*
Piraino, Russell Wayne *Law&B 92*
Piraino, Thomas A., Jr. *Law&B 92*
Piramal, Dilip Gopikrishna 1949- *WhoWor 93*
Piramowicz, Grzegorz 1735-1801 *PolBiDi*
Pirandello, Luigi 1867-1936 *MagSWL [port], WorLitC [port]*
Pirani, Adam *ScF&FL 92*
Pirani, Conrad Levi 1914- *WhoAm 92*
Pirani, Eugenio 1852-1939 *Baker 92*
Pirani, Vincenzo *WhoScE 91-3*
Piranian, Poozant 1910- *St&PR 93*
Pirard, Jean-Paul E. 1947- *WhoScE 91-2*
Pirard, Willy 1953- *WhoScE 91-2*
Pirazzoli, Paolo Antonio 1939- *WhoScE 91-2, WhoWor 93*
Pircher, Leo Joseph 1933- *WhoAm 92*
Pirchner, Franz 1927- *WhoScE 91-3*
Pirdavari, Houman *BioIn 17*
Pire, R. *WhoScE 91-2*
Pirelli, Leopoldo 1925- *WhoWor 93*
Pires, (Luis) Filipe 1934- *Baker 92*
Pires, Kenneth Michael 1956- *St&PR 93*
Pires, Maria-Joao 1944- *Baker 92*
Pires, Pedro Verona Rodrigues 1934- *WhoAfr*
Pires Da Costa, Jose Santos 1938- *WhoScE 91-3*
Pires-Hester, Laura J. 1939- *WhoE 93*
Piret, John J. 1938- *St&PR 93*
Piret, Marguerite Alice 1948- *WhoAm 92, WhoE 93*
Pirich, Donna Marie Bridget 1958- *WhoAmW 93*
Pirie, David 1946- *ScF&FL 92*
Pirie, Gordon 1931-1991 *AnObit 1991*
Pirie, Robert B. 1933- *St&PR 93*
Pirie, Robert Burns, Jr. 1933- *WhoAm 92*
Pirie, Robert Gordon 1936- *WhoSSW 93*
Pirie, Robert S. 1934- *St&PR 93, WhoAm 92*
Pirie, William Stewart 1938- *St&PR 93*
Pirilli, John 1943- *St&PR 93*
Pirinen, Onni *WhoScE 91-4*
Pirk, Hans A. *WhoScE 91-3*
Pirkl, James Joseph 1930- *WhoAm 92, WhoE 93*
Pirkle, Earl Charnell 1922- *WhoAm 92*
Pirkle, George Emory 1947- *WhoAm 92, WhoEmL 93*
Pirkle, John Ward 1937- *WhoAm 92*
Pirkle, William Arthur 1945- *WhoSSW 93*
Pirlot, Benoit *Law&B 92*
Pirnar, Turgrul *WhoScE 91-4*
Pirner, Connie White 1955- *SmATA 72 [port]*
Pirner, Miros 1928- *WhoScE 91-4*
Pirnes, Hannu Erkki 1945- *WhoWor 93*
Pirnie, Bruce 1935- *WhoWor 93*
Pirnie, Malcolm, Jr. 1917- *WhoAm 92*
Piro, Anthony John 1930- *WhoAm 92*
Pirodsky, Donald Max 1945- *WhoE 93*
Pirofsky, Bernard 1926- *WhoAm 92*
Pirogov, Alexander 1899-1964 *OxDcOp*
Pirogov, Alexander (Stepanovich) 1899-1964 *Baker 92*
Pirogov, Alexey 1895- *OxDcOp*
Pirogov, Grigory 1885-1931 *OxDcOp*
Pirogov, Mikhail 1887-1933 *OxDcOp*
Pirolli, Augustine Richard 1930- *WhoAm 92*
Piron, Constantin 1932- *WhoScE 91-4*
Piron, Georges Jacques 1959- *WhoWor 93*
Pirone, Thomas Pascal 1936- *WhoAm 92*
Pironio, Bruno *St&PR 93*
Pironio, Eduardo Cardinal 1920- *WhoAm 92, WhoWor 93*
Pironkoff, Simeon 1927- *Baker 92*
Pironneau, Olivier R. 1945- *WhoScE 91-2*
Piront, Andre 1943- *WhoScE 91-2*
Pirotte, John Keith 1950- *St&PR 93*
Pirotte, Pol L.R.J.J. 1936- *WhoScE 91-2*
Pirozynski, Jan 1936- *WhoWor 93*
Pirozynski, Michal P. 1953- *WhoScE 91-4*
Pirozzoli, Alexander 1922- *St&PR 93*
Pirozzoli, Richard William 1948- *St&PR 93*
Pirquet, Hans P. 1934- *St&PR 93*
Pirret, Joseph B. 1940- *St&PR 93*
Pirretti, James Joseph *Law&B 92*
Pirrie, William James 1847-1924 *BioIn 17*
Pirrin, Eusebio *HispAmA*
Pirro, Andre (Gabriel Edme) 1869-1943 *Baker 92*
Pirrotta, Nino 1908- *Baker 92*
Pirs, Joze Karl 1925- *WhoScE 91-4*
Pirsch, Carol McBride 1936- *WhoAmW 93*
Pirsch, Peter Joseph 1936- *St&PR 93*
Pirscher, Carl William 1924- *St&PR 93, WhoAm 92*
Pirschl, Anne D. 1963- *St&PR 93*
Pirschl, Gary 1958- *St&PR 93*
Pirsig, Robert M. *BioIn 17*
Pirsig, Robert M. 1928- *ConLC 73 [port]*
Pirsig, Robert Maynard 1928- *WhoAm 92, WhoWrEP 92*
Pirsig, Susan Marie 1953- *WhoAmW 93*
Pirt, Stanley John *WhoScE 91-1*
Pirtle, Jamie L. 1929- *St&PR 93*
Pirtle, William B. 1944- *St&PR 93*
Pirtle, Woody *BioIn 17*
Pirumov, Alexander 1930- *Baker 92*
Pirzadeh, Shahyar 1952- *WhoSSW 93*
Pirzio-Biroli, Corrado 1940- *WhoE 93*
Pisa, Agostino fl. 17th cent.- *Baker 92*
Pisa, John Charles 1944- *St&PR 93*
Pisacane, Ernie John 1937- *WhoWrEP 92*
Pisacich, Kevin Walter 1966- *WhoE 93*
Pisacrita, Marie Seliste 1946- *WhoEmL 93*
Pisador, Diego 1509?-1557? *Baker 92*
Pisan, Christine de c. 1364-c. 1431 *BioIn 17*
Pisani, Anthony J. d1992 *NewYTBS 92 [port]*
Pisani, Anthony J. 1911-1992 *BioIn 17*
Pisani, Anthony Michael 1943- *WhoE 93*
Pisani, Edgard 1918- *BioIn 17*
Pisani, Gerald V. 1940- *St&PR 93*
Pisani, Joseph Michael 1919- *WhoAm 92*
Pisani, Michael *Law&B 92*
Pisani, Robert Louis 1956- *WhoE 93, WhoWrEP 92*
Pisanko, Henry Jonathan 1925- *WhoE 93, WhoWor 93*
Pisano, A. Robert 1943- *WhoAm 92*
Pisano, Anthony M. 1940- *St&PR 93*
Pisano, Bernardo 1490-1548 *Baker 92*
Pisano, John Francis 1948- *WhoE 93*
Pisano, Judith Belushi 1951- *WhoEmL 93*
Pisano, Ronald George 1948- *WhoAm 92*
Pisapia, Ronn A. *Law&B 92*
Pisar, Samuel 1929- *WhoWrEP 92*
Pisari, Pasquale 1725-1778 *Baker 92*
Pisaroni, Benedetta Rosamunda 1793-1872 *OxDcOp*
Pisarski, Bohdan *WhoScE 91-4*
Pisasale, Roy Frank 1949- *St&PR 93*
Piscatelli, Nancy Marie 1953- *WhoAmW 93*

Pischinger, Franz Felix 1930- *WhoScE 91-3*
Pischl, Adolph John 1920- *WhoAm 92*
Pischna, Josef 1826-1896 *Baker 92*
Piscione, Joseph *St&PR 93*
Pisciotta, Anthony Vito 1921- *WhoAm 92*
Pisciotta, Charles 1933- *St&PR 93*
Piscitello, John Salvatore *Law&B 92*
Piscopo, Albert E. 1944- *St&PR 93*
Piscopo, Joseph A. 1944- *St&PR 93*
Piscopo, Joseph Charles 1951- *WhoAm 92*
Piscotta, Dolores *WhoE 93*
Pisek, Jan Krtitel 1814-1873 *OxDcOp*
Pisendel, Johann Georg 1687-1755 *Baker 92*
Pisent, Gualtiero 1930- *WhoScE 91-3*
Piser, Donald H. 1941- *St&PR 93*
Piser, Donald Harris 1941- *WhoAm 92*
Piserchia, Doris 1928- *BioIn 17, ScF&FL 92*
Piserchia, Doris Elaine 1928- *WhoAm 92*
Pisetzner, Emanuel 1926- *WhoAm 92*
Pishev, Ognian Raytchev 1951- *WhoWor 93*
Pishkin, Vladimir 1931- *WhoAm 92*
Pishny, Teresa Dawn 1959- *WhoAmW 93*
Pisier, Marie-France 1944- *MiSFD 9*
Pisier, Marie-France 1946?- *BioIn 17*
Pisk, Krunoslav 1943- *WhoScE 91-4*
Pisk, Paul A(madeus) 1893-1990 *Baker 92*
Piskacek, Vladimir Richard 1929- *WhoWor 93*
Piskurich, S.F. 1935- *St&PR 93*
Pisney, Raymond Frank 1940- *WhoAm 92, WhoWor 93*
Pissarides, Christopher Antoniou *WhoScE 91-1*
Pissarides, Christopher Antoniou 1948- *WhoWor 93*
Pissart, Albert J.G. 1930- *WhoScE 91-2*
Pisseleu, Anne de 1508-1580 *BioIn 17*
Pissocra, C.E. 1933- *St&PR 93*
Pistell, Peter C. 1945- *St&PR 93*
Pistella, Christine Ley 1949- *WhoAmW 93*
Pistella, Fabio *WhoScE 91-3*
Pister, Karl Stark 1925- *WhoAm 92*
Pistilli, Frederick M. *St&PR 93*
Pistilli, Philip 1926- *WhoAm 92*
Pistner, Stephen L. 1932- *St&PR 93*
Pistner, Stephen Lawrence 1932- *WhoAm 92, WhoE 93*
Pistocchi, Francesco Antonio 1659-1726 *OxDcOp*
Pistocchi, Francesco Antonio Mamiliano 1659-1726 *Baker 92*
Pistolakis, Nicholas S. 1933- *WhoE 93*
Pistole, Thomas Gordon 1942- *WhoAm 92, WhoE 93*
Pistolesi, Gianfranco 1927- *WhoScE 91-3*
Piston, Walter Hamor, Jr. 1894-1976 *Baker 92*
Pistone, Lisa Marian 1959- *WhoSSW 93*
Pistor, Charles H., Jr. 1930- *St&PR 93*
Pistor, Charles Herman, Jr. 1930- *WhoAm 92*
Pistorius, George 1922- *WhoAm 92*
Pistulka, Donald Joseph 1946- *St&PR 93*
Pi-Sunyer, F. Xavier 1933- *WhoE 93*
Pita, Dan 1938- *DrEEuF*
Pita, Marina K. *Law&B 92*
Pitagorsky, George 1942- *WhoE 93*
Pitanguy, Ivo *BioIn 17*
Pitaro, Nicholas R. *Law&B 92*
Pitaro, Vincent L. 1913-1991 *BioIn 17*
Pita Rodriguez, Felix 1909- *SpAmA*
Pitarresi, Frances Louise 1948- *WhoE 93*
Pitassy, Caesar L. 1914- *St&PR 93*
Pitblado, J.B. 1932- *St&PR 93*
Pitblado, Robin Maurice 1948- *St&PR 93*
Pitcairn, John 1722-1775 *HarEnMi*
Pitcairn, Sharon Rachel 1963- *WhoAmW 93*
Pitcel, Robert Allen 1932- *St&PR 93*
Pitchell, Loretta Ann 1942- *WhoSSW 93*
Pitchell, Robert J. *WhoAm 92*
Pitchenik, David E. *Law&B 92*
Pitcher, Desmond Henry 1935- *WhoWor 93*
Pitcher, Donald Folsom, Jr. 1938- *St&PR 93*
Pitcher, Frank E. *Law&B 92*
Pitcher, Griffith Fontaine 1937- *WhoSSW 93*
Pitcher, John Alfred 1935- *WhoSSW 93*
Pitcher, Max Grow 1935- *WhoAm 92*
Pitcher, Thomas B. 1937- *St&PR 93*
Pitcher, William Crawford *Law&B 92*
Pitchford, D.J. Watkins- 1905-1990 *BioIn 17*
Pitchie, R. Brooks *Law&B 92*
Pitchon, Daniel Nathan 1947- *WhoE 93*
Pitchumoni, Capecomorin Sankar 1938- *WhoAm 92*
Pitcock, Albert Richard 1938- *WhoE 93*
Pitcock, Charles Louis *Law&B 92*
Pitcock, James Kent 1951- *WhoAm 92*
Pitcock, John W. 1948- *St&PR 93*
Pitelka, Frank Alois 1916- *WhoAm 92*
Pitera, Jo-Ann Innocence 1953- *WhoSSW 93*
Piternick, Anne Brearley *WhoAm 92*
Pitet, Patrick G. *Law&B 92*
Pitfield, Peter Michael 1937- *WhoE 93*
Pitfield, Thomas B(aron) 1903- *Baker 92*
Pitfield, Ward C. 1925- *St&PR 93*
Pithart, Petr 1941- *WhoWor 93*
Pitino, Richard 1952- *WhoAm 92*
Pitino, Rick *BioIn 17*
Pitis, Marcela *WhoScE 91-4*
Pitkanen, Jorma Antero 1934- *WhoScE 91-4*
Pitkethley, Janice *ScF&FL 92*
Pitkin, Barbara Anne 1960- *WhoAmW 93*
Pitkin, Edward Meyer 1949- *St&PR 93*
Pitkin, Edward Thaddeus 1930- *WhoAm 92*
Pitkin, Patricia A. 1951- *WhoAm 92*
Pitkin, Roy Macbeth 1934- *WhoAm 92*
Pitkow, Howard Spencer 1941- *WhoE 93*
Pitkowsky, Murray 1931- *St&PR 93*
Pitler, Richard Kalman 1928- *WhoAm 92*
Pitman, Alyson Rock 1953- *WhoAmW 93*
Pitman, Betty Jean 1936- *WhoAmW 93*
Pitman, Grover Allen 1943- *WhoE 93*
Pitman, Kathryn Ann 1965- *WhoSSW 93*
Pitman, Mark Ira 1932- *WhoAm 92*
Pitman, Sharon Gail 1946- *WhoSSW 93*
Pitner, Albert William *Law&B 92*
Pitner, Samuel Ellis 1932- *WhoAm 92*
Pitner, Thomas J. 1941- *St&PR 93*
Pitney, Mahlon 1858-1924 *OxCSupC [port]*
Pitofsky, Robert 1929- *WhoAm 92*
Pitol, Sergio 1933- *DcMexL*
Pitoni, Giuseppe Ottavio 1657-1743 *Baker 92*
Pitoniak, Elizabeth Ann 1954- *WhoAmW 93*
Pitorak, Larry John 1946- *St&PR 93*
Pitot, Henry Clement 1930- *WhoAm 92*
Pitre, Giuseppe 1841-1916 *IntDcAn*
Pitre, Glen 1955- *MiSFD 9*
Pitre, Merline *WhoAmW 93*
Pitrolffy, Thomas Bela 1935- *St&PR 93*
Pitruzzella, Vincenzo D. *Law&B 92*
Pitsch, Larry H. 1941- *St&PR 93*
Pitsilos, Lenore-Staffieri *WhoE 93*
Pitstick, Leslie James 1935- *St&PR 93, WhoAm 92*
Pitsula, James (Michael) 1950- *ConAu 137*
Pitt, Bertram 1932- *WhoAm 92, WhoWor 93*
Pitt, Brad 1964?- *ConTFT 10*
Pitt, Brice Masterman Norman *WhoScE 91-1*
Pitt, Christine A. 1952- *WhoWrEP 92*
Pitt, Christopher W. *WhoScE 91-1*
Pitt, Connie Jean 1960- *WhoAmW 93*
Pitt, David C(harles) 1938- *ConAu 37NR*
Pitt, Donald Alfred 1926- *WhoSSW 93*
Pitt, Douglas Charles *WhoScE 91-1*
Pitt, Earle William 1923- *St&PR 93*
Pitt, Frederick J., Mrs. *AmWomPl*
Pitt, Gavin Alexander 1915- *WhoWor 93*
Pitt, George 1938- *WhoAm 92, WhoWor 93*
Pitt, Harvey Lloyd 1945- *WhoAm 92*
Pitt, Jane 1938- *WhoAmW 93*
Pitt, John P. 1944- *St&PR 93*
Pitt, Joseph B., Jr. *Law&B 92*
Pitt, Joseph Charles 1944- *WhoAm 92, WhoSSW 93*
Pitt, Lawrence B. *Law&B 92*
Pitt, Percy 1870-1932 *Baker 92, OxDcOp*
Pitt, Robert Healy, II 1924- *WhoAm 92*
Pitt, Suzanne Frances 1946- *WhoWrEP 92*
Pitt, Theo H., Jr. 1936- *St&PR 93*
Pitt, Theophilus Harper, Jr. 1936- *WhoAm 92*
Pitt, Tyrone Leslie *WhoScE 91-1*
Pitt, Valerie E. 1952- *WhoAmW 93*
Pitt, William 1708-1778 *BioIn 17, HarEnMi*
Pitt, William 1759-1806 *BioIn 17*
Pitt, William Arthur John, Jr. 1942- *WhoSSW 93*
Pittaluga, Ferruccio A. 1945- *WhoWor 93*
Pittaluga, Giovanna Giuseppina 1943- *WhoWor 93*
Pittaluga, Gustavo 1906- *Baker 92*
Pittard, Darrell Dennis 1948- *WhoAm 92*
Pittard, Marion Tralton 1939- *St&PR 93*
Pittas, John Francis 1932- *St&PR 93*
Pittas, Peggy Alice 1944- *WhoAmW 93*
Pittaway, David Bruce 1951- *WhoAm 92, WhoE 93*
Pittel, Harvey 1943- *Baker 92*
Pittelkow, Mark Robert 1952- *WhoAm 92*
Pittendrigh, Colin Stephenson 1918- *WhoAm 92*
Pittenger, Brad *Law&B 92*
Pittenger, Bruce R. 1946- *St&PR 93*
Pittenger, Jerrold W. 1942- *St&PR 93*
Pittenger, Kathleen Ann 1959- *WhoAmW 93*
Pittenger, Mark Charles 1959- *WhoSSW 93*
Pittenger, Richard F. 1935- *BioIn 17*
Pitter, Ruth 1897-1992 *ConAu 137*
Pitterich, Michael P. 1954- *St&PR 93*
Pitteway, Michael Lloyd Victor *WhoScE 91-1*
Pitteway, Michael Lloyd Victor 1934- *WhoWor 93*
Pitti, Donald Robert 1929- *St&PR 93, WhoAm 92*
Pittilo, R.N. *WhoScE 91-4*
Pitting Bin Haji Mohd Ali *WhoAsAP 91*
Pittinger, Wilbur Barke 1948- *WhoAm 92*
Pittius, Dolores Genevieve 1932- *WhoAmW 93*
Pittler, Marvin S. d1990 *BioIn 17*
Pittman, Al 1940- *WhoCanL 92*
Pittman, Bob *BioIn 17*
Pittman, Bruce 1950- *MiSFD 9*
Pittman, David Joshua 1927- *WhoAm 92, WhoWor 93*
Pittman, Debbie Lynn Odom 1949- *WhoWrEP 92*
Pittman, Donald George 1960- *WhoSSW 93*
Pittman, Edwin Lloyd 1935- *WhoAm 92, WhoSSW 93*
Pittman, G.C. 1921- *St&PR 93*
Pittman, Helena Clare 1945- *SmATA 71 [port]*
Pittman, Jacquelyn 1932- *WhoAmW 93, WhoSSW 93, WhoWor 93*
Pittman, James Allen, Jr. 1927- *WhoAm 92, WhoSSW 93, WhoWor 93*
Pittman, James David *Law&B 92*
Pittman, John Frank Townsend 1937- *WhoWor 93*
Pittman, Julia N. 1963- *St&PR 93*
Pittman, Key 1912-1940 *PolPar*
Pittman, Margaret 1901- *BioIn 17, WhoAmW 93*
Pittman, Natalie Anne 1952- *WhoAmW 93*
Pittman, Richard Frank, Jr. 1923- *St&PR 93*
Pittman, Robert C. *Law&B 92*
Pittman, Robert Turner 1929- *WhoAm 92*
Pittman, Robert Warren 1953- *WhoAm 92, WhoE 93*
Pittman, Sandy Hill *BioIn 17*
Pittman, Steuart Lansing 1919- *WhoAm 92*
Pittman, Thomas Franklin 1951- *WhoSSW 93*
Pittman, Tommy David 1948- *St&PR 93*
Pittman, Virgil 1916- *WhoAm 92, WhoSSW 93*
Pittman, Virgil Lee, Jr. 1941- *St&PR 93*
Pittman, William Claude 1921- *WhoSSW 93*
Pittman, William H. *Law&B 92*
Pittner, Heribert 1948- *WhoScE 91-4*
Pittock, Murray (G. H.) 1962- *ConAu 138*
Pittore, Carlo *WhoWrEP 92*
Pittore, Carlo 1943- *WhoE 93*
Pittrich, George Washington 1870-1934 *Baker 92*
Pitt-Rivers, Augustus Henry Lane-Fox 1827-1900 *BioIn 17, IntDcAn*
Pitts, Barbara Ann 1952- *WhoAmW 93*
Pitts, Bill 1934- *WhoAm 92*
Pitts, Carolyn 1924- *BioIn 17*
Pitts, Charlie d1876 *BioIn 17*
Pitts, Diane Castello 1955- *St&PR 93*
Pitts, Donald Graves 1926- *WhoSSW 93*
Pitts, Edward G. 1933- *St&PR 93*
Pitts, Eugene, III 1940- *WhoE 93, WhoWrEP 92*
Pitts, Greenfield 1918- *St&PR 93*
Pitts, James A. 1940- *St&PR 93*
Pitts, James Atwater 1940- *WhoAm 92*
Pitts, James D. 1938- *St&PR 93*
Pitts, Joe W., III 1960- *WhoWor 93*
Pitts, John Brantson *Law&B 92*
Pitts, John Wilson 1926- *St&PR 93*
Pitts, Karen Abernathy *Law&B 92*
Pitts, Lydia M. *Law&B 92*
Pitts, Marcellus Theadore 1957- *WhoSSW 93*
Pitts, Marvin Houston, Jr. 1952- *WhoSSW 93*
Pitts, Michael R. 1947- *ScF&FL 92*
Pitts, Richard D. 1950- *St&PR 93*
Pitts, Robert Eugene, Jr. 1948- *WhoAm 92*
Pitts, Robert Joseph 1932- *St&PR 93*
Pitts, S.R. 1937- *St&PR 93*
Pitts, Samuel R. *Law&B 92*
Pitts, Samuel Richard 1937- *WhoAm 92, WhoE 93*
Pitts, Sidney Clark 1950- *WhoSSW 93*
Pitts, Stephen James 1961- *WhoE 93*
Pitts, Thomas J. 1957- *St&PR 93*
Pitts, Vincent Joseph 1947- *WhoAm 92*
Pitts, Virginia 1953- *St&PR 93*
Pitts, Virginia M. 1953- *WhoAm 92*
Pitts, William 1925- *St&PR 93*
Pitts, ZaSu 1898-1963 *QDrFCA 92 [port]*
Pitty, Dimas Lidio 1941- *SpAmA*
Piturro, Marlene Cohen 1947- *WhoAmW 93*
Pitz, Peter E. 1941- *St&PR 93*
Pitzak, Marvin E. *Law&B 92*
Pitzer, Donald Elden 1936- *WhoAm 92*
Pitzer, George Lewis 1916- *St&PR 93*
Pitzer, Gloria *BioIn 17*
Pitzer, Kenneth Sanborn 1914- *BioIn 17, WhoAm 92*
Pitzer, Larry M. 1939- *St&PR 93*
Pitzinger, Gertrude 1904- *Baker 92*
Piunno, Frank R. 1948- *St&PR 93*
Pius, IX, Pope 1792-1878 *BioIn 17*
Pius, XII 1876-1958 *DcTwHis*
Piutti, Karl 1846-1902 *Baker 92*
Piva, Giulio 1940- *WhoWor 93*
Pivan, David B. 1921- *St&PR 93*
Pivan, David Bernard 1921- *WhoAm 92*
Pivar, Jack Joseph 1948- *WhoE 93*
Pivato, Joseph 1946- *WhoCanL 92*
Piven, Frances Fox 1932- *WhoAm 92*
Piven, Peter Anthony 1939- *WhoAm 92*
Piver, M. Steven 1934- *ConAu 138, WhoE 93*
Pivert, Marceau 1895-1958 *BioIn 17*
Pi Vila, Francesc 1959- *WhoWor 93*
Pivin, Jeanette Eva 1932- *WhoAmW 93*
Pivirotto, Richard Roy 1930- *St&PR 93, WhoAm 92*
Pivko, Ivan B. 1941- *St&PR 93*
Pivnick, Ben 1917- *St&PR 93*
Pivonka, Leonard Daniel 1951- *WhoAm 92*
Pivot, Bernard *BioIn 17*
Pivovar, Jennifer Ann 1957- *WhoAmW 93*
Piwocki, Franciszek Ksawery 1901-1974 *IntDcAn*
Piwocki, Marcin 1936- *WhoScE 91-4*
Piwowar, B. *WhoScE 91-4*
Piwowar, Jan 1947- *WhoScE 91-4*
Piwowarski, Radoslaw 1948- *DrEEuF*
Pixerecourt, Guilbert de 1773-1844 *NinCLC 39 [port], OxDcOp*
Pixis, Francilla 1816- *OxDcOp*
Pixis, Johann Peter 1788-1874 *Baker 92, OxDcOp*
Pixley, Carl Preston 1942- *WhoSSW 93*
Pixley, John Sherman, Sr. 1929- *WhoAm 92*
Pixley, Jorge V. 1937- *ConAu 37NR*
Pixley, Shirley 1936- *See* Shirley & Lee *SoulM*
Piyadasa, Godellewatte Arachchige 1940- *WhoWor 93*
Piyaoui, Chanut *BioIn 17*
Piyatissa, Mary Elizabeth 1946- *WhoWor 93*
Pi y Margall, Francisco 1824-1901 *BioIn 17*
Piza, Arthur Luiz 1928- *WhoWor 93*
Pizam, Abraham 1937- *WhoSSW 93*
Pizan, Christine de c. 1364-c. 1431 *BioIn 17*
Pizarnik, Alejandra 1936-1972 *BioIn 17, SpAmA*
Pizarro, Francisco c. 1471-1541 *OxDcOp*
Pizarro, Francisco c. 1475-1541 *BioIn 17, Expl 93 [port]*
Pizarro, Nicolas 1830-1895 *DcMexL*
Pizarro, Pete R. 1961- *St&PR 93*
Pizarro, Renato D. 1941- *St&PR 93*
Pizer, Donald 1929- *WhoAm 92, WhoWrEP 92*
Pizer, Howard Charles 1941- *WhoAm 92*
Pizer, Irwin H. 1934-1991 *BioIn 17*
Pizitz, Richard 1930- *St&PR 93*
Pizitz, Richard Alan 1930- *WhoAm 92*
Pizon, Andrzej Jacek 1936- *WhoScE 91-4*
Pizor, Faith K. 1943- *ScF&FL 92*
Pizza, Jack *Law&B 92*
Pizzamiglio, Nancy Alice 1936- *WhoAmW 93*
Pizzella, Anthony Nicola 1957- *WhoE 93, WhoEmL 93, WhoWor 93*
Pizzella, Guido 1933- *WhoScE 91-3*
Pizzetti, Ildebrando 1880-1968 *Baker 92, IntDcOp, OxDcOp*
Pizzey, Erin 1939- *BioIn 17*
Pizzi, Charles Peter 1950- *WhoAm 92*
Pizzi, Emilio 1861-1940 *Baker 92*
Pizzi, Pier Luigi 1930- *IntDcOp, WhoAm 92*
Pizzichil, William Paul, Jr. 1946- *St&PR 93*
Pizzini, Carlo Alberto 1905-1981 *Baker 92*
Pizzoferrato, Rudolph Cesidio 1931- *St&PR 93*
Pizzolato, Victor William 1932- *St&PR 93*
Pizzoli, Pasquale Vincenzo 1928- *WhoWor 93*
Pizzuto, Laura C. *Law&B 92*
Pjerrou, Mary 1945- *ConAu 137, ScF&FL 92*
Pla, Josefina *BioIn 17*
Pla, Josefina 1909- *SpAmA*
Plaa, Gabriel Leon 1930- *WhoAm 92*
Plaatje, Sol T. 1876-1932 *DcLB 125 [port]*
Plaatjes, Mark *BioIn 17*

Plabe, Howard C. *Law&B 92*
Place, Charles Michael 1951- *St&PR 93*
Place, Dale Hubert 1937- *WhoSSW 93*
Place, David Elliott 1921- *WhoAm 92*
Place, Douglas W. 1946- *St&PR 93*
Place, Geoffrey 1931- *WhoAm 92*
Place, Jack 1925- *St&PR 93*
Place, Janet K. *Law&B 92*
Place, John Bassett, Jr. 1953- *WhoE 93*
Place, Mary Kay *WhoAm 92*
Place, Phillip W. 1946- *St&PR 93*
Place, Robin (Mary) 1926- *SmATA 71 [port]*
Place, Susan Mary 1962- *WhoAmW 93*
Placek, William M. 1948- *St&PR 93*
Placencia, Alfredo R. 1873-1930 *DcMexL*
Placiente, Siony Araneta 1944- *WhoAmW 93*
Placier, Philip R. 1933- *WhoAm 92*
Placke, James Anthony 1935- *WhoAm 92*
Placotaris, Nicholas 1939- *WhoUN 92*
Placzek, Adolf Kurt 1913- *WhoAm 92*
Pladek, Robert W. *Law&B 92*
Plaeger, Frederick Joseph, II *Law&B 92*
Plaeger, Frederick Joseph, II 1953- *St&PR 93, WhoAm 92, WhoEmL 93*
Plagemann, Bentz 1913-1991 *BioIn 17*
Plagenhoef, Vern d1992 *BioIn 17*
Plagenz, George Richard 1923- *WhoAm 92*
Plager, Bob 1943- *WhoAm 92*
Plager, S. Jay *CngDr 91*
Plager, S. Jay 1931- *WhoAm 92, WhoE 93*
Plagge, Irene R. 1936- *St&PR 93*
Plagnet, Bernard 1946- *WhoWor 93*
Plaidy, Louis 1810-1874 *Baker 92*
Plail, Edgar Anton 1935- *WhoWor 93*
Plain, Belva *BioIn 17*
Plain, Mary Louise 1966- *WhoAmW 93*
Plaine, Lloyd Leva 1947- *WhoAmW 93*
Plainfosse, Marie Christine 1930- *WhoScE 91-2*
Plaisted, Carole Anne 1939- *WhoAmW 93*
Plaisted, Robert Leroy 1929- *WhoAm 92*
Plaisted, Suzette Lynne 1963- *WhoAmW 93*
Plake, Glen *BioIn 17*
Plakidis, Peteris 1947- *Baker 92*
Plaksin, Irving L. 1932- *St&PR 93*
Plamann, Alfred A. 1942- *St&PR 93*
Plambeck, Herbert Henry 1908- *WhoAm 92*
Plamenac, Dragan 1895-1983 *Baker 92*
Plamenevsky, Boris 1939- *WhoWor 93*
Plamondon, Linda Gail 1943- *WhoAmW 93*
Plamondon, Luc *Law&B 92*
Plamondon, Robert *ScF&FL 92*
Planalp, Jay C. 1944- *St&PR 93*
Planat, Michel Roland 1951- *WhoWor 93*
Planchart, Alejandro Enrique 1935- *WhoAm 92*
Planche, James Robinson 1796-1880 *OxDcOp*
Plancher, Robert L. 1932- *St&PR 93*
Plancher, Robert Lawrence 1932- *WhoAm 92, WhoE 93*
Planchet, Dominique-Charles 1857-1946 *Baker 92*
Planck, Annika 1941- *ConAu 139*
Planck, John Maurice 1946- *St&PR 93*
Planck, Robert D. 1948- *St&PR 93*
Plancon, Pol 1851-1914 *OxDcOp*
Plancon, Pol (-Henri) 1851-1914 *Baker 92*
Plander, Ivan 1928- *WhoWor 93*
Plane, Donald Ray 1938- *WhoAm 92*
Planer, Lillian H. d1990 *BioIn 17*
Planes, Antoni 1953- *WhoWor 93*
Plangere, Jules L., Jr. 1920- *St&PR 93*
Plangere, Jules Leon, Jr. 1920- *WhoAm 92*
Planit, Jan Holly 1961- *WhoAmW 93*
Planitzer, Russell E. *WhoAm 92*
Planitzer, Russell E. 1944- *St&PR 93*
Plank, Arno A.O. 1933- *WhoScE 91-3*
Plank, Betsy Ann 1924- *WhoAm 92*
Plank, Eddie 1875-1926 *BioIn 17*
Plank, Helene Elizabeth 1957- *WhoAmW 93*
Plank, Joanna Leonard 1957- *WhoSSW 93*
Plank, Laura S. *Law&B 92*
Plank, Peggy Lynn 1954- *WhoAmW 93*
Plank, Raymond 1922- *St&PR 93, WhoAm 92*
Plank, Richard H. 1948- *St&PR 93*
Plank, Robert 1907-1983 *ScF&FL 92*
Plank, Roger B. 1956- *St&PR 93*
Plankis, Joseph V. 1943- *St&PR 93*
Plano, Jack Charles 1921- *ConAu 39NR*
Plano, Richard James 1929- *WhoAm 92*
Planoudes, Maximos c. 1255-c. 1305 *OxDcByz*
Planquette, Robert 1848-1903 *OxDcOp*
Planquette, (Jean-) Robert 1848-1903 *Baker 92*
Plansker, Dennis H. 1940- *St&PR 93*
Planson, Rollie Joe 1945- *WhoWor 93*
Plant, Albin MacDonough 1937- *WhoAm 92*
Plant, Arnold I. 1931- *St&PR 93*
Plant, Forrest Albert 1924- *WhoAm 92*
Plant, Gregory E. 1949- *St&PR 93*
Plant, Maretta Moore 1937- *WhoAmW 93, WhoE 93*
Plant, Mark William 1955- *WhoE 93*
Plant, Michele Susan 1959- *WhoAmW 93*
Plant, Robert *BioIn 17*
Plant, Robert Anthony 1948- *WhoAm 92*
Plant, Ruth d1988 *BioIn 17*
Plant, William Joseph Jesse 1926- *WhoE 93*
Plantade, Charles-Henri 1764-1839 *Baker 92*
Plante, D.F. 1946- *St&PR 93*
Plante, David *BioIn 17*
Plante, David 1940- *ConGAN*
Plante, Edmund *ScF&FL 92*
Plante, Francis 1839-1934 *Baker 92*
Plante, Joseph H. 1932- *St&PR 93*
Plante, Kathleen Goulder 1944- *WhoSSW 93*
Plante, Raymond 1947- *WhoCanL 92*
Plante, Richard La *ScF&FL 92*
Plante, Robert *BioIn 17*
Plante, Robert J. *Law&B 92*
Plante, William Madden 1938- *WhoAm 92, WhoE 93*
Planterose, Rowan Michael 1954- *WhoWor 93*
Plantikow, Frances Kay 1947- *WhoAmW 93*
Planting, Charles O. 1923- *WhoAm 92*
Plantinga, Alvin 1932- *WhoAm 92, WhoWrEP 92*
Plantinga, Leon (Brooks) 1935- *Baker 92*
Plantos, Ted 1943- *WhoCanL 92*
Plantz, Bernard F. *Law&B 92*
Plapp, Bryce Vernon 1939- *WhoAm 92*
Plaschke, Friedrich 1875-1951 *Baker 92*
Plaschke, Friedrich 1875-1952 *OxDcOp*
Plaschko, Peter 1941- *WhoWor 93*
Plasencia, Philip Edward 1944- *St&PR 93*
Plasha, Michael, Jr. 1933- *St&PR 93*
Plashchina, Irina Germanovna 1946- *WhoWor 93*
Plaskacz, Roman Todd *Law&B 92*
Plaske, Bedrich 1875-1951 *Baker 92*
Plaskett, Thomas G. 1943- *St&PR 93, WhoAm 92*
Plass, Ludwig 1864-1946 *Baker 92*
Plass, Margaret Feurer d1990 *BioIn 17*
Plass, Neil Walton 1935- *St&PR 93*
Plassard, Jean 1955- *WhoWor 93*
Plasschaert, Alphons J.M. 1942- *WhoScE 91-3*
Plasschaert, Alphons Johannes Marie 1942- *WhoWor 93*
Plasson, Michel 1933- *Baker 92*
Plaster, Robert W. 1930- *St&PR 93*
Plasynski, James Michael *Law&B 92*
Plat, Richard Vertin 1929- *St&PR 93, WhoAm 92*
Plata, Horacio Rodriguez 1915-1987 *BioIn 17*
Platania, Pietro 1828-1907 *Baker 92*
Platarote, Francis R. *St&PR 93*
Plata-Salaman, Carlos Ramon 1959- *WhoE 93, WhoWor 93*
Plate, Erich J. 1929- *WhoScE 91-3*
Plate, Janet Margaret Dieterle 1943- *WhoAmW 93*
Plate, Thomas Gordon 1944- *WhoAm 92*
Platen, August von 1796-1835 *BioIn 17*
Plater, Emilia 1806-1831 *PolBiDi*
Plater, William M. 1945- *ScF&FL 92*
Plater, William Marmaduke 1945- *WhoAm 92*
Plater-Zyberk, Elizabeth 1950- *BioIn 17*
Plater-Zyberk, Elizabeth Maria 1950- *WhoAmW 93*
Plath, James Walter 1950- *WhoWrEP 92*
Plath, Peter Daniel 1937- *St&PR 93*
Plath, Sylvia *BioIn 17*
Plath, Sylvia 1932-1963 *MagSAmL [port], WorLitC [port]*
Plath, Wolfgang 1930- *Baker 92*
Platiere, Jeanne Manon Roland de la 1754-1793 *BioIn 17*
Platis, Jim George 1927- *WhoWor 93*
Platis, Tom G. *Law&B 92*
Platkin, Lawrence *Law&B 92*
Platner, Brian *St&PR 93*
Platner, John L. 1932- *St&PR 93*
Platner, John Leland 1932- *WhoAm 92*
Platner, Warren 1919- *WhoAm 92*
Platnick, Kenneth B. 1943- *WhoE 93*
Platnick, Norman I. 1951- *WhoAm 92*
Plato *BioIn 17, OxDcByz*
Plato c. 428BC-347?BC *Baker 92*
Plato 427BC-347BC *MagSWL [port]*
Plato, Dana *BioIn 17*
Plato, Sharyll Adelle 1935- *WhoSSW 93*
Platonov, Sergei Sergeevich 1954- *WhoWor 93*
Plato of Sakkoudion c. 735-814 *OxDcByz*
Platos, Stanley d1991 *BioIn 17*
Platou, Joanne Dode 1919- *WhoAm 92*
Platou, Valborg 1839-1928 *BioIn 17*
Platowski, Andrew C. 1947- *St&PR 93*
Platsoucas, Chris Dimitrios 1951- *WhoSSW 93*
Platt, Agnes Electra *AmWomPl*
Platt, Alan Arthur 1944- *WhoE 93*
Platt, Albert Edward *WhoScE 91-1*
Platt, Charles 1945- *ScF&FL 92*
Platt, Charles Adams 1932- *WhoAm 92*
Platt, Charles F. *Law&B 92*
Platt, Craig T. 1952- *St&PR 93*
Platt, Czeslaw 1925- *WhoWor 93*
Platt, David d1992 *NewYTBS 92*
Platt, David 1912- *St&PR 93*
Platt, Dieter 1936- *WhoScE 91-3*
Platt, Douglas G. 1944- *St&PR 93*
Platt, Edmund 1865-1939 *BioIn 17*
Platt, Elsie Hawley *AmWomPl*
Platt, Eugene 1939- *WhoWrEP 92*
Platt, Frank Hinchman 1913-1990 *BioIn 17*
Platt, Franklin Dewitt 1932- *WhoAm 92*
Platt, George R. 1954- *St&PR 93*
Platt, Harold 1923- *St&PR 93*
Platt, Harold Kirby 1942- *WhoE 93*
Platt, Harrison G., Jr. d1992 *NewYTBS 92*
Platt, Helen B. *St&PR 93*
Platt, Jerome Joseph 1941- *WhoE 93, WhoWor 93*
Platt, Joel R. *Law&B 92*
Platt, John R. d1992 *NewYTBS 92*
Platt, John Rader 1918-1992 *ConAu 138*
Platt, Jonathan James 1950- *WhoE 93, WhoWor 93*
Platt, Joseph Beaven 1915- *WhoAm 92*
Platt, Kin 1911- *DcAmChF 1960, ScF&FL 92*
Platt, Lewis Emmett 1941- *WhoAm 92*
Platt, Lucian Brewster 1931- *WhoAm 92*
Platt, Marc 1914- *ScF&FL 92*
Platt, Marcia Ellin 1947- *WhoAmW 93*
Platt, Mark E. *WhoAm 92*
Platt, Michael Elliott 1942- *St&PR 93*
Platt, Nicholas 1936- *WhoAm 92, WhoWor 93*
Platt, Nicolas W. 1953- *St&PR 93*
Platt, Peter Godfrey 1937- *WhoAm 92*
Platt, Randall Beth 1948- *ScF&FL 92*
Platt, Reginald, III 1928- *WhoSSW 93*
Platt, Richard Gordon 1930- *St&PR 93*
Platt, Robert Holmes 1920- *WhoAm 92*
Platt, Roger H. 1944- *WhoScE 91-1*
Platt, Ronald Eugene 1933- *WhoSSW 93*
Platt, Sherman Phelps, Jr. 1918- *WhoAm 92*
Platt, Thomas C. 1833-1910 *PolPar*
Platt, Thomas Collier 1925- *WhoAm 92, WhoE 93*
Platt, Trevor Charles 1942- *WhoAm 92*
Platt, William Rady 1915- *WhoAm 92*
Platte, James R. 1945- *St&PR 93*
Platten, Donald C. 1918-1991 *BioIn 17*
Platten, Peter M., III 1939- *St&PR 93*
Platten, Peter Michael, III 1939- *WhoAm 92*
Plattenteich, A.W. *WhoScE 91-3*
Platters *SoulM*
Platthy, Jeno 1920- *WhoAm 92, WhoWor 93*
Platti, Giovanni Benedetto 1697-1763 *Baker 92*
Platti, Rita Jane 1925- *WhoAmW 93, WhoWor 93*
Plattig, Karl-Heinz 1931- *WhoScE 91-3*
Plattner, Helmut 1939- *WhoScE 91-3*
Platto, Charles 1945- *WhoAm 92*
Platts-Mills, Thomas Alexander E. 1941- *WhoAm 92*
Platz, Theodore A., Jr. 1927- *St&PR 93*
Platzer, Ann R. *Law&B 92*
Platzer, Michael Karl Heinrich 1946- *WhoUN 92*
Platzer, Werner Oskar Franz 1929- *WhoScE 91-4*
Platzman, George William 1920- *WhoAm 92*
Plaue, Rudolf *Law&B 92*
Plaut, Eric Alfred 1927- *WhoAm 92*
Plaut, Gerhard Wolfgang Eugen 1921- *WhoAm 92*
Plaut, James Sachs 1912- *WhoAm 92*
Plaut, Martin Edward 1937- *WhoWrEP 92*
Plaut, Michael Felix *Law&B 92*
Plaut, Nathan Michael 1917- *WhoAm 92*
Plaut, Peter K. *Law&B 92*
Plaut, Roger David 1966- *WhoAm 92*
Plaut, Thomas Franz Alfred 1925- *WhoE 93*
Plaut, Wofl Gunther 1912- *WhoAm 92*
Plavoukos, Spencer 1936- *WhoAm 92, WhoE 93*
Plawecki, Judith Ann 1943- *WhoAmW 93*
Play *BioIn 17*
Play, M. *WhoScE 91-2*
Playe, George Louis 1917- *WhoAm 92*
Player, Gary E. *St&PR 93*
Player, Gary Jim 1935- *WhoAm 92, WhoWor 93*
Player, Mary Anne 1920- *WhoAmW 93*
Player, Mary Francine 1953- *WhoWrEP 92*
Player, Michael Antony *WhoScE 91-1*
Player, Thelma B. *WhoE 93, WhoWor 93*
Playfair, William Henry 1789-1857 *BioIn 17*
Playford, Henry 1657-c. 1707 *Baker 92*
Playford, John 1623-1686 *Baker 92*
Playnick, Judith Ann 1959- *WhoAmW 93*
Plaza (-Alfonzo), Juan Bautista 1898-1964 *Baker 92*
Plaza, Charito B. 1957- *WhoAsAP 91*
Plaza, Democrito O. 1921- *WhoAsAP 91*
Plaza, Fernando 1942- *WhoUN 92*
Plaza, Hector Hugo 1950- *WhoWor 93*
Plazak, Richard A. 1937- *WhoIns 93*
Plazek, Donald John 1931- *WhoE 93*
Plazyk, Judy Lynn 1960- *WhoWrEP 92*
Pleasant, Lillian *AmWomPl*
Pleasant, Richard 1909-1961 *BioIn 17*
Pleasant, Richard J. 1944- *St&PR 93*
Pleasant, Robert Dale 1946- *St&PR 93, WhoWor 93*
Pleas'ant, Tammy Jean 1962- *WhoE 93*
Pleasant, Ursula Gladys 1943- *WhoE 93*
Pleasanton, Alfred 1824-1897 *HarEnMi*
Pleasants, Elsie Walter 1915- *WhoAmW 93*
Pleasants, Henry 1910- *Baker 92, WhoAm 92*
Pleasants, Julian McIver 1938- *WhoSSW 93*
Pleasence, Donald 1919- *BioIn 17, IntDcF 2-3 [port], WhoAm 92, WhoWor 93*
Pleasure, King 1922-1981 *BioIn 17*
Pleasure, Robert Jonathan 1942- *WhoWor 93*
Pleat, Kenneth L. 1947- *St&PR 93*
Plebani, G.J. 1946- *St&PR 93*
Plebani, Thomas Joseph 1951- *WhoE 93*
Ple-Caussade, Simone 1897-1985 *Baker 92*
Plechko, Vladimir Yakovlevich 1934- *WhoWor 93*
Pledger, Carolyn Brastow Hughes 1932- *WhoSSW 93*
Pledger, Jim *BioIn 17*
Pledger, Reginald Harrison, Jr. 1934- *WhoAm 92*
Pledger, Thomas R. 1938- *St&PR 93*
Pledger, Thomas Rolon 1938- *WhoAm 92*
Pledger, Timothy Carter *Law&B 92*
Plehn-Mejia, Marcial 1941- *WhoUN 92*
Plehve, Vyacheslav Konstantinovich 1846-1904 *BioIn 17*
Plejdrup, Allyn Dean 1935- *St&PR 93*
Plekhanov, Georgi Valentinovich 1857-1918 *DcTwHis*
Plemmons, Gerald Thomas 1940- *St&PR 93*
Plens, Ole Emil 1948- *WhoWor 93*
Plenty, Royal Homer 1918- *WhoAm 92*
Plenty Coups, Chief of the Crows 1848-1932 *BioIn 17*
Plepler, Richard L. 1958- *WhoE 93*
Plersch, Jan Bogumil 1732-1817 *PolBiDi*
Pleshakov, Vladimir 1934- *Baker 92*
Pleshette, Norman 1902-1990 *BioIn 17*
Pleshette, Suzanne *WhoAm 92, WhoAmW 93*
Pleshette, Suzanne 1937- *BioIn 17*
Pleskow, Eric Roy *WhoAm 92, WhoE 93*
Pleskow, Raoul 1931- *Baker 92*
Plesniak, Wieslaw 1944- *WhoWor 93*
Plesnik, Jan 1925- *WhoScE 91-4*
Pleso, Joseph Frank 1936- *St&PR 93*
Pless, John Edward 1938- *WhoAm 92*
Pless, Robert Stephen 1939- *St&PR 93*
Pless, Vera 1931- *WhoAmW 93*
Plessas, Willibald 1949- *WhoWor 93*
Plessis, Hubert du 1922- *Baker 92*
Plessis-Belair, Michel 1942- *St&PR 93*
Plestina, Radovan 1934- *WhoUN 92*
Pleszko, E.J. 1930- *St&PR 93*
Pletcher, David Mitchell 1920- *WhoAm 92*
Pletcher, Eldon 1922- *WhoAm 92*
Pletcher, James Roger 1954- *WhoSSW 93*
Pletcher, John Harold, Jr. 1945- *WhoSSW 93*
Plethon, George Gemistos c. 1360-1452 *OxDcByz*
Pletsch, Carl (Erich) 1943- *ConAu 137*
Plettscher, Alfred 1917- *WhoScE 91-4*
Plett, Frederick Randall 1946- *St&PR 93*
Pletz, Arthur C. 1943- *WhoIns 93*
Pletz, Karen L. 1947- *WhoAmW 93*
Pletzer, K. Randall 1945- *St&PR 93*
Pletzke, Kathi Jean 1962- *WhoAmW 93*
Pleva, Jaroslav 1941- *WhoScE 91-4*
Pleve, Viacheslav Konstantinovich 1846-1904 *BioIn 17*
Pleven, Rene 1901- *BioIn 17*
Plevy, Arthur L. 1936- *WhoE 93*
Plew, Larry Eugene 1947- *WhoSSW 93*

Plewacki, Richard A. *Law&B 92*
Plewes, Donald E. 1942- *St&PR 93*
Plewes, Stanley Frank *Law&B 92*
Plexico, Walter Moore, Jr. 1945- *WhoSSW 93*
Plexman, Eric 1953- *St&PR 93*
Pleyel, (Joseph Stephen) Camille 1788-1855 *Baker 92*
Pleyel, Ignace Joseph 1757-1831 *Baker 92*
Pleyer, Klemens 1921- *WhoWor 93*
Plianbangchang, Samlee 1940- *WhoUN 92, WhoWor 93*
Plich, Henryk 1942- *WhoScE 91-4*
Plichta, Thomas Francis 1952- *WhoSSW 93*
Plietz, Clinton Charles 1955- *St&PR 93*
Plimer, Ian Rutherford 1946- *WhoWor 93*
Plimpton, Calvin Hastings 1918- *WhoAm 92*
Plimpton, George *BioIn 17*
Plimpton, George Ames 1927- *WhoAm 92, WhoE 93, WhoWrEP 92*
Plimpton, John Hamilton 1931- *WhoWor 93*
Plimpton, Martha *BioIn 17*
Plimpton, Pauline Ames 1901- *WhoAmW 93, WhoE 93, WhoWor 93*
Plimpton, Peggy Lucas 1931- *WhoAmW 93, WhoE 93, WhoWor 93*
Plimpton, Susan Blaine 1943- *St&PR 93*
Plimsoll, Samuel 1824-1898 *BioIn 17*
Plinski, Marcin 1943- *WhoScE 91-4*
Plischke, Elmer 1914- *ConAu 40NR, WhoAm 92*
Plischke, Le Moyne Wilfred 1922- *WhoWor 93*
Plishka, Paul *BioIn 17*
Plishka, Paul 1941- *OxDcOp*
Plishka, Paul (Peter) 1941- *Baker 92*
Pliskin, William Aaron 1920- *WhoAm 92*
Pliskoff, Stanley Stewart 1930- *WhoAm 92*
Plissonnier, Gaston 1913- *BioIn 17*
Plitch, Lawrence William *Law&B 92*
Plitt, Henry G. 1918- *WhoAm 92*
Plitt, Jane Ruth 1948- *WhoE 93*
Plitt, Jeanne Given 1927- *WhoAm 92, WhoAmW 93*
Plitt, Robert A. 1936- *St&PR 93*
Plochocki, Andrew Plato 1936- *WhoAm 92*
Plociak, Richard A. 1943- *St&PR 93*
Plocq, V. *WhoScE 91-2*
Ploeger, Katherine Marie 1955- *WhoWrEP 92*
Ploeser, Walter Christian 1907- *WhoAm 92*
Ploessel, Velma Dunn 1918- *WhoAmW 93*
Plog, Stanley Clement 1930- *St&PR 93*
Ploger, Robert Riis 1915- *WhoAm 92*
Ploke, Thomas P. 1962- *St&PR 93*
Plomer, William 1903-1973 *BioIn 17*
Plomgren, Ronald Arthur 1934- *St&PR 93, WhoAm 92*
Plommet, Michel 1927- *WhoScE 91-2*
Plommet, Michel Georges 1927- *WhoWor 93*
Plomp, Reinier 1929- *WhoScE 91-3*
Plomp, Teunis 1938- *WhoAm 92*
Plomp, Tjeerd 1938- *WhoWor 93*
Plonait, Hans *WhoScE 91-3*
Plone, Bernard Jay 1915- *WhoSSW 93*
Plonien, Cynthia G. 1953- *WhoWrEP 92*
Plonsey, Robert 1924- *WhoAm 92*
Plonski, Guilherme Ary 1948- *WhoWor 93*
Plopper, Charles George 1944- *WhoAm 92*
Ploss, Hanna Kaya Mirecka 1928- *WhoE 93*
Plosser, Charles Irving 1948- *WhoAm 92, WhoE 93, WhoWor 93*
Plossu, Bernard Pierre 1945- *WhoAm 92*
Ploszynski, Michal Antoni 1931- *WhoScE 91-4*
Plotch, Walter 1932- *WhoE 93*
Plotecher, Gary Robert *Law&B 92*
Plotinos 205-270 *OxDcByz*
Plotkin, Cary Howard 1950- *WhoE 93*
Plotkin, Harry Morris 1913- *WhoAm 92*
Plotkin, Irving H. 1941- *St&PR 93*
Plotkin, Manuel D. *WhoAm 92*
Plotkin, Martin 1922- *WhoAm 92*
Plotkin, Martin 1945- *WhoE 93*
Plotkin, Steven Michael *Law&B 92*
Plotnick, Gary David 1941- *WhoE 93*
Plotnick, Harvey Barry 1941- *WhoAm 92*
Plotnick, S. Maurice d1991 *BioIn 17, NewYTBS 92*
Plotnik, Arthur 1937- *JrnUS, WhoAm 92, WhoWrEP 92*
Plotnikov, Eugene 1877-1951 *Baker 92*
Plotnikova, Galina V. 1934- *WhoScE 91-2*
Plott, Brent *BioIn 17*
Plott, Charles R. 1938- *WhoAm 92*
Plott, Monte Glenn 1952- *WhoSSW 93*
Plotz, Charles Mindell 1921- *WhoAm 92, WhoE 93*
Plotz, John B. 1921- *St&PR 93*
Plotz, Paul Hunter 1937- *WhoE 93*
Plough, Charles Tobias, Jr. 1926- *WhoWor 93*
Plough, Francis Azzo 1923- *St&PR 93*
Plourde, Gerard 1916- *St&PR 93, WhoAm 92*
Plourde, Joseph Donald 1936- *WhoAm 92*
Plourde, Marc 1951- *WhoCanL 92*
Plourde, William A., Jr. *Law&B 92*
Plowcha, Charlene Snyder 1946- *WhoE 93*
Plowden, Tony Wendell 1959- *WhoSSW 93*
Plowgian, Alan Grix 1949- *WhoWor 93*
Plowman, Jack Wesley 1929- *WhoAm 92*
Plowman, R. Dean 1928- *WhoAm 92*
Plowman, Robert Jacob 1939- *WhoE 93*
Plowright, Joan Anne 1929- *WhoAm 92, WhoWor 93*
Plowright, Rosalind 1949- *Baker 92, OxDcOp*
Plowright, Teresa 1952- *ScF&FL 92*
Plows, G. *WhoScE 91-1*
Plows, Robert C. *Law&B 92*
Pluard, Gerald C., Jr. *Law&B 92*
Plubell, Ann Marie *Law&B 92*
Plubell, Ann Marie 1950- *St&PR 93*
Plubell, Susan Charlotte 1949- *WhoAmW 93*
Pluciennik, John T. *St&PR 93*
Pluckhan, F.J. 1933- *St&PR 93*
Pluddemann, Martin 1854-1897 *Baker 92*
Plueckhahn, Diana Lynn 1941- *WhoAmW 93*
Plueckhahn, Penny 1941- *St&PR 93*
Pluemer, Lutz Gunther 1951- *WhoWor 93*
Pluhar, Darwin Mark 1959- *WhoSSW 93*
Pluimer, Peggy Lee 1948- *WhoAmW 93*
Plukas, John Michael 1944- *St&PR 93*
Plum, Charles W. *BioIn 17*
Plum, Charles Walden 1914- *WhoAm 92*
Plum, Claude D., Jr. *ScF&FL 92*
Plum, Diane Woodman 1945- *WhoAmW 93*
Plum, Fred 1924- *BioIn 17, WhoAm 92*
Plum, Larry *St&PR 93*
Plum, Leo Augustus, Jr. *Law&B 92*
Plum, Michael 1954- *WhoWor 93*
Plum, Nancy Terhune 1953- *WhoWrEP 92*
Plum, Richard Eugene 1928- *WhoWor 93*
Plum, Stephen Haines, IV *Law&B 92*
Plumb, Benjamin Neely, Jr. 1943- *WhoSSW 93*
Plumb, Donna A. *Law&B 92*
Plumb, Eve 1958- *BioIn 17*
Plumb, John Harold 1911- *WhoWor 93*
Plumb, Max L. 1921- *St&PR 93*
Plumb, Pamela 1943- *St&PR 93*
Plumb, Pamela Pelton 1943- *WhoAm 92*
Plumb, Robert Charles 1926- *WhoAm 92*
Plumb, Robert Eugene, Jr. *Law&B 92*
Plumb, Roger Thomas 1944- *WhoScE 91-1*
Plumb, Todd K. 1952- *St&PR 93*
Plumber, Betty Joyce 1944- *WhoSSW 93*
Plumber, Harrison Patrick, Jr. 1939- *WhoSSW 93*
Plumbridge, Robin Allan 1935- *St&PR 93*
Plume, Nona Dextrose *WhoWrEP 92*
Plumer, Edward D. 1944- *St&PR 93*
Plumer, Elizabeth Ann 1940- *WhoAmW 93*
Plumer, Herbert Charles Onslow 1857-1932 *BioIn 17, HarEnMi*
Plumer, PattiSue *BioIn 17*
Plumez, Jean Paul 1939- *WhoAm 92*
Plumlee, Amanda Ruth 1956- *WhoSSW 93*
Plumlee, Kenneth B. *St&PR 93*
Plumley, Della Ruby 1926- *WhoAmW 93*
Plumley, Frank Edwin 1949- *St&PR 93*
Plumley, Michael Alan 1950- *St&PR 93*
Plumley, S. Patric 1949- *WhoAm 92*
Plumly, Anna C. 1925- *St&PR 93*
Plumme, Don E. *ConAu 37NR*
Plummer, Amanda 1957- *WhoAm 92*
Plummer, Benjamin Frank 1936- *WhoSSW 93*
Plummer, Bill 1947- *WhoAm 92*
Plummer, Carol Ann 1944- *WhoSSW 93*
Plummer, Christopher Orme 1929- *WhoAm 92, WhoWor 93*
Plummer, Cindy Marie 1957- *WhoAmW 93*
Plummer, Daniel C. 1927- *WhoIns 93*
Plummer, Daniel Clarence, III 1927- *WhoAm 92*
Plummer, Donald R. 1946- *St&PR 93*
Plummer, E. Bruce 1938- *WhoE 93*
Plummer, Edward G. 1949- *St&PR 93*
Plummer, Henry 1832-1864 *BioIn 17*
Plummer, J. Paul *Law&B 92*
Plummer, Jeffrey Robert 1966- *WhoSSW 93*
Plummer, Jerry L. 1941- *St&PR 93*
Plummer, Joseph Thornton 1941- *WhoAm 92*
Plummer, Kenneth Alexander 1928- *WhoWor 93*
Plummer, Lawrence L. 1933- *St&PR 93*
Plummer, Marcie Stern 1950- *WhoAm 92*
Plummer, Mary Wright 1856-1916 *BioIn 17*
Plummer, Michael Kenneth 1954- *WhoWor 93*
Plummer, Patricia Lynne Moore *WhoAmW 93*
Plummer, Richard B. 1945- *St&PR 93*
Plummer, Risque Wilson 1910- *WhoAm 92*
Plummer, Robert Lee 1927- *St&PR 93*
Plummer, Stephen Ray 1952- *WhoSSW 93*
Plummer, Thomas 1958- *St&PR 93*
Plummer, Vaughn Ray 1954- *WhoSSW 93*
Plummer, Walter A. 1916- *St&PR 93*
Plummer, William Francis 1947- *WhoAm 92*
Plummer, William Hamilton, III 1944- *WhoSSW 93*
Plumpton, John Martin 1946- *St&PR 93*
Plumstead, William Charles 1938- *WhoSSW 93*
Plum-Woehning, Huberta Marianne *AmWomPl*
Plunier, Guy Albert 1930- *WhoWor 93*
Plunk, Robert M. 1932- *WhoIns 93*
Plunk, Robert Malcolm 1932- *St&PR 93*
Plunk, Stephen D. 1950- *St&PR 93*
Plunket, Daniel Clark 1929- *WhoAm 92*
Plunket, Paul W., III *Law&B 92*
Plunkett, Andrew *Law&B 92*
Plunkett, Belinda Carol 1960- *WhoAmW 93*
Plunkett, D. Brian 1956- *St&PR 93*
Plunkett, Dianne *Law&B 92*
Plunkett, Donna Davis 1963- *WhoAmW 93*
Plunkett, Edward *ScF&FL 92*
Plunkett, Horace Curzon 1854-1932 *BioIn 17*
Plunkett, Jack William 1950- *WhoEmL 93, WhoSSW 93*
Plunkett, James 1947- *HispAmA [port]*
Plunkett, James William, Jr. 1947- *WhoAm 92*
Plunkett, John L. 1947- *St&PR 93*
Plunkett, Joseph Charles 1933- *WhoWor 93*
Plunkett, Larry Neil 1945- *St&PR 93*
Plunkett, Maryann 1953- *WhoAmW 93*
Plunkett, Melba Kathleen 1929- *WhoAmW 93, WhoWor 93*
Plunkett, Michael G. 1959- *St&PR 93*
Plunkett, Michael Stewart 1937- *St&PR 93, WhoAm 92*
Plunkett, Nancy Geraldine 1925- *WhoWrEP 92*
Plunkett, Oliver 1625-1681 *BioIn 17*
Plunkett, Paul Edward 1935- *WhoAm 92*
Plunkett, Robert 1919- *WhoAm 92*
Plunkett, Robert L. 1951- *ScF&FL 92*
Plunkett, Robert Wilson, Jr. 1950- *St&PR 93*
Plunkett, Ruth Anne 1917- *WhoWrEP 92*
Plunkett, Sherman *BioIn 17*
Plunkett, Stephen J. 1948- *St&PR 93*
Plunkett, Susan *ScF&FL 92*
Plunkett, Thomas P. 1950- *St&PR 93*
Plunkett, Thomas S. *St&PR 93*
Plunkett, Warren Francis 1920- *WhoIns 93*
Plunkitt, George Washington 1842-1924 *PolPar*
Plush, Vincent 1950- *Baker 92*
Plusk, Ronald Frank 1933- *St&PR 93, WhoAm 92*
Plusnick, Robert R. *St&PR 93*
Plusquellec, Jacques 1929- *WhoScE 91-2*
Pluta, Maria Elfride 1948- *WhoAmW 93*
Plutarch c. 46-c. 120 *MagSWL [port], OxDcByz*
Plutarch c. 46-c. 119 *Baker 92*
Plutzer, Martin David 1944- *WhoE 93*
Plutzik, Jonathan 1954- *St&PR 93*
Pluvinage, Guy 1942- *WhoScE 91-2*
Pluymen, Bert W. 1948- *WhoEmL 93*
Plybon, Jerry *St&PR 93*
Plyler, Edward C. 1949- *St&PR 93*
Plym, Lawrence J. 1906- *St&PR 93*
Plym, Lawrence John 1906- *WhoAm 92*
Plymale, Mary Jo 1920- *WhoAmW 93*
Plymat, William N. 1911- *WhoIns 93*
Plymen, Roger John 1943- *WhoWor 93*
Pniakowski, Andrew Frank 1930- *WhoE 93, WhoWor 93*
Pniewski, Bohdan 1897-1965 *PolBiDi*
Poad, William James 1930- *St&PR 93*
Poarch, James William 1938- *WhoSSW 93*
Pobedria, Borys Efim 1937- *WhoWor 93*
Pobell, Frank D.M. 1937- *WhoScE 91-3, WhoWor 93*
Pober, Zalmon 1939- *WhoE 93*
Pobiner, Joseph Andrew 1955- *WhoSSW 93*
Poblete, Rita Maria Bautista 1954- *WhoAmW 93, WhoEmL 93, WhoSSW 93, WhoWor 93*
Poblocki, John F. 1947- *St&PR 93*
Pobo, Kenneth George 1954- *WhoWrEP 92*
Pocahontas d1617 *BioIn 17*
Pocanic, Dinko 1955- *WhoSSW 93*
Pocar, Donato 1937- *WhoScE 91-3*
Pocaterra, Jose Rafael 1888-1955 *SpAmA*
Pocchiari, Francesco 1924- *WhoScE 91-3*
Pocci, Franz, Graf von 1807-1876 *Baker 92*
Poccia, Dominic Louis 1945- *WhoE 93*
Poch, Gerald 1932- *WhoScE 91-4*
Poch, Herbert Edward 1927- *WhoE 93*
Pocheptsov, Georgi Georgiyevich 1926- *WhoWor 93*
Pocher, Frank J. 1941- *St&PR 93*
Pochi, Peter Ernest 1929- *WhoAm 92*
Pochick, Francis Edward 1931- *WhoE 93*
Po-Chih, Leong *MiSFD 9*
Pochily, Barbara Ann 1959- *WhoAmW 93*
Pochoda, Elizabeth Turner 1941- *WhoWrEP 92*
Pochoda, Philip M. 1940- *WhoWrEP 92*
Pochon, Alfred 1878-1959 *Baker 92*
Pochyly, Donald Frederick 1934- *WhoAm 92*
Pociask, Stephen Bernard 1956- *WhoSSW 93*
Pocidalo, Jean-Jacques *WhoScE 91-2*
Pocino, Mark C. 1944- *St&PR 93*
Pocius, Gerald L(ewis) 1950- *ConAu 137*
Pockat, Alison Ann 1958- *WhoSSW 93*
Pockell, Leslie M. 1942- *WhoAm 92*
Pocker, Richard James 1954- *WhoAm 92*
Pocker, Yeshayau 1928- *WhoAm 92*
Pocklington, Peter H. 1941- *WhoAm 92*
Pocknett, Lawrence W. 1934- *WhoIns 93*
Pockney, Bertram P. *WhoScE 91-1*
Pockriss, Lee Julien 1927- *WhoE 93*
Pocock, Brian Lovel Reginald 1936- *WhoWor 93*
Pocock, F.J. *WhoScE 91-1*
Pocock, Frederick James 1923- *WhoAm 92*
Pocock, Jack E. 1925- *St&PR 93*
Pocock, John William 1916- *St&PR 93*
Pocock, Louise M. 1928- *WhoAmW 93, WhoSSW 93*
Pocs, Tamas 1933- *WhoScE 91-4*
Pocsai, Emil 1943- *WhoScE 91-4*
Podair, Arnold David 1948- *WhoSSW 93*
Podany, Amy Elizabeth 1961- *WhoAmW 93*
Podany, Clayton James 1943- *St&PR 93*
Podany, Gerald S. 1944- *St&PR 93*
Podar, Vinod R. 1963- *St&PR 93*
Podaras, Straton C. 1932- *St&PR 93*
Podboy, John Watts 1943- *WhoWor 93*
Poddar, R.K. 1930- *WhoAsAP 91*
Poddar, Vishwanath 1932- *WhoWor 93*
Podell, Howard Irwin 1917- *WhoE 93, WhoWor 93*
Podell, Richard Jay 1943- *WhoAm 92*
Podest, Ludvik 1921-1968 *Baker 92*
Podesta, Aldo Clement d1992 *NewYTBS 92*
Podesta, Aldo Clement 1919-1992 *BioIn 17*
Podesta, Robert Angelo 1912- *St&PR 93, WhoAm 92*
Podesva, Jaromir 1927- *Baker 92*
Podet, Allen Howard 1934- *WhoE 93*
Podewils, Robert C. *St&PR 93*
Podgorny, George 1934- *WhoAm 92, WhoWor 93*
Podgorny, Nikolay Viktorovich 1903-1983 *DcTwHis*
Podgorny, Richard Joseph 1944- *WhoAm 92*
Podgorski, Robert Paul 1943- *WhoWor 93*
Podgurski, Charles Vincent 1941- *WhoSSW 93*
Podgurski, Myron *BioIn 17*
Podhoretz, Harriette 1932- *WhoE 93*
Podhoretz, Norman *BioIn 17*
Podhoretz, Norman 1930- *ColdWar 1 [port], JeAmHC, WhoAm 92, WhoE 93, WhoWrEP 92*
Podimatas, Yiannis 1956- *WhoWor 93*
Podjarny, Alberto Daniel 1950- *WhoWor 93*
Podkowinski, Wladyslaw 1866-1895 *PolBiDi*
Podkowka, Witold 1929- *WhoScE 91-4*
Podlech, Dietrich 1931- *WhoScE 91-3*
Podles, Eleanor Pauline 1920- *WhoAmW 93*
Podlesak, Robert G. 1938- *St&PR 93*
Podlesakova, Eliska 1937- *WhoScE 91-4*
Podlesney, Francis A. *Law&B 92*
Podlesney, Francis A. 1932- *St&PR 93*
Podlich, William F. 1944- *WhoIns 93*
Podlich, William Frederick 1944- *St&PR 93*
Podmokly, Patricia Gayle 1940- *WhoAmW 93*

Podobinski, James R. *Law&B 92*
Podol, Beth Deniz 1963- *WhoAmW 93*
Podolak, Marian Andrzej 1939- *WhoWor 93*
Podolec, Richard 1948- *St&PR 93*
Podoloff, Donald Alan 1938- *WhoSSW 93*
Podolske, Diane Lynne 1966- *WhoAmW 93*
Podolsky, Milton 1921- *WhoAm 92*
Podolsky, Steven H. 1946- *WhoAm 92*
Podos, Steven Maurice 1937- *WhoAm 92*
Podosek, Frank Anthony 1941- *WhoAm 92*
Podratz, Wayne Owen 1940- *St&PR 93*
Podrazil, Patricia J. 1951- *St&PR 93*
Podskalsky, Zdenek 1923- *DrEEuF*
Podstawski, Robert Michael 1946- *WhoE 93*
Podufal, Joseph A. 1952- *St&PR 93*
Podufalov, Nikolai Dmitrievich 1949- *WhoWor 93*
Podurgiel, George *Law&B 92*
Poduska, Howard John 1920- *St&PR 93*
Poduska, John William, Sr. 1937- *ConEn*
Poduska, John William, Jr. 1937- *WhoAm 92*
Podwoski, Thomas Alan 1935- *St&PR 93*
Poe, Amos *MiSFD 9*
Poe, Charles Eugene 1928- *St&PR 93*
Poe, Crawford 1932- *St&PR 93*
Poe, David Russell 1948- *WhoAm 92*
Poe, Douglas Allan 1942- *WhoAm 92*
Poe, Edgar Allan 1809-1849 *BioIn 17, MagSAmL [port], ScF&FL 92, WorLitC [port]*
Poe, George Wilkinson 1952- *WhoSSW 93*
Poe, Howard Ritter 1934- *St&PR 93*
Poe, Jerry B. 1931- *WhoAm 92*
Poe, Katrine Laura 1958- *WhoWrEP 92*
Poe, Luke Harvey, Jr. 1916- *WhoAm 92*
Poe, Margaret W. 1897-1990 *BioIn 17*
Poe, Martin 1942- *WhoE 93*
Poe, Melissa Ellen *WhoSSW 93*
Poe, Nelson Crawford 1932- *St&PR 93*
Poe, Particia I. *Law&B 92*
Poe, Peggy *AmWomPl*
Poe, Reigh Kessen 1949- *WhoSSW 93*
Poe, Richard W. 1928- *St&PR 93*
Poe, Rose Lorene 1926- *WhoWrEP 92*
Poe, Sandra *Law&B 92*
Poe, Sheri 1952- *ConEn, St&PR 93*
Poe, Vera Ellen 1957- *WhoAmW 93*
Poe, William Edward, Jr. *Law&B 92*
Poe, William Frederick 1931- *WhoAm 92, WhoSSW 93*
Poehler, Theodore Otto 1935- *WhoE 93*
Poehling, Gerhard G. 1914- *St&PR 93*
Poehling, James M. 1948- *St&PR 93*
Poehling, Robert Edward 1944- *St&PR 93*
Poehlmann, Gerhard Manfred 1924- *WhoWor 93*
Poehlmann, John Joseph *Law&B 92*
Poehner, Raymond Glenn 1923- *WhoWor 93*
Poel, Robert Walter 1934- *WhoAm 92*
Poelaert, Jean 1942- *WhoScE 91-2*
Poellot, Raymond Albert 1955- *WhoWrEP 92*
Poelstra, G.J. *WhoScE 91-3*
Poeppel, Ernst 1940- *WhoWor 93*
Poer, Jerry Robert, Jr. 1953- *WhoSSW 93*
Poerio, Joseph Ross 1944- *WhoE 93*
Poersch, Enno d1990 *BioIn 17*
Poersch, Werner *WhoScE 91-3*
Poesch, Jessie Jean 1922- *WhoAm 92*
Poesnecker, Connie Jo 1959- *WhoAmW 93*
Poesse, Gerhard Johan 1928- *WhoScE 91-3*
Poessel, Sharon Ann 1964- *WhoAmW 93*
Poetis, Phytos Panteli 1937- *WhoWor 93*
Poet of Titchfield Street, The *ConAu 40NR*
Poett, Henry 1938- *St&PR 93*
Poettcker, Henry 1925- *WhoAm 92*
Poettmann, Fred Heinz 1919- *WhoAm 92*
Poff, Gregory V. 1948- *St&PR 93*
Poff, John Wayne, Sr. 1937- *St&PR 93*
Poff, N. Thomas 1937- *St&PR 93*
Poff, Richard Harding 1923- *WhoAm 92*
Poff, Robert L. 1952- *St&PR 93*
Poffenberger, Edith *AmWomPl*
Pofsky, Norma Louise 1945- *WhoE 93*
Pogach, Allan C. 1944- *St&PR 93*
Pogachnik, Robert Charles 1946- *WhoSSW 93*
Pogacic, Vladimir 1919- *DrEEuF*
Pogan, Eugenia 1919- *WhoScE 91-4*
Poganski, Daniel 1960- *St&PR 93*
Pogge, Jack *Law&B 92*
Poggensee, Mathilde d1991 *BioIn 17*
Poggi, Anne Walsh d1991 *BioIn 17*
Poggi, Antonio 1806-1875 *See* Frezzolini, Erminia 1818-1884 *OxDcOp*
Poggi, Gabriella 1939- *WhoScE 91-3*
Poggi, Gianfranco 1934- *WhoAm 92*
Poggi, Jean Charles *WhoScE 91-2*
Poggi, Jose Arturo 1949- *WhoWor 93*
Poggie, Robert *St&PR 93*
Poggio, Eugene C. 1945- *St&PR 93*
Poggio, Gian Franco 1927- *WhoAm 92*
Poggio, Joseph C. 1943- *St&PR 93*
Poggioli, Rosanna 1943- *WhoScE 91-3*
Poglia, Edo *WhoScE 91-4*
Poglietti, Alessandro d1683 *Baker 92*
Pogmore, James William 1936- *St&PR 93*
Pognonec, Yves Maurice 1948- *WhoSSW 93, WhoWor 93*
Pogo, Beatriz Teresa Garcia-Tunon 1932- *WhoAm 92*
Pogo, Gustave Javier 1957- *WhoE 93*
Pogoloff, Donald D. *Law&B 92*
Pogorelich, Ivo 1958- *Baker 92*
Pogoriler, Harvey W. *Law&B 92*
Pogorzelski, Witold Adam 1927- *WhoWor 93*
Pogostin, S. Lee *MiSFD 9*
Pogrebin, Letty Cottin *BioIn 17*
Pogrebin, Letty Cottin 1939- *WhoAm 92, WhoWrEP 92*
Pogson, Christopher Ian 1942- *WhoScE 91-1*
Pogue, Bill *ConAu 137*
Pogue, D. Eric 1949- *St&PR 93*
Pogue, Forrest Carlisle 1912- *WhoAm 92, WhoSSW 93, WhoWrEP 92*
Pogue, George Alexander *WhoScE 91-1*
Pogue, Jack D. 1933- *St&PR 93*
Pogue, L. Welch 1899- *EncABHB 8 [port]*
Pogue, Lloyd Welch 1899- *WhoAm 92*
Pogue, Mary Ellen E. 1904- *WhoWor 93*
Pogue, Richard Welch 1928- *WhoAm 92, WhoWor 93*
Pogue, Robert David 1929- *WhoWor 93*
Pogue, Thomas Franklin 1935- *WhoWor 93*
Pogue, William R. 1930- *ConAu 137*
Pogue, William Reid 1930- *WhoAm 92*
Pogue, William W. 1946- *St&PR 93*
Pohan, Armand 1944- *WhoAm 92*
Poher, Alain 1909- *BioIn 17*
Pohiva, Samuela Akilisi 1941- *WhoWor 93*
Pohjola, Leila Mirjami 1944- *WhoScE 91-4*
Pohl, Carl Ferdinand 1819-1887 *Baker 92*
Pohl, Carol *ScF&FL 92*
Pohl, Emma *AmWomPl*
Pohl, Frederik 1919- *BioIn 17, ConAu 37NR, ScF&FL 92, WhoAm 92, WhoWrEP 92*
Pohl, Frederik, IV 1956- *ScF&FL 92*
Pohl, Fritz M. 1939- *WhoScE 91-3*
Pohl, Gunther Erich 1925- *WhoAm 92*
Pohl, Henry Sidney 1946- *WhoE 93*
Pohl, Herbert A. 1932- *St&PR 93*
Pohl, John Joseph, Jr. 1927- *WhoSSW 93*
Pohl, Karl Otto 1929- *WhoWor 93*
Pohl, Kathleen Sharon 1951- *WhoWor 93*
Pohl, Pierre Henri Louis 1938- *WhoScE 91-2*
Pohl, Richard 1826-1896 *Baker 92*
Pohl, Richard Walter 1916- *WhoAm 92*
Pohl, Robert Otto 1929- *WhoAm 92*
Pohl, Stephan-Andreas 1956- *WhoWor 93*
Pohl, Victoria Mary 1930- *WhoAmW 93*
Pohl, Walter LeoPold 1941- *WhoWor 93*
Pohlad, Carl R. *WhoAm 92*
Pohlad, Carl R. 1915- *BioIn 17, St&PR 93*
Pohlad, William *MiSFD 9*
Pohle, Arthur R. 1929- *St&PR 93*
Pohle, Gerhard 1925- *WhoScE 91-3*
Pohle, Robert W., Jr. 1949- *ScF&FL 92*
Pohlenz, Joachim F.L. 1936- *WhoScE 91-3*
Pohlhammer, Mark Ellis 1960- *WhoSSW 93*
Pohli, Kate A. Jacoby *AmWomPl*
Pohlig, Karl 1858-1928 *Baker 92*
Pohlkamp, Francis W., Jr. *Law&B 92*
Pohlman, James A. 1928- *St&PR 93*
Pohlman, James Erwin 1932- *WhoAm 92, WhoWor 93*
Pohlman, Katherine J. *Law&B 92*
Pohlman, Randolph Allen 1944- *WhoAm 92*
Pohlman, Richard C. 1942- *St&PR 93*
Pohlmann, Gregory Luther 1948- *St&PR 93*
Pohlmann, William Albert 1939- *St&PR 93*
Pohlmeyer, Klaus 1944- *WhoScE 91-3*
Pohlsander, Hans Achim 1927- *WhoAm 92*
Pohly, Lawrence M. 1943- *St&PR 93*
Pohm, Arthur V. 1927- *WhoAm 92*
Pohmer, Dieter Joachim Walter 1925- *WhoWor 93*
Pohn, Gail W. *Law&B 92*
Pohn, Gail W. 1938- *St&PR 93*
Pohorecki, Ryszard 1936- *WhoScE 91-4*
Pohrer, William John *Law&B 92*
Pohrt, Tom *BioIn 17*
Pohs, Arnold C. 1928- *St&PR 93*
Pohtila, Eljas *WhoScE 91-4*
Pohto, Pentti 1938- *WhoScE 91-4*
Poian, Edward Licio 1946- *WhoE 93, WhoEmL 93, WhoWor 93*
Poiani, Eileen Louise 1943- *WhoAmW 93*
Poidevin, Ronald K. 1939- *St&PR 93*
Poignant, Alain-Francois 1931- *WhoScE 91-2*
Poignard, John M. 1948- *St&PR 93*
Poijarvi, Heikki *WhoScE 91-4*
Poikolainen, Kari 1945- *WhoScE 91-4*
Poilblanc, Rene 1933- *WhoScE 91-2*
Poillon, Arthur Jacques 1925- *WhoSSW 93*
Poinar, George Orlo, Jr. 1936- *WhoAm 92*
Poincare, Henri 1854-1912 *BioIn 17*
Poincare, Raymond 1860-1934 *BioIn 17, DcTwHis*
Poindexter, Chris Herndon 1938- *WhoAm 92*
Poindexter, John *DcCPCAm*
Poindexter, John A. *Law&B 92*
Poindexter, John Bruce 1944- *WhoAm 92*
Poindexter, John E. 1923- *St&PR 93*
Poindexter, John M. *BioIn 17*
Poindexter, Joseph Boyd 1935- *WhoAm 92, WhoWrEP 92*
Poindexter, Kenneth Wayne 1937- *WhoSSW 93*
Poindexter, William Mersereau 1925- *WhoAm 92*
Poindexter, Wm. 1925- *St&PR 93*
Poindexter, Zeb Ferdinand, III 1959- *WhoSSW 93*
Poinsett, Alexander Caesar 1926- *WhoAm 92*
Poinsette, Cheryl Lynne *Law&B 92*
Poinsette, Donald Eugene 1914- *WhoWor 93*
Poinso-Chapuis, Germaine 1901-1981 *BioIn 17*
Point, Flora S. 1953- *St&PR 93*
Point, Warren 1921- *WhoSSW 93*
Pointe de Sable, Jean Baptiste 1745?-1818 *BioIn 17*
Pointelin, Larry R. 1941- *St&PR 93*
Pointer, Anita 1948- *See* Pointer Sisters *SoulM*
Pointer, Anita 1949- *See* Pointer Sisters, The *ConMus 9*
Pointer, Bonnie 1950- *See* Pointer Sisters, The *ConMus 9* *See Also* Pointer Sisters *SoulM*
Pointer, David John 1937- *WhoWor 93*
Pointer, June 1953?- *See* Pointer Sisters, The *ConMus 9*
Pointer, June 1954- *See* Pointer Sisters *SoulM*
Pointer, Ruth 1946- *See* Pointer Sisters, The *ConMus 9*
Pointer, Sam Clyde, Jr. 1934- *WhoAm 92, WhoSSW 93*
Pointer, Thomas H. 1958- *St&PR 93*
Pointer Sisters *SoulM*
Pointer Sisters, The *ConMus 9 [port]*
Pointon, Anthony John *WhoScE 91-1*
Pointon, John 1951- *WhoWor 93*
Poiret, Jean d1992 *NewYTBS 92*
Poiret, Jean 1926-1992 *BioIn 17*
Poirier, Anne *BioIn 17*
Poirier, Charles Carroll, III 1936- *St&PR 93*
Poirier, Frank Eugene 1940- *WhoAm 92*
Poirier, Jean-Paul *WhoScE 91-2*
Poirier, John Kenneth *Law&B 92*
Poirier, Louis 1910- *BioIn 17*
Poirier, Louis Joseph 1918- *WhoAm 92*
Poirier, Patrick *BioIn 17*
Poirier, Richard 1925- *ConAu 40NR, WhoAm 92, WhoWrEP 92*
Poirier, Richard Oveila 1947- *WhoWor 93*
Poirier, Roger J. 1942- *St&PR 93*
Poirier, Vickie Hu 1946- *BioIn 17*
Poirier, Victor L. 1941- *St&PR 93*
Poirion, Daniel 1927- *WhoAm 92*
Poirot, James Wesley 1931- *St&PR 93, WhoAm 92*
Poiry, James R. 1944- *St&PR 93*
Pois, Joseph 1905- *WhoAm 92, WhoE 93, WhoWor 93*
Pois, Robert August 1940- *WhoAm 92, WhoWrEP 92*
Poise, (Jean Alexandre) Ferdinand 1828-1892 *Baker 92*
Poissant, Charles-Albert 1925- *St&PR 93, WhoAm 92, WhoE 93*
Poissant, Herve Julien 1930- *WhoE 93*
Poissl, Johann Nepomuk, Freiherr von 1783-1865 *Baker 92*
Poissl, Johann Nepomuk von 1783-1865 *OxDcOp*
Poister, John J. 1923- *St&PR 93*
Poitevin, J.P. *WhoScE 91-2*
Poitevin, Michel Jean-Marie 1944- *WhoWor 93*
Poitevint, A. Lloyd 1918- *St&PR 93*
Poitier, Cyril *BioIn 17*
Poitier, Sidney *BioIn 17, WhoAm 92*
Poitier, Sidney 1924- *AfrAmBi, IntDcF 2-3 [port], MiSFD 9*
Poitout, Dominique Gilbert M. 1946- *WhoWor 93*
Poitra, Patricia Diane 1955- *St&PR 93*
Poitras, Edward Whitney 1932- *WhoSSW 93*
Poitras, James W. 1939- *St&PR 93*
Poitras, Nancy Lou 1944- *WhoWor 93*
Poitras, Pierre 1934- *St&PR 93, WhoAm 92*
Poizat, Bruno 1946- *WhoWor 93*
Poja, Frank Joseph 1950- *St&PR 93*
Poje, Drazen 1924- *WhoScE 91-4*
Pojeta, John, Jr. 1935- *WhoAm 92*
Pojmanska, Teresa *WhoScE 91-4*
Pojucan 1957- *BioIn 17*
Poka, Terez 1935- *WhoScE 91-4*
Poka Laenui 1946- *WhoEmL 93*
Pokasai, James 1950- *WhoAsAP 91*
Pokelwaldt, Robert N. *WhoAm 92*
Pokempner, Joseph Kres 1936- *WhoAm 92*
Pokieser, Herbert 1930- *WhoScE 91-4*
Pokky, Eric Jon 1957- *WhoSSW 93*
Pokora, Jan 1928- *WhoScE 91-4*
Pokorny, Franz Xaver 1728-1794 *Baker 92*
Pokorny, Gerold E. 1928- *WhoAm 92*
Pokorny, Gerold Erwin 1928- *St&PR 93*
Pokorny, Ivo Camillo 1939- *WhoUN 92*
Pokorny, Jan Hird 1914- *WhoAm 92*
Pokorny, L. Robert 1947- *St&PR 93*
Pokorny, Michael John *WhoScE 91-1*
Pokorny, Vladimir 1922- *WhoScE 91-4*
Pokorski, Robert J. 1952- *St&PR 93*
Pokorski, Stefan 1942- *WhoScE 91-4*
Pokosh, Terri Lee 1952- *WhoAmW 93*
Pokras, Bruce A. *Law&B 92*
Pokras, Sheila Frances 1935- *WhoAmW 93*
Pokrass, Dimitri 1899-1978 *Baker 92*
Pokrovsky, Boris 1912- *OxDcOp*
Pol, Anne 1947- *WhoAmW 93*
Pol, Santiago 1945- *BioIn 17*
Pol, Wincenty 1807-1872 *IntDcAn, PolBiDi*
Pola, Robert M. 1947- *St&PR 93*
Polacco, Erseo 1929- *WhoScE 91-3*
Polacco, Giorgio 1873-1960 *Baker 92*
Polacco, Giorgio 1874-1960 *OxDcOp*
Polacco, Patricia *ChlBIID [port]*
Polacek, Deborah 1955- *WhoE 93*
Polach, Jaroslav George 1914- *WhoE 93, WhoWor 93*
Polach, Susan E. 1955- *St&PR 93*
Polacheck, Hilda Satt *AmWomPl*
Polacheck, Jerry H. 1943- *St&PR 93*
Polachek, Solomon William 1945- *WhoE 93*
Polack, Robert *Law&B 92*
Polacki, Zenon 1929- *WhoScE 91-4*
Polaczek, Stanislaw Marian 1915- *WhoWor 93*
Polaczyk, Gary E. *St&PR 93*
Poladian, Leon 1964- *WhoWor 93*
Polak, Elijah 1931- *WhoAm 92*
Polak, Jacques Jacobus 1914- *WhoAm 92, WhoE 93*
Polak, Julia Margaret *WhoScE 91-1*
Polak, Julie Stark 1945- *WhoWrEP 92*
Polak, Marek 1948- *WhoScE 91-4*
Polak, T.A. *WhoScE 91-1*
Polak, Vivian Louise 1952- *WhoAmW 93*
Polakas, Victoria V. 1936- *WhoAmW 93*
Polakoff, Abe *WhoAm 92*
Polakoff, Keith Ian 1941- *WhoAm 92*
Polakoff, Murray Emanuel 1922- *WhoAm 92*
Polakoski, Raymond Robert 1947- *WhoE 93*
Polakowski, Benon 1927- *WhoScE 91-4*
Polakowski, Kenneth Michael Joseph 1953- *WhoE 93*
Polan, Annette Lewis 1944- *WhoE 93*
Polan, David Jay 1951- *WhoEmL 93, WhoWor 93*
Polan, Lisa Gail *Law&B 92*
Polan, Morris 1924- *WhoAm 92*
Polan, Nancy Moore *WhoAm 92, WhoAmW 93, WhoSSW 93, WhoWor 93*
Polan, Steven M. *Law&B 92*
Polanco, Luis Enrique 1947- *WhoWor 93*
Poland, George *Law&B 92*
Poland, Helen Barbara 1942- *WhoAmW 93*
Poland, Peter J. *Law&B 92*
Poland, Robert Paul 1925- *WhoAm 92*
Poland, Susan L. *Law&B 92*
Poland, Thomas Mitchell 1949- *WhoSSW 93*
Polanek, Richard I. 1931- *St&PR 93*
Polanin, John, Jr. *Law&B 92*
Polanski, Benjamin H. 1951- *St&PR 93*
Polanski, Roman *BioIn 17*
Polanski, Roman 1933- *MiSFD 9, PolBiDi, WhoAm 92, WhoWor 93*
Polanski, S. Michael 1947- *St&PR 93*
Polansky, David Samuel 1945- *WhoE 93*
Polansky, Edwin Herbert 1932- *St&PR 93*

Polansky, Gerald A. BioIn 17
Polansky, Larry 1954- Baker 92
Polansky, Larry Paul 1932- WhoAm 92
Polansky, Michael D. Law&B 92
Polansky, Sheldon Law&B 92
Polansky, Sheldon 1949- St&PR 93
Polansky, Sol 1926- WhoAm 92
Polanyi, John Charles 1929- WhoAm 92, WhoE 93, WhoWor 93
Polanyi, Karl BioIn 17
Polanyi, Karl 1886-1964 IntDcAn
Polanyi, Michael 1891-1976 BioIn 17
Polark, James F. 1950- St&PR 93
Polascik, Mary Ann 1940- WhoAmW 93
Polasek, Edward John 1927- WhoSSW 93
Polasek, Edwin F. 1929- WhoSSW 93
Polasek, Wolfgang 1951- WhoWor 93
Polashock, Michael Stephen 1932- WhoSSW 93
Polaski, Anne Spencer Law&B 92
Polatnick, Jerome 1922- WhoE 93
Polavarapu, Prasad Leela 1952- WhoSSW 93
Polayes, Irving Marvin 1927- WhoAm 92, WhoE 93
Polayes, Maurice Benjamin 1923- WhoE 93
Polcari, Stephen 1945- WhoE 93
Polcaro, Vito Francesco 1945- WhoWor 93
Polcovar, Jane ScF&FL 92
Polder, Markus MajAI
Poldini, Ede (Eduard) 1869-1957 Baker 92
Poldowski 1879-1932 Baker 92
Poldowski, Dean Paul, Lady 1880-1932 PolBiDi
Polebaum, Mark Neal 1952- WhoAm 92
Polec, Stanley Walter 1930- WhoWrEP 92
Poledor, Theodore St&PR 93
Polemis, Augustis 1955- WhoWor 93
Polemitou, Olga Andrea 1950- WhoAmW 93, WhoE 93, WhoEmL 93, WhoWor 93
Polemius Silvius fl. 5th cent.- OxDcByz
Polen, G. Raymond 1931- St&PR 93
Polen, Thomas Morris 1935- St&PR 93
Polenberg, Richard 1937- WhoAm 92
Polen-Dorn, Linda Frances 1945- WhoAmW 93, WhoSSW 93
Polenov, Vasilii Dmitrievich 1844-1927 BioIn 17
Polenske, Karen Rosel 1937- WhoAm 92
Polenske, Richard Emil 1928- St&PR 93
Polenz, Joanna Magda 1936- WhoAmW 93, WhoE 93, WhoWor 93
Poler, Mira AmWomPl
Polese, Carolyn 1947- DcAmChF 1985
Polesinski, Zbigniew Jerzy 1932- WhoScE 91-4
Poleskie, Stephen Francis 1938- WhoAm 92, WhoWor 93
Polesky, Herbert Fred 1933- WhoAm 92
Polet, Jean Marie 1941- WhoWor 93
Polette, Nancy (Jane) 1930- WhoWrEP 92
Poletti, Charles 1903- WhoAm 92
Poletti, Syria 1921- BioIn 17
Poletti, Ugo Cardinal 1914- WhoWor 93
Polevoy, Nancy Tally 1944- WhoAmW 93, WhoE 93, WhoWor 93
Polezzo, Stefanin WhoScE 91-3
Polfanders, Janis Ivars Law&B 92
Polfer, Mary M. St&PR 93
Polgar, Antoine Jean 1940- WhoE 93
Polgar, Jean 1949- St&PR 93
Polgar, Judit 1976- NewYTBS 92 [port]
Polgar, Leslie George 1943- WhoE 93
Polgar, Tibor 1907- Baker 92
Polge, Christopher WhoScE 91-1
Polge, E.J.C. 1926- WhoScE 91-1
Polhamus, Sally Nelson 1947- St&PR 93
Polhemus, Mary Irene 1937- WhoAmW 93
Poli, Diego 1950- WhoWor 93
Poli, Kenneth Joseph 1921- WhoAm 92
Poli, Marco D. 1942- WhoScE 91-3
Poliak, Aaron 1925- WhoE 93
Poliakin, Miron 1895-1941 Baker 92
Poliakoff, Gary A. 1944- WhoSSW 93
Poliakoff, Stephen MiSFD 9
Poliakov, Valeri(an) 1913-1970 Baker 92
Polian, Bill 1942- WhoAm 92, WhoE 93
Policano, Joseph Daniel 1933- WhoAm 92
Policappelli, Nini BioIn 17
Polich, John Elliott 1946- WhoEmL 93
Polichino, Joseph Anthony, Jr. 1948- WhoSSW 93
Policinski, Henry J. Law&B 92
Policoff, Leonard David 1918- WhoAm 92
Policoff, Susan Lewis 1944- WhoWrEP 92
Policy, Carmen A. 1943- WhoAm 92
Polidori, John 1795-1821 ScF&FL 92
Polidori, John William 1795-1821 BioIn 17, DcLB 116 [port]
Polidoro, Caroline Ruth 1939- WhoAmW 93
Polignac, Armande de 1876-1962 Baker 92
Polihronov, N.I. 1938- WhoScE 91-4
Polikarov, Azarja Prizenti 1921- WhoScE 91-4
Polikarpus, Viido 1946- ScF&FL 92
Polikoff, Benet, Jr. 1936- WhoAm 92
Polimene, Frank Anthony 1946- St&PR 93
Polin, Claire WhoAm 92
Polin, Claire 1926- Baker 92
Poliner, Randall Edward 1955- St&PR 93
Poling, David L. 1932- St&PR 93
Poling, George Wesley 1935- WhoAm 92
Poling, Harold A. BioIn 17
Poling, Harold A. 1925- St&PR 93
Poling, Harold Arthur 1925- WhoAm 92
Poling, Jim BioIn 17
Poling, John Robert 1951- St&PR 93
Poling, John W. 1945- St&PR 93
Poling(-Kempes), Lesley 1954- ConAu 136
Poling, Marlene M. 1932- St&PR 93
Poling, Richard Duane 1955- WhoWor 93
Poling, Steven Clark Law&B 92
Poling, Wesley Henry 1945- WhoE 93
Polinsky, David B. Law&B 92
Polinsky, Janet Naboicheck 1930- WhoAmW 93
Polinsky, Joseph Thomas 1947- WhoE 93
Polinszky, Karoly 1922- WhoScE 91-4
Polio, Dennis C. 1945- St&PR 93
Poliquin, Jane d1992 BioIn 17
Polis, Anthony W. 1943- St&PR 93
Polis, Julian M. 1925- St&PR 93
Polis, Michael Philip 1943- WhoAm 92
Polis, Sheri Helene 1956- WhoAmW 93
Polisano, Enrico Joseph 1949- St&PR 93
Polisar, Barry Louis BioIn 17
Polisar, Barry Louis 1954- WhoE 93
Polisar, Leonard Myers 1929- WhoAm 92, WhoWor 93
Polish, Jacob d1991 BioIn 17
Polishan, Paul F. 1945- St&PR 93
Polishan, Paul Frank 1945- WhoAm 92
Polisi, Joseph W(illiam) 1947- Baker 92
Polisi, Joseph William 1947- WhoAm 92, WhoWor 93
Polisini, John Law&B 92
Polisseni, Eugene R. 1939- St&PR 93
Politakis, Lazarus 1927- St&PR 93
Politan, Nicholas H. 1935- WhoAm 92, WhoE 93
Politano, Frank L. Law&B 92
Politano, Victor Anthony 1919- WhoAm 92
Polite, Carlene Hatcher 1932- WhoWrEP 92
Polite, Edmonia Allen 1922- WhoAmW 93
Polite, Frank C. 1936- WhoWrEP 92
Politi, Beth Kukkonen 1949- WhoEmL 93
Politi, Leo 1908- ChlLR 29 [port], MajAI [port]
Politicus ConAu 37NR
Politiek, Rommert D. 1926- WhoScE 91-3
Polito, Edward 1944- St&PR 93
Polito, Susan Evans 1957- WhoAmW 93
Polito, William 1936-1991 BioIn 17
Polity, Leddy Smith 1936- WhoAmW 93, WhoE 93
Politz, Henry Anthony 1932- WhoAm 92, WhoSSW 93
Politzer, Hugh David 1949- WhoAm 92
Polivchak, Philip Michael 1933- WhoWor 93
Polivka, John Michael 1953- WhoSSW 93
Polivka, Vladimir 1896-1948 Baker 92
Polivnick, Paul 1947- WhoAm 92
Polivy, Gail L. Law&B 92
Polizotto, Bruce Alan 1941- WhoAm 92
Polizzi, D. Michael 1939- St&PR 93
Polizzi, Joseph Anthony 1938- WhoSSW 93
Polizzi, Rick BioIn 17
Polizzonto, Joseph Law&B 92
Poljak, Roberto J. 1932- WhoScE 91-2
Poljenoff, Wassilij Dmitrijewitsch 1844-1927 BioIn 17
Polk, Audrey Leigh Law&B 92
Polk, Beverly Benton 1947- WhoAmW 93
Polk, Cara Saylor 1945- ConAu 38NR
Polk, Charles 1920- WhoAm 92, WhoE 93
Polk, George BioIn 17
Polk, Hiram Carey, Jr. 1936- WhoAm 92, WhoSSW 93
Polk, James 1939- WhoCanL 92
Polk, James H. 1911-1992 BioIn 17, NewYTBS 92 [port]
Polk, James Hilliard, III 1942- St&PR 93
Polk, James K. DcCPCAm
Polk, James K. 1795-1849 BioIn 17, PolPar
Polk, James Ray 1937- WhoAm 92, WhoSSW 93
Polk, James Warren Law&B 92
Polk, John George 1932- WhoAm 92
Polk, John Robert 1934- St&PR 93
Polk, Lee 1923- WhoAm 92
Polk, Leonidas 1806-1864 BioIn 17, HarEnMi
Polk, Linda Donice 1938- WhoSSW 93
Polk, Louis Frederick, Jr. 1930- St&PR 93, WhoAm 92
Polk, Lucy J. 1949- St&PR 93
Polk, Manfred Law&B 92
Polk, Matthew Steele, Jr. 1949- St&PR 93
Polk, Noel Earl 1943- WhoSSW 93
Polk, Richard L. Law&B 92
Polk, Richard Lee Law&B 92
Polk, Robert Forrest 1947- WhoAm 92
Polk, Ronald Thomas 1958- WhoSSW 93
Polk, Samuel T., III Law&B 92
Polk, Samuel T., III 1950- St&PR 93
Polk, Sarah Childress 1803-1891 BioIn 17
Polk, Stephen R. 1955- WhoAm 92
Polk, William Merrill 1935- WhoAm 92
Polke, Sigmar BioIn 17
Polkey, C.E. WhoScE 91-1
Polking, Kirk 1925- WhoWrEP 92
Polking, Paul J. Law&B 92
Polkinghorn, William A., Jr. Law&B 92
Polkinghorne, Michael Aughey 1962- WhoWor 93
Polkinghorne, Patricia Ann 1948- WhoAmW 93
Polko, Elise 1822-1899 Baker 92
Polkowski, Delphine Theresa 1930- WhoWor 93
Poll, David Ian Alistair 1950- WhoWor 93
Poll, Heinz 1926- WhoAm 92
Poll, Joan Frances 1950- WhoE 93
Poll, Martin Harvey WhoAm 92
Poll, Max Henry 1946- WhoAm 92
Poll, Robert E. 1948- St&PR 93
Poll, Robert Eugene, Jr. 1948- WhoAm 92
Pollack, Barbara A. Law&B 92
Pollack, Barry MiSFD 9
Pollack, Ben 1903-1971 Baker 92
Pollack, Bruce 1951- WhoE 93
Pollack, Carol Lough 1924- WhoAmW 93
Pollack, Cindy Pam 1957- WhoAmW 93
Pollack, Dale WhoAm 92
Pollack, Daniel 1935- WhoAm 92
Pollack, David B. Law&B 92
Pollack, Eileen 1956- ConAu 138
Pollack, Ephram 1949- St&PR 93
Pollack, Gerald A. 1929- WhoAm 92
Pollack, Gerald Harvey 1940- WhoAm 92
Pollack, Gerald J. 1942- St&PR 93
Pollack, Gerald Leslie 1933- WhoAm 92
Pollack, Henry Nathan 1936- WhoAm 92
Pollack, Herbert William 1927- St&PR 93
Pollack, Herman 1919- WhoAm 92
Pollack, Irwin William 1927- WhoAm 92
Pollack, Jane S. Law&B 92
Pollack, Jeffrey S. 1953- St&PR 93
Pollack, Jeffrey Stuart 1956- WhoE 93
Pollack, Joe 1931- WhoAm 92
Pollack, Jordan Ellis 1934- WhoE 93
Pollack, Joseph 1917- WhoAm 92
Pollack, Joseph 1939- St&PR 93, WhoAm 92
Pollack, Lana 1942- WhoAmW 93
Pollack, Lester 1933- St&PR 93
Pollack, Louis 1920- WhoAm 92, WhoE 93
Pollack, Mark William 1958- WhoE 93
Pollack, Michael B. 1958- St&PR 93
Pollack, Michael J. Law&B 92
Pollack, Milton 1906- WhoAm 92, WhoE 93
Pollack, Morris I. Law&B 92
Pollack, Norman 1933- WhoAm 92
Pollack, Paul R. 1941- St&PR 93
Pollack, Paul Robert 1941- WhoAm 92
Pollack, Rachel 1945- ScF&FL 92
Pollack, Reginald Murray 1924- WhoAm 92
Pollack, Rhoda-Gale 1937- WhoAmW 93
Pollack, Rhoda Olanoff 1932- WhoAmW 93
Pollack, Richard A. ScF&FL 92
Pollack, Robert 1933- WhoIns 93
Pollack, Robert Elliot 1940- WhoAm 92
Pollack, Robert William 1947- WhoWor 93
Pollack, Robin Lynn Law&B 92
Pollack, Ronald Frank 1944- WhoAm 92
Pollack, Seymour Victor 1933- WhoAm 92
Pollack, Solomon Robert 1934- WhoAm 92
Pollack, Stanley P. Law&B 92
Pollack, Stanley P. 1928- St&PR 93
Pollack, Stephen J. 1937- WhoAm 92
Pollack, Susan F. Law&B 92
Pollack, Sydney 1934- MiSFD 9, WhoAm 92
Pollack, Sylvia Byrne 1940- WhoAmW 93
Pollack, William L. 1951- St&PR 93
Pollak, Anna 1912- OxDcOp
Pollak, David 1917- St&PR 93
Pollak, David Paul 1964- WhoE 93
Pollak, Edward Barry 1934- WhoAm 92
Pollak, Egon 1879-1933 Baker 92, OxDcOp
Pollak, Felix 1909- WhoWrEP 92
Pollak, Helga Katharina 1935- WhoWor 93
Pollak, Henry M. 1931- St&PR 93
Pollak, James Stephen 1940- WhoAm 92
Pollak, Lee Law&B 92
Pollak, Lisa Joan Law&B 92
Pollak, Louis Heilprin 1922- WhoE 93
Pollak, Martin M. 1927- St&PR 93
Pollak, Martin Marshall 1927- WhoAm 92
Pollak, Maurice A. d1990 BioIn 17
Pollak, Richard 1934- WhoAm 92, WhoWrEP 92
Pollak, Robert Andrew 1938- WhoAm 92
Pollak, Sanford Zachary 1941- WhoSSW 93
Pollak, Sarah Straas WhoAmW 93
Pollak, Thomas F. 1950- St&PR 93
Pollak, Tim WhoAm 92, WhoE 93
Pollak, Vivian R. 1938- ConAu 136
Pollak, Walter Heilprin 1887-1940 OxCSupC
Pollak, William F. 1942- St&PR 93
Pollan, Andrea Stefanie 1961- WhoE 93
Pollan, Carolyn Joan 1937- WhoAmW 93
Pollan, Lynn E. Law&B 92
Pollan, Michael BioIn 17
Pollan-Cohen, Shirley WhoWrEP 92
Polland, Madeleine A. 1918- BioIn 17
Polland, Madeleine A(ngela Cahill) 1918- ConAu 37NR, MajAI [port]
Pollanschutz, Josef WhoScE 91-4
Pollara, Bernard WhoAm 92
Pollara, John B. St&PR 93
Pollard, A. James 1935- St&PR 93
Pollard, C. William 1938- St&PR 93
Pollard, Carl F. 1938- WhoAm 92
Pollard, Carl Faulkner 1938- St&PR 93
Pollard, Charles E. 1932- St&PR 93
Pollard, Charles W. Law&B 92
Pollard, Charles William 1938- WhoWor 93
Pollard, Clint E. 1949- St&PR 93
Pollard, Connie Maria 1957- WhoSSW 93
Pollard, David Edward 1927- WhoAm 92
Pollard, David James WhoScE 91-1
Pollard, Edward Ellsberg 1945- WhoE 93
Pollard, Elizabeth Blitch 1939- WhoSSW 93
Pollard, Franklin Dawes 1934- WhoWor 93
Pollard, Fred Don 1931- WhoAm 92
Pollard, Geoffrey WhoScE 91-1
Pollard, George Marvin 1909- WhoAm 92
Pollard, Gerald Tilman 1940- WhoSSW 93
Pollard, Harvey B. 1943- WhoE 93
Pollard, Howard Frank 1920- WhoWor 93
Pollard, James Ashwell 1946- WhoSSW 93
Pollard, Jean Ann 1934- WhoAmW 93
Pollard, Jeanette Marie 1951- WhoAmW 93
Pollard, Jenal A. 1961- WhoAmW 93
Pollard, John WhoScE 91-1
Pollard, John F. d1990 BioIn 17
Pollard, John Oliver 1937- WhoSSW 93
Pollard, Joseph Augustine 1924- WhoAm 92
Pollard, Kathleen Kromer 1945- WhoAmW 93
Pollard, Margaret Louise 1934- WhoAmW 93
Pollard, Michael Ross 1947- WhoE 93, WhoEmL 93
Pollard, Morris 1916- WhoAm 92
Pollard, Nicholas Anthony, Sr. 1924- WhoWor 93
Pollard, Overton Price 1933- WhoAm 92
Pollard, Reed 1913- St&PR 93
Pollard, Richard F. 1933- St&PR 93
Pollard, Sam A., Jr. 1929- St&PR 93
Pollard, Shirley 1939- WhoAmW 93
Pollard, Snub 1886-1962 QDrFCA 92 [port]
Pollard, Thomas Dean 1942- WhoAm 92
Pollard, William Sherman, Jr. 1925- WhoAm 92
Pollaro, J.M. Law&B 92
Pollaro, Paul Philip 1921- WhoE 93
Pollarolo, (Giovanni) Antonio 1676?-1746 Baker 92
Pollarolo, Carlo Francesco c. 1653-1722 OxDcOp
Pollarolo, Carlo Francesco c. 1653-1723 Baker 92
Pollart, Dale Flavian 1932- WhoAm 92
Poller, Jeri 1952- WhoAmW 93
Pollert, William R. 1944- St&PR 93
Pollet, Elizabeth 1922- WhoWrEP 92
Pollet, Richard Law&B 92, WhoAm 92
Pollet, Sylvester 1939- WhoWrEP 92
Polley, April Marie 1942- WhoAmW 93
Polley, Douglas Craig 1958- WhoE 93
Polley, Edward Herman 1923- WhoAm 92
Polley, Howard Freeman 1913- WhoAm 92
Polley, John E. Law&B 92
Polley, Max Eugene 1928- WhoSSW 93
Polley, Michael H. Law&B 92
Polley, Paulette BioIn 17

Polley, Richard Donald 1937- *WhoSSW 93, WhoWor 93*
Polley, Sarah *BioIn 17*
Polley, Terry Lee 1947- *WhoEmL 93*
Polli, G. Patrick 1959- *WhoEmL 93*
Pollich, Peter Adam 1928- *St&PR 93*
Pollicino, Joseph Anthony 1939- *WhoAm 92*
Pollick, G. David 1947- *WhoAm 92*
Pollick, Richard Raymond 1939- *St&PR 93*
Pollicove, Harvey Myles 1944- *WhoE 93*
Pollihan, Thomas H. *Law&B 92*
Pollihan, Thomas H. 1949- *St&PR 93*
Pollikoff, Max 1904-1984 *Baker 92*
Pollin, Abe 1923- *WhoAm 92*
Pollin, Burton R. 1916- *ScF&FL 92*
Pollina, Ronald J. 1946- *St&PR 93*
Pollini, Bernhard 1838-1897 *Baker 92, OxDcOp*
Pollini, Cesare, Cavaliere de' 1858-1912 *Baker 92*
Pollini, Francesco (Giuseppe) 1762-1846 *Baker 92*
Pollini, Francis 1930- *WhoAm 92*
Pollini, Maurizio 1942- *Baker 92*
Pollino, Patrick A. 1942- *St&PR 93*
Pollino, Riccardo *WhoScE 91-3*
Pollins, Perry 1924- *St&PR 93*
Pollio, Howard Ronald 1937- *WhoSSW 93*
Pollio, John W. *Law&B 92*
Pollio, Ralph Thomas 1948- *WhoAm 92, WhoWor 93*
Pollitt, Christopher John *WhoScE 91-1*
Pollitt, Jerome Jordan 1934- *WhoAm 92*
Pollitt, John J. 1932- *St&PR 93*
Pollitt, Katha *BioIn 17*
Pollitt, Katha 1949- *WhoWrEP 92*
Pollitt, Ronald Eugene 1947- *St&PR 93*
Pollitzer, Anita 1894-1975 *BioIn 17*
Pollitzer, William Sprott 1923- *WhoAm 92*
Pollman, Cheryl Ellen *Law&B 92*
Pollmann, Johannes 1945- *WhoScE 91-3*
Pollmann, Peter 1935- *WhoScE 91-3*
Pollmer, Jost Udo 1954- *WhoWor 93*
Pollmer, W. Gerhard 1926- *WhoScE 91-3*
Pollmer, Wolfgang Gerhard 1926- *WhoWor 93*
Pollnow, Charles Francis 1932- *St&PR 93*
Pollnow, Jan L. *WhoIns 93*
Pollnow, Jan Lee 1944- *St&PR 93*
Pollock, Adam N. *Law&B 92*
Pollock, Alexander John 1943- *WhoAm 92*
Pollock, Alice Diane 1939- *WhoAmW 93*
Pollock, Alice Leal *AmWomPl*
Pollock, Charles Cecil 1902-1988 *BioIn 17*
Pollock, Dale *ScF&FL 92*
Pollock, David A. 1953- *St&PR 93*
Pollock, David Michael 1945- *St&PR 93*
Pollock, Don C. 1933- *St&PR 93*
Pollock, Earl Edward 1928- *WhoAm 92*
Pollock, Edward M. *Law&B 92*
Pollock, Eleanor d1991 *BioIn 17*
Pollock, Frederick 1845-1937 *BioIn 17*
Pollock, George 1772-1839 *BioIn 17*
Pollock, George Howard 1923- *WhoAm 92*
Pollock, Jack Paden 1920- *WhoSSW 93, WhoWor 93*
Pollock, Jackson 1912-1956 *BioIn 17, ModArCr 3 [port]*
Pollock, James 1810-1890 *BioIn 17*
Pollock, James Brooker *Law&B 92*
Pollock, James Valiant 1937- *WhoAm 92*
Pollock, John A. *St&PR 93*
Pollock, John Albon 1936- *WhoAm 92*
Pollock, John (Charles) 1923- *ConAu 40NR*
Pollock, John Crothers, III 1943- *WhoAm 92*
Pollock, John Glennon 1943- *WhoAm 92*
Pollock, John Phleger 1920- *WhoAm 92*
Pollock, Kenneth L. 1920- *St&PR 93*
Pollock, Larry Richard 1937- *WhoE 93*
Pollock, Lawrence J. *WhoAm 92*
Pollock, Linda A(nne) 1955- *ConAu 39NR*
Pollock, Luella Rebecca 1920- *WhoAm 92*
Pollock, M. Duncan 1943- *WhoAm 92*
Pollock, M.R. *WhoScE 91-1*
Pollock, Mark Stephen 1959- *WhoE 93*
Pollock, Marlene Patrick 1946- *WhoAmW 93*
Pollock, Marvin Erwin 1931- *WhoAm 92*
Pollock, Mary *MajAI*
Pollock, Michael Robert 1938- *WhoWor 93*
Pollock, Nancy J. 1934- *ConAu 139*
Pollock, Neal Jay 1947- *WhoE 93*
Pollock, Paul Jackson 1912-1956 *BioIn 17*
Pollock, Paul Robert 1950- *St&PR 93*
Pollock, Ray Jean 1931- *WhoSSW 93*
Pollock, Robert E. *Law&B 92*
Pollock, Robert Elwood 1936- *WhoAm 92*
Pollock, Roy Van Horn 1949- *WhoAm 92*
Pollock, S.E.N. *St&PR 93*
Pollock, Samuel Joseph 1932- *WhoE 93*
Pollock, Sharon *WhoCanL 92*
Pollock, Sheldon Ivan 1948- *WhoAm 92*
Pollock, Stephen Michael 1936- *WhoAm 92*
Pollock, Stewart Glasson 1932- *WhoAm 92*
Pollock, Thomas 1769-1803 *BioIn 17*
Pollock, Thomas P. 1943- *WhoAm 92*
Pollock, Walter Herries 1850-1926 *ScF&FL 92*
Pollock, Ward Robert 1943- *St&PR 93*
Pollock, William John 1943- *WhoE 93*
Pollock, William K. 1942- *St&PR 93*
Pollock-Ciampi, Judith *Law&B 92*
Pollotta, Nicholas A. *ScF&FL 92*
Pollotta, Nick 1954- *ScF&FL 92*
Pollsen, Robert Bruce 1953- *St&PR 93*
Polly, Dianne Kammerer 1951- *WhoSSW 93*
Polman, Gerrit Roelof 1868-1932 *BioIn 17*
Polnay, Peter de *ScF&FL 92*
Polner, Alex M. *St&PR 93*
Polner, Eli 1928- *St&PR 93*
Polner, Murray *BioIn 17*
Polo, Eddie 1875-1961 *BioIn 17*
Polo, Maffeo d1310?
See Polo, Nicolo d1300? & Polo, Maffeo d1310? *Expl 93*
Polo, Marco 1254-1323? *BioIn 17*
Polo, Marco 1254?-1324 *Expl 93 [port]*
Polo, Nicolo d1300? & Polo, Maffeo d1310? *Expl 93 [port]*
Polo, Roberto 1950- *BioIn 17*
Polo-Chiapolini, Claude 1942- *WhoScE 91-2*
Pologar, Alan Joseph 1950- *St&PR 93*
Pololanik, Zdenek 1935- *Baker 92*
Polome, Edgar Charles 1920- *WhoAm 92, WhoSSW 93, WhoWrEP 92*
Polon, Martin Ishiah 1942- *WhoE 93*
Polon, Steven 1919- *St&PR 93*
Polonio, Pedro *WhoScE 91-3*
Polonis, Douglas Hugh 1928- *WhoAm 92*
Polonovski, Jean-Pierre Jacques 1958- *WhoWor 93*
Polonsky, Abraham 1910- *ConTFT 10, MiSFD 9*
Polonsky, Arthur 1925- *WhoAm 92, WhoE 93*
Polonsky, Leonard S. 1927- *St&PR 93*
Polonsky, Michael Jay 1959- *WhoWor 93*
Polonyi, Stefan 1930- *WhoScE 91-3, WhoWor 93*
Poloukhine, Olga 1934- *WhoE 93*
Polovinkin, Leonid (Alexeievich) 1894-1949 *Baker 92*
Polowczyk, Grzegorz Adam 1950- *WhoUN 92*
Polowczyk, M. *WhoScE 91-4*
Polozola, Frank Joseph 1942- *WhoSSW 93*
Pol Pot *BioIn 17*
Pol Pot 1926- *WhoWor 93*
Pol Pot 1928- *ColdWar 2 [port], DcTwHis*
Pols, Cynthia Mary *WhoAmW 93*
Polsby, Nelson Woolf 1934- *WhoAm 92, WhoWrEP 92*
Polselli, Rocco Louis, Sr. 1943- *WhoE 93*
Polshek, James Stewart *BioIn 17*
Polshek, James Stewart 1930- *WhoAm 92*
Polsinelli, Perry *St&PR 93*
Polsky, Andrew J. 1955- *ConAu 139*
Polsky, Donald N. *St&PR 93*
Polsky, Laurence H. 1943- *St&PR 93*
Polsky, Louis Sanford 1932- *WhoE 93*
Polson, Donald 1934- *WhoCanL 92*
Polson, Margaret Ruth 1931- *WhoSSW 93*
Polson, William Jerry 1943- *WhoSSW 93*
Polster, Eugene Louis 1932- *St&PR 93*
Polster, Jerry 1936- *St&PR 93*
Polster, John J. 1956- *St&PR 93*
Polster, Robert W. *Law&B 92*
Poltawska, Wanda (Wiktoria) 1921- *ConAu 136*
Polter, Dirk Meints 1942- *WhoWor 93*
Polumsky, Dieter 1944- *WhoScE 91-3, WhoWor 93*
Polunin, Nicholas *WhoAm 92, WhoWor 93*
Polutchko, John Andrew 1933- *St&PR 93*
Poluzzi, Amleto 1919- *WhoWor 93*
Polvani, Filippo Maria 1926- *WhoScE 91-3*
Polverari, Paul *St&PR 93*
Polvino-Bodnar, Maryellen 1953- *WhoAmW 93*
Polyak, Boris T. 1935- *WhoWor 93*
Polyansky, Igor *BioIn 17*
Polychron, John P. 1936- *St&PR 93*
Polychron, John Philip 1936- *WhoAm 92*
Polydoris, Nicholas George 1930- *St&PR 93*
Polydoris, Steven Nicholas 1954- *WhoEmL 93, WhoWor 93*
Polydorou, Kyriakos 1932- *WhoScE 91-4*
Polyeuktos c. 900- *OxDcByz*
Polysperchon fl. c. 331BC-304BC *HarEnMi*
Polyzonis, Marios-B. 1928- *WhoScE 91-3*
Polyzopoulos, Nicholas A. 1920- *WhoScE 91-3*
Polzien, Paul Adalbert 1918- *WhoWor 93*
Polzin, John Theodore 1919- *WhoWor 93*
Polzin, Mark Frederick 1945- *St&PR 93*
Pomada, Elizabeth Luly 1940- *WhoWrEP 92*
Pombo, Alberto Alavar 1957- *WhoWor 93*
Pombo Alvarez, Selva 1956- *WhoWor 93*
Pomerance, Diane Linda 1951- *WhoAmW 93*
Pomerance, Norman 1926- *WhoAm 92*
Pomerance, Philip L. 1956- *St&PR 93*
Pomerance, Ralph 1907- *WhoAm 92*
Pomerantz, Adam L. *Law&B 92*
Pomerantz, Charlotte 1930- *ConAu 38NR, WhoWrEP 92*
Pomerantz, Edwin 1930- *St&PR 93*
Pomerantz, Ernest Harold *WhoAm 92*
Pomerantz, Jacob 1907- *WhoSSW 93*
Pomerantz, James Robert 1946- *WhoAm 92, WhoSSW 93, WhoWor 93*
Pomerantz, Jerald Michael 1954- *WhoEmL 93, WhoSSW 93*
Pomerantz, John J. 1933- *WhoAm 92*
Pomerantz, Laura 1948- *WhoAmW 93*
Pomerantz, Lawrence Stewart 1943- *St&PR 93*
Pomerantz, Lisa Renee *Law&B 92*
Pomerantz, Martin 1939- *WhoAm 92, WhoSSW 93*
Pomerantz, Marvin A. 1930- *St&PR 93*
Pomerantz, Marvin Alvin 1930- *WhoAm 92*
Pomerantz, Rhoda Silverstein 1937- *WhoAmW 93*
Pomeranz, Alfred J. *Law&B 92*
Pomeranz, Felix 1926- *WhoAm 92, WhoWor 93*
Pomeranz, Morton 1922- *WhoWor 93*
Pomeranz, Yeshajahu 1922- *WhoAm 92*
Pomerene, James Herbert 1920- *WhoAm 92*
Pomerenke, Michael John 1950- *WhoWor 93*
Pomerico, Thomas Michael 1954- *WhoE 93*
Pomerleau, Robert Raymond 1947- *St&PR 93*
Pomeroy, Brad Warren 1963- *St&PR 93*
Pomeroy, Claire *WhoWrEP 92*
Pomeroy, David Wardell 1939- *WhoE 93*
Pomeroy, Earl R. *BioIn 17*
Pomeroy, Ellen R.C. 1949- *WhoAmW 93*
Pomeroy, Harlan 1923- *WhoAm 92*
Pomeroy, Ira Lewis 1924- *WhoWrEP 92*
Pomeroy, James Seaton 1950- *WhoSSW 93*
Pomeroy, John J. *Law&B 92*
Pomeroy, Joseph H. *Law&B 92*
Pomeroy, Karl F. 1937- *St&PR 93*
Pomeroy, Kent Lytle 1935- *WhoWor 93*
Pomeroy, Leason Frederick, III 1937- *WhoAm 92*
Pomeroy, Lee Harris 1932- *WhoAm 92*
Pomeroy, Leslie Ann 1945- *WhoAm 92*
Pomeroy, Robert L. 1938- *St&PR 93*
Pomeroy, Robert Lee 1938- *WhoAm 92*
Pomeroy, Robert Watson, III 1935- *WhoE 93*
Pomeroy, Roxanne Kieda *Law&B 92*
Pomeroy, Theodore M. 1824-1905 *PolPar*
Pomeroy, Thomas Wilson, Jr. 1908- *WhoAm 92*
Pomeroy, William Henry, Jr. 1912- *St&PR 93*
Pomeroy, Wyman Burdette 1932- *WhoSSW 93*
Pomilla, Frank Rocco 1926- *WhoE 93*
Pommer, Richard *BioIn 17*
Pommer, Richard 1930- *ConAu 137*
Pommer, Richard 1930-1992 *NewYTBS 92 [port]*
Pommerening, Klaus Dieter 1946- *WhoWor 93*
Pommerville, Robert W. *Law&B 92, St&PR 93, WhoAm 92*
Pommier, Jean-Bernard 1944- *Baker 92*
Pommier de Santi, Patrice Robert 1945- *WhoWor 93*
Pommies, Robert Albert Jean 1941- *WhoWor 93*
Pomodoro, Carmelo d1992 *NewYTBS 92 [port]*
Pomorski, Krzysztof Roman 1945- *WhoScE 91-4*
Pomorski, Stanislaw 1934- *WhoAm 92*
Pomot, Claude Jean 1937- *WhoScE 91-2*
Pomp, Martin 1946- *St&PR 93*
Pompa, James Robert 1937- *WhoAm 92*
Pompa, Leonardo 1933- *WhoWor 93*
Pompadur, Edward R. *BioIn 17*
Pompadur, I. Martin *BioIn 17*
Pompadur, I. Martin 1935- *WhoAm 92*
Pompan, Jack Maurice 1926- *WhoE 93*
Pompe, Igor 1938- *WhoScE 91-4*
Pompea, Charles E. 1949- *St&PR 93*
Pompeiano, Ottavio 1927- *WhoWor 93*
Pompeius, Quintus fl. c. 144BC-131BC *HarEnMi*
Pompeius Magnus, Gnaeus c. 78BC-45BC *HarEnMi*
Pompeius Magnus Pius, Sextus c. 67BC-35BC *HarEnMi*
Pompeo, Bernard 1926- *St&PR 93*
Pomper, Philip 1936- *WhoAm 92*
Pomper, Victor Herbert 1923- *WhoAm 92*
Pompetti-Szul, Irene Catherine 1948- *WhoAmW 93*
Pompidou, Alain J. 1942- *WhoScE 91-2*
Pompidou, Georges 1911-1974 *BioIn 17*
Pompidou, Georges Jean Raymond 1911-1974 *DcTwHis*
Pomposello, Thomas Anthony 1949- *WhoE 93*
Pomraning, Gerald Carlton 1936- *WhoAm 92*
Pomroy, James F. 1934- *St&PR 93*
Pomus, Doc 1925-1991 *AnObit 1991, BioIn 17*
Pomus, Jerome 1925-1991 *SoulM*
Pomykalski, Zdzislaw 1917- *WhoScE 91-4*
Pon, Henry *Law&B 92*
Pon-Brown, Kay Migyoku 1956- *WhoAmW 93*
Ponc, Miroslav 1902-1976 *Baker 92*
Ponce, Carlos 1948- *WhoSSW 93*
Ponce, Edwin Canete 1959- *WhoWor 93*
Ponce, Federico *DcCPCAm*
Ponce, Joseph L. 1927- *St&PR 93*
Ponce, Manuel 1913- *DcMexL*
Ponce, Manuel (Maria) 1882-1948 *Baker 92*
Ponce, Mary Helen 1938- *DcLB 122 [port], NotHsAW 93 [port]*
Ponce, Norrato d1865 *BioIn 17*
Ponce, Rene Emilio *DcCPCAm, WhoWor 93*
Ponce, S. Daniel 1948- *St&PR 93*
Ponce, Theta Celeste 1947- *WhoWor 93*
Ponce De Leon, David A. 1950- *WhoAsAP 91*
Ponce de Leon, Juan 1474?-1521 *Expl 93 [port]*
Ponce de Leon, Michael 1922- *HispAmA, WhoAm 92*
Ponce-Montoya, Juanita 1949- *DcLB 122 [port]*
Poncet, Jean Francois- 1928- *BioIn 17*
Ponchak, Frank George 1934- *St&PR 93*
Ponchard, Antoine 1758-1827 *OxDcOp*
Ponchard, Charles Marie Auguste 1824-1891 *OxDcOp*
Ponchard, Louis Antoine Eleonore 1787-1866 *OxDcOp*
Ponchard, Marie Sophie Carrault- 1792-1873 *OxDcOp*
Ponchel, Pierre 1934- *WhoScE 91-2*
Ponchet, Jacques 1924- *WhoScE 91-2*
Ponchick, Rosanne Susan 1944- *WhoE 93*
Ponchielli, Amilcare 1834-1886 *Baker 92, IntDcOp [port], OxDcOp*
Pond, Albert Edward
See Pond, Sylvanus Billings 1792-1871 *Baker 92*
Pond, Byron O. 1936- *WhoAm 92*
Pond, Byron Oliver, Jr. 1936- *St&PR 93*
Pond, Daniel James 1949- *WhoAm 92*
Pond, Donald H., Jr. 1943- *WhoIns 93*
Pond, Donald Herbert, Jr. 1943- *St&PR 93*
Pond, Floyd H. 1918- *St&PR 93*
Pond, George Warren
See Pond, Sylvanus Billings 1792-1871 *Baker 92*
Pond, Gloria Dibble 1939- *WhoAmW 93, WhoE 93*
Pond, James B. 1838-1903 *GayN*
Pond, Jeffrey Genin 1947- *St&PR 93*
Pond, Jesse Earl 1917- *WhoSSW 93*
Pond, John F. 1948- *St&PR 93*
Pond, Larry C. *Law&B 92*
Pond, Martin Allen 1912- *WhoAm 92*
Pond, Norman H. 1938- *WhoAm 92*
Pond, Patricia Ann 1948- *WhoAmW 93*
Pond, Patricia Brown 1930- *WhoAm 92*
Pond, Peggy Ann 1951- *WhoE 93*
Pond, Richard L. 1911- *St&PR 93*
Pond, Sylvanus Billings 1792-1871 *Baker 92*
Pond, Thomas Alexander 1924- *WhoAm 92, WhoE 93*
Pond, William A. d1885
See Pond, Sylvanus Billings 1792-1871 *Baker 92*
Pond, William A., Jr. d1884
See Pond, Sylvanus Billings 1792-1871 *Baker 92*
Ponder, Bruce Anthony John *WhoScE 91-1*
Ponder, Catherine 1927- *WhoWor 93*
Ponder, Debra Lynn 1954- *WhoAmW 93*
Ponder, Herman 1928- *WhoAm 92*
Ponder, James Alton 1933- *WhoSSW 93*
Ponder, Kent 1932- *WhoWor 93*

Ponder, Lester McConnico 1912- *WhoAm 92*
Ponder, Thomas C. 1921- *WhoAm 92*
Ponder, Virginia Joyce 1952- *WhoAmW 93*
Ponder, William Milton, III 1946- *WhoSSW 93*
Pondman, Karel Willem 1923- *WhoScE 91-3*
Pondrom, Lee Girard 1933- *WhoAm 92*
Pone, Gundaris 1932- *Baker 92*
Pong, David Bertram Pak-Tang 1939- *WhoE 93*
Ponge, Francis (Jean Gaston Alfred) 1899-1988 *ConAu 40NR*
Pongpanit, Montree *WhoAsAP 91*
Pongpudpunth, Mayuree 1949- *WhoWor 93*
Pongracz, Helen Elaine 1932- *WhoAmW 93*
Pongracz, Zoltan 1912- *Baker 92*
Pongratz, Olaf Heinz 1937- *WhoWor 93*
Poniatowska, Elena *BioIn 17*
Poniatowska, Elena 1932- *SpAmA*
Poniatowska, Elena 1933- *DcMexL*
Poniatowski, Jozef 1816-1873 *OxDcOp*
Poniatowski, Jozef Antoni 1762-1813 *HarEnMi*
Poniatowski, Jozef Antoni 1763-1813 *PolBiDi*
Poniatowski, Jozef (Michal Xsawery Franciszek Jan) 1816-1873 *Baker 92*
Poniatowski, Kazimierz 1721-1800 *PolBiDi*
Poniatowski, Michael Jerzy 1736-1794 *PolBiDi*
Poniatowski, Michel 1922- *BioIn 17*
Poniatowski, Michel Casimir 1922- *WhoWor 93*
Poniatowski, Stanislaw 1677-1762 *PolBiDi*
Poniatowski, Stanislaw 1884-1945 *IntDcAn*
Poniatowski, Stanislaw Augustus 1732-1798 *PolBiDi*
Ponicsan, Darryl 1939- *WhoWrEP 92*
Poniewaz, Jeff 1946- *WhoWrEP 92*
Poniewaz, Kenneth Anthony 1949- *St&PR 93*
Poniridis, Georges 1892-1982 *Baker 92*
Ponitz, David H. 1931- *WhoAm 92*
Ponitz, John A. *Law&B 92*
Ponitz, John A. 1949- *St&PR 93*
Ponizovskii, Josef Solomonovich 1928- *WhoWor 93*
Ponka, Lawrence John 1949- *WhoWor 93*
Ponnamperuma, Cyril Andrew 1923- *WhoAm 92*
Ponnelle, Jean-Pierre 1932- *IntDcOp*
Ponnelle, Jean-Pierre 1932-1988 *Baker 92, OxDcOp*
Ponner, Johann Nikolaus Anton 1931- *WhoScE 91-3*
Ponosov, Arcady Vladimirovitch 1957- *WhoWor 93*
Ponquinette, Christine Poole 1941- *WhoAmW 93*
Pons, Alfonso Muzzo 1914- *WhoWor 93*
Pons, Bernard 1926- *WhoWor 93*
Pons, Charles 1870-1957 *Baker 92*
Pons, Dominique 1953- *WhoScE 91-2*
Pons, Francisco B. 1917- *St&PR 93*
Pons, Helene 1898-1990 *BioIn 17*
Pons, Jose 1918- *WhoScE 91-3*
Pons, Lily 1898-1976 *Baker 92, IntDcOp [port], OxDcOp*
Pons, Louis *BioIn 17*
Pons, Ted *ScF&FL 92*
Ponse, Luctor 1914- *Baker 92*
Ponselle, Carmela 1888-1977 *OxDcOp*
Ponselle, Carmela 1892-1977 *Baker 92*
Ponselle, Rosa 1897-1981 *IntDcOp [port], OxDcOp*
Ponselle, Rosa (Melba) 1897-1981 *Baker 92*
Ponseti, Ignacio Vives 1914- *WhoAm 92*
Ponsford, Bill 1900-1991 *AnObit 1991*
Pons Irazazabal, D. Felix 1942- *WhoWor 93*
Pons-Nunez, Victor Manuel 1935- *WhoAm 92, WhoSSW 93*
Ponsor, Kenneth C. 1936- *St&PR 93*
Pons Subicki, Jakub Piotr 1949- *WhoWor 93*
Ponstingl, Herwig 1939- *WhoScE 91-3*
Pont, Denise du *ScF&FL 92*
Pont, Diane du *ScF&FL 92*
Pont, John *BioIn 17*
Pont, John 1927- *WhoAm 92*
Pontarelli, Thomas *Law&B 92*
Pontarelli, Thomas 1949- *St&PR 93, WhoIns 93*
Pontbriand, Michael 1954- *St&PR 93*
Ponte, Charles Dennis 1953- *WhoSSW 93, WhoWor 93*
Ponte, Joseph Gonsalves, Jr. 1925- *WhoWrEP 92*
Ponte, Leonard Perry 1933- *St&PR 93*
Ponte, Richard 1934- *St&PR 93*
Ponte, Robert W. 1944-1991 *BioIn 17*
Ponte-Castaneda, Pedro 1961- *WhoE 93*
Pontecorvo, Gillo 1919- *MiSFD 9*
Pontecorvo, Giulio 1923- *WhoE 93*
Pontecoulant, Louis-Adolphe le Doulcet, Marquis de 1794-1882 *Baker 92*
Pontefract, Robert *St&PR 93*
Pontell, Irwin 1925- *St&PR 93*
Ponten, Jan A.B. 1926- *WhoScE 91-4*
Ponter, Alan Robert Sage *WhoScE 91-1*
Ponteri, Joseph R. 1943- *St&PR 93*
Pontes, Elicio Bezerra 1941- *WhoWor 93*
Ponti, Carlo 1913- *WhoWor 93*
Ponti, Michael 1937- *Baker 92, BioIn 17*
Pontiac c. 1720-1769 *HarEnMi*
Ponticello, Matthew 1948- *WhoWrEP 92*
Ponticello, Teresita Labastida *Law&B 92*
Pontier, Jacques F. 1938- *WhoScE 91-2*
Pontifell, Luke Ives *BioIn 17*
Pontiflet, Addie Roberson 1943- *WhoAmW 93*
Pontikes, Kenneth Nicholas 1940- *St&P93*
Pontes, Elicio Bezerra 1941- *WhoWor 93*
Ponti, Carlo 1913- *WhoWor 93*
Ponti, Michael 1937- *Baker 92, BioIn 17*
Pontiac c. 1720-1769 *HarEnMi*
Ponticello, Matthew 1948- *WhoWrEP 92*
Ponticello, Teresita Labastida *Law&B 92*
Pontier, Jacques F. 1938- *WhoScE 91-2*
Pontifell, Luke Ives *BioIn 17*
Pontiflet, Addie Roberson 1943- *WhoAmW 93*
Pontikes, Kenneth Nicholas 1940- *St&PR 93, WhoAm 92*
Pontious, Sharon Lynn 1946- *WhoAmW 93*
Pontiroli, Antonio Ettore 1947- *WhoWor 93*
Pontius, Gavius fl. 321BC-316BC *HarEnMi*
Pontius, Geraldine C. *BioIn 17*
Pontius, John Samuels 1945- *WhoE 93*
Pontius, Keith Don 1933- *St&PR 93*
Pont-Lezica, Rafael Fernando 1940- *WhoWor 93*
Pontnica, Joseph 1929- *St&PR 93*
Pontoglio, Cipriano 1831-1892 *Baker 92*
Ponton, Jack Wylie *WhoScE 91-1*
Ponton, Mark *WhoAm 92*
Ponton, Richard Edward 1937- *WhoAm 92*
Ponton, William Nigel 1943- *WhoWor 93*
Pontonnier, Georges *WhoScE 91-2*
Pontoppidan, Myanna 1959- *WhoE 93*
Pontow, Thomas M. 1949- *St&PR 93*
Pontrella, James 1956- *St&PR 93*
Pontriand, Michel 1954- *St&PR 93*
Ponturo, Anthony T. 1952- *St&PR 93*
Ponty, Jean-Luc 1942- *Baker 92, BioIn 17, ConMus 8 [port], WhoAm 92*
Pontz, Curtis Michael *Law&B 92*
Ponya, Jozsef *WhoScE 91-4*
Ponz, Francisco 1919- *WhoScE 91-3*
Ponzi, Charles *BioIn 17*
Ponzi, Marylou Bernadette 1950- *WhoAmW 93*
Ponzi, Maurizio 1939- *MiSFD 9*
Ponziani, Felice dc. 1826 *OxDcOp*
Ponzillo, Carmela 1892-1977 *Baker 92*
Ponzillo, Marie *BioIn 17*
Ponzillo, Rosa (Melba) 1897-1981 *Baker 92*
Ponzo, Santo Joseph 1948- *St&PR 93*
Pooch, Udo Walter 1943- *WhoSSW 93*
Poock, Ronald Bernard 1946- *St&PR 93*
Poojary, Janardhan 1937- *WhoAsAP 91*
Pook, Leslie Philip 1935- *WhoWor 93*
Pooka, I.M. *WhoWrEP 92*
Pool, David de Sola 1885-1970 *JeAmHC*
Pool, Douglas Vernon 1945- *St&PR 93, WhoAm 92*
Pool, Eugene K. *Law&B 92*
Pool, James Lewis 1946- *WhoSSW 93*
Pool, James William 1957- *WhoSSW 93*
Pool, Jan 1931- *WhoScE 91-3*
Pool, Jerome Marvin 1935- *St&PR 93*
Pool, Lea *MiSFD 9*
Pool, Mary Jane *WhoAm 92, WhoAmW 93, WhoWor 93*
Pool, Norman D. 1942- *St&PR 93*
Pool, Patricia Stewart 1946- *WhoAm 92, WhoAmW 93*
Pool, Philip Bemis, Jr. 1954- *WhoAm 92, WhoE 93*
Pool, Robert Allen *Law&B 92*
Pool, Timothy Kevin 1954- *WhoSSW 93*
Pool, William Robert 1937- *WhoE 93*
Poole, A.T. 1942- *St&PR 93*
Poole, Albert Mitchell, Jr. 1947- *WhoAm 92*
Poole, Anita Joyce 1950- *WhoSSW 93*
Poole, Anthony *Law&B 92*
Poole, Barney George 1923- *BiDAMSp 1989*
Poole, Carolyn Ann 1931- *WhoWrEP 92*
Poole, Cecil F. *WhoAm 92*
Poole, Daniel L. *Law&B 92*
Poole, David Armstrong 1921- *St&PR 93*
Poole, David B.R. 1933- *WhoScE 91-3*
Poole, Deborah Louise 1958- *WhoAmW 93*
Poole, Jay Martin 1934- *WhoAm 92, WhoWrEP 92*
Poole, John Jordan 1906- *WhoAm 92*
Poole, John Swanson 1946- *St&PR 93*
Poole, Jon Michael 1958- *WhoSSW 93*
Poole, Jonathan Gregory *Law&B 92*
Poole, Josephine 1933- *ScF&FL 92*
Poole, Kathleen Zada 1953- *WhoWrEP 92*
Poole, Laura Jean 1958- *WhoSSW 93*
Poole, Leslie Ann 1964- *WhoWor 93*
Poole, Madeline *AmWomPl*
Poole, Mary Beth Gaffney 1946- *WhoSSW 93*
Poole, Mary Elizabeth 1914- *BioIn 17*
Poole, Michael John Findlay *WhoScE 91-1*
Poole, Pamela 1952- *WhoAmW 93*
Poole, Patricia Mary 1965- *WhoAmW 93*
Poole, Richard William 1927- *WhoAm 92, WhoSSW 93*
Poole, Robert Sumner, III 1949- *WhoSSW 93*
Poole, Roger *BioIn 17*
Poole, Shawn W. 1959- *St&PR 93*
Poole, Thomas Marion 1961- *WhoSSW 93*
Poole, W. Kenneth 1939- *St&PR 93*
Poole, William 1937- *WhoAm 92*
Pooler, Ann *Law&B 92*
Poolet, Michelle Ann 1948- *WhoAmW 93*
Poole-Wilson, P. *WhoScE 91-1*
Poole-Wilson, Philip *WhoScE 91-1*
Pooley, Beverley John 1934- *WhoAm 92*
Pooley, Derek *WhoScE 91-1*
Pooley, Frederick David *WhoScE 91-1*
Pooley, James H.A. *St&PR 93*
Pooley, Lorraine Elizabeth 1953- *WhoWrEP 92*
Poolman, John C. *Law&B 92*
Poon, Chung-Kwong 1940- *WhoAsAP 91*
Poon, Linda *Law&B 92*
Poon, Peter Wing-Cheung 1934- *WhoAsAP 91*
Poon Chi-Fai 1951- *WhoAsAP 91*
Poonja, Mohamed 1948- *WhoEmL 93, WhoWor 93*
Poor, Alfred Easton 1951- *WhoE 93*
Poor, Anne 1918- *WhoAm 92*
Poor, Arthur G. d1990 *BioIn 17*
Poor, Charles N. 1947- *St&PR 93*
Poor, Charles R. 1935- *WhoSSW 93*
Poor, Harold Vincent 1951- *WhoAm 92*
Poor, James Seward 1937- *St&PR 93*
Poor, James T. 1932- *WhoIns 93*
Poor, Janet Meakin 1929- *WhoAmW 93*
Poor, Peter Varnum 1926- *WhoAm 92*
Poor, Thomas M. 1943- *St&PR 93*
Poor, William Russell 1928- *WhoAm 92*
Poorbaugh, Catherine K. 1935- *St&PR 93*
Poore, Benjamin Perley 1820-1887 *JrnUS*
Poore, Christine Hammarth *WhoAmW 93*
Poore, Edgar E. 1933- *St&PR 93*
Poore, Gregory R. 1945- *St&PR 93*
Poore, Gregory Robert *Law&B 92*
Poore, James Albert, III 1943- *WhoWor 93*
Poore, Nancye P. *St&PR 93*
Poore, Ralph Ezra, Jr. 1951- *WhoSSW 93*
Poore, Thomas William 1951- *WhoSSW 93*
Poorman, Omer Wayne 1949- *WhoSSW 93*
Poorman, Paul Arthur 1930- *WhoAm 92*
Poorman, Paul Arthur 1930-1992 *ConAu 136*
Poorman, Robert Lewis 1926- *WhoAm 92*
Poortvliet, Marien *ScF&FL 92*
Poortvliet, Rien *BioIn 17*
Poortvliet, Rien 1932- *ConAu 136*
Poortvliet, Rien 1933?- *ScF&FL 92*
Poortvliet, William G. 1931- *WhoIns 93*
Poortvliet, William George 1931- *St&PR 93, WhoAm 92*
Poos, Arthur 1931- *WhoScE 91-2*
Poos, George Ireland 1923- *WhoAm 92*
Poos, Jacques Francois 1935- *WhoWor 93*
Poot, Albert 1934- *WhoScE 91-2*
Poot, Marcel 1901-1988 *Baker 92*
Poots, Graham *WhoScE 91-1*
Pop, Emil 1939- *WhoWor 93*
Pop, Iggy 1947- *BioIn 17, WhoAm 92*
Pop, Teofil Faust Dumitru 1930- *WhoWor 93*
Popa, Octavian 1930- *WhoScE 91-4*
Popa, Petru 1938- *WhoWor 93*
Popa, Vasko 1922-1991 *BioIn 17*
Popaduik, Roman 1950- *WhoAm 92*
Popcorn, Faith *BioIn 17*
Pope d1690 *HarEnMi*
Pope, Albert Augustus 1944- *WhoE 93*
Pope, Alexander 1688-1744 *BioIn 17, MagSWL [port], WorLitC [port]*
Pope, Alexander H. 1929- *WhoAm 92*
Pope, Allan *Law&B 92*
Pope, Andrew Jackson, Jr. 1913- *WhoAm 92*
Pope, Anne Elizabeth 1942- *WhoE 93*
Pope, Arlette Farrar 1958- *WhoAmW 93*
Pope, Barbara Spyridon 1951- *WhoAm 92, WhoAmW 93*
Pope, Bill Jordan 1922- *WhoAm 92*
Pope, Britt H. 1948- *St&PR 93*
Pope, C. Larry 1954- *St&PR 93*
Pope, Cynthia A. *Law&B 92*
Pope, David Bruce *Law&B 92*
Pope, David E. 1920- *WhoAm 92*
Pope, David W. 1942- *St&PR 93*
Pope, Deborah *ConAu 136*
Pope, Douglas V. *Law&B 92*
Pope, Douglas V. 1945- *St&PR 93*
Pope, Eddie Michael 1950- *St&PR 93*
Pope, Edward John Andrew 1962- *WhoWor 93*
Pope, Elizabeth Marie 1917- *DcAmChF 1960, ScF&FL 92*
Pope, Francis Michael *WhoScE 91-1*
Pope, Frank H., Jr. *Law&B 92*
Pope, Gary W. *St&PR 93*
Pope, Generoso, Jr. *BioIn 17*
Pope, Guy B. 1936- *St&PR 93*
Pope, Harrison Graham, Jr. 1947- *WhoAm 92, WhoWor 93*
Pope, Harry Melville 1861-1950 *BioIn 17*
Pope, Howard E. *WhoIns 93*
Pope, Ingrid Bloomquist 1918- *WhoAmW 93, WhoE 93*
Pope, James R. *Law&B 92*
Pope, Jane Laird Miller 1942- *WhoAmW 93*
Pope, Jean 1942- *WhoSSW 93*
Pope, Jodie *BioIn 17*
Pope, John 1822-1892 *BioIn 17, HarEnMi*
Pope, John A. 1933- *St&PR 93*
Pope, John Charles 1949- *St&PR 93*
Pope, John E. *Law&B 92*
Pope, John Edwin, III 1928- *WhoAm 92*
Pope, John M. 1948- *WhoSSW 93*
Pope, John Russell 1874-1937 *BioIn 17*
Pope, Kerig Rodgers 1935- *WhoAm 92*
Pope, Lawrence S. *Law&B 92*
Pope, Leavitt Joseph 1924- *WhoAm 92*
Pope, Marjorie Jean 1947- *WhoSSW 93*
Pope, Mark A. *Law&B 92*
Pope, Mark C., III 1924- *St&PR 93, WhoSSW 93*
Pope, Martha S. *CngDr 91*
Pope, Marvin Hoyle 1916- *WhoAm 92, WhoE 93, WhoWor 93*
Pope, Michael 1924- *WhoAm 92*
Pope, Patricia *Law&B 92*
Pope, Peter T. 1934- *WhoAm 92*
Pope, Peter Talbot, Sr. 1934- *St&PR 93*
Pope, Ralph Kennedy *Law&B 92*
Pope, Raymond K. 1927- *St&PR 93*
Pope, Richard Downing, Jr. 1930- *St&PR 93*
Pope, Richard W. 1933- *WhoIns 93*
Pope, Robert Glynn 1935- *WhoAm 92*
Pope, Robert J. *Law&B 92*
Pope, Roslyn Elizabeth 1938- *WhoAmW 93*
Pope, Saxton Temple 1875-1926 *IntDcAn*
Pope, Stephen Bailey 1949- *WhoAm 92*
Pope, Steven Francois 1948- *WhoAm 92*
Pope, Theodore C., Jr. 1932- *St&PR 93*
Pope, Thomas Edward 1947- *WhoSSW 93*
Pope, Thomas Harrington, Jr. 1913- *WhoAm 92*
Pope, Tony L. *St&PR 93*
Pope, Vars Gage 1958- *WhoSSW 93*
Pope, William H. 1936- *St&PR 93*
Pope, William Ray 1935- *St&PR 93*
Pope, William T. *Law&B 92*
Popeck, Raymond John 1951- *WhoAm 92*
Popecki, Joseph Thomas 1924- *WhoE 93*
Pope-Hennessy, John *BioIn 17*
Pope-Hennessy, John Wyndham 1913- *WhoAm 92, WhoWor 93*
Popehn, Arthur John 1919- *St&PR 93*
Pope John, XXIII *DcCPCAm*
Pope John Paul, II *DcCPCAm*
Popel, Aleksander S. 1945- *WhoAm 92*
Popenoe, Hugh Llywelyn 1929- *WhoSSW 93*
Popenoe, John 1929- *WhoAm 92, WhoSSW 93*
Pope Paul, VI *DcCPCAm*
Popescu, C. Paul 1936- *WhoScE 91-2*
Popescu, Dumitru Radu 1935- *BioIn 17*
Popescu, Oreste 1913- *WhoWor 93*
Popescu, Petru *MiSFD 9*
Popescu, Petru 1929- *ScF&FL 92*
Popescu, Valerian 1912- *WhoWor 93*
Popescu, Vasile 1926- *WhoScE 91-4*
Popescu-Zeletin, Radu 1947- *WhoScE 91-3*
Popham, Arthur Cobb, Jr. 1915- *WhoAm 92*
Popham, Charles Ray 1951- *WhoSSW 93*
Popham, Lewis Charles, III 1928- *WhoAm 92*
Popham, Thomas Wayne 1939- *WhoSSW 93*
Popham, Wayne Gordon 1929- *WhoAm 92*
Popiela, Tadeusz 1933- *WhoScE 91-4*
Popieluszko, Jerzy 1947-1984 *PolBiDi*
Popivanov, Peter Radoev 1946- *WhoWor 93*

Popjak, George Joseph 1914- *WhoAm 92*
Popkave, Murray Warren 1941- *WhoE 93*
Popkes, Steven 1952- *ScF&FL 92*
Popkin, Joel 1932- *WhoE 93*
Popkin, Joyce Gail 1947- *WhoAmW 93, WhoE 93*
Popkin, Mark Anthony 1929- *WhoSSW 93*
Popkin, Michael Harlan 1950- *WhoSSW 93*
Popkin, Roy Sandor 1921- *WhoAm 92, WhoWrEP 92*
Popkin, Samuel L. *BioIn 17*
Poplack, Michael James *Law&B 92*
Poplar, Jacquelyn Ann 1964- *WhoAmW 93*
Poplawski, Paul Edwin 1949- *WhoE 93*
Pople, John Anthony 1925- *BioIn 17, WhoAm 92*
Poplin, Cecile M. 1938- *WhoScE 91-2*
Poplinger, James J. *Law&B 92*
Poploff, Michelle *BioIn 17*
Poploff, Michelle Jo 1956- *WhoAmW 93*
Popoff, Frank Peter 1935- *St&PR 93, WhoAm 92*
Popofsky, Melvin Laurence 1936- *WhoAm 92*
Popolizio, Eliseo 1938- *WhoWor 93*
Popolizio, Emanuel P. d1992 *NewYTBS 92 [port]*
Popov, Alexander 1927- *Baker 92*
Popov, Dimiter Petrov 1932- *WhoUN 92*
Popov, Dusko 1912-1981 *BioIn 17*
Popov, Egor Paul 1913- *WhoAm 92*
Popov, Evgueny Konstantinov *WhoWor 93*
Popov, Gavriil *BioIn 17*
Popov, Gavriil 1904-1972 *Baker 92*
Popov, George 1950- *St&PR 93*
Popov, Ivan Nikolov 1907- *WhoScE 91-4*
Popov, Kantcho Georgoev 1933- *WhoWor 93*
Popov, N.I. 1935- *WhoScE 91-4*
Popov, Peter *Law&B 92*
Popov, Peter N. 1951- *St&PR 93*
Popov, V. *WhoScE 91-4*
Popova, Alla Dmitriyevna 1952- *WhoWor 93*
Popova, Liubov 1889-1924 *BioIn 17*
Popova, Nina 1922- *WhoAm 92*
Popovic, Koca d1992 *NewYTBS 92*
Popovic, Kresimir 1940- *WhoScE 91-4*
Popovic, Stanko 1938- *WhoScE 91-4*
Popovich, Grigori *BioIn 17*
Popovich, Helen Houser 1935- *WhoAm 92, WhoAmW 93*
Popovich, Lisa A. *Law&B 92*
Popovich, Peter Stephen 1920- *WhoAm 92*
Popovici, Adrian 1942- *WhoAm 92*
Popovici, Doru 1932- *Baker 92*
Popowski, Linda Chowaniec 1952- *WhoAmW 93*
Popp, Alice W. 1948- *St&PR 93*
Popp, Anthony C. 1927- *St&PR 93*
Popp, Betty 1935- *St&PR 93*
Popp, Charlotte Louise 1946- *WhoAmW 93, WhoE 93, WhoWor 93*
Popp, Dorothy May 1930- *WhoAmW 93*
Popp, Hanns-Peter 1936- *WhoScE 91-3*
Popp, James Alan 1945- *WhoAm 92*
Popp, John M. 1948- *St&PR 93*
Popp, Lucia 1939- *Baker 92, IntDcOp, OxDcOp*
Popp, Nathaniel William George 1940- *WhoAm 92*
Popp, Pamela Lynn 1962- *WhoAmW 93*
Popp, Ralph William 1934- *St&PR 93*
Popp, Robin Renee 1965- *WhoE 93*
Popp, Rosanna Katherine 1955- *WhoAmW 93*
Poppa, Ryal R. 1933- *St&PR 93*
Poppa, Ryal Robert 1933- *WhoAm 92*
Poppe, Donna 1953- *WhoAmW 93*
Poppe, Fred Christoph 1923- *WhoAm 92*
Poppe, G.L. *Law&B 92*
Poppe, Gerald Wayne 1952- *WhoSSW 93*
Poppe, Magda 1931- *WhoScE 91-4*
Poppe, Rick 1947- *St&PR 93*
Poppe, Wassily 1918- *WhoAm 92*
Poppe, William G., Jr. 1942- *St&PR 93*
Poppel, Hans 1942- *SmATA 71 [port]*
Poppel, Harvey Lee 1937- *WhoAm 92*
Poppel, Seth R. 1944- *St&PR 93*
Poppel, Seth Raphael 1944- *WhoAm 92, WhoE 93, WhoWor 93*
Poppelbaum, Wolfgang Johann 1924- *WhoAm 92*
Poppele, June Patricia 1927- *St&PR 93*
Poppen, Robert G. 1934- *St&PR 93*
Poppensiek, George Charles 1918- *WhoAm 92*
Popper, Arthur N. 1943- *WhoAm 92*
Popper, Charlotte 1898- *BioIn 17*
Popper, David 1843-1913 *Baker 92*
Popper, Karl Raimund 1902- *BioIn 17*
Popper, Peter 1933- *WhoScE 91-4*
Popper, Richard H. 1948- *St&PR 93*
Popper, Robert 1932- *WhoAm 92*
Popper, Robert David 1927- *WhoE 93*
Popper, Walter Lincoln 1920- *St&PR 93*
Poppers, Paul Jules 1929- *WhoAm 92, WhoE 93*
Poppick, Harry M. 1917-1990 *BioIn 17*
Poppino, Allen G. 1925- *St&PR 93*
Popple, John A. 1945- *St&PR 93*
Poppler, Doris Swords 1924- *WhoAm 92, WhoAmW 93*
Poprawski, Tadeusz Jerzy 1947- *WhoE 93*
Poprick, Mary Ann 1939- *WhoAmW 93, WhoWor 93*
Pops, Richard F. *St&PR 93*
Populaire, Jacques G. A. 1952- *WhoWor 93*
Populer, C. *WhoScE 91-2*
Populus, Jacques 1953- *WhoScE 91-2*
Popwell, Vicki Evers 1956- *WhoSSW 93*
Pora, Paul Schmidt 1946- *WhoAsAP 91*
Porach, Richard A. *Law&B 92*
Porada, Edith 1912- *WhoAm 92*
Poradowski, Stefan (Boleslaw) 1902-1967 *Baker 92, PolBiDi*
Porat, Itzchak *WhoScE 91-1*
Porath, Ellen *ScF&FL 92*
Porath, Peter Joseph 1931- *St&PR 93*
Porcari, Damian *Law&B 92*
Porcaro, Jeffrey T. d1992 *NewYTBS 92*
Porcase, Frederic Frank, Jr. 1950- *WhoSSW 93*
Porceddu, Enrico 1938- *WhoScE 91-3*
Porcelijn, David 1947- *Baker 92*
Porcella, Arthur David 1918- *WhoSSW 93*
Porcelli, James G. *Law&B 92*
Porcelli, Joseph V. 1935- *St&PR 93*
Porcello, Joseph Edward 1952- *St&PR 93*
Porcello, Leonard Joseph 1934- *WhoAm 92*
Porczynska, Janina 1928- *PolBiDi*
Porczynski, Zbigniew 1919- *PolBiDi*
Pordan, George W. *Law&B 92*
Pordon, Susan Ann 1955- *WhoAmW 93*
Pordy, Leon 1919- *St&PR 93, WhoAm 92*
Poreba, Bohdan 1934- *DrEEuF*
Porebski, Wieslaw M. 1936- *WhoScE 91-4*
Porell, Richard D. 1933- *WhoIns 93*
Porembski, Priscilla E. *Law&B 92*
Porento, Gerald John *Law&B 92*
Porfeli, Joseph J. *BioIn 17*
Porfetye, Andreas 1927- *Baker 92*
Porfido, Stanley M. 1936- *St&PR 93*
Porges, Ellen R. *Law&B 92*
Porges, Irwin 1909- *ScF&FL 92*
Porges, K. Shelly *BioIn 17*
Porges, Walter Rudolf 1931- *WhoAm 92*
Pories, Walter Julius 1930- *WhoAm 92*
Porile, Norbert Thomas 1932- *WhoAm 92*
Poris, Marilyn Abby 1931- *WhoAmW 93*
Poriss, Emily Jane *Law&B 92*
Porkert, Manfred Bruno 1933- *WhoWor 93*
Porlingis, I.C. 1925- *WhoScE 91-3*
Porner, Hans J. W. A. 1942- *WhoWor 93*
Porosoff, Harold 1946- *St&PR 93, WhoAm 92*
Porowski, S. *WhoScE 91-4*
Porphyrios of Gaza c. 347-420 *OxDcByz*
Porphyrius Optatianus fl. 4th cent.- *OxDcByz*
Porphyry 233-c. 306 *OxDcByz*
Porpora, Nicola 1686-1768 *OxDcOp*
Porpora, Nicola (Antonio) 1686-1768 *Baker 92, IntDcOp*
Porpora, Peter 1934- *St&PR 93*
Porporati, Guido 1932- *St&PR 93*
Porraz, Mauricio Jimenez Labora 1938- *WhoWor 93*
Porreca, Raymond J., Jr. *Law&B 92*
Porrello, Joy Marie 1937- *WhoAmW 93*
Porrett, James D. 1953- *St&PR 93*
Porretta, Antonino 1927- *WhoScE 91-3*
Porretta, Emanuele 1942- *St&PR 93*
Porretta, Emanuele Peter 1942- *WhoAm 92*
Porreye, W. 1928- *WhoScE 91-2*
Porrino, Ennio 1910-1959 *Baker 92*
Porrino, Peter R. 1956- *WhoIns 93*
Porritt, Jonathon 1950- *BioIn 17*
Porro, Francesco Alessandro 1951- *WhoWor 93*
Porro, James E. *Law&B 92*
Porro, Massimo Riccardo 1950- *WhoWor 93*
Porro, Pierre-Jean 1750-1831 *Baker 92*
Porsche, Ferdinand Alexander *BioIn 17*
Porschen, Walter 1923- *WhoScE 91-3*
Porshnev, Georgii Ivanovich 1887-1937 *BioIn 17*
Porsile, Giuseppe 1680-1750 *Baker 92, OxDcOp*
Port, Arthur Tyler 1916- *WhoSSW 93*
Port, David H. *St&PR 93*
Port, Larry Neil *Law&B 92*
Port, Louise A. M. *WhoAmW 93, WhoSSW 93, WhoWor 93*
Port, Sidney Charles 1935- *WhoAm 92*
Port, Sidney Lawrence 1911- *St&PR 93*
Port, William S. *Law&B 92*
Porta, Antonio 1935-1989 *DcLB 128 [port]*
Porta, Carlo Cesare 1930- *WhoWor 93*
Porta, Costanzo 1528?-1601 *Baker 92*
Porta, Jaime 1944- *WhoScE 91-3*
Porta, John E. 1931- *WhoAm 92*
Porta, Piero *WhoScE 91-3*
Portal, Charles Frederick Algernon 1893-1971 *DcTwHis*
Portal, Ellis *WhoCanL 92*
Portal, Gilbert Marcel Adrien 1930- *WhoAm 92*
Portal, Jean-Claude 1941- *WhoWor 93*
Portal, Magda 1901-1989 *SpAmA*
Portal, Magda 1903-1989 *BioIn 17*
Portal, Marcel *WhoCanL 92*
Portalatin, Aida Cartagena 1918- *SpAmA*
Portale, Carl *BioIn 17*
Porte, Jean 1916- *WhoWor 93*
Porte, Joel Miles 1933- *WhoAm 92*
Portela, Antonio Gouvea 1918- *WhoWor 93*
Portela, Denis Charles 1952- *WhoWor 93*
Portela, Mary Green 1932- *WhoSSW 93, WhoWor 93*
Portele, Gerhard Ludwig 1933- *WhoWor 93*
Portell, Frank Raymond 1951- *WhoSSW 93*
Portella, Eduardo 1932- *WhoUN 92*
Portell Vila, Herminio 1901-1992 *BioIn 17*
Porten, Henny 1888-1960 *IntDcF 2-3*
Porteous, Andrew *WhoScE 91-1*
Porteous, Charles Robert, Jr. 1944- *WhoE 93*
Porteous, L. Robert, Jr. 1923- *St&PR 93*
Porteous, Thomas Clark 1910- *WhoSSW 93*
Porteous, Timothy 1933- *WhoAm 92*
Porter, A.P. 1945- *BioIn 17*
Porter, A(nthony) P(eyton) 1945- *ConAu 136*
Porter, Agnes *AmWomPl*
Porter, Allen Wayne 1936- *WhoSSW 93*
Porter, Andrew 1946- *ScF&FL 92*
Porter, Andrew (Brian) 1928- *Baker 92, WhoWor 93, WhoWrEP 92*
Porter, Anna Maria 1780-1832 *DcLB 116 [port]*
Porter, Arthur 1910- *WhoAm 92*
Porter, Arthur Kenneth *WhoScE 91-1*
Porter, Arthur Reno 1918- *WhoAm 92*
Porter, Audrey *WhoScE 91-1*
Porter, Barry *ScF&FL 92*
Porter, Barry M. 1953- *WhoE 93*
Porter, Barry Schuyler 1937- *St&PR 93, WhoAm 92*
Porter, Bern 1911- *WhoWrEP 92*
Porter, Bernard Harden 1911- *WhoE 93*
Porter, Bernard L. *St&PR 93*
Porter, Bertha Currier *AmWomPl*
Porter, Beverly Anne 1948- *WhoAmW 93*
Porter, Blaine Robert Milton 1922- *WhoAm 92*
Porter, Brian *WhoScE 91-1*
Porter, Bruce Douglas 1952- *WhoAm 92*
Porter, Burton Frederick 1936- *WhoAm 92, WhoE 93*
Porter, Charles Allan 1932- *WhoAm 92*
Porter, Charles W. 1930- *St&PR 93*
Porter, Christopher H. *St&PR 93*
Porter, Clyde C. 1938- *St&PR 93*
Porter, Cole 1891-1964 *Baker 92, BioIn 17, OxDcOp*
Porter, Colin Andrew 1956- *WhoWor 93*
Porter, Connie 1960- *ConLC 70 [port]*
Porter, Connie Rose *BioIn 17*
Porter, Curtis Hunter 1942- *WhoSSW 93*
Porter, Dale L. 1925- *St&PR 93*
Porter, Daniel Morris 1936- *WhoSSW 93*
Porter, Daniel Reed, III 1930- *WhoAm 92*
Porter, Darwin Fred 1937- *WhoAm 92, WhoE 93, WhoWor 93, WhoWrEP 92*
Porter, David 1780-1843 *HarEnMi*
Porter, David 1941- *SoulM*
Porter, David Dixon 1813-1891 *HarEnMi*
Porter, David Gray 1953- *WhoEmL 93*
Porter, David Hugh 1935- *WhoAm 92*
Porter, David L. 1938- *St&PR 93*
Porter, David Lindsay *Law&B 92*
Porter, David Lindsey 1941- *WhoAm 92*
Porter, David Rittenhouse 1788-1867 *BioIn 17*
Porter, David W. *Law&B 92*
Porter, Dean Allen 1939- *WhoAm 92*
Porter, Dennis Dudley 1933- *WhoAm 92*
Porter, Donald *ScF&FL 92*
Porter, Donald 1939- *BioIn 17, WhoAm 92, WhoWrEP 92*
Porter, Douglas K. *Law&B 92*
Porter, Dudley, Jr. 1915- *St&PR 93, WhoAm 92*
Porter, Dwight Johnson 1916- *WhoAm 92*
Porter, Edward A. *Law&B 92*
Porter, Edwin David 1912- *WhoE 93*
Porter, Edwin S. 1869?-1941 *BioIn 17, MiSFD 9N*
Porter, Eleanor Hodgman 1868-1920 *AmWomPl*
Porter, Eliot 1901-1990 *BioIn 17*
Porter, Elisabeth Scott 1942- *WhoAm 92, WhoAmW 93*
Porter, Elsa Allgood 1928- *WhoAm 92*
Porter, Eric Richard 1928- *WhoWor 93*
Porter, Eric William 1944- *St&PR 93*
Porter, Fitz-John 1822-1901 *HarEnMi*
Porter, Ford Davis, Jr. 1914- *WhoWor 93*
Porter, Francis A. 1920- *ScF&FL 92*
Porter, Frederick M. 1926- *St&PR 93*
Porter, Gary Lynn 1959- *WhoSSW 93*
Porter, Gene Stratton- 1863-1924 *BioIn 17*
Porter, George *WhoScE 91-1*
Porter, George 1920- *WhoAm 92, WhoWor 93*
Porter, George E. 1931- *St&PR 93*
Porter, George Homer, III 1933- *WhoSSW 93*
Porter, Gerald Joseph 1937- *WhoAm 92*
Porter, Glenn 1944- *WhoAm 92, WhoE 93*
Porter, Harlan David *WhoWrEP 92*
Porter, Hayden Samuel 1945- *WhoSSW 93*
Porter, Helen Fogwill *WhoCanL 92*
Porter, Helen Viney 1935- *WhoAm 92*
Porter, Henry Homes, Jr. *WhoAm 92*
Porter, Horace 1837-1921 *BioIn 17*
Porter, Howard Leonard, III 1945- *WhoSSW 93*
Porter, Ian Herbert 1929- *WhoE 93*
Porter, Irwin Freeman 1918- *St&PR 93*
Porter, Ivan 1947- *WhoAm 92*
Porter, J. *WhoScE 91-1*
Porter, J. Gregory *Law&B 92*
Porter, J(ene) M(iles) 1937- *WhoWrEP 92*
Porter, J.W. 1933- *BioIn 17*
Porter, J. Winston 1937- *WhoAm 92*
Porter, Jack E. 1934- *St&PR 93*
Porter, Jack Nusan 1944- *WhoAm 92, WhoE 93*
Porter, Jadranka *BioIn 17*
Porter, James *BioIn 17*
Porter, James A. 1905-1970 *BioIn 17*
Porter, James Alexander 1942- *WhoAm 92*
Porter, James Franklin 1935- *WhoSSW 93*
Porter, James H. 1933- *WhoE 93*
Porter, James Kenneth 1934- *WhoWor 93*
Porter, James Morris 1931- *WhoAm 92*
Porter, James R. 1935- *St&PR 93*
Porter, James Robert 1950- *WhoAsAP 91*
Porter, Jane 1776-1850 *DcLB 116 [port]*
Porter, Janet Kay 1945- *WhoWrEP 92*
Porter, Janet Mae 1941- *WhoAmW 93*
Porter, Janice Lee *BioIn 17*
Porter, Jay 1933- *BioIn 17*
Porter, Jeffery Scott 1961- *WhoSSW 93*
Porter, Jeffrey Alan 1955- *WhoSSW 93*
Porter, Jennifer Garner 1959- *WhoE 93*
Porter, Jermain B. 1925- *St&PR 93*
Porter, Jesse *AmWomPl*
Porter, Joan Margaret 1937- *WhoAmW 93*
Porter, Jody E. *Law&B 92*
Porter, Joe Ashby 1942- *ConGAN, WhoWrEP 92*
Porter, John D. 1948- *St&PR 93*
Porter, John Edward 1935- *CngDr 91, WhoAm 92*
Porter, John F., III 1934- *St&PR 93*
Porter, John Finley, Jr. 1927- *WhoAm 92*
Porter, John Francis, III 1934- *WhoAm 92*
Porter, John Hill 1933- *WhoAm 92, WhoE 93*
Porter, John Isaac 1949- *WhoEmL 93*
Porter, John M. *Law&B 92*
Porter, John Robert, Jr. 1935- *WhoAm 92, WhoWor 93*
Porter, John Stephen 1932- *WhoAm 92*
Porter, John W. 1931- *AfrAmBi [port]*
Porter, John Weston 1939- *WhoE 93*
Porter, John William 1926- *St&PR 93*
Porter, John Wilson A. 1931- *WhoAm 92*
Porter, Joseph Daniel *Law&B 92*
Porter, Joyce Klowden 1949- *WhoAmW 93*
Porter, Judith Deborah Revitch 1940- *WhoAm 92, WhoAmW 93*
Porter, Judson L. *St&PR 93*
Porter, Karen *BioIn 17*
Porter, Karen Meyer *Law&B 92*
Porter, Karl Hampton 1939- *WhoAm 92*
Porter, Katherine Anne 1890-1980 *BioIn 17, MagSAmL [port]*
Porter, Katherine Anne 1894-1980 *AmWomWr 92*
Porter, Kendall 1932- *WhoAm 92*
Porter, Kenneth Edwin *WhoScE 91-1*
Porter, Kevin 1950- *BiDAMSp 1989*
Porter, KT 1944- *WhoE 93*
Porter, Lana Garner 1943- *WhoAmW 93*
Porter, Larry Milton 1945- *St&PR 93*
Porter, Laura Spencer *AmWomPl*
Porter, Leah LeEarle 1963- *WhoAmW 93*

Porter, Leon Eugene, Jr. Law&B 92
Porter, Liliana Alicia 1941- WhoAm 92
Porter, Lisa Law&B 92
Porter, Lynn Keith 1929- WhoAm 92
Porter, Marcia Hoebel BioIn 17
Porter, Margaret Evans 1959- WhoWrEP 92
Porter, Mary Coppoletti 1936- WhoAmW 93
Porter, Mary E. Law&B 92
Porter, Mary L. Law&B 92
Porter, Mary Louise Wise Law&B 92
Porter, Michael A. 1949- St&PR 93
Porter, Michael E. 1947- BioIn 17
Porter, Milton 1911- WhoAm 92
Porter, Nancy Carol 1961- WhoAmW 93
Porter, Nora Roxanne 1949- WhoE 93
Porter, Norman Charles 1951- St&PR 93
Porter, Olive AmWomPl
Porter, Philip BioIn 17
Porter, Philip Thomas 1930- WhoAm 92
Porter, Philip Wayland 1928- WhoAm 92
Porter, (William) Quincy 1897-1966 Baker 92
Porter, Ralph Jefferson 1958- WhoSSW 93
Porter, Richard Frank 1943- WhoE 93
Porter, Richard H. Law&B 92
Porter, Richard James 1950- WhoE 93
Porter, Richard Kent 1948- St&PR 93
Porter, Richard Sterling 1929- WhoAm 92
Porter, Richard Worfolk 1959- WhoAm 92
Porter, Robert L. 1941- St&PR 93
Porter, Roberta Ann 1949- WhoAmW 93
Porter, Rodney Wayne 1946- WhoSSW 93
Porter, Roger Blaine 1946- WhoAm 92
Porter, Roger Eldridge 1957- St&PR 93
Porter, Roger John 1942- WhoAm 92
Porter, Roger Stephen 1928- WhoAm 92
Porter, Ronald C. Law&B 92
Porter, Ronald Philip 1944- St&PR 93
Porter, Roy 1923- BioIn 17
Porter, Rufus 1792-1884 BioIn 17
Porter, Russell W. d1949 BioIn 17
Porter, Russell W., Jr. Law&B 92
Porter, S.R. Law&B 92
Porter, Samuel Hamilton 1927- WhoAm 92
Porter, Scott D. 1947- St&PR 93
Porter, Scott Douglas Law&B 92
Porter, Sharon Ann 1953- WhoAmW 93, WhoEmL 93, WhoWor 93
Porter, Stephen Winthrop 1925- WhoAm 92
Porter, Steven Brian 1961- WhoE 93
Porter, Steven J. 1952- St&PR 93
Porter, Stuart Charles 1947- St&PR 93
Porter, Sue ConAu 37NR
Porter, Susan Smith 1954- WhoAmW 93
Porter, Sylvia 1913- WhoWrEP 92
Porter, Sylvia 1913-1991 AnObit 1991, JrnUS
Porter, Sylvia Field 1913-1991 BioIn 17
Porter, Thomas Nelson d1991 BioIn 17
Porter, Timothy L. Law&B 92
Porter, Verna Louise 1941- WhoAmW 93
Porter, W.R. Bruce d1991 BioIn 17
Porter, W. Thomas 1934- St&PR 93
Porter, Walter Arthur 1924- WhoAm 92
Porter, Walter Thomas, Jr. 1934- WhoAm 92
Porter, William 1935- St&PR 93
Porter, William B., III Law&B 92
Porter, William Francis, Jr. Law&B 92
Porter, William Joseph 1924- WhoE 93
Porter, William Larry Law&B 92
Porter, William Lyman 1934- WhoAm 92
Porter, William Moring 1913- St&PR 93
Porter, William Robert 1922- WhoE 93
Porter, William Sydney GayN
Porter, William Sydney 1862-1910 BioIn 17
Porter, William Trotter 1809-1858 JrnUS
Portera, Alan August 1951- WhoE 93
Portera, Steve 1949- St&PR 93
Porterfield, Amanda 1947- ConAu 138
Porterfield, Craig Allen 1955- WhoE 93
Porterfield, Dennis 1936- St&PR 93
Porterfield, Donald Richard 1934- St&PR 93
Porterfield, James Temple Starke 1920- WhoAm 92
Porterfield, Neil Harry 1936- WhoAm 92
Porterfield, William Wendell 1936- WhoAm 92, WhoSSW 93
Porter-O'Grady, Timothy 1947- WhoSSW 93
Portes Gil, Emilio DcCPCAm
Portfolio, Almerindo Gerard 1923- WhoAm 92
Porthouse, J. David 1938- St&PR 93
Portier, Josik 1939- WhoScE 91-2
Portier, Kenneth Michael 1951- WhoSSW 93
Portilla, Anselmo de la 1816-1879 DcMexL
Portillo, Frank 1933- St&PR 93
Portillo, Julio BioIn 17
Portillo, Michael Denzil Xavier 1953- WhoWor 93
Portillo Trambley, Estela 1936- AmWomWr 92, NotHsAW 93
Portin, Petter Erik 1940- WhoScE 91-4
Portis, Alan Mark 1926- WhoAm 92
Portis, Charles BioIn 17
Portis, Charles 1933- MagSAmL [port]
Portis, Charles McColl 1933- WhoAm 92
Portland, Rene BioIn 17
Portlock, Zna Y.D. Law&B 92
Portman, Barbara Lynn Law&B 92
Portman, Glenn Arthur 1949- WhoEmL 93, WhoSSW 93, WhoWor 93
Portman, Jerry A. 1928- St&PR 93
Portman, John Calvin, Jr. 1924- WhoAm 92
Portman, Mark 1952- St&PR 93
Portman, Robert George 1942- St&PR 93
Portman, Susan Newell Law&B 92
Portmann, J.E. 1940- WhoScE 91-1
Portner, Mark A. Law&B 92
Portnoff, Collice Henry 1898- WhoAm 92
Portnoff, Diane Louise 1941- WhoAmW 93
Portnow, Marjorie BioIn 17
Portnoy, Fern C. 1945- WhoAm 92
Portnoy, Howard N. 1946- ScF&FL 92
Portnoy, Libby B. Law&B 92
Portnoy, Martin Law&B 92
Portnoy, Sara S. 1926- WhoAm 92
Portnoy, Steven Albert Law&B 92
Portnoy, William Manos 1930- WhoAm 92
Portogallo, Marcos Antonio (da Fonseca) 1762-1830 Baker 92
Portoghese, Philip Salvatore 1931- WhoAm 92
Portos, Jean-Louis 1931- WhoScE 91-2
Ports, Michael Allan 1948- WhoE 93
Portsmouth, Thomas Edward Law&B 92
Portugal, Marcos Antonio 1762-1830 OxDcOp
Portugal, Marcos Antonio (da Fonseca) 1762-1830 Baker 92
Portugal, Pamela Rainbear WhoWrEP 92
Portugal Ferreira, Martim R. 1935- WhoScE 91-3
Portugalov, Nikolai S. BioIn 17
Portuondo, Bernardo Andres Law&B 92
Portway, Christopher ScF&FL 92
Portwood, John Harding 1928- WhoAm 92
Portwood, Robert E. 1922- St&PR 93
Portyrata, Raymond E. 1927- St&PR 93
Porumbescu, Ciprian 1853-1883 Baker 92
Porus fl. 4th cent.BC- HarEnMi
Porush, David 1952- ScF&FL 92
Porush, Jerome Gershon 1930- WhoE 93
Porwit-Bobr, Zofia 1924- WhoScE 91-4
Porybny, Zdenek 1945- WhoWor 93
Porzecanski, Arturo C. 1949- St&PR 93
Porzecanski, Arturo Cusiel 1949- WhoE 93
Porzecanski, Teresa 1945- SpAmA
Porzio, Anthony Joseph 1927- St&PR 93
Porzio, Patrick F. 1937- St&PR 93
Porzio, Patrick Francis 1937- WhoE 93
Porzio, William 1951- WhoWor 93
Posadas, Martin Posadas 1921- WhoWor 93
Posadas Ocampo, Juan Jesus 1926- WhoSSW 93
Posadas Ocampo, Juan Jesus Cardinal 1926- WhoWor 93
Posadskaya, Anastasya BioIn 17
Posamentier, Alfred Steven 1942- WhoAm 92
Posamentier, Evelyn 1951- WhoWrEP 92
Posch, Hubert WhoScE 91-4
Posch, Robert J., Jr. Law&B 92
Posch, Robert J., Jr. 1950- St&PR 93
Posekany, Lewis A., Jr. Law&B 92
Posen, Barry R. 1952- ConAu 137
Poser, Charles Marcel 1923- WhoAm 92
Poser, Ernest George 1921- WhoAm 92
Poser, Hans August Louis 1907- WhoWor 93
Poser, Joan Rapps 1940- WhoAmW 93, WhoE 93
Poser, Norman Stanley 1928- WhoAm 92
Poserina, John A. 1940- St&PR 93
Posey, Alexander 1873-1908 BioIn 17
Posey, Carl A. 1933- ScF&FL 92
Posey, Chester Nelson 1922- St&PR 93
Posey, Conrad Strother 1933- St&PR 93
Posey, Delma Powell 1937- WhoSSW 93
Posey, Earl A. 1928- St&PR 93
Posey, Edward W. 1927- AfrAmBi
Posey, Eldon Eugene 1921- WhoAm 92
Posey, John Alton, Jr. 1942- WhoSSW 93
Posey, Richard E. 1947- St&PR 93
Posey, Robert N. 1960- St&PR 93
Posey, Warren M. 1940- St&PR 93
Posgay, Karoly 1925- WhoScE 91-4
Poshard, Glenn 1945- CngDr 91, WhoAm 92
Posillico, Louis Francis 1946- St&PR 93
Posin, Daniel Q. 1909- WhoAm 92
Posin, Deborah A. Law&B 92
Posin, Melvin 1925- St&PR 93
Poskitt, T.J. WhoScE 91-1
Poskochil, Rodney Duane 1952- St&PR 93
Poskozim, James Gerard Law&B 92
Poskuta, Jerzy W. 1931- WhoScE 91-4
Posler, Gerry Lynn 1942- WhoAm 92
Posley, Lola Ray 1953- WhoAmW 93
Posluns, David 1959- St&PR 93
Posluns, Irving WhoAm 92
Posluns, Wilfred M. 1932- WhoAm 92
Posluns, Wilfred Murray 1932- St&PR 93
Posluszny, Joseph P. 1953- St&PR 93
Posnak, Robert Lincoln 1938- WhoIns 93
Posnansky, Merrick 1931- WhoAm 92, WhoWrEP 92
Posner, Amy K. Law&B 92
Posner, Bruce Frederick 1954- WhoE 93
Posner, David Mark 1945- WhoE 93
Posner, David S. Law&B 92
Posner, Donald 1931- WhoAm 92
Posner, Edward Charles 1933- WhoAm 92
Posner, Ernest Gary Law&B 92
Posner, Ernest Gary 1937- St&PR 93
Posner, Gary Herbert 1943- WhoAm 92
Posner, Gerald D. 1948- St&PR 93
Posner, Henry J. 1951- WhoE 93
Posner, Howard R. 1935- St&PR 93
Posner, James S. Law&B 92
Posner, James Stuart Law&B 92
Posner, Jerome Beebe 1932- WhoAm 92, WhoE 93
Posner, Kathy Robin 1952- WhoAmW 93
Posner, Kenneth Robert 1947- WhoAm 92
Posner, Linda Irene 1939- WhoAmW 93
Posner, Louis Joseph 1956- WhoE 93
Posner, Richard 1944- ScF&FL 92
Posner, Richard Allen 1939- WhoAm 92
Posner, Roy Edward 1933- St&PR 93, WhoAm 92
Posner, Sidney 1924- WhoAm 92
Posner, Steven 1943- WhoAm 92
Posner, Tracy 1962- WhoAmW 93
Posner, Victor 1918- WhoAm 92, WhoSSW 93
Posner, William M. Law&B 92
Posner-Cahill, Cheryl Lynn 1950- WhoSSW 93
Posnick, Adolph 1926- St&PR 93
Posnick, Paul ScF&FL 92
Poso, Simo 1938- WhoScE 91-4
Pospischil, Andreas 1948- WhoScE 91-4
Pospisil, Eva Holdridge 1953- WhoAmW 93
Pospisil, Frantisek WhoScE 91-4
Pospisil, George Curtis 1945- WhoAm 92, WhoWor 93
Pospisil, Jaromir 1930- WhoScE 91-4
Pospisil, Juraj 1931- Baker 92
Pospisil, Leopold Jaroslav 1923- WhoAm 92
Pospisilik, Jan Carl 1943- WhoUN 92
Pospisilova, Dorota 1930- WhoScE 91-4
Poss, John Claybron 1948- WhoAm 92
Poss, Stephen Daniel 1955- WhoEmL 93
Possati, Stefano 1950- WhoWor 93
Posse, Abel 1939- ScF&FL 92
Possehl, Jerry Roy 1942- WhoE 93
Posselt, Ruth 1914- Baker 92
Posselt, Ulrich K. 1943- WhoScE 91-3
Possinger, Frank St&PR 93
Possis, Zinon C. 1923- St&PR 93
Posso-Serrano, Abelardo 1943- WhoUN 92
Post, Alan 1914- WhoAm 92, WhoWor 93
Post, Alan R. Law&B 92
Post, Alfred 1936- WhoScE 91-3
Post, Anne Bretzfelder WhoE 93
Post, Avery Denison 1924- WhoAm 92
Post, Barbara Joan 1930- WhoAmW 93
Post, Barry A. 1943- St&PR 93
Post, Boyd Wallace 1928- WhoAm 92
Post, Cecella St&PR 93
Post, David Alan 1941- WhoAm 92, WhoE 93
Post, David Lyn 1959- St&PR 93
Post, Donna Matthews Law&B 92
Post, Edda S. Law&B 92
Post, Elizabeth Lindley 1920- WhoAm 92
Post, Emily 1873-1960 JrnUS
Post, Frederick 1962- WhoE 93
Post, G. Roger Law&B 92, St&PR 93
Post, Gerald Joseph 1925- WhoAm 92
Post, Glen Fleming, III 1952- St&PR 93, WhoAm 92
Post, Herschel 1939- WhoAm 92, WhoWor 93
Post, Howard Allen 1916- WhoAm 92
Post, Howard E. Law&B 92
Post, J.B. 1937- ScF&FL 92
Post, Jaap 1935- WhoScE 91-3
Post, Jackie E. 1928- St&PR 93
Post, Jackie Jackson 1928- WhoAm 92
Post, Jacqueline Kay 1945- WhoAmW 93
Post, James W. 1930- St&PR 93
Post, Jerald L. 1946- St&PR 93
Post, Jonathan F(rench) S(cott) 1947- ConAu 37NR
Post, Jonathan Vos 1951- WhoWrEP 92
Post, Joseph 1913- WhoAm 92
Post, Joseph A. Law&B 92
Post, Kenneth W. 1953- WhoE 93
Post, Lisa Ann 1954- WhoAmW 93
Post, Markie WhoAm 92
Post, Mike WhoAm 92
Post, Nancy 1957- WhoE 93
Post, Rick Alan 1962- WhoWrEP 92
Post, Robert Lickely 1920- WhoE 93
Post, Robert M. 1914- St&PR 93
Post, Robert M. 1914-1990 BioIn 17
Post, Rose Zimmerman 1926- WhoSSW 93
Post, Steven Michael Law&B 92
Post, Ted 1918- MiSFD 9
Post, Wiley 1899-1935 Expl 93
Post, Willem Steven 1938- WhoUN 92
Post, William J. 1950- St&PR 93
Post, William Joseph 1950- WhoAm 92
Postal, Andrew 1948- St&PR 93
Poste, George Henry 1944- WhoAm 92
Postel, Christian Heinrich 1658-1705 OxDcOp
Postel, Jacques 1927- WhoScE 91-2
Postel, John William 1953- WhoSSW 93
Postel, Wilhelm 1927- WhoScE 91-3, WhoWor 93
Postelle, Frederick Arnold 1945- St&PR 93
Postema, Richard Lee 1955- WhoEmL 93
Poster, Carol 1956- WhoWrEP 92
Poster, Don Steven 1950- WhoSSW 93
Poster, Evelyn BioIn 17
Poster, Karen BioIn 17
Posteraro, Anthony Francis 1915- WhoE 93
Posternak, Michel Alexandre 1942- WhoWor 93
Post-Gorden, Joan Carolyn 1932- WhoAmW 93
Posthoff, Christian 1943- WhoWor 93
Posthuma, Helen Marie 1920- WhoAmW 93
Posthumus, Adam C. 1934- WhoScE 91-3
Posthumus, Carol Laytham 1944- WhoE 93
Postiglione, Luigi 1926- WhoScE 91-3
Postle, Katherine J. AmWomPl
Postle, Robert Ross 1929- St&PR 93
Postlethwaite, Carl Albert 1905- St&PR 93
Postlethwaite, Ian WhoScE 91-1
Postlethwaite, Roy WhoScE 91-1
Postlewait, Harry Owen 1933- St&PR 93, WhoAm 92
Postma, Herman 1933- WhoAm 92
Postnikova, Viktoria (Valentinovna) 1944- Baker 92
Postol, Steven M. 1930- St&PR 93
Postolka, Milan 1932- Baker 92
Poston, Ann Genevieve 1936- WhoAmW 93
Poston, Charles Debrille 1825-1902 BioIn 17
Poston, David S. Law&B 92
Poston, Elizabeth 1905-1987 Baker 92
Poston, Frances Eddy 1923- WhoSSW 93
Poston, Gerald Connell 1936- St&PR 93
Poston, Gretchen BioIn 17
Poston, Gretchen Householder d1992 NewYTBS 92
Poston, Iona 1951- WhoSSW 93
Poston, James R. Law&B 92
Poston, Joe B. 1951- St&PR 93
Poston, John Michael 1935- WhoE 93
Poston, Larry (A.) 1952- ConAu 138
Poston, Theodore Roosevelt Augustus Major 1906-1974 EncAACR
Poston, Tom 1927- WhoAm 92
Postuma, Klaas Hoite 1926- WhoScE 91-3
Postumus, Marcus Cassianus Latinius d268 HarEnMi
Postupolski, Tomasz Wlodzimierz 1931- WhoWor 93
Post Wolcott, Marion Scott 1910-1990 BioIn 17
Postyn, Sol 1934- WhoAm 92
Poswick, Reginald-Ferdinand 1937- WhoWor 93
Poswillo, David Ernest WhoScE 91-1
Posy, David H. Law&B 92
Pot, Pol BioIn 17
Potamkin, Meyer P. 1909- WhoAm 92
Potapov, Alexander Serge 1948- WhoWor 93
Potapov, L.P. 1905- IntDcAn
Potasek, Mary Joyce 1945- WhoE 93
Potash, Jerome 1925- St&PR 93
Potash, Martin 1937- WhoUN 92
Potash, Michael Alan 1948- St&PR 93
Potash, Stephen Jon 1945- WhoAm 92
Potashnick, Barbara A. Law&B 92
Potate, John Spencer, Sr. 1934- WhoAm 92
Potchen, E. James 1932- WhoAm 92
Potchen, Joseph Anton 1931- WhoIns 93

Potdukhe, Shantaram 1933- *WhoAsAP 91*
Pote, Harold William 1946- *BioIn 17, WhoAm 92*
Poteat, Harry Towsley 1961- *WhoE 93*
Poteet, Daniel Powell, II 1940- *WhoAm 92*
Poteet, Thomas M., Jr. 1935- *WhoIns 93*
Poteete, Robert Arthur 1926- *WhoAm 92, WhoWrEP 92*
Potekhin, I.I. 1903-1964 *IntDcAn*
Potel, David H. *Law&B 92*
Potembski, Larry Michael 1958- *St&PR 93*
Potemkin, Gregori Aleksandrovich 1739-1791 *HarEnMi*
Potempa, Wayne C. 1949- *St&PR 93*
Potente, Eugene, Jr. 1921- *WhoWor 93*
Potente, Helmut M. 1939- *WhoScE 91-3*
Potente, Helmut Michael 1939- *WhoWor 93*
Potenza, Joseph Anthony 1941- *WhoAm 92*
Potesky, James Michael 1958- *St&PR 93*
Potesta, Rudolph M. 1932- *St&PR 93*
Potet, Francois *WhoScE 91-2*
Poth, Edward Cornelius 1927- *WhoAm 92*
Poth, Gregory E. 1945- *St&PR 93*
Poth, Harry Augustus, Jr. 1911- *St&PR 93*
Poth, Stefan Michael 1933- *St&PR 93, WhoAm 92*
Pothan, Kap 1929- *ScF&FL 92*
Potherat, Janine Simone *Law&B 92*
Pothier, Dick *BioIn 17*
Pothier, Joseph 1835-1923 *Baker 92*
Potier, Pierre *WhoScE 91-2*
Potiker, Howard M. 1927- *St&PR 93*
Potiker, Kenneth J. *St&PR 93*
Potiker, Sheila Millman 1929- *St&PR 93*
Potila, Antti 1938- *WhoWor 93*
Potkin, Harvey 1935- *St&PR 93*
Potkul, Karen M. *Law&B 92*
Potocka, Delfina 1805-1877 *PolBiDi*
Potocki, Ignacy 1750-1809 *PolBiDi*
Potocki, Jan 1761-1815 *PolBiDi, ScF&FL 92*
Potocki, Kenneth Anthony 1940- *WhoE 93*
Potocki, Waclaw 1625-1696 *PolBiDi*
Potocki, Walenty d1749 *PolBiDi*
Potocnik, William John 1936- *St&PR 93*
Potok, Andrew 1931- *ConAu 139*
Potok, Chaim 1929- *BioIn 17, JeAmFiW, JeAmHC, MagSAmL [port], WhoAm 92, WhoWrEP 92*
Potoker, Edward Martin 1931- *WhoAm 92, WhoWrEP 92*
Potoreiko, Jean Frances 1940- *WhoE 93*
Potorski, Robert L. 1937- *St&PR 93*
Potrebenko, Helen 1940- *WhoCanL 92*
Potron, Gerard 1936- *WhoScE 91-2*
Potsic, William Paul 1943- *WhoAm 92*
Pottabathni, Pandu Ranga 1947- *WhoWor 93*
Pottasch, Alan *BioIn 17*
Pottasch, Stuart Robert 1932- *WhoScE 91-3*
Pottash, A. Carter 1948- *WhoAm 92*
Potteiger, Paula Darlene 1969- *WhoAmW 93*
Pottenger, Charles 1950- *St&PR 93*
Potter, A(rchibald) J(ames) 1918-1980 *Baker 92*
Potter, Alfred D. 1926- *St&PR 93*
Potter, Alfred K. 1948- *St&PR 93*
Potter, Anthony Grahame 1949- *St&PR 93*
Potter, Anthony Nicholas, Jr. 1942- *WhoWor 93*
Potter, Barrett George 1929- *WhoAm 92*
Potter, Beatrix 1866-1943 *BioIn 17*
Potter, (Helen) Beatrix 1866-1943 *ConAu 137, MajAI [port]*
Potter, Benjamin Franklin, Jr. 1940- *WhoSSW 93*
Potter, Bronson *DcAmChF 1960*
Potter, Carol *BioIn 17*
Potter, Charles 1907-1989 *BioIn 17*
Potter, Charles Arthur, Jr. 1925- *WhoAm 92*
Potter, Christopher William *WhoScE 91-1*
Potter, (Philip) Cipriani (Hambley) 1792-1871 *Baker 92*
Potter, Clarkson Nott 1928- *WhoAm 92, WhoWrEP 92*
Potter, Clinton Ray 1936- *St&PR 93*
Potter, David C. *WhoScE 91-1*
Potter, David Marshall 1953- *WhoSSW 93*
Potter, David Samuel 1925- *WhoAm 92*
Potter, Dean Marion 1939- *St&PR 93*
Potter, Delcour Stephen, III 1935- *St&PR 93*
Potter, Dennis *BioIn 17*
Potter, Dennis 1935- *MiSFD 9, WhoWor 93*
Potter, Donald Albert 1922- *St&PR 93*
Potter, Donald Joseph, Jr. 1949- *WhoEmL 93, WhoSSW 93*
Potter, Dorothy *AmWomPl*
Potter, Douglas Ernest 1930- *St&PR 93*
Potter, Edmund Lysle 1924- *St&PR 93*
Potter, Edward Ralph 1946- *St&PR 93*
Potter, Elaine 1935-1991 *BioIn 17*
Potter, Eloise Fretz 1931- *WhoWrEP 92*
Potter, Emma Josephine Hill 1921- *WhoAmW 93, WhoE 93*
Potter, Ernest Luther 1940- *WhoAm 92, WhoSSW 93*
Potter, Frances B. *AmWomPl*
Potter, Fred Leon 1948- *WhoIns 93*
Potter, Fuller 1910-1990 *BioIn 17*
Potter, Gary Robert 1945- *St&PR 93*
Potter, George Harris 1936- *St&PR 93*
Potter, George William, Jr. 1930- *WhoWor 93*
Potter, Grace *AmWomPl*
Potter, Guy Dill 1928- *WhoAm 92*
Potter, H.C. 1904-1977 *MiSFD 9N*
Potter, Hamilton Fish, Jr. 1928- *WhoAm 92*
Potter, Harold d1992 *BioIn 17, NewYTBS 92*
Potter, Jacqueline Riley *WhoWrEP 92*
Potter, James *Law&B 92*
Potter, James Craig 1943- *WhoAm 92*
Potter, James Douglas 1944- *WhoAm 92*
Potter, James Earl 1933- *WhoAm 92*
Potter, Jeffrey K. *ScF&FL 92*
Potter, John Davis 1944- *WhoWor 93*
Potter, John Francis 1925- *WhoAm 92*
Potter, John Leith 1923- *WhoAm 92, WhoSSW 93*
Potter, John R. *Law&B 92*
Potter, John R. 1945- *St&PR 93*
Potter, John William 1918- *WhoAm 92*
Potter, June Anita 1938- *WhoAmW 93*
Potter, Karl Harrington 1927- *WhoAm 92*
Potter, Keith 1946- *St&PR 93*
Potter, Kenneth C. 1939- *St&PR 93*
Potter, Kenneth Nelson 1962- *WhoSSW 93*
Potter, Laurence A., III *Law&B 92*
Potter, Leroy Minteer 1936- *WhoE 93*
Potter, Lillian Florence 1912- *WhoAmW 93*
Potter, Lon G. *Law&B 92*
Potter, Marie Josephine Warren *AmWomPl*
Potter, Mark *WhoWrEP 92*
Potter, Mark James 1962- *WhoE 93*
Potter, Marshall Richard 1948- *WhoE 93*
Potter, Michael 1924- *WhoAm 92*
Potter, Nancy Dutton 1946- *WhoAmW 93*
Potter, Pat *BioIn 17*
Potter, Patricia Ann 1951- *WhoE 93*
Potter, Peggy Marie 1955- *WhoE 93*
Potter, Ralph Benajah, Jr. 1931- *WhoAm 92*
Potter, Richard E. *Law&B 92*
Potter, Richard Huddleston 1755-1821? *See* Potter, (Philip) Cipriani (Hambley) 1792-1871 *Baker 92*
Potter, Richard J. *Law&B 92*
Potter, Richard Kevin 1959- *WhoE 93*
Potter, Richard Thomas, Jr. *Law&B 92*
Potter, Robert A. 1951- *St&PR 93*
Potter, Robert Arthur 1938- *WhoE 93*
Potter, Robert Daniel 1923- *WhoSSW 93*
Potter, Robert Gene 1939- *St&PR 93, WhoAm 92*
Potter, Robert J. 1932- *St&PR 93*
Potter, Robert Joseph 1932- *WhoAm 92, WhoSSW 93*
Potter, Robert L. 1933- *St&PR 93*
Potter, Robert Wallace, Jr. 1947- *WhoEmL 93*
Potter, Robert William *WhoScE 91-1*
Potter, Ronald Cary *Law&B 92*
Potter, Sally *MiSFD 9*
Potter, Stephen 1900-1969 *BioIn 17*
Potter, Stephen Brent *Law&B 92*
Potter, Thomas A. *Law&B 92*
Potter, Thomas D. 1939- *WhoIns 93*
Potter, Trevor Alexander McClurg 1955- *WhoE 93*
Potter, Vincent George 1928- *WhoE 93*
Potter, Wayne Allen 1944- *St&PR 93*
Potter, William Bartlett 1938- *St&PR 93, WhoAm 92*
Potter, William Blake 1955- *WhoE 93*
Potter, William Gray 1950- *BioIn 17*
Potter, William Gray, Jr. 1950- *WhoAm 92*
Potter, William James 1948- *WhoAm 92, WhoE 93, WhoEmL 93, WhoWor 93*
Potter-Case, Genevieve *AmWomPl*
Potterfield, Joan Ellen 1953- *WhoE 93*
Potterfield, Peter *BioIn 17*
Potterfield, Peter Lounsbury 1949- *WhoWrEP 92*
Potter O'Connell, Alison Richey 1955- *WhoAmW 93*
Potters, Edward Paul 1951- *WhoE 93*
Potterton, Gerald 1931- *MiSFD 9*
Potthoff, Richard Frederick 1932- *WhoSSW 93*
Pottie, David Laren 1952- *WhoE 93*
Pottie, Roswell Francis 1933- *WhoAm 92*
Pottier, Michel Bernard 1938- *WhoScE 91-2*
Pottier, Pierre *WhoScE 91-2*
Pottinger, Audrey Marie 1962- *WhoAmW 93*
Pottle, Bruce W. 1939- *St&PR 93*
Pottle, Christopher 1932- *WhoE 93*
Pottle, Connie Sue 1953- *WhoAmW 93*
Pottle, Frederick Albert 1897-1987 *BioIn 17*
Pottmeyer, Jerome J. *Law&B 92*
Pottmeyer, Wayne G. 1947- *St&PR 93*
Pottorff, James Arthur 1959- *St&PR 93*
Pottorff, Jo Ann 1936- *WhoAmW 93*
Pottratz, Patricia Anne 1936- *WhoAmW 93*
Pottruck, David S. 1948- *WhoAm 92*
Pottruck, Garry R. 1956- *St&PR 93*
Potts, Annie *BioIn 17*
Potts, Annie 1952- *WhoAm 92*
Potts, Barbara Joyce 1932- *WhoAm 92, WhoAmW 93*
Potts, Bernard 1915- *WhoE 93*
Potts, Billye Marie 1961- *WhoSSW 93*
Potts, Bobby Eugene *Law&B 92*
Potts, Charles 1943- *WhoWrEP 92*
Potts, David Malcolm 1935- *WhoAm 92*
Potts, Donald Ralph 1930- *WhoSSW 93*
Potts, Douglas Gordon 1927- *WhoAm 92*
Potts, Erwin Rea 1932- *St&PR 93, WhoAm 92*
Potts, Floyd 1922- *WhoSSW 93*
Potts, Frederic A. 1904-1991 *BioIn 17*
Potts, G.R. *WhoScE 91-1*
Potts, G. Richard 1939- *WhoScE 91-1*
Potts, Gerald Neal 1933- *WhoAm 92*
Potts, Gilbert E. 1951- *WhoWor 93*
Potts, Harold Francis, Jr. 1955- *St&PR 93, WhoE 93, WhoEmL 93*
Potts, James P. *Law&B 92*
Potts, Janice E. *Law&B 92*
Potts, John Thomas, Jr. 1932- *WhoAm 92*
Potts, M. Dean 1926- *WhoAm 92*
Potts, Nancy Dee Needham 1947- *WhoEmL 93, WhoSSW 93*
Potts, Ramsay Douglas 1916- *WhoAm 92, WhoWor 93*
Potts, Renfrey Burnard 1925- *WhoWor 93*
Potts, Richard W. 1937- *St&PR 93*
Potts, Robert Anthony 1927- *WhoAm 92*
Potts, Robert H. *Law&B 92*
Potts, Robert Leslie 1944- *WhoAm 92, WhoSSW 93*
Potts, Starr Boggs 1956- *WhoAmW 93*
Potts, Stephen Deaderick 1930- *WhoAm 92*
Potts, Stephen W. 1949- *ScF&FL 92*
Potts, Timothy Alan 1951- *WhoE 93*
Potts, William Taylor Windle *WhoScE 91-1*
Potts-Guin, Marilyn d1989 *BioIn 17*
Potturi, Butchi Raju 1946- *WhoWor 93*
Potuznik, Charles Laddy 1947- *WhoAm 92*
Potvin, Alfred Raoul 1942- *WhoAm 92*
Potvin, D. Joseph *Law&B 92*
Potvin, Douglas Leo 1966- *WhoE 93*
Potvin, Philip N. 1946- *St&PR 93*
Potvin, Pierre 1932- *WhoAm 92*
Potvin, Raymond Herve 1924- *WhoAm 92*
Potvin, William Tracey 1951- *WhoAm 92*
Potwin, Connie Marie 1962- *WhoE 93*
Potwin, John M. *Law&B 92*
Potwin, John Martin 1943- *St&PR 93*
Potworowski, Piotr 1898-1962 *PolBiDi*
Poty, Patrick Georges 1946- *WhoWor 93*
Potztal, Eva H.I. 1924- *WhoScE 91-3*
Pou, Brenda Prine 1948- *WhoAmW 93*
Pou, Linda Alice 1942- *WhoAmW 93*
Poucher, John Scott 1945- *WhoE 93*
Poudrier, Lucinda Marie 1965- *WhoAmW 93*
Poudyal, Sri Ram 1950- *WhoWor 93*
Poueigh, Jean (Marie-Octave-Geraud) 1876-1958 *Baker 92*
Pouget, Emile 1860-1931 *BioIn 17*
Pough, Frederick Harvey 1906- *WhoAm 92*
Pough, Richard Hooper 1904- *WhoAm 92*
Pougin, Arthur 1834-1921 *OxDcOp*
Pougin, (Francois-Auguste-) Arthur 1834-1921 *Baker 92*
Pouillaude, Francois 1927- *WhoScE 91-2*
Pouillon, Nora Emanuela 1943- *WhoAmW 93*
Pouishnov, Lev 1891-1959 *Baker 92*
Poujade, Pierre 1920- *BioIn 17*
Poul, Franklin 1924- *WhoAm 92*
Poulakos, Constantine 1936- *WhoScE 91-3*
Poulard, Jean Rene Felix 1923- *WhoScE 91-2*
Poulenc, Francis 1899-1963 *BioIn 17, IntDcOp, OxDcOp*
Poulenc, Francis (Jean Marcel) 1899-1963 *Baker 92*
Poulet, Gaston 1892-1974 *Baker 92*
Poulet, Gerard 1938- *Baker 92*
Pouleur, Hubert Gustave 1948- *WhoWor 93*
Poulianos, Nickos 1956- *WhoWor 93*
Poulin, A., Jr. 1938- *WhoWrEP 92*
Poulin, Danielle *Law&B 92*
Poulin, Gerald Conrad 1942- *St&PR 93*
Poulin, Jacques 1961- *WhoCanL 92*
Poulin, Marie-Paule 1945- *WhoAm 92, WhoAmW 93*
Poulin, Ronald F. 1948- *WhoE 93*
Poulin, Stephane 1961- *ChlLR 28 [port]*
Poulin, Tracey Kay 1961- *St&PR 93*
Poulin-Kloehr, Lisa 1956- *WhoAmW 93*
Pouliot, Jean *St&PR 93*
Pouliot, John *Law&B 92*
Pouliquen, Yves *WhoScE 91-2*
Pouliquen, Yves Jean Marie 1931- *WhoScE 91-2*
Poulos, Harry G. 1940- *WhoWor 93*
Poulos, James Thomas 1938- *WhoWor 93*
Poulos, Michael J. 1931- *St&PR 93*
Poulos, Michael James 1931- *WhoAm 92, WhoIns 93, WhoSSW 93*
Poulos, Michael Stephen *Law&B 92*
Poulsen, Bruce Aberg *Law&B 92*
Poulsen, Dennis Robert 1946- *WhoWor 93*
Poulsen, Emil 1921- *WhoScE 91-2*
Poulsen, Erik *WhoScE 91-2*
Poulsen, Erik Fangel 1934- *WhoWor 93*
Poulsen, John *WhoScE 91-2*
Poulsen, Knud 1936- *WhoScE 91-2*
Poulsen, Niels 1950- *WhoScE 91-2*
Poulsen, Ove 1946- *WhoWor 93*
Poulson, Robert Dean 1927- *WhoAm 92*
Poulter, Roger Guy 1950- *WhoScE 91-1*
Poulterer, William Taylor, III 1938- *WhoSSW 93*
Poulton, Bruce Robert 1927- *WhoAm 92, WhoSSW 93*
Poulton, Charles Edgar 1917- *WhoAm 92*
Poulton, Daniel Gabriel 1951- *WhoScE 91-2*
Poulton, Kingsley Joseph 1966- *WhoWor 93*
Pouncey, Peter Richard 1937- *WhoAm 92, WhoE 93, WhoWor 93*
Pouncey, Philip 1910-1990 *BioIn 17*
Pouncy, Mattie Hunter 1924- *WhoWrEP 92*
Pound, Ezra 1885-1972 *BioIn 17, MagSAmL [port], WorLitC [port]*
Pound, Ezra (Loomis) 1885-1972 *Baker 92*
Pound, Ezra (Weston Loomis) 1885-1972 *ConAu 40NR*
Pound, Richard William Duncan 1942- *WhoAm 92*
Pound, Robert Vivian 1919- *WhoAm 92*
Pounder, Derrick John *WhoScE 91-1*
Pounder, Derrick John 1949- *WhoWor 93*
Pounds, Billy Dean 1930- *WhoSSW 93*
Pounds, Darryl D. 1949- *St&PR 93*
Pounds, Kenneth Alwyne 1934- *WhoWor 93*
Pounds, Rebecca L. 1961- *St&PR 93*
Pounds, Thomas Wade *Law&B 92*
Pounds, William Frank 1928- *WhoAm 92*
Poundstone, Sally *WhoAmW 93*
Poungui, Ange-Edouard 1942- *WhoAfr*
Pouns, Brauna E. *ScF&FL 92*
Pountney, David 1947- *IntDcOp, OxDcOp*
Pountney, David Charles *WhoScE 91-1*
Poupard, Henri-Pierre 1901-1989 *BioIn 17*
Poupard, James J. 1932- *WhoAm 92*
Poupart, Jean-Marie 1947- *WhoCanL 92*
Poupliniere *Baker 92*
Pour, Vladimir *WhoScE 91-4*
Pourbaix, Antoine J.E. 1939- *WhoScE 91-2*
Pourcelet, Michel Joseph 1934- *WhoUN 92*
Pourcelot, Leandre Georges 1940- *WhoScE 91-2*
Pourchot, Mary Ellen 1923- *WhoWrEP 92*
Pourciau, Charles Lee, Jr. *Law&B 92*
Pourciau, Lester John 1936- *WhoAm 92*
Pour-El, Marian Boykan *WhoAm 92, WhoAmW 93*
Pournelle, Jerry 1933- *BioIn 17, ScF&FL 92*
Pournelle, Jerry Eugene 1933- *WhoAm 92*
Pourrat, Jacques P. 1945- *WhoScE 91-2*
Pourtales, Guy (Guido James) de 1881-1941 *Baker 92*
Pourtois, Michel R.J.P. 1931- *WhoScE 91-2*
Pourvoyeur, Robert A.M.A. 1924- *WhoWor 93*
Pousa, Ricardo Daniel 1961- *WhoWor 93*
Pousette-Dart, Joanna *BioIn 17*
Pousette-Dart, Richard 1916- *BioIn 17, WhoAm 92*
Pousette-Dart, Richard 1916-1992 *NewYTBS 92 [port]*
Pousland, Annie E. *AmWomPl*
Poussaint, Alvin Francis 1934- *WhoAm 92*

Poussaint, Renee Francine 1944- *WhoAmW 93*
Poussart, Denis Jean-Marie 1940- *WhoAm 92*
Pousseur, Henri 1929- *IntDcOp*
Pousseur, Henri (Leon Marie Therese) 1929- *Baker 92*
Poutasse, Edmund Joseph 1931- *WhoE 93*
Poutiainen, Esko K. 1936- *WhoScE 91-4*
Poutrel, Bernard 1941- *WhoScE 91-2*
Poutsiaka, William J. 1952- *WhoIns 93*
Pouyat, Anna-Juliette 1941- *WhoUN 92*
Povall, Allie S., Jr. *Law&B 92*
Poveda, Gabriel 1931- *WhoWor 93*
Pover, Yvonne Worrell 1944- *WhoAmW 93*
Povero, Mary Borromeo 1920- *WhoE 93*
Povey, Thomas George 1920- *WhoAm 92, WhoE 93, WhoWor 93*
Povh, Bogdan 1932- *WhoScE 91-3*
Povich, Maury *BioIn 17, NewYTBS 92 [port]*
Povich, Maury 1939- *ConAu 138*
Povich, Maury Richard 1939- *WhoAm 92*
Povich, Shirley Lewis 1905- *WhoAm 92*
Povish, Kenneth Joseph 1924- *WhoAm 92*
Povman, Morton 1931- *WhoE 93*
Povod, Reinaldo 1959- *ConAu 136*
Povolny, Dalibor 1924- *WhoScE 91-4*
Povondra, Robert M. 1938- *St&PR 93*
Pow, Richard B. 1934- *St&PR 93*
Powderly, Robert G. 1947- *St&PR 93*
Powdermaker, Hortense 1896-1970 *IntDcAn*
Powders, Donna Jo 1942- *WhoWrEP 92*
Powdrill, Gary Leo 1945- *WhoWor 93*
Powe, B.W. 1955- *WhoCanL 92*
Powe, Bruce Allen 1925- *WhoCanL 92*
Powe, Ralph Elward 1944- *WhoAm 92*
Powe, Ronald *ScF&FL 92*
Powel, Nick *BioIn 17*
Powell, Adam Clayton 1908-1972 *BioIn 17*
Powell, Adam Clayton, Jr. 1908-1972 *ConBlB 3 [port], EncAACR, PolPar*
Powell, Alan 1928- *WhoAm 92*
Powell, Alma *BioIn 17*
Powell, Amy Tuck 1963- *WhoAmW 93, WhoSSW 93*
Powell, Andrew *Law&B 92*
Powell, Anice Carpenter 1928- *WhoAm 92, WhoSSW 93*
Powell, Anne Elizabeth 1951- *WhoAm 92*
Powell, Anthony 1905- *BioIn 17, MagSWL [port], ScF&FL 92*
Powell, Anthony Dymoke 1905- *WhoWor 93*
Powell, Barbara 1929- *WhoE 93*
Powell, Barry B. 1942- *ConAu 136*
Powell, Barry Bruce 1942- *WhoAm 92*
Powell, Benjamin Edward 1905-1981 *BioIn 17*
Powell, Betty Jean 1926- *WhoAmW 93*
Powell, Beverly Jo 1940- *WhoWrEP 92*
Powell, Bill Jake 1936- *WhoAm 92*
Powell, Billy 195-?- *See* Lynyrd Skynyrd *ConMus 9*
Powell, Bolling Raines, Jr. 1910- *WhoAm 92*
Powell, "Bud" (Earl) 1924-1966 *Baker 92*
Powell, Burnele Venable 1947- *WhoAm 92*
Powell, Carl E. 1945- *St&PR 93*
Powell, Charles M. 1934-1991 *BioIn 17*
Powell, Christine Pacelli 1961- *WhoSSW 93*
Powell, Claire *ScF&FL 92*
Powell, Clinton Cobb 1918- *WhoAm 92*
Powell, Colin 1937- *ColdWar 1 [port], ConHero 2 [port]*
Powell, Colin L. *BioIn 17*
Powell, Colin L. 1937- *AfrAmBi [port]*
Powell, Colin Luther 1937- *HarEnMi, WhoAm 92*
Powell, Cornelius Patrick 1931- *St&PR 93*
Powell, Curtis Everett 1961- *WhoSSW 93*
Powell, Cynthia Anne 1958- *WhoWrEP 92*
Powell, Daniel Thomas 1947- *St&PR 93*
Powell, Darrell M. 1950- *St&PR 93*
Powell, David *BioIn 17*
Powell, David Greatorex 1933- *St&PR 93, WhoAm 92*
Powell, David John 1945- *WhoAm 92*
Powell, David L. 1951- *St&PR 93*
Powell, David Thomas, Jr. 1941- *WhoSSW 93*
Powell, Dennis G. 1949- *St&PR 93*
Powell, Diane Elaine 1955- *WhoAmW 93*
Powell, Dick 1904-1963 *IntDcF 2-3 [port], MiSFD 9N*
Powell, Dick 1950- *St&PR 93*
Powell, Dilys 1901- *BioIn 17*
Powell, Don Graber 1939- *WhoAm 92*
Powell, Don Watson 1938- *WhoAm 92*
Powell, Donald George 1932- *St&PR 93*
Powell, Donald Richard, Jr. *Law&B 92*
Powell, Drexel Dwane, Jr. 1944- *WhoAm 92*
Powell, Durwood Royce 1951- *WhoAm 92, WhoEmL 93*
Powell, E. Sandy 1947- *SmATA 72 [port]*
Powell, Earl A., III *NewYTBS 92 [port]*
Powell, Earl Alexander, III 1943- *WhoAm 92*
Powell, Earl Dean 1938- *WhoSSW 93*
Powell, Edmund William 1922- *WhoAm 92*
Powell, Eleanor 1912-1982 *IntDcF 2-3 [port]*
Powell, Enid Levinger 1931- *WhoWrEP 92*
Powell, Enoch 1912- *BioIn 17*
Powell, Erin Feys 1950- *WhoAmW 93*
Powell, Ernestine Breisch 1906- *WhoAmW 93, WhoWor 93*
Powell, Frances R. *St&PR 93*
Powell, Frank James 1934- *St&PR 93*
Powell, Gene A. *Law&B 92*
Powell, George A. 1926- *St&PR 93*
Powell, George E., Jr. 1926- *St&PR 93*
Powell, George Everett, Jr. 1926- *WhoAm 92*
Powell, George Everett, III 1948- *St&PR 93, WhoAm 92*
Powell, George Howard 1943- *St&PR 93*
Powell, George T., III *Law&B 92*
Powell, George Van Tuyl 1910- *WhoAm 92*
Powell, Gregory A. 1950- *St&PR 93*
Powell, H. Robert 1926- *St&PR 93*
Powell, Hampton Oliver 1911- *WhoAm 92*
Powell, Harold Fryburg 1932- *WhoAm 92*
Powell, Harvard Wendell 1915- *WhoAm 92*
Powell, Hedy M. *Law&B 92*
Powell, Herbert J. 1898- *WhoAm 92*
Powell, Isabelle Reedy 1923- *WhoAmW 93*
Powell, Ivor 1910- *ConAu 38NR*
Powell, Jack Laverne 1959- *WhoE 93*
Powell, James Albert, Jr. 1948- *WhoSSW 93*
Powell, James Alfred *WhoScE 91-1*
Powell, James Bobbitt 1938- *St&PR 93, WhoAm 92, WhoSSW 93, WhoWor 93*
Powell, James Henry 1928- *WhoAm 92*
Powell, James Lawrence 1936- *WhoAm 92*
Powell, James Matthew 1930- *WhoAm 92*
Powell, James Vernon, Jr. 1922- *WhoSSW 93*
Powell, Jan P. 1944- *WhoAm 92*
Powell, Janet *BioIn 17*
Powell, Janet Frances 1942- *WhoAsAP 91*
Powell, Janice M. *Law&B 92*
Powell, Janice Margarete *Law&B 92*
Powell, Jeffrey David 1946- *St&PR 93*
Powell, Jerry T. 1933- *WhoAm 92*
Powell, Jerry W. *Law&B 92*
Powell, Jerry W. 1950- *St&PR 93*
Powell, Jim *BioIn 17*
Powell, Jody 1943- *WhoAm 92*
Powell, Joe Allen *Law&B 92*
Powell, John 1882-1963 *Baker 92*
Powell, John 1911-1991 *BioIn 17*
Powell, John Enoch 1912- *BioIn 17, DcTwHis*
Powell, John Henderson d1990 *BioIn 17*
Powell, John Jenkins Marklieu *WhoScE 91-1*
Powell, John Key 1925- *WhoSSW 93*
Powell, John Wesley 1834-1902 *BioIn 17, GayN, IntDcAn*
Powell, Joseph Edward 1952- *WhoWrEP 92*
Powell, Joseph Herbert 1926- *WhoAm 92*
Powell, Joseph Lester 1943- *WhoAm 92, WhoE 93*
Powell, Judith Anne 1944- *WhoSSW 93*
Powell, Judith E. 1939- *WhoAmW 93*
Powell, Julian Anthony 1945- *WhoSSW 93*
Powell, Karan Hinman 1953- *WhoAmW 93*
Powell, Karl C. 1943- *St&PR 93*
Powell, Kenneth Edward 1952- *WhoAm 92*
Powell, Kent D. 1946- *St&PR 93*
Powell, Larry Randall 1948- *WhoSSW 93*
Powell, Larson Merrill 1932- *WhoAm 92, WhoE 93*
Powell, Laurence 1899-1990 *Baker 92*
Powell, Lawrence Clark 1906- *ScF&FL 92*
Powell, Lee Jackson 1939- *St&PR 93*
Powell, Lesley Cameron 1924- *DcChlFi*
Powell, Leslie Charles, Jr. 1927- *WhoAm 92*
Powell, Lewis F., Jr. *BioIn 17*
Powell, Lewis Franklin, Jr. 1907- *CngDr 91, OxCSupC [port], WhoAm 92, WhoE 93*
Powell, Linda Rae 1947- *WhoAmW 93*
Powell, Lois Cecile 1941- *WhoE 93*
Powell, M.C. *WhoScE 91-1*
Powell, M. Elaine 1954- *WhoSSW 93*
Powell, Margaret Ann Simmons 1952- *WhoAmW 93*
Powell, Mary Atkeson 1944- *WhoAmW 93*
Powell, Mary Rudd 1933- *WhoSSW 93*
Powell, Mason *ScF&FL 92*
Powell, Maud 1868-1920 *Baker 92, BioIn 17*
Powell, Maxwell M. 1916- *St&PR 93*
Powell, Mel 1923- *BioIn 17, WhoAm 92*
Powell, Mel 1933- *Baker 92*
Powell, Melanie Jane *WhoScE 91-1*
Powell, Melchior Daniel 1935- *WhoWor 93*
Powell, Michael 1905-1990 *BioIn 17, MiSFD 9N*
Powell, Michael 1939- *DcCPCAm*
Powell, Michael C. 1946- *WhoScE 91-1*
Powell, Michael James David *WhoScE 91-1*
Powell, Mike *BioIn 17*
Powell, Mike 1964- *WhoAm 92*
Powell, Miles, Jr. 1926- *St&PR 93, WhoE 93*
Powell, Nancy *BioIn 17*
Powell, Nina Clark 1920- *WhoAmW 93*
Powell, Norborne Berkeley 1914- *WhoAm 92*
Powell, Norman R. *Law&B 92*
Powell, Norman R. 1939- *St&PR 93*
Powell, Oliver S. 1896-1963 *BioIn 17*
Powell, Patricia Ann 1956- *WhoAmW 93*
Powell, Paul A. 1912- *St&PR 93*
Powell, Peggy Nance 1940- *WhoAmW 93*
Powell, Peter Clive *WhoScE 91-1*
Powell, Philip 1921- *WhoWor 93*
Powell, Raymond Eugene 1936- *WhoSSW 93*
Powell, Richard Cortland 1953- *WhoE 93, WhoWor 93*
Powell, Richard Gordon 1918- *WhoAm 92*
Powell, Richard Pitts 1908- *WhoAm 92, WhoWor 93, WhoWrEP 92*
Powell, Robert Ellis 1936- *WhoAm 92*
Powell, Robert Eugene 1955- *WhoWor 93*
Powell, Robert J. *Law&B 92*
Powell, Robert J. 1948- *St&PR 93*
Powell, Robert Morgan 1934- *St&PR 93*
Powell, Robert Wendell, Jr. 1930- *St&PR 93, WhoAm 92*
Powell, Roger 1896-1990 *BioIn 17*
Powell, Romae Turner 1926-1990 *AfrAmBi*
Powell, Ronald W. *Law&B 92*
Powell, Rosalie 1947- *WhoAmW 93*
Powell, Ruth Lang 1930- *WhoAmW 93*
Powell, Sandra Black 1941- *WhoAmW 93*
Powell, Sandra Theresa 1944- *St&PR 93, WhoAm 92*
Powell, Scott R. 1948- *St&PR 93*
Powell, Sharon Lee 1940- *WhoAmW 93*
Powell, Shirley Jean 1946- *WhoSSW 93*
Powell, Stanley, Jr. 1917- *WhoAm 92*
Powell, Stephen Clarke 1950- *WhoE 93*
Powell, Steven D. 1951- *St&PR 93*
Powell, Susan Elaine 1954- *WhoAmW 93*
Powell, Sylvester d1877 *BioIn 17*
Powell, Theodore James Malcolm *St&PR 93*
Powell, Thomas Edward, III 1936- *St&PR 93, WhoAm 92*
Powell, Tina Joyce 1962- *WhoAmW 93*
Powell, Tristram 1940- *MiSFD 9*
Powell, Victoria A. *Law&B 92*
Powell, W. Kindred, Jr. 1946- *WhoSSW 93*
Powell, Walter Allen 1933- *WhoSSW 93*
Powell, Walter Hecht 1945- *WhoAm 92*
Powell, Watson, Jr. 1917- *WhoIns 93*
Powell, Wilfred *WhoScE 91-1*
Powell, Willard Rees 1926- *WhoAm 92*
Powell, William 1892-1984 *BioIn 17, IntDcF 2-3 [port]*
Powell, William Arnold, Jr. 1929- *St&PR 93, WhoAm 92, WhoSSW 93, WhoWor 93*
Powell, William Council, Sr. 1948- *WhoSSW 93, WhoWor 93*
Powell, William E. 1936- *AfrAmBi [port]*
Powell, William Robert 1936- *St&PR 93*
Powell, William Rossell, Jr. 1926- *WhoAm 92*
Powell, Williams Albert 1935- *St&PR 93*
Powell-Brown, Ann 1947- *WhoAmW 93*
Powelson, James S. 1931- *St&PR 93*
Power, Anthony John 1959- *WhoWor 93*
Power, Brian 1918- *ConAu 139*
Power, Caroline Marguerite *AmWomPl*
Power, Colin Nelson 1939- *WhoUN 92*
Power, Colleen Joyce 1945- *WhoAmW 93*
Power, David *ScF&FL 92*
Power, David J. *Law&B 92*
Power, Dennis Michael 1941- *WhoAm 92*
Power, Edwin Albert *WhoScE 91-1*
Power, Elizabeth Henry 1953- *WhoAmW 93*
Power, Eugene Barnum 1905- *WhoAm 92*
Power, F. William 1925- *St&PR 93, WhoAm 92*
Power, Ian D. 1954- *St&PR 93*
Power, J. Timothy *BioIn 17*
Power, Jenny Wilmarth Theresa 1960- *WhoWor 93*
Power, John Bruce 1936- *WhoAm 92*
Power, John G. 1932- *WhoIns 93*
Power, John George 1932- *St&PR 93*
Power, Joseph Edward 1938- *WhoAm 92*
Power, Jules 1921- *WhoAm 92*
Power, Kenneth D. 1927- *WhoAm 92*
Power, Leonel d1445 *Baker 92*
Power, M.S. 1935- *ScF&FL 92*
Power, Marjorie 1947- *WhoWrEP 92*
Power, Mark 1937- *WhoAm 92*
Power, Mary Susan 1935- *WhoAm 92*
Power, Michelle *Law&B 92*
Power, Richard Dunstan 1948- *St&PR 93*
Power, Robert Harbison 1926- *WhoAm 92*
Power, Sharon Andrews 1952- *St&PR 93*
Power, Stephen Charles *WhoScE 91-1*
Power, Stephen H. 1939- *St&PR 93*
Power, Susan H. *Law&B 92*
Power, Thomas Edward 1946- *WhoSSW 93*
Power, Thomas Francis, Jr. 1940- *St&PR 93, WhoAm 92*
Power, Thomas Michael 1940- *WhoAm 92*
Power, Tyrone 1913-1958 *BioIn 17*
Power, Tyrone 1914-1958 *IntDcF 2-3 [port]*
Power, Victor Pellot 1931- *BiDAMSp 1989*
Power, W. Gerard *Law&B 92*
Power, William Redmond 1945- *WhoAm 92*
Powero, Leonel d1445 *Baker 92*
Powers, Allen Edward 1939- *St&PR 93, WhoAm 92*
Powers, Amy Lynne 1961- *WhoAmW 93*
Powers, Ann 1946- *WhoAm 92*
Powers, Arthur 1947- *WhoAm 92, WhoSSW 93*
Powers, Arthur Sutherland 1947- *St&PR 93*
Powers, Bruce Raymond 1927- *WhoAm 92, WhoE 93*
Powers, Carla K. 1962- *St&PR 93*
Powers, Charles Henri 1945- *WhoAm 92*
Powers, Charles William 1941- *WhoE 93*
Powers, Claudia McKenna 1950- *WhoAmW 93*
Powers, David Alton 1948- *WhoSSW 93*
Powers, Dennis Alpha 1938- *WhoAm 92*
Powers, Dennis W. 1942- *St&PR 93*
Powers, Diane 1943- *St&PR 93*
Powers, Donald Matthew, Jr. 1941- *WhoE 93*
Powers, Doris Hurt 1927- *WhoAmW 93*
Powers, Duane C. 1934- *St&PR 93*
Powers, Dudley 1911- *WhoAm 92*
Powers, Edward Alton 1927- *WhoAm 92*
Powers, Edward D. 1932- *St&PR 93*
Powers, Edward John, Jr. 1938- *WhoE 93*
Powers, Edward Latell 1919- *WhoAm 92*
Powers, Edwin Malvin 1915- *WhoE 93*
Powers, Eric Randall 1947- *WhoAm 92*
Powers, Ernest Michael 1942- *WhoWor 93*
Powers, Eva Agoston 1938- *WhoE 93*
Powers, Francis Gary 1929-1977 *BioIn 17, ColdWar 1 [port]*
Powers, Frederick W. *Law&B 92*
Powers, Frederick Wayne 1951- *St&PR 93*
Powers, George Richard *Law&B 92*
Powers, Geraldine Dolan *WhoAmW 93*
Powers, Harold S(tone) 1928- *Baker 92*
Powers, Harris Pat 1934- *WhoAm 92*
Powers, Henry Martin 1932- *St&PR 93*
Powers, Henry Martin, Jr. 1932- *WhoAm 92*
Powers, Hiram 1805-1873 *BioIn 17*
Powers, Hugh J. *Law&B 92*
Powers, J.F. 1917- *BioIn 17, MagSAmL [port]*
Powers, James Bascom 1924- *WhoAm 92*
Powers, James Carter 1936- *WhoE 93*
Powers, James F. 1938- *WhoE 93*
Powers, James Farl 1917- *BioIn 17, WhoAm 92, WhoWrEP 92*
Powers, James Francis 1938- *St&PR 93, WhoAm 92*
Powers, James J. 1936- *WhoIns 93*
Powers, Jan *Law&B 92*
Powers, Jefrey R. 1959- *St&PR 93*
Powers, John A. 1926- *St&PR 93*
Powers, John Glenn, Jr. 1930- *WhoAm 92*
Powers, John J. 1912-1942 *BioIn 17*
Powers, John Joseph 1918- *WhoSSW 93*
Powers, John Joseph 1935- *St&PR 93, WhoAm 92*
Powers, John Kieran 1947- *WhoE 93, WhoWor 93*
Powers, John R. 1945- *WhoAm 92, WhoWrEP 92*
Powers, John W. 1938- *St&PR 93*

Powers, Kathleen Jay 1946- *WhoAmW 93*
Powers, Kenneth William 1930- *WhoE 93*
Powers, Kerns Harrington *BioIn 17*
Powers, Larry K. 1942- *St&PR 93*
Powers, Laura Beth 1950- *WhoAmW 93*
Powers, Lawrence M. 1931- *St&PR 93*
Powers, Lawrence Milton 1931- *WhoAm 92*
Powers, Leo J. 1909-1967 *BioIn 17*
Powers, Louise E. *ScF&FL 92*
Powers, Mala 1931- *BioIn 17, WhoAm 92*
Powers, Marcus E. *Law&B 92*
Powers, Marcus E. 1929- *St&PR 93*
Powers, Marcus Eugene 1929- *WhoAm 92, WhoWor 93*
Powers, Margaret Maura *Law&B 92*
Powers, Michael Francis *Law&B 92*
Powers, Michael Kevin 1948- *WhoAm 92, WhoE 93*
Powers, Odell E. d1991 *BioIn 17*
Powers, Onie H. 1907- *WhoWor 93*
Powers, Patricia Ann *Law&B 92*
Powers, Paul Joseph 1935- *St&PR 93, WhoAm 92*
Powers, Philip Hemsley 1937- *WhoSSW 93*
Powers, Ralph A., Jr. 1936- *St&PR 93*
Powers, Ramon Sidney 1939- *WhoAm 92*
Powers, Ray *St&PR 93*
Powers, Raymond E. 1937- *St&PR 93*
Powers, Richard 1921- *ScF&FL 92*
Powers, Richard 1957- *BioIn 17*
Powers, Richard Dale 1927- *WhoAm 92*
Powers, Richard F., III 1946- *WhoAm 92*
Powers, Richard Ralph 1940- *WhoAm 92*
Powers, Richard T. 1947- *St&PR 93*
Powers, Richard William *Law&B 92*
Powers, Robert Allan 1926- *St&PR 93*
Powers, Ronald George 1934- *WhoWor 93*
Powers, Samuel Joseph 1917-1991 *BioIn 17*
Powers, Sarah Ann 1958- *WhoAmW 93*
Powers, Scott 1948- *WhoE 93*
Powers, Shirley Marie 1930- *WhoAmW 93*
Powers, Sonia Nodle 1943- *WhoAmW 93*
Powers, Stefanie 1945- *WhoAm 92*
Powers, Suzi Elizabeth 1961- *WhoAmW 93*
Powers, T.W. *Law&B 92*
Powers, Theodore Richard 1932- *St&PR 93*
Powers, Thomas E. 1929- *St&PR 93*
Powers, Thomas J. *Law&B 92*
Powers, Thomas Moore 1940- *WhoAm 92, WhoWrEP 92*
Powers, Tim 1952- *ScF&FL 92*
Powers, Tom *ScF&FL 92*
Powers, Tom L. 1936- *WhoSSW 93*
Powers, Walter E. 1941- *St&PR 93*
Powers, William F. *BioIn 17*
Powers, William J., Jr. *Law&B 92*
Powers, William Jennings 1930- *WhoAm 92*
Powers, William Shotwell 1910- *WhoAm 92*
Powerscourt, Sheila *ConAu 136*
Powhatan, Becky A. *Law&B 92*
Powhatan, Becky A. 1952- *St&PR 93*
Powing, Maynard Walker 1931- *St&PR 93*
Powis, Alfred 1930- *St&PR 93, WhoAm 92, WhoWor 93*
Powlan, Rebecca *Law&B 92*
Powlędge, Fred Arlius 1935- *WhoE 93*
Powles, Jack Gordon *WhoScE 91-1*
Powles, John G. 1936- *St&PR 93, WhoIns 93*
Powles, Trevor J. 1938- *WhoScE 91-1*
Powley, George Reinhold 1916- *WhoAm 92*
Powlick, George E. 1944- *St&PR 93*
Powling, Chris 1943- *ChlFicS*
Powlson, David Stephen *WhoScE 91-1*
Powlus, JoAnn Y. *Law&B 92*
Pownall, (Marjorie) Eve(lyn Sheridan) *DcChlFi*
Pownall, James Richard 1951- *WhoWor 93*
Pownall, Malcolm Wilmor 1933- *WhoAm 92*
Pownall, Mary Ann 1751-1796 *Baker 92*
Pownall, Thomas G. 1922- *St&PR 93*
Powning, Maynard Walker 1931- *St&PR 93*
Powys, John Cowper 1872-1963 *BioIn 17, ScF&FL 92*
Powys, Llewelyn 1884-1939 *BioIn 17*
Poy, Glenn Derrick 1957- *WhoWor 93*
Poyarkov, Vasily Danilovich d1668 *Expl 93*
Poyart, Claude *WhoScE 91-2*
Poydasheff, Robert S. 1930- *St&PR 93*
Poydock, Mary Eymard 1910- *WhoAm 92*
Poyer, David 1949- *WhoWrEP 92*
Poyer, David C. 1949- *ScF&FL 92*
Poyer, Joe *ConAu 40NR*
Poyer, Joe 1939- *ScF&FL 92*
Poyer, Joseph *ScF&FL 92*
Poyer, Joseph John, Jr. 1939- *ConAu 40NR*
Poyner, James Marion 1914- *WhoAm 92*
Poynor, Deborah Ann 1952- *WhoAmW 93*
Poynor, Robert Allen, Jr. 1939- *WhoSSW 93*
Poynter, Beulah *AmWomPl*
Poynter, Daniel Frank 1938- *WhoWrEP 92*
Poynter, James Bradford 1950- *St&PR 93*
Poynter, James Morrison 1939- *WhoWor 93*
Poynter, Judy Fensterbusch 1950- *WhoAmW 93*
Poynter, Marion K. *BioIn 17*
Poynter, Marion Knauss 1926- *WhoAm 92*
Poynter, Melissa Venable 1949- *WhoAmW 93, WhoSSW 93*
Poynter, Nelson 1903-1978 *DcLB 127 [port]*
Poynter, Philip A. 1942- *WhoIns 93*
Poynter, Wandaleen *Law&B 92*
Poyntz, Juliet Stuart *BioIn 17*
Poyourow, Robert Lee *Law&B 92*
Poysa, H. *WhoScE 91-4*
Poythress, David Bryan 1943- *WhoAm 92*
Poythress, Stephanie Lynn 1964- *WhoAmW 93*
Pozar, Hrvoje 1916- *WhoScE 91-4*
Pozas Arciniega, Ricardo 1912- *DcMexL*
Pozdro, John (Walter) 1923- *Baker 92, WhoAm 92*
Pozen, Denise *Law&B 92*
Pozen, Robert Charles *Law&B 92*
Pozen, Robert Charles 1946- *St&PR 93*
Pozen, Walter 1933- *WhoAm 92*
Pozil, Paul L. 1938- *St&PR 93*
Poznanska, Krystyna 1954- *WhoWor 93*
Poznanski, Andrew Karol 1931- *WhoAm 92*
Pozner, Vladimir *BioIn 17*
Pozner, Vladimir 1934- *ConAu 136*
Pozos, Anthony Martin 1940- *St&PR 93*
Pozsgai, John *BioIn 17*
Pozsgay, Imre *BioIn 17*
Pozsgay, Imre 1933- *ColdWar 2 [port]*
Pozza, Duane Charles 1953- *St&PR 93*
Pozzatti, Rudy Otto 1925- *WhoAm 92*
Pozzessere, Heather *ScF&FL 92*
Pozzi, Angelo 1932- *WhoWor 93*
Pozzi, Luigi 1929- *WhoScE 91-3*
Pozzilli, Paolo Paride 1951- *WhoWor 93*
Pozzuoli, Joseph Anthony 1953- *WhoE 93*
Prabhakar, Sundaresan 1937- *WhoWor 93*
Prabhakaran, Ramamurthy 1943- *WhoSSW 93*
Prabhu, Catherine Dudley 1941- *WhoE 93*
Prabhu, R. 1947- *WhoAsAP 91*
Praca, Antonio Augusto Souza 1953- *WhoWor 93*
Prachick, Toni Thomas 1954- *WhoAmW 93*
Pracht, Drenda Kay 1952- *WhoAmW 93, WhoEmL 93*
Prada, Adrian 1960- *WhoWor 93*
Prada, Alberto Armando 1962- *WhoEmL 93, WhoWor 93*
Prada Oropeza, Renato 1937- *SpAmA*
Prade, Ernest La *ScF&FL 92*
Prade, Jean Noel Cresta 1946- *WhoSSW 93, WhoWor 93*
Pradella, Marco 1955- *WhoWor 93*
Pradere, Francois *WhoScE 91-2*
Pradham, Sahana *WhoAsAP 91*
Pradhan, Goraksha Bahadur N. 1929- *WhoWor 93*
Pradhan, Trilochan 1929- *WhoWor 93*
Pradhani, K. 1922- *WhoAsAP 91*
Pradier, Jerome Martin 1947- *WhoSSW 93*
Prado, Antonio G. 1945- *St&PR 93*
Prado, Edward C. 1947- *HispAmA*
Prado, Edward Charles 1947- *WhoAm 92, WhoSSW 93*
Prado, Gerald M. 1946- *St&PR 93, WhoAm 92*
Prado, Julio 1958- *WhoWor 93*
Prado, Pedro *Law&B 92*
Prado, William Manuel 1927- *WhoSSW 93*
Prados, Emilio 1899-1962 *DcMexL*
Prados, John William 1929- *WhoAm 92*
Pradt, Louis A. 1931- *St&PR 93*
Praed, Winthrop Mackworth 1802-1839 *BioIn 17*
Praeger, Cheryl Elisabeth 1948- *WhoWor 93*
Praeger, Frederick Amos 1915- *WhoAm 92*
Praeger, Herman Albert, Jr. 1920- *WhoWor 93*
Praeger, Otto 1871-1948 *EncABHB 8 [port]*
Praeger, Robert Lloyd 1865-1953 *BioIn 17*
Prael, Francis J. d1991 *BioIn 17*
Praestgaard, Eigil L. *WhoScE 91-2*
Praetextatus 31-?-384 *OxDcByz*
Praetorius *Baker 92*
Praetorius, Hieronymus 1560-1629 *Baker 92*
Praetorius, Jacob c. 1530-1586 *Baker 92*
Praetorius, Jacob 1586-1651 *Baker 92*
Praetorius, Johannes c. 1595-1660 *Baker 92*
Praetorius, Michael 1571-1621 *Baker 92*
Praetorius, William Albert, Sr. 1924- *WhoAm 92*
Pragacz, Susan Ann 1952- *WhoAmW 93*
Pragana, Rildo Jose Da Costa 1951- *WhoWor 93*
Pragay, Desider Alex 1921- *WhoWor 93*
Prager, Alan N. *Law&B 92*
Prager, Alice Heinecke 1930- *WhoAm 92*
Prager, David 1918- *WhoAm 92*
Prager, Herta 1909-1991 *BioIn 17*
Prager, Iris J. 1944- *St&PR 93*
Prager, Jean-Claude 1945- *WhoWor 93*
Prager, Jonas 1938- *WhoE 93*
Prager, Morton David 1927- *WhoSSW 93*
Prager, Paul G. 1941- *St&PR 93*
Prager, Stephen 1928- *WhoAm 92*
Prager, Susan Westerberg 1942- *WhoAm 92*
Prah, Pamela Marie 1963- *WhoE 93*
Prahl, Richard D. 1945- *St&PR 93*
Prahl-Andersen, Birte 1939- *WhoWor 93*
Prahler, Richard Joseph 1946- *St&PR 93*
Prahm, Lars Philipsen 1944- *WhoScE 91-2*
Prain, K.A.R. *WhoScE 91-1*
Prairie, Celia Esther Freda 1940- *WhoE 93*
Prairie, James R. 1926- *St&PR 93*
Prais, John Peter 1945- *St&PR 93*
Praisner, J.A. *St&PR 93*
Prajer-Janczewska, Lidia 1925- *WhoScE 91-4*
Prakap, William A. 1955- *St&PR 93*
Prakapas, Dorothy 1928- *WhoAmW 93*
Prakapas, Eugene Joseph 1932- *WhoAm 92*
Prakash, Ravi 1941- *WhoAm 92*
Prakash, Satya 1938- *WhoAm 92*
Prakup, Barbara Lynn 1957- *WhoAmW 93*
Pralle, Arlene *BioIn 17*
Pralong, Sandra 1958- *WhoAmW 93, WhoWor 93*
Pramar, Yashoda Vickram 1960- *WhoSSW 93*
Pramberg, James Cook 1955- *WhoSSW 93*
Pramer, David 1923- *WhoAm 92*
Pramer, Ulf 1938- *WhoWor 93*
Pramila, Antti V.J. 1951- *WhoScE 91-4*
Pran, Peter Christian 1935- *WhoAm 92*
Prance, G.T. *WhoScE 91-1*
Prance, Ghillean T. 1937- *BioIn 17*
Prance, Ghillean Tolmie 1937- *WhoScE 91-1*
Prance, June E. *WhoWrEP 92*
Prandl, Wolfram 1935- *WhoScE 91-3*
Prandle, David *WhoScE 91-1*
Prange, Arthur Jergen, Jr. 1926- *WhoAm 92*
Prange, Henry C. 1927- *St&PR 93*
Prange, Marnie 1953- *WhoWrEP 92*
Prange, Raymon A. 1921- *St&PR 93*
Prange, Richard Herman 1946- *St&PR 93*
Pranger, Louis John 1925- *WhoSSW 93*
Prangsma, Geert J. 1941- *WhoScE 91-3*
Pranses, Anthony Louis 1920- *WhoAm 92*
Prantera, Amanda 1942- *ScF&FL 92*
Prappas, Dempsey J. *Law&B 92*
Praquin, Pierre *BioIn 17*
Pras, Robert Thomas 1941- *St&PR 93, WhoAm 92*
Prasad, Ananda Shiva 1928- *WhoAm 92*
Prasad, Brij 1942- *St&PR 93*
Prasad, Chaudhury Mukesh 1946- *St&PR 93*
Prasad, Govind 1933- *WhoUN 92*
Prasad, Rajendra 1884-1963 *DcTwHis*
Prasad, Ramjee 1946- *WhoWor 93*
Prasad, Ramon 1940- *WhoWor 93*
Prasad, Sankarshan 1933- *St&PR 93*
Prasad, Surya Sattiraju *WhoWor 93*
Prasad, Udayan *MiSFD 9*
Prasad, Vishwanath 1949- *WhoE 93*
Prasertphon, Sothorn 1933- *WhoUN 92*
Prashker, Betty A. *WhoWrEP 92*
Prasse, Gene R. *Law&B 92*
Prasse, Ronald D. 1938- *St&PR 93*
Prassel, Frank G. 1912- *St&PR 93*
Prast, Robert F. 1939- *St&PR 93*
Prata, Eduardo L.A. 1950- *WhoScE 91-3*
Prat-Bartes, Albert 1942- *WhoScE 91-3*
Pratchett, Terry 1948- *ChlFicS, ScF&FL 92*
Pratella, Francesco Balilla 1880-1955 *Baker 92*
Prater, David 1937-1988 *See Sam and Dave ConMus 8*
See Also Sam & Dave *SoulM*
Prater, Jack Edward 1951- *WhoSSW 93*
Prater, John 1947- *SmATA 72*
Prater, John Edward 1938- *St&PR 93, WhoAm 92*
Prater, Penny L. *Law&B 92*
Prater, Robert W. 1930- *St&PR 93*
Prater, Ruby Marian 1915- *WhoWrEP 92*
Prater-Harvey, Peggy 1949- *St&PR 93*
Pratesi, Riccardo 1936- *WhoScE 91-3*
Prather, Donna Lynn 1946- *WhoAmW 93*
Prather, Gerald L. 1935- *WhoAm 92*
Prather, Jon L. 1939- *St&PR 93*
Prather, Jon Lee *Law&B 92*
Prather, Lenore Loving 1931- *WhoAm 92, WhoAmW 93, WhoSSW 93*
Prather, Nancy Nicole 1969- *WhoAmW 93*
Prather, Ray *BlkAuII 92*
Prather, Rita Catherine 1948- *WhoSSW 93*
Prather, Thomas Levi, Jr. 1940- *AfrAmBi, WhoAm 92*
Prather, William E., Jr. 1947- *WhoAm 92, WhoSSW 93*
Prati, Alessio 1750-1788 *OxDcOp*
Prati, Lauro 1937- *WhoScE 91-3*
Pratkanis, Lisa Ann 1965- *WhoSSW 93*
Pratney, William A. *ScF&FL 92*
Pratney, Winkie 1944- *ScF&FL 92*
Prato, Nancy Rutter Henry 1935- *WhoAmW 93*
Pratola, Stephanie 1952- *WhoSSW 93*
Pratolini, Vasco 1913-1991 *BioIn 17*
Prats, Michael 1925- *WhoAm 92*
Pratsch, Johann-Christian 1928- *WhoSSW 93*
Pratsolis, Stamatis 1949- *WhoWor 93*
Pratt, Addison d1872 *BioIn 17*
Pratt, Aileen M. *Law&B 92*
Pratt, Alan John 1927- *WhoWor 93*
Pratt, Albert 1911- *WhoAm 92*
Pratt, Alice Ford 1926- *WhoE 93*
Pratt, Alice Reynolds 1922- *WhoAmW 93, WhoWor 93*
Pratt, Anne Caroline 1953- *WhoAmW 93*
Pratt, Annis 1937- *ScF&FL 92*
Pratt, Billy Kenton 1948- *WhoSSW 93*
Pratt, Burt Carlton 1911- *WhoE 93*
Pratt, Charles McCready *Law&B 92*
Pratt, Christine 1961- *WhoAmW 93*
Pratt, Christopher John *WhoScE 91-1*
Pratt, Cindy Ann 1960- *WhoAmW 93*
Pratt, Dan Edwin 1924- *WhoAm 92*
Pratt, Dana Joseph 1926- *WhoAm 92*
Pratt, David D. 1936- *St&PR 93*
Pratt, David H. 1949- *St&PR 93*
Pratt, David Lee 1957- *WhoSSW 93*
Pratt, David Terry 1934- *WhoAm 92*
Pratt, Davis 1923-1991 *BioIn 17*
Pratt, Diane Adele 1951- *WhoAmW 93*
Pratt, Dianne Carol 1946- *WhoAmW 93*
Pratt, Donald Henry 1937- *St&PR 93*
Pratt, Dori 1955- *WhoAmW 93*
Pratt, E.J. 1882-1964 *BioIn 17*
Pratt, Edmund T., Jr. 1927- *St&PR 93*
Pratt, Edmund Taylor, Jr. 1927- *WhoAm 92, WhoE 93*
Pratt, Edward Taylor, Jr. 1923- *WhoAm 92*
Pratt, Edwin John 1882-1964 *BioIn 17*
Pratt, Eliza Jane 1902-1981 *BioIn 17*
Pratt, Fletcher 1897-1956 *ScF&FL 92*
Pratt, G.N. *Law&B 92*
Pratt, George 1932- *St&PR 93*
Pratt, George Cheney 1928- *WhoAm 92, WhoE 93*
Pratt, George Leonard Berry 1930- *WhoAm 92*
Pratt, Georgeanne C. *St&PR 93*
Pratt, Jane *BioIn 17*
Pratt, Jane c. 1963- *Au&Arts 9 [port], ConAu 138*
Pratt, John Adams, Jr. 1930- *St&PR 93, WhoAm 92*
Pratt, John Clark 1932- *ConAu 40NR, WhoWrEP 92*
Pratt, John Helm 1910- *CngDr 91, WhoAm 92*
Pratt, John Macdonald *WhoScE 91-1*
Pratt, John Rolla 1940- *WhoE 93*
Pratt, John Winsor 1931- *WhoAm 92*
Pratt, Joseph Hyde, Jr. 1911- *WhoAm 92*
Pratt, Julia *AmWomPl*
Pratt, Katherine Claire 1956- *WhoAmW 93*
Pratt, Lawrence Arthur 1907- *WhoAm 92, WhoWor 93*
Pratt, Linda 1948- *WhoE 93*
Pratt, Linda Ray 1943- *WhoAmW 93*
Pratt, M.S. *WhoScE 91-1*
Pratt, Margaret Wade 1925- *WhoWor 93*
Pratt, Marjorie Jean 1936- *WhoWrEP 92*
Pratt, Mark Ernest 1939- *WhoSSW 93*
Pratt, Marvin 1944- *AfrAmBi [port]*
Pratt, Mary *AmWomPl*
Pratt, Matthew Rick 1928- *WhoAm 92*
Pratt, Michael John *WhoScE 91-1*

Pratt, Michael John 1937- WhoWor 93
Pratt, Michael Theodore 1943- WhoAm 92
Pratt, Miles Robert 1942- St&PR 93
Pratt, Nancy Cameron 1960- WhoAmW 93
Pratt, P.L. WhoScE 91-1
Pratt, Paul W. 1946- WhoWrEP 92
Pratt, Peter Lynn WhoScE 91-1
Pratt, Philip Chase 1920- WhoAm 92
Pratt, Rachel Brook AmWomPl
Pratt, Richard Law&B 92
Pratt, Richard G. Law&B 92
Pratt, Richard Houghton 1934- WhoAm 92, WhoE 93
Pratt, Richardson, Jr. 1923- WhoAm 92, WhoE 93
Pratt, Robert Cranford 1926- WhoAm 92
Pratt, Robert Henry 1922- WhoSSW 93
Pratt, Robert Leonard 1947- WhoE 93
Pratt, Robert N. 1930- St&PR 93
Pratt, Robert Thomas, Jr. 1959- WhoSSW 93
Pratt, Robert Wayne 1967- WhoSSW 93
Pratt, Rosalie Rebollo 1933- WhoAmW 93
Pratt, Ruth Sears Baker 1877-1965 BioIn 17
Pratt, Sherwood L. 1932- St&PR 93
Pratt, Sherwood Lambertson 1932- WhoE 93
Pratt, Silas Gamaliel 1846-1916 Baker 92
Pratt, Stephen John WhoScE 91-1
Pratt, Terrence Wendall 1940- WhoAm 92
Pratt, Waldo Selden 1857-1939 Baker 92
Pratt, Walter E. 1927- St&PR 93
Pratt, Wendy Labreche 1951- WhoAmW 93
Pratt, William Crouch, Jr. 1927- WhoAm 92, WhoWrEP 92
Pratt, William Gordon 1954- WhoIns 93
Pratt, William Henry Law&B 92
Pratt, William Hunter 1913- WhoSSW 93
Pratte, Eugene J. Wyser- d1990 BioIn 17
Pratte, Lise 1950- St&PR 93, WhoAm 92
Pratte, Louis 1926- WhoE 93
Praus, Oldrich 1929- WhoScE 91-4
Prausnitz, Frederik 1920- Baker 92
Prausnitz, John Michael 1928- WhoAm 92
Pravdic, Velimir 1931- WhoScE 91-4
Pravel, Bernarr Roe 1924- WhoAm 92
Pravica, Petar 1931- WhoScE 91-4
Praw, Albert Z. Law&B 92
Praw, Albert Z. 1948- St&PR 93
Prawel, Sherwood P. 1932- WhoE 93
Prawer, Harvey Edwin 1938- St&PR 93
Prawer, Joshua 1917-1990 BioIn 17
Prawer, S.S. 1925- ScF&FL 92
Prawer, Siegbert Salomon 1925- WhoWor 93
Prawiro, Radius 1928- WhoAsAP 91
Prawl, Nancy Irene 1942- WhoAmW 93
Praxenthaler, Heinrich 1926- WhoScE 91-3
Pray, Charles Craig 1955- St&PR 93
Pray, David W. 1942- WhoIns 93
Pray, Glen A. St&PR 93
Pray, Janet Lorraine 1939- WhoAmW 93
Pray, Lloyd Charles 1919- WhoAm 92
Pray, Merle Evelyn 1931- WhoAmW 93
Pray, Ralph Marble, III 1938- WhoAm 92
Praytor, Margaret Aiken 1948- WhoAmW 93
Prazewska, Mieczyslawa 1931- WhoScE 91-4
Prazmark, Rob BioIn 17
Prcic, Midhat 1925- WhoScE 91-4
Preacher, Ronda Radford 1949- WhoAmW 93
Preate, Ernest D., Sr. 1909- WhoAm 92
Preate, Ernest D., Jr. 1940- WhoAm 92, WhoE 93
Preate, Joseph Gerard 1961- WhoE 93
Preato, Robert R. d1991 BioIn 17
Prebble, Richard William 1948- WhoAsAP 91
Prebich, Elizabeth Ann 1949- WhoAmW 93
Prebil, James M. St&PR 93
Prebisch, Raul 1901-1986 BioIn 17
Preble, Edward 1761-1807 HarEnMi
Preble, Laurence George 1939- WhoAm 92
Preble, Robert C., Jr. 1922- St&PR 93
Preble, Robert Curtis, Jr. 1922- WhoIns 93
Prebluda, Harry J. 1911-1990 BioIn 17
Precht, James David 1949- WhoAm 92
Precht, Witold 1928- WhoScE 91-4
Precht, Wolfgang 1938- WhoScE 91-4
Prechter, Robert Rougelot BioIn 17
Preciado, Cecilia de Burciago NotHsAW 93
Precizale, Shelley G. Law&B 92
Preckwinkle, George Thomas 1917- St&PR 93
Preckwinkle, George Wilburn 1956- St&PR 93
Preclik, Herbert Joachim 1951- WhoUN 92
Precopio, Frank Mario 1925- WhoAm 92
Precourt, Frank Arnold 1929- St&PR 93
Precourt, George Augustine 1934- WhoAm 92
Precourt, Jay A. 1937- St&PR 93
Precsenyi, I. 1926- WhoScE 91-4
Pred, Elenore BioIn 17
Pred, Nancy G. 1958- WhoAmW 93
Preda, Ileana 1924- WhoScE 91-3
Predan, Robert Arthur-Michael Law&B 92
Preddy, F.A. 1935- St&PR 93
Preddy, Raymond Randall 1940- WhoAm 92, WhoSSW 93
Predel, Bruno 1928- WhoScE 91-3
Predeleanu, Mircea 1929- WhoScE 91-2
Predieri Baker 92
Predieri, Antonio c. 1650-1710 Baker 92
Predieri, Giacomo Cesare 1671-1753 Baker 92
Predieri, Giacomo (Maria) 1611-1695 Baker 92
Predieri, Luca Antonio 1688-1767 Baker 92, OxDcOp
Predock, Antoine BioIn 17
Predock, Antoine 1936- News 93-2
Preece, Michael 1936- MiSFD 9
Preece, Nancy Ann 1960- WhoAmW 93
Preece, Paul Eric WhoScE 91-1
Preece, Robert S. Law&B 92
Preece, Timothy F. 1927- St&PR 93
Preece, Warren Eversleigh 1921- WhoAm 92
Preede, Nydia 1926- WhoE 93
Preeg, Ernest Henry 1934- WhoAm 92
Preer, John Randolph, Jr. 1918- WhoAm 92
Preetorius, Emil 1883-1973 OxDcOp
Prefontaine, Pierre Law&B 92
Prefontaine, Steve BioIn 17
Preger, Leo 1907-1965 Baker 92
Pregerson, Harry 1923- WhoAm 92
Pregger, Fred Titus 1924- WhoE 93
Pregill, Gregory Kent 1946- WhoAm 92
Pregnolato, John Anthony 1939- St&PR 93
Prego, Virginia 1958?- BioIn 17
Pregulman, Betsy A. Law&B 92
Pregulman, Mervin 1922- St&PR 93
Prehn, Edward C. 1910-1991 BioIn 17
Prehn, Ronald Scott 1953- WhoSSW 93
Prehoda, Robert W. 1929- ScF&FL 92
Preil, Gabriel BioIn 17
Preindl, Josef 1756-1823 Baker 92
Preining, Othmar 1927- WhoScE 91-4
Preis, Alexander George 1921- WhoWor 93
Preis, Paul H. 1933- St&PR 93
Preiser, Gert R. 1928- WhoScE 91-3
Preiser, Godfrey K., Jr. Law&B 92
Preiser, Wolfgang Friedrich Ernst 1941- WhoAm 92
Preiskel, Barbara Scott 1924- WhoAm 92, WhoE 93
Preiskel, Robert Howard 1922- WhoAm 92
Preisler, Jerome ScF&FL 92
Preiss, Beth 1954- WhoE 93
Preiss, Byron 1953- ScF&FL 92
Preiss, Cornelius 1884-1944 Baker 92
Preiss, David C. 1950- WhoE 93
Preiss, David Lee 1935- WhoAm 92
Preiss, Ivor Louis 1933- WhoE 93
Preiss, Jack 1932- WhoAm 92
Preisser, Bernhard F. 1947- St&PR 93
Preister, Mary Joan Cerny 1949- WhoAmW 93
Prejean, Dalton BioIn 17
Prejean, Jeanne Ellen 1949- WhoAmW 93
Prekop, Martin D. 1940- WhoAm 92
Prekopa, Andras 1929- WhoScE 91-4
Prelack, Steven 1957- St&PR 93
Prelinger, Catherine M. d1991 BioIn 17
Prell, Hermann Heinrich 1925- WhoScE 91-3
Prell, Michael Jack 1944- WhoAm 92
Prell, Owen Law&B 92
Prellberg, Joanne Marie 1960- WhoAmW 93
Prelog, Vladimir 1906- BioIn 17, WhoAm 92, WhoWor 93
Prelutsky, Jack BioIn 17
Prelutsky, Jack 1940- ConAu 38NR, MajAI [port], WhoAm 92
Prem, F. Herbert, Jr. 1932- WhoAm 92
Prem, Konald Arthur 1920- WhoAm 92
Premacanda 1880-1936 BioIn 17
Premack, David 1925- WhoAm 92
Premadasa, Ranasinghe 1924- WhoAsAP 91, WhoWor 93
Premchand 1880-1936 BioIn 17
Premecz, Gyorgy 1947- WhoScE 91-4
Premilat, Samuel 1938- WhoScE 91-2
Preminger, Otto 1906-1986 MiSFD 9N
Preminger, Robert Jay Law&B 92
Premo, Paul Mark 1942- WhoAm 92
Premont, Paul 1936- St&PR 93, WhoAm 92
Prempree, Thongbliew 1935- WhoSSW 93
Premru, Raymond (Eugene) 1934- Baker 92
Prendergast, D. Elizabeth Law&B 92
Prendergast, Maurice Brazil 1859-1924 BioIn 17
Prendergast, Michael H. 1913-1990 BioIn 17
Prendergast, Stephen D. Law&B 92
Prendergast, Stephen D. 1946- St&PR 93
Prendergast, Walter Gerard 1965- WhoWor 93
Preng, David Edward 1946- WhoAm 92
Prensky, Arthur Lawrence 1930- WhoAm 92
Prenter, Regin 1907-1991 BioIn 17
Prentice, Andrew Major WhoScE 91-1
Prentice, Ann Ethelynd 1933- WhoAm 92
Prentice, Bertha G. AmWomPl
Prentice, Bryant H., III 1940- St&PR 93
Prentice, David Ramage 1943- WhoAm 92
Prentice, Estar St&PR 93
Prentice, Eugene Miles, III 1942- WhoE 93, WhoWor 93
Prentice, George D. 1802-1870 JrnUS
Prentice, Irving John 1951- St&PR 93
Prentice, James Stuart 1944- WhoAm 92
Prentice, Norman Macdonald 1925- WhoAm 92
Prentice, Penelope Ann 1943- WhoWrEP 92
Prentice, Rena 1955- St&PR 93
Prentice, Sheldon Law&B 92
Prentice, Tim 1930- WhoAm 92
Prentiss, Augustin Mitchell, Jr. 1915- WhoAm 92
Prentiss, Benjamin Mayberry 1819-1901 HarEnMi
Prentiss, Janet AmWomPl
Prentiss, Michael V. BioIn 17
Prentiss, Robert Noble 1943- St&PR 93
Prentiss, Tina M. 1911- WhoWrEP 92
Preobrazhenskii, E.A. 1886-1937 BioIn 17
Preobrazhenskii, Evgenii Alekseevich 1886-1937 BioIn 17
Preobrazhensky, Anton (Viktorovich) 1870-1929 Baker 92
Preovolos, Penelope Athene 1955- WhoAm 92
Preparata, Franco Paolo 1935- WhoAm 92
Preparata, Giuliano M. 1942- WhoWor 93
Presby, J. Thomas 1940- WhoAm 92
Preschlack, John Edward 1933- WhoAm 92
Prescot, Dray ScF&FL 92
Prescott, Bruce Henry 1940- WhoWor 93
Prescott, Charles A. Law&B 92
Prescott, David Marshall 1926- WhoAm 92
Prescott, Gary M. Law&B 92
Prescott, Gerald James 1940- St&PR 93
Prescott, John Hernage 1935- WhoAm 92, WhoE 93
Prescott, John Mack 1921- WhoAm 92
Prescott, John Sherwin 1927- St&PR 93
Prescott, Laurie Francis WhoScE 91-1
Prescott, Laurie Francis 1934- WhoWor 93
Prescott, Lawrence Malcolm 1934- WhoWor 93
Prescott, Paul Ithel 1931- WhoSSW 93
Prescott, Peter Sherwin 1935- WhoAm 92
Prescott, Robert W. 1913-1978 EncABHB 8 [port]
Prescott, Robin John WhoScE 91-1
Prescott, Roger B., Jr. 1923- St&PR 93
Prescott, William Glenn 1936- WhoAm 92
Prescott, William Linzee 1917-1981 BioIn 17
Present, Raphael 1921- St&PR 93
Presgrove, Sharon Ruth 1946- WhoAmW 93
Presher, Gordon E. 1946- St&PR 93
President, Toni Elizabeth 1954- WhoAmW 93
Preska, Margaret Louise Robinson 1938- WhoAm 92, WhoAmW 93
Presle, Micheline 1922- IntDcF 2-3 [port]
Presley, Bobby W. 1931- WhoIns 93
Presley, Carole A. St&PR 93
Presley, Elvis 1935-1977 Baker 92, BioIn 17, IntDcF 2-3 [port]
Presley, Janet Passidomo 1952- WhoAmW 93
Presley, John Ralph WhoScE 91-1
Presley, Lisa Marie BioIn 17
Presley, Priscilla 1945- WhoAm 92
Presley, Priscilla Beaulieu BioIn 17
Presnar, Carol Ann 1959- St&PR 93
Presnar, Mark Steven 1952- St&PR 93
Presnell, W. Dale 1943- St&PR 93
Press, Aida Kabatznick 1926- WhoAmW 93
Press, Arthur I. 1934- WhoE 93
Press, Caren S. Law&B 92
Press, Charles 1922- WhoAm 92
Press, Debra Ann 1960- WhoAmW 93
Press, Edward 1913- WhoAm 92
Press, Frank 1924- WhoAm 92, WhoE 93
Press, Jeffery Bruce 1947- WhoAm 92
Press, Michael Warner 1947- St&PR 93, WhoAm 92
Press, Russell George, Jr. Law&B 92
Press, Simone Naomi Juda 1943- WhoWrEP 92
Press, William Henry 1948- WhoAm 92
Pressas, Wendy Forsht 1965- WhoAmW 93
Pressburger, Emeric 1902-1988 MiSFD 9N
Pressburger, Joyce Marie 1949- WhoSSW 93
Pressel, Ralph Richard 1945- WhoSSW 93
Pressense, Francis Dehaut de 1853-1914 BioIn 17
Presser, Cary 1952- WhoE 93
Presser, Dorothy Ann 1929- WhoSSW 93
Presser, Harriet Betty 1936- WhoAm 92
Presser, Sheldon Law&B 92
Presser, Stephen B. 1946- ConAu 139
Presser, Stephen Bruce 1946- WhoAm 92
Presser, Theodore 1848-1925 Baker 92
Pressey, Walter M. 1944- St&PR 93
Pressing, Kirk L. 1932-1991 BioIn 17
Pressler, Antone d1990 BioIn 17
Pressler, Herman Paul 1902- WhoAm 92
Pressler, Herman Paul, III 1930- WhoSSW 93
Pressler, Larry 1942- CngDr 91, WhoAm 92
Pressler, Menahem 1923- Baker 92
Pressler, Philip Bernard 1946- WhoE 93
Pressley, Carolyn Mullenax 1943- WhoAmW 93
Pressly, Barbara 1937- WhoAmW 93, WhoE 93
Pressly, Brantley Phillips 1949- WhoSSW 93
Pressly, Thomas James 1919- WhoAm 92
Pressly, William Laurens 1944- WhoE 93
Pressman, Alan 1941- WhoWor 93
Pressman, Barney 1894?-1991 BioIn 17
Pressman, Doc BioIn 17
Pressman, Edward BioIn 17
Pressman, Edward J. 1940- WhoE 93
Pressman, Fred 1923- BioIn 17
Pressman, Gene BioIn 17
Pressman, Harold B. 1913- St&PR 93
Pressman, Lisa Jo 1963- WhoAmW 93
Pressman, Michael 1950- MiSFD 9
Pressman, Richard Seth 1941- WhoSSW 93
Pressman, Robert BioIn 17
Pressman, Robert A. Law&B 92
Pressman, Steven 1952- WhoE 93
Pressman, Thelma 1921- WhoAmW 93
Pressman, Todd Evan 1960- WhoE 93
Presson, Gina 1959- WhoAmW 93
Pressouyre, Leon 1935- WhoWor 93
Pressprich, William O. 1956- St&PR 93
Presswood, Mary Theresa 1959- WhoAmW 93
Prest, Peckett 1810?-1859 ScF&FL 92
Prestage, James Jordan 1926- WhoAm 92
Prestage, Jewel Limar 1931- WhoAm 92, WhoAmW 93
Prestage, John Arthur Law&B 92
Prestage, Terri WhoIns 93
Prestamo, Felipe S. Law&B 92
Prestayko, Archie W. 1941- St&PR 93
Prestbo, John Andrew 1941- WhoAm 92, WhoWrEP 92
Prestegaard, Peter 1942- WhoAm 92
Prestemon, David L. Law&B 92
Prestera, Lauretta Anne 1947- WhoAmW 93
Prestes, Luis Carlos 1898-1990 BioIn 17
Presti, Geralyn M. Law&B 92
Presting, Hartmut 1956- WhoWor 93
Prestini, Elena 1949- WhoWor 93
Prestini, James Libero 1908- WhoAm 92
Prestipino, Anthony Charles 1947- St&PR 93
Prestley, Peter B. Law&B 92
Preston, Andrew Joseph 1922- WhoAm 92, WhoE 93, WhoWor 93
Preston, Beth Brown 1953- WhoE 93
Preston, Billy 1946- SoulM
Preston, C. Kathryn Law&B 92
Preston, Charles Brian 1937- WhoWor 93
Preston, Charles Milton 1918-1991 BioIn 17
Preston, Cheryl Gomez- BioIn 17
Preston, Colleen Ann 1955- WhoAmW 93
Preston, David Michael 1930- WhoAm 92
Preston, Effa Estelle 1884- AmWomPl
Preston, Elizabeth A. 1957- WhoAmW 93
Preston, Elizabeth Florence 1932- WhoAmW 93
Preston, Eugene Francis 1929- St&PR 93

Preston, Faith 1921- *WhoAm 92, WhoE 93*
Preston, Frances W. *WhoAm 92*
Preston, Frank N. 1928- *St&PR 93*
Preston, Frankie Lynn 1956- *WhoSSW 93*
Preston, Frederick Willard 1912- *WhoAm 92*
Preston, Gary Robert *Law&B 92*
Preston, Gaylene 1947- *MiSFD 9*
Preston, George *BioIn 17*
Preston, George W. *WhoAm 92*
Preston, Guy *ScF&FL 92*
Preston, Harry 1923- *ScF&FL 92*
Preston, Ida Reid *AmWomPl*
Preston, James E. 1933- *WhoAm 92*
Preston, James Edward 1933- *St&PR 93*
Preston, Jerome, Jr. 1922- *WhoAm 92*
Preston, John 1587-1628 *BioIn 17*
Preston, John 1945- *ConGAN, WhoWrEP 92*
Preston, John E. *Law&B 92*
Preston, John E. 1941- *St&PR 93*
Preston, John R. 1947- *St&PR 93*
Preston, Julia Jackson Christian 1887-1991 *BioIn 17*
Preston, Karen Yvonne *WhoAmW 93*
Preston, Kelly *BioIn 17*
Preston, Kendall, Jr. 1927- *WhoAm 92*
Preston, Lewis *BioIn 17*
Preston, Lewis T. 1926- *WhoUN 92*
Preston, Lewis Thompson 1926- *WhoAm 92*
Preston, Loyce Elaine 1929- *WhoAmW 93, WhoWor 93*
Preston, Malcolm 1919- *WhoAm 92*
Preston, Marcia 1944- *WhoWrEP 92*
Preston, Margaret Junkin 1820-1897 *BioIn 17*
Preston, Mark I. 1938- *St&PR 93*
Preston, Marvin 1944- *St&PR 93*
Preston, Mary Frances Johnson *AmWomPl*
Preston, Melvin Alexander 1921- *WhoAm 92*
Preston, Noel Gary 1947- *WhoSSW 93*
Preston, Norman Wyckoff 1932- *St&PR 93*
Preston, Richard Arthur 1910- *WhoAm 92*
Preston, Richard McCann 1954- *WhoE 93*
Preston, Robert 1918-1987 *IntDcF 2-3*
Preston, Robert Bruce 1926- *WhoAm 92*
Preston, Robert D. 1923- *WhoIns 93*
Preston, Robert F. *Law&B 92*
Preston, Robert Frank 1943- *St&PR 93*
Preston, Roy Charles 1944- *WhoScE 91-1*
Preston, Samuel Hulse 1943- *WhoAm 92*
Preston, Sara *AmWomPl*
Preston, Seymour Stotler, III 1933- *St&PR 93, WhoAm 92, WhoE 93*
Preston, Simon (John) 1938- *Baker 92*
Preston, Sondra Kay 1947- *WhoWrEP 92*
Preston, Stephen 1957- *WhoWor 93*
Preston, Susan Elliott *WhoAmW 93*
Preston, Susan Lee 1945- *WhoAmW 93*
Preston, Thomas Lyter 1934- *WhoSSW 93*
Preston, Thomas Ronald 1936- *WhoAm 92*
Preston, W. H., Mrs. *AmWomPl*
Preston, Wilbur Day, Jr. 1922- *WhoAm 92*
Preston, William *BioIn 17*
Preston, William Allen 1936- *St&PR 93*
Preston, William Hubbard 1920- *WhoAm 92*
Preston, William L. 1922- *St&PR 93*
Preston, William M. *Law&B 92*
Prestopino, Frank 1949- *St&PR 93*
Prestopino, Frank J. 1949- *WhoIns 93*
Prestopino, Robert Joseph 1937- *St&PR 93*
Prestowitz, Clyde Vincent 1941- *WhoAm 92*
Prestridge, Pamela Adair 1945- *WhoSSW 93, WhoWor 93*
Prestrud, Stuart Holmes 1919- *St&PR 93*
Prestwidge, Kathleen Joyce 1927- *WhoAmW 93*
Prestwood, John C., Jr. 1953- *St&PR 93*
Prete, Philip John 1955- *WhoSSW 93*
Pretenders, The *ConMus 8 [port]*
Preti, Carlo 1937- *WhoScE 91-3*
Pretipino, A.C. 1947- *St&PR 93*
Pretlow, Carol Jocelyn 1946- *WhoAmW 93*
Pretlow, Theresa P. 1939- *WhoAmW 93*
Pretnar, Igor 1924-1977 *DrEEuF*
Preto, G. 1942- *WhoScE 91-3*
Pretorius, Andries Wilhelmus Jacobus 1798-1853 *HarEnMi*
Pretorius, Marthinus Wessel 1819-1901 *HarEnMi*
Preto-Rodas, Richard Anthony 1936- *WhoAm 92*
Pretre, Georges 1924- *Baker 92, IntDcOp, OxDcOp*
Pretti, Bradford Joseph 1930- *WhoAm 92*
Prettl, Wilhelm 1939- *WhoScE 91-3*
Pretty, David Walter 1925- *WhoIns 93*
Prettyjohns, Richard Charles *WhoScE 91-1*
Prettyman, Elijah Barrett, Jr. 1925- *WhoAm 92*
Prettyman, Keith Arthur 1951- *St&PR 93, WhoIns 93*
Pretz, L. Dale *Law&B 92*
Pretzinger, Donald Leonard 1923- *WhoAm 92*
Pretzl, Klaus Peter 1940- *WhoWor 93*
Preus, Anthony 1936- *WhoE 93*
Preus, David Walter 1922- *WhoAm 92*
Preus, Jacob Aall Ottesen 1920- *WhoAm 92*
Preuschoft, Holger 1932- *WhoScE 91-3*
Preuss, Clifford W. 1931- *St&PR 93*
Preuss, Hans-Joachim 1932- *WhoScE 91-3*
Preuss, Heinzwerner 1925- *WhoScE 91-3*
Preuss, Konrad Theodor 1869-1938 *IntDcAn*
Preuss, Paul 1942- *ScF&FL 92*
Preuss, Roger Emil 1922- *WhoAm 92, WhoWor 93*
Preuss, Ronald Stephen 1935- *WhoWor 93*
Preuss, Ruben *MiSFD 9*
Preusser, Donald Harold 1957- *St&PR 93*
Preusser, E.F. 1946- *St&PR 93*
Preussler, Otfried 1923- *ScF&FL 92*
Preuter, W.R. *Law&B 92*
Preval, Rene *WhoWor 93*
Prevatte, Sheila Arrington 1953- *WhoAmW 93*
Preve, Roberta Jean 1954- *WhoAmW 93*
Prevert, Jacques 1900-1977 *BioIn 17*
Previato, Emma 1952- *WhoE 93*
Previdi, Peter P. 1943- *St&PR 93*
Previdi, Robert 1935- *WhoE 93*
Previll, Arthur Ernest 1921- *WhoE 93*
Previn, Andre 1929- *BioIn 17, WhoAm 92, WhoWor 93*
Previn, Andre (George) 1929- *Baker 92*
Previtali, Fernando 1907-1985 *Baker 92*
Previte, Richard 1935- *St&PR 93*
Previts, Gary John 1942- *WhoAm 92*
Prevor, Barry J. 1963- *St&PR 93*
Prevor, Michael 1936- *St&PR 93*
Prevost, (Joseph Gaston Charles) Andre 1934- *Baker 92*
Prevost, Antoine-Francois 1697-1763 *OxDcOp*
Prevost, Augustine 1723-1786 *HarEnMi*
Prevost, Edward James 1941- *WhoAm 92*
Prevost, Eugene-Prosper 1809-1872 *Baker 92*
Prevost, Louis-Constant 1787-1856 *BioIn 17*
Prevost, Philippe 1963- *WhoWor 93*
Prevost, Stephen M. 1938- *St&PR 93*
Prevost, Verbie Lovorn 1943- *WhoSSW 93*
Prevost, William M. 1945- *St&PR 93*
Prevot, Francois G. 1923- *WhoScE 91-2*
Prevot, Jean-Paul Henri 1928- *WhoScE 91-2*
Prevot, Michel *WhoScE 91-2*
Prevoznik, Stephen Joseph 1929- *WhoAm 92*
Prew, Diane Schmidt 1945- *WhoAmW 93*
Prew, Robert David *WhoScE 91-1*
Prewitt, Charles Thompson 1933- *WhoAm 92*
Prewitt, Joyce Ann 1938- *WhoSSW 93*
Prewitt, Kenneth 1936- *WhoAm 92*
Prewitt, Lena Burrell *WhoSSW 93*
Prewitt, Merle Rainey 1928- *WhoSSW 93*
Prewitt, Patricia Woods 1933- *WhoAmW 93, WhoSSW 93*
Prewitt, Taylor Archie, III 1938- *WhoSSW 93*
Prewoznik, Jerome Frank 1934- *WhoAm 92, WhoWor 93*
Prey, Claude 1925- *Baker 92, OxDcOp*
Prey, Hermann 1929- *Baker 92, IntDcOp, OxDcOp*
Preyer, Alvin O. 1945- *St&PR 93*
Preyer, Carl Adolph 1863-1947 *Baker 92*
Preyer, Gottfried von 1807-1901 *Baker 92*
Preyer, Robert Otto 1922- *WhoAm 92*
Preysner, John P. *Law&B 92*
Preysz, Louis Robert Fonss, III 1944- *WhoSSW 93*
Prezeau, Louis E. 1943- *St&PR 93*
Preziosi, Paolo 1931- *WhoScE 91-3*
Prezzano, Wilbur J. 1940- *St&PR 93*
Prezzano, Wilbur John 1940- *WhoAm 92*
Prian, Barbara Ann 1948- *WhoAmW 93*
Prianishnikov, Ippolit (Petrovich) 1847-1921 *Baker 92*
Priaulx, Allan 1940- *WhoAm 92*
Priaulx, David Lloyd 1949- *WhoSSW 93*
Pribble, Easton 1917- *WhoAm 92*
Pribila, L.W. *Law&B 92*
Pribor, Hugo Casimer 1928- *WhoWor 93*
Pribram, John G. 1924- *BioIn 17*
Pribram, John Karl 1941- *WhoE 93*
Pribyl, Vilem 1925-1990 *Baker 92, OxDcOp*
Pribyl, Wolfgang *WhoScE 91-4*
Price, Alan Thomas 1949- *WhoSSW 93*
Price, Albert 1930- *AfrAmBi*
Price, Alfred L. *Law&B 92*
Price, Alfred Lee 1935- *St&PR 93*
Price, Alvin Audis 1917- *WhoAm 92*
Price, Arthur Richard 1951- *WhoAm 92*
Price, B. Byron *WhoAm 92*
Price, B.R.L. *Law&B 92*
Price, Barbara Ann 1951- *WhoAmW 93*
Price, Barbara Graham 1965- *WhoE 93*
Price, Barbara Neff 1938- *WhoE 93*
Price, Ben A. 1938- *St&PR 93*
Price, Bradford F. 1956- *St&PR 93*
Price, Brian K. *Law&B 92*
Price, Bridgette Denise 1965- *WhoSSW 93*
Price, Caroline Leona 1947- *WhoSSW 93*
Price, Charles C. 1948- *St&PR 93*
Price, Charles H., II 1931- *WhoAm 92, WhoWor 93*
Price, Charles U. 1916- *WhoAm 92*
Price, Cheryl *St&PR 93*
Price, Christie Speir 1954- *WhoEmL 93*
Price, Christine Gundersen 1948- *WhoAmW 93*
Price, Christopher *BioIn 17*
Price, Christopher Philip *WhoScE 91-1*
Price, Clara B. *AmWomPl*
Price, Clarence L. *Law&B 92*
Price, Clifford B., Jr. *Law&B 92*
Price, Clifford Warren 1935- *WhoWor 93*
Price, Cynthia Ann 1957- *WhoEmL 93*
Price, Cynthia M. 1962- *WhoAmW 93*
Price, D.R.H. *WhoScE 91-1*
Price, Dalias Adolph 1913- *WhoAm 92*
Price, David B. 1945- *St&PR 93*
Price, David E. 1940- *CngDr 91*
Price, David Eugene 1940- *WhoAm 92, WhoSSW 93*
Price, David F. *MiSFD 9*
Price, David McClellan 1936- *WhoE 93*
Price, David Robert 1940- *St&PR 93*
Price, Dennis 1915-1973 *BioIn 17*
Price, Dennis Lee 1930- *WhoSSW 93*
Price, Derek de Solla 1922-1983 *BioIn 17*
Price, Don K. 1910- *WhoAm 92*
Price, Donald Albert 1919- *WhoAm 92*
Price, Donald E. *Law&B 92*
Price, Donald E. 1928- *St&PR 93*
Price, Donald George 1930- *WhoSSW 93*
Price, Donald Ray 1939- *WhoAm 92*
Price, Douglas Armstrong 1950- *WhoSSW 93, WhoWor 93*
Price, E.H., Jr. 1918- *St&PR 93*
Price, E. Hoffmann 1898-1988 *ScF&FL 92*
Price, Edgar Hilleary, Jr. 1918- *WhoAm 92*
Price, Edward Dean 1919- *WhoAm 92*
Price, Edward J. 1925- *BiDAMSp 1989*
Price, Elaine S. 1957- *WhoAmW 93*
Price, Emma *St&PR 93*
Price, Eugene 1929- *WhoSSW 93*
Price, Florence B(eatrice) 1888-1953 *Baker 92*
Price, Francis D., Jr. 1949- *St&PR 93*
Price, Frank 1930- *ConTFT 10, WhoAm 92*
Price, Gail Elizabeth 1940- *WhoAmW 93*
Price, Gary L. *Law&B 92*
Price, Gary L. 1944- *St&PR 93*
Price, Gary Layton 1947- *St&PR 93*
Price, Gary Lee 1954- *BioIn 17*
Price, George 1919- *DcCPCAm*
Price, George Cadle 1919- *WhoWor 93*
Price, Gerald F. *St&PR 93*
Price, Gilbert 1942-1991 *BioIn 17*
Price, Glenda Delores 1939- *WhoE 93*
Price, Glenn Albert 1923- *WhoE 93*
Price, Glenn Mason *Law&B 92*
Price, Gordon A. 1947- *St&PR 93*
Price, Grewyn *WhoScE 91-1*
Price, H. Lyons 1935- *St&PR 93*
Price, Harold A. 1893-1990 *BioIn 17*
Price, Harold James 1943- *WhoSSW 93*
Price, Harrison Alan 1921- *WhoAm 92*
Price, Harry S., Jr. 1910- *St&PR 93*
Price, Harry Steele, Jr. 1910- *WhoAm 92*
Price, Helena *St&PR 93*
Price, Henry E. 1947- *St&PR 93*
Price, Henry Locher 1922- *WhoAm 92*
Price, Hollister Anne Cawein 1954- *WhoEmL 93*
Price, Homer L. 1924- *St&PR 93*
Price, Humphrey Wallace 1954- *WhoWor 93*
Price, I. Edward 1942- *WhoAm 92*
Price, Irving Lanouette 1884-1976 *BioIn 17*
Price, J. C. 1854-1893 *EncAACR*
Price, Jacqueline S. 1952- *WhoAmW 93*
Price, James Edward 1941- *WhoE 93*
Price, James Eldridge 1952- *WhoSSW 93*
Price, James Gordon 1926- *WhoAm 92*
Price, James Huddleston 1950- *St&PR 93*
Price, James Ligon 1915- *WhoSSW 93*
Price, James Melford 1921- *WhoWor 93*
Price, James Ray 1939- *St&PR 93*
Price, Janet Isabel 1948- *WhoAmW 93*
Price, Janey Lou Ellen 1959- *WhoAmW 93*
Price, Janis *WhoAmW 93*
Price, Jay J. *Law&B 92*
Price, Jerome J. 1933- *St&PR 93*
Price, Jim *BioIn 17*
Price, Joan Webster 1931- *WhoE 93*
Price, Joanne 1938- *WhoAmW 93*
Price, Joe 1935- *WhoAm 92*
Price, Joe D. *BioIn 17*
Price, Joe Sealy 1933- *WhoSSW 93*
Price, John *WhoScE 91-1*
Price, John Aley 1947- *WhoAm 92*
Price, John-Allen 1954- *ScF&FL 92*
Price, John Bernard *Law&B 92*
Price, John J. 1951- *St&PR 93*
Price, John M. *Law&B 92*
Price, John Martin 1936- *St&PR 93*
Price, John Ronald 1951- *WhoSSW 93*
Price, John Roy 1938- *St&PR 93*
Price, John Roy, Jr. 1938- *WhoAm 92*
Price, John Stephen 1955- *WhoSSW 93*
Price, John William 1927- *WhoAm 92*
Price, Joseph Levering 1962- *WhoAm 92*
Price, Joyce Ann 1947- *WhoSSW 93*
Price, Judith Holm 1937- *WhoAmW 93*
Price, Julian 1943- *St&PR 93*
Price, Karen M. *Law&B 92*
Price, Keith 1950- *St&PR 93*
Price, Kenneth L. 1938- *St&PR 93*
Price, Kenneth M(arsden) 1954- *ConAu 38NR*
Price, Larry C. 1954- *WhoAm 92*
Price, Larry Dean 1954- *WhoSSW 93*
Price, Laura 1962- *WhoAmW 93*
Price, Leigh 1941- *WhoAmW 93*
Price, Leontyne *BioIn 17*
Price, Leontyne 1927- *EncAACR [port], IntDcOp [port], OxDcOp, WhoAm 92, WhoWor 93*
Price, (Mary Violet) Leontyne 1927- *Baker 92*
Price, Lester Lee 1955- *WhoE 93*
Price, Linda Rice 1948- *WhoAmW 93*
Price, Linda Susan 1946- *WhoAmW 93*
Price, Lloyd 1934- *SoulM*
Price, Lloyd M. 1931- *WhoAm 92*
Price, Lucile Brickner Brown 1902- *WhoWor 93*
Price, Margaret 1941- *IntDcOp, OxDcOp*
Price, Margaret Ann 1951- *WhoE 93*
Price, Margaret (Berenice) 1941- *Baker 92*
Price, Marian Whitlow 1943- *WhoSSW 93*
Price, Marilyn Jeanne 1948- *WhoWor 93*
Price, Marion Woodrow 1914- *WhoAm 92*
Price, Martin 1920- *WhoAm 92*
Price, Martin Burton 1928- *St&PR 93, WhoAm 92*
Price, Mary Alene *Law&B 92*
Price, Mary Leontyne 1927- *AfrAmBi*
Price, Mauricia 1925- *WhoWrEP 92*
Price, Michael *St&PR 93*
Price, Michael Clinton 1948- *WhoSSW 93*
Price, Michael F. 1951- *St&PR 93*
Price, Michael H. 1947- *ScF&FL 92*
Price, Monroe Edwin 1938- *WhoAm 92*
Price, Morgan Samuel *BioIn 17*
Price, Nicholas Charles *WhoScE 91-1*
Price, Olive M. *AmWomPl*
Price, Oscar A. 1931- *St&PR 93*
Price, Owen Gwyn *Law&B 92*
Price, Patrick L. *ScF&FL 92*
Price, Paul Buford 1932- *WhoAm 92*
Price, Paul E. 1934- *WhoAm 92*
Price, Paul Edward 1934- *St&PR 93*
Price, Paul Marnell 1959- *WhoE 93*
Price, Paul W. 1932- *WhoIns 93*
Price, Pete 1868-1951 *BioIn 17*
Price, Peter Jack *WhoE 93*
Price, Peter Michael 1946- *WhoE 93*
Price, Philip Adams 1917- *St&PR 93*
Price, Polly Selders 1922- *WhoWrEP 92*
Price, Powell B. 1947- *St&PR 93*
Price, Preston 1961- *WhoSSW 93*
Price, Randall Craig 1960- *WhoAm 92*
Price, Ray 1926- *WhoAm 92*
Price, (Noble) Ray 1926- *Baker 92*
Price, Raymond Alexander 1933- *WhoAm 92*
Price, Reynolds 1933- *BioIn 17, MagSAmL [port], WhoAm 92, WhoWrEP 92*
Price, (Edward) Reynolds 1933- *ConAu 37NR*
Price, Richard 1723-1791 *BioIn 17*
Price, Richard 1941- *WhoAm 92*
Price, Richard 1949- *BioIn 17, WhoWrEP 92*
Price, Richard J. *WhoAm 92*
Price, Richard Taylor 1930- *WhoE 93*
Price, Robert *Law&B 92*
Price, Robert 1929- *WhoAm 92*
Price, Robert 1932- *St&PR 93, WhoAm 92*
Price, Robert D. 1924- *St&PR 93*
Price, Robert Eben 1931- *WhoAm 92*
Price, Robert Edmunds 1926- *WhoE 93, WhoWor 93*

Price, Robert Harold 1926- *WhoSSW 93*
Price, Robert Ira 1921- *WhoAm 92*
Price, Robert John *WhoScE 91-1*
Price, Robert M. 1941- *ConAu 139*
Price, Robert M. 1954- *ScF&FL 92*
Price, Robert N. *Law&B 92*
Price, Roberta Faye 1937- *WhoAmW 93*
Price, Rodney Fredrick Walter 1940- *WhoWor 93*
Price, Roger d1990 *BioIn 17*
Price, Roger 1941- *ScF&FL 92*
Price, Roger 1945- *WhoAsAP 91*
Price, Roland John Stuart 1961- *WhoAm 92*
Price, Ronald D. *St&PR 93*
Price, Rosalie Pettus *WhoAmW 93, WhoSSW 93, WhoWor 93*
Price, Roy H. 1942- *St&PR 93*
Price, Ruth A. *Law&B 92*
Price, S. David 1943- *WhoWrEP 92*
Price, Sammy d1992 *NewYTBS 92 [port]*
Price, Sammy 1908-1992 *BioIn 17*
Price, Sarah Jones 1954- *WhoAmW 93*
Price, Seglenda Dawn 1962- *WhoAmW 93*
Price, Selma Brown 1915- *WhoAmW 93*
Price, Sol 1932- *St&PR 93*
Price, Stephanie Jo Wallace 1946- *WhoAmW 93*
Price, Stephen M. *Law&B 92*
Price, Sterling 1809-1867 *BioIn 17, HarEnMi*
Price, Steven 1962- *WhoE 93, WhoEmL 93*
Price, Steven D(avid) 1940- *ConAu 37NR*
Price, Steven S. 1955- *St&PR 93*
Price, Susan 1955- *ChlFicS, ScF&FL 92*
Price, Susan Carole 1959- *WhoAmW 93*
Price, Teresa Anne 1965- *WhoEmL 93*
Price, Theresa Alice 1950- *WhoAmW 93*
Price, Thomas Benjamin 1920- *WhoAm 92*
Price, Thomas Emile 1921- *WhoAm 92*
Price, Thomas Ransone 1934- *WhoAm 92*
Price, Timothy F. 1953- *St&PR 93*
Price, Trevor Robert Pryce 1943- *WhoAm 92, WhoE 93*
Price, V.B. 1940- *WhoWrEP 92*
Price, Vergie Gayle 1954- *WhoEmL 93*
Price, Vicki Jean 1955- *WhoE 93*
Price, Victor Edward *WhoScE 91-1*
Price, Victoria S. *Law&B 92*
Price, Vincent 1911- *BioIn 17, IntDcF 2-3 [port]*
Price, Vincent Leonard 1911- *WhoAm 92*
Price, Virginia S. *Law&B 92*
Price, W. James 1924- *St&PR 93*
Price, Walter *St&PR 93*
Price, Walter Lee 1914- *WhoSSW 93*
Price, Warren, III 1943- *WhoAm 92*
Price, Westcott Wilkin, III 1939- *WhoAm 92*
Price, William 1938- *WhoWrEP 92*
Price, William Anthony 1938- *WhoSSW 93*
Price, William David 1938- *WhoSSW 93*
Price, William Geraint *WhoScE 91-1*
Price, William Henry 1932- *WhoWor 93*
Price, William James 1918- *WhoAm 92, WhoE 93*
Price, William James, IV 1924- *WhoAm 92*
Price, William Joseph 1930- *St&PR 93*
Price, William Loyd 1959- *WhoSSW 93*
Price, William W. 1867-1931 *BioIn 17*
Price, Willis Joseph 1931- *WhoWor 93*
Price, Woodruff Murray 1935- *St&PR 93*
Price Boday, Mary Kathryn 1945- *WhoAmW 93, WhoE 93, WhoWor 93*
Pricer, Wilbur David 1935- *WhoAm 92*
Price-Wilson, Fannie E. *AmWomPl*
Prichard, Bob *BioIn 17*
Prichard, Edgar Allen 1920- *WhoAm 92, WhoWor 93*
Prichard, J. Robert S. *BioIn 17*
Prichard, John Franklin 1907- *WhoSSW 93, WhoWor 93*
Prichard, John Robert Stobo 1949- *WhoAm 92*
Prichard, John Stephens 1942- *WhoScE 91-3*
Prichard, Katharine Susannah 1884-1969 *BioIn 17*
Prichard, Peter S. 1944- *ConAu 139, WhoAm 92, WhoE 93*
Prichard, Robert Williams 1923- *WhoAm 92*
Prickett, F. Daniel 1946- *St&PR 93*
Prickett, Nancy Miriam 1950- *WhoAmW 93*
Prickett, Stephen 1939- *ScF&FL 92*
Prickett, Tom, Jr. 1921- *WhoSSW 93*
Prickett, Will Smith, Jr. 1950- *St&PR 93*
Prickett, William *WhoIns 93*
Pricola, Vito 1925- *St&PR 93, WhoAm 92*
Prida, Dolores 1943- *HispAmA, NotHsAW 93*
Priddle, Roland 1933- *WhoAm 92*
Priddy, Jerry F. 1937- *St&PR 93*
Priddy, Joseph E. *Law&B 92*
Priddy, Robert L. 1946- *St&PR 93*
Priddy, Susan Wachel 1962- *WhoAmW 93*
Pride, Benjamin David 1952- *WhoEmL 93*
Pride, Charley 1938- *Baker 92*
Pride, Charley 1939- *WhoAm 92*
Pride, Charley Frank 1938- *AfrAmBi*
Pride, Douglas Spencer 1959- *WhoE 93*
Pride, Fleetwood Martin, III 1948- *WhoSSW 93*
Pride, Harvey, Jr. 1947- *St&PR 93*
Pride, Miriam R. 1948- *WhoAmW 93*
Pride, Neil *WhoScE 91-1*
Prideaux, Gary Dean 1939- *WhoAm 92*
Prideaux, James 1935- *ConAu 138*
Prideaux, John Raymond, Jr. 1931- *WhoE 93*
Pridgen, Gary L. 1945- *St&PR 93*
Pridham, Geoffrey 1942- *ConAu 38NR*
Pridham, Herbert H. 1929- *WhoAm 92*
Pridham, John Brian *WhoScE 91-1*
Pridmore, Roy Davis 1925- *WhoAm 92*
Priebe, David C. *Law&B 92*
Priebe, Dennis *Law&B 92*
Priebe, Louis Victor 1941- *WhoSSW 93*
Priebe, Richard K. 1942- *WhoSSW 93*
Priebe, Richard O. 1927- *St&PR 93*
Priebe, Robert John 1928- *St&PR 93*
Priebe, Stefan 1953- *WhoWor 93*
Priebe, Waldemar Antoni 1948- *WhoSSW 93*
Priem, Ted L. 1940- *St&PR 93*
Prien, Alan Russel 1943- *WhoUN 92*
Prier, Raymond Adolph 1939- *WhoSSW 93*
Pries, C. *WhoScE 91-3*
Priesand, Sally Jane 1946- *WhoAm 92*
Priesol, Anthony Joseph 1941- *St&PR 93*
Priest, Christopher *BioIn 17*
Priest, Christopher 1943- *ScF&FL 92*
Priest, David Gerard 1938- *WhoSSW 93*
Priest, Eric R. *WhoScE 91-1*
Priest, Eric Ronald 1943- *WhoWor 93*
Priest, Eva Louise 1935- *WhoAmW 93*
Priest, George L. 1947- *WhoAm 92*
Priest, Gordon Webb, Jr. *Law&B 92*
Priest, Gregory A. *WhoIns 93*
Priest, Hartwell Wyse 1901- *WhoAm 92, WhoWor 93*
Priest, Ivy Baker 1905-1975 *PolPar*
Priest, James D. *ScF&FL 92*
Priest, Laurie *BioIn 17*
Priest, Mary Elizabeth 1868- *AmWomPl*
Priest, Melville Stanton 1912- *WhoAm 92, WhoWor 93*
Priest, Robert 1951- *WhoCanL 92*
Priest, Sharon Devlin *WhoAm 92, WhoAmW 93, WhoSSW 93*
Priester, Andre A. 1891-1955 *EncABHB 8*
Priester, Dudley B. 1923- *St&PR 93*
Priester, Gayle Boller 1912- *WhoWor 93*
Priestland, Gerald 1927-1991 *AnObit 1991*
Priestland, Robert Neal *WhoScE 91-1*
Priestley, Douglas Allen 1945- *St&PR 93*
Priestley, G.T.E. 1942- *St&PR 93*
Priestley, G. T. Eric 1942- *WhoSSW 93*
Priestley, J.B. 1894-1984 *BioIn 17, ScF&FL 92*
Priestley, Jason *BioIn 17*
Priestley, John Boynton 1894-1984 *BioIn 17*
Priestley, Margaret 1919?- *ScF&FL 92*
Priestley, Maurice Bertram *WhoScE 91-1*
Priestley, Maurice Bertram 1933- *WhoWor 93*
Priestley, Michael Linn 1953- *WhoEmL 93*
Priestley, Opal Lee 1904- *WhoWrEP 92*
Priestley, William Turk 1907- *WhoAm 92*
Priestly, Jason c. 1970- *News 93-2 [port]*
Priest-Mackie, Nancy Ray 1934- *WhoSSW 93*
Priestman, Brian 1927- *Baker 92*
Priestner, Edward B. 1936- *St&PR 93*
Priestner, Edward Bernard 1936- *WhoAm 92*
Priestner-Werte, Barbara Ann 1959- *WhoAmW 93*
Priest of Diokleia fl. 12th cent.- *OxDcByz*
Prieto, Carlos 1922- *DcMexL*
Prieto, Guillermo 1818-1897 *DcMexL*
Prieto, Jesus 1944- *WhoScE 91-3*
Prieto, Patricio 1932- *WhoWor 93*
Prieto, Ramon Ernesto 1948- *WhoWor 93*
Prieto, Robert 1954- *St&PR 93, WhoAm 92*
Prieto, Vicente 1947- *WhoEmL 93*
Prieto de Landazuri, Isabel 1833-1876 *DcMexL*
Prieur, Jean 1929- *WhoScE 91-2*
Prieux, Pierre 1952- *WhoWor 93*
Prieve, Dennis Charles 1947- *WhoE 93*
Prieve, Michael *BioIn 17*
Prigent, Pierre 1945- *WhoWor 93*
Prigge, Roger Leroy 1935- *St&PR 93*
Prigmore, Charles Samuel 1919- *WhoAm 92, WhoSSW 93, WhoWor 93*
Prigmore, L.T. 1920- *St&PR 93*
Prigmore, Maralee Sands 1930- *WhoAmW 93*
Prignot, Jacques Jules Nicolas Ghislain 1924- *WhoScE 91-2*
Prigogine, Alexandre 1913-1991 *BioIn 17*
Prigogine, Ilya 1917- *WhoScE 91-2, WhoWrEP 92*
Prigogine, Vicomte Ilya 1917- *WhoAm 92, WhoSSW 93, WhoWor 93*
Prigozhin, Lucian (Ambramovich) 1926- *Baker 92*
Prihoda, Alton Roy 1955- *WhoSSW 93*
Prihoda, Vasa 1900-1960 *Baker 92*
Prilepko, Aleksey Ivanovich 1935- *WhoWor 93*
Prillaman, Barbara Alison 1964- *WhoAmW 93*
Prillaman, Bob Maurice 1933- *WhoSSW 93*
Prillaman, Leslie I. 1943- *St&PR 93*
Prillaman, P. Miles *Law&B 92*
Prillhofer, Klaus *WhoScE 91-4*
Prima, Louis 1911-1978 *Baker 92, BioIn 17*
Primack, Leonard 1936- *WhoE 93*
Primakov, E.M. 1929- *BioIn 17*
Primakov, Evgenii Maksimovich 1929- *BioIn 17*
Primatesta, Raul Francisco Cardinal 1919- *WhoWor 93*
Primault, Bernard P. 1922- *WhoScE 91-4*
Primavesi, C.A. *WhoScE 91-3*
Prime, Henry Ashworth *WhoScE 91-1*
Prime, Penelope Benson 1954- *WhoSSW 93*
Primeaux, Henry, III 1941- *WhoWor 93*
Primeaux, Wilton 1935- *St&PR 93*
Primel, L. *WhoScE 91-2*
Primera, Irene C. *St&PR 93*
Primes *SoulM*
Primi, Don Alexis 1947- *WhoEmL 93*
Primich, Theodore 1915- *WhoWor 93*
Primis, Jeff 1949- *WhoE 93*
Primis, Lance Roy 1946- *WhoAm 92, WhoE 93*
Primm, Marcus Lee 1941- *St&PR 93*
Primmer, George Melvin, Jr. 1954- *WhoE 93*
Primo, Albert Thomas 1935- *WhoAm 92*
Primo, Quintin Ebenezer, Jr. 1913- *WhoAm 92*
Primo de Rivera, Miguel 1870-1930 *DcTwHis*
Primo de Rivera, Pilar d1991 *BioIn 17*
Primorac, Zarko-Tadija's 1937- *WhoWor 93*
Primozic, William *Law&B 92*
Primps, William Guthrie 1949- *WhoAm 92, WhoE 93*
Primrose, Archibald Philip 1847-1929 *BioIn 17*
Primrose, Diana fl. c. 1630- *DcLB 126*
Primrose, William 1903-1982 *Baker 92*
Primrose, William Robertson 1952- *WhoWor 93*
Primus, Barry 1938- *MiSFD 9*
Primus, Carol Jo 1955- *WhoAmW 93*
Primus, Francesca d1992 *BioIn 17, NewYTBS 92*
Primus, Marcus Antonius fl. 61-69 *HarEnMi*
Primus, Mary Jane Davis 1924- *WhoWor 93*
Primus, Pearl 1919- *BioIn 17*
Primus, Wendell 1946- *BioIn 17*
Primuth, David J. 1938- *St&PR 93*
Prin, Alice Ernestine 1901-1953? *BioIn 17*
Prina, Louis Edgar 1917- *WhoAm 92*
Prince *BioIn 17, MiSFD 9*
Prince 1958- *Baker 92, SoulM, WhoAm 92*
Prince, Alan Norton 1939- *St&PR 93*
Prince, Alan Theodore 1915- *WhoAm 92*
Prince, Alison 1931- *ScF&FL 92*
Prince, Andrew Steven *Law&B 92*
Prince, Andrew Steven 1943- *WhoAm 92*
Prince, Anna L. *WhoSSW 93, WhoWor 93*
Prince, Antoinette Odette 1946- *WhoAmW 93*
Prince, Bart 1947- *NewYTBS 92 [port]*
Prince, Betty 1942- *WhoAmW 93*
Prince, Carl E. 1934- *WhoAm 92*
Prince, Charles O., III *Law&B 92*
Prince, Christian H. d1991 *BioIn 17*
Prince, Daniel Lloyd 1955- *WhoAm 92*
Prince, David *Law&B 92*
Prince, Don 1903-1983 *ScF&FL 92*
Prince, E. Ted 1947- *St&PR 93*
Prince, Edward Rudolph, Jr. 1929- *St&PR 93*
Prince, Eugene Edward 1932- *St&PR 93*
Prince, Faith 1957- *BioIn 17*
Prince, Faith c. 1959- *News 93-2 [port]*
Prince, Frances Anne Kiely 1923- *WhoWor 93*
Prince, Garnett B., Jr. 1949- *WhoAm 92*
Prince, Gary A. 1954- *St&PR 93*
Prince, George Edward 1921- *WhoSSW 93*
Prince, George Richard 1944- *St&PR 93*
Prince, Gregory Smith, Jr. 1939- *WhoAm 92*
Prince, Harold 1928- *IntDcOp, MiSFD 9, WhoAm 92, WhoE 93*
Prince, Jacquelynne Bolander 1955- *WhoAmW 93*
Prince, James E. *Law&B 92*
Prince, John Luther, III 1941- *WhoAm 92*
Prince, Julius S. 1911- *WhoAm 92, WhoE 93*
Prince, Larry L. 1937- *WhoSSW 93*
Prince, Larry L. 1938- *St&PR 93*
Prince, Martin 1937- *St&PR 93*
Prince, Mary *BioIn 17*
Prince, Melvin 1932- *WhoE 93*
Prince, Milton S. 1912- *WhoAm 92*
Prince, Morris David 1926- *WhoAm 92*
Prince, Morton Bronenberg 1924- *WhoAm 92*
Prince, Peter (Alan) 1942- *ConAu 139*
Prince, Peter James d1991 *BioIn 17*
Prince, Peter Joseph *WhoScE 91-1*
Prince, Robb L. 1941- *St&PR 93*
Prince, Robb Lincoln 1941- *WhoAm 92*
Prince, Robert E. 1947- *St&PR 93*
Prince, Robert Ferris 1916-1985 *BiDAMSp 1989*
Prince, Robert George 1929- *WhoSSW 93*
Prince, Robert Mason 1914- *WhoWor 93*
Prince, Ronald Stanford 1931- *St&PR 93*
Prince, Stephen 1959- *WhoWor 93*
Prince, Thomas 1687-1758 *BioIn 17*
Prince, Thomas F. 1934- *St&PR 93*
Prince, Thomas Richard 1934- *WhoAm 92*
Prince, Warren Victor 1911- *WhoWor 93*
Prince, William Taliaferro 1929- *WhoAm 92*
Prince Akeem *BioIn 17*
Prince-Marable, Cynthia 1953- *WhoEmL 93*
Principal, Victoria *BioIn 17*
Principal, Victoria 1950- *WhoAm 92, WhoAmW 93*
Princz, Judith *WhoAm 92, WhoAmW 93*
Prindiville, Robert A. 1935- *St&PR 93*
Prindiville, Robert Andrew 1935- *WhoAm 92*
Prindiville, Terry Spencer 1935- *St&PR 93*
Prindl, Andreas Robert 1939- *WhoWor 93*
Prindle, Cheryl H. 1960- *WhoAmW 93, WhoWor 93*
Prindle, William Roscoe 1926- *WhoAm 92*
Prine, Andrew Lewis 1936- *WhoAm 92*
Prine, Charles W., Jr. 1926- *St&PR 93*
Prine, John 1946- *WhoAm 92*
Prineas, Ronald James 1937- *WhoAm 92*
Pring, Martin John 1943- *WhoE 93*
Pringle, Aileen 1895-1989 *BioIn 17*
Pringle, Barbara Carroll 1939- *WhoAmW 93*
Pringle, Charles P. 1944- *St&PR 93*
Pringle, Craig Robertson *WhoScE 91-1*
Pringle, David 1950- *ScF&FL 92*
Pringle, Edward E. 1914- *WhoAm 92*
Pringle, Edward Graves 1941- *WhoAm 92*
Pringle, Elisa M. 1959- *St&PR 93*
Pringle, Elizabeth W. Allston 1845-1921 *BioIn 17*
Pringle, Eric *ScF&FL 92*
Pringle, George Overton 1923- *WhoSSW 93*
Pringle, James Edward *WhoScE 91-1*
Pringle, John Alan 1949- *WhoEmL 93*
Pringle, Laurence *MajAI*
Pringle, Laurence P. *BioIn 17*
Pringle, Laurence P(atrick) 1935- *MajAI [port]*
Pringle, Laurence Patrick 1935- *WhoAm 92*
Pringle, Lewis Gordon 1941- *St&PR 93, WhoAm 92*
Pringle, Oran Allan 1923- *WhoAm 92*
Pringle, Peter Kilner 1941- *WhoSSW 93*
Pringle, Ricardo Blaine *Law&B 92*
Pringle, Robert Maxwell 1936- *WhoAm 92*
Pringle, Robert W. *WhoIns 93*
Pringle, Samuel W. *Law&B 92*
Pringle, Terrence Michael 1947- *ConAu 136*
Pringle, Terry *ConAu 136*
Pringle, Thomas Walker 1957- *WhoE 93, WhoEmL 93*
Pringle, William J. *St&PR 93*
Pringsheim, Klaus 1883-1972 *Baker 92*
Prinja, Anil Kant 1955- *WhoWor 93*
Prinkkila, Helena Marjatta 1938- *WhoScE 91-4*
Prinn, Charles Edward, III 1940- *St&PR 93*
Prinos, Monique E. 1957- *WhoEmL 93*
Prins, Albertus 1928- *WhoScE 91-3*
Prins, Arend Pieter A. 1946- *WhoScE 91-3*
Prins, David 1930- *WhoAm 92*

Prins, Jacob Egbert 1925- *WhoScE 91-3*
Prins, Jan *WhoWor 93*
Prins, L.A.J. *WhoScE 91-3*
Prins, LaVonne Kay 1957- *WhoAmW 93*
Prins, Richard Greenway 1936- *St&PR 93*
Prins, Robert Jack 1932- *WhoAm 92, WhoWor 93*
Prins, Rudolf A. 1939- *WhoScE 91-3*
Prins, W.H. 1939- *WhoScE 91-3*
Prinsky, Robert *St&PR 93*
Prinstein, Meyer 1880-1925 *BiDAMSp 1989*
Prinster, Anthony F. 1941- *St&PR 93*
Prinster, Leo T. 1928- *St&PR 93*
Printer, Alan Alfred 1929- *WhoSSW 93*
Printy, David L. 1946- *St&PR 93*
Printz, Philip Hallie 1947- *WhoE 93*
Printz, Stacey E. *Law&B 92*
Printz, Wolfgang Caspar 1641-1717 *Baker 92*
Printzlau, Olga *AmWomPl*
Prinz, B. *WhoScE 91-3*
Prinz, Matthias Leo 1956- *WhoWor 93*
Prinz, Wolfgang *WhoScE 91-3*
Prinze, Freddie 1954-1977 *BioIn 17*
Prinzen, F.W. 1954- *WhoScE 91-3*
Prinzi, Barbara Dolle 1938- *WhoAmW 93*
Prinzivalli, Joseph Anthony, Jr. 1955- *WhoE 93*
Priode, Len 1944- *St&PR 93*
Priola, Donald Victor 1938- *WhoAm 92*
Prioleau, H. Frost 1929- *St&PR 93*
Prioli, Carmine Andrew 1946- *WhoSSW 93*
Priolo, Toby A. 1939- *St&PR 93*
Prior, Boyd Thelman 1926- *WhoSSW 93*
Prior, Cornelius B., Jr. 1934- *St&PR 93*
Prior, David A. *MiSFD 9*
Prior, G. *WhoScE 91-1*
Prior, James Michael Leathes 1927- *WhoWor 93*
Prior, John Alan 1913- *WhoAm 92*
Prior, John C. *St&PR 93*
Prior, Katherine Faith 1949- *WhoE 93*
Prior, Matthew 1664-1721 *BioIn 17*
Prior, Nicholas J. *Law&B 92*
Prior, Peter N. 1933- *St&PR 93*
Prior, Richard Marion 1942- *WhoSSW 93*
Priore, Frank Vincent 1946- *WhoWrEP 92*
Priore, Roger L. 1938- *WhoAm 92*
Priory, Joseph Downs 1944- *WhoAm 92*
Priory, Richard Baldwin 1946- *St&PR 93*
Prio Socarras, Carlos *DcCPCAm*
Priour, Donald James 1946- *WhoSSW 93*
Priovolos, Theophilos 1952- *WhoWor 93*
Prisant, Louis Michael 1949- *WhoSSW 93*
Prisant, Millard B. 1935- *St&PR 93*
Prischak, Isabel J. 1936- *St&PR 93*
Prischak, Joseph J. 1931- *St&PR 93*
Priscian dc. 530 *OxDcByz*
Priscillian c. 335-c. 385 *OxDcByz*
Prisco, Dorothy DeSteno 1942- *WhoE 93*
Prisco, Douglas Louis 1945- *WhoE 93*
Prisco, Joseph d1990 *BioIn 17*
Priscu, D.J. 1923- *St&PR 93*
Prisk, Elaine Mary *WhoScE 91-1*
Priske, Daniel G. 1928- *St&PR 93*
Priskos dc. 612 *OxDcByz*
Priskos 41-?-c. 472 *OxDcByz*
Pristed, Bent 1945- *WhoWor 93*
Pritan, Amrita 1919- *WhoAsAP 91*
Pritchard, A.J. *WhoScE 91-1*
Pritchard, Alan S., Jr. 1941- *St&PR 93*
Pritchard, Anthony John *WhoScE 91-1*
Pritchard, Claudius Hornby, Jr. 1927- *WhoAm 92*
Pritchard, Constance Jenkins 1950- *WhoAmW 93, WhoSSW 93*
Pritchard, Dalton Harold 1921- *WhoAm 92*
Pritchard, David Edward 1941- *WhoAm 92*
Pritchard, David Peter 1944- *WhoWor 93*
Pritchard, Donald William 1922- *WhoAm 92*
Pritchard, Edward Arthur 1943- *WhoAm 92*
Pritchard, Elsie Tomlinson 1947- *WhoSSW 93*
Pritchard, Geoffrey *WhoScE 91-1*
Pritchard, Harmon Otis, Jr. 1930- *St&PR 93*
Pritchard, Huw Owen 1928- *WhoAm 92*
Pritchard, James Bennett 1909- *WhoAm 92*
Pritchard, Joel 1925- *WhoAm 92*
Pritchard, John 1921-1989 *IntDcOp, OxDcOp*
Pritchard, John (Michael) 1921-1989 *Baker 92*
Pritchard, John W. *ScF&FL 92*
Pritchard, Lucille Martin 1945- *WhoE 93*
Pritchard, Mary D'Ercole 1940- *WhoAmW 93*
Pritchard, Marylou 1948- *St&PR 93*
Pritchard, Melissa Brown 1948- *WhoWrEP 92*
Pritchard, Michael D. *St&PR 93*
Pritchard, Parm Frederick 1914- *WhoWrEP 92*
Pritchard, Paul Ralph 1950- *WhoSSW 93*
Pritchard, Paul William 1956- *WhoSSW 93*
Pritchard, Polly Ann *AmWomPl*
Pritchard, Ralph W. d1992 *BioIn 17*
Pritchard, Raymond John 1931- *WhoAm 92*
Pritchard, Raymond John 1932- *WhoSSW 93*
Pritchard, Sandra Jo 1943- *WhoAmW 93*
Pritchard, Thomas Iorwerth *WhoScE 91-1*
Pritchard, Wilbur Louis 1923- *WhoAm 92, WhoWor 93*
Pritchard, William Baker 1950- *WhoE 93*
Pritchard, William Grady, Jr. 1927- *WhoIns 93*
Pritchard, William H. *BioIn 17*
Pritchard, William Roy 1924- *WhoAm 92*
Pritchard, William W. *Law&B 92*
Pritchard, William Winther 1951- *WhoAm 92*
Pritchett, Betty J. Clark 1944- *WhoSSW 93*
Pritchett, C. Herman 1907- *BioIn 17*
Pritchett, Charles Herman 1907- *BioIn 17, WhoAm 92*
Pritchett, Jerry Coston 1940- *WhoE 93*
Pritchett, Joseph Everett 1948- *WhoWor 93*
Pritchett, Lafayette Bow 1934- *WhoWor 93*
Pritchett, Lois Jane *WhoSSW 93*
Pritchett, M. Jed, Jr. *Law&B 92*
Pritchett, Muriel Ellis 1945- *WhoAmW 93*
Pritchett, Ola Anne H. 1947- *WhoAmW 93*
Pritchett, Rita Joyce 1947- *WhoAmW 93*
Pritchett, Robert Lee 1948- *St&PR 93*
Pritchett, Rosemary *BioIn 17*
Pritchett, Samuel Travis 1938- *WhoIns 93*
Pritchett, Theodore Edward 1957- *WhoSSW 93*
Pritchett, Thomas Carroll 1952- *WhoSSW 93*
Pritchett, Thomas Henry 1954- *WhoE 93*
Pritchett, Thomas Keith 1946- *WhoSSW 93*
Pritchett, Thomas Ronald 1925- *WhoAm 92*
Pritchett, V.S. 1900- *BioIn 17, MagSWL [port]*
Pritchett, Victor Sawdon 1900- *BioIn 17, WhoAm 92, WhoWor 93*
Pritham, Howard George 1940- *WhoE 93*
Pritikin, Marvin E. 1922- *WhoIns 93*
Pritikin, Nathan *BioIn 17*
Pritikin, Roland I. 1906- *WhoAm 92*
Pritsker, A. Alan B. 1933- *WhoAm 92*
Pritts, Roger L. 1944- *St&PR 93*
Pritts, William E., II 1939- *St&PR 93*
Prittwitz und Graffron, Max von 1848-1917 *HarEnMi*
Pritz, Alan K. *WhoIns 93*
Pritz, Peter J. 1928- *St&PR 93*
Pritz, Tamas 1946- *WhoScE 91-4*
Pritzker, A. 1954- *St&PR 93*
Pritzker, A.N. 1896-1986 *BioIn 17*
Pritzker, Abram Nicholas 1896-1986 *BioIn 17*
Pritzker, Andreas Eugen Max 1945- *WhoWor 93*
Pritzker, Donald Nicholas 1932-1972 *BioIn 17*
Pritzker, Jack Nicholas 1904-1979 *BioIn 17*
Pritzker, Jay A. *BioIn 17*
Pritzker, Jay A. 1922- *St&PR 93*
Pritzker, Jay Arthur 1922- *WhoAm 92*
Pritzker, John *BioIn 17*
Pritzker, Leon 1922- *WhoAm 92*
Pritzker, Nicholas J. *WhoAm 92*
Pritzker, Nicholas J. 1945- *BioIn 17*
Pritzker, Robert A. *BioIn 17*
Pritzker, Robert A. 1926- *St&PR 93*
Pritzker, Robert Alan 1926- *WhoAm 92*
Pritzker, Thomas J. 1950- *St&PR 93*
Pritzker, Thomas Jay 1950- *BioIn 17, WhoAm 92*
Pritzkow, Ellen Elisabeth 1953- *WhoAmW 93*
Pritzlaff, John Charles, Jr. 1925- *WhoAm 92*
Privat, Jeannette Mary 1938- *WhoAm 92*
Privett, Donald F. 1955- *WhoIns 93*
Privett, Franklin D. 1937- *St&PR 93*
Privette, William Herbert 1949- *WhoWrEP 92*
Privitera, John Nathan 1944- *WhoE 93*
Privitere, Louis Philip 1925- *St&PR 93*
Prizer, Charles John 1924- *WhoAm 92*
Prizio, Betty J. 1928- *WhoAmW 93*
Prizzi, Jack Anthony 1935- *WhoAm 92, WhoWor 93*
Prizzi, John J. *Law&B 92*
Pro, Philip Martin 1946- *WhoAm 92*
Proakis, Anthony George 1940- *WhoE 93*
Probart, Claudia Kay 1945- *WhoSSW 93*
Probasco, Calvin Henry Charles 1926- *WhoAm 92*
Probasco, Kathleen Ruth Peck 1946- *WhoAmW 93*
Probasco, Scott Livingston 1928- *WhoAm 92*
Probelski, Kathy B. *St&PR 93*
Prober, Joanne S. 1938- *WhoAmW 93*
Probert, Barbara Stevenson 1929- *WhoSSW 93*
Probert, Sydney Douglas *WhoScE 91-1*
Probert, Walter 1925- *WhoAm 92*
Probst, Alane C. *Law&B 92*
Probst, Albert *WhoScE 91-3*
Probst, David S. 1939- *St&PR 93*
Probst, Helen B. *Law&B 92*
Probst, Lawrence F., Jr. 1925- *St&PR 93*
Probst, Nancy L. 1956- *St&PR 93*
Probst, Raymond *WhoScE 91-4*
Probstein, Ian Emil 1953- *WhoE 93*
Probstein, Ronald Filmore 1928- *WhoAm 92*
Probus 328?-388? *OxDcByz*
Probus, Marcus Aurelius 232-282 *HarEnMi*
Proceviat, Clifford Nicholas 1942- *St&PR 93*
Proch, Heinrich 1809-1878 *Baker 92*
Proch, Robert L. 1952- *St&PR 93*
Prochazka, Bohumil 1932- *WhoScE 91-4*
Prochazka, Rudolf von 1864-1936 *Baker 92*
Prochazka, Stanislav 1940- *WhoScE 91-4*
Prochazkova, Iva 1953- *BioIn 17*
Prochazkova, Olga 1947- *WhoScE 91-4*
Prochnau, William 1937- *ScF&FL 92*
Prochnow, Herbert Victor 1897- *WhoAm 92*
Prochorow, J. *WhoScE 91-4*
Procich, Julianne *BioIn 17*
Procidano, Mary Elizabeth 1954- *WhoEmL 93*
Procknow, Donald E. 1923- *St&PR 93*
Procknow, Donald Eugene 1923- *WhoAm 92*
Prockop, Darwin Johnson 1929- *WhoAm 92*
Procope, Ernesta Gertrude *AfrAmBi*
Procopio, Joseph Guydon 1940- *St&PR 93*
Procopius c. 326-366 *HarEnMi*
Procter, Alice McElroy 1915-1987 *Baker 92*
Procter, Bryan Waller 1787-1874 *BioIn 17*
Procter, Garry *WhoScE 91-1*
Procter, John Ernest 1918- *WhoAm 92*
Procter, Leland 1914- *Baker 92*
Procter, (Mary) Norma 1928- *Baker 92*
Procter, Page Sunderland d1991 *BioIn 17*
Procter, Robin Peter McGill *WhoScE 91-1*
Procter, William 1801?- *BioIn 17*
Proctor, Adelaide *BioIn 17*
Proctor, Barbara Gardner *WhoAm 92, WhoAmW 93*
Proctor, Bobby L. 1933- *St&PR 93*
Proctor, David Ray 1956- *WhoSSW 93*
Proctor, Donald Frederick 1913- *WhoAm 92*
Proctor, Dorcas *AmWomPl*
Proctor, Gary R. *Law&B 92*
Proctor, Geo W. 1946- *ScF&FL 92*
Proctor, Howard Maxwell Raymond *WhoScE 91-1*
Proctor, Janice Katherine *WhoAmW 93*
Proctor, Jesse Harris, Jr. 1924- *WhoAm 92*
Proctor, John Douglas 1949- *St&PR 93*
Proctor, John Franklin 1931- *WhoAm 92*
Proctor, John Howard 1931- *WhoSSW 93*
Proctor, Kenneth Donald 1944- *WhoAm 92*
Proctor, Kenneth W., Jr. 1929- *St&PR 93*
Proctor, Lester T., Jr. 1927- *St&PR 93*
Proctor, Mark Alan 1948- *WhoEmL 93, WhoSSW 93, WhoWor 93*
Proctor, Randall Wesley 1928- *St&PR 93, WhoAm 92, WhoWor 93*
Proctor, Richard Owen 1935- *WhoAm 92*
Proctor, Robert Alexander 1950- *WhoE 93*
Proctor, Robert N. 1954- *ConAu 138*
Proctor, Robert Swope 1922- *WhoAm 92*
Proctor, Samuel 1919- *WhoAm 92*
Proctor, Stanley Irving 1936- *WhoAm 92*
Proctor, Stanley Matthew 1920- *St&PR 93*
Proctor, Susan Dorothy *Law&B 92*
Proctor, Timothy D. *Law&B 92*
Proctor, Vilma d1990 *BioIn 17*
Proctor, William 1943- *WhoScE 91-1*
Proctor, William Lee 1933- *WhoAm 92*
Proctor, William Zinsmaster 1902- *WhoAm 92*
Proculus dc. 282 *HarEnMi*
Proczko, Taras R. *Law&B 92*
Prodan, John 1924- *WhoWor 93*
Prodaniuk, Roland George 1947- *WhoWor 93*
Prodanov, Elena *Law&B 92*
Prodanovic, A. Andy 1956- *St&PR 93*
Prodev, Stefan 1927- *WhoWor 93*
Prodhan, Bimal Kumar 1937- *WhoWor 93*
Prod'homme, J(acques)-G(abriel) 1871-1956 *Baker 92*
Prodi, Franco 1941- *WhoScE 91-3*
Prodromos, Manganeios fl. 12th cent.- *OxDcByz*
Prodromos, Theodore c. 1100-c. 1170 *OxDcByz*
Proefrock, Carl Kenneth 1928- *WhoAm 92*
Proell, Annemarie Moser- 1953- *BioIn 17*
Proemper, Herbert 1931- *WhoWor 93*
Proesch, Gilbert *BioIn 17*
Proeysen, Alf 1914-1970 *ConAu 136*
Profant, Allan Dale 1944- *WhoSSW 93*
Profe, Ambrosius 1589-1661 *Baker 92*
Professor Griff *BioIn 17*
Professor Longhair 1918- *SoulM*
Profeta, Laurentiu 1925- *Baker 92*
Profeta, Nicholas J. 1929- *St&PR 93*
Profeta, Salvatore, Jr. 1951- *WhoWor 93*
Proffer, Ellendea Catherine 1944- *WhoWrEP 92*
Proffer, Richard Samuel, Jr. 1955- *WhoSSW 93*
Proffit, William Robert 1936- *WhoAm 92*
Proffitt, David A. *St&PR 93*
Proffitt, David T. 1948- *St&PR 93*
Proffitt, James Nicholas, Jr. 1945- *WhoSSW 93*
Proffitt, John B. 1939- *St&PR 93*
Proffitt, John Richard 1930- *WhoAm 92, WhoE 93*
Proffitt, John Roscoe, Jr. 1924- *St&PR 93*
Proffitt, Josephine *ScF&FL 92*
Proffitt, Joyce Harrison 1925- *St&PR 93*
Proffitt, Merlyn L. 1930- *St&PR 93*
Proffitt, Nicholas (Charles) 1943- *ConAu 139*
Proffitt, Thomas Jefferson, Jr. 1932- *WhoSSW 93*
Profio, Winston Clarke 1931- *St&PR 93*
Profit, Betty Jean 1948- *WhoAmW 93*
Profitt, Glenn Arliss, II 1942- *WhoAm 92*
Profughi, Terence C. 1946- *St&PR 93*
Profumo, David 1955- *ConAu 137*
Profumo, John D. *BioIn 17*
Profuturus fl. c. 377- *HarEnMi*
Profy, Robert J. *Law&B 92*
Progar, Dorothy 1924- *WhoAm 92*
Progelhof, Richard Carl 1936- *WhoAm 92, WhoSSW 93*
Prohaska, Carl 1869-1927 *Baker 92*
Prohaska, Felix 1912-1987 *Baker 92*
Prohaska, Jaro 1891-1965 *OxDcOp*
Prohaska, Jaro(slav) 1891-1965 *Baker 92*
Prohaska, John William 1929- *St&PR 93*
Prohaszka, Janos 1920- *WhoScE 91-4*
Prohofsky, Dennis E. *Law&B 92*
Prohor of Pcinja fl. 11th cent.- *OxDcByz*
Proietti, Rose Marie 1948- *WhoE 93*
Proimos, Vasilios S. 1930- *WhoScE 91-3*
Projahn, Hans Juergen 1938- *WhoWor 93*
Prokasy, William Frederick 1930- *WhoAm 92*
Prokesch, Clemens Elias 1918- *WhoE 93*
Prokhorov, Aleksandr Mikhailovich 1916- *WhoWor 93*
Prokhorov, Vasili Alekseevich 1958- *WhoWor 93*
Proklos d446? *OxDcByz*
Proklos 410?-485 *OxDcByz*
Prokofieff, Sergei (Sergeievich) 1891-1953 *Baker 92*
Prokofiev, Sergei 1891-1953 *IntDcOp [port]*
Prokofiev, Sergei (Sergeievich) 1891-1953 *Baker 92*
Prokofiev, Sergey 1891-1953 *BioIn 17, OxDcOp*
Prokop, Bill P. *St&PR 93*
Prokop, Michael Andrew *Law&B 92*
Prokop, Michael Stephen 1953- *WhoWrEP 92*
Prokop, Otto 1921- *WhoScE 91-3*
Prokopchak, Steve David 1954- *WhoE 93*
Prokopenko, Joseph Ivanovich 1939 *WhoUN 92, WhoWor 93*
Prokopic, Jan *WhoScE 91-4*
Prokopios d303 *OxDcByz*
Prokopios c. 326-366 *OxDcByz*
Prokopios of Caesarea fl. 6th cent.- *OxDcByz*
Prokopios of Gaza c. 465-c. 528 *OxDcByz*
Prokopis, Emmanuel Charles 1942- *WhoAm 92*
Prokopoff, Stephen Stephen 1929- *WhoAm 92*
Prokopovich, S. Richard 1948- *WhoE 93*
Prokopowicz, Jan 1931- *WhoScE 91-4, WhoWor 93*
Prokopowicz, Jerzy 1936- *WhoScE 91-4*
Prokopy, John Alfred 1926- *WhoE 93*
Prokosch, Walther 1911-1991 *BioIn 17*
Prokoski, Francine J. 1948- *St&PR 93*
Proksch, Alfred 1942- *WhoScE 91-3*
Proksch, Emil 1932- *WhoScE 91-4*
Proksch, Josef 1794-1864 *Baker 92*

Proksza, Janos 1944- *WhoScE 91-4*
Prol, John H. 1937- *St&PR 93*
Proler, Herman 1927- *St&PR 93*
Proll, Douglas A. 1950- *St&PR 93*
Prom, Stephen George 1954- *WhoAm 92, WhoSSW 93*
Promisel, Nathan E. 1908- *WhoAm 92*
Promotus, Publius Flavius d391 *HarEnMi*
Pronaszko, Andrzej 1888-1961 *PolBiDi*
Pronaszko, Zbigniew 1885-1958 *PolBiDi*
Pronczuk, Slawomir *WhoScE 91-4*
Pronczuk de Garbino, Jenny 1947- *WhoUN 92*
Proner, Rochelle Celia 1965- *WhoAmW 93*
Proner, Sanford Clay 1955- *WhoE 93*
Pronier, Bernard 1929- *WhoScE 91-2*
Pronin, Barbara *ScF&FL 92*
Proniuk, Stefan T. *Law&B 92*
Pronko, Peter Paul 1938- *WhoAm 92*
Prontnicki, Janice 1960- *WhoAmW 93*
Prony, Gaspard-Claire-Francois-Marie-Riche, Baron de 1755-1839 *Baker 92*
Pronzini, Bill 1943- *ScF&FL 92*
Pronzini, Bill John 1943- *WhoAm 92, WhoWrEP 92*
Pronzini, William J. *ScF&FL 92*
Proost, Jos 1945- *WhoScE 91-2*
Proost, Robert Lee 1937- *WhoAm 92*
Propatto, Juan Carlos Aldo 1953- *WhoWor 93*
Proper, Dean D. 1936- *St&PR 93*
Prophet, Elizabeth Clare *BioIn 17*
Prophet, Matthew Waller, Jr. 1930- *WhoAm 92*
Propos, Herbert M. *St&PR 93*
Propp, Gail Dane Gomberg 1944- *WhoAmW 93*
Propp, Gina A. *Law&B 92*
Propp, V.IA. 1895-1970 *IntDcAn*
Propp, William Walker *Law&B 92*
Propper, Alain Y. 1941- *WhoScE 91-2*
Propper, Norman Sherwin 1923- *WhoSSW 93*
Propping, Peter 1942- *WhoScE 91-3*
Propst, Harold Dean 1934- *WhoSSW 93*
Propst, John Leake 1914- *St&PR 93, WhoAm 92*
Propst, Nell Brown 1925- *WhoWrEP 92*
Propst, Robert Bruce 1931- *WhoAm 92*
Proriol, Joseph 1931- *WhoWor 93*
Proschan, Frank 1921- *WhoAm 92*
Prose, Francine 1947- *BioIn 17, ScF&FL 92*
Prosen, Harry 1930- *WhoAm 92*
Prosen, Rose Mary *WhoWrEP 92*
Prosev, Toma 1931- *Baker 92*
Proshansky, Harold M. 1920-1990 *BioIn 17*
Prosho, Stephen *BioIn 17*
Proskauer, Eric S. 1903-1991 *BioIn 17*
Proske, Carl 1794-1861 *Baker 92*
Proske, Paul Edward 1932- *St&PR 93*
Proske, Robert *St&PR 93*
Proskouriakoff, Tatiana 1909-1985 *BioIn 17*
Prosky, Robert Joseph 1930- *WhoAm 92*
Prosnak, Wlodzimierz J. 1925- *WhoScE 91-4*
Prosnik, C.A. 1943- *St&PR 93*
Prosniz, Adolf 1829-1917 *Baker 92*
Prosperi, Robert 1942- *St&PR 93*
Prosperino, Robert 1966- *WhoE 93*
Pross, Lester Fred 1924- *WhoSSW 93*
Prosser, C. Ladd 1907- *WhoAm 92*
Prosser, Daniel Feigal 1949- *WhoSSW 93*
Prosser, Franklin Pierce 1935- *WhoAm 92*
Prosser, Geoffrey Daniel 1948- *WhoAsAP 91*
Prosser, H.L. 1944- *ScF&FL 92*
Prosser, Harold Lee 1944- *WhoWrEP 92*
Prosser, J.N. *WhoScE 91-1*
Prosser, John Martin 1932- *WhoAm 92*
Prosser, John Warren, Jr. 1945- *St&PR 93*
Prosser, Raymond L. *Law&B 92*
Prosser, Sarah S. *Law&B 92*
Prosser, Terrance Walsh 1946- *WhoE 93*
Prosser, Thomas E. 1935- *St&PR 93*
Prossman, Jennie *BioIn 17*
Prost, Andre 1944- *WhoUN 92*
Prost, Edmund K. 1921- *WhoScE 91-4*
Prost, Jean-Marc 1953- *WhoWor 93*
Prostano, Emanuel T. 1931- *WhoAm 92*
Prosterman, Roy L. 1935- *WhoAm 92*
Proszynski, Andrzej 1948- *WhoWor 93*
Proszynski, Witold 1942- *WhoScE 91-4*
Prota, Patrick A. 1943- *St&PR 93*
Prota, Ulisse *WhoScE 91-3*
Prota-Giurleo, Ulisse 1886-1966 *Baker 92*
Protas, Jean Norbert 1932- *WhoScE 91-2*
Protas, Ron *WhoAm 92*
Protas, Ronald *BioIn 17*
Protasio, Fortunata Layson 1950- *WhoWor 93*
Protasov, Igor Vladimir 1953- *WhoWor 93*
Proth, Jean-Marie 1938- *WhoScE 91-2*
Prothero, Charles Leslie 1932- *St&PR 93*
Protheroe, Daniel 1866-1934 *Baker 92*
Prothero-Smith, Joy Eddette 1952- *WhoAmW 93*
Prothro, Esther Jamieson 1913- *WhoWrEP 92*
Prothro, Jerry Robert 1946- *WhoSSW 93*
Protic, Radmilo 1919- *WhoScE 91-4*
Protigal, Stanley N. *Law&B 92*
Proto, Araceli Noemi 1944- *WhoWor 93*
Proto, Rodney Raymond 1948- *WhoWor 93*
Protopapadakis, Eftichios 1944- *WhoWor 93*
Protopopov, Aleksandr Dmitrievich 1864-1918 *BioIn 17*
Protopopov, Ludmila 1935- *BioIn 17*
Protopopov, Oleg 1932- *BioIn 17*
Protos, Arthur Paul 1951- *WhoWor 93*
Protovin, Richard M. d1991 *BioIn 17*
Prott, Jean Marie *WhoScE 91-2*
Prott, Lyndel Vivien 1940- *WhoUN 92*
Protter, Eric 1927- *ScF&FL 92*
Proud, James Richardson 1948- *St&PR 93*
Proudfit, Nancy Walker *Law&B 92*
Proudfoot, Bill 1953- *St&PR 93*
Proudfoot, George Wilfred 1921- *WhoWor 93*
Proudfoot, Lucy South *AmWomPl*
Proudfoot, V. Bruce *WhoScE 91-1*
Proudlock, Annabella Phyllis 1943- *WhoWor 93*
Proudlove, Ronald Keith *WhoScE 91-1*
Prough, Russell Allen 1943- *WhoAm 92*
Prouk, Gary *BioIn 17*
Proulx, Dana K. *Law&B 92*
Proulx, Edna Annie 1935- *WhoAmW 93*
Proulx, Roger Anthony 1932- *WhoAm 92*
Prousis, Theophilus C. *BioIn 17*
Proust, Jean-Paul 1940- *WhoWor 93*
Proust, Jeanne-Clemence Weil *BioIn 17*
Proust, Marcel 1871-1922 *BioIn 17, DcTwHis, MagSWL [port], WorLitC [port]*
Prout, C.K. *WhoScE 91-1*
Prout, Curtis 1915- *WhoAm 92*
Prout, Ebenezer 1835-1909 *Baker 92*
Prout, Francis J. d1992 *NewYTBS 92*
Prout, George Russell, Jr. 1924- *WhoAm 92*
Prout, Gerald Robert 1949- *WhoE 93*
Prout, Marilyn Eileen 1961- *St&PR 93*
Prout, Ralph Eugene 1933- *WhoAm 92*
Prouty, Howard H. *ScF&FL 92*
Prouty, Norman R. 1939- *WhoAm 92, WhoWor 93*
Provance, Holly Leann 1960- *WhoAmW 93*
Provasoli, Anthony Manuel 1953- *WhoWor 93*
Provasoli, Luigi d1992 *NewYTBS 92*
Provaznik, Marie d1991 *BioIn 17*
Proven, M.J. *WhoScE 91-1*
Provence, Joe Lee 1939- *WhoSSW 93*
Provencher, Roger Arthur 1923- *WhoAm 92*
Provencher, Stephen Wilfred 1942- *WhoScE 91-3*
Provencher, Thomas J. 1938- *St&PR 93*
Provencher-Kambour, Frances 1947- *WhoWor 93*
Provencio, Linda Kay 1955- *WhoAmW 93*
Provensen, Alice & Provensen, Martin 1916-1987 *ChlBIID [port]*
Provensen, Alice 1918- *MajAI [port], SmATA 70 [port]*
Provensen, Alice Rose Twitchell *WhoAm 92*
Provensen, Martin 1916-1987 *See* Provensen, Alice & Provensen, Martin 1916-1987 *ChlBIID*
Provensen, Martin (Elias) 1916-1987 *MajAI, SmATA 70 [port]*
Provenzale, Francesco c. 1626-1704 *Baker 92, OxDcOp*
Provenzale, Maryellen Kirby 1938- *WhoAm 92*
Provenzano, Vincent P. *Law&B 92*
Proverbio, Edoardo 1928- *WhoScE 91-3*
Province, Sharon *Law&B 92*
Provines, Michael Jack 1947- *St&PR 93*
Provo, W. Rodger 1944- *WhoWor 93*
Provorny, Frederick Alan 1946- *WhoAm 92, WhoE 93, WhoEmL 93, WhoWor 93*
Provost, Alain 1930- *WhoScE 91-2*
Provost, David Emile 1949- *St&PR 93*
Provost, Donald Moore 1941- *WhoE 93*
Provost, Eddy *BioIn 17*
Provost, Gail Levine- *BioIn 17*
Provost, Gary 1944- *BioIn 17*
Provost, Lloyd 1931- *WhoE 93, WhoIns 93*
Provost, Margo Suzan 1951- *WhoAmW 93, WhoEmL 93*
Provost, Mary Jacoba 1945- *WhoSSW 93*
Provost, Norman J. *Law&B 92*
Provost, Rhonda Marie 1948- *WhoEmL 93*
Provotorova, Elena Nikolayevna 1954- *WhoWor 93*
Provus, Barbara Lee 1949- *WhoAm 92*
Prowans, Stanislaw 1918- *WhoScE 91-4*
Prowell, Roy Walters, Jr. 1945- *WhoWor 93*
Prown, Jules David 1930- *WhoE 93*
Prowse, Andrew R. 1951- *St&PR 93*
Prowse, Christopher V. *WhoScE 91-1*
Prowse, David John 1941- *WhoAsAP 91*
Prox, Robert F., Jr. 1926- *St&PR 93*
Proxmire, William *BioIn 17*
Proxmire, William 1915- *PolPar, WhoAm 92*
Proyect, Martin H. 1932- *St&PR 93, WhoAm 92*
Proysen, Alf *ConAu 136*
Proysen, Alf 1914-1970 *BioIn 17*
Prozan, Lawrence Ira 1961- *WhoEmL 93*
Prpic, George J(ure) 1920- *ConAu 38NR*
Prpic, Ivan 1927- *WhoScE 91-4*
Pruc, Edward 1946- *St&PR 93*
Prucha, Francis Paul 1921- *ConAu 38NR*
Prucha, John James 1924- *WhoAm 92*
Pruchnicki, Jerzy 1935- *WhoScE 91-4*
Prucz, Jacky Carol 1949- *WhoSSW 93*
Prudden, George Alan 1953- *WhoE 93*
Prudden, John Fletcher 1920- *St&PR 93*
Prude, O. Cooper 1936- *St&PR 93*
Pruden, James Norfleet, III 1948- *WhoSSW 93*
Pruden, Peter DeWitt, III 1945- *St&PR 93*
Pruden, Samuel H. 1936- *St&PR 93*
Pruden, Terry Alan 1945- *St&PR 93*
Prudent, Emile (Racine Gauthier) 1817-1863 *Baker 92*
Prudenti, Anthony J. 1928-1990 *BioIn 17*
Prudentius 348-c. 405 *OxDcByz*
Prud'homme, Albert Fredric 1952- *WhoWor 93*
Prud'homme, Cindy Jo 1959- *WhoAmW 93*
Prud'homme, Hector Alexander 1961- *WhoE 93*
Prudhomme, Maryellen D. *Law&B 92*
Prudhomme, Michael P. 1943- *St&PR 93*
Prudhomme, William Charles 1950- *St&PR 93*
Prudky, Jiri 1946- *WhoScE 91-4*
Prueter, James M. 1947- *WhoIns 93*
Prueter, William R. *Law&B 92*
Pruett, Carl Russell 1955- *WhoSSW 93*
Pruett, Cheryl Lyn 1955- *WhoAmW 93*
Pruett, Clayton Dunklin 1935- *WhoWor 93*
Pruett, Donnie Ray 1948- *WhoAmW 93*
Pruett, Edwin Clark 1946- *St&PR 93*
Pruett, Gordon Earl 1941- *WhoE 93*
Pruett, James Daniel *Law&B 92*
Pruett, James W(orrell) 1932- *Baker 92*
Pruett, James Worrell 1932- *WhoAm 92*
Pruett, Jeanne *WhoAm 92*
Pruett, Kyle Dean 1943- *WhoAm 92, WhoE 93*
Pruett, Leo M. *Law&B 92*
Pruett, Samuel H. 1932- *St&PR 93, WhoAm 92*
Prufer, (Hermann Bernhard) Arthur 1860-1944 *Baker 92*
Pruger, Robert Joseph 1948- *St&PR 93*
Prugh, Dane G. 1918-1990 *BioIn 17*
Prugh, George Shipley 1920- *WhoAm 92*
Prugovecki, Eduard 1937- *WhoAm 92*
Pruim, E.G. 1933- *St&PR 93*
Pruis, John J. 1923- *WhoAm 92*
Pruitt, Alice Fay 1943- *WhoAmW 93*
Pruitt, Anne Loring 1929- *WhoAm 92*
Pruitt, Anne Smith *WhoAmW 93*
Pruitt, Basil Arthur, Jr. 1930- *WhoAm 92*
Pruitt, Cynthia Mitcham 1960- *WhoSSW 93*
Pruitt, Dean Garner 1930- *WhoAm 92*
Pruitt, Gary E. 1950- *St&PR 93*
Pruitt, George Albert 1946- *WhoAm 92*
Pruitt, J. Doug 1945- *WhoAm 92*
Pruitt, James E. 1935- *St&PR 93*
Pruitt, Jane O. 1939- *St&PR 93*
Pruitt, Kenneth Melvin 1933- *WhoSSW 93*
Pruitt, Peter Taliaferro 1932- *WhoAm 92*
Pruitt, Raymond Donald 1912- *WhoAm 92*
Pruitt, Tamara Ann 1935- *St&PR 93*
Pruitt, Thomas Pitts, Jr. 1922- *St&PR 93*
Pruitt, Tom F. *Law&B 92*
Pruitt, Vernon Kent 1934- *St&PR 93*
Pruitt, William H. 1947- *St&PR 93*
Prumier, Ange-Conrad 1820-1884 *See* Prumier, Antoine 1794-1868 *Baker 92*
Prumier, Antoine 1794-1868 *Baker 92*
Prummer, Rolf A. 1937- *WhoScE 91-3*
Pruneau, Tom 1945- *St&PR 93*
Prunella, Warren James 1941- *WhoAm 92*
Pruneski, James C. *St&PR 93*
Prunieres, Henry 1886-1942 *Baker 92*
Prunte, Thomas J. *Law&B 92*
Prunty, Marshall E., Jr. 1925- *St&PR 93*
Prunty, Patricia Louise 1962- *WhoE 93*
Prunty, Robert Earl 1926- *St&PR 93*
Prunty, Robin L. 1963- *St&PR 93*
Prupas, Melvern Irving 1926- *WhoE 93*
Pruppacher, Hans R. 1930- *WhoScE 91-3*
Prus, Boleslaw 1845-1912 *TwCLC 48 [port]*
Prus, Boleslaw 1847-1912 *PolBiDi*
Prus, Francis Vincent 1927- *WhoAm 92*
Prus, Joseph Stanley 1952- *WhoSSW 93*
Prus, Victor Marius 1917- *WhoAm 92*
Prusa, Harold A. 1928- *St&PR 93*
Prusa, James Graham 1948- *WhoAm 92*
Pruschek, Rudolf 1929- *WhoScE 91-3*
Prushan, Sheldon 1934- *St&PR 93*
Prushankin, Jim *BioIn 17*
Prusiner, Stanley Ben 1942- *WhoAm 92*
Prusinkiewicz, Zbigniew Andrzej 1923- *WhoScE 91-4*
Prusinski, Antoni 1925- *WhoScE 91-4*
Prusinski, Richard C. 1923- *St&PR 93*
Pruski, Ann Ward 1952- *WhoAmW 93*
Pruski, Richard John 1946- *St&PR 93*
Pruslin, Stephen (Lawrence) 1940- *Baker 92*
Prusnofsky, Jeff Scott *Law&B 92*
Prusoff, William Herman 1920- *WhoAm 92, WhoE 93*
Prussin, Jeffrey A. 1943- *WhoSSW 93*
Prussing, Laurel Lunt 1941- *WhoAmW 93*
Prust, Susan Luzader 1954- *WhoWrEP 92*
Pruszewicz, Antoni Narcyz 1931- *WhoScE 91-4, WhoWor 93*
Pruszko, Tadeusz 1943- *WhoWor 93*
Pruszynski, Bogdan 1934- *WhoScE 91-4*
Pruter, Karl Hugo 1920- *WhoAm 92*
Pruter, Margaret Franson *WhoAmW 93*
Pruter, Robert 1944- *ConAu 137*
Prutton, Martin *WhoScE 91-1*
Prutzman, Priscilla Rose 1946- *WhoE 93*
Pruwer, Julius 1874-1943 *Baker 92*
Pruyn, Leonard 1898-1973 *ScF&FL 92*
Pruyn, William J. 1922- *WhoAm 92*
Pruyne, Robert E. 1934- *St&PR 93*
Pruzan, Irene 1949- *WhoAmW 93, WhoEmL 93, WhoWor 93*
Pruzan, Paul Stephen 1940- *St&PR 93*
Pruzansky, Joshua Murdock 1940- *WhoE 93, WhoWor 93*
Pruzzo, Judith Josephine 1945- *WhoSSW 93*
Pry, Polly 1857-1938 *BioIn 17*
Pry, Robert H. *WhoScE 91-4*
Pryanishnikov, Ippolit 1847-1921 *OxDcOp*
Pryce, Deborah D. 1951- *WhoAmW 93*
Pryce, Edward Lyons 1914- *WhoAm 92*
Pryce, John Derwent 1941- *WhoWor 93*
Pryce, Jonathan *BioIn 17*
Pryce, Jonathan 1947- *WhoAm 92*
Pryce, Larry *ScF&FL 92*
Pryce, Richard James 1936- *WhoAm 92*
Pryce, William Thornton 1932- *WhoAm 92*
Pryce-Jones, Alan 1908- *BioIn 17*
Pryde, Marion Jackson 1911- *WhoWrEP 92*
Prydz, Hans P.B. 1933- *WhoScE 91-4*
Pryjmak, Peter Gothart 1949- *WhoE 93, WhoWor 93*
Prykarpatsky, Anatoly Karolevych 1953- *WhoWor 93*
Pryke, Ian *BioIn 17*
Pryke, Roy *BioIn 17*
Pryluck, Calvin 1924- *WhoE 93*
Prynne, J(eremy) H(alvard) 1936- *ConAu 39NR*
Pryor, Alan Mark 1949- *WhoAm 92*
Pryor, Arthur 1944- *WhoSSW 93*
Pryor, Arthur (Willard) 1870-1942 *Baker 92*
Pryor, Bonnie 1942- *SmATA 69 [port]*
Pryor, Brenda Rogers 1952- *St&PR 93, WhoAmW 93*
Pryor, Cabell Nicholas, Jr. 1938- *WhoSSW 93*
Pryor, Carol Graham *WhoAmW 93*
Pryor, Charles W. 1944- *St&PR 93*
Pryor, Dale 1929- *St&PR 93*
Pryor, David 1934- *CngDr 91*
Pryor, David Hampton 1934- *WhoAm 92, WhoSSW 93*
Pryor, Diana Mercer- *BioIn 17*
Pryor, Duaine 1930- *St&PR 93*
Pryor, Flynn Belaine *BioIn 17*
Pryor, Frederic L. 1933- *WhoE 93*
Pryor, Gerald W. 1931- *St&PR 93*
Pryor, Harold S. 1920- *WhoAm 92*
Pryor, Hubert 1916- *WhoAm 92, WhoWrEP 92*
Pryor, Jerry Dennis 1952- *WhoWor 93*
Pryor, John Thomas 1949- *WhoSSW 93*
Pryor, Joseph Ehrman 1918- *WhoAm 92*
Pryor, Juliette Williams *Law&B 92*
Pryor, Mark Wayne 1958- *WhoWrEP 92*
Pryor, Mary Condon *Law&B 92*
Pryor, Millard H., Jr. 1933- *St&PR 93*
Pryor, Millard Handley, Jr. 1933- *WhoAm 92*

Pryor, Peter Malachia 1926- *WhoE 93*
Pryor, Peter Patrick 1946- *WhoAm 92*
Pryor, Richard *BioIn 17*
Pryor, Richard 1940- *ConBlB 3 [port], IntDcF 2-3, MiSFD 9, QDrFCA 92 [port], WhoAm 92*
Pryor, Richard Edward, II *Law&B 92*
Pryor, Richard Walter 1932- *WhoAm 92*
Pryor, Sarah Sherman *AmWomPl*
Pryor, Shepherd Green, IV 1946- *WhoAm 92*
Pryor, Tony *Law&B 92*
Pryor, William Austin 1929- *WhoAm 92*
Pryor, William Daniel Lee 1926- *WhoSSW 93, WhoWor 93*
Pryor, William Lee, III 1933- *WhoAm 92*
Prystowsky, Harry 1925- *WhoAm 92*
Pryszmont, Jan 1919- *WhoWor 93*
Przegalinski, Edmund 1937- *WhoScE 91-4*
Przelomski, Anastasia Nemenyi 1918- *WhoAm 92*
Przemieniecki, Janusz Stanislaw 1927- *WhoAm 92*
Przeradzki, Bogdan 1953- *WhoWor 93*
Przesmycki, Zenon Miriam 1861-1941 *PolBiDi*
Przewlocka, Hanna 1923- *WhoScE 91-4*
Przewlocki, Ryszard 1943- *WhoScE 91-4*
Przeworska-Rolewicz, Danuta 1931- *WhoWor 93*
Przezdziecki, Franciszek 1926- *WhoScE 91-4*
Przheval'skii, Nikolai Mikhailovich 1839-1888 *BioIn 17*
Przhevalsky, Nikolai 1839-1888 *Expl 93 [port]*
Przybilski, Bronislaw K(azimierz) 1941- *Baker 92*
Przybycin, Jolanta 1954- *WhoWor 93*
Przybyla, Brenda Elizabeth 1966- *WhoAmW 93*
Przybylowicz, Carolyn Lyon 1947- *WhoEmL 93*
Przybylowicz, Edwin Paul 1933- *St&PR 93, WhoAm 92*
Przybylowski, Jan Wladyslaw 1928- *WhoWor 93*
Przybylski, Pamela Ann 1959- *WhoE 93*
Przybylski, Ryszard 1925- *WhoScE 91-4*
Przybylski, Wlodzimierz 1940- *WhoScE 91-4*
Przybylski, Zdzislaw 1929- *WhoScE 91-4*
Przybyszewska, Stanislawa 1901-1935 *PolBiDi*
Przybyszewski, Anthony R. *WhoIns 93*
Przybyszewski, Anthony R. 1943- *St&PR 93*
Przybyszewski, Stanislaw 1868-1927 *PolBiDi*
Przygodzki, Jacek Ryszard 1933- *WhoScE 91-4*
Przygodzki, Stanislaw 1938- *WhoUN 92*
Przygorzewski, Stanislaw 1929- *WhoScE 91-4*
Przylipiak, Stanislaw 1922- *WhoScE 91-4*
Przyluski, Jan S. 1930- *WhoScE 91-4*
Przypkowski, Felix 1872-1951 *PolBiDi*
Przytula, Marian 1928- *WhoScE 91-4*
Przytulski, Stanislaw 1924- *WhoScE 91-4*
Przytycki, Jozef Henryk 1953- *WhoWor 93*
Przywieczerski, Darius *BioIn 17*
Psaila, Walter 1930- *St&PR 93*
Psallidas, Peter G. 1936- *WhoScE 91-3*
Psallidas, Peter George 1936- *WhoWor 93*
Psaltakis, Gregory C. 1955- *WhoWor 93*
Psaltis, John Costas 1940- *St&PR 93, WhoAm 92*
Psarakis, Emanuel Nicholas 1932- *WhoAm 92*
Psaros-Hartigan, Denise Kay 1960- *WhoE 93*
Psarouthakis, John 1932- *St&PR 93*
Psarras, Ernest Con 1925- *St&PR 93*
Pschorn-Walcher, Hubert 1926- *WhoScE 91-3*
Psellos, Michael 1018-c. 1081 *OxDcByz*
Pshtissky, Yacov A. 1952- *St&PR 93*
Psiharis, Nicholas 1915- *WhoE 93*
Psilander, Valdemar 1884-1917 *IntDcF 2-3*
Psilas, Konstantinos G. 1938- *WhoScE 91-3*
Psomiades, Harry John 1928- *WhoAm 92*
Psuty, Norbert Phillip 1937- *WhoAm 92, WhoE 93*
Psychoyos, Alexandre 1927- *WhoScE 91-2*
Pszczolkowski, Robert E. 1946- *WhoAm 92*
Pszenny, Lawrence John 1943- *St&PR 93*
Ptacek, Kathryn 1952- *ScF&FL 92*
Ptak, Edwin A. *Law&B 92*
Ptak, Edwin A. 1951- *St&PR 93*
Ptak, Frank S. 1943- *WhoAm 92*
Ptak, Robert Charles 1946- *St&PR 93*
Ptak, Wlodzimierz 1928- *WhoScE 91-4*
Ptalis, Donald L. 1942- *St&PR 93*
Ptashkin, Barry Irwin 1944- *WhoWor 93*
Ptashne, Mark Steven 1940- *WhoAm 92*
Ptaszynska, Marta 1943- *Baker 92, BioIn 17*
Ptochoprodromos *OxDcByz*
Ptolemy fl. 130-175 *OxDcByz*
Ptolemy c. 83-c. 161 *Baker 92*
Ptolemy Soter, I c. 367BC-283BC *HarEnMi*
Ptusko, Aleksandr 1900-1973 *DrEEuF*
Pu, Shan 1923- *WhoWor 93*
Puaux, Frederic 1953- *WhoWor 93*
Pubillones, Jorge 1954- *WhoSSW 93*
Public Enemy *News 92 [port]*
Pucar, Zvonimir 1922- *WhoScE 91-4*
Puccetti, Dianna Dee 1949- *WhoAmW 93*
Puccetti, Roland Peter 1924- *WhoAm 92, WhoWrEP 92*
Pucci, Emilio *BioIn 17*
Pucci, Emilio d1992 *NewYTBS 92 [port]*
Pucci, Emilio 1914- *WhoWor 93*
Pucci, Patrice Anne *Law&B 92*
Puccia, J. Mark 1956- *St&PR 93*
Pucciarelli, Albert J. 1950- *St&PR 93*
Puccinelli, Alvin Emil 1938- *St&PR 93*
Puccinelli, Robert A. 1937- *WhoIns 93*
Puccinelli, Roger A. 1934- *St&PR 93*
Puccini *Baker 92*
Puccini, Antonio (Benedetto Maria) 1747-1832 *Baker 92*
Puccini, Arthur Victor 1932- *St&PR 93*
Puccini, Christopher John 1950- *WhoE 93*
Puccini, Domenico (Vencenzo Maria) 1772-1815 *Baker 92*
Puccini, Giacomo 1712?-1781 *Baker 92*
Puccini, Giacomo 1858-1924 *Baker 92, BioIn 17, IntDcOp [port], OxDcOp*
Puccini, Michele 1813-1864 *Baker 92*
Puccini, Tommaso 1749-1811 *BioIn 17*
Puccio, Joseph Anthony 1955- *WhoE 93*
Puccio, Peter James 1938- *St&PR 93*
Pucek, Zdzislaw K. 1930- *WhoScE 91-4*
Pucek, Zdzislaw Kazimierz 1930- *WhoWor 93*
Pucel, Jody M. *Law&B 92*
Pucel, Robert Albin 1926- *WhoAm 92*
Puchalka, Tadeusz 1929- *WhoScE 91-4*
Puchalski, Jerzy Tadeusz 1947- *WhoScE 91-4*
Puchalski, Lawrence C. 1938- *St&PR 93*
Puchalski, Wlodzimierz 1909-1979 *PolBiDi*
Puchalsky, Vladimir (Viacheslavovich) 1848-1933 *Baker 92*
Pu Chaozhu 1930- *WhoAsAP 91*
Puchat, Max 1859-1919 *Baker 92*
Puchebner, Alfred 1945- *St&PR 93*
Puchelle, Edith *WhoScE 91-2*
Pucheu, Pierre Firmin d1944 *BioIn 17*
Puchta, Charles George 1918- *WhoAm 92*
Puchtler, Holde 1920- *WhoAmW 93*
Pucik, Vladimir *WhoE 93*
Pucilowski, Joseph John, Jr. 1942- *WhoE 93*
Pucinski, Elizabeth Simpson 1920?-1990 *BioIn 17*
Pucinski, Lydia 1896-1984 *PolBiDi*
Pucitta, Vincenzo 1778-1861 *Baker 92*
Puck, Theodore Thomas 1916- *WhoAm 92*
Puck, Wolfgang *BioIn 17*
Pucker, Norbert 1934- *WhoScE 91-4*
Puckett, Allen E. 1919- *St&PR 93*
Puckett, Allen Weare 1942- *WhoAm 92*
Puckett, Cathy 1947- *WhoSSW 93*
Puckett, Charles L. *Law&B 92*
Puckett, Christine Starling 1922- *WhoSSW 93*
Puckett, Elsbeth Camille 1946- *WhoSSW 93*
Puckett, James Butler 1947- *WhoSSW 93*
Puckett, James Manuel, Jr. 1916- *WhoSSW 93, WhoWor 93*
Puckett, James Richard 1929- *St&PR 93*
Puckett, Janice Lee 1945- *WhoSSW 93*
Puckett, Kathleen T. *Law&B 92*
Puckett, Kirby *BioIn 17*
Puckett, Kirby 1961- *ConBlB 4 [port], WhoAm 92*
Puckett, Loyd 1928- *St&PR 93*
Puckett, Richard Edward 1932- *WhoWor 93*
Puckett, Robert Hugh 1935- *WhoAm 92*
Puckett, Ruby Parker 1932- *WhoSSW 93*
Puckett, Stanley Allen 1951- *WhoSSW 93*
Puckette, Miller Smith 1959- *WhoWor 93*
Puckette, Stephen Elliott 1927- *WhoAm 92*
Pucko, Diane Bowles 1940- *WhoAmW 93*
Puckorius, Theodore D. 1930- *St&PR 93*
Pucurs, Ilmars 1951- *St&PR 93*
Puddephatt, William 1951- *St&PR 93*
Puddington, Ira Edwin 1911- *WhoAm 92*
Pudenz Family *BioIn 17*
Pudim, D.R. 1950- *St&PR 93*
Pudles, Lynne 1951- *WhoAmW 93*
Pudlik, Wieslaw 1930- *WhoScE 91-4*
Pudlin, Helen Pomerantz *Law&B 92*
Pudney, Gary Laurence 1934- *WhoAm 92*
Pudnos, Stanley Herbert 1930- *WhoE 93, WhoIns 93*
Pudovkin, Vsevelod 1893-1953 *MiSFD 9N*
Pudvin, J.E. 1928- *St&PR 93*
Pudzianowski, Andrew Thaddeus 1947- *WhoE 93*
Puebla, Claudio Gabriel 1950- *WhoWor 93*
Puech, Claude P. 1942- *WhoScE 91-2*
Puech, Pierre-Francois Flavien 1941- *WhoWor 93*
Puel, Jacqueline 1936- *WhoWor 93*
Puelicher, John A. 1920- *St&PR 93, WhoAm 92*
Puello, Christopher Alan *WhoE 93*
Puening, Dennis T. 1948- *St&PR 93*
Puente, Antonio Enrique 1952- *WhoSSW 93*
Puente, Giuseppe Del 1841-1900 *Baker 92*
Puente, John George 1930- *St&PR 93, WhoAm 92*
Puente, Narciso 1919-1990 *BioIn 17*
Puente, Tito *BioIn 17*
Puente, Tito Anthony 1923- *WhoAm 92*
Puentes, Hernan P. 1942- *WhoUN 92*
Puenzo, Luis 1949- *MiSFD 9*
Puerner, Paul Raymond 1927- *WhoWor 93*
Puett, Charles Lynn 1947- *WhoSSW 93*
Puett, Tommy *BioIn 17*
Puette, Robert *BioIn 17*
Puetz, Pamela Ann 1949- *WhoAmW 93*
Puetz, Robert W. 1941- *St&PR 93*
Puey, Manuel H. 1947- *WhoAsAP 91*
Puff, Christian 1949- *WhoScE 91-4*
Puff, Jean Ellingwood 1924- *WhoAmW 93, WhoE 93*
Puffer, Barbara Warzecha 1951- *WhoAmW 93, WhoE 93*
Puffer, Richard Judson 1931- *WhoAm 92*
Puffer, Sharon Kaye 1944- *WhoAmW 93*
Puga, Maria Luisa 1944- *DcMexL, SpAmA*
Pugatch, Ernest 1928- *St&PR 93*
Pugay, Jeffrey Ibanez 1958- *WhoEmL 93*
Puga y Acal, Manuel 1860-1930 *DcMexL*
Puget, Paul-Charles-Marie 1848-1917 *Baker 92*
Pugh, Alan *WhoScE 91-1*
Pugh, Andrew Tucker 1959- *WhoE 93*
Pugh, Arthur James 1937- *WhoAm 92*
Pugh, David Arthur 1926- *WhoAm 92*
Pugh, Derek Salman *WhoScE 91-1*
Pugh, Emerson William 1929- *WhoAm 92*
Pugh, Howel G. *BioIn 17*
Pugh, James H., Jr. 1937- *St&PR 93*
Pugh, James R. *Law&B 92*
Pugh, James Whitworth 1946- *WhoE 93*
Pugh, Jim *BioIn 17*
Pugh, Joel Wilson, II 1932- *WhoSSW 93*
Pugh, Keith E., Jr. 1937- *WhoAm 92*
Pugh, Kenneth Duane 1937- *St&PR 93*
Pugh, Lawrence R. 1933- *St&PR 93, WhoAm 92, WhoE 93*
Pugh, Marion Stirling 1911- *WhoAm 92*
Pugh, Michael P. 1943- *WhoScE 91-1*
Pugh, Owen 1933- *WhoScE 91-1*
Pugh, Raymond Francis 1929- *WhoWor 93*
Pugh, Richard Crawford 1929- *WhoAm 92*
Pugh, Robert G. *St&PR 93*
Pugh, Robert Gahagan 1924- *WhoAm 92*
Pugh, Roderick Wellington 1919- *WhoAm 92*
Pugh, Roger V. 1929- *St&PR 93*
Pugh, Samuel Franklin 1904- *WhoWrEP 92*
Pugh, Stuart *WhoScE 91-1*
Pugh, Susan J. *Law&B 92*
Pugh Thomas, Michael *WhoScE 91-1*
Puglia, Naresh C. 1948- *WhoAsAP 91*
Puglia, Wayne Joseph 1950- *St&PR 93*
Pugliese, Anthony Paul 1942- *WhoE 93*
Pugliese, Elisa Maria *Law&B 92*
Pugliese, Frank A. *Law&B 92*
Pugliese, Joseph Sebastian 1943- *St&PR 93*
Pugliese, Michael (Gabriel) 1956- *Baker 92*
Pugliese, Paul Joseph 1952- *WhoE 93*
Pugliese, Robert F. *Law&B 92*
Pugliese, Robert Francis 1933- *St&PR 93, WhoAm 92*
Pugliese, Rocco Vincent 1953- *WhoE 93*
Puglisi, Angela Aurora 1949- *WhoWrEP 92*
Puglisi, Anthony Joseph 1949- *St&PR 93, WhoAm 92*
Pugnani, (Giulio) Gaetano (Gerolamo) 1731-1798 *Baker 92*
Pugnetti, Giuseppe 1935- *WhoUN 92*
Pugni, Cesare 1802-1870 *Baker 92*
Pugno, (Stephane) Raoul 1852-1914 *Baker 92*
Pugo, Boris *BioIn 17*
Pugo, Boris 1937-1991 *AnObit 1991*
Pugsley, Alfred Grenvile 1903- *WhoWor 93*
Pugsley, Paula Cyr *Law&B 92*
Puhala, James J. *Law&B 92*
Puhala, James Joseph 1942- *St&PR 93, WhoAm 92*
Puhl, Frances Pellegrino *Law&B 92*
Puhl, Michael Earl 1948- *St&PR 93*
Puhvel, Jaan 1932- *WhoAm 92*
Puhvel, Sirje Madli 1939- *WhoAmW 93*
Pui, Ching-Hon 1951- *WhoSSW 93*
Puia, I. *WhoScE 91-4*
Puig, Angela Renee 1966- *WhoE 93*
Puig, Janice Claire 1944- *WhoE 93*
Puig, Manuel *BioIn 17*
Puig, Manuel 1932-1990 *SpAmA*
Puig Casauranc, Jose Manuel 1888-1939 *DcMexL*
Puigdefabregas, Juan *WhoScE 91-3*
Puiggari, Jose Luis 1954- *WhoWor 93*
Puig i Cadafalch, Joseph 1869?-1957? *BioIn 17*
Puippe, J.C. 1950- *WhoScE 91-4*
Puisieux, Francis Henri 1934- *WhoScE 91-2*
Pujal Carrera, Marcos 1922- *WhoScE 91-3*
Pujin, Vlasta 1929- *WhoScE 91-4*
Pujo, Maurice 1872-1955 *BioIn 17*
Pujol, Francesco 1878-1945 *Baker 92*
Pujol, Henri *WhoScE 91-2*
Pujol, Jean-Pierre 1941- *WhoScE 91-2*
Pujol, Joaquin Pierre 1941- *WhoUN 92*
Pujol, Juan (Pablo) c. 1573-1626 *Baker 92*
Pujol, Laetitia *BioIn 17, NewYTBS 92 [port]*
Pujol, Remy 1939- *WhoScE 91-2*
Pukander, Juhani S. 1944- *WhoScE 91-4*
Pukkila, Tarmo M. 1946- *WhoScE 91-4*
Pukkila, Tarmo Mikko 1946- *WhoWor 93*
Pukl, Joseph Michael, Jr. 1953- *WhoSSW 93*
Pula, Augustinus Lekhotla *WhoWor 93*
Pulakesin, II d642 *HarEnMi*
Pulakos, A.C. 1926- *St&PR 93*
Pulakos, George A. 1964- *St&PR 93*
Pulaski, John B. 1939- *St&PR 93*
Pulaski, Kazimierz 1747-1779 *HarEnMi, PolBiDi [port]*
Pulaski, Mark L. *St&PR 93*
Pulaski, Mary Ann Spencer d1992 *NewYTBS 92*
Pulaski, Mary Ann Spencer 1916-1992 *BioIn 17, ConAu 137*
Pulcheria 399-453 *OxDcByz*
Pulcrano, James Thomas 1957- *St&PR 93*
Puleo, Frederick William 1951- *St&PR 93*
Puleo, Nancy W. *Law&B 92*
Puleo, Nunzio J. 1925- *St&PR 93*
Puleo, William Joseph 1955- *St&PR 93*
Pulford, Robert Edward 1938- *St&PR 93*
Pulgram, Ernst 1915- *WhoAm 92*
Pulgram, William Leopold 1921- *WhoAm 92*
Pulgram-Arthen, Lucia Deirdre 1956- *WhoE 93*
Pulhamus, Aaron Rae 1938- *WhoE 93*
Puliafico, G. Albert 1927- *St&PR 93*
Puliafito, Carmen Anthony 1951- *WhoE 93*
Pulido, Abraham 1953- *MiSFD 9*
Pulido, Miguel Lazaro 1934- *WhoSSW 93*
Pulina, Marian 1936- *WhoScE 91-4*
Pulis, Michael Patrick 1966- *WhoE 93*
Pulis, R.S. 1944- *St&PR 93*
Pulis, Ralph Stephen 1944- *WhoIns 93*
Pulisifer, Howard A. 1942- *St&PR 93*
Pulitzer, Emily S. Rauh 1933- *WhoAm 92, WhoAmW 93*
Pulitzer, Joseph 1847-1911 *BioIn 17, GayN, JrnUS, PolPar*
Pulitzer, Joseph, Jr. 1885-1955 *JrnUS*
Pulitzer, Joseph, Jr. 1913- *WhoAm 92*
Pulitzer, Michael Edgar 1930- *St&PR 93, WhoAm 92*
Pulitzer, Sidney C. 1934- *St&PR 93*
Pulizzi, Matthew S. 1943- *St&PR 93*
Pulker, Hans Karl 1933- *WhoWor 93*
Pulkkinen, Erkki J. 1924- *WhoScE 91-4*
Pulkkinen, Erkki Juhani 1944- *WhoWor 93*
Pulkonik, Kenneth J. *St&PR 93*
Pulkrabek, Larry A. *Law&B 92*
Pulkrabek, Larry Alster 1939- *St&PR 93, WhoAm 92*
Pullar, D.R. 1939- *St&PR 93*
Pullekines, Carol Anne 1955- *WhoAmW 93*
Pullen, David John 1936- *WhoE 93*
Pullen, Edwin Wesley 1923- *WhoAm 92*
Pullen, Janet Kaye 1954- *St&PR 93*
Pullen, Keats A., Jr. 1916- *WhoAm 92*
Pullen, Nancy Lynn 1965- *WhoAmW 93*
Pullen, Patrick Lee 1956- *WhoSSW 93*
Pullen, Penny Lynne 1947- *WhoAmW 93*
Pullen, Phillip Arden 1926- *St&PR 93*
Pullen, Randall L. 1948- *St&PR 93*
Pullen, Richard Owen 1944- *WhoE 93*
Puller, Lewis B., Jr. *BioIn 17*

Puller, Linda Todd 1945- *WhoAmW 93*
Pulles, Gregory J. *Law&B 92*
Pulles, Peter Cornells Wilhelm 1924- *WhoWor 93*
Pulley, Brenda Diane 1958- *WhoE 93*
Pulley, Jack I. *Law&B 92*
Pulley, Judith Poss 1940- *WhoAmW 93*
Pulley, Karl Emmanuel *Law&B 92*
Pulleyblank, Edwin George 1922- *WhoAm 92*
Pulleyn, Samuel Robert 1946- *WhoAm 92*
Pulli, Seppo Kalevi 1939- *WhoScE 91-4*
Pullia, Antonino 1935- *WhoScE 91-3*
Pulliainen, Erkki Ossi Olavi 1938- *WhoScE 91-4*
Pulliam, Della Denise 1963- *WhoWor 93*
Pulliam, Eugene C(ollins) 1889-1975 *DcLB 127 [port]*
Pulliam, Eugene Smith 1914- *WhoAm 92*
Pulliam, Evelyn Jean *Law&B 92*
Pulliam, Howard Ronald 1945- *WhoAm 92, WhoSSW 93*
Pulliam, Mark Stephen 1955- *WhoAm 92*
Pulliam, Martha 1891-1991 *BioIn 17*
Pulliam, Steve Cameron 1948- *WhoSSW 93*
Pulliam, Sylvia Clark 1945- *WhoSSW 93*
Pulliam, Virgil R. *Law&B 92*
Pullicino, Alberto c. 1719-c. 1765 *BioIn 17*
Pullin, Charles Russell 1923- *St&PR 93*
Pullin, Jorge Alfredo 1963- *WhoE 93, WhoWor 93*
Pulling, Edward 1898-1991 *BioIn 17*
Pulling, Rebecca Ann 1964- *WhoE 93*
Pulling, Ronald Wilson, Sr. 1919- *WhoAm 92*
Pulling, Thomas L. 1939- *St&PR 93*
Pulling, Thomas Leffingwell 1939- *WhoAm 92, WhoWor 93*
Pullman, Anthony J. 1945- *St&PR 93*
Pullman, George 1831-1897 *GayN*
Pullman, Maynard Edward 1927- *WhoAm 92*
Pullman, Philip 1946- *BioIn 17, ScF&FL 92*
Pullman, Philip (N.) 1946- *MajAI [port]*
Pullman, Philip Nicholas 1946- *WhoAm 92*
Pullmann, Ernst A. 1953- *WhoWor 93*
Pullum, Erin Lynn 1961- *WhoAmW 93*
Pullum, Geoffrey K(eith) 1945- *ConAu 138*
Pulos, Arthur Jon 1917- *WhoAm 92*
Pulos, Virginia Kate 1947- *WhoAmW 93*
Pulquerio, Manuel de Oliveira 1928- *WhoWor 93*
Puls, Richard John 1925- *WhoWor 93*
Pulsifer, Edgar D. 1934- *St&PR 93*
Pulsifer, Fay *AmWomPl*
Pulsifer, Howard A. *Law&B 92*
Pulsifer, Margaret Bigwood 1959- *WhoE 93*
Pulsifer, Roy 1931- *WhoSSW 93*
Pultorak, Jerzy 1932- *WhoScE 91-4*
Pultz, George S. *Law&B 92*
Pulutan, Rosalie Dorado 1960- *WhoWor 93*
Pulver, Mary Monica 1943- *ScF&FL 92*
Pulver, Robin 1945- *WhoWrEP 92*
Pulvertaft, T. Christopher R. 1932- *WhoScE 91-2*
Puma, Michael John 1946- *St&PR 93*
Puma, Samuel George, Jr. 1951- *WhoE 93*
Pumariega, Andres Julio 1953- *WhoSSW 93*
Pumariega, JoAnne Buttacavoli 1952- *WhoSSW 93*
Pumpalov, Atanas 1936- *WhoUN 92*
Pumper, Robert William 1921- *WhoAm 92*
Pumphrey, Hugh Charles 1964- *WhoWor 93*
Pumphrey, Janet Kay 1946- *WhoAmW 93, WhoE 93, WhoEmL 93*
Pumpian, Betty Ann G. 1935- *WhoAmW 93*
Punak, Debra Lynn 1959- *WhoAmW 93*
Punch, Gary Francis 1957- *WhoAsAP 91*
Punchard, Constance *ScF&FL 92*
Punches, Dennis 1936- *St&PR 93*
Puncochar, Pavel 1944- *WhoScE 91-4*
Pundole, K.N. 1949- *St&PR 93*
Pundsack, Fred L. 1925- *St&PR 93*
Puner, Helen W. 1915-1989 *BioIn 17*
Pung, Robert E. 1932- *St&PR 93*
Pung, Rosalyn Alyce 1948- *WhoAmW 93*
Pungor, Erno 1923- *WhoScE 91-4*
Punithalingam, Eliyathamby *WhoScE 91-1*
Punjabi, Rajesh Khemchand 1946- *WhoWor 93*
Punkar, Ronald E. 1933- *St&PR 93*
Punkkinen, Matti 1939- *WhoScE 91-4*
Punnapayak, Hunsa 1951- *WhoWor 93*
Punnett, Audrey Frances 1947- *WhoAmW 93*
Punnett, Milton B. 1930- *St&PR 93*
Punnonen, Juha *WhoScE 91-3*
Punnonen, Reijo Helge 1936- *WhoScE 91-4*
Punter, David 1949- *ScF&FL 92*
Punter, Pieter Herman 1947- *WhoWor 93*
Punto, Giovanni *Baker 92*
Punwani, Dharam V. 1942- *St&PR 93*
Punzak-Marcus, Anne 1958- *WhoAmW 93*
Punzalan, Jeses M. 1935- *WhoAsAP 91*
Puopolo, Lou *MiSFD 9*
Puotinen, Arthur Edwin 1941- *WhoAm 92*
Pupel, Daniel S., Jr. *Law&B 92*
Pupin, Michael 1858-1935 *GayN*
Puplick, Christopher John Guelph 1948- *WhoAsAP 91*
Pupo, Raul 1946- *St&PR 93*
Puppo, Giuseppe 1749-1827 *Baker 92*
Purcell, Ann Rushing 1945- *WhoAmW 93*
Purcell, Anne G. 1932- *ConAu 139*
Purcell, Arthur Henry 1944- *WhoAm 92*
Purcell, Ben(jamin H.) 1928- *ConAu 139*
Purcell, Bernice Marie 1963- *WhoEmL 93*
Purcell, Bradford Moore 1929- *WhoAm 92*
Purcell, C. William *Law&B 92*
Purcell, Dale 1919- *WhoAm 92*
Purcell, Daniel c. 1660-1717 *Baker 92*
Purcell, Daniel Shannon 1950- *St&PR 93*
Purcell, Edward Mills 1912- *WhoAm 92, WhoE 93, WhoWor 93*
Purcell, Evelyn *MiSFD 9*
Purcell, Francis Jerome 1939- *WhoAm 92*
Purcell, George Richard 1921- *WhoE 93, WhoWor 93*
Purcell, Gertrude 189-?-1963 *AmWomPl*
Purcell, Henry 1659-1695 *Baker 92, IntDcOp [port], OxDcOp*
Purcell, Henry, III 1929- *WhoSSW 93*
Purcell, James Edward 1932- *St&PR 93*
Purcell, James Francis 1920- *St&PR 93, WhoAm 92*
Purcell, James Lawrence 1929- *WhoAm 92*
Purcell, John C. *Law&B 92*
Purcell, John M. 1932- *WhoScE 91-3*
Purcell, John N. 1937- *St&PR 93*
Purcell, Joseph *MiSFD 9*
Purcell, Joseph Carroll 1921- *WhoSSW 93*
Purcell, Kenneth 1928- *WhoAm 92*
Purcell, Mary Hamilton *WhoAmW 93*
Purcell, Mary Louise Gerlinger 1923- *WhoAmW 93*
Purcell, P.J. *St&PR 93*
Purcell, Patrick B. 1943- *St&PR 93, WhoAm 92*
Purcell, Paul E. 1959- *WhoWrEP 92*
Purcell, Philip J. 1943- *St&PR 93*
Purcell, Philip James 1943- *WhoAm 92, WhoE 93*
Purcell, Richard Fick *Law&B 92*
Purcell, Richard Fick 1924- *St&PR 93, WhoAm 92*
Purcell, Robert E. *St&PR 93*
Purcell, Robert Harry 1935- *WhoAm 92*
Purcell, Robert Harry 1943- *St&PR 93*
Purcell, Robert R. *Law&B 92*
Purcell, Robert William 1911-1991 *BioIn 17*
Purcell, Royal 1921- *WhoWrEP 92*
Purcell, S. *Law&B 92*
Purcell, Steven Richard *WhoAm 92, WhoE 93, WhoWor 93*
Purcell, Thomas O., Jr. 1944- *St&PR 93*
Purcell, William Hugh 1942- *St&PR 93*
Purcell, William Paul 1935- *WhoAm 92*
Purcell, William Paxson, III 1953- *WhoSSW 93*
Purcell, William Riker *Law&B 92*
Purchas, Derek B. 1929- *WhoScE 91-1*
Purchase, Earl Ralph 1919- *WhoSSW 93*
Purchase, I.F.H. *WhoScE 91-1*
Purciful, Dan Elwood 1935- *WhoAm 92*
Purcifull, Robert Otis 1932- *WhoAm 92, WhoSSW 93*
Purcival, Julie Helene *AmWomPl*
Purczynski, Jan 1944- *WhoScE 91-4*
Purdes, Alice Marie 1931- *WhoAmW 93*
Purdew, Robert Cyril 1923-1990 *BioIn 17*
Purdie, Alexander M. 1945- *St&PR 93*
Purdie, Alexander M., Jr. 1945- *WhoAm 92*
Purdie, David Wilkie *WhoScE 91-1*
Purdie, John Hyndman 1770-1845 *BioIn 17*
Purdom, Paul Walton, Jr. 1940- *WhoAm 92*
Purdom, R. Don 1926- *WhoIns 93*
Purdom, Thomas James 1937- *WhoAm 92*
Purdue, Henry Michael *WhoScE 91-1*
Purdue, Jack Olen 1913- *WhoSSW 93*
Purdum, Robert L. 1935- *St&PR 93, WhoAm 92, WhoE 93*
Purdy, Al 1918- *BioIn 17, ConAu 17AS [port], WhoCanL 92*
Purdy, Alan Harris 1923- *WhoAm 92*
Purdy, Alan MacGregor 1940- *WhoAm 92*
Purdy, Carol *BioIn 17*
Purdy, Carol 1943- *ConAu 136*
Purdy, Charles Robert 1937- *WhoAm 92*
Purdy, David Lawrence 1928- *St&PR 93*
Purdy, Frank *Law&B 92*
Purdy, Frank Kerr, Jr. 1939- *WhoSSW 93*
Purdy, Frazier Rodney 1929- *WhoAm 92*
Purdy, George Donald, Jr. 1939- *WhoE 93*
Purdy, James 1923- *BioIn 17, WhoAm 92, WhoWrEP 92*
Purdy, James 1927- *ConGAN*
Purdy, Judith Bolyard 1949- *WhoSSW 93*
Purdy, Kenneth Rodman 1933- *WhoSSW 93*
Purdy, Laura M. 1946- *ConAu 137*
Purdy, Nannie Sutton *AmWomPl*
Purdy, Nina Sutherland 1889- *AmWomPl*
Purdy, P.D. *WhoScE 91-1*
Purdy, Ralph William 1924- *WhoAm 92*
Purdy, Richard Little 1904-1990 *BioIn 17*
Purdy, Robin Christopher 1951- *St&PR 93*
Purdy, Sherry M. *Law&B 92*
Purdy, Susan 1942- *WhoWrEP 92*
Purdy, William Crossley 1930- *WhoAm 92*
Purdy, William Marshall 1940- *WhoAm 92*
Purens, Ilmars Uldis 1947- *WhoWrEP 92*
Purewal, Satinder 1954- *WhoWor 93*
Purg, Franc 1955- *WhoWor 93*
Purgathofer, Werner 1955- *WhoWor 93*
Purgatori, Andrea 1953- *WhoWor 93*
Purgavie, Charles Samuel 1929- *WhoE 93*
Puri, Madan Lal 1929- *WhoAm 92*
Puri, Pratap 1938- *WhoSSW 93*
Puri, Rajendra Kumar 1932- *WhoSSW 93*
Purice, S. *WhoScE 91-4*
Purifoy, Stephen D. 1951- *St&PR 93*
Purify, James, & Bobby *SoulM*
Purin, Thomas 1941- *WhoSSW 93*
Purinton, Arthur L., II 1942- *St&PR 93*
Purinton, Michael Ray 1947- *WhoSSW 93*
Puris, Martin Ford 1939- *WhoAm 92*
Purishottaman, Vakhom 1928- *WhoAsAP 91*
Puritano, Vincent 1930- *WhoAm 92*
Purkiser, Westlake Taylor 1910- *WhoAm 92*
Purkiss, Linda M. *Law&B 92*
Purkiss, Richard Allen 1941- *St&PR 93, WhoAm 92*
Purkyne, Jan Evangelista 1787-1869 *IntDcAn*
Purl, O. Thomas 1924- *WhoAm 92*
Purmort, Francis Walworth, Jr. 1930- *WhoIns 93*
Purnell, Charles Rea 1922- *WhoAm 92*
Purnell, Colin James *WhoScE 91-1*
Purnell, Harry Sylvester 1933- *St&PR 93*
Purnell, John H. 1941- *WhoAm 92*
Purnell, John Harris 1941- *St&PR 93*
Purnell, John Howard 1925- *WhoWor 93*
Purnell, Margaret Montgomery 1963- *WhoAmW 93*
Purnell, Maurice Eugene, Jr. 1940- *WhoAm 92*
Purnhagen-Schaal, Jenne E. 1920- *St&PR 93*
Purple, Adam *BioIn 17*
Purpura, Dominick P. 1927- *WhoAm 92*
Purpura, Peter Joseph 1939- *WhoAm 92*
Purrington, Robert 1939- *WhoE 93*
Purrington, Robert Daniel 1936- *WhoSSW 93*
Purscell, Delano Benjamin 1934- *WhoAm 92*
Purse, Charles Roe 1960- *WhoEmL 93, WhoWor 93*
Purse, Robert Allgood 1930- *St&PR 93*
Pursel, David G. *Law&B 92*
Pursel, Robert Wayne, Jr. 1966- *WhoE 93*
Pursell, Carl D. 1932- *CngDr 91*
Pursell, Carl Duane 1932- *WhoAm 92*
Pursell, Carroll Wirth 1932- *WhoAm 92*
Pursell, Elliott Dearing 1945- *WhoSSW 93*
Purser, Bruce H. 1928- *WhoScE 91-2*
Purser, Charles A. *Law&B 92*
Purser, Donald Joseph 1954- *WhoEmL 93*
Purser, Lynda Christine *WhoScE 91-1*
Purser, Sarah 1848-1943 *BioIn 17*
Purser, Susan Joy Richardson 1949- *WhoSSW 93*
Pursey, Derek Lindsay 1927- *WhoAm 92*
Pursifull, Carmen Maria 1930- *WhoWrEP 92*
Pursinger, Marvin Gavin 1923- *WhoSSW 93, WhoWor 93*
Pursley, A.N. 1941- *St&PR 93*
Pursley, Aaron *BioIn 17*
Pursley, Michael Bader 1945- *WhoAm 92*
Pursley, Michael Gene 1958- *WhoSSW 93*
Purtell, Lawrence R. *Law&B 92*
Purtell, Lawrence R. 1947- *St&PR 93*
Purtell, Lawrence Robert 1947- *WhoAm 92*
Purtill, Patrick D. *Law&B 92*
Purtill, Richard 1931- *ScF&FL 92*
Purtilo, David T. d1992 *NewYTBS 92*
Purtle, John Ingram 1923- *WhoAm 92*
Purtle, Virginia Sue 1940- *WhoAmW 93, WhoSSW 93*
Purves, Alan Carroll 1931- *WhoAm 92, WhoWrEP 92*
Purves, John T. *Law&B 92*
Purves, William 1931- *WhoAsAP 91, WhoWor 93*
Purves, William Kirkwood 1934- *WhoAm 92*
Purviance, Edna 1894-1958 *IntDcF 2-3 [port]*
Purvin, Robert L. 1917- *St&PR 93*
Purvin, Robert L. 1917-1991 *BioIn 17*
Purvin, Theodore V. 1918- *St&PR 93*
Purvines, Verne E. *Law&B 92*
Purvines, Verne E., Jr. 1945- *St&PR 93*
Purvis, Alison M. 1961- *St&PR 93*
Purvis, Archie C., Jr. *St&PR 93*
Purvis, Darwin W. 1933- *St&PR 93*
Purvis, George Allen 1933- *St&PR 93*
Purvis, George Frank, Jr. 1914- *St&PR 93, WhoAm 92, WhoIns 93*
Purvis, Hoyt Hughes 1939- *WhoSSW 93*
Purvis, James M. *Law&B 92*
Purvis, Joseph A. *Law&B 92*
Purvis, Michael Blaikie 1952- *St&PR 93, WhoAm 92*
Purvis, Michael Curtis *Law&B 92*
Purvis, Ronald Scott 1928- *WhoSSW 93, WhoWor 93*
Purwin, Paul E. *Law&B 92*
Purwins, Hans-Georg 1939- *WhoScE 91-3*
Puryear, Alvin Nelson 1937- *WhoAm 92*
Puryear, James Burton 1938- *WhoSSW 93*
Puryear, Martin 1941- *BioIn 17, WhoAm 92*
Purze, Judy Suzanne 1953- *WhoSSW 93*
Pusaperi, David P. *Law&B 92*
Pusateri, Lawrence Xavier 1931- *WhoAm 92*
Pusch, Guenter 1941- *WhoScE 91-3*
Puscheck, Herbert Charles 1936- *WhoAm 92*
Puschel, Philip P. 1938- *St&PR 93*
Puschel, Roberta J. 1943- *St&PR 93*
Puschmann, Adam (Zacharias) 1532-1600 *Baker 92*
Puschra, Werner Friedrich 1952- *WhoWor 93*
Pusey, Ellen Pratt 1928- *WhoAmW 93*
Pusey, Gregory S. 1952- *St&PR 93*
Pusey, Paul Lawrence 1952- *WhoSSW 93*
Pusey, William Webb, III 1910- *WhoAm 92*
Pushkarev, Boris S. 1929- *WhoAm 92*
Pushkin, Aleksandr Sergeevich 1799-1837 *BioIn 17*
Pushkin, Alexander 1799-1837 *MagSWL [port], OxDcOp, WorLitC [port]*
Puska, Pekka 1945- *WhoScE 91-4*
Puskar, Janet K. 1943- *WhoAmW 93*
Puskar, Michael 1932- *St&PR 93*
Puskar, Patricia Ann 1932- *St&PR 93*
Puskarz, Stanley J. 1937- *St&PR 93*
Pussel, Franz, Jr. 1942- *St&PR 93*
Pust, L. *WhoScE 91-4*
Pust, Ladislav 1927- *WhoScE 91-4*
Pustelnik, Czeslaw 1916- *WhoScE 91-4*
Pusterla, Thomas Edward 1951- *WhoE 93*
Pustet, Friedrich 1798-1882 *Baker 92*
Pusti, Maureen S. *ScF&FL 92*
Pustilnik, David D. *Law&B 92*
Pustilnik, David Daniel 1931- *WhoAm 92*
Pustilnik, Jean Todd 1932- *WhoE 93*
Pustola, Jerzy 1923- *WhoScE 91-4*
Pusztai, Arpad *WhoScE 91-1*
Puta, Diane Fay 1947- *WhoAmW 93*
Pu Ta-Hai 1922- *WhoAsAP 91*
Puth, John W. 1929- *St&PR 93*
Puth, John Wells 1929- *WhoAm 92, WhoWor 93*
Puth, Robert Christian 1936- *WhoE 93*
Puthipiroj, Pisit *WhoWor 93*
Puthoff, Frank M. *Law&B 92*
Puthoff, Harold E. *WhoSSW 93*
Puthuff, Hanson 1875-1972 *BioIn 17*
Puthuff, Steven Henry 1940- *WhoAm 92*
Putilov, B.N. 1919- *IntDcAn*
Putka, Andrew Charles 1926- *WhoAm 92*
Putman, Andree *BioIn 17*
Putman, Anthony O'Neal 1945- *St&PR 93*
Putman, Charles Ed 1941- *WhoAm 92*
Putman, Dale Cornelius 1927- *WhoAm 92*
Putman, George Wendell 1929- *WhoE 93*
Putman, Linda Murray *Law&B 92*
Putman, Mark Frans 1944- *WhoWor 93*
Putman, Mary *BioIn 17*
Putman, Paul 1929- *St&PR 93*
Putman, Robert M. 1952- *St&PR 93*
Putman, Stephen R. 1950- *St&PR 93*
Putnam, Alice 1916- *BioIn 17*
Putnam, Allan Ray 1920- *WhoWor 93*
Putnam, Ashley 1952- *OxDcOp*
Putnam, Ashley (Elizabeth) 1952- *Baker 92*
Putnam, Barbara Deyo 1926- *WhoAmW 93*
Putnam, Charles Duane 1928- *St&PR 93*
Putnam, Cynthia Louise 1958- *WhoAmW 93*

Putnam, David Binney 1913-1992 *BioIn 17*
Putnam, David Binney, Sr. d1992 *NewYTBS 92*
Putnam, Donald B. 1932- *St&PR 93*
Putnam, Ella Jane *St&PR 93*
Putnam, Frank William 1917- *WhoAm 92*
Putnam, Frederic L., Jr. 1925- *St&PR 93*
Putnam, Frederic Ward 1839-1915 *BioIn 17, IntDcAn*
Putnam, Frederick Warren, Jr. 1917- *WhoAm 92*
Putnam, G. P. 1814-1872 *DcLB Y92 [port]*
Putnam, George 1926- *St&PR 93, WhoAm 92*
Putnam, George Endicott 1921- *WhoAm 92*
Putnam, George N. d1991 *BioIn 17*
Putnam, George Palmer 1814-1872 *BioIn 17*
Putnam, George W., Jr. 1920- *WhoAm 92*
Putnam, Harrington d1990 *BioIn 17*
Putnam, Israel 1718-1790 *HarEnMi*
Putnam, Joanne White 1945- *WhoSSW 93*
Putnam, John G., Jr. 1929- *St&PR 93*
Putnam, Kenneth J. 1938- *St&PR 93*
Putnam, Linda Lee 1945- *WhoAm 92*
Putnam, Lula M. *AmWomPl*
Putnam, Mark *BioIn 17*
Putnam, Martin S. *Law&B 92*
Putnam, Michael Courtney Jenkins 1933- *WhoAm 92*
Putnam, Nina Wilcox 1888-1962 *AmWomPl*
Putnam, Norbert *SoulM*
Putnam, Peter Brock 1920- *WhoAm 92*
Putnam, Robert E. 1933- *WhoAm 92, WhoWrEP 92*
Putnam, Rosalie B. *AmWomPl*
Putnam, Sarah Rockwell 1960- *WhoAmW 93*
Putnam, Terri *WhoWrEP 92*
Putnam, Thomas P. *St&PR 93*
Putnam, Virginia Ann 1927- *WhoAmW 93*
Putnam, William Lowell 1924- *WhoE 93*
Putney, John A. 1939- *St&PR 93*
Putney, John A., Jr. 1939- *WhoIns 93*
Putney, John Alden, Jr. 1939- *WhoAm 92*
Putney, John Fraser, II 1939- *WhoE 93*
Putney, Judith Eileen 1957- *WhoAmW 93*
Putney, Mark William 1929- *St&PR 93, WhoAm 92*
Putney, Mary Engler 1933- *WhoAmW 93*
Putney, Nancy Hoddinott 1960- *WhoSSW 93*
Putney, Robert E., III *Law&B 92*
Putnik, Cathy L. *St&PR 93*
Putnik, Radomir 1847-1917 *HarEnMi*
Putnoky-Krako, Janice 1951- *St&PR 93*
Putrimas, Donald J. 1952- *St&PR 93*
Putsep, Ervin Peeter 1921- *WhoWor 93*
Putsep, Peeter Ervin 1955- *WhoWor 93*
Putt, William Donald 1937- *St&PR 93*
Putter, Irving 1917- *WhoAm 92*
Putterman, Florence Grace 1927- *WhoAm 92*
Putterman, Lawrence E. 1948- *St&PR 93*
Putterman, Louis G. 1952- *WhoAm 92*
Puttick, Keith Ernest *WhoScE 91-1*
Puttnam, David 1941- *ConTFT 10*
Puttnam, David Terence 1941- *WhoAm 92, WhoWor 93*
Putukian, Lisa Ann 1959- *WhoE 93*
Putz, Charles *WhoScE 91-2*
Putz, Reinhard V. 1942- *WhoScE 91-3*
Putz, Walter Edwin 1924- *St&PR 93*
Putze, Louis 1916- *WhoAm 92*
Putzel, Constance Kellner 1922- *WhoAm 92*
Putzel, Henry, Jr. 1913- *OxCSupC*
Putzell, Edwin J., Jr. 1913- *St&PR 93*
Putzell, Edwin Joseph, Jr. 1913- *WhoAm 92*
Putzer, Agnes G. 1933- *St&PR 93*
Putzrath, Resha Mae 1949- *WhoE 93*
Puustinen, Kauko 1939- *WhoScE 91-4*
Puverel, Roland Marie Pierre 1913- *WhoWor 93*
Puy, Jean 1876-1960 *BioIn 17*
Puyana, Rafael 1931- *Baker 92*
Puyane, Ramon 1947- *WhoWor 93*
Puyat-Reyes, Ma. Consuelo 1937- *WhoAsAP 91*
Puyau, Francis Albert 1928- *WhoAm 92*
Puyenbroek, Marinus 1953- *WhoWor 93*
Pu Yi 1906-1967 *BioIn 17, DcTwHis*
Puz, Richard 1936- *St&PR 93*
Puzinas, James Joseph 1960- *St&PR 93*
Puzo, Dorothy Ann *MiSFD 9*
Puzo, Lisa L. 1957- *St&PR 93*
Puzo, Mario 1920- *BioIn 17, ConTFT 10, ScF&FL 92, WhoAm 92, WhoWor 93, WhoWrEP 92*
Puzon, Leoncio M. 1919- *WhoAsAP 91*
Puzon, Mary Bridget 1931- *WhoAmW 93*
Puzyna, Jan Kozielko 1842-1911 *PolBiDi*
Puzyrewski, Romuald Kazimierz 1935- *WhoScE 91-4*
Puzzele, James Albert 1951- *WhoE 93*
P. Vallal, Peruman 1949- *WhoAsAP 91*
Py, Pierre 1956- *St&PR 93*
P'ya Tashin d1782 *HarEnMi*
Pyatt, D.G. 1939- *WhoScE 91-1*
Pyatt, Everett Arno 1939- *WhoAm 92*
Pyatt, Francis Brian *WhoScE 91-1*
Pyatt, Frank Graham *WhoScE 91-1*
Pycard fl. c. 1400- *Baker 92*
Pyck, Karel L.G. 1938- *WhoScE 91-2*
Pye, August Kenneth 1931- *WhoAm 92, WhoSSW 93*
Pye, Gordon Bruce 1933- *WhoAm 92*
Pye, Joanne 1952- *WhoWor 93*
Pye, John David *WhoScE 91-1*
Pye, Lenwood David 1937- *WhoAm 92*
Pye, Lloyd 1946- *ScF&FL 92*
Pye, Lucian Wilmot 1921- *WhoAm 92*
Pye, Mort 1918- *WhoAm 92, WhoE 93*
Pyers, Paula A. 1962- *WhoAmW 93*
Pyett, Roger H. 1929- *St&PR 93*
Pyfer, John Frederick, Jr. 1946- *WhoEmL 93*
Pyhala, Mikko O. 1945- *WhoUN 92*
Pyhtila, Mauno J. 1934- *WhoScE 91-4*
Pyke, David (Alan) 1921- *ConAu 138*
Pyke, John S., Jr. *Law&B 92*
Pyke, John S., Jr. 1938- *St&PR 93*
Pyke, John Secrest, Jr. 1938- *WhoAm 92*
Pyke, Ronald 1931- *WhoAm 92*
Pyke, Steve 1957- *BioIn 17*
Pyke, Thomas Nicholas, Jr. 1942- *WhoAm 92*
Pyle, Alan James 1946- *WhoE 93*
Pyle, Artimus
See Lynyrd Skynyrd *ConMus 9*
Pyle, Caroline Michele 1964- *WhoAmW 93*
Pyle, David Leo *WhoScE 91-1*
Pyle, Ellen B.T. 1881-1936 *BioIn 17*
Pyle, Ernie 1900-1945 *BioIn 17, JrnUS*
Pyle, Franklin Ross 1951- *St&PR 93*
Pyle, George B. 1956- *St&PR 93*
Pyle, Gerald Fredric 1937- *WhoSSW 93*
Pyle, Gladys 1890-1989 *BioIn 17*
Pyle, Hilary 1936- *ScF&FL 92*
Pyle, Howard 1853-1911 *ConAu 137, GayN, MajAI [port]*
Pyle, James Harford 1947- *WhoE 93*
Pyle, John T. 1950- *St&PR 93*
Pyle, Katharine 1863-1938 *BioIn 17*
Pyle, Kenneth Birger 1936- *WhoAm 92, WhoWrEP 92*
Pyle, Kent C. 1958- *St&PR 93*
Pyle, Michael J. 1939- *St&PR 93*
Pyle, Michael Terry 1938- *WhoIns 93, WhoSSW 93, WhoWor 93*
Pyle, Pamela Jean *Law&B 92*
Pyle, Robert M. d1991 *BioIn 17*
Pyle, Robert M., Jr. 1938- *St&PR 93*
Pyle, Robert Milner, Jr. 1938- *WhoAm 92*
Pyle, Robert Noble 1926- *WhoAm 92*
Pyle, Ronald M. 1940- *St&PR 93*
Pyle, Susan Clinard 1960- *WhoAmW 93*
Pyle, Thomas A. 1933- *WhoSSW 93*
Pyle, Thomas Edward 1941- *WhoAm 92*
Pyle, Thomas Francis, Jr. 1941- *St&PR 93*
Pyles, Carol DeLong 1948- *WhoAmW 93, WhoEmL 93*
Pyles, Nancy Katherine 1941- *WhoAmW 93*
Pyles, Robert Phillip 1931- *WhoE 93*
Pyles, Rodney Allen 1945- *WhoAm 92*
Pyles, Susan Kay 1954- *WhoAmW 93*
Pylinski, Albert, Jr. 1953- *WhoE 93*
Pylipow, Stanley R. *BioIn 17*
Pylipow, Stanley Ross 1936- *WhoAm 92*
Pylkkanen, Tauno Kullervo 1918-1980 *Baker 92*
Pylkko, Kari Juhani 1945- *WhoScE 91-4*
Pym, Barbara *BioIn 17*
Pym, Barbara 1913-1980 *BritWr S2, MagSWL [port]*
Pym, John S. *WhoScE 91-1*
Pyman, Brian Clive 1942- *WhoWor 93*
Pymn, Bridget Ann *WhoScE 91-1*
Pynchon, Thomas *BioIn 17*
Pynchon, Thomas 1937- *ConLC 72 [port], MagSAmL, ScF&FL 92, WhoAm 92, WhoWrEP 92, WorLitC [port]*
Pyndus, Philip Richard 1921- *St&PR 93*
Pyne, Daniel 1955- *ConTFT 10*
Pyne, Eben W. 1917- *St&PR 93*
Pyne, Eben Wright 1917- *WhoAm 92*
Pyne, Louisa 1832-1904 *OxDcOp*
Pyne, Stephen Geoffrey 1954- *WhoWor 93*
Pynes, Penelope June 1954- *WhoSSW 93*
Pynn, Maria Elena 1941- *WhoE 93*
Pynn, Roger 1945- *WhoAm 92*
Pyorala, Kalevi 1930- *WhoScE 91-4*
Pyra, Thomas Marion 1952- *St&PR 93*
Pyrcioch, Tadeusz 1949- *WhoScE 91-4*
Pyr'ev, Ivan 1901-1968 *DrEEuF*
Pyriev, Ivan 1901-1968 *MiSFD 9N*
Pyros, John 1931- *WhoWrEP 92*
Pyrrhon c. 365BC-275?BC *OxDcByz*
Pyrrhos *OxDcByz*
Pyrrhus 319BC-272BC *HarEnMi*
Pyrros, James G. *Law&B 92*
Pysz, Donna Marie DiMauro 1952- *WhoEmL 93*
Pytasz, Marian 1923- *WhoScE 91-4*
Pytell, Robert Henry 1926- *WhoAm 92*
Pyt'ev, Yurii Petrovich 1935- *WhoWor 93*
Pythagoras c. 580BC-c. 500BC *Baker 92*
Pytheas 380?BC-300?BC *Expl 93*
Pytka, Joe *MiSFD 9*
Pytko, Stanislaw Jerzy 1929- *WhoWor 93*
Pytte, Agnar 1932- *WhoAm 92, WhoWor 93*
Pytynia, Thomas L. *Law&B 92*
Pyun, Albert *MiSFD 9*
Pyy, Lauri Jaakko 1941- *WhoScE 91-4*
Pyy, Pekka E. 1948- *WhoWor 93*
Pyykko, Pekka 1941- *WhoScE 91-4*
Pyysalo, Heikki Sakari 1946- *WhoScE 91-4*
Pyysalo, Tapani 1947- *WhoScE 91-4*

Q

Qaboos Bin Said Bin Taymour 1940- *WhoWor 93*
Qabus bin Said, Sultan of Oman 1940- *BioIn 17*
Qaddafi, Muammar al- 1942- *BioIn 17, ColdWar 2 [port]*
Qadeer, Abdul, Sheikh 1940- *WhoE 93*
Qadeer, Adnan *BioIn 17*
Qadhafi, Muammar al- 1942- *DcTwHis*
Qadi al-Nu'man, Al- c. 904-974 *OxDcByz*
Qaim, Syed Muhammad 1941- *WhoWor 93*
Qajar, Mahine Banou 1900-1990 *BioIn 17*
Qajar dynasty *DcTwHis*
Qasim, Syed Reazul 1938- *WhoAm 92*
Qassim, Abdul Karim 1914-1963 *BioIn 17*
Qays dc. 536 *OxDcByz*
Qazilbash, Imtiaz Ali 1934- *WhoWor 93*
Qazwini, Al- c. 1203-1283 *OxDcByz*
Qian, Zhaoming 1944- *WhoSSW 93*
Qian Guoliang *WhoAsAP 91*
Qian Liren 1925- *WhoAsAP 91*
Qian Qichen 1928- *WhoAsAP 91, WhoWor 93*
Qian Sanqiang *BioIn 17*
Qian Sanqiang 1913-1992 *NewYTBS 92*
Qian Shaojun *WhoAsAP 91*
Qian Shugen *WhoAsAP 91*
Qian Xuesen 1911- *BioIn 17*
Qian Yonchang 1933- *WhoAsAP 91*
Qiao Shi *BioIn 17*
Qiao Shi 1924- *WhoAsAP 91, WhoWor 93*
Qiao Zonghuai 1944- *WhoAsAP 91*
Qi Huaiyuan 1930- *WhoAsAP 91*
Qin, Meng Zhao 1937- *WhoWor 93*
Qin, Ning 1958- *WhoWor 93*
Qin, Zhengdi 1952- *WhoWor 93*
Qin Ben Li *BioIn 17*
Qin Benli 1917-1991 *AnObit 1991*
Qingpeng, Xue 1954- *WhoWor 93*
Qin Jiwei 1914- *WhoAsAP 91, WhoWor 93*
Qiu, Jinquan 1939- *WhoWor 93*
Qiu, Sen 1941- *WhoWor 93*
Qiu, Yuan 1919- *WhoWor 93*
Qiu, Zhong 1941- *WhoWor 93*
Qi Yuanjing 1929- *WhoAsAP 91*
Q-Tip 1970- See Tribe Called Quest, A *ConMus 8*
Qu, Frank Shi-Jing 1936- *WhoWor 93*
Qu, Liangsheng 1931- *WhoWor 93*
Quaal, Albert Lawrence 1933- *St&PR 93*
Quaal, Ward Louis 1919- *WhoAm 92, WhoWor 93*
Quack, Martin 1948- *WhoWor 93*
Quackenbush, Justin Lowe 1929- *WhoAm 92*
Quackenbush, Robert M. 1929- *ScF&FL 92*
Quackenbush, Robert M(ead) 1929- *ConAu 38NR, MajAI [port], SmATA 70 [port]*
Quackenbush, Robert Mead 1929- *WhoE 93*
Quackenbush, Robert S. 1903-1985 *BioIn 17*
Quacquarelli, Antonio 1936- *WhoScE 91-3*
Quade, Dennis H. *Law&B 92*
Quade, Horst W. 1935- *WhoScE 91-3*
Quade, Quentin Lon 1933- *WhoAm 92*
Quade, Victoria Catherine 1953- *WhoAm 92*
Quader, Noorul *BioIn 17*
Quadflieg, Roswitha 1949- *BioIn 17*
Quadrado, R.A. *WhoScE 91-3*
Quadri, Argeo 1911- *Baker 92*
Quadrio, Francesco Saverio 1695-1756 *OxDcOp*
Quadros, Janio *BioIn 17*
Quadros, Janio Da Silva 1917-1992 *CurBio 92N, NewYTBS 92 [port]*
Quadt, Raymond Adolph 1916- *WhoAm 92*
Quaglia, Louis Anthony 1930- *WhoAm 92*
Quagliana, Paul Michael 1967- *WhoE 93*
Quagliano, Anthony John 1941- *WhoWrEP 92*
Quagliata, John 1941- *St&PR 93*
Quagliati, Paolo c. 1555-1628 *Baker 92*
Quaglio, Angelo, I 1784-1815 *OxDcOp*
Quaglio, Angelo, II 1829-1890 *OxDcOp*
Quaglio, Angelo, III 1877-1917 *OxDcOp*
Quaglio, Carlo *OxDcOp*
Quaglio, Domenico, I 1708-1773 *OxDcOp*
Quaglio, Domenico, II 1787-1837 *OxDcOp*
Quaglio, Eugen 1857-1942 *OxDcOp*
Quaglio, Franz 1844-1920 *OxDcOp*
Quaglio, Giovanni Maria, II 1772-1813 *OxDcOp*
Quaglio, Giulio, I c. 1601-1668 *OxDcOp*
Quaglio, Giulio, II 1668-1751 *OxDcOp*
Quaglio, Giulio, III c. 1700-1765 *OxDcOp*
Quaglio, Giulio, IV 1764-1801 *OxDcOp*
Quaglio, Giuseppe 1747-1828 *OxDcOp*
Quaglio, Lorenzo, I 1730-1805 *OxDcOp*
Quaglio, Lorenzo, II 1793-1869 *OxDcOp*
Quaglio, Martin *OxDcOp*
Quaglio, Simon 1795-1878 *OxDcOp*
Quaid, Dennis *BioIn 17*
Quaid, Dennis 1954- *HolBB [port]*
Quaid, Dennis William 1954- *WhoAm 92*
Quaid, Randy 1950- *WhoAm 92*
Quaid, Randy 1953- *BioIn 17*
Quaife, Darlene Barry 1948- *ConAu 137*
Quaife, Elsie West 1870- *AmWomPl*
Quaife, Nancy J. *Law&B 92*
Quail, Kathleen A. *St&PR 93*
Quaile, Elizabeth 1874-1951 *Baker 92*
Quain, Mitchell I. 1951- *WhoAm 92*
Quaintance, Donald Charles, II *Law&B 92*
Quaintance, Douglas R. 1955- *St&PR 93*
Quainton, Anthony Cecil Eden 1934- *WhoAm 92, WhoWor 93*
Quaisain, Adrien 1766-1828 *OxDcOp*
Quaison-Sackey, Alex d1992 *NewYTBS 92*
Quakenbush, Edith M. *AmWomPl*
Qualen, Michael A. 1945- *St&PR 93*
Qualey, Terryl K. *Law&B 92*
Qualey, Thomas Leo, Jr. 1946- *WhoSSW 93*
Qualley, Charles Albert 1930- *WhoAm 92*
Qualls, Charles Robert 1936- *St&PR 93*
Qualls, Charles Wayne, Jr. 1949- *WhoSSW 93*
Qualls, Howard M. 1934- *St&PR 93*
Qualls, Robert Gerald 1952- *WhoWor 93*
Qualls, Robert L. 1933- *St&PR 93, WhoAm 92, WhoSSW 93*
Qualls, Robert M. 1950- *St&PR 93*
Qualls, Sandra Lee 1964- *WhoAmW 93*
Qualset, Calvin Odell 1937- *WhoAm 92*
Qualter, Terence Hall 1925- *WhoAm 92*
Qualtrough, Mary Louise 1941- *WhoAmW 93*
Quam, Robert Charles 1934- *St&PR 93*
Quamme, Jack O. 1927- *WhoAm 92*
Quan, John Joseph 1951- *WhoWor 93*
Quandt, Richard Emeric 1930- *WhoAm 92, WhoE 93*
Quandt, William Bauer 1941- *WhoAm 92*
Quane, Denis J. 1935-1990 *BioIn 17*
Quane, Michael T. 1949- *St&PR 93*
Quane, Terrence J. *Law&B 92*
Quann, Dorothy Ann *Law&B 92*
Quann, Joan Louise 1935- *WhoE 93*
Quan Shureu 1931- *WhoAsAP 91*
Quanstrom, Walter Roy 1942- *WhoAm 92*
Quant, Mary 1934- *BioIn 17, WhoWor 93*
Quantrill, William Clarke 1837-1865 *HarEnMi*
Quantz, Albert Theodore, Jr. 1939- *St&PR 93*
Quantz, Johann Joachim 1697-1773 *Baker 92*
Quaraeshi, Shahid 1948- *St&PR 93*
Quaranta, Alberto *WhoScE 91-3*
Quaranto, Leonard Anthony *Law&B 92*
Quarcelino, Nancy Lucia 1955- *WhoAmW 93*
Quarenghi, Guglielmo 1826-1882 *Baker 92*
Quarfoot, Arleen (Lee) 1951- *WhoWrEP 92*
Quarforth, J.S. 1954- *St&PR 93*
Quarles, Benjamin 1904- *EncAACR*
Quarles, Benjamin 1905- *BlkAuII 92*
Quarles, Carroll Adair, Jr. 1938- *WhoAm 92*
Quarles, Francis 1592-1644 *DcLB 126 [port]*
Quarles, James Cliv 1921- *WhoAm 92*
Quarles, James Linwood, III 1946- *WhoAm 92*
Quarles, John M. 1940- *St&PR 93*
Quarles, John Monroe 1942- *WhoSSW 93*
Quarles, Joseph V. 1908- *St&PR 93*
Quarles, Leo Thompson 1944- *St&PR 93*
Quarles, Ralph B. 1944- *St&PR 93*
Quarles, Rebecca Colwell 1939- *WhoAmW 93, WhoSSW 93*
Quarles, Thomas J. *Law&B 92*
Quarles, Thomas J. 1949- *St&PR 93*
Quarls, Harry F. 1952- *St&PR 93*
Quarracino, Antonio Cardinal 1923- *WhoWor 93*
Quarrell, John James 1948- *WhoWor 93*
Quarrie, Stephen Alexander *WhoScE 91-1*
Quarrington, Glenn Austin 1949- *St&PR 93*
Quarrington, Paul 1953- *WhoCanL 92*
Quarry, Robert 1928- *BioIn 17*
Quartaro, Nena 1910- *SweetSg C [port]*
Quartel, Donald Robert, Jr. *BioIn 17*
Quartel, Donald Robert, Jr. 1950- *WhoAm 92*
Quartermain, Peter (Allan) 1934- *ConAu 40NR*
Quartermain, Robert A. 1955- *St&PR 93*
Quartermaine, Gina R. *WhoAmW 93*
Quarterman, Lloyd Albert 1918-1982 *ConBlB 4 [port]*
Quarto, Roslyn A. *Law&B 92*
Quarton, Jean Elsa Rulf 1942- *WhoAmW 93*
Quarton, William Barlow 1903- *WhoAm 92*
Quasebarth, Werner Horton 1931- *St&PR 93*
Quasem, Mostafa Bin 1941- *WhoAsAP 91*
Quasha, Alan G. 1950- *WhoAm 92*
Quasha, William Howard 1912- *WhoWor 93*
Quasimodo, Salvatore 1901-1968 *BioIn 17*
Quast, David C. *Law&B 92*
Quast, Florence Edwina 1937- *WhoAmW 93*
Quast, Peter 1940- *WhoScE 91-3*
Quast, Richard Donald 1930- *St&PR 93*
Quast, William James 1938- *St&PR 93*
Quate, Calvin Forrest 1923- *WhoAm 92*
Quatrain, John *WhoWrEP 92*
Quatrefages, Armand de 1810-1892 *IntDcAn*
Quatremere de Quincy, Antoine-Chrysostome 1755-1849 *Baker 92*
Quatt, Mark B. *Law&B 92*
Quattlebaum, Donald Anderson 1953- *St&PR 93*
Quattlebaum, Walter Emmett, Jr. 1922- *WhoWor 93*
Quattlebaum, William Franklin 1953- *WhoSSW 93*
Quattrocchi, John Anthony 1962- *WhoE 93*
Quave, Gerald J. 1933- *St&PR 93*
Quay, James Stephen *Law&B 92*
Quay, Laurie Ann 1966- *WhoAmW 93*
Quay, Matthew S. 1833-1904 *PolPar*
Quay, Richard Dangerfield *Law&B 92*
Quay, Thomas Emery 1934- *WhoAm 92*
Quayle, Anthony 1913-1989 *BioIn 17, IntDcF 2-3 [port]*
Quayle, Dan *BioIn 17, NewYTBS 92 [port]*
Quayle, Dan 1947- *CngDr 91*
Quayle, J. Danforth 1947- *PolPar*
Quayle, James Danforth 1947- *WhoAm 92, WhoE 93, WhoEmL 93, WhoWor 93*
Quayle, Marilyn *BioIn 17*
Quayle, Marilyn 1949- *WhoAm 92, WhoAmW 93, WhoE 93, WhoEmL 93*
Quayle, Marilyn Tucker 1949- *NewYTBS 92 [port]*
Quaynor, Festus Kweitei 1934- *WhoUN 92*
Quaytman, Harvey *BioIn 17*
Quaytman, Rebecca *BioIn 17*
Quda'i, Al- d1062 *OxDcByz*
Qudama Ibn Ja'far c. 873-c. 932 *OxDcByz*
Qudrud-Din, Mian 1938- *WhoUN 92*
Que, Louise Emily 1967- *WhoAmW 93*
Quebe, Jerry Lee 1942- *WhoAm 92*
Quebedeaux, Bruno 1941- *WhoAm 92, WhoE 93*
Quednau, Marion 1952- *WhoCanL 92*
Queen, C.V. 1903- *St&PR 93*
Queen, Daniel 1934- *WhoE 93*
Queen, Ellery *ConAu 39NR, ScF&FL 92*
Queen, Ellery, Jr. *ConAu 39NR*
Queen, Gary L. *St&PR 93*
Queen, Gary W. 1947- *WhoAm 92*
Queen, Gary Wayne 1947- *St&PR 93*
Queen, James W. 1940- *St&PR 93*

Queen, Kay Wallace 1937- *WhoSSW 93*
Queen, Susan C. *Law&B 92*
Queenan, Edward P. *Law&B 92*
Queenan, John Thomas 1933- *WhoAm 92*
Queenan, John W. d1992 *NewYTBS 92 [port]*
Queenan, John William 1906-1992 *BioIn 17*
Queenan, Joseph Martin, Jr. 1950- *WhoAm 92, WhoWrEP 92*
Queenan, Linda Joyce *WhoWrEP 92*
Queeney, David 1957- *WhoWor 93*
Queen Ida 1929- *ConMus 9 [port]*
Queenin, Martha Jane 1961- *WhoAmW 93*
Queen Latifah *BioIn 17*
Queensryche *ConMus 8 [port]*
Quef, Charles 1873-1931 *Baker 92*
Queffelec, Anne (Tita) 1948- *Baker 92*
Queffelec, Denise A. 1957- *St&PR 93*
Queguiner, Guy 1938- *WhoScE 91-2*
Quehl, Gary Howard 1938- *WhoAm 92*
Queirolo, Peter Samuel 1964- *WhoSSW 93*
Queiros, Eca de 1845-1900 *ScF&FL 92*
Queisser, Hans Joachim 1931- *WhoScE 91-3*
Queler, Eve *WhoE 93*
Queler, Eve 1936- *Baker 92*
Quelle, Frederick William, Jr. 1934- *WhoAm 92*
Queller, Donald Edward 1925- *WhoAm 92*
Queller, Fred 1932- *WhoE 93*
Quellmalz, Frederick 1912- *WhoWor 93*
Quellmalz, Henry 1915- *St&PR 93, WhoAm 92, WhoE 93, WhoWor 93*
Quellmalz, Marion Lynch 1916- *St&PR 93*
Quello, James *BioIn 17*
Quello, James Henry 1914- *WhoAm 92*
Queneau, Patrice Michel 1938- *WhoScE 91-2*
Queneau, Paul Etienne 1911- *WhoAm 92*
Queneau, Raymond 1903-1976 *BioIn 17*
Quenec'hdu, Y. 1941- *WhoScE 91-2*
Quenelle, John Duff 1946- *WhoWrEP 92*
Queniart, Jean *WhoScE 91-2*
Quennell, Nicholas 1935- *WhoAm 92*
Quennell, Peter 1905- *WhoWor 93*
Quenneville, Gilles *St&PR 93*
Quenneville, Kathleen *Law&B 92*
Quenon, Robert Hagerty 1928- *WhoAm 92*
Quentel, Albert Drew 1934- *WhoAm 92*
Quentel, Charles E., III 1927- *St&PR 93*
Quentin, Philippe Gaston 1944- *WhoWor 93*
Quenzel, Heinrich 1932- *WhoScE 91-3*
Quenzer, Clinton Quenton 1935- *St&PR 93*
Queoff, Pamela Frances 1952- *WhoAmW 93*
Queralt, Michael 1962- *WhoE 93*
Queralt Teixido, Rafael 1924- *WhoScE 91-3*
Querbes, Betty-Lane Shipp *WhoAmW 93, WhoSSW 93*
Quere, Michel Jean Christian 1957- *WhoWor 93*
Querejeta, Carlos d1992 *NewYTBS 92*
Querido, Philip 1927- *WhoWor 93*
Quern, Arthur Foster 1942- *St&PR 93*
Querner, Gerhard Martin 1944- *WhoWor 93*
Querns, William R. *WhoScE 91-1*
Querol (Gavalda), Miguel 1912- *Baker 92*
Querrard, Charles *DcCPCAm*
Querry, Ronald Burns 1943- *WhoWrEP 92*
Querry, Simon *ScF&FL 92*
Quertermus, Carl John, Jr. 1943- *WhoSSW 93*
Query, David Leon 1949- *WhoEmL 93*
Query, Joy Marves Neale *WhoAm 92*
Quesada, Elwood R. 1904- *EncABHB 8 [port]*
Quesada, Eugenio 1927- *HispAmA*
Quesada, Maria Saenz *BioIn 17*
Quesenberry, Marcia Kay 1955- *WhoAmW 93*
Quesenberry, Michael Stephen 1963- *WhoE 93*
Quesenbery, Marion Irene *Law&B 92*
Quesnel, David John 1950- *WhoE 93*
Quesnel, Joseph *BioIn 17*
Quest, Charles Francis 1904- *WhoAm 92*
Quest, Donald Richard 1938- *St&PR 93*
Quest, James Howard 1934- *WhoAm 92*
Quested, John *MiSFD 9*
Questel, Mae 1908- *WhoAm 92*
Quester, George Herman 1936- *WhoAm 92*
Questrom, Allen I. 1941- *WhoAm 92, WhoSSW 93*
Quetelet, Adolphe 1796-1874 *IntDcAn*
Quetier, Francis 1944- *WhoScE 91-2*
Queuille, Henri 1884-1970 *BioIn 17*
Queux, William Le *ScF&FL 92*
Queva *WhoScE 91-2*
Quevedo, Fernando G. 1933- *WhoUN 92*
Quevedo Camacho, Rafael Isidro 1943- *WhoWor 93*
Quevedo y Zubieta, Salvador 1859-1935 *DcMexL*
Queyrouze, Mia C. 1964- *WhoAmW 93*
Quezada, Abel *BioIn 17*
Quezada, Leticia 1953- *NotHsAW 93*
Quezada, Milly *BioIn 17*
Quezel-Ambrunaz, Pierre Louis 1926- *WhoScE 91-2*
Quezergue, Wardell *SoulM*
Quezon, Manuel Luis 1874-1944 *DcTwHis*
Qui, Yingjue 1931- *WhoUN 92*
Quiambao, Dalisay Lelay 1945- *WhoSSW 93*
Quiat, Gerald M. 1924- *WhoAm 92*
Quiat, Mindy S. 1956- *St&PR 93*
Quick, Albert Thomas 1939- *WhoAm 92*
Quick, Edward Raymond 1943- *WhoAm 92*
Quick, Elaine L. *Law&B 92*
Quick, Howard Roland d1991 *BioIn 17*
Quick, James S. 1940- *WhoAm 92*
Quick, Joe Akers, Jr. 1945- *WhoE 93*
Quick, Joe Cecil 1935- *St&PR 93*
Quick, John Biery 1918- *St&PR 93*
Quick, L.C., Jr. *St&PR 93*
Quick, L.C., III 1956- *St&PR 93*
Quick, Leslie Charles, III 1953- *WhoAm 92*
Quick, Paddy 1945- *WhoAmW 93*
Quick, Perry Day 1945- *WhoAm 92*
Quick, Peter 1956- *St&PR 93*
Quick, Robert J. *Law&B 92*
Quick, Roy Dixon, Jr. 1951- *WhoEmL 93*
Quick, Thomas Clarkson 1955- *WhoAm 92*
Quick, W.T. *ScF&FL 92*
Quick, William K(ellon) 1933- *ConAu 137*
Quickel, James J. 1932- *St&PR 93*
Quickel, Kenneth Elwood, Jr. 1939- *WhoAm 92*
Quick-Smith, Tracey *Law&B 92*
Quidd, David Andrew 1954- *WhoEmL 93, WhoSSW 93*
Quie, Paul Gerhardt 1925- *WhoAm 92*
Quigg, Donald James 1916- *WhoAm 92*
Quigg, James R., Jr. 1933- *St&PR 93*
Quigg, Lemuel Ely 1863-1919 *JrnUS*
Quiggins, Richard Stone, II 1947- *St&PR 93*
Quigley, Ann M. *Law&B 92*
Quigley, Austin Edmund 1942- *WhoAm 92*
Quigley, Bryan M. *Law&B 92*
Quigley, Dianne Patricia 1955- *WhoE 93*
Quigley, Eileen B. *Law&B 92*
Quigley, Jack Allen 1914- *WhoAm 92*
Quigley, Joan *BioIn 17*
Quigley, John Bernard 1940- *WhoAm 92*
Quigley, John Michael 1942- *WhoAm 92*
Quigley, Joseph V. 1931- *St&PR 93*
Quigley, Martin Schofield 1917- *WhoAm 92*
Quigley, Martin (Schofield), Jr. 1917- *ConAu 38NR*
Quigley, Michael F. 1948- *St&PR 93*
Quigley, Michael J., III 1940- *St&PR 93*
Quigley, Michael Jerome 1937- *WhoSSW 93*
Quigley, Nancy Louise 1935- *WhoAmW 93*
Quigley, Peter W. *Law&B 92*
Quigley, Philip J. 1943- *WhoAm 92*
Quigley, Robert Alan 1943- *St&PR 93*
Quigley, Robert Murvin 1934- *WhoAm 92*
Quigley, Roger A. 1934- *WhoIns 93*
Quigley, Sherry Renee 1960- *WhoAmW 93*
Quigley, Thomas J. 1923- *WhoAm 92*
Quigley, W.H. 1926- *St&PR 93*
Quijano, Alejandro 1883-1957 *DcMexL*
Quijano, Margarita 1914- *DcMexL*
Quijano, Mary L. 1944- *ScF&FL 92*
Quijano, Raul *WhoUN 92*
Quijano, Raul Alberto 1923- *WhoWor 93*
Quiles, Paul 1942- *BioIn 17*
Quilici, Folco 1930- *MiSFD 9*
Quilico, Gino 1955- *OxDcOp*
Quilico, Louis 1925- *Baker 92*
Quilico, Louis 1929- *OxDcOp*
Quilico, Louis 1931- *WhoAm 92*
Quill, Ann L. 1950- *WhoAmW 93*
Quill, Barnaby *ConAu 38NR*
Quill, E. Spencer 1941- *St&PR 93*
Quill, Leonard Walter 1931- *WhoAm 92*
Quill, Shirley 1918-1991 *BioIn 17*
Quill, Stephen F. 1940- *St&PR 93*
Quillan, Eddie 1907-1990 *BioIn 17*
Quillen, Cecil D., Jr. *Law&B 92*
Quillen, Cecil Dyer 1937- *St&PR 93*
Quillen, Cecil Dyer, Jr. 1937- *WhoAm 92*
Quillen, D.G. *WhoScE 91-1*
Quillen, James H. 1916- *CngDr 91*
Quillen, James Henry 1916- *WhoAm 92, WhoSSW 93*
Quillen, Lloyd Douglas 1943- *WhoWor 93*
Quillen, William Tatem 1935- *WhoAm 92*
Quillet, Vitus Dean 1943- *St&PR 93*
Quillevere, Daniel 1945- *WhoUN 92*
Quillian, William Fletcher, Jr. 1913- *WhoAm 92*
Quilligan, Edward James 1925- *WhoAm 92*
Quillinan, Robert Joseph 1947- *St&PR 93*
Quillman, James Edward 1946- *St&PR 93*
Quilp, Jocelyn 1870-1932 *ScF&FL 92*
Quilter, Roger 1877-1953 *Baker 92*
Quilty, Rafe 1943- *ScF&FL 92*
Quimby, Bill 1936- *WhoWrEP 92*
Quimby, Fred William 1945- *WhoE 93*
Quimby, George Irving 1913- *WhoAm 92, WhoWor 93*
Quimby, Harriet 1884-1912 *BioIn 17*
Quimby, Marcel *BioIn 17*
Quimby, Robert Sherman 1916- *WhoAm 92*
Quimby, Walter 1946- *WhoE 93*
Quimby, William Robert 1936- *WhoWrEP 92*
Quin, Joseph Marvin 1947- *St&PR 93, WhoAm 92*
Quin, Louis DuBose 1928- *WhoAm 92*
Quina, La 1922- *DcCPCAm*
Quina, Richard D. 1924- *St&PR 93*
Quinan, Robert L. *Law&B 92*
Quinault, Jean-Baptiste-Maurice 1687-1745 *Baker 92*
Quinault, Philippe 1635-1688 *Baker 92, IntDcOp, OxDcOp*
Quinby, Charles E. 1943- *St&PR 93*
Quinby, Charles Edward, Jr. 1943- *WhoAm 92*
Quinby, Dawn Deleen 1948- *WhoAmW 93*
Quinby, William Albert 1941- *WhoAm 92*
Quincy, Josiah 1859-1919 *PolPar*
Quindel, Darlene Jean 1944- *WhoAmW 93*
Quindlen, Anna *BioIn 17*
Quindlen, Anna 1935- *WhoAm 92*
Quindlen, Anna 1952- *News 93-1 [port]*
Quindlen, Anna 1953- *ConAu 138, WhoAmW 93, WhoE 93*
Quindlen, John Joseph 1932- *St&PR 93*
Quine, Richard 1920-1989 *MiSFD 9N*
Quine, W.V. *BioIn 17, ConAu 37NR*
Quine, Willard V. *ConAu 37NR*
Quine, Willard Van Orman *BioIn 17*
Quine, Willard Van Orman 1908- *ConAu 37NR, WhoAm 92*
Quinell, Bruce Andrew 1949- *WhoAm 92*
Quinet, Fernand 1898-1971 *Baker 92*
Quinet, Marcel 1915-1986 *Baker 92*
Quiniton, Michael Wayne 1950- *St&PR 93*
Quinkert, Gerhard 1927- *WhoScE 91-3*
Quinlan, Brian E. *Law&B 92*
Quinlan, Denis J. *Law&B 92*
Quinlan, Diane M. *Law&B 92*
Quinlan, Donald P. 1931- *WhoAm 92*
Quinlan, Donald Paul 1931- *St&PR 93*
Quinlan, Francis X. 1928- *St&PR 93*
Quinlan, Georgianna McLoughlin *Law&B 92*
Quinlan, Guy Christian 1939- *WhoAm 92*
Quinlan, James E. 1938- *St&PR 93*
Quinlan, James Finbarr 1942- *WhoScE 91-3*
Quinlan, John Edward, Jr. 1946- *St&PR 93*
Quinlan, John J. 1925- *St&PR 93*
Quinlan, John Michael 1936- *St&PR 93*
Quinlan, Joseph Michael 1941- *WhoAm 92*
Quinlan, Michael D. *Law&B 92*
Quinlan, Michael E. *Law&B 92*
Quinlan, Michael J. 1938- *WhoIns 93*
Quinlan, Michael R. *BioIn 17*
Quinlan, Michael R. 1944- *St&PR 93*
Quinlan, Michael Robert 1944- *WhoAm 92*
Quinlan, Terrence E. *Law&B 92*
Quinlan, Thomas E., Jr. 1922- *WhoAm 92*
Quinlan, Thomas L. *Law&B 92*
Quinlan, William Joseph, Jr. 1939- *WhoAm 92*
Quinlisk, Warren 1924- *St&PR 93*
Quinliven, J.O. *ScF&FL 92*
Quinly, James Carlton 1931- *St&PR 93*
Quinn, A. Peter, Jr. 1923- *WhoIns 93*
Quinn, Aidan 1959- *WhoAm 92*
Quinn, Andrew Peter, Jr. 1923- *WhoAm 92*
Quinn, Andrew W. *Law&B 92*
Quinn, Anne M. *Law&B 92, St&PR 93*
Quinn, Anthony *BioIn 17*
Quinn, Anthony 1915- *DcLB 122 [port], HispAmA [port], IntDcF 2-3, MiSFD 9*
Quinn, Anthony Rudolph Oaxaca 1915- *WhoAm 92, WhoWor 93*
Quinn, Art Jay 1936- *WhoSSW 93*
Quinn, Arthur Hobson 1874-1944 *ScF&FL 92*
Quinn, Arthur J. d1991 *BioIn 17*
Quinn, Bernetta Viola 1915- *WhoWrEP 92*
Quinn, Betty Nye 1921- *WhoAm 92*
Quinn, C. Jack 1929- *WhoAm 92*
Quinn, Caroline G. 1949- *St&PR 93*
Quinn, Carroll Thomas 1946- *WhoE 93*
Quinn, Charles Andrew 1931- *WhoE 93*
Quinn, Charles C. 1924- *St&PR 93*
Quinn, Charles Nicholas 1930- *WhoAm 92*
Quinn, Cheri Lynne 1949- *WhoAmW 93*
Quinn, Cheryl E. 1947- *WhoAmW 93*
Quinn, Christi D. *Law&B 92*
Quinn, Colleen Elizabeth 1965- *WhoAmW 93*
Quinn, Cornelius P. *Law&B 92*
Quinn, Daniel 1935- *ConAu 137, ScF&FL 92*
Quinn, Daniel Joseph 1945- *St&PR 93*
Quinn, David W. 1942- *St&PR 93*
Quinn, Deborah Lee *Law&B 92*
Quinn, Dennis B. 1928- *WhoAm 92*
Quinn, Donald Edward, II 1947- *St&PR 93*
Quinn, Dorothy Ann 1956- *WhoE 93*
Quinn, Edel 1907-1944 *BioIn 17*
Quinn, Edward Francis, III 1944- *WhoE 93*
Quinn, Edward James 1942- *St&PR 93*
Quinn, Edward Leigh 1931- *St&PR 93*
Quinn, Edward W. 1941- *St&PR 93*
Quinn, Eugene Frederick 1935- *WhoAm 92*
Quinn, Francis A. 1921- *WhoAm 92*
Quinn, Francis Xavier 1932- *WhoSSW 93*
Quinn, Galen Warren 1922- *WhoAm 92*
Quinn, Gerald M. d1991 *BioIn 17*
Quinn, Gerald V. 1952- *WhoE 93*
Quinn, Hank *BioIn 17*
Quinn, Helen 1943- *BioIn 17*
Quinn, Helen Rhonda 1943- *WhoAmW 93*
Quinn, Jack *WhoAm 92*
Quinn, James David 1929- *WhoE 93*
Quinn, James Francis 1949- *WhoSSW 93*
Quinn, James M. *Law&B 92*
Quinn, James P. 1933- *WhoIns 93*
Quinn, James P. 1941- *St&PR 93*
Quinn, James V. 1946- *St&PR 93*
Quinn, Jane Bryant *BioIn 17*
Quinn, Jane Bryant 1939- *WhoAm 92, WhoAmW 93*
Quinn, Jarus William 1930- *WhoAm 92*
Quinn, Jeffry N. 1959- *St&PR 93*
Quinn, Jeffry Neal *Law&B 92*
Quinn, John 1870-1924 *BioIn 17*
Quinn, John Albert 1932- *WhoAm 92, WhoE 93*
Quinn, John Brian Patrick 1943- *WhoAm 92*
Quinn, John Collins 1925- *St&PR 93, WhoAm 92, WhoSSW 93, WhoWrEP 92*
Quinn, John F. 1935- *St&PR 93*
Quinn, John J. 1944- *St&PR 93*
Quinn, John J. 1945- *St&PR 93*
Quinn, John Joseph 1944- *WhoAm 92*
Quinn, John R. 1929- *WhoAm 92*
Quinn, Joseph Michael 1937- *WhoAm 92*
Quinn, Julia Province 1919- *WhoAmW 93, WhoSSW 93, WhoWor 93*
Quinn, Karen Marie 1949- *WhoAmW 93*
Quinn, Katherine B. 1951- *WhoE 93*
Quinn, Kathleen *BioIn 17*
Quinn, Keith A. 1951- *St&PR 93*
Quinn, Kelly 1962- *WhoAmW 93*
Quinn, Kenneth J. *Law&B 92*
Quinn, Kevin A. *Law&B 92*
Quinn, Kevin A. 1941- *St&PR 93*
Quinn, Lloyd 1917- *St&PR 93*
Quinn, Margaret Mary *WhoAmW 93*
Quinn, Martin Vincent 1948- *St&PR 93*
Quinn, Michael D. 1953- *St&PR 93*
Quinn, Michael Desmond 1936- *WhoAm 92*
Quinn, Michael F. 1932- *St&PR 93*
Quinn, Michael J. 1947- *St&PR 93*
Quinn, Michael K. *Law&B 92*
Quinn, Michael William 1949- *WhoSSW 93*
Quinn, Niall 1943- *ConAu 37NR*
Quinn, Patrick *WhoAm 92*
Quinn, Patrick 1950- *SmATA 73 [port]*
Quinn, Patrick F. 1918- *ScF&FL 92*
Quinn, Patrick James 1931- *WhoAm 92*
Quinn, Patrick John 1943- *St&PR 93*
Quinn, Paul J., Jr. 1932- *St&PR 93*
Quinn, Philip Francis 1932- *WhoSSW 93*
Quinn, Philip Lawrence 1940- *WhoAm 92*
Quinn, Revanell 1920- *St&PR 93*
Quinn, Richard Paul 1942- *WhoSSW 93*
Quinn, Robert Anthony 1947- *WhoSSW 93*
Quinn, Robert Charles 1930- *WhoE 93*
Quinn, Robert Henry 1919- *WhoAm 92*
Quinn, Robert J. *Law&B 92*
Quinn, Robert K. *Law&B 92*

Quinn, Robert K. 1934- *St&PR 93*
Quinn, Robert William 1912- *WhoWor 93*
Quinn, Rosemary *Law&B 92*
Quinn, Sally *BioIn 17*
Quinn, Sally 1941- *WhoAm 92, WhoAmW 93, WhoWrEP 92*
Quinn, Seabury 1889-1969 *ScF&FL 92*
Quinn, Susan *AmWomPl*
Quinn, T.J. *WhoScE 91-2*
Quinn, Thomas A. 1940- *WhoSSW 93*
Quinn, Thomas F. 1942- *St&PR 93*
Quinn, Thomas G. *Law&B 92*
Quinn, Thomas James 1933- *WhoScE 91-3*
Quinn, Thomas Joseph, Jr. 1951- *WhoE 93, WhoEmL 93*
Quinn, Tim 1953- *ScF&FL 92*
Quinn, Timothy Charles, Jr. 1936- *WhoE 93, WhoWor 93*
Quinn, Vicent K. 1931- *St&PR 93*
Quinn, Vincent Kevin 1931- *WhoIns 93*
Quinn, Virginia Nichols 1937- *WhoAmW 93*
Quinn, William A. 1928- *WhoIns 93*
Quinn, William Francis 1919- *WhoAm 92*
Quinn, William Wilson 1907- *WhoAm 92*
Quinnan, Edward Michael 1935- *WhoAm 92*
Quinnan, Gerald Vincent, Jr. 1947- *WhoAm 92*
Quinnan, Joseph Edward 1944- *St&PR 93*
Quinn-Cordero, Mary 1955- *WhoE 93*
Quinnell, Bruce A. 1949- *St&PR 93*
Quinnell, Bruce Andrew 1949- *WhoAm 92*
Quinnert, David Michael 1946- *St&PR 93*
Quinn-Musgrove, Sandra Lavern 1935- *WhoSSW 93*
Quinones, Carlos Ramon 1951- *St&PR 93*
Quinones, Miguel A. *Law&B 92*
Quinones, William Bill 1962- *WhoE 93*
Quinones-Lopez, Carlos 1927- *WhoWor 93*
Quinonez, Naomi 1951- *NotHsAW 93*
Quinsler, William Thomson 1924- *WhoAm 92*
Quinson, Bruno Andre 1938- *WhoAm 92*
Quint, Charles Z. *Law&B 92*
Quint, David P. 1950- *St&PR 93*
Quint, Ira 1930- *St&PR 93, WhoAm 92*
Quint, Ruth E. *Law&B 92*
Quintana, J.M. 1940- *WhoScE 91-3*
Quintana, Jorge Ovidio 1952- *WhoE 93*
Quintana, Jose *Law&B 92*
Quintana, Louie *BioIn 17*
Quintana, Marie Annette 1954- *WhoAmW 93*
Quintana, Miguel 1986- *BioIn 17*
Quintana, Patricia 1946- *BioIn 17*
Quintana, Sammy J. 1949- *WhoAm 92*
Quintanar, Hector 1936- *Baker 92*
Quintana Roo, Andres 1787-1851 *DcMexL*
Quintanilla, Antonio Paulet 1927- *WhoWor 93*
Quintanilla, Faustino 1948- *WhoE 93*
Quintanilla, Guadalupe C. 1937- *HispAmA [port]*
Quintanilla, Maria Aline Griffiths y Dexter *BioIn 17*
Quintano, Gene *MiSFD 9*
Quintart, Alain H.M.G. 1932- *WhoScE 91-2*
Quintasket, Christine 1888-1936 *BioIn 17*
Quintela, Alberto *BioIn 17*
Quintela, Helen Wells 1953- *BioIn 17*
Quintella, Thereza Maria M. 1938- *WhoUN 92*
Quinter, Ken John 1931- *St&PR 93*
Quintero, Charles G. 1942- *St&PR 93*
Quintero, Ednodio 1947- *SpAmA*
Quintero, Jose 1924- *MiSFD 9, WhoAm 92*
Quintero, Milagros S. Gabriel 1923- *WhoWor 93*
Quintero, Ronald Gary 1954- *WhoE 93*
Quinteros, Teresita Beatriz 1956- *WhoWor 93*
Quinton, Michael Wayne 1950- *St&PR 93*
Quinton, Paul Marquis 1944- *WhoAm 92*
Quinton, Pauline Brooks *AmWomPl*
Quintus of Smyrna *OxDcByz*
Quirarte, Jacinto 1931- *WhoAm 92*
Quirarte, Vicente 1954- *DcMexL*
Quirico, Francis Joseph 1911- *WhoAm 92*
Quirin, Albert J. 1948- *WhoIns 93*
Quirin, Albert Joseph 1948- *St&PR 93*
Quirin, Philip J. 1940- *WhoIns 93*
Quiring, Wayne R. 1927- *St&PR 93*
Quirino, Joe 1930- *ScF&FL 92*
Quirino, Jose *ScF&FL 92*
Quirion, Luc *BioIn 17*
Quirk, Brian J. 1960- *WhoSSW 93*
Quirk, Donna Hawkins 1955- *WhoAmW 93*
Quirk, Frank J. 1941- *St&PR 93*
Quirk, Frank Joseph 1941- *WhoAm 92*
Quirk, John James 1943- *St&PR 93, WhoAm 92*
Quirk, Kathryn Loretta *Law&B 92*
Quirk, Lawrence Joseph 1923- *WhoWrEP 92*
Quirk, Mary Isabel *AmWomPl*
Quirk, Peter Richard 1936- *WhoAm 92*
Quirk, Randolph 1920- *WhoWor 93*
Quirk, Robert Emmett 1950- *WhoAm 92*
Quirk, Thomas J., III 1938- *St&PR 93*
Quirke, Nicholas 1952- *WhoScE 91-1*
Quiroga, Dario O. 1941- *St&PR 93*
Quiroga, Elena *BioIn 17*
Quiroga, Horacio 1878-1937 *BioIn 17*
Quiroga, Manuel 1890-1961 *Baker 92*
Quiroga, Vivian P. *Law&B 92*
Quiros, Pedro Fernandez de 1565-1615 *Expl 93 [port]*
Quiroz, Antonio Castro 1933- *WhoSSW 93*
Quiroz, Roderick Sotelo 1923- *WhoE 93*
Quirozz Hernandez, Alberto 1907- *DcMexL*
Quisenberry, Dan Ray 1938- *WhoSSW 93*
Quisenberry, Mary Ellen 1954- *WhoAmW 93*
Quisenberry, Richard Keith 1934- *WhoAm 92*
Quisenberry, Robert B. 1936- *St&PR 93*
Quisgard, Liz Whitney 1929- *WhoAm 92, WhoE 93*
Quisling, Rolf W. *Law&B 92*
Quisling, Vidkun 1887-1945 *BioIn 17*
Quisling, Vidkun Abraham Lauritz Jonsson 1887-1945 *DcTwHis*
Quispe Tito, Diego *BioIn 17*
Quissell, Barbara Carolyn *Law&B 92*
Quist, Adrian 1913-1991 *BioIn 17*
Quist, Arvin Sigvard 1933- *WhoSSW 93*
Quist, Beth Dobson 1953- *WhoAmW 93*
Quist, Edwin Arnold, Jr. 1951- *WhoAm 92*
Quist, George R. 1920- *St&PR 93*
Quist, George Robert 1920- *WhoIns 93*
Quist, Jeanette Fitzgerald 1948- *WhoAmW 93*
Quist, Marinus *Law&B 92*
Quist, Scott Milton 1953- *St&PR 93*
Quitevis, Minda Altea 1937- *WhoAmW 93*
Quitiquit, Maxine Teresa 1935- *WhoAmW 93*
Quitman, John Anthony 1798-1858 *HarEnMi*
Quitmann, Dieter 1931- *WhoScE 91-3*
Quittard, C. *WhoScE 91-2*
Quittmeyer, Charles Loreaux 1917- *WhoAm 92*
Quittmeyer, Susan *BioIn 17*
Quivar, Florence 1944- *Baker 92*
Qun Zhongda 1923- *WhoAsAP 91*
Quock, Joan Marie 1941- *WhoWor 93*
Quogan, Anthony *WhoWrEP 92*
Quoirez, Francoise 1935- *BioIn 17, ConAu 39NR, WhoWor 93*
Quoyeser, Clement Louis 1899- *St&PR 93*
Quraishi, Mohammed Sayeed 1924- *WhoAm 92*
Qurashi, Mazhar Mahmood 1925- *WhoWor 93*
Qureshey, Safi U. 1951- *WhoAm 92*
Qureshey, Safi U. 1951- & Yuen, Thomas C.K. 1952- *ConEn*
Qureshi, A.W. 1934- *WhoScE 91-3*
Qureshi, Abdul Wahab 1934- *WhoUN 92*
Qureshi, Arshad Hasan 1940- *St&PR 93*
Qureshi, Azam Sajjad 1942- *St&PR 93*
Qureshi, Hazel 1949- *ConAu 138*
Qureshi, Iqbal Hussain 1936- *WhoWor 93*
Qureshi, Joan Viantha 1948- *WhoAmW 93*
Qureshi, Mahmud Akhtar 1944- *WhoWor 93*
Qureshi, Moeen A. 1930- *WhoUN 92*
Qureshi, Moeen Ahmad 1930- *St&PR 93*
Qureshi, Muhammad Abdur Rauf 1935- *WhoWor 93*
Qureshi, Shahid Ul Haq 1945- *WhoAm 92*
Qurusu, Allan 1949- *WhoAsAP 91*
Qutayba ibn Muslim d715 *HarEnMi*
Qutub, Musa Yacub 1940- *WhoAm 92*
Quwatli, Shukri al- 1891-1967 *BioIn 17*
Quyth, Gabriel 1928- *ScF&FL 92*
Qvale, Bjorn 1937- *WhoScE 91-2*
Qvist, Sven 1934- *WhoScE 91-2*

R

R., O. *ScF&FL 92*
Ra, Carol Fae 1939- *WhoWrEP 92*
Ra, Le Sony'r 1915- *WhoAm 92*
Raab, Cornel E. 1946- *St&PR 93*
Raab, G. Kirk 1935- *St&PR 93, WhoAm 92*
Raab, Herbert Norman 1925- *WhoAm 92, WhoE 93*
Raab, Hilary Albert, Jr. 1942- *St&PR 93*
Raab, Ira Jerry 1935- *WhoAm 92, WhoE 93, WhoWor 93*
Raab, John Joseph 1936- *St&PR 93*
Raab, Lawrence Edward 1946- *WhoE 93*
Raab, Leonard Frederick 1939- *St&PR 93*
Raab, Martin D. 1932- *St&PR 93*
Raab, Selwyn 1934- *WhoAm 92*
Raab, Sheldon 1937- *WhoAm 92*
Raab, Walter F. 1924- *St&PR 93*
Raab, Walter Ferdinand 1924- *WhoAm 92*
Raabe, James A. 1952- *St&PR 93*
Raabe, John 1930- *St&PR 93*
Raabe, Peter 1872-1945 *Baker 92*
Raabe, Wilhelm 1831-1910 *TwCLC 45 [port]*
Raad, Virginia 1925- *WhoAm 92*
Raaf, John Elbert 1905- *WhoAm 92*
Raaf, John Hart 1941- *WhoAm 92*
Raaf, Robert T. 1946- *St&PR 93*
Raaff, Anton 1714?-1797 *Baker 92, IntDcOp [port], OxDcOp*
Raaflaub, Kurt A. 1941- *WhoAm 92*
Raaflaub, Vernon Arthur 1938- *WhoWor 93*
Raalte, Albert van 1890-1952 *Baker 92*
Raam, Shanthi 1941- *WhoE 93*
Raasted, Niels Otto 1888-1966 *Baker 92*
Raats, Jaan 1932- *Baker 92*
Raats, Peter A.C. 1935- *WhoScE 91-3*
Raattamaa, Wilhelm 1921- *WhoWor 93*
Raatz, Patricia Anne Tirrell 1946- *WhoWrEP 92*
Rab, Attila 1942- *WhoScE 91-4*
Rabadeau, Mary Frances 1948- *WhoE 93*
Rabadjija, Neven *Law&B 92*
Rabar, Paul *BioIn 17*
Rabasa, Emilio 1856-1930 *DcMexL*
Rabasco Alvarez, Antonio Maria 1955- *WhoScE 91-3*
Rabassa, Gregory 1922- *WhoAm 92*
Rabate, Jean-Michel 1949- *ConAu 139*
Rabaud, Henri 1873-1949 *OxDcOp*
Rabaud, Henri (Benjamin) 1873-1949 *Baker 92*
Rabb, Bernard Paul 1939- *WhoAm 92*
Rabb, Bruce 1941- *WhoAm 92, WhoWor 93*
Rabb, Ellis 1930- *WhoAm 92*
Rabb, George Bernard 1930- *WhoAm 92*
Rabb, Harriet Schaffer 1941- *WhoAm 92*
Rabb, Kate Milner *AmWomPl*
Rabb, Maxwell M. 1910- *WhoAm 92*
Rabb, Nancy 1938- *St&PR 93*
Rabb, Richard Avery 1943- *St&PR 93*
Rabb, Stephen M. 1944- *St&PR 93*
Rabb, Theodore K. 1937- *WhoAm 92*
Rabb, Virg Sullivan 1932- *St&PR 93*
Rabbani, Burhanuddin 1940- *WhoWor 93*
Rabbani, Ruhiyyih 1910- *WhoWor 93*
Rabbinge, Roelof 1946- *WhoScE 91-3*
Rabbio, Salvatore Frank 1963- *WhoSSW 93*
Rabbit, John Michael 1941- *St&PR 93*
Rabbitt, Edward Thomas 1941- *WhoAm 92*
Rabbula d436 *OxDcByz*
Rabe, Berniece Louise 1928- *WhoWrEP 92*
Rabe, David William 1940- *WhoAm 92*
Rabe, Diane Marie 1959- *St&PR 93*
Rabe, Folke (Alvar Harald Reinhold) 1935- *Baker 92*
Rabe, Jean 1942- *ScF&FL 92*
Rabe, Jurgen P. 1955- *WhoWor 93*
Rabe, Margaret *AmWomPl*
Rabe, Robert L. d1990 *BioIn 17*
Rabel, William Huitt 1941- *WhoIns 93*
Rabelais, Francois c. 1494-1553 *MagSWL [port], OxDcOp, WorLitC [port]*
Rabeler, Steven Walter 1958- *WhoE 93*
Rabell, Arnaldo Roche *BioIn 17*
Rabelo, Leonardo Dutra 1956- *WhoWor 93*
Raben, Joseph 1924- *WhoE 93*
Rabenau, Albrecht 1922- *WhoScE 91-3*
Rabenhorst, Helmut *WhoScE 91-3*
Rabenstein, Dallas Leroy 1942- *WhoAm 92*
Rabensteiner, Gunther 1938- *WhoScE 91-4*
Raber, Donald R. 1943- *St&PR 93*
Raber, Douglas John 1942- *WhoE 93*
Raber, J. 1929- *WhoWor 93*
Raber, Marvin 1937- *WhoAm 92*
Raber, Robert Arthur *Law&B 92*
Rabetafika, Joseph A. Blaise 1932- *WhoUN 92*
Rabetafika, Joseph Albert Blaise 1932- *WhoWor 93*
Rabi, Isidor Isaac 1898-1988 *JeAmHC*
Rabideau, Peter Wayne 1940- *WhoAm 92*
Rabie, Mohamed 1940- *WhoE 93*
Rabig, Tony *ScF&FL 92*
Rabii, Patricia Berg 1942- *WhoAmW 93*
Rabil, Albert, Jr. 1934- *WhoE 93*
Rabil, Mitchell Joseph 1931- *WhoAm 92, WhoWor 93*
Rabil, Richard Joseph 1956- *WhoSSW 93*
Rabin, Bruce Stuart 1941- *WhoAm 92*
Rabin, Herbert 1928- *WhoAm 92*
Rabin, Jennifer *ScF&FL 92*
Rabin, Joseph Harry 1927- *WhoWor 93*
Rabin, Michael 1936-1972 *Baker 92*
Rabin, Mitchell Jay 1954- *WhoE 93*
Rabin, Myer *Law&B 92*
Rabin, Paul I. 1938- *St&PR 93*
Rabin, Paul Irwin 1938- *WhoIns 93*
Rabin, Stanley Arthur 1938- *St&PR 93*
Rabin, Trevor *See* Yes *ConMus 8*
Rabin, Walter D. *Law&B 92*
Rabin, Yitzhak *NewYTBS 92 [port]*
Rabin, Yitzhak 1922- *BioIn 17, ColdWar 2 [port], HarEnMi, News 93-1 [port], WhoWor 93*
Rabindranath Tagore 1861-1941 *BioIn 17*
Rabineau, Eli 1914-1991 *BioIn 17*
Rabineau, Louis 1924- *WhoAm 92*
Rabiner, Lawrence Richard 1943- *WhoAm 92, WhoE 93*
Rabiner, Susan 1948- *WhoAm 92, WhoWrEP 92*
Rabinof, Benno 1908-1975 *Baker 92*
Rabinovich, David 1900-1978 *Baker 92*
Rabinovich, Judith Paula 1944- *WhoAmW 93*
Rabinovich, Sergio 1928- *WhoAm 92*
Rabinovich, Vladimir Samuilovich 1940- *WhoWor 93*
Rabinovici, Benjamin M. 1922- *St&PR 93*
Rabinovitch, Benton Seymour 1919- *WhoAm 92*
Rabinovitch, Donald F. 1946- *St&PR 93*
Rabinovitz, Jason 1921- *WhoAm 92*
Rabinovitz, Mayer *Law&B 92*
Rabinow, Jacob 1910- *WhoAm 92*
Rabinowicz, Ernest 1926- *WhoAm 92*
Rabinowicz, Theodore 1919- *WhoWor 93*
Rabinowitch, David George 1943- *WhoE 93*
Rabinowitch, Victor 1934- *WhoAm 92*
Rabinowitz, Alan J. *Law&B 92*
Rabinowitz, Alan James *Law&B 92*
Rabinowitz, Allan Charles 1933- *St&PR 93*
Rabinowitz, Ann *ScF&FL 92*
Rabinowitz, Beryl *St&PR 93*
Rabinowitz, Harold Lawrence 1936- *St&PR 93*
Rabinowitz, Harry 1927- *St&PR 93*
Rabinowitz, Harvey Allen 1931- *WhoE 93*
Rabinowitz, Israel *St&PR 93*
Rabinowitz, Jack Grant 1927- *WhoAm 92*
Rabinowitz, Jay Andrew 1927- *WhoAm 92*
Rabinowitz, Joseph Loshak 1923- *WhoE 93*
Rabinowitz, Marvin 1939- *WhoAm 92*
Rabinowitz, Mayer E. 1939- *WhoAm 92*
Rabinowitz, Mayer Elya 1939- *WhoE 93*
Rabinowitz, Maynard *St&PR 93*
Rabinowitz, Michael Abraham 1940- *WhoE 93*
Rabinowitz, Peter Alan 1944- *WhoAm 92*
Rabinowitz, Rubin 1919- *St&PR 93*
Rabinowitz, Samuel Nathan 1932- *WhoAm 92*
Rabinowitz, Sholem Yakov 1859-1916 *BioIn 17*
Rabinowitz, Stanley Samuel 1917- *WhoAm 92*
Rabinowitz, Wilbur Melvin 1918- *St&PR 93*
Rabins, Michael Jerome 1932- *WhoAm 92*
Rabischong, Pierre 1932- *WhoScE 91-2*
Rabjohn, Norman 1915- *WhoAm 92*
Rabkin, Alan Brent *Law&B 92*
Rabkin, Eric S. 1946- *ScF&FL 92*
Rabkin, Lee W. *Law&B 92*
Rabkin, Leo 1919- *WhoAm 92*
Rabkin, Mitchell Thornton 1930- *WhoAm 92*
Rabkin, Peggy A. *Law&B 92*
Rabkin, Susan Marie *Law&B 92*
Rabl, Ari 1942- *WhoWor 93*
Rabl, Walter 1873-1940 *Baker 92*
Rablen, Elizabeth Charlotte 1924- *WhoAmW 93*
Rabo, Jule Anthony *WhoAm 92*
Rabold, Barbara Ann 1939- *WhoAmW 93*
Rabold, Robert E.H. *WhoIns 93*
Rabold, Robert Eh 1939- *St&PR 93*
Rabon, Ronald Ray 1955- *WhoE 93*
Rabon, Timothy Alan 1954- *St&PR 93, WhoSSW 93*
Rabon, William James, Jr. 1931- *WhoAm 92, WhoSSW 93, WhoWor 93*
Raboni, Giovanni 1932- *DcLB 128 [port]*
Raborg, Frederick Ashton, Jr. 1934- *WhoWrEP 92*
Raborn, Thomas Philip 1938- *St&PR 93*
Raborn, William Francis 1905-1990 *BioIn 17*
Rabosky, Joseph George 1944- *WhoE 93*
Rabotnov, Tikhon A. 1904- *WhoWor 93*
Raboy, David Geoffrey 1952- *WhoE 93*
Raboy, S. Caesar 1936- *St&PR 93, WhoAm 92, WhoIns 93*
Rabska, Zuzanna 1882-1960 *BioIn 17*
Rabstejnek, George J. 1932- *St&PR 93*
Rabuel, Pierre 1933- *WhoScE 91-2*
Rabuffo, Jeffrey Vincent 1939- *WhoE 93*
Rabuka, Sitiveni 1948- *BioIn 17*
Rabuka, Sitiveni Ligamamada 1948- *WhoWor 93*
Rabun, John Brewton, Jr. 1946- *WhoAm 92, WhoEmL 93*
Rabwin, Marcella 1908- *BioIn 17*
Raby, Elaine Miller 1938- *WhoWrEP 92*
Raby, Nancy E. *WhoAmW 93*
Raby, William Louis 1927- *WhoAm 92*
Racamier, Henry *BioIn 17*
Racamond, Julien 1885-1966 *BioIn 17*
Racanelli, Vito Peter *St&PR 93*
Raccah, Dominique Marcelle 1956- *WhoWrEP 92*
Raccah, Paul Mordechay 1933- *WhoAm 92*
Racchini, Robert L. 1945- *St&PR 93*
Race, Darrin 1965- *BioIn 17*
Race, David 1954- *WhoWor 93*
Race, David H. 1929- *St&PR 93*
Race, George Justice 1926- *WhoAm 92*
Race, Martha *AmWomPl*
Race, Paula Holmes *WhoAmW 93*
Race, Peter Kempton 1931- *St&PR 93*
Race, Robert K. 1956- *WhoIns 93*
Racek, Jan 1905-1979 *Baker 92*
Racer, James Harold 1939- *St&PR 93*
Racey, Paul Adrian *WhoScE 91-1*
Rachaiah, B. 1922- *WhoAsAP 91*
Rachals, Richard 1910- *St&PR 93*
Ra Chang Joo 1935- *WhoAsAP 91*
Rachel *BioIn 17*
Rachel, Louise 1951- *WhoWrEP 92*
Rachele, Julian d1992 *NewYTBS 92*
Rachelson, Joyce Ann 1946- *WhoEmL 93*
Rachford, Laurie A. *Law&B 92*
Rachie, Cyrus 1908- *WhoAm 92*
Rachilde 1860-1953 *BioIn 17, DcLB 123 [port]*
Rachins, Alan *WhoAm 92*
Rachinski, Howard Dale 1951- *WhoEmL 93, WhoWor 93*
Rachinsky, Joseph W. 1946- *WhoIns 93*
Rachleff, Jack 1913- *St&PR 93*
Rachleff, Owen S. 1934- *ScF&FL 92*
Rachleff, Owen S(pencer) 1934- *ConAu 40NR*
Rachleff, Owen Spencer 1934- *WhoAm 92*
Rachlin, Alan R. *St&PR 93*
Rachlin, Carol K. 1919- *BioIn 17*
Rachlin, Harvey 1951- *WhoWrEP 92*
Rachlin, Harvey Brant 1951- *WhoAm 92*
Rachlin, Jack 1923- *St&PR 93*
Rachlin, Nahid *BioIn 17, ConAu 17AS [port]*
Rachlin, Nahid 1944- *WhoWrEP 92*

Rachlin, Stephen Leonard 1939- *WhoAm 92, WhoE 93, WhoWor 93*
Rachman, Bradley Scott 1961- *WhoSSW 93*
Rachmaninoff, Sergei 1873-1943 *BioIn 17*
Rachmaninoff, Sergei (Vassilievich) 1873-1943 *Baker 92*
Rachmaninov, Sergey *OxDcOp*
Rachmeler, Louis 1923- *St&PR 93*
Rachmiel, George J. 1940- *St&PR 93*
Rachow, Louis August 1927- *WhoAm 92, WhoE 93*
Rachuta, Marian *WhoScE 91-4*
Rachwalski, Frank Joseph, Jr. 1945- *St&PR 93*
Racic, Frank-Josip 1947- *WhoEmL 93*
Racic, Robert Walter 1949- *St&PR 93*
Racicot, Marc F. 1948- *WhoAm 92*
Racina, Thom 1946- *ScF&FL 92, WhoAm 92*
Racine, Jean 1639-1699 *MagSWL [port], OxDcOp*
Racine, L.O. *Law&B 92*
Racine, Michel 1942- *ConAu 136*
Racine, Pierre 1909- *BioIn 17*
Racine, R. *WhoScE 91-2*
Racioppo, Stephen Gerard 1952- *WhoAm 92*
Raciti, Cherie 1942- *WhoAm 92*
Raciunas, Antanas 1905-1984 *Baker 92*
Rack, Peter Michael Horsman *WhoScE 91-1*
Racker, Efraim 1913-1991 *BioIn 17*
Rackerby, Thomas K. 1947- *St&PR 93*
Rackers, Thomas William 1955- *WhoEmL 93, WhoSSW 93*
Rackham, Arthur 1867-1939 *BioIn 17, MajAI [port]*
Rackham, Peggy Sue *BioIn 17*
Racki, Joan 1948- *WhoAmW 93*
Rackl, Donald George 1955- *St&PR 93*
Rackleff, Owen Spencer 1934- *WhoAm 92*
Rackleff, Robert Neal 1944- *WhoSSW 93*
Rackler, Jean Hope 1939- *WhoWrEP 92*
Rackley, Audie Neal 1934- *WhoAm 92, WhoWrEP 92*
Rackley, Clifford Walker 1923- *WhoAm 92*
Rackley, Frank Bailey, Jr. 1944- *St&PR 93*
Rackley, H. Wayne 1937- *WhoIns 93*
Rackman, Emanuel 1910- *JeAmHC*
Rackmil, Milton R. d1992 *NewYTBS 92 [port]*
Rackmil, Milton R. 1903-1992 *BioIn 17, CurBio 92N*
Rackow, Sylvia 1931- *WhoWrEP 92*
Raclin, Ernestine Morris 1927- *WhoAm 92*
Racoosin, Samuel Israel *Law&B 92*
Ractliffe, Robert E.G. 1943- *St&PR 93*
Racz, Andre 1916- *WhoAm 92*
Racz, Gabor Bela 1937- *WhoAm 92*
Racz, Istvan 1933- *WhoScE 91-4*
Racz, Zoltan 1930- *WhoScE 91-4*
Racz-Clough, Victoria Elizabeth 1955- *WhoAmW 93*
Raczka, Jan Stanislaw 1922- *WhoScE 91-4*
Raczkiewicz, Mac A. 1942- *St&PR 93*
Raczkiewicz, Wladyslaw 1885-1947 *PolBiDi*
Raczko, Waldemar Piotr 1938- *WhoScE 91-4*
Raczkowski, Dale John *Law&B 92*
Raczkowski, Jan Wlodzimierz 1926- *WhoWor 93*
Raczkowski, Jozef Wojciech 1930- *WhoScE 91-4*
Raczynska-Bojanowska, Konstancja 1922- *WhoScE 91-4*
Rada, Alexander 1923- *WhoWor 93*
Rada, John B. 1951- *St&PR 93*
Rada, Roy *WhoScE 91-1*
Rada, Thomas John 1941- *WhoAm 92*
Radabaugh, Michele Jo 1961- *WhoAmW 93*
Radach, Calvin L. 1928- *St&PR 93*
Radack, Frank Charles 1940- *WhoSSW 93*
Radaelli, Luciano *WhoScE 91-3*
Radakovich, Peter 1948- *St&PR 93*
Radan, G. T. *ConAu 39NR*
Radan, George T(ivadar) 1923- *ConAu 39NR*
Radandt, Friedhelm K. 1932- *WhoAm 92*
Radanovic, Dusan 1933- *WhoScE 91-4*
Radavich, David Allen 1949- *WhoWrEP 92*
Radcliff, Timothy L. 1955- *St&PR 93*
Radcliff, William 1768-1842 *BioIn 17*
Radcliff, William Franklin 1922- *WhoAm 92*
Radcliffe, Ann Ward 1764-1823 *BioIn 17*
Radcliffe, Courtney Lane 1962- *WhoEmL 93*
Radcliffe, Elsa J. 1935- *ScF&FL 92*
Radcliffe, Frederick R., Jr. 1939- *St&PR 93*
Radcliffe, Garnett 1899- *ScF&FL 92*
Radcliffe, George Grove 1924- *St&PR 93, WhoAm 92*
Radcliffe, Gerald Eugene 1923- *WhoWor 93*
Radcliffe, Janette *WhoWrEP 92*
Radcliffe, John Alfred *WhoScE 91-1*
Radcliffe, Phyllis E. 1926- *St&PR 93*
Radcliffe, R. Stephen 1945- *WhoIns 93*
Radcliffe, Redonia Wheeler *WhoAm 92*
Radcliffe, Robert D. 1934- *St&PR 93*
Radcliffe, S. Victor 1927- *WhoAm 92*
Radcliffe-Brown, A.R. 1881-1955 *IntDcAn*
Radcliffe-Smallwood, Cynthia 1946- *WhoAmW 93*
Radda, G.K. *WhoScE 91-1*
Raddall, Thomas Head 1903- *WhoCanL 92*
Raddatz, Robert H. 1926- *St&PR 93*
Radder, Joseph Henry 1920- *WhoE 93*
Radding, Edward 1941- *St&PR 93*
Raddysh, Garry *WhoCanL 92*
Radecke, Robert 1830-1911 *Baker 92*
Radecke, Rudolf 1829-1893 *Baker 92*
Radecki, Anthony Eugene 1939- *St&PR 93, WhoAm 92*
Radecki, Tadeusz 1950- *WhoWor 93*
Radek, Garald A. 1940- *St&PR 93*
Radek, Karl 1885-1941 *DcTwHis*
Radeka, Veljko 1930- *WhoAm 92*
Radeke, Sandra Kay *Law&B 92*
Radel, Dwayne C. *Law&B 92*
Radel, Eva 1934- *WhoAmW 93*
Radelaar, S. *WhoScE 91-3*
Radell, George Martin 1933- *St&PR 93*
Radell, Nicholas John 1930- *St&PR 93, WhoAm 92*
Rademacher, Betty Green 1935- *WhoAmW 93*
Rademacher, Franz 1899-1987 *BioIn 17*
Rademacher, Hans-Bert 1960- *WhoWor 93*
Rademacher, Hollis W. 1935- *St&PR 93*
Rademacher, Hollis William 1935- *WhoAm 92*
Rademacher, Paul 1940- *WhoWor 93*
Rademacher, Richard Glenn 1937- *St&PR 93*
Rademacher, Richard Joseph 1937- *WhoAm 92*
Rademaekers, Ed 1948- *WhoSSW 93*
Rademaker, Chris Theodorus 1934- *St&PR 93*
Rademaker, Stephen Geoffrey 1959- *WhoAm 92*
Rademakers, Fons 1920- *MiSFD 9*
Raden, Koestedjo 1916- *WhoWor 93*
Raden, Louis 1929- *WhoWor 93*
Radenbaugh, Dawn *BioIn 17*
Radenhausen, Russell Alan 1950- *WhoSSW 93*
Rader, Charles George 1946- *WhoAm 92*
Rader, Chovine Richardson, Jr. 1942- *St&PR 93*
Rader, Daniel S. 1959- *St&PR 93*
Rader, Darwin Joe 1951- *St&PR 93*
Rader, Dennis 1940- *WhoE 93*
Rader, Dick Allen 1940- *WhoSSW 93*
Rader, Dotson Carlyle 1942- *WhoAm 92*
Rader, Hannelore 1937- *WhoAmW 93*
Rader, Jack d1990 *BioIn 17*
Rader, John J. 1950- *St&PR 93*
Rader, John R. 1950- *St&PR 93*
Rader, K.C. 1948- *St&PR 93*
Rader, Louis T. 1911- *WhoAm 92*
Rader, Margaret O. 1914- *St&PR 93*
Rader, Nancy Louise de Villiers 1948- *WhoAmW 93, WhoE 93*
Rader, Peter *MiSFD 9*
Rader, Ralph Wilson 1930- *WhoAm 92*
Rader, Randall R. 1949- *CngDr 91*
Rader, Randall Ray 1949- *WhoAm 92, WhoE 93*
Rader, Rhoda Caswell 1945- *WhoE 93*
Radermacher, Frank James 1953- *St&PR 93*
Radesater, J. Tommy 1947- *WhoScE 91-4*
Radest, Howard Bernard 1928- *WhoAm 92*
Radest, Michael B. *Law&B 92*
Radetsky, Gregg E. *Law&B 92*
Radetzky, Josef Wenceslas 1766-1858 *HarEnMi*
Radev, Ivan Stefanov 1958- *WhoWor 93*
Radev, Vlo 1923- *DrEEuF*
Radewagen, Fred 1944- *WhoAm 92*
Radey, Richard Greger 1933- *St&PR 93, WhoAm 92*
Radez, William R. *Law&B 92*
Radford, Arthur William 1896-1973 *HarEnMi*
Radford, Basil 1897-1952 & Wayne, Naunton 1901-1970 *QDrFCA 92 [port]*
Radford, Dixie Ann 1941- *WhoAmW 93*
Radford, G. Lahrye 1943- *St&PR 93*
Radford, Gary Paul 1961- *WhoE 93*
Radford, Ken *ScF&FL 92*
Radford, Kenneth Charles 1941- *WhoE 93*
Radford, Linda Robertson 1944- *WhoAmW 93*
Radford, Michael 1950- *MiSFD 9*
Radford, Norman DePue, Jr. 1943- *WhoAm 92*
Radford, Peter Weston 1949- *St&PR 93*
Radford, Philip James 1938- *WhoScE 91-1*
Radford, Richard Francis, Jr. 1939- *WhoWrEP 92*
Radford, Robert 1874-1933 *Baker 92, OxDcOp*
Radford, Ruby Lorraine *AmWomPl*
Radford, Virginia Rodriguez 1917- *WhoAmW 93*
Radford, Winifred 1901- *OxDcOp*
Radha, Sivananda 1911- *BioIn 17*
Radhakrishna, Puttapaga 1944- *WhoAsAP 91*
Radhakrishnan, Sarvepalli 1888-1975 *DcTwHis*
Radic, Alicja 1933- *WhoScE 91-3*
Radic, Dusan 1929- *Baker 92*
Radica, Ruben 1931- *Baker 92*
Radicati Di Brozolo, Luigi Arialdo 1919- *WhoScE 91-3*
Radice, Anne-Imelda *NewYTBS 92 [port]*
Radice, Anne-Imelda 1948- *WhoAm 92, WhoAmW 93*
Radice, Frank A. 1930- *St&PR 93*
Radice, Frank J. 1949- *WhoWor 93*
Radice, Robert 1946- *WhoSSW 93*
Radice, Shirley Rosalind 1935- *WhoAmW 93*
Radice, Steven A. 1948- *St&PR 93*
Radicella, Renato 1934- *WhoUN 92*
Radiciotti, Giuseppe 1858-1931 *Baker 92*
Radies, Norman W. 1952- *St&PR 93*
Radig, Bernd M. 1944- *WhoScE 91-3*
Radigan, Frank Xavier 1933- *WhoE 93*
Radigan, J. Brian *Law&B 92*
Radigan, Joseph Richard 1939- *St&PR 93, WhoAm 92*
Radigan, Michael Gerard *Law&B 92*
Radil, Tomas 1930- *WhoScE 91-4*
Radin, Alex 1921- *WhoAm 92*
Radin, Laura Levine 1944- *WhoAmW 93*
Radin, Neila B. *Law&B 92*
Radin, Norman Samuel 1920- *WhoAm 92*
Radin, Paul 1883-1959 *IntDcAn*
Radin, Robert B. *Law&B 92*
Radin, Roy 1950-1983 *BioIn 17*
Radin, Stuart 1967- *St&PR 93*
Radin, Wendy Sue 1950- *WhoAmW 93*
Radinovic, Djuro 1929- *WhoScE 91-4*
Radinsky, Eliezer J. 1961- *St&PR 93*
Radison, Garry 1949- *WhoCanL 92*
Radisson, Pierre-Esprit 1636?-1710 *Expl 93*
Raditsa, Bogdan 1904- *WhoWrEP 92*
Radivojevic, Milos 1939- *DrEEuF*
Radix, Kendrick 1941- *DcCPCAm*
Radjai, Ahmad Agat Al-Kala 1933- *WhoUN 92*
Radke, Anna *AmWomPl*
Radke, Chris Alan *Law&B 92*
Radke, Jack William *Law&B 92*
Radke, Magdelente Craft *AmWomPl*
Radke, Margaret Hoffman 1923- *WhoAmW 93*
Radke, Richard *BioIn 17*
Radke, Vincent James 1948- *WhoSSW 93*
Radkowski, Margaret Louise 1951- *WhoAmW 93*
Radkowsky, Karen B. 1957- *WhoAmW 93*
Radlach, Robert 1958- *WhoSSW 93*
Radle, William D. 1932- *St&PR 93*
Radler, Bob *MiSFD 9*
Radler, Ferdinand 1929- *WhoScE 91-3*
Radler, Jeffrey Alan 1959- *St&PR 93*
Radler, Louis 1931- *St&PR 93*
Radler, Warren S. 1936- *WhoAm 92*
Radley, Virginia Louise 1927- *WhoAm 92*
Radlick, Janice Marie *Law&B 92*
Radlinska, Helena 1879-1954 *BioIn 17*
Radlinski, David V. *St&PR 93*
Radloff, Charles B. 1928- *St&PR 93*
Radloff, Robert Albert 1947- *WhoAm 92*
Radlov, V.V. 1837-1918 *IntDcAn*
Radmacher, Sally Ann 1937- *WhoAmW 93*
Radmer, Michael John 1945- *St&PR 93, WhoAm 92, WhoWor 93*
Radmin, Nancye *BioIn 17*
Radnai, Miklos 1892-1935 *Baker 92*
Radnay, Paul Andrew 1913- *WhoAm 92*
Radner, Gilda *QDrFCA 92*
Radner, Gilda 1946-1989 *BioIn 17*
Radner, Roy 1927- *WhoAm 92*
Radner, Sidney Hollis 1919- *WhoE 93*
Radnofsky, Barbara A. *WhoAmW 93*
Radnor, Alan *ScF&FL 92*
Rado, Aladar 1882-1914 *Baker 92*
Rado, Francis A. 1950- *St&PR 93*
Rado, Ladislav Leland 1909- *WhoAm 92*
Rado, Peter Thomas 1928- *St&PR 93*
Rado, Tony 1950- *St&PR 93*
Radocha, Daniel Joseph *Law&B 92*
Radocha, Dennis L. *Law&B 92*
Radock, Michael 1917- *WhoAm 92*
Radocy, Paul F. 1917- *St&PR 93*
Radoff, Leonard Irving 1927- *WhoAm 92*
Radoff, Linda R. *Law&B 92*
Radojcsics, Anne Parsons 1929- *WhoAmW 93*
Radojevic, Danilo *WhoAm 92*
Radomisli, Michel 1931- *WhoE 93*
Radomska, Maria Joanna 1925- *WhoScE 91-4*
Radomski, Jack London 1920- *WhoAm 92*
Radomski, Robyn L. 1954- *St&PR 93*
Radomski, Robyn Lynn 1954- *WhoAm 92*
Radomsky, Michael 1952- *St&PR 93*
Radon, Jenik Richard 1946- *WhoWor 93*
Radon, John Adolf 1919- *WhoWor 93*
Radonezhskii, Sergii *BioIn 17*
Radonic, Milovan 1921- *WhoScE 91-4*
Radonski, Gilbert Clemence 1936- *WhoAm 92*
Rados, Alexander Stephen 1928- *St&PR 93*
Rados, David Lee 1933- *WhoSSW 93*
Radosavljevic, Sasa 1962- *WhoWor 93*
Radoux, Gilbert 1820- *BioIn 17*
Radoux, Jean-Theodore 1835-1911 *Baker 92*
Radoux-Rogier, Charles 1877-1952 *Baker 92*
Radovan, Mary B. 1922- *St&PR 93*
Radovanovic, Vladan 1932- *Baker 92*
Radovsky, Frank Jay 1929- *WhoSSW 93*
Radsch, Richard T. *Law&B 92*
Radsch, Richard Thackery *Law&B 92*
Radstone, Graham Michael *Law&B 92*
Radt, Richard Louis 1932- *St&PR 93*
Radtke, Bruce Michael 1951- *WhoWrEP 92*
Radtke, Eldon *St&PR 93*
Radtke, H. Helmut 1946- *St&PR 93*
Radtke, James Paul 1951- *St&PR 93*
Radu, Kenneth *WhoCanL 92*
Raduchel, William James 1946- *WhoEmL 93*
Raduenz, Gary A. *Law&B 92*
Radulf of Caen c. 1080-c. 1131 *OxDcByz*
Radusch, Jenny *WhoScE 91-3*
Radvanyi, Pierre C. 1926- *WhoScE 91-2*
Radvanyi, Pierre Charles 1926- *WhoWor 93*
Radvial, P. *WhoScE 91-4*
Radwan, Ann Bos 1941- *WhoAmW 93*
Radwan, Samir Mohamed 1942- *WhoUN 92*
Radwanski, Andrzej 1709-1762 *PolBiDi*
Radway, Deborah Brooke 1956- *WhoE 93*
Radwill, Arthur Scott 1948- *St&PR 93*
Radwin, Howard M. 1931- *WhoAm 92*
Radycki, Diane Josephine 1946- *WhoE 93*
Radzicka, Anna Jolanta *WhoAmW 93*
Radzievskiy, Aleksei Ivanovich 1911-1978 *HarEnMi*
Radzik, Donna L. *Law&B 92*
Radzikowski, Czeslaw M. 1929- *WhoScE 91-4*
Radzinowicz, Leon 1906- *WhoWor 93*
Radzinowicz, Mary Ann 1925- *WhoAm 92*
Radzins, Edmund 1919- *St&PR 93*
Radzinsky, Edvard Stanislavovich 1936- *WhoWor 93*
Radziwill, Anton Heinrich 1775-1833 *Baker 92*
Radziwill, Barbara 1520-1551 *PolBiDi*
Radziwill, Jerzy 1556-1600 *PolBiDi*
Radzykewycz, Dan Theodore 1942- *WhoSSW 93, WhoWor 93*
Rae, Allan 1942- *Baker 92*
Rae, Allan Neville 1943- *WhoWor 93*
Rae, Barbara Joyce 1930- *WhoAmW 93*
Rae, Carolyn Williams 1952- *WhoAmW 93*
Rae, Charlotte 1926- *WhoAm 92*
Rae, David L. *Law&B 92*
Rae, Douglas Whiting 1939- *WhoAm 92*
Rae, E. Ann 1944- *WhoAm 92*
Rae, Earl F. 1929- *St&PR 93*
Rae, Fiona 1963- *BioIn 17*
Rae, Hugh C. 1935- *ScF&FL 92*
Rae, Ian G. 1936- *BioIn 17*
Rae, John *BioIn 17, WhoScE 91-1*
Rae, Matthew Sanderson, Jr. 1922- *WhoAm 92, WhoWor 93*
Rae, Michael *MiSFD 9*
Rae, Michelle Lauren 1968- *WhoWrEP 92*
Rae, Patricia *ScF&FL 92*
Rae, Peter Murdoch MacPhail 1944- *WhoE 93*
Rae, Robert *BioIn 17*
Rae, Robert Andrew 1944- *St&PR 93*
Rae, Robert Keith 1948- *WhoAm 92, WhoE 93*
Raeburn, Andrew Harvey 1933- *WhoAm 92, WhoSSW 93*
Raeburn, John Hay 1941- *WhoAm 92*
Raeburn, Michael 1943- *MiSFD 9*
Raeburn, Susan Delaney 1950- *WhoAmW 93*
Raedeke, Linda Dismore 1950- *WhoEmL 93*
Raeder, Erich 1876-1960 *HarEnMi*
Raeder, James Hamilton 1940- *St&PR 93*

Raeder, Morten Gustav 1939- *WhoWor 93*
Raeder, Myrna Sharon 1947- *WhoAmW 93*
Raedler, Dorothy Florence 1917- *WhoAm 92*
Raeff, Marc 1923- *WhoWrEP 92*
Raekallio, Jyrki Arno Johannes 1929- *WhoScE 91-4*
Raelin, Abby Phyllis 1947- *WhoAmW 93*
Raemer, Harold Roy 1924- *WhoAm 92*
Raeper, William 1959- *ScF&FL 92*
Raeschild, Sheila 1936- *WhoWrEP 92*
Raether, Edward W. 1936- *St&PR 93*
Raether, Friedrich 1958- *WhoScE 91-3*
Raeuchle, Ernest T. 1928- *St&PR 93*
Raezer, Sallie Stewart 1951- *WhoAmW 93*
Rafael, Don *WhoWrEP 92*
Rafael, Frederic 1931- *MiSFD 9*
Rafael, Georg *BioIn 17*
Rafael, Otalora 1955- *WhoE 93*
Rafael, Ruth Kelson 1929- *WhoAm 92*
Rafaelsen, Ole Jorgen 1930- *WhoScE 91-2*
Rafai, Pal 1940- *WhoScE 91-4*
Rafajko, Robert Richard 1931- *WhoAm 92*
Rafajlowicz, Ewaryst 1953- *WhoWor 93*
Rafalowicz, Jan 1931- *WhoScE 91-4*
Rafalowicz, Jerzy Antoni 1933- *WhoScE 91-4*
Rafalowska, Janina 1929- *WhoScE 91-4*
Rafalowski, Janice Ann 1950- *WhoE 93*
Rafalski, Henryk 1925- *WhoScE 91-4*
Rafalsky, Stephen Mark 1942- *WhoWrEP 92*
Rafanelli, Kenneth Robert 1937- *WhoAm 92*
Rafart, Juan 1934- *WhoWor 93*
Rafea, Ahmed Abdelwahed 1950- *WhoWor 93*
Rafeedie, Edward 1929- *WhoAm 92*
Rafeeuddin, Ahmed *WhoUN 92*
Rafei, Uton Muchtar 1935- *WhoUN 92*
Rafelson, Bob *BioIn 17*
Rafelson, Bob 1933- *WhoAm 92*
Rafelson, Bob 1935- *MiSFD 9*
Rafelson, Max Emanuel, Jr. 1921- *WhoAm 92*
Rafer, Ester Dayrit 1935- *St&PR 93*
Rafetto, John 1950- *WhoE 93*
Rafetto, Michele Minner 1960- *WhoAmW 93*
Raff, Gilbert 1928- *St&PR 93, WhoAm 92*
Raff, Joachim 1822-1882 *OxDcOp*
Raff, (Joseph) Joachim 1822-1882 *Baker 92*
Raff, Joseph Allen 1933- *WhoAm 92, WhoWor 93*
Raff, Raymond J. 1918- *St&PR 93*
Raff, Spencer J. *Law&B 92*
Raffa, Joseph 1947- *WhoWrEP 92*
Raffa, Louise Morrison 1932- *St&PR 93*
Raffa, Peter Eugene 1926- *St&PR 93*
Raffael, Joseph 1933- *WhoAm 92*
Raffaele, John Eugene 1948- *St&PR 93*
Raffay, Stephen Joseph 1927- *WhoAm 92*
Raffel, Burton Nathan 1928- *WhoWrEP 92*
Raffel, David Nathan 1929- *WhoSSW 93*
Raffel, Jeffrey Allen 1945- *WhoAm 92*
Raffel, Jerome 1925- *St&PR 93*
Raffel, Leroy B. 1927- *WhoAm 92*
Raffel, Louis B. 1933- *WhoAm 92*
Rafferty, Brian Joseph 1957- *WhoAm 92*
Rafferty, Carolyn Banks 1941- *WhoWrEP 92*
Rafferty, Chips 1909-1971 *IntDcF 2-3*
Rafferty, Frank Thomas 1925- *St&PR 93*
Rafferty, Gary Lee *Law&B 92*
Rafferty, James Patrick 1947- *WhoAm 92*
Rafferty, Jennifer Lee 1960- *WhoE 93*
Rafferty, Joanne M. *St&PR 93*
Rafferty, John T. *Law&B 92*
Rafferty, John T. 1932- *St&PR 93*
Rafferty, Kevin Patrick 1955- *WhoWrEP 92*
Rafferty, Larry E. 1942- *WhoWrEP 92*
Rafferty, Michael F. 1947- *St&PR 93*
Rafferty, Michael Griffin, Jr. 1935- *St&PR 93*
Rafferty, Michael Robert 1949- *WhoAm 92*
Rafferty, Nancy Schwarz 1930- *WhoAm 92*
Rafferty, Sherwood J. 1947- *St&PR 93*
Rafferty, William Bernard 1912- *WhoAm 92*
Rafferty, William Steven 1952- *St&PR 93*
Raffetto, Michael d1990 *BioIn 17*
Raffi *BioIn 17, ConAu 136*
Raffi 1948- *ConMus 8 [port]*
Raffi, Charles Louis, Jr. 1927- *St&PR 93*
Raffi, Rhonda Curtin 1953- *St&PR 93*
Raffiani, Jeanne M. *Law&B 92*
Raffill, Stewart *MiSFD 9*
Raffin, Bennett Lyon 1918- *St&PR 93*
Raffin, Thomas A. 1947- *WhoAm 92*
Raffini, James O. 1941- *ConAu 40NR*
Raffler, Hans 1930- *WhoIns 93*
Raffoux, Jean-Francois 1942- *WhoScE 91-2*
Rafi, Comrade Lieutenant General 1942- *WhoAsAP 91*
Rafi, Salahuddin 1955- *WhoWor 93*
Rafidah Aziz, Paduka Dato' Seri 1943- *WhoAsAP 91*
Rafique, Tariq 1957- *St&PR 93*
Rafique Alam 1929- *WhoAsAP 91*
Rafiroiu, D. Mihai 1931- *WhoScE 91-4*
Rafkin, Alan 1928- *WhoAm 92*
Rafkin, Alan 1938- *MiSFD 9*
Rafols, Juan M. 1959- *WhoSSW 93*
Rafos, Stuart A. 1945- *St&PR 93*
Rafsanjani, Ali Akbar *BioIn 17*
Rafsanjani, Hashemi *BioIn 17*
Rafsanjani, Hojatolislam Hashemi Ali Akbar 1934- *DcTwHis*
Rafshoon, Gerald Monroe 1934- *WhoAm 92*
Rafson, Harold 1927- *St&PR 93*
Raft, Carole Ruth 1940- *WhoSSW 93*
Raft, George 1895-1980 *IntDcF 2-3 [port]*
Rafter, John R. *Law&B 92*
Rafter, Sarah S. *AmWomPl*
Rafter, Thomas Daniel *Law&B 92*
Raftery, Joseph P. 1938- *St&PR 93*
Raftery, William A. 1925- *WhoE 93*
Rafti, Vincent James 1926- *WhoAm 92*
Raftis, George S. 1956- *St&PR 93*
Raftis, Spiros 1925- *St&PR 93*
Rafuse, Calvin Edward, Jr. *Law&B 92*
Rafuse, John R. 1951- *St&PR 93*
Rafuse, Wanda Jeanette 1957- *WhoAmW 93*
Raga, Francesco 1940- *WhoScE 91-3*
Ragals, William Charles, Jr. 1939- *WhoAm 92*
Ragan, Bob *BioIn 17*
Ragan, David 1925- *WhoAm 92*
Ragan, James 1944- *WhoWrEP 92*
Ragan, James Otis 1942- *WhoSSW 93*
Ragan, James Thomas 1929- *WhoAm 92*
Ragan, Roy Allen 1929- *WhoWrEP 92*
Ragan, Samuel Talmadge 1915- *WhoAm 92, WhoWrEP 92*
Ragan, Seaborn Bryant Timmons 1929- *WhoWor 93*
Ragan, Thomas Cameron 1904-1990 *BioIn 17*
Ragatz, Thomas George 1934- *WhoAm 92*
Ragavoy, Jerry 1935- *SoulM*
Ragazzo, Anthony, Jr. 1967- *WhoE 93*
Ragazzo, Richard 1952- *St&PR 93*
Ragen, Brooks Geer 1933- *St&PR 93*
Ragent, Boris 1924- *WhoAm 92*
Ragep, Marci Kelli 1964- *WhoAmW 93*
Rager, Charles E. 1928- *St&PR 93, WhoAm 92*
Rager, Greg 1946- *WhoSSW 93*
Rager, Gunter 1938- *WhoScE 91-4*
Rager, Richard Scott 1948- *WhoIns 93*
Ragetly, Paul Rene 1944- *WhoWor 93*
Raggi, Lisa *Law&B 92*
Raggi, Reena 1951- *WhoAm 92, WhoAmW 93, WhoE 93*
Raggio, Kenneth Gaylord 1949- *WhoAm 92*
Raggio, Louise Ballerstedt 1919- *WhoAm 92, WhoWor 93*
Raggio, Nora Genevieve 1958- *WhoAmW 93*
Raggio, Olga 1926- *BioIn 17*
Raggio, William Gerard 1956- *WhoE 93*
Raggio, William J. 1926- *St&PR 93*
Raggio-Amarilla, Miguel Mario 1926- *WhoWor 93*
Raghavan, Raghu 1948- *WhoWor 93*
Raghoebar, Maikel 1957- *WhoWor 93*
Raghupathi, P. S. 1945- *WhoAm 92, WhoSSW 93*
Ragin, Deborah Fish 1956- *WhoE 93*
Ragin, Derek Lee 1958- *WhoE 93*
Ragin, Luther M., Jr. 1955- *St&PR 93*
Ragin, Luther Mack, Jr. 1955- *WhoE 93*
Ragins, Herzl 1929- *WhoE 93*
Ragins, Marianne *BioIn 17*
Ragir, Norma L. *St&PR 93*
Raglan, Fitzroy James Henry Somerset 1788-1855 *HarEnMi*
Raglan, FitzRoy Richard Somerset 1885-1964 *IntDcAn*
Ragland, Alwine Mulhearn 1913- *WhoAmW 93*
Ragland, Douglas Lee 1947- *St&PR 93*
Ragland, Jack Whitney 1938- *WhoAm 92*
Ragland, James B. 1917- *St&PR 93*
Ragland, James Black 1917- *WhoAm 92*
Ragland, John C. 1939- *St&PR 93*
Ragland, Marianne 1961- *WhoAmW 93*
Ragland, Mary Ann 1933- *WhoSSW 93*
Ragland, Sherman Leon, II 1962- *WhoEmL 93*
Ragland, William Lauman, III 1934- *WhoSSW 93*
Ragland, William McKenzie, Jr. 1960- *WhoSSW 93*
Ragle, Joanne Feiger 1948- *WhoAmW 93*
Ragle, John Linn 1933- *WhoE 93*
Ragley, Michele G. *Law&B 92*
Ragnarsson, Ulf Ingemar 1934- *WhoScE 91-4*
Ragni, Gerome 1942-1991 *BioIn 17, ConTFT 10*
Ragnotti, Giovanni 1936- *WhoWor 93*
Rago, Alexis 1930- *Baker 92*
Rago, Daniel A. *Law&B 92*
Rago, John J. 1955- *St&PR 93*
Rago, Rosalinde Teresa 1952- *WhoAmW 93, WhoE 93*
Ragogna, Andrew Robert 1948- *St&PR 93*
Ragone, David Vincent 1930- *WhoAm 92, WhoWor 93*
Ragozzino, Antonio 1936- *WhoScE 91-3*
Ragsdale, Bertha Mae 1925- *WhoAmW 93*
Ragsdale, Carl Vandyke 1925- *WhoAm 92*
Ragsdale, Christina Ann 1956- *WhoAmW 93*
Ragsdale, James Marcus 1938- *WhoE 93*
Ragsdale, Nancy Nealy 1938- *WhoAmW 93*
Ragsdale, Richard Elliot 1943- *St&PR 93, WhoAm 92, WhoSSW 93*
Ragsdale, Thomas Ray 1960- *WhoSSW 93*
Ragusa, Joseph F. 1954- *St&PR 93*
Ragusa, Louis John *Law&B 92*
Ragusa, Olga Maria 1922- *WhoAm 92*
Ragusi, Sandra L. *Law&B 92*
Raguso, Sam L., Jr. 1941- *St&PR 93*
Rahal, Mary G. 1946- *WhoIns 93*
Rahal, Robert W. 1953- *WhoAm 92*
Rahal, Robert Woodward 1953- *BiDAMSp 1989*
Rahall, Nicholas J., II 1949- *WhoSSW 93*
Rahall, Nick J., II 1949- *WhoAm 92*
Rahall, Nick Joe, II 1949- *CngDr 91*
Raham, (R.) Gary 1946- *ConAu 136*
Rahardjo, Raden Wido 1950- *WhoWor 93*
Rahbar, Zita Ina 1937- *WhoAmW 93, WhoWor 93*
Rahe, Learld E. 1945- *St&PR 93*
Rahe, Lin Christine 1950- *WhoSSW 93*
Rahe, Maribeth S. 1948- *St&PR 93*
Rahe, Maribeth Sembach 1948- *WhoAm 92*
Raheem, Jehan 1935- *WhoUN 92*
Rahel 1771-1833 *BioIn 17*
Rahenkamp, Eric Edward 1961- *WhoSSW 93*
Rahenkamp, John Edward 1937- *WhoAm 92*
Rahhal, Talal Youssef 1953- *WhoWor 93*
Rahie, John G. *Law&B 92*
Rahim, Hussein 1932- *WhoUN 92*
Rahimian, Iradj 1934- *WhoScE 91-3*
Rahimtoola, Habib Ibrahim 1912-1991 *BioIn 17*
Rahimtoola, Shahbudin Hooseinally 1931- *WhoAm 92*
Rahjes, Doyle Dean 1930- *St&PR 93*
Rahka, Klaus Albert 1946- *WhoWor 93*
Rahkamaa, Erkki J. 1938- *WhoScE 91-4*
Rahko, Kauko Johan Samuel 1933- *WhoScE 91-4*
Rahko, Timo Kalevi 1939- *WhoScE 91-4*
Rahl, Cecilia May N. 1931- *WhoWrEP 92*
Rahl, James Andrew 1917- *WhoAm 92*
Rahl, Leslie Lynn 1950- *WhoE 93*
Rahm, Calvin R. 1923- *St&PR 93*
Rahm, David Alan 1941- *WhoAm 92, WhoE 93, WhoWor 93*
Rahm, Dianne 1951- *WhoAmW 93*
Rahm, Susan Berkman 1943- *WhoAm 92, WhoAmW 93*
Rahman, A.H.M. Mahfuzur 1935- *WhoUN 92*
Rahman, A. S. M. Mustafizur *WhoWor 93*
Rahman, Abdul 1903-1990 *BioIn 17*
Rahman, Abdul Putra 1903-1990 *DcTwHis*
Rahman, Abu T.R. 1936- *WhoUN 92*
Rahman, Abu Tayeb Rafiqur 1936- *WhoE 93*
Rahman, Atiqur 1950- *WhoUN 92*
Rahman, Azizur 1935- *WhoAsAP 91*
Rahman, Glenn *ScF&FL 92*
Rahman, Haji Zakaria Bin Abdul 1936- *WhoAsAP 91*
Rahman, Linda *BioIn 17*
Rahman, Linda Lou 1946- *WhoAmW 93*
Rahman, Mahboob Er 1933- *WhoUN 92*
Rahman, Mahbubur 1934- *WhoAsAP 91*
Rahman, Mirza Atiqur 1959- *WhoWor 93*
Rahman, Mohd. Khaleelur 1936- *WhoAsAP 91*
Rahman, Mujib-Ur 1938- *WhoWor 93*
Rahman, Mujibur 1920-1975 *DcTwHis*
Rahman, Rezaur 1957- *WhoWor 93*
Rahman, Sadiq Abdul 1936- *BioIn 17*
Rahman, Syed Khalid 1950- *WhoWor 93*
Rahman, Syed Mojib 1932- *WhoWor 93*
Rahman, Syedur A. H. 1936- *WhoWor 93*
Rahman, Yueh-Erh 1928- *WhoAm 92*
Rahman bin Bakar, Abdul *WhoAsAP 91*
Rahman Bin Dato Setia Haji Awang, Yang Berhormat Pehin Orang Kaya Setia *WhoAsAP 91*
Rahman-Garcia, Sabina Kaysree 1965- *WhoAmW 93*
Rahman Khan, Ataur 1905- *WhoAsAP 91*
Rahmann, Hinrich 1935- *WhoScE 91-3, WhoWor 93*
Rahmann, John Charles 1927- *St&PR 93*
Rahmas, Sigrid Johnson 1913- *WhoWrEP 92*
Rahmatullah, Mohammed 1940- *WhoUN 92*
Rahmel, Alfred 1927- *WhoScE 91-3*
Rahmig, William Conrad 1936- *WhoAm 92*
Rahn, Alvin Albert 1925- *WhoAm 92*
Rahn, Ernst W. 1934- *St&PR 93*
Rahn, Herbert George 1943- *St&PR 93*
Rahn, John 1944- *Baker 92*
Rahn, Richard William 1942- *WhoAm 92*
Rahner, Karl 1904-1984 *BioIn 17*
Rahner-Reimann, Patricia Anne 1957- *WhoE 93*
Rahoy, John D. *Law&B 92*
Rahr, Guido R., Jr. 1928- *St&PR 93*
Rai, Kalp Nath 1941- *WhoAsAP 91*
Rai, Kalpnath 1941- *WhoAsAP 91*
Rai, Raghu 1942- *St&PR 93*
Raia, Carl Bernard 1931- *WhoSSW 93*
Raia, Michele C. *Law&B 92*
Raia, Sam B., Jr. 1935- *St&PR 93*
Raia, Samuel Patrick *Law&B 92*
Raibley, David T. 1951- *St&PR 93*
Raiche, Herbert L. *Law&B 92*
Raichel, Daniel Richter 1935- *WhoE 93*
Raichev, Alexander 1922- *Baker 92*
Raichl, Miroslav 1930- *Baker 92*
Raichlen, Francine G. *Law&B 92*
Rai-Choudhury, Prosenjit 1937- *WhoE 93*
Raida, Karl Alexander 1852-1923 *Baker 92*
Raiden, Douglas L. *Law&B 92*
Raiden, Norman H. *Law&B 92*
Raider, Bernard *St&PR 93*
Raider, Donald Gene 1932- *St&PR 93*
Raider, Louis 1913- *WhoSSW 93, WhoWor 93*
Raidi 1938- *WhoAsAP 91*
Raidler, Bill 1865-1905? *BioIn 17*
Raif, Joshua 1946- *St&PR 93*
Raiff, Frederic Kaufman 1927- *St&PR 93*
Raiff, Robert M. *St&PR 93*
Raifsnider, Barbara *ScF&FL 92*
Raihall, Denis T. 1941- *WhoIns 93*
Raiken, Esther Cagen 1907- *WhoAmW 93*
Raikes, Charles F.G. *Law&B 92*
Raikes, Charles Fitzgerald 1930- *St&PR 93, WhoAm 92*
Raikher, Yuri L. 1948- *WhoWor 93*
Raikos, George K. 1934- *St&PR 93*
Raikov, George Dimitrov 1954- *WhoWor 93*
Raikov, Zahary Dimitrov 1936- *WhoWor 93*
Raila, Doug 1952- *St&PR 93*
Railey Bin Haji Jeffrey, Railey Bin Jeffrey 1945- *WhoAsAP 91*
Railkar, Sudhir Balkrishna 1956- *WhoE 93*
Railo, Eino *ScF&FL 92*
Railsback, Brian Evan 1959- *WhoSSW 93*
Railsback, David Phillips 1950- *WhoE 93*
Railsback, Sherrie L. 1942- *WhoAmW 93*
Railton, Jeremy *NewYTBS 92 [port]*
Railton, William Scott 1935- *WhoAm 92, WhoWor 93*
Raimann, Rudolf 1861-1913 *Baker 92*
Raimbault, Georges 1945- *WhoScE 91-2*
Raimbault, Ginette 1924- *WhoScE 91-2*
Raimi, Burton Louis 1938- *WhoAm 92*
Raimi, Sam *MiSFD 9*
Raimi, Sam 1959- *ConTFT 10*
Raimi, Samuel M. 1960- *BioIn 17*
Raimond, Jean *WhoScE 91-2*
Raimondi, Albert Anthony 1925- *WhoAm 92*
Raimondi, Gianni 1923- *Baker 92*
Raimondi, Ignazio c. 1735-1813 *Baker 92*
Raimondi, Peter John, III 1955- *WhoE 93*
Raimondi, Pietro 1786-1853 *Baker 92*
Raimondi, Ruggero 1941- *Baker 92, OxDcOp, WhoAm 92, WhoWor 93*
Raimu 1883-1946 *IntDcF 2-3 [port]*
Raimund, Ferdinand 1790-1836 *BioIn 17, OxDcOp*
Raimy, Victor 1913-1987 *BioIn 17*
Rain, Cheryl Ann 1950- *WhoAmW 93*
Rain, Maurice O. 1913- *St&PR 93*
Rain, Robert Louis 1933- *WhoAm 92*
Rain, Talbot 1920- *St&PR 93*
Rainard, Robert Lyn 1950- *WhoSSW 93*
Rainbolt, H.E. 1929- *St&PR 93*
Rainbolt, Hal E. *Law&B 92*
Rainbow, Thomas 1948- *WhoWrEP 92*
Raine, Kathleen 1908- *BioIn 17*
Raine, Stuart Alan *Law&B 92*
Rainear, Dennis H. *Law&B 92*
Rainelli, P. *WhoScE 91-2*

Rainer, Arnulf 1929- *BioIn 17*
Rainer, James W., Jr. 1943- *WhoSSW 93*
Rainer, John David 1921- *WhoAm 92*
Rainer, Luise 1910- *IntDcF 2-3 [port]*
Rainer, Rex Kelly 1924- *WhoAm 92*
Rainer, William Gerald 1927- *WhoAm 92*
Raines, Boyd W. 1950- *St&PR 93*
Raines, Charles A. 1927- *ScF&FL 92*
Raines, Edwin G. 1945- *St&PR 93*
Raines, Ellen *BioIn 17*
Raines, Franklin Delano 1949- *WhoAm 92*
Raines, Howell *BioIn 17*
Raines, Howell Hiram 1943- *WhoAm 92*
Raines, Irene Freeze 1924- *WhoSSW 93, WhoWor 93*
Raines, Jean Lee 1949- *WhoAmW 93*
Raines, Jeff 1943- *WhoAm 92, WhoSSW 93, WhoWor 93*
Raines, Jeffrey Hunt *Law&B 92*
Raines, Jo-Ann Ryan 1948- *WhoAmW 93*
Raines, John D. 1947- *St&PR 93*
Raines, Kathleen Jane 1946- *WhoWrEP 92*
Raines, Mary Elizabeth *Law&B 92*
Raines, Mary Elizabeth 1951- *WhoAm 92*
Raines, O.L., Jr. 1941- *St&PR 93*
Raines, Patricia Anne 1938- *WhoAmW 93*
Raines, Rosser R. 1938- *St&PR 93*
Raines, Stephen *Law&B 92*
Raines, Stephen 1938- *St&PR 93*
Raines, Stephen Samuel 1945- *WhoSSW 93*
Raines, Theron 1925- *ScF&FL 92*
Raines, Theron Wade 1925- *WhoE 93*
Raines, Tim 1959- *WhoAm 92*
Raines, Tim D. 1950- *WhoEmL 93, WhoSSW 93*
Raines, Timothy 1959- *BiDAMSp 1989*
Raines, William Thomas, Jr. 1960- *WhoSSW 93*
Rainess, Errol Jonathan 1947- *St&PR 93*
Rainey, Christine Rose 1952- *WhoAmW 93*
Rainey, Clark O. 1942- *St&PR 93*
Rainey, Claude Gladwin 1923- *WhoAm 92*
Rainey, Craig L. *Law&B 92*
Rainey, Froelich G. d1992 *NewYTBS 92*
Rainey, Gail Bivins 1950- *WhoSSW 93*
Rainey, Henry T. 1860-1934 *PolPar*
Rainey, Homer P. 1896-1985 *EncAACR*
Rainey, James A. 1929- *WhoAm 92, WhoSSW 93*
Rainey, Jean Osgood 1925- *WhoAm 92*
Rainey, John David 1945- *WhoAm 92, WhoSSW 93*
Rainey, Joseph Hayne 1832-1887 *BioIn 17*
Rainey, Julian D. 1889-1961 *EncAACR*
Rainey, Kenneth Tyler 1936- *WhoSSW 93*
Rainey, "Ma" 1886-1939 *Baker 92, BioIn 17*
Rainey, Meredith *BioIn 17*
Rainey, Rich *ScF&FL 92*
Rainey, Robert Edward 1943- *WhoSSW 93*
Rainey, Russ Wayne 1954- *WhoSSW 93*
Rainey, Sylvia L. *Law&B 92*
Rainey, Wayne *BioIn 17*
Rainey, William Joel *Law&B 92*
Rainey, William Joel 1946- *St&PR 93, WhoAm 92*
Rainford, B.D. *WhoScE 91-1*
Rainford, Roderick George 1940- *WhoWor 93*
Rainger, Charles Willam 1933- *St&PR 93*
Rainger, Ralph 1901-1942 *Baker 92*
Rainier, III 1923- *WhoWor 93*
Rainier, Priaulx 1903-1986 *Baker 92, BioIn 17*
Rainier, Robert Paul 1940- *WhoAm 92*
Rainieri, Riccardo 1960- *St&PR 93*
Raininko, Kyosti Kalevi 1934- *WhoScE 91-4*
Raininko, Sirkka 1940- *WhoScE 91-4*
Rainis, Eugene Charles 1940- *St&PR 93, WhoAm 92*
Rainone, Donald J. 1943- *St&PR 93*
Rainone, Michael Carmine 1918- *WhoE 93*
Rainone, Robert E. 1934- *St&PR 93*
Rains, Albert McKinley 1902-1991 *BioIn 17*
Rains, Catherine Burke 1959- *WhoAmW 93*
Rains, Claude 1889-1967 *BioIn 17, IntDcF 2-3*
Rains, Gloria Cann 1928- *WhoSSW 93*
Rains, Harry H. 1909- *St&PR 93*
Rains, Harry Hano 1909- *WhoAm 92*
Rains, Jack Morris 1937- *WhoAm 92, WhoSSW 93*
Rains, Jennifer Alyne 1960- *WhoAmW 93*
Rains, Leon 1870-1954 *Baker 92*
Rains, Mary Jo 1935- *WhoSSW 93*
Rains, Merritt Neal 1943- *WhoAm 92*
Rains, Muriel Barnes 1916- *WhoAmW 93*
Rains, Rob 1956- *ConAu 138*
Rains, Stephen A. *Law&B 92*
Rainsford, B.C. 1951- *St&PR 93*
Rainsford, George Nichols 1928- *WhoAm 92*
Rainson, Ronald L. 1940- *St&PR 93*
Raintree, Lee *ConAu 136, -37NR*
Rainville, Dewey 1923- *St&PR 93*
Rainville, Douglas L. 1952- *St&PR 93*
Rainville, William Anthony 1942- *St&PR 93*
Rainwater, Avie James, III 1955- *WhoSSW 93*
Rainwater, Crawford *St&PR 93*
Rainwater, Deanna Marie 1964- *WhoAmW 93*
Rainwater, Gregg *BioIn 17*
Rainwater, John L. *St&PR 93*
Rainwater, Mary Catherine 1953- *WhoAmW 93, WhoSSW 93*
Rainwater, Paul Edward 1953- *WhoSSW 93*
Rainwater, R. Steven 1962- *WhoSSW 93*
Rainwater, Richard E. *BioIn 17*
Raiola, Anthony J. *Law&B 92*
Raisa, Rosa 1893-1963 *Baker 92, IntDcOp [port], OxDcOp*
Raisanen, Seppo Olavi 1922- *WhoWor 93*
Raisbeck, Gordon 1925- *WhoAm 92*
Raisbeck, James David 1936- *WhoWor 93*
Raiselis, Richard 1951- *WhoE 93*
Raiser, C. Victor d1992 *NewYTBS 92*
Raiser, C. Victor, II 1940- *St&PR 93*
Raiser, Lane *BioIn 17*
Raisian, John 1949- *WhoAm 92*
Raisig, Paul Jones, Jr. 1932- *WhoAm 92*
Raisler, Herbert A. 1916- *St&PR 93*
Raisler, Kenneth Mark 1951- *WhoAm 92*
Raisler, Robert K. 1904- *St&PR 93*
Raisman, Geoffrey *WhoScE 91-1*
Raisner, Joseph Craig 1952- *WhoE 93*
Raison, Andre 1650?-1719 *Baker 92*
Raisor, Gary *ScF&FL 92*
Rais Yatim, Dato' 1942- *WhoAsAP 91*
Raisz, Ivan 1943- *WhoScE 91-4*
Raisz, Lawrence Gideon 1925- *WhoE 93*
Rait, S.R. 1947- *St&PR 93*
Raitala, Jouko Tapani 1949- *WhoScE 91-4*
Raiten, Daniel Jay 1951- *WhoE 93*
Raiteri, Maurizio 1935- *WhoScE 91-3*
Raith, Francis J. 1932- *St&PR 93*
Raithby, Paul Robert *WhoScE 91-1*
Raithel, Michael L. 1947- *St&PR 93*
Raiti, Lisa Maria 1956- *St&PR 93*
Raiti, Robert Joseph 1950- *St&PR 93*
Raitio, Pentti 1930- *Baker 92*
Raitio, Vaino (Eerikki) 1891-1945 *Baker 92*
Raitt, Bonnie *BioIn 17*
Raitt, Bonnie 1949- *Baker 92*
Raitt, Bonnie Lynn 1949- *WhoAm 92, WhoAmW 93*
Raitt, Jill 1931- *WhoAmW 93*
Raitt, John (Emmet) 1917- *Baker 92*
Raitz, Glenn Norman 1931- *St&PR 93*
Raitzin, Misha 1930-1990 *BioIn 17*
Raitzin, Shirley 1924- *St&PR 93*
Raives, Ann Leslie 1956- *St&PR 93*
Raizes, Sheldon F. *Law&B 92*
Raj, Bhim 1943- *WhoAsAP 91*
Rajadurai, Pathmanathan 1953- *WhoWor 93*
Rajagopal, Ranganatha 1930- *WhoScE 91-2*
Rajagopalachariar, Chakravarti 1878-1972 *DcTwHis*
Rajakovics, Gundolf Emil 1937- *WhoWor 93*
Rajala, Paavo Olavi 1932- *WhoScE 91-4*
Rajalingam, K. 1947- *St&PR 93*
Rajan, Periasamy Karivaratha 1942- *WhoSSW 93*
Rajaneesh, Acharya 1931-1990 *BioIn 17*
Rajangam, N. 1920- *WhoAsAP 91*
Rajani, Guli R. 1942- *WhoAm 92*
Rajani, Prem R. 1949- *St&PR 93, WhoAm 92*
Rajaram, Sanjaya 1943- *WhoAm 92*
Raja Rao *BioIn 17*
Rajaratnam, Daniel 1955- *WhoSSW 93*
Rajasekariah, G'Hall Rangappa 1943- *WhoWor 93*
Rajbhandary, Siba Bhakta 1939- *WhoUN 92*
Rajec, Andrew M. *Law&B 92*
Rajendran, V.K. Swamy 1958- *WhoWor 93*
Rajeshwaran, V. 1950- *WhoAsAP 91*
Rajewsky, Manfred Fedor 1934- *WhoWor 93*
Rajicic, Stanojlo 1910- *Baker 92*
Rajk, Laszlo 1909-1949 *DcTwHis*
Rajki, Walter Albert 1925- *WhoAm 92*
Rajki-Siklosi, Erzsebet 1946- *WhoScE 91-4*
Rajkovic, Dragoljub Stevan 1965- *WhoE 93*
Rajlich, Vaclav Thomas 1939- *WhoWor 93*
Rajna, Thomas 1928- *Baker 92*
Rajneesh, Bhagwan Shree 1931-1990 *BioIn 17*
Rajotte, Jean *Law&B 92, St&PR 93*
Rajpurohit, David Singh 1947- *WhoWor 93*
Rajs, Jovan 1933- *WhoScE 91-4*
Rajter, Ludovit 1906- *Baker 92*
Raju, Vijaya Kumar 1936- *WhoAsAP 91*
Rajzman, Julij 1903- *DrEEuF*
Rak, Andrew George *Law&B 92*
Rak, Bronislaw 1933- *WhoScE 91-4*
Rak, Hubert 1931- *WhoScE 91-4*
Rak, William *St&PR 93*
Rakay, William R. 1955- *WhoAm 92*
Rake, Heinrich 1936- *WhoScE 91-3*
Rakel, Robert Edwin 1932- *WhoAm 92*
Raker, Colleen M. *Law&B 92*
Raker, Gilbert D. *St&PR 93*
Rakers, Harry B. 1946- *St&PR 93*
Rakes, Ganas Kaye 1938- *WhoAm 92*
Rakestraw, Gregory Allen 1949- *WhoEmL 93*
Rakestraw, Warren Vincent 1940- *WhoAm 92*
Rakhmaninov, Sergey 1873-1943 *OxDcOp*
Rakic, Pasko 1933- *WhoAm 92*
Rakich, Robert T. 1937- *WhoAm 92*
Rakim c. 1968- *See* Eric B. c. 1965- & Rakim c. 1968- *ConMus 9*
Rakita, Louis 1922- *WhoAm 92*
Raknem, Ingvald 1910- *ScF&FL 92*
Rakoczy, Richard E. *Law&B 92*
Rakoff, Alvin 1937- *MiSFD 9*
Rakoff, Jed Saul 1943- *WhoAm 92*
Rakoff, Vivian Morris 1928- *WhoAm 92*
Rakonjac, Vojislav 1935-1969 *DrEEuF*
Rakos, Maria Eva *Law&B 92*
Rakos, Matej 1922- *WhoScE 91-4*
Rakosi, Carl 1903- *BioIn 17, WhoWrEP 92*
Rakosi, Matyas 1892-1971 *ColdWar 2 [port], DcTwHis*
Rakouskas, Michael Gerard 1944- *WhoSSW 93*
Rakov, Barbara Streem 1946- *WhoAmW 93*
Rakov, Nikolai 1908- *Baker 92*
Rakov, Robert Willis 1926- *WhoE 93*
Rakow, Thomas Stewart 1942- *St&PR 93*
Rakowicz, Stanislaw 1935- *WhoWor 93*
Rakowicz-Szulczynska, Ewa M. 1951- *WhoScE 91-4*
Rakowska, Elena 1878-1964 *See* Serafin, Tullio 1878-1968 *OxDcOp*
Rakowska, Maria 1923- *WhoScE 91-4*
Rakowski, Barbara Ann 1948- *WhoAmW 93*
Rakowski, Gustaw 1929- *WhoScE 91-4*
Rakowski, Marek 1956- *WhoSSW 93*
Rakowski, Mieczyslaw F. 1926- *BioIn 17*
Rakowski, Sharon S. 1948- *St&PR 93*
Rakowsky, Ihor G. *Law&B 92*
Rakshit, Ashok Kumar 1930- *WhoWor 93*
Raksin, David 1912- *Baker 92*
Rakusa-Suszczewski, Stanislaw 1938- *WhoScE 91-4*
Ralegh, Walter 1552?-1618 *BioIn 17*
Raleigh, Alfred 1926- *St&PR 93*
Raleigh, Cecil Baring 1934- *WhoAm 92*
Raleigh, Thomas L. d1990 *BioIn 17*
Raleigh, Walter 1552?-1618 *BioIn 17, Expl 93 [port]*
Rales, Steven M. *St&PR 93*
Rales, Steven M. 1951- *WhoE 93*
Raley, Gary Lynn 1946- *WhoSSW 93*
Raley, Harold Cecil 1934- *WhoSSW 93*
Raley, James Douglas 1956- *WhoSSW 93*
Raley, James Morris 1950- *St&PR 93*
Raley, Thomas P. 1903- *St&PR 93*
Ralf, Oscar 1881-1964 *OxDcOp*
Ralf, Oscar (Georg) 1881-1964 *Baker 92*
Ralf, Richard 1897-1977 *Baker 92*
Ralf, Torsten 1901-1954 *OxDcOp*
Ralf, Torsten (Ivar) 1901-1954 *Baker 92*
Rall, David Platt 1926- *WhoAm 92, WhoE 93*
Rall, Johann Gottlieb c. 1720-1776 *HarEnMi*
Rall, Joseph Edward 1920- *WhoAm 92*
Rall, Wilfrid 1922- *WhoE 93*
Ralles *OxDcByz*
Rallis, Chris A. *Law&B 92*
Rallo, Francesco *WhoScE 91-3*
Ralls, Julius Garrett, Jr. 1952- *WhoEmL 93, WhoSSW 93*
Ralls, Katherine 1939- *WhoAm 92*
Ralph, A. Laurence *Law&B 92*
Ralph, Andrew Quentin 1946- *WhoE 93*
Ralph, Brian *WhoScE 91-1*
Ralph, Brian 1939- *WhoWor 93*
Ralph, Charles Bradshaw 1944- *St&PR 93*
Ralph, Debra Eckstine 1958- *WhoAmW 93*
Ralph, E.J. 1940- *St&PR 93*
Ralph, Gerald R. *Law&B 92*
Ralph, Gwendolyn Mary *Law&B 92*
Ralph, Jan C. 1933- *WhoUN 92*
Ralph, Jean Dolores 1923- *WhoAmW 93*
Ralph, Julian 1853-1903 *JrnUS*
Ralph, M.C. *WhoScE 91-1*
Ralph, Robert A. *BioIn 17*
Ralph, Ronald J. 1937- *St&PR 93*
Ralph, Shea 1960- *St&PR 93*
Ralph, Sherri R. *Law&B 92*
Ralph, Sheryl Lee *BioIn 17*
Ralph, Sidney 1916- *St&PR 93*
Ralph, Stevan Bradley Graeme 1955- *WhoE 93*
Ralph, Thomas Gordon, Jr. 1933- *St&PR 93*
Ralphs, George L. *Law&B 92*
Ralston, Anthony 1930- *WhoAm 92*
Ralston, Clarice McDuffie 1932- *WhoAmW 93*
Ralston, David Cornell 1930- *WhoSSW 93*
Ralston, David Michael 1955- *WhoAm 92*
Ralston, Esther 1902- *SweetSg B [port]*
Ralston, Gilbert Alexander 1912- *WhoWor 93*
Ralston, Henry James, III 1935- *WhoAm 92*
Ralston, Hugh James 1958- *WhoEmL 93*
Ralston, James A. *Law&B 92*
Ralston, James A. 1946- *St&PR 93*
Ralston, James Allen 1946- *WhoAm 92*
Ralston, Joanne Smoot 1939- *WhoAm 92*
Ralston, John A. 1942- *St&PR 93*
Ralston, Ken *WhoAm 92*
Ralston, Lloyd Stanley 1919- *WhoAm 92*
Ralston, Lucy Virginia Gordon 1926- *WhoAmW 93*
Ralston, Lynda Claire 1948- *WhoAmW 93*
Ralston, Richard Dennis 1942- *BiDAMSp 1989*
Ralston, Steven Philip 1954- *WhoWor 93*
Ralston, Thomas *WhoScE 91-1*
Ralston, Vera Hruba *SweetSg D [port]*
Ralstor, Adam *WhoWrEP 92*
Ram, Buck 1907-1991 *BioIn 17*
Ram, Chitta Venkata 1948- *WhoSSW 93*
Ram, Hari fl. 19th cent.- *Expl 93*
Ram, Samuel 1907-1991 *BioIn 17*
Rama, I d1809 *HarEnMi*
Rama, Carlos M. 1921- *WhoWor 93*
Rama, John Carl 1958- *WhoSSW 93*
Ramacciotti, Aldo 1926- *WhoScE 91-3*
Ramachandran, Arcot 1923- *WhoUN 92*
Ramachandran, C.P. 1936- *WhoUN 92*
Ramachandran, Gopalasamudram Narayana 1922- *WhoWor 93*
Ramachandran, Krishnan 1946- *WhoE 93*
Ramachandran, Venkatanarayana Deekshit 1934- *WhoAm 92*
Ramadas, Shree 1947- *St&PR 93*
Ramade, Francois A.J. 1934- *WhoScE 91-2*
Ramadier, Paul 1888-1961 *BioIn 17*
Ramaekers, F.C.S. 1952- *WhoScE 91-3*
Ramaekers, J. 1943- *WhoScE 91-2*
Ramaekers, Jean 1943- *WhoWor 93*
Ramaema, Elias Phisoana 1933- *WhoWor 93*
Ramaema, Elias Phitsoane 1933- *WhoAfr*
Ramage, Jean Carol 1939- *WhoAmW 93*
Ramage, John c. 1748-1802 *BioIn 17*
Ramage, Lawson P. 1909-1990 *BioIn 17*
Ramage, Martis Donald, Jr. 1957- *WhoSSW 93*
Ramage, Robert *WhoScE 91-1*
Ramage, Robert Thomas 1928- *WhoAm 92*
Ramakavelo, Desire Philippe 1939- *WhoWor 93*
Ramakavelo, Maurice Philippe 1935- *WhoUN 92*
Ramaker, Dudley Don 1929- *St&PR 93*
Ramaker, M. Jolene 1948- *WhoAmW 93*
Ramakrishna 1836-1886 *BioIn 17*
Ramakrishna, Kilaparti 1955- *WhoE 93*
Ramakrishnan, Venkataswamy 1929- *WhoAm 92*
Ramakrishna Rao, Adapa 1927- *ScF&FL 92*
Ramal, Bill B. 1937- *WhoSSW 93*
Ramal, Walter *ConAu 137, MajAI*
Ramaley, Judith Aitken 1941- *WhoAm 92, WhoAmW 93*
Ramalho, Americo Costa 1921- *WhoWor 93*
Ramalho Ribeiro, Joao M.C. 1946- *WhoScE 91-3*
Rama Montaldo, Manuel D. *WhoUN 92*
Ramamoorthy, C. V. *WhoAm 92*
Ramamurthy, K. 1939- *WhoAsAP 91*
Ramamurthy, Subramanian 1948- *WhoEmL 93, WhoWor 93*
Ramamurthy, Thindivanam K. 1934- *WhoAsAP 91*
Ramamurti, Ravi 1952- *WhoE 93*
Raman, C.S. 1940- *St&PR 93*
Raman, Chandrasekhara Venkata 1888-1970 *BioIn 17*
Raman, Hafeez 1937- *St&PR 93*
Raman, Musarapakkam Samaram 1937- *WhoUN 92*

Ramana, Maharshi 1879-1950 *BioIn 17*
Ramanarayanan, Madhava Prabhu 1945- *WhoAm 92, WhoE 93*
Ramanathan, Kavasseri Vaidianatha 1932- *WhoAm 92*
Ramanathan, Muthiah 1936- *St&PR 93*
Ramanathan, V. 1933- *WhoAsAP 91*
Ramanayya, Iyyanki Venkata 1890-1979 *BioIn 17*
Ramann, Lina 1833-1912 *Baker 92*
Ramanujan, A. K. 1929- *WhoAm 92*
Ramanujan Aiyangar, Srinivasa 1887-1920 *BioIn 17*
Ramaphosa, Cyril 1952- *ConBlB 3 [port]*
Ramaprasad, Kackadasam Raghavachar 1938- *WhoE 93*
Ramassamy, Albert 1923- *WhoAsAP 91*
Ramaswamy, H.N. 1937- *WhoSSW 93*
Ramat, Charles S. 1951- *St&PR 93*
Ramat, Charles Samuel 1951- *WhoAm 92*
Ramat, Silvio 1939- *DcLB 128*
Ramati, Alexander *MiSFD 9*
Rama T'ibodi, II d1529 *HarEnMi*
Ram Awadh Prasad 1938- *WhoAsAP 91*
Ramazani, Jahan 1960- *WhoSSW 93*
Rambach, Francoise *BioIn 17*
Rambach, Harvey *BioIn 17*
Rambach, Peggy Diane 1958- *WhoWrEP 92*
Rambaldi, Victor J. *MiSFD 9*
Rambam, Cyvia 1888-1982 *PolBiDi*
Rambeau, Catharine *BioIn 17*
Ramberg, Christina 1946- *WhoAm 92*
Ramberg, Max 1936- *St&PR 93*
Ramberg, Patricia Lynn 1951- *WhoAmW 93*
Rambert, Charles Jean Julien 1924- *WhoWor 93*
Rambert, Marie 1888-1982 *PolBiDi*
Rambin, William R., Jr. 1938- *WhoSSW 93*
Rambis, Kurt *BioIn 17*
Rambo, Dee M. 1956- *St&PR 93*
Rambo, George Curtis 1928- *St&PR 93*
Rambo, Jean W. 1930- *St&PR 93*
Rambo, John William 1932- *St&PR 93*
Rambo, Lewis Mitchell 1937- *St&PR 93*
Rambo, Sylvia H. 1936- *WhoAm 92, WhoAmW 93, WhoE 93*
Rambousek, Joseph 1845-1901 *Baker 92*
Rambova, Natacha 1896?-1966 *BioIn 17*
Rambow, Gunter 1938- *BioIn 17*
Rambusch, Viggo Bech 1931- *St&PR 93*
Rambusch, Viggo F.E. 1900- *St&PR 93*
Ramcharan, Bertrand Gangapersaud 1943- *WhoUN 92*
Ram Dhan 1921- *WhoAsAP 91*
Ramdin, R.H. 1939- *St&PR 93*
Rameau, Guy Michel 1940- *WhoWor 93*
Rameau, Jean-Jacques 1934- *WhoScE 91-2*
Rameau, Jean-Philippe 1683?-1764 *Baker 92, IntDcOp [port], OxDcOp*
Ramee, Thomas Mark *Law&B 92*
Ramel, Baron Stig *WhoScE 91-4*
Ramel, Benita Saga 1928- *WhoWor 93*
Ramel, Stig 1927- *WhoWor 93*
Ramenofsky, Max Lantin 1939- *WhoE 93*
Ramer, Bruce 1933- *WhoAm 92*
Ramer, Claude O., II *Law&B 92*
Ramer, Donna Klein 1949- *WhoAmW 93*
Ramer, Hal Reed 1923- *WhoSSW 93*
Ramer, James LeRoy 1935- *WhoAm 92, WhoWor 93*
Ramer, John Robert 1934- *St&PR 93*
Ramer, Lawrence J. 1928- *St&PR 93*
Ramer, Paul 1942- *BioIn 17*
Ramer, Richard C. 1942- *WhoE 93*
Rameses, II, King of Egypt *BioIn 17*
Ramesh, Elaine Marie 1962- *WhoAmW 93*
Ramette, Richard Wales 1927- *WhoAm 92*
Ramey, Ann Marie 1942- *WhoAmW 93*
Ramey, Billy Joe 1926- *St&PR 93*
Ramey, Carl Robert 1941- *WhoE 93*
Ramey, Cecil Edward, Jr. 1923- *WhoAm 92, WhoSSW 93*
Ramey, Darol K. 1930- *St&PR 93*
Ramey, Denny L. 1947- *WhoAm 92*
Ramey, Diane Elfriede 1949- *WhoWrEP 92*
Ramey, Henry Jackson, Jr. 1925- *WhoAm 92*
Ramey, Joseph Frederick 1925- *WhoAm 92*
Ramey, Melvin Richard 1938- *WhoAm 92*
Ramey, Phillip 1939- *Baker 92*
Ramey, Samuel *BioIn 17*
Ramey, Samuel 1942- *OxDcOp*
Ramey, Samuel E. 1942- *IntDcOp*
Ramey, Samuel (Edward) 1942- *Baker 92, WhoAm 92*
Ramey, Sharon Landesman 1947- *WhoSSW 93*
Ramiah, Kirupananthan 1953- *WhoWor 93*
Ramie, Florence *ScF&FL 92*
Ramig, Alexander, Jr. 1941- *WhoAm 92*
Ramin, Bruce P. *Law&B 92*
Ramin, Gunther (Werner Hans) 1898-1956 *Baker 92*
Ramin, Kurt 1942- *WhoE 93*
Ramirez, Alexis 1937- *WhoWor 93*
Ramirez, Alice *ScF&FL 92*
Ramirez, Amanda-Jane 1958- *WhoWor 93*
Ramirez, Ana Milagros 1946- *WhoSSW 93*
Ramirez, Arthur Christopher 1937- *WhoE 93*
Ramirez, Blandina Cardenas 1944- *NotHsAW 93 [port]*
Ramirez, Domingo Victor 1932- *WhoAm 92*
Ramirez, Enrique Rene 1930- *WhoSSW 93*
Ramirez, Erick *DcCPCAm*
Ramirez, Fausto 1923- *HispAmA*
Ramirez, Ignacio 1818-1879 *DcMexL*
Ramirez, Janice L. 1947- *WhoAmW 93, WhoEmL 93*
Ramirez, Joan E. 1943- *WhoWrEP 92*
Ramirez, Joe *Law&B 92*
Ramirez, Jose Agustin *DcMexL*
Ramirez, Jose Ernesto 1954- *WhoWor 93*
Ramirez, Jose Maria 1834-1892 *DcMexL*
Ramirez, Jose T. 1934- *WhoAsAP 91*
Ramirez, Luis Antonio 1923- *Baker 92*
Ramirez, Maria Concepcion *WhoAmW 93*
Ramirez, Maria Fiorini 1948- *WhoAm 92*
Ramirez, Mario E. 1926- *HispAmA [port]*
Ramirez, Mario Efrain 1926- *WhoAm 92*
Ramirez, Medardo Figueroa *ScF&FL 92*
Ramirez, Paul Michael 1951- *WhoE 93*
Ramirez, Paul Robert 1950- *WhoE 93*
Ramirez, Ralph Henry 1949- *WhoWor 93*
Ramirez, Raul Anthony 1944- *HispAmA, WhoAm 92*
Ramirez, Raymond R. *Law&B 92*
Ramirez, Sara Estela 1881-1910 *NotHsAW 93*
Ramirez, Sergio 1942- *SpAmA*
Ramirez, Susan Elizabeth 1946- *NotHsAW 93, WhoAmW 93*
Ramirez, Tina *NotHsAW 93*
Ramirez, William Earl 1951- *WhoEmL 93*
Ramirez Bravo, Maria Elena 1957- *WhoWor 93*
Ramirez Cabanas, Joaquin 1886-1945 *DcMexL*
Ramirez de Arellano, Diana 1919- *NotHsAW 93*
Ramirez de Asbaje, Juana *DcMexL*
Ramirez-De la O, Rogelio 1948- *WhoWor 93*
Ramirez de la Piscina, Julian 1956- *WhoWor 93*
Ramirez Estrada, Alsino 1930- *SpAmA*
Ramirez-Garcia, Eduardo Agustin 1950- *WhoWor 93*
Ramirez Jaramillo, Arcesio 1927- *WhoWor 93*
Ramirez-Rivera, Jose 1929- *WhoAm 92*
Ramiro, Hilarion J., Jr. 1938- *WhoAsAP 91*
Ramis, Harold 1944- *ConTFT 10, MiSFD 9*
Ramis, Harold Allen 1944- *WhoAm 92*
Ramist, Roselyn B. 1939- *St&PR 93*
Ramistella, Robert 1945- *St&PR 93*
Ramiz, Alia 1925- *WhoWor 93*
Ramke, Bin 1947- *DcLB 120 [port]*
Ramler, Karl Wilhelm 1725-1798 *BioIn 17*
Ramm, Arthur Juergen 1949- *WhoWor 93*
Ramm, Kent Arthur 1935- *St&PR 93*
Ramm, Peter Henry *Law&B 92*
Ramm, Richard W. 1949- *St&PR 93, WhoAm 92*
Ramm, Vladimir Grigorievich 1937- *WhoWor 93*
Rammel, John Marshall 1942- *St&PR 93*
Rammell, Phelon Scott *Law&B 92*
Rammelt, Charles G. 1935- *St&PR 93*
Rammerstorfer, Franz G. 1948- *WhoScE 91-4*
Ram-Mohan, L. Ramdas 1944- *WhoE 93*
Ramo, Simon 1913- *WhoAm 92, WhoWor 93*
Ramo, Virginia M. Smith *WhoAmW 93, WhoWor 93*
Ramoi, Gabriel *WhoAsAP 91*
Ramond, Charles Knight, II 1930- *WhoAm 92*
Ramone, C.J. 1965- *See* Ramones, The *ConMus 9*
Ramone, Dee Dee 1952- *See* Ramones, The *ConMus 9*
Ramone, Joey 1952- *See* Ramones, The *ConMus 9*
Ramone, Johnny 1948- *See* Ramones, The *ConMus 9*
Ramone, Marky *See* Ramones, The *ConMus 9*
Ramone, Ritchie *See* Ramones, The *ConMus 9*
Ramone, Tommy *See* Ramones, The *ConMus 9*
Ramones, The *ConMus 9 [port]*
Ramonette, Richard *Law&B 92*
Ramon y Cajal, Santiago 1852-1934 *BioIn 17*
Ramon y Rivera, Luis Felipe 1913- *Baker 92*
Ramos, Alfredo *BioIn 17*
Ramos, Andres C. 1961- *St&PR 93*
Ramos, Andres R. 1914- *St&PR 93*
Ramos, Armando 1948- *HispAmA*
Ramos, Arthur 1903-1949 *IntDcAn*
Ramos, Carlos R. *Law&B 92*
Ramos, Celina *BioIn 17*
Ramos, Debi A. *Law&B 92*
Ramos, Eduardo 1952- *WhoWor 93*
Ramos, Elba *BioIn 17*
Ramos, Fabio D. 1940- *St&PR 93*
Ramos, Fidel V. *BioIn 17*
Ramos, Fidel V. 1928- *WhoAsAP 91*
Ramos, Fidel V. Eddie 1928- *WhoWor 93*
Ramos, Florence Hernandez *NotHsAW 93*
Ramos, Harold Smith 1928- *WhoSSW 93*
Ramos, Harvey Lee 1938- *St&PR 93*
Ramos, Hazel Balatero 1936- *WhoAmW 93, WhoSSW 93, WhoWor 93*
Ramos, J. Mario 1956- *WhoAm 92, WhoSSW 93*
Ramos, Jose Antonio *BioIn 17*
Ramos, Jose Maria Castellano 1945- *WhoWor 93*
Ramos, Joseph R(afael) 1938- *ConAu 139*
Ramos, Juan Antonio 1948- *SpAmA*
Ramos, Juan Ignacio 1953- *WhoE 93*
Ramos, Kleyde Mendes Lopes 1939- *WhoWor 93*
Ramos, Linda Marie 1961- *WhoWor 93*
Ramos, Lolita 1945- *WhoAmW 93*
Ramos, Manuel M. 1926- *WhoWor 93*
Ramos, Melvin John 1935- *WhoAm 92*
Ramos, Raymundo 1934- *DcMexL*
Ramos Alegre, Domingo 1919- *WhoScE 91-3*
Ramos de Pareia, Bartolome c. 1440-c. 1491 *Baker 92*
Ramos Soto, Oswaldo *DcCPCAm*
Ramous, Mario 1924- *DcLB 128*
Ramovs, Primoz 1921- *Baker 92*
Ramp, Marjorie Jean Sumerwell 1924- *WhoAmW 93*
Rampa, T. Lobsang *BioIn 17, ScF&FL 92*
Rampacek, Charles M. 1943- *WhoAm 92*
Rampal, Jean-Pierre (Louis) 1922- *Baker 92, WhoAm 92, WhoWor 93*
Rampal, Manohar Lal 1944- *WhoWor 93*
Ramparany, Fano 1959- *WhoWor 93*
Rampe, John F. 1908- *St&PR 93*
Rampen, Leonardus Eduard 1928- *WhoE 93*
Rampersad, Arnold *BioIn 17*
Rampersad, Peggy A. Snellings 1933- *WhoAmW 93*
Rampey, Denver Lee *Law&B 92*
Rampino, Louis J. 1952- *St&PR 93*
Rampley, Anthony M. 1947- *St&PR 93*
Rampling, Anne *BioIn 17*
Rampulla, Leonard Michael 1954- *WhoE 93*
Ramqvist, Lars Henry 1938- *WhoWor 93*
Rams, Dieter 1932- *BioIn 17, WhoWor 93*
Ramsahoye, Lyttleton Estil 1930- *WhoWor 93*
Ramsauer, Kirk L. *Law&B 92*
Ramsay, Allan 1685?-1758 *BioIn 17*
Ramsay, Annetta Jean 1956- *WhoAmW 93*
Ramsay, Colin David 1967- *WhoWor 93*
Ramsay, David 1749-1815 *BioIn 17*
Ramsay, David B. 1941- *St&PR 93*
Ramsay, Donald Allan 1922- *WhoAm 92*
Ramsay, Ernest Canaday 1939- *WhoAm 92*
Ramsay, Ethel Davis 1905- *WhoWrEP 92*
Ramsay, George Bowie, Jr. 1913- *St&PR 93*
Ramsay, Gustavus Remak 1937- *WhoAm 92*
Ramsay, Heather *BioIn 17*
Ramsay, Ian Allan 1942- *WhoWor 93*
Ramsay, Jay *ScF&FL 92*
Ramsay, John 1768?-1831 *BioIn 17*
Ramsay, John Erwin 1915- *WhoAm 92*
Ramsay, John Erwin, Jr. 1948- *WhoSSW 93*
Ramsay, John G. 1931- *WhoScE 91-4*
Ramsay, Louis Lafayette, Jr. 1918- *St&PR 93, WhoAm 92, WhoWor 93*
Ramsay, Martha Laurens 1759-1811 *BioIn 17*
Ramsay, Peggy *BioIn 17*
Ramsay, Penelope Joy 1945- *WhoAm 92*
Ramsay, Roland Thomas 1936- *WhoE 93*
Ramsay, Shirley Jeanne Good *WhoAmW 93*
Ramsay, William Charles 1930- *WhoE 93*
Ramsay, William McDowell 1922- *WhoSSW 93*
Ramsay, William Morrill 1955- *WhoE 93*
Ramsay, William Thaddaeus 1928- *WhoSSW 93*
Ramsbottom, John Edmund 1946- *WhoScE 91-1*
Ramsdale, Dan Jerry 1942- *WhoSSW 93*
Ramsdale, David Alan 1950- *WhoWrEP 92*
Ramsdell, Vittz-James 1921- *WhoAm 92*
Ramsden, Anthony Neil 1944- *St&PR 93*
Ramsden, Jeremy Joachim 1955- *WhoWor 93*
Ramsden, Katharine Lee 1958- *WhoE 93*
Ramses, II, King of Egypt *BioIn 17*
Ramseth, Douglas James 1941- *St&PR 93*
Ramseur, F.H., Jr. 1915- *St&PR 93*
Ramsey, Betty Foster 1937- *WhoAmW 93*
Ramsey, Bill 1931- *WhoAm 92*
Ramsey, Bonnie Jeanne 1952- *WhoAmW 93*
Ramsey, Bruce A. *Law&B 92*
Ramsey, Charles Eugene 1923- *WhoAm 92*
Ramsey, Charles Frederic, Jr. 1915- *WhoWrEP 92*
Ramsey, Claude Swanson, Jr. 1925- *WhoAm 92*
Ramsey, Craig R. 1951- *St&PR 93*
Ramsey, Craig Ray 1951- *WhoAm 92*
Ramsey, David Irving 1944- *St&PR 93*
Ramsey, David Lauren 1951- *St&PR 93*
Ramsey, David Selmer 1931- *WhoAm 92*
Ramsey, Dennis John 1966- *WhoSSW 93*
Ramsey, Donald David 1935- *WhoE 93*
Ramsey, Douglas K. 1951- *WhoE 93*
Ramsey, Edwin Price *BioIn 17*
Ramsey, Febbie Lee 1952- *WhoEmL 93*
Ramsey, Forrest Gladstone, Jr. 1930- *St&PR 93, WhoAm 92, WhoSSW 93*
Ramsey, Frances Mae 1925- *WhoAmW 93*
Ramsey, Frank Allen 1929- *WhoAm 92*
Ramsey, Frank B. 1902- *WhoWrEP 92*
Ramsey, Garrard 1920- *BiDAMSp 1989*
Ramsey, George Hamilton 1922- *WhoSSW 93*
Ramsey, Gloria Dawn 1950- *WhoSSW 93*
Ramsey, Greg W. 1922- *St&PR 93*
Ramsey, Gregory Arnold 1948- *WhoE 93*
Ramsey, Harry Edgar, Jr. 1943- *WhoE 93*
Ramsey, Henry, Jr. 1934- *WhoAm 92, WhoE 93*
Ramsey, Inez Linn 1938- *WhoAmW 93, WhoSSW 93, WhoWor 93*
Ramsey, Ira Clayton 1931- *St&PR 93, WhoAm 92, WhoSSW 93*
Ramsey, J. Kevin *Law&B 92*
Ramsey, Jackson Eugene 1938- *WhoSSW 93*
Ramsey, James Elbert, Jr. 1943- *WhoSSW 93*
Ramsey, Jarold W. 1937- *WhoWrEP 92*
Ramsey, Jarold William 1937- *WhoAm 92*
Ramsey, Jerry Dwain 1933- *WhoSSW 93*
Ramsey, Jettie Cecil 1925- *WhoWor 93*
Ramsey, John C. 1936- *St&PR 93*
Ramsey, John Colt 1951- *St&PR 93*
Ramsey, John Hansberry 1941- *WhoAm 92*
Ramsey, Katherine Brown 1946- *WhoAmW 93*
Ramsey, Katherine Coffin 1960- *WhoAmW 93*
Ramsey, Kathleen Sommer 1947- *WhoAmW 93, WhoSSW 93*
Ramsey, Kenneth Clive 1933- *St&PR 93*
Ramsey, Lloyd Brinkley 1918- *WhoAm 92*
Ramsey, Lloyd Hamilton 1921- *WhoAm 92*
Ramsey, Logan 1921- *ConTFT 10*
Ramsey, Lucille Avra 1942- *WhoAmW 93*
Ramsey, Lynn Allison 1944- *WhoE 93*
Ramsey, Margaret *BioIn 17*
Ramsey, Marjorie Elizabeth 1921- *WhoAm 92*
Ramsey, Mary Lou 1947- *WhoE 93*
Ramsey, Michael 1904-1988 *BioIn 17*
Ramsey, Michael Allen 1960- *BiDAMSp 1989*
Ramsey, Michael Kirby 1948- *WhoWrEP 92*
Ramsey, Norman 1915- *WhoAm 92, WhoE 93, WhoWor 93*
Ramsey, Norman Park 1922- *WhoAm 92, WhoE 93*
Ramsey, Patricia Longworth 1949- *WhoAmW 93*
Ramsey, Paul 1913-1988 *BioIn 17*
Ramsey, Paul Willard 1919- *WhoAm 92*
Ramsey, Peggy 1908-1991 *AnObit 1991*
Ramsey, Peter Christie 1942- *WhoAm 92, WhoE 93*
Ramsey, Peter Michael 1943- *St&PR 93*
Ramsey, Priscilla R. 1940- *WhoE 93*
Ramsey, Richard Alec 1949- *St&PR 93*
Ramsey, Richard L. 1947- *St&PR 93*
Ramsey, Robert c. 1595-1644? *Baker 92*
Ramsey, Robert Lee 1929- *WhoAm 92*
Ramsey, Robert Russell, Jr. 1929- *WhoSSW 93*

Ramsey, Robin *BioIn 17*
Ramsey, Roger A. 1938- *St&PR 93*
Ramsey, Sally Ann Seitz 1931- *WhoSSW 93*
Ramsey, Stephen D. 1947- *St&PR 93*
Ramsey, Stephen Douglas *Law&B 92*
Ramsey, Stephen Douglas 1947- *WhoAm 92*
Ramsey, Stephen T. 1949- *St&PR 93*
Ramsey, Terry Lane 1941- *WhoSSW 93*
Ramsey, Thomas H. 1948- *St&PR 93*
Ramsey, Wiley Fredrick 1940- *WhoSSW 93, WhoWor 93*
Ramsey, William Dale, Jr. 1936- *WhoSSW 93, WhoWor 93*
Ramsey, William Edward 1931- *WhoAm 92*
Ramsey, William F. 1951- *St&PR 93*
Ramsey, William P. 1936- *St&PR 93*
Ramsey, William Perry 1936- *WhoAm 92*
Ramsey, William Ray 1926- *WhoAm 92*
Ramseyer, Loretta L. *Law&B 92*
Ramseyer, Paul Edwards 1927- *WhoAm 92*
Ramseyer, Ronald L. 1942- *St&PR 93*
Ramsey-Goldman, Rosalind 1954- *WhoAmW 93*
Ramsier, Paul 1927- *WhoE 93*
Ramsin, Hakan 1945- *WhoWor 93*
Ramsland, Katherine 1953- *ConAu 136, ScF&FL 92*
Ramsour, David L. 1940- *St&PR 93*
Ramsour, James Larry 1936- *WhoSSW 93*
Ramspacher, Anna *AmWomPl*
Ramstack, Richard V. 1919- *St&PR 93*
Ramstad, Jim 1946- *CngDr 91, WhoAm 92*
Ramstad, Polly E. *Law&B 92*
Ramstein, William Louis 1950- *WhoWor 93*
Ramunni, Angelo Ugo 1927- *WhoScE 91-3*
Ramusack, Barbara Nell 1937- *WhoAmW 93*
Ramzy, Ishak d1992 *BioIn 17, NewYTBS 92*
Ran, Antonio *WhoScE 91-3*
Ran, Shulamit 1949- *Baker 92, WhoAm 92, WhoAmW 93*
Rana, J. *WhoCanL 92*
Rana, Kathleen Sehr 1965- *WhoAmW 93*
Rana, Kiranjit S., II 1946- *WhoWrEP 92*
Rana, Prabhakar Shumshere Jung Bahadur 1935- *WhoWor 93*
Rana, Prakriti Shumshere Jung Bakadur 1939- *WhoWor 93*
Rana, Swadesh M. 1939- *WhoUN 92*
Rana, Uttam S. 1934- *WhoUN 92*
Ranachowski, Jerzy Michal 1926- *WhoScE 91-4*
Ranada, Antonio Fernandez 1939- *WhoScE 91-3*
Ranade, Karen *ScF&FL 92*
Ranadive, Prakash K. 1940- *WhoUN 92*
Ranagan, Donald 1957- *St&PR 93*
Ranald, Ralph A. *ScF&FL 92*
Ranald, Ralph Arthur 1930- *WhoE 93*
Ranaldo, Lee c. 1959- *See* Sonic Youth *ConMus 9*
Ranalli, Daniel 1948- *WhoAm 92*
Ranalli, Michael Patrick 1933- *St&PR 93, WhoAm 92*
Ranallo, Edmund G. *Law&B 92*
Ranard, Donald L. 1917-1990 *BioIn 17*
Ranauro, John Nicholas 1945- *WhoE 93*
Ranc, Arthur 1831-1908 *BioIn 17*
Ranc, Georges *WhoScE 91-2*
Rance, Patrick 1918- *ConAu 138*
Rance, Sheila *BioIn 17*
Ranchet, Jean 1941- *WhoScE 91-2*
Ranchod, Bahadra Ghalloo 1944- *WhoWor 93*
Ranck, Christopher John *Law&B 92*
Ranck, James Byrne, Jr. 1930- *WhoE 93*
Ranck, Katherine Quintana 1942- *DcLB 122 [port]*
Ranck, Robert Dale 1934- *WhoE 93*
Ranck, Sandra Ann 1962- *WhoAmW 93*
Rancke, Robert Karl *Law&B 92*
Rancoita, Giorgio Maria 1927- *WhoScE 91-3*
Rancont, Diane Fraser 1936- *WhoAmW 93*
Rancour-Laferriere, Daniel *ConAu 138*
Rancourt, Jacques 1946- *WhoCanL 92*
Rancourt, John Herbert 1946- *WhoEmL 93*
Ranczak, Hildegard 1895-1987 *Baker 92*
Rand, Arthur Gorham, Jr. 1935- *WhoE 93*
Rand, Ayn 1905-1967 *JeAmHC*
Rand, Ayn 1905-1982 *Au&Arts 10 [port], BioIn 17, ScF&FL 92, WorLitC [port]*
Rand, B. *WhoScE 91-1*
Rand, Brian 1941- *WhoWor 93*
Rand, Calvin Gordon 1929- *WhoAm 92*
Rand, Christopher A. *Law&B 92*
Rand, D. *WhoScE 91-1*
Rand, David Alan *WhoScE 91-1*
Rand, Duncan D. 1940- *WhoAm 92*
Rand, Harry 1947- *ConAu 137*
Rand, Harry Israel 1912- *WhoAm 92*
Rand, Harry Zvi 1947- *WhoAm 92*
Rand, Helen *AmWomPl*
Rand, James Henry 1943- *WhoAm 92*
Rand, Joella M. 1932- *WhoE 93*
Rand, Joella Mae 1932- *WhoAmW 93*
Rand, John Born 1921- *WhoAm 92*
Rand, John Fay 1932- *WhoAm 92*
Rand, Kathy Sue 1945- *WhoAm 92*
Rand, Lawrence Anthony 1942- *WhoAm 92*
Rand, Leon 1930- *WhoAm 92*
Rand, Martha Elizabeth 1950- *WhoE 93*
Rand, Michael C. *Law&B 92*
Rand, Patrick *MiSFD 9*
Rand, Peter 1940- *ScF&FL 92*
Rand, Phillip Gordon 1934- *WhoAm 92*
Rand, Robert Wheeler 1923- *WhoAm 92*
Rand, Samuel 1953- *WhoAm 92*
Rand, Sidney Anders 1916- *WhoAm 92*
Rand, Stanley J. *Law&B 92*
Rand, Ted *ChlBIID [port]*
Randa, Larry 1948- *St&PR 93*
Randall, Alexander, V 1951- *WhoE 93*
Randall, Bob 1937- *ScF&FL 92, WhoAm 92*
Randall, Charles E. 1932- *St&PR 93*
Randall, Claire 1919- *WhoAm 92, WhoAmW 93*
Randall, Clifford Wendell 1936- *WhoAm 92*
Randall, Craig 1957- *WhoWor 93*
Randall, Dale Bertrand Jonas 1929- *WhoSSW 93*
Randall, David A. 1905-1975 *ScF&FL 92*
Randall, David Lawrence 1941- *WhoSSW 93*
Randall, Dean Bowman 1920- *WhoAm 92*
Randall, Dick *BioIn 17*
Randall, Dick J. 1931- *WhoAm 92*
Randall, E.W. *WhoScE 91-1*
Randall, Edward, III 1927- *St&PR 93*
Randall, Edward Vincent, Jr. 1932- *St&PR 93, WhoAm 92*
Randall, Elizabeth 1944- *WhoAmW 93*
Randall, Ethel Claire *AmWomPl*
Randall, Florence Engel 1917- *ScF&FL 92*
Randall, Francis Ballard 1931- *WhoAm 92*
Randall, Frederick Alvon 1945- *St&PR 93*
Randall, Gerald Jean 1931- *St&PR 93, WhoIns 93*
Randall, Gertrude Blanchard *AmWomPl*
Randall, Henry Thomas 1914- *WhoAm 92*
Randall, Hermine Maria 1927- *WhoAmW 93*
Randall, J(ames) K(irtland) 1929- *Baker 92*
Randall, Jacob S., Mrs. *AmWomPl*
Randall, James A. 1955- *St&PR 93*
Randall, James Grafton 1951- *WhoEmL 93*
Randall, James Ryden 1839-1908 *JrnUS*
Randall, James Thomas 1961- *WhoSSW 93*
Randall, John *Law&B 92*
Randall, John 1929- *MiSFD 9*
Randall, John D. 1944- *ScF&FL 92*
Randall, John M. 1944- *WhoScE 91-1*
Randall, John Stone 1912- *St&PR 93*
Randall, Karen Brigich *Law&B 92*
Randall, Kathleen Powers 1952- *WhoAmW 93*
Randall, Larry D. 1941- *St&PR 93*
Randall, Lee W. 1949- *St&PR 93*
Randall, Leslie Carl *Law&B 92*
Randall, Linda Lea 1946- *WhoAmW 93, WhoEmL 93*
Randall, Lolly 1952- *WhoAmW 93*
Randall, Lyman K. 1933- *St&PR 93*
Randall, Lynn Ellen 1946- *WhoAmW 93*
Randall, Madeline I. *AmWomPl*
Randall, Malcom 1916- *WhoAm 92, WhoSSW 93*
Randall, Mark R. *Law&B 92*
Randall, Marta *BioIn 17*
Randall, Marta 1948- *ScF&FL 92*
Randall, Mary Cecilia 1946- *WhoAmW 93*
Randall, Michael *BioIn 17*
Randall, Neil *ScF&FL 92*
Randall, Patricia Mary 1948- *WhoAmW 93*
Randall, Peggy 1961- *WhoE 93*
Randall, Phyllis Rosanna 1931- *WhoAmW 93, WhoSSW 93*
Randall, Priscilla Richmond 1926- *WhoAmW 93*
Randall, Richard Harding, Jr. 1926- *WhoAm 92*
Randall, Richard P. *Law&B 92*
Randall, Richard Rainier 1925- *WhoAm 92*
Randall, Richard Stuart 1935- *WhoE 93*
Randall, Richard William 1931- *WhoE 93, WhoWor 93*
Randall, Richard William 1950- *St&PR 93*
Randall, Robert *BioIn 17, MajAI*
Randall, Robert L. *Law&B 92*
Randall, Robert Lee 1936- *WhoE 93, WhoWor 93*
Randall, Robert W. 1916- *St&PR 93*
Randall, Roger D. 1953- *St&PR 93*
Randall, Ronald F. 1934- *St&PR 93*
Randall, Ronald Fisher 1934- *WhoAm 92*
Randall, Ronald R. *Law&B 92*
Randall, Ruth Jean 1937- *WhoAmW 93*
Randall, Samuel J. 1828-1890 *PolPar*
Randall, Sherri Lee 1959- *WhoAmW 93*
Randall, Thomas Joseph 1945- *WhoE 93*
Randall, Tony *BioIn 17*
Randall, Tony 1920- *QDrFCA 92 [port], WhoAm 92*
Randall, Trevor Jones *WhoScE 91-1*
Randall, William *BioIn 17*
Randall, William B. 1921- *WhoAm 92, WhoWor 93*
Randall, William S. *St&PR 93*
Randall, William Seymour 1933- *WhoAm 92*
Randall, William Theodore 1931- *WhoAm 92*
Randazzo, Anthony *WhoAm 92*
Randazzo, Anthony 1943- *St&PR 93*
Randazzo, Joseph C. 1950- *St&PR 93*
Randazzo, Michael d1991 *BioIn 17*
Randegger, Alberto 1832-1911 *OxDcOp*
Randegger, Alberto, Sr. 1832-1911 *Baker 92*
Randegger, Alberto, Jr. 1880-1918 *Baker 92*
Randel, Ronald Dean 1938- *WhoAm 92, WhoSSW 93*
Randel, Tony *MiSFD 9*
Randel, William Peirce 1909- *WhoE 93*
Randell, Brian *WhoScE 91-1*
Randell, Gerald Anthony *WhoScE 91-1*
Randell, Joseph David 1954- *WhoE 93*
Randell, Roger T. *St&PR 93*
Randelson, Mark 1957- *WhoSSW 93*
Randers, Nicholas *ScF&FL 92*
Randhawa, Bikkar Singh 1933- *WhoAm 92*
Randi, James *BioIn 17*
Randi, James 1928- *WhoAm 92, WhoWrEP 92*
Randich, Gene Martin 1929- *St&PR 93*
Randish, Joan Marie 1954- *WhoAmW 93*
Randisi, Elaine Marie 1926- *WhoAmW 93*
Randisi, Jennifer Lynn 1950- *WhoAmW 93*
Randisi, Robert J. 1951- *ScF&FL 92*
Randle, Annie Edith Keeling 1888- *AmWomPl*
Randle, Augustus B., III 1940- *St&PR 93*
Randle, Augustus Brown, III *Law&B 92*
Randle, Ellen Eugenia Foster 1948- *WhoAmW 93, WhoEmL 93*
Randle, Frank 1901-1957 *QDrFCA 92 [port]*
Randle, Kevin 1949- *ScF&FL 92*
Randle, Michael Charles 1952- *WhoWor 93*
Randle, Philip John *WhoScE 91-1*
Randle, Philip John 1926- *WhoWor 93*
Randle, Roger A. *WhoSSW 93*
Randle, William P. *Law&B 92*
Randleman, Sandra L. *Law&B 92*
Randles, Marianne Christine 1963- *WhoAmW 93*
Randles, Ronald Herman 1942- *WhoSSW 93*
Randlett, Richard Carl 1931- *St&PR 93*
Randolph, A. Philip 1889-1979 *ConBlB 3 [port], EncAACR, PolPar*
Randolph, A. Raymond 1943- *CngDr 91*
Randolph, Angus M.C. 1946- *St&PR 93*
Randolph, Arthur Raymond 1943- *WhoAm 92, WhoE 93*
Randolph, Asa Philip 1889-1979 *BioIn 17, DcTwHis*
Randolph, Barry R. 1958- *St&PR 93*
Randolph, Bernard P. 1933- *AfrAmBi [port]*
Randolph, Beverley 1951- *WhoAmW 93*
Randolph, Carl Lowell 1922- *WhoAm 92*
Randolph, Carole *Law&B 92*
Randolph, Christopher Craven 1956- *WhoWor 93*
Randolph, Clyde Clifton, Jr. 1928- *WhoWor 93*
Randolph, D. Edward, Jr. *Law&B 92*
Randolph, David 1914- *Baker 92, WhoAm 92*
Randolph, David M. 1948- *St&PR 93*
Randolph, Deborah Jean Greenway 1951- *WhoAmW 93*
Randolph, Edith *AmWomPl*
Randolph, Eleanor *BioIn 17*
Randolph, F.F. 1927- *St&PR 93*
Randolph, Francis Fitz, Jr. 1927- *WhoAm 92*
Randolph, Harrison 1916- *St&PR 93*
Randolph, Harry E. 1932- *St&PR 93*
Randolph, Jackson H. 1930- *St&PR 93*
Randolph, James H. 1947- *St&PR 93*
Randolph, James Harrison, Sr. 1917- *WhoSSW 93*
Randolph, Jean 1945- *WhoAmW 93*
Randolph, Jennings, Jr. 1934- *WhoAm 92*
Randolph, John 1773-1833 *PolPar*
Randolph, John 1915- *WhoAm 92*
Randolph, John 1931- *St&PR 93*
Randolph, John Denson 1938- *WhoAm 92, WhoWrEP 92*
Randolph, John Lind 1937- *WhoAm 92*
Randolph, John Maurice 1926- *WhoAm 92*
Randolph, John S. *Law&B 92*
Randolph, Judson Graves 1927- *WhoAm 92*
Randolph, Lee 1954- *St&PR 93*
Randolph, Malcolm Logan 1920- *WhoSSW 93*
Randolph, Michael E. 1956- *WhoSSW 93*
Randolph, Mickey Lane 1950- *WhoSSW 93*
Randolph, Mike 1937- *St&PR 93*
Randolph, Nancy Adele 1941- *WhoSSW 93*
Randolph, Richard 1770-1796 *BioIn 17*
Randolph, Robert D. 1935- *St&PR 93*
Randolph, Robert DeWitt 1929- *WhoAm 92*
Randolph, Robert Lee 1926- *WhoAm 92*
Randolph, Robert Raymond 1937- *WhoAm 92*
Randolph, Rodger Leon 1931- *St&PR 93*
Randolph, Ron 1940- *St&PR 93*
Randolph, Ross V. *BioIn 17*
Randolph, Susan C. 1938- *St&PR 93*
Randolph, Thomas 1605-1635 *DcLB 126*
Randolph, Thomas Jefferson 1792-1875 *BioIn 17*
Randolph, Velma Lois 1930- *WhoWrEP 92*
Randolph, Virginia Seal 1932- *WhoAmW 93*
Randolph, Walter R. 1926- *St&PR 93*
Randolph, Wendell G. 1895-1990 *BioIn 17*
Randolph, William Abbott 1923- *St&PR 93*
Randolphe, Arabella *ScF&FL 92*
Random, Alex *ScF&FL 92*
Randour, Paul Alfred 1935- *WhoAm 92*
Rands, Bernard 1934- *Baker 92, WhoAm 92*
Randt, Clark Thorp 1917- *WhoAm 92*
Randza, Jason Michael 1963- *WhoSSW 93*
Ranelli, John Raymond 1946- *WhoE 93, WhoEmL 93, WhoWor 93*
Ranelli, Raymond A. 1947- *WhoAm 92*
Raney, Charles Dewey 1939- *WhoSSW 93*
Raney, Hollaman Martin 1933- *St&PR 93*
Raney, Kenneth C., Jr. *Law&B 92*
Raney, Miriam Day 1922- *WhoAmW 93, WhoSSW 93, WhoWor 93*
Raney, R.H. 1928- *St&PR 93*
Ranft, Johannes 1933- *WhoWor 93*
Ranga, N.G. 1900- *WhoAsAP 91*
Ranganathan, Babu Gopal 1957- *WhoE 93*
Ranganathan, S.R. 1892-1972 *BioIn 17*
Ranganathan, Shiyali Ramamrita 1892-1972 *BioIn 17*
Range, A. J. 1950- *WhoSSW 93*
Range, Michele *Law&B 92*
Range, William d1992 *BioIn 17*
Rangel, Adolfo Larralde *St&PR 93*
Rangel, Charles 1930- *ConBlB 3 [port]*
Rangel, Charles B. *BioIn 17*
Rangel, Charles B. 1930- *AfrAmBi [port], CngDr 91*
Rangel, Charles Bernard 1930- *WhoAm 92, WhoE 93*
Rangel, Nicolas 1864-1935 *DcMexL*
Rangel, Rosalva Margarita 1967- *WhoAmW 93*
Rangel Guerra, Alfonso 1928- *DcMexL*
Rangel-Guerra, Ricardo Alberto 1934- *WhoWor 93*
Rangell, Leo 1913- *WhoAm 92*
Rangen, Christopher T. 1953- *St&PR 93*
Ranger, C.N. *St&PR 93*
Ranger, Charles 1727-1805 *BioIn 17*
Rangheard, Yves 1933- *WhoScE 91-2*
Rangkhasiri, Dusit *WhoAsAP 91*
Rangos, John *BioIn 17*
Rangos, John G. 1929- *WhoAm 92*
Rangos, John G., Sr. 1929- *St&PR 93*
Rangstrom, (Anders Johan) Ture 1884-1947 *Baker 92*
Ranguin *WhoScE 91-2*
Ranhand, Samuel 1915-1990 *BioIn 17*
Rania, Albert Nunzio 1966- *WhoWrEP 92*
Ranieri, Gregory C. *Law&B 92*
Ranieri, Lewis S. *WhoAm 92*
Ranieri, Lorraine Mary 1943- *WhoWrEP 92*
Raniolo, Frank Joseph 1934- *WhoE 93*
Ranis, Gustav 1929- *WhoAm 92, WhoE 93*
Ranjbaran, Abdolrasoul 1952- *WhoWor 93*

Ranjeva, Raymond 1942- WhoUN 92
Ranjit Singh, Maharaja of the Punjab 1780-1839 BioIn 17
Rank, Dieter 1940- WhoScE 91-4
Rank, Ernst Josef 1954- WhoWor 93
Rank, Everett George 1921- WhoAm 92
Rank, Jerry Dean 1935- St&PR 93
Rank, John Thomas 1947- WhoAm 92
Rank, Larry Gene 1935- WhoAm 92
Rank, Maureen Joy 1947- WhoWrEP 92
Rank, Robert Pomeroy 1941- WhoAm 92
Rankaitis, Susan 1949- WhoAm 92, WhoAmW 93
Ranke-Heinemann, Uta (Johanna Ingrid) 1927- ConAu 137
Rankel, Lillian Ann 1944- WhoE 93
Ranki, Dezso 1951- Baker 92
Ranki, Gyorgy 1907- Baker 92, OxDcOp
Rankin, Alan J. 1944- St&PR 93
Rankin, Alfred Marshall 1913- St&PR 93, WhoAm 92
Rankin, Alfred Marshall, Jr. 1941- St&PR 93, WhoAm 92
Rankin, Arthur, Jr. MiSFD 9
Rankin, B.M., Jr. 1941- St&PR 93
Rankin, Bonnie Lee 1953- WhoAmW 93
Rankin, Clyde Evan, III 1950- WhoE 93, WhoWor 93
Rankin, Donald T. 1941- St&PR 93
Rankin, Edward J. 1948- WhoIns 93
Rankin, Edward L., III Law&B 92
Rankin, Elizabeth Anne DeSalvo 1948- WhoAmW 93
Rankin, Harley, Jr. 1939- St&PR 93
Rankin, Helen Cross WhoAmW 93
Rankin, Henry Hollis, III 1944- WhoSSW 93
Rankin, Herb Lee 1957- St&PR 93
Rankin, Ian 1960- ScF&FL 92
Rankin, James A. 1928- St&PR 93
Rankin, James C. 1938- St&PR 93
Rankin, James Winton 1943- WhoAm 92
Rankin, Jean F. Law&B 92
Rankin, Jeannette BioIn 17
Rankin, Jeannette 1880-1973 PolPar
Rankin, Joanna Marie 1942- WhoAmW 93
Rankin, John J. 1943- St&PR 93
Rankin, Juanita Rose 1949- WhoE 93, WhoWor 93
Rankin, Karl Lott 1898-1991 BioIn 17
Rankin, Larry V. 1943- St&PR 93
Rankin, Michael BioIn 17
Rankin, Michael R. Law&B 92
Rankin, Nell 1926- Baker 92
Rankin, Robert 1915- WhoAm 92
Rankin, Robert 1949- ScF&FL 92
Rankin, Robert Allen, Jr. 1945- St&PR 93
Rankin, Robert Arthur 1949- WhoAm 92
Rankin, Susan Jewel 1949- WhoWrEP 92
Rankin, Thomas Robert 1947- WhoE 93
Rankin, Ulon Lon Willis 1945- WhoSSW 93
Rankin, W.L. 1937- St&PR 93
Rankin, William Chase, Jr. 1949- WhoAm 92
Rankin, Wilton Law&B 92
Rankin, Zinora Mitchell- BioIn 17
Rankine, B. James 1936- St&PR 93
Rankine, John ScF&FL 92
Rankin-Smith, Pamela 1918- WhoE 93
Rankl, Karl 1898-1968 Baker 92, OxDcOp
Ranko, Rebecca Marie 1966- WhoAmW 93
Rankovic, Milojko WhoScE 91-4
Rankovic, Milojko 1937- WhoScE 91-4
Ranks, Anne Elizabeth 1916- WhoAmW 93, WhoWor 93
Rannenberg, Wendy 1956- WhoAmW 93
Ranney, Austin BioIn 17
Ranney, Austin 1920- WhoAm 92
Ranney, George Alfred 1912- WhoAm 92
Ranney, Helen Margaret 1920- WhoAm 92, WhoAmW 93
Ranney, Maurice William 1934- WhoWor 93
Rannikko, Simo Juhani 1936- WhoScE 91-4
Ranody, Laszlo 1919-1983 DrEEuF
Ransby, E.J. 1942- St&PR 93
Ransdell, Lynda Beth 1963- WhoAmW 93
Ransdell, Ronald Eugene 1941- St&PR 93
Ranseen, John David 1955- WhoSSW 93
Ransford, John Gerard 1940- St&PR 93
Ranshaw, Jane Ellen 1944- WhoAmW 93
Ransier, Alonzo Jacob 1834-1882 BioIn 17
Ransil, Bernard Jerome 1929- WhoE 93, WhoWor 93
Ranske, Jutta Mordt Bell AmWomPl
Ransmayr, Christoph 1954- ScF&FL 92
Ransohoff, Martin 1927- WhoAm 92
Ransohoff, Priscilla Burnett 1912- WhoE 93
Ransom, Alan Brian 1940- St&PR 93
Ransom, Bill 1945- ScF&FL 92, WhoAm 92, WhoWrEP 92
Ransom, Dana WhoWrEP 92
Ransom, Daniel ConAu 138, ScF&FL 92
Ransom, Daniel Joseph 1951- WhoSSW 93
Ransom, Edward Charles Philip WhoScE 91-1
Ransom, Edward Duane 1914- WhoAm 92
Ransom, Freeman B. 1884-1947 EncAACR
Ransom, Jeremy WhoAm 92
Ransom, John Crowe 1888-1974 BioIn 17
Ransom, Nancy Alderman 1929- WhoAmW 93
Ransom, Reverdy C. 1861-1959 BioIn 17
Ransom, Reverdy Cassius 1861-1959 EncAACR
Ransom, Richard E. 1932- WhoAm 92
Ransom, Robert Edwin 1952- St&PR 93
Ransom, Ronald 1882-1947 BioIn 17
Ransom, Shirley A. Law&B 92
Ransom, Thomas Richard 1934- St&PR 93
Ransom, William M. ScF&FL 92
Ransome, Arthur (Michell) 1884-1967 ChlFicS, MajAI [port]
Ransome, Ernest Leslie, III WhoAm 92
Ransome, Ernest Leslie, III 1926- St&PR 93
Ransome, James 1961- BlkAuII 92
Ranson, Charles W. 1903-1988 BioIn 17
Ranson, Guy Harvey 1916- WhoAm 92
Ranson, Jeanette S. 1939- St&PR 93
Ranson, Lyle H. 1936- St&PR 93
Ranson, Nancy Sussman 1905- WhoAm 92, WhoAmW 93
Ranson, Stewart WhoScE 91-1
Ranson, William Joseph 1938- WhoSSW 93
Ransone, Robin Key 1933- WhoE 93
Ransopher, Ivan Allen 1960- WhoAm 92
Ranta, Aarne Uolevi 1943- WhoScE 91-4
Ranta, Hilkka M. 1941- WhoScE 91-4
Ranta, Matti A. 1932- WhoScE 91-4
Ranta, Richard Robert 1943- WhoAm 92
Ranta, Sulho 1901-1960 Baker 92
Ranta Aho, Martha Helen 1923- WhoAmW 93, WhoWor 93
Rantala, Veikko Reima 1933- WhoWor 93
Rantanen, Jorma WhoScE 91-4
Rantisi, Audeh G. BioIn 17
Rants, Carolyn Jean 1936- WhoAmW 93
Rantzau, Johann von 1492-1565 HarEnMi
Rantzau, Josias von 1609-1650 HarEnMi
Ranum, Jane Barnhardt 1947- WhoAmW 93
Ranum, Orest Allen 1933- WhoAm 92
Ranzahuer, Guillermo Gonzalez 1928- WhoAm 92
Ranzini, Joseph Louis 1929- St&PR 93
Ranzini, Mildred St&PR 93
Ranzini, Stelvio Milton Teixeira 1930- WhoWor 93
Ranzini, Stephen Lange 1965- St&PR 93
Rao, A. Narsimha 1927- St&PR 93
Rao, Adapa Ramakrishna ScF&FL 92
Rao, Arun d1991 BioIn 17
Rao, Challasree Rama St&PR 93
Rao, Chandra Rajeswara 1914- WhoAsAP 91
Rao, Chintamani Nagesa Ramachandra 1934- WhoWor 93
Rao, Desiraju Bhavanarayana 1936- WhoAm 92
Rao, Dhairyashil C. WhoUN 92
Rao, Dhananjaya K. 1949- St&PR 93
Rao, G. Kris 1951- St&PR 93
Rao, Ganti Lakshminarayana 1939- WhoUN 92
Rao, Gopala Rao 1937- WhoAsAP 91
Rao, H.V. WhoScE 91-1
Rao, J. Chokka 1923- WhoAsAP 91
Rao, J. Vengala 1922- WhoAsAP 91
Rao, Janakirama B.V. 1917- WhoSSW 93
Rao, K.S. 1943- WhoAsAP 91
Rao, Kellie Evans 1961- WhoAmW 93
Rao, Koneru Ramakrishna 1932- WhoSSW 93
Rao, Ming 1954- WhoWor 93
Rao, Moturu Hanumantha 1917- WhoAsAP 91
Rao, Mulki Padupanambur Umanath 1939- WhoWor 93
Rao, Musunuru Sambasiva 1939- WhoWor 93
Rao, Nannapaneni Narayana WhoAm 92
Rao, P.V. Narasimha BioIn 17
Rao, P. V. Narasimha 1921- CurBio 92 [port], News 93-2 [port]
Rao, Raja BioIn 17
Rao, Raja 1909- IntvWPC 92 [port]
Rao, Ramgopal Palakurthi 1942- WhoE 93
Rao, Sethuramiah Lakshminarayana 1942- WhoE 93, WhoUN 92
Rao, Tadikonda Lakshmi Kantha 1946- WhoWor 93
Rao, Tumkur Krishna Murthy Sreepada 1944- WhoE 93
Rao, V. Krishna 1925- WhoAsAP 91
Rao, Vaman 1933- WhoWor 93
Rao, Yalla Sesi Bhushana 1929- WhoAsAP 91
Raouf, Raouf Ali 1960- WhoE 93
Raoufi, Mehdi 1952- WhoSSW 93
Raoul OxDcByz
Raoul, Manuel fl. c. 1355-1369 OxDcByz
Raoulaina, Theodora c. 1240-1300 OxDcByz
Raoul of Caen OxDcByz
Raoult, Didier 1952- WhoScE 91-2
Raoux, Denis J. 1942- WhoScE 91-2
Rapaccioli, Donna Maria 1962- WhoAmW 93
Rapaccioli, Michel Antoine 1934- St&PR 93, WhoAm 92
Rapacciuolo, A.R. 1942- WhoScE 91-3
Rapacki, Ryszard 1949- WhoWor 93
Rapagnola, Mario 1927- St&PR 93
Rapaidus, David Martin 1956- WhoSSW 93
Rapalyea, Lisa BioIn 17
Rapanaro, Angelo 1929- St&PR 93
Rapaport, David A. 1942- St&PR 93
Rapaport, David Alan 1942- WhoAm 92
Rapaport, Felix Theodosius 1929- WhoAm 92
Rapaport, Robert M. 1931- WhoAm 92
Rapaport, Ronald L. 1945- St&PR 93
Rapaport, Samuel I. 1921- WhoAm 92
Rapaport, William Joseph 1946- WhoE 93
Rapawy, Walter 1944- St&PR 93
Rapchak, Lawrence 1951- Baker 92
Rapee, Erno 1891-1945 Baker 92
Rapeli, Antti Sakari 1948- WhoWor 93
Raper, Charles Albert 1926- WhoAm 92, WhoWor 93
Raper, James LeRoy, Sr. 1937- WhoSSW 93
Raper, Julius Rowan, III 1938- WhoSSW 93
Raper, William Burkette 1927- WhoAm 92
Rapf, Kurt 1922- Baker 92
Rapf, Matthew 1920-1991 BioIn 17, ConTFT 10
Raphael 1943?- BioIn 17
Raphael, Alan H. Law&B 92
Raphael, Albert Ash, Jr. 1925- WhoAm 92
Raphael, Alice AmWomPl
Raphael, Anne Wagner 1941- WhoAmW 93
Raphael, Coleman 1925- WhoAm 92
Raphael, Dan Ambrose 1952- WhoWrEP 92
Raphael, Dana WhoE 93
Raphael, David ben d1992 BioIn 17
Raphael, Frederic Michael 1931- WhoAm 92
Raphael, Gunter (Albert Rudolf) 1903-1960 Baker 92
Raphael, Joanne Hackett Law&B 92
Raphael, Kenneth J. Law&B 92
Raphael, Louise Arakelain 1937- WhoAmW 93
Raphael, Morris Charles 1917- WhoWrEP 92
Raphael, Oriel 1939- WhoAm 92
Raphael, Phyllis 1937- WhoWrEP 92
Raphael, Pierre BioIn 17
Raphael, Sally Jessy BioIn 17, WhoAm 92, WhoAmW 93
Raphael, Sally Jessy 1943- News 92 [port]
Raphael, Stuart I. 1938- WhoIns 93
Raphaelson, Arnold Herbert 1929- WhoE 93
Raphaelson, Joel 1928- WhoAm 92
Raphel, Gerald 1943- St&PR 93
Raphling, Sam(uel) 1910-1988 Baker 92
Rapholz, James Lewis, II 1939- St&PR 93
Rapidis, Alexander Demetrius 1948- WhoWor 93
Rapier, James Thomas 1837-1883 BioIn 17
Rapier, Lori King 1960- WhoSSW 93
Rapilly, Frantz 1937- WhoScE 91-2
Rapin, Charles Rene Jules 1935- WhoWor 93
Rapin, Isabelle 1927- WhoAm 92, WhoAmW 93
Rapin, Jean Robert 1942- WhoScE 91-2
Rapin, Lynn Suzanne 1946- WhoAmW 93
Rapin, Michel WhoScE 91-2
Rapin, Michel A. 1932- WhoScE 91-2
Rapke, Jack WhoAm 92
Rapkin, Grace Zucker 1958- WhoE 93
Rapkin, Jerome 1929- WhoE 93
Rapkine, Louis 1904-1948 BioIn 17
Rapo, Paul S. Law&B 92
Rapone, Alberto 1941- WhoWor 93
Rapoport, Anatol 1911- WhoAm 92
Rapoport, Benzion Jakob 1929- WhoE 93
Rapoport, Bernard 1917- St&PR 93, WhoAm 92, WhoIns 93
Rapoport, Bernard Robert 1919- WhoAm 92
Rapoport, Daniel 1933- WhoWrEP 92
Rapoport, I. C. MiSFD 9
Rapoport, Janis 1946- ConAu 40NR, WhoCanL 92
Rapoport, Judith 1933- WhoAmW 93
Rapoport, Morton I. 1934- WhoAm 92
Rapoport, Nancy L. 1945- St&PR 93
Rapoport, Natan 1911-1987 PolBiDi
Rapoport, Nessa BioIn 17
Rapoport, Robert Norman 1924- ConAu 39NR
Rapoport, Ronald Jon 1940- WhoAm 92
Raposeiro, Carlos 1935- WhoScE 91-3
Raposo, Joseph G. 1937-1989 BioIn 17
Raposo, Nancy BioIn 17
Rapoza, Edward J. 1936- St&PR 93
Rapoza, John F. Law&B 92
Rapp, Adolf 1933- WhoScE 91-3
Rapp, Augustus 1871-1961 BioIn 17
Rapp, Christian F. 1933- St&PR 93
Rapp, Christian Ferree 1933- WhoSSW 93, WhoWor 93
Rapp, David Abner 1931- WhoWor 93
Rapp, David M. Law&B 92
Rapp, Doris Jean 1940- WhoAmW 93
Rapp, Fred 1929- WhoAm 92
Rapp, Gerald Duane 1933- WhoAm 92, WhoWor 93
Rapp, Ilana Beth 1968- WhoE 93
Rapp, John 1920- WhoE 93
Rapp, John B. 1936- WhoAm 92
Rapp, John Buswell 1936- St&PR 93
Rapp, John P. Law&B 92
Rapp, Larry P. 1948- St&PR 93
Rapp, Lea Bayers 1946- WhoWrEP 92
Rapp, Richard Arlen, Jr. Law&B 92
Rapp, Richard Tilden 1944- WhoAm 92
Rapp, Robert Anthony 1934- WhoAm 92
Rapp, Robert Cullen, Jr. 1926- St&PR 93
Rapp, Ronald J. Law&B 92
Rapp, Steven M. Law&B 92
Rapp, William David Law&B 92
Rapp, William Edward 1924- St&PR 93
Rappaccioli, Mario DcCPCAm
Rappahahn, Ted L. 1955- St&PR 93
Rappaneau, Jean-Paul 1932- MiSFD 9
Rappaport, Anna Maria 1940- WhoIns 93
Rappaport, Carey Milford 1959- WhoE 93
Rappaport, David BioIn 17
Rappaport, Earle Samuel, Jr. 1935- WhoAm 92
Rappaport, Fred BioIn 17
Rappaport, Gary B. 1937- St&PR 93
Rappaport, Gary Burton 1937- WhoAm 92
Rappaport, Gary Dennis 1950- St&PR 93
Rappaport, Irving S. Law&B 92
Rappaport, Irwin 1932- St&PR 93
Rappaport, Janet Kay Law&B 92
Rappaport, Judith Ann 1955- WhoAmW 93
Rappaport, Lawrence 1928- WhoAm 92
Rappaport, Margaret M. 1947- WhoE 93
Rappaport, Mark 1942- WhoE 93
Rappaport, Martin Paul 1935- WhoAm 92, WhoSSW 93
Rappaport, Raphael 1932- WhoScE 91-2
Rappaport, Stephen S. WhoAm 92
Rappaport, Steven N. 1948- St&PR 93
Rapparlie, Evalyn Barbara 1931- WhoSSW 93
Rappel, Robert 1936- WhoSSW 93
Rappeport, Stephen Alan 1950- WhoSSW 93
Rapper, Irving 1898- MiSFD 9
Rapping, Leonard A. 1934-1991 BioIn 17
Rappleye, Richard K. 1940- St&PR 93
Rappleyea, Frederick A. 1918- WhoSSW 93
Rappleyea, Robert G. d1991 BioIn 17
Rappold, Charles E., II Law&B 92
Rappold, Marie c. 1873-1957 Baker 92
Rappoldi, Adrian 1876-1948 See Rappoldi, Eduard 1831-1903 Baker 92
Rappoldi, Eduard 1831-1903 Baker 92
Rappoldi, Laura 1853-1925 See Rappoldi, Eduard 1831-1903 Baker 92
Rappoport, Ronald A. Law&B 92
Rapport, Robin Schuman 1954- WhoAmW 93
Rapsey, A.N. WhoScE 91-1
Rapsomanikis, Antonis 1937- WhoWor 93
Rapson, Donald J. Law&B 92
Rapson, Kim Elizabeth 1963- WhoAmW 93
Rapson, Ralph 1914- WhoAm 92
Rapson, Richard L. 1937- WhoAm 92
Rapson, William Howard 1912- WhoAm 92
Raquepaw, Jayne Marie 1961- WhoAmW 93
Raquet, Bonnie E. Law&B 92
Raquet, Walter 1944- St&PR 93
Rare, Rico WhoWrEP 92
Rarey, Raymond Joseph 1948- WhoSSW 93
Raridon, Richard Jay 1931- WhoAm 92
Ras, Zbigniew Wieslaw 1947- WhoSSW 93

Rasalilananda, Gurudev Sri 1931- *WhoWor 93*
Rasanayagam, Angelo 1936- *WhoUN 92*
Rasanen, Eric K. 1946- *WhoIns 93*
Rasanen, Eric Konrad 1946- *St&PR 93*
Rasanen, Erkki 1940- *WhoScE 91-4*
Rasanen, Pentti K. *WhoScE 91-4*
Rasaputram, Warnasena 1927- *WhoUN 92*
Rasbach, James Harrison 1932- *St&PR 93*
Rasbach, Oscar 1888-1975 *Baker 92*
Rasberry, Rebecca Kay 1945- *WhoAmW 93*
Rascati, E. Joseph 1957- *WhoSSW 93*
Rasch, Bruce J. *Law&B 92*
Rasch, Douglas William *Law&B 92*
Rasch, Ellen Myrberg 1927- *WhoAmW 93*
Rasch, Robert William 1926- *WhoSSW 93*
Rasche, Gunther 1934- *WhoScE 91-4*
Rasche, Richard R. 1916- *WhoSSW 93*
Rasche, Robert Harold 1941- *WhoAm 92*
Rasched, Ihab R. 1938- *WhoScE 91-3*
Rascher, Sigurd (Manfred) 1907- *Baker 92*
Raschi, Victor John Angelo 1919-1988 *BiDAMSp 1989*
Raschke, Carl A. *BioIn 17*
Raschke, Ehrhard A. 1936- *WhoScE 91-3*
Raschko, Patrick P. 1940- *St&PR 93*
Raschko, Paula Katherine 1951- *WhoAmW 93*
Raschle, Bruno E. 1950- *WhoWor 93*
Rascio, Anthony A. *Law&B 92*
Rascio, Anthony A. 1942- *St&PR 93*
Rascoe, Eric 1932- *St&PR 93*
Rascon, Armando *BioIn 17*
Raselius, Andreas c. 1563-1602 *Baker 92*
Rasenick, Enid S. *Law&B 92*
Rash, Bryson B. d1992 *NewYTBS 92*
Rash, Bryson Brennan 1913- *WhoAm 92*
Rash, Nancy 1940- *ConAu 37NR*
Rash, Nancy Batson Nisbet 1940- *WhoAmW 93*
Rash, Richard Dale 1958- *St&PR 93*
Rash, Steve *MiSFD 9*
Rash, Steven Britton 1947- *WhoSSW 93*
Rashad, Ahmad *BioIn 17*
Rashad, Ahmad 1949- *WhoAm 92*
Rashad, Johari M(ahasin) 1951- *ConAu 138*
Rashad, Phylicia *BioIn 17, WhoAm 92*
Rasher, Steven M. *Law&B 92*
Rashford, Mercedes Avalyn 1962- *WhoE 93*
Rashi 1040-1105 *BioIn 17*
Rashid d1991 *BioIn 17*
Rashid, Abdul 1947- *WhoWor 93*
Rashid, James Mark *Law&B 92*
Rashid, Kazi Firoz *WhoAsAP 91*
Rashid, Mohammed *BioIn 17*
Rashid, Samir Yousef 1953- *WhoWor 93*
Rashid, Tariq 1949- *WhoWor 93*
Rashid, Zafar 1950- *WhoIns 93*
Rashid Ali al-Gailani 1892-1965 *DcTwHis*
Rashid bin Said al Maktum, Sheik 1912-1990 *BioIn 17*
Rashid Hussain *BioIn 17*
Rashid ibn Ahmad Al-Mualla, Sheikh 1930- *WhoWor 93*
Rashilla, Richard James, Jr. 1959- *WhoSSW 93*
Rashkes, Moshe 1928- *WhoWor 93*
Rashkow, Ronald 1940- *WhoAm 92*
Rashmir, Lewis P. 1925- *St&PR 93*
Rasi, Francesco 1574-c. 1620 *OxDcOp*
Rasi, Humberto Mario 1935- *WhoAm 92*
Rasiej, K. Steve 1926- *St&PR 93*
Rasin, I. Freeman 1833-1907 *PolPar*
Rasin, Rudolph Stephen 1930- *WhoAm 92*
Rasines, Isidoro 1927- *WhoScE 91-3, WhoWor 93*
Rask, Michael Raymond 1930- *WhoAm 92, WhoWor 93*
Raskas, Heschel J. 1941- *St&PR 93*
Raskevicius, V. Leo 1936- *St&PR 93*
Raskin, Allen 1926- *WhoE 93*
Raskin, Ben *BioIn 17*
Raskin, Ellen 1925?-1984 *DcAmChF 1960*
Raskin, Ellen 1928-1984 *ConAu 37NR, MajAI [port]*
Raskin, Fred Charles 1948- *St&PR 93, WhoAm 92*
Raskin, Judith 1928-1984 *Baker 92, IntDcOp*
Raskin, Marcus Goodman 1934- *WhoAm 92*
Raskin, Michael A. 1925- *WhoAm 92*
Raskin, Miriam Susan 1943- *WhoSSW 93*
Raskin, Noel Michael 1947- *WhoE 93*
Raskin, Rubin 1918- *St&PR 93*
Raskin, Walter 1913- *St&PR 93*
Raskind, Leo Joseph 1919- *WhoAm 92*
Raskind, Lisa *ScF&FL 92*
Rasko, Istvan 1939- *WhoScE 91-4*
Raskob, John J. 1879-1950 *PolPar*
Raskob, John Jakob 1879-1950 *BioIn 17*
Raskov, Daniel *MiSFD 9*
Rasky, Harry 1928- *MiSFD 9, WhoAm 92, WhoCanL 92*
Rasley, Alicia Todd 1955- *WhoWrEP 92*
Rasmus, John Avery 1954- *WhoAm 92*
Rasmuson, Brent Jacobsen 1950- *WhoWor 93*
Rasmuson, Edward Bernard 1940- *WhoAm 92*
Rasmuson, Elmer Edwin 1909- *WhoAm 92, WhoWor 93*
Rasmuson, Judith Ellen 1948- *WhoAmW 93*
Rasmussen, Alis A. 1958- *ScF&FL 92*
Rasmussen, Arthur E. 1922- *St&PR 93*
Rasmussen, C.F. *St&PR 93*
Rasmussen, Christopher L. *Law&B 92*
Rasmussen, D. Scott 1958- *WhoE 93*
Rasmussen, Dale L. 1950- *St&PR 93*
Rasmussen, David G. *Law&B 92*
Rasmussen, Dennis Loy 1940- *WhoSSW 93, WhoWor 93*
Rasmussen, Erik B. *WhoScE 91-2*
Rasmussen, Frank M. 1934- *St&PR 93*
Rasmussen, Gail Cunningham 1947- *WhoAmW 93*
Rasmussen, Gunnar 1925- *WhoWor 93*
Rasmussen, Hans 1934- *WhoScE 91-2*
Rasmussen, Harry Paul 1939- *WhoAm 92*
Rasmussen, J.A. 1945- *St&PR 93*
Rasmussen, James Laurence 1936- *WhoUN 92*
Rasmussen, Janet Elaine 1949- *WhoAmW 93*
Rasmussen, Jay A. 1928- *St&PR 93*
Rasmussen, Jens 1926- *WhoScE 91-2*
Rasmussen, Jessie K. 1945- *WhoAmW 93*
Rasmussen, Joe *BioIn 17*
Rasmussen, John A., Jr. *Law&B 92*
Rasmussen, John Oscar 1926- *WhoAm 92*
Rasmussen, John Robert 1957- *St&PR 93*
Rasmussen, Jutta 1931- *WhoScE 91-2*
Rasmussen, K.L. 1953- *WhoScE 91-2*
Rasmussen, Karl Aage 1947- *Baker 92*
Rasmussen, Kathleen Anne 1958- *WhoAmW 93, WhoSSW 93*
Rasmussen, Keith George 1928- *St&PR 93*
Rasmussen, Kjeld 1936- *WhoScE 91-2*
Rasmussen, Knud 1879-1933 *IntDcAn*
Rasmussen, Knut 1938- *WhoScE 91-4*
Rasmussen, Leif *WhoScE 91-2*
Rasmussen, Louis Charles 1928- *St&PR 93*
Rasmussen, Myron Gerald 1937- *St&PR 93*
Rasmussen, Neal Charles 1936- *St&PR 93*
Rasmussen, Neil E. 1955- *St&PR 93*
Rasmussen, Nestor Sigvard 1931- *WhoWor 93*
Rasmussen, Nicholas Roberts 1946- *St&PR 93, WhoAm 92*
Rasmussen, Norman Carl 1927- *WhoAm 92*
Rasmussen, Peter G. 1954- *St&PR 93*
Rasmussen, Richard Alan 1950- *St&PR 93*
Rasmussen, Richard Frank 1935- *St&PR 93*
Rasmussen, Richard Jones 1940- *St&PR 93*
Rasmussen, Richard R. *Law&B 92*
Rasmussen, Robert N. 1930- *St&PR 93*
Rasmussen, Roberta A. *WhoAmW 93*
Rasmussen, Scott William 1956- *WhoWor 93*
Rasmussen, Steen Eiler 1898-1990 *BioIn 17*
Rasmussen, Stephen Mark 1967- *WhoE 93*
Rasmussen, Stephen S. 1952- *St&PR 93*
Rasmussen, Susan Lee *Law&B 92*
Rasmussen, Sven Nybo 1939- *WhoScE 91-2*
Rasmussen, Teresa J. *Law&B 92*
Rasmussen, Victor Philip, Jr. 1950- *WhoWor 93*
Rasmussen, Waldemar E. *Law&B 92*
Rasmussen, Warren W. 1930- *St&PR 93*
Rasmusson, Eugene Martin 1929- *WhoE 93, WhoWor 93*
Rasmusson, Joseph Gabriel 1957- *St&PR 93*
Rasnic, Carol Daugherty 1941- *WhoSSW 93*
Raso, Margaret Mildred 1933- *WhoAmW 93, WhoE 93*
Raso-Kirstein, Melinda Adele 1955- *WhoAmW 93*
Rasor, Dina Lynn 1956- *WhoAm 92*
Rasor, Doris Lee 1929- *WhoAmW 93*
Rasor, Elizabeth Ann 1962- *WhoAmW 93*
Rasor, Richard Drew 1939- *St&PR 93*
Rasor, Robert L. 1922- *St&PR 93*
Rasp, Fritz 1891-1976 *IntDcF 2-3 [port]*
Raspail, Jean 1925- *ScF&FL 92*
Raspante, Anthony *St&PR 93*
Raspberry, William J. *BioIn 17*
Raspberry, William James 1935- *WhoAm 92*
Rasper, Deborah Young 1950- *WhoAmW 93*
Raspet, Richard 1947- *WhoSSW 93*
Rasporich, Anthony Walter 1940- *WhoAm 92*
Rasputin, Grigori Yefimovich 1871-1916 *DcTwHis*
Rasputin, Grigorii Efimovich 1871-1916 *BioIn 17*
Rasputin, Valentin Grigor'evich *BioIn 17*
Rass, Hans Heinrich 1936- *WhoWor 93*
Rass, Rebecca Rivka 1936- *WhoWrEP 92*
Rassam, Ghassan Noel 1942- *WhoE 93*
Rassbach, Herbert David 1944- *WhoAm 92*
Rasschaert, E.H. 1949- *St&PR 93*
Rasse, Francois (Adolphe Jean Jules) 1873-1955 *Baker 92*
Rasser, J.C. *Law&B 92*
Rassers, W.H. 1877-1973 *IntDcAn*
Rassieur, Charles L. 1931- *St&PR 93*
Rassin, Barry Jonathan 1947- *WhoWor 93*
Rassin, David Keith 1942- *WhoSSW 93*
Rassnick, Leopold S. 1939- *WhoAm 92*
Rassool, Bertrand Louis Maurice 1957- *WhoWor 93*
Rassou, Regis 1936- *WhoUN 92*
Rassweiler, James C. *Law&B 92*
Rast, Everette Duncan 1938- *WhoSSW 93*
Rast, Gary Fischer 1935- *St&PR 93*
Rast, Mendel Walker 1935- *St&PR 93, WhoAm 92*
Rast, Richard Randall 1958- *WhoSSW 93*
Rast, Walter, Jr. 1944- *WhoAm 92*
Rastegar, Farzad Ali 1956- *WhoE 93*
Rastegar, Nader Esmail 1953- *WhoEmL 93, WhoSSW 93, WhoWor 93*
Rastelli, Philip d1991 *BioIn 17*
Rastellini, Susan Infantine 1962- *WhoAmW 93*
Rastetter, William H. *St&PR 93*
Rastislav dc. 870 *OxDcByz*
Rastogi, Anil Kumar 1942- *WhoAm 92*
Rastogi, Pramod Kumar 1951- *WhoWor 93*
Rastrelli, Joseph 1799-1842 *Baker 92*
Rasul, Santanina Tillah 1930- *WhoAsAP 91*
Rasulala, Thalmus 1939-1991 *ConTFT 10*
Rasuli, Ghulam Rasul 1940- *WhoWor 93*
Rasulov, Mahir Abdulali Ogly 1950- *WhoWor 93*
Ras-Work, Terrefe 1936- *WhoUN 92, WhoWor 93*
Raszka, Terry Lee 1948- *WhoIns 93*
Rat, Marcel *WhoScE 91-2*
Rat, Marcel 1939- *WhoScE 91-2*
Rataj, Maciej 1884-1940 *PolBiDi*
Ratajac, Miomir 1926- *WhoScE 91-4*
Ratajczak, Aleksander 1931- *WhoScE 91-4*
Ratajczak, Henryk 1932- *WhoScE 91-4, WhoWor 93*
Ratajski, Magda A. 1950- *St&PR 93*
Ratajski, Magda Anne 1950- *WhoAmW 93, WhoSSW 93*
Ratalahti, Heikki *BioIn 17*
Ratana, Tahupotiki Wiremu 1873-1939 *DcTwHis*
Ratana-Rueangsri, Vararatana 1960- *WhoWor 93*
Ratan Kumari 1913- *WhoAsAP 91*
Ratch, Jerry 1944- *WhoWrEP 92*
Ratchford, Paul Courtney 1955- *St&PR 93*
Ratchford, Regena Stevens- *BioIn 17*
Ratchford, Roger Lionel 1933- *WhoE 93*
Ratchford, Thomas C. 1949- *St&PR 93*
Ratcliff, David L. 1938- *St&PR 93*
Ratcliff, G. *WhoScE 91-1*
Ratcliff, Gene A. 1930- *St&PR 93*
Ratcliff, Gene Austin 1930- *WhoAm 92*
Ratcliff, H.C. 1944- *St&PR 93*
Ratcliff, Hugh Chalfant, Jr. 1944- *WhoAm 92*
Ratcliff, James Lewis 1946- *WhoE 93*
Ratcliff, Reginald Alan 1955- *WhoSSW 93*
Ratcliff, Sara Boney 1957- *WhoAm 92, WhoAmW 93*
Ratcliffe, Ann Elizabeth 1963- *WhoAmW 93*
Ratcliffe, C. Kenneth 1920- *St&PR 93*
Ratcliffe, Christopher Thomas 1955- *WhoSSW 93*
Ratcliffe, David M. *St&PR 93*
Ratcliffe, David N. 1949- *WhoIns 93*
Ratcliffe, George Jackson, Jr. 1936- *St&PR 93*
Ratcliffe, Hazel 1946- *WhoWor 93*
Ratcliffe, John A. 1939- *St&PR 93*
Ratcliffe, Norman Arthur *WhoScE 91-1*
Ratcliffe, Philip George 1955- *WhoWor 93*
Ratcliffe, Ryan Cooper 1959- *WhoE 93, WhoWor 93*
Rateaver, Bargyla 1916- *WhoWrEP 92*
Raterman, Susan Marie 1956- *WhoAmW 93*
Ratez, Emile-Pierre 1851-1934 *Baker 92*
Rath, Alfred Gary 1946- *St&PR 93*
Rath, Alfred V. 1929- *WhoUN 92*
Rath, Antoinette Petrillo 1959- *WhoE 93*
Rath, Bernard Emil 1949- *WhoAm 92*
Rath, Felix vom 1866-1905 *Baker 92*
Rath, Francis Steven 1955- *WhoEmL 93*
Rath, George Edward 1913- *WhoAm 92*
Rath, Gerald Fred 1943- *WhoAm 92*
Rath, Hildegard 1909- *WhoAm 92*
Rath, Joseph P. *Law&B 92*
Rath, R. John 1910- *WhoAm 92*
Rath, Theodore A. 1904-1989 *BioIn 17*
Rath, Thomas David 1945- *WhoAm 92*
Rath, Vicky 1952- *St&PR 93*
Rath, William Collins 1946- *WhoE 93*
Rathakette, Pagarat 1947- *WhoWor 93*
Rathaus, Karol 1895-1954 *Baker 92, PolBiDi*
Rathblott, Paul L. *Law&B 92*
Rathblott, Paul L. 1940- *St&PR 93*
Rathblott, Paul Leon 1940- *WhoAm 92*
Rathbone, Basil 1892-1967 *BioIn 17, IntDcF 2-3*
Rathbone, Charles Stanley 1941- *WhoSSW 93*
Rathbone, David Lyell 1935- *WhoSSW 93*
Rathbone, Donald Earl 1929- *WhoAm 92*
Rathbone, Josephine Adams 1864-1941 *BioIn 17*
Rathbone, Lucy d1990 *BioIn 17*
Rathbone, Perry Townsend 1911- *WhoAm 92*
Rathbone, Peter Betts 1946- *St&PR 93*
Rathbone, Wendy *ScF&FL 92*
Rathborne, Tina *MiSFD 9*
Rathbun, John Wilbert 1924- *WhoAm 92*
Rathbun, Linda S. 1947- *St&PR 93*
Rathbun, Mark *ScF&FL 92*
Rathbun, Roger M. *Law&B 92*
Rathbun-Nealy, Melissa A. *BioIn 17*
Rathburn, Carl C. 1940- *St&PR 93*
Rathburn, Carlisle Baxter, Jr. 1924- *WhoSSW 93*
Rathburn, Carlisle Baxter, III 1957- *WhoSSW 93*
Rathburn, Eldon (Davis) 1916- *Baker 92*
Rathburn, James Patrick *Law&B 92*
Rathe, Gustave 1921- *ConAu 138*
Rathe, R.J. 1928- *St&PR 93*
Rathenau, Walther 1867-1922 *DcTwHis*
Rather, Dan *BioIn 17*
Rather, Dan 1931- *JrnUS, WhoAm 92*
Rather, Gordon Smeade, Jr. 1939- *WhoSSW 93*
Rather, Lois 1905- *ScF&FL 92*
Rather, Lucia Porcher Johnson 1934- *WhoAm 92*
Rather, Terry *BioIn 17*
Rathfon, Steven D. *Law&B 92*
Rathfurd, Michael *WhoE 93*
Rathgeb, Thomas Michael *Law&B 92*
Rathgeber, Frank S. 1935- *St&PR 93*
Rathgen, Gunther H. 1928- *WhoScE 91-3*
Rathje, Frank C. 1924- *St&PR 93*
Rathje, Judy Christine 1952- *WhoAmW 93*
Rathjen, Carl Henry 1909-1984 *ScF&FL 92*
Rathjens, George William 1925- *WhoAm 92*
Rathke, Robert W. *Law&B 92*
Rathke, Sheila Wells 1943- *WhoAmW 93*
Rathke, Wayne George 1931- *St&PR 93*
Rathkolb, Oliver Robert 1955- *WhoWor 93*
Rathkolb, Otto *WhoScE 91-4*
Rathman, Richard R. 1928- *BiDAMSp 1989*
Rathman, William Ernest 1927- *WhoAm 92*
Rathmann, George B. *St&PR 93*
Rathmayer, Werner 1937- *WhoScE 91-3*
Rathmell, Robert Day 1942- *St&PR 93*
Rathnam, Lincoln Yesu 1949- *WhoE 93*
Rathnam, Premila 1936- *WhoE 93*
Rathnow, Hans 1934- *WhoIns 93*
Rathod, David 1952- *MiSFD 9*
Rathod, Uttam B. 1928- *WhoAsAP 91*
Rathore, Uma Pandey 1950- *WhoWor 93*
Rathwa, Ramsinh 1951- *WhoAsAP 91*
Rathwell, Peter John 1943- *WhoAm 92*
Rathwell, Thomas Arnold 1944- *WhoWor 93*
Ratican, Peter J. 1943- *St&PR 93*
Ratiu, Adrian 1928- *Baker 92*
Ratiu, Indrei Stephen Pilkington 1946- *WhoWor 93*
Ratiu, Ion 1917- *WhoWor 93*
Ratkewitch, Samuel 1945- *St&PR 93*
Ratkovics, Ferenc 1931- *WhoScE 91-4*
Ratkowski, Donald J. 1938- *WhoAm 92*
Ratledge, Colin *WhoScE 91-1*
Ratliff, Cecil Wayne 1946- *WhoAm 92, WhoWor 93*
Ratliff, Charles Edward, Jr. 1926- *WhoAm 92, WhoSSW 93*
Ratliff, Cynthia Moore 1949- *WhoSSW 93*
Ratliff, Floyd 1919- *WhoAm 92*
Ratliff, Gerald Lee 1944- *WhoAm 92*

Ratliff, Janice Kay 1949- *WhoSSW 93*
Ratliff, John Charles 1956- *WhoSSW 93*
Ratliff, Leigh Ann 1961- *WhoAmW 93, WhoWor 93*
Ratliff, Louis Jackson, Jr. 1931- *WhoAm 92*
Ratliff, Mike Robert 1934- *St&PR 93*
Ratliff, Randy Lee 1957- *WhoSSW 93*
Ratliff, William D., III 1949- *WhoEmL 93*
Ratliff, William Durrah, Jr. 1921- *WhoAm 92, WhoSSW 93*
Ratner, Albert B. 1927- *St&PR 93*
Ratner, David Louis 1931- *WhoAm 92*
Ratner, Gerald *Law&B 92*
Ratner, Gerald 1913- *WhoAm 92*
Ratner, Gerald Irving 1949- *WhoWor 93*
Ratner, Hank J. *Law&B 92*
Ratner, Harold 1927- *WhoE 93*
Ratner, Harvey *WhoAm 92*
Ratner, Joel H. 1938- *St&PR 93*
Ratner, Joseph 1908-1991 *BioIn 17*
Ratner, Leonard Gilbert 1916- *Baker 92*
Ratner, Lillian Gross 1932- *WhoAmW 93, WhoE 93*
Ratner, Mark Alan 1942- *WhoAm 92*
Ratner, Max 1907- *St&PR 93, WhoAm 92*
Ratner, Michael Howard 1942- *St&PR 93*
Ratner, Milton D. 1918-1991 *BioIn 17*
Ratner, Paul 1936- *St&PR 93*
Ratner, Payne Harry 1896-1974 *BioIn 17*
Ratner, Phillip 1944- *St&PR 93*
Ratner, Robert J. 1950- *St&PR 93*
Ratner, Robert S. 1941- *St&PR 93*
Ratner, Rochelle 1948- *WhoWrEP 92*
Ratner, Wayne Elliot 1950- *WhoE 93*
Ratner-Gantshar, Barbara Grace *WhoAmW 93, WhoE 93*
Ratnoff, Oscar Davis 1916- *WhoAm 92*
Ratny, Ruth Lucille 1932- *WhoAm 92*
Ratoff, Gregory 1897-1960 *MiSFD 9N*
Ratoff, Steven Bernard 1942- *WhoAm 92*
Ratsiraka, Didier 1936- *WhoAfr, WhoWor 93*
Rattan, Arlene Ivy 1955- *WhoE 93*
Rattan, Suresh Inder Singh 1955- *WhoWor 93*
Rattazzi, Serena 1935- *WhoAm 92*
Rattee, David A. 1942- *St&PR 93*
Rattee, Michael Dennis 1953- *WhoWrEP 92*
Ratter, James A. 1934- *WhoScE 91-1*
Ratterman, David Burger 1946- *WhoAm 92*
Ratti, Ronald Andrew 1948- *WhoAm 92*
Ratti, Umberto 1938- *WhoScE 91-3*
Rattigan, Mary Therese 1933- *WhoAmW 93*
Rattigan, Terence *BioIn 17*
Rattigan, Thomas J. 1937- *St&PR 93*
Rattine, R. Ann 1949- *WhoAmW 93*
Rattle, Henry William Ernest *WhoScE 91-1*
Rattle, Simon *BioIn 17*
Rattle, Simon 1955- *NewYTBS 92 [port], OxDcOp, WhoAm 92*
Rattle, Simon (Denis) 1955- *Baker 92*
Rattley, Jessie Menifield 1929- *AfrAmBi, WhoAmW 93*
Rattner, Jack 1925- *St&PR 93*
Rattner, Justin *WhoAm 92*
Rattner, Robert Mitchell 1952- *WhoE 93*
Rattner, Selma *St&PR 93*
Rattner, Steven Lawrence 1952- *WhoAm 92*
Ratto, Eugene Joseph 1926- *WhoAm 92*
Rattoballi, James Philip 1942- *St&PR 93*
Rattoone, Elijah Dunham 1768-1810 *BioIn 17*
Rattray, Douglas C. 1944- *St&PR 93*
Rattray, Robert Sutherland 1881-1938 *IntDcAn*
Ratushinskaya, Irina *BioIn 17*
Raty, Hannu Olavi 1955- *WhoWor 93*
Ratynski, Wojciech *WhoScE 91-4*
Ratz, Ferenc 1942- *WhoScE 91-4*
Ratz, Steve 1920- *St&PR 93*
Ratzel, Friedrich 1844-1904 *IntDcAn*
Ratzenberg, Irving 1928- *St&PR 93*
Ratzenberger, John Dezso 1947- *WhoAm 92*
Ratzinger, Joseph *DcCPCAm*
Ratzinger, Joseph Alois Cardinal 1927- *WhoWor 93*
Ratzlaff, David Edward 1938- *WhoSSW 93*
Ratzlaff, James W. *WhoAm 92*
Ratzlaff, Larry Clifford 1952- *St&PR 93*
Ratzlaff, Stanley A. 1935- *St&PR 93*
Ratzlaff, Stanley Abe 1935- *WhoAm 92*
Ratzsch, Manfred 1933- *WhoScE 91-3*
Ratzsch, Margit Theresa 1934- *WhoScE 91-3*
Rau, Alfred 1927- *WhoAm 92*
Rau, Anantaswamy Ravi Prakash 1945- *WhoSSW 93*
Rau, Charles 1826-1887 *IntDcAn*
Rau, Charles W. 1937- *St&PR 93*
Rau, Cheryl A. 1946- *St&PR 93*
Rau, David E. 1956- *St&PR 93*
Rau, David Edward 1956- *WhoAm 92*
Rau, G. Randal *ScF&FL 92*
Rau, Guenter 1938- *WhoScE 91-3*
Rau, James P. 1943- *St&PR 93*
Rau, John Edward 1948- *St&PR 93, WhoAm 92*
Rau, Lawrence M. 1931- *St&PR 93*
Rau, Lee Arthur 1940- *WhoAm 92*
Rau, Ralph Ronald 1920- *WhoAm 92, WhoE 93*
Rau, Richard H. 1949- *St&PR 93*
Rau, Robert N. 1927- *St&PR 93*
Rau, Robert S. d1991 *BioIn 17*
Rau, Werner 1927- *WhoScE 91-3*
Rau, Werner Bernhard 1927- *WhoWor 93*
Rauam, Naima 1946- *WhoE 93*
Raub, Christoph J. 1932- *WhoScE 91-3*
Raub, Frieda Wright 1912- *WhoAmW 93*
Raub, Kim P. 1953- *St&PR 93*
Raub, Philip J. 1950- *St&PR 93*
Raub, William Fine 1939- *WhoAm 92*
Rauber, A. *WhoScE 91-3*
Rauber, Theresa C. *Law&B 92*
Raucci, Francis Joseph *Law&B 92*
Rauch, Abraham M. 1919- *St&PR 93*
Rauch, Charles Davis 1955- *St&PR 93*
Rauch, Charles Frederick, Jr. 1925- *WhoE 93*
Rauch, Charles Joseph 1922- *St&PR 93*
Rauch, Dudley Atkins 1941- *St&PR 93*
Rauch, Earl Mac 1949- *ScF&FL 92*
Rauch, Francis Clyde 1938- *St&PR 93*
Rauch, Frank W. 1935- *St&PR 93*
Rauch, George Washington 1919- *WhoAm 92*
Rauch, Helmut 1939- *WhoScE 91-4*
Rauch, Herbert Emil 1935- *WhoAm 92*
Rauch, Irmengard 1933- *WhoAm 92, WhoWrEP 92*
Rauch, Joan *WhoAmW 93*
Rauch, John Keiser, Jr. 1930- *WhoAm 92*
Rauch, Kathleen 1951- *WhoAmW 93*
Rauch, Lawrence Lee 1919- *WhoAm 92, WhoWor 93*
Rauch, Lillian H. 1925- *St&PR 93*
Rauch, Lisa Fay 1963- *WhoAmW 93*
Rauch, Mary Laurissa 1952- *WhoAmW 93*
Rauch, Melvin *St&PR 93*
Rauch, Paul David 1933- *WhoAm 92*
Rauch, Richard A. 1929- *St&PR 93*
Rauch, Richard Allan 1929- *WhoE 93*
Rauch, Rudolph Stewart, III 1943- *WhoAm 92*
Rauch, Wolf *WhoScE 91-4*
Rauchenecker, Georg Wilhelm 1844-1906 *Baker 92*
Raucher, Herman 1928- *ScF&FL 92, WhoAm 92*
Rauchle, Craig William 1955- *St&PR 93*
Rauchwerger, Deborah Ann *Law&B 92*
Raucina, Thomas Frank *ScF&FL 92*
Raucina, Thomas Frank 1946- *WhoAm 92*
Rauck, G. *WhoScE 91-3*
Rauck, Gert 1935- *WhoScE 91-3*
Rauck, Horst *WhoScE 91-3*
Raudabaugh, Joseph Luther 1956- *St&PR 93*
Raudales, Ramon *DcCPCAm*
Raue, Jorg Emil 1936- *WhoAm 92*
Rauen, Arnold John 1907- *WhoAm 92*
Rauenhorst, Gerald 1927- *WhoAm 92*
Rauf, Robert Charles, Sr. 1944- *WhoSSW 93, WhoWor 93*
Raugel, Felix 1881-1975 *Baker 92*
Raugust, Carol *BioIn 17*
Raugust, Thomas Anthony 1935- *St&PR 93*
Rauh, Carl Stephen 1940- *WhoAm 92*
Rauh, John David 1932- *WhoAm 92*
Rauh, Joseph, Jr. 1911- *EncAACR*
Rauh, Joseph L. 1911- *PolPar*
Rauh, Joseph L., Jr. 1911- *WhoAm 92*
Rauh, Joseph L., Jr. 1911-1992 *NewYTBS 92*
Rauh, Joseph L(ouis), Jr. 1911-1992 *CurBio 92N*
Rauh, Richard *St&PR 93*
Rauh, Richard Paul 1948- *WhoEmL 93, WhoWor 93*
Rauh, W. *WhoScE 91-3*
Rauhala, Veikko Tapio 1920- *WhoScE 91-4*
Raul, Alan Charles 1954- *WhoAm 92*
Raul, Robin 1958- *WhoE 93*
Raulee, Marcus *St&PR 93*
Raulinaitis, Pranas Algis 1927- *WhoAm 92*
Raullerson, Calvin Henry 1920- *WhoAm 92*
Rauls, Joseph Thomas *Law&B 92*
Rauls, Walter 1930- *WhoScE 91-3*
Rauls, Walter Matthias 1930- *WhoWor 93*
Raulston, Lucy 1936- *WhoSSW 93*
Raum, Arnold 1908- *CngDr 91, WhoAm 92*
Raum, Bernard Anthony 1944- *WhoE 93*
Raum, Johannes William 1931- *WhoWor 93*
Rauma, John Gunnar 1926- *WhoAm 92*
Raumolin, Heikki Ilmari 1944- *WhoScE 91-4*
Raunemaa, Taisto M. 1939- *WhoScE 91-4*
Rauner, Vincent Joseph 1927- *St&PR 93, WhoAm 92*
Rauniyar, Ganesh Prasad 1954- *WhoE 93*
Raup, David Malcolm 1933- *WhoAm 92*
Raupach, Hermann Friedrich 1728-1778 *Baker 92*
Rauppius, Lawrence Hugh 1937- *St&PR 93*
Rauramo, Jaakko Kaarle Mauno 1941- *WhoWor 93*
Raus, Calvin Hugh 1929- *St&PR 93*
Rausa, Giuseppe 1936- *WhoScE 91-3*
Rausch, George H. 1927- *St&PR 93*
Rausch, Howard 1928- *WhoAm 92*
Rausch, Jeffrey Lynn 1953- *WhoWor 93*
Rausch, Joan Brawner 1931- *WhoAmW 93*
Rausch, John Reed 1952- *St&PR 93*
Rausch, Maury K. 1927- *St&PR 93*
Rausch, Walter William 1914- *St&PR 93*
Rausch, William P. 1932- *St&PR 93*
Rauschenberg, Dale Eugene 1938- *WhoE 93, WhoWor 93*
Rauschenberg, Richard A. 1945- *St&PR 93*
Rauschenberg, Robert 1925- *BioIn 17, WhoAm 92, WhoWor 93*
Rauscher, Frank Joseph, Jr. 1931- *WhoWor 93*
Rauscher, John Howard, Jr. 1924- *St&PR 93, WhoAm 92*
Rauscher, Tomlinson Gene 1946- *WhoAm 92*
Rauschert, Gottfried Paul 1924- *WhoWor 93*
Raushenbush, Stephen 1896-1991 *BioIn 17*
Raushenbush, Walter Brandeis 1928- *WhoAm 92*
Rausing, Alf 1937- *WhoScE 91-4*
Rausser, Gordon C. *BioIn 17*
Rausser, Gordon Clyde 1943- *WhoAm 92*
Rauta, Corneliu *WhoScE 91-4*
Rauta, Mircea 1927- *WhoScE 91-4*
Rautavaara, Aulikki 1906-1990 *OxDcOp*
Rautavaara, Eino 1876-1939 *OxDcOp*
Rautavaara, Einojuhani 1928- *Baker 92, OxDcOp*
Rautavaara, Vaino 1872-1950 *OxDcOp*
Rautenbach, Robert 1931- *WhoScE 91-3*
Rautenberg, George David 1924- *St&PR 93*
Rautenberg, H. William 1930- *St&PR 93*
Rautenberg, Herbert Gustav 1935- *St&PR 93*
Rautenberg, Leonard J. 1920- *St&PR 93*
Rautenberg, Wolfgang 1936- *WhoWor 93*
Rauth, Robert Kenneth, Jr. 1960- *WhoSSW 93*
Rautin Ibrahim, Dato' Haji Mohammad Abu Bakar *WhoAsAP 91*
Rautio, H. Kristene 1947- *St&PR 93*
Rautio, Matti 1922-1986 *Baker 92*
Rautiola, Jordan 1961- *St&PR 93*
Rautiola, Norman 1932- *St&PR 93*
Rautman, Arthur Louis 1910- *WhoSSW 93*
Raux, Donald James 1949- *WhoE 93*
Rauzin, Erica Meyer 1949- *WhoWrEP 92*
Rauzzini, Venanzio 1746?-1810 *Baker 92, OxDcOp*
Rava, Susan Roudebush 1939- *WhoAmW 93*
Ravachol 1859-1892 *BioIn 17*
Ravaglioli, Antonio 1938- *WhoScE 91-3*
Ravaioli, Leonida 1921- *WhoScE 91-3*
Raval, Dilip N. *St&PR 93*
Ravanello, Oreste 1871-1938 *Baker 92*
Ravas, Andrea L. *Law&B 92*
Ravas, Paul George 1935- *St&PR 93*
Ravasenga, Carlo 1891-1964 *Baker 92*
Ravasi, Gianfranco 1942- *WhoWor 93*
Ravaud, Jean-Francois 1954- *WhoScE 91-2*
Raveche, Elizabeth Scott 1950- *WhoE 93*
Raveche, Harold Joseph 1943- *WhoAm 92*
Raveis, William *BioIn 17*
Ravel, Aviva *WhoCanL 92*
Ravel, Joanne Macow 1924- *WhoAm 92*
Ravel, Joseph Maurice 1875-1937 *BioIn 17*
Ravel, Maurice 1875-1937 *BioIn 17, IntDcOp [port], OxDcOp*
Ravel, (Joseph) Maurice 1875-1937 *Baker 92*
Raveling, Dennis Graff 1939- *WhoAm 92*
Raven, Anthony *ScF&FL 92*
Raven, Bertram Herbert 1926- *WhoAm 92*
Raven, Daniel *ScF&FL 92*
Raven, Gregory K. 1949- *St&PR 93*
Raven, Gregory Kurt 1949- *WhoAm 92*
Raven, J.E. 1951- *St&PR 93*
Raven, Jacques Robert 1933- *WhoE 93*
Raven, Joel F. 1951- *St&PR 93*
Raven, Jonathan Ezra *Law&B 92*
Raven, Mike 1924- *BioIn 17*
Raven, Peter Hamilton 1936- *WhoAm 92*
Raven, Robert Dunbar 1923- *WhoAm 92*
Raven, Ronald William 1904-1991 *ConAu 136*
Ravenal, Carol Bird Myers *WhoAmW 93*
Ravenal, Earl Cedric 1931- *WhoAm 92*
Ravenel, Arthur, Jr. 1927- *CngDr 91, WhoAm 92, WhoSSW 93*
Ravenel, Charles D. 1938- *St&PR 93*
Ravenel, Henry, Jr. 1934- *St&PR 93*
Ravenel, Shannon 1938- *WhoWrEP 92*
Ravenholt, Marjorie Severyns d1992 *BioIn 17, NewYTBS 92*
Ravenholt, Reimert Thorolf 1925- *WhoAm 92*
Raven-Riemann, Carolyn Sue 1945- *WhoE 93*
Ravenscroft, Arthur 1924-1989 *BioIn 17*
Ravenscroft, John dc. 1708 *Baker 92*
Ravenscroft, Thomas c. 1582-c. 1635 *Baker 92*
Ravenstein, Helga 1919- *WhoWor 93*
Ravenswood, Fritzen *ScF&FL 92*
Raven-Symone *BioIn 17*
Raventos, Antolin 1925- *WhoAm 92*
Raver, Leonard 1927-1992 *BioIn 17, NewYTBS 92 [port]*
Raver, William J. 1947- *St&PR 93*
Ravese, Theresa Geraldine 1958- *WhoAmW 93*
Ravetch, Irving *BioIn 17*
Ravez, Jean 1940- *WhoScE 91-2*
Ravich, Norman J. 1926- *St&PR 93*
Ravier *WhoScE 91-2*
Ravilious, Eric William 1903-1942 *BioIn 17*
Raville, Stephen E. *BioIn 17*
Raville, Stephen E. 1947- *St&PR 93*
Ravin, Richard M. 1943- *St&PR 93*
Ravin, Richard Michael 1943- *WhoIns 93*
Ravina, Jean-Henri 1818-1906 *Baker 92*
Ravindra, Dhurjety 1948- *WhoWor 93*
Ravindra, Mysore V. 1939- *St&PR 93*
Ravindra, Nuggehalli Muthanna 1955- *WhoE 93*
Ravine, Harris 1942- *St&PR 93*
Raviola, Elio 1932- *WhoAm 92*
Ravis, Howard Shepard 1934- *WhoAm 92*
Ravi Shankar 1920- *WhoAsAP 91*
Ravitch, Beverly *Law&B 92*
Ravitch, Diane *BioIn 17*
Ravitch, Diane Silvers 1938- *WhoAm 92, WhoE 93*
Ravitch, Norman 1936- *WhoAm 92*
Ravitch, Richard 1933- *WhoE 93*
Ravitsky, Charles 1917- *WhoSSW 93*
Ravitz, Amy L. *Law&B 92*
Ravitz, Leonard J., Jr. *WhoAm 92, WhoE 93, WhoSSW 93, WhoWor 93*
Ravitz, Robert Allan 1938- *WhoAm 92*
Ravitz, Tina A. *Law&B 92*
Ravitz, Tina A. 1954- *St&PR 93*
Raviv, Gabriel *St&PR 93*
Raviv, Gil 1955- *St&PR 93*
Ravizza, Eugene A. 1928- *St&PR 93*
Ravn, Michael E. *Law&B 92*
Ravvin, Norman 1963- *ConAu 138, WhoCanL 92*
Rawak, Pate *St&PR 93*
Rawat, Harish Chandra Singh 1949- *WhoAsAP 91*
Rawczynska-Englert, Irena 1932- *WhoWor 93*
Rawe, Francis Anthony 1941- *WhoWrEP 92*
Rawi, Ousama 1939- *MiSFD 9*
Rawicz, Andrew Peter 1934- *WhoE 93*
Rawiri, Georges 1932- *WhoAfr*
Rawis, William Bryant 1899-1991 *BioIn 17*
Rawitch, Robert Joe 1945- *WhoAm 92*
Rawl, Arthur Julian 1942- *WhoAm 92, WhoE 93, WhoWor 93*
Rawl, Lawrence G. *BioIn 17*
Rawl, Lawrence G. 1928- *CurBio 92 [port], St&PR 93, WhoAm 92, WhoSSW 93, WhoWor 93*
Rawl, Michael J. 1946- *St&PR 93*
Rawlence, Christopher *MiSFD 9*
Rawlence, Christopher 1945- *ConAu 136*
Rawley, Callman 1903- *BioIn 17*
Rawley, James Albert 1916- *WhoAm 92*
Rawlings, Boynton Mott 1935- *WhoWor 93*
Rawlings, Charles S. *Law&B 92*
Rawlings, David Lionel 1943- *St&PR 93*
Rawlings, Hunter Ripley, III 1944- *WhoAm 92, WhoWor 93*
Rawlings, James Scott 1922- *WhoAm 92*
Rawlings, Jerry J. *BioIn 17*
Rawlings, Jerry John 1947- *DcTwHis, WhoAfr, WhoWor 93*
Rawlings, Marjorie Kinnan 1896-1953 *BioIn 17, ConAu 137, MajAI [port]*
Rawlings, Mary 1936- *WhoAmW 93*
Rawlings, Paul C. 1928- *WhoAm 92*
Rawlings, Randall Adair 1952- *WhoSSW 93*

Rawlings, Robert Hoag 1924- WhoAm 92
Rawlings, Robert William 1941- St&PR 93
Rawlings, Roy M. 1944- St&PR 93
Rawlings, Samuel Craig 1938- WhoE 93
Rawlins, Christopher Brady 1964- WhoSSW 93
Rawlins, Christopher J. 1945- St&PR 93
Rawlins, Christopher John 1945- WhoAm 92
Rawlins, Donald R. Law&B 92
Rawlins, Harry Erle, Jr. 1907- WhoWor 93
Rawlins, Jack 1946- ScF&FL 92
Rawlins, Michael David WhoScE 91-1
Rawlins, Michael David 1941- WhoWor 93
Rawlins, Susan Elizabeth 1941- WhoWrEP 92
Rawlins, V. Lane WhoSSW 93
Rawlins, Wilson Terry 1949- WhoE 93
Rawlinson, Helen Ann 1948- WhoAm 92
Rawlinson, Herbert 1885-1953 BioIn 17
Rawlinson, Jane 1947- ConAu 138
Rawlinson, Richard 1690-1755 BioIn 17
Rawls, Benjamin M. 1940- St&PR 93
Rawls, Charles Allen 1905-1987 AfrAmBi
Rawls, Eugenia WhoAm 92
Rawls, James H. 1952- St&PR 93
Rawls, John 1921- OxCSupC
Rawls, Joyce Lynn Law&B 92
Rawls, Kathryn Stark 1950- WhoSSW 93
Rawls, Lou 1936- WhoAm 92
Rawls, Lou 1937- SoulM
Rawls, Lou(is Allen) 1936- Baker 92
Rawls, Louis Allen 1936- AfrAmBi
Rawls, Sol Waite, III 1948- WhoAm 92
Rawls, Thompson T., II Law&B 92
Rawluszko, Jozef 1944- WhoScE 91-4
Rawlyk, George A. BioIn 17
Rawn, Isabel Nanton AmWomPl
Rawn, Melanie 1953?- ScF&FL 92
Rawn, Stanley Ryle, Jr. 1928- St&PR 93, WhoAm 92
Rawnsley, Howard Melody 1925- WhoAm 92
Rawski, Conrad Henry 1914- WhoAm 92
Rawski, Evelyn Sakakida 1939- WhoAm 92, WhoAmW 93
Rawski, Thomas George 1943- WhoAm 92
Rawson, Charles E. 1925- St&PR 93
Rawson, Claude Julien 1935- WhoE 93
Rawson, Cynthia Ann 1958- WhoAmW 93
Rawson, Eleanor S. WhoAm 92, WhoAmW 93, WhoWrEP 92
Rawson, Elizabeth BioIn 17
Rawson, Jim Charles 1947- WhoSSW 93
Rawson, Kennett L. d1992 NewYTBS 92
Rawson, Kennett Longley 1911- WhoAm 92
Rawson, L.J. 1917- St&PR 93
Rawson, Michael James 1957- St&PR 93
Rawson, Raymond D. 1940- WhoAm 92
Rawson, Richard J. Law&B 92
Rawson, Robert Orrin 1917- WhoAm 92
Rawson, Thomas C. 1952- St&PR 93
Rawson, William Robert 1925- WhoAm 92
Rawsthorne, Alan 1905-1971 Baker 92
Raxach, Enrique 1932- Baker 92
Raxter, Alan R. 1951- St&PR 93
Ray, Aldo 1926-1991 AnObit 1991, BioIn 17
Ray, Allene 1901-1979 SweetSg B [port]
Ray, Arthur Wiley Law&B 92
Ray, Aviva Rosalind Law&B 92
Ray, Barbara Ann 1937- WhoAmW 93
Ray, Barbara Ann 1952- WhoAmW 93
Ray, Bernard J. d1944 BioIn 17
Ray, Billy Frank 1935- St&PR 93
Ray, Blanche H. AmWomPl
Ray, Bobbi WhoWrEP 92
Ray, Bonnie MacDougall 1947- WhoE 93
Ray, Bradley Stephen 1957- WhoEmL 93, WhoSSW 93, WhoWor 93
Ray, Brian WhoScE 91-1
Ray, Bruce D. Law&B 92
Ray, Bruce David 1955- WhoWor 93
Ray, Bryan H. 1945- St&PR 93
Ray, Carl 1943-1978 BioIn 17
Ray, Caroline Miller d1992 NewYTBS 92
Ray, Cecil Arthur, Jr. 1936- WhoAm 92
Ray, Charlene J. WhoAmW 93
Ray, Charles 1944- St&PR 93
Ray, Charles Kendall 1928- WhoAm 92
Ray, Charlotte K. 1954- St&PR 93
Ray, Craig 1960- St&PR 93
Ray, Cread L., Jr. 1931- WhoAm 92
Ray, Cyril 1908-1991 AnObit 1991
Ray, Dan Keith 1948- WhoE 93
Ray, Daniel 1939- St&PR 93
Ray, David ScF&FL 92
Ray, David A. 1926- St&PR 93
Ray, David Christian 1961- WhoWor 93
Ray, David Eugene 1932- WhoAm 92, WhoWrEP 92
Ray, David Gilbert 1952- WhoE 93
Ray, David L. 1957- St&PR 93
Ray, David Scott 1930- WhoAm 92
Ray, Deba Prasad 1949- WhoAsAP 91
Ray, Debasish 1954- WhoE 93
Ray, Deborah Kogan 1941- WhoWrEP 92
Ray, Delia 1963- ConAu 138, SmATA 70 [port]
Ray, Delores I. 1936- St&PR 93
Ray, Don Brandon 1926- Baker 92
Ray, Donald Hensley 1952- WhoAm 92
Ray, Donald Page 1916- WhoAm 92
Ray, Douglas K. 1947- St&PR 93
Ray, Dwight Wiley 1944- St&PR 93
Ray, Eddye Robert 1941- WhoSSW 93
Ray, Edgar Wayne, Jr. 1941- WhoAm 92
Ray, Edward 1932- St&PR 93
Ray, Edward John 1944- WhoAm 92
Ray, Ellen Gail Law&B 92
Ray, Eula Zoline WhoAmW 93
Ray, Eva Konig WhoE 93
Ray, Frank David 1940- WhoAm 92
Ray, Fred Olen MiSFD 9
Ray, Fred Olen 1954- ScF&FL 92
Ray, Gary L. 1941- St&PR 93
Ray, Gary Lee 1940- St&PR 93
Ray, Gene W. 1938- St&PR 93
Ray, Gene Wells 1938- WhoAm 92
Ray, George A. 1940- St&PR 93
Ray, George Allan 1951- St&PR 93
Ray, George Einar 1910- WhoAm 92
Ray, George Washington, III 1932- WhoAm 92
Ray, Gordon N. 1915-1986 ScF&FL 92
Ray, Gordon Norton 1915-1986 BioIn 17
Ray, Gordon Thompson 1928- WhoE 93
Ray, Gregory Ernest 1965- WhoSSW 93
Ray, H. M. 1924- WhoAm 92
Ray, Harold Byrd 1940- St&PR 93, WhoAm 92
Ray, Hugh 1884-1956 BioIn 17
Ray, Hugh Massey, Jr. 1943- WhoAm 92
Ray, J. Franklin 1905-1991 BioIn 17
Ray, Jack Harris 1924- WhoAm 92
Ray, James Butler, III 1954- WhoSSW 93
Ray, James Earl 1928- BioIn 17
Ray, James Phillip Law&B 92
Ray, Jane 1960- SmATA 72 [port]
Ray, Jane Zimrude 1937- WhoAmW 93
Ray, Jeanne Cullinan 1943- WhoAm 92, WhoAmW 93
Ray, Jesse Paul 1916- WhoSSW 93
Ray, John J., III Law&B 92
Ray, John S. Law&B 92
Ray, John Thomas, Jr. 1937- St&PR 93
Ray, John Walker 1936- WhoWor 93
Ray, Johnnie 1927-1990 Baker 92, BioIn 17
Ray, Judy Self 1946- WhoAmW 93, WhoEmL 93, WhoSSW 93, WhoWor 93
Ray, Juliet Man BioIn 17
Ray, Juliet Man 1911-1991 AnObit 1991
Ray, Kelley WhoAm 92
Ray, Kurt K. 1952- St&PR 93
Ray, Man 1890-1976 BioIn 17, MiSFD 9N
Ray, Marianne Yurasko 1934- WhoAmW 93
Ray, Marty A. 1943- WhoSSW 93
Ray, Michael E. Law&B 92
Ray, Michael E. 1945- St&PR 93
Ray, Michael Joseph 1937- WhoE 93
Ray, Michael Thomas 1954- WhoIns 93
Ray, Michele Lynn 1963- WhoSSW 93
Ray, Middleton P., Jr. Law&B 92
Ray, Nicholas 1911-1979 BioIn 17, MiSFD 9N
Ray, Norman H. St&PR 93
Ray, Norman Wilson 1942- WhoAm 92
Ray, Paul Leo 1946- WhoWor 93
Ray, Paul R., Jr. 1943- WhoAm 92
Ray, Rabi 1926- WhoWor 93
Ray, Randy T. 1959- WhoSSW 93
Ray, Rayburn Windham 1925- WhoSSW 93
Ray, Rene 1912- ScF&FL 92
Ray, Richard 1927- CngDr 91
Ray, Richard Archibald 1936- WhoAm 92
Ray, Richard Barney 1940- St&PR 93
Ray, Richard Belmont 1927- WhoAm 92, WhoSSW 93
Ray, Richard Eugene 1950- WhoWor 93
Ray, Richard F. 1937- St&PR 93
Ray, Ricky BioIn 17
Ray, Ricky d1992 NewYTBS 92
Ray, Robert 1928- ScF&FL 92
Ray, Robert D. 1914- WhoAm 92
Ray, Robert F. 1949- St&PR 93
Ray, Robert Francis 1947- WhoAsAP 91, WhoWor 93
Ray, Robert Franklin 1949- WhoAm 92
Ray, Robert Henry 1940- WhoSSW 93
Ray, Robert Owen 1949- WhoAm 92
Ray, Roger Buchanan 1935- WhoAm 92
Ray, Ronald Eric 1941- WhoAm 92
Ray, Roy Robert 1902- WhoAm 92
Ray, Ruth Alice Yancey 1931- WhoAmW 93, WhoSSW 93
Ray, Ruth Ann 1943- WhoAmW 93
Ray, Satyajit BioIn 17
Ray, Satyajit 1921- MiSFD 9
Ray, Satyajit 1921-1992 ConAu 137, CurBio 92N, NewYTBS 92 [port]
Ray, Satyajit 1922-1992 ScF&FL 92
Ray, Scott H. 1955- St&PR 93
Ray, Shirley G. 1934- WhoWrEP 92
Ray, Stephen John 1961- St&PR 93
Ray, Sudhir 1933- WhoAsAP 91
Ray, Susanne Gettings 1938- WhoAmW 93
Ray, Suzanne Judy 1939- WhoAmW 93, WhoWrEP 92
Ray, Ted 1909-1977 QDrFCA 92 [port]
Ray, Timothy Britt 1939- WhoSSW 93
Ray, Trevor 1934- ScF&FL 92
Ray, W. Harmon 1940- WhoAm 92
Ray, William F. 1915- St&PR 93, WhoAm 92, WhoE 93, WhoWor 93
Ray, William Jackson 1945- WhoAm 92
Raya, Marcos 1948- HispAmA
Rayan, Muhammad Fahim 1928- WhoWor 93
Raybeck, Michael Joseph 1945- WhoSSW 93
Raybon, Patricia A. 1943- St&PR 93
Raybuck, Joseph H. Law&B 92
Rayburn, Carole Mary Aida Ann 1938- WhoAm 92, WhoAmW 93
Rayburn, Clyde J. Law&B 92
Rayburn, Cynthia Speed 1947- WhoSSW 93
Rayburn, Gene WhoAm 92
Rayburn, George Marvin 1920- WhoAm 92
Rayburn, James L. 1944- St&PR 93
Rayburn, James T. Law&B 92
Rayburn, Jerry W. 1940- St&PR 93
Rayburn, Patricia AmWomPl
Rayburn, Samuel T. 1882-1961 PolPar
Raydio SoulM
Raydon, Max E. 1942- St&PR 93
Raye, Don 1946- WhoEmL 93
Raye, Gary 1963- BioIn 17
Raye, Jesse A. Law&B 92
Raye, Martha 1908- QDrFCA 92 [port]
Raye, Robert S. 1940- St&PR 93
Rayer, Francis G. 1921-1981 ScF&FL 92
Rayevsky, Robert ChlBIID [port]
Rayfiel, David 1923- ConAu 139
Rayfield, Allan Laverne 1935- WhoAm 92
Rayfield, Florence R. AmWomPl
Rayfield, Gordon Elliott 1950- WhoAm 92
Rayford, Alma SweetSg B [port]
Rayher, John 1946- WhoE 93
Rayl, Granville Monroe 1917- WhoWor 93
Rayl, India 1956- WhoAmW 93
Rayl, John Edward 1947- WhoAm 92
Raylesberg, Alan Ira 1950- WhoAm 92, WhoEmL 93
Rayman, S. Eric Law&B 92
Rayment, Robert WhoScE 91-1
Rayment, T. WhoScE 91-1
Raymer, Donald George 1924- St&PR 93, WhoAm 92
Raymer, Joel L. Law&B 92
Raymer, Steven Laurence 1945- WhoAm 92
Raymes, Frederick 1929- St&PR 93
Raymon, Gerald Law&B 92
Raymon, Paul M. 1927- St&PR 93
Raymond, Alice 1938- ScF&FL 92
Raymond, Arthur Joseph 1949- WhoE 93
Raymond, C. Elizabeth 1953- ConAu 139
Raymond, Charles M. Law&B 92
Raymond, Charles Michael 1953- WhoSSW 93
Raymond, Charles Walker, III 1937- WhoE 93
Raymond, Cynthia Diane Armstrong 1947- WhoAmW 93
Raymond, Dan 1937- St&PR 93
Raymond, David A. 1940- St&PR 93
Raymond, David Alan 1948- WhoAm 92
Raymond, David W. Law&B 92
Raymond, Donald Laurence 1931- WhoE 93
Raymond, Dorothy Gill 1954- St&PR 93, WhoAmW 93
Raymond, Elfie Stock 1931- WhoAm 92
Raymond, Eugene Thomas 1923- WhoWor 93
Raymond, F. Douglas, III 1958- WhoE 93
Raymond, George G., Jr. 1921- St&PR 93
Raymond, George Gamble, Jr. 1921- WhoAm 92
Raymond, George Leslie Law&B 92
Raymond, George Marc 1919- WhoAm 92
Raymond, Gerard Gabriel 1948- WhoUN 92
Raymond, Ginny Terry 1944- WhoAmW 93
Raymond, Guy 1911- WhoAm 92
Raymond, Harvey Francis 1915- WhoAm 92
Raymond, Henry 1820-1869 JrnUS
Raymond, Henry J. 1820-1869 PolPar
Raymond, Henry Jarvis 1820-1869 BioIn 17
Raymond, Ilene Helen 1954- WhoWrEP 92
Raymond, Jack 1918- WhoAm 92, WhoWor 93
Raymond, James C. 1940- WhoWrEP 92
Raymond, James Patrick 1935- WhoAm 92
Raymond, Joan M. 1936- WhoAm 92, WhoSSW 93
Raymond, John ScF&FL 92
Raymond, John A., Jr. 1918- St&PR 93
Raymond, Katherine Law&B 92
Raymond, Kenneth Norman 1942- WhoAm 92
Raymond, Lee R. 1938- St&PR 93, WhoAm 92, WhoWor 93
Raymond, Lucille J. 1943- St&PR 93
Raymond, Mark Wesley 1950- WhoWrEP 92
Raymond, Michael Lyons 1943- St&PR 93
Raymond, Michael William 1957- WhoE 93
Raymond, Monica E. 1949- WhoWrEP 92
Raymond, Norma Cohen 1931- WhoAmW 93
Raymond, Rene ScF&FL 92
Raymond, Rhoades Robert 1949- WhoSSW 93
Raymond, Richard G. Law&B 92
Raymond, Robert 1906- St&PR 93
Raymond, Robert G. Law&B 92
Raymond, Robert Pennal Law&B 92
Raymond, (Myrtle) Roby 1920- WhoWrEP 92
Raymond, Ronald Alan, III 1944- St&PR 93
Raymond, Samuel 1920- WhoE 93
Raymond, Samuel 1928- St&PR 93
Raymond, Sandra Lynn 1944- WhoAmW 93
Raymond, Spencer Henry 1926- WhoAm 92
Raymond, Teresa 1960- St&PR 93
Raymond, Theodore Alan 1927- St&PR 93
Raymond, Tim C. Law&B 92
Raymond, William Marshall 1934- St&PR 93
Raymonda, James Earl 1933- St&PR 93, WhoAm 92
Raymond-Bedore, Carrie A. Law&B 92
Raymond of Aguilers fl. c. 1100- OxDcByz
Raymond of Poitiers c. 1098-1149 OxDcByz
Raymond, of Poitiers, Prince of Antioch 1099?-1149 BioIn 17
Raymond of Toulouse c. 1041-1105 OxDcByz
Raymonds, Stephen C. Law&B 92
Raymore, Karen Lovell 1956- WhoAmW 93
Raymund, Steven 1955- WhoSSW 93
Raymundo, Adelisa A. 1934- WhoAsAP 91
Raynard, P. WhoScE 91-2
Raynaud, Dominique P.M. 1942- WhoScE 91-2
Raynaud, Jacques Francois 1946- WhoWor 93
Raynauld, Andre 1927- WhoAm 92
Rayner, Anthony John WhoScE 91-1
Rayner, Arno A. 1928- St&PR 93
Rayner, Bonnie Lou 1940- WhoAmW 93
Rayner, Donald Edward 1944- St&PR 93
Rayner, Kenneth 1808-1884 PolPar
Rayner, Michael 1943- BioIn 17
Rayner, Robert M. 1946- St&PR 93
Rayner, Robert Martin 1946- WhoE 93
Rayner, William 1929- ScF&FL 92
Rayner, William Alexander 1929- WhoAm 92
Raynes, Bruno 1944- St&PR 93
Raynes, Martin BioIn 17
Raynock, Joseph Francis 1924- St&PR 93
Raynolds, Eleanor H. d1992 NewYTBS 92 [port]
Raynolds, Harold, Jr. 1925- WhoAm 92, WhoE 93
Raynor, John Patrick 1923- WhoAm 92
Raynor, Richard Benjamin 1928- WhoAm 92, WhoE 93, WhoWor 93
Raynor, Richard D. 1935- St&PR 93
Raynor, William ScF&FL 92
Raynsford, Kathleen Johnson Law&B 92
Raynsford, Robert Wayne, Jr. 1935- WhoE 93
Rayome, Mark Francis 1960- WhoE 93
Rayson, Edwin Hope 1923- WhoAm 92
Rayson, Glendon Ennes 1915- WhoE 93, WhoWor 93
Rayson, Jack Henry 1931- WhoAm 92, WhoSSW 93
Raysor, Frank Wannamaker, II 1943- WhoE 93
Raytchev, Peter Petrov 1938- WhoWor 93
Rayvid, Douglas A. Law&B 92
Rayward, Warden Boyd 1939- WhoAm 92, WhoWor 93

Raz, Hilda 1938- WhoWrEP 92
Raz, Jo Anne WhoWrEP 92
Raz, Lawrence W. Law&B 92
Raz, Robert Eugene 1942- WhoAm 92
Razafimahatratra, Victor Cardinal 1921- WhoWor 93
Razafy, Robert Jean 1943- WhoUN 92
Razak, Dato' Seri Haji Mohd Najib Bin Tun Haji Abdul 1953- WhoAsAP 91
Razak Abu Samah, Datuk 1926- WhoAsAP 91
Razaleigh, Hamzah BioIn 17
Razaleigh Hamzah, Tengku 1937- WhoAsAP 91
Razali, Ismail 1939- WhoUN 92
Razanamasy, Guy WhoWor 93
Razatos, Spiro MiSFD 9
Razek, Adel 1945- WhoScE 91-2
Razey, Sandra Lynn 1963- WhoE 93
Razi, Kathleen Ann 1950- WhoAmW 93
Razin, Assaf 1941- ConAu 136
Raz Mohammad Paktin, Comrad Prof. 1941- WhoAsAP 91
Raznoff, Beverly Shultz 1946- WhoSSW 93
Razoharinoro 1936- WhoWor 93
Razon, Enrique K. 1960- WhoWor 93
Razowski, Jozef 1932- WhoScE 91-4
Razumovsky, Count 1752-1836 Baker 92
Razzano, Frank Charles 1948- WhoE 93, WhoEmL 93, WhoWor 93
Razzano, Pasquale Angelo 1943- WhoE 93, WhoWor 93
Razze, Gary 1953- St&PR 93
Razzell, Mary 1930- DcChlFi
Razzhevaikin, Valery Nicolaevitch 1954- WhoWor 93
Razzi, James 1931- ScF&FL 92
Razzi, Jim ScF&FL 92
Re, Edward D. 1920- CngDr 91, WhoAm 92, WhoE 93
Rea, Amadeo Michael 1939- WhoAm 92
Rea, Ann Hadley Kuehn 1962- WhoAmW 93
Rea, Charles A. Law&B 92
Rea, David 1949- St&PR 93
Rea, David B. 1926- St&PR 93
Rea, David K. 1919- St&PR 93
Rea, Graeme Francis 1935- WhoUN 92
Rea, John 1944- Baker 92
Rea, John 1947- WhoScE 91-1
Rea, Kerry Douglas 1958- St&PR 93
Rea, Margaret Eleanore 1935- WhoWor 93
Rea, Marina Ferreira 1946- WhoUN 92
Rea, Norman H. 1923- St&PR 93
Rea, Richard A. 1939- St&PR 93
Rea, Richard H. Law&B 92
Rea, S.N. Law&B 92
Rea, Stanley M. Law&B 92
Rea, William Edward 1936- St&PR 93
Reach, Barbara d1992 NewYTBS 92
Reach, Brian L. 1955- St&PR 93
Read, Al 1931- St&PR 93
Read, Allan Alexander 1923- WhoAm 92
Read, Anice BioIn 17
Read, Anne 1959- WhoWor 93
Read, Arthur William 1930- WhoAm 92
Read, Barbara Harris 1936- WhoSSW 93
Read, Benjamin Huger 1925- WhoAm 92, WhoWor 93
Read, Bryan E. 1934- WhoScE 91-1
Read, Cameron ScF&FL 92
Read, Daniel 1757-1836 Baker 92
Read, David Law&B 92
Read, David Haxton Carswell 1910- WhoAm 92
Read, E. WhoScE 91-1
Read, Elfreida 1920- WhoCanL 92
Read, Frank Henry WhoScE 91-1
Read, Frank Thompson 1938- WhoAm 92
Read, Frederick Wilson, Jr. 1908- WhoAm 92
Read, Gardner 1913- Baker 92
Read, Gregory Charles 1942- WhoAm 92
Read, Harold T. 1938- St&PR 93
Read, Harrison Andrew 1950- WhoSSW 93
Read, Herbert Edward 1893-1968 BioIn 17
Read, James Bond 1766-1841 BioIn 17
Read, Jennifer Lynn 1946- WhoSSW 93
Read, Joel WhoAm 92, WhoAmW 93
Read, John ScF&FL 92
Read, John 1769-1854 BioIn 17
Read, John Conyers 1947- St&PR 93, WhoAm 92
Read, John Douglas St&PR 93
Read, John Emms 1918- St&PR 93
Read, John Meredith 1797-1874 OxCSupC
Read, Jonathan Miles d1990 BioIn 17
Read, Mary Jane 1961- WhoAmW 93
Read, Michael J. Law&B 92
Read, Michael Oscar 1942- WhoSSW 93
Read, Nicholas C. Law&B 92
Read, Nicholas Wallace WhoScE 91-1
Read, Opie 1852-1939 JrnUS
Read, Paul Alfred WhoScE 91-1
Read, Paul E. 1937- WhoAm 92
Read, Philip Lloyd 1932- WhoAm 92
Read, Piers Paul 1941- ConAu 38NR, ScF&FL 92, WhoAm 92
Read, Richard Edward Harvey WhoScE 91-1
Read, Robert Gary 1947- St&PR 93
Read, Sanders Glover, Jr. 1940- WhoSSW 93
Read, Susan C. WhoAm 92
Read, Wallace W. 1932- St&PR 93
Read, William Edgar 1927- WhoAm 92, WhoWor 93
Read, William Edward 1953- St&PR 93
Read, William J. 1938- St&PR 93
Read, William Lawrence 1926- WhoAm 92
Read, William McClain 1918- WhoAm 92
Read, William T. 1938- WhoSSW 93
Reade, Claire Elizabeth 1952- WhoAm 92, WhoE 93
Reade, David M. 1927- St&PR 93
Reade, Deborah 1949- SmATA 69 [port]
Reade, Hamish 1936- BioIn 17
Reade, Richard 1922- St&PR 93
Reade, Richard Sill 1913- WhoAm 92
Reade, Robert B. 1918- St&PR 93
Reade, Robert Mellor 1940- WhoAm 92
Reade, Suzanne Joan Floss 1952- WhoAmW 93
Reader, Alec Harold 1957- WhoWor 93
Reader, Arthur Murray 1930- WhoSSW 93
Reader, Barbara 1955- WhoE 93
Reader, Chan B. Law&B 92
Reader, Charles M. 1928- St&PR 93
Reader, Dennis 1929- SmATA 71 [port]
Reader, Dennis Joel 1939- WhoWrEP 92
Reader, George Gordon 1919- WhoAm 92
Reader, Russell B. Law&B 92
Reader, Sydney Ralph 1918- WhoWor 93
Reader, W(illiam) J(oseph) 1920-1990 ConAu 39NR
Reading, Anthony John 1933- WhoAm 92
Reading, Bertice d1991 BioIn 17
Reading, Bertice 1933-1991 AnObit 1991
Reading, Charles Roland 1944- St&PR 93
Reading, George Paul 1929- WhoE 93
Reading, James Edward 1924- WhoAm 92
Reading, John c. 1645-1692 Baker 92
Reading, John c. 1685-1764 Baker 92
Reading, John W. Law&B 92
Reading, Kathleen Adell 1944- WhoE 93
Readings, Bill 1960- ConAu 139
Ready, Elizabeth M. 1953- WhoAmW 93
Ready, Robert James 1952- WhoAm 92
Ready, William B. 1914-1981 ScF&FL 92
Reagan, Barbara Benton WhoAm 92
Reagan, Bernida 1954- WhoAmW 93
Reagan, Floranne R. St&PR 93
Reagan, Georgia Ann 1949- WhoAmW 93
Reagan, Harry D. 1933- St&PR 93
Reagan, James C. 1958- St&PR 93
Reagan, James W. St&PR 93, WhoAm 92
Reagan, JoAnn Freiberg 1953- WhoAmW 93
Reagan, John J. Law&B 92
Reagan, Mark Edward 1949- St&PR 93
Reagan, Nancy 1923- BioIn 17
Reagan, Nancy Davis 1923- WhoAm 92, WhoAmW 93, WhoWor 93
Reagan, Patricia Ann BioIn 17
Reagan, Patrick Dennis 1953- WhoSSW 93
Reagan, Paul V. Law&B 92
Reagan, Peter L. 1944- St&PR 93
Reagan, Reginald Lee 1910- WhoWor 93
Reagan, Renee Gabrielle 1964- WhoAmW 93
Reagan, Ron BioIn 17
Reagan, Ron 1958- CurBio 92 [port]
Reagan, Ronald 1911- BioIn 17, ColdWar 1 [port], DcTwHis, IntDcF 2-3 [port], OxCSupC
Reagan, Ronald W. 1911- PolPar
Reagan, Ronald Wilson 1911- WhoAm 92, WhoWor 93
Reagin, Arthur H. Law&B 92
Reagin, Leslie Dyer, III 1943- WhoSSW 93
Reagin, Nancy Ruth 1960- WhoE 93
Reagin, Richard Stephen 1962- WhoSSW 93
Reagin, Thomas Gaby 1954- WhoSSW 93
Reagles, Kenneth W. 1940- WhoE 93
Reagon, Bernice Johnson 1942- WhoAm 92
Reagor, Craig St&PR 93
Real, Cathleen Clare 1934- WhoAmW 93
Real, Fernando N. Ferreira 1923- WhoScE 91-3
Real, Isidoro E., Jr. 1936- WhoAsAP 91
Real, James Cary 1951- St&PR 93
Real, Manuel L. 1924- HispAmA [port]
Real, Manuel Lawrence 1924- WhoAm 92
Real, William Jay 1948- St&PR 93
Reale, Carmine A. Law&B 92
Reale, Dianne Jennifer 1961- WhoAmW 93
Reale, Paul 1943- Baker 92
Reale, Richard Thomas 1939- St&PR 93
Reali, Janet L. Law&B 92
Reals, William Joseph 1920- WhoAm 92
Reals, Willis Braithwaite 1925- St&PR 93
Ream, David L. Law&B 92
Ream, Jeffrey L. 1946- St&PR 93
Ream, John K. 1934- St&PR 93
Ream, Juliet Lynn 1963- WhoAmW 93
Ream, Michael D. 1943- St&PR 93
Ream, Richard P. 1943- St&PR 93
Ream, Ronald Lee 1941- St&PR 93
Reamer, Norton H. 1935- St&PR 93
Reamer, Sharon Elizabeth 1953- WhoAmW 93
Reames, Richard R. 1942- St&PR 93
Reames, Stephen Anthony 1945- WhoSSW 93
Reames, Timothy Paul Law&B 92
Reames, Timothy Paul 1935- St&PR 93, WhoAm 92
Reams, Bernard Dinsmore, Jr. 1943- WhoAm 92, WhoWor 93
Reams, Gerald Brock 1929- WhoSSW 93
Reams, Hugh Douglas, Jr. Law&B 92
Reams, Radford M. Law&B 92
Reamy, Thomas E. ScF&FL 92
Reamy, Tom 1935-1977 ScF&FL 92
Reanda, Laura 1938- WhoUN 92
Reaney, Gilbert 1924- Baker 92, WhoAm 92
Reaney, James Crerar 1926- WhoAm 92, WhoCanL 92
Reap, Coleman R. Law&B 92
Reap, Mary Margaret 1941- WhoAm 92, WhoAmW 93
Reap, Norah Boyle 1947- WhoAmW 93
Reaph, Joseph V., Jr. Law&B 92
Rearden, Anna AmWomPl
Rearden, Jim 1925- ConAu 40NR
Reardon, Andrew Fitzpatrick 1945- WhoAm 92
Reardon, Anna Joyce 1910- WhoSSW 93
Reardon, Bryan Peter 1928- WhoAm 92
Reardon, D. Barry WhoAm 92
Reardon, Edward Hyland 1942- WhoWrEP 92
Reardon, Edward Joseph 1943- St&PR 93
Reardon, Edwin Everett, Jr. 1956- WhoSSW 93
Reardon, G. WhoScE 91-1
Reardon, Janet Mauk WhoWrEP 92
Reardon, Jeffrey James 1955- WhoAm 92
Reardon, John 1930-1988 Baker 92
Reardon, John Joseph 1938- St&PR 93
Reardon, Kathleen Mary 1958- WhoAmW 93
Reardon, Leonard W. 1940- St&PR 93
Reardon, Mark F. Law&B 92
Reardon, Mark W. Law&B 92
Reardon, Mary Agnes 1912- WhoE 93
Reardon, Michael J. Law&B 92
Reardon, Michael James 1956- WhoEmL 93
Reardon, Patrick C. 1937- St&PR 93
Reardon, Rebecca S. 1955- WhoAmW 93
Reardon, Robert J. 1928- St&PR 93
Reardon, Robert Joseph 1928- WhoAm 92
Rearick, Carolyn Sue 1949- WhoAmW 93
Reark, John Benson 1923- WhoSSW 93, WhoWor 93
Reaser, Vernon Neal, Jr. 1942- WhoWor 93
Reason, Joseph Paul 1941- AfrAmBi [port]
Reasoner, Charles F. ScF&FL 92
Reasoner, Elizabeth Diane 1949- WhoAmW 93
Reasoner, Harry 1923-1991 AnObit 1991, BioIn 17, ConTFT 10, JrnUS, News 92
Reasoner, Harry Max 1939- WhoAm 92
Reasoner, John William 1940- WhoSSW 93
Reasoner, Macey Hodges 1940- WhoAmW 93
Reasoner, Stephen M. 1944- WhoAm 92
Reasoner, Willis Irl, III 1951- WhoAm 92
Reasor, Janet M. Law&B 92
Reat, N(oble) Ross 1951- ConAu 139
Reategui, Julio Antonio 1956- WhoE 93
Reategui, Randolfo St&PR 93
Reath, George, Jr. Law&B 92
Reath, George, Jr. 1939- WhoAm 92, WhoE 93
Reaties, Betty Ann 1942- WhoSSW 93
Reau, Jean-Maurice 1940- WhoScE 91-2
Reaugh, O.H. 1913- St&PR 93
Reaume, David Michael 1941- WhoWor 93
Reaux, Angelina BioIn 17
Reaux, Gerald G. 1961- St&PR 93
Reaver, Chap 1935- ConAu 137, SmATA 69 [port]
Reaver, Herbert R. ConAu 137
Reaver, J. Russell 1915- WhoSSW 93
Reaves, Benjamin F. WhoAm 92
Reaves, Charles Edwin 1942- WhoSSW 93
Reaves, Frank McLeod 1924- St&PR 93
Reaves, Michael 1950- ScF&FL 92
Reaves, Mitchell W. 1954- St&PR 93
Reaves, Randal Moran Law&B 92
Reaves, Troy Albert, Jr. 1945- WhoSSW 93
Reaves, Wendy Wick 1950- WhoAm 92
Reaves, William B., III 1944- St&PR 93
Reavis, Charles G. 1948- WhoWrEP 92
Reavis-Freeman, Terry Kaye 1961- WhoSSW 93
Reavley, Thomas Morrow 1921- WhoAm 92, WhoSSW 93
Reavy, Colleen 1965- WhoE 93
Reay, D. WhoScE 91-1
Reay, J.S.S. WhoScE 91-1
Reback, Joyce Ellen 1948- WhoAm 92
Reback, Kathryn A. Law&B 92
Reback, Richard Neal 1954- WhoEmL 93
Reback, Shelley Wall Law&B 92
Rebal, James N. 1936- St&PR 93
Rebane, John T. Law&B 92
Rebane, John T. 1946- St&PR 93, WhoAm 92
Rebar, Robert William 1947- WhoAm 92
Rebay, Luciano 1928- WhoAm 92
Rebec, George Vincent 1949- WhoAm 92
Rebecca BioIn 17
Rebecca, Dan Joseph 1957- St&PR 93
Rebecchi, John Arnold 1954- WhoE 93
Rebeck, Daniel S. 1938- St&PR 93
Rebeil, Patricia Anne 1962- WhoAmW 93
Rebeiz, Constantin Anis 1936- WhoAm 92
Rebekah BioIn 17
Rebel Baker 92
Rebel, Andre 1934- WhoScE 91-2
Rebel, Anne-Renee 1663?-1722 Baker 92
Rebel, Francois 1701-1775 Baker 92
Rebel, Jean dc. 1692 Baker 92
Rebel, Jean-Fery 1666?-1747 Baker 92
Rebele, Anthony P. 1933- St&PR 93
Rebele, David E. 1928- St&PR 93
Rebello, Joao Soares 1610-1661 Baker 92
Rebello, Luiz Francisco 1924- WhoWor 93
Rebelo, Joao Soares 1610-1661 Baker 92
Rebenack, John Henry 1918- WhoAm 92
Rebenfeld, Ludwig 1928- WhoAm 92
Rebenko, Alexei Luckich 1945- WhoWor 93
Rebennack, Mac SoulM
Rebensdorf, John Law&B 92
Reber, Cheryl Ann 1956- WhoAmW 93
Reber, Denise Garibaldi 1961- WhoAmW 93
Reber, Gottlieb Friedrich 1880-1959 BioIn 17
Reber, (Napoleon-) Henri 1807-1880 Baker 92
Reber, Raymond Andrew 1942- WhoE 93
Reber, Ron R. 1947- WhoSSW 93
Reber, Stanley R. 1943- St&PR 93
Reber, Stanley Roy 1943- WhoAm 92
Rebernik, P. WhoScE 91-4
Rebernik, Peter 1950- WhoWor 93
Rebert, Bruce 1951- WhoE 93
Rebicek, Vincent Stass 1922- WhoE 93
Rebikov, Vladimir 1866-1920 OxDcOp
Rebikov, Vladimir (Ivanovich) 1866-1920 Baker 92
Rebman, John R. Law&B 92
Rebmann, Johannes 1820-1876 Expl 93
Rebne, Claudia Ann 1962- WhoAmW 93
Rebner, Adolf 1876-1967 Baker 92
Rebner, Ronald Marshall 1944- St&PR 93
Rebner, Wolfgang Eduard 1910- Baker 92
Rebolledo, Efren 1877-1929 DcMexL
Rebolledo, Tey Diana 1937- HispAmA, NotHsAW 93
Rebollo-Lopez, Francisco WhoSSW 93
Rebone, Joseph W. Law&B 92
Rebone, William Frederick 1931- St&PR 93
Rebora, Alfredo 1935- WhoScE 91-3
Reboul, Anne Colette 1956- WhoWor 93
Reboul, Jaques Regis 1947- WhoWor 93
Rebozo, Charles Gregory 1912- WhoAm 92
Reburn, John A. 1926- St&PR 93
Rebusmen, Richard Joseph 1944- St&PR 93
Recalde, Carlos M. BioIn 17
Recana, Jaime Red 1932- WhoWor 93
Recanati, Dimitri N. 1926- St&PR 93
Recanati, Elias Isaac 1932- WhoE 93
Recanati, Michael 1957- St&PR 93
Recasens, Francisco 1946- WhoScE 91-3
Recca, Carol Leslie 1957- WhoAmW 93
Recchia, Susan Margaret 1955- WhoAmW 93
Rech, Charles Louis 1938- St&PR 93
Rechard, Ottis William 1924- WhoAm 92
Rechard, Paul Albert 1927- WhoAm 92
Rechardt, A. Leena 1934- WhoScE 91-4
Rechberg, Burkard Mullenheim- 1910- BioIn 17
Rechberger, Herman(n) 1947- Baker 92
Rechcigl, Miloslav, Jr. 1930- WhoAm 92
Rechenberg, Peter 1933- WhoScE 91-4
Rechenmann, Roger WhoScE 91-2

Rechenmann, Roger Victor 1927- *WhoScE 91-2*
Recher, Louis *Law&B 92*
Rechholtz, Robert August 1937- *St&PR 93*
Rechka, Mary Emily 1937- *WhoAmW 93*
Rechkemmer, Gerhard 1951- *WhoScE 91-3*
Rechkemmer, Michael Louis 1949- *St&PR 93*
Rechsteiner, Emil B. 1931- *St&PR 93*
Recht, Milton Richard 1948- *WhoE 93*
Recht, Theresa Kerrigan 1954- *WhoAmW 93*
Rechter, Debbie Elizabeth 1961- *WhoAmW 93*
Rechter, Denise Marie *Law&B 92*
Rechter, Herbert Leslie 1932- *St&PR 93*
Rechter, Leo E. 1927- *WhoE 93*
Rechter, Richard P. 1939- *St&PR 93*
Rechtien, John Gerhardt 1937- *WhoSSW 93*
Rechtin, Eberhardt 1926- *WhoAm 92*
Rechy, John 1934- *ConGAN, DcLB 122 [port]*
Rechy, John Francisco *WhoAm 92*
Recine, Anthony F. *Law&B 92*
Recine, Bob *BioIn 17*
Recio, Irene M. 1968- *WhoAmW 93*
Reck, Andrew Joseph 1927- *WhoAm 92*
Reck, Gregory Milton 1946- *WhoE 93*
Reck, James Rodney 1938- *St&PR 93*
Reck, Norma Jean 1933- *WhoE 93*
Reck, Rima Drell 1933- *WhoSSW 93*
Reck, Saul I. 1918- *St&PR 93*
Reck, Thomas Carl 1914- *St&PR 93*
Reck, W(aldo) Emerson 1903- *WhoWrEP 92*
Reck, Waldo Emerson 1903- *WhoAm 92*
Recker, Kenneth Joseph 1947- *St&PR 93*
Recker, Ronald William 1949- *St&PR 93*
Reckeweg, Donald *St&PR 93*
Reckford, Thomas Joseph 1943- *WhoE 93*
Reckley, Charles S. *St&PR 93*
Recklies, Adele Rogers 1949- *WhoE 93*
Recknagel, Ekkehard 1931- *WhoScE 91-3*
Reclus, Elisee 1830-1905 *BioIn 17*
Recomendes, Joseph A. 1944- *St&PR 93*
Record, John Fordham 1942- *St&PR 93*
Record, Neil Peter 1953- *WhoWor 93*
Record, Patricia Louise 1956- *WhoAmW 93*
Record, Phillip Julius 1929- *WhoAm 92, WhoWor 93*
Records, George Jeffrey 1934- *St&PR 93*
Records, Susan Frances 1943- *WhoSSW 93*
Recsetar, Ernie Laszlo *Law&B 92*
Rectanus, Elizabeth Rehm *WhoAmW 93*
Rectenwald, Margaret Buck 1947- *WhoSSW 93*
Recto, Claro M. 1890-1960 *BioIn 17*
Rector, Bruce Johnson 1953- *WhoE 93*
Rector, Clark Ellsworth 1934- *WhoSSW 93*
Rector, Edward *BioIn 17*
Rector, Floyd Clinton, Jr. 1929- *WhoAm 92*
Rector, Harold E. 1946- *St&PR 93*
Rector, John Michael 1943- *WhoAm 92*
Rector, Liam 1949- *WhoWrEP 92*
Rector, Margaret Hayden 1916- *WhoAmW 93, WhoWor 93*
Rector, Melvin Hampton 1954- *WhoSSW 93*
Rector, Milton Gage 1918- *WhoAm 92*
Rector, Rebecca Ann 1949- *WhoAmW 93*
Rector, Richard Robert 1925- *WhoAm 92*
Rector, Robert Wayman 1916- *WhoAm 92*
Rector, Susan Darnell 1959- *WhoAmW 93*
Rector, Walter Tucker 1930- *St&PR 93*
Recupero, John 1931- *St&PR 93*
Red, Eric *MiSFD 9*
Red, John West, Jr. 1920- *WhoSSW 93*
Red, Ma Victoria Goyenechea 1951- *WhoWor 93*
Reda, Donald J. 1934- *WhoUN 92*
Reda, Ralph 1941- *St&PR 93*
Redaelli, Alberto Cesare 1941- *WhoWor 93*
Redai, Istvan 1922- *WhoScE 91-4*
Redalen, Gustav 1947- *WhoScE 91-4*
Redbird, Robert *BioIn 17*
Redbone, Leon *WhoAm 92*
Red Cloud 1822-1909 *BioIn 17, HarEnMi*
Redd, Catharine A. *Law&B 92*
Redd, Charles Appleton 1954- *WhoEmL 93*
Redd, Donald A. *Law&B 92*
Redd, J. Diane 1945- *WhoAmW 93*
Redd, John Gordon 1923- *WhoE 93*
Redd, Judy Ann 1939- *WhoAmW 93*
Redd, Radney Markel 1947- *WhoSSW 93*
Redd, Thomasina Atwater 1941- *WhoAmW 93*
Redda, Kinfe Ken 1948- *WhoAm 92, WhoSSW 93*
Reddan, Harold Jerome 1926- *WhoAm 92*
Redden, Bette Jo 1936- *WhoAmW 93*
Redden, Catherine McEachern 1949- *WhoE 93*
Redden, David Normand 1949- *St&PR 93, WhoAm 92*
Redden, Edward C. 1923- *St&PR 93*
Redden, F. David 1940- *St&PR 93*
Redden, Jack Allison 1926- *WhoAm 92*
Redden, James Anthony 1929- *WhoAm 92*
Redden, Kenneth Robert 1917- *WhoAm 92*
Redden, Lawrence Drew 1922- *WhoAm 92*
Redden, Richard A. 1943- *St&PR 93*
Redden, Roger Duffey 1932- *WhoAm 92*
Redder, Thomas H. 1948- *St&PR 93*
Reddick, Olive Irene *AmWomPl*
Reddick, Raymond 1932- *St&PR 93*
Reddick, Richard L. 1951- *St&PR 93*
Reddick, Robert John 1939- *WhoSSW 93*
Reddick, Walker Homer 1922- *WhoSSW 93, WhoWor 93*
Reddin, Ronald D. 1947- *St&PR 93*
Redding, Bloor, Jr. *Law&B 92*
Redding, David W. 1948- *St&PR 93*
Redding, Edward John 1941- *St&PR 93*
Redding, Edward Patrick 1926- *St&PR 93*
Redding, Evelyn A. 1945- *WhoAmW 93*
Redding, Foster Kinyon 1929- *WhoAm 92*
Redding, J. Saunders 1906-1988 *BioIn 17*
Redding, James Francis 1931- *WhoE 93*
Redding, Jay Saunders 1906-1988 *BioIn 17*
Redding, Joseph H. 1934- *St&PR 93*
Redding, Morris G. 1932- *WhoAm 92*
Redding, Otis 1941-1967 *Baker 92, SoulM*
Redding, P.S. 1938- *St&PR 93*
Redding, Peter Stoddard 1938- *WhoAm 92*
Redding, Roger William 1955- *WhoSSW 93*
Redding, Rogers Walker 1942- *WhoAm 92*
Redding, William Howard, Jr. 1936- *St&PR 93*
Redding, William Kern 1924- *WhoWor 93*
Reddinger, Richard H. 1946- *St&PR 93*
Reddington, Patrick Michael 1946- *St&PR 93*
Reddish, John Joseph 1946- *WhoEmL 93*
Redditt, Nina Belle 1923- *WhoAmW 93*
Reddoch, Claudette R. 1934- *St&PR 93*
Reddoch, Judy Mae 1947- *WhoAmW 93*
Reddout, Donna Jane 1947- *WhoWrEP 92*
Reddy, B.N. 1923- *WhoAsAP 91*
Reddy, B. Satyanarayan 1927- *WhoAsAP 91*
Reddy, D. Raj 1937- *WhoAm 92*
Reddy, G. Vijaya Mohan 1925- *WhoAsAP 91*
Reddy, Helen 1941?- *ConMus 9 [port]*
Reddy, Helen Maxine 1941- *WhoAm 92*
Reddy, Jai Ram *WhoAsAP 91*
Reddy, John W. *Law&B 92*
Reddy, K.V. Raghunath 1924- *WhoAsAP 91*
Reddy, Kalluru Jayarami 1953- *WhoE 93*
Reddy, Krishna Narayana 1925- *WhoAm 92*
Reddy, Muni Krishna Thukivakam 1945- *WhoWor 93*
Reddy, Narreddy Thulasi 1951- *WhoAsAP 91*
Reddy, Patrick D. 1941- *St&PR 93*
Reddy, Paul W. 1940- *WhoAm 92, WhoSSW 93*
Reddy, Pratap Chandupatla 1944- *WhoAm 92, WhoSSW 93*
Reddy, Raj *BioIn 17*
Reddy, Ramakrishna P. 1936- *St&PR 93*
Reddy, Richard L. 1946- *St&PR 93*
Reddy, Siva Prasad 1946- *St&PR 93*
Reddy, Suresh Baddam 1965- *WhoE 93*
Reddy, T. Chandrashekhar 1932- *WhoAsAP 91*
Reddy, Thomas Bradley 1933- *WhoE 93*
Reddyhough, Julian Nicholas 1962- *WhoWor 93*
Rede, Deborah Fae 1952- *WhoAmW 93*
Rede, John d1521 *BioIn 17*
Redeker, Allan Grant 1924- *WhoAm 92*
Redeker, Jerrald H. 1934- *St&PR 93*
Redeker, Jerrald Hale 1934- *WhoAm 92*
Redeker, Richard A. 1943- *St&PR 93*
Redekopp, Elsa *BioIn 17*
Redel, Kurt 1918- *Baker 92*
Redelbach, Andrzej 1946- *WhoWor 93*
Redemann, Louis C. 1938- *St&PR 93*
Redenius, Doug *BioIn 17*
Redenius, Mary Palmer 1942- *WhoWrEP 92*
Redepenning, Charles W. *Law&B 92*
Redepenning, Charles William, Jr. *Law&B 92*
Reder, Milton *BioIn 17*
Reder, Milton d1992 *NewYTBS 92*
Reder, Thomas J. 1949- *St&PR 93*
Reder, Walter d1991 *BioIn 17*
Redesdale, Baron of 1932-1991 *BioIn 17*
Redeske, James Floyd 1939- *St&PR 93*
Redetzki, Horst E. 1937- *St&PR 93*
Redfearn, Donald D. 1952- *St&PR 93*
Redfern, John D. 1936- *WhoAm 92*
Redfern, John Douglas 1935- *St&PR 93*
Redfern, John Joseph, III 1939- *St&PR 93, WhoSSW 93*
Redfern, John P. *WhoScE 91-1*
Redfield, Carol Ann Luckhardt 1958- *WhoSSW 93*
Redfield, James Michael 1935- *WhoAm 92*
Redfield, John H. 1924- *St&PR 93*
Redfield, Robert 1897-1958 *BioIn 17, IntDcAn*
Redfinn, Michael *ScF&FL 92*
Redford, Donald Bruce 1934- *WhoAm 92, WhoWrEP 92*
Redford, Emmette Shelburn 1904- *BioIn 17*
Redford, John c. 1485-1547 *Baker 92*
Redford, Robert 1936- *BioIn 17*
Redford, Robert 1937- *IntDcF 2-3 [port], MiSFD 9, News 93-2 [port], WhoAm 92*
Redgate, Susana Elizabeth 1963- *WhoAmW 93*
Redgrave, Lynn *BioIn 17*
Redgrave, Lynn 1943- *WhoAm 92, WhoAmW 93*
Redgrave, Michael 1908-1985 *IntDcF 2-3 [port]*
Redgrave, Vanessa 1937- *BioIn 17, IntDcF 2-3, WhoAm 92, WhoAmW 93, WhoWor 93*
Redgrove, Peter W. 1932- *ScF&FL 92*
Redgrove, Peter (William) 1932- *ConAu 39NR*
Redgwick, Hubert Arthur 1906- *St&PR 93*
Redhage, Darryl Keith 1938- *St&PR 93*
Redhage, James Herbert 1939- *St&PR 93*
Redhardt, Albrecht 1927- *WhoScE 91-3*
Redhead, M.F. *WhoScE 91-1*
Redhead, Paul Aveling 1924- *WhoAm 92*
Redheffer, Raymond Moos 1921- *WhoAm 92, WhoWor 93*
Red Hot Chili Peppers, The *News 93-1 [port]*
Redhouse, John Walter, Jr. 1937- *St&PR 93*
Redig, Dale Francis 1929- *WhoAm 92, WhoWor 93*
Rediger, Delmar Reid 1934- *St&PR 93*
Rediker, Dennis Louis 1944- *WhoAm 92*
Rediker, Robert Harmon 1924- *WhoAm 92*
Reding, Nicholas Lee 1934- *St&PR 93, WhoAm 92*
Reding, Robert W. 1949- *St&PR 93*
Reding, Sheila Marie 1942- *WhoAmW 93*
Reding, Stephen John 1946- *WhoWor 93*
Reding, Thomas M., Jr. 1951- *St&PR 93*
Redinger, James C. 1937- *St&PR 93*
Redington, Rowland Wells 1924- *WhoAm 92*
Redish, Edward Frederick 1942- *WhoE 93*
Redkey, Edwin Storer 1931- *WhoE 93*
Redl, Alfred 1864-1913 *BioIn 17*
Redler, Erica F. *Law&B 92*
Redler, Sherry Press 1933- *WhoAmW 93, WhoE 93*
Redlich, Donald Harold 1929- *WhoE 93*
Redlich, Hans F(erdinand) 1903-1968 *Baker 92*
Redlich, Marc 1946- *WhoE 93, WhoEmL 93*
Redlich, Norman 1925- *WhoAm 92*
Redlo, Rochelle Marcia 1949- *WhoE 93*
Redman, Barbara Klug *WhoAm 92*
Redman, Charles Bryson 1926- *St&PR 93*
Redman, Charles Edgar 1943- *WhoAm 92, WhoWor 93*
Redman, Clarence O. 1942- *St&PR 93*
Redman, Dale Edward 1948- *St&PR 93*
Redman, Don(ald Matthew) 1900-1964 *Baker 92*
Redman, Harry N(ewton) 1869-1958 *Baker 92*
Redman, John Robert 1950- *WhoE 93*
Redman, Karleen Krepps 1954- *WhoAmW 93*
Redman, Leon Earl *Law&B 92*
Redman, Mark William *Law&B 92*
Redman, Mary Y. *Law&B 92*
Redman, Peter 1935- *St&PR 93, WhoAm 92*
Redman, Robert Shelton 1935- *WhoE 93*
Redman, Sheila 1942- *WhoAm 92*
Redman, Timothy Paul 1950- *WhoAm 92*
Redman, William Charles 1923- *WhoAm 92*
Redman, William Walter, Jr. 1933- *WhoSSW 93*
Redmon, Anne 1943- *ScF&FL 92*
Redmon, Mike 1950- *St&PR 93*
Redmond, Daniel Mark 1957- *St&PR 93*
Redmond, Donald Eugene, Jr. 1939- *WhoAm 92*
Redmond, Douglas Michael 1954- *WhoE 93*
Redmond, Frances Harrietta 1921- *WhoAmW 93*
Redmond, Gail Elizabeth 1946- *WhoAmW 93, WhoEmL 93, WhoWor 93*
Redmond, Granville 1871-1935 *BioIn 17*
Redmond, Hope S. *Law&B 92*
Redmond, J. Woodward 1921- *St&PR 93*
Redmond, James N. *Law&B 92*
Redmond, James R. 1942- *St&PR 93*
Redmond, James Ronald 1928- *WhoAm 92*
Redmond, Joan Williams *WhoAmW 93*
Redmond, John Edward 1856-1918 *BioIn 17*
Redmond, John L. 1930- *St&PR 93*
Redmond, John M. *Law&B 92*
Redmond, Joseph C., Jr. *Law&B 92*
Redmond, Liam 1913-1989 *BioIn 17*
Redmond, Markus *BioIn 17*
Redmond, Michael P. *Law&B 92*
Redmond, Michael Peter *Law&B 92*
Redmond, Patricia Ann 1950- *WhoEmL 93*
Redmond, Paul Anthony 1937- *St&PR 93, WhoAm 92*
Redmond, Richard Joseph 1946- *St&PR 93*
Redmond, Sandra Lynn 1946- *WhoAmW 93*
Redmond, Sue Ann 1958- *WhoAmW 93*
Redmond, Velma A. *Law&B 92*
Redmond, Velma A. 1954- *St&PR 93*
Redmond, Virgie St. John 1919- *BioIn 17*
Redmond, William L. 1937- *St&PR 93*
Redmont, Bernard Sidney 1918- *WhoAm 92*
Redner, Robert P. 1929- *St&PR 93*
Redner, S. Alex 1929- *St&PR 93*
Redo, Maria Elaine 1925- *WhoWor 93*
Redo, Saverio Frank 1920- *WhoAm 92*
Redondo de Feldman, Susanna 1913- *NotHsAW 93*
Redoy, Patrick D. 1941- *St&PR 93*
Redpath, Alan 1949- *St&PR 93*
Redpath, James 1833-1891 *BioIn 17*
Redpath, John S., Jr. *Law&B 92*
Redpath, Thomas W. *WhoScE 91-1*
Redshaw, Peggy Ann 1948- *WhoSSW 93*
Red Star, Kevin 1943- *BioIn 17*
Redstone, Edward S. 1928- *St&PR 93*
Redstone, Louis Gordon 1903- *WhoAm 92*
Redstone, Sumner *BioIn 17*
Redstone, Sumner Murray 1923- *WhoAm 92, WhoE 93, WhoWor 93*
Red Virgin 1830-1905 *BioIn 17*
Redway, Alan Arthur Sydney 1935- *WhoAm 92*
Redway, Albert Sessions, Jr. 1929- *St&PR 93*
Redwine, Glynis Wheeler *Law&B 92*
Redwine, James M. *Law&B 92*
Redwine, Michael Dwain 1946- *WhoSSW 93*
Redwine, Susette Dalton 1956- *WhoAmW 93*
Redwine, William Howard 1957- *WhoSSW 93*
Red Wing, Princess 1884-1974 *SweetSg A [port]*
Redwood, Richard George 1936- *WhoAm 92*
Ree, Anton 1820-1886 *Baker 92*
Ree, Gerry de la *ScF&FL 92*
Ree, Harry d1991 *BioIn 17*
Ree, Harry 1914-1991 *AnObit 1991*
Ree, Jennie *AmWomPl*
Ree, Louis 1861-1939 *Baker 92*
Reeb, Harold B. 1936- *St&PR 93*
Reeb, James J. 1927-1965 *EncAACR*
Reece, Abigail Mayer- *BioIn 17*
Reece, B. Carroll 1889-1961 *PolPar*
Reece, Beth Pauley 1945- *WhoAmW 93*
Reece, Brazilla Carroll 1889-1961 *BioIn 17*
Reece, Daniel Boone, III *Law&B 92*
Reece, David N. 1920- *St&PR 93*
Reece, Ernest James 1881-1976 *BioIn 17*
Reece, Gabrielle *BioIn 17*
Reece, Harriet Lee 1930- *WhoAmW 93*
Reece, James Adolphus 1919- *St&PR 93*
Reece, Joe Wilson 1935- *WhoAm 92*
Reece, Karyn Lynn 1967- *WhoAmW 93*
Reece, Kathleen Deanne 1954- *WhoEmL 93*
Reece, Louise Goff 1898-1970 *BioIn 17*
Reece, Marshall Philip 1954- *WhoWor 93*
Reece, Maynard Fred 1920- *WhoAm 92*
Reece, Peggy *AmWomPl*
Reece, Randi Sue 1949- *WhoAmW 93*
Reece, Richard Terrance 1935- *WhoE 93*
Reece, Robert William 1942- *WhoAm 92*
Reece, Rodney Leon *WhoScE 91-1*
Reece, S. Richard 1933- *St&PR 93*
Reece, Sterling Richard 1933- *WhoAm 92*
Reece, Steven Lee 1951- *WhoWor 93*
Reece, Wanda G. 1956- *WhoEmL 93, WhoSSW 93, WhoWor 93*

Reece, Wayne Gail 1935- *WhoWrEP 92*
Reece Myron, Monique Elizabeth 1960- *WhoAmW 93*
Reed, Adam Victor 1946- *WhoAm 92*
Reed, Albert A. 1934- *St&PR 93*
Reed, Alfred 1921- *Baker 92, WhoAm 92*
Reed, Alfred Byron 1916- *WhoAm 92*
Reed, Alfred Douglas 1928- *WhoSSW 93, WhoWor 93*
Reed, Alison Touster 1952- *WhoWrEP 92*
Reed, Allen R. *Law&B 92*
Reed, Amelia Matz 1963- *WhoAmW 93*
Reed, Andrew M. 1952- *St&PR 93*
Reed, Austin F. *Law&B 92*
Reed, Austin F. 1951- *St&PR 93*
Reed, Barbara True 1946- *WhoAmW 93*
Reed, Berenice Anne 1934- *WhoAmW 93, WhoE 93, WhoWor 93*
Reed, Bill J. 1953- *St&PR 93*
Reed, Brenda *BioIn 17*
Reed, Bruce A. *Law&B 92*
Reed, Bruce Norman 1926- *St&PR 93*
Reed, C. Robert 1936- *St&PR 93*
Reed, Carol 1906-1976 *BioIn 17, MiSFD 9N*
Reed, Carol Louise 1938- *WhoAmW 93*
Reed, Carole *BioIn 17*
Reed, Charles 1944- *WhoSSW 93*
Reed, Charles A. 1912- *IntDcAn*
Reed, Charles Allen 1912- *WhoAm 92*
Reed, Charles Bass 1941- *WhoAm 92, WhoSSW 93*
Reed, Charles Emmett 1922- *WhoAm 92*
Reed, Charles Loren, Jr. 1940- *St&PR 93*
Reed, Charlie d1883? *BioIn 17*
Reed, Christopher *ScF&FL 92*
Reed, Christopher G. *BioIn 17*
Reed, Christopher Robert 1948- *WhoWor 93*
Reed, Clarence Raymond 1932- *WhoAm 92*
Reed, Clyde Martin 1871-1949 *BioIn 17*
Reed, Con Scott 1928- *WhoWor 93*
Reed, Constance Louise *WhoAmW 93*
Reed, Cordell 1938- *St&PR 93*
Reed, Curtis Michael 1948- *St&PR 93*
Reed, Dale D. 1931- *St&PR 93*
Reed, Dalpha Mae 1921- *WhoWrEP 92*
Reed, Dana *ScF&FL 92*
Reed, Darrel 1941- *St&PR 93*
Reed, Darwin Cramer 1915- *WhoAm 92*
Reed, David 1946- *WhoAm 92*
Reed, David A. 1950- *St&PR 93*
Reed, David Andrew 1933- *WhoAm 92*
Reed, David Benson 1927- *WhoAm 92*
Reed, David C. 1937- *WhoAm 92*
Reed, David George 1945- *WhoWor 93*
Reed, David J., Jr. 1936- *St&PR 93*
Reed, David P. 1952- *St&PR 93*
Reed, David Scudder 1931- *St&PR 93*
Reed, David Stuart 1950- *WhoWrEP 92*
Reed, Debra Lynn 1956- *St&PR 93*
Reed, Dena *AmWomPl*
Reed, Diana Lynn 1943- *WhoAmW 93*
Reed, Diane Gray 1945- *WhoAmW 93, WhoSSW 93*
Reed, Diane Marie 1934- *WhoAmW 93, WhoWor 93*
Reed, Donald A. 1935- *ScF&FL 92*
Reed, Donald B. 1944- *St&PR 93*
Reed, Donna 1921-1986 *BioIn 17, IntDcF 2-3 [port]*
Reed, Dwight Thomas 1955- *WhoWor 93*
Reed, Edward Cornelius, Jr. 1924- *WhoAm 92*
Reed, Eliot *ConAu 38NR*
Reed, Elizabeth May Millard 1919- *WhoSSW 93*
Reed, Emil *St&PR 93*
Reed, Emily Ann Fabrycki 1941- *WhoE 93*
Reed, Emma *BlkAmWO*
Reed, Ethel E. *AmWomPl*
Reed, Ethelyn *AmWomPl*
Reed, Everett C. 1916- *St&PR 93*
Reed, Frank *BioIn 17*
Reed, Frank Engelhart 1935- *WhoAm 92*
Reed, Fredric David 1937- *St&PR 93*
Reed, Gail Simon 1943- *WhoE 93*
Reed, Gareth La Verne 1932- *St&PR 93*
Reed, George Elliott 1923- *WhoE 93*
Reed, George F. 1935- *St&PR 93*
Reed, George Farrell 1922- *WhoAm 92*
Reed, George Francis 1928- *WhoAm 92*
Reed, George Lindmiller 1937- *WhoSSW 93*
Reed, Gordon W. 1899- *St&PR 93*
Reed, Gordon Wies 1899- *WhoAm 92*
Reed, Guy Dean 1922- *WhoSSW 93*
Reed, H. Carlyle 1915- *WhoAm 92*
Reed, H(erbert) Owen 1910- *Baker 92*
Reed, Harrietta Green 1950- *WhoAmW 93*
Reed, Harvey Jay *Law&B 92*
Reed, Helen Bernice 1917- *WhoAmW 93*
Reed, Horace Curtis 1917- *WhoAm 92*
Reed, Howard Alexander 1920- *WhoAm 92*
Reed, Ione *SweetSg B [port]*
Reed, Ishmael 1938- *BioIn 17, MagSAmL [port], ScF&FL 92*
Reed, Ishmael Scott 1938- *WhoAm 92, WhoWrEP 92*
Reed, Ivy Kellerman 1877-1968 *ScF&FL 92*
Reed, J. Ross 1949- *St&PR 93*
Reed, J. Walter 1933- *WhoAm 92*
Reed, Jack Louis 1945- *WhoAm 92*
Reed, Jake *BioIn 17*
Reed, James Anthony 1939- *WhoWor 93*
Reed, James C., Jr. *Law&B 92*
Reed, James Donald 1940- *WhoAm 92*
Reed, James Eddie *BioIn 17*
Reed, James Hugh, IV 1949- *St&PR 93*
Reed, James M. 1933- *St&PR 93*
Reed, James Rudolph 1938- *WhoSSW 93*
Reed, James Wesley 1944- *WhoAm 92*
Reed, James Whitfield 1935- *WhoAm 92*
Reed, James William, Jr. 1947- *WhoE 93*
Reed, James Wilson 1944- *WhoSSW 93*
Reed, Jane Garson 1948- *WhoEmL 93*
Reed, Jean Salas 1940- *WhoAmW 93*
Reed, Jeffrey *Law&B 92*
Reed, Jeffrey Garth 1948- *WhoE 93*
Reed, Jeremy *BioIn 17*
Reed, Jerry 1937- *Baker 92, MiSFD 9*
Reed, Jim *BioIn 17*
Reed, Jimmy 1925-1976 *BioIn 17*
Reed, Joan Spahr 1930- *WhoAmW 93*
Reed, Joel Leston 1951- *WhoAm 92, WhoSSW 93*
Reed, John 1887-1920 *BioIn 17, JrnUS*
Reed, John Alton 1931- *WhoAm 92*
Reed, John Calvin 1935- *WhoSSW 93*
Reed, John E. 1915- *St&PR 93*
Reed, John F. 1917- *St&PR 93*
Reed, John F. 1949- *CngDr 91*
Reed, John Francis 1949- *WhoAm 92, WhoE 93*
Reed, John Franklin 1917- *WhoAm 92*
Reed, John G. 1929- *WhoAm 92*
Reed, John Giveen, Jr. 1930- *St&PR 93*
Reed, John Hathaway 1921- *WhoAm 92*
Reed, John Joseph 1956- *St&PR 93*
Reed, John R. 1938- *ScF&FL 92*
Reed, John S. *BioIn 17*
Reed, John Shedd 1917- *WhoAm 92*
Reed, John Shepard 1939- *St&PR 93, WhoAm 92, WhoWor 93*
Reed, John Squires, II 1949- *WhoAm 92, WhoSSW 93*
Reed, John Theodore 1946- *WhoWrEP 92*
Reed, John Wesley 1918- *WhoAm 92*
Reed, Jon Stanley 1939- *St&PR 93*
Reed, Joseph, Jr. 1944- *WhoE 93*
Reed, Joseph Howard 1930- *WhoAm 92*
Reed, Joseph Verner *BioIn 17*
Reed, Joseph Verner, Jr. 1937- *WhoE 93*
Reed, Joseph Wayne 1932- *WhoAm 92*
Reed, Joseph Wayne, Jr. 1932- *WhoWrEP 92*
Reed, Joyce Ann Borden 1939- *WhoAm 92*
Reed, Kathlyn Louise 1940- *WhoAm 92*
Reed, Keith Allen 1939- *WhoAm 92*
Reed, Kenneth G. 1917- *WhoAm 92*
Reed, Kit *WhoWrEP 92*
Reed, Kit 1932- *ScF&FL 92*
Reed, Larry Douglas 1939- *St&PR 93*
Reed, Lary Lyn 1939- *WhoSSW 93*
Reed, Laurence A. 1939- *WhoAm 92*
Reed, Leon S. 1918- *St&PR 93*
Reed, Leon Samuel 1949- *WhoE 93*
Reed, Leonard 1907- *BioIn 17*
Reed, Leonard 1929- *St&PR 93*
Reed, Lester James 1925- *WhoAm 92*
Reed, Lester Willard, Jr. 1932- *WhoSSW 93*
Reed, Lillian *ScF&FL 92*
Reed, Linda 1955- *ConAu 137*
Reed, Lois Mary 1919- *WhoWrEP 92*
Reed, Lou *BioIn 17*
Reed, Lou 1942- *WhoAm 92*
Reed, Lou(is Alan) 1942- *Baker 92*
Reed, Lowell A., Jr. 1930- *WhoAm 92, WhoE 93*
Reed, Luman c. 1784-1836 *BioIn 17*
Reed, Margaret G. *Law&B 92*
Reed, Mark A. *BioIn 17*
Reed, Mary de Groat d1991 *BioIn 17*
Reed, Mary Lou *WhoAmW 93*
Reed, Merl Elwyn 1925- *WhoSSW 93*
Reed, Michael Charles 1942- *WhoAm 92*
Reed, Michael John 1940- *WhoAm 92*
Reed, Nell Donnelly 1889-1991 *BioIn 17*
Reed, Norman Bruce 1949- *WhoEmL 93, WhoWor 93*
Reed, Oliver 1938- *IntDcF 2-3 [port], WhoAm 92, WhoWor 93*
Reed, Pamela *BioIn 17*
Reed, Pamela 1949- *WhoAm 92*
Reed, Patricia Colleen 1939- *WhoAmW 93*
Reed, Paul *WhoScE 91-1*
Reed, Paul 1956- *ConGAN, WhoWrEP 92*
Reed, Paul Thomas 1927- *WhoAm 92*
Reed, Priscilla Horton 1818-1895 *See* Reed, Thomas German 1817-1888 *Baker 92*
Reed, Ralph Donald 1947- *WhoSSW 93*
Reed, Raymond Deryl 1930- *WhoAm 92*
Reed, Rebecca Casey *Law&B 92*
Reed, Rex 1938- *WhoE 93, WhoWrEP 92*
Reed, Rex Raymond 1922- *WhoAm 92*
Reed, Richard Anthony *Law&B 92*
Reed, Richard Baxter 1943- *WhoSSW 93*
Reed, Richard John 1922- *WhoAm 92*
Reed, Richard W. 1920- *St&PR 93*
Reed, Rick R. *ScF&FL 92*
Reed, Robert d1992 *NewYTBS 92 [port]*
Reed, Robert 1932-1992 *BioIn 17*
Reed, Robert c. 1933-1992 *News 92*
Reed, Robert 1956- *ScF&FL 92*
Reed, Robert A. *Law&B 92*
Reed, Robert Alan 1942- *St&PR 93, WhoAm 92*
Reed, Robert Daniel 1941- *WhoAm 92*
Reed, Robert Dixon 1927- *St&PR 93*
Reed, Robert G., III 1927- *St&PR 93*
Reed, Robert George, III 1927- *WhoAm 92*
Reed, Robert J.R. *WhoScE 91-1*
Reed, Robert Leonard 1932- *St&PR 93*
Reed, Robert Monroe 1932- *WhoAm 92*
Reed, Roberta Gable 1945- *WhoAmW 93*
Reed, Roger Harold 1941- *St&PR 93*
Reed, Ronald Steven 1948- *WhoSSW 93*
Reed, Sally Ann 1947- *WhoWrEP 92*
Reed, Samuel Benedict 1818-1891 *BioIn 17*
Reed, Sarah Rebecca 1914-1978 *BioIn 17*
Reed, Scott Eldridge 1948- *St&PR 93, WhoAm 92*
Reed, Scott William 1960- *WhoAm 92*
Reed, Seaton A., Jr. 1941- *St&PR 93*
Reed, Shanna *BioIn 17*
Reed, Shelley A. *Law&B 92*
Reed, Sherman Kennedy 1919- *WhoAm 92*
Reed, Simon *ConAu 39NR*
Reed, Stanley Forman 1884-1980 *OxCSupC [port]*
Reed, Stanley Foster 1917- *St&PR 93, WhoAm 92, WhoWor 93*
Reed, Steven Charles 1948- *WhoEmL 93*
Reed, Steven Robert *Law&B 92*
Reed, Stuart Bennett 1936- *WhoAsAP 91*
Reed, Terry *BioIn 17*
Reed, Terry Allen 1948- *WhoSSW 93*
Reed, Thomas A. *Law&B 92*
Reed, Thomas B. 1839-1902 *PolPar*
Reed, Thomas Care 1934- *WhoAm 92*
Reed, Thomas German 1817-1888 *Baker 92*
Reed, Thomas J. 1937- *St&PR 93*
Reed, Thomas James 1940- *WhoE 93*
Reed, Thomas Joseph 1937- *WhoAm 92*
Reed, Thomas Lloyd, Jr. 1947- *WhoE 93*
Reed, Todd Randall 1954- *WhoWor 93*
Reed, Toni 1944- *ScF&FL 92*
Reed, Tony 1962- *ScF&FL 92*
Reed, Tony Norman 1951- *WhoAm 92*
Reed, Travis Dean 1930- *WhoAm 92*
Reed, Vincent Emory 1928- *WhoAm 92*
Reed, W. Chad *Law&B 92*
Reed, Wallace Allison 1916- *WhoAm 92, WhoWor 93*
Reed, Wallace Smart 1945- *WhoWor 93*
Reed, Walt *ScF&FL 92*
Reed, Walter 1851-1902 *GayN, HarEnMi*
Reed, Walter Gurnee Dyer 1952- *WhoE 93*
Reed, William Burch 1928- *St&PR 93*
Reed, William C. 1951- *WhoE 93*
Reed, William Edward 1914- *WhoAm 92*
Reed, William H. *St&PR 93*
Reed, William Henry 1876-1942 *Baker 92*
Reed, William L(eonard) 1910- *Baker 92*
Reed, William R., Jr. 1946- *St&PR 93*
Reed, Willis 1942- *WhoAm 92*
Reed, Wilmer Handy, III 1925- *WhoSSW 93*
Reed, Wrightly Thompson 1945- *WhoSSW 93*
Reed-Clark, Larita Diane 1960- *WhoAmW 93*
Reeder, Andrew Horatio 1807-1864 *BioIn 17*
Reeder, Carolyn *DcAmChF 1985*
Reeder, Carolyn 1937- *BioIn 17*
Reeder, Charles Benton 1922- *WhoAm 92*
Reeder, Charles Edgar 1927- *WhoSSW 93*
Reeder, David Scott 1944- *St&PR 93*
Reeder, Donald Lee 1930- *St&PR 93*
Reeder, Douglas L. 1937- *St&PR 93*
Reeder, Ernestine Nichols *WhoAmW 93*
Reeder, Harley S. 1929- *St&PR 93*
Reeder, Hubert 1948- *WhoWrEP 92*
Reeder, Hugh Sidney 1930- *St&PR 93*
Reeder, James Arthur 1933- *WhoSSW 93*
Reeder, James Seymour, Jr. 1932- *St&PR 93*
Reeder, John A. *Law&B 92*
Reeder, John P., Jr. 1937- *WhoAm 92*
Reeder, Milton K. 1956- *St&PR 93*
Reeder, Oliver Howard 1916- *WhoAm 92*
Reeder, Paula B. 1950- *St&PR 93*
Reeder, Robert Harry 1930- *WhoAm 92*
Reeder, Stewart 1940- *St&PR 93*
Reeder, William Glase 1929- *WhoAm 92*
Reeder, William H. 1939- *St&PR 93*
Reed-Gross, Patricia Elaine 1952- *WhoWor 93*
Reedich, Douglas Edward *Law&B 92*
Reedijk, Jan 1943- *WhoWor 93*
Reed-Mackay, Pauline 1942- *WhoAmW 93*
Reed-Mackay, Pauline Reed 1942- *St&PR 93*
Reedy, Frances Starr 1948- *WhoAmW 93*
Reedy, George E. 1917- *PolPar*
Reedy, George Edward 1917- *WhoAm 92, WhoWrEP 92*
Reedy, Harry Lee 1945- *WhoE 93*
Reedy, Jerry Edward 1936- *WhoAm 92, WhoWrEP 92*
Reedy, Penelope Michal 1947- *WhoWrEP 92*
Reedy, Terrell Wayne 1941- *WhoSSW 93*
Reedy, William Marion 1862-1920 *BioIn 17*
Reef, Arthur 1916- *WhoAm 92*
Reef, Catherine 1951- *SmATA 73 [port]*
Reefer, Elizabeth D. *Law&B 92*
Reeg, Jay F. 1931- *St&PR 93*
Reeg, Ruth Zimmerman *Law&B 92*
Reeher, William Floyd 1933- *St&PR 93*
Reehling, Ronald E. 1935- *St&PR 93*
Reehm, Sue Plympton 1941- *WhoAmW 93*
Reeke, John Elliott 1964- *WhoSSW 93*
Reekers, Jeffery Patrick 1954- *WhoSSW 93*
Reekie, Charles Douglas 1924- *St&PR 93*
Reeling, Glenn Eugene 1930- *WhoE 93*
Reels, Donna Marie 1948- *WhoAmW 93*
Reely, Mary Katharine 1881- *AmWomPl*
Reely, Robert Harold, Jr. 1938- *WhoSSW 93*
Reeman, Douglas *BioIn 17*
Reemes, Dana M. *ScF&FL 92*
Reems, Harry 1947- *BioIn 17*
Reemtsen, September W. Presley 1956- *WhoSSW 93*
Reen, Jeremiah Joseph 1942- *WhoAm 92*
Reenberg, Anette 1948- *WhoScE 91-2*
Reenpaa, Heikki Allan 1922- *WhoWor 93*
Reents, Sue *WhoAmW 93*
Reents, William David 1954- *WhoE 93*
Reep, Gary E. *St&PR 93*
Reep, Sandra A. *St&PR 93*
Rees, Adrian 1956- *WhoWor 93*
Rees, Albert 1921-1992 *BioIn 17, NewYTBS 92*
Rees, Albert Everett 1921- *WhoAm 92*
Rees, Albert (Everett) 1921-1992 *ConAu 139*
Rees, Arthur John d1991 *BioIn 17*
Rees, C.W. *WhoScE 91-1*
Rees, Camilla Reilly Gallagher 1957- *WhoAmW 93*
Rees, Charles H. G. 1922- *WhoAm 92*
Rees, Clifford Harcourt, Jr. 1936- *WhoAm 92*
Rees, Clive *MiSFD 9*
Rees, D.A. *WhoScE 91-1*
Rees, David *WhoScE 91-1*
Rees, David 1936- *SmATA 69 [port]*
Rees, David (Bartlett) 1936- *MajAI [port]*
Rees, Diane DeMuro 1939- *WhoAmW 93*
Rees, Elmer Gethin *WhoScE 91-1*
Rees, Grover Joseph, III 1951- *WhoAm 92*
Rees, H. *WhoScE 91-1*
Rees, Helen *BioIn 17, ScF&FL 92*
Rees, Huw Hefin *WhoScE 91-1*
Rees, J.G. *WhoScE 91-1*
Rees, Jennifer Linda *WhoScE 91-1*
Rees, Jerry *MiSFD 9*
Rees, John Robert 1930- *WhoAm 92*
Rees, (George) Leslie (Clarke) 1905- *DcChlFi*
Rees, Margaret A(nn) 1933- *ConAu 39NR*
Rees, Martha L. *Law&B 92*
Rees, Martin John *WhoScE 91-1*
Rees, Mina Spiegel 1902- *WhoAm 92*
Rees, Norma S. 1929- *WhoAmW 93*
Rees, Paul Klein 1902- *WhoSSW 93*
Rees, Raymond F. 1944- *WhoAm 92*
Rees, Richard 1900-1970 *ScF&FL 92*
Rees, Rosemary *AmWomPl*
Rees, Sherrel Jerry Evans 1926- *WhoAm 92*
Rees, Simon 1958- *ScF&FL 92*
Rees, Warren A. 1926- *St&PR 93*
Rees, William B. *Law&B 92*
Rees, William Dewi *WhoScE 91-1*
Rees, William Lehigh 1900-1989 *BioIn 17*
Reesby, Carl Edwin 1926- *St&PR 93*
Reese, Andy Clare 1942- *WhoSSW 93*
Reese, Ann N. *WhoAmW 93*
Reese, Bernard P., Jr. 1925- *St&PR 93*
Reese, Bob 1938- *BioIn 17*
Reese, Bruce T. 1949- *St&PR 93*
Reese, Carolyn Johnson 1938- *BioIn 17*

Reese, Charles S. 1948- *St&PR 93*
Reese, Colin Bernard *WhoScE 91-1*
Reese, Colin Bernard 1930- *WhoWor 93*
Reese, Daniel William 1953- *WhoE 93*
Reese, David Jen 1963- *WhoSSW 93*
Reese, Deborah Decker 1950- *WhoWrEP 92*
Reese, Della *BioIn 17*
Reese, Della 1931- *WhoAm 92*
Reese, Della 1932- *Baker 92*
Reese, Errol Lynn 1939- *WhoAm 92, WhoE 93*
Reese, Francis Edward 1919- *WhoAm 92*
Reese, George E., Jr. *Law&B 92*
Reese, Glen A. 1939- *St&PR 93*
Reese, Glenn G. 1942- *WhoSSW 93*
Reese, Gustave 1899-1977 *Baker 92*
Reese, Harold, Jr. 1942- *WhoSSW 93, WhoWor 93*
Reese, Harry Edwin, Jr. 1928- *WhoAm 92*
Reese, Harry Eugene 1946- *WhoWrEP 92*
Reese, Hayne Waring 1931- *WhoAm 92*
Reese, James D. 1941- *St&PR 93*
Reese, James M. *BioIn 17*
Reese, James R. 1930- *St&PR 93*
Reese, Jimmy *BioIn 17*
Reese, John N. d1945 *BioIn 17*
Reese, John R. 1944- *St&PR 93*
Reese, John Rathbone 1944- *WhoAm 92*
Reese, John Robert 1939- *WhoAm 92*
Reese, John Russell 1948- *St&PR 93*
Reese, Joseph Hammond, Jr. 1928- *St&PR 93*
Reese, Jules Douglas 1952- *WhoE 93*
Reese, Jurgen 1942- *WhoWor 93*
Reese, Karen *BioIn 17*
Reese, Latricia *BioIn 17*
Reese, Lulu T. *AmWomPl*
Reese, Lymon Clifton 1917- *WhoAm 92*
Reese, Mamie Bynes 1913- *AfrAmBi*
Reese, Marcia Mitchell 1929- *WhoE 93*
Reese, Michael Joseph 1949- *St&PR 93*
Reese, Norma Carol 1946- *WhoAmW 93*
Reese, Patricia Ann 1954- *WhoSSW 93*
Reese, Paul L. 1925- *St&PR 93*
Reese, Paul S. 1951- *St&PR 93*
Reese, Pee Wee 1919- *BioIn 17*
Reese, Phyllis Thomas 1946- *WhoAmW 93*
Reese, Richard Bruce 1940- *St&PR 93*
Reese, Richard F. 1945- *St&PR 93*
Reese, Richard L. 1957- *St&PR 93*
Reese, Richard Page 1926- *WhoWrEP 92*
Reese, Robert M. *Law&B 92*
Reese, Ronald Craig *WhoE 93*
Reese, Roy Charles 1949- *WhoWor 93*
Reese, S. Howard 1944- *St&PR 93*
Reese, Ted M. 1959- *WhoEmL 93*
Reese, Terry W. 1942- *St&PR 93*
Reese, Thomas Sargent 1935- *WhoAm 92*
Reese, Thomas William 1924- *St&PR 93*
Reese, William Albert, III 1932- *WhoWor 93*
Reese, William Lewis 1921- *WhoAm 92*
Reese, William S. 1947- *St&PR 93*
Reese, William Sherman 1955- *WhoE 93*
Reese, William Willis 1940- *WhoE 93, WhoWor 93*
Reese, Willis L.M. *BioIn 17*
Reeser, (Hendrik) Eduard 1908- *Baker 92*
Reeser, Edward V. 1952- *St&PR 93*
Reeser, Jack B. 1947- *St&PR 93*
Reeser, Lyle Grant 1918- *WhoAm 92*
Reeside, Michelle Lee *Law&B 92*
Reesman, Jeanne Campbell 1955- *WhoSSW 93*
Reesman, Kenneth G. 1921- *St&PR 93*
Reeson, Richard Leonard *Law&B 92*
Rees-Potter, Lorna Katherine 1942- *WhoWor 93*
Reeth, George van *BioIn 17*
Reetz, Manfred T. 1943- *WhoScE 91-3*
Reeve, Adrian Grantley 1957- *WhoWor 93*
Reeve, Agnesa B. 1927- *ConAu 138*
Reeve, Agnesa Lufkin 1927- *WhoWrEP 92*
Reeve, Arthur B. 1880-1936 *ScF&FL 92*
Reeve, Christopher *BioIn 17*
Reeve, Christopher 1952- *HolBB [port], WhoAm 92*
Reeve, Douglas V. 1928- *St&PR 93*
Reeve, Edgar H. 1945- *St&PR 93*
Reeve, Edward John *Law&B 92*
Reeve, F.D. 1928- *WhoWrEP 92*
Reeve, Geoffrey 1932- *MiSFD 9*
Reeve, James Key *WhoAm 92*
Reeve, John Newton 1947- *WhoAm 92*
Reeve, John Samuel 1929- *WhoScE 91-1*
Reeve, Ken R. 1947- *St&PR 93*
Reeve, Mary Ruth 1952- *WhoAmW 93*
Reeve, Richard Robert 1948- *WhoE 93*
Reeve, Robert C. 1902-1980 *EncABHB 8 [port]*
Reeve, Ronald Cropper, Jr. 1943- *WhoAm 92*
Reeve, Scott d1990 *BioIn 17*
Reeve, Thomas Smith 1923- *WhoWor 93*
Reeve, William 1757-1815 *Baker 92*
Reeves, Barbara Ann 1949- *WhoAm 92, WhoAmW 93*
Reeves, Barry Lucas 1935- *WhoE 93*
Reeves, Bruce 1959- *WhoSSW 93*
Reeves, Carla Marianne 1949- *WhoAmW 93*
Reeves, Charles Banes, Jr. 1923- *WhoAm 92*
Reeves, Charles Howell 1915- *WhoAm 92*
Reeves, Charles Monroe, Jr. 1923- *St&PR 93*
Reeves, Charles Sherman 1927- *St&PR 93*
Reeves, Connie Lynn 1954- *WhoAmW 93*
Reeves, Daniel 1915- *BioIn 17*
Reeves, Daniel E. 1912-1971 *BioIn 17*
Reeves, Daniel Edward 1944- *WhoAm 92*
Reeves, David B. *Law&B 92*
Reeves, David M. d1991 *BioIn 17*
Reeves, David Nash Scott 1951- *WhoSSW 93*
Reeves, David Wallis 1838-1900 *Baker 92*
Reevés, Dianne *BioIn 17*
Reeves, Donald W. 1953- *WhoSSW 93*
Reeves, Dorothy Elizabeth McClure 1933- *WhoAmW 93*
Reeves, Douglas Michael *Law&B 92*
Reeves, Edmund Hoffman, III 1949- *WhoE 93*
Reeves, Frances Skinner 1926- *St&PR 93*
Reeves, Frank Blair 1922- *WhoAm 92*
Reeves, Frank Hough *Law&B 92*
Reeves, Garland Phillip 1944- *WhoSSW 93*
Reeves, Gary Wayne 1955- *WhoSSW 93*
Reeves, Gene 1930- *WhoSSW 93*
Reeves, George 1914-1959 *BioIn 17*
Reeves, George McMillan, Jr. 1921- *WhoAm 92*
Reeves, Ginger Ann 1949- *WhoWrEP 92*
Reeves, Gordon *WhoScE 91-1*
Reeves, Hannah *BioIn 17*
Reeves, James L. *Law&B 92*
Reeves, James Louis 1922- *WhoAm 92*
Reeves, John 1926- *WhoCanL 92*
Reeves, John Drummond 1914- *WhoE 93*
Reeves, John E. 1913-1990 *BioIn 17*
Reeves, John Mercer, II 1954- *WhoSSW 93*
Reeves, John P. 1934- *St&PR 93*
Reeves, Joseph William 1953- *WhoE 93*
Reeves, Kaye Lynn 1963- *WhoSSW 93*
Reeves, Keanu *BioIn 17*
Reeves, Keanu 1964- *News 92 [port]*
Reeves, L.P. 1937- *ScF&FL 92*
Reeves, Malcolm M. 1908- *St&PR 93*
Reeves, Margie Ann 1952- *WhoSSW 93*
Reeves, Mark Thomas 1955- *WhoSSW 93*
Reeves, Martha 1941- *Baker 92*
Reeves, Martha, & the Vandellas *SoulM*
Reeves, Marvin Coke 1911- *St&PR 93*
Reeves, Mary Jane W. 1949- *WhoAmW 93*
Reeves, Marylou 1959- *WhoE 93*
Reeves, Maud Pember d1953 *BioIn 17*
Reeves, Michael Stanley 1935- *St&PR 93, WhoAm 92*
Reeves, Micheal Aaron 1943- *WhoSSW 93*
Reeves, Michelle *BioIn 17*
Reeves, Patricia Ruth 1931- *WhoE 93*
Reeves, Paul Alfred 1932- *WhoAsAP 91, WhoWor 93*
Reeves, Ralph B., III 1947- *WhoAm 92*
Reeves, Richard Ackroyd 1927- *St&PR 93*
Reeves, Robert Grier LeFevre 1920- *WhoAm 92*
Reeves, Robert Michael 1942- *WhoUN 92*
Reeves, Roger DeForest 1949- *WhoE 93*
Reeves, Rosser Scott, III 1936- *WhoAm 92*
Reeves, Roy Russell 1952- *WhoEmL 93*
Reeves, Shirley Smith 1950- *WhoAmW 93*
Reeves, Sims 1818-1900 *OxDcOp*
Reeves, (John) Sims 1818-1900 *Baker 92*
Reeves, Stephen Bernard 1955- *WhoSSW 93*
Reeves, Susan Elizabeth Buchanan 1940- *WhoWrEP 92*
Reeves, Susan Leslie 1963- *WhoSSW 93*
Reeves, Timothy Scott 1953- *WhoWrEP 92*
Reeves, W. Colby, Jr. 1945- *St&PR 93*
Reeves, William Charles 1829- *BioIn 17*
Reeves-Marquardt, Dona Batty 1932- *WhoSSW 93*
Reeves-Stevens, Garfield 1953- *ScF&FL 92*
Reeves-Stevens, Judith 1953?- *ScF&FL 92*
Reevy, William Robert 1922- *WhoSSW 93*
Refalopei, Kalisto 1946- *WhoAsAP 91*
Refardt, Edgar 1877-1968 *Baker 92*
Refatti, Elvio 1921- *WhoScE 91-3*
Reffell, Derek 1928- *WhoWor 93*
Refice, Licinio 1883-1954 *Baker 92*
Refice, Licinio 1885-1954 *OxDcOp*
Refinski, Joseph Anthony 1954- *WhoE 93*
Refior, Everett Lee 1919- *WhoAm 92*
Refsell, Stephen T. *Law&B 92*
Refsnes, Joseph L. 1927- *St&PR 93*
Refsum, Harald E. 1924- *WhoScE 91-4*
Regal, Robert Denis 1941- *WhoWor 93*
Regalado, Antonio *DcCPCAm*
Regalado, Eloisa *Law&B 92*
Regalado, Kevin 1970- *WhoSSW 93*
Regalado, Nancy Nemencia 1945- *WhoAmW 93*
Regalado, Raul L. 1945- *WhoAm 92*
Regalbuto, Joe *BioIn 17, WhoAm 92*
Regalia, Nanzi *ScF&FL 92*
Regalmuto, Nancy Marie 1956- *WhoAmW 93*
Regamey, Constantin 1907-1982 *Baker 92*
Regan, Andrew Charles 1959- *WhoWor 93*
Regan, Basil *BioIn 17*
Regan, Catherine Marie *Law&B 92*
Regan, David 1935- *WhoAm 92*
Regan, David Michael 1955- *WhoE 93*
Regan, Deborah M. *Law&B 92*
Regan, Dian Curtis *ScF&FL 92*
Regan, Donald H. 1944- *WhoAm 92*
Regan, Donald Thomas 1918- *WhoAm 92*
Regan, Edward 1936- *WhoWor 93*
Regan, Edward C. 1935- *St&PR 93*
Regan, Edward Van Buren 1930- *WhoE 93*
Regan, Ellen Frances 1919- *WhoAmW 93*
Regan, F. Vincent 1922- *St&PR 93*
Regan, Frederic Dennis 1921- *WhoE 93*
Regan, Gerald Thomas 1931- *WhoSSW 93*
Regan, Harold 1943- *St&PR 93*
Regan, Jackie *ScF&FL 92*
Regan, James P. *Law&B 92*
Regan, John J. 1929- *WhoAm 92*
Regan, John MacVeign, Jr. 1921- *St&PR 93*
Regan, John N. 1898-1992 *BioIn 17*
Regan, Kenneth Michael 1951- *St&PR 93*
Regan, Linda Anne 1957- *WhoAmW 93*
Regan, Lynn *BioIn 17*
Regan, Mary B. *Law&B 92*
Regan, Muriel 1930- *BioIn 17, WhoAmW 93*
Regan, Nathan 1926- *St&PR 93*
Regan, Norma K. d1992 *NewYTBS 92*
Regan, Pascal 1914- *BioIn 17*
Regan, Patrick 1939- *MiSFD 9*
Regan, Patrick James 1949- *St&PR 93*
Regan, Paul Edward 1939- *St&PR 93*
Regan, Paul Erskine *WhoScE 91-1*
Regan, Paul J., Jr. 1940- *St&PR 93*
Regan, Peter C. 1940- *St&PR 93*
Regan, Peter Francis, III 1924- *WhoAm 92*
Regan, Peter John 1942- *WhoAm 92*
Regan, Richard Joseph 1930- *WhoE 93*
Regan, Robert *BioIn 17*
Regan, Robert 1930- *ScF&FL 92*
Regan, Robert Charles 1930- *WhoAm 92*
Regan, Rod 1950- *St&PR 93*
Regan, Sylvia 1908- *WhoAm 92*
Regan, Walter Joseph, Jr. 1936- *St&PR 93*
Regan, William Jerome 1943- *St&PR 93*
Regan, William Joseph, Jr. 1946- *WhoAm 92, WhoIns 93, WhoSSW 93*
Regan, William Marion 1938- *St&PR 93*
Regar, David Bennett 1939- *St&PR 93*
Regazzi, John H. 1921- *St&PR 93*
Regazzi, John Henry 1921- *WhoAm 92, WhoWor 93*
Regazzi, John James, III 1948- *WhoAm 92*
Regazzini, Eugenio 1946- *WhoWor 93*
Rege, Narayan R. 1932- *WhoUN 92*
Regeimbal, Neil Robert, Sr. 1929- *WhoAm 92*
Regelbrugge, Roger Rafael 1930- *St&PR 93, WhoAm 92*
Regen, Mark J. *Law&B 92*
Regenbaum, Shelly Haya 1941- *WhoE 93*
Regenbogen, Ellis Arnold 1946- *St&PR 93*
Regenbogen, Leslie Alan 1932- *St&PR 93*
Regensburg, Edward Alan 1953- *WhoE 93*
Regensburger, Dieter 1934- *WhoWor 93*
Regenstein, Barry I. 1956- *St&PR 93*
Regenstein, Lewis Graham 1943- *WhoAm 92*
Regenstein, Louis 1912- *St&PR 93, WhoAm 92*
Regensteiner, Else 1906- *BioIn 17*
Regenstreif, Herbert 1935- *WhoE 93, WhoWor 93*
Regenstreif, Samuel Peter 1936- *WhoAm 92*
Reger, George F. 1928- *St&PR 93*
Reger, Lawrence Lee 1939- *WhoAm 92*
Reger, (Johann Baptist Joseph) Max(imilian) 1873-1916 *Baker 92*
Reger, Paul A. 1926- *St&PR 93*
Reger, Ronald A. 1949- *St&PR 93*
Reges, Marianna Alice 1947- *WhoAm 92, WhoWor 93*
Reggia, Frank 1921- *WhoAm 92*
Reggiani, Serge 1922- *IntDcF 2-3*
Reggie, Catherine *ScF&FL 92*
Reggio, Godfrey *MiSFD 9*
Reggio, Vito Anthony 1929- *WhoWor 93*
Regier, Anna Lee Katherine 1926- *WhoWrEP 92*
Regier, Jon Louis 1922- *WhoWor 93*
Regier, Michael J. *Law&B 92*
Regillus, Lucius Aemilius fl. c. 190BC-189BC *HarEnMi*
Regina, Frank Joseph 1934- *St&PR 93*
Reginald, R. 1948- *ScF&FL 92*
Reginald, Robert 1948- *WhoWrEP 92*
Reginato, Robert Joseph 1935- *WhoAm 92*
Regini, Judith L. 1953- *WhoAmW 93*
Reginster, Jean-Yves Luc 1958- *WhoWor 93*
Regiomontanus, Johannes 1436-1476 *BioIn 17*
Region, Oscar *ConAu 139*
Regis, Johannes c. 1430-c. 1485 *Baker 92*
Register, Annette Rowan 1931- *WhoAmW 93*
Register, Benjamin Franklin, Jr. 1930- *WhoAm 92*
Register, David S. 1956- *St&PR 93*
Register, John 1939- *BioIn 17*
Register, John R. 1955- *St&PR 93*
Register, John Robert 1955- *WhoSSW 93*
Register, Ulma Doyle 1920- *WhoAm 92*
Register, Victoria Smith 1944- *WhoWrEP 92*
Regler, Meinhard 1941- *WhoScE 91-4*
Regli, Francesco 1802-1866 *Baker 92*
Regli, Patrick 1936- *WhoScE 91-2*
Regmi, Achyut Rad 1929- *WhoAsAP 91*
Regn, Bonnie Marie 1957- *WhoAmW 93*
Regnart, Jacob c. 1540-1599 *Baker 92*
Regnault, Phillips M. *Law&B 92*
Regnery, Alfred Scattergood 1942- *WhoAm 92*
Regnery, Henry 1912- *WhoAm 92*
Regnery, John Wallace *Law&B 92*
Regnery, Marcia Joan 1962- *WhoAmW 93*
Regnier, A. *WhoScE 91-3*
Regnier, Francois Jean 1933- *WhoWor 93*
Regnier, Gerald Anthony *Law&B 92*
Regnier, Gerard 1940- *BioIn 17*
Regnier, Marc *Law&B 92*
Regnier, Marc 1939- *St&PR 93*
Regnier, Marc Charles 1939- *WhoAm 92*
Regnier, Roland John 1953- *WhoE 93*
Regnier, Stephen Joseph 1950- *WhoWrEP 92*
Regnis, Michael *BioIn 17*
Rego, Edward John 1948- *St&PR 93*
Rego, Paula 1935- *BioIn 17*
Rego, Vincent Anthony 1924- *St&PR 93*
Regos, Annette Joanne *Law&B 92*
Regt, Hendrik de 1950- *Baker 92*
Regula, Ralph 1924- *CngDr 91, WhoAm 92*
Regulinski, David R. *Law&B 92*
Regulus, Gaius Atilius d224BC *HarEnMi*
Regulus, Marcus Atilius dc. 250BC *HarEnMi*
Reguly, Antal 1819-1858 *IntDcAn*
Reh, Thomas Edward 1943- *WhoWor 93*
Rehak, James Richard 1938- *WhoWor 93*
Rehak, Svatopluk 1926- *WhoScE 91-4*
Rehark, Russell John 1911- *St&PR 93*
Rehberg, Dennis R. 1955- *WhoAm 92*
Rehberg, Hans 1901-1963 *DcLB 124*
Rehberg, John T. *Law&B 92*
Rehberger, Gustav 1910- *WhoE 93, WhoWor 93*
Rehberger, Robert Lee 1949- *WhoEmL 93*
Rehbinder, Claes 1938- *WhoScE 91-4*
Rehbinder, Manfred Ernst 1935- *WhoWor 93*
Rehbock, Nancy E. 1959- *WhoWrEP 92*
Rehder, Dieter 1941- *WhoScE 91-3*
Rehder, Peter U. 1939- *WhoWor 93*
Reherman, Ronald Gilbert 1935- *St&PR 93, WhoAm 92*
Reheuser, Edward F. 1933- *St&PR 93*
Rehfeld, Beverly Dawna 1929- *WhoAmW 93*
Rehfeld, Jens Frederik 1941- *WhoScE 91-2, WhoWor 93*
Rehfisch, Hans Jose 1891-1960 *DcLB 124 [port]*
Rehfuess, Karl-Eugen 1933- *WhoScE 91-3*
Rehfuss, Heinz (Julius) 1917-1988 *Baker 92*
Rehkugler, Gerald Edwin 1935- *WhoAm 92*
Rehm, Allan Stanley 1936- *WhoSSW 93*
Rehm, Dieter 1938- *WhoScE 91-3*
Rehm, G. *WhoScE 91-3*
Rehm, Hans-Jurgen 1927- *WhoScE 91-3*
Rehm, Jack Daniel 1932- *St&PR 93, WhoAm 92*
Rehm, John Edwin 1924- *WhoWor 93*
Rehm, Karl M. 1935- *SmATA 72 [port]*
Rehm, Leo Frank 1916- *WhoAm 92*
Rehm, Lynn Paul 1941- *WhoSSW 93*
Rehm, Warren Stacey, Jr. 1907- *WhoAm 92*
Rehm, Wolfgang 1929- *Baker 92*

Rehmus, Charles Martin 1926- *WhoAm 92*
Rehn, Marta Elisabeth 1935- *WhoWor 93*
Rehnborg, Carl S. 1936- *St&PR 93*
Rehnquist, William H. *BioIn 17*
Rehnquist, William Hubbs 1924- *CngDr 91, OxCSupC [port], WhoAm 92, WhoE 93, WhoWor 93*
Rehnqvist-Ahlberg, Nina A.K. 1944- *WhoScE 91-4*
Rehns, Marsha Lee 1946- *WhoAmW 93*
Rehnstrom, J. Bernard 1930- *WhoAm 92*
Rehor, David G. 1939- *St&PR 93*
Rehor, David George 1939- *WhoAm 92*
Rehor, Raymond James 1929- *St&PR 93*
Rehote, Alphonse *WhoWor 93*
Rehrauer, Harold W. 1937- *St&PR 93*
Rehwald, R. Thomas 1938- *St&PR 93*
Reibel, Kurt 1926- *WhoAm 92*
Reibel, Martin A. 1942- *St&PR 93*
Reiber, Johan H.C. 1946- *WhoScE 91-3*
Reibman, Jeanette Fichman 1915- *WhoAm 92, WhoAmW 93, WhoE 93*
Reibman-Myers, Francine Lee 1949- *WhoAmW 93*
Reiboldt, James Max 1951- *St&PR 93, WhoSSW 93*
Reice, Gerard Charles 1946- *St&PR 93*
Reich, Alan Anderson 1930- *WhoAm 92*
Reich, Ali *ConAu 37NR*
Reich, Axel Manfred 1942- *WhoWor 93*
Reich, Barry Alan 1950- *WhoE 93*
Reich, Bernard 1926- *WhoAm 92*
Reich, Bernard 1941- *WhoAm 92*
Reich, Bruce P. 1956- *WhoIns 93*
Reich, Charles William 1930- *WhoAm 92*
Reich, Daniel 1943- *St&PR 93*
Reich, David Lee 1930- *WhoAm 92*
Reich, Ernest B. 1893-1922 *BiDAMSp 1989*
Reich, Ferenc 1930- *WhoE 93, WhoWor 93*
Reich, Garrett W. *Law&B 92*
Reich, Garrett Wayne 1951- *WhoEmL 93*
Reich, George Arthur *WhoSSW 93*
Reich, Gerhard Richard 1950- *WhoSSW 93*
Reich, Gloria *Law&B 92*
Reich, Hans-Joachim O. 1949- *St&PR 93*
Reich, Henry E., Jr. *Law&B 92*
Reich, Herb *WhoAm 92, WhoE 93, WhoWrEP 92*
Reich, Herbert J. 1900- *WhoE 93*
Reich, Ismar Meyer 1924- *St&PR 93*
Reich, J.E. 1910- *St&PR 93*
Reich, Jack E. 1910- *WhoIns 93*
Reich, Jack Egan 1910- *WhoAm 92*
Reich, Jay 1929- *St&PR 93*
Reich, Julie A. *Law&B 92*
Reich, Kenneth Irvin 1938- *WhoAm 92*
Reich, Michael *BioIn 17*
Reich, Michael William 1956- *WhoE 93*
Reich, Morton Melvyn 1939- *WhoAm 92*
Reich, Murray Herbert 1922- *WhoE 93*
Reich, Nathaniel Edwin 1907- *WhoAm 92*
Reich, Otto Juan 1945- *WhoAm 92*
Reich, Paul Seth 1955- *WhoE 93*
Reich, Pauline Carole 1946- *WhoAm 92*
Reich, Randi Ruth Novak 1954- *WhoAmW 93*
Reich, Richard M. 1947- *St&PR 93*
Reich, Robert B. *BioIn 17, NewYTBS 92 [port]*
Reich, Robert Bernard 1946- *WhoAm 92, WhoE 93*
Reich, Robert Claude 1929- *WhoWor 93*
Reich, Robert Sigmund 1913- *WhoAm 92*
Reich, Ronald 1945- *St&PR 93*
Reich, Rose Marie 1937- *WhoAmW 93*
Reich, Seymour David 1933- *WhoAm 92*
Reich, Sherri E. *Law&B 92*
Reich, Steve *BioIn 17*
Reich, Steve 1936- *Baker 92, ConMus 8 [port], WhoAm 92*
Reich, Walter 1943- *WhoE 93*
Reich, Willi 1898-1980 *Baker 92*
Reich, William Charles 1864-1924 *JrnUS*
Reich, William Michael 1943- *WhoE 93*
Reicha, Antoine (-Joseph) 1770-1836 *Baker 92*
Reichard, Gary Warren 1943- *WhoSSW 93*
Reichard, Gladys Amanda 1893-1955 *IntDcAn*
Reichard, Hugo Manley 1918- *WhoAm 92*
Reichard, John Francis 1924- *WhoAm 92, WhoE 93*
Reichard, John Louis 1930- *St&PR 93*
Reichard, John Mohr, Jr. 1934- *St&PR 93*
Reichard, Sherwood Marshall 1928- *WhoAm 92, WhoSSW 93*
Reichard, William Thomas 1943- *St&PR 93*
Reichard, William Thomas, III 1943- *WhoAm 92, WhoSSW 93*
Reichardt, Carl E. *BioIn 17*
Reichardt, Carl E. 1931- *St&PR 93, WhoAm 92*
Reichardt, Christian 1934- *WhoScE 91-3*
Reichardt, David L. *Law&B 92*
Reichardt, Delbert Dale 1927- *WhoAm 92*
Reichardt, Jasia 1933- *ScF&FL 92*
Reichardt, Johann Friedrich 1752-1814 *Baker 92, OxDcOp*
Reichardt, Juliane Benda 1752-1783 *BioIn 17*
Reichardt, Louise 1779-1826 *BioIn 17*
Reichardt, Luise 1779-1826 *Baker 92*
Reichardt, Werner *WhoScE 91-3*
Reichart, James P. 1949- *St&PR 93*
Reichart, Stuart Richard 1924- *WhoE 93*
Reichartz, W. Dan 1946- *WhoAm 92*
Reichbart, Howard Enoch 1943- *WhoSSW 93*
Reichblum, Audrey Rosenthal 1935- *WhoE 93*
Reiche, Frank Perley 1929- *WhoAm 92*
Reichek, Jesse 1916- *WhoAm 92*
Reichek, Morton Arthur 1924- *WhoAm 92*
Reichel, Charles Edward 1943- *WhoSSW 93*
Reichel, Francene Donna 1963- *WhoAmW 93*
Reichel, Friedrich 1833-1889 *Baker 92*
Reichel, Horst 1941- *WhoWor 93*
Reichel, Rhoda Ottmar Rebay 1878- *AmWomPl*
Reichel, Robert *BioIn 17*
Reichel, Walter Emil 1935- *WhoAm 92*
Reichelt, Fred 1941- *WhoAm 92, WhoWor 93*
Reichen, Jurg 1946- *WhoWor 93*
Reichenau, Walter von 1884-1942 *BioIn 17*
Reichenbach, Donald Philipp 1945- *WhoWor 93*
Reichenbach, Francois 1922- *MiSFD 9*
Reichenbach, George Sheridan 1929- *St&PR 93*
Reichenbach, Hans 1936- *WhoScE 91-3*
Reichenbach, M. J. Gertrude 1912- *WhoAmW 93*
Reichenbach, William F. *Law&B 92*
Reichenbecher, Vernon Edgar, Jr. 1948- *WhoSSW 93*
Reichenberg, William D. 1941- *St&PR 93*
Reichenberger, John F. *Law&B 92*
Reichenecker, David Robert 1950- *St&PR 93*
Reicher-Kindermann, Hedwig 1853-1883 *Baker 92, OxDcOp*
Reichert, Bruce Robert 1942- *WhoE 93*
Reichert, Charles M. 1937- *St&PR 93*
Reichert, Cheryl McBroom 1946- *WhoAmW 93*
Reichert, David 1929- *WhoAm 92*
Reichert, Jack Frank 1930- *St&PR 93, WhoAm 92*
Reichert, James P. *Law&B 92*
Reichert, James William 1944- *St&PR 93*
Reichert, Jean 1928- *WhoScE 91-2*
Reichert, Jon Douglas 1962- *St&PR 93*
Reichert, Julia *MiSFD 9*
Reichert, Konrad 1930- *WhoScE 91-4*
Reichert, Leo Edmund, Jr. 1932- *WhoAm 92, WhoE 93, WhoWor 93*
Reichert, Mark *MiSFD 9*
Reichert, Mickey Zucker 1962- *ScF&FL 92*
Reichert, Miriam Zucker *ScF&FL 92*
Reichert, Paul B. 1938- *St&PR 93*
Reichert, Robert F. 1945- *St&PR 93*
Reichert, William Mark *Law&B 92*
Reichert-Facilides, Otto Ernst 1925- *WhoAm 92*
Reichertz, Peter L. 1930- *WhoScE 91-3*
Reichgott, Ember Darlene 1953- *WhoAmW 93, WhoEmL 93*
Reichgott, Michael Joel 1940- *WhoE 93*
Reichhelm, Kim *BioIn 17*
Reichle, Frederick Adolph 1935- *WhoAm 92*
Reichle, Gail Ann 1937- *WhoAmW 93*
Reichle, Gregory Charles 1943- *St&PR 93*
Reichle, Linda Kimberly *Law&B 92*
Reichley, Charley Ann 1928- *WhoSSW 93*
Reichlin, Seymour 1924- *WhoAm 92*
Reichman, Allen 1932- *WhoE 93*
Reichman, Dawn Leslie 1951- *WhoAmW 93*
Reichman, Fredrick Thomas 1925- *WhoAm 92*
Reichman, George T. 1937- *St&PR 93*
Reichman, Jack Z. 1950- *St&PR 93*
Reichman, Lee Brodersohn 1938- *WhoAm 92*
Reichman, Neil *Law&B 92*
Reichman, Ronald *Law&B 92*
Reichman, Walter 1938- *WhoAm 92*
Reichmann, Albert *WhoAm 92, WhoWor 93*
Reichmann, David E. *Law&B 92*
Reichmann, Paul *BioIn 17, WhoAm 92*
Reichmann, Peter Ivan 1942- *WhoWor 93*
Reichmann, Ralph *WhoWor 93*
Reichmann, Renee d1990 *BioIn 17*
Reichmann, Theodor 1849-1903 *Baker 92, OxDcOp*
Reichmann, Thomas Josef 1938- *WhoWor 93*
Reichmann, Thomas M. 1940- *WhoUN 92*
Reichner, John S. *Law&B 92*
Reichstein, Tadeus 1897- *WhoAm 92, WhoWor 93*
Reichstein, Tadeusz 1897- *PolBiDi*
Reichstetter, Arthur Charles 1946- *St&PR 93, WhoAm 92*
Reichwalder, P. *WhoScE 91-4*
Reichwein, John H. 1909- *St&PR 93*
Reichwein, John Henry, Jr. 1954- *St&PR 93*
Reichwein, Leopold 1878-1945 *Baker 92*
Reicin, Ronald Ian 1942- *WhoAm 92*
Reick, Robert Alan 1947- *St&PR 93*
Reickert, Erick A. 1935- *St&PR 93*
Reickert, Erick Arthur 1935- *WhoAm 92*
Reid, Adrienne Wilder 1955- *WhoIns 93*
Reid, Alan David 1942- *WhoAm 92*
Reid, Alastair 1939- *MiSFD 9*
Reid, Alice L. *Law&B 92*
Reid, Amelia 1942- *WhoAmW 93*
Reid, Annie *BioIn 17*
Reid, Antonio *WhoAm 92*
Reid, Aubrey Karl, Jr. 1927- *St&PR 93*
Reid, B.L. 1918-1990 *BioIn 17*
Reid, Barbara 1936- *St&PR 93*
Reid, Barbara 1957- *ChlBIID [port]*
Reid, Barbara Addison 1943- *WhoE 93*
Reid, Benjamin Lawrence 1918- *WhoAm 92, WhoWrEP 92*
Reid, Benjamin Lawrence 1918-1990 *BioIn 17*
Reid, Bernadette P. *St&PR 93*
Reid, Beverly Ann 1949- *WhoE 93*
Reid, Bill J. 1931- *St&PR 93*
Reid, Carol McMillan *AmWomPl*
Reid, Carolyn Anne 1944- *WhoAmW 93*
Reid, Cedric Nicholas *WhoScE 91-1*
Reid, Charles Clark 1937- *WhoAm 92*
Reid, Charles Henry 1929- *WhoE 93*
Reid, Charles P. 1930- *St&PR 93*
Reid, Charles Phillip Patrick 1940- *WhoAm 92, WhoSSW 93*
Reid, Charlotte Thompson 1913- *BioIn 17*
Reid, Christopher *BioIn 17*
Reid, Clark L. 1925- *St&PR 93*
Reid, Cornelius J., Jr. 1924- *St&PR 93*
Reid, Cornelius L. 1911- *Baker 92*
Reid, Darlene Agar 1947- *WhoSSW 93*
Reid, David Evans 1943- *WhoAm 92*
Reid, David H. *Law&B 92*
Reid, Desmond *ConAu 38NR*
Reid, Desmond 1945- *BlkAull 92*
Reid, Don 1945- *See* Statler Brothers, The *ConMus 8*
Reid, Donald David *WhoWor 93*
Reid, Douglas MacKenzie 1935- *St&PR 93*
Reid, Douglas Stewart, Sr. 1932- *St&PR 93*
Reid, Edith Gittings 1863- *AmWomPl*
Reid, Edward Snover 1930- *WhoAm 92*
Reid, Elizabeth Sinkiewicz 1962- *WhoE 93*
Reid, Evans Burton 1913- *WhoAm 92*
Reid, Everett Coolidge, II 1957- *WhoE 93*
Reid, Forrest 1846-1947 *ScF&FL 92*
Reid, Frances *BioIn 17*
Reid, George Houston 1845-1918 *BioIn 17*
Reid, George Kell 1918- *WhoAm 92*
Reid, George Wayne 1930- *WhoE 93*
Reid, Glenn James *Law&B 92*
Reid, Gordon MacDonald 1935- *St&PR 93, WhoE 93*
Reid, Gordon Stanley 1923- *WhoAsAP 91*
Reid, Gregory L. *Law&B 92*
Reid, H.G. *Law&B 92*
Reid, Harold 1939- *See* Statler Brothers, The *ConMus 8*
Reid, Harry 1939- *CngDr 91, WhoAm 92*
Reid, Harvey L. 1928- *St&PR 93*
Reid, Helen Rogers 1882-1970 *JrnUS*
Reid, Helena Patricia 1959- *WhoE 93*
Reid, Herbert O. *BioIn 17*
Reid, Hoch 1909- *WhoAm 92*
Reid, Inez Smith 1937- *WhoAmW 93, WhoE 93*
Reid, Ira De A. 1901-1968 *EncAACR*
Reid, J. Frederick 1927- *St&PR 93, WhoIns 93*
Reid, J. Kirk 1946- *St&PR 93*
Reid, Jack Powell 1936- *WhoAm 92*
Reid, Jackson Brock 1921- *WhoAm 92*
Reid, James Dolan 1930- *WhoAm 92*
Reid, James M. 1944- *St&PR 93*
Reid, James S., Jr. 1926- *St&PR 93*
Reid, James T. 1935- *St&PR 93*
Reid, Janet Kay 1952- *WhoWrEP 92*
Reid, Jeanne Louise 1962- *WhoAmW 93*
Reid, Jill *Law&B 92*
Reid, Jim Frank 1933- *St&PR 93*
Reid, Joan Evangeline 1932- *WhoAmW 93*
Reid, John 1721-1807 *Baker 92*
Reid, John 1946- *MiSFD 9*
Reid, John B. 1940- *St&PR 93*
Reid, John Calvin 1901- *ScF&FL 92*
Reid, John F. *Law&B 92*
Reid, John L. *WhoScE 91-1*
Reid, John M. 1926- *St&PR 93*
Reid, John McArthur *WhoScE 91-1*
Reid, John Mitchell 1926- *WhoAm 92*
Reid, John Phillip 1930- *WhoAm 92*
Reid, Jonathan L. *Law&B 92*
Reid, Joseph Lee 1923- *WhoAm 92*
Reid, Joseph William 1955- *WhoSSW 93*
Reid, Joyce Edna 1941- *WhoWrEP 92*
Reid, Kathryn J. *Law&B 92*
Reid, Kenneth Bannerman Milne *WhoScE 91-1*
Reid, Kenneth Bannerman Milne 1943- *WhoWor 93*
Reid, Kenneth O. 1926- *St&PR 93*
Reid, Khartrell *BioIn 17*
Reid, Langhorne, III 1950- *WhoAm 92, WhoE 93, WhoEmL 93, WhoWor 93*
Reid, Lawrence Charles 1948- *WhoIns 93*
Reid, Leighton *Law&B 92*
Reid, Loren Dudley 1905- *WhoAm 92*
Reid, Louisa *AmWomPl*
Reid, Lyle 1930- *WhoAm 92, WhoSSW 93*
Reid, Lynne McArthur 1923- *WhoAm 92*
Reid, Malcolm *Law&B 92*
Reid, Malcolm 1943- *St&PR 93*
Reid, Margaret Elizabeth 1935- *WhoAsAP 91*
Reid, Margaret (Isabel) 1925-1992 *ConAu 139*
Reid, Marion L. 1929- *WhoAm 92, WhoAmW 93, WhoE 93*
Reid, Marita *HispAmA*
Reid, Martin R. 1942- *St&PR 93*
Reid, Max 1944- *MiSFD 9*
Reid, Michael B. *WhoIns 93*
Reid, Michael J. 1938- *WhoAm 92*
Reid, Mike *BioIn 17*
Reid, Neil Henry *Law&B 92*
Reid, Noal Douglas 1944- *St&PR 93*
Reid, Norman R. 1933- *WhoIns 93*
Reid, Octavius Ted, III 1964- *WhoE 93*
Reid, Oscar 1936- *St&PR 93*
Reid, Pamela Trotman 1946- *WhoAmW 93*
Reid, Philip Dean 1937- *WhoE 93*
Reid, Phillip Roger 1959- *St&PR 93*
Reid, Ralph Ralston, Jr. 1934- *WhoAm 92*
Reid, Ralph Waldo Emerson 1915- *WhoSSW 93, WhoWor 93*
Reid, Randal G. *Law&B 92*
Reid, Randall 1931- *WhoWrEP 92*
Reid, Richard Joseph 1932- *WhoWor 93*
Reid, Richard Stanley 1934- *WhoUN 92*
Reid, Robert Clark 1924- *WhoAm 92*
Reid, Robert John 1942- *WhoAm 92*
Reid, Robert John 1954- *St&PR 93*
Reid, Robert Lelon 1942- *WhoAm 92*
Reid, Robert Newton 1908- *WhoAm 92*
Reid, Rosemary Anne 1951- *WhoEmL 93*
Reid, Ross 1917- *St&PR 93*
Reid, Rust Endicott 1931- *WhoAm 92*
Reid, Ruth Hanford 1938- *WhoAmW 93*
Reid, Samuel Chester 1783-1861 *HarEnMi*
Reid, Sarah Layfield 1952- *WhoAmW 93*
Reid, Stanley Douglas 1945- *WhoWor 93*
Reid, Stephen Robert *WhoScE 91-1*
Reid, Steven J. *St&PR 93*
Reid, Sue Titus 1939- *WhoAmW 93*
Reid, Suzann Michell *Law&B 92*
Reid, Terence C. W. 1941- *WhoAm 92*
Reid, Terrence *St&PR 93*
Reid, Thomas H. *Law&B 92*
Reid, Tim *BioIn 17*
Reid, Timothy 1936- *WhoAm 92*
Reid, Tommy Jean 1945- *WhoAmW 93*
Reid, Toy Franklin 1924- *St&PR 93*
Reid, V. S. 1913-1987 *DcLB 125 [port]*
Reid, W. Malcolm 1910-1990 *BioIn 17*
Reid, Wallace 1891-1923 *IntDcF 2-3 [port]*
Reid, Whitelaw 1837-1912 *GayN, JrnUS*
Reid, Whitelaw 1913- *St&PR 93*
Reid, William H(oward) 1945- *ConAu 37NR*
Reid, William Hill 1926- *WhoAm 92*
Reid, William J(ames) 1928- *ConAu 39NR*
Reid, William James 1927- *WhoAm 92*
Reid, William James 1928- *WhoAm 92*
Reid, William James 1941- *WhoSSW 93*
Reid, William Michael 1954- *WhoSSW 93*
Reida, Alvah 1920-1975 *ScF&FL 92*
Reida-Allen, Pamela Anne 1944- *WhoAmW 93*
Reid Banks, Lynne 1929- *ScF&FL 92*
Reid Banks, Lynne 1929- *BioIn 17, ConAu 38NR, MajAI [port]*
Reid Cabral, Donald 1923- *DcCPCAm, WhoWor 93*
Reidel, Carl Hubert 1937- *WhoE 93*
Reidenbach, J.M. 1940- *WhoScE 91-2*
Reidenbach, J. Michael *Law&B 92*

Reidenbach, William J. *Law&B 92*
Reidenbach, William John 1930- *St&PR 93*
Reidenbaugh, Lowell Henry 1919- *WhoAm 92*
Reidenberg, Marcus Milton 1934- *WhoAm 92*
Reider, George M., Jr. 1940- *WhoIns 93*
Reider, Judith Barbara 1938- *WhoAmW 93*
Reider, Robert M. 1925- *St&PR 93*
Reidl, Otto 1939- *St&PR 93*
Reidler, Richard C. 1938- *St&PR 93*
Reid-Petty, Jane 1927- *WhoAmW 93*
Reid Scott, David Alexander Carroll 1947- *WhoWor 93*
Reid-Seidner, Kathleen L. *Law&B 92*
Reidy, Carolyn Kroll 1949- *WhoAm 92, WhoAmW 93*
Reidy, Gerald P. *Law&B 92*
Reidy, Gerald Patrick 1929- *WhoAm 92*
Reidy, James, Jr. 1929- *St&PR 93*
Reidy, James J. 1941- *St&PR 93*
Reidy, John Joseph, Jr. 1932- *St&PR 93*
Reidy, Richard F. 1935- *WhoIns 93*
Reidy, Richard J. *St&PR 93*
Reidy, Roger Patrick 1925- *WhoE 93*
Reidy, Sarah McCrea 1962- *WhoAmW 93*
Reidy, William P. 1932- *St&PR 93*
Reif, David Poynter 1953- *St&PR 93*
Reif, Eliot d1991 *BioIn 17*
Reif, Eric Peter 1942- *WhoAm 92*
Reif, John Henry 1951- *WhoSSW 93*
Reif, Louis R. 1923- *St&PR 93*
Reif, Louis Raymond 1923- *WhoAm 92*
Reif, Paul 1910-1978 *Baker 92*
Reif, Phyllis Heibel 1921- *WhoAmW 93*
Reif, Robert C. 1949- *St&PR 93*
Reif, Steven Jay 1947- *WhoSSW 93*
Reif, Winfried Herbert 1930- *WhoWor 93*
Reifenberg, Thomas P. 1930- *St&PR 93*
Reifenheiser, Thomas V. 1935- *WhoAm 92*
Reifer, Annemarie Theresa 1966- *WhoAmW 93*
Reifers, Richard Francis 1919- *WhoAm 92*
Reiff, Dovie Kate 1931- *WhoAmW 93*
Reiff, Gaston d1992 *BioIn 17*
Reiff, J. 1944- *WhoScE 91-3*
Reiff, Jack W. 1927- *St&PR 93*
Reiff, Patricia Hofer 1950- *WhoAmW 93*
Reiff, Philip L. 1947- *St&PR 93*
Reiff, Stephanie 1948- *ScF&FL 92*
Reiffel, Charles 1862-1942 *BioIn 17*
Reiffel, Leonard 1927- *ScF&FL 92, St&PR 93, WhoAm 92*
Reiff Sodano, Tana 1951- *WhoWrEP 92*
Reifler, Clifford Bruce 1931- *WhoAm 92*
Reifler, Samuel 1939- *WhoWrEP 92*
Reifschneider, Darrel 1933- *St&PR 93*
Reifsnider, Kenneth Leonard 1940- *WhoAm 92*
Reifsnyder, Mark W. 1951- *St&PR 93*
Reifsnyder, William Edward 1924- *WhoAm 92*
Reig, June Wilson 1933- *WhoAm 92*
Reigber, Christoph 1939- *WhoScE 91-3*
Reigel, Todd L. 1958- *St&PR 93*
Reighard, Catherine F. *AmWomPl*
Reighard, Clyde Waltz 1929- *WhoAm 92*
Reighard, Homer Leroy 1924- *WhoAm 92*
Reigle, Ruthann 1962- *WhoAmW 93*
Reignier, Jean G.M. 1933- *WhoScE 91-2*
Reigrod, Robert Hull 1941- *WhoAm 92*
Reigstad, Ruth Elaine 1923- *WhoAmW 93*
Reihl, Bruno 1954- *WhoWor 93*
Reijnen, Piet 1933- *WhoScE 91-3*
Reijsenbach de Haan, Frederik 1949- *WhoUN 92*
Reik, Rita Ann Fitzpatrick 1951- *WhoSSW 93*
Reik, Wolf Ulrich 1957- *WhoWor 93*
Reilert, Robert E. *Law&B 92*
Reiley, T. Phillip 1950- *WhoE 93, WhoEmL 93, WhoWor 93*
Reiling, David Joseph 1964- *WhoSSW 93*
Reiling, Henry Bernard 1938- *WhoAm 92*
Reilley, Dennen 1937- *WhoE 93*
Reilley, James Clark 1919- *WhoE 93*
Reilley, Michael J. 1954- *St&PR 93*
Reilly, Arlene L. *Law&B 92*
Reilly, Bernard J. *Law&B 92*
Reilly, Brendan Joseph d1992 *BioIn 17, NewYTBS 92*
Reilly, Charles A. 1947- *St&PR 93*
Reilly, Charles Nelson 1931- *BioIn 17, WhoAm 92*
Reilly, Charles Vincent 1939- *WhoWor 93*
Reilly, Cynthia Faithe 1952- *WhoAmW 93*
Reilly, Daniel Patrick 1928- *WhoAm 92, WhoE 93*
Reilly, David Henry 1936- *WhoAm 92, WhoSSW 93*
Reilly, David John *Law&B 92*
Reilly, David Robert *Law&B 92*
Reilly, Donald C. 1950- *St&PR 93*
Reilly, Dorna *BioIn 17*
Reilly, Edgar M. 1916-1991 *BioIn 17*
Reilly, Edward Arthur 1943- *WhoAm 92, WhoE 93*
Reilly, Edward John 1923- *WhoE 93*
Reilly, Edward Joseph 1916- *WhoWrEP 92*
Reilly, Edward T., Jr. 1946- *St&PR 93*
Reilly, Frank Kelly 1935- *WhoAm 92, WhoWor 93*
Reilly, Frank T. 1928- *St&PR 93*
Reilly, Frank Thomas 1928- *WhoAm 92*
Reilly, Frederick John 1961- *WhoSSW 93*
Reilly, George Love Anthony 1918- *WhoAm 92*
Reilly, Gerard Denis 1906- *WhoAm 92*
Reilly, Harold V. Pat 1924- *WhoE 93*
Reilly, Jack L. 1936- *St&PR 93*
Reilly, James E. *Law&B 92*
Reilly, James P. 1940- *St&PR 93*
Reilly, James P., Jr. 1946- *St&PR 93*
Reilly, James Patrick 1940- *WhoE 93*
Reilly, James Vincent 1926- *St&PR 93*
Reilly, Jeanette P. 1908- *WhoAmW 93, WhoWor 93*
Reilly, John E. *Law&B 92*
Reilly, John Hurford 1934- *WhoE 93*
Reilly, John Joseph 1938- *WhoAm 92*
Reilly, John L. 1940- *St&PR 93*
Reilly, John Lawrence 1940- *WhoAm 92*
Reilly, John Paul 1943- *St&PR 93*
Reilly, John Regis 1935- *WhoE 93*
Reilly, John Richard 1928- *WhoAm 92*
Reilly, Joy Harriman 1942- *WhoAmW 93*
Reilly, Kathleen *Law&B 92*
Reilly, Kathy Maurer 1949- *St&PR 93*
Reilly, Laura J. *Law&B 92*
Reilly, Lawrence Hugh 1928- *St&PR 93*
Reilly, Lawrence J. 1956- *St&PR 93*
Reilly, Lisa Ann 1957- *WhoAmW 93*
Reilly, Lois Ann Pelcarsky 1941- *WhoAmW 93*
Reilly, Louis E. *Law&B 92*
Reilly, M.T. *Law&B 92*
Reilly, Madelyn A. *Law&B 92*
Reilly, Mary Anne Sommers 1943- *WhoAm 92*
Reilly, Mary Ellen 1963- *WhoAmW 93*
Reilly, Michael Atlee 1948- *WhoEmL 93*
Reilly, Michael D. 1948- *St&PR 93*
Reilly, Michael J. 1954- *St&PR 93*
Reilly, Michael James 1944- *St&PR 93*
Reilly, Michael Martin 1957- *St&PR 93*
Reilly, Nancy O. 1951- *WhoWrEP 92*
Reilly, Noel M.P. 1902-1991 *BioIn 17*
Reilly, Patricia A. *Law&B 92*
Reilly, Patrick 1932- *ConAu 37NR*
Reilly, Patrick D. *ConAu 38NR*
Reilly, Paul 1912-1990 *BioIn 17*
Reilly, Paul F. d1992 *NewYTBS 92*
Reilly, Paul J. 1953- *St&PR 93*
Reilly, Peter *BioIn 17*
Reilly, Peter C. 1907- *St&PR 93*
Reilly, Peter Richard *Law&B 92*
Reilly, Robert 1933- *ScF&FL 92*
Reilly, Robert Francis 1921- *WhoAm 92*
Reilly, Robert Frederick 1952- *WhoEmL 93, WhoWor 93*
Reilly, Robert James 1945- *St&PR 93*
Reilly, Robert Kevin 1953- *WhoE 93*
Reilly, Sally S. *Law&B 92*
Reilly, Sara Slife *Law&B 92*
Reilly, Sean C. *Law&B 92*
Reilly, Sean F. *Law&B 92*
Reilly, Susan Moira 1948- *WhoAmW 93*
Reilly, T.H. *Law&B 92*
Reilly, Theresa *WhoAmW 93*
Reilly, Thomas *WhoScE 91-1*
Reilly, Thomas E. 1947- *St&PR 93*
Reilly, Thomas F. d1992 *NewYTBS 92*
Reilly, Thomas Michael 1941- *St&PR 93*
Reilly, Timothy G. 1950- *St&PR 93*
Reilly, Trudy P. *Law&B 92*
Reilly, William *MiSFD 9*
Reilly, William A. 1947- *St&PR 93*
Reilly, William D. 1930- *St&PR 93*
Reilly, William F. *BioIn 17*
Reilly, William Francis 1938- *WhoAm 92*
Reilly, William G., Jr. *Law&B 92*
Reilly, William K. 1940- *BioIn 17*
Reilly, William Kane 1940- *NewYTBS 92 [port], WhoAm 92, WhoE 93*
Reilly, William P. 1917-1991 *BioIn 17*
Reily, Jack P. 1950- *St&PR 93*
Reily, John C. 1907- *St&PR 93*
Reim, Gary Paul 1946- *St&PR 93*
Reim, Martin 1931- *WhoWor 93*
Reiman, Andre M. *Law&B 92*
Reiman, Donald Henry 1934- *WhoAm 92, WhoE 93, WhoWor 93*
Reiman, Joey 1953- *WhoAm 92*
Reiman, Roy J. *BioIn 17*
Reiman, Thomas Jay 1949- *St&PR 93*
Reimann, Aribert 1936- *Baker 92, IntDcOp, OxDcOp*
Reimann, Heinrich 1850-1906 *Baker 92*
Reimann, Ignaz 1820-1885 *Baker 92*
Reimann, Kathryn *Law&B 92*
Reimann, Kurt William 1944- *St&PR 93*
Reimann, Patricia Anne 1957- *WhoAmW 93*
Reimann, Ronald Hill 1939- *St&PR 93*
Reimann, William Page 1935- *WhoAm 92*
Reimann-Philipp, Rainer Georg Paul F. 1927- *WhoScE 91-3*
Reimdl, George 1940- *St&PR 93*
Reimer, Bennett 1932- *WhoAm 92*
Reimer, Daniel Peter 1946- *St&PR 93*
Reimer, Jeffrey Charles 1963- *WhoE 93*
Reimer, Linda M. *Law&B 92*
Reimer, Ronald Anthony 1945- *WhoSSW 93*
Reimer, Terry Allan 1945- *WhoAm 92*
Reimer, Wendy Gerard *Law&B 92*
Reimers, Dieter H. 1943- *WhoScE 91-3*
Reimers, Naomi Headley 1920- *WhoE 93*
Reimers, Paul 1878-1942 *Baker 92*
Reimonenq, Simeon Bernard, Jr. *Law&B 92*
Rein, Catherine Amelia 1943- *St&PR 93, WhoAm 92*
Rein, David M. 1960- *St&PR 93*
Rein, Dolores Elaine 1936- *WhoAmW 93*
Rein, Martin L. 1915- *WhoIns 93*
Rein, Michael David 1956- *WhoSSW 93*
Rein, William F. 1935- *St&PR 93*
Reina 1931- *WhoE 93*
Reina, Carlos Roberto *DcCPCAm*
Reina, Domenico 1797-1843 *Baker 92, OxDcOp*
Reina, Jack *BioIn 17*
Reina, Jorge Arturo See Reina, Carlos Roberto *DcCPCAm*
Reinach, Albert 1929- *St&PR 93*
Reinach, Jacquelyn (Krasne) 1930- *WhoWrEP 92*
Reinach, Joseph 1856-1921 *BioIn 17*
Reinach, (Salomon) Theodore 1860-1928 *Baker 92*
Reinagle, Alexander 1756?-1809 *Baker 92, OxDcOp*
Reinauer, B. Franklin, III 1941- *St&PR 93*
Reinauer, Hans 1933- *WhoScE 91-3*
Reinboth, Rudolf 1929- *WhoScE 91-3*
Reindel, Edna 1900- *BioIn 17*
Reindel, Susanne Edith 1959- *WhoWor 93*
Reinders, Gerrit Reinier 1952- *WhoWor 93*
Reinecke, Carl (Heinrich Carsten) 1824-1910 *Baker 92*
Reinecke, Daniel K. *Law&B 92*
Reinecke, Manfred G. 1935- *WhoAm 92*
Reinecke, Robert Dale 1929- *WhoAm 92*
Reinecke, Thomas J. *St&PR 93*
Reineker, Peter 1940- *WhoWor 93*
Reineman, Joseph Vilsack 1933- *St&PR 93*
Reinemann, Glenn N. 1931- *St&PR 93*
Reinemund, J.A. *WhoScE 91-4*
Reinemund, Steven S. 1948- *WhoAm 92*
Reiner, Carl 1922- *ConAu 138, MiSFD 9, WhoAm 92*
Reiner, Elsa 1930- *WhoScE 91-4*
Reiner, Fritz 1888-1963 *Baker 92, IntDcOp, OxDcOp*
Reiner, Gary M. 1954- *St&PR 93*
Reiner, Gladys Aisman 1926- *WhoE 93*
Reiner, Irma Moses 1922- *WhoAmW 93*
Reiner, Jeffrey *MiSFD 9*
Reiner, Jeffrey Alan *Law&B 92*
Reiner, John *BioIn 17*
Reiner, Karel 1910-1979 *Baker 92*
Reiner, Lucas *MiSFD 9*
Reiner, Mary Elisabeth 1931- *WhoAmW 93, WhoWor 93*
Reiner, Rob *BioIn 17, WhoAm 92*
Reiner, Rob 1945- *MiSFD 9*
Reiner, Rob(ert) 1945- *ConAu 138*
Reiner, Sidney d1991 *BioIn 17*
Reiner, Stephen R. 1940- *St&PR 93*
Reiners, Karlheinz 1950- *WhoWor 93*
Reiners, Rudolph 1931- *St&PR 93*
Reinert, A. Joe *Law&B 92*
Reinert, Al *MiSFD 9*
Reinert, Clifford Daniel 1946- *WhoE 93*
Reinert, Craig Gerard 1967- *WhoE 93*
Reinert, Erik Steenfeldt 1949- *WhoWor 93*
Reinert, James A. 1944- *WhoSSW 93*
Reinert, Kenneth Allen 1958- *WhoE 93*
Reinert, Norbert Frederick 1928- *WhoAm 92*
Reinert, Paul Clare 1910- *WhoAm 92*
Reinerts, Aivars Maris 1935- *St&PR 93*
Reinertsen, Norman 1934- *St&PR 93, WhoAm 92*
Reines, Bernard d1991 *BioIn 17*
Reines, Frederick 1918- *WhoAm 92*
Reinette, Luc 1950- *DcCPCAm*
Reinfeld, Abraham H. 1917- *St&PR 93*
Reinfelds, Rita *BioIn 17*
Reinfort, Ernest B. 1952- *St&PR 93*
Reinfurt, Donald William 1938- *WhoSSW 93*
Reinfuss, Roman 1910- *IntDcAn*
Reingold, Haim 1910- *WhoAm 92*
Reingold, Irving 1921- *WhoE 93*
Reingold, Iver David 1949- *WhoE 93*
Reingold, Mark S. *Law&B 92*
Reingold, Nathan 1927- *WhoAm 92*
Reinhard, Arthur Elliot 1933- *WhoE 93*
Reinhard, Christopher John 1953- *WhoAm 92*
Reinhard, Constance W. *Law&B 92*
Reinhard, Hans-Jurgen 1939- *WhoScE 91-3*
Reinhard, J. Pedro 1945- *St&PR 93*
Reinhard, Jeffrey P. *Law&B 92*
Reinhard, Keith Leon 1935- *WhoAm 92, WhoE 93*
Reinhard, Kurt 1914-1979 *Baker 92*
Reinhard, Marilyn Marjean 1933- *WhoAmW 93*
Reinhard, Mary Kathryn 1948- *WhoAmW 93*
Reinhard, Mary Marthe 1929- *WhoAm 92*
Reinhardt, Ad 1913-1967 *BioIn 17*
Reinhardt, Brian M. 1959- *WhoSSW 93*
Reinhardt, Bruce P. 1950- *St&PR 93*
Reinhardt, Delia 1892-1974 *Baker 92, OxDcOp*
Reinhardt, Django 1910-1953 *Baker 92*
Reinhardt, Hank *ScF&FL 92*
Reinhardt, Heinrich 1865-1922 *Baker 92*
Reinhardt, Herbert Paul 1932- *WhoSSW 93*
Reinhardt, J. Alec 1942- *St&PR 93*
Reinhardt, James Alec 1942- *WhoAm 92*
Reinhardt, John David *Law&B 92*
Reinhardt, John Edward 1920- *WhoAm 92*
Reinhardt, Kendall S. 1939- *St&PR 93*
Reinhardt, Kurt 1920- *WhoWor 93*
Reinhardt, Madge 1925- *WhoWrEP 92*
Reinhardt, Manfred E. 1927- *WhoScE 91-3*
Reinhardt, Mark Warren *Law&B 92*
Reinhardt, Max 1873-1943 *BioIn 17, IntDcOp, MiSFD 9N, OxDcOp*
Reinhardt, Max 1915- *WhoWor 93*
Reinhardt, Nicholas 1932- *WhoE 93*
Reinhardt, Stephen Roy 1931- *WhoAm 92*
Reinhardt, Uwe Ernst 1937- *WhoAm 92, WhoWor 93*
Reinhardt, William Parker 1942- *WhoAm 92*
Reinhart, Andrew J. 1923- *WhoAm 92*
Reinhart, Betty Louise 1943- *WhoAmW 93*
Reinhart, Charles 1844-1896 *GayN*
Reinhart, Dietrich Thomas 1949- *WhoAm 92*
Reinhart, Ewald 1936- *WhoScE 91-3*
Reinhart, Gregory Duncan 1951- *WhoSSW 93*
Reinhart, Kellee Connely 1951- *WhoAm 92*
Reinhart, Maria Sylvia 1952- *WhoAmW 93*
Reinhart, Peter 1950- *ConAu 136*
Reinhart, Peter S. *Law&B 92*
Reinhart, Peter S. 1950- *St&PR 93*
Reinhart, Peter Sargent 1950- *WhoAm 92*
Reinhart, Richard Mercer, Jr. 1942- *WhoE 93*
Reinhart, Theodore Russell 1938- *WhoSSW 93*
Reinharz, Jehuda 1944- *WhoAm 92*
Reinharz, Shulamit 1946- *ConAu 138*
Reinheimer, Robert, Jr. 1917- *WhoAm 92*
Reinherz, Helen Zarsky 1923- *WhoAm 92*
Reinhold, Charleen A. *Law&B 92*
Reinhold, Dennis *Law&B 92*
Reinhold, Heinz 1910- *WhoWor 93*
Reinhold, Hugo 1854-1935 *Baker 92*
Reinhold, Judge *WhoAm 92*
Reinhold, W.B. 1924- *St&PR 93*
Reinhold, Walter William 1939- *WhoE 93*
Reinhold, Warren R. 1925- *St&PR 93*
Reinholm, Gert 1928- *WhoWor 93*
Reinhorn, Andrei M. 1945- *WhoAm 92, WhoE 93*
Reinicke, Melinda June 1956- *WhoAmW 93*
Reinig, Gerd Ernst 1938- *St&PR 93*
Reinig, James William 1954- *WhoE 93*
Reiniger, Clair *BioIn 17*
Reining, Beth LaVerne 1921- *WhoAmW 93*
Reining, Francis E. 1940- *St&PR 93*
Reining, Maria 1903-1991 *Baker 92, OxDcOp*
Reining, Priscilla Copeland 1923- *WhoAmW 93*
Reining, William Norbert 1940- *St&PR 93*
Reininger, Paul Michael 1961- *WhoWor 93*
Reininghaus, Rolf K. *St&PR 93*
Reininghaus, Ruth 1922- *WhoAm 92*
Reinisch, Deborah *MiSFD 9*
Reinisch, June M(achover) 1943- *ConAu 138*
Reinisch, June Machover 1943- *WhoAm 92*
Reinisch, Morris Norman *Law&B 92*
Reinisch, Simon Leo 1832-1919 *IntDcAn*
Reinitz, Joyce Baraban 1945- *WhoE 93*

Reinius, Trish 1936- *ScF&FL 92*
Reinke, Alan M. *Law&B 92*
Reinke, Barbara Jean 1953- *WhoAmW 93*
Reinke, Doris Marie 1922- *WhoAmW 93*
Reinke, Jerome L. 1932- *St&PR 93*
Reinke, Leonard Herman 1918- *WhoAm 92*
Reinke, Mark A. *Law&B 92*
Reinke, Ralph Louis 1927- *WhoAm 92*
Reinke, Twila O'Such 1942- *WhoAmW 93*
Reinke, William John 1930- *WhoAm 92*
Reinken, Jan Adams 1623-1722 *Baker 92*
Reinke-Scorzelli, Mary Margaret 1949- *WhoAmW 93*
Reinking, Ann *BioIn 17*
Reinking, Ann H. 1950- *WhoAm 92*
Reinman, Jacob J. 1947- *WhoWrEP 92*
Reinmar, Hans 1895-1961 *Baker 92*
Reinmuth, Oscar MacNaughton 1927- *WhoAm 92*
Reinneck, Lori Anne 1960- *WhoSSW 93*
Reino, Fernando 1929- *WhoUN 92*
Reino, Joseph *ScF&FL 92*
Reinoehl, Richard Louis 1944- *WhoAm 92*
Reins, Ralph Erich 1940- *WhoAm 92*
Reinsberg, John Robert 1956- *WhoAm 92*
Reinsch, Ernst Albrecht 1931- *WhoScE 91-3*
Reinsch, J. Leonard 1908-1991 *AnObit 1991, BioIn 17*
Reinschke, Kurt Johannes 1940- *WhoWor 93*
Reinschmidt, Kenneth Frank 1938- *WhoAm 92*
Reinschmiedt, Anne Tierney 1932- *WhoAmW 93, WhoSSW 93, WhoWor 93*
Reinsdorf, Jerry Michael 1936- *WhoAm 92, WhoWor 93*
Reinsfeider, Donald Leo 1931- *St&PR 93*
Reinsma, Harold Lawrence 1928- *WhoWor 93*
Reinsmith, Richard 1930- *ScF&FL 92*
Reinstein, Alan 1947- *WhoAm 92*
Reinstein, Joel 1946- *WhoAm 92*
Reinstetle, Dwight Alan 1951- *St&PR 93*
Reinthaler, Karl (Martin) 1822-1896 *Baker 92*
Reintjes, R.C. 1936- *WhoScE 91-3*
Reintzel, Warren Andrew 1945- *WhoE 93*
Reinwald, Arthur Burton 1929- *WhoAm 92*
Reio, Lembitu 1924- *WhoScE 91-4*
Reirden, David W. 1939- *St&PR 93*
Reis, Arthur Henry, Jr. 1946- *WhoE 93*
Reis, Arthur Robert, Jr. 1916- *WhoAm 92*
Reis, Carolyn Whitelaw Carver 1959- *WhoSSW 93*
Reis, Curtis Sanford 1934- *St&PR 93*
Reis, David A. *St&PR 93*
Reis, Donald Jeffery 1931- *WhoAm 92, WhoE 93, WhoWor 93*
Reis, Frank L., Jr. 1946- *St&PR 93*
Reis, Irving 1906-1953 *MiSFD 9N*
Reis, Jean Stevenson 1914- *WhoAmW 93*
Reis, Joao Carlos Ribeiro 1945- *WhoWor 93*
Reis, Judson Patterson 1942- *WhoAm 92*
Reis, Leslee d1990 *BioIn 17*
Reis, Ricardo 1888-1935 *BioIn 17*
Reis, Richard H. 1930- *ScF&FL 92*
Reis, Robert Danforth 1950- *St&PR 93*
Reis, Robert Stanley 1916- *St&PR 93*
Reis, Ron *BioIn 17*
Reis, Samuel H. d1991 *BioIn 17*
Reis, Timothy Charles *Law&B 92*
Reisacher, Carl Raymond 1958- *WhoE 93*
Reisberg, Barry 1947- *WhoAm 92*
Reisberg, Leon Elton 1949- *WhoWor 93*
Reisberg, Richard S. 1941- *WhoAm 92*
Reisberg, Richard Stephen *BioIn 17*
Reisbord, Paul S.A. 1943- *St&PR 93*
Reisch, Gunter 1927- *DrEEuF*
Reisch, Walter d1983 *BioIn 17*
Reischauer, Edwin O. 1910-1990 *BioIn 17*
Reische, Alan Lawrence 1939- *WhoE 93*
Reischman, Gene 1918- *St&PR 93*
Reischman, Michael C. 1945- *St&PR 93*
Reisenauer, Alfred 1863-1907 *Baker 92*
Reisenbach, John d1990 *BioIn 17*
Reisenberg, John Ralph 1944- *St&PR 93*
Reisenberg, Nadia 1904-1983 *Baker 92*
Reisenbigler, David Richard 1942- *St&PR 93*
Reisenweber, Michael A. 1949- *St&PR 93*
Reiser, Alois 1887-1977 *Baker 92*
Reiser, Charles Edward, Jr. 1939- *WhoAm 92*
Reiser, David Richard 1959- *WhoE 93, WhoWor 93*
Reiser, Duane Dennis 1955- *St&PR 93*
Reiser, Evelyn Ellis 1941- *WhoE 93*
Reiser, Heinz *WhoScE 91-3*
Reiser, Leroy Franklin, Jr. 1921- *WhoAm 92*
Reiser, Morton Francis 1919- *WhoAm 92*
Reiser, Stephen Jay 1942- *St&PR 93*
Reisert, Mary E. *Law&B 92*
Reising, Richard P. *Law&B 92*
Reisinger, Barbara 1770-1806 *See* Gerl, Franz Xaver 1764-1827 *OxDcOp*
Reisinger, George Lambert 1930- *WhoAm 92*
Reisinger, John S. 1938- *St&PR 93*
Reisinger, Joy Ann 1934- *WhoAmW 93*
Reisinger, Karl 1964- *WhoWor 93*
Reisinger, Nicholas Joseph 1952- *St&PR 93*
Reisinger, Roy *BioIn 17*
Reisinger, William M. 1957- *ConAu 138*
Reiskytl, James Frank 1937- *St&PR 93*
Reisler, Raymond 1907-1992 *BioIn 17*
Reisman, Andrew *Law&B 92*
Reisman, Andy 1956- *St&PR 93*
Reisman, Arnold 1927- *WhoAm 92*
Reisman, Arnold 1934- *WhoAm 92*
Reisman, Averil 1942- *WhoAmW 93*
Reisman, David S. *Law&B 92*
Reisman, Fredricka Kauffman 1930- *WhoAm 92*
Reisman, George F. 1924- *St&PR 93*
Reisman, Glenn M. *Law&B 92*
Reisman, Harold Bernard 1935- *St&PR 93, WhoE 93*
Reisman, Kenneth P. *Law&B 92*
Reisman, Neil A. *Law&B 92*
Reisman, Otto Ignaz 1928- *WhoE 93*
Reisman, Philip 1904-1992 *NewYTBS 92*
Reisman, Richard Roy 1947- *WhoE 93*
Reisman, Robert D. 1930- *St&PR 93*
Reisman, Robert E. 1932- *WhoAm 92*
Reisman, Ronald H. *Law&B 92*
Reisman, Scott 1951- *WhoSSW 93*
Reismann, Herbert 1926- *WhoAm 92*
Reisner, Allen *MiSFD 9*
Reisner, Elena Mackay 1922- *WhoAmW 93*
Reisner, Gerald Seymour 1926- *WhoE 93*
Reisner, Phyllis 1934- *WhoAmW 93*
Reisner, Richard Hansen 1943- *St&PR 93*
Reiss, Albert 1870-1940 *Baker 92*
Reiss, Albert John, Jr. 1922- *WhoAm 92*
Reiss, Alvin 1932- *WhoAm 92, WhoWrEP 92*
Reiss, Alvin Herbert 1930- *WhoWrEP 92*
Reiss, Bonnie *BioIn 17*
Reiss, Claire Lee *Law&B 92*
Reiss, Claude J.R. 1934- *WhoScE 91-2*
Reiss, Clifford Earl, II 1942- *St&PR 93*
Reiss, D.T. 1932- *WhoScE 91-2*
Reiss, Elaine S. 1940- *St&PR 93*
Reiss, Ernest 1909- *St&PR 93*
Reiss, Glenda Carole 1935- *WhoAmW 93*
Reiss, Harry F. d1992 *BioIn 17*
Reiss, Howard 1922- *WhoAm 92*
Reiss, Ira Leonard 1925- *WhoAm 92*
Reiss, James 1941- *WhoWrEP 92*
Reiss, James Henry 1938- *WhoE 93*
Reiss, John Barlow 1939- *WhoAm 92, WhoE 93, WhoWor 93*
Reiss, John C. 1922- *WhoAm 92*
Reiss, Jozef (Wladyslaw) 1879-1956 *Baker 92*
Reiss, Kathryn *ScF&FL 92*
Reiss, Kenneth William 1959- *WhoWor 93*
Reiss, Marc *ScF&FL 92*
Reiss, Martin H. 1935- *St&PR 93*
Reiss, Martin Harold 1935- *WhoAm 92, WhoE 93*
Reiss, Matthias Burkhard 1948- *WhoWor 93*
Reiss, Nathan Morris 1940- *WhoE 93*
Reiss, Paul Jacob 1930- *WhoAm 92*
Reiss, Peter E. *Law&B 92*
Reiss, Pixie Eaves *BioIn 17*
Reiss, Richard T. 1918- *St&PR 93*
Reiss, Robert Cornell 1932- *WhoIns 93*
Reiss, Robert Marshall 1929- *WhoE 93*
Reiss, Russell A. 1944- *St&PR 93*
Reiss, Spencer Stephen 1952- *WhoSSW 93*
Reiss, Susan R. *Law&B 92*
Reiss, Theodore J. 1933- *St&PR 93*
Reiss, Timothy James 1942- *WhoAm 92, WhoWrEP 92*
Reissenweber, Beth Randerson 1961- *WhoAmW 93*
Reisserova, Julie 1888-1938 *Baker 92*
Reissig, Martha Tilton 1929- *WhoAmW 93*
Reissiger, Carl Gottlieb 1798-1859 *Baker 92*
Reissiger, Karl 1798-1859 *OxDcOp*
Reissman, Maurice L. *WhoAm 92*
Reissman, Max 1919- *St&PR 93*
Reissmann, August (Friedrich Wilhelm) 1825-1903 *Baker 92*
Reissmann, Thomas Lincoln 1920- *WhoE 93*
Reissmuller, Johann Georg 1932- *WhoWor 93*
Reissner, Eric Max Erich 1913- *WhoAm 92*
Reissner, Laura Anne 1965- *WhoAmW 93*
Reissner, Pierre Dale 1928- *WhoWrEP 92*
Reist, Andreas 1955- *WhoE 93*
Reistad, Dag Vilhelm 1941- *WhoWor 93*
Reister, Raymond Alex 1929- *WhoAm 92*
Reister, Ruth Alkema 1936- *WhoAm 92*
Reistle, Carl Ernest, Jr. 1901- *WhoAm 92*
Reistroffer, Douglas J. *Law&B 92*
Reisz, John A. 1915- *St&PR 93*
Reisz, Karel 1926- *MiSFD 9*
Reit, Seymour V. 1918- *ScF&FL 92*
Reitan, Daniel Kinseth 1921- *WhoAm 92*
Reitan, Paul Hartman 1928- *WhoAm 92*
Reitci, Rita *ScF&FL 92*
Reitemeier, Richard Joseph 1923- *WhoAm 92*
Reiten, Richard 1941- *WhoAm 92*
Reitenbach, Daniel *Law&B 92*
Reitenbach, Rudolf 1947- *WhoWor 93*
Reiter, Burton L. *Law&B 92*
Reiter, Edward J. 1939- *St&PR 93*
Reiter, Harold Braun 1942- *WhoSSW 93*
Reiter, Henry H. 1936- *WhoE 93*
Reiter, Howard Lee 1945- *WhoE 93*
Reiter, Howard S. *Law&B 92*
Reiter, James D. 1926- *St&PR 93*
Reiter, Josef 1862-1939 *Baker 92*
Reiter, Joseph Henry 1929- *WhoAm 92*
Reiter, Kenneth E. *Law&B 92*
Reiter, Lora K. 1939- *WhoWrEP 92*
Reiter, Norbert 1928- *WhoWor 93*
Reiter, Reinhold 1920- *WhoScE 91-3*
Reiter, Robert Edward 1943- *St&PR 93, WhoAm 92*
Reiter, Sandra D. 1947- *St&PR 93*
Reiter, Stanley 1925- *WhoAm 92*
Reiter, Steve *BioIn 17*
Reiter, Victoria (Kelrich) *ConAu 139*
Reith, Bob *Law&B 92*
Reith, Carl Joseph 1914- *WhoAm 92*
Reith, John Charles Walsham 1889-1971 *DcTwHis*
Reith, Marianne 1955- *WhoEmL 93*
Reith, Peter Keaston 1950- *WhoAsAP 91*
Reith, Roger John *Law&B 92*
Reithal, Georgia J. *Law&B 92*
Reither, Kenneth M. *Law&B 92*
Reitman, Edwin H. *Law&B 92*
Reitman, Ivan 1946- *MiSFD 9, WhoAm 92*
Reitman, Jack 1910- *St&PR 93*
Reitman, Jeffrey B. *Law&B 92*
Reitman, Jeremy Herman 1945- *St&PR 93*
Reitman, Jerry Irving 1938- *WhoAm 92*
Reitman, Paul *St&PR 93*
Reitman, Robert S. 1933- *St&PR 93*
Reitman, Robert Stanley 1933- *WhoAm 92*
Reitmyer, Jeffrey J. *Law&B 92*
Reitsch, Robert A. 1934- *St&PR 93*
Reitsch, Robert B. 1959- *St&PR 93*
Reitsma, Tjeerd 1941- *WhoScE 91-3*
Reitter, Charles Andrew 1956- *WhoAm 92*
Reittinger, Donna Lis 1949- *WhoE 93*
Reitz, Barbara Maurer 1931- *WhoAmW 93*
Reitz, Curtis Randall *WhoAm 92*
Reitz, David Walter *Law&B 92*
Reitz, Don 1929- *BioIn 17*
Reitz, Douglas John Frank 1955- *WhoSSW 93*
Reitz, Edgar *BioIn 17*
Reitz, Edgar 1932- *MiSFD 9*
Reitz, Elmer A. 1909- *WhoAm 92*
Reitz, Howard Wesley 1947- *WhoE 93*
Reitz, Kenneth W. *Law&B 92*
Reitz, Michelle Mastruserio 1954- *WhoWrEP 92*
Reitz, Paul A. 1928- *St&PR 93*
Reitz, Richard Elmer 1938- *WhoAm 92, WhoWor 93*
Reitz, Stephanie Karen 1968- *WhoAmW 93*
Reitz, William 1923- *St&PR 93*
Reitzel-Nielsen, Michael 1939- *WhoUN 92*
Reitzer, Lawrence Joseph 1951- *WhoSSW 93*
Reitzfeld, Robert 1937- *BioIn 17*
Reivitz, Leon Conrad *Law&B 92*
Reizenstein, Franz (Theodor) 1911-1968 *Baker 92*
Reizenstein, Peter G. 1928- *WhoScE 91-4*
Reizenstein, Peter Georg 1928- *WhoWor 93*
Rej, Mikolaj 1505-1569 *PolBiDi*
Rejai, Mostafa 1931- *WhoAm 92*
Rejano, Juan 1903-1976 *DcMexL*
Rejchan, Alojzy 1807-1860 *PolBiDi*
Rejeski, Philip J. 1958- *St&PR 93*
Rejewski, Marian 1937- *WhoScE 91-4*
Rejholec, Vaclav 1920- *WhoScE 91-4*
Rejman, Diane Louise 1956- *WhoAmW 93*
Rejman, Stefan Jozef 1942- *WhoScE 91-4*
Rejtan, Tadeusz 1746-1780 *PolBiDi*
Rekasius, Antanas 1928- *Baker 92*
Rekate, Albert C. 1916- *WhoAm 92*
Rekau, Richard Robert 1936- *WhoSSW 93*
Rekeczky, Jozsef 1930- *WhoScE 91-4*
Rekettye, Gabor 1944- *WhoWor 93*
Reklewski, Zygmunt *WhoScE 91-4*
Rekoff, Michael George, Jr. 1929- *WhoSSW 93*
Rekola, Kimmo Heikki Johannes *Law&B 92*
Reksc, Wladyslaw 1928- *WhoScE 91-4*
Reksten, Harold E. 1932- *St&PR 93*
Rektorik-Sprinkle, Patricia Jean 1941- *WhoSSW 93*
Relation, A. Joseph *Law&B 92*
Reldan, Robert Ronald 1942- *WhoWor 93*
Relf, Patricia 1954- *SmATA 71*
Relfe, C. Perry 1943- *St&PR 93*
Relfe, Charles Perry *Law&B 92*
Relfe, John 1763-c. 1837 *Baker 92*
Reljic, Mary E. 1933- *WhoAmW 93*
Relkin, Parris Craig 1954- *WhoE 93*
Rella, Joseph Victor 1951- *St&PR 93*
Rella, Rudolph d1991 *BioIn 17*
Relle, Ferenc Matyas 1922- *WhoAm 92, WhoWor 93*
Reller, Gary *BioIn 17*
Relling, William, Jr. 1954- *ScF&FL 92*
Rellstab, Caroline 1793-1813 *See* Rellstab, Johann Carl Friedrich 1759-1813 *Baker 92*
Rellstab, Johann Carl Friedrich 1759-1813 *Baker 92*
Rellstab, (Heinrich Friedrich) Ludwig 1799-1860 *Baker 92*
Relman, Arnold *BioIn 17*
Relman, Arnold Seymour 1923- *WhoAm 92, WhoE 93*
Relson, Morris 1915- *WhoAm 92*
Relyea, Mark A. 1960- *St&PR 93*
Relyea, Michael Stewart 1956- *St&PR 93*
Remacle, J.A.L. 1936- *WhoScE 91-2*
Remacle, Jose A.L. 1946- *WhoScE 91-2*
Remak, Jeannette Elizabeth 1952- *WhoAmW 93*
Remaley, Allen Richard 1939- *WhoE 93*
Remaley, Andrew Jacob 1951- *WhoE 93*
Remaley, Donald Frank 1931- *St&PR 93*
Remaly, Richard Carl 1939- *St&PR 93*
Remarque, Erich Maria 1898-1970 *BioIn 17*
Rembar, Charles Isaiah 1915- *WhoAm 92*
Rembar, James Carlson 1949- *WhoE 93*
Rembe, Toni 1936- *WhoAmW 93*
Rembert, Allen Jones 1945- *WhoSSW 93*
Rembert, Donald Mosby 1939- *WhoSSW 93*
Rembert, Paul 1930- *St&PR 93, WhoAm 92*
Rembert, Virginia Pitts 1921- *WhoAm 92*
Rembielinski, Jakub 1945- *WhoScE 91-4*
Remblier, Jean-Pierre 1938- *WhoScE 91-2*
Rembold, Ulrich 1929- *WhoScE 91-3*
Rembrandt Harmenszoon van Rijn 1606-1669 *BioIn 17*
Rembski, Stanislav *WhoAm 92, WhoWor 93*
Reme, Henri 1939- *WhoScE 91-2*
Remec, Cynthia Tavs *Law&B 92*
Remedios, Alberto 1935- *Baker 92, OxDcOp*
Remeika, James *Law&B 92*
Remeneski, Shirley Rodriguez 1938- *NotHsAW 93*
Remenick, Seymour 1923- *WhoAm 92*
Remenkov, Stefan 1923- *Baker 92*
Remenyi, Ede (Eduard) 1828-1898 *Baker 92*
Remenyi, Joseph Vincent 1946- *WhoWor 93*
Remenyi, Karoly 1934- *WhoScE 91-4*
Remer, Donald Sherwood 1943- *WhoAm 92*
Remer, James C. 1940- *St&PR 93*
Remer, John Higgins 1925- *St&PR 93*
Remer, Vernon Ralph 1918- *WhoAm 92*
Remes, Emily R. *Law&B 92*
Remeschatis, Frederick A. 1945- *St&PR 93*
Remeta, Esther Marie 1960- *WhoAmW 93*
Remetey-Fulopp, Gabor 1944- *WhoScE 91-4*
Remetta, Janet 1952- *WhoAmW 93*
Remick, Forrest Jerome, Jr. 1931- *WhoAm 92, WhoWor 93*
Remick, Lee 1935-1991 *AnObit 1991, BioIn 17, ConTFT 10, IntDcF 2-3 [port]*
Remick, Lee c. 1936-1991 *News 92*
Remick, Oscar Eugene 1932- *WhoAm 92, WhoWor 93*
Remijas, Andrew 1956- *St&PR 93*
Remijnse, J.D. *WhoScE 91-3*
Remillard, Lionel (Bud) *Law&B 92*
Remillieux, Joseph 1940- *WhoScE 91-2*
Remine, Debra Bjurquist *Law&B 92*
ReMine, Debra Bjurquist 1956- *WhoAmW 93*
ReMine, William Hervey, Jr. 1918- *WhoAm 92, WhoSSW 93*

Reminger, Richard Thomas 1931- WhoAm 92, WhoWor 93
Remington, Deborah Williams 1935- WhoAm 92
Remington, Delwin Woolley 1950- WhoWor 93
Remington, Frederic 1861-1909 BioIn 17, GayN
Remington, Jack Samuel 1931- WhoAm 92
Remington, Joan Janelle 1953- WhoAmW 93
Remington, John Addison 1941- WhoAm 92
Remington, Michael D. Law&B 92
Remington, Paul David 1959- St&PR 93
Remington, Thomas J. 1939- ScF&FL 92
Remington, Thomas R. 1927- St&PR 93
Remington, W. Bruce 1950- St&PR 93
Remini, Robert Vincent 1921- WhoAm 92
Remissong, Mark O. 1952- St&PR 93
Remitron, Naillil AmWomPl
Remler, Emily BioIn 17
Remley, Audrey Wright 1931- WhoAmW 93
Remley, Cynthia L. Law&B 92
Remley, John Frank, III 1941- St&PR 93
Remley, Richard J. Law&B 92
Remley, Theodore Phant, Jr. 1947- WhoAm 92
Remlinger, Frederick Endre 1957- WhoE 93
Remme, Jan Hendrick F. 1948- WhoUN 92
Remme, John d1992 BioIn 17, NewYTBS 92
Remmell, Robert E. 1931- St&PR 93
Remmenga, Merlin E. Law&B 92
Remmer, Harry Thomas, Jr. 1920- WhoSSW 93
Remmers, Kurt William 1944- WhoE 93
Remmers, William H. 1935- St&PR 93
Remmert, Hermann H. 1931- WhoScE 91-3
Remmert, Hermann Heinrich 1931- WhoWor 93
Remmert, John 1954- St&PR 93
Remmes, Richard Giles Law&B 92
Remondi, John J. 1937- St&PR 93
Remondiere, A. WhoScE 91-2
Remoortel, Edouard van 1926-1977 Baker 92
Remotti, Gianni 1928- WhoScE 91-3
Rempe, James H. Law&B 92
Rempe, James Henry 1930- St&PR 93
Rempel, Rudolph William 1932- St&PR 93
Rempert, Leonard Arthur 1930- St&PR 93
Rempp, Paul F. 1928- WhoScE 91-2
Rems, Jack 1955- ScF&FL 92
Remsburg, F. Raine Law&B 92
Remschmidt, Helmut Ernst 1938- WhoScE 91-3
Remsen, Alfred Soule 1942- St&PR 93
Remson, Irwin 1923- WhoAm 92
Remus, Dale Howard 1929- St&PR 93
Remus, Michael T. 1957- WhoE 93
Remusat, Jean 1815-1880 Baker 92
Remuzzi, Giuseppe 1949- WhoScE 91-3
Remy, Alfred 1870-1937 Baker 92
Remy, Caroline 1855-1929 BioIn 17
Remy, Guillaume 1856-1932 Baker 92
Remy, Jean Claude 1941- WhoScE 91-2
Remy, Jerald Carter 1932- St&PR 93
Remy, Pieree-Jean 1937- WhoWor 93
Remy, Ray WhoAm 92
Remy, Robert E. 1952- WhoIns 93
Ren, Chung-Li 1931- WhoE 93
Ren, Jian-Hua 1930- WhoWor 93
Ren, Yanxia 1965- WhoWor 93
Renahan, James Patrick 1944- St&PR 93
Renaille, Gerard 1932- WhoWor 93
Renaldo, Duncan 1904- HispAmA
Renaldo, John Joseph 1938- WhoSSW 93
Renan, Sheldon 1941- ScF&FL 92
Renard, H.A. 1926- WhoScE 91-2
Renard, Ian Andrew 1946- WhoWor 93
Renard, Jean 1936- WhoScE 91-2
Renard, Jean-Luc 1940- WhoScE 91-2
Renard, John Sanders 1938- St&PR 93
Renard, Joseph 1939- ScF&FL 92
Renard, Kenneth George 1934- WhoAm 92
Renard, Stephen J. 1939- St&PR 93
Renardy, Michael 1955- WhoSSW 93
Renart, Jaime 1947- WhoScE 91-3
Renaud, Audrey Cynthia 1957- WhoAmW 93
Renaud, Bernadette 1945- BioIn 17, WhoCanL 92
Renaud, Bernadette Marie Elise 1945- WhoAm 92
Renaud, David J. 1951- St&PR 93
Renaud, Gilles 1946- St&PR 93
Renaud, Johannes Everardus 1958- WhoWor 93
Renaud, Maurice 1861-1933 OxDcOp
Renaud, Maurice 1940- WhoScE 91-2
Renaud, Maurice (Arnold) 1861-1933 Baker 92
Renaud, Real H. 1946- St&PR 93
Renaud, Rita Ann 1953- WhoAmW 93
Renaud, Ronald K. Law&B 92
Renaud, Serge Charles 1927- WhoScE 91-2
Renaudin, William Sutcliffe 1935- WhoSSW 93
Renauld, Ron ScF&FL 92
Renault, Suzanne Law&B 92
Renbarger, Daniel Law&B 92
Renborg, Ulf B. 1920- WhoScE 91-4
Renchard, William S. 1908- St&PR 93
Renchof, Sharon A. Law&B 92
Renda, Dominic Phillip 1913- WhoAm 92
Renda, Randolph Bruce 1926- WhoAm 92
Renda, Tindaro G. 1940- WhoScE 91-3
Rendall, Steven 1939- ConAu 139
Rendeiro, James C., III Law&B 92
Rendel, Jan E.R. 1927- WhoScE 91-4
Rendell, Edward Gene 1944- WhoAm 92, WhoE 93
Rendell, Kenneth William 1943- WhoWor 93
Rendell, Ruth 1930- BioIn 17
Rendell, Ruth Barbara 1930- WhoAmW 93
Rendell-Baker, Leslie 1917- WhoAm 92
Render, Arlene WhoAm 92, WhoAmW 93, WhoWor 93
Render, Mattiline BlkAmWO
Render, Regina Alberta 1961- WhoAmW 93
Rendina, Tony P. 1927- St&PR 93
Rendino, Christine Marie 1968- WhoSSW 93
Rendl, Sebastian 1942- St&PR 93
Rendleman, Robert Terrence 1945- St&PR 93
Rendlen, Albert Lewis 1922- WhoAm 92
Rendl-Marcus, Mildred 1928- WhoE 93, WhoWor 93
Rendon, Mario Ivan 1938- WhoE 93
Rendon, Marta Ines 1957- WhoAmW 93
Rendulic, James Ronald 1946- St&PR 93
Rendulic, Klaus WhoScE 91-4
Rene, France-Albert 1935- WhoAfr, WhoWor 93
Rene, Norman MiSFD 9
Reneau, Daniel D. WhoAm 92, WhoSSW 93
Reneau, James T. St&PR 93
Reneau, Linda Rae 1948- WhoWrEP 92
Reneau, Marvin Bryan 1939- WhoSSW 93, WhoWor 93
Reneau, Susan Campbell 1952- WhoAmW 93
Renehan, Robert Francis Xavier 1935- WhoAm 92
Reneker, Maxine Hohman 1942- WhoAm 92
Reneson, Paul Matthew 1948- WhoSSW 93
Renfield, Richard Lee 1932- WhoUN 92
Renfrew, Andrew Colin 1937- WhoWor 93
Renfrew, Carolyn AmWomPl
Renfrew, Charles B. Law&B 92
Renfrew, Charles Byron 1928- St&PR 93, WhoAm 92
Renfrew, Colin 1937- BioIn 17
Renfrew, Glen McGarvie 1928- WhoAm 92
Renfrew, Malcolm MacKenzie 1910- WhoAm 92
Renfrew, Marion AmWomPl
Renfro, Beverly Jane 1944- WhoAmW 93
Renfro, Charles Gilliland 1943- WhoAm 92
Renfro, Edward Eugene, III 1925- WhoSSW 93
Renfro, Melvin Lacy 1941- BiDAMSp 1989
Renfro, Patricia Elise WhoE 93
Renfroe, Delwin D. 1939- St&PR 93
Renfroe, Iona A. Law&B 92
Renfroe, Martha Kay ScF&FL 92
Renfroe, Othello d1991 BioIn 17
Renfroe, Penny Lynne 1962- WhoAmW 93
Renfrow, Edward 1940- WhoAm 92
Renfrow, Judy Lynn 1965- WhoAmW 93
Renfrow, Randy BioIn 17
Renger, Eberhard 1940- WhoScE 91-3
Renger, Gernot 1937- WhoScE 91-3
Renger, James Dietrich 1940- St&PR 93
Renggli, Heinz H. 1936- WhoScE 91-3
Reni 1953- WhoAmW 93
Renick, Carol Bishop 1956- WhoAmW 93
Renick, Charles Mathew 1926- WhoE 93
Renick, Gary Steven Law&B 92
Renick, Ralph Apperson 1928-1991 BioIn 17
Renick, Virginia Shearer Law&B 92
Renick, William R. 1951- St&PR 93
Renicker, Robert Nolan 1944- St&PR 93
Renie, Henriette 1875-1956 Baker 92
Renier, James J. 1930- WhoAm 92
Renier, James Joseph 1930- St&PR 93
Renieri, Alberto 1943- WhoScE 91-3
Renier of Montferrat c. 1163-c. 1182 OxDcByz
Ren Jianxin WhoWor 93
Ren Jianxin 1925- WhoAsAP 91
Renjun, Zou 1927- WhoWor 93
Renka, Robert Joseph 1947- WhoSSW 93
Renkawitz, Rainer 1949- WhoScE 91-3
Renkema, Jan A. 1937- WhoScE 91-3
Renken, Albert K.E. 1941- WhoScE 91-4
Renkis, Alan Ilmars 1938- WhoWor 93
Renko, Sheri Ann 1958- WhoAmW 93
Renlund, Eric B.P. 1942- WhoUN 92
Renn, Daniel J. 1942- St&PR 93
Renn, Mark H. 1954- St&PR 93
Renna, Gary Steven Law&B 92
Rennaker, Wayne E. 1930- St&PR 93
Renne, Louise Hornbeck 1937- WhoAmW 93
Renne, Virgil L. St&PR 93
Renneberg, Jan 1956- WhoWor 93
Rennekamp, Rosemarie G. 1950- St&PR 93
Renneker, Frederick Weyman, III 1939- WhoAm 92
Rennels, Marshall Leigh 1939- WhoAm 92
Rennenkampf, Pavel Karlovich 1854-1918 HarEnMi
Renner, Arnold Edward Law&B 92
Renner, August N. 1921- St&PR 93
Renner, Barbara Jean 1957- WhoAmW 93
Renner, Carol Jean 1929- WhoAmW 93
Renner, E. Wayne 1947- St&PR 93
Renner, Edmund 1932- WhoScE 91-3
Renner, Gerald F. 1934- St&PR 93
Renner, Gerard William 1921- WhoE 93
Renner, Glenn Delmar 1925- WhoSSW 93
Renner, Greg St&PR 93
Renner, John F. 1946- St&PR 93
Renner, Josef 1832-1895 Baker 92
Renner, Karen Sue 1946- WhoSSW 93
Renner, Karl 1870-1950 DcTwHis
Renner, Kris Lynn Law&B 92
Renner, Lee H. Law&B 92
Renner, Richard Wilson Law&B 92
Renner, Robert George 1923- WhoAm 92
Renner, S. Edward 1934- St&PR 93
Renner, Simon Edward 1934- WhoAm 92, WhoE 93, WhoWor 93
Renner, Theresa ScF&FL 92
Rennert, Gunther 1911-1978 Baker 92, IntDcOp
Rennert, Hal Hellmut 1939- WhoSSW 93
Rennert, Owen Murray 1938- WhoAm 92
Rennhack, Rolf 1931- WhoScE 91-3
Rennie, Barbara MiSFD 9
Rennie, Carol Ann 1939- WhoIns 93
Rennie, David WhoScE 91-1
Rennie, Emma AmWomPl
Rennie, Heughan Bassett 1945- WhoWor 93
Rennie, Janet Saire WhoScE 91-1
Rennie, Janice G. 1957- St&PR 93
Rennie, John C. 1937- St&PR 93
Rennie, John Coyne 1937- WhoAm 92
Rennie, Michael John WhoScE 91-1
Rennie, Paul T. 1940- St&PR 93
Rennie, Thomas Howard 1943- WhoSSW 93
Renninger, Earl Eugene 1933- St&PR 93
Renninger, John H. 1939- St&PR 93
Renninger, John Park 1945- WhoUN 92
Renninger, Martin 1940- St&PR 93
Renninger, Mary Karen 1945- WhoAm 92
Renninger, Michael Alan 1958- St&PR 93
Renno, H. Eugene 1942- St&PR 93
Reno, Barbara M. 1946- St&PR 93
Reno, Cheryl St&PR 93
Reno, Edward A., Jr. 1943- St&PR 93
Reno, Janet 1938- WhoAm 92
Reno, John Findley 1939- WhoAm 92
Reno, Ottie Wayne 1929- WhoWor 93
Reno, Robert BioIn 17
Reno, Robert B. Law&B 92
Reno, Roger 1924- St&PR 93, WhoAm 92
Reno, Rosemary 1934- WhoAmW 93
Reno, Russell Ronald, Jr. 1933- WhoAm 92
Reno, Susan Bennekemper 1954- WhoWrEP 92
Reno, William Henry 1936- WhoAm 92
Renoff, Ronald Hamilton 1939- WhoE 93
Renoir, Auguste 1841-1919 BioIn 17
Renoir, Jean 1894-1979 BioIn 17, MiSFD 9N
Renon, G. WhoScE 91-2
Renosi, F. WhoScE 91-2
Renouf, Edda 1943- WhoAm 92
Renouf, Harold Augustus 1917- WhoAm 92
Renoux, Gerard Eugene 1915- WhoWor 93
Renoux, Mario 1933- WhoScE 91-2
Rensberger, Michael J. 1947- St&PR 93
Rensberry, Richard J. 1952- WhoWrEP 92
Rensch, Joseph R. 1923- St&PR 93
Rensch, Joseph Romaine 1923- WhoAm 92
Rense, Arthur F. d1990 BioIn 17
Rense, Paige BioIn 17
Renshaw, Amanda Frances 1934- WhoSSW 93
Renshaw, Charles Clark, Jr. 1920- WhoAm 92, WhoWrEP 92
Renshaw, John Graham, Jr. 1949- WhoWor 93
Renshaw, Lisa BioIn 17
Rensin, Hy d1991 BioIn 17
Rensing, Ludger 1932- WhoScE 91-3
Rensink, Jacqueline Rhea 1954- WhoSSW 93
Renson, Marcel Gilles 1926- WhoWor 93
Renstrom, Allison Law&B 92
Rent, Clyda Stokes 1942- WhoAm 92, WhoAmW 93
Rentenbach, Thomas J. 1911- St&PR 93
Rentenbach, Thomas Joseph 1911- WhoAm 92, WhoSSW 93
Rentenbach, Thomas Michael 1939- St&PR 93
Renteria, Cheryl Christina 1944- WhoAmW 93, WhoSSW 93
Renteria, Hermelinda 1960- NotHsAW 93 [port]
Ren Tie WhoAsAP 91
Rentmeester, Lawrence Raymond 1939- St&PR 93
Rentner, James David 1940- WhoSSW 93
Renton, Allan Hopkins 1926- St&PR 93
Renton, David 1830-1864 BioIn 17
Renton, Hollings C. 1946- St&PR 93
Rentoulas, Spiros Ohmhtrios 1968- WhoWor 93
Rentrop, Norman Frank 1957- WhoWor 93
Rentschler, Cathy 1947- WhoE 93
Rentschler, William Henry 1925- St&PR 93, WhoAm 92, WhoWor 93
Rentz, J. Fred 1924- St&PR 93
Rentzel, Del(os Wilson) 1909-1991 CurBio 92N
Rentzel, Delos Wilson 1909-1991 BioIn 17
Rentzepis, Peter M. 1934- WhoAm 92
Rentzsch, Ralph Vernon 1925- St&PR 93
Renvall, Johan WhoAm 92
Renwick, Gloria Rainey WhoWrEP 92
Renwick, James Brevoort 1949- St&PR 93
Renwick, James Harrison WhoScE 91-1
Renwick, James Harrison 1926- WhoWor 93
Renwick, John P. 1947- St&PR 93
Renwick, William J. 1948- St&PR 93
Renxia, Chang 1904- WhoWor 93
Reny, D.R. 1954- St&PR 93
Reny, L. Guy 1927- St&PR 93
Renyi, Gabor BioIn 17
Renyi, Tamas 1929-1980 DrEEuF
Renyi, Thomas A. 1946- St&PR 93
Renz, Frederick 1940- Baker 92
Renz, Ulrich Hartmut 1939- WhoScE 91-3
Renz, William Thomas 1938- St&PR 93
Renza, John Sebastian, Jr. 1948- WhoE 93
Renzetti, Attilio David 1920- WhoAm 92
Renzi, Paul WhoAm 92
Renzi, Virgie A. 1936- St&PR 93
Renzoni, Aristeo 1929- WhoScE 91-3
Reohr, Janet Ruth 1948- WhoE 93
Reoliquio, Edwin 1959- St&PR 93
Repa, George 1955- WhoSSW 93
Repa, Steven J. Law&B 92
Repapis, Christos WhoScE 91-3
Repasi, Stephen 1958- WhoE 93
Repaske, Roy 1925- WhoE 93
Repasky, Mark Edward 1956- WhoSSW 93
Repass, L. Donald 1938- St&PR 93
Repasy, Christine Hayer Law&B 92
Repetti, Joan H. Law&B 92
Rephan, Jack 1932- WhoAm 92
Repin, Il'ia Efimovich 1844-1930 BioIn 17
Repko, Cheryl Beatrice 1951- WhoAmW 93
Repko, William C. 1949- St&PR 93
Repko, William Clarke 1949- WhoAm 92, WhoE 93
Replansky, Naomi 1918- WhoWrEP 92
Replinger, John Gordon 1923- WhoAm 92
Replogle, David Robert 1931- WhoAm 92
Replogle, John C. 1945- St&PR 93
Repman, Judith Lavine 1954- WhoSSW 93
Repoli, Michael Gerald 1948- WhoAm 92, WhoIns 93
Reposa, Carol Coffee 1943- WhoWrEP 92
Repp, Ed Earl 1900-1979 ScF&FL 92
Repp, Paul H. Law&B 92
Repp, Sheldon D. Law&B 92
Repp, William E. 1943- St&PR 93
Repp, William S. 1933- St&PR 93
Reppen, Norbjorn Dag 1940- WhoAm 92
Reppert, Alfred R. 1919- St&PR 93
Reppert, Alfred Reed 1919- WhoAm 92
Reppert, D.L. 1943- St&PR 93
Reppert, Joan Garland Smith WhoE 93
Reppert, Nancy Lue 1933- WhoAmW 93
Reppert, Steven Marion 1946- WhoAm 92

Reppert, William Downing 1923- WhoE 93
Reppy, John David, Jr. 1931- WhoAm 92
Reps, David Nathan 1926- WhoE 93
Reps, John W(illiam) 1921- ConAu 39NR
Requarth, Harold William 1925- St&PR 93
Requarth, William Henry 1913- WhoAm 92
Requat, Klaus 1958- WhoWor 93
Requena, Jaime 1946- WhoWor 93
Requena, Manuel 1802-1876 HispAmA
Requena Legarreta, Pedro 1893-1918 DcMexL
Rerat, Alain Andre 1926- WhoScE 91-2
Rerek, Mark Edward 1956- WhoAm 92
Reres, Mary Epiphany 1941- WhoAm 92
Rericha, Karel WhoScE 91-4
Rerngprasertuit, Phol WhoAsAP 91
Rerolle, Vincent 1962- WhoWor 93
Rerup, Claus Christian 1924- WhoScE 91-4
Res, Zannis George WhoScE 91-1
Resch, Bela A. 1938- WhoScE 91-4
Resch, Cynthia Fortes 1951- WhoE 93
Resch, F.J. 1942- WhoScE 91-2
Resch, J.F. 1942- WhoScE 91-2
Resch, Joseph Anthony 1914- WhoAm 92
Resch, Joseph Bernard, Jr. 1918- St&PR 93
Resch, Kathleen ScF&FL 92
Resch, Klaus 1941- WhoWor 93
Resch, Mary Louise 1956- WhoAmW 93
Resch, Michael F. 1950- St&PR 93
Reschke, Claus 1935- WhoSSW 93
Reschke, Diethelm Frederic 1941- WhoWor 93
Reschke, Michael W. 1955- WhoAm 92
Rescigno, Peter James Law&B 92
Rescildo, Ralph J. 1941- St&PR 93
Resconich, Samuel 1933- WhoE 93
Rescorla, Robert Arthur 1940- WhoAm 92, WhoE 93
Resden, Dee Kronenberg 1948- WhoE 93
Resden, Ronald Everette 1944- WhoE 93
Resek, Robert William 1935- WhoAm 92
Reser, Bill J. 1933- St&PR 93
Reser, Michael R. 1953- St&PR 93
Reshetnikov, Fedor Grigor'evich 1919- WhoWor 93
Reshevsky, Samuel 1911-1992 BioIn 17, CurBio 92N, NewYTBS 92 [port]
Reshotko, Eli 1930- WhoAm 92
Resika, Paul 1928- WhoAm 92
Resinarius, Balthasar c. 1485-1544 Baker 92
Resler, Edward Charles Law&B 92
Resler, Edwin Louis, Jr. 1925- WhoE 93
Reslow, Leif Frederick 1952- St&PR 93
Resmini, Francesco 1938- WhoScE 91-3
Resnais, Alain 1922- MiSFD 9, WhoWor 93
Resnati, Giuseppe Paolo 1955- WhoWor 93
Resnekov, Leon 1928- WhoAm 92
Resnick, Alan Howard 1943- WhoAm 92
Resnick, Alice Robie 1939- WhoAm 92, WhoAmW 93
Resnick, Allan Mark Law&B 92
Resnick, Charles H. 1924- WhoAm 92
Resnick, Charles Henry Law&B 92
Resnick, Cindy 1949- WhoAmW 93
Resnick, Elaine Bette 1944- WhoE 93
Resnick, Harriette Ilene Law&B 92
Resnick, Henry Roy 1952- WhoE 93
Resnick, Idrian Navarre 1936- WhoAm 92
Resnick, Jack d1991 BioIn 17
Resnick, Jaquelyn Liss 1946- WhoAmW 93, WhoSSW 93
Resnick, Jeffrey Tyler 1956- St&PR 93
Resnick, Joel H. 1936- WhoAm 92
Resnick, Kenneth 1934- WhoWor 93
Resnick, Marcia Aylene 1950- WhoAm 92, WhoE 93
Resnick, Mark Law&B 92
Resnick, Mark H. Law&B 92
Resnick, Mark I. 1947- St&PR 93
Resnick, Michael D. ScF&FL 92
Resnick, Mike 1942- ScF&FL 92
Resnick, Milton 1917- WhoAm 92
Resnick, Myron J. 1931- St&PR 93, WhoAm 92
Resnick, Robert 1923- WhoAm 92
Resnick, Stephanie 1959- WhoAmW 93, WhoE 93
Resnick, Steven A. Law&B 92
Resnik, David Alan 1956- St&PR 93, WhoE 93, WhoEmL 93, WhoWor 93
Resnik, Frank Edward 1928- WhoAm 92
Resnik, Frank H. 1942- St&PR 93
Resnik, Harvey Lewis Paul 1930- WhoAm 92
Resnik, Judith A. 1949-1986 BioIn 17
Resnik, Linda Ilene 1950- WhoAm 92
Resnik, Marvin I. Law&B 92
Resnik, Regina 1922- Baker 92, IntDcOp, OxDcOp
Resnik, Regina 1924- WhoAm 92
Resnik, Robert 1938- WhoAm 92
Resnikoff, George Joseph 1915- WhoAm 92
Resnikoff, Robert MiSFD 9
Reso, Anthony 1934- WhoAm 92, WhoSSW 93
Reso, Sidney Joseph 1935- WhoAm 92
Resor, Stanley Rogers 1917- WhoAm 92
Respicio, Santiago P. 1931- WhoAsAP 91
Respighi, Elsa Olivieri Sangiacomo 1894- See Respighi, Ottorino 1879-1936 Baker 92
Respighi, Ottorino 1879-1936 Baker 92, OxDcOp
Respighi Olivieri-Sangiacomo, Elsa 1894- OxDcOp
Respondek, Erwin 1894-1971 BioIn 17
Ress, Charles William 1933- WhoWor 93
Ress, Joseph W. d1991 BioIn 17
Ress, Robert Joseph, Jr. Law&B 92
Ressel, Paul 1948- WhoWor 93
Ressler, Barry 1940- St&PR 93
Ressler, Harold Kirkby 1944- WhoE 93
Ressler, Parke Edward 1916- WhoSSW 93
Ressler, Richard James Law&B 92
Rest, Friedrich Otto 1913- ConAu 38NR
Restaino, Federico 1934- WhoScE 91-3
Restaino, Katherine Marie 1937- WhoAmW 93
Restaino, Thomas A. Law&B 92
Restall, Lawrence Jerry 1939- St&PR 93, WhoAm 92
Restani, Jane A. 1948- CngDr 91, WhoE 93
Restek, Ivan 1919- WhoScE 91-4
Restel, James D. 1935- St&PR 93
Restell, Madame 1812-1878 BioIn 17
Restell, Lawrence Jerry 1939- WhoAm 92
Restelli, James Charles 1941- St&PR 93
Rester, Alfred Carl, Jr. 1940- WhoAm 92, WhoSSW 93, WhoWor 93
Restiano, Richard Angelo 1948- WhoE 93
Restivo, James John, Jr. 1946- WhoAm 92
Reston, James 1909- BioIn 17, JrnUS
Reston, James Barrett 1909- WhoAm 92, WhoWor 93
Reston, Mary Jo 1937- WhoE 93
Restorff, Kathleen Ann 1949- WhoAmW 93
Restrepo, Jose Luis 1930- WhoE 93
Restrick, John K. Law&B 92
Reswick, James Bigelow 1922- WhoAm 92
Resz, Charles Dennis 1935- St&PR 93
Reszka, Alfons 1924- WhoAm 92
Reszke, Edouard de Baker 92
Reszke, Jean de Baker 92
Reszke, de OxDcOp
Retamozo, Juan Francisco 1945- WhoWor 93
Retes, Jose Ignacio 1918- DcMexL
Retey, Janos 1934- WhoScE 91-3
Rethberg, Elisabeth 1894-1976 Baker 92, IntDcOp, OxDcOp
Rethee, Kam Law&B 92
Retherford, John Clifford 1951- St&PR 93
Retherford, Stephen Ted 1951- WhoSSW 93
Rethore, Bernard Gabriel 1941- St&PR 93, WhoAm 92
Rethore, Bernard Michael Law&B 92
Reti, Gabriel Andrew 1930- St&PR 93
Reti, Richard 1889-1929 BioIn 17
Reti, Rudolph 1885-1957 Baker 92
Retkin, Harry WhoScE 91-1
Retore, Guy 1924- WhoWor 93
Retsas, Spyros 1942- WhoWor 93
Retsema, James Allan 1942- WhoE 93
Rett, Andreas WhoScE 91-4
Rettaliata, John B. d1991 BioIn 17
Rettani, Roberto 1953- WhoWor 93
Rettberg, Charles Clayland, Jr. Law&B 92
Rettberg, John R. 1937- St&PR 93
Rettek, Susan Ilsa 1958- WhoE 93
Retter, G.J. 1922- WhoScE 91-4
Retterstol, Nils 1924- WhoScE 91-4, WhoWor 93
Rettich, Wilhelm 1892-1988 Baker 92
Rettie, Alistair James Law&B 92
Rettie, John Garner 1949- WhoWrEP 92
Rettig, Carolyn Faith 1951- WhoE 93
Rettig, H. Lee 1954- St&PR 93
Rettig, Hans M. 1921- WhoScE 91-3
Rettig, Harald WhoScE 91-4
Rettig, R. Joseph 1943- St&PR 93
Rettig, Richard Allen 1936- WhoAm 92
Rettig, Terry 1947- WhoEmL 93, WhoSSW 93, WhoWor 93
Rettig, Tommy 1941- BioIn 17
Rettinger, Dale G. 1944- St&PR 93
Rettinger, Donald Henry 1933- St&PR 93
Rettke, Michael C. 1944- St&PR 93
Retton, Mary Lou BioIn 17
Rettstadt, Charles William 1946- WhoWor 93
Retty, Glen St&PR 93
Retvari, Laszlo 1936- WhoScE 91-4
Retz, William Andrew 1940- WhoAm 92
Retzer, William K. 1943- St&PR 93
Retzky, Allan Abraham 1937- St&PR 93, WhoE 93
Retzler, Kurt E. 1927- St&PR 93
Retzler, Kurt Egon 1927- WhoAm 92
Retzow, Ruth von Kleist- 1867-1945 BioIn 17
Reuben, Alvin Bernard 1940- WhoAm 92
Reuben, Betty Gene 1943- WhoAmW 93
Reuben, Don Harold 1928- WhoAm 92, WhoWor 93
Reuben, Jay R. Law&B 92
Reuben, Paula 1932- ScF&FL 92
Reuben, Shelly 1945- ScF&FL 92
Reubens, Paul BioIn 17
Reubens, Paul 1952- QDrFCA 92 [port]
Reuber, Grant Louis 1927- St&PR 93, WhoAm 92
Reubke, Adolf 1805-1875 Baker 92
Reubke, (Friedrich) Julius 1834-1858 See Reubke, Adolf 1805-1875 Baker 92
Reubke, Otto 1842-1913 Baker 92
Reudink, Douglas Otto John 1939- WhoAm 92
Reuhl, Mercedes WhoAm 92
Reul, Helmut M. 1942- WhoScE 91-3
Reul, Richard Philip 1921- WhoWrEP 92
Reul, Sylvia Law&B 92
Reulier, Christian BioIn 17
Reuling, Karl d1991 BioIn 17
Reuling, Michael Frederick 1946- St&PR 93
Reuling, (Ludwig) Wilhelm 1802-1879 Baker 92
Reum, W. Robert 1942- St&PR 93, WhoAm 92
Reuman, Robert Everett 1923- WhoAm 92
Reunala, Timo Lauri 1943- WhoScE 91-4
Reurs, John H. d1990 BioIn 17
Reusche, Robert F. 1927- St&PR 93, WhoAm 92
Reuschel, Ricky Eugene 1949- BiDAMSp 1989
Reuscher, Richard J. 1934- St&PR 93
Reuschlein, Harold Gill 1904- WhoAm 92
Reuse, Ronald 1946- WhoEmL 93, WhoWor 93
Reusner, Esaias 1636-1679 Baker 92
Reuss, August 1871-1935 Baker 92
Reuss, Daniel J. 1955- St&PR 93
Reuss, Eduard 1851-1911 See Reuss-Belce, Luise 1860-1945 Baker 92
Reuss, Jerry 1949- BiDAMSp 1989
Reuss, Robert P. 1918- St&PR 93
Reuss, Robert Pershing 1918- WhoAm 92
Reuss-Belce, Luise 1860-1945 Baker 92
Reussner, Esaias 1636-1679 Baker 92
Reuter, Bjarne 1950- BioIn 17
Reuter, Bjarne (B.) 1950- ConAu 137
Reuter, Carol Joan 1941- WhoAm 92, WhoAmW 93, WhoE 93, WhoWor 93
Reuter, Daniela Susanne 1964- WhoAmW 93
Reuter, Florizel von 1890-1985 Baker 92
Reuter, Frank Theodore 1926- WhoAm 92, WhoSSW 93, WhoWrEP 92
Reuter, Harald 1934- WhoScE 91-4, WhoWor 93
Reuter, Helmut 1925- WhoScE 91-3
Reuter, Judith Eileen Law&B 92
Reuter, Karl E. 1934- WhoScE 91-2
Reuter, Nancy Ann 1952- WhoAmW 93
Reuter, Paul 1911-1990 BioIn 17
Reuter, Rolf 1926- Baker 92
Reuter, Stewart Ralston 1934- WhoAm 92
Reuter, William Lee 1934- St&PR 93
Reuterskiold, Marianne Astrid 1946- WhoWor 93
Reutersward, Lars H.E. 1949- WhoScE 91-4
Reuther, David 1946- St&PR 93
Reuther, David Louis 1946- WhoAm 92, WhoWrEP 92
Reuther, Hans 1920-1989 BioIn 17
Reuther, Hans 1940- St&PR 93
Reuther, Jurgen Friedrich 1940- WhoWor 93
Reuther, Karl A.A. 1932- St&PR 93
Reuther, Rosann White 1943- WhoAmW 93
Reuther, Walter 1907-1970 EncAACR
Reuther, Walter 1911- WhoAm 92
Reuther, Walter P. 1907-1970 PolPar
Reuther, Walter Philip 1907-1970 BioIn 17, DcTwHis
Reutter, Eberhard Edmund, Jr. 1924- WhoAm 92, WhoE 93
Reutter, Georg (von) 1656?-1738 Baker 92
Reutter, (Johann Adam Joseph Karl) Georg von 1708?-1772 Baker 92
Reutter, Hermann 1900-1985 Baker 92, OxDcOp
Revalski, Julian Petrov 1956- WhoWor 93
Revane, Michael J. 1934- St&PR 93
Revay, Miklos 1933- WhoScE 91-4
Reveal, Ernest Ira 1915- WhoAm 92
Reveaux, Mark M. 1941- St&PR 93
Revel, Gary Neal 1949- WhoWor 93
Revel, Gilles WhoScE 91-2
Revel, Gilles F. 1937- WhoScE 91-2
Revel, Ricky Joe 1956- WhoSSW 93
Reveles, Robert Apodaca 1932- St&PR 93
Reveley, Jacob BioIn 17
Reveley, Walter Taylor, III 1943- WhoAm 92
Revell, Donald 1954- ConAu 39NR
Revell, Oliver Burgan 1938- WhoAm 92, WhoWor 93
ReVelle, Charles S. 1938- WhoAm 92
Revelle, Donald Gene 1930- WhoAm 92
ReVelle, Penelope Louise 1941- WhoE 93
Revelle, Roger 1909-1991 AnObit 1991, BioIn 17
Revelli, William D. BioIn 17
Revelli, William D(onald) 1902- Baker 92
Revels, Hiram R. 1827-1901 EncAACR [port]
Revels, Hiram Rhodes 1827-1901 BioIn 17
Revenko-Jones, Paul 1946- WhoWrEP 92
Revens, John Cosgrove, Jr. 1947- WhoE 93
Revercomb, George H. 1929- CngDr 91
Revercomb, George Hughes 1929- WhoAm 92, WhoE 93
Reverdin, Bernard J. 1919- WhoAm 92
Revere, Anne 1903-1990 BioIn 17
Revere, John D. ScF&FL 92
Revere, Paul 1735-1818 HarEnMi
Revere, Paul Joseph 1832-1863 BioIn 17
Revere, Virginia Lehr WhoSSW 93
Reversat, Marc 1947- WhoWor 93
Revesz, Geza 1878-1955 Baker 92
Revesz, Gyorgy 1927- DrEEuF
Revesz, Laszlo 1926- WhoScE 91-4
Reviczky, Janos 1954- WhoWor 93
Revier, Dorothy 1904- SweetSg B [port]
Reviglio, Giuseppe Domenico 1923- WhoWor 93
Revill, Clive 1930- ConTFT 10
Revilla, Carlos Law&B 92
Revillard, Jean-Pierre 1938- WhoScE 91-2
Reville, Georgiana Ford Law&B 92
Reville, Michael W. Law&B 92
Reville, Michael William 1959- WhoE 93
Revin, Bengt 1940- WhoWor 93
Revis, Stephen E. Law&B 92
Revitt, Joan Marie 1946- WhoAmW 93
Revoile, Charles P. 1934- St&PR 93
Revoile, Charles Patrick Law&B 92
Revoile, Charles Patrick 1934- WhoAm 92
Revollo Bravo, Mario Cardinal 1919- WhoWor 93
Revolta, John 1911-1991 BiDAMSp 1989
Revolta, Johnny 1911-1991 BioIn 17
Revoltella, R. WhoScE 91-3
Revoltella, Roberto Paolo 1939- WhoWor 93
Revolution SoulM
Revord, Francis Earle 1929- St&PR 93
Revsbech, Vicki SmATA 72
Revsine, Lawrence 1942- WhoAm 92
Revson, Alfred F., Jr. 1926- St&PR 93
Revson, Charles 1906-1975 BioIn 17
Revson, James A. BioIn 17
Revson, Lyn BioIn 17
Revuelta, Maria Dolores 1956- WhoWor 93
Revueltas, Jose 1914-1975 DcMexL
Revueltas, Jose 1914-1976 SpAmA
Revueltas, Silvestre 1899-1940 Baker 92
Revutsky, Lev(ko Mikolaievich) 1889-1977 Baker 92
Revzin, Philip Steven 1952- WhoWor 93
Rew, Tacie May Hanna AmWomPl
Rew, William Edmund 1923- WhoSSW 93, WhoWor 93
Rewaj, Tadeusz Mieczyslaw 1931- WhoScE 91-4, WhoWor 93
Rewak, William John 1933- WhoAm 92, WhoWor 93
Rewbotham, F. Dickson 1941- St&PR 93
Rewcastle, Neill Barry 1931- WhoAm 92
Rewerts, Carl R. Law&B 92
Rewey, Pamela S. 1946- WhoAmW 93
Rewey, Robert L. 1938- St&PR 93
Rewolinski, Leah ScF&FL 92
Rex, Christopher Davis 1951- WhoSSW 93
Rex, Dietrich 1934- WhoWor 93
Rex, Robert Richmond 1909- WhoWor 93
Rex, Roy A. 1926- St&PR 93
Rexine, John Efstratios 1929- WhoAm 92, WhoWrEP 92
Rex-Johnson, Braiden 1956- ConAu 139
Rexner, Romulus 1920- ScF&FL 92
Rexon, G. Frederick, Jr. 1956- St&PR 93
Rexroad, Kelley Lee 1957- St&PR 93
Rexroat, Charles Marion 1932- WhoAm 92
Rexroat, Dee Ann 1960- WhoAmW 93
Rexroth, Kenneth 1905-1982 BioIn 17
Rexroth, Nancy Louise 1946- WhoAm 92
Rey, Anthony M. 1916-1991 BioIn 17
Rey, Carmen Rosello 1923- WhoAm 92
Rey, Cemal Reshid 1904-1985 Baker 92

Rey, David Michael 1956- WhoSSW 93
Rey, (Louis-Etienne-) Ernest 1823-1909 Baker 92
Rey, Fernando 1917- IntDcF 2-3
Rey, Guido M. 1936- WhoScE 91-3
Rey, H. A. 1898-1977 SmATA 69 [port]
Rey, H(ans) A(ugusto) 1898-1977 MajAI [port]
Rey, Jean-Baptiste 1734-1810 Baker 92
Rey, Judy-Lynn del ScF&FL 92
Rey, Lester del ScF&FL 92
Rey, Louis-Charles-Joseph 1738-1811 Baker 92
Rey, Margret (Elisabeth) 1906- ConAu 38NR, MajAI
Rey, Martine Pamela 1958- WhoSSW 93
Rey, Pascal BioIn 17
Rey, Paule 1929- WhoScE 91-4
Rey, Russell ScF&FL 92
Rey, William Kenneth 1925- WhoAm 92
Reya, Ewald 1943- WhoScE 91-3
Reycraft, George Dewey 1924- WhoAm 92
Reyelts, Paul Courtney 1946- St&PR 93
Reyer, Allan Kent 1948- WhoE 93
Reyer, Ernest 1823-1909 OxDcOp
Reyer, (Louis-Etienne-) Ernest 1823-1909 Baker 92
Reyer, Randall William 1917- WhoSSW 93
Reyerson, Dennis Orville 1939- WhoWrEP 92
Reyes, Alfonso 1889-1959 DcMexL, SpAmA
Reyes, Alfonso Salita, Jr. 1955- St&PR 93
Reyes, Alma Law&B 92
Reyes, Andre WhoAm 92
See Also Gipsy Kings, The ConMus 8
Reyes, Baltazar Velasquez, Jr. 1927- WhoWor 93
Reyes, Canut
See Gipsy Kings, The ConMus 8
Reyes, Carlos 1935- WhoWrEP 92
Reyes, Carmen Rosa 1935- WhoSSW 93
Reyes, Carmencita O. WhoAsAP 91
Reyes, Eduardo Mendoza, III 1964- WhoE 93
Reyes, Ernie, Jr. BioIn 17
Reyes, Francisco I. 1935- WhoE 93
Reyes, Hernan Macaballug 1933- WhoWor 93
Reyes, Hernan Rodrigo 1951- WhoWor 93
Reyes, Juan 1962- WhoWor 93
Reyes, Luis Alberto 1924- WhoWor 93
Reyes, Marcia Stygles 1950- WhoAmW 93
Reyes, Marie BioIn 17
Reyes, Nancy Yvonne 1961- WhoSSW 93
Reyes, Nicolas
See Gipsy Kings, The ConMus 8
Reyes, Raul Gregorio 1928- WhoSSW 93
Reyes, Rodrigo Berenguer De Los 1924- WhoIns 93
Reyes, Shirley Norflin 1949- WhoAmW 93
Reyes de la Maza, Luis 1932- DcMexL
Reyes-Guerra, David Richard 1933- WhoAm 92
Reyes Matta, Jose Maria DcCPCAm
Reyes Nevares, Salvador 1922- DcMexL
Reyes Ruiz, Jesus 1908- DcMexL
Reyhner, Jon (Allan) 1944- ConAu 139
Reyment, Richard Arthur 1926- WhoScE 91-4
Reymeulen, Herwig R.T. 1944- WhoScE 91-2
Reymont, Wladyslaw 1868-1925 PolBiDi [port]
Reyna, Leo J. 1918- WhoWor 93
Reyna, Troy Michael 1950- WhoSSW 93
Reynal, Katherine Whelan d1992 BioIn 17
Reynard, Muriel Joyce Law&B 92
Reynaud, Ann Luckett Law&B 92
Reynaud, Paul 1878-1966 BioIn 17, DcTwHis
Reynaud, Rosie Sevilla 1949- WhoAmW 93
Reyniac, Maurice Druon de ScF&FL 92
Reynier, Jean-Pierre 1946- WhoScE 91-2
Reynolds, A. William 1933- St&PR 93, WhoAm 92
Reynolds, Aidan ScF&FL 92
Reynolds, Alan Anthony 1942- WhoAm 92
Reynolds, Alan James WhoScE 91-1
Reynolds, Alan Sidney 1928- St&PR 93
Reynolds, Albert NewYTBS 92 [port]
Reynolds, Albert 1932- BioIn 17, WhoWor 93
Reynolds, Albert Barnett 1931- WhoAm 92, WhoSSW 93
Reynolds, Alberta E. WhoAmW 93
Reynolds, Alfred ScF&FL 92
Reynolds, Angus Stuart, Jr. 1936- WhoE 93, WhoWor 93
Reynolds, Ann WhoWrEP 92
Reynolds, Anna 1931- Baker 92
Reynolds, Arlin BioIn 17
Reynolds, B. Gerald Law&B 92
Reynolds, Baillie, Mrs. ScF&FL 92
Reynolds, Beatrix AmWomPl
Reynolds, Ben Jeff 1950- St&PR 93
Reynolds, Benedict Michael 1925- WhoAm 92
Reynolds, Benjamin James 1952- WhoWrEP 92
Reynolds, Bertha Capen 1885- BioIn 17
Reynolds, Beverly M. 1948- WhoAmW 93
Reynolds, Bill ConTFT 10
Reynolds, Billie I. 1929- WhoAm 92
Reynolds, Billie Iles 1929- WhoWrEP 92
Reynolds, Bonnie Jones ScF&FL 92
Reynolds, Brenda Starr 1952- WhoAmW 93
Reynolds, Bruce H. 1939- St&PR 93
Reynolds, Burt BioIn 17
Reynolds, Burt 1936- IntDcF 2-3 [port], MiSFD 9, WhoAm 92
Reynolds, C.P. BioIn 17
Reynolds, Carl Christiansen 1934- WhoAm 92
Reynolds, Carl Robert 1948- St&PR 93
Reynolds, Carole Lee WhoAmW 93
Reynolds, Catherine M. Law&B 92
Reynolds, Charles H. St&PR 93, WhoSSW 93
Reynolds, Clark Andre 1951- St&PR 93
Reynolds, Clark Gilbert 1939- WhoSSW 93
Reynolds, Clarke E. 1921- St&PR 93
Reynolds, Claude Lewis, Jr. 1948- WhoE 93
Reynolds, (Richard) Clay 1949- ConAu 139
Reynolds, Clyde Richard David 1943- WhoUN 92
Reynolds, Colin S. WhoScE 91-1
Reynolds, Collins James, III 1937- WhoAm 92
Reynolds, Dallas McC. ScF&FL 92
Reynolds, Dana Drummond 1908- WhoAm 92
Reynolds, David WhoWrEP 92
Reynolds, David Alan 1947- WhoSSW 93
Reynolds, David George 1933- WhoAm 92
Reynolds, David J. 1957- St&PR 93
Reynolds, David Parham 1915- St&PR 93, WhoAm 92
Reynolds, David Robert WhoIns 93
Reynolds, David W. 1932- St&PR 93
Reynolds, Debbie 1932- IntDcF 2-3, WhoAm 92
Reynolds, Denise Annette 1960- WhoWrEP 92
Reynolds, Diane D. Law&B 92
Reynolds, Diane Marie 1954- WhoAmW 93
Reynolds, Don William 1926- WhoSSW 93, WhoWor 93
Reynolds, Donald Blair 1928- St&PR 93
Reynolds, Donald N. 1948- St&PR 93
Reynolds, Donald R. 1922- St&PR 93
Reynolds, Donald William 1929- St&PR 93
Reynolds, Donald Worthington 1906- WhoAm 92
Reynolds, Dorinda Lynn 1952- WhoSSW 93
Reynolds, Doris June 1929- WhoSSW 93
Reynolds, Dudley C. 1953- St&PR 93
Reynolds, Dudley Cole Law&B 92
Reynolds, Edward 1926- WhoAm 92
Reynolds, Edward Osmund Royle WhoScE 91-1
Reynolds, Edwin Wilfred, Jr. 1937- WhoE 93
Reynolds, Effie Ruth 1946- WhoAmW 93
Reynolds, Elizabeth Ann 1941- WhoAmW 93
Reynolds, Ernest West 1920- WhoAm 92
Reynolds, Frank 1923-1983 JrnUS
Reynolds, Frank Everett 1930- WhoAm 92
Reynolds, Frank Miller 1917- WhoAm 92
Reynolds, Frank Russell 1920- St&PR 93
Reynolds, Fred S. Law&B 92
Reynolds, Fred T. 1921- St&PR 93
Reynolds, G. W. M. 1814-1879 NinCLC 37 [port]
Reynolds, Gary A. d1990 BioIn 17
Reynolds, Gary Alan 1943- WhoAm 92
Reynolds, Gary Kemp 1944- WhoE 93
Reynolds, Gary N. 1940- St&PR 93
Reynolds, Gayle Marie 1943- WhoAmW 93
Reynolds, Gene 1925- MiSFD 9, WhoAm 92
Reynolds, George Thomas 1917- WhoAm 92
Reynolds, Glenn Francis 1928- St&PR 93
Reynolds, Graham 1944- ConAu 138
Reynolds, Gregg McClellan 1935- St&PR 93
Reynolds, H. Gerald Law&B 92
Reynolds, Harry Lincoln 1925- WhoAm 92
Reynolds, Helen M. AmWomPl
Reynolds, Herbert Hal 1930- WhoSSW 93
Reynolds, Herbert Young 1939- WhoE 93
Reynolds, Jack W. 1923- WhoAm 92
Reynolds, James A. 1929- WhoWrEP 92
Reynolds, James A. 1938- St&PR 93
Reynolds, James E., Jr. Law&B 92
Reynolds, James Glenn 1943- St&PR 93
Reynolds, Jan 1956- BioIn 17
Reynolds, Jean Edwards 1941- WhoAm 92, WhoE 93
Reynolds, Jeff H. BioIn 17
Reynolds, Jeff H. 1964- St&PR 93
Reynolds, Jerry Owen 1944- WhoAm 92
Reynolds, Jimmy Dale 1940- WhoSSW 93
Reynolds, John 1950- WhoScE 91-1
Reynolds, John Allen 1942- WhoAm 92
Reynolds, John Charles 1933- WhoAm 92
Reynolds, John Dana 1945- WhoWrEP 92
Reynolds, John Elliott, III 1952- WhoSSW 93
Reynolds, John Francis 1921- WhoAm 92
Reynolds, John Fulton 1820-1863 HarEnMi
Reynolds, John Hamilton 1794-1852 BioIn 17
Reynolds, John Hamilton 1923- WhoAm 92
Reynolds, John Hughes, IV 1940- WhoSSW 93
Reynolds, John James WhoScE 91-1
Reynolds, John R. Law&B 92
Reynolds, John W. 1921- WhoAm 92
Reynolds, Jonathan P. 1947- St&PR 93
Reynolds, Joseph Melvin 1924- WhoAm 92, WhoWor 93
Reynolds, Joseph Patrick, Jr. 1937- St&PR 93
Reynolds, Joshua 1723-1792 BioIn 17
Reynolds, Judith Eichmann 1942- WhoAmW 93
Reynolds, Julian Douglas 1942- WhoWor 93
Reynolds, Karen Perry 1945- WhoSSW 93
Reynolds, Kathleen N. ScF&FL 92
Reynolds, Kathy P. 1950- St&PR 93
Reynolds, Kay 1951- ScF&FL 92
Reynolds, Keith Allan 1951- WhoAm 92
Reynolds, Keith Lamar 1929- WhoE 93
Reynolds, Kenneth W. 1939- WhoAm 92
Reynolds, Kevin 1952- MiSFD 9
Reynolds, L. George BioIn 17
Reynolds, L.J. SoulM
Reynolds, Lana Kay 1959- WhoAmW 93
Reynolds, Laura Alberta 1931- WhoSSW 93
Reynolds, Leslie M. Law&B 92
Reynolds, Lloyd George 1910- WhoAm 92
Reynolds, Lola Sullivan Law&B 92
Reynolds, Lorraine Phyllis 1919- WhoWrEP 92
Reynolds, Lucinda A. Law&B 92
Reynolds, Mack 1917-1983 ScF&FL 92
Reynolds, Margaret 1941- WhoAsAP 91
Reynolds, Margery Jane 1966- WhoAmW 93
Reynolds, Marion Frances 1940- St&PR 93
Reynolds, Marjorie 1921- SweetSg C [port]
Reynolds, Mark Edward 1958- WhoSSW 93
Reynolds, Marshall Truman 1937- WhoAm 92
Reynolds, Mary Ann WhoAmW 93
Reynolds, Mary Elizabeth Fontaine 1931- WhoSSW 93
Reynolds, Mary Trackett 1913- WhoAm 92
Reynolds, Max J. 1939- St&PR 93
Reynolds, Michael BioIn 17
Reynolds, Michael D. St&PR 93
Reynolds, Michael David 1954- WhoSSW 93
Reynolds, (Marjorie) Moira Davison 1915- WhoWrEP 92
Reynolds, Nancy Bradford duPont 1919- WhoE 93
Reynolds, Nancy Hubbard 1923- WhoAmW 93
Reynolds, Nancy Remick 1938- WhoAmW 93, WhoWor 93
Reynolds, Nathaniel Dunton 1950- WhoSSW 93
Reynolds, Nick 1933-
See Kingston Trio, The ConMus 9
Reynolds, Norman BioIn 17
Reynolds, Norman Eben 1919- WhoAm 92, WhoSSW 93
Reynolds, Pamela Christine Schrom 1945- WhoWrEP 92
Reynolds, Patricia Ellen 1934- WhoE 93
Reynolds, Paul B. 1915- St&PR 93
Reynolds, Paul G. 1922- St&PR 93
Reynolds, Peter James 1949- WhoSSW 93
Reynolds, Peter Morgan Law&B 92
Reynolds, Philip N. Law&B 92
Reynolds, Quinton BioIn 17
Reynolds, R. John 1936- WhoAm 92
Reynolds, Randolph Nicklas 1941- St&PR 93, WhoAm 92, WhoSSW 93
Reynolds, Raymond S. St&PR 93
Reynolds, Renita Law&B 92
Reynolds, Rhonda E.F. Law&B 92
Reynolds, Richard Clyde 1929- WhoAm 92
Reynolds, Richard Kent 1956- WhoE 93
Reynolds, Richard Louis 1953- WhoSSW 93
Reynolds, Richard Morgan 1937- WhoAm 92
Reynolds, Richard Paulsen 1946- WhoWor 93
Reynolds, Richard Samuel, III 1934- St&PR 93, WhoSSW 93
Reynolds, Rick BioIn 17
Reynolds, Robert Arthur 1932- St&PR 93
Reynolds, Robert E. 1957- St&PR 93
Reynolds, Robert Edgar 1938- WhoAm 92
Reynolds, Robert Gregory 1952- WhoEmL 93
Reynolds, Robert H. 1913- St&PR 93
Reynolds, Robert Hugh 1937- WhoWor 93
Reynolds, Robert Joel 1944- WhoAm 92, WhoE 93, WhoWor 93
Reynolds, Robert Lester 1917- WhoAm 92
Reynolds, Robert Louis 1939- St&PR 93, WhoAm 92
Reynolds, Robert W. 1944- St&PR 93
Reynolds, Robert Webster 1941- WhoE 93
Reynolds, Roger Dale 1948- St&PR 93
Reynolds, Roger Dean Law&B 92
Reynolds, Roger (Lee) 1934- Baker 92, WhoAm 92
Reynolds, Roger Whitman 1926- WhoSSW 93
Reynolds, Ron R. 1939- WhoSSW 93
Reynolds, Russell Seaman, Jr. 1931- WhoAm 92
Reynolds, Ruth Lillian 1922- St&PR 93
Reynolds, Sallie Blackburn 1940- WhoAmW 93
Reynolds, Scott Walton 1941- St&PR 93, WhoAm 92
Reynolds, Sidney Rae 1956- WhoWrEP 92
Reynolds, Stephen Philip 1948- WhoAm 92
Reynolds, Ted 1938- ScF&FL 92
Reynolds, Terrence Edward 1938- St&PR 93
Reynolds, Theodore A. ScF&FL 92
Reynolds, Thomas St&PR 93, WhoScE 91-1
Reynolds, Thomas J. 1912-1990 BioIn 17
Reynolds, Thomas P. 1952- WhoE 93, WhoWor 93
Reynolds, Tom 1950- WhoE 93
Reynolds, Verne (Becker) 1926- Baker 92
Reynolds, W. Ann BioIn 17
Reynolds, Warren Jay 1918- WhoAm 92
Reynolds, Wayne C. 1940- St&PR 93
Reynolds, Wiley Richard 1917- WhoAm 92
Reynolds, William 1910- ConTFT 10
Reynolds, William Bradford 1942- WhoAm 92
Reynolds, William Everett 1938- St&PR 93
Reynolds, William F. 1938- St&PR 93
Reynolds, William Francis 1930- WhoAm 92
Reynolds, William Gray, Jr. 1939- St&PR 93
Reynolds, William H. ConTFT 10
Reynolds, William Harold 1925- WhoAm 92
Reynolds, William James 1956- WhoWrEP 92
Reynolds, William Leroy 1945- WhoAm 92
Reynolds, William T. Law&B 92
Reynolds, William T. 1933- WhoAm 92
Reynolds, William T. 1959- St&PR 93
Reynolds, William Thomas 1959- WhoSSW 93
Reynolds, Wynetka Ann 1937- WhoAm 92, WhoAmW 93, WhoE 93
Reynoldson, Walter Ward 1920- WhoAm 92
Reynoso, Cruz 1931- HispAmA
Rey Prendes, Julio Adolfo DcCPCAm
Reys, Philippe 1928- WhoScE 91-2
Reyzen, Mark 1895- OxDcOp
Reza, Abu 1944- WhoWor 93
Reza, Marilyn d1990 BioIn 17
Reza, Rini 1957- WhoWor 93
Reza, Robert BioIn 17
Rezac, Ivan 1924-1977 Baker 92
Rezai, Shahrzad 1949- St&PR 93
Reza-Morales, Lucy 1949- WhoSSW 93
Rezek, Ellen Marie 1952- WhoAmW 93
Rezek, Geoffrey Robert 1941- WhoE 93
Rezel, Ronald Glenn 1932- St&PR 93
Rezich, George F. 1927- St&PR 93, WhoAm 92
Rezlescu, Nicolae 1937- WhoScE 91-4
Reznack, Andrew V. 1931- St&PR 93

Rezneck, Daniel Albert 1935- WhoAm 92
Rezneck, Samuel BioIn 17
Rezner, Barbara Ann Law&B 92
Reznicek, Bernard William 1936- WhoAm 92
Reznicek, Emil Nikolaus von 1860-1945 Baker 92
Reznicek, Emil von 1860-1945 OxDcOp
Reznick, Robert 1919- St&PR 93
Reznor, Trent BioIn 17
Rezyka, Mark 1949- MiSFD 9
Rezzonico, Renzo 1929- WhoWor 93
Rezzori (d'Arezzo), Gregor von 1914- ConAu 136
Rezzori, Gregor von BioIn 17
Rhabdas, Nicholas Artabasdos fl. 14th cent.- OxDcByz
Rhaidestinos, David fl. 15th cent.- OxDcByz
Rhakendytes, Joseph OxDcByz
Rhame, Thomas Gene 1941- WhoAm 92
Rhame, William T. 1915- St&PR 93
Rhame, William Thomas 1915- WhoAm 92
Rhamy, Jennifer Frances 1954- WhoAmW 93
Rhatigan, Pamela Mossay 1953- WhoAmW 93
Rhau, Georg 1488-1548 Baker 92
Rhaw, Georg 1488-1548 Baker 92
Rhawn, Edward Woodward 1938- St&PR 93
Rhazaoui, Ahmed 1944- WhoUN 92
Rhea, Albert Lisle 1915- St&PR 93
Rhea, Ann Crawford 1940- WhoAmW 93
Rhea, Marcia Chandler 1956- WhoAmW 93
Rhea, Mildred Louise 1911- WhoAmW 93
Rhea, Ronald E. 1939- St&PR 93
Rhead, Michael Martin WhoScE 91-1
Rheam, Micheal C. St&PR 93
Rheaume, Manon NewYTBS 92 [port]
Rheaume, Myron 1944- St&PR 93
Rhedin, Judith A. 1948- WhoAmW 93
Rhee, Margaret Sue 1939- WhoAmW 93
Rhee, Syngman 1871-1965 DcTwHis
Rhee, Syngman 1875-1965 ColdWar 2 [port]
Rhee, Yang Ho 1943- WhoWor 93
Rhee Chi Ho 1940- WhoAsAP 91
Rhee In Je 1950- WhoAsAP 91
Rhees, Raymond C. 1914- St&PR 93
Rheims, Bettina BioIn 17
Rhein, Ezra A. 1952- St&PR 93
Rhein, John Hancock Willing, III 1931- St&PR 93
Rhein, Murray Harold 1912- WhoAm 92
Rhein, Timothy James 1941- St&PR 93
Rheinberger, Joseph (Gabriel) 1839-1901 Baker 92
Rheinboldt, Werner Carl 1927- WhoAm 92, WhoE 93
Rheinfrank, Lamson, Jr. 1940- St&PR 93
Rheingold, Arnold Morton 1931- WhoAm 92
Rheingold, Arthur D. Law&B 92
Rheingold, Harriet Lange 1908- WhoAmW 93, WhoSSW 93
Rheingold, Howard 1947- ScF&FL 92
Rheinheimer, Gerhard 1927- WhoScE 91-3
Rheinheimer, Kurt 1946- WhoSSW 93, WhoWrEP 92
Rheinlander, T.W. 1940- St&PR 93
Rheins, Carl Jeffrey 1945- WhoE 93
Rheinstein, John 1930- WhoE 93
Rheinstein, Linda Carol 1956- WhoAmW 93
Rheinstein, Peter Howard 1943- WhoAm 92, WhoE 93, WhoWor 93
Rhem, Durward D. 1927- St&PR 93
Rhemann, Eugene Evans 1941- WhoSSW 93
Rhen, Vuokko Hannele 1957- WhoScE 91-4
Rhenan-Segura, Jorge 1955- WhoUN 92
Rhene-Baton 1879-1940 Baker 92
Rhenisch, Harold 1958- WhoCanL 92
Rhetorios of Egypt fl. 7th cent.- OxDcByz
Rhett, Harry Moore, Jr. 1912- WhoSSW 93
Rhett, Haskell Emery Smith 1936- WhoAm 92, WhoE 93
Rhett, John Taylor, Jr. 1925- WhoAm 92
Rhett, Robert Barnwell 1800-1876 JrnUS
Rhetts, Paul Fisher 1946- WhoEmL 93
Rhi, Sang-Kyu 1933- WhoWor 93
Rhiew, Francis Changnam 1938- WhoE 93
Rhind, J. Christopher 1934- WhoIns 93
Rhind, James Thomas 1922- WhoAm 92
Rhind, John Arthur 1920- St&PR 93
Rhind, John Christopher 1934- WhoAm 92
Rhine, Jack G. 1933- St&PR 93
Rhine, Richard MajAI, SmATA 69
Rhinehart, David Andrew 1951- WhoSSW 93
Rhinehart, Luke 1932- ScF&FL 92
Rhinehart, Marilyn D. 1948- ConAu 139
Rhinelander, John Bassett 1933- St&PR 93, WhoAm 92
Rhinelander, Melvin A. 1950- St&PR 93
Rhines, Frederick WhoAm 92
Rhines, Peter Broomell 1942- WhoAm 92
Rhines, Walden Clark 1946- St&PR 93
Rhinesmith, Stephen Headley 1942- WhoAm 92
Rho, Lorraine Therese WhoWrEP 92
Rhoades, Amanda WhoWrEP 92
Rhoades, Barbara Barry 1948- WhoAmW 93
Rhoades, Dennis Keith 1944- WhoE 93
Rhoades, Dorothy G. 1953- St&PR 93
Rhoades, Jacqueline Jo 1941- WhoWrEP 92
Rhoades, James Lawrence 1933- WhoSSW 93
Rhoades, Jon Allen 1937- WhoIns 93
Rhoades, Kathleen M. Law&B 92
Rhoades, Kathleen Marie Law&B 92
Rhoades, Lawrence Woodruff 1922- WhoE 93
Rhoades, Leslie H. 1944- St&PR 93
Rhoades, Marye Frances 1937- WhoAmW 93
Rhoades, Nina 1863- AmWomPl
Rhoades, Sam J. 1908- St&PR 93
Rhoades, Sylvia Eileen 1936- WhoAmW 93
Rhoades, Timothy Gerard 1955- St&PR 93
Rhoades, Warren A., Jr. 1924- WhoAm 92
Rhoads, D. Dean 1927- St&PR 93
Rhoads, Daniel Lee Law&B 92
Rhoads, Diana Akers 1944- WhoSSW 93
Rhoads, Edwin A. 1936- St&PR 93
Rhoads, Eugenia Eckford BioIn 17
Rhoads, Gary L. 1954- St&PR 93
Rhoads, George Grant 1940- WhoE 93
Rhoads, Geraldine Emeline 1914- WhoAm 92
Rhoads, James Berton 1928- WhoAm 92
Rhoads, James Darius 1936- St&PR 93
Rhoads, Jeni F. Law&B 92
Rhoads, Jonathan Evans 1907- WhoAm 92, WhoE 93, WhoWor 93
Rhoads, Keating 1949- St&PR 93
Rhoads, Michael Dennis 1949- WhoE 93
Rhoads, Patricia Mary Gruenewald 1953- WhoAm 92
Rhoads, Paul Kelly 1940- WhoAm 92
Rhoads, Richard C. 1927- St&PR 93
Rhoads, Richard H. St&PR 93
Rhoads, Robert K. Law&B 92
Rhoads, Robert K. 1954- WhoAm 92
Rhoads, Steven Eric 1939- WhoAm 92
Rhoads, William Charles 1929- St&PR 93
Rhoda, Christopher Herbert 1966- WhoE 93
Rhoda, Johnny Keith 1950- WhoSSW 93
Rhoda, William F. 1944- St&PR 93
Rhodaberger, W.L. 1950- St&PR 93
Rhode, Alfred Shimon 1928- WhoAm 92
Rhode, David Leland 1950- WhoAm 92
Rhode, Deborah Lynn 1952- WhoAm 92
Rhode, Edward Albert 1926- WhoAm 92
Rhode, Gerald Kenneth 1929- St&PR 93
Rhode, James Arthur 1936- St&PR 93
Rhode, Kenneth George 1909- WhoIns 93
Rhode, Naomi Reed 1938- St&PR 93
Rhode, Robert Thomas 1954- WhoWrEP 92
Rhodeback, Melanie Joyce 1955- WhoSSW 93
Rhodebeck, Lyle Dean 1957- St&PR 93
Rhoden, Harold Hugh 1943- WhoAm 92
Rhoden, Jack 1925- St&PR 93
Rhoden, Ron E. 1953- St&PR 93
Rhodes, Alfred William 1922- WhoAm 92
Rhodes, Alice Graham 1941- WhoWor 93
Rhodes, Allen Franklin 1924- St&PR 93
Rhodes, Andrew James 1911- WhoAm 92
Rhodes, Ann Louise 1941- WhoAmW 93, WhoSSW 93
Rhodes, Ashby Marshall 1923- WhoAm 92
Rhodes, Barry 1947- WhoE 93
Rhodes, Betty Jane 1921- WhoAmW 93, WhoWor 93
Rhodes, Beverly Anisowicz 1947- WhoEmL 93
Rhodes, Bianca A. 1958- St&PR 93
Rhodes, Carol Jean 1936- WhoSSW 93
Rhodes, Cecil John 1853-1902 BioIn 17
Rhodes, Charles Harker, Jr. 1930- WhoAm 92
Rhodes, Charles Kirkham 1939- WhoAm 92
Rhodes, Clayton Bennett 1945- WhoSSW 93
Rhodes, Daniel ScF&FL 92
Rhodes, Daniel 1911-1989 BioIn 17
Rhodes, David Mark 1951- WhoWrEP 92
Rhodes, Donald Robert 1923- WhoAm 92
Rhodes, Elisha Hunt 1842-1917 BioIn 17
Rhodes, Eric Foster 1927- WhoAm 92
Rhodes, Erik 1906-1990 BioIn 17
Rhodes, Frank Harold Trevor 1926- WhoAm 92, WhoE 93, WhoWor 93
Rhodes, Gary L. 1941- St&PR 93
Rhodes, Gary Lynn 1941- WhoAm 92
Rhodes, Gary W. 1948- WhoAm 92
Rhodes, Gaylena Ruth 1960- WhoSSW 93
Rhodes, Gene Paul 1955- WhoSSW 93
Rhodes, Gordon Ellsworth 1927- St&PR 93, WhoIns 93
Rhodes, Gregory H. Law&B 92
Rhodes, Helen Mary 1921- WhoAmW 93
Rhodes, Jack Wright 1949- WhoSSW 93
Rhodes, James Devers 1955- WhoSSW 93
Rhodes, James Richard 1945- WhoWor 93
Rhodes, James Thomas 1941- St&PR 93
Rhodes, James Whitfield 1945- WhoAm 92
Rhodes, John WhoScE 91-1
Rhodes, John Bower 1925- WhoAm 92
Rhodes, John Bower, Jr. 1925- St&PR 93
Rhodes, John C. BioIn 17
Rhodes, John J. 1916- PolPar
Rhodes, John J., III 1943- CngDr 91, WhoAm 92
Rhodes, John Jacob 1916- WhoAm 92
Rhodes, Kenneth Anthony, Jr. 1930- WhoE 93
Rhodes, Kent 1912-1991 BioIn 17
Rhodes, Marc Alan 1958- WhoSSW 93
Rhodes, Mary WhoAmW 93
Rhodes, Mary Lee Sabourin 1959- WhoAmW 93
Rhodes, Michael MiSFD 9
Rhodes, Michael John Charles WhoScE 91-1
Rhodes, Milton 1945- WhoAm 92
Rhodes, Mitchell L. 1940- WhoAm 92
Rhodes, Nathaniel Richard 1936- WhoSSW 93
Rhodes, Norman Leonard 1942- WhoWrEP 92
Rhodes, Odella Jeanne 1934- WhoE 93
Rhodes, Paul Christian, III 1956- WhoSSW 93
Rhodes, Peter E. 1942- St&PR 93
Rhodes, Peter Edward 1942- WhoAm 92
Rhodes, Phillip (Carl) 1940- Baker 92
Rhodes, R.A.W. WhoScE 91-1
Rhodes, R. A. W. 1944- ConAu 139
Rhodes, Richard BioIn 17
Rhodes, Richard Lee 1937- WhoAm 92, WhoWrEP 92
Rhodes, Richard William Law&B 92
Rhodes, Robert Hunt 1937- ConAu 136
Rhodes, Rondell Horace 1918- WhoE 93
Rhodes, Russell L. ScF&FL 92
Rhodes, Samuel 1941- WhoAm 92
Rhodes, Sandra BioIn 17
Rhodes, Susan E. 1954- WhoAmW 93
Rhodes, Virgil Leonard 1928- WhoSSW 93
Rhodes, Willard d1992 NewYTBS 92
Rhodes, Willard 1901- Baker 92
Rhodes, Willard 1901-1992 BioIn 17
Rhodes, William Reginald 1935- St&PR 93, WhoAm 92
Rhody, Ronald Edward 1932- St&PR 93, WhoAm 92
Rhomaios, Eustathios OxDcByz
Rhondda, Viscountess 1883-1958 BioIn 17
Rhone, Sylvia BioIn 17
Rhonehouse, Don 1937- St&PR 93
Rhonehouse, Dorothy 1941- St&PR 93
Rhoney, Ann 1953- BioIn 17
Rhoten, Carey Douglas 1936- St&PR 93
Rhoton, Albert Loren, Jr. 1932- WhoAm 92
Rhudick, Diana 1962- WhoAmW 93
Rhue, Morton MajAI, SmATA 71, WhoWrEP 92
Rhule, Homer A. 1921- WhoIns 93
Rhule, Homer Albert 1921- WhoE 93
Rhulen, W.A. 1931- St&PR 93
Rhyne, Charles Sylvanus 1912- WhoAm 92, WhoE 93, WhoWor 93
Rhyne, Nancy 1926- BioIn 17
Rhyne, Neal Herbert 1945- St&PR 93
Rhyne, Theresa-Marie 1954- WhoAmW 93
Rhyne, Vernon Thomas 1942- WhoAm 92
Rhys, Hedley Howell 1910-1990 BioIn 17
Rhys, Jack ScF&FL 92
Rhys, Jean BioIn 17
Rhys, Jean 1890-1979 BritWr S2, DcLB 117 [port], IntLitE
Rhys, Sylvia Marjorie 1932- WhoWor 93
Rhys Jones, Griff 1953- See Smith, Mel 1952- & Rhys Jones, Griff 1953- QDrFCA 92
Riabov, Darelle Dee Lake 1951- WhoAmW 93
Riabtsev, Vladimir BioIn 17
Riach, Peter Andrew 1937- WhoWor 93
Riad, Mahmoud d1992 NewYTBS 92
Riad, Mahmoud 1917-1992 BioIn 17, ConAu 136, CurBio 92N
Riadis, Emilios 1885-1935 Baker 92
Riady, Mochtar BioIn 17
Riall, Phineas 1775-1850 HarEnMi
Rialp, Eduardo Augurio 1938- WhoWor 93
Rial-Planas, Ruben Victor 1943- WhoWor 93
Riano, Juan Facundo 1828-1901 Baker 92
Riano, Renie 1899-1971 See Yule, Joe 1888-1950 & Riano, Renie 1899-1971 QDrFCA 92
Rianto, Gunawan 1951- WhoWor 93
Riasanovsky, Nicholas Valentine 1923- WhoAm 92
Riback, Jeffrey L. Law&B 92
Ribadeneira, Mario 1933- WhoAm 92
Ribak, Louis Leon 1903-1979 BioIn 17
Ribakov, Anatolii BioIn 17
Ribakov, Sergei Gavrilovich 1867-1921 Baker 92
Ribalta, Francisco 1565?-1628 BioIn 17
Ribando, Brian L. Law&B 92
Ribari, Otto 1932- WhoScE 91-4
Ribaric, Marijan 1932- WhoScE 91-4, WhoWor 93
Ribary, Antal 1924- Baker 92
Ribas, Jorge Luis 1942- WhoAm 92
Ribbans, Geoffrey Wilfrid 1927- WhoAm 92
Ribbentrop, Joachim von 1893-1945 DcTwHis
Ribbing, Carl Gustaf 1942- WhoScE 91-4, WhoWor 93
Ribble, John Charles 1931- WhoAm 92
Ribble, Marland S. 1932- St&PR 93
Ribble, Ronald George 1937- WhoSSW 93
Ribbons, Douglas W. WhoScE 91-1
Ribbons, Justin Charles Law&B 92
Ribbs, Willy T. BioIn 17
Ribe, Martin Gustaf 1945- WhoWor 93
Ribeiro, Antonio Cardinal 1928- WhoAm 92, WhoWor 93
Ribeiro, Augusto R. De Castro 1950- WhoWor 93
Ribeiro, Celso Carneiro 1954- WhoWor 93
Ribeiro, Frank Henry 1949- WhoEmL 93
Ribeiro, Guilherme Alvares 1926- WhoWor 93
Ribeiro, Joaquim S.S. 1936- St&PR 93
Ribeiro, Lance Edward 1962- WhoE 93
Ribeiro, Rene 1914- IntDcAn
Ribeiro, Stella Carr ScF&FL 92
Ribeiro Filho, Aurino 1947- WhoWor 93
Ribelin, Herman A. 1927- St&PR 93
Ribenboim, Paulo 1928- WhoAm 92
Ribera, Fernando Enriquez y Afan de 1583-1637 BioIn 17
Ribera, Jusepe de 1591-1652 BioIn 17
Ribera (Maneja), Antonio 1873-1956 Baker 92
Ribera (y Tarrago), Julian 1858-1934 Baker 92
Riberio Pacheco, J.F.J. WhoScE 91-3
Ribero, Michael A. 1956- St&PR 93
Ribero, Michael Antonio 1956- WhoAm 92
Ribes, Jean-Claude WhoScE 91-2
Ribeyro, Julio Ramon 1929- SpAmA
Ribi, Nils Andrew 1955- St&PR 93
Ribicoff, Abraham A. 1910- WhoAm 92
Rible, Mortan Law&B 92
Rible, Morton 1938- WhoAm 92
Riblet, William Breeze 1938- St&PR 93
Ribman, Ronald Burt 1932- WhoAm 92
Ribner, Herbert Spencer 1913- WhoAm 92
Riboli, Elio 1951- WhoUN 92
Ribolla, Luigi 1937- WhoWor 93
Ribordy, Denis Eugene 1929- St&PR 93
Ribot, Alexandre Felix Joseph 1842-1923 BioIn 17
Ribot, Marc BioIn 17
Ricard, Andre 1938- WhoCanL 92
Ricard, Andre 1939- WhoScE 91-2
Ricard, Jacques 1929- WhoScE 91-2
Ricardi, Leon Joseph 1924- WhoAm 92
Ricardo 1903-1991 BioIn 17
Ricardo, David 1772-1823 BioIn 17
Ricardo, Richard Ledesma 1963- WhoWor 93
Ricardo-Campbell, Rita 1920- NotHsAW 93, WhoAm 92, WhoAmW 93
Ricardo Garcia, Joaquin 1952- WhoWor 93
Ricardou, Jean 1932- BioIn 17
Ricart, Fred BioIn 17
Ricca, Gregory J. Law&B 92
Ricca, John A. Law&B 92
Ricca, John J., Jr. Law&B 92
Ricca, Sergio 1938- WhoUN 92
Riccardi, Anthony 1941- St&PR 93
Riccardi, Richard V. 1940- St&PR 93
Riccardi, Susan 1958- St&PR 93
Riccardo, Martin V. ScF&FL 92
Riccards, Diana Marie 1950- WhoAmW 93
Riccards, Michael Patrick 1944- WhoAm 92, WhoWrEP 92
Ricceri, Myra Jane 1957- WhoAmW 93

Ricchiuti, James *Law&B 92*
Ricci, Adelaide 1850-1871 *OxDcOp*
Ricci, Adolfo 1922- *WhoScE 91-3*
Ricci, Aldo *WhoScE 91-3*
Ricci, Christina *BioIn 17*
Ricci, Costante 1925- *WhoScE 91-3*
Ricci, David A. 1945- *St&PR 93*
Ricci, Douglas M. 1945- *St&PR 93*
Ricci, Egidio *OxDcOp*
Ricci, Federico 1809-1877 *Baker 92, OxDcOp*
Ricci, Francesco Paolo *WhoScE 91-3*
Ricci, Francisco 1608-1685 *BioIn 17*
Ricci, Franco Maria Marchese 1937- *WhoWor 93*
Ricci, Giovanni Mario 1929- *WhoWor 93*
Ricci, Luigi 1805-1859 *Baker 92, OxDcOp*
Ricci, Luigi 1852-1906 *OxDcOp*
Ricci, Michael J. *St&PR 93*
Ricci, Naomic C. 1942- *WhoWrEP 92*
Ricci, Nino *BioIn 17*
Ricci, Nino 1959- *ConAu 137, ConLC 70 [port], WhoCanL 92*
Ricci, Renato Angelo 1927- *WhoScE 91-3*
Ricci, Robert Ronald 1945- *WhoSSW 93*
Ricci, Ruggiero 1918- *Baker 92, WhoAm 92*
Ricci, Steven Peter 1960- *WhoWrEP 92*
Ricci, Thomas Michael 1937- *St&PR 93*
Ricci, Vittore 1923- *WhoWor 93*
Ricciardelli, Carl F. 1931- *WhoIns 93*
Ricciardi, Christine Secola 1963- *WhoE 93*
Ricciardi, Frank Anthony 1950- *WhoE 93*
Ricciardi, Lawrence R. *Law&B 92, WhoAm 92*
Ricciardi, Louis Michael 1959- *WhoE 93*
Ricciardi, Lucy Rae *St&PR 93*
Ricciardi, Patrice Joan 1956- *WhoAmW 93*
Ricciardi, Walter G. *Law&B 92*
Ricciarelli, Katia 1946- *Baker 92, IntDcOp [port], OxDcOp, WhoAm 92, WhoWor 93*
Riccinto, Patrick John, Jr. 1943- *WhoWrEP 92*
Riccio, David Anthony 1947- *WhoE 93*
Riccio, Jerome Michael 1955- *WhoWor 93*
Riccio, Joseph F. 1939- *St&PR 93*
Riccio, Nicholas D. 1947- *St&PR 93*
Riccio, Peter M. 1898-1990 *BioIn 17*
Ricciotti, Carlo c. 1681-1756 *Baker 92*
Riccitelli, Primo 1875-1941 *Baker 92*
Riccius, August Ferdinand 1819-1886 *Baker 92*
Riccius, Karl August 1830-1893 *Baker 92*
Ricciuti, Annette A. 1956- *St&PR 93*
Ricciuto, Ildo *Law&B 92*
Riccoboni, Marie-Jeanne 1714-1792 *BioIn 17*
Riccobono, Donna L. *Law&B 92*
Rice, Alan Harrison 1963- *WhoE 93*
Rice, Alice Hegan 1870-1942 *BioIn 17*
Rice, Anita Marie 1947- *St&PR 93*
Rice, Ann 1933- *WhoAm 92*
Rice, (Ethel) Ann 1933- *WhoWrEP 92*
Rice, Anne 1941- *Au&Arts 9 [port], BioIn 17, ScF&FL 92, WhoAm 92, WhoAmW 93, WhoWrEP 92*
Rice, Argyll Pryor *WhoAmW 93, WhoE 93*
Rice, Barbara Lynn 1955- *WhoAmW 93, WhoE 93, WhoWor 93*
Rice, Beatrice E. *AmWomPl*
Rice, Ben Herbert, III 1918- *WhoAm 92*
Rice, Beva E. *AmWomPl*
Rice, Bruce Clarence 1947- *St&PR 93*
Rice, Carolyn Frances *AmWomPl*
Rice, Carolyn J. 1952- *WhoWrEP 92*
Rice, Cecil Spring 1859-1918 *BioIn 17*
Rice, Charles Duncan 1942- *WhoAm 92, WhoE 93*
Rice, Charles E. *Law&B 92*
Rice, Charles Edward 1935- *St&PR 93, WhoAm 92*
Rice, Charles Edward 1936- *WhoSSW 93*
Rice, Charles Owen 1908- *BioIn 17*
Rice, Christopher George *WhoScE 91-1*
Rice, Clare I. 1918- *WhoAm 92*
Rice, Clark Hammond, Jr. 1932- *WhoAm 92*
Rice, Clive Maitland *WhoScE 91-1*
Rice, Clovita 1929- *WhoWrEP 92*
Rice, Condoleezza *AfrAmBi*
Rice, Condoleezza 1954- *BioIn 17, ConBIB 3 [port]*
Rice, Cyrus Norman 1939- *WhoSSW 93*
Rice, David Ainsworth 1940- *WhoAm 92*
Rice, David Eugene, Jr. 1916- *WhoAm 92, WhoE 93, WhoWor 93*
Rice, David R. 1947- *St&PR 93*
Rice, Denis Timlin 1932- *WhoAm 92, WhoWor 93*
Rice, Dennis K. 1939- *St&PR 93*
Rice, Dennis Keith 1939- *WhoAm 92*
Rice, Donald Blessing 1939- *WhoAm 92, WhoE 93*
Rice, Donald Lee 1938- *WhoWrEP 92*
Rice, Donald Sands 1940- *WhoAm 92*
Rice, Donnellda L. *Law&B 92*
Rice, Dorothy Pechman 1922- *WhoAm 92, WhoAmW 93*
Rice, Douglas 1964- *BioIn 17*
Rice, E. Blair, Jr. *St&PR 93*
Rice, Edmund Ignatius 1762-1844 *BioIn 17*
Rice, Edward Earl 1909- *WhoAm 92*
Rice, Elmer L. 1892-1967 *BioIn 17*
Rice, Elroy Leon 1917- *WhoSSW 93*
Rice, Elva M. *AmWomPl*
Rice, Emily Marie 1922- *WhoAmW 93*
Rice, Emmett John 1919- *BioIn 17*
Rice, Erling E. 1915- *St&PR 93*
Rice, Esme *DcChlFi*
Rice, Ethel M. *AmWomPl*
Rice, Ferill Jeane 1926- *WhoAmW 93*
Rice, Frank C. 1943- *St&PR 93*
Rice, Frank Joseph 1924- *WhoE 93*
Rice, Garry Stephen *Law&B 92*
Rice, Gene E. 1930- *St&PR 93*
Rice, Georgeanne Tolley 1959- *WhoAmW 93*
Rice, Glen Edward 1933- *St&PR 93, WhoAm 92*
Rice, Grantland 1880-1954 *JrnUS*
Rice, Greg 1916-1991 *BioIn 17*
Rice, Harold Israel 1929- *St&PR 93*
Rice, Harry Glen 1954- *WhoSSW 93*
Rice, Haynes 1932- *WhoAm 92*
Rice, Henry Hart d1992 *BioIn 17, NewYTBS 92 [port]*
Rice, Howard A. *ScF&FL 92*
Rice, J. Andrew 1953- *WhoSSW 93*
Rice, J.T. 1922- *St&PR 93*
Rice, Jack *St&PR 93*
Rice, Jack 1948- *St&PR 93*
Rice, Jacqueline Ann 1947- *WhoSSW 93*
Rice, James Anderson 1932- *St&PR 93*
Rice, James H. *Law&B 92*
Rice, James H. 1926- *St&PR 93*
Rice, James Robert 1940- *WhoAm 92*
Rice, Jean Ann 1932- *WhoAmW 93*
Rice, Jean E. *Law&B 92*
Rice, Jerry *BioIn 17*
Rice, Jerry Lee 1962- *WhoAm 92*
Rice, Jerry Mercer 1940- *WhoE 93*
Rice, John C. 1936- *St&PR 93*
Rice, John D. *Law&B 92*
Rice, John L. 1951- *St&PR 93*
Rice, John R. 1895-1980 *BioIn 17*
Rice, John Rischard 1934- *WhoAm 92*
Rice, John Thomas 1931- *WhoAm 92*
Rice, Joseph Albert 1924- *WhoAm 92*
Rice, Joseph J. 1949- *St&PR 93*
Rice, Joseph Lee, III 1932- *St&PR 93, WhoAm 92*
Rice, Joy Katharine 1939- *WhoAm 92*
Rice, Joyce 1945- *ConEn*
Rice, Julian Casavant 1924- *WhoAm 92*
Rice, Katharine McDowell *AmWomPl*
Rice, Kathleen Louise 1961- *WhoAmW 93*
Rice, Kathleen Marie 1960- *WhoAmW 93*
Rice, Kathryn Wells Taffy 1960- *WhoAmW 93*
Rice, Kathy Strickland 1947- *WhoSSW 93*
Rice, Kenneth Lloyd 1937- *WhoWor 93*
Rice, Kimberely Anne Furgason 1958- *WhoEmL 93*
Rice, Lacy I., Jr. 1931- *St&PR 93, WhoAm 92*
Rice, Leland 1940- *BioIn 17*
Rice, Leo C. 1928- *St&PR 93*
Rice, Lester 1927- *WhoAm 92*
Rice, Linda Johnson *BioIn 17, WhoAm 92, WhoAmW 93*
Rice, Lindsay J. 1954- *St&PR 93*
Rice, Liston M., Jr. 1927- *St&PR 93*
Rice, Lois Dickson 1933- *WhoAm 92, WhoAmW 93*
Rice, Luanne 1955- *ConAu 139*
Rice, Margaret Leona 1921- *WhoAmW 93*
Rice, Margaret Mary 1959- *WhoE 93*
Rice, Marilyn Grace 1962- *WhoAmW 93*
Rice, Marvin Samuel 1936- *St&PR 93*
Rice, Mary F. 1902-1991 *BioIn 17*
Rice, Mary Joan 1931- *WhoAmW 93*
Rice, Mattie Mae 1925- *WhoAmW 93*
Rice, Melanie Ailene 1957- *WhoAmW 93*
Rice, Melva Gene 1918- *WhoAmW 93*
Rice, Michael 1928- *ConAu 137*
Rice, Michael Lewis 1943- *WhoAm 92*
Rice, Mitchell F. 1948- *ConAu 138*
Rice, Monte Dean 1956- *WhoEmL 93, WhoSSW 93*
Rice, Norman 1943- *WhoAm 92*
Rice, Norman B. 1943- *AfrAmBi [port]*
Rice, Norman R. *BioIn 17*
Rice, Patricia Anne 1949- *WhoWrEP 92*
Rice, Patricia D. 1943- *WhoE 93*
Rice, Patricia M. *Law&B 92*
Rice, Patricia Wegmann 1943- *WhoSSW 93*
Rice, Paul Jackson 1938- *WhoE 93*
Rice, Peter *ScF&FL 92*
Rice, Peter S. *Law&B 92*
Rice, Phyllis Mather 1942- *WhoAm 92*
Rice, Ramona Gail 1950- *WhoEmL 93*
Rice, Rebecca 1899- *AmWomPl*
Rice, Richard Campbell 1933- *WhoWor 93*
Rice, Richard Lee 1919- *WhoAm 92*
Rice, Robert Marshall 1930- *WhoAm 92*
Rice, Robert O. *Law&B 92*
Rice, Roger Douglas 1921- *WhoAm 92*
Rice, Ronald James 1944- *WhoSSW 93*
Rice, Sarah Bouchelle Shepard 1920- *WhoAmW 93*
Rice, Sharon Margaret 1943- *WhoAmW 93*
Rice, Sidney Ellis 1928- *St&PR 93*
Rice, Stanley Matthew 1927- *St&PR 93*
Rice, Stanley Travis, Jr. 1942- *WhoAm 92*
Rice, Stephen Landon 1941- *WhoAm 92, WhoSSW 93*
Rice, Steven Dale 1947- *WhoWor 93*
Rice, Stuart Alan 1932- *WhoAm 92*
Rice, Sue Ann 1934- *WhoAmW 93*
Rice, T. Maurice 1939- *WhoScE 91-4*
Rice, Ted 1932- *ConEn*
Rice, Timothy George *Law&B 92*
Rice, Timothy Miles Bindon 1944- *WhoWor 93*
Rice, Vernon R. *Law&B 92*
Rice, Victor 1941- *St&PR 93*
Rice, Victor Albert 1941- *WhoAm 92*
Rice, Walter Herbert 1937- *WhoAm 92*
Rice, Willard K. d1992 *BioIn 17*
Rice, William A. 1919- *St&PR 93*
Rice, William C. *St&PR 93*
Rice, William C. 1955- *WhoWrEP 92*
Rice, William D. 1934- *St&PR 93*
Rice, William Dent 1934- *WhoAm 92*
Rice, William Edward 1938- *WhoAm 92*
Rice, William Roy *Law&B 92*
Rice, Wm. Thomas 1912- *St&PR 93*
Riceman, John Patrick 1941- *St&PR 93*
Rice-Marko, Debbie *BioIn 17*
Rice-Ritchie, Sharon Marie 1953- *WhoAmW 93*
Rich, Adam *BioIn 17*
Rich, Adrienne *BioIn 17*
Rich, Adrienne 1929- *AmWomWr 92, ConLC 73 [port], MagSAmL [port], PoeCrit 5 [port], WhoAm 92, WhoWrEP 92*
Rich, Alan 1924- *Baker 92, WhoAm 92, WhoWrEP 92*
Rich, Albert Clark 1950- *WhoSSW 93, WhoWor 93*
Rich, Alexander 1924- *WhoAm 92*
Rich, Arthur 1937-1990 *BioIn 17*
Rich, Arthur George 1910- *WhoWor 93*
Rich, Arthur Gilbert 1936- *WhoE 93*
Rich, Arthur Lowndes 1905- *WhoAm 92*
Rich, Ben Arthur 1947- *WhoAm 92*
Rich, Ben Robert 1925- *BioIn 17, St&PR 93*
Rich, Beverly Cook 1924- *St&PR 93*
Rich, Buddy 1917-1987 *Baker 92, BioIn 17*
Rich, Charles Allan 1932- *WhoAm 92*
Rich, Charles Anthony 1951- *WhoWor 93*
Rich, Charlie 1932- *Baker 92*
Rich, Christine Estelle 1947- *WhoWrEP 92*
Rich, Coleman Reynolds 1954- *St&PR 93*
Rich, Craig R. *Law&B 92*
Rich, David A. *Law&B 92*
Rich, David A. 1944- *St&PR 93*
Rich, David Lowell 1920- *MiSFD 9*
Rich, David Thayer *Law&B 92*
Rich, Doris L. 1920- *ConAu 138*
Rich, Eric 1921- *WhoAm 92*
Rich, Frances Luther 1910- *WhoAm 92*
Rich, Frank *BioIn 17*
Rich, Frank D. d1990 *BioIn 17*
Rich, Frank Hart 1949- *WhoAm 92, WhoE 93, WhoWrEP 92*
Rich, Frederick Walter 1949- *St&PR 93*
Rich, George S. *St&PR 93*
Rich, Giles Sutherland 1904- *CngDr 91, WhoAm 92*
Rich, Harry E. 1940- *St&PR 93, WhoAm 92*
Rich, Harry Louis 1917- *WhoE 93*
Rich, Harry P. 1942- *St&PR 93*
Rich, Herbert 1915- *WhoE 93*
Rich, Hershel Maurice 1925- *WhoSSW 93*
Rich, Irene 1891-1988 *SweetSg B*
Rich, James A. *Law&B 92*
Rich, James Eric Antony 1929- *WhoAm 92*
Rich, James Joseph 1935- *St&PR 93*
Rich, Janet Lowry *Law&B 92*
Rich, Jimmy Ray 1950- *WhoSSW 93*
Rich, John 1691?-1761 *OxDcOp*
Rich, John 1925- *MiSFD 9, WhoAm 92*
Rich, John Krause 1957- *WhoE 93*
Rich, John Lewis *Law&B 92*
Rich, John Martin 1931- *WhoAm 92*
Rich, John Stanley 1943- *WhoSSW 93*
Rich, Jonathan F. *Law&B 92*
Rich, Joseph T. *Law&B 92*
Rich, Jude T. 1943- *WhoAm 92*
Rich, Kenneth Malcolm 1946- *WhoAm 92, WhoE 93, WhoEmL 93*
Rich, Lee *WhoAm 92*
Rich, Leonard Geary 1925- *St&PR 93*
Rich, Louise Dickinson 1903- *DcAmChF 1960*
Rich, Louise Dickinson 1903-1991 *BioIn 17*
Rich, Marc *BioIn 17*
Rich, Mark 1958- *ScF&FL 92*
Rich, Mark David 1958- *WhoWrEP 92*
Rich, Mary C. *Law&B 92*
Rich, Matty *BioIn 17, MiSFD 9*
Rich, Michael David 1953- *WhoAm 92*
Rich, Michael Joseph 1945- *WhoAm 92*
Rich, Michael L. 1942- *St&PR 93*
Rich, Milton 1913- *WhoE 93*
Rich, Mitchell Jeffrey 1954- *WhoE 93*
Rich, Patrick J.J. 1931- *St&PR 93*
Rich, Paul A. *Law&B 92*
Rich, Paul John 1938- *WhoWor 93*
Rich, Peter Hamilton 1939- *WhoE 93*
Rich, Peter R. *Law&B 92*
Rich, Philip Dewey 1940- *WhoE 93*
Rich, Phyllis Jeanne 1935- *WhoAmW 93*
Rich, Raphael Z. 1929- *WhoWor 93*
Rich, Richard *MiSFD 9*
Rich, Robert Bruce 1949- *WhoAm 92*
Rich, Robert E. *BioIn 17*
Rich, Robert E., Jr. 1941- *WhoAm 92*
Rich, Robert Edward 1913- *WhoAm 92*
Rich, Robert Edward 1944- *WhoAm 92*
Rich, Robert F. *WhoAm 92*
Rich, Robert Graham, Jr. 1930- *WhoAm 92*
Rich, Robert Peter 1919- *WhoE 93*
Rich, Robert Regier 1941- *WhoAm 92, WhoSSW 93, WhoWor 93*
Rich, Robert Stephen 1938- *WhoAm 92*
Rich, Roger Lee, Jr. 1934- *WhoAm 92*
Rich, Rolla Ross 1945- *WhoWor 93*
Rich, Rosan 1946- *WhoAmW 93*
Rich, S. Judith *St&PR 93, WhoAm 92, WhoAmW 93*
Rich, Sally K. *Law&B 92*
Rich, Sandra L. *Law&B 92*
Rich, Stephen 1954- *ScF&FL 92*
Rich, Steven F. 1960- *St&PR 93*
Rich, Susan Beth 1959- *WhoAmW 93*
Rich, Theodore 1932- *St&PR 93*
Rich, Thomas Hurblut 1946- *WhoAm 92*
Rich, Tracy L. *Law&B 92*
Rich, Tracy Shannon *Law&B 92*
Rich, Vivian 1893-1957 *SweetSg A [port]*
Rich, Walter George *BioIn 17*
Rich, Walter George 1946- *St&PR 93, WhoE 93*
Rich, Wayne Adrian 1912- *WhoWor 93*
Rich, William W.K. 1939- *St&PR 93*
Rich, Willis Frank, Jr. 1919- *WhoAm 92*
Richadson, William Cahill, Jr. 1936- *St&PR 93*
Richafort, Jean c. 1480-c. 1547 *Baker 92*
Richard, I 1157-1199 *HarEnMi*
Richard, I, King of England 1157-1199 *BioIn 17*
Richard, III 1452-1485 *HarEnMi*
Richard, III, King of England 1452-1485 *BioIn 17*
Richard, Adrienne 1921- *DcAmChF 1960*
Richard, Alain 1939- *WhoScE 91-2*
Richard, Alfred Leon 1860-1911 *BioIn 17*
Richard, Alice *WhoWrEP 92*
Richard, B. Loynd *WhoAm 92*
Richard, Betti 1916- *WhoAm 92*
Richard, David A. 1945- *St&PR 93*
Richard, Denis G. *Law&B 92*
Richard, Edward H. 1937- *St&PR 93, WhoAm 92*
Richard, Ellen 1957- *WhoAmW 93*
Richard, Firmine *BioIn 17*
Richard, Frederic Jean 1945- *WhoUN 92*
Richard, Frederick Hugh 1938- *WhoSSW 93*
Richard, George Victor 1956- *WhoSSW 93*
Richard, Gregory B. *St&PR 93*
Richard, Guy 1946- *St&PR 93*
Richard, Hubert M.J. 1938- *WhoScE 91-2*
Richard, James Rodney 1950- *BiDAMSp 1989*
Richard, Jean *St&PR 93*
Richard, John Benard 1932- *WhoAm 92*
Richard, Keith 1943- *Baker 92*
Richard, Marc *WhoScE 91-2*
Richard, Mark M. 1939- *WhoAm 92*
Richard, Michel Paul 1933- *WhoWrEP 92*
Richard, Neil M. 1925- *St&PR 93*
Richard, Oliver G., III 1952- *St&PR 93*
Richard, Philippe 1937- *WhoScE 91-2*
Richard, Pierre 1924- *WhoWor 93*
Richard, Pierre 1956- *St&PR 93*
Richard, Ralph Stephenson 1919- *St&PR 93*
Richard, Ralph Zachary *WhoSSW 93*
Richard, Rita 1928- *St&PR 93*
Richard, Sandra Clayton *WhoAmW 93, WhoSSW 93, WhoWor 93*
Richard, Scott F. 1946- *WhoAm 92*
Richard, Shirley A. 1947- *St&PR 93*
Richard, Susan Mathis 1949- *WhoAm 92*
Richard, Virginia Rynne 1943- *WhoE 93*

Richard, Warren *Law&B 92*
Richard, Yves *DcCPCAm*
Richard, Zachary 1950- *ConMus 9 [port]*
Richardi, Ralph Leonard 1947- *WhoAm 92*
Richard Lionheart, I 1157-1199 *OxDcByz*
Richards, Aleta Williams 1965- *WhoAmW 93*
Richards, Ann *BioIn 17*
Richards, Ann W. *NewYTBS 92 [port]*
Richards, Ann Willis 1933- *WhoAm 92, WhoAmW 93, WhoSSW 93*
Richards, Anthony Frank *WhoScE 91-1*
Richards, Arthur L. 1907-1991 *BioIn 17*
Richards, Arthur Mark 1955- *WhoWor 93*
Richards, Arthur V. 1939- *St&PR 93*
Richards, Ashby T., Jr. *Law&B 92*
Richards, Benjamin Franklin, Jr. 1941- *WhoE 93*
Richards, Benjamin T., Jr. *Law&B 92*
Richards, Bernard 1927- *St&PR 93, WhoAm 92*
Richards, Bill 1936- *WhoAm 92*
Richards, (Henry) Brinley 1817-1885 *Baker 92*
Richards, Bruce S. 1955- *St&PR 93*
Richards, Bruce Steven *Law&B 92*
Richards, Bryan Edward *WhoScE 91-1*
Richards, Burt 1930- *WhoAm 92*
Richards, Carl Steven 1949- *WhoE 93*
Richards, Carmeleete A. 1948- *WhoAmW 93*
Richards, Caroline *AmWomPl*
Richards, Carolyn Baxter 1926- *WhoWrEP 92*
Richards, Cecilia Dianne 1954- *WhoE 93*
Richards, Charlene Anna 1963- *WhoAmW 93*
Richards, Charles A. 1941- *St&PR 93*
Richards, Charles T. 1913- *St&PR 93*
Richards, Christine-Anne *BioIn 17*
Richards, Christine P. *Law&B 92*
Richards, Curtis *ScF&FL 92*
Richards, Curtis Vance 1932- *WhoSSW 93*
Richards, Cyndi *WhoWrEP 92*
Richards, Daniel J. 1961- *WhoSSW 93*
Richards, Darrie Hewitt 1921- *WhoWor 93*
Richards, David Adams 1950- *WhoCanL 92*
Richards, David Alan 1945- *WhoAm 92, WhoWor 93*
Richards, David George *Law&B 92*
Richards, David Gleyre 1935- *WhoAm 92*
Richards, David John 1948- *St&PR 93, WhoAm 92*
Richards, David Kimball 1939- *WhoAm 92*
Richards, David Zehner 1935- *St&PR 93*
Richards, Denzil Leonard *WhoScE 91-1*
Richards, Diana Lyn 1944- *WhoAmW 93*
Richards, Diane R. 1963- *WhoAmW 93*
Richards, Dick 1936- *MiSFD 9*
Richards, Donald *BioIn 17*
Richards, Donald C. 1932- *St&PR 93*
Richards, Doris Jean 1937- *St&PR 93*
Richards, Douglas Robert 1959- *WhoSSW 93*
Richards, E.J. *WhoScE 91-1*
Richards, Edgar Lester 1942- *WhoAm 92*
Richards, Edward *DcCPCAm*
Richards, Edward A. 1946- *St&PR 93*
Richards, Edward T. 1944- *St&PR 93*
Richards, Elfyn John 1914- *WhoWor 93*
Richards, Elizabeth Glazier 1959- *WhoWrEP 92*
Richards, Ellen Henrietta Swallow 1842-1911 *BioIn 17*
Richards, Evan *ScF&FL 92*
Richards, Fred Tracy 1914- *St&PR 93, WhoAm 92*
Richards, Frederic Middlebrook 1925- *WhoAm 92*
Richards, Gail Arbing 1939- *St&PR 93*
Richards, Gale Lee 1918- *WhoAm 92*
Richards, Gary Paul 1950- *WhoSSW 93*
Richards, George Leroy 1926- *St&PR 93*
Richards, George R. 1932- *St&PR 93*
Richards, George Thomas 1932- *WhoE 93*
Richards, George Whitfield, III 1941- *St&PR 93, WhoAm 92, WhoE 93*
Richards, Gerald A. 1940- *St&PR 93*
Richards, Gilbert 1927- *St&PR 93*
Richards, Gregory B. *Law&B 92, ScF&FL 92*
Richards, Guy 1905-1979 *ScF&FL 92*
Richards, H. Clive *MiSFD 9*
Richards, H. Leroy *Law&B 92*
Richards, Harold Linn 1931- *WhoSSW 93*
Richards, Herbert East 1919- *WhoAm 92*
Richards, Hilda 1936- *WhoAm 92, WhoE 93*
Richards, Holly Ann 1951- *WhoAmW 93*
Richards, Hugh Taylor 1918- *WhoAm 92, WhoWor 93*
Richards, I.A. 1893-1979 *BioIn 17, BritWr S2*
Richards, Irmagarde *AmWomPl*
Richards, Ivor James *WhoScE 91-1*
Richards, J.H. *WhoScE 91-1*
Richards, Jack William *Law&B 92*
Richards, James C. 1941- *St&PR 93*
Richards, James Edward 1952- *WhoSSW 93*
Richards, James H. 1943- *St&PR 93*
Richards, James John 1941- *WhoE 93*
Richards, James R. 1933- *WhoAm 92*
Richards, Janis C. 1960- *St&PR 93*
Richards, Jasmine Doreen 1942- *WhoAmW 93*
Richards, Jeanette P. 1924- *WhoAm 92*
Richards, Jeanne Herron 1923- *WhoAm 92*
Richards, Jeff 1944- *WhoWrEP 92*
Richards, Jeffrey Hamilton 1948- *WhoSSW 93*
Richards, Jeffrey Iven 1955- *WhoSSW 93*
Richards, Jeffrey Owen 1949- *WhoWor 93*
Richards, Jerrold Allen 1949- *WhoWrEP 92*
Richards, Jerry Lee 1939- *WhoAm 92*
Richards, Joe 1909-1992 *BioIn 17, ConAu 136*
Richards, Joel 1937- *ScF&FL 92*
Richards, John F. 1947- *St&PR 93*
Richards, John Irwyn 1944- *WhoUN 92*
Richards, John L.G. 1941- *St&PR 93*
Richards, John M. 1937- *WhoAm 92*
Richards, John R. 1920- *St&PR 93*
Richards, John Stewart 1892-1979 *BioIn 17*
Richards, John William, Jr. 1950- *WhoSSW 93, WhoWor 93*
Richards, Jonathan *ScF&FL 92*
Richards, Judith Olch 1947- *WhoE 93*
Richards, Keith 1943- *Baker 92, WhoAm 92*
Richards, Kenneth J. 1932- *St&PR 93*
Richards, LaClaire Lissetta Jones *WhoAmW 93, WhoWor 93*
Richards, Larry *BioIn 17*
Richards, Laura E(lizabeth Howe) 1850-1943 *ConAu 137, MajAI [port]*
Richards, Laura Elizabeth Howe 1850-1943 *AmWomPl*
Richards, Leonard Martin 1935- *St&PR 93, WhoSSW 93*
Richards, Lisle Frederick 1909- *WhoAm 92*
Richards, Lloyd *MiSFD 9*
Richards, Lloyd D. *Law&B 92*
Richards, Lloyd G. *BioIn 17*
Richards, Lloyd George *WhoAm 92*
Richards, Louise Sutermeister 1949- *WhoE 93*
Richards, Lynn 1949- *WhoAmW 93*
Richards, Mark Danner 1919- *St&PR 93*
Richards, Marta Alison 1952- *WhoSSW 93*
Richards, Martin 1932- *ConTFT 10*
Richards, Mary Fallon 1920- *WhoWrEP 92*
Richards, Mary Hinrichs 1954- *WhoAmW 93*
Richards, Mary Lea Johnson 1926-1990 *BioIn 17*
Richards, Max De Voe 1923- *WhoAm 92*
Richards, Merlon Foss 1920- *WhoAm 92*
Richards, Nancy Jill Schanfald 1961- *WhoAmW 93*
Richards, Nelson Glasgow 1924- *WhoSSW 93*
Richards, Nicki *BioIn 17*
Richards, Nita 1939- *WhoSSW 93*
Richards, Norman Blanchard 1924- *WhoAm 92*
Richards, Pamela Motter 1950- *WhoSSW 93*
Richards, Pamela Spence 1941- *WhoE 93*
Richards, Patricia Anne 1942- *WhoAmW 93*
Richards, Patricia N. 1958- *WhoAmW 93*
Richards, Paul *ScF&FL 92*
Richards, Paul E. *Law&B 92*
Richards, Paul Granston 1943- *WhoAm 92, WhoE 93*
Richards, Paul Linford 1934- *WhoAm 92*
Richards, Paul Rapier 1908-1986 *BiDAMSp 1989*
Richards, Paul William 1964- *WhoE 93*
Richards, Philip W. 1948- *St&PR 93*
Richards, Ramona Pope 1957- *WhoWrEP 92*
Richards, Raymond L. *WhoScE 91-1*
Richards, Reuben Francis 1929- *St&PR 93, WhoAm 92, WhoE 93*
Richards, Rhoda Root Wagner 1917- *WhoAmW 93, WhoE 93*
Richards, Richard 1932- *PolPar*
Richards, Richard Davison 1927- *WhoAm 92*
Richards, Riley Harry 1912- *WhoAm 92*
Richards, Robert Charles 1941- *WhoSSW 93*
Richards, Robert D. 1928- *St&PR 93*
Richards, Robert E. 1955- *St&PR 93*
Richards, Robert H.E. 1937- *St&PR 93*
Richards, Robert Leroy 1920- *WhoAm 92*
Richards, Robert Wadsworth 1921- *WhoAm 92*
Richards, Roger T. 1947- *St&PR 93*
Richards, Roger Thomas 1942- *WhoE 93, WhoWor 93*
Richards, Ross *ScF&FL 92*
Richards, Roy John 1944- *WhoWor 93*
Richards, Rupert Merrick 1923- *St&PR 93*
Richards, Sean *ScF&FL 92*
Richards, Shirley Mastin 1927- *WhoAmW 93*
Richards, Stanford Harvey 1932- *WhoAm 92*
Richards, Stanley Harold 1922- *St&PR 93*
Richards, Stanley K. *Law&B 92*
Richards, Stephen C. 1914- *St&PR 93*
Richards, Stephen F. 1948- *St&PR 93*
Richards, Stephen I. 1949- *St&PR 93*
Richards, Stephen M.G. *Law&B 92*
Richards, Susan Bridwell 1948- *WhoAmW 93*
Richards, Susan R. 1948- *WhoAmW 93*
Richards, Thomas Carl 1930- *WhoAm 92*
Richards, Thomas Lombard 1934- *St&PR 93*
Richards, Tony *ScF&FL 92*
Richards, Vicki *ScF&FL 92*
Richards, Victor 1918- *WhoAm 92*
Richards, Vincent Philip Haslewood 1933- *WhoAm 92*
Richards, Walter DuBois 1907- *WhoAm 92*
Richards, Wanda Jamie 1930- *WhoAmW 93*
Richards, Ward D. *Law&B 92*
Richards, William *BioIn 17*
Richards, William Alford 1849-1912 *BioIn 17*
Richards, William George 1920- *WhoSSW 93*
Richards, William J. 1927- *St&PR 93*
Richards, William Joseph 1936- *WhoSSW 93*
Richardson, Abby Sage 1837-1900 *AmWomPl*
Richardson, Abram Harding 1855-1931 *BiDAMSp 1989*
Richardson, Alan Douglas 1942- *WhoWor 93*
Richardson, Allyn St. Clair 1918- *WhoE 93*
Richardson, Andrew *WhoScE 91-1*
Richardson, Ann Bishop 1940- *WhoAm 92*
Richardson, Ann Marie 1952- *WhoAmW 93*
Richardson, Anna Steese Sausser 1865-1949 *AmWomPl*
Richardson, Artemas Partridge 1918- *WhoAm 92*
Richardson, Arthur Jerold 1938- *WhoSSW 93*
Richardson, Barbara Kathryn 1936- *WhoWor 93*
Richardson, Barbara Warren 1953- *WhoAmW 93*
Richardson, Ben M. *Law&B 92*
Richardson, Ben M. 1928- *St&PR 93*
Richardson, Betty 1935- *ScF&FL 92*
Richardson, Betty Joyce 1935- *WhoWrEP 92*
Richardson, Betty Kehl 1938- *WhoAmW 93*
Richardson, Bill 1947- *CngDr 91*
Richardson, Brenda Elouise 1955- *WhoAmW 93*
Richardson, Bryan D. *St&PR 93*
Richardson, C. Leonard 1926- *St&PR 93*
Richardson, Campbell 1930- *WhoAm 92*
Richardson, Carl C., Jr. 1941- *St&PR 93*
Richardson, Carol Elliott *St&PR 93*
Richardson, Cecil Antonio 1928-1991 *ConAu 136*
Richardson, Charles Clifton 1935- *WhoAm 92*
Richardson, Charles Marsh 1925- *WhoE 93*
Richardson, Charles P. 1946- *St&PR 93*
Richardson, Charles Ray 1964- *WhoSSW 93*
Richardson, Chester A. *Law&B 92*
Richardson, Clinton Dennis 1949- *WhoSSW 93*
Richardson, Clyta Faith 1915- *WhoAm 92*
Richardson, D. Lyneir *Law&B 92*
Richardson, Dana Theodore 1949- *St&PR 93*
Richardson, Daniel B. 1928- *St&PR 93*
Richardson, Daniel Charles 1937- *WhoAm 92*
Richardson, Darrell C. 1918- *ScF&FL 92*
Richardson, David Bacon 1916- *WhoE 93*
Richardson, David Horsfall Stuart 1942- *WhoScE 91-3*
Richardson, David I. 1943- *St&PR 93*
Richardson, David John 1943- *WhoAm 92*
Richardson, David Walthall 1925- *WhoAm 92*
Richardson, David William 1948- *WhoE 93*
Richardson, Davis Bates 1929- *St&PR 93*
Richardson, Dean Eugene 1927- *St&PR 93, WhoAm 92*
Richardson, Deanna Ruth 1956- *WhoAmW 93*
Richardson, Dee H. *Law&B 92*
Richardson, Delroy Mccoy 1938- *St&PR 93*
Richardson, Dennis Samuel 1950- *WhoSSW 93*
Richardson, Desmond *BioIn 17*
Richardson, Don Orland 1934- *WhoSSW 93*
Richardson, Don Ramon 1938- *WhoSSW 93*
Richardson, Donald Charles 1937- *WhoWor 93*
Richardson, Donald Edward 1931- *WhoAm 92*
Richardson, Dorsie Gillis *AmWomPl*
Richardson, Douglas Fielding 1929- *WhoAm 92*
Richardson, Earl Stanford *AfrAmBi [port]*
Richardson, Ed 1841- *BioIn 17*
Richardson, Edward Ewing 1941- *St&PR 93*
Richardson, Edward J. *St&PR 93*
Richardson, Edward James 1954- *WhoAm 92*
Richardson, Elizabeth Ann 1943- *WhoSSW 93*
Richardson, Elliot Lee 1920- *WhoAm 92*
Richardson, Elsie Helen 1918- *WhoAmW 93*
Richardson, Emilie White *WhoSSW 93*
Richardson, Esther Harbage Cole 1894- *WhoAm 92*
Richardson, Evelyn H. 1929- *St&PR 93*
Richardson, Everett Vern 1924- *WhoAm 92*
Richardson, F. C. 1936- *WhoAm 92, WhoE 93*
Richardson, Faye Collins 1946- *WhoAmW 93*
Richardson, Floyd Don 1932- *WhoSSW 93*
Richardson, Francis Joseph, III 1943- *WhoSSW 93*
Richardson, Frank H. 1933- *St&PR 93, WhoAm 92, WhoSSW 93, WhoWor 93*
Richardson, Frank Kellogg 1914- *WhoAm 92*
Richardson, Frederick Joseph 1926- *St&PR 93*
Richardson, Gail Marguerite 1955- *WhoAmW 93*
Richardson, Gary Albert 1949- *WhoSSW 93*
Richardson, Geoffrey *WhoScE 91-1*
Richardson, George *Law&B 92*
Richardson, George T. 1924- *St&PR 93*
Richardson, Gilbert Payton, Sr. 1926- *WhoAm 92*
Richardson, Gordon Banning 1937- *WhoWor 93*
Richardson, Grace *AmWomPl*
Richardson, Graham 1949- *WhoAsAP 91*
Richardson, Graham Frederick 1949- *WhoWor 93*
Richardson, H. Neil 1916-1988 *BioIn 17*
Richardson, Harold Dean 1934- *WhoSSW 93*
Richardson, Harriett Powell 1958- *WhoSSW 93*
Richardson, Harry A., Jr. 1929- *St&PR 93*
Richardson, Harry Van Buren 1901- *AfrAmBi*
Richardson, Helen *BioIn 17*
Richardson, Henry Handel 1870-1946 *IntLitE*
Richardson, Herbert Heath 1930- *WhoAm 92, WhoSSW 93*
Richardson, Howard L. 1909- *St&PR 93*
Richardson, Ian William 1934- *WhoWor 93*
Richardson, Isla Paschal 1886- *AmWomPl*
Richardson, James 1950- *WhoWrEP 92*
Richardson, James A. 1933- *WhoIns 93*
Richardson, James Abner, III 1908- *WhoAm 92*
Richardson, James Bitting, Jr. 1937- *St&PR 93*
Richardson, James Fairgrieve 1940- *St&PR 93, WhoIns 93*
Richardson, James Robert 1946- *WhoWrEP 92*
Richardson, James T. 1941- *ConAu 139*
Richardson, Jane Shelby 1941- *WhoAm 92*
Richardson, Jasper Edgar 1922- *WhoSSW 93*
Richardson, Jean *ScF&FL 92*
Richardson, Jean 1943- *WhoE 93*

Richardson, Jean Brooks 1940- *WhoSSW 93*
Richardson, Jenny *BioIn 17*
Richardson, Jerome J. 1936- *BioIn 17*
Richardson, Jerome Johnson 1936- *St&PR 93, WhoAm 92, WhoSSW 93*
Richardson, Jerry W. 1945- *St&PR 93*
Richardson, Joe William 1966- *WhoSSW 93*
Richardson, Joel Glenn 1955- *WhoSSW 93*
Richardson, John 1796-1852 *BioIn 17*
Richardson, John 1921- *WhoAm 92*
Richardson, John 1924- *BioIn 17*
Richardson, John Carroll 1932- *WhoAm 92*
Richardson, John E. 1933- *St&PR 93*
Richardson, John Francis *WhoScE 91-1*
Richardson, John Henry, Jr. 1948- *WhoSSW 93*
Richardson, John J. *Law&B 92*
Richardson, John Joseph 1926- *St&PR 93*
Richardson, John M. 1941- *St&PR 93*
Richardson, John Thomas 1923- *WhoAm 92*
Richardson, John Vinson, Jr. 1949- *WhoAm 92*
Richardson, Jonathan Lynde 1935- *WhoE 93*
Richardson, Joseph Blancet 1936- *WhoE 93, WhoWor 93*
Richardson, Joseph Blancet 1963- *WhoE 93*
Richardson, Joseph E., II 1929- *St&PR 93*
Richardson, Joseph Gerald 1923- *WhoAm 92*
Richardson, Josephine *ScF&FL 92*
Richardson, K. Scott 1951- *WhoEmL 93, WhoSSW 93, WhoWor 93*
Richardson, Kathryn *BioIn 17*
Richardson, Keith Edward 1947- *WhoWor 93*
Richardson, Ken Edgar 1952- *WhoWrEP 92*
Richardson, Kendrick Eugene 1965- *WhoSSW 93*
Richardson, Kevan Anthony 1958- *WhoWor 93*
Richardson, Larie K. 1941- *St&PR 93*
Richardson, Laurel Walum 1938- *WhoAm 92*
Richardson, Lawrence, Jr. 1920- *WhoAm 92*
Richardson, Legrand 1923- *St&PR 93*
Richardson, Linda *Law&B 92*
Richardson, Linda 1944- *ScF&FL 92*
Richardson, Linda F. 1951- *WhoWrEP 92*
Richardson, Luns C. *AfrAmBi [port]*
Richardson, Lunsford, Jr. 1924- *St&PR 93*
Richardson, Lynford M. 1932- *WhoIns 93*
Richardson, Malcolm Charles *WhoScE 91-1*
Richardson, Maria Renna *Law&B 92*
Richardson, Marian Evis Hartman 1941- *WhoAmW 93*
Richardson, Mark *MiSFD 9*
Richardson, Mark Edwin, III *Law&B 92*
Richardson, Martha 1917- *WhoAmW 93*
Richardson, Mary Elisabeth 1947- *WhoSSW 93*
Richardson, Mary Raleigh 1885?-1961 *BioIn 17*
Richardson, Melvin Orde Wingate *WhoScE 91-1*
Richardson, Michael *Law&B 92*
Richardson, Michael 1946- *ScF&FL 92*
Richardson, Michael G. 1940- *St&PR 93*
Richardson, Midge Turk 1930- *WhoAm 92, WhoE 93, WhoWrEP 92*
Richardson, Mildred Tourtillott 1907- *WhoAmW 93*
Richardson, Miles Edward 1932- *WhoSSW 93*
Richardson, Natasha *BioIn 17*
Richardson, Natasha Jane 1963- *WhoAm 92*
Richardson, Neville Vincent *WhoScE 91-1*
Richardson, Pamela Diane 1956- *WhoAmW 93*
Richardson, Paula Noel 1962- *WhoAmW 93*
Richardson, Peter *MiSFD 9*
Richardson, Peter Charles *Law&B 92*
Richardson, Polly Renee 1955- *WhoAmW 93*
Richardson, Ralph 1902-1983 *IntDcF 2-3 [port]*
Richardson, Ralph Ernest 1927- *WhoAm 92*
Richardson, Ralph H. *Law&B 92*
Richardson, Raymond J. 1946- *St&PR 93*
Richardson, Rexford Joseph 1955- *WhoSSW 93*
Richardson, Richard Judson 1935- *WhoAm 92*
Richardson, Richard Thomas 1933- *WhoAm 92, WhoWor 93*
Richardson, Robert Alvin 1951- *WhoSSW 93*
Richardson, Robert C. 1882-1954 *HarEnMi*
Richardson, Robert Charlwood, III 1918- *WhoAm 92*
Richardson, Robert Coleman 1937- *WhoAm 92*
Richardson, Robert Dale, Jr. 1934- *WhoAm 92*
Richardson, Robert Jules 1925- *WhoSSW 93*
Richardson, Robert S. 1902-1981 *ScF&FL 92*
Richardson, Robert W. 1939- *St&PR 93*
Richardson, Robert William 1935- *WhoAm 92*
Richardson, Roger K. 1909- *St&PR 93*
Richardson, Ronald A. 1943- *St&PR 93*
Richardson, Ronald James 1946- *St&PR 93*
Richardson, Rosemary *Law&B 92*
Richardson, Ross Frederick 1928- *WhoAm 92*
Richardson, Rudy James 1945- *WhoAm 92*
Richardson, Ruth *BioIn 17*
Richardson, Ruth 1951- *ConAu 136*
Richardson, Ruth Greene 1926- *WhoE 93*
Richardson, Ruth Margaret 1950- *WhoAsAP 91*
Richardson, Samuel 1689-1761 *MagSWL [port], WorLitC [port]*
Richardson, Samuel David 1942- *WhoE 93*
Richardson, Sandra Kay 1959- *WhoAmW 93*
Richardson, Sheryl Rose 1948- *WhoAmW 93*
Richardson, Shirley Emma 1925- *WhoAmW 93*
Richardson, Shirley Maxine 1931- *WhoAmW 93*
Richardson, Sylvia Onesti 1920- *WhoAm 92*
Richardson, Terry *Law&B 92*
Richardson, Thomas Legh 1941- *WhoUN 92*
Richardson, Tom 1948- *WhoEmL 93*
Richardson, Tony *BioIn 17, ConAu 136*
Richardson, Tony 1928-1991 *AnObit 1991, CurBio 92N, MiSFD 9N*
Richardson, Walter John 1926- *WhoAm 92*
Richardson, Willard 1802-1875 *JrnUS*
Richardson, William Allen 1959- *WhoSSW 93*
Richardson, William B. 1947- *HispAmA [port]*
Richardson, William Blaine 1947- *WhoAm 92*
Richardson, William Carlton 1927- *St&PR 93*
Richardson, William Charles 1943- *WhoSSW 93*
Richardson, William Chase 1940- *WhoAm 92, WhoE 93*
Richardson, William J. 1920- *ScF&FL 92*
Richardson, William M. 1934- *St&PR 93*
Richardson, William Wightman, III 1928- *WhoSSW 93*
Richardson, William Winfree, III 1939- *WhoSSW 93*
Richardson, Willis 1889-1977 *BioIn 17*
Richardson-Bourke, Christina 1958- *WhoAmW 93*
Richards-Wright, Genevieve Mercedes *WhoE 93*
Richard, the Lion Heart 1157-1199 *BioIn 17*
Richarme, Michael Thomas 1954- *WhoSSW 93*
Richart, Frank Edwin, Jr. 1918- *WhoAm 92*
Richart, Gerald R. 1947- *St&PR 93*
Richart, John Douglas 1947- *WhoAm 92, WhoE 93*
Richberg, John Eugene, III 1958- *WhoSSW 93*
Richbourg, John d1986 *SoulM*
Riche, Dominique 1946- *WhoWor 93*
Richebourg, J. Ron *Law&B 92*
Richefield, Genevieve *AmWomPl*
Richeimer, Mary Jane 1913- *WhoAmW 93*
Richel, Alan Lewis 1950- *WhoEmL 93*
Richel, Victor M. 1938- *St&PR 93*
Richelieu, Cardinal, duc de 1585-1642 *BioIn 17*
Richelieu, Armand Jean du Plessis, Cardinal and Duke of 1585-1642 *HarEnMi*
Richelson, Geraldine 1922- *ScF&FL 92*
Richelson, Paul William 1939- *WhoAm 92*
Richemont, Artur de Bretagne, Count of 1393-1458 *HarEnMi*
Richemont, Enid *ScF&FL 92*
Richenberg, Richard Edward 1935- *St&PR 93*
Richenburg, Robert Bartlett 1917- *WhoAm 92*
Richens, Muriel Whittaker *WhoAmW 93*
Richer, Alan B. *Law&B 92*
Richer, Alvin 1929- *St&PR 93*
Richer, Angelique
See Philidor, Francois-Andre Danican 1726-1795 *OxDcOp*
Richer, Cheryl E. 1951- *St&PR 93*
Richer, Jean Herbert 1918- *St&PR 93*
Richer, Roger Thomas 1952- *St&PR 93*
Richerson, Dennis Ray 1953- *WhoSSW 93*
Richerson, Hal Bates 1929- *WhoAm 92*
Richerson, Modesta Dorsett 1905- *WhoAmW 93*
Richert, Hans-Egon 1924- *WhoWor 93*
Richert, Harvey Miller, II 1948- *WhoSSW 93*
Richert, Maxine Harper 1947- *St&PR 93*
Richert, William *MiSFD 9*
Riches, Brenda 1942- *WhoCanL 92*
Riches, Kenneth William 1962- *WhoEmL 93, WhoWor 93*
Richeson, Cena Golder 1941- *WhoWrEP 92*
Richeson, Hugh Anthony, Jr. 1947- *WhoEmL 93, WhoSSW 93*
Richeson, John William 1945- *St&PR 93*
Richesson, Edward R. 1933- *St&PR 93*
Richette, Lisa Aversa 1928- *WhoAm 92*
Richetti, John Joseph 1938- *WhoE 93*
Richey, Albert L. 1949- *St&PR 93*
Richey, Alvan Edgar, Jr. 1936- *St&PR 93*
Richey, Annie Lou 1934- *WhoWrEP 92*
Richey, Charles R. 1923- *CngDr 91*
Richey, Charles Robert 1923- *WhoAm 92, WhoE 93, WhoWor 93*
Richey, Diane J. *Law&B 92*
Richey, Edith Rose 1932- *WhoAmW 93*
Richey, Esther Lavern 1909- *WhoAmW 93*
Richey, Everett Eldon 1923- *WhoWor 93*
Richey, Herbert Southall 1922- *WhoAm 92*
Richey, Kenneth L. 1941- *St&PR 93*
Richey, Leonard *St&PR 93*
Richey, Leroy Milburn, Jr. 1930- *St&PR 93*
Richey, Nancy *BiDAMSp 1989*
Richey, Phil Horace 1923- *WhoAm 92*
Richey, Robert Lee 1923- *WhoAm 92*
Richey, Rodney Paul 1957- *WhoWrEP 92*
Richey, Ronald H. 1950- *St&PR 93*
Richey, Ronald K. 1926- *St&PR 93*
Richey, Thomas Adam 1934- *WhoAm 92*
Richharia, Govind Das 1920- *WhoAsAP 91*
Richhart, James W. 1941- *St&PR 93*
Richie, Leroy C. *Law&B 92*
Richie, Lionel 1949- *AfrAmBi, Baker 92, SoulM*
Richie, Lionel B., Jr. 1949- *WhoAm 92*
Richie, Sharon Ivey 1949- *AfrAmBi*
Richier, J.L. *WhoScE 91-2*
Richieri, Kenneth A. *Law&B 92*
Richings, (Mary) Caroline 1827-1882 *Baker 92*
Richino, Martha Elisabeth 1942- *WhoE 93*
Richkind, Kathleen E. 1948- *St&PR 93*
Richkus, Peta Naylor 1947- *WhoAmW 93*
Richler, Daniel 1956- *ConAu 137, WhoCanL 92*
Richler, Mordecai 1931- *BioIn 17, ConLC 70 [port], DcChlFi, MagSWL [port], MajAI [port], WhoAm 92, WhoCanL 92, WhoWor 93, WhoWrEP 92*
Richley, Robert Douglas 1944- *WhoAm 92, WhoSSW 93*
Richlin, Maurice N. 1920-1990 *BioIn 17*
Richlin, W. Gar 1945- *WhoAm 92*
Richling, Mitchell David *Law&B 92*
Richlovsky, Thomas A. 1951- *St&PR 93*
Richlovsky, Thomas Andrew 1951- *WhoAm 92*
Richman, Alan *BioIn 17*
Richman, Alan 1939- *WhoAm 92, WhoWrEP 92*
Richman, Arthur L. 1921- *St&PR 93*
Richman, Beth 1964- *WhoAmW 93*
Richman, David 1946- *St&PR 93*
Richman, David Marc 1951- *WhoE 93*
Richman, David Paul 1943- *WhoAm 92*
Richman, Donald 1922- *WhoAm 92*
Richman, Elliot 1941- *WhoWrEP 92*
Richman, Frances Sharpe 1947- *WhoAmW 93*
Richman, Gertrude Gross 1908- *WhoAmW 93*
Richman, H.B. 1928- *St&PR 93*
Richman, Harold Alan 1937- *WhoAm 92*
Richman, Herbert J. 1935- *St&PR 93, WhoAm 92*
Richman, Jeffrey Elliot 1949- *WhoE 93*
Richman, Joan F. 1939- *WhoAm 92, WhoAmW 93*
Richman, John Emmett 1951- *WhoEmL 93, WhoWor 93*
Richman, John Marshall 1927- *WhoAm 92*
Richman, Jordan Paul 1931- *WhoWrEP 92*
Richman, Julia 1855-1912 *JeAmHC*
Richman, Laura K. 1948- *WhoE 93*
Richman, Lillian Beatrice 1924- *WhoE 93*
Richman, Marc Herbert 1936- *WhoAm 92, WhoE 93*
Richman, Martin Franklin 1930- *WhoAm 92*
Richman, Marvin Jordan 1939- *WhoAm 92*
Richman, Nancy E. *Law&B 92*
Richman, Paul 1942- *WhoAm 92*
Richman, Peter 1927- *St&PR 93, WhoAm 92, WhoE 93*
Richman, Peter Mark 1927- *WhoAm 92*
Richman, Phyllis Chasanow 1939- *WhoAm 92, WhoAmW 93*
Richman, Robert Michael 1950- *WhoE 93*
Richman, Sol 1914- *WhoSSW 93*
Richman, Stephen I. 1933- *WhoAm 92, WhoE 93*
Richman, Steven Mark 1955- *WhoWrEP 92*
Richman, William Sheldon 1921- *St&PR 93, WhoAm 92*
Richmond, Allen Wayne *Law&B 92*
Richmond, Anthony 1942- *MiSFD 9*
Richmond, Anthony Henry 1925- *WhoAm 92*
Richmond, Brian 1948- *St&PR 93*
Richmond, Bruce Timothy 1959- *St&PR 93*
Richmond, Charles Ronald 1939- *St&PR 93*
Richmond, David Walker 1914- *WhoAm 92*
Richmond, Dene 1924- *St&PR 93*
Richmond, Douglas Wertz 1946- *WhoSSW 93*
Richmond, Fiona *ScF&FL 92*
Richmond, Frederick William 1923- *WhoAm 92*
Richmond, George E. 1933- *St&PR 93*
Richmond, Grace Louise Smith 1866-1959 *AmWomPl*
Richmond, Harold Nicholas 1935- *WhoE 93*
Richmond, James Ellis 1938- *WhoAm 92*
Richmond, John Allen 1932- *St&PR 93*
Richmond, John Christopher Blake 1909-1990 *BioIn 17*
Richmond, John William 1955- *WhoSSW 93*
Richmond, Jon 1957- *WhoAm 92*
Richmond, Jonas Edward 1929- *WhoAm 92*
Richmond, Julius Benjamin 1916- *WhoAm 92*
Richmond, Keith Henry 1940- *WhoUN 92*
Richmond, L.A. 1944- *St&PR 93*
Richmond, Lee 1857-1929 *BioIn 17*
Richmond, Lee J. d1990 *BioIn 17*
Richmond, Lee Joyce 1934- *WhoAmW 93*
Richmond, Leigh 1911- *ScF&FL 92*
Richmond, Marilyn Susan 1949- *WhoAm 92, WhoAmW 93*
Richmond, Mary 1903-1973 *ScF&FL 92*
Richmond, Michael Lloyd 1945- *WhoSSW 93*
Richmond, Nancy M. 1944- *St&PR 93*
Richmond, P.J. *Law&B 92*
Richmond, Peter *WhoScE 91-1*
Richmond, Peter H. 1937- *St&PR 93*
Richmond, Phyllis Allen 1921- *WhoAm 92, WhoAmW 93*
Richmond, Robert Linn 1920- *WhoAm 92*
Richmond, Samuel Bernard 1919- *WhoAm 92*
Richmond, Stephen M. *Law&B 92*
Richmond, Steven Allan 1941- *WhoWrEP 92*
Richmond, Susan Mills *Law&B 92*
Richmond, Thomas G. 1957- *WhoAm 92*
Richmond, Tim *BioIn 17*
Richmond, Tyronza R. 1940- *WhoSSW 93*
Richmond, Victor J. 1932- *St&PR 93*
Richmond, Walt 1922-1977 *ScF&FL 92*
Richmond, William Patrick 1932- *WhoAm 92*
Richmond and Derby, Countess of 1443-1509 *BioIn 17*
Richnak, Barbara M. 1936- *WhoWrEP 92*
Richner, Clifford 1952- *WhoE 93*
Richo, Anna S. *Law&B 92*
Richstein, Abraham Richard 1919- *WhoAm 92*
Richstone, Douglas Orange 1949- *WhoAm 92*
Richstone, Ellen Blair 1951- *St&PR 93*
Richter, Achim 1940- *WhoScE 91-3*
Richter, Alan Marc 1955- *St&PR 93*
Richter, Alfred G., Jr. *Law&B 92*
Richter, Annette L. *Law&B 92*
Richter, Barbara Ann 1943- *WhoAmW 93*
Richter, Barry 1935- *St&PR 93*

Richter, Burton 1931- *WhoAm 92, WhoWor 93*
Richter, Carol Dean 1940- *WhoAmW 93*
Richter, Carol Roberta 1943- *WhoAmW 93*
Richter, Conrad 1890-1968 *BioIn 17, MagSAmL [port]*
Richter, Curt Paul 1894-1988 *BioIn 17*
Richter, David J. *Law&B 92*
Richter, Dieter Oswald 1947- *WhoWor 93*
Richter, Donald Paul 1924- *WhoAm 92*
Richter, Dorothy Anne 1948- *WhoAmW 93, WhoE 93*
Richter, Earl E. 1923- *St&PR 93*
Richter, Earl Edward 1923- *WhoAm 92*
Richter, Egon Walter 1928- *WhoScE 91-3*
Richter, Elmer Bud 1926- *St&PR 93*
Richter, Ernst Friedrich (Eduard) 1808-1879 *Baker 92*
Richter, Ferdinand Tobias 1651?-1711 *Baker 92*
Richter, Frank 1916- *WhoWrEP 92*
Richter, Franz Xaver 1709-1789 *Baker 92*
Richter, George Robert, Jr. 1910- *WhoAm 92*
Richter, Gerhard *BioIn 17*
Richter, Hans 1843-1916 *Baker 92, IntDcOp [port], OxDcOp*
Richter, Hans Joachim 1926- *WhoScE 91-3*
Richter, Hans Peter 1925- *MajAI [port]*
Richter, Harry Mark 1954- *WhoSSW 93*
Richter, Harvena 1919- *WhoWrEP 92*
Richter, Henry Andrew 1930- *WhoE 93*
Richter, Irvin E. 1944- *St&PR 93*
Richter, James Arthur 1942- *St&PR 93*
Richter, James Michael 1950- *WhoAm 92*
Richter, Joachim 1937- *WhoScE 91-3*
Richter, Johann Christoph 1689-1751 *BioIn 17*
Richter, Johann Gotthard 1924- *WhoScE 91-3*
Richter, Johann Paul Friedrich 1763-1825 *BioIn 17*
Richter, Jorg J. 1937- *WhoScE 91-3*
Richter, Judith Anne 1942- *WhoAmW 93*
Richter, Juliette *Law&B 92*
Richter, Karen June 1949- *WhoE 93*
Richter, Karl 1926-1981 *Baker 92*
Richter, Knut 1943- *WhoWor 93*
Richter, Linda Dale 1949- *WhoAmW 93*
Richter, Marc *Law&B 92*
Richter, Marga 1926- *Baker 92*
Richter, Mary Jane 1937- *WhoAmW 93*
Richter, Mike *BioIn 17*
Richter, Nico (Max) 1915-1945 *Baker 92*
Richter, Norman H. 1938- *St&PR 93*
Richter, Patti Quinn 1959- *WhoSSW 93*
Richter, Paul Robert 1948- *St&PR 93*
Richter, Peter Christian 1944- *WhoAm 92*
Richter, Peyton E. *ScF&FL 92*
Richter, R.G. 1945- *St&PR 93*
Richter, Reed Brannon 1949- *WhoSSW 93*
Richter, Richard Paul 1931- *WhoAm 92*
Richter, Robert 1929- *WhoE 93*
Richter, Robert E. 1947- *St&PR 93*
Richter, Rostislav 1938- *WhoScE 91-4*
Richter, Sviatoslav (Teofilovich) 1915- *Baker 92*
Richter, Sviatoslav Theofilovich 1915- *WhoWor 93*
Richter, Todd Benjamin 1957- *WhoE 93*
Richter, W.D. 1945- *MiSFD 9*
Richter, Wolfgang 1937- *WhoScE 91-3*
Richter, Z. *WhoScE 91-4*
Richter-Haaser, Hans 1912-1980 *Baker 92*
Richters, Edward M. *Law&B 92*
Richthofen, Manfred von 1892-1918 *HarEnMi*
Richtofen, Wolfram von 1895-1945 *HarEnMi*
Richtol, Herbert Harold 1932- *WhoAm 92*
Richwine, David Alan 1943- *WhoAm 92*
Rici, Francisco 1608-1685 *BioIn 17*
Ricigliano, James Vincent 1938- *St&PR 93*
Ricigliano, Robert *BioIn 17*
Ricimer d472 *OxDcByz*
Ricimer, Flavius d472 *HarEnMi*
Riciopo, Eric 1955 *WhoE 93*
Rick, Charles Madeira, Jr. 1915- *WhoAm 92*
Rick, Edward Albert 1930- *WhoSSW 93*
Rick, Susan Kay 1953- *WhoAmW 93*
Rick, Wirnt 1928- *WhoScE 91-3*
Rickaby, Lillian *AmWomPl*
Rickard, Bob 1932- *St&PR 93*
Rickard, Carroll M. 1929- *St&PR 93*
Rickard, David Terrence *WhoScE 91-1*
Rickard, Graham 1949- *SmATA 71 [port]*
Rickard, Jerry E. *Law&B 92*
Rickard, Joan Dee 1964- *WhoAmW 93*
Rickard, Joseph Conway 1926- *WhoSSW 93*
Rickard, Linda C. *Law&B 92*
Rickard, Lisa A. 1955- *WhoAmW 93*
Rickard, Norman Edward 1936- *WhoAm 92*
Rickard, Peter C. *WhoScE 91-1*
Rickard, Ruth David 1926- *WhoAmW 93*
Rickards, Catherine Isabella 1916- *WhoWrEP 92*
Rickards, Debra Jean 1952- *WhoE 93*
Rickards, Leonard Myron 1927- *WhoAm 92, WhoSSW 93*
Rickards, Michael Anthony 1930- *WhoSSW 93*
Rickart, Charles Earl 1913- *WhoAm 92*
Rickayzen, Gerald *WhoScE 91-1*
Rickayzen, Gerald 1929- *WhoWor 93*
Ricke, Barbara Ann 1952- *WhoAmW 93, WhoSSW 93*
Ricke, Dennis Frank 1948- *WhoWor 93*
Ricke, P. Scott 1948- *WhoWor 93*
Rickel, Annette Urso *WhoAmW 93*
Rickel, E.J. 1925- *St&PR 93*
Rickels, G. Rodney 1941- *St&PR 93*
Rickels, Karl 1924- *WhoAm 92*
Rickenbach, R.M. *St&PR 93*
Rickenbacher, Karl Anton 1940- *Baker 92*
Rickenbacker, Edward V. 1890-1973 *EncABHB 8 [port]*
Rickenbacker, Edward Vernon 1890-1973 *HarEnMi*
Ricker, John Boykin, Jr. 1917- *WhoAm 92*
Ricker, Margaret Wendy 1932- *WhoAmW 93*
Ricker, William Edwin 1908- *WhoAm 92*
Rickerby, David George 1952- *WhoWor 93*
Rickerby, Joseph d1850 *BioIn 17*
Rickerd, Donald Sheridan 1931- *WhoAm 92*
Rickershauser, Charles Edwin, Jr. 1928- *St&PR 93*
Rickerson, Stuart *Law&B 92*
Rickerson, Stuart Eugene 1949- *WhoE 93*
Rickert, Alfred E. 1930- *WhoE 93*
Rickert, David E. 1951- *St&PR 93*
Rickert, Edward Joseph 1936- *WhoSSW 93*
Rickert, Edwin Weimer 1914- *WhoE 93*
Rickert, Kenneth Wilson, Jr. 1946- *St&PR 93*
Rickert, Paul E. 1933- *St&PR 93*
Rickert, Robert Richard 1936- *WhoE 93*
Rickert, Wm. J. 1924- *St&PR 93*
Ricketson, James Doyle 1932- *St&PR 93*
Ricketson, Mary Alice 1948- *WhoSSW 93*
Ricketson, Richard D. 1936- *St&PR 93*
Rickett, Arthur Compton- *ScF&FL 92*
Rickett, Harold William 1896-1989 *BioIn 17*
Rickett, Joseph Compton- *ScF&FL 92*
Rickett, Robert R. *Law&B 92*
Ricketti, James Carmen 1955- *WhoE 93*
Ricketts, Barrie L. 1949- *St&PR 93*
Ricketts, Frederick J. 1881-1945 *Baker 92*
Ricketts, Gary Eugene 1935- *WhoAm 92*
Ricketts, Glenn W. 1921- *St&PR 93*
Ricketts, John Benjamin 1954- *WhoSSW 93, WhoWor 93*
Ricketts, John F. 1937- *St&PR 93*
Ricketts, Marijane Gnegy 1925- *WhoWrEP 92*
Ricketts, Martin *BioIn 17*
Ricketts, Richard Randall 1947- *WhoSSW 93*
Ricketts, Shirley C. *St&PR 93*
Ricketts, Steven Walter 1942- *St&PR 93*
Ricketts, Thomas Lee 1942- *WhoSSW 93*
Ricketts, Thomas R. 1931- *St&PR 93*
Ricketts, Thomas Roland 1931- *WhoAm 92*
Rickey, Branch 1881-1965 *BioIn 17*
Rickey, George Warren 1907- *WhoAm 92*
Rickey, Thomas 1954- *St&PR 93*
Rickey, Vickie L. 1952- *St&PR 93*
Rickhoff, Romayne Goranson 1934- *St&PR 93*
Rickin, Sheila Anne 1945- *WhoE 93*
Rickles, Donald Jay 1926- *WhoAm 92*
Ricklin, Arthur H. 1934- *WhoAm 92*
Rickman, Fred Dempsey, Jr. 1953- *St&PR 93*
Rickman, Gregg *ScF&FL 92*
Rickman, Percy d1989 *BioIn 17*
Rickman, Ray *AfrAmBi*
Rickman, Ray 1948- *WhoE 93*
Rickman, Tom *MiSFD 9*
Rickman, Wayne Lee 1957- *WhoEmL 93, WhoWor 93*
Rickman, William Warren 1942- *St&PR 93*
Rickords, David L. 1947- *St&PR 93*
Rickover, Hyman 1900-1986 *ColdWar 1 [port]*
Rickover, Hyman George 1900-1986 *BioIn 17, JeAmHC*
Ricks, Dallis Derrick Biehl 1938- *WhoSSW 93*
Ricks, Donald Jay 1936- *WhoAm 92*
Ricks, Glenn E. *Law&B 92*
Ricks, Glenn E. 1938- *St&PR 93*
Ricks, John Howard 1926- *St&PR 93*
Ricks, John Paul 1955- *WhoSSW 93*
Ricks, Joycia Camilla 1949- *WhoEmL 93*
Ricks, Ron 1949- *St&PR 93*
Ricks, Thomas E. 1946- *St&PR 93*
Ricks, Thomas Edwin 1955- *WhoE 93*
Rickter, Donald Oscar 1931- *WhoE 93*
Rickword, Edgell 1898-1982 *BioIn 17*
Rico, Andre 1929- *WhoScE 91-2*
Rico, Daniel P. 1955- *St&PR 93*
Rico, David M. 1951- *WhoSSW 93*
Rico, Don 1917-1985 *ScF&FL 92*
Rico, Ul de *ScF&FL 92*
Rico Cano, Tomas 1916- *DcMexL*
Ricolfi, Teresio 1940- *WhoScE 91-3*
Ricordi *Baker 92*
Ricordi, Giovanni 1785-1853 *Baker 92, OxDcOp*
Ricordi, Giulio 1840-1912 *OxDcOp*
Ricordi, Guilio 1840-1912 *Baker 92*
Ricordi, Tito 1811-1888 *Baker 92, OxDcOp*
Ricordi, Tito 1865-1933 *Baker 92, OxDcOp*
Ricotta, Edwin C. d1991 *BioIn 17*
Ricotta, Paul J. *Law&B 92*
Ricottilli, John, Jr. 1933- *St&PR 93*
Ricupero, Rubens 1937- *WhoUN 92*
Ridanovic, Josip 1929- *WhoScE 91-4*
Ridd, John Howard *WhoScE 91-1*
Riddell, Adaljiza Sosa *NotHsAW 93*
Riddell, C.H. *St&PR 93*
Riddell, Charlotte E. *ScF&FL 92*
Riddell, Grahame E. 1946- *St&PR 93*
Riddell, J.F. 1953- *St&PR 93*
Riddell, J.H., Mrs. 1832-1906 *ScF&FL 92*
Riddell, James H. 1925- *St&PR 93*
Riddell, Matthew Donald Rutherford 1918- *WhoAm 92*
Riddell, Mike *BioIn 17*
Riddell, Richard Anderson 1940- *WhoAm 92*
Riddell, Richard Harry 1916- *WhoAm 92*
Riddell, Ruth *ScF&FL 92*
Riddell, Tally D. 1946- *St&PR 93*
Ridden, Geoffrey M. *ScF&FL 92*
Ridder, Anton de 1929- *Baker 92*
Ridder, Bernard H., Jr. 1916- *St&PR 93*
Ridder, Bernard Herman, Jr. 1916- *WhoAm 92*
Ridder, Daniel Hickey 1922- *WhoAm 92*
Ridder, Eric 1918- *St&PR 93, WhoAm 92*
Ridder, Mary Jane d1991 *BioIn 17*
Ridder, Paul Anthony 1940- *WhoAm 92, WhoSSW 93*
Ridder, Victor L. d1991 *BioIn 17*
Ridder, Walter Thompson 1917-1990 *BioIn 17*
Ridder, Willem 1930- *St&PR 93*
Ridderbusch, Karl 1932- *Baker 92, OxDcOp*
Riddick, Andrea Celestine 1963- *WhoE 93*
Riddick, Daniel Howison 1941- *WhoAm 92*
Riddick, Douglas Smith 1942- *WhoSSW 93, WhoWor 93*
Riddick, Frank Adams, Jr. 1929- *WhoAm 92, WhoWor 93*
Riddick, Ron 1952- *BioIn 17*
Riddiford, Lynn Moorhead 1936- *WhoAmW 93*
Riddle, Carol Ann 1936- *WhoAmW 93*
Riddle, Charles Daniel 1945- *WhoSSW 93*
Riddle, Constance Christine 1923- *WhoAmW 93, WhoWor 93*
Riddle, Daniel Phillip 1953- *WhoSSW 93*
Riddle, Dennis Raymond 1933- *St&PR 93*
Riddle, Dennis Raymond 1934- *WhoAm 92*
Riddle, Dixie Lee *WhoAm 92*
Riddle, Donald Husted 1921- *WhoAm 92*
Riddle, Ervin Adril *Law&B 92*
Riddle, H. Marvin, III 1930- *St&PR 93*
Riddle, James Douglass 1933- *WhoE 93*
Riddle, John B. 1920- *St&PR 93*
Riddle, Judith Lee 1950- *WhoAmW 93*
Riddle, Judy Noel *Law&B 92*
Riddle, Katharine Parker 1919- *WhoAmW 93*
Riddle, Malcolm Graeme 1909- *St&PR 93*
Riddle, Mark Alan 1948- *WhoE 93*
Riddle, Maxwell 1907- *WhoWor 93*
Riddle, Nelson 1921-1985 *Baker 92*
Riddle, Rhonda Kiser 1960- *WhoAmW 93*
Riddle, Sturgis Lee 1909- *WhoAm 92*
Riddle, Veryl Lee 1921- *WhoAm 92*
Riddles, Libby *BioIn 17*
Riddlesperger, Anthony G. *Law&B 92*
Riddoch, Gregory Lee 1945- *WhoAm 92*
Riddoch, Hilda Johnson 1923- *WhoAmW 93, WhoWor 93*
Riddoch, Peter Roy 1947- *St&PR 93*
Riddoch, William G. *Law&B 92*
Riddoch-Gharbi, Isobel 1934- *WhoUN 92*
Riddolls, W.E. 1916- *St&PR 93*
Ride, Sally 1951- *Expl 93 [port]*
Ride, Sally K. *BioIn 17*
Ride, Sally Kristen 1951- *WhoAm 92, WhoAmW 93*
Rideau, Wilbert *BioIn 17*
Ridella, Gregory J. *Law&B 92*
Ridella, Sandro *WhoScE 91-3*
Riden, Michael David 1947- *WhoEmL 93, WhoSSW 93*
Ridenhour, Carlton *See* Public Enemy *News 92*
Ridenhour, Joseph Conrad 1920- *WhoAm 92*
Ridenour, Andy *BioIn 17*
Ridenour, Debora Ann 1961- *WhoAmW 93*
Ridenour, Jack Burl 1922- *WhoSSW 93*
Ridenour, Patricia *BioIn 17*
Ridenour, Windsor Allen 1938- *St&PR 93*
Ridenour-Jones, James Amburs 1939- *WhoSSW 93*
Rideout, Elmer William, III *Law&B 92*
Rideout, Patricia Irene 1931- *WhoAm 92*
Rideout, Philip Munroe 1936- *WhoAm 92, WhoWor 93*
Rideout, Phyllis McCain 1938- *WhoAmW 93*
Rideout, Roy P. 1947- *St&PR 93*
Rideout, Thomas Gerard 1948- *WhoAm 92*
Rideout, Walter Bates 1917- *WhoAm 92, WhoWrEP 92*
Rider, Betty L. *BioIn 17*
Rider, Brent Taylor 1942- *St&PR 93*
Rider, Gregory Ashford 1949- *WhoEmL 93*
Rider, Robert Bruce *Law&B 92*
Rider, Suzanne Costich 1935- *WhoSSW 93*
Rider-Kelsey, Corinne 1877-1947 *Baker 92*
Ridge, David C. *Law&B 92*
Ridge, Gavin C. 1947- *St&PR 93*
Ridge, Jean *AmWomPl*
Ridge, John Charles 1955- *WhoE 93*
Ridge, Kieran T. *Law&B 92*
Ridge, Thomas J. 1945- *CngDr 91*
Ridge, Thomas Joseph 1945- *WhoAm 92, WhoE 93*
Ridgeway, Fritzie 1898- *SweetSg B [port]*
Ridgeway, James Fowler 1936- *WhoAm 92, WhoWrEP 92*
Ridgley, Robert Louis 1934- *St&PR 93*
Ridgley, William 1837-1868 *BioIn 17*
Ridgway, Brock G. *Law&B 92*
Ridgway, Brunilde Sismondo 1929- *WhoAm 92*
Ridgway, C. David 1930- *St&PR 93*
Ridgway, Dave *BioIn 17*
Ridgway, David *BioIn 17*
Ridgway, David Wenzel 1904- *WhoWor 93*
Ridgway, George M. 1936- *St&PR 93*
Ridgway, George Martin 1936- *WhoWor 93*
Ridgway, Gerald Wesley 1918- *St&PR 93*
Ridgway, Helen Jane 1937- *WhoAmW 93*
Ridgway, James M. *ScF&FL 92*
Ridgway, James Stratman 1936- *WhoSSW 93*
Ridgway, Jim 1930- *ScF&FL 92*
Ridgway, Marcella Davies 1957- *WhoAmW 93*
Ridgway, Marion Vannett d1991 *BioIn 17*
Ridgway, Mark Cameron 1959- *WhoWor 93*
Ridgway, Matthew B. 1895- *ColdWar 1 [port]*
Ridgway, Matthew Bunker 1895- *CmdGen 1991 [port], DcTwHis, HarEnMi*
Ridgway, Priscilla 1943- *WhoE 93*
Ridgway, Rozanne LeJeanne 1935- *WhoAm 92, WhoAmW 93*
Ridgway, Sara R. 1944- *St&PR 93*
Ridick, Joyce Marie 1941- *WhoAmW 93, WhoE 93*
Riding, Deborah Renee 1962- *WhoSSW 93*
Riding, Julia *ScF&FL 92*
Riding, Karen Dorothy 1957- *WhoAmW 93*
Riding, Laura 1901-1991 *AnObit 1991, BioIn 17*
Ridinger, Jay George, VII 1934- *WhoWor 93*
Ridings, Barry W. 1952- *St&PR 93*
Ridings, Dorothy Sattes 1939- *WhoAm 92, WhoAmW 93*
Ridings, Susan Elizabeth 1949- *WhoAmW 93*
Ridington, Robin 1939- *ConAu 139*
Ridky, Jaroslav 1897-1956 *Baker 92*
Ridl, Jack Rogers 1944- *WhoWrEP 92*
Ridlen, Lillian May Heigle 1946- *WhoSSW 93*
Ridler, Des *BioIn 17*
Ridler, Gregory L. 1946- *St&PR 93*
Ridley, Anthony *WhoScE 91-1*
Ridley, Betty Ann 1926- *WhoAmW 93, WhoWor 93*
Ridley, Brian Kidd *WhoScE 91-1*
Ridley, Cecilia 1819-1845 *BioIn 17*
Ridley, Kevin L. *Law&B 92*
Ridley, Mark 1956- *WhoSSW 93*

Ridley, Mark L. 1957- *WhoWor 93*
Ridley, Nancy L. 1957- *WhoSSW 93*
Ridley, Nicholas 1929- *BioIn 17*
Ridley, Philip *MiSFD 9, ScF&FL 92*
Ridley-Thomas, Roger 1939- *WhoWor 93*
Ridloff, Richard 1948- *St&PR 93, WhoAm 92*
Ridlon, John Melville *Law&B 92*
Ridolphi, Lucy Elizabeth 1957- *WhoWrEP 92*
Ridout, Alan 1934- *ScF&FL 92*
Ridout, Godfrey 1918-1984 *Baker 92*
Ridout, Theodore Corner, Jr. 1942- *WhoE 93*
Ridout, Wayne Edward 1943- *WhoSSW 93*
Ridpath, M(ichael) G(errans) 1926- *ConAu 139*
Ridruejo, Dionisio 1912-1975 *BioIn 17*
Ridsdale, Angela M. 1927- *ScF&FL 92*
Ridsdale, Leone *WhoScE 91-1*
Ridwan, Mohammad 1939- *WhoUN 92*
Riead, William *MiSFD 9*
Riebe, Frederick Charles 1944- *St&PR 93*
Riebe, James Clifford 1942- *St&PR 93*
Riebe, Susan Jane 1955- *WhoAmW 93*
Rieber, Hans Paul 1934- *WhoScE 91-4*
Rieber, Jesse Alvin 1945- *WhoE 93*
Riebesehl, E. Allan 1938- *WhoE 93*
Riebling, Phillip R. *BioIn 17*
Riebman, Jesse Herman 1929- *St&PR 93*
Riebman, Leon 1920- *St&PR 93, WhoAm 92*
Riebsame, William Edward 1955- *WhoSSW 93*
Riechartz, W. Daniel 1946- *St&PR 93*
Riechel, Gerhard P. *Law&B 92*
Riechmann, Fred B. 1915- *WhoAm 92*
Rieck, Bruce William *Law&B 92*
Rieck, Edward Ernest *Law&B 92*
Rieck, Kim Alan *Law&B 92*
Rieck, Ray C. 1948- *St&PR 93*
Riecke, Hans Heinrich 1929- *WhoAm 92*
Riecken, Ernst-Otto 1932- *WhoScE 91-3*
Riecken, Henry William 1917- *WhoAm 92*
Rieckens, Faye Ann 1960- *WhoAmW 93*
Riecker, William H. 1924- *St&PR 93*
Ried, Glenda E. 1933- *WhoWrEP 92*
Ried, Walter Georg 1920- *WhoScE 91-3*
Riede, Ronald Frederick, Jr. 1957- *WhoEmL 93*
Riedeburg, Theodore 1912- *WhoAm 92*
Riedel, Alan E. 1930- *St&PR 93*
Riedel, Alan Ellis 1930- *WhoAm 92*
Riedel, Bernard Edward 1919- *WhoAm 92*
Riedel, Carl 1827-1888 *Baker 92*
Riedel, Chris C. *St&PR 93*
Riedel, Daniel P. 1939- *St&PR 93*
Riedel, Jack A. 1934- *St&PR 93*
Riedel, John 1940- *St&PR 93*
Riedel, Robert Ronald 1946- *St&PR 93*
Rieder, Corinne Jane 1939- *WhoE 93*
Rieder, Georg Leonhard 1939- *WhoWor 93*
Rieder, Helmut Franz 1950- *WhoWor 93*
Rieder, Ronald Frederic 1933- *WhoE 93*
Rieder, Th. *WhoScE 91-4*
Riederer, Donald Edward 1932- *St&PR 93*
Rieders, Fredric 1922- *WhoAm 92, WhoE 93*
Riedesel, Clark Alan 1930- *WhoE 93*
Riedesel, Donald Weston 1919- *St&PR 93*
Riedesel, Friedrich Adolphus von 1738-1800 *HarEnMi*
Riedhammer, Thomas Martin 1948- *WhoAm 92*
Riedinger, DeMeril A. 1928- *St&PR 93*
Riedinger, James Richard 1921- *St&PR 93*
Riedinger, Roland E. 1943- *WhoScE 91-2*
Riedl, Daniel A. *Law&B 92*
Riedl, Gayle James *Law&B 92*
Riedl, Rudolf George 1936- *St&PR 93*
Riedl, Steve L. 1955- *St&PR 93*
Riedl, Wm. R. 1940- *St&PR 93*
Riedler, W. *WhoScE 91-4*
Riedman, M. Suzanne *Law&B 92*
Riedman, Sarah R(egal) 1902- *ConAu 37NR*
Riedmann, Beth 1955- *WhoAmW 93*
Riedmiller, Matilda Anna 1938- *WhoAmW 93*
Riedner, Werner Ludwig Fritz 1924- *WhoWor 93*
Riedt, Friedrich Wilhelm 1710-1783 *Baker 92*
Riedy, John P. 1936- *St&PR 93*
Riedy, Mark Joseph 1942- *WhoAm 92*
Riedy, Mary Esther 1923- *WhoAmW 93*
Riefe, Alan 1925- *ScF&FL 92*
Riefe, Barbara *ScF&FL 92*
Riefenstahl, Leni 1902- *MiSFD 9, WhoWor 93*
Rieff, D.E. 1909- *St&PR 93*
Rieff, David *BioIn 17*
Rieff, Philip 1922- *WhoE 93*
Riefke, Robert Francis 1931- *St&PR 93*
Riefkohl, Ronald Edward 1947- *WhoSSW 93*
Riefler, Donald Brown 1927- *WhoAm 92*
Riefler, John Franklin, III 1947- *WhoE 93*
Riegel, Byron William 1938- *WhoAm 92, WhoWor 93*
Riegel, Henri Joseph 1741-1799 *Baker 92*
Riegel, J. Kent *Law&B 92*
Riegel, J. Kent 1938- *St&PR 93*
Riegel, John Kent 1938- *WhoAm 92*
Riegel, Kenneth 1938- *Baker 92*
Riegel, Kurt Wetherhold 1939- *WhoAm 92*
Riegels, Guy Anthony 1945- *WhoAm 92*
Riegemhautt, Ethan *Law&B 92*
Rieger, Audrey F. 1920- *WhoAmW 93*
Rieger, Fritz 1910-1978 *Baker 92*
Rieger, Michael Bernard 1949- *St&PR 93*
Rieger, Mitchell Sheridan 1922- *WhoAm 92*
Rieger, Philip Henri 1935- *WhoAm 92*
Rieger, Sam Lee 1946- *WhoSSW 93*
Riegert, Robert Adolf 1923- *WhoAm 92*
Riegger, Wallingford (Constantin) 1885-1961 *Baker 92*
Riegle, Donald W., Jr. *BioIn 17*
Riegle, Donald W., Jr. 1938- *CngDr 91*
Riegle, Donald Wayne, Jr. 1938- *WhoAm 92*
Riegle, Karen Dewald 1951- *WhoWrEP 92*
Riegle, Linda B. 1948- *WhoAmW 93*
Riegler, Josef 1938- *WhoWor 93*
Riegler, Lee Edward 1944- *St&PR 93*
Riegler, Peter 1940- *WhoScE 91-4*
Riegler, Richard Robert 1946- *St&PR 93*
Riegler, Susan Germaine 1960- *WhoE 93*
Riegner, Elizabeth Jane 1944- *WhoSSW 93*
Riehecky, Janet Ellen 1953- *WhoAm 92*
Riehl, Edward J. 1942- *St&PR 93*
Riehl, Edward Joseph *Law&B 92*
Riehl, Harry Ernest 1943- *St&PR 93*
Riehl, Wilhelm Heinrich 1823-1897 *IntDcAn*
Riehl, Wilhelm Heinrich von 1823-1897 *Baker 92*
Riehle, Gregory Robert *Law&B 92*
Riehm, Eckhard Wolfgang 1930- *WhoWor 93*
Riehm, J.W. 1920- *St&PR 93*
Riehm, Sarah Lawrence 1952- *WhoWrEP 92*
Riek, Jeanne Lanese *Law&B 92*
Rieke, Blaine Eugene 1933- *St&PR 93*
Rieke, Edward T. 1944- *St&PR 93*
Rieke, Kurt W. *Law&B 92*
Rieke, Marc Kimm 1948- *WhoAm 92*
Rieke, Regina Miller 1938- *WhoAmW 93*
Rieke, William Oliver 1931- *WhoAm 92*
Riekert, Lothar 1928- *WhoScE 91-3*
Riekkinen, Paavo Johannes 1936- *WhoScE 91-4, WhoWor 93*
Riel, Louis 1844-1885 *BioIn 17*
Rielley, Bernard D. 1937- *St&PR 93*
Rielley, David Joseph, III 1938- *St&PR 93*
Rielly, James Scott 1963- *WhoE 93*
Rielly, John Edward 1932- *WhoAm 92*
Riely, Caroline Armistead 1944- *WhoAmW 93*
Riely, Phyllis Eleanor 1918- *WhoAmW 93*
Riem, Friedrich Wilhelm 1779-1857 *Baker 92*
Rieman, Janece Marie 1929- *St&PR 93*
Rieman, Stephen Ralph 1946- *St&PR 93*
Riemann, Helmut E. 1926- *WhoScE 91-3*
Riemann, (Karl Wilhelm Julius) Hugo 1849-1919 *Baker 92*
Riemann, Mark L. 1956- *St&PR 93*
Riemens, Adriaan J. 1946- *WhoScE 91-3*
Riemenschneider, (Charles) Albert 1878-1950 *Baker 92*
Riemenschneider, Albert Louis 1936- *WhoAm 92*
Riemenschneider, Klaus Dieter 1943- *WhoWor 93*
Riemenschneider, Paul Arthur 1920- *WhoAm 92*
Riemenschneider, Ronald 1958- *St&PR 93*
Riemer, Amy Robin 1963- *WhoE 93*
Riemer, James D. *ScF&FL 92*
Riemer, John Richard 1953- *St&PR 93*
Riemer, Ruby 1924- *WhoWrEP 92*
Riemerschmid, Richard 1868-1957 *BioIn 17*
Riemersma, James Karl 1942- *St&PR 93*
Riemke, Richard Allan 1944- *WhoAm 92*
Riendeau, Dennis A. 1956- *St&PR 93*
Rienecker, Ronald J. 1957- *St&PR 93*
Riener, Thomas Clem 1947- *St&PR 93*
Rienhoff, Otto 1949- *WhoWor 93*
Rienner, Lynne Carol 1945- *WhoAm 92, WhoAmW 93*
Rienow, Leona Train 1903-1983 *ScF&FL 92*
Rienow, Robert 1909-1989 *ScF&FL 92*
Rienstra, Ellen Walker 1940- *WhoWrEP 92*
Rienzi, Anthony Thomas 1920- *WhoAm 92*
Rienzo, Robert James 1949- *WhoE 93*
Riepe, Dale Maurice 1918- *WhoAm 92*
Riepe, James Sellers 1943- *St&PR 93, WhoAm 92*
Riepel, Joseph 1709?-1782 *Baker 92*
Rieper, Alan George 1941- *St&PR 93*
Riepl, Francis Joseph 1936- *WhoAm 92*
Riera, Jordi 1951- *WhoScE 91-3*
Riera, Teresa 1950- *WhoScE 91-3*
Riera, Victor 1936- *WhoScE 91-3*
Riera-Diaz, Angel Ernesto 1953- *WhoWor 93*
Rierson, Robert Leak 1927- *WhoSSW 93*
Ries, Al *BioIn 17*
Ries, Alison Carolyn *WhoScE 91-1*
Ries, Cathy Gribble *Law&B 92*
Ries, Daniel Roland 1947- *St&PR 93*
Ries, Edward Richard 1918- *WhoAm 92, WhoSSW 93, WhoWor 93*
Ries, Ferdinand 1784?-1838 *Baker 92*
Ries, Franz 1846-1932 *Baker 92*
Ries, Franz (Anton) 1755-1846 *Baker 92*
Ries, Gunter A.M. 1933- *WhoScE 91-3*
Ries, (Pieter) Hubert 1802-1886 *Baker 92*
Ries, John Francis 1923- *St&PR 93*
Ries, Richard Ralph 1935- *WhoE 93*
Ries, Richard Raymond 1953- *WhoWrEP 92*
Ries, Stanley K. 1927- *WhoAm 92*
Ries, William Campbell 1948- *St&PR 93*
Ries, William Russell 1953- *WhoSSW 93*
Riesbeck, James E. 1942- *St&PR 93*
Riesbeck, James Edward 1942- *WhoAm 92*
Riesberg, Kenneth D. 1939- *St&PR 93*
Riese, Arthur Carl 1955- *WhoWor 93*
Riese, Beatrice 1917- *WhoE 93*
Riese, David John 1937- *St&PR 93*
Riese, Edna *AmWomPl*
Riese, Irving *BioIn 17*
Riese, Marilyn Laraine 1944- *WhoAmW 93, WhoSSW 93*
Riesel, Hans Ivar 1929- *WhoWor 93*
Riesenbach, Marvin S. 1929- *WhoAm 92*
Riesenberg, Mark Elliot 1947- *WhoE 93*
Riesenberger, John Richard 1948- *WhoWor 93*
Riesenfeld, Alphonse 1911-1989 *BioIn 17*
Riesenfeld, Harald Ernst 1913- *WhoWor 93*
Riesenfeld, Helen *AmWomPl*
Riesenfeld, James *Law&B 92*
Riesenfeld, Stefan Conrad 1948- *St&PR 93, WhoAm 92*
Riesenhuber, Heinz Friedrich Ruppert 1935- *WhoScE 91-3*
Rieser, Leonard Moos 1922- *WhoAm 92*
Rieser, Richard M., Jr. 1943- *WhoAm 92*
Riesman, David 1909- *WhoAm 92*
Riesmeyer, R.F. 1948- *St&PR 93*
Riesmeyer, William F., III *Law&B 92*
Riess, Dorothy Young 1931- *WhoAmW 93*
Riess, Gerard 1932- *WhoScE 91-2*
Riess, Gordon Sanderson 1928- *St&PR 93*
Riess, Jean G. 1936- *WhoScE 91-2*
Riessman, Frank 1924- *BioIn 17*
Riest, Uwe Wilhelm Karl 1938- *WhoScE 91-3*
Riester, J.L. *WhoScE 91-2*
Riester, Sharon Lee 1941- *WhoSSW 93*
Riestra, Gloria 1929- *DcMexL*
Riesz, Peter Charles 1937- *WhoAm 92*
Rieth, Otmar Hans 1916- *St&PR 93*
Rieth, Rodney Dale 1938- *St&PR 93*
Riether, Harold Landi 1941- *St&PR 93*
Riethle, William Edward, III 1948- *WhoE 93*
Riethman, Robert B. 1947- *St&PR 93*
Riethmiller, Marita Marlowe 1934- *WhoSSW 93*
Riethmuller, Gert 1934- *WhoScE 91-3*
Rieti, Vittorio 1898- *Baker 92*
Rietjens, Leonardus H.Th. 1929- *WhoScE 91-3*
Rietsch (Lowy), Heinrich 1860-1927 *Baker 92*
Rietz, John T. 1933- *St&PR 93*
Rietz, (August Wilhelm) Julius 1812-1877 *Baker 92*
Rietz, Siegfried 1936- *WhoScE 91-3*
Rieu, Jean F. 1937- *WhoScE 91-2*
Rieutord, E. *WhoScE 91-2*
Riew, Changkiu Keith 1928- *WhoWor 93*
Riezler, Kurt 1882-1955 *BioIn 17*
Rifai, Zein Samir 1944- *WhoWor 93*
Rifakes, George Peter 1934- *St&PR 93*
Rifbjerg, Klaus 1931- *ScF&FL 92*
Rifbjerg, Klaus (Thorvald) 1931- *ConAu 137, WhoWor 93*
Rife, Joanne T. 1932- *WhoAmW 93*
Rife, Joseph L. 1927- *St&PR 93*
Rife, Patricia Elizabeth 1957- *WhoAmW 93*
Rife, Richard C. *Law&B 92*
Rifelj, Carol de Dobay 1946- *WhoE 93*
Rifenburgh, Richard Philip 1932- *WhoAm 92*
Riff, Carrie S. 1899- *St&PR 93*
Riffaterre, Hermine *ScF&FL 92*
Riffaterre, Lee *Law&B 92*
Riffaterre, Michael 1924- *WhoAm 92*
Riffe, John Vernon 1951- *WhoWor 93*
Riffe, Vernal G., Jr. *WhoAm 92*
Riffel, Robert D. 1933- *St&PR 93*
Riffert, Robert John 1947- *St&PR 93*
Riffin, Irving M. 1913-1990 *BioIn 17*
Riffin, Thomas Kim 1952- *WhoE 93*
Riffle, Charles E. 1935- *St&PR 93*
Riffle, Juanita Maria Annette 1952- *WhoAmW 93*
Rifino, Crescenzio 1924- *St&PR 93*
Rifkin, Abraham 1920- *St&PR 93*
Rifkin, Adam *MiSFD 9*
Rifkin, Bernard M. *Law&B 92*
Rifkin, Harold 1916- *WhoAm 92*
Rifkin, Jeremy *BioIn 17*
Rifkin, Jeremy Chicago 1945- *WhoWrEP 92*
Rifkin, Joshua 1944- *Baker 92*
Rifkin, Larry Jay 1960- *WhoE 93*
Rifkin, Leonard 1931- *WhoAm 92*
Rifkin, Ned Lee 1949- *WhoAm 92, WhoSSW 93*
Rifkin, William 1920- *St&PR 93*
Rifkind, Arleen B. 1938- *WhoAmW 93, WhoE 93*
Rifkind, Malcolm Leslie 1946- *WhoWor 93*
Rifkind, Richard Allen 1930- *WhoWor 93*
Rifkind, Robert Singer 1936- *WhoAm 92*
Rifkind, Simon Hirsch 1901- *WhoAm 92*
Rifman, Eileen Nissenbaum 1944- *WhoAmW 93*
Riga, Kathleen Marie 1965- *WhoE 93*
Riga, Peter J(ohn) 1933- *ConAu 37NR*
Rigamonti, Attilio A. 1937- *WhoScE 91-3*
Rigamonti, Gianni C. 1937- *WhoScE 91-3*
Rigas, John Nicholas *Law&B 92*
Rigattieri, Lisa 1953- *WhoIns 93*
Rigault, Jean-Paul 1948- *WhoScE 91-2*
Rigaux, Christopher Michael 1960- *WhoE 93*
Rigaux-Bricmont, Benny Patrick 1943- *WhoE 93*
Rigby, Cathy 1952- *BioIn 17*
Rigby, Kathleen B. *AmWomPl*
Rigby, Kenneth 1925- *WhoWor 93*
Rigby, Marilyn K. 1927-1990 *BioIn 17*
Rigby, Martha Ward 1951- *WhoAmW 93*
Rigby, Perry Gardner 1932- *WhoAm 92*
Rigby, Peter William Jack *WhoScE 91-1*
Rigby, Richard Norris 1935- *WhoWrEP 92*
Rigdon, Charles *ScF&FL 92*
Rigdon, Edward Eugene 1953- *WhoSSW 93*
Rigdon, Imogene Stewart 1937- *WhoAmW 93*
Rigdon, Ronald Milton 1937- *WhoWor 93*
Rigdon, Thomas 1946- *St&PR 93*
Rigel, Darrell Spencer 1950- *WhoE 93*
Rigel, Henri-Jean 1772-1852 *Baker 92*
Rigelhof, T.F. 1944- *WhoCanL 92*
Riger, Robert Paris 1960- *St&PR 93*
Rigg, C. *WhoScE 91-1*
Rigg, Colin 1935- *WhoScE 91-1*
Rigg, Dewey Douglas 1953- *St&PR 93*
Rigg, Diana *BioIn 17*
Rigg, Diana 1938- *WhoAm 92, WhoWor 93*
Rigg, Donald Albert 1934- *WhoAm 92*
Rigg, Linda Dale 1944- *WhoSSW 93*
Rigg, Robert B. *ScF&FL 92*
Riggenbach, Christophe *WhoScE 91-4*
Riggin, Lee Pepper 1924- *WhoE 93*
Riggins, John *BioIn 17*
Riggins, Roderick Mark 1952- *WhoSSW 93*
Riggins, William G. *Law&B 92*
Riggins-Ezzell, Lois 1939- *WhoAm 92, WhoAmW 93*
Riggio, Anita 1952- *SmATA 73 [port]*
Riggio, Caroline A. *Law&B 92*
Riggio, Leonard *BioIn 17*
Riggs, Anthony L. d1991 *BioIn 17*
Riggs, Arthur Jordy 1916- *WhoAm 92*
Riggs, Barney d1900? *BioIn 17*
Riggs, Barry *St&PR 93*
Riggs, Benjamin C. d1992 *NewYTBS 92*
Riggs, Benjamin Clapp, Jr. 1945- *WhoAm 92*
Riggs, Bobby *BioIn 17*
Riggs, Byron Lawrence, Jr. 1931- *WhoAm 92, WhoWor 93*
Riggs, David F. 1950- *WhoSSW 93*
Riggs, David Lynn 1943- *WhoSSW 93, WhoWor 93*
Riggs, David N. 1929- *St&PR 93*
Riggs, Dionis Coffin 1898- *WhoWrEP 92*
Riggs, Donald Eugene 1942- *WhoAm 92, WhoWor 93*
Riggs, Douglas A. 1944- *St&PR 93, WhoAm 92*
Riggs, Frank *CngDr 91*
Riggs, Frank 1950- *WhoAm 92*
Riggs, Fred W. 1917- *BioIn 17*
Riggs, Gregory L. *Law&B 92*
Riggs, Gretchen *AmWomPl*

Riggs, Harvey 1914- *St&PR 93*
Riggs, Henry Earle 1935- *WhoAm 92*
Riggs, J.A., Jr. 1909- *St&PR 93*
Riggs, James A. 1936- *St&PR 93*
Riggs, James Arthur 1936- *WhoAm 92*
Riggs, Janet Catherine *Law&B 92*
Riggs, John A., III 1934- *St&PR 93*
Riggs, John E., III 1945- *St&PR 93*
Riggs, John R(aymond) 1945- *ConAu 37NR*
Riggs, Karl Alton, Jr. 1929- *WhoSSW 93*
Riggs, Lawrence Wilson 1943- *WhoSSW 93*
Riggs, Leonard, II 1943- *WhoAm 92*
Riggs, Lorrin Andrews 1912- *WhoAm 92, WhoE 93*
Riggs, Lynn 1899-1954 *BioIn 17*
Riggs, Lynn Spencer 1946- *WhoWrEP 92*
Riggs, Mary Lou 1927- *WhoSSW 93*
Riggs, Michael David 1951- *WhoAm 92*
Riggs, Michael L. *Law&B 92*
Riggs, Richard C. *St&PR 93*
Riggs, Robert Dale 1932- *WhoSSW 93*
Riggs, Rollie Lynn 1899-1954 *BioIn 17*
Riggs, Rollin Arthur 1960- *WhoSSW 93*
Riggs, Ronald L. 1944- *St&PR 93*
Riggs, Thomas Jeffries, Jr. 1916- *WhoAm 92*
Riggs, Toni *BioIn 17*
Riggsby, Dutchie Sellers 1940- *WhoAmW 93*
Riggulsford, Michael James 1956- *WhoWor 93*
Righelato, R.C. *WhoScE 91-1*
Righetti, Dave *BioIn 17*
Righetti-Giorgi, Geltrude *OxDcOp*
Righetti-Giorgi, Geltrude 1793-1862 *Baker 92*
Righi-Lambertini, Egano Cardinal 1906- *WhoAm 92, WhoWor 93*
Righini, Giancarlo C. 1944- *WhoScE 91-3*
Righini, Giancarlo Cesare 1944- *WhoWor 93*
Righini, Vincenzo 1756-1812 *Baker 92, OxDcOp*
Righteous Brothers *SoulM*
Righter, Walter Cameron 1923- *WhoAm 92*
Rights, Graham Henry 1935- *WhoSSW 93*
Rigler, Charles 1882-1936 *BiDAMSp 1989*
Rigler, Gail Charlotte *WhoSSW 93*
Rigler, John Barr 1921- *St&PR 93*
Rigney, Bill 1919- *BioIn 17*
Rigney, David Roth 1950- *WhoE 93*
Rigney, James *ScF&FL 92*
Rigney, James Oliver, Jr. 1948- *WhoWrEP 92*
Rigney, Michael E. *Law&B 92*
Rignold, Hugo (Henry) 1905-1976 *Baker 92*
Rigny, Paul J. 1939- *WhoScE 91-2*
Rigo, Jean-Marie 1950- *WhoScE 91-2*
Rigo, Marie-Odile 1943- *WhoScE 91-2*
Rigo, Marie-Odile Catherine 1943- *WhoWor 93*
Rigo, Marion Lee Bennett 1948- *WhoAmW 93, WhoSSW 93*
Rigo, Michael Maurice 1956- *WhoSSW 93*
Rigoglioso, Domenic *Law&B 92*
Rigo-Joseph, Sandra Luisa 1962- *WhoE 93*
Rigolot, Francois 1939- *WhoAm 92*
Rigoni, Robert J. 1936- *St&PR 93*
Rigor, Conrado Nicolas 1942- *WhoWrEP 92*
Rigout, Marcel 1928- *BioIn 17*
Rigsbee, Christopher Brooks *Law&B 92*
Rigsbee, Ned L. 1941- *St&PR 93*
Rigsbee, William A. 1926- *St&PR 93*
Rigsbee, William Alton 1926- *WhoAm 92*
Rigsby, Delbert Keith *Law&B 92*
Rigsby, Linda F. *Law&B 92*
Rigsby, Sheila G. 1955- *WhoWor 93*
Rigsby, Sheila Goree 1955- *WhoAmW 93*
Rigsby, Timothy Alan 1956- *WhoSSW 93*
Rigual, Antonio *BioIn 17*
Rigutti, Mario *WhoScE 91-3*
Riha, Jaroslav 1928- *WhoUN 92*
Riha, Karel 1949- *WhoWor 93*
Riha, William E. 1943- *St&PR 93*
Riha, William Edwin 1943- *WhoAm 92, WhoE 93*
Rihar, Gabrijel 1941- *WhoScE 91-4*
Riherd, John Robert *Law&B 92*
Rihm, Wolfgang 1952- *OxDcOp*
Rihm, Wolfgang (Michael) 1952- *Baker 92*
Rihs, Toni 1938- *WhoScE 91-4*
Riihentaus, Leo Juhani 1942- *WhoWor 93*
Riikola, Michael Edward 1951- *WhoEmL 93*
Riipi, Linda Ruth 1952- *WhoAmW 93*
Riis, Jacob 1849-1914 *GayN*
Riis, Jacob Augustus 1849-1914 *JrnUS*
Riis, Per Arne *St&PR 93*
Riis, Sharon 1947- *ConAu 136*
Riisager, Knudage 1897-1974 *Baker 92*
Riisgaard, Steen 1951- *St&PR 93*
Rijckaert, Marcel 1943- *WhoScE 91-2*
Rijkenbarg, G.J.H. *WhoScE 91-3*
Rijks, Derk Anne 1933- *WhoUN 92*
Rijksen, Herman D. 1942- *WhoScE 91-3*
Rijnberk, Ad 1938- *WhoScE 91-3*
Rijneveld, Reindert 1925- *WhoScE 91-3*
Rijnhart, Susie Carson 1868-1908 *Expl 93*
Rijniersce, K. 1950- *WhoScE 91-3*
Rijo, Jose *BioIn 17*
Rijpkema, Y.S. 1933- *WhoScE 91-3*
Rijtema, P.E. 1929- *WhoScE 91-3*
Rikala, Susan Carol 1955- *St&PR 93*
Rikard, Donald Allen 1928- *WhoSSW 93*
Rike, Linda Stokes 1949- *WhoSSW 93*
Rike, Susan 1952- *WhoAmW 93*
Riker, David Lewis 1958- *WhoSSW 93*
Riker, H. Charles 1921- *St&PR 93*
Riker, Harland Alexander, Jr. 1928- *St&PR 93*
Riker, R. Anthony *Law&B 92*
Riker, Walter F., Jr. 1916- *WhoAm 92*
Riker, William H. 1920- *PolPar*
Riker, William Harrison 1920- *WhoAm 92*
Riker, William Kay 1925- *WhoAm 92*
Rikhoff, Jean *WhoWrEP 92*
Rikhye, Ravi 1946- *ScF&FL 92*
Rikki *WhoCanL 92*
Riklin, Seth J. *Law&B 92*
Riklis, Meshulam 1923- *WhoAm 92*
Rikoski, Richard Anthony 1941- *WhoAm 92, WhoWor 93*
Rilander, Kenneth L. 1949- *St&PR 93*
Rile, Joanne Clarissa 1934- *WhoAm 92*
Rilea, Jack Dwight 1930- *St&PR 93*
Riles, Wilson Camanza 1917- *WhoAm 92*
Riley, Alice Cushing Donaldson 1867-1955 *AmWomPl*
Riley, Ann A. 1957- *St&PR 93*
Riley, Ann Peoples 1947- *WhoWor 93*
Riley, Anthony William 1929- *WhoAm 92, WhoWrEP 92*
Riley, B.J. 1925- *St&PR 93*
Riley, Barbara Polk 1928- *WhoWor 93*
Riley, Barry 1942- *ConAu 136*
Riley, Bonnie Galloway 1954- *WhoAmW 93*
Riley, Bridget Louise 1931- *WhoWor 93*
Riley, C. Ronald 1938- *WhoIns 93*
Riley, Carol J. Cusick *Law&B 92*
Riley, Carroll Lavern 1923- *WhoAm 92*
Riley, Catherine Irene 1947- *WhoAmW 93*
Riley, Charles Logan Rex 1946- *WhoWor 93*
Riley, Charles P. 1950- *St&PR 93*
Riley, Charles P., Jr. 1932- *St&PR 93*
Riley, Cheryl Pepsii *BioIn 17*
Riley, Corinne Boyd 1893-1979 *BioIn 17*
Riley, D.C. *WhoScE 91-1*
Riley, Daniel Edward 1915- *WhoAm 92*
Riley, Daniel Wayne 1949- *St&PR 93*
Riley, David Clyde 1926- *St&PR 93*
Riley, David D. 1961- *WhoE 93*
Riley, David E. *Law&B 92*
Riley, David Joseph 1942- *WhoE 93*
Riley, David Richard 1940- *WhoWor 93*
Riley, Denise Kathleen 1947- *WhoAmW 93*
Riley, Dick 1946- *ScF&FL 92*
Riley, Dolores Marie 1941- *WhoAmW 93*
Riley, Donald Neal 1948- *WhoSSW 93*
Riley, Dorothy Comstock 1924- *HispAmA [port], WhoAmW 93*
Riley, Dorothy Elaine *WhoAmW 93*
Riley, E.H. 1934- *St&PR 93*
Riley, Edgar Alsop 1919-1991 *BioIn 17*
Riley, Elaine 1923- *SweetSg C [port]*
Riley, Elizabeth Glynn 1956- *WhoAmW 93*
Riley, Francena 1957- *WhoAmW 93*
Riley, Frank J. 1928- *St&PR 93*
Riley, Gary M. 1955- *St&PR 93*
Riley, Gary Michael 1955- *WhoAm 92*
Riley, George Richardson, Jr. 1943- *WhoSSW 93*
Riley, Georgianne M. *Law&B 92*
Riley, H. John 1940- *St&PR 93*
Riley, H. Sanford *Law&B 92*
Riley, Harold E. 1928- *St&PR 93*
Riley, Harold Eugene 1928- *WhoIns 93*
Riley, Harold John, Jr. 1940- *WhoAm 92*
Riley, Harris DeWitt, Jr. 1924- *WhoAm 92*
Riley, Helene Maria Kastinger 1939- *WhoSSW 93*
Riley, Henry Charles 1932- *St&PR 93, WhoAm 92*
Riley, Ivers W. 1932- *St&PR 93*
Riley, Ivers Whitman 1932- *WhoAm 92*
Riley, J. Derek *St&PR 93*
Riley, J.P. *Law&B 92*
Riley, Jack 1935- *WhoAm 92*
Riley, Jame A. *ScF&FL 92*
Riley, James Arnold *WhoScE 91-1*
Riley, James Joseph 1919- *WhoAm 92, WhoE 93, WhoWor 93*
Riley, James Joseph 1948- *St&PR 93*
Riley, James Whitcomb 1849-1916 *ConAu 137, GayN, MajAI [port]*
Riley, Jeffrey A. 1949- *St&PR 93*
Riley, Jeremiah Anthony 1951- *WhoAm 92*
Riley, Jim 1853- *BioIn 17*
Riley, Jocelyn *BioIn 17*
Riley, Jocelyn (Carol) 1949- *ConAu 39NR, WhoWrEP 92*
Riley, John Edmund, Jr. 1952- *WhoSSW 93*
Riley, John F. *Law&B 92*
Riley, John F. 1943- *WhoIns 93*
Riley, John Francis 1936- *St&PR 93*
Riley, John Graham 1945- *WhoAm 92*
Riley, John Price *WhoScE 91-1*
Riley, John Thomas Joseph *Law&B 92*
Riley, John Winchell, Jr. 1908- *WhoAm 92*
Riley, Joseph E., Jr. *Law&B 92*
Riley, Joseph Harry 1922- *WhoAm 92*
Riley, Joseph John 1941- *St&PR 93*
Riley, Joshua Dean 1962- *WhoSSW 93*
Riley, Judith Merkle 1942- *ScF&FL 92*
Riley, Karen E. 1950- *St&PR 93*
Riley, Karen Lee 1958- *WhoE 93*
Riley, Kay Evon 1941- *St&PR 93*
Riley, Kevin Thomas 1943- *WhoIns 93*
Riley, Larry *BioIn 17*
Riley, Larry d1992 *NewYTBS 92*
Riley, Lawrence Joseph 1914- *WhoAm 92*
Riley, Leo Michael 1938- *WhoAm 92*
Riley, Leslie Walter, Jr. 1926- *WhoAm 92*
Riley, Louise 1904-1957 *DcChlFi*
Riley, Malcolm Wood 1927- *St&PR 93*
Riley, Margaret 1951- *WhoAmW 93*
Riley, Marilyn Gledhill 1954- *WhoE 93*
Riley, Mary Morgan 1946- *WhoAmW 93*
Riley, Matilda White 1911- *BioIn 17, WhoAm 92, WhoAmW 93*
Riley, Melissa 1956- *WhoSSW 93*
Riley, Michael David 1945- *WhoWrEP 92*
Riley, Millie Willett 1935- *WhoWrEP 92*
Riley, Norman *WhoScE 91-1*
Riley, Olive Murle 1932- *St&PR 93*
Riley, Pat *BioIn 17*
Riley, Patrick Anthony *WhoScE 91-1*
Riley, Patrick Gavan Duffy 1927- *WhoAm 92*
Riley, Patrick James 1936- *St&PR 93*
Riley, Patrick James 1945- *WhoAm 92, WhoE 93*
Riley, Philip *WhoScE 91-1*
Riley, Philip J. 1948- *ScF&FL 92*
Riley, Ramon R. 1935- *St&PR 93*
Riley, Randy James 1950- *WhoAm 92*
Riley, Rebecca *WhoWrEP 92*
Riley, Reed Farrar *Law&B 92*
Riley, Richard A. *ScF&FL 92*
Riley, Robert Annan, III 1955- *WhoE 93, WhoEmL 93, WhoWor 93*
Riley, Robert Bartlett 1931- *WhoAm 92*
Riley, Robert Bernard *Law&B 92*
Riley, Robert E. *Law&B 92*
Riley, Robert Edward 1930- *WhoAm 92*
Riley, Ron 1943- *St&PR 93*
Riley, Ronald P. 1948- *St&PR 93*
Riley, Ronald Patrick, Sr. 1948- *WhoSSW 93*
Riley, Rosetta *BioIn 17*
Riley, Rosetta M. 1940- *St&PR 93*
Riley, Sam G. 1939- *ConAu 136*
Riley, Stephen Thomas 1908- *WhoAm 92*
Riley, Susie Jackson 1948- *WhoSSW 93*
Riley, Teddy 1967- *SoulM*
Riley, Terry *BioIn 17*
Riley, Terry 1935- *WhoAm 92*
Riley, Terry (Mitchell) 1935- *Baker 92*
Riley, Thomas *WhoScE 91-1*
Riley, Thomas d1868 *BioIn 17*
Riley, Thomas Auraldo 1907- *WhoE 93*
Riley, Thomas C. *Law&B 92*
Riley, Thomas L. 1937- *St&PR 93*
Riley, Thomas Leslie 1927- *WhoSSW 93*
Riley, Victor J., Jr. 1931- *St&PR 93, WhoAm 92*
Riley, W. Joseph 1934- *St&PR 93*
Riley, Walter 1955- *ConEn*
Riley, William d1861 *BioIn 17*
Riley, William 1931- *St&PR 93, WhoE 93*
Riley, William Bell 1861-1947 *BioIn 17*
Riley, William D. *St&PR 93*
Riley, William Franklin 1925- *WhoAm 92*
Riley, William James, Jr. 1946- *WhoWor 93*
Rilke, Franco 1929- *WhoScE 91-3*
Rilke, Rainer Maria 1875-1926 *BioIn 17, MagSWL [port]*
Rill, James F. *BioIn 17*
Rill, James Franklin 1933- *WhoAm 92*
Rill, Lynda Reilly 1945- *WhoAmW 93*
Rilla, Wolf *MiSFD 9*
Rillieux, Norbert 1806-1894 *BioIn 17*
Rilling, Eugene Christopher 1962- *WhoSSW 93*
Rilling, Helmuth 1933- *Baker 92*
Rilling, John Robert 1932- *WhoSSW 93*
Rilly, Cheryl Ann 1952- *WhoWrEP 92*
Rima, Bertus Karel *WhoScE 91-1*
Rima, Ingrid Hahne *WhoAm 92*
Rima, Philip Woodring 1921- *WhoE 93*
Rimall, Bimal Nath 1944- *WhoWor 93*
Riman, J. *WhoScE 91-4*
Riman, Josef 1925- *WhoWor 93*
Riman, Joseph 1925- *WhoScE 91-4*
Rimarcik, Joseph Carl 1939- *St&PR 93*
Rimbach, Evangeline Lois 1932- *WhoAmW 93*
Rimbaud, Arthur 1854-1891 *BioIn 17, MagSWL [port], NinCLC 35 [port], WorLitC [port]*
Rimbaud, Jean Nicolas Arthur 1854-1891 *BioIn 17*
Rimbault, Edward (Francis) 1816-1876 *Baker 92*
Rimberg, Kjeld 1943- *WhoWor 93*
Rimel, Duane W. 1915- *ScF&FL 92*
Rimel, Rebecca Webster *WhoAmW 93*
Rimel, Rebecca Webster 1951- *WhoAm 92*
Rimer, Barbara K. 1949- *ConAu 136*
Rimer, John Thomas 1933- *WhoAm 92*
Rimerman, Ira Stephen 1938- *St&PR 93, WhoAm 92*
Rimerman, Morton W. 1929- *St&PR 93*
Rimerman, Morton Walter 1929- *WhoAm 92*
Rimerman, Thomas W. *BioIn 17*
Rimes, Myrtle L. 1938- *St&PR 93*
Rimiller, Ronald Wayne 1949- *WhoE 93*
Rimini, Emanuele 1940- *WhoScE 91-3*
Rimini, Giacomo 1887-1952 *See* Raisa, Rosa 1893-1963 *OxDcOp*
Rimland, Lisa Phillip 1954- *WhoE 93*
Rimler, Walter 1946- *ConAu 139*
Rimm, Sylvia Barkan 1935- *WhoAmW 93*
Rimm, Virginia Mary 1933- *WhoWrEP 92*
Rimmele, Frederick C. 1915- *St&PR 93*
Rimmer, A.J. *ScF&FL 92*
Rimmer, Alison *WhoScE 91-1*
Rimmer, Arthur 1926- *WhoScE 91-1*
Rimmer, Christine L. 1950- *WhoWrEP 92*
Rimmer, Jack 1921- *WhoAm 92*
Rimmer, James H. *BioIn 17*
Rimmer, Knud *WhoScE 91-2*
Rimmer, Robert H. 1917- *ScF&FL 92*
Rimmer, Stephen King 1948- *St&PR 93*
Rimmer, Steven W. *ScF&FL 92*
Rimmey, James L. 1940- *St&PR 93*
Rimmler, William F. 1932- *St&PR 93*
Rimoin, David Lawrence 1936- *WhoAm 92*
Rimon, Ranan Hilel 1938- *WhoScE 91-4*
Rimpel, Auguste Eugene, Jr. 1939- *WhoAm 92, WhoE 93, WhoWor 93*
Rimpler, Horst 1935- *WhoScE 91-3*
Rimrott, Friedrich Paul Johannes 1927- *WhoAm 92*
Rimsky-Korsakov, Andrei (Nikolaievich) 1878-1940 *Baker 92*
Rimsky-Korsakov, Georgi (Mikhailovich) 1901-1965 *Baker 92*
Rimsky-Korsakov, Nicolai 1844-1908 *IntDcOp*
Rimsky-Korsakov, Nikolai (Andreievich) 1844-1908 *Baker 92*
Rimsky-Korsakov, Nikolay 1844-1908 *OxDcOp*
Rimstad, Wynn H. 1944- *St&PR 93*
Rin, Zengi 1935- *WhoWor 93*
Rinaldi, Frank Robert *Law&B 92*
Rinaldi, Frank Robert 1927- *St&PR 93*
Rinaldi, Frank Thomas 1948- *WhoE 93*
Rinaldi, Fulvio Redento 1920- *WhoWor 93*
Rinaldi, Gail A. *Law&B 92*
Rinaldi, Gerard W. *WhoE 93*
Rinaldi, Jack Ismael 1946- *St&PR 93*
Rinaldi, Keith Stephen 1952- *WhoE 93*
Rinaldi, Nicholas Michael 1934- *WhoWrEP 92*
Rinaldi, Sergio 1940- *WhoScE 91-3*
Rinaldini, Luis E. 1953- *St&PR 93*
Rinaldini, Luis Emilio 1953- *WhoAm 92*
Rinaldi-Sandler, Ellen 1952- *St&PR 93*
Rinaldo, Helen 1922- *WhoE 93*
Rinaldo, Matthew J. 1931- *CngDr 91*
Rinaldo, Matthew John 1931- *WhoAm 92, WhoE 93*
Rinaldo di Capua c. 1705-c. 1780 *Baker 92, OxDcOp*
Rinaman, James Curtis, Jr. 1935- *WhoAm 92*
Rinard, R.E. 1950- *St&PR 93*
Rinaudo, Marguerite 1939- *WhoScE 91-2*
Rinauro, Paul D. 1943- *St&PR 93*
Rinck, Elizabeth Appel 1961- *WhoAmW 93*
Rinck, Johann Christian Heinrich 1770-1846 *Baker 92*
Rincon, Cathy E. *Law&B 92*
Rind, Kenneth William 1935- *St&PR 93*
Rind, Sherry 1952- *WhoWrEP 92*
Rinde, John Jacques 1935- *WhoSSW 93*
Rinder, George Greer 1921- *WhoAm 92*
Rindert, Birger 1928- *WhoScE 91-4*
Rindfuss, Ronald Richard 1946- *WhoSSW 93*
Rindge, Debora Anne 1956- *WhoE 93*

Rindi, Gianguido 1920- WhoScE 91-3, WhoWor 93
Rindlaub, Jean Wade BioIn 17
Rindlaub, John Wade 1934- WhoAm 92
Rindoks, Kurt Peter 1958- WhoSSW 93
Rinearson, Judith Law&B 92
Rinearson, Peter Mark 1954- WhoAm 92
Rineberg, Bill 1937- St&PR 93
Rineberg, William J. 1937- St&PR 93
Rinehart, Charles R. 1947- WhoAm 92
Rinehart, Charles Robert 1947- St&PR 93
Rinehart, Gary Lee 1940- St&PR 93
Rinehart, Harry Elmer 1921- WhoSSW 93
Rinehart, James Forrest 1950- WhoSSW 93
Rinehart, Kathryn Ann 1948- WhoAmW 93
Rinehart, Marie Vaughn 1937- WhoSSW 93
Rinehart, Mary Roberts 1876-1958 AmWomPl, ScF&FL 92
Rinehart, Nita WhoAmW 93
Rinehart, Patti Lynn Rawlins 1960- WhoSSW 93
Rinehart, Peggy J. 1950- St&PR 93
Rinehart, Raymond G. 1922- St&PR 93
Rinehart, Robert 1938- WhoE 93
Rinehart, Steven O. 1946- St&PR 93
Rinehart, William Francis 1925- St&PR 93
Rinek, Robert Pierson 1952- St&PR 93
Rines, Carol Mary Williamson 1943- WhoE 93
Rines, John Randolph 1947- WhoAm 92
Rines, Robert Harvey 1922- WhoWor 93
Rines, S. Melvin 1924- St&PR 93, WhoAm 92
Rines, Stanley E. 1921- St&PR 93
Rinesmith, Terry L. 1942- St&PR 93
Riney, Hal Patrick 1932- WhoWor 93
Ring, Alfred Adolf 1905- WhoSSW 93
Ring, Alice Ruth 1931- WhoSSW 93
Ring, Alvin Manuel 1933- WhoAm 92
Ring, Carl E. 1902-1991 BioIn 17
Ring, Caryle C., Jr. Law&B 92
Ring, Chester A., III 1927- St&PR 93
Ring, Dennis Randall 1952- WhoSSW 93
Ring, Gerald J. 1928- WhoAm 92
Ring, Hans 1927- WhoWor 93
Ring, Harold F. 1921- St&PR 93
Ring, Herbert Everett 1925- WhoWor 93
Ring, Jackson A. 1940- St&PR 93
Ring, James Edward Patrick 1940- WhoAm 92
Ring, James Walter 1929- WhoAm 92
Ring, John H. Law&B 92
Ring, John James 1928- WhoAm 92
Ring, Karen Ann 1962- WhoAmW 93
Ring, Kathleen Ann Law&B 92
Ring, Leonard M. 1923- WhoAm 92, WhoWor 93
Ring, Lina Barbara Taylor 1879-1941 AmWomPl
Ring, Liza G. Law&B 92
Ring, Margaret R. WhoWrEP 92
Ring, Martin 1918- St&PR 93
Ring, Michael Vincent 1965- WhoSSW 93
Ring, Millard A. d1992 NewYTBS 92
Ring, Richard R. Law&B 92
Ring, Robert G. 1926- St&PR 93
Ring, Stephen Douglas Law&B 92
Ring, Thomasina ScF&FL 92
Ringadoo, Veerasamy 1920- WhoWor 93
Ringbeck, Jurgen 1955- WhoWor 93
Ringbom, Hakan ScF&FL 92
Ringbom, Nils-Eric 1907-1988 Baker 92
Ringdal, Frode 1942- WhoScE 91-4
Ringden, Olle T.H. 1944- WhoScE 91-4
Ringe, Donald A. 1923- ScF&FL 92
Ringe, Henry Ralph 1936- WhoE 93
Ringe, Johann Diederich 1946- WhoWor 93
Ringel, Deborah Taper 1957- WhoAmW 93
Ringel, Harry ScF&FL 92
Ringel, Robert Lewis 1937- WhoAm 92
Ringelberg, Melvin Lee 1934- WhoSSW 93
Ringelblum, Emmanuel 1900-1944 PolBiDi
Ringen, Catherine Oleson 1943- WhoAm 92
Ringenberg, John Jay 1954- St&PR 93
Ringer, Alexander L(other) 1921- Baker 92
Ringer, James Milton 1943- WhoAm 92
Ringer, Jerome M. 1935- St&PR 93
Ringer, Larry Joel 1937- WhoSSW 93
Ringer, Pamela Glisson 1953- WhoSSW 93
Ringer, Thomas Latta 1931- WhoAm 92
Ringer, Walter M., III 1947- St&PR 93
Ringertz, Nils R. 1932- WhoScE 91-4
Ringgold, Faith BioIn 17
Ringgold, Faith 1930- BlkAuII 92, ConBlB 4 [port], SmATA 71 [port], WhoAm 92
Ringhaver, Lance Christian 1939- St&PR 93
Ringhaver, Randal St&PR 93
Ringhofer, Joseph Frank 1936- St&PR 93
Ringhofer, Richard Alan Law&B 92
Ringhofer, William Michael 1945- WhoIns 93
Ringle, Brett Adelbert 1951- WhoAm 92, WhoEmL 93, WhoSSW 93
Ringleb, Dietrich 1927- WhoScE 91-3
Ringlee, Robert James 1926- WhoAm 92
Ringler, David S. 1948- St&PR 93
Ringler, James M. 1945- WhoAm 92
Ringler, Lenore WhoAm 92
Ringler, Robin Lynn 1949- St&PR 93
Ringler, Sharon Mattila 1948- WhoWrEP 92
Ringlund, Kare 1934- WhoScE 91-4
Ringness, Ronald Christian 1949- St&PR 93
Ringo, Betty Penfold 1924- WhoAmW 93
Ringo, Jim 1932- BioIn 17
Ringo, John 1844-1882 BioIn 17
Ringo, Philip J. 1942- St&PR 93
Ringoen, Richard Miller 1926- St&PR 93
Ringoir, Severin 1931- WhoScE 91-2
Ringoir, Severin Maria Ghislenus 1931- WhoWor 93
Ringpfeil, Manfred Gustav 1932- WhoScE 91-3
Ringrose, David Robert 1938- WhoAm 92
Ringrose, Joanna J. Law&B 92
Ringrose, John Robert WhoScE 91-1
Ringrose, Nigel John Carter 1938- WhoUN 92
Ringswald, Michael Anthony 1950- St&PR 93
Ringuet 1895-1960 BioIn 17
Ringuette, Adrien L. Law&B 92
Ringuette, Adrien Lanthier 1925- St&PR 93
Ringuette, Domer BioIn 17, NewYTBS 92
Ringvald, Miguel Andres 1956- WhoE 93
Ringvold, Amund 1936- WhoScE 91-4
Ringwald, Molly 1968- WhoAm 92
Ring-Wilson, Kristine 1948- WhoE 93
Ringwood, Gwen 1910-1984 WhoCanL 92
Ringwood, Stephen B. Law&B 92
Rini, Donald Anthony 1935- St&PR 93
Rinicella, Randy Damian Law&B 92
Riniotis, Thomas 1938- WhoWor 93
Rink, Anthony Arnold 1942- WhoWor 93
Rink, Christopher Lee 1952- WhoSSW 93
Rink, John Felix 1927- St&PR 93
Rink, Lawrence Donald 1940- WhoAm 92
Rink, Robert Joseph 1942- St&PR 93
Rink, Wesley Winfred 1922- WhoAm 92
Rinkel, Margaret Elizabeth 1928- WhoWrEP 92
Rinkel, Sherman A. 1925- St&PR 93
Rinker, Marshall Edison 1904- St&PR 93
Rinker, Marshall Edison, Sr. 1904- WhoAm 92
Rinkevich, Charles Francis 1940- WhoAm 92
Rinkey, Benjamin S. 1941- St&PR 93
Rinkoff, Barbara 1923-1975 DcAmChF 1960, ScF&FL 92
Rinn, Louise A. Law&B 92
Rinn, Marvin L. 1933- St&PR 93
Rinnander, Philip H. 1944- St&PR 93
Rinne, Austin Dean 1919- WhoWor 93
Rinne, Kalle Antero 1935- WhoScE 91-4
Rinne, Risto WhoScE 91-4
Rinner, Ronald R. Law&B 92
Rinnooy Kan, Alexander Hendrik George 1949- WhoWor 93
Rinolfi, Rinaldo 1947- WhoScE 91-3
Rinsch, Charles E. 1932- St&PR 93
Rinsch, Charles Emil 1932- WhoAm 92
Rinser, Luise 1911- WhoWor 93
Rinsky, Judith Lynn 1941- WhoE 93
Rinsland, Roland DeLano 1933- WhoE 93, WhoWor 93
Rinsler, Norma Sybil 1927- WhoWor 93
Rinta, J. WhoScE 91-4
Rintamaki, John M. Law&B 92
Rintelmann, William Fred 1930- WhoAm 92
Rinuccini, Giovanni Battista 1592-1653 BioIn 17
Rinuccini, Ottavio 1562-1621 Baker 92, OxDcOp
Rinville, F. WhoScE 91-3, WhoUN 92
Rinzel, Daniel Francis 1942- WhoAm 92
Rinzler, Allan 1941- WhoAm 92
Rinzler, Carol Eisen BioIn 17
Rinzler, Carol Gene Eisen 1941- WhoWrEP 92
Rinzler, Kenneth Law&B 92
Rinzler, Ralph 1934- WhoAm 92
Rio, Dolores Del NotHsAW 93
Rio, Petra Barreras del NotHsAW 93
Rion, Fount H., Jr. 1920- St&PR 93
Riopel, Louis M. 1933- St&PR 93
Riopelle, Arthur Jean 1920- WhoAm 92, WhoSSW 93
Riopelle, Jean-Paul 1923- BioIn 17
Riordan, Bill d1991 BioIn 17
Riordan, Denis J. Law&B 92
Riordan, Denis J. 1936- St&PR 93
Riordan, George Nickerson 1933- WhoAm 92
Riordan, James Francis 1934- WhoE 93
Riordan, James Q. 1927- St&PR 93
Riordan, James Quentin 1927- WhoAm 92
Riordan, James William WhoScE 91-1
Riordan, John D. 1951- St&PR 93
Riordan, John Francis 1936- WhoAm 92
Riordan, John Thomas 1937- WhoAm 92
Riordan, John Thomas 1945- WhoAm 92
Riordan, Joseph Edward 1953- St&PR 93
Riordan, Michael 1946- ConAu 37NR, WhoWrEP 92
Riordan, Michael L. St&PR 93
Riordan, Robert F. 1942- St&PR 93
Riordan, Thomas J. 1950- St&PR 93
Riordan, Thomas Michael 1933- St&PR 93
Riordan, William F. 1941- WhoAm 92
Riordon, John Bernard 1947- WhoAm 92, WhoE 93
Rios, Alberto 1952- DcLB 122 [port]
Rios, Carlos A. 1943- St&PR 93
Rios, Carolina Susana 1966- WhoSSW 93
Rios, Evelyn Deerwester 1916- WhoSSW 93
Rios, Isabella NotHsAW 93
Rios, Jose R. Law&B 92
Rios, Juan 1914- WhoWor 93
Rios, Waldo de los 1934-1977 Baker 92
Rios Montt, Jose Efrain 1927- DcCPCAm
Rios R., Adolfo 1959- WhoWor 93
Riotte, Philipp Jakob 1776-1856 Baker 92, OxDcOp
Riou WhoScE 91-2
Rioukhine, Serguei N. 1949- WhoUN 92
Rioux, Claude 1935- WhoScE 91-2
Rioux, Helene 1949- WhoCanL 92
Ripa, Alberto da c. 1500-1551 Baker 92
Ripa, Cesare fl. 1600- BioIn 17
Ripa, Louis C. 1927- St&PR 93
Ripberger, Henry A. 1938- St&PR 93
Riperton, Minnie 1947-1979 BioIn 17
Riphahn, Wilhelm 1889-1963 BioIn 17
Ripka, G. Elizabeth 1924- WhoE 93
Ripken, Cal, Jr. BioIn 17
Ripken, Cal, Jr. 1960- CurBio 92 [port]
Ripken, Calvin Edwin 1935- WhoAm 92
Ripken, Calvin Edwin, Jr. 1960- WhoAm 92, WhoE 93
Ripley, Alexandra BioIn 17
Ripley, Alexandra 1934- ConAu 38NR, CurBio 92 [port], WhoAmW 93
Ripley, Betty Farrally 1915- WhoAm 92
Ripley, Brian David WhoScE 91-1
Ripley, Brian David 1952- WhoWor 93
Ripley, Craig Meredith 1961- St&PR 93
Ripley, Donald BioIn 17
Ripley, Edward Franklin 1927- WhoAm 92
Ripley, Francis Joseph 1912- ConAu 39NR
Ripley, George 1802-1880 JrnUS
Ripley, George W., II Law&B 92
Ripley, Karen ScF&FL 92
Ripley, Karen A. Law&B 92
Ripley, Lionel George WhoScE 91-1
Ripley, Mary Moncrieffe Livingston WhoE 93
Ripley, Melissa Louise Belote Hamlin 1956- BiDAMSp 1989
Ripley, Patricia F. 1927- St&PR 93
Ripley, Pida 1944- WhoWor 93
Ripley, Robert Leroy 1893-1949 JrnUS
Ripley, Stuart McKinnon 1930- WhoWor 93
Ripley, Thomas Charles 1946- St&PR 93
Ripley, Vickie Corbett 1950- WhoAmW 93
Ripley, Wayne E., Jr. Law&B 92
Ripling, Edward Joseph 1921- WhoAm 92
Ripoche, Jean 1934- WhoScE 91-2
Ripoll-Muntaner, Andres 1933- WhoScE 91-2
Ripp, James A. 1946- St&PR 93
Ripp, Marvin Law&B 92
Ripp, Richard J. St&PR 93
Rippe, Peter Marquart 1937- WhoAm 92, WhoSSW 93
Rippe, Robert D., Jr. Law&B 92
Rippee, Doyle R. 1948- St&PR 93
Rippel, Harry Conrad 1926- WhoAm 92
Rippel, Jeffrey Alan 1945- WhoAm 92, WhoSSW 93
Rippel, Julius A. 1901-1990 BioIn 17
Rippeon, Teresa Lynne 1965- WhoAmW 93
Rippeteau, Darrel Downing 1917- WhoAm 92
Rippey, Donald Taylor 1927- WhoAm 92
Rippin, David W.T. 1935- WhoScE 91-4
Rippin, Joseph P., III Law&B 92
Rippington, Geoff ScF&FL 92
Rippl, Bart H. 1966- St&PR 93
Rippl, George Allyn 1936- St&PR 93
Ripple, Kenneth Frances 1943- WhoAm 92
Ripple, Louis J. 1945- St&PR 93
Ripple, Raymond M. Law&B 92
Ripple, Ronald St&PR 93
Ripplinger, George Raymond, Jr. 1945- WhoAm 92
Ripps, Lewis S. 1932- St&PR 93
Ripps, Van 1958- St&PR 93
Rippy, Benjamin Wesley BiDAMSp 1989
Rippy, Bobby Gene 1930- WhoSSW 93
Rippy, Frances Marguerite Mayhew 1929- WhoAmW 93
Rippy, James P. 1943- St&PR 93, WhoIns 93
Rippy, Rodney Allen BioIn 17
Rips, Ervine Milton ScF&FL 92
Rips, Richard M. 1930- WhoScE 91-2
Rips, Richard Maurice 1930- WhoWor 93
Ripstein, Arturo 1943- MiSFD 9
Ripstein, Charles Benjamin 1913- WhoAm 92
Ripston, Robert G. 1929- St&PR 93
Ripullone, Shirley A. Law&B 92
Riq MajAI
Riquelme, Sonia Ines 1944- WhoSSW 93
Riquelme Ballesteros, Fernando 1948- WhoScE 91-3
Riquelmy, Edward S. Law&B 92
Riquier, Yves 1939- WhoScE 91-2
Ririe, Craig Martin 1943- WhoAm 92
Ris, Hans 1914- WhoAm 92
Ris, William Krakow 1915- WhoAm 92
Risberg, Gerald Lawrence 1930- St&PR 93
Risberg, John F. Law&B 92
Risberg, Ovind 1958- St&PR 93
Risbourg, Pascale BioIn 17
Risca, Maria Rodica 1937- WhoScE 91-4
Riscalla, Louise Beverly 1932- WhoAmW 93
Risch, James E. 1943- WhoAm 92
Risch, Martin Donald 1929- WhoAm 92
Risch, William H. 1938- St&PR 93
Rischard, Jean-Francois 1948- WhoUN 92
Riscica, Robert J. St&PR 93
Riscili, Catherine Lucinda 1964- WhoAmW 93
Risdon, David Lyon 1951- WhoEmL 93
Risdon, Vera Jane 1945- WhoAmW 93
Rise, Carl Halley 1915- St&PR 93
Risebrough, Doug 1954- WhoAm 92
Riseden, Joe Frank 1923- WhoSSW 93
Riseley, Martha Suzannah Heater 1916- WhoWor 93
Riseman, Susan G. Law&B 92
Risen, Paul Steven 1950- St&PR 93
Riser, Brenda Denice 1962- WhoAmW 93
Risgaard, Ernest Milton 1936- St&PR 93
Rish, L. David Law&B 92
Rish, Stephen A. 1946- St&PR 93
Rishel, Joseph J. 1940- WhoAm 92
Rishel, Mary Ann Malinchak 1940- WhoWrEP 92
Rishel, Richard Clinton 1943- St&PR 93, WhoAm 92
Rishell, William Arthur 1940- St&PR 93
Risher, Carol Adrienne Seeger 1946- WhoE 93
Risher, John Robert, Jr. 1938- WhoAm 92
Risher, Ronald D. 1956- St&PR 93
Rishpon, Moshe BioIn 17
Rishwain, Robert J. 1937- St&PR 93
Risi, Dino 1917- MiSFD 9
Risi, Louis J., Jr. 1936- WhoAm 92, WhoWor 93
Risi, Marco 1951- MiSFD 9
Risien, Cody 1957- WhoAm 92
Risimini, Ralph Dominick 1939- St&PR 93
Rising, Clara BioIn 17
Rising, Gerald Richard 1927- WhoE 93
Rising, Keith B. 1949- St&PR 93
Risinger, D. Michael 1945- WhoAm 92
Risinger, James A. 1948- St&PR 93
Risjord, Norman K. 1931- WhoWrEP 92
Risk, David Duncan Leslie WhoScE 91-1
Risk, J. Fred 1928- St&PR 93, WhoAm 92
Risk, James Muir Symington WhoScE 91-1
Risk, Ken R. 1948- St&PR 93
Risk, Sharon Clay d1991 BioIn 17
Risk, Thomas Neilson 1922- WhoWor 93
Riska, Dan Olof W. 1944- WhoScE 91-4
Riskin, Gerald H. St&PR 93
Riskin, Samuel F. d1992 NewYTBS 92
Riskind, Kenneth J. 1937- St&PR 93
Riskind, Kenneth Jay 1937- WhoAm 92
Riskind, Mary 1944- BioIn 17
Riskind, Reuben 1919- St&PR 93
Risko, Edward W. Law&B 92
Risku, Daniel M. Law&B 92
Risler, Edouard 1873-1929 Baker 92
Risley, Curtis Law&B 92
Risley, Henry Brainard 1946- WhoE 93, WhoEmL 93
Risley, Jean Funk 1945- WhoAmW 93
Risley, John Hollister 1919- WhoE 93
Risley, Rod BioIn 17
Risley, Rod Alan 1954- WhoSSW 93
Risley, Todd Robert 1937- WhoAm 92

Risman, Michael 1938- *WhoAm 92*
Risner, Ray David 1945- *WhoSSW 93*
Risner, Ronald Dean 1947- *WhoSSW 93*
Risnes, Helge Briseid 1948- *WhoWor 93*
Risness, E.J. *WhoScE 91-1*
Riso, David Adrian *Law&B 92*
Risom, Jens 1916- *WhoAm 92, WhoE 93*
Risom, Ole Christian 1919- *WhoAm 92*
Rison, Andre *BioIn 17*
Riss, E.S. 1949- *St&PR 93*
Riss, Eric 1929- *WhoAm 92, WhoE 93*
Riss, Micha *BioIn 17*
Riss, Murray 1940- *WhoAm 92*
Riss, Robert B. 1927- *St&PR 93*
Riss, Robert Bailey 1927- *WhoAm 92, WhoWor 93*
Risse, Guenter Bernhard 1932- *WhoAm 92*
Risse, Horst F.E. 1936- *St&PR 93*
Risse, Klaus Heinz 1929- *St&PR 93*
Risseeuw, Janet E. 1944- *WhoAmW 93*
Risser, Anne Maureen 1960- *WhoAmW 93*
Risser, Arthur Crane, Jr. 1938- *WhoAm 92*
Risser, James Vaulx, Jr. 1938- *WhoAm 92*
Risser, Paul Gillan 1939- *WhoAm 92*
Risset, Jean-Claude 1938- *WhoScE 91-2, WhoWor 93*
Rissi, William Thomas 1935- *St&PR 93*
Rissinger, Rollin Paul, Jr. 1943- *St&PR 93*
Rissman, Burton Richard 1927- *WhoAm 92*
Rissman, John A. *Law&B 92*
Rissman, Lawrence E. *Law&B 92*
Rissmann-Joyce, Stacie Lynn 1950- *WhoAmW 93*
Rissmeyer, Patricia Ann 1956- *WhoE 93*
Rist, Andre 1927- *WhoScE 91-2*
Rist, Johann 1607-1667 *Baker 92*
Rist, Robert G. 1946- *St&PR 93*
Rist, S. *WhoScE 91-4*
Ristau, Edsel Paul 1942- *WhoE 93*
Ristau, Kenneth Eugene, Jr. 1939- *WhoAm 92*
Ristau, Mark M. 1944- *St&PR 93*
Ristau, Ronald W. 1953- *St&PR 93*
Riste, Tormod 1925- *WhoScE 91-4*
Ristenpart, Karl 1900-1967 *Baker 92*
Ristic, Milan 1908-1982 *Baker 92*
Ristich, Miodrag 1938- *WhoE 93, WhoWor 93*
Ristig, Kyle Gregory 1954- *WhoSSW 93*
Ristig, Lynn Elizabeth *Law&B 92*
Ristino, Robert J. 1943- *WhoE 93*
Riston, Francois Xavier 1963- *WhoWor 93*
Ristori, Allan John 1936- *WhoE 93*
Ristori, Giovanni Alberto 1692-1753 *Baker 92, OxDcOp*
Ristori, Tommaso *OxDcOp*
Ristow, Gail Ross 1949- *WhoAmW 93*
Ristow, George Edward 1943- *WhoAm 92*
Rita, William Edward 1941- *St&PR 93*
Ritardi, Albert F. 1936- *St&PR 93*
Ritardi, Albert Francis 1936- *WhoAm 92, WhoWor 93*
Ritcey, Paul L. *St&PR 93*
Ritch, Herald LaVern 1951- *WhoAm 92, WhoE 93*
Ritch, James Earle, Jr. 1931- *WhoWor 93*
Ritch, Joe H. 1950- *St&PR 93*
Ritch, Kathleen 1943- *St&PR 93, WhoAm 92, WhoAmW 93*
Ritch, Robert Harry 1942- *WhoWor 93*
Ritch, Thomas Alden 1955- *WhoE 93*
Ritchel, Raymond B., Jr. *Law&B 92*
Ritcheson, Charles Ray 1925- *WhoAm 92*
Ritchey, Alan *WhoScE 91-1*
Ritchey, Belle MacDiarmid *AmWomPl*
Ritchey, David 1940- *WhoWrEP 92*
Ritchey, David Anthony 1949- *WhoSSW 93*
Ritchey, Jeanette Mayer 1945- *WhoAmW 93, WhoSSW 93*
Ritchey, Jeanne Louise 1942- *WhoAmW 93*
Ritchey, John J. *Law&B 92*
Ritchey, John J. 1947- *St&PR 93*
Ritchey, Kenneth James 1926- *St&PR 93*
Ritchey, Michael R. 1939- *St&PR 93*
Ritchey, Paul Andrew 1950- *WhoWor 93*
Ritchey, William Michael 1925- *WhoAm 92*
Ritchie, Alan Alfred 1939- *St&PR 93*
Ritchie, Alan Isaac 1941- *St&PR 93*
Ritchie, Alan Joseph 1942- *St&PR 93*
Ritchie, Albert 1939- *WhoAm 92*
Ritchie, Catherine Dlorah 1954- *WhoAmW 93*
Ritchie, Cedric *BioIn 17*
Ritchie, Cedric Elmer 1927- *St&PR 93, WhoAm 92, WhoWor 93*
Ritchie, Charles Jackson, Jr. 1933- *St&PR 93, WhoAm 92*
Ritchie, Cindy Lou 1955- *WhoWor 93*
Ritchie, Daniel Goodhue 1942- *WhoUN 92*
Ritchie, Daniel Lee 1931- *WhoAm 92*
Ritchie, David J. *Law&B 92*
Ritchie, David Malcolm 1950- *WhoE 93*
Ritchie, Donald Andrew *WhoScE 91-1*
Ritchie, E.D. 1926- *St&PR 93*
Ritchie, Earl J. 1944- *St&PR 93*
Ritchie, Fred P. 1924- *St&PR 93*
Ritchie, G.S. 1939- *WhoScE 91-1*
Ritchie, Garry Harlan 1938- *WhoE 93, WhoWor 93*
Ritchie, J. Murdoch 1925- *WhoE 93*
Ritchie, Jack 1924- *St&PR 93*
Ritchie, James J. 1954- *WhoIns 93*
Ritchie, James Timothy *Law&B 92*
Ritchie, Karen *BioIn 17, WhoAmW 93*
Ritchie, Karen 1943- *St&PR 93*
Ritchie, Kenneth A. *Law&B 92*
Ritchie, Lisa 1961- *WhoSSW 93*
Ritchie, Mark A. *BioIn 17*
Ritchie, Michael 1938- *MiSFD 9*
Ritchie, Michael Brunswick 1938- *WhoAm 92*
Ritchie, Michael Karl 1946- *WhoWrEP 92*
Ritchie, Norman Robert 1933- *WhoAm 92*
Ritchie, Paul 1923- *ScF&FL 92*
Ritchie, Paul O'Neal 1931- *St&PR 93*
Ritchie, Rex E. 1938- *St&PR 93*
Ritchie, Richard L. 1946- *St&PR 93*
Ritchie, Richard Lee 1946- *WhoAm 92*
Ritchie, Rita 1930- *ScF&FL 92*
Ritchie, Robert C. 1929- *St&PR 93*
Ritchie, Robert F. 1917- *St&PR 93*
Ritchie, Robert Field 1917- *WhoAm 92, WhoSSW 93*
Ritchie, Robert Jamieson 1944- *WhoAm 92*
Ritchie, Ronald Stuart 1918- *WhoAm 92*
Ritchie, Royal Daniel 1945- *WhoAm 92, WhoE 93*
Ritchie, Rufus Haynes 1924- *WhoSSW 93*
Ritchie, Stanley (John) 1935- *Baker 92*
Ritchie, Stephen Holland 1951- *WhoSSW 93*
Ritchie, Thomas 1778-1854 *JrnUS, PolPar*
Ritchie, W. 1932- *St&PR 93*
Ritchie, (Harry) Ward 1905- *WhoWrEP 92*
Ritchie, William *WhoScE 91-1*
Ritchin, Barbara Sue 1940- *WhoAmW 93*
Ritchlin, Martha Ann 1953- *WhoAmW 93*
Ritenour, Lee *BioIn 17*
Riter, Stephen 1940- *WhoAm 92*
Ritger, William J. 1949- *St&PR 93*
Rithauddeen Bin Tengku Ismail, Tengku Dato' Ahmad 1932- *WhoAsAP 91*
Rither, Alan Craig *Law&B 92*
Ritholz, Jules 1925- *WhoAm 92*
Ritins, Ilmars 1937- *St&PR 93*
Ritner, Joseph 1780-1869 *BioIn 17*
Ritondaro, G.H. 1946- *St&PR 93*
Ritsch, Frederick Field 1935- *WhoAm 92*
Ritschel, James Allan 1930- *WhoWor 93*
Ritsema, A. Reinier 1923- *WhoScE 91-3*
Ritsema, Larry James 1950- *St&PR 93*
Ritson, Richard 1931- *St&PR 93*
Ritsos, Giannes *ConAu 39NR*
Ritsos, Giannes 1909-1990 *BioIn 17*
Ritsos, Yannis 1909-1990 *BioIn 17, ConAu 39NR*
Ritt, Albert E. 1908- *St&PR 93*
Ritt, James William *Law&B 92*
Ritt, John A. 1941- *St&PR 93*
Ritt, Martin *BioIn 17*
Ritt, Martin 1913-1990 *MiSFD 9N*
Ritt, Paul Edward 1928- *WhoAm 92*
Ritt, W.W., Jr. *Law&B 92*
Rittaporn, Atip 1957- *WhoWor 93*
Rittberg, Ellen Pober 1952- *WhoWrEP 92*
Rittberger, Volker 1941- *WhoWor 93*
Rittberger, Werner Heinz 1927- *WhoWor 93*
Rittenbach, Karen Joan 1959- *WhoE 93*
Rittenberg, Arthur 1904- *WhoSSW 93*
Rittenberg, Richard M. *Law&B 92*
Rittenberg, Vladimir I. 1934- *WhoScE 91-3*
Rittenhouse, Bruce Dean 1951- *WhoSSW 93*
Rittenhouse, Dicie M. *AmWomPl*
Rittenhouse, Jack D. 1912-1991 *BioIn 17*
Rittenhouse, Joseph Wilson 1917- *WhoAm 92*
Rittenhouse, Thomas Scott 1941- *St&PR 93*
Ritter, Alexander 1833-1896 *Baker 92*
Ritter, Alfred 1923- *WhoAm 92, WhoSSW 93*
Ritter, Alfred F., Jr. 1946- *St&PR 93*
Ritter, Alfred Francis, Jr. 1946- *WhoAm 92*
Ritter, Andrew K. *Law&B 92*
Ritter, Ann L. 1933- *WhoAmW 93, WhoE 93, WhoWor 93*
Ritter, Anna Marie 1961- *WhoAmW 93*
Ritter, August Gottfried 1811-1885 *Baker 92*
Ritter, Bruce 1927- *BioIn 17*
Ritter, Carl Alan 1932- *WhoE 93*
Ritter, Carole *Law&B 92*
Ritter, Carolyn S. 1934- *St&PR 93*
Ritter, Charles Edward 1938- *WhoAm 92*
Ritter, Charles W., Jr. 1933- *St&PR 93*
Ritter, Dale William 1919- *WhoWor 93*
Ritter, Daniel Benjamin 1937- *WhoAm 92*
Ritter, David Allen 1954- *WhoWor 93*
Ritter, Don 1940- *CngDr 91*
Ritter, Donald Lawrence 1940- *WhoAm 92, WhoE 93*
Ritter, Doris Standring 1926- *WhoAmW 93*
Ritter, Edward S. 1954- *WhoIns 93*
Ritter, Erika *WhoCanL 92*
Ritter, F. Richard 1932- *St&PR 93*
Ritter, Fanny Raymond 1840-1890 *See* Ritter, Frederic Louis 1826-1891 *Baker 92*
Ritter, Frank Nicholas 1928- *WhoAm 92*
Ritter, Frederic Louis 1826-1891 *Baker 92*
Ritter, Georg Wenzel 1748-1808 *OxDcOp*
Ritter, Gerhard A. 1929- *WhoWor 93*
Ritter, Gordon Louis 1942- *St&PR 93*
Ritter, Harwood Hugo, II 1935- *St&PR 93*
Ritter, Heinrich fl. 1779-1793 *OxDcOp*
Ritter, Henry L. 1941- *St&PR 93*
Ritter, Hermann 1849-1926 *Baker 92*
Ritter, James 1945- *St&PR 93*
Ritter, James Michael *WhoScE 91-1*
Ritter, James William 1942- *WhoAm 92*
Ritter, Jean Marie 1959- *WhoAmW 93*
Ritter, Jerry E. 1935- *St&PR 93, WhoAm 92*
Ritter, Joe *MiSFD 9*
Ritter, John 1948- *ConTFT 10, HolBB [port]*
Ritter, Johnathan Southworth 1948- *WhoAm 92*
Ritter, Joseph M. 1950- *WhoIns 93*
Ritter, Juergen 1943- *WhoWor 93*
Ritter, Karen Anne 1953- *WhoAmW 93*
Ritter, Karen Lynn 1962- *WhoAmW 93*
Ritter, Katrina Dania 1963- *WhoAmW 93*
Ritter, Lawrence (Stanley) 1922- *WhoWrEP 92*
Ritter, Malcolm Frank 1954- *WhoE 93*
Ritter, Mary Carol 1962- *WhoAmW 93*
Ritter, Merrie Dawn 1957- *WhoAmW 93*
Ritter, Michelle Ivy *Law&B 92*
Ritter, Naomi 1937- *ConAu 138*
Ritter, Peter 1763-1846 *Baker 92, OxDcOp*
Ritter, Robert Forcier 1943- *WhoAm 92*
Ritter, Robert Henry *Law&B 92*
Ritter, Robert J. 1959- *St&PR 93*
Ritter, Robert Joseph 1925- *WhoAm 92, WhoE 93*
Ritter, Thelma 1905-1969 *IntDcF 2-3 [port]*
Ritter, Theodore 1841-1886 *Baker 92*
Ritter, William Frederick 1942- *WhoE 93*
Ritter-Clough, Elise Dawn 1952- *WhoAmW 93*
Ritterhoff, Charles William 1921- *WhoAm 92, WhoSSW 93, WhoWor 93*
Ritterman, Judith Lynn *WhoE 93*
Ritterman, Sharen Bruneau 1949- *WhoEmL 93*
Ritterman, Stuart I. 1937- *WhoAm 92*
Rittgers, Donald L. 1947- *St&PR 93*
Rittgers, Rubye Elizabeth 1928- *St&PR 93*
Ritthaler, Gerald Irvin 1930- *WhoAm 92, WhoWor 93*
Rittinger, Martha Gerber 1933- *WhoAmW 93*
Rittmaster, Robert 1925- *St&PR 93*
Rittner, Carl Frederick 1914- *WhoE 93*
Rittner, Edmund Sidney 1919- *WhoAm 92*
Rittner, Tadeusz 1873-1921 *PolBiDi*
Rittof, Paul Raymond 1955- *WhoSSW 93*
Ritts, Christy 1957- *St&PR 93*
Ritts, Herb c. 1954- *News 92 [port]*
Ritts, Herbert I. 1912- *St&PR 93*
Rittwage, William *St&PR 93*
Ritvo, Edward Ross 1930- *WhoAm 92*
Ritvo, Roger Alan 1944- *WhoAm 92*
Ritz, Al 1901-1965 *See* Ritz Brothers, The *QDrFCA 92*
Ritz, Cesar 1850-1918 *BioIn 17*
Ritz, Charles 1891-1976 *BioIn 17*
Ritz, Dan *BioIn 17*
Ritz, David 1943- *ConAu 40NR*
Ritz, Esther Leah 1918- *WhoAm 92*
Ritz, Harry 1906-1986 *See* Ritz Brothers, The *QDrFCA 92*
Ritz, Irving *Law&B 92*
Ritz, Irving 1928- *St&PR 93*
Ritz, Jimmy 1903-1985 *See* Ritz Brothers, The *QDrFCA 92*
Ritz, Joseph P. 1929- *WhoWrEP 92*
Ritz, Richard Ellison 1919- *WhoAm 92*
Ritz, Richard L. 1953- *St&PR 93*
Ritz Brothers, The *QDrFCA 92 [port]*
Ritzel, Bud 1943- *St&PR 93*
Ritzel, Dennis A. 1937- *St&PR 93*
Ritzel, Joseph William 1958- *St&PR 93*
Ritzenberg, Frederick *MiSFD 9*
Ritzenthaler, Robert Eugene 1911-1980 *IntDcAn*
Ritzer, Lonnie Mark 1954- *WhoE 93*
Ritzer, Philip J. 1942- *St&PR 93*
Ritzer, Teri Ann *WhoAm 92*
Ritzman, Laura L. *Law&B 92*
Ritzman, Thomas Alexander 1914- *WhoE 93*
Ritzu, Barbara Jean 1951- *WhoAmW 93*
Rius, Luis 1930- *DcMexL*
Rius y Taulet, Francisco de Paula 1833-1889 *BioIn 17*
Riva, Alessandro 1939- *WhoScE 91-3*
Riva, Alessandro Lodovico 1939- *WhoWor 93*
Riva, Amadeo 1937- *WhoWor 93*
Riva, H.J. *Law&B 92*
Riva, Silvano 1939- *WhoScE 91-3*
Rivail, Jean-Louis 1937- *WhoScE 91-2, WhoWor 93*
Rival, Steven E. 1952- *WhoSSW 93*
Rivals, Jean 1935- *WhoUN 92*
Riva Palacio y Guerrero, Vicente 1832-1896 *DcMexL*
Rivard, Adjutor 1868-1945 *BioIn 17*
Rivard, George Henry 1931- *St&PR 93*
Rivard, Jean 1926- *WhoAm 92*
Rivard, Jean 1940- *St&PR 93*
Rivard, Ken 1947- *WhoCanL 92*
Rivard, Michael Louis 1956- *St&PR 93*
Rivard, Paul Edmund 1943- *WhoE 93*
Rivard, William Charles 1942- *WhoAm 92, WhoE 93*
Rivard, Yvon 1945- *WhoCanL 92*
Rivas, Frank T. *Law&B 92*
Rivas, Marian Lucy 1943- *HispAmA*
Rivas Garcia, Oscar Humberto *DcCPCAm*
Rivas Gasteazoro, Eduardo *DcCPCAm*
Rivas Salmon, Alfonso 1912- *WhoWor 93*
Rivas-Vazquez, Ana Victoria 1963- *WhoSSW 93*
Rive, Richard (Moore) 1931-1989 *DcLB 125 [port]*
Rive-King, Julie 1854-1937 *Baker 92*
Rivelli, William Raymond Allan 1935- *WhoE 93*
Rivenbank, Rembert Reginald, Jr. 1939- *St&PR 93*
Rivenbark, Jan Meredith 1950- *WhoWor 93*
Rivera, Angel Luis 1950- *WhoEmL 93, WhoSSW 93*
Rivera, Antonio T. *WhoIns 93*
Rivera, Brooklyn *DcCPCAm*
Rivera, Chita *BioIn 17*
Rivera, Chita 1933- *NotHsAW 93 [port], WhoAm 92, WhoAmW 93*
Rivera, Daniel Carlos 1931- *WhoIns 93*
Rivera, Daniel James 1954- *WhoSSW 93*
Rivera, Dennis *BioIn 17, NewYTBS 92 [port]*
Rivera, Diana Cynthia *Law&B 92*
Rivera, Diego *DcCPCAm*
Rivera, Diego 1886-1957 *BioIn 17*
Rivera, Eida Luz 1957- *WhoE 93*
Rivera, Evelyn Margaret 1929- *HispAmA, WhoAmW 93*
Rivera, Frida Kahlo 1907-1954 *BioIn 17*
Rivera, Geraldo *BioIn 17*
Rivera, Geraldo 1943- *HispAmA, WhoAm 92*
Rivera, Ignacio *Law&B 92*
Rivera, Jose Eustasio 1888-1928 *SpAmA*
Rivera, Julio Adalberto *DcCPCAm*
Rivera, Kathleen M. *Law&B 92*
Rivera, Louis Reyes 1945- *WhoWrEP 92*
Rivera, Luis d1992 *NewYTBS 92*
Rivera, Luis Ernesto 1950- *St&PR 93*
Rivera, Lutgardo Ferrer 1933- *WhoWor 93*
Rivera, Marina 1942- *DcLB 122 [port]*
Rivera, Mario *Law&B 92*
Rivera, Matea Usero 1927- *WhoWor 93*
Rivera, Michael P. *Law&B 92*
Rivera, Miquela Carleen 1954- *WhoWrEP 92*
Rivera, Oscar R. 1956- *WhoEmL 93, WhoSSW 93*
Rivera, Pilar Primo de d1991 *BioIn 17*
Rivera, Richard E. 1947- *St&PR 93, WhoAm 92*
Rivera, Robert A. 1940- *St&PR 93*
Rivera, Toni Luisa 1959- *WhoAmW 93*
Rivera, Vicente C., Jr. 1931- *WhoAsAP 91*
Rivera, Vicki Laura 1945- *WhoWrEP 92*
Rivera-Almentero, Daisy 1958- *WhoAmW 93*
Rivera-Colon, Lucas 1918- *St&PR 93*
Rivera Martinez, Edgardo 1933- *SpAmA*
Rivera-Morales, Roberto 1953- *WhoWor 93*
Rivera-Munich, Fernando *Law&B 92*
Rivera-Ortiz, Gilberto 1932- *WhoSSW 93*
Rivera-Soto, Roberto A. *Law&B 92*
Rivera-Soto, Roberto Andres 1953- *St&PR 93*
Rivera-Urrutia, Beatriz Dalila 1951- *WhoAmW 93*

Riverin, Bruno 1941- *WhoAm 92, WhoE 93, WhoWor 93*
Rivero, Andres 1936- *WhoWrEP 92*
Rivero, Eliana 1940- *HispAmA*
Rivero, Jose Antonio 1931- *St&PR 93*
Rivero, Pedro 1938- *WhoWor 93*
Rivero Aguero, Andres *DcCPCAm*
Rivers, Augustus Henry Lane-Fox Pitt- 1827-1900 *BioIn 17*
Rivers, Caryl 1937- *WhoWrEP 92*
Rivers, Caryl Ann 1937- *WhoE 93*
Rivers, Cheryl P. *WhoAmW 93*
Rivers, Diana 1931- *ScF&FL 92*
Rivers, Douglas Bernard 1951- *WhoSSW 93*
Rivers, Gary Clinton 1951-1990 *BioIn 17*
Rivers, Jessie Mae 1933- *WhoWor 93*
Rivers, Joan 1933?- *ConTFT 10, MiSFD 9, WhoAm 92, WhoAmW 93*
Rivers, Joan 1937- *BioIn 17, WhoWrEP 92*
Rivers, John Minott, Jr. 1945- *WhoSSW 93*
Rivers, Joyce Mansfield *Law&B 92*
Rivers, Kathryn Shields 1931- *WhoAmW 93*
Rivers, Kenneth Jay 1938- *WhoE 93*
Rivers, Larry *BioIn 17*
Rivers, Marie Bie 1928- *WhoAm 92, WhoAmW 93, WhoWor 93*
Rivers, Marilyn Luciw 1960- *WhoAmW 93*
Rivers, Marion P. *St&PR 93*
Rivers, Mary Shipes 1927- *WhoAmW 93*
Rivers, Mickey 1948- *BioIn 17*
Rivers, Miriam Wooding *WhoAmW 93*
Rivers, Otis Thomas 1961- *WhoSSW 93*
Rivers, Pamela Susan 1966- *WhoE 93*
Rivers, Porter, Jr. 1927- *St&PR 93*
Rivers, Richard D. *Law&B 92*
Rivers, Richard Davis 1934- *St&PR 93, WhoAm 92*
Rivers, Richard Robinson 1942- *WhoAm 92*
Rivers, Robert Alfred 1923- *WhoAm 92*
Rivers, Ronald D. 1933- *WhoAm 92*
Rivers, Sam 1930- *BioIn 17*
Rivers, Sherry Diane 1948- *WhoSSW 93*
Rivers, W.H.R. 1864-1922 *IntDcAn*
Rivers, Wilga Marie 1919- *WhoAm 92*
Riverside, John *MajAI, SmATA 69*
Rivers-Kennedy, Elizabeth Keville 1944- *WhoSSW 93*
Riverso, Renato 1934- *St&PR 93*
Riverso, Renato M. 1934- *WhoAm 92*
Rives, Amelie *AmWomPl*
Rives, Harry Clayton 1920- *St&PR 93*
Rives, James Claude, Jr. 1956- *St&PR 93*
Rives, John Cook 1795-1864 *JrnUS*
Rives, Richard Taylor 1895-1982 *EncAACR*
Rives, Robert Landon 1933- *St&PR 93, WhoAm 92*
Rives, Stanley Gene 1930- *WhoAm 92*
Rivest, F. *Law&B 92*
Rivest, Francois *Law&B 92*
Rivet, David Michael *Law&B 92*
Rivet, Diana Wittmer 1931- *WhoE 93*
Rivet, Jeannine M. 1948- *St&PR 93*
Rivet, Paul 1876-1958 *IntDcAn*
Rivet, Simon *Law&B 92*
Rivette, Gerard Bertram 1932- *WhoAm 92, WhoWor 93*
Rivette, Jacques *MiSFD 9*
Rivetti, Antonio *WhoScE 91-3*
Riviello Bazan, Antonio 1926- *WhoWor 93*
Rivier, Jean 1896-1987 *Baker 92*
Riviera, Daniel John 1927- *WhoAm 92*
Riviere, Bill *DcCPCAm*
Riviere, Georges Henri 1897-1985 *IntDcAn*
Riviere, J.P. 1945- *WhoScE 91-2*
Riviere, Joan 1883-1962 *BioIn 17*
Rivin, Donald 1934- *WhoE 93*
Rivin, Susan *Law&B 92*
Rivin, Zelma Goodman *WhoAmW 93*
Rivington, James c. 1724-1802 *JrnUS*
Rivinus, Francis Markoe 1915- *WhoE 93*
Rivizzigno, Victoria Lynne 1947- *WhoSSW 93*
Rivkin, Allen 1903-1990 *BioIn 17*
Rivkin, Donald Herschel 1924- *WhoAm 92*
Rivkin, J.F. *ScF&FL 92*
Rivkin, Jack Leon 1940- *WhoAm 92*
Rivkind, Melvin 1919- *St&PR 93*
Rivkind, Perry Abbot 1930- *WhoAm 92*
Rivkis, Renee H. *Law&B 92*
Rivlin, Alice Mitchell 1931- *WhoAm 92, WhoAmW 93*
Rivlin, Benjamin 1921- *WhoAm 92*
Rivlin, Elisa M. *Law&B 92*
Rivlin, Gary 1958- *ConAu 139*
Rivlin, Gerald B. 1929- *St&PR 93*
Rivlin, Harry N. 1904-1991 *BioIn 17*
Rivlin, Rachel *Law&B 92*
Rivlin, Ronald Samuel 1915- *WhoAm 92*
Rivnak-McAdam, Julie Anne 1956- *WhoSSW 93*
Rivoli, Pauline 1817-1881 *PolBiDi*
Rivolier, Jean 1923- *WhoScE 91-2*
Rix, Brian 1924- *QDrFCA 92 [port]*
Rix, Donald Melvin 1930- *St&PR 93*
Rix, John 1947- *St&PR 93*
Rix, Steven Carl 1939- *WhoAm 92*
Rixhon, L. *WhoScE 91-2*
Rixon, James Michael 1945- *WhoE 93*
Rixon, Peter A.R. *Law&B 92*
Rixon, Robert N. 1948- *WhoWrEP 92*
Riza, Iqbal 1934- *WhoUN 92*
Rizai, Matthew M. 1956- *WhoWor 93*
Rizal, Jose 1861-1896 *BioIn 17*
Rizam, Ihsan 1939- *St&PR 93*
Rizer, E. Lloyd 1930- *St&PR 93*
Rizer, Edward Nash *Law&B 92*
Rizi, Francisco 1608-1685 *BioIn 17*
Rizi, Juan 1600-1681 *BioIn 17*
Rizk, Farouk Aboul Makarem 1934- *WhoAm 92*
Rizk, Hikmat Youssef 1947- *WhoWor 93*
Rizk, Laila Galal 1961- *WhoWor 93*
Riznic, Jovica Radomir 1951- *WhoWor 93*
Rizowy, Carlos Guillermo 1949- *WhoEmL 93*
Rizvanov, Krum 1922- *WhoScE 91-4*
Rizvi, Syed Mohammed Nasir Raza 1953- *WhoWor 93*
Rizvi, Tanzeem R. 1949- *WhoWor 93*
Rizza, Charles Rocco 1930- *WhoWor 93*
Rizza, Joseph M. 1924- *St&PR 93*
Rizzardi, Anton 1919- *St&PR 93*
Rizzello, Claudio 1950- *WhoScE 91-3*
Rizzetta, Carolyn Teresa 1942- *WhoSSW 93*
Rizzi, Alfredo 1933- *WhoWor 93*
Rizzi, Deborah L. 1955- *WhoE 93*
Rizzi, Louis Leon 1932- *St&PR 93*
Rizzi, Paul C., Jr. 1946- *St&PR 93*
Rizziello, Patricia Derrickson 1940- *WhoE 93*
Rizzieri, L. Stephen *Law&B 92*
Rizzitello, Nicholas Anthony 1953- *WhoE 93*
Rizzo, Antonio fl. 1465-1498 *BioIn 17*
Rizzo, Caroline Frances 1958- *WhoAmW 93*
Rizzo, Edward Michael 1945- *St&PR 93*
Rizzo, Francis 1936- *WhoAm 92*
Rizzo, Frank 1920-1991 *AnObit 1991, News 92*
Rizzo, Frank L. 1920- *PolPar*
Rizzo, Frank Lazarro *BioIn 17*
Rizzo, Frank Simon 1944- *St&PR 93*
Rizzo, Gary Edward 1944- *WhoE 93*
Rizzo, James J. 1934- *St&PR 93*
Rizzo, James M. 1938- *WhoIns 93*
Rizzo, Jeffrey Francis 1954- *St&PR 93*
Rizzo, Jilly 1917-1992 *BioIn 17, NewYTBS 92*
Rizzo, Joseph L. 1942- *WhoIns 93*
Rizzo, Lawrence A. *Law&B 92*
Rizzo, Lynne M. 1961- *St&PR 93*
Rizzo, Mary Ann Frances 1942- *WhoAmW 93*
Rizzo, Paul J. 1928- *St&PR 93*
Rizzo, Richard David 1944- *WhoAm 92*
Rizzo, Richard John 1943- *St&PR 93*
Rizzo, Ronald Stephen 1941- *WhoAm 92, WhoWor 93*
Rizzo, Terrie Lorraine Heinrich 1946- *WhoWor 93*
Rizzo, Thomas Dignan 1931- *WhoE 93*
Rizzo, Vincenzo 1937- *WhoScE 91-3*
Rizzolatti, Giacomo 1937- *WhoWor 93*
Rizzuto, Ana-Maria 1932- *WhoAmW 93*
Rizzuto, C.R. 1937- *WhoScE 91-3*
Rizzuto, James Joseph 1939- *WhoWrEP 92*
Rizzuto, Leandro Peter 1938- *WhoAm 92*
Rizzuto, Phil 1918- *BioIn 17*
Rizzuto, Sharida Ann 1948- *WhoWrEP 92*
Rjazanov, El'dar 1927- *DrEEuF*
Rjndt, Philippe Van *ScF&FL 92*
Roa, Benedicta B. 1929- *WhoAsAP 91*
Roa, Fred *WhoE 93*
Roa Barcena, Jose Maria 1827-1908 *DcMexL*
Roa Bastos, Augusto 1917- *SpAmA*
Roa Bastos, Augusto Antonio *BioIn 17*
Roach, Alfred J. 1915- *St&PR 93*
Roach, Allene Z. d1992 *NewYTBS 92*
Roach, Arvid Edward, II 1951- *WhoAm 92*
Roach, Bonnie Lee 1957- *WhoAmW 93*
Roach, Charles James 1925- *St&PR 93*
Roach, Christopher Lane *Law&B 92*
Roach, Deborah Taylor 1965- *WhoAmW 93*
Roach, Don H. 1942- *St&PR 93*
Roach, Donald A. 1930- *St&PR 93*
Roach, Doris Terrer *Law&B 92*
Roach, Ed D. *WhoAm 92*
Roach, Edgar Mayo, Jr. 1948- *WhoAm 92*
Roach, Eleanor Marie 1932- *WhoAmW 93*
Roach, Gary DeLano 1940- *WhoSSW 93*
Roach, Glenn Allen 1954- *WhoSSW 93*
Roach, Hal 1892- *BioIn 17*
Roach, Hal 1892-1992 *NewYTBS 92 [port]*
Roach, Herbert R., Jr. 1946- *St&PR 93*
Roach, Irene K. 1934- *WhoAmW 93*
Roach, J. Phillip 1939- *WhoSSW 93*
Roach, J. Thurston 1941- *St&PR 93*
Roach, James Edward 1917- *St&PR 93*
Roach, James Patrick *WhoScE 91-1*
Roach, James R. *Law&B 92*
Roach, James Robert 1922- *WhoAm 92*
Roach, John 1943- *St&PR 93*
Roach, John D. C. 1943- *WhoAm 92*
Roach, John Hendee, Jr. 1941- *WhoAm 92*
Roach, John Marvil 1920- *WhoAm 92*
Roach, John Robert 1921- *WhoAm 92*
Roach, John V. 1938- *St&PR 93*
Roach, John Vinson, II 1938- *WhoAm 92*
Roach, Joyce Gibson 1935- *ConAu 40NR*
Roach, Larry W. 1949- *St&PR 93*
Roach, Margot Ruth 1934- *WhoAm 92*
Roach, Marilynne K. 1946- *ScF&FL 92*
Roach, Mark Carlton 1954- *St&PR 93*
Roach, Max *BioIn 17*
Roach, Max 1924- *Baker 92*
Roach, Maxwell Lemuel 1924- *WhoAm 92*
Roach, Ralph Lee 1957- *WhoE 93, WhoEmL 93*
Roach, Robert J. 1941- *St&PR 93*
Roach, Thomas Adair 1929- *WhoAm 92*
Roach, Timothy J. 1947- *St&PR 93*
Roach, Walter P. *Law&B 92*
Roach, Wesley Linville 1931- *WhoAm 92*
Roach, William Russell 1940- *WhoAm 92, WhoWor 93*
Roache, Edward Francis 1923- *WhoAm 92*
Roache, Gregory Paul 1957- *St&PR 93*
Roache, Patrick Michael, Jr. 1946- *WhoEmL 93*
Roach-Wheeler, Margaret 1942- *BioIn 17*
Road, Alan *ScF&FL 92*
Roadarmel, Paul Douglas 1942- *WhoWrEP 92*
Roaden, Arliss L. 1930- *BioIn 17*
Roaden, Arliss Lloyd 1930- *WhoAm 92*
Roaldset, Elen 1944- *WhoWor 93*
Roaman, Chet 1939- *ScF&FL 92*
Roan, James Cortland, Jr. 1937- *WhoAm 92*
Roan, John A. 1945- *St&PR 93*
Roan, Tattie Mae Williams 1928- *WhoSSW 93*
Roane, Kenneth I. 1946- *St&PR 93*
Roane, Martha Kotila 1921- *WhoAmW 93*
Roantree, T.C., III *Law&B 92*
Roark, Carl Oliver 1948- *St&PR 93*
Roark, David T. *Law&B 92*
Roark, Glenn Earnest 1929- *WhoSSW 93*
Roark, Helen Wills 1905- *BioIn 17*
Roark, Janice Kay *Law&B 92*
Roark, Roderic Bruce 1949- *WhoSSW 93*
Roark, Terry Paul 1938- *WhoAm 92*
Roarke, Adam *MiSFD 9*
Roat, Bruce W. *St&PR 93*
Roath, K.B. 1935- *St&PR 93*
Rob, Joseph M. 1942- *St&PR 93*
Rob, Oldrich 1931- *WhoScE 91-4*
Robach, Michael Charles 1953- *WhoSSW 93*
Robach, Roger J. d1991 *BioIn 17*
Robacker, Earl Francis 1904- *ConAu 37NR*
Robak, Rostyslaw Wsewolod 1948- *WhoE 93*
Robakiewicz, Wojciech 1932- *WhoScE 91-4*
Robalino, Cesar Raul 1936- *WhoWor 93*
Robalo Silva, J. 1945- *WhoScE 91-3*
Robards, Anthony William *WhoScE 91-1*
Robards, Donald Lynn 1941- *St&PR 93*
Robards, Frank Benjamin, Jr. 1929- *WhoAm 92*
Robards, Jason 1922- *BioIn 17, IntDcF 2-3*
Robards, Jason Nelson, Jr. 1922- *WhoAm 92*
Robards, Sherman M(arshall) 1939- *ConAu 37NR*
Robards, Thomas Frederick 1946- *St&PR 93, WhoAm 92*
Robarts, John Tremaine 1940- *WhoE 93*
Robaska, P. Gordon 1936- *St&PR 93*
Robaye Ali, Salem 1934-1978 *BioIn 17*
Robb, Bruce 1919- *WhoAm 92*
Robb, Bryan J. *Law&B 92*
Robb, Charles S. *BioIn 17*
Robb, Charles S. 1939- *CngDr 91*
Robb, Charles Spittal 1939- *NewYTBS 92 [port], WhoAm 92, WhoSSW 93*
Robb, David Buzby, Jr. 1935- *WhoAm 92*
Robb, David G. *Law&B 92*
Robb, David Metheny, Jr. 1937- *WhoAm 92*
Robb, Edward Haupt 1912- *St&PR 93*
Robb, Felix Compton 1914- *WhoAm 92*
Robb, Graham 1958- *ConAu 136*
Robb, James Alexander 1930- *WhoAm 92*
Robb, James Willis 1918- *WhoAm 92, WhoE 93*
Robb, Janette Consuela 1956- *WhoE 93*
Robb, John Harold 1940- *St&PR 93*
Robb, John Wesley 1919- *WhoAm 92*
Robb, Kenneth *ConAu 139*
Robb, Lynda Bird Johnson 1943- *BioIn 17*
Robb, Lynda Johnson 1944- *WhoAmW 93*
Robb, Mary Ann 1957- *St&PR 93*
Robb, Michael S. *WhoIns 93*
Robb, Michael S. 1947- *St&PR 93*
Robb, Nathaniel Heyward, Jr. 1942- *WhoAm 92*
Robb, Raymond R. 1942- *St&PR 93*
Robb, Richard Arlin 1942- *WhoAm 92*
Robb, Richard Irving 1935- *WhoWrEP 92*
Robb, Thomas Bradley 1932- *WhoWrEP 92*
Robb, Walter E., III 1926- *St&PR 93*
Robb, Walter L. 1928- *St&PR 93*
Robb, Walter Lee 1928- *WhoAm 92*
Robb, William G. *Law&B 92*
Robbe-Grillet, Alain 1922- *BioIn 17, MiSFD 9, WhoWor 93*
Robbelen, Gerhard P.K. 1929- *WhoScE 91-3*
Robbert, Louise Buenger 1925- *WhoAmW 93*
Robbibaro, Joanne C. 1961- *WhoSSW 93, WhoWor 93*
Robbie, J. Michael 1948- *WhoAm 92*
Robbie, Seymour *MiSFD 9*
Robbie, Timothy John 1955- *WhoAm 92, WhoSSW 93*
Robbin, Barry M. 1948- *St&PR 93*
Robbin, Harry J. 1916- *St&PR 93*
Robbin, Tony 1943- *WhoE 93*
Robbins, Allen Bishop 1930- *WhoAm 92*
Robbins, Anne Francis 1923- *WhoAmW 93, WhoWor 93*
Robbins, Archie Lew *Law&B 92*
Robbins, Arthur S. *St&PR 93*
Robbins, Augustus, III 1926- *WhoE 93*
Robbins, Barbara *BioIn 17*
Robbins, Betty Lorraine 1950- *WhoAmW 93*
Robbins, Bruce E. 1944- *St&PR 93*
Robbins, Carole Rita 1937- *WhoE 93*
Robbins, Catherine Codispoti 1941- *WhoWrEP 92*
Robbins, Chandler Seymour 1918- *WhoAm 92*
Robbins, Charles F. 1921- *St&PR 93*
Robbins, Charles K. *Law&B 92*
Robbins, Cheryl Lenore 1963- *WhoAmW 93*
Robbins, Clarence Ralph 1938- *WhoE 93*
Robbins, Cornelius Van Vorse 1931- *WhoAm 92, WhoE 93*
Robbins, Cynthia Bilt Resnick 1946- *WhoAmW 93*
Robbins, Daniel 1933- *WhoAm 92*
Robbins, David 1950- *ScF&FL 92*
Robbins, David Arthur 1944- *WhoSSW 93*
Robbins, David Walter, Jr. 1919- *WhoAm 92*
Robbins, Deborah Thatcher 1953- *WhoE 93*
Robbins, Deena Jane 1944- *WhoAmW 93*
Robbins, Donald M. *Law&B 92*
Robbins, Donald M. 1935- *St&PR 93*
Robbins, Donald Michael 1935- *WhoAm 92*
Robbins, Doren Richard 1949- *WhoWrEP 92*
Robbins, Douglas Ernest 1953- *WhoSSW 93*
Robbins, E. Petri 1940- *St&PR 93*
Robbins, Earl L. 1921- *WhoSSW 93*
Robbins, Edwin 1931- *St&PR 93*
Robbins, Edwin Boyd 1925- *St&PR 93*
Robbins, Elliott Charles 1946- *St&PR 93*
Robbins, Emmett Todd 1962- *WhoSSW 93*
Robbins, Enoch G. 1906- *St&PR 93*
Robbins, Estelle Harriet *AmWomPl*
Robbins, Francis F. 1942- *St&PR 93*
Robbins, Fred d1992 *NewYTBS 92*
Robbins, Frederick Chapman 1916- *WhoAm 92, WhoWor 93*
Robbins, Geoffrey Ralph 1929- *WhoE 93*
Robbins, George William 1940- *St&PR 93*
Robbins, Gerald H. 1924- *St&PR 93*
Robbins, Greg M. 1943- *St&PR 93*
Robbins, Harold 1912- *BioIn 17*
Robbins, Harold 1916- *WhoAm 92, WhoWrEP 92*
Robbins, Harold W. d1990 *BioIn 17*
Robbins, Henry Zane 1930- *WhoAm 92*
Robbins, Honey-Miam 1930- *WhoWor 93*
Robbins, Hulda Dornblatt 1910- *WhoAm 92*
Robbins, Jack Rian 1941- *WhoWor 93*
Robbins, Jack W. *Law&B 92*

Robbins, Jacob 1922- WhoE 93
Robbins, James A. 1952- WhoIns 93
Robbins, James Arnold, Jr. 1957- St&PR 93
Robbins, James Bryce, II 1953- St&PR 93
Robbins, James Edward 1931- WhoWor 93
Robbins, James Tate 1945- WhoSSW 93
Robbins, Jane (Borsch) 1939- ConAu 38NR, WhoAm 92, WhoAmW 93
Robbins, Jeffrey Howard 1941- WhoE 93
Robbins, Jerome BioIn 17
Robbins, Jerome 1918- MiSFD 9, WhoAm 92, WhoE 93, WhoWor 93
Robbins, Jerome G. 1934- St&PR 93
Robbins, Jerry Hal 1939- WhoAm 92
Robbins, Joan Raff WhoAmW 93
Robbins, John Clapp 1921- WhoAm 92
Robbins, John Michael, Jr. 1947- WhoAm 92
Robbins, John William 1914- WhoSSW 93
Robbins, John William 1948- WhoE 93
Robbins, Jon N. Law&B 92
Robbins, Joseph E. 1922- St&PR 93
Robbins, Joseph H. 1924- St&PR 93
Robbins, Keith David Law&B 92
Robbins, Ken BioIn 17
Robbins, Kenneth L. WhoAm 92, WhoE 93
Robbins, Kevin F. Law&B 92
Robbins, Larry Jack 1935- WhoSSW 93
Robbins, Lawrence Harry 1938- WhoAm 92
Robbins, Lee David 1953- WhoE 93
Robbins, Leonard A. 1921- ScF&FL 92
Robbins, Lewis C. 1909-1990 BioIn 17
Robbins, Lillian Cukier 1933- WhoE 93
Robbins, Lionel 1928- St&PR 93
Robbins, Lionel Charles 1898-1984 BioIn 17
Robbins, Marjorie Jean Gilmartin 1940- WhoAmW 93
Robbins, Martha Ann 1942- WhoAmW 93
Robbins, Martha Louise 1952- WhoAmW 93
Robbins, Martin 1931- WhoWrEP 92
Robbins, Marty 1925-1982 Baker 92, BioIn 17, ConMus 9 [port]
Robbins, Matthew MiSFD 9
Robbins, Melvin Lloyd 1928- St&PR 93
Robbins, Michelle Edwards 1958- WhoAmW 93
Robbins, Milan 1934- St&PR 93
Robbins, Milan B. Law&B 92
Robbins, Nina 1965- WhoAmW 93
Robbins, Orem O. 1915- WhoIns 93
Robbins, Orem Olford 1915- St&PR 93
Robbins, Orren Bourne 1932- WhoAm 92, WhoE 93
Robbins, Paul Reuben 1918- WhoSSW 93
Robbins, Philip 1931- WhoE 93
Robbins, Phillips Wesley 1930- WhoAm 92
Robbins, Phyllis B. 1934- St&PR 93
Robbins, Rachel F. Law&B 92
Robbins, Ray Charles 1920- St&PR 93, WhoAm 92
Robbins, Richard BioIn 17
Robbins, Richard Leroy 1953- WhoWrEP 92
Robbins, Robert St&PR 93
Robbins, Ron G. Law&B 92
Robbins, Ruth Rhea 1949- WhoSSW 93
Robbins, Stanley Leonard 1915- WhoE 93
Robbins, Steaven Dwain 1953- WhoSSW 93
Robbins, Susan T. Law&B 92
Robbins, Thomas E. ScF&FL 92
Robbins, Tim BioIn 17, WhoAm 92
Robbins, Tim 1958- MiSFD 9
Robbins, Tim 1959- News 93-1 [port]
Robbins, Tom BioIn 17
Robbins, Tom 1936- ScF&FL 92, WhoAm 92, WhoWrEP 92
Robbins, Vernon Kay 1939- WhoSSW 93
Robbins, Wayne P. 1944- St&PR 93
Robbins, William Curtis, Jr. 1948- WhoWor 93
Robbins, William Michael 1946- St&PR 93
Robbins, William Randolph 1912- WhoAm 92, WhoE 93
Robbins-Carter, Jane ConAu 38NR
Robbins-Wilf, Marcia 1949- WhoAmW 93, WhoE 93, WhoEmL 93, WhoWor 93
Robe, Mike MiSFD 9
Robe, Thurlow Richard 1934- WhoAm 92
Robecchi Bricchetti, Luigi 1855-1926 IntDcAn
Robeck, Gordon Gurney 1923- WhoAm 92
Robeck, Mildred Coen 1915- WhoAmW 93
Robedeau, William Frank 1939- St&PR 93
Robek, Mary Frances 1927- WhoAm 92
Robelo Callejas, Alfonso DcCPCAm
Robenalt, John Alton 1922- WhoAm 92, WhoWor 93
Robens, Howard ScF&FL 92
Robenseifner, Robert Stephen 1930- WhoUN 92
Robenstine, Rance M. 1950- St&PR 93
Roberge, Jill Quigley 1955- WhoAmW 93
Roberge, Lisa Hebb WhoAmW 93
Roberge, M. Sheila WhoAmW 93
Roberge, Sue 1949- WhoAmW 93
Robers, Gregory James Law&B 92
Roberson, Bruce H. 1941- WhoAm 92
Roberson, Charles R. 1933- St&PR 93
Roberson, Constance Belinda 1948- WhoAmW 93
Roberson, David E. 1951- St&PR 93
Roberson, Dennis Walter 1958- WhoSSW 93
Roberson, Donald Thomas 1935- St&PR 93
Roberson, Fred O., Jr. 1947- WhoSSW 93
Roberson, G. Gale, Jr. 1933- St&PR 93
Roberson, Howard A. 1926-1991 BioIn 17
Roberson, James MiSFD 9
Roberson, James O. WhoSSW 93
Roberson, Jennifer 1953- ScF&FL 92, SmATA 72 [port]
Roberson, Kathryn Watson 1947- WhoSSW 93
Roberson, Marvin R. Law&B 92
Roberson, Michael L. Law&B 92
Roberson, Nathan Russell 1930- WhoAm 92
Roberson, Patt Foster 1934- WhoAmW 93
Roberson, Richard W. 1947- St&PR 93
Roberson, Rick 1956- ScF&FL 92
Roberson, Robert Stephen 1942- WhoWor 93
Roberson, Roger Truman 1941- St&PR 93
Roberson, S. Paulette 1946- WhoAmW 93
Robert, Cameron Terrance 1948- St&PR 93
Robert, Daniel 1940- WhoScE 91-2
Robert, Daniel Winans 1942- St&PR 93
Robert, Didier L.C. 1945- WhoScE 91-2
Robert, Felix 1862-1916 BioIn 17
Robert, Genevieve MiSFD 9
Robert, Gilbert Oday 1925- St&PR 93, WhoAm 92
Robert, Jacques 1949- WhoScE 91-2
Robert, Jean-Louis 1949- WhoScE 91-2
Robert, Joseph Clarke 1906- WhoSSW 93
Robert, Lawrence Wood, IV 1937- St&PR 93
Robert, Leslie Ladislas 1924- WhoWor 93
Robert, Patrick 1937- WhoAm 92
Robert, Paul L. Law&B 92
Robert, Paul Leo 1955- WhoE 93
Robert, Philippe Alain 1938- WhoScE 91-4
Robert, Samuel K. 1908- St&PR 93
Robert, Yves 1920- MiSFD 9
Robertazzi, Thomas Joseph 1928- St&PR 93
Robert-Baudouy, J. WhoScE 91-2
Robert Carteret, Jean-Yves 1948- WhoWor 93
Robert de Clari dc. 1216 OxDcByz
Robert Guiscard c. 1015-1085 OxDcByz
Robert-Houdin, Jean-Eugene 1805-1871 BioIn 17
Roberti, Mario A. Law&B 92
Roberti, Mario Andrew 1935- St&PR 93, WhoAm 92
Roberti, William V. 1946- St&PR 93
Roberti, William Vincent 1946- WhoAm 92
Roberto, Albert Gene 1943- WhoE 93
Roberto, Douglas P. Law&B 92
Roberto, Vito 1951- WhoWor 93
Robert of Courtenay d1228 OxDcByz
Robert of Flanders c. 1013-1093 OxDcByz
Robert of Normandy c. 1054-1134 OxDcByz
Robert of Torigny d1186 OxDcByz
Roberton, Donald K. 1941- St&PR 93
Roberton, Hugh (Stevenson) 1874-1952 Baker 92
Roberts, A. Addison 1915- St&PR 93
Roberts, A.D. WhoScE 91-1
Roberts, A.F. 1935- WhoScE 91-1
Roberts, Adrian Phair WhoScE 91-1
Roberts, Alan MiSFD 9
Roberts, Alan S. 1947- St&PR 93
Roberts, Albert Roy 1944- WhoAm 92
Roberts, Alfred Wheeler, III 1938- WhoAm 92
Roberts, Andrew L. d1878 BioIn 17
Roberts, Andrew Timothy 1966- WhoWor 93
Roberts, Andrew Vaughan WhoScE 91-1
Roberts, Archibald Edward 1915- WhoWor 93
Roberts, B. K. 1907- WhoAm 92, WhoWor 93
Roberts, Barbara 1936- WhoAm 92, WhoAmW 93
Roberts, Barbara Baker 1934- WhoSSW 93, WhoWrEP 92
Roberts, Barbara Gale Law&B 92
Roberts, Bert C., Jr. 1942- WhoAm 92
Roberts, Betty Jo 1927- WhoAmW 93
Roberts, Bill Glen 1938- WhoAm 92, WhoSSW 93, WhoWor 93
Roberts, Bob Alan 1962- WhoSSW 93
Roberts, Bonnie Leslie 1949- WhoWrEP 92
Roberts, Boyd O. 1947- St&PR 93
Roberts, Brian Leon 1959- WhoAm 92
Roberts, Brian P. Law&B 92
Roberts, Bruce Everett 1917- WhoAm 92
Roberts, Bruce G. 1949- St&PR 93
Roberts, Burnell R. 1927- St&PR 93
Roberts, Burnell Richard 1927- WhoAm 92
Roberts, Burton Bennett 1922- WhoAm 92
Roberts, C. Kenneth Law&B 92
Roberts, C. Kenneth 1930- WhoAm 92
Roberts, C. Pinckney Law&B 92
Roberts, C. Wesley 1903-1975 BioIn 17, PolPar
Roberts, Carter Dale 1944- WhoIns 93
Roberts, Catherine Stephanie 1962- WhoAmW 93
Roberts, Cecil Johnson d1990 BioIn 17
Roberts, Celia Ann 1935- WhoAmW 93, WhoE 93
Roberts, Chalmers McGeagh 1910- WhoAm 92
Roberts, Charles Corwin 1924- St&PR 93
Roberts, Charles E. 1950- St&PR 93
Roberts, Charles G.D. 1860-1943 BioIn 17
Roberts, Charles Patrick 1936- WhoAm 92
Roberts, Charles S. 1918- St&PR 93
Roberts, Charles Wesley 1903-1975 BioIn 17
Roberts, Charles Wesley 1916-1992 BioIn 17, ConAu 136
Roberts, Charles Wood, Jr. 1962- WhoSSW 93
Roberts, Christian Bruce 1947- WhoSSW 93
Roberts, Christopher Ross 1957- WhoWor 93
Roberts, Clarence Lewis, Jr. 1934- St&PR 93
Roberts, Claudia Dorgan Law&B 92
Roberts, Clyde Francis 1924- WhoAm 92
Roberts, Cokie BioIn 17, WhoE 93
Roberts, Cokie 1943- WhoAm 92
Roberts, Colin 1909-1990 ScF&FL 92
Roberts, Corinne Boggs 1943- WhoAm 92, WhoAmW 93
Roberts, Curtis Bush 1933- WhoIns 93
Roberts, Curtis M. Law&B 92
Roberts, Dale 1946- St&PR 93
Roberts, Dale H. 1941- St&PR 93
Roberts, Daryl Trent 1956- WhoSSW 93
Roberts, David Caron 1944- WhoE 93, WhoWor 93
Roberts, David Glen 1952- WhoSSW 93
Roberts, David Glendenning 1928- WhoAm 92
Roberts, David Gordon WhoScE 91-1
Roberts, David Harrill 1944- WhoAm 92, WhoSSW 93
Roberts, David Hugh WhoScE 91-1
Roberts, David J. 1944- St&PR 93
Roberts, David Lee 1934- St&PR 93
Roberts, Deborah MiSFD 9
Roberts, Debra J. 1954- WhoIns 93
Roberts, Debra Lynn 1954- WhoAmW 93
Roberts, Delmar L. 1933- WhoWrEP 92
Roberts, Dennis H. 1954- St&PR 93
Roberts, Dennis J. 1942- St&PR 93
Roberts, Derrell Clayton 1927- WhoSSW 93
Roberts, Diane WhoScE 91-1
Roberts, Diane Hill 1947- WhoWrEP 92
Roberts, Don E. 1934- WhoSSW 93
Roberts, Donald Albert 1935- WhoE 93
Roberts, Donald John 1945- WhoAm 92
Roberts, Donald Munier 1935- WhoAm 92
Roberts, Donna J. 1935- St&PR 93
Roberts, Donna Joyce 1935- WhoAm 92
Roberts, Doris 1930- WhoAm 92
Roberts, Doris Emma 1915- WhoAm 92, WhoAmW 93
Roberts, Dorothy 1906- WhoCanL 92
Roberts, Dorothy H. BioIn 17
Roberts, Dorothy H. 1928- St&PR 93
Roberts, Dorothy Hyman 1928- WhoAmW 93
Roberts, Dorothy James 1903-1990 BioIn 17
Roberts, Douglas B. WhoAm 92
Roberts, Douglas Earl 1948- St&PR 93
Roberts, Dwight Loren 1949- WhoEmL 93, WhoWor 93
Roberts, Dwight V. 1935- St&PR 93
Roberts, E. F. 1930- WhoAm 92
Roberts, Earl K. 1928- St&PR 93
Roberts, Edward Baer 1935- WhoAm 92, WhoE 93, WhoWor 93
Roberts, Edward C. Law&B 92
Roberts, Edward Calhoun 1937- WhoAm 92, WhoSSW 93
Roberts, Edward Graham WhoAm 92
Roberts, Edwin Albert, Jr. 1932- WhoAm 92
Roberts, Edwin G. d1992 NewYTBS 92
Roberts, Elena Yolanda 1963- WhoSSW 93
Roberts, Elizabeth Ann 1943- WhoE 93
Roberts, Elizabeth Madox 1881-1941 BioIn 17
Roberts, Ellen Jo 1954- WhoAmW 93
Roberts, Emyr Wyn 1950- WhoScE 91-1
Roberts, Enoch G. 1940- WhoIns 93
Roberts, Eric 1956- WhoAm 92
Roberts, Eric Hywel WhoScE 91-1
Roberts, Ernst Edward 1926- St&PR 93, WhoAm 92
Roberts, Ernst Edward, II 1951- WhoSSW 93
Roberts, Ethan Shawn 1954- WhoE 93
Roberts, Eugene L. BioIn 17
Roberts, Eugenie Bodick 1950- WhoSSW 93
Roberts, Eunice Jane 1936- WhoAmW 93
Roberts, Frances Cabaniss 1916- WhoAm 92
Roberts, Francis Donald 1938- WhoAm 92
Roberts, Francis Joseph 1918- WhoAm 92
Roberts, Francis Stone 1944- St&PR 93, WhoAm 92
Roberts, Frank 1907- BioIn 17
Roberts, Frank Emmett 1930- WhoAm 92
Roberts, Frank H.H., Jr. 1897-1966 IntDcAn
Roberts, Fred T. 1941- WhoIns 93
Roberts, Frederick J. 1949- St&PR 93
Roberts, Frederick Sleigh 1832-1914 HarEnMi
Roberts, G.G. WhoScE 91-1
Roberts, Gail Ann 1961- WhoE 93
Roberts, Garrett W. 1942- St&PR 93
Roberts, Gary C. 1938- St&PR 93
Roberts, Gary William 1958- WhoSSW 93
Roberts, George Adam 1919- St&PR 93, WhoAm 92
Roberts, George Bernard, Jr. 1939- WhoAm 92
Roberts, George Harrison 1944- St&PR 93, WhoIns 93
Roberts, George P. 1937- St&PR 93
Roberts, George R. BioIn 17
Roberts, George T. 1917- St&PR 93
Roberts, George Truett, Jr. Law&B 92
Roberts, Gerald Franklin 1938- WhoSSW 93
Roberts, Gerald J. 1931- St&PR 93
Roberts, Gerald Jeffrey 1949- WhoAm 92
Roberts, Gerald W. 1952- St&PR 93
Roberts, Gerry Rea 1940- WhoAmW 93, WhoSSW 93
Roberts, Gilbert B. 1941- WhoAm 92
Roberts, Glenn Eric 1947- WhoE 93
Roberts, Godwin 1939- WhoWor 93
Roberts, Gordon C.K. WhoScE 91-1
Roberts, Granville Oral 1918- WhoAm 92
Roberts, Gregory A. Law&B 92
Roberts, Gwyn WhoScE 91-1
Roberts, Harry Morris, Jr. 1938- WhoAm 92, WhoSSW 93, WhoWor 93
Roberts, Harry Vivian 1923- WhoAm 92
Roberts, Henry Reginald 1916- WhoAm 92, WhoIns 93
Roberts, Howard Leslie 1922- St&PR 93
Roberts, Howard Topol Law&B 92
Roberts, Howard Topol 1931- St&PR 93
Roberts, Hubert H. Law&B 92
Roberts, Hubert Wilson, Jr. 1944- WhoSSW 93
Roberts, Hugh Evan 1923- WhoAm 92
Roberts, Hyman Jacob 1924- WhoAm 92, WhoSSW 93, WhoWor 93
Roberts, Ida Marie 1942- St&PR 93
Roberts, Ina Brevoort Deane 1874- AmWomPl
Roberts, Irene C. WhoAm 92
Roberts, Irene C. 1944- St&PR 93
Roberts, J. Lamar BioIn 17
Roberts, J.R. ScF&FL 92
Roberts, J. William 1942- WhoAm 92
Roberts, Jack Earle 1928- WhoAm 92
Roberts, James Allen 1934- WhoAm 92
Roberts, James C. 1924- St&PR 93
Roberts, James Cleveland 1946- WhoAm 92
Roberts, James E. 1934- St&PR 93
Roberts, James Edward 1945- St&PR 93
Roberts, James G. 1922- WhoAm 92
Roberts, James Kitto 1952- WhoSSW 93
Roberts, James L. BioIn 17, WhoSSW 93
Roberts, James L. 1942- WhoAm 92
Roberts, James McGregor 1923- WhoAm 92
Roberts, James Michael 1948- WhoSSW 93
Roberts, James Milnor, Jr. 1918- WhoAm 92
Roberts, Jane 1929-1984 ScF&FL 92

Roberts, Janet Louise 1925- WhoWrEP 92
Roberts, Janet Louise 1925-1982 ScF&FL 92
Roberts, Janet Marie 1947- WhoAmW 93, WhoWrEP 92
Roberts, Janine 1947- WhoE 93
Roberts, Jared I. Law&B 92
Roberts, Jay 1927- WhoAm 92
Roberts, Jeane M. 1926- WhoAmW 93
Roberts, Jeanne Addison WhoAm 92
Roberts, Jeffery David 1943- WhoWor 93
Roberts, Jeri Lynn 1963- WhoAmW 93
Roberts, Jim 1859-1934 BioIn 17
Roberts, Jo Ann Wooden 1948- WhoAmW 93
Roberts, John B. 1944- St&PR 93
Roberts, John Benjamin, II 1955- WhoAm 92, WhoWrEP 92
Roberts, John Bennett 1935- WhoSSW 93
Roberts, John Brian WhoScE 91-1
Roberts, John Charles 1938- St&PR 93
Roberts, John Chester 1947- WhoAm 92
Roberts, John D. BioIn 17
Roberts, John D. 1918- WhoAm 92
Roberts, John Glover, Jr. 1955- WhoAm 92
Roberts, John Heath 1949- WhoWor 93
Roberts, John Joseph 1922- St&PR 93, WhoAm 92, WhoIns 93
Roberts, John K. 1961- St&PR 93
Roberts, John K., Jr. 1936- St&PR 93
Roberts, John Kenneth, Jr. 1936- WhoAm 92, WhoIns 93
Roberts, John Laing 1939- WhoUN 92
Roberts, John Maddox 1947- ScF&FL 92
Roberts, John Noel 1951- WhoWor 93
Roberts, John Peter WhoScE 91-1
Roberts, John Peter Lee 1930- WhoAm 92
Roberts, John S. 1953- St&PR 93
Roberts, John Sauls, Jr. 1954- WhoSSW 93
Roberts, John Watts 1918- St&PR 93
Roberts, Joseph St&PR 93
Roberts, Josephine Anastasia 1948- WhoAmW 93, WhoSSW 93
Roberts, Judd d1887 BioIn 17
Roberts, Judith Marie 1939- WhoAmW 93
Roberts, Julia BioIn 17
Roberts, Julia 1967- IntDcF 2-3 [port], WhoAm 92, WhoAmW 93
Roberts, June E. Law&B 92
Roberts, Justin 1919- WhoAm 92
Roberts, K(enneth) B(ryson) 1923- ConAu 139
Roberts, Karen Barbara 1953- WhoSSW 93
Roberts, Karlene Ann 1937- WhoAmW 93
Roberts, Kathleen Joy Doty 1951- WhoE 93, WhoWor 93
Roberts, Kathleen Mary 1947- WhoAmW 93
Roberts, Kay K. 1940- WhoAmW 93
Roberts, Kaye Virginia 1958- WhoAmW 93
Roberts, Keith WhoScE 91-1
Roberts, Keith 1935- ScF&FL 92
Roberts, Kenneth WhoScE 91-1
Roberts, Kenneth Barris 1954- WhoE 93
Roberts, Kenneth Boyett 1944- WhoSSW 93
Roberts, Kenneth D. 1933- St&PR 93
Roberts, Kenneth Douglas 1949- WhoE 93
Roberts, Kenneth Lewis 1932- WhoAm 92
Roberts, Kenneth S. 1930- St&PR 93
Roberts, Kenneth Somers 1930- WhoAm 92, WhoWor 93
Roberts, Kevin 1940- WhoCanL 92
Roberts, Kevin Frances 1948- WhoE 93
Roberts, Larry Paul 1950- WhoAm 92
Roberts, Larry Spurgeon 1935- WhoAm 92
Roberts, Lee R. 1939- St&PR 93
Roberts, Leigh Milton 1925- WhoAm 92, WhoWor 93
Roberts, Leonard H. BioIn 17
Roberts, Leonard H. 1949- St&PR 93, WhoAm 92, WhoSSW 93
Roberts, Leonard Robert 1947- WhoWrEP 92
Roberts, Leonidas Howard 1921- WhoSSW 93
Roberts, Lesa Phillip 1890- BioIn 17
Roberts, Letitia 1943- St&PR 93
Roberts, Lewis Edward John WhoScE 91-1
Roberts, Lewis H. WhoIns 93
Roberts, Linda Sue McCallister 1947- WhoAmW 93
Roberts, Lloyd Eugene 1943- WhoSSW 93
Roberts, Lon 1948- WhoSSW 93
Roberts, Lorin Watson 1923- WhoAm 92
Roberts, Lorraine Marie 1930- WhoAmW 93
Roberts, Louis A. St&PR 93
Roberts, Louis Douglas 1918- WhoAm 92, WhoSSW 93
Roberts, Louis Wright 1913- WhoAm 92
Roberts, Louise Nisbet 1919- WhoAm 92
Roberts, Lucy Whitty 1965- WhoAmW 93
Roberts, Lynn Springer 1943- WhoAm 92
Roberts, Lynne 1919?-1978 SweetSg C [port]
Roberts, Marcus BioIn 17
Roberts, Margaret Harold 1928- WhoAm 92
Roberts, Margaret Rose 1948- WhoSSW 93
Roberts, Margaret Rose 1957- WhoAmW 93
Roberts, Marie Dyer 1943- WhoAmW 93, WhoWor 93
Roberts, Marion Munsell 1961- WhoAmW 93
Roberts, Marjorie Helen 1938- WhoAmW 93
Roberts, Mark K. 1936- ScF&FL 92
Roberts, Mark Owen 1911- WhoIns 93
Roberts, Mark Scott 1951- WhoEmL 93, WhoWor 93
Roberts, Markley 1930- WhoAm 92
Roberts, Mary Elizabeth AmWomPl
Roberts, Mary Lou 1950- WhoSSW 93
Roberts, Meade d1992 NewYTBS 92
Roberts, Meade 1930-1992 BioIn 17
Roberts, Megan 1952- Baker 92
Roberts, Meirion Wyn WhoScE 91-1
Roberts, Meirion Wyn 1931- WhoWor 93
Roberts, Melville Parker, Jr. 1931- WhoAm 92, WhoWor 93
Roberts, Merrill Joseph 1915- WhoAm 92
Roberts, Michael 1946- WhoWor 93
Roberts, Michael D. 1952- St&PR 93
Roberts, Michael Dennis 1949- WhoEmL 93
Roberts, Michael Murphy 1940- St&PR 93
Roberts, Michael Wells 1941- WhoSSW 93
Roberts, Mitchell 1913- St&PR 93
Roberts, Morfudd 1922-1991 BioIn 17
Roberts, Morris Henry, Jr. 1940- WhoAm 92
Roberts, Morton Spitz 1926- WhoAm 92
Roberts, Moss 1937- ScF&FL 92
Roberts, Myron 1923-1992 ConAu 139
Roberts, Nadine ScF&FL 92
Roberts, Nancy 1938- WhoAmW 93
Roberts, Nancy A. Law&B 92
Roberts, Nancy Carolyn 1935- WhoSSW 93
Roberts, Nancy Correll WhoAm 92
Roberts, Neil Fletcher 1914- WhoAm 92
Roberts, Nora ScF&FL 92
Roberts, Norbert J. 1916-1990 BioIn 17
Roberts, Norman L. Law&B 92
Roberts, Norman Leslie 1935- WhoAm 92
Roberts, Octavia AmWomPl
Roberts, Oral BioIn 17
Roberts, Oral 1918- WhoAm 92
Roberts, Owen Josephus 1875-1955 OxCSupC [port]
Roberts, P.A. 1940- WhoScE 91-3
Roberts, P.F.P. WhoScE 91-1
Roberts, Pam BioIn 17
Roberts, Pat 1936- CngDr 91
Roberts, Paul A. d1991 BioIn 17
Roberts, Paul Craig, III 1939- WhoAm 92
Roberts, Paul J. 1937- St&PR 93
Roberts, Pauline 1958- WhoAmW 93
Roberts, Pernell WhoAm 92
Roberts, Peter 1950- ScF&FL 92
Roberts, Peter A. 1951- WhoAm 92, WhoE 93, WhoWor 93
Roberts, Peter David WhoScE 91-1
Roberts, Peter James 1942- WhoSSW 93
Roberts, Peter Job 1944- WhoAm 92
Roberts, Peter S. 1937- WhoIns 93
Roberts, Peter William Law&B 92
Roberts, Philip Gwynne, Jr. 1939- WhoE 93
Roberts, Philip Kenneth 1945- St&PR 93
Roberts, Philip Richard 1942- St&PR 93
Roberts, Priscilla Warren 1916- WhoAm 92
Roberts, Rachel 1927-1980 IntDcF 2-3 [port]
Roberts, Ralph F. 1918- St&PR 93
Roberts, Ralph Henry, Jr. 1936- St&PR 93
Roberts, Ralph J. 1920- St&PR 93
Roberts, Ralph Joel 1920- WhoAm 92
Roberts, Randal 1951- St&PR 93
Roberts, Randolph Wilson 1946- WhoE 93
Roberts, Ray BioIn 17
Roberts, Ray Crouse, Jr. 1929- WhoSSW 93
Roberts, Raymond Paul 1923- St&PR 93
Roberts, Raymond Url 1949- WhoSSW 93
Roberts, Rex H. Law&B 92
Roberts, Richard 1941- ScF&FL 92
Roberts, Richard A.J. 1940- WhoUN 92
Roberts, Richard Allen 1933- St&PR 93
Roberts, Richard E. 1944- St&PR 93
Roberts, Richard F. 1945- St&PR 93
Roberts, Richard G., Jr. 1939- St&PR 93
Roberts, Richard Harris 1924- WhoSSW 93
Roberts, Richard Heilbron 1925- WhoAm 92
Roberts, Richard James 1922- WhoAm 92
Roberts, Richard Robert 1941- WhoE 93
Roberts, Richard S. 1929- St&PR 93
Roberts, Richard Stewart 1945- WhoAm 92
Roberts, Richard Stuart 1942- WhoSSW 93
Roberts, Rita Frances 1929- WhoAmW 93
Roberts, Robert Richard, III 1944- WhoIns 93
Roberts, Robert Winston 1932- WhoAm 92
Roberts, Robin BioIn 17
Roberts, Roger Andrew WhoScE 91-1
Roberts, Roger P. 1948- WhoIns 93
Roberts, Ronald John WhoScE 91-1
Roberts, Ross H. 1938- St&PR 93
Roberts, Russell Alfred 1953- WhoSSW 93
Roberts, Samuel Smith 1936- WhoAm 92, WhoE 93
Roberts, Sandra 1951- WhoAmW 93
Roberts, Sarah Meeks Law&B 92
Roberts, Scott Alan Law&B 92
Roberts, Seymour M. 1934- WhoAm 92
Roberts, Shawn 1959- WhoSSW 93
Roberts, Sidney 1918- WhoAm 92
Roberts, Sidney I. 1913- WhoAm 92
Roberts, Stanley H. 1917- St&PR 93
Roberts, Stanley Michael WhoScE 91-1
Roberts, Stephen Earl 1948- St&PR 93
Roberts, Steven D. 1956- St&PR 93
Roberts, Steven K. 1952- BioIn 17, News 92 [port]
Roberts, Steven V. BioIn 17
Roberts, Steven Victor 1943- WhoAm 92
Roberts, Susan Ellen 1949- WhoAmW 93
Roberts, Susan Moody 1956- WhoSSW 93
Roberts, Suzanne Emily 1946- WhoAmW 93
Roberts, Terrie Lynn 1953- WhoAmW 93
Roberts, Terry Allen Law&B 92
Roberts, Theodore Goodridge 1877-1953 BioIn 17
Roberts, Theodore H. 1929- St&PR 93
Roberts, Thomas Law&B 92
Roberts, Thomas George 1929- WhoWor 93
Roberts, Thomas H., Jr. 1924- St&PR 93
Roberts, Thomas Morgan 1937- WhoWor 93
Roberts, Thomasene Blount 1943- WhoAmW 93
Roberts, Tom AfrAmBi [port]
Roberts, Toni Dale 1949- WhoAmW 93
Roberts, Tony 1939- WhoAm 92
Roberts, Valerie BioIn 17
Roberts, Valerie A. Law&B 92
Roberts, Victor Colin WhoScE 91-1
Roberts, Victoria Lynn Parmer 1953- WhoAmW 93
Roberts, Virgil Patrick 1947- WhoAm 92
Roberts, Virginia Sykes WhoSSW 93
Roberts, W. WhoScE 91-1
Roberts, Walter Herbert Beatty 1915- WhoAm 92
Roberts, Walter Orr 1915-1990 BioIn 17
Roberts, Walter Ronald 1916- WhoAm 92
Roberts, Warren Errol 1933- WhoAm 92
Roberts, Warren Hoyle, Jr. 1955- WhoSSW 93
Roberts, Willard John 1933- WhoSSW 93
Roberts, William 1945- WhoE 93, WhoScE 91-4
Roberts, William Allan 1930- WhoE 93
Roberts, William Allen 1949- WhoSSW 93
Roberts, William B. 1939- WhoAm 92
Roberts, William Everett 1926- WhoAm 92
Roberts, William H. Law&B 92, WhoScE 91-1
Roberts, William H. 1929- WhoScE 91-1
Roberts, William H. 1945- WhoIns 93
Roberts, William Hooton, IV 1953- WhoE 93
Roberts, William Hugh, III 1936- WhoAm 92
Roberts, William J. 1920- St&PR 93
Roberts, William J. 1944- St&PR 93
Roberts, William James Cynfab 1938- WhoWor 93
Roberts, William Michael Eugene 1950- WhoSSW 93
Roberts, William O. 1942- St&PR 93
Roberts, William Prowting 1806-1871 BioIn 17
Roberts, Willo Davis 1928- DcAmChF 1960, DcAmChF 1985, MajAI [port], ScF&FL 92, SmATA 70 [port]
Roberts-DeGennaro, Maria 1947- WhoAmW 93
Robertshaw, Thomas Stevens 1947- St&PR 93
Robertson, A. Haeworth 1930- WhoAm 92, WhoWor 93
Robertson, Abel L., Jr. 1926- WhoAm 92
Robertson, Adam Patrick WhoScE 91-1
Robertson, Alan 1920-1989 BioIn 17
Robertson, Alan Gordon 1928- WhoE 93
Robertson, Alastair 1949- WhoScE 91-1
Robertson, Alec 1892-1982 Baker 92
Robertson, Alice A. ScF&FL 92
Robertson, Alice Mary 1854-1931 BioIn 17
Robertson, Alice O. Law&B 92
Robertson, Alvin 1962- BioIn 17
Robertson, Alvin Cyrrale 1962- WhoAm 92
Robertson, Andrew 1936- WhoE 93
Robertson, Armand James, II 1937- WhoAm 92, WhoWor 93
Robertson, Arthur Kenneth, Jr. 1937- WhoE 93
Robertson, Baldwin 1934- WhoE 93
Robertson, Ben F. 1854-1884 BioIn 17
Robertson, Beverly Carruth 1922- WhoAm 92
Robertson, Bill 1956- BioIn 17
Robertson, Brent Parish 1961- WhoE 93
Robertson, Brian F. 1958- St&PR 93
Robertson, Bruce 1934- ScF&FL 92
Robertson, C. R. 1930- WhoAm 92
Robertson, Carol A. Law&B 92
Robertson, Caroline Bullock 1955- WhoWor 93
Robertson, Charles 1927- ScF&FL 92
Robertson, Charles Garland 1941- St&PR 93
Robertson, Charles James 1934- WhoE 93
Robertson, Charles Morven 1954- WhoWor 93
Robertson, Charlie 1896-1984 BioIn 17
Robertson, Christine Blalock 1960- WhoAmW 93
Robertson, Cliff 1925- IntDcF 2-3, MiSFD 9, WhoAm 92
Robertson, Clifford Houston 1912- WhoSSW 93
Robertson, D.I. WhoScE 91-1
Robertson, D.S. WhoScE 91-1
Robertson, D(urant) W(aite), Jr. 1914-1992 ConAu 139
Robertson, Darrell 1942- St&PR 93
Robertson, David 1947- WhoAm 92, WhoWor 93
Robertson, David Alan 1950- WhoE 93
Robertson, David L. 1942- St&PR 93
Robertson, David Wyatt 1937- WhoAm 92
Robertson, Dirk Briscoe 1953- WhoWor 93
Robertson, Durant Waite, Jr. d1992 NewYTBS 92 [port]
Robertson, Durant Waite, Jr. 1914- WhoAm 92
Robertson, E.A. 1903-1961 ScF&FL 92
Robertson, Edward D., Jr. 1952- WhoAm 92
Robertson, Edward Dunbar, Jr. 1942- St&PR 93
Robertson, Edwin David 1946- WhoAm 92, WhoE 93, WhoEmL 93, WhoWor 93
Robertson, Edwin Oscar 1923- St&PR 93
Robertson, Ellis MajAI
Robertson, Frank J. 1948- St&PR 93
Robertson, Franklin Lee 1934- St&PR 93
Robertson, Gavin Douglas 1932- St&PR 93
Robertson, George Leven 1921- WhoAm 92
Robertson, George O. 1930- St&PR 93
Robertson, Grace BioIn 17
Robertson, Gregg W. 1934- St&PR 93
Robertson, Gregg Westland 1934- WhoAm 92
Robertson, Heather Margaret 1942- ConAu 37NR, WhoCanL 92
Robertson, Henry Howard 1950- WhoSSW 93
Robertson, Herbert Chapman, Jr. 1928- WhoSSW 93
Robertson, Horace Bascomb, Jr. 1923- WhoAm 92
Robertson, Howard Wayne 1947- WhoWrEP 92
Robertson, Hugh Duff 1957- WhoAm 92, WhoWor 93
Robertson, Ian 1947- WhoWor 93
Robertson, J.R. ScF&FL 92
Robertson, Jack Clark 1943- WhoAm 92
Robertson, Jack Westbrook, Jr. 1929- St&PR 93
Robertson, Jaime Robbie 1944- See Band, The ConMus 9
Robertson, James c. 1813-1881 BioIn 17
Robertson, James 1912-1991 OxDcOp
Robertson, James 1938- WhoAm 92
Robertson, James Burrough, II 1944- WhoE 93
Robertson, James Cole 1929- WhoSSW 93
Robertson, James Colvert 1932- St&PR 93, WhoAm 92

Robinson, Chris *BioIn 17*
Robinson, Christine Marie *WhoSSW 93*
Robinson, Christopher Douglas 1925-1990 *BioIn 17*
Robinson, Christopher Thomas 1951- *WhoAm 92*
Robinson, Claire *Law&B 92*
Robinson, Colin *WhoScE 91-1*
Robinson, Colleen McC. *ScF&FL 92*
Robinson, Cora Guinn 1958- *WhoWrEP 92*
Robinson, Crabb 1775-1867 *BioIn 17*
Robinson, D.W. *WhoScE 91-1*
Robinson, Dana C. 1957- *St&PR 93*
Robinson, Daniel Baruch 1937- *WhoAm 92*
Robinson, Daniel Thomas 1925- *WhoAm 92*
Robinson, David *BioIn 17, WhoScE 91-1*
Robinson, David 1965- *WhoAm 92*
Robinson, David Adair 1925- *WhoAm 92*
Robinson, David Bradford 1937- *WhoSSW 93, WhoWor 93*
Robinson, David Brooks 1939- *WhoAm 92*
Robinson, David J. 1951- *WhoAsAP 91*
Robinson, David Kenneth 1951- *St&PR 93*
Robinson, David Mason 1932- *WhoAm 92, WhoWor 93*
Robinson, David Maurice 1965- *BiDAMSp 1989*
Robinson, David Stuart *WhoScE 91-1*
Robinson, David W. 1928- *WhoScE 91-3*
Robinson, David Weaver 1914- *WhoAm 92*
Robinson, David Z. 1927- *WhoAm 92*
Robinson, Davis Rowland 1940- *WhoAm 92*
Robinson, Dean Wentworth 1929- *WhoAm 92*
Robinson, Deanna Campbell 1938- *WhoAmW 93*
Robinson, Debora Sue 1956- *WhoAmW 93*
Robinson, Deborah L. *Law&B 92*
Robinson, DeRhon *BioIn 17*
Robinson, Dolores *BioIn 17*
Robinson, Donald *WhoScE 91-1*
Robinson, Donald 1913-1991 *BioIn 17*
Robinson, Donald Joseph *WhoScE 91-1*
Robinson, Donald Keith 1932- *WhoAm 92*
Robinson, Donald Leonard 1936- *WhoAm 92*
Robinson, Donald Louis 1936- *WhoE 93*
Robinson, Donald Sewart *WhoScE 91-1*
Robinson, Donald T. 1942- *St&PR 93*
Robinson, Donald Walter *WhoAm 92*
Robinson, Donald Warren 1932- *WhoE 93*
Robinson, Doris Herbert 1942- *WhoAmW 93*
Robinson, Dorothy Carol Jones 1930- *WhoAmW 93*
Robinson, Dorothy Washington 1929- *BlkAuII 92*
Robinson, Douglas 1954- *ScF&FL 92*
Robinson, Douglas W. 1928- *St&PR 93*
Robinson, Duncan 1943- *WhoAm 92, WhoE 93*
Robinson, Dwight G. 1935- *St&PR 93*
Robinson, E. B., Jr. 1941- *WhoAm 92, WhoSSW 93*
Robinson, Earl 1910-1991 *AnObit 1991, News 92*
Robinson, Earl David 1948- *St&PR 93*
Robinson, Earl (Hawley) 1910-1991 *Baker 92, BioIn 17*
Robinson, Eddie Day *WhoAm 92*
Robinson, Edgar Allen 1933- *St&PR 93, WhoAm 92*
Robinson, Edna L. 1938- *St&PR 93*
Robinson, Edward A. 1932- *St&PR 93*
Robinson, Edward G. *BioIn 17*
Robinson, Edward G. 1893-1973 *IntDcF 2-3 [port]*
Robinson, Edward Joseph 1940- *St&PR 93, WhoSSW 93*
Robinson, Edward Murray 1959- *St&PR 93*
Robinson, Edward N. 1945- *St&PR 93*
Robinson, Edwin Arlington 1869-1935 *BioIn 17, GayN*
Robinson, Edwin O. *Law&B 92*
Robinson, Edwin O., Jr. 1939- *WhoAm 92*
Robinson, Eleanor *ScF&FL 92*
Robinson, Eliot Steele 1942- *St&PR 93*
Robinson, Elizabeth *BiDAMSp 1989*
Robinson, Emyre Barrios 1926- *HispAmA [port]*
Robinson, Enders Anthony 1930- *WhoAm 92, WhoSSW 93, WhoWor 93*
Robinson, F. George 1911- *St&PR 93*
Robinson, Farrel Richard 1927- *WhoAm 92*
Robinson, Faye 1943- *Baker 92*
Robinson, Florence Claire Crim 1932- *WhoAm 92*
Robinson, Florine Samantha 1935- *WhoAmW 93, WhoE 93, WhoWor 93*
Robinson, Floyd Walter, Jr. 1947- *WhoSSW 93*
Robinson, Forbes 1926-1987 *OxDcOp*
Robinson, (Peter) Forbes 1926-1987 *Baker 92*
Robinson, Frank *BioIn 17*
Robinson, Frank 1935- *AfrAmBi, WhoAm 92, WhoE 93*
Robinson, Frank Brooks, Sr. 1931- *WhoE 93*
Robinson, Frank M. 1926- *ScF&FL 92*
Robinson, Frank S. 1947- *ScF&FL 92*
Robinson, Franklin *BioIn 17*
Robinson, Franklin Westcott 1939- *WhoAm 92, WhoE 93*
Robinson, Fred, Mrs. *AmWomPl*
Robinson, Fred Colson 1930- *WhoAm 92*
Robinson, Frederic Murray 1934- *St&PR 93*
Robinson, G. Wilse 1924- *WhoAm 92*
Robinson, Gail J. *Law&B 92*
Robinson, Gary C. 1940- *St&PR 93*
Robinson, Gary Dale 1938- *WhoWor 93*
Robinson, Gene *St&PR 93*
Robinson, George Cottman, Jr. 1934- *St&PR 93*
Robinson, George Waller 1949- *WhoSSW 93*
Robinson, Glen Parmelee, Jr. 1923- *St&PR 93*
Robinson, Glynne 1934- *WhoE 93*
Robinson, Grenville Arthur *WhoScE 91-1*
Robinson, Gwynn Herndon 1920- *WhoAm 92*
Robinson, Halbert B. 1925-1981 *BioIn 17*
Robinson, Hamilton, Jr. 1934- *St&PR 93*
Robinson, Harold Ivens 1951- *WhoSSW 93*
Robinson, Harry Granville, III 1942- *WhoAm 92*
Robinson, Harry L. 1929- *St&PR 93*
Robinson, Harry S. 1947- *St&PR 93*
Robinson, Hazel *BioIn 17*
Robinson, Hazel M. *AmWomPl*
Robinson, Henry *AfrAmBi*
Robinson, Henry Crabb 1775-1867 *BioIn 17*
Robinson, Henry John 1943- *St&PR 93*
Robinson, Henry Peach 1830-1901 *BioIn 17*
Robinson, Herbert 1916- *St&PR 93*
Robinson, Hobart Krum 1937- *WhoAm 92*
Robinson, Hugh Granville 1932- *St&PR 93*
Robinson, Hugh Latham 1929- *St&PR 93*
Robinson, Hugh R. 1922- *WhoAm 92*
Robinson, Ian Crawford *WhoScE 91-1*
Robinson, Ian Louis 1927- *WhoAsAP 91*
Robinson, Imogene Decrow 1901- *WhoE 93*
Robinson, Ingrid Elizabeth 1947- *WhoAmW 93*
Robinson, Ira L. *Law&B 92*
Robinson, Irwin Jay 1928- *WhoAm 92, WhoE 93*
Robinson, Ivan E. 1920- *St&PR 93*
Robinson, J. Fletcher *BioIn 17*
Robinson, J. Kenneth 1916-1990 *BioIn 17*
Robinson, J.M. *WhoScE 91-1*
Robinson, J. Mack 1923- *St&PR 93, WhoIns 93*
Robinson, Jack A. 1930- *St&PR 93*
Robinson, Jack Albert 1930- *WhoAm 92*
Robinson, Jackie 1919-1972 *BioIn 17, EncAACR*
Robinson, Jacqueline Carter 1944- *WhoAmW 93*
Robinson, Jacques Alan 1947- *WhoAm 92*
Robinson, James *WhoAm 92*
Robinson, James A. *Law&B 92*
Robinson, James Allen 1927- *WhoSSW 93*
Robinson, James Arthur 1932- *WhoAm 92, WhoWrEP 92*
Robinson, James Arthur 1949- *WhoIns 93*
Robinson, James Brian *Law&B 92*
Robinson, James D., III *BioIn 17*
Robinson, James D., III 1935- *St&PR 93*
Robinson, James Dixon, III 1935- *WhoAm 92*
Robinson, James Ford 1955- *WhoWrEP 92*
Robinson, James G. *BioIn 17*
Robinson, James Harvey 1863-1936 *BioIn 17*
Robinson, James Keith 1916- *WhoWrEP 92*
Robinson, James Kenneth 1943- *WhoAm 92*
Robinson, James LeRoy 1940- *WhoAm 92, WhoE 93*
Robinson, James S. 1947- *St&PR 93*
Robinson, James V. *Law&B 92*
Robinson, James Victor 1927- *St&PR 93*
Robinson, James Wayne 1946- *St&PR 93*
Robinson, James William 1919- *WhoAm 92*
Robinson, James William 1934- *St&PR 93*
Robinson, Jan Sue 1945- *St&PR 93*
Robinson, Jane Butler 1934- *WhoAmW 93*
Robinson, Jane Jenifer Ann *WhoScE 91-1*
Robinson, Janet Lee 1955- *WhoE 93*
Robinson, Jara Baxter 1935- *WhoSSW 93*
Robinson, Jay 1915- *WhoAm 92*
Robinson, Jay Luke 1932- *WhoAm 92*
Robinson, Jeanne 1948- *ScF&FL 92*
Robinson, Jeffery Herbert 1956- *WhoEmL 93, WhoSSW 93*
Robinson, Jeffrey 1945- *ConAu 37NR*
Robinson, Jeffrey Brian 1946- *St&PR 93*
Robinson, Jerome David 1941- *WhoE 93*
Robinson, Jerome Lawrence 1922- *St&PR 93*
Robinson, Jerry Allen 1939- *WhoSSW 93*
Robinson, Jerry H. 1932- *WhoAm 92*
Robinson, Jerry La Mar *Law&B 92*
Robinson, Jerry Mason 1938- *WhoSSW 93*
Robinson, Joan 1903-1983 *BioIn 17*
Robinson, Joan 1963- *WhoAmW 93*
Robinson, Joan E. *Law&B 92*
Robinson, John 1575?-1625 *BioIn 17*
Robinson, John A. 1935- *St&PR 93*
Robinson, John Alan 1930- *WhoAm 92*
Robinson, John Alan 1946- *St&PR 93*
Robinson, John Alexander 1935- *BiDAMSp 1989, WhoAm 92*
Robinson, John Beckwith 1922- *WhoAm 92*
Robinson, John Bowers, Jr. 1946- *St&PR 93, WhoAm 92, WhoE 93*
Robinson, John David 1937- *WhoAm 92*
Robinson, John Delyn 1946- *WhoWrEP 92*
Robinson, John H. *BioIn 17*
Robinson, John Hamilton 1927- *WhoAm 92*
Robinson, John Jeffrey 1941- *WhoE 93*
Robinson, John Joseph *WhoScE 91-1*
Robinson, John Lewis 1918- *WhoAm 92*
Robinson, John Louis 1935- *WhoSSW 93*
Robinson, John Mark 1949- *MiSFD 9*
Robinson, John Minor 1910- *WhoAm 92, WhoWor 93*
Robinson, John Nathaniel 1912- *WhoE 93*
Robinson, John Rowland 1935- *WhoE 93*
Robinson, Johnny Nolan 1938- *BiDAMSp 1989*
Robinson, Jon R. *Law&B 92*
Robinson, Joseph A. 1938- *St&PR 93*
Robinson, Joseph Albert 1938- *WhoAm 92*
Robinson, Joseph Daniel 1943- *WhoE 93*
Robinson, Joseph Edward 1925- *WhoAm 92*
Robinson, Joseph T. 1872-1937 *BioIn 17, PolPar*
Robinson, JulieNell Napier 1950- *WhoAmW 93*
Robinson, Katherine Prentis Woodroofe 1939- *WhoWrEP 92*
Robinson, Kathleen Shelley 1948- *WhoAmW 93, WhoWrEP 92*
Robinson, Kaylaine 1933- *WhoWrEP 92*
Robinson, Keith 1948- *WhoSSW 93*
Robinson, Keith Burney 1954- *St&PR 93*
Robinson, Kenneth James 1944- *St&PR 93*
Robinson, Kenneth Larry 1944- *WhoSSW 93*
Robinson, Kenneth Patrick 1933- *St&PR 93*
Robinson, Kim Stanley 1952- *ScF&FL 92*
Robinson, Larry R. 1936- *St&PR 93*
Robinson, Larry Robert 1936- *WhoAm 92, WhoIns 93*
Robinson, Laura Hales 1956- *St&PR 93*
Robinson, LaVaughn 1927- *BioIn 17*
Robinson, Lawrence Brandon 1932- *WhoWor 93*
Robinson, Lawrence Donald *BioIn 17*
Robinson, Lawrence Vernon, Jr. 1934- *St&PR 93*
Robinson, Lee Harris 1939- *WhoAm 92*
Robinson, Leila Bridger 1926- *St&PR 93*
Robinson, Leland Walter 1942- *WhoSSW 93*
Robinson, Leonard Harrison, Jr. 1943- *WhoAm 92*
Robinson, Leonard Wallace 1912- *WhoWrEP 92*
Robinson, Leonardo DaVinci *Law&B 92*
Robinson, Leroy *Law&B 92*
Robinson, Lewis J., Jr. *Law&B 92*
Robinson, Lillian Sara 1941- *WhoSSW 93*
Robinson, Linda Gosden 1953- *BioIn 17, WhoAm 92, WhoAmW 93*
Robinson, Lisa M. *Law&B 92, St&PR 93*
Robinson, Lloyd *MajAI*
Robinson, Lloyd O. 1923- *St&PR 93*
Robinson, Logan 1949- *ScF&FL 92*
Robinson, Logan G. *Law&B 92*
Robinson, Lorna Jane 1957- *WhoAmW 93*
Robinson, Louie, Jr. 1926- *BlkAuII 92*
Robinson, Louise Evette 1952- *WhoAmW 93*
Robinson, M. John 1938- *St&PR 93*
Robinson, Maggie Comer d1992 *NewYTBS 92*
Robinson, Malcolm *BioIn 17*
Robinson, Malcolm 1942- *WhoSSW 93*
Robinson, Marc Alan 1951- *St&PR 93*
Robinson, Marcela *WhoWrEP 92*
Robinson, Marcella Louise 1928- *WhoAmW 93*
Robinson, Margaret Louise 1952- *WhoAmW 93*
Robinson, Marguerite Stern 1935- *WhoAm 92*
Robinson, Marietta Sebree 1951- *WhoAmW 93*
Robinson, Mark E. *Law&B 92*
Robinson, Mark E. 1955- *St&PR 93*
Robinson, Marshall Alan 1922- *WhoAm 92*
Robinson, Martha Stewart 1914- *WhoAm 92*
Robinson, Martin d1992 *BioIn 17, NewYTBS 92*
Robinson, Marvin Stuart 1933- *WhoAm 92*
Robinson, Mary 1944- *BioIn 17, News 93-1 [port]*
Robinson, Mary 1945- *WhoWor 93*
Robinson, Mary Anna *Law&B 92*
Robinson, Mary Close *AmWomPl*
Robinson, Mary E. Goff 1925- *WhoAmW 93*
Robinson, Mary Jean 1929- *WhoSSW 93*
Robinson, Mary Lou 1926- *WhoAm 92, WhoAmW 93, WhoSSW 93*
Robinson, Mary Louise *AmWomPl*
Robinson, Maurice Richard, Jr. 1937- *WhoAm 92*
Robinson, Max *WhoScE 91-1*
Robinson, Max 1939-1988 *ConBlB 3 [port]*
Robinson, Meghan d1990 *BioIn 17*
Robinson, Melvyn Roland 1933- *WhoWor 93*
Robinson, Meyer H. d1992 *NewYTBS 92 [port]*
Robinson, Michael *BioIn 17*
Robinson, Michael F. 1948- *St&PR 93*
Robinson, Michael Francis 1954- *WhoE 93*
Robinson, Michael Hill 1929- *WhoAm 92, WhoE 93*
Robinson, Michael J. *Law&B 92*
Robinson, Michael J. 1932- *St&PR 93*
Robinson, Michelle Elaine 1957- *WhoAmW 93*
Robinson, Mildred Ann 1938- *WhoAmW 93*
Robinson, Mildred Wigfall 1944- *WhoAm 92*
Robinson, Minnie Lenetha *WhoAmW 93, WhoWor 93*
Robinson, Nan Senior 1932- *WhoAmW 93*
Robinson, Nathaniel David 1904- *WhoSSW 93, WhoWor 93*
Robinson, Neal E. 1951- *St&PR 93*
Robinson, Nell Bryant 1925- *WhoAmW 93*
Robinson, Nigel *ScF&FL 92*
Robinson, Opal Anne 1936- *WhoAmW 93*
Robinson, Ormsbee Wright 1910- *WhoSSW 93*
Robinson, Patricia Ann 1952- *WhoSSW 93*
Robinson, Patricia B. 1952- *St&PR 93*
Robinson, Patricia Snyder 1952- *WhoE 93*
Robinson, Paul *ScF&FL 92*
Robinson, Paul 1956- *WhoSSW 93*
Robinson, Paul Arnold 1940- *WhoAm 92*
Robinson, Paul Frank *Law&B 92*
Robinson, Peggie Crose 1944- *WhoAmW 93*
Robinson, Peter *WhoScE 91-1*
Robinson, Peter 1932- *WhoAm 92*
Robinson, Peter 1950- *WhoCanL 92*
Robinson, Peter Bullene 1949- *WhoE 93*
Robinson, Peter C. 1938- *St&PR 93*
Robinson, Peter Clark 1938- *WhoAm 92*
Robinson, Peter E. *Law&B 92*
Robinson, Peter John 1944- *WhoSSW 93*
Robinson, Peter Michael *WhoScE 91-1*
Robinson, Peter Philip *WhoScE 91-1*
Robinson, Phil Alden *MiSFD 9*
Robinson, Phil Alden 1950?- *ConAu 139*
Robinson, Philip 1950- *WhoWor 93*
Robinson, Prezell Russell 1922- *WhoSSW 93*
Robinson, Priscilla Lutresia 1951- *WhoSSW 93*
Robinson, R.C. 1940- *St&PR 93*
Robinson, R.W. *St&PR 93*
Robinson, Ralph C. 1957- *WhoE 93*
Robinson, Randall *BioIn 17*
Robinson, Ray 1932- *Baker 92*
Robinson, Raymond Edwin 1932- *WhoAm 92, WhoSSW 93*
Robinson, Raymond G. *Law&B 92*
Robinson, Raymond J. 1956- *St&PR 93*

Robinson, Raymond Kenneth 1920- *WhoWrEP 92*
Robinson, Reba Genell *Law&B 92*
Robinson, Rich *BioIn 17*
Robinson, Richard 1937- *WhoAm 92*
Robinson, Richard D.B. *WhoScE 91-1*
Robinson, Richard Edwin 1938- *St&PR 93*
Robinson, Richard Francis 1941- *WhoSSW 93*
Robinson, Richard Garwood 1915- *WhoWor 93*
Robinson, Richard Irvine 1930- *St&PR 93, WhoAm 92*
Robinson, Richard James 1952- *WhoE 93*
Robinson, Richard L. *Law&B 92*
Robinson, Richard L. 1930- *St&PR 93*
Robinson, Richard S. *Law&B 92*
Robinson, Rick J. 1951- *WhoE 93*
Robinson, Robert 1886-1975 *BioIn 17*
Robinson, Robert A. 1914-1990 *BioIn 17*
Robinson, Robert Armstrong 1925- *St&PR 93, WhoAm 92, WhoE 93, WhoWor 93*
Robinson, Robert Blacque 1927- *WhoAm 92*
Robinson, Robert Earl 1927- *WhoSSW 93*
Robinson, Robert Edward 1924- *St&PR 93*
Robinson, Robert H. *Law&B 92*
Robinson, Robert J. 1935- *WhoAm 92*
Robinson, Robert James 1935- *WhoAm 92*
Robinson, Robert James 1943- *St&PR 93*
Robinson, Robert L. *Law&B 92*
Robinson, Robert L. 1936- *WhoAm 92*
Robinson, Roger 1943- *ScF&FL 92*
Robinson, Ronald Alan 1952- *WhoAm 92*
Robinson, Ronald Allen 1943- *St&PR 93*
Robinson, Ronald Franklin 1936- *St&PR 93*
Robinson, Ronald James 1946- *WhoEmL 93*
Robinson, Ronald Michael 1942- *WhoAm 92*
Robinson, Roscoe 1928- *BioIn 17*
Robinson, Roscoe, Jr. 1928- *AfrAmBi*
Robinson, Roscoe Ross 1929- *WhoAm 92, WhoSSW 93, WhoWor 93*
Robinson, Ross A. *Law&B 92*
Robinson, Roy S. *St&PR 93*
Robinson, Rudyard Livingstone 1951- *WhoWor 93*
Robinson, Russell Lee 1931- *WhoSSW 93*
Robinson, Sally 1959- *ScF&FL 92*
Robinson, Sally Winston 1924- *WhoAmW 93, WhoWor 93*
Robinson, Samuel Charles 1931- *St&PR 93*
Robinson, Samuel L. *WhoAm 92*
Robinson, Samuel Lee 1939- *St&PR 93*
Robinson, Sandra Dee 1960- *WhoAmW 93*
Robinson, Sandra L. *Law&B 92*
Robinson, Saundra A. *AfrAmBi*
Robinson, Sharleen 1950- *WhoAmW 93*
Robinson, Sharon Beth 1959- *WhoE 93*
Robinson, Sherman 1942- *WhoAm 92*
Robinson, Sherman Monte 1924- *WhoAm 92*
Robinson, Simon Courtney 1964- *St&PR 93*
Robinson, Smokey *WhoAm 92*
Robinson, "Smokey" 1940- *Baker 92, ConBlB 3 [port]*
See Also Robinson, Smokey, & the Miracles *SoulM*
Robinson, Smokey, & the Miracles *SoulM*
Robinson, Spencer T. Herk 1940- *WhoAm 92*
Robinson, Spider *BioIn 17*
Robinson, Spider 1948- *ScF&FL 92, WhoCanL 92*
Robinson, Spotswood W., III 1916- *CngDr 91*
Robinson, Spottswood William, III 1916- *WhoAm 92*
Robinson, Stanford 1904-1984 *Baker 92*
Robinson, Stanley Daniel 1926- *WhoAm 92*
Robinson, Stephen *BioIn 17*
Robinson, Stephen J. 1950- *St&PR 93*
Robinson, Stephen Michael 1942- *WhoAm 92*
Robinson, Stuart Keven *WhoScE 91-1*
Robinson, Sue *ScF&FL 92*
Robinson, Sugar Ray *BioIn 17*
Robinson, Sumner Martin 1928- *WhoAm 92*
Robinson, Susan *BioIn 17*
Robinson, Susan Estes 1950- *WhoSSW 93*
Robinson, Susan Hand 1942- *WhoWrEP 92*
Robinson, Susan M. 1941- *WhoAmW 93*
Robinson, Sylvia *SoulM*
Robinson, T.A. *Law&B 92*
Robinson, Terence Edward 1959- *St&PR 93*
Robinson, Thomas Bullene 1917- *WhoAm 92*
Robinson, Thomas Christopher 1944- *WhoAm 92*
Robinson, Thomas E. d1992 *NewYTBS 92 [port]*
Robinson, Thomas G. *Law&B 92*
Robinson, Thomas George 1929- *St&PR 93*
Robinson, Thomas P. d1990 *BioIn 17*
Robinson, Thurston 1915- *WhoAm 92*
Robinson, Timothy *Law&B 92*
Robinson, Toni Patricia 1948- *WhoAmW 93*
Robinson, Trevor *BioIn 17*
Robinson, Ursula *ScF&FL 92*
Robinson, Violet *AmWomPl*
Robinson, Violet Marie 1935- *WhoAmW 93*
Robinson, Virginia A. 1942- *St&PR 93*
Robinson, W. Lee 1943- *WhoSSW 93*
Robinson, Walker Lee 1941- *WhoE 93*
Robinson, Walter George 1911- *WhoAm 92*
Robinson, Walter Stitt, Jr. 1917- *WhoAm 92*
Robinson, Warren L. 1950- *St&PR 93*
Robinson, Wayne A. *Law&B 92*
Robinson, Wendy *Law&B 92*
Robinson, Wendy R. *Law&B 92*
Robinson, Wilburn Vaughn 1934- *St&PR 93*
Robinson, Wilkes Coleman 1925- *CngDr 91, WhoAm 92, WhoE 93*
Robinson, William d1990 *BioIn 17*
Robinson, William 1848- *BioIn 17*
Robinson, William A. 1934- *WhoAm 92*
Robinson, William Andrew 1944- *WhoAm 92*
Robinson, William Erigen 1814-1892 *JrnUS*
Robinson, William Franklin 1916- *WhoAm 92*
Robinson, William Gregory 1928- *St&PR 93*
Robinson, William Ingraham 1909- *WhoAm 92*
Robinson, William J. 1918- *WhoIns 93*
Robinson, William James 1953- *WhoWor 93*
Robinson, William P. 1949- *WhoAm 92*
Robinson, William Peter *WhoScE 91-1*
Robinson, William T. *Law&B 92*
Robinson, William Walker 1950- *WhoAm 92*
Robinson, William Wheeler 1918- *WhoAm 92, WhoWrEP 92*
Robinson, Willie Clarence 1934- *WhoAm 92*
Robinson, Windsor Calvert 1950- *WhoE 93*
Robinson, Winfield F. 1938- *St&PR 93*
Robirosa, Mercedes 1951- *BioIn 17*
Robish, Dennis Michael 1944- *St&PR 93*
Robison, Andrew Cliffe, Jr. 1940- *WhoAm 92*
Robison, Charles B. 1913- *WhoIns 93*
Robison, Clarence, Jr. 1924- *WhoAm 92, WhoSSW 93*
Robison, Clyde Francis 1930- *St&PR 93*
Robison, David Alan 1937- *St&PR 93*
Robison, Frederick Mason 1934- *WhoAm 92*
Robison, James E. 1915- *St&PR 93*
Robison, James Everett 1915- *WhoAm 92, WhoE 93*
Robison, Kenneth Gerald 1938- *WhoE 93, WhoWor 93*
Robison, Odis Wayne 1934- *WhoSSW 93*
Robison, Olan Randle d1992 *BioIn 17*
Robison, Olin Clyde 1936- *WhoAm 92, WhoE 93*
Robison, Paul Frederick 1919- *WhoAm 92*
Robison, Paula (Judith) 1941- *Baker 92, WhoAm 92*
Robison, Richard Eugene 1951- *WhoSSW 93*
Robison, Susan Miller 1945- *WhoAmW 93, WhoE 93*
Robison, Vince *BioIn 17*
Robison, William Thomas 1924- *WhoAm 92*
Robitaille, Denis A. *Law&B 92*
Robitaille, Julie *ScF&FL 92*
Robitaille, Luc *BioIn 17*
Robitaille, Luc 1966- *WhoAm 92*
Robitaille, Stephen John 1949- *WhoSSW 93*
Robitelle, Clifford C. 1947- *St&PR 93*
Robke, Kevin Gerard 1961- *WhoSSW 93*
Robkin, Maurice Abraham 1931- *WhoAm 92*
Roble, Carole Marcia 1938- *WhoAmW 93*
Roble, M.A. 1955- *St&PR 93*
Roble, Roger Harold 1941- *St&PR 93*
Roblek, Branko 1934- *WhoWor 93*
Robles, Alfonso Garcia 1911-1991 *BioIn 17*
Robles, Antonio 1897- *DcMexL*
Robles, Daniel Alomias 1871-1942 *Baker 92*
Robles, Emmanuel 1914- *BioIn 17*
Robles, Fernando 1887- *DcMexL*
Robles, German *BioIn 17*
Robles, Jose Canovas d1992 *BioIn 17*
Robles, Marco Aurelio 1905-1990 *BioIn 17*
Robles, Mireya 1934- *NotHsAW 93*
Robles, Rosalie Miranda 1942- *WhoAmW 93*
Robles, Virgilio P. 1937- *WhoAsAP 91*
Robles Jimenez, Jose Esaul 1925- *WhoAm 92*
Robles Pariente, Rafael 1939- *WhoScE 91-3*
Roblick, Wolfgang Rudi 1945- *WhoWor 93*
Roblin, Duff 1917- *WhoAm 92*
Robnak, David Zack 1957- *St&PR 93*
Robock, Alan 1949- *WhoE 93*
Robock, Stefan Hyman 1915- *WhoAm 92*
Robohm, Karl-Friedrich 1938- *WhoScE 91-3*
Robohm, Peggy Adler 1942- *WhoAmW 93, WhoE 93, WhoWor 93*
Robold, Alice Ilene 1928- *WhoAm 92, WhoAmW 93*
Robotham, Lascelles Lister 1923- *WhoWor 93*
Robotti, Dorene E. *Law&B 92*
Robottom, John 1934- *ConAu 38NR*
Robredo, Raimundo 1925- *WhoWor 93*
Robrock, Richard Barker, II 1941- *WhoE 93*
Robshaw, Alan 1950-1991 *BioIn 17*
Robshaw, James Dale 1942- *WhoAm 92*
Robsjohn-Gibbings, Terence Harold 1905-1976 *BioIn 17*
Robson, Andrew John *Law&B 92*
Robson, Ann 1958-1990 *BioIn 17*
Robson, Antony Robert Orpen d1991 *BioIn 17*
Robson, Barry *WhoScE 91-1*
Robson, Brian A. 1937- *St&PR 93*
Robson, Christopher 1953- *OxDcOp*
Robson, Donald S. 1952- *St&PR 93*
Robson, Edward H. *WhoScE 91-1*
Robson, Eleanor *AmWomPl*
Robson, Elizabeth Browel *WhoScE 91-1*
Robson, Ethel Hedley *AmWomPl*
Robson, Fred Lee 1936- *WhoE 93*
Robson, Geoffrey Robert 1929- *WhoWor 93*
Robson, Gordon *WhoScE 91-1*
Robson, James Christopher *WhoScE 91-1*
Robson, John Edwin 1930- *St&PR 93*
Robson, Kathleen Patricia 1960- *WhoAmW 93*
Robson, Mark 1913-1978 *MiSFD 9N*
Robson, May 1858-1942 *AmWomPl*
Robson, Michael 1931- *ScF&FL 92*
Robson, Morton S. 1923- *St&PR 93*
Robson, P.J. *WhoScE 91-1*
Robson, Peter 1934- *WhoScE 91-4*
Robson, Peter Neville *WhoScE 91-1*
Robson, Regina M. David *Law&B 92*
Robson, Ruthann 1956- *ConAu 139*
Robson, Sybil Ann 1956- *WhoAmW 93, WhoEmL 93*
Robson, Terry Patrick 1943- *WhoSSW 93*
Robustelli, Andy *BioIn 17*
Roby, Christina Yen *WhoAmW 93, WhoE 93*
Roby, Donald Franklin 1929- *St&PR 93*
Roby, Douglas d1992 *NewYTBS 92*
Roby, Douglas 1898-1992 *BioIn 17*
Roby, Edgar Maclin 1931- *WhoAm 92*
Roby, Kinley Edmund 1929- *WhoWrEP 92*
Robyn, Alfred George 1860-1935 *Baker 92*
Roca, Blas *DcCPCAm*
Roca, Carlos Manuel 1962- *WhoE 93*
Roca, Rafael A. 1928- *WhoIns 93*
Roca, Roberto *DcCPCAm*
Roca, Sergio G. 1961- *HispAmA*
Roca de Torres, Irma Eneida 1942- *WhoAmW 93*
Rocard, Michel *BioIn 17*
Rocard, Michel 1930- *ColdWar 1 [port]*
Rocard, Michel Louis Leon 1930- *WhoWor 93*
Rocard, Yves d1992 *NewYTBS 92*
Rocard, Yves 1903-1992 *BioIn 17*
Rocca, Curtis M., III 1962- *St&PR 93*
Rocca, F.H. 1939- *St&PR 93*
Rocca, Lodovico 1895-1986 *Baker 92, OxDcOp*
Rocca, Robert Angelo 1954- *WhoE 93*
Roccanova, Louis Patrick 1965- *WhoE 93*
Rocchi, Al *Law&B 92*
Rocchi, Raniero 1932- *WhoScE 91-3*
Rocchini, Richard Allan *Law&B 92*
Rocchi Pellegrini, Fulvia 1949- *WhoWor 93*
Rocco, Alex 1936- *WhoAm 92*
Rocco, Ellen Jane 1946- *WhoAmW 93*
Rocco, Frank W. *Law&B 92*
Rocco, James Robert 1953- *WhoEmL 93*
Rocco, Joseph Eugene 1960- *St&PR 93*
Rocco, Marc *MiSFD 9*
Rocco, Mildred Jeffries 1938- *WhoAmW 93*
Rocco, Vincent Anthony 1945- *St&PR 93, WhoAm 92*
Rocek, Ivan 1932- *WhoScE 91-4*
Rocek, Jan 1924- *WhoAm 92*
Roch, Jeanette *Law&B 92*
Roch, Kenneth Malcolm *WhoScE 91-1*
Rocha, Denise Michele *Law&B 92*
Rocha, Glauber 1938-1981 *MiSFD 9N*
Rocha, Patrica S. *Law&B 92*
Rocha, Rene Fernandez 1948- *WhoSSW 93*
Rochaix, Jean-David 1944- *WhoScE 91-4*
Rochambeau, Jean Baptiste Donatien de Vimeur, Count of 1725-1807 *HarEnMi*
Rochant, Eric *MiSFD 9*
Rocha-Pereira, Maria Helena Monteiro 1925- *WhoWor 93*
Rochas, Michel *WhoScE 91-2*
Rochat, Herve 1937- *WhoScE 91-2*
Rochat, Jean-Paul 1943- *WhoWor 93*
Rochat, Philippe H.P. 1942- *WhoUN 92*
Rochberg, George 1918- *Baker 92, WhoAm 92*
Roche, Alain Andre 1948- *WhoWor 93*
Roche, Antonio 1944- *WhoWor 93*
Roche, Burke B. 1913- *St&PR 93*
Roche, David Alan 1946- *WhoAm 92*
Roche, David H. 1947- *St&PR 93*
Roche, Denise Ann 1942- *WhoAmW 93*
Roche, Douglas David 1936- *WhoAm 92*
Roche, Edward J. *Law&B 92*
Roche, F. *WhoScE 91-2*
Roche, Genevieve Harris *Law&B 92*
Roche, George A. 1941- *St&PR 93*
Roche, George Augustine 1941- *WhoAm 92*
Roche, George Charles, III 1935- *WhoAm 92*
Roche, Gerard R. 1931- *St&PR 93*
Roche, Gerard Raymond 1931- *WhoAm 92*
Roche, Henri Pierre 1879-1959 *BioIn 17*
Roche, Jack d1991 *BioIn 17*
Roche, James F. 1943- *WhoScE 91-3*
Roche, James G. 1939- *St&PR 93*
Roche, James Joseph 1953- *WhoE 93*
Roche, James M. 1906- *St&PR 93*
Roche, James McMillan 1934- *WhoAm 92*
Roche, James Richard 1924- *WhoWor 93*
Roche, Jerome (Lawrence Alexander) 1942- *Baker 92*
Roche, Joan Denise 1961- *St&PR 93*
Roche, John E. 1946- *St&PR 93*
Roche, John Edward 1946- *WhoE 93*
Roche, John J. *Law&B 92, WhoAm 92*
Roche, John J. 1942- *WhoAm 92*
Roche, John Jefferson 1934- *WhoAm 92*
Roche, John P. 1923- *WhoAm 92*
Roche, Joyce *St&PR 93*
Roche, Joyce M. *BioIn 17*
Roche, Karen Marie *Law&B 92*
Roche, Kevin 1922- *WhoAm 92, WhoWor 93*
Roche, Kevin Joseph 1935- *St&PR 93, WhoAm 92*
Roche, Lynn F. 1960- *WhoE 93*
Roche, Mark A. *Law&B 92*
Roche, Mary-Lisa Favret *Law&B 92*
Roche, Myles John 1941- *St&PR 93*
Roche, Patrick W. 1948- *St&PR 93*
Roche, Paul C. 1915- *St&PR 93*
Roche, Paul Hoop, Jr. 1945- *St&PR 93*
Roche, Robert Francis 1942- *St&PR 93*
Roche, Stephen Michael 1959- *St&PR 93*
Roche, Thomas M. *Law&B 92*
Roche, William John 1953- *WhoE 93*
Roche, Winston M. *BioIn 17*
Rochebouet, Gaetan de Grimaudet de 1813-1899 *BioIn 17*
Rochefort, Christiane 1917- *BioIn 17*
Rochefort, Henri *WhoScE 91-2*
Rochefort, Henri 1831-1913 *BioIn 17*
Rochefort, John Spencer 1924- *WhoAm 92*
Rocheleau, Barbara Schwartz 1944- *WhoAmW 93*
Rocheleau, Beth Ann 1963- *WhoEmL 93*
Rocheleau, Donald 1933- *St&PR 93*
Rocheleau, James Romig 1940- *WhoAm 92*
Rocheleau, Norman J. *St&PR 93*
Rocheleau, Serge 1942- *St&PR 93*
Rochelle, Claire d1981 *SweetSg C [port]*
Rochelle, J. 1930- *St&PR 93*
Rochelle, James Monroe 1930- *WhoE 93*
Rochelle, Leone Castles 1951- *WhoAmW 93*
Rocher, Allan Charles 1936- *WhoAsAP 91*
Rocher, Ludo 1926- *WhoAm 92*
Roche Rabell, Arnaldo *BioIn 17*
Roche Rabell, Arnaldo 1955- *HispAmA*
Rochereau de La Sabliere, Jean-Marc 1946- *WhoUN 92*
Rochester, Colin H. *WhoScE 91-1*
Rochester, Dudley Fortescue 1928- *WhoAm 92*

Rochester, Michael Grant 1932- WhoAm 92
Rochester, Richard James 1950- WhoSSW 93
Rochet, Claude 1949- WhoWor 93
Rochet, Waldeck 1905-1983 BioIn 17
Rochette, Jean-Francois 1939- WhoWor 93
Rochette, Louis 1923- St&PR 93, WhoAm 92
Rochetto, Evelyn Marie 1906- WhoWor 93
Rochford, Paul E. Law&B 92
Rochford, Sheri Renae 1955- WhoAmW 93
Rochford, Walter 1943- St&PR 93
Rochira, Nancy Mary 1944- WhoAmW 93
Rochlin, Doris 1932- ScF&FL 92
Rochlin, Joyce Tretick 1941- WhoAmW 93
Rochlin, Phillip 1923- WhoE 93
Rochlis, James J. 1916- St&PR 93
Rochlitz, (Johann) Friedrich 1769-1842 Baker 92
Rochman, Alan L. 1945- St&PR 93
Rochois, Marthe c. 1658-1728 OxDcOp
Rochon, Edwin Waterbury 1918- WhoWrEP 92
Rochon, Esther 1948- ScF&FL 92
Rochon, Jean 1938- WhoUN 92
Rochon, Lela BioIn 17
Rochon, Pierre Paul 1944- WhoWor 93
Rochus, Pierre Leon 1950- WhoWor 93
Rochwarger, Jeffrey Alan 1953- WhoAm 92
Rochwarger, Leonard 1925- St&PR 93, WhoAm 92
Rochwerger, Leonard Leslie 1942- St&PR 93
Rocio, Quesada Castillo 1949- WhoWor 93
Rock, Arthur 1926- St&PR 93, WhoAm 92
Rock, Bradley E. 1952- St&PR 93
Rock, Chris BioIn 17
Rock, Chris 1967?- ConBlB 3 [port]
Rock, Douglas L. 1947- St&PR 93
Rock, Harold L. 1932- WhoAm 92
Rock, Howard 1911-1976 DcLB 127 [port]
Rock, Howard B. 1944- ConAu 139
Rock, James A. 1929- ScF&FL 92
Rock, John Aubrey 1946- WhoAm 92
Rock, John Van Hassel 1939- St&PR 93
Rock, Leslie S. 1957- St&PR 93
Rock, Michael J. BioIn 17
Rock, Monti, III BioIn 17
Rock, Paul Elliot WhoScE 91-1
Rock, Peter Alfred 1939- WhoAm 92
Rock, Ronald A.P. Law&B 92
Rock, Sabra Leigh 1952- WhoAmW 93
Rock, Sally BioIn 17
Rock, Sally S. Law&B 92
Rock, Sandra Kaye 1952- WhoE 93
Rock, Terrence L. BioIn 17
Rock, Thomas P. 1943- St&PR 93
Rock, William Booth 1947- WhoWor 93
Rockafellow, Deborah Susan 1954- WhoE 93
Rockafellow, Virginia L. Law&B 92
Rockart, John Fralick 1931- WhoE 93
Rockas, Leo 1928- WhoE 93
Rockaway, David Edwin 1958- WhoSSW 93
Rockburne, Dorothea 1934- BioIn 17
Rockburne, Dorothea G. WhoAm 92, WhoAmW 93
Rocke, David Morton 1946- WhoAm 92
Rocke, Richard A. 1942- St&PR 93
Rocke, William J. 1924- St&PR 93
Rockefeller, Blanchette Ferry Hooker 1909-1992 NewYTBS 92 [port]
Rockefeller, Blanchette Hooker 1909- WhoAm 92
Rockefeller, David 1915- WhoAm 92, WhoE 93
Rockefeller, David, Jr. BioIn 17
Rockefeller, Edwin Shaffer 1927- WhoAm 92
Rockefeller, Frederic Lincoln 1921- St&PR 93
Rockefeller, Happy WhoAm 92
Rockefeller, Jay 1937- BioIn 17
Rockefeller, John D. 1839-1937 GayN
Rockefeller, John D. 1937- BioIn 17
Rockefeller, John D., IV 1937- CngDr 91
Rockefeller, John Davison 1839-1937 See Rockefeller family DcTwHis
Rockefeller, John Davison, Jr. 1874-1960 See Rockefeller family DcTwHis
Rockefeller, John Davison, IV 1937- WhoAm 92, WhoSSW 93
Rockefeller, Laurance S. 1910- WhoWor 93
Rockefeller, Margaretta Fitler Murphy WhoAm 92
Rockefeller, Martha Baird 1895-1971 Baker 92
Rockefeller, Mary French 1910- WhoAm 92
Rockefeller, Nelson A. 1908-1979 BioIn 17, PolPar
Rockefeller, Nelson Aldrich 1908-1979 See Rockefeller family DcTwHis
Rockefeller, Rodman Clark 1932- WhoAm 92
Rockefeller, Sharon Percy 1944- WhoAm 92, WhoAmW 93
Rockefeller, William 1918-1990 BioIn 17
Rockefeller family DcTwHis
Rockemer, Kevin George 1952- WhoWor 93
Rockenfield, Scott See Queensryche ConMus 8
Rockenschaub, Alfred 1920- WhoScE 91-4
Rockensies, John William 1932- WhoE 93
Rockenstein, William J. 1949- WhoIns 93
Rockert, Hans O.E. 1932- WhoScE 91-4
Rockett, David Everett 1953- WhoSSW 93
Rockey, Dawn 1961- WhoAm 92, WhoAmW 93
Rockey, Edward M. 1912-1991 BioIn 17
Rockey, Ernest Arthur St&PR 93
Rockey, Jay WhoAm 92
Rockfeld, Michael 1951- WhoE 93
Rockhill, Alvin Turner Law&B 92
Rockhill, William Woodville 1854-1914 GayN
Rockhold, William L. 1932- St&PR 93
Rockingham, Constance Theresa 1949- WhoAmW 93
Rockland, Barry 1943- St&PR 93
Rockland, Barry Clifford 1943- WhoAm 92
Rocklen, Kathy Hellenbrand 1951- St&PR 93, WhoAmW 93
Rockler, Walter James 1920- WhoAm 92
Rocklin, I.J. 1907- St&PR 93
Rocklin, Isadore J. 1907- WhoAm 92
Rocklin, Ross ScF&FL 92
Rocklynne, Ross 1913-1988 ScF&FL 92
Rockmore, Clara 1911- Baker 92
Rockmore, Daniel Nahum 1961- WhoE 93
Rockmore, Julie E. Law&B 92
Rockmore, Martin F. d1992 NewYTBS 92
Rockne, Knute 1888-1931 BioIn 17
Rocko, Chester Joseph 1952- St&PR 93
Rockoff, Alan Law&B 92
Rockoff, S. David 1931- WhoAm 92, WhoE 93
Rockola, David C. 1897- St&PR 93
Rockower, Marc S. Law&B 92
Rockowitz, Noah E. Law&B 92
Rockowitz, Noah E. 1949- St&PR 93
Rockrise, George Thomas 1916- WhoAm 92
Rockrise, Sally Scott 1929- WhoAmW 93
Rocks, Bernard Francis 1946- WhoWor 93
Rockstein, Morris 1916- WhoAm 92
Rockstro, William (Smith) 1823-1895 Baker 92
Rockstroh, Dennis John 1942- WhoWor 93
Rockwell, Alexandre MiSFD 9
Rockwell, Alvin John 1908- WhoAm 92
Rockwell, Amy L.H. Law&B 92
Rockwell, Anne 1934- WhoAm 92
Rockwell, Anne F. 1934- MajAI [port], SmATA 71 [port]
Rockwell, Bruce McKee 1922- St&PR 93, WhoAm 92
Rockwell, Burton Lowe 1920- WhoAm 92
Rockwell, Don Arthur 1938- WhoAm 92, WhoWor 93
Rockwell, Elizabeth Dennis 1921- WhoAm 92, WhoAmW 93, WhoSSW 93
Rockwell, Elizabeth Goode 1920- WhoAmW 93, WhoE 93, WhoWor 93
Rockwell, Ethel Gesner AmWomPl
Rockwell, Ethel Theodora 1884- AmWomPl
Rockwell, Francis Warren 1886-1979 HarEnMi
Rockwell, George 1922- St&PR 93
Rockwell, George Barcus 1926- WhoAm 92
Rockwell, John Sargent 1940- WhoAm 92
Rockwell, Norman 1927- St&PR 93, WhoE 93
Rockwell, Ronald James, Jr. 1937- WhoAm 92, WhoWor 93
Rockwell, S. Kent 1944- St&PR 93
Rockwell, Sara Campbell 1943- WhoE 93
Rockwell, Sherman Ralph, Jr. 1949- WhoSSW 93
Rockwell, Theodore 1922- WhoAm 92
Rockwell, Thomas 1933- MajAI [port], SmATA 70 [port]
Rockwell, Virginia Considine 1940- WhoAmW 93
Rockwell, W. Barron d1990 BioIn 17
Rockwell, Willard F., Jr. d1992 NewYTBS 92 [port]
Rockwell, Willard F., Jr. 1914- St&PR 93
Rockwell, Willard Frederick, Jr. 1914- WhoAm 92
Rockwood, Beth BioIn 17
Rockwood, Frederick Whitney 1947- St&PR 93
Rockwood, Joyce 1947- DcAmChF 1960
Rockwood, Roy ConAu 37NR, MajAI, ScF&FL 92
Rockwood, Ruth H. 1906- WhoAm 92
Rockwood, S.D. 1943- St&PR 93
Rockwood, William A., Jr. 1947- St&PR 93
Rocmans, Pierre Arthur 1937- WhoScE 91-2
Roco, Mihail Constantin 1947- WhoWor 93
Roco, Raul S. 1941- WhoAsAP 91
Rocour, Jean Luc 1935- WhoWor 93
Rocque, Vincent Joseph 1945- WhoAm 92
Rocquelin, Gerard 1938- WhoScE 91-2
Roczen, Marko 1947- WhoWor 93
Rod, Einar M. Law&B 92
Roda, Cesare WhoScE 91-3
Roda, John Law&B 92
Rodak, Dawn Allison 1963- WhoSSW 93
Rodakowski, Henryk 1823-1894 PolBiDi
Rodal, Monica B. Law&B 92
Rodale, Ardath BioIn 17
Rodale, J.I. 1898-1971 BioIn 17
Rodale, Jerome Irving 1898-1971 BioIn 17
Rodale, Robert BioIn 17
Rodan, Brian Joseph Law&B 92
Rodan, Mendi 1929- Baker 92
Rodas, Mary BioIn 17
Rodas Alvarado, Modesto DcCPCAm
Rodbell, Clyde A. 1927- St&PR 93
Rodbell, Clyde Armand 1927- WhoAm 92
Rodbell, Martin 1925- WhoAm 92
Rodbell, Sidney Philip 1946- St&PR 93
Rodby, Craig Robert 1949- St&PR 93
Rodby, Steve BioIn 17
Rodd, Allan Keith 1932- St&PR 93
Rodd, Bert 1930- St&PR 93
Rodd, Michael Godfrey WhoScE 91-1
Rodd, Tom BioIn 17
Rodda, Bruce Edward 1942- WhoE 93
Rodda, Emily 1948- ScF&FL 92
Rodda, Emily (Jennifer Rowe) 1948- DcChlFi
Rodda, J. WhoScE 91-1, -91-2
Rodda, John Carrol 1934- WhoUN 92
Rodda, Kenn Stryker- 1903-1990 BioIn 17
Rodda, Luca 1960- WhoWor 93
Rodda-London, Daisy Hyacinth Henrietta 1923- WhoWor 93
Roddam, Franc 1946- MiSFD 9
Rodden, John James 1933- WhoAm 92
Roddenberry, Eugene W. ScF&FL 92
Roddenberry, Eugene Wesley 1921-1991 ConAu 37NR
Roddenberry, Gene ConAu 37NR
Roddenberry, Gene 1921-1991 AnObit 1991, BioIn 17, ConLC 70, ConTFT 10, News 92, ScF&FL 92, SmATA 69
Roddenbery, Ralph J. 1925- St&PR 93
Roddey, Alyce 1932- WhoE 93
Roddick, Anita BioIn 17
Roddick, Anita 1942- CurBio 92 [port]
Roddick, David B. 1948- St&PR 93
Roddick, David Bruce 1948- WhoEmL 93
Roddick, John Francis 1959- WhoWor 93
Roddin, Michael Ian 1955- WhoWrEP 92
Roddis, Louis H. 1918-1991 BioIn 17
Roddis, Richard Stiles Law 1930- WhoAm 92, WhoIns 93
Roddy, Ardith Janine Hollis 1942- WhoSSW 93
Roddy, Carol R. 1960- St&PR 93
Roddy, Carol Roberts 1960- WhoAmW 93
Roddy, Dermot James 1960- WhoWor 93
Roddy, Edward 1931- St&PR 93
Roddy, Francis L. 1931- St&PR 93
Roddy, Jessica Law&B 92
Rode, Albert 1930- St&PR 93
Rode, Clifford J. 1941- St&PR 93
Rode, Hans 1943- WhoScE 91-4
Rode, Henry J., II Law&B 92
Rode, James D. 1948- St&PR 93
Rode, James Dean 1948- WhoAm 92
Rode, Leif 1926- WhoAm 92, WhoWor 93
Rode, Michael K. Law&B 92
Rode, (Jacques-) Pierre (Joseph) 1774-1830 Baker 92
Rode, Wilhelm 1887-1959 Baker 92, OxDcOp
Rodecape, Marjorie ScF&FL 92
Rodeck, William Martin 1929- St&PR 93
Rodefeld, Gary H. 1953- St&PR 93
Rodefeld, James A. 1938- St&PR 93
Rodefer, Joanne Marie 1953- WhoE 93
Rodeheaver, Homer A(lvan) 1880-1955 Baker 92
Rodeheffer, Jonathan Paul 1942- WhoSSW 93
Rodeheffer, Martha Ann 1937- WhoAmW 93
Roden, Jon-Paul 1943- WhoE 93
Rodenas, Paula SmATA 73
Rodenas, Sandra Hamilton 1961- WhoAmW 93
Rodenberg, Richard Theodore 1920- St&PR 93
Rodenberg, Rudolf Hubert Anton 1929- WhoScE 91-3, WhoWor 93
Rodenberger, Charles Alvard 1926- WhoAm 92
Rodenburg, Clifton Glenn 1949- WhoEmL 93
Rodenhizer, Harry Edwin, Jr. 1927- WhoAm 92
Rodenhouse, Curtis W. 1954- St&PR 93
Rodenkirch, John Jeffrey 1950- St&PR 93
Roder, Carl Gottlieb 1812-1883 Baker 92
Roder, Martin 1851-1895 Baker 92
Roder, Ronald E. 1948- St&PR 93
Roder, Tommy 1948- WhoWor 93
Roderburg, Kjell WhoScE 91-4
Roderburg, T.K. 1929- WhoScE 91-4
Roderich, Hans Harold 1926- St&PR 93
Roderick, Bruce Anthony 1958- St&PR 93
Roderick, David M. 1924- St&PR 93
Roderick, Dorothy Paetel 1935- WhoAmW 93
Roderick, G.J. WhoScE 91-1
Roderick, Richard Michael 1948- St&PR 93, WhoAm 92
Roderick, Robert Gene 1944- WhoSSW 93
Roderick, Robert Lee 1925- WhoAm 92
Roderus, Frank 1942- ConAu 38NR
Rodes, Barbara Knauft 1938- WhoAmW 93
Rodewald, Alexander-Ludwig 1943- WhoScE 91-3
Rodewald, Alice AmWomPl
Rodewald, Georg W. 1921- WhoScE 91-3
Rodewald, Paul Gerhard 1899- WhoAm 92
Rodewald, William Young 1928- WhoAm 92
Rodewald-Fout, April J. Law&B 92
Rodewig, John Stuart 1933- St&PR 93
Rodger, David WhoScE 91-1
Rodger, Ian William WhoScE 91-1
Rodger, Linda Joan Macintosh 1940- WhoAmW 93
Rodger, Stanley Joseph 1940- WhoAsAP 91
Rodger, Susan Hatcher 1961- WhoAmW 93
Rodger, Wallace G. Law&B 92
Rodgers, Aggie Guerard WhoAm 92
Rodgers, Alan 1959- ScF&FL 92
Rodgers, Allen Wade 1937- WhoSSW 93
Rodgers, Antoinette Yvetta 1959- WhoAmW 93
Rodgers, B.D. 1924- St&PR 93
Rodgers, Betty L. 1930- St&PR 93
Rodgers, Buck 1938- WhoAm 92
Rodgers, Calbraith Perry BioIn 17
Rodgers, Carolyn M. 1945- BioIn 17
Rodgers, D.G. Law&B 92
Rodgers, Daniel Tracy 1942- WhoAm 92
Rodgers, Dorothy d1992 NewYTBS 92 [port]
Rodgers, Dorothy F(einer) 1909-1992 ConAu 139
Rodgers, Ed BioIn 17
Rodgers, Eugene 1939- WhoAm 92
Rodgers, Frank 1927- WhoAm 92
Rodgers, Frank 1944- ConAu 137, SmATA 69 [port]
Rodgers, Frank Judson, Jr. 1930- St&PR 93
Rodgers, Frederic Barker 1940- WhoAm 92
Rodgers, George D. 1933- St&PR 93
Rodgers, Gerry B. 1946- WhoUN 92
Rodgers, Gregg Law&B 92
Rodgers, Hugh Irman 1934- WhoSSW 93
Rodgers, Imogene Sevin 1945- WhoE 93
Rodgers, Jack Alexander 1938- WhoSSW 93
Rodgers, James A. Law&B 92
Rodgers, James Foster 1951- WhoAm 92
Rodgers, James Turner 1934- St&PR 93
Rodgers, Jeffrey Warren 1951- WhoSSW 93
Rodgers, Jesse ScF&FL 92
Rodgers, Jim WhoAm 92
Rodgers, Jimmie 1897-1933 Baker 92
Rodgers, Joe M. 1933- WhoAm 92
Rodgers, John 1772-1838 HarEnMi
Rodgers, John 1914- WhoAm 92
Rodgers, John Ex 1935- St&PR 93
Rodgers, John H. 1944- St&PR 93
Rodgers, John Hunter Law&B 92
Rodgers, John Hunter 1944- WhoAm 92
Rodgers, John S. Law&B 92
Rodgers, John T. Law&B 92
Rodgers, Johnathan BioIn 17
Rodgers, Johnathan 1946- WhoAm 92
Rodgers, Johnathan Arlin 1946- AfrAmBi
Rodgers, Joseph F. 1932- St&PR 93
Rodgers, Katherine McNair 1947- WhoSSW 93
Rodgers, Kenneth William, Jr. 1957- St&PR 93

Rodgers, Kevin Charles 1956- *WhoSSW 93*
Rodgers, Kirk Procter 1932- *WhoE 93*
Rodgers, Larry William 1950- *WhoSSW 93*
Rodgers, Lawrence Rodney 1920- *WhoAm 92*
Rodgers, Mark L. *Law&B 92*
Rodgers, Mary 1931- *DcAmChF 1960, MajAI [port], OxDcOp, ScF&FL 92, WhoAm 92*
Rodgers, Mary Columbro 1925- *WhoAm 92, WhoE 93, WhoWrEP 92*
Rodgers, Nancy Lucille 1934- *WhoAmW 93*
Rodgers, Neomia *BioIn 17, BlkAmWO*
Rodgers, Nile 1952- *ConMus 8 [port], SoulM*
Rodgers, Paul 1933- *WhoAm 92*
Rodgers, Quincy *Law&B 92*
Rodgers, R. Wayne 1928- *St&PR 93*
Rodgers, Rhonda Lee 1939- *WhoE 93*
Rodgers, Richard 1902-1972 *ConMus 9 [port]*
Rodgers, Richard 1902-1979 *BioIn 17, OxDcOp*
Rodgers, Richard (Charles) 1902-1979 *Baker 92*
Rodgers, Robert Allen 1939- *WhoE 93*
Rodgers, Ronald W. *St&PR 93*
Rodgers, Rowland *St&PR 93*
Rodgers, Royce W. 1933- *St&PR 93*
Rodgers, Sandra Jean 1966- *WhoAmW 93*
Rodgers, Sharon Lynette *Law&B 92*
Rodgers, Stephen L. *Law&B 92*
Rodgers, Suzanne Hooker 1939- *WhoE 93*
Rodgers, Sylvia Amanda *AmWomPl*
Rodgers, Thelma Elaine *WhoE 93*
Rodgers, Thomas H. *Law&B 92*
Rodgers, Thomas H. 1944- *St&PR 93*
Rodgers, Thomas J. 1946- *St&PR 93*
Rodgers, Thurman John *BioIn 17*
Rodgers, Thurman John 1948- *ConEn*
Rodgers, Will 1879-1935 *IntDcF 2-3 [port]*
Rodgers, William, Jr. 1950- *St&PR 93*
Rodgers, William Henry 1947- *WhoAm 92*
Rodgers, William M. 1926- *WhoAm 92*
Rodgers, William Michael 1926- *St&PR 93*
Rodgers-Barstack, Renee Elizabeth 1949- *WhoAmW 93*
Rodgerson, Dewey A. 1928- *St&PR 93*
Rodgman, Alan 1924- *WhoAm 92*
Rodhain, Francois 1939- *WhoWor 93*
Rodhe, K. Henning 1941- *WhoScE 91-4*
Rodhe, Peder Magnus 1945- *WhoWor 93*
Rodich, Michael E. 1952- *St&PR 93*
Rodich-Hodges, Nancy Ann 1931- *WhoAmW 93*
Rodie, Andrew *Law&B 92*
Rodie, Edward B. 1921- *St&PR 93*
Rodier, Christopher Peter *Law&B 92*
Rodier, D.G. 1931- *St&PR 93*
Rodighiero, Giovanni 1921- *WhoScE 91-3*
Rodimer, Frank Joseph 1927- *WhoAm 92*
Rodimtseva, Irina Aleksandrova 1934- *WhoWor 93*
Rodin, Alvin Eli 1926- *WhoAm 92*
Rodin, Auguste 1840-1917 *BioIn 17*
Rodin, Ervin Yechiel Laszlo 1932- *WhoAm 92*
Rodin, Geraldine W. 1938- *St&PR 93*
Rodin, Howard Alan 1942- *WhoWor 93*
Rodin, Judith Seitz 1944- *WhoAm 92, WhoAmW 93*
Rodin, Michael F. *Law&B 92*
Rodino, Peter Wallace, Jr. 1909- *WhoAm 92, WhoE 93*
Rodino, Vincent Louis 1929- *WhoE 93*
Rodio, Rocco c. 1535-1615? *Baker 92*
Rodis, Nicholas 1924- *WhoE 93*
Rodis, Theodore George *Law&B 92*
Rodisch, Robert Joseph 1919- *WhoAm 92*
Rodis-Jamero, Nilo *ScF&FL 92*
Roditi, Claudio Braga 1946- *WhoE 93*
Roditi, Edouard *BioIn 17*
Roditi, Edouard d1992 *NewYTBS 92*
Roditi, Edouard Herbert 1910-1992 *ConAu 137*
Roditis, George Christofis 1949- *WhoWor 93*
Rodkiewicz, Bohdan 1925- *WhoScE 91-4*
Rodland, Arild 1947- *WhoScE 91-4*
Rodler, Miklos 1927- *WhoScE 91-4*
Rodloff, Arne C. 1953- *WhoScE 91-3*
Rodman, Alan George 1933- *WhoE 93*
Rodman, Alpine Clarence 1952- *WhoEmL 93, WhoWor 93*
Rodman, Angela Faye 1963- *WhoAmW 93*
Rodman, Dennis *BioIn 17*
Rodman, Dennis Keith 1961- *WhoAm 92*
Rodman, Eric *MajAI*
Rodman, Harry Eugene 1913- *WhoAm 92*
Rodman, James Purcell 1926- *WhoWor 93*
Rodman, John Gray 1951- *WhoE 93*
Rodman, Leroy E. 1914- *St&PR 93*
Rodman, Leroy Eli 1914- *WhoAm 92*
Rodman, Maia *MajAI*
Rodman, Michael Alan 1940- *WhoE 93*
Rodman, Michael R. 1949- *St&PR 93*
Rodman, Peter Warren 1943- *WhoAm 92*
Rodman, Sarah Jane 1952- *WhoAmW 93*
Rodman, Sue Arlene 1951- *WhoAmW 93, WhoEmL 93, WhoWor 93*
Rodman, Sumner 1915- *WhoAm 92*
Rodman, Thomas Jackson 1815-1871 *HarEnMi*
Rodne, Kjell John 1948- *WhoEmL 93*
Rodner, Kim 1931- *WhoAm 92*
Rodney, Burton *Law&B 92*
Rodney, George Brydges 1718-1792 *HarEnMi*
Rodney, Jim Anthony 1962- *WhoE 93*
Rodney, Joel Morris 1937- *WhoAm 92*
Rodney, Martina B. *AmWomPl*
Rodney, Paul Frederick 1944- *WhoSSW 93*
Rodney, Red *BioIn 17*
Rodney, Walter 1942-1980 *DcCPCAm*
Rodnick, Eliot Herman 1911- *WhoAm 92*
Rodnina, Irina 1949- *BioIn 17*
Rodning, Charles Bernard 1943- *WhoSSW 93*
Rodnite, Andrew John 1935- *WhoSSW 93*
Rodnunsky, Sidney 1946- *WhoWor 93*
Rodolitz, Gary Michael 1950- *WhoE 93, WhoEmL 93, WhoWor 93*
Rodolphe, Jean Joseph 1730-1812 *Baker 92*
Rodoreda, Merce 1909- *BioIn 17*
Rodoreda Fiol, Jose Maria 1952- *WhoWor 93*
Rodos, Joseph Jerry 1933- *WhoWor 93*
Rodowicz, Henry A. 1930- *St&PR 93*
Rodowicz, Stanley A. 1930- *St&PR 93*
Rodowsky, Colby 1932- *ScF&FL 92*
Rodowsky, Lawrence Francis 1930- *WhoAm 92*
Rodrick, Richard J. *Law&B 92*
Rodrick, Robert M. *Law&B 92*
Rodrigo, marques de Castel- d1651 *BioIn 17*
Rodrigo, F. Guerra 1937- *WhoScE 91-3*
Rodrigo, Joaquin 1901- *Baker 92*
Rodrigo, Rafael 1953- *WhoScE 91-3*
Rodrigue, Charlotte Marie 1947- *WhoAmW 93*
Rodrigue, George Pierre 1931- *WhoAm 92*
Rodrigue, Lionel Gerard 1942- *St&PR 93*
Rodrigue, Marie *Law&B 92*
Rodrigues, Alexandre Manuel Duarte Kito *WhoAfr*
Rodrigues, Anil N. 1942- *St&PR 93*
Rodrigues, Antonio *BioIn 17*
Rodrigues, Carol Maria 1947- *WhoE 93*
Rodrigues, Clarence Constancio 1958- *WhoE 93*
Rodrigues, Claudio 1939- *WhoWor 93*
Rodrigues, F. Carvalho *WhoScE 91-3*
Rodrigues, Joe E. 1936- *St&PR 93*
Rodrigues, Jose Delgado 1945- *WhoScE 91-3*
Rodrigues, M. *Law&B 92*
Rodrigues, Maria Adeline 1964- *WhoAmW 93*
Rodrigues, Raimundo Nina *IntDcAn*
Rodrigues, Raymond J. *ScF&FL 92*
Rodrigues de Ledesma, Mariano 1779-1848 *Baker 92*
Rodrigues Grande, Nuno L. 1932- *WhoScE 91-3*
Rodrigues Junior, Carlos Jose *WhoScE 91-3*
Rodriguez, Abelardo *DcCPCAm*
Rodriguez, Alberto F. 1945- *WhoIns 93*
Rodriguez, Alberto Hernandez 1948- *WhoWor 93*
Rodriguez (Amador), Augusto (Alejandro) 1904- *Baker 92*
Rodriguez, Andres *BioIn 17*
Rodriguez, Beatriz *WhoAm 92*
Rodriguez, Belgica 1941- *NotHsAW 93, WhoAm 92, WhoAmW 93*
Rodriguez, Carlos Rafael 1913- *WhoWor 93*
Rodriguez, Carmen 1956- *WhoWor 93*
Rodriguez, Cassandra Jean 1957- *WhoAmW 93*
Rodriguez, Catherine de Leon 1959- *WhoSSW 93*
Rodriguez, Christine *ScF&FL 92*
Rodriguez, Clara 1944- *HispAmA*
Rodriguez, Cleto *BioIn 17*
Rodriguez, Cyril A. *Law&B 92*
Rodriguez, Edgardo E. 1944- *St&PR 93*
Rodriguez, Eduardo A. 1955- *St&PR 93*
Rodriguez, Eduardo Ariel *Law&B 92*
Rodriguez, Eladio R. 1937- *St&PR 93*
Rodriguez, Elaine Flud *Law&B 92*
Rodriguez, Elizabeth 1953- *HispAmA*
Rodriguez, Eloy 1947- *WhoAm 92*
Rodriguez, Estelita d1966 *SweetSg C [port]*
Rodriguez, Esther Lilia 1941- *WhoAmW 93*
Rodriguez, Felipe 1759-1814 *Baker 92*
Rodriguez, Felix I. *BioIn 17*
Rodriguez, Ferdinand 1928- *WhoAm 92*
Rodriguez, Geno 1940- *WhoAm 92*
Rodriguez, Gloria 1948- *NotHsAW 93 [port]*
Rodriguez, Gloria Fuentebella 1928- *WhoWor 93*
Rodriguez, Gloria G. 1948- *HispAmA*
Rodriguez, Helen 1929- *NotHsAW 93 [port]*
Rodriguez, Humberto 1948- *WhoWor 93*
Rodriguez, Isabel L. *Law&B 92*
Rodriguez, Janis Parkison *Law&B 92*
Rodriguez, Jean Bates 1943- *WhoWor 93*
Rodriguez, Jeffrey *Law&B 92*
Rodriguez, Joaquin 1934- *WhoE 93*
Rodriguez, Joel De Jesus 1957- *WhoE 93*
Rodriguez, John 1958- *HispAmA*
Rodriguez, Jose Fco 1949- *WhoWor 93*
Rodriguez, Jose Manuel 1945- *WhoE 93*
Rodriguez, Joseph 1942- *St&PR 93*
Rodriguez, Joseph H. 1930- *HispAmA [port]*
Rodriguez, Joseph Martin 1937- *St&PR 93*
Rodriguez, Juan 1935- *HispAmA [port]*
Rodriguez, Juan Alfonso 1941- *WhoAm 92*
Rodriguez, Juan Carlos 1958- *WhoSSW 93*
Rodriguez, Juan Guadalupe 1920- *HispAmA, WhoAm 92, WhoSSW 93*
Rodriguez, Juan Jose 1959- *WhoSSW 93*
Rodriguez, Leonard 1944- *WhoWor 93*
Rodriguez, Lina S. 1949- *NotHsAW 93 [port]*
Rodriguez, Linda Roberson 1963- *WhoAmW 93*
Rodriguez, Lorraine Ditzler 1920- *WhoAmW 93*
Rodriguez, Louis Joseph 1933- *WhoAm 92, WhoSSW 93*
Rodriguez, Luis De Jesus 1963- *WhoWor 93*
Rodriguez, Manny Jesus 1943- *WhoSSW 93*
Rodriguez, Manuel *Law&B 92*
Rodriguez, Maria Lourdes 1958- *WhoSSW 93*
Rodriguez, Marianne 1940- *St&PR 93*
Rodriguez, Martha Cecilia 1957- *WhoE 93*
Rodriguez, Matt L. *WhoAm 92*
Rodriguez, Michael *Law&B 92*
Rodriguez, Miguel 1931- *WhoAm 92*
Rodriguez, Moises-Enrique 1962- *WhoWor 93*
Rodriguez, Nelson 1952- *WhoSSW 93*
Rodriguez, Olga de los Angeles 1959- *WhoAmW 93*
Rodriguez, Oscar *HispAmA*
Rodriguez, Oscar S. 1945- *WhoAsAP 91*
Rodriguez, Patricia 1944- *HispAmA, NotHsAW 93*
Rodriguez, Paul 20th cent.- *HispAmA [port]*
Rodriguez, Paul Henry 1937- *WhoAm 92, WhoSSW 93*
Rodriguez, Peter 1926- *HispAmA*
Rodriguez, Ralph 1943- *St&PR 93*
Rodriguez, Ralph 1961- *WhoSSW 93*
Rodriguez, Ramiro de Jesus *BioIn 17*
Rodriguez, Ramon Joseph 1938- *WhoE 93*
Rodriguez, Randall Saul *Law&B 92*
Rodriguez, Raul 1950- *WhoE 93*
Rodriguez, Ray 1951- *WhoWor 93*
Rodriguez, Raymond *WhoAm 92*
Rodriguez, Ricky *BioIn 17*
Rodriguez, Rita M. 1942- *NotHsAW 93*
Rodriguez, Rita Maria 1944- *WhoE 93*
Rodriguez, Robert L. 1948- *St&PR 93*
Rodriguez, Robert W. *Law&B 92*
Rodriguez, Robert Xavier 1946- *Baker 92*
Rodriguez, Roman 1951- *WhoAm 92*
Rodriguez, Santiago 1952- *Baker 92*
Rodriguez, Steve *BioIn 17*
Rodriguez, Tomas Manuel 1959- *WhoSSW 93*
Rodriguez, Veronica Hanglin 1944- *WhoUN 92*
Rodriguez, Vicente c. 1685-1760? *Baker 92*
Rodriguez, Victor *WhoAm 92, WhoSSW 93*
Rodriguez, Vincent Angel 1921- *WhoAm 92*
Rodriguez Alcala, Guido 1946- *SpAmA*
Rodriguez-Alcala, Hugo 1917- *SpAmA*
Rodriguez-Arnaiz, Rosario 1945- *WhoWor 93*
Rodriguez-Atkatz, Jonathan *Law&B 92*
Rodriguez-Barrueco, Claudino 1937- *WhoScE 91-3*
Rodriguez Beltran, Cayetano 1866-1939 *DcMexL*
Rodriguez-Boulan, Enrique Javier 1946- *WhoAm 92*
Rodriguez-Camilloni, Humberto Leonardo 1945- *WhoAm 92, WhoSSW 93*
Rodriguez-Campoamor, Hernan 1921- *WhoWor 93*
Rodriguez Chicharro, Cesar 1930- *DcMexL*
Rodriguez de Hita, Antonio c. 1724-1787 *Baker 92*
Rodriguez-Diaz, Juan E. 1941- *WhoSSW 93, WhoWor 93*
Rodriguez-Erdmann, Franz 1935- *WhoAm 92*
Rodriguez Espinosa, Jose Miguel 1953- *WhoWor 93*
Rodriguez Galvan, Ignacio 1816-1842 *DcMexL*
Rodriguez Garcia De Muro, J. Marcelo 1937- *WhoScE 91-3*
Rodriguez-Iturbe, Jose Benjamin 1940- *WhoWor 93*
Rodriguez Julia, Edgardo 1946- *SpAmA*
Rodriguez Martin, Antonio 1946- *WhoScE 91-3*
Rodriguez Monegal, Emir 1921-1985 *ScF&FL 92*
Rodriguez-Munguia, Juan Climaco 1938- *WhoE 93*
Rodriguez Orejuela, Gilberto *BioIn 17*
Rodriguez Paul, Ricardo Francisco 1921- *WhoWor 93*
Rodriguez Pedotti, Andres 1923- *WhoWor 93*
Rodriguez-Peralta, Phyllis White 1923- *WhoAmW 93*
Rodriguez Plata, Horacio 1915-1987 *BioIn 17*
Rodriguez-Reinoso, Francisco 1941- *WhoScE 91-3*
Rodriguez Remeneski, Shirley *NotHsAW 93*
Rodriguez Rodriguez, Carlos Rafael 1913- *DcCPCAm*
Rodriguez-Sains, Rene S. 1952- *WhoE 93, WhoEmL 93*
Rodriguez-Servera, Rafael Joaquin 1946- *WhoAm 92*
Rodriguez Trevino, Juan Victor 1950- *WhoWor 93*
Rodriques, Gene E. *Law&B 92*
Rodriquez, Andrew 1933- *St&PR 93*
Rodriquez, C. Felice 1953- *St&PR 93*
Rodriquez, Charles Joseph 1932- *St&PR 93*
Rodstein, Richard Michael 1954- *St&PR 93*
Rodwell, George 1800-1852 *OxDcOp*
Rodwell, J.D. 1946- *St&PR 93*
Rodwell, John Dennis 1946- *WhoAm 92*
Rodysill, Jerome O. 1929- *St&PR 93*
Rodysill, Jerome Otto 1929- *WhoAm 92*
Rodzianko, Paul 1945- *WhoAm 92, WhoE 93, WhoWor 93*
Rodzianko, Vladimir 1915- *BioIn 17*
Rodzinski, Artur 1891-1958 *PolBiDi*
Rodzinski, Artur 1892-1958 *Baker 92, OxDcOp*
Roe, Allie Jones 1950- *WhoAmW 93*
Roe, Anne 1904-1991 *BioIn 17*
Roe, Benson Bertheau 1918- *WhoAm 92*
Roe, Betty Joyce 1944- *WhoSSW 93, WhoWrEP 92*
Roe, Byron Paul 1934- *WhoAm 92*
Roe, Chang Hee 1938- *WhoUN 92*
Roe, Charles Richard 1940- *WhoAm 92*
Roe, Christopher John 1954- *WhoWor 93*
Roe, Clifford Ashley, Jr. 1942- *WhoAm 92*
Roe, D.H. 1946- *St&PR 93*
Roe, David 1938- *St&PR 93*
Roe, David Allen 1955- *WhoE 93*
Roe, Elwin Charles 1915- *BiDAMSp 1989*
Roe, Enid Adrian Talton 1921- *WhoAmW 93*
Roe, Eunice Marie 1942- *WhoAmW 93*
Roe, Frances d1920 *BioIn 17*
Roe, Fred, Jr. 1954- *St&PR 93*
Roe, Gene 1928- *St&PR 93*
Roe, Georgeanne Thomas 1945- *WhoE 93*
Roe, Ina Lea 1930- *WhoWrEP 92*
Roe, J. Harvie 1949- *St&PR 93*
Roe, Jack Willhoit 1945- *WhoAm 92*
Roe, Jo Ann *WhoWrEP 92*
Roe, John H. 1939- *St&PR 93*
Roe, Kenneth A 1916-1991 *BioIn 17*
Roe, Kenneth Keith 1945- *WhoAm 92*
Roe, Kenneth Mark 1949- *St&PR 93*
Roe, Lou D. 1936- *St&PR 93*
Roe, Mary E. *AmWomPl*
Roe, Michael Henry 1944- *WhoSSW 93*
Roe, Norman J.E. 1922- *St&PR 93*
Roe, Orpha V. *AmWomPl*
Roe, Pamela Kay 1960- *WhoAmW 93*
Roe, Philip Lawrence *WhoScE 91-1*
Roe, Radie Lynn 1962- *WhoAmW 93*
Roe, Ramona Jeraldean 1942- *WhoSSW 93*
Roe, Rebecca *BioIn 17*
Roe, Richard C. 1930- *WhoAm 92, WhoWor 93*
Roe, Richard L. 1936- *ScF&FL 92*
Roe, Robert A. *BioIn 17*
Roe, Robert A. 1924- *CngDr 91, WhoAm 92, WhoE 93*
Roe, Thomas Anderson 1927- *WhoAm 92*

Rogers, Howard Jeffords 1955- *St&PR 93*
Rogers, Irene 1932- *WhoAmW 93, WhoE 93*
Rogers, Isabel Wood 1924- *WhoAm 92, WhoAmW 93*
Rogers, Ivor A. *ScF&FL 92*
Rogers, J.E. *Law&B 92*
Rogers, J. Kenneth 1939- *St&PR 93*
Rogers, Jack A. 1945- *St&PR 93*
Rogers, Jack Eugene 1957- *WhoSSW 93*
Rogers, Jacqueline 1960- *WhoAmW 93*
Rogers, Jacqueline H. *BioIn 17*
Rogers, Jacqueline Jeanette 1961- *WhoAmW 93*
Rogers, James Albert 1944- *WhoAm 92*
Rogers, James Devitt 1929- *WhoAm 92*
Rogers, James E., Jr. 1947- *St&PR 93*
Rogers, James Edwin 1929- *WhoSSW 93*
Rogers, James Eugene, Jr. 1947- *WhoAm 92*
Rogers, James Frederick 1935- *WhoAm 92*
Rogers, James Gardiner 1952- *WhoE 93*
Rogers, James Keith 1931- *St&PR 93*
Rogers, James P. 1951- *St&PR 93*
Rogers, James Robert 1947- *WhoSSW 93*
Rogers, James Thomas 1941- *WhoWor 93*
Rogers, James Tracey *Law&B 92*
Rogers, James Virgil, Jr. 1922- *WhoSSW 93*
Rogers, Jane Hooks 1941- *WhoAmW 93*
Rogers, Jean 1916-1991 *BioIn 17*
Rogers, Jeanette D. *Law&B 92*
Rogers, Jeffrey Craig 1951- *St&PR 93*
Rogers, Jerome Walter *Law&B 92*
Rogers, Jill Suzanne 1968- *WhoAmW 93*
Rogers, Jimmy 1924- *BioIn 17*
Rogers, Jimmy C. 1934- *St&PR 93*
Rogers, Joan Gerdau 1938- *St&PR 93*
Rogers, Joe E. 1933- *St&PR 93*
Rogers, John, Jr. *BioIn 17*
Rogers, John Alvin 1946- *WhoEmL 93, WhoSSW 93*
Rogers, John Arnold 1945- *St&PR 93*
Rogers, John Charles 1949- *WhoSSW 93*
Rogers, John James William 1930- *WhoAm 92*
Rogers, John Patrick *Law&B 92*
Rogers, John S. 1930- *WhoAm 92*
Rogers, John W., Jr. *WhoAm 92*
Rogers, Jon Martin 1942- *WhoSSW 93*
Rogers, Judith W. *WhoAm 92, WhoAmW 93, WhoE 93*
Rogers, Judy Ann 1948- *WhoEmL 93*
Rogers, Judy R. 1943- *WhoSSW 93*
Rogers, Julia Anne *AmWomPl*
Rogers, Juliette Marie 1961- *WhoE 93*
Rogers, Justin Towner, Jr. 1929- *St&PR 93, WhoAm 92*
Rogers, Karl David 1959- *St&PR 93*
Rogers, Katharine Munzer 1932- *WhoE 93*
Rogers, Kathryn Johanna *Law&B 92*
Rogers, Ken *BioIn 17*
Rogers, Ken E. 1951- *WhoSSW 93*
Rogers, Kenneth Cannicott 1929- *WhoAm 92, WhoE 93, WhoWor 93*
Rogers, Kenneth Edward *Law&B 92*
Rogers, Kenneth Norman 1931- *WhoAm 92*
Rogers, Kenneth R. *WhoAm 92, WhoE 93*
Rogers, Kenneth Ray 1938- *WhoAm 92*
Rogers, Kenny 1938- *Baker 92*
Rogers, Kipp Alan d1990 *BioIn 17*
Rogers, Laura Jane 1960- *WhoAmW 93*
Rogers, Lawrence A. 1947- *St&PR 93*
Rogers, Lawrence H., II 1921- *WhoAm 92*
Rogers, Lee Frank 1934- *WhoAm 92*
Rogers, Lee Jasper 1955- *WhoAm 92, WhoE 93, WhoEmL 93, WhoWor 93*
Rogers, Leo Joseph, Jr. 1936- *St&PR 93, WhoAm 92*
Rogers, Leonard Charles *WhoAm 92*
Rogers, Leonard Christopher Gordon *WhoScE 91-1*
Rogers, Leonard John 1931- *WhoWor 93*
Rogers, Lewis Henry 1910- *WhoSSW 93*
Rogers, Linda 1944- *WhoCanL 92*
Rogers, Lon Brown 1905- *WhoSSW 93*
Rogers, Lorene Lane 1914- *WhoAm 92*
Rogers, M. Weldon, III 1941- *St&PR 93*
Rogers, Margaret Ellen Jonsson 1938- *WhoAmW 93, WhoSSW 93*
Rogers, Marie Marguerite 1933- *WhoAmW 93*
Rogers, Mark *ScF&FL 92*
Rogers, Mark Charles 1942- *WhoAm 92*
Rogers, Mark E. 1952- *ScF&FL 92*
Rogers, Martha Elizabeth 1914- *WhoAm 92*
Rogers, Mary Anne Henley 1856-1937 *BioIn 17*
Rogers, Mary Brigid *Law&B 92*
Rogers, Mary Elizabeth *WhoScE 91-1*
Rogers, Mary Frances 1937- *WhoSSW 93*
Rogers, Megan Elizabeth *WhoAmW 93*
Rogers, Michael 1950- *BioIn 17, ScF&FL 92*
Rogers, Michael 1952- *WhoSSW 93*
Rogers, Michael Howard *WhoScE 91-1*
Rogers, Michael Ray 1951- *St&PR 93, WhoAm 92*
Rogers, Michael Thomas 1941- *WhoAm 92*
Rogers, Michelle M. *Law&B 92*
Rogers, Millard Foster, Jr. 1932- *WhoAm 92*
Rogers, Minor Lee 1930-1991 *BioIn 17*
Rogers, N. Kay 1940- *WhoAmW 93*
Rogers, N. Stewart 1930- *St&PR 93, WhoAm 92*
Rogers, Nathaniel Sims 1919- *WhoAm 92*
Rogers, Nigel (David) 1935- *Baker 92*
Rogers, Norman
See Public Enemy *News 92*
Rogers, Oliver Van Naarden 1953- *WhoSSW 93*
Rogers, P. Jay, III 1951- *WhoSSW 93*
Rogers, Patricia Morris 1950- *WhoAmW 93*
Rogers, Patrick F. *ScF&FL 92*
Rogers, Pattiann 1940- *BioIn 17, WhoWrEP 92*
Rogers, Paul Grant 1921- *WhoAm 92*
Rogers, Paul W. 1926- *WhoAm 92*
Rogers, Peggy Jean 1944- *WhoAmW 93*
Rogers, Peter D(amien) 1942- *ConAu 38NR*
Rogers, Peter Norman 1938- *St&PR 93, WhoAm 92*
Rogers, Peter Philips 1937- *WhoAm 92*
Rogers, Peter Thomas 1952- *St&PR 93*
Rogers, Peter Vance 1955- *St&PR 93*
Rogers, Phil G. *Law&B 92*
Rogers, Philip 1951- *BioIn 17*
Rogers, Philip O. 1913- *St&PR 93*
Rogers, Philip Sydney *WhoScE 91-1*
Rogers, Ralph B. 1909- *St&PR 93, WhoAm 92, WhoSSW 93*
Rogers, Ralph Withrow 1932- *St&PR 93*
Rogers, Raymond Jesse 1941- *WhoAm 92*
Rogers, Rex R. *Law&B 92*
Rogers, Richard B. *Law&B 92*
Rogers, Richard Dean 1921- *WhoAm 92*
Rogers, Richard George 1933- *WhoWor 93*
Rogers, Richard Hilton 1935- *WhoAm 92*
Rogers, Richard Hunter 1939- *WhoAm 92*
Rogers, Richard Mead 1942- *St&PR 93, WhoAm 92*
Rogers, Richard R. 1943- *St&PR 93*
Rogers, Richard Wayne 1943- *WhoIns 93*
Rogers, Robert 1731-1795 *HarEnMi*
Rogers, Robert Burnett 1931- *WhoAm 92*
Rogers, Robert Burnett 1935- *St&PR 93*
Rogers, Robert D. 1936- *WhoAm 92, WhoSSW 93*
Rogers, Robert David 1936- *St&PR 93*
Rogers, Robert Ernest 1928- *WhoAm 92*
Rogers, Robert J. *Law&B 92*
Rogers, Robert M. *BioIn 17*
Rogers, Robert M. 1926- *St&PR 93*
Rogers, Robert Mark 1933- *WhoAm 92*
Rogers, Robert Reed 1929- *WhoWor 93*
Rogers, Robert Wentworth 1914- *WhoWrEP 92*
Rogers, Robert Willis 1912- *WhoWrEP 92*
Rogers, Rodney Albert 1926- *WhoAm 92*
Rogers, Ronald D. 1918- *WhoIns 93*
Rogers, Ronald Gene 1950- *WhoSSW 93*
Rogers, Ronald W. 1955- *St&PR 93*
Rogers, Rosemary 1932- *BioIn 17, WhoAm 92, WhoWrEP 92*
Rogers, Roy 1911- *Baker 92, ConMus 9 [port], IntDcF 2-3*
Rogers, Ruth Ann 1946- *WhoE 93*
Rogers, Ruthanne Chadwick 1931- *WhoAmW 93*
Rogers, Rutherford David 1915- *WhoAm 92*
Rogers, Samuel 1763-1855 *BioIn 17*
Rogers, Samuel M. 1917- *St&PR 93*
Rogers, Seleta Justine 1950- *WhoAmW 93*
Rogers, Sharon J. 1941- *WhoAm 92, WhoAmW 93, WhoE 93*
Rogers, Shelby R. 1949- *St&PR 93*
Rogers, Shelby R., Jr. *Law&B 92*
Rogers, "Shorty" 1924- *Baker 92*
Rogers, Stanley C. 1946- *St&PR 93*
Rogers, Stearns Walter 1934- *WhoSSW 93*
Rogers, Stephen 1912- *St&PR 93*
Rogers, Stephen C. *Law&B 92*
Rogers, Stephen Hitchcock 1930- *WhoWor 93*
Rogers, Stephen Hitchock 1930- *WhoAm 92*
Rogers, Steven Bennett 1955- *WhoAm 92*
Rogers, Steven Bruce *Law&B 92*
Rogers, Sue *BioIn 17*
Rogers, Suzanne Wilson 1933- *WhoAmW 93*
Rogers, Sydney Michael, Jr. 1925- *St&PR 93*
Rogers, Tami Walker *Law&B 92*
Rogers, Teresa Ann 1956- *WhoAmW 93*
Rogers, Theodore Courtney 1934- *WhoAm 92, WhoE 93, WhoWor 93*
Rogers, Thomas C. 1950- *St&PR 93*
Rogers, Thomas Francis 1923- *WhoAm 92*
Rogers, Thomas McLemore 1948- *St&PR 93*
Rogers, Thomas N.R. *WhoWrEP 92*
Rogers, Thomas Paul 1932- *St&PR 93*
Rogers, Timothy Folk 1947- *WhoSSW 93*
Rogers, Timothy S. 1950- *St&PR 93*
Rogers, Timothy Wayne *Law&B 92*
Rogers, Tom 1948- *ScF&FL 92*
Rogers, Trumbull 1939- *WhoWrEP 92*
Rogers, Vance Donald 1917- *WhoAm 92*
Rogers, Vera Barbara *St&PR 93*
Rogers, Virgil Madison 1898-1990 *BioIn 17*
Rogers, Walter Russell 1945- *WhoSSW 93*
Rogers, Warren Joseph, Jr. 1922- *WhoAm 92*
Rogers, Wayne *ScF&FL 92*
Rogers, Wayne 1933- *WhoAm 92*
Rogers, Werner *WhoAm 92*
Rogers, Will 1879-1935 *BioIn 17, JrnUS, QDrFCA 92 [port]*
Rogers, William Brookins 1938- *WhoSSW 93*
Rogers, William Cecil 1919- *WhoAm 92*
Rogers, William Cushing 1959- *WhoE 93*
Rogers, William Dill 1927- *WhoAm 92*
Rogers, William Edward 1947- *WhoE 93*
Rogers, William Fenna, Jr. 1912- *WhoWor 93*
Rogers, William Forrest 1938- *WhoSSW 93*
Rogers, William Irvine 1927- *WhoE 93*
Rogers, William Raymond 1932- *WhoAm 92, WhoSSW 93*
Rogers, William Z. 1950- *St&PR 93*
Rogers, Wilma Messer 1931- *WhoAmW 93*
Rogers-Aregger, Susan Vicki 1951- *WhoAmW 93*
Rogers-Lafferty, Sarah Jeanne 1956- *WhoAm 92*
Rogersohn, William *ScF&FL 92*
Rogerson, Carol E. *St&PR 93*
Rogerson, Donald *BioIn 17*
Rogerson, J(ohn) W(illiam) 1935- *ConAu 38NR*
Rogerson, Jess A. 1938- *St&PR 93*
Rogerson, John *ConAu 38NR*
Rogerson, John H. *WhoScE 91-1*
Rogerson, John William 1935- *WhoWor 93*
Rogerson, Kenneth Francis 1948- *WhoSSW 93*
Rogerson, Larry Richard 1943- *St&PR 93*
Rogerson, Lynda Gail 1948- *WhoWrEP 92*
Rogerson, William Durie 1934- *St&PR 93*
Rogerwick, Edward Anthony 1938- *WhoAm 92, WhoE 93*
Roget, Henriette 1910- *Baker 92*
Roget, Peter Mark 1779-1869 *BioIn 17*
Rogg, Lionel 1936- *Baker 92*
Rogge, Dwaine William 1938- *WhoWor 93*
Rogge, Joel Jay 1934- *WhoE 93*
Rogge, Lothar Ernst 1942- *WhoWor 93*
Rogge, Susan Marie Andresen 1953- *WhoAmW 93*
Roggendorf, Hans 1953- *WhoScE 91-3*
Roggenkamp, Karen Lee 1956- *WhoE 93*
Rogger, Hans Jack 1923- *WhoAm 92*
Roggeveen, Jacob 1659-1729 *Expl 93*
Roggio, Sergio Oscar 1957- *WhoWor 93*
Rogich, Sig *WhoAm 92*
Rogiers, Fernand Hippolyte Francois 1928- *WhoWor 93*
Rogin, Gilbert Leslie 1929- *WhoAm 92, WhoWrEP 92*
Rogin, Lawrence M. 1909-1988 *BioIn 17*
Roginski, Raymond Stephen 1955- *WhoE 93*
Rogister, Andre Lambert 1940- *WhoWor 93*
Rogister, Jean (Francois Toussaint) 1879-1964 *Baker 92*
Rogliano, Aldo Thomas 1925- *WhoAm 92*
Rogne, Odd 1942- *WhoScE 91-4*
Rogner, Heinz 1929- *Baker 92*
Rognerud, Gudrun Queseth 1937- *WhoScE 91-4*
Rogness, Kurt E. 1943- *St&PR 93*
Rognoni, Paulina Amelia 1947- *WhoWor 93*
Rogo, D. Scott *BioIn 17*
Rogo, Kathleen 1952- *WhoSSW 93*
Rogoff, Carol Vernice *Law&B 92*
Rogoff, Jerome Howard 1938- *WhoAm 92*
Rogoff, Jonathan Michael *Law&B 92*
Rogoff, Richard A. *Law&B 92*
Rogol, Martin Howard 1945- *WhoSSW 93*
Rogolsky, Robert L. 1922- *St&PR 93*
Rogos, Roger B. 1940- *St&PR 93*
Rogosheske, Walter Frederick 1914- *WhoAm 92*
Rogosin, Lionel 1924- *MiSFD 9*
Rogoski, Patricia Diana 1939- *St&PR 93, WhoAm 92, WhoAmW 93, WhoSSW 93*
Rogov, Igor Mikhailovitch 1927- *WhoWor 93*
Rogov, Voldemar-Berngard 1938- *WhoWor 93*
Rogovchenko, Yuri Vasiljevich 1961- *WhoWor 93*
Rogovin, Mitchell 1930- *WhoAm 92*
Rogow, Bruce Joel 1945- *WhoAm 92*
Rogow, Louis Michael 1944- *WhoE 93*
Rogow, Roberta 1942- *ScF&FL 92*
Rogow, Zack 1952- *WhoWrEP 92*
Rogowicki, John T. 1941- *St&PR 93*
Rogowski, Jerzy 1942- *WhoScE 91-4*
Rogowski, Ludomir (Michal) 1881-1954 *Baker 92*
Rogozinska, Janina Halina 1925- *WhoScE 91-4*
Rogstad, Astri 1943- *WhoWor 93*
Rogstad, Mark Roland 1957- *WhoEmL 93, WhoWor 93*
Rogula, Dominik 1936- *WhoScE 91-4*
Rogula, James Leroy 1933- *WhoAm 92*
Rogulski, Jan Stanislaw 1951- *WhoWor 93*
Rogus, Casimir A. 1905-1991 *BioIn 17*
Rogus, Katherine Olivia 1962- *WhoAmW 93*
Rogus, Robert Ronald 1941- *St&PR 93*
Roguski, Antoni Teofil 1927- *WhoScE 91-4, WhoWor 93*
Roguski, Gustav 1839-1921 *Baker 92*
Roguski, Wladyslaw 1890-1940 *PolBiDi*
Roh, Jae Kyung 1949- *WhoWor 93*
Roh, Milan Samuel 1931- *St&PR 93*
Roh, Tae Woo *BioIn 17*
Rohack, John James 1954- *WhoSSW 93*
Rohan, Henri de Rohan, Duke of 1579-1638 *HarEnMi*
Rohan, Jean de d1571? *BioIn 17*
Rohan, Kenneth E. 1953- *St&PR 93*
Rohan, Luther Jean 1921- *WhoWor 93*
Rohan, Michael Scott 1951- *ScF&FL 92*
Rohan, Virginia Bartholome 1939- *WhoE 93*
Rohan, Zina 1946- *ConAu 137*
Rohart, Jean Serge 1945- *WhoWor 93*
Rohatyn, Felix G. 1928- *St&PR 93*
Rohatyn, Felix George 1928- *WhoAm 92*
Rohda, Rodney Raymond 1942- *St&PR 93, WhoAm 92*
Rohde, Barbara E. *Law&B 92*
Rohde, Barbara Jo 1952- *WhoE 93*
Rohde, David William 1944- *WhoAm 92*
Rohde, Fritz G. 1935- *WhoScE 91-3*
Rohde, Gil C., Jr. 1948- *WhoIns 93*
Rohde, John Hans 1929- *WhoE 93*
Rohde, Linda Dianne 1945- *St&PR 93*
Rohde, (Friedrich) Wilhelm 1856-1928 *Baker 92*
Rohde, William L. *ScF&FL 92*
Rohe, Ludwig Mies van der 1886-1969 *BioIn 17*
Rohe, Ronald F. 1943- *St&PR 93*
Rohe, William Michael 1950- *WhoSSW 93*
Roheim, Geza 1891-1953 *IntDcAn*
Rohen, Johannes W. 1921- *WhoScE 91-3*
Roher, J.W. 1921- *WhoScE 91-3*
Roher, Marjorie Mae 1963- *WhoE 93*
Rohfeld, Michael D. *Law&B 92*
Roh In Hwan 1933- *WhoAsAP 91*
Rohleder, Jozef Wladyslaw 1925- *WhoScE 91-4*
Rohlf, Marvin Eugene 1927- *St&PR 93*
Rohlffs, Duke 1937- *St&PR 93*
Rohlfs, Christian 1849-1938 *BioIn 17*
Rohlfs, Friedrich Gerhard 1831-1896 *Expl 93 [port]*
Rohlfs, Kristen 1930- *WhoScE 91-3*
Rohlich, Pal 1929- *WhoScE 91-4*
Rohlin, Diane Elizabeth 1958- *WhoAm 92*
Rohlin, Madeleine I.-L. 1945- *WhoScE 91-4*
Rohlin, Toby L. 1944- *St&PR 93*
Rohling, Gregory C. *Law&B 92*
Rohlman, Frances B. *Law&B 92*
Rohloff, Albert Christian 1926- *WhoE 93*
Rohloff, Claire Marie 1945- *WhoAmW 93*
Rohloff, Ernst 1899-1983 *Baker 92*
Rohloff, George Douglas 1945- *St&PR 93*
Rohm, Charles E. 1935- *WhoIns 93*
Rohm, Charles Edward 1935- *St&PR 93, WhoAm 92*
Rohm, Eberhard 1940- *WhoE 93*
Rohm, Jeffrey P. *Law&B 92*
Rohm, Robert Hermann 1934- *WhoAm 92*
Rohman, Patricia Ann 1967- *WhoSSW 93*
Rohmann, Gerd 1940- *WhoWor 93*
Rohmann, Paul Henry 1918- *WhoWrEP 92*
Rohmer, Eric *BioIn 17*
Rohmer, Eric 1920- *MiSFD 9, WhoAm 92, WhoWor 93*
Rohmer, Michel 1948- *WhoScE 91-2*
Rohmer, Richard 1924- *ScF&FL 92, WhoCanL 92*
Rohmer, Sax 1883-1959 *ScF&FL 92*
Rohmert, W. 1929- *WhoScE 91-3*

Rohn, William R. 1943- *St&PR 93*
Rohner, Adrien 1929- *WhoScE 91-4*
Rohner, Gerrit John 1922- *St&PR 93*
Rohner, Paul E. 1937- *St&PR 93, WhoAm 92*
Rohner, Ralph John 1938- *WhoAm 92*
Rohner, Ronald Preston 1935- *WhoE 93*
Rohner, Thomas John, Jr. 1936- *WhoAm 92*
Rohovsky, Michael William 1937- *WhoE 93*
Rohr, Brian P. 1947- *WhoIns 93*
Rohr, Daniel C. 1946- *WhoAm 92*
Rohr, David Baker 1933- *WhoAm 92*
Rohr, Davis Charles 1929- *WhoAm 92*
Rohr, Donald Gerard 1920- *WhoAm 92*
Rohr, Hugo 1866-1937 *Baker 92*
Rohr, James E. 1948- *St&PR 93*
Rohr, James Edward 1948- *WhoAm 92*
Rohr, K. *WhoScE 91-3*
Rohr, Max 1931- *WhoScE 91-4*
Rohr, Michael Egan 1950- *WhoSSW 93*
Rohrabacher, Dana 1947- *BioIn 17, CngDr 91, WhoAm 92*
Rohrbach, Hans Joachim 1903- *WhoWor 93*
Rohrbach, Heidi A. *Law&B 92*
Rohrbach, Lewis Bunker 1941- *WhoE 93*
Rohrbach, Mary Kay *Law&B 92*
Rohrbach, Peter Thomas 1926- *WhoWrEP 92*
Rohrbach, Richard Paul 1930- *St&PR 93*
Rohrbach, Roger Phillip 1942- *WhoSSW 93*
Rohrbach, Susan Windett 1947- *WhoAmW 93*
Rohrbach, Thomas 1931- *St&PR 93*
Rohrbach, W. Thomas 1947- *St&PR 93*
Rohrbach, Walter Allen 1934- *St&PR 93*
Rohrbach, William Thomas 1947- *WhoE 93*
Rohrbacher, Karl Joseph *Law&B 92*
Rohrbacher, Ronald 1945- *St&PR 93*
Rohrbacker, Raymond B. 1940- *St&PR 93*
Rohrbaugh, Lisa Anne 1956- *WhoAmW 93*
Rohrbaugh, Randolph Lee 1950- *WhoIns 93*
Rohrberger, Mary 1929- *WhoWrEP 92*
Rohrberger, Mary Helen 1929- *WhoSSW 93*
Rohrbough, Elsa Claire 1915- *WhoAmW 93*
Rohrbough, Linda Jandecka 1947- *WhoAmW 93*
Rohren, Brenda Marie Anderson 1959- *WhoAmW 93*
Rohrer, Dean C. *Law&B 92*
Rohrer, Edna 1942- *WhoAmW 93*
Rohrer, Gertrude Martin 1875- *AmWomPl*
Rohrer, Heinrich 1933- *WhoAm 92, WhoScE 91-4, WhoWor 93*
Rohrer, Jeffrey Thomas 1952- *St&PR 93*
Rohrer, Joanne Elaine 1956- *St&PR 93*
Rohrer, Josephine N. 1924- *St&PR 93*
Rohrer, Lila Borg 1929- *WhoWrEP 92*
Rohrer, Philip L., Jr. *St&PR 93*
Rohrer, Richard C., Jr. 1946- *St&PR 93*
Rohrer, Richard Raymond 1958- *St&PR 93*
Rohrer, Robert Lee 1939- *WhoSSW 93*
Rohrer, Ronald Alan 1939- *WhoAm 92*
Rohrer, Susan *MiSFD 9*
Rohrich, Clarence George 1920- *St&PR 93*
Rohrich, Eugene S. 1922- *St&PR 93*
Rohrich, Robert D. 1915- *St&PR 93*
Rohrich, Thomas R. 1948- *St&PR 93*
Rohrig, Emil 1882-1954 *Baker 92*
Rohrig, Ernst 1921- *WhoScE 91-3*
Rohrkemper, Paul H. *WhoAm 92*
Rohrlich, Fritz 1921- *WhoE 93*
Rohrlich, George Friedrich 1914- *WhoAm 92, WhoE 93*
Rohrman, Nicholas Leroy 1937- *WhoAm 92*
Rohrmann, Guenter 1939- *St&PR 93*
Rohrs, Elizabeth Vincent 1959- *WhoAmW 93*
Rohrs, Gustav Werner 1931- *WhoAm 92*
Rohrs, Wilhelm Hermann 1932- *WhoWrEP 92*
Rohs, Thomas Joseph 1941- *St&PR 93*
Rohsenow, Warren M. 1921- *St&PR 93*
Rohsenow, Warren Max 1921- *WhoAm 92, WhoE 93*
Roh Sung Hwan 1928- *WhoAsAP 91*
Roh Tae Woo 1932- *WhoWor 93*
Roh Tae Woo, His Excellency 1932- *WhoAsAP 91*
Rohwedder, Detlev *BioIn 17*
Rohwedder, Donald Charles 1928- *St&PR 93*
Rohwedder, James L. *Law&B 92*
Rohwetter, Carl B. 1931- *St&PR 93*
Roider, Karl Andrew, Jr. 1943- *WhoSSW 93*
Roig, Gonzalo 1890-1970 *Baker 92*
Roig, Montserrat 1946- *BioIn 17*
Roijen, Jan Herman van 1905-1991 *BioIn 17*
Roiland, Gary K. 1948- *St&PR 93*
Roiland, Jacques *Law&B 92*
Roilos, Minas 1930- *WhoScE 91-3*
Roine, Unto Kalevi 1930- *WhoScE 91-4*
Roisin, Jean-Didier 1946- *WhoWor 93*
Roisin, Paul L.H.R. 1926- *WhoScE 91-2*
Roisler, Glenn Harvey 1952- *WhoEmL 93, WhoSSW 93, WhoWor 93*
Roisman, Hanna Maslovski 1948- *WhoAmW 93*
Roisman, Richard *Law&B 92*
Roithmayr, Carlos Michael 1960- *WhoSSW 93*
Roitman, Isaac 1939- *WhoWor 93*
Roitman, Judith 1945- *WhoAmW 93*
Roitsch, Paul Albert 1926- *WhoE 93*
Roiz, Myriam 1938- *WhoWor 93*
Roizin, Leon 1912-1991 *BioIn 17*
Roizman, Bernard 1929- *WhoAm 92, WhoWor 93*
Roizman, Owen 1936- *ConTFT 10*
Rojahn, Theodore C. 1938- *St&PR 93*
Rojak, Rebecca Lee 1957- *WhoAmW 93*
Rojanschi, Vladimir 1941- *WhoScE 91-4*
Rojas, Ann Marie *Law&B 92*
Rojas, Carlos 1928- *WhoAm 92*
Rojas, Francisco Gomez Sandoval y 1552-1625 *BioIn 17*
Rojas, Gonzalo 1917- *SpAmA*
Rojas, Jaime 1940- *WhoUN 92*
Rojas, Kristine Briggs 1947- *WhoAmW 93*
Rojas, Louis Edward 1947- *WhoE 93*
Rojas, Manuel 1896-1973 *SpAmA*
Rojas, Patricio Ivan 1945- *WhoUN 92*
Rojas, Raul 1942- *WhoWor 93*
Rojas, Richard Raimond 1931- *WhoAm 92*
Rojas, Saavedra Patricio *WhoWor 93*
Rojas Garciduenas, Jose 1912-1981 *DcMexL*
Rojas Gonzalez, Francisco 1904-1951 *DcMexL*
Rojas-Gonzalez, Raul 1955- *WhoWor 93*
Rojas-Lombardi, Felipe d1991 *BioIn 17*
Rojas Samanez, Alvaro 1946- *WhoWor 93*
Rojek, Mark A. 1957- *St&PR 93*
Rojer, Olga Elaine 1953- *WhoE 93*
Rojo, Hector Julio 1941- *WhoWor 93*
Rojo, Jesus 1950- *WhoWor 93*
Rojo, Salvador Madariaga y *ScF&FL 92*
Rojo Olalla, Casiano 1877-1931 *Baker 92*
Roka, Attila Michael 1935- *St&PR 93*
Roka, Ladislaus 1919- *WhoScE 91-3*
Rokeach, Milton *BioIn 17*
Roker, Al *NewYTBS 92 [port]*
Rokes, Willis Park 1926- *WhoIns 93*
Rokeya, Begum 1880-1932 *ScF&FL 92*
Rokha, Pablo de 1894-1968 *SpAmA*
Rokich, Paul *BioIn 17*
Rokicki, Eligiusz 1934- *WhoWor 93*
Rokkanen, Pentti U. 1927- *WhoScE 91-4*
Rokkanen, Seppo Olavi 1945- *WhoWor 93*
Rokke, Ervin Jerome 1939- *WhoAm 92*
Rokoff, June L. 1946- *St&PR 93*
Rokossovski, Konstantin 1896-1968 *ColdWar 2 [port]*
Rokossovski, Konstantin Konstantinovich 1896-1968 *HarEnMi*
Rokossovsky, Konstantin Konstantinovich 1887-1968 *DcTwHis*
Rokosz, Andrzej 1927- *WhoScE 91-4*
Rokosz, Andrzej Mateusz 1927- *WhoWor 93*
Rokowsky, Morris d1991 *BioIn 17*
Rokseth, Yvonne 1890-1948 *Baker 92*
Rokus, Josef Wilhelm 1942- *St&PR 93*
Rokyta, Richard 1938- *WhoScE 91-4*
Roland fl. c. 778- *HarEnMi*
Roland, Betty 1903- *DcChlFi*
Roland, Billy Ray 1926- *WhoSSW 93*
Roland, Catherine Dixon 1936- *WhoAmW 93, WhoWor 93*
Roland, Charles Gordon 1933- *WhoAm 92*
Roland, Claude-Robert 1935- *Baker 92*
Roland, Craig Williamson 1935- *WhoAm 92*
Roland, Donald E. 1942- *St&PR 93*
Roland, Donald Edward 1942- *WhoAm 92*
Roland, Eleanor Joyce 1940- *WhoAmW 93*
Roland, Frank H. 1935- *St&PR 93*
Roland, Gilbert 1905- *HispAmA*
Roland, Howell, Jr. *ScF&FL 92*
Roland, Kjell 1953- *WhoWor 93*
Roland, Melissa Montgomery 1961- *WhoSSW 93*
Roland, Michel 1932- *WhoScE 91-2*
Roland, P.E. 1943- *WhoScE 91-4*
Roland, Paul *ScF&FL 92*
Roland, Ruth 1892?-1937 *SweetSg B [port]*
Roland, Ruth 1894-1937 *BioIn 17*
Roland, William L. 1953- *St&PR 93*
Roland, Yves Georges Isidore 1951- *WhoWor 93*
Roland-Billecart, Yves 1926- *WhoWor 93*
Roland de la Platiere, Jeanne Manon 1754-1793 *BioIn 17*
Rolandi, Gianna 1952- *Baker 92, WhoAm 92*
Roland-Manuel 1891-1966 *Baker 92*
Roldan, Amadeo 1900-1939 *Baker 92*
Roldan, Margaret Dobos 1958- *WhoAmW 93*
Roldan, Mario Reni *DcCPCAm*
Roldan, Simeon Yee *Law&B 92*
Rolen, Stanley Robert 1934- *WhoE 93*
Rolett, Ellis Lawrence 1930- *WhoAm 92, WhoE 93*
Rolewicz, Stefan 1932- *WhoWor 93*
Roley, Sutton *MiSFD 9*
Rolf, Howard Leroy 1928- *WhoSSW 93*
Rolf, Randolph K. 1942- *St&PR 93*
Rolfe, A.G. *WhoScE 91-1*
Rolfe, Bari 1916- *WhoWrEP 92*
Rolfe, Christopher 1938- *ScF&FL 92*
Rolfe, Edwin 1909-1954 *BioIn 17*
Rolfe, Gerald T. 1936- *St&PR 93*
Rolfe, Harold Edward *Law&B 92*
Rolfe, Michael N. 1937- *WhoAm 92*
Rolfe, Paula Grace 1942- *WhoSSW 93*
Rolfe, Peter *WhoScE 91-1*
Rolfe, Robert Abial 1908-1969 *BiDAMSp 1989*
Rolfe, Robin Ann 1949- *WhoAm 92*
Rolfe, Ronald Stuart 1945- *WhoAm 92*
Rolfe, Stanley Theodore 1934- *WhoAm 92*
Rolfe Johnson, Anthony 1940- *Baker 92, OxDcOp*
Rolfs, Robert T. 1926- *St&PR 93*
Rolfs, Thomas John 1922- *St&PR 93*
Rolf the Granger fl. c. 890-911 *HarEnMi*
Rolian, Paul 1945- *WhoUN 92*
Rolih, Joan Marie 1961- *WhoAmW 93*
Roline, Alan C. *Law&B 92*
Roline, Eric Alfred 1955- *WhoSSW 93*
Rolinski, Zbigniew 1931- *WhoScE 91-4*
Rolison, Elizabeth Norwood 1960- *WhoSSW 93*
Rolison, Patricia Jane Maertens 1964- *WhoSSW 93*
Roll, Gerald A. 1933- *St&PR 93*
Roll, Irwin C. 1925- *St&PR 93*
Roll, Irwin Clifford 1925- *WhoAm 92*
Roll, Janet Blair 1945- *WhoAmW 93*
Rolla, Adrienne Marie 1959- *St&PR 93*
Rolla, Alessandro 1757-1841 *Baker 92*
Rolla, Giuseppe Antonio 1798-1837 *Baker 92*
Rolland, Albert *St&PR 93*
Rolland, Albert 1919- *WhoWor 93*
Rolland, Christopher Lars 1947- *WhoAm 92*
Rolland, Donna Josephine 1952- *WhoAmW 93*
Rolland, Ian McKenzie *WhoIns 93*
Rolland, Ian McKenzie 1933- *St&PR 93, WhoAm 92*
Rolland, Kenneth S. 1930- *St&PR 93*
Rolland, Lucien G. 1916- *St&PR 93, WhoAm 92, WhoE 93*
Rolland, Michel Didier 1949- *St&PR 93*
Rolland, Peter George 1930- *WhoAm 92*
Rolland, Romain 1866-1944 *Baker 92, BioIn 17*
Rolland, Rune 1944- *WhoWor 93*
Rollans, James O. 1942- *WhoAm 92*
Rollans, James Ora 1942- *St&PR 93*
Rollason, W. Peter 1939- *WhoAm 92*
Rollason, William J. *Law&B 92*
Rollberg, Jeanne Norton 1957- *WhoAmW 93*
Rolle, Andrew 1922- *WhoWrEP 92*
Rolle, Andrew F. 1922- *WhoAm 92*
Rolle, Christian Friedrich 1681-1751 *See* Rolle, Johann Heinrich 1716-1785 *Baker 92*
Rolle, Darrell Erwin 1943- *WhoWor 93*
Rolle, Dietrich Otto August 1929- *WhoWor 93*
Rolle, Esther *BioIn 17, WhoAm 92, WhoAmW 93*
Rolle, Johann Heinrich 1716-1785 *Baker 92*
Rolle, Lillian *AmWomPl*
Rolle, Myra Moss 1937- *WhoAmW 93, WhoWor 93*
Rollefson, Richard Carl 1948- *WhoAm 92*
Rollence, Michele Lynette 1955- *WhoAmW 93*
Roller, Alfred 1864-1935 *IntDcOp, OxDcOp*
Roller, Duane Henry DuBose 1920- *WhoAm 92*
Roller, Herbert Alfred 1927- *WhoAm 92*
Roller, Larry L. *Law&B 92*
Roller, Maurice L. 1946- *St&PR 93*
Roller, Robert Douglas, III 1928- *WhoAm 92*
Roller, Stanley *Law&B 92*
Roller, Thomas Benjamin 1950- *WhoAm 92, WhoEmL 93*
Rollet, Christine G. 1939- *WhoUN 92*
Rollet, M. 1928- *WhoScE 91-2*
Rollgen, Franz W. 1937- *WhoScE 91-3*
Roll-Hansen, Nils Diderik 1938- *WhoWor 93*
Rollhaus, Philip E., Jr. 1934- *St&PR 93*
Rollhaus, Philip Edward, Jr. 1934- *WhoAm 92, WhoWor 93*
Rolli, John Mario Albert 1942- *WhoSSW 93*
Rolli, Paolo Antonio 1687-1765 *IntDcOp, OxDcOp*
Rollier, Jack Albert 1940- *St&PR 93*
Rollig, Carl Leopold c. 1735-1804 *Baker 92*
Rollin, Bernard Elliot 1943- *WhoAm 92*
Rollin, Betty *BioIn 17*
Rollin, Betty 1936- *WhoAm 92*
Rollin, Grant E. 1947- *St&PR 93*
Rollin, Ida 1908-1983 *BioIn 17*
Rollin, Jean 1906-1977 *Baker 92*
Rollin, Stephen H. 1925- *St&PR 93*
Rolling, Danny Harold *BioIn 17*
Rollinghoff, Martin 1941- *WhoScE 91-3*
Rollings, Alane *WhoWrEP 92*
Rollings, David 1953- *St&PR 93*
Rollings, James Robert, III 1948- *WhoSSW 93*
Rollins, Albert Williamson 1930- *WhoSSW 93*
Rollins, Alden M(ilton) 1946- *ConAu 139*
Rollins, Alfred Brooks, Jr. 1921- *WhoAm 92*
Rollins, Charlemae 1897-1979 *BioIn 17, BlkAull 92*
Rollins, Edward John 1943- *NewYTBS 92 [port]*
Rollins, Elaine G. *Law&B 92*
Rollins, Gary Wayne 1944- *WhoAm 92, WhoSSW 93*
Rollins, Henry Moak 1921- *WhoAm 92*
Rollins, Howard Ellsworth, Jr. 1950- *WhoAm 92*
Rollins, Jack 1914- *WhoAm 92*
Rollins, James D., III 1958- *St&PR 93*
Rollins, Jay Neil 1960- *WhoSSW 93*
Rollins, John David 1964- *WhoSSW 93*
Rollins, John W. 1916- *St&PR 93*
Rollins, John William, Sr. 1916- *WhoAm 92*
Rollins, Judith Ann *WhoE 93*
Rollins, Marcus Wayne 1953- *WhoSSW 93*
Rollins, Patti Diane 1959- *WhoSSW 93*
Rollins, Raymond Lee *Law&B 92*
Rollins, Richard L. 1936- *St&PR 93*
Rollins, Richard William 1930- *St&PR 93*
Rollins, Sherrie Sandy 1958- *NewYTBS 92 [port], WhoAm 92*
Rollins, Sonny *BioIn 17*
Rollins, "Sonny" 1929- *Baker 92*
Rollins, Sonny 1930- *WhoAm 92*
Rollins, Thomas Christian 1959- *WhoE 93*
Rollins, Timothy *BioIn 17*
Rollins-Garcia, Lisa D. 1960- *WhoSSW 93*
Rollinson, Mark 1935- *WhoSSW 93*
Rollinson, Simeon Harrison, III 1939- *St&PR 93*
Roll-Kerwick, Teresa *Law&B 92*
Rollo, F. David 1939- *St&PR 93, WhoAm 92*
Rollo, William *ScF&FL 92*
Rollock, Barbara d1992 *NewYTBS 92*
Rollock, Barbara T. 1924- *BioIn 17*
Rolloff Langworthy, Carol Lemay 1942- *WhoWrEP 92*
Rolloos, Marinus 1944- *WhoScE 91-3*
Rolls, Charles Stewart 1877-1910 *BioIn 17*
Rolls, Dana Kramer- *ScF&FL 92*
Rolls, Maurice John *WhoScE 91-1*
Rolls, Robert Earl 1942- *St&PR 93*
Rollwagen, John A. 1940- *St&PR 93*
Rollyson, Carl 1948- *WhoWrEP 92*
Rolnicki, Thomas Edward 1949- *WhoAm 92*
Roloff, Hans-Gert 1932- *WhoWor 93*
Roloff, M.E., Jr. 1931- *St&PR 93*
Roloff, Michael 1937- *WhoWrEP 92*
Roloff, ReBecca Koenig 1954- *WhoIns 93*
Rolofson, Kristine Nancy 1951- *WhoWrEP 92*
Rolon, Jose 1883-1945 *Baker 92*
Rolontz, Robert 1920- *WhoAm 92*
Rolow-Mialowski, Karol 1842-1907 *PolBiDi*
Rolph, Juanita Lu 1937- *WhoWrEP 92*
Rolston, Benedict Francis d1991 *BioIn 17*
Rolston, Holmes, III 1932- *WhoWor 93*
Rolston, Ken *ScF&FL 92*
Rolston, Kenneth Stuart 1928- *WhoAm 92*
Rolston, Matthew *BioIn 17*
Rolston, Richard Gerard 1947- *WhoE 93*
Rolston, Robert L. *St&PR 93*
Rolvaag, Karl Fritjof 1913-1990 *BioIn 17*
Rolwing, Francis David 1934- *St&PR 93*
Rolwing, Robert Eugene 1926- *St&PR 93*

Rom, Irving 1923- *WhoAm 92*
Rom, Martin 1946- *WhoAm 92*
Roma, John R. 1940- *St&PR 93*
Roma de Albuquerque, Luis Octavio 1937- *WhoUN 92*
Romagnole, Anthony J. 1959- *St&PR 93*
Romagosa, Elmo Lawrence 1924- *WhoAm 92*
Romagosa, Jerome J. 1917- *WhoSSW 93*
Romaguera, Enrique 1942- *WhoWor 93*
Romaguera, Mariano Antonio 1928- *WhoWor 93*
Romain, James d1864 *BioIn 17*
Romaine, Henry S. 1933- *St&PR 93, WhoIns 93*
Romaine, Henry Simmons 1933- *WhoAm 92, WhoSSW 93*
Romaine, Ralph O. 1918- *St&PR 93*
Romains, Jules 1885-1972 *BioIn 17, ScF&FL 92*
Roman, Cecelia Florence 1956- *WhoAmW 93*
Roman, Edward S. *Law&B 92*
Roman, Ernan 1950- *WhoE 93*
Roman, Frederick *St&PR 93*
Roman, Gilberto d1990 *BioIn 17*
Roman, Harold 1926- *WhoWor 93*
Roman, Herschel Lewis 1914-1989 *BioIn 17*
Roman, Johan Helmich 1694-1758 *Baker 92*
Roman, John Joseph 1950- *WhoE 93*
Roman, Juan Manuel 1941- *WhoWor 93*
Roman, Kenneth, Jr. 1930- *WhoAm 92*
Roman, Kenneth J. 1930- *St&PR 93*
Roman, Marek 1931- *WhoScE 91-4*
Roman, Mark B. *BioIn 17*
Roman, Mary Broumas 1932- *WhoAmW 93*
Roman, Michael M. 1947- *St&PR 93*
Roman, Nancy Grace 1925- *WhoAmW 93*
Roman, Petre 1946- *WhoWor 93*
Roman, Phil *MiSFD 9*
Roman, Robert E., Jr. *Law&B 92*
Roman, Ronald Peter 1945- *WhoSSW 93*
Roman, Ruth 1923- *SweetSg D [port]*
Roman, Spencer Myles 1949- *WhoIns 93*
Roman, Stanford Augustus, Jr. *WhoE 93*
Roman, Stella d1992 *NewYTBS 92 [port]*
Roman, Stella 1904- *Baker 92*
Roman, Stella 1910-1992 *BioIn 17*
Roman, Stephen E. 1947- *St&PR 93*
Roman, Tony *MiSFD 9*
Roman, W.S. 1943- *St&PR 93*
Roman, William Edward 1955- *WhoAm 92*
Romanansky, Marcia Canzoneri 1941- *WhoAmW 93*
Roman-Barber, Helen 1946- *WhoAm 92, WhoAmW 93, WhoE 93*
Romance, Viviane 1909-1991 *AnObit 1991*
Romanchenko, Vladimir Aleksandrovich 1932- *WhoWor 93*
Romanchych, V.E. *St&PR 93*
Romand, Maurice J. 1936- *WhoScE 91-2*
Romanek, Mark *MiSFD 9*
Romanell, Patrick 1912- *WhoAm 92*
Romanelli, Felice 1751-1839 *OxDcOp*
Romanello, Marguerite Marie 1939- *WhoAmW 93*
Romanese, Gino 1957- *WhoE 93*
Romani, Carlo 1824-1875 *Baker 92*
Romani, Felice 1788-1865 *Baker 92, IntDcOp*
Romani, John Henry 1925- *WhoAm 92*
Romani, Luigi 1788-1865 *OxDcOp*
Romani, Pietro 1791-1877 *Baker 92, OxDcOp*
Romanies, Michael Edward 1962- *WhoE 93*
Romanini, Attilio 1921- *WhoScE 91-3*
Romaniuk, Andrzej 1931- *WhoWor 93*
Romaniuk, Jozef *WhoScE 91-4*
Romaniuk, Ryszard Stanislaw 1952- *WhoWor 93*
Romaniuk, William G. 1949- *St&PR 93*
Romaniw, Sania K.Y. *Law&B 92*
Roman-Lagunas, Jorge 1943- *WhoSSW 93*
Romano, Andrew Anthony 1940- *St&PR 93*
Romano, Benito 1949- *WhoAm 92*
Romano, Daniel 1927- *St&PR 93*
Romano, Daniel A. *St&PR 93*
Romano, Frank J. 1941- *WhoWrEP 92*
Romano, Fred M. *Law&B 92*
Romano, Geraldine 1937- *WhoE 93*
Romano, Giovanni 1905-1990 *BioIn 17*
Romano, Jack d1991 *BioIn 17*
Romano, Joan Michele 1951- *WhoAmW 93*
Romano, John 1908- *WhoAm 92*
Romano, John Joseph 1942- *WhoAm 92*
Romano, Joseph Anthony 1946- *WhoE 93*
Romano, Linda E. 1953- *St&PR 93*
Romano, Malcolm Joseph *Law&B 92*
Romano, Marjorie Jean 1933- *WhoE 93*
Romano, Nick Joseph 1951- *WhoWrEP 92*
Romano, Octavio 1923- *DcLB 122*
Romano, Robert Steven *Law&B 92*
Romano, Roberta 1952- *WhoAm 92*
Romano, Vincent J. 1928- *St&PR 93*
Romanoff, Douglas Preston 1950- *WhoSSW 93*
Romanoff, Milford Martin 1921- *WhoAm 92*
Romano-Magner, Patricia R. 1928- *WhoAmW 93*
Romanones, Aline Griffith *BioIn 17*
Romanos, II 939-963 *OxDcByz*
Romanos, John, Jr. 1942- *WhoAm 92*
Romanos, Nabil Elias 1965- *WhoWor 93*
Romanos Argyros, III c. 968-1034 *OxDcByz*
Romanos Diogenes, IV d1072 *OxDcByz*
Romanos Lekapenos, I c. 870-948 *OxDcByz*
Romanos the Melode dc. 555 *OxDcByz*
Romanov, Boris Georgievich 1891-1957 *BioIn 17*
Romanov, Nikolai 1868-1918 *BioIn 17*
Romano-V., Octavio I. 1932- *BioIn 17*
Romanov, Victor *Law&B 92*
Romanov, Vladimir Gavrilovich 1938- *WhoWor 93*
Romanov, Vladimir Kirillovich *BioIn 17*
Romanov, Vladimir Kirillovich 1917-1992 *NewYTBS 92*
Romanovsky, Alexander Boris 1954- *WhoWor 93*
Romanow, Joseph S. *Law&B 92*
Romanow, Roy J. *BioIn 17*
Romanow, Roy John *WhoAm 92*
Romanow, Theodore Mayer 1955- *St&PR 93*
Romanowitz, Byron Foster 1929- *WhoAm 92*
Romanowski, Richard Ronald 1932- *WhoE 93*
Romanowski, Thomas Andrew 1925- *WhoAm 92*
Romans, Donald B. 1931- *St&PR 93*
Romans, Donald Bishop 1931- *WhoAm 92*
Romans, John Niebrugge 1942- *WhoAm 92*
Romansky, Monroe James 1911- *WhoAm 92*
Romanus Diogenes, IV d1072 *HarEnMi*
Romariz, Carlos 1920- *WhoScE 91-3*
Romas, Elaine 1966- *WhoAmW 93*
Romauldi, James Philip 1929- *WhoAm 92*
Rombach, Louis H. *Law&B 92*
Rombaux, J.P. *WhoScE 91-2*
Romberg, Andreas Jakob 1767-1821 *Baker 92*
Romberg, Bernhard Heinrich 1767-1841 *Baker 92*
Romberg, Bernhardine 1803-1878 *Baker 92*
Romberg, Ciprian Friedrich 1807-1865 *See* Romberg, Andreas Jakob 1767-1821 *Baker 92*
Romberg, Gerhard Heinrich 1745-1819 *See* Romberg, Andreas Jakob 1767-1821 *Baker 92*
Romberg, Heinrich Maria 1802-1859 *See* Romberg, Andreas Jakob 1767-1821 *Baker 92*
Romberg, Karl 1811-1897 *Baker 92*
Romberg, Nina *ScF&FL 92*
Romberg, Sigmund 1887-1951 *Baker 92, OxDcOp*
Romberg, Wayne D. 1946- *St&PR 93*
Romberger, John Albert 1925- *WhoE 93, WhoWor 93*
Rombert, Palmira C. 1922- *WhoScE 91-3*
Rombola, Anthony Mario Stephen 1953- *WhoE 93*
Rombough, Bartlett B. 1924- *St&PR 93, WhoAm 92*
Rombouts, Jean-Jacques 1941- *WhoScE 91-2*
Romcevic, Ljubomir 1926- *WhoScE 91-4*
Rome, David Andrew *Law&B 92*
Rome, Donald Lee 1929- *WhoAm 92*
Rome, Elaine *ConAu 138*
Rome, Gerald Francis 1926- *WhoAm 92*
Rome, Harold Jacob 1908- *WhoAm 92*
Rome, Herbert Mark 1926- *St&PR 93, WhoAm 92*
Rome, James Alan 1942- *WhoSSW 93*
Rome, John L. 1954- *St&PR 93*
Romefelt, Mark W. *Law&B 92*
Romei, Lura Knachel 1947- *WhoAm 92*
Romeis, Ronald Alan 1947- *WhoE 93*
Romeling, Waldemar Briggs 1909- *WhoE 93*
Romelus, Willy *DcCPCAm*
Romeo, Aurelio 1923- *WhoScE 91-3*
Romeo, Garet Martin 1938- *St&PR 93*
Romeo, Laura Elizabeth 1955- *WhoAmW 93*
Romeo, Luigi 1926- *WhoAm 92*
Romeo, Marian Victoria *Law&B 92*
Romeo, Michael, Jr. 1947- *WhoSSW 93*
Romeo, Nicola 1940- *WhoScE 91-3*
Romeo, Paulo *DcCPCAm*
Romeo, Ross Victor 1958- *WhoE 93*
Romeos *SoulM*
Romer, Claude Jean 1943- *WhoUN 92*
Romer, Emma 1814-1868 *OxDcOp*
Romer, Franz Josef 1943- *WhoWor 93*
Romer, Klaus 1940- *St&PR 93*
Romer, Peter John 1944- *St&PR 93*
Romer, Roy *BioIn 17, NewYTBS 92 [port]*
Romer, Roy R. 1928- *WhoAm 92, WhoWor 93*
Romerio, Giovanni Francesco 1935- *WhoUN 92*
Romero *Baker 92*
Romero, Angel 1926- *WhoScE 91-3*
Romero, Angel 1946- *Baker 92*
Romero, Armando Paul 1943- *St&PR 93*
Romero, Celedonio 1918- *Baker 92*
Romero, Celin 1940- *Baker 92*
Romero, Cesar 1907- *HispAmA*
Romero, Clemente *WhoScE 91-3*
Romero, Eddie 1924- *MiSFD 9*
Romero, Emilio Felipe 1946- *WhoSSW 93*
Romero, Frank 1941- *HispAmA*
Romero, George A. 1940- *MiSFD 9, ScF&FL 92*
Romero, Javier, Jr. 1954- *WhoWor 93*
Romero, Jesus d1992 *BioIn 17*
Romero, Joaquim J.B. 1928- *WhoScE 91-3*
Romero, Joaquin 1946- *St&PR 93*
Romero, Jose Ruben 1890-1952 *DcMexL, SpAmA*
Romero, Juan Carlos 1937- *HispAmA*
Romero, Leo 1950- *DcLB 122 [port]*
Romero, Leo M. 1943- *HispAmA*
Romero, Lin 1947- *DcLB 122 [port]*
Romero, Linda Gayle 1950- *WhoAmW 93*
Romero, Martha Gandert 1940- *WhoAmW 93*
Romero, Mateo 1575?-1647 *Baker 92*
Romero, Miguel L. 1941- *WhoAsAP 91*
Romero, Omhny *BioIn 17*
Romero, Oscar A. 1917-1980 *BioIn 17*
Romero, Oscar Arnulfo 1917-1980 *DcCPCAm*
Romero, Pepe 1944- *Baker 92*
Romero, Randall Keith 1959- *St&PR 93*
Romero, Serapio *DcCPCAm*
Romero Barcelo, Carlos 1932- *DcCPCAm*
Romero-Barcelo, Carlos Antonio 1932- *WhoAm 92, WhoSSW 93*
Romero Bosque, Pio *DcCPCAm*
Romero Mena, Carlos Humberto c. 1926- *DcCPCAm*
Romeu, Eddie N. 1960- *St&PR 93*
Romeu, Luis 1874-1937 *Baker 92*
Romey, William Dowden 1930- *WhoAm 92*
Romeyn, Jonathan W. *Law&B 92*
Romhild, Johann Theodor 1684-1756 *Baker 92*
Romhildt, Johann Theodor 1684-1756 *Baker 92*
Romich, Kelly M. *Law&B 92*
Romich, Sharon 1946- *St&PR 93*
Romig, Charles Stuart 1946- *St&PR 93*
Romig, George C. 1931- *St&PR 93*
Romig, Joseph Howard 1941- *BiDAMSp 1989*
Romig, Karl A. 1926- *St&PR 93*
Romig, Michael Victor 1943- *St&PR 93*
Romig, Phillip Richardson 1938- *WhoAm 92*
Romig, William James 1944- *St&PR 93*
Romijn, Hanna Kooyker- *ScF&FL 92*
Romilly, Jacqueline de *BioIn 17*
Romilus, Arn *ScF&FL 92*
Romine, Aden F. *ScF&FL 92*
Romine, Joan Marie 1951- *WhoAmW 93*
Romine, Mary C. *ScF&FL 92*
Romine, Maurice G. 1941- *St&PR 93*
Romine, Thomas Beeson, Jr. 1925- *WhoAm 92, WhoSSW 93, WhoWor 93*
Rominger, Tom *BioIn 17*
Rominiecki, Ronald R. 1953- *St&PR 93*
Romita, Augusto 1934- *WhoScE 91-3*
Romjue, John Lawson 1936- *WhoWrEP 92*
Romkes-Sparks, Marjorie 1962- *WhoAmW 93*
Romkey, Michael *ScF&FL 92*
Romley, Derek Vanderbilt 1935- *WhoE 93*
Romley, Richard S. 1944- *St&PR 93*
Romm, Ethel Grodzins 1925- *WhoAmW 93*
Romm, Mihail 1901-1971 *DrEEuF*
Rommel, Erwin 1891-1944 *BioIn 17, DcTwHis*
Rommel, Erwin Johannes Eugen 1891-1944 *HarEnMi*
Rommel, Frederick Allen 1935- *WhoE 93*
Rommelspacher, Hans 1942- *WhoWor 93*
Rommer, James Andrew 1952- *WhoE 93*
Romness, Mark D. *Law&B 92*
Romney, Carl F. 1924- *WhoAm 92*
Romney, Cyril 1931- *DcCPCAm*
Romney, David Stewart *Law&B 92*
Romney, George 1907- *WhoAm 92*
Romney, George W. 1907- *PolPar*
Romney, Richard Bruce 1942- *WhoAm 92*
Romney, Seymour Leonard 1917- *WhoAm 92*
Romo, Angel M. 1955- *WhoScE 91-3*
Romo, Cheryl Annette 1944- *WhoSSW 93*
Romo, Gene David 1947- *WhoAm 92*
Romo, Jose Leon 1930- *WhoSSW 93*
Romo, Ricardo 1943- *HispAmA [port]*
Romoda, Tibor 1921- *WhoScE 91-4*
Romoff, Jeffrey Alan 1945- *WhoAm 92*
Romoser, George Kenneth 1929- *WhoAm 92*
Romoser, W. David *Law&B 92*
Romozer, W. David *Law&B 92*
Rompf, Clifford G., Jr. 1930- *St&PR 93, WhoAm 92*
Rompis, Robert James 1951- *WhoWor 93*
Rompkey, Ronald (George) 1943- *ConAu 37NR*
Romrell, Larry E. 1939- *St&PR 93*
Romrell, Lynn John 1944- *WhoSSW 93*
Romrell, Randall L. *Law&B 92*
Romsdahl, Marvin Magnus 1930- *WhoAm 92, WhoSSW 93*
Romsek, Thomas Anton 1938- *St&PR 93*
Romski, Mary Ann 1952- *WhoAmW 93*
Romslo, Inge 1938- *WhoScE 91-4*
Romtvedt, David William 1950- *WhoWrEP 92*
Romuald, II *OxDcByz*
Romualdez Marcos, Imelda *BioIn 17*
Romualdo, Alejandro 1926- *SpAmA*
Romualdo, Pedro P. 1935- *WhoAsAP 91*
Romulo, Alberto Gatmaitan 1933- *WhoAsAP 91*
Romulo, Beth Day *ConAu 40NR*
Romulo, Carlos Pena 1899-1985 *DcTwHis*
Romulo, Roberto Rey 1938- *WhoWor 93*
Romulus Augustulus dc. 507 *OxDcByz*
Romyanond, Prathuan *WhoAsAP 91*
Romylos dc. 1381 *OxDcByz*
Ron, William 1943- *St&PR 93*
Rona, Agnes *Law&B 92*
Rona, Donna C. 1954- *WhoWrEP 92*
Rona, George 1924- *WhoAm 92*
Rona, Peter 1946- *St&PR 93*
Ronai, Ferenc 1926- *WhoScE 91-4*
Ronald, Allan Ross 1938- *WhoAm 92*
Ronald, Christopher John 1945- *WhoUN 92*
Ronald, F. Eugene, Jr. 1930- *St&PR 93*
Ronald, Landon 1873-1938 *Baker 92*
Ronald, Mark *ScF&FL 92*
Ronald, Martin *WhoScE 91-1*
Ronald, Peter 1926- *WhoAm 92*
Ronald, Thomas Iain 1933- *St&PR 93*
Ronald, William 1926- *WhoAm 92*
Ronalds, Leigh 1923- *St&PR 93*
Ronan, Elena Vinade *WhoWor 93*
Ronan, Frank 1963- *ConAu 138*
Ronan, John Thomas 1936- *WhoAm 92*
Ronan, Joseph E., Jr. *Law&B 92*
Ronan, Peter William 1944- *St&PR 93*
Ronan, William J. 1912- *St&PR 93*
Ronan, William John 1912- *WhoAm 92, WhoSSW 93, WhoWor 93*
Ronayne, Joan Bernice 1966- *WhoE 93*
Ronayne, Michael Richard, Jr. 1937- *WhoAm 92, WhoE 93*
Ronc, Michael Joseph 1944- *WhoWor 93*
Ronca, Luciano Bruno 1935- *WhoAm 92*
Roncada, E. 1943- *WhoScE 91-3*
Roncador, Italo A.M. 1943- *WhoScE 91-3*
Roncaglia, Gino 1883-1968 *Baker 92*
Roncalli, Angelo Giuseppe 1881-1963 *BioIn 17*
Ronchetti, Giulio 1931- *WhoScE 91-3*
Ronchetti, Joseph Franklin 1940- *WhoAm 92*
Ronchetti, S.V. 1939- *St&PR 93*
Ronchi-Proja, Francesca 1924- *WhoScE 91-3*
Ronco, Bradley Eugene 1946- *St&PR 93*
Ronconi *Baker 92*
Ronconi, Domenico 1772-1839 *Baker 92, OxDcOp*
Ronconi, Felice 1811-1875 *Baker 92*
Ronconi, Giorgio 1810-1890 *Baker 92, OxDcOp*
Ronconi, Sebastiano 1814-1900 *Baker 92, OxDcOp*
Rondeau, Cheryl MaryAnn 1952- *WhoAmW 93*
Rondeau, Clement Robert 1928- *WhoSSW 93*
Rondeau, Doris Jean 1941- *WhoWor 93*
Rondeau, Edmond Paul 1945- *WhoSSW 93*
Rondeau, Eugene E. *BioIn 17*
Rondeau, John *BioIn 17*
Rondepierre, Edmond 1930- *St&PR 93*
Rondepierre, Edmond F. *Law&B 92*
Rondepierre, Edmond F. 1930- *WhoIns 93*
Rondepierre, Edmond Francois 1930- *WhoAm 92*
Rondeux, Jacques M.H. 1944- *WhoScE 91-2*
Rondileau, Adrian 1912- *WhoAm 92*
Rondinelli, Dennis August 1943- *WhoSSW 93*

Rondon, Candido 1865-1958 *Expl 93*
Rone, B.J. 1942- *St&PR 93*
Rone, Charles Curtis 1946- *St&PR 93*
Rone, David B. *Law&B 92*
Rone, Dinah Annette 1954- *WhoSSW 93*
Rone, William Eugene, Jr. 1926- *WhoAm 92, WhoWrEP 92*
Ronel, Samuel H. 1936- *St&PR 93*
Ronemus, Alan David 1955- *WhoSSW 93*
Ronettes *SoulM*
Roney, John Harvey 1932- *WhoAm 92, WhoWor 93*
Roney, Paul H. 1921- *WhoAm 92, WhoSSW 93*
Roney, Robert Kenneth 1922- *WhoAm 92*
Roney, Scott Allen *Law&B 92*
Roney, Stephen Christopher 1951- *St&PR 93*
Roney, Thomas F. 1945- *St&PR 93*
Roney, Wallace *BioIn 17*
Roney, Wallace 1960- *WhoAm 92*
Roney, William C., Jr. 1924- *St&PR 93*
Ronga, Luigi 1901- *Baker 92*
Ronge, Jean-Baptiste 1825-1882 *Baker 92*
Rong Yiren 1916- *WhoAsAP 91*
Rongzhen, Nie 1899-1992 *NewYTBS 92*
Roniewicz, Piotr 1936- *WhoScE 91-4*
Roningen, Robert N. 1935- *St&PR 93*
Ronis, Willy 1910- *BioIn 17*
Ronk, Glenn Emery 1925- *WhoAm 92*
Ronkin, Alan Marshall 1941- *WhoE 93*
Ronkin, Bruce Edward 1957- *WhoE 93*
Ronn, Ehud Israel 1950- *WhoSSW 93, WhoWor 93*
Ronn, Joshua Imrich 1915- *St&PR 93*
Ronn, Lars Erik 1940- *WhoWor 93*
Ronn, Yuval *ScF&FL 92*
Ronne, Tove *WhoScE 91-2*
Ronnefeld, Peter 1935-1965 *Baker 92*
Ronnel, Jacob 1956- *WhoWor 93*
Ronnick, Herbert *St&PR 93*
Ronning, Royal N., Jr. *Law&B 92*
Ronningen, Knut 1938- *WhoScE 91-4*
Ronnmark, Kjell *WhoScE 91-4*
Ronnow, Robert William 1924- *WhoE 93*
Rono, Jose A. *WhoAsAP 91*
Ronquillo, Allan L. *Law&B 92*
Ronquillo, Allan Louis 1941- *WhoAm 92*
Ronsheim, Sally 1917-1990 *BioIn 17*
Ronson, Mark *ScF&FL 92*
Ronson, Raoul R. 1931- *WhoE 93, WhoWor 93*
Ronson, Susan 1940- *WhoE 93*
Ronstadt, Karl Graves 1929- *St&PR 93*
Ronstadt, Linda *BioIn 17*
Ronstadt, Linda 1946- *NotHsAW 93 [port]*
Ronstadt, (Maria) Linda 1946- *Baker 92*
Ronstadt, Linda Marie 1946- *WhoAm 92, WhoAmW 93*
Ronstadt, Peter 1942- *WhoAm 92*
Rontal, Joseph 1909- *St&PR 93*
Rontgen, Julius 1855-1932 *Baker 92*
Ronto, Gyorgyi 1934- *WhoScE 91-4*
Ronty, Bruno George 1922- *WhoE 93*
Ronveaux, Andre 1932- *WhoScE 91-2*
Ronyak, David Michael *Law&B 92*
Ronzi, Giuseppina *OxDcOp*
Roobol, Norman Richard 1934- *WhoAm 92*
Rood, David S. 1940- *WhoAm 92*
Rood, Don D. 1930- *St&PR 93, WhoIns 93*
Rood, Frank William 1905- *WhoWrEP 92*
Rood, George Ashley 1936- *St&PR 93*
Rood, Henry F. 1906- *St&PR 93*
Rood, Hope Thornton Thompson 1933- *WhoAmW 93*
Roodenko, Igal d1991 *BioIn 17*
Roodin, Paul A. 1943- *WhoE 93*
Roodt, Darrell James *MiSFD 9*
Roof, Betty Sams 1926- *WhoAmW 93*
Roof, James Sheldon 1947- *WhoE 93*
Roof, Katherine Metcalf *AmWomPl*
Roofner, M. Robert *Law&B 92*
Roofner, M. Robert 1946- *St&PR 93*
Rook, Jean 1931-1991 *AnObit 1991*
Rook, Pearl Newton 1923- *WhoWrEP 92*
Rooke, Allen Driscoll, Jr. 1924- *WhoSSW 93*
Rooke, Ben G. 1949- *St&PR 93*
Rooke, David Lee 1923- *WhoAm 92*
Rooke, Donald Bruce 1929- *St&PR 93*
Rooke, Leon 1934- *WhoCanL 92*
Rooke, Susan Ann 1959- *WhoAmW 93*
Rooker, C. Keith *Law&B 92*
Rooker, Dennis S. *Law&B 92*
Rooker, Michael *BioIn 17*
Rooker, Paul George 1943- *St&PR 93*
Rookey, Thomas Jerome 1944- *WhoE 93*
Rook-Green, Peter G. 1940- *St&PR 93*
Rooks, Charles Shelby 1924- *WhoAm 92*
Rooks, Conrad *MiSFD 9*
Rooks, Floyd Jefferson 1923- *WhoSSW 93, WhoWor 93*
Rooks, George (M.) 1951- *WhoWrEP 92*
Rooley, Anthony 1944- *Baker 92*
Roomann, Hugo 1923- *WhoAm 92*
Roomberg, Lila Goldstein 1929- *WhoAm 92*
Roomberg, Susan Kelly 1961- *WhoSSW 93*
Roome, Katherine Davis *Law&B 92*
Roome, Peter D. 1937- *St&PR 93*
Roon, Albrecht Theodor Emil, Count von 1803-1879 *HarEnMi*
Rooney, Andrew A. *BioIn 17*
Rooney, Andrew Aitken 1919- *WhoAm 92, WhoE 93, WhoWrEP 92*
Rooney, Andy *BioIn 17*
Rooney, Art 1901-1988 *BioIn 17*
Rooney, Bernard J. *Law&B 92*
Rooney, Bethany *MiSFD 9*
Rooney, Carol Bruns 1940- *WhoAmW 93, WhoWor 93*
Rooney, Charles J. 1935- *ScF&FL 92*
Rooney, Daniel M. 1932- *WhoAm 92*
Rooney, David 1962- *BioIn 17*
Rooney, Donald R. *Law&B 92*
Rooney, Francis C., Jr. 1921- *St&PR 93*
Rooney, Gail Schields 1947- *WhoAmW 93*
Rooney, Gerard P. *Law&B 92*
Rooney, J. Patrick 1927- *WhoIns 93*
Rooney, James Patrick 1938- *WhoWor 93*
Rooney, Jeffrey L. 1942- *St&PR 93*
Rooney, John E. 1942- *St&PR 93*
Rooney, John Edward, Jr. 1942- *WhoAm 92*
Rooney, John Francis 1960- *St&PR 93*
Rooney, John Henry, Jr. 1952- *St&PR 93*
Rooney, John Jerome d1991 *BioIn 17*
Rooney, John Joseph 1915- *WhoAm 92*
Rooney, Kevin Davitt 1944- *WhoAm 92*
Rooney, M. Shawn 1946- *St&PR 93*
Rooney, Margaret Louise 1951- *WhoE 93*
Rooney, Martin Michael 1943- *St&PR 93*
Rooney, Michael *BioIn 17*
Rooney, Michael 1946- *WhoE 93*
Rooney, Michael J. 1941- *St&PR 93, WhoAm 92, WhoE 93*
Rooney, Mickey *BioIn 17*
Rooney, Mickey 1920- *IntDcF 2-3 [port], QDrFCA 92 [port], WhoAm 92*
Rooney, Patricia Jane 1936- *WhoAmW 93*
Rooney, Patrick D. *Law&B 92*
Rooney, Patrick Edward 1946- *St&PR 93*
Rooney, Patrick Michael 1957- *WhoE 93*
Rooney, Paul George 1925- *WhoAm 92*
Rooney, Paul Monroe 1918- *WhoAm 92*
Rooney, Phillip Bernard 1944- *St&PR 93, WhoAm 92*
Rooney, Robert D. *Law&B 92*
Rooney, Steven D. 1947- *St&PR 93*
Rooney, Thomas David 1946- *St&PR 93*
Rooney, Thomas Michael 1947- *St&PR 93*
Rooney, William J. *Law&B 92*
Rooney, William Richard 1938- *WhoAm 92*
Roop, James J. 1949- *WhoAm 92*
Roop, Joseph McLeod 1941- *WhoWor 93*
Roop, Ralph G. 1915- *St&PR 93*
Roop, Ralph Goodwin 1915- *WhoAm 92, WhoSSW 93*
Roorbach, Bill 1953- *ConAu 137*
Roorbach, Douglas E. 1959- *WhoWrEP 92*
Roorbach, George B. 1926- *St&PR 93*
Roorbach, George Brett 1926- *WhoE 93*
Roorda, John Francis, Jr. 1923- *WhoAm 92*
Roos, B. *WhoScE 91-4*
Roos, Bjorn Olof 1937- *WhoWor 93*
Roos, Casper 1925- *WhoAm 92*
Roos, Daniel 1939- *WhoAm 92*
Roos, Dirk 1941- *WhoScE 91-3*
Roos, Frederick Ried 1934- *WhoAm 92*
Roos, Gerrit 1944- *WhoWor 93*
Roos, Gretchen L. *Law&B 92*
Roos, Jean Carolyn 1891-1982 *BioIn 17*
Roos, Jef R. 1943- *WhoScE 91-2*
Roos, Juanita E. 1878- *AmWomPl*
Roos, Kathleen Susan 1949- *WhoAmW 93*
Roos, Matts G.W. 1931- *WhoScE 91-4*
Roos, Philip 1930- *WhoAm 92, WhoSSW 93*
Roos, Robert C., Jr. *Law&B 92*
Roos, Robert de 1907-1976 *Baker 92*
Roos, Roger Antoine 1931- *WhoWor 93*
Roos, Ron 1952- *WhoE 93*
Roos, Sybil Friedenthal 1924- *WhoAmW 93*
Roos, Thomas Bloom 1930- *WhoAm 92*
Roosa, James K. *Law&B 92*
Roosa, Robert V. 1918- *St&PR 93*
Roosa, Robert Vincent 1918- *WhoAm 92*
Roosa, Stuart 1933- *WhoAm 92*
Roose, Christina 1944- *WhoWrEP 92*
Roose-Church, Lisa Anno 1964- *WhoWrEP 92*
Roose-Evans, James *BioIn 17*
Roosen, Carol H. 1931- *St&PR 93*
Roosen, Jean-Paul 1945- *WhoScE 91-2*
Roosen, Robert C. *St&PR 93*
Roosenboom, Derk *St&PR 93*
Roosendaal, Eddy Maria Cyrille 1931- *WhoWor 93*
Roosevelt, Archibald 1918-1990 *BioIn 17*
Roosevelt, Cornelius V.S. *BioIn 17*
Roosevelt, Edith Kermit Carow 1861-1948 *BioIn 17*
Roosevelt, Eleanor 1884-1962 *BioIn 17, DcTwHis, EncAACR, JrnUS, PolPar*
Roosevelt, Elliott 1910-1990 *BioIn 17*
Roosevelt, Franklin D. *DcCPCAm*
Roosevelt, Franklin D. 1882-1945 *BioIn 17*
Roosevelt, Franklin Delano 1882-1945 *ColdWar 1 [port], ConHero 2 [port], DcTwHis, HarEnMi, OxCSupC, PolPar*
Roosevelt, J(oseph) Willard 1918- *Baker 92*
Roosevelt, James 1907-1991 *AnObit 1991, BioIn 17*
Roosevelt, James M. *Law&B 92*
Roosevelt, Selwa *BioIn 17*
Roosevelt, Theodore *DcCPCAm*
Roosevelt, Theodore 1858-1919 *BioIn 17, Expl 93 [port], GayN, PolPar*
Roosevelt, Theodore, IV 1942- *St&PR 93, WhoAm 92*
Roosevelt, W. Emlen 1917- *St&PR 93*
Roosje, G.S. 1928- *WhoScE 91-3*
Root, Alan Charles 1925- *WhoAm 92*
Root, Albert 1891-1990 *ScF&FL 92*
Root, Allen William 1933- *WhoAm 92*
Root, Betty *WhoScE 91-1*
Root, Chapman Shaw 1925-1990 *BioIn 17*
Root, David A. 1942- *WhoE 93*
Root, Edward Lakin 1940- *WhoE 93*
Root, Elihu 1845-1937 *DcTwHis, HarEnMi*
Root, Elihu 1845-1938 *PolPar*
Root, Franklin Russell 1923- *WhoAm 92*
Root, Frederick L. 1943- *St&PR 93*
Root, Frederick W(oodman) 1846-1916 *Baker 92*
Root, George Frederick 1820-1895 *Baker 92*
Root, Ivy Ashton *AmWomPl*
Root, John Alan 1933- *St&PR 93*
Root, Joseph E. *Law&B 92*
Root, Kathleen Jean 1964- *WhoAmW 93*
Root, L. Allen *WhoAm 92*
Root, L. Allen 1943- *St&PR 93*
Root, L. Eugene d1992 *NewYTBS 92*
Root, Larry Donald 1936- *St&PR 93*
Root, Leonard Eugene 1910-1992 *BioIn 17*
Root, Louis D., Jr. 1922- *St&PR 93*
Root, Lynal A. 1930- *St&PR 93, WhoAm 92*
Root, M. Belinda 1957- *WhoSSW 93*
Root, Nathan J. 1911- *St&PR 93*
Root, Nile 1926- *WhoWor 93*
Root, Nina J. 1934- *WhoAm 92*
Root, Oren 1911- *WhoAm 92*
Root, Pamela P. *Law&B 92*
Root, Peter T. 1951- *St&PR 93*
Root, Raymond Francis 1948- *WhoSSW 93*
Root, Sherwin F. *Law&B 92*
Root, Stanley William, Jr. 1923- *WhoAm 92*
Root, Steven E. 1951- *St&PR 93*
Root, Stuart Dowling 1932- *WhoAm 92, WhoWor 93*
Root, Timothy L. 1956- *St&PR 93*
Root, William Alden 1923- *WhoAm 92*
Root, William Lucas 1919- *WhoAm 92*
Root, William Pitt 1941- *DcLB 120 [port], WhoAm 92, WhoWrEP 92*
Root-Bernstein, Robert Scott 1953- *WhoAm 92*
Rootenberg, Jacob 1936-1991 *BioIn 17*
Rootes, Charles Wesley 1927- *WhoAm 92*
Rootham, Cyril (Bradley) 1875-1938 *Baker 92*
Roots, Ernest Frederick 1923- *WhoAm 92*
Roots, William 1946- *WhoWor 93*
Roover, Charles A. *Law&B 92*
Rooy, Anton van 1870-1932 *OxDcOp*
Ropars, Claude 1937- *WhoScE 91-2*
Ropartz, Joseph Guy (Marie) 1864-1955 *Baker 92*
Ropchan, Jim R. 1950- *WhoWor 93*
Rope, William Frederick 1940- *WhoAm 92*
Ropelewski, Tom *MiSFD 9*
Roper, Bert E. 1923- *St&PR 93*
Roper, Beryl Cain 1931- *WhoSSW 93*
Roper, Burns Worthington 1925- *St&PR 93, WhoAm 92*
Roper, Clyde Forrest Eugene 1937- *WhoAm 92*
Roper, David J. *Law&B 92*
Roper, David J. 1937- *St&PR 93*
Roper, Elmo 1900-1981 *PolPar*
Roper, Francis John 1933- *WhoWor 93*
Roper, George Clay 1930- *WhoSSW 93*
Roper, George H. *Law&B 92*
Roper, J.L., IV 1953- *St&PR 93*
Roper, Jane Anderson 1946- *WhoAmW 93*
Roper, John Edgar 1962- *WhoWrEP 92*
Roper, John Joseph 1946- *WhoE 93*
Roper, John Lonsdale, III 1927- *St&PR 93, WhoAm 92, WhoSSW 93*
Roper, John M. *Law&B 92*
Roper, Joseph Alan *WhoScE 91-1*
Roper, Lanning 1912-1983 *BioIn 17*
Roper, Laroy R. 1943- *St&PR 93*
Roper, Louis L. 1931- *St&PR 93*
Roper, Michael 1932- *WhoWor 93*
Roper, Norman Allen 1936- *St&PR 93*
Roper, Robert William 1800-1845 *BioIn 17*
Roper, William A. 1946- *WhoAm 92*
Roper, William Alford, Jr. 1946- *St&PR 93*
Roper, William H. 1929- *St&PR 93*
Roper, William Lee 1948- *WhoAm 92*
Ropes, John S. 1938- *St&PR 93*
Ropka, Mary Elizabeth 1949- *WhoAmW 93*
Roppolo, John Wayne 1939- *WhoSSW 93*
Roppolo, Sharon T. 1944- *St&PR 93*
Roque, David Raul 1959- *WhoSSW 93*
Roque, Elaine Marie 1960- *WhoAmW 93*
Roque, Francisco Victorino Henson 1942- *WhoUN 92*
Roque, Jean-Louis 1948- *WhoWor 93*
Roque, Margarita 1946- *NotHsAW 93*
Roque, Victor A. *Law&B 92*
Roque, Victor A. 1946- *St&PR 93*
Roquelaure, A.N. *ScF&FL 92*
Roquelaure, A.N. 1941- *BioIn 17*
Roquemore, Anne Mickler 1950- *WhoWrEP 92*
Roquemore, Elizabeth Anne *WhoSSW 93*
Roquemour, Grayson 1942- *WhoAmW 93*
Roquero, Carlos 1924- *WhoScE 91-3*
Roques, Bernard *WhoScE 91-2*
Roquette-Pinto, Edgar 1884-1954 *IntDcAn*
Roque Villada, Daniel Alfredo 1938- *WhoWor 93*
Roraback, J. Henry 1870-1937 *PolPar*
Roraback, Thomas Joseph 1943- *WhoIns 93*
Rordorf, Alwin Willy 1933- *WhoWor 93*
Rore, Cipriano de 1515?-1565 *Baker 92*
Rorem, Ned 1923- *Baker 92, WhoAm 92, WhoWrEP 92*
Rorer, Leonard George 1932- *WhoWor 93*
Rorholt, Arnold 1951- *WhoWor 93*
Rorick, Alan Green 1918- *WhoAm 92*
Rorie, Durwood G., Jr. 1933- *St&PR 93*
Rorig, Kurt Joachim 1920- *WhoAm 92*
Rorimer, Louis 1872-1939 *BioIn 17*
Rorison, I.H. *WhoScE 91-1*
Rorison, Margaret Lippitt 1925- *WhoSSW 93*
Rork, Allen W. 1944- *St&PR 93*
Rork, Allen Wright 1944- *WhoIns 93*
Rorke, Edwin Grant 1923- *St&PR 93*
Rorke, James 1944- *WhoSSW 93*
Rorke, Kevin C. 1949- *St&PR 93*
Rorke, Kevin H. 1949- *St&PR 93*
Rorke, Kevin Hayden 1949- *WhoAm 92*
Rorke, Lucy Balian 1929- *WhoAm 92*
Rorschach, Carol Ann 1940- *St&PR 93*
Rorschach, Richard Gordon 1928- *WhoAm 92*
Rorschach, Robert Louis 1922- *St&PR 93*
Rorsman, Hans 1930- *WhoScE 91-4*
Rorty, Richard *BioIn 17*
Rorty, Richard McKay 1931- *WhoAm 92*
Rorvik, David 1946- *ScF&FL 92*
Rorvik, David M(ichael) 1946- *ConAu 38NR*
Ros, Amanda McKittrick 1860-1939 *BioIn 17*
Ros, Carl Wilhelm 1941- *WhoWor 93*
Ros, Ernest A. 1925- *St&PR 93*
Rosa, Alfred Felix 1942- *WhoE 93*
Rosa, Carl 1842-1889 *Baker 92, OxDcOp*
Rosa, Daniel C. 1951- *St&PR 93*
Rosa, Donald J. 1949- *St&PR 93*
Rosa, George Machado 1949- *WhoE 93*
Rosa, Javier de la *BioIn 17*
Rosa, Jean *WhoScE 91-2*
Rosa, Kenneth J. 1926- *St&PR 93*
Rosa, Margarita 1953- *WhoAmW 93*
Rosa, Michael Richard 1953- *WhoWor 93*
Rosa, Nick *BioIn 17*
Rosa, Peter Manuel 1946- *WhoE 93*
Rosa, Raymond Ulric 1927- *WhoAm 92*
Rosa, Roberto 1965- *WhoSSW 93*
Rosa, Salvator(e) 1615-1673 *Baker 92*
Rosa, Sylvio Goulart, Jr. 1940- *WhoWor 93*
Rosa, Tina Maria 1956- *WhoAmW 93*
Rosa, Vicky Lynn 1953- *WhoAmW 93*
Rosa, William F. 1960- *St&PR 93*
Rosabal, Nelson John 1943- *St&PR 93*
Rosada, Rosemary *St&PR 93*
Rosado, Carlos G. 1941- *WhoWor 93*
Rosado-Schmucker, Patricia Virginia 1958- *WhoAmW 93*
Rosado Vega, Luis 1873-1958 *DcMexL*
Rosal', Grigorij 1898-1983 *DrEEuF*
Rosaldo, Renato Ignacio, Jr. 1941- *WhoAm 92*
Rosales, Denise M. *Law&B 92*
Rosales, Francisco 1937- *WhoWor 93*
Rosales, Richard Anthony *Law&B 92*
Rosales, Terso R. *Law&B 92*

Rosalsky, Andrew James 1948- *WhoSSW 93*
Rosalsky, Mercedes C. 1956- *WhoSSW 93*
Rosamond, John Bell 1936- *WhoAm 92, WhoE 93*
Rosamond, Patricia A. 1947- *St&PR 93*
Rosamond, Samuel M., Jr. 1937- *St&PR 93*
Rosamond, Sandra Pauline 1947- *WhoAmW 93, WhoEmL 93, WhoSSW 93*
Rosan, Richard Marshall 1942- *WhoAm 92*
Rosand, Aaron 1927- *Baker 92*
Rosand, David 1938- *WhoAm 92*
Rosander, Mats E. 1957- *WhoScE 91-4*
Rosandich, Thomas James 1954- *WhoWor 93*
Rosane, Edwin L. 1936- *WhoIns 93*
Rosario, Alejandro Jose Villanueva 1924- *WhoWor 93*
Rosas, Joan Xicota 1958- *WhoE 93*
Rosasco, Stephen J. *Law&B 92*
Rosas Moreno, Jose 1838-1883 *DcMexL*
Rosatelli, Dennis 1948- *St&PR 93*
Rosati, Beth Ann 1964- *WhoAmW 93*
Rosati, Dariusz Kajetan 1946- *WhoWor 93*
Rosati, Mario 1928- *WhoWor 93*
Rosati, Pasquale 1937- *WhoScE 91-3*
Rosati, Phillis C. 1925- *St&PR 93*
Rosati, R.S. 1939- *St&PR 93*
Rosati, Richie 1968- *WhoE 93*
Rosato, Francis Ernest 1934- *WhoAm 92*
Rosato, Lucia *Law&B 92*
Rosato, Margaret Ann 1964- *WhoAmW 93*
Rosato, Peter Charles 1948- *WhoE 93*
Rosay, Francoise 1891-1974 *IntDcF 2-3 [port]*
Rosbaud, Hans 1895-1962 *Baker 92, BioIn 17, IntDcOp, OxDcOp*
Rosberg, Carl Gustaf 1923- *WhoAm 92*
Rosberg, David William 1919- *WhoAm 92*
Rosberg, Rose *WhoWrEP 92*
Rosborough, E. Marie 1951- *WhoSSW 93*
Rosborough, Susan L. *Law&B 92*
Rosbottom, Ronald Carlisle 1942- *WhoAm 92*
Rosca, Radu Rochas 1909- *WhoWor 93*
Rosch, Friedrich 1862-1925 *Baker 92*
Rosch, John Thomas 1939- *WhoAm 92*
Rosch, Notker 1943- *WhoWor 93*
Rosch, Paul John 1927- *WhoAm 92, WhoE 93, WhoWor 93*
Roschenthaler, Gerd-Volker 1944- *WhoScE 91-3*
Roscher, Nina Matheny 1938- *WhoAmW 93, WhoE 93*
Roschman, Georgiann 1940- *St&PR 93*
Roscia, John J. 1920- *WhoAm 92*
Roscian, Francis A. 1938- *WhoScE 91-3*
Roscioni, Remo 1951- *WhoWor 93*
Rosciszewska, Danuta Helena 1926- *WhoScE 91-4*
Rosciszewski, Marcin 1929- *WhoScE 91-4*
Roscoe, Albert 1888-1933 *BioIn 17*
Roscoe, Dvosha G. *Law&B 92*
Roscoe, Stanley Nelson 1920- *WhoAm 92*
Roscoe, Theodore 1906-1992 *ScF&FL 92*
Roscopf, Charles Buford 1928- *WhoAm 92*
Roscower, Emma *AmWomPl*
Rosdeitcher, Sidney S. 1936- *WhoAm 92*
Rose, Abigail Jayne 1960- *WhoE 93*
Rose, Adam Zachary 1948- *WhoAm 92*
Rose, Adrianne Lenore *WhoAmW 93*
Rose, Albert 1910-1990 *BioIn 17*
Rose, Alec 1908-1991 *AnObit 1991, BioIn 17*
Rose, Alex 1898-1976 *PolPar*
Rose, Andrew (Wyness) 1944- *ConAu 136*
Rose, Anita Carroll 1922- *WhoAmW 93, WhoE 93, WhoWor 93*
Rose, Anthony C. 1925- *St&PR 93*
Rose, Arnold (Josef) 1863-1946 *Baker 92*
Rose, Axl *BioIn 17*
Rose, Axl c. 1962- *News 92 [port]*
Rose, Barbara Jean 1945- *WhoAmW 93*
Rose, Barry Leon 1955- *WhoSSW 93*
Rose, Beatrice Schroeder 1922- *WhoAm 92*
Rose, Bernard *MiSFD 9*
Rose, Bernard (William George) 1916- *Baker 92*
Rose, Billy 1899-1966 *BioIn 17, JeAmHC*
Rose, Bonnie Lou 1951- *WhoAmW 93*
Rose, C. Robert F. 1938- *St&PR 93*
Rose, Carol Ann 1942- *WhoAmW 93*
Rose, Caroline Baer 1913-1975 *BioIn 17*
Rose, Charles *WhoAm 92, WhoE 93*
Rose, Charles C. 1934- *St&PR 93*
Rose, Charles Grandison, III 1939- *WhoAm 92, WhoSSW 93*
Rose, Charles I. *WhoSSW 93*
Rose, Charlie 1939- *CngDr 91*
Rose, Cheryl Romprey 1949- *WhoSSW 93*
Rose, Christine Brooke- *ScF&FL 92*
Rose, Claudia J. *Law&B 92*
Rose, Curtis G. *Law&B 92*
Rose, D.W. 1925- *St&PR 93*
Rose, Daniel 1929- *WhoAm 92*
Rose, Daniel Asa *BioIn 17*
Rose, Daniel Asa 1949- *WhoWrEP 92*
Rose, Daniel Meredith 1940- *WhoAm 92*
Rose, David 1910-1990 *BioIn 17*
Rose, David Alan 1949- *WhoSSW 93*
Rose, David Cameron 1942- *WhoAm 92*
Rose, David E. *Law&B 92*
Rose, David E. 1944- *St&PR 93*
Rose, David H. 1955- *St&PR 93*
Rose, David L. *Law&B 92*
Rose, Deborah Elizabeth 1956- *WhoAmW 93*
Rose, Deborah Lee 1955- *SmATA 71 [port]*
Rose, Donald James 1944- *WhoAm 92*
Rose, Donald McGregor 1933- *WhoAm 92*
Rose, Donna Gay 1946- *WhoAmW 93*
Rose, Edward W. *WhoSSW 93*
Rose, Edward W. 1941- *St&PR 93*
Rose, Eleanor *WhoWrEP 92*
Rose, Elihu 1933- *WhoAm 92*
Rose, Elizabeth 1933- *BioIn 17*
Rose, Eric Allen 1951- *WhoAm 92*
Rose, Eric Cellu *Law&B 92*
Rose, Ernestine 1810-1892 *BioIn 17*
Rose, Ernestine 1880-1961 *BioIn 17*
Rose, Ernestine Louise Siismondi Powtowski 1809-1892 *JeAmHC*
Rose, Eugene V. 1937- *WhoAm 92*
Rose, Evans, Jr. 1932- *WhoAm 92*
Rose, F. Tore 1943- *WhoUN 92, WhoWor 93*
Rose, Francis David *WhoScE 91-1*
Rose, Frank Anthony 1920-1991 *BioIn 17*
Rose, Frederick 1915-1991 *BioIn 17*
Rose, Frederick Andrew *WhoScE 91-1*
Rose, Frederick Phineas 1923- *WhoAm 92, WhoWor 93*
Rose, Gail Elaine 1949- *WhoEmL 93*
Rose, Garland P., Jr. 1944- *St&PR 93*
Rose, Gerald 1935- *BioIn 17*
Rose, Gervase R. 1936- *St&PR 93*
Rose, Gilbert Jacob 1923- *WhoE 93, WhoWor 93*
Rose, Gilbert Paul 1939- *WhoWrEP 92*
Rose, Gloria *WhoE 93*
Rose, Guy 1867-1925 *BioIn 17*
Rose, H. Chapman 1907-1990 *BioIn 17*
Rose, Herman 1909- *WhoAm 92*
Rose, Howard Claude 1934- *St&PR 93*
Rose, Israel Harold 1917- *WhoAm 92*
Rose, James E., Jr. *Law&B 92*
Rose, James E., Jr. 1942- *St&PR 93*
Rose, James McKinley, Jr. 1927- *WhoAm 92*
Rose, James Turner 1935- *WhoAm 92*
Rose, James W. *Law&B 92*
Rose, James W. 1935- *WhoAm 92*
Rose, Jeffrey Raymond 1946- *WhoAm 92*
Rose, Jerome 1938- *Baker 92*
Rose, Jerzy Edwin 1909- *WhoAm 92*
Rose, Joanna Semel 1930- *WhoAmW 93*
Rose, Joanne W. *Law&B 92, St&PR 93*
Rose, Joel 1948- *WhoWrEP 92*
Rose, John Allison 1943- *WhoSSW 93*
Rose, John Brewster 1927- *WhoWor 93*
Rose, John Charles 1924- *WhoAm 92*
Rose, John K. *Law&B 92*
Rose, John Marek 1916- *WhoAm 92*
Rose, John Robert 1937- *WhoSSW 93*
Rose, John Schaefer *WhoSSW 93*
Rose, John Thomas 1943- *WhoAm 92*
Rose, John Winston *WhoScE 91-1*
Rose, Jonathan Chapman 1941- *WhoAm 92*
Rose, Jules Freed 1936- *BioIn 17*
Rose, June H. 1949- *WhoEmL 93*
Rose, Justin 1932- *St&PR 93*
Rose, Kenneth Edward 1939- *WhoSSW 93*
Rose, Kenneth Jon 1954- *ConAu 38NR*
Rose, Kenneth Leon 1936- *St&PR 93*
Rose, Kenny Wyndell 1964- *WhoSSW 93*
Rose, Kenton R. *Law&B 92*
Rose, Larry Lee 1943- *WhoSSW 93*
Rose, Leonard (Joseph) 1918-1984 *Baker 92*
Rose, Les *MiSFD 9*
Rose, Leslie *Law&B 92*
Rose, Lewis Norman 1959- *St&PR 93*
Rose, Lloyd *BioIn 17*
Rose, Louise Blecher 1943- *WhoWrEP 92*
Rose, Margaret A. 1947- *ConAu 138*
Rose, Marian Henrietta *WhoE 93*
Rose, Marian Jean 1953- *WhoSSW 93*
Rose, Mark 1939- *ScF&FL 92*
Rose, Mark 1956- *WhoE 93*
Rose, Mark Allen 1939- *WhoAm 92, WhoWrEP 92*
Rose, Mark Edward 1963- *St&PR 93*
Rose, Mark Howard 1945- *WhoSSW 93*
Rose, Marshall 1937- *WhoAm 92*
Rose, Melissa Eva Anderson 1959- *WhoAmW 93*
Rose, Michael *Law&B 92*
Rose, Michael D. 1942- *St&PR 93*
Rose, Michael David 1942- *WhoWor 93*
Rose, Michael Dean 1937- *WhoAm 92*
Rose, Michael E. 1947- *St&PR 93*
Rose, Michael George 1937- *WhoWor 93*
Rose, Michael L. 1948- *WhoSSW 93*
Rose, Michael Leonard 1952- *WhoWor 93*
Rose, Mickey *MiSFD 9*
Rose, Milton C. 1904- *St&PR 93*
Rose, Milton Curtiss 1904- *WhoAm 92*
Rose, Neal Nicholas 1950- *WhoSSW 93*
Rose, Noel Richard 1927- *WhoAm 92*
Rose, Pamela *ScF&FL 92*
Rose, Pamela S. 1954- *St&PR 93*
Rose, Patricia Anthone 1930- *WhoWrEP 92*
Rose, Paul E. 1947- *St&PR 93*
Rose, Paul Edward 1947- *WhoAm 92, WhoWor 93*
Rose, Pete 1941- *BioIn 17*
Rose, Peter Edward 1941- *WhoAm 92*
Rose, Peter Isaac 1933- *WhoAm 92*
Rose, Peter Shepard 1940- *WhoAm 92*
Rose, Phyllis 1942- *WhoAm 92, WhoWrEP 92*
Rose, Phyllis Kay 1955- *WhoAmW 93*
Rose, Porter Brawley 1942- *St&PR 93*
Rose, Raymond David 1937- *WhoE 93*
Rose, Reginald 1920- *ConTFT 10, WhoAm 92, WhoWrEP 92*
Rose, Renwick *DcCPCAm*
Rose, Richard 1933- *ScF&FL 92*
Rose, Richard Channon 1947- *St&PR 93*
Rose, Richard D. 1954- *St&PR 93*
Rose, Richard J. *St&PR 93*
Rose, Richard L. 1936- *St&PR 93*
Rose, Richard Loomis 1936- *WhoAm 92*
Rose, Robert Carlisle 1917- *WhoAm 92*
Rose, Robert Charles 1943- *St&PR 93*
Rose, Robert E. 1939- *WhoAm 92*
Rose, Robert Ernest 1938- *St&PR 93*
Rose, Robert G., III 1957- *St&PR 93*
Rose, Robert H. 1927- *St&PR 93*
Rose, Robert John 1930- *WhoAm 92*
Rose, Robert L. 1931- *St&PR 93*
Rose, Robert Lawrence 1945- *WhoAm 92, WhoE 93*
Rose, Robert Michael 1937- *WhoAm 92*
Rose, Robert Neal 1951- *WhoAm 92, WhoE 93, WhoEmL 93, WhoWor 93*
Rose, Robert R., Jr. 1915- *WhoAm 92*
Rose, Roslyn 1929- *WhoE 93*
Rose, Rowland G. 1916- *St&PR 93*
Rose, Rubye Blevins *WhoAm 92*
Rose, Selwyn H. 1933- *WhoWor 93*
Rose, Stephen 1936- *ScF&FL 92*
Rose, Stephen Jay 1925- *WhoAm 92*
Rose, Steven Peter Russell *WhoScE 91-1*
Rose, Susan Porter 1941- *WhoAm 92, WhoAmW 93*
Rose, Thomas Albert 1942- *WhoAm 92*
Rose, Thomas G. 1957- *St&PR 93*
Rose, Velma Annette 1953- *WhoAmW 93*
Rose, Verlinda Catherine *Law&B 92*
Rose, Vincent Celmer 1930- *WhoE 93*
Rose, Vincent Harold 1931- *St&PR 93*
Rose, Virginia Rogers 1942- *WhoAmW 93*
Rose, Virginia Shottenhamer 1924- *WhoAmW 93*
Rose, Wayne Myron 1946- *St&PR 93*
Rose, Wendy (Bronwen) Elizabeth 1948- *WhoWrEP 92*
Rose, William Allen, Jr. 1938- *WhoAm 92, WhoE 93, WhoWor 93*
Rose, William Dake 1928- *WhoSSW 93*
Rose, William H. *Law&B 92*
Rose, William Louis 1925- *St&PR 93*
Rose, William Shepard, Jr. 1948- *WhoAm 92*
Rose, Zeke 1932- *St&PR 93*
Rose, Zeldon E. 1932- *WhoAm 92*
Rose-Ackerman, Susan 1942- *WhoAm 92*
Rosebaum, Peter Andrew 1952- *WhoE 93*
Roseberg, Carl Andersson 1916- *WhoAm 92, WhoWor 93*
Roseberry, Richard Lee 1953- *WhoE 93*
Rosebery, Earl of 1847-1929 *BioIn 17*
Rosebery, Richard J. 1935- *St&PR 93*
Roseborough, Joseph Anthony *Law&B 92*
Rosebrough, Carol Delville 1940- *WhoAmW 93*
Rosebrough, Walter M., Jr. 1954- *WhoAm 92*
Rosebury, Amy L. 1918- *WhoE 93*
Rosebush, James Scott 1949- *WhoAm 92*
Rosecrans, Clarence Jacob, Jr. 1927- *WhoSSW 93*
Rosecrans, William Starke 1819-1898 *HarEnMi*
Rosedahl, David Evans *Law&B 92*
Rosedahl, David Evans 1947- *St&PR 93*
Rosefeldt, Paul Nagim 1944- *WhoSSW 93*
Rosefield, Herbert Aaron, Jr. 1943- *WhoSSW 93*
Rosefielde, Alan Paul 1946- *WhoSSW 93*
Rosegger, Gerhard 1930- *WhoAm 92*
Rose-Hansen, John 1937- *WhoWor 93*
Rosehart, Robert George 1943- *WhoAm 92*
Rose-Hayes, Karla Lavon 1947- *WhoAmW 93, WhoEmL 93, WhoSSW 93, WhoWor 93*
Rosei, Maria Anna 1946- *WhoWor 93*
Roseig, Esther Marian 1917- *WhoWor 93*
Rosel, Artur 1859-1934 *Baker 92*
Rosel, Peter 1945- *Baker 92*
Roselaers, Frans 1946- *WhoUN 92*
Roseliep, Robert Edward 1934- *St&PR 93*
Roselinsky, Alan 1945- *St&PR 93*
Rosell, Lars-Erik 1944- *Baker 92*
Rosell, Robert Stewart 1961- *WhoScE 91-1*
Rosell, Sune *WhoScE 91-4*
Rosella, John Daniel 1938- *WhoWor 93*
Roselle, David Paul 1939- *WhoAm 92, WhoE 93*
Roselle, James E. *Law&B 92*
Roselle, Richard Donaldson 1916- *WhoWor 93*
Roselle, Robert Paul 1925- *St&PR 93*
Roselle, William Charles 1936- *WhoAm 92*
Rosellen, Henri 1811-1876 *Baker 92*
Roselli, Daniel *St&PR 93*
Roselli, Evelyn *St&PR 93*
Roselli, Rina *Law&B 92*
Roselli, Victor J. *St&PR 93*
Rosellini, Robert Amerigo 1946- *WhoE 93*
Roseman, Carey Schwartz *Law&B 92*
Roseman, Catherine R. *Law&B 92*
Roseman, George H. 1937- *St&PR 93*
Roseman, Mill 1921- *St&PR 93*
Roseman, Saul 1921- *WhoAm 92*
Roseman, Susan Carol 1950- *WhoAmW 93, WhoE 93*
Roseman, Walda *BioIn 17*
Rosemann, Gerd E. *WhoScE 91-3*
Rosemberg, Eugenia 1918- *WhoAm 92*
Rosemon, Mabel J. *AmWomPl*
Rosemond, Bruce W. 1934- *St&PR 93*
Rosemont, Franklin 1943- *WhoWrEP 92*
Rosemont, Norman 1924- *WhoAm 92*
Rosemore, Fredric Michael 1923- *St&PR 93*
Rosen, A. Eric *Law&B 92*
Rosen, Albert Leonard 1924- *BiDAMSp 1989, WhoAm 92*
Rosen, Andrew Mayer 1951- *St&PR 93, WhoAm 92*
Rosen, Andrew S. *Law&B 92*
Rosen, Ann Kelly *Law&B 92*
Rosen, Arthur Marvin 1930- *WhoAm 92*
Rosen, Arthur S. *Law&B 92*
Rosen, Barrie *Law&B 92*
Rosen, Barry 1944- *ConAu 136*
Rosen, Barry Howard 1942- *WhoAm 92*
Rosen, Benjamin Maurice 1933- *WhoAm 92, WhoSSW 93*
Rosen, Benson 1942- *WhoAm 92*
Rosen, Bernard 1927- *St&PR 93*
Rosen, Bernard 1934- *WhoE 93*
Rosen, Bernard H. 1922- *WhoAm 92*
Rosen, Bertram Howard 1933- *WhoE 93*
Rosen, Beth Dee 1945- *WhoAmW 93*
Rosen, Beverly Doris 1924- *WhoAmW 93*
Rosen, Bruce D. *Law&B 92*
Rosen, Bruce David 1946- *St&PR 93*
Rosen, Calvin R. *Law&B 92*
Rosen, Carol Mendes 1933- *WhoE 93*
Rosen, Catherine Elkin 1927- *WhoSSW 93*
Rosen, Charles, II 1925- *WhoAm 92*
Rosen, Charles (Welles) 1927- *Baker 92, WhoAm 92*
Rosen, Cheryl Hope 1963- *WhoE 93*
Rosen, Corey 1948- *ConAu 138*
Rosen, Craig H. *BioIn 17*
Rosen, Daniel Allan 1952- *WhoSSW 93*
Rosen, David Bruce 1958- *St&PR 93*
Rosen, David Henry 1945- *WhoWrEP 92*
Rosen, David Michael 1945- *WhoE 93*
Rosen, Deborah A. *Law&B 92*
Rosen, Deborah Ann 1944- *WhoAmW 93*
Rosen, Dolly 1950- *St&PR 93*
Rosen, Donald Jules 1933- *WhoE 93*
Rosen, Edith S. *Law&B 92*
Rosen, Ellen Freda 1941- *WhoSSW 93*
Rosen, Ellen Israel d1991 *BioIn 17*
Rosen, Ellen S. *Law&B 92*
Rosen, Eric von 1879-1948 *IntDcAn*
Rosen, Esther *St&PR 93*
Rosen, Eve Cutler 1952- *WhoIns 93*
Rosen, Frank Stanley 1937- *WhoE 93*
Rosen, Fred Saul 1930- *WhoAm 92*
Rosen, Gary 1947- *See* Rosenshontz *ConMus 9*
Rosen, George 1920- *WhoAm 92*
Rosen, George M. 1936- *WhoAm 92*
Rosen, George Michel 1950- *WhoE 93*
Rosen, Gerald Ellis 1951- *WhoAm 92*
Rosen, Gerald Harris 1933- *WhoAm 92*
Rosen, Gerald M. 1940- *St&PR 93*
Rosen, Gerald Robert 1930- *WhoAm 92*
Rosen, Harvey Sheldon 1949- *WhoE 93*
Rosen, Herbert Irving 1922- *St&PR 93, WhoAm 92*
Rosen, Howard 1929- *St&PR 93*
Rosen, Irving 1928- *St&PR 93*
Rosen, Irving Louis 1928- *WhoSSW 93*

Rosen, J. *WhoScE 91-2*
Rosen, James Carl 1949- *WhoE 93*
Rosen, Jay M. *Law&B 92*
Rosen, Jay Martin 1937- *St&PR 93*
Rosen, Jeffrey S. *Law&B 92*
Rosen, Jeffrey Solomon 1954- *WhoE 93*
Rosen, Jeffrey Stuart 1946- *WhoE 93*
Rosen, Jerome 1921- *WhoAm 92*
Rosen, Jerome (William) 1921- *Baker 92*
Rosen, Joel D. *Law&B 92*
Rosen, John 1957- *St&PR 93*
Rosen, John William 1948- *WhoSSW 93*
Rosen, Jonathan Martin 1954- *WhoE 93*
Rosen, Joshua Philip 1956- *WhoAm 92*
Rosen, Judah Ben 1922- *WhoAm 92*
Rosen, Judy R. 1942- *St&PR 93*
Rosen, Kaj V. 1949- *WhoScE 91-4*
Rosen, Kenneth Roy 1950- *St&PR 93, WhoIns 93*
Rosen, Lawrence 1937- *WhoE 93*
Rosen, Lawrence 1941- *WhoAm 92*
Rosen, Lawrence J. 1943- *St&PR 93*
Rosen, Lawrence Ronald 1938- *WhoSSW 93*
Rosen, Leonard William 1917- *St&PR 93*
Rosen, Lillian 1928- *BioIn 17*
Rosen, Louis 1918- *WhoAm 92*
Rosen, Manuel Morrison 1926- *WhoAm 92*
Rosen, Marcella 1934- *St&PR 93*
Rosen, Marcella Jung 1934- *WhoAm 92*
Rosen, Mark L. 1943-1991 *BioIn 17*
Rosen, Mark Lawrence 1948- *St&PR 93*
Rosen, Marta 1939- *WhoWor 93*
Rosen, Martin *MiSFD 9*
Rosen, Marvin 1947- *St&PR 93*
Rosen, Maurice M. 1920- *St&PR 93*
Rosen, Max 1900-1956 *Baker 92*
Rosen, Mel *BioIn 17*
Rosen, Melvin L. d1992 *NewYTBS 92 [port]*
Rosen, Michael Elliott 1942- *WhoSSW 93*
Rosen, Michael J. 1954- *WhoWrEP 92*
Rosen, Michael Jordon 1961- *WhoE 93*
Rosen, Michael Robert 1961- *WhoWor 93*
Rosen, Milton Jacques 1920- *WhoE 93*
Rosen, Milton William 1915- *WhoE 93*
Rosen, Molly Ann 1941- *WhoAmW 93*
Rosen, Morris 1932- *WhoUN 92*
Rosen, Mortimer G. d1992 *NewYTBS 92*
Rosen, Mortimer Gilbert 1931- *WhoAm 92*
Rosen, Myor 1917- *WhoAm 92*
Rosen, Nathan 1914- *St&PR 93*
Rosen, Nathan B. *Law&B 92*
Rosen, Nathaniel (Kent) 1948- *Baker 92, WhoAm 92*
Rosen, Norma *WhoWrEP 92*
Rosen, Norman E. *Law&B 92*
Rosen, Norman Edward 1938- *WhoAm 92*
Rosen, Norman H. *Law&B 92*
Rosen, Ora M. 1935-1990 *BioIn 17*
Rosen, Phillip 1955- *St&PR 93*
Rosen, Rhoda 1933- *WhoAmW 93*
Rosen, Richard 1917- *WhoSSW 93*
Rosen, Richard Lewis 1943- *WhoAm 92*
Rosen, Richard M. 1935-1991 *BioIn 17*
Rosen, Robert Arnold 1936- *St&PR 93, WhoAm 92*
Rosen, Robert H. 1955- *ConAu 139*
Rosen, Robert L. 1937- *MiSFD 9*
Rosen, Robert L. 1946- *St&PR 93*
Rosen, Robert Lewis 1935- *WhoE 93*
Rosen, Robert Stanley 1936- *WhoSSW 93*
Rosen, Robert Stephen 1947- *WhoE 93*
Rosen, Robert Thomas 1941- *WhoE 93*
Rosen, Robin L. *Law&B 92*
Rosen, Sam 1920- *WhoAm 92*
Rosen, Saul d1990 *BioIn 17*
Rosen, Seymour 1927- *WhoE 93*
Rosen, Sherman David 1930- *St&PR 93*
Rosen, Sherwin 1938- *WhoAm 92*
Rosen, Sidney 1926- *WhoE 93*
Rosen, Sindey 1913- *St&PR 93*
Rosen, Stanley Howard 1929- *WhoAm 92*
Rosen, Stanley W. 1932- *St&PR 93*
Rosen, Stephen R. *Law&B 92*
Rosen, Steven 1950- *WhoAm 92*
Rosen, Sue-Ann *Law&B 92*
Rosen, Theodore Howard 1947- *WhoE 93*
Rosen, William 1926- *WhoAm 92*
Rosen, William M. 1935- *St&PR 93*
Rosen, William Warren 1936- *WhoAm 92, WhoSSW 93*
Rosenak, Chuck *BioIn 17*
Rosenak, Jan *BioIn 17*
Rosenau, Blanche Gottardo 1918- *WhoAmW 93*
Rosenau, James Nathan 1924- *WhoAm 92, WhoWrEP 92*
Rosenau, John Rudolph 1943- *WhoE 93*
Rosenau, William W. 1928-1991 *BioIn 17*
Rosenauer, Libby Lois 1930- *WhoAmW 93*
Rosenbalm, Richard L. 1952- *St&PR 93*
Rosenband, Debra E. *Law&B 92*
Rosenbauer, Helmut 1936- *WhoScE 91-3*
Rosenbaum, Albert B. 1949- *St&PR 93*
Rosenbaum, Allen 1937- *WhoAm 92*
Rosenbaum, Arthur Elihu 1935- *WhoAm 92*
Rosenbaum, Arthur Saul 1953- *WhoE 93*
Rosenbaum, Belle Sara 1922- *WhoE 93*
Rosenbaum, Bruce T. *Law&B 92*
Rosenbaum, Carl S. 1934- *St&PR 93*
Rosenbaum, David d1991 *BioIn 17*
Rosenbaum, Edward E. 1915- *BioIn 17, ConAu 139*
Rosenbaum, Emanuel *St&PR 93*
Rosenbaum, F. Rainer 1945- *WhoUN 92*
Rosenbaum, Greg Alan 1952- *St&PR 93*
Rosenbaum, H.K. 1916- *St&PR 93*
Rosenbaum, Hope Elizabeth *Law&B 92*
Rosenbaum, Howard Stewart 1949- *WhoE 93*
Rosenbaum, Irving M. 1921- *WhoAm 92*
Rosenbaum, Jacob I. 1927- *St&PR 93, WhoAm 92*
Rosenbaum, Joan Hannah 1942- *WhoAm 92, WhoAmW 93, WhoE 93*
Rosenbaum, Joseph I. *Law&B 92*
Rosenbaum, Keith 1945- *WhoSSW 93*
Rosenbaum, Maj-Britt Anita Sofia 1937- *WhoAmW 93*
Rosenbaum, Martin M. 1923- *WhoIns 93*
Rosenbaum, Martin Michael 1923- *St&PR 93*
Rosenbaum, Michael A. 1953- *WhoAm 92*
Rosenbaum, Michael F. *Law&B 92*
Rosenbaum, Paul Leonard 1937- *WhoAm 92*
Rosenbaum, Richard Merrill 1931- *WhoAm 92*
Rosenbaum, Robert Abraham 1915- *WhoAm 92*
Rosenbaum, Sheldon A. 1948- *WhoE 93*
Rosenbaum, Steven Ira 1946- *WhoAm 92, WhoE 93*
Rosenbaum, Stuart Evan 1943- *WhoSSW 93*
Rosenbaum, Sylvia P. *WhoWrEP 92*
Rosenbaum, Therese Maria 1774-1837 *See* Gassmann, Florian Leopold 1729-1774 *OxDcOp*
Rosenberg, A. Richard 1938- *WhoAm 92*
Rosenberg, Aaron Edward 1937- *WhoAm 92*
Rosenberg, Alan Stewart 1930- *WhoAm 92*
Rosenberg, Alberto 1937- *WhoAm 92*
Rosenberg, Alex 1926- *WhoAm 92*
Rosenberg, Alex Jacob 1919- *WhoAm 92, WhoWor 93*
Rosenberg, Alexander 1946- *WhoAm 92*
Rosenberg, Alfred 1893-1946 *DcTwHis*
Rosenberg, Alison P. 1945- *WhoAm 92, WhoAmW 93*
Rosenberg, Allen E. 1935- *St&PR 93*
Rosenberg, Allison Anne 1959- *WhoE 93*
Rosenberg, Anita *MiSFD 9*
Rosenberg, Arnold 1941- *St&PR 93*
Rosenberg, Arthur Donald 1939- *WhoE 93*
Rosenberg, Arthur James 1926- *St&PR 93, WhoAm 92*
Rosenberg, Barbara Hatch 1928- *WhoE 93*
Rosenberg, Barnett 1944- *St&PR 93*
Rosenberg, Barr Marvin 1942- *WhoAm 92*
Rosenberg, Bernard *St&PR 93*
Rosenberg, Bernard 1928- *WhoAm 92*
Rosenberg, Betty 1916- *ScF&FL 92*
Rosenberg, Bruce Alan 1934- *WhoAm 92, WhoWrEP 92*
Rosenberg, Bruce M. 1947- *St&PR 93*
Rosenberg, Bruce Michael *Law&B 92*
Rosenberg, Burton M. *WhoAm 92*
Rosenberg, Carole 1936- *WhoE 93*
Rosenberg, Carolyn M. 1956- *WhoSSW 93*
Rosenberg, Charles Ernest 1936- *WhoAm 92, WhoWrEP 92*
Rosenberg, Charles Harvey 1919- *WhoE 93*
Rosenberg, Charles Michael 1945- *WhoAm 92*
Rosenberg, Claude N. *BioIn 17*
Rosenberg, Claude Newman, Jr. 1928- *WhoAm 92*
Rosenberg, Cy *St&PR 93*
Rosenberg, Dan 1944- *St&PR 93, WhoE 93*
Rosenberg, David *Law&B 92*
Rosenberg, David 1934- *St&PR 93*
Rosenberg, David Alan 1948- *WhoAm 92, WhoE 93*
Rosenberg, David Howard 1941- *WhoAm 92*
Rosenberg, Dennis Melville Leo 1921- *WhoAm 92*
Rosenberg, Donald C. *Law&B 92*
Rosenberg, Donald Jay *Law&B 92*
Rosenberg, Donald M. 1933- *St&PR 93*
Rosenberg, Donald Martin 1933- *WhoAm 92*
Rosenberg, Edgar *BioIn 17*
Rosenberg, Edgar 1925- *WhoAm 92*
Rosenberg, Eduardo German 1939- *St&PR 93*
Rosenberg, Eric M. *Law&B 92*
Rosenberg, Ethel 1915-1953 *BioIn 17, ColdWar 1 [port]*
Rosenberg, Frank Louis 1940- *St&PR 93*
Rosenberg, Fred Allan 1932- *WhoE 93*
Rosenberg, Gary Aron 1940- *WhoAm 92*
Rosenberg, George *WhoAm 92*
Rosenberg, Gerald Alan 1944- *WhoAm 92*
Rosenberg, Glenda Lerner 1939- *WhoAmW 93*
Rosenberg, Harold 1906-1978 *ConAu 39NR*
Rosenberg, Harry 1940- *WhoAm 92*
Rosenberg, Henry A., Jr. 1929- *St&PR 93, WhoAm 92, WhoE 93*
Rosenberg, Hernan 1947- *WhoUN 92*
Rosenberg, Hilding 1892-1985 *OxDcOp*
Rosenberg, Hilding (Constantin) 1892-1985 *Baker 92*
Rosenberg, Ira S. *Law&B 92*
Rosenberg, Irene Vera 1936- *WhoAmW 93*
Rosenberg, Irwin Harold 1935- *WhoAm 92*
Rosenberg, Jack *BioIn 17*
Rosenberg, Jacob Joseph 1947- *WhoE 93*
Rosenberg, James William 1958- *WhoE 93*
Rosenberg, Jay Arthur 1939- *WhoAm 92*
Rosenberg, Jay Frank 1942- *WhoWrEP 92*
Rosenberg, Jeffrey Stephen 1954- *St&PR 93*
Rosenberg, Jerome I. 1931- *WhoAm 92*
Rosenberg, Jerome Laib 1921- *WhoAm 92, WhoE 93*
Rosenberg, Jerome Roy 1926- *WhoWor 93*
Rosenberg, Jerry Martin 1935- *WhoAm 92, WhoWrEP 92*
Rosenberg, Joel 1954- *ScF&FL 92*
Rosenberg, John David 1929- *WhoAm 92, WhoWrEP 92*
Rosenberg, John K. *Law&B 92*
Rosenberg, John K. 1945- *St&PR 93, WhoAm 92*
Rosenberg, Jonathan *St&PR 93*
Rosenberg, Joseph Lawrence 1949- *WhoE 93*
Rosenberg, Joshua *Law&B 92*
Rosenberg, Judith Frima 1946- *WhoAmW 93*
Rosenberg, Judith M. *Law&B 92*
Rosenberg, Judith Meta 1964- *WhoAmW 93*
Rosenberg, Julian D. d1989 *BioIn 17*
Rosenberg, Julius 1918-1953 *BioIn 17, ColdWar 1 [port]*
Rosenberg, Katherine B. *Law&B 92*
Rosenberg, Kenneth 1946- *St&PR 93*
Rosenberg, Lawrence Joseph 1941- *WhoE 93*
Rosenberg, Leon E. 1933- *WhoAm 92*
Rosenberg, Leon Joseph 1918- *WhoAm 92*
Rosenberg, Leslie Karen 1949- *WhoAmW 93*
Rosenberg, Lisa 1953- *WhoAmW 93*
Rosenberg, Liz *NewYTBS 92*
Rosenberg, Louis 1898- *WhoAm 92*
Rosenberg, Lyndon Harvey *Law&B 92*
Rosenberg, Manuel 1930- *WhoAm 92*
Rosenberg, Marianne 1954- *WhoAmW 93*
Rosenberg, Mark H. d1992 *NewYTBS 92*
Rosenberg, Marshal E. 1936- *WhoSSW 93*
Rosenberg, Marshall *Law&B 92*
Rosenberg, Marvin B. *Law&B 92*
Rosenberg, Maurice 1919- *WhoAm 92, WhoWrEP 92*
Rosenberg, Michael 1927- *WhoScE 91-3*
Rosenberg, Michael 1928- *St&PR 93*
Rosenberg, Michael 1937- *WhoAm 92*
Rosenberg, Michael A. *Law&B 92*
Rosenberg, Michael Joseph 1928- *WhoAm 92, WhoE 93*
Rosenberg, Michael L. 1944- *WhoAm 92*
Rosenberg, Milton Hertz 1912- *WhoE 93*
Rosenberg, Milton J. 1925- *WhoAm 92*
Rosenberg, Mordechai 1933- *St&PR 93*
Rosenberg, Morris *BioIn 17*
Rosenberg, Morton David 1929- *WhoE 93*
Rosenberg, Morton Yale 1932- *WhoAm 92*
Rosenberg, Nancy Sherman 1931- *WhoWrEP 92*
Rosenberg, Nathan 1927- *WhoAm 92*
Rosenberg, Neal W. *Law&B 92*
Rosenberg, Norman 1916- *WhoAm 92*
Rosenberg, Norman Jack 1930- *WhoAm 92*
Rosenberg, Paul 1910- *WhoAm 92*
Rosenberg, Paul B. 1932- *St&PR 93*
Rosenberg, Peter A. 1943- *St&PR 93*
Rosenberg, Peter David 1942- *WhoE 93*
Rosenberg, Priscilla Elliott *Law&B 92*
Rosenberg, Raben 1946- *WhoWor 93*
Rosenberg, Ralph S. 1931- *St&PR 93*
Rosenberg, Raymond 1922- *St&PR 93*
Rosenberg, Raymond David 1951- *WhoE 93*
Rosenberg, Richard M. *BioIn 17*
Rosenberg, Richard Morris 1930- *St&PR 93, WhoAm 92, WhoWor 93*
Rosenberg, Robert *Law&B 92, St&PR 93*
Rosenberg, Robert Allen 1935- *WhoE 93*
Rosenberg, Robert Brinkmann 1937- *WhoAm 92*
Rosenberg, Robert C. 1934- *St&PR 93*
Rosenberg, Robert Craig 1951- *WhoE 93*
Rosenberg, Robert D. *Law&B 92*
Rosenberg, Robert M. 1938- *St&PR 93*
Rosenberg, Robert Michael 1938- *WhoAm 92*
Rosenberg, Roger Newman 1939- *WhoAm 92*
Rosenberg, Ronald I. 1936- *St&PR 93*
Rosenberg, Rudy 1930- *St&PR 93, WhoE 93*
Rosenberg, Rutger 1943- *WhoScE 91-4*
Rosenberg, Ruth Helen Borsuk 1935- *WhoAm 92*
Rosenberg, S. Lee 1949- *St&PR 93*
Rosenberg, Samuel Nathan 1936- *WhoAm 92*
Rosenberg, Sandor 1946- *St&PR 93*
Rosenberg, Sarah Zacher 1931- *WhoAm 92*
Rosenberg, Saul Allen 1927- *WhoAm 92*
Rosenberg, Seymour 1917- *St&PR 93*
Rosenberg, Seymour 1926- *WhoAm 92*
Rosenberg, Shelby 1942- *St&PR 93*
Rosenberg, Sheli *Law&B 92*
Rosenberg, Sheli Z. *Law&B 92*
Rosenberg, Sheli Zysman 1942- *WhoAm 92*
Rosenberg, Shirley Sirota *WhoE 93*
Rosenberg, Sigmond *St&PR 93*
Rosenberg, Steven A. *BioIn 17*
Rosenberg, Steven Aaron 1940- *WhoAm 92*
Rosenberg, Steven M. *Law&B 92*
Rosenberg, Steven Mark 1947- *WhoE 93*
Rosenberg, Steven Neil *Law&B 92*
Rosenberg, Stuart 1927- *ConTFT 10, WhoAm 92*
Rosenberg, Stuart 1928- *MiSFD 9*
Rosenberg, Stuart E. 1922-1990 *BioIn 17*
Rosenberg, Suzanne 1915- *BioIn 17*
Rosenberg, Sydney J. 1914- *St&PR 93*
Rosenberg, Theodore T. 1909- *St&PR 93*
Rosenberg, Thomas *WhoScE 91-2*
Rosenberg, Thomas M. *Law&B 92*
Rosenberg, Tina 1960- *ConAu 136*
Rosenberg, Victor I. 1936- *WhoE 93*
Rosenberg, Victor Laurence 1944- *WhoE 93, WhoWor 93*
Rosenberg, Warren 1954- *WhoE 93*
Rosenberg, William *BioIn 17*
Rosenberg, William Harry 1949- *WhoE 93*
Rosenberg, William S. *Law&B 92*
Rosenberg, Zena 1918- *St&PR 93*
Rosenberger, Alice Lynn 1962- *WhoAmW 93*
Rosenberger, Carol 1935- *WhoAm 92*
Rosenberger, Charles Meredith *Law&B 92*
Rosenberger, Donald Markley 1913- *WhoAm 92*
Rosenberger, Ernst Hey 1931- *WhoAm 92*
Rosenberger, Francis Coleman 1915- *WhoWrEP 92*
Rosenberger, Frank Joseph 1947- *St&PR 93*
Rosenberger, Franz Ernst 1933- *WhoSSW 93*
Rosenberger, Joseph *ScF&FL 92*
Rosenberger, Marcus L. *St&PR 93*
Rosenberger, Patricia Hirt 1955- *WhoAmW 93*
Rosenberger, Walter Emerson 1918- *WhoAm 92*
Rosenberg Family *BioIn 17*
Rosenberry, Frank A. 1937- *St&PR 93*
Rosenblatt, Albert Martin 1936- *WhoAm 92*
Rosenblatt, Alice 1948- *St&PR 93*
Rosenblatt, Arthur Isaac 1931- *WhoAm 92*
Rosenblatt, Arthur S. 1938- *BioIn 17*
Rosenblatt, Charles B. 1926- *St&PR 93*
Rosenblatt, Daniel Charles 1946- *WhoSSW 93*
Rosenblatt, Gerd Matthew 1933- *WhoAm 92*
Rosenblatt, Gregory S. *Law&B 92*
Rosenblatt, Harvey 1939- *St&PR 93*
Rosenblatt, Howard 1933- *St&PR 93*
Rosenblatt, Howard Marshall 1947- *WhoSSW 93*
Rosenblatt, Jason P. 1941- *ConAu 137*
Rosenblatt, Jason Philip 1941- *WhoE 93*
Rosenblatt, Joan Raup 1926- *WhoAmW 93*
Rosenblatt, Joe 1933- *WhoCanL 92*
Rosenblatt, Joel I. *Law&B 92*
Rosenblatt, Joseph 1933- *WhoAm 92*
Rosenblatt, Julia Carlson 1940- *WhoE 93*
Rosenblatt, Leonard 1929-1990 *BioIn 17*

Rosenblatt, Lester 1920- *WhoAm 92, WhoWor 93*
Rosenblatt, Louis 1928- *WhoAm 92*
Rosenblatt, Marc Saul 1950- *St&PR 93*
Rosenblatt, Michael 1947- *WhoAm 92*
Rosenblatt, Murray 1926- *WhoAm 92*
Rosenblatt, Paul 1928- *WhoWrEP 92*
Rosenblatt, Peter Ronald 1933- *WhoAm 92*
Rosenblatt, Robert John 1956- *WhoE 93*
Rosenblatt, Roger *BioIn 17*
Rosenblatt, Roger 1940- *WhoAm 92*
Rosenblatt, Roger Alan 1945- *WhoAm 92*
Rosenblatt, Ruth 1934- *WhoWrEP 92*
Rosenblatt, Sidney Marvin 1939- *WhoE 93*
Rosenblatt, Sol 1929- *St&PR 93*
Rosenblatt, Stephen Paul 1935- *WhoAm 92*
Rosenbleeth, Michael *WhoIns 93*
Rosenbleeth, Richard Marvin 1932- *WhoAm 92*
Rosenblith, Robert Michael *Law&B 92*
Rosenblith, Walter Alter 1913- *WhoAm 92*
Rosenbloom, Alan B. *Law&B 92*
Rosenbloom, Arlan Lee 1934- *WhoAm 92*
Rosenbloom, Bert 1944- *WhoAm 92, WhoE 93*
Rosenbloom, Daniel 1930- *St&PR 93, WhoAm 92*
Rosenbloom, H. David 1941- *WhoAm 92*
Rosenbloom, Jerry Samuel 1939- *WhoIns 93*
Rosenbloom, Morris Victor 1915- *WhoAm 92, WhoWor 93*
Rosenbloom, Oscar Alan *Law&B 92*
Rosenbloom, Peter C. *Law&B 92*
Rosenbloom, Richard H. 1939- *St&PR 93*
Rosenbloom, Richard Selig 1933- *WhoAm 92*
Rosenbloom, Samuel *Law&B 92*
Rosenbloom, Samuel M. *Law&B 92*
Rosenbloom, Sanford M. 1928- *WhoAm 92*
Rosenblueth, Emilio 1926- *WhoAm 92*
Rosenblum, A. 1943-1991 *BioIn 17*
Rosenblum, Arnold 1935- *St&PR 93*
Rosenblum, Arnold 1943-1991 *BioIn 17*
Rosenblum, Bernard William 1948- *WhoE 93*
Rosenblum, Bruce *BioIn 17*
Rosenblum, Cynthia Shipman 1954- *WhoAmW 93*
Rosenblum, David Marcus *Law&B 92*
Rosenblum, Harold *Law&B 92*
Rosenblum, Harold 1918- *WhoSSW 93*
Rosenblum, Harold Arthur 1923- *WhoAm 92*
Rosenblum, Harvey 1943- *St&PR 93*
Rosenblum, Jerald E. 1935- *St&PR 93*
Rosenblum, Jerold H. *Law&B 92*
Rosenblum, John William 1944- *WhoAm 92*
Rosenblum, Joseph 1952- *St&PR 93*
Rosenblum, Judith Barbara 1951- *WhoAmW 93*
Rosenblum, Leonard Allen 1936- *WhoE 93*
Rosenblum, M. Edgar 1932- *WhoAm 92*
Rosenblum, Mark C. *Law&B 92*
Rosenblum, Marshall 1947- *WhoE 93*
Rosenblum, Martin J(ack) 1946- *ConAu 40NR*
Rosenblum, Martin Jack 1946- *WhoWrEP 92*
Rosenblum, Martin Jerome 1948- *WhoEmL 93, WhoSSW 93*
Rosenblum, Marvin 1926- *WhoAm 92*
Rosenblum, Mathew 1954- *Baker 92*
Rosenblum, Mindy Fleischer 1951- *WhoAmW 93*
Rosenblum, Myron 1925- *WhoAm 92*
Rosenblum, Ralph 1925- *MiSFD 9*
Rosenblum, Robert *ScF&FL 92, WhoAm 92*
Rosenblum, Robert 1927- *WhoAm 92*
Rosenblum, Stewart Irwin *WhoWor 93*
Rosenblum, Victor Gregory 1925- *WhoAm 92*
Rosenblum, William F., Jr. *Law&B 92*
Rosenblum, William Franklin, Jr. 1935- *St&PR 93*
Rosenbluth, J. William d1991 *BioIn 17*
Rosenbluth, Leon d1990 *BioIn 17*
Rosenbluth, Leonard Robert 1933- *BiDAMSp 1989*
Rosenbluth, Marshall Nicholas 1927- *WhoAm 92*
Rosenbluth, Michael Albert 1930- *WhoAm 92*
Rosenbluth, Morton 1924- *WhoAm 92*
Rosenbluth, Sidney Alan 1933- *WhoAm 92*
Rosenbohm, Elimar 1916- *WhoWor 93*
Rosenbohm, Kay F. *Law&B 92*
Rosenboom, David (Charles) 1947- *Baker 92*
Rosenborg, Ralph 1913-1992 *NewYTBS 92*
Rosenborg, Ralph Mozart 1913- *WhoAm 92*
Rosenburg, Robert Kemper 1920- *WhoWrEP 92*
Rosenburgh, Dwayne Maurice 1960- *WhoE 93*
Rosenbury, W. Mark 1947- *St&PR 93*
Rosenbusch, Jurg P. 1938- *WhoScE 91-3*
Rosencrans, Chip 1952- *St&PR 93*
Rosencrans, Evan William 1926- *WhoAm 92*
Rosencrantz, Lawrence 1945- *St&PR 93, WhoAm 92*
Rosendal, Ib 1934- *WhoScE 91-2*
Rosendhal, Jeffrey David 1941- *WhoAm 92*
Rosendin, Raymond Joseph 1929- *St&PR 93, WhoAm 92*
Rosene, Linda Roberts 1938- *WhoSSW 93*
Rosene, Ralph Walfred 1938- *WhoSSW 93*
Rosener, Judy Bogen 1929- *WhoAmW 93*
Rosenfalck, Annelise 1922- *WhoWor 93*
Rosenfarb, Chava *WhoCanL 92*
Rosenfeld, A. Victor 1916- *St&PR 93*
Rosenfeld, Alvin Z. d1992 *NewYTBS 92*
Rosenfeld, Alvin (Z.) 1919-1992 *ConAu 139*
Rosenfeld, Arnold Solomon 1933- *WhoAm 92, WhoWrEP 92*
Rosenfeld, Arthur H. 1926- *WhoAm 92*
Rosenfeld, Arthur H. 1930- *WhoAm 92*
Rosenfeld, Azriel 1931- *WhoAm 92*
Rosenfeld, Boris Abramovich 1917- *WhoE 93*
Rosenfeld, Charles Richard 1941- *WhoSSW 93*
Rosenfeld, Claude 1933- *WhoScE 91-2*
Rosenfeld, Eric R. *BioIn 17*
Rosenfeld, Franklyn P. *Law&B 92*
Rosenfeld, Harold E. *Law&B 92*
Rosenfeld, Harold E. 1951- *St&PR 93*
Rosenfeld, Herbert *St&PR 93*
Rosenfeld, Isaac 1918-1956 *JeAmFiW*
Rosenfeld, Isadore 1926- *ConAu 40NR*
Rosenfeld, J.A. 1932- *St&PR 93*
Rosenfeld, Jerold Charles 1943- *WhoE 93*
Rosenfeld, Joel 1957- *WhoWor 93*
Rosenfeld, Joseph 1907- *WhoE 93, WhoWor 93*
Rosenfeld, Leonard Sidney 1913-1990 *BioIn 17*
Rosenfeld, Leopold 1850-1909 *Baker 92*
Rosenfeld, Mark Allan d1991 *BioIn 17*
Rosenfeld, Mark K. 1946- *St&PR 93*
Rosenfeld, Mark Kenneth 1946- *WhoAm 92*
Rosenfeld, Nancy *WhoAm 92*
Rosenfeld, Nancy P. *Law&B 92*
Rosenfeld, Norman H. 1919- *St&PR 93*
Rosenfeld, Paul (Leopold) 1890-1946 *Baker 92*
Rosenfeld, Robert Maurice 1928- *St&PR 93*
Rosenfeld, Ronald Norman *WhoE 93*
Rosenfeld, Stephen Samuel 1932- *WhoAm 92*
Rosenfeld, Steven Ira 1949- *WhoE 93, WhoEmL 93*
Rosenfeld, Susan *BioIn 17*
Rosenfeld, Walter David, Jr. 1930- *WhoAm 92*
Rosenfeld, William Peter 1936- *St&PR 93*
Rosenfeld, Yechiel 1948- *St&PR 93*
Rosenfelder, Alfred S. 1916- *St&PR 93, WhoIns 93*
Rosenfelder, Michael 1935- *St&PR 93*
Rosenfelt, Frank Edward 1921- *WhoAm 92*
Rosenfelt, Scott *MiSFD 9*
Rosenfield, Allan 1933- *WhoAm 92*
Rosenfield, Arthur Ted 1942- *WhoE 93*
Rosenfield, George *BioIn 17*
Rosenfield, James Alexander 1938- *WhoSSW 93*
Rosenfield, James H. 1929- *St&PR 93*
Rosenfield, James Harold 1929- *WhoAm 92*
Rosenfield, James R. *BioIn 17*
Rosenfield, Jay 1948- *St&PR 93*
Rosenfield, Jay Gary 1948- *WhoAm 92*
Rosenfield, John Max 1924- *WhoAm 92, WhoWor 93*
Rosenfield, Maurice Lillman 1909- *St&PR 93*
Rosenfield, Maurice Ullman 1909- *WhoAm 92*
Rosenfield, Paul 1948- *ConAu 139*
Rosenfield, Paul William *Law&B 92*
Rosenfield, Robert Lee 1934- *WhoAm 92*
Rosenfield, Sheryl *BioIn 17*
Rosengarten, Alfred d1990 *BioIn 17*
Rosengarten, Herbert (J.) 1940- *ConAu 138*
Rosengren, Bengt Henrik Oscar 1927- *WhoScE 91-4*
Rosengren, Jenny 1965- *WhoWor 93*
Rosengren, Paul G. *Law&B 92*
Rosengren, William R. *Law&B 92*
Rosengren, William R. 1934- *WhoAm 92*
Rosengren, William Roy 1934- *St&PR 93*
Rosenhagen, Ronald Wayne 1934- *WhoSSW 93*
Rosenhain, Eduard 1818-1861 See Rosenhain, Jacob 1813-1894 *Baker 92*
Rosenhain, Jacob 1813-1894 *Baker 92*
Rosenhan, Alvin Kirk 1940- *WhoSSW 93*
Rosenhauer, Matthias 1940- *WhoScE 91-3*
Rosenhead, Jonathan Vivian *WhoScE 91-1*
Rosenheim, Andrew 1955- *ConAu 139*
Rosenheim, Daniel Edward 1949- *WhoAm 92*
Rosenheim, Donald Edwin 1926- *WhoAm 92*
Rosenheim, Edward Weil 1918- *WhoAm 92*
Rosenheim, Howard Harris 1915- *WhoAm 92*
Rosenheim, Margaret Keeney 1926- *WhoAm 92*
Rosenhoffer, Chris 1913- *WhoWor 93*
Rosenholm, Jarl B. 1946- *WhoScE 91-4*
Rosenholtz, Jerome 1932- *St&PR 93*
Rosenhouse, Irwin *WhoE 93*
Rosenhouse, Michael Allan 1946- *WhoE 93*
Rosenker, Mark Victor 1946- *WhoAm 92*
Rosenkilde, Per 1930- *WhoScE 91-2*
Rosenkoetter, Gerald E. 1927- *St&PR 93*
Rosenkoetter, Gerald Edwin 1927- *WhoAm 92*
Rosenkrantz, Amy *Law&B 92*
Rosenkrantz, Barbara Gutmann 1923- *WhoAm 92*
Rosenkrantz, Carol M. 1947- *St&PR 93*
Rosenkrantz, Daniel J. 1943- *WhoAm 92*
Rosenkrantz, Linda 1934- *WhoAmW 93*
Rosenkrantz, Rita R. 1934- *WhoAmW 93*
Rosenkrantz, Robert 1947- *St&PR 93*
Rosenkranz, Franklin Daniel 1945- *St&PR 93*
Rosenkranz, Gerardo Miguel 1951- *WhoE 93*
Rosenkranz, Herbert S. 1933- *WhoAm 92, WhoE 93*
Rosenkranz, Morty 1928- *St&PR 93*
Rosenkranz, Robert 1942- *St&PR 93*
Rosenkranz, Robert Bernard 1939- *WhoAm 92*
Rosenkranz, Stanley William 1933- *WhoAm 92*
Rosenman, Dorothy 1900-1991 *BioIn 17*
Rosenman, John Brown 1941- *WhoWrEP 92*
Rosenman, Leonard 1924- *Baker 92*
Rosenman, Stanley 1923- *WhoE 93*
Rosenman, Stephen David 1945- *WhoE 93*
Rosenmuller, Johann c. 1619-1684 *Baker 92*
Rosenn, Harold 1917- *WhoAm 92, WhoE 93*
Rosenn, Keith Samuel 1938- *WhoAm 92*
Rosenn, Max 1910- *WhoAm 92, WhoE 93*
Rosenne, Meir 1931- *WhoAm 92*
Rosenoer, Jonathan *Law&B 92*
Rosenow, Edward Carl, III 1934- *WhoAm 92*
Rosenow, James F. *Law&B 92*
Rosenow, John Edward 1949- *WhoAm 92*
Rosenow, John Henry 1913- *WhoAm 92*
Rosenquist, Glenn Carl 1931- *WhoAm 92*
Rosenquist, J.B. 1939- *WhoScE 91-4*
Rosenquist, James Albert 1933- *WhoAm 92*
Rosenquist, James W. *Law&B 92*
Rosenquist, Kay-Sune 1937- *WhoWor 93*
Rosenquit, Bernard 1923-1991 *BioIn 17*
Rosenqvist, Heikki J. 1942- *WhoScE 91-4*
Rosensaft, Menachem Z. *Law&B 92*
Rosensaft, Menachem Zwi 1948- *WhoAm 92, WhoE 93, WhoWor 93*
Rosenschein, Guy Raoul 1953- *WhoWor 93*
Rosenshein, Neil 1947- *Baker 92*
Rosenshine, Allen Gilbert 1939- *St&PR 93, WhoAm 92, WhoE 93*
Rosenshontz *ConMus 9 [port]*
Rosenspire, Karen Cheryl 1951- *WhoAmW 93*
Rosensteel, George T. 1947- *WhoAm 92, WhoSSW 93*
Rosensteel, John William 1940- *St&PR 93*
Rosensteele, James William 1948- *St&PR 93*
Rosenstein, Allen Bertram 1920- *WhoAm 92, WhoWor 93*
Rosenstein, Arnold 1953- *St&PR 93*
Rosenstein, Arthur *Law&B 92*
Rosenstein, Beryl Joel 1937- *WhoAm 92*
Rosenstein, Conrad 1910-1978 *BioIn 17*
Rosenstein, David H. 1933- *St&PR 93*
Rosenstein, Earl 1932- *St&PR 93*
Rosenstein, Henri 1941- *WhoWor 93*
Rosenstein, Irwin B. *Law&B 92*
Rosenstein, Irwin Lawrence 1936- *St&PR 93*
Rosenstein, James Alfred 1939- *WhoAm 92*
Rosenstein, Laurence S. 1943- *WhoE 93*
Rosenstein, Neil Howard 1926- *St&PR 93*
Rosenstein, Perry 1926- *St&PR 93*
Rosenstein, Robert Bryce 1954- *WhoEmL 93*
Rosenstein, Samuel M. 1909- *CngDr 91, WhoAm 92*
Rosenstein, Walter S. *Law&B 92*
Rosenstiel, Leonie *WhoWrEP 92*
Rosenstock, Francyne N. 1951- *WhoWrEP 92*
Rosenstock, Harvey Allan 1940- *WhoSSW 93*
Rosenstock, Jack I. *WhoAm 92*
Rosenstock, Jerome *Law&B 92*
Rosenstock, Joseph 1895-1985 *Baker 92*
Rosenstock, Milton d1992 *NewYTBS 92*
Rosenstock, Milton 1917-1992 *BioIn 17*
Rosenstock, Morton 1929- *WhoE 93*
Rosenstock, Stanley C. 1923- *St&PR 93*
Rosenstreich, David Leon 1942- *WhoE 93*
Rosen-Supnick, Elaine Renee 1951- *WhoAmW 93*
Rosensweig, Ronald Ellis 1932- *WhoAm 92*
Rosensweig, Stanley Harold 1918- *WhoAm 92*
Rosensweig, Tod 1950- *St&PR 93*
Rosenswig, Deanna *BioIn 17*
Rosenthal, A. Ralph *WhoScE 91-1*
Rosenthal, Aaron 1914- *WhoAm 92*
Rosenthal, Abigail Laura 1937- *WhoE 93*
Rosenthal, Abraham M. 1922- *JrnUS*
Rosenthal, Abraham Michael 1922- *WhoAm 92, WhoWor 93, WhoWrEP 92*
Rosenthal, Alan Sayre 1926- *WhoAm 92*
Rosenthal, Alan Stephen 1939- *WhoAm 92*
Rosenthal, Albert Jay 1928- *WhoAm 92*
Rosenthal, Albert Joseph 1919- *WhoAm 92*
Rosenthal, Alexander E. 1912- *WhoIns 93*
Rosenthal, Amir *Law&B 92*
Rosenthal, Amnon 1934- *WhoAm 92*
Rosenthal, Andrew 1958- *St&PR 93*
Rosenthal, Arnold H. 1933- *WhoAm 92*
Rosenthal, Arnold Joseph 1922- *WhoE 93*
Rosenthal, Arnold R. 1942- *St&PR 93*
Rosenthal, Arthur Frederick 1931- *WhoE 93*
Rosenthal, Arthur Jesse 1919- *WhoAm 92*
Rosenthal, Bernard 1934- *ScF&FL 92*
Rosenthal, Bette Lee 1951- *WhoSSW 93*
Rosenthal, Carla F. *AmWomPl*
Rosenthal, Cary 1940- *St&PR 93*
Rosenthal, Charles M. 1935- *St&PR 93*
Rosenthal, David 1943- *St&PR 93*
Rosenthal, David H. 1945- *WhoWrEP 92*
Rosenthal, David Hershel d1992 *NewYTBS 92*
Rosenthal, David Michael 1961- *WhoE 93, WhoWor 93*
Rosenthal, Donald B. 1937- *WhoAm 92*
Rosenthal, Donna Myra 1944- *WhoE 93*
Rosenthal, Doris d1971 *BioIn 17*
Rosenthal, Douglas Eurico 1940- *WhoAm 92, WhoWrEP 92*
Rosenthal, Earl Edgar 1921- *WhoAm 92*
Rosenthal, Edward d1991 *BioIn 17*
Rosenthal, Eleanor *WhoAmW 93*
Rosenthal, Ely Manuel 1922- *WhoAm 92, WhoWor 93*
Rosenthal, Emily d1991 *BioIn 17*
Rosenthal, Felix 1925- *WhoE 93*
Rosenthal, Frank Vernon 1908- *WhoIns 93*
Rosenthal, Franz 1914- *WhoAm 92*
Rosenthal, Gary L. *St&PR 93*
Rosenthal, Gert 1935- *WhoUN 92, WhoWor 93*
Rosenthal, Halina d1991 *BioIn 17*
Rosenthal, Harold (David) 1917-1987 *Baker 92*
Rosenthal, Harold Leslie 1922- *WhoAm 92*
Rosenthal, Henry Bernard 1917- *WhoSSW 93*
Rosenthal, Herbert M. 1922- *St&PR 93*
Rosenthal, Herbert Marshall *WhoAm 92*
Rosenthal, Howard Landau *Law&B 92*
Rosenthal, Howard Lewis 1939- *WhoAm 92*
Rosenthal, Hubert Daniel Jean 1933- *WhoWor 93*
Rosenthal, Ira Maurice 1920- *WhoAm 92*
Rosenthal, Irving d1990 *BioIn 17*
Rosenthal, Irving 1931- *St&PR 93*
Rosenthal, J. William 1922- *WhoSSW 93*
Rosenthal, Jack 1930- *WhoAm 92, WhoWor 93*
Rosenthal, Jacob 1935- *WhoAm 92, WhoWrEP 92*
Rosenthal, Jaime Rolando 1936- *WhoWor 93*

Rosenthal, James D. 1932- *WhoAm 92*
Rosenthal, James Edward 1942- *WhoIns 93*
Rosenthal, Jim *St&PR 93*
Rosenthal, Julian Bernard 1908- *WhoAm 92*
Rosenthal, Leighton A. 1915- *WhoAm 92*
Rosenthal, Leonard 1947- *WhoE 93*
Rosenthal, Louis S. 1928- *St&PR 93*
Rosenthal, Lucy Gabrielle *WhoAm 92*
Rosenthal, M.L. 1917- *WhoWrEP 92*
Rosenthal, Macha Louis 1917- *WhoAm 92*
Rosenthal, Manuel 1904- *Baker 92*
Rosenthal, Marc 1946- *St&PR 93*
Rosenthal, Mark *MiSFD 9*
Rosenthal, Mark 1946- *BioIn 17*
Rosenthal, Mark Lawrence 1945- *WhoE 93*
Rosenthal, Martha Newman 1956- *WhoAmW 93*
Rosenthal, Martin Alek 1928- *St&PR 93*
Rosenthal, Marvin Bernard 1930- *WhoE 93*
Rosenthal, Michael A. 1955- *St&PR 93*
Rosenthal, Michael Ross 1939- *WhoAm 92*
Rosenthal, Milton Frederick 1913- *WhoAm 92*
Rosenthal, Mitchell Stephen 1935- *WhoWor 93*
Rosenthal, Moriz 1862-1946 *Baker 92*
Rosenthal, Morton H. *St&PR 93*
Rosenthal, Moses d1991 *BioIn 17*
Rosenthal, Moshe 1941- *WhoWor 93*
Rosenthal, Murray Wilford 1926- *WhoAm 92*
Rosenthal, Myron Martin 1930- *WhoAm 92*
Rosenthal, Nan 1937- *WhoAm 92*
Rosenthal, Peter 1946- *WhoAm 92*
Rosenthal, Ralph J. *Law&B 92*
Rosenthal, Rhoda *Law&B 92*
Rosenthal, Richard A. 1933- *St&PR 93*
Rosenthal, Richard A., Jr. *Law&B 92*
Rosenthal, Richard H. 1933- *St&PR 93*
Rosenthal, Richard L. 1916- *St&PR 93*
Rosenthal, Richard Scott *Law&B 92*
Rosenthal, Rick 1950- *MiSFD 9*
Rosenthal, Robert 1926-1989 *BioIn 17*
Rosenthal, Robert 1933- *WhoAm 92, WhoWrEP 92*
Rosenthal, Robert C. 1933- *St&PR 93*
Rosenthal, Robert E. 1945- *AfrAmBi*
Rosenthal, Robert J. *MiSFD 9*
Rosenthal, Rosa *AmWomPl*
Rosenthal, Shirley Florence Lord *WhoE 93*
Rosenthal, Sol 1934- *WhoAm 92*
Rosenthal, Sol Roy *WhoAm 92*
Rosenthal, Stanley Lawrence 1929- *WhoAm 92*
Rosenthal, Steven Siegmund 1949- *WhoAm 92*
Rosenthal, Stuart Alan 1945- *St&PR 93*
Rosenthal, Susan Barbara 1946- *WhoSSW 93*
Rosenthal, Susan Leslie 1956- *WhoAmW 93*
Rosenthal, Tomme N. 1926- *St&PR 93*
Rosenthal, Warren W. 1923- *WhoAm 92*
Rosenthal, Warren Weil 1923- *St&PR 93*
Rosenthal, William E. *Law&B 92*
Rosenthal, William Forshaw 1933- *WhoAm 92*
Rosenthal, William J. 1920- *WhoAm 92*
Rosenus, Alan Harvey 1940- *WhoWrEP 92*
Rosenwald, E. John, Jr. 1930- *St&PR 93*
Rosenwald, Julius 1862-1932 *BioIn 17, EncAACR*
Rosenwald, Peter Joseph 1935- *WhoWor 93*
Rosenwald, William 1903- *WhoAm 92*
Rosenzweig, Alexander 1948- *St&PR 93*
Rosenzweig, David 1940- *WhoAm 92*
Rosenzweig, Franz 1886-1929 *BioIn 17*
Rosenzweig, Fred 1935- *WhoE 93*
Rosenzweig, Mark Richard 1922- *WhoAm 92*
Rosenzweig, Norman 1924- *WhoWor 93*
Rosenzweig, Peter M. 1949- *ConAu 139*
Rosenzweig, Phyllis D. 1943- *WhoWrEP 92*
Rosenzweig, Richard S. 1935- *St&PR 93*
Rosenzweig, Richard Stuart 1935- *WhoAm 92*
Rosenzweig, Roy Alan 1950- *WhoSSW 93*
Rosenzweig, Saul 1907- *WhoAm 92*
Rosenzweig, Stanley Paul 1928- *WhoE 93*
Rosenzweig, William David 1946- *WhoE 93*
Roser, Herman E. 1922-1990 *BioIn 17*
Roser, Thomas *WhoScE 91-3*
Rose Royce *SoulM*
Roses, Otmaro Enrique 1935- *WhoWor 93*
Rose-Siegel, Darlene 1951- *St&PR 93*
Rosett, Ann Doyle 1955- *WhoAmW 93*
Rosett, Arthur Irwin 1934- *WhoAm 92*
Rosett, Jacqueline Berlin 1945- *WhoAmW 93*
Rosett, Richard Nathaniel 1928- *WhoAm 92, WhoE 93*
Rosette, Marion Savage d1991 *BioIn 17*
Rosetti, (Francesco) Antonio c. 1750-1792 *Baker 92*
Rosewater, Edward 1841-1906 *BioIn 17*
Rosewater, Victor 1871-1940 *BioIn 17, PolPar*
Roshanraven, Mel 1945- *St&PR 93*
Rosheim, David L. *ScF&FL 92*
Roshel, John Albert, Jr. 1941- *WhoWor 93*
Roshkind, David Michael 1950- *WhoSSW 93*
Roshon, George Kenneth 1942- *WhoAm 92, WhoE 93*
Roshong, Dee Ann Daniels 1936- *WhoAmW 93*
Rosi, Eugene Joseph 1931- *WhoAm 92*
Rosi, Francesco 1922- *MiSFD 9*
Rosica, Gabriel Adam 1940- *St&PR 93, WhoAm 92*
Rosicky, Bohumir 1922- *WhoWor 93*
Rosicky, John Anton 1940- *St&PR 93*
Rosiello, Thomas A. *Law&B 92*
Rosier, Carl 1640-1725? *Baker 92*
Rosier, Frederick David Stewart 1951- *WhoWor 93*
Rosier, James Louis 1932- *WhoAm 92, WhoE 93, WhoWrEP 92*
Rosignolo, Beverly Ann 1950- *WhoAmW 93*
Rosilier, Glenn D. 1948- *St&PR 93*
Rosin, Lindsay Zweig 1954- *WhoEmL 93, WhoSSW 93*
Rosin, Morris 1924- *WhoSSW 93*
Rosin, Nadine L. *Law&B 92*
Rosin, Robert Fisher 1936- *WhoE 93*
Rosing, Vladimir 1890-1963 *Baker 92, OxDcOp*
Rosini, Joseph 1939- *WhoE 93*
Rosino, Leonida S. 1915- *WhoScE 91-3*
Rosinski, Edwin Francis 1928- *WhoAm 92*
Rosinski, Leonard Daniel 1951- *St&PR 93*
Rosinski, Martin J. 1938- *St&PR 93*
Rosinski, Thaddeus Julian 1930- *St&PR 93*
Rosinsky, Natalie M. 1951- *ScF&FL 92*
Rosinsky, Rebecca M. *Law&B 92*
Rosival, Ladislav 1924- *WhoScE 91-4*
Roska, Tamas 1940- *WhoScE 91-4*
Roskam, Jan 1930- *WhoAm 92*
Roskam, Verlyn Ronald 1929- *St&PR 93*
Roskelley, John *BioIn 17*
Roskens, Ronald William 1932- *WhoAm 92*
Roskies, Arthur 1927- *St&PR 93*
Roskies, Ethel 1933- *WhoAm 92*
Roskin, Lewis Ross 1920- *WhoAm 92*
Roskind, Susan Reimer 1951- *WhoAmW 93*
Rosko, Michael Daniel 1949- *WhoAm 92*
Roskolenko, Harry 1907-1980 *ScF&FL 92*
Roskos, Donald Paul 1945- *WhoAm 92*
Roskoski, Robert, Jr. 1939- *WhoAm 92*
Roskoz, Jack Houston 1938- *St&PR 93*
Rosky, Burton Seymour 1927- *WhoAm 92*
Rosky, Theodore Samuel 1937- *WhoAm 92, WhoSSW 93*
Roslanowski, Kazimierz 1926- *WhoScE 91-4*
Roslavetz, Nikolai (Andreievich) 1881-1944 *Baker 92*
Ros-Lehtinen, Ileana *BioIn 17*
Ros-Lehtinen, Ileana 1952- *CngDr 91, HispAmA [port], NotHsAW 93 [port], WhoAm 92, WhoAmW 93, WhoSSW 93*
Rosler, Henry M. *Law&B 92*
Rosler, Joachim Peter 1956- *St&PR 93*
Rosler, Johann Joseph 1771-1813 *Baker 92*
Rosler, Martha 1943- *BioIn 17*
Rosler, Uwe 1950- *WhoScE 91-3*
Rosling, Mats Otto 1939- *WhoWor 93*
Roslow, Sydney 1910- *WhoSSW 93, WhoWor 93*
Roslund, Carol L. *Law&B 92*
Roslund, Carol L. 1943- *WhoAmW 93*
Rosman, Mark *MiSFD 9*
Rosman, Riko 1927- *WhoScE 91-4*
Rosmanith, Olga 1893-1978 *ScF&FL 92*
Ros-Marba, Antoni 1937- *Baker 92*
Rosmarin, Susan Gresser 1954- *St&PR 93*
Rosmarin, Trude Weiss- 1908- *BioIn 17*
Rosmundsson, Olafur Ingi 1941- *WhoWor 93*
Rosmus, Anja *BioIn 17*
Rosnell, Tara M. *Law&B 92*
Rosner, Anthony Leopold 1943- *WhoE 93*
Rosner, Arnold 1945- *Baker 92*
Rosner, B.S. *WhoScE 91-1*
Rosner, Bernat *Law&B 92*
Rosner, Bernat 1932- *St&PR 93*
Rosner, Carl Heinz 1929- *St&PR 93*
Rosner, Diane A. 1949- *WhoE 93*
Rosner, Fred 1935- *WhoAm 92*
Rosner, Jonathan Lincoln 1941- *WhoAm 92*
Rosner, Jorge 1921- *WhoAm 92*
Rosner, Lawrence 1912- *St&PR 93*
Rosner, M. Norton 1931- *WhoAm 92*
Rosner, Mark *MiSFD 9*
Rosner, Michael Jeffrey 1953- *WhoE 93*
Rosner, N.J. *Law&B 92*
Rosner, Norman H. *Law&B 92*
Rosner, Richard 1941- *WhoAm 92*
Rosner, Stanley 1928- *WhoE 93*
Rosner, William 1933- *WhoE 93*
Rosnes, Renee *BioIn 17*
Rosness, Betty June 1924- *WhoAmW 93, WhoWor 93*
Rosnow, Ralph Leon 1936- *WhoE 93*
Rosny, J.-H. 1856-1940 *ScF&FL 92*
Rosoff, Elayne Sandra *WhoAmW 93*
Rosoff, Leonard, Sr. 1912- *WhoAm 92*
Rosoff, Michael Howard *Law&B 92*
Rosoff, William A. 1943- *WhoAm 92, WhoE 93, WhoWor 93*
Rosomoff, Hubert Lawrence 1927- *WhoAm 92*
Rosovaky, Henry 1927- *St&PR 93*
Rosovsky, Henry 1927- *WhoAm 92*
Rosow, Jerome Morris 1919- *WhoAm 92*
Rosowicz, Theodore John 1945- *St&PR 93*
Rosowski, Robert B. 1940- *St&PR 93*
Rosowski, Robert Bernard 1940- *WhoAm 92*
Rosowsky, Andre 1936- *WhoE 93*
Rosowsky, Solomon 1878-1962 *Baker 92*
Rospigliosi, Giulio 1600-1669 *BioIn 17, IntDcOp, OxDcOp*
Rosqui, Tom 1928- *ConTFT 10*
Ross, A. Frank 1911-1989 *BioIn 17*
Ross, A. Joseph *ScF&FL 92*
Ross, Adrian E. 1912- *St&PR 93, WhoAm 92*
Ross, Alan *WhoScE 91-1*
Ross, Alan Dale 1956- *WhoE 93*
Ross, Alan Marshall 1944- *WhoE 93*
Ross, Alan Otto 1921- *WhoAm 92, WhoE 93*
Ross, Alexander S. 1929- *St&PR 93*
Ross, Allan Anderson 1939- *WhoAm 92*
Ross, Allan Michael 1939- *WhoAm 92*
Ross, Alvin 1922- *WhoWor 93*
Ross, Andrea Patricia *WhoWrEP 92*
Ross, Anna Marie *BioIn 17*
Ross, Annie 1930- *BioIn 17*
Ross, Arthur 1910- *St&PR 93*
Ross, Ashley M. 1938- *St&PR 93*
Ross, Barbara Ellen *Law&B 92*
Ross, Barbara June 1947- *WhoAmW 93*
Ross, Barnaby *ConAu 39NR*
Ross, Barry Joel 1948- *St&PR 93*
Ross, Beatrice Brook 1927- *WhoAm 92*
Ross, Bernard Harris 1927- *WhoAm 92, WhoWor 93*
Ross, Bernard L. *ScF&FL 92*
Ross, Bernard Rogan 1827-1874 *IntDcAn*
Ross, Bert A. 1926- *St&PR 93*
Ross, Betty Grace 1931- *WhoAmW 93*
Ross, Blair Arthur 1927- *St&PR 93*
Ross, Bob *BioIn 17*
Ross, Bob 1942- *BioIn 17*
Ross, Bobby *WhoAm 92*
Ross, Brian Elliott 1948- *WhoAm 92*
Ross, Bruce 1945- *WhoE 93*
Ross, C. Ian 1942- *St&PR 93*
Ross, Carol Fein *Law&B 92*
Ross, Carolyn Thayer 1948- *WhoAm 92*
Ross, Carrie Chrisann Wolfgang 1961- *WhoAmW 93*
Ross, Carson 1946- *AfrAmBi [port]*
Ross, Charles 1937- *WhoAm 92*
Ross, Charles N. *Law&B 92*
Ross, Charles Robert 1920- *WhoAm 92*
Ross, Charles Worthington, IV 1933- *WhoAm 92*
Ross, Charlotte Pack 1932- *WhoAmW 93*
Ross, Christopher Wade Stelyan 1943- *WhoAm 92, WhoWor 93*
Ross, Clarissa *ScF&FL 92*
Ross, Coleman DeVane 1943- *WhoAm 92, WhoE 93, WhoWor 93*
Ross, Conrad Harold 1931- *WhoSSW 93*
Ross, Courtney Sale *MiSFD 9*
Ross, Cynthia Marie 1966- *WhoSSW 93*
Ross, Dan 1912- *ScF&FL 92*
Ross, Daniel Manuel 1918- *WhoE 93*
Ross, Darlene Y. *Law&B 92*
Ross, David d1992 *NewYTBS 92*
Ross, David 1929- *WhoWrEP 92*
Ross, David 1949- *BioIn 17*
Ross, David A. 1949- *WhoAm 92, WhoE 93*
Ross, David D. 1949?- *ScF&FL 92*
Ross, David E. *Law&B 92*
Ross, David Ewall 1945- *St&PR 93*
Ross, David Frank *Law&B 92*
Ross, David Stanley 1947- *WhoE 93*
Ross, Debra Benita 1956- *WhoAmW 93, WhoEmL 93, WhoWor 93*
Ross, Delmer Gerrard 1942- *WhoAm 92*
Ross, Deloy C. 1925- *St&PR 93*
Ross, Diana *BioIn 17*
Ross, Diana 1944- *Baker 92, SoulM, WhoAm 92, WhoAmW 93, WhoWor 93*
Ross, Dolores Anne 1952- *WhoAmW 93, WhoE 93*
Ross, Don Carl *Law&B 92*
Ross, Donald, Jr. 1941- *WhoAm 92*
Ross, Donald A. *Law&B 92*
Ross, Donald Edward 1930- *WhoAm 92, WhoE 93, WhoWor 93*
Ross, Donald K. d1992 *NewYTBS 92*
Ross, Donald Keith 1925- *St&PR 93, WhoAm 92*
Ross, Donald Kenneth 1925- *WhoAm 92*
Ross, Donald Kirby 1910-1992 *BioIn 17*
Ross, Donald Roe 1922- *WhoAm 92*
Ross, Doris D. 1946- *St&PR 93*
Ross, Doris G. 1919- *WhoAmW 93, WhoE 93, WhoWor 93*
Ross, Doris Laune 1926- *WhoSSW 93*
Ross, Dorothy 1936- *ConAu 137, WhoAmW 93*
Ross, Dorthy Marcussen 1933- *WhoWrEP 92*
Ross, Douglas Taylor 1929- *St&PR 93, WhoAm 92*
Ross, E.R. 1937- *WhoIns 93*
Ross, E. Wayne 1956- *WhoE 93*
Ross, E. William 1938- *St&PR 93*
Ross, Edward *ConTFT 10*
Ross, Edward 1937- *WhoAm 92, WhoWor 93*
Ross, Edward Joseph 1934- *WhoAm 92, WhoE 93*
Ross, Edward W. *WhoAm 92*
Ross, Edward W. 1920- *St&PR 93*
Ross, Edwin Francis 1917- *WhoAm 92*
Ross, Elinor 1932- *WhoAm 92*
Ross, Elinor Parry 1932- *WhoSSW 93*
Ross, Elise J. 1943- *St&PR 93*
Ross, Elise Jane 1943- *WhoAm 92*
Ross, Enrique 1938- *WhoWor 93*
Ross, Ernest E. 1948- *St&PR 93*
Ross, Euan Macdonald 1937- *WhoWor 93*
Ross, Eunice Latshaw 1923- *WhoAmW 93*
Ross, Frank 1904-1990 *BioIn 17*
Ross, Frank Howard, III 1946- *WhoEmL 93, WhoWor 93*
Ross, Fred d1992 *NewYTBS 92*
Ross, G.A. *WhoScE 91-1*
Ross, Gary 1948- *ConAu 38NR, WhoCanL 92*
Ross, Gary Earl 1951- *WhoE 93*
Ross, Gavin James Stirling *WhoScE 91-1*
Ross, George Everett 1947- *St&PR 93*
Ross, George Martin 1933- *WhoAm 92, WhoE 93*
Ross, George William 1940- *WhoAm 92*
Ross, Gerald Elliott 1941- *WhoE 93*
Ross, Gerald Fred 1930- *WhoAm 92, WhoSSW 93*
Ross, Gilbert Stuart 1930- *WhoAm 92*
Ross, Glen 1929- *BioIn 17*
Ross, Glen Ernest 1929- *WhoWrEP 92*
Ross, Glenn Evan 1958- *WhoE 93*
Ross, Glynn 1914- *WhoAm 92*
Ross, Guy Matthews, Jr. 1933- *WhoAm 92*
Ross, Harold 1892-1951 *JrnUS*
Ross, Harold Wallace 1892-1951 *BioIn 17*
Ross, Harry L. *St&PR 93*
Ross, Harvey M. 1927- *St&PR 93*
Ross, Heidi A. 1954- *WhoE 93*
Ross, Helen S. *Law&B 92*
Ross, Henry 1901-1991 *BioIn 17*
Ross, Henry, III 1954- *WhoE 93*
Ross, Henry Raymond 1919- *WhoAm 92*
Ross, Herbert 1927- *MiSFD 9*
Ross, Herbert David 1927- *WhoAm 92*
Ross, Howard 1943- *St&PR 93*
Ross, Howard Philip 1939- *WhoWor 93*
Ross, Hugh *BioIn 17*
Ross, Hugh A. *St&PR 93*
Ross, Hugh C. 1929- *St&PR 93*
Ross, Hugh Courtney 1923- *WhoAm 92*
Ross, Hugh (Cuthbert Melville) 1898-1990 *Baker 92*
Ross, Ian *ScF&FL 92*
Ross, Ian Munro 1927- *WhoAm 92*
Ross, Idajane McDowell 1919- *WhoAm 92*
Ross, J. Pat 1929- *St&PR 93*
Ross, Jack Lewis 1932- *WhoAm 92*
Ross, Jack Stafford, III 1965- *WhoSSW 93*
Ross, Jackie 1946- *BioIn 17*
Ross, Jacob J., Jr. *Law&B 92*
Ross, James Adrian 1936- *St&PR 93*
Ross, James B. 1936- *St&PR 93*
Ross, James Barrett 1930- *WhoAm 92*
Ross, James Clark 1800-1862 *Expl 93 [port]*
Ross, James Donald 1948- *St&PR 93*
Ross, James Elmer 1931- *WhoAm 92*
Ross, James Francis 1931- *WhoAm 92, WhoWrEP 92*
Ross, James H. 1938- *WhoAm 92*
Ross, James H. 1953- *St&PR 93*
Ross, James J. 1943- *WhoE 93*

Ross, James Neil, Jr. 1940- *WhoAm 92*
Ross, James Patrick 1929- *WhoAm 92*
Ross, James Sinclair 1908- *WhoCanL 92*
Ross, James Ulric 1941- *WhoSSW 93, WhoWor 93*
Ross, Jane Bennett d1990 *BioIn 17*
Ross, Jayne M. 1956- *St&PR 93*
Ross, Jean *AmWomPl*
Ross, Jeffrey Allan 1947- *WhoAm 92, WhoEmL 93*
Ross, Jerilyn 1946- *WhoAmW 93*
Ross, Jerrold 1935- *WhoE 93*
Ross, Jerry W. *Law&B 92*
Ross, Jesse 1921- *St&PR 93*
Ross, Jill A. *WhoAmW 93*
Ross, Jimmy Douglas 1936- *WhoAm 92*
Ross, Joe *ScF&FL 92*
Ross, John 1777-1856 *Expl 93 [port]*
Ross, John 1790-1866 *BioIn 17*
Ross, John 1926- *WhoAm 92*
Ross, John, Jr. 1928- *WhoAm 92*
Ross, John E. *Law&B 92*
Ross, John H., III *Law&B 92*
Ross, John J. *BioIn 17, Law&B 92*
Ross, John Joseph 1927- *WhoAm 92*
Ross, John M. *Law&B 92*
Ross, John Mershon 1931- *St&PR 93*
Ross, John Michael 1919- *WhoAm 92, WhoWor 93*
Ross, John Thompson, Jr. 1942- *WhoAm 92*
Ross, Jon Andrew 1949- *WhoWor 93*
Ross, Joseph Charles, Jr. 1925- *St&PR 93*
Ross, Joseph Comer 1927- *WhoAm 92, WhoWor 93*
Ross, Joseph E. 1923- *WhoAm 92*
Ross, Joseph Foster 1910- *WhoAm 92*
Ross, Joseph J. 1945- *St&PR 93*
Ross, Julian Richard Huxham 1941- *WhoWor 93*
Ross, June Rosa Pitt 1931- *WhoAmW 93*
Ross, Karen Susan 1957- *WhoAmW 93*
Ross, Katharine 1943- *SweetSg D [port], WhoAm 92*
Ross, Kathleen Anne 1941- *WhoAmW 93*
Ross, Kenneth E. 1952- *St&PR 93*
Ross, Kenneth Ray 1955- *WhoSSW 93*
Ross, Kenton Eugene 1930- *WhoAm 92*
Ross, Kevin G. *Law&B 92*
Ross, L.C. *Law&B 92*
Ross, L.C. 1947- *St&PR 93*
Ross, L. Michael 1954- *WhoE 93, WhoEmL 93*
Ross, Lara *ScF&FL 92*
Ross, Lawrence John 1942- *WhoAm 92*
Ross, Lawrence Jules 1939- *WhoAm 92*
Ross, Lee A. 1945- *WhoWrEP 92*
Ross, Leona C. 1953- *ScF&FL 92*
Ross, Leona Curtis 1953- *WhoWrEP 92*
Ross, Leonard Lester 1927- *WhoAm 92*
Ross, Leonard Q. 1908- *WhoAm 92*
Ross, Leonard Stanley 1928- *WhoE 93*
Ross, Lesa Moore 1959- *WhoAmW 93, WhoEmL 93, WhoSSW 93, WhoWor 93*
Ross, Lester Keith 1946-1991 *AfrAmBi [port]*
Ross, Lillian Hammer 1925- *SmATA 72 [port]*
Ross, Lisa Angela 1963- *WhoAmW 93*
Ross, Lois Ina 1947- *WhoAmW 93*
Ross, Lorraine G. 1935- *WhoAmW 93*
Ross, Louis Joseph Norman *WhoScE 91-1*
Ross, Louise L. 1928- *St&PR 93*
Ross, Lynn Pearl 1940- *WhoSSW 93*
Ross, Madelyn Ann 1949- *WhoAm 92, WhoAmW 93*
Ross, Malcolm 1911- *WhoCanL 92*
Ross, Malcolm 1929- *WhoAm 92*
Ross, Maria Luisa 188-?-1945 *DcMexL*
Ross, Marie Heise 1930- *WhoAmW 93*
Ross, Marilyn *ScF&FL 92*
Ross, Marilyn Ann (Ann Markham) 1939- *WhoWrEP 92*
Ross, Marilyn Jane 1944- *WhoAmW 93*
Ross, Marion *WhoAm 92*
Ross, Marisela S. *Law&B 92*
Ross, Martin 1862-1915 *BioIn 17*
Ross, Mary Adelaide Eden *ConAu 37NR*
Ross, Mary Caslin 1953- *WhoE 93*
Ross, Mary Ellen 1950- *WhoSSW 93*
Ross, Mary Jane 1961- *WhoAmW 93*
Ross, Mary Riepma Cowell 1910- *WhoAmW 93*
Ross, Mason Greene 1944- *St&PR 93*
Ross, Matthew *Law&B 92*
Ross, Michael A. 1950- *WhoSSW 93*
Ross, Michael Aaron 1941- *WhoAm 92*
Ross, Michael Frederick 1950- *WhoE 93, WhoEmL 93, WhoWor 93*
Ross, Michael I. 1926- *St&PR 93*
Ross, Michael James 1965- *WhoSSW 93*
Ross, Michael McLean 1944- *WhoWor 93*
Ross, Michael R. *Law&B 92*
Ross, Mildred R. *BioIn 17*
Ross, Miriam A. *Law&B 92*
Ross, Molly Owings 1954- *WhoAmW 93, WhoWor 93*
Ross, Monte 1932- *WhoAm 92*
Ross, Morton M. 1925- *St&PR 93*
Ross, Murray George 1910- *WhoAm 92*
Ross, Murray L. 1947- *St&PR 93*
Ross, N.C. *WhoScE 91-1*
Ross, Nancy Lawrence 1947- *WhoAmW 93*
Ross, Nancy Scandrett 1932- *WhoAmW 93*
Ross, Nell Triplett 1922- *WhoWor 93*
Ross, Norman Alan 1942- *WhoAm 92*
Ross, Norman Alexander 1922- *WhoAm 92, WhoSSW 93*
Ross, Norman E. 1941- *St&PR 93*
Ross, Norman Everett 1930- *WhoE 93*
Ross, Otho B., III *Law&B 92*
Ross, Otho Bescent 1951- *WhoWor 93*
Ross, Pat L. *St&PR 93*
Ross, Patricia Cleland 1950- *St&PR 93*
Ross, Patti Jayne 1946- *WhoAmW 93, WhoSSW 93*
Ross, Paul 1927- *WhoAm 92*
Ross, Paul Frederic 1926- *WhoE 93*
Ross, Percy Nathan 1916- *WhoAm 92*
Ross, Peter Adam 1954- *WhoSSW 93*
Ross, Peter M. *Law&B 92*
Ross, Ramon Royal 1930- *BioIn 17*
Ross, Randall Howard 1942- *St&PR 93*
Ross, Randolph Ernest 1955- *WhoEmL 93*
Ross, Raymond J. *ScF&FL 92*
Ross, Raymond Samuel 1925- *WhoWrEP 92*
Ross, Rhoda 1941- *WhoAmW 93*
Ross, Richard 1937- *St&PR 93*
Ross, Richard Deloy 1953- *St&PR 93*
Ross, Richard Francis 1935- *WhoAm 92*
Ross, Richard L. 1928- *St&PR 93*
Ross, Richard L. 1935- *St&PR 93*
Ross, Richard M., Jr. 1929- *St&PR 93*
Ross, Richard Robert *Law&B 92*
Ross, Richard Starr 1924- *WhoAm 92*
Ross, Robert 1766-1814 *HarEnMi*
Ross, Robert Baldwin 1869-1918 *BioIn 17*
Ross, Robert Bruce, IV 1945- *WhoSSW 93*
Ross, Robert Curtis *Law&B 92*
Ross, Robert E. 1944- *WhoWrEP 92*
Ross, Robert Edgar 1948- *WhoE 93*
Ross, Robert Edward 1929- *St&PR 93*
Ross, Robert Gaylord- 1945-1990 *BioIn 17*
Ross, Robert J. 1936- *WhoAm 92*
Ross, Robert LeRoy 1934- *WhoSSW 93*
Ross, Robert Martin 1943- *WhoAm 92*
Ross, Robert Oberholtzer 1945- *WhoE 93*
Ross, Robert Page 1942- *St&PR 93*
Ross, Robert S. 1920- *St&PR 93*
Ross, Robert Thomas 1924- *WhoAm 92*
Ross, Robinette Davis 1952- *WhoAmW 93, WhoE 93, WhoWor 93*
Ross, Roderic Henry 1930- *St&PR 93, WhoAm 92*
Ross, Rogard Thomas 1967- *WhoSSW 93*
Ross, Roger 1929- *WhoE 93*
Ross, Ronald J. *Law&B 92*
Ross, Ronald S. 1949- *WhoE 93*
Ross, Ronnie 1933-1991 *AnObit 1991*
Ross, Roseanna Gaye 1949- *WhoWrEP 92*
Ross, Russell 1929- *WhoAm 92*
Ross, Russell Marion 1921- *WhoAm 92*
Ross, Samuel A. *BioIn 17*
Ross, Samuel Jay, Jr. *WhoSSW 93*
Ross, Scott Alan 1951- *WhoAm 92*
Ross, Scott Lamond 1948- *WhoE 93*
Ross, Sheila Maureen Holmes 1951- *WhoAmW 93*
Ross, Sheldon Jules 1924- *WhoAm 92*
Ross, Sherman 1919- *WhoAm 92*
Ross, Sheryl Jean 1954- *WhoEmL 93*
Ross, Spencer Irwin 1924- *WhoE 93*
Ross, Stanford G. 1931- *WhoAm 92*
Ross, Stanley d1992 *NewYTBS 92*
Ross, Stanley Clark 1948- *WhoE 93*
Ross, Stanley Ralph 1940- *WhoAm 92*
Ross, Stephen 1948- *St&PR 93*
Ross, Stephen Addison 1940- *WhoE 93*
Ross, Stephen Bruce 1944- *WhoAm 92*
Ross, Stephen Cael 1962- *WhoSSW 93*
Ross, Stephen Carl 1947- *WhoE 93*
Ross, Stephen David 1935- *ConAu 39NR*
Ross, Steven Charles 1947- *WhoEmL 93*
Ross, Steven J. *BioIn 17*
Ross, Steven J. 1927- *St&PR 93, WhoAm 92, WhoE 93*
Ross, Steven J. 1927-1992 *NewYTBS 92 [port]*
Ross, Steven Jay 1965- *WhoWor 93*
Ross, Steven S. 1958- *St&PR 93*
Ross, Steven Sander 1946- *WhoWrEP 92*
Ross, Stuart B. 1937- *St&PR 93*
Ross, Stuart Dunning 1936- *WhoE 93*
Ross, Stuart Tennent 1907- *WhoAm 92*
Ross, Sue Iris 1948- *WhoAmW 93, WhoEmL 93*
Ross, Sueellen *BioIn 17*
Ross, Susan *WhoWrEP 92*
Ross, Susan L. *Law&B 92*
Ross, Susan Standart 1947- *WhoAmW 93*
Ross, Ted 1931- *St&PR 93*
Ross, Terence William 1935- *WhoWor 93*
Ross, Theodore John 1924- *WhoWrEP 92*
Ross, Thomas 1928- *WhoSSW 93*
Ross, Thomas Bernard 1929- *St&PR 93, WhoAm 92, WhoWor 93*
Ross, Thomas Edward 1942- *WhoSSW 93*
Ross, Thomas Hugh 1927- *WhoE 93, WhoWor 93*
Ross, Thomas McCallum 1931- *WhoE 93, WhoWor 93*
Ross, Thomas R. *St&PR 93*
Ross, Thomas Warren 1950- *WhoSSW 93*
Ross, Tony 1938- *BioIn 17, MajAI*
Ross, Veronica 1946- *WhoCanL 92*
Ross, Vivian Lee *Law&B 92*
Ross, W.A. 1926- *St&PR 93*
Ross, W.E.D. *ScF&FL 92*
Ross, Walter (Beghtol) 1936- *Baker 92*
Ross, Walter Marion 1903-1990 *BioIn 17*
Ross, Warren Reinhard 1926- *WhoAm 92*
Ross, Wendy Clucas 1942- *WhoAm 92*
Ross, Wesley Frederick 1941- *WhoSSW 93*
Ross, Wilbur L. *BioIn 17*
Ross, Wilbur Louis, Jr. 1937- *St&PR 93, WhoAm 92, WhoE 93*
Ross, William D. *Law&B 92*
Ross, William Jarboe 1930- *WhoAm 92, WhoWor 93*
Ross, William Thomas 1927- *St&PR 93*
Ross, William Warfield 1926- *WhoAm 92*
Rossa, Glynn Michael 1937- *St&PR 93*
Rossa, Robert Frank 1942- *WhoSSW 93*
Rossano, August Thomas 1916- *WhoAm 92*
Rossano, Kenneth R. 1934- *St&PR 93*
Rossant, James Stephane 1928- *WhoAm 92*
Rossant, John Sinclair 1955- *WhoWor 93*
Rossat-Mignod, Jean 1944- *WhoScE 91-2*
Rossavik, Ivar Kristian 1936- *WhoSSW 93*
Rossbach, Ed 1914- *BioIn 17*
Rossbach, Paul Robert 1946- *WhoSSW 93*
Rossbach, Susan K. *Law&B 92*
Rossberg, Hans-Joachim 1927- *WhoWor 93*
Rossberg, Robert Howard 1926- *WhoAm 92*
Ross-Breggin, Virginia (Ginger) Faye 1951- *WhoWrEP 92*
Rosse, James Nelson 1931- *WhoAm 92*
Rosse, Jeanie Quinton *AmWomPl*
Rosse, Wendell Franklyn 1933- *WhoAm 92*
Rosseau, Norbert (Oscar Claude) 1907-1975 *Baker 92*
Rosseel, John G. 1930- *St&PR 93*
Rosseel-Jones, Mary L. *Law&B 92*
Rossel, Jean 1918- *WhoScE 91-4*
Rossel, Pierre 1943- *WhoScE 91-2*
Rossel, Sven H(akon) 1943- *WhoWrEP 92*
Rosseland, Wanda Jane 1949- *WhoWrEP 92*
Rosselin, Gabriel 1929- *WhoScE 91-2*
Rossell, Sune 1932- *WhoScE 91-4*
Rosselle, E. *WhoScE 91-2*
Rosselli, Amelia 1930- *DcLB 128*
Rossellini, Isabella *BioIn 17*
Rossellini, Isabella 1952- *WhoAm 92*
Rossellini, Renzo 1908-1982 *Baker 92, OxDcOp*
Rossellini, Roberto 1906-1977 *MiSFD 9N*
Rossello, Carlos 1953- *WhoWor 93*
Rossello, Joseph Anthony 1959- *WhoE 93*
Rossello, Randolph Joseph 1962- *St&PR 93*
Rosselot, Mim 1954- *WhoSSW 93*
Rosselot, Richard G. 1934- *St&PR 93*
Rossen, Janice Adelle 1955- *WhoSSW 93*
Rossen, Jordan 1934- *WhoAm 92*
Rossen, Robert 1908-1966 *MiSFD 9N*
Rossen, Selma 1936- *St&PR 93*
Rossen, Ted 1920- *St&PR 93*
Rosser, Annetta Hamilton 1913- *WhoAmW 93*
Rosser, Charles D. 1935- *WhoAm 92*
Rosser, Darryl 1951- *St&PR 93*
Rosser, David Pendleton 1945- *WhoSSW 93*
Rosser, Donna Colwell 1954- *WhoWrEP 92*
Rosser, Janis L. *Law&B 92*
Rosser, Janis L. 1939- *St&PR 93*
Rosser, Joy Lynn 1950- *WhoSSW 93*
Rosser, Richard Franklin 1929- *WhoAm 92*
Rosset, Barnet Lee, Jr. 1922- *WhoAm 92*
Rosset, Barney *BioIn 17*
Rosset, Claude Roland 1942- *WhoWor 93*
Rosset, Lisa Krug 1952- *WhoAm 92, WhoWrEP 92*
Rosset, Robert Henri 1933- *WhoWor 93*
Rosseter, Philip 1567?-1623 *Baker 92*
Rossetti, Christina 1830-1894 *WorLitC [port]*
Rossetti, Christina (Georgina) 1830-1894 *MajAI [port]*
Rossetti, Dante Gabriel 1828-1882 *BioIn 17, WorLitC [port]*
Rossetti, Frank G. d1992 *NewYTBS 92 [port]*
Rossetti, Louis A. 1934- *St&PR 93*
Rossetti, Lucy Maddox 1843-1894 *ScF&FL 92*
Rossetti, Paul 1948- *St&PR 93*
Rossetti, Paul P. 1923- *WhoIns 93*
Rossetti, Richard P. 1946- *St&PR 93*
Rossetti, Ronald Louis 1943- *St&PR 93*
Rossetto, Gilberto 1949- *WhoScE 91-3*
Rossetto, Louis d1991 *BioIn 17*
Rossettos, John Nicholas 1932- *WhoE 93*
Rossey, Paul William 1926- *WhoAm 92, WhoWor 93*
Ross-Gordon, Jovita M. 1952- *WhoE 93*
Rossi, Agnelo Cardinal 1913- *WhoWor 93*
Rossi, Alan Juan 1948- *St&PR 93*
Rossi, Aldo 1931- *BioIn 17, WhoAm 92, WhoWor 93*
Rossi, Alice S. 1922- *BioIn 17, WhoAm 92*
Rossi, Amadeo Joseph 1954- *WhoEmL 93*
Rossi, Andre 1938- *WhoScE 91-2*
Rossi, Anthony Gerald 1935- *WhoAm 92*
Rossi, Anthony J. *Law&B 92*
Rossi, Bruno 1905- *WhoAm 92, WhoWor 93*
Rossi, Bruno Benedetto 1905- *BioIn 17*
Rossi, Carlo Eugenio *WhoScE 91-3*
Rossi, Cheryl Lynn 1960- *WhoAmW 93*
Rossi, Christina 1955- *WhoAmW 93*
Rossi, Columbia Rose 1908- *WhoE 93*
Rossi, Cristina Peri 1941- *BioIn 17*
Rossi, Dino A. 1954- *St&PR 93*
Rossi, Dominick F., Jr. 1941- *WhoAm 92*
Rossi, Elena Agata 1962- *WhoWor 93*
Rossi, Erno Delano 1936- *WhoWrEP 92*
Rossi, Faust F. 1932- *WhoAm 92*
Rossi, Francesco c. 1645- *Baker 92*
Rossi, Francis Steven *Law&B 92*
Rossi, Francis Vincent 1925- *WhoE 93*
Rossi, Frank Arthur 1937- *WhoAm 92*
Rossi, Gaetano 1774-1855 *OxDcOp*
Rossi, Giovanni (Gaetano) 1828-1886 *Baker 92*
Rossi, Giulio 1865-1931 *Baker 92*
Rossi, Giuseppe 1938- *WhoScE 91-3*
Rossi, Guido Antonio 1944- *WhoWor 93*
Rossi, Harald Hermann 1917- *WhoAm 92*
Rossi, Harry 1919- *St&PR 93, WhoAm 92*
Rossi, Irving d1991 *BioIn 17*
Rossi, James *Law&B 92*
Rossi, John B., Jr. *Law&B 92*
Rossi, John Paul 1967- *BioIn 17*
Rossi, Jorge *DcCPCAm*
Rossi, Jose Welisson 1945- *WhoWor 93*
Rossi, Joseph H. 1950- *St&PR 93*
Rossi, Joseph O. *WhoE 93*
Rossi, Lauro 1810-1885 *Baker 92*
Rossi, Lauro 1812-1885 *OxDcOp*
Rossi, Lee D. 1946- *ScF&FL 92*
Rossi, Linda Jean 1956- *WhoAmW 93*
Rossi, Louis D. 1944- *St&PR 93*
Rossi, Lucian J. 1920- *WhoWrEP 92*
Rossi, Luigi c. 1597-1653 *Baker 92, OxDcOp*
Rossi, Marie T. *BioIn 17*
Rossi, Mario *WhoScE 91-3*
Rossi, Mario 1902- *Baker 92*
Rossi, Mario Alexander 1931- *WhoAm 92*
Rossi, Mark A. *Law&B 92*
Rossi, Michel Angelo 1601?-1656? *Baker 92*
Rossi, Michelangelo 1601?-1656 *OxDcOp*
Rossi, Mose 1938- *WhoScE 91-3*
Rossi, Opilio Cardinal 1910- *WhoWor 93*
Rossi, Peter Henry 1921- *WhoAm 92*
Rossi, Philip M. 1958- *St&PR 93*
Rossi, Ralph L. 1928- *St&PR 93, WhoAm 92*
Rossi, Roberta *WhoWor 93*
Rossi, Roberto A.S. 1943- *St&PR 93*
Rossi, Ronald Aldo 1956- *WhoE 93*
Rossi, Salamone 1570-c. 1630 *Baker 92*
Rossi, Steven 1954- *WhoE 93*
Rossi, Tino 1907-1983 *Baker 92*
Rossi-Bernardi, Luigi P. 1932- *WhoScE 91-3*
Rossides, Eugene Telemachus 1927- *WhoAm 92*
Rossides, Zenon 1895-1990 *BioIn 17*
Rossi Di Montelera, Luigi 1946- *WhoWor 93*
Rossier, Jean Pierre 1944- *WhoWor 93*
Rossi-Espagnet, Gianfranco 1947- *St&PR 93, WhoAm 92*
Rossif, Frederic *BioIn 17*
Rossignol, Felix Ludger *Baker 92*
Rossignol, Jean-Francois 1943- *St&PR 93*
Rossignol, Jean-Louis *WhoScE 91-2*
Rossignol, Jean Luc 1939- *WhoWor 93*
Rossignol, Roger John 1941- *WhoE 93*
Rossi-Lemeni, Nicola 1920-1991 *Baker 92, IntDcOp, OxDcOp*
Rossi-Lemeni, Nicola Makedon 1920-1991 *BioIn 17*
Rossing, Thomas D. 1929- *BioIn 17*

Rossington, David Ralph 1932- WhoAm 92, WhoE 93
Rossington, Gary c. 1949- See Lynyrd Skynyrd ConMus 9
Rossini, Edwin R. Law&B 92
Rossini, Gioachino 1792-1868 IntDcOp [port], OxDcOp
Rossini, Gioachino (Antonio) 1792-1868 Baker 92
Rossini, Louis Sebastian 1957- St&PR 93
Rossinot, Andre 1939- BioIn 17
Rossio, Robert D. 1929- St&PR 93
Rossitch, Eugene 1934- St&PR 93
Rossiter, Alexander, Jr. 1936- WhoAm 92
Rossiter, Bruce St&PR 93
Rossiter, Charles M. 1942- WhoWrEP 92
Rossiter, Daniel H. 1925- St&PR 93
Rossiter, Margaret Walsh 1944- WhoAm 92
Rossiter, Oscar 1918- ScF&FL 92
Rossiter, Phyllis Jo 1938- WhoWrEP 92
Rossiter, Robert E. 1946- WhoAm 92
Rossiter, Sarah 1942- ConAu 136
Ross-Jacobs, Ruth Ann 1934- WhoAmW 93
Rosskamm, Alan 1950- St&PR 93
Rosskamm, Martin 1915- St&PR 93, WhoAm 92
Ross-Kilkelly, Cloteen 1939- St&PR 93
Rossky, William 1917- WhoE 93
Rossler, Ernst Karl 1909-1980 Baker 92
Rossler, K. Helmut 1922- WhoScE 91-3
Rossler, Willis Kenneth, Jr. 1946- WhoSSW 93
Rossley, Paul R. 1938- WhoIns 93
Rossley, Paul Robert 1938- St&PR 93, WhoAm 92
Rossl-Majdan, Hildegard 1921- Baker 92
Rossman, Charles E. ScF&FL 92
Rossman, Charles Raymond 1938- WhoSSW 93
Rossman, Cynthia A. 1956- St&PR 93
Rossman, Douglas A. 1936- ScF&FL 92
Rossman, Howard David 1945- WhoE 93
Rossman, Isadore 1913- WhoE 93
Rossman, Parker 1919- WhoWrEP 92
Rossman, Richard Alan 1939- WhoAm 92
Rossman, Robert Harris 1932- WhoE 93
Rossman, Ruth Scharff WhoAm 92
Rossman, Toby Gale 1942- WhoAmW 93
Rossman, William J. 1941- St&PR 93
Rossmann, John F. 1942- ScF&FL 92
Rossmann, Michael George 1930- WhoAm 92
Rossmann, Rudolph Alexander 1939- St&PR 93
Rossmann, Tatiana 1944- WhoWor 93
Rossmeisl, Leslie A. 1961- St&PR 93
Rossmiller, George Eddie 1935- WhoAm 92
Rossner, Judith BioIn 17
Rossner, Judith 1935- WhoAm 92, WhoWrEP 92
Rossner, Stephan 1942- WhoScE 91-4
Rosso, David John 1938- WhoAm 92
Rosso, Julee 1944- ConAu 139
Rosso, Louis T. 1933- St&PR 93
Rosso, Renzo Luigi 1950- WhoWor 93
Rosso de Irizarry, Carmen 1947- WhoAmW 93
Rossomando, Robert 1938- St&PR 93
Rosson, Glenn Richard 1937- WhoAm 92
Rosson, Mary Beth 1955- WhoAmW 93
Rosson, Peggy 1935- WhoAmW 93
Rosson, William Mimms 1922- St&PR 93
Rosson-Davis, Barbara Ann 1946- WhoWrEP 92
Rossoni, Edmondo 1884-1965 BioIn 17
Rossotti, Barbara Jill Margulies 1940- WhoAm 92, WhoAmW 93
Rossotti, Charles C. St&PR 93
Rossotti, Charles O. 1941- St&PR 93
Rossotti, Charles Ossola 1941- WhoAm 92
Rossotti, F.J.C. WhoScE 91-1
Rossow, Mark Matthew Law&B 92
Rossow, William B. 1947- ScF&FL 92
Rossowski, Wladyslaw 1857-1930 PolBiDi
Ross-Rhoades, Vicki Ann 1957- WhoAmW 93
Rosston, Edward William 1918- WhoAm 92
Rossum, Frederik (Leon Hendrik) van 1939- Baker 92
Rossum, Ralph Arthur 1946- WhoAm 92
Rosswall, P. Thomas 1941- WhoWor 93
Rosswork, Paul Burton Law&B 92
Rosswork, Sandra Goody 1939- WhoAmW 93
Rossy, Richard Paul 1949- St&PR 93
Rost, Andrew J. 1908- St&PR 93
Rost, Stephen H. 1949- St&PR 93
Rost, Thomas Lowell 1941- WhoAm 92
Rost, William Joseph 1926- WhoAm 92
Rostad, Kenneth Leif 1941- WhoAm 92
Rostagno, Derrick BioIn 17
Rostaing, Michel 1944- WhoWor 93
Rostal, Max 1905- Baker 92
Rostami, Abdolmohamad 1948- WhoE 93
Rostan, John P., III 1943- St&PR 93
Rostand, Claude 1912-1970 Baker 92
Rostand, Edmond 1868-1918 BioIn 17, OxDcOp
Rostand, Robert ConAu 38NR
Rostanski, Krzysztof 1930- WhoScE 91-4
Rosten, Irwin 1924- WhoAm 92
Rosten, Leo Calvin 1908- WhoAm 92
Rostenkowski, Dan CngDr 91
Rostenkowski, Dan 1928- WhoAm 92
Roster, Michael 1945- WhoAm 92
Rostetter, Alice AmWomPl
Rostetter, Carolyn Margaret 1961- WhoAmW 93
Rostgaard, Jorgen 1932- WhoScE 91-2
Rosthip, Chinda 1933- WhoWor 93
Rostick, Edward Anthony 1930- St&PR 93
Rostkowski, Margaret I. 1945- DcAmChF 1985
Rostky, George Harold 1926- WhoAm 92, WhoWrEP 92
Rostockij, Stanislav 1922- DrEEuF
Rostoker, Gordon 1940- WhoAm 92
Rostoker, Guy Pascal Francis 1956- WhoWor 93
Rostollan, Donovan M. 1959- St&PR 93
Roston, Arnold 1923- WhoAm 92
Roston, Robert A. 1926- St&PR 93
Rostov, Charles I. d1989 BioIn 17
Rostovsky, Alla Grigorievna 1941- WhoE 93
Rostow, Charles Nicholas 1950- WhoAm 92
Rostow, Elspeth Davies WhoAm 92
Rostow, Eugene Victor 1913- WhoAm 92
Rostow, W.W. 1916- BioIn 17
Rostow, Walt 1916- ColdWar 1 [port]
Rostow, Walt Whitman 1916- BioIn 17, WhoAm 92
Rostropovich, Leopold 1892-1942 Baker 92
Rostropovich, Mstislav 1926- See Vishnevskaya, Galina 1926- OxDcOp
Rostropovich, Mstislav 1927- BioIn 17
Rostropovich, Mstislav (Leopoldovich) 1927- Baker 92, WhoAm 92, WhoWor 93
Rostroprovich, Mstislav WhoE 93
Rostrup, Kaspar MiSFD 9
Rostrup-Nielsen, Jens R. 1939- WhoScE 91-2
Rosuck, Jordan I. WhoAm 92
Rosvaenge, Helge 1897-1972 Baker 92, OxDcOp
Rosvaenge, Helge Anton Hansen 1897-1971 IntDcOp [port]
Rosvik, A. 1934- WhoScE 91-4
Rosvoll, Randi Veie 1928- WhoAm 92
Roswaenge, Helge 1897-1972 Baker 92
Roswaenge, Helge Anton Hansen 1897-1971 IntDcOp [port]
Roswick, Elmer Julius 1919- St&PR 93
Roswick, John T. 1946- St&PR 93
Rosypal, Kathryn Gayle 1949- WhoAmW 93
Roszak, Michele Lee 1963- WhoSSW 93
Roszak, Theodore 1933- ScF&FL 92
Roszkowski, Jacek 1931- WhoScE 91-4
Roszkowski, Michael Joseph 1950- WhoE 93
Roszkowski, Waldemar 1946- WhoScE 91-4
Rosztoczy, Ferenc Erno 1932- WhoWor 93
Rota, Enrico C. Law&B 92
Rota, Ezio 1924- WhoScE 91-3
Rota, Gian-Carlo 1932- WhoAm 92, WhoWor 93
Rota, Marian Loren 1958- WhoE 93
Rota, Nino 1911-1979 Baker 92, OxDcOp
Rota, Robert V. 1935- CngDr 91
Rotar, Vladimir Ilyich 1942- WhoWor 93
Rotatori, Arthur J. Law&B 92
Rotberg, Eugene Harvey 1930- WhoAm 92
Rotberg, Robert Irwin 1935- WhoAm 92
Rotch, Helen Gilman Ludington AmWomPl
Rotch, William 1929- WhoAm 92
Rote, Andrew Bendler 1928- St&PR 93
Rote, Carey Clements 1957- WhoSSW 93
Rote, Frank Conrad, Jr. Law&B 92
Rote, Gunter 1960- WhoWor 93
Rote, William Kyle, Sr. 1928- BiDAMSp 1989
Rotella, Robert F. Law&B 92
Rotelli, Claudio Raffaello 1939- WhoWor 93
Rotemberg, Julio Jacobo 1953- WhoE 93
Roten, M. 1933- WhoScE 91-4
Roten, Robert Darrel 1946- St&PR 93
Rotenberg, Marc Steven 1960- WhoE 93
Rotenberg, Marvin R. 1944- St&PR 93
Rotenberg, Sheldon 1917- WhoAm 92
Rotenberry, William John Law&B 92
Rotenstreich, Jon W. BioIn 17
Rotenstreich, Jon W. 1943- St&PR 93
Rotenstreich, Jon Wallace 1943- WhoAm 92
Roter, Benjamin St&PR 93
Roterman-Konieczna, Irena Krystyna 1950- WhoWor 93
Roters, Ernst 1892-1961 Baker 92
Rotert, Charles Henry, Jr. 1933- WhoAm 92
Rotert, Denise Anne 1949- WhoAmW 93
Rotfeld, Herbert Jack 1950- WhoSSW 93
Roth, Alan d1992 BioIn 17, NewYTBS 92
Roth, Allan E. Law&B 92
Roth, Allan Robert 1931- WhoAm 92
Roth, Alvin Eliot 1951- WhoAm 92
Roth, Andre 1933- WhoScE 91-4
Roth, Ann WhoAm 92
Roth, Arthur 1921- ScF&FL 92
Roth, Audrey Joan 1927- WhoAmW 93, WhoSSW 93
Roth, Barry L. 1951- St&PR 93
Roth, Bernard 1933- WhoAm 92
Roth, Bernard B. 1915- St&PR 93
Roth, Bobby MiSFD 9
Roth, Carol Jean Law&B 92
Roth, Charles Francis, Jr. 1946- WhoE 93
Roth, Christian Francis BioIn 17
Roth, Daniel 1942- Baker 92
Roth, Daniel Benjamin 1929- WhoAm 92
Roth, David Lee 1955- See Van Halen ConMus 8
Roth, Debra J. Law&B 92
Roth, Duane A. 1957- WhoWrEP 92
Roth, Duane J. 1949- St&PR 93
Roth, Edna Laura 1934- WhoAmW 93
Roth, Edward Emil 1945- WhoE 93
Roth, Edwin Morton 1927- WhoAm 92
Roth, Ellen Carlstein St&PR 93
Roth, Ellen Rochelle 1961- WhoAmW 93
Roth, Eugene 1935- WhoWor 93
Roth, Feri 1899-1969 Baker 92
Roth, Fredric E., Jr. Law&B 92
Roth, George Stanley 1946- WhoAm 92
Roth, Gerald Bart 1941- St&PR 93
Roth, Gerhard 1942- DcLB 124 [port]
Roth, Gloria Ingram 1922- WhoAmW 93
Roth, Hannah BioIn 17
Roth, Harold 1934- WhoAm 92
Roth, Harold Philmore 1915- WhoAm 92
Roth, Harvey Paul 1933- St&PR 93, WhoAm 92
Roth, Henry 1906- BioIn 17, ConAu 38NR, JeAmFiW, JeAmHC
Roth, Henry H. 1933- WhoWrEP 92
Roth, Herbert, Jr. 1928- WhoAm 92
Roth, Herbert Fredrick 1930- WhoAm 92
Roth, Herman 1901-1989 BioIn 17
Roth, I. 1940- St&PR 93
Roth, Irving 1934- WhoWrEP 92
Roth, Ivan 1935- St&PR 93
Roth, Jack Joseph 1920- WhoAm 92
Roth, James Chesley 1959- WhoAm 92
Roth, James Frank 1925- WhoAm 92
Roth, James H. 1934- St&PR 93
Roth, James Seymour 1934- WhoAm 92
Roth, Jane Richards 1935- WhoAm 92, WhoAmW 93, WhoE 93
Roth, Jean-Pierre WhoScE 91-2
Roth, Jeffrey Lee Law&B 92
Roth, Jerome Allan 1943- WhoE 93
Roth, Jim Craig 1934- St&PR 93
Roth, Joe BioIn 17, NewYTBS 92 [port]
Roth, Joe 1948- MiSFD 9, WhoAm 92
Roth, John Austin 1934- WhoAm 92
Roth, John E. 1928- St&PR 93
Roth, John King 1940- WhoAm 92, WhoWrEP 92
Roth, John Reece 1937- WhoAm 92, WhoSSW 93
Roth, John Roger 1939- WhoAm 92
Roth, Joseph 1894-1939 BioIn 17
Roth, Judith Paris 1949- WhoWrEP 92
Roth, Jules K. Law&B 92
Roth, Julian d1992 NewYTBS 92
Roth, June 1926-1990 BioIn 17
Roth, June Doris Spiewak 1926- WhoAm 92
Roth, Karlheinz 1919- WhoScE 91-3
Roth, Kathie C. 1962- WhoAmW 93
Roth, Kathryn Gaie 1964- WhoAmW 93
Roth, Klaus Friedrich WhoScE 91-1
Roth, Laura Maurer 1930- WhoAm 92, WhoE 93
Roth, Lawrence Frederick, Jr. 1948- WhoWor 93, WhoWrEP 92
Roth, Lawrence H. Law&B 92
Roth, Lawrence Max 1936- WhoAm 92
Roth, Loren 1939- WhoAm 92
Roth, Loren Dennis 1943- St&PR 93
Roth, M. Augustine 1926- WhoAmW 93
Roth, Margarete Maria 1938- WhoAmW 93
Roth, Martha 1938- WhoWrEP 92
Roth, Martin G. 1937- St&PR 93
Roth, Mary Jane 1942- WhoAmW 93
Roth, Michael 1931- WhoAm 92
Roth, Michael I. BioIn 17
Roth, Michael I. 1945- St&PR 93, WhoAm 92
Roth, Michael J. Law&B 92
Roth, Monica A. Law&B 92
Roth, Morton 1952- St&PR 93
Roth, Muriel Parker d1990 BioIn 17
Roth, Nancy Louise 1955- WhoAmW 93
Roth, Patricia Sue 1961- WhoAmW 93
Roth, Patty Jane 1955- St&PR 93
Roth, Paul Norman 1939- WhoAm 92
Roth, Peter T. 1957- St&PR 93
Roth, Philip BioIn 17
Roth, Philip 1933- AmWrS3, MagSAmL [port], WhoAm 92, WhoE 93, WhoWor 93, WhoWrEP 92, WorLitC [port]
Roth, Philip Milton 1933- JeAmHC
Roth, Phyllis A. 1945- ScF&FL 92
Roth, Phyllis Irene 1937- WhoE 93
Roth, R.E. Law&B 92
Roth, Rhoda Steindler Law&B 92
Roth, Richard, Jr. 1933- St&PR 93, WhoAm 92
Roth, Richard J. 1936- WhoAm 92
Roth, Richard J. 1941- WhoIns 93
Roth, Richard J., Jr. 1942- WhoIns 93
Roth, Richard James, Sr. 1919- WhoIns 93
Roth, Richard Joseph 1941- St&PR 93
Roth, Richard Lee 1931- WhoAm 92
Roth, Robert A. 1943- WhoE 93
Roth, Robert Alan 1950-1990 BioIn 17
Roth, Robert Earl 1937- WhoAm 92
Roth, Robert George 1925- St&PR 93
Roth, Robert Howard 1933- WhoE 93
Roth, Robert Steele 1930- WhoE 93
Roth, Robert W. 1923- St&PR 93
Roth, Robert William 1953- WhoSSW 93
Roth, Roger Z. 1938- St&PR 93
Roth, Russell Robert 1946- St&PR 93
Roth, Sanford Harold 1934- WhoAm 92
Roth, Sanford Irwin 1932- WhoAm 92
Roth, Scott Alan 1949- WhoE 93
Roth, Sherri BioIn 17
Roth, Sol 1927- WhoAm 92
Roth, Stacia Lynn 1960- WhoAmW 93
Roth, Stanley 1929- St&PR 93
Roth, Stanley W. 1932- WhoE 93
Roth, Steven H. Law&B 92
Roth, Steven William Law&B 92
Roth, Stuart N. Law&B 92
Roth, Susan Nance Law&B 92
Roth, Terry Dumas 1958- WhoSSW 93
Roth, Thomas James Law&B 92
Roth, Toby 1938- CngDr 91, WhoAm 92
Roth (Vanceburg), Martha 1938- ConAu 137
Roth, Walter L. 1921- St&PR 93
Roth, Wesley A. 1932- St&PR 93
Roth, William George 1938- WhoAm 92
Roth, William Matson 1916- WhoAm 92
Roth, William V., Jr. 1921- CngDr 91, WhoAm 92, WhoE 93
Roth, Wolfgang 1910-1988 BioIn 17
Rothacher, Albrecht Friedrich 1955- WhoWor 93
Rothbard, Abe 1918- St&PR 93
Rothbard, Fran 1953- WhoSSW 93
Rothbard, Richard Wintman 1947- St&PR 93
Rothbard, Sanford Harvey 1936- St&PR 93
Rothbardt, Patricia A. Law&B 92
Rothbart, Herbert Lawrence 1937- WhoE 93
Rothbart, Marian 1942- WhoAmW 93
Rothbaum, Fred Mark 1949- WhoE 93
Rothbaum, Ira WhoAm 92
Rothbein, Sylvia 1951- WhoAmW 93
Rothberg, Abraham 1922- WhoAm 92, WhoWrEP 92
Rothberg, David A. 1954- St&PR 93
Rothberg, Edward Law&B 92
Rothberg, Falk 1916- St&PR 93
Rothberg, Gerald 1937- WhoAm 92
Rothberg, June Simmonds 1923- WhoAm 92
Rothberg, Karen S. Law&B 92
Rothberg, Lea Gremm 1955- WhoSSW 93
Rothberg, Sol 1910- St&PR 93, WhoAm 92
Rothblatt, Donald Noah 1935- WhoAm 92
Rothblatt, Emma Alden 1918- WhoWor 93
Rothblum, Egon Gotthilf 1915- WhoWor 93
Rothblum, Lisa S. Law&B 92
Rothchild, Herbert E. 1921- St&PR 93
Rothchild, Howard Leslie 1929- WhoAm 92
Rothchild, John St&PR 93
Rothchild, Joseph F. 1918- St&PR 93
Rothdeutsch, Thomas Carl 1948- WhoSSW 93
Rothe, Ann Toulmin- BioIn 17
Rothe, Guenter Hans 1928- WhoSSW 93
Rothe, William S., Jr. St&PR 93
Rothel, James W. 1945- St&PR 93
Rothemeyer, H. WhoScE 91-3
Rothenberg, Alan B. 1907-1977 ScF&FL 92

Rothenberg, Alan I. 1939- *WhoAm 92*
Rothenberg, Alan Miles 1941- *WhoE 93*
Rothenberg, Albert 1930- *WhoAm 92*
Rothenberg, Barbara Meyer *Law&B 92*
Rothenberg, Charles *BioIn 17*
Rothenberg, Charles 1903-1992 *BioIn 17*
Rothenberg, Elliot Calvin 1939- *WhoAm 92, WhoWor 93*
Rothenberg, Francine M. 1945- *WhoAmW 93*
Rothenberg, Frederick M. 1942- *WhoAm 92, WhoWor 93*
Rothenberg, Gilbert A. 1930- *St&PR 93*
Rothenberg, Gunther Erich 1923- *WhoAm 92*
Rothenberg, Jerome 1931- *WhoAm 92*
Rothenberg, Jerome Dennis 1931- *WhoWrEP 92*
Rothenberg, Jerome Samuel *Law&B 92*
Rothenberg, Joseph Lawrence 1940- *St&PR 93*
Rothenberg, Julia Christine Johnson 1941- *WhoE 93*
Rothenberg, Leonard 1940- *St&PR 93*
Rothenberg, Leslie Steven 1941- *WhoAm 92*
Rothenberg, Marc *Law&B 92*
Rothenberg, Mark 1949- *St&PR 93*
Rothenberg, Robert Edward 1908- *WhoAm 92, WhoWor 93*
Rothenberg, Robert Philip 1936- *WhoAm 92*
Rothenberg, Sandra Myers *St&PR 93*
Rothenberg, Steve *BioIn 17*
Rothenberg, Steven A. *St&PR 93*
Rothenberg, Susan *BioIn 17*
Rothenberg, Susan 1945- *WhoAm 92, WhoAmW 93*
Rothenberger, Anneliese 1924- *Baker 92, IntDcOp, OxDcOp*
Rothenberger, Harold A. 1943- *St&PR 93*
Rothenberger, James E. 1947- *St&PR 93*
Rother, Artur (Martin) 1885-1972 *Baker 92*
Rother, John Charles 1947- *WhoAm 92*
Rothermel, Daniel Krott 1938- *St&PR 93, WhoAm 92*
Rothermel, John Kindig *Law&B 92*
Rothermel, Joseph Jackson 1918- *WhoE 93*
Rothermel, Rodman S. 1932- *St&PR 93*
Rothermel, Timothy Simes 1945- *WhoUN 92*
Rothermere, Lady d1992 *NewYTBS 92 [port]*
Rother-Simmonds, Helga Elisabeth 1954- *WhoWor 93*
Rothert, Heinrich 1938- *WhoScE 91-3*
Rothery, Agnes Edwards 1888- *AmWomPl*
Rotheval *WhoScE 91-2*
Rothfarb, Ruth *BioIn 17*
Rothfeld, Michael B. 1947- *St&PR 93*
Rothfeld, Neil S. 1936- *St&PR 93*
Rothfield, Lawrence I. 1927- *WhoAm 92*
Rothfield, Naomi Fox 1929- *WhoAm 92, WhoAmW 93*
Rothfus, John Arden 1932- *WhoAm 92*
Rothfuss, Barry *BioIn 17*
Rothgeb, Russell 1936- *St&PR 93*
Rothhaar, John C. *Law&B 92*
Rothholz, Peter Lutz 1929- *WhoAm 92*
Rothier, Leon 1874-1951 *Baker 92*
Rothing, Frank John 1924- *WhoAm 92*
Rothko, Mark 1903-1970 *BioIn 17*
Rothkopf, David Jochanan 1955- *WhoWor 93*
Rothlein, Lee Alan 1944- *St&PR 93*
Rothlisberger, Dana John 1952- *WhoE 93*
Rothlisberger, Hans 1923- *WhoScE 91-4*
Roth-Maier, Dora A. 1940- *WhoScE 91-3*
Rothman, Allen S. 1943- *WhoE 93*
Rothman, Bernard 1932- *WhoAm 92, WhoE 93*
Rothman, Beulah d1990 *BioIn 17*
Rothman, Charles W. *ScF&FL 92*
Rothman, Chuck 1952- *ScF&FL 92*
Rothman, Deanna 1938- *WhoAmW 93*
Rothman, Edward M. *Law&B 92*
Rothman, Esther Pomeranz 1919- *WhoAmW 93, WhoE 93*
Rothman, Frances Dektor 1932- *WhoAmW 93*
Rothman, Frank 1926- *St&PR 93, WhoAm 92*
Rothman, Frank George 1930- *WhoAm 92*
Rothman, Gerald 1937- *St&PR 93*
Rothman, Henry Isaac 1943- *WhoAm 92*
Rothman, Herbert B. 1924- *WhoAm 92*
Rothman, Howard 1953- *WhoWrEP 92*
Rothman, Howard Barry 1938- *WhoSSW 93*
Rothman, Howard E. *Law&B 92*
Rothman, Howard Joel 1945- *WhoAm 92, WhoWor 93*
Rothman, I.H. *St&PR 93*
Rothman, James Edward 1950- *WhoAm 92*
Rothman, James S. 1961- *St&PR 93*
Rothman, Judith Lee 1940- *WhoAmW 93*
Rothman, Julius Lawrence 1920- *WhoWor 93*
Rothman, Laurence Sidney 1940- *WhoE 93*
Rothman, Louis James 1932- *WhoWor 93*
Rothman, Martin 1946- *St&PR 93*
Rothman, Melvin L. 1930- *WhoAm 92*
Rothman, Patricia Mary 1946- *WhoAmW 93*
Rothman, R.H. 1941- *St&PR 93*
Rothman, Robert L. *Law&B 92*
Rothman, Sidney 1918- *WhoE 93*
Rothman, Stephanie *MiSFD 9*
Rothman, Stewart Neil 1930- *WhoWor 93*
Rothman, Tony 1953- *ScF&FL 92*
Rothman, William B. *St&PR 93*
Rothman-Denes, Lucia Beatriz 1943- *WhoAmW 93*
Rothmeier, Steven George 1946- *St&PR 93, WhoAm 92*
Rothmuller, Marko 1908- *OxDcOp*
Rothmuller, (Aron) Marko 1908- *Baker 92*
Rothovius, Iska 1926- *WhoE 93, WhoWor 93*
Rothrauff, Guido A., Jr. *Law&B 92*
Rothrock, Jan Campbell 1935- *WhoWor 93*
Rothrock, Lori Anne *Law&B 92*
Rothrock, Ronald Edward 1952- *St&PR 93*
Roths, Tarcisia 1930- *WhoAmW 93*
Rothschild, Alan Friend 1925- *WhoAm 92*
Rothschild, Amalie Randolph 1945- *WhoAmW 93*
Rothschild, Amalie Rosenfeld 1916- *WhoAm 92*
Rothschild, Anthony Joseph 1953- *WhoE 93*
Rothschild, Bernhard A., Jr. 1913- *St&PR 93*
Rothschild, Bruce I. *Law&B 92*
Rothschild, Carol Louise 1946- *WhoE 93*
Rothschild, Carolyn Anita 1939- *WhoE 93*
Rothschild, Charles Joseph, Jr. 1921- *St&PR 93, WhoAm 92*
Rothschild, Cheryl Lynn 1967- *WhoAmW 93*
Rothschild, Diane 1943- *WhoAmW 93*
Rothschild, Ernest Leo 1922- *WhoAm 92*
Rothschild, George H., Jr. *Law&B 92*
Rothschild, George William 1917- *WhoAm 92*
Rothschild, Guy de *BioIn 17*
Rothschild, Henry 1932- *WhoSSW 93*
Rothschild, Irene Celia 1931- *WhoAmW 93*
Rothschild, Jacob *BioIn 17*
Rothschild, James Alan 1946- *WhoE 93*
Rothschild, Jeffrey L. 1945- *St&PR 93*
Rothschild, John Albert 1943- *WhoE 93*
Rothschild, Kurt W. 1914- *BioIn 17*
Rothschild, Loran Robert 1938- *St&PR 93*
Rothschild, Loren Robert 1938- *WhoAm 92*
Rothschild, Marie-Helene de *BioIn 17*
Rothschild, Michael 1942- *WhoAm 92*
Rothschild, Miriam *BioIn 17*
Rothschild, Miriam 1908- *CurBio 92 [port]*
Rothschild, Nathaniel Charles Jacob *BioIn 17*
Rothschild, Nathaniel Mayer Victor 1910-1990 *BioIn 17*
Rothschild, Paul H. 1937- *St&PR 93*
Rothschild, Richard Kahn *Law&B 92*
Rothschild, Robert 1945- *WhoWor 93*
Rothschild, Rona R. 1941- *St&PR 93*
Rothschild, Sigmund *BioIn 17*
Rothschild, Steven B. 1953- *St&PR 93*
Rothschild, Steven James 1944- *WhoAm 92, WhoE 93*
Rothschild, V. Henry 1908-1991 *BioIn 17*
Rothschild Family *BioIn 17*
Rothstein, Allan *ScF&FL 92*
Rothstein, Anne L. *BioIn 17*
Rothstein, Arnold d1928 *BioIn 17*
Rothstein, Aser 1918- *WhoAm 92*
Rothstein, Barbara A. *Law&B 92*
Rothstein, Barbara Jacobs 1939- *WhoAm 92, WhoAmW 93*
Rothstein, Cy 1934- *WhoWor 93*
Rothstein, David 1955- *St&PR 93*
Rothstein, Edward 1952- *ConAu 136*
Rothstein, Eric 1936- *WhoAm 92, WhoWrEP 92*
Rothstein, Fred H. *WhoAm 92*
Rothstein, Gerald Alan 1941- *St&PR 93, WhoAm 92*
Rothstein, Hannah Rebecca 1951- *WhoAmW 93*
Rothstein, L. *St&PR 93*
Rothstein, Lawrence I. 1952- *St&PR 93*
Rothstein, Marilyn E. 1938- *WhoWrEP 92*
Rothstein, Marilyn Simon 1953- *WhoAmW 93*
Rothstein, Morton 1926- *WhoAm 92*
Rothstein, Phyllis A. 1957- *St&PR 93*
Rothstein, Richard *MiSFD 9*
Rothstein, Ron *WhoAm 92*
Rothstein, Samuel 1921- *WhoAm 92*
Rothstein, Sheldon *Law&B 92*
Rothuizen, Jasper Warner 1939- *WhoWor 93*
Rothwarf, Allen 1935- *WhoAm 92, WhoE 93*
Rothwell, Albert Falcon 1926- *WhoAm 92*
Rothwell, Evelyn 1911- *Baker 92*
Rothwell, James Harold 1945- *St&PR 93*
Rothwell, Kenneth Sprague, Jr. 1955- *WhoE 93*
Rothwell, P.J. *WhoScE 91-1*
Rothwell, Peter Sutherland *Law&B 92*
Rothwell, Robert Clark 1939- *St&PR 93, WhoAm 92*
Rothwell, T.A. 1931- *St&PR 93*
Rothwell, Timothy Gordon 1951- *WhoAm 92*
Rothwell, Walter Henry 1872-1927 *Baker 92*
Rothwell, Warren Randall 1917- *St&PR 93*
Rothzeid, Bernard 1925- *WhoAm 92*
Roti, Thomas D. *Law&B 92*
Rotili, P. *WhoScE 91-3*
Rotimi, Ola 1938- *BioIn 17*
Rotimi, (Emmanuel Gladstone) Ola(wale) 1938?- *DcLB 125 [port]*
Rotman, Arthur 1926- *WhoAm 92*
Rotman, Jesse Louis 1947- *WhoAm 92*
Rotman, Morris Bernard 1918- *WhoAm 92*
Rotmer, Edward Donald 1939- *WhoE 93*
Rotner, Robert Alan 1944- *WhoAm 92*
Rotolo, Vilma Stolfi 1930- *WhoWor 93*
Rotondaro, Antonio Luis Pacheco 1965- *WhoWor 93*
Rotondi, Charles A. 1949- *St&PR 93*
Rotondi, Marie A. 1924- *St&PR 93*
Rotroff, Stephen R. *St&PR 93*
Rotsler, William 1926- *ScF&FL 92*
Rott, Hans 1858-1884 *Baker 92*
Rott, Hans-Dieter 1940- *WhoScE 91-3*
Rottas, Ray 1927- *WhoAm 92*
Rottenberg, Dan(iel) 1942- *ConAu 40NR*
Rottenberg, Ludwig 1864-1932 *Baker 92*
Rottensteiner, Franz 1942- *ScF&FL 92*
Rotter, Clara d1992 *NewYTBS 92 [port]*
Rotter, David A. 1950- *St&PR 93*
Rotter, Doris M. 1936- *WhoAmW 93*
Rotter, Paul Talbott 1918- *WhoAm 92, WhoWor 93*
Rotter, Robert Reynold 1946- *St&PR 93*
Rotter, Russell J. *Law&B 92*
Rotter, Steven Jeffrey 1955- *WhoE 93*
Rotter, William R. 1953- *St&PR 93*
Rottger, Jurgen *WhoScE 91-4*
Rottino, Antonio 1903-1991 *BioIn 17*
Rottluff, Karl Schmidt- 1884-1976 *BioIn 17*
Rottman, Ellis 1930- *WhoAm 92*
Rottman, Fritz M. 1937- *WhoAm 92*
Rottman, Gordon 1947- *ScF&FL 92*
Rottman, Gordon Leroy 1947- *WhoWrEP 92*
Rottman, Howard 1922- *St&PR 93*
Rottmann, Betty Cook *BioIn 17*
Rottner, Susan A. 1945- *St&PR 93*
Rotton, James 1944- *WhoSSW 93*
Rottunda, Lawrence H. *Law&B 92*
Rotunda, Donald Theodore 1945- *WhoE 93, WhoWor 93*
Rotunda, Ronald Daniel 1945- *WhoAm 92*
Rotunno, Joseph R. 1928- *St&PR 93*
Rotunno, Phyllis di Buono 1929- *WhoAmW 93*
Rotz, Anna Overcash 1940- *WhoAmW 93*
Rotz, John Robert 1950- *St&PR 93*
Rotzal, Walter E. 1914- *St&PR 93*
Rotzien, William A. *Law&B 92*
Rotzinger-Padden, Karin Marie 1962- *WhoWrEP 92*
Rotzoll, Kim Brewer 1935- *WhoAm 92*
Rotzsch, Hans-Joachim 1929- *Baker 92*
Rou, Henry Jennings, II 1935- *St&PR 93*
Rouan, Brigitte *MiSFD 9*
Rouault, Georges 1871-1958 *BioIn 17*
Roub, Bryan R. 1941- *St&PR 93*
Roub, Bryan Roger 1941- *WhoAm 92*
Roubik, Susanne Eileen 1959- *WhoEmL 93*
Roubitchek, Donald A. 1950- *St&PR 93*
Roubos, Gary Lynn 1936- *St&PR 93, WhoAm 92, WhoE 93*
Rouch, James *ScF&FL 92*
Rouch, Jean 1917- *IntDcAn*
Roucolle, Adrienne 1875- *AmWomPl*
Roud, Richard 1929-1989 *BioIn 17*
Rouda, Mitchell Bruce 1957- *WhoAm 92*
Roudabush, Aaron Paul 1965- *WhoE 93*
Roudakov, Vladimir Ivanovitch 1954- *WhoUN 92*
Roudebush, Brooks 1926- *St&PR 93*
Roudebush, George M. 1894- *WhoAm 92*
Roudier, Jean Alex 1953- *WhoWor 93*
Roudiez, Cecelia T. *Law&B 92*
Roudy, Yvette 1929- *BioIn 17*
Roudybush, Alexandra 1911- *WhoAmW 93, WhoWor 93*
Roudybush, Franklin 1906- *WhoWor 93*
Roueche, Berton 1911- *WhoAm 92, WhoWrEP 92*
Roueche, John Edward, II 1938- *WhoAm 92, WhoWor 93*
Rouff, Benjamin 1914- *St&PR 93*
Roufs, J.A.J. 1929- *WhoScE 91-3*
Rouge, Francois Claude Jacques 1961- *WhoWor 93*
Rouge, J.C.J. 1931- *WhoScE 91-2*
Rougelot, Rodney S. 1933- *St&PR 93*
Rouget, Gilbert 1916- *Baker 92*
Rouget de l'Isle, Claude-Joseph 1760-1836 *Baker 92*
Rough, David S. 1933- *WhoWor 93*
Rough, Herbert Louis 1935- *WhoSSW 93*
Roughton, William L., Jr. *Law&B 92*
Rougier-Chapman, Alwyn Spencer Doug- 1939- *St&PR 93*
Rougier-Chapman, Alwyn Spencer Douglas, Sr. 1939- *WhoAm 92*
Rougny, Robert 1938- *WhoScE 91-2*
Rougraff, Maurice E. 1926- *St&PR 93, WhoIns 93*
Rouh, Edwin H., Jr. *Law&B 92*
Rouhana, William J., Jr. 1952- *St&PR 93*
Rouhana, William Joseph, Jr. 1952- *WhoE 93, WhoWor 93*
Rouher, Jean Charles 1939- *WhoUN 92*
Rouhesmaa, Juhani *WhoScE 91-4*
Rouillon, Annik *WhoScE 91-2*
Roukema, Margaret Scafati 1929- *WhoAm 92, WhoAmW 93, WhoE 93*
Roukema, Marge *BioIn 17*
Roukema, Marge 1929- *CngDr 91*
Roulac, Stephen E. *BioIn 17*
Roulac, Stephen E. 1945- *WhoAm 92*
Rouland, Jay Thomas 1935- *WhoAm 92*
Rouleau, Eric 1926- *WhoWor 93*
Rouleau, Ernest 1916-1991 *BioIn 17*
Rouleau, Guy 1939- *St&PR 93*
Rouleau, Jean Claude 1921- *WhoWor 93*
Rouleau, Joseph (Alfred Pierre) 1929- *Baker 92*
Rouleau, Monique Lucille 1964- *WhoE 93*
Rouleau, R. Michael *St&PR 93*
Rouleau, Wilfred Thomas 1929- *WhoE 93*
Roulet, Claude-Alain 1941- *WhoScE 91-4*
Roulet, L.C. *Law&B 92*
Roulier, Joy Roulier 1960- *WhoWrEP 92*
Roulier, Richard 1947- *St&PR 93*
Roulson, Lee C. 1943- *St&PR 93*
Roulston, Charles Robert 1930- *WhoSSW 93*
Roulston, David John 1936- *WhoWor 93*
Roulston, J.F. 1948- *WhoScE 91-1*
Roulston, John Frank Clement 1941- *WhoWor 93*
Roulston, Keith 1947- *WhoCanL 92*
Roulston, Laurie Laidlaw *Law&B 92*
Roulston, Thomas Henry 1933- *WhoAm 92, WhoWor 93*
Roulstone, George 1767-1804 *JrnUS*
Roumain, Jacques *DcCPCAm*
Roumm, Phyllis Evelyn Gensbigler 1927- *WhoAmW 93*
Round, Frank Eric *WhoScE 91-1*
Round, Joan M. *WhoScE 91-1*
Round, Lawrence Allen 1928- *St&PR 93*
Rounds, Donald Edwin 1926- *WhoAm 92*
Rounds, Glen 1906- *ChlBIID [port]*
Rounds, Glen (Harold) 1906- *MajAI [port], SmATA 70 [port]*
Rounds, John S. 1927- *St&PR 93*
Rounds, Kathleen Linda 1948- *WhoWrEP 92*
Rounds, Kevin Thomas 1951- *WhoAm 92*
Rounds, Linda Louise Charley 1949- *WhoAmW 93*
Rounds, Nadine Forster 1938- *WhoAmW 93*
Roundtree, Deborah *BioIn 17*
Roundtree, Eugene Van Nostrand 1927- *St&PR 93*
Roundtree, Phil Robert *St&PR 93*
Roundtree, Richard 1942- *WhoAm 92*
Rounick, Jack A. 1935- *St&PR 93, WhoAm 92*
Rounsaville, Guy, Jr. *Law&B 92*
Rounsaville, Guy, Jr. 1943- *St&PR 93*
Rountree, Asa 1927- *WhoAm 92*
Rountree, Frank Cox 1944- *St&PR 93*
Rountree, Janet Caryl 1937- *WhoAm 92*
Rountree, Jeanie Sue 1960- *WhoSSW 93*
Rountree, John Griffin Richardson 1936- *WhoSSW 93*
Rountree, Michael Allen 1942- *St&PR 93*
Rountree, Neal Thomas *Law&B 92*
Rountree, Neva Dixon 1943- *WhoAm 92*
Rountree, William C. 1941- *St&PR 93*
Rountree, William F., Jr. 1944- *St&PR 93*
Roup, Brenda Jacobs 1948- *WhoAmW 93*
Roupe, James Paul 1957- *WhoE 93*
Rouquerol, Jean 1937- *WhoScE 91-2*
Roure, Jean-Claude 1938- *WhoWor 93*
Rourk, Thomas Lee 1935- *St&PR 93*

Rourke, Arlene Carol 1944- *WhoAmW 93, WhoWor 93*
Rourke, Charles Kane 1932- *St&PR 93*
Rourke, Evan Charles 1964- *WhoE 93*
Rourke, Michael J. 1934- *St&PR 93*
Rourke, Michael James 1934- *WhoAm 92*
Rourke, Mickey *BioIn 17, WhoAm 92*
Rourke, Mickey 1950- *HolBB [port]*
Rourke, Mickey 1956- *IntDcF 2-3 [port]*
Rourke, Raymond Robert 1940- *St&PR 93*
Rourke, Stanley A. 1936- *St&PR 93*
Rous, Robert Kenneth 1944- *St&PR 93*
Rous, Stephen Norman 1931- *WhoAm 92, WhoWor 93*
Rousakis, John Paul 1929- *WhoAm 92, WhoSSW 93*
Rousch, C.E. *ScF&FL 92*
Rouse, Andrew Miles 1928- *WhoAm 92*
Rouse, Christopher (Chapman) 1949- *Baker 92*
Rouse, Doris Jane 1948- *WhoAm 92*
Rouse, Fenella *BioIn 17*
Rouse, Gregory Stanley 1954- *WhoWor 93*
Rouse, Irving 1913- *WhoAm 92*
Rouse, James R. 1942- *St&PR 93*
Rouse, James W. *BioIn 17*
Rouse, Jeffrey Taylor 1958- *WhoSSW 93*
Rouse, John W., Jr. 1937- *St&PR 93*
Rouse, John Wilson, Jr. 1937- *WhoAm 92*
Rouse, Juanita Andre 1943- *WhoAmW 93*
Rouse, Michael J. *WhoScE 91-1*
Rouse, Michael John 1939- *WhoScE 91-1*
Rouse, Michael William 1941- *WhoSSW 93*
Rouse, Richard Hunter 1933- *WhoAm 92*
Rouse, Robert A. 1949- *St&PR 93*
Rouse, Robert Sumner 1930- *WhoAm 92, WhoE 93*
Rouse, Roscoe, Jr. 1919- *WhoAm 92*
Rouse, Roy Dennis 1920- *WhoAm 92*
Rouse, Russell 1915-1987 *MiSFD 9N*
Rouse, Ted D. 1935- *St&PR 93*
Rouse, William Bradford 1947- *WhoAm 92*
Rouse, William S. 1931- *St&PR 93*
Rousell, Ralph Henry 1933- *WhoWor 93*
Roush, Annette Marie 1957- *WhoE 93*
Roush, Esther *AmWomPl*
Roush, Jack *BioIn 17*
Rousi, Arne H. 1931- *WhoScE 91-4*
Rousmaniere, John 1944- *ConAu 38NR*
Rousmaniere, John Pierce 1944- *WhoE 93*
Rouson, Vivian Reissland 1929- *WhoAmW 93*
Rousos, Elizabeth T. *Law&B 92*
Rousos, Peter C. *Law&B 92*
Rouss, Ruth 1914- *WhoAm 92*
Roussakis, Nicolas 1934- *Baker 92, WhoAm 92*
Rousse, David Edmond 1953- *St&PR 93*
Rousse, Georges *BioIn 17*
Rousseau, Conrad Ernest, Jr. 1937- *WhoIns 93*
Rousseau, Eugene 1932- *Baker 92*
Rousseau, Eugene Ellsworth 1932- *WhoAm 92*
Rousseau, Gabriel Argy- 1885-1953 *BioIn 17*
Rousseau, George Sebastian 1941- *WhoAm 92*
Rousseau, Guy G. 1939- *WhoScE 91-2*
Rousseau, Irene Victoria *WhoE 93*
Rousseau, Jacques Ambroise 1933- *St&PR 93*
Rousseau, Jean-Jacques 1712-1778 *Baker 92, BioIn 17, IntDcAn, IntDcOp, MagSWL [port], OxDcOp, WorLitC [port]*
Rousseau, Jeannine Marie 1941- *WhoAm 92*
Rousseau, John F. 1943- *St&PR 93*
Rousseau, Leodor Edgar 1933- *St&PR 93*
Rousseau, Marcel (-Auguste-Louis) 1882-1955 *Baker 92*
Rousseau, Norman P. *Law&B 92*
Rousseau, Normand 1939- *WhoCanL 92*
Rousseau, Pierre *Law&B 92*
Rousseau, Pierre Marie Rene Ernest Waldeck- 1846-1904 *BioIn 17*
Rousseau, Ronald Joseph 1935- *St&PR 93*
Rousseau, Ronald William 1943- *WhoAm 92*
Rousseau, Samuel-Alexandre 1853-1904 *Baker 92*
Rousseau, Victor 1879-1960 *ScF&FL 92*
Rousseau-Finelli, Sharon 1964- *WhoE 93*
Roussel, Alain M. 1949- *WhoWor 93*
Roussel, Alain Rene 1938- *WhoScE 91-2*
Roussel, Albert 1869-1937 *OxDcOp*
Roussel, Albert (Charles Paul Marie) 1869-1937 *Baker 92*
Roussel, Athina *BioIn 17*
Roussel, George A. 1920- *St&PR 93*
Roussel, Normand Lucien 1934- *WhoE 93*
Roussel, Thierry *BioIn 17*
Roussel De Bailleul d1078 *OxDcByz*
Rousselet, Francois Jean 1929- *WhoScE 91-2*
Rousseliere, Charles 1875-1950 *Baker 92, OxDcOp*
Roussell, Norward *BioIn 17*
Rousset, A.C.M. 1938- *WhoScE 91-2*
Rousset, Alain *WhoAm 92*
Roussey, Robert Stanley 1935- *WhoWor 93*
Roussier, Pierre-Joseph 1716-1792 *Baker 92*
Roussin, Richard A. 1932- *St&PR 93*
Rousso, Eli L. 1920- *St&PR 93*
Rousso, Eli Louis 1920-1990 *BioIn 17*
Roussos, David G. *Law&B 92*
Roussy, Georges 1938- *WhoScE 91-2*
Routcliffe, Robert Henry *Law&B 92*
Route, Deborah A. 1953- *WhoWrEP 92*
Routh, Donald Kent 1937- *WhoAm 92*
Routh, Francis (John) 1927- *Baker 92*
Routhier, Adolphe-Basile 1839-1920 *BioIn 17*
Routien, John Broderick 1913- *WhoAm 92*
Routledge, Lee H. *Law&B 92*
Routray, Nilamoni 1920- *WhoAsAP 91*
Routson, Clell Dennis 1946- *St&PR 93*
Routti, Jorma Tapio 1938- *WhoScE 91-4*
Routzahn, Nancy Gloria *Law&B 92*
Rouve, Gerhard A.K. 1927- *WhoScE 91-3*
Rouverol, Aurania Ellerbeck 1885-1955 *AmWomPl*
Rouvier, Pierre Maurice 1842-1911 *BioIn 17*
Rouvinen, Hannu Matti 1951- *WhoWor 93*
Roux, Ambroise Marie Casimir 1921- *WhoAm 92, WhoWor 93*
Roux, Jean Claude 1936- *WhoScE 91-2*
Roux, Jean-Louis 1923- *WhoAm 92*
Roux, Joseph Edward 1958- *WhoSSW 93*
Roux, Marc Charles 1943- *WhoScE 91-2*
Roux, Michel *BioIn 17*
Roux, Michel 1943- *WhoScE 91-2*
Roux, Michel 1944- *WhoScE 91-2*
Roux, Mildred Anna 1914- *WhoAmW 93, WhoE 93*
Roux, Stephane 1960- *WhoWor 93*
Rouxel, Jean 1935- *WhoScE 91-2*
Rouxel, Vincent Yves 1948- *St&PR 93*
Rouxhet, Paul G.F.G. 1941- *WhoScE 91-2*
Rouze, Jeffrey Alan 1952- *WhoWor 93*
Rovansek, Gary John 1942- *St&PR 93*
Rove, Karl Christian 1950- *WhoSSW 93*
Roveda, John Gregory 1938- *St&PR 93*
Rovegno, George F. 1948- *St&PR 93*
Rovell, Michael Jay 1949- *WhoEmL 93*
Rovelli, Pietro 1793-1838 *Baker 92*
Rovelo, Jaime O. 1943- *St&PR 93*
Rovelstad, Mathilde Verner 1920- *WhoAm 92*
Roven, Milton Dean 1916- *WhoE 93*
Rover, Cecelia Mary 1938- *WhoAmW 93*
Rover, Edward Frank 1938- *WhoAm 92*
Rovere, Agostino 1804-1865 *Baker 92*
Rovere, Richard H. 1915-1979 *JrnUS*
Roveri, Aldo 1937- *WhoScE 91-3*
Roversi, Roberto 1923- *DcLB 128 [port]*
Roverud, Eleanor 1912- *WhoWor 93*
Rovery, Mireille 1922- *WhoScE 91-2*
Roveto, Connie Ida *WhoE 93*
Rovetta, Giovanni c. 1595-1668 *Baker 92, OxDcOp*
Rovin, Jeff 1951- *ScF&FL 92*
Rovin, Leo 1914- *St&PR 93*
Rovine, Arthur William 1937- *WhoAm 92, WhoWor 93*
Rovinski, Michael E. *Law&B 92*
Rovinskii, Dmitrii Aleksandrovich 1824-1895 *BioIn 17*
Rovinsky, Joseph Judah 1927- *WhoAm 92*
Rovira, Luis D. 1923- *HispAmA [port]*
Rovira, Luis Dario 1923- *WhoAm 92*
Rovira-Paoli, Alba *Law&B 92*
Rovito, Janice M. 1954- *St&PR 93*
Rovner, Arkady 1940- *WhoWrEP 92*
Rovner, David Richard 1930- *WhoAm 92*
Rovner, Ilana Kara Diamond 1938- *WhoAm 92, WhoAmW 93*
Rovzar, Alexis E. 1951- *WhoWor 93*
Row, Barry Lynn 1952- *WhoSSW 93*
Row, Clark 1934- *WhoE 93*
Row, David 1949- *WhoE 93*
Row, Orion Y. 1915- *St&PR 93*
Row, Peter L. *WhoAm 92*
Row, Susan A. *Law&B 92*
Rowady, Edward P. 1928- *St&PR 93*
Rowan, Arnold 1954- *WhoE 93*
Rowan, Bruce Clayton 1952- *St&PR 93*
Rowan, Carl Thomas 1925- *BioIn 17, JrnUS, WhoAm 92, WhoWrEP 92*
Rowan, E. Charles, Jr. *Law&B 92*
Rowan, Edward Walter 1947- *St&PR 93*
Rowan, Gerald Burdette 1916- *WhoAm 92*
Rowan, James P. *Law&B 92*
Rowan, James P. 1933- *St&PR 93*
Rowan, John Robert 1919- *WhoAm 92, WhoSSW 93*
Rowan, Marie Downey 1960- *WhoAmW 93*
Rowan, Phyllis Hobbs *BioIn 17*
Rowan, Rena Jung 1928- *WhoAm 92*
Rowan, Richard Lamar 1931- *WhoAm 92*
Rowan, Robert Dale 1922- *WhoAm 92*
Rowan, Roy *BioIn 17*
Rowand, Edward W. 1942- *St&PR 93*
Rowan-Robinson, Michael *WhoScE 91-1*
Rowark, Maureen 1933- *WhoAm 92*
Rowatt, Robert Watson *WhoScE 91-1*
Rowden, Gwen A. *Law&B 92*
Rowden, Gwen Alison 1954- *WhoE 93*
Rowden, Marcus Aubrey 1928- *WhoAm 92*
Rowden, William Henry 1930- *WhoAm 92*
Rowder, William Louis 1937- *WhoAm 92*
Rowe, A. Prescott 1938- *St&PR 93*
Rowe, Adrian Harold Redfern *WhoScE 91-1*
Rowe, Alan M. 1956- *St&PR 93*
Rowe, Allan D. 1951- *St&PR 93*
Rowe, Allan Duncan 1951- *WhoAm 92*
Rowe, Arthur Edgar 1929- *St&PR 93, WhoAm 92*
Rowe, Audrey 1958- *WhoAmW 93*
Rowe, Barbara Marie 1953- *St&PR 93*
Rowe, Bertrand R. 1947- *WhoScE 91-2*
Rowe, Beverly Hope 1933- *WhoWrEP 92*
Rowe, Bonnie Gordon 1922- *WhoWor 93*
Rowe, Brian Peter 1953- *WhoSSW 93*
Rowe, Charles Alfred 1934- *WhoAm 92*
Rowe, Charles S. 1925- *St&PR 93*
Rowe, Charles Spurgeon 1925- *WhoAm 92*
Rowe, Clair Devere 1924- *WhoAm 92*
Rowe, Clarence John 1916- *WhoAm 92*
Rowe, Clyde C. *Law&B 92*
Rowe, David John 1936- *WhoAm 92*
Rowe, David Lawrence 1952- *WhoE 93*
Rowe, Donald A. *Law&B 92*
Rowe, Donald A. 1937- *WhoAm 92*
Rowe, Edgar Riley 1922- *WhoSSW 93*
Rowe, Elizabeth 1674-1737 *BioIn 17*
Rowe, Elizabeth Ulman 1912-1991 *BioIn 17*
Rowe, Elizabeth Webb 1957- *WhoE 93*
Rowe, G. Steven *Law&B 92*
Rowe, George 1938- *MiSFD 9*
Rowe, George Giles 1921- *WhoAm 92*
Rowe, Grace *AmWomPl*
Rowe, Harris 1923- *St&PR 93*
Rowe, Harrison Edward 1927- *WhoAm 92*
Rowe, Helen *ScF&FL 92*
Rowe, Henry Theodore, Jr. 1932- *WhoSSW 93*
Rowe, Herbert Joseph 1924- *WhoAm 92*
Rowe, Jack Field 1927- *St&PR 93, WhoAm 92*
Rowe, James David 1957- *WhoSSW 93*
Rowe, James Gordon 1857-1929 *BiDAMSp 1989*
Rowe, James Walter 1923- *St&PR 93*
Rowe, James Wilmot 1928- *WhoWor 93*
Rowe, Jason *NewYTBS 92 [port]*
Rowe, Jean Ann 1959- *WhoAmW 93*
Rowe, Jennifer *ScF&FL 92*
Rowe, Jody Raye *Law&B 92*
Rowe, John Howland 1918- *WhoAm 92*
Rowe, John J. 1951- *St&PR 93*
Rowe, John R. *Law&B 92*
Rowe, John R., Jr. 1939- *St&PR 93*
Rowe, John Wallis 1944- *WhoAm 92*
Rowe, John Westel 1924- *WhoAm 92*
Rowe, John William 1945- *WhoAm 92*
Rowe, Joseph Everett 1927- *WhoAm 92*
Rowe, Josiah Pollard 1928- *St&PR 93*
Rowe, Kevin Ian 1961- *WhoWor 93*
Rowe, Kevin S. 1938- *WhoAm 92, WhoE 93*
Rowe, Lynn Tayul 1955- *WhoE 93*
Rowe, Lynwood Thomas 1910-1961 *BiDAMSp 1989*
Rowe, Marieli Dorothy *WhoAmW 93*
Rowe, Marvin Wayne 1937- *WhoSSW 93*
Rowe, Max L. 1921- *WhoAm 92*
Rowe, Melanie *WhoWrEP 92*
Rowe, Michael George 1940- *St&PR 93*
Rowe, Michael T. 1953- *WhoScE 91-1*
Rowe, Myra 1927- *WhoWrEP 92*
Rowe, Nathaniel Hawthorne 1931- *WhoAm 92*
Rowe, Nicholas 1664-1718 *BioIn 17*
Rowe, Nigel 1964- *ScF&FL 92*
Rowe, O. Reagan, Jr. 1929- *St&PR 93*
Rowe, Peter 1947- *MiSFD 9*
Rowe, Peter Grimmond 1945- *WhoAm 92*
Rowe, Peter John 1947- *WhoWor 93*
Rowe, Peter Joseph 1938- *WhoAm 92*
Rowe, Richard Lloyd 1926- *WhoAm 92*
Rowe, Richard Roy 1933- *St&PR 93*
Rowe, Robert Hetsley 1929- *WhoIns 93*
Rowe, Russell P. *Law&B 92*
Rowe, Sandra Mims 1948- *WhoAm 92*
Rowe, Teresa Marie 1959- *WhoAmW 93*
Rowe, Thomas Dudley, Jr. 1942- *WhoAm 92*
Rowe, Thomas Lee *Law&B 92*
Rowe, W. Bayless *Law&B 92*
Rowe, W.W. 1934- *ScF&FL 92*
Rowe, Wanda Sue 1941- *WhoAmW 93*
Rowe, William Brian *WhoScE 91-1*
Rowe, William Brian 1939- *WhoWor 93*
Rowe, William Davis 1937- *WhoAm 92*
Rowe, William Jeffrey 1954- *WhoSSW 93*
Rowe, William John 1936- *WhoE 93*
Rowe, William Morford, Jr. 1937- *WhoWrEP 92*
Rowe, William Neil 1942- *WhoCanL 92*
Rowecki, Stefan 1895-1944 *PolBiDi*
Rowek, Joseph F. *Law&B 92*
Rowekamp, Edward A. 1949- *St&PR 93*
Rowell, Adelaide Corinne 1887- *AmWomPl*
Rowell, C.H.F. 1933- *WhoScE 91-4*
Rowell, Charles Frederick 1935- *WhoAm 92*
Rowell, David Benton 1939- *WhoE 93*
Rowell, Dean W. *St&PR 93*
Rowell, Edward Morgan 1931- *WhoAm 92, WhoWor 93*
Rowell, Edward S., Jr. 1945- *St&PR 93*
Rowell, Galen A. *BioIn 17*
Rowell, George (Rignall) 1923- *ConAu 39NR*
Rowell, Harry B., Jr. 1941- *St&PR 93*
Rowell, Harry Brown, Jr. 1941- *WhoAm 92, WhoE 93*
Rowell, John Thomas 1920- *WhoSSW 93*
Rowell, Lester John, Jr. 1932- *St&PR 93, WhoAm 92, WhoE 93*
Rowell, Melissa C. *St&PR 93*
Rowe-Maas, Betty Lu 1925- *WhoAmW 93, WhoWor 93*
Rowen, Francis Augustine, Jr. *Law&B 92*
Rowen, Gary M. *Law&B 92*
Rowen, Harold Charles 1931- *St&PR 93*
Rowen, Henry Stanislaus 1925- *WhoAm 92*
Rowen, Hobart 1918- *JrnUS, WhoAm 92*
Rowen, Ida M. *AmWomPl*
Rowen, Marshall *WhoAm 92*
Rowen, Michael J. 1956- *St&PR 93*
Rowen, Robert M. *Law&B 92*
Rowen, Rose Lee 1917- *WhoAmW 93, WhoE 93*
Rowen, Ruth Halle 1918- *Baker 92, WhoAm 92, WhoAmW 93, WhoE 93, WhoWor 93*
Rowicki, Witold 1914-1989 *Baker 92*
Rowland, Allen Ray 1944- *St&PR 93*
Rowland, Arthur Ray 1930- *WhoAm 92, WhoSSW 93*
Rowland, Bertram I. *St&PR 93*
Rowland, Brian A. *Law&B 92*
Rowland, David Jack 1921- *WhoSSW 93*
Rowland, David Lawrence 1949- *WhoSSW 93*
Rowland, Dermot F. 1937- *St&PR 93*
Rowland, Donald M. 1926- *St&PR 93*
Rowland, Donald S. 1928- *ScF&FL 92*
Rowland, Dorothy Esther 1914- *WhoAmW 93*
Rowland, Edna 1922- *ConAu 139*
Rowland, Edwin W. *Law&B 92*
Rowland, Esther Edelman 1926- *WhoAm 92*
Rowland, Frank Sherwood *BioIn 17*
Rowland, Frank Sherwood 1927- *WhoAm 92*
Rowland, George E. 1937- *WhoSSW 93*
Rowland, Ivan Wendell 1910- *WhoAm 92*
Rowland, J. Roy 1926- *CngDr 91*
Rowland, James Anthony 1922- *WhoAsAP 91*
Rowland, James Morten 1948- *WhoE 93*
Rowland, James Richard 1940- *WhoAm 92*
Rowland, James Roy 1926- *WhoAm 92*
Rowland, James Roy Roy 1926- *WhoSSW 93*
Rowland, Jan Brownstein *WhoAmW 93*
Rowland, Jan Reagan 1944- *WhoSSW 93*
Rowland, John G. 1957- *WhoE 93*
Rowland, Karen C. *Law&B 92*
Rowland, Landon Hill 1937- *St&PR 93, WhoAm 92*
Rowland, Lewis Phillip 1925- *WhoAm 92*
Rowland, Lori Pruitt *Law&B 92*
Rowland, Lucy Minogue 1948- *WhoSSW 93*
Rowland, Pleasant *News 92 [port], -92-3 [port]*
Rowland, Ralph Thomas 1920- *WhoAm 92*
Rowland, Robert Charles 1946- *WhoSSW 93*
Rowland, Robin F. 1950- *ConAu 136*
Rowland, Sherry *BioIn 17*
Rowland, Theodore Justin 1927- *WhoAm 92*
Rowland, Thomas W. *Law&B 92*
Rowland, Thomas W. 1948- *St&PR 93*
Rowland, Thomas William 1942- *St&PR 93*
Rowland, Thomas William 1948- *WhoAm 92*
Rowland, Walter S. *Law&B 92*
Rowland, William B., Jr. *Law&B 92*
Rowland, William L. 1946- *WhoIns 93*

Rowland, William Lachell 1946- *St&PR 93*
Rowland Payne, Christopher Melville Edwin 1955- *WhoWor 93*
Rowlands, Brian James *WhoScE 91-1*
Rowlands, D.G. 1941- *ScF&FL 92*
Rowlands, David George 1941- *WhoScE 91-1*
Rowlands, David Thomas 1930- *WhoAm 92*
Rowlands, Gena 1934?- *IntDcF 2-3*
Rowlands, Gena 1936- *WhoAm 92, WhoAmW 93*
Rowlands, George 1932- *WhoWor 93*
Rowlands, June *WhoE 93*
Rowlands, Marvin Lloyd, Jr. 1926- *WhoAm 92*
Rowlands, Robert Edward 1936- *WhoAm 92*
Rowlands, Samuel c. 1570-1630 *DcLB 121*
Rowlands, T. Dewi 1939- *WhoAm 92*
Rowlandson, Mary White c. 1637-1710? *BioIn 17*
Rowlenson, Richard C. *Law&B 92*
Rowlenson, Richard C. 1949- *St&PR 93*
Rowles, Charles A. 1915- *WhoAm 92*
Rowles, Peter Alexander 1954- *St&PR 93*
Rowlett, Bobby N. 1952- *St&PR 93*
Rowlett, Dale K. 1955- *St&PR 93*
Rowlett, Ralph Morgan 1934- *WhoAm 92*
Rowley, Alec 1892-1958 *Baker 92*
Rowley, Barbara *BioIn 17*
Rowley, Beverley Davies 1941- *WhoAm 92, WhoAmW 93*
Rowley, Charlene Marie 1943- *WhoAmW 93*
Rowley, Charles G. 1936- *St&PR 93*
Rowley, Charles Kershaw 1939- *WhoSSW 93*
Rowley, Christopher *BioIn 17*
Rowley, Christopher 1948- *ScF&FL 92*
Rowley, Christopher Andrew *WhoScE 91-1*
Rowley, Frank Selby, Jr. 1913- *WhoSSW 93, WhoWor 93*
Rowley, Glenn Harry 1948- *WhoE 93*
Rowley, H.L. 1945- *St&PR 93*
Rowley, James J. d1992 *NewYTBS 92 [port]*
Rowley, James Max 1943- *WhoE 93*
Rowley, James Walton 1925- *WhoAm 92*
Rowley, Janet Davison 1925- *WhoAm 92, WhoAmW 93*
Rowley, Jean F. 1933- *WhoAm 92*
Rowley, Kathleen Dorothy 1941- *WhoAmW 93*
Rowley, L. Dale 1939- *St&PR 93*
Rowley, Michael Fitzgerald 1949- *St&PR 93*
Rowley, Peter Templeton 1929- *WhoAm 92*
Rowley, R. Casey 1932- *St&PR 93*
Rowley, Rezia *AmWomPl*
Rowley, Stephen John *Law&B 92*
Rowley, William Richard Charlton 1935- *WhoScE 91-1*
Rowley, William Robert 1943- *WhoAm 92*
Rowlings, Donald George 1929- *WhoAm 92*
Rowlingson, John Clyde 1948- *WhoAm 92, WhoSSW 93*
Rowlinson, John Shipley *WhoScE 91-1*
Rowlinson, Peter 1944- *WhoWor 93*
Rownak, John Joseph, Jr. 1946- *St&PR 93*
Rowney, John A. 1945- *St&PR 93*
Rowney, John Adalbert 1945- *WhoIns 93*
Rowntree, B. Seebohm 1871-1954 *BioIn 17*
Rowntree, Benjamin Seebohm 1871-1954 *BioIn 17, DcTwHis*
Rowntree, O. Cedric d1990 *BioIn 17*
Rowohlt, Heinrich Maria Ledig- 1908-1992 *BioIn 17*
Rowold, Carl A. *Law&B 92*
Rowse, Alfred Leslie 1903- *WhoWor 93*
Rowson, Henry M. 1936- *WhoScE 91-1*
Rowson, Richard Cavanagh 1926- *WhoAm 92*
Rowswell, Mark *BioIn 17*
Roxas, Edmund R. 1949- *WhoWor 93*
Roxas, Emilia Bien-Bien *BioIn 17*
Roxas, Gerardo A., Jr. 1960- *WhoAsAP 91*
Roxas, Manuel 1892-1948 *DcTwHis*
Roxas, Sofronio Pongos 1938-1984 *BioIn 17*
Roxas, Virginia Palicpic 1964- *WhoWor 93*
Roxburgh, Edwin 1937- *Baker 92*
Roxburgh, Ian Walter *WhoScE 91-1*
Roxburgh, Ian Walter 1939- *WhoWor 93*
Roxe, Joseph D. 1936- *St&PR 93*
Roy, Allan George 1937- *St&PR 93*
Roy, Andre *Law&B 92*
Roy, Andre 1944- *WhoCanL 92*
Roy, Ann G. *Law&B 92*
Roy, Archibald *ScF&FL 92*
Roy, Archie 1924- *ScF&FL 92*
Roy, Archie E. *WhoScE 91-1*
Roy, Armand Joseph 1942- *WhoAm 92*
Roy, Barbeau A. *Law&B 92*
Roy, Bimalendu Narayan *WhoWor 93*
Roy, Camille 1870-1944 *BioIn 17*
Roy, Catherine Elizabeth 1948- *WhoEmL 93*
Roy, Charles Robert 1930- *St&PR 93, WhoAm 92*
Roy, Chunilal 1935- *WhoAm 92, WhoWor 93*
Roy, Concetta Cornacchia d1991 *BioIn 17*
Roy, David Tod 1933- *WhoAm 92*
Roy, Dean Paul *Law&B 92*
Roy, Della Martin 1926- *WhoAm 92, WhoAmW 93, WhoE 93*
Roy, Delwin Adams 1937- *WhoE 93*
Roy, Dennis J. 1954- *WhoE 93*
Roy, Dev Kumar 1951- *WhoSSW 93*
Roy, Douglas 1947- *BioIn 17*
Roy, Elsijane Trimble 1916- *WhoAm 92, WhoAmW 93, WhoSSW 93*
Roy, Emil Lawrence 1933- *WhoSSW 93*
Roy, Frances Breen 1956- *WhoSSW 93*
Roy, Francois R. 1955- *St&PR 93*
Roy, Gabriel Delvis 1939- *WhoSSW 93*
Roy, Gabrielle 1909-1983 *BioIn 17, MagSWL [port]*
Roy, Gordon J. 1949- *St&PR 93*
Roy, Harold Edward 1921- *WhoWor 93*
Roy, Helen Antoinette 1933- *St&PR 93*
Roy, Henri A. 1947- *WhoAm 92*
Roy, James DeWall 1940- *St&PR 93*
Roy, James Stapleton 1935- *WhoAm 92, WhoWor 93*
Roy, Jean-Denis *Law&B 92*
Roy, Jean-Yves 1940- *WhoCanL 92*
Roy, Jeffrey 1955- *St&PR 93*
Roy, John Flint 1913- *ScF&FL 92*
Roy, John L. 1929- *St&PR 93*
Roy, Jules 1907- *BioIn 17*
Roy, Klaus George 1924- *Baker 92*
Roy, Madeleine *Law&B 92*
Roy, Melinda *BioIn 17, WhoAm 92*
Roy, Michelle 1936- *WhoCanL 92*
Roy, Norman E. 1926- *WhoAm 92*
Roy, Norman Ernest 1926- *St&PR 93*
Roy, P. Norman 1934- *St&PR 93*
Roy, Patricia E. *ConAu 137*
Roy, Patrick 1965- *WhoAm 92*
Roy, Paul *BioIn 17*
Roy, Paul Henri 1924- *WhoAm 92*
Roy, Philip Franklin 1921- *St&PR 93*
Roy, Radha Raman 1921- *WhoAm 92*
Roy, Real O. 1938- *St&PR 93*
Roy, Richard 1955- *St&PR 93*
Roy, Robert 1927-1990 *BioIn 17*
Roy, Roberto Ramon 1948- *WhoWor 93*
Roy, Ronald Dwayne 1956- *WhoE 93*
Roy, Rustum 1924- *WhoAm 92*
Roy, Sue *ScF&FL 92*
Roy, Thomas (Albert) *DcChlFi*
Roy, Tuhin Kumar 1923- *WhoWor 93*
Roy, William Gordon Begg 1943- *WhoWor 93*
Roya, Randy *BioIn 17*
Royal, Brian James *ScF&FL 92*
Royal, Darrell K. 1924- *WhoAm 92, WhoSSW 93*
Royal, Lyssa 1961- *WhoWrEP 92*
Royal, Richard M. 1935- *WhoIns 93*
Royal, Sharon Gail *Law&B 92*
Royal, William Henry 1924- *WhoWor 93*
Royall, Anne 1769-1854 *JrnUS*
Royall, Anne Newport 1769-1854 *BioIn 17*
Royal Spades *SoulM*
Royalty, David *Law&B 92*
Royalty, Jane Swaim 1920- *WhoAmW 93*
Roy-Arcelin, Nicole *WhoAmW 93*
Roybal, Edward R. 1916- *CngDr 91, HispAmA [port], WhoAm 92*
Roybal, Timmy *BioIn 17*
Roybal-Allard, Lucille 1941- *NotHsAW 93 [port], WhoAmW 93*
Royce, Anya Peterson *BioIn 17*
Royce, Barrie Saunders Hart 1933- *WhoAm 92*
Royce, C.C. 1845-1923 *IntDcAn*
Royce, Donald d1990 *BioIn 17*
Royce, Edward 1886-1963 *Baker 92*
Royce, Joseph R. *BioIn 17*
Royce, Josiah 1855-1916 *BioIn 17, GayN*
Royce, Paul C. 1928- *WhoAm 92, WhoE 93*
Royce, Raymond Watson 1936- *WhoAm 92*
Royce, Robert Coolidge 1930- *St&PR 93*
Royce, Rolland D. 1953- *St&PR 93*
Royce, Ruth 1893-1971 *SweetSg B*
Roychoudhuri, Chandrasekhar 1942- *WhoE 93, WhoWor 93*
Roychoudhury, Prodyot Kumar 1932- *WhoUN 92*
Roycroft, Howard Francis 1930- *WhoAm 92*
Roycroft, Richard Wallace 1963- *WhoSSW 93*
Royden, Halsey Lawrence 1928- *WhoAm 92*
Royds, Robert Bruce 1944- *WhoE 93, WhoWor 93*
Roye, Nancy L. 1923- *St&PR 93*
Royer, Charles Theodore 1939- *WhoAm 92*
Royer, David Lee 1950- *St&PR 93, WhoIns 93*
Royer, Donald E. *Law&B 92*
Royer, Donald E. 1949- *WhoAm 92*
Royer, Etienne 1882-1928 *Baker 92*
Royer, Henry 1931- *St&PR 93*
Royer, Jean 1920- *BioIn 17*
Royer, Joseph-Nicolas-Pancrace c. 1705-1755 *Baker 92*
Royer, Kathleen Rose 1949- *WhoAmW 93*
Royer, Kenneth W. 1928- *St&PR 93*
Royer, Linda Mary 1949- *WhoE 93*
Royer, Marilyn Ann 1948- *WhoE 93*
Royer, Mark P. *Law&B 92*
Royer, Raymond *WhoAm 92*
Royer, Rene Jean 1931- *WhoScE 91-2*
Royer, Robert Lewis 1928- *WhoAm 92*
Royer, Susan Cort 1964- *WhoAmW 93*
Royer, Thomas Jerry 1943- *WhoWor 93*
Royko, Mike 1932- *JrnUS, WhoAm 92, WhoWrEP 92*
Royko, Raymond T. 1946- *St&PR 93*
Royko, Raymond Thomas *Law&B 92*
Roylance, Peter James 1928- *WhoE 93*
Royle, David Johnston *WhoScE 91-1*
Royle, Nicholas *ScF&FL 92*
Royle, Richard Dwight 1937- *WhoAm 92*
Royo, Aristides *DcCPCAm*
Royo, Joaquin 1926- *WhoScE 91-3*
Royon, Rene Jean Maurice 1931- *WhoWor 93*
Roy Pradhan, Amar 1930- *WhoAsAP 91*
Royse, Charles David 1954- *St&PR 93*
Royse, James Charles 1945- *WhoSSW 93*
Royse, Mary Kay 1949- *WhoAmW 93*
Royse, Morton W. d1992 *NewYTBS 92*
Royster, David Calvin 1952- *WhoSSW 93*
Royster, Jacqueline Jones 1950- *WhoSSW 93*
Royster, Vermont (Connecticut) 1914- *DcLB 127 [port], JrnUS, WhoAm 92*
Royster, Wimberly Calvin 1925- *WhoSSW 93*
Royston, Dawn Marie 1953- *WhoAmW 93*
Royston, Dick Coombs 1940- *WhoSSW 93*
Royston, Jonathan Whitney *Law&B 92*
Royston, Richard John 1931- *WhoAm 92*
Roytek, Thomas E. 1938- *St&PR 93*
Roz, Gian Piero T. 1946- *WhoUN 92*
Rozak, Kevin F. 1950- *St&PR 93*
Rozak, Theodore 1907-1981 *PolBiDi*
Rozakis, Robert H. 1951- *WhoWrEP 92*
Rozanczyk, Gary A. 1952- *St&PR 93*
Rozanski, Edward Casimir 1915- *WhoWor 93*
Rozanski, Raphaela Patricia 1945- *WhoE 93*
Roze, Claude 1936- *WhoScE 91-2*
Roze, Marie 1846-1926 *Baker 92*
Roze, Raymond 1875-1920 *Baker 92*
Rozee, Patricia *BioIn 17*
Rozel, Samuel Joseph 1935- *St&PR 93, WhoAm 92*
Rozell, Walter Henry d1991 *BioIn 17*
Rozelle, Lee Theodore 1933- *WhoAm 92, WhoWor 93*
Rozelle, Mark Albert 1960- *WhoE 93*
Rozelle, Pete *BioIn 17*
Rozelle, Pete 1926- *WhoAm 92*
Rozelot, Jean-Pierre 1942- *WhoScE 91-2*
Rozema, Patricia *BioIn 17*
Rozema, Patricia 1958- *MiSFD 9*
Rozen, Jerome George, Jr. 1928- *WhoAm 92*
Rozen, Milton A. 1921- *St&PR 93*
Rozen, Wayne A. *St&PR 93*
Rozenbaum, Najman 1945- *WhoWor 93*
Rozenberg, Michael Albert 1949- *WhoIns 93*
Rozenblum, Maurice J. 1935- *St&PR 93*
Rozenblum, Raquel L. *St&PR 93*
Rozenblyum, Alexander Veniaminovich 1948- *WhoWor 93*
Rozenblyum, Gregory Vladimirovich 1948- *WhoWor 93*
Rozendal, Silvius *DcCPCAm*
Rozenfeld, Bronislaw 1922- *WhoScE 91-4*
Rozengurt, Juan Enrique 1942- *WhoScE 91-1*
Rozett, Walter P. 1923- *St&PR 93*
Rozewicz, Paul J. 1941- *St&PR 93*
Rozewicz, Stanislaw 1924- *DrEEuF*
Rozewicz, Tadeusz 1921- *BioIn 17*
Rozhdestvensky, Gennadi Nikolaevich 1931- *WhoWor 93*
Rozhdestvensky, Gennadi (Nikolaievich) 1931- *Baker 92*
Rozhdestvensky, Robert Ivanovich 1932- *WhoWor 93*
Rozich, Ileene Shaffer 1932- *WhoWor 93*
Rozier, Dick *BioIn 17*
Rozier, Jacques E.Y. 1934- *WhoScE 91-2*
Rozin, Skip *BioIn 17*
Rozkosny, Josef 1833-1913 *OxDcOp*
Rozkosny, Josef Richard 1833-1913 *Baker 92*
Rozlo, Jan Kazimierz 1936- *WhoScE 91-4*
Rozmajzl, James A. *Law&B 92*
Rozman, Gilbert Friedell 1943- *WhoAm 92*
Rozman, Sheryl Ann 1956- *WhoAmW 93*
Rozniecki, Jerzy 1929- *WhoScE 91-4*
Rozovski, Samuel Jaime 1944- *WhoE 93*
Rozsa, Gyorgy 1922- *WhoWor 93*
Rozsa, Gyula 1941- *WhoWor 93*
Rozsa, Janos 1937- *DrEEuF*
Rozsa, Miklos 1907- *Baker 92, BioIn 17, CurBio 92 [port], WhoAm 92*
Rozsnyai, Zoltan 1927-1990 *Baker 92, BioIn 17*
Roztropowicz, Stanislava 1927- *WhoScE 91-4*
Rozumova, Bela 1903- *See* Chalabala, Zdenek 1899-1962 *OxDcOp*
Rozwadowski, Michal Stanislaw 1936- *WhoScE 91-4*
Rozwadowski, Mikolaj 1930- *WhoWor 93*
Rozycki, Ludomir 1884-1953 *Baker 92, PolBiDi*
Rozycki, William Eugene 1940- *St&PR 93*
Rozzell, George McAllaster 1926- *WhoSSW 93*
Rozzell, Scott Ellis 1949- *WhoAm 92*
Rozzi, P.D. *ScF&FL 92*
Rozzi, Samuel J. d1992 *NewYTBS 92 [port]*
Rozzi, Tullio *WhoScE 91-1*
Rozzini, Paul Joseph 1940- *St&PR 93*
Rozzoli, Kevin Richard 1937- *WhoAsAP 91*
Ru, Ju-Chieh 1935- *St&PR 93*
Ru, Min 1963- *WhoWor 93*
Rua, Milton Francisco 1919- *WhoSSW 93, WhoWor 93*
Ruan, Bao Gen 1951- *WhoWor 93*
Ruan, John 1771-1849 *BioIn 17*
Ruan, John, III 1943- *St&PR 93*
Ruan Chongwu 1933- *WhoAsAP 91*
Ruane, John Patrick, Jr. 1939- *St&PR 93*
Ruane, Joseph Edward 1929- *WhoIns 93*
Ruane, Maureen Muriel 1945- *WhoAmW 93*
Ruane, Thomas G. 1942- *St&PR 93*
Ruane, William J. *Law&B 92*
Ruano-Gil, Domingo 1932- *WhoScE 91-3*
Ruark, Gibbons 1941- *DcLB 120 [port], WhoWrEP 92*
Ruasen, Aaron Reuben 1930- *WhoE 93*
Rub, Louis John 1915- *WhoAm 92*
Rubach, Peggy 1947- *WhoAm 92*
Rubalcaba, Gonzalo *BioIn 17*
Rubalcava, Dulcie *Law&B 92*
Rubash, Joyce Newborn 1930- *WhoSSW 93*
Rubash, Norman Joseph 1932- *WhoAm 92*
Rubasingam, Sellathurai 1933- *WhoWor 93*
Rubayi, Salah 1942- *WhoWor 93*
Rubb, Peggy-Grace Plourd 1931- *WhoAmW 93, WhoE 93*
Rubben, Alfred 1940- *WhoScE 91-3*
Rubbert, William R. *Law&B 92*
Rubbia, Carlo 1934- *WhoAm 92, WhoScE 91-4, WhoWor 93*
Rubbo, Michael 1938- *MiSFD 9*
Rubbra, (Charles) Edmund 1901-1986 *Baker 92*
Rubel, Arthur 1940- *WhoE 93*
Rubel, Arthur Joseph 1924- *WhoAm 92*
Rubel, David Michael 1917- *WhoAm 92*
Rubel, Jeffrey *Law&B 92*
Rubel, Paul *WhoScE 91-2*
Rubel, Paula Glicksman 1933- *WhoAmW 93*
Rubel, Saundra Kae 1959- *WhoAmW 93*
Rubel, Stanislaw Jan 1922- *WhoScE 91-4*
Rubel, Walter Paul *Law&B 92*
Rubell, Steve *BioIn 17*
Ruben, Alan Miles 1931- *WhoAm 92*
Ruben, Ann Moliver 1925- *WhoSSW 93, WhoWrEP 92*
Ruben, Audrey H. *WhoAmW 93*
Ruben, Brent David 1944- *WhoAm 92*
Ruben, David Hillel 1943- *WhoWor 93*
Ruben, Gary A. 1924- *WhoAm 92*
Ruben, Ida G. 1929- *WhoAmW 93*
Ruben, Joseph 1951- *MiSFD 9*
Ruben, Katt Shea *MiSFD 9*
Ruben, Lawrence 1926- *WhoAm 92*
Ruben, Leonard 1921- *WhoAm 92*
Ruben, Richards 1925- *WhoE 93*
Ruben, Robert J. 1923- *St&PR 93*
Ruben, Robert Joel 1933- *WhoAm 92*
Ruben, Robert Joseph 1923- *WhoAm 92*
Ruben, Sharon *BioIn 17*
Ruben, Sonnino 1948- *WhoSSW 93*
Ruben, William S. *ScF&FL 92*

Ruben, William Samuel 1927- *St&PR 93, WhoAm 92*
Rubendall, Howard L. 1910-1991 *BioIn 17*
Rubenfeld, Joseph 1927- *St&PR 93*
Rubenfeld, Louis Allen 1941- *St&PR 93*
Rubenfeld, Michael 1948- *St&PR 93*
Rubenfeld, Stanley Irwin 1930- *WhoAm 92*
Rubenids *OxDcByz*
Rubenowitz, Sigvard 1925- *WhoWor 93*
Rubens, Bernice *BioIn 17*
Rubens, Bernice 1928- *ScF&FL 92*
Rubens, Jeff(rey Peter) 1941- *ConAu 39NR*
Rubens, Leonard 1928- *WhoUN 92*
Rubens, Paul (Alfred) 1875-1917 *Baker 92*
Rubens, Percival *MiSFD 9*
Rubens, Robert 1943- *WhoWor 93*
Rubens, Robert David *WhoScE 91-1*
Rubens, Robert David 1943- *WhoWor 93*
Rubens, Sidney Michel 1910- *WhoAm 92*
Rubens, William Stewart 1927- *WhoAm 92*
Rubenson, Albert 1826-1901 *Baker 92*
Rubenson, James R. 1937- *St&PR 93*
Rubenstein, Albert 1913-1991 *BioIn 17*
Rubenstein, Allan Earl 1944- *WhoE 93*
Rubenstein, Arthur Harold 1937- *WhoAm 92*
Rubenstein, Barnet *BioIn 17*
Rubenstein, Barry J. 1950- *St&PR 93*
Rubenstein, Barry John *Law&B 92*
Rubenstein, Bernard 1937- *WhoAm 92, WhoSSW 93*
Rubenstein, Byron d1990 *BioIn 17*
Rubenstein, Charles 1895-1990 *BioIn 17*
Rubenstein, Charles Philip 1947- *WhoE 93*
Rubenstein, Edward 1924- *WhoAm 92*
Rubenstein, Edward M. *Law&B 92*
Rubenstein, Elaine J. 1949- *WhoWrEP 92*
Rubenstein, Eric Davis 1952- *WhoWor 93*
Rubenstein, Farrell 1930- *WhoAm 92*
Rubenstein, Gillian *DcChlFi*
Rubenstein, Howard J. 1932- *BioIn 17*
Rubenstein, Howard Joseph 1932- *WhoAm 92*
Rubenstein, Jerome Max 1927- *WhoAm 92*
Rubenstein, Joshua Seth 1954- *WhoAm 92, WhoE 93, WhoEmL 93, WhoWor 93*
Rubenstein, Laurence D. *Law&B 92*
Rubenstein, Leonard Mark 1946- *St&PR 93, WhoAm 92*
Rubenstein, Lewis W. 1908- *WhoE 93*
Rubenstein, M.D. 1924- *St&PR 93*
Rubenstein, Neil Joseph *Law&B 92*
Rubenstein, Richard 1946- *St&PR 93*
Rubenstein, Richard L. 1924- *JeAmHC*
Rubenstein, Richard Lowell 1924- *WhoAm 92*
Rubenstein, Roberta 1944- *ScF&FL 92*
Rubenstein, Roberta Ann 1941- *WhoAmW 93*
Rubenstein, Sarah *Law&B 92*
Rubenstein, Sharon Lynn 1945- *WhoWrEP 92*
Rubenstein, Stanley Ellis 1930- *WhoAm 92, WhoE 93*
Rubenstein, Steven B. 1959- *St&PR 93*
Rubenstein, Steven Paul 1951- *WhoAm 92*
Rubertone, Donna J. 1958- *St&PR 93*
Rubie, Peter 1950- *ScF&FL 92*
Rubieri, Ermolao 1818-1879 *IntDcAn*
Rubies, Pedro 1949- *WhoScE 91-3*
Rubies-Autonell, Concepcion 1947- *WhoWor 93*
Rubin, Alan A. 1926- *WhoAm 92*
Rubin, Alan J. 1934- *WhoAm 92*
Rubin, Alvin B. 1920-1991 *BioIn 17*
Rubin, Andrej 1937- *WhoWor 93*
Rubin, Anne Loughran 1955- *WhoAmW 93*
Rubin, Arnold 1937-1988 *BioIn 17*
Rubin, Arnold Jesse 1924- *WhoAm 92*
Rubin, Arthur Herman 1927- *WhoE 93, WhoWor 93*
Rubin, Barry Mitchel 1950- *WhoAm 92*
Rubin, Benjamin Arnold 1917- *WhoE 93*
Rubin, Benjamin H. 1962- *St&PR 93*
Rubin, Benny 1899-1986 *QDrFCA 92 [port]*
Rubin, Bent 1943- *WhoScE 91-2*
Rubin, Bernard 1919- *WhoE 93*
Rubin, Bruce Joel *BioIn 17, WhoAm 92*
Rubin, Carl Bernard 1920- *WhoAm 92*
Rubin, Carl M. *Law&B 92*
Rubin, Cathy Ann 1948- *WhoAmW 93, WhoEmL 93*
Rubin, Charles Elliott 1947- *WhoAm 92*
Rubin, Daniel John 1949- *St&PR 93*
Rubin, David Albert 1950- *WhoE 93*
Rubin, David Lee 1939- *WhoSSW 93*
Rubin, David Lee 1943- *WhoAm 92*
Rubin, David M. 1945- *WhoWrEP 92*
Rubin, David Robert 1933- *WhoAm 92*
Rubin, David Stephen 1944- *WhoSSW 93*
Rubin, Diana Kwiatkowski 1958- *WhoWrEP 92*
Rubin, Donald Bruce 1943- *WhoE 93*
Rubin, Donald S. 1934- *St&PR 93*
Rubin, Dorothy Molly 1932- *WhoE 93*
Rubin, Edward Stephen 1941- *WhoAm 92*
Rubin, Edwin Manning 1927- *WhoAm 92*
Rubin, Emanuel 1928- *WhoAm 92*
Rubin, Eric 1955- *St&PR 93*
Rubin, Gabriel Kevi 1927- *WhoE 93*
Rubin, George F. 1943- *St&PR 93*
Rubin, Gerald H. *Law&B 92*
Rubin, Gerald J. 1943- *St&PR 93*
Rubin, Gustav 1913- *WhoAm 92*
Rubin, Harold Richard 1927- *St&PR 93*
Rubin, Harris B. 1932- *WhoAm 92*
Rubin, Harry M. 1952- *St&PR 93*
Rubin, Harry Meyer 1952- *WhoAm 92*
Rubin, Henry Park 1943- *WhoSSW 93*
Rubin, Herbert 1918- *WhoAm 92*
Rubin, Irvin I. 1919- *WhoE 93*
Rubin, Irving 1911- *St&PR 93*
Rubin, Irving 1916- *WhoAm 92, WhoWor 93*
Rubin, Izhak 1942- *WhoAm 92*
Rubin, Jacob Carl 1926- *WhoAm 92, WhoE 93*
Rubin, James B. *St&PR 93*
Rubin, Jane Lockhart Gregory 1944- *WhoE 93*
Rubin, Jay d1990 *BioIn 17*
Rubin, Jean Estelle 1926- *WhoAm 92*
Rubin, Jeffery Seth 1943- *St&PR 93*
Rubin, Jeffrey Ellis 1959- *WhoAm 92*
Rubin, Jeffrey Zachary 1941- *WhoAm 92, WhoE 93*
Rubin, Jennifer *BioIn 17*
Rubin, Jerome Sanford 1925- *St&PR 93, WhoAm 92, WhoWor 93*
Rubin, Joan Shelley 1947- *ConAu 139*
Rubin, Joanne Leslie 1950- *WhoAmW 93*
Rubin, Joel 1926- *St&PR 93*
Rubin, Joel Edward 1928- *WhoAm 92, WhoE 93*
Rubin, Joseph H. 1942- *St&PR 93*
Rubin, Karen 1951- *WhoWrEP 92*
Rubin, Karen Beth 1951- *WhoAmW 93*
Rubin, Karen E. *Law&B 92*
Rubin, Larry Bruce 1958- *WhoEmL 93, WhoWor 93*
Rubin, Larry Jerome 1930- *WhoSSW 93, WhoWrEP 92*
Rubin, Laura V. *St&PR 93*
Rubin, Lawrence 1933- *St&PR 93*
Rubin, Lawrence Edward 1933- *WhoAm 92*
Rubin, Lawrence Gilbert 1925- *WhoAm 92*
Rubin, Leah Plonchak 1957- *WhoWor 93*
Rubin, Lenore Borzak 1938- *WhoE 93*
Rubin, Lillian B(reslow) 1924- *ConAu 37NR*
Rubin, Lori Sue *Law&B 92*
Rubin, Louis Decimus, Jr. 1923- *WhoAm 92, WhoWrEP 92*
Rubin, Mahlon 1924- *St&PR 93*
Rubin, Marc 1955- *WhoSSW 93*
Rubin, Marcel 1905- *Baker 92*
Rubin, Marci R. *Law&B 92*
Rubin, Maria Victoria 1962- *WhoAmW 93*
Rubin, Marilyn Ruth 1946- *WhoE 93*
Rubin, Mark Evan 1947- *St&PR 93*
Rubin, Mark S. 1941- *St&PR 93*
Rubin, Mark Stephen 1946- *WhoSSW 93, WhoWor 93*
Rubin, Martin N. 1928- *WhoE 93, WhoWor 93*
Rubin, Marty *ScF&FL 92*
Rubin, Marvin Joseph 1928- *WhoE 93*
Rubin, Melvin Lynne 1932- *WhoAm 92*
Rubin, Meyer I. 1918- *St&PR 93*
Rubin, Michael 1946- *St&PR 93, WhoAm 92*
Rubin, Michele Barrie 1944- *WhoE 93*
Rubin, Mitchell D. *Law&B 92*
Rubin, Muriel 1927- *St&PR 93*
Rubin, Nancy Ruth Zimman 1944- *WhoE 93*
Rubin, Neville Nordav 1935- *WhoUN 92*
Rubin, Norman Julius 1923- *WhoE 93*
Rubin, Paul Harold 1942- *WhoE 93*
Rubin, Philip 1927- *WhoAm 92*
Rubin, Ramon 1912- *DcMexL*
Rubin, Richard Allan 1942- *WhoAm 92*
Rubin, Richard H. *Law&B 92*
Rubin, Richard I. 1903- *St&PR 93*
Rubin, Richard Lee 1946- *WhoSSW 93*
Rubin, Richard P. *Law&B 92*
Rubin, Rick *MiSFD 9*
Rubin, Rick 1949- *BioIn 17*
Rubin, Rick c. 1963- *ConMus 9*
Rubin, Robert E. *BioIn 17*
Rubin, Robert E. 1938- *St&PR 93*
Rubin, Robert Edward 1938- *WhoAm 92*
Rubin, Robert Irving 1922- *St&PR 93*
Rubin, Robert Joseph 1946- *WhoAm 92*
Rubin, Robert Melvin 1925- *St&PR 93*
Rubin, Rose Mohr 1939- *WhoSSW 93*
Rubin, S. Robert 1943- *WhoSSW 93*
Rubin, Samuel Harold 1916- *WhoAm 92*
Rubin, Seymour Jeffrey 1914- *WhoAm 92*
Rubin, Sharon Goldman 1944- *WhoE 93*
Rubin, Sheldon 1938- *St&PR 93*
Rubin, Stanley 1943- *WhoE 93*
Rubin, Stanley B. 1928- *St&PR 93*
Rubin, Stanley Creamer 1917- *WhoAm 92*
Rubin, Stanley Gerald 1938- *WhoAm 92*
Rubin, Stephen 1938-1991 *BioIn 17*
Rubin, Stephen Edward 1941- *WhoAm 92*
Rubin, Steve *BioIn 17*
Rubin, Steven *Law&B 92*
Rubin, Steven 1947- *St&PR 93*
Rubin, Stuart A. 1958- *St&PR 93*
Rubin, Susan *BioIn 17*
Rubin, Theodore Isaac 1923- *WhoAm 92*
Rubin, Thomas A. 1947- *St&PR 93*
Rubin, Tibor *BioIn 17*
Rubin, Vera 1911-1985 *IntDcAn*
Rubin, Vera 1928- *BioIn 17*
Rubin, Vera Cooper 1928- *WhoAm 92, WhoAmW 93*
Rubin, Wendy Lee 1958- *WhoAmW 93*
Rubin, William 1927- *WhoAm 92*
Rubin, William 1928- *WhoAm 92*
Rubin, William Stanley *BioIn 17*
Rubin, Wladyslaw 1917-1990 *BioIn 17, PolBiDi*
Rubin, Zick 1944- *WhoAm 92*
Rubincik, Valerij 1940- *DrEEuF*
Rubiner, Walter J. 1930- *St&PR 93*
Rubinett, Arthur E. *Law&B 92*
Rubinfeld, Abraham N. *Law&B 92*
Rubinfeld, Abraham Norman 1952- *St&PR 93*
Rubinger, Robert S. 1942- *St&PR 93*
Rubini, Adelaide Comelli- 1798?-1874 *OxDcOp*
Rubini, Giovanni Battista 1794-1854 *Baker 92, IntDcOp [port], OxDcOp*
Rubini, Nancy Beth 1956- *St&PR 93*
Rubini, Roberto 1930- *St&PR 93*
Rubino, Anthony August 1931- *St&PR 93*
Rubino, Frank *BioIn 17*
Rubino, Frank 1919- *St&PR 93*
Rubino, Giovanni F. 1918- *WhoScE 91-3*
Rubino, John Anthony 1956- *WhoE 93*
Rubino, John Anthony, III *Law&B 92*
Rubino, Michael *St&PR 93*
Rubino, Richard Gregory 1926- *St&PR 93*
Rubino, Victor Joseph 1940- *WhoAm 92*
Rubinoff, Ira 1938- *WhoAm 92, WhoWor 93*
Rubino-Sammartano, Mauro 1937- *WhoWor 93*
Rubinovitz, Samuel 1929- *St&PR 93, WhoAm 92, WhoE 93*
Rubinowicz, Claude Jean-Pierre 1947- *WhoWor 93*
Rubins, Roy Selwyn 1935- *WhoSSW 93*
Rubinsky, Holley 1943- *WhoCanL 92*
Rubinson, Alan M. *Law&B 92*
Rubinstein, Akiba 1882-1961 *BioIn 17*
Rubinstein, Alvin Zachary 1927- *ConAu 39NR, WhoAm 92*
Rubinstein, Aniela 1911- *PolBiDi*
Rubinstein, Anton 1829-1894 *IntDcOp [port], OxDcOp*
Rubinstein, Anton (Grigorievich) 1829-1894 *Baker 92*
Rubinstein, Arthur 1887-1982 *Baker 92*
Rubinstein, Artur 1887-1982 *PolBiDi*
Rubinstein, Arye *WhoE 93*
Rubinstein, Beryl 1898-1952 *Baker 92*
Rubinstein, Betsy Anne 1951- *WhoE 93*
Rubinstein, Carol d1991 *BioIn 17*
Rubinstein, Charlotte *Law&B 92*
Rubinstein, Dorothy Lee 1948- *WhoAmW 93*
Rubinstein, Elaine Perle 1953- *WhoEmL 93*
Rubinstein, Eli A. *BioIn 17*
Rubinstein, Eva Anna 1933- *WhoAm 92*
Rubinstein, Frank 1922- *St&PR 93*
Rubinstein, Frank M. 1924- *St&PR 93*
Rubinstein, G. Edward 1949- *WhoE 93*
Rubinstein, Georges Robert 1932- *WhoUN 92*
Rubinstein, Gillian *BioIn 17*
Rubinstein, Gillian 1942- *ScF&FL 92*
Rubinstein, Gillian (Margaret) 1942- *ConAu 136*
Rubinstein, Hyman Solomon 1904- *WhoAm 92*
Rubinstein, Jack Herbert 1925- *WhoAm 92*
Rubinstein, Jerold H. 1938- *St&PR 93*
Rubinstein, John Arthur 1946- *WhoAm 92*
Rubinstein, John B. 1946- *St&PR 93*
Rubinstein, Joseph 1847-1884 *Baker 92*
Rubinstein, Joseph Harris 1936- *WhoSSW 93*
Rubinstein, Michael Henry *WhoScE 91-1*
Rubinstein, Moshe Fajwel 1930- *WhoAm 92*
Rubinstein, Nikolai (Grigorievich) 1835-1881 *Baker 92*
Rubinstein, Richard Paul 1947- *St&PR 93*
Rubinstein, Steven David 1952- *St&PR 93*
Rubinstein, William M. *Law&B 92*
Rubinstein, William Morris 1923- *St&PR 93*
Rubinyi-Anderson, Susan J. *ScF&FL 92*
Rubio, Elenita Ignacio 1943- *WhoWor 93*
Rubio, J.L. 1947- *WhoScE 91-3*
Rubio, Jane *Law&B 92*
Rubio, Juan Antonio 1944- *WhoScE 91-3*
Rubio, Pedro A. 1944- *WhoSSW 93, WhoWor 93*
Rubio, Robert B. 1955- *WhoSSW 93*
Rubio, Vicente 1949- *WhoScE 91-3*
Ruble, Ann 1953- *WhoEmL 93*
Ruble, Charles 1946- *St&PR 93*
Ruble, Elizabeth Lynnette 1955- *WhoAmW 93*
Ruble, Randall Tucker 1932- *WhoAm 92*
Rubley, Charles Ronald *Law&B 92*
Rublowsky, John 1928- *BioIn 17*
Rubner, Cornelius *Baker 92*
Rubner, Roland 1939- *WhoScE 91-3*
Rubnitz, Myron Ethan 1924- *WhoWor 93*
Rubnitz, Thomas Block d1992 *NewYTBS 92*
Rubottom, Donald Julian 1926- *WhoSSW 93*
Rubottom, Roy Richard, Jr. 1912- *WhoAm 92*
Rubow, Charles L. *Law&B 92*
Rubow, Steven 1941- *St&PR 93*
Rubow, Thomas W. 1937- *WhoScE 91-2*
Rubright, Royal Cushing 1909- *WhoAm 92*
Rubritz, Timothy G. 1954- *St&PR 93*
Rubsam, Wolfgang 1946- *Baker 92*
Rubsamen, Walter (Howard) 1911-1973 *Baker 92*
Ruby, Burton Bennett 1919- *St&PR 93*
Ruby, Charles H. 1909-1990 *EncABHB 8*
Ruby, Charles Leroy 1900- *WhoAm 92, WhoWor 93*
Ruby, Jay 1935- *ConAu 136*
Ruby, Lois F. 1942- *ConAu 39NR*
Ruby, Maureen Frances 1955- *WhoAmW 93*
Ruby, Michael *WhoAm 92*
Ruby, Russell Glenn 1911- *WhoAm 92*
Rucci, Anthony Joseph 1950- *St&PR 93, WhoAm 92*
Ruccius, Elizabeth Anne 1952- *WhoE 93*
Ruch, Jean Victor 1935- *WhoScE 91-2*
Ruch, Peggy Ann F. 1940- *WhoAmW 93*
Ruch, Richard H. 1930- *St&PR 93*
Ruch, Richard Hurley 1930- *WhoAm 92*
Ruch, Wayne Eugene 1946- *WhoWor 93*
Ruch, William Vaughn 1937- *WhoE 93*
Ruchardt, Christoph J. 1929- *WhoScE 91-3*
Ruchelman, Leonard Isadore 1933- *WhoSSW 93*
Ruchlis, Hy(man) 1913-1992 *ConAu 139, SmATA 72*
Ruchlis, Hyman d1992 *NewYTBS 92*
Ruchman, Isaac 1909- *WhoSSW 93*
Ruchman, Marshall Doran 1934- *St&PR 93*
Ruchti, Ulrich *ScF&FL 92*
Rucier, Robin Arthur 1951- *St&PR 93*
Rucinski, Jerzy Jakub 1920- *WhoScE 91-4*
Rucinski, Walter Paul 1944- *St&PR 93*
Ruck, Amy *ScF&FL 92*
Ruck, Andrew J. 1930- *WhoIns 93*
Ruck, Berta 1878- *AmWomPl*
Ruck, Berta 1878-1978 *ScF&FL 92*
Ruck, Peter F. Carter- 1914- *BioIn 17*
Ruck, Sigridur T. 1937- *St&PR 93*
Ruckauf, Anton 1855-1903 *Baker 92*
Ruckdeschel Hibbard, Mary Josephine 1945- *WhoE 93*
Ruckebusch, Yves 1931- *WhoScE 91-2*
Ruckelshaus, William D. *BioIn 17*
Ruckelshaus, William D. 1932- *St&PR 93*
Ruckelshaus, William Doyle 1932- *WhoAm 92, WhoSSW 93, WhoWor 93*
Ruckenbauer, Peter 1939- *WhoScE 91-3*
Ruckenstein, Eli 1925- *WhoAm 92*
Rucker, Charles Thomas 1931- *WhoAm 92*
Rucker, Della Lee 1921- *WhoAmW 93*
Rucker, Gerhard 1931- *WhoScE 91-3*
Rucker, John G., III *Law&B 92*
Rucker, Kevin M. *Law&B 92*
Rucker, Paula Elaine 1964- *WhoE 93*
Rucker, Robert Mark 1958- *WhoSSW 93*
Rucker, Rudolf *ScF&FL 92*
Rucker, Rudy 1946- *ScF&FL 92*
Rucker, Steven M. *Law&B 92*
Rucker, Sylvia Mary 1934- *WhoSSW 93*
Rucker, Thomas J. *Law&B 92*
Rucker, Wilie J., Jr. 1920- *St&PR 93*
Ruckers *Baker 92*
Ruckers, Andreas 1579?-1645? *Baker 92*
Ruckers, Andreas 1607?-1667? *Baker 92*
Ruckers, Hans c. 1545-1598 *Baker 92*
Ruckers, Johannes 1578?-1643 *Baker 92*
Ruckman, Frederick L. 1949- *St&PR 93*
Ruckman, Mark Warren 1954- *WhoE 93*

Ruckman, Robert Mackereth 1949- *WhoAm 92*
Ruckman, Shelley J. *Law&B 92*
Ruckman-Bowers, Teresia Rose 1957- *WhoAmW 93*
Rucksdashel, Rex Neil *Law&B 92*
Rud, Anthony 1893-1942 *ScF&FL 92*
Rud, Victor *Law&B 92*
Ruda, Charles Ross 1962- *St&PR 93*
Ruda, Jerome 1943- *St&PR 93*
Ruda, Jose Maria 1924- *WhoWor 93*
Ruda, Neil Michael 1957- *WhoSSW 93*
Rudabaugh, Dave 1840-1886 *BioIn 17*
Rudall, P.J. 1954- *WhoScE 91-1*
Rudat, Jane Hildenbrand 1955- *WhoAmW 93*
Rudbach, Jon Anthony 1937- *St&PR 93, WhoAm 92*
Rudd, Andrew *St&PR 93*
Rudd, Charles Leo 1936- *St&PR 93*
Rudd, Dale Frederick 1935- *WhoAm 92*
Rudd, David William 1931- *WhoE 93*
Rudd, Eldon *WhoAm 92*
Rudd, Ellison C. 1944- *St&PR 93*
Rudd, Gerald Ray 1929- *St&PR 93*
Rudd, Gillian Barr d1992 *BioIn 17*
Rudd, Howard F., Jr. 1944- *WhoSSW 93*
Rudd, Hughes d1992 *NewYTBS 92 [port]*
Rudd, Hughes (Day) 1921-1992 *ConAu 139*
Rudd, Hynda L. 1936- *WhoAmW 93*
Rudd, John William 1934- *WhoSSW 93*
Rudd, Leo Slaton 1924- *WhoSSW 93*
Rudd, Nicholas 1943- *WhoAm 92, WhoWor 93*
Rudd, Paul Ryan 1940- *WhoAm 92*
Ruddaka, Andrew 1962- *WhoAsAP 91*
Ruddell, Gary Ronald 1948- *WhoAm 92*
Rudden, David Philip 1935- *St&PR 93*
Rudder, Brian L. 1944- *WhoIns 93*
Rudder, Kenneth Wayne 1949- *WhoSSW 93*
Rudder, Paul R. 1938- *WhoSSW 93*
Rudder-Taylor, Marva M. *Law&B 92*
Ruddick, Bob *ScF&FL 92*
Ruddick, Bruce d1992 *NewYTBS 92*
Ruddick, J. Perry 1936- *St&PR 93, WhoAm 92*
Ruddick, Nicholas 1952- *ScF&FL 92*
Ruddle, Nancy Hartman 1940- *WhoAmW 93*
Ruddley, John 1912- *WhoE 93*
Ruddock, K.H. *WhoScE 91-1*
Ruddock, Philip Maxwell 1943- *WhoAsAP 91*
Ruddock, Ted 1930- *ConAu 139*
Ruddon, Raymond Walter, Jr. 1936- *WhoAm 92*
Ruddy, Don 1954?-1992 *BioIn 17*
Ruddy, Donald P. d1992 *NewYTBS 92*
Ruddy, E. Peter, Jr. 1940- *WhoAm 92*
Ruddy, Frank S. 1937- *WhoAm 92, WhoE 93, WhoWor 93*
Ruddy, James P. 1922- *St&PR 93*
Ruddy, James W. *Law&B 92*
Ruddy, Jon *ScF&FL 92*
Ruddy, Kenneth Edward 1925- *St&PR 93*
Ruddy, Michael E. 1934- *WhoUN 92*
Rudecki, Walter J., Jr. *Law&B 92*
Rudee, Mervyn Lea 1935- *WhoAm 92*
Rudeen, Louisa *ScF&FL 92*
Rudel, Hans Ulrich 1916-1982 *BioIn 17*
Rudel, Julius 1921- *Baker 92, IntDcOp, OxDcOp, WhoAm 92*
Rudel, Lawrence Lee 1941- *WhoAm 92*
Rudelic-Fernandez, Zvjezdana Dana 1959- *WhoWor 93*
Rudell, Milton Wesley 1920- *WhoAm 92*
Rudellat, Yvonne 1897-1945 *BioIn 17*
Rudenberg, Frank Hermann 1927- *WhoSSW 93*
Rudenberg, Hermann Gunther 1920- *WhoE 93*
Rudenstine, Angelica Zander 1937- *WhoE 93*
Rudenstine, Neil Leon 1935- *BioIn 17, WhoAm 92, WhoE 93*
Ruder, Brian 1954- *St&PR 93*
Ruder, David Sturtevant 1929- *WhoAm 92*
Ruder, Helen Finn d1990 *BioIn 17*
Ruder, Juergen Karl Max 1940- *WhoWor 93*
Ruder, Melvin Harvey 1915- *WhoAm 92*
Ruder, William 1921- *St&PR 93, WhoAm 92*
Ruderman, Armand Peter 1923- *WhoAm 92*
Ruderman, Irving Warren 1920- *WhoE 93*
Ruderman, Ronald 1943- *St&PR 93*
Ruderman, Warren 1920- *St&PR 93*
Ruders, Poul 1949- *Baker 92*
Rudert, Heinrich 1935- *WhoScE 91-3*
Rudge, Christopher *Law&B 92*
Rudge, Christopher 1937- *St&PR 93*
Rudge, Howard J. *Law&B 92*
Rudgers, Anthony Joseph 1938- *WhoSSW 93*
Rudhart, Peter 1939- *WhoSSW 93*
Rudhyar, Dane 1895-1985 *Baker 92, ScF&FL 92*
Rudiak, Mary Helen Crawley 1941- *WhoAmW 93*
Rudick, M.J. 1938- *St&PR 93*
Rudick, Michael J. *Law&B 92*
Rudie, Donald Duane 1935- *St&PR 93*
Rudikoff, Michael T. 1946- *WhoE 93*
Rudin, Anne Noto 1924- *WhoAm 92, WhoAmW 93*
Rudin, Arnold James 1934- *WhoWrEP 92*
Rudin, Jeffrey *Law&B 92*
Rudin, John F. 1945- *St&PR 93*
Rudin, May d1992 *NewYTBS 92*
Rudin, Scott *BioIn 17*
Rudin, Scott 1958- *ConTFT 10*
Rudin, Werner 1945- *WhoScE 91-4*
Ruding, Herman Onno 1939- *WhoAm 92, WhoWor 93*
Rudinger, Gottfried 1886-1946 *Baker 92*
Rudinger, Warren Craig 1945- *St&PR 93*
Rudini 1929- *WhoAsAP 91*
Rudins, Leonids 1928- *WhoE 93, WhoWor 93*
Rudisaile, Stanley Edward 1963- *WhoSSW 93*
Rudisch, Louis d1992 *NewYTBS 92*
Rudisill, Robert Grant 1922- *St&PR 93*
Rudisill, Robert Mack, Jr. 1945- *WhoAm 92, WhoWor 93*
Rudkin, Margaret Fogarty 1897-1967 *BioIn 17*
Rudland, Philip Spencer *WhoScE 91-1*
Rudland, William P. *Law&B 92*
Rudlin, David Alan 1947- *WhoAm 92*
Rudloff, Rainer 1939- *WhoWor 93*
Rudloff, Robert William, Jr. 1958- *WhoE 93*
Rudloff, William Joseph 1941- *WhoSSW 93*
Rudman, Duke *BioIn 17*
Rudman, Frances *St&PR 93*
Rudman, Herbert Charles 1923- *WhoAm 92*
Rudman, John S. *Law&B 92*
Rudman, Mark 1948- *WhoWrEP 92*
Rudman, Michael P. 1950- *St&PR 93*
Rudman, Reuben 1937- *WhoE 93*
Rudman, Richard James *Law&B 92*
Rudman, Richard James 1927- *St&PR 93*
Rudman, Solomon Kal 1930- *WhoWor 93*
Rudman, Stephen Todd *Law&B 92*
Rudman, Warren B. *BioIn 17*
Rudman, Warren B. 1930- *CngDr 91*
Rudman, Warren Bruce 1930- *WhoAm 92, WhoE 93*
Rudmin, Joseph Webster 1942- *WhoSSW 93*
Rudner, Rita *BioIn 17*
Rudner, Rita 1956- *News 93-2 [port]*
Rudner, Sara 1944- *WhoAm 92*
Rudney, Harry 1918- *WhoAm 92*
Rudnick, Alan A. *Law&B 92*
Rudnick, Alan A. 1947- *St&PR 93*
Rudnick, David Lawrence 1940- *St&PR 93*
Rudnick, Ellen Ava *WhoAm 92*
Rudnick, Ellen Ava 1950- *St&PR 93*
Rudnick, Gary William 1946- *WhoE 93*
Rudnick, Irene Krugman 1929- *WhoAmW 93*
Rudnick, M. Jack *Law&B 92*
Rudnick, Paul 1957?- *ConAu 139*
Rudnick, Paul David 1940- *WhoAm 92*
Rudnick, Rebecca Sophie 1952- *WhoAmW 93*
Rudnick, Wilhelm 1850-1927 *Baker 92*
Rudnicki, Adolf 1912-1990 *BioIn 17*
Rudnicki, Barbara Anne 1942- *WhoAmW 93*
Rudnicki, Cezary Aleksander 1942- *WhoWor 93*
Rudnicki, Konrad M. Pawel 1926- *WhoScE 91-4*
Rudnicki, Marian (Teofil) 1888-1944 *Baker 92*
Rudnicki, Robert Michael *Law&B 92*
Rudnicki, Ryszard Jan 1957- *WhoWor 93*
Rudnicki, Ryszard Maciej 1940- *WhoScE 91-4*
Rudnik, Stanislaw 1923- *WhoScE 91-4, WhoWor 93*
Rudning, Charles Rodger 1930- *WhoAm 92*
Rudnytsky, Antin 1902-1975 *Baker 92*
Rudo, Frieda Galindo 1923- *WhoE 93*
Rudo, Milton 1919- *WhoAm 92*
Rudofker, Robert C. 1934- *St&PR 93*
Rudofsky, Bernard 1905-1988 *BioIn 17*
Rudolf, II, Holy Roman Emperor 1552-1612 *BioIn 17*
Rudolf, Max *BioIn 17*
Rudolf, Max 1902- *Baker 92, WhoAm 92, WhoWor 93*
Rudolph, Abraham Morris 1924- *WhoAm 92*
Rudolph, Alan 1943- *MiSFD 9*
Rudolph, Andrew Henry 1943- *WhoWor 93*
Rudolph, Arnold Jack 1918- *WhoAm 92*
Rudolph, Arthur 1928- *St&PR 93*
Rudolph, Bernd 1944- *WhoWor 93*
Rudolph, Brian Albert 1961- *WhoWor 93*
Rudolph, Carl J. 1945- *St&PR 93*
Rudolph, Deborah Ann 1958- *WhoAmW 93*
Rudolph, Eberhard Ernst 1941- *WhoWor 93*
Rudolph, Elaine Taylor 1926- *WhoAmW 93*
Rudolph, Eric B. *Law&B 92*
Rudolph, Frederick 1920- *WhoAm 92*
Rudolph, Frederick W. 1929- *St&PR 93*
Rudolph, Fritz 1926- *WhoWor 93*
Rudolph, George Cooper 1951- *WhoEmL 93*
Rudolph, Karin 1941- *WhoUN 92*
Rudolph, Lavere Christian 1921- *WhoAm 92*
Rudolph, Lloyd Irving 1927- *WhoAm 92*
Rudolph, Louis 1943- *MiSFD 9*
Rudolph, Malcolm R. 1924- *St&PR 93*
Rudolph, Malcolm Rome 1924- *WhoAm 92*
Rudolph, Marguerite Hannah 1942- *WhoSSW 93*
Rudolph, Mendy d1979 *NewYTBS 92 [port]*
Rudolph, Paul 1918- *BioIn 17, WhoAm 92*
Rudolph, Piet *BioIn 17*
Rudolph, Ralph A. 1926- *St&PR 93*
Rudolph, Rebecca Ann 1953- *WhoAmW 93*
Rudolph, Robert E. 1936- *St&PR 93*
Rudolph, Robert R. 1937- *St&PR 93*
Rudolph, Roland Lutz 1939- *WhoScE 91-3*
Rudolph, Ronald Alvin 1949- *WhoWor 93*
Rudolph, Ronald W. *St&PR 93*
Rudolph, Scot Alan 1957- *WhoSSW 93*
Rudolph, Stephen E. 1945- *St&PR 93*
Rudolph, Susanne Hoeber 1930- *WhoAm 92*
Rudolph, Theodore J. 1937- *St&PR 93*
Rudolph, Wallace Morton 1930- *WhoAm 92*
Rudolph, William D. *Law&B 92*
Rudolph, Wilma *BioIn 17*
Rudolph, Wilma 1940- *BlkAmWO [port], ConBlB 4 [port], ConHero 2 [port]*
Rudolphy, J.W. 1934- *WhoScE 91-3*
Rudomin, Esther *MajAI*
Rudomino, Margarita Ivanovna 1900-1990 *BioIn 17*
Rudorff, Ernst (Friedrich Karl) 1840-1916 *Baker 92*
Rudov, Melvin Howard 1933- *WhoE 93*
Rudowicz, Czeslaw Zygmunt 1948- *WhoWor 93*
Rudowski, Witold J. 1918- *WhoScE 91-4*
Rudstam, Sven Gosta 1925- *WhoScE 91-4*
Rudstein, David Stewart 1946- *WhoAm 92*
Ru Dusky, Basil Michael 1933- *WhoAm 92*
Rudwall, John C. 1929- *St&PR 93*
Rudy, Bruce C. 1943- *St&PR 93*
Rudy, Cynthia Ann 1959- *WhoAmW 93*
Rudy, Cynthia Jo 1958- *WhoAmW 93*
Rudy, David Robert 1934- *WhoAm 92*
Rudy, Dorothy L. 1924- *WhoWrEP 92*
Rudy, Douglas Warren *Law&B 92*
Rudy, George Warren 1911- *St&PR 93*
Rudy, Lester Howard 1918- *WhoAm 92*
Rudy, Michael H. *Law&B 92*
Rudy, Raymond Bruce, Jr. 1931- *WhoAm 92*
Rudy, Sylvia June 1939- *St&PR 93*
Rudy, Willis 1920- *WhoAm 92*
Rudyak, Yuli Borisovitch 1948- *WhoWor 93*
Rudzinski, Jerzy Marek 1958- *WhoWor 93*
Rudzinski, John J. *St&PR 93*
Rudzinski, Kenneth William 1947- *WhoE 93*
Rudzinski, Witold 1913- *Baker 92*
Rudzinski, Zbigniew 1935- *Baker 92*
Rudzinsky, Louis 1933- *WhoE 93*
Rudzki, Eugeniusz Maciej 1914- *WhoE 93*
Rue, C.J. 1945- *St&PR 93*
Rue, Carl C. 1938- *St&PR 93*
Rue, Elizabeth G. *Law&B 92*
Rue, T. Steve 1946- *St&PR 93*
Rue, Thomas Scott 1958- *WhoE 93*
Rue, William B. *St&PR 93*
Ruebensaal, Clayton Frederick 1918- *St&PR 93*
Ruebhausen, Oscar Melick 1912- *WhoAm 92*
Rueble, Jeffrey Scott *Law&B 92*
Ruechardt, Christoph Johannes 1929- *WhoWor 93*
Rueck, Jon Michael 1940- *WhoAm 92*
Rueckert, Frederic 1921- *WhoE 93*
Rueckert, Roland Rudyard 1931- *WhoAm 92*
Rueda Medina, Gustavo 1905-1959 *DcMexL*
Rueden, Henry Anthony 1949- *WhoEmL 93*
Ruedenberg, Klaus 1920- *WhoAm 92*
Ruedin, James Messer, Sr. 1928- *St&PR 93*
Ruedisueli, Richard L. 1940- *St&PR 93*
Rueff, Jacques 1896-1978 *BioIn 17*
Ruegamer, Lana 1941- *WhoAmW 93*
Ruegamer, William Raymond 1922- *WhoSSW 93*
Rueger, Lauren John 1921- *WhoAm 92*
Ruegg, Donald George 1924- *WhoAm 92*
Ruegg, Henri 1930- *WhoScE 91-4*
Ruegg, Johann Caspar 1930- *WhoScE 91-3*
Ruegg, Max W. 1942- *WhoScE 91-4*
Ruegsegger, Martin C. *Law&B 92*
Ruehl, Mercedes *WhoAm 92, WhoAmW 93, WhoE 93*
Ruehle, Charles Joseph 1943- *WhoE 93, WhoWor 93*
Ruehle, Gregory J. *St&PR 93*
Ruehmann, Albert C., III *Law&B 92*
Ruehr, Ben B. 1933- *St&PR 93*
Ruekert, Linda Fennema 1953- *WhoAmW 93*
Ruel, Linda S. *Law&B 92*
Ruellan, Alain Jean 1943- *WhoWor 93*
Ruellan, Andree 1905- *BioIn 17, WhoAm 92*
Ruelle, David Pierre 1935- *WhoWor 93*
Ruemelin, Charles R. *St&PR 93*
Ruemelin, Robert J. *St&PR 93*
Ruemmler, John David *ScF&FL 92*
Rue-Potter, Joyce 1942- *WhoAmW 93, WhoSSW 93*
Rues, T. Dietrich 1930- *WhoScE 91-3*
Ruesch, Margaret Ann 1950- *WhoAmW 93*
Ruesink, Albert William 1940- *WhoAm 92*
Rueth, Alora Lynn 1958- *WhoWrEP 92*
Ruether, Rosemary Radford 1936- *ConAu 39NR, WhoAmW 93*
Ruether, Walter Henry 1893-1970 *BiDAMSp 1989*
Ruettgers, Michael C. 1942- *St&PR 93*
Ruetz, George J. 1925- *St&PR 93*
Ruetz, James Peter 1957- *St&PR 93*
Ruetz, William Joseph 1949- *St&PR 93*
Rueve, Charles E. 1937- *St&PR 93*
Ruf, Dave G., Jr. 1938- *St&PR 93*
Ruf, Ernst Hermann *Law&B 92*
Ruf, Gerhard 1939- *WhoScE 91-4*
Ruf, H. William *Law&B 92*
Ruf, John A. 1939- *St&PR 93*
Rufa, Robert Henry 1943- *WhoAm 92*
Rufe, R. Kane 1930- *St&PR 93*
Rufeh, Firooz *St&PR 93*
Rufelt, L.G. Snorre 1950- *WhoScE 91-4*
Rufer, Josef (Leopold) 1893-1985 *Baker 92*
Rufer, Philippe (-Barthelemy) 1844-1919 *Baker 92*
Ruff, Charles F. C. 1939- *WhoAm 92*
Ruff, Donald E. 1936- *St&PR 93*
Ruff, Edward C. 1939- *St&PR 93*
Ruff, Ellen T. *Law&B 92*
Ruff, George E. *Law&B 92*
Ruff, Howard Joseph 1930- *WhoAm 92, WhoWrEP 92*
Ruff, Imre 1938- *WhoScE 91-4*
Ruff, Jean-Paul A. 1934- *St&PR 93*
Ruff, John Douglass *Law&B 92*
Ruff, Katheryn Lorene 1954- *WhoAmW 93*
Ruff, Lorraine Marie 1947- *WhoE 93*
Ruff, Marie Nancy 1934- *St&PR 93*
Ruff, Matt *ScF&FL 92*
Ruff, Nancy Rae 1946- *WhoSSW 93*
Ruff, Robert Louis 1950- *WhoEmL 93, WhoWor 93*
Ruff, Tilman Alfred 1955- *WhoWor 93*
Ruff, Willie *BioIn 17*
Ruff, Willie 1931- *Baker 92*
Ruffalo, Alan Michael 1943- *St&PR 93*
Ruffalo, James Anthony 1949- *St&PR 93*
Ruffalo, Maria Therese 1963- *WhoAmW 93*
Ruffell, Ann 1941- *ScF&FL 92*
Ruffelle, Frances 1966- *WhoAmW 93*
Ruffer, David Gray 1937- *WhoAm 92*
Ruffier, Joan Dial 1939- *WhoSSW 93*
Ruffin, Bruce E. 1944- *St&PR 93*
Ruffin, Clovis *BioIn 17*
Ruffin, Clovis d1992 *NewYTBS 92 [port]*
Ruffin, David *BioIn 17*
Ruffin, David 1941- *SoulM*
Ruffin, David 1941-1991 *AnObit 1991*
Ruffin, Edmund 1794-1865 *BioIn 17*
Ruffin, Jimmy 1939- *SoulM*
Ruffin, Josephine St. Pierre 1842-1924 *EncAACR*
Ruffin, Julian M. 1946- *St&PR 93*
Ruffin, Margaret Ann 1934- *WhoAmW 93*
Ruffin, Mark Anthony 1956- *WhoWrEP 92*

Ruffin, Paul Dean 1941- WhoWrEP 92
Ruffing, Anne Elizabeth WhoAm 92
Ruffing, Gregory Joseph Law&B 92
Ruffing, Janet Kathryn 1945- WhoAmW 93
Ruffing, Kenneth G. 1943- WhoUN 92
Ruffini, Nina Law&B 92
Ruffins, Reynold 1930- BlkAuII 92, MajAI [port]
Ruffle, John Frederick 1937- WhoAm 92
Ruffley, Herbert Elsworth 1929- St&PR 93
Ruffner, Charles Louis 1936- WhoSSW 93
Ruffner, Frederick G., Jr. 1926- WhoAm 92, WhoWor 93
Ruffner, George 1862?-1933 BioIn 17
Ruffner, Jay S. 1941- WhoAm 92
Ruffo, Ernesto DcCPCAm
Ruffo, Titta 1877-1953 Baker 92, IntDcOp [port], OxDcOp
Ruffo, Vincenzo c. 1508-1587 Baker 92
Ruffolo, Lisa M. 1956- WhoWrEP 92
Ruffus, Stephen 1949- WhoWrEP 92
Rufino, Ernesto Baltazar, Jr. 1941- WhoWor 93
Rufinus d395 OxDcByz
Rufinus of Aquileia c. 345-410 OxDcByz
Rufli, Kurt 1945- WhoWor 93
Rufolo, Regina S. 1961- St&PR 93
Rufus SoulM
Rufus, Lucius Vibullius fl. 56BC-48BC HarEnMi
Rufus Festus OxDcByz
Ruga, Publius 1927- St&PR 93
Rugaber, Walter Feucht, Jr. 1938- WhoAm 92
Rugambwa, Laurean Cardinal 1912- WhoWor 93
Rugambwa-Otim 1960- WhoWor 93
Rugani, Maria Louise 1956- WhoAmW 93
Ruge, Clara 1856- AmWomPl
Ruge, Daniel August 1917- WhoAm 92
Ruge, I. WhoScE 91-3
Ruge, Michael Helmuth 1962- WhoEmL 93
Ruge, Neil Marshall 1913- WhoAm 92, WhoWor 93
Rugeles, Manuel Felipe 1903-1959 SpAmA
Ruger, James Richard Law&B 92
Ruger, Stephen Lewis 1950- WhoE 93
Ruger, William Batterman 1916- BioIn 17, St&PR 93, WhoAm 92
Rugeroni, Ian WhoAm 92
Rugg, Kenneth L. 1942- St&PR 93
Rugg, Marjorie Alice 1916- WhoAmW 93
Rugge, Henry Ferdinand 1936- WhoAm 92
Rugge, Hugo Robert 1935- WhoAm 92
Rugger, Gerald Klein 1916- St&PR 93
Ruggera, Paul Stephen 1944- WhoWor 93
Ruggeri, Agnes Clementine 1881- AmWomPl
Ruggeri, Andrea Pietro 1943- WhoWor 93
Ruggeri, Edward St&PR 93
Ruggeri, Tommaso Antonio 1947- WhoWor 93
Ruggerio, Michael John 1936- WhoSSW 93
Rugg-Gunn, Andrew John WhoScE 91-1
Ruggi, Francesco 1767-1845 Baker 92
Ruggia, James Charles 1954- WhoWrEP 92
Ruggieri, Elaine 1933- WhoSSW 93
Ruggieri, Giovanni Maria fl. c. 1690-1720 OxDcOp
Ruggieri, Helen 1938- WhoWrEP 92
Ruggieri, John Thomas 1956- St&PR 93
Ruggieri, Pamela Joy 1944- WhoAmW 93
Ruggieri, Patricia 1947- WhoE 93
Ruggiero, Anthony William 1941- St&PR 93, WhoAm 92, WhoWor 93
Ruggiero, Edward B. St&PR 93
Ruggiero, Greg BioIn 17, NewYTBS 92 [port]
Ruggiero, John A. 1936- St&PR 93
Ruggiero, Laurence Joseph 1948- WhoAm 92, WhoSSW 93
Ruggiero, Matthew John 1932- WhoAm 92
Ruggiero, Mike BioIn 17
Ruggiero, Murray Anthony, Jr. 1963- WhoE 93
Ruggiero, Richard Salvador 1944- WhoE 93
Ruggio, Joseph P. 1943- St&PR 93
Ruggirello, Gaspare G. Law&B 92
Ruggles, Carl 1876-1971 Baker 92, BioIn 17
Ruggles, Charles 1886-1970 QDrFCA 92 [port]
Ruggles, Donald Francis 1936- St&PR 93
Ruggles, Donald M. 1926- St&PR 93
Ruggles, Gordon St&PR 93
Ruggles, Larry Leon 1940- WhoSSW 93
Ruggles, Robert Thomas 1931- St&PR 93
Ruggles, Rudy Lamont, Jr. 1938- WhoAm 92
Ruggles, Wesley 1889-1972 MiSFD 9N
Rugh, John F. 1934- St&PR 93
Rugh, William Arthur 1936- WhoAm 92
Rugheimer, John H. Law&B 92
Rugina, Anghel N. 1913- WhoE 93
Rugina, Valeriu WhoScE 91-4
Rugnetta, Joseph Francis, Jr. 1957- WhoIns 93
Rugo, Paul R. 1933- WhoAm 92
Rugolo, Pete 1915- Baker 92, BioIn 17
Ruh, Edwin 1924- WhoE 93
Ruh, Joseph F., Jr. Law&B 92
Ruhe, Axel 1942- WhoScE 91-4, WhoWor 93
Ruhen, Carl 1937- ScF&FL 92
Ruhfus, Jurgen 1930- WhoWor 93
Ruhkala, Peter D. 1940- St&PR 93
Ruhl, Donald J. d1945 BioIn 17
Ruhl, Douglas L. 1948- St&PR 93
Ruhl, Robert Charles 1941- St&PR 93
Ruhl, Ronald F. 1947- St&PR 93
Ruhl, Steven 1954- WhoWrEP 92
Ruhl, Werner 1937- WhoScE 91-3
Ruhland, Charles Melvin 1943- St&PR 93
Ruhland, Elizabeth A. WhoWrEP 92
Ruhle, Manfred 1938- WhoScE 91-3
Ruhling, Werner 1939- WhoScE 91-3
Ruhlman, Jon Randall 1927- St&PR 93
Ruhlman, Terrell Louis 1926- WhoAm 92
Ruhlmann, Frans 1868-1948 Baker 92
Ruhlmann, (Adolf) Julius 1816-1877 Baker 92
Ruhm, Friedrich 1936- WhoScE 91-4
Ruhm, Thomas F. Law&B 92
Ruhm, Thomas Francis 1935- WhoE 93, WhoWor 93
Ruhrup, Clifton Brown 1916- WhoSSW 93
Ruhs, Christian 1961- WhoWor 93
Ruibal, Charles Adrian 1947- WhoAm 92, WhoE 93
Ruijs, Joseph Henricus Joannes 1934- WhoWor 93
Ruijs, Mary Law&B 92
Ruina, Jack Philip 1923- WhoAm 92
Ruina, Lisa A. Law&B 92
Ruini, Camillo Cardinal 1931- WhoWor 93
Ruis, Helmut 1940- WhoScE 91-4
Ruis, Janet Wood 1945- WhoSSW 93
Ruis, Stanley W. 1936- St&PR 93
Ruisi, Christopher S. 1949- WhoIns 93
Ruisi, Christopher Salvatore 1949- St&PR 93
Ruitenberg, E. Joost 1937- WhoScE 91-3
Ruitenberg, Nicholas 1957- St&PR 93
Ruiter, Adriaan 1934- WhoScE 91-3
Ruiter, Wim de 1943- Baker 92
Ruivo, Mario WhoScE 91-2
Rui Xingwen 1928- WhoAsAP 91
Ruiz, Antonio Maria 1952- WhoWor 93
Ruiz, Emilio 1944- WhoE 93
Ruiz, Fernando A. Law&B 92
Ruiz, Henry DcCPCAm
Ruiz, Hipolito 1752-1808 Expl 93
Ruiz, John 1954- WhoE 93
Ruiz, Jose Garcia 1947- WhoEmL 93, WhoWor 93
Ruiz, Jose Philicho 1960- WhoSSW 93
Ruiz, Jose Ricardo d1992 BioIn 17
Ruiz, Julio Cesar 1951- WhoWor 93
Ruiz, Manuel Blasco, Jr. 1945- WhoWor 93
Ruiz, Othon 1943- WhoWor 93
Ruiz, Ralph 1948- St&PR 93
Ruiz, Ramon Eduardo 1921- HispAmA [port], WhoAm 92
Ruiz, Raul 1941- MiSFD 9
Ruiz, Vicki 1955- NotHsAW 93
Ruiz, Vicki L. 1955- HispAmA
Ruiz-Conforto, Tracie BioIn 17
Ruiz Cortines, Adolfo 1891- DcCPCAm
Ruiz de Alarcon, Juan 1580-1639 DcMexL
Ruiz De Alegria Arratibel, Jesus 1943- WhoWor 93
Ruiz de Angulo y Martinez, Dionisio 1933- WhoUN 92
Ruiz-de-Conde, Justina 1909- WhoAm 92
Ruiz-Fornells, Enrique 1925- WhoSSW 93
Ruiz-Marcos, Antonio 1940- WhoScE 91-3
Ruiz Nestosa, Jesus 1941- SpAmA
Ruiz-Quintanilla, Segundo Antonio 1951- WhoWor 93
Ruiz-Valera, Phoebe Lucile 1950- WhoAmW 93
Ruiz-Zuniga, Angel 1954- WhoWor 93
Rujevcan, Holly Anne 1960- WhoAmW 93
Ruka, Ed BioIn 17
Ruka, Marie BioIn 17
Rukavina, Daniel 1937- WhoScE 91-4
Rukavishnikov, Victor Anotolevich 1956- WhoWor 93
Rukeyser, Louis 1933- JrnUS
Rukeyser, Louis Richard 1933- WhoAm 92, WhoE 93
Rukeyser, M. S., Jr. 1931- WhoAm 92
Rukeyser, Muriel 1913-1980 BioIn 17
Rukeyser, Robert James 1942- St&PR 93, WhoAm 92
Rukeyser, William Simon 1939- ConAu 37NR, WhoAm 92
Rukh d1447 HarEnMi
Ruland, Donald Bert 1942- St&PR 93
Ruland, Midlred Ardelia 1918- WhoAmW 93
Ruland, Richard Eugene 1932- WhoAm 92
Rule, Adrian O., III 1927- St&PR 93
Rule, Ann BioIn 17, WhoAmW 93
Rule, Charles Frederick 1955- WhoAm 92
Rule, Daniel Rhodes 1940- WhoAm 92
Rule, Elton H. 1916-1990 BioIn 17
Rule, Elton H. 1917-1990 ConTFT 10
Rule, Jane 1931- ScF&FL 92, WhoCanL 92
Rule, John Corwin 1929- WhoAm 92
Rule, Peter W. Law&B 92
Rule, Peter William 1939- WhoAm 92
Rulfo, Juan 1917-1986 SpAmA
Rulfo, Juan 1918-1986 BioIn 17, DcMexL
Rulis, Raymond Joseph 1924- WhoAm 92
Rull, Luis F. 1949- WhoWor 93
Rulnick, Adrienne A. 1945- WhoAmW 93
Rulon, Robert E. 1943- St&PR 93
Rulon-Miller, Robert, Jr. 1952- St&PR 93
Rulon-Miller, William Lippincott 1948- St&PR 93
Rumack, Barry H. 1942- WhoAm 92
Rumack, Frederick W. Law&B 92
Rumage, Joseph Paul 1927- WhoSSW 93
Ruman, Robert S. 1942- St&PR 93
Rumbarger, Charles D. WhoIns 93
Rumbaugh, Max Elden, Jr. 1937- WhoAm 92, WhoWor 93
Rumbaugh, Melvin Dale 1929- WhoAm 92
Rumbaugh, Paul Ernest 1919- St&PR 93
Rumbaugh, Ross St. Clair 1922- St&PR 93
Rumberger, Regina 1921- WhoAmW 93, WhoSSW 93
Rumble, Adrian 1945- ConAu 137
Rumbo, L. Law&B 92
Rumbold, Charlotte AmWomPl
Rumbough, Leah BioIn 17
Rumbough, Stan BioIn 17
Rumbough, Stanley Maddox, Jr. 1920- WhoAm 92, WhoSSW 93
Rumbough, Stanley Moddox, Jr. 1920- St&PR 93
Rumelhart, David Everett 1942- WhoAm 92
Rumelhart, Joann Weslie 1953- St&PR 93, WhoIns 93
Rumely, John Winn, Jr. Law&B 92
Rumens, Carol BioIn 17
Rumery, Michael 1947- WhoSSW 93
Rumfelt, Harvey Lesley 1949- WhoSSW 93
Rumford, Debora Dawn 1957- WhoAmW 93
Rumi, Jalal al-Din 1207-1273 BioIn 17
Rumilly, Bernard Sebastian 1935- WhoE 93
Ruml, Beardsley BioIn 17
Rumler, Robert Hoke 1915- WhoAm 92
Rumley, Michael T. 1943- St&PR 93
Rumman, Wadi 1926- WhoAm 92
Rummel Baker 92
Rummel, August 1824-1886 Baker 92
Rummel, Christian 1787-1849 Baker 92
Rummel, Franz 1853-1901 Baker 92
Rummel, George T. Law&B 92
Rummel, Harold Edwin 1940- WhoSSW 93
Rummel, Joseph 1818-1880 Baker 92
Rummel, Josephine 1812-1877 Baker 92
Rummel, Robert Wiland 1915- WhoAm 92
Rummel, Walter Morse 1887-1953 Baker 92
Rummel-Bulska, Iwona Maria 1948- WhoUN 92
Rummelhardt, Jacques Antoine 1941- WhoWor 93
Rummell, Grant D. 1937- St&PR 93
Rummery, T.E. St&PR 93
Rummler, William R. 1940- St&PR 93
Rumor, Mariano 1915-1990 BioIn 17
Rump, Donald Alan Law&B 92
Rump, Michael A. Law&B 92
Rump, Siegfried Michael 1955- WhoWor 93
Rumpa, William St&PR 93
Rumpel, Dieter A.N. 1932- WhoScE 91-3
Rumpel, Peter Loyd 1939- WhoAm 92
Rumpeltin, Frank E. 1945- St&PR 93
Rumpf, John Louis 1921- WhoAm 92
Rumph, Lee C. 1921- WhoAm 92
Rumple, Margaret AmWomPl
Rumpler, Yves 1938- WhoScE 91-2
Rumpp, Carl St&PR 93
Rumsey, Daniel W. Law&B 92
Rumsey, R. Douglas 1918- WhoE 93
Rumsey, Victor Henry 1919- WhoAm 92
Rumsfeld, Donald H. 1932- WhoAm 92
Rumsfeld, Donald Henry 1932- WhoE 93
Rumzie, Kenneth Hubbard 1931- St&PR 93
Runac, Pamela Joan 1948- WhoAmW 93
Runcie, Robert BioIn 17
Runcie, Robert Alexander Kennedy 1921- WhoWor 93
Runciman, Herbert Morrison 1941- WhoWor 93
Runciman, John F. 1866-1916 Baker 92
Runciman, Lex 1951- WhoWrEP 92
Runciman, Steven 1903- WhoWor 93
Runciman, Walter 1870-1949 BioIn 17
Runck, Robert Ridgway 1935- WhoE 93
Runcorn, Stanley Keith 1922- WhoWor 93
Rund, Douglas Andrew 1945- WhoWor 93
Rundblom, James Cloyd Law&B 92
Runde, James A. 1946- WhoAm 92
Runde, William C. 1929- St&PR 93
Rundel, Pamela Ann 1957- WhoAmW 93
Rundell, Bob Ray 1933- WhoSSW 93
Rundell, C.A., Jr. 1931- St&PR 93
Rundell, David Richard WhoScE 91-1
Rundell, Jeffrey Edwin 1951- WhoE 93
Rundgren, Todd 1948- WhoAm 92
Rundle, Anne ScF&FL 92
Rundle, Henry Maurice Palmerston 1938- WhoWor 93
Rundle, Philip Sterling 1953- St&PR 93
Rundle, Steven M. d1990 BioIn 17
Rundquist, Howard Irving 1929- WhoAm 92
Rundquist, Richard Allyn 1927- St&PR 93
Rundqvist, Stig Olov 1929- WhoScE 91-4
Rundstedt, Karl Rudolf Gerd von 1875-1953 BioIn 17, DcTwHis, HarEnMi
Rune, E.J. Valle 1936- WhoScE 91-4
Rune, V. 1936- WhoScE 91-4
Runes, Richard Norton 1944- WhoWor 93
Rung, Frederik 1854-1914 Baker 92
Rung, Henrik 1807-1871 Baker 92
Rung, Richard Allen 1929- WhoAm 92
Runge, A.H. 1935- WhoScE 91-3
Runge, Bjorn 1937- WhoWor 93
Runge, De Lyle Paul 1918- WhoAm 92
Runge, Donald Edward 1938- WhoAm 92
Runge, John Scott 1927- St&PR 93
Runge, Kay Kretschmar 1946- WhoEmL 93
Runge, Linda Jacob 1947- WhoAmW 93
Rungenhagen, Carl Friedrich 1778-1851 Baker 92
Runham, S.R. WhoScE 91-1
Runk, Fred J. 1942- St&PR 93
Runk, John W. 1938- St&PR 93
Runk, Judith Ann 1938- St&PR 93
Runk, Lee H. 1940- St&PR 93
Runk, Lee Hammond 1940- WhoAm 92
Runkel, Francis J. 1949- St&PR 93
Runkle, Bertha AmWomPl
Runkle, Martin 1937- BioIn 17
Runkle, Martin Davey 1937- WhoAm 92
Runkle, Mary Arvella 1934- WhoWrEP 92
Runkle, Robert S. 1936- St&PR 93
Runkle, Robert Scott 1936- WhoE 93
Runnalls, John Clyve 1924- WhoAm 92
Runne, Herbert Rein Law&B 92
Runne, Jeanne K. Law&B 92
Runnells, Clive 1926- WhoSSW 93
Runnells, David L. 1945- St&PR 93
Runnels, Charles Duke 1953- St&PR 93
Runnels, G. Tyler 1956- St&PR 93
Runnels, Jerry Spencer 1940- St&PR 93, WhoIns 93
Runnels, Pete 1928-1991 BioIn 17
Runner, Ada Kellogg AmWomPl
Runner, David Clark 1948- WhoSSW 93
Runnicles, Donald 1954- WhoAm 92
Running, Joseph Martin, Jr. 1945- WhoSSW 93
Running Rabbit 1943- BioIn 17
Runnion, Cynthia Prosser 1948- St&PR 93
Runnion, Daniel Thomas 1949- WhoIns 93
Runnion, Howard J., Jr. 1930- WhoAm 92
Runnion, Howard Jackson 1930- St&PR 93
Runolfsson, Karl Otto 1900-1970 Baker 92
Runolfsson, Sveinn 1946- WhoScE 91-4
Runolfsson, Thordur 1959- WhoE 93
Runsdorf, H. Norman 1908-1991 BioIn 17
Runstadler, Peter W. 1934- St&PR 93
Runtagh, Hellene S. St&PR 93
Runte, Roseann 1948- WhoAmW 93
Runyan, Anita Karen 1955- WhoAmW 93
Runyan, C.F. ScF&FL 92
Runyan, Charles Alan 1951- WhoEmL 93
Runyan, John William, Jr. 1924- WhoAm 92
Runyan, Roger A. 1952- St&PR 93
Runyan, Thomas Earl 1932- WhoSSW 93
Runyan, William Marion 1924- St&PR 93
Runyeon, Jennifer BioIn 17
Runyon, Alfred Damon 1880-1946 BioIn 17
Runyon, Catherine 1947- BioIn 17
Runyon, Charles W. 1928-1987 ScF&FL 92
Runyon, Cornelia BioIn 17

Runyon, Damon 1880-1946 BioIn 17
Runyon, Damon 1884-1946 JrnUS
Runyon, Floyd Lawrence 1936- WhoAm 92
Runyon, Guy Eric 1945- WhoE 93, WhoWor 93
Runyon, John Charles 1944- WhoSSW 93
Runyon, Kim BioIn 17
Runyon, Marvin Travis 1924- WhoAm 92, WhoE 93
Runyon, Theodore Hubert, Jr. 1930- WhoSSW 93
Runzheimer, Lee 1942- St&PR 93
Ruocchio, Patricia Jeanne 1958- WhoWrEP 92
Ruof, Richard Alan 1932- WhoE 93
Ruoff, Abby BioIn 17
Ruoff, Andrew Christian, III 1919- WhoAm 92
Ruoff, Arthur Louis 1930- WhoAm 92
Ruoff, Carl F. Law&B 92
Ruoff, James A. Law&B 92
Ruolz-Montchal, Henri, Comte de 1808-1887 Baker 92
Rupard, G. Marion, Sr. 1905- St&PR 93
Rupe, Art 1919- SoulM
Rupe, Shirley Ann 1942- WhoAmW 93
Rupercht, Adrienne M. 1946- St&PR 93
Rupert, Prince 1619-1682 HarEnMi
Rupert, Prince, Count Palatine 1619-1682 BioIn 17
Rupert, Donald William 1946- WhoAm 92
Rupert, Elizabeth Anastasia 1918- WhoAm 92
Rupert, Frederick E. Law&B 92
Rupert, Hoover 1917- WhoAm 92
Rupert, J. Paul 1942- St&PR 93
Rupert, James C(layton), II 1957- ConAu 136
Rupert, Johann P. BioIn 17
Rupert, John Edward 1927- WhoAm 92
Rupert, Karen Martin 1961- St&PR 93
Rupert, Wayne W. Law&B 92
Rupert of Deutz c. 1075-1129 OxDcByz
Rupilius, Publius fl. c. 132BC- HarEnMi
Rupke, Jerry I. 1938- St&PR 93
Rupley, Agnes Emmott 1960- WhoAmW 93
Rupley, Theodore J. 1939- WhoIns 93
Rupley, William Henry, III 1945- WhoSSW 93
Rupnik, Ivan 1911- Baker 92
Rupnik, Louis John 1942- St&PR 93
Rupnow, Alma AmWomPl
Rupp, Adolph 1901-1977 BioIn 17
Rupp, Augustus ScF&FL 92
Rupp, Daniel R. Law&B 92
Rupp, Dean Edward 1941- St&PR 93
Rupp, Elaine Helen 1944- WhoAmW 93
Rupp, Franz 1901-1992 BioIn 17, NewYTBS 92 [port]
Rupp, George Erik 1942- WhoAm 92, WhoSSW 93, WhoWor 93
Rupp, George W. 1949- St&PR 93
Rupp, Geraldlynn Sue 1946- WhoAmW 93
Rupp, Glenn N. 1944- St&PR 93, WhoAm 92
Rupp, James M. 1935- St&PR 93, WhoAm 92
Rupp, James McElroy Law&B 92
Rupp, John Anthony Law&B 92
Rupp, John Norris 1913- WhoAm 92
Rupp, Leila Jane 1950- WhoAmW 93
Rupp, Monica Cecilia 1956- WhoEmL 93
Rupp, Ralph Russell 1929- WhoAm 92
Rupp, Richard W. 1918- St&PR 93
Rupp, Sharen Lynn 1941- WhoSSW 93
Rupp, William John 1927- WhoAm 92
Ruppe, Arthur Maxwell 1928- WhoSSW 93
Ruppe, Dianne Kay 1944- WhoSSW 93
Ruppe, Harry O. 1929- WhoScE 91-3
Ruppe, Loret Miller 1936- WhoAm 92, WhoAmW 93, WhoWor 93
Ruppel, George Robert 1911- WhoAm 92
Ruppel, Howard James, Jr. 1941- WhoWor 93
Ruppel, Wayne D. 1940- St&PR 93
Ruppel, Wolfgang 1929- WhoScE 91-3
Ruppelli, Todd P. 1927- St&PR 93
Rupper, Gerold Robert 1908- WhoWor 93
Ruppert, Christine M. 1956- St&PR 93
Ruppert, David Paul 1934- St&PR 93
Ruppert, Gary Lee 1944- St&PR 93
Ruppert, James K. 1949- WhoWrEP 92
Ruppert, John Lawrence 1953- WhoEmL 93
Ruppert, Leonard Harvey 1929- WhoE 93
Ruppert, Paul Richard 1958- WhoE 93
Ruppert, Peter 1941- ScF&FL 92
Ruppin, Richard C. Law&B 92
Rupprecht, Crown Prince of Bavaria 1869-1955 HarEnMi
Rupprecht, Carol Schreier 1939- WhoAmW 93
Rupprecht, Hans S. 1930- WhoScE 91-3
Rupprecht, Herbert Harald 1936- WhoScE 91-3
Rupprecht, Nancy Ellen 1948- WhoAmW 93
Ruprecht, Martin c. 1758-1800 OxDcOp
Ruprecht, Thomas G. 1941- WhoIns 93
Ruqba, Hamud 'Abdallah al- 1951- WhoWor 93
Rurik dc. 879 HarEnMi
Rurode, Louise Joyce 1948- WhoWrEP 92
Rusak, Halina Rodko WhoAmW 93
Rusbridge, M.G. WhoScE 91-1
Rusbridger, James 1928- ConAu 39NR
Rusca, Francesco fl. 17th cent.- Baker 92
Ruscalla, Giovenale Vegezzi IntDcAn
Ruscetta, Harold Pasquale, Jr. 1945- WhoE 93
Rusch, Bruce R. 1943- St&PR 93
Rusch, Hugh Leonard 1902- WhoAm 92
Rusch, Kristine Kathryn 1960- ScF&FL 92
Rusch, Shari Lyn 1966- BioIn 17
Rusch, Thomas William 1946- WhoAm 92, WhoWor 93
Rusch, Willard Van Tuyl 1933- WhoAm 92
Rusch, William B. 1951- St&PR 93
Rusch, William Graham 1937- WhoAm 92
Ruscha, Edward BioIn 17
Ruscha, Edward 1937- WhoAm 92
Rusche, Edmund W., Jr. Law&B 92
Ruschi, Augusto 1915-1986 BioIn 17
Ruschp, Sepp d1990 BioIn 17
Rusciano, Anthony 1944- WhoE 93
Rusciano, Anthony J. St&PR 93
Ruscica, Dorothy P. 1934- St&PR 93
Ruscitella, Maria Martha Law&B 92
Ruscitti, Donald R. St&PR 93
Rusco, Linda Suzanne 1951- WhoAmW 93
Rusconi, Gerardo 1922-1974 Baker 92
Rusconi, Steven A. Law&B 92
Ruse, Gary Alan 1946- ScF&FL 92
Ruse, Paul William, Jr. 1943- WhoAm 92, WhoE 93
Ruser, John M. 1937- St&PR 93
Rush ConMus 8 [port]
Rush, Aiken P., Jr. 1939- WhoIns 93
Rush, Albert F. Law&B 92
Rush, Alison 1951- ScF&FL 92
Rush, Andrew Wilson 1931- WhoAm 92
Rush, Avery, Jr. 1922- St&PR 93
Rush, Bobby 1940- BioIn 17
Rush, Carl V. 1955- St&PR 93
Rush, Catherine Patricia 1944- WhoAmW 93
Rush, Cecil Archer 1917- WhoE 93
Rush, David 1934- WhoAm 92, WhoE 93
Rush, David Geoffrey WhoScE 91-1
Rush, David H. 1918- St&PR 93
Rush, Fletcher Grey, Jr. 1917- WhoAm 92
Rush, Herman 1929- St&PR 93
Rush, Herman E. 1929- WhoAm 92
Rush, Jeffrey S. 1950- WhoWrEP 92
Rush, John 1782-1853 BioIn 17
Rush, John Lawrence 1934- St&PR 93
Rush, Julia Ann Halloran 1927- WhoAmW 93
Rush, Kenneth 1910- WhoAm 92, WhoWor 93
Rush, Kenneth Wayne 1939- WhoE 93
Rush, Loren 1935- Baker 92
Rush, Margaret Dana AmWomPl
Rush, Max Wilson 1936- St&PR 93
Rush, Michael David WhoScE 91-1
Rush, Norman BioIn 17
Rush, Norman 1933- WhoAm 92
Rush, Otis BioIn 17
Rush, Pamela Jeanne Turbow 1958- WhoSSW 93
Rush, Patricia L. Law&B 92
Rush, Peter 1949- WhoAm 92
Rush, Rebecca Lynn 1948- St&PR 93
Rush, Richard 1930- MiSFD 9
Rush, Richard Henry 1915- WhoAm 92, WhoWor 93
Rush, Richard P. 1945- WhoSSW 93
Rush, Roseann Novosel 1958 WhoSSW 93
Rush, Rosemary 1944- WhoAmW 93
Rush, Thomas Michael Law&B 92
Rush, William John 1936- WhoAm 92
Rush, William Louis 1955- WhoWrEP 92
Rushalko, Kevin B. 1950- St&PR 93
Rushby, George 1900- BioIn 17
Rushdie, Salman BioIn 17
Rushdie, Salman 1947- IntLitE, MagSWL [port], ScF&FL 92, WhoWor 93
Rushefsky, Norman Law&B 92
Rushen, Frank Joseph 1940- St&PR 93
Rusher, William A. 1923- PolPar
Rusher, William Allen 1923- WhoAm 92, WhoE 93
Rushford, Donald L. Law&B 92
Rushford, Donald Lawrence 1930- St&PR 93
Rushford, Patricia H(elen) 1943- ConAu 37NR
Rushforth, Marjorie Alice 1943- WhoAmW 93
Rushin, Lester, III Law&B 92
Rushin, Steve BioIn 17
Rushing, Allen Ingram 1949- St&PR 93
Rushing, Byron 1942- WhoE 93
Rushing, Dorothy Marie 1925- WhoAmW 93
Rushing, Felder BioIn 17
Rushing, Henry H. 1943- St&PR 93
Rushing, Jane Gilmore 1925- WhoAm 92, WhoWrEP 92
Rushing, Jimmy 1903-1972 Baker 92, BioIn 17
Rushing, Joe Bob 1921- WhoAm 92
Rushing, Natalia Moehle 1950- WhoAmW 93
Rushing, Norma Hodges 1944- WhoAmW 93
Rushing, Roy Eugene 1943- St&PR 93
Rushing, Zella Ann 1940- St&PR 93
Rushinsky, Michael J. 1933- St&PR 93
Rushkoff, Marvin 1929- WhoAm 92
Rushnell, Squire Derrick 1938- WhoAm 92
Rushton, A. WhoScE 91-1
Rushton, Brian Mandel 1933- St&PR 93, WhoAm 92, WhoE 93
Rushton, Brian Norman 1932- WhoWor 93
Rushton, Darrell M. St&PR 93
Rushton, Julian (Gordon) 1941- Baker 92
Rushton, Kenneth Ralph WhoScE 91-1
Rushton, Nan Michelle 1964- WhoAmW 93
Rushton, Neil WhoScE 91-1
Rushton, Theodore Allan 1938- WhoWrEP 92
Rushton, William J., III 1929- St&PR 93
Rushton, William James, III 1929- WhoAm 92, WhoIns 93
Rushworth, Robert Aitken 1924- WhoAm 92
Rusie, Sue Coffee 1954- WhoEmL 93
Rusiecki, Kanuty 1801-1860 PolBiDi
Rusiewski, Mark 1961- St&PR 93
Rusin, Alan Law&B 92
Rusin, Edward A. 1922- WhoAm 92
Rusin, Karel 1937- WhoScE 91-4
Rusin, William Aloysius 1938- WhoE 93
Rusinak, Ronald Peter Law&B 92
Rusine, James Michael 1948- St&PR 93
Rusing, Rick BioIn 17
Rusiniak, Yvonne Lubov 1945- WhoWrEP 92
Rusinko, Frank, Jr. 1930- WhoE 93
Rusinol, Santiago 1861-1931 BioIn 17
Rusinski, Michat 1948- WhoUN 92
Rusis, Robert Law&B 92
Rusis, Robert 1933- St&PR 93
Rusk, Barbara Joan 1926- St&PR 93
Rusk, Brian Dwight 1955- WhoE 93
Rusk, Charles Edward 1964- WhoSSW 93
Rusk, David Dean 1909- DcTwHis
Rusk, Dean 1909- BioIn 17, ColdWar 1 [port], WhoAm 92
Rusk, Howard Archibald 1901-1989 BioIn 17
Rusk, James, Jr. ScF&FL 92
Rusk, Linda Baugher 1947- WhoAmW 93
Rusk, Nance J. 1957- WhoWrEP 92
Rusk, Ralph L. 1803-1882 BioIn 17
Rusk, Richard (Geary) 1946- ConAu 138
Rusk, Willard C. 1921- St&PR 93
Ruska, Ernst 1906-1988 BioIn 17
Ruskai, Mary Beth 1944- WhoAmW 93
Ruskauff, Catherine 1967- WhoAmW 93
Ruskay, Richard A. d1992 BioIn 17
Ruskell, Gordon Leonard WhoScE 91-1
Ruskin, Adam Jay 1963- WhoE 93
Ruskin, Jerome 1936- WhoSSW 93
Ruskin, John 1819-1900 BioIn 17, MagSWL [port]
Ruskin, Joseph Richard 1924- WhoAm 92
Ruskin, Les D. 1960- WhoSSW 93
Ruskin, Robert Sterling 1945- WhoE 93
Ruskin, Ronald ScF&FL 92
Rusler, Robert BioIn 17
Rusling, Barbara Neubert 1945- WhoSSW 93
Rusling, Thomas Griswold 1941- St&PR 93
Rusnak, Martha Hendrick 1938- WhoAmW 93
Rusnell, Joanne D. Law&B 92
Rusnell, Joanne D. 1954- St&PR 93, WhoAm 92
Rusnock, James Albert 1946- WhoE 93
Rusnock, John A. 1939- St&PR 93
Rusoff, Garry ScF&FL 92
Rusoff, Irving Isadore 1915- WhoE 93
Russ, Charles P., III Law&B 92
Russ, Charles P., III 1944- St&PR 93
Russ, Charles Paul, III 1944- WhoAm 92
Russ, Gerald Allen 1936- WhoE 93
Russ, Gina S. Law&B 92
Russ, Jack BioIn 17, CngDr 91
Russ, Jack 1945- NewYTBS 92 [port]
Russ, Joanna 1937- BioIn 17, ScF&FL 92, WhoAm 92, WhoWrEP 92
Russ, John C. 1949- St&PR 93
Russ, Lavinia 1904-1992 BioIn 17
Russ, Lavinia Faxon d1992 NewYTBS 92
Russ, Lavinia (Faxon) 1904-1992 ConAu 137
Russ, Lawrence 1950- WhoWrEP 92
Russ, Lisa WhoWrEP 92
Russ, Ronald G. 1954- St&PR 93
Russ, Sherman B. 1937- St&PR 93
Russ, Thomas Ashley 1964- WhoSSW 93
Russ, William BioIn 17
Russac, Randall Joseph 1947- WhoEmL 93, WhoSSW 93
Russakovskii, Alexander Mironovitch 1957- WhoWor 93
Russam, K. WhoScE 91-1
Russamano, Dean Michael 1956- St&PR 93
Russavage, Janet Marie 1962- WhoAmW 93
Russe, Conrad Thomas Campbell 1954- WhoSSW 93
Russe, Meinhard Werner 1928- WhoScE 91-3
Russek, Henry I. 1911-1990 BioIn 17
Russel, Marjorie Ellen 1944- WhoAmW 93
Russel, Richard Gordon 1943- St&PR 93
Russell, A.A., Jr. 1927- St&PR 93
Russell, Alan K. ScF&FL 92
Russell, Albert Edward 1941- St&PR 93
Russell, (George) Alexander 1880-1953 Baker 92
Russell, Allan David 1924- WhoAm 92
Russell, Allen Stevenson 1915- WhoAm 92
Russell, Amanda ConAu 39NR
Russell, Amy Requa AmWomPl
Russell, Andy d1992 BioIn 17, NewYTBS 92
Russell, Angela V. 1943- WhoAmW 93
Russell, Armistead Goode 1913- St&PR 93
Russell, Attie Yvonne 1923- WhoAmW 93
Russell, Barbara Dalton 1952- WhoE 93
Russell, Benjamin 1761-1845 JrnUS
Russell, Bert SoulM
Russell, Bertha M. AmWomPl
Russell, Bertrand 1872-1970 BioIn 17
Russell, Bertrand Arthur William 1872-1970 DcTwHis
Russell, Beverly 1941- St&PR 93
Russell, Bill BioIn 17
Russell, Bill 1905-1992 NewYTBS 92
Russell, Bill 1934- WhoAm 92
Russell, Bobby d1992 NewYTBS 92
Russell, Carlton Parrish, Jr. 1935- WhoSSW 93
Russell, Carol Ann 1943- WhoAmW 93
Russell, Carolann Marie 1951- WhoWrEP 92
Russell, Caryl L. Law&B 92
Russell, Charles 1832-1900 BioIn 17
Russell, Charles A. 1933- St&PR 93
Russell, Charles Arthur d1992 BioIn 17
Russell, Charles Arthur, Jr. d1992 NewYTBS 92
Russell, Charles Edward 1860-1941 JrnUS
Russell, Charles Ellsworth 1906-1969 Baker 92
Russell, Charles M. 1864-1926 BioIn 17
Russell, Charles Marion 1864-1926 GayN
Russell, Charles Mead, Jr. 1937- St&PR 93
Russell, Charles Ray 1941- WhoAm 92
Russell, Charles Stevens 1926- WhoAm 92
Russell, Charlotte Sananes 1927- WhoAmW 93
Russell, Chester David, Jr. 1933- St&PR 93
Russell, Chuck MiSFD 9
Russell, Clifford Springer 1938- WhoSSW 93
Russell, Colette H. BioIn 17
Russell, Craig d1990 BioIn 17
Russell, Dan M., Jr. 1913- WhoAm 92, WhoSSW 93
Russell, Daniel Joseph, Jr. 1959- WhoE 93
Russell, Daniel Lindsay, Jr. 1845-1908 EncAACR
Russell, David Allison 1935- WhoAm 92
Russell, David B. Law&B 92
Russell, David Gray 1937- WhoWor 93
Russell, David L. 1942- WhoAm 92, WhoSSW 93
Russell, David Lawson 1921- WhoAm 92
Russell, David Williams 1945- WhoWor 93
Russell, Diane E. Law&B 92
Russell, Dominique WhoAmW 93, WhoE 93, WhoWor 93
Russell, Donald A. 1935- St&PR 93
Russell, Donald Glenn 1931- WhoAm 92
Russell, Donald L. 1943- St&PR 93

Russell, Donald Ray 1926- St&PR 93
Russell, Donald Stuart 1906- WhoAm 92, WhoSSW 93
Russell, Donnie BioIn 17
Russell, Dora Winifred Black 1894-1986 BioIn 17
Russell, Dorothy Miller Law&B 92
Russell, Dorothy Schoeberlein 1935- WhoAmW 93
Russell, Douglas Campbell 1945- WhoAm 92
Russell, Douglas Henry 1948- WhoSSW 93
Russell, Douglas Muir Galloway 1958- WhoWor 93
Russell, E(nid) S(herry) 1924- ConAu 139
Russell, Edwin F. 1914- St&PR 93
Russell, Edwin Fairman 1914- WhoAm 92
Russell, Edwin Fortune 1910-1990 BioIn 17
Russell, Elbert Winslow 1929- WhoSSW 93
Russell, Elizabeth Dougherty 1961- WhoAmW 93
Russell, Elizabeth G. 1958- WhoAmW 93, WhoEmL 93
Russell, Emma G. Watson Winfield 1921- WhoAmW 93
Russell, Eric Frank 1905-1978 BioIn 17, ScF&FL 92
Russell, Ernest Everett 1923- WhoSSW 93
Russell, Fabian LeVan 1953- WhoE 93
Russell, Fay L. 1944- St&PR 93
Russell, Francia 1938- WhoAm 92, WhoAmW 93
Russell, Frank E. 1920- St&PR 93
Russell, Frank Eli 1920- WhoAm 92
Russell, Fred McFerrin 1906- WhoAm 92, WhoSSW 93
Russell, Frederick William 1923- WhoAm 92, WhoE 93
Russell, G.T. WhoScE 91-1
Russell, Gaylord L. 1942- St&PR 93
Russell, Gene 1942- St&PR 93
Russell, George Albert 1921- WhoAm 92
Russell, George Albert 1947- St&PR 93
Russell, George (Allan) 1923- Baker 92
Russell, George Allen 1923- WhoAm 92
Russell, George E., Jr. 1944- St&PR 93
Russell, George Haw 1945- WhoSSW 93, WhoWor 93
Russell, George Keith 1937- WhoE 93
Russell, George William 1867-1935 BioIn 17
Russell, Glen Allan 1925- WhoAm 92
Russell, Gloria Mary 1936- WhoSSW 93
Russell, Grace Jarrell Williams 1924- WhoWrEP 92
Russell, Grant Neil 1953- St&PR 93
Russell, H. Diane 1936- WhoAm 92
Russell, Harold Louis 1916- WhoAm 92
Russell, Harriet Shaw 1952- WhoEmL 93
Russell, Helen Ross 1915- WhoWrEP 92
Russell, Henry 1812-1900 Baker 92
Russell, Henry 1871-1937 Baker 92
Russell, Henry George 1941- WhoAm 92
Russell, Henry William 1937- WhoWor 93
Russell, Herman J. BioIn 17
Russell, Herman Jerome 1930- AfrAmBi, WhoAm 92
Russell, Howard Lewis 1962- ConAu 136
Russell, Ian John WhoScE 91-1
Russell, Inez Snyder 1951- WhoAmW 93, WhoSSW 93, WhoWor 93
Russell, Irwin E. 1926- St&PR 93
Russell, J.H. WhoScE 91-1
Russell, James Alvin, Jr. 1917- WhoAm 92, WhoSSW 93
Russell, James E. 1943- St&PR 93
Russell, James F. 1941- St&PR 93
Russell, James Franklin, Jr. 1935- St&PR 93
Russell, James Miller, III 1935- St&PR 93
Russell, James R. 1946- St&PR 93
Russell, James Sargent 1903- WhoWor 93
Russell, James Webster, Jr. 1921- WhoAm 92, WhoSSW 93
Russell, Jane 1921- IntDcF 2-3 [port], SweetSg D [port]
Russell, Jay MiSFD 9
Russell, Jean 1939-1982? ScF&FL 92
Russell, Jeanne Y. St&PR 93
Russell, Jeffrey Burton BioIn 17
Russell, Jeffrey Burton 1934- WhoAm 92
Russell, Joann M. Law&B 92
Russell, John 1919- BioIn 17
Russell, John A. 1931- St&PR 93
Russell, John David 1928- WhoAm 92
Russell, John Fintan 1934- WhoE 93
Russell, John Francis 1929- WhoSSW 93
Russell, John G. 1928- St&PR 93
Russell, John Gordon 1928- WhoScE 91-3
Russell, John Robert ScF&FL 92
Russell, John St. Clair, Jr. 1917- WhoAm 92
Russell, John William 1952- WhoE 93
Russell, Joseph 1922- St&PR 93
Russell, Joseph M. Law&B 92
Russell, Josette Renee 1964- WhoAmW 93
Russell, Josiah Cox 1900- WhoAm 92, WhoSSW 93, WhoWor 93
Russell, Joyce Anne Rogers 1920- WhoAm 92
Russell, Joyce M. Law&B 92
Russell, Juanita Renner 1951- WhoE 93
Russell, Katharine A. 1948- St&PR 93
Russell, Keith P. 1945- St&PR 93
Russell, Keith Palmer 1916- WhoAm 92
Russell, Keith Palmer, Jr. 1945- WhoAm 92
Russell, Ken 1927- MiSFD 9, WhoAm 92
Russell, Kenneth Calvin 1936- WhoAm 92
Russell, Kenneth J. Law&B 92
Russell, Kevin Patrick 1952- WhoE 93
Russell, Kurt BioIn 17
Russell, Kurt 1951- HolBB [port]
Russell, Kurt Von Vogel 1951- WhoAm 92
Russell, L. Michael Law&B 92
Russell, Lawrence 1941- WhoCanL 92
Russell, Leeolin Vance Law&B 92
Russell, Leon 1941- Baker 92
Russell, Leonard H. 1927- St&PR 93
Russell, Liane Brauch 1923- WhoAm 92
Russell, Lillian 1861-1922 Baker 92, BioIn 17
Russell, Linda K. Law&B 92
Russell, Louise 1931- WhoAmW 93
Russell, Louise Bennett 1942- WhoAm 92
Russell, Lynn Darnell 1937- WhoAm 92, WhoSSW 93
Russell, M.F. WhoScE 91-1
Russell, Mariann Barbara 1935- WhoAmW 93, WhoE 93
Russell, Marjorie Rose 1925- WhoAmW 93
Russell, Mark 1932- WhoAm 92
Russell, Marlou 1956- WhoEmL 93
Russell, Mary 1947- BioIn 17
Russell, Mary C. AmWomPl
Russell, Mary McSorley 1881- AmWomPl
Russell, Mason Webster 1956- WhoE 93
Russell, Maud d1989 BioIn 17
Russell, Micahel A. St&PR 93
Russell, Michael Anthony Hamilton WhoScE 91-1
Russell, Michael James 1958- WhoE 93, WhoEmL 93, WhoWor 93
Russell, Michael John WhoScE 91-1
Russell, Michael R. 1942- St&PR 93
Russell, Michael Thomas 1950- St&PR 93
Russell, Michael William 1944- WhoSSW 93
Russell, Morgan 1886-1953 BioIn 17
Russell, Nellie Stuart AmWomPl
Russell, Odo William Leopold 1829-1884 BioIn 17
Russell, Olga Wester 1913- WhoE 93
Russell, Olive AmWomPl
Russell, Oris Stanley 1922- WhoWor 93
Russell, Oscar Cecil, Jr. 1945- WhoAm 92
Russell, Pamela A. 1955- St&PR 93
Russell, Patti E. Law&B 92
Russell, Paul BioIn 17
Russell, Paul 1956- ConGAN
Russell, Paul Edgar 1924- WhoAm 92
Russell, Paul Edwin Law&B 92
Russell, Paul Snowden 1925- WhoAm 92
Russell, Peggy Taylor 1927- WhoSSW 93, WhoWor 93
Russell, Peter 1921- BioIn 17
Russell, Phillip Ray 1953- WhoSSW 93
Russell, R. Scott Law&B 92
Russell, Ralph Timothy 1948- WhoIns 93, WhoSSW 93
Russell, Randall L.C. 1945- St&PR 93
Russell, Ray 1924- ScF&FL 92, WhoAm 92
Russell, Richard A. Law&B 92
Russell, Richard B. 1897-1971 BioIn 17, PolPar
Russell, Richard Doncaster 1929- WhoAm 92
Russell, Richard Frederick 1950- St&PR 93
Russell, Richard G. 1943- St&PR 93
Russell, Richard John 1953- WhoE 93
Russell, Richard L. Law&B 92
Russell, Richard Lawson 1940- WhoE 93
Russell, Richard Olney, Jr. 1932- WhoAm 92
Russell, Rinaldina 1934- WhoE 93
Russell, Robert Alan 1946- WhoSSW 93
Russell, Robert Anderson 1927- St&PR 93
Russell, Robert Gilmore 1928- WhoAm 92, WhoWor 93
Russell, Robert Henry 1956- WhoSSW 93
Russell, Robert Hilton 1927- WhoAm 92
Russell, Robert J. 1942- St&PR 93
Russell, Robert Larry 1942- St&PR 93
Russell, Robert Leonard 1916- WhoWor 93
Russell, Robert M. 1925- St&PR 93
Russell, Robert Mitchell 1941- WhoE 93
Russell, Robert Pritchard 1945- WhoSSW 93
Russell, Robert W. d1992 NewYTBS 92
Russell, Robert W. 1912-1992 BioIn 17
Russell, Robert W. 1942- WhoUN 92
Russell, Roger Allen 1952- WhoSSW 93
Russell, Rosalind 1908-1976 IntDcF 2-3
Russell, Rossi Alexis Law&B 92
Russell, Scott BioIn 17
Russell, Scott Charles 1936- WhoE 93
Russell, Scott Daniel 1952- WhoSSW 93
Russell, Sean ScF&FL 92
Russell, Seena WhoE 93
Russell, Sharman Apt 1954- WhoWrEP 92
Russell, Sheryl Peterson 1943- WhoSSW 93
Russell, Shirley 1935- ConTFT 10
Russell, Sol Smith 1848-1902 BioIn 17
Russell, Stanley G., Jr. WhoAm 92
Russell, Susan B. Law&B 92
Russell, Ted McKinnies 1943- WhoE 93
Russell, Theresa BioIn 17
Russell, Theresa 1957- ConTFT 10
Russell, Theresa Lynn 1957- WhoAm 92
Russell, Thomas Edgie, III 1942- St&PR 93
Russell, Thomas Frank 1924- St&PR 93
Russell, Thomas Lyon 1946- WhoWrEP 92
Russell, Thomas William Fraser 1934- WhoAm 92
Russell, Thomas Wright, Jr. 1916- WhoAm 92, WhoWor 93
Russell, Timothy 1951- WhoWrEP 92
Russell, Timothy Ross 1942- WhoE 93
Russell, Tomas Morgan 1934- WhoAm 92, WhoIns 93
Russell, Turner Alan 1944- WhoAm 92
Russell, Virginia Willis 1913- WhoAmW 93
Russell, Wallace Dee 1933- St&PR 93
Russell, Ward BioIn 17
Russell, Wendell Phillip, Jr. Law&B 92
Russell, William 1884-1929 BioIn 17
Russell, William 1905- Baker 92
Russell, William A. 1972- St&PR 93
Russell, William Alexander, Jr. 1946- WhoE 93
Russell, William B. WhoE 93
Russell, William Blanton 1934- WhoSSW 93
Russell, William Clelland WhoScE 91-1
Russell, William Douglas 1949- St&PR 93
Russell, William Edward 1944- St&PR 93
Russell, William Ellis 1948- BiDAMSp 1989
Russell, William Felton 1934- AfrAmBi
Russell, William Fletcher, III 1950- WhoAm 92
Russell, William Joseph 1941- WhoAm 92
Russell, William Richard, Jr. 1930- St&PR 93
Russell, William Steven 1948- St&PR 93, WhoAm 92
Russell, William Thomas, III 1958- St&PR 93
Russell-Hunter, William Devigne 1926- WhoAm 92, WhoWor 93
Russell of Killowen, Baron 1832-1900 BioIn 17
Russell Taylor, Elisabeth 1930- ScF&FL 92
Russell-Wood, Anthony John R. 1939- WhoAm 92
Russer, Peter 1943- WhoScE 91-3
Russert, Charlene A. 1946- St&PR 93
Russeth, Richard Quentin Law&B 92
Russian, David H. 1952- St&PR 93
Russian, Rhonda Lee Law&B 92
Russian Bill d1881 BioIn 17
Russiano, John 1942- WhoAm 92
Russianoff, Leon 1916-1990 BioIn 17
Russin, F. Stanley 1951- St&PR 93
Russin, Jonathan 1937- WhoAm 92, WhoWor 93
Russin, Richard J. Law&B 92
Russin, Robert Isaiah 1914- WhoAm 92
Russler, David James 1948- St&PR 93
Russler, Diana Elena 1953- WhoUN 92
Russman, Thomas Anthony 1944- WhoAm 92, WhoSSW 93
Russ-Mohl, Stephan 1950- WhoWor 93
Russo, Aaron MiSFD 9
Russo, Alexander Peter 1922- WhoAm 92
Russo, Anthony F. d1990 BioIn 17
Russo, Anthony J. 1938- St&PR 93
Russo, Anthony Joseph, Jr. Law&B 92
Russo, Anthony Michael 1935- WhoE 93
Russo, Celia Mireille Russo 1944- WhoWor 93
Russo, Christine Lou 1958- WhoSSW 93
Russo, Claire Marie 1943- WhoAmW 93
Russo, Dennis Charles 1950- WhoE 93
Russo, Diane St&PR 93
Russo, Elizabeth Louise 1950- St&PR 93
Russo, Francis Bennett 1948- WhoE 93
Russo, Francis John 1953- WhoSSW 93
Russo, Frank Raymond, Jr. 1958- WhoSSW 93
Russo, Fred Anthony 1941- St&PR 93
Russo, Gennaro 1940- WhoScE 91-3
Russo, Gregory T. Law&B 92
Russo, Gregory T. 1949- St&PR 93
Russo, Gregory Thomas 1949- WhoAm 92
Russo, Harry A. Law&B 92
Russo, Irma Haydee Alvarez de 1942- WhoAmW 93, WhoWor 93
Russo, James P. 1943- St&PR 93
Russo, Joe Duane 1947- St&PR 93
Russo, John 1939- ScF&FL 92
Russo, John Marc Law&B 92
Russo, John N. 1936- St&PR 93
Russo, Jordan A. 1932- St&PR 93
Russo, Jose 1942- WhoAm 92
Russo, Joseph Donald 1935- St&PR 93
Russo, Joseph Frank 1924- WhoAm 92
Russo, Joseph Salvatore 1954- WhoE 93
Russo, Josephine Marie 1948- WhoAmW 93
Russo, Karen L. St&PR 93
Russo, Kathleen Marie 1947- WhoAm 92, WhoSSW 93
Russo, Marisabina ChlBIID [port]
Russo, Martin A. 1944- WhoAm 92
Russo, Marty 1944- CngDr 91
Russo, Michael L. 1948- St&PR 93
Russo, Monica Martin 1964- WhoSSW 93
Russo, Nick BioIn 17
Russo, Peter Francis 1932- St&PR 93, WhoAm 92
Russo, Peter J. 1946- St&PR 93
Russo, Rene BioIn 17
Russo, Richard 1949- WhoWrEP 92
Russo, Richard A. 1945- St&PR 93
Russo, Richard A. 1946- ScF&FL 92
Russo, Richard Paul 1954- ScF&FL 92
Russo, Robert Nicholas 1936- WhoE 93
Russo, Rosemary 1951- WhoAmW 93
Russo, Roy Lawrence 1935- WhoAm 92
Russo, Thomas Anthony 1943- WhoAm 92
Russo, Thomas Joseph 1941- WhoAm 92
Russo, Thomas M. Law&B 92
Russo, Vincent Francis 1948- WhoE 93
Russo, Vito 1946-1990 BioIn 17
Russo, William (Joseph) 1928- Baker 92
Russo-Caia, Salvatore 1929- WhoScE 91-3
Russo Frattasi, Alberto 1922- WhoScE 91-3
Russolo, Luigi 1885-1947 Baker 92
Russom, Philip Wade 1955- WhoE 93
Russomanno, Lee 1953- WhoE 93
Russo-Marie, Francoise 1945- WhoWor 93
Russotto, Thomas Vincent 1945- WhoE 93
Russum, John Law&B 92
Russwurm, Hellmut WhoScE 91-4
Rust Baker 92
Rust, David Edward 1929- WhoAm 92, WhoE 93
Rust, David H. 1947- St&PR 93
Rust, Edward B., Jr. 1950- St&PR 93, WhoIns 93
Rust, Edward Barry, Jr. 1950- WhoAm 92
Rust, Friedrich Wilhelm 1739-1796 Baker 92
Rust, Jennifer Lynn 1967- WhoAmW 93
Rust, Lynn Eugene 1952- WhoWor 93
Rust, Mathias BioIn 17
Rust, Philip C. 1944- St&PR 93
Rust, Philip Frederick 1947- WhoSSW 93
Rust, Robert Francis 1927- WhoSSW 93
Rust, Robert Warren 1928- WhoSSW 93
Rust, Wilhelm 1822-1892 Baker 92
Rust, Wilhelm Karl 1787-1855 Baker 92
Rust, William J. 1929- St&PR 93
Rust, William James 1929- WhoAm 92
Rusta, "B" WhoWrEP 92
Rustad, Noreen BioIn 17
Rustagi, Jagdish Sharan 1923- WhoAm 92
Rustagi, Raghuvir Sharan 1936- WhoE 93
Rustand, Jon Arthur 1963- WhoSSW 93
Rustanto Law&B 92
Rustgi, Eileen Boyle 1955- WhoE 93
Rustgi, Moti Lal 1929- WhoAm 92
Rustgi, Vinod Kumar 1954- WhoE 93
Rusthoven, Peter James 1951- WhoAm 92
Rusticus ConAu 38NR
Rustin, Bayard 1910-1987 ConBlB 4 [port], PolPar
Rustin, Bayard 1912-1987 EncAACR
Ruston, Perry L. d1992 NewYTBS 92
Rusu, Alexandru 1940- WhoScE 91-4
Rusu, George 1932- WhoScE 91-4
Rusu, Mircea 1920- WhoScE 91-4
Rusu, Stefan 1942- WhoScE 91-4
Rusuku, Simon 1948- WhoAfr
Rusz, Joe BioIn 17
Ruszkowska, Maria 1926- WhoScE 91-4
Ruszkowski, Andrzej 1928- WhoScE 91-4
Ruszkowski, Ivo 1921- WhoScE 91-4
Ruszkowski, Marek 1925- WhoScE 91-4
Ruszkowski, Robert Lee 1947- WhoE 93
Rusznak, Istvan 1920- WhoScE 91-4

Ruta, Philip Ralph 1931- WhoE 93
Rutan, Burt BioIn 17
Rutan, Dick 1939- & Yeager, Jeana 1952- Expl 93 [port]
Rutan, Edwin P., II Law&B 92
Rutan, Elbert L. 1943- WhoAm 92
Rutan, Richard Glenn 1938- WhoAm 92
Rutan, Thomas Carl 1954- WhoSSW 93
Rutenberg-Rosenberg, Sharon Leslie 1951- WhoAm 92
Ruter, Christiaan Frederik 1938- WhoWor 93
Ruter, Horst 1942- WhoScE 91-3
Ruter, Ingo 1962- WhoWor 93
Rutes, Walter Alan 1928- WhoAm 92
Rutford, Robert Hoxie 1933- WhoAm 92, WhoSSW 93
Rutgard, Lorraine Levin 1925- WhoAmW 93
Rutgers, Katharine Phillips 1910- WhoAmW 93, WhoE 93, WhoWor 93
Ruth BioIn 17
Ruth, Alisa Michaelovna 1936- WhoAmW 93
Ruth, Alpheus Landis 1915- WhoAm 92
Ruth, Ann Alva 1964- WhoAmW 93
Ruth, Babe 1895-1948 BioIn 17
Ruth, Carol A. 1942- WhoAm 92
Ruth, Charles Wallace 1922- St&PR 93
Ruth, Daniel John 1949- WhoAm 92
Ruth, George Herman 1895-1948 BioIn 17
Ruth, Jack H. St&PR 93
Ruth, James C. Law&B 92
Ruth, James M. 1952- St&PR 93
Ruth, James Perry 1946- WhoAm 92
Ruth, John Homer 1936- WhoAm 92
Ruth, JoLinda S. 1956- WhoE 93
Ruth, Lois-Jean 1931- WhoAmW 93
Ruth, Marc D. Law&B 92
Ruth, Marsha Diane 1950- WhoAmW 93
Ruth, Martha Cruz 1948- WhoAmW 93
Ruth, Richard I. 1953- WhoE 93
Ruth, Robert Douglas 1943- WhoSSW 93
Ruth, Terry P. St&PR 93
Ruth, Volker 1932- WhoScE 91-3
Ruth, William Edward 1926- WhoAm 92
Ruthardt, Adolf 1849-1934 Baker 92
Ruthchild, Geraldine Quietlake WhoAmW 93
Ruthenburg, Grace Dorcas 1897- AmWomPl
Rutherfood, Marc Eugene 1958- St&PR 93
Rutherford, Ann 1917?- SweetSg C [port]
Rutherford, Brett 1947- ScF&FL 92, WhoWrEP 92
Rutherford, Brian William John 1956- WhoWor 93
Rutherford, Christopher A. 1962- St&PR 93
Rutherford, Clyde E. 1939- WhoAm 92
Rutherford, David L. Law&B 92
Rutherford, Donald W.S. 1939- St&PR 93
Rutherford, Edward ConAu 139
Rutherford, Ernest 1871-1937 BioIn 17
Rutherford, G.W. 1920- St&PR 93
Rutherford, J.H. 1930- St&PR 93
Rutherford, John Sherman, III 1938- WhoAm 92
Rutherford, Leo Herschel 1929- St&PR 93
Rutherford, Linda Lucas Law&B 92
Rutherford, Lucy Page Mercer 1891?-1948 BioIn 17
Rutherford, Margaret 1892-1972 BioIn 17, IntDcF 2-3 [port], QDrFCA 92 [port]
Rutherford, Michael 1946- ScF&FL 92
Rutherford, Paul Harding 1938- WhoAm 92
Rutherford, Rana Hunter 1952- St&PR 93
Rutherford, Reid 1952- WhoEmL 93
Rutherford, Robert Barry 1931- WhoAm 92
Rutherford, Romilly T. 1908- St&PR 93
Rutherford, Sally Jane 1959- St&PR 93
Rutherford, Samuel J. 1928- St&PR 93
Rutherford, Sherrie Nichols Law&B 92
Rutherford, William Drake 1939- WhoAm 92, WhoWor 93
Rutherglen, George A. 1949- WhoAm 92
Ruthin, Margaret ConAu 38NR, MajAI
Ruthizer, Jeffrey Law&B 92
Ruthman, Thomas R. 1933- St&PR 93
Ruthven, Becky 1947- WhoAmW 93
Ruthven, Douglas Morris 1938- WhoAm 92
Ruthven, Patrick Leo Brer 1964- WhoWor 93
Rutigliano, Barbara A. Law&B 92
Rutigliano, Barbara A. 1951- St&PR 93
Rutigliano, Deborah Gail 1964- WhoE 93
Rutigliano, Sam 1932- BioIn 17
Rutilius Claudius Namatianus fl. 5th cent.- OxDcByz
Rutilius Rufus, Publius c. 154BC-c. 75BC HarEnMi
Rutini, Giovanni Marco 1723-1797 Baker 92
Rutins, Karlis Visvaldis 1937- WhoE 93
Rutishauser, Wilhelm Jakob 1931- WhoScE 91-4
Rutkin, Edward Eugene 1951- WhoSSW 93
Rutkin, Richard 1938- WhoE 93
Rutkin, Seymour 1927- WhoAm 92
Rutkoff, Peter M. 1942- ConAu 39NR
Rutkofske, Randall L. Law&B 92
Rutkovsky, Paul Michael 1947- WhoWrEP 92
Rutkowski, Antoni 1920- WhoScE 91-4
Rutkowski, David John 1951- St&PR 93
Rutkowski, Jan 1924- WhoScE 91-4
Rutkowski, Jerzy 1920- WhoScE 91-4
Rutkowski, Witold Maksymilian 1947- WhoWor 93
Rutland, George Patrick 1932- WhoAm 92
Rutland, Lucile AmWomPl
Rutland, Mark MiSFD 9
Rutledge, Ann d1835 BioIn 17
Rutledge, Arthur Clayton, Jr. 1944- St&PR 93, WhoE 93
Rutledge, Charles Ozwin 1937- WhoAm 92
Rutledge, E. Peter 1940- St&PR 93
Rutledge, Felix Noah 1917- WhoAm 92
Rutledge, Ivan Cate 1915- WhoAm 92
Rutledge, James Joseph 1948- WhoSSW 93
Rutledge, Jerry Eugene 1936- WhoIns 93
Rutledge, John 1739-1800 OxCSupC [port]
Rutledge, John William 1923- WhoAm 92
Rutledge, Louella Whicker 1953- WhoAmW 93
Rutledge, Mary Jayne 1962- WhoAmW 93
Rutledge, Myra-Ann 1952- WhoE 93
Rutledge, Paul Edmund, III 1953- WhoIns 93
Rutledge, Perry 1930- St&PR 93
Rutledge, Philip C. 1906-1990 BioIn 17
Rutledge, Robert William 1950- WhoSSW 93
Rutledge, Wiley Blount, Jr. 1894-1949 OxCSupC [port]
Rutledge, William J. 1932- St&PR 93
Rutledge, William P. 1942- WhoAm 92
Rutman, Gregory L. Law&B 92
Rutman, Leo 1935- ScF&FL 92
Rutman, Mark Charles 1930- WhoAm 92
Rutman, Roanne Beth Cline 1941- WhoAmW 93
Rutman, Robert Jesse 1919- WhoAm 92, WhoE 93
Rutsala, Vern 1934- WhoWrEP 92
Rutsala, Vern A. 1934- WhoAm 92
Rutsey, John
See Rush ConMus 8
Rutskoy, Aleksandr WhoWor 93
Rutsky, Curtiss Alan 1944- St&PR 93
Rutsky, Lester 1924- WhoWrEP 92
Rutstein, David W. Law&B 92
Rutstein, David W. 1944- St&PR 93, WhoAm 92
Rutstein, Hazel Kleban 1927- WhoE 93
Rutstein, Sheldon 1934- St&PR 93, WhoAm 92
Rutstein, Stanley Harold 1941- WhoAm 92
Ruttan, Susan BioIn 17, WhoAm 92
Ruttan, Vernon Wesley 1924- WhoAm 92
Rutten, F.F.H. 1948- WhoScE 91-3
Rutten, W.P.F. 1946- WhoScE 91-3
Ruttenber, Timothy Tyson d1992 BioIn 17
Ruttenberg, Harold Joseph 1914- St&PR 93, WhoAm 92
Ruttenberg, Harold S. 1941- St&PR 93
Ruttenberg, Harvey Nolan 1942- WhoSSW 93
Ruttenberg, Reid 1936- St&PR 93
Ruttenberg, Stanley Harvey 1917- WhoAm 92
Ruttenberg, Valerie H. Law&B 92
Ruttencutter, Brian B. 1953- St&PR 93
Rutter, Deborah Frances 1956- WhoAmW 93
Rutter, Eileen ScF&FL 92
Rutter, Elizabeth J. 1937- St&PR 93
Rutter, Elizabeth Jane 1937- WhoAm 92
Rutter, Frances Tompson 1920- WhoAm 92
Rutter, Frank Mowbray 1911-1989 BioIn 17
Rutter, James E. 1933- WhoAm 92
Rutter, John (Milford) 1945- Baker 92
Rutter, M. WhoScE 91-1
Rutter, Michael BioIn 17
Rutter, Michael Llewellyn WhoScE 91-1
Rutter, N.W. WhoScE 91-4
Rutter, Nathaniel Westlund 1932- WhoAm 92
Rutter, William J. 1928- WhoAm 92
Rutterer, Paul J.M. Law&B 92
Rutterer, Paul James 1948- St&PR 93
Rutter Giappone, Anthony 1954- WhoWor 93
Ruttimann, Rene 1948- WhoWor 93
Ruttner, Albert A. 1937- WhoAm 92
Rutyna, Richard Albert 1937- WhoSSW 93
Rutz, Rebecca Ruth 1948- WhoAmW 93, WhoEmL 93, WhoSSW 93
Rutz, Richard Frederick 1919- WhoAm 92
Rutzen, Arthur Cooper, Jr. 1947- WhoAm 92
Ruud, Clayton Olaf 1934- WhoAm 92
Ruud, Millard Harrington 1917- WhoAm 92
Ruus, Veronica 1905- WhoWrEP 92
Ruutel, Arnold Fedorovich 1928- WhoWor 93
Ruuth, Marianne 1933- ScF&FL 92
Ruvalds, John 1940- WhoSSW 93
Ruvane, Anne Julie Law&B 92
Ruvane, John Austin 1935- WhoAm 92
Ruvane, Joseph J., Jr. St&PR 93
Ruvelson, Alan K. 1915- St&PR 93
Ruvigny, marquis de 1648-1720 BioIn 17
Ruvolo, Felix 1912- WhoAm 92
Ruvolo, John J. 1938- St&PR 93
Ruvolo, Louis Salvatore 1940- WhoE 93
Ruwayha, Faysal Amin 1935- WhoUN 92
Ruwe, Dean Melvin 1938- St&PR 93
Ruwe, L. Nicholas 1933-1990 BioIn 17
Ruwe, Robert Paul 1941- CngDr 91
Ruwet, Nicolas 1932- Baker 92
Ruxin, Robert Harris Law&B 92
Ruyle-Hullinger, Elizabeth Smith 1946- WhoEmL 93
Ruyneman, Daniel 1886-1963 Baker 92
Ruysser, Bernard J. 1919- St&PR 93
Ruyten, Wilhelmus Maria 1959- WhoSSW 93
Ruyter, Michel Adriaanszoon de 1607-1676 HarEnMi
Ruzek, Peter R. Law&B 92
Ruzek, Sheryl Burt 1945- WhoE 93
Ruzic, Neil P. 1930- ConAu 39NR
Ruzic, Neil Pierce 1930- WhoAm 92, WhoWrEP 92
Ruzick, S., Jr. 1945- St&PR 93
Ruzicka, Jaromir 1934- WhoScE 91-2
Ruzicka, Mary Frances 1943- WhoAmW 93, WhoE 93
Ruzicka, Peter 1948- Baker 92
Ruzicka, Rudolf 1941- Baker 92
Ruzicka, Thomas 1952- WhoWor 93
Ruzickova, Zuzana 1928- Baker 92
Ruzie, David Raymond 1933- WhoWor 93
Ruzimatov, Faruk BioIn 17
Ruzitska, Jozsef c. 1775-c. 1823 OxDcOp
Ruzow, Miriam Gottlieb BioIn 17
Ruzsanyi, Laszlo 1937- WhoScE 91-4
Rwegellera, George Gregory Celestine 1936- WhoUN 92
Ryabko, Boris Yakov 1949- WhoWor 93
Ryabov, Gennady G. 1936- WhoWor 93
Ryabukhin, Yuri Sergeevitch 1931- WhoUN 92
Ryall, Jo-Ellyn M. 1949- WhoAmW 93
Ryall, Michael John WhoScE 91-1
Ryals, Clyde de Loache 1928- WhoAm 92, WhoSSW 93
Ryals, Vicki Elaina 1947- WhoAmW 93
Ryan, Alan 1943- ScF&FL 92
Ryan, Alice J. 1959- St&PR 93
Ryan, Allan Andrew, Jr. 1945- WhoAm 92
Ryan, Arthur F. 1942- St&PR 93
Ryan, Arthur Norman 1938- St&PR 93
Ryan, Arthur S. 1945- St&PR 93
Ryan, Ashton J. 1947- St&PR 93
Ryan, Barbara Battle 1928- WhoWrEP 92
Ryan, Barry Ronelle 1934- St&PR 93
Ryan, Brenda Kay 1962- WhoAmW 93
Ryan, Bruce J. 1943- St&PR 93, WhoAm 92
Ryan, Buddy BioIn 17
Ryan, Buddy 1934- WhoAm 92
Ryan, Carl Ray 1938- WhoAm 92
Ryan, Charles 1937- ScF&FL 92
Ryan, Charles C. 1946- ScF&FL 92
Ryan, Charles Carroll 1947- WhoSSW 93
Ryan, Charles Edward 1940- WhoAm 92
Ryan, Charles Patrick, Jr. 1939- St&PR 93
Ryan, Charlton 1935- WhoSSW 93
Ryan, Christopher J. St&PR 93
Ryan, Clarence Augustine, Jr. 1931- WhoAm 92
Ryan, Clifford Charles Law&B 92
Ryan, Cornelius (John) 1920-1974 ConAu 38NR
Ryan, Cornelius Michael 1933- WhoAm 92
Ryan, Cornelius O'Brien 1917- WhoAm 92
Ryan, Daniel John 1960- WhoE 93
Ryan, Daniel Joseph 1961- WhoIns 93
Ryan, Daniel Leo 1930- WhoAm 92
Ryan, Daniel N. 1930- St&PR 93
Ryan, Daniel Nolan 1930- WhoAm 92, WhoWor 93
Ryan, Daniel P. 1940- St&PR 93
Ryan, David Thomas 1939- WhoAm 92
Ryan, Dennis John Law&B 92
Ryan, Dennis Joseph 1951- WhoSSW 93
Ryan, Dennis Patrick 1946- St&PR 93
Ryan, Desmond 1943- ScF&FL 92
Ryan, Diane Phyllis 1954- WhoE 93
Ryan, Donald Francis 1942- WhoE 93
Ryan, Donnell Michael 1941- WhoWor 93
Ryan, Edward A. Law&B 92
Ryan, Edward J., Jr. 1957- St&PR 93
Ryan, Edward V. 1928- St&PR 93
Ryan, Edward W. 1928- WhoScE 91-3
Ryan, Edward W. 1932- WhoAm 92
Ryan, Edwin L., Jr. Law&B 92
Ryan, Edwin L., Jr. 1930- St&PR 93
Ryan, Eileen Law&B 92
Ryan, Elizabeth Anne 1943- WhoAmW 93
Ryan, Ellen Bouchard 1947- WhoAm 92
Ryan, Ellie Louise 1945- WhoAmW 93
Ryan, Estelle L. 1890- AmWomPl
Ryan, Frances Mary 1920- WhoAm 92
Ryan, Francis Patrick 1944- WhoWor 93
Ryan, Frank 1902-1944 BioIn 17
Ryan, Frank J. 1935- St&PR 93
Ryan, Frederick Joseph, Jr. 1955- WhoAm 92
Ryan, G. Thomas Law&B 92
Ryan, Gary L. Law&B 92
Ryan, Gaynor J. Law&B 92
Ryan, George H., Sr. 1934- WhoAm 92
Ryan, Gerald A. 1935- St&PR 93
Ryan, Gerard Spencer 1926- WhoAm 92
Ryan, Halford Ross 1943- WhoSSW 93
Ryan, Harold J. 1945- St&PR 93
Ryan, Harold L. 1923- WhoAm 92
Ryan, Helen P. AmWomPl
Ryan, Hewson A. 1922-1991 BioIn 17
Ryan, Holly Anne 1945- WhoAmW 93
Ryan, Howard Chris 1916- WhoAm 92
Ryan, Ione Jean Alohilani 1926- WhoAmW 93
Ryan, J. Bruce 1944- WhoSSW 93, WhoWor 93
Ryan, J. Richard 1929- St&PR 93
Ryan, Jack d1991 BioIn 17
Ryan, Jack 1926-1991 AnObit 1991
Ryan, James C. 1938- St&PR 93
Ryan, James Edwin 1919- WhoAm 92
Ryan, James Francis 1928- WhoAm 92
Ryan, James Francis 1943- WhoE 93
Ryan, James Franklin 1948- WhoAm 92
Ryan, James J. 1948- St&PR 93
Ryan, James Joseph 1929- WhoAm 92
Ryan, James Leo 1932- WhoAm 92
Ryan, James Neal 1931- St&PR 93
Ryan, James Stephen 1944- WhoSSW 93
Ryan, James Thomas 1931- St&PR 93
Ryan, James Vincent d1990 BioIn 17
Ryan, James Walter 1935- WhoAm 92, WhoSSW 93, WhoWor 93
Ryan, Jane Touhey Hammes 1925- WhoSSW 93
Ryan, Janice E. WhoAmW 93
Ryan, Jerry William 1928- WhoAm 92
Ryan, Jillian BioIn 17
Ryan, John Augustine 1869-1945 BioIn 17
Ryan, John C. Law&B 92
Ryan, John Dale 1915-1983 HarEnMi
Ryan, John E., Jr. 1939- WhoIns 93
Ryan, John F. Law&B 92
Ryan, John Francis 1946- St&PR 93
Ryan, John Francis, III 1953- St&PR 93
Ryan, John Franklin 1925- WhoAm 92
Ryan, John G. Law&B 92
Ryan, John Gerald 1952- St&PR 93, WhoAm 92
Ryan, John J. Law&B 92
Ryan, John Lester, Jr. 1936- St&PR 93
Ryan, John M. Law&B 92
Ryan, John M. 1936- WhoSSW 93
Ryan, John T., Jr. 1912- St&PR 93
Ryan, John Thomas, Jr. 1912- WhoAm 92, WhoWor 93
Ryan, John Thomas, III 1943- St&PR 93, WhoAm 92
Ryan, John Vincent Law&B 92
Ryan, John William 1929- WhoAm 92
Ryan, John William 1937- WhoAm 92, WhoWor 93
Ryan, John William, Jr. 1940- WhoAm 92
Ryan, Joseph A. 1920- ConAu 138
Ryan, Joseph Edwin 1929- St&PR 93
Ryan, Joseph Thomas 1913- WhoAm 92
Ryan, Judith Andre 1936- WhoAm 92
Ryan, Kara Mary Frances 1935- WhoAmW 93
Ryan, Kenneth John 1926- WhoAm 92
Ryan, Kenneth Robert, Jr. 1947- WhoSSW 93
Ryan, Kevin 1952- WhoE 93
Ryan, Kevin James 1940- St&PR 93
Ryan, Kitty BioIn 17
Ryan, Lee Thomas 1949- WhoE 93
Ryan, Lehan Jerome 1935- WhoAm 92
Ryan, Leo Vincent 1927- WhoAm 92, WhoWor 93
Ryan, Leonard Eames 1930- WhoAm 92, WhoWor 93
Ryan, Linda Smith 1951- WhoEmL 93
Ryan, Liz 1959- WhoAmW 93
Ryan, Louis Farthing Law&B 92
Ryan, Louis Farthing 1947- St&PR 93, WhoAm 92

Ryan, M. Andrea *Law&B 92*
Ryan, M. Kevin *Law&B 92*
Ryan, Marc James *Law&B 92*
Ryan, Margaret 1950- *WhoWrEP 92*
Ryan, Marian Teresa 1954- *WhoAmW 93*
Ryan, Marilyn Grams 1932- *WhoAmW 93*
Ryan, Marleigh Grayer 1930- *WhoAm 92, WhoAmW 93*
Ryan, Mary A. 1940- *WhoAmW 93*
Ryan, Mary E. *BioIn 17*
Ryan, Mary Elizabeth 1953- *WhoWrEP 92*
Ryan, Mary Gene 1953- *WhoSSW 93*
Ryan, Mary Louise *Law&B 92*
Ryan, Maureen Ann 1957- *WhoE 93*
Ryan, Maurice J. *Law&B 92*
Ryan, Maurice William 1924- *WhoE 93*
Ryan, Max J. 1927- *WhoScE 91-3*
Ryan, Meg *BioIn 17*
Ryan, Meg 1961- *WhoAm 92*
Ryan, Michael *BioIn 17*
Ryan, Michael 1952- *WhoEmL 93*
Ryan, Michael A. 1949- *St&PR 93*
Ryan, Michael Beecher 1936- *WhoAm 92*
Ryan, Michael Clifford 1948- *WhoE 93*
Ryan, Michael D. *Law&B 92*
Ryan, Michael E. 1938- *St&PR 93*
Ryan, Michael Edmond 1938- *WhoAm 92*
Ryan, Michael H. *Law&B 92*
Ryan, Michael J. *Law&B 92*
Ryan, Michael J. 1947- *WhoIns 93*
Ryan, Michael J. 1952- *St&PR 93*
Ryan, Michael J., Jr. *Law&B 92*
Ryan, Michael Joseph 1953- *WhoWrEP 92*
Ryan, Michael Louis 1945- *WhoWor 93*
Ryan, Michael P. 1942- *WhoScE 91-3*
Ryan, Michael T. *Law&B 92*
Ryan, Mike, II 1951- *WhoEmL 93*
Ryan, Mike Herbert 1951- *WhoSSW 93*
Ryan, Nancy D. d1990 *BioIn 17*
Ryan, Nancy Marie *WhoWrEP 92*
Ryan, Neil Joseph 1930- *WhoWor 93*
Ryan, Noel 1925- *WhoAm 92*
Ryan, Nolan *BioIn 17*
Ryan, Nolan 1947- *WhoAm 92*
Ryan, Pat *WhoWrEP 92*
Ryan, Patrick G. 1937- *St&PR 93, WhoAm 92, WhoIns 93*
Ryan, Patrick J. 1937- *St&PR 93*
Ryan, Patrick J. 1938- *WhoAm 92*
Ryan, Patrick M. *BioIn 17*
Ryan, Patrick Michael 1937- *St&PR 93, WhoAm 92*
Ryan, Patrick Michael 1944- *WhoAm 92*
Ryan, Patrick W. 1937- *St&PR 93*
Ryan, Paul F. 1938- *St&PR 93*
Ryan, Paul H. *Law&B 92*
Ryan, Paul J. 1925- *St&PR 93*
Ryan, Paul Louis 1943- *WhoE 93*
Ryan, Paul Phillip 1946- *WhoE 93*
Ryan, Paul Ryder, Jr. 1932- *WhoAm 92, WhoE 93*
Ryan, Peggy 1924- *BioIn 17*
Ryan, Peter John 1922- *WhoAm 92*
Ryan, Peter M. 1948- *St&PR 93, WhoAm 92*
Ryan, Philip Glennon 1945- *WhoE 93*
Ryan, Pierce 1928- *WhoScE 91-3*
Ryan, Porter K. *Law&B 92*
Ryan, R.A. *Law&B 92*
Ryan, Rachel *ConAu 139*
Ryan, Raymond D. 1922- *WhoAm 92*
Ryan, Reade Haines, Jr. 1937- *WhoAm 92, WhoWor 93*
Ryan, Regina Claire 1938- *WhoAm 92*
Ryan, Richard 1935- *WhoE 93*
Ryan, Richard G. 1953- *St&PR 93*
Ryan, Richard K. 1937- *St&PR 93*
Ryan, Richard Matthew 1945- *St&PR 93*
Ryan, Robert 1909-1973 *IntDcF 2-3*
Ryan, Robert Collins 1953- *WhoWor 93*
Ryan, Robert Seibert 1922- *WhoAm 92*
Ryan, Rocky *BioIn 17*
Ryan, Sandra Belcher 1943- *WhoAmW 93*
Ryan, Sheila *Law&B 92*
Ryan, Sheila 1921-1975 *SweetSg C [port]*
Ryan, Sherry Lynn 1944- *WhoAmW 93*
Ryan, Stephen F. 1935- *St&PR 93*
Ryan, Stephen Joseph, Jr. 1940- *WhoAm 92*
Ryan, Susan Maree 1942- *WhoAsAP 91*
Ryan, Suzanne Irene 1939- *WhoAmW 93*
Ryan, Theresa Ann Julia 1962- *WhoAmW 93*
Ryan, Thomas 1827-1903 *Baker 92*
Ryan, Thomas Anthony 1951- *WhoWor 93*
Ryan, Thomas D. 1939- *WhoAm 92*
Ryan, Thomas J. *Law&B 92*
Ryan, Thomas J. 1942- *ScF&FL 92*
Ryan, Thomas Joseph 1945- *WhoAm 92*
Ryan, Thomas L. *Law&B 92*
Ryan, Thomas M. 1948- *St&PR 93*
Ryan, Thomas P. 1938- *St&PR 93*
Ryan, Thomas Patrick, Jr. 1929- *WhoAm 92*
Ryan, Thomas Timothy, Jr. 1945- *WhoAm 92*
Ryan, Thomas W. *St&PR 93*
Ryan, Thomas William, III 1947- *WhoSSW 93*
Ryan, Tim *BioIn 17, Law&B 92*
Ryan, Tom Kreusch 1926- *WhoAm 92*
Ryan, Tula Fleshman 1927- *WhoAmW 93, WhoWor 93*
Ryan, Walter James 1931- *WhoAm 92*
Ryan, William *WhoScE 91-1*
Ryan, William Anthony 1926- *St&PR 93*
Ryan, William Francis 1925- *WhoAm 92*
Ryan, William Frank 1924- *WhoWor 93*
Ryan, William Grady 1942- *WhoSSW 93*
Ryan, William John, Jr. 1954- *WhoE 93*
Ryan, William Joseph 1932- *WhoAm 92, WhoWor 93*
Ryan, William Paul 1930- *St&PR 93*
Ryan, William R. 1911- *St&PR 93*
Ryan-Reinking, Mary E. *Law&B 92*
Ryans, Charles H., Jr. *Law&B 92*
Ryavec, Karl W(illiam) 1936- *ConAu 137*
Ryba, Earle Richard 1934- *WhoE 93*
Ryba, Jakub (Simon) Jan 1765-1815 *Baker 92*
Ryba, Jeanie Ruth 1947- *WhoAmW 93*
Ryba, John W. 1944- *St&PR 93*
Rybak-Chmielewska, Helena 1946- *WhoScE 91-4*
Rybakov, Anatolii Naumovich *BioIn 17*
Rybakov, Yuri M. 1930- *WhoWor 93*
Rybalka, Michel 1933- *WhoAm 92*
Rybar, Valerian S. 1918-1990 *BioIn 17*
Rybczynski, Witold *BioIn 17*
Rybczynski, Witold Marian 1943- *WhoAm 92*
Rybeck, Bo 1935- *WhoScE 91-4*
Ryberg, Jean E. 1932- *St&PR 93*
Rybicki, Alexander Andrew, Jr. 1944- *St&PR 93*
Rybicki, Clarice Annette 1959- *WhoEmL 93*
Rybka, Vratislav 1940- *WhoScE 91-4*
Rybkowski, Jan 1912-1987 *DrEEuF*
Rybner, (Peter Martin) Cornelius 1855-1929 *Baker 92*
Rybolt, Robert Marsh 1913- *WhoAm 92*
Rybolt, Thomas R. *BioIn 17*
Ryburn, Samuel McChesney 1914- *WhoAm 92, WhoWor 93*
Rycerski, Aleksander 1825-1866 *PolBiDi*
Rychecky, Helen Rose 1922- *WhoAmW 93*
Rychetnik, Jurgen J. 1933- *WhoScE 91-4*
Rychlak, Joseph Frank 1928- *WhoAm 92*
Rychlik, Jan 1916-1964 *Baker 92*
Rychlik, Jozef 1946- *Baker 92*
Rychman, Ladislav 1922- *DrEEuF*
Rychter, Mauro 1952- *WhoWor 93*
Ryckman, DeVere Wellington 1924- *WhoAm 92*
Rycombel, Thomas J. 1940- *WhoE 93*
Rycroft, Donald C. 1938- *St&PR 93, WhoIns 93*
Rycroft, Donald Cahill 1938- *WhoAm 92*
Rycroft, Donald James *Law&B 92*
Rycroft, Michael J. 1938- *WhoScE 91-1*
Rycus, Mitchell Julian 1932- *WhoAm 92*
Rydahl, Thorkild 1939- *WhoWor 93*
Rydberg, Jan 1923- *WhoScE 91-4*
Rydberg, Per Axel 1860-1931 *BioIn 17*
Rydberg, Sven 1933- *WhoWor 93*
Rydberg, Ulf S. 1940- *WhoScE 91-4*
Ryde, Hans B. 1931- *WhoScE 91-4*
Rydel, Lucjan 1870-1918 *PolBiDi*
Rydel, Stefan 1920- *WhoScE 91-4*
Rydell, Bengt 1950- *WhoScE 91-3*
Rydell, Chris *BioIn 17*
Rydell, Mark *WhoAm 92*
Rydell, Mark 1934- *MiSFD 9*
Ryden, John Graham 1939- *St&PR 93, WhoAm 92*
Ryden, Katherine 1947- *St&PR 93, WhoAmW 93*
Ryden, Lars 1939- *WhoScE 91-4*
Ryden, Mats Lennart Edvard 1929- *WhoWor 93*
Ryden, Stig 1908-1965 *IntDcAn*
Ryden, Susan Kay 1945- *WhoAmW 93*
Ryden, T.E. 1936- *St&PR 93*
Rydeng, Carl Enemark 1933- *WhoUN 92*
Ryder, Albert Pinkham 1847-1917 *BioIn 17*
Ryder, Albert Pinkham 1847-1919 *GayN*
Ryder, Birthe *Law&B 92*
Ryder, C.C. 1947- *St&PR 93*
Ryder, Carl *See* Public Enemy *News 92*
Ryder, Donald Porter 1926- *WhoAm 92*
Ryder, Edward Breyer, IV 1955- *WhoE 93*
Ryder, Edward Francis 1931- *WhoE 93*
Ryder, Elizabeth Godbey 1943- *WhoAmW 93*
Ryder, Frank A. 1939- *St&PR 93*
Ryder, Harl Edgar 1938- *WhoAm 92*
Ryder, Henry Clay 1928- *WhoAm 92*
Ryder, Jack McBride 1928- *WhoAm 92*
Ryder, James *ScF&FL 92*
Ryder, Joanne *BioIn 17*
Ryder, Joanne (Rose) 1946- *MajAI [port]*
Ryder, John Douglass 1907- *WhoAm 92*
Ryder, Kay Hatton 1935- *WhoAmW 93*
Ryder, M. Lynn 1937- *St&PR 93*
Ryder, Mahler d1992 *NewYTBS 92*
Ryder, Mahler 1937-1992 *BioIn 17*
Ryder, Oliver Allison 1946- *WhoWor 93*
Ryder, Richard D. 1940- *ConAu 139*
Ryder, Sandra Smith 1949- *WhoSSW 93*
Ryder, Stephen Willis, Jr. 1923- *St&PR 93*
Ryder, Thomas G. *Law&B 92*
Ryder, Thomas Michael 1934- *WhoAm 92*
Ryder, Thomas O. 1944- *WhoE 93*
Ryder, Timothy Thomas 1930- *WhoWor 93*
Ryder, Winona *BioIn 17*
Ryder, Winona 1971- *WhoAm 92*
Ryder Richardson, Edward Colin 1929- *WhoWor 93*
Rydesky, Mary Margaret 1952- *WhoAmW 93*
Rydholm, Nancy Lynn 1958- *WhoAmW 93*
Rydholm, Ralph Williams 1937- *St&PR 93, WhoAm 92*
Rydman, John Alan 1950- *WhoSSW 93*
Rydman, Kari 1936- *Baker 92*
Rydstrom, Carlton Lionel 1928- *WhoSSW 93*
Rydz, John S. 1925- *WhoAm 92*
Rydzewski, J.R. *WhoScE 91-1*
Rydzewski, Robert Stanley *St&PR 93*
Rydzewski, Robert Stanley 1931- *WhoE 93*
Rye, Anthony *ConAu 37NR, MajAI*
Rye, Walter L., Jr. 1930- *St&PR 93*
Ryelandt, Joseph 1870-1965 *Baker 92*
Ryer, David F. *Law&B 92*
Ryerse, Dorance D., Jr. 1932- *St&PR 93*
Ryerse, William C. 1929- *St&PR 93*
Ryerson, Florence Willard 1894?-1965 *AmWomPl*
Ryerson, Jay W. 1935- *St&PR 93*
Ryerson, Joseph Leslie 1918- *WhoAm 92*
Ryerson, W. Newton 1902- *WhoE 93*
Ryerson, William Newton 1945- *WhoE 93*
Ryga, George 1932-1987 *WhoCanL 92*
Rygh, Ole B. 1944- *St&PR 93*
Rygor, Stanley 1926- *St&PR 93*
Ryhanen, Pauli T. 1939- *WhoScE 91-4*
Ryherd, Geraldine Schneider 1929- *WhoAmW 93*
Ryherd, Larry Earl 1940- *WhoAm 92*
Ryker, Charles Edwin 1920- *WhoAm 92*
Ryker, Norman J., Jr. 1926- *St&PR 93, WhoAm 92*
Rykhoek, Philip M. 1956- *St&PR 93*
Rykiel, Sonia *BioIn 17*
Rykwert, Joseph 1926- *WhoAm 92*
Rylaarsdam, J. Coert *BioIn 17*
Ryland, Cally Thomas 1871- *AmWomPl*
Ryland, Greaner Neal 1941- *St&PR 93, WhoAm 92*
Ryland, John Stanley *WhoScE 91-1*
Ryland, William Hugh 1934- *St&PR 93*
Rylander, Edith May 1935- *WhoWrEP 92*
Rylander, Henry Grady, Jr. 1921- *WhoAm 92*
Rylander, Michael Kent 1935- *WhoSSW 93*
Rylant, Cynthia 1954- *Au&Arts 10 [port], ConAu 136, DcAmChF 1985, MajAI [port]*
Ryle, Joseph Donald 1910- *WhoAm 92*
Rylee, R.T. 1930- *St&PR 93*
Ryles, Gerald Fay 1936- *WhoAm 92*
Ryles, John Arnold 1945- *St&PR 93*
Ryles, Tim 1941- *WhoIns 93*
Ryley, Madeleine Lucette 1868-1934 *AmWomPl*
Ryman, Geoff 1951- *ScF&FL 92*
Ryman, John *MiSFD 9*
Ryman, Ras *ScF&FL 92*
Ryman, Robert 1930- *BioIn 17*
Ryman, Robert Tracy 1930- *WhoAm 92*
Ryman, Roger Gerald 1932- *St&PR 93*
Rymar, Julian Wencel 1919- *St&PR 93*
Rymarowicz, Andrzej 1929- *WhoScE 91-4*
Rymarz, Aleksander 1925- *WhoScE 91-4*
Rymer, James Malcolm 1814-1884 *ScF&FL 92*
Rymer, Jeanne Stockdale 1928- *WhoAmW 93, WhoE 93*
Rymer, Pamela Ann 1941- *WhoAm 92, WhoAmW 93*
Rymer, R.A. 1939- *St&PR 93*
Rymer, S. Bradford, Jr. 1915- *WhoAm 92*
Rymer, Thomas 1641-1713 *BioIn 17*
Rymkiewicz, Danuta 1927- *WhoScE 91-4*
Rymo, Lars 1940- *WhoScE 91-4*
Rymuza, Zygmunt 1944- *WhoWor 93*
Ryn, Claes Gosta 1943- *WhoAm 92*
Rynberk, Gilbert J. 1930- *St&PR 93*
Ryncarz, Tadeusz 1927- *WhoScE 91-4*
Rynd, Frank Barlow *Law&B 92*
Ryndak, Richard B. *Law&B 92*
Rynearson, Gary M. 1940- *St&PR 93*
Rynes, Ralph Edmond 1954- *WhoSSW 93*
Ryniker, Bruce Walter Durland 1940- *WhoWor 93*
Rynja, Hendrik Adrian Joan 1926- *WhoWor 93*
Rynja, J.C.F. 1935- *WhoScE 91-3*
Rynkiewicz, John Paul *Law&B 92*
Rynn, John A. *St&PR 93*
Rynn, Nathan 1923- *WhoAm 92*
Rynne, David John 1940- *St&PR 93*
Rynning, Elvind Pryoz 1943- *St&PR 93*
Rynning, Thomas H. 1866-1941 *BioIn 17*
Ryno, H. Bruce 1949- *St&PR 93*
Rynone, Richard T. 1957- *St&PR 93*
Ryon, H. Perry *Law&B 92*
Ryon, John Lesley, Jr. 1926- *St&PR 93*
Ryon, John Walker, III 1940- *WhoE 93*
Ryon, Margaret Stevens 1951- *WhoAmW 93*
Ryon, Mortimer 1929- *St&PR 93*
Ryota, Shinohara 1947- *WhoWor 93*
Rypacek, Frantisek 1947- *WhoScE 91-4*
Rypczyk, Candice Leigh 1949- *WhoAmW 93*
Rypel, T.C. 1949- *ScF&FL 92*
Rypel, Thaddeus Chester 1949- *WhoWrEP 92*
Rypien, Mark *BioIn 17*
Rypien, Mark 1962- *News 92 [port], -92-3 [port]*
Rypien, Mark Robert 1962- *WhoAm 92*
Rypkema, Richard G. 1939- *St&PR 93*
Ryrie, Charles C(aldwell) 1925- *ConAu 39NR*
Ryrie, William S. *WhoUN 92*
Ryrie, William Sinclair 1928- *St&PR 93*
Rys, Jan 1941- *WhoScE 91-4*
Rys, Premysl 1919- *WhoScE 91-4*
Rysanek, Leonie 1926- *Baker 92, IntDcOp, OxDcOp, WhoAm 92*
Rysanek, Lotte 1928- *See* Rysanek, Leonie 1926- *Baker 92*
Ryseff, Carolyn B. *Law&B 92*
Ryser, Hugues Jean-Paul 1926- *WhoAm 92*
Ryskamp, Bruce Edward 1941- *St&PR 93*
Ryskamp, Carroll Joseph 1930- *WhoE 93, WhoWor 93*
Ryskamp, Charles Andrew 1928- *WhoAm 92*
Ryskamp, Kenneth L. *BioIn 17*
Ryskamp, Kenneth Lee 1932- *WhoSSW 93*
Ryske, Paul R. *Law&B 92*
Ryskind, Morrie 1895-1985 *BioIn 17*
Rystrom, David Wayne 1942- *WhoWor 93*
Rystrom, Nancy A. *Law&B 92*
Rystsov, Igor Constantinovich 1949- *WhoWor 93*
Ryszkiewicz, Alicja 1951- *WhoWor 93*
Ryszkowski, Lech 1931- *WhoScE 91-4*
Rytel, Piotr 1884-1970 *Baker 92, PolBiDi*
Ryterband, Roman 1914-1979 *Baker 92*
Ryterski, Jurand Pawel 1924- *WhoScE 91-4*
Ryttenberg, Anita *AmWomPl*
Rytter, Jakob 1932- *WhoWor 93*
Rytter, Lawrence Jensen 1945- *WhoE 93*
Rytter, Wojciech Maciej 1948- *WhoWor 93*
Ryu, Chishu 1906- *IntDcF 2-3 [port]*
Ryu, Eung Kul 1937- *WhoWor 93*
Ryu Don Woo 1934- *WhoAsAP 91*
Ryu Seung Beon 1927- *WhoAsAP 91*
Ryu Seung Kyu 1947- *WhoAsAP 91*
Ryvarden, Leif 1935- *WhoScE 91-4*
Rywalski, Robert F. *Law&B 92*
Rywkin, Michael 1925- *WhoE 93*
Ryzynski, Andrzej Rajmund 1926- *WhoScE 91-4*
Rzad, James Joseph 1948- *St&PR 93*
Rzasa, Marie M. 1954- *St&PR 93*
Rzazewski, Kazimierz Maria 1943- *WhoWor 93*
Rzedowski, Wieslaw 1926- *WhoScE 91-4*
Rzedzicki, Jerzy 1940- *WhoScE 91-4*
Rzeminski, Peter Joseph 1947- *WhoEmL 93*
Rzepinski, John E. 1961- *St&PR 93*
Rzepka, Charles Julian 1949- *WhoE 93*
Rzepka, Joseph L. 1953- *St&PR 93*
Rzepka, Peter 1928- *St&PR 93*
Rzeszewski, Samuel Herman 1911-1992 *BioIn 17*
Rzevski, George *WhoScE 91-1*
Rzewnicki, Janet C. 1953- *WhoAm 92, WhoAmW 93, WhoE 93*
Rzewski, Frederic (Anthony) 1938- *Baker 92*
Rzhevskii, Sergei Vladimirovich 1951- *WhoWor 93*

S

S., I. *ScF&FL 92*
S. L. C. *MajAI*
Sa, Khun *BioIn 17*
Saab, Deanne Keltum 1945- *WhoAmW 93, WhoE 93, WhoWor 93*
Saab, Ghassan M. 1944- *St&PR 93*
Saad, Edson Abdalla 1935- *WhoWor 93*
Saad, Edward Theodore 1923- *WhoE 93*
Saad, Elizabeth L. 1940- *St&PR 93*
Saad, Joseph K. 1948- *St&PR 93*
Saad, Kamal N. 1931- *St&PR 93*
Sa'ad, Nabil Theodore 1936- *WhoWor 93*
Saad, Natan Mayer 1953- *St&PR 93*
Saad, Theodore S. 1920- *St&PR 93*
Saad, Theodore Shafick 1920- *WhoAm 92*
Saada, Adel Selim 1934- *WhoAm 92*
Saad Al-Abdallah Al-Salim Al-Sabah, Sheikh 1924- *WhoWor 93*
Saadawi, Nawal el- *BioIn 17*
Saade, Jose A. 1947- *St&PR 93*
Saadiah ben Joseph, Gaon 892?-942 *BioIn 17*
Saadiah Gaon 892?-942 *BioIn 17*
Saage, Gary 1960- *St&PR 93*
Saal, Carol 1929- *WhoScE 91-4*
Saal, Elias 1952- *St&PR 93*
Saal, Hubert Daniel 1924- *WhoAm 92*
Saalbach, William Frederick 1921- *WhoE 93*
Saalfeld, Clem J. 1942- *St&PR 93*
Saalfeld, Fred Erich 1935- *WhoSSW 93*
Saalfeld, Richard L. 1944- *WhoAm 92*
Saalfield, James A. 1946- *St&PR 93*
Saalman, Howard 1928- *WhoAm 92*
Saar, Alison *BioIn 17*
Saar, Betye 1926- *BioIn 17, WhoAm 92*
Saar, James 1949-1988 *WhoCanL 92*
Saar, Louis Victor (Franz) 1868-1937 *Baker 92*
Saar, Mart 1882-1963 *Baker 92*
Saarela, Aino Annikki 1944- *WhoWor 93*
Saarelma, Hannu J. 1948- *WhoScE 91-4*
Saarenmaa, Hannu T. 1954- *WhoScE 91-4*
Saari, Albin Toivo 1930- *WhoWor 93*
Saari, Donald Gene 1940- *WhoAm 92*
Saari, Esko Olavi 1938- *WhoScE 91-4*
Saari, Jorma T. 1944- *WhoScE 91-4*
Saari, Leonard M. *Law&B 92*
Saari, Leonard Mathew 1938- *St&PR 93, WhoAm 92*
Saariaho, Kaija 1952- *Baker 92*
Saarialho, Antti Vainamo 1933- *WhoScE 91-4*
Saarimaa, Juho *WhoScE 91-4*
Saarinen, Arthur W., Jr. 1927- *St&PR 93*
Saarinen, Arthur William, Jr. 1927- *WhoAm 92*
Saarinen, Aulis Veli Artturi 1939- *WhoScE 91-4*
Saarinen, Kimmo Veli 1950- *WhoWor 93*
Saarinen, Lauri H. 1943- *WhoScE 91-4*
Saario, Vaino Sakari 1942- *WhoWor 93*
Saario, Vesa Lasse 1952- *WhoWor 93*
Saarnak, Ago 1933- *WhoScE 91-2*
Saas, William J. 1940- *St&PR 93*
Saastamoinen, Olli 1945- *WhoScE 91-4*
Saatchi, Charles 1943- *WhoAm 92, WhoWor 93*
Saatchi, Maurice 1946- *WhoAm 92, WhoWor 93*
Saathoff, Patricia Lee 1954- *WhoAmW 93*
Saaty, Thomas Lorie 1926- *WhoAm 92*
Saavedra, Agustin Weise 1943- *WhoWor 93*
Saavedra, Antonio del Castillo y 1603-1667 *BioIn 17*
Saavedra, C. James 1941- *St&PR 93*
Saavedra, Cecile B. 1947- *St&PR 93*
Saavedra, Daniel Ortega *BioIn 17*
Saavedra, Julio 1944- *WhoScE 91-3*
Saavedra, Louis E. 1933- *HispAmA [port], WhoAm 92*
Saavedra y Ceron, Alvaro de d1529 *Expl 93*
Saba, Bettye Miller 1917- *WhoAmW 93*
Saba, Gabriel N. 1930- *WhoWor 93*
Saba, Shoichi 1919- *WhoWor 93*
Sabadie, Patrick Alfonso 1946- *WhoSSW 93*
Sabah, Abdullah al-Salem al- 1895-1965 *BioIn 17*
Sabah, Jaber al-Ahmad al-Jaber al- 1926- *BioIn 17*
Sabah, Salim al-Sabah al-Salim al- 1937- *WhoWor 93*
Sabala, James A. 1954- *St&PR 93*
Sabalat, Jean-Robert *WhoWor 93*
Sabalot, Richard Alexander *Law&B 92*
Saban, Haim *BioIn 17*
Sabanas-Wells, Alvina Olga 1914- *WhoAmW 93*
Sabanci, Sakip *BioIn 17*
Sabaneyev, Leonid 1881-1968 *Baker 92*
Sabanos, Michael P. 1956- *St&PR 93*
Sabaroff, Rose Epstein 1918- *WhoAm 92*
Sabas 439-532 *OxDcByz*
Sabas the Goth 334-372 *OxDcByz*
Sabat, Julia Riera 1913- *St&PR 93*
Sabat, Rosemary Ann 1944- *WhoAmW 93*
Sabata, Victor de *Baker 92, OxDcOp*
Sabatell, Henry Paul 1937- *St&PR 93*
Sabater, Bartolome 1946- *WhoScE 91-3*
Sabat Ercasty, Carlos 1887-1982 *SpAmA*
Sabater-Tobella, Juan 1934- *WhoScE 91-3*
Sabates, Felix Nabor 1930- *WhoAm 92*
Sabath, Jerrold 1947- *St&PR 93*
Sabath, Leon David 1930- *WhoAm 92*
Sabath, Robert Edward 1943- *St&PR 93*
Sabatier, Robert 1923- *ConAu 39NR, WhoWor 93*
Sabatine, Jean Ann 1941- *WhoWrEP 92*
Sabatine, Paul L. *Law&B 92*
Sabatini, Albert, Jr. *Law&B 92*
Sabatini, Carolyn Ann *Law&B 92*
Sabatini, Frank Carmine 1932- *WhoAm 92*
Sabatini, Gabriela *BioIn 17*
Sabatini, Gabriela 1970- *CurBio 92 [port], NewYTBS 92 [port], WhoAm 92, WhoAmW 93, WhoWor 93*
Sabatini, Nelson John 1940- *WhoAm 92*
Sabatini, Rafael 1875-1950 *TwCLC 47 [port]*
Sabatino, Frank George 1948- *WhoAm 92*
Sabato, Ernesto 1911- *SpAmA, WhoWor 93*
Sabato, Ernesto R. 1911- *BioIn 17*
Sabattani, Aurelio Cardinal 1912- *WhoWor 93*
Sabaut, J.J. *WhoScE 91-2*
Sabbag, Allen L. 1944- *St&PR 93*
Sabbag, Randa Chahal *MiSFD 9*
Sabbagh, Sheraine Kay 1959- *WhoAmW 93*
Sabbah, Alfred 1935- *WhoScE 91-2*
Sabbaruddin Chik, Dato' Haji 1941- *WhoAsAP 91*
Sabbath, Wendy June 1956- *WhoAmW 93*
Sabbatini, Galeazzo 1597-1662 *Baker 92*
Sabbatini, Luigi Antonio 1732-1809 *Baker 92*
Sabbatino, Pat Joseph 1942- *St&PR 93*
Sabbeth, Stephen 1947- *St&PR 93*
Sabbeth, Stephen J. 1947- *WhoAm 92*
Sabean, Joel Arthur 1947- *WhoEmL 93*
Sabean, Richard 1956- *BioIn 17*
Sabec, Drago 1930- *WhoScE 91-4*
Sabel, Bernhard August Maria 1957- *WhoWor 93*
Sabel, Bradley Kent 1948- *WhoAm 92*
Sabel, David G. 1952- *St&PR 93*
Sabel, Ivan R. 1945- *St&PR 93*
Sabela, Wladyslaw Jan 1925- *WhoWor 93*
Sabell, Wallace S. 1951- *St&PR 93*
Sabella, John A. 1959- *St&PR 93*
Sabella, William d1992 *NewYTBS 92*
Sabelli, Cesare *WhoScE 91-3*
Saben, Hugh Simon 1939- *St&PR 93*
Saben, Lionel *ScF&FL 92*
Saber, Terry Ann 1953- *St&PR 93*
Saberg, Ove *WhoScE 91-2*
Saberhagen, Bret *BioIn 17*
Saberhagen, Bret 1964- *WhoAm 92*
Saberhagen, Fred 1930- *BioIn 17, ScF&FL 92*
Saberhagen, Joan *ScF&FL 92*
Saber-Lane, Sally B. *Law&B 92*
Sabers, Richard Wayne 1938- *WhoAm 92*
Sabersky, Rolf Heinrich 1920- *WhoAm 92*
Sabet, Habib d1990 *BioIn 17*
Sabey, David R. *Law&B 92*
Sabharwal, Ranjit Singh 1925- *WhoAm 92, WhoWor 93*
Sabiani, Simon *BioIn 17*
Sabicas d1990 *BioIn 17*
Sabido, Almeda Alice 1928- *WhoE 93*
Sabik, Monica Marian 1965- *WhoAmW 93*
Sabin, Albert *BioIn 17*
Sabin, Albert B. 1906- *JeAmHC*
Sabin, Albert Bruce 1906- *WhoAm 92, WhoWor 93*
Sabin, Arnold Leonard 1926- *WhoWor 93*
Sabin, Arthur J. 1930- *WhoWrEP 92*
Sabin, Clifford G. 1908- *St&PR 93*
Sabin, David C. *St&PR 93*
Sabin, Dwight M. 1843-1902 *PolPar*
Sabin, Edwin L. 1870-1952 *ScF&FL 92*
Sabin, Florence Rena 1871-1953 *BioIn 17*
Sabin, Gary B. 1947- *St&PR 93*
Sabin, James Thomas 1943- *St&PR 93, WhoAm 92*
Sabin, John Rogers 1940- *WhoSSW 93*
Sabin, Marc Leslie 1944- *WhoE 93*
Sabin, Wallace Arthur 1860-1937 *Baker 92*
Sabin, William Albert 1931- *WhoAm 92*
Sabina, Frank James 1951- *WhoWrEP 92*
Sabin-Abrahamson, Ellen *Law&B 92*
Sabine, Gordon Arthur 1917- *WhoAm 92*
Sabine, Lillian Keal 1880- *AmWomPl*
Sabine, Ted *ScF&FL 92*
Sabines, Jaime 1926- *SpAmA*
Sabinin, Lev Vasilevich 1932- *WhoWor 93*
Sabino, Francis V. 1935- *St&PR 93*
Sabino, Mary Kay *Law&B 92*
Sabinson, Harvey Barnett 1924- *WhoAm 92*
Sabinson, Lee 1911-1991 *BioIn 17*
Sabinus, Quintus Titurius d54BC *HarEnMi*
Sabiston, David Coston, Jr. 1924- *WhoAm 92, WhoWor 93*
Sable, Barbara Kinsey 1927- *WhoAmW 93, WhoWrEP 92*
Sable, Edith d1992 *NewYTBS 92 [port]*
Sable, Henry Zodoc 1918- *WhoAm 92*
Sable, Jean Baptiste Pointe de 1745?-1818 *BioIn 17*
Sable, John E. 1939- *St&PR 93*
Sable, Robert 1904-1990 *BioIn 17*
Sable, Ronald K. 1941- *St&PR 93*
Sablik, Martin John 1939- *WhoSSW 93*
Sabloff, Jeremy Arac 1944- *WhoAm 92*
Sablone, Frank Anthony 1946- *WhoE 93*
Sablotsky, Noreen 1955- *St&PR 93*
Sablotsky, Steven 1955- *St&PR 93*
Sablowksy, Robert 1938- *St&PR 93*
Sabo, Alexander *BioIn 17*
Sabo, Chris *BioIn 17*
Sabo, Jack Charles 1936- *WhoE 93*
Sabo, Mark Andrew 1950- *St&PR 93*
Sabo, Martin Olav 1938- *CngDr 91, WhoAm 92*
Sabo, Mary Ann 1962- *WhoAmW 93*
Sabo, Richard Steven 1934- *WhoAm 92*
Sabo, Walter Richard, Jr. 1952- *WhoAm 92*
Sabo, William D. *Law&B 92*
Sabol, Albert Thomas 1952- *St&PR 93*
Sabol, Paul William 1926- *St&PR 93*
Sabonis, Arvidas *BioIn 17*
Saborios fl. 7th cent.- *OxDcByz*
Sabosik, Patricia Elizabeth 1949- *WhoAm 92, WhoAmW 93*
Sabot, Emmanuele 1967- *WhoWor 93*
Sabot, Richard Henry 1944- *WhoE 93*
Sabota, Catherine Marie 1949- *WhoAmW 93*
Sabounghi, Joseph M. *Law&B 92*
Sabourin, Dennis M. 1940- *St&PR 93*
Sabourin, Steven Mark 1960- *WhoE 93*
Sabra, Paul F. *Law&B 92*
Sabri, Belgacem 1948- *WhoUN 92*
Sabrin, Joseph 1942- *St&PR 93*
Sabrina *ScF&FL 92*
Sabri-Tabrizi, Gholam-Reza *BioIn 17*
Sabroe, Svend 1942- *WhoScE 91-2*
Sabry, Aly 1920-1991 *BioIn 17*
Sabsevitz, Abraham Meyer 1907- *WhoAm 92*
Sabshin, Melvin 1925- *WhoAm 92*
Sabumeri, Benais 1949- *WhoAsAP 91*
Sabwa, Matanda A. 1939- *WhoUN 92*
Saby, John Sanford 1921- *WhoAm 92*
Saca, David Peter 1933- *WhoUN 92*
Saca, Jose M. 1942- *WhoWor 93*
Sacadura, Jean Francois 1941- *WhoScE 91-2*
Sacagawea 1786-1884 *BioIn 17*
Sacasa, Juan Bautista *DcCPCAm*
Sacasa Guerrero, Ramiro *DcCPCAm*
Sacastru, Martin 1914- *BioIn 17*
Saccente, Vincent Ulysses 1946- *WhoE 93*
Sacchet, Edward M. 1936- *WhoAm 92*
Sacchetti, Liberius 1852-1916 *Baker 92*
Sacchi, Giovenale 1726-1789 *Baker 92*

Sacchi, Luigi Francesco 1940- *WhoScE 91-3*
Sacchini, Antonio 1730-1786 *Baker 92, IntDcOp [port], OxDcOp*
Sacco, Bessie *Law&B 92*
Sacco, Bessie A. *Law&B 92*
Sacco, Donald John 1941- *WhoAm 92*
Sacco, John Michael 1952- *WhoE 93*
Sacco, Nicola 1891-1927 *BioIn 17*
Sacco, P(atrick) Peter 1928- *Baker 92*
Sacco, Rita 1937- *WhoE 93*
Sacco, Russell 1944- *WhoE 93*
Sacco, Thomas Anthony 1953- *WhoSSW 93, WhoWor 93*
Sacco, Thomas N. *Law&B 92*
Saccoccia, Stephen A. *BioIn 17*
Saccoccio, August J. 1937- *St&PR 93*
Saccoccio, Louis A. 1932- *St&PR 93*
Saccone, Girolamo M. *Law&B 92*
Sacconi, Attilio 1945- *WhoScE 91-3*
Sacerdote, George S. 1945- *St&PR 93*
Sacerdote, Manuel Ricardo 1943- *St&PR 93, WhoAm 92*
Sacerdote, Pearl d1990 *BioIn 17*
Sacerdote, Peter M. 1937- *St&PR 93, WhoAm 92*
Sacha, Krzysztof Michal 1951- *WhoWor 93*
Sacha, Robert Frank 1946- *WhoAm 92*
Sachar, Abram Leon 1899- *WhoAm 92*
Sachar, David Bernard 1940- *WhoE 93, WhoWor 93*
Sachar, Howard Morley 1928- *WhoAm 92*
Sachar, Louis 1954- *BioIn 17, ChlLR 28 [port]*
Sacharow, Stanley 1935- *WhoE 93*
Sachdev, Mohindar Singh 1928- *WhoAm 92*
Sachdev, Tirath Ram 1935- *WhoSSW 93*
Sachdev, Ved Parkash 1932- *WhoE 93*
Sacher, Alex 1922- *WhoE 93*
Sacher, Michael C. 1934- *St&PR 93*
Sacher, Paul 1906- *Baker 92*
Sacher, Steven Jay 1942- *WhoAm 92*
Sachere, Andrew B. *WhoE 93*
Sachetto, Jean-Pierre Louis 1942- *WhoWor 93*
Sachkar, Catharine Mollica 1921- *St&PR 93*
Sachlikes, Stephen c. 1331-c. 1391 *OxDcByz*
Sachner, Paul M. d1992 *NewYTBS 92*
Sachnoff, Katherine Mildred 1961- *WhoAmW 93*
Sachs, Alan A. *Law&B 92*
Sachs, Alan A. 1947- *St&PR 93*
Sachs, Alan Arthur 1947- *WhoAm 92*
Sachs, Albie 1933- *BioIn 17*
Sachs, Allan M. 1921-1989 *BioIn 17*
Sachs, Arthur Samuel 1927- *St&PR 93*
Sachs, Blanche 1933- *WhoWrEP 92*
Sachs, Charles E. 1930- *WhoScE 91-2*
Sachs, Curt 1881-1959 *Baker 92*
Sachs, David d1992 *NewYTBS 92*
Sachs, David 1933- *WhoAm 92*
Sachs, David Howard 1942- *WhoE 93*
Sachs, David Stanley 1942- *St&PR 93*
Sachs, Eugene 1933-1990 *BioIn 17*
Sachs, H. *WhoScE 91-3*
Sachs, Hans 1494-1576 *Baker 92, OxDcOp*
Sachs, Horst 1927- *WhoWor 93*
Sachs, Howard Frederic 1925- *WhoAm 92*
Sachs, Ilan 1947- *WhoWor 93*
Sachs, Irwin M. 1932- *St&PR 93*
Sachs, Janet *BioIn 17*
Sachs, Jeffrey D. *BioIn 17*
Sachs, Jeremy *Law&B 92*
Sachs, Jerry *WhoAm 92*
Sachs, Joel 1939- *Baker 92*
Sachs, John Andre 1936- *WhoWor 93*
Sachs, John Peter 1926- *WhoAm 92*
Sachs, Keith Lee 1945- *St&PR 93*
Sachs, Ken 1914- *St&PR 93*
Sachs, Lee Robert 1960- *WhoE 93*
Sachs, Leo 1856-1930 *Baker 92*
Sachs, Lloyd Robert 1950- *WhoAm 92*
Sachs, Lorraine Phyllis 1936- *WhoE 93*
Sachs, Louis S. 1928- *St&PR 93*
Sachs, Marilyn 1927- *BioIn 17*
Sachs, Marilyn (Stickle) 1927- *DcAmChF 1960, DcAmChF 1985, MajAI [port], WhoAm 92*
Sachs, Mary Parmly Koues 1882- *AmWomPl*
Sachs, Mendel 1927- *WhoE 93*
Sachs, Michael L(eo) 1951- *ConAu 37NR*
Sachs, Michael Leo 1951- *WhoE 93*
Sachs, Nancy Lyn 1957- *St&PR 93*
Sachs, Ned R. *Law&B 92*
Sachs, Patricia Susan *WhoAmW 93*
Sachs, Paul J. *BioIn 17*
Sachs, Robert *Law&B 92*
Sachs, Robert A. 1942- *St&PR 93*
Sachs, Robert Green 1916- *WhoAm 92*
Sachs, Robert H. 1939- *St&PR 93*
Sachs, Rose *BioIn 17*
Sachs, Samuel, II 1935- *WhoAm 92*
Sachs, Sidney Stanley 1916- *WhoAm 92*
Sachs, Steven W. 1947- *St&PR 93*
Sachs, Steven Warren 1947- *WhoIns 93*
Sachs, William *MiSFD 9*
Sachse, Armin Michael 1940- *St&PR 93*
Sachse, Guenther 1949- *WhoWor 93*
Sachse, Leopold 1880-1961 *Baker 92*
Sachsman, Theodore *Law&B 92*
Sachsse, Walter 1932- *WhoScE 91-3*
Sachtjen, Wilbur Manley 1927- *WhoE 93*
Sachtleben, Alan T. 1942- *St&PR 93*
Sachtler, Wolfgang Max Hugo 1924- *WhoAm 92*
Sacino, Christine *Law&B 92*
Sacino, D.F. 1930- *WhoIns 93*
Sacino, Dick F. 1930- *St&PR 93*
Saciuk, Olena H. 1940- *ScF&FL 92*
Sack, Alan Lawrence 1926- *St&PR 93*
Sack, Alvin Lee 1949- *WhoE 93*
Sack, Burton Marshall 1937- *St&PR 93, WhoAm 92*
Sack, Edgar Albert 1930- *WhoAm 92*
Sack, Erna 1898-1972 *Baker 92, OxDcOp*
Sack, George Henry, Jr. 1943- *WhoE 93*
Sack, Horst 1935- *WhoScE 91-3*
Sack, J. Erica *Law&B 92*
Sack, Larry E. 1937- *St&PR 93*
Sack, Lucy Ann 1945- *WhoE 93*
Sack, Michael Roland 1957- *WhoE 93*
Sack, R.G. 1933- *St&PR 93*
Sack, R.J. 1903- *St&PR 93*
Sack, Robert David 1939- *WhoAm 92*
Sack, Sylvan Hanan 1932- *WhoAm 92*
Sack, Thomas F. 1927- *St&PR 93*
Sackeim, Harold 1951- *WhoAm 92, WhoE 93*
Sackel, Sol 1924- *St&PR 93*
Sackett, Clara Elizabeth *AmWomPl*
Sackett, Dennis Anthony 1950- *St&PR 93*
Sackett, Ernest L. 1928- *WhoWrEP 92*
Sackett, Gary G. *Law&B 92*
Sackett, Gary G. 1940- *St&PR 93*
Sackett, Hugh F. 1930- *WhoE 93*
Sackett, Jeffrey 1949- *ScF&FL 92*
Sackett, Michael Anthony 1947- *WhoUN 92*
Sackett, Peter John *WhoScE 91-1*
Sackett, Richard 1934- *St&PR 93*
Sackett, Ross DeForest 1930- *WhoAm 92*
Sackett, Susan 1943- *ScF&FL 92, WhoWrEP 92*
Sackett, Susan Deanna 1943- *WhoAmW 93*
Sackett, Walter James, Jr. 1932- *St&PR 93*
Sackett, William Tecumseh, Jr. 1921- *WhoAm 92*
Sackin, Erwin R. 1915- *St&PR 93*
Sackin, Eugene M. 1920- *St&PR 93*
Sackin, Kenneth C. 1952- *St&PR 93*
Sackler, Arthur Brian 1950- *WhoAm 92*
Sackler, Arthur M. 1913-1987 *BioIn 17*
Sackler, Seymour S. *Law&B 92*
Sackley, Martha V. 1959- *WhoAmW 93*
Sacklow, Harriette Lynn 1944- *WhoAmW 93*
Sacklow, Stewart Irwin 1942- *WhoAm 92, WhoE 93*
Sacklowski, Jurgen F.K. 1937- *WhoUN 92*
Sackmann, Erich 1934- *WhoScE 91-3*
Sackmann, Peter C. 1942- *St&PR 93*
Sackner, Marvin A. *BioIn 17*
Sackner, Marvin A. 1932- *St&PR 93*
Sackner, Marvin Arthur 1932- *WhoAm 92*
Sackner, Ruth *BioIn 17*
Sacks, Alan *MiSFD 9*
Sacks, Albert M. 1920-1991 *BioIn 17*
Sacks, Barbara M. *Law&B 92*
Sacks, Bernard L. *Law&B 92*
Sacks, David G. 1924- *St&PR 93, WhoAm 92*
Sacks, David Gregory 1950- *WhoE 93*
Sacks, David Harris 1942- *ConAu 139*
Sacks, Herbert Simeon 1926- *WhoAm 92*
Sacks, Janet *ScF&FL 92*
Sacks, Mark I. 1965- *St&PR 93*
Sacks, Martin 1959- *St&PR 93*
Sacks, Mary Kathleen 1945- *WhoAmW 93, WhoSSW 93*
Sacks, Michael B. *Law&B 92*
Sacks, Oliver W. *BioIn 17*
Sacks, Oliver Wolf 1933- *WhoAm 92, WhoWrEP 92*
Sacks, Roberta B. *Law&B 92*
Sacks, Rodney C. *St&PR 93*
Sacks, Roslyn 1932- *St&PR 93*
Sacks, Stuart 1941- *Baker 92*
Sacks, Susan Riemer 1936- *WhoAmW 93*
Sacks, Temi J. *WhoAm 92*
Sacks, William Bennett 1954- *WhoAm 92*
Sacksteder, Frederick Henry 1924- *WhoAm 92*
Sackton, Frank Joseph 1912- *WhoAm 92*
Sackville, Charles 1638?-1706 *BioIn 17*
Sackville, Edward 1591-1652 *BioIn 17*
Sackville Germain, George 1716-1785 *HarEnMi*
Sackville-West, V. 1892-1962 *BioIn 17*
Sackville-West, V(ictoria Mary) 1892-1962 *ConAu 40NR*
Sackville-West, Victoria 1892-1962 *BioIn 17*
Sacona, Harry M. 1927- *St&PR 93*
Sacranie, Raj *ScF&FL 92*
Sacrati, Francesco 1605?-1650 *Baker 92, OxDcOp*
Sacre, Mary Alice 1933- *WhoAmW 93*
Saculla, William F. 1951- *St&PR 93*
Sada, Concepcion 1899- *DcMexL*
Sadacca, Stephen Sol *Law&B 92*
Sadagic, Amela 1963- *WhoWor 93*
Sadai, Yizhak 1935- *Baker 92*
Sadat, Anwar 1918-1981 *BioIn 17*
Sadat, Muhammad Anwar 1918-1981 *DcTwHis*
Sa'dawi, Nawal *BioIn 17*
Sadd, William Wheeler 1935- *WhoAm 92*
Saddam Hussein *BioIn 17*
Saddlemyer, Ann 1932- *WhoAm 92, WhoAmW 93*
Saddlemyer, (Eleanor) Ann 1932- *WhoWrEP 92*
Saddler, Donald Edward 1920- *WhoAm 92*
Saddler, Patricia Boyd *BioIn 17*
Saddler, Toni Elaine 1962- *WhoAmW 93*
Saddock, Harry G. 1929- *WhoAm 92*
Saddock, Harry George 1929- *St&PR 93*
Sade 1959- *Baker 92, News 93-2 [port], SoulM*
Sade, marquis de 1740-1814 *BioIn 17*
Sade, marquise de d1810 *BioIn 17*
Sade, Donald Stone 1937- *WhoAm 92*
Sadel, Hans L. 1920- *St&PR 93*
Sader, Carol Hope 1935- *WhoAmW 93*
Sader, Pablo E. 1958- *WhoUN 92*
Sader, Ronald Joseph 1934- *St&PR 93*
Sadi, Marcus Vinicius 1956- *WhoWor 93*
Sa'd Ibn Abi Waqqas c. 596-c. 660 *HarEnMi*
Sadick, Neil (S.) 1951- *ConAu 138*
Sadie, Stanley (John) 1930- *Baker 92, WhoWor 93*
Sadik, Marvin Sherwood 1932- *WhoAm 92*
Sadik, Nafis I. 1929- *WhoUN 92*
Sadik-Khan, Orhan Idris 1929- *WhoAm 92*
Sadiq, Nazneen *BioIn 17*
Sadiq Ali, Jam d1992 *BioIn 17, NewYTBS 92*
Sadja, Elliott Daniel 1919- *St&PR 93*
Sadka, David *BioIn 17*
Sadker, Myra Pollack 1943- *WhoWrEP 92*
Sadkin, David Michael *Law&B 92*
Sadlej, Andrzej Jerzy 1941- *WhoWor 93*
Sadler, Barbara Ann 1955- *WhoE 93*
Sadler, Barry *BioIn 17*
Sadler, Barry 1940-1989 *ScF&FL 92*
Sadler, Carol Jeane 1934- *WhoAmW 93*
Sadler, Catherine Edwards 1952- *BioIn 17*
Sadler, Charles Benjamin, Jr. 1939- *WhoSSW 93, WhoWor 93*
Sadler, Charles Randolph 1928- *WhoE 93*
Sadler, Christopher John *WhoScE 91-1*
Sadler, Clifford Lincoln *Law&B 92*
Sadler, David G. 1939- *WhoAm 92*
Sadler, Dolores Ann 1945- *WhoSSW 93*
Sadler, Eric
See Public Enemy *News 92*
Sadler, Frank 1939- *ScF&FL 92*
Sadler, Glenn Edward 1935- *WhoE 93*
Sadler, Graham Hydrick 1931- *WhoAm 92*
Sadler, Joan Lorraine 1964- *WhoAmW 93*
Sadler, Kenneth Marvin 1949- *WhoWor 93*
Sadler, Mark *WhoWrEP 92*
Sadler, Norma Jean 1944- *WhoWrEP 92*
Sadler, Orin Winslow, IV 1941- *WhoSSW 93*
Sadler, Robert Alexander 1938- *St&PR 93*
Sadler, Robert K. *St&PR 93*
Sadler, Robert Livingston 1935- *St&PR 93, WhoAm 92*
Sadler, Stanley Gene 1938- *WhoSSW 93*
Sadler, Theodore R., Jr. 1930- *WhoAm 92*
Sadler, Tommy Joe 1954- *WhoSSW 93*
Sadlier, Darlene J. 1950- *ConAu 139*
Sadlier, James, Mrs. 1820-1903 *BioIn 17*
Sadlier, Mary Anne Madden 1820-1903 *BioIn 17*
Sadlon, Richard Dale 1933- *St&PR 93*
Sadlowski, Dennis Allen *Law&B 92*
Sadlowski, Dennis Allen 1940- *St&PR 93*
Sadlucki-Rakaczewski, Carol Ann 1946- *WhoAmW 93*
Sadock, Benjamin James 1933- *WhoAm 92*
Sadock, Virginia Alcott 1938- *WhoE 93*
Sadock, William M. 1925- *St&PR 93*
Sadoff, Ira 1945- *DcLB 120 [port], WhoWrEP 92*
Sadoff, Micky 1944- *WhoAmW 93*
Sadoff, Robert Leslie 1936- *WhoAm 92, WhoWor 93*
Sadok, Lucjan 1941- *WhoScE 91-4*
Sadosky, Cora Susana 1940- *WhoAmW 93*
Sadoul, Jacques 1934- *ScF&FL 92*
Sadourny, R. *WhoScE 91-2*
Sadourny, Robert 1939- *WhoScE 91-2*
Sadove, Stephen Irving 1951- *WhoE 93*
Sadow, Elliot S. 1940- *St&PR 93*
Sadow, Eric S. *Law&B 92*
Sadow, Harvey S. 1922- *St&PR 93, WhoAm 92, WhoWor 93*
Sadowey, John Peter 1925- *St&PR 93*
Sadowska-Wroblewska, Maria *WhoScE 91-4*
Sadowski, A.J. 1938- *St&PR 93*
Sadowski, Anthony *Law&B 92*
Sadowski, Anthony James 1938- *WhoAm 92*
Sadowski, Chester Philip 1946- *St&PR 93*
Sadowski, David *BioIn 17*
Sadowski, Francis William *Law&B 92*
Sadowski, John Stanley 1948- *WhoEmL 93, WhoWor 93*
Sadowski, Marek Jan 1937- *WhoScE 91-4*
Sadowski, Mark Victor *Law&B 92*
Sadowski, Stanislaw 1928- *WhoScE 91-4*
Sadr, Musa *BioIn 17*
Sadra, I. Wayan 1953- *Baker 92*
Sadruddin, Moe 1943- *WhoWor 93*
Sadruddin Aga Khan 1933- *BioIn 17*
Sadry, Behrooz 1936- *WhoUN 92*
Sadun, Alfredo Arrigo 1950- *WhoWor 93*
Sadwith, Geoffrey Richard 1946- *St&PR 93*
Sadwith, Howard Marvin 1916- *St&PR 93*
Sadwith, James Steven 1952- *MiSFD 9*
Sadybekov, Makhmud Abdysametovich 1963- *WhoWor 93*
Sadyrbaev, Felix 1951- *WhoWor 93*
Sae, Hong Gay 1968- *WhoWor 93*
Saeboe, Hans Viggo 1947- *WhoScE 91-4*
Saedler, Heinz 1941- *WhoScE 91-3*
Saeedpour, Vera Beaudin 1930- *WhoE 93*
Saefke, Steven Charles 1945- *St&PR 93*
Saeger, William T. 1931- *St&PR 93*
Saegusa, Michio 1939- *WhoWor 93*
Saeks, Allen Irving 1932- *WhoAm 92*
Saeks, Richard Ephraim 1941- *WhoAm 92*
Saemala, Francis J. 1944- *WhoAsAP 91*
Saemann, Robert Alan 1964- *St&PR 93*
Saemundsson, Thorsteinn 1935- *WhoScE 91-4*
Saenger, Bruce W. 1943- *WhoIns 93*
Saenger, Eugene Lange 1917- *WhoAm 92*
Saenger, Gustav 1865-1935 *Baker 92*
Saenger, Oscar 1868-1929 *Baker 92*
Saenger, Wolfram Heinrich Edmund 1939- *WhoWor 93*
Saenjaroen, Nikhom *WhoAsAP 91*
Saent-Johns, Geraldine McCormick 1930- *WhoWor 93*
Saenz, Albert William 1923- *HispAmA*
Saenz, Manuela *BioIn 17*
Saenz, Martha 1942- *NotHsAW 93*
Saenz, Pedro 1915- *Baker 92*
Saenz, Rodolfo Forero 1934- *WhoE 93*
Saenz, Roel 1925- *St&PR 93*
Saenz, Rolando Ernesto 1937- *WhoSSW 93*
Saenz Klinsky, Alberto *WhoWor 93*
Saenz Lain, Concepcion *WhoScE 91-3*
Saenz Quesada, Maria *BioIn 17*
Saenz-Ramirez, Alejandro 1949- *WhoWor 93*
Saer, Juan Jose 1937- *SpAmA*
Saether, Ole A. 1936- *WhoScE 91-4*
Saevarsson, Torfi Dan 1960- *WhoWor 93*
Saeverud, Harald (Sigurd Johan) 1897- *Baker 92*
Saeverud, Ketil *Baker 92*
Saewulf *OxDcByz*
Saey, Jean-Claude 1943- *WhoScE 91-2*
Saez, Alberto Mariano 1922- *WhoWor 93*
Saez, Jose M. 1934- *WhoScE 91-2*
Safa, Sanchez *WhoScE 91-3*
Safa, Ali Mohammad 1944- *WhoSSW 93*
Safadi, Ayman A. 1962- *WhoWor 93*
Safar, Mahmoud Mohammad 1940- *WhoWor 93*
Safar, Michel 1937- *WhoScE 91-2*
Safarik, Allan 1948- *WhoCanL 92*
Safars, Berta 1928- *WhoAm 92, WhoAmW 93*
Safdie, Moshe 1938- *WhoAm 92, WhoWor 93*
Safe, Kenneth Shaw, Jr. 1929- *WhoE 93, WhoWor 93*
Safenowitz, Howard B. *Law&B 92*
Safenowitz, Milton 1927- *St&PR 93*
Safer, Edward George 1927- *St&PR 93*
Safer, John 1922- *WhoAm 92*
Safer, Morley *BioIn 17*
Safer, Morley 1931- *JrnUS, WhoAm 92, WhoE 93*
Safer, Phyllis *Law&B 92*

Saff, Edward Barry 1944- *WhoAm 92, WhoSSW 93*
Saffa, Sheila Marie Madden 1958- *WhoAmW 93*
Saffan, Benjamin David 1928- *WhoSSW 93*
Saffar, Jean-Louis 1948- *WhoScE 91-2*
Saffar, Muhammad 19th cent.- *BioIn 17*
Saffeir, Harvey J. 1929- *St&PR 93, WhoIns 93*
Saffeir, Harvey Joseph 1929- *WhoAm 92*
Saffell, Karl Louis 1955- *WhoSSW 93*
Saffels, Dale Emerson 1921- *WhoAm 92*
Saffer, Alfred 1918- *WhoAm 92*
Safferman, Robert Samuel 1932- *WhoAm 92*
Saffiotti, Umberto 1928- *WhoAm 92*
Saffir, Cynthia *Law&B 92*
Saffir, Herbert Seymour 1917- *WhoAm 92, WhoWor 93*
Saffle, Michael 1946- *ConAu 139*
Saffle, Sherry Wood 1959- *WhoAmW 93*
Saffman, Philip G. 1931- *WhoAm 92*
Saffo *OxDcOp*
Saffold, Shirley Strickland *AfrAmBi [port]*
Safford, Bob 1958- *St&PR 93*
Safford, Dan Scott 1950- *WhoWrEP 92*
Safford, John Lugton 1947- *WhoSSW 93*
Safford, Robert O. 1934- *WhoIns 93*
Saffran, Bernard 1936- *WhoAm 92*
Saffran, Kalman 1947- *WhoAm 92*
Saffran, Murray 1924- *WhoAm 92*
Saffron, Morris Harold 1905- *WhoAm 92, WhoE 93*
Saffron, Robert 1918-1985 *ScF&FL 92*
Safft, Stuart J. 1941- *St&PR 93, WhoE 93*
Safi, George Fredric *Law&B 92*
Safian, Leroy Scheller 1916- *WhoE 93*
Safian, Shelley Carole 1954- *WhoAmW 93*
Safiol, George E. 1932- *St&PR 93, WhoAm 92, WhoE 93*
Safir, Andrew Jeffrey 1948- *WhoAm 92*
Safir, Leonard d1992 *NewYTBS 92 [port]*
Safire, William *BioIn 17*
Safire, William 1929- *JrnUS, WhoAm 92, WhoE 93, WhoWrEP 92*
Safley, James Robert 1943- *WhoAm 92*
Safonov, Michael George 1948- *WhoAm 92*
Safonov, Vasili (Ilich) 1852-1918 *Baker 92*
Safora, Isabel R. *Law&B 92*
Safra, Edmund J. *WhoAm 92*
Safran, Claire *WhoAm 92*
Safran, Claire 1958- *WhoWrEP 92*
Safran, Edward Myron 1937- *WhoAm 92*
Safran, Gordon Howard 1935- *St&PR 93*
Safran, Henri 1932- *MiSFD 9*
Safran, Laura Marilyn *Law&B 92*
Safran, Verna *WhoWrEP 92*
Safranek, Thomas William 1951- *WhoSSW 93*
Safranek-Kavic, Lujo 1882-1940 *Baker 92*
Safransky, Sy 1945- *WhoSSW 93, WhoWrEP 92*
Safrata, R.S. 1925- *WhoScE 91-4*
Safron, Monte M. 1929- *St&PR 93*
Safron, Terry *Law&B 92*
Safronchuk, Vasiliy Stepanovich 1925- *WhoUN 92*
Safronov, Serguei Vladimirovich 1937- *WhoUN 92*
Saft, Virginia Colebeck 1928- *WhoAmW 93*
Sagaev, Dimiter 1915- *Baker 92*
Sagal, Boris 1923-1981 *MiSFD 9N*
Sagal, Katey *BioIn 17*
Sagalkin, Sanford 1942- *WhoAm 92*
Sagalyn, Irwin 1916- *St&PR 93*
Sagalyn, James M. 1945- *St&PR 93*
Sagami, Kim *WhoAm 92*
Sagan, Carl 1934- *BioIn 17, ScF&FL 92*
Sagan, Carl Edward 1934- *WhoAm 92, WhoE 93, WhoWor 93, WhoWrEP 92*
Sagan, Francoise *ConAu 39NR*
Sagan, Francoise 1935- *BioIn 17, WhoWor 93*
Sagan, Gene Hill d1991 *BioIn 17*
Sagan, Hans 1928- *WhoAm 92, WhoSSW 93*
Sagan, John 1921- *WhoAm 92*
Sagan, Kathyrne V. 1952- *WhoWrEP 92*
Sagan, Miriam Anna 1954- *WhoWrEP 92*
Sagan, Stanley Daniel 1916- *WhoSSW 93*
Sagansky, Jeff *BioIn 17, WhoAm 92*
Sagansky, Jeff 1952- *News 93-2 [port]*
Sagar, R. Brian 1927-1990 *BioIn 17*
Sagara, Junji 1943- *WhoWor 93*
Sagara, Koichi 1929- *WhoWor 93*
Sagara, Michele M. *ScF&FL 92*
Sagara, Noriaki 1943- *WhoUN 92*
Sagarin, Edward 1913-1986 *ScF&FL 92*
Sagarminaga, Antonio 1928- *WhoUN 92*
Sagawa, Yoneo 1926- *WhoAm 92*
Sagdeev, R.Z. *BioIn 17*
Sagdeyev, Roald Zinnurovich *BioIn 17*
Sage, Alison *ScF&FL 92*
Sage, Andrew G.C., II 1926- *St&PR 93*
Sage, Andrew Gregg Curtin, II 1926- *WhoAm 92*
Sage, Andrew Patrick, Jr. 1933- *WhoAm 92, WhoSSW 93, WhoWor 93*
Sage, Darold R. *St&PR 93*
Sage, Jay Peter 1943- *WhoE 93*
Sage, John A. 1935- *St&PR 93*
Sage, Juniper *ConAu 136, MajAI*
Sage, Morley W. 1930- *WhoScE 91-1*
Sage, Myron Alvin 1920- *St&PR 93*
Sage, Paula Winsor 1942- *WhoAmW 93*
Sage, Peter J. 1941- *St&PR 93*
Sage, Victor 1942- *ScF&FL 92*
Sagebrecht, Marianne 1945- *ConTFT 10*
Sagen, Johan, Jr. 1918- *WhoWor 93*
Sagendorf, Bud 1915- *WhoAm 92*
Sager, Al Carl *WhoWor 93*
Sager, Bert *St&PR 93*
Sager, Carole Bayer *BioIn 17*
Sager, Carole Bayer 1947- *WhoAm 92*
Sager, Catherine 1835-1910 *BioIn 17*
Sager, Clifford Julius *WhoAm 92*
Sager, David Rolland 1951- *WhoWor 93*
Sager, Donald Allen 1930- *WhoIns 93*
Sager, Donald Jack 1938- *WhoAm 92*
Sager, Donna Layne 1956- *WhoWrEP 92*
Sager, Gilbert Landis 1947- *WhoE 93*
Sager, Harry Charles 1930- *St&PR 93*
Sager, J.C. *WhoScE 91-1*
Sager, Jonathan Ward *Law&B 92*
Sager, Patricia Wells 1930- *St&PR 93*
Sager, Richard *St&PR 93*
Sager, Roderick Cooper 1923- *WhoAm 92*
Sager, Ruth 1918- *WhoAm 92, WhoAmW 93*
Sager, Thomas L. *Law&B 92*
Sager, William F. 1918- *WhoAm 92*
Sagerholm, James Alvin 1927- *WhoAm 92*
Saget, Bob *BioIn 17, WhoAm 92*
Sagett, Jan Jeffrey 1943- *WhoAm 92*
Saggau, David Jon *Law&B 92*
Saggers, Geoffrey *WhoIns 93*
Saggese, Aldo E. 1928- *St&PR 93*
Saggese, Enrico 1949- *WhoScE 91-3*
Saggus, James Sutton 1925- *WhoSSW 93*
Saghir, Adel Jamil 1930- *WhoE 93*
Sagi, Ferenc 1927- *WhoScE 91-4*
Saginaw, Robert Benjamin *Law&B 92*
Sagir, Abuzer 1949- *WhoScE 91-4*
Sagittarius *Baker 92*
Sagiuchi, Toshiyuki 1950- *WhoAm 92*
Sagl, Nancy Leigh Ann 1958- *WhoE 93*
Sagmeister, Heinz 1940- *WhoScE 91-4*
Sagness, Richard Lee 1937- *WhoAm 92*
Sagnier, Thierry J. 1946- *ScF&FL 92*
Sago, Anthony E.W. 1946- *WhoE 93*
Sago, Paul Edward 1931- *WhoAm 92*
Sagoff, Mark 1941- *WhoE 93*
Sagolla, Lisa Jo 1959- *WhoAmW 93*
Sagraves, Allan Todd 1930- *WhoE 93*
Sagraves, Rosalie 1945- *WhoAmW 93, WhoSSW 93*
Saguchi, Shichiro 1917- *WhoWor 93*
Saguisag, Rene Augusto Verceluz 1939- *WhoAsAP 91*
Sagul, Bernadette Anne 1932- *WhoSSW 93*
Sagun, Stanley Joseph *Law&B 92*
Sah, Chih-Tang 1932- *WhoAm 92*
Saha, Anita Rani 1964- *WhoAmW 93*
Saha, Arthur W. 1923- *ScF&FL 92*
Saha, Asis Kumar 1941- *WhoWor 93*
Saha, Debabrata 1955- *WhoE 93*
Saha, Murari Mohan 1947- *WhoWor 93*
Saha, Pabitra Kumar 1949- *WhoSSW 93*
Sahadtjian, Steven 1964- *St&PR 93*
Sahagun, Bernardo de 1500?-1590 *DcMexL*
Sahagun, Carlos 1938- *BioIn 17*
Sahai, Hardeo 1942- *WhoSSW 93*
Sahakian, Henry D. 1937- *St&PR 93*
Sahalos, John 1943- *WhoScE 91-3*
Sahanek, Tatana 1922- *WhoAm 92, WhoE 93*
Sahatdjian, Haig Aram 1922- *St&PR 93*
Sahatdjian, Victor S. 1949- *St&PR 93*
Sahay, Dayanand 1932- *WhoAsAP 91*
Sahgal, Nayantara 1927- *IntLitE*
Sahgal, Pavan 1949- *St&PR 93, WhoWrEP 92*
Sahin, Irfan 1932- *WhoScE 91-4*
Sahin, Sumer 1942- *WhoScE 91-4*
Sahini, Victor Emanuel 1927- *WhoScE 91-4*
Sahl, Morton Lyon 1927- *WhoAm 92*
Sahl, Richard Joachim 1919- *WhoWor 93*
Sahl, William Jay, Jr. 1940- *WhoSSW 93*
Sahlberg, John T. *Law&B 92*
Sahlberg, Robert Donald 1926- *St&PR 93, WhoAm 92*
Sahlem, James Robert 1948- *WhoE 93*
Sahli, Asem Al 1956- *WhoSSW 93*
Sahli, Edward Augustus, Jr. 1936- *St&PR 93*
Sahlie, Richard Scott 1929- *St&PR 93*
Sahlie, William Finley 1933- *WhoSSW 93*
Sahlin, Leland John 1925- *St&PR 93*
Sahlin, Michelle 1959- *WhoAmW 93*
Sahlin, Sven 1926- *WhoScE 91-4, WhoWor 93*
Sahlman, Charles Wesley 1926- *St&PR 93*
Sahloul, Ali Ahmed *WhoWor 93*
Sahlstrom, Elmer Bernard 1918- *WhoAm 92*
Sahm, Doug
 See Texas Tornados, The *ConMus 8*
Sahm, Peter R. 1934- *WhoScE 91-3*
Sahn, John G. *Law&B 92*
Sahn, John G. 1946- *St&PR 93*
Sahnazarov, Karne 1952- *DrEEuF*
Sahoo, Prasanna 1951- *WhoSSW 93*
Sahota, Gurcharn Singh 1940- *WhoE 93*
Sahr, Morris G. 1928- *WhoSSW 93*
Sahu, Baikuntha Nath 1950- *WhoAsAP 91*
Sahu, Rajni Ranjan 1934- *WhoAsAP 91*
Sahu, Santosh Kumar 1935- *WhoAsAP 91*
Sahuc, Richard C., Jr. 1949- *WhoSSW 93*
Sahu Khan, Muhammad Shamsud-Dean 1940- *WhoWor 93*
Sahula-Dycke, Ignatz 1900-1982 *ScF&FL 92*
Sahulka, Stuart *BioIn 17, NewYTBS 92 [port]*
Saia, Albert Steve 1933- *St&PR 93, WhoAm 92*
Saia, Vincent Joseph 1958- *St&PR 93*
Saibini, John 1921- *St&PR 93*
Saibou, Ali *WhoWor 93*
Saibou, Ali 1940- *WhoAfr*
Said, Abdul Aziz 1930- *WhoAm 92*
Said, Edward W. 1935- *WhoAm 92, WhoWrEP 92*
Said, Fahad bin Mahmoud al- 1944- *WhoWor 93*
Said, Fahr bin Taimur al- 1926- *WhoWor 93*
Said, Mark C. *Law&B 92*
Said, Mohsin M. 1954- *WhoEmL 93*
Sa'id, Nuri al- 1888-1958 *BioIn 17*
Said bin Taimur, Sultan of Muscat and Oman 1910-1972 *BioIn 17*
Saidenberg, Rebecca Marshall 1958- *WhoE 93*
Sa'id Ibn Batriq *OxDcByz*
Saidman, Gary K. 1952- *WhoSSW 93*
Saido, Kiichiro 1942- *WhoWor 93*
Saied, J. Robert *St&PR 93*
Saifer, Mark Gary 1938- *St&PR 93*
Saifer, Mark Gary Pierce 1938- *WhoAm 92*
Saigal, Shiv Nath 1934- *WhoUN 92*
Saigo, Megumi 1936- *WhoWor 93*
Saigo, Takamori 1827-1877 *HarEnMi*
Saigo, Tsugumichi 1843-1902 *HarEnMi*
Saijo, Takao 1942- *WhoWor 93*
Saiki, Jessica K(awasuna) 1928- *ConAu 138*
Saiki, Patricia *BioIn 17*
Saiki, Patricia 1930- *WhoAm 92, WhoAmW 93*
Saikia, Nagen 1941- *WhoAsAP 91*
Saikkola, Lauri 1906- *Baker 92*
Saikkonen, Pekka Juhani 1946- *WhoWor 93*
Saikowski, Ronald Alexander 1950- *WhoSSW 93*
Saikusa, Satoshi 1959- *BioIn 17*
Sailas, Vaino Henrik 1928- *WhoScE 91-4*
Saile, John C., Jr. *Law&B 92*
Sailele, Tuilaepa 1945- *WhoAsAP 91*
Sailer, Anton 1935?- *BioIn 17*
Sailer, Christopher Aldrich 1946- *St&PR 93*
Sailer, Henry Powers 1929- *WhoAm 92*
Sailer, Hermann F. 1943- *WhoScE 91-4*
Sailer, Jerrold D. 1956- *St&PR 93*
Sailer, Lynne Barger 1956- *WhoAmW 93*
Sailer, Nicholaos 1951- *WhoWor 93*
Sailer, Randolph C., II *Law&B 92*
Sailer, Rosemarie *Law&B 92*
Sailer, Toni 1935?- *BioIn 17*
Sailer, William Franklin 1930- *WhoE 93*
Sailing, Roberta Lynn *Law&B 92*
Saillon, Alfred 1944- *WhoWor 93*
Sailly, Francis Antoine 1942- *WhoWor 93*
Sailor, Charles 1947- *ScF&FL 92*
Sailor, Dennis I. 1939- *St&PR 93*
Sailors, Susanne Creech 1913- *WhoAmW 93*
Saima, Atsushi 1923- *WhoWor 93*
Saiman, Martin S. 1932- *WhoAm 92*
Saimes, George Thomas 1941- *BiDAMSp 1989*
Saimoto, Hiroyuki 1956- *WhoWor 93*
Sain, John Franklin 1917- *BiDAMSp 1989*
Sain, Michael Kent 1937- *WhoAm 92*
Sainani, Ram Hariram 1925- *St&PR 93, WhoE 93*
Sainburg, Richard B. 1924- *St&PR 93*
Saindon, Alfred Louis 1923- *St&PR 93*
Saine, Carroll Lee 1934- *St&PR 93, WhoAm 92*
Sainer, Arthur 1924- *WhoAm 92, WhoWrEP 92*
Saini, Gulshan Rai 1924- *WhoE 93*
Saini, Vasant Durgadas 1952- *WhoE 93, WhoWor 93*
Sainju, Indra Raj 1960- *WhoWor 93*
Saino, Joseph Neuhoff 1933- *St&PR 93*
Saint, Crosbie Edgerton 1936- *WhoAm 92*
Saint, Eva Marie 1924- *IntDcF 2-3 [port], WhoAm 92*
Saint, H.F. 1941- *ScF&FL 92*
Saint, Lerinda Ruth *Law&B 92*
Saint Adalbert 956-997 *PolBiDi*
St. Alcorn, Lloyd *ScF&FL 92*
St. Amand, Normand Gerard 1939- *St&PR 93*
St. Amand, Pierre 1920- *WhoAm 92*
St. Andre, Ken 1947- *ScF&FL 92*
Saint Andrew Bobola 1591-1657 *PolBiDi*
St. Andrews, Barbara *WhoAmW 93*
St. Angelo, Allen Joseph 1932- *WhoSSW 93*
St. Antoine, Theodore Joseph 1929- *WhoAm 92*
St. Armand, Barton Levi 1943- *ScF&FL 92*
Saint-Arnaud, Louis *Law&B 92*
Saint-Arnaud, Louis 1946- *St&PR 93*
Saint-Aubin, Alexandrine 1793- *OxDcOp*
Saint-Aubin, Gabriel Jacques de 1724-1780 *BioIn 17*
St. Aubin, Helen Callaghan Candaele d1992 *NewYTBS 92 [port]*
Saint-Aubin, Horace de *ScF&FL 92*
Saint-Aubin, Jeanne-Charlotte Schroeder 1764-1850 *OxDcOp*
St. Aubin de Teran, Lisa 1953- *BioIn 17*
Saint-Aubin Duret, Cecile 1785-1862 *OxDcOp*
St. Bernard, Ian *DcCPCAm*
Saintbury, Elizabeth 1913- *ScF&FL 92*
Saint Casimir 1458-1484 *PolBiDi [port]*
St. Charles, Annell 1951- *WhoSSW 93*
St. Clair, Arthur 1736-1818 *CmdGen 1991 [port], HarEnMi*
St. Clair, Basil S. *Law&B 92*
St. Clair, Bob 1931- *BioIn 17*
St. Clair, Byron Wagner 1924- *St&PR 93*
St. Clair, Carl *WhoAm 92*
St. Clair, David 1932- *ScF&FL 92*
St. Clair, Elizabeth 1938- *ScF&FL 92*
St. Clair, Hal Kay 1925- *WhoAm 92*
St. Clair, Henry *ScF&FL 92*
St. Clair, James 1920- *OxCSupC*
St. Clair, James Draper 1920- *WhoAm 92*
St. Clair, Jane Elizabeth 1944- *WhoAmW 93*
St. Clair, Jesse Walton, Jr. 1930- *St&PR 93, WhoAm 92*
St. Clair, John M. *St&PR 93*
St. Clair, John Norman 1905- *St&PR 93*
St. Clair, Margaret 1911- *BioIn 17, ScF&FL 92*
St. Clair, Michael 1912- *WhoAm 92, WhoE 93*
St. Clair, Philip 1944- *WhoWrEP 92*
St. Clair, Rita Erika *WhoAm 92*
St. Clair, Thomas McBryar 1935- *WhoAm 92*
St. Clair, William *ScF&FL 92*
St. Clair, Winifred *AmWomPl*
St. Claire, Adelaide *AmWomPl*
St. Claire, Erin *ConAu 139*
St. Claire, Frank Arthur 1949- *WhoAm 92, WhoSSW 93, WhoWor 93*
St. Clement, Courtney Tolson 1951- *WhoE 93, WhoEmL 93*
St. Cloud, Alden *WhoWrEP 92*
St. Cyr, Henry P. 1944- *St&PR 93*
St. Cyr, John Albert, II 1949- *WhoWor 93*
Saint-Cyr, Laurent Gouvion, Marquis of 1764-1830 *HarEnMi*
St. Cyr, Napoleon Joseph 1924- *WhoWrEP 92*
St. Denis, Ruth 1880-1968 *BioIn 17*
St. Dennis, Jerry A. 1942- *WhoAm 92*
Sainten, Kim V. *Law&B 92*
Saint-Evremond, Charles de Saint-Denis 1614?-1703 *OxDcOp*
Saint-Exupery, Antoine de 1900-1944 *BioIn 17*
Saint-Exupery, Antoine (Jean Baptiste Marie Roger) de 1900-1944 *MajAI [port]*
St. Florian, Friedrich Gartler 1932- *WhoAm 92*
Saint-Foix, Georges, Comte de 1874-1954 *Baker 92*
Saint-Gaudens, Augustus 1848-1907 *BioIn 17, GayN*
St. George, Ardelle Catherine *Law&B 92*
St. George, David *ScF&FL 92*
St. George, E.A. 1937- *ScF&FL 92*
Saint-George, George 1841-1924 *Baker 92*
Saint-George, Henry 1866-1917 *Baker 92*
St. George, Judith 1931- *ScF&FL 92*
St. George, Judith Alexander 1931- *WhoAm 92*
St. George, Katharine 1896-1983 *BioIn 17*
St. George, Margaret *ConAu 40NR, WhoWrEP 92*

St. George, Nicholas James 1939- *St&PR 93, WhoAm 92, WhoSSW 93*
St. George, William Ross 1924- *WhoAm 92*
Saint-Georges, Joseph Boulogne, Chevalier de c. 1739-1799 *Baker 92*
St. Gerard, Michael *BioIn 17*
St. Germain, Fernand Joseph *WhoAm 92*
St. Germain, Jean Mary *WhoAmW 93, WhoE 93*
St. Goar, Edward 1955- *St&PR 93, WhoAm 92*
St. Goar, Herbert 1916- *St&PR 93, WhoAm 92*
Saint Hedwig 1174-1243 *PolBiDi*
St. Hilaire, Donald 1945- *St&PR 93*
St. Hilaire, Sheila Barbara 1951- *St&PR 93*
St. Hubbins, David c. 1948- *See* Spinal Tap *ConMus 8*
Saint-Huberty 1756-1812 *OxDcOp*
Saint-Huberty, Mme. de 1756-1812 *Baker 92*
Saint Hyacinth 1185-1257 *PolBiDi*
Saint-Jacques, Alfred Joseph 1956- *WhoWrEP 92*
St. Jacques, Alice *WhoCanL 92*
Saint-Jacques, Bernard 1928- *ConAu 37NR, WhoAm 92, WhoWrEP 92*
St. Jacques, Raymond 1930-1990 *BioIn 17*
St. Jacques, Robert H. 1924- *St&PR 93, WhoE 93*
St. James, Blakely *ScF&FL 92*
St. James, Brian R. *Law&B 92*
St. James, Dana Juan *Law&B 92*
Saint-James, Daniel 1927- *WhoScE 91-2*
St. James, Lionel David 1926- *WhoWor 93*
St. James, Lyn 1947- *News 93-2 [port], WhoAmW 93*
St. James, Ronald Leon 1947- *WhoE 93*
Saint James, Susan 1946- *HolBB [port], WhoAm 92*
St. Jean, Catherine Avery 1950- *WhoAm 92, WhoAmW 93*
St. Jean, Denis L. 1933- *St&PR 93*
St. Jean, Gary *WhoAm 92*
St. Jean, Guy 1941- *WhoAm 92*
St. Jean, Joseph, Jr. 1923- *WhoAm 92*
St. John, Adrian, II 1921- *WhoAm 92, WhoWor 93*
St. John, Al 1893-1963 *QDrFCA 92 [port]*
St. John, Anthony Paul 1937- *WhoAm 92*
St. John, B.D. 1931- *St&PR 93*
St. John, Bernard *DcCPCAm*
St. John, Bill Dean 1931- *WhoAm 92, WhoSSW 93*
St. John, Billy Eugene 1932- *WhoAm 92*
St. John, Charles Virgil 1922- *WhoWor 93*
St. John, Christopher *MiSFD 9*
St. John, Dale W. 1924- *St&PR 93*
St. John, Dan *BioIn 17*
St. John, Henry 1678-1751 *BioIn 17*
St. John, Howard C. 1923- *St&PR 93*
St. John, Howard Chambers *WhoAm 92*
St. John, Jill 1940- *BioIn 17, WhoAm 92*
St. John, John 1921- *WhoAm 92*
St. John, John Pierce 1833-1916 *BioIn 17*
St. John, Judy Kay 1949- *WhoAmW 93*
St. John, Kenneth Raymond 1953- *WhoSSW 93*
Saint-John, Kristine *ScF&FL 92*
St. John, Nancy Marie 1953- *WhoAmW 93*
St. John, Nicole *ScF&FL 92*
St. John, Richard Joseph 1936- *St&PR 93*
St. John, Robert 1941- *St&PR 93*
St. John, Sarah 1902-1991 *BioIn 17*
St. John, Spenser Buckingham 1825-1910 *IntDcAn*
St. John, William B. *BioIn 17*
St. John, Wylly Folk 1908- *DcAmChF 1960*
St. John De La Salle Eno, Brian Peter George 1948- *WhoAm 92*
St. John-Foster, Keith Edward *BioIn 17*
Saint John of Kanti c. 1390-1473 *PolBiDi*
St. Johns, Adela Rogers 1894-1988 *JrnUS*
Saint Josaphat 1580-1623 *PolBiDi*
St. Julian, Horace *Law&B 92*
Saint-Just 1767-1794 *BioIn 17*
St. Just, Maria *BioIn 17*
St. Landau, Norman 1925- *WhoE 93, WhoWor 93*
St. Laurent, Henry Alexander 1925- *St&PR 93*
St. Laurent, Louis Stephen 1882-1973 *DcTwHis*
St. Laurent, Yves *BioIn 17*
Saint Laurent, Yves 1936- *WhoWor 93*
St. Leger, Barry 1737-1789 *HarEnMi*
St. Leon, Ernest d1891 *BioIn 17*
Saint-Louis, Acedius 1938- *WhoWor 93*
St. Louis, M.R. *Law&B 92*
Saint-Lubin, Leon de 1805-1850 *Baker 92*
St. Luz, Berthe 1871-1968 *ScF&FL 92*
Saint Maksymilian Kolbe 1894-1941 *PolBiDi*
Saint-Marc, Andre J. 1944- *WhoScE 91-2*
Saint Marc, Michele 1935- *WhoWor 93*
Saint Marc, Philippe 1927- *WhoWor 93*
Saint-Marcoux, Micheline Coulombe 1938-1985 *Baker 92*
St. Marie, Satenig 1927- *WhoAm 92*
St. Mark, Carole C. *BioIn 17*
St. Mark, Carole F. *St&PR 93, WhoAmW 93*
St. Martin, John Roger 1956- *St&PR 93*
St. Mary, Edward Sylvester 1941- *WhoAm 92*
St. Maur, Edward 1924-1991 *BioIn 17*
St. Meyer, Ned *MajAI*
Saint-Mleux, Andre Francois 1956- *WhoWor 93*
St. Omer, Garth 1931- *DcLB 117 [port]*
Sainton, Prosper (Philippe Catherine) 1813-1890 *Baker 92*
Sainton-Dolby, Charlotte 1821-1885 *See* Sainton, Prosper (Philippe Catherine) 1813-1890 *Baker 92*
St. Onge, Hubert Jules 1946- *WhoWor 93*
St. Onge, John J. *St&PR 93*
St. Onge, Keith R. 1920- *ConAu 139*
St. Onge, Mary Frances 1939- *WhoE 93*
Saint-Paul, Raymond Henri 1927- *WhoScE 91-2*
St. Pe, Gerald J. *WhoAm 92*
St. Pierre, Barry Joseph 1946- *St&PR 93*
St. Pierre, Beverly Jane 1949- *WhoE 93*
St. Pierre, Dennis *ScF&FL 92*
St. Pierre, George Roland, Jr. 1930- *WhoAm 92*
Saint-Pierre, Guy 1934- *WhoE 93*
St.-Pierre, Jacques 1920- *WhoAm 92*
Saint-Pierre, Michael Robert 1947- *WhoEmL 93*
Saint Pierre, Michel de 1916-1987 *BioIn 17*
St. Pierre, Paul 1923- *WhoCanL 92*
St. Pierre, Richard William 1940- *St&PR 93*
St. Pierre, Ronald Leo 1955- *WhoE 93*
St. Pierre, Ronald Leslie 1938- *WhoAm 92*
Saint-Requier, Leon 1872-1964 *Baker 92*
St. Romain Coussens, Janice Marie 1955- *WhoSSW 93*
Saint-Saens, Camille 1835-1921 *IntDcOp, OxDcOp*
Saint-Saens, (Charles-) Camille 1835-1921 *Baker 92*
St. Sauveur, John Harold 1932- *St&PR 93*
St. Sauveur, Kimberly *Law&B 92*
St. Schell, Josef *WhoScE 91-3*
Saint-Simon, duc de 1675-1755 *BioIn 17*
Saint Stanislaw 1030-1079 *PolBiDi*
Saint Stanislaw Kostka 1550-1568 *PolBiDi*
St. Thomas, James W. 1927- *St&PR 93*
St. Thomas, William H. 1901- *St&PR 93*
Sainty, Guy Stair 1950- *WhoAm 92, WhoE 93*
Sainz, Gustavo 1940- *DcMexL, SpAmA*
Sainz De Cueto Torres, Francisco Javier 1950- *WhoScE 91-3*
Sais, Marin 1887- *SweetSg A [port]*
Saisselin, Remy Gilbert 1925- *WhoAm 92*
Saisto, Jarkko 1932- *WhoScE 91-4*
Sait, Ebrahim Sulaiman 1922- *WhoAsAP 91*
Saita, Keiji 1938- *WhoUN 92*
Saito, Dennis Katsuji *Law&B 92*
Saito, Eizaburo 1913- *WhoAsAP 91*
Saito, Fumio 1928- *WhoAsAP 91*
Saito, Hidehiko 1939- *WhoWor 93*
Saito, Hideo 1902-1974 *Baker 92*
Saito, Isao 1941- *WhoWor 93*
Saito, Joichi 1935- *St&PR 93*
Saito, Juro 1940- *WhoAsAP 91*
Saito, Kazuo 1925- *WhoAsAP 91*
Saito, Kiyomi 1950- *WhoAmW 93*
Saito, Kunikichi 1909- *WhoAsAP 91*
Saito, Makoto 1930- *WhoAsAP 91*
Saito, Milton K. 1942- *St&PR 93*
Saito, Minoru 1932- *St&PR 93*
Saito, Mitsuru 1951- *WhoWor 93*
Saito, Norio 1935- *WhoWor 93*
Saito, Osamu 1950- *WhoWor 93*
Saito, R. 1950- *St&PR 93*
Saito, Shizuki 1942- *WhoWor 93*
Saito, Shuzo 1924- *WhoWor 93*
Saito, Taiichi 1931- *WhoWor 93*
Saito, Toshitsugu 1944- *WhoAsAP 91*
Saito, Yoshitaka 1926- *WhoWor 93*
Saito, Yoshitsugu 1890-1944 *HarEnMi*
Saitoh, Mamoru 1935- *WhoWor 93*
Saitoh, Tamotsu 1938- *WhoWor 93*
Saitoti, George 1944- *WhoAfr*
Saitta, Peter Andrew 1942- *St&PR 93*
Saive, Robert G.M. 1939- *WhoScE 91-2*
Saizan, Paula Theresa 1947- *WhoAmW 93, WhoEmL 93*
Saiz De Bustamante, A. 1932- *WhoScE 91-3*
Saiz-Garcia, Fernando 1944- *WhoWor 93*
Saizon, Anthony L. 1953- *WhoE 93*
Sajak, Pat *BioIn 17*
Sajak, Pat 1947- *WhoAm 92*
Sajaniemi, Jorma Kalevi 1950- *WhoScE 91-4*
Sajewski, William Thomas Christopher 1950- *WhoE 93*
Sajgo, Mihaly 1933- *WhoScE 91-4*
Sajjad, Wasim 1941- *WhoAsAP 91*
Sajovec, Frank M., Jr. *Law&B 92*
Sajovic, Dusan 1928- *WhoScE 91-4*
Sajtinac, Borislav 1943- *BioIn 17*
Sajus, Lucien Henri 1935- *WhoScE 91-2*
Sak, Peter Joseph 1933- *St&PR 93*
Sakac, Branimir 1918-1979 *Baker 92*
Sakada, Daryll M. 1941- *St&PR 93*
Sakagawa, Richard M. 1943- *St&PR 93*
Sakaguchi, Genji 1927- *WhoWor 93*
Sakaguchi, Shukichi 1926- *WhoWor 93*
Sakai, Hiroichi 1929- *WhoAsAP 91*
Sakai, Hiroko 1939- *WhoAmW 93*
Sakai, James T. 1926- *St&PR 93*
Sakai, Katsuo 1942- *WhoWor 93*
Sakai, Kunikazu 1941- *WhoWor 93*
Sakai, Ryozi 1945- *WhoWor 93*
Sakai, Shogo 1948- *WhoWor 93*
Sakai, Tadao 1944- *WhoWor 93*
Sakai, Takanori 1947- *WhoAsAP 91*
Sakai, Takashi 1887-1946 *HarEnMi*
Sakai, Tomoya 1933- *WhoWor 93*
Sakai, Toshihiko 1943- *WhoWor 93*
Sakai, Yasuhiro 1940- *WhoWor 93*
Sakaida, Takashi 1940- *WhoWor 93*
Sakakibara, Naohiko 1951- *WhoWor 93*
Sakall, S. Z. 1884-1955 *QDrFCA 92 [port]*
Sakamoto, Goji 1944- *WhoAsAP 91*
Sakamoto, Ichitaro 1926- *WhoWor 93*
Sakamoto, Jun 1933- *WhoWor 93*
Sakamoto, Misoji 1949- *WhoAsAP 91*
Sakamoto, Munenori 1936- *WhoWor 93*
Sakamoto, Naoto 1939- *WhoWor 93*
Sakamoto, Sandra L. *Law&B 92*
Sakamoto, Tadanobu 1931- *WhoWor 93*
Sakamoto, Toshiatsu 1858-1941 *HarEnMi*
Sakamoto, Yoshiichi 1937- *WhoWor 93*
Sakamoto, Yukio 1929- *WhoWor 93*
Sakamura, Sadao 1925- *WhoWor 93*
Sakanashi, Matao 1943- *WhoWor 93*
Sakano, Shigenobu 1917- *WhoAsAP 91*
Sakaran Bin Dandai, Haji 1930- *WhoAsAP 91*
Sakarias, Wayne Philip *Law&B 92*
Sakata, Terry Masateru 1948- *WhoWor 93*
Sakbani, M. Michael *WhoUN 92*
Sakellarios, Alekos d1991 *BioIn 17*
Sakellaropoulos, George Panayotis 1944- *WhoWor 93*
Sakelliou-Schultz, Liana 1956- *WhoWor 93*
Saker, Joseph J. 1929- *WhoAm 92*
Saker, S.A. 1946- *St&PR 93*
Sakers, Don 1958- *ScF&FL 92, SmATA 72*
Sakharnov, Svyatoslav 1923- *BioIn 17*
Sakharov, Andrei 1921-1989 *ColdWar 2 [port]*
Sakharov, Andrei Dmitrievich 1921-1989 *BioIn 17*
Sakharov, Andrey Dmitrievich 1921-1989 *DcTwHis*
Sakharov, Elena Bonner *BioIn 17*
Sakharov, Igor' Vasil'evich *BioIn 17*
Sakheim, David Kurt 1956- *WhoE 93*
Saki 1870-1916 *BioIn 17, WorLitC [port]*
Sakiewicz, Linda Anne 1961- *WhoAmW 93*
Sakin, Benita A. *Law&B 92*
Sakin, Gary *BioIn 17*
Sakires, Nicholas James 1928- *St&PR 93*
Sakita, Bunji 1930- *WhoAm 92*
Sakiz, Edouard 1926- *WhoScE 91-2, WhoWor 93*
Sakkas, John 1932- *WhoScE 91-3*
Sakkas, John George 1932- *WhoWor 93*
Sakkopoulos, Sotirios A. 1945- *WhoScE 91-3*
Saklad, Daniel A. 1943- *St&PR 93*
Saklad, Stephen Ross 1953- *WhoSSW 93*
Saklofsky, Robert Frederick 1930- *St&PR 93*
Sakmann, Bert *WhoScE 91-3, WhoWor 93*
Sakmann, Bert 1942- *BioIn 17*
Sakmar, Ismail Aydin 1925- *WhoWor 93*
Sakmyster, Joseph R. *Law&B 92*
Sako, Soumana 1950- *WhoWor 93*
Sakon, Masao 1936- *WhoAsAP 91*
Sakosits, John Joseph 1934- *St&PR 93*
Sakoutis, Steve 1930- *St&PR 93*
Sakowitz, Richard 1939- *St&PR 93*
Sakowitz, Robert 1938- *St&PR 93*
Sakowitz, Robert T. *BioIn 17*
Sakowitz, Robert Tobias 1938- *WhoAm 92, WhoWor 93*
Sakowski, Robert Joseph 1942- *WhoE 93*
Saks, A. George *Law&B 92*
Saks, A. George 1937- *St&PR 93*
Saks, Arnold 1931- *WhoAm 92*
Saks, Gene *WhoAm 92*
Saks, Gene 1921- *MiSFD 9*
Saks, Judith-Ann 1943- *WhoAmW 93*
Saks, Mary Louise 1914-1990 *BioIn 17*
Saks, Michael Jay 1947- *WhoAm 92*
Saks, Stephen Howard 1941- *WhoAm 92*
Saksela, Eero 1937- *WhoScE 91-4*
Saksida, Marino F. 1939- *WhoScE 91-3*
Sakson, Sharon Rose 1952- *WhoAmW 93*
Sakuma, Tsutomi 1879-1910 *HarEnMi*
Sakurai, Isamu 1933- *WhoWor 93*
Sakurai, Kijun 1935- *WhoAsAP 91*
Sakurai, Kiyoshi 1934- *WhoWor 93*
Sakurai, Kunitomo 1933- *BioIn 17*
Sakurai, Seizo 1889- *HarEnMi*
Sakurai, Shin 1933- *WhoAsAP 91*
Sakurai, Tadamitsu 1947- *WhoWor 93*
Sakurai, Takeo 1938- *WhoWor 93*
Sakurai, Teruo 1931- *WhoWor 93*
Sakurauchi, Yoshio 1912- *WhoAsAP 91*
Sakuta, Manabu 1947- *WhoEmL 93, WhoWor 93*
Sakya, Gautam Man 1938- *WhoUN 92*
Sakya, Jamyang 1934- *BioIn 17*
Sakya, Manju Ratna 1946- *WhoWor 93*
Sakyamuni *BioIn 17*
Sal, Jack 1954- *WhoE 93*
Sala, Luis Francisco 1919- *WhoAm 92*
Sala, Nicola 1713-1801 *Baker 92*
Sala, Osvaldo Esteban 1950- *WhoWor 93*
Sala, Tadeusz 1925- *WhoScE 91-4*
Salabarria, Berarda 1934- *WhoWor 93*
Salabe, Giovanni Battista 1932- *WhoWor 93*
Salabert, Edouard 1838-1903 *See* Salabert, Francis 1884-1946 *Baker 92*
Salabert, Francis 1884-1946 *Baker 92*
Salabounis, Manuel 1935- *WhoWor 93*
Salacuse, Jeswald William 1938- *WhoAm 92*
Salada, Maurice Regan *Law&B 92*
Saladin 1138-1193 *HarEnMi, OxDcByz*
Saladino, Anthony Joseph 1959- *WhoSSW 93*
Saladino, John A. 1954- *St&PR 93*
Saladrigas, Carlos *DcCPCAm*
Salagean, Traian 1929- *WhoScE 91-4*
Salagi, Doris 1947- *WhoAmW 93*
Salah, Abdullah A. 1922- *WhoUN 92*
Salah, Joseph Elias 1944- *WhoAm 92*
Salahuddin Abdul Aziz Shah 1926- *WhoWor 93*
Salahuddin Abul Aziz Shah Ibni Almarhum, Sultan 1926- *WhoAsAP 91*
Salai, Andrea *DcAmChF 1960*
Salam, Abdus *WhoScE 91-1*
Salam, Abdus 1926- *WhoAm 92, WhoScE 91-3, WhoWor 93*
Salam, Debera Jean 1957- *WhoAmW 93, WhoEmL 93, WhoWor 93*
Salama, Amin Hanna 1941- *WhoUN 92*
Salama, C. Andre Tewfik 1938- *WhoAm 92*
Salama, Claude 1936- *St&PR 93*
Salama, Guy 1930- *St&PR 93*
Salama, Hussein Samir Abdel Rahman 1936- *WhoWor 93*
Salamacha, Judy Anne 1944- *WhoAmW 93*
Salaman, Charles (Kensington) 1814-1901 *Baker 92*
Salaman, Ricardo *Law&B 92*
Salamanca, Lucy d1989 *BioIn 17*
Salami, 'Alawi Salih al- *WhoWor 93*
Salamini, Francesco *WhoScE 91-3*
Salamon, Isaac 1933- *St&PR 93*
Salamon, Itamar 1934- *WhoE 93*
Salamon, Julie *BioIn 17*
Salamon, Julie 1953- *ConAu 136*
Salamon, Linda Bradley 1941- *WhoAm 92, WhoAmW 93*
Salamon, Michael Jacob 1951- *WhoEmL 93*
Salamon, Miklos Dezso Gyorgy 1933- *WhoAm 92, WhoWor 93*
Salamon, Myron Ben 1939- *WhoAm 92*
Salamon, Pearl *Law&B 92*
Salamon, Renay 1948- *WhoAmW 93, WhoE 93, WhoEmL 93, WhoWor 93*
Salamone, Anthony A. 1944- *St&PR 93*
Salamone, Jean Smith 1929- *St&PR 93*
Salamone, Jodie *BioIn 17*
Salamone, Joseph Charles 1939- *WhoAm 92*
Salamone, Thomas W. 1944- *St&PR 93*
Salamone-Kochowicz, Jean Gloria 1929- *WhoAmW 93*
Salan, Beryl R. 1936- *St&PR 93*
Salan, Raoul Albin Louis 1899-1984 *DcTwHis*
Salan, Raoul Louis 1899-1984 *BioIn 17*
Saland, Linda Carol 1942- *WhoAmW 93*
Saland, Stephanie *WhoAm 92*
Salandre *WhoScE 91-2*
Salane, Linda Burton 1947- *WhoAmW 93*
Salaneck, William R. 1941- *WhoScE 91-4*
Salang Siden, Thomas 1945- *WhoAsAP 91*
Salanki, Janos 1929- *WhoScE 91-4*

Salanne, Simo *WhoScE 91-4*
Salans, Carl Fredric 1933- *WhoAm 92*
Salans, Lester Barry 1936- *WhoAm 92*
Salanski, Charles William 1935- *WhoAm 92*
Salant, Nathan Nathaniel 1955- *WhoE 93*
Salant, Walter S. 1911- *WhoAm 92*
Salanter, Israel 1810-1883 *BioIn 17*
Salanthe, R.P. 1944- *WhoScE 91-4*
Salantrie, Frank 1926- *WhoWrEP 92*
Salarrue 1899-1975 *SpAmA*
Salas, Floyd Francis 1931- *WhoWrEP 92*
Salas, George Rafael 1946- *WhoWor 93*
Salas, Lauro 1927- *HispAmA*
Salas, Mario Marcel 1949- *WhoSSW 93*
Salas, Rafael Angel 1956- *WhoSSW 93*
Salas, Randall Nouel 1945- *WhoWor 93*
Salaspuro, Mikko P.J. 1939- *WhoScE 91-4*
Salas-Ramirez, Francisco Heriberto 1960- *WhoWor 93*
Salassa, Robert Maurice 1914- *WhoAm 92*
Salas Viu, Vicente 1911-1967 *Baker 92*
Salas y Castro, Esteban 1725-1803 *Baker 92*
Salat, Jordi 1951- *WhoScE 91-3*
Salata, Gerard A. 1944- *St&PR 93*
Salathe, John, Jr. 1928- *WhoAm 92*
Salathe, John Jr. 1928- *St&PR 93*
Salatic, Dusan 1929- *WhoScE 91-4*
Salatich, Donald C. 1946- *St&PR 93*
Salatich, John Smyth 1926- *WhoSSW 93*
Salatich, William G. 1922- *St&PR 93*
Salatka, Charles Alexander 1918- *WhoAm 92, WhoSSW 93*
Salaverria, Helena Clara 1923- *WhoAmW 93*
Salay, Carolyn Jeanne *WhoAmW 93, WhoSSW 93, WhoWor 93*
Salay, Cindy Rolston 1955- *WhoAmW 93*
Salay, Tedd *ScF&FL 92*
Salazar, Abel *BioIn 17*
Salazar, Adolfo 1890-1958 *Baker 92*
Salazar, Alberto 1958- *WhoAm 92*
Salazar, Alberto Bauduy 1958- *HispAmA [port]*
Salazar, Antonio de Oliveira 1889-1970 *BioIn 17, DcTwHis*
Salazar, Barbara M. 1949- *WhoWrEP 92*
Salazar, Carlos J. *Law&B 92*
Salazar, Daniel Reynolds 1942- *WhoWor 93*
Salazar, Deborah *BioIn 17*
Salazar, Debra 1952- *WhoAmW 93*
Salazar, Freddy 1940- *WhoWor 93*
Salazar, George Alberto 1953- *WhoSSW 93*
Salazar, Jose Ramiro *Law&B 92*
Salazar, Melito Sison, Jr. 1949- *WhoWor 93*
Salazar, Ramiro 1954- *WhoAm 92*
Salazar, Rogelio Colendrino 1935- *WhoWor 93*
Salazar, Valentin 1934- *WhoScE 91-3*
Salazar, Yginio 1863-1936 *BioIn 17*
Salazar Bondy, Sebastian 1924-1965 *SpAmA*
Salazar-Carrillo, Jorge 1938- *WhoAm 92, WhoSSW 93, WhoWor 93*
Salazar de Alarcon, Eugenio 1530-1605? *DcMexL*
Salazar Lopez, Jose 1910-1991 *BioIn 17*
Salazar Mallen, Ruben 1905- *DcMexL*
Salaz-Marquez, Ruben 1935- *DcLB 122 [port]*
Salbaing, M.P. 1945- *St&PR 93*
Salbaing, Pierre Alcee 1914- *WhoAm 92*
Salber, Hubert Wilhelm 1928- *WhoWor 93*
Salberg, Batsheva 1953- *WhoAmW 93*
Salberg, Howard J. 1954- *WhoE 93*
Salberg, Joel L. 1936- *St&PR 93*
Salce, Luciano 1922-1989 *MiSFD 9N*
Salcedo Fernandez Del Castillo, Tomas De 1946- *WhoWor 93*
Salch, Steven Charles 1943- *WhoAm 92*
Salchert, Brian Arthur 1941- *WhoWrEP 92*
Salci, Larry Eugene 1946- *WhoAm 92*
Salcido, Angela *BioIn 17*
Salcido, Ramon *BioIn 17*
Salcman, Michael 1946- *WhoE 93*
Salcudean, Martha Eva 1934- *WhoAm 92*
Saldanha, Desmond Joseph 1933- *WhoUN 92*
Saldanha, Luiz Vieira Caldas 1937- *WhoScE 91-3*
Saldarriaga, Alexander 1960- *WhoSSW 93*
Saldeen, Ake 1937- *WhoWor 93*
Saldich, Robert Joseph 1933- *St&PR 93, WhoAm 92*
Saldin, Thomas R. *Law&B 92*
Saldin, Thomas R. 1946- *St&PR 93*
Saldivar, Vicente 1943- *HispAmA*
Saldoni, Baltasar 1807-1889 *Baker 92*
Sale, Arthur Harry John *WhoWor 93*
Sale, Frank Robert *WhoScE 91-1*
Sale, James Prowant, Jr. 1947- *WhoAm 92*
Sale, John Morton- 1901-1990 *BioIn 17*
Sale, Kirkpatrick *BioIn 17*
Sale, Kirkpatrick 1937- *WhoAm 92*
Sale, Marilyn Mills 1928- *WhoWrEP 92*
Sale, Roger 1932- *ScF&FL 92*
Sale, Sara Lee 1954- *WhoAmW 93*
Sale, Tom S. 1942- *WhoSSW 93, WhoWor 93*
Sale, Virginia d1992 *NewYTBS 92 [port]*
Sale, William Merritt 1929- *WhoAm 92*
Saleda, Marion Eugene 1935- *St&PR 93*
Salee, Adrian Michael 1936- *WhoE 93*
Saleeby, Raymond G. 1945- *St&PR 93*
Saleeby, Robert W. 1951- *WhoWor 93*
Saleem, A. U. 1934- *WhoWor 93*
Saleem, Ab 1940- *St&PR 93*
Saleem, Mohammad Yunus 1912- *WhoAsAP 91*
Saleem, Syed Mohammed 1940- *WhoWor 93*
Saleh, Bahaa E. A. 1944- *WhoAm 92*
Saleh, Dennis 1942- *ScF&FL 92, WhoWrEP 92*
Saleh, Ismail 1926- *WhoAsAP 91*
Saleh, Jaime 1941- *WhoWor 93*
Saleh, Salim 1957- *WhoAfr*
Saleh, Samir A. 1932- *WhoWor 93*
Saleh, Suhayl Shukri 1937- *WhoWor 93*
Salei, Thomas Apa 1931- *St&PR 93*
Salei, Yevgeni Vladimirovich *BioIn 17*
Salek, Mustapha Ould Mohammed c. 1928- *WhoAfr*
Salem, Charles Louis 1935- *St&PR 93*
Salem, David Andrew 1956- *WhoE 93*
Salem, E. 1936- *St&PR 93*
Salem, George Richard 1953- *WhoAm 92*
Salem, Harry 1929- *WhoE 93*
Salem, John Joseph 1920- *WhoSSW 93*
Salem, Richard *ScF&FL 92*
Salem, Samuel 1923- *St&PR 93*
Salembier, Valerie *BioIn 17*
Salembier, Valerie Birnbaum 1945- *WhoAm 92, WhoAmW 93, WhoE 93*
Salembier, Walter Charles 1940- *St&PR 93*
Saleme, Salvatore Alphonse 1923- *WhoSSW 93*
Salemi, Joseph R. 1941- *St&PR 93*
Salemme, Antonio 1892- *BioIn 17, WhoE 93*
Salemme, Lucia 1919- *WhoE 93*
Salemme, Martha Anne Caroline 1912- *WhoE 93*
Salen, Wayne Louis 1954- *WhoE 93*
Salenger, Lucy Lee 1938- *WhoAmW 93*
Salengro, Roger 1890-1936 *BioIn 17*
Salenstedt, Carl-Rune 1929- *WhoScE 91-4*
Salentine, Thomas James 1939- *St&PR 93, WhoAm 92*
Salerno, Anthony 1911-1992 *NewYTBS 92 [port]*
Salerno, Frank Gregory 1956- *WhoSSW 93*
Salerno, Leon Alexander 1933- *St&PR 93*
Salerno, Michael J. 1936- *St&PR 93*
Salerno, Nicholas Andrew 1936- *WhoWrEP 92*
Salerno, Nicholas James 1927- *St&PR 93*
Salerno, Peter Charles *Law&B 92*
Salerno, Peter Thomas 1941- *St&PR 93*
Salerno, Philip Adams 1953- *WhoSSW 93*
Salerno-Sonnenberg, Nadja *BioIn 17*
Salerno-Sonnenberg, Nadja 1961- *Baker 92, WhoAmW 93*
Sales, A. R. 1948- *WhoAm 92*
Sales, Christian G. 1949- *WhoScE 91-2*
Sales, Eugenio de Araujo Cardinal 1920- *WhoAm 92, WhoWor 93*
Sales, Franz c. 1550-1599 *Baker 92*
Sales, Jack Christian *Law&B 92*
Sales, James Bohus 1934- *WhoAm 92, WhoSSW 93, WhoWor 93*
Sales, James J. *Law&B 92*
Sales, Michael 1928- *WhoIns 93*
Sales, Michael W. *Law&B 92*
Sales, Michel 1928- *WhoAm 92*
Sales, Milton S. *Law&B 92*
Sales, Nikolaus c. 1550-1606 *See* Sales, Franz c. 1550-1599 *Baker 92*
Sales, Pietro Pompeo c. 1729-1797 *Baker 92*
Salese, Irene 1930- *St&PR 93*
Saleski, Felicitas *AmWomPl*
Salesky, Charles d1991 *BioIn 17*
Saless, Mehdi Akhavan 1928-1990 *BioIn 17*
Salesses, John Joseph 1933- *WhoAm 92*
Salet, Eugene Albert 1911- *WhoSSW 93*
Saletta, John Steven *Law&B 92*
Salette, Jean E. 1936- *WhoScE 91-2*
Saley, Albert d1991 *BioIn 17*
Saleza, Albert 1867-1916 *Baker 92*
Salgado, Alfredo Garcia 1951- *St&PR 93*
Salgado, Antonio de Pareda y c. 1599-c. 1678 *BioIn 17*
Salgado, Carmelita Garcia 1939- *WhoWor 93*
Salgado, Lissette *WhoAm 92*
Salgado, Maria Antonia 1933- *WhoSSW 93*
Salgado, Sebastiao *BioIn 17*
Salganicoff, Leon 1924- *WhoE 93*
Salgia, Tansukh J. 1937- *WhoWor 93*
Salgueiro, Alex 1954- *WhoSSW 93*
Salguero, Carlos Eduardo 1929- *St&PR 93, WhoAm 92*
Salguero, Ricardo Arturo 1954- *St&PR 93*
Salha, Rhett Herman 1959- *St&PR 93*
Salhanick, Brenda Crane 1951- *WhoAmW 93*
Salhany, Gary T. 1954- *St&PR 93*
Salhany, Lucie *BioIn 17, St&PR 93*
Salhany, Lucille S. *WhoAm 92, WhoAmW 93*
Salhus, Victoria D. *Law&B 92*
Salib, Adolph B. *Law&B 92*
Salib, Maher Badie 1934- *WhoWor 93*
Saliba, David R. 1949- *ScF&FL 92*
Saliba, Jacob 1913- *St&PR 93*
Saliba, John H. 1938- *St&PR 93, WhoIns 93*
Saliba, Louis John 1935- *WhoUN 92*
Saliba, Philip 1931- *BioIn 17*
Saliba, Philip E. 1931- *WhoAm 92*
Salibra, Lawrence A. *Law&B 92*
Salice, Barbara Farenga 1944- *WhoAmW 93*
Salick, Bernard 1939- *St&PR 93*
Salieri, Antonio 1750-1825 *Baker 92, IntDcOp, OxDcOp*
Saliers, Anne Burr 1954- *WhoAmW 93*
Salig, Joram C. *Law&B 92*
Saliga, Marie T. 1934- *St&PR 93*
Saligman, Harvey 1938- *WhoAm 92*
Salignac, Thomas 1867-1945 *OxDcOp*
Salih, Ali Abdallah 1942- *BioIn 17*
Salih, Ali Abdullah 1942- *WhoWor 93*
Salih, Faisal Ali Abu 1944- *WhoAfr*
Salih, Halil Ibrahim 1939- *WhoSSW 93*
Salik *ScF&FL 92*
Salikof, K.S. *ScF&FL 92*
Salim, Ahmed Salim 1942- *WhoAfr*
Salim, Emil 1930- *WhoAsAP 91*
Salim, Hassan Kamau 1950- *WhoE 93*
Salimbeni, Felice 1712-1751 *OxDcOp*
Salimi, Wasim *Law&B 92*
Salin, Pascal Marie 1939- *WhoWor 93*
Salin, William N. 1931- *St&PR 93*
Salina, David M. *St&PR 93*
Salinari, Piero 1943- *WhoScE 91-3*
Salinas, Carlos 1948- *News 92 [port]*
Salinas, Francisco de 1513-1590 *Baker 92*
Salinas, Gloria M. *Law&B 92*
Salinas, Luciano, Jr. 1950- *WhoSSW 93*
Salinas, Lucila Mercedes 1953- *WhoSSW 93*
Salinas, Pedro 1892-1951 *BioIn 17*
Salinas, Trinidad Cervantes 1940- *St&PR 93*
Salinas de Gortari, Carlos *BioIn 17*
Salinas de Gortari, Carlos 1948- *DcCPCAm, WhoSSW 93*
Salinas Duron, Mary 1952- *NotHsAW 93*
Saline, Carol *BioIn 17*
Saline, Lindon Edgar 1924- *WhoAm 92*
Salinger, Anthony Wilshire 1938- *WhoWor 93*
Salinger, J.D. 1919- *BioIn 17, MagSAmL [port], WorLitC [port]*
Salinger, J(erome) D(avid) 1919- *ConAu 39NR, MajAI [port]*
Salinger, Jerome David 1919- *BioIn 17, WhoAm 92, WhoWrEP 92*
Salinger, Marion Casting 1917- *WhoAmW 93*
Salinger, Pierre 1925- *JrnUS*
Salinger, Pierre Emil George 1925- *WhoAm 92, WhoWrEP 92*
Salinger, Robert M. *Law&B 92*
Salinger, Robert Meredith 1950- *WhoAm 92*
Salinger, Ruth Angier 1931- *WhoAmW 93, WhoE 93*
Salino, Jeffrey Alan 1960- *WhoSSW 93*
Saliola, Frances 1921- *St&PR 93, WhoE 93*
Salipante, Robert C. *WhoIns 93*
Salis, Jean Rodolphe de 1901- *BioIn 17*
Salisbury, Marquis of 1830-1903 *BioIn 17*
Salisbury, Alan Blanchard 1937- *WhoSSW 93*
Salisbury, Alicia Laing 1939- *WhoAmW 93*
Salisbury, Carla Ann 1964- *WhoAmW 93*
Salisbury, Donald Charles 1946- *WhoSSW 93*
Salisbury, Douglas Lee 1946- *St&PR 93*
Salisbury, Frank Boyer 1926- *WhoAm 92*
Salisbury, Franklin Cary 1910- *WhoAm 92, WhoE 93*
Salisbury, Harrison E. 1908- *JrnUS*
Salisbury, Harrison Evans 1908- *BioIn 17, WhoAm 92*
Salisbury, Harry Lawton, Jr. 1933- *WhoSSW 93*
Salisbury, Helen Holland 1923- *WhoE 93*
Salisbury, Irving Daniel 1936- *WhoE 93*
Salisbury, John Eagan 1931- *St&PR 93*
Salisbury, John F. *Law&B 92*
Salisbury, John Francis 1930- *St&PR 93, WhoAm 92*
Salisbury, Kevin M. *Law&B 92*
Salisbury, Kevin M. 1935- *St&PR 93*
Salisbury, Kevin Mahon 1935- *WhoAm 92*
Salisbury, LuAnn Joyce 1959- *WhoE 93*
Salisbury, Marianne Hart 1929- *St&PR 93*
Salisbury, Mike 1942- *ConAu 136*
Salisbury, Ralph James 1926- *WhoWrEP 92*
Salisbury, Robert Cameron 1943- *WhoAm 92*
Salisbury, Robert Cecil, Earl of 1563-1612 *BioIn 17*
Salisbury, Robert Holt 1930- *WhoAm 92*
Salisbury, Susan D. *Law&B 92*
Salisbury, Terri 1953- *WhoAmW 93*
Salisian, Neal S. 1938- *St&PR 93*
Salit, Gary S. *Law&B 92*
Salitore, Robert Angelo 1948- *St&PR 93*
Salius, Michael W. 1947- *St&PR 93*
Salizzoni, Frank L. 1938- *St&PR 93*
Salje, E. *WhoScE 91-1*
Salk, Ahmet 1940- *WhoScE 91-4*
Salk, Darrell J. 1947- *St&PR 93*
Salk, Howard A. *Law&B 92*
Salk, Jane Ellen 1957- *WhoAmW 93*
Salk, Jonas 1914- *BioIn 17*
Salk, Jonas Edward 1914- *JeAmHC, WhoAm 92, WhoWor 93*
Salk, Lee 1926-1992 *BioIn 17, ConAu 137, CurBio 92N, NewYTBS 92 [port]*
Salkey, Andrew 1928- *BlkAuII 92*
Salkey, (Felix) Andrew (Alexander) 1928- *DcLB 125 [port]*
Salkiewicz, Ewa Stanislawa Alicja 1950- *WhoWor 93*
Salkin, Maureen Ada 1943- *WhoE 93*
Salkin, Paul 1932- *WhoE 93*
Salkind, Alvin J. 1927- *WhoAm 92*
Salkind, Malvin Ronald *WhoScE 91-1*
Salkind, Neil J. 1947- *WhoAm 92*
Salkind, Neil Joseph 1947- *WhoWrEP 92*
Sallah, Majeed 1920- *WhoWor 93*
Sallah, Ousman Ahmadou 1938- *WhoWor 93*
Sallai, Gyula 1945- *WhoScE 91-4*
Sallami, Marion Davis 1918- *WhoE 93, WhoWor 93*
Sallani, Werner, Mrs. 1918- *WhoE 93, WhoWor 93*
Sallas, Anita Maria 1959- *WhoSSW 93*
Salle, Bernard Louis 1931- *WhoScE 91-2*
Salle, David *BioIn 17*
Salle, David 1952- *WhoAm 92*
Salle, Victor La *ScF&FL 92*
Sallee, Bill 1929- *WhoSSW 93*
Sallee, Harry Franklin 1885-1950 *BiDAMSp 1989*
Sallee, Marilyn 1948- *WhoWrEP 92*
Sallee, Robb Kameron *Law&B 92*
Salleh, Wan Yahya B. Wan 1951- *WhoWor 93*
Sallen, David Urban 1952- *WhoEmL 93*
Sallen, Ira Bruce 1954- *WhoE 93, WhoWor 93*
Sallen, Melvin J. 1928- *St&PR 93*
Sallen, Melvin Julius 1928- *WhoAm 92*
Saller, Richard Paul 1952- *WhoAm 92*
Salles, Maurice J.M.M. 1930- *WhoScE 91-2*
Salles, Walter, Jr. *MiSFD 9*
Salley, J. Ronald 1939- *St&PR 93*
Salley, John *BioIn 17*
Salley, John Jones 1926- *WhoAm 92*
Salley, Thomas R., III *Law&B 92*
Sallinen, Aulis 1935- *Baker 92, IntDcOp, OxDcOp*
Sallmann, Hans-Peter 1939- *WhoScE 91-3*
Salloukh, Fawzi Hassan 1931- *WhoUN 92*
Salloum, Gary M. *Law&B 92*
Salloum, Maroun H. *BioIn 17*
Salloum, Salim George 1956- *WhoE 93*
Salloustios fl. 4th cent.- *OxDcByz*
Sallye, Frederick Isaac, I 1949- *WhoSSW 93*
Salm, Bruno 1932- *WhoScE 91-4*
Salm, Bruno Walter 1932- *WhoWor 93*
Salm, Nicholas von 1459-1530 *HarEnMi*
Salm, Peter 1919-1990 *BioIn 17*
Salm, Rick D. 1952- *St&PR 93*
Salmaggi, Felix W. d1990 *BioIn 17*
Salman, Steven L. 1947- *St&PR 93, WhoIns 93*
Salmanov, Vadim (Nikolaievich) 1912-1978 *Baker 92*
Salmans, Charles Gardiner 1945- *WhoAm 92*
Salmans, James Lee 1935- *St&PR 93*
Salmelin, Bror Johan 1956- *WhoWor 93*
Salmen, Larry James 1947- *St&PR 93*
Salmen, Stanley 1914- *St&PR 93*
Salmen, Walter 1926- *Baker 92*

Salmenhaara, Erkki (Olavi) 1941- Baker 92
Salmenpera, Hannu 1941- WhoScE 91-4
Salmeron, Antonio 1963- WhoWor 93
Salmeron, Jose Luis 1948- WhoWor 93
Salmhofer, Franz 1900-1975 Baker 92, OxDcOp
Salmi, Albert 1928-1990 BioIn 17
Salmi, Maurizio 1947- WhoScE 91-3
Salminen, A. Lotta M. 1939- WhoScE 91-4
Salminen, Hannu Antero 1947- WhoWor 93
Salminen, Kari Olavi 1937- WhoScE 91-4
Salminen, Matti 1945- Baker 92, OxDcOp
Salminen, Pekka 1938- WhoScE 91-4
Salminen, Reijo K. 1943- WhoScE 91-4
Salmoiraghi, Gian Carlo 1924- WhoAm 92, WhoWor 93
Salmon, Lord 1903-1991 AnObit 1991
Salmon, Benjamin Thomas 1889-1932 BioIn 17
Salmon, Charles P. 1925- WhoScE 91-2
Salmon, Dena K. BioIn 17
Salmon, Garland Russell 1930- St&PR 93
Salmon, George Arthur WhoScE 91-1
Salmon, J.F. Law&B 92
Salmon, J.T. Law&B 92
Salmon, J.T. 1927- St&PR 93
Salmon, John Hearsey Mc Millan 1925- WhoWrEP 92
Salmon, John Hearsey McMillan 1925- WhoAm 92
Salmon, Jon W. 1952- St&PR 93
Salmon, Jon Wheaton 1952- WhoAm 92
Salmon, Joseph Thaddeus 1927- WhoAm 92
Salmon, Judith Elaine 1940- WhoSSW 93
Salmon, L.T.J. 1946- WhoScE 91-1
Salmon, Laura Beth 1938- WhoAmW 93
Salmon, Louis 1923- WhoAm 92
Salmon, Mark Howard 1949- WhoWor 93
Salmon, Michael C. Law&B 92
Salmon, Phyllis Ward 1948- WhoAmW 93
Salmon, Robin Robertson 1952- WhoSSW 93
Salmon, Thomas Paul 1932- WhoAm 92
Salmon, Vincent 1912- WhoAm 92
Salmon, Walter J. WhoAm 92
Salmon, Walter Lawrence, Jr. 1930- St&PR 93
Salmon, William Cooper 1935- WhoAm 92
Salmon, William Gordon 1946- St&PR 93
Salmond, Alex 1954- BioIn 17
Salmond, Felix (Adrian Norman) 1888-1952 Baker 92
Salmon Legagneur, Emmanuel R.C.M. 1929- WhoScE 91-2
Salmons, Arthur W. 1940- St&PR 93
Salmons, Hugh I. 1940- St&PR 93
Salmons, Joanna 1931- WhoWor 93
Salmonson, Amos ScF&FL 92
Salmonson, Jessica Amanda 1950- ScF&FL 92
Salner, Marcia Beck 1938- WhoAmW 93
Salnikov, Nikolai Nikolaevich 1954- WhoWor 93
Salnikov, Vladimir BioIn 17
Salo, Ernest Olavi 1919-1989 BioIn 17
Salo, Gasparo da Baker 92
Salo, James D. Law&B 92
Salo, John E. 1947- St&PR 93
Salo, Markku BioIn 17
Salo, Matti Sakari 1938- WhoScE 91-4
Salo, Seppo Kullervo 1950- WhoWor 93
Salogga, Frederick William 1908- WhoAm 92
Salois, M. Elizabeth AmWomPl
Salojarvi, Pekka Tapani 1940- WhoWor 93
Salokangas, Raimo Juhani 1934- WhoScE 91-4
Salokangas, Raimo K.R. 1944- WhoScE 91-4
Salokar, Rebecca Mae 1956- WhoSSW 93
Saloman, Siegfried 1816-1899 Baker 92
Salome 1954- BioIn 17
Salome, Jo Ann 1951- WhoAmW 93
Salome, Lou Andreas- 1861-1937 BioIn 17
Salome, William C., III 1929- St&PR 93
Salomon Baker 92
Salomon, Allan 1939- St&PR 93
Salomon, Edward S. 1836-1913 BioIn 17
Salomon, Haym 1740-1785 BioIn 17, PolBiDi
Salomon, Janet Lynn Nowicki 1953- WhoAm 92, WhoEmL 93
Salomon, Johann Peter 1745?-1815 Baker 92
Salomon, Johanna 1944- WhoAmW 93
Salomon, Leon Edward 1936- WhoAm 92
Salomon, Lucy 1925- WhoE 93
Salomon, Mikael WhoAm 92
Salomon, Mikael 1945- ConTFT 10
Salomon, Richard 1912- WhoAm 92
Salomon, Richard Adley 1953- WhoAm 92
Salomon, Roger Blaine 1928- WhoAm 92
Salomon, William R. BioIn 17
Salomone, J.G. 1940- St&PR 93
Salomone, William Gerald 1948- WhoSSW 93
Salomonis Baker 92
Salomons, Dirk 1940- WhoUN 92
Salomons, W. 1945- WhoScE 91-3
Salonen, Esa-Pekka 1958- Baker 92, WhoAm 92, WhoWor 93
Salonen, Heikki Olavi 1933- WhoAm 92
Salonen, Jukka T. 1953- WhoScE 91-4
Salonen, Sulo (Nikolai) 1899-1976 Baker 92
Salonga, Jovito Reyes 1920- WhoAsAP 91
Salonga, Lea BioIn 17
Saloniemi, Hannu 1944- WhoScE 91-4
Saloom, Joseph A. 1921- WhoAm 92
Saloom, Joseph Michael 1950- WhoSSW 93
Saloom, Kaliste Joseph, Jr. 1918- WhoWor 93
Salop, Arnold 1923- WhoE 93
Salopek, Daniel F. 1938- St&PR 93
Salosa, Melkianus d1991 BioIn 17
Salovaara, Timo WhoScE 91-4
Salovey, Peter BioIn 17
Salowitz, Charles B. Law&B 92
Salpeter, Edwin Ernest 1924- WhoAm 92
Salpeter, Miriam Mark 1929- WhoAm 92
Salsberg, Arthur Philip 1929- WhoAm 92
Salsburg, Donald M. Law&B 92
Salsbury, Larry G. 1940- St&PR 93
Salsbury, Phillip James 1942- St&PR 93
Salsbury, Sherrod 1915- St&PR 93
Salsbury, Stephen Matthew 1931- WhoAm 92
Salsieder, Michael W. Law&B 92
Salsitz, Amalie Petranker 1922- BioIn 17
Salsitz, Norman 1920- BioIn 17
Salsitz, R.A.V. ScF&FL 92
Salsitz, Rhondi ScF&FL 92
Salt, Alger Dean 1955- WhoSSW 93
Salt, Henry Stephens 1851-1939 BioIn 17
Salt, Julia Ann 1955- WhoWor 93
Saltamachia, Joe G. 1930- St&PR 93
Saltarelli, Eugene A. 1923- WhoAm 92
Saltarelli, Martin O. 1935- St&PR 93
Salten, David George 1913- WhoAm 92
Salten, Felix ConAu 137, MajAI
Saltenberger, Pamela Guay 1944- St&PR 93
Salter, Carla Todd 1958- WhoAmW 93
Salter, Charles E. BioIn 17
Salter, Dianne S. Law&B 92
Salter, Edwin Carroll 1927- WhoAm 92
Salter, James BioIn 17, MiSFD 9
Salter, John Rotherham 1932- WhoWor 93
Salter, Leo Guilford 1937- WhoSSW 93
Salter, Lester Herbert 1918- WhoAm 92
Salter, Lionel (Paul) 1914- Baker 92
Salter, Mary Elizabeth 1856-1938 Baker 92
Salter, Mary Jo 1954- DcLB 120 [port]
Salter, Mavis Juliette 1946- WhoWor 93
Salter, Maxwell Hillary 1920- St&PR 93
Salter, Michael Laurie 1949- St&PR 93
Salter, Patrick M. WhoScE 91-1
Salter, Robert Bruce 1924- WhoAm 92
Salter, Robert Mundhenk, Jr. 1920- WhoAm 92
Salterberg, B.J. 1934- ScF&FL 92
Salterberg, Susan Kay 1960- WhoWrEP 92
Salterio, Joseph Louis, Jr. 1944- St&PR 93
Salters, Richard Stewart 1951- WhoSSW 93
Saltford, Herbert Wetherbee 1911- WhoWrEP 92
Saltich, Jack L. 1943- St&PR 93
Saltiel, Alan Robert 1953- WhoWor 93
Saltiel-Berzin, Rita Aime 1953- WhoAmW 93
Saltin, Bengt 1935- WhoScE 91-4
Saltman, David 1912- WhoWor 93
Saltman, David J. 1951- WhoSSW 93
Saltman, Judith BioIn 17
Saltman, Judith 1947- WhoCanL 92
Saltman, Roy Gilbert 1932- WhoE 93
Saltman, Stuart I. Law&B 92
Saltmarsh, P. David 1939- St&PR 93
Salt 'N' Pepa SoulM
Saltoglu, Senai 1934- WhoScE 91-4
Salton, Albin 1916- WhoAm 92
Salton, Gerard 1927- WhoAm 92, WhoE 93
Salton, Linda M. 1949- St&PR 93
Saltonstall, Frances A. F. AmWomPl
Saltoun, Julie A. Law&B 92
Saltus, Edgar 1855-1921 GayN
Saltus, Phyllis Borzelliere 1931- WhoAmW 93, WhoE 93
Saltus, Scott M. 1953- St&PR 93
Saltwell, E.R. 1924- St&PR 93
Saltykov, Aleksej 1934- DrEEuF
Saltz, Carole Pogrebin 1949- WhoAm 92, WhoAmW 93
Saltz, Ivan Kenneth 1949- WhoSSW 93
Saltz, James G. 1932- St&PR 93
Saltz, Ralph Law&B 92
Saltz, Ralph 1948- St&PR 93, WhoAm 92
Saltzberg, Burton Reuben 1933- WhoAm 92
Saltzburg, Stephen Allan 1945- WhoAm 92, WhoE 93
Saltzer, Jerome Howard 1939- WhoAm 92, WhoE 93
Saltzman, Arnold Asa 1916- WhoAm 92
Saltzman, Arthur M(ichael) 1953- ConAu 136
Saltzman, Barry 1931- WhoAm 92, WhoE 93
Saltzman, Benjamin Nathan 1914- WhoAm 92, WhoWor 93
Saltzman, Carol Lipton Law&B 92
Saltzman, Charles E. 1903- St&PR 93
Saltzman, Charles Eskridge 1903- WhoAm 92
Saltzman, Deepa Mehta MiSFD 9
Saltzman, George 1927- St&PR 93
Saltzman, Glenn Alan 1935- WhoAm 92
Saltzman, Harry 1915- WhoAm 92
Saltzman, Irene Cameron 1927- WhoWor 93
Saltzman, Joseph 1939- WhoAm 92
Saltzman, Lee Stephen 1948- WhoE 93
Saltzman, Nancy Elise 1965- WhoAmW 93
Saltzman, Paul Law&B 92
Saltzman, Paul 1943- MiSFD 9
Saltzman, Philip 1928- WhoAm 92
Saltzman, Rachelle Hope 1956- WhoE 93
Saltzman, Richard Alan 1947- WhoE 93
Saltzman, Robert P. 1942- St&PR 93
Saltzman, Robert Paul 1942- WhoAm 92, WhoIns 93
Saltzman, Russell Edward 1947- WhoSSW 93
Saltzman, Sidney 1926- WhoAm 92
Saltzman, William 1916- WhoAm 92
Saltzman, William H. Law&B 92
Saltzmann-Stevens, Minnie 1874-1950 Baker 92
Salu, Mary 1919- ScF&FL 92
Salucci, Anthony 1942- St&PR 93
Salup, Stephen Law&B 92
Salusjarvi, Markku Rafael 1947- WhoScE 91-4
Salustro, Larry J. Law&B 92
Salutin, Rick 1942- WhoCanL 92
Saluzzo, Ludovico, Marquis of d1504 HarEnMi
Salva, Tadeas 1937- Baker 92
Salvador, Armindo Jose Alves Silva 1965- WhoWor 93
Salvador, Francis 1747-1776 BioIn 17
Salvador, Richard A. 1927- St&PR 93
Salvador, Sal 1925- BioIn 17, WhoAm 92, WhoWor 93
Salvador, Santiago BioIn 17
Salvadore, Michael A. St&PR 93
Salvadore, Michael Andrew, Jr. 1957- WhoE 93
Salvadori, Andrea 1591-1635 OxDcOp
Salvadori, Massimo ConAu 138
Salvadori, Max W. d1992 NewYTBS 92 [port]
Salvadori, Max (William) ConAu 138
Salvadori, Piero 1935- WhoScE 91-3
Salvadori, Tedfilo Alexander 1899- WhoWor 93
Salvadori-Paleotti, Massimo 1908-1992 ConAu 138
Salvage, Jane Elizabeth 1953- WhoUN 92
Salvaggio, John Edmond 1933- WhoAm 92, WhoWor 93
Salvaggio, Ruth 1951- ScF&FL 92
Salvagni, C.A. 1936- St&PR 93
Salvaneschi, Luigi 1929- WhoAm 92, WhoSSW 93
Salvant, Paulette Marie 1960- WhoSSW 93
Salvati, Marco 1948- WhoScE 91-3
Salvati, Serafina WhoScE 91-3
Salvati, Stephen James Law&B 92
Salvato, Leonard 1952-1992 NewYTBS 92
Salvato, Sharon ScF&FL 92
Salvatore, Anne Theresa 1941- WhoAmW 93
Salvatore, Diane 1960- ConAu 139
Salvatore, Donna Ann 1953- WhoAmW 93
Salvatore, Frank A. 1922- WhoE 93
Salvatore, Gaetano WhoScE 91-3
Salvatore, Michael Joseph 1934- WhoWrEP 92
Salvatore, Nicholas D. 1941- St&PR 93
Salvatore, R.A. 1959- ScF&FL 92
Salvatore, Roco BioIn 17
Salvatores, Gabriele 1950- MiSFD 9
Salvatori, G. WhoScE 91-2
Salvatori, Grace Ford d1990 BioIn 17
Salvatori, Vincent L. 1932- St&PR 93
Salvayre, Gaston 1847-1916 Baker 92
Salve, N.K.P. 1921- WhoAsAP 91
Salve, Patrick J. Law&B 92
Salvendy, Gavriel 1938- WhoAm 92
Salverson, Laura Goodman 1890-1970 BioIn 17
Salvesen, Bonnie Forbes 1944- WhoAmW 93, WhoWor 93
Salvesen, Robert Henry 1924- WhoE 93
Salveter, Sharon Caroline 1949- WhoAmW 93
Salvi, Antonio 1742- OxDcOp
Salvi, Lorenzo 1810-1879 Baker 92
Salvia, Rita A. Law&B 92
Salvia, Robert F. Law&B 92
Salvian c. 400-c. 480 OxDcByz
Salvidio, Emanuele P. 1922- WhoScE 91-3
Salvini-Donatelli, Fanny 1815-1891 Baker 92, OxDcOp
Salvino, S.M. 1928- St&PR 93, WhoAm 92
Salviucci, Giovanni 1907-1937 Baker 92
Salvo, Joseph Charles, Jr. 1941- St&PR 93
Salvo, Lori M. Law&B 92
Salwak, Dale 1947- ScF&FL 92
Salwak, Dale (Francis) 1947- ConAu 137
Salwasser, Hal 1945- WhoE 93
Salway, Lance ScF&FL 92
Salwen, Barry David 1955- WhoE 93
Salwen, Edward 1924- St&PR 93
Salwen, Harry St&PR 93
Salwen, Richard 1942- St&PR 93
Salwi, Dilip M. 1952- DcChlFi
Salwin, Arthur Elliott 1948- WhoE 93
Salwin, Harold 1915- WhoE 93
Salyer, Mark Walton 1959- WhoSSW 93
Salyer, Robert L. 1949- St&PR 93
Salyer, Stephen BioIn 17
Salyer, Stephen Lee 1950- WhoAm 92
Salyers, Thomas Edwin 1963- WhoSSW 93
Saly Vongkhamsao d1991 BioIn 17
Salz, Leon A. St&PR 93
Salza, Hermann von c. 1170-1239 HarEnMi
Salzarulo, Leonard Michael 1927- WhoAm 92
Salzberg, Allan Michael 1939- WhoE 93
Salzberg, Allen 1953- ConAu 137
Salzberg, Betty Joan 1944- WhoAmW 93
Salzberg, Harry L. 1948- St&PR 93
Salzberg, Robert Lewis Law&B 92
Salzedo, (Leon) Carlos 1885-1961 Baker 92
Salzedo, P. WhoScE 91-2
Salzen, Eric Arthur WhoScE 91-1
Salzer, Felix 1904-1986 Baker 92
Salzer, John Michael 1917- WhoAm 92
Salzer, Louis William 1918- WhoWor 93
Salzer, Thomas Benjamin Law&B 92
Salzer-Pagan, Joan Elizabeth 1934- WhoAmW 93
Salzhandler, Henry Law&B 92
Salzinger, Kurt 1929- WhoE 93
Salzman, Arthur George 1929- WhoAm 92
Salzman, David Elliot 1943- WhoAm 92
Salzman, Edwin William 1928- WhoE 93
Salzman, Eric 1933- Baker 92
Salzman, Eva (Frances) 1960- ConAu 139
Salzman, Glen 1951- MiSFD 9
Salzman, Herbert 1916-1990 BioIn 17
Salzman, Mark BioIn 17
Salzman, Mark (Joseph) 1959- ConAu 136
Salzman, Neil 1940- ConAu 139
Salzman, Stanley 1924-1991 BioIn 17
Salzman, Stephen Philip 1937- St&PR 93, WhoAm 92
Salzmann, George Stephen 1948- WhoE 93
Salzmann, Jacob A. d1992 NewYTBS 92
Salzmann, Siegmund 1869-1945 ConAu 137, MajAI [port]
Salzstein, Richard Alan 1959- WhoAm 92
Sam, Alfred Chief 1879- EncAACR
Sam, David 1933- WhoAm 92
Sam, Farzad 1957- WhoWor 93
Sam, Joseph 1923- WhoAm 92
Sama, Robert F. 1931- St&PR 93, WhoAm 92
Sama, Victoria E. 1962- WhoAmW 93
Samaan, Naguib Abdelmalik 1925- WhoAm 92, WhoWor 93
Samach, Michael Alan 1947- WhoE 93
Sa-Machado, Victor Nunes 1933- WhoWor 93
Samachson, Joseph 1906-1980 ScF&FL 92
Samaha, Emile Kozhaya 1933- WhoUN 92
Samaha, Francis Joseph 1928- WhoAm 92
Samaha, Richard John 1938- WhoE 93
Samaja, Michele 1951- WhoWor 93
Samake, Cyr Mathieu 1939- WhoUN 92
Samal, Jean 1928- WhoScE 91-2
Samalin, Edwin 1935- WhoWor 93
Samalman, Alexander ScF&FL 92
Samana, Utula 1951- WhoAsAP 91
Sam and Dave ConMus 8 [port], SoulM
Samanids OxDcByz
Samanin, Rosario 1938- WhoScE 91-3
Samara, Brenda Mary 1941- WhoAmW 93
Samara, Spiro 1861-1917 Baker 92

Samarakis, Antonis 1919- *ConAu 16AS [port]*
Samaranch, Juan Antonio 1920- *WhoWor 93*
Samaras, Antonis *BioIn 17*
Samaras, John Michael 1946- *WhoSSW 93*
Samaras, Lucas 1936- *BioIn 17*
Samaras, Spiridon 1861-1917 *OxDcOp*
Samaras, Zoe 1935- *WhoWor 93*
Samardich, Gordon R. *St&PR 93*
Samardzhiev, Dimitar *WhoScE 91-4*
Samargya, Michael J. 1934- *St&PR 93*
Samaritani, Pier Luigi 1942- *WhoWor 93*
Samaroff, Olga 1882-1948 *Baker 92*
Samarrai, Ahmad Husayn Khudayir Al *WhoWor 93*
Samartin, Avelino 1939- *WhoScE 91-3*
Samartin, Avelino Quiroga 1939- *WhoWor 93*
Samartini, James Rogers 1935- *St&PR 93, WhoAm 92*
Samat, Ramkishin Kanu 1945- *WhoE 93*
Samater, Ali Mohammed 1931- *WhoAfr*
Samawi, Khalil Khalil 1936- *WhoUN 92*
Samayoa, John F. 1930- *St&PR 93*
Samazeuilh, Gustave (Marie Victor Fernand) 1877-1967 *Baker 92*
Samba, Ebrahim Malick 1932- *WhoUN 92*
Sambach, Warren Austin, Jr. 1945- *WhoE 93*
Sambaluk, Nicholas Wayne 1955- *WhoSSW 93*
Sambasivam, Era 1924- *WhoAsAP 91*
Samber, David Mark 1949- *St&PR 93*
Samber, Richard Allan 1938- *St&PR 93*
Samber, Robert 1682-1745? *BioIn 17*
Samber, Roland Hayes 1924- *WhoSSW 93*
Samborski, Daniel J. 1922-1989 *BioIn 17*
Samborsky, Sergey Nikolaevitch 1944- *WhoWor 93*
Sambre, Christopher 1937- *WhoAsAP 91*
Sambrook, Arthur James 1931- *ConAu 40NR*
Sambur, Ned Elliot 1949- *St&PR 93*
Sambwa, Pida Nbagui 1940- *WhoAfr*
Samdal, John Erik 1927- *WhoScE 91-4*
Samejima, Fumiko *BioIn 17*
Samejima, Shigeo 1849-1928 *HarEnMi*
Samejima, Tomoshige 1889-1966 *HarEnMi*
Samek, Andrzej 1924- *WhoScE 91-4*
Samek, Edward L. 1936- *St&PR 93*
Samek, Michael Johann 1920- *WhoAm 92*
Samelson, Lincoln Russell 1926- *St&PR 93, WhoAm 92, WhoWor 93*
Samelson, William 1928- *ConAu 37NR*
Samenfeld, Herbert William 1924- *WhoE 93*
Sameroff, Arnold Joshua 1937- *WhoAm 92*
Samers, Bernard Norman 1934- *WhoE 93*
Samers, Edith 1938- *St&PR 93*
Samet, Andrew B. *Law&B 92*
Samet, Andrew B. 1941- *St&PR 93*
Samet, Andrew Benjamin 1941- *WhoAm 92*
Samet, Harry 1932- *St&PR 93*
Samet, Jack I. 1940- *WhoAm 92*
Sameth, Patricia A. *Law&B 92*
Sametz, Arnold William 1919- *WhoE 93*
Samford, Dan A. *Law&B 92*
Samford, Karen Elaine 1941- *WhoSSW 93*
Samford, Thomas Drake, III 1934- *WhoAm 92*
Samford, Yetta Glenn, Jr. 1923- *WhoAm 92*
Samide, M.R. 1944- *St&PR 93*
Samii, Abdol Hossein 1930- *WhoE 93, WhoWor 93*
Samilowitz, Hazel Faye 1940- *WhoE 93*
Samin, Ana Delia 1959- *WhoAmW 93*
Saminsky, Lazare 1882-1959 *Baker 92*
Samios, Nicholas Peter 1932- *WhoAm 92*
Samis, Gust A. 1936- *St&PR 93*
Samis, M.S. *St&PR 93*
Samko, Stefan Grigorievich 1941- *WhoWor 93*
Samloff, I. Michael 1932- *WhoAm 92*
Samlowski, Martin A. F. 1938- *WhoWor 93*
Sammad, Mohamed Abdel 1953- *WhoWor 93*
Samman, George 1946- *WhoAm 92*
Sammarco, Mario 1867-1930 *IntDcOp [port]*
Sammarco, Mario 1868-1930 *OxDcOp*
Sammarco, (Giuseppe) Mario 1868-1930 *Baker 92*
Sammarco, Paul William 1948- *WhoEmL 93*
Sammartin, Lawrence J. 1939- *St&PR 93*
Sammartini, Giovanni Battista 1700?-1775 *Baker 92, OxDcOp*
Sammartini, Giuseppe 1695-1750 *Baker 92*
Sammartino, Bruno *BioIn 17*
Sammartino, Peter d1992 *NewYTBS 92 [port]*
Sammartino, Peter 1904-1992 *BioIn 17, ConAu 137, CurBio 92N, WhoAm 92*
Sammartino, Sylvia 1903-1992 *WhoAm 92*
Sammataro, John Anthony 1931- *St&PR 93*
Sammataro, Nelva M. Weber d1990 *BioIn 17*
Sammes, Peter G. *WhoScE 91-1*
Sammet, Jean E. *WhoAm 92, WhoAmW 93*
Sammet, Rolf 1920- *WhoWor 93*
Sammis, Edward R. d1990 *BioIn 17*
Sammis, Stuart Keith 1954- *WhoE 93*
Sammon, Grace Marie 1953- *WhoE 93*
Sammon, Kevin Michael 1942- *WhoSSW 93*
Sammon, Paul M. 1949- *ScF&FL 92*
Sammond, John Stowell 1928- *WhoAm 92*
Sammons, Albert (Edward) 1886-1957 *Baker 92*
Sammons, Dennis M. 1948- *St&PR 93*
Sammons, Elaine D. *WhoAm 92*
Sammons, James E. 1933- *St&PR 93*
Sammons, Kristan Rodger *WhoE 93*
Sammons, Lenny H. 1954- *WhoAm 92*
Sammons, Martha C. 1949- *ScF&FL 92*
Sammons, Mary F. 1946- *WhoAm 92*
Sammons, Ronald C. 1943- *WhoIns 93*
Sammons, Ronald Colin 1943- *St&PR 93*
Sammut, Joe 1957- *WhoWor 93*
Samochocka, Krystyna Maria 1932- *WhoScE 91-4*
Samoggia, Giorgio 1934- *WhoScE 91-3*
Samojla, Scott Anthony 1955- *WhoEmL 93*
Samokhin, Alexey Vasilievitch 1947- *WhoWor 93*
Samolinska, Teofila 1848-1913 *PolBiDi*
Samolis, John Richard 1947- *St&PR 93*
Samonas *See* Gourias, Samonas, and Abibas *OxDcByz*
Samonas c. 875-c. 908 *OxDcByz*
Samora, Julian 1920- *HispAmA*
Samori Toure c. 1835-1900 *HarEnMi*
Samosky, Robert J. 1944- *St&PR 93*
Samostrzelnik, Stanislaw 1506-1541 *PolBiDi*
Samosud, Samuil (Abramovich) 1884-1964 *Baker 92*
Samotus, Alina Jozefa 1932- *WhoScE 91-4*
Samozwaniec, Magdalena 1899-1972 *PolBiDi*
Samp, Frederick S. *Law&B 92*
Samp, Nancy Carolyn 1946- *WhoAmW 93*
Sampaio, A. *WhoScE 91-3*
Sampas, Dorothy M. 1933- *WhoAmW 93, WhoWor 93*
Sampath, Elizabeth D. *Law&B 92*
Sampedro, Hortensia Edelmira 1950- *WhoEmL 93*
Sampedro, Jose Luis 1917- *WhoWor 93*
Sampel, James Richard 1932- *St&PR 93*
Samper, J. Phillip 1934- *St&PR 93*
Samper, Joseph Phillip 1934- *WhoAm 92*
Samperi, Frank V. 1933- *WhoWrEP 92*
Sampey, James J. 1933- *St&PR 93*
Sampias, Ernest J. 1951- *St&PR 93*
Sample, Dale 1945- *St&PR 93*
Sample, David *St&PR 93*
Sample, Frederick Palmer 1930- *WhoAm 92*
Sample, Joe *BioIn 17*
Sample, Joe 1939- *SoulM*
Sample, Joseph Scanlon 1923- *WhoAm 92*
Sample, Mary McGuire *Law&B 92*
Sample, Michael J. *Law&B 92*
Sample, Michael M. 1952- *St&PR 93*
Sample, Nathaniel Welshire 1918- *WhoAm 92*
Sample, Steven Browning 1940- *WhoAm 92, WhoWor 93*
Samples, Jerry Wayne 1947- *WhoE 93, WhoEmL 93*
Samples, Lenina Joy 1958- *WhoAmW 93*
Samples, Martina 1942- *WhoSSW 93*
Samples, Ronald Eugene 1926- *WhoAm 92*
Sampliner, Linda Hodes 1945- *WhoAmW 93*
Sampo, Roanld Lee 1932- *St&PR 93*
Sampou, Andre Peter 1931- *St&PR 93*
Sampras, Pete *BioIn 17*
Sampras, Pete 1971- *WhoAm 92*
Sampsell, Charles K. 1924- *St&PR 93*
Sampsell, David Fenner 1938- *WhoSSW 93*
Sampsell, Robert Bruce 1941- *St&PR 93*
Sampson, Anthony Terrell Seward 1926- *WhoWor 93*
Sampson, Bill *ConTFT 10*
Sampson, Bonnie P. 1942- *WhoAmW 93*
Sampson, Carol Ann 1942- *WhoWrEP 92*
Sampson, Curt 1952- *ConAu 139*
Sampson, Curtis A. 1933- *St&PR 93*
Sampson, Daniel Lee 1951- *WhoSSW 93*
Sampson, Daphne Rae 1943- *WhoAmW 93*
Sampson, David Synnott 1942- *WhoE 93*
Sampson, Edith S. 1901-1979 *ConBlB 4 [port]*
Sampson, Emma Speed 1868-1947 *BioIn 17*
Sampson, Fay *ChlFicS*
Sampson, Fay 1935- *ScF&FL 92*
Sampson, Fay (Elizabeth) 1935- *ConAu 40NR*
Sampson, Gail Elizabeth *AmWomPl*
Sampson, Gary Phillip 1943- *WhoUN 92*
Sampson, Geoffrey Richard *WhoScE 91-1*
Sampson, Gladys B. *AmWomPl*
Sampson, Harvey, Jr. 1929- *St&PR 93*
Sampson, Herschel Wayne 1944- *WhoSSW 93*
Sampson, John Eugene 1941- *St&PR 93, WhoAm 92*
Sampson, John Pierce 1940- *St&PR 93*
Sampson, Karen Leigh 1950- *WhoAmW 93*
Sampson, Kurt D. 1963- *St&PR 93*
Sampson, Larry B. *Law&B 92*
Sampson, Patsy Hallock 1932- *WhoAm 92, WhoAmW 93*
Sampson, Robert 1927- *ScF&FL 92*
Sampson, Robert Carl, Jr. 1948- *WhoE 93*
Sampson, Robert Neil 1938- *WhoAm 92*
Sampson, Ronald G. *Law&B 92*
Sampson, Ronald Gary 1942- *St&PR 93*
Sampson, Samuel Franklin 1934- *WhoAm 92*
Sampson, Steven Curtis 1958- *St&PR 93*
Sampson, Thyra Ann 1948- *WhoAmW 93*
Sampson, Vincent Louis 1946- *St&PR 93*
Sampson, William Thomas 1840-1902 *HarEnMi*
Sampson the Xenodochos *OxDcByz*
Sampter, Jessie Ethel 1883-1938 *AmWomPl*
Sampugna, Joseph 1931- *WhoE 93*
Samra, Cal *BioIn 17*
Samra, Victor M., Jr. 1941- *St&PR 93*
Samrin, Heng 1934- *ColdWar 2 [port]*
Sams, Carl Earnest 1951- *WhoSSW 93*
Sams, Cathy R. *Law&B 92*
Sams, David E., Jr. 1943- *St&PR 93*
Sams, David R. 1958- *ConAu 138*
Sams, David Ronald 1958- *WhoWor 93*
Sams, Eric 1926- *Baker 92*
Sams, Eristus d1990 *BioIn 17*
Sams, Ferrol 1922- *BioIn 17*
Sams, James F. *Law&B 92*
Sams, James Farid 1932- *WhoE 93, WhoWor 93*
Sams, John Roland 1922- *WhoAm 92*
Sams, Kenneth Dorsey 1951- *St&PR 93*
Sams, L. Wayne *Law&B 92*
Sams, Ross Martin, Jr. 1927- *St&PR 93*
Samsel, Maebell Scroggins 1940- *WhoSSW 93*
Samsiev, Bolotbek 1941- *DrEEuF*
Samsil, D. M. 1946- *WhoSSW 93*
Samson *BioIn 17*
Samson, Alain R. 1953- *St&PR 93*
Samson, Alexander M., Jr. *Law&B 92*
Samson, Allen Lawrence 1939- *WhoAm 92*
Samson, Alvin 1917- *WhoAm 92*
Samson, Carla Elaine 1951- *WhoAmW 93*
Samson, Charles Harold, Jr. 1924- *WhoAm 92*
Samson, Eugene Gabor *Law&B 92*
Samson, Frederick Eugene, Jr. 1918- *WhoWor 93*
Samson, James A. 1949- *St&PR 93*
Samson, Joan 1937-1976 *ScF&FL 92*
Samson, M.S. 1941- *St&PR 93*
Samson, Richard Max 1946- *WhoAm 92*
Samson, Solomon B. 1947- *St&PR 93*
Samson-Doel, Michelle 1958- *St&PR 93*
Samsonov, Aleksandr Vasilievich 1859-1914 *HarEnMi*
Samsonov, Samson 1921- *DrEEuF*
Samter, Max 1908- *WhoAm 92*
Samudio, David *DcCPCAm*
Samudio, Maria Mercedes 1965- *WhoAmW 93*
Samudragupta d375 *HarEnMi*
Samuel *BioIn 17*
Samuel, Adolphe (-Abraham) 1824-1898 *Baker 92*
Samuel, Alan E(douard) 1932- *ConAu 37NR*
Samuel, Arthur L. 1901-1990 *BioIn 17*
Samuel, Athanasius Yeshue 1907- *WhoAm 92*
Samuel, Dan Judah 1925- *WhoE 93, WhoWor 93*
Samuel, Edmond 1929- *WhoScE 91-2*
Samuel, Gerhard 1924- *Baker 92, WhoAm 92*
Samuel, Harold 1879-1937 *Baker 92*
Samuel, Howard David 1924- *WhoAm 92*
Samuel, Irene 1915-1991 *BioIn 17*
Samuel, Joseph H. 1925- *St&PR 93*
Samuel, K. 1953- *St&PR 93*
Samuel, Leopold 1883-1975 *Baker 92*
Samuel, Maurice 1895-1972 *JeAmFiW*
Samuel, Ralph David 1945- *WhoWor 93*
Samuel, Robert Thompson 1944- *WhoWor 93*
Samuel, Sally *Law&B 92*
Samuel, Stuart Alan 1953- *WhoE 93*
Samuel, Taraja Fraser *BioIn 17*
Samuel, Taraja Linda Fraser d1992 *NewYTBS 92*
Samuel, Thevapalan David 1940- *WhoWor 93*
Samuel, Valerie Jane 1957- *WhoAmW 93*
Samuel of Ani *OxDcByz*
Samuel of Bulgaria d1014 *OxDcByz*
Samuel-Rousseau, Marcel *Baker 92*
Samuels, Abram 1920- *WhoAm 92*
Samuels, Alfred Putnam, Jr. 1926- *WhoWrEP 92*
Samuels, Andrew Albert, Jr. 1937- *St&PR 93*
Samuels, Anne D. *Law&B 92*
Samuels, Carl Eugene 1953- *WhoE 93*
Samuels, Cynthia Kalish 1946- *WhoAmW 93, WhoEmL 93*
Samuels, Donald 1943- *St&PR 93*
Samuels, Ellen R. *Law&B 92*
Samuels, Eloise Wood 1950- *WhoAmW 93*
Samuels, Ernest 1903- *BioIn 17, WhoAm 92*
Samuels, Gloria Heard *BioIn 17*
Samuels, Helen 1931- *St&PR 93*
Samuels, J. Victor 1940- *St&PR 93*
Samuels, Jerald M. 1936- *WhoE 93*
Samuels, John M. *Law&B 92*
Samuels, John Malcolm *WhoScE 91-1*
Samuels, Jonathan *Law&B 92*
Samuels, Leslie Eugene 1929- *WhoWor 93*
Samuels, Louis P. 1922- *St&PR 93*
Samuels, Morton 1925- *St&PR 93*
Samuels, Nathaniel 1908- *WhoAm 92*
Samuels, Paul E. *Law&B 92*
Samuels, Richard Mel 1943- *WhoE 93, WhoWor 93*
Samuels, Robert 1957- *St&PR 93*
Samuels, Robert J. *BioIn 17*
Samuels, Robert Walter 1929- *St&PR 93*
Samuels, Ronald Larry 1946- *St&PR 93*
Samuels, Sandor E. 1952- *St&PR 93*
Samuels, Sandor Eli *Law&B 92*
Samuels, Seymour, Jr. 1912- *WhoAm 92, WhoSSW 93*
Samuels, Sheldon Wilfred 1929- *WhoAm 92*
Samuels, Sherwin L. 1935- *St&PR 93, WhoAm 92*
Samuels, Shirley Chasins 1930- *WhoAmW 93*
Samuels, Stephen Edmund 1949- *WhoWor 93*
Samuels, Walter 1950- *St&PR 93*
Samuels, Warren J. 1933- *BioIn 17*
Samuels, William Mason 1929- *WhoAm 92*
Samuelsen, Ragnar T. 1942- *WhoScE 91-4*
Samuelsen, Roy 1933- *WhoAm 92*
Samuelson, Bernard J. 1942- *St&PR 93*
Samuelson, Carl Gustaf Ebbe 1948- *WhoWor 93*
Samuelson, Charles Harry 1929- *WhoSSW 93*
Samuelson, David N. 1939- *ScF&FL 92*
Samuelson, Derrick W. 1929- *St&PR 93*
Samuelson, Derrick William *Law&B 92*
Samuelson, Derrick William 1929- *WhoAm 92*
Samuelson, Ellen Banman 1930- *WhoAmW 93*
Samuelson, Georgia Jamie 1950- *WhoWrEP 92*
Samuelson, Joan *BioIn 17*
Samuelson, Karl-Rune 1927- *WhoScE 91-4*
Samuelson, Kenneth Lee 1946- *WhoE 93, WhoEmL 93*
Samuelson, Lance Denzel 1944- *St&PR 93*
Samuelson, Marvin Lee 1931- *WhoAm 92*
Samuelson, Paul A(nthony) 1915- *ConAu 40NR*
Samuelson, Paul Anthony 1915- *BioIn 17, JeAmHC, WhoAm 92, WhoE 93, WhoWor 93*
Samuelson, Robert Jacob 1945- *WhoAm 92*
Samuelson, Robert L. 1928- *St&PR 93*
Samuelson, Robert William 1933- *St&PR 93*
Samuelson, Sue 1956-1991 *BioIn 17*
Samuelson, Sylvia Heller *WhoE 93*
Samuelsson, Alf G. 1929- *WhoScE 91-4*
Samuelsson, Alf George 1929- *WhoWor 93*
Samuelsson, Arne 1933- *St&PR 93*
Samuelsson, Bengt I. 1934- *WhoScE 91-4*
Samuelsson, Bengt Ingemar 1934- *WhoAm 92, WhoWor 93*
Samuelsson, Gunnar 1925- *WhoScE 91-4*

Samyn, Gilbert L.J.H. 1946- *WhoScE 91-2*
Samy Vellu, Dato' 1936- *WhoAsAP 91*
Samz, Jane Dede *WhoWor 93*
San, Hlaing Myint 1939- *WhoWor 93*
San, Nguyen Duy 1932- *WhoWor 93*
Sanabria, Victor *DcCPCAm*
Sanadi, D. Rao 1920- *WhoE 93*
Sananman, Michael Lawrence 1939- *WhoE 93*
San Antonio, Joel 1952- *St&PR 93*
Sanator, Robert Joseph 1930- *St&PR 93*
Sanaullah, Andrew Suleman 1916- *WhoWor 93*
Sanbar, Samir H. 1934- *WhoUN 92*
Sanberg, Paul Ronald 1955- *WhoWrEP 92*
San Biagio, Pier Luigi 1952- *WhoWor 93*
Sanborn, Anna Lucille 1924- *WhoAmW 93*
Sanborn, Benjamin Franklin 1831-1917 *JrnUS*
Sanborn, David *BioIn 17*
Sanborn, David 1945- *CurBio 92 [port], SoulM*
Sanborn, Doreen Kay 1948- *WhoWor 93*
Sanborn, L.T. 1928- *St&PR 93*
Sanborn, Margaret 1915- *St&PR 93*
Sanborn, Robert Burns 1929- *WhoIns 93*
Sanborn, Robert Charles 1914- *St&PR 93*
Sanborn, Robert Harvey 1949- *WhoSSW 93*
Sanborn, Russell *BioIn 17*
Sanborn, Terry L. 1943- *St&PR 93*
Sanborn, Theodore 1921- *St&PR 93*
Sanborn, Theodore S. 1921- *WhoAm 92*
Sanborn, Walter D., III 1943- *St&PR 93*
Sanc, Ivo 1955- *WhoScE 91-4*
Sancak, Bedia 1932- *WhoScE 91-4*
Sances, Giovanni Felice c. 1600-1679 *Baker 92, OxDcOp*
Sancetta, Constance Antonina 1949- *WhoAmW 93*
Sanchelli, Charles Raymond 1951- *WhoSSW 93*
Sanches, Aderito Alain 1945- *WhoScE 91-2*
Sanches Furtado, A.F. 1930- *WhoScE 91-3*
Sanchez, Antonio R., Sr. *St&PR 93*
Sanchez, Beatrice Rivas 1941- *WhoAmW 93*
Sanchez, Berta 1960- *WhoWor 93*
Sanchez, Carol A. 1961- *NotHsAW 93*
Sanchez, D. Jean 1948- *WhoAmW 93*
Sanchez, David Alan 1933- *WhoAm 92*
Sanchez, Dennis *Law&B 92*
Sanchez, Dolores 1936- *NotHsAW 93*
Sanchez, Eduardo B. *Law&B 92*
Sanchez, Eugenio 1951- *WhoSSW 93*
Sanchez, Fernando V. 1953- *St&PR 93*
Sanchez, Francisco 1936- *WhoScE 91-3*
Sanchez, Francisco P. 1960- *WhoWrEP 92*
Sanchez, Gali 1951- *ScF&FL 92*
Sanchez, George I. 1906-1972 *HispAmA*
Sanchez, Gilbert 1938- *WhoAm 92*
Sanchez, Gilberto 1942- *WhoWor 93*
Sanchez, Hortensia O. 1947- *WhoSSW 93*
Sanchez, Isaac Cornelius 1941- *WhoSSW 93*
Sanchez, Isis Rubio 1956- *WhoAmW 93*
Sanchez, J. Jose 1927- *WhoScE 91-3*
Sanchez, Janice Patterson 1948- *WhoAmW 93*
Sanchez, Laura Balverde *NotHsAW 93*
Sanchez, Leonedes Monarrize W. 1951- *WhoEmL 93, WhoWor 93*
Sanchez, Luis Rafael 1936- *SpAmA*
Sanchez, Manuel A. 1959- *St&PR 93*
Sanchez, Maria d1989 *BioIn 17*
Sanchez, Maria E. 1927- *NotHsAW 93*
Sanchez, Marla Rena 1956- *WhoAmW 93, WhoWor 93*
Sanchez, Marta *WhoAm 92*
Sanchez, Maurice *Law&B 92*
Sanchez, Nancy Eileen 1956- *WhoWrEP 92*
Sanchez, Olga Jonas *Law&B 92*
Sanchez, Orlando Edmundo 1938- *WhoWor 93*
Sanchez, Oscar Arias *BioIn 17*
Sanchez, Osmundo, Jr. 1939- *WhoWor 93*
Sanchez, Pancho *BioIn 17*
Sanchez, Paul J. *St&PR 93*
Sanchez, Pedro Antonio 1940- *HispAmA [port]*
Sanchez, Philomeno 1917- *DcLB 122 [port]*
Sanchez, Rafael Camilo 1919- *WhoAm 92*
Sanchez, Ralph H. *St&PR 93*
Sanchez, Raymond G. 1941- *WhoAm 92*
Sanchez, Ricardo 1941- *HispAmA [port], WhoWrEP 92*
Sanchez, Robert Fortune 1934- *WhoAm 92*
Sanchez, Robert Francis 1938- *WhoAm 92*
Sanchez, Rosaura 1941- *HispAmA*
Sanchez, Ruben Dario 1943- *WhoWor 93*
Sanchez, Sonia 1934- *BioIn 17, MajAI [port]*
Sanchez, Susan B. *Law&B 92*
Sanchez, Sylvia Deleon 1951- *St&PR 93*
Sanchez, Terence Michael *Law&B 92*
Sanchez, Vanessa Mia 1963- *WhoAmW 93*
Sanchez, Virginia Korrol 20th cent.- *HispAmA*
Sanchez, Wanda Ivette 1956- *WhoAmW 93*
Sanchez, William Arthur 1936- *St&PR 93*
Sanchez-Arcilla, Agustin 1955- *WhoScE 91-3*
Sanchez-Atzel, Alejandro 1964- *WhoEmL 93*
Sanchez Camazano, Maria 1933- *WhoScE 91-3*
Sanchez Coello, Alonso 1531?-1588 *BioIn 17*
Sanchez de Fuentes, Eduardo 1874-1944 *Baker 92*
Sanchez De La Puente, Luis 1932- *WhoScE 91-3*
Sanchez Del Rio, Carlos 1924- *WhoScE 91-3*
Sanchez-Diaz, Manuel F. 1942- *WhoScE 91-3*
Sanchez Flores, Daniel d1990 *BioIn 17*
Sanchez Gutierrez, Abelardo 1943- *WhoUN 92*
Sanchez-Imizcoz, Ruth 1960- *WhoSSW 93*
Sanchez-Llaca, Juan 1960- *WhoAm 92*
Sanchez Lujan, Gilbert 1940- *HispAmA*
Sanchez Marmol, Manuel 1839-1912 *DcMexL*
Sanchez Osuna, Mayra Regina 1947- *WhoUN 92*
Sanchez-Perez, Angel M. 1944- *WhoScE 91-3*
Sanchez-Salinero, Ignacio 1954- *WhoWor 93*
Sanchez-Scott, Milcha 1953- *NotHsAW 93*
Sanchez-Silva, Jose Maria 1911- *MajAI [port]*
Sanchez-Torrento, Eugenio 1928- *WhoSSW 93*
Sanchez Vilella, Roberto *DcCPCAm*
Sanchini, Dominick J. d1990 *BioIn 17*
Sancho, Jose Maria 1948- *WhoWor 93*
Sancho-Garnier, Helene *WhoScE 91-2*
Sancho-Garnier, Helene 1939- *WhoWor 93*
Sand, Benno G. 1954- *St&PR 93*
Sand, George 1804-1876 *BioIn 17, DcLB 119 [port], WorLitC [port]*
Sand, George X. *WhoWrEP 92*
Sand, Leonard B. 1928- *WhoE 93*
Sand, Margaret 1932- *ScF&FL 92*
Sand, Peter H. 1936- *WhoUN 92*
Sand, Robert H. *Law&B 92*
Sand, William 1945- *WhoSSW 93*
Sanda, Dominique 1948- *BioIn 17, IntDcF 2-3 [port]*
Sandage, Allan Rex 1926- *WhoAm 92*
Sandage, Charles Harold 1902- *WhoAm 92*
Sandage, Elizabeth Anthea 1930- *WhoWor 93*
Sandahl, Bonnie Beardsley 1939- *WhoAmW 93*
Sandahl, Skov K. 1922- *WhoScE 91-2*
Sandalls, William Thomas, Jr. 1944- *WhoAm 92*
Sandalow, Terrance 1934- *WhoAm 92*
Sandarg, Janet Icenhour 1949- *WhoSSW 93*
Sandars, P.G.H. *WhoScE 91-1*
Sandback, Frederick Lane 1943- *WhoAm 92*
Sandbank, Henry 1932- *WhoAm 92*
Sandberg, Carolyn Masami *Law&B 92*
Sandberg, Hans Torbjorn 1946- *WhoWor 93*
Sandberg, Irwin David 1935- *St&PR 93, WhoAm 92*
Sandberg, Irwin Walter 1934- *WhoAm 92*
Sandberg, Job B.B. 1946- *St&PR 93*
Sandberg, Joel E. 1950- *St&PR 93*
Sandberg, John A. *Law&B 92*
Sandberg, John Ronald *Law&B 92*
Sandberg, Jorgen 1950- *WhoWor 93*
Sandberg, Kathy 1964- *WhoAmW 93*
Sandberg, Mordecai 1897-1973 *Baker 92*
Sandberg, Ray 1940- *BioIn 17*
Sandberg, Richard A. 1942- *St&PR 93*
Sandberg, Richard J. 1927- *St&PR 93*
Sandberg, Robert Alexis 1914- *WhoAm 92*
Sandberg, Robert Gustave 1939- *WhoE 93*
Sandberg, Ryne *BioIn 17*
Sandberg, Ryne 1959- *WhoAm 92*
Sandberg, Stevan A. *Law&B 92*
Sandberg, Stevan A. 1952- *St&PR 93*
Sandberg, Torbjorn *WhoScE 91-4*
Sandberg, Ulf S.I. 1946- *WhoWor 93*
Sandberg, W. Gary 1946- *St&PR 93*
Sandberger, Adolf 1864-1943 *Baker 92*
Sandbo, John H. 1931- *St&PR 93*
Sandbulte, Arend John 1933- *St&PR 93, WhoAm 92*
Sandburg, Carl 1878-1967 *BioIn 17, MagSAmL [port], WorLitC [port]*
Sandburg, Carl (August) 1878-1967 *MajAI [port]*
Sandburg, Charles *MajAI*
Sandburg, Charles A. *MajAI*
Sandburg, Helga 1918- *WhoAm 92, WhoWrEP 92*
Sandburg, Richard Rex 1925- *St&PR 93*
Sandby, Hermann 1881-1965 *Baker 92*
Sande, Barbara 1939- *WhoWor 93*
Sande, Ervin Elder 1932- *St&PR 93*
Sande, Gunvald 1918- *St&PR 93*
Sande, Ronald Gene 1941- *St&PR 93*
Sande, Theodore Anton 1933- *WhoAm 92*
Sandebring, Hans 1944- *WhoScE 91-4*
Sandeelo, Zeeba Karim 1949- *WhoWor 93*
Sandefur, James Daniel 1941- *WhoSSW 93*
Sandefur, Thomas E., Jr. *St&PR 93*
Sandefur, Thomas Edwin, Jr. 1939- *WhoAm 92, WhoSSW 93*
Sandel, Charles R. *Law&B 92*
Sandel, Cora 1880-1974 *BioIn 17*
Sandelin, Clarence K. 1915- *ScF&FL 92*
Sandelin, Karl R. 1928- *St&PR 93*
Sandell, Hakan A. 1944- *WhoScE 91-4*
Sandell, Richard Arnold 1937- *WhoAm 92, WhoE 93, WhoWor 93*
Sandell, William *BioIn 17*
Sandelman, Sanford Melvyn 1925- *St&PR 93*
Sandeman, Mina *ScF&FL 92*
Sandeman, T.C. 1947- *St&PR 93*
Sandeman, Thomas J. 1948- *St&PR 93*
Sanden, Bo Ingvar 1946- *WhoSSW 93*
Sander, Donald Henry 1933- *WhoAm 92*
Sander, Dorothy L. *Law&B 92*
Sander, Gary H. 1949- *St&PR 93*
Sander, Hans-Joerg 1941- *WhoWor 93*
Sander, Klaus 1929- *WhoScE 91-3*
Sander, Lawrence D. *WhoWrEP 92*
Sander, Lincoln Raymond 1939- *St&PR 93*
Sander, Malvin G. *Law&B 92*
Sander, Malvin Gustav 1946- *St&PR 93, WhoAm 92*
Sander, Raymond John 1944- *WhoAm 92*
Sander, Rudolph Charles 1930- *WhoAm 92*
Sander, Volkmar 1929- *WhoAm 92*
Sander, Wilhelm 1929- *WhoScE 91-3*
Sander, William August, III 1942- *WhoSSW 93*
Sandercox, Robert Allen 1932- *WhoAm 92*
Sandergaard, Theordore Jorgensen 1946- *WhoWor 93*
Sanderlin, Eva Slover 1924- *WhoWrEP 92*
Sanderlin, George 1915- *WhoWrEP 92*
Sanderlin, M.L. 1946- *St&PR 93*
Sanderlin, Owenita Harrah 1916- *WhoWrEP 92*
Sanderling, Kurt 1912- *Baker 92*
Sanderling, Thomas 1942- *Baker 92*
Sanders, Aaron Perry 1924- *WhoAm 92*
Sanders, Andra Danielle *Law&B 92*
Sanders, Barbara Heeb 1938- *WhoSSW 93*
Sanders, Barefoot 1925- *WhoAm 92*
Sanders, Barry *BioIn 17*
Sanders, Barry 1968- *News 92 [port], WhoAm 92*
Sanders, Barry David 1968- *BiDAMSp 1989*
Sanders, Benjamin Elbert 1918- *WhoAm 92*
Sanders, Bernard *BioIn 17*
Sanders, Bernard 1941- *CngDr 91, WhoAm 92, WhoE 93*
Sanders, Bill 1951- *ConAu 137*
Sanders, Billiesue Tankersley 1952- *WhoAmW 93*
Sanders, Bobby Lee 1935- *WhoSSW 93*
Sanders, Brice Sidney 1930- *WhoAm 92*
Sanders, Bryan Henry 1937- *St&PR 93*
Sanders, Carol R. *Law&B 92*
Sanders, Charlene Lorla Heflinger 1924- *WhoAmW 93*
Sanders, Charles A. 1933- *WhoSSW 93*
Sanders, Charles Addison 1932- *St&PR 93, WhoAm 92*
Sanders, Charles Franklin 1931- *WhoAm 92*
Sanders, Charles G. 1943- *St&PR 93*
Sanders, Charles Leonard *BioIn 17*
Sanders, Charles Martin, Jr. 1939- *St&PR 93*
Sanders, Charmaine Yevette 1966- *WhoSSW 93*
Sanders, Clinton R. 1944- *ConAu 139*
Sanders, Colonel 1890-1980 *BioIn 17*
Sanders, Cora A. *AmWomPl*
Sanders, David E. *Law&B 92*
Sanders, Debra Faye 1952- *WhoWrEP 92*
Sanders, Deion *BioIn 17*
Sanders, Deion 1967- *ConBlB 4 [port], News 92 [port]*
Sanders, Deion Luwynn 1967- *WhoAm 92*
Sanders, Dori *BioIn 17*
Sanders, Dwain Dupree 1947- *St&PR 93*
Sanders, Ed 1939- *BioIn 17*
Sanders, Edith Anne 1934- *WhoAmW 93*
Sanders, Elmer Blair 1923- *St&PR 93*
Sanders, Esther Jeannette 1926- *WhoWrEP 92*
Sanders, Eugene Thomas 1950- *St&PR 93*
Sanders, Evelyn Beatrice 1931- *WhoAmW 93*
Sanders, Everett 1882-1950 *BioIn 17, PolPar*
Sanders, Franklin D. 1935- *St&PR 93, WhoAm 92, WhoIns 93*
Sanders, Fred Joseph 1928- *WhoAm 92*
Sanders, Frederick 1923- *WhoAm 92*
Sanders, Gary Glenn 1944- *WhoWor 93*
Sanders, Gary Wayne 1949- *WhoAm 92*
Sanders, Geoff *WhoScE 91-1*
Sanders, George 1906-1973 *IntDcF 2-3 [port]*
Sanders, George Douglas 1933- *BiDAMSp 1989*
Sanders, Georgia Elizabeth 1933- *WhoSSW 93, WhoWor 93*
Sanders, Gerald Hollie 1924- *WhoWor 93*
Sanders, Gerald Martin 1947- *WhoSSW 93*
Sanders, Gilbert Otis 1945- *WhoWor 93*
Sanders, Glenn R. 1926- *WhoAm 92*
Sanders, H.R., Jr. 1932- *St&PR 93*
Sanders, Harland 1890-1980 *BioIn 17*
Sanders, Harold August, Jr. 1930- *WhoSSW 93*
Sanders, Harold Barefoot, Jr. 1925- *WhoAm 92, WhoSSW 93*
Sanders, Hassel Marteen 1930- *St&PR 93, WhoAm 92*
Sanders, Howard 1941- *WhoAm 92*
Sanders, Howard R. 1947- *St&PR 93*
Sanders, I.S. 1947- *WhoScE 91-3*
Sanders, Irwin Taylor 1909- *WhoAm 92*
Sanders, J.R. *ScF&FL 92*
Sanders, Jack Ford 1918- *WhoAm 92*
Sanders, Jack Thomas 1935- *WhoAm 92*
Sanders, Jacquelyn Seevak 1931- *WhoAmW 93*
Sanders, James Alvin 1927- *WhoAm 92*
Sanders, James Grady 1951- *WhoE 93*
Sanders, James Joseph 1946- *St&PR 93*
Sanders, James W. *Law&B 92*
Sanders, Jay William 1924- *WhoAm 92*
Sanders, Jean Marie 1939- *WhoAmW 93*
Sanders, Jeff Davis 1931- *WhoSSW 93*
Sanders, Jerome *St&PR 93*
Sanders, Jill Marie 1964- *WhoAmW 93*
Sanders, Joann Johnson 1935- *WhoSSW 93*
Sanders, John *Law&B 92*
Sanders, John David 1938- *WhoSSW 93*
Sanders, John Grayson 1940- *St&PR 93*
Sanders, John Lassiter 1927- *WhoAm 92*
Sanders, John Theodore 1941- *WhoAm 92*
Sanders, Johnny d1990 *BioIn 17*
Sanders, Joseph L. 1940- *ScF&FL 92*
Sanders, Joseph M. *Law&B 92*
Sanders, Joseph Stanley 1942- *WhoAm 92*
Sanders, Judith Mabel 1951- *WhoAmW 93*
Sanders, Karl 1930- *St&PR 93*
Sanders, Kay Marie 1947- *WhoAmW 93*
Sanders, Keith R. 1939- *WhoAm 92*
Sanders, Kinney L. 1934- *St&PR 93*
Sanders, Laura Beth 1952- *WhoAmW 93*
Sanders, Lawrence 1920- *BioIn 17, ScF&FL 92, WhoAm 92, WhoWrEP 92*
Sanders, Leonard Marion, Jr. 1929- *WhoWrEP 92*
Sanders, Linda 1950- *WhoAmW 93*
Sanders, Louisa Ann Vilensky 1956- *WhoE 93*
Sanders, Luzetta *AmWomPl*
Sanders, Mabelle P. *AmWomPl*
Sanders, Marc Andrew 1947- *WhoSSW 93*
Sanders, Margaret Webb *AmWomPl*
Sanders, Marguerite Dees 1914- *WhoSSW 93*
Sanders, Marilyn Miller 1932- *WhoSSW 93*
Sanders, Marlene *BioIn 17*
Sanders, Marlene 1931- *WhoAm 92, WhoAmW 93*
Sanders, Mary Elizabeth 1917- *WhoAmW 93*
Sanders, Mary Louise 1951- *WhoAmW 93*
Sanders, Melanie 1955- *WhoAmW 93*
Sanders, Morton *BioIn 17*
Sanders, Norman Karl 1932- *WhoAsAP 91*
Sanders, Ona Carol 1939- *WhoAmW 93*
Sanders, Paul 1891-1986 *Baker 92*
Sanders, Paul Hampton 1909- *WhoAm 92*
Sanders, Peggy Jean 1928- *WhoAmW 93*

Sanders, Peter *Law&B 92*
Sanders, Pharoah 1940- *BioIn 17, WhoAm 92*
Sanders, Phyllis Aden 1919- *WhoAmW 93*
Sanders, Randolph Kent 1952- *WhoSSW 93*
Sanders, Randy W. 1948- *St&PR 93*
Sanders, Richard Henry 1944- *WhoAm 92*
Sanders, Richard Kinard 1940- *WhoAm 92*
Sanders, Richard L. 1937- *WhoE 93*
Sanders, Richard Louis 1949- *WhoAm 92*
Sanders, Richard Scott 1950- *St&PR 93*
Sanders, Robert H. *Law&B 92*
Sanders, Robert L(evine) 1906-1974 *Baker 92*
Sanders, Robert Martin 1928- *WhoAm 92*
Sanders, Roger Cobban 1936- *WhoAm 92*
Sanders, Ronald *BioIn 17*
Sanders, Russell Edward 1949- *WhoSSW 93*
Sanders, Ruth Ann Nomathemba Sidzumo 1941- *WhoAmW 93*
Sanders, Ruth Manning- *ScF&FL 92*
Sanders, Samuel 1937- *Baker 92*
Sanders, Scott R. 1945- *BioIn 17*
Sanders, Scott Russell 1945- *ScF&FL 92, WhoWrEP 92*
Sanders, Sharon *WhoWrEP 92*
Sanders, Sharon Michelle 1955- *WhoEmL 93*
Sanders, Steve *WhoAm 92*
Sanders, Steve A. 1951- *St&PR 93*
Sanders, Steven Gill 1936- *WhoSSW 93, WhoWor 93*
Sanders, Stuart Anthony Compton *WhoScE 91-1*
Sanders, Summer 1972- *WhoAmW 93*
Sanders, Teressa Irene 1951- *WhoE 93*
Sanders, Thomas Joseph, Sr. 1942- *WhoAm 92*
Sanders, Vernon Charles 1930- *St&PR 93*
Sanders, Wallace Wolfred, Jr. 1933- *WhoAm 92*
Sanders, Walter J., III 1936- *St&PR 93*
Sanders, Walter Jeremiah, III 1936- *WhoAm 92*
Sanders, Wayne R. 1947- *St&PR 93, WhoAm 92, WhoSSW 93*
Sanders, William *ScF&FL 92*
Sanders, William Beauregarde *WhoSSW 93*
Sanders, William Eugene 1933- *WhoSSW 93, WhoWor 93*
Sanders, William Eugene, Jr. 1934- *WhoAm 92*
Sanders, William George 1932- *WhoAm 92*
Sanders, William H. d1992 *NewYTBS 92*
Sanderson, Arthur Clark 1946- *WhoE 93*
Sanderson, Christian C. d1966 *BioIn 17*
Sanderson, Chuck 1943- *St&PR 93*
Sanderson, Dave *BioIn 17*
Sanderson, David Alan 1951- *WhoWor 93*
Sanderson, David Odell 1956- *WhoSSW 93*
Sanderson, Dawn A. 1954- *WhoAmW 93*
Sanderson, Dennis Darrell 1944- *St&PR 93*
Sanderson, Diana Lee 1957- *WhoAmW 93, WhoSSW 93*
Sanderson, Eric George 1948- *WhoE 93*
Sanderson, Eric W. 1950- *St&PR 93*
Sanderson, Frank H. *WhoScE 91-1*
Sanderson, Fred Hugo 1914- *WhoAm 92*
Sanderson, Gary Warner 1934- *St&PR 93, WhoAm 92*
Sanderson, George Edmond 1951- *St&PR 93*
Sanderson, George H. 1927- *St&PR 93*
Sanderson, Irma 1912- *BioIn 17*
Sanderson, Jack T. 1936- *St&PR 93*
Sanderson, James Richard 1925- *WhoAm 92*
Sanderson, Jeffrey John *WhoScE 91-1*
Sanderson, Jerrell Dee 1959- *WhoSSW 93*
Sanderson, Joe Frank 1925- *St&PR 93*
Sanderson, John M., Jr. 1938- *St&PR 93*
Sanderson, Lester E. 1920- *St&PR 93*
Sanderson, Philip James *WhoScE 91-1*
Sanderson, Richard D. 1941- *St&PR 93*
Sanderson, Richard Elmer 1936- *WhoAm 92*
Sanderson, Richard Lewis, Jr. *Law&B 92*
Sanderson, Robert C. 1939- *St&PR 93*
Sanderson, Robert G. 1941- *St&PR 93*
Sanderson, Robert George 1943- *WhoWor 93*
Sanderson, Sandra B. 1943- *St&PR 93*
Sanderson, Sibyl 1865-1903 *Baker 92, OxDcOp*
Sanderson, Sybil 1865-1903 *IntDcOp [port]*
Sanderson, Virginia *AmWomPl*
Sanderson, Walter H., Jr. *AfrAmBi*
Sandeson, William Seymour 1913- *WhoAm 92*
Sandford, Emily White *AmWomPl*
Sandford, Frank W. 1862-1948 *BioIn 17*
Sandford, Herbert Adolphus 1927- *WhoWor 93*
Sandford, John *ConAu 138*
Sandford, John 1944- *BioIn 17*
Sandfort, Peter H., Jr. 1944- *St&PR 93*
Sandgrund, David M. *Law&B 92*
Sandham, William Allan 1952- *WhoWor 93*
Sandhas, Werner E. 1934- *WhoScE 91-3*
Sandhaus, Ronald Evan *Law&B 92*
Sandhoff, Konrad 1939- *WhoScE 91-3*
Sandholm, Markus W. 1943- *WhoScE 91-4*
Sandhouse, Mark Eric 1961- *WhoSSW 93*
Sandhu, Bachittar Singh 1935- *WhoWor 93*
Sandhu, Hargurpal Singh 1936- *WhoWor 93*
Sandhu, James *WhoScE 91-1*
Sandhu, Rajpal 1962- *WhoE 93*
Sandi, Horea Mircea Ioan 1932- *WhoScE 91-4*
Sandi, Luis 1905- *Baker 92*
Sandidge, Kanita Durice 1947- *WhoAmW 93, WhoE 93, WhoWor 93*
Sandifer, Linda P. 1951- *WhoWrEP 92*
Sandifer, Rosie *BioIn 17*
Sandifer, Wallace L. 1926- *St&PR 93*
Sandiford, Cedric d1991 *BioIn 17*
Sandiford, Erskine 1937- *DcCPCAm*
Sandiford, Kimberly Elyse 1965- *WhoAmW 93*
Sandiford, Lloyd Erskine 1937- *WhoWor 93*
Sandifur, C. Paul, Sr. 1903- *St&PR 93*
Sandifur, C. Paul, Jr. 1941- *St&PR 93*
Sandifur, Cantwell Paul 1903- *WhoIns 93*
Sandifur, Cantwell Paul, Sr. 1903- *WhoAm 92*
Sandilands, Emma Louise 1966- *WhoWor 93*
Sandilos, Robert J. *Law&B 92*
Sandin, Benedict 1918-1982 *IntDcAn*
Sandin, W.T. 1934- *St&PR 93*
Sandino, Augusto Cesar 1895-1934 *BioIn 17, DcCPCAm*
Sandino, Augusto Cesar 1896-1934 *DcTwHis*
Sandison, Alan 1932- *ScF&FL 92*
Sanditen, Edgar Richard 1920- *WhoAm 92*
Sandklef, Stig 1937- *WhoScE 91-4*
Sandkuhler, Robert J. *Law&B 92*
Sandland, Eric Michael 1938- *WhoWor 93*
Sandland, Paul 1941- *St&PR 93*
Sandler, Aaron E. 1926- *St&PR 93*
Sandler, Bernice Resnick 1928- *WhoAmW 93*
Sandler, Fulton William 1923- *St&PR 93*
Sandler, Gerald H. 1934- *St&PR 93*
Sandler, Gerald Howard 1934- *WhoE 93*
Sandler, Guillermo Alberto 1933- *WhoWor 93*
Sandler, Herbert M. 1931- *St&PR 93, WhoAm 92*
Sandler, Irving Harry 1925- *WhoAm 92, WhoWrEP 92*
Sandler, Jenny *WhoAm 92*
Sandler, Jon L. *Law&B 92*
Sandler, Kay W. *Law&B 92*
Sandler, Kenneth Bruce 1942- *WhoE 93*
Sandler, Les *BioIn 17*
Sandler, Lewis H. 1936- *St&PR 93*
Sandler, Lucy Freeman 1930- *WhoAm 92, WhoWrEP 92*
Sandler, Marion O. 1930- *St&PR 93*
Sandler, Marion Osher 1930- *WhoAm 92, WhoAmW 93*
Sandler, Mark Jay 1957- *WhoSSW 93*
Sandler, Merton *WhoScE 91-1*
Sandler, Paul *Law&B 92*
Sandler, Robert A. *Law&B 92*
Sandler, Robert Michael 1942- *WhoAm 92*
Sandler, Roberta 1943- *WhoWrEP 92*
Sandler, Scott Eric 1954- *St&PR 93*
Sandler, Stanley Irving 1940- *WhoAm 92, WhoWor 93*
Sandler, Susan J. *Law&B 92*
Sandler, Thomas R. 1946- *WhoAm 92*
Sandler, Vicki Gene *Law&B 92*
Sandlin, Ann Marie 1940- *WhoSSW 93*
Sandlin, Joseph Ernest 1919- *WhoAm 92*
Sandlin, Steven Monroe 1935- *WhoWor 93*
Sandlin, Tim *BioIn 17*
Sandlin, Tim 1950- *WhoWrEP 92*
Sandman, Alan George 1947- *WhoSSW 93*
Sandman, Dan David *Law&B 92*
Sandman, Paul W. *Law&B 92*
Sandman, Paul William 1947- *St&PR 93*
Sandman, Robert L. 1927- *St&PR 93*
Sandman Lilius, Irmelin *ScF&FL 92*
Sandmeier, Ruedi Beat 1945- *WhoAm 92*
Sandmeyer, Robert Lee 1929- *WhoAm 92*
Sandmo, Agnar 1938- *WhoWor 93*
Sandner, Frank X., Jr. 1918- *St&PR 93*
Sandner, John Francis 1941- *WhoAm 92*
Sandnes, Kjartan 1953- *WhoScE 91-4*
Sandnes, Ron David 1942- *St&PR 93*
Sandness, Arne Olaf 1951- *WhoE 93*
Sandness, Paul Kent *Law&B 92*
Sando, Ernest 1941- *St&PR 93*
Sando, William Jasper 1927- *WhoSSW 93*
Sandok, Burton Alan 1937- *WhoAm 92*
Sandom, J. Gregory 1956- *ConAu 137*
Sandor, Arpad 1896-1972 *Baker 92*
Sandor, George Nason 1912- *WhoAm 92*
Sandor, Gyorgy *WhoAm 92*
Sandor, Gyorgy 1912- *Baker 92*
Sandor, Kenneth V. 1947- *St&PR 93*
Sandor, Leslie Thomas 1927- *St&PR 93*
Sandor, Pal 1939- *DrEEuF*
Sandor, Richard Laurence 1941- *WhoAm 92*
Sandor, Stefan 1927- *WhoScE 91-4*
Sandor, Thomas 1924- *WhoAm 92*
Sandorfy, Camille 1920- *WhoAm 92*
Sandorse, Donna Irene 1957- *WhoAmW 93*
Sandoval, Alicia 1943- *NotHsAW 93*
Sandoval, Anthony *BioIn 17*
Sandoval, Arturo *BioIn 17*
Sandoval, Carlos J. *Law&B 92*
Sandoval, Jose I. *Law&B 92*
Sandoval, Maria Olga 1964- *WhoWor 93*
Sandoval, Maureen *BioIn 17*
Sandoval, Miguel 1903-1953 *Baker 92*
Sandoval Alarcon, Mario 1923- *DcCPCAm*
Sandoval y Rojas, Francisco Gomez 1552-1625 *BioIn 17*
Sandow, Bruce Arnold 1945- *WhoSSW 93*
Sandowski, Norma Jewell 1940- *WhoAmW 93, WhoWor 93*
Sandoz, Mari 1896-1966 *BioIn 17*
Sandoz, Mari (Susette) 1901-1966 *DcAmChF 1960*
Sandoz, Rodney Joseph 1939- *St&PR 93*
Sandquist, Elroy Charles, Jr. 1922- *WhoAm 92*
Sandquist, Eric G. 1935- *St&PR 93*
Sandquist, Gary Marlin 1936- *WhoAm 92*
Sandqvist, Aage 1939- *WhoWor 93*
Sandrev, Ivan *WhoScE 91-4*
Sandrich, Jay 1932- *MiSFD 9*
Sandrich, Jay H. 1932- *WhoAm 92*
Sandrich, Mark 1900-1945 *MiSFD 9N*
Sandridge, Margaret Ruth *Law&B 92*
Sandridge, Russell L. *Law&B 92*
Sandridge, Sidney Edwin 1927- *WhoAm 92*
Sandridge, T.L. 1936- *St&PR 93*
Sandrock, E. Thomas 1951- *St&PR 93*
Sandroff, Ronni *BioIn 17*
Sandrow, Hope 1951- *WhoE 93*
Sandru, Emil 1938- *WhoScE 91-4*
Sandry, Karla Kay Foreman 1961- *WhoAmW 93*
Sands, Arthur William, Jr. *BioIn 17*
Sands, Barbara Williams 1944- *WhoSSW 93*
Sands, Bob 1950- *WhoSSW 93*
Sands, Bobby d1981 *BioIn 17*
Sands, Cecile Ruth d1992 *NewYTBS 92*
Sands, Cecile Ruth 1900-1992 *BioIn 17*
Sands, Charles Francis 1938- *WhoWor 93*
Sands, Don W. 1926- *St&PR 93*
Sands, Don William 1926- *WhoAm 92, WhoSSW 93*
Sands, Donald Edgar 1929- *WhoAm 92, WhoSSW 93*
Sands, Edith Sylvia Abeloff *WhoAm 92, WhoWrEP 92*
Sands, Edward A. 1939- *WhoE 93*
Sands, Edward Theodore 1913- *St&PR 93*
Sands, Gary Luther 1962- *WhoE 93*
Sands, I. Jay *WhoAm 92, WhoE 93*
Sands, Jerome D., Jr. 1939- *St&PR 93*
Sands, John Eliot 1941- *WhoAm 92*
Sands, Julian *BioIn 17*
Sands, Marvin 1924- *WhoAm 92*
Sands, Matthew Linzee 1919- *WhoAm 92*
Sands, Melody Gail 1955- *WhoWrEP 92*
Sands, Meredith Barbanell 1965- *WhoE 93*
Sands, Peter P. *St&PR 93*
Sands, Raoul L. 1928- *St&PR 93*
Sands, Richard 1951- *St&PR 93*
Sands, Richard E. 1951- *WhoAm 92*
Sands, Robert Charles 1799-1832 *JrnUS*
Sands, Robert-John H. *Law&B 92*
Sands, Robert-John H. 1954- *WhoIns 93*
Sands, Robert S. *Law&B 92*
Sands, Roberta Alyse 1937- *WhoAmW 93*
Sands, Ronald Gene 1943- *WhoSSW 93*
Sands, Sharon Louise 1944- *WhoAmW 93*
Sands, Thomas Allen 1935- *WhoAm 92*
Sands, Tony *BioIn 17*
Sandson, John I. 1927- *WhoAm 92*
Sandstad, Kenneth D. 1946- *WhoAm 92*
Sandstead, Harold Hilton 1932- *WhoAm 92*
Sandstede, Gerd 1929- *WhoScE 91-3*
Sandstedt, Becky *BioIn 17*
Sandstedt, John Philip 1940- *WhoE 93*
Sandstrom, Alan R(ussell) 1945- *ConAu 139*
Sandstrom, Alice Wilhelmina 1914- *WhoAmW 93*
Sandstrom, Arne Sven Gustaf 1949- *WhoWor 93*
Sandstrom, Boden C. 1945- *WhoAmW 93*
Sandstrom, Clas G. 1945- *WhoUN 92*
Sandstrom, Dale Vernon 1950- *WhoWor 93*
Sandstrom, Gunnar Emanuel 1951- *WhoWor 93*
Sandstrom, Pamela Effrein 1954- *ConAu 139*
Sandstrom, Philip William 1952- *WhoE 93*
Sandstrom, Robert Edward 1946- *WhoWor 93*
Sandstrom, Rolf J.V. 1943- *WhoScE 91-4*
Sandstrom, Sven-David 1942- *Baker 92*
Sandstrom, Thomas J. *Law&B 92*
Sandstrom, Ulf Teddy 1952- *WhoSSW 93*
Sandstrom, William M. 1946- *St&PR 93*
Sandt, Maximilian van de 1863-1934 *Baker 92*
Sandt, Sara A. *AmWomPl*
Sanduja, Mohan L. 1935- *WhoAm 92*
Sandulescu, Dumitru 1922- *WhoScE 91-4*
Sandunova, Elizaveta 1772?-1826 *OxDcOp*
Sandusky, Harold William 1949- *WhoE 93*
Sandvig, Karen Joy 1956- *WhoAmW 93*
Sandvik, Karl Oscar 1945- *WhoScE 91-4*
Sandvik, Knut Lyng 1938- *WhoScE 91-4*
Sandvik, Ole Mork 1875-1976 *Baker 92*
Sandvik, Peter B.J. 1953- *WhoScE 91-4*
Sandweiss, Jack 1930- *WhoAm 92*
Sandweiss, Martha A. 1954- *WhoAm 92, WhoAmW 93, WhoE 93*
Sandweiss, Martha A(nn) 1954- *ConAu 136*
Sandwell, B.K. 1876-1954 *BioIn 17*
Sandwell, Bernard Keble 1876-1954 *BioIn 17*
Sandwich, Edward Montagu, Earl of 1625-1672 *HarEnMi*
Sandwich, John Montagu, Earl of 1718-1792 *BioIn 17*
Sandy, Donald *BioIn 17*
Sandy, Edward Allen 1958- *WhoWor 93*
Sandy, Leo Robert 1943- *WhoE 93*
Sandy, Milton Larimore, Sr. 1916- *St&PR 93*
Sandy, Stephen 1934- *WhoAm 92*
Sandy, Stephen Merrill 1934- *WhoWrEP 92*
Sandy, Steven C. 1942- *St&PR 93*
Sandy, Vickie Lynne 1962- *WhoAmW 93*
Sandy, William H. 1929- *St&PR 93*
Sandy, William Haskell 1929- *WhoAm 92*
Sandys, Edwina Kaplan 1938- *WhoE 93*
Sandys, George 1578-1644 *DcLB 121 [port]*
Sanefuji, Takashi 1937- *WhoWor 93*
Sanejouand, Renaud *WhoScE 91-2*
Sanelli, Teresa *Law&B 92*
Sanem, Michael L. 1942- *WhoAm 92*
Saner, Joseph P. 1934- *St&PR 93*
Sanese, Ralph, Jr. 1953- *St&PR 93*
Saneto, Russell Patrick 1950- *WhoEmL 93*
Sanetti, Stephen Louis *Law&B 92*
Saneyev, Viktor 1945- *BioIn 17*
Sanfelici, Arthur Hugo 1934- *WhoAm 92, WhoSSW 93, WhoWrEP 92*
Sanfelippo, Peter Michael 1938- *WhoAm 92*
Sanfield, Steve 1937- *WhoWrEP 92*
Sanfilip, Thomas 1952- *WhoWrEP 92*
Sanfilippo, Janet Thompson 1949- *WhoSSW 93*
San Fillipo, Mariane 1944- *St&PR 93*
Sanford, Agnes Mary White 1897-1976 *BioIn 17*
Sanford, Amelia *AmWomPl*
Sanford, Anne Dorman 1921- *WhoAmW 93*
Sanford, Anne Putnam *AmWomPl*
Sanford, Bascom N. 1917- *St&PR 93*
Sanford, Carl Thomas 1932- *St&PR 93*
Sanford, Charles David 1939- *St&PR 93*
Sanford, Charles Steadman, Jr. 1936- *St&PR 93, WhoAm 92*
Sanford, Dan L. *Law&B 92*
Sanford, David Boyer 1943- *WhoAm 92, WhoWrEP 92*
Sanford, David Hawley 1937- *WhoAm 92*
Sanford, Delores Mae 1931- *WhoAmW 93*
Sanford, Donald G. 1938- *WhoSSW 93*
Sanford, Doris 1937- *ConAu 138, SmATA 69 [port]*
Sanford, Dorothy Zerzan 1924- *WhoAmW 93*
Sanford, Edmund Eyers 1959- *St&PR 93*
Sanford, Edmund Philip, Jr. 1923- *WhoSSW 93*
Sanford, Edward Terry 1865-1930 *OxCSupC [port]*

Sanford, Elias Benjamin 1843-1932 BioIn 17
Sanford, Elise 1948- WhoAmW 93
Sanford, Frank Wadsworth 1955- St&PR 93
Sanford, Frederick Goodman WhoAm 92
Sanford, Geraldine A. 1928- WhoWrEP 92
Sanford, Glenna Griffin 1968- WhoAmW 93
Sanford, Howard S. 1933- WhoSSW 93
Sanford, Isabel Gwendolyn WhoAm 92, WhoAmW 93
Sanford, James Kenneth 1932- WhoSSW 93
Sanford, Janet Carol 1930- St&PR 93
Sanford, Jay Philip 1928- WhoAm 92
Sanford, John A. 1954- St&PR 93
Sanford, John B. 1904- BioIn 17
Sanford, Joseph P. 1937- St&PR 93
Sanford, Katherine Koontz 1915- WhoAmW 93
Sanford, Kendall T. Law&B 92
Sanford, Larry E. Law&B 92
Sanford, Larry E. 1946- St&PR 93
Sanford, Richard ScF&FL 92
Sanford, Richard D. 1944- ConEn
Sanford, Robert Preston 1959- St&PR 93
Sanford, Robert Wadsworth 1920- St&PR 93
Sanford, Roy Leon 1946- WhoAm 92
Sanford, Ruth B. 1925- St&PR 93
Sanford, Sarah J. 1949- WhoAm 92, WhoAmW 93
Sanford, Sharon Ann 1946- WhoAmW 93
Sanford, Stephen R. Law&B 92
Sanford, Susan Haspel 1944- WhoAmW 93
Sanford, Terrance 1917- WhoSSW 93
Sanford, Terry 1917- CngDr 91, PolPar, WhoAm 92, WhoWrEP 92
Sanford, Valerius 1923- WhoAm 92
Sanford, Willard C. 1932- WhoIns 93
Sanford, William Anthony 1933- St&PR 93
Sanford, William F. 1935- St&PR 93
Sanford, William R. 1927- ScF&FL 92
Sang, Barbara Ellen 1937- WhoAmW 93
Sang, Heng-Kang WhoE 93
Sangalis, Gregory Theodore Law&B 92
Sangalli, Scott Robert 1950- St&PR 93
Sanger, Alexander C. 1947- St&PR 93
Sanger, Alexander Campbell 1947- WhoE 93
Sanger, David E. 1960- ConAu 136
Sanger, Eleanor 1929- WhoAm 92, WhoAmW 93
Sanger, Frederick 1918- WhoAm 92, WhoWor 93
Sanger, Heinz Ludwig WhoScE 91-3
Sanger, Herbert Shelton, Jr. 1936- WhoAm 92
Sanger, John WhoScE 91-1
Sanger, Jonathan MiSFD 9
Sanger, Margaret 1879-1966 BioIn 17, ConHero 2 [port], WomChHR [port]
Sanger, Susan M. Law&B 92
Sangha, Hariqbal Singh 1958- WhoWor 93
Sangha, Jangbir 1945- St&PR 93
Sanghavi, D.K. 1938- St&PR 93
San Giacomo, Rose-Marie Carla 1950- WhoAmW 93
Sangiocomo, Thomas G. 1949- St&PR 93
Sangiolo, Joseph B. 1928- St&PR 93
Sangiovanni, Antonio 1831-1892 Baker 92
Sangiuliano, Jerry MiSFD 9
Sangmeister, George E. 1931- CngDr 91
Sangmeister, George Edward 1931- WhoAm 92
Sangnier, Marc 1873-1950 BioIn 17
Sangree, Walter Hinchman 1926- WhoAm 92
Sangster, Alan John WhoScE 91-1
Sangster, Charles 1822-1893 BioIn 17
Sangster, Donald DcCPCAm
Sangster, James Allan 1954- St&PR 93
Sangster, Jimmy 1927- MiSFD 9
Sangster, John Fraser 1942- WhoWor 93
Sangster, K.J. WhoScE 91-1
Sangster, Margaret Elizabeth 1894- AmWomPl
Sangster, Robert Edmund 1936- WhoWor 93
Sangsue, Daniel 1955- WhoWor 93
Sanguineti, Edoardo 1930- DcLB 128 [port], WhoWor 93
Sanguineti, Vittorio 1940- St&PR 93
Sanguinetti, Alexandre 1913-1981 BioIn 17
Sanguinetti, Eugene Frank 1917- WhoAm 92
Sanguszko, Wladyslaw 1803-1870 PolBiDi
Sangweni, Stanislaus S. 1933- WhoUN 92
Sanhueza, Pablo Reyes 1954- WhoWor 93
Sani, Robert LeRoy 1935- WhoAm 92
Saniewski, Wieslaw 1948- DrEEuF
Saniff, Sidek Bin 1938- WhoAsAP 91
Sanii, A.E. 1936- St&PR 93
Sanin Posada, Nohemi WhoWor 93
Sanji, Shigenobu 1917- WhoAsAP 91
Sanjian, Avedis Krikor 1921- WhoAm 92
Sanjines, Jorge 1936- MiSFD 9
San Juan, German Moral 1940- WhoWor 93
San Juan, Javier 1951- St&PR 93
San Juan, Manuel, Jr. 1920- WhoIns 93
San Juan, Manuel H. 1864-1917 DcMexL
Sanjuan, Pedro 1886-1976 Baker 92
Sanjust, Filippo 1925- OxDcOp
Sankala, Pekka Tor Olavi 1942- WhoUN 92
Sankalia, Hasmukhlal Dhirajlal 1908-1989 BioIn 17
Sankar, Andrea (Patrice) 1948- ConAu 139
Sankey, Ira D(avid) 1840-1908 Baker 92
Sankey, John 1920- St&PR 93
Sankey, Kenneth 1946- St&PR 93
Sankey, Vernon L. 1949- St&PR 93
Sankhyan, Anek Ram 1951- WhoWor 93
Sankies, Austen Melvyn Bernard 1938- WhoWor 93
Sankiewicz, Marianna 1921- WhoScE 91-4
Sankner, Sheri Warren 1959- WhoE 93
Sankovitz, James Leo 1934- WhoWor 93
Sankpill, L. Alan 1942- St&PR 93
Sanks, Charles Randolph, Jr. 1928- WhoAm 92, WhoE 93
Sanks, Robert Leland 1916- WhoAm 92
Sanladerer, Loren K. 1936- St&PR 93
San Leocadio, Pablo de 1447-1520 BioIn 17
San Martin, Jose de 1778?-1850 BioIn 17, HarEnMi
Sanmartin, Juan R. 1941- WhoScE 91-3
San Miguel, Manuel 1930- WhoWor 93
San Miguel, Sandra Bonilla 1944- WhoSSW 93
Sanmuganathan, K. 1937- WhoScE 91-1
Sanmuganathan, Muttusamy 1932- WhoUN 92
Sann, Paul 1914-1986 ScF&FL 92
Sann, Ted BioIn 17
Sannella, Lee Sherman 1916- St&PR 93
Sanner, G. Bradley 1953- St&PR 93
Sanner, George Elwood 1929- WhoE 93, WhoSSW 93, WhoWor 93
Sanner, Jay W. Law&B 92
Sanner, Royce N. Law&B 92
Sanner, Royce N. 1931- WhoIns 93
Sanner, Royce Norman 1931- St&PR 93, WhoAm 92
Sannuti, Peddapullaiah 1941- WhoAm 92
Sannwald, William Walter 1940- WhoAm 92
Sanny, Charles Gordon 1947- WhoSSW 93
Sano, Keiji 1920- WhoWor 93
Sano, Nobuo 1936- WhoWor 93
Sano, Roy I. WhoAm 92
Sano, Tadayoshi 1889-1945 HarEnMi
Sano, Tetsuro 1931- WhoWor 93
Sanocki, Edward John, Jr. 1950- WhoE 93
Sanoff, Alvin P. 1941- ConAu 136
Sanoff, Henry 1934- WhoSSW 93
Sanoussi, Zainoul Abidine 1944- WhoUN 92
San Pedro, Enrique 1926- WhoAm 92
San Pedro, Ofelia 1953- WhoSSW 93
San Qimeng 1911- WhoAsAP 91
Sanquirico, Alessandro 1777-1849 IntDcOp, OxDcOp
Sanquist, Nancy Johnson 1947- WhoAmW 93
Sanroma, Jesus Maria 1902-1984 Baker 92
Sans, Nick 1949- St&PR 93
Sansaverino, Joseph Frank 1937- St&PR 93
Sansavini, Silviero 1933- WhoScE 91-3, WhoWor 93
Sansbury, Olin Bennett, Jr. 1937- WhoAm 92
San Sebastian, Jose Antonio de Baker 92
Sansen, Willy M.C. 1943- WhoScE 91-2
Sanseverino, Raymond Anthony 1947- WhoEmL 93
Sanseverino, Vincenzo 1951- St&PR 93
Sans i Miret, Rosanna 1959- WhoWor 93
Sansing, John BioIn 17
Sansing, Nancy Jean Yarbrough 1951- WhoSSW 93
Sanslone, William Robert 1931- WhoE 93
Sanso, Fernando 1945- WhoScE 91-3
Sansom, Chip BioIn 17
Sansom, Matt Rudiger 1950- WhoWor 93
Sansom, William 1912-1976 BioIn 17
Sanson, Edward J. 1951- St&PR 93
Sanson, Phil 1941- St&PR 93
Sanson, Rudolph J., Jr. 1937- St&PR 93
Sansone, Eric Brandfon 1939- WhoE 93
Sansone, John C. 1955- St&PR 93
Sansone, Robert 1942-1991 BioIn 17
Sansone, Rocco Carl 1950- WhoIns 93
Sanson Flores, Jesus 1909-1966 DcMexL
San Souci, Robert D. 1946- ScF&FL 92
Sansovino, Jacopo 1486-1570 BioIn 17
Sanstead, Wayne Godfrey 1935- WhoAm 92
Sansweet, Stephen Jay 1945- WhoAm 92
Sant, John Talbot 1932- St&PR 93, WhoAm 92
Sant, Joni Rose 1963- WhoAmW 93
Sant, Moreshwar Dattatraya 1932- WhoUN 92
Sant, Roger W. St&PR 93
Sant, Thomas 1948- ConAu 136
Sant, Thomas D. 1948- WhoAm 92
Santa, Ferenc 1927- BioIn 17
Santa, Sharon Aichele 1953- St&PR 93
Santa Anna, Antonio Lopez de 1794?-1876 BioIn 17, HarEnMi
Santabarenos, Theodore d914? OxDcByz
Santacana, Guido E. 1952- WhoAm 92
Santacilia, Pedro 1826-1910 DcMexL
Santacroce, Donald Paul 1932- St&PR 93
Santacroct, R. WhoScE 91-3
Santa Cruz, Alvaro de Bazan, Marquis of 1526-1588 HarEnMi
Santa Cruz (Wilson), Domingo 1899-1987 Baker 92
Santa-Cruz Bendezu, Carlos Enrique 1955- WhoWor 93
Santaella, Irma Vidal 1924- NotHsAW 93 [port], WhoAmW 93
Santaferrara, Michael Joseph 1961- WhoE 93
Santalainen, Timo Juhani 1946- WhoWor 93
Santa Maria, Carmen Law&B 92
Santa Maria, Dario Atehortua 1943- WhoE 93
Santamaria, Jose Luis 1931- WhoUN 92
Santamaria, Marco Giulio 1965- St&PR 93
Santa Maria, Odilyn Archie Litonjua WhoSSW 93
SantaMaria, Phillip 1943- WhoE 93
Santamaria, Phillip Hunt 1940- St&PR 93
Santa Maria, Tomas de c. 1510-1570 Baker 92
Santana, Aracelly A. 1946- WhoUN 92
Santana, Carlos 1947- Baker 92, BioIn 17, WhoAm 92
Santana, Jose Antonio 1942- WhoWor 93
Santander, Cesar BioIn 17
Santandrea, Mary Frances 1952- WhoAmW 93
Santandrea, Stefano 1904- IntDcAn
Santangeli, Frank 1934- WhoAm 92
Santangelo, Arlene E. 1947- St&PR 93
Santangelo, Betty J. Law&B 92
Santangelo, Charles Edward 1927- St&PR 93
Santangelo, Joseph Anthony 1954- St&PR 93
Santangelo, Mario Vincent 1931- WhoWor 93
Santangelo, Stephen J. 1953- St&PR 93
Santaniello, Angelo Gary 1924- WhoAm 92
Santaniello, Joseph M. Law&B 92
Sant'Anna, Veraldo Augusto 1929- WhoWor 93
Santarella, Joseph Michael 1939- WhoSSW 93
Santarelli, Carlo Henry, Jr. 1950- St&PR 93
Santarelli, Donald Eugene 1937- WhoAm 92
Santarelli, Eugene David 1944- WhoAm 92
Santarelli, Marino J. 1951- St&PR 93
Santarello, Piero Enrico 1942- WhoWor 93
Santarius, Kurt Adolf 1933- WhoScE 91-3, WhoWor 93
Santarlasci, Stephen M. 1952- WhoWrEP 92
Santavicca, Donald Gene 1943- St&PR 93
Santayana, George 1863-1952 GayN
Sante, William Arthur, II 1943- St&PR 93, WhoAm 92
Santee, Dale William 1953- WhoWor 93
Santee, Richard Ellis, Jr. 1951- WhoE 93
Santeiro, Luis BioIn 17
Santeiro, Luis 1947- HispAmA [port]
Santelices, Bernabe 1945- WhoWor 93
Santell, Alfred 1895-1981 MiSFD 9N
Santelli, Heidi Lux 1963- WhoE 93
Santelmann, William Henry 1863-1932 Baker 92
Santemma, Jon Noel 1937- WhoE 93
Santer, James Owen 1931- WhoE 93
Santer, Jean Jacques 1937- WhoWor 93
Santerre, Marc Law&B 92
Santesson, Johan 1944- WhoWor 93
Santeusanio, Peter E. 1948- St&PR 93
Santez, David Lewis Law&B 92
Santhuff, Carol Jean 1946- WhoAmW 93
Santi, Nello BioIn 17
Santi, Nello 1931- Baker 92, OxDcOp, WhoWor 93
Santi, Victor Amerigo 1948- WhoSSW 93
Santiago, Andreas Juan BioIn 17
Santiago, Anita Muller WhoAmW 93
Santiago, Benito BioIn 17
Santiago, Benito Rivera 1965- WhoAm 92
Santiago, Cheryl Brownstein NotHsAW 93
Santiago, Cirio H. 1936- MiSFD 9
Santiago, Danny 1911-1988 DcLB 122 [port]
Santiago, Eduardo G. 1949- HispAmA
Santiago, Fabiola 1959- NotHsAW 93
Santiago, Gloria Bonilla NotHsAW 93
Santiago, Isagani Ocampo 1921- WhoWor 93
Santiago, Isaura 1946- NotHsAW 93 [port]
Santiago, Miriam Defensor- BioIn 17
Santiago, Ron BioIn 17
Santiago, Saundra 1957- NotHsAW 93
Santiago-Noa, Victor Manuel 1944- WhoE 93
Santic, Ante Spiro 1928- WhoScE 91-4
Santilli, Arthur Attilio 1929- WhoE 93
Santilli, Paul T. Law&B 92
Santilli, Paul Thomas 1929- St&PR 93
Santilli, Vincent Edward 1962- WhoE 93
Santillo, Carl John 1949- St&PR 93, WhoIns 93
Santin, Jean 1938- WhoAmW 93
Santini, Anthony M. Law&B 92
Santini, Christina Ann 1950- WhoAmW 93
Santini, Dennis P. Law&B 92
Santini, Fortunato 1778-1861 Baker 92
Santini, Fred Law&B 92
Santini, Gabriele 1886-1964 Baker 92, OxDcOp
Santini, Gilles Francois-Marie 1947- WhoWor 93
Santini, John Amedeo 1926- WhoAm 92
Santini, Roger Louis 1939- WhoScE 91-2
Santini, Rosemarie WhoWrEP 92
Santini, William Andrew, Jr. 1931- St&PR 93
Santirocco, Laura A. Law&B 92
Santley, Charles 1834-1922 Baker 92, OxDcOp
Santman, Leon Duane 1930- WhoAm 92
Santmyer, Helen Hooven 1895-1986 BioIn 17
Santner, Mary Patricia 1956- WhoAmW 93
Santo d1984 BioIn 17
Santo, Akiko 1942- WhoAsAP 91
Santo, Harold Paul 1947- WhoWor 93
Santo, James M. Law&B 92
Santo, James Matthew 1941- St&PR 93
Santo, James R. 1937- St&PR 93
Santo, Tetsuo 1919- WhoWor 93
Santo, Tomaz Rebelo Espirito WhoScE 91-3
Santola, Daniel Ralph 1949- WhoWor 93
Santolalla, Irene Silva de d1992 NewYTBS 92
Santolalla, Irene Silva De 1904-1992 CurBio 92N
Santoli, Dennis Raymond Law&B 92
Santoli, Vittorio 1901-1971 IntDcAn
Santoliquido, Francesco 1883-1971 Baker 92
Santolucito, Joseph Anthony 1946- WhoAm 92
Santomaa, Veli August 1936- WhoScE 91-4
Santomasso, Antoinette Therese 1949- WhoE 93
Santomauro, Mary Elizabeth 1935- WhoWrEP 92
Santomero, Anthony M. 1946- WhoAm 92
Santomieri, David M. 1945- WhoIns 93
Santona, Gloria Law&B 92
Santoni, Ronald Ernest 1931- WhoAm 92
Santonio, Joel San 1952- St&PR 93
Santonocito, Patricia Percz Law&B 92
Santopietro, Joseph C. 1941- WhoE 93
Santora, Donna Maria 1949- WhoAmW 93
Santora, Joseph Christopher 1950- WhoE 93
Santora, Kathleen Curry 1958- WhoAm 92
Santorelli, Thomas J. 1941- St&PR 93
Santoro, Anthony Richard 1939- WhoAm 92
Santoro, Armando 1950- WhoWor 93
Santoro, Carlo Maria 1935- WhoWor 93
Santoro, Charles William 1959- WhoWor 93
Santoro, Claudio 1919-1989 Baker 92
Santoro, Elissa Jeanne 1938- WhoE 93
Santoro, Eugene Anthony 1935- WhoE 93
Santoro, Ferruccio Fontes 1952- WhoWor 93
Santoro, John R. 1939- St&PR 93
Santoro, Joseph Lewis 1936- WhoE 93
Santoro, Paul M. 1949- St&PR 93
Santoro, Piero 1942- WhoScE 91-3
Santorsola, Giuseppe Guglielmo 1954- WhoWor 93
Santorum, Richard John 1958- CngDr 91

Santorum, Rick 1958- *WhoAm 92, WhoE 93*
Santos, Adele Naude 1938- *WhoAm 92*
Santos, Alfredo *BioIn 17*
Santos, Andres 1956- *WhoWor 93*
Santos, Antonio Mendes 1950- *WhoWor 93*
Santos, Arthur Magno 1946- *WhoE 93*
Santos, Dianne S. 1941- *St&PR 93*
Santos, Eduardo Cerqueira 1958- *WhoSSW 93*
Santos, Elizabeth A. *Law&B 92*
Santos, Emilio 1935- *WhoWor 93*
Santos, Eugene Sy, Jr. 1968- *WhoE 93*
Santos, Filipe Duarte 1942- *WhoScE 91-3*
Santos, George Wesley 1928- *WhoAm 92, WhoE 93*
Santos, Jim *BioIn 17*
Santos, Joaquim Jorge 1951- *WhoWor 93*
Santos, (Jose Manuel) Joly Brãga 1924-1988 *Baker 92*
Santos, Jose Eduardo dos 1942- *BioIn 17, ColdWar 2 [port]*
Santos, Joseph 1916- *St&PR 93*
Santos, Luis T. 1924- *WhoAsAP 91*
Santos, Miriam 1956- *NotHsAW 93 [port]*
Santos, Murillo 1932- *WhoUN 92*
Santos, Oscar F. 1930- *WhoAsAP 91*
Santos, Quirino D. Abad, Jr. *WhoAsAP 91*
Santos, Ruth *BioIn 17*
Santos, Sherod 1948- *WhoWrEP 92*
Santos, Tharcisio Damy de Souza 1912- *WhoWor 93*
Santos Alvite, Eduardo 1940- *WhoUN 92*
Santos-Martinez, Jesus 1924- *WhoSSW 93*
Santostefano, Damon *MiSFD 9*
Santowski, Jerome George 1936- *St&PR 93*
Santroni, A. *WhoScE 91-3*
Santry, Arthur Joseph, Jr. 1918- *St&PR 93*
Santry, J.E. 1934- *St&PR 93*
Santschi, Peter Hans 1943- *WhoAm 92, WhoSSW 93, WhoWor 93*
Santschi, Tom 1876-1931 *BioIn 17*
Santucci, Marco 1762-1843 *Baker 92*
Santullano, Luis A. 1879-1952 *DcMexL*
Santulli, Andrew Philip 1947- *St&PR 93*
Santulli, Thomas Vincent 1915- *WhoAm 92*
Santulli, Vincent F. 1942- *St&PR 93*
Santus, Rene Claude 1941- *WhoWor 93*
Santuyo, Ricardo Taytay 1931- *WhoWor 93*
Santy, Albert Christy 1948- *WhoE 93*
Sanudo Torsello, Marino c. 1270-1343 *OxDcByz*
Sanusi Bin Junid, Data' Seri 1943- *WhoAsAP 91*
Sanyal, Bikas Chandra 1938- *WhoUN 92*
Sanyal, Manik 1934- *WhoAsAP 91*
Sanyour, Michael Louis 1930- *St&PR 93*
Sanyour, Michael Louis, Jr. 1930- *WhoAm 92*
Sanz, Gaspar fl. 17th cent.-18th cent. *Baker 92*
Sanz, Kathleen Marie 1955- *WhoAmW 93*
Sanz, Lorenzo 1946- *WhoScE 91-3*
Sanzari, Paul V. 1949- *St&PR 93*
Sanzogno, Nino 1911-1983 *Baker 92, IntDcOp, OxDcOp*
Sanzone, Donna 1949- *WhoAmW 93*
Sanzone, John C. *Law&B 92*
Sanzone, Marla Marisa 1962- *WhoAmW 93*
Sanz-Perez, Bernabe 1926- *WhoScE 91-3*
Sanz Sanchez, Felix *WhoScE 91-3*
Saoud, Edmond Raja 1944- *WhoWor 93*
Saouma, Edouard 1926- *WhoScE 91-3, WhoUN 92, WhoWor 93*
Sapaden, Glenn Patrick *Law&B 92*
Sapadin, Linda Alice 1940- *WhoAmW 93, WhoE 93*
Sapala, Donald J. *Law&B 92*
Sapan, Melissa Robin 1962- *WhoAmW 93*
Sapanski, John William 1930- *St&PR 93*
Sapelli, Arthur A. *Law&B 92*
Sapelnikov, Vasili 1867-1941 *Baker 92*
Sapenter, Deborah *BlkAmWO*
Saper, Clifford Baird 1952- *WhoAm 92*
Saper, Lawrence 1928- *WhoAm 92*
Sapera, Samuel M. *Law&B 92*
Sapergia, Barbara *WhoCanL 92*
Sapers, Carl Martin 1932- *WhoAm 92*
Saperstein, David *MiSFD 9*
Saperstein, David 1900-1990 *BioIn 17*
Saperstein, David 1937- *ScF&FL 92*
Saperstein, David Allan 1937- *WhoAm 92*
Saperstein, Jonathan I. *Law&B 92*
Saperstein, Lee Waldo 1943- *WhoAm 92*
Saperstein, Marc Eli 1944- *WhoAm 92*
Saperston, Howard Truman, Sr. 1899- *WhoAm 92*
Saperston, Howard Truman, Jr. 1939- *WhoE 93*
Saperton, David 1889-1970 *Baker 92*
Sapeta, Robert G. 1947- *St&PR 93*
Sapharas, Stella 1929- *WhoAmW 93*
Saphiere, Dianne Marie 1960- *WhoAmW 93*
Saphir, Richard Louis 1933- *WhoE 93*
Saphire, Gary Steven 1952- *WhoE 93*
Saphire, Naomi Carrol 1938- *WhoAmW 93*
Sapho *OxDcOp*
Sapico, Francisco Lejano 1940- *WhoAm 92*
Sapieha, Adam Stefan 1867-1951 *PolBiDi*
Sapienza, C. *WhoScE 91-2*
Sapienza, John Thomas 1913- *WhoAm 92*
Sapienza, Michael *St&PR 93*
Sapienza, Stephen L. *Law&B 92*
Sapieyevski, Anne L. *ScF&FL 92*
Sapin, Cory Roberta 1951- *WhoAmW 93, WhoWor 93*
Sapinsky, Joseph Charles 1923- *WhoAm 92*
Sapinsley, Barbara *ConAu 137*
Sapinsley, Lila Manfield 1922- *WhoAmW 93*
Sapinsley, Milton d1990 *BioIn 17*
Sapio, David A. 1945- *St&PR 93*
Sapir, Boris M. 1902-1989 *BioIn 17*
Sapir, Edward 1884-1939 *BioIn 17, IntDcAn*
Sapir, Richard 1936-1987 *ScF&FL 92*
Sapirie, Samuel Ralph 1909-1991 *BioIn 17*
Sapirif, Stephen Alan 1936- *WhoUN 92*
Sapiro, Anna Merchant *AmWomPl*
Sapiro, Leland 1924- *WhoSSW 93*
Saplagio, Eleanor Enriquez 1964- *WhoWor 93*
Saplywyj, Ihor 1955- *St&PR 93*
Sapoff, Meyer 1927- *St&PR 93, WhoE 93, WhoWor 93*
Sapolsky, Harvey Morton 1939- *WhoAm 92*
Saponara, Eduardo Milligan 1948- *WhoE 93*
Saponaro, Joseph A. 1939- *WhoAm 92*
Saponaro, Joseph Anthony 1939- *St&PR 93*
Sapone, Antonio *BioIn 17*
Sapora, Joe d1992 *BioIn 17, NewYTBS 92*
Saporiti, Antonia *OxDcOp*
Saporiti, Teresa c. 1763-1869 *Baker 92, OxDcOp*
Saporito, Patricia L. 1949- *WhoIns 93*
Saporta, Marc 1923- *WhoWor 93*
Sapos, Mary Ann *WhoAmW 93*
Sapountzis, Elias 1931- *WhoScE 91-3*
Sapozhenko, Alexanr Antonovich 1939- *WhoWor 93*
Sapp, A. Eugene 1936- *St&PR 93*
Sapp, A. Eugene, Jr. 1933- *WhoSSW 93*
Sapp, Allan D. 1956- *St&PR 93*
Sapp, Allen *BioIn 17*
Sapp, Allen Dwight 1922- *Baker 92*
Sapp, Carolyn Suzanne *BioIn 17*
Sapp, Clayton H. *St&PR 93*
Sapp, Eva Jo 1944- *WhoWrEP 92*
Sapp, George David 1946- *WhoIns 93*
Sapp, Mary Manley 1949- *WhoAmW 93*
Sapp, Neil Carleton 1939- *WhoSSW 93, WhoWor 93*
Sapp, Peggy Brotherton 1942- *WhoAmW 93*
Sapp, Samuel Dee 1948- *WhoSSW 93*
Sapp, Stanley C. 1961- *St&PR 93*
Sapp, Walter William *Law&B 92*
Sapp, Walter William 1930- *WhoAm 92*
Sapp, William Darlo 1932- *St&PR 93*
Sappenfield, Charles Madison 1930- *WhoAm 92*
Sapper 1888-1937 *ScF&FL 92*
Sapper, Neil Gary 1941- *WhoSSW 93*
Sappho *BioIn 17, OxDcByz*
Sappho fl. c. 7th cent.BC- *OxDcOp*
Sappho fl. 6th cent.BC- *PoeCrit 5*
Sappia, Alfred E. 1930- *St&PR 93*
Sappington, Michael Lee 1949- *St&PR 93*
Sapsford, Ralph Neville 1938- *WhoWor 93*
Sapsowitz, Sidney H. 1936- *St&PR 93, WhoAm 92*
Sapuppo, Victor 1938- *St&PR 93*
Saqr bin Muhammad Al-Qasimi, Sheikh 1920- *WhoWor 93*
Sarabande, William *ScF&FL 92*
Sarabi, Abdul Wahed 1926- *WhoAsAP 91*
Sarabia, Antonio R., II *Law&B 92*
Saracci, Rodolfo 1936- *WhoScE 91-2, WhoUN 92*
Saracco, Guillermo Jorge 1964- *WhoWor 93*
Sarachchandra, Ediriwira 1914- *IntLitE*
Sarachik, Myriam Paula 1933- *WhoAmW 93, WhoE 93*
Sarachik, Philip Eugene 1931- *WhoE 93*
Saracho, Victor 1949- *WhoWor 93*
Saracino, Arthur Michael 1949- *St&PR 93*
Saracoglu, Rusdu 1948- *WhoWor 93*
Saraff, Hari Mohan 1942- *WhoWor 93*
Sarafian, Deran *MiSFD 9*
Sarafian, Richard C. 1932- *MiSFD 9*
Sarafian, Robert K. *Law&B 92*
Sarafoglou, Nikias 1954- *WhoWor 93*
Sarah *BioIn 17*
Sarah, Duchess of York 1959- *BioIn 17*
Sarah, Robyn 1949- *WhoCanL 92*
Sarai, Tibor 1919- *Baker 92*
Sarajian, Lisa R. 1959- *St&PR 93*
Saral, Tulsi B. 1928- *WhoSSW 93*
Saralegui, Cristina 1948- *HispAmA [port], NotHsAW 93 [port]*
Saralegui, Jorge *ScF&FL 92*
Saraliev, Borislav 1922- *DrEEuF*
Sarama, John Anthony 1951- *St&PR 93*
Saramago, Jose 1922- *ScF&FL 92*
Saramaki, Jussi Paavo 1946- *WhoScE 91-4*
Saran, Deo 1955- *WhoWor 93*
Saran, Sam H. 1924- *St&PR 93*
Saranasena, Gamage 1933- *WhoWor 93*
Sarandon, Susan *BioIn 17*
Sarandon, Susan 1946- *ConTFT 10, HolBB [port], IntDcF 2-3 [port]*
Sarandon, Susan Abigail 1946- *WhoAm 92, WhoAmW 93*
Saranin, Alexander Peter 1921- *WhoWor 93*
Saranovic, Milinko 1929- *WhoScE 91-4*
Saranpaa, Pekka T. 1959- *WhoScE 91-4*
Sarantenos *OxDcByz*
Sarantides, James 1954- *WhoE 93*
Sarantides, Stylianos 1936- *WhoWor 93*
Sarantopoulos, Theodore 1961- *WhoWor 93*
Sarantos, Athena Apanomith 1930- *WhoAmW 93*
Sarantos, Susan Elizabeth 1958- *WhoE 93*
Saranummi, Niilo K. 1946- *WhoScE 91-4*
Sarapata, Susan Lee 1950- *WhoEmL 93*
Sarasate, Pablo de 1844-1908 *Baker 92*
Sarasin, Arsa 1936- *WhoAsAP 91, WhoWor 93*
Sarasin, Pow 1907- *WhoAsAP 91*
Sarasohn-Kahn, Jane 1955- *WhoE 93*
Sarason, Esther Kroop 1918- *WhoAmW 93, WhoE 93*
Sarason, Irwin G. 1929- *WhoAm 92*
Sarason, Seymour Bernard 1919- *BioIn 17*
Saraste, Jukka-Pekka 1956- *Baker 92*
Sarasvati, Dayananda 1824-1883 *BioIn 17*
Sarat, Austin D. 1947- *WhoAm 92*
Sarath, Maria A. *Law&B 92*
Saratz, Gian 1944- *WhoWor 93*
Saravay, Stacey Chapman *Law&B 92*
Saravia, Alvaro Rafael *DcCPCAm*
Sarazen, Nicholas *ScF&FL 92*
Sarazen, Richard Allen 1933- *WhoAm 92, WhoE 93*
Sarazin, Marc Simon 1955- *WhoWor 93*
Sarback, Susan A. 1955- *WhoAmW 93*
Sarban 1910-1989 *ScF&FL 92*
Sarbanes, Paul S. 1933- *CngDr 91*
Sarbanes, Paul Spyros 1933- *WhoAm 92, WhoE 93*
Sarbello, Michael Charles 1943- *St&PR 93*
Sarbiewski, Maciej Kazimierz 1595-1640 *PolBiDi [port]*
Sarbin, Hershel B. 1924- *St&PR 93*
Sarbin, Hershel Benjamin 1924- *WhoAm 92*
Sarchet-Waller, Paul Robert 1947- *WhoWor 93*
Sarchio, Andrew Philip 1943- *WhoE 93*
Sarcia, Giovanni 1941- *WhoWor 93*
Sarcia, James F. 1931- *St&PR 93*
Sarcka, Elizabeth Man d1992 *BioIn 17, NewYTBS 92*
Sard, George *WhoAm 92*
Sard, George 1953- *WhoE 93*
Sarda, Alain Georges 1947- *WhoWor 93*
Sarda, F. 1951- *WhoScE 91-3*
Sarda, Rabin M. 1942- *WhoUN 92*
Sardachuk, Grant R. 1958- *St&PR 93*
Sardas, Jacques Raphael 1930- *St&PR 93*
Sarde, Philippe 1945- *ConTFT 10*
Sardegna, Nicholas John 1939- *WhoUN 92*
Sarden, Claudia 1958- *WhoWrEP 92*
Sardi, Dorotea 1763-c. 1810 See Bussani, Francesco 1743-c. 1807 *OxDcOp*
Sardi, Maurice Charles 1935- *WhoAm 92, WhoE 93*
Sardilli, David Bruce 1945- *WhoAm 92*
Sardinas, Eligio 1910- *HispAmA*
Sardinha, R. *WhoScE 91-3*
Sardone, Vincent Paul 1953- *St&PR 93*
Sardou, Victorien 1831-1908 *OxDcOp*
Sarduy, Severo 1937- *SpAmA*
Sareeram, Ray Rupchand 1938- *WhoAm 92*
Saren, Glenn Edward 1948- *St&PR 93*
Sarett, Herbert Paul 1916- *WhoSSW 93*
Sarett, Judith Ann 1941- *WhoAmW 93*
Saretzky, Simon 1908- *St&PR 93*
Sareyan, Alexander 1913- *WhoE 93*
Sarf, Peter Francis 1922- *St&PR 93*
Sarfaty, Wayne Allen 1951- *WhoE 93, WhoWor 93*
Sargeant, Ernest James 1918- *WhoAm 92*
Sargeant, Nancy Reardon 1933- *WhoWrEP 92*
Sargeant, Robert 1924- *St&PR 93*
Sargeant, Winthrop 1903-1986 *Baker 92*
Sargent, Barbara Elaine 1963- *WhoAmW 93*
Sargent, Ben 1948- *WhoAm 92*
Sargent, Benson Collins 1943- *WhoAm 92*
Sargent, Carl Robert 1952- *St&PR 93*
Sargent, Charles Gary 1943- *St&PR 93*
Sargent, Charles Lee 1937- *St&PR 93, WhoWor 93*
Sargent, Chauncey Forward 1828-1904 *BioIn 17*
Sargent, Craig *ScF&FL 92*
Sargent, David Jasper 1931- *WhoAm 92*
Sargent, David R. *Law&B 92*
Sargent, Dennis Michael 1950- *WhoE 93*
Sargent, Dick 1933- *BioIn 17*
Sargent, Edward Vincent 1951- *WhoE 93*
Sargent, Epes 1813-1880 *JrnUS*
Sargent, Ernest Douglas 1931- *WhoAm 92*
Sargent, Francis Williams, Jr. 1946- *WhoE 93*
Sargent, George Henry 1867-1931 *JrnUS*
Sargent, H.B. *ScF&FL 92*
Sargent, Henry B., Jr. 1934- *St&PR 93*
Sargent, Herbert E. 1906- *St&PR 93*
Sargent, James Cunningham 1916- *WhoAm 92*
Sargent, John Allston, Jr. 1937- *WhoAm 92*
Sargent, John Morgan 1939- *WhoE 93*
Sargent, John Reid *WhoScE 91-1*
Sargent, John Richard 1925- *WhoWor 93*
Sargent, John Singer 1856-1925 *GayN*
Sargent, John Turner 1924- *WhoAm 92*
Sargent, Joseph 1925- *MiSFD 9*
Sargent, Joseph Denny 1929- *WhoAm 92*
Sargent, Joseph Dudley 1937- *WhoAm 92*
Sargent, Linda C. *Law&B 92*
Sargent, Liz Elaine 1942- *WhoAmW 93*
Sargent, Lyman Tower 1940- *ScF&FL 92*
Sargent, Malcolm 1895-1967 *OxDcOp*
Sargent, (Harold) Malcolm (Watts) 1895-1967 *Baker 92*
Sargent, Maud d1992 *NewYTBS 92*
Sargent, Pamela 1948- *ScF&FL 92, WhoE 93*
Sargent, Patrick *BioIn 17*
Sargent, Peter B. 1952- *St&PR 93*
Sargent, Robert George 1937- *WhoAm 92*
Sargent, Robert Strong 1912- *WhoWrEP 92*
Sargent, Roger William Herbert *WhoScE 91-1*
Sargent, Rose-Mary 1950- *WhoE 93*
Sargent, Sarah 1937- *ScF&FL 92*
Sargent, Seth Richard 1941- *St&PR 93*
Sargent, Shirley *BioIn 17*
Sargent, Stewart William 1945- *WhoWor 93*
Sargent, Thomas Andrew 1933- *WhoAm 92*
Sargent, Thomas John 1943- *WhoAm 92*
Sargent, Wallace Leslie William 1935- *WhoAm 92*
Sargent, William Copley 1928- *St&PR 93*
Sargent, William Leroy 1947- *St&PR 93*
Sargenti, Marina *MiSFD 9*
Sargentini, Aurelia 1936- *WhoScE 91-3*
Sargeson, Frank 1903-1982 *ConAu 38NR*
Sargon, I, King of Agade fl. c. 2500BC- *BioIn 17*
Sargon, Simon 1938- *Baker 92*
Sargrad, Gita D. *Law&B 92*
Sari, Ada 1886-1968 *Baker 92, PolBiDi*
Sari, Keith J. 1948- *St&PR 93*
Saria, Sarah Namnama 1965- *WhoAmW 93*
Saric, Marko 1924- *WhoScE 91-4*
Sarich, Ralph *BioIn 17*
Sarich, Vincent M. 1934- *WhoAm 92*
Saricks, Ambrose 1915- *WhoAm 92*
Saricks, Joyce Goering 1948- *WhoAmW 93*
Saridis, George Nicholas 1931- *WhoAm 92, WhoE 93*
Sarin, Henrik H. 1946- *WhoScE 91-4*
Sarini, N.J. 1927- *St&PR 93*
Saris, F.W. *WhoScE 91-3*
Saris, Nils-Erik Leo 1928- *WhoScE 91-4*
Saris, Wim H.M. 1949- *WhoScE 91-3*
Sarja, Asko Erkki *WhoScE 91-4*
Sarjeant, Lawrence E. *Law&B 92*
Sarjeant, Walter James 1944- *WhoAm 92, WhoE 93*
Sarkar, Chitto Priyo 1951- *WhoSSW 93*
Sarkar, Patricia Anne 1953- *WhoAmW 93*
Sarkar, S. 1928- *WhoScE 91-3*
Sarkar, Sasanka Sekhar 1908-1969 *IntDcAn*
Sarkas, Albert Harry 1930- *WhoE 93*
Sarkett, Joann Lynn 1959- *WhoWrEP 92*
Sarkisian, Cherilyn 1946- *WhoAmW 93*

Sarkisian, Pamela Outlaw 1941- *WhoAmW 93*
Sarkisian, Richard Gabriel 1952- *WhoE 93*
Sarkisyan, Vazgen *WhoWor 93*
Sarkodie-Mensah, Kwasi 1955- *WhoE 93*
Sarkomaa, Pertti Juhani 1941- *WhoScE 91-4*
Sarkowski, Michael S. 1949- *St&PR 93*
Sarkozy, Istvan 1920- *Baker 92*
Sarlabous, Marie Antoinette *AmWomPl*
Sarlandziev, Ljubomir 1931-1979 *DrEEuF*
Sarlat, Noah 1918- *WhoAm 92*
Sarle, William A. 1948- *St&PR 93*
Sarles, Jean Claude 1930- *WhoScE 91-2*
Sarley, Mary Patricia 1955- *WhoAmW 93*
Sarli, Robert J. 1950- *St&PR 93*
Sarlin, Kristel 1946- *WhoScE 91-4*
Sarlo, Arnold F. 1927- *St&PR 93*
Sarlos, Andy *BioIn 17*
Sarlow, Michael-Tyler Curtis 1952- *WhoWor 93*
Sarly, Henry 1883-1954 *Baker 92*
Sarma, Amardeo Christian 1955- *WhoWor 93*
Sarma, Gabbita Sundara Rama 1937- *WhoWor 93*
Sarma, Vimala Devi 1947- *WhoWor 93*
Sarmanian, Peter 1934- *St&PR 93*
Sarmento, Joaquim Ribeiro 1916- *WhoWor 93*
Sarmiento, Domingo Faustino 1811-1888 *BioIn 17*
Sarmiento, Justino 1885-1937 *DcMexL*
Sarmiento, Lorenzo S. 1909- *WhoAsAP 91*
Sarmiento, Valeria *MiSFD 9*
Sarmiento Galan, Antonio Fernando 1954- *WhoWor 93*
Sarna, Bal K. 1931- *WhoUN 92*
Sarna, Nahum Mattathias 1923- *WhoAm 92*
Sarna, Seppo J. 1943- *WhoScE 91-4*
Sarnat, Bernard George 1912- *WhoAm 92*
Sarnat, Marshall 1929- *WhoWor 93*
Sarne, Michael 1939- *MiSFD 9*
Sarnecki, Linda *BioIn 17*
Sarnecki, Tom *BioIn 17*
Sarnelle, Joseph R. 1951- *WhoAm 92*
Sarner, Erik G. 1943- *WhoScE 91-4*
Sarner, George 1931- *St&PR 93*
Sarner, James George 1949- *St&PR 93*
Sarney, George W. 1939- *St&PR 93*
Sarni, Vincent A. 1928- *St&PR 93*
Sarni, Vincent Anthony 1928- *WhoAm 92, WhoE 93*
Sarno, Gerald D. 1928- *St&PR 93*
Sarno, John E. 1923- *BioIn 17*
Sarno, Patricia Ann 1947- *WhoAmW 93, WhoE 93, WhoEmL 93, WhoWor 93*
Sarno, Sam 1946- *St&PR 93*
Sarnoff, Albert 1925- *St&PR 93, WhoAm 92*
Sarnoff, David 1891-1971 *BioIn 17, JeAmHC*
Sarnoff, Jill Robin *Law&B 92*
Sarnoff, Lili-Charlotte Dreyfus 1916- *WhoAmW 93, WhoWor 93*
Sarnoff, Pam Martin d1991 *BioIn 17*
Sarnoff, Paul 1918- *ConAu 40NR, WhoE 93*
Sarnoff, Robert W. *BioIn 17*
Sarnoff, Stanley J. 1917-1990 *BioIn 17*
Sarnoff, Thomas Warren 1927- *WhoAm 92*
Sarnoff, William 1929- *St&PR 93, WhoAm 92, WhoE 93*
Sarnowski, Stanley John 1940- *St&PR 93*
Saro, J. Heinrich 1827-1891 *Baker 92*
Saroff, Marie S. 1928- *WhoE 93*
Sarofim, Adel Fares 1934- *WhoAm 92*
Sarofim, Fayez *BioIn 17*
Sarokin, H. Lee 1928- *WhoAm 92*
Sarosi, Balint 1925- *Baker 92*
Sarosiek, James J. *Law&B 92*
Sarosiek, James J. 1946- *St&PR 93*
Sarosiek, James John 1946- *WhoAm 92*
Sarov, Israel d1989 *BioIn 17*
Saroyan, William 1908-1981 *BioIn 17, MagSAmL [port], WorLitC [port]*
Sarpalius, Bill 1948- *CngDr 91, WhoAm 92*
Sarpalius, William 1948- *WhoSSW 93*
Sarpaneva, Timo Tapani 1926- *WhoWor 93*
Sarpila, Antti Juhani 1964- *WhoWor 93*
Sarpkaya, Turgut 1928- *WhoAm 92*
Sarpy, Courtney-Anne 1939- *WhoSSW 93*
Sarpy, Leon 1907- *WhoAm 92*
Sarr, Robert 1943- *WhoUN 92*
Sarra, Martha Cutright *Law&B 92*
Sarrade-Loucheur, Bernard Louis 1945- *WhoWor 93*
Sarraf, Roberta Jean 1945- *WhoE 93, WhoWor 93*
Sarran, Wallace E., Jr. 1928- *St&PR 93*
Sarrantonio, Al 1952- *ScF&FL 92*
Sarraut, Albert 1872-1962 *BioIn 17*
Sarraut, Maurice 1869-1943 *BioIn 17*
Sarraute, Nathalie *BioIn 17*
Sarraute, Nathalie 1900- *WhoWor 93*
Sarrazin, Albertine 1937-1967 *BioIn 17*
Sarrazin, Bernard P. 1937- *St&PR 93*
Sarrazin, Hubertus O. 1942- *St&PR 93*
Sarrette, Bernard 1765-1858 *Baker 92*
Sarri, Domenico Natale 1679-1744 *Baker 92*
Sarri, Rosemary Conzemius Alcuin 1926- *WhoAmW 93*
Sarrien, Jean Marie Ferdinand 1840-1915 *BioIn 17*
Sarris, Andrew *BioIn 17*
Sarris, Andrew George 1928- *WhoAm 92, WhoE 93, WhoWrEP 92*
Sarris, Emmanuel T. 1945- *WhoScE 91-3*
Sarris, Evangelos 1949- *WhoWor 93*
Sarro, Domenico Natale 1679-1744 *Baker 92, OxDcOp*
Sarry, Christine 1946- *WhoAm 92*
Sarsfield, Luke Aloysius 1925- *WhoE 93*
Sarsfield, Patrick 1650-1693 *BioIn 17*
Sarson, Evelyn Patricia *WhoWrEP 92*
Sarson, Evelyn Patricia 1937- *WhoAm 92*
Sarson, John Christopher 1935- *WhoAm 92*
Sarsten, Gunnar E. 1937- *St&PR 93*
Sarsten, Gunnar Edward 1937- *WhoAm 92*
Sartain, Aaron Quinn 1905- *WhoSSW 93*
Sartain, David Carter *WhoScE 91-1*
Sartain, E.P. 1963- *St&PR 93*
Sartain, James Edward 1941- *WhoWor 93*
Sarte, Elfren R. 1924- *WhoAsAP 91*
Sartelli, Deborah Nelson 1953- *WhoAmW 93*
Sarther, Lynette Kay 1947- *WhoEmL 93*
Sarti, Giuseppe 1729?-1802 *Baker 92, OxDcOp*
Sarti, Laura 1925- *OxDcOp*
Sartisky, Michael Jeffrey 1951- *WhoSSW 93*
Sarto, Gloria Elizabeth 1929- *WhoAm 92*
Sartoga, Susan G. *Law&B 92*
Sarto I Monteys, Victor 1957- *WhoWor 93*
Sarton, May 1912- *BioIn 17, WhoAm 92, WhoAmW 93*
Sartor, Anthony Joseph 1943- *WhoAm 92*
Sartor, Daniel Ryan, Jr. 1932- *WhoAm 92*
Sartor, Doris Patricia 1957- *WhoAmW 93*
Sartorelli, Alan Clayton 1931- *WhoAm 92*
Sartoretto, Flavio 1956- *WhoWor 93*
Sartori, Claudio 1913- *Baker 92*
Sartori, Franco Felice 1922- *WhoWor 93*
Sartori, Giovanni 1924- *ConAu 38NR, WhoAm 92*
Sartori, Helfred Edwin 1939- *WhoE 93*
Sartori, James *St&PR 93*
Sartori, Joseph *St&PR 93*
Sartori, Mario d1990 *BioIn 17*
Sartori, Peter 1931- *WhoScE 91-3*
Sartori, Silvio 1957- *St&PR 93*
Sartori, Stephen *St&PR 93*
Sartorio, Anthony Thomas 1962- *WhoE 93*
Sartorio, Antonio 1630-1680 *Baker 92, OxDcOp*
Sartorio, Jose Manuel 1746-1829 *DcMexL*
Sartorius, Norman 1935- *WhoUN 92*
Sartorius, Paul 1569?-1609 *Baker 92*
Sartre, Jean Paul 1905-1980 *BioIn 17, DramC 3 [port], MagSWL [port], ScF&FL 92, WorLitC [port]*
Sartwell, Philip Earl 1908- *WhoE 93*
Sartzetakis, Christos 1929- *WhoWor 93*
Saru, George 1920- *WhoE 93*
Sarubbi, Thomas F. 1922- *St&PR 93*
Sarudy, Richard J. 1940- *St&PR 93*
Sarukhan, Jose Aristeo 1940- *WhoWor 93*
Sarukhanian, Eduard Iosifovitch 1940- *WhoUN 92*
Sarusky, Jaime 1931- *SpAmA*
Sarvala, Jouko 1945- *WhoScE 91-4*
Sarvanto, Kari Tapani 1961- *WhoWor 93*
Sarvas, Matti Olavi 1940- *WhoScE 91-4*
Sarver, Eugene 1943- *WhoE 93*
Sarver, J. William *Law&B 92*
Sarver, Jerry L. 1938- *St&PR 93*
Sarver, Robert Dean 1938- *St&PR 93*
Sarvetnick, H. 1929- *St&PR 93*
Sarwar, Mohammed *WhoScE 91-1*
Sarwer-Foner, Gerald Jacob 1924- *WhoAm 92*
Sary, Laszlo 1940- *Baker 92*
Sarychev, Andrei V. 1956- *WhoWor 93*
Sas, Chr. *WhoScE 91-3*
Sas, Louis J. 1937- *St&PR 93*
Sas, Mihaly 1924- *WhoScE 91-4*
Sas (Orchassal), Andres 1900-1967 *Baker 92*
Sasagawa, Takashi 1935- *WhoAsAP 91*
Sasahara, Arthur Asao 1927- *WhoAm 92, WhoWor 93*
Sasaki, Clarence Takashi 1941- *WhoAm 92*
Sasaki, Hidenori 1934- *WhoAsAP 91*
Sasaki, J.K. *Law&B 92*
Sasaki, Ken 1936- *WhoWor 93*
Sasaki, Koichi 1943- *St&PR 93*
Sasaki, Man 1926- *WhoAsAP 91*
Sasaki, Masafumi 1929- *WhoWor 93*
Sasaki, Nobuo 1949- *WhoWor 93*
Sasaki, R. A. 1952- *ConAu 136*
Sasaki, Robert J. 1962- *WhoWor 93*
Sasaki, Robert K. 1941- *St&PR 93*
Sasaki, Sadako 1943-1955 *BioIn 17*
Sasaki, Shin-Ichi 1925- *WhoWor 93*
Sasaki, Tadahiro 1940- *WhoWor 93*
Sasaki, Taizo 1925- *WhoWor 93*
Sasaki, Tatsuo 1944- *WhoAm 92, WhoWor 93*
Sasaki, Toshiaki 1934- *WhoWor 93*
Sasaki, Wataru 1923- *WhoWor 93*
Sasanians *OxDcByz*
Sasano, Teiko 1933- *WhoAsAP 91*
Sasayama, Takao 1937- *WhoE 93*
Sasdelli, Renato 1943- *WhoScE 91-3*
Sasdi, George P. 1934- *St&PR 93, WhoAm 92*
Sasdy, Peter *MiSFD 9*
Saseen, Sharon Louise 1949- *WhoSSW 93*
Sasek, Gloria Burns 1926- *WhoAmW 93, WhoSSW 93*
Sasenick, Joseph Anthony 1940- *WhoAm 92*
Sasiadek, John D. 1943- *St&PR 93*
Sasich, Rose Kordich 1945- *WhoAmW 93*
Sasko, Nancy Ann 1956- *WhoSSW 93*
Saslaw, Dianne Capps *Law&B 92*
Saslaw, Leonard David 1927- *WhoE 93*
Sasloff, Alan I. 1935- *St&PR 93*
Saslow, Jerome A. 1938- *St&PR 93*
Sasmor, James Cecil 1920- *WhoSSW 93*
Sass, Arthur Harold 1928- *WhoWor 93*
Sass, Barbara 1936- *DrEEuF*
Sass, Bob 1939- *WhoEmL 93*
Sass, Daniel Benjamin 1919- *WhoE 93*
Sass, David Werner 1935- *WhoE 93*
Sass, Gray William 1947- *WhoSSW 93*
Sass, Henning 1944- *WhoWor 93*
Sass, Jan 1886-1951 *PolBiDi*
Sass, Lorna J. *BioIn 17*
Sass, Marie Constance 1834-1907 *Baker 92, OxDcOp*
Sass, Mary Martha *WhoAmW 93*
Sass, Pal 1937- *WhoScE 91-4*
Sass, Ronald Lewis 1932- *WhoSSW 93*
Sass, Stephen J. *Law&B 92*
Sass, Sylvia 1951- *Baker 92, IntDcOp*
Sassa, Masataka 1948- *WhoWor 93*
Sassa, Scott Michael 1959- *BioIn 17*
Sassano, Karen Elizabeth 1966- *WhoAmW 93*
Sassard, Jean 1942- *WhoScE 91-2*
Sasse, C. Dieter 1934- *WhoScE 91-4*
Sasseen, George Thiery 1928- *WhoAm 92, WhoSSW 93*
Sasseen, Robert Francis 1932- *WhoAm 92*
Sassen, Georgia 1949- *WhoAmW 93*
Sassen, Saskia 1947- *HispAmA*
Sasser, Bob 1951- *St&PR 93*
Sasser, Charles Eugene 1946- *St&PR 93*
Sasser, Donald E. 1949- *St&PR 93*
Sasser, Edward Rhone 1937- *St&PR 93, WhoAm 92*
Sasser, Jacqueline Hurst 1954- *WhoAmW 93*
Sasser, James R. *BioIn 17*
Sasser, James Ralph 1936- *WhoAm 92*
Sasser, James Ralph Jim 1936- *WhoSSW 93*
Sasser, Jim 1936- *CngDr 91*
Sasser, Jonathan Drew 1956- *WhoSSW 93*
Sasser, Michael D. *Law&B 92*
Sasser, Ruth *BioIn 17*
Sasser, William David 1962- *WhoSSW 93, WhoWor 93*
Sasseville, J. Serge *Law&B 92*
Sasseville, Katherine E. *Law&B 92*
Sassi, Francesco P. 1935- *WhoScE 91-3*
Sassi, Henry D. *St&PR 93*
Sassi, Richard M. *Law&B 92*
Sasso, Eleanor Catherine 1934- *WhoAmW 93*
Sasso, Phillip D. *Law&B 92*
Sasso, Ruth Maryann 1928- *WhoE 93*
Sassoli, Ada 1886-1946 *Baker 92*
Sasson, Albert 1935- *WhoUN 92*
Sasson, Michel 1935- *WhoAm 92*
Sassone, Oley *MiSFD 9*
Sassone, Ralph John 1926- *St&PR 93*
Sassoon, Andre Gabriel 1936- *WhoE 93, WhoWor 93*
Sassoon, Humphrey Frederick 1920- *WhoSSW 93*
Sassoon, Siegfried 1886-1967 *BioIn 17*
Sassoon, Vidal 1928- *WhoAm 92*
Sassou-Nguesso, Denis 1943- *WhoAfr, WhoWor 93*
Sassou-Nguesso, Edith Lucie *BioIn 17*
Sassouni, Maral *BioIn 17*
Sastre Munoz, Roberto 1943- *WhoScE 91-3*
Sas-Uhrynowski, Andrzej 1933- *WhoScE 91-4*
Sata, Genichiro 1952- *WhoAsAP 91*
Sata, Lindbergh Saburo 1928- *WhoAm 92*
Satake, Yoshishige 1547-1612 *HarEnMi*
Satanowski, Robert 1918- *WhoWor 93*
Satchel, Dorethea Browning 1942- *WhoAmW 93*
Satchell, Carol Alexis 1945- *WhoWrEP 92*
Satchell, Derek Peter Norman *WhoScE 91-1*
Satcher, David 1941- *St&PR 93, WhoAm 92*
Satchler, George Raymond 1926- *WhoAm 92*
Sateler, Ricardo 1955- *WhoUN 92*
Satell, Edward Michael 1936- *WhoE 93*
Sateren, Terry 1943- *WhoWor 93*
Saterfiel, Thomas Horne 1950- *WhoAm 92*
Satern, Miriam Nella 1951- *WhoAmW 93*
Sathe, Sharad Somnath 1940- *WhoAm 92*
Sathe, Vasant 1925- *WhoAsAP 91*
Sather, David S. *Law&B 92*
Sather, Duane 1944- *WhoAm 92*
Sather, Edward B. 1945- *St&PR 93*
Sather, Glen *BioIn 17*
Sather, Glen Cameron 1943- *WhoAm 92*
Satiacum, Robert d1991 *BioIn 17*
Satian, Sarkis 1938- *WhoWor 93*
Satie, Erik 1866-1925 *BioIn 17, OxDcOp*
Satie, Erik (Alfred-Leslie) 1866-1925 *Baker 92*
Satin, Elaine *WhoE 93*
Satin, Joseph 1920- *WhoAm 92*
Satin, Karen W. 1938- *WhoAmW 93*
Satina, Donald L. *Law&B 92*
Satinover, Jeffrey Burke 1947- *WhoAm 92, WhoE 93*
Satinskas, Henry A. 1936- *St&PR 93*
Satinskas, Henry Anthony 1936- *WhoAm 92*
Satisky, Donald B. 1938- *St&PR 93*
Satlof, Ron *MiSFD 9*
Satmar Rebbe 1886-1979 *JeAmHC*
Sato, Akio 1934- *WhoWor 93*
Sato, Eunice Noda 1921- *WhoAm 92*
Sato, Frank Saburo 1929- *WhoAm 92*
Sato, Gordon Hisashi 1927- *WhoAm 92*
Sato, Gordon Leslie 1950- *WhoSSW 93*
Sato, Heidi Darlene 1965- *WhoAmW 93*
Sato, Hiroshi 1918- *WhoAm 92*
Sato, Hisayuki 1916- *WhoWor 93*
Sato, Jun 1936- *WhoWor 93*
Sato, Junya *MiSFD 9*
Sato, Kanju 1942- *WhoAsAP 91*
Sato, Kazuya 1942- *WhoSSW 93*
Sato, Kazuyoshi 1930- *WhoE 93, WhoWor 93*
Sato, Keiji 1920- *WhoAsAP 91*
Sato, Kenichiro 1947- *WhoAsAP 91*
Sato, Kitaru 1939- *St&PR 93, WhoAm 92*
Sato, Koichi 1934- *WhoWor 93*
Sato, Kojiro 1862-1927 *HarEnMi*
Sato, Koko 1928- *WhoAsAP 91*
Sato, Kotoku 1893-1959 *HarEnMi*
Sato, Megumu 1924- *WhoAsAP 91*
Sato, Michael Kei 1958- *WhoWor 93*
Sato, Moriyoshi 1922- *WhoAsAP 91*
Sato, Motoaki 1929- *WhoAm 92, WhoSSW 93, WhoWor 93*
Sato, Norio 1927- *WhoWor 93*
Sato, Sango 1929- *WhoAsAP 91*
Sato, Shinji 1932- *WhoAsAP 91*
Sato, Sukehiro 1933- *WhoAsAP 91*
Sato, Susumu *BioIn 17*
Sato, Tadashi 1923- *WhoAm 92*
Sato, Taiji *BioIn 17*
Sato, Taisuke 1943- *WhoAsAP 91*
Sato, Takao 1935- *WhoAsAP 91*
Sato, Takashi 1927- *WhoAsAP 91*
Sato, Takeshi Ken 1938- *WhoWor 93*
Sato, Tetsutaro 1866-1942 *HarEnMi*
Sato, Tokuo 1928- *WhoAsAP 91*
Sato, Tsuneharu 1935- *WhoAsAP 91*
Sato Eisaku 1901-1975 *DcTwHis*
Satoh, Yoshiharu 1928- *St&PR 93, WhoAm 92*
Sato Kenryo 1895-1975 *HarEnMi*
Satolli, Roberto 1948- *WhoWor 93*
Sator, Baltazar A. 1937- *WhoAsAP 91*
Satoria, Jan 1936- *WhoScE 91-4*
Satovsky, Abraham 1907- *WhoAm 92*
Satow, Clayton L. *Law&B 92*
Satowaki, Joseph Asajiro Cardinal 1904- *WhoWor 93*
Satre, Philip Glen 1949- *WhoAm 92*
Satre, Wendell Julian 1918- *St&PR 93*
Satrum, Jerry R. 1933- *WhoSSW 93*
Satsumabayashi, Koko 1940- *WhoWor 93*
Satsumabayashi, Sadayoshi 1935- *WhoWor 93*
Satt, Hilda *AmWomPl*
Sattar, Abdus 1941- *WhoWor 93*
Sattar, Mohamed Abdus 1935- *WhoWor 93*
Sattelle, David Barry *WhoScE 91-1*
Sattelmeyer, Robert Dale, Jr. 1946- *WhoSSW 93*
Satten, Sara L. *Law&B 92*
Satter, Gustav 1832- *Baker 92*

Satter, Marlene Yvonne 1952- *WhoWrEP 92*
Satter, Robert 1919- *ConAu 139*
Satter, Susan Edel 1949- *WhoAmW 93*
Satterfield, Ben 1945- *WhoWrEP 92*
Satterfield, Charles *ConAu 37NR*
Satterfield, Charles Nelson 1921- *WhoAm 92*
Satterfield, Douglas Stewart 1944- *WhoSSW 93*
Satterfield, Lee A. *Law&B 92*
Satterfield, Mark Edward 1955- *WhoSSW 93*
Satterfield, Pamela Stever 1962- *WhoAmW 93*
Satterfield, Robert Wayne 1926- *St&PR 93*
Satterfield, Russell L. 1911- *St&PR 93*
Satterfield, Terry Lee 1948- *WhoE 93*
Satterfield-Harris, Rita 1949- *WhoAmW 93, WhoE 93*
Satterford, Robert B. *Law&B 92*
Satterlee, Anna Eliza Hickox 1851- *AmWomPl*
Satterlee, Karen Boring *Law&B 92*
Satterlee, W. Bryan, Jr. 1934- *St&PR 93*
Satterlund, Frederic Paul 1956- *St&PR 93*
Satterly, Jack 1906- *WhoAm 92*
Satterly, Kenneth Roland *Law&B 92*
Satterthwaite, Cameron B. 1920- *WhoAm 92*
Satterthwaite, George, II 1935- *WhoE 93*
Satterthwaite, Helen Foster 1928- *WhoAmW 93*
Satterthwaite, Joseph C. 1900-1990 *BioIn 17*
Satterwhite, Cynthia Bennett 1955- *WhoSSW 93*
Satterwhite, R. Scott 1962- *WhoEmL 93, WhoWor 93*
Satterwhite, Ramon Scott 1962- *WhoSSW 93*
Satterwhite, Ramon Stewart 1940- *WhoSSW 93*
Satterwhite, Robert Boyd 1938- *WhoSSW 93*
Satterwhite, W.T. *Law&B 92*
Satterwhite, William T. 1933- *St&PR 93, WhoAm 92*
Satti, Venkata Subbireddy 1939- *WhoE 93*
Sattinger, Jack M. *Law&B 92*
Sattler, Ernst Ludwig 1927- *WhoScE 91-3*
Sattler, Heinrich 1811-1891 *Baker 92*
Sattler, Helen Roney 1921- *WhoWrEP 92*
Sattler, Joseph Peter 1940- *WhoE 93*
Sattler, Lee A. 1920- *St&PR 93*
Sattler, Nancy Joan 1950- *WhoAmW 93*
Sattler, Philipp Klaus 1923- *WhoScE 91-3*
Sattler, Rolf 1936- *WhoAm 92*
Sattran, Vladimir 1930- *WhoScE 91-4*
Satty, Harvey J. 1936- *ScF&FL 92*
Satuloff, Barth 1945- *WhoSSW 93*
Satya Bahin 1944- *WhoAsAP 91*
Satyapriya, Combatore Keshavamurthy 1949- *WhoAm 92*
Satz, Ilya 1875-1912 *Baker 92*
Satz, Louis K. 1927- *WhoAm 92*
Satz, Phyllis Robyne Sdoia 1935- *WhoSSW 93*
Satz, Steven L. *Law&B 92*
Satzger, Douglas A. *Law&B 92*
Satzinger, Walter 1924- *WhoScE 91-3*
Sauar, Tor O. *WhoScE 91-4*
Saucedo, Robert 1932- *WhoAm 92*
Saucedo-Galvan, Beatriz *Law&B 92*
Saucier, Albert Pierre, Jr. 1959- *WhoSSW 93*
Saucier, Randolph Joseph 1939- *WhoSSW 93*
Saucke, M.M. 1927- *St&PR 93*
Sa'ud, 'Abd al-'Aziz ibn-'Abd al-Rahman ibn Faisal c. 1880-1953 *HarEnMi*
Sa'ud, Ibn 1880-1953 *BioIn 17*
Saud Al-Faisal, Prince 1941- *WhoWor 93*
Saudek, Karen Fogg 1943- *St&PR 93*
Sauder, Erie Joseph 1904- *WhoAm 92*
Sauder, Michael Hockensmith 1948- *WhoSSW 93*
Saudinos, Jean *WhoScE 91-2*
Sauer, Bernard d1991 *BioIn 17*
Sauer, Carl 1889-1975 *IntDcAn*
Sauer, Claire Johnson 1960- *WhoAmW 93*
Sauer, Conrad Frederick, III 1923- *St&PR 93*
Sauer, Conrad Frederick, IV 1949- *WhoSSW 93*
Sauer, D. *WhoScE 91-4*
Sauer, David Andrew 1948- *WhoE 93*
Sauer, Douglas C. 1943- *St&PR 93*
Sauer, Elaine 1935- *St&PR 93*
Sauer, Emil (Georg Konrad) von 1862-1942 *Baker 92*
Sauer, George H., Jr. *Law&B 92*
Sauer, George Henry, Sr. 1910- *BiDAMSp 1989*
Sauer, George William 1931- *WhoE 93*
Sauer, Gerhard 1932- *WhoScE 91-3*
Sauer, Gordon Chenoweth 1921- *WhoAm 92, WhoWor 93*
Sauer, Harold 1918- *St&PR 93*
Sauer, Harold John 1953- *WhoEmL 93, WhoWor 93*
Sauer, Harry John, Jr. 1935- *WhoAm 92*
Sauer, Henry E. 1932- *St&PR 93*
Sauer, Henry John 1917- *BiDAMSp 1989*
Sauer, J. George 1916- *St&PR 93*
Sauer, Jeanne Marie 1948- *WhoE 93*
Sauer, Joe Dean 1948- *WhoSSW 93*
Sauer, Jonathan Deininger 1918- *WhoAm 92*
Sauer, Julia L. 1891-1983 *ScF&FL 92*
Sauer, Kenneth 1931- *WhoAm 92*
Sauer, Louis E. 1915- *St&PR 93*
Sauer, Paul Alan 1945- *WhoE 93*
Sauer, Peter 1937- *ConAu 139*
Sauer, Peter Fred 1955- *WhoSSW 93*
Sauer, Richard John 1939- *WhoAm 92*
Sauer, Robert Thomas 1948- *WhoE 93*
Sauer, Susan D. 1965- *WhoAmW 93*
Sauer, Timothy David 1966- *WhoWor 93*
Sauer, Walter R. 1936- *St&PR 93*
Sauerbeck, Dieter R. 1927- *WhoScE 91-3*
Sauerberg, Robert Allen 1930- *St&PR 93*
Sauerbrey, Ellen Elaine Richmond 1937- *WhoAmW 93*
Sauerbrey, G. *WhoScE 91-3*
Sauereisen, Phil F. 1930- *St&PR 93*
Sauerhaft, Stan 1926- *WhoAm 92*
Sauerland, Jeff Michael 1958- *St&PR 93*
Sauers, Edward S. 1941- *St&PR 93*
Sauerwein, Robert A. 1936- *St&PR 93*
Sauey, William R. 1927- *St&PR 93*
Saufley, William Edward *Law&B 92*
Saufley, William Edward 1956- *St&PR 93, WhoAm 92*
Saugerud, Odd Tore 1943- *WhoScE 91-4*
Saugier, Bernard 1943- *WhoScE 91-2*
Sauguet, Henri 1901-1989 *Baker 92, BioIn 17, OxDcOp*
Sauk, Jimson Papak 1944- *WhoAsAP 91*
Saukerson, Eleanor *WhoAmW 93*
Saul, King of Israel *BioIn 17*
Saul, B. Francis, II 1932- *WhoAm 92*
Saul, Barbara Ann 1940- *WhoAmW 93*
Saul, Bradley Scott 1960- *WhoEmL 93*
Saul, Bruce H. *Law&B 92*
Saul, Connie Cline 1954- *WhoAmW 93, WhoSSW 93*
Saul, David John 1950- *WhoIns 93*
Saul, Franklin Robert 1929- *St&PR 93*
Saul, George Brandon 1901-1986 *ScF&FL 92*
Saul, George Brandon, II 1928- *WhoAm 92, WhoE 93*
Saul, John 1942- *Au&Arts 10 [port], ScF&FL 92*
Saul, John Ralston 1947- *WhoCanL 92*
Saul, John (W.), III 1942- *ConAu 40NR*
Saul, John Woodruff, III 1942- *WhoAm 92, WhoWrEP 92*
Saul, Kathryn Bernice 1960- *WhoSSW 93*
Saul, Kenneth Louis 1923- *WhoAm 92*
Saul, Leslie *St&PR 93*
Saul, Mark E. 1948- *WhoE 93*
Saul, Myra Leslie *Law&B 92*
Saul, Nancy Quigley 1950- *WhoAmW 93*
Saul, Norman Eugene 1932- *WhoAm 92*
Saul, Ralph Southey 1922- *St&PR 93, WhoAm 92*
Saul, Ronald John 1947- *St&PR 93*
Saul, W. James 1923- *St&PR 93*
Saul, William Edward 1934- *WhoAm 92*
Saulino, John Louis 1944- *St&PR 93*
Saull, Laura Ann 1960- *WhoAmW 93*
Saulnier, Jean-Pierre Claude 1937- *WhoUN 92*
Saulnier, Jon *St&PR 93*
Sauls, Edna *BioIn 17*
Saulsberry, Belinda T. *Law&B 92*
Saulters, Robert Lockhart 1958- *WhoSSW 93*
Saum, Elizabeth Pape 1930- *WhoAmW 93*
Saum, Hugh H., III *Law&B 92*
Saum, Karen 1935- *ConAu 137*
Saumagne, Pierre 1929- *WhoScE 91-2*
Saumarokov, Leonid *WhoUN 92*
Saumier, Andre 1933- *WhoAm 92*
Saunby, John Brian 1933- *WhoAm 92*
Saunders, A. *WhoScE 91-1*
Saunders, Adrian *DcCPCAm*
Saunders, Alan J. 1943- *St&PR 93*
Saunders, Alan Keith 1947- *WhoAm 92*
Saunders, Albert Henry, II 1950- *St&PR 93*
Saunders, Alexander Hall 1941- *WhoSSW 93*
Saunders, Alexander W. 1941- *St&PR 93*
Saunders, Arlene 1930- *OxDcOp*
Saunders, Arlene 1935- *Baker 92, WhoAm 92*
Saunders, B. Anthony *Law&B 92*
Saunders, Barry Wayne 1944- *WhoSSW 93*
Saunders, Beatrice Nair 1915- *WhoE 93*
Saunders, Bradd *MiSFD 9*
Saunders, Brenda M. 1947- *WhoAmW 93*
Saunders, C.M. 1929- *St&PR 93*
Saunders, Caleb *MajAI, SmATA 69*
Saunders, Catharine Irvine 1872- *AmWomPl*
Saunders, Catherine Hoover 1948- *WhoE 93*
Saunders, Catherine Ruggie 1951- *WhoWrEP 92*
Saunders, Charles, Jr. *Law&B 92*
Saunders, Charles Baskerville, Jr. 1928- *WhoAm 92*
Saunders, Charles Edward 1932- *St&PR 93*
Saunders, Charles Joseph 1938- *WhoSSW 93*
Saunders, Charles R. 1946- *ScF&FL 92*
Saunders, Cicely *BioIn 17*
Saunders, David 1948- *ScF&FL 92*
Saunders, David C. *St&PR 93*
Saunders, David Stanley *WhoScE 91-1*
Saunders, Deborah Lynne 1949- *WhoAmW 93*
Saunders, Dero Ames 1913- *WhoAm 92, WhoWrEP 92*
Saunders, Donald Draper 1935- *WhoWor 93*
Saunders, Donald H. 1935- *St&PR 93*
Saunders, Donald Herbert 1935- *WhoAm 92*
Saunders, Donald Lee *Law&B 92*
Saunders, Donald Leslie 1935- *WhoAm 92*
Saunders, Doris Evans 1921- *WhoAm 92, WhoWrEP 92*
Saunders, Douglas J. 1942- *St&PR 93*
Saunders, Edgar Bogue, Jr. 1933- *St&PR 93*
Saunders, Elizabeth A. 1948- *ScF&FL 92*
Saunders, Elizabeth Ann 1965- *WhoE 93*
Saunders, Eric Don 1942- *WhoAm 92*
Saunders, F. Guy 1940- *St&PR 93*
Saunders, Florence Wenderoth *AmWomPl*
Saunders, Frank Henry 1934- *WhoWor 93*
Saunders, G.K. *ScF&FL 92*
Saunders, George Lawton, Jr. 1931- *WhoAm 92, WhoWor 93*
Saunders, George Wendell 1917- *WhoE 93*
Saunders, Gina Renee 1963- *WhoAmW 93*
Saunders, Gregory Stephen *Law&B 92*
Saunders, Gregory T. 1956- *St&PR 93*
Saunders, Harold E. 1925- *St&PR 93*
Saunders, Harold Henry 1930- *WhoAm 92*
Saunders, Harry D. *Law&B 92*
Saunders, Herbert G. 1937- *St&PR 93*
Saunders, Hilary *ScF&FL 92*
Saunders, Iris Elaine *WhoAmW 93*
Saunders, J(ohn) W(hiteside) 1920- *ConAu 39NR*
Saunders, Jake 1947- *ScF&FL 92*
Saunders, James (Arthur) 1925- *ConAu 139*
Saunders, James C. 1941- *WhoE 93*
Saunders, James Harwood 1948- *WhoWor 93*
Saunders, James S. 1943- *St&PR 93*
Saunders, John *WhoScE 91-1*
Saunders, John 1947- *WhoWor 93*
Saunders, John D. 1926- *St&PR 93*
Saunders, John Harvey 1939- *WhoAm 92*
Saunders, John Howard 1957- *WhoSSW 93*
Saunders, John Louis 1937- *WhoSSW 93*
Saunders, John Martin 1916- *WhoWor 93*
Saunders, John Richard 1925- *WhoE 93*
Saunders, Jon I. 1944- *St&PR 93*
Saunders, Joseph Arthur 1926- *St&PR 93, WhoE 93*
Saunders, Joseph Francis 1950- *WhoAm 92*
Saunders, Joyce Carol 1938- *WhoAmW 93*
Saunders, Judith Anne 1963- *WhoAmW 93*
Saunders, Karen Estelle 1941- *WhoWor 93*
Saunders, Kathryn A. 1920- *WhoAmW 93*
Saunders, Keith C. 1942- *St&PR 93*
Saunders, Kenneth B. *WhoScE 91-1*
Saunders, Kenneth D. 1927- *WhoAm 92*
Saunders, Lillian *AmWomPl*
Saunders, Linda Juanita 1949- *WhoAmW 93*
Saunders, Lonna Jeanne *WhoWor 93*
Saunders, Louise 1893- *AmWomPl*
Saunders, Margaret Marshall 1861-1947 *BioIn 17*
Saunders, Martha Ann 1930- *WhoSSW 93*
Saunders, Mary Sue Susie 1943- *WhoAmW 93*
Saunders, Nancy 1925- *SweetSg C [port]*
Saunders, Norman 1943- *DcCPCAm*
Saunders, Owen Alfred 1904- *WhoWor 93*
Saunders, Patricia Gene 1946- *WhoAmW 93*
Saunders, Paul Christopher 1941- *WhoAm 92*
Saunders, Peter Paul 1928- *St&PR 93, WhoAm 92*
Saunders, R.W. *WhoScE 91-1*
Saunders, Raymond Jennings 1934- *WhoAm 92*
Saunders, Rebecca Ann 1949- *WhoE 93*
Saunders, Richard 1947- *ScF&FL 92*
Saunders, Richard Faye 1919- *St&PR 93*
Saunders, Richard P. 1901-1990 *BioIn 17*
Saunders, Robert Mallough 1915- *WhoAm 92*
Saunders, Robert Samuel 1951- *WhoE 93, WhoWor 93*
Saunders, Roger Alfred 1929- *WhoAm 92*
Saunders, Rubie Agnes 1929- *WhoAm 92, WhoAmW 93, WhoWrEP 92*
Saunders, Russell Joseph 1937- *WhoAm 92*
Saunders, Sally Love 1940- *WhoAm 92, WhoAmW 93, WhoWrEP 92*
Saunders, Sam Cundiff 1931- *WhoAm 92*
Saunders, Samuel Paul 1914- *St&PR 93*
Saunders, Sharyn Elizabeth 1952- *WhoAmW 93*
Saunders, Steven Lawrence 1955- *WhoE 93*
Saunders, Stuart Thomas, Jr. 1941- *St&PR 93, WhoAm 92*
Saunders, Susan Presley 1956- *WhoAmW 93*
Saunders, Ted Elliott 1952- *WhoSSW 93*
Saunders, Terry Rose 1942- *WhoAmW 93*
Saunders, Thomas R. 1946- *St&PR 93*
Saunders, Toni Lynne 1949- *WhoAmW 93*
Saunders, V. Lamoine 1941- *St&PR 93*
Saunders, Virginia Fox 1938- *WhoAmW 93*
Saunders, Ward Bishop, Jr. 1919- *WhoAm 92*
Saunders, William Hundley, Jr. 1926- *WhoAm 92, WhoE 93*
Saunders, William John 1943- *St&PR 93*
Saunders, William Lockwood 1911- *WhoAm 92*
Saunders, Winnie *AmWomPl*
Saunderson, John 1948- *WhoAsAP 91*
Saundry, Susan L. *Law&B 92*
Saunier, Jacques 1948- *WhoWor 93*
Saunier-Seite, Alice 1925- *BioIn 17*
Saunt, Trevor James *WhoScE 91-1*
Sauntry, Susan Schaefer 1943- *WhoAm 92, WhoAmW 93*
Sauntson, B.J. *WhoScE 91-1*
Saupe, Ronald F. *Law&B 92*
Saupe, William A. 1928- *St&PR 93*
Saur, Hans Gunter 1939- *WhoWor 93*
Saur, Karl Otto 1902-1966 *BioIn 17*
Saur, Karl Otto 1944- *BioIn 17*
Saur, Karl W. *Law&B 92*
Saur, Klaus 1941- *BioIn 17*
Saur, Klaus G. 1941- *WhoAm 92*
Saur, Ronald Garlin 1950- *WhoSSW 93*
Saura, Carlos *BioIn 17*
Saura, Carlos 1932- *MiSFD 9*
Saurat, Jean-Hillaire 1943- *WhoScE 91-4*
Sauret, Emile 1852-1920 *Baker 92*
Sauro, Frank *Law&B 92*
Sauro, Frank A. 1958- *St&PR 93*
Sauro, Joseph Pio 1927- *WhoE 93*
Saus, Alfons 1931- *WhoScE 91-3*
Sausen, Allen A. 1948- *St&PR 93*
Sausen, Len Gary 1943- *St&PR 93*
Sausser, Robert Gary 1941- *WhoAm 92*
Saussure, Ferdinand de 1857-1913 *IntDcAn*
Sauter, Charles H. 1942- *St&PR 93*
Sauter, Charles Herman *WhoAm 92*
Sauter, Eric 1948- *ScF&FL 92*
Sauter, Franz Fabian 1933- *WhoWor 93*
Sauter, Friedrich H. 1930- *WhoScE 91-4*
Sauter, Jorg J. 1937- *WhoScE 91-3*
Sauter, Richard S. *St&PR 93*
Sauter, Roy Jacob 1930- *St&PR 93*
Sauter, Van Gordon 1935- *WhoAm 92*
Sauter, Walter August 1925- *St&PR 93*
Sautet, Claude 1924- *MiSFD 9*
Sautter, Dorothy Ann 1946- *WhoAmW 93*
Sautter, R. Craig 1947- *WhoWrEP 92*
Sautter, Richard Daniel 1926- *WhoAm 92*
Sautter, Scott Willard 1957- *WhoSSW 93*
Sauvage, Dominique 1942- *WhoScE 91-2*
Sauvage, Michael 1948- *WhoWor 93*
Sauvage, Pierre *MiSFD 9*
Sauvant, Karl P. 1944- *WhoUN 92*
Sauve, Georges 1925- *WhoWor 93*
Sauve, Jacqueline Annmary 1943- *WhoAmW 93*
Sauve, Jeanne 1922- *WhoAm 92, WhoAmW 93, WhoE 93*
Sauve, Maurice d1992 *NewYTBS 92*
Sauve, Maurice 1923-1992 *BioIn 17*
Sauveur, Bernard 1942- *WhoScE 91-2*
Sauveur, Joseph 1653-1716 *Baker 92*
Sauvey, Donald Robert 1924- *WhoAm 92*
Sauvey, Marian Weilert *Law&B 92*

Sauvy, Alfred 1898-1990 *BioIn 17*
Sauzay, (Charles-) Eugene 1809-1901 *Baker 92*
Savadov, Arsen 1962- *BioIn 17*
Savage, Adrian *ScF&FL 92*
Savage, Arthur L. 1951- *WhoAm 92*
Savage, Arthur P. *Law&B 92*
Savage, Blair deWillis 1941- *WhoAm 92*
Savage, Blake 1914-1990 *BioIn 17*
Savage, Carl d1991 *BioIn 17*
Savage, Charles *Law&B 92*
Savage, Christopher William *Law&B 92*
Savage, D.J. 1950- *ScF&FL 92*
Savage, Dave 1948- *St&PR 93*
Savage, David B. 1954- *St&PR 93*
Savage, David S. 1910- *ScF&FL 92*
Savage, Deborah *DcAmChF 1985*
Savage, Deborah Ann 1963- *WhoAmW 93*
Savage, Donald C. *WhoWrEP 92*
Savage, Donald George 1925- *St&PR 93*
Savage, Dorothy *AmWomPl*
Savage, Edward James 1943- *WhoAm 92*
Savage, Edward Warren, Jr. 1933- *WhoAm 92*
Savage, Eugene Arnold 1934- *WhoE 93*
Savage, Frank 1938- *WhoAm 92*
Savage, Fred *BioIn 17*
Savage, Gale Eleanor *WhoAmW 93*
Savage, Georgia *ConAu 138*
Savage, Gregg J. *St&PR 93*
Savage, Gus *BioIn 17*
Savage, Gus 1925- *CngDr 91, WhoAm 92*
Savage, Henry 1859-1927 *OxDcOp*
Savage, Henry, Jr. 1903- *WhoAm 92*
Savage, Henry W(ilson) 1859-1927 *Baker 92*
Savage, James Amos 1949- *WhoSSW 93*
Savage, James Cathey, III 1947- *WhoE 93*
Savage, James Francis 1939- *WhoAm 92*
Savage, Janet Marie *Law&B 92*
Savage, Jill 1960- *WhoAmW 93*
Savage, John Edmund 1939- *WhoAm 92*
Savage, Joseph George *WhoE 93*
Savage, Joy Marie 1961- *WhoAmW 93*
Savage, Katharine James 1905-1989 *BioIn 17*
Savage, Kay Webb 1942- *WhoAmW 93, WhoSSW 93, WhoWor 93*
Savage, Marcia A. *WhoAmW 93*
Savage, Michael Howard 1938- *WhoE 93*
Savage, Michael Joseph 1872-1940 *DcTwHis*
Savage, Naomi 1927- *WhoAm 92*
Savage, Neve Richard 1944- *WhoAm 92*
Savage, Phyllis *Law&B 92*
Savage, Ralph M. *Law&B 92*
Savage, Randall Ernest 1939- *WhoAm 92*
Savage, Raymond C. 1938- *St&PR 93*
Savage, Richard d1743 *BioIn 17*
Savage, Richard Mark 1950- *WhoSSW 93*
Savage, Richard R. 1925- *St&PR 93*
Savage, Richard Rudolph 1925- *WhoAm 92*
Savage, Richard Temple 1909- *BioIn 17*
Savage, Robert Heath 1929- *WhoAm 92*
Savage, Robert J. 1951- *St&PR 93*
Savage, Robert Joseph Gay *WhoScE 91-1*
Savage, Robert L. 1939- *ScF&FL 92, WhoSSW 93*
Savage, Russell T. *Law&B 92*
Savage, Scott David 1954- *WhoAm 92*
Savage, Stephen Edman 1940- *WhoE 93*
Savage, Stephen J. *Law&B 92*
Savage, Stephen William 1953- *WhoE 93*
Savage, Terry L. 1952- *St&PR 93*
Savage, Thomas Hixon 1928- *WhoAm 92*
Savage, Thomas Joseph 1947- *WhoAm 92*
Savage, Thomas R. *Law&B 92*
Savage, Thomas U. 1948- *WhoWrEP 92*
Savage, Wallace Hamilton 1912- *WhoAm 92*
Savage, Whitney Lee 1928- *WhoAm 92*
Savage, William Woodrow 1914- *WhoAm 92*
Savage, Xyla Ruth 1937- *WhoAm 92*
Savageau, Michael Antonio 1940- *WhoAm 92*
Savalas, Telly 1926- *MiSFD 9*
Savalas, Telly Aristoteles 1926- *WhoAm 92*
Savanauskas, Linda Sue 1959- *WhoAmW 93, WhoE 93*
Savang Vatthana 1907-1981? *DcTwHis*
Savano, Anthony T. *Law&B 92*
Savant, Doug *ConTFT 10*
Sava of Serbia 1175-1235 *OxDcByz*
Savarain, Magdalena Fajardo 1938- *WhoUN 92*
Savard, (Marie-Gabriel-) Augustin 1814-1881 *Baker 92*
Savard, Denis *BioIn 17*
Savard, Denis 1961- *WhoAm 92*
Savard, Edward Victor 1939- *WhoSSW 93*
Savard, Felix Antoine 1896-1982 *BioIn 17, WhoCanL 92*
Savard, Marie-Emmanuel-Augustin 1861-1942 *Baker 92*
Savard, Michel J. *Law&B 92*
Savard, Pierre 1936- *WhoWrEP 92*
Savard, Serge 1946- *WhoAm 92*
Savarese, E.W. *St&PR 93*
Savarese, Louis A. 1926- *St&PR 93*
Savariego, Berta Kozolchyk 1946- *WhoSSW 93*
Savarin, Julian Jay *ScF&FL 92*
Savarino, Samuel Joseph 1958- *WhoE 93*
Savart, Felix 1791-1841 *Baker 92*
Savary, Alain 1918-1988 *BioIn 17*
Savaryn, Peter 1926- *WhoAm 92*
Savas, Emanuel S. 1931- *WhoAm 92*
Savatiel, Karl Robert 1943- *BioIn 17*
Savchenko, Vladimir 1933- *ScF&FL 92*
Savchenko, Vladimir Kirillovich 1939- *WhoUN 92*
Savci Beg d1385? *OxDcByz*
Saveant, J.M. 1933- *WhoScE 91-2*
Savedge, Anne Creery 1947- *WhoSSW 93*
Savedge, Henry S. 1933- *St&PR 93*
Saveland, Robert Nelson 1921- *WhoWrEP 92*
Saveliev, Vladimir Leonidovich 1949- *WhoWor 93*
Savelkoul, Donald Charles 1917- *WhoAm 92*
Savell, Edward Lupo 1921- *WhoAm 92*
Savelli, Angelo 1911- *WhoAm 92*
Saveriano, G.J. 1922- *St&PR 93*
Saverimuttu, Clarence S. B. 1945- *WhoWor 93*
Saverin, Ronald F. 1950- *St&PR 93*
Saverino, Joseph A. 1959- *St&PR 93*
Savesky, Robert S. 1940- *St&PR 93*
Saveth, Edward Norman 1915- *WhoAm 92, WhoWrEP 92*
Saviano, Carl Rocco 1940- *WhoE 93*
Saviano, John Paul 1940- *St&PR 93*
Savic, Dragoslav 1927- *WhoScE 91-4*
Savic, Isidor 1919- *WhoScE 91-4*
Savic, Michael 1929- *WhoE 93*
Savicky, Randolph Philip 1953- *WhoWrEP 92*
Savidge, Benjamin 1929- *St&PR 93*
Savidge, Geoffrey Francis *WhoScE 91-1*
Savier, Etta *AmWomPl*
Saviers, William P., Jr. *Law&B 92*
Savignac, Antonio Enriquez *WhoUN 92*
Saville, Dudley Albert 1933- *WhoAm 92*
Saville, Eric Joseph 1919- *St&PR 93*
Saville, Frances 1863-1935 *Baker 92*
Saville, Malcolm 1901-1982 *ScF&FL 92*
Saville, Philip *MiSFD 9*
Saville, Royce Blair 1948- *WhoEmL 93*
Saville, Thorndike, Jr. 1925- *WhoAm 92*
Saville, Victor d1979 *MiSFD 9N*
Saville-Troike, Muriel Renee 1936- *WhoAm 92*
Savillo, Robert Louis 1953- *WhoE 93*
Savimbi, Jonas 1934- *BioIn 17, ColdWar 2 [port]*
Savimbi, Jonas Malheiro 1934- *DcTwHis, WhoAfr*
Savin, Francisco 1929- *Baker 92*
Savin, Robert Shevryn 1925- *WhoAm 92*
Savin, Ronald Richard 1926- *WhoWor 93*
Savin, Samuel Marvin 1940- *WhoAm 92*
Savine, Alexander 1881-1949 *Baker 92*
Savinelli, Emilio Alfred 1930- *WhoAm 92*
Savini, Donato Antonio 1939- *WhoAm 92*
Savini, Tom *MiSFD 9*
Savini, Tom 1950- *ScF&FL 92*
Savinio, Alberto 1891-1952 *BioIn 17*
Savinkov, Boris 1879-1925 *BioIn 17*
Savino, Frank John 1930- *St&PR 93*
Savino, Peter J. 1942- *WhoAm 92*
Savino, Salvatore M. 1943- *St&PR 93*
Savino-Jones, Marie Dauphine 1961- *WhoAmW 93*
Savio, Robert F. *Law&B 92*
Savioli, Lorenzo 1952- *WhoUN 92*
Saviskas, Judson P. 1953- *St&PR 93*
Saviskas, Judson Peter 1953- *WhoAm 92*
Savit, Carl Hertz 1922- *WhoAm 92*
Savitch, Jessica 1947-1983 *JrnUS*
Savitripriya, Swami 1930- *WhoAmW 93*
Savits, Thomas H. 1938- *WhoE 93*
Savitske, M.B. 1941- *St&PR 93*
Savitsky, Arlene B. *Law&B 92*
Savitsky, Daniel 1921- *WhoAm 92*
Savitsky, David R. 1948- *St&PR 93*
Savitsky, Gerald S. *Law&B 92*
Savitsky, Mordecai d1991 *BioIn 17*
Savitsky, Stephen J. 1945- *St&PR 93*
Savitsky, Thomas R. *Law&B 92*
Savitt, Richard 1927- *BiDAMSp 1989*
Savitt, Sidney Allan 1920- *WhoAm 92*
Savitz, Gerald L. 1936- *St&PR 93*
Savitz, Harriet May 1933- *MajAI [port], SmATA 72 [port]*
Savitz, Jack 1951- *St&PR 93*
Savitz, Joseph J. 1922- *WhoE 93*
Savitz, Martin Harold 1942- *WhoE 93, WhoWor 93*
Savitz, Maxine Lazarus 1937- *WhoAm 92, WhoAmW 93*
Savitz, Richard J. 1946- *St&PR 93*
Savitz, Samuel J. 1936- *WhoAm 92*
Savoca, Antonio Litterio 1923- *WhoAm 92*
Savoca, Carmen Salvatore 1924- *WhoE 93*
Savoca, Nancy *BioIn 17, MiSFD 9*
Savocchio, Joyce A. *WhoAm 92, WhoE 93*
Savoie, Leonard M. 1923-1991 *BioIn 17*
Savoie, Leonard Norman 1928- *St&PR 93, WhoAm 92*
Savoie, Paul 1946- *WhoCanL 92*
Savoie, Terrence Maurice 1946- *WhoWrEP 92*
Savoie, Thomas R. *Law&B 92*
Savolainen, Kai M. 1950- *WhoScE 91-4*
Savolainen, Kaisa 1940- *WhoUN 92*
Savolainen, Vesa Valter 1944- *WhoWor 93*
Savona, Michael Richard 1947- *WhoEmL 93, WhoWor 93*
Savonarola, Girolamo 1452-1498 *BioIn 17*
Savory, Gerald *ScF&FL 92*
Savory, Monica *AmWomPl*
Savory, Teo 1909-1989 *ScF&FL 92*
Savoy, Douglas Eugene 1927- *WhoAm 92, WhoWor 93, WhoWrEP 92*
Savoy, Edward Thomas 1945- *WhoSSW 93*
Savoy, Harold 1924- *St&PR 93*
Savoy, Lauret E. *ConAu 139*
Savoy, Paul 1930- *St&PR 93*
Savoy, Suzanne Marie 1946- *WhoEmL 93*
Savoyka, Lydia d1991 *BioIn 17*
Savrann, Richard Allen 1935- *WhoAm 92*
Savransky, Semen Davidovich 1958- *WhoWor 93*
Savren, Shelley 1949- *WhoWrEP 92*
Savrin, Louis 1927- *WhoAm 92*
Savrun, Ender 1953- *WhoWor 93*
Savtchenko, Victor Gavrilovich 1937- *WhoUN 92*
Saw, Asquith 1949- *WhoWor 93*
Sawabini, Nabil George 1951- *WhoAm 92, WhoE 93*
Sawabini, Wadi Issa 1917- *WhoAm 92*
Sawada, Hideo 1934- *WhoWor 93*
Sawada, Hiroshi 1918- *WhoAsAP 91*
Sawada, Issei 1921- *WhoAsAP 91*
Sawada, Toshio 1933- *WhoWor 93*
Sawafuji, Reijiro 1928- *WhoAsAP 91*
Sawai, Gloria *WhoCanL 92*
Sawai, Teruo 1917- *WhoWor 93*
Sawaki, Yasuhiko 1939- *WhoWor 93*
Sawall, Richard P. *Law&B 92*
Sawallisch, Wolfgang 1923- *Baker 92, IntDcOp, OxDcOp, WhoAm 92, WhoWor 93*
Sawamoto, Mitsuo 1951- *WhoWor 93*
Saward, Eric *ScF&FL 92*
Sawasi, Babadi 1947- *WhoAsAP 91*
Sawatsky, John *BioIn 17*
Sawaya, Michael George 1949- *WhoWor 93*
Sawayanagi, Masataro 1865-1927 *BioIn 17*
Sawbridge, John 1732?-1795 *BioIn 17*
Sawchuck, Ann M. *Law&B 92*
Sawchuk, Ronald John 1940- *WhoAm 92*
Sawde, Derek *ScF&FL 92*
Sawdei, Milan A. *Law&B 92*
Sawdei, Milan A. 1946- *St&PR 93*
Sawdey, Richard M. 1943- *St&PR 93*
Sawdey, Richard Marshall 1943- *WhoAm 92*
Sawdon, Frank B. d1991 *BioIn 17*
Sawey, George Vincent 1928- *St&PR 93*
Sawey, Mary Jean 1955- *WhoAmW 93*
Sawh, Lall Ramnath 1951- *WhoWor 93*
Sawhill, Isabel Van Devanter 1937- *WhoAm 92, WhoE 93*
Sawhill, John Crittenden 1936- *WhoAm 92*
Sawhney, Ravi 1944- *WhoUN 92*
Sawicki, Craig Randall 1959- *St&PR 93*
Sawicki, Jerzy 1927- *WhoScE 91-4*
Sawicki, John Edward 1944- *WhoE 93*
Sawicki, Katherine Rivas 1929- *WhoAmW 93*
Sawicki, Thomas 1945- *St&PR 93*
Sawicz, Thomas Theodore 1951- *WhoAm 92*
Sawin, Craig B. 1956- *St&PR 93*
Sawin, Edward Adams 1937-1990 *BioIn 17*
Sawin, Nancy Churchman 1917- *WhoAm 92*
Sawin, Philip 1933- *ConAu 137*
Sawinski, Vincent John 1925- *WhoAm 92*
Sawiris, Milad Youssef 1922- *WhoAm 92*
Sawkill, J. *WhoScE 91-1*
Sawle, William S., III 1924- *St&PR 93*
Saw Maung, Gen. *WhoAsAP 91*
Saworotnow, Parfeny Pavlovich 1924- *WhoE 93*
Sawran, William R. 1944- *St&PR 93*
Sawtell, Stephen M. 1931- *WhoAm 92*
Sawtelle, Carl S. 1927- *WhoWor 93*
Sawtelle, Gilbert Goss, III 1957- *WhoSSW 93*
Sawtelle, Nancy Lucille 1952- *WhoSSW 93*
Sawyer, Amos *WhoWor 93*
Sawyer, Amos 1945- *BioIn 17, WhoAfr*
Sawyer, Ana Maria Ramirez 1954- *WhoSSW 93*
Sawyer, Annita Perez 1943- *WhoAmW 93, WhoE 93*
Sawyer, Barbara Jean 1920- *WhoWrEP 92*
Sawyer, Barbara Jo 1948- *WhoAmW 93*
Sawyer, Bonnie Louise 1948- *WhoE 93*
Sawyer, Bruce P. 1939- *St&PR 93*
Sawyer, C. Wilson 1945- *St&PR 93*
Sawyer, Charles Henry 1915- *WhoAm 92*
Sawyer, Corinne Holt 1924- *WhoWrEP 92*
Sawyer, David Neal 1940- *WhoSSW 93*
Sawyer, David T. *Law&B 92*
Sawyer, Diane *BioIn 17*
Sawyer, Diane 1945- *ConTFT 10, JrnUS, WhoAm 92, WhoAmW 93*
Sawyer, (Frederick) Don(ald) 1947- *SmATA 72 [port]*
Sawyer, Donald D. 1933- *WhoWor 93*
Sawyer, Donald Keith, Jr. 1930- *St&PR 93*
Sawyer, Dwight Wesley 1933- *St&PR 93*
Sawyer, Ellen Dupuy 1950- *WhoAmW 93*
Sawyer, Forrest *WhoAm 92*
Sawyer, Frederick W. 1950- *St&PR 93*
Sawyer, George Albert 1931- *WhoAm 92*
Sawyer, George C., Sr. d1992 *NewYTBS 92*
Sawyer, Grant 1918- *WhoWor 93*
Sawyer, Helen 1900- *BioIn 17*
Sawyer, Helen Alton *WhoAm 92, WhoAmW 93*
Sawyer, Herman Rudolph, Jr. 1951- *WhoWor 93*
Sawyer, Howard Jerome 1929- *WhoAm 92*
Sawyer, James *BioIn 17*
Sawyer, James E. *BioIn 17*
Sawyer, James Hobart 1960- *WhoSSW 93*
Sawyer, James Lawrence 1947- *WhoE 93*
Sawyer, Jessie M. 1951- *WhoSSW 93*
Sawyer, Joe 1901-1982
See Tracy, William 1917-1967 & Sawyer, Joe 1901-1982 *QDrFCA 92*
Sawyer, John *WhoAm 92*
Sawyer, John Edward 1917- *WhoAm 92*
Sawyer, Joseph Alvin, Jr. *Law&B 92*
Sawyer, Lorraine McPherson 1940- *WhoAmW 93*
Sawyer, Lucy M. *AmWomPl*
Sawyer, Marian K. 1955- *WhoAmW 93*
Sawyer, Mary-Jo Powell 1958- *WhoSSW 93*
Sawyer, R. Scott *Law&B 92*
Sawyer, Raymond Lee, Jr. 1935- *WhoAm 92*
Sawyer, Raymond Terry 1943- *WhoAm 92*
Sawyer, Robert *Law&B 92*
Sawyer, Robert E. *Law&B 92*
Sawyer, Robert G. 1938- *St&PR 93*
Sawyer, Robert J. 1960- *ScF&FL 92*
Sawyer, Robert McLaran 1929- *WhoAm 92*
Sawyer, Robert Noel 1946- *WhoIns 93*
Sawyer, Ruth 1880-1970 *AmWomPl, ConAu 37NR, MajAI [port]*
Sawyer, Samuel Locke 1922- *St&PR 93*
Sawyer, Sandra Lee *Law&B 92*
Sawyer, Stephen P. *Law&B 92*
Sawyer, Sydney White 1960- *WhoAmW 93*
Sawyer, Thomas C. 1945- *CngDr 91, WhoAm 92*
Sawyer, Thomas Edgar 1932- *WhoWor 93*
Sawyer, Thomas H.W. *Law&B 92*
Sawyer, Thomas William 1933- *WhoAm 92*
Sawyer, Warren Allen d1989 *BioIn 17*
Sawyer, Wilbur Henderson 1921- *WhoAm 92*
Sawyer, William Curtis 1933- *WhoWor 93*
Sawyer, William Dale 1929- *WhoAm 92*
Sawyer-Laucanno, Christopher David 1951- *WhoE 93*
Sawyers, Elizabeth Joan 1936- *WhoAm 92*
Sawyers, John Lazelle 1925- *WhoAm 92, WhoWor 93*
Sawyers, Julia Edwards 1964- *WhoAmW 93*
Sawyers, June 1957- *WhoWrEP 92*
Sax, Adolphe 1814-1894 *Baker 92*
Sax, Carol *AmWomPl*
Sax, Charles-Joseph 1791-1865 *Baker 92*
Sax, Geoffrey *MiSFD 9*
Sax, Helen Spigel 1915- *WhoAm 92*
Sax, Joseph Lawrence 1936- *WhoAm 92*
Sax, M. Beth *Law&B 92*
Sax, Mary Randolph 1925- *WhoAmW 93, WhoWor 93*
Sax, Robert A. 1930- *St&PR 93*
Sax, Stanley P. 1925- *St&PR 93*
Sax, Stanley Paul 1925- *WhoAm 92*
Sax, Steve *BioIn 17*
Saxbe, William Bart 1916- *WhoAm 92*
Saxberg, Borje Osvald 1928- *WhoAm 92*

Saxby, Brian John Liddiard *WhoScE 91-1*
Saxby, Lewis Weyburn, Jr. 1924- *St&PR 93*
Saxby, (Henry) Maurice 1924- *SmATA 71 [port]*
Saxby, Stephen John 1950- *WhoWor 93*
Saxby, William *ScF&FL 92*
Saxe, Adrian Anthony 1943- *WhoAm 92*
Saxe, Alan J. *Law&B 92*
Saxe, Diane d1990 *BioIn 17*
Saxe, H. Laurence 1951- *St&PR 93*
Saxe, Hermann Maurice, Count de 1696-1750 *HarEnMi*
Saxe, Jessica Schorr 1951- *WhoSSW 93*
Saxe, Jon S. 1936- *St&PR 93*
Saxe, Jon Sheldon 1936- *WhoAm 92*
Saxe, Leonard *BioIn 17*
Saxe, Leonard 1947- *WhoAm 92*
Saxe, Natalie 1923- *WhoE 93*
Saxe, Richard H. *Law&B 92*
Saxe, Thelma Richards 1941- *WhoAmW 93, WhoE 93, WhoWor 93*
Saxegaard, Finn 1933- *WhoScE 91-4*
Saxena, Amol 1962- *WhoWor 93*
Saxena, Arjun Nath 1932- *WhoWor 93*
Saxena, Brij B. *WhoAm 92*
Saxena, Pramod R. 1939- *WhoScE 91-3*
Saxena, Rakesh Kumar 1957- *WhoWor 93*
Saxena, Subhash Chandra *WhoSSW 93*
Saxer, Richard Karl 1928- *WhoAm 92, WhoWor 93*
Saxod, Raymond 1938- *WhoScE 91-2*
Saxon, A(rthur) H(artley) 1935- *ConAu 37NR*
Saxon, David Stephen 1920- *WhoAm 92*
Saxon, Dirk *WhoWrEP 92*
Saxon, Edward G. 1959- *St&PR 93*
Saxon, Franklin N. 1952- *St&PR 93*
Saxon, George Edward 1932- *WhoWor 93*
Saxon, Grady Sue Loftin *WhoSSW 93*
Saxon, Isabelle fl. 1861-1866 *BioIn 17*
Saxon, James 1954- *WhoE 93*
Saxon, Jerome A. *Law&B 92*
Saxon, John 1936- *MiSFD 9*
Saxon, John David 1950- *WhoAm 92*
Saxon, Peter *ScF&FL 92*
Saxon, Robert Edwin 1947- *WhoSSW 93*
Saxon, Steven Dee 1955- *St&PR 93*
Saxon, William 1927- *ScF&FL 92*
Saxon, William John 1949- *St&PR 93*
Saxonhouse, W. Jack 1941- *WhoSSW 93*
Saxton, Carolyn Virginia 1948- *WhoAmW 93*
Saxton, H. James 1943- *WhoAm 92, WhoE 93*
Saxton, Harold E. *Law&B 92*
Saxton, Jim 1943- *CngDr 91*
Saxton, Josephine 1935- *ScF&FL 92*
Saxton, La Verne Young 1921- *WhoWrEP 92*
Saxton, Mark 1914-1988 *ScF&FL 92*
Saxton, Mary Jane 1953- *WhoAmW 93*
Saxton, Pamela L. 1952- *St&PR 93*
Saxton, Paul Allen 1938- *St&PR 93*
Saxton, Peter *ScF&FL 92*
Saxton, Robert 1953- *Baker 92*
Saxton, Robert F. 1922- *St&PR 93*
Saxton, William Marvin 1927- *WhoAm 92*
Saxum, Gregory A. *Law&B 92*
Say, Allen 1937- *BioIn 17, ChlBIID [port], MajAI [port], SmATA 69 [port]*
Say, Leon 1826-1896 *BioIn 17*
Say, Marlys Mortensen 1924- *WhoAmW 93, WhoWor 93*
Say, P.J. *WhoScE 91-1*
Say, Peggy *BioIn 17*
Sayad, Homer Elisha 1915- *WhoAm 92*
Sayag, Hadida Aigueline 1931- *WhoWor 93*
Sayaji Rao Gaekwar, III, Maharaja of Baroda 1863-1939 *BioIn 17*
Sayao, Bidu 1902- *Baker 92, IntDcOp, OxDcOp*
Sayare, Mitchel 1948- *St&PR 93*
Sayasov, Yuri Stepanovich 1927- *WhoWor 93*
Sayatovic, Wayne Peter 1946- *St&PR 93, WhoAm 92*
Saybolt, Thomas Lawrence *Law&B 92*
Sayce, I.G. *WhoScE 91-1*
Sayed, Mushahid Hussain 1952- *WhoWor 93*
Sayed, Mustafa Kamal 1946- *WhoWor 93*
Sayed, Nisar Ahmad Shah 1930- *WhoWor 93*
Sayeed, Mufti Mohamad *WhoAsAP 91*
Sayeed, P.M. 1941- *WhoAsAP 91*
Sayegh, Glenda Faye 1953- *WhoSSW 93*
Sayegh, Juliette A. 1933- *WhoUN 92*
Sayegh, Nazar 1960- *BioIn 17*
Sayegh, Paul S. 1943- *St&PR 93*
Sayen, Clarence N. 1919-1965 *EncABHB 8 [port]*
Sayen, David Winpenny 1955- *WhoE 93*
Sayen, William Henry 1921- *WhoE 93*
Sayenju, Om Sundar 1956- *WhoWor 93*
Sayer, George *ScF&FL 92*
Sayer, Ian (Keith Terence) 1945- *ConAu 139*
Sayer, John Samuel 1917- *WhoWor 93*
Sayer, Michael 1935- *WhoAm 92*
Sayer, Peter Edwin *Law&B 92*
Sayer, Philip George *WhoScE 91-1*
Sayers, Bruce McArthur *WhoScE 91-1*
Sayers, Chera Lee 1959- *WhoSSW 93*
Sayers, Dorothy L. 1893-1957 *BioIn 17, MagSWL [port]*
Sayers, Frances Clarke 1897-1989 *BioIn 17*
Sayers, Gale 1943- *BioIn 17, WhoAm 92*
Sayers, Hazel Jean 1927- *WhoAmW 93*
Sayers, John *ScF&FL 92*
Sayers, Martin Peter 1922- *WhoAm 92*
Sayers, Peig 1873-1958 *BioIn 17*
Sayers, Roger *WhoSSW 93*
Sayetta, Thomas Charles 1937- *WhoSSW 93*
Sayettat *WhoScE 91-2*
Sayf Al-Dawla 916-967 *OxDcByz*
Sayfie, Eugene Joe 1934- *WhoSSW 93*
Saygili, Hikmet 1941- *WhoScE 91-4*
Saygun, Ahmed Adnan 1907-1991 *Baker 92, BioIn 17*
Sayin, Erol R. 1954- *WhoScE 91-4*
Sayir, Mahir 1940- *WhoScE 91-4*
Sayk, Johannes 1923- *WhoWor 93*
Sayka, Anthony 1957- *WhoWor 93*
Saykally, Richard James 1947- *WhoAm 92*
Sayko, Andrew F., Jr. *Law&B 92*
Sayko, Gene J. 1939- *WhoWrEP 92*
Sayle, Alexei 1952- *QDrFCA 92 [port]*
Sayle, John Gilbert 1939- *St&PR 93*
Sayler, J. William 1935- *WhoIns 93*
Sayler, Jane *BioIn 17*
Sayler, John William, Jr. 1935- *St&PR 93*
Sayles, Dean *BioIn 17*
Sayles, Frank Edward, Jr. 1954- *WhoSSW 93*
Sayles, Helen E.R. 1950- *St&PR 93*
Sayles, John 1950- *BioIn 17, MiSFD 9*
Sayles, John Thomas 1950- *WhoAm 92*
Sayles, Johnny 1937- *BioIn 17*
Sayles, Leah Silberzan d1991 *BioIn 17*
Sayles, Leonard Robert 1926- *WhoAm 92*
Sayles, Michael C. *St&PR 93*
Sayles, Michael J. *Law&B 92*
Sayles, Thomas D., Jr. 1932- *St&PR 93*
Sayles, Thomas Dyke, Jr. 1932- *WhoAm 92*
Saylor, Alice Crane *Law&B 92*
Saylor, Bruce (Stuart) 1946- *Baker 92*
Saylor, Charles D. 1932- *St&PR 93*
Saylor, David J. 1952- *St&PR 93*
Saylor, Henry S. 1930- *St&PR 93*
Saylor, J. Galen 1902- *BioIn 17*
Saylor, Jeannie Watson 1967- *WhoSSW 93*
Saylor, Joan Nesenkar 1950- *WhoAmW 93*
Saylor, John W. 1945- *St&PR 93*
Saylor, Peter M. 1941- *WhoAm 92*
Sayman, Yuksul *WhoScE 91-4*
Saynor, Derek 1955- *WhoScE 91-1*
Sayn-Wittgenstein, Carolyne de 1819-1887 *BioIn 17*
Sayn-Wittgenstein-Berleburg, Friedrich Ernst 1837-1915 *Baker 92*
Sayn-Wittgenstein-Sayn, Marianne *BioIn 17*
Sayre, Cheryl *ScF&FL 92*
Sayre, Clifford M. *BioIn 17*
Sayre, David 1924- *WhoAm 92*
Sayre, Francis Bowes, Jr. 1915- *WhoAm 92*
Sayre, George Edward 1935- *WhoAm 92*
Sayre, Gregg C. *Law&B 92*
Sayre, J.L. 1936- *St&PR 93*
Sayre, Jerry Wayne 1949- *WhoSSW 93*
Sayre, John Marshall 1921- *WhoAm 92, WhoWor 93*
Sayre, Kathleen Pope 1950- *WhoIns 93*
Sayre, Kenneth Malcolm 1928- *WhoAm 92*
Sayre, Nancy Ellen 1943- *WhoE 93*
Sayre, Peter Brent *Law&B 92*
Sayre, Philip Robinson 1946- *WhoE 93*
Sayre, Philip Russell 1932- *St&PR 93*
Sayre, Robert Freeman 1933- *WhoAm 92, WhoWrEP 92*
Sayre, Robert H. 1922- *WhoAm 92, WhoWor 93*
Sayre, Robert Heysham 1939- *St&PR 93*
Sayre, Robert Marion 1924- *WhoAm 92, WhoWor 93*
Sayre, Rose *ScF&FL 92*
Sayre, Scott E. *Law&B 92*
Sayre, William Heysham 1933- *WhoAm 92*
Sayre-McCord, Geoffrey 1956- *WhoSSW 93*
Sayres, William Cortlandt 1927- *WhoAm 92*
Sayve, Lambert de 1548?-1614 *Baker 92*
Saywell, William George Gabriel 1936- *WhoAm 92*
Saywer, John J. 1950- *WhoSSW 93*
Sazama, James F. 1942- *St&PR 93*
Sazama, Kathleen 1941- *WhoAmW 93*
Sazdanoff, Catherine A. *Law&B 92*
Sazegar, Morteza 1933- *WhoAm 92*
Sazima, Henry John 1927- *WhoAm 92*
Sazonov, Vjacheslav Vasily 1935- *WhoWor 93*
Sbar, P.S. *Law&B 92*
Sbar, Sandra Carol 1942- *WhoAmW 93*
Sbaratta, Richard M. *Law&B 92*
Sbarbaro, Richard D. 1946- *St&PR 93*
Sbarbaro, Richard Donald 1946- *WhoAm 92*
Sbarbaro, Robert Arthur 1933- *St&PR 93, WhoAm 92*
Sbarra, Donald 1930- *St&PR 93*
Sbarra, Francesco 1611-1668 *OxDcOp*
Sbarra, Robert Anthony 1934- *WhoE 93*
Sbarra, Robert D. 1945- *St&PR 93*
Sbarro, Mario 1942- *St&PR 93*
Sbo, Stein *WhoScE 91-4*
Sbordon, William G. 1928- *WhoAm 92*
Sbordone, Louise *St&PR 93*
Sbragia, Gary W. 1941- *WhoWor 93*
Sbriglia, Giovanni 1829-1916 *Baker 92, OxDcOp*
Sbriglio, Robert Patrick 1953- *WhoE 93, WhoWor 93*
Sbuttoni, Michael James 1953- *WhoE 93*
Scaasi, Arnold 1932?- *BioIn 17*
Scaasi, Arnold Martin *WhoAm 92*
Scacchi, Greta *BioIn 17*
Scacchi, Marco c. 1600-c. 1684 *Baker 92*
Scaccia, Carmelo Anthony 1930- *St&PR 93*
Scacciati, Bianca 1894-1948 *Baker 92*
Scacco, Linda Ann 1954- *WhoAmW 93*
Scace, Albert Walter 1948- *WhoWrEP 92*
Scaduto, James A. *Law&B 92*
Scaduto, Patricia M. *Law&B 92*
Scafe, Kenneth R. 1936- *St&PR 93*
Scafetta, Joseph, Jr. 1947- *WhoSSW 93*
Scaffidi, Judith Ann 1950- *WhoAmW 93, WhoE 93, WhoEmL 93, WhoWor 93*
Scaffidi, Marie Ann 1961- *St&PR 93*
Scafidel, James R. *ScF&FL 92*
Scafidi, Frank Anthony 1961- *WhoSSW 93*
Scafura, Angelo Thomas 1937- *St&PR 93*
Scaggs, Boz 1944- *SoulM, WhoAm 92*
Scaggs, Howard Irwin 1921- *WhoAm 92*
Scaggs, Roger T. 1939- *St&PR 93*
Scaglione, Aldo Domenico 1925- *WhoAm 92*
Scaglione, Janet 1950- *WhoSSW 93*
Scaglione, Joseph Maria d1992 *NewYTBS 92*
Scagliuso, Mark J. 1959- *St&PR 93*
Scagnetti, Jack James 1924- *WhoWrEP 92*
Scahill, Edward Joseph, Jr. *Law&B 92*
Scaia, Mary Julie 1953- *WhoE 93*
Scaiano, Donald A. 1932- *WhoIns 93*
Scaife, Brendan Kevin Patrick 1928- *WhoScE 91-3*
Scaife, John Graham *WhoScE 91-1*
Scaife, William Arthur 1947- *WhoSSW 93*
Scaife, William Oliver, Jr. *Law&B 92*
Scaillet, Michel V.C. 1935- *WhoUN 92*
Scairpon, Sharon Cecilia 1946- *WhoAmW 93*
Scala, Francis (Maria) 1819?-1903 *Baker 92*
Scala, James 1934- *WhoAm 92*
Scala, Joseph Anthony, Jr. 1940- *WhoAm 92*
Scala, Ralph John 1949- *St&PR 93*
Scalapino, Douglas James 1933- *WhoAm 92*
Scalapino, Robert A(nthony) 1919- *ConAu 40NR*
Scalchi, Sofia 1850-1922 *Baker 92*
Scalchunes, Peter 1937- *St&PR 93*
Scalchunes, William 1935- *St&PR 93*
Scalcucci, Frank S. 1943- *St&PR 93*
Scalercio, Eugene Nicholas 1940- *St&PR 93*
Scalero, Rosario 1870-1954 *Baker 92*
Scales, Althea E. 1951- *WhoWrEP 92*
Scales, Ann *Law&B 92*
Scales, Derek P. 1921- *ScF&FL 92*
Scales, Diann Roylette 1945- *WhoAmW 93*
Scales, George Walter 1900-1976 *BiDAMSp 1989*
Scales, James Ralph 1919- *WhoAm 92*
Scales, Jean Norris 1930- *WhoAmW 93, WhoSSW 93*
Scales, Jeffrey M. 1953- *St&PR 93*
Scales, Laura Lord 1879-1990 *BioIn 17*
Scales, Peter Craig 1949- *WhoSSW 93*
Scaletta, Helen Marguerite 1927- *WhoAmW 93, WhoWor 93*
Scaletta, Phillip Jasper 1925- *WhoWor 93*
Scalfano, Jennie Lou 1956- *WhoAmW 93*
Scalfaro, Luigi 1918- *WhoWor 93*
Scalfi, Carlo Guiseppe 1932- *WhoWor 93*
Scalia, Antonin 1936- *BioIn 17, CngDr 91, OxCSupC [port], WhoAm 92, WhoE 93, WhoWor 93*
Scalia, Jack *BioIn 17*
Scalia, John Cazes 1947- *WhoE 93*
Scalia, Rebeka J. 1942- *St&PR 93*
Scalia, William Charles 1944- *St&PR 93*
Scaling, G. Wilson, II 1938- *WhoAm 92*
Scalise, Carol Jeanne 1936- *WhoAmW 93*
Scalise, Charles Joseph 1950- *WhoSSW 93*
Scalise, Osvaldo Hector 1940- *WhoWor 93*
Scalish, Frank Anthony 1940- *WhoWor 93*
Scall, P. 1936- *St&PR 93*
Scalla, Rene 1940- *WhoScE 91-2*
Scallan, James Bernard *Law&B 92*
Scallen, Thomas K. 1926- *St&PR 93*
Scallen, Thomas Kaine 1925- *WhoAm 92, WhoWor 93*
Scalley, John J. 1930- *WhoSSW 93*
Scallon, Timothy Phillip 1957- *WhoSSW 93*
Scalo, Joseph F. *Law&B 92*
Scalzi, Carlo fl. 1719-1738 *OxDcOp*
Scaminace, Joseph M. *St&PR 93*
Scamman, W. Douglas, Jr. 1941- *WhoAm 92*
Scammell, Barry Edward 1941- *St&PR 93, WhoAm 92*
Scammell, Bill *ScF&FL 92*
Scammon, Richard Montgomery 1915- *WhoAm 92*
Scampini, Constantino 1951- *WhoWor 93*
Scanavino, N. H. Marco 1953- *WhoWor 93*
Scandalios, George N. *WhoAm 92*
Scandalios, John George 1934- *WhoAm 92*
Scandary, E. Jane 1923- *WhoAmW 93*
Scandello, Antonio 1517-1580 *Baker 92*
Scandling, William Fredric 1922- *WhoAm 92*
Scandura, Jani *BioIn 17*
Scandura, Joseph Michael 1932- *WhoAm 92*
Scandurra, Roberto 1935- *WhoScE 91-3*
Scanes, Colin Guy 1947- *WhoE 93*
Scanlan, Eugene Richard 1923- *WhoAm 92*
Scanlan, Francis X. 1949- *St&PR 93*
Scanlan, J.O. 1937- *WhoScE 91-3*
Scanlan, James Patrick 1927- *WhoAm 92*
Scanlan, John Douglas 1927- *WhoAm 92*
Scanlan, John E., Jr. 1961- *St&PR 93*
Scanlan, John Joseph 1906- *WhoAm 92*
Scanlan, John Thomas *WhoE 93*
Scanlan, Joseph L. *MiSFD 9*
Scanlan, Mary Ellen 1942- *WhoAmW 93*
Scanlan, P. Douglas *St&PR 93*
Scanlan, Papali'i Tommy 1953- *WhoWor 93*
Scanlan, Richard Thomas 1928- *WhoAm 92*
Scanlan, Stephanie *Law&B 92*
Scanlan, Thomas Cleary 1957- *WhoAm 92*
Scanlan, Thomas Joseph 1945- *WhoAm 92, WhoE 93*
Scanlan, Thomas M., Jr. 1935- *St&PR 93*
Scanling, Frederick Hamilton 1942- *WhoSSW 93*
Scanlon, Anthony John 1951- *WhoE 93*
Scanlon, Carlene Myers 1937- *WhoSSW 93*
Scanlon, Charles Francis 1935- *WhoAm 92*
Scanlon, Charles J. 1915-1990 *BioIn 17*
Scanlon, David G. 1921-1990 *BioIn 17*
Scanlon, Dorothy Therese 1928- *WhoAmW 93*
Scanlon, Edward F. 1918- *WhoAm 92*
Scanlon, James Thomas 1946- *St&PR 93*
Scanlon, Jane Cronin 1922- *WhoAm 92, WhoAmW 93, WhoE 93*
Scanlon, John *BioIn 17*
Scanlon, John James, III *Law&B 92*
Scanlon, Laurie Ann 1961- *WhoWor 93*
Scanlon, Mary Agnes 1954- *WhoAmW 93*
Scanlon, Michael J. 1954- *WhoSSW 93*
Scanlon, Noel *ScF&FL 92*
Scanlon, Patrick Michael 1940- *WhoAm 92*
Scanlon, Patrick R. *Law&B 92*
Scanlon, Paul *ScF&FL 92*
Scanlon, Peter Redmond 1931- *WhoAm 92*
Scanlon, Rosemary 1939- *WhoAm 92*
Scanlon, Terrence Maurice 1939- *WhoAm 92*
Scanlon, Thomas Michael 1909- *WhoAm 92*
Scannapieco, Pasquale Joseph 1942- *WhoE 93*
Scannell, Dale Paul 1929- *WhoAm 92*
Scannell, Gerard F. *BioIn 17*
Scannell, Joan P. *Law&B 92*

Scannell, Philip Lawrence, Jr. 1919- St&PR 93
Scannell, Robert E. Law&B 92
Scannell, Robert E. 1939- St&PR 93, WhoAm 92
Scannell, Thomas John 1954- WhoWor 93
Scannell, William Edward 1934- WhoWor 93
Scannerini, Silvano Idelio Ezio 1940- WhoWor 93
Scano, Joan S. 1944- St&PR 93
Scantland, Donald Maurice 1931- St&PR 93
Scanziani, Piero d1908 ScF&FL 92
Scaparro, Jack ScF&FL 92
Scapicchio, Frank A. Law&B 92
Scapula, Publius Ostorius dc. 52 HarEnMi
Scar, Howard S. 1930- St&PR 93
Scarabelli, Diamante Maria fl. 1695-1718 OxDcOp
Scaramuzzi, Franco 1926- WhoScE 91-3, WhoWor 93
Scarano, Eduardo WhoScE 91-3
Scarantino, Sal E. Law&B 92
Scaravaglione, Concetta 1900-1975 BioIn 17
Scarbath, Horst G. 1938- WhoWor 93
Scarbinsky, Mark Joseph 1949- St&PR 93
Scarboro, Edwin Mosgrove 1931- St&PR 93
Scarborough, Carl Arthur 1940- St&PR 93
Scarborough, Charles ScF&FL 92
Scarborough, Charles Bishop, III 1943- WhoAm 92, WhoWor 93
Scarborough, Chuck 1943- ScF&FL 92
Scarborough, Elizabeth 1947- ScF&FL 92
Scarborough, Frances Songer 1957- WhoAmW 93
Scarborough, George Adolphus 1859-1900 BioIn 17
Scarborough, George W. d1900 BioIn 17
Scarborough, Isabel Willena 1898- WhoWrEP 92
Scarborough, Jack William 1946- WhoSSW 93
Scarborough, June D. Law&B 92
Scarborough, Mary Gosman 1895- BioIn 17
Scarborough, Robert Bowman 1928- St&PR 93
Scarborough, Robert Henry, Jr. 1923- WhoAm 92
Scarborough, Ruth 1939- WhoE 93
Scarborough, Vernon L(ee) 1950- ConAu 139
Scarborough, William Sanders 1852-1926 EncAACR
Scarborough, Yancey Wilcox, Jr. 1922- St&PR 93
Scarbrough, Arlan Earl 1936- St&PR 93
Scarbrough, Cleve Knox, Jr. 1939- WhoAm 92, WhoSSW 93
Scarbrough, Ernest Earl 1947- WhoWor 93
Scarbrough, George (Addison) 1915- ConAu 38NR, WhoWrEP 92
Scarbrough, Patsy Ann Wurth 1947- WhoEmL 93
Scardefield, Amelia F. AmWomPl
Scardellato, Adriano 1955- WhoWor 93
Scardera, Michael 1935- WhoE 93
Scardino, Albert James 1948- WhoAm 92
Scardino, Don MiSFD 9, WhoE 93
Scardino, James J. 1953- St&PR 93
Scardino, John, Jr. 1950- St&PR 93
Scardino, Marjorie Morris 1947- WhoE 93
Scardino, Michael Christopher 1948- WhoAm 92
Scardocchia, Gaetano 1937- WhoE 93
Scarf, Herbert Eli 1930- WhoAm 92
Scarf, Maggie 1932- WhoWrEP 92
Scarf, Margaret 1932- WhoAm 92
Scarfia, Michael Louis 1928- St&PR 93
Scarfo, Nicodemo Law&B 92
Scarfone, Anthony C. Law&B 92
Scarfone, Jay ScF&FL 92
Scaria, Emil 1838-1886 Baker 92, OxDcOp
Scarino, Marianne Cannava 1951- WhoWrEP 92
Scarlata, Antonia Ellen L. 1944- WhoE 93
Scarlatesco, Ion 1872-1922 Baker 92
Scarlato, Orest Alexandrovich 1920- WhoWor 93
Scarlatti, Alessandro 1660-1725 IntDcOp [port], OxDcOp
Scarlatti, (Pietro) Alessandro (Gaspare) 1660-1725 Baker 92
Scarlatti, Domenico 1685-1757 OxDcOp
Scarlatti, (Giuseppe) Domenico 1685-1757 Baker 92
Scarlatti, Giuseppe c. 1718-1777 Baker 92
Scarlatti, Giuseppe c. 1720-1777 OxDcOp
Scarlett, Harold O. WhoAm 92
Scarlett, John Archibald 1951- St&PR 93
Scarlett, John Donald 1923- WhoAm 92
Scarlett, Robert H. 1943- St&PR 93
Scarlett, Susan MajAI
Scarman, George ScF&FL 92
Scarman, Leslie George BioIn 17
Scarminach, Charles Anthony 1944- WhoAm 92
Scarmolin, (Anthony) Louis 1890-1969 Baker 92
Scarne, John 1903- WhoAm 92
Scarne, Paul Thomas 1947- WhoAm 92, WhoWor 93
Scaros, Constantine St&PR 93
Scarpa, Anthony F. WhoAm 92
Scarpa, Antonio 1942- WhoAm 92
Scarpati, Daniele Francesco 1947- WhoWor 93
Scarpelli, Dante Giovanni 1927- WhoAm 92
Scarpini, Pietro 1911- Baker 92
Scarpino, John J. 1966- WhoE 93
Scarpino, Pasquale Valentine 1932- WhoAm 92
Scarpitti, Frank Roland 1936- WhoAm 92
Scarpone, Frank R. 1947- St&PR 93
Scarr, Sandra Wood 1936- WhoAm 92
Scarrett, Douglas WhoScE 91-1
Scarritt, James Richard 1935- WhoAm 92
Scarrow, Pamela Kay 1949- WhoAmW 93
Scarry, Elaine (Margaret) 1946- ConAu 137
Scarry, Richard (McClure) 1919- ConAu 39NR, MajAI [port], WhoAm 92
Scarsdale, Richard Bouten 1931- St&PR 93
Scarsdale, Sybil S. 1933- St&PR 93
Scarsdale, William M. 1952- St&PR 93
Scarsi, Livio 1927- WhoScE 91-3, WhoWor 93
Scasta, David Lynn 1949- WhoE 93, WhoWor 93
Scatena, Lorraine Borba 1924- WhoAmW 93
Scates, Carol Moore 1943- WhoAmW 93
Scates, Eva Winifred AmWomPl
Scattergood, Harold F. 1948- St&PR 93
Scaturro, Philip David 1938- WhoAm 92
Scavullo, Charles, Jr. 1953- St&PR 93
Scavullo, Francesco 1929- BioIn 17, WhoAm 92
Sce, Doug F. 1954- St&PR 93
Scearce, Michael A. Law&B 92
Scearce, William Russell 1930- WhoWrEP 92
Scearse, Patricia Dotson 1931- WhoAm 92, WhoWor 93
Scedrov, Andre 1955- WhoE 93, WhoWor 93
Sceery, Beverly Davis WhoAmW 93
Scek, Danuta WhoScE 91-4
Scelba, Mario 1901-1991 BioIn 17, CurBio 92N
Scelsi, Giacinto 1905-1988 Baker 92
Scemons, Donna J. WhoAmW 93
Scepanski, Jordan Michael 1942- WhoAm 92
Sceppaguercio, Maria Ann 1962- WhoAmW 93
Scerbo, Joseph E. 1934- St&PR 93
Scerra, Robert A. 1955- St&PR 93
Schaab, Arnold J. 1939- WhoE 93
Schaab, Robert 1817-1887 Baker 92
Schaack, Philip Anthony 1921- WhoAm 92
Schaad, Dieter 1928- WhoUN 92
Schaaf, Allen 1942- MiSFD 9
Schaaf, Barbara Carol WhoAmW 93
Schaaf, Bradford Perkins 1942- St&PR 93
Schaaf, Carl Hart 1912- WhoAm 92
Schaaf, Donald Martin 1961- WhoE 93
Schaaf, Eileen AmWomPl
Schaaf, Eric William 1956- WhoE 93
Schaaf, Frederick Carl 1954- WhoWrEP 92
Schaaf, Kathryn Ann 1954- WhoAmW 93
Schaaf, M.B. Goffstein BioIn 17
Schaaf, Richard Edmund 1949- WhoWrEP 92
Schaaf, Robert E. 1935- WhoIns 93
Schaafsma, Paul E. Law&B 92
Schaafsma, Tjeerd J. 1937- WhoScE 91-3
Schaag, Carolyn Louise 1936- WhoSSW 93
Schaake, Paul E. 1946- St&PR 93
Schaal, Allyson Brooke 1965- WhoE 93
Schaal, Daniel A., Jr. 1941- St&PR 93
Schaal, Ernest A. Law&B 92
Schaal, Herbert Rudolf 1940- WhoAm 92
Schaal, John Eric Law&B 92
Schaal, Peter 1935- WhoWor 93
Schaal, Werner Georg Hans 1934- WhoWor 93
Schaap, James Calvin 1948- WhoWrEP 92
Schaap, Richard Jay 1934- WhoAm 92, WhoWrEP 92
Schaap, William Herman 1940- WhoE 93
Schaar, Frances Elizabeth 1911- WhoWrEP 92
Schaar, Gunter 1932- WhoWor 93
Schaar, Susan Clarke 1949- WhoAmW 93
Schaar, William Henry 1938- St&PR 93
Schab, Thomas J. Law&B 92
Schaber, Gordon Duane 1927- WhoAm 92
Schaberg, S. Donald 1938- St&PR 93
Schabert, Peter 1939- St&PR 93
Schachar, Ronald A. 1941- WhoSSW 93
Schachat, Walter S. 1916-1990 BioIn 17
Schachinger, Ewald 1943- WhoScE 91-4
Schachman, Howard Kapnek 1918- WhoAm 92
Schachne, Gary 1950- St&PR 93, WhoE 93
Schachner, Carol B. Law&B 92
Schachner, Dianne Joyce WhoE 93
Schachner, E. Douglas M. 1935- St&PR 93
Schachner, Robert David 1955- WhoSSW 93
Schachner, Robert Wahl 1940- WhoSSW 93
Schachner, Rudolf Joseph 1821-1896 Baker 92
Schachner-Camartin, Melitta 1943- WhoScE 91-3
Schacht, Chrisopher Cleland 1946- WhoAsAP 91
Schacht, Cordula 1943- BioIn 17
Schacht, Henry B. 1934- St&PR 93
Schacht, Henry Brewer 1934- WhoAm 92
Schacht, Henry Mevis 1916- WhoAm 92
Schacht, Henry Neil 1930- WhoSSW 93
Schacht, Hjalmar 1877-1970 BioIn 17, DcTwHis
Schacht, Jochen Heinrich 1939- WhoAm 92
Schacht, John Michael 1959- St&PR 93
Schacht, Matthias Henriksen 1660-1700 Baker 92
Schacht, Michael A. BioIn 17
Schacht, Richard Lawrence 1941- WhoAm 92, WhoWrEP 92
Schacht, Ronald Stuart 1932- WhoAm 92
Schacht, Theodor, Freiherr von 1748-1823 Baker 92
Schachte, Henry M. d1991 BioIn 17
Schachte, John Jacob 1933- St&PR 93
Schachte, William Leon, Jr. 1940- WhoAm 92
Schachtel, Barbara Harriet Levin 1921- WhoAmW 93, WhoWor 93
Schachter, Edwin Neil 1943- WhoE 93
Schachter, Frances Fuchs 1930-1991 BioIn 17
Schachter, Harry 1933- WhoAm 92
Schachter, Hindy Lauer 1945- WhoWrEP 92
Schachter, Judith Spector 1928- WhoAmW 93
Schachter, Julius 1936- WhoAm 92
Schachter, Madeleine Law&B 92
Schachter, Max 1913- WhoAm 92
Schachter, Michael Ben 1941- WhoE 93
Schachter, Milton Jay 1953- WhoSSW 93
Schachter, Oscar 1915- WhoAm 92, WhoE 93
Schachter, Oscar H. 1933- St&PR 93
Schachter, Rozalie 1946- WhoAmW 93
Schachter, Sheldon Jay 1943- St&PR 93
Schachter, Stanley 1922- WhoAm 92
Schachter, Steven MiSFD 9
Schack, Benedikt 1758-1826 OxDcOp
Schack, Benedikt (Emanuel) 1758?-1826 Baker 92
Schacker, Barbara BioIn 17
Schacknow, Rosalind Koss 1925- St&PR 93
Schacter, Daniel L. BioIn 17
Schacter, Daniel Lawrence 1952- WhoAm 92
Schacter, Janice Lynn 1963- WhoAmW 93
Schad, Joseph 1812-1879 Baker 92
Schad, Theodore George, Jr. 1927- St&PR 93, WhoAm 92, WhoSSW 93, WhoWor 93
Schad, Theodore MacNeeve 1918- WhoAm 92, WhoE 93
Schade, Ardith Ann 1945- WhoAmW 93
Schade, Edward P. 1941- St&PR 93
Schade, Emil A.G.M. Law&B 92
Schaden, Egon 1913- IntDcAn
Schadewitz, Carl 1887-1945 Baker 92
Schadler, Harvey Walter 1931- WhoE 93
Schadler, Thomas E. 1951- St&PR 93
Schadrack, Frederick Charles 1926- St&PR 93
Schadt, James P. 1938- St&PR 93
Schaeberle, Timothy Michael Law&B 92
Schaechter, Moselio 1928- WhoAm 92
Schaedler, Russell William 1927- WhoAm 92
Schaefer, Adolph O., Jr. 1932- WhoAm 92
Schaefer, Bonnie Maclay 1961- WhoAmW 93
Schaefer, C. Barry 1939- WhoAm 92
Schaefer, Carl Fellman 1903- WhoAm 92
Schaefer, Carl George Lewis WhoAm 92
Schaefer, Charles James, III 1926- WhoAm 92, WhoWor 93
Schaefer, Charles V., Jr. 1914- St&PR 93
Schaefer, Dan 1936- CngDr 91
Schaefer, Dan L. 1936- WhoAm 92
Schaefer, Diane BioIn 17
Schaefer, Ephraim A. 1926- St&PR 93
Schaefer, Erhardt H. 1928- St&PR 93
Schaefer, Ethelinda AmWomPl
Schaefer, George 1920- MiSFD 9
Schaefer, George A. 1945- St&PR 93
Schaefer, George Anthony 1928- BioIn 17, St&PR 93, WhoAm 92
Schaefer, George J., III 1942- St&PR 93
Schaefer, George Louis 1920- WhoAm 92
Schaefer, George Peter 1950- WhoE 93
Schaefer, Georgette A. Law&B 92
Schaefer, Gordon Emory 1932- WhoAm 92
Schaefer, Hans K. 1935- St&PR 93
Schaefer, Hans Michael 1940- St&PR 93
Schaefer, Harry G. 1936- St&PR 93
Schaefer, Harry George 1936- WhoAm 92
Schaefer, Helmut 1926- WhoScE 91-3
Schaefer, Henry 1930- St&PR 93
Schaefer, Henry Frederick, III 1944- WhoAm 92, WhoSSW 93
Schaefer, Herbert G. BioIn 17
Schaefer, Jack 1907-1991 AnObit 1991, ScF&FL 92
Schaefer, Jack Warner 1907- DcAmChF 1960
Schaefer, Jack Warner 1907-1991 BioIn 17
Schaefer, Jacob Wernli 1919- WhoAm 92
Schaefer, James Simeon 1948- St&PR 93
Schaefer, Jimmie Wayne, Jr. 1951- WhoAm 92
Schaefer, John Bock 1937- WhoE 93
Schaefer, John Edward 1948- WhoSSW 93
Schaefer, John Paul 1934- WhoAm 92
Schaefer, Jon Patrick 1948- WhoWor 93
Schaefer, Kristi Ann Schmidt 1953- WhoAmW 93
Schaefer, Leslye BioIn 17
Schaefer, Lois Elizabeth 1924- WhoAm 92
Schaefer, Marcia Sontz 1938- WhoE 93
Schaefer, Marilyn Louise 1933- WhoAmW 93
Schaefer, Mary Ann 1942- WhoAmW 93
Schaefer, Mary B. 1932- WhoAmW 93
Schaefer, Matthias Dietrich 1942- WhoWor 93
Schaefer, Michael R. 1949- St&PR 93
Schaefer, P. James 1918- St&PR 93
Schaefer, Paul BioIn 17
Schaefer, Philip S. Law&B 92
Schaefer, Philip W. Law&B 92
Schaefer, Philip William 1935- WhoSSW 93
Schaefer, Rhoda Pesner 1947- WhoE 93
Schaefer, Robert 1928- St&PR 93
Schaefer, Robert A. 1961- St&PR 93
Schaefer, Robert James 1939- WhoE 93
Schaefer, Robert L. Law&B 92
Schaefer, Robert L. 1939- St&PR 93
Schaefer, Robert Wayne 1934- WhoAm 92
Schaefer, Roland Michael 1954- WhoWor 93
Schaefer, Rowland 1916- St&PR 93
Schaefer, Scott Michael 1955- St&PR 93
Schaefer, Stephen Martin 1946- WhoWor 93
Schaefer, Steven Joseph 1950- WhoSSW 93
Schaefer, Terry William 1946- St&PR 93
Schaefer, Theodor 1904-1969 Baker 92
Schaefer, Theodore Peter 1933- WhoAm 92
Schaefer, Thomas Carl 1939- St&PR 93
Schaefer, Thomas Felix 1955- WhoWor 93
Schaefer, Thomas Reuben 1950- St&PR 93
Schaefer, William David 1928- WhoAm 92
Schaefer, William Donald BioIn 17
Schaefer, William Donald 1921- WhoAm 92, WhoE 93, WhoWor 93
Schaefer, Wolfgang 1952- WhoWor 93
Schaeffer, Andrew L. Law&B 92
Schaeffer, Barbara Hamilton 1926- WhoAmW 93, WhoSSW 93, WhoWor 93
Schaeffer, Bayard G. d1991 BioIn 17
Schaeffer, Boguslaw (Julien) 1929- Baker 92
Schaeffer, Donald Thomas 1926- WhoSSW 93
Schaeffer, Edwin Frank, Jr. 1930- St&PR 93, WhoAm 92
Schaeffer, Francis MiSFD 9
Schaeffer, Franky BioIn 17
Schaeffer, Glen Law&B 92
Schaeffer, Glenn William 1953- WhoAm 92

Schaeffer, Helmut A. 1938- WhoScE 91-3
Schaeffer, Henri 1954- WhoWor 93
Schaeffer, Ina Elaine 1947- WhoE 93
Schaeffer, J.D. Law&B 92
Schaeffer, Neil Jerome 1940- WhoE 93
Schaeffer, Peter N. 1951- St&PR 93
Schaeffer, Pierre 1910- Baker 92
Schaeffer, Pierre Henri Marie 1910- WhoWor 93
Schaeffer, Piotr (Mikolaj) 1958- See Schaeffer, Boguslaw (Julien) 1929- Baker 92
Schaeffer, R. 1945- St&PR 93
Schaeffer, Rebecca BioIn 17
Schaeffer, Reiner Horst 1938- WhoAm 92
Schaeffer, Susan Fromberg BioIn 17
Schaeffer, Susan Fromberg 1941- JeAmFiW, ScF&FL 92, WhoAmW 93, WhoWrEP 92
Schaeffer, Tyler BioIn 17
Schaeffer, Vernon Joseph 1919- WhoWrEP 92
Schaeffer, Wayne G. 1946- St&PR 93
Schaeffer, Wendell Gordon 1917- WhoWor 93
Schaeffner, Andre 1895-1980 Baker 92, IntDcAn
Schaefgen, Philip P. 1958- WhoSSW 93, WhoWor 93
Schaefler, Leon 1903- WhoAm 92
Schaeidt, Helmut 1927- WhoWor 93
Schaen, Frederic Warren 1937- St&PR 93
Schaen, Lawrence L. 1929- St&PR 93
Schaeneman, Lewis G., Jr. 1930- WhoAm 92
Schaenen, Lee Joel 1925- WhoAm 92
Schaer, Michelle Leann 1962- WhoAmW 93
Schaer, Werner 1940- St&PR 93
Schaerf, Frederick Warren 1951- WhoSSW 93
Schaeter, Gary L. 1947- St&PR 93
Schaetzel, Wendy 1950- ConAu 136
Schafenacker, James A. 1930- St&PR 93
Schafer, Alan Bruce St&PR 93
Schafer, Albert C. 1935- St&PR 93
Schafer, Alice Turner 1915- WhoAmW 93, WhoSSW 93
Schafer, Barbara Louise AmWomPl
Schafer, Becky BioIn 17
Schafer, Carl Walter 1936- WhoAm 92
Schafer, Dirk 1873-1931 Baker 92
Schafer, Edward Albert, Jr. 1939- WhoWor 93
Schafer, Edward H. BioIn 17
Schafer, Edward Hetzel 1913- WhoWrEP 92
Schafer, Frederick Ferdinand 1839-1927 BioIn 17
Schafer, G.E. 1922- St&PR 93
Schafer, Glenn S. 1949- WhoIns 93
Schafer, Glenn Stanley 1949- St&PR 93
Schafer, Gunter G.W. 1935- WhoScE 91-3
Schafer, Hans J. 1937- WhoScE 91-3
Schafer, Harold BioIn 17
Schafer, James Henry 1945- WhoAm 92
Schafer, Janice Oakes Law&B 92
Schafer, Jerry MiSFD 9
Schafer, Jerry Sanford 1934- WhoWor 93
Schafer, John Charles 1948- WhoE 93
Schafer, John Francis 1921- WhoAm 92
Schafer, John Stephen 1934- WhoAm 92
Schafer, Karlheinz 1935- WhoScE 91-3
Schafer, Kenneth C. 1907- St&PR 93
Schafer, Larry Gordon Law&B 92
Schafer, Larry W. 1952- WhoE 93
Schafer, Marvel Virginia 1931- WhoAmW 93
Schafer, Michael Eugene 1940- WhoAm 92
Schafer, Michael Frederick 1942- WhoAm 92
Schafer, Michael Moore 1957- WhoSSW 93
Schafer, Mike 1948- BioIn 17
Schafer, Natalie d1991 BioIn 17
Schafer, Natalie 1900-1991 ConTFT 10
Schafer, Neil Joseph 1945- St&PR 93
Schafer, R(aymond) Murray 1933- Baker 92
Schafer, Raette Marie 1963- WhoSSW 93
Schafer, Raymond Murray 1933- WhoAm 92
Schafer, Robert E. 1938- St&PR 93
Schafer, Robert Louis 1937- WhoAm 92
Schafer, Roger S. d1991 BioIn 17
Schafer, Ronald William 1938- WhoAm 92
Schafer, Seymour Jay 1933- WhoE 93
Schafer, Suanne 1952- WhoAmW 93
Schafer, Tami Lou 1960- WhoAmW 93
Schafer, Thomas Wilson 1939- St&PR 93, WhoAm 92
Schafer, Walter L. 1929- St&PR 93
Schafer, William Harry 1936- WhoWor 93
Schaferdiek, Knut 1930- WhoWor 93
Schaff, Adam 1913- WhoWor 93
Schaff, Philip 1819-1893 BioIn 17
Schaff, Philip H., Jr. 1920- St&PR 93
Schaff, Zsuzsanna 1943- WhoScE 91-4
Schaffel, Lewis WhoAm 92
Schaffeld, Daniel J. 1957- St&PR 93
Schaffer, Alan L. 1942- St&PR 93
Schaffer, August 1814-1879 Baker 92
Schaffer, Bonnie Lynn 1957- WhoAmW 93
Schaffer, David Irving 1935- WhoAm 92
Schaffer, Debra Simon 1936- WhoE 93
Schaffer, Diane Maximoff 1946- WhoEmL 93
Schaffer, Donald J. 1956- St&PR 93
Schaffer, Edmund John 1925- WhoAm 92
Schaffer, Franklin Edwin 1924- WhoAm 92
Schaffer, Gene 1941- ScF&FL 92
Schaffer, Irene Elizabeth 1923- St&PR 93
Schaffer, Irving 1922- St&PR 93
Schaffer, Joel Lance 1945- WhoWor 93
Schaffer, Julius 1823-1902 Baker 92
Schaffer, Kenny BioIn 17
Schaffer, Kirk Law&B 92
Schaffer, Michael J. 1944- WhoE 93
Schaffer, Monroe 1917- St&PR 93
Schaffer, Peter 1940- St&PR 93
Schaffer, Raimund 1948- WhoScE 91-3
Schaffer, Robert Jay 1960- WhoE 93
Schaffer, Robert W. St&PR 93
Schaffer, Rosanne Strunsky 1922- WhoE 93
Schaffer, Scott A. St&PR 93
Schaffer, Stephen L. 1955- St&PR 93
Schaffer, Teresita Currie 1945- WhoAm 92, WhoAmW 93
Schaffhausen, Paul James Law&B 92
Schaffhausen, Paul Vincent 1929- St&PR 93
Schaffhauser, Horst WhoScE 91-4
Schaffhauser, Robert J. 1938- St&PR 93
Schaffner, Bernard P. 1936- St&PR 93
Schaffner, Charles Etzel 1919- WhoAm 92
Schaffner, Fenton 1920- WhoAm 92
Schaffner, Franklin J. 1920-1989 MiSFD 9N
Schaffner, Fred C. 1926- St&PR 93
Schaffner, George A., II 1921- St&PR 93
Schaffner, Joan Elsa 1957- WhoAmW 93
Schaffner, Kurt 1931- WhoScE 91-3
Schaffner, Kurt Walter 1931- WhoWor 93
Schaffner, Linda Carol 1954- WhoAmW 93
Schaffner, Melissa Anne 1963- WhoAmW 93
Schaffner, Nicholas 1953-1991 BioIn 17
Schaffner, Robert Thomas, Jr. 1937- WhoE 93
Schaffner, Walter 1944- WhoScE 91-4
Schaffran, Thomas Foxhall 1941- St&PR 93
Schaffrath, Christoph 1709-1763 Baker 92
Schaffrath, Kurt Alexander Law&B 92
Schaffstall, Charles Francis 1926- St&PR 93
Schaffzin, Richard Alan 1944- St&PR 93
Schafler, Samuel d1991 BioIn 17
Schafran, Lynn Hecht 1941- WhoE 93
Schafran, Walter BioIn 17
Schafrank, Michael S. 1935- WhoE 93
Schafrick, Rick BioIn 17
Schafron, Laura Lynn 1964- WhoAmW 93
Schaftel, Robert B. 1940- WhoE 93
Schaible, John Edward 1938- St&PR 93
Schaible, Mary Kay 1965- WhoAmW 93
Schaible, Michael BioIn 17
Schaible, Ronald David 1947- WhoE 93
Schaible, Steven Reinhold 1958- WhoE 93
Schaie, Klaus Warner 1928- WhoAm 92
Schaik, Anton Van 1944- WhoWor 93
Schain, Don MiSFD 9
Schainholz, Herbert d1991 BioIn 17
Schainholz, Jay D. 1959- St&PR 93
Schairer, George Swift 1913- WhoAm 92
Schaitkin, Mark R. Law&B 92
Schake, Lowell Martin 1938- WhoAm 92
Schake, Robert H. 1932- St&PR 93
Schakel, Peter J. 1941- ScF&FL 92
Schalck, Christopher Allen 1948- St&PR 93
Schalcosky, S. Richard 1947- WhoEmL 93
Schaleben, Arville 1907- WhoAm 92
Schalekamp, Jacob Cornelis 1942- WhoWor 93
Schalekamp, William A. Law&B 92
Schalin, Olle WhoScE 91-4
Schalk, Eugene Norbert 1932- St&PR 93
Schalk, Franz 1863-1931 Baker 92, IntDcOp [port], OxDcOp
Schalk, Josef 1857-1900 Baker 92
Schalk, Rene 1955- WhoWor 93
Schalk, Thomas G. 1932- St&PR 93
Schalk, Thomas William 1952- St&PR 93
Schalk, Willi BioIn 17
Schalkowsky, Samuel 1925- St&PR 93
Schalkwijk, J. Pieter M. 1936- WhoScE 91-3
Schall, Claus Nielsen 1757-1835 Baker 92
Schall, Debra Jean 1952- WhoAmW 93
Schall, Fred R. 1948- St&PR 93
Schall, Joseph Julian 1946- WhoE 93
Schall, Richard 1922- Baker 92
Schallenkamp, Kay 1949- WhoAm 92, WhoAmW 93
Schaller, Alfred Friedrich 1930- WhoScE 91-4
Schaller, Christopher L. WhoAm 92
Schaller, Daryl Richard 1943- St&PR 93, WhoAm 92
Schaller, George Beals 1933- WhoAm 92, WhoWrEP 92
Schaller, H.W. 1905- St&PR 93
Schaller, Jane Green 1934- WhoAm 92, WhoAmW 93
Schaller, Joanne Frances 1943- WhoAmW 93
Schaller, Klaus 1943- WhoScE 91-3
Schaller, Oskar Heinrich 1923- WhoScE 91-4
Schaller, Sandra J. Law&B 92
Schallert, Donovan H. 1924- WhoIns 93
Schallert, James B. 1948- St&PR 93
Schallert, James Britton 1948- WhoIns 93
Schallert, William Joseph 1922- WhoAm 92
Schalles, George W., III Law&B 92
Schallhorn, Susan Kelley 1945- WhoSSW 93
Schallibaum, Melchior 1947- WhoScE 91-4
Schallich, Terrence James 1961- WhoE 93
Schally, Andrew Victor 1926- PolBiDi, WhoAm 92, WhoSSW 93, WhoWor 93
Schalm, Solko W. 1940- WhoScE 91-3
Schalm, Solko Walle 1940- WhoWor 93
Schalow, Gayle Jean 1951- WhoAmW 93
Schaltenbrand, Philip Edward 1944- WhoE 93
Schama, Simon BioIn 17
Schama, Simon 1945- WhoWor 93
Schama, Simon (Michael) 1945- ConAu 39NR
Schamber, J.G. 1938- St&PR 93
Schamberg, Morton 1881-1918 BioIn 17
Schamberger, Lucille AmWomPl
Schamberger, William George, Jr. 1943- WhoE 93
Schambra, Philip Ellis 1934- WhoAm 92
Schamer, Paul James 1945- St&PR 93
Schamore, Terry B. 1932- St&PR 93
Schamp, Niceas Maurice 1937- WhoWor 93
Schamps, Joel 1945- WhoScE 91-2
Schanbacher, Walter W. Law&B 92
Schanbaum, Gene T. 1928- St&PR 93
Schanberg, Saul Murray 1933- WhoAm 92
Schanberg, Sydney BioIn 17
Schanberg, Sydney Hillel 1934- WhoAm 92
Schanberger, Jean M. Law&B 92
Schanck, Francis Raber 1907-1991 BioIn 17
Schanck, Jack W. 1951- St&PR 93
Schanck, Jordan Thomas 1931- St&PR 93
Schanda, Erwin 1931- WhoScE 91-4, WhoWor 93
Schanda, Janos 1932- WhoScE 91-4
Schanely, Patricia Ann 1953- WhoE 93
Schang, Frederick 1893-1990 BioIn 17
Schang, Kenneth William 1941- St&PR 93
Schang, Walter Henry 1889-1965 BiDAMSp 1989
Schank, Bernard Lynn 1921- WhoSSW 93
Schank, Roger Carl 1946- WhoAm 92
Schank, Stanley Cox 1932- WhoSSW 93
Schanker, Louis 1903-1981 BioIn 17
Schankman, Alan Robert 1947- WhoEmL 93
Schannep, John Dwight 1934- WhoAm 92
Schanstra, Carla Ross 1954- WhoAmW 93, WhoWrEP 92
Schantl, Joachim G. 1937- WhoScE 91-4
Schantz, Birger WhoScE 91-4
Schantz, Birger 1932- WhoScE 91-4
Schantz, Daniel Dean 1942- WhoWrEP 92
Schantz, Michael William 1948- WhoE 93
Schantzenbach, William Kerchner 1941- St&PR 93, WhoAm 92
Schanzer, Henry Isaac Law&B 92
Schanzer, Mark Joseph 1957- WhoSSW 93
Schanzer, Rosalyn Good 1942- WhoSSW 93
Schap, Louis R. 1928- St&PR 93
Schaper, Edzard 1908-1984 ScF&FL 92
Schaper, Joseph A. Law&B 92
Schaper, Jutta 1937- WhoWor 93
Schaper, Laurence T. 1936- St&PR 93
Schaper, Louise Levy 1950- WhoE 93
Schaper, Martin W. 1956- St&PR 93
Schaper, Richard J. 1957- St&PR 93
Schaper, Ron A. St&PR 93
Schaper, Wolfgang 1934- WhoScE 91-3
Schapera, Isaac 1905- IntDcAn
Schapery, Richard Allan 1935- WhoAm 92
Schaphorst, William K. Law&B 92
Schapira, Allan Max 1949- WhoUN 92
Schapira, Morey R. 1949- St&PR 93
Schapira, Morey Rael 1949- WhoEmL 93
Schapiro, Donald 1925- WhoAm 92
Schapiro, Edith K. 1929- St&PR 93
Schapiro, Herb 1929- WhoAm 92
Schapiro, Jerome B. 1930- St&PR 93
Schapiro, Jerome Bentley 1930- WhoE 93, WhoWor 93
Schapiro, Martin BioIn 17
Schapiro, Mary WhoAm 92
Schapiro, Mary 1955- WhoAmW 93
Schapiro, Meyer 1904- BioIn 17, WhoAm 92
Schapiro, Miriam 1923- WhoAm 92
Schapiro, Morris A. 1903- St&PR 93, WhoAm 92
Schapiro, Nancy 1929- WhoWrEP 92
Schapiro, Rolf Lutz 1933- WhoE 93
Schapiro, Ruth G. 1926-1991 BioIn 17
Schaplowsky, Ellen H. 1946- St&PR 93
Schaplowsky, Richard Lee Law&B 92
Schappals, Julia A. Law&B 92
Schappel, Marion F. d1992 BioIn 17, NewYTBS 92
Schapperle, Robert Francis 1946- WhoE 93
Schappes, Morris U(rman) 1907- WhoWrEP 92
Schar, Dwight C. BioIn 17
Schar, Dwight C. 1942- WhoSSW 93
Schar, Stuart 1941- WhoE 93
Schara, Charles G. 1952- St&PR 93
Schara, Charles Gerard 1952- WhoAm 92
Schardein, Sandra Wild (Katherine Selby) 1946- WhoWrEP 92
Schardt, James Eric Law&B 92
Scharer, A.J. WhoScE 91-1
Scharf, Bertram 1931- WhoE 93
Scharf, Charles BioIn 17
Scharf, Charles F. 1947- St&PR 93
Scharf, Cheryl Hile 1948- WhoAmW 93
Scharf, Daniel W. 1959- St&PR 93
Scharf, Heino W. Law&B 92
Scharf, Irwin 1935- St&PR 93
Scharf, Jesse 1939- St&PR 93
Scharf, Kenny BioIn 17
Scharf, Steven 1953- St&PR 93
Scharf, Waldemar Henryk 1930- WhoWor 93
Scharf, William 1927- WhoAm 92
Scharfenberg, Doris Ann 1917- WhoAm 92
Scharfenberg, Kirk d1992 NewYTBS 92
Scharfenberg, Margaret Ellan 1924- WhoAmW 93
Scharfenberger, George T. 1919- St&PR 93
Scharfenberger, John George 1939- WhoSSW 93
Scharfetter, Christian F. 1936- WhoScE 91-4
Scharfetter, Donald L. 1934- WhoAm 92
Scharff, Constance Kramer WhoAmW 93, WhoE 93
Scharff, Jean-Pierre 1941- WhoScE 91-2
Scharff, Joseph Laurent 1935- WhoAm 92
Scharff, Matthew Daniel 1932- WhoAm 92
Scharff, Monroe Bernard 1923- WhoE 93
Scharffenberger, George Thomas 1919- WhoAm 92
Scharffenberger, William J. 1921- St&PR 93, WhoAm 92
Scharfman, Scott Phillip 1962- WhoE 93
Scharfsten, Alan J. 1953- St&PR 93
Scharin, Ann 1921- St&PR 93
Scharin, Lesile A. 1945- St&PR 93
Scharlach, David Arthur Law&B 92
Scharlau, Charles Edward 1927- St&PR 93
Scharlau, Charles Edward, III 1927- WhoAm 92, WhoSSW 93
Scharlemann, Robert Paul 1929- WhoAm 92
Scharmann, Arthur 1928- WhoScE 91-3
Scharmer, Neal R. Law&B 92
Scharnberg, Charles J. Law&B 92
Scharnhorst, Gerhard Johann David von 1755-1813 HarEnMi
Scharp, Anders 1934- WhoAm 92
Scharpe, Simon 1944- WhoScE 91-2
Scharpe, Simon Lodewijk WhoWor 93
Scharpf, A. WhoScE 91-4
Scharpf, Hans Christoph 1938- WhoScE 91-3
Scharpf, Michael J. Law&B 92
Scharpf, Tad 1946- St&PR 93
Scharrer, August 1866-1936 Baker 92
Scharrer, Berta Vogel 1906- WhoAm 92, WhoAmW 93
Scharrer, Edwin 1937- WhoScE 91-4
Scharrer, Irene 1888-1971 Baker 92
Schartner, Albert Lyman 1931- WhoWor 93

Schartner, Karl-Heinz 1939- *WhoScE 91-3*
Scharwenka, (Ludwig) Philipp 1847-1917 *Baker 92*
Scharwenka, (Franz) Xaver 1850-1924 *Baker 92*
Schary, Dore 1905-1980 *BioIn 17, MiSFD 9N*
Schary, Ed 1925- *St&PR 93*
Schary, Emanuel 1924- *WhoAm 92, WhoE 93*
Schary, William Lee 1948- *WhoE 93*
Schat, Peter 1935- *Baker 92*
Schatell, Brian *BioIn 17*
Schatt, Stanley 1943- *ScF&FL 92*
Schatte, Peter Karl 1938- *WhoWor 93*
Schatten, William E. 1928- *St&PR 93*
Schattinger, James Henry 1935- *St&PR 93*
Schattner, Robert L. 1938- *St&PR 93*
Schatton, Norman P. 1917- *St&PR 93*
Schattschneider, David Allen 1939- *WhoE 93*
Schattschneider, Doris Jean 1939- *WhoE 93*
Schattschneider, E. E. 1892-1971 *PolPar*
Schattschneider, Peter 1950- *WhoWor 93*
Schatvet, Halfdan 1929- *St&PR 93*
Schatz, A. *WhoScE 91-3*
Schatz, Arthur J. 1940- *WhoSSW 93*
Schatz, E. Gary 1929- *St&PR 93*
Schatz, Gottfried 1936- *WhoScE 91-4, WhoWor 93*
Schatz, Helmut 1937- *WhoScE 91-3, WhoWor 93*
Schatz, Irwin Jacob 1931- *WhoAm 92*
Schatz, Jill C. *Law&B 92*
Schatz, Jules Leonard 1920- *WhoE 93*
Schatz, Julius 1915- *WhoE 93*
Schatz, Martin 1936- *WhoSSW 93*
Schatz, S. Michael 1921- *WhoAm 92*
Schatzberg, Alan Frederic 1944- *WhoAm 92*
Schatzberg, Jerry 1927- *MiSFD 9*
Schatzberg, Jerry Ned 1927- *WhoAm 92*
Schatzberg, Richard K. 1954- *St&PR 93*
Schatzberg, Theodore 1929- *St&PR 93*
Schatzel, Kim E. *BioIn 17*
Schatzki, Erich 1898-1991 *BioIn 17*
Schatzki, George 1933- *WhoAm 92*
Schatzmann, Hans Jurg 1924- *WhoScE 91-4*
Schaub, Edward H. 1931- *St&PR 93*
Schaub, Hans 1880-1965 *Baker 92*
Schaub, Harry Carl 1929- *St&PR 93, WhoAm 92*
Schaub, James Hamilton 1925- *WhoAm 92*
Schaub, Jurgen 1936- *WhoScE 91-3*
Schaub, Marcus C. 1936- *WhoScE 91-4*
Schaub, Marilyn McNamara 1928- *WhoAm 92, WhoAmW 93*
Schaub, Sherwood Anhder, Jr. 1942- *WhoAm 92*
Schaubelt, F.J. *ScF&FL 92*
Schaubert, Daniel Harold 1947- *WhoAm 92, WhoE 93*
Schaubert, Stephen Jay 1946- *WhoAm 92*
Schauble, Wolfgang *BioIn 17*
Schauble, Wolfgang 1942- *WhoWor 93*
Schaubroeck, Armand P. *St&PR 93*
Schaubroeck, Blaine *St&PR 93*
Schaubroeck, Bruce *St&PR 93*
Schaudies, Jesse P., Jr. 1954- *WhoSSW 93*
Schaudinn, Ligeth A. 1940- *WhoUN 92*
Schaudt, Peter Lindsay *BioIn 17*
Schauenberg, Susan Kay 1945- *WhoAmW 93*
Schauer, Albert Christian 1942- *St&PR 93*
Schauer, Catharine Guberman 1945- *WhoAmW 93*
Schauer, David A. 1945- *St&PR 93*
Schauer, Frederick Franklin 1946- *WhoAm 92*
Schauer, Louis Frank 1928- *WhoAm 92*
Schauer, Lynne Ballantyne 1939- *WhoAmW 93*
Schauer, Michael D. 1961- *St&PR 93*
Schauer, Nancy Ruth 1950- *WhoAmW 93*
Schauer, Richard Costello 1937- *WhoE 93*
Schauer, Roland 1936- *WhoScE 91-3*
Schauer, Thomas Alfred 1927- *WhoWor 93*
Schauer, Wilbert Edward, Jr. 1926- *WhoAm 92*
Schauerte, C. M. 1928- *WhoAm 92*
Schauf, Carolyn Jane 1946- *WhoAmW 93*
Schauf, Lawrence E. *Law&B 92, WhoAm 92*
Schauf, Susan Marie 1951- *WhoWor 93*
Schauf, Victoria 1943- *WhoAmW 93*
Schaufelberger, Walter 1940- *WhoScE 91-4*
Schaufele, Walter R. 1937- *WhoScE 91-3*
Schaufele, William E., Jr. 1923- *WhoE 93*
Schaufuss, Peter 1950- *WhoAm 92, WhoWor 93*
Schaum, J. Michael 1949- *St&PR 93*
Schaum, John W. 1905-1988 *Baker 92*
Schauman, Melba Sally 1937- *WhoAm 92, WhoAmW 93*
Schaumann, Ernst 1943- *WhoScE 91-3, WhoWor 93*
Schaumann, Wolfgang 1926- *WhoScE 91-3*
Schaumburg, Herbert Howard 1932- *WhoAm 92*
Schaumburg, Ronald G. 1936- *St&PR 93*
Schaumburger, Joseph Zalmon 1930- *WhoE 93*
Schaumburg-Lever, Gundula Maria 1942- *WhoWor 93*
Schaupp, Joan Pomprowitz 1932- *WhoAmW 93*
Schaupp, Richard 1936- *St&PR 93*
Schaut, Joseph William 1928- *WhoAm 92*
Schauwecker, Margaret Liddie 1934- *WhoAmW 93*
Schaw, Walter Allan 1934- *WhoAm 92*
Schawk, Clarence W. 1926- *St&PR 93*
Schawlow, Arthur Leonard 1921- *WhoAm 92, WhoWor 93*
Schayes, Wendy Lucero *NotHsAW 93*
Schcoley, Virginia G. 1946- *St&PR 93*
Schebesta, Paul Joachim 1887-1967 *IntDcAn*
Schebler, Steven J. 1948- *St&PR 93*
Schech, Marianne 1914- *Baker 92*
Schechner, Richard 1934- *WhoAm 92*
Schechter, Allen Edward 1935- *St&PR 93, WhoAm 92*
Schechter, Alvin H. 1933- *WhoAm 92*
Schechter, Bernard Alvin 1923- *St&PR 93*
Schechter, Clifford 1958- *WhoE 93, WhoWor 93*
Schechter, Danny *BioIn 17*
Schechter, David Alan *Law&B 92*
Schechter, Dov S. *Law&B 92*
Schechter, Geraldine Poppa 1938- *WhoAmW 93*
Schechter, Harold A. 1944- *St&PR 93*
Schechter, Hope Mendoza 1921- *NotHsAW 93*
Schechter, Joseph Michael 1938- *WhoE 93*
Schechter, Marc David *Law&B 92*
Schechter, Marshall David 1921- *WhoE 93*
Schechter, Peter David 1959- *WhoE 93*
Schechter, Robert Samuel 1929- *WhoAm 92*
Schechter, Robin P. *Law&B 92*
Schechter, Saul 1933- *St&PR 93*
Schechter, Sol 1916- *WhoAm 92*
Schechter, Solomon 1847-1915 *BioIn 17, JeAmHC*
Schechter, Stephen Lloyd 1945- *WhoAm 92*
Schechter, Sue A. 1952- *WhoAmW 93*
Schechtman, Marsha Ilene 1958- *WhoAmW 93*
Scheck, Florian A. 1936- *WhoScE 91-3*
Scheck, Jay T., Jr. *Law&B 92*
Scheckner, Barry *St&PR 93*
Scheckner, Sy 1924- *WhoAm 92*
Schecter, Erline Dian 1956- *WhoAmW 93*
Schecter, Joel R. 1947- *WhoWrEP 92*
Schecter, Julie S. *Law&B 92*
Schecter, Manny Wade *Law&B 92*
Schecter, Roger A. *Law&B 92*
Schecter, Scott M. 1956- *St&PR 93*
Schecter, William H. *WhoAm 92*
Schecter, Winifred *ScF&FL 92*
Schectman, Herbert A. 1930- *St&PR 93, WhoAm 92*
Schectman, Stephen Barry 1947- *WhoE 93, WhoEmL 93*
Schedler, Gilbert Walter 1935- *WhoWrEP 92*
Schedler, Spencer Jaime 1933- *WhoE 93*
Scheeberger, Don R. 1930- *St&PR 93*
Scheeder, Louis 1946- *WhoAm 92*
Scheel, Chester Timothy 1947- *WhoSSW 93*
Scheel, Fritz 1852-1907 *Baker 92*
Scheel, Georg 1950- *WhoWor 93*
Scheel, Mark W. 1943- *WhoWrEP 92*
Scheel, Nels Earl 1925- *WhoAm 92*
Scheel, Walter 1919- *WhoWor 93*
Scheele, Roy Martin 1942- *WhoWrEP 92*
Scheelen, Andre Joannes 1964- *WhoWor 93*
Scheeler, Charles 1925- *WhoAm 92*
Scheeler, James Arthur 1927- *WhoAm 92*
Scheeler, Milford C. 1949- *St&PR 93*
Scheels, John M. *Law&B 92*
Scheepmaker, A. *WhoScE 91-3*
Scheepmaker, Hans *MiSFD 9*
Scheer, Christian 1942- *WhoWor 93*
Scheer, Hugo 1942- *WhoScE 91-3, WhoWor 93*
Scheer, Jerry *BioIn 17*
Scheer, Julian *St&PR 93*
Scheer, Julian Weisel 1926- *WhoAm 92*
Scheer, K.H. 1928-1991 *ScF&FL 92*
Scheer, Milton David 1922- *WhoAm 92*
Scheer, R. Scott 1938- *WhoE 93*
Scheer, Reinhard 1863-1928 *DcTwHis, HarEnMi*
Scheer, Robert Gijs Van Der 1959- *WhoWor 93*
Scheer, Ruth C. 1940- *St&PR 93*
Scheer, Thomas F. *Law&B 92*
Scheer, Thomas N. 1934- *St&PR 93*
Scheer, Ulrich 1942- *WhoScE 91-3*
Scheer, Verlin Harold 1949- *WhoIns 93*
Scheeren, Judith Anne 1947- *WhoAmW 93*
Scheerenberger, Richard Charles 1930- *WhoAm 92*
Scheerer, Robert *MiSFD 9*
Scheetz, Linda Jean 1947- *WhoAmW 93*
Scheetz, Mary JoEllen 1926- *WhoAm 92, WhoAmW 93*
Scheetz, Thomas S. 1935- *St&PR 93*
Schefe, Burton Harold 1935- *St&PR 93*
Scheff, Fritzi 1879-1954 *Baker 92*
Scheff, Steven R. 1937- *St&PR 93*
Scheffel, John, III *Law&B 92*
Scheffel, Pablo G. 1946- *St&PR 93*
Scheffer, B. *WhoScE 91-3*
Scheffler, Eckart Arthur 1941- *WhoAm 92*
Scheffler, Ingolf 1943- *WhoScE 91-3*
Scheffler, Israel *WhoAm 92*
Scheffler, Lewis Francis 1928- *WhoWor 93*
Scheffler, Samuel 1951- *WhoAm 92*
Scheffler, Siegfried 1892-1969 *Baker 92*
Scheffler, Stuart Jay 1950- *WhoEmL 93*
Scheffman, David Theodore 1943- *WhoAm 92, WhoSSW 93*
Schefold, Bertram 1943- *BioIn 17*
Schefstad, Steven R. *Law&B 92*
Schefstad, Theresa 1958- *WhoSSW 93*
Scheftel, Herbert 1907- *St&PR 93*
Schefter, Robert J. 1937- *St&PR 93*
Scheftner, Gerold 1937- *WhoAm 92*
Schehr, Lawrence Robins 1954- *WhoSSW 93*
Schei, Anders 1930- *WhoScE 91-4*
Scheib, Earl A. *BioIn 17*
Scheib, Earl A. 1907-1992 *NewYTBS 92 [port]*
Scheibe, Frederick A. *Law&B 92*
Scheibe, Johann c. 1680-1748 *See* Scheibe, Johann Adolf 1708-1776 *Baker 92*
Scheibe, Johann Adolf 1708-1776 *Baker 92*
Scheibe, Karl Edward 1937- *WhoAm 92*
Scheibel, Arnold Bernard 1923- *WhoAm 92*
Scheibel, Jim 1947- *WhoAm 92*
Scheibel, Kenneth Maynard 1920- *WhoAm 92*
Scheibel, Leonard William 1938- *WhoE 93*
Scheiber, Donald Edwin 1926- *St&PR 93*
Scheiber, Harry N. 1935- *WhoAm 92*
Scheiber, Pal 1942- *WhoScE 91-4*
Scheiber, Stephen Carl 1938- *WhoAm 92*
Scheibl, Jerome A. 1930- *WhoIns 93*
Scheibl, Jerome Alois 1930- *St&PR 93*
Scheible, Douglas Laverne 1962- *St&PR 93*
Scheiblechner, Hartmann 1939- *WhoScE 91-3*
Scheibler, Edward G., Jr. *Law&B 92*
Scheibler, Johann Heinrich 1777-1837 *Baker 92*
Scheibling, Norman John 1932- *St&PR 93*
Scheibner, Henry W. 1913- *St&PR 93*
Scheich, John F. 1942- *WhoE 93, WhoWor 93*
Scheick, William J. 1941- *ScF&FL 92*
Scheick, William J(oseph) 1941- *ConAu 38NR*
Scheick, William Joseph 1941- *WhoSSW 93*
Scheid, Francis 1920- *WhoAm 92*
Scheid, Harald 1939- *WhoWor 93*
Scheid, Peter *WhoScE 91-3*
Scheid, Werner 1938- *WhoScE 91-3*
Scheid, Werner Fritz 1938- *WhoWor 93*
Scheide, Richard Gilson 1929- *St&PR 93, WhoAm 92*
Scheidel, Thomas Maynard 1931- *WhoAm 92*
Scheideler, Albert L. 1926- *St&PR 93*
Scheidemann, Heinrich c. 1595-1663 *Baker 92*
Scheidemantel, Karl 1859-1923 *Baker 92, OxDcOp*
Scheider, Roy 1935- *BioIn 17, IntDcF 2-3*
Scheider, Wilhelm 1928- *WhoWor 93*
Scheidereit, Claus 1954- *WhoScE 91-3*
Scheidhauer, Lynn Irene 1955- *WhoWrEP 92*
Scheidig, Kenneth C. *Law&B 92*
Scheidler, John B. *Law&B 92*
Scheidt, Karl 1934- *St&PR 93*
Scheidt, Samuel 1587?-1654 *Baker 92*
Scheidt, W. Robert 1942- *WhoAm 92*
Scheie, Harold G. 1909-1990 *BioIn 17*
Scheie, Paul Olaf 1933- *WhoSSW 93*
Scheier, Libby 1946- *ConAu 136, WhoCanL 92*
Scheifele, Richard Paul 1934- *St&PR 93, WhoAm 92*
Scheifly, John Edward 1925- *WhoAm 92*
Scheimer, Louis 1928- *WhoAm 92*
Schein, Ann 1939- *Baker 92*
Schein, Boris Moiseyevich 1938- *WhoSSW 93*
Schein, Harvey L. 1927- *WhoAm 92*
Schein, Jacob M. d1989 *BioIn 17*
Schein, Jerome 1923- *WhoWrEP 92*
Schein, Johann Hermann 1586-1630 *Baker 92*
Schein, Jonah Walter 1945- *WhoE 93*
Schein, Philip Samuel 1939- *WhoAm 92*
Schein, Sally Joy 1930- *WhoAmW 93*
Schein, Steven M. 1949- *St&PR 93*
Schein, Virginia Ellen 1943- *WhoAmW 93*
Schein, W.M. 1958- *St&PR 93*
Scheinbaum, David 1951- *WhoAm 92*
Scheinbaum, Sandra Lynn 1950- *WhoAmW 93*
Scheinberg, Alfred L. d1992 *BioIn 17*
Scheinberg, Peritz 1920- *WhoAm 92*
Scheinberg, Steven Eliot 1952- *WhoAm 92*
Scheindlin, Raymond Paul 1940- *WhoAm 92*
Scheine, Arnold J. 1937- *St&PR 93*
Scheiner, Amy Rose 1960- *WhoAmW 93*
Scheiner, David Charles 1945- *St&PR 93*
Scheiner, Leon 1937- *St&PR 93*
Scheiner, Lillian Claire 1937- *WhoE 93*
Scheiner, Martin *BioIn 17*
Scheiner, Martin L. d1992 *NewYTBS 92*
Scheinert, Lindsey Gray 1950- *St&PR 93*
Scheinfeld, James D. 1926- *St&PR 93*
Scheinfeld, James David 1926- *WhoAm 92, WhoWor 93*
Scheinfeldt, Jerry K. *Law&B 92*
Scheinholtz, Leonard Louis 1927- *WhoAm 92*
Scheinin, Arje 1923- *WhoScE 91-4*
Scheininger, Lester 1947- *WhoAm 92*
Scheinkman, Alan David 1950- *WhoE 93*
Scheinkman, Jose Alexandre 1948- *WhoAm 92*
Scheinman, David A. 1942- *St&PR 93*
Scheinman, Nancy Jane 1955- *WhoAmW 93*
Scheinman, Stanley Bruce 1933- *WhoAm 92*
Scheinpflug, Paul 1875-1937 *Baker 92*
Scheiring, Michael James 1949- *WhoE 93*
Scheitlin, Constance Joy 1949- *WhoSSW 93*
Scheja, Johann Wolfgang 1940- *WhoScE 91-3*
Schelar, Virginia Mae 1924- *WhoAmW 93, WhoWor 93*
Schelble, Johann Nepomuk 1789-1837 *Baker 92*
Scheld, Karl A. 1930- *St&PR 93*
Scheld, Robert William 1920- *WhoIns 93*
Schelde, Per 1945- *WhoE 93*
Schele, Linda *BioIn 17*
Scheler, Brad Eric 1953- *WhoAm 92*
Scheler, James R., Sr. 1940- *St&PR 93*
Scheler, Manfred 1926- *WhoWor 93*
Scheler, Werner 1923- *WhoScE 91-3, WhoWor 93*
Schelin, Richard Wayne *Law&B 92*
Schelke, Charles W. 1939- *St&PR 93*
Schelkunoff, Sergei A. d1992 *NewYTBS 92*
Schelkunoff, Sergei A. 1907-1992 *BioIn 17*
Schell, Allan Carter 1934- *WhoAm 92*
Schell, Augustus 1812-1884 *BioIn 17, PolPar*
Schell, Bonnie Jo 1944- *WhoAmW 93*
Schell, Braxton 1924- *WhoAm 92*
Schell, Charles A. 1959- *WhoWor 93*
Schell, Edgar Thomas 1931- *WhoAm 92*
Schell, Herman 1850-1906 *BioIn 17*
Schell, James Munson 1944- *WhoAm 92*
Schell, Jonathan 1943- *CurBio 92 [port]*
Schell, Jonathan Edward 1943- *WhoWrEP 92*
Schell, Jozef 1935- *WhoScE 91-2*
Schell, Jozef Stephaan 1935- *WhoScE 91-3*
Schell, Karel Johan 1940- *WhoWor 93*
Schell, Maria 1926- *BioIn 17, IntDcF 2-3*
Schell, Mark Edward 1957- *St&PR 93*
Schell, Maximilian 1930- *BioIn 17, IntDcF 2-3, MiSFD 9, WhoAm 92, WhoWor 93*
Schell, Richard A. 1950- *WhoAm 92, WhoSSW 93*
Schell, Rolfe F(inch) 1916- *WhoWrEP 92*
Schell, Sherrie Virginia *Law&B 92*
Schell, Willa H.B. *Law&B 92*
Schelle, Johann 1648?-1701 *Baker 92*
Schelle, Michael 1950- *Baker 92*
Schellekens, H. 1949- *WhoScE 91-3*
Schellekens, Hubertus 1949- *WhoWor 93*
Schellenberg, Ernest 1932- *St&PR 93*

Schellenberg, Karl Abraham 1931- *WhoAm 92*
Schellenberg, Peter Joseph 1931- *WhoE 93*
Schellenberger, Robert Earl 1932- *WhoSSW 93*
Schellenger, James P. 1919- *St&PR 93*
Schellentrager, James E. *Law&B 92*
Scheller, Ernest, Jr. 1929- *St&PR 93*
Scheller, Melanie *BioIn 17*
Scheller, Sanford Gregory 1931- *St&PR 93, WhoAm 92*
Schellerup, Henning *MiSFD 9*
Schellhaas, Linda Jean 1956- *WhoSSW 93*
Schellhaas, Robert Wesley 1952- *WhoSSW 93*
Schellhas, Edward William 1920- *St&PR 93*
Schellhas, Paul 1859-1945 *IntDcAn*
Schellhase, Jodi Ann 1966- *WhoE 93*
Schellhorn, Alice Hope 1945- *WhoE 93*
Schellin, Leonilda Marta 1946- *WhoWor 93*
Schelling, Christoph *Law&B 92*
Schelling, Ernest (Henry) 1876-1939 *Baker 92*
Schelling, Friedrich Wilhelm Joseph von 1775-1854 *BioIn 17*
Schelling, Hans Peter 1938- *WhoScE 91-4*
Schelling, John P. 1924- *St&PR 93*
Schelling, John Paul 1924- *WhoAm 92*
Schelling, Joyce Elaine 1937- *WhoAmW 93*
Schelling, Thomas C. 1921- *ColdWar 1 [port]*
Schelling, Thomas Crombie 1921- *WhoE 93*
Schellinger, Paul E. 1962- *ScF&FL 92*
Schellman, John A. 1924- *WhoAm 92*
Schellmann, Hans-Joachim Werner Egbert 1944- *WhoWor 93*
Schellpeper, Gene H. 1941- *St&PR 93*
Schelm, Roger Leonard 1936- *WhoAm 92*
Schelp, Richard Herbert 1936- *WhoSSW 93*
Schelske, Claire L. 1932- *WhoAm 92*
Scheludko, Aleksej Dimitrov 1920- *WhoScE 91-4*
Scheman, L. Ronald 1931- *WhoE 93*
Schembechler, Bo *BioIn 17*
Schembechler, Bo 1929- *ConAu 139, WhoAm 92*
Schembra, Philip A. 1945- *WhoSSW 93*
Schemel, David Joseph 1951- *WhoE 93*
Schemelli, Georg Christian c. 1676-1762 *Baker 92*
Schemmel, Janet Eleanor *WhoAmW 93*
Schemmer, Benjamin F. 1932- *WhoAm 92*
Schempp, Paul G. *BioIn 17*
Schena, Francesco Paolo 1940- *WhoWor 93*
Schenck, A.W., Jr. 1916- *St&PR 93*
Schenck, A. William, III 1943- *WhoAm 92*
Schenck, Andrew *BioIn 17*
Schenck, Andrew 1941-1992 *NewYTBS 92*
Schenck, Andrew Craig 1941- *WhoAm 92*
Schenck, Benjamin Robinson 1938- *St&PR 93, WhoAm 92*
Schenck, Bill 1947- *BioIn 17*
Schenck, Daniel W. *Law&B 92*
Schenck, Dorothy *AmWomPl*
Schenck, Frederick A. 1928- *WhoAm 92*
Schenck, Harvey Norman 1937- *WhoE 93*
Schenck, Henry Paul 1929- *WhoE 93*
Schenck, Hilbert 1926- *ScF&FL 92*
Schenck, Jack Lee 1938- *St&PR 93, WhoAm 92, WhoWor 93*
Schenck, Johannes 1660?-c. 1712 *Baker 92*
Schenck, John Franklin, III 1921- *St&PR 93*
Schenck, John Richardson 1935- *St&PR 93*
Schenck, Margaret Anna 1938- *WhoE 93*
Schenck, Pieter A. 1928- *WhoScE 91-3*
Schenck, Pyotr 1870-1915 *Baker 92*
Schenck, Raymond H. *Law&B 92*
Schenck, Steven James 1948- *St&PR 93*
Schend, Bernd 1956- *WhoWor 93*
Schendel, Dan Eldon 1934- *WhoAm 92*
Schendel, Ward C. *Law&B 92*
Schene, Arthur V. 1916- *St&PR 93*
Schenek, Siegfried 1957- *WhoWor 93*
Schenk, Erich 1902-1974 *Baker 92*
Schenk, George 1934- *St&PR 93*
Schenk, George (Walden) 1929- *ConAu 139*
Schenk, Hendrik 1939- *WhoScE 91-3*
Schenk, Johann Baptist 1753-1836 *Baker 92, OxDcOp*
Schenk, Lynn *WhoAmW 93*
Schenk, Manfred K. 1947- *WhoScE 91-3*
Schenk, Norman Frederick 1949- *St&PR 93*
Schenk, Otto 1930- *IntDcOp*
Schenk, Peter Cornelius 1928- *WhoWor 93*
Schenk, Quentin Frederick 1922- *WhoAm 92*
Schenk, Richard 1926- *WhoSSW 93*
Schenk, Roland *BioIn 17*
Schenk, Winfried *WhoScE 91-4*
Schenk, Worthington George, Jr. 1922- *WhoAm 92*
Schenkein, William F. *Law&B 92*
Schenkel, Andrew James 1962- *WhoWor 93*
Schenkel, Carl *MiSFD 9*
Schenkel, Suzanne Chance 1940- *WhoAmW 93*
Schenkelaars, Godefridus J. 1939- *WhoUN 92*
Schenkenberg, Mary Martin 1944- *WhoAmW 93*
Schenkenfelder, John Charles 1952- *WhoSSW 93*
Schenker, Alexander Marian 1924- *WhoAm 92*
Schenker, Dona 1947- *BioIn 17*
Schenker, Eric 1931- *WhoAm 92*
Schenker, Heinrich 1868-1935 *Baker 92*
Schenker, Henry Hans 1926- *WhoE 93*
Schenker, Leo 1922- *WhoAm 92*
Schenker, Steven 1929- *WhoAm 92*
Schenkkan, Judith L. *Law&B 92*
Schenkkan, Pieter Meade 1947- *WhoAm 92*
Schenkkan, Robert Frederic 1953- *WhoAm 92*
Schenkman, John Boris 1936- *WhoAm 92, WhoE 93*
Schenk von Stauffenberg, Franz-Ludwig, Graf 1938- *BioIn 17*
Schenk von Stauffenberg, Klaus Philipp, Graf 1907-1944 *BioIn 17*
Schensted, M.A. 1943- *St&PR 93*
Schenstrom, Carl 1881-1942 *See* Madsen, Harald 1890-1949 & Schenstrom, Carl 1881-1942 *IntDcF 2-3*
Schenz, Anne Filer 1945- *WhoAmW 93*
Scheopner, Cynthia Ann 1953- *WhoAmW 93*
Schepard, Eric d1991 *BioIn 17*
Schepers, Donald Herbert 1951- *WhoWor 93*
Schepis, Guy A. *St&PR 93*
Schepis, Joseph Michael 1953- *St&PR 93*
Schepisi, Fred 1939- *MiSFD 9*
Schepker, Donald Joseph 1949- *St&PR 93*
Schepman, Berne Adair 1926- *St&PR 93*
Schepp, Brad Jeffrey 1955- *WhoWrEP 92*
Schepp, George Phillip, Jr. 1955- *WhoWor 93*
Scheppach, Raymond Carl, Jr. 1940- *WhoAm 92*
Scheppner, Kathleen 1949- *WhoAmW 93*
Schepps, Phil J. 1918- *St&PR 93*
Scheps, Esther 1941- *WhoE 93*
Scher, Allan Joseph 1935- *WhoE 93*
Scher, Allen Myron 1921- *WhoAm 92*
Scher, Coby Allyn 1942- *WhoSSW 93*
Scher, David Lawrence 1963- *WhoE 93*
Scher, Herbert Irwin 1928- *St&PR 93*
Scher, Irving 1933- *WhoAm 92*
Scher, J. Douglas 1959- *St&PR 93*
Scher, Jeffrey Noyes *MiSFD 9*
Scher, John *BioIn 17*
Scher, Martin M. 1922- *St&PR 93*
Scher, Monica Marcia 1951- *WhoAmW 93*
Scher, Murray Howard 1942- *WhoSSW 93*
Scher, Norman A. 1937- *St&PR 93*
Scher, Paula Joan 1948- *WhoAm 92*
Scher, Robert Elliott 1926-1991 *BioIn 17*
Scher, Robert Sander 1934- *WhoE 93*
Scher, Stanley Jules 1929- *WhoAm 92*
Scher, Stephen Karl 1934- *St&PR 93*
Scher, Steven Paul 1936- *WhoAm 92*
Scher, Werner 1940- *WhoAm 92*
Scheraga, Harold Abraham 1921- *WhoAm 92*
Scheraga, Joel Dov 1955- *WhoE 93*
Scherb, Joan C. 1937- *St&PR 93*
Scherb, Peter 1944- *St&PR 93*
Scherba, Elaine Louise 1949- *WhoAm 92*
Scherba, Elaine P. 1949- *St&PR 93*
Scherba, John E. 1928- *St&PR 93*
Scherban, Dwight Michael 1948- *WhoE 93*
Scherber, Anthony L. 1934- *St&PR 93*
Scherber, Catherine A. 1947- *WhoAmW 93*
Scherbina, Vladimir Iljich 1942- *WhoWor 93*
Scherchen, Hermann 1891-1966 *Baker 92, OxDcOp*
Scherchen, Tona 1938- *Baker 92*
Scherdin, Mary Jane Liskovec 1940- *WhoAmW 93*
Schere, Jonathan Lawrence 1938- *WhoAm 92*
Scheremetiev, Alexander *Baker 92*
Scherer, A. Edward 1942- *WhoE 93*
Scherer, Alfredo Vicente Cardinal 1903- *WhoWor 93*
Scherer, Barbara Elizabeth 1958- *WhoWor 93*
Scherer, Barbara Vaughn 1956- *St&PR 93*
Scherer, Donald Richard 1939- *WhoAm 92*
Scherer, Frederic Michael 1932- *WhoAm 92*
Scherer, Harold N., Jr. 1929- *St&PR 93*
Scherer, Harold Nicholas, Jr. 1929- *WhoAm 92, WhoE 93*
Scherer, Henri Joseph 1920- *WhoWor 93*
Scherer, J. Peter 1949- *St&PR 93*
Scherer, Jacqueline Rita 1931- *WhoAmW 93*
Scherer, Karla 1937- *WhoAmW 93*
Scherer, Klaus Rainer 1943- *WhoWor 93*
Scherer, Margaret Mary *WhoSSW 93*
Scherer, Maurice 1920- *WhoAm 92*
Scherer, Michael Joseph 1951- *St&PR 93*
Scherer, Nancy Ann 1935- *WhoAmW 93*
Scherer, Otto E. 1915- *St&PR 93*
Scherer, Peter R. 1956- *St&PR 93*
Scherer, Robert B. 1941- *St&PR 93*
Scherer, Robert Davisson 1929- *WhoAm 92*
Scherer, Robert Grainger 1929- *St&PR 93*
Scherer, Robert T. *Law&B 92*
Scherer, Roger Henry 1935- *St&PR 93*
Scherer, Roy 1925-1985 *BioIn 17*
Scherer, Steven J. *Law&B 92*
Scherer, Theodore M. 1934- *St&PR 93*
Scherf, Christopher N. 1950- *WhoAm 92*
Scherf, Margaret (Louise) 1908-1979 *DcAmChF 1960*
Scherff, Scott Alan *Law&B 92*
Schergens, Becky Lou 1940- *WhoAmW 93, WhoSSW 93*
Scherger, Dave Frank 1946- *St&PR 93*
Scherger, Joseph E. 1950- *WhoAm 92*
Scheri, Allen I. 1940- *St&PR 93*
Scherich, Edward Baptiste 1923- *WhoAm 92*
Scherich, Erwin Thomas 1918- *WhoAm 92*
Schering, Arnold 1877-1941 *Baker 92*
Scherker, Michael d1990 *BioIn 17*
Scherl, Donald Jacob *WhoAm 92*
Scherling, Sarah *ScF&FL 92*
Scherm, Reinhard 1937- *WhoScE 91-3*
Scherman, Susan Louise 1953- *WhoWrEP 92*
Scherman, Thomas 1917-1979 *OxDcOp*
Scherman, Thomas (Kielty) 1917-1979 *Baker 92*
Schermer, Harry Angus 1942- *St&PR 93*
Schermer, Judith Kahn 1949- *WhoAmW 93*
Schermer, Lloyd *BioIn 17*
Schermer, Lloyd G. 1927- *St&PR 93*
Schermerhorn, John Watson 1920- *WhoAm 92*
Schermerhorn, Kenneth (de Witt) 1929- *Baker 92*
Schermerhorn, Kenneth Dewitt 1929- *WhoAm 92, WhoSSW 93*
Schermerhorn, Lee Van Dyke, Jr. 1928- *St&PR 93*
Schermerhorn, Neal Y. 1936- *St&PR 93*
Scherpe, Claus Rudiger 1939- *WhoWor 93*
Scherpenberg, Theodore Anthony 1924- *St&PR 93*
Scherpf, Joseph Charles 1943- *St&PR 93*
Scherr, Allan Lee 1940- *WhoAm 92*
Scherr, Barbara Nadle 1946- *St&PR 93*
Scherr, Bruce Avrim 1948- *WhoSSW 93*
Scherr, David Edward 1948- *St&PR 93*
Scherr, Harry, III 1944- *St&PR 93*
Scherr, Lawrence 1928- *WhoAm 92*
Scherr, Marvin Gerald 1940- *WhoE 93*
Scherrer, Charles Lee 1948- *St&PR 93*
Scherrer, Deborah King 1946- *WhoAmW 93*
Scherrer, Everett John 1942- *St&PR 93*
Scherrmann, J.M. 1948- *WhoScE 91-2*
Schersten, H. Donald 1919- *WhoAm 92*
Schersten, Tore 1930- *WhoScE 91-4*
Schertenleib, Roland 1945- *WhoScE 91-4*
Schertle, Alice Marguerite 1941- *WhoAm 92*
Schertler, Nancy *BioIn 17*
Schertz, Doris Ethel 1938- *WhoAmW 93*
Schertz, Jeffrey 1941- *St&PR 93*
Schertzer, Robert John 1951- *WhoE 93, WhoEmL 93*
Schertzinger, Victor 1880-1941 *MiSFD 9N*
Scherubel, Ronald L. *Law&B 92*
Scherzer, Harry S. 1935- *St&PR 93*
Scherzer, Saul M. 1937- *WhoE 93*
Schetky, Johann Georg Christoph 1737-1824 *Baker 92*
Schetky, Laurence McDonald 1922- *St&PR 93, WhoAm 92*
Schetlin, Eleanor M. 1920- *WhoAmW 93, WhoE 93, WhoWor 93*
Schettini, Francesco 1930- *WhoScE 91-3*
Schettkat, Ronald 1954- *WhoWor 93*
Schetzen, Martin 1928- *WhoE 93*
Scheuber, Theodor Schmidt 1934- *St&PR 93*
Scheuch, Donald Ralph 1918- *St&PR 93*
Scheuer, James H. 1920- *CngDr 91*
Scheuer, James Haas 1920- *WhoAm 92, WhoE 93*
Scheuer, Jill *Law&B 92*
Scheuer, Katherine Dunn 1937- *WhoAm 92, WhoAmW 93*
Scheuer, P.A.G. *WhoScE 91-1*
Scheuer, Paul Josef 1915- *WhoAm 92*
Scheuer, Peter Joseph *WhoScE 91-1*
Scheuer, Thomas *Law&B 92*
Scheuer Family *BioIn 17*
Scheuerman, Richard R. 1954- *St&PR 93*
Scheuerman, Thomas J. *Law&B 92*
Scheuermann, Dietrich Wilhelm 1939- *WhoScE 91-2*
Scheuermann, Milton George, Jr. 1933- *WhoSSW 93*
Scheuermann, Sarah Melissa 1968- *WhoSSW 93*
Scheufele, W. Joseph 1948- *St&PR 93*
Scheuing, Richard A. 1927- *St&PR 93*
Scheuing, Richard Albert 1927- *WhoAm 92*
Scheurer, Charles B. 1941- *St&PR 93*
Scheurer-Kestner, Auguste 1833-1899 *BioIn 17*
Scheuring, David Keith 1947- *WhoE 93*
Scheuring, Garry J. 1939- *St&PR 93*
Scheuring, Garry Joseph 1939- *WhoAm 92*
Scheuring, Helen 1940- *WhoAmW 93, WhoWor 93*
Scheurle, Jurgen Karl 1951- *WhoWor 93*
Scheurleer, Daniel Francois 1855-1927 *Baker 92*
Scheuzger, Thomas Peter 1960- *WhoE 93*
Schevill, James Erwin 1920- *WhoAm 92, WhoWrEP 92*
Scheving, Lawrence Einar 1920- *WhoAm 92*
Schewel, Marc Allen 1948- *St&PR 93*
Schewel, Rosel Hoffberger 1928- *WhoAmW 93*
Schewel, Stanford 1918- *WhoAm 92*
Schexnayder, Brian Edward 1953- *WhoAm 92*
Schexnayder, Charlotte Tillar 1923- *WhoAmW 93*
Schey, John Anthony 1922- *WhoAm 92*
Schey, Ralph Edward 1924- *WhoAm 92*
Scheyd, Charles Phillip 1960- *St&PR 93*
Scheye, Klaus G. 1923- *St&PR 93*
Scheyer, Galka 1889-1945 *BioIn 17*
Scheyer, Lawrence W. *Law&B 92*
Scheyer, Stuart R. 1930- *St&PR 93*
Schiaffino, Silvio Stephen 1927- *WhoAm 92, WhoE 93*
Schiaffino, Stefano *WhoScE 91-3*
Schiano, Tony 1951- *St&PR 93*
Schiaparelli, Giovanni Virginio 1835-1910 *BioIn 17*
Schiappa, Janice Miller 1950- *WhoAmW 93*
Schiavelli, Melvyn David 1942- *WhoAm 92*
Schiavi, Anthony Romeo 1950- *WhoEmL 93*
Schiavi, Raul Constante 1930- *WhoE 93, WhoWor 93*
Schiavina, Laura Margaret 1917- *WhoAm 92*
Schiavo, A. Mary Sterling 1955- *WhoAmW 93*
Schiavog, Mary Sterling 1955- *WhoAm 92*
Schiavone, James d1991 *BioIn 17*
Schiavone, James 1929- *St&PR 93*
Schiavone-Gurule, Theresa Ann 1949- *WhoAmW 93*
Schiavoni, Giorgio *Law&B 92*
Schiavoni, Robert Patrick 1949- *WhoE 93*
Schiazza, Guido Domenic 1930- *WhoE 93, WhoWor 93*
Schibler, Armin 1920-1986 *Baker 92*
Schibler, Ulrich 1947- *WhoScE 91-4*
Schibley, James V. *Law&B 92*
Schibli, Paul *MiSFD 9*
Schichler, Rebecca Potter 1951- *WhoWrEP 92*
Schicht, Johann Gottfried 1753-1823 *Baker 92*
Schiciano, Joseph S. 1927- *St&PR 93*
Schick, August 1940- *WhoWor 93*
Schick, Bela 1877-1967 *JeAmHC*
Schick, Edgar Brehob 1934- *WhoAm 92*
Schick, Elliot 1924- *St&PR 93*
Schick, Frank Leopold 1918-1992 *BioIn 17*
Schick, George 1908-1985 *Baker 92*
Schick, Hans 1937- *WhoScE 91-3*
Schick, Harry L. 1927- *St&PR 93*
Schick, Irvin Henry 1924- *WhoE 93, WhoWor 93*
Schick, James Baldwin Mc Donald 1940- *WhoWrEP 92*

Schick, Joseph Carl 1930- *St&PR 93*
Schick, Lawrence 1953- *ScF&FL 92*
Schick, Lawrence 1955- *ConAu 139*
Schick, Margarete (Luise) 1773-1809 *Baker 92*
Schick, Rene *DcCPCAm*
Schick, Thomas Edward 1941- *St&PR 93*
Schickel, Richard *BioIn 17, MiSFD 9*
Schickel, Richard 1933- *ConTFT 10, WhoAm 92, WhoWrEP 92*
Schickele, Peter *BioIn 17*
Schickele, Peter 1935- *Baker 92, WhoAm 92*
Schickele, Sandra Eloise 1939- *WhoAmW 93*
Schicker, Dona Roberta 1939- *WhoSSW 93*
Schicker, Glenn Earl 1950- *WhoWrEP 92*
Schickler, W.J. 1934- *St&PR 93*
Schidlovsky, John 1948- *WhoWor 93*
Schidlowsky, Leon 1931- *Baker 92*
Schiebel, Herman Max 1909- *WhoSSW 93*
Schieber, Allen Dale 1948- *St&PR 93*
Schieber, Judith A. *Law&B 92*
Schieber, Marc Elliot 1948- *WhoUN 92*
Schieber, William D. 1940- *WhoUN 92*
Schiebler, Gerold Ludwig 1928- *WhoAm 92*
Schiebler, Theodor H. 1923- *WhoScE 91-3*
Schied, Peter J. 1944- *St&PR 93*
Schieder, Joseph Eugene 1908- *WhoAm 92*
Schiedermair, Ludwig 1876-1957 *Baker 92*
Schiedermayer, Johann Baptist 1779-1840 *Baker 92*
Schiedmayer *Baker 92*
Schiedmayer, Adolf 1819-1890 *Baker 92*
Schiedmayer, Balthasar 1711-1781 *Baker 92*
Schiedmayer, Hermann 1820-1861 *Baker 92*
Schiedmayer, Johann David 1753-1805 *Baker 92*
Schiedmayer, Johann Lorenz 1786-1860 *Baker 92*
Schiedmayer, Julius 1822-1878 *Baker 92*
Schiedmayer, Max Julius *Baker 92*
Schiedmayer, Paul 1829-1890 *Baker 92*
Schiefelbein, Ernesto F. 1934- *WhoUN 92*
Schiefelbein, Lester W. *Law&B 92*
Schiefelbusch, A.J. Wim 1939- *WhoUN 92*
Schiefelbusch, Richard L. 1918- *WhoAm 92*
Schiefer, Hans Gerd 1935- *WhoScE 91-3, WhoWor 93*
Schieferdecker, G. Peter 1925- *St&PR 93*
Schieferdecker, Johann Christian 1679-1732 *Baker 92*
Schieffelin, Edward 1848?-1898? *BioIn 17*
Schieffelin, George Richard 1930- *WhoSSW 93, WhoWor 93*
Schieffelin, Laurie Graham 1941- *WhoAm 92, WhoWrEP 92*
Schieffelin, Thomas Lawrence 1936- *WhoWor 93*
Schieffer, Bob *WhoAm 92*
Schieffer, Bob 1937- *JrnUS*
Schiehlen, Werner O. 1938- *WhoScE 91-3*
Schieke, Herman Edward, Jr. 1937- *St&PR 93*
Schieken, Richard Merrill 1939- *WhoSSW 93*
Schiel, Ulrich 1945- *WhoWor 93*
Schield, Marshall Lew 1946- *St&PR 93*
Schield, Michael F. 1948- *St&PR 93*
Schield, William H., Jr. 1926- *St&PR 93*
Schiele, Egon 1890-1918 *BioIn 17*
Schiele, Henry F. 1922- *St&PR 93*
Schiele, James E. 1929- *St&PR 93*
Schiele, Paul Ellsworth, Jr. 1924- *WhoWor 93*
Schieler, Calvin Louis 1932- *St&PR 93*
Schieler, Jean Marie L. *Law&B 92*
Schielke, Kent John *Law&B 92*
Schiemann, Don A. *Law&B 92*
Schier, Donald Stephen 1914- *WhoAm 92*
Schier, Ernest Leonard 1918- *WhoE 93*
Schier, Neil 1968- *WhoE 93*
Schiera, Roger J. *Law&B 92*
Schierbeck, Poul (Julius Ouscher) 1888-1949 *Baker 92*
Schiereck, P. 1943- *WhoScE 91-3*
Schieren, George A. *Law&B 92*
Schierholz, William Francis, Jr. 1921- *WhoAm 92*
Schierholz, Wm. F., Jr. 1921- *St&PR 93*
Schiering, John H. 1946- *St&PR 93*
Schierl, Paul J. 1935- *St&PR 93*
Schierlman, Dixie Lee 1951- *WhoAmW 93*
Schierloh, Harold A. 1945- *St&PR 93*
Schierloh, James Edward 1929- *St&PR 93*
Schierow, Linda-Jo 1947- *WhoAmW 93*
Schieser, Hans Alois 1931- *WhoAm 92*
Schiesl, Joseph P. 1952- *St&PR 93*
Schiess, Betty Bone 1923- *WhoAmW 93*
Schiess, Kenneth R. 1947- *St&PR 93*
Schiessl, Peter 1943- *WhoScE 91-3*
Schiessler, Robert Walter 1918- *WhoAm 92*
Schieszler, Augustus J. 1918- *St&PR 93*
Schieszler, Joseph F. 1939- *St&PR 93*
Schievelbein, Thomas Clayton 1953- *WhoSSW 93*
Schiff, Alan Dana 1950- *St&PR 93*
Schiff, Andras 1953- *Baker 92*
Schiff, April 1957- *WhoAmW 93*
Schiff, David S.T. *Law&B 92*
Schiff, David Tevele 1936- *WhoAm 92*
Schiff, Davida Lynne 1954- *WhoAmW 93*
Schiff, Dobbie G. *WhoAm 92*
Schiff, Donald Wilfred 1925- *WhoAm 92*
Schiff, Dorothy 1903-1989 *DcLB 127 [port]*
Schiff, Elliot Donald 1957- *WhoSSW 93*
Schiff, Eugene Roger 1937- *WhoAm 92*
Schiff, Gert 1926-1990 *BioIn 17, ScF&FL 92*
Schiff, Gunther Hans 1927- *WhoAm 92*
Schiff, Harold Irvin 1923- *WhoAm 92*
Schiff, Heinrich 1951- *Baker 92*
Schiff, Heinrich 1952- *BioIn 17*
Schiff, Isaac 1944- *WhoAm 92*
Schiff, Jacob Henry 1847-1920 *BioIn 17*
Schiff, Jamieson M. *Law&B 92*
Schiff, Jayne Nemerow 1945- *WhoAmW 93, WhoE 93*
Schiff, Jerome Arnold 1931- *WhoAm 92, WhoE 93*
Schiff, John J. 1916- *St&PR 93*
Schiff, John Jefferson 1916- *WhoAm 92, WhoIns 93*
Schiff, Joseph *WhoAm 92*
Schiff, Laurence Elliot 1950- *WhoE 93*
Schiff, Laurie 1960- *WhoAmW 93*
Schiff, Leonard Norman 1938- *WhoE 93*
Schiff, Lonny 1929- *WhoE 93*
Schiff, Marlene Sandler *WhoAmW 93, WhoE 93*
Schiff, Martin 1922- *WhoAm 92*
Schiff, Michael 1915- *WhoE 93*
Schiff, Morton 1934- *St&PR 93*
Schiff, Stefan Otto 1930- *WhoAm 92*
Schiff, Stephen *WhoAm 92*
Schiff, Steven 1947- *CngDr 91*
Schiff, Stuart David 1946- *ScF&FL 92*
Schiffel, D.D. 1943- *St&PR 93*
Schiffel, Dennis Duane 1943- *WhoWor 93*
Schiffelbein, Wayne Lloyd 1939- *WhoE 93*
Schiffer, Claudia *BioIn 17*
Schiffer, Daniel L. *WhoAm 92*
Schiffer, Daniel L. 1943- *St&PR 93*
Schiffer, John Paul 1930- *WhoAm 92*
Schiffer, Michael C. *Law&B 92*
Schifferle, Klaudia 1955- *BioIn 17*
Schiffhorst, Gerald J. 1940- *ConAu 38NR*
Schiffman, Alan Theodore 1942- *WhoE 93*
Schiffman, David 1926- *WhoE 93*
Schiffman, Gerald 1926- *WhoAm 92, WhoE 93, WhoWor 93*
Schiffman, Harold Fosdick 1938- *WhoAm 92*
Schiffman, Joseph Harris 1914- *WhoAm 92, WhoE 93*
Schiffman, Lawrence Steven 1950- *WhoE 93*
Schiffman, Louis F. 1927- *WhoE 93, WhoWor 93*
Schiffman, Mark E. *Law&B 92*
Schiffman, Mia Helen 1953- *WhoAmW 93*
Schiffman, Michael 1965- *St&PR 93*
Schiffman, Mindy Rae 1952- *WhoAmW 93, WhoE 93*
Schiffman, Richard Gary *WhoE 93*
Schiffman, Robert S. 1944- *WhoAm 92*
Schiffman, Robert Stanley 1944- *St&PR 93*
Schiffman, Samuel A. *Law&B 92*
Schiffman, Saul S. 1914- *St&PR 93*
Schiffman, Stephan 1946- *WhoE 93*
Schiffman, Susan Stolte 1940- *WhoAmW 93*
Schiffman, Suzanne *MiSFD 9*
Schiffmann, Yoram 1941- *WhoWor 93*
Schiffner, Charles Robert 1948- *WhoEmL 93*
Schiffner, Klaus Joachim 1937- *WhoScE 91-3*
Schiffres, Michael E. *Law&B 92*
Schiffrin, Andre 1935- *WhoAm 92*
Schiffrin, David J. *WhoScE 91-1*
Schiffrin, Milton Julius 1914- *WhoWor 93*
Schifman, Edward Joseph 1949- *WhoEmL 93*
Schifrin, Lalo 1932- *WhoAm 92*
Schifrin, Lalo (Boris) 1932- *Baker 92*
Schift, Craig M. *St&PR 93*
Schifter, Craig Robert 1952- *St&PR 93*
Schifter, Richard 1923- *WhoAm 92*
Schijve, Jacobus 1927- *WhoScE 91-3*
Schikaneder, Emanuel 1751-1812 *Baker 92, BioIn 17, IntDcOp [port], OxDcOp*
Schilcher, Heinz 1930- *WhoScE 91-3*
Schilcher, Sabrina *BioIn 17*
Schild, G.C. *WhoScE 91-1*
Schild, Joyce Anna 1931- *WhoAmW 93*
Schild, Wayne L. 1945- *St&PR 93*
Schildbach, Reinhold 1933- *WhoScE 91-3*
Schildberg, Friedrich Wilhelm 1934- *WhoScE 91-3*
Schilder, Ellie Bryce 1936- *WhoAmW 93*
Schilder, J. Michael 1943- *St&PR 93*
Schildgen, Gordon Wayne 1943- *St&PR 93*
Schildhouse, Burton *St&PR 93*
Schildkraut, Carl Louis 1937- *WhoAm 92*
Schildkraut, Joseph Jacob 1934- *WhoAm 92, WhoE 93*
Schildkraut, Peter Jeremy 1968- *WhoE 93*
Schildwachter, Eric Francis 1960- *WhoSSW 93*
Schildwachter, Fred Henry, III 1949- *St&PR 93*
Schilizzi, Richard T. 1945- *WhoScE 91-3*
Schill, Wolf-B. 1939- *WhoScE 91-3*
Schill, Wolf-Bernhard 1939- *WhoWor 93*
Schiller, Alfred George 1918- *WhoAm 92*
Schiller, Arthur A. 1910- *WhoAm 92*
Schiller, Donald Charles 1942- *WhoAm 92*
Schiller, Francis 1909- *WhoAm 92*
Schiller, Friedrich 1759-1805 *BioIn 17, MagSWL [port], NinCLC 39 [port]*
Schiller, Friedrich von 1759-1805 *OxDcOp*
Schiller, (Johann Christian) Friedrich von 1759-1805 *Baker 92*
Schiller, Gabrielle Antonia 1962- *WhoAmW 93*
Schiller, Ginnell M. 1955- *St&PR 93*
Schiller, Herbert I. 1919- *WhoWrEP 92*
Schiller, Herbert Irving 1919- *WhoAm 92*
Schiller, Herbert Miles 1943- *WhoSSW 93*
Schiller, J.P. *Law&B 92*
Schiller, Jerome Paul 1934- *WhoAm 92*
Schiller, Jerry A. 1932- *St&PR 93, WhoAm 92*
Schiller, Lawrence J. 1936- *MiSFD 9*
Schiller, Lawrence Julian 1936- *WhoAm 92*
Schiller, Leon 1887-1954 *PolBiDi*
Schiller, M. Sharon *Law&B 92*
Schiller, Madeline 1845-1911 *Baker 92*
Schiller, Marilyn 1951- *WhoE 93*
Schiller, Martin David 1938- *WhoAm 92*
Schiller, Marvin 1933- *St&PR 93*
Schiller, Michael 1933- *St&PR 93*
Schiller, Pieter Jon 1938- *WhoAm 92*
Schiller, Sherry Lynne 1948- *WhoAmW 93*
Schiller, Thomas George 1956- *St&PR 93*
Schiller, Tom *MiSFD 9*
Schiller, William Charles 1923- *St&PR 93*
Schiller, William E. 1909-1990 *BioIn 17*
Schiller, William H. *St&PR 93*
Schiller, William Joseph 1946- *WhoSSW 93*
Schiller, William Richard 1937- *WhoAm 92*
Schillhahn, Michael Vaughn 1952- *WhoSSW 93*
Schillhammer, Richard W. 1914- *St&PR 93*
Schilling, Albert Henry 1943- *WhoAm 92*
Schilling, Allan Dale 1942- *St&PR 93*
Schilling, Arlo L. 1924- *St&PR 93*
Schilling, Arlo Leonard 1924- *WhoAm 92*
Schilling, Carl F. 1923- *St&PR 93*
Schilling, Charles Henry 1918- *WhoSSW 93*
Schilling, Deborah Jan 1951- *WhoAmW 93*
Schilling, Dennis L. *Law&B 92*
Schilling, Edward George 1931- *WhoE 93*
Schilling, Franklin Charles, Jr. 1958- *WhoE 93, WhoEmL 93, WhoWor 93*
Schilling, Frederick C. 1941- *St&PR 93*
Schilling, Gustav 1805-1880 *Baker 92*
Schilling, James Joseph *WhoE 93*
Schilling, John Albert 1917- *WhoAm 92*
Schilling, John Michael 1951- *WhoAm 92*
Schilling, Kenneth Lee 1946- *St&PR 93*
Schilling, Kurt Von 1939- *St&PR 93*
Schilling, Marie Battelle *AmWomPl*
Schilling, Ralph Franklin 1921- *WhoAm 92*
Schilling, Richard M. *Law&B 92*
Schilling, Richard M. 1937- *WhoAm 92*
Schilling, Richard Merlin 1937- *St&PR 93*
Schilling, Stacey Lynn 1964- *WhoEmL 93*
Schilling, Sue Belevich 1953- *WhoAmW 93*
Schilling, William Richard 1933- *WhoSSW 93, WhoWor 93*
Schillinger, Beat 1945- *St&PR 93*
Schillinger, Edwin Joseph 1923- *WhoAm 92*
Schillinger, Joseph (Moiseievich) 1895-1943 *Baker 92*
Schillings, Max von 1868-1933 *Baker 92, OxDcOp*
Schillingsfurst, Chlodwig Karl Viktor Hohenlohe-, Furst zu *BioIn 17*
Schilpp, Paul Arthur 1897- *WhoAm 92*
Schilson, Arno 1945- *WhoWor 93*
Schilt, Alexander Frank 1941- *WhoSSW 93*
Schiltberger, Johann 1380- *OxDcByz*
Schilthuis, Willem C. d1990 *BioIn 17*
Schiltz, James 1962- *St&PR 93*
Schiltz, Kenneth *St&PR 93*
Schiltz, Marlin *St&PR 93*
Schiltz, Pierre 1936- *WhoScE 91-2*
Schiltz, Richard *St&PR 93*
Schimberg, Armand Bruce 1927- *WhoAm 92, WhoWor 93*
Schimberg, Henry Aaron 1933- *St&PR 93, WhoAm 92*
Schimbor, Mark Anderson 1945- *St&PR 93*
Schimek, Dianna R. 1940- *WhoAmW 93*
Schimel, John L. d1991 *NewYTBS 92*
Schimel, John L. 1916-1991 *BioIn 17*
Schimelpfenig, Danny Alfred 1945- *St&PR 93*
Schimelpfenig, Glen Herbert 1929- *St&PR 93*
Schimer, John Francis 1934- *St&PR 93*
Schimidt, Eric 1960- *St&PR 93*
Schimizzi, Ned Vincent 1936- *WhoE 93, WhoWor 93*
Schimke, Robert Tod 1932- *WhoAm 92*
Schimmel, Allan 1940- *St&PR 93, WhoAm 92, WhoE 93*
Schimmel, David M. 1934- *WhoE 93*
Schimmel, Norbert 1904-1990 *BioIn 17*
Schimmel, Paul Reinhard 1940- *WhoAm 92, WhoE 93*
Schimmel, Robert H. 1937- *St&PR 93*
Schimmel, Solomon 1941- *ConAu 139*
Schimmel, Walter Paul 1938- *WhoSSW 93*
Schimmenti, Michael Ronald 1932- *St&PR 93*
Schimmer, John, Jr. 1933- *WhoSSW 93*
Schimming, Rainer 1944- *WhoWor 93*
Schimmoeller, Gerald M. 1943- *St&PR 93*
Schimon, Adolf 1820-1887 *Baker 92*
Schimon-Regan, Anna 1841-1902 *Baker 92*
Schimpf, Barbara *St&PR 93*
Schimpf, John J. 1949- *St&PR 93*
Schimpf, John Joseph 1949- *WhoAm 92*
Schimpff, Stephen Callender 1941- *WhoAm 92*
Schinagl, Erich F. 1932- *St&PR 93*
Schinagl, Erich Friedrich 1932- *WhoAm 92*
Schindel, Donald A. 1933- *St&PR 93*
Schindel, Donald Marvin 1932- *WhoAm 92, WhoWor 93*
Schindelman, Joseph 1923- *BioIn 17*
Schindelmeisser, Louis 1811-1864 *Baker 92, OxDcOp*
Schinderle, Robert Frank 1923- *WhoAm 92*
Schindewolf, Darcy Doyle 1947- *St&PR 93*
Schindewolf, Ulrich 1927- *WhoScE 91-3*
Schindler, Adolf Eduard 1936- *WhoWor 93*
Schindler, Albert Isadore 1927- *WhoAm 92*
Schindler, Alexander Moshe 1925- *WhoAm 92*
Schindler, Alfred N. *BioIn 17*
Schindler, Anton Felix 1795-1864 *Baker 92*
Schindler, David L. 1945- *St&PR 93*
Schindler, David William 1940- *WhoAm 92*
Schindler, Dennis 1944- *St&PR 93*
Schindler, Donald Warren 1925- *WhoE 93*
Schindler, Jerome R. *Law&B 92*
Schindler, Karl 1931- *WhoScE 91-3*
Schindler, Kurt 1882-1935 *Baker 92*
Schindler, Mark 1921- *St&PR 93*
Schindler, Marvin Samuel 1932- *WhoAm 92*
Schindler, Norbert 1918- *WhoWor 93*
Schindler, Peter David 1931- *WhoAm 92*
Schindler, Ralph Joseph, Jr. 1948- *St&PR 93*
Schindler, Ralph N. 1931- *WhoScE 91-3*
Schindler, Ronald Louis 1944- *WhoSSW 93*
Schindler, Rose M. *Law&B 92*
Schindler, William Stanley 1933- *WhoAm 92*
Schindler-Mahler, Alma Maria 1879-1964 *BioIn 17*
Schine, Gerard David 1927- *WhoAm 92*
Schine, Joan Goldwasser 1923- *WhoE 93*
Schine, Wendy Wachtell 1961- *WhoAmW 93*
Schinelli, Guillermo Carlos *Law&B 92*

Schingler, Steve Lee 1952- *St&PR 93*
Schink, Frank Edward 1922- *WhoAm 92*
Schinkel, J.W. 1937- *WhoScE 91-3*
Schinkel, Karl Friedrich 1781-1841 *OxDcOp*
Schinman, Henry Lawrence 1943- *St&PR 93*
Schinzel, Andrzej Bobola Maria 1937- *WhoWor 93*
Schinzel, Britta A. 1943- *WhoWor 93*
Schinzer, Michael H. 1957- *St&PR 93*
Schioler, Victor 1899-1967 *Baker 92*
Schiorring, Nils 1910- *Baker 92*
Schiotz, Aksel (Hauch) 1906-1975 *Baker 92*
Schiotz, Arne *WhoScE 91-2*
Schipa, Tito 1888-1965 *Baker 92, IntDcOp [port], OxDcOp*
Schiper, Ignacy 1884-1943 *PolBiDi*
Schipitsch, Douglas Anthony 1950- *WhoE 93*
Schipke, Roger W. *WhoAm 92*
Schippel, John E. *Law&B 92*
Schippel, John E. 1934- *St&PR 93*
Schipper, Emil (Zacharias) 1882-1957 *Baker 92*
Schipper, Kevin D. *St&PR 93*
Schipper, Paul *BioIn 17*
Schippereit, Merrie E. 1952- *St&PR 93*
Schippers, B. 1934- *WhoScE 91-3*
Schippers, David Philip 1929- *WhoAm 92*
Schippers, J.M. *WhoScE 91-3*
Schippers, Louis 1938- *WhoE 93*
Schippers, Thomas 1930-1977 *Baker 92, IntDcOp, OxDcOp*
Schira, Francesco 1809-1883 *OxDcOp*
Schira, Jeffrey Scot *Law&B 92*
Schirach, Baldur von 1907-1974 *DcTwHis*
Schirato, Robert J. 1930- *St&PR 93*
Schirick, Edward Arthur 1948- *WhoE 93*
Schirick, Robert John 1928- *WhoE 93*
Schirm, Karen Marie 1946- *WhoWrEP 92*
Schirmacher, Peter 1961- *WhoWor 93*
Schirmang, William Peter 1923- *St&PR 93*
Schirmer *Baker 92*
Schirmer, Ernest Charles 1865-1958 *Baker 92*
Schirmer, Ernst Ludwig Rudolf 1784- *Baker 92*
Schirmer, Gustav 1829-1893 *Baker 92*
Schirmer, Gustave 1864-1907 *Baker 92*
Schirmer, Gustave, Jr. d1992 *NewYTBS 92*
Schirmer, Gustave, III 1890-1965 *Baker 92*
Schirmer, Henry William 1922- *WhoAm 92*
Schirmer, Howard August, Jr. 1942- *WhoAm 92*
Schirmer, Johann Georg *Baker 92*
Schirmer, Marilyn Marie 1938- *St&PR 93*
Schirmer, R. Heiner 1942- *WhoScE 91-3*
Schirmer, Robert H. 1940- *St&PR 93*
Schirmer, Robert Hamilton 1940- *WhoAm 92*
Schirmer, Rudolph Edward 1859-1919 *Baker 92*
Schirmer, Rudolph Edward 1919- *Baker 92*
Schirn, Janet Sugerman *WhoAm 92*
Schiro-Geist, Chrisann 1946- *WhoAmW 93*
Schirra, John Ross 1937- *WhoSSW 93*
Schirra, Walter Marty, Jr. 1923- *WhoAm 92, WhoWor 93*
Schirrmacher, Volker 1943- *WhoScE 91-3*
Schisgal, Murray Joseph 1926- *WhoAm 92*
Schiske, Karl (Hubert Rudolf) 1916-1969 *Baker 92*
Schisler, Floyd 1926- *St&PR 93*
Schissler, Jean Marie 1934- *WhoWor 93*
Schiuma, Alfredo 1885-1963 *Baker 92*
Schiva, Tito 1941- *WhoScE 91-3*
Schivek, Elaine Rona 1930- *WhoE 93, WhoWor 93*
Schiweck, Hubert 1929- *WhoScE 91-3*
Schiweck, Hubert M. 1929- *WhoScE 91-3*
Schjelderup, Gerhard (Rosenkrone) 1859-1933 *Baker 92*
Schjerning, E.J. *Law&B 92*
Schjetne, Karl G. 1935- *WhoScE 91-4*
Schjonning, Per 1953- *WhoScE 91-2*
Schkeeper, Peter A., II 1944- *St&PR 93*
Schlaak, Max W. 1934- *WhoScE 91-3*
Schlabach, Tom Daniel 1924- *WhoE 93*
Schlackman, Neil 1943- *WhoE 93*
Schlactenhaufen, John E. 1939- *St&PR 93*
Schlader, Donald Richard 1933- *St&PR 93*
Schlaeger, Gary D. 1938- *St&PR 93*
Schlaeger, Wolfgang 1942- *WhoIns 93*
Schlaepfer, R. *WhoScE 91-4*
Schlaepfer, Rodolphe-Rene 1940- *WhoScE 91-4*
Schlaf, Johannes 1862-1941 *DcLB 118 [port]*
Schlafer, Donald Hughes 1948- *WhoAm 92*
Schlafke, Ethelda Bleibtrey MacRobert 1902-1978 *BiDAMSp 1989*
Schlafly, Hubert Joseph 1919- *St&PR 93*
Schlafly, Hubert Joseph, Jr. 1919- *WhoAm 92*
Schlafly, John Byrne *Law&B 92*
Schlafly, Phyllis *BioIn 17*
Schlafly, Phyllis S. 1924- *PolPar*
Schlafly, Phyllis Stewart 1924- *WhoAm 92, WhoAmW 93, WhoWrEP 92*
Schlag, Edward William 1932- *WhoScE 91-3*
Schlag, Gunther *WhoScE 91-4*
Schlagel, Clarence R. 1928- *St&PR 93*
Schlagel, Richard H. 1925- *WhoAm 92*
Schlager, Hans 1820-1885 *Baker 92*
Schlager, John J. *Law&B 92*
Schlager, Maynard Morton 1928- *WhoE 93*
Schlageter, Gunter N. 1943- *WhoScE 91-3*
Schlageter, Robert William 1925- *WhoAm 92*
Schlaifer, Charles 1909- *WhoAm 92*
Schlaifer, Marissa Carla 1964- *WhoSSW 93*
Schlaifer, Robert Osher 1914- *WhoAm 92*
Schlaile, Barry F. 1953- *St&PR 93*
Schlain, Barbara E. *Law&B 92*
Schlain, Barbara E. 1948- *St&PR 93*
Schlain, Barbara Ellen 1948- *WhoAmW 93*
Schlain, David 1910- *WhoE 93*
Schlakman, Geoffrey Craig 1954- *WhoE 93*
Schlam, Mark Howard 1951- *WhoE 93, WhoWor 93*
Schlammadinger, Joseph 1938- *WhoScE 91-4*
Schlamme, Thomas *MiSFD 9*
Schlamowitz, Isadore 1915-1991 *BioIn 17*
Schlang, Alan Leslie 1942- *St&PR 93*
Schlang, David 1912- *WhoE 93, WhoWor 93*
Schlang, Elliott L. 1934- *St&PR 93, WhoAm 92*
Schlang, Joseph 1911- *WhoAm 92, WhoE 93, WhoWor 93*
Schlange, Richard Walter 1935- *St&PR 93*
Schlanger, Bernard B. 1915-1991 *BioIn 17*
Schlanger, Eugene Joseph 1925- *St&PR 93*
Schlanger, Jacob L. 1951- *St&PR 93*
Schlanger, Norman R. 1937- *St&PR 93*
Schlant, Robert Carl 1929- *WhoAm 92, WhoSSW 93*
Schlapfer, K. *WhoScE 91-4*
Schlapp, Andrew Thomas, Jr. 1951- *WhoE 93*
Schlappack, Otto Kurt 1956- *WhoWor 93*
Schlarb, Roger James 1943- *St&PR 93*
Schlater, Herb 1919- *St&PR 93*
Schlatmann, J.L.M.A. 1927- *WhoScE 91-3*
Schlatter, Charlie *BioIn 17*
Schlatter, Donald Allan 1929- *St&PR 93*
Schlatter, George 1932- *MiSFD 9*
Schlatter, Herman H. 1912- *St&PR 93*
Schlatter, Konard 1935- *St&PR 93*
Schlauch, Paul John 1942- *WhoAm 92*
Schlauch, Walter F. 1941- *St&PR 93*
Schlecht, Matthew Fred 1953- *WhoE 93*
Schlecht, William R. *Law&B 92*
Schleck, Roth Stephen 1915- *WhoAm 92*
Schlee, Ann 1934- *ScF&FL 92*
Schlee, John 1943- *WhoAm 92*
Schlee, Susan *ConAu 40NR*
Schlee, Walter 1942- *WhoWor 93*
Schleede, Glenn R. 1933- *St&PR 93*
Schleede, Glenn Roy 1933- *WhoAm 92*
Schleef, Helen Ida 1914- *WhoWrEP 92*
Schleenvoigt, Carole VanderWiel 1950- *WhoSSW 93*
Schlegel, August Wilhelm von 1767-1845 *BioIn 17*
Schlegel, Beverly Faye 1950- *WhoAmW 93, WhoEmL 93*
Schlegel, Donald E. 1941- *St&PR 93*
Schlegel, Dorothea Mendelssohn von 1763-1839 *BioIn 17*
Schlegel, Friedrich von 1772-1829 *BioIn 17*
Schlegel, Hans-Gunter 1924- *WhoScE 91-3*
Schlegel, Jack *BioIn 17*
Schlegel, John F. *BioIn 17*
Schlegel, John Frederick 1944- *WhoAm 92, WhoE 93*
Schlegel, John Peter 1943- *WhoAm 92*
Schlegel, Justin J. 1922- *WhoWor 93*
Schlegel, Leander 1844-1913 *Baker 92*
Schlegel, Nancy Browning 1929- *WhoAmW 93*
Schlegel, Robert Philip 1929- *St&PR 93*
Schleger, Walter *WhoScE 91-4*
Schleh, Eugene 1939- *ConAu 137*
Schleh, Eugene Paul Anderson 1939- *WhoE 93*
Schlehofer, Bernd 1936- *WhoScE 91-3*
Schlei, Norbert Anthony 1929- *WhoAm 92*
Schleich, Donald Max 1950- *WhoE 93*
Schleich, Wolfgang Peter 1957- *WhoWor 93*
Schleicher, August 1821-1868 *IntDcAn*
Schleicher, Dennis J. 1945- *St&PR 93*
Schleicher, Joel Arthur 1952- *WhoAm 92*
Schleicher, Kurt von 1882-1934 *DcTwHis*
Schleicher, Nora Elizabeth 1952- *WhoAmW 93*
Schleiermacher, Friedrich 1768-1834 *BioIn 17*
Schleif, Robert F. 1940- *WhoE 93*
Schleifer, Karin Faith *Law&B 92*
Schleifer, Karl Heinz 1939- *WhoScE 91-3*
Schleifer, Ronald 1948- *WhoAm 92*
Schleifer, Trudy R. 1944- *St&PR 93*
Schleiff, Henry Stephan 1948- *St&PR 93*
Schleimer, Joseph 1930- *WhoE 93*
Schlein, Dov C. 1947- *St&PR 93*
Schlein, Miriam *WhoAmW 93*
Schlein, Stephen 1944- *St&PR 93*
Schlembach, John Michael 1947- *WhoWor 93*
Schlemmer, Alfred E., Jr. 1931- *St&PR 93*
Schlemmer, Frederick Charles, II 1943- *WhoSSW 93*
Schlemmer, Nancy L. 1936- *St&PR 93*
Schlemmer, Oskar 1888-1943 *BioIn 17*
Schlemmer, Roger P. 1933- *St&PR 93*
Schlender, Bodo H.W. 1931- *WhoScE 91-3*
Schlender, William Elmer 1920- *WhoAm 92*
Schlenker, Barry Richard 1947- *WhoSSW 93*
Schlenker, Claire 1940- *WhoScE 91-2*
Schlenker, David James 1948- *WhoSSW 93*
Schlenker, Ralph F. 1928- *St&PR 93*
Schlenker, Ralph P. 1945- *St&PR 93*
Schlensker, Gary Chris 1950- *WhoAm 92*
Schleppi, W. Joseph *Law&B 92*
Schler, Sue Hope 1955- *WhoAmW 93*
Schlesch, Ronald Duane 1929- *St&PR 93*
Schlesing, Hendrik 1944- *WhoWor 93*
Schlesinger, Adolph Martin 1769-1838 *Baker 92*
Schlesinger, Alan M. *Law&B 92*
Schlesinger, Albert R. 1941- *St&PR 93*
Schlesinger, Albert Reuben 1941- *WhoAm 92*
Schlesinger, Arthur M. 1917- *BioIn 17*
Schlesinger, Arthur M., Jr. 1917- *ColdWar 1 [port]*
Schlesinger, Arthur Meier, Jr. 1917- *WhoAm 92, WhoWor 93, WhoWrEP 92*
Schlesinger, B. Frank 1925- *WhoAm 92*
Schlesinger, Barbara Joyce 1945- *WhoAmW 93*
Schlesinger, Benjamin 1928- *WhoWrEP 92*
Schlesinger, David Harvey 1939- *WhoAm 92, WhoE 93*
Schlesinger, Edward Bruce 1913- *WhoAm 92*
Schlesinger, Helmut 1924- *WhoWor 93*
Schlesinger, Jacques Louis 1942- *WhoWor 93*
Schlesinger, James G. 1943- *St&PR 93*
Schlesinger, James R. 1929- *ColdWar 1 [port]*
Schlesinger, James Rodney 1929- *WhoAm 92, WhoWor 93*
Schlesinger, Jeffrey Lance *Law&B 92*
Schlesinger, John 1926- *BioIn 17, MiSFD 9*
Schlesinger, John Richard 1926- *WhoAm 92, WhoWor 93*
Schlesinger, Joseph Abraham 1922- *WhoAm 92*
Schlesinger, Kathleen 1862-1953 *Baker 92*
Schlesinger, Lee 1926- *St&PR 93*
Schlesinger, Maurice *BioIn 17*
Schlesinger, Maurice Adolphe 1797-1871 *Baker 92*
Schlesinger, Otto J. 1924- *St&PR 93*
Schlesinger, Otto J., III 1949- *St&PR 93*
Schlesinger, Patrick Jerome *Law&B 92*
Schlesinger, Philip Ronald *WhoScE 91-1*
Schlesinger, Robert Walter 1913- *WhoAm 92*
Schlesinger, Rudolf Berthold 1909- *WhoAm 92, WhoWor 93*
Schlesinger, Sanford Joel 1943- *WhoE 93, WhoWor 93*
Schlesinger, Sebastian Benson 1837-1917 *Baker 92*
Schlesinger, Stephen Lyons 1940- *WhoAm 92*
Schlesinger, Steven Roger 1944- *WhoAm 92*
Schlesinger, Victor H. 1925- *St&PR 93*
Schlesinger, Zigmund d1928 *BioIn 17*
Schless, Guy Lacy 1929- *WhoWor 93*
Schless, James Murray 1918- *WhoSSW 93, WhoWor 93*
Schless, Phyllis Ross *WhoAm 92*
Schlessel, Walter *St&PR 93*
Schlesser, E. *WhoScE 91-3*
Schlesser, Jean-Marc Robert 1962- *WhoWor 93*
Schlessinger, Bernard S. 1930- *WhoAm 92, WhoSSW 93*
Schlessinger, Joseph *WhoE 93*
Schlessinger, June Hirsch 1933- *WhoSSW 93*
Schletterer, Hans Michel 1824-1893 *Baker 92*
Schleunes, Brenda Pursel 1939- *WhoSSW 93*
Schleusener, Horst P.R. 1933- *WhoScE 91-3*
Schleusener, Richard August 1926- *WhoAm 92*
Schley, Charles C. 1923- *St&PR 93*
Schley, Christian *Law&B 92*
Schley, James Powrie 1956- *WhoWrEP 92*
Schley, Michael D. 1955- *St&PR 93*
Schley, Michael Dodson 1955- *WhoAm 92*
Schley, Reeve, III 1936- *WhoAm 92*
Schley, Winfield Scott 1839-1909 *HarEnMi*
Schleyer, Paul von Rague 1930- *WhoAm 92, WhoScE 91-3, WhoWor 93*
Schlich, Roland 1932- *WhoScE 91-2*
Schlicht, Ekkehart Johannes 1945- *WhoWor 93*
Schlichting, Diane Marie 1946- *WhoAmW 93*
Schlick, Arnolt c. 1460-1521 *Baker 92*
Schlickau, George Hans 1922- *WhoAm 92*
Schlicting, Julia A. *Law&B 92*
Schlieffen, Alfred von 1833-1913 *HarEnMi*
Schliemann, Analucia Dias 1943- *WhoWor 93*
Schliemann, Heinrich 1822-1890 *BioIn 17*
Schliemann, Peter C. 1945- *St&PR 93*
Schlier, Christoph G. 1930- *WhoScE 91-3*
Schlierf, Gregory Norbert 1964- *WhoE 93*
Schlimbach, William *Law&B 92*
Schlimme, E. *WhoScE 91-3*
Schlindwein, James A. 1929- *WhoAm 92*
Schlingensiepen, Georg Hermann 1928- *WhoWor 93*
Schlinger, Robin E. *Law&B 92*
Schlinger, Warren Gleason 1923- *WhoAm 92*
Schlipf, Frank Joseph 1938- *St&PR 93*
Schlipf, Frederick A. 1941- *WhoWrEP 92*
Schlipkoter, Hans-Werner 1924- *WhoScE 91-3*
Schlissel, Joanne 1953- *St&PR 93*
Schlissel, Theodore 1940- *St&PR 93*
Schlitt, Jacob 1927- *WhoE 93*
Schlitt, Klaus 1938- *WhoWor 93*
Schlitt, Ludwig 1939- *WhoWor 93*
Schlittler-Silva, Gilberto Bueno 1934- *WhoUN 92*
Schlitzkus, Jolly Maddox 1940- *WhoSSW 93*
Schlobin, Roger C. 1944- *ScF&FL 92*
Schlobohm, Raymond William 1943- *WhoE 93*
Schloegel, George Anthony 1940- *St&PR 93, WhoAm 92*
Schloemann, Ernst Fritz 1926- *WhoAm 92, WhoWor 93*
Schloemer, Kristin S. *Law&B 92*
Schloemer, Paul George 1928- *St&PR 93, WhoAm 92*
Schloendorff, Georg H.G. 1931- *WhoScE 91-3*
Schloerb, Paul Richard 1919- *WhoAm 92*
Schloeter-Paredes, Maryluz 1932- *WhoUN 92*
Schloezer, Boris de 1881-1969 *Baker 92*
Schlogel, Xavier 1854-1889 *Baker 92*
Schlogl, Friedrich Christian Otto 1917- *WhoScE 91-3*
Schlogl, Karl 1924- *WhoScE 91-4*
Schlomann, James Martin 1949- *St&PR 93*
Schlondorff, Volker 1939- *MiSFD 9, WhoWor 93*
Schloop, Clinton P. 1942- *St&PR 93*
Schloot, Werner 1937- *WhoScE 91-3*
Schlorff, Donald Joseph 1955- *St&PR 93*
Schlosberg, Hilton H. *St&PR 93*
Schlose, William Timothy 1948- *WhoEmL 93*
Schloss, B. Stephen 1954- *St&PR 93*
Schloss, Bruce M. *Law&B 92*
Schloss, Carolyn Dina 1963- *WhoAmW 93*
Schloss, Eugene M., Jr. *Law&B 92*
Schloss, Eugene M., Jr. 1932- *St&PR 93*
Schloss, Fredlyn D. 1936- *St&PR 93*
Schloss, Henry *St&PR 93*
Schloss, Howard Michael 1952- *St&PR 93*
Schloss, Jo Ann Bock 1932- *WhoAmW 93, WhoWor 93*

Schloss, Lawrence Michael Van Daelen 1954- *WhoAm 92*
Schloss, Martin E. *Law&B 92*
Schloss, Max 1933- *St&PR 93*
Schloss, Milton Joseph 1913- *WhoAm 92*
Schloss, Myron A. 1948- *St&PR 93*
Schloss, Samuel Leopold 1926- *St&PR 93*
Schloss, Samuel Leopold, Jr. 1926- *WhoAm 92*
Schloss, Walter Amson 1914- *WhoE 93*
Schlossberg, Jerry d1991 *BioIn 17*
Schlossberg, Julian *MiSFD 9*
Schlossberg, Mark A. *Law&B 92*
Schlossberg, Nancy Kamin 1929- *WhoAmW 93*
Schlossberg, Stephen I. 1921- *WhoAm 92*
Schlosser, (Karl Wilhelm) Adolf 1830-1913 *Baker 92*
Schlosser, Anne Griffin 1939- *WhoAmW 93*
Schlosser, Debra Jean 1954- *WhoAmW 93*
Schlosser, Francois M. 1938- *WhoScE 91-2*
Schlosser, Frank Roger 1941- *St&PR 93*
Schlosser, Franklin Roger 1941- *WhoAm 92*
Schlosser, Herbert S. 1926- *WhoAm 92*
Schlosser, John A. *Law&B 92*
Schlosser, Leonard B. 1925-1991 *BioIn 17*
Schlosser, Louis 1800-1886 *Baker 92*
Schlosser, Max 1835-1916 *Baker 92*
Schlosser, Max Karl 1835-1916 *OxDcOp*
Schlosser, Peter 1955- *WhoE 93*
Schlosser, Scott *St&PR 93*
SchlOsser, Willem Martin Jozef 1927- *WhoWor 93*
Schlossmacher, Norbert 1956- *WhoWor 93*
Schlossman, Beryl Fern *WhoSSW 93*
Schlossman, David Yale 1960- *St&PR 93*
Schlossman, John Isaac 1931- *WhoAm 92*
Schlossman, Mark 1958- *St&PR 93*
Schlossman, Stuart Franklin 1935- *WhoAm 92, WhoE 93*
Schlossstein, Steven *BioIn 17*
Schlossstein, Steven 1941- *WhoAm 92*
Schlote, Karl-Heinz 1949- *WhoWor 93*
Schlotfeldt, Rozella May 1914- *WhoAm 92, WhoAmW 93*
Schloth, Edward C. 1929- *St&PR 93*
Schlotman, Edward A. *Law&B 92*
Schlott, Richard J. *Law&B 92*
Schlott, Richard William, III 1939- *WhoE 93*
Schlotter, Rene de Leon *DcCPCAm*
Schlotterback, David Lee 1932- *St&PR 93*
Schlotterbeck, Walter Albert 1926- *WhoAm 92*
Schlotthauer, Julius P. 1937- *WhoWor 93*
Schlottmann, Louis 1826-1905 *Baker 92*
Schlotz, Randy Craig 1947- *WhoSSW 93*
Schlough, Paul W. 1937- *St&PR 93*
Schlozman, Kay Lehman 1946- *WhoAmW 93*
Schlueter, David Arnold 1946- *WhoAm 92, WhoEmL 93*
Schlueter, John J. 1939- *St&PR 93*
Schlueter, John William 1943- *WhoE 93*
Schlueter, June Mayer 1942- *WhoE 93*
Schlueter, Linda Lee 1947- *WhoAm 92, WhoAmW 93, WhoEmL 93, WhoSSW 93, WhoWor 93*
Schlueter, Paul 1933- *ScF&FL 92, WhoE 93*
Schlumberger, Jean *BioIn 17*
Schlumberger, Robert Ernest 1951- *WhoSSW 93*
Schlundt, Donald 1933-1985 *BiDAMSp 1989*
Schlunk, Jurgen Eckart 1944- *WhoSSW 93*
Schlusnus, Heinrich 1888-1952 *Baker 92, IntDcOp, OxDcOp*
Schlussel, Joseph Lazar 1935- *WhoE 93*
Schlussel, Murray *Law&B 92*
Schlussel, Neil 1945- *WhoSSW 93*
Schluter, Arnulf *WhoScE 91-3*
Schluter, Gerald Emil 1942- *WhoE 93*
Schluter, H.B.K. 1922- *WhoScE 91-3*
Schluter, Kathleen Hyland *Law&B 92*
Schluter, Klaus 1943- *WhoScE 91-3*
Schluter, Peter Mueller 1933- *St&PR 93, WhoAm 92, WhoE 93*
Schluter, Poul Holmskov 1929- *WhoWor 93*
Schlyer, Lyle J. *Law&B 92*
Schmadeka, Delores 1933- *WhoWrEP 92*
Schmader, Michael T. 1948- *St&PR 93*
Schmahl, Dietrich *WhoScE 91-3*
Schmalbeck, Richard Louis 1947- *WhoAm 92*
Schmalbruch, T. Dankward 1932- *St&PR 93*
Schmalenberger, Jerry Lew 1934- *WhoAm 92*
Schmalensee, Diane H. 1946- *St&PR 93*
Schmalensee, Richard Lee 1944- *WhoAm 92*
Schmall, Arthur J. 1927- *St&PR 93*
Schmalreck, Arno Ferdinand 1945- *WhoWor 93*
Schmalscheidt, Walter 1931- *WhoScE 91-3*
Schmalstieg, William Riegel 1929- *WhoAm 92, WhoWor 93*
Schmaltz, Kathleen Mary 1958- *WhoAmW 93*
Schmaltz, Lawrence Gerard 1957- *WhoSSW 93*
Schmaltz, Richard R. 1940- *St&PR 93*
Schmaltz, Richard Robert 1940- *WhoE 93*
Schmalz, Alfred Chandler 1924- *WhoSSW 93*
Schmalz, Carl Nelson, Jr. 1926- *WhoAm 92*
Schmalz, Hans-Gunther 1957- *WhoWor 93*
Schmalz, Randall John 1952- *WhoEmL 93*
Schmalz, Richard Lee *Law&B 92*
Schmalz, Robert Fowler 1929- *WhoE 93*
Schmalz, Robert L. 1940- *St&PR 93*
Schmalz, Roman 1927- *St&PR 93*
Schmalz, William A. 1921- *St&PR 93*
Schmalzer, Victor David 1941- *WhoAm 92*
Schmalzried, Hermann 1932- *WhoScE 91-3*
Schmalzried, Marvin E. 1924- *St&PR 93*
Schmalzried, Marvin Eugene 1924- *WhoAm 92*
Schmalzriedt, Gary 1946- *WhoIns 93*
Schmandke, Horst 1935- *WhoScE 91-3*
Schmandt, Jurgen 1929- *WhoSSW 93*
Schmandt-Besserat, Denise 1933- *WhoAm 92*
Schmank, James R. 1953- *St&PR 93*
Schmaus, Siegfried H. A. 1915- *WhoE 93, WhoWor 93*
Schmautz, Harald 1953- *WhoWor 93*
Schmechel, Warren P. 1927- *WhoAm 92*
Schmechel, Warren Paul 1927- *St&PR 93*
Schmedes, Erik 1866-1931 *OxDcOp*
Schmedes, Erik 1868-1931 *Baker 92*
Schmee, Josef 1945- *WhoE 93*
Schmeer, Arline Catherine 1929- *WhoAmW 93*
Schmehl, Kenneth Gordan 1942- *St&PR 93*
Schmeidler, Felix 1920- *WhoWor 93*
Schmeidler, Gertrude Raffel 1912- *WhoAmW 93, WhoE 93*
Schmeidler, Neal Francis 1948- *WhoSSW 93*
Schmeiser, Stephen George 1943- *WhoSSW 93*
Schmeisser, Jorg 1942- *WhoWor 93*
Schmeisser, Peter C. d1992 *NewYTBS 92*
Schmekel, Johannes S.A. 1935- *WhoScE 91-4*
Schmelder, William James, Jr. 1958- *St&PR 93*
Schmeling, Gareth 1940- *WhoAm 92*
Schmelkin, Benjamin 1910- *WhoWor 93*
Schmelovsky, Karl-Heinz 1930- *WhoScE 91-3*
Schmeltz, Edward James 1949- *WhoE 93*
Schmeltzer, David 1930- *WhoAm 92*
Schmeltzer, Edward 1923- *WhoAm 92*
Schmeltzle, Dale R. 1954- *St&PR 93*
Schmelz, Brenda Lea 1958- *WhoAmW 93*
Schmelz, Julius Wirth 1931- *St&PR 93*
Schmelzer, Andreas Anton 1653?-1701 *See* Schmelzer, Johann Heinrich c. 1621-1680 *Baker 92*
Schmelzer, Francine *St&PR 93*
Schmelzer, Georg Joseph 1655-c. 1700 *See* Schmelzer, Johann Heinrich c. 1621-1680 *Baker 92*
Schmelzer, Henry Louis Phillip 1943- *St&PR 93, WhoAm 92*
Schmelzer, Johann Heinrich c. 1621-1680 *Baker 92*
Schmelzer, Joseph John, III 1946- *St&PR 93*
Schmelzer, Peter Clemens 1672?-1746 *See* Schmelzer, Johann Heinrich c. 1621-1680 *Baker 92*
Schmelzl, Wolfgang c. 1500-c. 1561 *Baker 92*
Schmelzle, Christian George 1944- *St&PR 93*
Schmemann, Serge 1945- *ConAu 136, WhoAm 92, WhoWor 93*
Schmergel, Gabriel 1940- *St&PR 93, WhoAm 92*
Schmerler, Barbara Ann 1957- *WhoAmW 93*
Schmerling, Erwin Robert 1929- *WhoAm 92, WhoE 93*
Schmerling, Philippe-Charles 1791-1836 *IntDcAn*
Schmerr, Mary Jo 1945- *WhoAmW 93*
Schmertmann, John Henry 1928- *WhoAm 92, WhoSSW 93*
Schmertz, Eric Joseph 1925- *WhoAm 92, WhoWor 93*
Schmertz, Herbert 1930- *WhoAm 92*
Schmertz, Ida F. S. *WhoAm 92*
Schmertz, Mildred F. *BioIn 17*
Schmertz, Mildred Floyd 1925- *WhoAm 92*
Schmets, Jean Francois 1940- *WhoWor 93*
Schmetterer, Robert Allen 1943- *WhoAm 92*
Schmetzer, Alan David 1946- *WhoEmL 93*
Schmeyer, Jon Eric 1955- *WhoE 93*
Schmick, Dennis Wayne 1946- *WhoSSW 93*
Schmick, Marianne 1955- *WhoAmW 93*
Schmid, Albert 1929- *WhoScE 91-3*
Schmid, Andrew Michael, Jr. 1957- *WhoE 93*
Schmid, Anton 1787-1857 *Baker 92*
Schmid, Calvin Eric 1950- *WhoE 93*
Schmid, Christoph 1937- *WhoWor 93*
Schmid, Christoph H. 1937- *WhoScE 91-4*
Schmid, Erich 1907- *Baker 92*
Schmid, Ernst Fritz 1904-1960 *Baker 92*
Schmid, Frank Richard 1924- *WhoAm 92*
Schmid, Frederic Werner 1948- *WhoWor 93*
Schmid, H. Dankward 1937- *WhoScE 91-3*
Schmid, Hans Dieter 1939- *WhoWor 93*
Schmid, Hans Fred 1933- *St&PR 93*
Schmid, Hans Heinrich 1937- *WhoScE 91-4, WhoWor 93*
Schmid, Heinrich Kaspar 1874-1953 *Baker 92*
Schmid, Herbert Karl Jakob 1927- *WhoWor 93*
Schmid, Ingobert Christian 1936- *WhoScE 91-3*
Schmid, Jack T. *Law&B 92*
Schmid, James Addison 1945- *WhoE 93*
Schmid, John L. *Law&B 92*
Schmid, Juergen 1944- *WhoScE 91-3*
Schmid, Nancy 1942- *St&PR 93*
Schmid, Patricia E. *Law&B 92*
Schmid, Paul A. 1912- *St&PR 93*
Schmid, Paul Albert, III 1943- *St&PR 93*
Schmid, Richard Jay 1929- *St&PR 93, WhoIns 93*
Schmid, Roberto 1938- *WhoScE 91-3*
Schmid, Rolf D. 1942- *WhoScE 91-3*
Schmid, Roman G. 1928- *St&PR 93, WhoIns 93*
Schmid, Ron Jay 1945- *St&PR 93*
Schmid, Rudi 1922- *WhoAm 92, WhoWor 93*
Schmid, Susan *Law&B 92*
Schmid, Uwe 1963- *WhoWor 93*
Schmid, Wilfried 1943- *WhoAm 92, WhoE 93*
Schmidbaur, Hubert 1934- *WhoScE 91-3*
Schmidek, Henry Hans-Heinz 1937- *WhoAm 92*
Schmid-Frazee, Carol A. *Law&B 92*
Schmid-Haas, Paul 1930- *WhoScE 91-4*
Schmidhauser, John Richard 1922- *WhoAm 92*
Schmidhauser, Paul *Law&B 92*
Schmidhuber de la Mora, Guillermo 1943- *DcMexL*
Schmidinger, Kim *BioIn 17*
Schmidinger, Krista *BioIn 17*
Schmidl, Antonio 1814-1880 *See* Schmidl, Carlo 1859-1943 *Baker 92*
Schmidl, Carlo 1859-1943 *Baker 92*
Schmidley, Eugenia M. *Law&B 92*
Schmidlin, Fred William 1925- *WhoE 93*
Schmidmaier, Dieter 1938- *WhoWor 93*
Schmidpeter, Alfred 1929- *WhoScE 91-3*
Schmid-Schonbein, Holger 1937- *WhoScE 91-3*
Schmidt, Adolph William 1904- *WhoAm 92*
Schmidt, Ahlert 1940- *WhoScE 91-3*
Schmidt, Albert Daniel 1925- *St&PR 93, WhoAm 92*
Schmidt, Albert Julius 1937- *WhoSSW 93*
Schmidt, Alexander Mackay 1930-1991 *BioIn 17*
Schmidt, Alfred 1928- *WhoScE 91-4, WhoWor 93*
Schmidt, Alfred Otto 1906- *WhoE 93*
Schmidt, Annerose 1936- *Baker 92*
Schmidt, Annie M.G. 1911- *BioIn 17*
Schmidt, Arno 1914-1979 *ScF&FL 92*
Schmidt, Arnold Johann 1938- *WhoWor 93*
Schmidt, Arthur Louis 1927- *WhoSSW 93*
Schmidt, Arthur P(aul) 1846-1921 *Baker 92*
Schmidt, Baldwin Stephen 1942- *St&PR 93*
Schmidt, Barbara Maria 1962- *WhoWor 93*
Schmidt, Benno C. *BioIn 17, St&PR 93*
Schmidt, Benno Charles 1913- *St&PR 93, WhoAm 92*
Schmidt, Benno Charles, Jr. 1942- *WhoAm 92, WhoWor 93*
Schmidt, Berlie Louis 1932- *WhoAm 92*
Schmidt, Bernhard 1928- *WhoScE 91-3*
Schmidt, Bianca Rosemarie 1964- *WhoAmW 93*
Schmidt, C. L. Mike 1940- *WhoSSW 93*
Schmidt, C. Oscar, Jr. *St&PR 93*
Schmidt, Carl Walter 1925- *WhoIns 93*
Schmidt, Carlos E. 1913- *St&PR 93*
Schmidt, Carolyn Marie 1948- *WhoE 93*
Schmidt, Cecilia Johanna 1932- *WhoUN 92*
Schmidt, Charles 1939- *WhoE 93*
Schmidt, Charles Edwin 1943- *WhoSSW 93*
Schmidt, Charles Lloyd 1944- *WhoSSW 93*
Schmidt, Charles Lynn 1936- *St&PR 93*
Schmidt, Charles Wilson 1928- *WhoAm 92*
Schmidt, Chauncey E. 1931- *St&PR 93*
Schmidt, Chauncey Everett 1931- *WhoAm 92*
Schmidt, Chuck 1947- *WhoAm 92*
Schmidt, Claude Henri 1924- *WhoAm 92*
Schmidt, Claudene Louise Philley 1946- *WhoSSW 93*
Schmidt, Cyril James 1939- *WhoAm 92*
Schmidt, Dan *ScF&FL 92*
Schmidt, Dana Murray *Law&B 92*
Schmidt, Daniel Edward, IV 1946- *WhoIns 93*
Schmidt, David G. 1939- *St&PR 93*
Schmidt, David Robert 1954- *St&PR 93*
Schmidt, Deborah Thyng 1955- *WhoE 93*
Schmidt, Debra Jean *WhoAmW 93*
Schmidt, Dennis *ScF&FL 92*
Schmidt, Diana V. *Law&B 92*
Schmidt, Diane 1953- *SmATA 70 [port]*
Schmidt, Diane Joy 1953- *WhoWrEP 92*
Schmidt, Dieter Willy 1931- *WhoWor 93*
Schmidt, Donald L. 1945- *St&PR 93*
Schmidt, Dorothy Sherman 1931- *WhoSSW 93*
Schmidt, E. Richard 1939- *St&PR 93*
Schmidt, Edward Conrad 1932- *St&PR 93*
Schmidt, Edward Craig 1947- *WhoEmL 93*
Schmidt, Edward Frank 1941- *St&PR 93*
Schmidt, Ellen *AmWomPl*
Schmidt, Ferenc Joseph 1921- *St&PR 93*
Schmidt, Franklin W. 1914- *St&PR 93*
Schmidt, Franz 1874-1939 *Baker 92, IntDcOp*
Schmidt, Fred 1915-1991 *BioIn 17*
Schmidt, Fred 1922- *WhoAm 92*
Schmidt, Frederick Eberhard 1940- *WhoE 93*
Schmidt, Gary P. *Law&B 92*
Schmidt, George 1926- *WhoAm 92*
Schmidt, Gerald D. 1934-1990 *BioIn 17*
Schmidt, Gladys *AmWomPl*
Schmidt, Glenda Bottoms 1949- *WhoAmW 93*
Schmidt, Glenn W. 1943- *St&PR 93*
Schmidt, Gregory Martin 1952- *WhoSSW 93*
Schmidt, Gunther Wolfgang 1939- *WhoWor 93*
Schmidt, Gustav 1816-1882 *Baker 92*
Schmidt, Hans E. *WhoScE 91-3*
Schmidt, Hans Ludwig 1926- *WhoScE 91-3*
Schmidt, Harold Eugene 1925- *WhoAm 92*
Schmidt, Harvey E. 1942- *St&PR 93*
Schmidt, Harvey Martin 1925- *WhoWor 93*
Schmidt, Helmut 1918- *ColdWar 1 [port], DcTwHis*
Schmidt, Henry J. 1943-1990 *BioIn 17*
Schmidt, Herman J. 1917- *St&PR 93, WhoAm 92*
Schmidt, Hermann Ulrich 1926- *WhoScE 91-3*
Schmidt, Hugo 1929- *WhoAm 92*
Schmidt, Ingo Lothar Ottokar 1932- *WhoWor 93*
Schmidt, Jakob Edward 1906- *WhoAm 92, WhoWor 93*
Schmidt, James A. 1950- *WhoSSW 93*
Schmidt, James Craig 1927- *WhoAm 92*
Schmidt, James Richard 1933- *St&PR 93*
Schmidt, Jean Marie 1938- *WhoAmW 93*
Schmidt, Jerome C. 1949- *St&PR 93*
Schmidt, Jerome W. 1951- *St&PR 93*
Schmidt, Joanne Harper 1938- *WhoSSW 93*
Schmidt, Joe 1932- *BioIn 17*
Schmidt, Johann Christoph 1664-1728 *Baker 92*
Schmidt, Johann Philipp Samuel 1779-1853 *Baker 92*
Schmidt, John C. *WhoAm 92*
Schmidt, John Edward 1946- *WhoAm 92*
Schmidt, John Henry fl. 18th cent.- *Baker 92*
Schmidt, John J. 1928- *St&PR 93*
Schmidt, John Joseph 1946- *WhoSSW 93*
Schmidt, John K. 1959- *St&PR 93*
Schmidt, John Nicholas 1947- *St&PR 93*

Schmidt, John Richard 1929- WhoAm 92
Schmidt, John T. Law&B 92
Schmidt, John Wesley 1917- WhoAm 92
Schmidt, Josef Johannes 1931- WhoScE 91-4, WhoUN 92
Schmidt, Joseph 1904-1942 Baker 92
Schmidt, Julie Beth 1959- WhoAmW 93
Schmidt, Julius 1923- WhoAm 92
Schmidt, K.-H. WhoScE 91-3
Schmidt, Karen Anne 1945- WhoAmW 93
Schmidt, Karl J. 1953- St&PR 93
Schmidt, Katherine E. Law&B 92
Schmidt, Klaus WhoScE 91-1
Schmidt, Klaus D. 1951- WhoWor 93
Schmidt, Klaus Dieter 1930- WhoAm 92
Schmidt, Klaus Franz 1928- WhoAm 92
Schmidt, Klaus L. 1936- WhoScE 91-3
Schmidt, L. Lee, Jr. 1937- WhoAm 92
Schmidt, Lail William, Jr. 1936- WhoWor 93
Schmidt, Laverne Frederick 1940- St&PR 93
Schmidt, Lothar R. 1936- WhoScE 91-3
Schmidt, Maarten 1929- WhoAm 92
Schmidt, Mark Alan 1948- WhoSSW 93
Schmidt, Martha Marie 1912- WhoAmW 93
Schmidt, Max 1874-1950 IntDcAn
Schmidt, Max 1925- WhoScE 91-3
Schmidt, Michael Jack 1949- WhoAm 92
Schmidt, Mike 1949- BioIn 17
Schmidt, Nancy Charlene Linder 1940- WhoAmW 93
Schmidt, Nancy J. 1936- WhoAm 92
Schmidt, Nancy Jean 1958- WhoAmW 93
Schmidt, Nelson Edward Law&B 92
Schmidt, Olaf 1943- WhoScE 91-3
Schmidt, Ole 1928- Baker 92
Schmidt, Paul G. 1944- St&PR 93
Schmidt, Paul Joseph 1925- WhoWor 93
Schmidt, Pavel 1933- WhoScE 91-3
Schmidt, Peter 1927- WhoAm 92
Schmidt, Peter Gustav 1921- St&PR 93, WhoAm 92
Schmidt, Peter R. WhoScE 91-3
Schmidt, Peter R. 1934- St&PR 93
Schmidt, Pieter H. 1926- WhoScE 91-3
Schmidt, Ralph S. 1947- WhoUN 92
Schmidt, Raymond A. Law&B 92
Schmidt, Raymond Paul 1937- WhoE 93
Schmidt, Richard David Law&B 92
Schmidt, Richard E. 1932- St&PR 93
Schmidt, Richard Edward 1932- WhoAm 92
Schmidt, Richard Marten, Jr. 1924- WhoAm 92
Schmidt, Richard R. 1935- WhoScE 91-3
Schmidt, Robert 1927- WhoAm 92, WhoWor 93
Schmidt, Robert Charles, Jr. 1942- WhoAm 92
Schmidt, Robert F. 1932- WhoScE 91-3
Schmidt, Robert Franz 1932- WhoScE 91-3, WhoWor 93
Schmidt, Robert Milton 1944- WhoAm 92
Schmidt, Robert W. 1916- St&PR 93
Schmidt, Russel Alan, II 1953- WhoEmL 93, WhoWor 93
Schmidt, Ruth Ann 1930- WhoAm 92, WhoAmW 93
Schmidt, Ruth Anna Marie 1916- WhoAmW 93
Schmidt, Sandra Jean 1955- WhoE 93
Schmidt, Sherri Ann 1960- WhoAmW 93
Schmidt, Shiela B. Law&B 92
Schmidt, Stanley 1944- ScF&FL 92
Schmidt, Stanley Albert 1944- WhoAm 92
Schmidt, Stefan 1950- WhoWor 93
Schmidt, Stephen C. 1945- WhoAm 92
Schmidt, Stephen Christopher 1920- WhoAm 92, WhoWor 93
Schmidt, Stephen Wilfred 1944- St&PR 93
Schmidt, Susan Mary WhoSSW 93
Schmidt, Terry Lane 1943- WhoAm 92
Schmidt, Thomas Carson 1930- WhoAm 92
Schmidt, Thomas Frank 1944- WhoWor 93
Schmidt, Thomas J., Jr. Law&B 92
Schmidt, Tom V. 1939- WhoWrEP 92
Schmidt, Trudeliese 1943- Baker 92
Schmidt, Ulrich Stephan 1968- WhoAm 92
Schmidt, V. WhoScE 91-3
Schmidt, Veronica Jean 1961- WhoAmW 93
Schmidt, Violet Danielson 1920- St&PR 93
Schmidt, Walter J. 1923- WhoWor 93
Schmidt, Werner 1929- WhoScE 91-3
Schmidt, Werner A. 1925- WhoE 93
Schmidt, Werner Rolf 1941- WhoWor 93
Schmidt, Wilhelm 1868-1954 IntDcAn
Schmidt, William 1926- Baker 92
Schmidt, William C. 1938- WhoAm 92
Schmidt, William Fredric 1928- St&PR 93
Schmidt, William James 1932- WhoE 93
Schmidt, William Joseph 1946- WhoWor 93
Schmidt, Winsor Chase, Jr. 1949- WhoSSW 93
Schmidt, Wolfgang BioIn 17
Schmidt, Wulf BioIn 17
Schmidt-Bleek, Karlheinz Friedrich 1932- WhoScE 91-4
Schmidtbonn, Wilhelm August 1876-1952 DcLB 118 [port]
Schmidt-Clausen, Hans Joachim 1935- WhoScE 91-3
Schmidt-Effing, Reinhard 1943- WhoScE 91-3
Schmidt-Falkenberg, Heinz 1926- WhoScE 91-3
Schmidtgall, William Harold 1946- St&PR 93
Schmidt-Gorg, Joseph 1897-1981 Baker 92
Schmidt-Isserstedt, Hans 1900-1973 Baker 92, OxDcOp
Schmidt-Kaler, Theodor 1930- WhoScE 91-3
Schmidtke, Hans-Herbert 1929- WhoScE 91-3, WhoWor 93
Schmidtke, Richard Allen 1925- WhoSSW 93
Schmidtlein, Frank Allen 1932- WhoE 93
Schmidtlein, Mary Virginia Law&B 92
Schmidt-Lorenz, Wilhelm 1922- WhoScE 91-4
Schmidtmann, Lucie Ann 1963- WhoAmW 93, WhoE 93, WhoEmL 93, WhoWor 93
Schmidt-Nielsen, Astrid 1941- WhoAmW 93
Schmidt-Nielsen, Bodil Mimi 1918- WhoAm 92
Schmidt-Nielsen, Knut 1915- WhoAm 92, WhoSSW 93
Schmidt-Rohr, Ulrich 1926- WhoScE 91-3
Schmidt-Rottluff, Karl 1884-1976 BioIn 17
Schmiechen, Michael 1932- WhoScE 91-3
Schmiedeker, Ronald Edward 1946- WhoE 93
Schmieder, Carl 1938- WhoWor 93
Schmieder, Frank J. 1941- St&PR 93
Schmieder, Frank Joseph 1941- WhoAm 92
Schmieder, Luke R. 1943- St&PR 93
Schmieder, Valerie Mary 1953- WhoAmW 93
Schmieder, Wolfgang 1901-1990 Baker 92
Schmiedeskamp, Kathy D. 1958- St&PR 93
Schmiedt, Donald Allen 1945- St&PR 93
Schmiege, Robert 1941- St&PR 93, WhoAm 92
Schmiegelow, Christian 1950- WhoWor 93
Schmieler, Claire R. 1942- WhoAmW 93
Schmilovici, Ina WhoAmW 93
Schmincke, Donald Randolph, Jr. 1956- WhoE 93
Schmincke, Hans-Ulrich 1937- WhoScE 91-3
Schmink, Marianne Camp 1949- WhoSSW 93
Schmit, Herman H. 1939- WhoIns 93
Schmit, Lucien Andre, Jr. 1928- WhoAm 92
Schmit, Patricia Brady ConAu 136
Schmit, Thomas S. 1943- St&PR 93
Schmits, Sharon 1940- St&PR 93
Schmitt, Alfred A. 1938- WhoScE 91-3
Schmitt, Alfred Martin 1936- WhoScE 91-3
Schmitt, Aloys 1788-1866 Baker 92
Schmitt, Bernard W. WhoAm 92, WhoSSW 93
Schmitt, Betty J. 1936- WhoWrEP 92
Schmitt, Camille 1908-1976 Baker 92
Schmitt, Carl 1888-1985 BioIn 17
Schmitt, Carol Sue 1960- WhoAmW 93
Schmitt, Cynthia Lynn 1956- WhoSSW 93
Schmitt, Eric J. 1950- St&PR 93
Schmitt, Florent 1870-1958 Baker 92
Schmitt, Francis Otto 1903- BioIn 17, WhoAm 92
Schmitt, Frederick Adrian 1953- WhoSSW 93, WhoWor 93
Schmitt, Gary D. 1957- St&PR 93
Schmitt, Georg Aloys 1827-1902 Baker 92
Schmitt, George BioIn 17
Schmitt, George Frederick 1943- WhoWor 93
Schmitt, George Frederick, Jr. 1939- WhoAm 92
Schmitt, George Herbert 1939- WhoAm 92
Schmitt, George Joseph 1928- WhoAm 92
Schmitt, Guenther 1928- WhoScE 91-3
Schmitt, Hans 1835-1907 Baker 92
Schmitt, Hans Jurgen 1930- WhoScE 91-3
Schmitt, Harrison Hagan 1935- WhoAm 92
Schmitt, Heinz-Josef 1954- WhoWor 93
Schmitt, Henri-Lucien WhoScE 91-2
Schmitt, Jacob 1803-1853 Baker 92
Schmitt, Jeffrey L. St&PR 93
Schmitt, John Edward 1938- St&PR 93, WhoAm 92
Schmitt, John R. 1958- St&PR 93
Schmitt, Judy Piper 1954- WhoAmW 93
Schmitt, Karl Michael 1922- WhoAm 92
Schmitt, Lee 1933- St&PR 93
Schmitt, Louis Charles 1946- St&PR 93
Schmitt, Madeline Hubbard 1943- WhoAmW 93
Schmitt, Margaret Schomburg 1927- WhoAmW 93
Schmitt, Mark F. 1923- WhoAm 92
Schmitt, Nicholas L. Law&B 92
Schmitt, Raymond J. 1934- St&PR 93
Schmitt, Raymond M. 1942- St&PR 93
Schmitt, Richard George 1948- WhoEmL 93
Schmitt, Robert Lee 1948- WhoE 93
Schmitt, Roland W. BioIn 17
Schmitt, Roland Walter 1923- St&PR 93, WhoAm 92, WhoE 93, WhoWor 93
Schmitt, Rudiger W. 1936- WhoScE 91-3
Schmitt, Ruediger 1939- WhoWor 93
Schmitt, Sara Green 1962- WhoE 93
Schmitt, Stephen Richard 1948- WhoEmL 93
Schmitt, Timothy J. Law&B 92
Schmitt, William Howard 1936- St&PR 93, WhoAm 92
Schmitt, William Robert 1948- St&PR 93
Schmitt, Wolfgang R. 1944- St&PR 93
Schmitt, Wolfgang Rudolph 1944- WhoAm 92
Schmitter, Charles Harry 1928- WhoAm 92
Schmitter, Elizabeth 1884-1980 BioIn 17
Schmitter, Henrietta Beatrice 1887-1973 BioIn 17
Schmitt-Walter, Karl 1900-1985 Baker 92
Schmitz, Arno L. 1927- WhoScE 91-3
Schmitz, (Franz) Arnold 1893-1980 Baker 92
Schmitz, Birger 1955- WhoWor 93
Schmitz, Charles Edison 1919- WhoWor 93
Schmitz, Dennis 1937- WhoWrEP 92
Schmitz, Dennis Mathew 1937- WhoAm 92
Schmitz, Dolores Jean 1931- WhoAmW 93
Schmitz, Don William Law&B 92
Schmitz, Edward Henry 1929- St&PR 93
Schmitz, Elie Robert 1889-1949 Baker 92
Schmitz, Elio BioIn 17
Schmitz, Ernst 1928- WhoScE 91-3
Schmitz, Ettore 1861-1928 BioIn 17
Schmitz, Eugen 1882-1959 Baker 92
Schmitz, Gunter 1956- WhoScE 91-3
Schmitz, Guy 1942- WhoScE 91-2
Schmitz, Heinz 1951- WhoWor 93
Schmitz, Homer H. BioIn 17
Schmitz, James H. 1911- BioIn 17
Schmitz, James H. 1911-1981 ScF&FL 92
Schmitz, Jochen 1943- St&PR 93
Schmitz, John Albert 1940- WhoAm 92
Schmitz, John G. 1930- PolPar
Schmitz, Josef Gotthard 1926- WhoWor 93
Schmitz, Lelde Martha 1951- WhoUN 92
Schmitz, Lizabeth Moriarty 1951- WhoAmW 93
Schmitz, Michael David Law&B 92
Schmitz, Nancy Ann 1929- WhoAmW 93
Schmitz, Norbert 1933- WhoScE 91-3
Schmitz, Oliver MiSFD 9
Schmitz, Ralph K. 1932- St&PR 93
Schmitz, Robert Allen 1941- WhoAm 92
Schmitz, Roger Anthony 1934- WhoAm 92
Schmitz, Stephen L. 1953- St&PR 93
Schmitz, Walter Douglas 1930- St&PR 93, WhoAm 92
Schmitz, Wolfgang 1949- WhoWor 93
Schmoeller, David MiSFD 9
Schmoke, Kurt BioIn 17
Schmoke, Kurt 1949- WhoAm 92, WhoE 93
Schmoke, Kurt L. 1949- AfrAmBi [port]
Schmoker, Jane Anne Law&B 92
Schmoker, John Benjamin d1991 BioIn 17
Schmoldt, Uwe 1941- WhoScE 91-3
Schmolka, Leo Louis 1939- WhoAm 92
Schmoll, Harry F., Jr. 1939- WhoE 93
Schmoller, Eberhard G.H. Law&B 92
Schmonsees, William Law&B 92
Schmoyer, Terrence K. 1939- St&PR 93
Schmucker, Ulrich 1930- WhoWor 93
Schmucker, William Albert 1931- St&PR 93
Schmucki, Ross F. Law&B 92
Schmuckler, Stanley Lloyd 1925- St&PR 93
Schmudde, Lee G. Law&B 92
Schmude, Richard Willis, Jr. 1958- WhoWor 93
Schmued, Edgar d1985 BioIn 17
Schmuhl, Marian Hobbs 1945- WhoWrEP 92
Schmuhl, William John, Jr. 1943- St&PR 93
Schmuller, Alexander 1880-1933 Baker 92
Schmults, Edward C. Law&B 92
Schmults, Edward Charles 1931- St&PR 93, WhoAm 92
Schmus, William G. Law&B 92
Schmus, William G. 1949- WhoAm 92
Schmutterer, Heinrich Johannes 1926- WhoScE 91-3
Schmutz, Arthur Walter 1921- WhoAm 92
Schmutz, John F. Law&B 92, WhoAm 92
Schmutz, W. WhoScE 91-3
Schmutzenhofer, Heinrich 1939- WhoScE 91-4
Schmutzhart, Berthold Josef 1928- WhoAm 92
Schmutzler, David Lee 1939- St&PR 93
Schmutzler, Reinhard 1934- WhoScE 91-3, WhoWor 93
Schnabel, Artur 1882-1951 Baker 92
Schnabel, Brian Thomas 1952- WhoAm 92
Schnabel, Deborah Jane 1955- WhoAmW 93
Schnabel, E. Eugene 1936- St&PR 93
Schnabel, John Henry 1915- WhoAm 92
Schnabel, Joseph Ignaz 1767-1831 Baker 92
Schnabel, Julian BioIn 17
Schnabel, Julian 1951- WhoAm 92
Schnabel, Karl 1809-1881 See Schnabel, Joseph Ignaz 1767-1831 Baker 92
Schnabel, Karl Ulrich 1909- Baker 92, WhoAm 92
Schnabel, Linda Rosanne Westlund 1953- WhoAmW 93
Schnabel, Michael 1775-1842 See Schnabel, Joseph Ignaz 1767-1831 Baker 92
Schnabel, Robert Victor 1922- WhoAm 92
Schnabel, Rockwell A. BioIn 17
Schnabel, Rockwell Anthony 1936- St&PR 93, WhoAm 92
Schnabel, Stefan Artur 1912- WhoAm 92
Schnabel, Walter 1927- St&PR 93
Schnabel, Wolfram Karl Anton 1931- WhoWor 93
Schnaberth, Gernot WhoScE 91-4
Schnack, Dietrich 1943- WhoScE 91-3
Schnack, Eckart 1941- WhoScE 91-3
Schnack, Larry Gene 1937- WhoAm 92
Schnackenberg, Gjertrud 1953- DcLB 120 [port]
Schnackenberg, Roy Lee 1934- WhoAm 92
Schnacker, R. Kent 1956- St&PR 93
Schnadelbach, Klaus 1934- WhoScE 91-3
Schnadelbach, R.T. 1939- St&PR 93
Schnadig, Lawrence K. 1908- St&PR 93
Schnaiberg, Allan 1939- WhoAm 92
Schnaitman, William Kenneth 1926- WhoAm 92
Schnakenberg, Donald G. 1939- WhoE 93
Schnakenburg, Barry Allen 1947- St&PR 93
Schnakenburg, Otto H. 1916- St&PR 93
Schnall, Edith Lea 1922- WhoAm 92, WhoAmW 93, WhoE 93
Schnall, Mimi d1991 BioIn 17
Schnapf, Abraham 1921- WhoE 93
Schnapf, Abraham 1921-1990 BioIn 17
Schnapf, Donald Jeffrey 1946- WhoE 93
Schnapp, Roger Herbert 1946- WhoEmL 93, WhoWor 93
Schnarr, Nicole Brinker 1945- WhoAmW 93
Schnarr, Richard A. 1929- St&PR 93
Schnars, Linda L. 1963- St&PR 93
Schnatterly, Robert Christopher 1952- WhoE 93
Schnatterly, Stephen E. 1938- WhoAm 92
Schnebel, Dieter 1930- Baker 92
Schnebel, Robert 1943- St&PR 93
Schnebelen, Pierre 1935- WhoWor 93
Schnebli, Hans Peter 1940- WhoScE 91-4
Schneck, Daniel Julio 1941- WhoAm 92
Schneck, Eric Milo 1954- WhoE 93
Schneck, Ernest 1929- St&PR 93
Schneck, James Anthony 1953- WhoE 93
Schneck, Jerome M. 1920- WhoAm 92, WhoWor 93
Schneck, Keith D. St&PR 93
Schneck, Paul D. 1952- ScF&FL 92
Schneck, Stuart Austin 1929- WhoAm 92
Schneck, Stuart B. Law&B 92
Schneckenburger, Karen Lynne 1949- WhoSSW 93
Schnecko, Hans W. 1931- WhoWor 93
Schnee, Daniel J. Law&B 92
Schnee, David Z. 1941- WhoE 93
Schneebacher, Alexander T. 1944- St&PR 93
Schneebaum, Marc R. St&PR 93
Schneebaum, Tobias 1922- WhoWrEP 92

Schneeberger, Don Roy 1930- St&PR 93
Schneeberger, Stephen A. Law&B 92
Schneekluth, Herbert 1921- WhoScE 91-3
Schneeman, Barbara Olds 1948- WhoAmW 93
Schneeman, Peter Henry 1937- WhoWrEP 92
Schneemann, Carolee 1939- BioIn 17, WhoWrEP 92
Schneerson, Grigori 1901-1982 Baker 92
Schneerson, Menachem 1902- NewYTBS 92 [port]
Schneerson, Menachem M. BioIn 17
Schneerson, Menachem Mendel JeAmHC
Schneerson, Menachem Mendel 1902- News 92 [port]
Schneerson-Mishkovsky, Zelda 1915?- BioIn 17
Schneevoigt, Georg (Lennart) 1872-1947 Baker 92
Schneewind, Jerome Borges 1930- WhoAm 92
Schneid, Thomas David 1956- WhoSSW 93
Schneidau, Tom Rodger 1942- St&PR 93
Schneider, A. WhoScE 91-4
Schneider, Adam Louis 1956- WhoWor 93
Schneider, Alan J. 1945- St&PR 93
Schneider, Alexander 1908- WhoAm 92
Schneider, (Abraham) Alexander 1908- Baker 92
Schneider, Allan M. d1991 BioIn 17
Schneider, Allan Stanford 1940- WhoAm 92
Schneider, Arthur 1947- WhoSSW 93, WhoWor 93
Schneider, Arthur Paul 1930- WhoAm 92
Schneider, Arthur Sanford 1929- WhoAm 92
Schneider, Barry 1935- St&PR 93
Schneider, Barry J. 1944- WhoSSW 93
Schneider, Ben Ross, Jr. WhoWrEP 92
Schneider, Benjamin 1938- WhoAm 92
Schneider, Birger WhoScE 91-2
Schneider, Bob R. St&PR 93
Schneider, Bobby Dean 1937- WhoSSW 93
Schneider, Brenda L. 1946- St&PR 93
Schneider, Bruce Stanley Law&B 92
Schneider, C. Leon WhoIns 93
Schneider, C. Rex 1937- WhoWrEP 92
Schneider, Calvin 1924- WhoWor 93
Schneider, Calvin Dwaine 1931- WhoSSW 93
Schneider, Carl W. 1932- WhoAm 92
Schneider, Carol Joyce 1938- WhoAmW 93
Schneider, Charles I. 1923- WhoAm 92
Schneider, Charles R. 1940- St&PR 93
Schneider, Cheryl Law&B 92
Schneider, Christine Lynn 1960- WhoAmW 93
Schneider, Cindy Ann 1959- WhoAmW 93
Schneider, Clara Garbus 1955- WhoSSW 93
Schneider, Claudia 1962- WhoAmW 93
Schneider, Claudine BioIn 17
Schneider, Cyril M. 1929- WhoAm 92
Schneider, Dan 1948- St&PR 93
Schneider, David M. 1918- IntDcAn
Schneider, David M. 1937- St&PR 93
Schneider, David Miller Law&B 92
Schneider, David Miller 1937- WhoAm 92
Schneider, David Theodore 1949- WhoE 93
Schneider, Dennis Eugene 1957- WhoEmL 93, WhoWor 93
Schneider, Dennis Ray 1952- WhoSSW 93
Schneider, Dietrich 1919- WhoScE 91-3
Schneider, Donald Alfred 1951- St&PR 93
Schneider, Donald Frederic 1939- WhoAm 92
Schneider, Donald S. 1947- St&PR 93
Schneider, Donald Wike 1930- St&PR 93
Schneider, Duane Bernard 1937- WhoAm 92, WhoWrEP 92
Schneider, Edward Faber 1872-1950 Baker 92
Schneider, Edward Lewis 1940- WhoAm 92
Schneider, Eleonora Frey 1921- WhoAmW 93
Schneider, Elisa Anne 1960- WhoAmW 93
Schneider, Elke 1940- WhoWor 93
Schneider, Emory Hugh 1940- St&PR 93
Schneider, Eric N. Law&B 92
Schneider, Eric N. 1951- St&PR 93
Schneider, Florian 1947- See Kraftwerk ConMus 9
Schneider, Frank 1940- WhoScE 91-3
Schneider, Frederick H. d1991 BioIn 17
Schneider, Frederick Howard 1938- WhoE 93
Schneider, Frederick William, Jr. 1923- WhoAm 92
Schneider, Friedhelm 1928- WhoScE 91-3, WhoWor 93
Schneider, (Johann Christian) Friedrich 1786-1853 See Schneider family Baker 92
Schneider, Fritz 1930- WhoScE 91-3
Schneider, Gene W. 1926- St&PR 93, WhoAm 92
Schneider, Georg Abraham 1770-1839 Baker 92
Schneider, George 1890-1963 BioIn 17
Schneider, George Alan Law&B 92
Schneider, George T. WhoAm 92
Schneider, George W. 1923- St&PR 93
Schneider, George William 1916- WhoAm 92
Schneider, George William 1923- WhoSSW 93
Schneider, Gerald Edward 1940- WhoAm 92
Schneider, Gerhard 1930- St&PR 93
Schneider, Gerhard M. 1932- WhoScE 91-3
Schneider, Gertrude 1928- WhoE 93
Schneider, Gottlieb 1797-1856 See Schneider family Baker 92
Schneider, Greta Sara 1954- WhoE 93, WhoWor 93
Schneider, Gunter 1918- WhoWor 93
Schneider, Hans 1929- WhoScE 91-3
Schneider, Hans-Jorg 1935- WhoScE 91-3
Schneider, Hans Juergen 1937- WhoScE 91-3
Schneider, Harald 1958- WhoWor 93
Schneider, Harold Joel 1923- WhoAm 92
Schneider, Harold N. 1950- St&PR 93
Schneider, Harvey B. 1922- St&PR 93
Schneider, Heinz Werner 1924- WhoWor 93
Schneider, Helmut F. 1936- WhoWor 93
Schneider, Herbert Carpenter 1945- WhoE 93
Schneider, Herbert J. Law&B 92
Schneider, Herbert J. 1926- St&PR 93
Schneider, Herbert William 1930- WhoAm 92
Schneider, Hermann 1935- WhoScE 91-3
Schneider, Hermann P.G. 1934- WhoScE 91-3
Schneider, Hortense 1833-1920 OxDcOp
Schneider, Howard 1935- WhoAm 92
Schneider, Howard M. 1943- St&PR 93
Schneider, Howard Stewart 1945- WhoAm 92
Schneider, Isidor 1896-1977 ScF&FL 92
Schneider, Jack 1917- WhoE 93
Schneider, Jack Ward 1943- WhoSSW 93
Schneider, Jacquelyn Jo 1942- WhoAmW 93
Schneider, James G. 1925- St&PR 93
Schneider, Jan 1933- WhoAm 92
Schneider, Janet M. 1950- WhoAm 92
Schneider, Janice Linnea 1938- WhoAmW 93
Schneider, Jean WhoWor 93
Schneider, Jeffrey H. Law&B 92
Schneider, Jeffrey M. 1955- St&PR 93
Schneider, JoAnne 1919- WhoAm 92
Schneider, Joel Alan 1938- WhoSSW 93
Schneider, Johann 1753-1840 See Schneider family Baker 92
Schneider, Johann 1789-1864 See Schneider family Baker 92
Schneider, John Arnold 1926- WhoAm 92
Schneider, John Edward Law&B 92
Schneider, John Francis Law&B 92
Schneider, John Hoke 1931- WhoAm 92
Schneider, John K. 1964- WhoE 93
Schneider, Jon David 1939- St&PR 93
Schneider, Joseph R. 1929- St&PR 93
Schneider, Joyce Anne 1942- ScF&FL 92
Schneider, Judith Lynn 1944- WhoAmW 93
Schneider, Jules Edouard, Jr. 1930- St&PR 93
Schneider, Julius 1805-1885 Baker 92
Schneider, Jurgen 1936- WhoAm 92
Schneider, Keith Hilary 1956- WhoAm 92
Schneider, Larry R. 1946- St&PR 93
Schneider, Lawrence Frank 1949- WhoEmL 93
Schneider, Laz Levkoff 1939- WhoSSW 93
Schneider, Leann St&PR 93
Schneider, Lewis 1941- St&PR 93
Schneider, Linda Ann 1945- WhoAmW 93
Schneider, Linda F. Law&B 92
Schneider, Louise Romero de Martinez 1943- WhoAmW 93, WhoWor 93
Schneider, Mahlon C. Law&B 92
Schneider, Mahlon Craig 1939- St&PR 93
Schneider, Maria 1952- BioIn 17
Schneider, Marius 1903-1982 Baker 92
Schneider, Mark 1946- WhoAm 92
Schneider, Mark L. 1941- WhoUN 92
Schneider, Mark Lewis 1941- WhoAm 92
Schneider, Martin Aaron 1926- WhoE 93
Schneider, Maryann W. 1946- St&PR 93
Schneider, Max 1875-1967 Baker 92
Schneider, Meg ScF&FL 92
Schneider, Melvin 1927- St&PR 93
Schneider, Michael Gerard 1957- St&PR 93
Schneider, Michael Ira 1936- St&PR 93
Schneider, Michael Joseph 1938- WhoAm 92
Schneider, Michael Wilmarth 1942- St&PR 93
Schneider, Michel 1943- WhoScE 91-2
Schneider, Norman M. 1911- WhoAm 92
Schneider, Pamela Cole 1954- WhoAmW 93
Schneider, Pamela Rolnick Law&B 92
Schneider, Paul MiSFD 9
Schneider, Paul L. 1954- St&PR 93, WhoIns 93
Schneider, Peter Raymond 1939- WhoAm 92
Schneider, Philip Allen 1938- WhoE 93
Schneider, Philip James 1949- WhoE 93
Schneider, Phyllis Leah 1947- WhoAm 92
Schneider, Pina R. 1941- St&PR 93
Schneider, Raymond Clinton 1920- WhoAm 92
Schneider, Richard Graham 1930- WhoAm 92
Schneider, Richard H. 1956- St&PR 93
Schneider, Richard Harold 1947- WhoSSW 93
Schneider, Richard Theodore 1927- WhoAm 92, WhoSSW 93
Schneider, Richard William 1946- WhoAm 92
Schneider, Rob BioIn 17
Schneider, Robert E. Law&B 92
Schneider, Robert Edward 1950- St&PR 93
Schneider, Rochelle J. Law&B 92
Schneider, Rolf 1940- WhoWor 93
Schneider, Romy 1938-1982 BioIn 17, IntDcF 2-3 [port]
Schneider, Rose E. St&PR 93
Schneider, Rudy L. 1949- St&PR 93
Schneider, Sandra Lee 1944- WhoAmW 93
Schneider, Sharon Kay 1950- WhoSSW 93
Schneider, Sol 1924- WhoAm 92
Schneider, Stephen Gary 1945- St&PR 93
Schneider, Stephen Henry 1945- WhoAm 92
Schneider, Steven D. Law&B 92
Schneider, Steven F. 1953- St&PR 93
Schneider, Steven P. Law&B 92
Schneider, Susan Marguerite 1958- WhoAmW 93
Schneider, Theodor 1827-1909 See Schneider family Baker 92
Schneider, Valerie Lois 1941- WhoAmW 93, WhoSSW 93
Schneider, Virginia Dee 1914- WhoWrEP 92
Schneider, Walter O. St&PR 93
Schneider, Wilhelm 1938- WhoScE 91-4
Schneider, William Alfred Law&B 92
Schneider, William Charles 1923- WhoAm 92
Schneider, William George 1915- WhoAm 92
Schneider, William George 1919- WhoAm 92
Schneider, William Henry 1934- WhoAm 92
Schneider, William James 1943- WhoSSW 93
Schneider, William Martin 1940- WhoSSW 93
Schneider, Wolf 1953- WhoAm 92
Schneider, Wolf-Dieter 1944- WhoWor 93
Schneider, Yvette E. WhoWrEP 92
Schneider-Criezis, Susan Marie 1953- WhoAmW 93, WhoWor 93
Schneidereith, C. Wm., Jr. 1938- St&PR 93
Schneider family Baker 92
Schneiderhan, Wolfgang (Eduard) 1915- Baker 92
Schneiderman, Bob Allen 1963- WhoE 93
Schneiderman, David Abbott 1947- WhoAm 92
Schneiderman, Gerald St&PR 93
Schneiderman, Herbert B. 1945- WhoAm 92
Schneiderman, Howard A. BioIn 17
Schneiderman, Howard Gary 1949- WhoE 93
Schneiderman, Irwin 1923- St&PR 93, WhoAm 92
Schneiderman, Michael Law&B 92
Schneiderman, Richard Steven 1948- WhoAm 92
Schneider-Maunoury, Michel 1931- St&PR 93, WhoAm 92, WhoE 93
Schneider-Siemssen, Gunther 1926- IntDcOp, OxDcOp
Schneidersmann, Ernst-Otto 1921- WhoScE 91-3
Schneider-Trnavsky, Mikulas 1881-1958 Baker 92
Schneiderwind, Barry J. Law&B 92
Schneidhofer, Adolf 1938- WhoScE 91-4
Schneidt, Hanns-Martin 1930- Baker 92
Schneier, Arthur 1930- WhoAm 92, WhoE 93
Schneier, Michael L. 1940- St&PR 93
Schneier, Paul Russ Law&B 92
Schneitzhoeffer, Jean 1785-1852 Baker 92
Schnekenburger, Ferdinand 1930- WhoScE 91-3
Schnell, Albert J. 1928- St&PR 93
Schnell, Carlton Bryce 1932- WhoAm 92
Schnell, Donald F. 1932- St&PR 93
Schnell, George Adam 1931- WhoAm 92
Schnell, Jane Milner 1930- WhoAmW 93
Schnell, John Arthur 1933- St&PR 93
Schnell, Joseph WhoAm 92
Schnell, K.F. 1936- WhoScE 91-3
Schnell, Laszlo 1923- WhoScE 91-4
Schnell, Nancy L. Law&B 92
Schnell, Roger Thomas 1936- WhoWor 93
Schnell, Terry L. Law&B 92
Schnell, Walter L. 1924- WhoScE 91-3
Schnelle, Jean BioIn 17
Schnelle, Karl Benjamin, Jr. 1930- WhoAm 92
Schneller, Marina V. Law&B 92
Schnelling, Anthony Hendrik Nehemiah 1947- WhoE 93
Schnelwar, Bruce M. St&PR 93
Schnepel, Roland 1957- WhoWor 93
Schnepf, Dale BioIn 17
Schnepf, Max Owen 1941- WhoWrEP 92
Schneps, Henry G. 1946- St&PR 93
Schneps, Jack 1929- WhoAm 92
Schnering, Philip Blessed 1917- WhoAm 92
Schnering, Philip Scott 1947- WhoE 93
Schnerr, Gunter Helmut 1944- WhoWor 93
Schnetter, Reinhard 1936- WhoScE 91-3
Schneyer, Charlotte Alper 1923- WhoAm 92, WhoAmW 93
Schneyer, Gene S. 1953- St&PR 93
Schnick, Thomas H. 1940- St&PR 93, WhoSSW 93
Schnick, Wolfgang 1957- WhoWor 93
Schnidman, Richard J. Law&B 92
Schnidrig, Herman Edward 1930- St&PR 93
Schnieders, Bernhard 1933- WhoScE 91-3
Schnieders, Charles Louis 1945- St&PR 93
Schniedewind, Jeanne Marie 1963- WhoAmW 93
Schnip, John I. 1927- St&PR 93
Schnipper, Lowell Elliot 1943- WhoAm 92
Schnirring, William Richard 1929- St&PR 93
Schnitger, Arp 1648-1719 Baker 92
Schnitger, Franz Caspar 1693?-1729 See Schnitger, Arp 1648-1719 Baker 92
Schnitger, Johann Georg 1690?-1733? See Schnitger, Arp 1648-1719 Baker 92
Schnitt, Jack 1955- St&PR 93
Schnittke, Alfred 1934- CurBio 92 [port]
Schnittke, Alfred (Garsievich) 1934- Baker 92
Schnitzer, Anne Ward 1954- St&PR 93
Schnitzer, Bruce W. 1944- St&PR 93
Schnitzer, Christine A. 1955- WhoWrEP 92
Schnitzer, Frances Sider 1917- WhoAmW 93
Schnitzer, Howard Joel 1934- WhoAm 92
Schnitzer, Iris Taymore 1943- WhoAmW 93
Schnitzer, Jeshaia 1918- WhoE 93
Schnitzer, Leonard Elliott 1924- St&PR 93
Schnitzer, Martin Colby 1925- WhoAm 92
Schnitzer, Morris 1922- BioIn 17
Schnitzer, Moshe 1921- WhoWor 93
Schnitzer, Robert A. MiSFD 9
Schnitzer, Robert Bruce 1949- WhoE 93
Schnitzer, Robert C. 1906- WhoAm 92
Schnitzlein, Harold Norman 1927- WhoAm 92, WhoSSW 93
Schnitzler, Arthur 1862-1931 DcLB 118 [port]
Schnitzler, Beverly Jeanne WhoAmW 93
Schnitzler, Ronald Michael 1939- WhoE 93
Schnizer, Bernhard 1935- WhoScE 91-4
Schnobrich, Roger William 1929- WhoAm 92
Schnoes, Robert F. 1926- St&PR 93
Schnog, Suzanne Adlerstein 1934- WhoAmW 93
Schnoll, Howard Manuel 1935- WhoAm 92
Schnoll, Steven 1946- St&PR 93
Schnoor, Hans 1893-1976 Baker 92
Schnoor, Jerald Lee 1950- WhoAm 92

Schnoor, Steven R. 1952- St&PR 93
Schnopper, Herbert W. 1933- WhoScE 91-2
Schnorf, James Roy 1954- St&PR 93
Schnorr, Donna Lynn 1963- WhoSSW 93
Schnorr, Wolfgang Reinhold 1949- WhoWor 93
Schnorr von Carolsfeld, Ludwig 1836-1865 Baker 92, OxDcOp
Schnorr von Carolsfeld, Malvina 1825-1904 Baker 92
Schnuck, Terry E. Law&B 92
Schnupp, Peter Hans 1934- WhoWor 93
Schnur, Daniel R. Law&B 92
Schnur, Jerome 1923- WhoAm 92
Schnur, Jerome 1923-1990 BioIn 17
Schnur, Louis S. 1940- St&PR 93
Schnurnberger, Lynn Edelman 1949- ScF&FL 92
Schnurr, Constance Burke 1932- WhoWrEP 92
Schnurr, Kenneth Eugene 1933- St&PR 93
Schnurr, Mary Jankousky Law&B 92
Schnurr, William Bernhardt WhoWrEP 92
Schnurre, Wolfdietrich 1920-1989 BioIn 17
Schnyder, Pierre WhoScE 91-4
Schnyder, Sandra Elizabeth Eddy 1939- WhoE 93
Schnyder, U.W. 1923- WhoScE 91-4
Schnyder von Wartensee, (Franz) Xaver 1786-1868 Baker 92
Schnydrig, Andrew J. BioIn 17
Schobel, James Edward Law&B 92
Schober, Charles Coleman, III 1924- WhoAm 92
Schober, Milton W. Law&B 92
Schober, Robert Charles 1940- WhoWor 93
Schoberlechner, Franz 1797-1843 Baker 92
Schobert, Johann c. 1735-1767 Baker 92
Schoch, Alexander Cochran Law&B 92
Schoch, Claude Martin 1955- WhoAm 92
Schoch, Laurence William 1934- St&PR 93
Schoch, Tim ScF&FL 92
Schochet, Victoria ScF&FL 92
Schochet, William A. Law&B 92
Schochor, Jonathan 1946- WhoEmL 93, WhoWor 93
Schock, Eberhard 1939- WhoWor 93
Schock, George Aloysius 1907- St&PR 93
Schock, Gunther 1928- WhoScE 91-4
Schock, Jacqui Virginia 1938- WhoAmW 93
Schock, Robert Norman 1939- WhoAm 92
Schock, Robert W. 1933- St&PR 93
Schock, Todd Alan 1960- St&PR 93
Schock, William Wallace 1923- WhoE 93
Schockaert, Barbara Ann 1938- WhoAmW 93
Schockaert, Ernest R. 1942- WhoScE 91-2
Schocken, Gershom 1912-1990 BioIn 17
Schoder, Barron Warren, Jr. 1930- St&PR 93
Schoder, Judith ScF&FL 92
Schoebel, Nancy 1952-1990 BioIn 17
Schoeberl, Robert R. 1936- St&PR 93
Schoeberlein, William Francis 1932- WhoAm 92
Schoech, Gerhard Konrad 1936- WhoScE 91-3
Schoeck, Clyde C. 1939- WhoIns 93
Schoeck, Helmut 1922- WhoAm 92
Schoeck, Othmar 1886-1957 Baker 92, OxDcOp
Schoeck, Peter Alfred 1926- WhoWor 93
Schoeck, Richard Joseph 1920- WhoAm 92, WhoWor 93
Schoedl, Renate Wilhelm 1937- WhoAmW 93
Schoedsack, Ernest B. 1893-1979 MiSFD 9N
Schoeffel, Jon Michael Law&B 92
Schoeffer, Rosemarie R. d1990 BioIn 17
Schoefs, Benoit 1965- WhoWor 93
Schoelcher, Victor 1804-1893 Baker 92
Schoelkopf, Dean Harold 1932- WhoAm 92
Schoelkopf, Robert 1927-1991 BioIn 17
Schoell, William 1951- ScF&FL 92, WhoWrEP 92
Schoeller, Francois 1934- WhoWor 93
Schoellkopf, Paul Arthur 1916- St&PR 93
Schoellkopf, Wolfgang 1932- St&PR 93, WhoAm 92
Schoelly, Marie-Louise 1915-1991 BioIn 17
Schoemaker, Hubert J.P. 1950- St&PR 93
Schoemaker, Maurice 1890-1964 Baker 92
Schoeman, Karel 1939- ScF&FL 92
Schoemehl, Vincent Charles, Jr. 1946- WhoAm 92
Schoemperlen, Diane 1954- WhoCanL 92
Schoen, Allen Harry 1936- WhoE 93
Schoen, Arthur Boyer, Jr. 1953- WhoAm 92
Schoen, Barbara Taylor 1924- WhoE 93
Schoen, Donald Philip 1938- St&PR 93
Schoen, Herbert Martin 1928- WhoE 93
Schoen, Kenneth Aloys 1927- St&PR 93
Schoen, Kurt L. 1927- St&PR 93
Schoen, LaDonna Faye 1945- WhoAmW 93
Schoen, Laurence Peter 1944- St&PR 93
Schoen, Linda Allen 1936- WhoAmW 93
Schoen, Marc Alan 1938- WhoWor 93
Schoen, Max Howard 1922- WhoAm 92
Schoen, Michael Arthur 1956- WhoSSW 93
Schoen, Paul G. 1944- St&PR 93
Schoen, Regina Neiman 1949- WhoAmW 93
Schoen, Richard Melvin 1950- WhoAm 92
Schoen, Robert 1930- WhoSSW 93
Schoen, Robert E. Law&B 92
Schoen, Robert Edward 1946- St&PR 93
Schoen, Ronald H. 1950- St&PR 93
Schoen, Roy Miles 1940- WhoE 93
Schoen, Scott Joseph Law&B 92
Schoen, Siegfried Ewald 1934- WhoUN 92
Schoen, William Jack 1935- WhoAm 92
Schoenauer, Thomas E. 1937- St&PR 93
Schoenbach, Peter Julian 1941- WhoAm 92
Schoenbach, Ronald A. 1947- St&PR 93
Schoenbaum, Alex 1915- St&PR 93
Schoenbaum, David Leon 1935- WhoAm 92
Schoenbaum, Samuel 1927- WhoAm 92, WhoWrEP 92
Schoenbeck, James Edwin 1944- St&PR 93
Schoenbeck-Temesy, Eva 1930- WhoScE 91-4
Schoenberg, Arnold 1874-1951 BioIn 17, IntDcOp [port], OxDcOp
Schoenberg, Arnold (Franz Walter) 1874-1951 Baker 92
Schoenberg, Harry W. 1927- WhoAm 92
Schoenberg, Herbert M. Law&B 92
Schoenberg, Lawrence Joseph 1932- WhoAm 92
Schoenberg, Mark George 1947- WhoAm 92, WhoSSW 93
Schoenberger, James Edwin 1947- WhoAm 92
Schoenberger, Michael 1940- WhoSSW 93
Schoenberger, Nancy WhoWrEP 92
Schoenberger, Nancy Jane 1950- WhoAmW 93
Schoenberger, Robert Joseph 1938- St&PR 93
Schoenberg-Swartchild, Coco 1939- WhoAmW 93
Schoenborn, Benno P. 1936- WhoE 93
Schoenborn, C. Scott 1960- WhoSSW 93
Schoenbrun, Larry Lynn 1940- WhoAm 92
Schoenbrunn, Erwin Frederick 1921- WhoE 93
Schoenbucher, Karen Ann 1948- St&PR 93
Schoendienst, Albert Fred 1923- WhoAm 92
Schoendienst, Red 1923- WhoAm 92
Schoendoerffer, Pierre MiSFD 9
Schoendorf, Judson Raymond 1942- WhoWor 93
Schoendorf, Walter John 1927- WhoAm 92
Schoendorf, William H. 1936- St&PR 93
Schoene, Armin Joachim 1932- WhoWor 93
Schoene, Kathleen Snyder 1953- WhoAmW 93, WhoEmL 93
Schoeneck, David Lee 1946- WhoWor 93
Schoenefeld, Henry 1857-1936 Baker 92
Schoener, Harvey 1943- St&PR 93
Schoener, Thomas William 1943- WhoAm 92
Schoenewolf, Gerald 1941- ConAu 136
Schoenfein, Benjamin P. 1899-1990 BioIn 17
Schoenfein, Robert 1937- St&PR 93
Schoenfein, Robert A. 1937- WhoAm 92
Schoenfeld, Hanns-Martin Walter 1928- WhoAm 92
Schoenfeld, Henry F. 1928- WhoE 93
Schoenfeld, Joel M. Law&B 92
Schoenfeld, Lawrence Steven 1941- WhoSSW 93
Schoenfeld, Lee 1952- St&PR 93
Schoenfeld, Michael P. 1935- WhoE 93, WhoWor 93
Schoenfeld, Myron R. 1928- WhoWrEP 92
Schoenfeld, Stanley 1932- WhoAm 92
Schoenfeld, Walter Edwin 1930- WhoAm 92
Schoenfelder, John Frederick 1940- St&PR 93
Schoenfelder, Peg Ann Law&B 92
Schoenhals, Alvin J. 1913- St&PR 93
Schoenhals, Marvin N. 1947- St&PR 93
Schoenhard, William Charles, Jr. 1949- WhoWor 93
Schoenharting, Guenther 1942- WhoScE 91-2
Schoenheimer, Pierre L. 1933- St&PR 93
Schoenheimer, Rudolf 1898-1941 BioIn 17
Schoenheit, Edward William, Jr. 1926- WhoE 93
Schoenheit, Marian Beauchamp 1927- WhoE 93
Schoenheit, Thomas Edward Law&B 92
Schoenherr, David Wilbert 1939- WhoE 93
Schoenherr, John ChlBIID [port]
Schoenherr, John 1935- BioIn 17
Schoenherr, John (Carl) 1935- ConAu 136, MajAI [port], WhoAm 92
Schoenherr, Karl 1867-1943 DcLB 118 [port]
Schoenherr, Russell W. 1940- St&PR 93
Schoenhut, George W. d1990 BioIn 17
Schoenig, Vincent Werner 1964- WhoSSW 93, WhoWor 93
Schoening, Mary D. Law&B 92
Schoeninger, Terrence T. Law&B 92
Schoenke, A.J. 1930- St&PR 93
Schoenke, Richard Warren 1943- WhoAm 92
Schoenle, Paul D. Law&B 92
Schoenly, Fred R. 1955- St&PR 93
Schoen-Rene, Anna 1864-1942 Baker 92
Schoenstadt, Steven E. 1939- St&PR 93
Schoenwald, David Jay 1949- St&PR 93
Schoenwald, Ernest Theodore 1923- WhoSSW 93
Schoenwald, Maurice Louis 1920- St&PR 93
Schoenwandt, Thomas Raymond 1944- WhoE 93
Schoenwetter, Janet Loree 1956- WhoEmL 93
Schoenwetter, L.J. 1939- St&PR 93
Schoenwetter, Rick P. 1952- St&PR 93
Schoenwetter, Sara Carolyn Law&B 92
Schoep, John Clifford 1933- St&PR 93
Schoep, Robert Leon 1946- St&PR 93
Schoepf, Albin Francis 1822-1886 PolBiDi
Schoepfer, Joseph Otto Law&B 92
Schoepfle, Otto Benjamin, Jr. 1910- WhoAm 92
Schoepflin, Harold ScF&FL 92
Schoepke, William 1924- St&PR 93
Schoeppel, Andrew Frank 1894-1962 BioIn 17
Schoer, Renee Kristine 1956- WhoAmW 93
Schoettger, Theodore Leo 1920- WhoAm 92
Schoettle, Ekkehard Law&B 92
Schoettle, Frederick John 1939- St&PR 93
Schoettle, Michael A. 1946- St&PR 93
Schoettler, Gail Sinton 1943- WhoAm 92, WhoAmW 93
Schoevers, H.W.C.L. 1934- WhoScE 91-3
Schofe, Kathy Davis 1949- WhoAmW 93
Schoff, Dennis L. Law&B 92
Schoffa, Georg 1922- WhoScE 91-3
Schoffeniels, Ernest 1927- WhoScE 91-2
Schoffler, Paul 1897-1977 Baker 92, OxDcOp
Schoffman, Nachum 1930- ConAu 137
Schoffstall, David Wayne 1950- WhoAm 92
Schoffstall, Kathleen 1943- St&PR 93
Schofield, Alfred Taylor 1846-1929 ScF&FL 92
Schofield, Andrew Noel WhoScE 91-1
Schofield, Charles Patrick WhoScE 91-1
Schofield, Donald S. 1928- St&PR 93
Schofield, Donald Stewart 1928- WhoAm 92
Schofield, George H. 1929- St&PR 93, WhoE 93
Schofield, Harley C. Law&B 92
Schofield, Jack H. 1923- St&PR 93
Schofield, James 1909-1990 BioIn 17
Schofield, Janet Ward WhoAmW 93
Schofield, Jennifer Lee 1963- WhoAmW 93
Schofield, John-David Mercer 1938- WhoAm 92
Schofield, John Marcus 1913- WhoSSW 93
Schofield, John McAllister 1831-1906 CmdGen 1991 [port], HarEnMi
Schofield, John T. 1936- St&PR 93
Schofield, John Trevor 1938- WhoAm 92
Schofield, Keitha Tullos 1951- St&PR 93
Schofield, Marsha Kovarsky 1958- WhoSSW 93
Schofield, Paul M. 1937- St&PR 93
Schofield, Robert Edwin 1923- WhoAm 92
Schofield, Roberta 1945- WhoSSW 93
Schofield, S. Gene 1947- WhoIns 93
Schofield, Seth E. 1939- St&PR 93
Schofield, Seth Eugene 1939- WhoAm 92
Schofield, Stephen ScF&FL 92
Schofield, Susan R.S. WhoAmW 93
Schofield, Wilfred WhoScE 91-1
Schofield, William 1921- WhoAm 92
Schofield, Wyvonna L. 1943- WhoWor 93
Schoggen, Joe G. 1922- St&PR 93
Schoggen, Phil Howard 1923- WhoAm 92
Schogt, Henry Gilius 1927- WhoAm 92
Schohl, John M. Law&B 92
Schohl, John Maison 1958- St&PR 93
Schohn, Joseph Louis Law&B 92
Schoknecht, Gunter 1930- WhoScE 91-3
Scholder, Fritz 1937- BioIn 17, WhoAm 92, WhoWor 93
Schole, Jurgen H. 1927- WhoScE 91-3
Scholefield, Adeline Peggy 1932- WhoAmW 93
Scholefield, Alan BioIn 17
Scholefield, Edmund O. ConAu 40NR
Scholefield, Peter Gordon 1925- WhoAm 92
Scholem, Gershom Gerhard 1897-1982 BioIn 17, ConAu 39NR
Scholer, Bo 1954- WhoWor 93
Scholer, Heinz-Friedrich 1948- WhoScE 91-3
Scholer, Sue Wyant 1936- WhoAmW 93
Scholes, Clifford R. 1927- St&PR 93
Scholes, Cynthia Marie 1958- WhoE 93
Scholes, Edison Earl 1939- WhoAm 92
Scholes, Gorden Glen Denton 1931- WhoAsAP 91
Scholes, I.R. WhoScE 91-1
Scholes, Katherine 1959- ScF&FL 92
Scholes, Kevan WhoScE 91-1
Scholes, Myron S. 1941- WhoAm 92
Scholes, Percy (Alfred) 1877-1958 Baker 92
Scholes, Robert 1929- ScF&FL 92
Scholes, Robert Edward 1929- WhoAm 92
Scholfield, A.F. 1884- ScF&FL 92
Scholfield, C. Norman WhoScE 91-1
Scholfield, Harvey H., Jr. 1922- St&PR 93
Scholl, David Carl 1956- WhoIns 93
Scholl, John P. Law&B 92
Scholl, Kenneth M. 1947- St&PR 93
Scholl, Lester J. 1915- St&PR 93
Scholl, Marilyn Darby 1942- WhoAmW 93
Scholl, Nevin Harold 1954- St&PR 93
Scholl, Robert Reinhard 1928- St&PR 93
Scholl, Ruth H. 1925- St&PR 93
Scholl, William C. 1947- St&PR 93
Scholl, William V. 1922- St&PR 93
Schollander, Wendell Leslie, Jr. 1943- WhoAm 92
Scholle, Roger Hal 1936- WhoAm 92
Scholler, Karl-Ludwig 1925- WhoScE 91-3
Schollmaier, Edgar H. 1933- WhoAm 92
Schollmeyer, E. WhoScE 91-3
Schollmeyer, H. Edward 1925- St&PR 93
Schollmeyer, Hartmut 1950- WhoWor 93
Schollum, Robert 1913-1987 Baker 92
Scholly, Francis J. 1939- St&PR 93
Scholmerich, Paul 1916- WhoScE 91-3
Scholsky, Martin Joseph 1930- WhoE 93, WhoWor 93
Scholssman, David Yale 1960- St&PR 93
Scholte, H.R. 1938- WhoScE 91-3
Scholten, Michael D. 1955- St&PR 93
Scholten, Rodney Dale 1956- WhoSSW 93
Scholten, Roger K. Law&B 92
Scholten, Willem 1927- ScF&FL 92
Scholtens, Clarence 1922- St&PR 93
Scholtens, Martin A. 1942- St&PR 93
Scholtes, Berthold 1950- WhoWor 93
Scholtes, Wayne Henry 1917- WhoAm 92
Scholtis, R.J.H. 1924- WhoScE 91-3
Scholtissek, Christoph 1929- WhoScE 91-3
Scholtmeijer, Roelof J. 1929- WhoScE 91-3
Scholtyssek, Karl-Heinz 1931- WhoWor 93
Scholtz, Elizabeth 1921- WhoAm 92, WhoAmW 93
Scholtz, Herrmann 1845-1918 Baker 92
Scholtz, Peter 1936- WhoScE 91-4
Scholtz, Robert Arno 1936- WhoAm 92
Scholz, Bernhard E. 1835-1916 Baker 92
Scholz, Carter 1953- ScF&FL 92
Scholz, D. WhoScE 91-3
Scholz, Franz 1928- WhoScE 91-3
Scholz, Garret Arthur 1939- St&PR 93, WhoAm 92
Scholz, Hans-Joachim 1927- WhoWor 93
Scholz, Hildemar Wolfgang 1928- WhoScE 91-3
Scholz, Markie Louise 1947- WhoAmW 93
Scholz, Mary E. 1958- St&PR 93
Scholz, Walter K. 1936- St&PR 93
Schomaker, Verner 1914- WhoAm 92
Schomberg, Charles de 1601-1656 HarEnMi
Schomberg, Friedrich Hermann 1615-1690 HarEnMi
Schomberg, M.G. WhoScE 91-1

Schomburg, Alex 1905- *ScF&FL 92*
Schomburg, Roger John 1935- *St&PR 93*
Schomburgk, Hans Hermann 1880-1967 *BioIn 17*
Schomburgk, Robert Hermann 1804-1865 *Expl 93*
Schomer, Fred Joseph 1931- *St&PR 93*
Schomer, Fred K. 1939- *WhoAm 92*
Schomer, Howard 1915- *WhoAm 92, WhoWor 93*
Schomers, Mike *BioIn 17*
Schon, Donald Alan 1930- *WhoAm 92*
Schon, Gerd 1948- *WhoWor 93*
Schon, Hans 1940- *WhoScE 91-3*
Schon, Isabel 1940- *NotHsAW 93*
Schon, Joseph Stephen 1942- *St&PR 93*
Schon, Nancy Quint 1928- *WhoAmW 93*
Schonath, G.R. 1941- *St&PR 93*
Schonbach, Bernard H. 1948- *St&PR 93*
Schonbach, Bernard Harvey 1948- *WhoE 93*
Schonbach, Dave Irwin 1947- *WhoE 93*
Schonbach, Dieter 1931- *Baker 92*
Schonbachler, James J. 1943- *St&PR 93*
Schonbaum, E. *WhoScE 91-3*
Schonbek, Andrew J. *St&PR 93*
Schonberg, Alan Robert 1928- *St&PR 93*
Schonberg, Arnold 1874-1951 *BioIn 17, IntDcOp [port]*
Schonberg, Arnold Franz Walter *Baker 92*
Schonberg, Bessie *BioIn 17*
Schonberg, Harold C(harles) 1915- *Baker 92*
Schonberg, Harold Charles 1915- *WhoAm 92*
Schonberg, Stig Gustav 1933- *Baker 92*
Schonberg, William Peter 1960- *WhoSSW 93*
Schonberger, Benno 1863-1930 *Baker 92*
Schonberger, Rachel Ann Pomerantz 1941- *WhoAmW 93, WhoSSW 93*
Schonberger, Winfried Josef 1940- *WhoWor 93*
Schonbohm, Ekkehard 1934- *WhoScE 91-3*
Schonborn, Hans-Hellmuth 1923- *WhoScE 91-3*
Schonbrun, Michael Keith 1948- *WhoAm 92*
Schone, John Ernest *Law&B 92*
Schone, Lotte 1891-1977 *Baker 92*
Schonebaum, Alfred 1914- *WhoE 93*
Schonebeck, Eugen 1936- *BioIn 17*
Schoneman, Richard Edwin 1933- *St&PR 93*
Schonemann, Peter Hans 1929- *WhoAm 92*
Schonenberger, Helmut 1924- *WhoScE 91-3*
Schonenberger, Walter 1944- *WhoScE 91-4*
Schoner, Gregor 1958- *WhoWor 93*
Schoner, Helmut 1930- *WhoScE 91-3*
Schoner, Wilhelm 1935- *WhoScE 91-3*
Schonewald, Ottilie 1883-1961 *BioIn 17*
Schonewetter, Dennis Ray 1947- *St&PR 93*
Schonfeld, Irvin Sam *WhoE 93*
Schonfeld, Klaus 1941- *St&PR 93*
Schonfeld, Ruth d1990 *BioIn 17*
Schonfeld, Sy 1939- *St&PR 93*
Schonfeld, William Rost 1942- *WhoAm 92*
Schonfelder, John Lawrence *WhoScE 91-1*
Schonhammer, Kurt E.P. 1946- *WhoScE 91-3*
Schonherr, Max 1903-1984 *Baker 92*
Schonhoff, Kathleen Marie 1923- *WhoSSW 93*
Schonholtz, George Jerome 1930- *WhoE 93*
Schonholtz, Joan Sondra Hirsch 1933- *WhoAm 92*
Schonhorn, Harold 1928- *WhoAm 92, WhoE 93*
Schoning, Klaus 1936- *Baker 92*
Schonke, D.W. 1933- *St&PR 93*
Schonstein, Karl 1797-1876 *Baker 92*
Schonwald, Gary Alan 1942- *St&PR 93*
Schonwiese, Christian-D. 1940- *WhoScE 91-3*
Schonzeler, Hans-Hubert 1925- *Baker 92*
Schoof, C. John, II *St&PR 93*
Schoof, Leslie Earl 1951- *WhoAm 92*
Schook, Jesse *BioIn 17*
Schoolar, Joseph Clayton 1928- *WhoAm 92*
Schoolar, Larry L. 1933- *St&PR 93*
Schoolcraft, Henry Rowe 1793-1864 *IntDcAn*
Schooler, Edmund *St&PR 93*
Schooley, Charles Earl 1905- *WhoAm 92, WhoWor 93*
Schooley, Dolores Harter 1905- *WhoWor 93*
Schooley, Elmer Wayne 1916- *BioIn 17*
Schooley, Virginia G. *St&PR 93*
Schoolfield, Henry Palmer, Jr. 1928- *WhoWrEP 92*
Schools, Charles Hughlette 1929- *WhoWor 93*
Schools, Randolph Robert 1945- *WhoE 93*
Schoon, Craig Gerald 1942- *WhoE 93*
Schoon, Susan Wylie 1948- *WhoAm 92*
Schooner, Heidi M. *Law&B 92*
Schoonheim, Jacobus A. 1940- *WhoScE 91-3*
Schoonhoven, Ray James 1921- *WhoAm 92*
Schoonmaker, Samuel Vail, III 1935- *WhoAm 92*
Schoonmaker, Thelma *BioIn 17*
Schoonman, Adelbert 1934- *WhoScE 91-3*
Schoonover, Garry Gene 1950- *WhoSSW 93*
Schoonover, Hugh James 1942- *WhoSSW 93*
Schoonover, Jack Ronald 1934- *WhoSSW 93, WhoWor 93*
Schoonover, Jean Way *WhoAm 92, WhoAmW 93*
Schoonover, Lawrence 1906-1980 *ScF&FL 92*
Schoonover, Nicholas Jerome, III 1961- *WhoE 93*
Schoonover, Rodney Lee 1950- *St&PR 93*
Schoonover, Thomas David 1936- *WhoSSW 93*
Schoop, Paul 1909-1976 *Baker 92*
Schooping, Fred W. 1942- *St&PR 93*
Schoor, Gerald W. 1934- *St&PR 93*
Schoor, Howard M. 1939- *WhoWor 93*
Schoor, Michael Mercier 1942- *WhoAm 92*
Schoors, Antoon Maria Jozef 1934- *WhoWor 93*
Schopenhauer, Arthur 1788-1860 *Baker 92, BioIn 17*
Schopenhauer, Artur 1788-1860 *OxDcOp*
Schopenhauer, Johanna 1766-1838 *BioIn 17*
Schopfer, Peter 1938- *WhoScE 91-3*
Schopler, John Henry 1930- *WhoAm 92*
Schopp, Lawrence M. *Law&B 92*
Schoppe, Michael Timothy 1951- *WhoSSW 93*
Schoppenhorst, William 1931- *St&PR 93*
Schopper, Herwig Franz 1924- *WhoScE 91-4*
Schopper, Jurgen R. 1925- *WhoScE 91-3*
Schoppmeyer, Martin William 1929- *WhoAm 92, WhoSSW 93, WhoWor 93*
Schor, Edward *Law&B 92*
Schor, Joseph Martin 1929- *St&PR 93, WhoAm 92*
Schor, Laurence 1942- *WhoE 93*
Schor, Lynda 1938- *WhoWrEP 92*
Schor, Olga Seemann 1951- *WhoAmW 93*
Schor, Sandra *BioIn 17*
Schor, Stanley Sidney 1922- *WhoAm 92*
Schor, William *Law&B 92*
Schorer, Mark 1908-1977 *BioIn 17*
Schorer, Suki *WhoAm 92*
Schorgl, Thomas Barry 1950- *WhoAm 92*
Schori, Jan *Law&B 92*
Schork, Rudolph Joseph, Jr. 1933- *WhoAm 92*
Schorling, William Harrison 1949- *WhoWor 93*
Schorm, Evald 1931-1988 *DrEEuF*
Schornack, John James 1930- *WhoAm 92*
Schorr, Alan Edward 1945- *WhoAm 92*
Schorr, Alvin Louis 1921- *WhoAm 92*
Schorr, Daniel Louis 1916- *JrnUS, WhoAm 92*
Schorr, Friedrich 1888-1953 *Baker 92, IntDcOp, OxDcOp*
Schorr, Jeffrey Michael 1963- *WhoE 93*
Schorr, Justin 1928- *WhoE 93*
Schorr, Kathy Staico *BioIn 17*
Schorr, Lisbeth B. 1931- *ConAu 136*
Schorr, Lisbeth Bamberger 1931- *WhoAm 92, WhoAmW 93*
Schorr, Martin Mark 1923- *WhoWor 93*
Schorr, Martyn Laurence 1936- *WhoE 93*
Schorr, Marvin Gerald 1925- *St&PR 93*
Schorr, Phillip Andrew 1936- *St&PR 93, WhoAm 92*
Schorr, Renen *MiSFD 9*
Schorr, S. L. 1930- *WhoAm 92*
Schorr, Stephen I. 1945- *St&PR 93*
Schorr, Thelma M. 1924- *St&PR 93*
Schorr, Todd *BioIn 17*
Schorre, Louis Charles, Jr. 1925- *WhoAm 92*
Schorsch, Emil 1899-1982 *BioIn 17*
Schorsch, Ismar 1935- *WhoAm 92*
Schorske, Carl Emil 1915- *WhoAm 92*
Schotanus, Eugene Leroy 1937- *St&PR 93, WhoAm 92*
Schotland, Donald Lewis 1930- *WhoAm 92*
Schotland, Roy Arnold 1933- *WhoAm 92*
Schotland, Sara Deutch 1948- *WhoAmW 93*
Schotsky, Samuel A. 1943- *St&PR 93*
Schotsmans, Paul Trifon 1950- *WhoWor 93*
Schott, Anton 1846-1913 *Baker 92*
Schott, Art *St&PR 93*
Schott, Bernhard 1748-1809 *Baker 92*
Schott, Charles George, III *BioIn 17*
Schott, Dale *MiSFD 9*
Schott, Edward E. 1931- *St&PR 93*
Schott, Emil H. 1902- *St&PR 93*
Schott, Frank W. *Law&B 92*
Schott, Franz Philipp 1811-1874 *Baker 92*
Schott, George E. 1936- *WhoAm 92*
Schott, Howard Mansfield 1923- *WhoE 93*
Schott, Johann Andreas 1781-1840 *Baker 92*
Schott, Johann Joseph 1782-1855 *Baker 92*
Schott, John Robert 1936- *WhoAm 92, WhoE 93*
Schott, Joseph Lawrence 1933- *WhoSSW 93*
Schott, Marcia Whitney d1989 *BioIn 17*
Schott, Marge *BioIn 17*
Schott, Marge 1928- *WhoAm 92, WhoAmW 93*
Schott, Melvin 1925- *St&PR 93*
Schott, Michael B. 1948- *St&PR 93*
Schott, Nancy L. *Law&B 92*
Schott, Newton B., Jr. *Law&B 92*
Schott, Penelope Scambly 1942- *WhoWrEP 92*
Schott, Peter d1894 *Baker 92*
Schott, Rudiger 1927- *WhoWor 93*
Schott, Stephen Harold 1961- *WhoWor 93*
Schotta, Charles 1935- *WhoAm 92*
Schottelkotte, Albert Joseph 1927- *St&PR 93, WhoAm 92*
Schottelkotte, William F. 1945- *St&PR 93*
Schottenfeld, Alvin C. 1916- *St&PR 93*
Schottenfeld, David 1931- *WhoAm 92*
Schottenfeld, Milton 1923- *St&PR 93*
Schottenfeld, Steven Richard 1954- *St&PR 93*
Schottenheimer, Martin Edward 1943- *WhoAm 92*
Schottenstein, Jerome M. d1992 *NewYTBS 92*
Schottenstein, Jerome M. 1926-1992 *BioIn 17*
Schottenstein, Saul 1924- *WhoAm 92*
Schotter, Andrew Roye 1947- *WhoAm 92*
Schotters, Bernard William 1944- *WhoAm 92*
Schottky, Walter 1886-1976 *BioIn 17*
Schottland, Charles Irwin 1906- *WhoAm 92*
Schotz, Jon P. 1955- *St&PR 93*
Schoubye, Peter 1939- *WhoScE 91-2*
Schoultz, A.C., III 1940- *St&PR 93*
Schousboe, Inger 1944- *WhoScE 91-2*
Schouten, M.J.W. 1945- *WhoScE 91-3*
Schouten, Willem 1567-1625 & Le Maire, Jacob 1585-1616 *Expl 93*
Schouweiler, Steven Harvey 1946- *St&PR 93*
Schouwman, Hans 1902-1967 *Baker 92*
Schow, David J. 1955- *ScF&FL 92*
Schow, Horace, II 1932- *WhoSSW 93*
Schowalter, Ellen Lefferts 1937- *WhoAmW 93, WhoE 93*
Schowalter, John Erwin 1936- *WhoAm 92*
Schowalter, Toni Lee 1948- *WhoE 93*
Schowalter, William Raymond 1929- *WhoAm 92*
Schowe, Sheral Lee Speaks 1953- *WhoAmW 93*
Schowen, Richard Lyle 1934- *WhoAm 92*
Schowengerdt, C.D. *St&PR 93*
Schowengerdt, Henry Albert 1930- *WhoAm 92*
Schoyer, David Kennedy *Law&B 92*
Schoyer, David Kennedy 1946- *St&PR 93*
Schrack, Harold Price, III 1959- *WhoSSW 93*
Schrack, James M. 1958- *St&PR 93*
Schrad, Dale 1945- *St&PR 93*
Schrade, Leo 1903-1964 *Baker 92*
Schrader, Achim 1934- *WhoWor 93*
Schrader, Arnold C. 1933- *St&PR 93*
Schrader, Barry 1945- *Baker 92*
Schrader, David Eugene 1947- *WhoE 93*
Schrader, Harry Christian, Jr. 1932- *WhoAm 92*
Schrader, Henry Carl 1918- *WhoAm 92, WhoE 93, WhoSSW 93*
Schrader, James M. 1955- *St&PR 93*
Schrader, Jeffrey L. *Law&B 92*
Schrader, Keith William 1938- *WhoAm 92*
Schrader, Lawrence Edwin 1941- *WhoAm 92*
Schrader, Lee Frederick 1933- *WhoAm 92*
Schrader, Leonard *MiSFD 9*
Schrader, Lynwood 1930- *St&PR 93*
Schrader, Martin Harry 1924- *WhoAm 92, WhoE 93*
Schrader, Otto W. 1914- *St&PR 93*
Schrader, Paul *BioIn 17*
Schrader, Paul 1946- *MiSFD 9*
Schrader, Paul Joseph 1946- *WhoAm 92*
Schrader, Peter Harmon 1945- *WhoE 93*
Schrader, Richard James 1941- *WhoE 93*
Schrader, Russell W. *Law&B 92*
Schrader, Thomas F. 1950- *St&PR 93, WhoAm 92*
Schrader, William C. 1933- *St&PR 93*
Schrader, William Christian, III 1940- *WhoSSW 93*
Schrader, William Joseph 1929- *WhoAm 92*
Schradieck, Ernst-Peter 1952- *WhoScE 91-3*
Schradieck, Henry 1846-1918 *Baker 92*
Schrady, David Alan 1939- *WhoAm 92*
Schraeger, Maurice 1907- *St&PR 93*
Schraer, Rosemary S. J. d1992 *NewYTBS 92*
Schraer, Rosemary S.J. 1924-1992 *BioIn 17*
Schrafel, Richard B. 1951- *St&PR 93*
Schraff, Anne E. 1939- *ScF&FL 92*
Schraff, Anne E(laine) 1939- *ConAu 39NR*
Schraft, Rolf Dieter 1942- *WhoScE 91-3*
Schraft, William C. 1921-1990 *BioIn 17*
Schrag, Adele Frisbie 1921- *WhoAm 92*
Schrag, Crystal Blythe 1965- *WhoAmW 93, WhoWor 93*
Schrag, Edward A., Jr. 1932- *WhoAm 92*
Schrag, Karl 1912- *WhoAm 92*
Schrag, Peter 1931- *WhoAm 92, WhoWrEP 92*
Schrage, Martin Henry 1941- *WhoE 93*
Schrage, Paul Daniel 1935- *St&PR 93, WhoAm 92*
Schrage, Rose 1942- *WhoAmW 93, WhoWor 93*
Schrager, Harley Dean 1947- *St&PR 93*
Schrager, Ian *BioIn 17*
Schrager, Mindy Rae 1958- *WhoEmL 93*
Schraibman, Sandra Marguerite Milner 1947- *WhoE 93*
Schram, C. Ronald 1942- *St&PR 93*
Schram, Daniel C. 1940- *WhoScE 91-3*
Schram, Donald Edward 1925- *St&PR 93*
Schram, Henry B. *WhoAm 92*
Schram, James L. 1947- *St&PR 93*
Schram, Martin Jay 1942- *WhoAm 92*
Schram, Norma Cheryl 1957- *WhoEmL 93*
Schram, Pieter P.J.M. 1934- *WhoScE 91-3*
Schram, William Thomas 1949- *St&PR 93*
Schrame, Larry G. 1940- *St&PR 93*
Schramek, Tomas 1944- *WhoAm 92*
Schramm, Bernard Charles, Jr. 1928- *WhoAm 92*
Schramm, Bernhard F. 1937- *WhoScE 91-3*
Schramm, Darrell G.H. 1943- *WhoWrEP 92*
Schramm, David Arden 1947- *WhoSSW 93*
Schramm, David Norman 1945- *WhoAm 92*
Schramm, Frederick Cullen 1942- *St&PR 93*
Schramm, Gregory Paul 1953- *WhoSSW 93*
Schramm, Gunter 1929- *WhoE 93, WhoWor 93*
Schramm, Heinz-Helmut 1936- *WhoScE 91-3*
Schramm, Howard Murfee, Jr. 1942- *St&PR 93*
Schramm, John Clarendon 1908- *WhoAm 92*
Schramm, Karin 1940- *WhoUN 92*
Schramm, Louis C. d1990 *BioIn 17*
Schramm, Margit 1935- *Baker 92*
Schramm, Marilyn J. *Law&B 92*
Schramm, Marilyn Jean 1951- *WhoAmW 93*
Schramm, Melchior c. 1553-1619 *Baker 92*
Schramm, Patricia Cain 1937- *WhoE 93*
Schramm, Rachel Fleischmann 1929- *WhoWrEP 92*
Schramm, Richard M. 1940- *St&PR 93*
Schramm, Ryszard Wiktor 1920- *WhoWor 93*
Schramm, Tex *BioIn 17*
Schramm, Texas E. 1920- *WhoAm 92*
Schramm, Texas Ernest, Jr. 1920- *BiDAMSp 1989*
Schramm, W.M. *St&PR 93*
Schramm, Werner 1939- *WhoScE 91-3*
Schramm, Werner Alfred 1939- *WhoWor 93*
Schramm, Wilbur 1907-1987 *ScF&FL 92*
Schramm, Wilbur Lang 1907-1987 *BioIn 17*
Schrandt, David T. 1947- *St&PR 93*
Schrang, Michael Scott *Law&B 92*
Schrank, Philip 1957- *St&PR 93*
Schrankel, Kenneth Reinhold 1945- *WhoE 93*
Schrantz, G. Mons 1936- *St&PR 93*

Schrantz, Stephen J. 1949- *St&PR 93*
Schratz, Walter Alfred 1922- *WhoE 93*
Schraut, Kenneth Charles 1913- *WhoAm 92*
Schrauth, William Lawrence 1935- *WhoAm 92*
Schrayer, Diane Wightman 1943- *St&PR 93*
Schreadley, Richard Lee 1931- *WhoAm 92, WhoSSW 93*
Schreber, Daniel Paul 1842-1911 *BioIn 17*
Schreck, George Charles *Law&B 92*
Schreck, Gustav 1849-1918 *Baker 92*
Schreck, James F. 1940- *St&PR 93*
Schreck, Patricia A. *Law&B 92*
Schreck, Richard Henry 1934- *St&PR 93*
Schreckenberg, Gervasia Mary 1916- *WhoAmW 93*
Schreckinger, Sy Edward 1937- *WhoAm 92*
Schrecongost, James Ray 1946- *St&PR 93*
Schreer, Andrew *Law&B 92*
Schreffler, Samuel John 1945- *St&PR 93*
Schrefler, Bernhard A. 1942- *WhoScE 91-3*
Schrefler, Bernhard Aribo 1942- *WhoWor 93*
Schregenberger, Martin Niklaus Wilhelm 1947- *WhoWor 93*
Schreger, I. *Law&B 92*
Schrei, Rudolph L. 1909- *St&PR 93*
Schreiber, Alfred Lawrence 1945- *WhoAm 92*
Schreiber, Bertram Manuel 1940- *WhoAm 92*
Schreiber, Charlotte Elizabeth Bertie Guest 1812-1895 *BioIn 17*
Schreiber, Clayton John 1946- *St&PR 93*
Schreiber, David N. *St&PR 93*
Schreiber, Donald R. *St&PR 93*
Schreiber, Edward 1930-1991 *BioIn 17*
Schreiber, Edward 1943- *WhoWor 93*
Schreiber, Eileen Sher 1925- *WhoAmW 93*
Schreiber, Elliott Harold 1933- *WhoE 93*
Schreiber, Eugene Ralph 1939- *WhoE 93*
Schreiber, Frederick 1895-1985 *Baker 92*
Schreiber, Friedrich Gustav 1817-1889 *Baker 92*
Schreiber, Gaby c. 1912-1991 *AnObit 1991*
Schreiber, George Richard 1922- *WhoAm 92*
Schreiber, Gerard T. 1942- *St&PR 93*
Schreiber, Gus 1915- *WhoSSW 93*
Schreiber, H. Mark 1950- *WhoE 93*
Schreiber, Harvey K. *ScF&FL 92*
Schreiber, Hope Ellen 1951- *WhoAmW 93*
Schreiber, James G. 1949- *St&PR 93*
Schreiber, Jean-Jacques Servan- *BioIn 17*
Schreiber, Joachim 1956- *St&PR 93*
Schreiber, Judy Ann 1952- *WhoE 93*
Schreiber, Klaus 1927- *WhoScE 91-3*
Schreiber, Kurt Clark 1922- *WhoE 93*
Schreiber, Kurt G. *Law&B 92*
Schreiber, Kurt Gilbert 1946- *St&PR 93*
Schreiber, Larry L. 1949- *WhoIns 93*
Schreiber, Larry S. 1941- *St&PR 93*
Schreiber, Leonard Irwin 1914- *St&PR 93*
Schreiber, Marc Elliot 1951- *St&PR 93*
Schreiber, Mark 1960- *WhoWrEP 92*
Schreiber, Marvin Mandel 1925- *WhoAm 92*
Schreiber, Melvyn Hirsh 1931- *WhoAm 92*
Schreiber, Michel 1937- *WhoScE 91-2*
Schreiber, Paul Solomon 1941- *WhoAm 92*
Schreiber, Raymond Gary 1940- *St&PR 93*
Schreiber, Robert R. 1942- *St&PR 93*
Schreiber, Ron 1934- *WhoWrEP 92*
Schreiber, Ronald 1938- *WhoSSW 93*
Schreiber, Selma Emdin 1918- *St&PR 93*
Schreiber, Sharron Kay 1951- *WhoSSW 93*
Schreiber, Sol Joseph 1916- *St&PR 93*
Schreiber, Steven L. 1942- *WhoE 93, WhoWor 93*
Schreiber, Suydam Van Zandt 1939- *St&PR 93*
Schreiber, Suzanne E. 1936- *WhoWrEP 92*
Schreiber, Thelma 1918- *St&PR 93*
Schreiber, William Francis 1925- *WhoAm 92*
Schreiber, Wolfgang 1935- *WhoScE 91-3*
Schreibman, Myrl A. *MiSFD 9*
Schreick, Josef *BioIn 17*
Schreick, Josef A. 1951- *WhoE 93*
Schreier, Gunter 1958- *WhoWor 93*
Schreier, Jeffrey B. *Law&B 92*
Schreier, Leonard 1934- *WhoAm 92*
Schreier, Peter 1935- *OxDcOp, WhoAm 92*
Schreier, Peter 1942- *WhoScE 91-3*
Schreier, Peter (Max) 1935- *Baker 92, IntDcOp*
Schreiner, Adolf 1929- *WhoScE 91-3*
Schreiner, Albert William 1926- *WhoAm 92*
Schreiner, Christopher Stephen 1956- *WhoE 93*
Schreiner, David Nathan 1921-1945 *BiDAMSp 1989*
Schreiner, Edward A. 1926- *St&PR 93*
Schreiner, Frances Homer *AmWomPl*
Schreiner, George E. 1922- *WhoAm 92*
Schreiner, John Chambers *Law&B 92*
Schreiner, John Christian 1933- *WhoAm 92*
Schreiner, Lillian Stair *AmWomPl*
Schreiner, Olive 1855-1920 *BioIn 17, BritWr S2, IntLitE*
Schreiner, Richard *St&PR 93*
Schreiner, Robert George 1925- *WhoAm 92*
Schreiner, Robert K. 1948- *St&PR 93*
Schreiner, Samuel A(gnew), Jr. 1921- *SmATA 70 [port]*
Schreiner, Thomas Edward *Law&B 92*
Schreiner, Werner E. 1921- *WhoScE 91-4*
Schreiner, William *MiSFD 9*
Schreiter, James G. *Law&B 92*
Schreitmueller, John Paul 1953- *WhoSSW 93*
Schreker, Franz 1878-1934 *Baker 92, BioIn 17, IntDcOp [port], OxDcOp*
Schremp, Faith Maryanne 1921- *WhoAmW 93*
Schrempf, Robert J. 1932- *St&PR 93*
Schrenk, Edward L. 1940- *WhoIns 93*
Schrenk, Roger L. *Law&B 92*
Schrenk, Willi Juergen 1945- *WhoAm 92*
Schrett, Roy F. 1937- *St&PR 93*
Schretzmann, Charles F. 1943- *WhoAm 92*
Schreuder, Hein 1951- *WhoWor 93*
Schreurs, Dale Kenneth 1931- *St&PR 93*
Schreurs, Wil. H.P. 1942- *WhoScE 91-3*
Schrevel, Joseph 1939- *WhoScE 91-2*
Schrevel, Joseph Desire 1939- *WhoWor 93*
Schrevens, Eddie 1955- *WhoScE 91-2*
Schreyer, George 1739-1819 *BioIn 17*
Schreyer, George 1771?- *BioIn 17*
Schreyer, Lothar 1886-1966 *BioIn 17*
Schreyer, Nancy Kraft 1952- *WhoAmW 93*
Schreyer, Richard *BioIn 17*
Schreyer, Werner Friedrich 1930- *WhoScE 91-3*
Schreyer, William A. 1928- *St&PR 93*
Schriber, Jonathan David 1951- *WhoE 93*
Schriber, Thomas Jude 1935- *WhoAm 92*
Schrichte, Dellzell 1962- *WhoWrEP 92*
Schricker, David E. *Law&B 92*
Schridde, Daniel *BioIn 17*
Schrider, Leo A. 1939- *WhoAm 92*
Schrieber, Leslie 1948- *WhoWor 93*
Schriefer, Dirk 1943- *WhoUN 92*
Schriefers, Herbert 1924- *WhoScE 91-3*
Schrieffer, John Robert 1931- *WhoAm 92, WhoSSW 93, WhoWor 93*
Schriener, Judy A. 1949- *WhoWrEP 92*
Schrier, Arnold 1925- *WhoAm 92, WhoWrEP 92*
Schrier, Helene T. 1963- *WhoAmW 93*
Schrier, Jack Joseph 1932- *WhoE 93*
Schrier, Robert William 1936- *WhoAm 92*
Schrier, Stan 1935- *St&PR 93*
Schrier, Stanley Leonard 1929- *WhoAm 92*
Schriesheim, Alan 1930- *WhoAm 92*
Schriever, Bernard A. *BioIn 17*
Schriever, Bernard Adolph 1910- *WhoAm 92*
Schriever, Fred M. 1930- *St&PR 93*
Schriever, Fred Martin 1930- *WhoAm 92*
Schrimpe, Maureen 1945- *WhoAmW 93*
Schrimper, Vernon L. 1933- *St&PR 93, WhoAm 92*
Schrimpf, Sherry Ann 1957- *St&PR 93*
Schriner, Sweeney 1911-1990 *BioIn 17*
Schriver, Byron, Jr. 1936- *St&PR 93*
Schrock, Harold Arthur 1915- *WhoAm 92*
Schrock, Rosalind 1937- *WhoAmW 93*
Schrock, Virgil Edwin 1926- *WhoAm 92*
Schroder *Baker 92*
Schroder, Alwin 1855-1928 *Baker 92*
Schroder, Dieter Karl 1935- *WhoAm 92*
Schroder, Donald K. *St&PR 93*
Schroder, E. *WhoScE 91-3*
Schroder, Friedrich 1744-1816 *OxDcOp*
Schroder, Friedrich Gerhard 1929- *WhoScE 91-3*
Schroder, Gerhard 1910-1989 *BioIn 17*
Schroder, Hanning 1896-1987 *Baker 92*
Schroder, Harald Bertel 1924- *WhoAm 92*
Schroder, Hermann 1843-1909 *Baker 92*
Schroder, J. Michael 1937- *WhoScE 91-3*
Schroder, Jaap 1925- *Baker 92*
Schroder, Jens 1909- *Baker 92*
Schroder, Josef 1937- *WhoWor 93*
Schroder, Karl 1816-1890 *Baker 92*
Schroder, Karl 1848-1935 *Baker 92*
Schroder, Richard F. 1955- *St&PR 93*
Schroder, Robert Lanzon *Law&B 92*
Schroder, Sophie Burger 1781-1868 *OxDcOp*
Schroder, Ulrich 1935- *WhoScE 91-3*
Schroder Alphons, Emile 1942- *WhoWor 93*
Schroder-Devrient, Wilhelmine 1804-1860 *Baker 92, IntDcOp [port], OxDcOp*
Schroder-Feinen, Ursula 1936- *Baker 92*
Schrodinger, Erwin 1887-1961 *BioIn 17*
Schrodt, Ariel G. 1927- *St&PR 93*
Schrodt, George Randolph 1928- *WhoAm 92*
Schroedel, Herman L. 1931- *St&PR 93*
Schroedel, Lou 1931- *St&PR 93*
Schroeder, A. *WhoScE 91-2*
Schroeder, Aaron Harold 1926- *WhoAm 92*
Schroeder, Alan 1961- *BioIn 17*
Schroeder, Alfred Christian 1915- *WhoAm 92*
Schroeder, Andreas 1946- *WhoCanL 92*
Schroeder, Andreas (Peter) 1946- *ConAu 37NR*
Schroeder, Barbet 1941- *MiSFD 9*
Schroeder, Binette 1939- *BioIn 17*
Schroeder, Charles E. 1935- *St&PR 93*
Schroeder, Charles Edgar 1935- *WhoAm 92*
Schroeder, Charles Henry 1942- *WhoAm 92*
Schroeder, Cheryl Ann 1960- *WhoAmW 93, WhoWrEP 92*
Schroeder, Christian 1945- *WhoScE 91-2*
Schroeder, David Harold 1940- *WhoWor 93*
Schroeder, David J. Dean 1942- *WhoSSW 93*
Schroeder, David Lawrence 1945- *WhoE 93*
Schroeder, David Lawrence 1954- *St&PR 93*
Schroeder, Denny *St&PR 93*
Schroeder, Dirk Philipp 1953- *WhoWor 93*
Schroeder, Dolores K. *Law&B 92*
Schroeder, Don R. 1948- *St&PR 93*
Schroeder, Donald Perry 1930- *WhoAm 92*
Schroeder, Douglas Fredrick 1935- *WhoAm 92*
Schroeder, Edward Herman 1935- *St&PR 93*
Schroeder, Frank C. *MiSFD 9*
Schroeder, Fred Erich Harald 1932- *WhoAm 92*
Schroeder, Frederick John, Jr. 1934- *St&PR 93*
Schroeder, Frederick William 1928- *WhoSSW 93*
Schroeder, Fritz H. 1937- *WhoScE 91-3*
Schroeder, G.A. *WhoScE 91-3*
Schroeder, Gary Steven 1951- *WhoWrEP 92*
Schroeder, Gary William 1958- *WhoSSW 93*
Schroeder, H.B.W. *St&PR 93*
Schroeder, Han d1992 *BioIn 17*
Schroeder, Harold Kenneth, Jr. 1936- *WhoAm 92*
Schroeder, Harry William, Jr. 1952- *WhoSSW 93*
Schroeder, Henry, Jr. 1932- *WhoE 93*
Schroeder, Herman Elbert 1915- *WhoAm 92*
Schroeder, Herman F. *Law&B 92*
Schroeder, Hubert Ernst 1931- *WhoScE 91-4*
Schroeder, Jack Walter 1925- *WhoAm 92*
Schroeder, James C. *Law&B 92*
Schroeder, Jean William 1916- *WhoWor 93*
Schroeder, John G. *St&PR 93*
Schroeder, John H. 1920- *St&PR 93*
Schroeder, John H. 1943- *WhoAm 92*
Schroeder, John Louis 1930- *WhoAm 92*
Schroeder, John Speer 1937- *WhoAm 92*
Schroeder, John W. *Law&B 92*
Schroeder, Jorg-Ulrich 1953- *WhoWor 93*
Schroeder, Joseph James 1960- *WhoSSW 93*
Schroeder, Kathleen Audrey 1959- *WhoWrEP 92*
Schroeder, Keith Carl 1936- *St&PR 93*
Schroeder, Kenneth 1943- *WhoAm 92*
Schroeder, Lawrence R. 1941- *St&PR 93*
Schroeder, Leila Obier 1925- *WhoWor 93*
Schroeder, M.R. 1926- *BioIn 17*
Schroeder, Manfred Franz 1930- *St&PR 93*
Schroeder, Manfred Robert 1926- *BioIn 17, ConAu 138, WhoScE 91-3*
Schroeder, Mary E. *Law&B 92*
Schroeder, Mary Margaret *Law&B 92*
Schroeder, Mary Murphy 1940- *WhoAm 92, WhoAmW 93*
Schroeder, Michael 1952- *MiSFD 9*
Schroeder, Michael J. 1957- *St&PR 93*
Schroeder, Mike F. 1957- *WhoWrEP 92*
Schroeder, Neil Rolf 1930- *WhoE 93*
Schroeder, Patricia *BioIn 17*
Schroeder, Patricia 1940- *CngDr 91*
Schroeder, Patricia Richards 1951- *WhoAmW 93*
Schroeder, Patricia Scott 1940- *WhoAm 92, WhoAmW 93*
Schroeder, Richard Philip 1951- *WhoE 93, WhoEmL 93*
Schroeder, Rita Iilene 1935- *WhoAmW 93*
Schroeder, Rita Molthen 1922- *WhoAmW 93, WhoWor 93*
Schroeder, Robert Anthony 1912- *WhoAm 92, WhoWor 93*
Schroeder, Robert Engle 1929- *WhoWrEP 92*
Schroeder, Robert L. 1927- *St&PR 93*
Schroeder, Robert R. *Law&B 92*
Schroeder, Roland M. 1936- *St&PR 93*
Schroeder, Roy George 1936- *St&PR 93*
Schroeder, Stephanie Lynn 1962- *WhoSSW 93*
Schroeder, Stephen Kenneth *Law&B 92*
Schroeder, Steven Alfred 1939- *WhoAm 92*
Schroeder, Steven Clifford 1958- *St&PR 93*
Schroeder, Steven Forrest 1957- *WhoSSW 93*
Schroeder, Susan Hill 1948- *WhoAmW 93*
Schroeder, W.F. 1932- *St&PR 93*
Schroeder, Wayne Harold 1944- *WhoWor 93*
Schroeder, William 1947- *St&PR 93*
Schroeder, William Henry 1929- *St&PR 93*
Schroeder, William John 1944- *St&PR 93, WhoAm 92*
Schroeder, William Paul 1953- *WhoSSW 93*
Schroeder, Wolfgang 1941- *WhoScE 91-3*
Schroeder-Kurth, Traute M. 1930- *WhoScE 91-3*
Schroedter, Thomas P. *Law&B 92*
Schroeer, Dietrich 1938- *WhoAm 92*
Schroeher, Bruce Charles 1940- *WhoIns 93*
Schroeher, Kathy Jean *Law&B 92*
Schroepfer, George John, Jr. 1932- *WhoAm 92, WhoWor 93*
Schroepfer, Laurence James *Law&B 92*
Schroer, Barbara Claire 1958- *WhoAmW 93*
Schroer, Edmund A. 1928- *St&PR 93*
Schroer, Edmund Armin 1928- *WhoAm 92*
Schroer, Gene Eldon 1927- *WhoWor 93*
Schroer, Heinz J.A. 1922- *WhoScE 91-3*
Schroer, Richard Allen 1944- *WhoE 93*
Schroer-Lamont, Anne Christine 1944- *WhoAmW 93, WhoSSW 93*
Schroeter, Arnold L. 1936- *WhoAm 92*
Schroeter, Johann Samuel c. 1752-1788 *Baker 92*
Schroeter, Louis C. 1929- *WhoAm 92*
Schroeter, Louis Clarence 1929- *St&PR 93*
Schroetter, Gina Marie 1960- *WhoAmW 93*
Schroff, Peter David 1926- *WhoE 93*
Schroit, Joel 1945- *St&PR 93*
Schroll, Carol A. 1947- *St&PR 93*
Schroll, Edwin John 1941- *WhoE 93*
Schroll, Eleanor Allen *AmWomPl*
Schroll, Erich 1923- *WhoScE 91-4*
Schroll, Loren E. *St&PR 93*
Schroller, Christine Marie 1950- *WhoAmW 93, WhoEmL 93*
Schrom, Elizabeth Ann 1941- *WhoAmW 93, WhoWor 93*
Schron, Dean *Law&B 92*
Schronk, Wendell Earl 1951- *WhoSSW 93*
Schropfer, David Waldron 1939- *WhoE 93*
Schropp, James Howard 1943- *WhoAm 92*
Schropp, Mary Lou 1947- *WhoAmW 93*
Schrote, John Ellis 1936- *WhoAm 92, WhoE 93*
Schroter *Baker 92*
Schroter, Christoph Gottlieb 1699-1782 *Baker 92*
Schroter, Corona 1751-1802 *Baker 92, BioIn 17, OxDcOp*
Schroter, Egon Horst 1928- *WhoScE 91-3*
Schroter, Heinrich c. 1760-1782 *Baker 92*
Schroter, Joachim 1931- *WhoScE 91-3*
Schroter, Johann Friedrich 1724-1811 *Baker 92*
Schroter, Leonhart c. 1532-c. 1601 *Baker 92*
Schroter, Marie Henriette 1766-c. 1804 *Baker 92*
Schroth, C. William 1948- *St&PR 93*
Schroth, James L. 1933- *St&PR 93*
Schroth, Peter W. *Law&B 92*

Schroth, Peter William 1946- *WhoAm 92, WhoE 93, WhoWor 93*
Schroth, Thomas Nolan 1920- *WhoAm 92*
Schrott, John D. 1947- *St&PR 93*
Schrottky, Oleda *AmWomPl*
Schrottmaier, Johann 1948- *WhoScE 91-4*
Schroyer, Connie Joan 1962- *WhoAmW 93*
Schruben, Johanna Stenzel 1944- *WhoSSW 93*
Schruben, John Henry 1926- *WhoAm 92*
Schrum, Ed P. 1927- *WhoAm 92*
Schrumpf, David W. *Law&B 92*
Schrumpf, Jane R. *Law&B 92*
Schrumpf, Robyn Lynn 1959- *WhoAmW 93, WhoEmL 93, WhoWor 93*
Schryer, William Martin 1951- *St&PR 93*
Schryock, Buren 1881-1974 *Baker 92*
Schryver, Richard E. 1931- *St&PR 93*
Schu, Michael E. *Law&B 92*
Schub, Andre-Michel 1952- *Baker 92*
Schuback, Marc G. *Law&B 92*
Schubart, Christian Friedrich Daniel 1739-1791 *Baker 92, BioIn 17*
Schubart, Mark Allen 1918- *WhoAm 92*
Schubarth, Glena Lynne Needham 1957- *WhoAmW 93*
Schubauer, James W. 1934- *St&PR 93*
Schubauer, James William 1934- *WhoAm 92*
Schubaur, Johann Lukas 1749?-1815 *Baker 92*
Schubel, Frederick P. 1932- *St&PR 93*
Schubel, Jerry Robert 1936- *WhoAm 92*
Schubel, Max 1932- *Baker 92*
Schuber, Francis J. 1941- *WhoScE 91-2*
Schubert, Anton 1766-1853 *Baker 92*
Schubert, Barbara Schuele 1939- *WhoAm 92*
Schubert, Clayton 1937- *St&PR 93*
Schubert, Deane E. 1941- *WhoAm 92*
Schubert, Dieter 1947- *BioIn 17*
Schubert, Edmund F., Jr. 1936- *St&PR 93, WhoIns 93*
Schubert, Elaine Elisabeth 1947- *St&PR 93*
Schubert, Esther Virginia 1945- *WhoAmW 93*
Schubert, Ferdinand (Lukas) 1794-1859 *Baker 92*
Schubert, Franz 1797-1828 *BioIn 17, IntDcOp, OxDcOp*
Schubert, Franz 1808-1878 *Baker 92*
Schubert, Franz Anton 1768-1827 *Baker 92*
Schubert, Franz (Peter) 1797-1828 *Baker 92*
Schubert, Georgine 1840-1878 *Baker 92*
Schubert, Glendon 1918- *WhoAm 92*
Schubert, Gotthilf Heinrich 1780-1860 *BioIn 17*
Schubert, Guenther Erich 1930- *WhoWor 93*
Schubert, Helen C. *WhoAmW 93*
Schubert, Helmar 1939- *WhoScE 91-3*
Schubert, Helmut Josef 1950- *WhoWor 93*
Schubert, Hiltmar A.O. 1927- *WhoScE 91-3*
Schubert, Ingrid 1953- *BioIn 17*
Schubert, James Ronald 1932- *St&PR 93*
Schubert, Janet Lee 1952- *WhoAmW 93*
Schubert, John Edward 1912- *WhoAm 92*
Schubert, Joseph H. 1938- *St&PR 93*
Schubert, Kathryn Ilyne 1941- *WhoAmW 93*
Schubert, Klaus R. 1939- *WhoScE 91-3*
Schubert, Kurt Heinrich 1926- *WhoWor 93*
Schubert, Leo Gilbert 1954- *WhoSSW 93*
Schubert, Louis 1828-1884 *Baker 92*
Schubert, Maschinka 1815-1882 *See* Schubert family *Baker 92*
Schubert, Richard Francis 1936- *WhoAm 92*
Schubert, Robert William, Jr. 1952- *WhoWor 93*
Schubert, Ronald Walter 1937- *WhoE 93*
Schubert, Ulrich *WhoScE 91-3*
Schubert, William C. *Law&B 92*
Schubert, William C. 1940- *St&PR 93*
Schubert, William Kuenneth 1926- *WhoAm 92*
Schubert, William L. 1943- *St&PR 93*
Schubert family *Baker 92*
Schuberth *Baker 92*
Schuberth, Carl 1811-1863 *Baker 92*
Schuberth, Friedrich (Wilhelm August) 1817-c. 1890 *Baker 92*
Schuberth, Gottlob 1778-1846 *Baker 92*
Schuberth, Julius (Ferdinand Georg) 1804-1875 *Baker 92*
Schuberth, Ludwig 1806-1850 *Baker 92*
Schubiger, Anselm 1815-1888 *Baker 92*
Schubring, Wolf-Dietrich 1941- *WhoWor 93*
Schuch, Ernst von 1846-1914 *Baker 92, IntDcOp, OxDcOp*
Schuch, Liesel von 1891-1990 *OxDcOp* *See Also* Schuch, Ernst von 1846-1914 *Baker 92*
Schuchardt, Daniel Norman 1937- *St&PR 93*
Schuchart, John Albert 1929- *St&PR 93*
Schuchart, John Albert, Jr. 1929- *WhoAm 92*
Schuchart, Wayne Joseph 1949- *St&PR 93*
Schuchinski, Luis *Law&B 92*
Schuchman, Ellen 1953- *WhoAmW 93*
Schuchman, Frederick E., III *Law&B 92*
Schuch-Proska, Klementine 1850-1932 *OxDcOp*
Schucht, John F. 1944- *St&PR 93*
Schuchter, Wilhelm 1911-1974 *Baker 92*
Schuck, Carl Joseph 1915- *WhoAm 92*
Schuck, Marjorie Massey 1921- *WhoAmW 93, WhoWrEP 92*
Schuck, Mary *BioIn 17*
Schuck, Peter H. 1940- *WhoAm 92*
Schuck, Robert Nelson 1936- *St&PR 93*
Schuck, Victoria 1909- *WhoAm 92, WhoAmW 93, WhoE 93, WhoWor 93*
Schuckard, John Daryle 1947- *St&PR 93*
Schucker, Charles 1908- *WhoE 93*
Schucker, Gerald Delano 1936- *WhoE 93*
Schuckman, Nancy Lee 1939- *WhoAmW 93*
Schudel, Hansjoerg 1937- *WhoAm 92*
Schudel, Thomas 1937- *Baker 92*
Schuder, Raymond Francis 1926- *WhoSSW 93*
Schudmak, Mel E. 1948- *St&PR 93*
Schudrich, David d1990 *BioIn 17*
Schudy, Patricia Hellingen 1939- *WhoWrEP 92*
Schuebelin, Peter Walter 1940- *WhoWor 93*
Schuecker, Edmund 1860-1911 *Baker 92*
Schueffel, Dieter Wolfram 1938- *WhoScE 91-3*
Schueffner, Dale Willard 1947- *WhoIns 93*
Schuehle, Jake *St&PR 93*
Schuele, Alban Wilhelm 1944- *WhoE 93*
Schuele, Donald Edward 1934- *WhoAm 92*
Schueler, Carey *BioIn 17*
Schueler, Carrol Guerrant 1949- *St&PR 93*
Schueler, Horst *Law&B 92*
Schueler, James Robert 1947- *St&PR 93*
Schueler, Jon 1916-1992 *NewYTBS 92 [port]*
Schueler, T.M. 1963- *St&PR 93*
Schuelka, B. Leora Davis 1931- *WhoAmW 93*
Schuelke, Constance Patricia 1953- *WhoAmW 93, WhoSSW 93, WhoWor 93*
Schuellein, Robert Joseph 1920- *WhoE 93*
Schueller, Thomas George 1936- *WhoAm 92*
Schuemann, Douglas L. 1939- *St&PR 93*
Schuenke, Donald J. 1929- *St&PR 93, WhoIns 93*
Schueppert, George L. 1938- *St&PR 93*
Schueppert, George Louis 1938- *WhoAm 92*
Schuerer, Ernst 1933- *ConAu 37NR*
Schuerholz, John Boland, Jr. 1940- *WhoAm 92, WhoSSW 93*
Schuerman, Janice Constance 1947- *St&PR 93*
Schuerman, John Richard 1938- *WhoAm 92*
Schuermann, David C. 1943- *St&PR 93*
Schuermann, Frederick L. 1946- *St&PR 93*
Schuermann, Kay Uwe 1939- *WhoWor 93*
Schuermann, Lisa Ann 1958- *WhoAmW 93*
Schuessler, Annemarie 1951- *WhoAmW 93*
Schuessler, Arthur P., Jr. 1947- *WhoIns 93*
Schuessler, John T. 1950- *St&PR 93*
Schuessler, Karl Frederick 1915- *WhoAm 92*
Schuessler, Morgan McGueen 1935- *St&PR 93*
Schuessler, Morgan McQueen 1935- *WhoAm 92*
Schuessler, Richard D. 1942- *St&PR 93*
Schuessler, Richard Jay 1938- *WhoE 93*
Schuessler, Robert W. 1946- *St&PR 93*
Schuessler, Walter E. 1913- *St&PR 93*
Schuessler Fiorenza, Elisabeth 1938- *WhoAm 92, WhoAmW 93*
Schueth, Steven Jerome 1954- *WhoE 93*
Schuette, Henry William 1923- *St&PR 93*
Schuette, Janice J. *St&PR 93*
Schuette, John H., Jr. 1924- *St&PR 93*
Schuette, Mary Kathryn *Law&B 92*
Schuette, Michael 1937- *WhoAm 92*
Schuette, Richard Francis *Law&B 92*
Schuette, Timothy Mark 1955- *St&PR 93*
Schuetterle, Georg 1928- *WhoScE 91-3*
Schuetz, Michael David 1959- *WhoE 93*
Schuetze, Frederik Edwin 1947- *WhoE 93*
Schuetzenduebel, Wolfram Gerhard 1932- *WhoAm 92, WhoSSW 93*
Schuetz-Mueller, Ingolf R. 1939- *WhoUN 92*
Schuff, H.O. *WhoScE 91-3*
Schuff, Karen Elizabeth 1937- *WhoWrEP 92*
Schuftan, Gideon *St&PR 93*
Schug, Kenneth Robert 1924- *WhoAm 92*
Schug, Linda Louise 1951- *St&PR 93*
Schug, Ric Andrew 1951- *WhoE 93*
Schuh, Erich *WhoScE 91-4*
Schuh, Frank Joseph 1935- *WhoAm 92*
Schuh, George Edward 1930- *WhoAm 92*
Schuh, Willi 1900-1986 *Baker 92*
Schuhmann, Reinhardt, Jr. 1914- *WhoAm 92*
Schuiling, Roelof Louis 1935- *WhoSSW 93*
Schuitema, David L. 1954- *St&PR 93*
Schuitemaker, Jan Jacob 1924- *WhoScE 91-3*
Schuk, Linda Lee 1946- *WhoAmW 93*
Schukai, Robert Joseph 1938- *St&PR 93*
Schukar, Harry T. 1933- *St&PR 93*
Schuker, Eleanor Sheila 1941- *WhoE 93*
Schuker, Stephen Alan 1939- *WhoAm 92*
Schukken, Folkert 1935- *WhoAm 92*
Schuknecht, Harold Frederick 1917- *WhoAm 92*
Schukraft, Scott Alan 1960- *WhoE 93*
Schul, Robert Keyser 1937- *BiDAMSp 1989*
Schulberg, Arnold L. 1952- *WhoE 93*
Schulberg, Budd *BioIn 17*
Schulberg, Budd 1914- *JeAmFiW, WhoAm 92, WhoWrEP 92*
Schulberg, Herbert Charles 1934- *WhoE 93*
Schulberg, Jay William 1939- *WhoAm 92*
Schuldiner, Arthur P. 1930- *St&PR 93*
Schuldner, Tiberius H. 1940- *St&PR 93*
Schuldt, Michael Bruce 1951- *WhoWrEP 92*
Schule, Wolfgang 1930- *WhoWor 93*
Schulenburg, Toni Phillips 1958- *WhoAmW 93*
Schuler, Burton Silverman 1950- *WhoEmL 93, WhoSSW 93*
Schuler, C. Barr 1940- *St&PR 93*
Schuler, Daretia Mary Usselman 1953- *WhoAmW 93*
Schuler, Dezso 1927- *WhoScE 91-4*
Schuler, Dorthy Ann 1927- *WhoE 93*
Schuler, George Albert 1933- *WhoSSW 93*
Schuler, Herbert F. 1940- *St&PR 93*
Schuler, Jack William 1940- *St&PR 93, WhoAm 92*
Schuler, James Terry 1948- *WhoE 93*
Schuler, Johannes 1894-1966 *Baker 92*
Schuler, John Albert 1942- *St&PR 93*
Schuler, John Neville 1927- *St&PR 93*
Schuler, Lawrence D. *Law&B 92*
Schuler, Melvin L. 1944- *St&PR 93*
Schuler, Michael Aloysius 1950- *St&PR 93*
Schuler, Michael Harold 1940- *WhoAm 92*
Schuler, Paul A. 1933- *St&PR 93*
Schuler, Paul George *Law&B 92*
Schuler, Peter *Law&B 92*
Schuler, Richard Edward 1937- *WhoE 93*
Schuler, Robert Hugo 1926- *WhoAm 92*
Schuler, Robert Jordan 1939- *WhoWrEP 92*
Schuler, Ruth Wildes 1933- *WhoWrEP 92*
Schuler, Steven T. 1951- *St&PR 93*
Schuler, Theodore Anthony 1934- *WhoSSW 93*
Schuler, Wolfgang Alec 1942- *WhoWor 93*
Schulert, Arthur Robert 1922- *WhoSSW 93, WhoWor 93*
Schulfer, Roche Edward 1951- *WhoAm 92*
Schulhof, H. Tuck *Law&B 92*
Schulhof, Hugh Tuck 1936- *St&PR 93*
Schulhof, Michael P. *BioIn 17*
Schulhof, Michael Peter 1942- *WhoAm 92, WhoE 93*
Schulhofer, Stephen Joseph 1942- *WhoAm 92*
Schulhoff, Erwin 1894-1942 *Baker 92*
Schulhoff, Julius 1825-1898 *Baker 92*
Schulhoff, Petr 1922-1986 *DrEEuF*
Schulian, John 1945- *WhoAm 92*
Schulke, Gerald J. *Law&B 92*
Schulke, Herbert Ardis, Jr. 1923- *WhoAm 92*
Schulke, Lothar 1935- *WhoScE 91-3*
Schulkins, Andrew *WhoScE 91-1*
Schuller, Diane Ethel 1943- *WhoE 93, WhoWor 93*
Schuller, Frederik Christiaan 1940- *WhoScE 91-3*
Schuller, Gunther (Alexander) 1925- *Baker 92, WhoAm 92*
Schuller, Kevin C. *Law&B 92*
Schuller, Kevin Carl 1948- *St&PR 93*
Schuller, Kirby B. 1953- *St&PR 93*
Schuller, Mary Ann 1952- *WhoWrEP 92*
Schuller, Robert Harold *BioIn 17*
Schuller, Rodolfo R. 1873-1932 *BioIn 17*
Schuller, Stephen Arthur 1951- *WhoSSW 93*
Schully, Sherwin H. 1918- *St&PR 93*
Schulman, Barbara Jean 1954- *WhoSSW 93*
Schulman, Bruce David 1950- *WhoE 93*
Schulman, Claude C. 1943- *WhoScE 91-2*
Schulman, Harold 1930- *WhoAm 92*
Schulman, Harry D. 1951- *St&PR 93*
Schulman, Irving 1922- *WhoAm 92*
Schulman, J. Neil 1953- *ScF&FL 92*
Schulman, Janet Carol 1933- *WhoAm 92*
Schulman, John A. *Law&B 92*
Schulman, Joseph Daniel 1941- *WhoAm 92*
Schulman, LaDonne H. d1992 *NewYTBS 92*
Schulman, Lawrence S. 1941- *WhoE 93*
Schulman, Lester Martin *ScF&FL 92*
Schulman, Martin Fred 1943- *WhoE 93*
Schulman, Marvin 1927- *WhoE 93*
Schulman, Mary 1910- *WhoWrEP 92*
Schulman, Melvin Louis 1921- *St&PR 93*
Schulman, Michael D. 1948- *ConAu 137*
Schulman, Paul H. *ScF&FL 92*
Schulman, Paul Martin 1940- *WhoAm 92*
Schulman, Rachelle Stern *Law&B 92*
Schulman, Robert Glen 1952- *WhoE 93*
Schulman, Robert Ivan 1946- *WhoAm 92*
Schulman, Robert P. 1927- *St&PR 93*
Schulman, Sarah M. 1958- *WhoWrEP 92*
Schulman, Sidney 1923- *WhoAm 92*
Schulman, Tammy Beth 1960- *WhoWor 93*
Schulman, Tom *WhoAm 92*
Schulmann, Horst 1933- *WhoE 93*
Schulmeyer, Gerhard *BioIn 17*
Schulsinger, Michael Alan 1952- *WhoWor 93*
Schulson, Stephen S. *Law&B 92*
Schult, R.W. 1949- *St&PR 93*
Schult, Susan Marie 1961- *WhoAmW 93*
Schulte, David Michael 1946- *WhoAm 92*
Schulte, Erhard 1941- *WhoScE 91-3*
Schulte, Francis B. 1926- *WhoAm 92, WhoSSW 93*
Schulte, Frank 1882-1949 *BiDAMSp 1989*
Schulte, Fred C. 1946- *St&PR 93*
Schulte, Gary Richard 1940- *WhoAm 92*
Schulte, Gerard J., Jr. *Law&B 92*
Schulte, Henry Clyde 1921- *St&PR 93*
Schulte, Henry Frank 1924- *WhoAm 92*
Schulte, Horst 1949- *WhoScE 91-3*
Schulte, Jeffrey Lewis 1949- *WhoE 93*
Schulte, Jerome Frank 1931- *St&PR 93*
Schulte, John Kemp 1932- *WhoSSW 93*
Schulte, John W. 1949- *St&PR 93*
Schulte, Joseph Leonard Jr., Jr. 1943- *WhoAm 92*
Schulte, Joseph W. 1941- *St&PR 93*
Schulte, Josephine Helen 1929- *WhoSSW 93*
Schulte, Karl 1946- *WhoWor 93*
Schulte, Kathleen B. *Law&B 92*
Schulte, Loretta 1927- *WhoAmW 93*
Schulte, Nancy M. 1956- *WhoSSW 93*
Schulte, Patrick Leo 1933- *St&PR 93*
Schulte, Rainer 1937- *WhoWrEP 92*
Schulte, Stephen John 1938- *WhoAm 92*
Schulte, Thomas E. 1950- *WhoWor 93*
Schulte, Tim *Law&B 92*
Schulte-Hermann, Rolf 1939- *WhoScE 91-4*
Schulteis, Herm C. 1928- *St&PR 93*
Schulter, Albert Jack 1933- *WhoE 93*
Schulter-Ellis, Frances Pierce 1923- *WhoAm 92*
Schultes, Richard Evans *BioIn 17*
Schultes, Richard Evans 1915- *WhoAm 92*
Schultetus, Treft William 1916- *WhoSSW 93*
Schultheis, Carl Frank, Jr. 1930- *WhoE 93*
Schultheis, Edwin Milford 1928- *WhoE 93, WhoWor 93*
Schultheisz, Emil 1923- *WhoScE 91-4*
Schulthess, Walter 1894-1971 *Baker 92*
Schulthies, Ronald A. 1943- *St&PR 93*
Schulties, Charles Walter 1936- *St&PR 93*
Schultz, Albert Barry 1933- *WhoAm 92*
Schultz, Alexander *Law&B 92*
Schultz, Allen M. 1932- *St&PR 93*
Schultz, Alvin Leroy 1921- *WhoWor 93*
Schultz, Andrew Edward 1949- *WhoE 93*
Schultz, Andrew Schultz, Jr. 1913- *WhoAm 92*
Schultz, Arthur Joseph, Jr. 1918- *WhoAm 92, WhoWor 93*
Schultz, Arthur LeRoy 1928- *WhoWor 93*
Schultz, Arthur Warren 1922- *St&PR 93, WhoAm 92, WhoWor 93*

Schultz, Barbara Townsend 1929- WhoE 93
Schultz, Barry C. 1964- St&PR 93
Schultz, Blake BioIn 17
Schultz, Carl 1939- MiSFD 9
Schultz, Carl Herbert 1925- St&PR 93, WhoAm 92
Schultz, Carole Lamb 1946- WhoAmW 93
Schultz, Charles L. 1928- St&PR 93, WhoIns 93
Schultz, Clarence Carven, Jr. 1924- WhoAm 92, WhoSSW 93
Schultz, Curtis A. Law&B 92
Schultz, Daniel Joseph 1951- St&PR 93
Schultz, Darlene Kay 1952- WhoAm 92
Schultz, David E. 1952- ScF&FL 92
Schultz, Dina Renee 1966- WhoAmW 93
Schultz, Douglas George 1947- WhoAm 92, WhoE 93
Schultz, Edwin 1827-1907 Baker 92
Schultz, Eileen Hedy WhoAm 92
Schultz, Estelle Peterson 1935- WhoAmW 93
Schultz, Finis W. 1937- St&PR 93
Schultz, Frank 1938- St&PR 93
Schultz, Franklin M. 1917- WhoAm 92
Schultz, Frederick Carl 1929- St&PR 93
Schultz, Frederick H. BioIn 17
Schultz, Frederick Henry 1929- WhoAm 92
Schultz, George E. 1921- St&PR 93
Schultz, Gerald Alfred 1941- WhoE 93
Schultz, Gerald Emil 1929- St&PR 93
Schultz, Gerald Ernest 1941- WhoAm 92
Schultz, Gernot 1929- WhoScE 91-3
Schultz, Gert A. 1936- WhoScE 91-3
Schultz, H.W. 1934- St&PR 93
Schultz, Hans-Georg 1929- WhoScE 91-3
Schultz, Harald 1909-1965 IntDcAn
Schultz, Heidi Flynn 1949- WhoAm 92, WhoAmW 93
Schultz, J. WhoScE 91-2
Schultz, Jackson L. 1924- WhoAm 92
Schultz, Jackson L. 1925- St&PR 93
Schultz, James Clement 1934- St&PR 93
Schultz, James H. 1948- St&PR 93
Schultz, Jane Schwartz 1932- WhoE 93
Schultz, Jane Streimer Law&B 92
Schultz, Janet Darlene 1942- WhoAmW 93
Schultz, Jay Ward 1937- St&PR 93
Schultz, Jeffrey Eric 1948- WhoEmL 93
Schultz, Jerome Samson 1933- WhoAm 92
Schultz, K. David 1949- WhoE 93
Schultz, L. Ron 1932- St&PR 93
Schultz, Leland Duane Law&B 92
Schultz, Leslie Brown 1936- WhoAmW 93
Schultz, Leslie Page 1918- St&PR 93
Schultz, Linda Jane 1962- WhoAmW 93
Schultz, Linda Kathryn 1961- WhoAmW 93
Schultz, Lisa Claire 1958- WhoEmL 93
Schultz, Louis Michael 1944- WhoAm 92
Schultz, Louis William 1927- WhoAm 92
Schultz, Lucy J. 1962- WhoAmW 93
Schultz, Lynette Carol 1951- WhoSSW 93
Schultz, Manuel 1928- WhoAm 92
Schultz, Mary Lou 1943- WhoAmW 93
Schultz, Michael BioIn 17
Schultz, Michael 1938- MiSFD 9, WhoAm 92
Schultz, Michael A. 1938- ConTFT 10
Schultz, Michael Edward 1953- WhoWrEP 92
Schultz, Michael Victor 1951- WhoE 93
Schultz, Nancy Lusignan 1956- WhoWrEP 92
Schultz, Paul Oesterle 1958- WhoSSW 93
Schultz, Paull C. 1938- St&PR 93
Schultz, Per-Olov 1932- WhoWor 93
Schultz, Peter G. BioIn 17
Schultz, Philip 1945- WhoAm 92
Schultz, Philip (Arnold) 1945- WhoWrEP 92
Schultz, Philip Stephen 1947- WhoWor 93
Schultz, Phyllis May 1933- WhoAmW 93
Schultz, Richard Arthur 1936- WhoAm 92
Schultz, Richard Carlton 1927- WhoAm 92
Schultz, Richard D. 1929- BioIn 17
Schultz, Richard Dale 1929- WhoAm 92
Schultz, Richard Lang 1948- WhoSSW 93
Schultz, Richard Otto 1930- WhoAm 92
Schultz, Robert A. 1940- St&PR 93
Schultz, Robert J. 1930- WhoAm 92
Schultz, Robert L. BioIn 17
Schultz, Robert Vernon 1936- WhoWor 93
Schultz, Robert William 1938- WhoAm 92
Schultz, Ruby Ethel 1934- WhoAmW 93
Schultz, Ruth Anne 1953- WhoAmW 93
Schultz, Samuel Jacob 1914- WhoAm 92
Schultz, Sandra S. Law&B 92
Schultz, Shelly Irene 1953- WhoAmW 93, WhoWor 93
Schultz, Stanley George 1931- WhoAm 92
Schultz, Steven Alan 1953- WhoIns 93
Schultz, Svend (Simon) 1913- Baker 92
Schultz, T. Paul 1940- WhoAm 92
Schultz, Theodore Edward 1945- St&PR 93, WhoAm 92
Schultz, Theodore William 1902- WhoAm 92, WhoWor 93
Schultz, Thomas A. 1957- St&PR 93
Schultz, Thomas S. 1944- WhoE 93
Schultz, Timothy P. 1945- St&PR 93
Schultz, Trevor S. 1942- St&PR 93
Schultz, Ward Guy 1958- St&PR 93
Schultz, William Louis 1923- WhoAm 92
Schultze, Antoinette Prien 1944- WhoE 93
Schultze, Bernard 1915- BioIn 17
Schultze, Charles Louis 1924- WhoAm 92
Schultze, Ernst Eugene 1944- WhoWor 93
Schultze, Helmuth W. 1927- St&PR 93
Schultze, Joachim Walter 1937- WhoWor 93
Schultze, Norbert 1911- Baker 92
Schultze, Robert William 1939- St&PR 93
Schultze, Ronald D. 1937- St&PR 93
Schultze, Ulrich 1938- WhoScE 91-4
Schultze-Bluhm, Ursula BioIn 17
Schultze Jena, Leonhard 1872-1955 IntDcAn
Schulweis, Harold M. 1925- BioIn 17
Schulz, Alfred Adalbert 1926- WhoWor 93
Schulz, Bonnie Lou 1951- WhoAmW 93
Schulz, Bruno 1892-1942 PolBiDi
Schulz, Charles M. BioIn 17
Schulz, Charles M. 1922- JrnUS
Schulz, Charles Monroe 1922- WhoAm 92, WhoWor 93
Schulz, Christine June 1960- WhoAmW 93
Schulz, Dale Valdyn 1950- St&PR 93
Schulz, David M. 1945- St&PR 93
Schulz, Deborah Craft 1949- WhoAmW 93
Schulz, Douglas William Law&B 92
Schulz, Emma AmWomPl
Schulz, Gail Frances Law&B 92
Schulz, Georg E. 1939- WhoScE 91-3
Schulz, George D. 1938- St&PR 93
Schulz, Gerhard E. O. 1928- WhoWor 93
Schulz, Gretchen Kline 1948- WhoSSW 93
Schulz, Hartmut S.G. 1940- WhoScE 91-3
Schulz, Helmut Wilhelm 1912- WhoE 93, WhoWor 93
Schulz, Herbert 1936- WhoScE 91-3
Schulz, Horst 1924- WhoScE 91-3
Schulz, James F. 1940- St&PR 93
Schulz, James Lawrence 1937- St&PR 93
Schulz, Jill BioIn 17
Schulz, Joann R. BioIn 17
Schulz, Joann Rene 1945- WhoAmW 93
Schulz, Johann Abraham Peter 1747-1800 Baker 92, OxDcOp
Schulz, Johann Philipp Christian 1773-1827 Baker 92
Schulz, Juergen 1927- WhoE 93
Schulz, Karen Gayle 1959- WhoEmL 93
Schulz, Keith Donald 1938- WhoAm 92
Schulz, Leo-Clemens 1923- WhoScE 91-3
Schulz, Mary Elizabeth Law&B 92
Schulz, Max J. 1939- WhoScE 91-3
Schulz, Michael Anthony, Jr. 1934- WhoSSW 93
Schulz, Oskar 1923- WhoScE 91-4
Schulz, Otto 1902- St&PR 93
Schulz, Otto G. 1930- St&PR 93, WhoIns 93
Schulz, Pablo Carlos 1943- WhoWor 93
Schulz, Patricia Lynn 1957- WhoAmW 93
Schulz, Rainer Walter 1942- WhoWor 93
Schulz, Ralph Richard 1928- WhoAm 92
Schulz, Richard Burkart 1920- WhoAm 92, WhoSSW 93
Schulz, Robert Francis 1936- St&PR 93
Schulz, Robert P. Law&B 92
Schulz, Rockwell Irwin 1929- WhoAm 92
Schulz, Rudolph Walter 1930- WhoAm 92
Schulz, Wilfried 1939- WhoWor 93
Schulz, William J. 1946- St&PR 93
Schulz, William John Law&B 92
Schulz, William John 1946- WhoAm 92
Schulz-Beuthen, Heinrich 1838-1915 Baker 92
Schulze, Arthur Edward 1938- WhoSSW 93
Schulze, Arthur Robert 1931- St&PR 93
Schulze, Beth Lucille 1951- WhoAmW 93
Schulze, Catherine Ann 1950- WhoAmW 93
Schulze, Christian Andreas c. 1660-1699 Baker 92
Schulze, Dallas ScF&FL 92
Schulze, Doris ScF&FL 92
Schulze, Enika Hermine 1938- WhoWrEP 92
Schulze, Erwin E. 1925- St&PR 93
Schulze, Franz, Jr. 1927- WhoAm 92
Schulze, Franz, Jr. 1972- WhoWrEP 92
Schulze, Hans-Joachim 1934- Baker 92
Schulze, Herbert Ernest, Jr. 1932- St&PR 93
Schulze, Herbert Richard Law&B 92
Schulze, Horst BioIn 17, WhoAm 92
Schulze, Howard L. 1942- St&PR 93
Schulze, J. Andrew 1775-1852 BioIn 17
Schulze, John B. WhoAm 92
Schulze, Kenneth W. 1951- WhoWrEP 92
Schulze, Mark Levon 1958- WhoWor 93
Schulze, Matthias Michael 1964- WhoWor 93
Schulze, Max H. Law&B 92
Schulze, Max Henry 1939- St&PR 93
Schulze, R.A.P.J. WhoScE 91-3
Schulze, Richard T. 1929- CngDr 91
Schulze, Richard Taylor 1929- WhoAm 92, WhoE 93
Schulze, Richard Wilfred 1937- St&PR 93, WhoAm 92
Schulze, Robert Oscar 1922- WhoAm 92
Schulze, Suzanne McDaniel 1967- WhoSSW 93
Schulz-Ekloff, Gunter W.R. 1936- WhoScE 91-3
Schulz-Evler, Andrei 1852-1905 Baker 92
Schulz-Schwerin, Karl 1845-1913 Baker 92
Schulz-Widmar, Russell Eugene 1944- WhoAm 92
Schum, Stephen J. 1956- St&PR 93
Schumacher, Alan T. 1912-1991 BioIn 17
Schumacher, Charles W. 1915- St&PR 93
Schumacher, Cynthia Jo 1928- WhoAmW 93
Schumacher, Diane K. 1953- St&PR 93
Schumacher, Diane Kosmach Law&B 92
Schumacher, Edward W. 1916- St&PR 93
Schumacher, Emery Robert 1935- St&PR 93
Schumacher, Frederick Carl 1911- WhoAm 92
Schumacher, Gebhard Friederich Bernhard 1924- WhoAm 92
Schumacher, Genny WhoWrEP 92
Schumacher, Hans Heinrich 1933- WhoAm 92
Schumacher, Harold Henry 1910- BiDAMSp 1989
Schumacher, Harry Ralph 1933- WhoAm 92, WhoWor 93
Schumacher, Henry Jerold 1934- WhoAm 92
Schumacher, Howard S. 1935- St&PR 93
Schumacher, Jacques BioIn 17
Schumacher, Jessica Robins Law&B 92
Schumacher, Joel 1942- MiSFD 9
Schumacher, John C. 1935- St&PR 93
Schumacher, John Christian 1935- WhoAm 92
Schumacher, John William 1934- WhoE 93
Schumacher, Jon Lee 1937- WhoAm 92
Schumacher, Jon Robert 1937- St&PR 93
Schumacher, Joseph Charles 1911- WhoAm 92
Schumacher, Julie Alison 1958- WhoWrEP 92
Schumacher, Kevin V.B. Law&B 92
Schumacher, Kurt 1895-1952 ColdWar 1 [port], DcTwHis
Schumacher, Leslie Smith 1956- St&PR 93
Schumacher, Norbert 1936- St&PR 93
Schumacher, Ray Fred 1942- WhoSSW 93
Schumacher, Richard H. 1955- St&PR 93
Schumacher, Robert 1929- WhoScE 91-4
Schumacher, Robert Denison 1933- WhoAm 92
Schumacher, Robert Joseph 1929- WhoAm 92
Schumacher, Sarah Sue 1949- WhoAmW 93
Schumacher, Stephen Joseph 1942- WhoWor 93
Schumacher, Udo WhoScE 91-1
Schumacher, Walter H. Law&B 92
Schumacher, Walter H. 1924- St&PR 93
Schumacher, Wilhelm 1928- WhoScE 91-3
Schumacher, William Jacob 1938- WhoAm 92
Schumack, Joan Maria 1953- WhoAmW 93, WhoWrEP 92
Schumacker, R.L.A. 1937- WhoScE 91-2
Schumaker, Dale H. 1933- St&PR 93
Schumaker, Larry Lee 1939- WhoAm 92, WhoSSW 93
Schumaker, Paul 1946- ConAu 139
Schumaker, W. James St&PR 93
Schuman, Chester D. 1949- WhoE 93
Schuman, David Feller 1942- WhoE 93
Schuman, David J. Law&B 92
Schuman, Diana C. WhoE 93
Schuman, Edwin Z. 1929- WhoAm 92
Schuman, Frank Albert 1944- St&PR 93
Schuman, Gary Law&B 92
Schuman, Gerald Eugene 1944- WhoAm 92
Schuman, Howard 1928- WhoAm 92
Schuman, Patricia 1943- BioIn 17
Schuman, Patricia Glass 1943- News 93-2 [port], WhoAmW 93
Schuman, Robert 1886-1963 BioIn 17, DcTwHis
Schuman, Robert James 1956- WhoE 93
Schuman, Sandor Paul 1951- WhoE 93
Schuman, Sid W., Jr. St&PR 93
Schuman, Thomas R. Law&B 92
Schuman, Wilfred Nicolaas 1952- WhoWor 93
Schuman, William d1992 NewYTBS 92
Schuman, William 1910-1992 BioIn 17, OxDcOp
Schuman, William (Howard) 1910- Baker 92
Schuman, William (Howard) 1910-1992 CurBio 92N
Schumann, Camillo 1872-1946 Baker 92
Schumann, Carole Ann 1959- WhoE 93
Schumann, Clara 1819-1896 BioIn 17
Schumann, Clara (Josephine) 1819-1896 Baker 92
Schumann, Elisabeth 1885-1952 IntDcOp [port]
Schumann, Elisabeth 1888-1952 Baker 92, OxDcOp
Schumann, Florence Ford d1991 BioIn 17
Schumann, Fritz 1939- WhoScE 91-3
Schumann, Georg (Alfred) 1866-1952 Baker 92
Schumann, Hans 1962- WhoWor 93
Schumann, Jim 1949- WhoWor 93
Schumann, Malcolm E. 1942- St&PR 93
Schumann, Maurice 1911- BioIn 17, WhoWor 93
Schumann, Merlin J. 1943- St&PR 93
Schumann, P. Richard St&PR 93
Schumann, Peter ScF&FL 92
Schumann, Robert 1810-1856 BioIn 17, OxDcOp
Schumann, Robert (Alexander) 1810-1856 Baker 92, IntDcOp
Schumann, Ulrich 1945- WhoScE 91-3
Schumann, Walter 1913-1958 Baker 92
Schumann, Walter 1927- WhoScE 91-4
Schumann, William F. 1939- St&PR 93
Schumann, William Frederick 1939- WhoAm 92
Schumann, William H. 1950- St&PR 93
Schumann, William Henry, III 1950- WhoAm 92
Schumann, William Robert 1942- WhoIns 93
Schumann, Willy 1927- BioIn 17
Schumann-Heink, Ernestine 1861-1936 Baker 92, GayN, IntDcOp, OxDcOp
Schumer, Arlen ScF&FL 92
Schumer, Charles E. BioIn 17
Schumer, Charles E. 1950- CngDr 91
Schumer, Charles Ellis 1950- WhoAm 92, WhoE 93
Schumer, Douglas Brian 1951- St&PR 93
Schumer, Gary BioIn 17
Schumer, Irwin P. 1931- St&PR 93
Schumer, William 1926- WhoAm 92
Schumitz, Elizabeth Dorothy 1935- WhoAmW 93
Schumm, Joseph J., Jr. 1944- St&PR 93
Schumm, Margot Kalberman 1929- WhoAmW 93
Schumm, Stanley Alfred 1927- WhoAm 92
Schumpe, Karl Gunter 1940- WhoScE 91-3
Schumpeter, Joseph Alois 1883-1950 BioIn 17
Schundler, Bruce E. 1948- St&PR 93
Schundler, Michael F. 1955- St&PR 93
Schundler, Peter Otto Law&B 92
Schundler, Robert Jeffrey 1945- St&PR 93
Schuneman, Norman Douglas 1942- St&PR 93
Schunemann, Georg 1884-1945 Baker 92
Schunemann, K.D. WhoScE 91-3
Schunke, Karl 1801-1839 Baker 92
Schunke, Ludwig 1810-1834 Baker 92
Schunke, Michael 1778-1821 See Schunke, Karl 1801-1839 Baker 92
Schupack, Andrew Larry 1953- St&PR 93
Schupack, Mark Barry 1931- WhoAm 92
Schupak, Leslie Allen 1945- WhoAm 92
Schupbach, Cortlan R., Jr. Law&B 92
Schupbach, Michelle Dee 1967- WhoAmW 93
Schupbach, Robecca F. Law&B 92
Schupp, Albert O. 1932- St&PR 93
Schupp, John R. Law&B 92
Schupp, Ronald Irving 1951- WhoWor 93
Schuppanzigh, Ignaz 1776-1830 Baker 92
Schur, Barbara E. Law&B 92
Schur, Jeffrey 1946- WhoAm 92
Schur, Leon Milton 1923- WhoAm 92
Schur, Norman W. BioIn 17
Schur, Norman W. d1992 NewYTBS 92
Schur, Norman W(arren) 1907- ConAu 37NR
Schur, Peter Henry 1933- WhoE 93
Schur, Susan Dorfman 1940- WhoAmW 93
Schur, Thomas P. Law&B 92

Schur, Walter Robert 1914- WhoE 93, WhoWor 93
Schure, Alexander 1921- WhoAm 92
Schure, Edouard 1841-1929 Baker 92
Schure, Matthew 1948- WhoAm 92
Schure, Teri WhoAmW 93
Schurer, Johann Georg c. 1720-1786 Baker 92
Schurer, K. 1931- WhoScE 91-3
Schurgast, Anselm W. 1921- WhoE 93
Schurger, Robert J. 1929- St&PR 93
Schuricht, Carl 1880-1967 Baker 92
Schuricht, Volkmar Adolf 1932- WhoUN 92
Schurig, Klaus 1942- WhoWor 93
Schurig, Volkmar (Julius Wilhelm) 1822-1899 Baker 92
Schurin, Ronald Charles 1949- WhoE 93
Schuring, Donna Hubbard 1938- WhoAmW 93
Schurman, Charles E. Law&B 92
Schurman, Donald Glenn 1933- WhoAm 92
Schurman, Joseph Rathborne 1924- WhoAm 92
Schurman, Juana M. Law&B 92
Schurman, Valerie K. Law&B 92
Schurmann, Georg Caspar 1672?-1751 Baker 92, OxDcOp
Schurmann, (Eduard) Gerard 1924- Baker 92
Schurmann, Gregor R. 1957- WhoWor 93
Schurmeier, L. Jon 1937- WhoAm 92
Schurr, Carolyn Law&B 92
Schurr, Gerald 1915-1989 BioIn 17
Schurr, Thierry Marie 1957- WhoWor 93
Schurre, Jacques 1902-1990 BioIn 17
Schursky, Melvin D. 1945- St&PR 93
Schurter, Bette Jo 1932- WhoAmW 93
Schurter, Dennis Dean 1942- WhoSSW 93
Schurz, Carl 1829-1906 BioIn 17, JrnUS, PolPar
Schurz, Franklin D., Jr. 1931- St&PR 93
Schurz, Franklin Dunn, Jr. 1931- WhoAm 92
Schurz, James Montgomery 1933- St&PR 93
Schurz, Josef 1924- WhoScE 91-4
Schuschnigg, Kurt von 1897-1977 DcTwHis
Schusler, Herbert Henry, II 1936- WhoSSW 93
Schussler, Irwin 1943- WhoSSW 93, WhoWor 93
Schussler, Samuel 1936- St&PR 93
Schussler, Theodore 1934- WhoAm 92, WhoE 93, WhoWor 93
Schuster, Allan D. St&PR 93, WhoAm 92, WhoIns 93
Schuster, Bernhard 1870-1934 Baker 92
Schuster, Charles Roberts 1930- WhoAm 92
Schuster, Elaine 1947- WhoAm 92
Schuster, Elizabeth K. Law&B 92
Schuster, Eugene I. 1936- St&PR 93
Schuster, Gary Benjamin 1946- WhoAm 92
Schuster, Gary F. 1942- St&PR 93
Schuster, Gary Francis 1942- WhoAm 92
Schuster, Gunter 1940- WhoScE 91-4
Schuster, Hal 1955- ScF&FL 92
Schuster, Hal Jan 1955- WhoWor 93
Schuster, Hans-Uwe 1930- WhoScE 91-3
Schuster, Harold d1986 MiSFD 9N
Schuster, Heinz 1927- WhoScE 91-3
Schuster, Helen Merci AmWomPl
Schuster, Ignaz 1779-1835 OxDcOp
Schuster, Ingeborg Ida 1937- WhoAmW 93
Schuster, Ingrid Hanna 1940- WhoWor 93
Schuster, Jack Clayton 1944- WhoWor 93
Schuster, Joseph 1748-1812 Baker 92
Schuster, Kenneth P. St&PR 93
Schuster, Lee R. 1934- St&PR 93
Schuster, Lois 1937- WhoAmW 93
Schuster, Melvin L. 1925- St&PR 93
Schuster, Monis 1931- St&PR 93
Schuster, Philip Arend Law&B 92
Schuster, Philip Frederick, II 1945- WhoWor 93
Schuster, Richard John 1944- St&PR 93
Schuster, Richard Louis 1945- WhoE 93
Schuster, Robert D. St&PR 93
Schuster, Robert Parks 1945- WhoAm 92, WhoWor 93
Schuster, Sarah Fletcher 1929- WhoAmW 93
Schuster, Seymour 1926- WhoAm 92
Schuster, Stephen M. Law&B 92
Schuster, Steven D. 1956- St&PR 93
Schuster, Todd Mervyn 1933- WhoAm 92
Schuster, William P. Law&B 92
Schuster, Willy Gottfried 1923- WhoWor 93
Schuth, Mary McDougle 1942- WhoAmW 93, WhoSSW 93
Schutrumpf, Eckart Ernst 1939- WhoWor 93
Schutt, Eduard 1856-1933 Baker 92
Schutt, Mary Ellen 1864-1956 BioIn 17
Schutt, Robert William 1953- WhoSSW 93
Schutt, Walter Eugene 1917- WhoWor 93
Schutta, Henry Szczesny 1928- WhoAm 92
Schutte, Anne Jacobson 1940- ConAu 139
Schutte, Giles W. 1931- St&PR 93, WhoAm 92, WhoE 93, WhoWor 93
Schutte, Howard J. 1909- St&PR 93
Schutte, Nicola S. 1959- WhoSSW 93
Schutte, Ron 1956- St&PR 93
Schutte, Thomas Frederick 1935- WhoAm 92
Schutte, William Metcalf 1919- WhoWrEP 92
Schuttish, Thomas R. Law&B 92
Schutz, Barbara Foster 1932- WhoSSW 93
Schutz, Bernard F. WhoScE 91-1
Schutz, Bernard Frederick 1946- WhoWor 93
Schutz, Donald Frank 1934- WhoAm 92
Schutz, Heinrich 1585-1672 Baker 92, BioIn 17, OxDcOp
Schutz, Helmut Georg 1938- WhoWor 93
Schutz, Herbert Dietrich 1922- WhoAm 92
Schutz, J.W. 1912-1984 ScF&FL 92
Schutz, James E. 1950- St&PR 93
Schutz, Jean-Philippe 1939- WhoScE 91-4
Schutz, John Adolph 1919- WhoAm 92, WhoWor 93
Schutz, John Edwin 1935- St&PR 93
Schutz, John Howard 1933- WhoAm 92
Schutz, Prescott D. d1990 BioIn 17
Schutz, Richard Phillip 1951- WhoSSW 93
Schutz, Robert J. 1946- St&PR 93
Schutz, Rudolf-M. WhoScE 91-3
Schutz, Sidney 1915-1990 BioIn 17
Schutzendorf Baker 92
Schutzendorf, Alfons 1882-1946 Baker 92, OxDcOp
Schutzendorf, Guido 1880-1967 Baker 92, OxDcOp
Schutzendorf, Gustav 1883-1937 Baker 92, OxDcOp
Schutzendorf, Leo 1886-1931 Baker 92, OxDcOp
Schutzendorf an der Mayr 1880-1967 Baker 92
Schutzenhofer, Joseph William 1936- St&PR 93
Schutzer, Daniel M. 1940- WhoE 93
Schutzman, Lee A. Law&B 92
Schutzman, Leonard 1946- St&PR 93
Schutzmann, Roy Louis 1931- WhoSSW 93
Schuur, Diane Joan 1953- WhoAm 92, WhoAmW 93
Schuur, Robert George 1931- WhoAm 92
Schuyler, Christopher J. Law&B 92
Schuyler, Daniel Merrick 1912- WhoAm 92, WhoWor 93
Schuyler, George S. 1895-1977 EncAACR, JrnUS, ScF&FL 92
Schuyler, James BioIn 17
Schuyler, James 1923-1991 AnObit 1991
Schuyler, James Marcus 1923- WhoWrEP 92
Schuyler, James Marcus 1923-1991 ConLC 70
Schuyler, Jane 1943- WhoAmW 93, WhoE 93, WhoWor 93
Schuyler, Linda BioIn 17
Schuyler, Michael Robert 1949- WhoEmL 93
Schuyler, Montgomery 1843-1914 JrnUS
Schuyler, Philip John 1733-1804 HarEnMi
Schuyler, Philippa Duke 1931-1967 Baker 92
Schuyler, Robert Len 1936- WhoAm 92
Schuyler, William L. 1952- St&PR 93
Schuyt, Cornelis (Floriszoon) 1557-1616 Baker 92
Schuyt, Nico(laas) 1922- Baker 92
Schvey, Norman I. d1992 NewYTBS 92
Schwaar, Pierre Georges 1921- WhoE 93
Schwab, Adolf Josef 1937- WhoWor 93
Schwab, Albert St&PR 93
Schwab, Anne T. Law&B 92
Schwab, Buddy d1992 NewYTBS 92
Schwab, Carl Edwin 1929- St&PR 93
Schwab, Carol Ann 1953- WhoEmL 93, WhoSSW 93
Schwab, Charles BioIn 17
Schwab, Charles G. 1947- St&PR 93
Schwab, Charles M. 1862-1939 BioIn 17, GayN
Schwab, Charles R. WhoAm 92
Schwab, Charles R. 1937- St&PR 93
Schwab, Charlotte A. Law&B 92
Schwab, Evan Lynn 1938- WhoAm 92
Schwab, Frank John 1895-1965 BiDAMSp 1989
Schwab, George 1931- ConAu 37NR
Schwab, George David 1931- WhoAm 92, WhoE 93
Schwab, Glenn Orville 1919- WhoAm 92
Schwab, Harold Lee 1932- WhoE 93, WhoWor 93
Schwab, Hermann Caspar 1920- WhoAm 92
Schwab, Israel 1935- St&PR 93
Schwab, James Charles 1949- WhoWrEP 92
Schwab, John Harris 1927- WhoAm 92
Schwab, John Joseph 1923- WhoAm 92
Schwab, Katharine Fisher d1990 BioIn 17
Schwab, Klaus Martin 1938- WhoWor 93
Schwab, Larry 1940- WhoE 93
Schwab, Leo BioIn 17
Schwab, Leonard C. 1922- St&PR 93
Schwab, Leonard Charles 1922- WhoE 93
Schwab, Manfred Reinhard 1945- WhoScE 91-3
Schwab, Martin Ernst 1949- WhoWor 93
Schwab, Mary J. 1938- St&PR 93
Schwab, Michael R. 1949- WhoSSW 93
Schwab, Morris St&PR 93
Schwab, Paul A. 1929- St&PR 93
Schwab, Philip Walter 1940- St&PR 93
Schwab, Ralph G. 1932- St&PR 93
Schwab, Richard B. Law&B 92
Schwab, Richard D. 1926- St&PR 93
Schwab, Roland Friedrich 1930- St&PR 93
Schwab, Samuel Charles 1951- St&PR 93
Schwab, Shelly 1936- WhoAm 92
Schwab, Susan Carol WhoAm 92
Schwab, Thomas Charles 1953- WhoE 93
Schwab, Winthrop deV 1918- St&PR 93
Schwabe, Arthur David 1924- WhoAm 92
Schwabe, Calvin Walter 1927- WhoAm 92
Schwabe, Carl 1891-1967 BioIn 17
Schwabe, George Blaine, III 1947- WhoEmL 93, WhoSSW 93
Schwabe, John Bennett, II 1946- WhoEmL 93, WhoWor 93
Schwabe, Walter W. WhoScE 91-1
Schwaber, Mitchell Keith 1951- WhoSSW 93
Schwabero, Mark D. 1952- St&PR 93
Schwabik, Robert John 1943- St&PR 93
Schwabsky, Barry 1957- WhoE 93
Schwade, Jack Lester 1940- WhoSSW 93
Schwader, Ann K. 1960- ScF&FL 92
Schwager, Edith Cohen 1916- WhoAmW 93
Schwager, Greg L. Law&B 92
Schwager, John L. 1948- St&PR 93
Schwager, Robert 1917- St&PR 93
Schwager, Robert Solomon 1935- St&PR 93
Schwager, Ronny Joel 1950- St&PR 93
Schwager, Thomas Edward 1951- St&PR 93
Schwahn, Dietmar Gerhard Jurgen 1943- WhoWor 93
Schwaidelson, Bruce R. 1949- St&PR 93
Schwaiger, Walt N. 1937- St&PR 93
Schwain, David G. 1945- St&PR 93
Schwalb, Miklos 1903-1981 Baker 92
Schwalbach, Glen R. 1945- St&PR 93
Schwalbach, Joachim 1948- WhoWor 93
Schwalba-Hoth, Frank 1952- WhoWor 93
Schwalbe, Jim P. 1944- St&PR 93
Schwalje, Joseph Louis 1922- WhoAm 92
Schwaller, John Frederick 1948- WhoSSW 93
Schwalm, Fritz Ekkehardt 1936- WhoAm 92
Schwam, Marvin Albert 1942- WhoAm 92
Schwamb, Donald F., Jr. 1940- St&PR 93
Schwamm, Justin M., Sr. Law&B 92
Schwan, Carl C. 1937- St&PR 93
Schwan, Charles A. Law&B 92
Schwan, Herman Paul 1915- WhoAm 92, WhoWor 93
Schwan, Judith Alecia 1925- WhoAmW 93
Schwan, Mark David Law&B 92
Schwanauer, Francis 1933- WhoE 93
Schwandt, Stephen BioIn 17
Schwanecke, Helmut 1927- WhoScE 91-3
Schwanenberg, Johann Gottfried c. 1740-1804 Baker 92
Schwaner, Marilyn Palm 1930- WhoSSW 93
Schwanitz, Gesa 1938- WhoScE 91-3
Schwank, Johannes Walter 1950- WhoWor 93
Schwann, William (Joseph) 1913- Baker 92, WhoAm 92
Schwantes, Carlos Arnaldo 1945- WhoWor 93
Schwantes, William Ray 1932- St&PR 93
Schwantner, Joseph 1943- Baker 92, WhoAm 92
Schwanz, H. Lee 1923- WhoWrEP 92
Schwanz, Herman Lee 1923- WhoAm 92
Schwappach, Edgar WhoScE 91-3
Schwarcz, Henry Philip 1933- WhoAm 92
Schwarcz, Steven Lance 1949- WhoAm 92
Schwardt, Susan Kelly 1936- WhoAmW 93
Schwark, Eberhard 1939- WhoWor 93
Schwark, Howard Edward 1917- WhoWor 93
Schwarte, David A. Law&B 92
Schwarting, Arthur Ernest 1917- WhoAm 92
Schwartz, A.J. 1947- St&PR 93
Schwartz, Aaron Robert 1926- WhoAm 92
Schwartz, Alan David 1950- St&PR 93, WhoAm 92
Schwartz, Alan E. 1925- St&PR 93, WhoAm 92
Schwartz, Alan Leigh 1948- WhoAm 92
Schwartz, Alan Stuart 1943- WhoAm 92
Schwartz, Alan Uriel 1933- WhoAm 92
Schwartz, Albert 1923- WhoSSW 93
Schwartz, Alfred 1922- WhoAm 92
Schwartz, Alice M. St&PR 93
Schwartz, Alice P.L. Law&B 92
Schwartz, Allen G. 1934- WhoAm 92
Schwartz, Allyson Y. 1948- WhoAmW 93
Schwartz, Aloysius d1992 BioIn 17
Schwartz, Alvin d1992 NewYTBS 92 [port]
Schwartz, Alvin 1927-1992 BioIn 17, ConAu 137, MajAI [port], SmATA 71
Schwartz, Alyse Bett 1960- WhoAmW 93
Schwartz, Amy ChlBIID [port]
Schwartz, Amy 1954- BioIn 17
Schwartz, Andrew H. Law&B 92
Schwartz, Anna J. 1915- WhoAm 92
Schwartz, Anthony 1940- WhoAm 92, WhoE 93
Schwartz, Arnold 1929- WhoAm 92
Schwartz, Arnold C. 1932- St&PR 93
Schwartz, Arthur 1900-1984 Baker 92, BioIn 17
Schwartz, Arthur H. 1903-1990 BioIn 17
Schwartz, Arthur Ira 1950- WhoE 93
Schwartz, Arthur J. d1991 BioIn 17
Schwartz, Arthur L. Law&B 92
Schwartz, Arthur Leonard 1941- WhoAm 92
Schwartz, Arthur Robert 1947- WhoAm 92
Schwartz, Aubrey Earl 1928- WhoAm 92
Schwartz, Barry 1942?- BioIn 17
Schwartz, Benjamin L. 1926- WhoSSW 93
Schwartz, Bennett W. 1949- St&PR 93
Schwartz, Bernard 1905- St&PR 93
Schwartz, Bernard 1923- WhoAm 92
Schwartz, Bernard 1927- WhoAm 92
Schwartz, Bernard L. 1925- St&PR 93, WhoAm 92
Schwartz, Bertram 1934- St&PR 93
Schwartz, Betty Ann 1927- ScF&FL 92
Schwartz, Brad E. 1962- St&PR 93
Schwartz, Bruce F. 1952- WhoE 93
Schwartz, Carl Edward 1935- WhoAm 92
Schwartz, Carol A. 1953- WhoAmW 93
Schwartz, Carol Halpert 1939- WhoAmW 93
Schwartz, Carol V. Law&B 92
Schwartz, Charles, Jr. 1922- WhoAm 92, WhoSSW 93
Schwartz, Charles Frederick 1916- WhoAm 92
Schwartz, Charles J. 1944- WhoE 93
Schwartz, Charles P., Jr. 1927- St&PR 93
Schwartz, Charles Phineas, Jr. 1927- WhoAm 92
Schwartz, Charles Walter 1953- WhoAm 92
Schwartz, Charlotte M. 1921- St&PR 93
Schwartz, Clarin S. Law&B 92
Schwartz, Constance Law&B 92
Schwartz, Craig 1953- St&PR 93
Schwartz, Dale Marvin 1942- WhoAm 92, WhoSSW 93
Schwartz, Daniel Bennett 1929- WhoAm 92
Schwartz, Daniel M. 1956- St&PR 93
Schwartz, David A. Law&B 92
Schwartz, David Arlen Law&B 92
Schwartz, David G. Law&B 92
Schwartz, David Howard 1957- WhoE 93
Schwartz, David M. 1948- St&PR 93
Schwartz, David Stough 1931- St&PR 93
Schwartz, Dean A. 1962- St&PR 93
Schwartz, Deborah Lynne 1961- WhoAmW 93
Schwartz, Delmore 1913-1966 BioIn 17, JeAmFiW
Schwartz, Donald 1927- WhoAm 92
Schwartz, Donald Franklin 1935- WhoAm 92
Schwartz, Doris Ruhbel 1915- WhoAm 92, WhoAmW 93
Schwartz, Douglas Wright 1929- BioIn 17, WhoAm 92
Schwartz, Eddie Simon 1937- WhoWor 93
Schwartz, Edward 1932- WhoE 93
Schwartz, Edward 1949- WhoSSW 93
Schwartz, Edward A. 1955- WhoE 93
Schwartz, Edward Arthur 1937- WhoAm 92
Schwartz, Edward F. 1927- St&PR 93
Schwartz, Edward J. WhoAm 92

Schwartz, Edward Malcolm 1928- *WhoAm 92*
Schwartz, Edward R. 1910- *St&PR 93*
Schwartz, Eleanor Brantley 1937- *WhoAm 92, WhoAmW 93*
Schwartz, Eli 1921- *WhoAm 92*
Schwartz, Elizabeth Robinson 1911- *BiDAMSp 1989*
Schwartz, Ellen Elizabeth English 1949- *WhoAmW 93*
Schwartz, Elliot *BioIn 17*
Schwartz, Elliott (Shelling) 1936- *Baker 92, WhoAm 92*
Schwartz, Estar Alma 1950- *WhoAmW 93*
Schwartz, Esther Dresden *AmWomPl*
Schwartz, Eugene J. *Law&B 92*
Schwartz, Felice N. *BioIn 17*
Schwartz, Felice N. 1925- *WhoAmW 93*
Schwartz, Francis 1940- *Baker 92*
Schwartz, Frederic W. 1916- *St&PR 93*
Schwartz, Frederick G. 1928- *St&PR 93*
Schwartz, Frederick Steven *Law&B 92*
Schwartz, Gary Alan 1952- *St&PR 93*
Schwartz, Gary Ray 1939- *WhoE 93*
Schwartz, George Edwin 1924- *St&PR 93*
Schwartz, Gerald 1927- *WhoWor 93*
Schwartz, Gerald Arthur 1946- *WhoE 93*
Schwartz, Gerri E. *WhoAmW 93*
Schwartz, Gilson 1960- *WhoWor 93*
Schwartz, Gordon Francis 1935- *WhoAm 92, WhoWor 93*
Schwartz, Harold 1920-1990 *BioIn 17*
Schwartz, Harold Albert 1913- *WhoAm 92*
Schwartz, Harold Lloyd 1936- *WhoE 93*
Schwartz, Harry 1919- *WhoAm 92*
Schwartz, Harry Kane 1934- *WhoAm 92*
Schwartz, Harvey Joel 1951- *WhoE 93*
Schwartz, Henry 1927- *WhoE 93*
Schwartz, Henry G., Jr. 1938- *St&PR 93*
Schwartz, Henry Gerard 1909- *WhoAm 92*
Schwartz, Herbert 1927- *St&PR 93*
Schwartz, Herbert Charles 1926- *WhoAm 92*
Schwartz, Herman 1916- *St&PR 93*
Schwartz, Hilda 1923- *St&PR 93*
Schwartz, Hilda G. *WhoAmW 93, WhoE 93, WhoWor 93*
Schwartz, Howard 1919-1990 *BioIn 17*
Schwartz, Howard Alan 1944- *WhoE 93*
Schwartz, Ilsa Roslow 1941- *WhoAmW 93*
Schwartz, Irving Donn 1927- *WhoAm 92*
Schwartz, Irving Leon 1918- *WhoAm 92*
Schwartz, Jack 1931- *WhoE 93*
Schwartz, Jack Theodore 1914- *WhoAm 92, WhoWor 93*
Schwartz, Jacob T. 1930- *WhoAm 92*
Schwartz, Jacques Paul 1928- *WhoAm 92*
Schwartz, James D., Jr. 1950- *St&PR 93*
Schwartz, James Frederick 1929- *WhoAm 92*
Schwartz, James Harris 1932- *WhoE 93*
Schwartz, James Peter 1919- *WhoWor 93*
Schwartz, Jane Andrews 1952- *WhoAmW 93*
Schwartz, Jean-Charles *WhoScE 91-2*
Schwartz, Jeffrey 1952- *WhoWrEP 92*
Schwartz, Jeffrey Byron 1940- *WhoWor 93*
Schwartz, Jeffrey Stephen 1943- *WhoE 93*
Schwartz, Jesse M. 1947- *St&PR 93*
Schwartz, Joan Lam 1928- *WhoAmW 93*
Schwartz, Joel 1955- *WhoE 93*
Schwartz, John C. 1947- *WhoIns 93*
Schwartz, John James 1919- *WhoAm 92, WhoE 93*
Schwartz, John Norman 1945- *WhoAm 92*
Schwartz, Jonathan *BioIn 17*
Schwartz, Joseph 1911- *WhoAm 92*
Schwartz, Joseph 1925- *WhoAm 92, WhoWrEP 92*
Schwartz, Joseph Adam 1938- *WhoWor 93*
Schwartz, Joshua Adam 1963- *WhoSSW 93*
Schwartz, Jules Jacob 1932- *WhoAm 92*
Schwartz, Julia A. *Law&B 92*
Schwartz, Kenneth Ernst 1922- *WhoWor 93*
Schwartz, Kessel 1920- *WhoAm 92, WhoWrEP 92*
Schwartz, Ketty 1937- *WhoScE 91-2*
Schwartz, Kevin Alan 1961- *WhoSSW 93*
Schwartz, Kove Jerome 1938- *WhoE 93*
Schwartz, L.M. 1910- *St&PR 93*
Schwartz, Lanny A. *Law&B 92*
Schwartz, Laurence M. *Law&B 92*
Schwartz, Laurie Koller 1947- *WhoAmW 93*
Schwartz, Lawrence 1935- *WhoWor 93*
Schwartz, Lawrence B. 1929- *St&PR 93, WhoAm 92*
Schwartz, Leah *BioIn 17*
Schwartz, Leon 1922- *WhoAm 92*
Schwartz, Leonard 1925- *WhoE 93*
Schwartz, Lillian 1927- *BioIn 17*
Schwartz, Lillian Feldman 1927- *WhoAm 92*
Schwartz, Lita Linzer 1930- *WhoAmW 93*
Schwartz, Lloyd 1941- *WhoWrEP 92*
Schwartz, Lloyd Marvin 1923- *WhoAm 92*
Schwartz, Lonn R. 1946- *St&PR 93*
Schwartz, Louis Brown 1913- *WhoAm 92*
Schwartz, Louis Martin 1926- *St&PR 93*
Schwartz, Louis O. 1927- *WhoE 93*
Schwartz, Louis Winn 1942- *WhoE 93*
Schwartz, Lucy McCallum 1944- *WhoAmW 93*
Schwartz, Lyle H. 1936- *WhoAm 92*
Schwartz, Lynne Sharon *BioIn 17*
Schwartz, Lynne Sharon 1939- *WhoWrEP 92*
Schwartz, Marchmont 1909-1991 *BioIn 17*
Schwartz, Marshall Zane 1945- *WhoAm 92*
Schwartz, Martha 1950- *WhoAm 92*
Schwartz, Martin 1923- *St&PR 93*
Schwartz, Martin V. *Law&B 92*
Schwartz, Martin Weber 1944- *WhoWrEP 92*
Schwartz, Marvin 1922- *WhoAm 92*
Schwartz, Maryln *BioIn 17*
Schwartz, Maureen W. 1946- *St&PR 93*
Schwartz, Mel M. 1929- *WhoE 93*
Schwartz, Melvin 1932- *WhoAm 92, WhoWor 93*
Schwartz, Meyer 1904- *WhoAm 92*
Schwartz, Michael 1937- *WhoAm 92*
Schwartz, Michael Allen 1946- *WhoE 93*
Schwartz, Michael B. *Law&B 92*
Schwartz, Michael Benjamin 1954- *WhoWor 93*
Schwartz, Michael I. 1939- *St&PR 93*
Schwartz, Michael Robinson 1940- *WhoAm 92*
Schwartz, Milton 1923- *St&PR 93*
Schwartz, Milton Lewis 1920- *WhoAm 92*
Schwartz, Mischa 1926- *WhoAm 92*
Schwartz, Morton Z. 1931- *St&PR 93*
Schwartz, Murray Louis 1920- *WhoAm 92*
Schwartz, Murray Merle 1931- *WhoAm 92, WhoE 93*
Schwartz, Nate *St&PR 93*
Schwartz, Nathan R. 1913- *St&PR 93*
Schwartz, Neena Betty 1926- *WhoAm 92, WhoAmW 93*
Schwartz, Neil D. 1942- *St&PR 93, WhoIns 93*
Schwartz, Norman David 1950- *St&PR 93*
Schwartz, Norman L. 1935- *WhoAm 92*
Schwartz, Patrick D. *Law&B 92*
Schwartz, Paul Arthur 1956- *WhoE 93*
Schwartz, Paul Michael 1959- *WhoSSW 93*
Schwartz, Paul Norman 1946- *St&PR 93*
Schwartz, Paula 1953- *WhoE 93*
Schwartz, Paula Ruth Oboler d1992 *BioIn 17, NewYTBS 92*
Schwartz, Peggy 1943- *WhoAmW 93*
Schwartz, Perry H. 1938- *St&PR 93*
Schwartz, Perry Lester 1939- *WhoAm 92*
Schwartz, Perry Thomas 1940- *WhoE 93*
Schwartz, Peter *BioIn 17, Law&B 92*
Schwartz, Peter 1960- *St&PR 93*
Schwartz, Peter A. *St&PR 93*
Schwartz, Peter Edward 1941- *WhoAm 92*
Schwartz, Philip C. 1925- *St&PR 93*
Schwartz, Philip L. 1940- *St&PR 93*
Schwartz, R. Malcolm 1934- *WhoAm 92*
Schwartz, Rachael Ellen *Law&B 92*
Schwartz, Rafael E. 1955- *WhoWor 93*
Schwartz, Renee Gerstler 1933- *WhoAm 92*
Schwartz, Richard *Law&B 92*
Schwartz, Richard A. *Law&B 92*
Schwartz, Richard Alan 1951- *WhoSSW 93*
Schwartz, Richard Brenton 1941- *WhoAm 92, WhoWor 93*
Schwartz, Richard D. 1944- *St&PR 93*
Schwartz, Richard Derecktor 1925- *WhoAm 92, WhoWor 93*
Schwartz, Richard Frederick 1922- *WhoE 93*
Schwartz, Richard Harold 1934- *WhoE 93*
Schwartz, Richard John 1935- *WhoAm 92*
Schwartz, Richard M. *Law&B 92*
Schwartz, Richard M. 1939- *St&PR 93*
Schwartz, Rick 1948- *WhoE 93*
Schwartz, Robert *Law&B 92*
Schwartz, Robert 1939- *WhoAm 92*
Schwartz, Robert 1946- *St&PR 93*
Schwartz, Robert Bernard 1929- *WhoE 93*
Schwartz, Robert E. *Law&B 92*
Schwartz, Robert G. 1928- *St&PR 93*
Schwartz, Robert George 1928- *WhoAm 92, WhoE 93, WhoIns 93*
Schwartz, Robert Glenn 1956- *WhoSSW 93*
Schwartz, Robert L. *Law&B 92*
Schwartz, Robert Maury *Law&B 92*
Schwartz, Robert R. 1941- *St&PR 93*
Schwartz, Robert Terry 1950- *WhoAm 92*
Schwartz, Robert William 1944- *WhoE 93, WhoWor 93*
Schwartz, Roberta Christine *WhoWrEP 92*
Schwartz, Robyn Rosalind 1944- *WhoWor 93*
Schwartz, Roger Alan 1945- *WhoWor 93*
Schwartz, Ronald A. *Law&B 92*
Schwartz, Ronald Herman 1956- *WhoSSW 93*
Schwartz, Roselind Shirley Grant 1922- *WhoAmW 93*
Schwartz, Roy R. *Law&B 92*
Schwartz, Roy Richard 1943- *St&PR 93, WhoAm 92*
Schwartz, Ruth Wainer *WhoAmW 93*
Schwartz, Sam D. 1940- *St&PR 93*
Schwartz, Samuel 1927- *WhoAm 92*
Schwartz, Sanford Louis 1950- *St&PR 93*
Schwartz, Sanford Mark 1951- *St&PR 93*
Schwartz, Scott M. *Law&B 92*
Schwartz, Seymour Ira 1928- *WhoAm 92*
Schwartz, Seymour N. 1937- *St&PR 93*
Schwartz, Sheila 1929- *ScF&FL 92*
Schwartz, Sheila Ruth 1936- *WhoE 93*
Schwartz, Sherwood *BioIn 17*
Schwartz, Shirley Eckwall 1935- *WhoAm 92, WhoAmW 93*
Schwartz, Sidney d1991 *BioIn 17*
Schwartz, Sol *Law&B 92*
Schwartz, Sol 1925- *St&PR 93*
Schwartz, Sorell Lee 1937- *WhoE 93*
Schwartz, Stephen Blair 1934- *St&PR 93, WhoAm 92*
Schwartz, Stephen C. 1942- *St&PR 93*
Schwartz, Stephen Eugene 1941- *WhoE 93*
Schwartz, Stephen Lawrence 1948- *WhoAm 92*
Schwartz, Steven 1946- *WhoWor 93*
Schwartz, Steven 1947- *St&PR 93*
Schwartz, Steven Arden 1953- *WhoSSW 93*
Schwartz, Steven H. *Law&B 92*
Schwartz, Steven Harvey 1948- *WhoE 93*
Schwartz, Steven R. 1950- *WhoWrEP 92*
Schwartz, Stuart 1925- *St&PR 93*
Schwartz, Stuart Charles 1943- *WhoSSW 93*
Schwartz, Susan Elisabeth Braloff 1956- *WhoE 93*
Schwartz, Susan J. *Law&B 92*
Schwartz, Susan Lynn Hill 1951- *WhoAmW 93*
Schwartz, Sylvan, Jr. 1946- *St&PR 93*
Schwartz, Ted 1947- *St&PR 93*
Schwartz, Teri Jean 1949- *WhoE 93*
Schwartz, Terry Walter 1950- *WhoWrEP 92*
Schwartz, Theodore A. 1929- *St&PR 93*
Schwartz, Theodore B. 1918- *WhoAm 92*
Schwartz, Thomas *Law&B 92*
Schwartz, Thomas Alan 1951- *St&PR 93, WhoE 93*
Schwartz, Tony (Anthony) 1923- *WhoWrEP 92*
Schwartz, Valerie Breuer 1912- *WhoAmW 93, WhoE 93*
Schwartz, Victoria W. *Law&B 92*
Schwartz, Vivian L. *Law&B 92*
Schwartz, Walter S. *Law&B 92*
Schwartz, Werner W. 1914- *St&PR 93*
Schwartz, William 1933- *WhoAm 92, WhoE 93, WhoWor 93*
Schwartz, William Allen 1938- *WhoAm 92*
Schwartz, William B., Jr. 1921- *WhoAm 92*
Schwartz, William Benjamin 1922- *WhoAm 92*
Schwartz, William Lewis 1931- *WhoSSW 93*
Schwartz-Barker, Lynne Susanne 1950- *WhoSSW 93*
Schwartzberg, Allan Zelig 1930- *WhoAm 92*
Schwartzberg, Gil N. 1942- *WhoAm 92*
Schwartzberg, Joanne Gilbert 1933- *WhoWor 93*
Schwartzberg, Linda Kay 1949- *WhoAmW 93*
Schwartzberg, Martin M. 1935- *St&PR 93, WhoAm 92*
Schwartzberg, Neala Spiegel 1947- *WhoAmW 93*
Schwartzberg, Roger Kerry 1948- *WhoSSW 93*
Schwartzberg, Wendy June 1965- *St&PR 93*
Schwartzburg, David Curtiss 1936- *St&PR 93*
Schwartzel, Charles Boone 1950- *WhoAm 92*
Schwartzhoff, James P. 1937- *St&PR 93*
Schwartzhoff, James Paul 1937- *WhoAm 92*
Schwartzlow, Jerry Ernest 1941- *St&PR 93*
Schwartzman, Alan 1923- *WhoAm 92*
Schwartzman, Andrew Jay 1946- *WhoAm 92*
Schwartzman, Arnold *BioIn 17, MiSFD 9*
Schwartzman, David 1924- *WhoAm 92*
Schwartzman, Jack 1912- *WhoE 93, WhoWor 93*
Schwartzman, Jacqueline d1990 *BioIn 17*
Schwartzman, Joan Wilck 1931- *WhoAmW 93*
Schwartzman, Joseph 1905-1990 *BioIn 17*
Schwartzman, Leon 1931- *WhoAm 92*
Schwartzman, Lois Phoebe 1937- *WhoWrEP 92*
Schwartzman, Peter 1936- *St&PR 93*
Schwartzman, Robert J. 1939- *WhoAm 92*
Schwartzman, Ronald Neil 1953- *WhoE 93*
Schwartzott, Paul Richard 1946- *WhoIns 93*
Schwartzstein, Daniel *St&PR 93*
Schwartzstein, Marvin 1931- *St&PR 93*
Schwartzwald, David W. 1949- *St&PR 93*
Schwary, Ronald Louis 1944- *WhoAm 92*
Schwarz, Alan d1990 *BioIn 17*
Schwarz, Barbara Ruth Ballou 1930- *WhoAmW 93*
Schwarz, Barbara Tova 1958- *WhoAmW 93*
Schwarz, Boris 1906-1983 *Baker 92*
Schwarz, Cindy Beth 1958- *WhoAmW 93*
Schwarz, Daniel Roger 1941- *WhoE 93*
Schwarz, Daniel Tracy 1938- *WhoAm 92*
Schwarz, Edward Lester *Law&B 92*
Schwarz, Egon 1922- *WhoAm 92*
Schwarz, Ekkehart Richard Johannes 1938- *WhoE 93*
Schwarz, Eric R. 1954- *St&PR 93*
Schwarz, Esther Doris 1933- *WhoWor 93*
Schwarz, Ferdinand Fred 1939- *WhoSSW 93*
Schwarz, Florine *AmWomPl*
Schwarz, Frederick August Otto, Jr. 1935- *WhoAm 92*
Schwarz, Gary M. 1946- *St&PR 93*
Schwarz, Gene 1941- *St&PR 93*
Schwarz, George Arthur 1951- *St&PR 93*
Schwarz, Gerard (Ralph) 1947- *Baker 92, WhoAm 92*
Schwarz, Gerhard 1930- *WhoScE 91-4*
Schwarz, Gerta 1914-1990 *BioIn 17*
Schwarz, H. Marshall 1936- *St&PR 93, WhoAm 92*
Schwarz, Hanna 1943- *Baker 92*
Schwarz, Harry 1949- *WhoSSW 93*
Schwarz, Harry Heinz 1924- *WhoWor 93*
Schwarz, Helmut 1931- *WhoScE 91-3*
Schwarz, J.J. *WhoScE 91-3*
Schwarz, James Nicholas 1945- *St&PR 93*
Schwarz, John H. 1938- *St&PR 93*
Schwarz, Joseph Edmund 1929- *WhoAm 92*
Schwarz, Josephine Lindeman 1908- *WhoAm 92*
Schwarz, Joyce A. *WhoWrEP 92*
Schwarz, Joyce Ann 1946- *WhoAmW 93, WhoWor 93*
Schwarz, Karen 1957- *ConAu 138*
Schwarz, Karl Otto 1949- *WhoE 93*
Schwarz, Karlheinz 1941- *WhoWor 93*
Schwarz, Kathleen Ann Brogan 1942- *WhoE 93*
Schwarz, Kurt Karl 1926- *WhoWor 93*
Schwarz, Larry Michael 1950- *WhoWor 93*
Schwarz, M. Roy 1936- *WhoAm 92*
Schwarz, Mary Katherine *Law&B 92*
Schwarz, Maurice Jacob 1939- *WhoE 93*
Schwarz, Michael 1952- *WhoEmL 93*
Schwarz, Michael Gideon *Law&B 92*
Schwarz, Michael J. *Law&B 92*
Schwarz, Ottmar 1921- *WhoScE 91-3*
Schwarz, Patricia Tzuanos 1948- *WhoAmW 93*
Schwarz, Peter C. *Law&B 92*
Schwarz, Peter Karl 1944- *WhoE 93*
Schwarz, Ralph Jacques 1922- *WhoAm 92*
Schwarz, Ray Paul 1948- *WhoSSW 93*
Schwarz, Richard *BioIn 17*
Schwarz, Richard Howard 1931- *WhoAm 92*
Schwarz, Richard William 1925- *WhoAm 92*
Schwarz, Rudolf 1905- *Baker 92*
Schwarz, Sanford 1920- *WhoAm 92*
Schwarz, Stephan 1932- *WhoWor 93*
Schwarz, Thomas Ralph 1936- *St&PR 93*
Schwarz, Uli 1934- *WhoScE 91-3*
Schwarz, Vera 1889-1964 *Baker 92*
Schwarz, W.H. Eugen 1937- *WhoScE 91-3*
Schwarz, Wilhelm 1937- *WhoScE 91-3*
Schwarz, Wolfgang 1926- *WhoAm 92, WhoWor 93*
Schwarzbart, Gunter 1932- *WhoSSW 93*
Schwarz-Bart, Simone 1938- *ScF&FL 92*
Schwarzbauer, Gerd E. 1943- *WhoScE 91-4*
Schwarze, Jochen 1937- *WhoScE 91-3, WhoWor 93*

Schwarzenbach, Dieter 1936- *WhoScE 91-4*
Schwarzenbek, Eugene E. 1943- *St&PR 93*
Schwarzenbek, Eugene Evan 1943- *WhoAm 92*
Schwarzenberg, Karl Philip, Prince of 1771-1820 *HarEnMi*
Schwarzenberger, Rolph Ludwig Edward *WhoScE 91-1*
Schwarzenegger, Arnold *BioIn 17*
Schwarzenegger, Arnold 1947- *HolBB [port], IntDcF 2-3 [port], MiSFD 9*
Schwarzenegger, Arnold Alois 1947- *WhoAm 92*
Schwarzer, W. *WhoScE 91-3*
Schwarzer, William W. 1925- *WhoAm 92*
Schwarzkopf, Elisabeth *BioIn 17*
Schwarzkopf, Elisabeth 1915- *Baker 92, IntDcOp [port], OxDcOp, WhoWor 93*
Schwarzkopf, H. Norman *BioIn 17*
Schwarzkopf, H. Norman 1934- *ConHero 2 [port], HarEnMi, WhoAm 92, WhoWor 93*
Schwarzkopf, Kurt Ian *Law&B 92*
Schwarzkopf, LeRoy C(arl) 1920- *ConAu 38NR*
Schwarzkopf, Richard M. 1939- *St&PR 93*
Schwarzman, Stephen Allen 1947- *WhoAm 92*
Schwarzschild, Karl 1873-1916 *BioIn 17*
Schwarzschild, Martin 1912- *WhoAm 92*
Schwarzschild, William Harry, Jr. 1903- *WhoAm 92*
Schwarztrauber, Sayre Archie 1929- *WhoWor 93*
Schwarzwalder, Daniel Robert 1948- *St&PR 93, WhoE 93*
Schwarzwalder, John Carl 1917- *WhoAm 92*
Schwarzwalder, R. *WhoScE 91-3*
Schwass, Gary L. 1945- *St&PR 93, WhoAm 92*
Schwatka, Mark Andrew 1950- *WhoAm 92*
Schwatschko, Arnold 1938- *WhoUN 92*
Schwebel, Andrew I. 1943- *WhoAm 92*
Schwebel, Jack P. 1925- *St&PR 93, WhoAm 92*
Schwebel, Joseph 1939- *St&PR 93*
Schwebel, Milton 1914- *WhoAm 92, WhoE 93*
Schwebel, Stephen Myron 1929- *WhoAm 92, WhoUN 92*
Schweber, Silvan Samuel 1928- *WhoAm 92*
Schwed, Pedro E. 1931- *St&PR 93*
Schwed, Peter 1911- *WhoAm 92, WhoWrEP 92*
Schwedel, Alan R. 1942- *St&PR 93*
Schwedel, Nat N. 1910- *St&PR 93*
Schwedes, Jorg 1938- *WhoScE 91-3*
Schwedhelm, Raymond Gustav 1944- *St&PR 93*
Schwedler, Donald James 1923- *St&PR 93*
Schweers, John Ray 1945- *St&PR 93*
Schwefel, Detlef Leonhard 1942- *WhoScE 91-3*
Schwefel, Lauri *BioIn 17*
Schweger, Donald E. *Law&B 92*
Schwegler, Helmut 1938- *WhoWor 93*
Schwegmann, Melinda 1946- *WhoAm 92, WhoAmW 93, WhoSSW 93*
Schwehm, Jerry Kenneth *WhoSSW 93*
Schwei, Russell Paul 1959- *St&PR 93*
Schweich, Robert Joseph 1934- *WhoAm 92*
Schweickart, Jim 1950- *WhoAm 92*
Schweickart, Patrocinio P. 1942- *ConAu 138*
Schweickart, Russell L. 1935- *WhoWor 93*
Schweid, Bernard d1990 *BioIn 17*
Schweig, Armin 1937- *WhoScE 91-3*
Schweig, Margaret Berris 1928- *WhoAmW 93*
Schweiger, Anthony Walter 1941- *WhoE 93*
Schweiger, Donald J. 1942- *St&PR 93*
Schweiger, Gladys Julia 1939- *WhoAmW 93*
Schweiger, Manfred F.W. 1936- *WhoScE 91-4*
Schweiger, Paul *WhoScE 91-3*
Schweigert, B.S. 1921-1989 *BioIn 17*
Schweigert, Florian Johannes 1958- *WhoWor 93*
Schweighardt, Frank Kenneth 1944- *WhoWor 93*
Schweiker, Richard Schultz 1926- *WhoAm 92, WhoIns 93*
Schweikert, David H. 1941- *St&PR 93*
Schweikert, Edgar Oskar 1938- *WhoE 93*
Schweikert, Norman Carl 1937- *WhoAm 92*
Schweikhart, Kenneth Arthur 1938- *St&PR 93*
Schweiner, Louie Edward *Law&B 92*
Schweinfurth, Georg 1836-1925 *IntDcAn*
Schweinfurth, Georg August 1836-1925 *Expl 93 [port]*
Schweingruber, Fritz Hans 1936- *WhoScE 91-4*
Schweinhart, Donald Lee 1954- *WhoSSW 93*
Schweinhart, Richard A. 1949- *St&PR 93*
Schweinhart, Richard Alexander 1949- *WhoAm 92*
Schweinhart, Sharon K. *Law&B 92*
Schweinitz, Wolfgang von 1953- *Baker 92*
Schweinshaut, Louise K. 1918- *St&PR 93*
Schweinshaut, Max, Jr. 1918- *St&PR 93*
Schweisthal, Karl Ludwig 1939- *St&PR 93*
Schweitzer, Albert 1875-1965 *Baker 92, BioIn 17, ConHero 2 [port], DcTwHis*
Schweitzer, Anton 1735?-1787 *Baker 92*
Schweitzer, Arlette *BioIn 17*
Schweitzer, Barbara Michele 1965- *WhoE 93*
Schweitzer, Byrd Baylor *MajAI, SmATA 69*
Schweitzer, Carl-Christoph 1924- *WhoWor 93*
Schweitzer, Carl Lawrence 1929- *St&PR 93*
Schweitzer, Christoph Eugen 1922- *WhoSSW 93*
Schweitzer, Darrell 1952- *ConAu 39NR, ScF&FL 92*
Schweitzer, Darrell Charles 1952- *WhoWrEP 92*
Schweitzer, Don Alan 1941- *WhoAm 92*
Schweitzer, Ferenc 1939- *WhoScE 91-4*
Schweitzer, Frank Weaver 1932- *St&PR 93*
Schweitzer, George F. *BioIn 17*
Schweitzer, George Keene 1924- *WhoAm 92, WhoSSW 93*
Schweitzer, Hans-Joachim 1928- *WhoScE 91-3*
Schweitzer, John Stephens 1929- *St&PR 93*
Schweitzer, Mark Brian 1957- *St&PR 93*
Schweitzer, Mitchell D. d1991 *NewYTBS 92 [port]*
Schweitzer, Mitchell D. 1905-1991 *BioIn 17*
Schweitzer, N. Tina 1941- *WhoAm 92, WhoAmW 93*
Schweitzer, Paul Jerome 1941- *WhoE 93*
Schweitzer, Peter 1939- *WhoAm 92*
Schweitzer, Peter A. *St&PR 93*
Schweitzer, Pierre-Paul 1912- *WhoAm 92*
Schweitzer, Sarah L. 1950- *WhoAmW 93*
Schweitzer, Ulrich 1920- *WhoAm 92*
Schweizer, Albert Edward 1943- *WhoSSW 93*
Schweizer, Charles Thomas 1935- *WhoE 93*
Schweizer, Eckhart 1936- *WhoScE 91-3*
Schweizer, Erhard Karl 1957- *WhoWor 93*
Schweizer, Karl W. 1946- *ConAu 136*
Schweizer, Kenneth Martin 1960- *WhoSSW 93*
Schweizer, Paul A. 1913- *St&PR 93*
Schweizer, Paul Douglas 1946- *WhoAm 92, WhoE 93*
Schweizer, Raymond C. 1921- *St&PR 93*
Schweizer, Ricki J. *Law&B 92*
Schweizer, William Stuart 1944- *St&PR 93*
Schweke, Mark A. 1951- *St&PR 93*
Schwemm, Henry Christian, Jr. 1941- *St&PR 93*
Schwemm, John B. 1934- *St&PR 93*
Schwemm, John Butler 1934- *WhoAm 92*
Schwemmer, Geary Karl 1953- *WhoE 93*
Schwemmle, Konrad Erwin Hildebrand 1934- *WhoScE 91-3*
Schwenck, Charles E. 1945- *St&PR 93*
Schwenck, Charles Ernest *Law&B 92*
Schwencke *Baker 92*
Schwencke, Christian Fredrich Gottlieb 1767-1822 *Baker 92*
Schwencke, Friedrich Gottlieb 1823-1896 *Baker 92*
Schwencke, Johann Friedrich 1792-1852 *Baker 92*
Schwencke, Johann Gottlieb 1744-1823 *Baker 92*
Schwencke, Karl 1797-1870 *Baker 92*
Schwendener, Benjamin O., Jr. *Law&B 92*
Schwendenmann, Steven C. *Law&B 92*
Schwender, Charles F. 1937- *St&PR 93*
Schwendiman, Donald L. *Law&B 92*
Schwendinger, Charles Joseph 1931- *WhoSSW 93*
Schwenk, Harold S. 1941- *St&PR 93*
Schwenk, Richard C. *St&PR 93*
Schwenk, Thomas James 1956- *WhoSSW 93*
Schwenke, Roger Dean 1944- *WhoAm 92*
Schwenke, Wolfgang Fritz 1921- *WhoScE 91-3*
Schwenn, Edwin George 1928- *WhoWor 93*
Schwenn, Lee William 1925- *WhoAm 92*
Schwensfeir, Robert James, Jr. 1934- *WhoE 93*
Schwenzer, Kristine Ann 1957- *WhoWrEP 92*
Schweppe, Henry Nelson, III 1963- *WhoE 93*
Schweppe, Joseph Louis 1921- *WhoSSW 93*
Schweppe, Richard J. *St&PR 93*
Schwer, William F. *Law&B 92*
Schwerd, Wolfgang *WhoScE 91-3*
Schwerdt, John d1989 *BioIn 17*
Schwerdt, Lisa Mary 1953- *WhoE 93*
Schwerdtfeger, Walter Kurt 1949- *WhoWor 93*
Schwerdtle, Edward S. 1933- *St&PR 93*
Schwerin, Alfred 1892-1977 *BioIn 17*
Schwerin, Doris *BioIn 17*
Schwerin, Doris 1922- *ScF&FL 92, WhoWrEP 92*
Schwerin, Horace S. 1914- *WhoAm 92*
Schwerin, Karl Henry 1936- *WhoAm 92*
Schwering, Felix Karl 1930- *WhoAm 92*
Schwerke, Irving 1893-1975 *Baker 92*
Schwerm, Gerald 1933- *WhoAm 92*
Schwerman, Jack F. 1952- *St&PR 93*
Schwerner, Armand 1927- *WhoWrEP 92*
Schwerner, Michael Henry 1939-1964 *EncAACR*
Schwerner, Nathan H. d1991 *BioIn 17*
Schwers, J.F. 1930- *WhoScE 91-2*
Schwert, George William, III 1950- *WhoE 93*
Schwertfeger, Robert E. 1943- *St&PR 93*
Schwertfeger, Timothy R. 1949- *St&PR 93*
Schwertly, Gary W. 1947- *St&PR 93*
Schwertmann, Udo 1927- *WhoScE 91-3*
Schwertner, Ray 1948- *St&PR 93*
Schwertsik, Kurt 1935- *Baker 92*
Schwesig, Claude Rudolf Emil 1945- *WhoE 93*
Schwesig, Norman Lee 1942- *WhoAm 92*
Schwetman, John William 1942- *WhoSSW 93*
Schwettmann, Juergen 1954- *WhoUN 92*
Schwetz, Karl-Alex 1940- *WhoScE 91-3, WhoWor 93*
Schwgitzer, Len 1947- *St&PR 93*
Schwieder, Bruce 1950- *St&PR 93*
Schwieger, Hans 1906- *Baker 92*
Schwier, Frederick Warren 1923- *WhoAm 92*
Schwier, James W. 1928- *St&PR 93*
Schwiesow, David R. *Law&B 92*
Schwietz, Roger L. *WhoAm 92*
Schwimmer, David 1913- *WhoAm 92, WhoWor 93*
Schwimmer, Rosika 1877-1948 *BioIn 17*
Schwind, Hermann 1923- *WhoScE 91-3*
Schwind, Michael Angelo 1924- *WhoAm 92*
Schwind, William F., Jr. *Law&B 92*
Schwindl, Friedrich 1737-1786 *Baker 92*
Schwindt, Robert F. 1929- *St&PR 93*
Schwing, Carol Elizabeth 1950- *WhoAmW 93*
Schwing, Charles E. 1929- *WhoAm 92*
Schwinger, Julian 1918- *WhoAm 92, WhoWor 93*
Schwinghamer, Robert John 1928- *WhoAm 92*
Schwinghammer, Arch C.L. 1926- *St&PR 93*
Schwinn, Edward R., Jr. *WhoAm 92*
Schwinn, Robert James 1930- *WhoAm 92*
Schwintowski, Hans-Peter 1947- *WhoWor 93*
Schwippert, G.A. 1935- *WhoScE 91-3*
Schwirian, Ann 1934- *WhoWrEP 92*
Schwisberg, Samuel E. *Law&B 92*
Schwister, Jay Edward 1962- *WhoE 93, WhoWor 93*
Schwitalla, Stephen Edward 1953- *WhoAm 92*
Schwitters, Ernst 1920- *BioIn 17*
Schwob, Marcel 1867-1905 *DcLB 123 [port]*
Schwoerer, Carol Ann 1943- *St&PR 93*
Schwoerer, Markus V.H. 1937- *WhoScE 91-3*
Schwuger, Milan Johann 1938- *WhoScE 91-3*
Schwyn, Charles Edward 1932- *WhoAm 92, WhoWor 93*
Schwyn, James Milton 1938- *St&PR 93*
Schygulla, Hanna *BioIn 17*
Schygulla, Hanna 1943- *IntDcF 2-3 [port]*
Schytte, Ludvig (Theodor) 1848-1909 *Baker 92*
Sciacca, Con 1947- *WhoAsAP 91*
Sciacca, Kathleen 1943- *WhoAmW 93, WhoE 93*
Sciackitano, Carmen *Law&B 92*
Scialabba, Arthur Joseph 1966- *WhoE 93*
Scialfa, Patti *BioIn 17*
Scialo, John Joseph *Law&B 92*
Scialoja, Mario 1930- *WhoUN 92*
Sciame, Joseph 1941- *WhoE 93*
Sciammarella, Valdo 1924- *Baker 92*
Sciammas, Jacques Daniel 1956- *WhoWor 93*
Scianandre, Dominick Thomas 1949- *St&PR 93*
Sciance, Carroll Thomas 1939- *WhoSSW 93*
Sciandra, Maria Theresa 1967- *WhoE 93*
Scianna, Cosimo 1941- *WhoE 93*
Sciarratta, Patrick Louis 1951- *WhoE 93*
Sciarrino, Salvatore 1947- *Baker 92*
Sciascia, Leonardo *BioIn 17*
Sciba, JoAnn 1946- *WhoAmW 93*
Scibelli, Joe 1939-1991 *BioIn 17*
Scibor-Marchocki, Romuald Ireneus 1926- *WhoWor 93*
Scicchitano, Edward A. 1930- *St&PR 93*
Scicutella, John Vincent 1949- *St&PR 93*
Sciegaj, Mark 1960- *WhoSSW 93*
Scielzo, Nicholas Henry 1941- *St&PR 93, WhoSSW 93*
Scieszka, Jon 1954- *BioIn 17, ChlLR 27 [port]*
Scifres, Don R. *WhoAm 92*
Scigliano, J. Michael 1941- *WhoE 93*
Scileppi, James d1992 *BioIn 17*
Scileppi, James G. d1992 *NewYTBS 92*
Scilken, Marvin *BioIn 17*
Scilley, Hugh Mason *Law&B 92*
Scime, Samuel Gene 1937- *WhoSSW 93*
Scimone, Claudio 1934- *Baker 92*
Scindia, Madhavrao J. 1945- *WhoAsAP 91*
Scindia, Vijaya Raje 1919- *WhoAsAP 91*
Scinta, Carol Rankins 1959- *WhoAmW 93*
Scio, Julie Angelique 1768-1807 *OxDcOp*
Sciocchetti, Peter Augusto 1957- *WhoE 93*
Scionti, Silvio 1882-1973 *BioIn 17*
Sciorra, Annabella *BioIn 17, ConTFT 10*
Sciortino, J. Paul 1958- *WhoE 93*
Scioscia, Mary 1926- *BioIn 17*
Scioscia, Mike *BioIn 17*
Scipio, Beverly Yvette 1951- *WhoAmW 93*
Scipio, Louis Albert, II 1922- *WhoAm 92, WhoWor 93*
Scipio, Publius Cornelius d211BC *HarEnMi*
Scipio Aemilianus Africanus Minor Numantinus, Publius Cornelius c. 184BC-129BC *HarEnMi*
Scipio Africanus Major, Publius Cornelius c. 236BC-184BC *HarEnMi*
Scipio Asiaticus, Lucius Cornelius fl. 207BC-184BC *HarEnMi*
Scipio Asina, Gnaeus Cornelius fl. 260BC-254BC *HarEnMi*
Scipio Barbatus, Lucius Cornelius fl. 304BC-280BC *HarEnMi*
Scipio Calvus, Gnaeus Cornelius d211BC *HarEnMi*
Scipione, Marianne 1946- *St&PR 93*
Scipione, Richard Stephen *Law&B 92*
Scipione, Richard Stephen 1937- *St&PR 93, WhoAm 92*
Scippa, Antonio 1942- *St&PR 93*
Scire, Giuseppe 1947- *WhoScE 91-3*
Scirica, Anthony Joseph 1940- *WhoAm 92, WhoE 93*
Scisco, Peter Leon 1956- *WhoAm 92*
Scism, Daniel Reed 1936- *WhoAm 92*
Scisson, Sidney E. 1917- *St&PR 93*
Scissors, Richard Curtis 1935- *WhoAm 92*
Scites, Janice L. 1950- *St&PR 93, WhoIns 93*
Scithers, George H. 1929- *ScF&FL 92*
Scitovsky, Anne Aickelin 1915- *WhoAm 92*
Scitovsky, Tibor *BioIn 17*
Sciubba, James John 1942- *WhoE 93*
Sciullo, John J. 1931- *WhoAm 92*
Sciuto, John J. 1945- *St&PR 93*
Sciutti, Graziella 1927- *Baker 92, OxDcOp*
Scivally, Bart Murnane 1944- *WhoSSW 93*
Sclafani, Accursio Peter 1947- *WhoE 93*
Sclafani, Frances Ann 1949- *WhoAm 92, WhoAmW 93*
Sclafani, Luciano V. d1991 *BioIn 17*
Sclar, Charles Bertram 1925- *WhoAm 92*
Sclarow, Barbara Harriet 1946- *WhoAmW 93*
Sclater, John *BioIn 17*
Sclater, John George 1940- *WhoAm 92*
Sclawy, Mary P. *Law&B 92*
Scliar, Moacyr *BioIn 17*
Scliar, Moacyr 1937- *ConAu 136, ScF&FL 92*
Sclufer, Nicholas George 1919- *WhoE 93*
Scobba, Judy 1944- *WhoAmW 93*
Scobbo, James Joseph 1962- *WhoE 93*
Scobell, Elizabeth Hight *WhoSSW 93*
Scobell, George Albert 1930- *St&PR 93*
Scobey, Brad Preston 1957- *WhoSSW 93*
Scobey, Heather *BioIn 17*
Scobey, Joan Moisseiff *WhoAmW 93*

Scobie, David G. 1947- *St&PR 93*
Scobie, Itha 1950- *WhoWrEP 92*
Scobie, Stephen 1943- *WhoCanL 92*
Scoblick, John J., Jr. *Law&B 92*
Scoby, Gloria *WhoAm 92*
Scocchio, Jeffrey V. 1944- *St&PR 93*
Scocco, Anthony Vincent 1958- *St&PR 93*
Scoco, Priscilla Rellas *Law&B 92*
Scocozza, Matthew Vincent 1948- *WhoAm 92*
Scodari, Nicholas F. 1927- *St&PR 93*
Scoff, Paul Allen *Law&B 92*
Scofffield, Kelly H. *Law&B 92*
Scoffone, A. Vincent 1943- *WhoAm 92*
Scoffone, Roy S. 1938- *St&PR 93*
Scofield, C.I. 1843-1921 *BioIn 17*
Scofield, Cyrus Ingerson 1843-1921 *BioIn 17*
Scofield, Gary Lee 1944- *St&PR 93*
Scofield, Gordon Lloyd 1925- *WhoAm 92*
Scofield, John *BioIn 17*
Scofield, John D. 1908- *St&PR 93*
Scofield, Larry Allan 1952- *WhoWor 93*
Scofield, Milton N. 1911- *St&PR 93*
Scofield, Paul 1922- *WhoWor 93*
Scofield, Penrod 1933- *BioIn 17*
Scofield, Richard Kenneth *Law&B 92*
Scofield, Richard Melbourne 1938- *WhoAm 92*
Scofield, Sandra Kay 1947- *WhoAmW 93*
Scofield, W. Richard 1952- *St&PR 93*
Scofield, William B. 1928- *St&PR 93*
Scoggan, John Kenneth 1953- *St&PR 93*
Scoggin, Charles H. *St&PR 93*
Scogin, Troy Pope 1932- *WhoSSW 93*
Scogland, William Lee 1949- *WhoEmL 93*
Scogna, Jared *BioIn 17*
Scognamiglio Pasini, Carlo 1944- *WhoWor 93*
Scola, Diane E. 1937- *St&PR 93*
Scola, Ettore 1931- *MiSFD 9*
Scola, Ralph Joseph 1943- *WhoWor 93*
Scola, Richard J. 1942- *St&PR 93*
Scola, Richard John *Law&B 92*
Scolari, Giuseppe 1720?-c. 1774 *OxDcOp*
Scolastico, Carlo P.N. 1936- *WhoScE 91-3*
Scoles, Clyde Sheldon 1949- *WhoAm 92*
Scoles, Eugene Francis 1921- *WhoAm 92*
Scoll, Geraldine R. *Law&B 92*
Scollan, Paul F. *Law&B 92*
Scollard, Diane Louise 1945- *WhoAmW 93*
Scollard, Jeannette Reddish *WhoWor 93*
Scollard, Patrick John 1937- *St&PR 93, WhoAm 92*
Scolnick, Edward M. *BioIn 17*
Scolnick, Edward Mark 1940- *WhoE 93*
Scolnick, Melvin J. *Law&B 92*
Scoltock, Jack 1942- *SmATA 72 [port]*
Sconfitto, Gerard Carl 1942- *WhoE 93, WhoWor 93*
Scontrino, Antonio 1850-1922 *Baker 92*
Sconyers, Hal W. 1928- *St&PR 93*
Sconyo, Philip 1951- *WhoE 93*
Scoon, Paul *DcCPCAm*
Scoon, Paul 1935- *WhoWor 93*
Scoones, Charlotte *AmWomPl*
Scopa, Frank J. 1923- *St&PR 93*
Scopaz, John M. 1948- *St&PR 93*
Scopaz, John Matthew 1948- *WhoAm 92*
Scopelliti, Joseph Anthony 1933- *WhoAm 92*
Scopes, Gary Martin 1947- *WhoAm 92*
Scopes, Jon Wilfred *WhoScE 91-1*
Scopino, Tony d1991 *BioIn 17*
Scopp, Irwin Walter 1909- *WhoWor 93*
Scopp, Kathleen H. *Law&B 92*
Scoppa, Pietro 1929- *WhoScE 91-3*
Scoppechio, Robert Anthony 1948- *WhoE 93*
Scoppettone, Sandra 1936- *DcAmChF 1985*
Scoppettone, Sandra Valerie 1936- *WhoWrEP 92*
Scorca, Marc Azzolini 1957- *WhoAm 92*
Scorce, Richard Anthony 1942- *St&PR 93*
Scordelis, Alexander Costicas 1923- *WhoAm 92*
Score, Herbert Jude 1933- *BiDAMSp 1989*
Scorer, Richard Segar *WhoScE 91-1*
Scorrano, Gianfranco 1939- *WhoScE 91-3*
Scorsese, Martin *BioIn 17*
Scorsese, Martin 1942- *MiSFD 9, WhoAm 92, WhoWor 93*
Scorsone, Vincent Robert 1935- *WhoAm 92*
Scortia, Thomas N. 1926- *BioIn 17*
Scortia, Thomas N. 1926-1986 *ScF&FL 92*
Scorza, Sylvio Joseph 1923- *WhoAm 92*
Scorzelli, James Francis 1943- *WhoE 93*
Scot, Anna *ScF&FL 92*
Scot, Michael *ScF&FL 92*
Scotellaro, Rocco 1923-1953 *DcLB 128 [port]*
Scothorn, Donald L. 1929- *St&PR 93*
Scott, A.G. *ScF&FL 92*
Scott, Alan 1947- *ScF&FL 92*
Scott, Alan James 1934- *WhoWor 93*
Scott, Alastair Ian 1928- *WhoAm 92*
Scott, Alexander Robinson 1941- *WhoAm 92*
Scott, Alice H. *WhoAm 92*
Scott, Allan *ConAu 136*
Scott, Allan 1952- *ScF&FL 92*
Scott, Amanda *WhoWrEP 92*
Scott, Amy Annette Holloway 1916- *WhoAmW 93, WhoWor 93*
Scott, Andrea Kay 1948- *WhoAmW 93*
Scott, Andrew 1928- *St&PR 93, WhoAm 92*
Scott, Anita Irma 1949- *WhoAmW 93*
Scott, Anna *ScF&FL 92*
Scott, Anna Marie Porter Wall *WhoAmW 93, WhoWor 93*
Scott, Anne Byrd Firor 1921- *WhoAm 92, WhoAmW 93*
Scott, Annetta Elizabeth 1960- *WhoAmW 93, WhoE 93*
Scott, Arnold D. 1942- *St&PR 93*
Scott, Arthur Ward 1936- *WhoSSW 93*
Scott, Audrey Ebba 1935- *WhoAm 92*
Scott, Ava Marie 1963- *WhoAmW 93*
Scott, Barbara Ann *BioIn 17*
Scott, Barbara Ann 1937- *WhoAmW 93*
Scott, Barbara S. 1948- *WhoWrEP 92*
Scott, Benjamin L. 1949- *WhoAm 92*
Scott, Bennett Norton 1926- *WhoSSW 93*
Scott, Bess Whitehead 1890- *BioIn 17*
Scott, Bill 1923- *DcChlFi, ScF&FL 92*
Scott, Bill 1949- *WhoAm 92*
Scott, Blaine W., III 1927- *St&PR 93*
Scott, Blaine Wahab, III 1927- *WhoE 93*
Scott, Bob Gerald 1938- *St&PR 93, WhoAm 92*
Scott, Bobby 1937-1990 *BioIn 17*
Scott, Bonnie Kime 1944- *WhoAmW 93*
Scott, Bradley Neil 1950- *St&PR 93*
Scott, Bradley S. *St&PR 93*
Scott, Bradley Sterling 1948- *WhoEmL 93, WhoWor 93*
Scott, Brian E. 1936- *WhoAm 92*
Scott, Brian Edward 1936- *St&PR 93, WhoIns 93*
Scott, Brian Walter 1935- *WhoWor 93*
Scott, Britt Stephen 1951- *WhoSSW 93*
Scott, Bruce Douglas 1958- *WhoWor 93*
Scott, Calvin *SoulM*
Scott, Campbell *BioIn 17*
Scott, Campbell 1930- *WhoAm 92*
Scott, Carl Werner 1953- *WhoSSW 93*
Scott, Carol Lee 1944- *WhoSSW 93*
Scott, Carole Elizabeth 1937- *WhoAmW 93*
Scott, Caroline Georgina Mary 1944- *WhoAmW 93*
Scott, Carolyn Alice 1965- *WhoE 93*
Scott, Charles David 1929- *WhoAm 92*
Scott, Charles Edward 1935- *WhoAm 92*
Scott, Charles Ellis, Jr. 1946- *WhoEmL 93*
Scott, Charles Kennedy 1876-1965 *Baker 92*
Scott, Charles Lewis 1924- *WhoAm 92*
Scott, Charles Prestwich 1846-1932 *BioIn 17*
Scott, Charles R. *WhoScE 91-1*
Scott, Charles R. 1928- *BioIn 17, St&PR 93, WhoAm 92, WhoSSW 93*
Scott, Charles S. 1932- *WhoIns 93*
Scott, Charles Wesley 1932- *WhoSSW 93*
Scott, Charlotte H. 1925- *WhoSSW 93*
Scott, Chris 1945- *WhoCanL 92*
Scott, Christopher 1930- *WhoSSW 93*
Scott, Cornelius Adolphus 1908- *BioIn 17*
Scott, Cynthia 1939- *MiSFD 9*
Scott, Cyril (Meir) 1879-1970 *Baker 92*
Scott, Daniel Joyner, III 1954- *WhoSSW 93*
Scott, Daniel Thomas 1944- *St&PR 93*
Scott, Danny Eugene 1947- *WhoSSW 93*
Scott, Darla Jean 1945- *WhoAmW 93*
Scott, David Bytovetzski 1919- *WhoAm 92*
Scott, David Evans 1938- *WhoAm 92*
Scott, David Irvin 1947- *WhoEmL 93*
Scott, David Janvier 1923-1991 *BioIn 17*
Scott, David Knight 1940- *WhoAm 92*
Scott, David McClure 1930- *WhoAm 92*
Scott, David R. 1932- *WhoAm 92*
Scott, David Richard Alexander 1954- *WhoWor 93*
Scott, David W. 1950- *St&PR 93*
Scott, David Warren 1950- *WhoAm 92, WhoSSW 93*
Scott, David William 1943- *WhoAm 92, WhoE 93*
Scott, Deborah Emont *WhoAm 92*
Scott, Dennis *WhoScE 91-1*
Scott, Dennis 1939-1991 *BioIn 17, DcLB 125 [port]*
Scott, Derek B. 1950- *ConAu 137*
Scott, Dianna Gay 1956- *WhoAmW 93*
Scott, Dixon 1881-1915 *BioIn 17*
Scott, Donald Allison 1929- *WhoAm 92*
Scott, Donald Charles 1920- *WhoSSW 93*
Scott, Donald John 1940- *WhoAm 92*
Scott, Donald L. 1933- *St&PR 93*
Scott, Donald Lavern 1938- *WhoAm 92*
Scott, Donald Laverne 1938- *AfrAmBi*
Scott, Donald Ray 1934- *WhoSSW 93*
Scott, Donald Rector 1905- *WhoAm 92*
Scott, Donald Wayne 1946- *St&PR 93*
Scott, Dorothy Marie 1921- *WhoAmW 93*
Scott, Douglas 1913-1990 *BioIn 17*
Scott, Douglas Edward *Law&B 92*
Scott, Douglas George *WhoScE 91-1*
Scott, Douglas W. *BioIn 17, St&PR 93*
Scott, Dread *BioIn 17*
Scott, Duncan Campbell 1862-1947 *BioIn 17*
Scott, Eddie E. *Law&B 92*
Scott, Eddie Elmer 1939- *WhoSSW 93*
Scott, Edward B., II *Law&B 92*
Scott, Edward Hofert 1929- *St&PR 93*
Scott, Edward William, Jr. 1938- *WhoAm 92*
Scott, Edwin D. *Law&B 92*
Scott, Edwin W. *Law&B 92*
Scott, Elaine Darlene 1952- *WhoAmW 93*
Scott, Eldred H. 1903- *St&PR 93*
Scott, Eleanor *ScF&FL 92*
Scott, Elizabeth Ann 1951- *WhoWrEP 92*
Scott, Emma G. *Law&B 92*
Scott, Emmett Jay 1873-1957 *EncAACR*
Scott, Eric *DcAmChF 1960*
Scott, Evelyn 1893-1963 *AmWomPl, BioIn 17*
Scott, Everett B. 1931- *St&PR 93*
Scott, F. Brantley 1930-1991 *BioIn 17*
Scott, F.L. *Law&B 92*
Scott, F.R. d1985 *WhoCanL 92*
Scott, Fenton 1927- *St&PR 93*
Scott, Francis George 1880-1958 *Baker 92*
Scott, Frank Edward 1920- *St&PR 93, WhoAm 92*
Scott, Franklin Daniel 1901- *WhoAm 92*
Scott, Frederick George 1861-1944 *BioIn 17*
Scott, Frederick Isadore, Jr. 1927- *WhoAm 92*
Scott, Frona *AmWomPl*
Scott, Gail C. 1958- *St&PR 93*
Scott, Gary D. *Law&B 92*
Scott, Gary Kuper 1933- *WhoAm 92*
Scott, Gary LeRoy 1954- *WhoEmL 93, WhoSSW 93, WhoWor 93*
Scott, Gene Dwight 1942- *St&PR 93*
Scott, George C. 1927- *BioIn 17, IntDcF 2-3 [port], MiSFD 9*
Scott, George Campbell 1927- *WhoAm 92*
Scott, George Charles, Jr. 1943- *BiDAMSp 1989*
Scott, George Cole, III 1937- *WhoSSW 93*
Scott, George Edmond 1924- *WhoAm 92*
Scott, George Ernest 1924- *WhoAm 92*
Scott, George Gallmann 1928- *WhoSSW 93*
Scott, Gerald *WhoScE 91-1*
Scott, Gerald David 1952- *WhoE 93*
Scott, Gerald Joseph 1947- *WhoWrEP 92*
Scott, Geraldine 1934- *St&PR 93*
Scott, Gloria 1927- *WhoAmW 93*
Scott, Gloria Dean Randle 1938- *AfrAmBi [port]*
Scott, Gloria R. *BioIn 17*
Scott, Gloria Romona 1927- *WhoE 93*
Scott, Gregory *BioIn 17*
Scott, H. Glen 1923- *St&PR 93*
Scott, Hal S. 1943- *WhoAm 92*
Scott, Harley Earle 1934- *WhoE 93*
Scott, Harold Bartlett 1917- *WhoAm 92*
Scott, Harvey W. 1838-1910 *JrnUS*
Scott, Hazel (Dorothy) 1920-1981 *Baker 92*
Scott, Henderson 1929- *St&PR 93*
Scott, Henry Edwards 1900-1990 *BioIn 17*
Scott, Henry Lawrence 1908- *WhoAm 92, WhoWor 93*
Scott, Henry William, Jr. 1916- *WhoAm 92*
Scott, Herbert Lee 1933- *St&PR 93*
Scott, Herman E. 1940- *WhoAm 92*
Scott, Howard Winfield, Jr. 1935- *WhoE 93*
Scott, Hugh *ScF&FL 92*
Scott, Hugh 1900- *WhoAm 92*
Scott, Hugh D., Jr. 1900- *PolPar*
Scott, Hugh Doggett 1900- *BioIn 17*
Scott, Hugh Lenox 1853-1934 *CmdGen 1991 [port], HarEnMi*
Scott, Hugh Nevin 1928- *WhoUN 92*
Scott, Hugh Patrick 1938- *WhoAm 92*
Scott, I. B. 1930- *WhoAm 92, WhoE 93*
Scott, Ian A. 1940- *WhoUN 92*
Scott, Irene Feagin 1912- *CngDr 91, WhoAm 92*
Scott, Isaac Alexander, Jr. 1934- *WhoWor 93*
Scott, Isadore Meyer 1912- *WhoAm 92*
Scott, J.D. 1931- *St&PR 93*
Scott, J.E. 1911- *ScF&FL 92*
Scott, J.T. *WhoScE 91-1*
Scott, J. Thomas *Law&B 92*
Scott, Jack Denton 1915- *MajAI [port]*
Scott, Jack P. 1946- *St&PR 93*
Scott, Jacqueline Delmar Parker 1947- *WhoAmW 93*
Scott, James *BioIn 17*
Scott, James 1941- *MiSFD 9*
Scott, James C. 1948- *St&PR 93*
Scott, James E. *Law&B 92*
Scott, James E., Mrs. *AmWomPl*
Scott, James Frazier 1934- *WhoWrEP 92*
Scott, James Hobbs, III 1938- *St&PR 93*
Scott, James Hunter, Jr. 1945- *WhoE 93, WhoWor 93*
Scott, James Leander 1814-1889? *BioIn 17*
Scott, James M. 1934- *St&PR 93, WhoIns 93*
Scott, James Owen 1936- *St&PR 93*
Scott, James Raymond 1937- *WhoAm 92*
Scott, James Steel *WhoScE 91-1*
Scott, James (Sylvester) 1885-1938 *Baker 92*
Scott, James Sylvester 1886-1938 *BioIn 17*
Scott, James White 1926- *WhoAm 92*
Scott, James Wilmot 1849-1895 *JrnUS*
Scott, Jan *St&PR 93*
Scott, Jane Ellen 1943- *WhoAmW 93*
Scott, Jane Harrington 1931- *WhoWrEP 92*
Scott, Jason *BioIn 17*
Scott, Jay 1949- *WhoAm 92*
Scott, Jayne Faye Bruno 1961- *WhoAmW 93*
Scott, Jeremy *ScF&FL 92*
Scott, Joan 1948- *WhoAmW 93*
Scott, Jody 1923- *ScF&FL 92*
Scott, John 1912-1976 *BioIn 17*
Scott, John A. *Law&B 92*
Scott, John Andrew *Law&B 92*
Scott, John Auston 1957- *WhoWor 93*
Scott, John B. 1944- *WhoIns 93*
Scott, John Brooks 1931- *WhoAm 92*
Scott, John Clark, Jr. 1953- *WhoE 93*
Scott, John Constante 1941- *WhoAm 92*
Scott, John E. 1939- *St&PR 93*
Scott, John Edward 1920- *WhoAm 92*
Scott, John Edward Smith 1936- *WhoAm 92, WhoWor 93*
Scott, John Ernest *WhoScE 91-1*
Scott, John J. *Law&B 92*
Scott, John Lenard 1921- *WhoAm 92, WhoE 93, WhoWor 93*
Scott, John Lyden 1934- *WhoAsAP 91*
Scott, John M. 1940- *WhoScE 91-3*
Scott, John N. 1930- *St&PR 93*
Scott, John Paul 1909- *WhoAm 92*
Scott, John Roland *Law&B 92*
Scott, John Roland 1937- *St&PR 93, WhoWor 93*
Scott, John Walter 1919- *WhoAm 92*
Scott, John William 1935- *WhoAm 92*
Scott, Jonathan L. 1930- *St&PR 93*
Scott, Jonathan LaVon 1930- *WhoAm 92*
Scott, Jonnie Melia Dean 1957- *WhoWrEP 92*
Scott, Joseph M. 1945- *St&PR 93*
Scott, Joseph Vernon 1926- *St&PR 93*
Scott, Joyce Alaine 1943- *WhoAm 92*
Scott, Judith Hulseberg *Law&B 92*
Scott, Judith Sugg 1945- *WhoSSW 93*
Scott, K.T. *Law&B 92*
Scott, Kathey Elaine 1945- *WhoAmW 93*
Scott, Kathryn Leigh 1943- *ScF&FL 92*
Scott, Kem Wayne 1948- *St&PR 93*
Scott, Ken 1918-1991 *BioIn 17*
Scott, Kenneth C. 1940- *St&PR 93, WhoAm 92*
Scott, Kenneth Elsner 1926- *WhoAm 92*
Scott, Kenneth Eugene 1928- *WhoAm 92*
Scott, Kenneth Pleasant, Jr. 1946- *WhoSSW 93*
Scott, Kerrigan Davis 1941- *WhoSSW 93*
Scott, Kristen 1946- *WhoAmW 93*
Scott, Larry Edwin 1948- *St&PR 93*
Scott, Larry Zant 1952- *WhoSSW 93*
Scott, Lawrence Vernon 1917- *WhoAm 92*
Scott, Lee Hansen 1926- *WhoAm 92*
Scott, Leigh 1888-1963 *BioIn 17*
Scott, Linda Preston 1941- *WhoAmW 93*
Scott, Loretta L. *Law&B 92*
Scott, Lottie Bell 1936- *WhoE 93*
Scott, Louis Edward 1923- *WhoAm 92*
Scott, Louis R. 1927- *St&PR 93*
Scott, Lurell Vaden 1942- *St&PR 93*
Scott, Lynn Edward 1933- *St&PR 93*
Scott, M.A. *WhoScE 91-1*
Scott, M. Gladys 1905-1990 *BioIn 17*
Scott, M. Lee 1910- *St&PR 93*
Scott, Malora Courtney 1949- *WhoAmW 93*
Scott, Marcia Nell 1938- *WhoAmW 93*
Scott, Margaret A. 1944- *WhoScE 91-1*
Scott, Margaret Daphne 1934- *WhoWor 93*
Scott, Margaret Simon 1934- *WhoAmW 93*
Scott, Margaretta *AmWomPl*
Scott, Marianne Florence 1928- *WhoAm 92, WhoAmW 93*
Scott, Marie Claudine 1953- *WhoAmW 93*

Scott, Marion (Margaret) 1877-1953 *Baker 92*
Scott, Marshal Logan 1909-1991 *BioIn 17*
Scott, Martha 1914?- *ConTFT 10*
Scott, Martha Sue 1961- *WhoAmW 93, WhoEmL 93*
Scott, Mary *ScF&FL 92*
Scott, Mary Davies 1944- *WhoAmW 93*
Scott, Mary Elizabeth 1940- *WhoAmW 93*
Scott, Mary Elizabeth 1951- *WhoEmL 93*
Scott, Mary Elizabeth 1959- *WhoEmL 93*
Scott, Mary Francis 1954- *WhoAmW 93*
Scott, Mary Jane Gomez 1944- *WhoE 93*
Scott, Mary Shy 1929- *WhoAmW 93*
Scott, Mary Theresa 1946- *WhoAmW 93*
Scott, Melissa *ScF&FL 92*
Scott, Michael *ScF&FL 92*
Scott, Michael 1924-1989 *BioIn 17*
Scott, Michael 1942- *MiSFD 9*
Scott, Michael 1959- *ScF&FL 92*
Scott, Michael David 1963- *WhoE 93*
Scott, Michael Dennis 1945- *WhoAm 92*
Scott, Michael Douglas *Law&B 92*
Scott, Michael George *WhoScE 91-1*
Scott, Michael J. *Law&B 92*
Scott, Michelle P. *Law&B 92*
Scott, Mike *BioIn 17*
Scott, Milcha Sanchez *NotHsAW 93*
Scott, Milton Leonard 1915- *WhoE 93*
Scott, Mimi Koblenz 1940- *WhoE 93*
Scott, Munroe *WhoCanL 92*
Scott, Myrtle 1937- *WhoAmW 93*
Scott, Myrtle Gladys 1905-1990 *BioIn 17*
Scott, N. Kenneth, Jr. *Law&B 92*
Scott, Nancy Ellen 1960- *WhoE 93, WhoWor 93*
Scott, Natalie Vivian 1890- *AmWomPl*
Scott, Nathan Alexander, Jr. 1925- *WhoAm 92*
Scott, Nelson 1835-1862 *BioIn 17*
Scott, Norman Bruce St. Clair 1933- *WhoUN 92*
Scott, Norman Roy 1936- *WhoAm 92*
Scott, Owen Myers, Jr. 1952- *WhoSSW 93*
Scott, Oz *MiSFD 9*
Scott, P.F. *WhoScE 91-1*
Scott, Pamela Moyers 1961- *WhoAmW 93*
Scott, Patricia Jeanne 1942- *WhoWrEP 92*
Scott, Patricia M. *Law&B 92*
Scott, Patrick Noel 1956- *WhoWor 93*
Scott, Paul 1920-1978 *BioIn 17*
Scott, Paul G. 1947- *St&PR 93*
Scott, Peter Bryan 1947- *WhoEmL 93*
Scott, Peter Hamilton 1936- *St&PR 93*
Scott, Peter John 1920- *St&PR 93*
Scott, Peter Markham 1909-1989 *BioIn 17*
Scott, Peter T. *Law&B 92*
Scott, Philip John 1931- *WhoWor 93*
Scott, Phillip J. *St&PR 93*
Scott, Phillip Randall *Law&B 92*
Scott, R.C. *ScF&FL 92*
Scott, R. J. *WhoAm 92*
Scott, R.T.M. 1882- *ScF&FL 92*
Scott, Ralph 1952- *WhoAm 92*
Scott, Ralph C. 1921- *WhoAm 92, WhoWor 93*
Scott, Ralph Mason 1921- *WhoAm 92*
Scott, Randolph 1903-1987 *IntDcF 2-3 [port]*
Scott, Raymond Peter William 1924- *WhoAm 92*
Scott, Reva Marvene Mann 1918- *WhoWrEP 92*
Scott, Richard 1956- *BioIn 17*
Scott, Richard Albert, Jr. 1957- *WhoE 93*
Scott, Richard E. 1942- *St&PR 93*
Scott, Richard Eugene 1950- *WhoE 93*
Scott, Richard P. *ScF&FL 92*
Scott, Ridley *BioIn 17*
Scott, Ridley 1939- *MiSFD 9, WhoAm 92*
Scott, Robert *BioIn 17*
Scott, Robert A. *Law&B 92, WhoIns 93*
Scott, Robert Allyn 1939- *WhoAm 92, WhoE 93, WhoWor 93*
Scott, Robert Cortez 1947- *WhoSSW 93*
Scott, Robert Falcon 1868-1912 *BioIn 17, Expl 93 [port]*
Scott, Robert Garth 1957- *ConAu 137*
Scott, Robert Kent 1936- *WhoAm 92*
Scott, Robert Lane 1922- *WhoAm 92*
Scott, Robert Lee 1908- *BioIn 17*
Scott, Robert Lee 1928- *WhoAm 92*
Scott, Robert Lee 1957- *WhoSSW 93*
Scott, Robert Lee, Jr. 1908- *WhoAm 92*
Scott, Robert Montgomery 1929- *WhoAm 92, WhoE 93, WhoWor 93*
Scott, Roderic MacDonald 1916- *WhoAm 92*
Scott, Rodger Gene 1931- *WhoAm 92*
Scott, Roger Davidson *WhoScE 91-1*
Scott, Roger Wilkin 1960- *WhoSSW 93*
Scott, Ronald Fraser 1929- *WhoAm 92*
Scott, Ronald H. 1932- *St&PR 93*
Scott, Ronald John 1936- *WhoE 93*
Scott, Ronald L. *Law&B 92*
Scott, Ronald William 1951- *WhoSSW 93*
Scott, Roney *ConAu 37NR*
Scott, Ross R. *Law&B 92*
Scott, Roy A. 1940- *St&PR 93*
Scott, Roy Vernon 1927- *WhoSSW 93*
Scott, Rufus S. *Law&B 92*
Scott, Russell William 1957- *WhoE 93*
Scott, Sam *St&PR 93*
Scott, Sandra *ScF&FL 92*
Scott, Sandra Louise 1944- *WhoAmW 93*
Scott, Sandy 1943- *BioIn 17*
Scott, Sarah Elizabeth 1959- *WhoAmW 93*
Scott, Sharon Kay 1940- *St&PR 93*
Scott, Sheila 1927-1988 *BioIn 17*
Scott, Sherry 1944- *St&PR 93*
Scott, Sidney Buford 1933- *WhoSSW 93*
Scott, Stanley DeForest 1926- *WhoE 93*
Scott, Stanley S. *BioIn 17*
Scott, Stanley S. d1992 *NewYTBS 92*
Scott, Stephen 1944- *Baker 92*
Scott, Stephen Carlos 1949- *WhoSSW 93*
Scott, Steven Donald 1941- *WhoAm 92*
Scott, Steven M. *St&PR 93*
Scott, Stuart Nash d1992 *NewYTBS 92 [port]*
Scott, Stuart Nash 1906-1992 *BioIn 17*
Scott, Sue 1951- *WhoScE 91-1*
Scott, Susan Rice 1942- *WhoAmW 93*
Scott, Susan Samples 1955- *WhoSSW 93*
Scott, Swayne F. 1933- *WhoUN 92*
Scott, Sylvia Rachel Jeanne 1949- *WhoAmW 93*
Scott, Tanya Gardiner- *ScF&FL 92*
Scott, Taryn *WhoWrEP 92*
Scott, Terry 1927- *QDrFCA 92 [port]*
Scott, Terry L. *St&PR 93*
Scott, Theodore R. 1924- *WhoAm 92*
Scott, Thomas Clevenger 1936- *WhoAm 92*
Scott, Thomas G., Sr. *Law&B 92*
Scott, Thomas H. *St&PR 93*
Scott, Thomas Wright 1948- *WhoAm 92*
Scott, Tim 1937- *BioIn 17*
Scott, Timothy Leighton 1944- *St&PR 93*
Scott, Tom 1912-1961 *Baker 92*
Scott, Tom Keck 1931- *WhoAm 92*
Scott, Tony *MiSFD 9, WhoAm 92*
Scott, Valerie Ann 1955- *WhoAmW 93*
Scott, Valerie Don 1949- *WhoAmW 93*
Scott, Velma 1950- *WhoAmW 93*
Scott, Vernita Lynn 1958- *WhoAmW 93*
Scott, Vernon G. *Law&B 92*
Scott, Victor Denis *WhoScE 91-1*
Scott, Victor Richard 1950- *St&PR 93*
Scott, Vikki *BioIn 17*
Scott, W. Russell, Jr. 1937- *St&PR 93*
Scott, Wade Addison 1937- *WhoSSW 93*
Scott, Wade T. *Law&B 92*
Scott, Waldron 1929- *WhoAm 92*
Scott, Walter 1771-1832 *BioIn 17, DcLB 116 [port], MagSWL [port], OxDcOp, ScF&FL 92, WorLitC [port]*
Scott, Walter, Jr. 1931- *WhoAm 92*
Scott, Walter Anthony John 1964- *WhoWor 93*
Scott, Walter Coke 1919- *WhoAm 92*
Scott, Walter Decker 1915- *WhoAm 92*
Scott, Walter Dill 1931- *WhoAm 92*
Scott, Walter Gerard, Jr. 1941- *St&PR 93*
Scott, Walter Neil 1935- *WhoE 93*
Scott, Walter Ray 1913- *WhoWrEP 92*
Scott, Wendell *BioIn 17*
Scott, Wendell Oliver, Sr. 1921-1990 *AfrAmBi*
Scott, Wiley Anthony, Jr. 1955- *WhoE 93*
Scott, Willard Herman 1934- *WhoAm 92*
Scott, Willard Philip 1909- *WhoAm 92*
Scott, William 1913-1989 *BioIn 17*
Scott, William Addison, III 1940- *WhoE 93*
Scott, William Beverley 1917- *WhoAm 92*
Scott, William Clement, III 1934- *WhoAm 92*
Scott, William Coryell 1920- *WhoAm 92, WhoWor 93*
Scott, William F. *St&PR 93*
Scott, William Fred 1953- *WhoAm 92*
Scott, William James 1944- *WhoE 93*
Scott, William Lloyd 1915- *WhoAm 92*
Scott, William N. *ScF&FL 92*
Scott, William P. 1930- *St&PR 93*
Scott, William Paul 1928- *WhoAm 92*
Scott, William R(alph) 1918-1992 *ConAu 136*
Scott, William Richard 1932- *WhoAm 92*
Scott, William T. 1953- *St&PR 93*
Scott, William Thomas d1990 *BioIn 17*
Scott, William W., Jr. 1944- *St&PR 93*
Scott, Winfield 1786-1866 *CmdGen 1991 [port], HarEnMi, PolPar*
Scott, Winfield Allen 1934- *WhoE 93*
Scott, Winfield H(arker) 1932-1992 *ConAu 136*
Scott-Conner, Carol Elizabeth Hoffman 1946- *WhoSSW 93*
Scott-Drennan, Lynne Ellen 1944- *WhoWrEP 92*
Scotte, Brandon *WhoWrEP 92*
Scotten, Cordell 1921- *ScF&FL 92*
Scott-Finan, Nancy Isabella 1949- *WhoAmW 93, WhoE 93*
Scotti, Anna *SmATA 73*
Scotti, Antonio 1866-1936 *Baker 92, IntDcOp [port], OxDcOp*
Scotti, Michael John, Jr. 1938- *WhoAm 92*
Scott-James, Anne 1913- *BioIn 17*
Scott-McBride, Nancy Forsyth 1940- *WhoWrEP 92*
Scott Moncrieff, D. 1907-1987 *ScF&FL 92*
Scotto, David A. 1943- *St&PR 93*
Scotto, Joseph V. 1934- *St&PR 93*
Scotto, Renata 1933- *Baker 92, OxDcOp*
Scotto, Renata 1934- *IntDcOp [port]*
Scotto, Renata 1935- *WhoAm 92, WhoWor 93*
Scotto, Sal 1936- *St&PR 93*
Scotto La Massese, Claude 1926- *WhoScE 91-2*
Scott-Roache, Ella Marie *WhoAmW 93*
Scott-Williams, Nigel Simon 1955- *WhoE 93*
Scott-Williams, Stephanie 1947- *WhoAmW 93*
Scott-Wilson, Sheryl Susette 1966- *WhoAmW 93*
Scotus, John *Baker 92*
Scotus, John Duns c. 1266-1308 *BioIn 17*
Scoular, Robert Frank 1942- *WhoAm 92, WhoWor 93*
Scoular, Tolmie Alexander 1926- *WhoWor 93*
Scoumanne, Florent 1884-1981 *BioIn 17*
Scouras, Tana Aline *WhoAmW 93*
Scouten, William Henry 1942- *WhoAm 92, WhoSSW 93*
Scovel, Mary Alice 1936- *WhoAmW 93*
Scovel, Sylvester 1869-1905 *GayN*
Scovel, Thomas Richard *Law&B 92*
Scovell, E(dith) J(oy) 1907- *ConAu 136*
Scovil, H. Raymond 1925- *WhoE 93*
Scovil, Roger Morris 1929- *WhoAm 92, WhoSSW 93*
Scovil, Samuel K. 1923- *St&PR 93*
Scovil, Samuel Kingston 1923- *WhoAm 92*
Scovill, Brian W. *Law&B 92*
Scoville, Barrett 1936-1991 *BioIn 17*
Scoville, E.N. 1941- *St&PR 93*
Scoville, James Griffin 1940- *WhoAm 92*
Scoville, John J. 1935- *St&PR 93*
Scoville, Jonathan Armstrong 1937- *WhoE 93*
Scoville, Ronald Robert 1927- *St&PR 93*
Scoville, Wayne W. 1937- *St&PR 93*
Scovotti, Jeanette 1936- *Baker 92*
Scowcroft, Alan Eric 1956- *WhoWor 93*
Scowcroft, Brent *BioIn 17*
Scowcroft, Brent 1925- *ColdWar 1 [port], WhoAm 92, WhoE 93*
Scowcroft, Jerome Chilwell 1947- *WhoAm 92, WhoEmL 93*
Scowcroft, John A. 1955- *St&PR 93*
Scowcroft, John Arthur 1954- *WhoAm 92*
Scowcroft, Richard Mark 1951- *WhoE 93*
Scoza, Robert H. 1947- *St&PR 93*
Scozzafava, Romano 1935- *WhoWor 93*
Scragg, George Henry, Jr. 1934- *WhoSSW 93*
Scragg, Thomas William 1940- *WhoWor 93*
Scragg, William W. 1941- *St&PR 93*
Scrantom, John Gardner 1928- *WhoSSW 93*
Scranton, Robert J. 1940- *St&PR 93*
Scranton, William Maxwell 1921- *St&PR 93, WhoAm 92*
Scranton, William W. 1917- *PolPar*
Scranton, William Warren 1917- *BioIn 17*
Scrase, David Anthony 1939- *WhoE 93*
Scratcherd, Thomas *WhoScE 91-1*
Screpetis, Dennis 1930- *WhoE 93*
Screvane, Paul Rogers 1914- *WhoAm 92*
Scriabin, Alexander (Nikolaievich) 1872-1915 *Baker 92*
Scriabine, Alexander 1926- *WhoE 93*
Scriabine, Marina 1911- *Baker 92*
Scriban, Rene 1920- *WhoScE 91-2*
Scribano, Angelo 1942- *WhoScE 91-3*
Scribe, Eugene 1791-1861 *IntDcOp [port], OxDcOp*
Scribe, (Augustin) Eugene 1791-1861 *Baker 92*
Scribner, Barbara Colvin 1926- *WhoAm 92*
Scribner, Belding Hibbard 1921- *WhoAm 92*
Scribner, Charles 1921- *BioIn 17*
Scribner, Charles, Jr. 1921- *WhoAm 92*
Scribner, Charles, III 1951- *WhoAm 92*
Scribner, David 1906-1991 *BioIn 17*
Scribner, Fred Clark, Jr. 1908- *St&PR 93, WhoAm 92*
Scribner, George *MiSFD 9*
Scribner, Jean Elizabeth 1922- *WhoAmW 93*
Scribner, Kimball J. 1917- *BioIn 17*
Scribner, Lizzie B. *AmWomPl*
Scribner, Margaret Ellen 1948- *WhoEmL 93*
Scribner, Norman (Orville) 1936- *Baker 92*
Scribner, Richard Orestes 1936- *WhoAm 92*
Scribner, Ronald Kent 1948- *WhoSSW 93*
Scribner, Sylvia 1925-1991 *BioIn 17*
Scricca, Diane Bernadette 1951- *WhoAmW 93*
Scriffignano, Rosanne Sally 1961- *WhoAmW 93*
Scriggins, Larry Palmer 1936- *WhoAm 92*
Scrignar, Chester Bruno 1934- *WhoSSW 93*
Scrim, Russel C. 1918- *St&PR 93*
Scrimenti, Belinda Jayne 1956- *WhoAmW 93*
Scrimgeour, James Richard 1938- *WhoWrEP 92*
Scrimshaw, Nevin Stewart 1918- *WhoAm 92*
Scrine, G.R. *WhoScE 91-1*
Scripcaru, Gheorghe *WhoScE 91-4*
Scripps, Charles E. 1920- *St&PR 93*
Scripps, Charles Edward 1920- *WhoAm 92*
Scripps, E.W. 1854-1926 *BioIn 17, JrnUS*
Scripps, Edward Wyllis 1854-1926 *BioIn 17*
Scripps, Edward Wyllis 1909- *WhoAm 92*
Scrire. O.T.O. 4=7 1884-1964 *ScF&FL 92*
Scritchfield, Randy Lawrence 1956- *WhoE 93*
Scritchfield, Shirley Ann 1947- *WhoAmW 93*
Scriven, L. Edward 1931- *WhoAm 92*
Scriven, Robert Geoffrey *WhoScE 91-1*
Scrivener, Olivier 1938- *WhoScE 91-2*
Scrivens, Patrick 1953- *St&PR 93*
Scriver, Charles Robert 1930- *WhoAm 92*
Scriver, John *Law&B 92*
Scriver, Robert Macfie 1914- *WhoAm 92*
Scrivner, Barbara E. 1931- *WhoAmW 93*
Scrivner, Douglas G. *Law&B 92*
Scrocco Zrzavy, Phyllis Ann 1960- *WhoE 93*
Scroeder, Darrell H. 1923- *St&PR 93*
Scroggie, Wayne Lee 1949- *WhoWor 93*
Scroggins, Carol D. 1933- *St&PR 93*
Scroggins, Carol Dean *WhoAmW 93*
Scroggins, Deborah Lane 1961- *WhoAm 92*
Scroggins, Nancy J. 1950- *WhoAmW 93*
Scroggins, Randy 1950- *St&PR 93*
Scroggins, Richard Muir 1932- *St&PR 93, WhoAm 92*
Scroggy, Hal *BioIn 17*
Scrone, Daniel 1939- *St&PR 93*
Scruggs, Charles G. 1923- *WhoAm 92*
Scruggs, Donald O. 1939- *WhoIns 93*
Scruggs, Earl (Eugene) 1924- *Baker 92, WhoAm 92*
Scruggs, Edwin Noel, Jr. 1953- *WhoSSW 93*
Scruggs, Ima Sue 1936- *St&PR 93*
Scruggs, Jack Gilbert 1930- *St&PR 93, WhoAm 92*
Scruggs, James Harry 1920- *WhoSSW 93*
Scruggs, John Dudley 1911- *WhoAm 92*
Scruggs, John Floyd 1955- *WhoE 93*
Scruggs, Paul Cecil 1937- *WhoSSW 93*
Scruitsky, Robert Lee 1963- *WhoE 93*
Scrushy, Richard M. 1952- *ConEn*
Scruton, George Stephen 1926- *St&PR 93*
Scruton, Kathleen A. *Law&B 92*
Scruton, Michelle P. *Law&B 92*
Scruton, Roger 1944- *ConAu 39NR*
Scrutton, Keith Robert 1932- *St&PR 93*
Scrutton, Michael Christopher *WhoScE 91-1*
Scrymsour, Ella 1888- *ScF&FL 92*
Scrysmour, Ella *AmWomPl*
Scudamore of Sligo, Viscount 1601-1671 *BioIn 17*
Scudder, Antoinette Quinby 1898- *AmWomPl*
Scudder, Daniel F. *Law&B 92*
Scudder, David Witherspoon 1936- *St&PR 93*
Scudder, Edna Drake *AmWomPl*
Scudder, Edward Wallace, Jr. 1911- *WhoAm 92*
Scudder, Geoffrey George Edgar 1934- *WhoAm 92*
Scudder, Ruby J. Smith 1935- *WhoSSW 93*
Scudder, Thayer 1930- *WhoAm 92*
Scudder, Theodore T. *BioIn 17*
Scudder, William 1739-1804 *BioIn 17*
Scuderi, Anthony Joseph 1958- *WhoE 93*
Scuderi, Filomena Perone 1930- *WhoAmW 93*
Scudery, Madeleine de 1607-1701 *BioIn 17*
Scudieri, Lorraine Alberto 1940- *WhoE 93*
Scudo, P(ietro) 1806-1864 *Baker 92*
Scuffham, J.B. *WhoScE 91-1*
Sculco, Lois Jean 1938- *WhoE 93*
Sculfort, Jean-Lou 1944- *WhoWor 93*

Sculfort, Maurice Charles 1925- *WhoAm 92*
Scull, Dorothy Mae 1948- *WhoAmW 93*
Scull, James Gregory 1961- *WhoSSW 93*
Scullen, Peter Raymond *Law&B 92*
Sculley, David W. 1946- *WhoAm 92, WhoE 93*
Sculley, John *BioIn 17*
Sculley, John 1939- *St&PR 93, WhoAm 92*
Scullin, Frederick James, Jr. 1939- *WhoAm 92*
Scullin, James Henry 1876-1953 *DcTwHis*
Scullion, Annette Murphy 1926- *WhoAmW 93*
Scullion, William Joseph 1932- *St&PR 93*
Scully, Colleen Mary 1969- *WhoAmW 93*
Scully, Crispian Michael 1945- *WhoWor 93*
Scully, Geoffrey Ballenger 1959- *St&PR 93*
Scully, James Joseph 1937- *WhoWrEP 92*
Scully, John C. 1932- *WhoIns 93*
Scully, John Carroll 1932- *WhoAm 92*
Scully, John Edward 1943- *St&PR 93*
Scully, John Robert 1949- *WhoEmL 93*
Scully, John Thomas 1931- *WhoAm 92*
Scully, Joseph C. 1940- *St&PR 93*
Scully, Lawrence A. 1922- *St&PR 93*
Scully, Marlan Orvil 1939- *WhoAm 92*
Scully, Monya Frances 1921- *WhoE 93*
Scully, Robert G. 1926- *St&PR 93*
Scully, Roger Tehan *Law&B 92*
Scully, Roger Tehan 1948- *WhoE 93, WhoEmL 93, WhoWor 93*
Scully, Sean Paul 1945- *WhoAm 92*
Scully, Susan 1950- *WhoE 93*
Scully, Vincent Edward 1927- *WhoAm 92*
Scully, Vincent Joseph 1920- *BioIn 17*
Scult, Lawrence N. *Law&B 92*
Sculthorpe, Peter 1929- *BioIn 17*
Sculthorpe, Peter (Joshua) 1929- *Baker 92, WhoWor 93*
Sculti, Leon 1934- *St&PR 93*
Scuorzo, Linda Marie *Law&B 92*
Scupham, A.G. *ScF&FL 92*
Scura, Dorothy McInnis 1933- *WhoSSW 93*
Scuralli, Joseph P. *St&PR 93*
Scurci, Daniel James 1925- *St&PR 93*
Scurfield, Robert M. *Law&B 92*
Scurlock, Arch Chilton 1920- *St&PR 93, WhoAm 92*
Scurlock, Doc d1882 *BioIn 17*
Scurlock, Ralph Geoffrey *WhoScE 91-1*
Scurlock, Robert Edward 1933- *St&PR 93*
Scuro, Vincent 1951- *ConAu 40NR*
Scurry, Richardson Gano 1938- *St&PR 93*
Scurry, Richardson Gano, Jr. 1938- *WhoAm 92*
Scurry, Rod d1992 *NewYTBS 92*
Scutt, Gerald Arthur 1929- *St&PR 93*
Scutta, Andreas 1806-1863 *OxDcOp*
Scylax fl. c. 516BC-509BC *HarEnMi*
Scylax of Caryanda fl. 6th cent.- *Expl 93*
Scyoc, Sydney J. Van *ScF&FL 92*
Szech, Marilyn J. 1948- *St&PR 93*
Sdoukos, Antonios 1939- *WhoScE 91-3*
Sdouz, Gert 1950- *WhoWor 93*
Seaberg, Ladd M. 1946- *St&PR 93*
Seaberry, Macarthur 1948- *WhoSSW 93*
Seaborg, Glenn Theodore 1912- *WhoAm 92, WhoWor 93*
Seaborn, A. Hardeman 1953- *St&PR 93*
Seaborn, J.L. 1923- *St&PR 93*
Seaborn, James Byrd 1932- *WhoSSW 93*
Seaborn, John Robert 1940- *St&PR 93*
Seabourn, Danny 1951- *St&PR 93*
Seabright, Idris 1911- *BioIn 17*
Seabrook, John Martin 1917- *WhoAm 92*
Seabrook, Robert Childs 1919- *WhoIns 93*
Seabrook, William B. 1886-1945 *BioIn 17*
Seabrooks, John R. 1947- *St&PR 93*
Seabrooks, Nettie Harris 1934- *WhoAmW 93*
Seaburg, Paul Allen 1934- *WhoAm 92*
Seaburg, Robert E. 1933- *St&PR 93*
Seabury, Caroline 1827-1893 *BioIn 17*
Seabury, Paul *BioIn 17*
Seabury, Richard Williams, III 1937- *St&PR 93*
Seaby, David Allen *WhoScE 91-1*
Seacat, Sandra *MiSFD 9*
Seachrest, Effie *AmWomPl*
Seacord, Stephanie Therese 1952- *WhoAmW 93*
Seade, Jesus 1946- *WhoUN 92*
Seaden, George 1936- *WhoAm 92*
Seader, Junior DeVere 1927- *WhoAm 92*
Seader, Paul A. *Law&B 92*
Seadle, Michael Steven 1950- *WhoE 93*
Seadler, Stephen Edward 1926- *WhoE 93, WhoWor 93*
Seaga, Edward 1930- *DcCPCAm, DcTwHis*
Seagal, Steven *BioIn 17*
Seagal, Steven 1952- *ConTFT 10*
Seager, Daniel Albert 1920- *WhoAm 92*
Seager, Elizabeth *Law&B 92*
Seager, John C.R. 1934- *WhoScE 91-3*
Seager, Stephen B. *BioIn 17*
Seager, Stephen B. 1950- *ConAu 139*
Seagle, Oscar 1877-1945 *Baker 92*
Seagle, Victor Ryland 1945- *WhoSSW 93*
Seagram, Norman Meredith 1934- *WhoAm 92*
Seagrave, James Edward 1949- *St&PR 93*
Seagrove, Jenny *BioIn 17*
Seagull, Barbara *ConTFT 10*
Seagull, Elizabeth Ann 1947- *WhoAmW 93*
Seah, Martin P. 1941- *WhoScE 91-1*
Seal *BioIn 17*
Seal, B.G. 1934- *St&PR 93*
Seal, John Charles 1950- *WhoAm 92*
Seal, John S., Jr. 1944- *WhoE 93, WhoWor 93*
Seal, Lawton Anthony 1950- *WhoSSW 93*
Seal, Leo W., Jr. 1924- *St&PR 93*
Seal, Leo William, Jr. 1924- *WhoAm 92*
Seal, Lester Paul 1932- *St&PR 93*
Seal, Robert Hutcheson 1923- *St&PR 93*
Seal, Thomas F. 1953- *St&PR 93*
Sealby, Susan Diane 1965- *WhoAmW 93*
Seale, Bobby 1936- *ConBlB 3 [port], EncAACR*
Seale, H. Patrick 1953- *St&PR 93*
Seale, J. William 1943- *St&PR 93*
Seale, James Lawrence, Jr. 1949- *WhoWor 93*
Seale, Jan Epton 1939- *WhoWrEP 92*
Seale, John *MiSFD 9*
Seale, Joseph Lloyd 1919- *WhoWrEP 92*
Seale, Robert L. 1941- *WhoAm 92*
Seale, William Edward 1941- *WhoAm 92*
Sealey, Barbara Edith 1939- *WhoAmW 93*
"Sea-Lion" 1909-1983 *ScF&FL 92*
Seall, Michael Eugene 1947- *St&PR 93*
Seall, Stephen Albert 1940- *WhoAm 92*
Seall-Sasiain, Jorge 1952- *WhoE 93*
Sealock, Ronald F. 1934- *St&PR 93*
Sealock, Thelma W. *AmWomPl*
Seals, Dan 1948- *ConMus 9 [port]*
Seals, Ernest C. 1937- *St&PR 93*
Seals, Henry Chaim 1924- *St&PR 93*
Seals, Mary Jane 1946- *WhoSSW 93*
Seals, Ryan Brown 1920- *WhoSSW 93*
Seals, Woodrow Bradley 1917-1990 *BioIn 17*
Sealy, Albert Henry 1917- *WhoAm 92, WhoWor 93*
Sealy, Brian John *WhoScE 91-1*
Sealy, George Paul 1926- *St&PR 93*
Sealy, I(rwin) Allan 1951- *ConAu 136*
Sealy, Malik *BioIn 17*
Sealy, Ruby *WhoWrEP 92*
Sealy, Sheila Ivoline 1961- *WhoUN 92*
Sealy, Tom 1909- *WhoAm 92*
Seaman, Alfred Jarvis 1912- *WhoAm 92*
Seaman, Allan M. *Law&B 92*
Seaman, Barbara 1935- *WhoAm 92*
Seaman, Byron James 1923- *St&PR 93, WhoAm 92*
Seaman, Charles Wilson 1946- *WhoEmL 93*
Seaman, Christopher 1942- *Baker 92*
Seaman, Daryl Kenneth 1922- *St&PR 93, WhoWor 93*
Seaman, David Michael 1962- *WhoSSW 93*
Seaman, Debra Beth 1959- *WhoAmW 93*
Seaman, Donald Roy 1925- *St&PR 93, WhoAm 92*
Seaman, Elizabeth Cochrane *GayN*
Seaman, Gerald Roberts 1934- *WhoWor 93*
Seaman, Gordy Carmichael 1950- *WhoSSW 93*
Seaman, Irving, Jr. 1923- *St&PR 93, WhoAm 92*
Seaman, James David 1930- *St&PR 93*
Seaman, James Richard 1941- *St&PR 93*
Seaman, Janet W. 1934- *St&PR 93*
Seaman, John Gates 1919- *WhoSSW 93*
Seaman, Mike *BioIn 17*
Seaman, Miles Andrew 1942- *WhoScE 91-1*
Seaman, Peggy Jean 1949- *WhoE 93*
Seaman, Peter B. 1952- *St&PR 93*
Seaman, Peter W. 1949- *St&PR 93*
Seaman, Robert E., III 1947- *WhoAm 92, WhoWor 93*
Seaman, Robert Lee 1942- *WhoAm 92*
Seaman, Ronald Leon 1947- *WhoSSW 93*
Seaman, Rosemarie *BioIn 17*
Seaman, William Bernard 1917- *WhoAm 92*
Seaman, William Casper 1925- *WhoAm 92*
Seamans, Andrew Charles 1937- *WhoE 93, WhoSSW 93, WhoWor 93, WhoWrEP 92*
Seamans, Richard C. *Law&B 92*
Seamans, Robert C., Jr. 1918- *St&PR 93*
Seamans, Robert Channing, Jr. 1918- *WhoAm 92, WhoE 93*
Seamans, Warren Arthur 1935- *WhoAm 92*
Seamans, William 1925- *WhoAm 92*
Seamark, Robert Frederick 1937- *WhoWor 93*
Seamen, James D. d1990 *BioIn 17*
Seamon, Mannie 1897-1983 *BioIn 17*
Seamon, William d1992 *BioIn 17, NewYTBS 92*
Seapker, Janet Kay 1947- *WhoAmW 93, WhoSSW 93*
Seaquist, Ernest Raymond 1938- *WhoAm 92*
Seaquist, Gwen 1952- *WhoAmW 93*
Sear, Morey Leonard 1929- *WhoAm 92, WhoSSW 93*
Sear, Robert J. 1936- *WhoIns 93*
Searby, Richard Henry 1931- *WhoWor 93*
Search, Frederick Preston 1889-1959 *Baker 92*
Searcy, Alan Winn 1925- *WhoAm 92*
Searcy, Chris Jackson 1953- *WhoSSW 93*
Searcy, James F. 1938- *St&PR 93*
Searcy, Jarrell D. Jay 1934- *WhoAm 92*
Searcy, John Cicero, III 1949- *WhoSSW 93*
Searcy, William Michael 1943- *St&PR 93*
Searfoss, David William 1951- *St&PR 93*
Searight, Carol Chipman 1942- *WhoAmW 93*
Searight, Mary Dell 1918- *WhoWor 93*
Searing, Marjory Ellen 1945- *WhoAm 92, WhoAmW 93*
Searl, John Roy Robert 1932- *WhoWor 93*
Searle, Clara *AmWomPl*
Searle, Daniel C. 1926- *St&PR 93*
Searle, David *WhoScE 91-1*
Searle, Eleanor Millard 1926- *WhoAm 92*
Searle, George Baldwin 1933- *St&PR 93*
Searle, Humphrey 1915-1982 *Baker 92, OxDcOp*
Searle, James Elmhurst 1929- *WhoWor 93*
Searle, John Gideon 1901-1978 *BioIn 17*
Searle, Katharine *AmWomPl*
Searle, Margaret Cassie *AmWomPl*
Searle, Nigel Hilton 1946- *WhoE 93*
Searle, Philip Ford 1924- *WhoAm 92*
Searle, Q.R. 1937- *St&PR 93*
Searle, Robert *Law&B 92*
Searle, Robert A. 1944- *St&PR 93*
Searle, Rodney Newell 1920- *WhoAm 92*
Searle, Ronald 1920- *BioIn 17, WhoAm 92*
Searle, Ronald (William Fordham) 1920- *MajAI [port], SmATA 70 [port]*
Searle, Stewart A., III *WhoIns 93*
Searle, William Louis 1928- *St&PR 93, WhoAm 92*
Searles, Baird 1934- *ScF&FL 92*
Searles, David Sewall, Jr. 1946- *WhoSSW 93*
Searles, Dewitt Richard 1920- *WhoAm 92*
Searles, John Rumney, Jr. 1912- *WhoSSW 93*
Searles, Michael M. 1949- *St&PR 93*
Searles, Richard B. 1936- *ConAu 139*
Searles, Richard Brownlee 1936- *WhoAm 92*
Searles, T.M., Jr. 1921- *St&PR 93*
Searles, Thomas Daniel 1937- *WhoE 93*
Searles, William Harris 1956- *WhoE 93*
Searls, Eileen Haughey 1925- *WhoAmW 93*
Searls, Frederick Taylor 1912- *WhoAm 92*
Searls, Hank 1922- *ScF&FL 92*
Searls, Henry *ScF&FL 92*
Searls, James Paul 1937- *WhoE 93*
Searls, Melvin William, Jr. 1935- *WhoAm 92*
Searls, Robert Louarn 1931- *WhoE 93*
Sears, A.H. *Law&B 92*
Sears, Al 1910-1990 *BioIn 17*
Sears, Bill W. 1947- *St&PR 93*
Sears, Bradford George 1915- *WhoAm 92*
Sears, Catherine Marie 1955- *WhoSSW 93*
Sears, Curtis Thornton, Jr. 1938- *WhoAm 92, WhoSSW 93*
Sears, Derek William George 1948- *WhoSSW 93*
Sears, Edward Milner, Jr. 1944- *WhoAm 92*
Sears, Eleonora Randolph 1881-1968 *BioIn 17*
Sears, Ernest R. 1910-1991 *BioIn 17*
Sears, George Ames 1926- *WhoAm 92*
Sears, George W., Jr. 1917- *St&PR 93*
Sears, Herbert T. *Law&B 92*
Sears, James Thomas 1951- *WhoSSW 93*
Sears, John Patrick 1940- *WhoAm 92*
Sears, John Winthrop 1930- *WhoAm 92, WhoE 93*
Sears, Kelley Dean *Law&B 92*
Sears, Lucius J., Jr. 1916- *St&PR 93*
Sears, Marvin *St&PR 93*
Sears, Marvin 1928- *WhoE 93*
Sears, Max 1925- *St&PR 93*
Sears, Mildred Bradley 1933- *WhoAmW 93, WhoSSW 93*
Sears, Pauline Snedden 1908- *BioIn 17*
Sears, Richard C. 1936- *St&PR 93*
Sears, Richard W., Jr. 1942- *WhoIns 93*
Sears, Richard Warren *BioIn 17*
Sears, Richard Warren, Jr. 1942- *St&PR 93*
Sears, Robert Needham 1915- *St&PR 93*
Sears, Robert Richardson 1908-1989 *BioIn 17*
Sears, Robert Stephen 1950- *WhoEmL 93, WhoSSW 93*
Sears, Ruth A. *Law&B 92*
Sears, Sandra Lee 1952- *WhoAmW 93*
Sears, Thomas Anthony *WhoScE 91-1*
Sears, William d1992 *BioIn 17, NewYTBS 92*
Sears, William Joseph *Law&B 92*
Sears, William Rees 1913- *WhoAm 92*
Sears, William Robert 1920- *WhoAm 92*
Sears, Zelda 1873-1935 *AmWomPl*
Sears-Collins, Leah J. 1955- *AfrAmBi, WhoAmW 93, WhoSSW 93*
Searstone, Kenneth *WhoScE 91-1*
Seary, Lawrence Anthony 1951- *WhoE 93*
Sease, Gene Elwood 1931- *WhoAm 92*
Sease, John William 1920- *WhoAm 92*
Seashore, Carl Emil 1866-1949 *Baker 92*
Season, James Hobson 1944- *WhoE 93*
Seastrom, James Russell *Law&B 92*
Seastrom, Victor *MiSFD 9N*
Seat, Elizabeth Ferguson *AmWomPl*
Seath, Olga Winnifred Hanna 1899- *WhoWrEP 92*
Seaton, Anthony *WhoScE 91-1*
Seaton, David Wayland 1953- *WhoSSW 93*
Seaton, Douglass 1950- *WhoSSW 93*
Seaton, Edward Lee 1943- *WhoAm 92*
Seaton, George 1911-1979 *MiSFD 9N*
Seaton, Jean Robarts 1931- *WhoAmW 93*
Seaton, John Richard 1934- *St&PR 93*
Seaton, Kenneth Duncan 1929- *WhoAm 92*
Seaton, Lloyd, Jr. 1929- *WhoAm 92*
Seaton, Richard Melvin 1913- *WhoAm 92*
Seaton, Robert Finlayson 1930- *WhoAm 92*
Seaton, W. B. 1925- *WhoAm 92*
Seaton, William Winston 1785-1866 *BioIn 17, JrnUS*
Seator, Lynette Hubbard 1929- *WhoWrEP 92*
Seats, Peggy Chisolm 1951- *WhoAmW 93, WhoE 93, WhoEmL 93*
Seaver, Danny Wade 1954- *WhoSSW 93*
Seaver, James Everett 1918- *WhoAm 92, WhoWrEP 92*
Seaver, John C. *St&PR 93*
Seaver, Richard Carlton 1922- *St&PR 93, WhoAm 92*
Seaver, Tom *BioIn 17*
Seaver, Tom 1944- *WhoAm 92*
Seaver, W. Burleigh 1944- *St&PR 93*
Seavey, A.W. 1928- *St&PR 93*
Seavey, Marion Webster *AmWomPl*
Seavey, Martha M. *AmWomPl*
Seavey, Nealle B. *Law&B 92*
Seavey, Richard Curtis 1956- *St&PR 93*
Seavy, Mary Ethel Ingle 1910- *WhoAmW 93*
Seavy, Mary Lynn 1942- *WhoWrEP 92*
Seawell, A. Brook *St&PR 93*
Seawell, Donald R. 1912- *St&PR 93*
Seawell, Donald Ray 1912- *WhoAm 92*
Seawell, Jess 1938- *St&PR 93*
Seawell, Molly Elliot 1860-1916 *AmWomPl*
Seawell, Thomas Robert 1936- *WhoAm 92*
Seawell, William Thomas 1918- *WhoAm 92*
Seawright, James L., Jr. 1936- *WhoAm 92*
Seay, Catherine Williams 1948- *WhoSSW 93*
Seay, Frank H. 1938- *WhoAm 92*
Seay, Frank Howell 1938- *WhoSSW 93*
Seay, Lonnie Edward 1943- *WhoSSW 93*
Seay, Mark *BioIn 17*
Seay, Solomon S. 1899-1988 *BioIn 17*
Seay, Thomas Patrick 1941- *St&PR 93*
Seay, William Curtis 1946- *WhoSSW 93*
Sebag Montefiore, Simon *ConAu 136*
Sebag-Montefiore, Simon 1965- *ConAu 136*
Sebald, Albrecht Martin 1957- *WhoWor 93*
Sebaly, Jon M. *Law&B 92*
Seban, Georges 1928- *WhoWor 93*
Sebanek, Jiri 1926- *WhoScE 91-4*
Sebaoun, Albert 1939- *WhoScE 91-2*
Sebastian, Georges 1903-1989 *Baker 92, OxDcOp*
Sebastian, Jesus 1941- *WhoScE 91-3*
Sebastian, John 1944- *Baker 92*
Sebastian, John Victor 1942- *St&PR 93*
Sebastian, Lee *BioIn 17, MajAI*

Sebastian, Marcus 1963- WhoWor 93
Sebastian, Michael James 1930- St&PR 93, WhoAm 92, WhoSSW 93
Sebastian, Paul E. 1934- St&PR 93
Sebastian, Peter 1926- WhoAm 92
Sebastian, Richard Lee 1942- WhoAm 92
Sebastian, Robert L. Law&B 92
Sebastian, Stuart BioIn 17
Sebastian, Thomas Anthony 1947- St&PR 93
Sebastian, Tim 1952- ConAu 139, ScF&FL 92
Sebastiani, Johann 1622-1683 Baker 92
Sebastiano, Frank Anthony 1945- St&PR 93
Sebastianus d378 HarEnMi
Sebela, Vicki Dawn 1964- WhoAmW 93, WhoEmL 93, WhoWor 93
Sebeok, Thomas A. 1920- ScF&FL 92
Sebeok, Thomas Albert 1920- WhoAm 92, WhoWrEP 92
Sebeos fl. 7th cent.- OxDcByz
Seberg, Jean 1938-1979 BioIn 17, IntDcF 2-3 [port]
Seberger, Donald Law&B 92
Seberry, Jennifer 1944- WhoWor 93
Sebesky, Douglas C. 1951- St&PR 93
Sebesta, Charles Joseph, Jr. 1940- WhoAm 92
Sebestyen, Gyorgy 1903-1989 Baker 92
Sebestyen, Igen MajAI
Sebestyen, Imre 1945- WhoScE 91-4
Sebestyen, Istvan 1947- WhoWor 93
Sebestyen, Janos 1931- Baker 92
Sebestyen, Ouida 1923- DcAmChF 1960
Sebestyen, Ouida 1924- ConAu 40NR, MajAI [port]
Sebille, Bernard F. 1936- WhoScE 91-2
Sebillotte, Michel 1934- WhoScE 91-2
Seblatnigg, Gerhard H. 1934- St&PR 93
Sebok, Gyorgy 1922- Baker 92, WhoAm 92
Sebold, Duane David 1945- WhoAm 92
Sebold, Russell Perry, III 1928- WhoAm 92
Sebold, Thomas Edward 1951- WhoE 93
Sebor, Karel 1843-1905 OxDcOp
Sebor, Karl 1843-1903 Baker 92
Sebrell, Thomas E. 1942- St&PR 93
Sebrell, W(illiam) H(enry), Jr. 1901-1992 CurBio 92N
Sebrell, W. Henry, Jr. d1992 NewYTBS 92
Sebrell, William Henry, Jr. 1901- WhoAm 92
Sebren, Lucille Griggs 1922- WhoAmW 93, WhoSSW 93
Sebring, Betty Stainback 1942- WhoSSW 93
Sebring, Joseph Bernard 1947- St&PR 93
Sebring, Marjorie Marie Allison 1926- WhoAmW 93
Sebrow, Yaakov 1944- St&PR 93
Sebunya, James Musisi 1945- WhoWor 93
Seburyamo, Benoit 1946- WhoUN 92
Seccafico, John 1948- WhoE 93
Secchia, Peter F. WhoAm 92, WhoWor 93
Seccombe, Jarvis W. Law&B 92
Secher, Ole 1918- WhoScE 91-2
Sechrest, William B. 1942- WhoAm 92
Sechrist, Chalmers F., Jr. 1930- WhoAm 92
Sechrist, Elizabeth Hough 1902-1991 ScF&FL 92
Sechter, Simon 1788-1867 Baker 92
Seckel, Cornelia 1946- WhoE 93
Seckendorff, Karl Siegmund, Freiherr von 1744-1785 Baker 92
Seckers, Daniel M. Law&B 92
Seckinger, Harold Eugene 1926- WhoSSW 93
Secola, Jane Austin 1929- WhoE 93
Secombe, Harry 1925- QDrFCA 92 [port]
Secondari, Helen Jean Rogers WhoAm 92
Seconi, G. WhoScE 91-3
Secoquian, Mary Lou 1953- St&PR 93
Secor, Donald Terry, Jr. 1934- WhoAm 92, WhoSSW 93
Secor, Glen Michael 1960- WhoE 93
Secor, Richard A. 1930- St&PR 93
Secor, Rosalyn Barbara 1945- WhoSSW 93
Secor, William B. 1931- St&PR 93
Secord, Richard DcCPCAm
Secrest, Larry 1941- St&PR 93
Secrest, Stephen Frederick Law&B 92
Secrist, Denise Rosmaita 1964- WhoAmW 93
Secrist, Lois Jean 1929- WhoAmW 93
Secrist, Richard A. 1945- St&PR 93
Secrist, Steven Ronald Law&B 92
Secroun, Claude L. 1943- WhoScE 91-2
Secunda, Arthur 1927- WhoAm 92
Secunda, Eugene 1934- WhoAm 92
Secunda, Holland 1927- WhoAm 92
Secunda, Sholom 1894-1974 Baker 92
Secunde, Nadine Claire 1951- WhoAm 92
Sedaine, Michel-Jean 1719-1797 OxDcOp
Sedaka, Neil 1939- WhoAm 92
Sedam, Mary Ann 1943- WhoAmW 93
Sedares, James L. 1956- WhoAm 92
Sedberry, Donald C. 1934- St&PR 93
Seddelmeyer, John E. Law&B 92
Sedding, Howard Gillison 1959- WhoWor 93
Seddon, Anne Marie St&PR 93
Seddon, Margaret Rhea 1947- WhoAmW 93
Seddon, Melvin E. St&PR 93
Seddon, Rhea BioIn 17
Seddon, Robert Edward 1942- St&PR 93
Sedelmaier, J. J. 1956- WhoE 93
Sedelmaier, John Josef 1933- WhoAm 92
Sedelow, Sally Ann Yeates 1931- WhoAm 92, WhoSSW 93
Sedelow, Walter Alfred, Jr. 1928- WhoAm 92
Sedeno, Eugene Raymond 1952- WhoEmL 93
Seder, Arthur Raymond, Jr. 1920- WhoAm 92
Seder, Herschel Lewis 1918- St&PR 93
Seder, Steve Dennis 1955- St&PR 93
Sederbaum, William 1914- WhoAm 92
Sederholm, Don 1930- WhoWrEP 92
Sedgeman, Catherine Monica 1941- WhoAmW 93
Sedgfield, W. Russell 1826-1902 BioIn 17
Sedgwick, Alexander 1930- WhoAm 92
Sedgwick, Eileen 1899- SweetSg B [port]
Sedgwick, Ellery 1872-1960 BioIn 17
Sedgwick, Ellery 1908-1991 BioIn 17
Sedgwick, Ellery, Jr. 1908- St&PR 93
Sedgwick, Henry D. 1928- St&PR 93
Sedgwick, James L. Law&B 92
Sedgwick, James L. 1939- WhoIns 93
Sedgwick, Josie 1898-1973 SweetSg B [port]
Sedgwick, K. WhoScE 91-1
Sedgwick, Kyra BioIn 17
Sedgwick, Theodore 1746-1813 BioIn 17, PolPar
Sedie, Enrico delle OxDcOp
Sedin, Mary Jane 1943- WhoAmW 93
Sediyama, Gilberto Chohaku 1946- WhoWor 93
Sedky, Atef 1930- WhoWor 93
Sedlacek, Evelyn Ann 1919- WhoAmW 93, WhoWor 93
Sedlacek, Gerhard H. 1939- WhoScE 91-3
Sedlacek, John 1925- St&PR 93
Sedlacek, Keith Wayne 1944- WhoE 93
Sedlacek, Robert G. Law&B 92
Sedlack, Robert J. 1935- St&PR 93
Sedlack, Russell L., II 1955- WhoSSW 93
Sedlak, Joseph Anthony, III 1952- WhoEmL 93
Sedlak, Stephen A. 1941- St&PR 93
Sedlak, Valerie Frances 1934- WhoAmW 93, WhoE 93
Sedlak, Viisha BioIn 17
Sedlarz, Karl H. 1937- St&PR 93
Sedler, Herbert L. 1930- St&PR 93
Sedlin, Elias David 1932- WhoAm 92
Sedmak, Giorgio 1942- WhoScE 91-3
Sedmak, Pamela Sue 1961- WhoAmW 93
Sedor, Robert Steven 1954- St&PR 93
Sedory, Allen R. Law&B 92
Sedov, Leonid Ivanovich 1907- WhoWor 93
Sedra, Adel S. 1943- WhoAm 92
Sedvall, Carl Goran 1936- WhoScE 91-4
Sedwick, Frank 1924- WhoAm 92
Sedwick, Robert Curtis 1926- WhoAm 92
Sedykh, Vyacheslav Dmitrievich 1955- WhoWor 93
Sedziwy, Stanislaw 1934- WhoWor 93
See, Alan Jeffery 1959- WhoSSW 93, WhoWor 93
See, Anna Phillips AmWomPl
See, Carolyn BioIn 17
See, Carolyn 1934- ScF&FL 92
See, Chak Mun 1941- WhoUN 92
See, French Augustus 1908- WhoSSW 93
See, Gary H. St&PR 93
See, Henry Wesselman 1923- St&PR 93
See, John R. 1949- St&PR 93
See, Karen Mason 1952- WhoAmW 93
See, Pamela Jineen 1966- WhoAmW 93
Seeba, Hinrich Claassen 1940- WhoAm 92
Seebach, Daisy F. Law&B 92
Seebach, Dieter 1937- WhoScE 91-4, WhoWor 93
Seebach, Elizabeth Emily 1960- WhoAmW 93
Seebach, Gerald Lawrence 1944- WhoSSW 93
Seebart, George E. 1928- St&PR 93, WhoIns 93
Seebass, Alfred Richard, III 1936- WhoAm 92
Seebeek, Gerold Eugene 1945- St&PR 93
Seeber, Gerhard 1925- WhoScE 91-4
Seeberg, Harald WhoScE 91-3
Seeberger, Edward J. 1951- St&PR 93
Seebert, Kathleen Anne 1949- WhoAmW 93
Seeburger, John 1923- St&PR 93
Seeckt, Hans von 1866-1936 DcTwHis, HarEnMi
Seed, David 1946- ScF&FL 92
Seed, Harris Waller 1927- St&PR 93
Seed, Paul 1947- MiSFD 9
Seedlock, Robert Francis 1913- WhoAm 92
Seedo c. 1700-c. 1754 Baker 92, OxDcOp
Seefehlner, Egon Hugo 1912- WhoWor 93
Seeff, Adele 1938- WhoE 93
Seefried, Carl George, Jr. 1944- WhoAm 92
Seefried, Irmgard 1919-1988 Baker 92, IntDcOp, OxDcOp
Seefried, Philip W. 1935- St&PR 93, WhoAm 92
Seegal, Frederic Milton BioIn 17
Seegal, Herbert Leonard 1915- St&PR 93, WhoAm 92
Seegar, Sara d1990 BioIn 17
Seeger, Alfred WhoScE 91-3
Seeger, Barbara Murro 1952- WhoAmW 93
Seeger, Charles L. 1912- BioIn 17
Seeger, Charles (Louis) 1886-1979 Baker 92
Seeger, D. WhoScE 91-3
Seeger, Edward Bethel 1945- WhoSSW 93
Seeger, H. WhoScE 91-3
Seeger, Horst 1926- Baker 92
Seeger, John Adam 1933- WhoE 93
Seeger, John Watts 1927- WhoSSW 93
Seeger, Josef 1716?-1782 Baker 92
Seeger, Karlheinz WhoScE 91-4
Seeger, Kevin Cedric WhoScE 91-1
Seeger, Michael 1933- WhoAm 92
Seeger, Mike 1933- See Seeger, Charles (Louis) 1886-1979 Baker 92
Seeger, Murray A. 1929- WhoUN 92
Seeger, Peggy 1935- See Seeger, Charles (Louis) 1886-1979 Baker 92
Seeger, Pete BioIn 17
Seeger, Pete 1919- ConHero 2 [port], PolPar, WhoAm 92
See Also Weavers, The ConMus 8
Seeger, Pete(r) 1919- Baker 92
Seeger, Ruth Crawford Baker 92
Seeger, Ruth Crawford 1901-1953 BioIn 17
Seeger, Walter August, Jr. 1932- St&PR 93
Seeger, Winifred AmWomPl
Seegers, Paul R. 1930- WhoAm 92, WhoSSW 93
Seegers, Walter Henry 1910- WhoAm 92
Seegman, Irvin P. 1921- St&PR 93, WhoAm 92
Seegmiller, Wan 1926- St&PR 93
Seegr, Josef 1716?-1782 Baker 92
Seegull, Stanley L. 1934- St&PR 93
Seehafer, Herbert Milton 1930- St&PR 93
Seehase, Robert James 1924- St&PR 93
Seeherman, Julian M. BioIn 17
Seel, Bernie Monroe 1947- St&PR 93
Seel, Jeffery W. 1947- St&PR 93
Seel, Martin Anthony 1933- St&PR 93
Seelander, John Marshall 1940- St&PR 93
Seelbinder, G. Arthur 1943- ConEn
Seele, Stephen Edward Law&B 92
Seelenberger, Sergio Hernan 1942- WhoWor 93
Seelenfreund, Alan 1936- WhoAm 92
Seelenfreund, Alan Jay 1936- St&PR 93
Seeler, Marcia Drake Law&B 92
Seeler, Richard W. 1919- St&PR 93
Seeler, Robert S. 1935- St&PR 93
Seeley, Benjamin Jackson 1945- St&PR 93, WhoE 93
Seeley, Bob MiSFD 9
Seeley, Chester L. 1913- St&PR 93
Seeley, David William 1944- WhoSSW 93, WhoWor 93
Seeley, Dwight C. Law&B 92
Seeley, Frederick Cooley 1942- St&PR 93
Seeley, Harry Wilbur, Jr. 1917- WhoAm 92
Seeley, John George 1915- WhoE 93
Seeley, Kimberley Ann 1960- WhoAmW 93
Seeley, Laura L. 1958- SmATA 71 [port]
Seeley, Rod Ralph 1945- WhoAm 92
Seelig, Clover Hartz AmWomPl
Seelig, Gerard Leo 1926- WhoAm 92
Seelig, Patrick Kelly 1950- WhoSSW 93
Seelig, Wolfgang 1939- WhoScE 91-3
Seeliger, Dieter Reinhard 1939- WhoWor 93
Seeliger, Heinz P.R. 1920- WhoScE 91-3
Seeligson, Molly Fulton 1942- WhoAmW 93
Seeling, Hans 1828-1862 Baker 92
Seelman, Gerald William 1936- St&PR 93
Seelman, Robert Norman 1934- St&PR 93
Seely, Dennis Jack 1952- WhoSSW 93
Seely, James Michael 1932- WhoAm 92
Seely, Robert Daniel 1923- WhoAm 92, WhoWor 93
Seely, Robert Eugene 1941- St&PR 93
Seely, Samuel 1909- WhoE 93
Seeman, Clara Lewis AmWomPl
Seeman, Linda Kamsky 1950- WhoAmW 93
Seeman, Melvin 1918- WhoAm 92
Seeman, Nadrian Charles 1945- WhoE 93
Seeman, Philip 1934- WhoAm 92
Seemann, Charles Henry, Jr. 1946- WhoSSW 93
Seemann, Ernest Albright 1929- WhoAm 92
Seemann, Horst 1937- DrEEuF
Seemann, Rosalie Mary 1942- WhoWor 93
Seemiller, Mark Louis 1957- St&PR 93
Seereeram, Shaym 1958- WhoWor 93
Seerey-Lester, John 1945- BioIn 17
Seers, Dudley BioIn 17
Seers, Eugene 1865-1945 BioIn 17
Seery, Peter WhoScE 91-3
Sees, Mary Carolyn 1931- WhoAm 92
Seeser, James W. 1943- St&PR 93
Seessel, Adam H. 1964- WhoAm 92
Seessel, Thomas Vining 1937- WhoAm 92
Seet, Joe Lip Poh 1952- WhoWor 93
Seet Ai Mee, Dr. 1943- WhoAsAP 91
Seethaler, William Charles 1937- WhoWor 93
Seetoo, Amy Dah Sun 1946- WhoWor 93
Seets, Lynn D. Law&B 92
Seevak, Sheldon 1929- WhoAm 92
Seevers, Charles Junior 1925- WhoAm 92
Seevers, Gary Leonard 1937- WhoAm 92
Seevers, Henning 1951- WhoWor 93
Seewagen, George d1990 BioIn 17
Seewald, Jeffrey R. Law&B 92
Seewald, Randal Ray Law&B 92
Sefcik, James Francis 1943- WhoAm 92, WhoSSW 93
Seferian, John W. 1949- St&PR 93
Seferis, George 1900-1971 BioIn 17
Seferis, James Constantine 1950- WhoWor 93
Seff, Leslie S. 1950- WhoAm 92
Seffrin, John Reese 1944- WhoAm 92
Seftenberg, Stephen Longfellow 1935- WhoSSW 93
Seftick, Ronald Gregory 1952- St&PR 93
Sefton, Amelia Kathleen 1950- WhoAmW 93
Sefton, Catherine ChlFicS
Sefton, Catherine 1941- ScF&FL 92
Sega, Gary Andrew 1941- WhoSSW 93
Segal, Allan 1948- WhoE 93
Segal, Anne L. Law&B 92
Segal, Benjamin David St&PR 93
Segal, Bernard Gerard 1907- WhoAm 92, WhoE 93, WhoWor 93
Segal, Bernard Louis 1929- WhoAm 92
Segal, Brian 1943- WhoWor 93
Segal, C. Brad 1935- WhoScE 91-4
Segal, Charles Paul 1936- ConAu 39NR, WhoAm 92, WhoWrEP 92
Segal, D. Robert 1920- WhoAm 92, WhoWor 93
Segal, David Michael Law&B 92
Segal, David P. 1931- St&PR 93
Segal, Donald Henry Gilbert 1928- WhoE 93, WhoWor 93
Segal, Eric Bruce 1942- St&PR 93
Segal, Erich 1937- BioIn 17, WhoAm 92, WhoWrEP 92
Segal, Evan J. St&PR 93
Segal, George 1924- WhoAm 92
Segal, George 1934- WhoAm 92
Segal, George 1936- IntDcF 2-3
Segal, Geraldine Rosenbaum 1908- WhoAmW 93, WhoE 93, WhoWor 93
Segal, Gil 1952- St&PR 93
Segal, Harold Lewis 1924- WhoAm 92
Segal, Harry Law&B 92
Segal, Herb 1924- St&PR 93
Segal, Herbert Erwin 1941- WhoSSW 93
Segal, Herman 1918- St&PR 93
Segal, Irving Ezra 1918- WhoAm 92
Segal, Irving Randall 1914- WhoAm 92
Segal, Jack 1934- WhoAm 92
Segal, Jerome J. 1929- St&PR 93
Segal, JoAn Smyth 1930- WhoAm 92
Segal, Joel Michael 1933- WhoAm 92
Segal, Jonathan Bruce 1946- WhoAm 92, WhoWrEP 92
Segal, Joyce Trager 1943- WhoAmW 93
Segal, Judith Z. 1948- ScF&FL 92
Segal, Julie Dee 1947- WhoSSW 93
Segal, Karen R. 1954- WhoE 93
Segal, Lore 1928- WhoAm 92, WhoWrEP 92
Segal, Lore Groszmann BioIn 17
Segal, Lynne Nicolau 1957- WhoAmW 93
Segal, Marilyn Mailman 1927- WhoSSW 93
Segal, Martin Eli 1916- WhoAm 92, WhoWor 93
Segal, Martin M. 1926- St&PR 93
Segal, Mendal 1914- St&PR 93

Segal, Merton Joseph 1929- *St&PR 93*
Segal, Milton *Law&B 92*
Segal, Patricia Bateman 1946- *WhoAmW 93*
Segal, Paul 1944- *WhoAm 92*
Segal, Peter Wyman 1943- *WhoE 93*
Segal, Philip A., Jr. 1926- *St&PR 93*
Segal, Philippe 1940- *WhoScE 91-2*
Segal, Robert B. 1944- *St&PR 93*
Segal, Robert Mandal 1915- *WhoAm 92*
Segal, Robert Martin 1935- *WhoAm 92*
Segal, Ronald 1938- *St&PR 93*
Segal, Ronald Michael 1932- *WhoWor 93*
Segal, Sanford Leonard 1937- *WhoE 93*
Segal, Sheldon Jerome 1926- *WhoAm 92*
Segal, Stephen Martin 1938- *WhoE 93*
Segal, Uri 1944- *Baker 92*
Segal, Vivienne d1992 *NewYTBS 92 [port]*
Segal, Zalman 1938- *St&PR 93*
Segalas, Hercules Anthony 1935- *WhoAm 92*
Segale, Atenogenes 1868-1903 *DcMexL*
Segall, Harold Abraham 1918- *WhoAm 92*
Segall, James Arnold 1956- *WhoEmL 93, WhoSSW 93*
Segall, John Louis 1926- *St&PR 93, WhoAm 92*
Segall, Jules Peter 1954- *WhoE 93*
Segall, Lasar 1891?-1957 *BioIn 17*
Segall, Mark *Law&B 92*
Segall, Marshall H. 1930- *WhoAm 92*
Segall, Ralph Simon 1926- *WhoSSW 93*
Segall, Samson 1920- *St&PR 93*
Segall, William Edwin *WhoSSW 93*
Segalman, Joel Scott 1963- *WhoE 93*
Segalman, Richard *BioIn 17*
Segal-Oppenheimer, Lori S. *Law&B 92*
Segar, Elzie Crisler 1894-1938 *BioIn 17*
Segar, Geoffrey 1926- *WhoAm 92*
Segar, James Henry 1938- *WhoE 93*
Segar, Timothy Crisler *Law&B 92*
Segarra, Juan E. 1937- *WhoScE 91-3*
Segarra, Robert 1959- *WhoE 93*
Segars, Alvin John 1953- *St&PR 93*
Segars, Dwayne R. *St&PR 93*
Segars, Kelly Scott 1930- *WhoSSW 93*
Segatta, Joseph John 1930- *St&PR 93*
Segatto, Bernard Gordon 1931- *WhoAm 92*
Segatto, Peter Richard 1928- *WhoE 93*
Sege, Ronald Alexander 1957- *St&PR 93*
Sege, Thomas Davis 1926- *St&PR 93*
Segel, Arnold Lester 1911- *WhoE 93*
Segel, J.M. 1931- *St&PR 93*
Segel', Jakov 1923- *DrEEuF*
Segel, Joseph M. 1931- *WhoAm 92*
Segel, Karen Lynn Joseph 1947- *WhoAmW 93*
Segel, Richard M. 1940- *St&PR 93*
Segel, Ronald G. 1935-1991 *BioIn 17*
Seger, Bob 1945- *WhoAm 92*
Seger, Charles Frederick, 3rd 1943- *St&PR 93*
Seger, George Wilbur 1938- *St&PR 93*
Seger, John *WhoIns 93*
Seger, Jon Allen 1946- *WhoAm 92*
Seger, Josef 1716?-1782 *Baker 92*
Seger, Joyce Ellen 1947- *WhoSSW 93*
Seger, Martha *BioIn 17*
Seger, Martha R. 1932- *St&PR 93*
Seger, Martha Romayne 1932- *WhoAm 92*
Seger, Maura *ScF&FL 92*
Segerberg, Karl Krister 1936- *WhoWor 93*
Segerblom, Bjorn Axel 1940- *WhoWor 93*
Segeren, A.J.M. 1944- *WhoScE 91-3*
Segeren, W.A. 1935- *WhoScE 91-3*
Segerstam, Leif (Selim) 1944- *Baker 92*
Segersten, Robert Hagy 1941- *WhoAm 92*
Segerstrom, Jane Archer 1930- *WhoWrEP 92*
Segert, Josef 1716?-1782 *Baker 92*
Seges, Phillip G. 1934- *St&PR 93*
Segger, Martin Joseph 1946- *WhoAm 92*
Seggerman, Anne B. *Law&B 92*
Seggerman, Harry Gurney Atha 1927- *WhoAm 92*
Seggerman, M.K. *St&PR 93*
Seggev, Meir 1939- *WhoE 93, WhoWor 93*
Seggewiss, Wilhelm 1937- *WhoScE 91-3*
Seghers, Francois-Jean-Baptiste 1801-1881 *Baker 92*
Seglem, Christopher King 1946- *St&PR 93*
Seglin, Lisa S. *Law&B 92*
Segmen, John Robert 1937- *WhoE 93*
Segnar, Samuel Frederick 1927- *St&PR 93*
Segner, Edmund Peter, Jr. 1928- *WhoSSW 93*
Segner, Edmund Peter, III 1953- *St&PR 93, WhoAm 92*
Segni, Julio 1498-1561 *Baker 92*
Segota, Tomislav 1929- *WhoScE 91-4*
Segovia, Andres 1893-1987 *Baker 92*
Segovia, Andrew *Law&B 92*
Segovia, Claudio Gaston 1933- *WhoAm 92*
Segovia, Tomas 1927- *DcMexL*
Segraves, Kathleen Blindt 1947- *WhoAmW 93*
Segraves, Kelly L. 1942- *ScF&FL 92*
Segre, Claudio 1932- *WhoWor 93*
Segre, Emilio *BioIn 17*
Segrin, Richard d1990 *BioIn 17*
Segsworth, Katherine Jane *Law&B 92*
Seguela, Jean Paul Marie 1938- *WhoScE 91-2*
Segui, Juan 1940- *WhoScE 91-2*
Seguin, Arthur 1809-1852 *OxDcOp*
Seguin, Gerard 1936- *WhoScE 91-2*
Seguin, Gilles 1939- *St&PR 93*
Seguin, J. Herve 1950- *St&PR 93*
Seguin, Juan N. 1806-1889? *BioIn 17*
Seguin, Philippe 1943- *BioIn 17*
Seguin, Robert Edgar 1960- *WhoWor 93*
Segun, Mabel D(orothy) 1930- *DcChlFi*
Segur, Sophie Rostopchine, Comtesse de 1799-1874 *BioIn 17*
Segura, Ana Isabel 1949- *WhoAmW 93*
Segura, Edilberto L. 1942- *WhoUN 92*
Segura, Jose Sebastian 1822-1889 *DcMexL*
Segura, Ricardo O. 1957- *St&PR 93*
Segura Najera, Jose 1933- *WhoWor 93*
Segurola, Andres de 1873-1953 *BioIn 17*
Seguy, Georges 1927- *BioIn 17*
Seher, Robert R. 1935- *St&PR 93*
Seheult, Malcolm McDonald Richardson 1949- *WhoEmL 93*
Sehgal, Amar Nath 1922- *WhoWor 93*
Sehgal, Raghbir Kumar 1937- *St&PR 93*
Sehlin, Arthur Andrew 1931- *St&PR 93*
Sehlmeyer, Richard George 1934- *WhoE 93*
Sehmi, Naginder Singh 1937- *WhoUN 92*
Sehnert, Charles Fredrick 1931- *St&PR 93*
Sehnert, Walter 1946- *WhoWor 93*
Sehon, Clarette L. *AmWomPl*
Sehovic, Enver 1938- *WhoWor 93*
Sehr, Alois 1923- *WhoScE 91-4*
Sehring, Hope Hutchison *WhoAmW 93, WhoE 93, WhoWor 93*
Seibel, Hugo Rudolf 1937- *WhoSSW 93*
Seibel, John Carl 1955- *St&PR 93*
Seibel, Mark Edward 1953- *WhoSSW 93*
Seibel, Monroe 1933- *St&PR 93*
Seibel, Morris H. 1900- *St&PR 93*
Seibel, Susan J. *Law&B 92*
Seibel, Wilfried P.A. 1930- *WhoScE 91-3*
Seiber, Matyas (Gyorgy) 1905-1960 *Baker 92*
Seiberlich, Carl Joseph 1921- *WhoAm 92, WhoWor 93*
Seiberling, John Frederick 1918- *WhoAm 92*
Seibert, Constance Jean 1932- *WhoAmW 93*
Seibert, Edward P. 1939- *St&PR 93*
Seibert, Florence 1897-1991 *BioIn 17*
Seibert, Jakob 1939- *WhoWor 93*
Seibert, John F. 1951- *WhoIns 93*
Seibert, Laura Louise 1956- *WhoSSW 93*
Seibert, Mary Lee 1942- *WhoE 93*
Seibert, Paul J. 1935- *St&PR 93*
Seibert, Peter Swift 1965- *WhoE 93*
Seibert, Robin A. 1956- *St&PR 93*
Seibert, Rudolph David 1926- *St&PR 93*
Seibert, Russell Jacob 1914- *WhoAm 92*
Seibert, Scott E. 1939- *St&PR 93*
Seibert, Wilson A., Jr. 1927- *WhoAm 92*
Seibold, Donald Lewis 1944- *WhoSSW 93*
Seibold, Eugen 1918- *WhoScE 91-3*
Seibold, Jenny Hopkins *AmWomPl*
Seibold, Philip William, Jr. 1937- *WhoAm 92*
Seid, Jay D. 1960- *St&PR 93*
Seid, Ruth 1913- *WhoAm 92, WhoWrEP 92*
Seide, Bruce Harold 1945- *WhoAm 92*
Seide, Leonard M. 1929- *St&PR 93*
Seide, Paul 1926- *WhoAm 92*
Seide, Robert G. *Law&B 92*
Seidel, Andrew David 1949- *WhoSSW 93*
Seidel, Arthur Harris 1923- *WhoAm 92*
Seidel, Barry S. 1956- *St&PR 93*
Seidel, Dianne Marie 1959- *WhoAmW 93*
Seidel, Donna L. *Law&B 92*
Seidel, Frederick Lewis 1936- *WhoAm 92, WhoWrEP 92*
Seidel, Friedrich Ludwig 1765-1831 *Baker 92*
Seidel, George Elias, Jr. 1943- *WhoAm 92*
Seidel, Hans *WhoScE 91-4*
Seidel, Jan 1908- *Baker 92*
Seidel, Joan Broude 1933- *WhoAmW 93*
Seidel, Richard Maurice 1926- *St&PR 93*
Seidel, Robert B. 1926- *St&PR 93*
Seidel, Selvyn 1942- *WhoE 93, WhoWor 93*
Seidel, Toscha 1899-1962 *Baker 92*
Seidel, William P. 1931- *St&PR 93*
Seidel, Wolfhart 1929- *WhoScE 91-3*
Seidel-Debrick, Carolyn Sue 1956- *WhoAmW 93, WhoWor 93*
Seidelman, Arthur Allan *MiSFD 9*
Seidelman, Susan *BioIn 17*
Seidelman, Susan 1952- *MiSFD 9, WhoAm 92, WhoAmW 93*
Seidelmann, Christoph 1943- *WhoScE 91-3*
Seidel-Zoller, Rosemarie 1950- *WhoWor 93*
Seiden, Bill A. 1955- *WhoE 93*
Seiden, Elliott M. 1945- *St&PR 93*
Seiden, Eric A. 1965- *WhoSSW 93*
Seiden, Henry 1928- *St&PR 93, WhoAm 92, WhoE 93*
Seiden, Katie 1936- *WhoE 93*
Seiden, Richard Steven 1938- *WhoE 93*
Seiden, Sharon Lynn 1963- *WhoE 93*
Seiden, Stella Bodner 1919- *WhoAmW 93*
Seiden, Steven A. 1936- *St&PR 93*
Seiden, Steven Arnold 1936- *WhoAm 92*
Seiden, Steven Jay 1960- *WhoE 93*
Seidenbaum, Art 1930-1990 *BioIn 17*
Seidenberg, Edward 1949- *WhoSSW 93*
Seidenberg, Ivan G. 1946- *St&PR 93, WhoAm 92*
Seidenfeld, Glenn Kenneth 1914- *WhoAm 92*
Seidenfeld, Glenn Kenneth, Jr. 1944- *WhoAm 92*
Seidenfeld, Mark *Law&B 92*
Seidenfrau, Steven 1945- *St&PR 93*
Seidenfus, Hellmuth Stephan 1924- *WhoWor 93*
Seidenglanz, J. *WhoScE 91-4*
Seidenglanz, Robert E. *St&PR 93*
Seidensticker, Edward George 1921- *WhoAm 92, WhoWor 93*
Seidensticker, Louis Peter 1930- *St&PR 93*
Seidensticker, Robert Beach 1929- *St&PR 93*
Seider, J. Paul 1926- *St&PR 93*
Seider, Julia Liane 1907- *WhoE 93*
Seiderer, Franz Rolf 1933- *WhoWor 93*
Seiderman, Bernard d1990 *BioIn 17*
Seiders, Joseph R. *Law&B 92*
Seiders, Joseph Robert 1948- *St&PR 93*
Seides, Niketas fl. 12th cent.- *OxDcByz*
Seidl, Anton 1850-1898 *Baker 92, IntDcOp, OxDcOp*
Seidl, Arthur 1863-1928 *Baker 92*
Seidl, Christian A.L. 1940- *WhoWor 93*
Seidl, Fredrick William 1940- *WhoAm 92, WhoE 93*
Seidl, Gerald Dorsey 1933- *St&PR 93*
Seidl, Gunther Bernhard 1931- *WhoWor 93*
Seidl, John Michael 1939- *St&PR 93, WhoAm 92*
Seidl, M. *WhoScE 91-3*
Seidl, Peter Rudolf 1941- *WhoWor 93*
Seidle, Joseph Worrell 1946- *St&PR 93*
Seidler, Bonnie Frank 1942- *WhoAmW 93*
Seidler, Doris 1912- *WhoAm 92*
Seidler, Harry 1923- *WhoWor 93*
Seidler, Horst 1944- *WhoScE 91-4*
Seidler, I. Marshall 1934- *WhoAm 92*
Seidler, Isidor 1906-1991 *BioIn 17*
Seidler, James F. 1942- *St&PR 93*
Seidler, Lee J. 1935- *St&PR 93*
Seidler, Maria 1925- *WhoScE 91-4*
Seidler, Stefan Adam 1915- *WhoScE 91-4*
Seidling, Susan Mary 1929- *WhoE 93*
Seidl-Kraus, Auguste *OxDcOp*
Seidman, Dorine R. *Law&B 92*
Seidman, Edward *BioIn 17*
Seidman, Eric *ScF&FL 92*
Seidman, Hugh 1940- *WhoWrEP 92*
Seidman, L. William 1921- *BioIn 17*
Seidman, Lewis William 1921- *BioIn 17, WhoAm 92*
Seidman, Marshall Jacob 1925- *WhoSSW 93*
Seidner, David *BioIn 17*
Seidner, Frederic Jay 1931- *WhoAm 92*
Seidner, Joel Philip 1947- *WhoSSW 93*
Seiersen, Nicholas Steen 1955- *WhoWor 93*
Seifart, Klaus H. 1937- *WhoScE 91-3*
Seifer, Amy D. *Law&B 92*
Seifer, Ronald Leslie 1942- *WhoSSW 93*
Seiferheld, David Froehlich 1904- *WhoAm 92*
Seiferle, Rebecca Ann 1951- *WhoWrEP 92*
Seifert, Arthur G. *Law&B 92*
Seifert, Bo Leopold 1945- *WhoWor 93*
Seifert, Carol Joy 1953- *WhoAmW 93*
Seifert, Friedrich A. 1941- *WhoScE 91-3*
Seifert, George *BioIn 17*
Seifert, George 1940- *WhoAm 92*
Seifert, Hans-Joachim 1930- *WhoScE 91-3*
Seifert, Horst Hans 1937- *St&PR 93*
Seifert, Horst S.H. 1930- *WhoScE 91-3*
Seifert, James J. *Law&B 92*
Seifert, Jaroslav 1901-1986 *BioIn 17*
Seifert, Jaroslav 1932- *WhoScE 91-4*
Seifert, Laurence Curt 1938- *WhoAm 92*
Seifert, Lori Ann 1961- *WhoAmW 93*
Seifert, Thomas Lloyd 1940- *WhoAm 92, WhoWor 93*
Seifert, William Walther 1920- *WhoAm 92*
Seiff, Alvin 1922- *WhoAm 92*
Seiffert, Leslie 1934-1990 *BioIn 17*
Seiffert, Manfred 1924- *WhoScE 91-3*
Seiffert, Margaret Kramer *Law&B 92*
Seiffert, Marjory Allen *AmWomPl*
Seiffert, Max 1868-1948 *Baker 92*
Seiffert, Ulrich W. 1941- *WhoScE 91-3*
Seifman, Eli 1936- *WhoE 93*
Seiford, Lawrence Martin 1945- *WhoE 93*
Seifrid, Thomas 1956- *ConAu 139*
Seifried, Linda Miller 1945- *WhoSSW 93*
Seifriz, Max 1827-1885 *Baker 92*
Seigel, Allen S. 1942- *WhoE 93*
Seigel, Arthur Michael 1944- *WhoE 93*
Seigel, Harold O. 1924- *St&PR 93*
Seigel, Hersch 1927- *St&PR 93*
Seigel, Jerrold Edward 1936- *WhoAm 92*
Seigel, Michael H. 1947- *St&PR 93*
Seigel, Robert Charles 1947- *WhoAm 92*
Seigel, Robert J. *MiSFD 9*
Seigel, Stuart Evan 1933- *WhoAm 92*
Seigelman, Harry 1930- *St&PR 93*
Seigenthaler, John (Lawrence) 1927- *DcLB 127 [port], WhoWor 93*
Seiger, Eileen Schor *Law&B 92*
Seigle, Harold T. 1908- *St&PR 93*
Seigle, Harry Jay 1946- *WhoAm 92*
Seigle, John William 1929- *WhoAm 92*
Seigle, Mark Steven 1958- *St&PR 93*
Seigle-Murandi, Francoise 1941- *WhoScE 91-2*
Seigler, David Stanley 1940- *WhoAm 92*
Seigler, Jane *Law&B 92*
Seigler, Ruth Queen 1942- *WhoAmW 93*
Seigler, William David 1934- *St&PR 93*
Seigneurin, Jean-Marie 1944- *WhoScE 91-2*
Seignolle, Claude 1917- *ScF&FL 92*
Seignoret, Clarence 1919- *WhoWor 93*
Seikaly, Rony *BioIn 17*
Seikel, George R., III 1933- *WhoWor 93*
Seikel, Oliver Edward 1937- *St&PR 93, WhoAm 92*
Seil, Fredrick John 1933- *WhoAm 92*
Seilacher, Adolf 1925- *WhoScE 91-3*
Seiler, Armin 1939- *WhoWor 93*
Seiler, George J. 1941- *WhoIns 93*
Seiler, George Roberts 1934- *WhoE 93*
Seiler, Gwendolen Logan *AmWomPl*
Seiler, H. *WhoScE 91-3*
Seiler, James E. *Law&B 92*
Seiler, John Gray, Jr. 1933- *St&PR 93*
Seiler, Lewis 1891-1963 *MiSFD 9N*
Seiler, Mark J. 1958- *St&PR 93*
Seiler, Michael J. *Law&B 92*
Seiler, Robert Edward 1925- *WhoAm 92*
Seiler, Wolfgang 1940- *WhoScE 91-3*
Seilheimer, Robert 1939- *St&PR 93*
Seiling, Josephine A. *WhoAmW 93*
Seilliere de Laborde, Ernest-Antoine 1937- *WhoWor 93*
Seils, William G. 1935- *St&PR 93*
Seils, William George *Law&B 92*
Seils, William George 1935- *WhoAm 92*
Seimiginowski, Jerzy Eleuter 1660-1711 *PolBiDi*
Seinberg, Saul A. *Law&B 92*
Seinemeyer, Meta 1895-1929 *Baker 92*
Seinfeld, Jerry *BioIn 17*
Seinfeld, Jerry 1954?- *ConTFT 10, CurBio 92 [port], News 92 [port]*
Seinfeld, Jerry 1955- *WhoAm 92*
Seinfeld, John Hersh 1942- *WhoAm 92*
Seinfeld, Robert D. 1931- *St&PR 93*
Seingalt, Giacomo Casanova de *ScF&FL 92*
Seinsheimer, J.F., Jr. 1913- *WhoIns 93*
Seinsheimer, Joseph Fellman, Jr. 1913- *St&PR 93, WhoAm 92*
Seinsheimer, Joseph Fellman, III 1940- *St&PR 93, WhoIns 93*
Seip, Hans Martin 1937- *WhoScE 91-4*
Seip, Martin Fredrik 1921- *WhoScE 91-4*
Seip, Tom D. 1950- *St&PR 93*
Seipel, Ignaz 1876-1932 *DcTwHis*
Seipel, John Howard 1925- *WhoSSW 93*
Seipel, Teresa Marie 1954- *WhoAmW 93*
Seiple, Stephen Bradley *Law&B 92*
Seipler, Maurice Russell 1926- *St&PR 93*
Seipp, Henry F. 1925- *St&PR 93*
Seireg, Ali Abdel Hay 1927- *WhoAm 92*
Seiss, Isodor (Wilhelm) 1840-1905 *Baker 92*
Seita, Trudy Rannells 1943- *WhoSSW 93*
Seitchik, Richard J. *St&PR 93*
Seite, Alice Saunier- 1925- *BioIn 17*
Seitel, Fraser P. 1946- *St&PR 93*
Seitel, Fraser Paul 1946- *WhoAm 92*
Seitelberger, F. *WhoScE 91-4*
Seitelman, Leon Harold 1940- *WhoE 93*
Seiter, James Julian 1941- *St&PR 93*
Seiter, William A. 1892-1964 *MiSFD 9N*
Seith, Alex R. 1934- *St&PR 93*
Seith, Alex Robert 1934- *WhoAm 92*

Seith, Nancy Lou 1928- *WhoAmW 93*
Seitschek, Viktor Rudolf 1943- *WhoWor 93*
Seittelman, Elizabeth Edith 1922- *WhoAm 92*
Seitter, Dellmer Bernheim, III 1965- *WhoSSW 93*
Seitter, Robert P. *Law&B 92*
Seitz, Charles Lewis 1943- *WhoAm 92*
Seitz, Collins Jacques 1914- *WhoAm 92*
Seitz, David Francis 1954- *WhoE 93*
Seitz, David Frederick 1944- *St&PR 93*
Seitz, Donn Philip 1948- *St&PR 93*
Seitz, Frederick 1911- *WhoAm 92*
Seitz, G.L. 1909- *St&PR 93*
Seitz, Gary Francis 1961- *WhoEmL 93*
Seitz, George B. 1888-1944 *MiSFD 9N*
Seitz, Gunther H.R. 1936- *WhoScE 91-3*
Seitz, Hanns Martin 1938- *WhoScE 91-3*
Seitz, Hanns Ulrich 1939- *WhoScE 91-3*
Seitz, Hans Joachim 1940- *WhoScE 91-3*
Seitz, Harold A. 1938- *WhoAm 92*
Seitz, Howard Alexander 1907- *WhoAm 92*
Seitz, James W. *Law&B 92*
Seitz, Jay Alfred 1954- *WhoE 93*
Seitz, Joan Glawe 1949- *WhoAmW 93*
Seitz, Joel Neil 1941- *St&PR 93*
Seitz, Karl Raymond 1943- *WhoSSW 93*
Seitz, Kim Witko *St&PR 93*
Seitz, M.N. 1945- *St&PR 93*
Seitz, Maria Catalina 1955- *WhoAmW 93*
Seitz, Melvin Christian, Jr. 1939- *St&PR 93*
Seitz, Nicholas Joseph 1939- *WhoAm 92, WhoWrEP 92*
Seitz, Raymond Carlton 1936- *WhoE 93*
Seitz, Raymond George Hardenbergh 1940- *WhoAm 92, WhoWor 93*
Seitz, Rosalie Fern 1927- *WhoAmW 93*
Seitz, Tadd C. 1941- *St&PR 93*
Seitz, Victoria Ann 1956- *WhoEmL 93*
Seitz, Wesley Donald 1940- *WhoAm 92*
Seitzman, Markell *Law&B 92*
Seiverling, Richard *BioIn 17*
Seixas, (Jose Antonio) Carlos de 1704-1742 *Baker 92*
Seixas, Frank A. d1992 *NewYTBS 92 [port]*
Seixas, Frank A. 1919-1992 *BioIn 17*
Seixas, Gershom Mendes 1745-1816 *BioIn 17*
Seiyama, Tetsuro 1920- *WhoWor 93*
Sejan, Nicolas 1745-1819 *Baker 92*
Sejanus, Lucius Aelius c. 18BC-31AD *HarEnMi*
Sejna, Karel 1896-1982 *Baker 92*
Sejpal, David 1958- *St&PR 93*
Sek, Danuta 1935- *WhoScE 91-4*
Sekas, Gus N. 1932- *St&PR 93*
Sekas, Nicholas 1963- *St&PR 93*
Sekely, Steve 1899-1979 *MiSFD 9N*
Sekerak, Deborah Janelle 1966- *WhoAmW 93*
Sekerak, Raymond Joseph 1938- *St&PR 93*
Sekeris, Constantine 1933- *WhoScE 91-3*
Sekeris, Constantine Evangelos 1933- *WhoWor 93*
Sekerka, Robert Floyd 1937- *WhoAm 92, WhoE 93*
Sekhar, B.C. *WhoScE 91-1*
Sekhonyana, Evaristus Retselisitsoe 1937- *WhoAfr*
Seki, Haremasa 1923- *WhoAsAP 91*
Seki, Hiroharu 1927- *WhoWor 93*
Seki, Hozen d1991 *BioIn 17*
Seki, Kenji 1959- *WhoWor 93*
Seki, Masahiro 1934- *WhoWor 93*
Seki, Shinji 1920- *BioIn 17*
Sekiguchi, Keizo 1926- *WhoAsAP 91*
Sekiguchi, Toyozo 1929- *WhoWor 93*
Sekimoto, Tadahiro 1926- *St&PR 93, WhoWor 93*
Sekimura, Toshio 1947- *WhoWor 93*
Sekiya, Gerald Yoshinori 1942- *WhoWor 93*
Sekiya, Jiro 1945- *WhoWor 93*
Sekiya, Katsutsugu 1938- *WhoAsAP 91*
Sekiyama, Nobuyuki 1934- *WhoAsAP 91*
Sekizawa, Masami 1944- *WhoWor 93*
Sekler, Eduard Franz 1920- *WhoAm 92, WhoWrEP 92*
Sekles, Bernhard 1872-1934 *Baker 92*
Seko, Masataka 1923- *WhoAsAP 91*
Seko, Mobutu Sese 1930- *BioIn 17*
Sekoll, June Louise 1931- *WhoSSW 93, WhoWrEP 92*
Sekoundinos, Nicholas 1402-1464 *OxDcByz*
Sekovski, Blaze 1954- *WhoE 93*
Sekowski, Boleslaw 1922- *WhoScE 91-4*
Sekowski, Cynthia Jean 1953- *WhoAmW 93*
Sekse, Per Arild 1956- *WhoWor 93*
Sekula, Edward Joseph, Jr. 1937- *WhoAm 92*
Sekula, John William *Law&B 92*
Sekula, Stanley *BioIn 17*
Sekuler, Robert William 1939- *WhoAm 92, WhoE 93*
Sekulic, Ante 1920- *WhoWor 93*
Sekulic, Dusko 1947- *WhoWor 93*
Sekulic, Sava 1931- *WhoScE 91-4*
Sekulic, Sava St. 1931- *WhoScE 91-4*
Sekulovich, Malden 1916- *WhoAm 92*
Sekyra, Hugo Michael 1941- *WhoWor 93*
Selak, Barbara S. *WhoWrEP 92*
Selakovic, Marko 1933- *WhoScE 91-4*
Selander, Lesley 1900-1979 *MiSFD 9N*
Selander, Lorraine Fyda 1927- *WhoAmW 93*
Selander, Stephen *Law&B 92*
Selbach, Albert Karl 1872-1956 *BiDAMSp 1989*
Selbach, Scott C. 1955- *St&PR 93*
Selbach, Willard M. *St&PR 93*
Selber, Arlene Bork 1942- *WhoSSW 93*
Selberg, Ingrid 1950- *BioIn 17*
Selberg, Ingrid (Maria) 1950- *ConAu 136*
Selberg, Janice Kay 1953- *WhoAmW 93*
Selberherr, Siegfried 1955- *WhoEmL 93*
Selbie, Evelyn 1882-1950 *SweetSg A [port]*
Selbin, Joel 1931- *WhoAm 92, WhoSSW 93*
Selborne, Earl of 1859-1942 *BioIn 17*
Selbourne, David 1937- *ConAu 38NR*
Selbourne, Hugh 1906- *BioIn 17*
Selby, Bertram Luard 1853-1918 *Baker 92*
Selby, Brian *WhoScE 91-1*
Selby, Cecily Cannan 1927- *WhoAm 92, WhoAmW 93*
Selby, Clark Linwood, Jr. 1936- *WhoSSW 93, WhoWor 93*
Selby, Curt *ScF&FL 92*
Selby, Gwendolyn Maxine Wallin 1940- *WhoAmW 93*
Selby, Hubert 1928- *BioIn 17*
Selby, Hubert, Jr. 1928- *WhoAm 92*
Selby, Janet S. Groshart 1927- *WhoAmW 93*
Selby, Jerome M. 1948- *WhoEmL 93, WhoWor 93*
Selby, John fl. 1772-1776 *BioIn 17*
Selby, John Ashley 1944- *WhoScE 91-4*
Selby, John Horace 1919- *WhoSSW 93*
Selby, John Rodney 1929- *St&PR 93*
Selby, Katherine *WhoWrEP 92*
Selby, Mary Ellen 1960- *WhoAmW 93*
Selby, Nancy Chizek 1935- *WhoSSW 93*
Selby, Robert Norman 1932- *WhoE 93*
Selby, Roger Lowell 1933- *WhoAm 92*
Selby, Roy Clifton, Jr. 1930- *WhoAm 92, WhoSSW 93*
Selby, Stephen P. 1940- *St&PR 93*
Selby, William c. 1738-1798 *Baker 92, BioIn 17*
Selby-Wright, Sonya d1990 *BioIn 17*
Selcer, David Mark 1943- *WhoAm 92*
Selcer, Richard F. 1950- *ConAu 139*
Selchow, Roger Hoffman 1911- *WhoE 93*
Selcov, Jay Adlai *Law&B 92*
Selden, Annie Alexander 1938- *WhoSSW 93*
Selden, David Edward 1960- *WhoE 93*
Selden, Gara *AmWomPl*
Selden, George *ConAu 37NR, MajAI, SmATA 73*
Selden, George 1929- *DcAmChF 1960*
Selden, George 1929-1989 *BioIn 17, ScF&FL 92*
Selden, John 1934- *WhoSSW 93*
Selden, Lawrence V. 1922- *WhoE 93*
Selden, Neil R. 1931- *BioIn 17, ScF&FL 92*
Selden, Phoebe Serena 1955- *WhoAmW 93*
Selden, Richard Thomas 1922- *WhoAm 92*
Selden, Robert Wentworth 1936- *WhoAm 92*
Selden, Stephen James *Law&B 92*
Selden, William Kirkpatrick 1911- *WhoAm 92*
Seldes, George 1890- *BioIn 17, WhoAm 92*
Seldes, Marian *WhoAm 92*
Seldin, Donald Wayne 1920- *WhoAm 92*
Seldon, Anthony 1953- *ConAu 136*
Seldon, Keith *ScF&FL 92*
Seldowitz, Steven R. *Law&B 92*
Selecman, Barbara Ann 1942- *WhoAmW 93*
Selecman, Charles Edward 1928- *WhoAm 92, WhoWor 93*
Seledee, Craig *Law&B 92*
Selegue, John Paul 1952- *WhoSSW 93*
Selenka, Fidelis 1930- *WhoScE 91-3*
Selenow, Harvey Steven 1943- *St&PR 93*
Seler, Eduard 1849-1922 *IntDcAn*
Seles, Monica *BioIn 17*
Seles, Monica 1973- *CurBio 92 [port], WhoAm 92, WhoWor 93*
Seley, Etta Squier *AmWomPl*
Self, Charles Edwin 1934- *WhoAm 92*
Self, Edwin Forbes 1920- *WhoAm 92, WhoWrEP 92*
Self, George Doyle 1943- *St&PR 93*
Self, Glen 1938- *St&PR 93*
Self, James C. 1919- *St&PR 93*
Self, James Reed 1944- *WhoAm 92*
Self, Madison Allen 1921- *WhoAm 92*
Self, Mark Edward 1955- *WhoEmL 93, WhoSSW 93, WhoWor 93*
Self, Ron *WhoScE 91-1*
Self, W. M. *WhoAm 92*
Self, William Edwin 1921- *WhoAm 92*
Self, William Lee 1932- *WhoSSW 93*
Selfe, Edward M. 1921- *St&PR 93*
Selfridge, George Dever 1924- *WhoAm 92*
Selfridge, Steven G. 1955- *St&PR 93*
Selhorst, L.O. 1933- *St&PR 93*
Selhorst, Lawrence O'Hare 1933- *WhoAm 92*
Selick, David Alan 1933- *St&PR 93*
Selig, Allan H. 1934- *WhoAm 92*
Selig, David George 1955- *WhoE 93*
Selig, Elaine Booth 1935- *ScF&FL 92*
Selig, Karl-Ludwig 1926- *WhoAm 92, WhoWor 93, WhoWrEP 92*
Selig, Kenneth Mishara 1950- *WhoE 93*
Selig, Marvin 1923- *WhoAm 92*
Selig, Phil 1943- *St&PR 93*
Selig, Phyllis Sims 1931- *WhoAmW 93*
Selig, Renee Jeanette *Law&B 92*
Selig, Robert Leigh 1939-1984 *Baker 92*
Selig, S. Stephen, III 1943- *St&PR 93*
Seliger, Charles 1926- *WhoAm 92*
Seliger, Gunther 1947- *WhoScE 91-3*
Seliger, Hendrik Gunther 1965- *WhoWor 93*
Seligman, Brenda Z. 1882-1965 *IntDcAn*
Seligman, C.G. 1873-1940 *IntDcAn*
Seligman, Daniel 1924- *WhoAm 92, WhoWrEP 92*
Seligman, David A. *Law&B 92*
Seligman, Henry 1909- *WhoWor 93*
Seligman, Linda Helen 1944- *WhoAmW 93*
Seligman, Mac 1918- *St&PR 93*
Seligman, Rachel *BioIn 17*
Seligman, Raphael David 1919- *WhoWor 93*
Seligman, Rudolph Frank 1943- *WhoAm 92*
Seligman, Shelly W. *Law&B 92*
Seligman, Thomas Knowles 1944- *WhoAm 92*
Seligmann, Gustav Leonard 1934- *WhoSSW 93*
Seligmann, Hippolyte-Prosper 1817-1882 *Baker 92*
Seligmann, Maxime G. 1927- *WhoScE 91-2*
Seligmann, Maxime Gerard 1927- *WhoWor 93*
Seligmann, Moses 1809-1887 *BioIn 17*
Selignac, Arnaud *MiSFD 9*
Seligsohn, Sheldon *Law&B 92*
Seligson, Carl H. 1935- *WhoAm 92*
Seligson, Charles D. 1942- *St&PR 93*
Seligson, Frances Hess 1949- *WhoE 93*
Seligson, Garry R. *Law&B 92*
Seligson, M. Ross 1949- *WhoSSW 93*
Seligson, Theodore H. 1930- *WhoAm 92*
Seligson, Thomas Frank *Law&B 92*
Selikoff, Irving J. *BioIn 17*
Selikoff, Irving J. d1992 *NewYTBS 92 [port]*
Selin, Ivan 1937- *BioIn 17, WhoAm 92, WhoE 93, WhoWor 93*
Selinger, Anton F. 1940- *St&PR 93*
Selinger, Bernard 1949- *ScF&FL 92*
Selinske, Charles E. 1933- *St&PR 93*
Selis, John L. *Law&B 92*
Selis, John Leon 1936- *St&PR 93*
Selis, Pamela Anne 1942- *WhoAmW 93*
Selis, Stuart L. 1951- *WhoEmL 93*
Seljuks *OxDcByz*
Selk, Eleanor Hutton 1918- *WhoAmW 93*
Selke, Gary Peter 1954- *St&PR 93*
Selke, William August 1922- *WhoE 93*
Selke-Kern, Barbara Ellen 1950- *WhoEmL 93, WhoSSW 93*
Selkirk, James Kirkwood 1938- *WhoAm 92*
Selko, Soll Leonard 1923- *St&PR 93*
Selkoe, Dennis J. 1943- *WhoAm 92*
Selkow, Paula *WhoE 93*
Selkowitz, Arthur 1943- *WhoAm 92*
Selkowitz, Judith 1944- *WhoE 93*
Selky, John Lee 1937- *St&PR 93*
Sell, Douglas P. 1948- *St&PR 93*
Sell, Edward Scott, Jr. 1917- *St&PR 93, WhoAm 92*
Sell, Floyd E. 1933- *St&PR 93*
Sell, Frederick O. Paul *St&PR 93*
Sell, Friedrich Leopold 1954- *WhoWor 93*
Sell, Helmut Lienhard 1939- *WhoUN 92*
Sell, Jack M. 1954- *MiSFD 9*
Sell, Jill 1950- *WhoWrEP 92*
Sell, Joan Isobel 1936- *WhoAmW 93*
Sell, Jurgen 1939- *WhoScE 91-4*
Sell, Kenneth Walter 1931- *WhoAm 92*
Sell, Neil I. 1941- *St&PR 93*
Sell, Robert Demeusy 1954- *WhoE 93*
Sell, Steven Ray 1941- *St&PR 93*
Sell, William Edward 1923- *WhoAm 92*
Sell, Wolfgang *WhoScE 91-3*
Sella, Edward Gerard 1933- *WhoE 93*
Sella, Emmanuel 1924- *WhoE 93*
Sella, George John, Jr. 1928- *St&PR 93, WhoAm 92*
Sella, Jeanne Geyer 1930- *WhoAmW 93*
Sellami-Meslem, Chafika 1934- *WhoUN 92*
Selland, Christopher Scott 1964- *WhoWor 93*
Sellar, Ian *MiSFD 9*
Sellars, Christopher Michael *WhoScE 91-1*
Sellars, Gilbert Fitzgerald 1932- *WhoSSW 93*
Sellars, James Allen 1958- *WhoWor 93*
Sellars, Nigel Anthony 1954- *WhoSSW 93, WhoWrEP 92*
Sellars, Peter *BioIn 17, MiSFD 9*
Sellars, Peter 1957- *Baker 92, IntDcOp, OxDcOp, WhoAm 92*
Sellberg, Sven U. 1943- *WhoUN 92*
Selldorff, J. Thomas 1928- *St&PR 93*
Selle, Burkhardt Herbert Richard 1938- *WhoWor 93*
Selle, Thomas 1599-1663 *Baker 92*
Sellecca, Connie *BioIn 17*
Sellecca, Connie 1955- *WhoAm 92*
Selleck, Anne *AmWomPl*
Selleck, Marilyn Ann 1958- *WhoAmW 93*
Selleck, Tom *BioIn 17*
Selleck, Tom 1945- *WhoAm 92*
Selleck, Virginia Mildred 1948- *WhoAmW 93*
Seller, Robert Herman 1931- *WhoAm 92*
Seller, Steven Mark 1952- *WhoE 93*
Seller, William Frank 1934- *St&PR 93*
Sellers, Alan 1948- *St&PR 93*
Sellers, Alan B. *Law&B 92*
Sellers, Alfred Mayer 1924- *WhoE 93*
Sellers, Arlene Maae 1944- *WhoAmW 93*
Sellers, Barbara Jackson 1940- *WhoAmW 93*
Sellers, Bettie Mixon 1926- *WhoWrEP 92*
Sellers, Beverly Burch 1962- *WhoSSW 93*
Sellers, Carolyn Cook *Law&B 92*
Sellers, Catherine Louise 1953- *WhoAmW 93*
Sellers, Cleveland 1944- *BioIn 17*
Sellers, Con 1922-1992 *ScF&FL 92*
Sellers, Con(nie Leslie, Jr.) 1922- *ConAu 37NR*
Sellers, Con(nie Leslie, Jr.) 1922-1992 *ConAu 136*
Sellers, Dennis Aaron 1956- *WhoWrEP 92*
Sellers, Donna Reiman 1954- *WhoE 93*
Sellers, Errica 1956- *WhoAmW 93*
Sellers, Fred Evans 1941- *WhoSSW 93*
Sellers, Fred Wilson 1942- *St&PR 93, WhoAm 92*
Sellers, Gary Richard 1954- *St&PR 93*
Sellers, Georgeanna 1955- *WhoSSW 93*
Sellers, Gregory Jude 1947- *WhoEmL 93, WhoWor 93*
Sellers, Irma Peixotto *AmWomPl*
Sellers, James Earl 1926- *WhoAm 92*
Sellers, Karen Anne 1945- *WhoE 93*
Sellers, Macklyn Rhett, Jr. 1962- *WhoSSW 93*
Sellers, Mary 1925- *ScF&FL 92*
Sellers, Mary Bailey 1948- *St&PR 93*
Sellers, Michele Renee 1962- *WhoAmW 93*
Sellers, Peter 1925-1980 *BioIn 17, IntDcF 2-3 [port], QDrFCA 92 [port]*
Sellers, Peter Hoadley 1930- *WhoAm 92*
Sellers, Philip A. 1920- *St&PR 93*
Sellers, Richard Wesley 1938- *St&PR 93*
Sellers, Shirley Nesbit 1926- *WhoAmW 93*
Sellers, Steve 1936- *St&PR 93*
Sellers, Wallace O. 1929- *St&PR 93*
Sellers, William E. 1934- *St&PR 93*
Sellery, J'nan Morse 1928- *WhoAmW 93, WhoWrEP 92*
Sellett, Mike *BioIn 17*
Selley, Ferenc 1936- *WhoScE 91-4*
Selley, Richard Curtis *WhoScE 91-1*
Sellick, John F. 1934- *St&PR 93, WhoIns 93*
Sellick, John Francis 1934- *WhoAm 92*
Sellier, Charles E., Jr. *MiSFD 9*
Sellier, Charles E., Jr. 1925?-1983? *ScF&FL 92*
Sellier, Henri 1883-1943 *BioIn 17*
Sellier, Karl 1924- *WhoScE 91-3*
Sellier, Louis 1885-1978 *BioIn 17*
Sellig, Robert George 1941- *WhoE 93*
Sellin, Bernard *ScF&FL 92*
Sellin, Eric 1933- *WhoAm 92, WhoWrEP 92*
Sellin, Michelle Lynn 1965- *WhoAmW 93*
Sellin, Robert Henry John *WhoScE 91-1*
Sellin, Theodore 1928- *WhoAm 92*
Selling, Hendrik Anne 1943- *WhoUN 92*
Sellinger, Barbara A. *Law&B 92*
Sellinger, Elaine 1931- *WhoE 93*

Sellinger, Joseph Anthony 1921- *WhoE 93*
Sellinger, Scott Michael 1953- *St&PR 93*
Sellinschegg, Wolf Dieter 1941- *WhoUN 92*
Sellke, Frank William 1956- *WhoE 93*
Sellman, Charles Harwood 1934- *St&PR 93*
Sellman, Kirk S. 1949- *St&PR 93*
Sellmeyer, J.B. 1947- *WhoScE 91-3*
Sellner, Joseph 1787-1843 *Baker 92*
Sello, A.R. 1939- *St&PR 93*
Sello, Allen Ralph 1939- *WhoAm 92*
Sello, Judy *Law&B 92*
Sellon, John A. 1910- *St&PR 93*
Sellover, R. Edwin *Law&B 92*
Sells, Boake Anthony 1937- *St&PR 93, WhoAm 92*
Sells, Bruce Howard 1930- *WhoAm 92*
Sells, Dan 1939- *St&PR 93*
Sells, Harold E. 1928- *St&PR 93, WhoAm 92*
Sells, Marcia Lynn *BioIn 17*
Sells, Richard T. 1939- *St&PR 93*
Sells, Robert Anthony *WhoScE 91-1*
Sells, Robert Anthony 1938- *WhoWor 93*
Sells, Trine Lise 1945- *WhoWor 93*
Selly, Joseph P. 1905-1991 *BioIn 17*
Selman, David H. 1933- *St&PR 93*
Selman, J.D. *WhoScE 91-1*
Selman, Jan Collins *BioIn 17*
Selman, Joe B. 1946- *WhoSSW 93*
Selman, John 1839-1896 *BioIn 17*
Selman, Murray 1926- *St&PR 93*
Selman, Randy S. 1956- *St&PR 93*
Selman, Ruth *AmWomPl*
Selman, T.C. 1950- *St&PR 93*
Selmar, Bonnie Jean 1953- *WhoAmW 93*
Selmeier, Richard James 1943- *WhoAm 92*
Selmer, Johan Peter 1844-1910 *Baker 92*
Selmes, B.A. *WhoScE 91-1*
Selmi, William, Jr. 1937- *WhoSSW 93*
Selnau, Edward Walter 1929- *St&PR 93*
Selonick, James Bennett 1925- *St&PR 93*
Selous, Frederick Courteney 1851-1917 *BioIn 17*
Selover, R. Edwin *Law&B 92*
Selover, R. Edwin 1945- *WhoAm 92*
Selover, William C. 1938- *St&PR 93*
Selsam, Milicent Ellis *WhoWrEP 92*
Selsam, Millicent E(llis) 1912- *MajAI [port]*
Selsam, Millicent Ellis 1912- *ConAu 38NR*
Selser, Gregorio d1991 *BioIn 17*
Selski, William E. 1953- *WhoE 93*
Selsor, Jeff 1961- *St&PR 93*
Selter, Edith *AmWomPl*
Selter, Eric Jay *Law&B 92*
Seltman, Mark Allan 1947- *WhoE 93*
Seltser, Raymond 1923- *WhoAm 92*
Seltz, Alfred Carl 1931- *St&PR 93*
Seltz, Paul H. 1921- *St&PR 93*
Seltz, Raymond 1934- *WhoScE 91-2*
Seltzer, Craig H. 1954- *St&PR 93*
Seltzer, David *MiSFD 9*
Seltzer, David 1920?- *ScF&FL 92*
Seltzer, Edward Charles 1927- *St&PR 93*
Seltzer, Jeffrey Lloyd 1956- *WhoE 93, WhoEmL 93*
Seltzer, Joanne 1929- *WhoWrEP 92*
Seltzer, Joanne Lynn 1946- *WhoEmL 93*
Seltzer, Leo 1910- *WhoAm 92*
Seltzer, Loretta Mae 1936- *WhoAmW 93*
Seltzer, Madeline 1942- *WhoAmW 93*
Seltzer, Margaret A. *Law&B 92*
Seltzer, Matthew D. *St&PR 93*
Seltzer, Mildred M. 1921- *WhoAm 92*
Seltzer, Mitchell Sherman 1948- *WhoE 93*
Seltzer, Neal L. 1937- *St&PR 93*
Seltzer, Phyllis Estelle 1928- *WhoAm 92, WhoAmW 93*
Seltzer, Richard Warren, Jr. 1946- *WhoE 93*
Seltzer, Ronald 1931- *WhoAm 92*
Seltzer, Ronald Anthony 1935- *WhoAm 92*
Seltzer, Samuel M. 1926- *WhoE 93*
Seltzer, Samuel Marvin 1926- *St&PR 93*
Seltzer, Sherwin Paul 1934- *WhoE 93*
Seltzer, Vicki Lynn 1949- *WhoAm 92, WhoAmW 93*
Seltzer, Vivian Center 1931- *WhoAmW 93*
Seltzer, William 1934- *WhoAm 92, WhoUN 92*
Selub, Clarice *WhoAmW 93*
Selub, Doris *WhoAmW 93*
Seluka, Alesana 1933- *WhoAsAP 91*
Selva, Blanche 1884-1942 *Baker 92*
Selva, Mauricio de la 1930- *DcMexL*
Selva, Salomon de la 1893-1959 *DcMexL*
Selvadurai, Antony Patrick Sinnappa 1942- *WhoAm 92*
Selvaggi, Rito 1898-1972 *Baker 92*
Selvaggio, Andrea W. *Law&B 92*
Selvanathan, Arputham 1942- *WhoUN 92*
Selvaraj, Kingsley 1964- *WhoWor 93*
Selvaraj, Parthasarathy 1947- *WhoWor 93*
Selvendran, Robert Rasiah *WhoScE 91-1*
Selvera, Norma Brito 1947- *NotHsAW 93*
Selves, David 1949- *ScF&FL 92*
Selvig, Knut A. *WhoScE 91-4*
Selvig, William Norman 1932- *St&PR 93*
Selvin, Harold *St&PR 93*
Selvon, Sam 1923- *DcLB 125 [port], IntvWPC 92 [port]*
Selvon, Samuel 1923- *BioIn 17, WhoCanL 92*
Selvy, Barbara 1938- *WhoSSW 93*
Selvy, Franklin Delano 1932- *BiDAMSp 1989*
Selwood, Peter John 1942- *WhoE 93*
Selwood, Pierce Taylor 1939- *WhoAm 92*
Selwyn, Donald 1936- *WhoAm 92*
Selya, Bruce Marshall 1934- *WhoAm 92, WhoE 93*
Selya, Robert P. *Law&B 92*
Selz, B.T. 1940- *St&PR 93*
Selz, Bernard 1940- *WhoAm 92*
Selz, Peter Howard 1919- *WhoAm 92*
Selzer, Michael David 1947- *WhoSSW 93*
Selzer, Richard *BioIn 17*
Selzer, Richard 1928- *ConLC 74 [port]*
Selzer, William Henry 1925- *St&PR 93*
Selzler, Bernard John 1939- *WhoWrEP 92*
Selznick, Arna 1948- *MiSFD 9*
Selznick, Brian *BioIn 17*
Selznick, David O. 1902-1965 *BioIn 17*
Selznick, Irene Mayer 1907-1990 *BioIn 17*
Semadeni, Zbigniew Wladyslaw 1934- *WhoWor 93*
Semak, David P. 1948- *St&PR 93*
Semak, Michael William 1934- *WhoAm 92*
Seman, Constantin 1943- *St&PR 93*
Seman, Robert J. *Law&B 92*
Semanov, Vladimir Ivanovitch 1933- *WhoWor 93*
Semans, Truman Thomas 1926- *WhoAm 92*
Semard, Pierre 1887-1942 *BioIn 17*
Semark, Philip Norman 1945- *WhoAm 92*
Semas, Philip Wayne 1946- *WhoAm 92*
Sembat, Marcel 1862-1922 *BioIn 17*
Sembdner, Gunther 1931- *WhoScE 91-3*
Sembene, Ousmane 1923- *BioIn 17, MiSFD 9*
Sember, Joseph Alexander 1923- *St&PR 93*
Sember, June Elizabeth 1932- *WhoE 93*
Sember, Shirley Anne 1944- *WhoAmW 93*
Sembery, Peter 1940- *WhoScE 91-4*
Semb-Johansson, Arne 1919- *WhoScE 91-4*
Sembler, Melvin 1930- *WhoAm 92, WhoWor 93*
Sembo, William George 1953- *St&PR 93*
Sembrich, Marcella 1858-1935 *Baker 92, IntDcOp, OxDcOp*
Sembrich-Kochanska, Marcella 1858-1935 *PolBiDi*
Semcken, Kevin R. *St&PR 93*
Semczuk, Boleslaw 1928- *WhoScE 91-4*
Seme, Joseph P. 1953- *St&PR 93*
Semedo, Joan Della 1938- *WhoE 93*
Semegen, Patrick W. 1946- *St&PR 93*
Semegen, Patrick William *Law&B 92*
Semegen, Patrick William 1946- *WhoAm 92*
Semegram, Harriet Rita 1933- *WhoE 93*
Semeiko, Nick Grigorevich 1948- *WhoWor 93*
Semel, Ann 1932- *WhoAmW 93*
Semel, Julie Maris/ *BioIn 17*
Semel, Scott N. *St&PR 93*
Semel, Terry 1943- *ConTFT 10, WhoAm 92*
Semelka, Joy Elaine 1954- *WhoSSW 93*
Semelsberger, Kenneth J. 1936- *St&PR 93*
Semenoff, Ivan 1917-1972 *OxDcOp*
Semenov, Boris A. 1930- *WhoUN 92*
Semenov, Vladimir Iosifovich 1950- *WhoWor 93*
Semeonoff, Boris 1910- *WhoWor 93*
Semerad, Roger Dale 1940- *WhoAm 92*
Semerjian, Hratch Gregory 1943- *WhoE 93*
Semerjian, Madelle Hegeler d1991 *BioIn 17*
Semer-Purzycki, Jeanne Claire 1948- *WhoAmW 93*
Semet, Theophile (-Aime-Emile) 1824-1888 *Baker 92*
Semhon, Gerard 1936- *St&PR 93*
Semichi, Abdelhamid 1937- *WhoUN 92*
Seminario, Alejandro Luis 1937- *WhoWor 93*
Semisi Maya *BioIn 17*
Semizorova, Nina *BioIn 17*
Semke, L.K. 1936- *St&PR 93*
Semko, Nancy Elaine 1963- *WhoAmW 93*
Semkow, Jerzy 1928- *Baker 92*
Semkow, Jerzy Stanislaw 1928- *WhoWor 93*
Semla-Pulaski, Halina Maria *WhoE 93*
Semler, Dean *WhoAm 92*
Semler, Dean R. 1929- *St&PR 93*
Semler, Jerry D. 1937- *St&PR 93, WhoAm 92, WhoIns 93*
Semler, Johannes 1923- *WhoWor 93*
Semlow, Bruce E. 1938- *St&PR 93*
Semlyen, Adam 1923- *WhoAm 92*
Semm, Kurt Karl Stephan 1927- *WhoScE 91-3*
Semmel, Arno 1929- *WhoScE 91-3*
Semmel, Bernard 1928- *WhoAm 92, WhoWrEP 92*
Semmel, David Robert 1957- *St&PR 93*
Semmelman, Andrew T. *Law&B 92*
Semmelmeyer, Kristin Leigh 1958- *WhoE 93*
Semmelweis, Ignac Fulop 1818-1865 *BioIn 17*
Semmens, James Pike 1919- *WhoSSW 93*
Semmes, Francis B. *Law&B 92*
Semmler, Carl D. *Law&B 92*
Semon, Larry 1889-1928 *MiSFD 9N, QDrFCA 92 [port]*
Semon, Michael Glenn 1958- *WhoSSW 93*
Semon, Warren Lloyd 1921- *WhoAm 92*
Semonelli, Christopher T. *St&PR 93*
Semonian, Robert Alexander 1939- *WhoAm 92, WhoE 93*
Semonin, Richard Gerard 1930- *WhoAm 92*
Semonin, William J. 1930- *St&PR 93*
Semonoff, Ralph Perlow 1918- *WhoAm 92*
Semons, Charles Williams *Law&B 92*
Semos, Chris Victor 1936- *WhoSSW 93*
Semowich, Charles John *WhoE 93*
Sempad Connetable *OxDcByz*
Sempe *WhoScE 91-2*
Sempere, Julian 1956- *WhoScE 91-3*
Semple, Cecil Snowdon 1917- *WhoAm 92, WhoE 93*
Semple, Harton Singer 1920-1990 *BioIn 17*
Semple, Lloyd Ashby 1939- *WhoAm 92*
Semple, Muriel Virginia 1915- *WhoWor 93*
Semple, Nathaniel Meacon 1946- *WhoE 93*
Semple, Robert Baylor, Jr. 1936- *WhoAm 92*
Semple, Robert Warren 1950- *St&PR 93*
Semple, Stephen John Greenhill *WhoScE 91-1*
Semple, T. Darrington, Jr. 1926- *WhoIns 93*
Sempliner, John Alexander 1953- *WhoWor 93*
Semprun, Jorge *BioIn 17*
Semrad, John B. 1923- *St&PR 93*
Semrad, Myron L. 1945- *St&PR 93*
Semrad, Myron Leslie 1945- *WhoSSW 93*
Semrad, Robert 1926- *WhoAm 92, WhoSSW 93*
Semrod, T. Joseph 1936- *WhoAm 92*
Semrod, Theodore Joseph 1936- *St&PR 93*
Semyonov, Alexey I. 1956- *WhoE 93*
Semyonov, Moshe 1946- *ConAu 139*
Semyonova, Marina 1908- *BioIn 17*
Sen, Amartya Kumar *BioIn 17*
Sen, Amartya Kumar 1933- *WhoWor 93*
Sen, Ashis 1922- *WhoAsAP 91*
Sen, Ashish Kumar 1942- *WhoAm 92*
Sen, Colleen Taylor 1944- *WhoAmW 93*
Sen, Dipankar 1939- *WhoSSW 93*
Sen, Mrinal 1923- *MiSFD 9*
Sen, Paresh Chandra 1938- *WhoAm 92*
Sen, Pranab Kumar 1937- *WhoSSW 93*
Sen, Selcuk 1965- *WhoWor 93*
Sen, Sondra Kotzin 1939- *WhoAmW 93*
Sen, Sukomal 1934- *WhoAsAP 91*
Sen, Tapas Kumar 1933- *WhoE 93*
Sena, Donald Thomas 1948- *WhoE 93*
Senacherim *OxDcByz*
Senaille, Jean Baptiste 1687-1730 *Baker 92*
Senaillie, Jean Baptiste 1687-1730 *Baker 92*
Senallie, Jean Baptiste 1687-1730 *Baker 92*
Senanayake, Don Stephen 1884-1952 *DcTwHis*
Senanayake, Piyasiri Suranimala 1944- *WhoWor 93*
Senanayake, Yakallakankanamge Don A. 1932- *WhoWor 93*
Senancour, Etienne Pivert de 1770-1846 *DcLB 119 [port]*
Senaratna, Tissa *BioIn 17*
Senaratne, Upali Susanta Philip 1935- *WhoWor 93*
Sencak, John Lee *Law&B 92*
Senchenko, Georgii 1962- *BioIn 17*
Sendak, Maurice *BioIn 17*
Sendak, Maurice 1928- *IntDcOp*
Sendak, Maurice (Bernard) 1928- *ConAu 39NR, MajAI [port], WhoAm 92, WhoWrEP 92*
Sendax, Victor Irven 1930- *WhoAm 92, WhoWor 93*
Sendell, Stuart Daniel 1942- *St&PR 93*
Sender (Barayon), Ramon 1934- *Baker 92*
Sender, Ramon Jose 1901-1982 *BioIn 17*
Sender, Ruth Minsky 1926- *BioIn 17*
Senderling, Jon Townsend *WhoAm 92*
Senders, Rita Lea 1949- *WhoAmW 93*
Senders, Virginia Loftus 1923- *WhoE 93*
Sendlein, Lyle V. A. 1933- *WhoAm 92, WhoSSW 93*
Sendler, David A. 1938- *WhoWrEP 92*
Sendov, Blagovest Hristov 1932- *WhoScE 91-4*
Sendrey, Albert Richard 1911- *Baker 92*
Sendrey, Alfred *Baker 92*
Sendrovic, Israel 1947- *St&PR 93, WhoAm 92*
Sendstad, Erling 1948- *WhoScE 91-4*
Sene, Malick 1943- *WhoUN 92*
Seneca 4BC-65AD *MagSWL [port]*
Seneca, Lucius Annaeus c. 4BC-65AD *BioIn 17*
Senecal, Eva 1905- *BioIn 17*
Senecal, Louise-Helene *Law&B 92*
Senecal-Tremblay, Marie *Law&B 92*
Senechal, Michel 1927- *OxDcOp*
Senechal, Philip J. 1946- *St&PR 93*
Seneker, Stanley A. *WhoAm 92*
Senelick, Laurence P(hilip) 1942- *WhoWrEP 92*
Senensky, Ralph 1923- *MiSFD 9*
Sener, Joseph W., Jr. 1926- *St&PR 93*
Sener, Joseph Ward, Jr. 1926- *WhoAm 92*
Sener, Robert N.H. 1933- *WhoIns 93*
Senerius, Norman H. *St&PR 93*
Senescu, Stuart *Law&B 92*
Senese, Donald Joseph 1942- *WhoAm 92*
Senesen, Ferial D. *Law&B 92*
Senesh, Hannah 1921-1944 *BioIn 17*
Senesi, Nicola 1943- *WhoWor 93*
Senesino d1759 *IntDcOp*
Senesino c. 1680-c. 1759 *Baker 92, OxDcOp*
Senezhak, Diana M. *Law&B 92*
Senf, Carol A. *ScF&FL 92*
Senff, Bartholf (Wilhelm) 1815-1900 *Baker 92*
Senfl, Ludwig c. 1486-c. 1542 *Baker 92*
Senft, Bodo E. 1931- *WhoScE 91-3*
Senft, Dexter E. 1952- *St&PR 93*
Senft, Mason George 1942- *WhoE 93, WhoWor 93*
Senftinger, Berthold Kilian 1960- *WhoWor 93*
Senftleben, Richard A. *Law&B 92*
Seng, Ann Frances 1936- *WhoAmW 93*
Seng, Thomas N. 1947- *St&PR 93*
Sengelaja, El'dar 1933- *DrEEuF*
Sengelaja, Giorgi 1937- *DrEEuF*
Sengenberger, Werner Otto 1941- *WhoUN 92*
Senger, Horst 1931- *WhoScE 91-3*
Senger, John David 1922- *WhoWor 93*
Senger und Etterlin, Frido von 1891-1963 *BioIn 17*
Senger Und Etterlin, Fridolin R. T. von 1891-1963 *HarEnMi*
Senghor, Leopold Sedar 1906- *BioIn 17, DcTwHis*
Seng-Kuo-Lin-Ch'in d1865 *HarEnMi*
Sengoku, Yoshito 1946- *WhoAsAP 91*
Sengpiehl, June Shirley *WhoWrEP 92*
Sengstack, David Kells 1922- *WhoE 93*
Sengstacke, John H. 1912- *EncAACR, St&PR 93*
Sengstacke, John H(erman Henry) 1912- *DcLB 127 [port]*
Sengstacke, John Herman Henry 1912- *WhoAm 92*
Sengstacke, Robert A. 1943- *St&PR 93*
Sengupta, Abhijit *DcChlFi*
Sengupta, Dipak Lal 1931- *WhoAm 92*
Sengupta, Poile (Ambika) 1948- *DcChlFi*
Sengwe, Ngoni Francis 1949- *WhoWor 93*
Senhauser, Donald Albert 1927- *WhoAm 92*
Senica, Carl Gerard 1933- *WhoE 93*
Senich, Donald 1929- *WhoAm 92*
Senilov, Vladimir 1875-1918 *Baker 92*
Senio, Ronald M. *Law&B 92*
Senior, David 1948- *St&PR 93, WhoAm 92*
Senior, Enrique F. 1943- *St&PR 93*
Senior, Gerald *BioIn 17*
Senior, Howard B., III *Law&B 92*
Senior, John *WhoScE 91-1*
Senior, John Michael *WhoScE 91-1*
Senior, John Robert 1927- *WhoE 93*
Senior, P.J. *WhoScE 91-1*
Senior, Thomas Bryan A. 1928- *WhoAm 92*
Senior, William C. 1926- *St&PR 93*
Senju, Shizuo 1923- *WhoWor 93*
Senker, Linda E. *Law&B 92*
Senkier, Robert Joseph 1916- *WhoAm 92*
Senn, Frank C(olvin) 1943- *ConAu 39NR*
Senn, Gregory R. 1954- *St&PR 93*
Senn, Marilyn Helene 1939- *WhoAmW 93*
Senn, Milton John Edward 1902-1990 *BioIn 17*

SerVaas, Margaret Ann 1952- *WhoAmW 93, WhoEmL 93*
Servais, Donna J. 1946- *WhoWrEP 92*
Servais, Francois c. 1847-1901 *Baker 92*
Servais, (Adrien-) Francois 1807-1866 *Baker 92*
Servais, Jean-Michel 1945- *WhoUN 92*
Servais, Joseph 1850-1885 *Baker 92*
Servan-Schreiber, Jean-Jacques *BioIn 17*
Servan-Schreiber, Jean-Jacques 1924- *WhoWor 93*
Servantez, Felix *Law&B 92*
Servedio, Dominick M. 1940- *St&PR 93*
Servedio, Dominick Michael 1940- *WhoE 93*
Servetus, Michael 1511?-1553 *BioIn 17*
Service, Kenneth Patrick 1946- *WhoE 93*
Service, Pamela F. *BioIn 17*
Service, Pamela F. 1945- *ScF&FL 92*
Service, Robert W. 1874-1958 *BioIn 17, WorLitC [port]*
Service, Thomas Howard 1952- *WhoE 93*
Servilius Geminus, Gnaeus d216BC *HarEnMi*
Servison, Roger Theodore 1945- *St&PR 93, WhoAm 92*
Serviss, Garrett P. 1851-1929 *ScF&FL 92*
Servitto, Matt *BioIn 17*
Servius Tullius dc. 535BC *HarEnMi*
Servodidio, Pat A. 1937- *St&PR 93*
Servodidio, Pat Anthony 1937- *WhoAm 92*
Serwadda, William Moses 1931- *BlkAull 92*
Serwer, Alan Michael 1944- *WhoAm 92*
Serwich, T. Gregory, II *Law&B 92*
Serwinski, Jerzy 1949- *WhoScE 91-4*
Serwy, Robert Anthony 1950- *WhoEmL 93*
Sery, Theodore Wilson 1924- *WhoE 93*
Sesler, Timothy W. *Law&B 92*
Sesody, John J. 1946- *St&PR 93*
Sesok, Michele Ann 1965- *WhoAmW 93*
Sesonske, Alexander 1921- *WhoAm 92*
Sessa, Aldo 1939- *BioIn 17, ScF&FL 92*
Sessa, Alex 1944- *MiSFD 9*
Sessa, Salvatore 1950- *WhoWor 93*
Sessan Pereira, Rafael *DcCPCAm*
Sesselmeier, Werner 1960- *WhoWor 93*
Sessions, Amasa *BioIn 17*
Sessions, George Purd 1931- *WhoSSW 93*
Sessions, Jean E. 1946- *WhoAm 92*
Sessions, Jefferson Beauregard, III 1946- *WhoAm 92*
Sessions, Judith Ann 1947- *WhoAmW 93*
Sessions, Larry C. 1952- *St&PR 93*
Sessions, Olin Thomas *Law&B 92*
Sessions, Robert Morris 1927- *St&PR 93*
Sessions, Robert Paul 1926- *WhoAm 92*
Sessions, Roger 1896-1985 *IntDcOp, OxDcOp*
Sessions, Roger Carl 1944- *WhoSSW 93*
Sessions, Roger (Huntington) 1896-1985 *Baker 92*
Sessions, T.M.B. *WhoScE 91-1*
Sessions, William Steele *BioIn 17*
Sessions, William Steele 1930- *WhoAm 92*
Sessle, Barry John 1941- *WhoAm 92*
Sessler, Albert Louis, Jr. *Law&B 92*
Sessler, Andrew Marienhoff 1928- *WhoAm 92*
Sessler, Gerhard Martin 1931- *WhoScE 91-3, WhoWor 93*
Sessler, John Charles 1932- *WhoE 93*
Sessler, John George 1920- *WhoE 93*
Sessler, Linda Rowland *Law&B 92*
Sessoms, Lawrence R. *Law&B 92*
Sessoms, Stuart McGuire 1921- *WhoAm 92*
Sessoms, Walter Woodrow 1934- *WhoAm 92*
Sestak, Regina M. *Law&B 92*
Sestak, Thomas Joseph 1936- *BiDAMSp 1989*
Sestak, Zdenek 1925- *Baker 92*
Sesti, Giuseppe Maria 1942- *ConAu 137*
Sestina, John E. 1942- *WhoWor 93*
Sestini, Virgil Andrew 1936- *WhoWor 93*
Sesvold, Ronald Louis 1941- *WhoWor 93*
Setaccioli, Giacomo 1868-1925 *Baker 92*
Setapen, James Anthony 1948- *WhoSSW 93*
Setatou, Helen 1938- *WhoScE 91-3*
Setbon, Philip *MiSFD 9*
Seter, Mordecai 1916- *Baker 92*
Seth, E.A. *Law&B 92*
Seth, Manomar Lal 1943- *WhoWor 93*
Seth, Marie *ScF&FL 92*
Seth, Oliver 1915- *WhoAm 92*
Seth, Suresh C. 1935- *St&PR 93*
Seth, Symeon fl. 11th cent.- *OxDcByz*
Seth, Vikram 1952- *DcLB 120 [port], WhoWrEP 92*
Sethi, Deepak 1945- *WhoE 93*
Sethi, Ramesh Kumar 1943- *WhoWor 93*
Sethna, Beheruz Nariman 1948- *WhoAm 92, WhoSSW 93, WhoWor 93*
Sethna, Rohinton 1939- *WhoUN 92*
Sethness, Charles Olin 1941- *WhoAm 92*
Sethuraman, Salem V. 1935- *WhoUN 92*
Sethy, Andreas 1932- *WhoScE 91-4*
Seti, I d1299BC *HarEnMi*
Setien, Miguel Delibes *BioIn 17*
Setler, Paulette E. *St&PR 93*
Setliff, Dorothy Ellen 1958- *WhoAmW 93*
Setlow, Richard Burton 1921- *WhoAm 92*
Setlowe, Richard *ScF&FL 92*
Seto, Muriel Elizabeth 1924- *WhoAmW 93*
Seto, Robert Mahealani Ming 1936- *WhoWor 93*
Seto, William Roderick 1954- *WhoEmL 93, WhoSSW 93*
Seton, Anya d1990 *BioIn 17*
Seton, Anya 1904?-1990 *ScF&FL 92*
Seton, Charles B. 1910- *WhoAm 92*
Seton, Cynthia Propper 1926-1982 *BioIn 17*
Seton, Elizabeth Ann 1774-1821 *BioIn 17*
Seton, Ernest Thompson 1860-1946 *BioIn 17, GayN*
Seton, Fenmore Roger 1917- *WhoAm 92, WhoWor 93*
Seton, Sue d1991 *BioIn 17*
Setrakian, Berge 1949- *WhoE 93, WhoWor 93*
Setser, Carole Sue 1940- *WhoAmW 93*
Setser, Donald Wayne 1935- *WhoAm 92*
Sett'at'irat d1571 *HarEnMi*
Settele, Walter G. 1928- *WhoScE 91-4*
Settembrini, Sara Charlotte 1949- *St&PR 93*
Setterlin, Ralph F. 1961- *St&PR 93*
Setterlin, Ralph F., Jr. 1937- *St&PR 93*
Setterstrom, William N. 1942- *St&PR 93*
Setterwall, N. Fredrik F. 1934- *WhoScE 91-4*
Setti, Giancarlo *WhoScE 91-3*
Settineri, Cyrus 1952- *WhoE 93*
Settle, Frank Alexander, Jr. 1937- *WhoSSW 93*
Settle, George Warren 1926- *WhoE 93*
Settle, Larry D. 1942- *St&PR 93*
Settle, Mary Alice 1941- *WhoSSW 93*
Settle, Mary Lee *BioIn 17*
Settle, Mary Lee 1918- *WhoAm 92, WhoAmW 93*
Settle, Noel A. 1934- *WhoAm 92*
Settle, Peveril O., III *Law&B 92*
Settle, Ray Leonard 1944- *WhoE 93*
Settle, Robert Burton 1934- *WhoE 93*
Settle, William Sydnor 1933- *WhoAm 92*
Settlemier, B.R. 1934- *St&PR 93*
Settles, Cheryl Lynne 1947- *WhoWrEP 92*
Settles, F. Stan, Jr. 1938- *WhoAm 92*
Settles, G. Patrick *Law&B 92*
Settles, G. Patrick 1949- *St&PR 93*
Settles, Joseph Hays 1954- *WhoSSW 93*
Settles, Linda *Law&B 92*
Settles, Lois Ellen 1933- *WhoSSW 93*
Settles, Thomas Edward 1951- *WhoAm 92, WhoSSW 93*
Settles, William Frederick 1937- *WhoWrEP 92*
Setton, Kenneth M. 1914- *ConAu 39NR, WhoAm 92, WhoWor 93*
Setzer, Gene Willis 1918- *WhoAm 92*
Setzer, H.C. 1919- *St&PR 93*
Setzer, Herbert John 1928- *WhoAm 92, WhoE 93, WhoWor 93*
Setzer, Lewis F. 1922- *St&PR 93*
Setzer, Mitchell R. 1949- *St&PR 93*
Setzer, Pearl *AmWomPl*
Setzer, Rick A. 1946- *WhoSSW 93*
Setzer, Robert D. 1947- *St&PR 93*
Setzer, Robert L. 1943- *St&PR 93*
Setzler, Frank M. 1902-1975 *IntDcAn*
Setzler, William Edward 1926- *WhoAm 92*
Seul, Heinrich Lorenz 1960- *WhoWor 93*
Seume, Johann Gottfried 1763-1810 *BioIn 17*
Seung, Thomas Kaehao 1930- *WhoAm 92, WhoWrEP 92*
Seurat, Georges Pierre 1859-1891 *BioIn 17*
Seurkamp, F.J. 1950- *St&PR 93*
Seuss, Dr. *BioIn 17*
Seuss, Dr. 1904-1991 *AnObit 1991*
Seuster, Horst 1930- *WhoScE 91-3*
Seutin, E. *WhoScE 91-2*
Sevald, Robert J. 1929- *St&PR 93*
Sevall, Joseph Roy, III 1941- *St&PR 93*
Sevan, Benon 1937- *WhoUN 92*
Sevandal, Marciana Asis Sagun 1912- *WhoWrEP 92*
Sevareid, Arnold Eric 1912- *JrnUS, WhoAm 92*
Sevareid, Eric 1912-1992 *NewYTBS 92 [port], News 93-1*
Sevareid, Eric (Arnold) 1912-1992 *CurBio 92N*
Sevcenko, Ihor 1922- *WhoAm 92*
Sevcik, Edward J. 1936- *St&PR 93*
Sevcik, Otakar 1852-1934 *Baker 92*
Sevekow, Fredrick M., Jr. *Law&B 92*
Sevel, Torben *WhoScE 91-2*
Sevem, James C. *Law&B 92*
Seven, John Anthony 1926- *St&PR 93*
Sevenich, David Mark 1961- *WhoSSW 93*
Severac, Deodat de 1872-1921 *Baker 92, OxDcOp*
Severance, Carol 1944- *ScF&FL 92*
Severance, Malcolm Floyd 1924- *St&PR 93*
Severe, John Thomas 1951- *WhoSSW 93, WhoWor 93*
Severe, Paula Rue 1935- *WhoAmW 93*
Severianos dc. 430 *OxDcByz*
Severin, Claude-A. 1942- *WhoScE 91-2*
Severin, Dieter 1940- *WhoScE 91-3*
Severin, Jean 1911-1987 *ScF&FL 92*
Severin, Steven c. 1959- *See* Siouxsie and the Banshees *ConMus 8*
Severine 1855-1929 *BioIn 17*
Severinghaus, Charles William 1916- *WhoE 93*
Severinghaus, Nelson 1929- *St&PR 93*
Severinghaus, Nelson, Jr. 1929- *WhoSSW 93*
Severini, Carl T. *Law&B 92*
Severini, Gino 1883-1966 *BioIn 17*
Severini, Joseph John 1931- *St&PR 93*
Severino, Alexandrino Eusebio 1931- *WhoAm 92*
Severino, Paul J. *St&PR 93*
Severinsen, Doc *BioIn 17*
Severinsen, "Doc" 1927- *Baker 92, WhoAm 92*
Severinus d482 *OxDcByz*
Severn, Edmund 1862-1942 *Baker 92*
Severn, Margaret *AmWomPl*
Severn, Roy Thomas *WhoScE 91-1*
Severne, G. 1931- *WhoScE 91-2*
Severns, Penny L. 1952- *WhoAmW 93*
Severo, Armanda *WhoScE 91-3*
Severo, Richard 1932- *WhoAm 92*
Severos c. 465-538 *OxDcByz*
Severs, Deborah Reed *Law&B 92*
Severs, Drew H. *Law&B 92*
Severs, Walter Bruce 1938- *WhoAm 92*
Severs, William Floyd 1932- *WhoE 93*
Severseike, Gary L. 1940- *St&PR 93*
Severson, Herbert Henry 1944- *WhoAm 92*
Severson, James Martin 1934- *St&PR 93*
Severson, Jerry W. 1942- *St&PR 93*
Severson, John Robert 1955- *St&PR 93*
Severson, Mark Anthony 1954- *St&PR 93*
Severson, Richard Henry 1932- *St&PR 93*
Severson, Roger A. 1932- *St&PR 93*
Severson, Roger Allan 1932- *WhoAm 92*
Severus Pius Pertinax, Lucius Septimius 146-211 *HarEnMi*
Severy, Janaki Gayle 1948- *WhoEmL 93*
Severy, Lawrence James 1943- *WhoAm 92, WhoSSW 93*
Severy, Richard 1944- *ChlFicS*
Sevey, John C. 1913- *St&PR 93*
Sevier, Ernest Youle 1932- *WhoAm 92*
Sevier, Francis Aloysius Charles 1924- *WhoSSW 93*
Sevier, Landers 1945- *St&PR 93*
Sevier, Vernon A. *Law&B 92*
Sevigne, marquise de 1626-1696 *BioIn 17*
Sevigny, Joseph A. 1927- *St&PR 93*
Sevigny, Joseph Pierre Albert 1917- *BioIn 17*
Sevigny, Therese Paquet 1934- *WhoUN 92*
Sevik, Maurice 1923- *WhoAm 92*
Sevilla, Mario Alfonso 1931- *WhoWor 93*
Sevilla, Roque Simon 1947- *WhoWor 93*
Sevilla, Stanley 1920- *WhoAm 92*
Sevilla-Gardinier, Josefina Zialcita 1931- *WhoAmW 93*
Seville, Jack James, Jr. 1938- *WhoWrEP 92*
Sevimsoy, Mahmut 1936- *WhoScE 91-4*
Sevin, Dieter Hermann 1938- *WhoSSW 93*
Sevin, Eugene 1928- *WhoAm 92*
Sevin, Irik Peter 1947- *St&PR 93*
Sevitzky, Fabien 1891-1967 *Baker 92*
Sevold, Gordon James 1926- *WhoAm 92*
Sevon, William David, III 1933- *WhoE 93*
Sevringhaus, Grace *AmWomPl*
Sevryuk, Mikhail Borisovich 1962- *WhoWor 93*
Sevy, Roger Warren 1923- *WhoAm 92*
Sewall, Edward R. 1927- *St&PR 93*
Sewall, Marcia *ChlBIID [port]*
Sewall, Marcia 1935- *MajAI [port], SmATA 69 [port]*
Sewall, Richard Benson 1908- *BioIn 17, WhoWrEP 92*
Sewall, Stanley Joseph 1944- *St&PR 93*
Sewall, Tingey H. 1940- *St&PR 93*
Sewall, Tingey Haig 1940- *WhoAm 92*
Sewall, Warren 1941- *WhoE 93*
Sewall, William Dana 1948- *St&PR 93*
Seward, Billie d1982 *SweetSg C [port]*
Seward, Doyle Adam, Jr. 1956- *WhoWrEP 92*
Seward, George Chester 1910- *WhoAm 92*
Seward, Gordon B. *Law&B 92*
Seward, John E., Jr. 1943- *WhoIns 93*
Seward, John E., Jr. 1948- *St&PR 93*
Seward, Perry *Law&B 92*
Seward, R.J. *Law&B 92*
Seward, Rudy Ray 1944- *WhoSSW 93*
Seward, Troilen Gainey 1941- *WhoSSW 93*
Seward, William H. 1801-1872 *PolPar*
Seward, William Henry 1801-1872 *BioIn 17*
Seward, William Ward, Jr. 1913- *WhoAm 92, WhoWrEP 92*
Sewards, Geoffrey Brian *WhoScE 91-1*
Sewell, Adrian Clive 1950- *WhoWor 93*
Sewell, Anna 1820-1878 *MajAI [port]*
Sewell, Ben Gardner 1911- *WhoAm 92*
Sewell, Beverly Jean 1942- *WhoAmW 93*
Sewell, Brocard 1912- *ScF&FL 92*
Sewell, Cecil W. 1946- *St&PR 93*
Sewell, Charles Haslett 1928- *WhoAm 92, WhoSSW 93*
Sewell, Darrel Leslie 1939- *WhoAm 92*
Sewell, Edna Belle Scott 1881-1967 *AmWomPl*
Sewell, Edward M. 1923-1990 *BioIn 17*
Sewell, Elizabeth 1919- *WhoWrEP 92*
Sewell, Geoffrey Leon *WhoScE 91-1*
Sewell, Helen (Moore) 1896-1957 *ConAu 137, MajAI [port]*
Sewell, Ike d1990 *BioIn 17*
Sewell, Isabel Fowler 1920- *St&PR 93*
Sewell, James Leslie 1903- *WhoAm 92*
Sewell, Joan Marshall 1936- *WhoWrEP 92*
Sewell, Joe 1898-1990 *BioIn 17*
Sewell, John Isaac *WhoScE 91-1*
Sewell, John Williamson 1935- *WhoAm 92*
Sewell, Michael John *WhoScE 91-1*
Sewell, Milton Ray 1942- *WhoSSW 93*
Sewell, Phyllis Shapiro 1930- *WhoAm 92*
Sewell, Richard Herbert 1931- *WhoAm 92*
Sewell, S. Scott 1953- *WhoAm 92*
Sewell, Stephen A. *Law&B 92*
Sewell, Truett Banks 1907-1989 *BiDAMSp 1989*
Sewell, V. Lawrence *Law&B 92*
Sewell, William Gerald 1941- *St&PR 93*
Sewell, William Hamilton 1909- *WhoAm 92*
Sewell, Winifred 1917- *WhoAm 92*
Sewer-Lewandowska, Barbara 1930- *WhoScE 91-4*
Seweryn, Nancy Market *Law&B 92*
Seweryn, Tadeusz 1894-1975 *IntDcAn*
Sewpershad, Lionel 1940- *WhoSSW 93, WhoWor 93*
Sexauer, Robert S. 1923- *St&PR 93*
Sexsmith, David Randal 1933- *St&PR 93*
Sexsmith, Jillian Diane *Law&B 92*
Sexson, Ward Earl 1933- *St&PR 93*
Sexton, Amy Manerbino 1957- *WhoAmW 93*
Sexton, Anne *BioIn 17*
Sexton, Anne 1928-1974 *WorLitC [port]*
Sexton, Brendan 1911-1988 *BioIn 17*
Sexton, Carol Burke 1939- *WhoAmW 93*
Sexton, David F. 1943- *St&PR 93*
Sexton, David Farrington 1943- *WhoAm 92*
Sexton, David John 1939- *WhoAm 92*
Sexton, Dixie Irene 1959- *WhoAmW 93*
Sexton, Donald Lee 1932- *WhoAm 92*
Sexton, Edward William, Jr. 1931- *St&PR 93*
Sexton, Ella May *AmWomPl*
Sexton, Ethelyn *AmWomPl*
Sexton, J.F. 1918- *St&PR 93*
Sexton, Janet Sieders 1949- *WhoAmW 93*
Sexton, Jeanne Lee *Law&B 92*
Sexton, Jo Ann 1933- *WhoAmW 93*
Sexton, John *MiSFD 9*
Sexton, John Edward 1942- *WhoAm 92*
Sexton, John F. 1932- *St&PR 93*
Sexton, John Q. 1937- *St&PR 93*
Sexton, John W., Jr. 1926- *St&PR 93*
Sexton, Karla K. *Law&B 92*
Sexton, Ken 1949- *WhoAm 92*
Sexton, Lance Albert 1960- *WhoSSW 93*
Sexton, Linda Gray 1953- *BioIn 17*
Sexton, Mark 1930- *WhoE 93*
Sexton, Mark S. 1956- *St&PR 93*
Sexton, Mary Catherine *Law&B 92*
Sexton, Miriam Elaine 1949- *WhoE 93*
Sexton, Owen James 1926- *WhoAm 92*
Sexton, Peter F. *Law&B 92*
Sexton, Richard 1929- *WhoAm 92*
Sexton, Thomas 1944- *St&PR 93*
Sexton, Virginia Staudt 1916- *BioIn 17*
Sexton, William Cottrell 1928- *WhoAm 92*
Sextus Julius Africanus *OxDcByz*
Seya, Hideyuki 1919- *WhoAsAP 91*
Seybert, Janet Rose 1944- *WhoWor 93*
Seybold, Artur 1868-1948 *Baker 92*
Seybold, H. Robert 1949- *St&PR 93*
Seybold, Karen Colapietro 1964- *WhoE 93*

Seydel, Rudiger Ulrich 1947- WhoWor 93
Seydel, Scott O'Sullivan 1940- WhoSSW 93
Seydelmann, Franz 1748-1806 Baker 92, OxDcOp
Seyden-Penne, Jacqueline 1930- WhoScE 91-2
Seyed-Yagoobi, Jamal 1956- WhoSSW 93
Seyfarth, Theodore Harold Law&B 92
Seyfert, Judith Lynn 1952- WhoAmW 93
Seyferth, Dietmar 1929- WhoAm 92
Seyffardt, Ernst (Hermann) 1859-1942 Baker 92
Seyffarth, Linda Jean Wilcox 1948- WhoAmW 93
Seyfried, Ignaz 1776-1841 OxDcOp
Seyfried, Ignaz (Xaver), Ritter von 1776-1841 Baker 92
Seyfried, Peter 1929- WhoScE 91-3
Seyhoun, Houshang 1920- WhoWor 93
Seykora, David G. Law&B 92
Seylaz, Jacques WhoScE 91-2
Seyler, Abel 1730-1800 OxDcOp
Seyler, Athene 1889-1990 BioIn 17
Seymore, William A. 1943- St&PR 93
Seymour, Alta Halverson 1893- AmWomPl
Seymour, Arabella Stuart 1575-1615 BioIn 17
Seymour, Arthur Hallock 1928- WhoAm 92
Seymour, Arthur T., Mrs. AmWomPl
Seymour, Brian Richard 1944- WhoAm 92
Seymour, Carol Anne WhoScE 91-1
Seymour, Charles 1944- WhoE 93
Seymour, Charles Burch 1932- St&PR 93
Seymour, Charles F. 1921- St&PR 93
Seymour, Christopher H. Law&B 92
Seymour, Dale Joseph 1947- WhoEmL 93
Seymour, Daniel J. Law&B 92
Seymour, Deborah Carol 1960- WhoAmW 93
Seymour, Edward Hobart 1840-1929 HarEnMi
Seymour, Elizabeth Halsey 1949- WhoSSW 93
Seymour, Ella AmWomPl
Seymour, Emma Carter AmWomPl
Seymour, Everett Hedden, Jr. 1958- WhoE 93, WhoWor 93
Seymour, Gerald 1933- St&PR 93, WhoE 93
Seymour, Harold 1910- ConAu 138
Seymour, Harold 1910-1992 NewYTBS 92
Seymour, Horatio 1810-1886 PolPar
Seymour, Jane BioIn 17
Seymour, Jane 1951- HolBB [port], WhoAm 92, WhoAmW 93
Seymour, Janet Martha 1957- WhoAmW 93
Seymour, Jeffrey Alan 1950- WhoEmL 93
Seymour, John BioIn 17
Seymour, John 1937- CngDr 91, WhoAm 92
Seymour, John Herbert 1945- WhoAm 92
Seymour, John Laurence 1893-1986 Baker 92
Seymour, Jon WhoAm 92
Seymour, Lee ScF&FL 92
Seymour, Lynn 1939- WhoWor 93
Seymour, Mary AmWomPl
Seymour, Mary Frances 1948- WhoEmL 93
Seymour, Mary Powell 1922- WhoAmW 93, WhoSSW 93
Seymour, Mayce F. AmWomPl
Seymour, McNeil Vernam 1934- WhoAm 92
Seymour, Miranda 1948- ScF&FL 92
Seymour, Percy Albertus Henry WhoScE 91-1
Seymour, Philip Herschel Kean WhoScE 91-1
Seymour, Raymond Benedict 1912-1991 WhoAm 92
Seymour, Richard BioIn 17
Seymour, Richard D. BioIn 17
Seymour, Richard Kellogg 1930- WhoAm 92
Seymour, Robert J. Law&B 92
Seymour, Robert J. 1933- St&PR 93
Seymour, Sandford Edwin 1950- WhoSSW 93
Seymour, Stephanie Kulp 1940- WhoAm 92, WhoAmW 93, WhoSSW 93
Seymour, Sylvia Joan 1937- WhoAmW 93
Seymour, Thaddeus 1928- WhoAm 92
Seymour, Wanda Sue 1938- WhoAmW 93
Seymour, Whitney North, Jr. 1923- WhoAm 92
Seymour, William J. BioIn 17
Seypidin Aze, Gen. 1916- WhoAsAP 91
Seyrig, Delphine 1932-1990 BioIn 17, IntDcF 2-3 [port]
Seyss-Inquart, Arthur 1892-1946 DcTwHis
Seznec, Alain 1930- WhoAm 92
Sfakiotakis, Evangelos 1936- WhoScE 91-3
Sfar, Rachid 1933- WhoWor 93
Sferrazza, Peter Joseph 1945- WhoAm 92
Sficas, Achilles George 1926- WhoScE 91-3
Sfikakis, Paul 1926- WhoWor 93
Sfikas, Peter Michael 1937- WhoAm 92
Sforza, Bona 1494-1557 PolBiDi
Sforza, Francesco 1401-1466 HarEnMi
Sforza, Pasquale Michael 1941- WhoE 93
Sforzini, Mario WhoScE 91-3
Sforzo, Robert Joseph 1947- WhoAm 92
Sgambati, Giovanni 1841-1914 Baker 92
Sganga, John B. 1931- St&PR 93, WhoAm 92, WhoWor 93
Sgarlata, Anthony Law&B 92
Sgarlata, F. 1926- WhoScE 91-3
Sgarro, Nicholas MiSFD 9
Sgarzi, Judith Marie 1945- WhoAmW 93
Sgouropoulos OxDcByz
Sgouros, Dimitris 1969- Baker 92
Sgouros, Leo d1207? OxDcByz
Sgrizzi, Luciano 1910- Baker 92
Sgro, Beverly Huston 1941- WhoAmW 93
Sgro, Joseph Anthony 1937- WhoAm 92
Sgroi, Donald Angelo 1943- WhoE 93
Sgroi, Joseph Nicholas 1937- St&PR 93
Sgroi, Rosemary Jane 1940- WhoE 93
Sgrosso, Vincent L. Law&B 92
Sguotas, Alexander T. 1942- WhoAm 92
Sgut, Martin Eduardo 1951- WhoWor 93
Sha, Chin-Kang 1949- WhoWor 93
Shaaban, Bouthaina 1953- ConAu 137
Shaar, H. Erik WhoAm 92
Shaar, Michael Vincent 1933- St&PR 93
Shaara, Michael 1929-1988 ScF&FL 92
Shabanov, Dimitar Stoyanov 1920- WhoScE 91-4
Shabat, Richard Gary 1940- St&PR 93
Shabaz, John C. 1931- WhoAm 92
Shabbethai Tzevi 1626-1676 BioIn 17
Shabbir, Mahnaz Mehdi 1959- WhoAmW 93
Shabino, Allen N. Law&B 92
Shabtai, Yaakov BioIn 17
Shachoy, Norman James 1937- WhoAm 92
Shack, Donald D. 1928- St&PR 93
Shack, Peter Donald 1953- WhoAsAP 91
Shack, William Alfred 1923- WhoAm 92
Shackelford, Alphonso Leon 1920- WhoSSW 93, WhoWrEP 92
Shackelford, Barton Warren 1920- St&PR 93, WhoAm 92
Shackelford, Charles Lewis 1918- WhoE 93
Shackelford, Donald Bruce 1932- WhoAm 92
Shackelford, Frederic Owen 1949- St&PR 93
Shackelford, George Green 1920- WhoAm 92, WhoSSW 93
Shackelford, Kim R. 1959- St&PR 93
Shackelford, Lottie H. 1941- AfrAmBi
Shackelford, Lottie Holt 1941- WhoAm 92, WhoAmW 93
Shackelford, Lynne Piper 1953- WhoSSW 93
Shackelford, Ted 1946- WhoAm 92
Shackelford, William Edwin 1927- St&PR 93
Shackelton, Norman John, Jr. 1939- WhoE 93
Shackett, Ricky Warren 1946- WhoWor 93
Shackett, Thomas Charles 1938- St&PR 93
Shackford, Paul R. 1950- St&PR 93
Shackle, G.L.S. 1903- BioIn 17
Shackle, G(eorge) L(ennox) S(harman) 1903-1992 ConAu 137
Shackle, George Lennox Sharman 1903- BioIn 17
Shackleford, Covington Law&B 92
Shackleford, Covington 1924- St&PR 93, WhoAm 92
Shackleford, Jack D. 1938- ScF&FL 92
Shackleford, Ruby P. 1913- WhoWrEP 92
Shackleton, Ernest 1874-1922 Expl 93 [port]
Shackleton, Ernest Henry 1874-1922 BioIn 17
Shackleton, Jenny BioIn 17
Shackleton, Michael MiSFD 9
Shackleton-Hill, Angela ScF&FL 92
Shacklett, Lyle Kent 1938- WhoSSW 93
Shacklett, Mary Eberle 1952- WhoAmW 93
Shacklett, Mildred D. AmWomPl
Shacochis, Bob 1951- ScF&FL 92
Shacochis, Robert G. ScF&FL 92
Shacter, Joseph Bernard Law&B 92
Shad, John 1923- St&PR 93, WhoAm 92
Shadbolt, Douglas 1925- WhoAm 92
Shadbolt, Jack BioIn 17
Shadburne, Susan MiSFD 9
Shadd, Mary Ann 1823-1893 BioIn 17
Shaddix, James W. Law&B 92
Shaddix, James W. 1946- St&PR 93
Shaddix, W.J. 1928- St&PR 93
Shaddock, David Robert 1948- WhoWrEP 92
Shaddock, Pamela Kerrigan 1948- WhoAmW 93
Shade, Michael W. 1954- St&PR 93
Shade, Sarah AmWomPl
Shadegg, Stephen 1909-1990 BioIn 17
Shadegg, Stephen C. 1909-1990 ScF&FL 92
Shader, Melvin Aaron 1925- St&PR 93
Shader, Richard Irwin 1935- WhoAm 92
Shaderowfsky, Eva Maria 1938- WhoAmW 93
Shadi, Ali Elsayed 1940- WhoUN 92
Shadid, George D. 1954- St&PR 93
Shadid, Michael A. 1882- BioIn 17
Shadley, Lafayette d1893 BioIn 17
Shadmi, Rena Margoshes 1926- WhoAmW 93
Shadoan, George Woodson 1933- WhoAm 92
Shadoian, Holly Lynn 1952- WhoE 93
Shadovitz, David Jay 1954- WhoWrEP 92
Shadur, Milton I. 1924- WhoAm 92
Shadwell, Delvenia Gail 1938- WhoWrEP 92
Shadwell, Thomas ScF&FL 92
Shadwick, Gerald 1931- St&PR 93
Shadyac, Tom MiSFD 9
Shaeffer, Charles Wayne 1910- WhoAm 92
Shaer, Ellen Ruth 1961- WhoAmW 93
Shaer, Milton 1923- St&PR 93
Shaer, Patricia Ann Blacha 1941- WhoAmW 93
Shaevsky, Mark 1935- St&PR 93, WhoAm 92, WhoWor 93
Shafarevich, I.R. 1923- BioIn 17
Shafarevich, Igor' Rostislavovich 1923- BioIn 17
Shafer, Alma Mater Wilson AmWomPl
Shafer, B. Lyle 1924- St&PR 93
Shafer, Byron Alvin 1938- St&PR 93
Shafer, David J. 1965- WhoSSW 93
Shafer, Everett Earl 1925- WhoAm 92
Shafer, Ingrid Hedwig 1939- WhoSSW 93
Shafer, Jack L. 1945- St&PR 93
Shafer, Jonathan Stickley 1936- WhoE 93
Shafer, Joseph Ernest 1903- WhoAm 92
Shafer, Michael Joe 1948- St&PR 93
Shafer, Patricia Moore 1945- WhoAmW 93
Shafer, Randall Jay 1965- St&PR 93
Shafer, Raymond Philip 1917- BioIn 17, WhoAm 92
Shafer, Robert 1920- ScF&FL 92
Shafer, Robert J. Law&B 92
Shafer, Robert L. 1932- St&PR 93
Shafer, Robert Tinsley, Jr. 1929- WhoWor 93
Shafer, Ronald G. BioIn 17
Shafer, Ryan BioIn 17
Shafer, Susan Wright 1941- WhoAmW 93
Shaff, Alan Martin 1958- WhoSSW 93
Shaff, Gerald H. 1933- St&PR 93
Shaff, Robert Myrven 1929- St&PR 93
Shaffer, Alan Lee 1950- WhoAm 92
Shaffer, Albert Jay 1953- St&PR 93
Shaffer, Anita Mohrland 1939- WhoSSW 93
Shaffer, Anthony 1926- ScF&FL 92
Shaffer, Bernard William 1924- WhoAm 92
Shaffer, Boyd Jensen 1925- WhoWor 93
Shaffer, Carolyn G. 1943- St&PR 93
Shaffer, Clyde H. d1990 BioIn 17
Shaffer, David 1936- WhoAm 92, WhoWor 93
Shaffer, David Clarence 1955- WhoE 93
Shaffer, David Ellsworth 1947- WhoSSW 93
Shaffer, David H. 1942- WhoAm 92, WhoWor 93
Shaffer, Dean W. 1926- St&PR 93
Shaffer, Donald Stephen 1929- WhoE 93
Shaffer, Dorothy Tien 1956- WhoAmW 93
Shaffer, Eric Paul 1955- WhoWor 93
Shaffer, Eugene Carl ScF&FL 92
Shaffer, Frances Annette 1946- WhoAmW 93
Shaffer, Fred W. Law&B 92
Shaffer, Fred Whittaker 1932- St&PR 93
Shaffer, Gail S. 1948- WhoAm 92, WhoAmW 93, WhoE 93
Shaffer, Harry G., Jr. 1926- St&PR 93
Shaffer, Henry R. Law&B 92
Shaffer, J.M. 1901- St&PR 93
Shaffer, J. Scott Law&B 92
Shaffer, James 1945- St&PR 93
Shaffer, James Burgess 1945- WhoAm 92
Shaffer, Jane Gloria 1944- WhoAmW 93
Shaffer, Janice Dawn 1946- St&PR 93
Shaffer, Jerome Arthur 1929- WhoAm 92
Shaffer, Jill 1958- WhoAmW 93
Shaffer, John Christopher 1937- St&PR 93
Shaffer, John Robert 1928- WhoWor 93
Shaffer, Karl Upton 1948- WhoSSW 93
Shaffer, Lewis A. Law&B 92
Shaffer, Margaret Minor 1940- WhoAmW 93
Shaffer, Mark S. Law&B 92
Shaffer, Michael L. 1945- St&PR 93, WhoAm 92
Shaffer, Nancy L. 1938- WhoE 93
Shaffer, Nancy Ruth 1954- WhoAmW 93
Shaffer, Nelson Jay 1951- WhoE 93
Shaffer, Paul 1949- WhoAm 92
Shaffer, Paul E. 1926- St&PR 93, WhoAm 92
Shaffer, Peter BioIn 17
Shaffer, Peter Levin 1926- WhoAm 92, WhoWor 93
Shaffer, Raymond F. 1912-1991 BioIn 17
Shaffer, Richard James 1931- WhoAm 92
Shaffer, Richard Paul 1949- WhoEmL 93, WhoSSW 93
Shaffer, Robert D. 1952- St&PR 93
Shaffer, Robert Howard 1915- WhoSSW 93
Shaffer, Roberta Ivy 1953- WhoAmW 93
Shaffer, Russell K. 1933- WhoAm 92
Shaffer, Samuel Holmes 1946- St&PR 93
Shaffer, Sherrill Lynn 1952- WhoE 93
Shaffer, Stephen M. 1954- WhoWor 93
Shaffer, Thomas H. 1948- St&PR 93
Shaffer, Thomas Lindsay 1934- WhoAm 92
Shaffet, Michael 1935- St&PR 93
Shaffner, Randolph Preston 1940- WhoSSW 93
Shaffner, Robert Christopher 1944- St&PR 93
Shafia, Georgia 1936- St&PR 93
Shafiezadeh, Sylvia Macia 1964- WhoAmW 93
Shafir, Michail Kleyner 1943- WhoE 93
Shafir, Pavel Evseevitch 1964- WhoWor 93
Shafran, Daniel (Borisovich) 1923- Baker 92
Shafran, Grace Brenda Law&B 92
Shafran, Hank 1945- WhoAm 92
Shafritz, David Andrew 1940- WhoAm 92
Shafroth, Will 1894-1991 BioIn 17
Shaftel, Oscar Hamilton 1912- WhoE 93
Shafter, Robert L. Law&B 92
Shafter, William Rufus 1835-1906 HarEnMi
Shaftesbury, Earl of 1671-1713 BioIn 17
Shaftman, Fredrick Krisch 1948- WhoSSW 93
Shafto, Robert Austin 1935- St&PR 93, WhoAm 92, WhoE 93
Shagam, Marvin Huckel-Berri WhoWor 93
Shagan, Steve 1927- ScF&FL 92, WhoAm 92
Shagari, Shehu (Alhaji) 1925- WhoAfr
Shagass, Charles 1920- WhoAm 92
Shager, Merrie Carolyn 1946- WhoAmW 93
Shagin, Tracy Dean 1952- WhoE 93
Shah, Amritlal Jivraj 1941- WhoWor 93
Shah, Anwar Muhammad Chaudry 1948- WhoE 93
Shah, Arvind V. WhoScE 91-4
Shah, Bipin A. 1943- St&PR 93
Shah, Bipin Chandra 1938- WhoAm 92
Shah, Caroline Teresa 1961- St&PR 93
Shah, Daksha Rajnikant 1945- WhoE 93
Shah, Haresh C. 1937- WhoAm 92
Shah, Haşmukh BioIn 17
Shah, Hemendra K. 1945- St&PR 93
Shah, Khalil Urrahman 1944- WhoWor 93
Shah, Krishna 1938- MiSFD 9
Shah, Kumar 1949- St&PR 93
Shah, Mubarik Ahmad 1949- WhoE 93
Shah, Naren Natwarlal 1934- WhoE 93
Shah, Natverlal Jagjivandas 1926- WhoWor 93
Shah, Pramod J. 1956- St&PR 93
Shah, Purushottam Mulji 1934- WhoUN 92
Shah, Raffique DcCPCAm
Shah, Rajesh K. 1951- St&PR 93
Shah, Rajnikant S. 1946- WhoE 93
Shah, Ramesh Keshavlal 1941- WhoAm 92
Shah, Ramesh Ranchhoddas 1931- WhoWor 93
Shah, Reza Sayed 1953- St&PR 93
Shah, Satish C. 1941- St&PR 93
Shah, Shirish Kalyanbhai 1942- WhoE 93
Shah, Sudhir Vithalbhai 1947- WhoAm 92, WhoSSW 93
Shah, Surendra P. 1937- St&PR 93
Shah, Surendra Poonamchand 1936- WhoAm 92
Shah, Swarupchand Mohanlal 1905- WhoSSW 93

Shah, Vikram Jayvaden 1938- *WhoUN 92*
Shahan, Norman Dean 1934- *WhoAm 92*
Shahan, Sherry Jean 1949- *WhoAmW 93*
Shahan, William R. 1939- *St&PR 93*
Shahani, Comila 1961- *WhoE 93*
Shahani, Leticia Ramos 1929- *WhoAsAP 91*
Shahar, Eluki bes *ScF&FL 92*
Shahbakian, Michael B. 1947- *St&PR 93*
Shaheed, Zafar Ahmad 1949- *WhoUN 92*
Shaheen, Jack G. 1935- *ScF&FL 92*
Shaheen, Jeanne 1947- *WhoAmW 93*
Shaheen, Michael Edmund, Jr. 1940- *WhoAm 92*
Shaheen, Shaheen Azeez 1928- *WhoAm 92, WhoWor 93*
Shaheen, Shouky Azeez 1929- *WhoSSW 93*
Shahen, Timothy 1943- *St&PR 93*
Shahidi, S.A. Salam d1992 *NewYTBS 92*
Shahin d625? *OxDcByz*
Shahin, Majdi Musa 1936- *WhoWor 93*
Shahin, Mamoun Shahin Amin 1966- *WhoWor 93*
Shah-Jahan, M. M. 1943- *WhoE 93*
Shahmanesh, Jane *Law&B 92*
Shahn, Ben 1898-1969 *BioIn 17, ModArCr 3 [port]*
Shahnavaz, Houshang 1936- *WhoScE 91-4, WhoWor 93*
Shahon, Laurie Meryl 1952- *WhoE 93*
Shahon, Susan Valerie 1948- *WhoEmL 93*
Shahrbaraz d630 *OxDcByz*
Shahryar, Suheil 1955- *WhoWor 93*
Shahwan, Mashour Darwish 1951- *WhoWor 93*
Shaia, Jacquelyn S. *Law&B 92*
Shaievitz, Sidney 1935- *WhoE 93*
Shaifer, Norman 1931- *WhoAm 92*
Shaikh, Anwar M. 1945- *BioIn 17*
Shaikh, Naz Ahmed 1939- *WhoWor 93*
Shaikh, Zahir Ahmad 1945- *WhoE 93*
Shaikhzadeh, Ayaz Aman 1960- *WhoWor 93*
Shail, Linda Grace 1947- *WhoWrEP 92*
Shailer, John Lawrence *Law&B 92*
Shain, Harold 1953- *St&PR 93*
Shain, Irving 1926- *St&PR 93, WhoAm 92*
Shain, Jonathan David *Law&B 92*
Shain, Kenneth Stephen 1952- *WhoSSW 93*
Shain, Myron Raymond 1940- *St&PR 93*
Shain, Russell Earl 1944- *WhoAm 92*
Shain, Steven M. *St&PR 93*
Shainberg, Lawrence 1936- *ConAu 137*
Shaine, Frederick Mordecai 1916- *WhoE 93*
Shainis, Murray J. 1926- *WhoWrEP 92*
Shainman, Barry J. *Law&B 92*
Shainman, Irwin 1921- *WhoAm 92*
Shainman, Jack 1957- *WhoE 93*
Shair, David I. 1921- *St&PR 93*
Sha Jiansun 1934- *WhoAsAP 91*
Shaka c. 1787-1828 *HarEnMi*
Shake, Ann O'Malley 1947- *WhoAmW 93*
Shakely, John Bower 1940- *WhoAm 92*
Shaker, Abdullah Jassim al- d1989 *BioIn 17*
Shakeshaft, J.R. *WhoScE 91-1*
Shakespear, Olivia *BioIn 17*
Shakespeare, Easton Geoffrey 1946- *WhoE 93*
Shakespeare, Frank 1925- *WhoAm 92*
Shakespeare, Jennifer K. d1992 *NewYTBS 92*
Shakespeare, William 1564-1616 *BioIn 17, MagSWL [port], OxDcOp, WorLitC [port]*
Shakespeare, William 1849-1931 *Baker 92*
Shakhashiri, Bassam Z. *BioIn 17*
Shakhashiri, Bassam Zekin 1939- *WhoAm 92*
Shakhmatov, Dmitri Borisovich 1961- *WhoWor 93*
Shakhnazarov, Georgii Khosroevich *BioIn 17*
Shakhray, Sergey Mikhailovich 1951 *WhoWor 93*
Shakin, Elisabeth Jeanne *WhoAmW 93*
Shaklan, Allen Yale 1945- *WhoAm 92*
Shaklovitz, Robert D. *Law&B 92*
Shakno, Robert Julian 1937- *WhoAm 92*
Shakoor, Adam A. *AfrAmBi [port]*
Shakow, Alexander 1937- *WhoUN 92*
Shakunle, Lere Oyebisi 1954- *WhoWor 93*
Shakya, Jnan Kaji 1943- *WhoWor 93*
Shalabi, Mazen Ahmad 1946- *WhoWor 93*
Shalack, Joan Helen 1932- *WhoAmW 93*
Shalagan, W.S. *Law&B 92*
Shalala, Donna *BioIn 17*
Shalala, Donna 1941- *News 92 [port], -92-3 [port]*
Shalala, Donna E. 1941- *NewYTBS 92 [port]*
Shalala, Donna Edna 1941- *WhoAm 92, WhoAmW 93, WhoWor 93*
Shalam, John J. 1933- *St&PR 93*
Shalam, John Joseph 1933- *WhoAm 92*
Shalamanov, Neum *BioIn 17*
Shalamar *SoulM*
Shalaty, James J. *St&PR 93*
Shaldon, Stanley 1931- *WhoWor 93*
Shaler, Eleanor *AmWomPl*
Shales, Thomas William 1948- *WhoAm 92, WhoE 93*
Shalette, Michael Alan 1935- *St&PR 93, WhoAm 92*
Shalikashvili, John Malchase 1936- *WhoAm 92*
Shalit, Bernard Lawrence 1920- *WhoE 93, WhoWor 93*
Shalit, Gene *BioIn 17*
Shalit, Hanoch 1953- *WhoE 93*
Shalita, Alan Remi 1936- *WhoAm 92*
Shalk, Robert J. *Law&B 92*
Shalkop, Robert Leroy 1922- *WhoAm 92*
Shallcross, Doris Jane 1933- *WhoE 93*
Shallcross, Helen Clanahan 1913- *WhoWor 93*
Shallcross, Russell G. *St&PR 93*
Shalleck, Benjamin d1992 *NewYTBS 92 [port]*
Shalleck, Benjamin 1896-1992 *BioIn 17*
Shallenberger, John B. 1917- *St&PR 93*
Shallis, Michael *ScF&FL 92*
Shallish, Robert 1948- *St&PR 93*
Shallon, David 1950- *Baker 92*
Shally, Brian J. *Law&B 92*
Shalof, William *St&PR 93*
Shalom, Liliane Winn 1940- *WhoAmW 93*
Shalom, Mordechai Ish- 1902-1991 *BioIn 17*
Shalowitz, Erwin Emmanuel 1924- *WhoAm 92*
Shalvarjian, Haig J. *Law&B 92*
Shalyapin, Fyodor 1873-1938 *OxDcOp*
Sham, Lu Jeu 1938- *WhoAm 92*
Shamapande, Yobert Kananga 1944- *WhoUN 92*
Shamas, Barry Neil 1947- *St&PR 93*
Shamas, James E. 1934- *WhoAm 92*
Shamas, Jimmy Ellis, Jr. *Law&B 92*
Shamash, Jack 1924-1990 *BioIn 17*
Shambarger, James Allen 1950- *St&PR 93*
Shambaugh, George Elmer, III 1931- *WhoAm 92*
Shambaugh, Irvin Calvin, Jr. 1943- *WhoSSW 93, WhoWor 93*
Shambaugh, Mark P. 1954- *St&PR 93*
Shambaugh, Max Paul 1922- *St&PR 93*
Shamberger, James M. 1940- *WhoIns 93*
Shamberg-Weisberg, Barbara Ann 1953- *WhoE 93*
Shamblin, A. Kent 1935- *St&PR 93*
Shamblin, Arnold Kent 1935- *WhoAm 92*
Shamblin, P. Richard 1946- *St&PR 93*
Shamburek, Roland Howard 1928- *WhoAm 92*
Shamburger, Sally C. 1953- *WhoIns 93*
Shamekh, Saleh Abdulrahman 1956- *WhoWor 93*
Shames, Abraham 1920- *WhoSSW 93*
Shames, Ervin Richard 1940- *St&PR 93, WhoAm 92, WhoE 93*
Shames, George Herbert 1926- *WhoE 93*
Shames, Harold 1924- *St&PR 93*
Shames, Henry Joseph 1921- *WhoAm 92*
Shames, Irving Herman 1923- *WhoAm 92*
Shames, Jeffrey L. 1955- *St&PR 93*
Shames, Jordan Nelson 1949- *WhoE 93, WhoEmL 93*
Shames, Mitchell Harrison *Law&B 92*
Shames, Sidney J. 1917- *St&PR 93*
Shames, William H. d1991 *BioIn 17*
Shamess, Alfred E. *Law&B 92*
Shamgar, Meir 1925- *WhoWor 93*
Shamieh, Fredric A. 1933- *St&PR 93*
Shamilzadeh, David 1946- *St&PR 93*
Shamir, Yitzak *BioIn 17*
Shamir, Yitzhak 1915- *DcTwHis, WhoWor 93*
Shamitoff, Daryl Lawrence 1950- *St&PR 93*
Shamlaye, Conrad Francois 1952- *WhoWor 93*
Shamlin, Rose 1918- *WhoAmW 93*
Shamma, Ronald L. *St&PR 93*
Shammas, Anton *BioIn 17*
Shamo, Igor 1925-1982 *Baker 92*
Shamoo, Adil Elias 1941- *WhoAm 92*
Shamos, Morris H. 1917- *St&PR 93*
Shamos, Morris Herbert 1917- *WhoAm 92, WhoE 93*
Sham Pak, Patrick 1935- *WhoAsAP 91*
Shams, Hadi 1942- *WhoUN 92*
Shamsavari, Ali 1944- *WhoWor 93*
Shamsi, Irfan Haider 1939- *WhoWor 93*
Shamurin, Evgenii Ivanovich 1889-1962 *BioIn 17*
Shamuyarira, Nathan 1930- *WhoAfr*
Shamuyarira, Nathan Marwirakuwa 1930- *WhoWor 93*
Shamy, Robert George 1945- *WhoE 93*
Shan, Linhua d1991 *BioIn 17*
Shan, Robert Kuocheng 1927- *WhoSSW 93*
Shanaberger, Melody Ann 1956- *WhoAmW 93*
Shanahan, Brien W. *Law&B 92*
Shanahan, Daniel (A.) 1947- *ConAu 139*
Shanahan, Danny *BioIn 17*
Shanahan, Edmond M. 1926- *St&PR 93*
Shanahan, Edmond Michael 1926- *WhoAm 92*
Shanahan, Eileen 1924- *WhoAmW 93*
Shanahan, Eileen Frances 1949- *WhoAmW 93*
Shanahan, Elizabeth Anne 1950- *WhoAmW 93*
Shanahan, Eugene Miles 1946- *WhoAm 92*
Shanahan, Frances d1991 *BioIn 17*
Shanahan, James Anthony 1898- *WhoAm 92*
Shanahan, James P. *Law&B 92*
Shanahan, James P. 1933- *WhoIns 93*
Shanahan, James Patrick 1933- *St&PR 93*
Shanahan, Michael F. 1939- *St&PR 93*
Shanahan, Mike *WhoAm 92*
Shanahan, R. Michael 1939- *St&PR 93*
Shanahan, Robert B. 1928- *WhoAm 92*
Shanahan, Thomas J. 1932- *WhoAm 92*
Shanahan, Thomas Joseph *Law&B 92*
Shanahan, Thomas Joseph 1932- *St&PR 93*
Shanahan, William Oswald 1913-1990 *BioIn 17*
Shananin, Alexander Alexeevich 1955- *WhoWor 93*
Shanard, G.H. 1926- *St&PR 93*
Shanas, Ethel 1914- *BioIn 17, WhoAm 92, WhoAmW 93*
Shanbacker, Frank Morse, III 1946- *WhoE 93*
Shanbacker, Kiamil Edward 1952- *WhoE 93*
Shanbhag, Damodar Nagesh 1937- *WhoWor 93*
Shand, Donna Lynn 1953- *WhoAmW 93*
Shand, Douglas Grosh 1956- *St&PR 93*
Shand, Mark 1951- *BioIn 17*
Shandler, Alan Robert 1944- *St&PR 93*
Shandles, H. Martin *Law&B 92*
Shandles, Ira David 1949- *WhoSSW 93*
Shandling, Garry *NewYTBS 92 [port]*
Shands, Courtney, Jr. 1929- *WhoAm 92*
Shands, Henry Lee 1935- *WhoAm 92*
Shands, William Ridley, Jr. 1929- *WhoAm 92*
Shane, Alan R. *Law&B 92*
Shane, Bob 1934- *WhoAm 92*
See Also Kingston Trio, The *ConMus 9*
Shane, Charles N., Jr. *Law&B 92*
Shane, Charles N., Jr. 1936- *St&PR 93*
Shane, Donald Eugene 1935- *St&PR 93*
Shane, Eleanor 1932- *WhoAmW 93*
Shane, Harold David 1936- *WhoAm 92*
Shane, Harold Gray 1914- *BioIn 17*
Shane, J. Lawrence 1935- *St&PR 93*
Shane, Jeffrey N. 1941- *WhoAm 92*
Shane, Joel H. 1945- *St&PR 93*
Shane, John Marder 1942- *WhoSSW 93*
Shane, Joseph Lawrence 1935- *WhoAm 92*
Shane, Michael B. *Law&B 92*
Shane, Michael B. 1941- *St&PR 93*
Shane, Paul E. 1944- *St&PR 93*
Shane, Raymond Edward *Law&B 92*
Shane, Rita *WhoAm 92*
Shane, Robert Samuel 1910- *WhoE 93*
Shane, Ronald 1953- *WhoAm 92*
Shane, Sheldon Richard 1929- *WhoAm 92*
Shane, William Whitney 1928- *WhoScE 91-3, WhoWor 93*
Shanebrook, John Richard 1938- *WhoE 93*
Shanefield, Daniel Jay 1930- *WhoE 93*
Shaner, David *BioIn 17*
Shaner, Peyton Nash 1928- *St&PR 93*
Shaner, Richard Clark 1948- *WhoWrEP 92*
Shaner, Robert H., Jr. 1920- *St&PR 93*
Shanes, E. *St&PR 93*
Shanet, Howard 1918- *Baker 92*
Shaney, Kevin R. *Law&B 92*
Shanfari, Said Ahmad al 1939- *WhoWor 93*
Shange, Ntozake *BioIn 17*
Shange, Ntozake 1948- *Au&Arts 9 [port], ConLC 74 [port], DramC 3 [port], MagSAmL [port], WhoAm 92, WhoWrEP 92*
Shangraw, Clarence Frank 1935- *WhoAm 92*
Shanholtz, Judy Lee 1947- *WhoAmW 93*
Shanis, Joseph *Law&B 92*
Shanis, Joseph 1919- *St&PR 93*
Shanji, Li *ScF&FL 92*
Shank, Allison *Law&B 92*
Shank, Brenda M. 1939- *WhoAmW 93, WhoE 93*
Shank, Bryon E. 1928- *St&PR 93*
Shank, Bud *BioIn 17*
Shank, Clare Brown Williams 1909- *WhoAm 92, WhoSSW 93*
Shank, Cleo Bernard 1927- *St&PR 93*
Shank, Fred Ross 1940- *WhoAm 92*
Shank, Jeffrey J. *Law&B 92*
Shank, John L. *Law&B 92*
Shank, Maurice Edwin 1921- *WhoAm 92*
Shank, Peter Rabe 1946- *WhoE 93*
Shank, Robert Ely 1914- *WhoAm 92*
Shank, Russell 1925- *WhoAm 92*
Shank, Stephen George 1943- *St&PR 93*
Shank, Suzanne Adams 1946- *WhoWor 93*
Shank, William O. 1924- *WhoAm 92*
Shankanga, Anderson Bonham 1939- *WhoUN 92*
Shankar (Lakshminarayana) 1950- *Baker 92*
Shankar, R. Sam 1942- *St&PR 93*
Shankar, Ratnaswamy 1942- *WhoE 93*
Shankar, Ravi 1920- *Baker 92, ConMus 9 [port], WhoWor 93*
Shankaranand, B. 1923- *WhoAsAP 91*
Shanker, Albert *BioIn 17*
Shanker, Albert 1928- *WhoAm 92*
Shanker, Morris Gerald 1926- *WhoAm 92*
Shankin, Stephen 1943- *St&PR 93*
Shanklin, Christopher Bryan 1946- *WhoSSW 93*
Shanklin, Douglas Radford 1930- *WhoAm 92, WhoSSW 93, WhoWor 93*
Shanklin, Evelyn *BioIn 17*
Shanklin, Lina *MiSFD 9*
Shanklin, Richard *BioIn 17*
Shanklin, Richard Vair, III 1937- *WhoAm 92*
Shankman, Gary Charles 1950- *WhoE 93, WhoEmL 93, WhoWor 93*
Shankman, K. 1943- *St&PR 93*
Shankman, Robert 1943- *St&PR 93*
Shanks, Ann *MiSFD 9*
Shanks, Ann Zane *WhoAmW 93*
Shanks, Carroll Dean 1927- *St&PR 93*
Shanks, Colin *St&PR 93*
Shanks, David C. 1939- *St&PR 93*
Shanks, Donald Gordon 1933- *St&PR 93*
Shanks, Donald K. 1934- *St&PR 93*
Shanks, Edward 1892-1953 *ScF&FL 92*
Shanks, Eugene Baylis 1913- *WhoAm 92, WhoSSW 93, WhoWor 93*
Shanks, Hershel 1930- *WhoAm 92, WhoWrEP 92*
Shanks, I.A. *WhoScE 91-1*
Shanks, Ian Alexander 1948- *WhoScE 91-1*
Shanks, Judith Weil 1941- *WhoAmW 93, WhoE 93, WhoWor 93*
Shanks, Lawrence Edward 1946- *St&PR 93*
Shanks, Russell *Law&B 92*
Shanks, Tom *BioIn 17*
Shanley, Bernard M. d1992 *NewYTBS 92*
Shanley, Bernard Michael 1903-1992 *BioIn 17*
Shanley, Diarmuid B. 1942- *WhoScE 91-3*
Shanley, James 1940- *St&PR 93*
Shanley, John Patrick 1950- *ConLC 75 [port], MiSFD 9*
Shanley, Kevin 1942- *St&PR 93, WhoAm 92*
Shanley, Mary Kay 1943- *WhoAmW 93*
Shanley, P.G. 1945- *St&PR 93*
Shanley, Robert Michael 1942- *WhoSSW 93*
Shanley, W. Joseph *Law&B 92*
Shanley, William C., III 1925- *WhoAm 92*
Shanman, James Alan 1942- *WhoAm 92, WhoE 93, WhoWor 93*
Shanmugam, P. 1927- *WhoAsAP 91*
Shanmugam, Subbiah 1958- *WhoWor 93*
Shanmugan, K. Sam 1943- *WhoAm 92*
Shann, Frank Athol 1944- *WhoWor 93*
Shann, Mary Halligan 1945- *WhoE 93*
Shannahan, Franklin M. 1928- *St&PR 93*
Shannahan, John Henry Kelly 1913- *WhoAm 92*
Shanno, David Francis 1938- *WhoAm 92*
Shannon, Albert P. 1951- *St&PR 93*
Shannon, Barbara K. *Law&B 92*
Shannon, Bernard Joseph 1930- *WhoSSW 93*
Shannon, Cheryl 1945- *St&PR 93*
Shannon, Christina *WhoWrEP 92*
Shannon, Claude Elwood 1916- *BioIn 17, WhoAm 92*
Shannon, Clayton P. 1934- *St&PR 93*
Shannon, Daniel Gerard 1946- *St&PR 93*
Shannon, David H. 1937- *St&PR 93*
Shannon, David Thomas 1933- *WhoAm 92, WhoSSW 93*
Shannon, Del 1939-1990 *BioIn 17*
Shannon, Don Michael 1948- *WhoWrEP 92*
Shannon, Donald Hawkins 1923- *WhoAm 92, WhoWor 93*

Shannon, Doris 1924- *ScF&FL 92*
Shannon, Douglas 1942- *WhoIns 93*
Shannon, Edgar Finley, Jr. 1918- *WhoAm 92, WhoSSW 93*
Shannon, Fred *ScF&FL 92*
Shannon, G. Michael 1938- *St&PR 93*
Shannon, George Albert 1934- *WhoSSW 93*
Shannon, George Ward, Jr. 1954- *WhoSSW 93*
Shannon, Gerald 1935- *WhoUN 92*
Shannon, Gerald T. 1923- *St&PR 93*
Shannon, Harry Alexander, III 1957- *WhoWor 93*
Shannon, Iris Reed *WhoAm 92, WhoAmW 93*
Shannon, Jacqueline *BioIn 17*
Shannon, James A. 1904- *WhoAm 92*
Shannon, James Patrick 1921- *WhoAm 92*
Shannon, James William 1938- *St&PR 93*
Shannon, Jean 1966- *WhoAmW 93*
Shannon, Jeremiah Stephen *Law&B 92*
Shannon, John Raymond 1895-1986 *BioIn 17*
Shannon, John S. *Law&B 92*
Shannon, John Sanford 1931- *St&PR 93*
Shannon, John T. 1902-1990 *BioIn 17*
Shannon, John W. 1933- *AfrAmBi [port], WhoAm 92*
Shannon, Judith L. 1942- *St&PR 93*
Shannon, Kathleen Eshleman *Law&B 92*
Shannon, Larry Redding 1949- *WhoSSW 93*
Shannon, Len Broughton, Jr. 1936- *St&PR 93*
Shannon, Lyle William 1920- *WhoAm 92*
Shannon, Malcolm L., Jr. *Law&B 92*
Shannon, Marc *Law&B 92*
Shannon, Margaret Rita *WhoAm 92*
Shannon, Mattie Bayly 1885- *AmWomPl*
Shannon, Michael Edward 1936- *St&PR 93, WhoAm 92*
Shannon, Michael K. *Law&B 92*
Shannon, Michael L. *Law&B 92*
Shannon, Michael R. 1950- *WhoSSW 93*
Shannon, Pat A. *Law&B 92*
Shannon, R.W.E. *WhoScE 91-1*
Shannon, Rex Byron 1930- *St&PR 93*
Shannon, Robert *BioIn 17*
Shannon, Robert Allen, Jr. 1945- *St&PR 93*
Shannon, Robert E. *Law&B 92*
Shannon, Robert Fudge 1933- *WhoSSW 93*
Shannon, Robert Rennie 1932- *WhoAm 92*
Shannon, Stephen Quinby, Jr. *WhoAm 92*
Shannon, Terrence J. 1941- *St&PR 93*
Shannon, Thomas Alfred 1932- *WhoAm 92*
Shannon, William C. *Law&B 92*
Shannon, William John 1953- *WhoSSW 93*
Shannon, William Norman, III 1937- *WhoAm 92, WhoWor 93*
Shannon, Wilson 1802-1877 *BioIn 17*
Shannonhouse, Robin *BioIn 17*
Shanok, Larry F. 1947- *St&PR 93*
Shanor, Donald Read 1927- *WhoAm 92*
Shansby, John Gary 1937- *WhoAm 92*
Shanshal, Abdul Jabbar Khalil 1920- *WhoWor 93*
Shanshal, Mohammed Sidiq d1990 *BioIn 17*
Shanstrom, Jack D. 1932- *WhoAm 92*
Shanta Kumar 1934- *WhoAsAP 91*
Shante, Roxanne *BioIn 17*
Shanteau, Virginia Joye 1957- *WhoAmW 93*
Shantz, Carolyn Uhlinger 1935- *WhoAmW 93*
Shantz, Robert Clayton 1925- *BiDAMSp 1989*
Shao, Otis Hung-I 1923- *WhoAm 92*
Shapar, Howard K. 1923- *WhoScE 91-2*
Shapell, Nathan *BioIn 17*
Shapell, Nathan 1922- *St&PR 93, WhoAm 92*
Shaper, Andrew Gerald *WhoScE 91-1*
Shaper, Christopher Thorne 1955- *WhoE 93*
Shaper, Stephen J. 1936- *St&PR 93*
Shapere, Dudley 1928- *WhoAm 92*
Shapero, Harold (Samuel) 1920- *Baker 92*
Shapero, Norman 1948- *St&PR 93*
Shapero, Sanford Marvin 1929- *WhoAm 92*
Shapey, Ralph 1921- *Baker 92*
Shapi, Alex Kaunda 1932- *WhoAfr*
Shapira, Dahlia 1939- *WhoWor 93*
Shapira, Max L. 1944- *St&PR 93*
Shapira, Meir 1887-1934 *PolBiDi*
Shapiro, Alan *MiSFD 9*
Shapiro, Alan M. 1956- *St&PR 93*
Shapiro, Alexander M. d1992 *NewYTBS 92 [port]*
Shapiro, Alvin Philip 1920- *WhoAm 92*
Shapiro, Amy M. 1953- *St&PR 93*
Shapiro, Amy Rosemarie 1949- *WhoAmW 93*
Shapiro, Andra L. *Law&B 92*
Shapiro, Arthur Joseph 1952- *WhoE 93*
Shapiro, Ascher Herman 1916- *WhoAm 92, WhoE 93*
Shapiro, Avraham 1918- *WhoWor 93*
Shapiro, Babe 1937- *WhoAm 92*
Shapiro, Barry David 1954- *WhoSSW 93*
Shapiro, Bennett Michaels 1939- *WhoAm 92, WhoE 93*
Shapiro, Bernard d1991 *BioIn 17*
Shapiro, Bernard J. 1930- *St&PR 93*
Shapiro, Beth Janet 1946- *WhoAm 92, WhoAmW 93, WhoSSW 93*
Shapiro, Blanche *BioIn 17*
Shapiro, Burton Leonard 1934- *WhoAm 92*
Shapiro, Charlotte *Law&B 92*
Shapiro, Cheryl Beth *Law&B 92*
Shapiro, Clifford Jay *Law&B 92*
Shapiro, Constantine d1992 *BioIn 17, NewYTBS 92*
Shapiro, Cynthia Rose 1946- *WhoAmW 93*
Shapiro, Daniel J. *Law&B 92*
Shapiro, David 1916- *WhoAm 92*
Shapiro, David 1951- *St&PR 93*
Shapiro, David 1954- *WhoIns 93*
Shapiro, David J. *Law&B 92*
Shapiro, David Joel 1947- *WhoE 93*
Shapiro, David Louis 1932- *WhoAm 92*
Shapiro, Debbie Lynn *WhoAm 92, WhoAmW 93*
Shapiro, Dianne Williams 1944- *WhoAmW 93*
Shapiro, E. Donald 1931- *WhoAm 92*
Shapiro, Edward Robert 1941- *WhoAm 92*
Shapiro, Eileen C. 1949- *WhoWor 93*
Shapiro, Elaine 1925- *WhoE 93*
Shapiro, Eli 1916- *WhoAm 92, WhoE 93*
Shapiro, Ellen 1948- *BioIn 17*
Shapiro, Ellen Marie 1948- *WhoAmW 93*
Shapiro, Florence 1948- *WhoAm 92, WhoAmW 93*
Shapiro, Fred David 1926- *WhoAm 92*
Shapiro, Fred Louis 1934- *WhoAm 92*
Shapiro, Gary D. *Law&B 92*
Shapiro, Gary H. *Law&B 92*
Shapiro, Gary Michael 1941- *WhoAm 92*
Shapiro, George Howard 1936- *WhoAm 92*
Shapiro, George M. 1919- *WhoAm 92, WhoE 93, WhoWor 93*
Shapiro, Harold Benjamin 1937- *St&PR 93, WhoAm 92*
Shapiro, Harold D. 1930- *St&PR 93*
Shapiro, Harold David 1927- *WhoAm 92*
Shapiro, Harold M. 1927- *St&PR 93*
Shapiro, Harold Tafler 1935- *WhoAm 92, WhoE 93, WhoWor 93*
Shapiro, Harry Dean 1940- *WhoAm 92*
Shapiro, Harry Lionel 1902-1990 *BioIn 17, IntDcAn*
Shapiro, Harvey 1924- *BioIn 17, WhoAm 92, WhoE 93*
Shapiro, Harvey 1937- *WhoE 93*
Shapiro, Henry 1906-1991 *AnObit 1991, BioIn 17*
Shapiro, Howard *Law&B 92*
Shapiro, Howard Allan 1930- *WhoAm 92*
Shapiro, Howard Irwin 1932- *WhoE 93*
Shapiro, Howard Lee 1948- *St&PR 93*
Shapiro, Irving S. *BioIn 17*
Shapiro, Irving Saul 1916- *WhoAm 92*
Shapiro, Irwin Ira 1929- *WhoAm 92*
Shapiro, Isadore 1916- *WhoWor 93*
Shapiro, Ivan 1928- *WhoAm 92*
Shapiro, James Eliot 1957- *WhoE 93*
Shapiro, Jerald Steven 1943- *WhoWor 93*
Shapiro, Jerome Gerson 1924- *WhoAm 92*
Shapiro, Jerome Herbert 1924- *WhoAm 92*
Shapiro, Jerome Leonard 1925- *St&PR 93*
Shapiro, Joan Isabelle 1943- *WhoAmW 93, WhoWor 93*
Shapiro, Joan Poliner 1942- *WhoAmW 93*
Shapiro, Joe *WhoAm 92*
Shapiro, Joel *BioIn 17*
Shapiro, Joel Elias 1941- *WhoAm 92*
Shapiro, Joel H. 1939- *St&PR 93*
Shapiro, Jonathan 1949- *WhoE 93*
Shapiro, Joseph C. *Law&B 92*
Shapiro, Judith R. 1942- *WhoAm 92, WhoAmW 93*
Shapiro, Julian L. 1904- *BioIn 17*
Shapiro, Karl Jay 1913- *BioIn 17, WhoAm 92*
Shapiro, Kathryn O'Shields *Law&B 92*
Shapiro, Ken 1943- *MiSFD 9*
Shapiro, Kenneth Paul 1946- *WhoE 93*
Shapiro, Laurence David 1941- *WhoAm 92*
Shapiro, Lee Tobey 1943- *WhoAm 92*
Shapiro, Leonard 1928- *St&PR 93, WhoAm 92*
Shapiro, Leslie Alan 1945- *WhoE 93*
Shapiro, Lester 1912- *St&PR 93*
Shapiro, Lisa Susan 1963- *WhoAmW 93*
Shapiro, Louis 1905-1991 *BioIn 17*
Shapiro, Lucille 1940- *WhoAm 92*
Shapiro, Lynn Huberman 1942- *WhoE 93*
Shapiro, Marc J. 1947- *St&PR 93*
Shapiro, Marc Jed 1953- *WhoWor 93*
Shapiro, Marian Kaplun 1939- *WhoAmW 93, WhoE 93*
Shapiro, Marjorie Mackay 1929- *WhoAmW 93*
Shapiro, Mark 1955- *WhoE 93*
Shapiro, Mark Howard 1940- *WhoAm 92*
Shapiro, Mark L. 1944- *St&PR 93*
Shapiro, Mark Lawrence 1944- *WhoAm 92*
Shapiro, Martin 1933- *WhoAm 92*
Shapiro, Marvin Lincoln 1923- *WhoAm 92*
Shapiro, Marvin Seymour 1936- *WhoAm 92*
Shapiro, Mary J. 1945- *WhoAmW 93*
Shapiro, Mathilde *AmWomPl*
Shapiro, Maurice Mandel 1915- *WhoAm 92*
Shapiro, Melvin *MiSFD 9*
Shapiro, Michael 1942- *WhoAm 92*
Shapiro, Michael Edward 1949- *WhoAm 92*
Shapiro, Milton Stanley 1922- *WhoAm 92, WhoWor 93*
Shapiro, Moses 1910-1990 *BioIn 17*
Shapiro, Myra Stein 1932- *WhoAmW 93*
Shapiro, Naomi K. 1941- *WhoWrEP 92*
Shapiro, Naomi Phyllis 1942- *WhoAmW 93*
Shapiro, Neil *ScF&FL 92*
Shapiro, Neil Robert 1962- *WhoE 93*
Shapiro, Nella Irene 1947- *WhoE 93*
Shapiro, Nils A. *St&PR 93*
Shapiro, Norma Sondra Levy 1928- *WhoAm 92, WhoE 93*
Shapiro, Norman Richard 1930- *WhoAm 92*
Shapiro, Paul *Law&B 92*
Shapiro, Paul 1955- *MiSFD 9*
Shapiro, Paul David 1940- *St&PR 93*
Shapiro, Perry 1941- *WhoAm 92*
Shapiro, Philip Alan 1940- *WhoWor 93*
Shapiro, Rashi Yisroel 1953- *WhoE 93*
Shapiro, Raymond L. 1934- *WhoAm 92*
Shapiro, Richard F. 1937- *St&PR 93*
Shapiro, Richard Gerald 1924- *WhoAm 92*
Shapiro, Richard Scott *Law&B 92*
Shapiro, Richard Stanley 1925- *WhoAm 92*
Shapiro, Robert Alan 1946- *WhoAm 92*
Shapiro, Robert B. 1938- *St&PR 93, WhoAm 92*
Shapiro, Robert D. 1928- *St&PR 93*
Shapiro, Robert Frank 1934- *WhoAm 92*
Shapiro, Robert M. 1945- *WhoWor 93*
Shapiro, Ronald 1946- *St&PR 93*
Shapiro, Ronald M. 1948- *St&PR 93*
Shapiro, Ronald Maurice 1943- *WhoAm 92*
Shapiro, Ruth 1926- *WhoE 93*
Shapiro, Sam 1914- *WhoAm 92*
Shapiro, Samuel Bernard 1909- *WhoAm 92*
Shapiro, Samuel David 1927- *WhoAm 92*
Shapiro, Samuel Oliver 1902-1990 *BioIn 17*
Shapiro, Sander Wolf 1929- *WhoAm 92*
Shapiro, Sandra 1944- *WhoAm 92, WhoAmW 93*
Shapiro, Sandra Libby Rosenberg 1946- *WhoE 93*
Shapiro, Sandra M. 1938- *WhoAmW 93*
Shapiro, Sheri Lynn 1959- *WhoAmW 93*
Shapiro, Sidney 1915- *ConAu 136*
Shapiro, Sidney 1931- *WhoAm 92*
Shapiro, Sidney Robert 1919- *St&PR 93*
Shapiro, Stanley 1925-1990 *BioIn 17, ScF&FL 92*
Shapiro, Stanley 1937- *WhoAm 92*
Shapiro, Stanton J. *Law&B 92*
Shapiro, Stephen R. 1934- *WhoAm 92*
Shapiro, Stuart Charles 1944- *WhoAm 92, WhoE 93*
Shapiro, Sumner 1923- *St&PR 93*
Shapiro, Sumner 1926- *WhoAm 92*
Shapiro, Susan 1955- *WhoAmW 93*
Shapiro, Susan Jane 1950- *WhoAmW 93*
Shapiro, Theodore 1932- *WhoAm 92*
Shapiro, Victor Lenard 1924- *WhoAm 92, WhoWor 93*
Shapiro, William D. *Law&B 92*
Shapiro-Ross, Debra 1955- *WhoAmW 93, WhoE 93*
Shapleigh, Bertram 1871-1940 *Baker 92*
Shapleigh, Donald Snowden 1948- *St&PR 93*
Shaplen, Robert 1917-1988 *JrnUS*
Shapley, Lloyd Stowell 1923- *WhoAm 92*
Shapley, Robert Martin 1944- *WhoAm 92*
Shapo, Marshall Schambelan 1936- *WhoAm 92*
Shapoff, Stephen H. 1944- *St&PR 93, WhoAm 92*
Shaporin, Yuri (Alexandrovich) 1887-1966 *Baker 92*
Shaporin, Yury 1887-1966 *OxDcOp*
Shaposhnikov, Yevgeny *BioIn 17*
Shapp, Charles M. 1906-1989 *BioIn 17*
Shapp, Milton J. 1912- *PolPar*
Shapp, Milton Jerrold 1912- *BioIn 17*
Shappirio, David Gordon 1930- *WhoAm 92*
Shapur the Great, II 310-379 *HarEnMi*
Sharad 1945- *WhoAsAP 91*
Sharaiha, Zeyad Khalil 1943- *WhoWor 93*
Sharan, Dina Nath 1938- *WhoWor 93*
Sharan, Rahoul 1961- *St&PR 93*
Sharansky, Natan *BioIn 17, NewYTBS 92*
Sharansky, Natan 1948- *WhoWor 93*
Sharapudinov, Idris Idrisovich 1948- *WhoWor 93*
Sharat Chandra, G.S. 1938- *WhoWrEP 92*
Sharbaugh, Amandus Harry 1919- *WhoAm 92*
Sharbaugh, H. Robert 1928- *St&PR 93*
Sharbaugh, Joseph Edward 1947- *St&PR 93*
Sharbel, Jean M. *WhoAm 92*
Sharbel, Paul J. 1940- *St&PR 93*
Sharber, Ann Boutwell 1948- *St&PR 93*
Sharboneau, Lorna Rosina 1935- *WhoAmW 93, WhoWor 93*
Sharbutt, Jay F. d1992 *BioIn 17, NewYTBS 92*
Share, Donald Seth 1957- *WhoWrEP 92*
Share, William Fremont 1926- *WhoAm 92*
Sharee, Keith *ScF&FL 92*
Sharer, Elmer Eugene 1933- *St&PR 93*
Sharer, Robert L. 1946- *WhoUN 92*
Sharett, Alan Richard 1943- *WhoSSW 93, WhoWor 93*
Sharf, Donald Jack 1927- *WhoAm 92*
Sharf, Stephan 1920- *WhoAm 92*
Sharff, Curtis M. 1949- *St&PR 93*
Sharff, Karl Edward 1934- *St&PR 93*
Sharfman, Herbert d1992 *NewYTBS 92 [port]*
Sharfman, Herbert 1909-1992 *BioIn 17*
Sharfman, William Lee 1942- *WhoE 93*
Sharfstein, Steven Samuel 1942- *WhoAm 92*
Shargal, Susan K. Y. 1948- *WhoE 93*
Shargel, Leon David 1941- *WhoE 93*
Sharick, Merle Dayton, Jr. 1946- *WhoEmL 93, WhoSSW 93*
Sharif, Mohammad 1933- *WhoUN 92*
Sharif, Mohammad Nowaz 1948- *WhoWor 93*
Sharif, Omar 1932- *IntDcF 2-3 [port], WhoAm 92*
Sharif, Y.N. *St&PR 93*
Sharif-Emami, Ali 1955- *St&PR 93*
Sharif-Emami, Jafar 1910- *WhoAm 92, WhoWor 93*
Sharify, Nasser 1925- *WhoAm 92, WhoE 93, WhoWor 93, WhoWrEP 92*
Sharin, Samuel 1924- *St&PR 93*
Sharir, Yacov 1940- *WhoAm 92*
Sharkansky, Richard M. *Law&B 92*
Sharkany, Edward J. 1931- *St&PR 93*
Sharkey, Charles W. 1932- *St&PR 93*
Sharkey, John Bernard 1940- *WhoE 93*
Sharkey, John F. 1943- *St&PR 93*
Sharkey, Joseph T. 1895-1991 *BioIn 17*
Sharkey, Kenneth George 1938- *St&PR 93*
Sharkey, Philip J. *WhoIns 93*
Sharkey, William J. *Law&B 92*
Sharkin, Gerald D. *Law&B 92*
Sharma, A.B. 1948- *WhoScE 91-4*
Sharma, Anand 1953- *WhoAsAP 91*
Sharma, Arjun D. 1953- *WhoWor 93*
Sharma, Bhu Dev 1938- *WhoAm 92*
Sharma, Chaman Lal 1932- *WhoUN 92*
Sharma, Chandan 1948- *WhoAsAP 91*
Sharma, Chandra Shekhar *WhoScE 91-1*
Sharma, Chiranji Lal 1923- *WhoAsAP 91*
Sharma, Dharm Paul 1947- *WhoWor 93*
Sharma, H.S.S. 1956- *WhoScE 91-1*
Sharma, Harish *WhoAsAP 91*
Sharma, Motilal 1942- *WhoWor 93*
Sharma, Neelam Kumar 1956- *WhoWor 93*
Sharma, Parashu Ram 1946- *WhoSSW 93*
Sharma, Prem Vallabh 1932- *WhoScE 91-2*
Sharma, R. *WhoScE 91-1*
Sharma, Ran S. 1937- *WhoE 93*
Sharma, S.C. 1941- *WhoScE 91-3*
Sharma, Santosh Devraj 1934- *WhoAmW 93*
Sharma, Satish Kumar 1947- *WhoAsAP 91*
Sharma, Shankar Dayal 1918- *WhoAsAP 91, WhoWor 93*
Sharma, Shiv K. 1941- *St&PR 93, WhoAm 92*
Sharma, Sitaram 1946- *WhoUN 92*
Sharma, Somesh D. *St&PR 93*

Sharma, Sushil 1956- WhoE 93, WhoWor 93
Sharma, Ursula Marion WhoScE 91-1
Sharma, Vijai P. 1941- WhoWrEP 92
Sharma, Vijai Prakash 1941- WhoSSW 93
Sharma, Yagya Datt 1921- WhoAsAP 91
Sharman, Alison ConAu 138, SmATA 70
Sharman, Dick 1934- St&PR 93
Sharman, Jim MiSFD 9
Sharman, Leslie Law&B 92
Sharman, Nick 1952- ScF&FL 92
Sharman, Pamela Mary 1934- WhoWor 93
Sharman, Richard Lee 1932- WhoSSW 93
Sharman, William 1926- WhoAm 92
Sharmat, Marjorie Weinman 1928- ConAu 39NR, MajAI [port]
Sharmat, Mitchell 1927- ScF&FL 92
Sharmel, Theolynpekrul WhoWrEP 92
Sharon, Ariel BioIn 17
Sharon, Ariel 1928- ColdWar 2 [port], HarEnMi, WhoWor 93
Sharon, Dennis Paul 1935- St&PR 93, WhoSSW 93
Sharon, Jeffrey D. 1949- St&PR 93
Sharon, Neva BioIn 17
Sharon, Yitzhak Yaakov 1936- WhoE 93
Sharp, Aaron John 1904- WhoAm 92
Sharp, Alan MiSFD 9
Sharp, Alfred Jay 1929- WhoE 93
Sharp, Allen ScF&FL 92
Sharp, Allen 1932- WhoAm 92
Sharp, Anne Catherine 1943- WhoAmW 93
Sharp, Arthur Glynn 1941- WhoWrEP 92
Sharp, Barry J. St&PR 93
Sharp, Bert Lavon 1926- WhoAm 92
Sharp, Cecil (James) 1859-1924 Baker 92
Sharp, Charles R. Law&B 92
Sharp, Dan BioIn 17
Sharp, Daniel Asher 1932- WhoAm 92
Sharp, David A. 1950- St&PR 93
Sharp, David Lee 1952- WhoEmL 93
Sharp, David William Arthur WhoScE 91-1
Sharp, David William Arthur 1931- WhoWor 93
Sharp, Don 1922- MiSFD 9
Sharp, Donald Douglas 1945- St&PR 93
Sharp, Donald Young 1937- St&PR 93
Sharp, Douglas Andrew 1945- WhoSSW 93
Sharp, Edith Lambert 1917- DcChlFi
Sharp, Elliott 1951- Baker 92
Sharp, Esther L. Law&B 92
Sharp, Gail M. St&PR 93
Sharp, Gary Lynn 1956- WhoSSW 93
Sharp, George Baldwin 1941- WhoE 93
Sharp, George Kendall 1934- WhoAm 92
Sharp, Herbert Cecil 1923- St&PR 93
Sharp, Ian 1946- MiSFD 9
Sharp, Ian Roger WhoScE 91-1
Sharp, Isadore BioIn 17
Sharp, J. Anthony 1946- WhoSSW 93
Sharp, James Franklin 1938- WhoAm 92, WhoE 93, WhoWor 93
Sharp, James R. 1945- St&PR 93
Sharp, James Roger 1936- WhoE 93
Sharp, Jane Ellyn 1934- WhoAmW 93
Sharp, Jane Shriver 1931- WhoAmW 93
Sharp, Jeanette Poppa 1945- WhoAmW 93
Sharp, Jerrilyn Sue 1957- WhoAmW 93
Sharp, Jessie BioIn 17
Sharp, John Alan WhoScE 91-1
Sharp, John Malcolm, Jr. 1944- WhoAm 92
Sharp, John Mark 1958- WhoAm 92
Sharp, John Randall 1954- WhoAsAP 91
Sharp, Karl Olin 1936- St&PR 93
Sharp, Kathy Lynn 1958- WhoAmW 93
Sharp, Kay Frances 1945- WhoAmW 93
Sharp, Lauriston 1907- IntDcAn
Sharp, Lemuel, III 1951- St&PR 93
Sharp, Lincoln V., Jr. Law&B 92
Sharp, Lisa Carole 1959- WhoAmW 93
Sharp, Luke ScF&FL 92
Sharp, Lyle Duane 1931- St&PR 93
Sharp, Margery 1905-1991 BioIn 17, ChlLR 27 [port], MajAI [port], ScF&FL 92
Sharp, Mary Pawling 1947- St&PR 93
Sharp, Mitchell BioIn 17
Sharp, Mitchell William 1911- WhoAm 92
Sharp, Nancy Weatherly 1936- WhoAmW 93
Sharp, Paul Frederick 1918- WhoAm 92, WhoSSW 93
Sharp, Paul M. 1957- WhoScE 91-3
Sharp, Peter BioIn 17
Sharp, Peter Jay d1992 NewYTBS 92 [port]
Sharp, Philip R. 1942- CngDr 91, WhoAm 92
Sharp, Phillip Allen 1944- WhoAm 92
Sharp, Renate Maria Law&B 92
Sharp, Richard L. 1947- St&PR 93, WhoAm 92, WhoSSW 93
Sharp, Robert A. 1932- St&PR 93
Sharp, Robert Charles 1936- St&PR 93, WhoAm 92
Sharp, Robert G. 1935- St&PR 93
Sharp, Robert L. 1945- St&PR 93
Sharp, Robert Phillip 1911- WhoAm 92
Sharp, Robert R. 1945- St&PR 93
Sharp, Robert Sutcliffe Dunstan Law&B 92
Sharp, Robert Weimer 1917- WhoAm 92
Sharp, Rodney Yorke WhoScE 91-1
Sharp, Ronald Alan 1945- WhoAm 92
Sharp, Sharon Annette Andrews 1952- WhoSSW 93, WhoWrEP 92
Sharp, Stephen Alan 1947- WhoAm 92
Sharp, Terance K. Law&B 92
Sharp, Walter M. 1916- St&PR 93
Sharp, Warren Donald 1939- St&PR 93
Sharp, William 1929- WhoAm 92
Sharp, William Edward 1961- WhoAm 92
Sharp, William F. 1942- St&PR 93
Sharp, William R. 1936- St&PR 93
Sharp, William Roy Law&B 92
Sharp, William Wheeler 1923- WhoSSW 93, WhoWor 93
Sharpe, Aubrey Dean 1944- WhoSSW 93
Sharpe, Beverly A. Law&B 92
Sharpe, C. Richard 1925- St&PR 93
Sharpe, Carla Jane Law&B 92
Sharpe, Charles Norval, Jr. 1927- WhoIns 93
Sharpe, Clyde E. 1928- St&PR 93
Sharpe, Damon 1973- BioIn 17
Sharpe, David A. 1951- St&PR 93
Sharpe, Debra Fetterman 1954- WhoSSW 93
Sharpe, Donald Edward 1937- WhoAm 92
Sharpe, Edward Cary 1938- WhoSSW 93
Sharpe, Frederick Richard 1950- WhoScE 91-1
Sharpe, Henry Dexter, Jr. 1923- St&PR 93
Sharpe, James M. 1950- St&PR 93
Sharpe, James Shelby 1940- WhoSSW 93, WhoWor 93
Sharpe, Jean Elizabeth WhoAm 92
Sharpe, John DcCPCAm
Sharpe, John H. Law&B 92
Sharpe, John Henry 1921- WhoWor 93
Sharpe, John I. 1934- St&PR 93
Sharpe, John Rufus, III ScF&FL 92
Sharpe, John T. 1936- St&PR 93
Sharpe, Judith Louise 1942- WhoAmW 93
Sharpe, Kathryn Moye 1922- WhoAmW 93
Sharpe, Kathy St&PR 93
Sharpe, Keith Yount 1930- WhoAm 92
Sharpe, Kevin 1949- ConAu 136
Sharpe, Logan Garnett 1952- St&PR 93
Sharpe, Louis Haughton 1927- WhoSSW 93
Sharpe, Louis Kerre 1944- St&PR 93
Sharpe, Margaret AmWomPl
Sharpe, Mary G. AmWomPl
Sharpe, Michael Douglas 1954- St&PR 93
Sharpe, Mitchell Raymond 1924- WhoSSW 93
Sharpe, Myron E(manuel) 1928- ConAu 136
Sharpe, Myron Emanuel 1928- WhoAm 92, WhoWrEP 92
Sharpe, P. WhoScE 91-1
Sharpe, R.S. WhoScE 91-1
Sharpe, Richard Samuel 1930- WhoAm 92
Sharpe, Robert F., Jr. Law&B 92
Sharpe, Robert F., Jr. 1953- WhoWor 93
Sharpe, Robert Francis 1921- St&PR 93, WhoAm 92
Sharpe, Robert Francis, Jr. 1952- WhoAm 92
Sharpe, Rochelle WhoSSW 93
Sharpe, Rochelle Phyllis 1956- WhoAmW 93
Sharpe, Roland Leonard 1923- WhoAm 92
Sharpe, Roosevelt, Jr. 1951- WhoE 93
Sharpe, Sara Buzze 1955- St&PR 93
Sharpe, Susan 1946- SmATA 71 [port]
Sharpe, Tom BioIn 17
Sharpe, Vera ScF&FL 92
Sharpe, Virginia Deegan 1935- WhoAmW 93, WhoSSW 93
Sharpe, William Chapman 1951- ConAu 139
Sharpe, William F. BioIn 17
Sharpe, William Forsyth 1934- WhoAm 92, WhoWor 93
Sharpe, William Norman, Jr. 1938- WhoAm 92
Sharpey-Schafer, John Francis WhoScE 91-1
Sharpf, Larry K. 1938- St&PR 93
Sharples, Dianne I. 1941- WhoAmW 93
Sharples, Richard DcCPCAm
Sharples, Winston Singleton 1932- WhoSSW 93
Sharpless, Jananne NewYTBS 92
Sharpless, Joseph Benjamin 1933- WhoE 93
Sharpless, K. Barry 1941- WhoAm 92
Sharpless, Richard Kennedy 1911- WhoAm 92
Sharpless, Samuel H. St&PR 93
Sharpnack, Sharon BioIn 17
Sharpstein, Richard Alan 1950- WhoSSW 93
Sharpton, Al BioIn 17
Sharrer, Cherry Tabb 1960- WhoAmW 93
Sharrock, David B. 1936- St&PR 93
Sharrow, Diane Marie 1959- WhoAmW 93
Sharrow, Leonard 1915- Baker 92
Sharrow, Marilyn Jane WhoAm 92, WhoAmW 93
Sharshan, Randall John 1955- WhoE 93
Shartle, Keith WhoAm 92
Shartle, Mark W. 1948- St&PR 93
Sharvelle, Eric G. 1908-1989 BioIn 17
Sharwell, William G. 1920- St&PR 93
Sharwell, William Gay 1920- WhoAm 92
Shasha, Alfred A. St&PR 93
Shashaani, Avideh WhoE 93
Shashkin, Yurii Alexeevich 1931- WhoWor 93
Shashoua, Ezra Law&B 92
Shashua-Hasson, Rena 1935- WhoUN 92
Shashy, Paul Moses 1925- WhoSSW 93
Shaskan, George F., Jr. 1917- St&PR 93
Shasteen, Donald Eugene 1928- WhoAm 92
Shastid, Jon Barton 1914- WhoAm 92
Shastri, Lal Bahadur 1904-1966 DcTwHis
Shatalin, Stanislav BioIn 17
Shatalow, Peter MiSFD 9
Shatan, Chaim Felix 1924- WhoAm 92
Shatkin, Aaron Jeffrey 1934- WhoAm 92
Shatner, Lisabeth ScF&FL 92
Shatner, William 1931- BioIn 17, MiSFD 9, ScF&FL 92, WhoAm 92
Shatoff, Larry D. 1944- WhoIns 93
Shattil, Siegfried 1914- St&PR 93
Shatto, Gloria McDermith 1931- WhoAm 92, WhoAmW 93
Shatto, James M. Law&B 92
Shatto, John Frederick 1957- WhoE 93
Shattuck, Cathie Ann 1945- WhoAm 92, WhoAmW 93
Shattuck, Charles H. 1910-1992 NewYTBS 92
Shattuck, Charles H(arlen) 1910-1992 ConAu 139
Shattuck, Curtis G. 1907- WhoIns 93
Shattuck, George C. 1927- ConAu 137
Shattuck, John H.F. BioIn 17
Shattuck, Mayo A., III 1954- St&PR 93
Shattuck, Paul C. 1944- St&PR 93
Shattuck, Roger BioIn 17
Shattuck, Roger Whitney 1923- WhoAm 92, WhoWrEP 92
Shattuck, Ruth M. d1990 BioIn 17
Shatz, Marilyn Joyce 1939- WhoAmW 93
Shatz, Ruth d1991 BioIn 17
Shatz, Stephen Sidney 1937- WhoAm 92
Shatzkin, Leonard 1919- WhoAm 92
Shatzky, Jacob 1893-1956 PolBiDi
Shatzky, Joel Lawrence 1943- WhoE 93
Shatzman, Aaron Mark 1946- WhoE 93
Shaub, Harold Arthur 1915- WhoAm 92
Shauck, Edwin W. 1926- St&PR 93
Shaud, Grant WhoAm 92
Shaud, John Albert 1933- WhoAm 92
Shaughnessy, Dennis R. Law&B 92
Shaughnessy, James Edward Law&B 92
Shaughnessy, James Michael 1945- WhoAm 92, WhoE 93
Shaughnessy, James P. Law&B 92
Shaughnessy, Marie Kaneko 1924- WhoAmW 93
Shaughnessy, Michael Kevin 1949- St&PR 93
Shaughnessy, Molly Clements 1949- St&PR 93
Shaughnessy, Paul V. 1938- St&PR 93
Shaughnessy, Phyllis B. 1934- WhoWrEP 92
Shaughnessy, Robert J. Law&B 92
Shaughnessy, Robert Michael 1940- St&PR 93
Shaughnessy, Thomas William 1938- WhoAm 92
Shaul, Janice Lee 1944- St&PR 93
Shaul, Roger Louis, Jr. 1948- WhoSSW 93
Shaull, Richard 1919- WhoAm 92
Shauman, R. William 1939- St&PR 93
Shaunnessey, Robert Lawrence 1947- St&PR 93
Shaunnessy, George Daniel 1948- WhoEmL 93
Shave, Michael John Ramage WhoScE 91-1
Shave, Robert E. 1952- St&PR 93
Shavelson, Kenneth M. 1949- St&PR 93
Shavelson, Melville 1917- MiSFD 9, WhoAm 92
Shaver, Beverly BioIn 17
Shaver, Carl B. 1935- St&PR 93
Shaver, Carl H. 1913- St&PR 93
Shaver, Clement L. 1867-1954 PolPar
Shaver, Clement Lawrence 1867-1954 BioIn 17
Shaver, Dennis George 1949- St&PR 93
Shaver, Donald LaVergne 1927- WhoAm 92
Shaver, Dorothy 1897-1959 BioIn 17
Shaver, Edwards Boone 1948- WhoEmL 93, WhoSSW 93, WhoWor 93
Shaver, Harold C. 1938- WhoSSW 93
Shaver, James Porter 1933- WhoAm 92
Shaver, Jesse M. 1919- St&PR 93
Shaver, Jesse Milton 1919- WhoAm 92
Shaver, Kimberly Ann 1959- WhoAmW 93, WhoWor 93
Shaver, Peter Albert 1943- WhoWor 93
Shaver, Phillip Robert 1944- WhoE 93
Shaver, Richard William 1940- St&PR 93
Shaver, Robert W. 1938- St&PR 93
Shaver, Scott Owen 1956- St&PR 93
Shaver, Sharon Rusch 1952- WhoSSW 93
Shaver, Stephen Blaise 1962- WhoSSW 93
Shaver, T.W. St&PR 93
Shaver, William 1927- St&PR 93
Shaverzashvili, Alexander 1919- Baker 92
Shaw, Alan Law&B 92
Shaw, Alan 1930- St&PR 93, WhoAm 92
Shaw, Alan J. 1949- St&PR 93, WhoAm 92
Shaw, Alan Roger 1938- WhoAm 92
Shaw, Albert 1857-1947 BioIn 17
Shaw, Allan d1990 BioIn 17
Shaw, Allen D. 1947- St&PR 93
Shaw, Amy BioIn 17
Shaw, Andrew, Jr. 1931- WhoAm 92
Shaw, Anna Howard 1847-1919 BioIn 17
Shaw, Anthony Edward 1955- WhoE 93
Shaw, Arnold BioIn 17
Shaw, Arnold 1909-1989 Baker 92, ScF&FL 92
Shaw, Artie 1910- Baker 92, BioIn 17, ConMus 8 [port], WhoAm 92
Shaw, Barbara Ann 1943- St&PR 93
Shaw, Barbara Ramsay 1943- WhoAmW 93
Shaw, Barry N. 1940- WhoE 93
Shaw, Bernard BioIn 17
Shaw, Bernard 1856-1950 BioIn 17, OxDcOp, TwCLC 45 [port], WorLitC [port]
Shaw, Bernard 1940- WhoAm 92, WhoE 93
Shaw, Bernard Heughes 1941- St&PR 93
Shaw, Bernard Leslie WhoScE 91-1
Shaw, Bob 1931- ScF&FL 92
Shaw, Brian ScF&FL 92
Shaw, Brian 1928-1992 BioIn 17
Shaw, Brigitte Wusten 1959- WhoAmW 93
Shaw, Bruce Jennings 1952- WhoSSW 93
Shaw, Bryan P. H. 1921- WhoAm 92
Shaw, Bynum Gillette 1923- WhoSSW 93, WhoWrEP 92
Shaw, Cameron BioIn 17
Shaw, Carole 1936- WhoAm 92, WhoAmW 93
Shaw, Catherine L. Law&B 92
Shaw, Charles Lemmon 1924- St&PR 93
Shaw, Charles Timothy WhoScE 91-1
Shaw, Chris MiSFD 9
Shaw, Christopher Ariel 1950- WhoWor 93
Shaw, Clayton Thomas 1941- WhoSSW 93
Shaw, Curtis S. Law&B 92
Shaw, Daniel Forrest Law&B 92
Shaw, David E. St&PR 93
Shaw, David George WhoScE 91-1
Shaw, David Lee 1947- WhoSSW 93
Shaw, David Lyle 1943- WhoAm 92
Shaw, David Mitchell 1958- WhoSSW 93
Shaw, David Peter 1941- St&PR 93
Shaw, David Tai-Ko 1938- WhoAm 92
Shaw, Denis Martin 1923- WhoAm 92
Shaw, Dennis Frederick 1924- WhoWor 93
Shaw, Don Wayne 1937- WhoAm 92
Shaw, Donald Hardy 1922- WhoAm 92
Shaw, Donald Leslie 1930- WhoAm 92
Shaw, Donna Gail 1955- WhoAmW 93
Shaw, Dorene Lee 1925- WhoWrEP 92
Shaw, Doris 1921- WhoAm 92
Shaw, Douglas Ian 1954- St&PR 93
Shaw, Douglas R. 1943- St&PR 93
Shaw, Duncan Frederic WhoScE 91-1
Shaw, E. Clay, Jr. 1939- CngDr 91, WhoAm 92, WhoSSW 93
Shaw, Edgar Albert George 1921- WhoAm 92
Shaw, Edward T. Law&B 92
Shaw, Eleanor Jane 1949- WhoAmW 93
Shaw, Ellsworth 1920- WhoWor 93
Shaw, Ernest G. 1929- St&PR 93
Shaw, Fran Weber 1947- WhoWrEP 92
Shaw, Frances Wells 1872-1937 AmWomPl
Shaw, Frank 1926- St&PR 93

Shaw, Garreth E. *Law&B 92*
Shaw, George Bernard 1856-1950 *Baker 92, BioIn 17, DcTwHis, MagSWL [port]*
Shaw, George Vincent 1928- *St&PR 93*
Shaw, Ghita Milgrom 1929- *WhoWor 93*
Shaw, Gina Louise 1960- *WhoAmW 93*
Shaw, Glen Byam 1904-1986 *IntDcOp, OxDcOp*
Shaw, Gloria Doris 1928- *WhoAmW 93*
Shaw, Gordon *WhoScE 91-1*
Shaw, Grace Goodfriend *WhoAm 92, WhoAmW 93, WhoE 93, WhoWor 93, WhoWrEP 92*
Shaw, Graham George 1944- *WhoScE 91-3*
Shaw, Harold 1923- *WhoAm 92*
Shaw, Harry Alexander, III 1937- *St&PR 93, WhoAm 92*
Shaw, Helen Lester Anderson 1936- *WhoAmW 93*
Shaw, Helen Louise Haith 1931- *WhoAmW 93*
Shaw, Henry Davis 1933- *St&PR 93*
Shaw, Herbert John 1918- *WhoAm 92*
Shaw, Herbert Weller 1935- *WhoE 93*
Shaw, Hugh J. 1949- *St&PR 93*
Shaw, Ian Alexander 1940- *WhoAm 92*
Shaw, Irwin 1913-1984 *BioIn 17, JeAmFiW*
Shaw, Isabel *WhoE 93*
Shaw, Jack Allen 1939- *WhoAm 92*
Shaw, James 1944- *WhoSSW 93*
Shaw, James Headon 1918- *WhoAm 92*
Shaw, James Renfrew 1930- *WhoE 93*
Shaw, Jane Elizabeth 1939- *St&PR 93*
Shaw, Janet 1937- *WhoWrEP 92*
Shaw, Janet Beeler 1937- *BioIn 17*
Shaw, Janine Ann 1955- *WhoAmW 93, WhoSSW 93*
Shaw, Jeanne Slotin 1935- *WhoSSW 93*
Shaw, Jerome 1926- *St&PR 93*
Shaw, Joan Fern 1938- *WhoCanL 92*
Shaw, John Andrew 1957- *WhoWor 93*
Shaw, John Arthur 1922- *WhoAm 92*
Shaw, John Firth 1948- *WhoAm 92*
Shaw, John Frederick 1938- *WhoAm 92*
Shaw, John Robert 1940- *St&PR 93*
Shaw, Joseph Francis 1932- *WhoUN 92*
Shaw, Josephine 1930- *WhoWor 93*
Shaw, Julius C. 1929- *WhoSSW 93*
Shaw, Karen Lee 1953- *WhoSSW 93*
Shaw, Keith Moffatt 1944- *WhoWor 93*
Shaw, Kendall 1924- *WhoAm 92, WhoE 93*
Shaw, Kenneth Alan 1939- *WhoAm 92*
Shaw, Kenneth Roger 1952- *WhoSSW 93*
Shaw, Kirk Cordell 1944- *WhoSSW 93*
Shaw, L. Edward, Jr. *Law&B 92*
Shaw, L. Edward, Jr. 1944- *St&PR 93*
Shaw, Larry *MiSFD 9*
Shaw, Larry 1948- *WhoSSW 93*
Shaw, Larry Don 1953- *WhoSSW 93*
Shaw, Larry T. 1924-1985 *ScF&FL 92*
Shaw, Lawrence Everett 1947- *WhoE 93*
Shaw, Lawrence T. *ScF&FL 92*
Shaw, Leander J., Jr. 1930- *AfrAmBi [port]*
Shaw, Leander Jerry, Jr. 1930- *WhoAm 92, WhoSSW 93*
Shaw, Lee Charles 1913- *WhoAm 92*
Shaw, Leon 1927- *St&PR 93*
Shaw, Leonard D. d1808? *BioIn 17*
Shaw, Leonard Glazer 1934- *WhoAm 92*
Shaw, Leroy Robert 1923- *WhoWrEP 92*
Shaw, Li Kung 1915- *WhoWrEP 92*
Shaw, Linda Louise 1938- *WhoWrEP 92*
Shaw, Luci N(orthcote) 1928- *ConAu 39NR*
Shaw, M. Allan 1940- *St&PR 93*
Shaw, M. Elizabeth *Law&B 92*
Shaw, M. Jane 1951- *WhoAmW 93*
Shaw, Manford Avis 1906- *WhoAm 92*
Shaw, Margery Wayne Schlamp 1923- *WhoAm 92*
Shaw, Margret *BioIn 17*
Shaw, Margret 1940- *ConAu 136*
Shaw, Marjorie Betts 1938- *WhoAm 92*
Shaw, Mark 1939- *St&PR 93*
Shaw, Martha L. 1961- *WhoWrEP 92*
Shaw, Martin Andrew 1944- *WhoE 93*
Shaw, Martin (Edward Fallas) 1875-1958 *Baker 92*
Shaw, Mary 1814-1876 *Baker 92*
Shaw, Mary 1854-1929 *AmWomPl*
Shaw, Mary Brown 1928- *St&PR 93*
Shaw, Mary Elizabeth 1929- *WhoAmW 93*
Shaw, Mary M. 1943- *WhoAm 92*
Shaw, Maurice Kenneth 1939- *St&PR 93, WhoAm 92*
Shaw, Melvin Phillip 1936- *WhoAm 92*
Shaw, Melvin Robert 1948- *WhoEmL 93*
Shaw, Michael 1924- *WhoAm 92*
Shaw, Michael 1944- *WhoWor 93*
Shaw, Michael Allan 1940- *WhoAm 92*
Shaw, Michael Joseph 1946- *WhoSSW 93*
Shaw, Michael S. 1954- *St&PR 93*
Shaw, Milton Clayton 1915- *WhoAm 92*
Shaw, Milton Herbert 1918- *WhoAm 92*
Shaw, Montgomery Throop 1943- *WhoE 93*
Shaw, Nancy 1946- *SmATA 71 [port]*
Shaw, Nancy Berry Keeling 1950- *WhoSSW 93*
Shaw, Nancy Rivard *WhoAm 92*
Shaw, Ned W. 1929- *St&PR 93*
Shaw, Neil McGowan 1929- *WhoAm 92, WhoWor 93*
Shaw, Norman E. 1929- *St&PR 93*
Shaw, Oliver 1779-1848 *Baker 92*
Shaw, Paul Whit 1952- *St&PR 93*
Shaw, Peter James *WhoScE 91-1*
Shaw, Philip Eugene 1934- *WhoSSW 93*
Shaw, Richard 1941- *WhoAm 92*
Shaw, Richard John 1939- *WhoE 93*
Shaw, Richard John Gildroy 1936- *WhoWor 93*
Shaw, Richard Leslie 1927- *St&PR 93*
Shaw, Richard M. *Law&B 92*
Shaw, Richard Melvin 1947- *WhoWor 93*
Shaw, Richard Paul 1933- *WhoE 93*
Shaw, Richard Wallace, Jr. 1962- *WhoE 93*
Shaw, Robert *ScF&FL 92, WhoScE 91-1*
Shaw, Robert 1927-1978 *IntDcF 2-3*
Shaw, Robert Alfred *WhoScE 91-1*
Shaw, Robert B. 1947- *ConAu 137, DcLB 120 [port]*
Shaw, Robert D. 1930- *St&PR 93*
Shaw, Robert E. 1931- *WhoAm 92, WhoSSW 93*
Shaw, Robert E. 1946- *St&PR 93*
Shaw, Robert Fletcher 1910- *WhoAm 92*
Shaw, Robert George 1947- *WhoSSW 93*
Shaw, Robert Gould 1837-1863 *BioIn 17*
Shaw, Robert Harold 1919- *WhoAm 92*
Shaw, Robert Hill *Law&B 92*
Shaw, Robert (Lawson) 1916- *Baker 92, WhoAm 92*
Shaw, Robert Samuel 1952- *WhoE 93*
Shaw, Robert T. *WhoAm 92*
Shaw, Robert W. 1913- *St&PR 93*
Shaw, Robert William, Jr. 1941- *WhoAm 92*
Shaw, Ronald *WhoScE 91-1*
Shaw, Ronald 1929- *WhoWor 93*
Shaw, Ronald Ahrend 1946- *WhoAm 92*
Shaw, Ronald G. 1938- *St&PR 93*
Shaw, Ronald Gordon 1938- *WhoAm 92*
Shaw, Run Run 1907- *BioIn 17*
Shaw, Russell Burnham 1935- *WhoAm 92*
Shaw, Russell Clyde 1940- *WhoAm 92*
Shaw, Ruth Jean 1943- *WhoAmW 93*
Shaw, Samuel E. 1943- *St&PR 93*
Shaw, Samuel Ervine, II 1933- *St&PR 93, WhoAm 92*
Shaw, Sandy *BioIn 17*
Shaw, Sondra A. 1944- *WhoWrEP 92*
Shaw, Spencer 1946- *WhoAm 92*
Shaw, Stanford Jay 1930- *WhoWrEP 92*
Shaw, Stanley Miner 1935- *WhoAm 92*
Shaw, Stephen Ragsdale 1945- *WhoSSW 93*
Shaw, Steven 1937- *WhoE 93*
Shaw, Steven John 1918- *WhoAm 92*
Shaw, Steven R. 1950- *St&PR 93*
Shaw, Talbert O. *WhoAm 92*
Shaw, Thelma 1901- *WhoAmW 93, WhoSSW 93*
Shaw, Thomas Gregory 1958- *WhoSSW 93*
Shaw, Thomas Jensen 1942- *St&PR 93*
Shaw, Trevor Henry Montague 1933- *St&PR 93*
Shaw, Valerine R. *WhoWrEP 92*
Shaw, Virginia Ruth 1952- *WhoAmW 93, WhoSSW 93*
Shaw, Wade Harrison, Jr. 1955- *WhoSSW 93*
Shaw, Walter Baxter 1942- *WhoSSW 93*
Shaw, (Harold) Watkins 1911- *Baker 92*
Shaw, William 1924- *St&PR 93*
Shaw, William Frederick 1920- *WhoAm 92*
Shaw, William H. 1927- *St&PR 93*
Shaw, William J. *BioIn 17*
Shaw, William James 1947- *WhoEmL 93*
Shaw, William Lewis 1938- *BiDAMSp 1989*
Shaw, William M. 1944- *St&PR 93*
Shaw, William V. *WhoScE 91-1*
Shaw, William Vaughan 1924- *WhoAm 92*
Shawber, Lloyd Oberlin 1926- *St&PR 93*
Shaw-Cohen, Lori Eve 1959- *WhoAm 92*
Shawe, Jan 1949- *WhoWor 93*
Shaw Elliot, Kimberly *Law&B 92*
Shawe-Taylor, Desmond (Christopher) 1907- *Baker 92*
Shaw-Galvez, Enrique *WhoWrEP 92*
Shawhan, Samuel Frazier, Jr. 1932- *WhoAm 92*
Shawl, Harry Michael 1947- *WhoSSW 93*
Shawn, Michael *BioIn 17*
Shawn, Ted 1891-1972 *BioIn 17*
Shawn, Wallace 1943- *WhoAm 92*
Shawn, William 1907- *WhoAm 92*
Shawn, William 1907-1992 *NewYTBS 92 [port]*
Shaw Yu-Ming 1938- *WhoAsAP 91*
Shay, Adell Leslie 1958- *WhoAmW 93*
Shay, Bernard E. *Law&B 92*
Shay, Don *ScF&FL 92*
Shay, John E., Jr. 1933- *WhoAm 92*
Shay, John J., Jr. *Law&B 92*
Shay, Martin Edward 1948- *WhoAm 92*
Shay, Paul Richard *Law&B 92*
Shay, Paul Richard 1954- *St&PR 93*
Shay, Philipp Wendell 1914- *WhoE 93, WhoWor 93*
Shay, Robert Michael 1936- *St&PR 93, WhoE 93, WhoWor 93*
Shay, Stephen Elliott 1951- *WhoE 93*
Shay, Thomas K. 1938- *St&PR 93*
Shaye, Robert *MiSFD 9*
Shaye, Robert Kenneth 1939- *St&PR 93, WhoAm 92*
Shaycvitz-Kellman, Jessie Rebecca 1960- *WhoAmW 93*
Shayler, Paul John *WhoScE 91-1*
Shayne, Arnie 1929- *WhoAm 92*
Shayne, David 1934- *WhoAm 92*
Shayne, Herbert M. 1926- *St&PR 93*
Shayne, Linda *MiSFD 9*
Shayne, Robert d1992 *NewYTBS 92*
Shayne, Robert 1910?- *BioIn 17*
Shayner, John Anthony 1945- *WhoE 93*
Shays, Christopher 1945- *CngDr 91, WhoAm 92, WhoE 93*
Shbib, Bashar *MiSFD 9*
Shcharansky, Anatoly *BioIn 17*
Shcharansky, Anatoly 1948- *WhoWor 93*
Shchedrin, Rodion (Konstantinovich) 1932- *Baker 92, WhoWor 93*
Shcherba, Anatoli Ivanovich 1960- *WhoWor 93*
Shcherbachev, Vladimir (Vladimirovich) 1889-1952 *Baker 92*
Shcherbak, IUrii 1934- *BioIn 17*
Shcherbakov, Boris Alexeevich 1924- *WhoWor 93*
Shcherbakov, Ivan Alexandrovich 1944- *WhoWor 93*
Shcherbin, Vasiliy Matveevich 1937- *WhoWor 93*
Shcherbitskii, V.V. 1918-1990 *BioIn 17*
Shcherbitskii, Vladimir Vasil'evich 1918-1990 *BioIn 17*
Shea, Ann Marie 1939- *WhoE 93*
Shea, Anne Joan 1907- *WhoAmW 93*
Shea, Christopher Lane 1959- *WhoWor 93*
Shea, Daniel Bartholomew, Jr. 1936- *WhoAm 92*
Shea, David Michael 1922- *WhoAm 92*
Shea, Dion Warren Joseph 1937- *WhoAm 92*
Shea, Donald Francis 1925- *WhoAm 92*
Shea, Donald Richard 1926- *WhoAm 92, WhoWrEP 92*
Shea, Donald William 1936- *WhoAm 92*
Shea, Edward Emmett 1932- *WhoAm 92*
Shea, Edward J. 1951- *St&PR 93*
Shea, Edward M. *Law&B 92*
Shea, Emmett Andrew 1930- *WhoE 93*
Shea, Everett D., Jr. 1930- *St&PR 93*
Shea, Francis Raymond 1913- *WhoAm 92*
Shea, Francis X. 1941- *St&PR 93*
Shea, Francis Xavier 1941- *WhoAm 92*
Shea, G. Leonard 1933- *St&PR 93*
Shea, George 1940- *ScF&FL 92*
Shea, George P. 1938- *St&PR 93*
Shea, George P., Jr. 1938- *WhoIns 93*
Shea, Gerald James 1949- *WhoWrEP 92*
Shea, Gloria 1913- *SweetSg C [port]*
Shea, Gregory Michael 1946- *St&PR 93*
Shea, J. Vernon 1912-1981 *ScF&FL 92*
Shea, Jack 1928- *MiSFD 9*
Shea, James L. 1943- *St&PR 93*
Shea, James William 1936- *WhoAm 92*
Shea, Jamie Patrick 1953- *WhoWor 93*
Shea, Jeremiah P. 1926- *St&PR 93*
Shea, John Dwane 1939- *WhoWor 93*
Shea, John Edward 1943- *WhoE 93*
Shea, John Francis 1928- *St&PR 93*
Shea, John J. 1938- *St&PR 93, WhoAm 92*
Shea, John Joseph 1924- *WhoAm 92*
Shea, John Martin, Jr. 1922- *WhoAm 92, WhoWor 93*
Shea, Joseph William, III 1947- *WhoEmL 93*
Shea, Kathleen T. 1950- *St&PR 93*
Shea, Kathryn Selleck 1958- *WhoAmW 93*
Shea, Linda Brownell 1951- *St&PR 93*
Shea, Maurice P., III *WhoAm 92*
Shea, Michael 1938- *ScF&FL 92*
Shea, Michael 1946- *ScF&FL 92*
Shea, Michael W. 1947- *St&PR 93*
Shea, R.M. *Law&B 92*
Shea, Richard J. 1936- *St&PR 93*
Shea, Richard Michael *Law&B 92*
Shea, Robert 1933- *ScF&FL 92*
Shea, Robert McConnell 1924- *WhoAm 92*
Shea, Stephen Michael 1926- *WhoAm 92*
Shea, Terence Joseph 1932- *St&PR 93*
Shea, Terrence W. 1941- *WhoIns 93*
Shea, Thomas D., Jr. 1931- *St&PR 93*
Shea, Thomas E. 1949- *St&PR 93*
Shea, Thomas Edward 1940- *WhoUN 92*
Shea, Thomas James 1949- *WhoE 93*
Shea, Timothy T. 1944- *St&PR 93*
Shea, Walter James 1929- *WhoAm 92*
Shea, William 1907-1991 *AnObit 1991*
Shea, William Alfred 1907-1991 *BioIn 17*
Shea, William Anthony 1933- *St&PR 93*
Shea, William Francis d1991 *BioIn 17*
Shea, William Rene 1937- *WhoAm 92*
Sheafer, William L. 1943- *St&PR 93*
Sheaffer, Carey Nelson 1947- *WhoE 93*
Sheaffer, James W. *St&PR 93*
Sheaffer, Louis 1912- *BioIn 17, WhoAm 92*
Sheaffer, M.P.A. *WhoWrEP 92*
Sheaffer, Richard Allen 1950- *WhoEmL 93*
Sheaffer, Theodore Campbell 1902- *St&PR 93*
Sheahan, Brian J. 1940- *WhoScE 91-3*
Sheahan, Edward Heffernan, III 1954- *WhoSSW 93*
Sheahan, John Bernard 1923- *WhoAm 92*
Sheahan, Joseph D. 1946- *WhoEmL 93*
Sheahan, Kathleen M. *Law&B 92*
Sheahan, Melody Ann 1959- *WhoSSW 93*
Sheahan, Robert Emmett 1942- *WhoSSW 93*
Sheahen, Allan 1932- *WhoWrEP 92*
Sheahin, John Matthew 1942- *St&PR 93*
Shealy, Alan Wardwell 1953- *WhoE 93*
Shealy, Clyde Norman 1932- *WhoAm 92*
Shealy, David Lee 1944- *WhoAm 92, WhoSSW 93*
Shealy, Ramon Lee 1940- *St&PR 93*
Shealy, Stanley Esthern 1947- *WhoSSW 93*
Shealy, Wallace *BioIn 17*
Shealy, William Ross 1925- *WhoSSW 93*
Shealy, William W. 1934- *WhoIns 93*
Shealy, William Walter 1934- *St&PR 93*
Shealy, Y. Fulmer 1923- *WhoWor 93*
Shean, Patricia *Law&B 92*
Shean, Timothy Joseph 1945- *WhoSSW 93, WhoWor 93*
Shear, Barry d1979 *MiSFD 9N*
Shear, Benjamin D. 1910- *St&PR 93*
Shear, Charles Robert 1942- *WhoE 93*
Shear, David *Law&B 92*
Shear, Edward Phillip 1923- *St&PR 93*
Shear, Henry Herbert 1935- *St&PR 93*
Shear, Ione Mylonas 1936- *WhoAmW 93, WhoE 93*
Shear, Kenneth 1945- *WhoAm 92*
Shear, Matthew Joel 1955- *WhoAm 92*
Shear, Natalie Pickus 1940- *WhoAmW 93, WhoE 93*
Shear, Richard H. *Law&B 92*
Shear, Theodore Leslie, Jr. 1938- *WhoAm 92, WhoWor 93*
Shear, Virginia Marguerite 1950- *WhoE 93*
Shearburn, Donald E. 1925- *St&PR 93*
Shearburn, E. Brice *St&PR 93*
Sheard, Charles, III 1914- *WhoE 93*
Sheard, Christopher K. *Law&B 92*
Sheard, Norma Fae Voorhees 1936- *WhoAmW 93*
Sheard, R. Cassandra 1939- *WhoAmW 93*
Sheard, Sarah 1953- *WhoCanL 92*
Sheard, Wendy Stedman 1935- *WhoE 93*
Shearer, Anthony Patrick 1948- *WhoWor 93*
Shearer, Beth Jane 1955- *WhoAmW 93*
Shearer, Burt A. 1923- *St&PR 93*
Shearer, Charles Livingston 1942- *WhoAm 92*
Shearer, David Paul 1940- *St&PR 93*
Shearer, Georgia Elizabeth 1929- *WhoAmW 93*
Shearer, Harry Julius 1943- *WhoAm 92*
Shearer, Hugh 1923- *DcCPCAm*
Shearer, John 1947- *BlkAuII 92*
Shearer, John Clyde 1928- *WhoAm 92*
Shearer, Jonathan Turbitt 1945- *WhoSSW 93*
Shearer, Martin Pogue 1947- *St&PR 93*
Shearer, Michael Charles 1957- *St&PR 93*
Shearer, Norma 1900-1983 *BioIn 17, IntDcF 2-3 [port]*
Shearer, Richard Eugene 1919- *WhoAm 92*
Shearer, Ronald Alexander 1932- *WhoAm 92*
Shearer, Ted d1992 *NewYTBS 92*
Shearer, Walter C. 1944- *WhoUN 92*
Shearer, William Kennedy 1931- *WhoAm 92*
Sheares, Reuben A. d1992 *NewYTBS 92 [port]*
Shearin, Betty Spurlock 1931- *WhoAmW 93*
Shearin, Frank D. *Law&B 92*
Shearin, Kathryn Kay 1946- *WhoE 93*

Shearin, Ronald Vance *Law&B 92*
Shearing, George (Albert) 1919- *Baker 92, WhoAm 92*
Shearing, Joseph *ScF&FL 92*
Shearman, Jeffrey Lynn 1957- *WhoE 93*
Shearon, Forrest Bedford 1934- *WhoSSW 93*
Shearon, George Buard 1932- *St&PR 93*
Shearouse, Lillian *AmWomPl*
Shearrer, Mary Anderson 1950- *WhoAmW 93*
Sheasby, J. Michael 1936- *St&PR 93*
Sheasgreen, Gerald *Law&B 92*
Shebalin, Vissarion (Yakovlevich) 1902-1963 *Baker 92*
Shebib, Donald 1938- *MiSFD 9*
Shechter, Ben-Zion 1940- *WhoAm 92*
Shechter, Emanuel 1937- *WhoScE 91-2*
Shechter, Floyd 1954- *St&PR 93*
Shechter, Laura Judith 1944- *WhoAm 92*
Shechtman, George Henoch 1941- *WhoE 93*
Shechtman, Michael Alan 1951- *WhoE 93*
Shechtman, Stephen 1946- *St&PR 93*
Sheckley, Robert 1928- *BioIn 17, ScF&FL 92*
Shecter, Ben 1935- *ScF&FL 92*
Shecter, Jon *BioIn 17*
Shecter, Jonathan Miles 1968- *WhoAm 92*
Shectman, Robin 1948- *WhoWrEP 92*
Shedd, Ben Alvin 1947- *WhoAm 92*
Shedd, Dennis W. 1953- *WhoSSW 93*
Shedd, Donald Pomroy 1922- *WhoAm 92, WhoE 93*
Shedd, Francis William 1922- *WhoE 93*
Shedd, George Joel 1922- *WhoE 93*
Sheddan, Marylin Kellett 1942- *WhoSSW 93*
Shedden, John A. *Law&B 92*
Shediac, Rawy Roy 1950- *St&PR 93*
Shedlawski, Joseph Ferdinand 1954- *WhoE 93*
Shedley, Ethan I. 1934- *ScF&FL 92*
Shedlock, J(ohn) S(outh) 1843-1919 *Baker 92*
Shedrick, Alberta Loretta 1936- *WhoAmW 93*
Shedrick, Mary Bernice 1940- *WhoAmW 93*
Sheed, Wilfrid *BioIn 17*
Sheed, Wilfrid John Joseph 1930- *WhoAm 92*
Sheedy, Ally *BioIn 17*
Sheedy, Ally 1962- *WhoAm 92, WhoAmW 93*
Sheedy, Janice Liberator 1951- *WhoE 93*
Sheedy, Katherine A. 1948- *St&PR 93*
Sheedy, Kathleen A. *Law&B 92*
Sheedy, Kenneth John 1945- *St&PR 93, WhoE 93*
Sheedy, Madelon Unkovic 1936- *WhoE 93*
Sheehan, Anne Marie 1952- *WhoAmW 93*
Sheehan, Charles Vincent 1930- *WhoAm 92*
Sheehan, Daniel Eugene 1917- *WhoAm 92*
Sheehan, Daniel Michael 1944- *WhoSSW 93*
Sheehan, Deborah Ann 1953- *WhoAmW 93*
Sheehan, Dennis E. *Law&B 92*
Sheehan, Dennis William 1934- *St&PR 93, WhoAm 92*
Sheehan, Diane M. *Law&B 92*
Sheehan, Donald Thomas 1911- *WhoAm 92*
Sheehan, Edward James 1935- *WhoAm 92*
Sheehan, George *BioIn 17*
Sheehan, Gerald Joseph 1944- *WhoIns 93*
Sheehan, Gerard Francis 1952- *WhoE 93*
Sheehan, J.D. 1924- *WhoScE 91-3*
Sheehan, James C. 1946- *St&PR 93*
Sheehan, James John 1937- *WhoAm 92*
Sheehan, James Patrick 1942- *St&PR 93, WhoAm 92*
Sheehan, John C. *BioIn 17*
Sheehan, John Clark d1992 *NewYTBS 92 [port]*
Sheehan, John Eugene 1929- *BioIn 17*
Sheehan, John Francis 1906- *WhoAm 92*
Sheehan, John Joseph 1899- *WhoAm 92*
Sheehan, John Michael *Law&B 92*
Sheehan, John Michael 1929- *WhoE 93*
Sheehan, John Patrick 1933- *St&PR 93*
Sheehan, John Wilfred, Jr. 1941- *WhoE 93*
Sheehan, Kathleen Therese 1953- *WhoAm 92*
Sheehan, Kevin Edward 1945- *St&PR 93*
Sheehan, Kevin John 1951- *St&PR 93*
Sheehan, Lawrence James 1932- *WhoAm 92*
Sheehan, Margaret *Law&B 92*
Sheehan, Mary Anderson 1932- *WhoE 93*
Sheehan, Maura *BioIn 17*
Sheehan, Michael Jarboe 1939- *WhoAm 92, WhoSSW 93*
Sheehan, Monica Mary 1955- *WhoWor 93*
Sheehan, Neil *BioIn 17*
Sheehan, Neil 1936- *ConAu 40NR, WhoAm 92, WhoE 93, WhoWrEP 92*
Sheehan, Patricia Leslie 1956- *BiDAMSp 1989*
Sheehan, Patty *BioIn 17, WhoAmW 93*
Sheehan, Paul Robert 1951- *WhoE 93*
Sheehan, Richard H., Jr. *Law&B 92*
Sheehan, Richard J. 1934- *St&PR 93*
Sheehan, Robert James, II 1937- *WhoE 93*
Sheehan, Robert R. *Law&B 92*
Sheehan, Shawn *BioIn 17*
Sheehan, Susan *BioIn 17*
Sheehan, Susan 1937- *ConAu 40NR, WhoAm 92, WhoAmW 93*
Sheehan, Thomas Francis, Jr. 1958- *WhoE 93*
Sheehan, Thomas Gerard 1956- *WhoE 93*
Sheehan, Thomas J. 1943- *St&PR 93*
Sheehan, Timothy G. d1992 *NewYTBS 92*
Sheehan, Virginia Mary 1945- *WhoAmW 93*
Sheehan, William 1954- *ConAu 139*
Sheehan, William G. 1938- *St&PR 93*
Sheehan, William J. 1943- *St&PR 93*
Sheehan, William Joseph 1944- *WhoAm 92*
Sheehan-Byrns, Edward Vincent, Jr. 1963- *WhoSSW 93*
Sheehy, Eugene Paul 1922- *WhoAm 92*
Sheehy, Gail *BioIn 17*
Sheehy, Gail Henion 1937- *WhoAm 92, WhoAmW 93, WhoWrEP 92*
Sheehy, Harriet *BioIn 17*
Sheehy, Helen Probst 1948- *WhoAmW 93*
Sheehy, Howard Sherman, Jr. 1934- *WhoAm 92*
Sheehy, James William 1949- *WhoEmL 93*
Sheehy, John Patrick 1942- *WhoAm 92, WhoWor 93*
Sheehy, Kevin T. *Law&B 92*
Sheehy, Patricia Ann 1960- *WhoAmW 93*
Sheehy, Patrick 1930- *St&PR 93, WhoAm 92, WhoSSW 93*
Sheehy, Robert Francis 1950- *St&PR 93*
Sheehy, Thomas Daniel 1946- *St&PR 93, WhoAm 92*
Sheehy, Veronica Garvey 1937- *WhoAmW 93*
Sheeler, Donald Eugene 1952- *St&PR 93, WhoAm 92*
Sheeley, Michael Kenneth 1955- *WhoSSW 93*
Sheeley, Rachel Evelyn 1966- *WhoAmW 93, WhoWor 93*
Sheeline, Paul C. 1921- *St&PR 93*
Sheeline, Paul Cushing 1921- *WhoAm 92*
Sheely, David G. 1958- *St&PR 93*
Sheen, Charlie *BioIn 17*
Sheen, Charlie 1965- *ConTFT 10*
Sheen, Fulton J. 1895-1979 *BioIn 17*
Sheen, Martin 1940- *BioIn 17, HispAmA, IntDcF 2-3, MiSFD 9, WhoAm 92*
Sheen, Robert Tilton 1909- *WhoAm 92*
Sheepshanks, Mary 1872-1958 *BioIn 17*
Sheer, Irwin Ronald 1960- *WhoWor 93*
Sheer, Leo R. *Law&B 92*
Sheeran, John Francis 1937- *WhoAm 92*
Sheeran, Maureen Flynn 1946- *WhoE 93*
Sheeran, Patrick J. *Law&B 92*
Sheeran, William J. *BioIn 17*
Sheeran, William James 1938- *WhoAm 92*
Sheeran-Emory, Kathleen Mary 1948- *WhoEmL 93*
Sheerin, John B. d1992 *NewYTBS 92 [port]*
Sheerin, John B. 1906-1992 *BioIn 17*
Sheerin, John Basil 1906-1992 *ConAu 136*
Sheerin, Maggie 1940- *WhoAmW 93*
Sheerin, Walter J. d1992 *BioIn 17*
Sheerin, William Eugene 1946- *WhoE 93*
Sheets, Herman Ernest 1908- *WhoAm 92*
Sheets, James Ross 1938- *St&PR 93*
Sheets, Jeffrey Lynn 1949- *WhoWor 93*
Sheets, John Wesley, Jr. 1953- *WhoEmL 93*
Sheets, Kenneth Ray 1936- *ConAu 136*
Sheets, Martha Louise 1923- *WhoAmW 93*
Sheets, Michael Jay 1930- *WhoAm 92*
Sheets, Millard 1907-1989 *BioIn 17*
Sheets, Phillip Lewis 1939- *WhoSSW 93*
Sheets, Robert C. *BioIn 17*
Sheets, Ron 1947- *St&PR 93*
Sheetz, Christine Ninfa 1940- *WhoAmW 93, WhoWor 93*
Sheetz, Ralph Albert 1908- *WhoE 93, WhoWor 93*
Sheetz, Richard LaTrelle 1906- *WhoAm 92*
Sheetz, Richard Smedley 1924- *St&PR 93*
Shefcik, Kenneth S. 1947- *WhoIns 93*
Shefcik, Kenneth Stanley 1947- *St&PR 93*
Sheff, Stanley *MiSFD 9*
Sheffe, Edward Devereux, III 1950- *WhoE 93*
Sheffel, Irving Eugene 1916- *WhoAm 92*
Sheffer, Donald Alger 1917- *St&PR 93*
Sheffer, Ralph Lin, Jr. *St&PR 93*
Sheffer, Sandra J. 1947- *St&PR 93*
Sheffer, Sandra Jean *Law&B 92*
Sheffey, Fred C., Jr. 1928- *AfrAmBi*
Sheffey, Steven R. *Law&B 92*
Sheffield, Ann *BioIn 17*
Sheffield, Benita Carroll 1950- *WhoAmW 93*
Sheffield, Charles 1935- *ScF&FL 92*
Sheffield, Don B. 1935- *WhoAm 92*
Sheffield, George Daniel 1940- *WhoSSW 93*
Sheffield, Horace Lindsey, Jr. 1916- *WhoAm 92*
Sheffield, James Rockwell 1936- *WhoE 93*
Sheffield, Leslie Floyd 1925- *WhoAm 92*
Sheffield, Linda Gail 1944- *WhoSSW 93*
Sheffield, Linda Jensen 1949- *WhoSSW 93*
Sheffield, Martin P. 1950- *St&PR 93*
Sheffield, Rena Cary, Mrs. *AmWomPl*
Sheffield, Scott D. 1952- *St&PR 93*
Sheffield, W.H. *St&PR 93*
Sheffler, Larry N. 1939- *St&PR 93*
Shefler, Deborah S. *Law&B 92*
Shefner, Evelyn 1919- *ScF&FL 92*
Shefner, Vadim 1915- *ScF&FL 92*
Sheft, Peter Ian 1956- *WhoE 93, WhoWor 93*
Sheftall, Mordecai 1735-1797 *BioIn 17*
Shefte, James Francis 1943- *St&PR 93*
Sheftel, Beatrice K. 1945- *WhoWrEP 92*
Sheftel, Harry Bernard 1906- *WhoE 93*
Sheftel, Roger Terry 1941- *WhoE 93*
Sheftel, Steven J. 1945- *St&PR 93*
Sheftell, Fred D. 1941- *ConAu 137*
Shefter, Martin 1943- *ConAu 136*
Sheh, Robert Bardhyl 1939- *St&PR 93*
Shehan, James C. *Law&B 92*
Shehee, A.B. 1926- *St&PR 93*
Sheheen, Robert J. 1943- *WhoSSW 93*
Shei, Juliana Chiang 1948- *WhoAmW 93*
Sheid, Christiane Valentine 1957- *WhoE 93*
Sheiffer, Arnold 1934- *St&PR 93*
Sheih, Samuel C. 1919- *WhoAsAP 91*
Sheikh, Atique Zafar 1940- *WhoWor 93*
Sheikh, Mohammad Islam 1933- *WhoUN 92*
Sheikh, Naseer Ud-Din 1937- *WhoWor 93*
Sheikh, Ramsey U. 1930- *St&PR 93*
Sheikh, Saad Raheem 1936- *WhoUN 92*
Sheil, Glenister 1929- *WhoAsAP 91*
Sheils, Melodee H. *Law&B 92*
Sheils, Paul T. *Law&B 92*
Sheil-Small, Terence Brian *WhoScE 91-1*
Sheiman, Ronald Lee 1948- *WhoE 93, WhoWor 93*
Shein, Brian 1947- *WhoCanL 92*
Shein, Ida *BioIn 17*
Shein, Kin 1938- *WhoUN 92*
Shein, Samuel T. 1932- *WhoE 93*
Shein, Simra Ezra 1931- *WhoE 93*
Shein, Soe Myint 1960- *WhoWor 93*
Sheinbaum, Richard Louis 1935- *St&PR 93*
Sheinbaum, Stanley K. 1920- *WhoWor 93*
Sheinberg, Israel 1932- *St&PR 93, WhoAm 92*
Sheinberg, Sidney 1935- *ConTFT 10*
Sheinberg, Sidney Jay 1935- *WhoAm 92*
Sheinfeld, David 1906- *Baker 92, WhoAm 92*
Sheinfeld, Myron M. 1930- *WhoSSW 93*
Sheingold, Daniel H. 1928- *WhoAm 92*
Sheinin, Rose 1930- *WhoAm 92, WhoAmW 93*
Sheinman, Eugene 1929- *St&PR 93*
Sheinman, Jerome *Law&B 92*
Sheinman, Yardin *St&PR 93*
Sheinwold, Alfred *WhoAm 92*
Shekhar, Chandra *BioIn 17*
Shekhar, Chandra 1927- *WhoWor 93*
Shekhter, Boris (Semyonovich) 1900-1961 *Baker 92*
Shelach, Riki *MiSFD 9*
Shelanski, Michael L. 1941- *WhoAm 92*
Shelato, Robert 1923- *St&PR 93*
Shelby, Ann *AmWomPl*
Shelby, Antonio McGee 1941- *St&PR 93*
Shelby, Carroll 1923- *BioIn 17*
Shelby, James Stanford 1934- *WhoSSW 93, WhoWor 93*
Shelby, Jerome 1930- *St&PR 93, WhoAm 92*
Shelby, Joyce Young 1947- *WhoWrEP 92*
Shelby, Kelly Russell 1925- *St&PR 93*
Shelby, Linda L. *Law&B 92*
Shelby, Peggy Louise 1950- *WhoAmW 93*
Shelby, Richard C. 1934- *CngDr 91*
Shelby, Richard Craig 1934- *WhoAm 92, WhoSSW 93*
Shelby, Robin *Law&B 92*
Shelby, Roselle Price 1929- *WhoAmW 93*
Shelden, Deborah Jean 1946- *WhoAmW 93*
Shelden, Michael *ScF&FL 92*
Sheldija, Lazer *BioIn 17*
Sheldon, Alice *AmWomPl, ScF&FL 92*
Sheldon, Alice Hastings Bradley 1916-1987 *BioIn 17*
Sheldon, Barbara L. 1946- *St&PR 93*
Sheldon, Brooke Earle 1931- *WhoAm 92, WhoAmW 93*
Sheldon, Charles Harvey 1929- *WhoAm 92*
Sheldon, Charles M. 1857-1946 *BioIn 17, GayN*
Sheldon, Charlie *ScF&FL 92*
Sheldon, Clifford George 1942- *St&PR 93*
Sheldon, Connie Isabelle 1953- *St&PR 93*
Sheldon, Curtiss Samuel 1941- *St&PR 93*
Sheldon, David Frederick 1929- *WhoAm 92, WhoE 93*
Sheldon, Don 1921-1975 *BioIn 17*
Sheldon, Donald R. 1945- *St&PR 93*
Sheldon, Eleanor Harriet Bernert 1920- *WhoAm 92, WhoAmW 93*
Sheldon, Elizabeth Joyce 1955- *WhoAmW 93*
Sheldon, Eric 1930- *WhoAm 92, WhoE 93*
Sheldon, Frances Dorothy Gigante 1949- *WhoAmW 93*
Sheldon, Garrett Ward 1954- *ConAu 139*
Sheldon, Gary 1953- *WhoAm 92*
Sheldon, George F. *WhoAm 92*
Sheldon, George William, III 1957- *WhoE 93*
Sheldon, Ingrid Kristina 1945- *WhoAmW 93*
Sheldon, J. Michael 1951- *WhoE 93*
Sheldon, James *MiSFD 9*
Sheldon, John Arthur 1935- *St&PR 93*
Sheldon, John Mahlon 1937- *St&PR 93*
Sheldon, L. Philip, Jr. *WhoSSW 93*
Sheldon, Lita *ScF&FL 92*
Sheldon, Mary Abby Merriam 1864- *AmWomPl*
Sheldon, May *AmWomPl*
Sheldon, May French 1847-1936 *Expl 93*
Sheldon, Michael L. *Law&B 92*
Sheldon, Nancy Way 1944- *WhoWor 93*
Sheldon, Peter Spafford 1939- *WhoAm 92*
Sheldon, Raccoona 1916-1987 *BioIn 17*
Sheldon, Richard Jay 1935- *St&PR 93*
Sheldon, Richard Robert 1932- *WhoAm 92*
Sheldon, Robert Howard d1991 *BioIn 17*
Sheldon, Roy *ScF&FL 92*
Sheldon, Sidney 1917- *BioIn 17, MiSFD 9, ScF&FL 92, WhoAm 92, WhoWrEP 92*
Sheldon, Terry Edwin 1945- *WhoAm 92*
Sheldon, Thomas Donald 1920- *WhoAm 92, WhoWor 93*
Sheldon, Walter J. 1917-1979? *ScF&FL 92*
Sheldon, William Charles 1943- *WhoAm 92*
Sheldon, William D. 1915- *ScF&FL 92*
Sheldon, William Douglas 1941- *WhoIns 93*
Sheleski, Stanley John 1931- *WhoE 93, WhoWor 93*
Shelesnyak, Moses Chaim 1909- *WhoAm 92*
Shelet, Dawn Ardelle 1954- *WhoSSW 93*
Sheley, Donald R., Jr. 1942- *St&PR 93*
Sheley, Donald Ray, Jr. 1942- *WhoAm 92*
Sheley, Kathy Ann 1951- *WhoAmW 93, WhoSSW 93*
Shelfer, A. Gordon, Jr. 1943- *St&PR 93*
Shelger, James M. *Law&B 92*
Shelhamer, John H. 1947- *St&PR 93*
Shelhamer, Linda K. 1952- *St&PR 93*
Shelhamer, Lloyd 1923- *St&PR 93*
Shelkovich, Vladimir Michailovich 1949- *WhoWor 93*
Shelkrot, Elliot Louis 1943- *WhoAm 92*
Shell, A.J. 1949- *St&PR 93*
Shell, Art *BioIn 17, WhoAm 92*
Shell, Bernard Ray 1925- *WhoSSW 93*
Shell, Billy Joe 1925- *WhoAm 92*
Shell, Courtney *WhoWrEP 92*
Shell, Ellen Ruppel 1952- *ConAu 138*
Shell, Glenn Harmen 1943- *St&PR 93*
Shell, Karl 1938- *WhoAm 92*
Shell, Kayla Paige *Law&B 92*
Shell, Leslie G., III 1946- *St&PR 93*
Shell, Owen G. 1936- *St&PR 93*
Shell, Owen G., Jr. 1936- *WhoAm 92, WhoSSW 93*
Shell, Robert Edward Lee 1946- *WhoEmL 93, WhoSSW 93, WhoWor 93*
Shellenback, Frank Victor 1898-1969 *BiDAMSp 1989*
Shellenberger, Verna S. 1915- *WhoWrEP 92*
Sheller, John O. *Law&B 92*
Shelley, Adrian D. 1949- *St&PR 93*
Shelley, Carole Augusta 1939- *WhoAm 92, WhoAmW 93*

Shelley, Edward Herman, Jr. 1919- *WhoAm 92*
Shelley, Er *BioIn 17*
Shelley, Harry Rowe 1858-1947 *Baker 92*
Shelley, Jaime Augusto 1939- *DcMexL*
Shelley, James H. *Law&B 92*
Shelley, James LaMar 1915- *WhoAm 92*
Shelley, John Fletcher 1943- *WhoAm 92*
Shelley, Mary 1797-1851 *MagSWL [port]*
Shelley, Mary Wollstonecraft 1797-1851 *BioIn 17, DcLB 116 [port], ScF&FL 92*
Shelley, Mary Wollstonecraft Godwin 1797-1851 *WorLitC [port]*
Shelley, Noreen (Walker) 1920- *DcChlFi*
Shelley, Percy Bysshe 1792-1822 *BioIn 17, MagSWL [port], WorLitC [port]*
Shelley, Peter c. 1956- *See* Buzzcocks, The *ConMus 9*
Shelley, Richard M. *ScF&FL 92*
Shelley, Rick 1947- *ScF&FL 92*
Shelley, Sally Swing 1924- *WhoWor 93*
Shelley, Stefanie Lisa 1962- *WhoAmW 93*
Shelley, Steve c. 1953- *See* Sonic Youth *ConMus 9*
Shelley, Steven Marius 1920- *WhoWor 93*
Shelley, Sue H. 1954- *St&PR 93*
Shelley, Walter Brown 1917- *WhoAm 92*
Shellhase, Leslie John 1924- *WhoAm 92*
Shellhorn, Ruth Patricia 1909- *WhoAm 92*
Shellman, Claudette Louise 1952- *WhoAmW 93*
Shellman, Eddie J. 1956- *WhoAm 92*
Shellman, Jolene Lang *Law&B 92*
Shellnut, Thomas Cochran 1940- *St&PR 93*
Shellow, James Myers 1926- *WhoAm 92*
Shellow, Robert 1929- *WhoAm 92*
Shellstrom, Scott 1958- *BioIn 17*
Shelly, Adrienne *BioIn 17*
Shelly, Douglas P. 1961- *St&PR 93*
Shelly, James Harold 1932- *WhoSSW 93*
Shelly, Judith A(llen) 1944- *ConAu 38NR*
Shelly, Thomas J., Jr. *Law&B 92*
Shelly, Walter Myers 1933- *WhoSSW 93*
Shelnitz, Mark A. *Law&B 92*
Shelnutt, Eve B. 1941- *WhoWrEP 92*
Shelnutt, Robert Curtis 1928- *WhoSSW 93*
Shelow, David P. *Law&B 92*
Shelp, D.L. *St&PR 93*
Shelp, Ronald Kent 1941- *WhoAm 92*
Shelton, Ann Walker 1934- *WhoAmW 93*
Shelton, Anne B. 1957- *WhoAmW 93*
Shelton, Betty Clare 1940- *WhoSSW 93, WhoWor 93*
Shelton, Bonnie Lee *WhoE 93*
Shelton, Carl F. 1931- *St&PR 93*
Shelton, Catherine Elizabeth 1956- *WhoAmW 93*
Shelton, Charles B., III 1941- *St&PR 93*
Shelton, David Houston 1928- *St&PR 93*
Shelton, David Howard 1928- *WhoAm 92*
Shelton, Deborah Jackson 1942- *WhoSSW 93*
Shelton, Delbert A. 1944- *St&PR 93*
Shelton, Donald Charles 1933- *St&PR 93*
Shelton, Edward Norman, Jr. 1958- *WhoSSW 93*
Shelton, Gary Richard 1947- *WhoSSW 93*
Shelton, Gene 1942- *St&PR 93*
Shelton, George Hallett 1933- *St&PR 93*
Shelton, Grady 1928- *St&PR 93*
Shelton, Harry C. 1929- *St&PR 93*
Shelton, Huntly Elberto, III 1957- *WhoSSW 93*
Shelton, James Joseph 1916- *St&PR 93*
Shelton, Jammi M. 1947- *WhoAmW 93*
Shelton, Jerrell Wilson 1945- *St&PR 93*
Shelton, Jerry Lynn 1952- *St&PR 93*
Shelton, Julie A. *Law&B 92*
Shelton, Karen Wallach *Law&B 92*
Shelton, Karl Mason 1933- *WhoAm 92*
Shelton, Lucy *WhoAmW 93*
Shelton, Lucy (Alden) 1944- *Baker 92*
Shelton, Marilyn J. 1955- *WhoSSW 93*
Shelton, Mark Logan 1958- *WhoWrEP 92*
Shelton, Michael Leo 1947- *St&PR 93*
Shelton, Nancy Britton 1946- *WhoSSW 93*
Shelton, Nicolina (Nikki) *WhoWrEP 92*
Shelton, Paul G. 1950- *St&PR 93*
Shelton, R.G.J. *WhoScE 91-1*
Shelton, Reid Leroy 1924- *WhoAm 92*
Shelton, Reuben Anderson *Law&B 92*
Shelton, Richard 1933- *WhoWrEP 92*
Shelton, Richard Fottrell 1929- *WhoAm 92*
Shelton, Robert Neal 1948- *WhoAm 92*
Shelton, Robert Warren 1943- *WhoSSW 93, WhoWor 93*
Shelton, Ron 1945- *MiSFD 9*
Shelton, Ruth Gaines *AmWomPl*
Shelton, Sandra Idele 1954- *WhoAmW 93*
Shelton, Sandra Lee 1952- *WhoAmW 93*
Shelton, Sloane 1934- *WhoAm 92*
Shelton, Stephani *WhoAm 92*
Shelton, Stephen Eugene 1947- *St&PR 93*
Shelton, Susan Willey 1938- *WhoSSW 93*
Shelton, Thomas L. *Law&B 92*
Shelton, Timothy Edwin 1948- *St&PR 93*
Shelton, Turner Blair 1915- *WhoAm 92*
Shelton, Vern R. 1938- *WhoIns 93*
Shelton, Wayne Vernon 1932- *WhoAm 92*
Shelton, William M. 1937- *St&PR 93*
Shelton-Foy, Holly 1956- *WhoSSW 93*
Sheluck, William, Jr. 1940- *St&PR 93*
Shelvankar, Krishnaro S. *ScF&FL 92*
Shemancik, John Allen 1948- *St&PR 93*
Shembarger, Donald Eugene 1938- *St&PR 93*
Shemel, Sidney d1992 *NewYTBS 92*
Shemel, Sidney 1913-1992 *BioIn 17*
Shemely, Charles Louis 1938- *St&PR 93, WhoAm 92*
Shemenski, Kenneth L. 1945- *St&PR 93*
Shemer, Jack Evvard 1940- *WhoAm 92*
Shemilt, John Michael *WhoScE 91-1*
Shemin, Barry L. 1942- *St&PR 93, WhoAm 92*
Shemin, David 1911-1991 *BioIn 17*
Shemin, Margaretha (Hoeneveld) 1928- *DcAmChF 1960*
Shemirani, Jamal 1932- *WhoUN 92*
Shemitz, Sylvan R. 1925- *St&PR 93*
Shemo, John Palmer David 1948- *WhoSSW 93*
Shemo, Thomas E. 1950- *St&PR 93*
Shemorry, Corinne Joynes 1920- *WhoAmW 93*
Shemtob, Richard 1940- *St&PR 93*
Shemuel, Yehuda Even- 1886-1976 *BioIn 17*
Shemwell, Sylvia *SoulM*
Shen, Benjamin Shih-Ping 1931- *WhoAm 92*
Shen, Chang-Jiang 1933- *WhoWor 93*
Shen, Chi-Kuo 1948- *WhoUN 92*
Shen, Chia Theng 1913- *WhoAm 92, WhoWor 93*
Shen, Eugenie *Law&B 92*
Shen, Fuxing 1945- *WhoWor 93*
Shen, George Clement 1929- *WhoWor 93*
Shen, Guang Yu 1932- *WhoWor 93*
Shen, Jinchang 1925- *WhoWor 93*
Shen, Liang Chi 1939- *WhoAm 92*
Shen, Mason Ming-Sun 1945- *WhoWor 93*
Shen, Shan-Fu 1921- *WhoAm 92*
Shen, Shue Chu Xuechu 1938- *WhoWor 93*
Shen, Steve Yu-Liang 1946- *WhoE 93*
Shen, Theodore Ping 1945- *St&PR 93, WhoAm 92*
Shen, Tsung Ying 1924- *WhoAm 92*
Shen, Yi-Bing 1939- *WhoWor 93*
Shen, Yuan-Yuan 1954- *WhoE 93*
Shen, Yueh 441-513 *BioIn 17*
Shen, Yujin 1949- *WhoE 93*
Shen, Zuhe 1933- *WhoWor 93*
Shen, Zuo Rui 1944- *WhoWor 93*
Shenar, Paul 1936- *WhoAm 92*
Shen Daren 1928- *WhoAsAP 91*
Shendow, Harry S. 1933- *St&PR 93*
Shenefelt, Lloyd Harrison, III *Law&B 92*
Shenefelt, Philip David 1943- *WhoSSW 93*
Shenefield, John Hale 1939- *WhoAm 92*
Shenefield, Mary Peterson 1929- *WhoAmW 93*
Sheneman, Victoria Laverne 1949- *WhoAmW 93*
Sheneman, Wayne E. 1933- *St&PR 93*
Shenfield, Arthur A. 1909-1990 *BioIn 17*
Sheng, Bright 1955- *Baker 92*
Sheng, Caiwei 1943- *WhoWor 93*
Sheng, Jean F. *St&PR 93*
Sheng, Shu Yun 1934- *WhoWor 93*
Shengold, Leonard 1925- *ConAu 136*
Shenier, Henry L. 1902-1991 *BioIn 17*
Shenk, John C., Jr. 1926- *St&PR 93*
Shenk, John Christian, Jr. 1926- *WhoAm 92*
Shenk, Thomas Eugene 1947- *WhoAm 92*
Shenk, Wilbur, III 1941- *St&PR 93*
Shenk, Willis Weidman 1915- *St&PR 93, WhoAm 92*
Shenkarow, Barry *WhoAm 92*
Shenker, Lewis 1927-1991 *BioIn 17*
Shenker, Nina O. *Law&B 92*
Shenkin, Alan *WhoScE 91-1*
Shenkin, Henry Arnold 1915- *WhoE 93*
Shenkir, William Gary 1938- *WhoAm 92*
Shennan, James G. 1910- *St&PR 93*
Shennan, Margaret 1933- *ScF&FL 92*
Shennum, Robert Herman 1922- *WhoAm 92*
Shenon, Philip 1959- *ConAu 136*
Shenouda, Anba, III 1923- *WhoWor 93*
Shenouda, George Samaan 1943- *WhoE 93*
Shenoute c. 350-466 *OxDcByz*
Shenoy, Sudhakar Venkatraya 1947- *St&PR 93*
Shen Rong 1935- *BioIn 17*
Shenshin, Alexander 1890-1944 *Baker 92*
Shensky, Davida Ann 1951- *WhoSSW 93*
Shenstone, William 1714-1763 *BioIn 17*
Shen Tong *BioIn 17*
Shen Zulun 1931- *WhoAsAP 91*
Sheon, Aaron 1937- *WhoAm 92*
Shepard, A. Courtenay 1939-1991 *BioIn 17*
Shepard, Alan B., Jr. *BioIn 17*
Shepard, Alan Bartlett, Jr. 1923- *WhoAm 92, WhoWor 93*
Shepard, Allyn C. *Law&B 92*
Shepard, Andrew J. 1924- *St&PR 93*
Shepard, Anna Osler 1903-1973 *IntDcAn*
Shepard, Barry 1931- *St&PR 93*
Shepard, Charles Frank 1935- *St&PR 93*
Shepard, Charles Virgil 1940- *WhoSSW 93*
Shepard, Charles Wayne *St&PR 93*
Shepard, David *BioIn 17*
Shepard, Dean Warren 1930- *St&PR 93*
Shepard, Donald James 1946- *St&PR 93*
Shepard, Earl Alden 1932- *WhoWor 93*
Shepard, Ednah *AmWomPl*
Shepard, Elaine Elizabeth *WhoAm 92*
Shepard, Elizabeth Lee *AmWomPl*
Shepard, Ernest H(oward) 1879-1976 *ChlLR 27 [port]*
Shepard, Ernest Howard 1879-1976 *MajAI [port]*
Shepard, Francis B. 1940- *St&PR 93*
Shepard, Geoffrey C. *Law&B 92*
Shepard, Geoffrey C. 1944- *St&PR 93*
Shepard, Geoffrey Carroll 1944- *WhoAm 92*
Shepard, George Leo 1947- *WhoE 93, WhoWor 93*
Shepard, Gregory Mark 1955- *WhoIns 93*
Shepard, Ivan Albert 1925- *WhoWor 93*
Shepard, James Dudley 1938- *St&PR 93*
Shepard, James J. 1931- *WhoAm 92*
Shepard, Jan B. *Law&B 92*
Shepard, Janie Ray 1954- *WhoAmW 93, WhoSSW 93*
Shepard, Jeffrey A. 1950- *St&PR 93*
Shepard, Jim 1956- *ConAu 137*
Shepard, Jon Max 1939- *WhoAm 92*
Shepard, Juliet *Law&B 92*
Shepard, Leroy Grenville 1920- *St&PR 93*
Shepard, Leslie 1917- *ScF&FL 92*
Shepard, Lucius 1947- *ScF&FL 92*
Shepard, Mary *MajAI*
Shepard, Mikki Maureen Allison 1951- *WhoAmW 93*
Shepard, Nancy Eiges *Law&B 92*
Shepard, Paul Howe 1925- *WhoAm 92*
Shepard, Paul M., Jr. 1930- *St&PR 93*
Shepard, Peggy Ellen 1953- *WhoAmW 93*
Shepard, Randall Terry 1946- *WhoAm 92, WhoEmL 93*
Shepard, Richard *MiSFD 9*
Shepard, Robert M. 1932- *WhoAm 92*
Shepard, Roger Newland 1929- *WhoAm 92*
Shepard, Rosemary T. *Law&B 92*
Shepard, Sam 1943- *AmWrS3, BioIn 17, MagSAmL [port], MiSFD 9, WhoAm 92*
Shepard, Samuel E. 1931- *St&PR 93*
Shepard, Scott 1948- *WhoE 93*
Shepard, Stephen Benjamin 1939- *St&PR 93, WhoAm 92*
Shepard, Thomas 1605-1649 *BioIn 17*
Shepard, Thomas 1939- *WhoUN 92*
Shepard, Thomas Hill 1923- *WhoAm 92*
Shepard, Thomas Rockwell, Jr. 1918- *WhoAm 92*
Shepard, Thomas Rockwell, III 1951- *WhoAm 92*
Shepard, Tracy Morgan 1957- *WhoIns 93*
Shepard, William Seth 1935- *WhoAm 92*
Shepardson, Charles Noah 1896-1975 *BioIn 17*
Shepardson, Elizabeth Prentiss 1953- *WhoE 93*
Shepardson, John Upham 1920- *WhoE 93*
Shepardson, Lucille D. 1937- *St&PR 93*
Shepela, Glenda R. 1951- *WhoAmW 93*
Sheperd, Lemuel Cornick, Jr. 1896-1990 *HarEnMi*
Shephard, Bruce Dennis 1944- *WhoSSW 93, WhoWor 93*
Shephard, Esther *AmWomPl*
Shephard, Gillian 1940- *WhoWor 93*
Shephard, Jacqueline 1946- *St&PR 93*
Shepherd, Alan A. *WhoScE 91-1*
Shepherd, Alan J. 1942- *WhoAm 92*
Shepherd, Alice Grant 1949- *St&PR 93*
Shepherd, Arthur 1880-1958 *Baker 92*
Shepherd, Carl Lee 1952- *WhoAm 92*
Shepherd, Catherine 1915- *WhoWrEP 92*
Shepherd, Charles Clinton 1929- *WhoSSW 93*
Shepherd, Charles Edward 1920- *St&PR 93*
Shepherd, Charles L. 1928- *St&PR 93*
Shepherd, Christopher Hart 1952- *St&PR 93*
Shepherd, Clark W. 1933- *WhoIns 93*
Shepherd, Clayton A. 1929-1990 *BioIn 17*
Shepherd, Cybill *BioIn 17*
Shepherd, Cybill 1950?- *HolBB [port], WhoAm 92*
Shepherd, David 1931- *BioIn 17*
Shepherd, Donald Ray 1935- *WhoSSW 93*
Shepherd, Elizabeth Poole 1937- *WhoSSW 93*
Shepherd, Emilie Kay 1934- *WhoAmW 93*
Shepherd, Forest Cecil 1941- *St&PR 93*
Shepherd, Gary Gene 1940- *St&PR 93*
Shepherd, Gary Kevin 1957- *WhoWrEP 92*
Shepherd, George E., Jr. *Law&B 92*
Shepherd, Jack Edwin 1937- *WhoE 93*
Shepherd, James *WhoScE 91-1*
Shepherd, James Lloyd *Law&B 92*
Shepherd, Janet E. *BioIn 17*
Shepherd, John Barron 1933- *St&PR 93*
Shepherd, John Calvin 1925- *WhoAm 92, WhoWor 93*
Shepherd, John Thompson 1919- *WhoAm 92*
Shepherd, Judy Carlile *WhoWor 93*
Shepherd, Karen 1940- *WhoAmW 93*
Shepherd, Keith Leslie *WhoScE 91-1*
Shepherd, Lemuel C. 1896-1990 *BioIn 17*
Shepherd, LeRoy Bryan 1957- *WhoSSW 93*
Shepherd, Linda A. 1959- *WhoIns 93*
Shepherd, Mark, Jr. 1923- *St&PR 93, WhoAm 92*
Shepherd, Murray C. 1938- *WhoAm 92*
Shepherd, Oliver d1868 *BioIn 17*
Shepherd, Paula Virginia 1964- *WhoWor 93*
Shepherd, Penelope Elaine *Law&B 92*
Shepherd, R. Patrick *Law&B 92*
Shepherd, Richard *WhoScE 91-1*
Shepherd, Robert 1949- *ConAu 136*
Shepherd, Robert James 1930- *WhoAm 92*
Shepherd, Saundra D. d1992 *NewYTBS 92 [port]*
Shepherd, Saundra Dianne 1945- *WhoE 93*
Shepherd, Steven Stewart 1956- *WhoSSW 93*
Shepherd, Suzanne Moore 1952- *WhoEmL 93*
Shepherd, Willard Nelson 1957- *WhoSSW 93*
Shepherd, William C. 1939- *WhoAm 92*
Shepherd, William G. *Law&B 92*
Shepherd, William J. 1926- *WhoAm 92*
Shepherd, William Smythe 1916- *St&PR 93*
Shepherdson, David 1955- *WhoWor 93*
Shepherdson, J.C. *WhoScE 91-1*
Shepitko, Larissa *BioIn 17*
Shepler, Donald C. *Law&B 92*
Shepler, John Edward 1950- *WhoEmL 93*
Shepler, Robert O. 1923-1990 *BioIn 17*
Shepley, George A. 1922- *St&PR 93*
Shepley, Hugh 1928- *WhoAm 92*
Shepley, Lewis Baker 1939- *St&PR 93*
Shepley, Robert Gardiner 1953- *St&PR 93*
Shepp, Allan 1928- *WhoAm 92*
Shepp, Bryan Eugene 1932- *WhoAm 92*
Shepp, Lawrence Alan 1936- *WhoAm 92*
Sheppard, Albert Parker, Jr. 1936- *WhoAm 92*
Sheppard, Allen J. G. 1932- *WhoWor 93*
Sheppard, Andy *BioIn 17*
Sheppard, Bob *BioIn 17*
Sheppard, Brian L. 1940- *WhoScE 91-3*
Sheppard, Claude-Armand 1935- *WhoAm 92*
Sheppard, Don(ald D.) 1930- *ConAu 138*
Sheppard, Edward Richard 1934- *St&PR 93*
Sheppard, Frederick G. 1935- *St&PR 93*
Sheppard, Harry Whittaker d1992 *BioIn 17, NewYTBS 92*
Sheppard, Helen B. 1927- *WhoAmW 93*
Sheppard, Jack W. 1931- *WhoAm 92*
Sheppard, James C. 1936- *St&PR 93*
Sheppard, John c. 1515-c. 1559 *Baker 92*
Sheppard, John 1956- *MiSFD 9*
Sheppard, John Chester 1925- *St&PR 93*
Sheppard, John Gavin 1916- *St&PR 93*
Sheppard, John W., Jr. 1946- *St&PR 93*
Sheppard, Joseph Sherly 1930- *WhoE 93*
Sheppard, Juliet *WhoScE 91-1*
Sheppard, Lesley *WhoScE 91-1*
Sheppard, Lesley Margaret 1955- *WhoWor 93*
Sheppard, Louis Clarke 1933- *WhoAm 92, WhoSSW 93, WhoWor 93*
Sheppard, Lynne S. 1951- *St&PR 93*
Sheppard, Matthew 1951- *St&PR 93*
Sheppard, Michael Charles *WhoScE 91-1*
Sheppard, Mubin 1905- *IntDcAn*
Sheppard, Norman *WhoScE 91-1*
Sheppard, Posy 1916- *WhoAm 92, WhoE 93*
Sheppard, Robert Charles *WhoScE 91-1*
Sheppard, Ronald John 1939- *WhoE 93*
Sheppard, S.M.F. *WhoScE 91-2*

Sheppard, Sherri Yvonne 1949- *WhoE 93*
Sheppard, Thomas Frederick 1935- *WhoSSW 93*
Sheppard, Thomas J. 1947- *St&PR 93*
Sheppard, Thomas Richard 1934- *WhoAm 92*
Sheppard, Walter Lee, Jr. 1911- *WhoE 93*
Sheppard, Warren J., Jr. *Law&B 92*
Sheppard, William J. 1937- *St&PR 93*
Sheppard, William Stevens 1930- *WhoAm 92*
Sheppard, William Vernon 1941- *WhoWor 93*
Sheppard-Fidler, Alwyn 1909-1990 *BioIn 17*
Sheppard-Goerke, Carrol Sahodra 1947- *WhoE 93*
Shepperd, Frederick Metz 1954- *WhoWor 93*
Shepperson, Wilbur Stanley 1919- *WhoAm 92*
Sheps, Cecil George 1913- *WhoAm 92, WhoSSW 93*
Sheps, Cynthia *Law&B 92*
Sheptock, Lisa Ann 1964- *WhoAmW 93*
Sheptyts'kyi, Andrii 1865-1944 *BioIn 17*
Sher, Ada Elizabeth 1948- *WhoSSW 93*
Sher, Allan L. 1931- *WhoAm 92*
Sher, Harold T. 1927- *St&PR 93*
Sher, Jack 1913-1988 *MiSFD 9N*
Sher, Jaimes *Law&B 92*
Sher, JoAnn Giffuni 1942- *WhoAmW 93*
Sher, Joanna d1992 *NewYTBS 92*
Sher, Joanna Ruth Hollenberg 1933- *WhoAmW 93*
Sher, Linda Rosenberg 1938- *WhoAmW 93*
Sher, Michael Stephen 1941- *WhoE 93*
Sher, Patricia Ruth 1931- *WhoAmW 93*
Sher, Paul Phillip 1939- *WhoAm 92*
Sher, Steven J. 1949- *WhoWrEP 92*
Shera, Jesse Hauk 1903-1982 *BioIn 17*
Shera, Joyce Ann 1944- *WhoAmW 93, WhoWor 93*
Sherak, Thomas Mitchell 1945- *WhoAm 92*
Sher Ali Khan 1825-1879 *HarEnMi*
Sherar, J. William 1930- *WhoIns 93*
Sherar, Joseph William 1930- *WhoWor 93*
Sherard, Joel W. 1946- *St&PR 93*
Sherard, Robert Douglas 1922- *WhoSSW 93*
Sherard, Thomas Rodney 1951- *St&PR 93*
Sheras, Peter Loren 1948- *WhoSSW 93*
Sheraton, Mimi *BioIn 17*
Sherba, John 1954- *See* Kronos Quartet, The *News 93-1*
Sherbell, Rhoda *WhoAm 92, WhoAmW 93*
Sherber, Kenneth 1948- *St&PR 93*
Sherbet, Gaja *WhoScE 91-1*
Sherbin, John M., II 1949- *St&PR 93*
Sherbin, Robert Joel 1957- *WhoWor 93*
Sherblom, James Peter 1955- *St&PR 93*
Sherbon, John Walter 1933- *WhoE 93*
Sherbourne, Archibald Norbert 1929- *WhoAm 92*
Sherburn, James R. 1936- *St&PR 93*
Sherburne, Donald Wynne 1929- *WhoAm 92, WhoWrEP 92*
Sherburne, Mary Lela 1926- *WhoAmW 93*
Sherburne, Robert C. 1920- *St&PR 93*
Sherburne, Zoa (Morin) 1912- *ConAu 37NR, MajAI [port]*
Shere, Charles 1935- *Baker 92*
Shere, Dennis 1940- *WhoAm 92*
Sheredos, Carol Ann 1944- *WhoE 93*
Shereff, Harry 1913- *St&PR 93*
Sheremeta, Myroslaw Nikolayevich 1943- *WhoWor 93*
Sheremetev, Nikolay Petrovich *BioIn 17*
Sheremetiev, Alexander 1859-1931 *Baker 92*
Sherer, Billee Jean 1948- *WhoWrEP 92*
Sherer, Edward Frank *Law&B 92*
Sherer, Elaine Winifred 1947- *WhoAmW 93*
Sherer, Frank A., Jr. *Law&B 92*
Sherer, Joseph F. 1949- *St&PR 93*
Sherer, Ronald Brian *Law&B 92*
Sherer, Samuel Ayers 1944- *WhoE 93*
Shereshevsky, Mark Alexandrovich 1964- *WhoWor 93*
Sheretov, Vladimir Georgievich 1938- *WhoWor 93*
Sherf, Arden F. *BioIn 17*
Sherfey, Geraldine Richards 1929- *WhoAmW 93*
Sherfey, James Daniel 1934- *St&PR 93*
Shergold, Adrian *MiSFD 9*
Shergold, Craig *BioIn 17*
Shergold, Harold E. 1936- *St&PR 93*
Shergold, Harold Edward 1936- *WhoIns 93*
Sherick, Donald R. 1941- *St&PR 93*
Sherick, Jack Matthew 1941- *St&PR 93*
Sheridan, Albert Jackson 1924- *WhoSSW 93*
Sheridan, Andrew James, III 1944- *WhoSSW 93*
Sheridan, Ann 1915-1967 *IntDcF 2-3 [port], SweetSg D [port]*
Sheridan, Ann Louise 1940- *WhoE 93*
Sheridan, Charles Fitzgerald, Jr. 1928- *WhoE 93*
Sheridan, Charles Steve 1958- *WhoWrEP 92*
Sheridan, Christopher Francis *Law&B 92*
Sheridan, Christopher Frederick 1953- *WhoAm 92*
Sheridan, Daniel J. *Law&B 92*
Sheridan, David *BioIn 17*
Sheridan, David S. 1908- *St&PR 93*
Sheridan, Diane L. *Law&B 92*
Sheridan, Dixie M. 1943- *WhoE 93*
Sheridan, Donald Patrick 1947- *WhoWor 93*
Sheridan, Donna Richards 1946- *WhoAmW 93*
Sheridan, Doreen J. 1949- *WhoAm 92*
Sheridan, Edward Patrick 1937- *WhoSSW 93*
Sheridan, Elsie L. *ScF&FL 92*
Sheridan, Emma *AmWomPl*
Sheridan, Frances Chamberlaine 1724-1766 *BioIn 17*
Sheridan, Frank P. d1990 *BioIn 17*
Sheridan, Harriet W. d1992 *NewYTBS 92*
Sheridan, James Edward 1922- *WhoAm 92*
Sheridan, James Michael *Law&B 92*
Sheridan, James Michael 1940- *St&PR 93*
Sheridan, Jamey 1951- *ConTFT 10*
Sheridan, Jim 1949- *MiSFD 9*
Sheridan, Joan Ruth 1956- *WhoE 93*
Sheridan, John Bernard 1935- *WhoAm 92*
Sheridan, John Brian 1947- *WhoAm 92*
Sheridan, John F. 1852-1914 *BiDAMSp 1989*
Sheridan, John Philip *Law&B 92*
Sheridan, Joseph Francis 1960- *St&PR 93*
Sheridan, Kathleen Regis 1947- *WhoAmW 93*
Sheridan, Lee Arthur 1943- *St&PR 93*
Sheridan, Linda Mary 1953- *WhoAmW 93*
Sheridan, Margaret Burke 1889-1958 *BioIn 17*
Sheridan, Marion C. d1979 *BioIn 17*
Sheridan, Martin F. 1942- *St&PR 93*
Sheridan, Mary *BioIn 17*
Sheridan, Mary Elizabeth 1951- *WhoAmW 93*
Sheridan, Michael J. *Law&B 92*
Sheridan, Neil Wallace 1941- *WhoE 93*
Sheridan, Nicollette *BioIn 17*
Sheridan, Nicollette 1963- *ConTFT 10*
Sheridan, Patrick M. 1940- *St&PR 93*
Sheridan, Patrick Michael 1940- *WhoAm 92*
Sheridan, Paul Matthew 1950- *St&PR 93*
Sheridan, Peter B. d1992 *NewYTBS 92*
Sheridan, Philip Henry 1831-1888 *BioIn 17, CmdGen 1991 [port], HarEnMi*
Sheridan, Philp Henry 1950- *WhoAm 92*
Sheridan, R. Champlin 1930- *St&PR 93*
Sheridan, Richard Bert 1918- *WhoAm 92, WhoWor 93*
Sheridan, Richard Brinsley 1751-1816 *OxDcOp, WorLitC [port]*
Sheridan, Richard Brinsley Butler 1751-1816 *BioIn 17*
Sheridan, Richard J. *Law&B 92*
Sheridan, Richard Jonathan 1956- *WhoWor 93*
Sheridan, Sonia Landy 1925- *WhoAm 92*
Sheridan, Susan M. 1961- *WhoSSW 93*
Sheridan, Thomas *ScF&FL 92*
Sheridan, Thomas Brown 1929- *WhoAm 92*
Sheridan, Thomas Joseph 1960- *St&PR 93*
Sheridan, Thomas R. 1929-1990 *BioIn 17*
Sherif, Ahmed Mohamed 1958- *WhoWor 93*
Sherif, Carolyn W. 1922-1982 *BioIn 17*
Sherif, Mahmoud Mohamed 1930- *WhoUN 92*
Sherif, S. A. 1952- *WhoSSW 93*
Sheriff, Leonard S. 1915- *St&PR 93*
Sheriff, Leonard S. 1915-1991 *BioIn 17*
Sheriff, Linda Lepper 1954- *WhoAmW 93*
Sheriff, Matthew *BioIn 17*
Sheriff, Noam 1935- *Baker 92*
Sherifis, Michael Eleftheriou 1937- *WhoWor 93*
Sherin, Edwin 1930- *MiSFD 9, WhoAm 92*
Sherington, Geoffrey Edgar 1945- *WhoWor 93*
Sherkow, Judith Ann 1949- *WhoAmW 93*
Sherlock, David *BioIn 17*
Sherlock, Gary Fuller 1945- *WhoE 93*
Sherlock, Holly Lisabeth 1958- *WhoAmW 93*
Sherlock, Mary Eva 1958- *WhoAmW 93*
Sherlock, Michael J. 1937- *St&PR 93*
Sherlock, Patti *SmATA 71 [port]*
Sherlock, Peter Allen 1960- *St&PR 93*
Sherlock, Philip 1902- *BlkAull 92*
Sherman, Abraham 1918- *St&PR 93*
Sherman, Albert K., Jr. 1943- *St&PR 93*
Sherman, Arlene 1947- *WhoAmW 93*
Sherman, Arnold *St&PR 93*
Sherman, Arthur *MiSFD 9*
Sherman, Barbara D. *Law&B 92*
Sherman, Barry M. 1941- *St&PR 93*
Sherman, Bradford Sterling 1956- *WhoWor 93*
Sherman, Bruce H. 1949- *St&PR 93*
Sherman, Burton Stuart 1930- *WhoE 93*
Sherman, C.L. 1931- *St&PR 93*
Sherman, Charles Daniel, Jr. 1920- *WhoAm 92, WhoWor 93*
Sherman, Charles Donald 1929- *St&PR 93*
Sherman, Charles Edwin 1934- *WhoAm 92*
Sherman, Cindy *BioIn 17*
Sherman, Cindy 1954- *News 92 [port], -92-3 [port], WhoAm 92*
Sherman, Cordelia C. *ScF&FL 92*
Sherman, D. Terrell *Law&B 92*
Sherman, Dan 1950- *ScF&FL 92*
Sherman, David *Law&B 92*
Sherman, David 1952- *St&PR 93*
Sherman, Dean F. 1908-1991 *BioIn 17*
Sherman, Dean J. 1956- *St&PR 93*
Sherman, Delia 1951- *ScF&FL 92*
Sherman, Dick *ConTFT 10*
Sherman, Donald Roger 1930- *WhoAm 92*
Sherman, Edmund 1927- *ConAu 139*
Sherman, Edward Francis 1937- *WhoAm 92, WhoSSW 93*
Sherman, Elaine *WhoAmW 93*
Sherman, Elaine C. 1938- *WhoAm 92, WhoAmW 93*
Sherman, Ellen Burns 1867- *AmWomPl*
Sherman, Emilia d1992 *BioIn 17*
Sherman, Eugene Jay 1935- *WhoAm 92*
Sherman, Forrest Percival 1896-1951 *HarEnMi*
Sherman, Frances J. 1918- *St&PR 93*
Sherman, Francis 1871-1926 *BioIn 17*
Sherman, Frank H. 1916- *St&PR 93*
Sherman, Frank Lynn 1931- *St&PR 93*
Sherman, Fred 1932- *WhoAm 92*
Sherman, Frederick Carl 1888-1957 *HarEnMi*
Sherman, Fredrick T. *BioIn 17*
Sherman, Gary A. *MiSFD 9*
Sherman, Geoffrey Kimmett 1961- *WhoE 93*
Sherman, George 1908-1991 *BioIn 17, MiSFD 9N*
Sherman, George M. 1941- *St&PR 93*
Sherman, Gerald *Law&B 92*
Sherman, Gerald M. 1951- *St&PR 93*
Sherman, Gilbert 1906-1990 *BioIn 17*
Sherman, Gordon B. 1927-1987 *BioIn 17*
Sherman, Gordon Rae 1928- *WhoAm 92, WhoSSW 93*
Sherman, Harold M. 1898-1987 *ScF&FL 92*
Sherman, Harry W. 1930- *St&PR 93*
Sherman, Helen Hoyt *AmWomPl*
Sherman, Henry Thomas 1908- *WhoSSW 93*
Sherman, Howard J. *BioIn 17*
Sherman, Howard Jay 1931- *WhoAm 92*
Sherman, Irwin William 1933- *WhoAm 92*
Sherman, J. Walter 1917- *St&PR 93*
Sherman, Jack *See* Red Hot Chili Peppers, The *News 93-1*
Sherman, James D. d1896 *BioIn 17*
Sherman, James E. *Law&B 92*
Sherman, James Richard 1935- *WhoWrEP 92*
Sherman, James S. 1855-1912 *PolPar*
Sherman, Jeffrey S. *Law&B 92*
Sherman, Jerome Kalman 1925- *WhoSSW 93*
Sherman, Jerome Nathaniel 1936- *WhoSSW 93*
Sherman, Joe 1945- *ConAu 137, WhoWrEP 92*
Sherman, Joel Henry 1957- *ScF&FL 92*
Sherman, John 1823-1900 *PolPar*
Sherman, John Clinton 1916- *WhoAm 92*
Sherman, John F., III *Law&B 92*
Sherman, John Foord 1919- *WhoAm 92*
Sherman, Jonathan Marc *BioIn 17*
Sherman, Jory 1932- *ScF&FL 92*
Sherman, Joseph 1945- *WhoCanL 92*
Sherman, Josepha *ScF&FL 92*
Sherman, Kenneth 1950- *ConAu 40NR, WhoCanL 92*
Sherman, Larry Ray 1934- *WhoE 93*
Sherman, Lawrence M. 1940- *WhoAm 92*
Sherman, Lee M. 1947- *St&PR 93*
Sherman, Lorraine R. *Law&B 92*
Sherman, Louis Allen 1943- *WhoAm 92*
Sherman, Malcolm Lee 1931- *St&PR 93*
Sherman, Mark A. 1951- *St&PR 93*
Sherman, Mark T. *Law&B 92*
Sherman, Martin 1920- *WhoAm 92*
Sherman, Mary 1947- *WhoAmW 93*
Sherman, Mary Angus 1937- *WhoAmW 93*
Sherman, Max B. *Law&B 92*
Sherman, Max Ray 1935- *WhoAm 92*
Sherman, Michael H. 1935- *St&PR 93*
Sherman, Michael P. *Law&B 92*
Sherman, Michael Paul 1952- *WhoAm 92*
Sherman, Michael Stuart 1947- *WhoAm 92*
Sherman, Milton d1990 *BioIn 17*
Sherman, Nat d1990 *BioIn 17*
Sherman, Nate H. d1980 *BioIn 17*
Sherman, Neil E. 1942- *St&PR 93*
Sherman, Norman 1926- *Baker 92*
Sherman, Norman Mark 1948- *WhoAm 92*
Sherman, Patricia A. *Law&B 92*
Sherman, Pauline *Law&B 92*
Sherman, Peter M. 1952- *St&PR 93*
Sherman, Philip D. 1941- *St&PR 93*
Sherman, Philip Martin 1930- *WhoE 93*
Sherman, Richard *Law&B 92*
Sherman, Richard Beatty 1929- *WhoSSW 93*
Sherman, Richard M. 1928- *ConTFT 10*
Sherman, Richard M., Jr. *Law&B 92*
Sherman, Richard Max 1940- *St&PR 93*
Sherman, Richard W. *Law&B 92*
Sherman, Robert A. 1942- *St&PR 93, WhoAm 92*
Sherman, Robert B. 1925- *ConTFT 10*
Sherman, Robert Bernard 1925- *WhoAm 92*
Sherman, Robert Irving 1923- *St&PR 93*
Sherman, Robert Martin 1949- *WhoE 93*
Sherman, Robert Stuart 1939- *WhoSSW 93*
Sherman, Robert T. 1937- *WhoWrEP 92*
Sherman, Roger 1930- *WhoAm 92*
Sherman, Roger E. 1934- *St&PR 93*
Sherman, Roger Talbot 1923- *WhoAm 92*
Sherman, Russell 1930- *Baker 92*
Sherman, Ruth April 1921- *WhoAmW 93*
Sherman, Ruth Cohen d1992 *BioIn 17*
Sherman, Ruth Tenzer 1920- *WhoE 93*
Sherman, Saul Lawrence 1926- *WhoAm 92*
Sherman, Saul S. 1917- *WhoAm 92*
Sherman, Scott 1954- *St&PR 93*
Sherman, Sherrill A. *Law&B 92*
Sherman, Signe Lidfeldt 1913- *WhoAmW 93, WhoWor 93*
Sherman, Steve Barry 1938- *WhoWrEP 92*
Sherman, Steven Lloyd 1947- *WhoE 93*
Sherman, Steven M. *Law&B 92*
Sherman, Stratford Pressley 1952- *WhoE 93*
Sherman, Stuart S. *Law&B 92*
Sherman, Suzette 1954- *WhoAm 92*
Sherman, Sylvia *AmWomPl*
Sherman, T.J. 1906- *St&PR 93*
Sherman, Theodore I. 1926- *St&PR 93*
Sherman, Thomas d1991 *BioIn 17*
Sherman, Thomas Brooks 1950- *WhoE 93*
Sherman, Thomas White 1940- *St&PR 93*
Sherman, Vincent 1906- *MiSFD 9*
Sherman, William Courtney 1923- *WhoAm 92*
Sherman, William David 1940- *WhoWrEP 92*
Sherman, William Delano 1942- *WhoAm 92*
Sherman, William Francis *WhoScE 91-1*
Sherman, William T. 1820-1891 *BioIn 17*
Sherman, William Tecumseh 1820-1891 *CmdGen 1991 [port], HarEnMi*
Sherman, Zachary 1922- *WhoE 93*
Sherman-Appel, Lori Rae 1955- *WhoAmW 93*
Sherman-Bircher, Ruth Faye 1956- *WhoSSW 93*
Shermoen, Richard Eugene 1930- *WhoAm 92*
Shern, Stephanie Marie 1948- *WhoAmW 93*
Sherner, Stephen D. 1950- *St&PR 93*
Shero, Fred 1925-1990 *BioIn 17*
Shero, John Paul, Jr. 1929- *WhoSSW 93*
Sheron, H. *WhoScE 91-1*
Sheronas, Victor F., Jr. 1941- *St&PR 93*
Sherouse, Deborah Lynn 1955- *WhoAmW 93, WhoSSW 93*
Sherowski, Henry John 1942- *St&PR 93*
Sherr, Paul E. 1933- *St&PR 93, WhoAm 92*
Sherraden, Michael (Wayne) 1948- *ConAu 137*
Sherrard, William Allen 1942- *WhoSSW 93*
Sherratt, David John *WhoScE 91-1*

Sherratt, Gerald Robert 1931- WhoAm 92, WhoWor 93
Sherred, T.L. 1915-1985 ScF&FL 92
Sherrell, Carl 1929-1990 ScF&FL 92
Sherren, Anne Terry 1936- WhoAmW 93, WhoWor 93
Sherrer, Charles David 1935- WhoAm 92
Sherrer, James Wylie 1935- St&PR 93
Sherrerd, John J.F. 1930- St&PR 93
Sherrick, Carl Edwin 1924- WhoE 93
Sherrick, Daniel N. 1929- St&PR 93
Sherrick, Daniel Noah 1929- WhoAm 92, WhoWor 93
Sherriff, David J. Law&B 92
Sherriffs, Ronald Everett 1934- WhoAm 92
Sherrill, Betty BioIn 17
Sherrill, Betty Pearson 1928- WhoAmW 93
Sherrill, Dorothy AmWomPl
Sherrill, Fred Lee, Jr. 1934- St&PR 93
Sherrill, H. Virgil 1920- WhoAm 92
Sherrill, Hugh Virgil 1920- St&PR 93
Sherrill, Jackie Wayne 1944- BiDAMSp 1989
Sherrill, Jeanette Rogers 1941- WhoAmW 93
Sherrill, Joseph H., Jr. 1941- St&PR 93
Sherrill, Joseph Newton, Jr. 1929- St&PR 93
Sherrill, Richard C. 1938- St&PR 93
Sherrill, Sabrina Rawlinson 1957- WhoAmW 93, WhoSSW 93
Sherrill, Stephen BioIn 17
Sherrill, Thomas B. 1930- St&PR 93
Sherrill, Thomas Boykin, III 1930- WhoAm 92, WhoWor 93
Sherrill, William Wayne 1926- BioIn 17
Sherringham, Philip R. St&PR 93
Sherrington, D. WhoScE 91-1
Sherrington, David 1941- WhoWor 93
Sherrington, David Colin WhoScE 91-1
Sherrington, Helen Baker 92
Sherrington, Paul William 1949- WhoSSW 93
Sherritt, George M. 1927- WhoIns 93
Sherrod, Anthony BioIn 17
Sherrod, Lonnie Ray 1950- WhoE 93
Sherrod, Robert Lee 1909- BioIn 17, WhoAm 92
Sherron, Walter Frederick 1931- St&PR 93
Sherry, Edna AmWomPl
Sherry, Fred (Richard) 1948- Baker 92
Sherry, George L. 1924- WhoUN 92
Sherry, George Leon 1924- WhoAm 92
Sherry, James Terence 1946- WhoWrEP 92
Sherry, John E(rnest) H(orwath) 1932- ConAu 37NR
Sherry, John Ernest Horwath 1932- WhoAm 92
Sherry, John P. Law&B 92
Sherry, John Sebastian 1946- WhoEmL 93
Sherry, Laura Case AmWomPl
Sherry, Lee 1948- WhoSSW 93
Sherry, Owen Edward 1918- St&PR 93
Sherry, Patrick 1938- ConAu 138
Sherry, Paul Henry 1933- WhoAm 92
Sherry, Richard James 1949- WhoSSW 93
Sherry, Sol 1916- WhoE 93
Sherry, Vincent B(ernard), Jr. 1948- ConAu 39NR
Sher Shah c. 1472-1545 HarEnMi
Shershin, Carmen Baytan 1944- WhoSSW 93
Shertukde, Hemchandra Madhusudan 1953- WhoE 93
Shertzer, Bruce Eldon 1928- WhoAm 92
Sherva, Dennis G. 1942- WhoAm 92
Shervheim, Lloyd Oliver 1928- WhoAm 92
Sherwan, Roy Glenn 1930- WhoWor 93
Sherwat, Harlan Law&B 92
Sherwin, Chalmers William 1916- WhoAm 92
Sherwin, George Rhodes 1941- St&PR 93
Sherwin, James Leland 1950- WhoWrEP 92
Sherwin, James Terry 1933- WhoAm 92
Sherwin, John Martin 1929- WhoE 93
Sherwin, Jonathan S. 1951- St&PR 93
Sherwin, Judith Johnson WhoWrEP 92
Sherwin, Lanny 1950- WhoWrEP 92
Sherwin, Marie-Louise Schoelly 1915-1991 BioIn 17
Sherwin, Michael Dennis 1939- WhoAm 92
Sherwin, Richard Joseph 1943- WhoAm 92
Sherwin, Richard P. 1948- St&PR 93
Sherwin, Richard Paul 1948- WhoAm 92
Sherwin, William F(isk) 1826-1888 Baker 92
Sherwood, Aaron Wiley 1915- WhoAm 92
Sherwood, Allen Joseph 1909- WhoAm 92
Sherwood, Annie AmWomPl
Sherwood, Arthur Lawrence 1943- WhoAm 92
Sherwood, Arthur Morley 1939- WhoAm 92
Sherwood, Bette Wilson 1920- WhoAm 92, WhoWor 93
Sherwood, Brent 1958- WhoSSW 93
Sherwood, Carrie Potter AmWomPl
Sherwood, David William 1943- WhoIns 93
Sherwood, Deborah ScF&FL 92
Sherwood, Dolly ConAu 138
Sherwood, Don Hugh 1935- WhoAm 92
Sherwood, Edward Charles 1941- WhoSSW 93
Sherwood, Evelyn Ruth 1929- WhoWrEP 92
Sherwood, George Kenneth 1939- St&PR 93
Sherwood, George R. 1939- St&PR 93
Sherwood, Hollace BioIn 17
Sherwood, Ila BioIn 17
Sherwood, James Blair 1933- St&PR 93, WhoAm 92
Sherwood, James Webster, III 1936- WhoE 93
Sherwood, John Neil WhoScE 91-1
Sherwood, Josephine AmWomPl
Sherwood, Keith R. 1944- St&PR 93
Sherwood, Kelly S. Law&B 92
Sherwood, Kenneth Parker, Jr. 1945- WhoE 93
Sherwood, Kenneth Wesley 1943- WhoSSW 93
Sherwood, Lawrence B. 1945- St&PR 93
Sherwood, Lillian Anna 1928- WhoAmW 93
Sherwood, Louis 1941- WhoAm 92
Sherwood, Louis Maier 1937- WhoAm 92, WhoE 93
Sherwood, Malcolm Harvey, Jr. 1930- St&PR 93
Sherwood, Margaret Pollock 1864-1955 AmWomPl
Sherwood, Martin 1942- ScF&FL 92
Sherwood, Mary Pasco 1906- WhoE 93
Sherwood, Pat BioIn 17
Sherwood, Peter W. Law&B 92
Sherwood, Rhonda Griffin 1953- WhoSSW 93
Sherwood, Richard Edwin 1928- WhoAm 92
Sherwood, Sam C., Jr. 1923- St&PR 93
Sherwood, Thomas WhoScE 91-1
Sherwood, Thomas Anderson 1942- St&PR 93
Sherwood, Thorne 1910- WhoAm 92
Sherwood, Tina Lou Law&B 92
Sherwood, William Bradley 1946- WhoE 93
Sherwood, William Hall 1854-1911 Baker 92
Sherzer, William Martin 1946- WhoE 93
Shesol, Jeff BioIn 17
Shestack, Alan 1938- WhoAm 92, WhoE 93, WhoWor 93
Shestack, Jerome Joseph 1925- WhoAm 92, WhoWor 93
Shestack, Melvin Bernard 1931- WhoAm 92, WhoWrEP 92
Shestakov, Ivan Pavlovich 1947- WhoWor 93
Shestokas, David John Law&B 92
Shestokas, Jill Barbara 1955- WhoEmL 93
Sheth, Jagdish Nanchand 1938- WhoAm 92
Sheth, Nila Amarish 1946- WhoE 93
Shetler, H.L. 1932- St&PR 93
Shetterly, Emma ScF&FL 92
Shetterly, Robert Browne 1915- WhoAm 92
Shetterly, Will 1955- ScF&FL 92
Shetterly, William Howard 1955- WhoWrEP 92
Shettle, Andrea ScF&FL 92
Shettles, Landrum Brewer 1909- WhoAm 92
Shetty, Ashok Kolkebail 1945- WhoE 93
Shetty, Kalidas 1959- WhoWor 93
Shetty, Mulki Radhakrishna 1940- WhoWor 93
Shetty, Romita 1966- St&PR 93
Sheumg, Chou Sui St&PR 93
Shevach, Ethan Menahem 1943- WhoE 93
Shevack, Brett BioIn 17
Shevardnadze, Eduard BioIn 17
Shevardnadze, Eduard Amvrosiyevich 1928- ColdWar 2 [port], WhoWor 93
Shevchuck, Harry 1924- WhoE 93
Shevel, W. Lee 1932- St&PR 93
Shevel, Wilbert Lee 1932- WhoAm 92
Shevin, David A. 1951- WhoWrEP 92
Shevin, Kenneth Ira 1935- WhoSSW 93
Shevin, Robert Lewis 1934- WhoAm 92
Shevitz, Mark H. 1955- WhoWor 93
Shevlin, Robert A. 1960- St&PR 93
Shevoroshkin, Vitaly 1932- WhoAm 92
Shew, Louis Glen 1932- St&PR 93
Shew, Sherman Law&B 92
Shewan, David Alexander WhoWor 93
Shewchuk, Robert John 1950- WhoE 93
Shewmake, C.B. 1916- St&PR 93
Shewmake, Donna Griffith Law&B 92
Shewmaker, Jack Clifford 1938- WhoAm 92
Shewmaker, John R. Law&B 92
Shewry, Peter Robert WhoScE 91-1
Sheyka, Robert Felix Law&B 92
Shi, Ding-Hua 1941- WhoWor 93
Shi, Guangchang 1936- WhoUN 92
Shi, Guoliang 1938- WhoWor 93
Shi, Jian-Yi 1948- WhoWor 93
Shi, Jiuxi 1929- WhoWor 93
Shi, Ning-Zhong 1950- WhoWor 93
Shi, Richard Hui 1963- WhoAm 92
Shi, Wujie 1943- WhoWor 93
Shi, Ying Guang 1942- WhoWor 93
Shi, Yong Bing 1947- WhoWor 93
Shiach, Allan G. 1941- ConAu 136
Shiao, Yee-foo 1907- BioIn 17
Shiau, H. Lin Law&B 92
Shiaw, Emma 1954- WhoE 93
Shiba, Junji 1948- WhoWor 93
Shibasaki, Sosuke 1916- WhoWor 93
Shibata, Akikazu 1935- WhoWor 93
Shibata, Eileen Aiko Law&B 92
Shibata, Hirofumi 1929- WhoWor 93
Shibata, Katsuie 1522-1583 HarEnMi
Shibata, Minao 1916- Baker 92, WhoWor 93
Shibata, Shoji 1915- WhoWor 93
Shibata, Susumu 1942- WhoWor 93
Shibata, Takumi 1953- WhoWor 93
Shibayama, Mitsuhiro 1954- WhoWor 93
Shibayama, Yahachi 1850-1924 HarEnMi
Shibib, M. Ayman 1953- WhoE 93
Shibley, Raymond Nadeem 1925- WhoAm 92
Shibley, Robert Gordon 1946- WhoAm 92
Shibukawa, Masami 1953- WhoWor 93
Shibusawa, Rikyu 1928- WhoAsAP 91
Shibutani, Osamu 1950- WhoAsAP 91
Shibuya, Hironobu 1946- WhoAm 92
Shibuya, Naoaki 1941- St&PR 93
Shick, Bradley Ullin 1956- WhoE 93
Shick, Daniel S. Law&B 92
Shick, Eloise K. 1950- WhoWrEP 92
Shickle, Richard Charles 1951- WhoSSW 93
Shicoff, Neil 1949- Baker 92
Shi Dazhen 1932- WhoAsAP 91
Shidehara, Francesco Eichi 1935- WhoWor 93
Shideler, Howard H. 1932- St&PR 93
Shideler, Ross Patrick 1936- WhoAm 92, WhoWrEP 92
Shideler, Shirley Ann Williams 1930- WhoAm 92
Shidrawi, George Romanos 1932- WhoUN 92
Shieh, Francis 1926- WhoE 93
Shieh, John Shunen 1946- WhoWor 93
Shieh, John Ting-chung 1935- WhoAm 92
Shieh, Samuel BioIn 17
Shieh, Yang Taur 1953- WhoE 93
Shiel, M. P. 1865-1947 ScF&FL 92
Shiel, Thomas William 1941- WhoE 93
Shiel, William A. 1950- St&PR 93
Shield, Richard Thorpe 1929- WhoAm 92
Shield, William 1748-1829 Baker 92, OxDcOp
Shields, Allan Edwin 1919- WhoAm 92
Shields, Allen L. 1927-1989 BioIn 17
Shields, Barbara Maria 1945- WhoE 93
Shields, Brooke BioIn 17
Shields, Brooke Christa Camille 1965- WhoAm 92
Shields, Bruce Maclean 1922- WhoE 93
Shields, Carol 1935- WhoCanL 92
Shields, Carolyn Mercer 1965- WhoAmW 93
Shields, Charles H. St&PR 93
Shields, Cynthia Rose 1954- WhoAmW 93
Shields, Dale BioIn 17
Shields, David J. 1956- WhoWrEP 92
Shields, Evelyn 1938- WhoAmW 93
Shields, Frank MiSFD 9
Shields, George W. 1951- WhoSSW 93
Shields, Gerald N. 1937- St&PR 93
Shields, Gregory Alan 1946- WhoAm 92
Shields, H. Richard WhoAm 92
Shields, Hattiebell AmWomPl
Shields, Ivine AmWomPl
Shields, J. Hugh St&PR 93
Shields, James Joseph, Jr. 1935- WhoE 93
Shields, James P. 1947- St&PR 93
Shields, Jean Harder Ryan d1991 BioIn 17
Shields, Jeffrey Patrick 1951- St&PR 93
Shields, Jerry Allen 1937- WhoAm 92, WhoWor 93
Shields, Jill BioIn 17
Shields, John A. 1943- St&PR 93
Shields, John Joseph 1938- St&PR 93
Shields, Laurene AmWomPl
Shields, Lawrence Thornton 1935- WhoAm 92, WhoE 93, WhoWor 93
Shields, Louis P. 1943- St&PR 93
Shields, Margaret WhoUN 92
Shields, Margaret 1941- WhoAsAP 91
Shields, Margaret Agnes 1946- WhoAmW 93
Shields, Martin T. d1991 BioIn 17
Shields, Patricia Lynn WhoE 93
Shields, Paul Keith 1949- WhoSSW 93
Shields, Paula Blair 1950- WhoAmW 93
Shields, Perry 1925- CngDr 91
Shields, Randy Joe 1953- WhoE 93
Shields, Richard Lee 1955- WhoSSW 93
Shields, Robert WhoScE 91-1
Shields, Robert 1930- WhoWor 93
Shields, Robert Emmet 1942- WhoAm 92
Shields, Robert Francis 1923- WhoWor 93
Shields, Robert H. d1991 BioIn 17
Shields, Robert M., Jr. 1938- St&PR 93
Shields, Robert Michael 1952- WhoE 93
Shields, Roy B. 1931- St&PR 93
Shields, Tamara West-O'Kelley 1948- WhoAmW 93
Shields, Thomas Charles 1941- WhoAm 92
Shields, Thomas E. 1931- St&PR 93
Shields, Thomas Ford 1930- WhoE 93
Shields, Thomas M. Law&B 92
Shields, Thomas Todhunter 1873-1955 BioIn 17
Shields, Thomas William 1922- WhoAm 92
Shields, Walter W. 1935- WhoWor 93
Shields, William A., III 1948- WhoAm 92
Shields, William M. 1937- St&PR 93
Shields, William Walker, III Law&B 92
Shiell, John A. 1919- St&PR 93
Shiels, Robert John 1927- St&PR 93
Shiely, John Stephen Law&B 92
Shiely, John Stephen 1952- WhoAm 92
Shiely, Joseph Leo, III 1941- St&PR 93
Shientag, Florence Perlow WhoAm 92, WhoWor 93
Shier, David G. 1940- St&PR 93
Shier, John Wellington 1923- St&PR 93
Shier, Jonathan Fraser 1947- WhoWor 93
Shier, Milton 1917- St&PR 93
Shierry, Robert Stephen 1932- St&PR 93
Shiff, Alan Howard William 1934- WhoAm 92
Shiff, Murray J. d1991 BioIn 17
Shiffer, James David 1938- St&PR 93, WhoAm 92
Shiffman, Bernard 1942- WhoAm 92
Shiflet, Donald L. 1947- St&PR 93
Shiflett, Pendleton M., III 1946- WhoIns 93
Shifley, Ralph Louis 1910- WhoAm 92, WhoWor 93
Shi Fong 1942- WhoAm 92
Shifrin, Kenneth Steven 1949- St&PR 93
Shifrin, Seymour 1926-1979 Baker 92
Shiga, Kazuo 1925- WhoAsAP 91
Shiga, Setsu 1933- WhoAsAP 91
Shiga, Takeshi 1931- WhoWor 93
Shigemoto, Takashi 1945- WhoWor 93
Shigemura, Rose Kamuri St&PR 93
Shigemura, Thomas S. St&PR 93
Shigenaka, Yoshinobu 1932- WhoWor 93
Shigeru, Mori 1937- St&PR 93
Shigeru, Takagi 1956- WhoWor 93
Shigesada, Nanako 1941- WhoWor 93
Shigley, Klaus O. 1945- St&PR 93
Shih, Benedict Chesang 1935- WhoWor 93
Shih, Chi-Yang 1935- WhoWor 93
Shih, Chiang 1956- WhoSSW 93
Shih, Dawei 1964- WhoWor 93
Shih, Helen 1953- WhoAmW 93
Shih, J. Chung-wen WhoAm 92
Shih, Jason Cheng 1942- WhoAm 92
Shih, Joan Chung-Wen 1948- WhoWrEP 92
Shih, Lucy 1957- WhoAmW 93
Shih, Marie 1959- WhoAmW 93
Shih, Symong 1950- WhoSSW 93
Shih, Vivian Ean 1934- WhoAmW 93
Shihada, Hani BioIn 17
Shihadeh, Christine Law&B 92
Shihadeh, Steve 1954- WhoE 93
Shihata, Ibrahim Fahmy Ibrahim 1937- WhoAm 92, WhoUN 92
Shih Carducci, Joan Chia-mo 1933- WhoAmW 93, WhoE 93, WhoWor 93
Shih Chi-Yang WhoAsAP 91
Shih Huang-Ti 259BC-210BC HarEnMi
Shih K'o-fa d1645 HarEnMi
Shih-Sen Chang, Shi-Sheng Zhang 1935- WhoWor 93
Shih Ta-k'ai 1821-1863 HarEnMi
Shikama, Tatsuo 1949- WhoWor 93
Shikanai, Nobutaka 1911-1990 BioIn 17
Shikanai, Rhonda BioIn 17
Shikarkhane, Naren Shriram 1954- WhoWor 93
Shikata, Jun-ichi 1926- WhoWor 93
Shikatani, Gerry 1950- WhoCanL 92

Shike, John Wesley 1955- *St&PR 93*
Shikes, Ralph E. 1912-1992 *BioIn 17, ConAu 137, NewYTBS 92*
Shikibu, Murasaki 978?- *BioIn 17*
Shikiko, Saitoh 1944- *WhoWor 93*
Shikler, Aaron 1922- *BioIn 17, WhoAm 92*
Shikuma, Eugene Yujin 1948- *WhoWor 93*
Shi-Kuo, Chang *ScF&FL 92*
Shiland, William, Jr. *Law&B 92*
Shildneck, Barbara Jean 1937- *WhoAm 92, WhoAmW 93, WhoE 93*
Shilepsky, Arnold Charles 1944- *WhoE 93*
Shilepsky, Carol Carter 1943- *WhoAmW 93*
Shilhavy, Jack C. *Law&B 92*
Shilkoff, Marilyn Leader 1932- *WhoAmW 93, WhoE 93*
Shilkret, Nat(haniel) 1895-1982 *Baker 92*
Shill, Todd Jeffrey 1967- *WhoE 93*
Shilladey, Ann 1933- *WhoAmW 93*
Shiller, Ed *BioIn 17*
Shiller, Robert J. 1946- *ConAu 136*
Shillestad, John G. 1934- *St&PR 93, WhoIns 93*
Shillestad, John Gardner 1934- *WhoAm 92*
Shilling, A. Gary 1937- *WhoAm 92*
Shilling, J.W. 1943- *St&PR 93*
Shilling, Kay Marlene 1953- *WhoEmL 93*
Shilling, Marion 1914- *SweetSg C [port]*
Shilling, Roy Bryant, Jr. 1931- *WhoAm 92*
Shillingburg, Herbert Thompson, Jr. 1938- *WhoWor 93*
Shillinger, Michael J. 1948- *St&PR 93*
Shillingford, Peter *MiSFD 9*
Shillinglaw, Fawn *BioIn 17*
Shillinglaw, Gordon 1925- *WhoAm 92*
Shillinglaw, Thomas L. *Law&B 92*
Shillingsburg, Miriam Jones 1943- *WhoAmW 93*
Shillingsburg, Peter L(eRoy) 1943- *ConAu 139*
Shillito, Barry James 1921- *St&PR 93*
Shillito, D.E. *WhoScE 91-1*
Shillitoe, Edward John 1947- *WhoSSW 93*
Shiloah, Amnon 1928- *Baker 92*
Shiloh, Allen 1947- *WhoWor 93*
Shils, Barry *MiSFD 9*
Shils, Edward B. 1915- *WhoAm 92*
Shilstone, Sandra Sciacca 1956- *WhoEmL 93*
Shilton, Gilbert 1945- *MiSFD 9*
Shilts, Randy *BioIn 17*
Shim, Young Joon 1944- *WhoWor 93*
Shima, Amy *BioIn 17*
Shima, Etsuzo 1927- *WhoWor 93*
Shima, Hiromu 1929- *WhoWor 93*
Shima, Kensuke 1935- *WhoWor 93*
Shima, Mikiko 1929- *WhoWor 93*
Shimabuku, Norris M. d1991 *BioIn 17*
Shimabukuro, Richard K. *Law&B 92*
Shimada, Brent H. *Law&B 92*
Shimada, Hitomi 1946- *WhoWor 93*
Shimada, Kazuhito 1959- *WhoWor 93*
Shimada, Shigeru 1916- *WhoWor 93*
Shimada, Shigetaro 1883- *HarEnMi*
Shimada, Shinji 1952- *WhoWor 93*
Shimada, Toshio *BioIn 17*
Shimada, Toshiyuki 1951- *WhoAm 92*
Shimahara, Kenzo 1928- *WhoWor 93*
Shimamura, Kaoru 1930- *WhoWor 93*
Shimamura, Yoshinobu 1934- *WhoAsAP 91*
Shimansky, Richard Anthony 1959- *WhoE 93*
Shimanura, Hayao 1858-1923 *HarEnMi*
Shimaoka, Tatsuzo 1919- *BioIn 17*
Shimark, P.E. 1932- *St&PR 93*
Shimasaki, Lynn Mitsugi 1953- *St&PR 93*
Shimasaki, Yuzuru 1925- *WhoAsAP 91*
Shimazaki, Yasuhisa 1946- *WhoWor 93*
Shimazu, Ichiro 1921- *WhoWor 93*
Shimazu, Shogo 1955- *WhoWor 93*
Shimazu, Takashi 1948- *St&PR 93*
Shimazu, Yoshihiro 1535-1619 *HarEnMi*
Shimazu, Yoshihisa 1533-1611 *HarEnMi*
Shimbo, Masaki 1914- *WhoWor 93*
Shimbo, Osamu 1931- *WhoAm 92*
Shim Chung Ku 1933- *WhoAsAP 91*
Shimeall, Warren Glen 1925- *WhoWor 93*
Shimei, Barbara A. *Law&B 92*
Shimer, Alice Marie 1926- *WhoE 93*
Shimer, Brian *BioIn 17*
Shimer, Dale J. 1935- *St&PR 93*
Shimer, Daniel Lewis 1944- *WhoAm 92*
Shimer, Zachary 1933- *WhoAm 92*
Shimin, Symeon 1902- *MajAI [port]*
Shimin, Tonia 1942- *WhoAmW 93*
Shimizu, Akira 1933- *St&PR 93*
Shimizu, Bunshichi 1932- *WhoWor 93*
Shimizu, Isamu 1925- *WhoAsAP 91*
Shimizu, Kayoko 1935- *WhoAsAP 91*
Shimizu, Keiichi 1936- *WhoWor 93*
Shimizu, Osamu 1911- *Baker 92*
Shimizu, P.H. 1935- *St&PR 93*
Shimizu, Sumiko 1928- *WhoAsAP 91*
Shimizu, Taisuke 1936- *WhoAm 92*
Shimizu, Tatsuo 1936- *WhoWor 93*
Shimizu, Toyotaro 1927- *WhoWor 93*
Shimizu, Yoshiaki 1936- *WhoAm 92*
Shimkat, Lynne Levien 1948- *WhoAmW 93*
Shimkin, Demitri Boris 1916- *WhoAm 92*
Shimkin, Demitri Boris 1916-1992 *NewYTBS 92*
Shimkonis, Deborah Ann 1957- *WhoE 93*
Shimkos, P. Dan 1949- *St&PR 93*
Shimkus, Robert J. 1946- *St&PR 93*
Shimm, Melvin Gerald 1926- *WhoAm 92*
Shimmin, C. Gary 1945- *WhoIns 93*
Shim Myung-Bo 1928- *WhoAsAP 91*
Shi Mo *ConAu 139*
Shimohsa, Tadayoshi 1924- *WhoWor 93*
Shimoinaba, Kokichi 1926- *WhoAsAP 91*
Shimoji, Koki 1935- *WhoWor 93*
Shimojima, Hiroyuki *BioIn 17*
Shimojo, Shinichiro 1920- *WhoAsAP 91*
Shimomura, Yutaka 1922- *WhoAsAP 91*
Shimonaka, Yasaburo 1878-1961 *BioIn 17*
Shimose, Pedro 1940- *SpAmA*
Shimoyama, Hifumi 1930- *Baker 92*
Shimoyama, Masanori 1936- *WhoWor 93*
Shimp, Karen Ann 1959- *WhoAmW 93*
Shimp, Richard Lee 1942- *WhoWor 93*
Shimp, Robert Everett, Jr. 1942- *WhoAm 92*
Shimrak, Peter Eli 1932- *WhoAm 92*
Shimrat, Niusia d1990 *BioIn 17*
Shimura, Takashi 1905-1982 *IntDcF 2-3*
Shim Wan-Gu 1940- *WhoAsAP 91*
Shin 1926- *WhoAsAP 91*
Shin, Kee Bock 1935- *WhoUN 92*
Shin, Nelson *MiSFD 9*
Shin, Seok Hwan 1955- *WhoWor 93*
Shin, Sook Florence *Law&B 92*
Shin, Yoon Sook 1946- *WhoWor 93*
Shinabarger, Bruce Winter 1925- *St&PR 93*
Shinagel, Michael 1934- *WhoAm 92, WhoE 93*
Shinal, Frank A. 1940- *St&PR 93*
Shinano, Kozo 1910- *WhoWor 93*
Shinar, Eva Hanski 1946- *WhoAmW 93*
Shinawatra, Thaksin *BioIn 17*
Shindell, Sidney 1923- *WhoAm 92*
Shinderman, William 1914- *BioIn 17*
Shindler, Elaine Rosalie G. 1934- *WhoAm 92*
Shindler, George Rudolph 1935- *St&PR 93*
Shindler, Michael C. *Law&B 92*
Shindo, Akio 1926- *WhoWor 93*
Shindo, Eitaro 1899-1977 *IntDcF 2-3*
Shindo, Kaneto 1922- *MiSFD 9*
Shindo, Yasuhide 1949- *WhoWor 93*
Shine, Deborah 1932- *ScF&FL 92, SmATA 71*
Shine, George W. d1990 *BioIn 17*
Shine, John T. 1935- *St&PR 93*
Shine, Kenneth I. 1935- *WhoAm 92*
Shine, Kevin Z. 1955- *St&PR 93*
Shine, Mike *BioIn 17*
Shine, Neal James 1930- *WhoAm 92*
Shine, Richard 1950- *ConAu 139*
Shine, Robert John 1941- *WhoE 93*
Shine, William Morton 1912- *WhoE 93*
Shinefield, Henry Robert 1925- *WhoAm 92*
Shineman, Edward W., Jr. 1915- *St&PR 93*
Shineman, Edward William, Jr. 1915- *WhoAm 92*
Shiner, Farley C. 1956- *St&PR 93*
Shiner, John Stewart 1949- *WhoWor 93*
Shiner, Kenneth S. *Law&B 92*
Shiner, Lewis 1950- *ScF&FL 92*
Shiner, Ronald 1903-1966 *QDrFCA 92 [port]*
Shines, Johnny *BioIn 17*
Shines, Johnny d1992 *NewYTBS 92*
Shiney, Richard Delmar 1929- *St&PR 93*
Shinfuku, Naotaka 1942- *WhoUN 92*
Shingles, Godfrey Stephen 1939- *WhoAm 92*
Shingleton, Beverly A. 1936- *WhoAmW 93*
Shingleton, Hugh Maurice 1931- *WhoAm 92*
Shingleton, John D. *ConAu 37NR*
Shingo, Shigeo *BioIn 17*
Shingu, Yasuo 1926- *WhoWor 93*
Shin Ha Chul 1935- *WhoAsAP 91*
Shin Jae Ki 1934- *WhoAsAP 91*
Shin Jin Soo 1943- *WhoAsAP 91*
Shinker, William M. 1947- *St&PR 93*
Shin Ki Ha 1942- *WhoAsAP 91*
Shinkle, John Thomas *Law&B 92*
Shin Kyung Shik 1940- *WhoAsAP 91*
Shinmori, Tatsuo 1926- *WhoAsAP 91*
Shinmura, Katsuo 1918- *WhoAsAP 91*
Shinn, Allen Mayhew 1908- *WhoAm 92*
Shinn, Clinton Wesley 1947- *WhoAm 92, WhoEmL 93, WhoSSW 93, WhoWor 93*
Shinn, David Hamilton 1940- *WhoAm 92*
Shinn, Douglas Brian 1957- *St&PR 93*
Shinn, Duane 1938- *WhoWrEP 92*
Shinn, George *WhoAm 92*
Shinn, George L. 1923- *St&PR 93*
Shinn, George Latimer 1923- *WhoAm 92*
Shinn, Linda Jane 1948- *WhoAmW 93*
Shinn, Michael Robert 1947- *WhoEmL 93, WhoWor 93*
Shinn, Richard R. 1918- *St&PR 93*
Shinn, Richard Randolph 1918- *WhoAm 92*
Shinn, Roger L(incoln) 1917- *ConAu 40NR*
Shinn, Roger Lincoln 1917- *WhoE 93*
Shinn, Susa Jane 1940- *WhoAmW 93*
Shinn, Thelma J. 1942- *ScF&FL 92*
Shinn, William Townsley, Jr. 1936- *WhoAm 92, WhoWor 93*
Shinnar, Reuel 1923- *WhoAm 92*
Shinners, Edward M. 1930- *St&PR 93*
Shinners, Jeffrey G. 1941- *St&PR 93*
Shinners, Stanley Marvin 1933- *WhoAm 92, WhoWor 93*
Shinnock, John B. *Law&B 92*
Shinoda, Kozo 1926- *WhoWor 93*
Shinoda, Masahiro 1931- *MiSFD 9, WhoWor 93*
Shinoda, Sumio 1939- *WhoWor 93*
Shinofield, Richard E. *Law&B 92*
Shinohara, Kazumitsu 1938- *WhoWor 93*
Shinohara, Kazuo *BioIn 17*
Shinohara, Makota 1931- *Baker 92*
Shin Oh-Chul 1939- *WhoAsAP 91*
Shinotsuka, Eiko 1942- *WhoWor 93*
Shinozaki, Akihiko 1927- *St&PR 93*
Shinozaki, Toshiko 1918- *WhoAsAP 91*
Shinozuka, Masanobu 1930- *WhoAm 92*
Shinsaka, Kazuo 1939- *WhoAsAP 91*
Shin Sang Sik 1938- *WhoAsAP 91*
Shin Sang Woo 1937- *WhoAsAP 91*
Shinsato, Francis G. 1951- *St&PR 93*
Shin Soon Beom 1936- *WhoAsAP 91*
Shinstine, Drucella Gayle 1943- *WhoAmW 93*
Shinton, N.K. *WhoScE 91-1*
Shinwell, Emanuel 1884-1986 *DcTwHis*
Shin Young Soon, Dr. 1938- *WhoAsAP 91*
Shin Yung Kook 1944- *WhoAsAP 91*
Shioiri, Takayuki 1935- *WhoWor 93*
Shiokawa, Masajuro *WhoAsAP 91*
Shionoya, Ruy 1950- *WhoAsAP 91*
Shiota, Kunihiro 1937- *WhoWor 93*
Shiozaki, Jun 1917- *WhoAsAP 91*
Shiozaki, Masao 1941- *WhoWor 93*
Shiozawa, Koichi 1881-1943 *HarEnMi*
Shipanga, Andreas Zak 1931- *WhoAfr*
Shipe, Don 1933- *St&PR 93*
Shipe, Jerry Miller 1944- *St&PR 93*
Shipler, David Karr 1942- *WhoAm 92, WhoE 93, WhoWrEP 92*
Shiplett, June Elizabeth Lund 1930- *WhoWrEP 92*
Shipley, Alden Peverly 1946- *WhoSSW 93*
Shipley, Cheryl Lentz 1947- *WhoAmW 93*
Shipley, David Elliott 1950- *WhoAm 92, WhoSSW 93*
Shipley, Donald W. 1945- *St&PR 93*
Shipley, James E. *Law&B 92*
Shipley, Jenny *WhoAsAP 91*
Shipley, Karl L. 1953- *WhoE 93*
Shipley, Keith 1932- *St&PR 93*
Shipley, L. Parks 1905- *St&PR 93*
Shipley, L. Parks, Jr. 1931- *WhoAm 92*
Shipley, Linwood Parks 1905- *WhoAm 92*
Shipley, Lucia Helene 1920- *WhoAm 92*
Shipley, Lyman Charles 1934- *St&PR 93*
Shipley, Margaret Rebecca Foxwell 1947- *WhoSSW 93*
Shipley, Nancy Louise 1950- *WhoEmL 93*
Shipley, Reginald Alden 1905- *WhoE 93*
Shipley, Robert Hopkins 1945- *WhoWrEP 92*
Shipley, Samuel Lynn 1929- *WhoAm 92*
Shipley, Thomas A. 1945- *St&PR 93*
Shipley, Thomas E., Jr. 1924- *WhoWrEP 92*
Shipley, Vergil Alan 1922- *WhoAm 92*
Shipley, Walter Vincent 1935- *St&PR 93, WhoAm 92, WhoE 93*
Shipley, William S. 1956- *St&PR 93*
Shipman, Charles d1989 *BioIn 17*
Shipman, Charles William 1924- *WhoAm 92*
Shipman, David 1932- *ScF&FL 92*
Shipman, David Norval 1939- *WhoAm 92*
Shipman, Dede 1950- *St&PR 93*
Shipman, Derek James *WhoScE 91-1*
Shipman, J. Darrel 1948- *St&PR 93*
Shipman, Jack Hewitt 1937- *St&PR 93*
Shipman, Jeffrey Roger 1956- *WhoSSW 93*
Shipman, Nell 1892-1970 *SweetSg A [port]*
Shipman, Robert J. *Law&B 92*
Shipman, Robert Jack 1933- *St&PR 93, WhoIns 93*
Shipman, Ross Lovelace 1926- *WhoSSW 93*
Shipman, Stephanie Louise 1954- *WhoE 93*
Shipon, Marc Benjamin *Law&B 92*
Shipp, Barry Eugene 1937- *WhoAm 92*
Shipp, Jacquelyn Adams 1931- *WhoAmW 93*
Shipp, John Wesley *BioIn 17, ConTFT 10*
Shipp, Melvin Douglas 1948- *WhoSSW 93*
Shipp, Robert L. 1928- *St&PR 93*
Shipp, Roger Lee 1948- *St&PR 93, WhoAm 92*
Shippee, Eva Becker *AmWomPl*
Shippen, Elizabeth Blount *AmWomPl*
Shippey, Frederick Alexander 1908- *WhoWrEP 92*
Shippey, Juanita Waters 1946- *WhoWrEP 92*
Shippey, Sandra L. *Law&B 92*
Shippey, Sandra Lee 1957- *WhoEmL 93*
Shippey, T.A. 1943- *ScF&FL 92*
Shiprek, Joseph Edward 1933- *St&PR 93*
Shipton, Alyn *ScF&FL 92*
Shipton, Harold William 1920- *WhoAm 92*
Shipton, John David *WhoScE 91-1*
Shipton, Oran Frederick 1933- *St&PR 93*
Shipton, Roger Francis 1936- *WhoAsAP 91*
Shipula, Anthony James, II 1956- *WhoE 93*
Shipway, M.R. *WhoScE 91-1*
Shipwright, Adrian John 1950- *WhoWor 93*
Shira, Francesco 1808-1883 *Baker 92*
Shira, Gerald Dee, II 1933- *WhoE 93*
Shira, Robert Bruce 1910- *WhoAm 92*
Shirah, Gordon H., II *St&PR 93*
Shirahama, Kazuyoshi 1947- *WhoAsAP 91*
Shirai, Atsushi 1930- *WhoWor 93*
Shirai, Claude Ryo 1937- *St&PR 93*
Shirai, Kiyohide *BioIn 17*
Shirai, Yasuto 1961- *WhoWor 93*
Shirai, Yoshiaki 1941- *WhoWor 93*
Shiraiwa, Kenichi 1928- *WhoWor 93*
Shirakawa, Yoshinori 1868-1932 *HarEnMi*
Shiraki, Keizo 1936- *WhoWor 93*
Shiras, George, Jr. 1832-1924 *OxCSupC [port]*
Shiras, Leif *BioIn 17*
Shiras, Wilmar H. 1908-1990 *ScF&FL 92*
Shirawi, Yousuf Ahmed 1927- *WhoWor 93*
Shirbroun, Richard Elmer 1929- *WhoAm 92*
Shircliff, Robert T. 1928- *St&PR 93*
Shircliff, Wayne Joseph 1949- *St&PR 93*
Shire, David Lee 1937- *WhoAm 92*
Shire, Donald Thomas 1930- *St&PR 93, WhoAm 92*
Shire, Helena (Mary) Mennie 1912-1991 *ConAu 136*
Shire, John Gavin Mennie *WhoScE 91-1*
Shire, Talia Rose 1946- *WhoAm 92*
Shire, Tanya Lee 1951- *WhoAmW 93*
Shirek, John Richard 1926- *WhoSSW 93*
Shirel, Douglas L. 1958- *St&PR 93*
Shirelles *SoulM*
Shirer, William L. *BioIn 17*
Shirer, William Lawrence 1904- *JrnUS, WhoAm 92, WhoWrEP 92*
Shires, George Thomas 1925- *WhoAm 92, WhoWor 93*
Shirey, David 1932- *St&PR 93*
Shirey, Ronald O. 1940- *St&PR 93*
Shirilau, Mark Steven 1955- *WhoEmL 93*
Shirinsky, Sergei 1903-1974 *See* Shirinsky, Vasili (Petrovich) 1901-1965 *Baker 92*
Shirinsky, Vasili (Petrovich) 1901-1965 *Baker 92*
Shirk, Annadora Vesper 1918- *WhoAmW 93*
Shirk, Evelyn Urban 1918- *WhoAmW 93*
Shirk, Everett L. 1930- *St&PR 93*
Shirk, Paul David 1948- *WhoSSW 93*
Shirley, Barbara Anne 1936- *WhoSSW 93*
Shirley, Charles Franklin 1952- *WhoSSW 93*
Shirley, Charles William 1954- *WhoSSW 93*
Shirley, Dennis 1955- *ConAu 137*
Shirley, George 1934- *IntDcOp, OxDcOp*
Shirley, George (Irving) 1934- *Baker 92*
Shirley, George Michael *Law&B 92*
Shirley, George Milton, Jr. 1939- *WhoSSW 93*
Shirley, Glenn Dean 1916- *WhoAm 92, WhoWrEP 92*
Shirley, Graham Edward 1943- *WhoAm 92*
Shirley, Jean 1919- *ConAu 138, SmATA 70 [port]*
Shirley, John 1953- *ScF&FL 92*
Shirley, Katherine 1942- *WhoAmW 93*
Shirley, Kenneth D. *Law&B 92*
Shirley, Lawrence Hoyt 1947- *WhoE 93*

Shirley, M. Jeff 1938- *St&PR 93*
Shirley, Michael James 1941- *St&PR 93*
Shirley, Norma 1935- *WhoAmW 93, WhoE 93*
Shirley, Richard E. 1937- *St&PR 93*
Shirley, Sara 1939- *St&PR 93*
Shirley, Steve 1933- *WhoWor 93*
Shirley, Virginia Lee 1936- *WhoAm 92*
Shirley & Company *SoulM*
Shirley & Lee *SoulM*
Shirley-Quirk, John 1931- *OxDcOp, WhoAm 92*
Shirley-Quirk, John (Stanton) 1931- *Baker 92, IntDcOp*
Shirokogorov, S.M. 1887-1939 *IntDcAn*
Shirpser, Clara 1901- *WhoAm 92, WhoWor 93*
Shirrell, Rick D. 1957- *St&PR 93*
Shirtcliff, John Delzell 1948- *WhoWor 93*
Shirtcliffe, G. Peter *St&PR 93*
Shirts, Morris A. 1922- *BioIn 17*
Shirtz, Joseph F. *Law&B 92*
Shirvani, Hamid 1950- *WhoAm 92, WhoEmL 93, WhoWor 93*
Shishido, Fumitake 1960- *WhoWor 93*
Shishkov, Dimitar P. 1939- *WhoScE 91-4*
Shishoo, Roshan L. 1938- *WhoScE 91-4*
Shishoo, Roshan Lal 1938- *WhoWor 93*
Shishov, Ivan 1888-1947 *Baker 92*
Shishov, Vasily *BioIn 17*
Shisler, Geoffrey Wayne 1947- *WhoIns 93*
Shisler, Mary Paul 1948- *WhoAmW 93*
Shister, Joseph 1917- *WhoAm 92*
Shivaji, Raja 1627-1680 *BioIn 17*
Shivakumar, Kunigal Nanjundaiah 1951- *WhoSSW 93*
Shivanandan, Mary 1932- *WhoE 93*
Shive, Dan Myles 1944- *WhoSSW 93*
Shive, Richard Byron 1933- *WhoE 93, WhoWor 93*
Shive, T.M. 1924- *St&PR 93*
Shive, Thomas M. 1924- *WhoAm 92*
Shivek, Herbert L. 1921- *St&PR 93*
Shiveley, Marcus H. 1958- *St&PR 93*
Shively, Carol Ann 1955- *WhoAmW 93*
Shively, Catherine E. *Law&B 92*
Shively, George S. *Law&B 92*
Shively, John Adrian 1922- *WhoAm 92*
Shively, Josephine *AmWomPl*
Shively, Judith Carolyn 1962- *WhoAmW 93*
Shively, Paul A. 1943- *St&PR 93*
Shively, Rita Gail 1954- *WhoSSW 93*
Shively, William Phillips 1942- *WhoAm 92*
Shiver, Elizabeth N. 1932- *St&PR 93*
Shiver, Gertrude 1954- *WhoAmW 93*
Shiverick, Margaret Brown 1954- *WhoAmW 93*
Shivers, Allan, Jr. 1946- *St&PR 93*
Shivers, Edward Thomas 1939- *St&PR 93*
Shivers, Jane 1943- *WhoAm 92, WhoAmW 93*
Shivers, Louise 1929- *ConAu 136*
Shivers, Ralph D. 1942- *St&PR 93*
Shivers, Richard Douglas 1930- *St&PR 93*
Shivers, Todd L. *Law&B 92*
Shivery, Charles W. 1945- *St&PR 93*
Shives, Agnes Bush 1943- *WhoAmW 93*
Shives, David W., Jr. 1947- *St&PR 93*
Shives, Paula J. *Law&B 92*
Shives, Ronald D. 1934- *St&PR 93*
Shives, Ronald Dean 1934- *WhoAm 92, WhoIns 93*
Shivler, James Fletcher, Jr. 1918- *WhoAm 92, WhoSSW 93*
Shiv Shankar, P. 1929- *WhoAsAP 91*
Shivtiel, Avihai *WhoScE 91-1*
Shi Yuxiao 1929- *WhoAsAP 91*
Shizawa, Masahiko 1961- *WhoWor 93*
Shizuri, Yoshikazu 1945- *WhoWor 93*
Shkenderov, Stefan 1928- *WhoScE 91-4*
Shklanka, Roman 1932- *St&PR 93*
Shklar, Gerald 1924- *WhoAm 92*
Shklar, Judith Nisse 1928- *WhoAm 92*
Shklovsky, Iosif S. 1916-1985 *BioIn 17*
Shkolnik, Sheldon d1990 *BioIn 17*
Shlaim, Avi 1945- *ConAu 136*
Shlaudeman, Harry Walter 1926- *WhoAm 92, WhoWor 93*
Shlesinger, Samuel Barry 1946- *St&PR 93*
Shlien, Helen Snower 1919- *WhoE 93*
Shlisky, Theodore M. 1939- *St&PR 93*
Shlomm, Boris 1939- *St&PR 93*
Shlora, Raymond Bernard 1919- *St&PR 93*
Shmanske, Stephen 1954- *ConAu 139*
Shmaruk, Julius 1938- *St&PR 93*
Shmavonian, Gerald S. 1945- *WhoAm 92*
Shmikler, David Joel 1948- *St&PR 93*
Shmikler, Michael Charles 1952- *St&PR 93*
Shmikler, Robert Gordon 1945- *St&PR 93*
Shmith, Athol 1914-1990 *BioIn 17*
Shmoys, Jerry 1923- *WhoAm 92*
Shmueli, Herzl 1920- *Baker 92*
Shmurak, Carole B. 1944- *WhoAmW 93*
Shnayerson, Robert Beahan 1925- *WhoAm 92, WhoWrEP 92*
Shneerson, John Michael *WhoScE 91-1*
Shneidman, Edwin S. 1918- *WhoAm 92*
Shneidman, J. Lee 1929- *WhoAm 92*
Shneidman, N(oah) N(orman) 1924- *ConAu 136*
Shneour, Elie Alexis 1925- *WhoAm 92*
Shniderman, Harry Louis 1916- *WhoAm 92*
Shnier, Alan 1928- *WhoAm 92*
Shnier, Allan Joseph 1928- *St&PR 93*
Shnier, Cecil 1913- *St&PR 93*
Shnier, Mark Allen 1954- *St&PR 93*
Shnier, Philip 1925- *St&PR 93*
Shnitke, Alfred *Baker 92*
Shnitkin, David F. 1957- *St&PR 93*
Shoaf, Charles J. *Law&B 92*
Shoaf, Robert Innes *Law&B 92*
Shoafstall, Earl Fred 1936- *WhoWor 93*
Shoal, Dale *WhoWrEP 92*
Shoap, Kenneth Edmund 1949- *St&PR 93*
Shobe, D.W. 1925- *St&PR 93*
Shobe, Harry Rodgers 1946- *St&PR 93*
Shober, Joyce Lee 1932- *ScF&FL 92*
Shober, Wharton 1927- *WhoAm 92*
Shobert, Erle Irwin, II 1913- *WhoAm 92*
Shobin, David 1945- *ScF&FL 92*
Shock, Julian *ScF&FL 92*
Shock, Nathan Wetherill 1906-1989 *BioIn 17*
Shockcor, Urbain Jacques *BiDAMSp 1989*
Shocked, Michelle *BioIn 17*
Shocker, Urban James 1890-1928 *BiDAMSp 1989*
Shockey, Helen A. *Law&B 92*
Shockey, Thomas Edward 1926- *WhoSSW 93, WhoWor 93*
Shock-G *BioIn 17*
Shocklee, Hank
See Public Enemy *News 92*
Shocklee, Keith
See Public Enemy *News 92*
Shockley, Alonzo Hilton, Jr. 1920- *WhoE 93*
Shockley, Ann Allen 1927- *WhoWrEP 92*
Shockley, Carol Frances 1948- *WhoSSW 93*
Shockley, Edward Julian 1924- *WhoAm 92, WhoSSW 93*
Shockley, Joe T., Jr. 1951- *St&PR 93*
Shockley, Leila Mahshi 1958- *WhoAmW 93*
Shockley, Lyn 1957- *St&PR 93*
Shockley, P. Norris, Jr. 1941- *St&PR 93*
Shockley, Susan Evelyn 1957- *WhoE 93*
Shockley, Thomas Dewey 1923- *WhoAm 92*
Shockley, Uriah B. 1925- *St&PR 93*
Shockley, W. Ray 1924- *WhoAm 92*
Shockley, William *BioIn 17*
Shockman, Gerald David 1925- *WhoAm 92*
Shoctor, Joseph Harvey 1922- *WhoAm 92*
Shoda, Koichiro 1931- *WhoWor 93*
Shoeless Joe Jackson 1887?-1951 *BioIn 17*
Shoemake, Peggy Lee 1933- *WhoAmW 93*
Shoemake, Thomas Roark 1949- *WhoWrEP 92*
Shoemaker, Alison J. 1948- *St&PR 93*
Shoemaker, Bill 1931- *BioIn 17, WhoAm 92*
Shoemaker, Blanche W. *AmWomPl*
Shoemaker, Carolie J. 1963- *Baker 92*
Shoemaker, Carrie Glassman 1952- *BioIn 17*
Shoemaker, Clara Brink 1921- *WhoAmW 93*
Shoemaker, Daniel J. 1943- *St&PR 93*
Shoemaker, David Powell 1920- *WhoAm 92*
Shoemaker, Don 1912- *WhoAm 92*
Shoemaker, Donald John 1928- *St&PR 93*
Shoemaker, Dora Adele *AmWomPl*
Shoemaker, E.I. 1938- *St&PR 93*
Shoemaker, Eleanor Boggs 1935- *WhoAmW 93, WhoE 93, WhoWor 93*
Shoemaker, Eugene Merle 1928- *BioIn 17, WhoAm 92*
Shoemaker, Faith Elaine 1952- *WhoAm 92*
Shoemaker, Frank Crawford 1922- *WhoAm 92*
Shoemaker, Gradus Lawrence 1921- *WhoAm 92*
Shoemaker, Harold Lloyd 1923- *WhoWor 93*
Shoemaker, Helen E. Martin Achor 1915- *WhoWor 93*
Shoemaker, Innis Howe *WhoAm 92*
Shoemaker, John L. *Law&B 92*
Shoemaker, John Michael 1933- *WhoAm 92*
Shoemaker, Jon Philip 1936- *WhoSSW 93*
Shoemaker, Kent 1961- *St&PR 93*
Shoemaker, Lynn Henry 1939- *WhoWrEP 92*
Shoemaker, Mary E. *Law&B 92*
Shoemaker, Phillip A. 1948- *St&PR 93*
Shoemaker, Rachel Walter Hinkle 1838-1915 *AmWomPl*
Shoemaker, Ralph Colin 1943- *St&PR 93*
Shoemaker, Richard D. 1947- *WhoE 93*
Shoemaker, Richard L. 1931- *WhoSSW 93*
Shoemaker, Richard W. 1944- *St&PR 93*
Shoemaker, Robert Harold 1921- *St&PR 93*
Shoemaker, Robert Morin 1924- *WhoAm 92*
Shoemaker, Roger L. 1947- *St&PR 93*
Shoemaker, Sydney S. 1931- *WhoAm 92*
Shoemaker, Vaughn 1902-1991 *BioIn 17*
Shoemaker, William Duane, Jr. 1946- *St&PR 93*
Shoemaker, William Edward 1945- *WhoE 93*
Shoemaker, William G. 1916- *St&PR 93*
Shoemaker, Willie 1931- *BioIn 17*
Shoemate, Charles R. 1939- *St&PR 93*
Shoemate, Charles Richard 1939- *WhoAm 92, WhoE 93*
Shoen, Edward J. 1949- *St&PR 93*
Shoen, L.S. *BioIn 17*
Shoen, Samuel W. 1945- *WhoAm 92*
Shoenberg, David *WhoScE 91-1*
Shoener, Arthur Lee 1946- *WhoAm 92*
Shoenfeld, Alayne 1947- *WhoAmW 93*
Shoenight, Pauline Aloise Souers 1914- *WhoSSW 93*
Shoer, Louis 1928- *St&PR 93*
Shoffner, Harry L. 1940- *St&PR 93*
Shoffner, Mary Barbara 1963- *WhoE 93*
Shoffner, Nancy Stafford Spoon 1834-1906? *BioIn 17*
Shofner, Jim 1935- *WhoAm 92*
Shofstahl, Robert Maxwell 1942- *WhoSSW 93*
Shogan, John Kristen *WhoWor 93*
Shogan, Robert *WhoAm 92*
Shoham, Daniel Maxwell 1934- *St&PR 93*
Shohet, Juda Leon 1937- *WhoAm 92*
Shohet, Morris 1936- *St&PR 93*
Shohet, Stephen Byron 1934- *WhoAm 92*
Shohoji, Takao 1938- *WhoWor 93*
Shoji, Ataru 1926- *WhoAsAP 91*
Shoji, Ichiro 1920- *WhoWor 93*
Shoji, June Midori 1957- *WhoAmW 93, WhoEmL 93, WhoWor 93*
Shoji, Uehara 1927- *WhoWor 93*
Shokeir, Mohamed Hassan Kamel 1938- *WhoAm 92*
Sholakh, Marwan *St&PR 93*
Sholander, Mark Canon *Law&B 92*
Shold, David Martin *Law&B 92*
Sholder, Frederic R. 1917- *St&PR 93*
Sholder, Jack *MiSFD 9*
Sholder, Kevin Leonard 1963- *WhoEmL 93, WhoWor 93*
Sholem Aleichem 1859-1916 *BioIn 17*
Sholes, Christopher Latham 1819-1890 *JrnUS*
Sholes, Christopher Warren 1953- *WhoSSW 93*
Sholes, David H. 1943- *WhoE 93*
Sholes, Ronald W. 1939- *WhoIns 93*
Sholes, Ronald William 1939- *St&PR 93*
Sholl, Betsy 1945- *WhoWrEP 92*
Sholl, Carol Converse 1931- *WhoAmW 93, WhoSSW 93*
Sholl, Elizabeth Neary 1945- *WhoWrEP 92*
Sholl, Howard Alfred 1938- *WhoE 93*
Sholl, Jack 1941- *St&PR 93*
Shollenberger, Bradly Scott 1959- *WhoE 93*
Shollenberger, Brian D. 1949- *St&PR 93*
Sholokhov, Mikhail Aleksandrovich 1905-1984 *BioIn 17*
Shols, W.W. *ScF&FL 92*
Sholty, Mary Janet 1942- *WhoSSW 93*
Shomaker, Gordon Alexander, Jr. 1926- *WhoWrEP 92*
Shoman, Abdul Majeed Abdul Hameed 1912- *WhoWor 93*
Shoman, Assad *DcCPCAm*
Shome, Partho 1950- *WhoUN 92*
Shomer, Enid 1944- *WhoWrEP 92*
Shomo, William *BioIn 17*
Shomper, James D., Jr. *Law&B 92*
Shon, Frederick John 1926- *WhoAm 92*
Shonberger, Mallory Frank 1945- *WhoSSW 93*
Shone, John R. 1962- *St&PR 93*
Shone, Phyllis B. 1929- *St&PR 93*
Shone, William E., Jr. 1926- *St&PR 93*
Shonfeld, Willard L. 1931- *St&PR 93*
Shoniker, Fintan Raymond 1914- *WhoAm 92*
Shonk, Albert Davenport, Jr. 1932- *WhoWor 93*
Shonsey, Mike *BioIn 17*
Shontz, Bill
See Rosenshontz *ConMus 9*
Shoob, Marvin H. 1923- *NewYTBS 92 [port], WhoAm 92*
Shook, Don P. 1938- *St&PR 93*
Shook, George E. 1934- *WhoSSW 93*
Shook, Gregory Ralph 1950- *St&PR 93*
Shook, Marie *BioIn 17*
Shook, Mark Roger 1954- *St&PR 93*
Shook, Richard G. *Law&B 92*
Shook, Robert Louis 1938- *WhoAm 92*
Shook, Stephen H. *Law&B 92*
Shoolman, Alan Robert 1929- *WhoE 93*
Shooman, Martin Lawrence 1934- *WhoAm 92*
Shooner, Pierre 1935- *St&PR 93*
Shoop, Deborah *Law&B 92*
Shoop, Glenn Powell 1920- *WhoSSW 93*
Shooter, Eric Manvers 1924- *WhoAm 92*
Shooter, James (Charles) 1951- *ConAu 136*
Shooter, Jim *ConAu 136*
Shooter, Tom 1941- *WhoE 93*
Shope, Ralph Wesley 1925- *St&PR 93*
Shope, Theresa Rachael 1963- *WhoAmW 93*
Shopiro, Eleanor Marchigiani 1929- *WhoAm 92*
Shopiro, Paula *Law&B 92*
Shopkorn, Stanley B. *St&PR 93*
Shopmaker, Michael Louis 1958- *St&PR 93*
Shopov, Dimitar Markov 1922- *WhoScE 91-4*
Shoptaw, Marilee Sue 1937- *WhoSSW 93*
Shor, Cynthia Lynch 1947- *WhoWrEP 92*
Shor, Murray 1932- *WhoWrEP 92*
Shor, Samuel Wendell Williston 1920- *WhoAm 92*
Shor, Stan 1948- *St&PR 93*
Shorb, Eugene Murray 1920- *St&PR 93, WhoAm 92*
Shorb, Mary Shaw 1907-1990 *BioIn 17*
Shorb, Robert David 1955- *WhoE 93*
Shore, Allan *St&PR 93*
Shore, Anthony D. *Law&B 92*
Shore, Betty Apple 1936- *WhoAmW 93*
Shore, Brian Keith *Law&B 92*
Shore, Carole Jean 1948- *WhoE 93*
Shore, Carolyn Sue 1948- *WhoSSW 93*
Shore, Cindy Brockman 1956- *WhoAmW 93*
Shore, Delia Kathleen Roberts 1938- *WhoSSW 93*
Shore, "Dinah" 1917- *Baker 92*
Shore, Dinah 1920- *BioIn 17*
Shore, Dinah 1921- *WhoAm 92*
Shore, Ellis M. 1939- *St&PR 93*
Shore, Emily 1819-1839 *BioIn 17*
Shore, Eric Eugene 1948- *WhoE 93*
Shore, Ernie 1891-1980 *BioIn 17*
Shore, Ferdinand John 1919- *WhoAm 92*
Shore, Harold B. *Law&B 92*
Shore, Harold B. 1937- *St&PR 93*
Shore, Harvey Harris 1940- *WhoE 93, WhoWor 93*
Shore, Herbert 1924- *WhoAm 92, WhoWrEP 92*
Shore, Howard *ConTFT 10*
Shore, Howard Leslie 1946- *WhoAm 92*
Shore, James Henry 1940- *WhoAm 92*
Shore, Janet 1951- *St&PR 93*
Shore, John c. 1662-1752 *Baker 92*
Shore, Lawrence Arthur 1928- *WhoIns 93*
Shore, Marcus S. *Law&B 92*
Shore, Miles Frederick 1929- *WhoAm 92*
Shore, Pauly *BioIn 17*
Shore, Philip R. 1957- *WhoScE 91-1*
Shore, Richard Arnold 1946- *WhoAm 92*
Shore, Samuel 1924- *WhoAm 92*
Shore, Sherman 1931- *St&PR 93*
Shore, Sig *MiSFD 9*
Shore, Stephen 1947- *WhoAm 92*
Shore, Thomas Spencer, Jr. 1939- *WhoAm 92*
Shore, Viola Brothers 1891-1970 *AmWomPl*
Shores, Cynthia Lucia 1961- *WhoSSW 93*
Shores, Dann C. 1949- *St&PR 93*
Shores, Doc 1844-1934 *BioIn 17*
Shores, Jack D. *St&PR 93*
Shores, Janie Ledlow 1932- *WhoAmW 93, WhoSSW 93*
Shores, Louis 1904-1981 *BioIn 17, ScF&FL 92*
Shores, Mae Jennifer 1959- *WhoAmW 93*
Shores, Pearl Marie 1946- *WhoAmW 93*
Shores, Veronica Lynn 1964- *WhoAmW 93*
Shorin, Abram J. d1990 *BioIn 17*
Shorin, Arthur T. 1935- *St&PR 93*
Shorney, George Herbert 1931- *WhoWor 93*
Shorr, Bernard 1928- *St&PR 93*
Shorr, Miriam Kronfeldt *WhoAmW 93*
Shorr, William Eugene 1926- *WhoSSW 93*
Shors, Clayton Marion 1925- *WhoAm 92*
Short, Alonzo E., Jr. 1939- *AfrAmBi*
Short, Arthur William 1941- *St&PR 93*
Short, Barry Arnold 1940- *WhoAm 92*
Short, Bobby *BioIn 17*
Short, "Bobby" 1926- *Baker 92*
Short, Brant Alison 1933- *St&PR 93*
Short, Brian (Michael) 1944- *ConAu 136*
Short, Bryan C. *ConAu 139*

Short, Byron Elliott 1901- *WhoAm 92*
Short, Charles E. 1937- *St&PR 93*
Short, Cheryl K. *Law&B 92*
Short, Chris 1937-1991 *BioIn 17*
Short, Christine 1944- *WhoAmW 93*
Short, David Bruce 1953- *WhoWor 93*
Short, David Gaines 1939- *St&PR 93, WhoAm 92*
Short, Debra Carpenter 1953- *WhoAmW 93*
Short, Dorothy *SweetSg C [port]*
Short, George Oscar, III 1957- *WhoEmL 93*
Short, Harold Harvey 1917- *St&PR 93*
Short, Harry William 1947- *WhoAm 92*
Short, J. Edward *Law&B 92*
Short, James Franklin, Jr. 1924- *WhoAm 92*
Short, James H. 1948- *St&PR 93*
Short, James Robert 1936- *WhoAsAP 91*
Short, Janet Marie 1939- *WhoE 93*
Short, Jeffrey R., Jr. 1913- *St&PR 93*
Short, John A. *Law&B 92*
Short, Joseph Norton 1939- *WhoE 93*
Short, K. Lowell, Jr. 1956- *St&PR 93*
Short, Keith Christopher *WhoScE 91-1*
Short, Kenneth Malcolm *WhoScE 91-1*
Short, Kenneth Richard MacDonald 1936- *WhoSSW 93*
Short, Leo N., Jr. 1926- *St&PR 93*
Short, Leonard V. 1959- *St&PR 93*
Short, Luke L. 1854-1893 *BioIn 17*
Short, Marion *AmWomPl*
Short, Marion Priscilla 1951- *WhoAmW 93*
Short, Martin 1950- *CurBio 92 [port]*
Short, Martin 1951- *QDrFCA 92 [port], WhoAm 92*
Short, Michael 1937- *BioIn 17*
Short, Michael Macgregor 1940- *WhoAm 92*
Short, R. Alastair 1953- *WhoE 93*
Short, R.W. *WhoScE 91-2*
Short, Ray Everett 1919- *WhoAm 92*
Short, Robert 1950- *MiSFD 9*
Short, Robert Henry 1924- *WhoAm 92*
Short, Robert L. 1932- *ScF&FL 92*
Short, Robert Trent 1950- *WhoSSW 93*
Short, Robert Waltrip 1924- *WhoAm 92*
Short, Roger, Jr. *ConTFT 10*
Short, Shirley Annette 1949- *WhoAmW 93*
Short, Thomas E. 1928- *St&PR 93, WhoAm 92*
Short, Walter Campbell 1880-1949 *HarEnMi*
Short, Walter J. 1918- *St&PR 93*
Short, William E. 1938- *St&PR 93*
Short, William H. 1924-1991 *BioIn 17*
Short, William Leigh 1935- *WhoE 93*
Short, Winthrop Allen 1919- *WhoAm 92*
Shortal, Helen Mary 1961- *WhoAmW 93*
Shortal, Terence Michael 1937- *WhoSSW 93, WhoWor 93*
Shortell, Stephen M. *BioIn 17*
Shorten, Harry d1991 *BioIn 17*
Shorter, Barbara Lucile 1936- *WhoAmW 93*
Shorter, Hazle Jeffries *BioIn 17*
Shorter, John 1926- *WhoWor 93*
Shorter, Philip *ScF&FL 92*
Shorter, Walter Wyatt 1932- *St&PR 93, WhoAm 92*
Shorter, Wayne 1933- *WhoAm 92*
Shortess, Edwin Steevin 1920- *WhoE 93, WhoWor 93*
Shortland, Michael *ScF&FL 92*
Shortley, George M. 1940- *WhoAm 92*
Shortley, George Melvin 1940- *St&PR 93*
Shortley, Michael J. *Law&B 92*
Shortliffe, Edward Hance 1947- *WhoAm 92*
Shortliffe, Glen Scott 1937- *WhoAm 92*
Short-Mayfield, Patricia Ahlene 1955- *WhoAmW 93*
Shortridge, Charles Emil 1941- *WhoWrEP 92*
Shortridge, James R. 1944- *ConAu 136*
Shortridge, Wayne Hall 1938- *WhoAm 92*
Shorts, Binkley Calhoun 1943- *St&PR 93*
Shortt, Rae Michael 1957- *WhoE 93*
Shory, Naseeb Lein 1925- *WhoAm 92*
Shoshitaishvili, Alexander Nikolaievich 1948- *WhoWor 93*
Shosid, Joseph Lewis 1927- *WhoAm 92*
Shosky, John Edwin 1955- *WhoE 93, WhoWor 93*
Shoss, Cynthia Renee 1950- *WhoAmW 93*
Shostak, Aleksander Peter 1948- *WhoWor 93*
Shostak, Ed Bennett 1941- *WhoE 93*
Shostak, Stanley Richard 1931- *WhoWor 93*
Shostakovich, Dmitri 1906-1975 *Baker 92, IntDcOp [port]*
Shostakovich, Dmitri 1961- *Baker 92*
Shostakovich, Dmitrii Dmitrievich 1906-1975 *BioIn 17*
Shostakovich, Dmitry 1906-1975 *OxDcOp*
Shostakovich, Maxim 1938- *Baker 92*
Shostakovich, Maxim Dmitriyevich 1938- *WhoAm 92, WhoSSW 93, WhoWor 93*
Shot, Danny 1957- *WhoWrEP 92*
Shotel, Barbra M. *Law&B 92*
Shotell, Richard G. 1937- *St&PR 93*
Shott, Edward Earl 1946- *WhoWor 93*
Shott, Gerald Lee 1934- *St&PR 93*
Shott, James R. 1925- *ConAu 139*
Shott, Robert B. 1922- *St&PR 93*
Shott, Sandra Kay 1960- *WhoSSW 93*
Shott, Scott 1926- *St&PR 93*
Shotton, Burton Kent, Jr. 1937- *St&PR 93*
Shotton, Darian Heather 1946- *WhoWor 93*
Shotton, K.C. *WhoScE 91-1*
Shotts, David Allison 1941- *WhoAm 92*
Shotwell, Charles Bland 1955- *WhoE 93*
Shotwell, J.P. *Law&B 92*
Shotwell, Larry R. 1938- *St&PR 93*
Shotwell, Louisa R(ossiter) 1902- *DcAmChF 1960*
Shotzberger, Martin Luther 1923- *WhoAm 92*
Shou, Sharon Louise Wikoff 1946- *WhoAmW 93*
Shoub, Earle Phelps 1915- *WhoE 93, WhoWor 93*
Shoudy, Emma *AmWomPl*
Shoujing, Zhuang 1931- *WhoWor 93*
Shoulberg, Harry 1903- *WhoAm 92*
Shoulders, John F. 1947- *St&PR 93*
Shoulders, Warren E. 1944- *St&PR 93*
Shoumatoff, Elizabeth 1888-1980 *BioIn 17*
Shoup, Andrew James, Jr. 1935- *St&PR 93, WhoAm 92*
Shoup, Carl Sumner 1902- *WhoAm 92, WhoE 93, WhoWor 93*
Shoup, Charles *BioIn 17*
Shoup, Charles Samuel, Jr. 1935- *WhoAm 92*
Shoup, Charlotte F. 1947- *St&PR 93*
Shoup, David M. *BioIn 17*
Shoup, David Monroe 1904-1983 *HarEnMi*
Shoup, Donald Albert 1929- *St&PR 93*
Shoup, Harold Arthur 1930- *WhoAm 92*
Shoup, Michael C. 1940- *WhoAm 92*
Shoup, Paul Connelly 1938- *St&PR 93*
Shoup, Robert W. 1920- *St&PR 93*
Shoup, Ronald Edward 1951- *WhoAm 92*
Shoup, Walter C. 1951- *St&PR 93*
Shouse, David Sinclair 1952- *WhoSSW 93*
Shouse, Karon Rogers 1964- *WhoAmW 93*
Shoushanian, Hrant H. 1936- *St&PR 93*
Shouvlin, Daniel Robert, Jr. 1919- *St&PR 93*
Shoval, Zalman 1930- *BioIn 17*
Shovald, Arlene Elizabeth 1940- *WhoWrEP 92*
Shovell, Cloudesley 1650-1707 *HarEnMi*
Shovelton, David Scott *WhoScE 91-1*
Show, Grant *BioIn 17*
Showalter, Buck 1956- *WhoAm 92*
Showalter, Denise Susan 1955- *WhoAmW 93*
Showalter, E. Lee *St&PR 93*
Showalter, English, Jr. 1935- *WhoAm 92*
Showalter, Jerry Newbern 1940- *WhoWor 93*
Showalter, Joan Frances 1933- *St&PR 93*
Showalter, John 1950- *St&PR 93*
Showalter, John A. *Law&B 92*
Showalter, Louis Reverdy 1931- *St&PR 93*
Showalter, Ralph Roland 1925- *St&PR 93*
Showalter, Robert Earl 1937- *WhoAm 92*
Showalter, William Nathaniel, III 1956- *WhoAm 92*
Showalter-Keefe, Jean 1938- *WhoSSW 93*
Showcross, Matthew J. *St&PR 93*
Showe, Jonathan 1945- *WhoE 93*
Showen, Robert 1924- *St&PR 93*
Shower, Robert Wesley 1937- *WhoAm 92*
Showers, April *WhoWrEP 92*
Showers, James Allen 1955- *St&PR 93*
Showers, Paul C. 1910- *ConAu 38NR, MajAI [port]*
Showers, Ralph Morris 1918- *WhoAm 92*
Showers, Wayne Allen 1932- *St&PR 93*
Showmen *SoulM*
Shows, Clarence Oliver 1920- *WhoWor 93*
Shows, Marshall T. *Law&B 92*
Shows, Regina P. *St&PR 93*
Shows, Thomas Byron 1938- *WhoAm 92*
Shparlinski, Igor 1956- *WhoWor 93*
Shpilrain, Vladimir Evald 1960- *WhoWor 93*
Shpuntoff, Albert Frank 1950- *WhoE 93*
Shrader, Alan Ross *ScF&FL 92*
Shrader, Dorothy Markham 1951- *WhoSSW 93*
Shrader, Marjorie A. *St&PR 93*
Shrader, William Whitney 1930- *WhoAm 92*
Shrager, Robert Neil 1948- *WhoWor 93*
Shragin, Boris *BioIn 17*
Shragin, Isaac Veniaminovich 1927- *WhoWor 93*
Shrallow, Dane A. *Law&B 92*
Shrapnel, Henry 1761-1842 *HarEnMi*
Shrauner, Barbara Wayne Abraham 1934- *WhoAm 92, WhoAmW 93*
Shrawder, Elsie June 1938- *WhoAmW 93*
Shrawder, J. Edward 1937- *St&PR 93*
Shrednick, Harvey R. 1940- *St&PR 93*
Shreeve, Arvin *BioIn 17*
Shreeve, Jean'ne Marie 1933- *WhoAm 92, WhoAmW 93*
Shreffler, Philip A. *ScF&FL 92*
Shreffler, Philip A. 1948- *ConAu 138*
Shreiber, Gerald B. *BioIn 17*
Shreiber, Gerald B. 1941- *WhoAm 92*
Shrem, Charles J. 1930- *St&PR 93*
Shrem, Charles Joseph 1930- *WhoAm 92, WhoE 93, WhoWor 93*
Shrem, Henry J. 1936- *St&PR 93*
Shrestha, Birendra Bahadur 1949- *WhoWor 93*
Shrestha, Mahesh Man 1945- *WhoWor 93*
Shrestha, Mathura *WhoAsAP 91*
Shrestha, Purushottam Narayan 1939- *WhoUN 92*
Shrestha, Surjit Prasad 1948- *WhoWor 93*
Shreve, Anita *BioIn 17*
Shreve, Anita 1947?- *ConAu 139*
Shreve, Eugenia Love 1960- *WhoSSW 93*
Shreve, Herb *BioIn 17*
Shreve, Jack 1949- *WhoE 93*
Shreve, Kevin Lee 1964- *WhoSSW 93*
Shreve, Peg 1927- *WhoAmW 93*
Shreve, Susan Richards 1939- *ConAu 38NR, DcAmChF 1985, MajAI [port], ScF&FL 92, WhoAm 92, WhoAmW 93*
Shrewsbury, John Talbot, Earl of c. 1384-1453 *HarEnMi*
Shriber, Leon Albert 1928- *St&PR 93*
Shriber, Maurice Norden 1943- *WhoAm 92*
Shrider, Bruce J. 1952- *St&PR 93*
Shridharani, Vasant Nanalal 1937- *WhoE 93*
Shrier, Adam Louis 1938- *WhoAm 92*
Shrier, Diane Kesler 1941- *WhoAmW 93*
Shrier, Joann *Law&B 92*
Shrier, Stefan 1942- *WhoAm 92*
Shrimpton, James Robert 1956- *WhoEmL 93*
Shrimpton, Roger 1948- *WhoUN 92*
Shriner, Robert Dale 1937- *WhoWor 93*
Shriner, Sara Venore *AmWomPl*
Shrivastava, Animesh 1962- *WhoWor 93*
Shrivastava, Santosh Kumar *WhoScE 91-1*
Shriver, Anthony 1965- *BioIn 17*
Shriver, Charles 1941- *St&PR 93*
Shriver, David A. 1942- *WhoE 93*
Shriver, Donald Woods, Jr. 1927- *WhoAm 92*
Shriver, Duward Felix 1934- *WhoAm 92*
Shriver, Eunice Kennedy *BioIn 17*
Shriver, Eunice Mary Kennedy *WhoAm 92, WhoAmW 93*
Shriver, Garner Edward 1912- *WhoAm 92*
Shriver, George Hite 1931- *WhoSSW 93*
Shriver, Harry Roland 1932- *St&PR 93*
Shriver, Jennifer M. 1950- *St&PR 93*
Shriver, Maria *BioIn 17*
Shriver, Norman 1943- *St&PR 93*
Shriver, Pam *BioIn 17*
Shriver, Pamela Howard 1962- *WhoAm 92, WhoAmW 93*
Shriver, Phillip Raymond 1922- *WhoAm 92*
Shriver, R. Sargent 1915- *PolPar*
Shriver, Robert Sargent, Jr. 1915- *WhoAm 92*
Shroads, James L. *Law&B 92*
Shroads, James Lawrence *Law&B 92*
Shroat, Jerry T. 1941- *WhoIns 93*
Shrock, Robert Rakes 1904- *WhoAm 92*
Shrodes, Caroline *WhoWrEP 92*
Shroeder, Janet Gregg Wallace 1902- *WhoE 93*
Shroff, David N. *St&PR 93*
Shroff, Firoz Sardar 1950- *WhoWor 93*
Shroff, Vipin R. 1935- *St&PR 93*
Shrontz, Frank Anderson 1931- *St&PR 93, WhoAm 92, WhoWor 93*
Shropshire, Donald Gray 1927- *WhoAm 92, WhoWor 93*
Shropshire, James Kenneth *Law&B 92*
Shropshire, Walter, Jr. 1932- *WhoAm 92*
Shropshire, William S. 1957- *St&PR 93*
Shrosbree, Robert C. *Law&B 92*
Shroup, Robert Lewis 1935- *St&PR 93*
Shrout, Lois Glenn 1941- *WhoSSW 93*
Shroyer, James Stanford 1946- *St&PR 93*
Shroyer, Keith L. 1949- *St&PR 93*
Shroyer, Norman Charles 1931- *St&PR 93*
Shrum, Christine Ruth 1949- *WhoWrEP 92*
Shrum, James R. *St&PR 93*
Shrut, Howard *St&PR 93*
Shryack, Dennis *ScF&FL 92*
Shryock, Carol D. d1990 *BioIn 17*
Shternberg, Leo 1861-1927 *IntDcAn*
Shtofman, Norman Maurice 1928- *WhoSSW 93*
Shtogarenko, Andrei (Yakovlevich) 1902- *Baker 92*
Shtohryn, Dmytro Michael 1923- *WhoAm 92*
Shu, Chi-Wang 1957- *WhoE 93*
Shu, Frank Hsia-San 1943- *WhoAm 92*
Shu, Qi-Qing 1944- *WhoWor 93*
Shu, Zhongzhou 1924- *WhoWor 93*
Shuard, Amy 1924-1975 *OxDcOp*
Shuard, Hilary Bertha 1928- *WhoWor 93*
Shuart, James Martin 1931- *WhoAm 92, WhoE 93*
Shub, Elizabeth *BioIn 17*
Shub, Meyer *BioIn 17*
Shubatt, Jacqueline Ann *Law&B 92*
Shube, Eugene E. 1927- *St&PR 93*
Shubert, Beth Cohen 1941- *WhoWor 93*
Shubert, Clarence M. 1940- *WhoUN 92*
Shubert, Duane Doyle 1962- *WhoE 93*
Shubert, Gary Michael 1948- *WhoWor 93*
Shubert, Gustave Harry 1929- *WhoAm 92*
Shubert, Irwin J. 1931- *St&PR 93*
Shubert, Jacob J. 1880-1963 *BioIn 17*
Shubert, Joseph Francis 1928- *WhoAm 92*
Shubert, Lee 1875-1953 *BioIn 17*
Shubert, Sam S. 1875-1905 *BioIn 17*
Shubik, Irene *ScF&FL 92*
Shubik, Martin 1926- *WhoAm 92*
Shubik, Philippe 1921- *WhoWor 93*
Shubin, Seymour 1921- *WhoWrEP 92*
Shubsda, Thaddeus A. 1925-1991 *BioIn 17*
Shucart, Evelyn Ann 1942- *WhoAmW 93, WhoWor 93*
Shuck, Bill C. 1941- *St&PR 93*
Shuck, Jerry Mark 1934- *WhoAm 92*
Shuck, John D. 1951- *WhoIns 93*
Shuck, Robert Fletcher 1937- *St&PR 93*
Shuck, Robert Fletcher, III 1937- *WhoAm 92*
Shuck, Yvonne M. *St&PR 93*
Shuckra, David W. *Law&B 92*
Shudi, Burkhard *Baker 92*
Shudtz, Peter Joseph *Law&B 92*
Shudy, John George, Jr. *Law&B 92*
Shue, Elisabeth *BioIn 17*
Shue, Elisabeth 1964?- *ConTFT 10*
Shue, Eugene William 1931- *WhoAm 92*
Shue, Robert Sidney 1943- *WhoSSW 93*
Shuebrook, Ronald Lee 1943- *WhoE 93*
Shuell, Thomas John 1938- *WhoE 93*
Shuey, Andrea Lee *WhoWrEP 92*
Shuey, Carolyn A. *Law&B 92*
Shuey, Elaine M. 1956- *WhoE 93*
Shuey, John Henry 1946- *WhoAm 92*
Shuey, Judith Lewis 1946- *WhoAmW 93, WhoSSW 93*
Shuey, Sidney Lee 1936- *St&PR 93*
Shufeldt, R. Charles 1950- *St&PR 93*
Shufeldt, Robert Charles 1950- *WhoAm 92*
Shuff, Herbert R. 1919- *WhoIns 93*
Shuff, Lily *WhoAm 92*
Shuffelton, Frank 1940- *ConAu 38NR*
Shuford, A. Alex 1944- *St&PR 93*
Shuford, Harley F. 1912- *St&PR 93*
Shuford, Harley Ferguson, Jr. 1937- *WhoAm 92*
Shuford, Harry L. 1941- *St&PR 93*
Shuford, R.F. 1937- *St&PR 93*
Shuford, William Harris 1932- *WhoSSW 93*
Shufro, Salwyn 1905- *St&PR 93, WhoE 93*
Shugarman, Richard Gerald 1940- *WhoSSW 93*
Shugars, Anne O'Donnell 1961- *WhoE 93*
Shugart, Alan F. 1930- *ConEn, St&PR 93, WhoAm 92*
Shugart, Cecil Glenn 1930- *WhoAm 92*
Shugart, Donna Lea 1948- *WhoAmW 93*
Shugart, Herman Henry 1944- *WhoAm 92*
Shugart, Howard Alan 1931- *WhoAm 92*
Shugart, Jill 1940- *WhoSSW 93*
Shugg, Carleton d1992 *NewYTBS 92 [port]*
Shugg, Carleton 1899-1992 *BioIn 17*
Shughart, Dale Franklin 1913- *WhoE 93*
Shugoll, Eugene L. *St&PR 93*
Shugoll, Joan S. 1928- *WhoE 93*
Shugrue, James Leonard 1948- *WhoWrEP 92*
Shugrue, Martin Roger, Jr. 1940- *WhoAm 92, WhoSSW 93*
Shugrue, Noreen Anne *Law&B 92*
Shukan, Donald Craine 1937- *WhoE 93*
Shuker, Gregory Brown 1932- *WhoAm 92*
Shukla, Pradip Kantilal 1956- *WhoWor 93*
Shukla, Rahul B. 1947- *St&PR 93*
Shukla, Vidya Charan 1929- *WhoAsAP 91*
Shukoski, Vernon Joseph 1951- *St&PR 93*

Shukshin, Vasily 1929-1974 *IntDcF 2-3 [port]*
Shula *ConAu 138*
Shula, David D. 1959- *WhoAm 92*
Shula, Don 1930- *News 92 [port]*
Shula, Don Francis 1930- *WhoAm 92, WhoSSW 93*
Shula, Robert Joseph 1936- *WhoAm 92*
Shulaia, Dazmir Alexandr 1945- *WhoWor 93*
Shulby, Bill *BioIn 17*
Shuldiner, Herbert 1929- *WhoWrEP 92*
Shulenberger, Cheryl Rene 1950- *WhoWrEP 92*
Shuler, Bill 1946- *St&PR 93*
Shuler, Ellie Givan, Jr. 1936- *WhoAm 92*
Shuler, George Nixon, Jr. 1952- *WhoSSW 93*
Shuler, Jerry B. 1933- *St&PR 93*
Shuler, John H. 1927- *St&PR 93*
Shuler, Kurt Egon 1922- *WhoAm 92*
Shuler, Linda Lay *ScF&FL 92*
Shuler, Michael Louis 1947- *WhoAm 92, WhoE 93*
Shuler, Sally Ann Smith 1934- *WhoAmW 93*
Shuler, Scott 1952- *WhoAm 92*
Shuler, Wilbur Burrnel 1943- *WhoSSW 93*
Shulevitz, Deborah G. *Law&B 92*
Shulevitz, Uri *ChlBIID [port]*
Shulevitz, Uri 1935- *MajAI [port], WhoAm 92, WhoWrEP 92*
Shulga, Cynthia Lee 1953- *St&PR 93*
Shul'gin, V.V. 1878- *BioIn 17*
Shul'gin, Vasilii Vital'evich 1878- *BioIn 17*
Shulkin, David *BioIn 17*
Shulko, Patsy Lee 1934- *WhoSSW 93*
Shull, Clifford G. 1915- *WhoAm 92*
Shull, David Scott 1946- *WhoEmL 93*
Shull, Ellen M. 1937- *WhoWrEP 92*
Shull, Frank Taylor, IV 1967- *WhoE 93*
Shull, George *BioIn 17*
Shull, Harrison 1923- *WhoAm 92*
Shull, Leon 1913- *PolPar*
Shull, Mary Jean 1923- *WhoAmW 93*
Shull, Noel J. *St&PR 93*
Shull, Richard Bruce 1929- *WhoAm 92*
Shull, Willard Charles, III 1940- *St&PR 93*
Shulman, Alan 1915- *Baker 92*
Shulman, Alix Kates 1932- *JeAmFiW*
Shulman, Arnold 1914- *WhoAm 92*
Shulman, Arnold G. *Law&B 92*
Shulman, Arnold M. 1933- *St&PR 93*
Shulman, Fay Stanley 1925-1990 *BioIn 17*
Shulman, Gary A. *Law&B 92*
Shulman, Irving 1913- *WhoAm 92, WhoWrEP 92*
Shulman, Jack Arnold 1952- *WhoE 93*
Shulman, Lawrence Edward 1919- *WhoAm 92, WhoE 93*
Shulman, Lenore 1934- *St&PR 93*
Shulman, Martin 1921- *St&PR 93*
Shulman, Max L. 1908- *St&PR 93, WhoAm 92*
Shulman, Michael Eben 1958- *WhoSSW 93*
Shulman, Morton P. 1925- *St&PR 93*
Shulman, Oscar 1911- *St&PR 93*
Shulman, Robert Gerson 1924- *WhoAm 92*
Shulman, Robert S. 1951- *St&PR 93*
Shulman, Roy A. *Law&B 92*
Shulman, Stephanie J. *Law&B 92*
Shulman, Stephen Neal 1933- *WhoAm 92*
Shulman, Steven 1941- *St&PR 93*
Shultis, Robert Lynn 1924- *WhoAm 92, WhoWor 93*
Shults, John R., Jr. 1926- *St&PR 93*
Shults, Robert L. 1936- *St&PR 93*
Shults, Robert Lee 1936- *WhoSSW 93, WhoWor 93*
Shults, Robert Luther, Jr. 1925- *WhoAm 92*
Shultz, Alvin 1929- *St&PR 93*
Shultz, Cathleen Michaele *WhoAmW 93*
Shultz, Emmet L. 1934- *St&PR 93*
Shultz, Emmet Lavel 1934- *WhoWor 93*
Shultz, Eveline Spooner *AmWomPl*
Shultz, George *DcCPCAm*
Shultz, George P. 1920- *ColdWar 1 [port]*
Shultz, George Pratt 1920- *WhoAm 92, WhoWor 93*
Shultz, Jack Ray 1942- *WhoSSW 93*
Shultz, Joseph Randolph 1927- *WhoAm 92*
Shultz, Lebert Dean *Law&B 92*
Shultz, Lebert Dean 1942- *St&PR 93*
Shultz, Leila McReynolds 1946- *WhoAmW 93*
Shultz, Leonard Donald 1945- *WhoE 93*
Shultz, Martha Jane 1916- *WhoAm 92, WhoAmW 93*
Shultz, Paul Albert 1954- *St&PR 93*
Shultz, Rick John 1952- *St&PR 93*
Shultz, Rosemarie Margaret 1930- *St&PR 93*
Shultz, Susan Kent Fried 1943- *WhoAmW 93*
Shum, Paul P. 1929- *St&PR 93*
Shumacker, Harris B., Jr. 1908- *WhoAm 92*
Shumadine, William F., Jr. 1944- *St&PR 93*
Shumaker, John William 1942- *WhoE 93*
Shumaker, L.E. *Law&B 92*
Shumaker, Nancy Worrell 1946- *WhoSSW 93*
Shumaker, Wayne Louis, Jr. *Law&B 92*
Shumaker-Holland, Judith B. *Law&B 92*
Shuman, Bonnie L. *Law&B 92*
Shuman, Deanne 1953- *WhoAmW 93, WhoEmL 93*
Shuman, Earl Stanley 1923- *WhoE 93*
Shuman, Hyman B. *St&PR 93*
Shuman, James Burrow 1932- *WhoE 93, WhoWor 93*
Shuman, Joseph O. 1944- *St&PR 93*
Shuman, Mark Samuel 1936- *WhoAm 92*
Shuman, Michael Harrison 1956- *WhoE 93*
Shuman, Mort d1991 *BioIn 17*
Shuman, Mort 1936- *SoulM*
Shuman, Mort 1938-1991 *AnObit 1991*
Shuman, Nicholas Roman 1921- *WhoAm 92*
Shuman, Robert Baird 1929- *WhoAm 92*
Shuman, Samuel A. 1927- *St&PR 93*
Shuman, Samuel Irving 1925- *WhoAm 92*
Shuman, Stanley S. 1935- *WhoAm 92*
Shuman, Willard Edward 1943- *WhoIns 93*
Shumate, Anderson Everett, III 1936- *St&PR 93*
Shumate, Douglas Omer 1936- *WhoSSW 93*
Shumate, Gloria Jones 1927- *WhoAmW 93*
Shumate, J. Bernard *WhoIns 93*
Shumate, James Bernard 1929- *St&PR 93*
Shumate, John Page 1934- *WhoE 93*
Shumate, Mack H., Jr. *Law&B 92*
Shumate, Minerva 1949- *WhoAmW 93*
Shumate, Paul William, Jr. 1941- *WhoAm 92*
Shumick, Diana Lynn 1951- *WhoAmW 93*
Shumila, Michael John 1947- *WhoWor 93*
Shump, Michael Eugene 1943- *St&PR 93*
Shumrick, Donald A. 1925- *WhoAm 92*
Shumsky, Oscar 1917- *Baker 92*
Shumsky, Zena *WhoWrEP 92*
Shumway, David Robert 1952- *WhoE 93*
Shumway, Frank Ritter d1992 *NewYTBS 92 [port]*
Shumway, Frank Ritter 1906-1992 *BioIn 17*
Shumway, Garrett P. *Law&B 92*
Shumway, Gary Scott 1949- *WhoWrEP 92*
Shumway, Harry Irving 1883-1974 *ScF&FL 92*
Shumway, Lucy C. *AmWomPl*
Shumway, Matthew F. *Law&B 92*
Shumway, Norman D. 1934- *WhoAm 92*
Shumway, Norman Edward 1923- *WhoAm 92*
Shumway, Spence A. 1955- *WhoSSW 93*
Shunk, Francis Rawn 1788-1848 *BioIn 17*
Shunkov, Vladimir Petrovich 1932- *WhoWor 93*
Shunsky, Vincent 1949- *St&PR 93*
Shuntich, Douglas John 1966- *WhoWor 93*
Shuntich, Louis Steven *Law&B 92*
Shupack, Harold 1936- *St&PR 93*
Shupack, Sheila Diane 1940- *St&PR 93*
Shupe, Charles B. 1933- *St&PR 93*
Shupe, Dorothy Brigman 1918- *WhoAmW 93*
Shupe, John Wallace 1924- *WhoAm 92*
Shupe, Mark *BioIn 17*
Shupenko, John Michael 1958- *WhoSSW 93*
Shupler, Ronald Steven 1954- *WhoSSW 93*
Shupp, Franklin Richard 1934- *WhoAm 92*
Shupp, Mike 1946- *ScF&FL 92*
Shur, Irene Ginsburg 1921- *WhoE 93*
Shur, Irwin M. *Law&B 92*
Shur, Michael 1942- *WhoAm 92*
Shur, Mikhail Grigorievich 1938- *WhoWor 93*
Shur, Steven Elliot 1947- *St&PR 93*
Shur, Walter 1929- *St&PR 93, WhoAm 92, WhoIns 93*
Shura (Craig), Mary Frances 1923-1991 *DcAmChF 1985*
Shura, Mary Francis *WhoWrEP 92*
Shura, Mary Francis 1923-1991 *BioIn 17*
Shure, Leonard 1910- *Baker 92*
Shure, Myrna Beth 1937- *WhoAmW 93*
Shurick, Edward Palmes 1912- *WhoAm 92*
Shurkin, Joel N. 1938- *ScF&FL 92*
Shurkin, Lorna Greene 1944- *WhoAmW 93, WhoE 93*
Shurley, Jay Talmadge 1917- *WhoAm 92*
Shurman, Rick *BioIn 17*
Shurr, Georgia Grey Hooks 1942- *WhoSSW 93*
Shurr, Gertrude d1992 *BioIn 17, NewYTBS 92 [port]*
Shurr, William Howard 1932- *WhoSSW 93*
Shurrager, Phil Sheridan 1907- *WhoAm 92, WhoWor 93*
Shurson, Debra Jean *Law&B 92*
Shurtleff, Jennifer Guze *Law&B 92*
Shurtleff, Leonard Grant 1940- *WhoAm 92*
Shurtleff, William Roy 1941- *WhoWrEP 92*
Shurtliff, Marvin Karl 1939- *WhoAm 92*
Shurupoff, Lawrence J. *Law&B 92*
Shushunova, Elena *BioIn 17*
Shust, Nestor W. *Law&B 92*
Shustek, Leonard J. 1948- *St&PR 93*
Shuster, Alvin 1930- *WhoAm 92*
Shuster, Bud *ConAu 138*
Shuster, Bud 1932- *CngDr 91*
Shuster, E. G. 1932- *ConAu 138*
Shuster, E. G. Bud 1932- *WhoAm 92, WhoE 93*
Shuster, George Whitcomb 1946- *St&PR 93*
Shuster, Herbert Victor 1924- *WhoAm 92*
Shuster, John Michael 1952- *St&PR 93*
Shuster, Joseph d1992 *NewYTBS 92 [port]*
Shuster, Lewis J. *WhoAm 92*
Shuster, Lynn A. 1942- *St&PR 93*
Shuster, Lynne Merrill 1939- *WhoAmW 93*
Shuster, Marc Ronald 1946- *WhoE 93*
Shuster, Robert G. 1927- *WhoAm 92*
Shuster, Sam *WhoScE 91-1*
Shuster, Sam 1927- *WhoWor 93*
Shusterman, Arnold Jerome 1937- *St&PR 93*
Shusterman, Nathan 1927- *WhoSSW 93, WhoWor 93*
Shusterman, Neal Douglas 1962- *WhoAm 92*
Shusterman, Richard (M.) 1949- *ConAu 136*
Shusterman, Ronald Stephen 1953- *WhoWor 93*
Shustin, Eugenii Isaakovich 1957- *WhoWor 93*
Shute, Celia E. *AmWomPl*
Shute, David *Law&B 92*
Shute, David 1931- *WhoAm 92*
Shute, Jenefer 1956- *ConAu 138*
Shute, Nevil 1899-1960 *BioIn 17, ScF&FL 92*
Shute, Richard Emil 1938- *WhoAm 92*
Shute, Sally *AmWomPl*
Shutiak, James 1932- *WhoAm 92*
Shutkin, John A. *Law&B 92*
Shutler, K. Eugene 1938- *St&PR 93*
Shutler, Kenneth Eugene 1938- *WhoAm 92*
Shutler, Mary Elizabeth 1929- *WhoAm 92*
Shutsky, Robert 1938- *St&PR 93*
Shutt, Edwin Holmes, Jr. 1927- *WhoAm 92*
Shutt, Harry James 1932- *St&PR 93*
Shutt, Jay W. 1951- *St&PR 93*
Shutt, Ward S., Jr. 1948- *St&PR 93*
Shuttee, Anne Katherine *Law&B 92*
Shuttle, Penelope 1947- *ScF&FL 92*
Shuttle, Penelope (Diane) 1947- *ConAu 39NR*
Shuttle, Robert J. 1934- *St&PR 93*
Shuttlesworth, Fred L. 1922- *EncAACR*
Shuttleworth, Anne Margaret 1931- *WhoWor 93*
Shuttleworth, Carol L. 1941- *St&PR 93*
Shuttleworth, Rebecca Scott 1919- *WhoAmW 93*
Shutts, Kenneth R. *Law&B 92*
Shutts, Kenneth Robertson 1922- *St&PR 93*
Shutty, Robert John 1937- *St&PR 93*
Shutz, Byron Christopher 1928- *St&PR 93, WhoAm 92*
Shutze, Virgil Cox 1944- *WhoAm 92*
Shuyler, Richard Harlan 1947- *St&PR 93*
Shvartsman, Ossip 1946- *WhoWor 93*
Shwartz, Kenneth A. 1955- *St&PR 93*
Shwartz, Merrill D. 1922- *St&PR 93*
Shwartz, Susan 1949- *ScF&FL 92*
Shwayder, Elizabeth Yanish 1922- *WhoAmW 93*
Shwide, Herman 1925- *WhoIns 93*
Shy, John Willard 1931- *WhoWrEP 92*
Shy, Paul N. 1939- *St&PR 93*
Shyer, Charles 1941- *MiSFD 9*
Shyer, Charles (Richard) 1941- *ConAu 138, WhoAm 92*
Shyers, Larry Edward 1948- *WhoEmL 93, WhoSSW 93*
Shyjka, Frank 1944- *St&PR 93*
Shyne, Ellen *AmWomPl*
Shyre, Paul *BioIn 17*
Shyu, Heidi 1953- *WhoAmW 93*
Si, Li Geng 1931- *WhoWor 93*
Siack, Steven D. 1946- *St&PR 93*
Siad Barre, Mohamed 1919- *ColdWar 2 [port]*
Siagian, Rizaldi 195-?- *Baker 92*
Siakotos, Ellen Catherine *Law&B 92*
Sialom, Sedat Sami 1940- *WhoWor 93*
Siamon, Sharon 1942- *WhoCanL 92*
Siano, Jerry J. *WhoAm 92*
Siano, Jerry J. 1935- *St&PR 93*
Siantz, Mary Lou deLeon 1947- *WhoAm 92*
Siapno, William David 1926- *WhoSSW 93*
Siarniak, Richard A. 1953- *St&PR 93*
Siart, William E.B. 1946- *St&PR 93*
Siart, William Eric Baxter 1946- *WhoAm 92*
Sias, Dennis *BioIn 17*
Sias, John B. 1927- *WhoAm 92*
Siatos, Thomas John 1923- *WhoWrEP 92*
Siau, John Finn 1921- *WhoAm 92*
Siazon, Domingo L., Jr. *WhoUN 92*
Sibal, Abner Woodruff 1921- *WhoAm 92*
Sibal, Louis Richard 1927- *WhoE 93*
Sibal, Virander Kumar 1937- *WhoUN 92*
Sibalszky, Zoltan Georg 1926- *WhoScE 91-4*
Sibaoka, Takao 1919- *WhoWor 93*
Sibay, Mussef *MiSFD 9*
Sibbet, Lorraine Alberta 1939- *WhoAmW 93*
Sibbett, Jane *BioIn 17*
Sibbett, Wilson *WhoScE 91-1*
Sibbett, Wilson 1948- *WhoWor 93*
Sibbio, Michael Gregory 1955- *WhoEmL 93*
Sibelius, Jean 1865-1957 *Baker 92, BioIn 17, OxDcOp*
Siber, Victor *Law&B 92*
Sibert, Ernest 1941- *WhoAm 92*
Sibert, Franklin Cummings 1891- *HarEnMi*
Sibert, Melissa Ann 1954- *WhoAmW 93*
Sibert, Sharon Rogers 1959- *WhoSSW 93*
Sibigtroth, Alan Ward 1950- *St&PR 93*
Sibigtroth, Joseph Clarence 1915- *WhoAm 92*
Sibley, Agnes 1914-1979 *ScF&FL 92*
Sibley, Alden Kingsland 1911- *WhoAm 92*
Sibley, Brian 1949- *ScF&FL 92*
Sibley, Charles Gald 1917- *WhoAm 92*
Sibley, David Emile 1935- *St&PR 93, WhoAm 92*
Sibley, Dawn Bunnell 1939- *WhoAm 92, WhoAmW 93*
Sibley, Earl A. 1929- *St&PR 93*
Sibley, Edgar Henry 1926- *WhoSSW 93*
Sibley, Elizabeth *Law&B 92*
Sibley, Ellen *St&PR 93*
Sibley, Gerry Ogden 1937- *St&PR 93*
Sibley, James Malcolm 1919- *WhoAm 92, WhoWor 93*
Sibley, Jerry Dan 1941- *WhoSSW 93*
Sibley, John Joseph *Law&B 92*
Sibley, Lewis Branch 1931- *WhoE 93*
Sibley, Mark Anderson 1950- *WhoAm 92*
Sibley, Richard Carl 1951- *WhoSSW 93*
Sibley, William Arthur 1932- *WhoAm 92*
Sibley, William Austin 1925- *WhoAm 92*
Sibley, Willis Elbridge 1930- *WhoAm 92*
Sibold, Robert H. 1941- *St&PR 93*
Sibole, Richard R. 1942- *St&PR 93*
Sibolski, Elizabeth Hawley 1950- *WhoAmW 93*
Sibolski, John Alfred, Jr. 1946- *WhoEmL 93*
Sibomana, Adrien 1953- *WhoAfr*
Sibomana, Andre 1954- *WhoWor 93*
Siboni, Erik (Anthon Valdemar) 1828-1892 *Baker 92*
Siboni, Giuseppe 1780-1839 *Baker 92*
Sibraa, Kerry Walter 1937- *WhoAsAP 91*
Sibson, Francis H. 1899- *ScF&FL 92*
Sibson, Robin *WhoScE 91-1*
Sibt Ibn Al-Jawzi 1186-1257 *OxDcByz*
Sibylle, Helene Marie Louise 1949- *WhoWor 93*
Sicard, Didier Philippe 1938- *WhoWor 93*
Sicard, M. 1932- *WhoScE 91-2*
Sichel, Arthur Gutman 1945- *WhoE 93*
Sichel, Beatrice Bonne 1934- *WhoAmW 93*
Sichel, Enid Keil 1946- *WhoAmW 93, WhoE 93*
Sichel, Leonard Joseph 1936- *St&PR 93*
Sichenze, Celeste Marie 1937- *WhoAmW 93*
Sicher, John D. *Law&B 92*
Sicherl, Pavle 1935- *WhoWor 93*
Sicherman, Marvin Allen 1934- *WhoAm 92*
Sichert, Paul O. 1933- *St&PR 93*
Sichewski, Vernon Roger 1942- *WhoSSW 93, WhoWor 93*

Sichi, Harry J. 1937- St&PR 93
Sichler, Edward H. 1935- St&PR 93
Sichler, Joseph E. 1941- St&PR 93
Sichler, Joseph Eberhardt, III 1941- WhoAm 92
Sichulski, Kazimierz 1879-1943 PolBiDi
Sicilian, Joseph Michael 1948- WhoAm 92
Siciliano, Harold Richard 1922- WhoSSW 93
Siciliano, Rocco Carmine 1922- St&PR 93, WhoAm 92
Siciliano, Sam 1947- ScF&FL 92
Sicilianos, Yorgos 1922- Baker 92
Sicinski, Andrzej 1924- ConAu 40NR
Sick, Helmut 1910-1991 BioIn 17
Sick, Henri 1936- WhoScE 91-2
Sick, William Norman, Jr. 1935- WhoAm 92
Sickels, David W. St&PR 93
Sickels, Robert Judd 1931- WhoAm 92
Sickle, Charlotte 1934- St&PR 93
Sickle, Cody T. 1949- St&PR 93, WhoAm 92
Sickler, Don BioIn 17
Sickler, Francis Edgar 1928- St&PR 93
Sickler, John Joseph 1942- St&PR 93
Sickles, Daniel E. BioIn 17
Sickles, Donna Howell- 1949- BioIn 17
Sicks, James N. Law&B 92
Siclari, Joseph D. ScF&FL 92
Sicotte, Luc 1955- St&PR 93
Sicotte, Sylvie 1936-1988 WhoCanL 92
Sicular, Terry 1955- WhoE 93
Sicuro, Natale Anthony 1934- WhoAm 92
Sida, Art Law&B 92
Sid Ahmed, Abdelkader 1942- WhoWor 93
Sidamon-Eristoff, Anne Phipps 1932- WhoAm 92
Sidamon-Eristoff, Constantine 1930- WhoAm 92, WhoWor 93
Sidar, Thomas Wilson 1949- WhoE 93
Sidare, Lynn Catherine 1958- WhoE 93
Sidaris, Andy 1933- MiSFD 9
Sidarta, Otok Bima 1960- Baker 92
Sidarweck, William John 1950- WhoE 93
Siddall, David L. Law&B 92
Siddall, Patricia Ann 1947- WhoE 93
Siddall, Sidney Stewart 1936- WhoWor 93
Siddall, Yvonne Robena 1946- WhoSSW 93
Siddayao, Corazon Morales 1932- WhoE 93
Sidders, Patrick M. 1940- St&PR 93
Sidders, Patrick Michael 1940- WhoAm 92
Siddhartha BioIn 17
Siddik, Harith 1949- WhoWor 93
Siddiqi, Jawed Iqbal Ahmed 1951- WhoWor 93
Siddiqi, Shamin Ahmad 1940- WhoAsAP 91
Siddiqui, Abdul Samad 1939- WhoAsAP 91
Siddiqui, Maqbool Ahmad 1941- WhoWor 93
Siddiqui, Waajid Law&B 92
Siddon, Thomas Edward 1941- WhoAm 92, WhoE 93
Siddons, Anne Rivers BioIn 17
Siddons, Anne Rivers 1936- ScF&FL 92
Siddons, Ernest George 1933- St&PR 93, WhoAm 92
Siddons, Ian 1942- WhoAm 92
Sidebottom, Eric WhoScE 91-1
Sidebottom, William George 1948- WhoEmL 93, WhoSSW 93
Sidel, Barrett Newman Law&B 92
Sidel, Enid Ruth 1936- WhoE 93
Sidel, Michael Kent 1950- WhoSSW 93
Sidel, Victor William 1931- WhoE 93
Sidell, Moss M. Law&B 92
Sidells, Arthur F. 1907- WhoAm 92
Sideman, Eva Stern WhoAmW 93
Sider, Richard Law&B 92
Sider, Ronald J(ames) 1939- ConAu 39NR
Sideri, Anthony H. 1925- St&PR 93
Sideris, George J. 1926- St&PR 93
Sideris, N. George 1944- WhoScE 91-3
Siderman, Richard Siderman 1952- St&PR 93
Sides, Barbara Joye 1933- WhoAmW 93
Sides, Brian Arthur WhoScE 91-1
Sides, Harold L. 1941- St&PR 93
Sides, Holly Harned 1957- WhoAmW 93
Sides, James Ralph 1936- WhoAm 92
Sides, John Quincy 1918- St&PR 93
Sides, Kermit Franklin 1932- WhoSSW 93
Sides, W(ade) Hampton 1962- ConAu 139
Sidewater, Samuel 1938- St&PR 93
Sidey, Hugh Swanson 1927- WhoAm 92
Sidhisunthorn, Arthasidhi 1913- WhoAsAP 91
Sidhu, Gurmail Singh 1955- WhoWor 93
Sidhwa, Bapsi BioIn 17
Sidhwa, Bapsi 1938- IntLitE
Sidhwa, Bapsi 1939- IntvWPC 92 [port]
Sidjakov, Nicolas 1924- WhoAm 92
Sidlauskas, Val 1927- St&PR 93
Sidle, Paul Robert 1925- St&PR 93
Sidlin, Murry 1940- Baker 92
Sidlowe, David A. St&PR 93
Sidman, Alice Fleming AmWomPl
Sidman, Evelyn 1914- St&PR 93
Sidman, James S. Law&B 92
Sidman, Marshall B. 1914- St&PR 93
Sidnal, Shamukhappa Basappa 1936- WhoAsAP 91
Sidnam, Caroline Northcote 1952- WhoE 93
Sidney, Algernon 1622-1683 BioIn 17
Sidney, George 1876-1945 & Murray, Charlie 1872-1941 QDrFCA 92 [port]
Sidney, George 1916- MiSFD 9
Sidney, Kathleen M. 1944- ScF&FL 92
Sidney, Mary 1561-1621 LitC 19 [port]
Sidney, Philip 1554-1586 BioIn 17, LitC 19 [port], MagSWL [port]
Sidney, Sylvia 1910- IntDcF 2-3 [port], WhoAm 92
Sidney, William Wright 1929- WhoWor 93
Sidney-Fryer, Donald 1934- ScF&FL 92
Sidonia, Alonso Perez de Guzman Medina 1550-1619 BioIn 17
Sidonius c. 431-c. 490 OxDcByz
Sidor, Ciril 1920- WhoScE 91-4
Sidor, Ellen Sutherland 1940- WhoE 93
Sidor, Karl V. Law&B 92
Sidorczyk, Zygmunt 1940- WhoScE 91-4
Sidoroff, Francois 1945- WhoScE 91-2
Sidorov, Vasiliy Sergeevich 1945- WhoUN 92
Sidorsky, Arthur 1933- St&PR 93
Sidoti, Christopher Alexander 1952- WhoE 93
Sidowski, Joseph Boleslaus 1925- WhoSSW 93
Sidran, Miriam 1920- WhoAmW 93
Sidrane, Michelle Diana 1948- WhoAm 92
Sidrane, Steven D. 1954- St&PR 93
Sidransky, Herschel 1925- WhoAm 92, WhoE 93
Sidransky, Ruth BioIn 17
Sidun, Nancy Marie 1955- WhoAmW 93
Sidwell, Robert C. Law&B 92
Sidwell, Robert Chandler Law&B 92
Sidwell, Robert William 1937- WhoAm 92
Sieban, Henry E. 1937- St&PR 93
Siebein, Gary Walter 1951- WhoSSW 93
Siebel, Mathias Paul WhoAm 92
Siebels, Scott A. Law&B 92
Sieben, Paul G. 1947- St&PR 93
Siebenberg, Henry Norman 1940- WhoE 93
Siebenga, David J. 1960- St&PR 93
Siebenschuh, William Robert 1942- WhoAm 92
Siebenthal, Paul Leroy 1938- St&PR 93
Siebenthall, Curtis Alan 1929- WhoSSW 93
Sieber, Albert 1844-1907 BioIn 17
Sieber, Claudia E. Law&B 92
Sieber, Ferdinand 1822-1895 Baker 92
Sieber, James Leo 1936- WhoE 93
Sieber, Robert P. 1945- St&PR 93
Sieber, Suzanne Mahoney 1963- WhoAmW 93
Sieber, Ulrich 1950- WhoWor 93
Siebers, Tobin 1953- ScF&FL 92
Siebert, Calvin D. 1934- WhoAm 92
Siebert, Caryn Brenna Law&B 92
Siebert, Diane Dolores 1948- WhoAm 92, WhoWor 93
Siebert, Donald Robert 1946- WhoE 93
Siebert, Douglas Kent 1943- WhoE 93
Siebert, George William 1943- WhoAm 92
Siebert, Harold L. St&PR 93
Siebert, Horst 1938- WhoWor 93
Siebert, Karl Joseph 1945- WhoAm 92
Siebert, Manfred 1925- WhoWor 93
Siebert, Muriel WhoAm 92, WhoAmW 93
Siebert, Raymond Nicholas 1947- St&PR 93
Siebert, Richard Walther 1912-1978 BiDAMSp 1989
Siebert, Stephanie Ray 1949- WhoAmW 93, WhoEmL 93, WhoWor 93
Siebert, Stephen Warner 1957- WhoE 93
Siebert, Wilhelm Dieter 1931- Baker 92
Siebert, William McConway 1925- WhoAm 92
Sieberth, Heinz-Gunter 1934- WhoScE 91-3, WhoWor 93
Sieberth, John F. Law&B 92
Sieberts, Jan Kristian 1942- St&PR 93
Siebold, Bert Allen 1951- WhoSSW 93
Siebold, Margaret A. 1939- WhoAm 92
Siebold, Philipp Franz von 1796-1866 IntDcAn
Siebrand, Willem 1932- WhoAm 92
Siebrasse, Kathy Ann 1954- WhoAmW 93
Siebrasse, Renate WhoScE 91-1
Siebrasse, Richard W. 1926- WhoAm 92
Sieburth, Janice Fae 1927- WhoAmW 93
Sieck, A. Gerard Law&B 92
Sieckmann, Gordon Fred Law&B 92
Sieczkarek, Mark M. 1954- St&PR 93
Siedlarz, John Edward 1942- St&PR 93
Siedlecki, Janusz A. 1947- WhoScE 91-4
Siedlecki-Grzymala, Adam 1876-1967 PolBiDi
Siedler, Arthur James 1927- WhoAm 92
Siedler, Gerold 1933- WhoScE 91-3
Siedlewski, Janusz Mieczyslaw 1929- WhoScE 91-4
Siedliska, Frances 1842-1902 PolBiDi
Siedlyk, Leon Lavern 1924- St&PR 93
Siedor, Greig Robert Law&B 92
Siefers, Robert George 1945- St&PR 93, WhoAm 92
Siefert, David Michael 1951- WhoWor 93
Siefert, Gerhard 1929- WhoScE 91-3
Siefert, Richard Maurice 1939- WhoSSW 93
Siefert, Robert George 1931- St&PR 93, WhoAm 92
Siefert, Tina Gilbert 1965- WhoAmW 93
Siefert-Kazanjian, Donna WhoAmW 93, WhoE 93
Sieff, John 1928- St&PR 93
Sieff, John Alexander 1923- WhoAm 92
Siefken, Kenneth C. 1949- St&PR 93
Siefkin, William Charles 1946- WhoEmL 93, WhoSSW 93, WhoWor 93
Sieg, Albert Louis 1930- St&PR 93, WhoAm 92
Sieg, Dennis A. 1932- St&PR 93
Sieg, George D., Jr. 1934- St&PR 93
Sieg, Judy Kesig 1955- WhoSSW 93
Sieg, Manfred 1944- WhoWor 93
Siegal, Allan Marshall 1940- WhoAm 92
Siegal, Burton Lee 1931- WhoAm 92
Siegal, Jacob J. 1929- WhoAm 92
Siegal, Janis c. 1953- See Manhattan Transfer, The ConMus 8
Siegal, John BioIn 17
Siegal, Rita Goran 1934- WhoAm 92
Siegan, Bernard Herbert 1924- WhoAm 92
Siegbahn, Kai Manne Borje 1918- WhoAm 92, WhoScE 91-4, WhoWor 93
Siegel, Alan BioIn 17
Siegel, Alan 1963- St&PR 93
Siegel, Alan E. Law&B 92
Siegel, Alan Michael 1938- WhoAm 92
Siegel, Alan Roger 1931- WhoE 93
Siegel, Allen George 1934- WhoAm 92
Siegel, Alvan 1934- St&PR 93
Siegel, Andrew J. Law&B 92
Siegel, Arnold 1928- St&PR 93
Siegel, Arnold 1931- St&PR 93
Siegel, Arthur 1908- WhoAm 92
Siegel, Arthur J. 1943- St&PR 93
Siegel, Barbara 1952?- ScF&FL 92
Siegel, Barbara Zenz 1931- WhoAmW 93
Siegel, Beatrice ConAu 40NR
Siegel, Benjamin 1914-1991 BioIn 17
Siegel, Benjamin Morton 1916-1990 BioIn 17
Siegel, Betty Lentz 1931- WhoAm 92, WhoAmW 93, WhoSSW 93
Siegel, Carl F.W. d1869 Baker 92
Siegel, Carole Ethel 1936- WhoAmW 93
Siegel, Carolyn Lee 1951- WhoWrEP 92
Siegel, Charles Law&B 92
Siegel, Charles 1944- WhoAm 92
Siegel, Charles Holladay 1941- WhoSSW 93
Siegel, Corky BioIn 17
Siegel, Cynthia Allison 1964- WhoAmW 93
Siegel, David B. Law&B 92
Siegel, David Donald 1931- WhoAm 92
Siegel, David J. 1948- St&PR 93, WhoIns 93
Siegel, Don 1912-1991 AnObit 1991, BioIn 17, ConTFT 10, MiSFD 9N
Siegel, Donald Bert 1935- St&PR 93
Siegel, Dorothy Paula 1932- WhoWrEP 92
Siegel, Edward J. 1944- St&PR 93
Siegel, Edward M. 1934- St&PR 93
Siegel, Erika Janet 1962- WhoE 93
Siegel, Faibel 1807-1887 BioIn 17
Siegel, Fred 1941- WhoE 93
Siegel, Frederic Richard 1932- WhoAm 92
Siegel, Gail Law&B 92
Siegel, Gary Michael 1947- St&PR 93
Siegel, Gary Morton 1930- St&PR 93
Siegel, George Henry 1926- WhoAm 92
Siegel, George Lewis 1934- WhoE 93
Siegel, Glenn Ernest 1958- WhoE 93
Siegel, Harold Aryai 1931- St&PR 93
Siegel, Herbert Bernard 1934- WhoAm 92
Siegel, Herbert J. 1928- St&PR 93
Siegel, Herbert Jay 1928- WhoAm 92, WhoE 93, WhoWor 93
Siegel, Ira B. 1943- St&PR 93
Siegel, Ira Theodore 1944- WhoAm 92, WhoE 93
Siegel, Isabelle BioIn 17
Siegel, Isabelle d1992 NewYTBS 92
Siegel, Jack Morton 1922- WhoAm 92
Siegel, Janis 1952- Baker 92
Siegel, Jeanne Ferris Law&B 92
Siegel, Jeff K. 1958- WhoE 93
Siegel, Jeffrey 1942- Baker 92
Siegel, Jeffrey Stuart 1942- St&PR 93
Siegel, Jeremy James 1945- WhoE 93
Siegel, Jerome Harold 1932- WhoE 93
Siegel, Jerome Samuel 1944- WhoE 93
Siegel, Jill Leslie 1953- WhoAmW 93
Siegel, Joel BioIn 17
Siegel, Jonathan A. Law&B 92
Siegel, Kathy 1947- St&PR 93
Siegel, Kenneth Ian 1957- WhoAm 92
Siegel, Larry 1935- WhoSSW 93
Siegel, Laurence 1928- WhoAm 92
Siegel, Lawrence 1931- WhoSSW 93
Siegel, Lawrence J. 1943- WhoE 93
Siegel, Leonard I. 1926- St&PR 93
Siegel, Lloyd H. 1928- WhoAm 92
Siegel, Louis 1902- St&PR 93
Siegel, Louis Pendleton 1942- WhoAm 92
Siegel, Lucy Boswell 1950- WhoAmW 93
Siegel, Lynne Elise Moore 1957- WhoAmW 93
Siegel, Marc Monroe 1916- WhoAm 92
Siegel, Marcia B. 1932- ConAu 37NR
Siegel, Margaret Ann 1947- WhoAmW 93
Siegel, Mark 1949- ScF&FL 92
Siegel, Mark Jordan 1949- WhoSSW 93, WhoWor 93
Siegel, Martin 1925- WhoWrEP 92
Siegel, Martin 1938-1972 ScF&FL 92
Siegel, Martin A. BioIn 17
Siegel, Martin Edward 1946- St&PR 93
Siegel, Martin Jay 1942- WhoAm 92
Siegel, Marvin Ira 1946- WhoE 93
Siegel, Mary-Ellen 1932- WhoE 93
Siegel, Mary-Ellen (Kulkin) 1932- ConAu 40NR
Siegel, Mary Goldburt 1896-1991 BioIn 17
Siegel, Michael D. 1937- St&PR 93
Siegel, Michael Elliot 1942- WhoWor 93
Siegel, Michael Eric 1950- WhoE 93
Siegel, Milt B. St&PR 93
Siegel, Milton P. 1911- WhoAm 92, WhoSSW 93, WhoWor 93
Siegel, Mo BioIn 17
Siegel, Mo J. 1949- WhoAm 92
Siegel, Nathaniel Harold 1929- WhoAm 92
Siegel, Ned Lawrence 1951- WhoSSW 93
Siegel, Norman Joseph 1943- WhoE 93
Siegel, Owen R. 1919- St&PR 93
Siegel, Paul 1938- WhoWor 93
Siegel, Paul Barton Law&B 92
Siegel, Paul Benjamin 1932- WhoSSW 93
Siegel, Paul Marc 1948- St&PR 93
Siegel, Randy 1955- WhoAm 92, WhoSSW 93
Siegel, Raymond John 1947- St&PR 93
Siegel, Richard ScF&FL 92
Siegel, Richard A. 1947- WhoE 93
Siegel, Richard Allen 1927- WhoE 93
Siegel, Richard David 1939- WhoAm 92
Siegel, Richard S. Law&B 92
Siegel, RitaSue WhoE 93
Siegel, Robert BioIn 17, WhoE 93
Siegel, Robert 1939- ScF&FL 92
Siegel, Robert B. 1924- St&PR 93
Siegel, Robert Harold 1939- WhoWrEP 92
Siegel, Robert James 1929- WhoSSW 93, WhoWor 93
Siegel, Robert Ted 1928- WhoAm 92
Siegel, Ronald Elliot Law&B 92
Siegel, Samuel 1930- St&PR 93, WhoAm 92
Siegel, Scott 1951- ScF&FL 92
Siegel, Scott Adam 1957- WhoE 93
Siegel, Seymour Louis 1933- WhoE 93
Siegel, Sheldon C. 1922- WhoAm 92
Siegel, Sid 1927- WhoAm 92
Siegel, Simon B. d1991 BioIn 17
Siegel, Stanley 1941- WhoAm 92
Siegel, Steven F. Law&B 92
Siegel, Sylvia 1946- WhoAmW 93
Siegel, Thomas Joseph 1935- St&PR 93, WhoE 93
Siegel, Thomas Louis 1939- WhoAm 92
Siegel, Victor J. d1990 BioIn 17
Siegel, William H. 1948- St&PR 93
Siegel, William Mordecai 1950- WhoWrEP 92
Siegele, H.H. 1883-1983 ScF&FL 92
Siegell, Barbara C. Law&B 92
Siegelman, Allison Stacey 1962- WhoAmW 93
Siegel-Tabori, Kristoffer ConTFT 10
Siegenthaler, Paul Andre 1931- WhoScE 91-4, WhoWor 93

Siegenthaler, Walter Ernst 1923- *WhoWor 93*
Sieger, Charles Martin 1946- *WhoAm 92*
Sieger, Dieter *BioIn 17*
Sieger, John A. 1942- *St&PR 93*
Siegert, Barbara Marie 1935- *WhoE 93*
Siegert, Joachim Heinrich 1956- *WhoWor 93*
Siegert, Marvin Giles 1948- *St&PR 93*
Siegfried, David Lars 1949- *St&PR 93*
Siegfried, John Paul 1938- *St&PR 93*
Siegfried, Peter Charles *Law&B 92*
Siegfried, Robert E. 1922- *St&PR 93*
Siegfried, Robert Edwin 1922- *WhoAm 92*
Siegfried and Roy *BioIn 17*
Siegl, Otto 1896-1978 *Baker 92*
Siegle, Richard E. 1929- *St&PR 93*
Siegler, Ava Lee 1939- *WhoAmW 93*
Siegler, Howard Matthew 1932- *WhoAm 92*
Siegler, Ilene C. 1946- *WhoAmW 93*
Siegler, Ira I. 1943- *St&PR 93*
Siegler, Mark 1941- *WhoAm 92, WhoWor 93*
Siegler, Morton Abraham 1922- *WhoE 93*
Siegler, Scott Merrill 1947- *St&PR 93*
Siegler, Thomas E. 1934- *St&PR 93*
Siegler, Thomas Edmund 1934- *WhoAm 92*
Siegler-Lathrop, Patrick 1942- *WhoWor 93*
Siegman, Aaron D. *Law&B 92*
Siegman, Anthony Edward 1931- *WhoAm 92*
Siegman, Ellen I. *Law&B 92*
Siegman, Marion Joyce 1933- *WhoAmW 93*
Siegman, Meryl *ScF&FL 92*
Siegmeister, Elie 1909-1991 *Baker 92, BioIn 17*
Siegmund, Melinda Gayle 1962- *WhoAmW 93*
Siegmund, Richard W. 1944- *St&PR 93*
Siegmund, Walter Paul 1925- *WhoE 93*
Siegmund-Schultze, Walther 1916- *Baker 92*
Siegner, Alan L. 1939- *St&PR 93*
Siegriest, Louis B. 1899-1989 *BioIn 17*
Siegrist, Johannes 1943- *WhoScE 91-3*
Siegrist, Michele Anne 1961- *WhoAmW 93*
Siegrist, Robert R. *ScF&FL 92*
Sieh, David Henry 1947- *WhoE 93*
Siehr, Gustav 1837-1896 *Baker 92, OxDcOp*
Sieke, Eric T. *Law&B 92*
Sieker, Friedhelm 1933- *WhoScE 91-3*
Siekert, Harold Richard 1928- *St&PR 93*
Siekert, Robert George 1924- *WhoAm 92, WhoWrEP 92*
Siekevitz, Philip 1918- *WhoAm 92*
Siekman, Elizabeth Nancy Ann 1942- *WhoAmW 93*
Siekman, Thomas C. *Law&B 92*
Siekmann, Donald Charles 1938- *WhoAm 92, WhoSSW 93, WhoWor 93*
Siekmann, Frank Herman 1925- *WhoE 93*
Siekmann, Jorg Hans 1941- *WhoWor 93*
Siekmann, Julius Wilhelm Dietrich 1925- *WhoScE 91-3*
Siekmann, Lothar 1942- *WhoScE 91-3, WhoWor 93*
Sielczak, Marek W. 1935- *WhoSSW 93*
Sielicki-Korczak, Boris Zdzislaw 1939- *WhoSSW 93*
Siem, Frederick Meyers 1949- *WhoSSW 93*
Siemankowski, Francis Theodore 1914- *WhoE 93*
Siemans, Lloyd *ScF&FL 92*
Siembab, Kevin J. 1955- *St&PR 93*
Siemek, Jakub-Kazimierz 1937- *WhoWor 93*
Siemens, Alfred H. 1932- *ConAu 139*
Siemer, Deanne Clemence 1940- *WhoAm 92, WhoAmW 93*
Siemer, Paul Jennings 1946- *WhoAm 92*
Siemer, Richard Clemens 1949- *St&PR 93*
Siemer, Robert Clemens 1952- *St&PR 93*
Siemers, Laurel T. *Law&B 92*
Siemes, Heinrich 1929- *WhoScE 91-3*
Siemiatycki, Jack 1946- *WhoAm 92*
Sieminski, Alfred Dennis 1911-1990 *BioIn 17*
Siemion, Ignacy Zenon 1932- *WhoScE 91-4*
Siemiradzki, Henryk 1843-1902 *PolBiDi*
Siemon, Carl 1922- *St&PR 93*
Siemon, John Austin 1959- *St&PR 93*
Siemon, Robert Lawrence 1949- *St&PR 93*
Siems, Margarethe 1879-1952 *Baker 92, IntDcOp, OxDcOp*
Siems, Rolf 1930- *WhoScE 91-3*
Siemssen, Rolf Hendrik 1933- *WhoScE 91-3*
Siem Tjam, Ferdinand Theo T.J. 1943- *WhoUN 92*
Siena, John J. *Law&B 92*
Siena, John R., Jr. *Law&B 92*
Siener, William Harold 1945- *WhoAm 92, WhoE 93*
Sienicki, Dennis J. 1949- *WhoE 93*
Sieniutycz, Stanislaw 1940- *WhoWor 93*
Sienkiewicz, Henryk 1846-1916 *BioIn 17, PolBiDi*
Sienkiewicz, John Casimir 1933- *St&PR 93*
Sienkiewicz, Julian *WhoWrEP 92*
Sienkiewicz, Julian M. 1929- *WhoAm 92*
Sienkiewicz-Mercer, Ruth 1950- *ConAu 136*
Siep, Carolyn Sue 1942- *WhoAmW 93*
Siepi, Cesare 1920- *OxDcOp*
Siepi, Cesare 1923- *Baker 92, IntDcOp, WhoAm 92*
Siepiola, James W. 1953- *St&PR 93*
Sieracki, Paul S. *Law&B 92*
Sieren, David Joseph 1941- *WhoSSW 93*
Siering, Joel R. 1936- *St&PR 93*
Sierk, James E. 1938- *St&PR 93*
Sierles, Frederick Stephen 1942- *WhoAm 92*
Sierpinski, Waclaw 1882-1969 *PolBiDi*
Sierra, Justo 1848-1912 *DcMexL*
Sierra, Roberto 1953- *Baker 92*
Sierra, Ruben *BioIn 17*
Sierra, Ruben 1946- *DcLB 122 [port]*
Sierra, Ruben Angel 1965- *WhoAm 92*
Sierra, Stella 1917- *SpAmA*
Sierra-Hill, Lazaro Marcelino 1955- *WhoSSW 93*
Sierra O'Reilly, Justo 1814-1861 *DcMexL*
Sierro, Jean-Marc 1946- *WhoWor 93*
Sierro, Jerome 1936- *WhoScE 91-4*
Siers, Charles Larry 1942- *St&PR 93*
Sies, Helmut 1942- *WhoScE 91-3*
Siesjo, Bo 1930- *WhoScE 91-4*
Siess, Alfred Albert, Jr. 1935- *WhoE 93*
Siess, Charles P., Jr. *WhoAm 92*
Siess, Chester Paul 1916- *WhoAm 92*
Siess, Judith Ann 1947- *WhoAmW 93*
Siess, Robert D. 1943- *St&PR 93*
Siesto, Vincenzo 1928- *WhoScE 91-3*
Sieveking, Martinus 1867-1950 *Baker 92*
Sieveking, Michelle Lynne *Law&B 92*
Sievel-Otten, Lisa Ann 1962- *WhoAmW 93*
Siever, Raymond 1923- *WhoAm 92, WhoWrEP 92*
Sievers, H.J. 1930- *St&PR 93*
Sievers, Lieselotte 1928- *WhoWor 93*
Sievers, Mark Paul *Law&B 92*
Sievers, Michael A. 1945- *St&PR 93*
Sievers, Philip C. 1936- *St&PR 93*
Sievers, Robert H. 1941- *WhoAm 92*
Sievers, Robert J. 1933- *St&PR 93*
Sievers, Roy 1926- *BioIn 17*
Sievers, Roy Edward 1926- *BiDAMSp 1989*
Sievert, Dorothy Carlton 1946- *WhoAmW 93*
Sievert, Frederick J. 1948- *WhoIns 93*
Sievert, James Lee 1934- *St&PR 93*
Sievert, Johannes D. 1935- *WhoScE 91-3*
Sievert, John *ScF&FL 92*
Sievert, Ken 1935- *St&PR 93*
Sievert, Wayne R. 1938- *St&PR 93*
Sieverts, Frank Arne 1933- *WhoAm 92*
Sievwright, Georgia Hastings *Law&B 92*
Sievwright, J.K. *Law&B 92*
Siew, Vincent 1939- *WhoAsAP 91*
Siewers, C. Nathaniel 1947- *St&PR 93*
Siewert, Cyrill R. 1943- *St&PR 93*
Siewert, Edgar Allen 1927- *WhoSSW 93, WhoWor 93*
Siewert, Jeffrey Paul 1947- *St&PR 93*
Siewert, Mark S. 1953- *St&PR 93*
Siewert, Raymond Francis, Jr. 1931- *WhoE 93*
Siewiorek, Daniel Paul 1946- *WhoAm 92*
Siezen, R.J. 1945- *WhoScE 91-3*
Siface 1653-1697 *Baker 92*
Siff, Ira *BioIn 17*
Siff, Jesse d1991 *BioIn 17*
Siff, Karen Ann 1960- *WhoAmW 93*
Siff, Lawrence A. 1962- *St&PR 93*
Siff, Marlene Ida 1936- *WhoAmW 93, WhoE 93*
Siff, Robert M. 1924- *St&PR 93*
Sifferman, Thomas Raymond 1941- *WhoSSW 93*
Siffert *WhoScE 91-2*
Siffert, John Sand 1947- *WhoWor 93*
Siffert, Robert Spencer 1918- *WhoAm 92*
Sifflard, Nancy Nichols 1964- *WhoE 93*
Sifford, Charlie 1922- *ConBlB 4 [port]*
Sifford, Darrell 1931-1992 *BioIn 17*
Sifford, Darrell Charles 1931- *WhoAm 92*
Sifkovic, Franc *WhoScE 91-4*
Sifneos, Peter Emanuel 1920- *WhoAm 92*
Sifre, Antonio R. 1944- *WhoAm 92*
Sifton, Claire Ginsburg 1897- *AmWomPl*
Sifton, David Whittier 1940- *WhoAm 92*
Sifton, Elisabeth 1939- *WhoAm 92*
Sifton, Michael Clifford 1931- *St&PR 93, WhoAm 92*
Sigal, Clancy 1926- *BioIn 17*
Sigal, Michael Stephen 1942- *WhoAm 92*
Sigal, Roland Lee 1925- *St&PR 93*
Sigall, Harold Fred 1943- *WhoAm 92*
Sigband, Norman Bruce 1920- *WhoAm 92*
Sigel, Efrem 1943- *WhoWrEP 92*
Sigel, Louis Paul, Jr. 1921- *WhoE 93*
Sigel, Marshall Elliot 1941- *WhoSSW 93*
Sigel, Mola Michael 1920- *WhoAm 92*
Sigelbaum, Harvey C. 1937- *WhoIns 93*
Sigety, Charles Edward 1922- *WhoAm 92, WhoSSW 93, WhoWor 93*
Sigfrids, James A. 1929- *St&PR 93*
Sigfried, Stefan Bertil 1955- *WhoWor 93*
Sigfusson, Arni 1956- *WhoWor 93*
Sigfusson, Stefan Hilmar 1934- *WhoScE 91-4*
Siggaard-Andersen, Ole 1932- *WhoScE 91-2*
Siggins, Jack Arthur 1938- *WhoAm 92*
Sigismondi, Giuseppe 1739-1826 *Baker 92*
Sigl, Rudolf 1928- *WhoScE 91-3*
Siglain, Helen 1950- *WhoAmW 93, WhoEmL 93, WhoWor 93*
Sigler, Andrew Clark 1931- *St&PR 93, WhoAm 92, WhoE 93*
Sigler, Donald H. 1946- *St&PR 93*
Sigler, Jay Adrian 1933- *WhoAm 92*
Sigler, LeRoy Walter 1926- *WhoAm 92*
Sigler, Lois Oliver 1923- *WhoSSW 93*
Sigler, Paul Benjamin 1934- *WhoAm 92*
Sigler, Richard 1945- *St&PR 93*
Sigler, William Franklin 1909- *WhoAm 92*
Sigli, Daniele 1945- *WhoScE 91-2*
Sigman, Christine W. *Law&B 92*
Sigman, David D. *Law&B 92*
Sigman, Eugene M. 1928- *WhoAm 92*
Sigman, Helene Hannah 1946- *WhoAmW 93*
Sigman, John Herbert 1943- *St&PR 93*
Sigman, Karl 1957- *WhoE 93*
Sigman, Mark 1950- *St&PR 93*
Sigman, Seymour 1925- *St&PR 93*
Sigman, Stuart Jay 1955- *WhoE 93*
Sigmon, Daniel Ray 1949- *WhoSSW 93*
Sigmon, James Edward 1948- *St&PR 93*
Sigmon, Scott B. 1946- *WhoEmL 93*
Sigmond, Richard Brian 1944- *WhoE 93, WhoWor 93*
Sigmond, Robert M. 1920- *WhoAm 92*
Sigmund, Barbara *BioIn 17*
Sigmund, Paul E(ugene) 1929- *ConAu 39NR*
Sigmund, Paul Eugene 1929- *WhoAm 92*
Sigmund, Peter 1936- *WhoScE 91-2*
Signer, Billie Touchstone 1930- *WhoWrEP 92*
Signer, Harry 1910- *St&PR 93*
Signer, Robert Andrew 1942- *WhoAm 92*
Signet, Bradford R. *Law&B 92*
Signor, Florence Rae *AmWomPl*
Signor, Said G. 1951- *St&PR 93*
Signor, Sharon Smith 1943- *WhoAmW 93, WhoE 93*
Signorelli, James *MiSFD 9*
Signorelli, Lindo A. 1937- *WhoE 93*
Signorelli, Pat *BioIn 17*
Signoret, Jean-Pierre 1929- *WhoScE 91-2*
Signoret, Pierre A. 1932- *WhoScE 91-2*
Signoret, Simone 1921-1985 *BioIn 17, IntDcF 2-3 [port]*
Signorile, Martha Anne 1949- *WhoAmW 93*
Signorile, Michelangelo *BioIn 17*
Signorile, Vincent Anthony 1959- *WhoE 93, WhoWor 93*
Signorini, Cosimo 1943- *WhoScE 91-3*
Signorini, John Ernest 1945- *St&PR 93*
Signorini, L. Federico 1923- *WhoScE 91-3*
Signorino, Charles A. 1932- *St&PR 93*
Signorovitch, Dennis James 1945- *WhoWor 93*
Sigoloff, Sanford Charles 1930- *St&PR 93*
Sigrest, Bobby Reed 1932- *St&PR 93*
Sigsbee, H. James 1949- *St&PR 93*
Sigtenhorst-Meyer, Bernhard van den 1888-1953 *Baker 92*
Sigua, Tengiz *WhoWor 93*
Siguenza, Silvia 1943- *DcMexL*
Siguion-Reyna, Leonardo 1921- *WhoWor 93*
Siguler, George William 1947- *St&PR 93, WhoAm 92*
Sigulogo, Gerard Temekapau 1945- *WhoAsAP 91*
Sigur, Wanda Anne Alexander 1958- *WhoSSW 93*
Sigurbjornsson, Bjorn 1931- *WhoScE 91-4, WhoUN 92*
Sigurbjornsson, Thorkell 1938- *Baker 92*
Sigurdardottir, Johanna 1942- *WhoWor 93*
Sigurdson, J.M. *Law&B 92*
Sigurdsson, Gunnar 1946- *WhoScE 91-4*
Sigurdsson, Haraldur 1939- *WhoAm 92*
Sigurdsson, Jon 1941- *WhoWor 93*
Sigurdsson, Jon 1946- *WhoWor 93*
Sigurdsson, Thordur Baldur 1929- *WhoWor 93*
Sigurgestsson, Hordur 1938- *WhoWor 93*
Sigurjonsson, Sturla 1958- *WhoWor 93*
Sigusch, Volkmar 1940- *WhoScE 91-3*
Sigwart, Botho 1884-1915 *Baker 92*
Sigworth, Craig L. *Law&B 92*
Sigworth, Mary Ann 1938- *WhoAmW 93*
Sih, Julius Wei Wu 1922- *WhoAm 92*
Sihanouk 1922- *BioIn 17*
Sihanouk, Norodom 1922- *ColdWar 2 [port], DcTwHis, WhoWor 93*
Sihler, William Wooding 1937- *WhoAm 92*
Siikarla, Neal 1947- *St&PR 93*
Sij, John William, Jr. 1943- *WhoSSW 93*
Sijan, Lance *BioIn 17*
Sijan, Slobodan *MiSFD 9*
Sijan, Slobodan 1946- *DrEEuF*
Sik, Tibor H. 1928- *WhoScE 91-4*
Sikarskie, David Lawrence 1937- *WhoAm 92*
Sikder, Firoze Shah 1953- *WhoWor 93*
Siker, Ephraim S. 1926- *WhoAm 92*
Siker, Estelle 1918- *WhoAmW 93*
Sikes, Alfred *BioIn 17*
Sikes, Alfred C. 1939- *WhoAm 92, WhoE 93, WhoWor 93*
Sikes, Cynthia Lee 1954- *WhoAmW 93*
Sikes, David Glenn 1942- *WhoWrEP 92*
Sikes, O.J. 1941- *WhoUN 92*
Sikes, Robert L. F. 1906- *WhoAm 92*
Sikes, Ruth Cox 1952- *WhoSSW 93*
Sikes, Shirley Ruth 1928- *WhoWrEP 92*
Sikes, William Wirt 1836-1883 *JrnUS*
Siket, Paul 1945- *St&PR 93*
Siki, Bela 1923- *Baker 92*
Sikkander, Nagoorpitchai 1945- *WhoUN 92*
Sikkema, Karen Ann 1946- *St&PR 93*
Sikkema, William D. 1949- *St&PR 93*
Sikkenga, William Jay *Law&B 92*
Sikking, James B. *BioIn 17*
Siklos, Albert 1878-1942 *Baker 92*
Siklossy, Laurent 1941- *WhoWor 93*
Sikora, Eugene Stanley 1924- *WhoSSW 93*
Sikora, Frank J(oseph) 1936- *ConAu 40NR*
Sikora, Jerzy Stanislaw 1925- *WhoScE 91-4*
Sikora, Karol *WhoScE 91-1*
Sikora, Richard Innes 1927- *WhoAm 92*
Sikora, Richard Paul 1931- *St&PR 93*
Sikora, Ryszard 1932- *WhoScE 91-4*
Sikorovsky, Eugene F. *Law&B 92*
Sikorovsky, Eugene Frank 1927- *St&PR 93, WhoAm 92*
Sikorski, Gerry 1948- *CngDr 91, WhoAm 92*
Sikorski, Irene Joyce 1947- *WhoAmW 93*
Sikorski, Kazimierz 1895-1986 *Baker 92*
Sikorski, Nicholas G. 1945- *St&PR 93*
Sikorski, Radek *BioIn 17*
Sikorski, Tomasz 1939- *Baker 92*
Sikorski, Wladislaw 1881-1943 *DcTwHis*
Sikorski, Wladyslaw 1881-1943 *PolBiDi*
Sikorski, Zdzislaw Edmund 1930- *WhoScE 91-4*
Sikorski-Tuerpe, Laura Mary 1950- *WhoAmW 93*
Sikorsky, Igor *BioIn 17*
Sikula, John Paul 1944- *WhoAm 92*
Sikyta, Bohumil 1932- *WhoScE 91-4*
Silag, Bill 1946- *WhoWrEP 92*
Silagi, Barbara Weibler 1930- *WhoAmW 93*
Silagi, Selma 1916- *WhoAm 92*
Silak, John L. *Law&B 92*
Silani, Vincenzo 1952- *WhoWor 93*
Silano, Robert Anthony 1942- *WhoE 93*
Silanyo, Ahmed Mohammed 1936- *WhoAfr*
Silard, Stephen A. 1938- *WhoUN 92*
Silas, A.E. *ScF&FL 92*
Silas, Cecil Jesse 1932- *St&PR 93, WhoAm 92, WhoSSW 93, WhoWor 93*
Silas, Edouard 1827-1909 *Baker 92*
Silas, Richard A. 1938- *WhoIns 93*
Silas, Stanley *Law&B 92*
Silayev, Ivan 1930- *BioIn 17*
Silbajoris, Frank Rimvydas 1926- *WhoAm 92*
Silbaugh, Preston Norwood 1918- *WhoAm 92, WhoWor 93*
Silber, Bernard d1990 *BioIn 17*
Silber, David 1943- *St&PR 93*
Silber, David E. 1935- *WhoE 93*
Silber, Diana *ScF&FL 92*
Silber, Frederic S. *Law&B 92*
Silber, John Karen 1945- *WhoWrEP 92*
Silber, John R. *BioIn 17*
Silber, John Robert 1926- *WhoAm 92, WhoE 93*
Silber, Jonathan Sanford *Law&B 92*
Silber, Norman Jules 1945- *WhoAm 92, WhoSSW 93*
Silber, Sam *BioIn 17*
Silberberg, Charles T. *Law&B 92*

Silberberg, Donald H. 1934- WhoAm 92
Silberberg, Inga 1934- WhoAmW 93
Silberberg, Mary Bickley 1956- WhoIns 93
Silberberg, Rein 1932- WhoWor 93
Silberberg, Sophie 1913-1991 BioIn 17
Silberg, Carol Ann Schwartz 1948- WhoE 93
Silberg, Jay Eliot 1941- WhoAm 92
Silberg, Joel MiSFD 9
Silbergeld, Arthur F. 1942- WhoAm 92
Silbergeld, Ellen Kovner 1945- WhoAm 92
Silbergeld, Mae D. d1990 BioIn 17
Silbergeld, Sam 1918- WhoE 93
Silbergleit, Alexander Samuilovich 1948- WhoWor 93
Silberlicht, Albert 1946- St&PR 93
Silberman, Alan Harvey 1940- WhoAm 92
Silberman, Allan David 1935- St&PR 93
Silberman, Arnold David 1935- St&PR 93
Silberman, Arthur 1929- WhoSSW 93
Silberman, Charles Eliot 1925- WhoAm 92, WhoWrEP 92
Silberman, Charles I. 1949- St&PR 93
Silberman, David B., Jr. 1920- St&PR 93
Silberman, Eugene Irvin 1930- St&PR 93
Silberman, Gregory Alan 1953- WhoSSW 93
Silberman, H. Lee 1919- WhoAm 92, WhoE 93
Silberman, Henri Casimir 1925- WhoWor 93
Silberman, Ira J. 1936- St&PR 93
Silberman, James Henry 1927- WhoAm 92, WhoE 93
Silberman, Laurence Hirsch 1935- CngDr 91, WhoAm 92, WhoE 93
Silberman, Lloyd Paul 1954- St&PR 93
Silberman, Mark S. 1950- St&PR 93
Silberman, Michael Jay 1954- WhoE 93
Silberman, Rebecca Louise 1957- WhoAmW 93, WhoE 93
Silberman, Rosalie Gaull 1937- WhoAmW 93
Silbermann Baker 92
Silbermann, Andreas 1678-1734 Baker 92
Silbermann, Eduard 1851- BioIn 17
Silbermann, Gottfried 1683-1753 Baker 92
Silbermann, Johann Andreas 1712-1783 Baker 92
Silbermann, Johann Daniel 1717-1766 Baker 92
Silbermann, Johann Friedrich 1762-1817 Baker 92
Silbermann, Johann Heinrich 1727-1799 Baker 92
Silbermann, Peter Thomas 1941- St&PR 93
Silbernagel, Walter 1924- St&PR 93
Silbernagel, Walter Eric 1961- St&PR 93
Silbernagl, Stefan 1939- WhoScE 91-3
Silbersack, John 1954- ScF&FL 92
Silbersack, Mark Louis 1946- WhoAm 92
Silbersack, Walter Roy 1926- WhoE 93
Silberstein, Alan Mark 1947- WhoAm 92
Silberstein, Charles K. 1929- St&PR 93
Silberstein, Jascha BioIn 17
Silberstein, Kenneth 1920- St&PR 93
Silberstein, Lynn 1951- WhoAmW 93
Silberstein, N. Ronald Law&B 92
Silberston, Zangwill Aubrey WhoScE 91-1
Silbert, Julie Parelman Law&B 92
Silbert, Layle WhoWrEP 92
Silbert, Theodore H. d1992 BioIn 17, NewYTBS 92 [port]
Silbert, Theodore H. 1904- WhoAm 92, WhoE 93
Silbert, William C. 1924- St&PR 93
Silbey, Joel Henry 1933- WhoAm 92
Silbey, Paula J. 1946- WhoWrEP 92
Silbey, Robert James 1940- WhoAm 92
Silbiger, Alexander 1935- ConAu 136
Silburn, Elaine Gwendolyn 1937- WhoAmW 93
Silburn, Richard L. WhoScE 91-1
Silby, D. Wayne 1948- WhoAm 92
Silby, Donald Wayne 1948- St&PR 93
Silcher, (Philipp) Friedrich 1789-1860 Baker 92
Silcock, D. Henry 1952- St&PR 93
Silcott, George Reed 1925- St&PR 93
Silcox, Marcia Fine 1954- WhoAmW 93
Silcox, Sharon Faye 1951- St&PR 93
Silcox, Teresa Law&B 92
Silen, William 1927- WhoAm 92
Silence, Cheryl Denise 1962- WhoAmW 93
Silence, Judith Olson 1940- WhoAmW 93
Sileo, Helena Estes 1948- WhoAmW 93
Siler, Eugene Edward, Jr. 1936- WhoAm 92, WhoSSW 93
Siler, Todd BioIn 17
Siler, Todd Lael 1953- WhoE 93, WhoEmL 93
Siler, Walter Orlando, Jr. 1920- WhoAm 92
Silesky, Barry 1949- WhoWrEP 92
Silets, Harvey Marvin 1931- WhoAm 92, WhoWor 93
Siletti, Mario d1991 BioIn 17
Silfen, Roberta Dawn 1932- WhoAmW 93
Silfvast, William T. 1937- WhoAm 92
Silha, Otto A. 1919- St&PR 93
Silha, Otto Adelbert 1919- WhoWor 93
Silhacek, Robert J. 1958- St&PR 93
Silhavy, Thomas Joseph 1948- WhoAm 92
Siliceo, Aguilar Alfonso 1945- WhoWor 93
Siligmueller, Dale Scott 1949- St&PR 93
Silin, Andrejs Roberts 1940- WhoWor 93
Silin, Dmitry Borisovitch 1957- WhoWor 93
Silins, Astrida Ilga 1928- WhoAmW 93
Silipigni, Alfredo 1931- WhoAm 92
Silja, Anja 1935- Baker 92, OxDcOp
Silja, Anja 1940- IntDcOp
Siljak, Dragoslav D. 1933- WhoAm 92
Silk, Alvin John 1935- WhoAm 92, WhoE 93
Silk, Bertram Edward 1931- St&PR 93, WhoAm 92
Silk, Frederick C.Z. 1934- St&PR 93
Silk, Frederick Charles Ziervogel 1934- WhoAm 92
Silk, George 1916- WhoAm 92
Silk, Gerald Douglas 1947- WhoE 93
Silk, James Paul Law&B 92
Silk, John Kevin 1938- WhoE 93
Silk, Leonard Solomon 1918- WhoAm 92
Silk, Robert Kilroy- ScF&FL 92
Silka, Linda Kay 1951- WhoE 93
Silke, Gary 1938- St&PR 93
Silke, James R. ScF&FL 92
Silkenat, James Robert 1947- WhoAm 92
Silkett, Robert Tillson 1929- WhoAm 92
Silkey, Sandra C. Law&B 92
Silkin, Jon 1930- WhoWor 93
Silkiner, Benjamin Nahum 1882-1933 BioIn 17
Silko, Leslie Marmon 1948- AmWomWr 92, ConLC 74 [port], MagSAmL [port]
Silkotch, Mary Ellen 1911- WhoAmW 93
Sill, Louise M. AmWomPl
Sill, Stephen E. 1945- St&PR 93
Silla, Ousmane 1931- WhoUN 92
Sillanpaa, Frans Eemil 1888-1964 BioIn 17
Sillanpaa, Matti Lauri 1936- WhoWor 93
Sillanpaa, Mikko 1925- WhoScE 91-4
Sillari, Ralph C. 1954- St&PR 93
Sillars, Malcolm Osgood 1928- WhoAm 92
Sillcox, John H. 1924- St&PR 93
Sillcox, Robert Lewis 1931- St&PR 93
Silleck, Harry Garrison 1921- WhoAm 92
Siller, Stephen I. 1949- WhoEmL 93
Sillerman, Robert F.X. BioIn 17
Sillero, Antonio 1938- WhoScE 91-3
Sillers, Donald A., Jr. 1926- St&PR 93
Sillery, Stephanie Felicite, marquise de 1746-1830 BioIn 17
Silles, Victor 1940- St&PR 93
Silletti, Susan Elizabeth 1941- WhoAmW 93
Silliman, Benjamin 1779-1864 BioIn 17
Silliman, Henry H., III Law&B 92
Silliman, Richard D. Law&B 92
Silliman, Richard George 1922- WhoAm 92
Silliman, Richard L. 1951- St&PR 93
Silliman, Ron 1946- WhoWrEP 92
Sillin, Lelan Flor 1945- WhoE 93
Sillin, Lelan Flor, Jr. 1918- WhoAm 92
Silliphant, Stirling Dale 1918- WhoAm 92
Sillitoe, Alan BioIn 17
Sillitoe, Alan 1928- WhoWor 93
Sillman, Arnold Joel 1940- WhoAm 92
Sillman, Emmanuel 1915- WhoE 93
Sillman, Herbert Phillip 1927- WhoAm 92
Sillman, Sewell 1924-1992 BioIn 17, NewYTBS 92
Silloway, James E. 1935- St&PR 93
Silloway, Richard Frank 1941- WhoSSW 93
Sills, Barbara A. 1946- St&PR 93
Sills, Beverly BioIn 17
Sills, Beverly 1929- Baker 92, IntDcOp, OxDcOp, WhoAm 92, WhoAmW 93, WhoWor 93
Sills, David Lawrence 1920- WhoAm 92
Sills, Gene Ellis 1950- WhoSSW 93
Sills, Harold Law&B 92
Sills, Joe Byrns 1938- WhoUN 92
Sills, Judith Robin WhoE 93
Sills, Laurel Anne 1960- WhoAmW 93
Sills, Lawrence Ira 1939- St&PR 93
Sills, Lillian Ross Seymour 1928- WhoAmW 93
Sills, Loretta 1947- St&PR 93
Sills, Milton 1882-1930 BioIn 17
Sills, Milton D. 1933- WhoAm 92
Sills, Myron A. 1927- St&PR 93
Sills, Richard Reynolds 1946- WhoE 93, WhoEmL 93, WhoWor 93
Sills, Sallie Alexander 1916- WhoAmW 93
Sills, Stanley S. 1925- WhoAm 92
Sills, Stephen BioIn 17
Sills, William Henry, III 1936- WhoWor 93
Silly, E. S. MajAI
Silman, Roberta (Karpel) 1934- DcAmChF 1960
Silmon, Patricia Ann 1959- WhoAmW 93
Silny, Frederick G. 1950- St&PR 93
Silobrcic, Vlatko 1935- WhoScE 91-4
Silone, Ignazio 1900-1978 BioIn 17
Siloti, Alexander 1863-1945 Baker 92
Silovic, Darko 1934- WhoUN 92
Silsbe, Brenda 1953- SmATA 73 [port]
Silsby, John P., II 1955- St&PR 93
Silsky, Edward 1843-1938 BioIn 17
Siltanen, Pentti Kustaa Pietari 1926- WhoWor 93
Silton, Laura A. 1951- WhoAmW 93
Silva, Abilio Marques 1933- WhoWor 93
Silva, Angel 1946- WhoUN 92
Silva, Anibal Cavaco 1939- BioIn 17
Silva, Benedicto Alves de Castro 1927- WhoWor 93
Silva, Beverly WhoWrEP 92
Silva, Beverly 1930- DcLB 122 [port]
Silva, Chris 1962?-1990 BioIn 17
Silva, David B. 1950- ScF&FL 92
Silva, Donna Steedle 1957- WhoAmW 93
Silva, Felipe 1919- WhoAm 92
Silva, Fernando Arturo 1942- WhoWor 93
Silva, Francisco Manuel da 1795-1865 Baker 92
Silva, Henriquez Raul Cardinal 1907- WhoWor 93
Silva, Hilda 1954- WhoAmW 93
Silva, John Yvonne WhoWrEP 92
Silva, Jorge Neves da 1935- WhoScE 91-3
Silva, Jose 1914- BioIn 17
Silva, Joseph ScF&FL 92
Silva, Joseph Donald 1935- WhoAm 92
Silva, Joseph S. 1959- St&PR 93
Silva, Laura J. M. 1949- WhoAmW 93, WhoE 93
Silva, Luigi 1903-1961 Baker 92
Silva, Maria Helena Vieira da 1908-1992 BioIn 17
Silva, Mark Robert 1954- WhoE 93
Silva, Omega Logan 1936- WhoAmW 93
Silva, Oscar da 1870-1958 Baker 92
Silva, P. Antonio 1934- WhoWor 93
Silva, Patricio 1939- WhoE 93
Silva, (David) Poll da 1834-1875 Baker 92
Silva, Rufino 1919- HispAmA
Silva, Ruth Caridad WhoAm 92, WhoAmW 93
Silva, Steven 1965- St&PR 93
Silva, Ubirajara Da Costa E. 1921- WhoWor 93
Silva, Yon Moreira, Jr. 1961- WhoWor 93
Silva Cimma, Enrique 1918- WhoWor 93
Silva Herzog, Jesus BioIn 17, DcCPCAm
Silva-Hunter, Margarita 1915- HispAmA
Silvani, Al 1910?- BioIn 17
Silvani, Carlos Alberto 1942- WhoUN 92
Silvani, Francesco d18th cent. OxDcOp
Silvano, Sandro WhoScE 91-3
Silva Villalobos, Antonio 1929- DcMexL
Silveira, Augustine, Jr. 1934- WhoAm 92
Silveira, Luiz Brandao 1951- WhoWor 93
Silveira, Mark Henry 1954- WhoAm 92
Silveira, Milton Anthony 1929- WhoAm 92, WhoSSW 93
Silvennoinen, Pekka Olavi 1945- WhoScE 91-4
Silver, Abba Hillel 1893-1963 JeAmHC
Silver, Alain 1947- ScF&FL 92
Silver, Alfred 1951- WhoCanL 92
Silver, Allan L. 1928- St&PR 93
Silver, Alvin M. 1931- WhoE 93
Silver, Amanda BioIn 17
Silver, Andrew MiSFD 9
Silver, Andrew J. 1956- St&PR 93
Silver, Andrew James 1956- WhoAm 92
Silver, Barnard Stewart 1933- WhoWor 93
Silver, Barry Stephen 1940- St&PR 93
Silver, Barry William 1946- WhoE 93
Silver, Bradley Scott 1956- St&PR 93
Silver, Brian David 1944- WhoAm 92
Silver, Brian Quayle 1942- WhoE 93, WhoWor 93
Silver, Carole 1937- ScF&FL 92
Silver, Charles 1868-1949 Baker 92
Silver, Charles Morton 1929- WhoAm 92
Silver, Cortland J., Jr. Law&B 92
Silver, Daniel B. 1941- WhoAm 92
Silver, Daniel Jeremy 1928-1989 BioIn 17
Silver, David 1931- WhoAm 92
Silver, David Francis 1957- WhoWrEP 92
Silver, David Mayer 1915- WhoAm 92
Silver, Diane MiSFD 9
Silver, Don A. St&PR 93
Silver, Donald 1929- WhoAm 92
Silver, Edward Lawrence 1969- WhoE 93
Silver, Elliott P. 1935- St&PR 93
Silver, Gary Lee 1948- WhoWrEP 92
Silver, George 1918- WhoSSW 93, WhoWor 93
Silver, George Albert 1913- WhoAm 92
Silver, Grace Verne 1889- AmWomPl
Silver, Greta B. 1934- WhoWrEP 92
Silver, Helene Marcia 1947- WhoAmW 93
Silver, Henry K. 1918-1991 BioIn 17
Silver, Horace (Ward Martin Tavares) 1928- Baker 92, WhoAm 92
Silver, Howard Findlay 1930- WhoAm 92
Silver, Howard Ira 1939- WhoE 93
Silver, Howard Joel 1949- WhoE 93
Silver, Ian Adair 1927- WhoWor 93
Silver, James Wesley 1907-1988 EncAACR
Silver, Jean 1926- WhoAmW 93
Silver, Jeff 1942- St&PR 93
Silver, Jerry H. 1930- St&PR 93
Silver, Joan Micklin 1935- MiSFD 9, WhoAm 92
Silver, Joel WhoAm 92
Silver, John J. St&PR 93
Silver, Jonathan 1937-1992 NewYTBS 92
Silver, Jonathan 1953- WhoAm 92
Silver, Joy Elaine 1951- WhoAmW 93
Silver, Julius 1900- WhoAm 92
Silver, Karin Joyce 1958- WhoSSW 93
Silver, Kenneth Alan 1927- WhoE 93
Silver, Malcolm David 1933- WhoAm 92
Silver, Marc S. 1951- WhoWrEP 92
Silver, Marian Ida 1932- WhoAmW 93
Silver, Marisa 1960- MiSFD 9
Silver, Martin 1940- St&PR 93
Silver, Mary Wilcox 1941- WhoAmW 93
Silver, Meagan Conway Law&B 92
Silver, Melvyn A. Law&B 92
Silver, Meyer 1926- WhoSSW 93
Silver, Michael G. Law&B 92
Silver, Michael Stanley WhoScE 91-1
Silver, Monty 1933- WhoE 93
Silver, Morris 1931- WhoAm 92
Silver, Morris Lewis Law&B 92
Silver, Nina Gail 1951- WhoE 93
Silver, Patricia Ann 1955- WhoAmW 93, WhoE 93
Silver, Paul 1937- WhoAm 92
Silver, Paul Joseph 1951- WhoE 93
Silver, Paul Robert 1931- WhoE 93, WhoSSW 93, WhoWor 93
Silver, Paul Samuel 1953- WhoSSW 93
Silver, Peter A. Law&B 92
Silver, R. Bruce 1923- St&PR 93
Silver, Ralph D. 1924- St&PR 93
Silver, Ralph David 1924- WhoAm 92
Silver, Raphael D. MiSFD 9
Silver, Richard B. Law&B 92
Silver, Richard Ludwig 1920- St&PR 93
Silver, Richard Tobias 1929- WhoAm 92, WhoE 93
Silver, Richard Victor Law&B 92
Silver, Robert Stephen 1951- St&PR 93
Silver, Ron 1946- BioIn 17, WhoAm 92
Silver, Rugenia Law&B 92
Silver, Samuel Manuel 1912- WhoAm 92
Silver, Saul Zee 1925- St&PR 93
Silver, Sheila 1946- Baker 92
Silver, Sheila Jane 1946- WhoE 93
Silver, Stephen Chaitt 1946- WhoE 93
Silver, Steve 1944- WhoWor 93
Silver, Steven J. Law&B 92
Silver, Sylvia 1942- WhoAmW 93
Silver, T. WhoScE 91-1
Silver, William H. 1954- St&PR 93
Silver, William Robert 1947- St&PR 93
Silvera, C. 1935- WhoAsAP 91
Silvera, Terilyn Ann 1963- WhoAmW 93
Silverberg, Ira 1962- ConAu 139
Silverberg, Janet L. Law&B 92
Silverberg, Karen ScF&FL 92
Silverberg, Larry 1957- WhoSSW 93
Silverberg, Robert BioIn 17, WhoWrEP 92
Silverberg, Robert 1935- MajAI [port], ScF&FL 92, WhoAm 92
Silverberg, Stanley J. Law&B 92
Silverberg, Stuart Owen 1931- WhoAm 92
Silver Brown, Susan BioIn 17
Silvercloud, Beth Norton 1937- WhoAmW 93
Silvere, Jean WhoScE 91-2
Silverglide, Edythe L. 1948- WhoAmW 93
Silverio, Robert W. 1945- St&PR 93
Silverlight, Irwin Joseph 1924- WhoAm 92
Silverlight, Terry Bennet 1957- WhoE 93
Silver-Lillywhite, Eileen 1953- WhoWrEP 92
Silverman, Al 1926- WhoAm 92, WhoWrEP 92
Silverman, Alan H. Law&B 92
Silverman, Alan H. 1954- St&PR 93, WhoEmL 93, WhoWor 93
Silverman, Albert A. 1908- St&PR 93, WhoAm 92, WhoWor 93
Silverman, Albert Jack 1925- WhoAm 92
Silverman, Albert James 1906- WhoWrEP 92
Silverman, Alice Ruth 1922- St&PR 93
Silverman, Althea Osber AmWomPl

Silverman, Alvin Michaels 1912- *WhoAm 92*
Silverman, Amy Gentry 1964- *WhoAmW 93*
Silverman, Arnold 1933- *WhoAm 92*
Silverman, Arnold Barry 1937- *WhoAm 92, WhoWor 93*
Silverman, Barry 1934-1991 *BioIn 17*
Silverman, Barry G. 1952- *WhoAm 92*
Silverman, Barry J. *Law&B 92*
Silverman, Bennet Hugh 1938- *WhoE 93*
Silverman, Bernard Walter *WhoScE 91-1*
Silverman, Bernard Walter 1952- *WhoWor 93*
Silverman, Bruce Gary 1945- *WhoAm 92*
Silverman, Burton Philip 1928- *WhoAm 92*
Silverman, Chuck *BioIn 17*
Silverman, Daniel N., III 1951- *St&PR 93*
Silverman, David Irving 1954- *WhoE 93*
Silverman, Elaine Roslyn 1941- *WhoSSW 93*
Silverman, Ellen 1942- *WhoAmW 93*
Silverman, Ellen Louise 1940- *WhoE 93*
Silverman, Frederic Noah 1914- *WhoAm 92*
Silverman, George Alan 1946- *WhoAm 92*
Silverman, Harold I. 1928- *WhoE 93*
Silverman, Henry 1940- *BioIn 17*
Silverman, Henry Jacob 1934- *WhoAm 92*
Silverman, Herbert Philip 1924- *WhoAm 92*
Silverman, Herbert R. 1914- *St&PR 93, WhoAm 92*
Silverman, Herschel 1926- *WhoWrEP 92*
Silverman, Hiram M. 1933- *St&PR 93*
Silverman, Hirsch Lazaar 1915- *WhoWrEP 92*
Silverman, Howard A. *Law&B 92*
Silverman, Howard Burton 1938- *WhoAm 92*
Silverman, Hugh J. 1945- *WhoAm 92*
Silverman, Hugh Richard *WhoScE 91-1*
Silverman, Ira 1945-1991 *BioIn 17*
Silverman, Ira Norton 1935- *WhoAm 92, WhoE 93*
Silverman, Isabelle d1990 *BioIn 17*
Silverman, Israel Abraham *Law&B 92*
Silverman, Jack Jacob 1911- *WhoE 93*
Silverman, Jason Howard 1952- *WhoSSW 93*
Silverman, Jeffrey Stuart 1945- *St&PR 93*
Silverman, Jerome B. 1927- *St&PR 93*
Silverman, Joel 1952- *St&PR 93*
Silverman, Joel A. *Law&B 92*
Silverman, Jonathan 1955- *ConAu 138*
Silverman, Jonathan 1966- *WhoAm 92*
Silverman, Joseph 1922- *WhoAm 92*
Silverman, Joshua Henry 1954- *WhoSSW 93*
Silverman, Kenneth *BioIn 17*
Silverman, Kenneth 1936- *ScF&FL 92*
Silverman, Kenneth Eugene 1936- *WhoAm 92, WhoWrEP 92*
Silverman, Leonard M. *WhoAm 92*
Silverman, Lester 1947- *St&PR 93*
Silverman, Lester Paul 1947- *WhoE 93*
Silverman, Linda Kreger 1941- *WhoAmW 93*
Silverman, Manny *BioIn 17*
Silverman, Marc *MiSFD 9*
Silverman, Marc Nelson 1941- *St&PR 93*
Silverman, Mark H. 1934- *St&PR 93*
Silverman, Marshall M. *Law&B 92*
Silverman, Martin Bernard 1936- *WhoE 93*
Silverman, Martin J. *Law&B 92*
Silverman, Mary Delson *WhoE 93*
Silverman, Marylin A. 1941- *WhoAm 92*
Silverman, Michael 1957- *WhoAm 92*
Silverman, Michael David 1946- *St&PR 93, WhoAm 92*
Silverman, Michael Harris 1949- *WhoE 93*
Silverman, Morris 1923- *St&PR 93*
Silverman, Morris 1924- *WhoE 93*
Silverman, Paul Hyman 1924- *WhoAm 92*
Silverman, Paul Leonard 1937- *WhoE 93*
Silverman, Peter Jay *Law&B 92*
Silverman, Richard 1925- *WhoE 93*
Silverman, Richard Bruce 1946- *WhoAm 92*
Silverman, Richard D. 1938- *St&PR 93*
Silverman, Richard F. d1992 *NewYTBS 92*
Silverman, Richard H. *Law&B 92*
Silverman, Robert Alan 1947- *WhoE 93*
Silverman, Robert Joseph 1942- *WhoAm 92*
Silverman, Robert M. *Law&B 92, St&PR 93*
Silverman, Robert P. 1944- *St&PR 93*
Silverman, Sam Mendel 1925- *WhoE 93*
Silverman, Samuel Joshua 1908- *WhoAm 92*
Silverman, Sidney d1991 *BioIn 17*
Silverman, Stanley W. 1947- *St&PR 93*
Silverman, Stephen M. *Law&B 92*
Silverman, Stephen Meredith 1951- *WhoE 93*
Silverman, Susan Emily *Law&B 92*
Silverman, Sylvia W. 1907-1992 *ConAu 139*
Silverman, Vicki Spelton 1946- *St&PR 93*
Silverman, Zita 1949- *St&PR 93, WhoIns 93*
Silvern, Steven Bruce 1949- *WhoSSW 93*
Silvernail, Lisa Anne Phipps 1958- *WhoAmW 93*
Silvernail, Robert F. 1943- *St&PR 93*
Silvers, Anne L. *Law&B 92*
Silvers, David 1949- *St&PR 93, WhoAm 92*
Silvers, Eileen S. 1948- *WhoAmW 93*
Silvers, Gerald T. 1937- *St&PR 93*
Silvers, Phil 1911-1985 *QDrFCA 92 [port]*
Silvers, Robert B. 1929- *WhoWrEP 92*
Silvers, Robert Benjamin 1929- *WhoAm 92, WhoE 93*
Silvers, Willys Kent 1929- *WhoAm 92*
Silverstein, Alan L. *Law&B 92*
Silverstein, Alvin 1933- *MajAI [port], SmATA 69 [port], WhoE 93*
Silverstein, Andrew *BioIn 17*
Silverstein, Anne *Law&B 92*
Silverstein, Arthur A. *Law&B 92*
Silverstein, Arthur Matthew 1928- *WhoAm 92*
Silverstein, Barbara *BioIn 17*
Silverstein, Barbara Ann 1947- *WhoAm 92*
Silverstein, Benjamin 1925- *St&PR 93*
Silverstein, Elizabeth Blume d1991 *BioIn 17*
Silverstein, Elliot 1927- *MiSFD 9*
Silverstein, Elliot M. 1947- *WhoSSW 93*
Silverstein, Emanuel 1930- *WhoE 93*
Silverstein, Ethel Bold 1924- *WhoAmW 93*
Silverstein, Herma 1937- *ScF&FL 92*
Silverstein, Howard Alan 1947- *WhoAm 92*
Silverstein, Jo Ann 1935- *WhoE 93*
Silverstein, Joseph 1932- *Baker 92*
Silverstein, Joseph H. 1927- *St&PR 93*
Silverstein, Joseph Harry 1932- *WhoAm 92*
Silverstein, Judith Lynn 1946- *WhoE 93*
Silverstein, Leonard Lewis 1922- *WhoAm 92*
Silverstein, Louis 1919- *WhoAm 92*
Silverstein, Marc A. 1952- *St&PR 93*
Silverstein, Marc Alan *Law&B 92*
Silverstein, Melvin Saul 1925- *WhoE 93*
Silverstein, Michael A. 1933- *WhoAm 92*
Silverstein, Robert M. *Law&B 92*
Silverstein, Samuel Charles 1937- *WhoAm 92*
Silverstein, Seth 1939- *WhoE 93*
Silverstein, Shel(by) 1932- *MajAI [port]*
Silverstein, Shelby 1932- *WhoAm 92, WhoWrEP 92*
Silverstein, Stanley P. *Law&B 92*
Silverstein, Stanley Parker 1952- *St&PR 93*
Silverstein, Suzanne Gubow 1963- *WhoSSW 93*
Silverstein, Virginia B. 1937- *SmATA 69*
Silverstein, Virginia B(arbara Opshelor) 1937- *MajAI*
Silverstein, Virginia Barbara 1937- *WhoE 93*
Silversten, Ronald Keith *Law&B 92*
Silverstone, David 1932- *WhoAm 92*
Silverstone, David Edward 1948- *WhoE 93*
Silverstone, Donald 1928- *St&PR 93*
Silverstone, Felix Abraham 1919- *WhoE 93*
Silverstone, Leon Martin 1939- *WhoAm 92*
Silverstone, Paul Harold 1931- *WhoE 93*
Silverthorn, Richard Jay *ScF&FL 92*
Silverthorn, Robert Sterner, Jr. 1948- *WhoAm 92, WhoSSW 93*
Silverthorne, Jeffrey 1963- *WhoSSW 93*
Silverthorne, Michael James 1941- *WhoAm 92*
Silverton, Leigh 1956- *WhoAmW 93*
Silverton, Michael John 1935- *WhoWrEP 92*
Silverton, Nancy *BioIn 17*
Silvester, I d335 *OxDcByz*
Silvester, David James *WhoScE 91-1*
Silvester, Peter J., Jr. 1946- *St&PR 93*
Silvester, Peter Peet 1935- *WhoAm 92*
Silvestri, Alan 1950- *BioIn 17*
Silvestri, Constantin 1913-1969 *Baker 92*
Silvestri, Lawrence A. *Law&B 92*
Silvestrini, Achille Cardinal 1923- *WhoWor 93*
Silvestrini, Giuseppe Vittorio 1935- *WhoWor 93*
Silvestrini, Rosella 1930- *WhoScE 91-3*
Silvestro, Clement Mario 1924- *WhoAm 92*
Silvestro, John Richard 1946- *WhoE 93*
Silvestro, Joy 1939- *St&PR 93*
Silvestroy, Valentin (Vasilievich) 1937- *Baker 92*
Silvette, Herbert *ScF&FL 92*
Silvetti, Jorge 1942- *BioIn 17*
Silveus, Mari L. 1957- *WhoWrEP 92*
Silvey, Anita Lynne 1947- *WhoAmW 93*
Silvey, Donald Kenneth *Law&B 92*
Silvey, James Madison, Jr. 1909- *WhoAm 92*
Silvey, Robyn Lee 1951- *St&PR 93*
Silvi, John L. 1954- *St&PR 93*
Silvi, Laurence J., II 1956- *St&PR 93*
Silvia, Her Majesty 1943- *WhoWor 93*
Silvia, John Edwin 1948- *St&PR 93*
Silvia, Kathleen 1958- *WhoAmW 93*
Silvia, Robert Charles 1942- *St&PR 93*
Silvia, William Frank 1933- *WhoE 93*
Silving Ryu, Helen 1906- *WhoAmW 93*
Silvis, Randall 1950- *ConAu 136*
Silvius, Donald Joe 1932- *WhoWor 93*
Silvius, Eric L. 1951- *St&PR 93*
Silvius, Eric Lane 1951- *WhoAm 92*
Silvoso, Joseph Anton 1917- *WhoAm 92*
Silzer, Frank S. 1954- *St&PR 93*
Sim, Ah Tee 1944- *WhoWor 93*
Sim, Alastair 1900-1976 *IntDcF 2-3 [port], QDrFCA 92 [port]*
Sim, Craig Stephen 1942- *WhoAm 92, WhoWor 93*
Sim, George Andrew *WhoScE 91-1*
Sim, John Cameron 1911-1990 *BioIn 17*
Sim, Peng Choon 1932- *WhoWor 93*
Sim, Richard G. 1944- *St&PR 93*
Sim, William J. 1944- *St&PR 93*
Simaan, Marwan A. 1946- *WhoAm 92*
Simaga, Richard C. 1949- *St&PR 93*
Simai, Pavol 1930- *Baker 92*
Simaitis, David E. *Law&B 92*
Simak, Clifford D. 1904-1988 *BioIn 17, ScF&FL 92*
Simak, Milan 1922- *WhoScE 91-4*
Simalarides, Anastasios 1955- *WhoWor 93*
Simanaitis, Dennis *BioIn 17*
Simandi, Laszlo I. 1935- *WhoScE 91-4*
Simandl, Franz 1840-1912 *Baker 92*
Simandl, Robert H. 1928- *St&PR 93*
Simandonis, John 1944- *WhoScE 91-3*
Simanton, Mark Donald 1958- *St&PR 93*
Simao, Joao E.J. 1929- *WhoScE 91-3*
Simard, Joanne M. *Law&B 92*
Simari, Osvaldo Antonio 1933- *WhoWor 93*
Simasathien, Panas 1932- *WhoWor 93*
Simatos, Nicholas Jerry 1948- *WhoSSW 93*
Simbeye, Adam Njanga 1942- *WhoUN 92*
Simches, Seymour Oliver 1919- *WhoAm 92*
Simcoe, Annell Lacy 1941- *WhoWrEP 92*
Simcoe, Elizabeth 1762-1850 *BioIn 17*
Simcoe, John Graves 1752-1806 *HarEnMi*
Simcox, Craig Dennis 1939- *WhoAm 92*
Simcox, Flavel L. 1924- *St&PR 93*
Simcox, William C. 1930- *St&PR 93*
Sime, Donald Rae 1926- *WhoAm 92*
Sime, James Thomson 1927- *WhoWor 93*
Sime, Jessie Georgina 1868-1958 *BioIn 17*
Sime, S.H. 1867-1941 *ScF&FL 92*
Simecka, Betty Jean 1935- *WhoAmW 93*
Simek, Ivo 1941- *WhoScE 91-4*
Simek, Joseph Ladislav 1926- *St&PR 93*
Simenon, Georges 1903-1989 *BioIn 17*
Simeon *OxDcByz*
Simeon, II, King 1937- *NewYTBS 92*
Simeon, II, King of Bulgaria 1937- *BioIn 17*
Simeon, Vladimir 1939- *WhoScE 91-4*
Simeona, Iosia 1954- *WhoWor 93*
Simeonidis, Nicholas *Law&B 92*
Simeonov, Jordan Todorov 1922- *WhoScE 91-4*
Simeonov, Konstantin (Arsenievich) 1910-1987 *Baker 92*
Simer, Cheryl 1948- *WhoAmW 93*
Simeral, Bartley R. *Law&B 92*
Simeral, William Goodrich 1926- *WhoAm 92*
Simermeyer, John Lawrence 1928- *St&PR 93*
Simes, Dimitri Konstantin 1947- *WhoAm 92*
Simes, Stephen M. 1951- *St&PR 93*
Sim Gi Sob 1945- *WhoAsAP 91*
Simic, Charles 1938- *BioIn 17, WhoAm 92, WhoE 93, WhoWrEP 92*
Simic, Dusan 1928- *WhoScE 91-4*
Simic, Radomir 1939- *WhoScE 91-4*
Simicsak, Robert Allen 1948- *WhoE 93*
Simila, Martti 1898-1958 *Baker 92*
Simin, Liu 1941- *WhoWor 93*
Siminerio, Andrew C. *Law&B 92*
Simino, Darrell W. 1942- *St&PR 93*
Siminoff, Bruce G. 1936- *St&PR 93*
Siminoff, Faren Rhea *Law&B 92*
Siminovitch, Louis 1920- *WhoAm 92*
Siminski, Philip Mark 1941- *St&PR 93*
Simionato, Giulietta 1910- *Baker 92, IntDcOp, OxDcOp*
Simionescu, Cristofor I. 1920- *WhoScE 91-4*
Simis, Theodore Luckey 1924- *WhoAm 92*
Simiskey, Patrick LeRoy 1940- *WhoSSW 93*
Simister, Leslie Thomas *WhoScE 91-1*
Simiti, Ioan 1928- *WhoScE 91-4*
Simkhovitch, Mary Melinda Kingsbury 1867-1951 *BioIn 17*
Simkin, Penelope Payson 1938- *WhoWrEP 92*
Simkin, Peter Anthony 1935- *WhoAm 92*
Simkin, Peter Lewis 1934- *WhoUN 92*
Simkin, Richard Graham 1952- *WhoWor 93*
Simkin, Thomas Edward 1933- *WhoE 93*
Simkin, William E. d1992 *NewYTBS 92*
Simkin, William E. 1907-1992 *BioIn 17*
Simkin, William E(dward) 1907-1992 *CurBio 92N*
Simkins, Dan Gene 1940- *St&PR 93*
Simkins, Joel E. *Law&B 92*
Simkins, John Anthony Benjamin 1944- *WhoWor 93*
Simkins, Leon J. 1927- *St&PR 93*
Simkins, Leon Jack 1927- *WhoAm 92*
Simkins, Morton H. 1937- *St&PR 93*
Simkins, Richard C. 1942- *St&PR 93*
Simkiss, Kenneth *WhoScE 91-1*
Simko, John S. *Law&B 92*
Simko, John Stephen 1939- *St&PR 93*
Simko, Paul R. 1952- *St&PR 93*
Simko, Vincent M. 1926- *St&PR 93*
Simkova-Plivova, Vera 1934- *DrEEuF*
Simkowitz, Michael Abraham 1938- *WhoAm 92*
Sim Kwang Yang 1948- *WhoAsAP 91*
Simler, Shellie Kenna 1950- *WhoSSW 93*
Simm, David J. 1934- *St&PR 93*
Simm, James Timothy 1959- *WhoSSW 93*
Simma, Willi *WhoScE 91-4*
Simmel, Gerhard Frederick 1930- *WhoWor 93*
Simmel, Marianne Lenore *WhoAm 92*
Simmelsgaard, Svend Erik 1945- *WhoScE 91-2*
Simmer-Brown, Judith Ann 1946- *WhoAmW 93*
Simmerman, Gary F. 1934- *St&PR 93*
Simmerman, George M. *Law&B 92*
Simmerman, Jim 1952- *WhoWrEP 92*
Simmermon, James Everett 1926- *WhoAm 92*
Simmermon, Robert David 1946- *WhoSSW 93*
Simmers, Ian 1937- *WhoScE 91-3*
Simmers, Terry Wayne 1946- *St&PR 93, WhoAm 92*
Simmet, John L. 1927- *St&PR 93*
Simmie, James Martin 1941- *ConAu 38NR*
Simmie, Lois 1932- *WhoCanL 92*
Simmler, Jozef 1823-1868 *PolBiDi*
Simmler, Otto A. 1933- *WhoScE 91-4*
Simmon, Vincent Fowler 1943- *St&PR 93*
Simmonds, Hermione Anne *WhoScE 91-1*
Simmonds, James Gordon 1935- *WhoAm 92*
Simmonds, Kennedy 1936- *DcCPCAm*
Simmonds, Kennedy Alphonse 1936- *WhoWor 93*
Simmonds, Kenneth 1935- *WhoWor 93*
Simmonds, Mattie Frances *AmWomPl*
Simmonds, Monique S.J. 1950- *WhoScE 91-1*
Simmonds, Norman Willison *WhoScE 91-1*
Simmonds, Posy *BioIn 17*
Simmononds, Geoffrey R. *St&PR 93*
Simmons, Adele Smith 1941- *BioIn 17, WhoAm 92, WhoAmW 93*
Simmons, Alan Jay 1924- *WhoAm 92*
Simmons, Alan John 1950- *WhoAm 92*
Simmons, Aldred John 1917- *St&PR 93*
Simmons, Almo B. 1933- *St&PR 93*
Simmons, Althea *BioIn 17*
Simmons, Amy Carol 1963- *WhoAmW 93*
Simmons, Anthony *MiSFD 9*
Simmons, Barbara J. *Law&B 92*
Simmons, Barry Putnam 1939- *WhoE 93*
Simmons, Barry William 1950- *WhoSSW 93*
Simmons, Ben D. 1950- *St&PR 93*
Simmons, Betty Jo 1936- *WhoAmW 93*
Simmons, Betty-Jo Whitaker 1939- *WhoSSW 93*
Simmons, Bonnie K. *Law&B 92*
Simmons, Bonnie Sue *WhoAmW 93*
Simmons, Bradley Williams 1941- *WhoAm 92, WhoWor 93*
Simmons, Bryan A. 1933- *St&PR 93*
Simmons, Bryan John *Law&B 92*
Simmons, Calvin (Eugene) 1950-1982 *Baker 92*
Simmons, Carl Kenneth 1914- *WhoWor 93*
Simmons, Caroline Thompson 1910- *WhoAmW 93*

Simmons, Carolyn Caudry 1951- *WhoAmW 93*
Simmons, Carolyn House 1940- *WhoAmW 93*
Simmons, Chad Jeffrey 1953- *St&PR 93*
Simmons, Charles 1924- *WhoAm 92*
Simmons, Charles Alan 1935- *St&PR 93*
Simmons, Charles Bedford, Jr. 1956- *WhoSSW 93*
Simmons, Charles William Bruce 1934- *WhoWor 93*
Simmons, Clarence George 1953- *St&PR 93*
Simmons, Curtis Thomas 1929- *BiDAMSp 1989*
Simmons, D. Ramsay, Jr. 1931- *St&PR 93*
Simmons, Dan *BioIn 17*
Simmons, Dan 1948- *ConAu 138, ScF&FL 92*
Simmons, David Jeffrey 1961- *WhoSSW 93*
Simmons, David Ramsay, Jr. 1931- *WhoSSW 93*
Simmons, David William 1947- *WhoAsAP 91*
Simmons, Deidre Warner 1955- *WhoAmW 93*
Simmons, Diane Eileen 1950- *WhoWor 93*
Simmons, Dick Bedford 1937- *WhoAm 92*
Simmons, Donald E. 1944- *St&PR 93*
Simmons, Edwin Howard 1921- *WhoAm 92, WhoE 93*
Simmons, Elizabeth E. 1947- *St&PR 93*
Simmons, Elroy, Jr. 1928- *WhoAm 92*
Simmons, Ernest Joseph 1903-1972 *BioIn 17*
Simmons, Esther Grace 1961- *WhoAmW 93*
Simmons, Eugene 1943- *WhoE 93*
Simmons, Fielding 1939- *St&PR 93*
Simmons, Francis Blair 1930- *WhoAm 92*
Simmons, Frederic Rudolph, Jr. 1956- *WhoSSW 93*
Simmons, Frederick J. 1937- *St&PR 93*
Simmons, Furnifold M. 1854-1940 *PolPar*
Simmons, Gary L. 1945- *St&PR 93*
Simmons, Gary Paul 1941- *WhoSSW 93*
Simmons, Gene 1949- *WhoAm 92*
Simmons, Geoffrey 1943?- *ScF&FL 92*
Simmons, George *WhoWrEP 92*
Simmons, George L. 1942- *St&PR 93*
Simmons, Gloria Harrill 1951- *WhoAmW 93*
Simmons, Greg *Law&B 92*
Simmons, Harold C. 1931- *WhoSSW 93*
Simmons, Harold Clark 1931- *St&PR 93*
Simmons, Harold Joseph 1940- *St&PR 93*
Simmons, Harris H. *BioIn 17*
Simmons, Harris H. 1954- *St&PR 93, WhoAm 92*
Simmons, Harry A. d1990 *BioIn 17*
Simmons, Harry David 1947- *WhoSSW 93*
Simmons, Harvey O., III *Law&B 92*
Simmons, Heather Patricia 1969- *WhoE 93*
Simmons, Helen L. 1946- *St&PR 93*
Simmons, Howard Ensign, Jr. 1929- *St&PR 93, WhoAm 92*
Simmons, Howard L. *WhoE 93, WhoWor 93*
Simmons, Howard Wilson 1918- *St&PR 93*
Simmons, Ian Gordon *WhoScE 91-1*
Simmons, J. Edgar 1921-1979 *BioIn 17*
Simmons, J. Gerald 1929- *WhoAm 92*
Simmons, Jack 1915- *ConAu 38NR*
Simmons, James 1933- *BioIn 17*
Simmons, James C. *Law&B 92*
Simmons, James Edwin 1923- *WhoAm 92*
Simmons, James P. 1924- *St&PR 93*
Simmons, James Pat 1949- *St&PR 93*
Simmons, Jay B. *Law&B 92*
Simmons, Jean 1929- *IntDcF 2-3 [port], WhoAm 92, WhoAmW 93*
Simmons, Jean Elizabeth Margaret 1914- *WhoAm 92*
Simmons, Joe A. *Law&B 92*
Simmons, John *ScF&FL 92*
Simmons, John Barry Eves 1937- *WhoScE 91-1*
Simmons, John Derek 1931- *WhoE 93, WhoWor 93*
Simmons, John E. *St&PR 93*
Simmons, John Franklin 1945- *WhoWor 93*
Simmons, John Kaul 1938- *WhoAm 92*
Simmons, John M. 1938- *St&PR 93*
Simmons, John Wesley 1918- *WhoAm 92*
Simmons, Joseph Jacob, III 1925- *WhoAm 92*
Simmons, Joseph Thomas 1936- *WhoWor 93*
Simmons, Keith 1948- *St&PR 93*
Simmons, Kenneth C. 1942- *St&PR 93*
Simmons, L.V. 1925- *St&PR 93*
Simmons, L. Whitley 1925- *St&PR 93*
Simmons, Larry G. 1948- *WhoIns 93*
Simmons, Lee Guyton, Jr. 1938- *WhoAm 92*
Simmons, Lee Howard 1935- *WhoAm 92*
Simmons, Lee Thomas 1953- *St&PR 93*
Simmons, Lezlle J. 1944- *St&PR 93*
Simmons, Marguerite Saffold 1954- *WhoAmW 93*
Simmons, Mark Golden 1960- *WhoSSW 93*
Simmons, Marshall Francis 1936- *WhoIns 93*
Simmons, Marvin Gene 1929- *WhoAm 92, WhoE 93*
Simmons, Mary K. *Law&B 92*
Simmons, Merle Edwin 1918- *WhoAm 92*
Simmons, Michael *BioIn 17*
Simmons, Michael A. *Law&B 92*
Simmons, Miriam Quinn 1928- *WhoAmW 93*
Simmons, Norman Sarney 1929- *WhoE 93*
Simmons, Obadiah Jerone Keith, Jr. 1953- *WhoSSW 93*
Simmons, Paul Allen 1921- *WhoE 93*
Simmons, Paul Barrett 1942- *WhoAm 92*
Simmons, Peter 1931- *WhoAm 92, WhoE 93*
Simmons, Peter Jeremy *WhoScE 91-1*
Simmons, Ralph Terrell 1938- *St&PR 93*
Simmons, Randy Neil 1946- *WhoWrEP 92*
Simmons, Richard B. 1947- *St&PR 93*
Simmons, Richard De Lacey 1934- *WhoAm 92, WhoE 93*
Simmons, Richard DeLacey 1934- *St&PR 93*
Simmons, Richard Milton Teagle 1948- *WhoAm 92*
Simmons, Richard Morgan, Jr. 1926- *St&PR 93*
Simmons, Richard Sheridan 1928- *St&PR 93*
Simmons, Richard Sheridan 1928-1991 *BioIn 17*
Simmons, Richard W. *Law&B 92*
Simmons, Robert Anthony 1939- *WhoWor 93*
Simmons, Robert Malcolm *WhoScE 91-1*
Simmons, Robert Malcolm 1938- *WhoWor 93*
Simmons, Robert Orrin, Jr. 1950- *WhoSSW 93*
Simmons, Roy W. 1916- *St&PR 93*
Simmons, Roy William 1916- *WhoAm 92*
Simmons, Russell *BioIn 17*
Simmons, S. Dallas 1940- *WhoAm 92*
Simmons, St. John *WhoCanL 92*
Simmons, Samuel Lee 1929- *St&PR 93, WhoAm 92*
Simmons, Seymour 1920- *St&PR 93*
Simmons, Sheldon B. 1908- *EncABHB 8 [port]*
Simmons, Sherwin Palmer 1931- *St&PR 93*
Simmons, Shirley J(oyce Leslie) *WhoWrEP 92*
Simmons, Simtec 1944- *BioIn 17*
Simmons, Stephen H. 1950- *WhoAm 92*
Simmons, Susan Annette 1947- *WhoSSW 93*
Simmons, Suzanne *WhoWrEP 92*
Simmons, Sylvia Jeanne Quarles 1935- *WhoAmW 93*
Simmons, Sylvia N. 1946- *WhoSSW 93*
Simmons, T. Dean *Law&B 92*
Simmons, Ted 1916- *ScF&FL 92*
Simmons, Ted Conrad 1916- *WhoWor 93*
Simmons, Ted Lyle 1949- *WhoAm 92*
Simmons, Thomas Edward 1925- *WhoSSW 93*
Simmons, Tim *St&PR 93*
Simmons, Vaughan Pippen 1922- *WhoAm 92*
Simmons, Virginia Anne *WhoWrEP 92*
Simmons, Virginia Barber 1913- *WhoAmW 93*
Simmons, Wendy *BioIn 17*
Simmons, William 1932- *WhoAm 92*
Simmons, William J., Jr. *Law&B 92*
Simmons, Wm. Mark *ScF&FL 92*
Simmons-Gill, Catherine *Law&B 92*
Simmons-Sixto, Camille Ann 1953- *WhoAmW 93*
Simmrock, Karl Hans 1930- *WhoScE 91-3*
Simms, Albert Egerton 1918- *WhoSSW 93*
Simms, Amelia Moss 1954- *WhoAmW 93*
Simms, Ami 1954- *WhoWrEP 92*
Simms, Amy Lang 1964- *WhoAmW 93*
Simms, Arthur Benjamin 1921- *St&PR 93, WhoAm 92*
Simms, Charles Averill 1937- *WhoAm 92*
Simms, Evelyn *AmWomPl*
Simms, George (Otto) 1910-1991 *ConAu 136*
Simms, James F. d1992 *BioIn 17, NewYTBS 92*
Simms, John Carson 1952- *WhoWor 93*
Simms, Julia J. 1931- *St&PR 93*
Simms, Maria Ester 1938- *WhoWor 93*
Simms, Mary Clay 1926- *St&PR 93*
Simms, Orville, Jr. 1934- *St&PR 93*
Simms, Phil 1955- *BioIn 17*
Simms, Phillip 1956- *WhoAm 92*
Simms, Robert Alderson, Sr. 1938- *WhoAm 92*
Simms, Robert D. 1926- *WhoSSW 93*
Simms, Senia Julia 1931- *St&PR 93*
Simms, Stephen G. 1940- *St&PR 93*
Simms, William E. *Law&B 92*
Simms, William Edward 1944- *St&PR 93*
Simnel, Lambert c. 1476-1534 *HarEnMi*
Simnett, George William 1943- *WhoWor 93*
Simoes, Luis Miguel Cruz 1955- *WhoWor 93*
Simoes, Luis Miguel da Cruz 1955- *WhoScE 91-3*
Simoes, Ronald Alan 1949- *St&PR 93*
Simoes De Carvalho, Armando A.M. 1920- *WhoScE 91-3*
Simojoki, Paavo Iisakki 1932- *WhoScE 91-4*
Simokaitis, Frank Joseph 1922- *WhoAm 92*
Simokattes, Theophylaktos 6th cent.- *OxDcByz*
Simola, Liisa Kaarina 1938- *WhoScE 91-4*
Simola, O. *WhoScE 91-4*
Simon, Abbey 1922- *Baker 92*
Simon, Adam *MiSFD 9*
Simon, Albert 1924- *WhoAm 92*
Simon, Alfred E. 1907-1991 *BioIn 17*
Simon, Alicja 1879-1957 *Baker 92*
Simon, Andrea G. *Law&B 92*
Simon, Andrea Judith 1946- *St&PR 93*
Simon, Anne Elizabeth 1956- *WhoE 93*
Simon, Anton 1850-1916 *Baker 92*
Simon, Arndt 1940- *WhoScE 91-3*
Simon, Arthur 1942- *WhoAm 92*
Simon, Arthur James 1927- *St&PR 93*
Simon, Arthur R. *BioIn 17*
Simon, Barbara Colby 1930- *St&PR 93*
Simon, Barry P. *Law&B 92*
Simon, Barry P. 1942- *St&PR 93*
Simon, Barry Philip 1942- *WhoAm 92*
Simon, Bernece Kern 1914- *WhoAm 92*
Simon, Bob *BioIn 17*
Simon, Carl Julian 1923- *St&PR 93*
Simon, Carly *BioIn 17*
Simon, Carly 1945- *WhoAm 92, WhoAmW 93*
Simon, Carol Ann 1951- *WhoAmW 93*
Simon, Caroline Klein *WhoAmW 93*
Simon, Cathy Jensen 1943- *WhoAm 92*
Simon, Charles *Law&B 92*
Simon, Charlotte Tulchin 1925- *WhoAmW 93, WhoE 93*
Simon, Claude *BioIn 17*
Simon, Claude 1913- *CurBio 92 [port]*
Simon, Claude Eugene Henri 1913- *WhoWor 93*
Simon, D.F. *St&PR 93*
Simon, Daniel J. 1949- *St&PR 93*
Simon, David 1960- *ConAu 136*
Simon, David A. 1952- *St&PR 93*
Simon, David Alec Gwyn 1939- *WhoWor 93*
Simon, David F. *Law&B 92*
Simon, David F. 1953- *WhoE 93*
Simon, David Harold 1930- *WhoAm 92*
Simon, David Judah 1960- *WhoE 93*
Simon, David L. 1921- *St&PR 93*
Simon, David Sidney 1941- *WhoAm 92*
Simon, Detlef L. 1930- *WhoScE 91-3*
Simon, Dolph B.H. *Law&B 92*
Simon, Dolph B.H. 1933- *St&PR 93*
Simon, Donald Arthur 1936- *WhoSSW 93*
Simon, Donald R. 1926- *St&PR 93*
Simon, Donald S. 1922- *St&PR 93*
Simon, Doris Marie Tyler 1932- *WhoAmW 93, WhoSSW 93, WhoWor 93*
Simon, Dorothy Martin 1919- *St&PR 93*
Simon, Eckehard Peter 1939- *WhoAm 92*
Simon, Edward D. 1927- *St&PR 93*
Simon, Edward Herbert 1928- *St&PR 93*
Simon, Edwin J. 1927- *St&PR 93*
Simon, Ellen McMurtrie 1919- *WhoAmW 93*
Simon, Eric Jacob 1924- *WhoAm 92*
Simon, Ernest Martin 1932- *St&PR 93*
Simon, Esther Annenberg d1992 *BioIn 17, NewYTBS 92*
Simon, Esther Janett *AmWomPl*
Simon, Evelyn 1943- *WhoAm 92*
Simon, Ferenc 1934- *WhoScE 91-4*
Simon, Francis *MiSFD 9*
Simon, Francis Malcolm 1928- *WhoSSW 93*
Simon, Franklin d1991 *BioIn 17*
Simon, Fred *BioIn 17*
Simon, Gary D. 1948- *St&PR 93*
Simon, Gary Richard *Law&B 92*
Simon, George T. *Law&B 92*
Simon, Harold 1930- *WhoAm 92*
Simon, Harold 1953- *WhoWrEP 92*
Simon, Heather *ScF&FL 92*
Simon, Helene L. 1929- *St&PR 93*
Simon, Helmut 1927- *WhoScE 91-3*
Simon, Helmut Franz 1927- *WhoWor 93*
Simon, Henry T. *St&PR 93*
Simon, Herbert *WhoAm 92*
Simon, Herbert Alexander 1916- *BioIn 17, WhoAm 92, WhoE 93, WhoWor 93*
Simon, Hermann E. 1900-1990 *BioIn 17*
Simon, Hilary Beth 1962- *WhoSSW 93*
Simon, Howard M. 1953- *St&PR 93*
Simon, Huey Paul 1923- *WhoAm 92, WhoSSW 93*
Simon, Ira Jonathan 1959- *St&PR 93*
Simon, Jack Aaron 1919- *WhoAm 92*
Simon, Jacqueline Albert *WhoAm 92, WhoE 93, WhoWor 93*
Simon, Jacqueline Ann 1943- *WhoWrEP 92*
Simon, James 1880-1944 *Baker 92*
Simon, James Lowell 1944- *WhoAm 92, WhoSSW 93*
Simon, Janice Myles 1956- *WhoAmW 93*
Simon, Jay *Law&B 92*
Simon, Jean *ScF&FL 92*
Simon, Jean Claude *WhoScE 91-2*
Simon, Jean-Francois 1932- *WhoScE 91-2*
Simon, Jeno *WhoScE 91-4*
Simon, Jerome B. 1927- *St&PR 93*
Simon, Jewel Woodard 1911- *WhoAmW 93*
Simon, Jimmy Louis 1930- *WhoAm 92*
Simon, Jo Ann 1946- *ScF&FL 92, WhoWrEP 92*
Simon, Joanna 1940- *WhoAm 92*
Simon, Joe 1943- *SoulM*
Simon, John *BioIn 17*
Simon, John Allsebrook 1873-1951 *DcTwHis*
Simon, John Bern 1942- *WhoAm 92, WhoWor 93*
Simon, John Gerald 1928- *WhoAm 92*
Simon, John Ivan 1925- *WhoAm 92*
Simon, John Lewis 1947- *WhoE 93*
Simon, John Louis 1946- *St&PR 93*
Simon, John Oliver 1942- *WhoWrEP 92*
Simon, John Roger 1939- *WhoAm 92*
Simon, Jolan 1935- *WhoScE 91-4*
Simon, Jonathan Edward 1949- *WhoWor 93*
Simon, Joseph B. 1928- *St&PR 93*
Simon, Joseph Patrick 1932- *WhoAm 92*
Simon, Judith F. *Law&B 92*
Simon, Jules 1814-1896 *BioIn 17*
Simon, Julian L. *BioIn 17*
Simon, Julian Lincoln 1932- *WhoAm 92*
Simon, K.R. 1887-1966 *BioIn 17*
Simon, Karen Jordan 1953- *WhoAm 92*
Simon, Kate *BioIn 17*
Simon, Kathryn Irene 1953- *WhoAmW 93, WhoWor 93*
Simon, Keith R. 1955- *WhoEmL 93, WhoSSW 93, WhoWor 93*
Simon, Kenneth Cyril 1917- *WhoWor 93*
Simon, Kenneth D. 1918- *St&PR 93*
Simon, Kevin Charles 1956- *St&PR 93*
Simon, Konstantin Romanovich 1887-1966 *BioIn 17*
Simon, Lawrence F. *St&PR 93*
Simon, Lee Will 1940- *WhoAm 92*
Simon, Leonard 1937- *ScF&FL 92*
Simon, Leonard S. *Law&B 92*
Simon, Leonard S. 1936- *St&PR 93*
Simon, Leonard Samuel 1936- *WhoAm 92*
Simon, Leslie Norman 1944- *St&PR 93*
Simon, Linda 1946- *WhoE 93*
Simon, Loretta L. 1948- *St&PR 93*
Simon, Lothar 1938- *WhoAm 92*
Simon, Louise Marie 1903- *BioIn 17*
Simon, Lowrell 1943- *BioIn 17*
Simon, Lucy *BioIn 17*
Simon, Madeleine *ScF&FL 92*
Simon, Marc Paul 1936- *WhoUN 92*
Simon, Marilyn W. 1927- *WhoAmW 93, WhoE 93*
Simon, Mark 1946- *WhoAm 92*
Simon, Mark William 1939- *St&PR 93*
Simon, Martin S. 1926- *St&PR 93*
Simon, Martin Stanley 1926- *WhoAm 92*
Simon, Martin Thomas 1950- *St&PR 93*
Simon, Marvin Kenneth 1939- *WhoAm 92*
Simon, Mary Elizabeth 1963- *WhoSSW 93*
Simon, Maurya 1950- *WhoWrEP 92*
Simon, Melvin 1926- *WhoAm 92*
Simon, Melvin I. 1937- *WhoAm 92*
Simon, Michael Alexander 1936- *WhoAm 92*
Simon, Michael F. 1951- *St&PR 93*
Simon, Michael Richard 1951- *St&PR 93*
Simon, Michel 1895-1975 *IntDcF 2-3 [port]*
Simon, Michele Johanna 1957- *WhoAmW 93*
Simon, Mordecai 1925- *WhoAm 92*
Simon, Morris *ScF&FL 92*
Simon, Morton S. *Law&B 92*
Simon, Myron Sydney 1926- *WhoE 93*
Simon, Nancy L. 1928- *St&PR 93*
Simon, Neil *BioIn 17*

Simon, Neil 1927- *ConLC 70 [port], JeAmHC, MagSAmL [port], WhoAm 92, WhoE 93, WhoWor 93*
Simon, Nicolas 1855-1923
See Simon-Girard, Juliette 1859-1959 *Baker 92*
Simon, Norma *BioIn 17*
Simon, Norma (Feldstein) 1927- *MajAI [port]*
Simon, Norma Plavnick 1930- *WhoAmW 93*
Simon, Norton *BioIn 17*
Simon, Paul *BioIn 17*
Simon, Paul 1928- *CngDr 91, WhoAm 92, WhoWrEP 92*
Simon, Paul 1941- *Baker 92, WhoAm 92*
Simon, Paul 1942?- *News 92 [port]*
Simon, Paul Jerome 1954- *WhoWor 93*
Simon, Paul S. 1931- *St&PR 93*
Simon, Peter J. 1948- *WhoScE 91-2*
Simon, Philippe Jean-Marie 1954- *WhoE 93*
Simon, Phyllis K. 1955- *St&PR 93*
Simon, Rainer 1941- *DrEEuF*
Simon, Ralph 1906- *WhoAm 92*
Simon, Richard A. 1938- *St&PR 93*
Simon, Richard Alan 1938- *WhoIns 93*
Simon, Richard Eric 1951- *St&PR 93*
Simon, Richard Michael 1942- *St&PR 93*
Simon, Richard S. 1921- *St&PR 93*
Simon, Robert G. *Law&B 92*
Simon, Robert G. 1927- *WhoAm 92*
Simon, Robert J. *St&PR 93*
Simon, Robert L. 1941- *WhoWrEP 92*
Simon, Robert S. 1946- *St&PR 93*
Simon, Robert W. 1947- *St&PR 93*
Simon, Robert Wayne 1947- *WhoIns 93*
Simon, Roger L. *MiSFD 9*
Simon, Roger L(ichtenberg) 1943- *ConAu 137*
Simon, Roger Mitchell 1948- *WhoAm 92, WhoWrEP 92*
Simon, Roger Scott 1956- *St&PR 93*
Simon, Ronald A. 1957- *St&PR 93*
Simon, Ronald Charles 1951- *WhoAm 92*
Simon, Ronald I. 1938- *WhoAm 92*
Simon, Ronald Isaac 1938- *St&PR 93*
Simon, Rowena *AmWomPl*
Simon, Ruth *Law&B 92*
Simon, Samuel J. *Law&B 92*
Simon, Seymour 1915- *WhoAm 92*
Simon, Seymour 1931- *MajAI [port], ScF&FL 92, SmATA 73 [port]*
Simon, Seymour B. 1927- *St&PR 93*
Simon, Sheldon Weiss 1937- *WhoAm 92*
Simon, Shena 1883-1972 *BioIn 17*
Simon, Sheridan Alan 1947- *WhoSSW 93*
Simon, Simone 1910?- *IntDcF 2-3 [port]*
Simon, Simone 1911- *WhoWor 93*
Simon, Sophie *BioIn 17*
Simon, Stanley 1917- *St&PR 93*
Simon, Stephen (Anthony) 1937- *Baker 92*
Simon, Steven 1945- *St&PR 93*
Simon, Steven Cliff 1945- *St&PR 93*
Simon, Sunka 1962- *WhoWor 93*
Simon, Susan Hewitt 1961- *WhoAmW 93*
Simon, Ted J. 1931- *St&PR 93*
Simon, Teri R. *Law&B 92*
Simon, Theodore Ronald 1949- *WhoWor 93*
Simon, Thomas Haskell 1936- *WhoE 93*
Simon, Thomas Shahean 1952- *WhoE 93*
Simon, Uwe *WhoScE 91-3*
Simon, Werner 1914- *WhoWrEP 92*
Simon, Werner Franz Heinz 1950- *WhoWor 93*
Simon, Wilhelm 1929- *WhoScE 91-4*
Simon, William 1929- *WhoAm 92*
Simon, William A., Jr. *Law&B 92*
Simon, William E. 1927- *BioIn 17*
Simon, William Edward 1927- *WhoAm 92*
Simon, Xavier 1962- *WhoScE 91-2*
Simonaitis, Richard Ambrose 1930- *WhoWor 93*
Simonalle, Eugene *Law&B 92*
Simonalle, Eugene 1931- *St&PR 93*
Simonard, Stephanie Harmon 1950- *WhoWor 93*
Simond, Andree Yvette 1939- *WhoUN 92*
Simonds, Bruce 1895-1989 *Baker 92*
Simonds, Charles *BioIn 17*
Simonds, Gary Lee 1941- *St&PR 93*
Simonds, John Edward 1935- *WhoAm 92*
Simonds, John Ormsbee 1913- *WhoAm 92*
Simonds, Karen Lynn 1962- *WhoAmW 93*
Simonds, Kenneth W. 1935- *St&PR 93*
Simonds, Marie Celeste 1947- *WhoAmW 93*
Simonds, Marshall 1930- *WhoAm 92*
Simonds, Philip George 1940- *St&PR 93*
Simonds, Robert James 1924- *St&PR 93*
Simone, Albert Joseph 1935- *WhoAm 92*
Simone, Elizabeth Ortiz 1951- *WhoE 93*
Simone, Frank J., Jr. *Law&B 92*
Simone, Gail Elisabeth 1944- *WhoAmW 93, WhoE 93, WhoWor 93*
Simone, John Joseph 1941- *St&PR 93, WhoAm 92*
Simone, Joseph Vincent 1935- *WhoAm 92*
Simone, Nina *BioIn 17*
Simone, Nina 1933- *Baker 92, SoulM*
Simone, Peter James 1947- *St&PR 93*
Simone, Sharon *BioIn 17*
Simone, Thomas B. 1942- *St&PR 93, WhoAm 92*
Simoneau, John J. 1925- *St&PR 93*
Simoneau, Leopold 1918- *Baker 92, IntDcOp, OxDcOp*
Simoneau, Yves *BioIn 17, MiSFD 9*
Simonelli, Charles Francis 1925- *WhoAm 92*
Simonelli, John 1946- *St&PR 93*
Simonelli, Marco Sergio 1942- *WhoWor 93*
Simonet, Jacques Louis 1940- *WhoWor 93*
Simonet, John Thomas 1926- *WhoAm 92*
Simonett, Davis S. 1926-1990 *BioIn 17*
Simonetta, Nicholas B. *Law&B 92*
Simonetti, Achille 1857-1928 *Baker 92*
Simonetti, Ignazio 1949- *WhoWor 93*
Simonetti, John A. *Law&B 92*
Simonetto, Joseph Ambrose 1943- *St&PR 93*
Simon-Girard, Juliette 1859-1959 *Baker 92*
Simoni, Francesco 1949- *WhoWor 93*
Simoni, Hugo Alberto 1943- *WhoWor 93*
Simoni, John Peter 1911- *WhoAm 92*
Simonian, David A. 1945- *St&PR 93*
Simonian, Simon John 1932- *WhoAm 92, WhoWor 93*
Simonich, Dennis Eugene 1945- *St&PR 93*
Simonides, Richard *St&PR 93*
Simonis 1294-c. 1336 *OxDcByz*
Simonis, Adrianus Johannes Cardinal 1931- *WhoWor 93*
Simonis, Asterios 1932- *WhoScE 91-3*
Simonis, Jean-Marie 1931- *Baker 92*
Simonis, John Charles 1940- *WhoSSW 93*
Simonis, Udo Ernst 1937- *WhoWor 93*
Simonnard, Michel A. 1933- *St&PR 93*
Simonnard, Michel Andre 1933- *WhoAm 92*
Simonotti, Lucio 1941- *WhoScE 91-4*
Simonov, Konstantin Mikhailovich 1915-1979 *BioIn 17*
Simonov, Yuri (Ivanovich) 1941- *Baker 92, WhoWor 93*
Simons, Albert, Jr. 1918- *WhoAm 92*
Simons, Algie Martin 1870-1950 *BioIn 17*
Simons, Beverly 1938- *WhoCanL 92*
Simons, Beverly A. *St&PR 93*
Simons, Charles Earl, Jr. 1916- *WhoAm 92*
Simons, Charles Franklin, III 1950- *WhoSSW 93*
Simons, Charles John 1918- *St&PR 93*
Simons, Dale Edward 1931- *WhoWrEP 92*
Simons, Dolph C., Jr. 1930- *St&PR 93*
Simons, Dolph Collins, Jr. 1930- *WhoAm 92*
Simons, Donald L. *BioIn 17*
Simons, Donald L. 1945- *ConAu 138*
Simons, Elizabeth Reiman 1929- *WhoAm 92, WhoAmW 93*
Simons, Elwyn LaVerne 1930- *WhoAm 92*
Simons, Evelyn *AmWomPl*
Simons, Frank Holmes 1932- *WhoSSW 93*
Simons, Gale Gene 1939- *WhoAm 92*
Simons, Gordon Donald, Jr. 1938- *WhoAm 92*
Simons, Helen 1930- *WhoAmW 93*
Simons, Jay R. 1930- *St&PR 93*
Simons, Jean E. *Law&B 92*
Simons, John C. *Law&B 92*
Simons, John H. 1939- *WhoAm 92*
Simons, John P. *WhoScE 91-1*
Simons, Joseph M. 1914- *St&PR 93*
Simons, Kai Lennart 1938- *WhoScE 91-3*
Simons, Kent Cobb 1935- *WhoAm 92*
Simons, Lawrence Brook 1924- *WhoAm 92*
Simons, Leonard Norman Rashall 1904- *WhoAm 92*
Simons, Leonard R. 1928- *St&PR 93*
Simons, Les *ScF&FL 92*
Simons, Lewis Martin 1939- *WhoWor 93*
Simons, Linnea M. *Law&B 92*
Simons, Lois Anne 1917- *WhoAmW 93*
Simons, Lynn Osborn 1934- *WhoAm 92, WhoAmW 93*
Simons, Marc V. 1948- *WhoAm 92*
Simons, Marlene J. 1935- *WhoAmW 93*
Simons, Paul William 1948- *St&PR 93*
Simons, Peter J. 1933- *WhoScE 91-1*
Simons, Ray D. 1946- *St&PR 93*
Simons, Renee V.H. *BioIn 17*
Simons, Richard A. 1936- *St&PR 93*
Simons, Richard Duncan 1927- *WhoAm 92, WhoE 93*
Simons, Robert A. *Law&B 92*
Simons, Robert A. 1947- *St&PR 93*
Simons, Roland F. d1990 *BioIn 17*
Simons, Roland S. 1955- *St&PR 93*
Simons, Samuel Stoney, Jr. 1945- *WhoE 93*
Simons, Sarah Emma 1867- *AmWomPl*
Simons, Stephen 1938- *WhoAm 92*
Simons, Thomas W., Jr. 1938- *WhoAm 92, WhoWor 93*
Simons, William A. *Law&B 92*
Simonsen, Asmund 1933- *WhoWor 93*
Simonsen, Eric A. 1945- *WhoIns 93*
Simonsen, Gregory Mark 1957- *WhoEmL 93*
Simonsen, Jeffry Scott 1953- *St&PR 93*
Simonsen, Mark Warren 1946- *St&PR 93*
Simonsen, Morten 1921- *WhoScE 91-2*
Simonsen, Rudolph (Hermann) 1889-1947 *Baker 92*
Simonsmeier, Larry Marvin 1944- *WhoWrEP 92*
Simonson, Arthur Francis 1964- *St&PR 93*
Simonson, David C. 1927- *WhoAm 92*
Simonson, Donna Jeanne 1947- *WhoAmW 93*
Simonson, Gerald Wallace 1930- *St&PR 93*
Simonson, Hana Malka 1929- *WhoAmW 93*
Simonson, John Alexander 1945- *St&PR 93, WhoAm 92*
Simonson, Joy Rosenheim 1919- *WhoAmW 93*
Simonson, Lee J. 1953- *WhoE 93*
Simonson, Lee Stuart 1948- *WhoAm 92*
Simonson, Miles Kevin 1950- *WhoWor 93*
Simonson, Rune G.W. 1935- *WhoScE 91-4*
Simonson, Solomon S. d1991 *BioIn 17*
Simonson, W. Thomas 1935- *St&PR 93*
Simonson, William L. 1943- *St&PR 93*
Simonson-Mohle, Brenda Kay 1959- *WhoSSW 93*
Simon-Spada, Susan Mindy 1957- *WhoE 93*
Simonsuuri, Kirsti Katariina 1945- *WhoWor 93*
Simonsz, Huibert Jan 1951- *WhoWor 93*
Simont, Marc 1915- *ConAu 38NR, MajAI [port], SmATA 73 [port], WhoAm 92*
Simonton, James William 1823-1882 *JrnUS*
Simonton, John W. 1945- *St&PR 93*
Simonton, Pamela A. *Law&B 92*
Simonton, Robert Bennet 1933- *WhoAm 92*
Simonton, Ronald Joseph 1939- *WhoSSW 93*
Simony, Maggy *WhoWrEP 92*
Simonyan, Gary *BioIn 17*
Simonyan, Gary 1935- *St&PR 93*
Simonyi-Gindele, Steven J. 1945- *St&PR 93*
Simopoulos, Artemis Panageotis 1933- *WhoAm 92, WhoE 93*
Simos, Anthony Efstathiou 1931- *WhoWor 93*
Simoson, William E. *Law&B 92*
Simova-Tosic, Dusanka 1934- *WhoScE 91-4*
Simovich, Roman 1901-1984 *Baker 92*
Simovici, Dan 1943- *WhoE 93*
Simpao, Ellen Grace 1964- *WhoAmW 93*
Simpfenderfer, Susan Lee 1963- *WhoAmW 93*
Simpich, William Morris 1924- *WhoAm 92*
Simpkin, Andrew Gordon 1947- *WhoWor 93*
Simpkin, Lawrence James 1933- *WhoAm 92*
Simpkins, Anne Eddleman 1950- *WhoAmW 93*
Simpkins, Lucille Angelique 1944- *WhoE 93*
Simpkins, William Daniel 1953- *WhoSSW 93*
Simplicio Durarte, Augusto *WhoScE 91-3*
Simplikios 6th cent.- *OxDcByz*
Simplot, Jack *BioIn 17*
Simplot, John R. 1909- *WhoAm 92*
Simpson, Adele 1908- *WhoAm 92*
Simpson, Alan K. *BioIn 17*
Simpson, Alan K. 1931- *CngDr 91*
Simpson, Alan Kooi 1931- *WhoAm 92*
Simpson, Albert Dee, III *Law&B 92*
Simpson, Alex Francis 1932- *St&PR 93*
Simpson, Allan Boyd 1948- *WhoEmL 93*
Simpson, Allan C. *WhoScE 91-1*
Simpson, Andrea Lynn 1948- *St&PR 93, WhoAmW 93, WhoEmL 93*
Simpson, Anne Roe 1904-1991 *BioIn 17*
Simpson, Audrey 1952- *WhoAmW 93*
Simpson, Barbara L. 1947- *WhoAmW 93, WhoE 93*
Simpson, Bart Tinsley *BioIn 17*
Simpson, Beverly Taylor 1937- *WhoAmW 93*
Simpson, Billie Faye 1938- *WhoSSW 93*
Simpson, Bruce C. 1939- *St&PR 93*
Simpson, Bruce Howard 1921- *WhoAm 92*
Simpson, Carla *ScF&FL 92*
Simpson, Carol Louise 1937- *WhoAmW 93, WhoE 93, WhoWor 93*
Simpson, Carole 1940- *WhoAm 92*
Simpson, Carter B. *Law&B 92*
Simpson, Cary Hatcher 1927- *WhoAm 92*
Simpson, Charles A. *St&PR 93*
Simpson, Charles Eugene 1950- *WhoSSW 93*
Simpson, Charles Herbert 1933- *WhoAm 92*
Simpson, Charles R., Jr. *St&PR 93*
Simpson, Charles R., III 1945- *WhoAm 92*
Simpson, Charles Reagan 1921- *WhoAm 92*
Simpson, Christopher c. 1605-1669 *Baker 92*
Simpson, Dan *WhoScE 91-1*
Simpson, Daniel H. 1939- *WhoAm 92, WhoWor 93*
Simpson, Daniel Reid 1927- *WhoSSW 93*
Simpson, David John 1946- *St&PR 93, WhoAm 92*
Simpson, David Louis, III *Law&B 92*
Simpson, David Louis, III 1936- *St&PR 93*
Simpson, David W. *Law&B 92*
Simpson, David William 1928- *WhoAm 92*
Simpson, Dennis Arden 1944- *WhoSSW 93*
Simpson, Derek Stanley *WhoScE 91-1*
Simpson, Diane Jeannette 1952- *WhoAmW 93*
Simpson, Don *WhoAm 92*
Simpson, Don 1945- *BioIn 17*
Simpson, Donald Bruce 1942- *WhoAm 92*
Simpson, Donnie 1954- *AfrAmBi*
Simpson, Dorothy 1933- *BioIn 17*
Simpson, Douglas H. *Law&B 92*
Simpson, Douglas Jackson 1940- *WhoAm 92*
Simpson, Douglas Knox *Law&B 92*
Simpson, Ducan S. 1946- *St&PR 93*
Simpson, Edna Oakes 1891-1984 *BioIn 17*
Simpson, Edward W. 1904- *St&PR 93*
Simpson, Edwin L. 1948- *WhoWrEP 92*
Simpson, Eileen B. *ConAu 139*
Simpson, Elizabeth 1939- *WhoScE 91-1*
Simpson, Elizabeth Ann 1941- *WhoAmW 93*
Simpson, Ethel Chachere 1937- *WhoWrEP 92*
Simpson, Eugenia M. *St&PR 93*
Simpson, Frank William 1920- *St&PR 93*
Simpson, Frankie Joe 1933- *WhoAmW 93*
Simpson, Frederick James 1922- *WhoAm 92*
Simpson, Gary Eldridge 1937- *St&PR 93*
Simpson, Gary Lee *Law&B 92*
Simpson, Geddes Wilson 1908- *WhoWrEP 92*
Simpson, George Charles 1961- *WhoE 93*
Simpson, George E. 1944- *ScF&FL 92*
Simpson, George Gaylord 1902-1984 *BioIn 17*
Simpson, H. Richard 1930- *WhoWor 93*
Simpson, Hatton William 1913- *WhoSSW 93*
Simpson, Hilda 1956- *St&PR 93*
Simpson, Howard 1922- *St&PR 93*
Simpson, Hugh Walter *WhoScE 91-1*
Simpson, Ian James 1942- *WhoWor 93*
Simpson, J. Kirk 1949- *WhoAm 92*
Simpson, Jack Ward 1941- *WhoAm 92*
Simpson, James A. *Law&B 92*
Simpson, James D., III 1940- *St&PR 93*
Simpson, James E. 1933- *St&PR 93*
Simpson, James Edward 1933- *WhoAm 92*
Simpson, James Rigg 1940- *St&PR 93*
Simpson, James Roche 1946- *WhoSSW 93*
Simpson, James Roger 1945- *WhoE 93*
Simpson, Janella K. *Law&B 92*
Simpson, Janet A. 1936- *St&PR 93*
Simpson, Jay A. 1947- *St&PR 93*
Simpson, Jay E. *Law&B 92*
Simpson, Jean Marie 1927- *WhoAmW 93*
Simpson, Jerry 1842-1905 *PolPar*
Simpson, Jerry H(oward, Jr.) 1925- *ConAu 138*
Simpson, Jess Richard 1924- *St&PR 93*
Simpson, Joan Y. 1952- *WhoAmW 93*
Simpson, Joanne Malkus 1923- *WhoAm 92, WhoAmW 93*
Simpson, Joe Leigh 1943- *WhoAm 92*
Simpson, John Alexander 1916- *WhoAm 92*
Simpson, John Arol 1923- *WhoAm 92*
Simpson, John Harold *WhoScE 91-1*
Simpson, John Joseph 1939- *WhoAm 92*
Simpson, John Mathes 1948- *WhoAm 92*
Simpson, John S. 1941- *St&PR 93*
Simpson, John Wistar 1914- *WhoAm 92*
Simpson, Judy Ann 1949- *WhoSSW 93*
Simpson, Karin S. *Law&B 92*
Simpson, Kenneth Lee 1931- *WhoE 93*

Simpson, Kenneth Warren 1944- *WhoAm 92*
Simpson, L. Bruce 1955- *WhoSSW 93*
Simpson, L.W. 1916- *St&PR 93*
Simpson, Larry L. 1949- *St&PR 93*
Simpson, Laura K. *Law&B 92*
Simpson, Lee C. 1934- *St&PR 93*
Simpson, Leo *WhoCanL 92*
Simpson, Leo 1934- *ScF&FL 92*
Simpson, Leo A. *Law&B 92*
Simpson, Lillie *AmWomPl*
Simpson, Lizzie Lou 1939- *WhoAmW 93*
Simpson, Lorna 1960- *ConBlB 4 [port]*
Simpson, Lorna 1961- *BioIn 17*
Simpson, Louis A. 1936- *WhoAm 92*
Simpson, Louis Allen 1936- *St&PR 93, WhoIns 93*
Simpson, Louis Aston Marantz 1923- *BioIn 17, WhoAm 92, WhoWrEP 92*
Simpson, Lucy Picco 1940- *WhoAmW 93*
Simpson, Lyle Lee 1937- *WhoWor 93*
Simpson, Mabel P. *AmWomPl*
Simpson, Mark S. *ScF&FL 92*
Simpson, Martyn William 1948- *WhoSSW 93*
Simpson, Mary Michael 1925- *WhoAmW 93*
Simpson, Michael 1938- *WhoAm 92*
Simpson, Michael A. *MiSFD 9*
Simpson, Michael J. 1953- *St&PR 93*
Simpson, Michael Kevin 1949- *WhoAm 92*
Simpson, Michael Marcial 1954- *WhoE 93*
Simpson, Michael Wayne 1959- *WhoEmL 93, WhoWor 93*
Simpson, Milton Crawford 1963- *WhoWor 93*
Simpson, Mona *BioIn 17*
Simpson, Murray 1921- *WhoAm 92, WhoE 93, WhoWor 93*
Simpson, Nancy Carolyn 1938- *WhoWrEP 92*
Simpson, O.J. *BioIn 17*
Simpson, O. J. 1947- *WhoAm 92*
Simpson, O. Strother 1910- *St&PR 93*
Simpson, Pamela *ScF&FL 92*
Simpson, Pamela Hemenway 1946- *WhoAmW 93*
Simpson, Patricia *ScF&FL 92*
Simpson, Phil 1935- *St&PR 93*
Simpson, Philip Francis 1923- *WhoWor 93*
Simpson, R.E. *Law&B 92*
Simpson, Ralph Michael 1937- *St&PR 93*
Simpson, Randolph Linsly d1992 *BioIn 17*
Simpson, Reid Edward 1957- *St&PR 93*
Simpson, Richard D., Jr. *Law&B 92*
Simpson, Richard Lee 1929- *WhoAm 92*
Simpson, Richard Vernon 1935- *WhoE 93*
Simpson, Robert C. 1942- *St&PR 93*
Simpson, Robert Edward 1917- *WhoAm 92*
Simpson, Robert G. 1952- *St&PR 93*
Simpson, Robert Glenn 1932- *WhoAm 92*
Simpson, Robert James *WhoScE 91-1*
Simpson, Robert Leatham 1915- *WhoAm 92*
Simpson, Robert Reynolds 1937- *WhoSSW 93*
Simpson, Robert Smith 1906- *WhoAm 92*
Simpson, Robert (Wilfred Levick) 1921- *Baker 92, WhoWor 93*
Simpson, Ruby Laird 1910- *WhoAmW 93, WhoWor 93*
Simpson, Russell 1880-1959 *BioIn 17*
Simpson, Russell Gordon 1927- *WhoAm 92*
Simpson, Samuel Ford, Jr. 1950- *WhoE 93*
Simpson, Scott W. 1951- *St&PR 93*
Simpson, Thomas 1582?-1630? *Baker 92*
Simpson, Thomas James *WhoScE 91-1*
Simpson, Thomas Joel 1931- *WhoSSW 93*
Simpson, Thomas John 1958- *St&PR 93*
Simpson, Thomas S. *Law&B 92*
Simpson, Thomas W(illiam) 1957- *ConAu 137*
Simpson, Tim *BioIn 17*
Simpson, V. Kathryn 1945- *WhoAmW 93*
Simpson, Valerie 1948- See Ashford & Simpson *SoulM*
Simpson, Vi 1946- *WhoAmW 93*
Simpson, Vinson Raleigh 1928- *WhoAm 92*
Simpson, Virginia White 1907- *WhoAmW 93*
Simpson, Wade Bland 1937- *St&PR 93*
Simpson, Wallis Warfield 1896-1986 *BioIn 17*
Simpson, Warren Edwin *Law&B 92*
Simpson, Wesley D. 1958- *St&PR 93*
Simpson, Willard Kempton, Jr. 1954- *WhoSSW 93*
Simpson, William Anderson 1941- *St&PR 93*
Simpson, William Arthur 1939- *WhoAm 92, WhoIns 93*
Simpson, William Cyril 1945- *WhoSSW 93*
Simpson, William Fulton 1945- *St&PR 93*
Simpson, William Gary 1943- *WhoAm 92*
Simpson, William H. 1938- *WhoIns 93*
Simpson, William H. 1941- *St&PR 93*
Simpson, William Henry 1924- *WhoE 93*
Simpson, William Hood 1888-1980 *HarEnMi*
Simpson, William Kelly 1928- *WhoAm 92*
Simpson, William Renton 1939- *WhoUN 92*
Simpson, William Stewart 1924- *WhoAm 92*
Simpson, Winifred Rouse 1937- *WhoWrEP 92*
Simpson, Zelma Alene 1923- *WhoAm 92*
Simpson-Hebert, Mayling 1946- *WhoUN 92*
Simrall, Dorothy Van Winkle 1917- *WhoAmW 93, WhoWor 93*
Simrock, "Fritz" 1837-1901 See Simrock, Nikolaus 1751-1832 *Baker 92*
Simrock, Fritz Auckenthaler 1893-1973 See Simrock, Nikolaus 1751-1832 *Baker 92*
Simrock, "Hans" 1861-1910 See Simrock, Nikolaus 1751-1832 *Baker 92*
Simrock, Nikolaus 1751-1832 *Baker 92*
Simrock, Peter Joseph 1792-1868 See Simrock, Nikolaus 1751-1832 *Baker 92*
Sims, Algie Wright, III *Law&B 92*
Sims, Andrew Charles Petter *WhoScE 91-1*
Sims, August Charles 1948- *WhoAm 92, WhoEmL 93*
Sims, Bennett Jones 1920- *WhoAm 92*
Sims, Bernard J. 1948- *St&PR 93*
Sims, Brian G. 1943- *WhoScE 91-1*
Sims, C. Paul 1951- *St&PR 93*
Sims, Carole Patricia *Law&B 92*
Sims, Carolyn Denise 1960- *WhoAmW 93*
Sims, Christopher Albert 1942- *WhoAm 92*
Sims, D.N. 1940- *ScF&FL 92*
Sims, David Suthern 1965- *WhoEmL 93, WhoSSW 93*
Sims, Deborah G. *BioIn 17*
Sims, Edward Howell 1923- *WhoAm 92*
Sims, Edward S. 1946- *St&PR 93*
Sims, Everett Martin 1920- *WhoAm 92*
Sims, Ezra 1928- *Baker 92*
Sims, Frank Mcnair 1932- *St&PR 93*
Sims, Fred William, Sr. 1915- *WhoSSW 93*
Sims, Garland D. *Law&B 92*
Sims, Gerald 1940- *BioIn 17*
Sims, Gregory Evans 1946- *WhoSSW 93*
Sims, Herman Christie 1960- *WhoSSW 93*
Sims, Iris Kathleen *Law&B 92*
Sims, Ivor Donald 1912- *WhoAm 92*
Sims, Jack Robert *WhoSSW 93*
Sims, James Hylbert 1924- *WhoAm 92, WhoWrEP 92*
Sims, James M. 1934- *St&PR 93*
Sims, Jennifer Emily 1953- *WhoAmW 93*
Sims, Joan *BioIn 17*
Sims, Joan 1930- *QDrFCA 92 [port]*
Sims, Joe 1944- *WhoAm 92*
Sims, John Dunaway 1962- *WhoSSW 93*
Sims, John R. *Law&B 92*
Sims, John Rogers, Jr. 1924- *WhoAm 92*
Sims, John William 1917- *WhoAm 92*
Sims, Jon Reed 1947-1984 *Baker 92*
Sims, Judy D.O. *St&PR 93*
Sims, Kent Otway 1940- *WhoAm 92*
Sims, Lois Lang- *BioIn 17*
Sims, Loretta James 1948- *WhoWor 93*
Sims, M.P.N. 1952- *ScF&FL 92*
Sims, Marcy J. 1946- *WhoSSW 93*
Sims, Margaret Church 1949- *WhoAmW 93*
Sims, Mari Kristine *Law&B 92*
Sims, Maude B. *AmWomPl*
Sims, Michael Hall *Law&B 92*
Sims, Michael Hall 1956- *St&PR 93*
Sims, Patterson *BioIn 17*
Sims, Patterson 1947- *WhoAm 92*
Sims, Paul Kibler 1918- *WhoAm 92*
Sims, Peter George 1941- *WhoWor 93*
Sims, Randy D. *Law&B 92*
Sims, Richard Edward 1941- *St&PR 93*
Sims, Richard G. *St&PR 93*
Sims, Richard Lee 1929- *WhoAm 92*
Sims, Riley V. 1903- *St&PR 93, WhoAm 92*
Sims, Robert B. *Law&B 92*
Sims, Robert Barry 1942- *WhoAm 92*
Sims, Robert Bell 1934- *WhoAm 92*
Sims, Robert McNeill 1928- *WhoSSW 93, WhoWor 93*
Sims, Robert Warren 1934- *WhoSSW 93*
Sims, Roberta Willis *Law&B 92*
Sims, Ronald Louis *Law&B 92*
Sims, Sandra Eola *Law&B 92*
Sims, Seymour E. 1914- *St&PR 93*
Sims, Stephen Paul 1947- *St&PR 93*
Sims, Thaddeus Michael 1943- *WhoSSW 93*
Sims, Thomas Auburn 1925- *WhoSSW 93*
Sims, Victor Dwayne 1959- *WhoWor 93*
Sims, William Dale 1941- *St&PR 93, WhoIns 93*
Sims, William Marquis 1944- *St&PR 93, WhoAm 92*
Sims, William Riley, Jr. 1938- *WhoAm 92*
Sims, William Sowden 1858-1936 *HarEnMi*
Sims, Wilson 1924- *WhoAm 92*
Sims, "Zoot" (John Haley) 1925-1985 *Baker 92*
Simsek, Ziya 1948- *WhoScE 91-4*
Simshauser, Philip Dale 1937- *St&PR 93*
Simshaw, Calvin K. *Law&B 92*
Simson, Daniel 1942- *WhoWor 93*
Simson, Gary Joseph 1950- *WhoAm 92*
Simson, Jo Anne 1936- *WhoAm 92, WhoAmW 93, WhoSSW 93*
Simson, Joanne 1936- *WhoWrEP 92*
Simson, Renate Maria 1934- *WhoAmW 93*
Simson, Rosalind Slivka 1952- *WhoAmW 93, WhoE 93*
Simundsson, Elva 1950- *BioIn 17*
Simutis, Leonard Joseph 1944- *WhoAm 92*
Sin, Jaime Lachica Cardinal 1928- *WhoWor 93*
Sin, Otakar 1881-1943 *Baker 92*
Sinaceur, Hourya 1940- *WhoWor 93*
Sinacore-Guinn, Ada Louise 1959- *WhoAmW 93*
Sinai, Allen 1939- *St&PR 93*
Sinai, Allen Leo 1939- *WhoAm 92, WhoWor 93*
Sinamoi, Brown 1951- *WhoAsAP 91*
Sinan, Rogelio 1902- *SpAmA*
Sinatra, Frank 1915- *Baker 92, BioIn 17, IntDcF 2-3 [port], MiSFD 9, WhoAm 92, WhoWor 93*
Sinatra, Richard Charles 1938- *WhoE 93*
Sinay, Hershel David 1938- *WhoAm 92*
Sinay, Joseph 1920- *WhoAm 92*
Sinbad *BioIn 17*
Sinbad 1956- *ConTFT 10*
Sincaglia, Frank Paul 1943- *St&PR 93*
Sincerbeaux, Robert A. 1913- *BioIn 17*
Sincerbeaux, Robert Abbott 1913- *WhoE 93*
Sinche, Robert Miller 1952- *WhoE 93*
Sinclair, Alastair James 1935- *WhoAm 92*
Sinclair, Alford C. 1930- *St&PR 93*
Sinclair, Andrew *BioIn 17, MiSFD 9*
Sinclair, Andrew 1935- *ScF&FL 92*
Sinclair, Andrew (Annandale) 1935- *ConAu 38NR*
Sinclair, Bertrand William 1881-1972 *BioIn 17*
Sinclair, Bill *BioIn 17*
Sinclair, Bradley H. 1957- *St&PR 93*
Sinclair, Bruce 1929- *WhoWrEP 92*
Sinclair, Carole 1942- *WhoAm 92, WhoAmW 93*
Sinclair, Clive 1948- *ScF&FL 92*
Sinclair, Daisy 1941- *WhoAmW 93*
Sinclair, Diane *Law&B 92*
Sinclair, Duncan Gordon 1933- *WhoAm 92*
Sinclair, Edward L., Jr. 1947- *St&PR 93*
Sinclair, Gavin *Law&B 92*
Sinclair, George 1912- *WhoAm 92*
Sinclair, George Robertson 1863-1917 *Baker 92*
Sinclair, Gregory Lynn *WhoSSW 93*
Sinclair, Howard S. 1945- *St&PR 93*
Sinclair, Hugh 1910-1990 *BioIn 17*
Sinclair, Iain 1943- *ScF&FL 92*
Sinclair, Ian McCahon 1929- *WhoAsAP 91*
Sinclair, James Garner 1952- *St&PR 93*
Sinclair, Jane *Law&B 92*
Sinclair, John 1920?- *BioIn 17*
Sinclair, John Alan 1948- *St&PR 93*
Sinclair, John David 1943- *WhoWor 93*
Sinclair, John Luther 1960- *WhoE 93*
Sinclair, Joseph Samuels 1922- *St&PR 93, WhoAm 92*
Sinclair, Judson Mark 1949- *WhoSSW 93*
Sinclair, K. Richard C. 1946- *St&PR 93*
Sinclair, Kenneth Richard Coates 1946- *WhoSSW 93*
Sinclair, Kenneth Roger 1927- *St&PR 93*
Sinclair, Madge 1940- *WhoAmW 93*
Sinclair, Margaret Nieland 1949- *WhoAmW 93*
Sinclair, Marjorie *AmWomPl*
Sinclair, Marjorie Putnam 1913- *WhoWrEP 92*
Sinclair, Mary *BioIn 17*
Sinclair, Miranda *ScF&FL 92*
Sinclair, Quinn *ScF&FL 92*
Sinclair, R.M. *St&PR 93*
Sinclair, Randolph Kyle 1950- *WhoSSW 93*
Sinclair, Raymond Allen 1946- *St&PR 93*
Sinclair, Richard Carroll 1948- *WhoEmL 93, WhoWor 93*
Sinclair, Robert J. *Law&B 92*
Sinclair, Robert P. 1961- *St&PR 93*
Sinclair, Rolf Malcolm 1929- *WhoAm 92, WhoE 93*
Sinclair, Sara Voris 1942- *WhoAmW 93, WhoWor 93*
Sinclair, Steven Allen 1953- *WhoSSW 93*
Sinclair, Upton 1878-1968 *BioIn 17, WorLitC [port]*
Sinclair, Upton B. 1878-1968 *PolPar*
Sinclair, Upton Beall 1878-1968 *JrnUS*
Sinclair, Warren Keith 1924- *WhoAm 92*
Sinclair, William F. *BioIn 17*
Sincoff, Jay Mitchell 1949- *WhoE 93*
Sincoff, Michael Z. 1943- *WhoAm 92*
Sindal, Helge 1938- *WhoWor 93*
Sindall, Teresa Lee 1954- *WhoE 93*
Sindeband, Seymour J. 1916- *St&PR 93*
Sindelar, Charles J. 1937- *St&PR 93*
Sindelar, Iris Petersen 1943- *WhoAmW 93*
Sindelar, Jody Louise 1951- *WhoE 93*
Sindelar, Peggy L. 1951- *WhoSSW 93*
Sindelar, William Francis 1945- *WhoAm 92, WhoE 93, WhoWor 93*
Sindell, Gerald Seth 1944- *MiSFD 9*
Sindell, Stuart L. *Law&B 92*
Sinden, Harry *BioIn 17*
Sinden, Howard Bruce 1958- *WhoSSW 93*
Sinden, K.W. 1935- *WhoScE 91-1*
Sinden, Robert E. *WhoScE 91-1*
Sindermann, Carl J(ames) *ConAu 138*
Sinderoff, Rita Joyce 1932- *WhoAmW 93*
Sinding, Christian (August) 1856-1941 *Baker 92*
Sinding, James E. *Law&B 92*
Sinding, Richard Victor 1946- *WhoAm 92*
Sindle, Harvey Bertrand 1930- *WhoWor 93*
Sindler, Millard S. 1918- *St&PR 93*
Sindoni, Elio 1937- *WhoWor 93*
Sindram, Hendrik J. 1906- *St&PR 93*
Sine, Jeffrey Alan 1954- *WhoAm 92*
Sineath, Timothy Wayne 1940- *WhoAm 92*
Sinegal, James 1936- *St&PR 93*
Sinegal, James D. 1936- *WhoAm 92*
Sinel, Norman Mark 1941- *WhoAm 92*
Sinell, Hans-Jurgen 1926- *WhoScE 91-3*
Sinel'shchikov, Sergey Dmitriyevich 1960- *WhoWor 93*
Sines, James Willam 1936- *St&PR 93*
Sines, Jay *BioIn 17*
Sines, Vonda Jean 1947- *WhoEmL 93*
Sinex, Francis Marott 1923- *WhoAm 92*
Sinfelt, John Henry 1931- *WhoAm 92*
Sing, Carol Jean 1939- *WhoAmW 93*
Sing, Kenneth Stafford 1925- *WhoWor 93*
Sing, Kenneth Stafford William *WhoScE 91-1*
Sing, Robert Fong 1953- *WhoE 93*
Singa Boyembe Mosambay 1932- *WhoAfr*
Singan, Michael 1950- *WhoAsAP 91*
Singaravadivel, S. 1934- *WhoAsAP 91*
Singel, Mark Stephen 1953- *WhoAm 92, WhoE 93, WhoWor 93*
Singelee, Jean-Baptiste 1812-1875 *Baker 92*
Singer, A.L. *ScF&FL 92, SmATA 72*
Singer, Alexander 1932- *MiSFD 9*
Singer, Alfred Richard Eric *WhoScE 91-1*
Singer, Allen Morris 1923- *WhoAm 92*
Singer, Amanda *ConAu 39NR*
Singer, Armand Edwards 1914- *WhoAm 92, WhoSSW 93, WhoWor 93*
Singer, Arthur 1917-1990 *BioIn 17*
Singer, Arthur Louis, Jr. 1929- *WhoAm 92*
Singer, Beth Yvonne 1965- *WhoAmW 93, WhoEmL 93*
Singer, Bradley Ray 1956- *St&PR 93*
Singer, Bryna L. *Law&B 92*
Singer, Burton Herbert 1938- *WhoAm 92*
Singer, Carl Norman 1916- *St&PR 93*
Singer, Cecile D. *WhoAmW 93*
Singer, Charles Blanton 1927- *WhoSSW 93*
Singer, Craig 1947- *WhoAm 92*
Singer, Daniel Eugene 1943- *WhoSSW 93*
Singer, Daniel Morris 1930- *WhoAm 92*
Singer, David A. *Law&B 92*
Singer, David Michael 1957- *WhoE 93, WhoEmL 93, WhoWor 93*
Singer, David Steven 1948- *WhoSSW 93*
Singer, David V. 1955- *St&PR 93*
Singer, Donald Ivan 1938- *WhoAm 92*
Singer, Donna Lea 1944- *WhoAmW 93*
Singer, Edmund 1830-1912 *Baker 92*
Singer, Edwin Z. 1930- *St&PR 93*
Singer, Eleanor 1930- *WhoAm 92*
Singer, Ezra D. *Law&B 92*
Singer, Fred M. 1947- *St&PR 93*
Singer, Frederick Raphael 1939- *WhoAm 92*
Singer, Frieda *WhoWrEP 92*
Singer, Garold G. 1930- *St&PR 93*
Singer, George 1908-1980 *Baker 92*
Singer, George Alan 1948- *WhoAm 92*
Singer, Gladys Montgomery *WhoAmW 93*
Singer, Hans Wolfgang 1910- *BioIn 17*

Singer, Hedy Karen 1954- *WhoAmW 93*
Singer, Hellmut 1936- *WhoScE 91-3*
Singer, Henry A. 1919- *WhoAm 92*
Singer, Herbert M. 1906- *St&PR 93*
Singer, Hermann 1941- *WhoScE 91-3*
Singer, Howard Jack 1940- *WhoE 93*
Singer, Howard Jay 1943- *St&PR 93*
Singer, I.J. 1893-1944 *JeAmHC*
Singer, Irving 1925- *WhoAm 92*
Singer, Irving Lewis 1922- *St&PR 93*
Singer, Irwin 1935- *St&PR 93*
Singer, Isaac *ConAu 39NR, MajAI*
Singer, Isaac Bashevis 1904-1991 *AnObit 1991, BioIn 17, ConAu 39NR, ConLC 70, JeAmHC, MagSWL [port], MajAI [port], News 92, PolBiDi, ScF&FL 92, WorLitC [port]*
Singer, Isaac Merritt 1811-1875 *BioIn 17*
Singer, Isadore Manuel 1924- *WhoAm 92*
Singer, Israel Joshua 1893-1944 *PolBiDi*
Singer, Jacques Mauriciu 1914- *WhoWor 93*
Singer, Jay 1950- *St&PR 93*
Singer, Jeanne 1924- *WhoAmW 93*
Singer, Jill *BioIn 17*
Singer, Joel David 1925- *WhoAm 92*
Singer, John J., Jr. 1921- *St&PR 93*
Singer, Jordana L. *Law&B 92*
Singer, Judith 1926- *ScF&FL 92*
Singer, Judith D. 1955- *WhoE 93*
Singer, Kenneth Edward *WhoScE 91-1*
Singer, Klaus *WhoScE 91-2*
Singer, Kurt 1911- *ScF&FL 92*
Singer, Kurt Deutsch 1911- *WhoAm 92, WhoWrEP 92*
Singer, Lawrence E. 1924- *St&PR 93*
Singer, Leonard 1923- *WhoScE 91-2*
Singer, Lewis 1934- *St&PR 93*
Singer, Lewis Abraham *Law&B 92*
Singer, Linda Ellen 1948- *St&PR 93*
Singer, Louis P. d1990 *BioIn 17*
Singer, Marcus George 1926- *WhoAm 92, WhoWrEP 92*
Singer, Marilyn 1948- *ConAu 39NR, MajAI [port], ScF&FL 92*
Singer, Marilyn Jean 1955- *WhoAmW 93*
Singer, Mark 1950- *ConAu 138*
Singer, Markus Morton 1917- *WhoAm 92*
Singer, Martina Beth 1960- *WhoAmW 93*
Singer, Matthew Ross 1961- *WhoE 93*
Singer, Max 1931- *WhoE 93*
Singer, Max E. 1943- *St&PR 93*
Singer, Maxine *BioIn 17*
Singer, Maxine Frank 1931- *WhoAm 92, WhoAmW 93, WhoWor 93*
Singer, Melissa *ScF&FL 92*
Singer, Michael Howard 1941- *WhoWor 93*
Singer, Michael I. *Law&B 92*
Singer, Michael Norman 1946- *WhoE 93*
Singer, Milton B. 1912- *IntDcAn*
Singer, Miriam 1959- *WhoAmW 93*
Singer, Mitchell F. *Law&B 92*
Singer, Monroe S. *Law&B 92*
Singer, Monroe S. 1927- *St&PR 93*
Singer, Nancy Lawrence 1946- *WhoSSW 93*
Singer, Norman 1932- *WhoWrEP 92*
Singer, Norman 1941- *St&PR 93*
Singer, Paul H. 1936- *St&PR 93*
Singer, Peter *BioIn 17*
Singer, Peter (Alkantara) 1810-1882 *Baker 92*
Singer, Peter D. 1927- *St&PR 93*
Singer, Ray d1992 *NewYTBS 92*
Singer, Rick H. 1954- *WhoAm 92*
Singer, Rita H. *St&PR 93*
Singer, Robert B. 1931- *St&PR 93*
Singer, Robert Joel *Law&B 92*
Singer, Robert N. *BioIn 17*
Singer, Robert Norman 1936- *WhoAm 92*
Singer, Rochelle 1939- *ScF&FL 92*
Singer, Roger M. *Law&B 92*
Singer, Ronald Leonard 1944- *St&PR 93*
Singer, Rose M. d1991 *BioIn 17*
Singer, Samuel Loewenberg 1911- *WhoAm 92*
Singer, Sandra Manes 1942- *WhoAmW 93*
Singer, Sanford Robert 1930- *St&PR 93, WhoAm 92, WhoSSW 93*
Singer, Sarah Beth 1915- *WhoAm 92, WhoWor 93, WhoWrEP 92*
Singer, Shelley *ScF&FL 92*
Singer, Siegfried Fred 1924- *WhoAm 92*
Singer, Stanley Gerald 1937- *St&PR 93*
Singer, Steven Richard 1956- *WhoE 93*
Singer, Susan Anderman 1947- *WhoAmW 93*
Singer, Susan Jennifer Rundell 1959- *WhoAmW 93*
Singer, Suzanne Fried 1935- *WhoAmW 93*
Singer, Thomas D. *Law&B 92*
Singer, Thomas D. 1952- *St&PR 93*
Singer, Thomas Eric 1926- *WhoAm 92*
Singer, Thomas Kenyon 1932- *St&PR 93, WhoAm 92*
Singer, William James 1946- *WhoEmL 93*
Singer, Wolf Joachim 1943- *WhoScE 91-3*
Singer-Leone, Mallory Ann 1950- *WhoAmW 93*
Singer-Magdoff, Laura Joan Silver 1917- *WhoAm 92*
Singg, Sangeeta 1950- *WhoSSW 93*
Singh, Ajit *BioIn 17*
Singh, Ajit 1939- *WhoAsAP 91*
Singh, Ajit 1940- *WhoWor 93*
Singh, Amarjit 1924- *WhoAm 92*
Singh, Amritjit 1945- *WhoE 93*
Singh, Arindra 1947- *St&PR 93*
Singh, Bhagat *BioIn 17*
Singh, Bir Bahadur 1935- *WhoAsAP 91*
Singh, Bir Bhadra Pratap 1931- *WhoAsAP 91*
Singh, Braj Kishore 1955- *WhoWor 93*
Singh, Chaitram 1949- *WhoSSW 93*
Singh, Chetan 1955- *ConAu 138*
Singh, Davbara 1916- *WhoAsAP 91*
Singh, Dhanwant 1946- *WhoE 93*
Singh, Dheerajlall Baramlall Seetul 1948- *WhoWor 93*
Singh, Dushyant Chanan 1938- *WhoAm 92, WhoUN 92*
Singh, Gajendra 1944- *WhoWor 93*
Singh, Gurpartap 1946- *WhoWor 93*
Singh, Hardev 1938- *St&PR 93*
Singh, Jyoti Shankar 1935- *WhoE 93, WhoUN 92, WhoWor 93*
Singh, Kanwal 1957- *St&PR 93*
Singh, Kanwar Kultar 1931- *St&PR 93*
Singh, Khushwant 1915- *WhoWor 93*
Singh, Kirpal *ScF&FL 92*
Singh, Kishen 1850-1921 *Expl 93*
Singh, Krishan G. 1932- *WhoUN 92*
Singh, Madan Gopal *WhoScE 91-1*
Singh, N. Tombi 1926- *WhoAsAP 91*
Singh, Nain 1830?-1882? *Expl 93*
Singh, Nirbhay Nand 1952- *WhoWor 93*
Singh, Param I. 1946- *St&PR 93*
Singh, Pargat 1954- *WhoWor 93*
Singh, Pratibha 1929- *WhoAsAP 91*
Singh, R.K. Dorendra 1934- *WhoAsAP 91*
Singh, Ram Awadhesh 1937- *WhoAsAP 91*
Singh, Ramendra P. *WhoSSW 93*
Singh, Ranjit 1780-1839 *BioIn 17*
Singh, Rickey 1937- *DcCPCAm*
Singh, Rudra Pratap 1936- *WhoAsAP 91*
Singh, Sampuran 1949- *WhoScE 91-1*
Singh, Sarup 1917- *WhoAsAP 91*
Singh, Satish Kumar 1960- *WhoWor 93*
Singh, Satwant 1953- *WhoWor 93*
Singh, Satyanarain *ScF&FL 92*
Singh, Seebalack 1952- *WhoWor 93*
Singh, Sukhjit 1941- *WhoSSW 93*
Singh, Sundar 1889-1929 *BioIn 17*
Singh, Sunita 1953- *St&PR 93*
Singh, Surender 1946- *WhoAsAP 91*
Singh, Swayam Prabha 1945- *WhoWrEP 92*
Singh, Tara 1921- *WhoWor 93*
Singh, Thakur Kamakhya Prasad 1925- *WhoAsAP 91*
Singh, Udai Kumar 1947- *WhoScE 91-1*
Singh, Vishvjit P. 1946- *WhoAsAP 91*
Singh, Vishwanath Pratap *BioIn 17*
Singh, Vishwanath Pratap 1931- *WhoAsAP 91*
Singh, Zail 1916- *WhoWor 93*
Singhadej, Orapin Srisuchart 1942- *WhoWor 93*
Singhal, Avinash Chandra 1941- *WhoWor 93*
Singhal, Jaya Asthana 1952- *WhoE 93*
Singhal, Kalyan 1946- *WhoE 93*
Singhal, Kishore 1944- *WhoAm 92*
Singhal, Radhey Lal 1940- *WhoAm 92*
Singham, A.W. *BioIn 17*
Singhasaheh, Suther 1928- *WhoAsAP 91*
Singhellakis, Panagiotis Nicolaos 1941- *WhoWor 93*
Singher, Martial *BioIn 17*
Singher, Martial (Jean-Paul) 1904-1990 *Baker 92, IntDcOp*
Singhvi, Sampat Manakchand 1947- *WhoE 93*
Singhvi, Surendra S. 1942- *St&PR 93*
Singhvi, Surendra Singh 1942- *WhoAm 92*
Singlaub, John *BioIn 17, DcCPCAm*
Single, Richard W., Sr. *Law&B 92*
Single, Richard Wayne 1938- *St&PR 93*
Single, Richard Wayne, Sr. 1938- *WhoAm 92*
Singlehurst, Dona G. 1928- *St&PR 93*
Singler, Frances D. *AmWomPl*
Singletary, Charlene Hansen 1953- *WhoSSW 93*
Singletary, J. Noland *Law&B 92*
Singletary, J. Noland 1929- *St&PR 93*
Singletary, Michael 1958- *WhoAm 92*
Singletary, Michael James 1950- *WhoE 93, WhoWor 93*
Singletary, Mike 1958- *ConBlB 4 [port]*
Singletary, Otis Arnold, Jr. 1921- *WhoAm 92*
Singletary, Patricia Ann 1948- *WhoAmW 93, WhoEmL 93, WhoWor 93*
Singletary, Robert Lombard 1941- *WhoE 93*
Singleterry, Gary Lee 1948- *WhoAm 92*
Singleton, Alvin (Elliot) 1940- *Baker 92*
Singleton, Alvin W. d1991 *BioIn 17*
Singleton, Benjamin 1809-1892 *EncAACR*
Singleton, Donald Edward 1936- *WhoAm 92*
Singleton, Donna Marie 1960- *WhoAmW 93*
Singleton, Harry Michael 1949- *WhoAm 92*
Singleton, Henry E. *BioIn 17*
Singleton, Henry Earl 1916- *WhoAm 92*
Singleton, Ina Duvall *AmWomPl*
Singleton, James Daniel, Jr. 1959- *WhoEmL 93*
Singleton, James Keith 1939- *WhoAm 92*
Singleton, John *BioIn 17, MiSFD 9*
Singleton, John 1930- *WhoE 93*
Singleton, John c. 1968- *ConAu 138*
Singleton, John A. 1940- *St&PR 93*
Singleton, John Vietor 1951- *WhoWrEP 92*
Singleton, John Virgil, Jr. 1918- *WhoAm 92*
Singleton, Kenneth P. *Law&B 92*
Singleton, Larry William 1950- *WhoAm 92*
Singleton, Lester Brian 1942- *WhoSSW 93*
Singleton, Lucile Powell d1992 *BioIn 17*
Singleton, Ogle Ridout, Jr. 1929- *WhoSSW 93*
Singleton, Paul Lester 1933- *WhoSSW 93*
Singleton, Penny 1908- *QDrFCA 92 [port]*
Singleton, Philip Arthur 1914- *WhoAm 92*
Singleton, Ralph S. *MiSFD 9*
Singleton, Raymund 1946- *St&PR 93*
Singleton, Raynoma Gordy *BioIn 17*
Singleton, Richard Lynn 1944- *St&PR 93*
Singleton, Robert William 1948- *St&PR 93*
Singleton, Ronald Edward 1950- *WhoSSW 93*
Singleton, Royce Alan, Jr. 1944- *WhoE 93*
Singleton, Samuel Winston 1928- *WhoAm 92*
Singleton, Sara 1940- *WhoAmW 93*
Singleton, Shelby 1931- *SoulM*
Singleton, Shelby S. 1931- *St&PR 93*
Singleton, Steven D. 1948- *WhoAm 92*
Singleton, Susan Merrimac 1955- *WhoAmW 93*
Singleton, Teresa Eileen 1960- *St&PR 93*
Singleton, W.B. *WhoScE 91-1*
Singleton, William 1941- *St&PR 93*
Singleton, William A. 1946- *St&PR 93*
Singleton, William Dean 1951- *WhoAm 92, WhoSSW 93*
Singleton, "Zutty" 1898-1975 *Baker 92*
Singleton-Wood, Allan James 1933- *WhoAm 92*
Singley, Dale Mitchell 1952- *St&PR 93*
Singley, John Edward, Jr. 1924- *WhoAm 92*
Singley, Mark Eldridge 1921- *WhoAm 92*
Singley, Robert Stephen *Law&B 92*
Singreen, Shirley Ann Basile 1941- *WhoAmW 93*
Singson, Eric D. 1948- *WhoAsAP 91*
Singson, Luis 1941- *WhoAsAP 91*
Singson, Rogelio L. *WhoAsAP 91*
Singstock, David John 1940- *WhoWor 93*
Sington, Fredric W., Jr. 1935- *St&PR 93*
Singular, Stephen 1950- *ConAu 139*
Sinha, Drew 1951- *WhoSSW 93*
Sinha, Nilima *DcChlFi*
Sinha, Pradip Kumar *WhoScE 91-1*
Sinha, Ramesh Chandra 1934- *WhoAm 92*
Sinha, Sarojini 1922- *DcChlFi*
Sinha, Tapen 1957- *WhoWor 93*
Sinha, Yashwant 1937- *WhoAsAP 91, WhoWor 93*
Sinhaseni, Norachit 1954- *WhoUN 92*
Sini, Jean-Francois Alain 1951- *WhoWor 93*
Sinicki, Sheila Jeanne 1952- *WhoEmL 93*
Sinico, Francesco 1810-1865 *Baker 92*
Sinico, Giuseppe 1836-1907 *See* Sinico, Francesco 1810-1865 *Baker 92*
Sinicropi, Anthony Vincent 1931- *WhoAm 92*
Sinigaglia, Leone 1868-1944 *Baker 92*
Sinise, Gary *MiSFD 9, WhoAm 92*
Sinisi, Ethna M. *Law&B 92*
Sink, Charles Stanley 1923- *WhoAm 92*
Sink, John Davis 1934- *WhoAm 92*
Sink, Joseph Steven, Jr. 1954- *St&PR 93*
Sink, Loren Gregory 1962- *WhoSSW 93*
Sink, Richard Alden 1934- *St&PR 93*
Sinke, Sharon *BioIn 17*
Sinkel, Bernhard *MiSFD 9*
Sinkford, Jeanne Craig 1933- *WhoAm 92, WhoAmW 93, WhoWor 93*
Sinkhorn, Mary Jean 1941- *WhoAmW 93*
Sinkinson, A.G. *WhoScE 91-1*
Sinkinson, Anne Judith 1951- *WhoWor 93*
Sinkler, Marzetta Fitts 1939- *WhoSSW 93*
Sinkoe, Morris Benjamin 1936- *WhoSSW 93*
Sinkovics, Joseph Geza 1924- *WhoSSW 93*
Sinkula, William J. 1930- *St&PR 93*
Sinkus, Michael F. 1952- *St&PR 93*
Sinkwich, Frank 1920-1990 *BioIn 17*
Sinman, Sadrettin 1925- *WhoScE 91-4*
Sinn, James Micheal 1950- *WhoEmL 93*
Sinnathamby, Thillainathan 1937- *WhoWor 93*
Sinner, George A. 1928- *St&PR 93*
Sinner, George Albert 1928- *WhoAm 92, WhoWor 93*
Sinnett, Clifford H. 1919- *St&PR 93*
Sinnett, Peter Frank 1934- *WhoWor 93*
Sinni, Huseyin 1926- *WhoScE 91-4*
Sinnott, Bethany Strong 1941- *WhoSSW 93*
Sinnott, Daniel 1934- *St&PR 93*
Sinnott, Donald Hugh 1944- *WhoWor 93*
Sinnott, Jessica M. *Law&B 92*
Sinnott, John P. *Law&B 92*
Sinnott, John T. 1939- *St&PR 93*
Sinnott, John William 1938- *St&PR 93*
Sinnott, Roger J. 1913- *St&PR 93*
Sinnott, Tom E. 1949- *St&PR 93*
Sinnreich-Levi, Deborah Margaret 1957- *WhoE 93*
Sinopoli, Giuseppe *BioIn 17*
Sinopoli, Giuseppe 1946- *Baker 92, IntDcOp*
Sinopoli, Richard C. 1956- *ConAu 138*
Sinor, Denis 1916- *WhoAm 92, WhoWor 93*
Sinor, John 1930- *ScF&FL 92*
Sinor, Norris L. *Law&B 92*
Sinoros-Szabo, Botond 1948- *WhoScE 91-4*
Sinou, Denis 1942- *WhoScE 91-2*
Sinsheimer, Joseph G. 1928- *St&PR 93*
Sinsheimer, Robert Louis 1920- *WhoAm 92*
Sinsheimer, Warren Jack 1927- *WhoAm 92*
Sinsigalli, Gerald E. 1938- *St&PR 93*
Sintes, Jorge Luis 1948- *WhoE 93*
Sinton, Richard J. *Law&B 92*
Sintonen, Leo 1938- *WhoScE 91-4*
Sintz, Edward Francis 1924- *WhoAm 92, WhoSSW 93*
Sintzoff, Michel 1938- *WhoWor 93*
Sinyard, David Blair 1956- *WhoSSW 93*
Sinykin, Gordon *BioIn 17*
Sinykin, Sheri Cooper 1950- *SmATA 72 [port]*
Sinzinger, Helmut F. 1948- *WhoScE 91-4*
Siock, Robert S. 1948- *St&PR 93*
Siodmak, Kurt 1902- *BioIn 17*
Siodmak, Robert 1900-1973 *MiSFD 9N*
Siohan, Robert (-Lucien) 1894-1985 *Baker 92*
Siok, Mary Anne 1966- *WhoAmW 93*
Sion, Edward Michael 1946- *WhoE 93*
Sion, Maurice 1928- *WhoAm 92*
Sione, Sifuiva 1932- *WhoAsAP 91*
Sioui, Richard Henry 1937- *WhoAm 92*
Sioux, Siouxsie c. 1958- *See* Siouxsie and the Banshees *ConMus 8*
Siouxsie and the Banshees *ConMus 8 [port]*
Sipan, Bernita M. *Law&B 92*
Sipe, Gary H. 1936- *St&PR 93*
Sipe, Herbert James, Jr. 1940- *WhoSSW 93*
Sipe, Nicholas Poovey 1946- *WhoSSW 93*
Sipe, Reginald Richard 1942- *St&PR 93*
Sipe, Richard E. 1931- *St&PR 93*
Siperstein, E. Barry 1942- *St&PR 93*
Siperstein, H.B. 1923- *St&PR 93*
Sipes, J. Richard 1946- *St&PR 93*
Sipes, Jeffrey W. 1954- *WhoEmL 93*
Sipes, Paul E. 1944- *St&PR 93*
Sipila, Eero (Aukusti) 1918-1972 *Baker 92*
Sipila, Kai 1951- *WhoScE 91-4*
Sipinen, Seppo Antero 1946- *WhoWor 93*
Sipiora, Leonard Paul 1934- *WhoSSW 93*
Sipley, Nancy E. Young 1929- *WhoAmW 93*
Siporin, Steve 1947- *ConAu 139*
Sipos, Attila 1951- *WhoScE 91-4*
Sipos, Jacqueline Ella 1953- *WhoAmW 93*
Sipp, G. Robert 1950- *WhoE 93*
Sippel, William Leroy 1948- *WhoAm 92*
Sipper, Mark A. *Law&B 92*
Sippl, James G. 1947- *St&PR 93*
Sipple, Constance S. 1962- *WhoAmW 93*
Sippy, David Dean 1953- *WhoWor 93*
Sippy, Larry G. 1943- *St&PR 93*
Sippy, Lon D. 1948- *St&PR 93*
Sippy, W.A. *St&PR 93*

Sipress, Jack Myron 1935- *WhoAm 92*
Sipusich, Susan G. 1948- *WhoAmW 93*
Siqueira, Ethevaldo Mello 1932- *WhoWor 93*
Siqueira, Jose (de Lima) 1907- *Baker 92*
Siqueiros, David Alfaro *DcCPCAm*
Siracusano, Luciano Vincenzo, III 1965- *WhoE 93*
Siragusa, Gregory J. 1928- *St&PR 93*
Siragusa, John R. 1932- *St&PR 93*
Siragusa, Ross D., Jr. 1930- *St&PR 93*
Siragusa, Ross David 1906- *WhoAm 92*
Siranni, Joseph F., Jr. 1945- *St&PR 93*
Sirat, Gabriel Yeshoua 1955- *WhoWor 93*
Siraut, Philippe C. 1961- *WhoWor 93*
Sirch, Bernhard Anton 1943- *WhoWor 93*
Sirchio, Connie Loyce 1942- *St&PR 93*
Sirchio, Cosmo d1992 *NewYTBS 92 [port]*
Sircy, Bob Clay, Jr. 1951- *St&PR 93*
Siregar, Arifin M. 1934- *WhoAsAP 91*
Siren, Heikki 1918- *WhoWor 93*
Siren, Katri Anna-Maija Helena 1920- *WhoWor 93*
Siress, Donald T. 1944- *St&PR 93*
Sirey, Aileen Riotto 1935- *WhoAmW 93*
Sirhal, Robert James 1946- *St&PR 93*
Sirhan, Sirhan 1944- *BioIn 17*
Siri, William Emil 1919- *WhoAm 92*
Sirianni, Fred A. 1926- *St&PR 93*
Sirica, John 1904-1992 *News 93-2*
Sirica, John J. 1904- *WhoAm 92*
Sirica, John J(oseph) 1904-1992 *CurBio 92N*
Sirica, John Joseph 1904-1992 *NewYTBS 92 [port]*
Sirico, John A. *Law&B 92*
Sirico, John P. *Law&B 92*
Sirignano, William Alfonso 1938- *WhoAm 92*
Sirilli, Giorgio 1949- *WhoScE 91-3*
Sirk, Douglas 1900-1987 *MiSFD 9N*
Sirkin, Alan Nelson 1944- *WhoSSW 93*
Sirkin, Sara Rachel 1942- *WhoAmW 93*
Sirkus, Robert 1947- *St&PR 93*
Sirmans, Dan Lamar 1941- *WhoE 93*
Sirmans, J.T. 1943- *St&PR 93*
Sirmon, Gordon C. 1941- *St&PR 93*
Sirna, Anthony Alfred, III 1924- *WhoAm 92*
Sirof, Harriet Toby 1930- *WhoWrEP 92*
Sirois, Allen Louis 1950- *WhoE 93*
Sirois, Ann M. *Law&B 92*
Sirois, Gerard 1934- *WhoAm 92*
Sirois, Herman Arnold 1945- *WhoE 93*
Sirois, L. Frank 1936- *St&PR 93*
Sirois, Raymond 1927- *St&PR 93, WhoAm 92*
Sirola, Bozidar 1889-1956 *Baker 92*
Sironi, Giovanni 1927- *WhoScE 91-3*
Sironi, Mario 1885-1961 *BioIn 17*
Sirota, B.I. *Law&B 92*
Sirota, Mark A. *Law&B 92*
Sirota, Michael B. *ScF&FL 92*
Sirota, Michael L. *Law&B 92*
Sirota, Mike 1946- *ScF&FL 92*
Sirota, Milton Stanley 1928- *St&PR 93*
Sirota, Mitch *WhoSSW 93*
Sirotic, Zvonimir 1921- *WhoScE 91-4*
Sirotkin, Phillip Leonard 1923- *WhoAm 92*
Sirow, Melvin 1924- *St&PR 93*
Sirow, Richard Lawrence 1950- *St&PR 93*
Sirower, Bonnie Fox 1949- *WhoAmW 93, WhoE 93*
Sirowitz, Leonard 1932- *WhoAm 92*
Sirtori, Cesare R. 1943- *WhoScE 91-3*
Sirvis, Barbara Pickard 1946- *WhoAmW 93*
Siry, JoAnne Michaele 1947- *WhoE 93*
Sis, Peter *BioIn 17, ChlBIID [port]*
Sis, Raymond Francis 1931- *WhoAm 92*
Sischy, Ingrid *BioIn 17*
Sischy, Ingrid Barbara 1952- *WhoAm 92*
Sisco, Joseph John 1919- *WhoAm 92*
Siscoe, George Leonard 1937- *WhoAm 92*
Sise, Michael J. *Law&B 92*
Sisel, Myrna M. 1936- *WhoAmW 93*
Sisemore, Claudia 1937- *WhoAmW 93*
Sisioka, Pawa P. 1955- *WhoAsAP 91*
Sisisky, Norman 1927- *CngDr 91, WhoAm 92, WhoSSW 93*
Sisk, Daniel Arthur 1927- *WhoAm 92*
Sisk, Fred Dean 1940- *WhoSSW 93*
Sisk, Laura A. 1954- *St&PR 93*
Sisk, Paul Douglas 1950- *WhoE 93*
Sisk, Philip Laurence 1914- *WhoAm 92*
Sisk, Zenobia Ann 1938- *WhoSSW 93*
Siska, Charles William, Jr. 1948- *St&PR 93*
Siska, Peter Emil 1943- *WhoE 93*
Siska, Richard Stanly 1948- *WhoEmL 93*
Siske, Roger Charles 1944- *WhoAm 92*
Siskel, Gene 1946- *ConTFT 10, WhoAm 92*
Siskin, Edward Joseph 1941- *WhoAm 92*
Siskin, Mitchell H. 1925- *St&PR 93*
Siskin, Susie F. *Law&B 92*
Siskind, Aaron *BioIn 17*
Siskind, Aaron 1903-1991 *AnObit 1991*
Siskind, Authur *Law&B 92*
Siskind, David Arthur *Law&B 92*
Siskind, Donald Henry 1937- *WhoAm 92*
Siskind, Gregory William 1934- *WhoE 93*
Siskind, Marvin S. *Law&B 92*
Sisko, Marie Ferraris *WhoAmW 93*
Sisko, Wendy Lee 1957- *WhoAmW 93*
Sisler, David *Law&B 92*
Sisler, David M. 1931- *St&PR 93*
Sisler, George 1893-1973 *BioIn 17*
Sisler, George Cooper 1923- *WhoAm 92*
Sisler, Harry Hall 1917- *WhoAm 92*
Sisler, William Philip 1947- *WhoAm 92*
Sisley, Becky Lynn 1939- *WhoAmW 93*
Sisley, Emily Lucretia 1930- *WhoAmW 93, WhoE 93*
Sisley, G. William 1944- *WhoAm 92*
Sisley, Nina Mae 1924- *WhoAmW 93*
Sislian, Robert Jan 1938- *St&PR 93*
Sismondo, Peter R. 1955- *St&PR 93*
Sisniega, Leonel *DcCPCAm*
Sisolak, Edward R. 1951- *St&PR 93*
Sison, Fabian S. 1916- *WhoAsAP 91*
Sissel, George Allen *Law&B 92*
Sissel, George Allen 1936- *St&PR 93, WhoAm 92*
Sisselman, Murray 1930- *WhoSSW 93*
Sissener, Einar W. *St&PR 93*
Sissle, Noble 1889-1975 *EncAACR*
Sissle, Noble (Lee) 1889-1975 *Baker 92*
Sissman, Lucille *AmWomPl*
Sissom, Leighton Esten 1934- *WhoAm 92*
Sisson, Breta Cora 1935- *WhoE 93*
Sisson, David H. 1936- *St&PR 93*
Sisson, Everett A. 1920- *St&PR 93*
Sisson, Everett Arnold 1920- *WhoAm 92, WhoWor 93*
Sisson, George Allen, Sr. 1920- *WhoAm 92*
Sisson, Jerry Tripp 1938- *St&PR 93*
Sisson, John Edward 1956- *St&PR 93*
Sisson, Kenneth S. *St&PR 93*
Sisson, Ray L. 1934- *WhoAm 92*
Sisson, Richard Hampton 1932- *St&PR 93*
Sisson, Robert F. 1923- *WhoAm 92*
Sisson, Virginia Baker 1957- *WhoAmW 93*
Sissons, John Gerald Patrick *WhoScE 91-1*
Sistar, James Leon, Jr. 1953- *WhoSSW 93*
Sistek, Walter J. 1940- *St&PR 93*
Sister Carol Anne O'Marie *ConAu 136*
Sister Harmony *BioIn 17*
Sistermans, Anton 1865-1926 *Baker 92*
Sister Sledge *SoulM*
Sisterson, Janet Margot 1940- *WhoE 93*
Sister Souljah *BioIn 17*
Sisto, Donato 1950- *WhoE 93*
Sisto, Elena 1952- *WhoE 93*
Sisto, Fernando 1924- *WhoAm 92*
Sistrunk, Catherine Eileen 1958- *WhoAmW 93*
Sistrunk, Max Nolen 1937- *St&PR 93*
Sistrunk, William Hicks 1937- *WhoAm 92*
Sisulu, Albertina *BioIn 17*
Sisulu, Walter *BioIn 17*
Sisulu, Walter Max Ulyate 1912- *WhoAfr*
Sit, Kingsley Ho-Yin 1949- *WhoAsAP 91*
Sitai, David 1949- *WhoAsAP 91*
Sitar, Andrew A. 1928- *St&PR 93*
Sitar, Thomas *St&PR 93*
Sitarz, Anneliese Lotte 1928- *WhoAmW 93*
Sitarz, Daniel 1948- *WhoWrEP 92*
Sitarz, Paula Gaj 1955- *WhoAmW 93*
Sitasz, Denise Maria 1960- *WhoAmW 93*
Sitek, Zbigniew 1928- *WhoScE 91-4*
Siteman, Alvin J. 1928- *St&PR 93*
Siteman, Alvin Jerome 1928- *WhoAm 92*
Sites, Edward J. *Law&B 92*
Sites, Howard Fred 1938- *St&PR 93*
Sites, Katherine Pauline 1947- *WhoAmW 93*
Siti Zaharah Hj Sulaiman, Datuk Dr. 1949- *WhoAsAP 91*
Sitka, Emil *BioIn 17*
Sitka, Warren *WhoWrEP 92*
Sitkei, Gyorgy 1931- *WhoScE 91-4*
Sitko, Emil Martin 1923-1973 *BiDAMSp 1989*
Sitko, Margaret K. *Law&B 92*
Sitkovetsky, Dmitry 1954- *Baker 92*
Sitkowski, Matthew J. *Law&B 92*
Sitlani, Ranjit 1939- *St&PR 93*
Sitowitz, Hal *MiSFD 9*
Sitrick, David H. *Law&B 92*
Sitrick, James Baker 1935- *WhoAm 92*
Sitrick, Michael S. 1947- *St&PR 93*
Sitrick, Michael Steven 1947- *WhoAm 92*
Sitrin, Sherman Allen *Law&B 92*
Sitsky, Larry 1934- *Baker 92*
Sitt, Hans 1850-1922 *Baker 92*
Sittason, Charles Rex 1944- *St&PR 93*
Sitte, Kurt 1910- *WhoWor 93*
Sitte, Peter 1929- *WhoScE 91-3*
Sittel, Karl 1916- *WhoE 93*
Sittenfeld, Curtis Joseph 1931- *St&PR 93*
Sitter, Deborah Ayer 1946- *WhoSSW 93*
Sitter, John Edward 1944- *WhoAm 92*
Sitter, Kathryn Anne 1965- *WhoE 93*
Sitter, R.M. 1940- *St&PR 93*
Sitterle, Scott Kinnear 1964- *WhoSSW 93*
Sitterly, Charlotte Moore 1898-1990 *BioIn 17*
Sitterly, Connie Sue 1953- *WhoAmW 93*
Sittig, John Joseph 1937- *St&PR 93*
Sitting Bull 1831-1890 *BioIn 17, GayN, HarEnMi*
Sittler, Claude M. 1930- *WhoScE 91-2*
Sittler, Douglas Ealey *Law&B 92*
Sitton, Claude Fox 1925- *WhoAm 92*
Sitton, Larry Bruce 1940- *WhoAm 92*
Sitton, Myron H. 1922- *St&PR 93*
Sitton, Rizamari *Law&B 92*
Sitton, Sarah Clydette 1943- *WhoSSW 93*
Situ, Rong 1935- *WhoWor 93*
Sitver, Robin Susan *WhoE 93*
Sitwell, Edith 1887-1964 *BioIn 17*
Sitwell, Francis Osbert Sacheverell 1892-1969 *BioIn 17*
Sitwell, Osbert 1892-1969 *BioIn 17, ScF&FL 92*
Sitzer, Resa R.H. *Law&B 92*
Sitzes, Steven L. *Law&B 92*
Sitzmann, Christopher Gregory *Law&B 92*
Siu, Kenneth Kwong Chee 1928- *WhoAm 92*
Siudela, Daniel M. 1938- *St&PR 93*
Siu Kwing-Chue, Gordon 1945- *WhoAsAP 91*
Siuru, William Dennis, Jr. 1938- *WhoWrEP 92*
Siv, Sichan *BioIn 17*
Siv, Sichan Aun 1948- *WhoAm 92*
Siva, Albert Jean 1946- *St&PR 93*
Sivack, Denis 1942- *WhoWrEP 92*
Sivadas, Iraja 1950- *WhoWor 93*
Sivaji 1627-1680 *BioIn 17*
Sivaji, Yelamanchili 1947- *WhoAsAP 91*
Sivak, Andrew 1931- *St&PR 93*
Sivalls, Charles Richard 1934- *St&PR 93*
Sivananda Radha, Swami 1911- *BioIn 17*
Sivard, Ruth Leger *BioIn 17*
Sive, David 1922- *WhoAm 92*
Sive, Rebecca Anne 1950- *WhoAm 92*
Siver, Chester A. 1912- *St&PR 93*
Siver, James Anthony *Law&B 92*
Siverd, Bonnie 1949- *WhoWrEP 92*
Siverd, Robert J. *Law&B 92*
Siverd, Robert J. 1948- *St&PR 93*
Siverd, Robert Joseph 1948- *WhoEmL 93*
Siverson, Randolph M. 1940- *ConAu 138*
Siverson, Randolph Martin 1940- *WhoAm 92*
Sivertsen, John B. *Law&B 92*
Sivic, Ciril 1925- *WhoScE 91-4*
Sivin, Nathan 1931- *WhoAm 92*
Sivinski, David Michael 1950- *St&PR 93*
Sivori, (Ernesto) Camillo 1815-1894 *Baker 92*
Sivright, John Avery 1929- *St&PR 93*
Sivsithamparam, Murugesu 1923- *WhoAsAP 91*
Sivulich, Stephen 1936- *WhoE 93*
Siwale, Sichilindi Harold 1940- *WhoUN 92*
Siwecki, Ryszard J. 1939- *WhoScE 91-4*
Siwek, Edward 1933- *WhoScE 91-4*
Siwek, Reuben Mark 1919- *St&PR 93*
Siwinski, Dale J. 1953- *St&PR 93*
Siwinski, Wlodzimierz 1939- *WhoWor 93*
Six, Don E. 1928- *St&PR 93*
Six, Fred N. 1929- *WhoAm 92*
Six, Marvin L. 1948- *St&PR 93*
Six, Robert F. 1907-1986 *EncABHB 8 [port]*
Six, Sean *BioIn 17*
Sixel, Jerome A. 1933- *St&PR 93*
Sixel, Lois Cabalek 1927- *WhoAmW 93*
Sixt, Johann Abraham 1757-1797 *Baker 92*
Sixta, Donald Joseph 1948- *WhoSSW 93*
Sixta, Jozef 1940- *Baker 92*
Sixto, Ramiro Ares 1935- *WhoWor 93*
Siyan, Karanjit Saint Germain Singh 1954- *WhoWor 93*
Sizemore, Barbara Ann 1927- *WhoAmW 93*
Sizemore, Carolyn Lee 1945- *WhoAmW 93*
Sizemore, Dale H. 1922- *St&PR 93*
Sizemore, Deborah Lightfoot 1956- *ConAu 138, WhoSSW 93, WhoWrEP 92*
Sizemore, Douglas Reece 1947- *WhoSSW 93*
Sizemore, Helen Joyce 1935- *WhoAmW 93*
Sizemore, Herman Mason, Jr. 1941- *WhoAm 92*
Sizemore, James Middleton, Jr. 1942- *WhoSSW 93*
Sizemore, N.C., Jr. 1937- *St&PR 93*
Sizemore, Richard Ellsworth 1936- *WhoWor 93*
Sizemore, Robert Carlen 1951- *WhoSSW 93, WhoWor 93*
Sizemore, William Christian 1938- *WhoAm 92*
Sizer, Irwin Whiting 1910- *WhoAm 92*
Sizer, Phillip Spelman 1926- *St&PR 93, WhoAm 92*
Sizer, Thomas R. *Law&B 92*
Sizmann, Andreas Franz Ludwig 1961- *WhoWor 93*
Sizonenko, Pierre-Claude 1932- *WhoScE 91-4, WhoWor 93*
Sjadzali, Haji Munawir 1925- *WhoAsAP 91*
Sjerven, Melvin Stanley 1921- *St&PR 93*
Sjoberg, Alf 1903-1980 *MiSFD 9N*
Sjoberg, Anders 1935- *WhoScE 91-4*
Sjoberg, Berndt O.H. 1931- *WhoScE 91-4*
Sjoberg, Bo 1941- *WhoScE 91-4*
Sjoberg, Britt-Marie K. 1944- *WhoScE 91-4*
Sjoberg, Earl Dwain 1932- *St&PR 93*
Sjoberg, Lennart 1939- *WhoWor 93*
Sjoberg, Per Arvid Stefan 1961- *WhoWor 93*
Sjoberg, Svante Leonard 1873-1935 *Baker 92*
Sjodin, Jan 1934- *WhoScE 91-4*
Sjoegren, Bo Gustaf 1930- *WhoWor 93*
Sjoerdsma, Albert 1924- *WhoAm 92*
Sjogren, Bengt 1949- *St&PR 93*
Sjogren, Clifford Steven 1945- *St&PR 93*
Sjogren, (Johan Gustaf) Emil 1853-1918 *Baker 92*
Sjogren, John C. 1916-1987 *BioIn 17*
Sjogren, Walter R. 1928- *St&PR 93*
Sjoholm, Bertil H. 1947- *WhoScE 91-4*
Sjoholm, Ingvar G.H. 1933- *WhoScE 91-4*
Sjoholm, Jack F., Jr. *Law&B 92*
Sjojstrom, Eero Vilhelm 1924- *WhoScE 91-4*
Sjolander, Alf 1927- *WhoScE 91-4*
Sjolander, Barbara Johnston 1944- *WhoAmW 93*
Sjolinder, Ann Lynch 1938- *WhoAmW 93*
Sjolund, Per-A. 1942- *WhoE 93*
Sjoman, Vilgot 1924- *MiSFD 9*
Sjorgren, Per N. 1936- *WhoUN 92*
Sjostedt, Lars Allan Vilhelm 1942- *WhoWor 93*
Sjostedt, Lars E. 1939- *WhoScE 91-4*
Sjostrand, Fritiof Stig 1912- *WhoAm 92*
Sjostrand, Johan 1936- *WhoScE 91-4*
Sjostrand, Nils G.F. 1925- *WhoScE 91-4*
Sjostrom, Christer 1944- *WhoScE 91-4*
Sjostrom, J. Ake 1943- *WhoScE 91-4*
Sjostrom, Olof Carl 1940- *WhoWor 93*
Sjostrom, Victor 1879-1960 *MiSFD 9N*
Sjovold, Torstein 1946- *WhoScE 91-4*
Sjursen, Constance Frederika 1959- *WhoAmW 93*
Skaar, Sarah Henson 1958- *WhoAmW 93*
Skaare, K. *WhoScE 91-4*
Skaaren, Warren d1990 *BioIn 17*
Skadden, Donald Harvey 1925- *WhoAm 92*
Skadden, Michael *Law&B 92*
Skadow, Ronald R. *Law&B 92*
Skadow, Ronald Robert 1942- *St&PR 93*
Skaf, Robert *ScF&FL 92*
Skaff, Andrew Joseph 1945- *WhoAm 92*
Skaff, Joseph John 1930- *WhoAm 92, WhoSSW 93*
Skafides, Thomas Michael 1952- *WhoSSW 93*
Skafte, Marjorie Doris 1921- *WhoWrEP 92*
Skagen, James H. *St&PR 93*
Skagfield, Hilmar Sigurdsson 1923- *WhoSSW 93*
Skaggs, Arline Dotson 1935- *WhoAmW 93*
Skaggs, Barbara Welch *Law&B 92*
Skaggs, Calvin *MiSFD 9*
Skaggs, Calvin Lee 1937- *WhoE 93*
Skaggs, David E. 1943- *CngDr 91, WhoAm 92*
Skaggs, Gary L. 1944- *St&PR 93*
Skaggs, James B. 1937- *St&PR 93*
Skaggs, James E. 1927- *St&PR 93*
Skaggs, Jimmy M(arion) 1940- *ConAu 39NR*
Skaggs, Johnny R. 1952- *St&PR 93*
Skaggs, Karen Gayle 1956- *WhoSSW 93*
Skaggs, Karla B. 1953- *St&PR 93*
Skaggs, Merrill Maguire 1937- *WhoE 93*
Skaggs, Richard Wayne 1942- *WhoAm 92*
Skaggs, Ricky *WhoAm 92*
Skaggs, Ricky 1954- *Baker 92*
Skaggs, Sanford Merle 1939- *WhoAm 92*
Skaggs, Susan Elizabeth 1960- *WhoSSW 93*
Skaggs, Wayne Gerard 1929- *WhoAm 92*
Skahan, Paul Laurence 1925- *WhoAm 92*
Skahen, Thomas M. 1942- *St&PR 93*
Skahill, Carolyn Marie 1941- *St&PR 93*
Skahill, Thomas B. 1963- *St&PR 93*
Skains, Thomas E. 1956- *St&PR 93*
Skaist, Howard A. *Law&B 92*

Skal, David J. ScF&FL 92
Skala, David James 1953- St&PR 93
Skala, Gary Dennis 1946- WhoEmL 93, WhoWor 93
Skala, Mary Jane 1948- WhoWrEP 92
Skalak, Richard 1923- WhoAm 92
Skaldaspillir, Sigfriour ScF&FL 92
Skalicky, Steven S. 1948- St&PR 93
Skalitzky, David Alfred 1936- St&PR 93
Skalka, Harold Walter 1941- WhoAm 92
Skalka, Stanley 1939- St&PR 93
Skalko, Louise Luchetti 1938- WhoSSW 93
Skalko, Richard Gallant 1936- WhoAm 92
Skalkottas, Nikos 1904-1949 Baker 92
Skalla, Bob BioIn 17
Skaller, Laurence D. 1932- St&PR 93
Skalniak, Joseph William Law&B 92
Skaloud, Ferdinand 1903-1984 IntDcAn
Skalski, Joanne Dorothy 1934- WhoAmW 93
Skamene, Emil 1941- WhoWor 93
Skan, Martin 1934- WhoWor 93
Skanchy, Rex Karren 1930- WhoSSW 93
Skandera-Trombley, Laura Elise 1960- WhoE 93
Skanderbeg c. 1405-1468 OxDcByz
Skands, Michael Henrik Vallo 1961- WhoWor 93
Skansen, Anita 1933- WhoWor 93
Skaperdas, Wesley J. 1953- St&PR 93
Skapik, Catherine Welch 1963- WhoAmW 93
Skar, Rolf WhoScE 91-3
Skarda, Patricia L. 1946- ScF&FL 92
Skarda, Patricia Lyn 1946- WhoAmW 93
Skarda, Richard Joseph 1952- WhoEmL 93
Skarda, Rudolf 1927- WhoScE 91-4
Skare, Robert M. 1930- St&PR 93
Skare, Robert Martin 1930- WhoWor 93
Skarendahl, Ake WhoScE 91-4
Skarga, Piotr 1536-1612 PolBiDi
Skaric, Vinko 1923- WhoScE 91-4
Skarmeta, Antonio 1940- SpAmA
Skarp, Sven-Uno 1934- WhoScE 91-4
Skarsaune, Oskar 1946- ConAu 136
Skarsten, James O. Law&B 92
Skaryna, Frantsysk c. 1490-c. 1535 BioIn 17
Skarzynska, Krystyna Maria 1934- WhoWor 93
Skarzynski, Stanislaw 1899-1942 PolBiDi
Skates, Ronald L. 1943- St&PR 93
Skates, Ronald Louis 1941- WhoAm 92, WhoE 93
Skattebol, Lars 1927- WhoScE 91-4
Skawin, Michael A. Law&B 92
Skeary, Michael J. Law&B 92
Skeat, Walter-William 1866-1953 IntDcAn
Skeates, William Busby 1926- St&PR 93
Skebe, Stanley Andrew 1953- WhoE 93
Skeel, Judy Ann 1957- WhoAmW 93
Skeels, Vernon ScF&FL 92
Skeen, Joe 1927- CngDr 91
Skeen, John K. 1941- St&PR 93
Skeen, John Kenneth 1941- WhoAm 92
Skeen, Joseph Richard 1927- WhoAm 92
Skeen, Richard 1950- St&PR 93
Skeen, Thomas L. 1947- St&PR 93
Skeens, Deborah M. Law&B 92
Skeens, Martha Evelyn 1940- WhoAmW 93
Skeer, Martin Henry WhoE 93
Skees, William Leonard, Jr. 1947- WhoAm 92
Skeete, F. Herbert 1930- WhoAm 92
Skeeter, Tommy Ray 1932- St&PR 93
Skeeters, Paul W. 1905-1983 ScF&FL 92
Skef, Zafer 1948- WhoWor 93
Skefos, Catherine Hetos 1952- WhoAmW 93
Skefos, James J. 1954- St&PR 93
Skehel, John James WhoScE 91-1
Skeie, L.J. 1942- St&PR 93
Skeist, S. Merrill 1918- St&PR 93
Skellchock, Leo H. 1927- St&PR 93
Skelley, Gary Allen 1944- St&PR 93
Skelley, George Calvin 1937- WhoSSW 93
Skelley, Robert D. 1948- St&PR 93
Skelley, William Martin, Jr. 1948- St&PR 93
Skelly, June Avon 1946- WhoAmW 93
Skelly, Kenneth Blair Law&B 92
Skelly, Richard Francis 1937- WhoE 93, WhoWor 93
Skelly, Richard Michael Law&B 92
Skelly, Ronald William 1939- WhoWor 93
Skelly, Thomas Francis 1934- St&PR 93
Skelly, Thomas Michael Law&B 92
Skelly-Gonzalez, Ralph Thomas 1945- WhoE 93
Skelsey, Henry F. St&PR 93
Skelskie, Arthur N. Law&B 92
Skelton, Allyn R., II 1951- St&PR 93
Skelton, Barbara 1918- ConAu 136
Skelton, Byron G. 1905- CngDr 91
Skelton, Byron George 1905- WhoAm 92
Skelton, Dennis Lee 1951- WhoE 93
Skelton, Don Richard 1931- WhoAm 92, WhoIns 93
Skelton, Dorothy Geneva Simmons WhoAmW 93, WhoSSW 93, WhoWor 93
Skelton, Earl Franklin 1940- WhoE 93
Skelton, Geoffrey (David) 1916- ConAu 40NR
Skelton, Gordon William 1949- WhoSSW 93
Skelton, Howard Clifton 1932- WhoSSW 93
Skelton, Ike 1931- CngDr 91
Skelton, Ira Steven 1949- WhoWrEP 92
Skelton, Isaac Newton, IV 1931- WhoAm 92
Skelton, James Anderson, II 1949- WhoE 93
Skelton, James Maurice 1939- WhoIns 93
Skelton, James W., Jr. Law&B 92
Skelton, Janice Kenmore 1918- WhoAmW 93
Skelton, John WhoScE 91-1
Skelton, John 1460?-1529 BioIn 17
Skelton, Melinda Ann 1949- WhoAmW 93
Skelton, Michael D. 1947- St&PR 93
Skelton, Monty Wayne 1941- WhoIns 93
Skelton, Red 1910- QDrFCA 92 [port]
Skelton, Red 1913- WhoAm 92
Skelton, Robert Beattie 1913- WhoAm 92
Skelton, Robert W. Law&B 92
Skelton, Robin 1925- ScF&FL 92, WhoCanL 92
Skelton, Shirley Ann 1943- St&PR 93
Skelton, Steven Patrick 1956- St&PR 93
Skelton, Thomas Allen 1947- St&PR 93
Skemer, Arnold Marius 1946- WhoWrEP 92
Skemer, Don Cornel 1948- WhoE 93
Skemp, Richard R. 1919- BioIn 17
Skemp, William F. 1939- St&PR 93
Skenderian, Donald Erwin 1941- WhoE 93
Skene, Allan Michael WhoScE 91-1
Skene, George Neil 1951- WhoAm 92
Skene, Jeremy F. 1949- St&PR 93
Skepides OxDcByz
Skerfving, Staffan B. 1940- WhoScE 91-4
Skerjanc, Lucijan Marija 1900-1973 Baker 92
Skerl, Dane 1931- Baker 92
Skerl, Jennie ScF&FL 92
Skerratt, Ralph William, Jr. 1918- St&PR 93
Skewes, Richard S. 1935- WhoIns 93
Skewes, Richard Stevenson 1935- St&PR 93
Skewes-Cox, Bennet 1918- WhoWor 93
Skiados, Deborah Ann 1958- WhoE 93
Skibinski, Marie Anne 1947- WhoE 93
Skibniewska, Halina 1921- WhoWor 93
Skibo, Charles Michael 1938- St&PR 93
Skibsted, Arnold 1950- WhoUN 92
Skibsted, Leif Horsfelt 1947- WhoWor 93
Skidd, Thomas Patrick, Jr. 1936- WhoAm 92
Skiddell, Elliot Lewis 1951- WhoSSW 93
Skidmore, Arthur 1922- St&PR 93
Skidmore, David Theodore 1952- WhoE 93
Skidmore, Donald Earl, Jr. 1944- WhoWor 93
Skidmore, E. Stewart 1916- St&PR 93
Skidmore, Howard Franklyn 1917- WhoAm 92
Skidmore, Ian 1929- ScF&FL 92
Skidmore, James A., Jr. 1932- St&PR 93
Skidmore, James Albert, Jr. 1932- WhoAm 92
Skidmore, Joel A. Law&B 92
Skidmore, Joel A. 1929- St&PR 93
Skidmore, Kenneth Franklin 1929- WhoE 93
Skidmore, Lemuel, III 1947- WhoE 93
Skidmore, Leon B. 1940- St&PR 93
Skidmore, Max Joseph 1933- WhoAm 92
Skidmore, Paul Harold 1918- WhoWor 93
Skidmore, Philip M. 1940- St&PR 93
Skidmore, Rex Austin 1914- WhoAm 92
Skidmore, Rex O. 1947- WhoIns 93
Skie, C.M. 1938- St&PR 93
Skierkowski, Jerzy 1928- WhoScE 91-4
Skierowski, J. WhoScE 91-4
Skiff, Brian A. BioIn 17
Skiff, Peter Duane 1938- WhoE 93
Skiffington, Guy 1940- St&PR 93
Skiffington-Simpson, Karen Anna 1958- WhoWor 93
Skifstad, Barbara Marie 1939- WhoAmW 93
Skigen, Patricia Sue 1942- WhoAmW 93
Skiles, James Jean 1928- WhoAm 92
Skiles, Michael L. 1946- St&PR 93
Skillern, Frank Lloyd, Jr. 1936- St&PR 93
Skillin, Edward Simeon 1904- WhoAm 92
Skilling, David Van Diest 1933- St&PR 93, WhoAm 92
Skilling, John Bower 1921- WhoAm 92
Skilling, Raymond I. Law&B 92
Skilling, Raymond I. 1939- WhoIns 93
Skillman, Becky Sue 1950- WhoAmW 93
Skillman, Ernest Edward, Jr. 1937- WhoWor 93
Skillman, John Harold 1927- WhoE 93, WhoWor 93
Skillman, Thomas Grant 1925- WhoAm 92
Skillman, William Alfred 1928- WhoAm 92
Skilton, Charles Sanford 1868-1941 Baker 92
Skimin, Robert 1929-1990 ScF&FL 92
Skimin, Robert Elwayne 1929- WhoWrEP 92
Skimina, Timothy Anthony 1960- WhoWor 93
Skinkle, Dorothy E. 1906?-1983? ScF&FL 92
Skinnemoen, Helge 1934- WhoScE 91-4
Skinner, Ada Maria 1878- AmWomPl
Skinner, Ainslie 1939- ScF&FL 92
Skinner, Alastair 1936- WhoAm 92
Skinner, Andrew Charles 1951- WhoEmL 93
Skinner, Anita Marier 1933- WhoAmW 93
Skinner, B.F. 1904-1990 BioIn 17
Skinner, B. Franklin 1931- WhoAm 92
Skinner, Burrhus Frederic 1904-1990 BioIn 17
Skinner, C. 1920- St&PR 93
Skinner, Charles Gordon 1923- WhoAm 92
Skinner, Charles Scofield 1940- WhoAm 92, WhoWor 93
Skinner, Constance Lindsay 1877-1939 AmWomPl
Skinner, Constance Lindsay 1882-1939 BioIn 17
Skinner, Cornelia Bennett 1928- WhoAmW 93
Skinner, Cornelia Otis 1901-1979 AmWomPl
Skinner, David Bernt 1935- WhoAm 92
Skinner, David H. 1927- St&PR 93
Skinner, David Lynn 1947- WhoSSW 93
Skinner, David N. 1947- St&PR 93
Skinner, Dennis BioIn 17
Skinner, Donald D. Law&B 92
Skinner, Dorothy M. 1930- WhoAm 92
Skinner, Edward Folland 1909- WhoSSW 93
Skinner, Eleanor Louise 1872- AmWomPl
Skinner, Ernest M(artin) 1866-1960 Baker 92
Skinner, Florence W. AmWomPl
Skinner, George 1832-1856 BioIn 17
Skinner, George Anthony WhoScE 91-1
Skinner, George William 1925- WhoAm 92
Skinner, Grant BioIn 17
Skinner, Harry Bryant 1943- WhoAm 92
Skinner, Helen Catherine Wild 1931- WhoAmW 93
Skinner, Irene AmWomPl
Skinner, John R. 1947- St&PR 93
Skinner, Knute Rumsey 1929- WhoAm 92, WhoWrEP 92
Skinner, L.M. WhoScE 91-1
Skinner, L. Michael Law&B 92
Skinner, Linda Walkup 1947- WhoAmW 93, WhoSSW 93
Skinner, Mary Evelyn 1955- WhoAmW 93
Skinner, Mary Just 1946- WhoAmW 93
Skinner, Mary Victoria 1954- WhoAmW 93
Skinner, Maud AmWomPl
Skinner, Maurice Edward, IV 1962- WhoE 93
Skinner, Michael 1953- ScF&FL 92
Skinner, Michael F. Law&B 92
Skinner, Odie Gary 1899- St&PR 93
Skinner, Orin Ensign 1892- WhoE 93
Skinner, Owen H., Jr. St&PR 93
Skinner, Patricia Morag 1932- WhoAmW 93
Skinner, Paul Elliot 1943- WhoE 93
Skinner, Peter Graeme Law&B 92
Skinner, Peter Graeme 1944- St&PR 93, WhoAm 92
Skinner, Robert Earle 1948- WhoSSW 93
Skinner, Robert G. 1946- WhoScE 91-2
Skinner, Sam 1938- News 92 [port], -92-3 [port]
Skinner, Samuel Ballou, III 1936- WhoSSW 93
Skinner, Samuel K. BioIn 17
Skinner, Samuel Knox 1938- CngDr 91, WhoAm 92, WhoE 93, WhoWor 93
Skinner, Stanley Thayer 1937- St&PR 93, WhoAm 92
Skinner, Thomas 1934- WhoAm 92
Skinner, Walter I. Law&B 92
Skinner, Wickham 1924- WhoAm 92
Skinner, William E. 1947- St&PR 93
Skinner, William Lea 1934- St&PR 93
Skinner-Klee, Jorge 1923- WhoWor 93
Skinner-Morris, Sarah Jane 1955- WhoAmW 93
Skipp, John 1957- ScF&FL 92
Skipper, Barbara Louise 1946- WhoAmW 93
Skipper, Donald Bruce 1945- WhoWrEP 92
Skipper, Harold Dallas, Jr. 1947- WhoWor 93
Skipper, James Everett 1920- WhoAm 92
Skipper, Nathan Richard, Jr. 1934- WhoAm 92
Skippings, Oswald 1953- DcCPCAm
Skippon, Philip c. 1600-1660 HarEnMi
Skiptunis, Raymond J. 1943- St&PR 93
Skira, Albert 1904-1973 BioIn 17
Skirbekk, Gunnar Bjorn 1937- WhoWor 93
Skirmunt, Konstanty 1866-1949 PolBiDi
Skirnick, Robert Andrew 1938- WhoE 93, WhoWor 93
Skitka, Linda Jean 1961- WhoAmW 93
Skivington, Dale E. Law&B 92
Skjaerstad, Ragnar 1944- WhoWor 93
Skjelbred, Perry Werner 1947- St&PR 93
Skjoldebrand, Christina 1945- WhoScE 91-4
Skjorten, Einar 1933- WhoWor 93
Skladal, Elizabeth Lee 1937- WhoAmW 93
Skladany, Joseph P. 1911-1972 BiDAMSp 1989
Skladony, William P. Law&B 92
Sklaire, Richard Michael 1948- WhoSSW 93
Sklamberg, Marvin S. Law&B 92
Sklansky, Jack 1928- WhoAm 92
Sklar, Alexander 1915- WhoWor 93
Sklar, Benjamin B. Law&B 92
Sklar, Corinne L. Law&B 92
Sklar, Doris Roslyn 1936- WhoAmW 93
Sklar, Dusty 1928- WhoWrEP 92
Sklar, Holly L 1955- WhoAmW 93
Sklar, Kathryn Kish 1939- ConAu 40NR, WhoAmW 93
Sklar, Lawrence E. Law&B 92
Sklar, Louis Selman 1939- St&PR 93
Sklar, Marvin Allen 1937- St&PR 93
Sklar, Morty E. 1935- WhoWrEP 92
Sklar, Richard 1930- ScF&FL 92
Sklar, Richard J. 1929- WhoAm 92
Sklar, Richard Lawrence 1930- WhoAm 92
Sklar, Rick d1992 NewYTBS 92 [port]
Sklar, Robert Anthony 1936- WhoWrEP 92
Sklar, Scott 1950- WhoE 93
Sklar, Steven J. 1956- St&PR 93
Sklare, Marshall d1992 NewYTBS 92
Sklare, Marshall 1921- WhoWrEP 92
Sklare, Marshall 1921-1992 BioIn 17, ConAu 137
Sklarek, Norma 1928- BioIn 17
Sklarek, Norma Merrick 1928- WhoAm 92
Sklaren, Cary Stewart 1943- WhoAm 92
Sklarew, Robert Jay 1941- WhoWor 93
Sklarin, Burton S. 1932- WhoAm 92
Sklarski, Bonnie 1943- BioIn 17
Sklavos, George 1888-1976 Baker 92
Sklenar, Caroline Sue 1956- WhoAmW 93
Sklenar, Herbert Anthony 1931- St&PR 93, WhoAm 92, WhoSSW 93
Skleraina dc. 1045 OxDcByz
Skleros OxDcByz
Skloot, Floyd BioIn 17
Sklover, Theodora K. d1992 BioIn 17, NewYTBS 92
Sklovsky, Robert Joel 1952- WhoEmL 93
Sklut, Josef 1928- St&PR 93
Sklute, Adam WhoAm 92
Skluzacek, Gayle Marie 1953- WhoAmW 93, WhoEmL 93
Skoblikova, Lydia 1939- BioIn 17
Skoblow, David V. Law&B 92
Skochlas, John 1949- WhoWrEP 92
Skoczen, John J. 1942- St&PR 93
Skoczowski, Stanislaw 1936- WhoScE 91-4
Skoczylas, Edward Joseph 1938- St&PR 93
Skoczylas, Wladyslaw 1883-1934 PolBiDi
Skoda, Dan 1946- St&PR 93
Skoda, Jan 1925- WhoScE 91-4
Skodras, Vicki Herring 1958- WhoAmW 93
Skofronick, Bruce David 1937- St&PR 93
Skog, Laurence Edgar 1943- WhoAm 92
Skog, Ole-Jorgen WhoScE 91-4
Skogan, John Kristen 1942- WhoWor 93
Skogen, Haven Sherman 1927- WhoWor 93
Skogerboe, Charles M. 1935- St&PR 93

Skogerboe, Rodney Kenneth 1931- WhoAm 92
Skoglund, Sandy 1946- BioIn 17
Skohlnik, Marten 1951- WhoE 93
Skok, Martin John 1928- St&PR 93
Skok, Wallace Thomas Law&B 92
Skok, Walter WhoScE 91-1
Skok, William Henry 1938- WhoWor 93
Skokan, Ralph J. 1943- St&PR 93
Skoklefald, Sverre Olav Brochmann 1931- WhoScE 91-4
Skol, Michael M. 1942- WhoAm 92, WhoWor 93
Skolan-Logue, Amanda Law&B 92
Skold, Kurt 1938- WhoScE 91-4
Skold, Ola E. 1933- WhoScE 91-4
Skold, (Karl) Yngve 1899- Baker 92
Skoldberg, Svante 1931- WhoWor 93
Skoler, Celia Rebecca 1931- WhoE 93
Skoler, Louis 1920- WhoAm 92
Skoler, Steven Frederick 1959- St&PR 93
Skolimowski, Jerzy 1938- ConTFT 10, DrEEuF, MiSFD 9, WhoWor 93
Skollar, Robert Alan 1949- WhoAm 92
Skoller, Richard M. Law&B 92
Skoller, Ronald A. Law&B 92
Skolnekovich, Dorothy Ann 1941- WhoE 93
Skolnick, Barry G. Law&B 92
Skolnick, Malcolm Harris 1935- WhoAm 92, WhoSSW 93
Skolnick, Nathan d1992 BioIn 17, NewYTBS 92
Skolnick, Phil 1947- WhoE 93
Skolnick, Steven E. Law&B 92
Skolnik, Barnet David 1941- WhoAm 92
Skolnik, Herman 1914- WhoE 93
Skolnik, Jinny 1934- WhoE 93
Skolnik, Merrill I. 1927- WhoAm 92
Skolnik, Richard Alan 1951- WhoE 93
Skolnik, Richard S. 1945- WhoIns 93
Skolnik, Sandra Rita 1946- WhoAmW 93
Skolnikoff, Eugene B. 1928- WhoAm 92, WhoE 93
Skolovsky, Zadel WhoAm 92, WhoWor 93
Skolsky, Syd 1917- ScF&FL 92
Skolyszewski, Jan 1935- WhoScE 91-4
Skomal, Edward Nelson 1926- WhoAm 92
Skoney, Sophie Essa 1929- WhoWor 93
Skonieczny, Juliusz Karol 1932- WhoScE 91-4
Skonord, Douglas H. 1943- St&PR 93
Skoog, Donald Paul 1931- WhoAm 92
Skoog, Folke Karl 1908- WhoAm 92
Skoog, Gerald Duane 1936- WhoAm 92
Skoog, Norma Law&B 92
Skoog, Ralph Edward 1929- WhoAm 92
Skoog, William Arthur 1925- WhoAm 92, WhoWor 93
Skoog de Lamas, Lisa Marie 1957- WhoE 93
Skopec, Adam Leslaw 1931- WhoWor 93
Skopic, Beverly Jane 1959- WhoE 93
Skopil, Otto Richard, Jr. 1919- WhoAm 92
Skopp, Douglas Bret 1960- WhoSSW 93
Skora, Susan Sundman 1947- WhoAmW 93
Skora, Wayne Philip 1944- WhoSSW 93
Skord, Jennifer Lynne Law&B 92
Skordal, Lynn M. Law&B 92
Skordal, Lynn M. 1949- St&PR 93
Skordev, Gencho 1943- WhoScE 91-4
Skorepa, Jiri 1921- WhoScE 91-4
Skoric, Arso 1922- WhoScE 91-4
Skorich, Arlene Rita Mae 1936- WhoAmW 93
Skorich, James Milan Law&B 92
Skorin, Yurii Law&B 92
Skorina, Franciscus c. 1490-c. 1535 BioIn 17
Skorka, Darlene McDonald 1942- WhoAmW 93
Skorna, Hans Juergen 1926- WhoWor 93
Skornia, Mark Douglas 1957- St&PR 93
Skorobogatov, German Alexandrovitch 1937- WhoWor 93
Skorping, Arne 1948- WhoScE 91-4
Skorpinski, Casimir J. 1944- St&PR 93
Skorton, David Jan 1949- WhoAm 92
Skorzeny, Otto 1908-1975 HarEnMi
Skotak, Bob MiSFD 9
Skotak, Robert ScF&FL 92
Skotak, Robert F. WhoAm 92
Skotheim, Robert Allen 1933- WhoAm 92
Skou, Bent 1931- WhoE 93
Skou, Jens Christian 1918- WhoWor 93
Skouby, Alan Douglas 1937- St&PR 93
Skouby, Knud Erik 1946- WhoWor 93
Skoufalos, Jim 1934- St&PR 93
Skouge, Richard J. 1941- St&PR 93
Skoulikidis, Theodore 1925- WhoScE 91-3
Skoulios, Antoine 1934- WhoScE 91-2
Skoultchi, Martin Milton 1933- WhoE 93
Skoupy, Jiri 1932- WhoUN 92
Skouras, Spyros Solon 1923- WhoAm 92
Skouse, Douglas 1953- WhoWor 93
Skoutariotes, Theodore c. 1230- OxDcByz
Skoutelas, John Serafin Law&B 92
Skov, Arlie Mason 1928- WhoAm 92, WhoSSW 93
Skov, K. Sandahl WhoScE 91-2
Skov, Leif 1946- WhoWor 93
Skov, Lisbeth Andersen 1949- WhoWor 93
Skov, Mildred Jane 1932- WhoAmW 93
Skovborg, E. Bulow WhoScE 91-2
Skove, Malcolm John 1931- WhoSSW 93
Skove, Thomas M. Law&B 92
Skove, Thomas Malcolm 1925- WhoAm 92
Skovgaard, Niels Peder 1924- WhoScE 91-2
Skovgaard Nielsen, Knud 1947- WhoScE 91-2, WhoWor 93
Skovron, David A. 1939- St&PR 93
Skower, Walter J. d1992 BioIn 17
Skown, Bernard 1940- St&PR 93
Skowron, Donald J. 1941- St&PR 93
Skowron, Tadeusz Adam 1950- WhoWor 93
Skowron, William Joseph 1930- BiDAMSp 1989
Skowronek, Maurice 1930- WhoWor 93
Skowronek, Miroslaw Stanislaw 1938- WhoScE 91-4
Skowronek, Wojciech 1940- WhoScE 91-4
Skowronski, Boleslaw 1933- WhoScE 91-4
Skowronski, Dan Ray Law&B 92
Skowronski, Jan Marian 1945- WhoScE 91-4
Skowronski, Thomas E. Law&B 92
Skowronski, Thomas Edward 1942- St&PR 93
Skowronski, Vincent Paul 1944- WhoAm 92
Skoyles, John 1949- WhoWrEP 92
Skrabacz, Mark Andrew 1949- WhoSSW 93
Skrabanek, Donald W. 1951- WhoWrEP 92
Skrabec, David Joseph Law&B 92
Skrable, Russell James 1946- St&PR 93
Skrajewski, Dennis John 1954- WhoE 93
Skramstad, Harold Kenneth 1941- WhoAm 92
Skramstad, Harold Kenneth, Jr. 1941- St&PR 93
Skramstad, Robert Allen 1937- WhoSSW 93
Skramstad, Sherry 1942- WhoWrEP 92
Skramstad, Susan 1942- ConAu 139
Skrapec, Candice Ann 1952- WhoE 93
Skratek, Sylvia Paulette 1950- WhoAmW 93
Skrebneski, Victor 1929- WhoAm 92
Skrepenak, Greg BioIn 17
Skriabin, Alexander (Nikolaievich) Baker 92
Skriganov, Maxim Michailovich 1948- WhoWor 93
Skrimshire, Anthony J.H. WhoScE 91-1
Skrine, Bruce Edward Law&B 92
Skriner, Edward St&PR 93
Skriniar, Jan 1923- WhoScE 91-4
Skrinjaric, Ilija WhoScE 91-4
Skritek, Paul 1952- WhoWor 93
Skrivanek, Britt Edward 1948- St&PR 93
Skroch, Walter Arthur 1937- WhoSSW 93
Skromme, Lawrence H. 1913- WhoAm 92
Skroumbelos, Nicholas George 1952- WhoE 93, WhoEmL 93
Skroup, Dominik Josef 1766-1830 See Skroup, Frantisek Jan 1801-1862 Baker 92
Skroup, Frantisek 1801-1862 OxDcOp
Skroup, Frantisek Jan 1801-1862 Baker 92
Skroup, Jan Nepomuk 1811-1892 Baker 92
Skrowaczewski, Stanislaw 1923- Baker 92, WhoAm 92, WhoWor 93
Skrucany, Rudolf 1925- WhoScE 91-4
Skrypak, John K. Law&B 92
Skrypnik, Wolodymyr Ivanovich 1948- WhoWor 93
Skrypnyk, Mstyslav Stepan 1898- WhoAm 92, WhoWor 93
Skrzymowski, Eugeniusz 1925- WhoScE 91-4
Skrzynecki, Lech 1937- WhoScE 91-4
Skrzypczak, Casimir S. 1941- St&PR 93
Skrzypczak, Ewa 1929- WhoScE 91-4
Skrzypczak, Jozef Aleksander 1938- WhoWor 93
Skuba, William C. 1955- St&PR 93
Skubachevskii, Alexander 1953- WhoWor 93
Skubak, Bernard 1951- St&PR 93
Skubala, Weislaw 1932- WhoScE 91-4
Skubas, Charles E. 1944- St&PR 93
Skubco, Yuri BioIn 17
Skubis, Jerzy 1950- WhoScE 91-4
Skubiszewski, Krzysztof 1926- WhoWor 93
Skucinska, Barbara Maria 1930- WhoScE 91-4
Skudrzyk, Eugen J. 1913-1990 BioIn 17
Skuhersky, Frantisek Zdenek (Xavier Alois) 1830-1892 Baker 92
Skula, Emil Richard Law&B 92
Skulachev, Vladimir Petrovich 1935- WhoWor 93
Skulberg, Anton 1921- WhoScE 91-4
Skulina, Thomas Raymond 1933- WhoAm 92
Skully, Michael Thomas WhoWor 93
Skully, Richard Patrick 1921- WhoAm 92
Skulsky, Harold Lawrence 1935- WhoE 93
Skult, Nils Henrik 1923- WhoScE 91-4
Skup, Daniel 1951- WhoAm 92
Skup, David Alan 1952- WhoSSW 93
Skupinski, Bogdan Kazimierz 1942- WhoAm 92
Skurdenis, Juliann Veronica 1942- WhoAmW 93, WhoE 93
Skurich, Monica Mary 1942- WhoAmW 93
Skuris, Stephen John Law&B 92
Skurka, Kathleen 1947- WhoSSW 93
Skurla, Laurus 1928- WhoAm 92
Skurnick, David 1942- WhoIns 93
Skurnick, Sam 1915- WhoSSW 93
Skurray, Geoffrey Richard 1945- WhoWor 93
Skurski, Michael J. 1949- WhoWor 93
Skurzynski, Gloria 1930- DcAmChF 1960, DcAmChF 1985
Skuse, George W. 1943- St&PR 93
Skuse, Robert William 1952- St&PR 93
Skutch, Alexander Frank 1904- BioIn 17
Skutch, William G. 1924- St&PR 93
Skutt, Anne-Marguerite 1924- WhoWrEP 92
Skutt, Thomas J. 1930- WhoIns 93
Skutt, Thomas James 1930- St&PR 93, WhoAm 92
Skutt, V.J. WhoIns 93
Skutt, V.J. 1902- St&PR 93
Skutt, Vestor Joseph 1902- WhoAm 92
Skvorecky, Josef BioIn 17, WhoCanL 92
Skvorecky, Josef Vaclav 1924- WhoAm 92
Skvortsov, Valentin Anatoljevich 1935- WhoWor 93
Skwarski, Tadeusz Jan 1922- WhoScE 91-4
Skwaryk, Robert Francis 1948- WhoE 93
Skwiertz, Albert A., Jr. Law&B 92
Skwiertz, Albert A., Jr. 1945- St&PR 93
Sky, Kathleen 1943- ScF&FL 92
Sky, Mickey WhoWrEP 92
Skylar, Grigory Mikchailovich 1957- WhoWor 93
Skyler, Marc Norman 1945- WhoE 93
Skylitzes, George fl. 12th cent.- OxDcByz
Skylitzes, John fl. 11th cent.- OxDcByz
Skylstad, William S. 1934- WhoAm 92
Skylv, Grethe Krogh 1938- WhoWor 93
Skypeck, Walter T. 1923- St&PR 93
Skywatcher, Justin Bertrand Galen 1942- WhoSSW 93
Slaatte, Howard Alexander 1919- WhoAm 92
Slabaugh, William F. Law&B 92
Slabbers, P.J. 1940- WhoScE 91-3
Slabe, James F. 1940- St&PR 93, WhoE 93
Slabon, Roland Michael 1941- WhoE 93
Slaby, Alexander 1952- WhoUN 92
Slaby, Andrew Edmund 1942- WhoE 93
Slaby, Lillian Frances 1931- WhoSSW 93
Slachta, Michael, Jr. 1944- WhoE 93
Slack, D. Stephen 1949- St&PR 93
Slack, Douglas M. 1947- St&PR 93
Slack, Elaine M. BioIn 17
Slack, Fred Philip 1946- St&PR 93
Slack, Frederick Ford 1917- WhoE 93
Slack, George H. 1926- St&PR 93
Slack, John L. 1938- St&PR 93
Slack, John M. 1948- St&PR 93
Slack, Karen Kershner 1951- WhoSSW 93
Slack, Lewis 1924- WhoAm 92
Slack, Marguerite Bickel 1908- WhoSSW 93
Slack, Nigel Douglas Cedric WhoScE 91-1
Slack, Paul D. 1932- St&PR 93
Slack, Stephen T. 1941- WhoAm 92
Slack, Steve D. 1946- St&PR 93
Slaczka, Andrzej 1931- WhoScE 91-4
Slade, Bernard 1930- WhoAm 92
Slade, Bernard Newton 1923- WhoE 93
Slade, Bonnie Batter 1951- WhoAmW 93
Slade, Corinne Sue 1945- WhoE 93
Slade, Derek ScF&FL 92
Slade, Diann Stukes 1956- WhoAmW 93
Slade, Dorinda Moody Salmon Goheen 1808-1895 BioIn 17
Slade, Edward Colin 1935- WhoSSW 93
Slade, Elizabeth Ohman Law&B 92
Slade, Gerald Jack 1919- WhoAm 92
Slade, Hutton Davison 1912- WhoAm 92
Slade, Jack 1829-1864 BioIn 17
Slade, James L. St&PR 93
Slade, Jarvis J. 1926- St&PR 93
Slade, Joseph Alfred 1829-1864 BioIn 17
Slade, Joseph W. 1941- ScF&FL 92
Slade, Llewellyn Eugene 1911- WhoAm 92
Slade, Mark E. Law&B 92
Slade, Mark J. 1959- St&PR 93
Slade, Michael ScF&FL 92, St&PR 93
Slade, Norma Marie Headrick 1922- WhoAmW 93
Slade, Paul Graham 1941- WhoAm 92
Slade, Peter 1912- BioIn 17
Slade, Peter David WhoScE 91-1
Slade, Robert Charles T. 1953- WhoWor 93
Slade, Roy 1933- WhoAm 92
Slade, Thomas Bog, III 1931- WhoSSW 93
Slade, Winton Lee 1927- WhoSSW 93
Sladek, John 1937- ScF&FL 92
Sladek, John R., Jr. 1943- WhoAm 92
Sladek, Lyle Virgil 1923- WhoAm 92
Sladek, Martha J. 1946- WhoAmW 93
Sladek, Ronald John 1926- WhoAm 92
Sladkevicius, Vincentas Cardinal 1920- WhoWor 93
Sladkus, Harvey Ira 1929- WhoE 93
Sladkus, John K. 1923- St&PR 93
Sladoljev, Zelimir 1932- WhoScE 91-4
Sladon, Donna J. 1957- St&PR 93
Sladon, Ronald B. 1929- St&PR 93
Sladzinski, Marianne 1942- WhoE 93
Slagel, Robert Clayton 1937- WhoAm 92
Slagel, Steven L. Law&B 92
Slaggie, Stephen M. 1939- St&PR 93
Slagle, Alton H. d1992 NewYTBS 92
Slagle, Jacob Winebrenner, Jr. 1945- WhoE 93
Slagle, James Robert 1934- WhoAm 92
Slagle, Judith Bailey 1949- WhoSSW 93
Slagle, Kerry D. 1948- WhoAm 92
Slagle, Larry B. 1934- WhoE 93
Slagle, Robert F. 1940- St&PR 93
Slagle, Robert Fred 1940- WhoAm 92
Slagle, Steve Bryce 1952- WhoE 93
Slagle, William F. 1929- WhoAm 92, WhoSSW 93
Slagowitz, Martin Barry 1941- St&PR 93
Slagsvold, Bjorn Johan 1936- WhoWor 93
Slagsvold, Tore 1947- WhoScE 91-4
Slagter, Wicher Jan 1923- WhoWor 93
Slahor, Ludomir Ivan 1947- WhoWor 93
Slaiby, Theodore George 1929- WhoAm 92
Slaight, Gary John 1951- St&PR 93
Slain, George Cedric 1950- WhoAm 92
Slain, John Joseph 1927- WhoAm 92
Slakey, Linda Louise 1939- WhoAm 92
Slakis, Albert G. 1929- WhoIns 93
Slama WhoScE 91-2
Slama, Abdelmajid 1943- WhoUN 92
Slama, Murray Alfred 1925- WhoAm 92
Slane, Charles J. Law&B 92
Slane, Charles J. 1947- St&PR 93
Slane, Charles Joseph 1947- WhoAm 92
Slane, Henry Pindell 1920- St&PR 93, WhoAm 92
Slaney, Mary Decker BioIn 17
Slanger, Frances d1944 BioIn 17
Slania, Czeslaw 1921- PolBiDi
Slanina, Ludovit 1928- WhoScE 91-4
Slansky, Jerry William 1947- WhoAm 92
Slansky, Jill Ann 1945- WhoAmW 93
Slansky, Rudolf 1901-1952 ColdWar 2 [port]
Slap, Joseph William 1927- WhoE 93
Slape, Lori Dale 1964- St&PR 93
Slapins, Andris d1991 BioIn 17
Slapnicar, Petar 1932- WhoScE 91-4
Slappey, Mary Mc Gowan 1914- WhoWrEP 92
Slappey, Sterling Greene 1917- WhoAm 92
Slash BioIn 17
Slaski, Cathleen Ann 1956- WhoWor 93
Slatcher, Edward G. 1932- St&PR 93
Slate, Douglas St&PR 93
Slate, Floyd Owen 1920- WhoAm 92, WhoE 93
Slate, Joe Hutson 1930- WhoAm 92
Slate, John Butler 1953- WhoAm 92
Slate, John R. 1955- WhoSSW 93
Slate, Lane MiSFD 9
Slate, Robert Wesley 1938- WhoSSW 93
Slaten, Charles Kent 1961- WhoSSW 93
Slaten, Jeff ScF&FL 92
Slaten, Paul Edward 1933- St&PR 93
Slaten, Troy BioIn 17
Slater, Alan T. 1945- WhoE 93
Slater, Alfred Terry, Jr. 1944- WhoUN 92
Slater, Amy E. Law&B 92
Slater, Anthony Ian WhoScE 91-1
Slater, Billy Ray 1946- St&PR 93
Slater, C. Stewart 1957- WhoE 93
Slater, Carl Howard 1941- WhoSSW 93
Slater, Christian BioIn 17
Slater, D. WhoScE 91-1
Slater, David H. 1940- St&PR 93
Slater, Don 1940- WhoAm 92
Slater, Doris Ernestine Wilke WhoWor 93

Slater, Edward Nathan 1941- *St&PR 93*
Slater, Gary 1947- *BioIn 17*
Slater, George R. 1924- *St&PR 93*
Slater, George Richard 1924- *WhoAm 92*
Slater, Ian 1941- *ScF&FL 92, WhoCanL 92*
Slater, James Alexander 1920- *WhoE 93*
Slater, James Howard *WhoScE 91-1*
Slater, James Munro 1929- *WhoAm 92*
Slater, Jerome William, Jr. 1936- *St&PR 93*
Slater, Jill Sherry 1943- *WhoAmW 93*
Slater, Jim 1929- *ScF&FL 92*
Slater, John Blackwell 1943- *WhoAm 92*
Slater, John Edmund 1922- *St&PR 93, WhoAm 92*
Slater, John Greenleaf 1935- *WhoAm 92*
Slater, Joseph Elliott 1922- *WhoAm 92*
Slater, Kelly *BioIn 17*
Slater, Ken 1917- *ScF&FL 92*
Slater, Kristie 1957- *WhoAmW 93*
Slater, Mandel E. *Law&B 92*
Slater, Manning 1917- *WhoAm 92*
Slater, Marilee Hebert 1949- *WhoSSW 93*
Slater, Martin Johns 1892-1990 *BioIn 17*
Slater, Michael R. 1940- *WhoIns 93*
Slater, Oliver Eugene 1906- *WhoAm 92*
Slater, Peter James Bramwell *WhoScE 91-1*
Slater, Philip E(lliot) 1927- *ConAu 40NR*
Slater, Ralph Evan 1948- *WhoE 93*
Slater, Richard James 1946- *St&PR 93, WhoAm 92*
Slater, Robert James 1923- *WhoAm 92*
Slater, Robert R. 1934- *St&PR 93*
Slater, Samuel 1768-1835 *BioIn 17*
Slater, Schuyler George 1923- *WhoE 93*
Slater, Terry 1937-1991 *BioIn 17*
Slater, Timothy T. *Law&B 92*
Slater, Trevor Frank *WhoScE 91-1*
Slater, William S. 1946- *St&PR 93*
Slatin, Alfred 1929- *St&PR 93*
Slatis, Par E.V. 1932- *WhoScE 91-4*
Slatkin, Burton 1920- *St&PR 93*
Slatkin, Daniel Nathan 1934- *WhoE 93*
Slatkin, Felix 1915-1963 *Baker 92*
Slatkin, Leonard *BioIn 17*
Slatkin, Leonard (Edward) 1944- *Baker 92, WhoAm 92*
Slatkin, Marcia 1943- *WhoWrEP 92*
Slatkin, Murray 1905- *St&PR 93, WhoAm 92*
Slatoff, Walter J. 1922-1991 *BioIn 17*
Slatoff, Walter Jacob 1922- *WhoWrEP 92*
Slaton, Gwendolyn Childs 1945- *WhoE 93*
Slaton, John William 1924- *St&PR 93*
Slatt, Roger Malcolm 1941- *WhoSSW 93*
Slatter, Jane *Law&B 92*
Slatter, Jane L. *Law&B 92*
Slatter, Sarah Piteo 1952- *St&PR 93*
Slattern, Lillian *AmWomPl*
Slattery, Charles Wilbur 1937- *WhoAm 92*
Slattery, Eugene William *WhoIns 93*
Slattery, Frank P., Jr. 1937- *St&PR 93*
Slattery, James A. 1942- *St&PR 93*
Slattery, James Arthur 1930- *WhoE 93*
Slattery, James Arthur 1942- *WhoAm 92*
Slattery, James Charles 1948- *WhoAm 92*
Slattery, James Joseph 1922- *WhoAm 92*
Slattery, James L. *Law&B 92*
Slattery, James P. *WhoIns 93*
Slattery, Jim 1948- *CngDr 91*
Slattery, Matthew Thomas, III 1936- *WhoWrEP 92*
Slattery, Michael K. *Law&B 92*
Slattery, Paul Francis 1940- *WhoAm 92*
Slattery, Paul Vincent Owen 1948- *WhoWor 93*
Slattery, Raymond Joseph, III *Law&B 92*
Slattery, Richard *Law&B 92*
Slattery, Roger Timothy *Law&B 92*
Slattery, William H. 1943- *St&PR 93*
Slattery, William Henry *Law&B 92*
Slattery, William Henry 1943- *WhoAm 92*
Slaughter, Arthur P. *Law&B 92*
Slaughter, Christopher Ray 1946- *St&PR 93*
Slaughter, D. French, Jr. 1925- *CngDr 91*
Slaughter, Edward Ratliff, Jr. 1931- *WhoAm 92*
Slaughter, Enos 1916- *BioIn 17*
Slaughter, Eugene Edward 1909- *WhoSSW 93*
Slaughter, Frank G. 1908- *ScF&FL 92*
Slaughter, Frank Gill 1908- *WhoAm 92*
Slaughter, Freeman Cluff 1926- *WhoSSW 93*
Slaughter, John 1841-1922 *BioIn 17*
Slaughter, John B. *BioIn 17*
Slaughter, John Brooks 1934- *WhoAm 92, WhoWor 93*
Slaughter, Louise M. 1929- *BioIn 17*
Slaughter, Louise McIntosh 1929- *CngDr 91, WhoAm 92, WhoAmW 93, WhoE 93*
Slaughter, Margo Ann 1951- *WhoAmW 93*
Slaughter, Mary Ann Elizabeth 1939- *WhoAmW 93*
Slaughter, Michie Paris 1941- *St&PR 93*
Slaughter, Pamela *ScF&FL 92*
Slaughter, Phillip Howard 1948- *WhoSSW 93*
Slaughter, Richard G. 1944- *St&PR 93*
Slaughter, Robert R. 1924-1992 *BioIn 17*
Slaughter, Robert S. 1947- *St&PR 93*
Slaughter, Thomas L. *Law&B 92*
Slaughter, Tod 1885-1956 *BioIn 17*
Slaus, Ivo 1931- *WhoScE 91-4*
Slaven, Bettye DeJon 1946- *WhoWor 93*
Slaven, Robert Michael *Law&B 92*
Slaven, Tony *BioIn 17*
Slavens, Thomas Paul 1928- *WhoAm 92*
Slavenski, Josip 1896-1955 *Baker 92*
Slavich, Denis Michael 1940- *WhoAm 92*
Slavich, Ivan Lewis, III 1956- *WhoSSW 93*
Slavicky, Klement 1910- *Baker 92*
Slavicsek, Bill *ScF&FL 92*
Slavik, Bohdan 1924- *WhoScE 91-4*
Slavik, Josef 1806-1833 *Baker 92*
Slavik, Ladislav 1933- *WhoScE 91-4*
Slavik, Milan Frank 1930- *WhoWor 93*
Slavik, Vladimir Jan 1921- *WhoWor 93*
Slavin, Alexandra Nadal 1943- *WhoSSW 93*
Slavin, Brenda Mary *WhoScE 91-1*
Slavin, Joanne Louise 1952- *WhoAmW 93*
Slavin, John Jeremiah 1921- *St&PR 93*
Slavin, Lesley Anne 1955- *WhoSSW 93*
Slavin, Neal 1941- *WhoAm 92*
Slavin, Raymond Granam 1930- *WhoAm 92*
Slavin, Roberta Landau 1929- *WhoAmW 93*
Slavin, Rosanne Singer 1930- *WhoAmW 93, WhoWor 93*
Slavin, Roy H. *St&PR 93*
Slavin, Simon 1916- *WhoAm 92*
Slavina, Maria 1858-1951 *OxDcOp*
Slavinskas, Darius Domas 1933- *WhoE 93*
Slavinsky, Tadeo 1901-1945 *PolBiDi*
Slavitt, David R. *ScF&FL 92*
Slavitt, David Rytman 1935- *WhoWrEP 92*
Slavitt, David Walton 1931- *WhoAm 92*
Slavitt, Earl Benton 1939- *WhoAm 92*
Slavitt, Jacob 1907-1990 *BioIn 17*
Slavkay, Miroslav 1933- *WhoScE 91-4*
Slavos, Alexios dc. 1229 *OxDcByz*
Slavutin, Debra Claire 1951- *WhoAmW 93*
Slavutin, Lee Jacob 1951- *WhoE 93, WhoWor 93*
Slavutskii, Ilia Shevelevich 1935- *WhoWor 93*
Slavutych, Yar 1918- *ConAu 38NR, WhoCanL 92*
Slawek, Walery 1879-1939 *PolBiDi*
Slawinski, Lora Ann 1952- *WhoAmW 93*
Slawsky, Milton M. *BioIn 17*
Slawsky, Zaka I. *BioIn 17*
Slawson, Wayne 1932- *Baker 92*
Slawy-Sutton, Catherine 1950- *WhoSSW 93*
Slaybaugh, Jon 1943- *St&PR 93*
Slayden, James Bragdon 1924- *WhoAm 92*
Slayden, John Paul 1952- *St&PR 93*
Slaydon, Jeanne Miller *WhoSSW 93*
Slaymaker, Gene Arthur 1928- *WhoAm 92*
Slayman, Carolyn Walch 1937- *WhoAm 92*
Slayman, Clifford Leroy, Jr. 1936- *WhoE 93*
Slayton, David Lee 1962- *St&PR 93*
Slayton, Deke 1924- *BioIn 17*
Slayton, Donald Kent 1924- *BioIn 17, WhoAm 92, WhoSSW 93*
Slayton, Gus 1937- *WhoAm 92*
Slayton, Joel *BioIn 17*
Slayton, John A. 1918- *St&PR 93*
Slayton, John Arthur 1918- *WhoAm 92*
Slayton, Lee E. 1926- *St&PR 93*
Slayton, Ransom Dunn 1917- *WhoWor 93*
Slayton, Ronald Alfred 1910- *WhoE 93, WhoWor 93*
Slayton, Ronald Edwin 1940- *WhoSSW 93*
Slayton, Scott H. *Law&B 92*
Slayton, Thomas Kennedy 1941- *WhoE 93*
Slayton, William Larew 1916- *WhoAm 92*
Slazinski, Darleen Marian 1938- *St&PR 93*
Slazinski, Stanley H. *Law&B 92*
Slease, Clyde Harold, III 1944- *WhoE 93*
Sleath, Martin David 1946- *St&PR 93*
Sleator, William *BioIn 17*
Sleator, William 1945- *ChlLR 29 [port], ScF&FL 92*
Sleator, William Warner, III *WhoAm 92*
Sleator, William Warner, (III) 1945- *DcAmChF 1985, MajAI [port]*
Sleavin, F. Richard 1938- *St&PR 93*
Slechta, Jiri 1939- *WhoWor 93*
Slechta, Robert Frank 1928- *WhoAm 92*
Sledd, James Hinton 1914- *WhoWrEP 92*
Sledge, Brian D. 1959- *St&PR 93*
Sledge, Clement Blount 1930- *WhoAm 92*
Sledge, Donald E. 1942- *St&PR 93*
Sledge, E.B. 1923- *BioIn 17*
Sledge, Eugene Bondurant 1923- *BioIn 17*
Sledge, Gary *BioIn 17*
Sledge, James Scott 1947- *WhoWor 93*
Sledge, Kim *Law&B 92*
Sledge, Levin Alexander 1913- *St&PR 93*
Sledge, Percy 1940- *SoulM*
Sledge, Reginald Leon 1954- *WhoE 93*
Sledzinski, Janusz 1931- *WhoScE 91-4*
Slee, Richard *BioIn 17*
Sleek, Harry T. 1943- *St&PR 93*
Sleek, Sewell Irwin 1936- *St&PR 93*
Sleeman, B.D. *WhoScE 91-1*
Sleeman, D. *WhoScE 91-1*
Sleeman, Thomas Barrett 1932- *St&PR 93, WhoAm 92*
Sleeman, William Clifford, Jr. 1923- *WhoSSW 93*
Sleep, Michael Ronan *WhoScE 91-1*
Sleepeck, William H., Jr. 1918- *St&PR 93*
Sleeper, Frank Harold 1927- *WhoE 93*
Sleeper, Henry Dike 1865-1948 *Baker 92*
Sleeper, Ruth d1992 *NewYTBS 92*
Sleet, Robert Emmett 1946- *St&PR 93*
Sleeth, Natalie W. 1930-1991 *BioIn 17*
Sleeth, Walter J. *Law&B 92*
Slehofer, Richard Charles 1957- *St&PR 93*
Sleicher, Charles Albert 1924- *WhoAm 92*
Sleicher, Harry K. 1925- *St&PR 93*
Sleigh, Barbara 1906-1982 *ScF&FL 92*
Sleigh, Burrows Willcocks Arthur 1821-1869 *BioIn 17*
Sleigh, James Douglas *WhoScE 91-1*
Sleigh, Michael Alfred *WhoScE 91-1*
Sleigh, Sylvia *WhoAm 92*
Sleight, A. *WhoScE 91-1*
Sleight, Arthur William 1939- *WhoAm 92*
Sleight, Thomas Perry 1943- *WhoE 93*
Sleik, Thomas S. *St&PR 93*
Sleisenger, Marvin Herbert 1924- *WhoAm 92*
Slejko, Dario 1949- *WhoScE 91-3*
Slemko, Morris Peter 1952- *St&PR 93*
Slemon, Gordon Richard 1924- *WhoAm 92*
Slenczka, Werner Georg 1934- *WhoWor 93*
Slenczynska, Ruth 1925- *Baker 92*
Slendzinski, Ludomir 1889-1980 *PolBiDi*
Slenker, Paul L. 1925- *St&PR 93*
Slenker, Richard Dreyer, Jr. 1957- *WhoE 93*
Slepchuk, Nicholas I., Jr. *Law&B 92*
Slepian, David 1923- *WhoAm 92*
Slepian, Jan 1921- *DcAmChF 1960*
Slepian, Jan(ice B.) 1921- *ConAu 136, MajAI [port]*
Slepian, Paul 1923- *WhoAm 92*
Slesicki, Wladyslaw 1927- *DrEEuF*
Slesin, Aviva 1946- *MiSFD 9*
Slesinger, Jacques Isidore 1930- *WhoE 93*
Slesinger, Larry Howard 1954- *WhoE 93*
Slesinger, Tess 1905-1945 *BioIn 17, JeAmFiW*
Slesinski, Mary Lucy 1923- *WhoAmW 93*
Slesnick, William Ellis 1925- *WhoAm 92, WhoE 93*
Slesser, Malcolm *WhoScE 91-1*
Slessman, Donald B. 1917- *St&PR 93*
Slessor, John Cotesworth 1897-1979 *HarEnMi*
Slessor, Kenneth 1901-1971 *BioIn 17*
Slettebak, Arne 1925- *WhoAm 92*
Sletten, John Robert 1932- *WhoAm 92*
Slev, Monica *Law&B 92*
Sleven, Marvin Owen 1925- *St&PR 93*
Sleven, Robert L. 1932- *WhoAm 92*
Slevin, Joseph Raymond 1918- *WhoE 93*
Slevin, Maurice Louis 1949- *WhoWor 93*
Slevin, Patrick Joseph 1951- *WhoE 93*
Slevin, Robert P. *Law&B 92*
Slewinski, Wladyslaw 1855-1919 *PolBiDi*
Slewitzke, Connie Lee 1931- *WhoAm 92, WhoAmW 93, WhoE 93*
Slezak, David G. *Law&B 92*
Slezak, Erika *BioIn 17*
Slezak, Erika Alma 1946- *WhoAm 92*
Slezak, Gary M. 1955- *St&PR 93*
Slezak, Leo 1873-1946 *Baker 92, IntDcOp, OxDcOp*
Slezak, Margaret 1901-1953 *OxDcOp*
Slezak, Steven Eugene 1959- *WhoE 93*
Slezak, Walter 1902-1983 *OxDcOp*
Slichter, Charles Pence 1924- *WhoAm 92*
Slichter, William P. 1922-1990 *BioIn 17*
Slick, Earl F. 1920- *EncABHB 8 [port]*
Slick, Grace 1939- *Baker 92, BioIn 17*
Slick, Grace Wing 1939- *WhoAm 92*
Slidell, John 1793-1871 *PolPar*
Sliepcevich, Cedomir M. 1920- *WhoAm 92*
Slier, Debby *SmATA 71*
Slifer, Karl R. *Law&B 92*
Slifka, Alan B. 1929- *St&PR 93*
Slifkin, Lawrence Myer 1925- *WhoAm 92*
Sliger, Bernard Francis 1924- *WhoWor 93*
Sliger, Herbert J., Jr. *Law&B 92*
Sligh, Charles Robert, Jr. 1906- *St&PR 93*
Sligh, Clarissa *BioIn 17*
Sligh, Lucile Crites *AmWomPl*
Sligh, Robert Lewis 1928- *St&PR 93*
Slijepcevic, Vladan 1930-1989 *DrEEuF*
Sliker, Thomas R. 1951- *St&PR 93, WhoAm 92*
Slim, Memphis *WhoWrEP 92*
Slim, William Joseph 1891-1970 *BioIn 17, DcTwHis, HarEnMi*
Sliman, Edward Anthony 1935- *WhoSSW 93*
Slim Helu, Carlos *BioIn 17*
Slimmer, John Earl 1940- *WhoE 93*
Slimmer, Richard B. 1953- *St&PR 93*
Slimp, Beverly B. 1916- *St&PR 93*
Slimp, Mickey Mantle 1954- *WhoSSW 93*
Sliney, David L. 1936- *St&PR 93*
Slingerman, Raymond Joseph, Jr. 1924- *St&PR 93*
Slingluff, Charles H., Jr. 1929- *St&PR 93*
Slipka, Jaroslav 1926- *WhoScE 91-4*
Slipman, Ronald 1939- *WhoSSW 93*
Slippen, Michael 1942- *WhoE 93*
Slipsager, Henrik Christian 1955- *St&PR 93*
Sliter, John E. 1937- *St&PR 93*
Sliter, John W. 1934- *WhoAm 92*
Slitt, Wayne L. *Law&B 92*
Slive, Seymour 1920- *WhoAm 92*
Slivinski, Robert Michael 1949- *WhoE 93*
Slivinsky, Vladimir 1894-1949 *OxDcOp*
Slivon, F.P., Jr. 1930- *St&PR 93*
Sliwa, Curtis *NewYTBS 92 [port]*
Sliwa, Henri 1938- *WhoScE 91-2*
Sliwa, Steven Mark *WhoSSW 93*
Sliwinski, Gerard *WhoScE 91-4*
Sliwinski, Tadeusz 1922- *WhoWor 93*
Sliwiok, Jozef 1934- *WhoScE 91-4*
Sljaka, Mary Tomica 1950- *WhoAmW 93*
Sloan, Benson B. d1990 *BioIn 17*
Sloan, Carolyn 1937- *ScF&FL 92*
Sloan, Christopher K. *Law&B 92*
Sloan, David Edward 1922- *St&PR 93, WhoAm 92*
Sloan, David Leighton 1946- *St&PR 93*
Sloan, David McPheator *WhoScE 91-1*
Sloan, David Walter 1937- *WhoSSW 93*
Sloan, Elaine Frank 1938- *WhoAm 92*
Sloan, Frank Allen 1942- *WhoAm 92*
Sloan, Frank Blaine 1920- *WhoE 93, WhoWor 93*
Sloan, Frank Keenan 1921- *WhoAm 92*
Sloan, Gerald Eugene Jerry 1942- *WhoAm 92*
Sloan, Herbert Elias 1914- *WhoAm 92, WhoWor 93*
Sloan, Hiram Cooper 1929- *WhoWor 93*
Sloan, Hugh Walter, Jr. 1940- *WhoAm 92*
Sloan, Jackson 1939- *St&PR 93*
Sloan, James E. *Law&B 92*
Sloan, James Park 1944- *WhoWrEP 92*
Sloan, Jeanette Pasin 1946- *WhoAm 92, WhoAmW 93*
Sloan, John E. 1937- *St&PR 93*
Sloan, Joseph d1990 *BioIn 17*
Sloan, Joseph Jay White, II 1958- *WhoSSW 93*
Sloan, Joyce *WhoAm 92*
Sloan, L. Lawrence 1922- *St&PR 93*
Sloan, Lane E. 1947- *St&PR 93*
Sloan, Lane Everett 1947- *WhoAm 92*
Sloan, Maceo Kennedy 1949- *WhoSSW 93, WhoWor 93*
Sloan, Marilyn D. *Law&B 92*
Sloan, Mary Jean 1927- *WhoSSW 93, WhoWor 93*
Sloan, Melanie Isa 1965- *WhoAmW 93*
Sloan, Michael *BioIn 17*
Sloan, Michael 1946- *ScF&FL 92*
Sloan, Michael Dana 1960- *WhoEmL 93, WhoWor 93*
Sloan, Mike *Law&B 92*
Sloan, Nanci Oliver *Law&B 92*
Sloan, Norman 1926- *BioIn 17*
Sloan, Norton Q. *St&PR 93*
Sloan, O. Temple, Jr. 1939- *WhoAm 92*
Sloan, Orris Temple, Jr. 1939- *St&PR 93*
Sloan, Reba Faye 1955- *WhoSSW 93*
Sloan, Rebecca L. *Law&B 92*
Sloan, Richard John 1938- *WhoAm 92*
Sloan, Robert Blake 1941- *St&PR 93*
Sloan, Robert E. *Law&B 92*
Sloan, Robert Hood, Jr. 1953- *WhoE 93*
Sloan, Robert Love 1947- *WhoSSW 93*
Sloan, Robert Smullyan 1915- *WhoE 93*
Sloan, Robert Wesley 1924- *WhoE 93*
Sloan, Robert Wesley 1930- *St&PR 93*
Sloan, Rosalind 1953- *WhoAmW 93*
Sloan, Stanley 1943- *WhoAm 92*
Sloan, Stephen 1932- *WhoAm 92*

Sloan, Stephen Stehly 1948- WhoAm 92
Sloan, Steven Kent Law&B 92
Sloan, Suzanne Barkin 1959- WhoAmW 93
Sloan, Timothy James 1957- WhoSSW 93
Sloan, Walter F. d1990 BioIn 17
Sloane, Ben ScF&FL 92
Sloane, Beverly LeBov 1936- WhoAmW 93, WhoWor 93
Sloane, Carl Stuart 1937- WhoAm 92
Sloane, David Edward Edison 1943- WhoE 93
Sloane, David Jonathan 1950- St&PR 93
Sloane, Eric BioIn 17
Sloane, Everett 1909-1965 IntDcF 2-3
Sloane, G. Michael WhoIns 93
Sloane, G. Michael 1952- St&PR 93
Sloane, Hans 1660-1753 BioIn 17
Sloane, John Edison d1990 BioIn 17
Sloane, John Hunt 1933- St&PR 93, WhoAm 92
Sloane, Marshall M. 1926- WhoAm 92
Sloane, Michael A. 1936- St&PR 93
Sloane, N.J.A. 1939- BioIn 17
Sloane, Neil James Alexander 1939- BioIn 17, WhoAm 92
Sloane, Peter Donald Law&B 92
Sloane, Peter J. WhoScE 91-1
Sloane, Phyllis Lester 1921- WhoAmW 93
Sloane, Robert C. ScF&FL 92
Sloane, Robert L. 1940- St&PR 93
Sloane, Robert Lindley 1940- WhoE 93
Sloane, Robert Malcolm 1933- WhoAm 92
Sloane, Thomas Charles 1922- WhoAm 92
Sloane, Thomas Edison, Jr. 1940- WhoE 93
Sloane, Thomas O. 1929- WhoAm 92
Sloane, William Martin 1951- WhoE 93
Sloas, Harold Andrew, Jr. 1942- WhoSSW 93
Sloat, Barbara Furin 1942- WhoAmW 93
Sloat, Cheri Lyn Brueggemann 1951- WhoAmW 93
Sloat, Jane Roberts DeGraff 1939- WhoE 93
Sloat, John Drake 1781-1867 HarEnMi
Sloat, Lauren Beth Law&B 92
Sloat, Robert Earl Law&B 92
Sloat, Teri 1948- ConAu 138, SmATA 70 [port]
Sloate, Alan R. Law&B 92
Sloate, Daniel 1931- WhoCanL 92
Slobadin, Stephen 1918- WhoE 93
Sloben, Donald Paul 1941- St&PR 93
Slobodianik, Alexander 1941- Baker 92
Slobodien, Howard David 1923- WhoE 93, WhoWor 93
Slobodin, Alex 1914- St&PR 93
Slobodin, Vadim Igorvich 1962- WhoWor 93
Slobodkin, Lawrence (B.) 1928- ConAu 137
Slobodkin, Louis 1903-1975 MajAI [port]
Slobodskaya, Oda 1888-1970 Baker 92, OxDcOp
Slochower, Harry 1900-1991 BioIn 17
Slochower, Joyce Anne 1950- WhoE 93
Slocombe, Douglas 1913- ConTFT 10
Slocombe, Walter Becker 1941- WhoAm 92
Slocum, Barclay 1942- WhoAm 92
Slocum, Donald Warren WhoAm 92, WhoSSW 93
Slocum, Frank 1925- ConAu 136
Slocum, Gail L. Law&B 92
Slocum, George Sigman 1940- St&PR 93, WhoSSW 93
Slocum, Henry Warner 1827-1894 HarEnMi
Slocum, Jack D. 1930- St&PR 93
Slocum, James MiSFD 9
Slocum, Jean B. 1920- St&PR 93
Slocum, Joyce Law&B 92
Slocum, Philip Carroll 1951- WhoSSW 93
Slocum, Richard D. 1927- St&PR 93
Slocum, Robert Bigney 1922- WhoE 93
Slocum, Rosemarie R. 1948- WhoAmW 93, WhoEmL 93, WhoWor 93
Slocum, Russell Huntington 1949- WhoE 93
Slocumb, Eudora Hollinshead AmWomPl
Slocumb, Margaret Elizabeth 1908- WhoAmW 93, WhoSSW 93, WhoWor 93
Sloe, John Edward 1953- St&PR 93, WhoWor 93
Sloggy, John Edward 1952- WhoSSW 93
Slogoff, Stephen 1942- WhoAm 92
Slomack, Michael J. Law&B 92
Sloman, Aaron WhoScE 91-1
Sloman, Aaron 1936- WhoWor 93
Sloman, Inta Law&B 92
Slomanson, William Reed 1945- WhoWor 93
Slominski, Leon 1935- WhoScE 91-4
Slomovitz, Carmi Malachi 1933- WhoSSW 93
Slomovitz, Philip 1896- BioIn 17
Slomski, Ryszard 1950- WhoScE 91-4
Slonaker, Larry ScF&FL 92
Slonczewski, Joan 1956- ScF&FL 92
Slone, Carol Deming 1948- WhoAmW 93
Slone, R. Wayne WhoAm 92
Slone, Richard Allen 1937- St&PR 93
Slone, Sandi 1939- WhoAm 92, WhoAmW 93
Slonecker, Charles Edward 1938- WhoAm 92
Slonecker, Michael L. Law&B 92
Sloneker, William Sauer 1953- St&PR 93
Slonem, Hunt 1951- WhoE 93
Slonim, Gilven M. 1913- WhoSSW 93
Slonimski, Antoni 1896-1976 PolBiDi
Slonimski, Piotr 1922- WhoScE 91-2
Slonimsky, Nicolas 1894- Baker 92, BioIn 17, WhoAm 92
Slonimsky, Sergei (Mikhailovich) 1932- Baker 92
Slonimsky, Yuri 1902-1978 Baker 92
Slonina, Werner 1926- WhoScE 91-3
Sloninkiewicz, Ludwik 1831-1855 PolBiDi
Slonov, Mikhail 1869-1930 Baker 92
Slooff, J.W. 1941- WhoScE 91-3
Slooff, Rudolf 1934- WhoUN 92
Slook, George F. 1946- St&PR 93
Sloper, (Edward Hugh) Lindsay 1826-1887 Baker 92
Slorach, Stuart Alexander 1939- WhoScE 91-4
Slorah, Patricia Perkins 1940- WhoAmW 93
Slorick, Michael Alexander 1938- WhoWor 93
Slosar, John M. 1938- St&PR 93
Slosberg, Michael BioIn 17
Slosberg, Mike 1934- WhoAm 92
Slosberg, Myles J. 1937- St&PR 93
Slosberg, Myles Joseph 1937- WhoE 93
Slosberg, Robert Harvey 1930- St&PR 93
Slosman, Everett Lawrence 1935- WhoWrEP 92
Slosman, Fred N. 1939- St&PR 93
Sloss, Carl H.T. d1991 BioIn 17
Sloss, Laurence Louis 1913- WhoAm 92
Sloss, Lesley Lord 1965- SmATA 72 [port]
Slosser, Jeffery Eric 1943- WhoSSW 93
Slot, Larry Lee 1947- WhoE 93, WhoEmL 93, WhoWor 93
Slote, Alfred 1926- DcAmChF 1960, MajAI [port], ScF&FL 92, SmATA 72 [port]
Slotemaker, Judy Ann 1941- WhoWrEP 92
Slotfeldt-Ellingsen, Dag 1943- WhoScE 91-4
Slotkin, Richard Sidney 1942- WhoWrEP 92
Slotnick, Barry Ivan 1939- WhoAm 92
Slotnick, Jules B. 1931- St&PR 93
Slotnick, Mortimer H. 1920- WhoAm 92
Slotnick, Robert 1929- St&PR 93
Slots, Jorgen 1944- WhoScE 91-4
Slott, Michael P. 1950- St&PR 93
Slotte, Peter Johan 1956- WhoWor 93
Slotten, LeRoy Ben 1927- St&PR 93
Slough, Robert Allan 1955- WhoSSW 93
Slovak, Hillel c. 1963-1988 See Red Hot Chili Peppers, The News 93-1
Slovak, Ladislav 1919- Baker 92
Slove, Martin L. 1936- St&PR 93
Slover, Claud Wesley 1924- WhoSSW 93
Sloves, Marvin 1933- WhoAm 92
Slovin, Bruce 1935- St&PR 93
Slovinsky, Louis J. 1937- St&PR 93
Sloviter, Dolores Korman 1932- WhoAm 92, WhoAmW 93
Sloviter, Henry Allan 1914- WhoAm 92
Slovo, Joe BioIn 17
Slovo, Joe 1926- WhoAfr
Slowacki, Julius 1809-1849 PolBiDi [port]
Slowey, Brian Aodh 1933- WhoWor 93
Slowey, William B. Law&B 92
Slowick, Daniel William 1952- WhoE 93
Slowik, Richard Andrew 1939- WhoSSW 93, WhoWor 93
Slowikowski, William Henry 1943- St&PR 93
Slowinski, Emil John 1922- WhoWrEP 92
Slowinski, Roman 1952- WhoWor 93
Slowronski, Boleslaw WhoScE 91-4
Sloyan, Gerard Stephen 1919- ConAu 40NR, WhoAm 92
Sloyan, Patrick Joseph 1937- WhoAm 92
Sloyan, Stephanie 1918- WhoAmW 93
Slucher, Rosemary Dawson 1950- WhoAmW 93
Sluchin, Benny 1948- WhoWor 93
Slud, Eric Victor 1953- WhoE 93
Sludikoff, Ann Paula 1947- St&PR 93
Sludikoff, Stanley Robert 1935- St&PR 93, WhoAm 92, WhoWrEP 92
Sluijter, Frans Willem 1936- WhoScE 91-3
Slung, Michele 1947- ScF&FL 92
Slurzberg, Elihu 1929- WhoE 93
Slusarz, Bernard Francis 1937- St&PR 93
Slusher, Marianne 1963- WhoAmW 93
Slusher, Ruth Varner 1945- WhoAmW 93
Slusher, William Preston 1915- WhoSSW 93
Slusky, Ronald D. Law&B 92
Sluss, Mollie Ann 1952- WhoAmW 93
Slusser, Daniel E. 1938- St&PR 93
Slusser, Eugene A. 1922- St&PR 93
Slusser, Eugene Alvin 1922- WhoE 93
Slusser, George Edgar 1939- ScF&FL 92
Slusser, Mark D. 1957- St&PR 93
Sluter, Claus c. 1340-1405? BioIn 17
Slutsky, Lorie Ann 1953- WhoAm 92, WhoAmW 93
Slutzky, Charles B. 1944- St&PR 93
Slutzky, Jack 1937- WhoE 93
Slutzky, Richard Owen 1956- WhoE 93
Sluyser, Mels 1930- WhoScE 91-3
Sluzalec, Adolf Roman 1927- WhoScE 91-4
Sly, John Eugene 1917- WhoE 93
Sly, Ridge Michael 1933- WhoAm 92
Sly, Sue 1953- WhoAmW 93
Sly & the Family Stone SoulM
Slyde, Jimmy BioIn 17
Slye, Donald M. 1951- St&PR 93
Slykhuis, John Timothy 1920- WhoAm 92
Slyter, Leonard Leroy 1933- WhoE 93
Slyter, Ronald L. Law&B 92
Smadbeck, Louis d1992 NewYTBS 92 [port]
Smadbeck, Louis 1920- St&PR 93
Smading, Daniel E. Law&B 92
Smaga, Kenneth C. 1959- WhoSSW 93
Smaglick, Paul William 1932- WhoAm 92
Smagorinsky, Joseph 1924- WhoAm 92
Smagorzewski-Schermann, Antoni 1818-1900 PolBiDi
Smaha, Francis Walter 1959- WhoE 93
Smaha, James 1935- WhoAm 92
Smaha, Joseph John 1951- WhoE 93
Smail, Richard Frank 1921- St&PR 93
Smail, Tamra Ann Law&B 92
Smaistrla, Jean Ann 1936- WhoSSW 93
Smaje, Laurence H. 1936- WhoScE 91-1
Smaldone, Edward Michael 1956- WhoE 93
Smaldone, Gerald Christopher 1947- WhoE 93
Smale, Graham 1945- WhoScE 91-1
Smale, J.A. Law&B 92
Smale, John Gray 1927- St&PR 93
Smales, Fred Benson 1914- St&PR 93, WhoAm 92
Smalheiser, Harvey 1942- WhoAm 92
Smalis, Gregory C. 1952- St&PR 93
Smalkin, Frederic N. WhoAm 92, WhoE 93
Small, A. Neil 1951- St&PR 93
Small, Adam BioIn 17
Small, Albert Harrison 1925- WhoWor 93
Small, Andrew Thomas 1958- WhoSSW 93
Small, Arline St&PR 93
Small, Austin J. 1894-1929 ScF&FL 92
Small, Barbara E. Law&B 92
Small, Beatrice 1937- ScF&FL 92
Small, Benjamin F. Law&B 92
Small, Christopher 1919- ScF&FL 92
Small, Clay G. Law&B 92
Small, David 1937- ConAu 39NR
Small, David 1945- ScF&FL 92
Small, Deborah Thomasine 1952- WhoAmW 93
Small, Doreen G. Law&B 92
Small, Edward Law&B 92
Small, Edward 1945- St&PR 93
Small, Edwin Warren Law&B 92
Small, Elaine Dolores 1954- WhoAmW 93
Small, Elisabeth Chan 1934- WhoAmW 93
Small, Ernest MajAI
Small, Erwin 1924- WhoAm 92
Small, George LeRoy 1924- WhoAm 92
Small, George M. 1944- St&PR 93
Small, Graham Newton 1939- WhoUN 92
Small, Greg T. 1955- St&PR 93
Small, Henry Gilbert 1941- WhoAm 92
Small, Herb 1951- St&PR 93
Small, John Grant, Jr. 1946- St&PR 93
Small, Jon MiSFD 9
Small, Jonathan Andrew Law&B 92
Small, Jonathan Andrew 1942- WhoAm 92
Small, Joyce Graham 1931- WhoAmW 93
Small, Kenneth Lawrence 1941- WhoE 93
Small, Kent Daniel 1965- WhoSSW 93
Small, Lawrence Farnsworth 1925- WhoAm 92
Small, Marshall Lee 1927- WhoAm 92
Small, Melvin 1939- WhoAm 92
Small, Parker Adams, Jr. 1932- WhoAm 92, WhoSSW 93
Small, Parker Adams, III 1958- WhoE 93
Small, Philip M. Law&B 92
Small, Ralph B. 1942- St&PR 93
Small, Ralph Edward 1950- WhoSSW 93
Small, Ralph Milton 1917- WhoAm 92
Small, Randy ScF&FL 92
Small, Rebecca Elaine 1946- WhoAmW 93
Small, Richard David 1945- WhoAm 92
Small, Ronald John WhoScE 91-1
Small, Sarah Mae 1923- WhoAmW 93, WhoE 93, WhoWor 93
Small, Saul Mouchly 1913- WhoAm 92
Small, Sharon Stevens 1954- WhoSSW 93
Small, Stephen Jay Law&B 92
Small, Stuart 1935- St&PR 93
Small, Sylvia Adamson 1952- WhoSSW 93
Small, Theodore D. d1992 BioIn 17
Small, Walter 1931- St&PR 93
Small, Wilfred Thomas 1920- WhoWor 93
Small, William Andrew 1914- WhoAm 92
Small, William Edwin, Jr. 1937- WhoAm 92
Small, William R. 1935- St&PR 93
Smallacombe, Robert J. 1933- St&PR 93
Smallacombe, Robert Joseph 1933- WhoE 93
Smallcombe, John MiSFD 9
Smalldon, Jeffrey 1953- ScF&FL 92
Smallenberger, James A. Law&B 92
Smallenberger, James Andrew 1942- St&PR 93
Smallenburg, Harry Russell 1942- WhoWrEP 92
Smallens, Alexander 1889-1972 Baker 92, OxDcOp
Smalley, Christopher Joseph 1953- WhoE 93
Smalley, David A. 1809-1877 PolPar
Smalley, David Allen fl. 19th cent.- BioIn 17
Smalley, Eugene Byron 1926- WhoAm 92
Smalley, George Washburn 1833-1916 JrnUS
Smalley, Henry 1765-1839 BioIn 17
Smalley, James Carl 1947- WhoE 93
Smalley, Joseph E. d1991 BioIn 17
Smalley, Kenneth Lee 1930- St&PR 93, WhoAm 92
Smalley, Larry Lee 1937- WhoSSW 93
Smalley, Maureen WhoScE 91-1
Smalley, Penny Judith 1947- WhoAmW 93
Smalley, Philip Adam, Jr. 1941- St&PR 93
Smalley, Randall Steven 1949- St&PR 93
Smalley, Richard Errett 1943- WhoAm 92
Smalley, Robert Arthur 1923- St&PR 93
Smalley, Robert Manning 1925- WhoAm 92
Smalley, Roger 1943- Baker 92
Smalley, Roy Frederick, III 1952- BiDAMSp 1989
Smalley, Scott Anthony 1953- St&PR 93
Smalley, William Edward 1940- WhoAm 92
Smallman, Beverley N. 1913- WhoAm 92
Smallman, Joseph Dempster 1955- WhoSSW 93
Smallman, Raymond Edward WhoScE 91-1
Smalls, Derek 1943- See Spinal Tap ConMus 8
Smalls, Robert 1839-1915 BioIn 17, EncAACR [port]
Smalls-Hector, Irene 1950- SmATA 73 [port]
Small-Weil, Susan B. 1954- WhoAm 92
Smallwood, Carol Ann 1939- WhoWrEP 92
Smallwood, Edmund Warren 1932- St&PR 93
Smallwood, Edward Hugh, Jr. 1926- WhoSSW 93
Smallwood, Franklin 1927- WhoAm 92, WhoWor 93
Smallwood, Genevieve Charlene 1942- WhoE 93
Smallwood, Glenn Walter, Jr. 1956- WhoEmL 93, WhoWor 93
Smallwood, Joey 1900-1991 AnObit 1991
Smallwood, Joseph R. 1900-1991 BioIn 17
Smallwood, Joseph R(oberts) 1900-1991 CurBio 92N
Smallwood, Michelle Anusbigian 1960- WhoAmW 93
Smallwood, Robert Albian, Jr. 1946- WhoE 93, WhoEmL 93
Smallwood, Robert L. 1948- St&PR 93
Smallwood, Williams 1831-1897 Baker 92
Smally, Donald Jay 1922- WhoAm 92
Smals, Bryan BioIn 17
Smaltz, Hugh M., II 1929- St&PR 93
Smarandache, Florentin 1954- WhoWrEP 92
Smarda, Jan Jiri 1930- WhoScE 91-4
Smardon, Richard Clay 1948- WhoE 93

Smareglia, Antonio 1854-1929 *Baker 92, OxDcOp*
Smarinsky, Michael *Law&B 92*
Smario, Thomas Michael 1950- *WhoWrEP 92*
Smarr, Larry *BioIn 17*
Smarr, Larry Lee 1948- *WhoAm 92, WhoWor 93*
Smars, Erik Algot 1923- *WhoWor 93*
Smart *Baker 92*
Smart, Allen Rich, II 1934- *WhoAm 92*
Smart, Ashlynn M. 1950- *WhoAmW 93*
Smart, B.G.D. *WhoScE 91-1*
Smart, Brian *ScF&FL 92*
Smart, Carol 1948- *ConAu 37NR*
Smart, Carolyn 1952- *WhoCanL 92*
Smart, Carolyn (Alexandra) 1952- *ConAu 38NR*
Smart, Charles Rich 1926- *WhoAm 92*
Smart, Christopher 1722-1771 *BioIn 17*
Smart, Clifton Murray, Jr. 1933- *WhoAm 92*
Smart, David A. *BioIn 17*
Smart, David Louis 1941- *WhoAm 92*
Smart, Denise Torvik 1951- *WhoSSW 93*
Smart, Dorothy Caroline *WhoAmW 93*
Smart, Edith Merrill 1929- *WhoAmW 93*
Smart, Elizabeth 1913-1985 *BioIn 17*
Smart, Elizabeth 1913-1986 *WhoCanL 92*
Smart, George 1776-1867 *OxDcOp*
Smart, George MacArthur 1945- *St&PR 93*
Smart, George (Thomas) 1776-1867 *Baker 92*
Smart, Gordon Musgrove 1929- *St&PR 93*
Smart, Gregg d1990 *BioIn 17*
Smart, Henry 1778-1823 *Baker 92*
Smart, Henry Thomas 1813-1879 *Baker 92*
Smart, Ian E.L. 1945- *St&PR 93*
Smart, Jackson W., Jr. 1930- *St&PR 93*
Smart, Jackson Wyman, Jr. 1930- *WhoAm 92*
Smart, Jacob Edward 1909- *WhoAm 92*
Smart, James D. 1932- *St&PR 93*
Smart, Jean *BioIn 17*
Smart, L. Edwin 1923- *St&PR 93*
Smart, Louis Edwin, Jr. 1923- *WhoAm 92, WhoWor 93*
Smart, Marriott Wieckhoff 1935- *WhoAmW 93*
Smart, Mary-Leigh Call 1917- *WhoAmW 93, WhoE 93, WhoWor 93*
Smart, Michael A.R. 1942- *WhoUN 92*
Smart, Pamela *BioIn 17*
Smart, Patricia 1940- *WhoCanL 92*
Smart, Paul M. 1929- *WhoAm 92*
Smart, Richard d1992 *NewYTBS 92 [port]*
Smart, Stephen Bruce, Jr. 1923- *WhoAm 92*
Smart, Steven Paul 1954- *St&PR 93*
Smart, Steven Tracy 1958- *WhoEmL 93*
Smart, William Buckwalter 1922- *WhoAm 92*
Smart, William Edward, Jr. 1933- *WhoWrEP 92*
Smart, William Robertson 1920- *St&PR 93*
Smartt, J(oseph) 1931- *ConAu 138*
Smarzewski, Ryszard 1949- *WhoWor 93*
Smathers, Ben d1990 *BioIn 17*
Smathers, Frank, Jr. 1909- *WhoAm 92*
Smathers, James Burton 1935- *WhoAm 92*
Smatresk, Neal Joseph 1951- *WhoSSW 93*
Smawley, Robert J. *MiSFD 9*
Smayling, Lyda Mozella 1923- *WhoAmW 93*
Smbat the Constable 1208-1276 *OxDcByz*
Smead, Eric Michael 1947- *WhoSSW 93*
Smeal, Eleanor C. 1939- *PolPar*
Smeal, Eleanor Cutri 1939- *WhoAm 92, WhoAmW 93*
Smeal, Frank P. 1918- *St&PR 93*
Smeal, Paul Lester 1932- *WhoAm 92, WhoSSW 93*
Smeaton, Doug 1949- *St&PR 93*
Smeaton, Melvin Douglas 1949- *WhoAm 92*
Smedberg, Staffan Gunnar 1941- *WhoWor 93*
Smedegaard, Norman H. 1916- *WhoAm 92*
Smedegaard, V. 1933- *WhoScE 91-2*
Smedira, Nicholas A. 1933- *St&PR 93*
Smedley, Agnes 1890-1950 *BioIn 17*
Smedley, Agnes 1892-1950 *AmWomWr 92*
Smedley, Bernard R. 1936- *St&PR 93*
Smedley, Bernard Ronald 1936- *WhoAm 92*
Smedley, Charles Vincent 1955- *WhoWor 93*
Smedley, Harold A. 1935- *St&PR 93*
Smedley, Katharine E. *AmWomPl*
Smedley, Raymond William 1940- *St&PR 93*
Smeds, Dave 1955- *ScF&FL 92*
Smeds, Edward William 1936- *St&PR 93, WhoAm 92*
Smedsfelt, K. Sigvard 1921- *WhoScE 91-4*
Smedsrud, Rick G. 1949- *St&PR 93*
Smee, K.L.B. *Law&B 92*
Smeekes, J.P. *WhoScE 91-3*
Smejkal, Joseph Frank 1921- *St&PR 93*
Smelewicz, Frank A. 1922- *St&PR 93*
Smelick, Robert Malcolm 1942- *St&PR 93, WhoWor 93*
Smelik, Pieter G. 1928- *WhoScE 91-3*
Smelkinson, Robert N. 1929- *St&PR 93*
Smelser, Emmett K. 1942- *St&PR 93*
Smelser, Neil Joseph 1930- *WhoWrEP 92*
Smelt, Ronald 1913- *WhoAm 92*
Smelter, Katherine Vafakas 1941- *WhoAmW 93*
Smeltzer, David P. 1958- *St&PR 93*
Smeltzer, Debra Jean 1953- *WhoSSW 93*
Smeltzer, Percy J. 1918- *St&PR 93*
Smeltzer, Walter William 1924- *WhoAm 92*
Smend, Friedrich 1893-1980 *Baker 92*
Smend, Rudolf 1932- *WhoWor 93*
Smeraldi, Florence G. Stark 1938- *WhoWrEP 92*
Smerdel, Stanislav 1935- *WhoScE 91-4*
Smerdon, Ernest Thomas 1930- *WhoAm 92*
Smerge, Raymond G. *Law&B 92*
Smerge, Raymond Gene 1944- *St&PR 93*
Smerlas, Donna 1949- *WhoAmW 93*
Smerlas, Fred *BioIn 17*
Smerling, Julian M. 1928- *St&PR 93*
Smerling, Julian Melvin 1928- *WhoAm 92*
Smernoff, Richard Louis 1941- *WhoAm 92*
Smestad, Russell Ray 1952- *St&PR 93*
Smetacek, Vaclav 1906-1986 *Baker 92*
Smetacek, Victor S. 1946- *WhoScE 91-3*
Smetana, Andrew Frank 1930- *WhoE 93*
Smetana, Bedrich 1824-1884 *Baker 92, IntDcOp [port], OxDcOp*
Smetana, Frederick O. 1928- *WhoSSW 93*
Smetana, Joseph C. 1937- *WhoIns 93*
Smeterlin, Jan 1892-1967 *Baker 92*
Smetheram, Herbert Edwin 1934- *WhoSSW 93*
Smethers, Lyle E. 1942- *St&PR 93*
Smethills, Harold R. 1948- *St&PR 93*
Smethills, Harold Reginald 1948- *WhoAm 92*
Smethurst, Edward William, Jr. 1930- *WhoAm 92*
Smethurst, Robert Guy 1929- *WhoAm 92*
Smethurst, William J. 1946- *St&PR 93*
Smetko, Craig N. *Law&B 92*
Smets, Georges 1915- *WhoScE 91-2*
Smets, Joannes Louis *WhoScE 91-2*
Smets, Philippe 1938- *WhoScE 91-2*
Smette, Darryl G. 1947- *St&PR 93*
Smetzer, Michael Bernie 1948- *WhoWrEP 92*
Smeyne, Fred Gary 1940- *St&PR 93*
Smialek, Ralph T. *Law&B 92*
Smialek, Robert Louis 1948- *St&PR 93, WhoIns 93*
Smialek, Thomas Walter, Jr. 1955- *WhoE 93*
Smiddy, Charles J. 1926- *St&PR 93*
Smiddy, Joseph Charles 1920- *WhoAm 92*
Smidof, Michel-Leon 1917- *WhoWor 93*
Smidt, Diedrich T. 1931- *WhoScE 91-3*
Smidt, Helio d1990 *BioIn 17*
Smidt, Seymour 1928- *WhoAm 92, WhoE 93*
Smidt, Stefan 1948- *WhoScE 91-4*
Smidt Olsen, Helge 1933- *WhoScE 91-4*
Smieszek, Zbigniew 1933- *WhoScE 91-4*
Smiga, David L. *Law&B 92*
Smigel, Irwin Elliot 1924- *WhoE 93*
Smight, Jack 1926- *MiSFD 9*
Smigielski, Jozef 1927- *WhoScE 91-4*
Smigly-Ridz, Edward 1886-1939 *DcTwHis*
Smigly-Rydz, Edward 1886-1941 *PolBiDi*
Smigrod, Claudia Merin 1949- *WhoAmW 93*
Smigrod, Daniel Lee 1956- *WhoSSW 93*
Smih, Gary L. 1945- *St&PR 93*
Smijers, Albert(us Antonius) 1888-1957 *Baker 92*
Smilde, K.W. 1933- *WhoScE 91-3*
Smiles, Linda Janet 1942- *WhoAmW 93*
Smiley, Albert Keith 1944- *WhoE 93*
Smiley, D. E. *WhoAm 92*
Smiley, David Bruce 1942- *WhoWor 93*
Smiley, Gail Sander 1964- *WhoAmW 93*
Smiley, Glenn 1910- *EncAACR*
Smiley, Irwin 1928- *WhoE 93*
Smiley, Jane 1949- *BioIn 17*
Smiley, Jane Graves 1949- *WhoAm 92, WhoAmW 93*
Smiley, Joseph Elbert, Jr. 1922- *WhoSSW 93, WhoWor 93*
Smiley, Karen Jane 1961- *WhoEmL 93*
Smiley, Kathryn A. *BioIn 17*
Smiley, Marilynn Jean 1932- *WhoAm 92*
Smiley, Michael S. *Law&B 92*
Smiley, Raymond E. *Law&B 92*
Smiley, Reed J. 1946- *St&PR 93*
Smiley, Robert Herschel 1943- *WhoAm 92*
Smiley, Robert William 1919- *WhoAm 92*
Smiley, Robert William, Jr. 1943- *WhoAm 92*
Smiley, Robert Wilson 1921- *St&PR 93*
Smiley, Ronald Michael 1949- *WhoE 93, WhoEmL 93, WhoWor 93*
Smiley, Terah Leroy 1914- *WhoAm 92, WhoWrEP 92*
Smiley, Virginia Kester 1923- *WhoWrEP 92*
Smiley, Vyron A. 1936- *St&PR 93*
Smiljanic, Gabro 1928- *WhoScE 91-4*
Smilley-Weiner, Debra Ann *Law&B 92*
Smillie, Chas. M., III 1934- *St&PR 93*
Smillie, Thomson John 1942- *WhoAm 92*
Smilowitz, Bertha *WhoAmW 93*
Smilowitz, Henry Martin 1946- *WhoE 93*
Smirfitt, J.A. *WhoScE 91-1*
Smirni, Allan D. *Law&B 92*
Smirni, Allan D. 1939- *St&PR 93*
Smirni, Allan Desmond 1939- *WhoAm 92*
Smirnoff, Mark 1951- *BioIn 17*
Smirnov, Dmitri 1882-1944 *IntDcOp [port]*
Smirnov, Dmitri 1948- *Baker 92*
Smirnov, Dmitri (Alexeievich) 1882-1944 *Baker 92*
Smirnov, Dmitry 1882-1944 *OxDcOp*
Smirnov, Dmitry 1948- *OxDcOp*
Smirnov, Stanislav 1939- *WhoUN 92*
Smirnova, Vera Borisovna 1946- *WhoWor 93*
Smirnova-Chikina, Ekaterina Sergeevna 1893-1979 *BioIn 17*
Smirnov-Sokol'skii, Nikolai Pavlovich *BioIn 17*
Smiszko, Stephan Emil 1929- *St&PR 93*
Smit, Alan Edward 1952- *WhoSSW 93*
Smit, Christian Jacobus Bester 1927- *WhoSSW 93*
Smit, Cor J. 1948- *WhoScE 91-3*
Smit, Jacobus Wilhelmus 1930- *WhoAm 92*
Smit, Leo 1900-1943 *Baker 92*
Smit, Leo 1921- *Baker 92*
Smit, Wilhelm 1933- *WhoScE 91-3*
Smit, Wim Andries 1943- *WhoWor 93*
Smith, A.C. 1925- *ScF&FL 92*
Smith, A.C.H. 1935- *ScF&FL 92*
Smith, A. David *WhoScE 91-1*
Smith, A(lbert) J(ames) 1924-1991 *ConAu 136*
Smith, A. Jeffrey *Law&B 92*
Smith, A.R. *St&PR 93*
Smith, A. Robert 1925- *WhoAm 92, WhoWrEP 92*
Smith, A. Thomas, III *Law&B 92*
Smith, Ada 1894-1984 *Baker 92*
Smith, Ada L. *AfrAmBi [port]*
Smith, Ada L. 1945- *WhoAmW 93*
Smith, Adam 1723-1790 *BioIn 17*
Smith, Adam 1930- *WhoAm 92*
Smith, Adrian Devaun 1944- *WhoAm 92*
Smith, Adrian F.M. *WhoScE 91-1*
Smith, Adrian John *WhoScE 91-1*
Smith, Agnes *WhoAm 92*
Smith, Agnes Monroe 1920- *WhoAmW 93*
Smith, Al 1873-1944 *PolPar*
Smith, Al 1928- *BioIn 17*
Smith, Alan *WhoScE 91-1*
Smith, Alan F. 1939- *St&PR 93*
Smith, Alan Frederick 1939- *WhoAm 92*
Smith, Alan Harvey 1920- *WhoAm 92, WhoWrEP 92*
Smith, Alan Jay 1949- *WhoAm 92*
Smith, Alan Lamont 1925- *WhoE 93*
Smith, Alan McKinley 1937- *WhoAm 92*
Smith, Albert Aldous 1944- *St&PR 93*
Smith, Albert Aloysius, Jr. 1935- *WhoAm 92*
Smith, Albert Brewster 1930- *ScF&FL 92*
Smith, Albert Carl 1934- *WhoSSW 93*
Smith, Albert Charles 1906- *WhoAm 92*
Smith, Albert Edward 1935- *St&PR 93*
Smith, Albert K. 1925- *St&PR 93*
Smith, Albert Matthews 1927- *WhoE 93*
Smith, Alec James *WhoScE 91-1*
Smith, Alexander, Jr. 1944- *WhoIns 93*
Smith, Alexander Forbes 1929- *St&PR 93*
Smith, Alexander Forbes, III 1929- *WhoAm 92*
Smith, Alexander Goudy 1919- *WhoAm 92, WhoSSW 93, WhoWor 93*
Smith, Alexander John Court 1934- *WhoAm 92*
Smith, Alexander Wyly, Jr. 1923- *WhoAm 92*
Smith, Alexis 1921- *WhoAm 92*
Smith, Alfred *BioIn 17*
Smith, Alfred Emanuel 1873-1944 *DcTwHis*
Smith, Alfred Goud 1921- *WhoAm 92*
Smith, Alfred P. 1954- *St&PR 93*
Smith, Alice Jean 1934- *WhoWrEP 92*
Smith, Alice K(imball) 1907- *ConAu 138*
Smith, Alice Mary 1839-1884 *Baker 92*
Smith, Alice Mary 1879- *AmWomPl*
Smith, Alice Murray 1930- *WhoAmW 93*
Smith, Alison 1932- *DcAmChF 1960*
Smith, Alison M. *WhoScE 91-1*
Smith, Alistair *WhoScE 91-1*
Smith, Allan 1949- *WhoE 93*
Smith, Allan Frederick 1911- *WhoAm 92*
Smith, Allan Lloyd- *ScF&FL 92*
Smith, Allen Anderson 1939- *WhoSSW 93*
Smith, Allen E. 1949- *BioIn 17*
Smith, Allen Elmer 1932- *WhoAm 92*
Smith, Allen F. 1939- *St&PR 93*
Smith, Allen Harold 1925- *WhoWor 93*
Smith, Allen Marion 1929- *St&PR 93*
Smith, Allen O. 1931- *St&PR 93*
Smith, Allie Maitland 1934- *WhoAm 92, WhoSSW 93*
Smith, Althea Marie 1950- *WhoE 93*
Smith, Alvin A. 1938- *St&PR 93*
Smith, Alvin James 1942- *WhoScE 91-1*
Smith, Amanda *WhoAm 92*
Smith, Amanda Joan Mackay 1940- *WhoSSW 93*
Smith, Amos Brittain, III 1944- *WhoAm 92*
Smith, Amy Abernethy 1964- *WhoAmW 93*
Smith, Andrea Pedersen 1944- *WhoAmW 93*
Smith, Andrew *BioIn 17, ScF&FL 92*
Smith, Andrew Alfred, Jr. 1947- *WhoE 93, WhoEmL 93*
Smith, Andrew Charles *WhoScE 91-1*
Smith, Andrew Creighton 1953- *WhoSSW 93*
Smith, Andrew Leonard 1949- *WhoWor 93*
Smith, Andrew Paul *WhoScE 91-1*
Smith, Andrew V. 1924- *St&PR 93*
Smith, Andrew Vaughn 1924- *WhoAm 92*
Smith, Angus Frank 1941- *St&PR 93, WhoAm 92*
Smith, Anita 1954- *WhoAmW 93*
Smith, Anna Deavere 1950- *WhoAmW 93*
Smith, Anna Lois *BlkAmWO*
Smith, Anna Maria 1958- *WhoAmW 93*
Smith, Anne Bowman 1934- *WhoAmW 93, WhoE 93*
Smith, Anne Mollegen *WhoWrEP 92*
Smith, Anne Mollegen 1940- *WhoAm 92, WhoAmW 93*
Smith, Annette Huggins 1942- *WhoSSW 93*
Smith, Annette L. *AmWomPl*
Smith, Annie *WhoWrEP 92*
Smith, Anthony David *WhoScE 91-1*
Smith, Anthony Wayne d1992 *NewYTBS 92*
Smith, Anthony Wayne 1906-1992 *BioIn 17*
Smith, Anthony Wayne 1954- *WhoSSW 93*
Smith, Apollo Milton Olin 1911- *WhoAm 92*
Smith, Arlene *SoulM*
Smith, Arnold Lowell 1954- *WhoSSW 93*
Smith, Arthur 1921- *WhoAm 92*
Smith, Arthur Beverly, Jr. 1944- *WhoAm 92*
Smith, Arthur H. *Law&B 92*
Smith, Arthur J. 1938- *St&PR 93*
Smith, Arthur John Stewart 1938- *WhoAm 92*
Smith, Arthur Kittredge, Jr. 1937- *WhoAm 92*
Smith, Arthur L. 1952- *St&PR 93*
Smith, Arthur Mathews, Jr. 1922- *WhoAm 92*
Smith, Arthur Ronald 1941- *St&PR 93*
Smith, Arvin H. 1929- *St&PR 93*
Smith, Azariah d1912 *BioIn 17*
Smith, Baker Armstrong 1947- *WhoAm 92*
Smith, Barbara *Law&B 92*
Smith, Barbara 1947- *BioIn 17*
Smith, Barbara 1952- *WhoAmW 93*
Smith, Barbara Anne 1941- *WhoAmW 93*
Smith, Barbara Barnard 1920- *WhoAm 92, WhoWor 93*
Smith, Barbara Burnham 1949- *WhoAmW 93*
Smith, Barbara Dail 1949- *WhoEmL 93*
Smith, Barbara Darling 1954- *WhoE 93*
Smith, Barbara Elaine Attaya 1963- *WhoAmW 93*
Smith, Barbara Gail 1957- *WhoWor 93*
Smith, Barbara Herrnstein 1932- *WhoWrEP 92*
Smith, Barbara Jeanne 1939- *WhoAm 92*
Smith, Barbara Roderick 1948- *WhoAmW 93*
Smith, Barbara T. 1931- *BioIn 17*
Smith, Barnard Elliot 1926- *WhoAm 92*
Smith, Barry *WhoScE 91-1*
Smith, Barry Alan 1945- *WhoSSW 93*

Smith, Barry David 1938- WhoAm 92, WhoE 93
Smith, Barry Decker 1940- WhoE 93
Smith, Barry Dell 1951- WhoSSW 93
Smith, Barry E. WhoScE 91-1
Smith, Barry H. 1949- WhoIns 93
Smith, Barry Hamilton 1943- WhoWor 93
Smith, Barry Paul Law&B 92
Smith, Barry Richard Law&B 92
Smith, Barton A. Law&B 92
Smith, Barton D. 1947- WhoIns 93
Smith, Barton Douglas 1947- St&PR 93
Smith, Basil A. 1908-1969 ScF&FL 92
Smith, Basil F.L. WhoScE 91-1
Smith, Benjamin BioIn 17
Smith, Benjamin 1776-1857 BioIn 17
Smith, Benjamin A. 1916-1991 BioIn 17
Smith, Benjamin A., III 1943- St&PR 93
Smith, Benjamin F. 1922- St&PR 93
Smith, Bernard d1991 BioIn 17
Smith, Bernard c. 1630-1708 Baker 92
Smith, Bernard Brussel- 1914- BioIn 17
Smith, Bernice Driskell 1916- WhoAmW 93, WhoE 93, WhoWor 93
Smith, Bernita Louise 1952- WhoWrEP 92
Smith, Bert Kruger 1915- WhoAm 92, WhoAmW 93
Smith, Bertie Reece 1913- WhoWrEP 92
Smith, Bertrand Dean 1929- WhoE 93
Smith, Beryl Kircaldie 1935- WhoAmW 93
Smith, Bess Foster AmWomPl
Smith, Bessie BioIn 17
Smith, Bessie 1894-1937 Baker 92, ConBlB 3 [port]
Smith, Bessie Blair AmWomPl
Smith, Betsi BioIn 17
Smith, Betsy Keiser 1960- WhoSSW 93
Smith, Bettie Jones 1951- WhoAmW 93
Smith, Betty WhoAmW 93, WhoE 93
Smith, Betty Denny 1932- WhoAmW 93
Smith, Betty Faye 1930- WhoAm 92
Smith, Betty Loretta 1937- WhoWor 93
Smith, Beverly Ann 1950- WhoAmW 93
Smith, Beverly Ann Evans 1948- WhoSSW 93
Smith, Bill d1902 BioIn 17
Smith, Billie M. 1933- WhoAm 92
Smith, Blake, Jr. 1912- St&PR 93
Smith, Bobbi ConAu 137
Smith, Bobby BioIn 17
Smith, Bobby Lee BioIn 17
Smith, Bonnie Beatrice 1948- WhoAmW 93
Smith, Bonnie Lou 1944- WhoE 93
Smith, Bradford, III 1937- St&PR 93
Smith, Bradford T. Law&B 92
Smith, Brenda Grumblatt WhoAmW 93
Smith, Brenda Thompson 1944- WhoSSW 93
Smith, Brian BioIn 17
Smith, Brian 1949- ConAu 139
Smith, Brian Douglas 1945- St&PR 93
Smith, Brian Francis Law&B 92
Smith, Brian J. Law&B 92
Smith, Brian Richard 1952- WhoE 93, WhoEmL 93, WhoWor 93
Smith, Brian William 1947- WhoE 93, WhoEmL 93
Smith, Brice Reynolds, Jr. WhoAm 92
Smith, Bridget Ann 1949- WhoWrEP 92
Smith, Brigitte 1938- BioIn 17
Smith, Bruce BioIn 17, MiSFD 9, WhoScE 91-1
Smith, Bruce 1963- WhoAm 92
Smith, Bruce Alfred 1943- St&PR 93
Smith, Bruce David 1946- WhoAm 92
Smith, Bruce N. 1930- St&PR 93
Smith, Bruce R. 1946- ConAu 139
Smith, Bruce Stewart 1954- WhoSSW 93
Smith, Bruce Warren 1952- WhoEmL 93
Smith, Bryan F., Jr. Law&B 92
Smith, Bryan W. 1948- St&PR 93
Smith, Bud MiSFD 9
Smith, Buddy BioIn 17
Smith, Buelah AmWomPl
Smith, Buffalo Bob 1917- BioIn 17
Smith, Buster 1904-1991 BioIn 17
Smith, Byron C. 1908-1990 BioIn 17
Smith, Byron Capleese 1908- WhoAm 92
Smith, Byron Owen 1916- WhoAm 92
Smith, C. Alan 1944- St&PR 93
Smith, C. Alphonso 1864-1924 ScF&FL 92
Smith, C. Kenneth 1918- WhoAm 92
Smith, C.L. 1938- St&PR 93
Smith, C. LeMoyne 1934- St&PR 93, WhoAm 92
Smith, C.R. BioIn 17
Smith, C. R. 1899-1990 EncABHB 8 [port]
Smith, C. Thomas, Jr. 1938- WhoAm 92
Smith, C. Vandiver Law&B 92
Smith, C.W. St&PR 93
Smith, C. Wendell 1908- St&PR 93
Smith, Cal Joseph 1955- WhoSSW 93
Smith, Calvert H. AfrAmBi [port]
Smith, Calvin Bruce 1940- WhoAm 92
Smith, Calvin C. 1920- St&PR 93
Smith, Calvin J. St&PR 93
Smith, Capers F., Jr. 1945- WhoIns 93
Smith, Cara Lockhart ScF&FL 92
Smith, Carl Dean, Jr. 1949- WhoE 93
Smith, Carl E. 1948- St&PR 93
Smith, Carl Edward Law&B 92
Smith, Carl Edwin 1954- WhoSSW 93
Smith, Carl Hofland 1942- WhoE 93
Smith, Carl O. 1942- St&PR 93
Smith, Carl Richard 1933- WhoAm 92
Smith, Carl Walter, Jr. 1927- WhoAm 92
Smith, Carla Walser 1953- WhoSSW 93
Smith, Carleton Sprague 1905- Baker 92, BioIn 17
Smith, Carlos C. Law&B 92
Smith, Carmela Vito 1950- WhoE 93
Smith, Carol Ann 1941- WhoAm 92
Smith, Carol Ann 1951- WhoEmL 93
Smith, Carol Denise 1961- WhoAmW 93
Smith, Carol E. Law&B 92
Smith, Carol Miller 1938- WhoAmW 93
Smith, Carol Sturm 1938- WhoWrEP 92
Smith, Carole J. 1949- St&PR 93
Smith, Carolyn Jane Hostetter 1938- WhoE 93
Smith, Carolyn Jeanne 1946- WhoAmW 93
Smith, Carolyn Robinson 1968- WhoAmW 93
Smith, Carolyn Sue 1935- WhoAmW 93
Smith, Carroll B. 1936- WhoIns 93
Smith, Catherine Frances 1931- WhoAmW 93
Smith, Catherine Weinrich 1953- St&PR 93
Smith, Catherine Yore 1944- WhoWrEP 92
Smith, Cathy L. Law&B 92
Smith, Cece 1944- WhoAm 92
Smith, Cedric Martin 1927- WhoE 93
Smith, Celeste A. Law&B 92
Smith, Chad BioIn 17
Smith, Chad c. 1963- See Red Hot Chili Peppers, The News 93-1
Smith, Charlene 1938- WhoAmW 93
Smith, Charles 1767-1848 BioIn 17
Smith, Charles 1947- WhoWrEP 92
Smith, Charles A. 1908- St&PR 93
Smith, Charles Alphonso 1909- WhoAm 92
Smith, Charles Alvah 1866-1946 BioIn 17
Smith, Charles Bradford 1916- HarEnMi
Smith, Charles C., Jr. 1948- WhoEmL 93
Smith, Charles E. Law&B 92
Smith, Charles Edward 1939- WhoAm 92, WhoSSW 93
Smith, Charles Emory 1842-1908 JrnUS
Smith, Charles Evan 1960- WhoE 93
Smith, Charles F. 1940- St&PR 93
Smith, Charles Francis 1932- St&PR 93
Smith, Charles Gordon, Jr. 1942- St&PR 93
Smith, Charles Haddon 1926- WhoAm 92
Smith, Charles Hayden 1933- St&PR 93
Smith, Charles Henry 1826-1903 JrnUS
Smith, Charles Henry, Jr. 1920- St&PR 93, WhoAm 92
Smith, Charles Isaac 1931- WhoAm 92
Smith, Charles J. 1927- St&PR 93
Smith, Charles Joe, Sr. 1951- WhoEmL 93
Smith, Charles Kent 1938- WhoAm 92
Smith, Charles L. 1928-1990 BioIn 17
Smith, Charles L., Jr. 1928- St&PR 93
Smith, Charles Madison 1948- WhoSSW 93, WhoWor 93
Smith, Charles Martin 1953- MiSFD 9
Smith, Charles Owen, Jr. 1921- St&PR 93
Smith, Charles Paul 1926- WhoAm 92
Smith, Charles Philip 1932- WhoAm 92
Smith, Charles Quinton 1939- WhoE 93
Smith, Charles Ronald Cooper 1946- WhoSSW 93
Smith, Charles T. Law&B 92
Smith, Charles Thomas 1914- WhoAm 92
Smith, Charles Whitley 1913- WhoAm 92
Smith, Charles William 1926- WhoSSW 93
Smith, Charles William 1936- WhoE 93
Smith, Charles Wilson, Jr 1949- WhoAm 92
Smith, Charles Z. 1927- AfrAmBi, WhoAm 92
Smith, Charlotte Mitchell Law&B 92
Smith, Charlotte Reed 1921- WhoAmW 93
Smith, Charlotte Turner 1749-1806 BioIn 17
Smith, Chas 1948- Baker 92
Smith, Cheryl BioIn 17
Smith, Cheryl A. ScF&FL 92
Smith, Cheryl Ann 1964- WhoAmW 93
Smith, Cheryl Deon-Newton 1956- WhoAmW 93
Smith, Cheryl S. 1949- WhoWrEP 92
Smith, Chester 1930- WhoWor 93
Smith, Chester Leo 1922- WhoAm 92, WhoWrEP 92
Smith, Chris BioIn 17, NewYTBS 92 [port]
Smith, Christina Ann 1947- WhoWrEP 92
Smith, Christine Donohue 1948- WhoE 93
Smith, Christine M. Law&B 92
Smith, Christopher Case 1934- WhoAm 92
Smith, Christopher H. 1953- BioIn 17, CngDr 91
Smith, Christopher Henry 1953- WhoAm 92, WhoE 93
Smith, Christopher Joe 1955- St&PR 93
Smith, Christopher Robin 1959- WhoE 93
Smith, Christopher Russell 1953- WhoE 93
Smith, Christopher St. John BioIn 17
Smith, Cindy T. Law&B 92
Smith, Clara May Freeman 1912- WhoWrEP 92
Smith, Clarence 1904-1929 Baker 92
Smith, Clarence Lavett 1927- WhoAm 92
Smith, Clark Ashton 1893-1961 ScF&FL 92
Smith, Claude D. 1925- St&PR 93
Smith, Clay M. Law&B 92
Smith, Clayton Alexander 1959- WhoE 93
Smith, Clayton Benke- 1959- BioIn 17
Smith, Clayton G. Law&B 92
Smith, Clive A. MiSFD 9
Smith, Clodus Ray 1928- WhoAm 92
Smith, Colin WhoScE 91-1
Smith, Colin Stansfield BioIn 17
Smith, Connie Umland WhoAmW 93
Smith, Constance Fletcher Law&B 92
Smith, Constance O'Neta 1935- WhoAmW 93
Smith, Cordwainer 1913-1966 ScF&FL 92
Smith, Corinne Roth 1945- WhoE 93
Smith, Corlies Morgan 1929- WhoAm 92
Smith, Cornelia Marschall 1895- WhoAmW 93
Smith, Cornelius C., Jr. 1941- St&PR 93, WhoAm 92
Smith, Cotter BioIn 17
Smith, Courtland Clement, Jr. 1927- WhoSSW 93
Smith, Courtney Charles 1947- WhoIns 93
Smith, Covey Leroy 1942- WhoIns 93
Smith, Craig I. Law&B 92
Smith, Craig R. 1940- St&PR 93
Smith, Craig Richards 1940- WhoAm 92
Smith, Craig T. Law&B 92
Smith, Craig W. Law&B 92
Smith, Cullen 1925- WhoAm 92
Smith, Curtis ScF&FL 92
Smith, Curtis C. 1939- ScF&FL 92
Smith, Curtis Johnston 1947- WhoAm 92
Smith, Curtis O(tto) B(ismarck) Curtis- Baker 92
Smith, Cynthia St&PR 93
Smith, Cynthia Dodd Law&B 92
Smith, Cynthia E. Law&B 92
Smith, Cynthia Lou 1953- WhoAmW 93
Smith, Cynthia Marlene 1951- WhoAmW 93
Smith, Cynthia Mary Law&B 92
Smith, Cyril (James) 1909-1974 Baker 92
Smith, Cyril James 1930- St&PR 93, WhoAm 92
Smith, Cyril Stanley d1992 NewYTBS 92 [port]
Smith, Cyril Stanley 1903-1992 CurBio 92N
Smith, Cyrus Rowlett BioIn 17
Smith, D. Alexander 1953- ScF&FL 92
Smith, D. Geoffrey WhoScE 91-1
Smith, D. Lamar 1936- St&PR 93
Smith, D.M. WhoScE 91-1
Smith, D. Richard 1930- WhoAm 92
Smith, DaCosta, Jr. 1917- WhoAm 92, WhoSSW 93
Smith, Dale Austin 1952- WhoE 93
Smith, Dale B. 1944- St&PR 93, WhoAm 92
Smith, Dan F. WhoSSW 93
Smith, Daniel 1765-1810 BioIn 17
Smith, Daniel Albert 1951- WhoE 93
Smith, Daniel Carpenter Law&B 92
Smith, Daniel Curtis 1948- WhoSSW 93
Smith, Daniel James 1944- WhoE 93
Smith, Daniel James 1957- WhoSSW 93
Smith, Daniel R. 1934- St&PR 93, WhoAm 92
Smith, Daniel S.M. Law&B 92
Smith, Danny Leon 1958- WhoSSW 93
Smith, Danny LeRoy 1953- WhoSSW 93
Smith, Danny Ray 1954- WhoSSW 93
Smith, Darlene St&PR 93
Smith, Darwin Eatna 1926- WhoAm 92, WhoSSW 93, WhoWor 93
Smith, Daryl D. 1940- St&PR 93
Smith, Datus Clifford, Jr. 1907- WhoAm 92
Smith, Dave 1942- BioIn 17
Smith, David Albert 1952- WhoSSW 93
Smith, David B. d1992 NewYTBS 92
Smith, David Brookman 1951- WhoAm 92
Smith, David C. Law&B 92
Smith, David C. 1929- ScF&FL 92
Smith, David C. 1952- ScF&FL 92
Smith, David Callaway 1941- WhoAm 92
Smith, David Carr 1944- WhoWor 93
Smith, David Charles WhoWrEP 92
Smith, David Claiborne 1953- WhoSSW 93
Smith, David Clark 1937- WhoAm 92
Smith, David Clayton 1929- WhoE 93
Smith, David D. 1923- St&PR 93
Smith, David Doyle 1956- WhoSSW 93
Smith, David E. 1952- St&PR 93
Smith, David Edmund 1934- WhoAm 92
Smith, David Edward 1939- WhoSSW 93, WhoWor 93
Smith, David Elvin 1939- WhoWor 93
Smith, David English 1920- WhoAm 92
Smith, David Ernest 1934- WhoUN 92
Smith, David F. Law&B 92
Smith, David Gilbert 1926- WhoAm 92
Smith, David Haughton 1947- St&PR 93
Smith, David J.H. 1941- WhoScE 91-1
Smith, David J.M. WhoScE 91-1
Smith, David James Law&B 92
Smith, David Jeddie 1942- BioIn 17, WhoAm 92, WhoWrEP 92
Smith, David John WhoScE 91-1
Smith, David K. Law&B 92
Smith, David Kingman 1928- St&PR 93
Smith, David Larry 1943- WhoE 93
Smith, David Lee 1939- WhoAm 92
Smith, David Lionel 1954- WhoE 93, WhoWrEP 92
Smith, David Martin 1948- WhoAm 92
Smith, David Martyn 1921- WhoAm 92
Smith, David N. 1952- ScF&FL 92
Smith, David Paul 1944- WhoSSW 93
Smith, David R. 1946- St&PR 93
Smith, David Richard, Jr. 1925- St&PR 93
Smith, David Rollins 1950- WhoWor 93
Smith, David Ryan 1952- WhoSSW 93
Smith, David Shiverick 1918- WhoAm 92
Smith, David Stanley 1877-1949 Baker 92
Smith, David Stephen 1943- WhoSSW 93
Smith, David Thornton 1935- WhoAm 92
Smith, David Todd 1953- St&PR 93, WhoAm 92
Smith, David Tyler 1953- St&PR 93
Smith, David VanMeter ScF&FL 92
Smith, David Waldo Edward 1934- WhoAm 92
Smith, David Warren WhoScE 91-1
Smith, David Wayne 1927- WhoAm 92
Smith, David Wayne 1955- WhoSSW 93
Smith, David William Law&B 92
Smith, Dean 1925- WhoE 93, WhoWor 93
Smith, Dean 1931- BioIn 17
Smith, Dean Edwards 1931- WhoAm 92, WhoSSW 93
Smith, Dean Wesley 1950- ScF&FL 92
Smith, Debbi Lynn 1959- WhoWrEP 92
Smith, Deborah Ann 1948- WhoAmW 93
Smith, Deborah Ann King 1951- WhoAmW 93
Smith, Deborah Lynn 1954- WhoEmL 93
Smith, Deborah Nieman 1951- WhoAmW 93
Smith, Debra R. Law&B 92
Smith, Delford Michael 1930- St&PR 93
Smith, Denis L. 1942- WhoScE 91-1
Smith, Denis Mack 1920- BioIn 17
Smith, Denise Groleau 1951- WhoAmW 93, WhoE 93, WhoEmL 93
Smith, Denise Lockett 1951- WhoAmW 93
Smith, Denise Myrtle 1955- WhoAmW 93
Smith, Dennis C. Law&B 92
Smith, Dennis C. 1933- St&PR 93
Smith, Dennis Dustin 1949- WhoWor 93
Smith, Dennis E. 1947- St&PR 93
Smith, Dennis Edward 1940- WhoAm 92
Smith, Dennis Edward 1945- WhoE 93
Smith, Dennis J. 1940- St&PR 93
Smith, Dennis Lee 1945- WhoSSW 93
Smith, Dennis Paul Law&B 92
Smith, Dennis R. Law&B 92
Smith, Derek Austin WhoScE 91-1
Smith, Derek V. WhoIns 93
Smith, Diane B. 1947- St&PR 93
Smith, Diane Elizabeth 1967- WhoAmW 93
Smith, Diane Valerie 1961- WhoAmW 93
Smith, Diann DeWeese BioIn 17
Smith, Dianna Lynne 1945- WhoSSW 93
Smith, Dick King- ScF&FL 92
Smith, Dickinson M. 1933- St&PR 93
Smith, Dinitia 1945- ConAu 136
Smith, Dodie ConAu 37NR, MajAI
Smith, Dodie 1896-1990 BioIn 17, ScF&FL 92
Smith, Dolores Maxine Plunk 1926- WhoWor 93
Smith, Dolores Snyder 1937- WhoSSW 93
Smith, Don A. Law&B 92
Smith, Donald A. Law&B 92
Smith, Donald Albert 1931- WhoSSW 93
Smith, Donald Bruce 1942- WhoAm 92

Smith, Donald C. 1935- *WhoE 93*
Smith, Donald Charles 1957- *WhoE 93*
Smith, Donald E. 1926- *St&PR 93*
Smith, Donald Eugene 1926- *WhoAm 92*
Smith, Donald Eugene 1934- *WhoSSW 93*
Smith, Donald Everett 1945- *WhoSSW 93*
Smith, Donald Gene 1941- *WhoAm 92*
Smith, Donald Hugh 1932- *WhoE 93*
Smith, Donald Kaye *Law&B 92*
Smith, Donald Kaye 1932- *St&PR 93, WhoAm 92, WhoIns 93*
Smith, Donald L., Jr. 1921- *St&PR 93*
Smith, Donald Raymond 1946- *WhoSSW 93*
Smith, Donald S. *Law&B 92*
Smith, Donald William 1906-1991 *BioIn 17*
Smith, Donald William 1933- *WhoAm 92*
Smith, Donald William 1934- *WhoSSW 93*
Smith, Donn L. 1915- *WhoAm 92*
Smith, Donna 1954- *WhoAm 92, WhoAmW 93*
Smith, Donna Beck 1954- *WhoAmW 93*
Smith, Donna Dearman 1949- *WhoSSW 93*
Smith, Donna Dyer *Law&B 92*
Smith, Donna Emerson 1958- *WhoSSW 93*
Smith, Donna Marie 1958- *WhoAmW 93, WhoSSW 93*
Smith, Donnetta Kay 1944- *WhoWrEP 92*
Smith, Donnie Louise 1952- *WhoAmW 93*
Smith, Dora V. *BioIn 17*
Smith, Dora Valentine 1893- *AmWomPl*
Smith, Doris *AmWomPl*
Smith, Doris Anita 1935- *St&PR 93*
Smith, Doris Balckwell 1945- *WhoAmW 93*
Smith, Doris Buchanan 1934- *DcAmChF 1960, DcAmChF 1985, MajAI [port], ScF&FL 92*
Smith, Doris Corinne Kemp 1919- *WhoAmW 93*
Smith, Doris Helen 1930- *WhoAmW 93*
Smith, Dorland Worth 1931- *St&PR 93*
Smith, Dorothy E. 1926- *BioIn 17*
Smith, Dorothy G. *ScF&FL 92*
Smith, Dorothy Gladys 1896-1990 *ConAu 37NR, MajAI*
Smith, Dorothy H. 1920- *St&PR 93*
Smith, Dorothy Louise 1946- *WhoSSW 93*
Smith, Dorothy Ottinger 1922- *WhoWor 93*
Smith, Douglas A. 1960- *WhoIns 93*
Smith, Douglas Burnet 1949- *WhoCanL 92*
Smith, Douglas Donel *Law&B 92*
Smith, Douglas G. 1940- *St&PR 93*
Smith, Douglas Gordon *WhoScE 91-1*
Smith, Douglas James 1965- *WhoE 93*
Smith, Douglas Oakley *Law&B 92*
Smith, Douglas Oster 1942- *St&PR 93*
Smith, Douglas R. 1915- *St&PR 93*
Smith, Douglas Sydney 1929- *WhoAm 92*
Smith, Drayton Beecher, II 1949- *WhoSSW 93*
Smith, Duckie *AmWomPl*
Smith, Dudley R. 1937- *St&PR 93*
Smith, Dudley Renwick 1937- *WhoAm 92, WhoIns 93*
Smith, Dwight Leon 1946- *St&PR 93*
Smith, Dwight Morrell 1931- *WhoAm 92*
Smith, Dwight Raymond 1921- *WhoAm 92*
Smith, E. E. 1890-1965 *BioIn 17, ScF&FL 92*
Smith, E. Everett d1991 *BioIn 17*
Smith, E.G. *BioIn 17*
Smith, E. Harlin 1933- *St&PR 93*
Smith, Earl Edward Tailer 1903-1991 *BioIn 17*
Smith, Earl Harold 1939- *WhoE 93*
Smith, Earl Pearson 1931- *WhoSSW 93*
Smith, Eberle Minard 1905- *WhoAm 92*
Smith, Eddie 1932- *WhoSSW 93*
Smith, Edgar A. *Law&B 92*
Smith, Edgar Benton 1932- *WhoAm 92*
Smith, Edgar Eugene 1934- *WhoAm 92*
Smith, Edgar J., Jr. *Law&B 92*
Smith, Edgar James, Jr. 1934- *WhoAm 92*
Smith, Edmund Kirby- 1824-1893 *BioIn 17*
Smith, Edward 1819-1874 *BioIn 17*
Smith, Edward A. 1918- *St&PR 93*
Smith, Edward Byron 1909- *St&PR 93*
Smith, Edward C. 1948- *St&PR 93*
Smith, Edward Elmer 1890-1965 *BioIn 17*
Smith, Edward Hardin, Jr. 1934- *WhoSSW 93*
Smith, Edward Herbert 1936- *WhoAm 92*
Smith, Edward Hughes *WhoScE 91-1*
Smith, Edward K. 1922- *WhoAm 92, WhoE 93*
Smith, Edward Lee *Law&B 92*
Smith, Edward Michael 1932- *WhoUN 92*
Smith, Edward Reaugh 1932- *WhoAm 92, WhoSSW 93*
Smith, Edward Samuel 1919- *CngDr 91, WhoAm 92*
Smith, Edwin *WhoScE 91-1*
Smith, Edwin Ely 1914- *St&PR 93*
Smith, Edwin Ide 1924- *WhoAm 92, WhoSSW 93*
Smith, Edwin Lee 1956- *WhoE 93*
Smith, Elaine Diana 1924- *WhoAm 92*
Smith, Elden Leroy 1940- *St&PR 93, WhoAm 92*
Smith, Eldred Gee 1907- *WhoAm 92*
Smith, Eldred Reid 1931- *WhoAm 92*
Smith, Eleanor R. 1932- *St&PR 93*
Smith, Elise Fiber 1932- *WhoAm 92, WhoAmW 93*
Smith, Elizabeth 1943- *WhoE 93*
Smith, Elizabeth Ann *Law&B 92*
Smith, Elizabeth Anne 1934- *WhoAmW 93*
Smith, Elizabeth Eugenia 1960- *WhoAmW 93*
Smith, Elizabeth Hull 1956- *WhoAmW 93*
Smith, Elizabeth M. 1951- *St&PR 93*
Smith, Elizabeth Patience 1949- *WhoAm 92*
Smith, Ella 1933- *ScF&FL 92*
Smith, Ellen M. 1949- *St&PR 93*
Smith, Ellen Margaret 1950- *WhoAmW 93*
Smith, Elliott L. 1934- *St&PR 93*
Smith, Elmer L. 1943- *St&PR 93*
Smith, Elouise Beard 1920- *WhoSSW 93*
Smith, Elske Van Panhuys 1929- *WhoAmW 93*
Smith, Elton Edward 1915- *WhoSSW 93*
Smith, Elva E. *Law&B 92*
Smith, Elvie Lawrence 1926- *WhoAm 92*
Smith, Elvin E. 1943- *St&PR 93*
Smith, Elwin Earl 1922- *WhoAm 92*
Smith, Emerson Warfield 1922- *WhoE 93*
Smith, Emery William *Law&B 92*
Smith, Emil L. 1911- *WhoAm 92*
Smith, Emmet Carter 1948- *WhoAm 92*
Smith, Emmitt *BioIn 17*
Smith, Emmitt J., III 1969- *WhoAm 92*
Smith, Ephraim Philip 1942- *WhoAm 92*
Smith, Eric Lyndon *WhoScE 91-1*
Smith, Eric Morgan 1953- *WhoSSW 93*
Smith, Eric Parkman 1910- *WhoE 93, WhoWor 93*
Smith, Eric Trent 1959- *WhoAm 92*
Smith, Eric Wilburn, Jr. 1916- *WhoAm 92*
Smith, Ernest Ketcham 1922- *WhoAm 92, WhoWor 93*
Smith, Ernest V. *WhoScE 91-1*
Smith, Esther Thomas 1939- *WhoAmW 93, WhoWor 93*
Smith, Ethel M. *AmWomPl*
Smith, Eugene F. 1933- *St&PR 93*
Smith, Eugene P. 1921- *WhoAm 92*
Smith, Eugene Willis 1947- *WhoE 93*
Smith, Eugene Wilson 1930- *WhoAm 92, WhoSSW 93*
Smith, Eugenia Sewell 1922- *WhoWor 93*
Smith, Evajune *BioIn 17*
Smith, Evelyn 1952- *St&PR 93*
Smith, Evelyn E. 1927- *ScF&FL 92*
Smith, Everett 1892-1991 *BioIn 17*
Smith, Everett G. 1909- *St&PR 93*
Smith, Everett Raymond 1929- *St&PR 93*
Smith, Evieline Lates *ScF&FL 92*
Smith, Ezra Sheldon 1931- *WhoE 93*
Smith, F.G. Walton *BioIn 17*
Smith, F.W. *WhoScE 91-1*
Smith, Felice A. 1935- *WhoSSW 93*
Smith, Felix C. 1918- *St&PR 93*
Smith, Fern M. 1933- *WhoAm 92, WhoAmW 93*
Smith, Florence F. *AmWomPl*
Smith, Florence Margaret 1902-1971 *BioIn 17*
Smith, Floyd Leslie 1931- *St&PR 93, WhoAm 92*
Smith, Floyd Rodenback 1913- *WhoAm 92*
Smith, Floyd W. *Law&B 92*
Smith, Forrest M. *Law&B 92*
Smith, Fran d1990 *BioIn 17*
Smith, Frances L. 1942- *WhoSSW 93*
Smith, Francie Larrieu 1953?- *BioIn 17*
Smith, Francine Denise 1949- *WhoWrEP 92*
Smith, Francis 1723-1791 *HarEnMi*
Smith, Francis Bradford, Jr. 1942- *WhoAm 92*
Smith, Francis Carlton 1938- *St&PR 93*
Smith, Francis Graham *WhoScE 91-1*
Smith, Francis John *WhoScE 91-1*
Smith, Francis John 1932- *WhoWor 93*
Smith, Francis Peterson 1934- *St&PR 93*
Smith, Frank A. *Law&B 92*
Smith, Frank Ackroyd 1919- *WhoE 93*
Smith, Frank Earl 1931- *WhoAm 92*
Smith, Frank Edward 1912- *WhoAm 92*
Smith, Frank Ellis 1918- *EncAACR*
Smith, Frank G. 1922- *St&PR 93*
Smith, Frank Houston 1903- *WhoSSW 93*
Smith, Frank Kingston 1919- *WhoWrEP 92*
Smith, Frank M. *BioIn 17*
Smith, Frank P. 1938- *St&PR 93*
Smith, Frank S., Jr. 1924- *St&PR 93*
Smith, Frank Thomas *WhoScE 91-1*
Smith, Franklin 1807- *BioIn 17*
Smith, Franklin H., Jr. 1951- *St&PR 93*
Smith, Franklin L. 1943- *WhoE 93*
Smith, Franklin Sumner, Jr. 1924- *WhoAm 92*
Smith, Fred 1948- See MC5, The *ConMus 9*
Smith, Fred Clifton, Jr. 1961- *WhoE 93*
Smith, Fred E. 1929- *St&PR 93*
Smith, Fred L. 1932- *WhoAm 92*
Smith, Fred O. 1934- *St&PR 93*
Smith, Freda L. 1923- *WhoAmW 93*
Smith, Frederick Coe 1916- *WhoAm 92*
Smith, Frederick Edwin 1872-1930 *BioIn 17*
Smith, Frederick Robert, Jr. 1929- *WhoAm 92*
Smith, Frederick Rutledge 1925- *WhoAm 92*
Smith, Frederick W. 1944- *BioIn 17, EncABHB 8 [port], St&PR 93*
Smith, Frederick Wallace 1944- *WhoAm 92, WhoSSW 93*
Smith, Frederik N. 1940- *ScF&FL 92*
Smith, Fredric Homer 1938- *St&PR 93*
Smith, Fredrick H. 1942- *St&PR 93*
Smith, G. E. Kidder 1913- *WhoAm 92*
Smith, G. Emmett *Law&B 92*
Smith, G. Emmett 1928- *St&PR 93*
Smith, G.R. *WhoScE 91-1*
Smith, G. Roysce, Jr. *BioIn 17*
Smith, G. Scott 1951- *St&PR 93*
Smith, Gail Hunter 1948- *WhoE 93, WhoWor 93*
Smith, Gale Eugene 1933- *WhoE 93*
Smith, Gardner Watkins 1931- *WhoAm 92*
Smith, Gary *ScF&FL 92*
Smith, Gary A. 1943- *St&PR 93*
Smith, Gary Ernest 1942- *BioIn 17*
Smith, Gary Evan *Law&B 92*
Smith, Gary F. 1948- *WhoE 93*
Smith, Gary H. 1949- *WhoE 93*
Smith, Gary K. 1938- *St&PR 93*
Smith, Gary L. *Law&B 92*
Smith, Gary M. *Law&B 92*
Smith, Gary Robert 1943- *St&PR 93*
Smith, Gary Vincent 1943- *WhoSSW 93*
Smith, Gary W. 1947- *WhoIns 93*
Smith, Gavin H. *Law&B 92*
Smith, Gavin H. 1945- *St&PR 93*
Smith, Genevieve Douglas 1923- *WhoWrEP 92*
Smith, Genevieve Thompson *AmWomPl*
Smith, Genny Hall 1921- *WhoWrEP 92*
Smith, Geoffrey A. *Law&B 92*
Smith, Geoffrey Adams 1947- *St&PR 93, WhoAm 92*
Smith, Geoffrey Allan *WhoScE 91-1*
Smith, Geoffrey Robin *WhoScE 91-1*
Smith, George Colin 1944- *WhoWor 93*
Smith, George Curtis 1935- *WhoAm 92*
Smith, George Dee 1929- *St&PR 93*
Smith, George Drury 1927- *WhoAm 92*
Smith, George E. *BioIn 17*
Smith, George E. 1916- *St&PR 93*
Smith, George F. *Law&B 92*
Smith, George Foster 1922- *WhoAm 92*
Smith, George H. 1922- *ScF&FL 92*
Smith, George Henry 1873-1931 *JrnUS*
Smith, George Henry 1922- *WhoAm 92*
Smith, George Leonard, Jr. 1935- *WhoAm 92*
Smith, George Monroe 1952- *WhoSSW 93*
Smith, George O. 1911-1981 *ScF&FL 92*
Smith, George Patrick, II 1939- *WhoAm 92*
Smith, George Robert 1936- *WhoSSW 93*
Smith, George S., Jr. *BioIn 17*
Smith, George S., Jr. 1948- *St&PR 93, WhoAm 92*
Smith, George Thornewell 1916- *WhoAm 92, WhoSSW 93*
Smith, George V.R. 1937- *WhoIns 93*
Smith, George Wolfram 1932- *WhoAm 92*
Smith, Georges *Law&B 92*
Smith, Gerald C. *St&PR 93*
Smith, Gerald John *WhoScE 91-1*
Smith, Gerald K. 1950- *St&PR 93*
Smith, Gerald Kendall 1936- *WhoAm 92*
Smith, Gerald M. *Law&B 92*
Smith, Gerald R., Jr. 1953- *St&PR 93*
Smith, Gerald Steven 1962- *WhoE 93*
Smith, Gerard Albert 1929- *St&PR 93*
Smith, Gerard Peter 1935- *WhoAm 92*
Smith, Gerrit 1797-1874 *PolPar*
Smith, Gertrude L. 1910- *St&PR 93*
Smith, Gilbert P. 1937- *St&PR 93*
Smith, Gina Morton 1966- *WhoAmW 93*
Smith, Glee Sidney, Jr. 1921- *WhoAm 92*
Smith, Glen A. *Law&B 92*
Smith, Glenda Faye 1948- *WhoAmW 93*
Smith, Glenn A. 1945- *St&PR 93*
Smith, Glenn Stanley 1945- *WhoAm 92*
Smith, Glenna Virginia 1949- *WhoSSW 93*
Smith, Gloria Richardson 1934- *WhoAm 92*
Smith, Godfrey Taylor 1935- *WhoAm 92*
Smith, Goff 1916- *WhoAm 92*
Smith, Goldwin 1823-1910 *BioIn 17*
Smith, Gordon 1907- *ScF&FL 92*
Smith, Gordon C. 1929- *WhoAm 92*
Smith, Gordon D. 1938- *St&PR 93*
Smith, Gordon Frederick *WhoScE 91-1*
Smith, Gordon H. 1936- *St&PR 93*
Smith, Gordon Howell 1915- *WhoAm 92*
Smith, Gordon L. 1935- *St&PR 93*
Smith, Gordon Laidlaw, Jr. 1926- *St&PR 93, WhoAm 92*
Smith, Gordon Paul 1916- *WhoAm 92, WhoWor 93*
Smith, Gordon R. 1948- *St&PR 93*
Smith, Gordon Ross 1917- *WhoAm 92, WhoWrEP 92*
Smith, Grace E. *AmWomPl*
Smith, Grace Jervis *AmWomPl*
Smith, Grafton Elliot 1871-1937 *IntDcAn*
Smith, Graham *WhoScE 91-1*
Smith, Graham Monro 1947- *WhoE 93*
Smith, Graham Sydney *WhoScE 91-1*
Smith, Grant Warren, II 1941- *WhoAm 92, WhoSSW 93*
Smith, Gregg 1931- *Baker 92*
Smith, Gregory Allgire 1951- *WhoSSW 93*
Smith, Gregory Alling 1950- *St&PR 93*
Smith, Gregory Blake 1951- *ScF&FL 92*
Smith, Gregory Dean 1948- *WhoE 93*
Smith, Gregory Dean 1956- *WhoSSW 93*
Smith, Gregory J. *ScF&FL 92*
Smith, Gregory L. 1917- *St&PR 93*
Smith, Gregory Michael 1941- *WhoE 93*
Smith, Gregory Stuart 1959- *WhoSSW 93*
Smith, Gregory Taylor 1957- *WhoSSW 93*
Smith, Grover Cleveland 1923- *WhoAm 92*
Smith, Gudmund J.W. 1920- *WhoScE 91-4*
Smith, Guy L. 1949- *St&PR 93*
Smith, Guy Lincoln, IV 1949- *WhoAm 92*
Smith, Guy N. 1939- *ScF&FL 92*
Smith, Guy William 1940- *St&PR 93*
Smith, H. *WhoScE 91-1*
Smith, H. Allen 1906-1976 *JrnUS*
Smith, H. Gene 1934- *St&PR 93*
Smith, H. Morgan 1942- *St&PR 93*
Smith, H. Russell 1914- *St&PR 93*
Smith, H. Shelton 1893-1987 *BioIn 17*
Smith, Hal H., III 1931- *St&PR 93*
Smith, Hal W. 1946- *WhoAm 92*
Smith, Hale 1925- *Baker 92*
Smith, Hallett Darius 1907- *WhoAm 92*
Smith, Hamilton *WhoScE 91-1*
Smith, Hamilton Othanel 1931- *WhoAm 92, WhoE 93, WhoWor 93*
Smith, Harlan 1872-1940 *BioIn 17*
Smith, Harlan J. *BioIn 17*
Smith, Harley M. *Law&B 92*
Smith, Harmon Lee, Jr. 1930- *WhoAm 92*
Smith, Harold Allen 1944- *WhoSSW 93, WhoWor 93*
Smith, Harold B. 1909-1990 *BioIn 17*
Smith, Harold Byron 1909- *St&PR 93*
Smith, Harold Byron, Jr. 1933- *St&PR 93, WhoAm 92*
Smith, Harold Charles 1934- *WhoE 93, WhoWor 93*
Smith, Harold H. 1925- *St&PR 93*
Smith, Harold Hill 1910- *WhoAm 92*
Smith, Harold Lee 1930- *WhoWrEP 92*
Smith, Harold Webster 1911- *St&PR 93*
Smith, Harriet D. *AmWomPl*
Smith, Harriet E. *AmWomPl*
Smith, Harriet Gwendolyn Gurley 1927- *WhoSSW 93*
Smith, Harrison Harvey 1915- *WhoSSW 93, WhoWor 93*
Smith, Harry *BioIn 17*
Smith, Harry Alcide 1925- *WhoSSW 93*
Smith, Harry B. *WhoAm 92*
Smith, Harry Clay 1863-1941 *BioIn 17*
Smith, Harry Davis, Jr. 1943- *WhoSSW 93*
Smith, Harry E. 1933- *St&PR 93*
Smith, Harry Joseph 1936- *WhoE 93*
Smith, Harvey Alvin 1932- *WhoAm 92*
Smith, Harvey Frank, Jr. 1927- *St&PR 93*
Smith, Harvey R. *Law&B 92*
Smith, Harwell Fitzhugh, III 1951- *WhoSSW 93*
Smith, Haydn William 1920-1990 *BioIn 17*
Smith, Haywood Clark, Jr. 1945- *WhoSSW 93*
Smith, Hazel Brannon 1914- *DcLB 127 [port], JrnUS*
Smith, Hazel L. *ScF&FL 92*
Smith, Hazel M. 1931- *St&PR 93*
Smith, Heather Kay 1964- *WhoAmW 93*
Smith, Hedrick *BioIn 17*
Smith, Hedrick L. 1933- *JrnUS*
Smith, Hedrick Laurence 1933- *WhoAm 92*

Smith, Heidi Suzanne 1968- WhoAmW 93
Smith, Helen Dibell 1941- WhoAmW 93
Smith, Helen Elizabeth 1946- WhoAmW 93, WhoSSW 93
Smith, Helen Jeanne 1947- WhoAmW 93
Smith, Helene Catherine 1935- WhoE 93
Smith, Henry Charles, III 1931- WhoAm 92
Smith, Henry Clay 1913- WhoAm 92
Smith, Henry Clay 1945- WhoAm 92
Smith, Henry George Wakelyn 1787-1860 HarEnMi
Smith, Henry Lewis 1945- WhoSSW 93
Smith, Henry Linton, Jr. Law&B 92
Smith, Herbert Charles 1946- WhoE 93
Smith, Herbert Furrer Law&B 92
Smith, Herbert Furrer 1938- St&PR 93, WhoAm 92
Smith, Herbert Leary, Jr. 1923- WhoAm 92
Smith, Herrick Hayner 1930- WhoAm 92
Smith, Hilrie Shelton 1893-1987 BioIn 17
Smith, Hoke LaFollette 1931- WhoAm 92, WhoE 93
Smith, Holland McTyeire 1882-1967 HarEnMi
Smith, Horace 1779-1849 BioIn 17
Smith, Horace E. BioIn 17
Smith, Horace Zack, Jr. 1924- WhoSSW 93
Smith, Horatio 1779-1849 BioIn 17, DcLB 116 [port]
Smith, Howard MiSFD 9
Smith, Howard A. Law&B 92
Smith, Howard Alan 1944- WhoE 93
Smith, Howard E. 1934- St&PR 93
Smith, Howard Franklin 1930- WhoE 93
Smith, Howard J., Jr. Law&B 92
Smith, Howard Kingsbury 1914- JrnUS
Smith, Howard McQueen 1919- WhoAm 92
Smith, Howard R. 1910- St&PR 93
Smith, Howard Ross 1917- WhoAm 92
Smith, Howard Russell 1914- WhoAm 92
Smith, Howard Thompson 1937- WhoAm 92, WhoSSW 93
Smith, Howard W. 1883-1976 PolPar
Smith, Howard Wesley 1929- WhoAm 92
Smith, Hudson Day 1951- St&PR 93
Smith, Hueston Merriam 1912- WhoWor 93
Smith, Huey 1934- SoulM
Smith, Hugh Davies 1929- St&PR 93
Smith, Hurley David Law&B 92
Smith, Hurley David 1940- St&PR 93
Smith, Hyacinthe Stoddart AmWomPl
Smith, I.R. WhoScE 91-1
Smith, Ian 1919- ColdWar 2 [port]
Smith, Ian Cormack Palmer 1939- WhoAm 92
Smith, Ian Douglas 1919- DcTwHis
Smith, Ian Edward WhoScE 91-1
Smith, Ian Michael 1944- WhoScE 91-2
Smith, Ian William Murison WhoScE 91-1
Smith, Ileene Andrea 1953- WhoAmW 93
Smith, Iris E. 1950- WhoSSW 93
Smith, Israel A. 1876-1958 BioIn 17
Smith, Ivan Huron 1907- WhoAm 92
Smith, J. Albert, Jr. 1940- St&PR 93
Smith, J. Dan 1925- St&PR 93
Smith, J.H. WhoScE 91-1
Smith, J. Kellum, Jr. 1927- WhoAm 92
Smith, J. Leon 1938- St&PR 93
Smith, J. Otis 1941- WhoE 93
Smith, J. Read d1991 BioIn 17
Smith, J. Richard Law&B 92
Smith, J. Roy 1936- WhoSSW 93
Smith, J. Thomas 1947- WhoSSW 93
Smith, Jabbo 1908-1991 AnObit 1991, Baker 92, BioIn 17
Smith, Jack d1890 BioIn 17
Smith, Jack C. 1923- St&PR 93
Smith, Jack Carl 1928- WhoAm 92, WhoWor 93
Smith, Jack Clifford 1916- WhoAm 92, WhoWrEP 92
Smith, Jack Everett 1937- WhoSSW 93
Smith, Jack Lee 1931- St&PR 93
Smith, Jack Louis 1934- WhoE 93
Smith, Jack Prescott 1945- WhoAm 92
Smith, Jack Wilkinson 1873?-1949 BioIn 17
Smith, Jaclyn BioIn 17
Smith, Jaclyn 1947- HolBB [port], WhoAm 92
Smith, Jacqueline d1992 NewYTBS 92
Smith, James 1775-1839 BioIn 17
Smith, James 1930- St&PR 93
Smith, James A. 1914-1983? ConAu 39NR
Smith, James A. 1930- WhoAm 92
Smith, James Alan 1942- WhoE 93
Smith, James Almer, Jr. 1923- WhoE 93, WhoWor 93
Smith, James B., Jr. 1948- WhoIns 93
Smith, James Barker d1990 BioIn 17
Smith, James Bigelow, Sr. 1908- WhoE 93
Smith, James Bonner 1950- WhoSSW 93
Smith, James Brian 1943- WhoE 93
Smith, James C. 1937- WhoIns 93
Smith, James C. 1940- WhoAm 92
Smith, James C. 1945- St&PR 93
Smith, James Charles 1948- WhoSSW 93
Smith, James Charles, Jr. 1950- WhoSSW 93
Smith, James Copeland 1945- WhoAm 92
Smith, James D. 1937- St&PR 93
Smith, James Donaldson 1922- WhoE 93
Smith, James Emory 1951- WhoEmL 93
Smith, James Ervin 1949- WhoE 93
Smith, James Everett Keith 1928- WhoAm 92
Smith, James F. 1932- WhoAm 92
Smith, James Finley 1938- WhoAm 92
Smith, James Forest, Jr. 1929- WhoAm 92, WhoSSW 93
Smith, James Francis 1936- St&PR 93, WhoAm 92
Smith, James Franklin 1946- St&PR 93
Smith, James Frederick 1944- WhoE 93, WhoWor 93
Smith, James Gilbert 1930- WhoAm 92
Smith, James H. St&PR 93
Smith, James Hamilton 1931- WhoAm 92
Smith, James Herbert 1947- WhoWor 93
Smith, James Howard 1947- WhoE 93
Smith, James Howell 1936- WhoSSW 93
Smith, James J., Jr. 1936- St&PR 93
Smith, James John 1914- WhoAm 92
Smith, James Kirk 1950- WhoAm 92
Smith, James L. 1938- St&PR 93
Smith, James Larkin 1949- St&PR 93
Smith, James Lavon 1928- WhoSSW 93
Smith, James Lawrence 1933- St&PR 93
Smith, James Lawrence 1943- WhoAm 92
Smith, James Lawrence, III 1960- WhoAm 92
Smith, James M. 1927- St&PR 93
Smith, James O. 1933- St&PR 93
Smith, James Oscar 1928- WhoAm 92
Smith, James Parker 1959- WhoE 93
Smith, James Pembroke 1950- WhoE 93
Smith, James Peyton 1956- WhoSSW 93
Smith, James Robert 1945- St&PR 93
Smith, James Ronald Law&B 92
Smith, James S. 1926- St&PR 93
Smith, James Todd BioIn 17
Smith, James V., Jr. ScF&FL 92
Smith, James Walter BioIn 17
Smith, James William 1932- St&PR 93
Smith, Jamesetta Delorise 1942- WhoAmW 93
Smith, Jane Davis 1949- WhoWrEP 92
Smith, Jane Farwell WhoAm 92
Smith, Janet Adam 1905- BioIn 17
Smith, Janet Diane Law&B 92
Smith, Janet Fay 1948- WhoSSW 93
Smith, Janet Marie 1957- BioIn 17, WhoAmW 93
Smith, Janet Patton ScF&FL 92
Smith, Janet Sue 1945- WhoE 93
Smith, Janie Lomax 1939- WhoSSW 93
Smith, Janine A. Law&B 92
Smith, Jason BioIn 17
Smith, Jasper ScF&FL 92
Smith, Jay D. 1940- St&PR 93
Smith, Jay Lawrence 1954- WhoWor 93
Smith, Jay Lester 1945- WhoE 93
Smith, Jay Maurice 1947- WhoWor 93
Smith, Jean Chandler 1918- WhoAm 92
Smith, Jean G. 1946- St&PR 93
Smith, Jean Kennedy BioIn 17
Smith, Jean Webb WhoAmW 93
Smith, Jeanie Oliver Davidson 1836-1925 AmWomPl
Smith, Jedediah 1799-1831 Expl 93
Smith, Jedediah Strong 1798-1831 BioIn 17
Smith, Jeff BioIn 17
Smith, Jeff David 1969- WhoWrEP 92
Smith, Jefferson Verne 1925- WhoSSW 93
Smith, Jeffery Steven 1945- WhoE 93
Smith, Jeffrey Alan 1953- WhoSSW 93
Smith, Jeffrey Bordeaux 1926- WhoAm 92
Smith, Jeffrey C. Law&B 92
Smith, Jeffrey D. ScF&FL 92
Smith, Jeffrey E. St&PR 93
Smith, Jeffrey Eugene 1947- WhoSSW 93
Smith, Jeffrey Greenwood 1921- WhoAm 92
Smith, Jeffrey H. Law&B 92
Smith, Jeffrey K. 1948- WhoAm 92
Smith, Jeffrey Kirk Law&B 92
Smith, Jeffrey L. Law&B 92
Smith, Jeffrey L. 1956- St&PR 93
Smith, Jeffrey M. 1961- St&PR 93
Smith, Jeffrey Michael 1947- WhoAm 92, WhoWor 93
Smith, Jeffrey Michael 1952- St&PR 93
Smith, Jeffry Alan 1943- WhoWor 93
Smith, Jennie S. AmWomPl
Smith, Jennifer C. 1952- WhoAmW 93
Smith, Jennings T. Law&B 92
Smith, Jeri Lynn 1952- WhoE 93
Smith, Jerome A. 1943- St&PR 93
Smith, Jerome Hazen 1936- WhoAm 92
Smith, Jerome Michael 1942- WhoSSW 93
Smith, Jerry Don 1940- WhoSSW 93
Smith, Jerry Edgar 1941- St&PR 93
Smith, Jerry Edwin 1944- WhoE 93
Smith, Jerry Edwin 1946- WhoAm 92
Smith, Jerry Wayne 1936- WhoSSW 93
Smith, Jerry Wayne 1949- St&PR 93
Smith, Jesse Graham, Jr. 1928- WhoAm 92, WhoSSW 93, WhoWor 93
Smith, Jesse Graham, III 1954- WhoSSW 93
Smith, Jesse R. 1939- St&PR 93
Smith, Jessica Belle Welborn AmWomPl
Smith, Jessie Carney WhoAmW 93
Smith, Jessie Carney 1930- ConAu 39NR, WhoWrEP 92
Smith, Jessie Willcox 1863-1935 MajAI [port]
Smith, Jill A. Law&B 92
Smith, Jim 1920- BioIn 17
Smith, Jo Ann Law&B 92
Smith, Jo Anne 1930- WhoAm 92
Smith, Jo Lynn 1961- WhoAmW 93
Smith, Joachim 1929- WhoAm 92
Smith, Joan Elizabeth 1962- WhoAmW 93
Smith, Joanne Jocelyn 1939- WhoAmW 93
Smith, JoAnne Marie 1962- WhoAmW 93
Smith, Joanne Smith 1927- WhoSSW 93
Smith, Jody Brant 1943- WhoWor 93
Smith, Joe 1884-1980 & Dale, Charlie 1881-1971 QDrFCA 92 [port]
Smith, Joe 1902-1937 Baker 92
Smith, Joe Dorsey, Jr. 1922- St&PR 93, WhoAm 92
Smith, Joe Mauk 1916- WhoAm 92
Smith, Joe W., Jr. 1944- St&PR 93
Smith, Joel 1925- WhoAm 92
Smith, Joel Bradley 1963- WhoWrEP 92
Smith, John ScF&FL 92
Smith, John 1580-1631 BioIn 17, Expl 93 [port]
Smith, John 1924- WhoAm 92
Smith, John 1927- WhoCanL 92
Smith, John 1938- WhoWor 93
Smith, John, Jr. 1917- St&PR 93
Smith, John Alec Sydney WhoScE 91-1
Smith, John Brewster 1937- WhoAm 92
Smith, John Bruce, Jr. 1942- WhoE 93
Smith, John Bundy Law&B 92
Smith, John Bundy 1939- St&PR 93, WhoAm 92
Smith, John Burnside 1931- St&PR 93, WhoAm 92
Smith, John Charles Law&B 92
Smith, John Christopher 1712-1795 Baker 92, OxDcOp
Smith, John D. 1938- St&PR 93
Smith, John Dorrance 1951- WhoAm 92
Smith, John E., II Law&B 92
Smith, John Edwin 1921- WhoAm 92, WhoWrEP 92
Smith, John Edwin 1924- WhoAm 92
Smith, John Ewing 1906- St&PR 93
Smith, John F. BioIn 17, St&PR 93
Smith, John Francis 1923- WhoAm 92
Smith, John Francis, Jr. d1938 NewYTBS 92 [port]
Smith, John Francis, Jr. 1938- WhoAm 92
Smith, John Francis, III 1941- WhoAm 92
Smith, John Gelston 1923- WhoAm 92
Smith, John H. Law&B 92
Smith, John Holmes, IV 1949- WhoSSW 93
Smith, John J. Law&B 92, WhoAm 92
Smith, John J. 1911- St&PR 93, WhoAm 92
Smith, John J. 1947- St&PR 93
Smith, John Joseph 1911- WhoAm 92
Smith, John Joseph 1913- WhoAm 92
Smith, John Kerwin 1926- WhoWor 93
Smith, John L. d1972 BioIn 17
Smith, John L., Jr. d1992 NewYTBS 92
Smith, John Lee, Jr. 1920- WhoAm 92
Smith, John M. 1931- WhoScE 91-3
Smith, John M. 1942- ConAu 139
Smith, John Malcolm WhoScE 91-1
Smith, John Marriott WhoScE 91-1
Smith, John Marvin, III 1947- WhoWor 93
Smith, John Matthew 1936- St&PR 93, WhoAm 92
Smith, John McNeill, Jr. 1918- WhoAm 92
Smith, John Morton WhoSSW 93
Smith, John Pierre 1956- WhoSSW 93
Smith, John Rhea 1767- BioIn 17
Smith, John Selby ScF&FL 92
Smith, John Stafford 1750?-1836 Baker 92
Smith, John Standbridge, Jr. 1955- WhoE 93
Smith, John Stephen 1938- WhoSSW 93
Smith, John Stuart WhoScE 91-1
Smith, John Sylvester 1914- WhoAm 92
Smith, John T., Jr. 1944- WhoE 93
Smith, John Thomson WhoScE 91-1
Smith, John Willis 1935- WhoAm 92
Smith, Jos(eph) A. 1936- SmATA 73 [port]
Smith, Jose I. 1943- St&PR 93
Smith, Josef Riley 1926- WhoAm 92
Smith, Joseph 1805-1844 BioIn 17
Smith, Joseph Benjamin 1928- WhoAm 92
Smith, Joseph C. 1946- St&PR 93
Smith, Joseph Judson, III 1938- WhoE 93
Smith, Joseph LeConte, Jr. 1929- WhoAm 92
Smith, Joseph Newton, III 1925- WhoAm 92
Smith, Joseph Patrick 1951- WhoSSW 93
Smith, Joseph Phelan WhoAm 92
Smith, Joseph Robert 1927- St&PR 93
Smith, Joseph Seton 1925- WhoAm 92
Smith, Joseph W. 1926- St&PR 93
Smith, Joshua Isaac 1941- AfrAmBi
Smith, Judith Allyson 1948- WhoAmW 93
Smith, Judith Ann 1950- WhoAmW 93
Smith, Judith Day 1949- WhoSSW 93
Smith, Judith Eleanor 1954- WhoAmW 93
Smith, Juel Hickman Shannon 1944- WhoSSW 93
Smith, Julia ScF&FL 92
Smith, Julia Amelia 1935- WhoAmW 93, WhoSSW 93
Smith, Julia Floyd 1914- WhoSSW 93
Smith, Julia (Frances) 1911-1989 Baker 92
Smith, Julian C. 1885- HarEnMi
Smith, Julian Cleveland, Jr. 1919- WhoAm 92, WhoE 93
Smith, Julian Payne 1930- WhoAm 92
Smith, Julie Dean 1960- ScF&FL 92
Smith, June WhoE 93
Smith, June Burlingame 1935- WhoAmW 93
Smith, Justina AmWomPl
Smith, K. Wayne 1938- BioIn 17, St&PR 93
Smith, Karen Groom 1952- WhoSSW 93
Smith, Karen H. 1949- WhoSSW 93
Smith, Karen Irons 1964- WhoAmW 93
Smith, Karen Jo 1952- WhoAmW 93
Smith, Karen Kelley 1961- WhoAmW 93
Smith, Karen Lynn 1965- WhoAmW 93
Smith, Karen Michelle 1959- WhoAmW 93
Smith, Kate 1907-1986 Baker 92
Smith, Katherine E. 1954- WhoE 93
Smith, Kathleen Dana 1947- WhoAmW 93
Smith, Kathleen Diane 1951- WhoAmW 93
Smith, Kathleen Goodpasture Law&B 92
Smith, Kathleen Keer McGowan 1918- WhoWrEP 92
Smith, Kathleen L. 1948- St&PR 93
Smith, Kathleen Maurer 1953- WhoAmW 93
Smith, Kathleen Therese 1943- WhoSSW 93
Smith, Kathryn Ann 1955- WhoAmW 93
Smith, Kathryn Baker 1946- WhoSSW 93
Smith, Kathryn Juanita McKay 1943- WhoAmW 93
Smith, Kathryn Leigh 1956- WhoAmW 93
Smith, Kathy Ann 1944- WhoAmW 93
Smith, Kathy Ann 1961- WhoAmW 93
Smith, Kathy Sue 1953- WhoAmW 93
Smith, Katie 1961- WhoAmW 93
Smith, Kay BioIn 17
Smith, Kay Darlene 1960- WhoAmW 93
Smith, Kay Nolte 1932- ScF&FL 92
Smith, Keith ScF&FL 92, WhoScE 91-1
Smith, Keith A. 1938- WhoAm 92
Smith, Keith A. 1940- WhoScE 91-1
Smith, Keith Anthony WhoScE 91-1
Smith, Keith Dryden, Jr. 1951- WhoE 93
Smith, Keith W. Law&B 92
Smith, Kellie Michelle 1965- WhoWrEP 92
Smith, Ken(neth John) 1938- ConAu 39NR
Smith, Kendall B. Law&B 92
Smith, Kennedy 1922- St&PR 93
Smith, Kenneth Alan 1936- WhoAm 92
Smith, Kenneth Blose 1926- WhoAm 92
Smith, Kenneth Bryant 1931- WhoAm 92
Smith, Kenneth Carless 1932- WhoAm 92
Smith, Kenneth Judson, Jr. 1930- WhoAm 92, WhoWor 93
Smith, Kenneth W. Law&B 92
Smith, Kent MiSFD 9, ScF&FL 92
Smith, Kermit Wayne 1938- WhoAm 92
Smith, Kerri S. 1960- ConAu 139
Smith, Kerry Clark 1935- WhoAm 92
Smith, Kevin Andrew 1962- WhoSSW 93
Smith, Kevin Zane 1957- WhoSSW 93
Smith, Kiki 1954- BioIn 17
Smith, Killian Middleton 1934- WhoSSW 93
Smith, Kim Oliphant 1955- St&PR 93
Smith, Kimberly Oliphant Law&B 92
Smith, Kristine Jensen 1949- WhoAmW 93

Smith, Kurt Landon 1963- WhoSSW 93
Smith, L.A., Jr. 1925- St&PR 93
Smith, L.J. ScF&FL 92
Smith, L.K. ScF&FL 92
Smith, L.L. 1936- St&PR 93
Smith, L. Neil 1946- ScF&FL 92
Smith, L. Russell 1933- St&PR 93
Smith, Lacey Baldwin 1922- WhoAm 92
Smith, Lachlan M. 1948- St&PR 93
Smith, Lamar 1892-1955 EncAACR
Smith, Lamar 1947- CngDr 91
Smith, Lamar Seeligson 1947- WhoAm 92, WhoSSW 93
Smith, Lane BioIn 17, ChlBIID [port]
Smith, Lanty L. 1942- St&PR 93
Smith, Lanty Lloyd 1942- WhoAm 92
Smith, LaPreal Monson 1920- WhoE 93
Smith, Larry Dennis 1954- WhoE 93
Smith, Larry Glenn 1924- WhoSSW 93
Smith, Larry R. 1943- WhoWrEP 92
Smith, Larry Steven 1950- WhoSSW 93, WhoWor 93
Smith, Larry Wayne 1954- WhoWrEP 92
Smith, Laura Lee Whitely Weisbrodt 1903- WhoAmW 93
Smith, Laura Rountree 1876-1924 AmWomPl
Smith, Laure ScF&FL 92
Smith, Laurel Ann 1955- WhoAmW 93
Smith, Laurel Diane 1953- WhoWrEP 92
Smith, Lauren Ashley 1924- WhoWor 93
Smith, Laurence Roger 1939- WhoE 93, WhoWor 93
Smith, Laurie J. St&PR 93
Smith, Laurie Macmillan 1960- WhoAmW 93
Smith, Lawrence A. Law&B 92
Smith, Lawrence Barrett, IV 1952- WhoE 93
Smith, Lawrence Earl, III 1919- St&PR 93
Smith, Lawrence F. 1938- WhoIns 93
Smith, Lawrence Hartley 1934- WhoAm 92
Smith, Lawrence J. 1941- CngDr 91
Smith, Lawrence Jack 1941- WhoAm 92, WhoSSW 93
Smith, Lawrence Leighton 1936- Baker 92, WhoAm 92
Smith, Lawrence M. 1921- St&PR 93
Smith, Lawrence Norfleet 1937- St&PR 93
Smith, Lawrence Ralph 1928- WhoWor 93
Smith, Lawrence Stewart Ainslie WhoScE 91-1
Smith, Le Sueur G., Jr. 1919- St&PR 93
Smith, Leah Johnson 1943- WhoAmW 93, WhoE 93
Smith, Lee 1944- ConLC 73 [port]
Smith, Lee Arthur 1957- WhoAm 92
Smith, Lee Arthur, Jr. 1957- BiDAMSp 1989
Smith, Lee Clark 1942- WhoAm 92
Smith, Lee Herman 1935- WhoAm 92
Smith, Lee L. 1936- WhoWor 93
Smith, Lee M. Law&B 92
Smith, Leighton Warren, Jr. 1939- WhoAm 92
Smith, Leila Hentzen 1932- WhoAmW 93, WhoWor 93
Smith, Leland (Clayton) 1925- Baker 92
Smith, Leland D., Jr. 1931- St&PR 93
Smith, Lena R. AmWomPl
Smith, Lendon H. 1921- BioIn 17
Smith, Lenore St&PR 93
Smith, Lenworth Law&B 92
Smith, Leo Gilbert 1929- WhoAm 92
Smith, Leon L., Sr. 1931- WhoWrEP 92
Smith, Leon Polk 1906- WhoAm 92
Smith, Leona Agatha 1942- WhoAmW 93
Smith, Leonard Bingley 1915- WhoAm 92
Smith, Leonard Clinton Geoffrey 1944- WhoIns 93
Smith, Leonard S. 1918- St&PR 93
Smith, Leroy Harrington, Jr. 1928- WhoAm 92
Smith, LeRoy T. 1922- St&PR 93
Smith, Leslie C. BioIn 17
Smith, Leslie D. Law&B 92
Smith, Leslie Donald 1947- St&PR 93
Smith, Leslie Roper 1928- WhoAm 92
Smith, Lester J. 1929- St&PR 93
Smith, Lewis Dennis 1938- WhoAm 92
Smith, Lewis Motter, Jr. 1932- WhoAm 92
Smith, Lewis O., III 1936- St&PR 93
Smith, Ley S. 1934- St&PR 93
Smith, Lilian AmWomPl
Smith, Lilli Huger AmWomPl
Smith, Lillian 1887-1966 EncAACR
Smith, Lillian H. 1887-1983 BioIn 17
Smith, Linda A. WhoAmW 93
Smith, Linda D. Law&B 92
Smith, Linda Mitchum 1946- WhoAmW 93
Smith, Lindsay ScF&FL 92
Smith, Lindsey Fairfield 1940- WhoWor 93
Smith, Lisa Andrews 1951- WhoSSW 93
Smith, Liz WhoAm 92, WhoE 93, WhoWrEP 92
Smith, Liz 1923- JrnUS
Smith, Lloyd 1941- WhoAm 92
Smith, Lloyd B. 1920- St&PR 93
Smith, Lloyd Bruce 1920- WhoAm 92
Smith, Lloyd Hilton 1905- WhoAm 92, WhoWor 93
Smith, Lockwood 1948- WhoAsAP 91
Smith, Logan Pearsall 1865-1946 BioIn 17
Smith, Lois Arlene 1930- WhoAm 92
Smith, Lon A. 1939- WhoIns 93
Smith, Lonnie M. 1944- St&PR 93
Smith, Lonnie Max 1944- WhoAm 92
Smith, Loren Allan 1944- CngDr 91
Smith, Lorie Jane 1959- WhoAmW 93
Smith, Lorna Watson 1935- WhoAmW 93
Smith, Lorraine Nancy WhoScE 91-1
Smith, Louis 1934- WhoWor 93
Smith, Louis M., Jr. 1937- WhoIns 93
Smith, Louis Roycraft, Jr. 1945- WhoSSW 93
Smith, Louise Ann 1951- WhoAmW 93
Smith, Louise Fink Law&B 92
Smith, Louise Hamilton 1926- WhoWrEP 92
Smith, Lowell WhoAm 92
Smith, Lowell Cyrus 1931- WhoAm 92, WhoWor 93
Smith, Lowndes A. 1939- St&PR 93
Smith, Lucien T. 1913- St&PR 93, WhoAm 92
Smith, Lyman Lee, Jr. 1933- WhoSSW 93
Smith, Lynn Howard 1936- WhoAm 92
Smith, Lynn S. ScF&FL 92
Smith, M. WhoScE 91-1
Smith, M. Alasdair M. WhoScE 91-1
Smith, M.D. Law&B 92
Smith, M.E., Jr. St&PR 93
Smith, M. Gregory 1947- WhoSSW 93
Smith, M. Hue, III Law&B 92
Smith, Macon Strother 1919- WhoAm 92
Smith, Maggie BioIn 17
Smith, Maggie 1934- IntDcF 2-3 [port], WhoAm 92, WhoAmW 93, WhoWor 93
Smith, Mahlon Brewster 1919- WhoAm 92
Smith, Malcolm d1990 BioIn 17
Smith, Malcolm B. 1923- St&PR 93
Smith, Malcolm Barry Estes 1939- WhoAm 92
Smith, Malcolm Bernard 1923- WhoAm 92
Smith, Malcolm N. 1921- St&PR 93
Smith, Malcolm Norman 1921- WhoAm 92
Smith, Malcolm Sommerville 1933- WhoAm 92
Smith, Mandy BioIn 17
Smith, Manning Lee 1943- WhoE 93
Smith, Mara A. 1945- WhoAmW 93
Smith, Marc BioIn 17
Smith, Marcia Ann Twomey 1938- WhoAmW 93
Smith, Marcia Jean 1947- WhoAmW 93, WhoE 93, WhoEmL 93
Smith, Marcia Jeanne 1935- WhoAmW 93
Smith, Marcia Sue 1951- WhoWor 93
Smith, Margaret Law&B 92, WhoAmW 93
Smith, Margaret A. 1951- WhoAmW 93
Smith, Margaret Brand 1911- WhoAmW 93
Smith, Margaret Butzler 1931- WhoAmW 93
Smith, Margaret Chase 1897- BioIn 17, PolPar
Smith, Margaret Dennis 1939- WhoAmW 93
Smith, Margaret Dill 1949- WhoSSW 93
Smith, Margaret Hamilton Donald 1915- WhoAm 92
Smith, Margaret Holbrook AmWomPl
Smith, Margaret Phyllis 1925- WhoAmW 93, WhoE 93, WhoWor 93
Smith, Margaret Riley 1960- WhoAmW 93
Smith, Margherita 1922- WhoAmW 93
Smith, Mari Lynn 1946- WhoSSW 93
Smith, Maria Wilkins AmWomPl
Smith, Marian Spencer AmWomPl
Smith, Marian Wesley 1907-1961 IntDcAn
Smith, Marilyn Diane Law&B 92
Smith, Marilyn Lynne 1944- WhoSSW 93
Smith, Marilyn Patricia 1942- WhoAmW 93, WhoE 93
Smith, Marilynn Jane 1944- WhoAmW 93, WhoSSW 93
Smith, Marion Pafford 1925- WhoAm 92
Smith, Marjorie Watkins 1921- WhoAmW 93
Smith, Mark Law&B 92, ScF&FL 92
Smith, Mark A. Law&B 92
Smith, Mark A., Jr. Law&B 92
Smith, Mark Alan 1934- WhoE 93
Smith, Mark Andrew Law&B 92
Smith, Mark Anthony 1956- WhoSSW 93
Smith, Mark Eugene 1951- WhoSSW 93
Smith, Mark L. Law&B 92
Smith, Mark L. 1961- St&PR 93
Smith, Mark Landon 1964- WhoSSW 93
Smith, Mark R. Law&B 92
Smith, Mark R. 1945- St&PR 93
Smith, Mark Richard 1935- WhoWrEP 92
Smith, Mark Wayne 1960- WhoSSW 93
Smith, Mark William Law&B 92
Smith, Markwick Kern, Jr. 1928- WhoAm 92
Smith, Marlan Reed 1943- St&PR 93
Smith, Marschall I. Law&B 92
Smith, Marschall Imboden 1944- WhoAm 92
Smith, Marshall Jay 1931- St&PR 93
Smith, Marshall Savidge 1937- WhoAm 92
Smith, Marshall Wayne 1931- WhoSSW 93
Smith, Martha BioIn 17
Smith, Martha Lewis 1942- WhoAmW 93
Smith, Martha Oliver- ScF&FL 92
Smith, Martha Stribling 1924- WhoSSW 93
Smith, Martian Law&B 92
Smith, Martin Bernhard 1930- WhoAm 92
Smith, Martin Cruz BioIn 17
Smith, Martin Cruz 1942- ScF&FL 92, WhoAm 92
Smith, Martin Henry 1921- WhoAm 92
Smith, Martin Jay 1942- WhoAm 92
Smith, Marvin 1940- BioIn 17
Smith, Marvin Wayne 1938- WhoAm 92
Smith, Mary Alice 1941- WhoAm 92, WhoAmW 93
Smith, Mary Alice 1944- WhoE 93
Smith, Mary-Ann Tirone 1944- ConAu 136
Smith, Mary Askew Backer 1897- WhoAmW 93
Smith, Mary Brainerd 1871- AmWomPl
Smith, Mary Elinor 1913- WhoAmW 93
Smith, Mary Elizabeth Roberts 1860-1945 BioIn 17
Smith, Mary Ellen 1952- WhoAmW 93
Smith, Mary Frances 1927- WhoWrEP 92
Smith, Mary Hart 1937- WhoAmW 93
Smith, Mary Howard Harding 1944- WhoAmW 93
Smith, Mary Louise 1914- PolPar, WhoAm 92
Smith, Mary R. 1920- St&PR 93
Smith, Mary Stafford 1859?-1934 AmWomPl
Smith, Marya 1945- WhoWrEP 92
Smith, Marya Jean 1945- WhoAmW 93
Smith, Matthew J. 1951- St&PR 93
Smith, Maude Sumner AmWomPl
Smith, Maurice Edward 1919- WhoAm 92
Smith, Maxwell P. 1924- St&PR 93
Smith, Maxwell Paul 1924- WhoWor 93
Smith, Maynard H. 1911-1984 BioIn 17
Smith, Mel 1952- MiSFD 9
Smith, Mel 1952- & Rhys Jones, Griff 1953- QDrFCA 92 [port]
Smith, Melissa Jane 1969- WhoAmW 93
Smith, Melody L. 1951- St&PR 93
Smith, Merilyn Roberta 1933- WhoAmW 93, WhoWor 93
Smith, Merle J. Law&B 92
Smith, Merlin Gale 1928- WhoAm 92
Smith, Merritt Roe 1940- WhoAm 92
Smith, Merritt Wayne 1929- St&PR 93
Smith, Micah P. 1916- St&PR 93
Smith, Micah Pearce, Jr. 1916- WhoSSW 93
Smith, Michael BioIn 17, St&PR 93
Smith, Michael 1962- BioIn 17
Smith, Michael A. Law&B 92
Smith, Michael Alan Law&B 92
Smith, Michael Alexis 1944- WhoAm 92
Smith, Michael Andrew WhoScE 91-1
Smith, Michael Anthony 1945- WhoAm 92
Smith, Michael B. Law&B 92
Smith, Michael C. Law&B 92
Smith, Michael C. B. 1955- WhoAm 92
Smith, Michael Carl 1963- WhoSSW 93
Smith, Michael D. 1940- St&PR 93
Smith, Michael David 1945- St&PR 93
Smith, Michael Edward Law&B 92
Smith, Michael Elwin 1948- WhoEmL 93
Smith, Michael F. Law&B 92
Smith, Michael F. 1961- St&PR 93
Smith, Michael H. Law&B 92
Smith, Michael Howard 1938- WhoAm 92
Smith, Michael James 1945- WhoAm 92
Smith, Michael Kelly 1959- WhoSSW 93
Smith, Michael Kenneth 1952- WhoSSW 93
Smith, Michael Peter 1942- WhoAm 92
Smith, Michael Peter 1949- WhoE 93
Smith, Michael Phillip 1964- WhoSSW 93
Smith, Michael Proctor 1937- WhoSSW 93
Smith, Michael R. 1938- St&PR 93
Smith, Michael Steven BioIn 17
Smith, Michael Steven 1956- WhoEmL 93, WhoWor 93
Smith, Michael Timothy 1943- St&PR 93
Smith, Michael Townsend 1935- WhoAm 92, WhoWrEP 92
Smith, Michael Vincent 1957- WhoE 93
Smith, Michael W. BioIn 17
Smith, Michael William 1944- WhoSSW 93
Smith, Michele E. Law&B 92
Smith, Michelle L. 1956- St&PR 93
Smith, Michelle Lynnette 1962- WhoSSW 93
Smith, Mildred Cassandra WhoAmW 93
Smith, Mildred Free 1942- WhoE 93
Smith, Mildred Katharine AmWomPl
Smith, Milledge Stevenson 1949- WhoSSW 93
Smith, Milton Frank, Jr. Law&B 92
Smith, Milton Ray 1935- St&PR 93, WhoAm 92
Smith, Miriam Estella 1966- WhoAmW 93
Smith, Miriam Spencer AmWomPl
Smith, Mitchell 1935- ConAu 136
Smith, Mitchell Brian 1955- WhoSSW 93
Smith, Moishe 1929- WhoAm 92
Smith, Moncrieff Hynson 1917- WhoAm 92
Smith, Monte WhoWrEP 92
Smith, Montgomery Luther Law&B 92
Smith, Montgomery W. Law&B 92
Smith, Morgan Kinmonth 1912- WhoAm 92
Smith, Morris BioIn 17
Smith, Morris J. 1928- St&PR 93
Smith, Morris J. 1957- WhoAm 92
Smith, Morton BioIn 17
Smith, Morton Howison 1923- WhoAm 92
Smith, Morton T. 1934- WhoSSW 93
Smith, Moses 1901-1964 Baker 92
Smith, Muriel Joan 1936- WhoWrEP 92
Smith, Murl Edward Law&B 92
Smith, Murray Livingstone 1937- WhoAm 92
Smith, Murray Thomas 1939- WhoAm 92
Smith, Murray W. 1943- St&PR 93
Smith, Myron E. Law&B 92
Smith, Myron J(ohn), Jr. 1944- ConAu 38NR
Smith, Myron John, Jr. 1944- WhoAm 92
Smith, Myrtle Harris AmWomPl
Smith, N. William, Jr. Law&B 92
Smith, Nancy BioIn 17
Smith, Nancy A.F. Law&B 92
Smith, Nancy DuVergne 1951- WhoAmW 93
Smith, Nancy Hohendorf 1943- WhoAm 92, WhoWor 93
Smith, Nancy Lynne 1947- WhoAmW 93
Smith, Nancy Marks Law&B 92
Smith, Nancy Napoletan Law&B 92
Smith, Nancy Pauline 1940- WhoAmW 93
Smith, Nancy R. 1929-1990 BioIn 17
Smith, Nancy Weitman 1950- WhoAmW 93
Smith, Nathan 1928- St&PR 93
Smith, Nathan L. Law&B 92
Smith, Nathan McKay 1935- WhoAm 92
Smith, Neal 1920- CngDr 91
Smith, Neal Edward 1920- WhoAm 92
Smith, Neal F. 1938- St&PR 93
Smith, Neil 1936- WhoWor 93
Smith, Nell Whitley 1929- WhoAmW 93
Smith, Nelson F. 1937- WhoE 93
Smith, Nelson W. 1931- St&PR 93
Smith, Neville Vincent 1942- WhoAm 92
Smith, Nicholas D. 1949- ConAu 137, ScF&FL 92
Smith, Nora Archibald AmWomPl
Smith, Nora Del AmWomPl
Smith, Norbert J. Law&B 92
Smith, Norman Clark 1917- WhoAm 92
Smith, Norman Cutler 1915- WhoAm 92
Smith, Norman F. 1920- SmATA 70 [port]
Smith, Norman Obed 1914- WhoAm 92
Smith, Norman Raymond 1946- WhoAm 92
Smith, Norman T. 1935- WhoAm 92
Smith, Numa Lamar, Jr. 1915- WhoAm 92
Smith, O.M. BioIn 17
Smith, Okla Bennett 1941- St&PR 93
Smith, Olcott Damon 1907- St&PR 93
Smith, Olen D. 1952- St&PR 93
Smith, Olive Irene Perry 1924- WhoAmW 93
Smith, Oliver 1918- WhoAm 92, WhoE 93
Smith, Oliver Prince 1893- HarEnMi
Smith, Ora L. AmWomPl
Smith, Orin R. 1935- St&PR 93
Smith, Orin Robert 1935- WhoAm 92, WhoE 93, WhoWor 93
Smith, Orville Auverne 1927- WhoAm 92
Smith, Orville Richard 1959- WhoSSW 93

Smith, Osborne Earl 1954- BiDAMSp 1989
Smith, Otis Milton 1922- St&PR 93
Smith, Owen C. Law&B 92
Smith, Ozzie BioIn 17
Smith, Ozzie 1954- WhoAm 92
Smith, P. Carter 1934- St&PR 93
Smith, Page BioIn 17
Smith, Pamela Ann 1956- WhoAmW 93
Smith, Pamela Anne Law&B 92
Smith, Pamela Colleen 1952- WhoAmW 93
Smith, Pamela Pearman 1958- WhoSSW 93
Smith, Patricia 1952- WhoAmW 93
Smith, Patricia Grace 1947- WhoAmW 93
Smith, Patricia J. 1946- WhoAmW 93
Smith, Patricia Jacquline 1944- WhoAmW 93
Smith, Patricia K. 1934- WhoAmW 93
Smith, Patricia Marie 1952- WhoSSW 93
Smith, Patricia Ruth 1932- WhoWrEP 92
Smith, Patricia T. Law&B 92
Smith, Patrick D. 1927- WhoSSW 93
Smith, Patrick Davis 1927- WhoWrEP 92
Smith, Patrick J(ohn) 1932- Baker 92
Smith, Patrick S. 1952- St&PR 93
Smith, Patsy BioIn 17
Smith, Patti Sanders 1954- WhoAmW 93
Smith, Paul BioIn 17
Smith, Paul Abraham 1912- WhoSSW 93
Smith, Paul C. 1930- St&PR 93
Smith, Paul David 1936- WhoE 93
Smith, Paul Edmund, Jr. 1927- WhoSSW 93
Smith, Paul Frederick 1916- WhoAm 92, WhoSSW 93
Smith, Paul John 1945- WhoWor 93
Smith, Paul Julian 1956- ConAu 138
Smith, Paul L. St&PR 93
Smith, Paul Lester 1935- WhoAm 92
Smith, Paul Lowell 1940- WhoSSW 93
Smith, Paul T. 1938- St&PR 93
Smith, Paul Thomas 1938- WhoAm 92
Smith, Paul Traylor 1923- WhoAm 92
Smith, Paul V. 1924- St&PR 93
Smith, Paul Vergon, Jr. 1921- WhoAm 92
Smith, Paula Marie 1960- WhoAmW 93
Smith, Payton 1932- WhoAm 92
Smith, Pearl Miller AmWomPl
Smith, Peggy Collins 1938- WhoAmW 93
Smith, Peggy Marie 1940- WhoWor 93
Smith, Penelope A. Law&B 92
Smith, Persifor Frazer 1798-1858 HarEnMi
Smith, Peter WhoScE 91-1
Smith, Peter 1924- WhoAm 92, WhoWor 93
Smith, Peter 1945- BioIn 17
Smith, Peter 1956- WhoWor 93
Smith, Peter 1962- WhoE 93
Smith, Peter B. 1934- St&PR 93
Smith, Peter Bennett 1934- WhoAm 92
Smith, Peter C. 1940- ScF&FL 92
Smith, Peter G. WhoScE 91-1
Smith, Peter Garthwaite 1923- WhoAm 92
Smith, Peter Harmon Law&B 92
Smith, Peter J. 1947- St&PR 93
Smith, Peter James 1950- WhoWor 93
Smith, Peter John 1931- WhoAm 92, WhoWor 93
Smith, Peter Kenelm 1943- WhoWor 93
Smith, Peter Lawrence 1942- WhoAm 92
Smith, Peter P., III d1992 NewYTBS 92 [port]
Smith, Peter Walker 1923- WhoAm 92, WhoWor 93
Smith, Peter William Ebblewhite 1937- WhoAm 92
Smith, Peter Wilson 1938- WhoAm 92
Smith, Phil ScF&FL 92
Smith, Philip Daniel 1933- WhoAm 92
Smith, Philip Dodd, Jr. 1933- WhoE 93
Smith, Philip E. BioIn 17
Smith, Philip Edward Lake 1927- WhoAm 92
Smith, Philip Meek 1932- WhoAm 92
Smith, Philip S. 1936- St&PR 93, WhoAm 92
Smith, Philip Swing 1926- St&PR 93
Smith, Philip W. 1947- St&PR 93
Smith, Philip Wayne 1945- WhoSSW 93
Smith, Phillip G. 1948- St&PR 93
Smith, Phillip Hartley 1927- WhoAm 92
Smith, Phillip N., Jr. Law&B 92
Smith, Phillips G. 1946- St&PR 93
Smith, Phillips Guy 1946- WhoAm 92
Smith, Phronia Eckes AmWomPl
Smith, Phyllis Mae 1935- WhoWor 93
Smith, Pierce Reiland 1943- St&PR 93
Smith, Preston Gibson 1941- WhoE 93
Smith, Preston Leete 1930- St&PR 93
Smith, Priscilla Agnes 1941- WhoAmW 93
Smith, Priscilla Sue Robinson 1919- WhoAmW 93
Smith, Quentin Ted 1937- WhoSSW 93
Smith, R.A. WhoScE 91-1
Smith, R.A. 1905-1959 ScF&FL 92
Smith, R. Anthony 1938- St&PR 93
Smith, R. Dixon 1944- ScF&FL 92
Smith, R.E. WhoScE 91-1
Smith, R(obert) E., Jr. 1943- WhoWrEP 92
Smith, R. Mark 1941- St&PR 93
Smith, R. Terry 1954- WhoSSW 93
Smith, R.V. WhoScE 91-1
Smith, Ralph 1919- WhoSSW 93, WhoWor 93
Smith, Ralph Alexander 1929- WhoAm 92
Smith, Ralph Corbett 1893- HarEnMi
Smith, Ralph Earl 1940- WhoWor 93
Smith, Ralph Lee 1927- WhoAm 92
Smith, Randall Nolen 1946- St&PR 93
Smith, Randall Paul 1957- WhoSSW 93
Smith, Randall Wayne 1958- WhoEmL 93
Smith, Randolph J. 1946- St&PR 93
Smith, Randolph Nunnally 1917- WhoSSW 93
Smith, Randolph Relihan 1944- WhoWor 93
Smith, Randy J. Law&B 92
Smith, Randy J. 1948- St&PR 93
Smith, Rankin McEachern, Sr. 1925- WhoAm 92, WhoSSW 93
Smith, Ray BioIn 17
Smith, Ray 1941- WhoCanL 92
Smith, Raymond WhoAm 92
Smith, Raymond Dupuy, Jr. 1933- St&PR 93, WhoAm 92
Smith, Raymond George WhoScE 91-1
Smith, Raymond J. 1938- St&PR 93
Smith, Raymond Leigh 1940- WhoE 93
Smith, Raymond Lloyd 1917- WhoAm 92
Smith, Raymond Thomas 1925- WhoAm 92
Smith, Raymond W. BioIn 17
Smith, Raymond W. 1937- St&PR 93, WhoAm 92, WhoE 93
Smith, Raymond Walter 1942- WhoE 93
Smith, Reagan Craig 1949- WhoSSW 93
Smith, Rebecca A. 1954- WhoSSW 93
Smith, Rebecca Ashworth 1967- WhoAmW 93
Smith, Rebecca Beach 1949- WhoAm 92, WhoAmW 93, WhoSSW 93
Smith, Rebecca C. Law&B 92
Smith, Rebecca McCulloch 1928- WhoAmW 93
Smith, Rebecca Sue 1950- WhoAmW 93
Smith, Rebecca Virtue 1953- WhoAmW 93
Smith, Red 1905-1982 BioIn 17, JrnUS
Smith, Reginald Brian Furness 1931- WhoAm 92, WhoSSW 93
Smith, Rene Nixon 1966- WhoSSW 93
Smith, Renee Corey 1932- WhoAmW 93
Smith, Rex G. 1956- WhoSSW 93
Smith, Rex William 1952- WhoAm 92
Smith, Reynold E. 1932- St&PR 93
Smith, Richard 1931- WhoWor 93
Smith, Richard A. Law&B 92
Smith, Richard A. 1941- St&PR 93
Smith, Richard A. 1943- St&PR 93
Smith, Richard Alan 1924- St&PR 93, WhoWor 93
Smith, Richard Allan 1949- WhoSSW 93
Smith, Richard Anthony 1939- WhoE 93
Smith, Richard Austin 1911- WhoE 93
Smith, Richard Bowen 1938- WhoAm 92
Smith, Richard C. 1949- St&PR 93
Smith, Richard Carlisle 1930- WhoAm 92
Smith, Richard D. 1954- WhoAm 92
Smith, Richard Donald 1928- WhoIns 93
Smith, Richard Dowlen 1938- WhoAm 92
Smith, Richard E. Law&B 92
Smith, Richard Edward 1948- St&PR 93
Smith, Richard Emerson 1922- WhoAm 92, WhoWor 93
Smith, Richard Ernest 1935- WhoAm 92
Smith, Richard Granger 1930- St&PR 93
Smith, Richard Grant 1937- WhoAm 92
Smith, Richard H. Law&B 92
Smith, Richard Howard 1927- WhoAm 92
Smith, Richard J. 1936- St&PR 93
Smith, Richard Jay 1930- WhoWrEP 92
Smith, Richard Joseph Law&B 92
Smith, Richard Joseph 1932- WhoAm 92
Smith, Richard Joseph 1944- WhoSSW 93
Smith, Richard Joyce 1903- WhoAm 92
Smith, Richard Keane 1942- WhoWrEP 92
Smith, Richard L. Law&B 92, WhoScE 91-1
Smith, Richard L. 1924- St&PR 93
Smith, Richard L. 1940- St&PR 93
Smith, Richard Lawrence 1933- WhoAm 92
Smith, Richard Lee, Jr. 1956- WhoSSW 93
Smith, Richard M. 1923- St&PR 93
Smith, Richard Melvyn 1940- WhoAm 92
Smith, Richard Mills 1946- WhoAm 92
Smith, Richard Muldrow 1939- WhoAm 92
Smith, Richard N. 1946- St&PR 93
Smith, Richard Norton 1953- WhoAm 92
Smith, Richard O. 1918- St&PR 93
Smith, Richard P. Law&B 92, WhoAm 92
Smith, Richard P. 1951- St&PR 93
Smith, Richard Pierson 1947- St&PR 93
Smith, Richard R. ScF&FL 92
Smith, Richard R.S. 1955- St&PR 93
Smith, Richard S. 1930- St&PR 93
Smith, Richard Thomas 1925- WhoAm 92
Smith, Richard Warren 1952- WhoE 93
Smith, Richard Worthington 1920- St&PR 93
Smith, Richey 1933- St&PR 93, WhoAm 92
Smith, Rick Montgomery 1953- WhoSSW 93
Smith, Rita Creighton AmWomPl
Smith, Rita Webb BioIn 17
Smith, Robert BioIn 17
Smith, Robert 1921- WhoAm 92
Smith, Robert, III 1939- WhoAm 92
Smith, Robert Alan d1991 BioIn 17
Smith, Robert Allen 1936- WhoE 93
Smith, Robert Arthur 1944- ScF&FL 92
Smith, Robert B. 1937- WhoAm 92
Smith, Robert Boulware, III 1933- WhoAm 92
Smith, Robert Bruce 1920- WhoAm 92
Smith, Robert Bruce 1937- WhoAm 92
Smith, Robert Burns 1929- WhoAm 92
Smith, Robert C. 1941- BioIn 17, CngDr 91
Smith, Robert Cathcart 1914- WhoSSW 93
Smith, Robert Charles ScF&FL 92
Smith, Robert Charles 1931- St&PR 93
Smith, Robert Clarke 1940- WhoWrEP 92
Smith, Robert Clinton 1941- WhoAm 92, WhoE 93
Smith, Robert Drake 1944- WhoAm 92
Smith, Robert Earl 1923- WhoAm 92, WhoSSW 93
Smith, Robert Ellis 1940- WhoWrEP 92
Smith, Robert Ellsworth 1921- WhoAm 92, WhoWor 93
Smith, Robert Everett 1936- WhoAm 92, WhoWor 93
Smith, Robert F. 1931- CngDr 91
Smith, Robert Forman Law&B 92
Smith, Robert Frank 1917- WhoWor 93
Smith, Robert Frederick 1958- WhoWor 93
Smith, Robert Freeman 1930- WhoWor 93
Smith, Robert Freeman 1931- WhoAm 92
Smith, Robert H. Law&B 92
Smith, Robert H. 1935- St&PR 93
Smith, Robert Harold 1924- WhoAm 92
Smith, Robert Harvey 1955- WhoSSW 93
Smith, Robert Houston 1931- ScF&FL 92, WhoAm 92
Smith, Robert Imbrie 1931- WhoAm 92, WhoWor 93
Smith, Robert J. Law&B 92
Smith, Robert James 1944- WhoAm 92
Smith, Robert James 1960- WhoE 93
Smith, Robert John 1927- WhoAm 92
Smith, Robert Kimmel 1930- WhoAm 92
Smith, Robert L. St&PR 93
Smith, Robert Lee 1923- WhoAm 92
Smith, Robert Lee 1939- WhoAm 92
Smith, Robert Lee, Jr. 1940- WhoSSW 93
Smith, Robert Leo 1925- WhoAm 92
Smith, Robert Letton 1928- WhoWrEP 92
Smith, Robert London 1919- WhoAm 92
Smith, Robert Louis 1922- WhoAm 92
Smith, Robert Louis 1932- WhoAm 92
Smith, Robert Luther 1927- WhoE 93
Smith, Robert M. Law&B 92
Smith, Robert Mason 1945- WhoWor 93
Smith, Robert McNeil 1932- WhoAm 92
Smith, Robert Michael 1940- WhoWor 93
Smith, Robert Milton 1932- St&PR 93
Smith, Robert Moors 1912- WhoAm 92
Smith, Robert Nathaniel 1944- WhoAm 92, WhoWor 93
Smith, Robert Nelson 1920- WhoAm 92
Smith, Robert O. 1932- St&PR 93
Smith, Robert Peter ScF&FL 92
Smith, Robert Powell 1929- WhoAm 92
Smith, Robert Rutherford 1933- WhoAm 92
Smith, Robert S. 1916- St&PR 93
Smith, Robert Samuel 1920- WhoAm 92
Smith, Robert Scott Law&B 92
Smith, Robert Sellers 1931- WhoAm 92
Smith, Robert Stanley 1934- WhoAm 92
Smith, Robert Victor 1942- WhoAm 92
Smith, Robert Walter 1937- WhoAm 92
Smith, Robert Weston 1938- WhoAm 92
Smith, Robert William Law&B 92
Smith, Robert William 1923- WhoAm 92
Smith, Roberta BioIn 17
Smith, Roberta Ann Pointer 1944- WhoAmW 93
Smith, Roberta Hawkins 1945- WhoAmW 93
Smith, Robin M. Law&B 92
Smith, Robin Wynclyffe 1942- WhoWor 93
Smith, Robyn Doyal 1947- WhoSSW 93
Smith, Roch Charles 1941- WhoSSW 93
Smith, Roderick James Hollas 1957- WhoWor 93
Smith, Rodney A. 1947- St&PR 93
Smith, Rodney Frank 1940- St&PR 93
Smith, Rodney R. 1946- St&PR 93
Smith, Rodney T. 1948- WhoWrEP 92
Smith, Rodney W., Jr. 1943- St&PR 93
Smith, Rodney Wike 1944- WhoSSW 93, WhoWor 93
Smith, Roger B. BioIn 17
Smith, Roger Bonham 1925- St&PR 93, WhoAm 92
Smith, Roger Crichton 1937- St&PR 93
Smith, Roger Dean 1932- WhoAm 92
Smith, Roger Drummond 1945- WhoScE 91-1
Smith, Roger Dwain 1937- WhoSSW 93
Smith, Roger G. BioIn 17
Smith, Roger Graham 1945- WhoWor 93
Smith, Roger Paul Law&B 92
Smith, Roger Powell 1932- WhoE 93
Smith, Roger S. Law&B 92
Smith, Roger W., III Law&B 92
Smith, Roger Winston 1936- WhoAm 92
Smith, Roland B., Jr. AfrAmBi [port]
Smith, Roland F. St&PR 93
Smith, Rona 1944- WhoE 93
Smith, Ronald 1922- Baker 92
Smith, Ronald Arthur 1943- St&PR 93
Smith, Ronald Clive WhoScE 91-1
Smith, Ronald Ehlbert 1947- WhoSSW 93
Smith, Ronald Emory 1950- WhoAm 92
Smith, Ronald H. St&PR 93
Smith, Ronald James John 1941- WhoWor 93
Smith, Ronald L. 1942- St&PR 93
Smith, Ronald L. 1952- ScF&FL 92
Smith, Ronald Lee 1937- WhoAm 92
Smith, Ronald Lee 1951- WhoE 93
Smith, Ronald Lynn 1940- WhoAm 92, WhoSSW 93
Smith, Ronald M. WhoIns 93
Smith, Ronald William WhoScE 91-1
Smith, Rory Dean Law&B 92
Smith, Rosamond 1938- ScF&FL 92
Smith, Rosie 1954- ConAu 139
Smith, Ross Menefee Law&B 92
Smith, Rowland James 1938- WhoAm 92, WhoWrEP 92
Smith, Roy WhoScE 91-1
Smith, Roy C. 1938- St&PR 93
Smith, Roy Leonard WhoE 93
Smith, Roy Philip 1933- WhoAm 92, WhoE 93
Smith, Rufus Albert, Jr. 1932- WhoSSW 93
Smith, Rufus Z. 1921-1991 BioIn 17
Smith, Rush Blackfan 1941- St&PR 93
Smith, Russell Aubrey 1936- WhoE 93
Smith, Russell Bryan 1936- WhoSSW 93
Smith, Russell David 1950- WhoE 93
Smith, Russell Eugene 1944- WhoSSW 93
Smith, Russell Francis 1944- WhoWor 93
Smith, Russell Jack BioIn 17
Smith, Russell Jack 1913- WhoAm 92
Smith, Russell Lynn, Jr. 1919- WhoAm 92
Smith, Ruth St&PR 93
Smith, Ruth Lillian Schluchter 1917- WhoAm 92
Smith, Ruth R. 1924- WhoAmW 93
Smith, S. WhoScE 91-1
Smith, S.D. WhoScE 91-1
Smith, S. Denny 1932- St&PR 93
Smith, S. Jennie AmWomPl
Smith, Saddie L. Law&B 92
Smith, Sally J. 1958- St&PR 93
Smith, Sallye Wrye 1923- WhoAmW 93
Smith, Sam AfrAmBi [port]
Smith, Samuel 1752-1839 HarEnMi, PolPar
Smith, Samuel Boyd 1929- WhoAm 92
Smith, Samuel David 1918- WhoAm 92
Smith, Samuel David 1955- WhoE 93
Smith, Samuel Harrison 1772-1845 JrnUS
Smith, Samuel Howard 1940- WhoAm 92
Smith, Samuel Joseph 1939- WhoAm 92
Smith, Samuel Reese, Jr. 1964- WhoSSW 93
Smith, Sandford D. 1947- St&PR 93
Smith, Sandra G. 1954- WhoSSW 93
Smith, Sandra Jane 1963- WhoAmW 93
Smith, Sandra L. Law&B 92
Smith, Sandra Louise 1950- WhoAmW 93
Smith, Sandra Metheny 1940- WhoAmW 93
Smith, Sandra Williams Law&B 92
Smith, Sara Elizabeth Cushing 1950- WhoSSW 93
Smith, Sarah Bixby- 1871-1935 BioIn 17
Smith, Sarah Lindsay 1951- WhoSSW 93
Smith, Sarah M. St&PR 93
Smith, Scott C. Law&B 92
Smith, Scott Clybourn 1950- WhoAm 92
Smith, Scott F. 1952- St&PR 93
Smith, Scott Lee 1926- St&PR 93

Smith, Sedgwick E. 1914-1990 *BioIn 17*
Smith, Selby Robert 1933- *St&PR 93*
Smith, Serafina Gangemi 1919- *WhoAmW 93*
Smith, Seymour David 1922- *WhoSSW 93*
Smith, Seymour Howard *Law&B 92*
Smith, Seymour M. 1941- *St&PR 93*
Smith, Seymour Maslin 1941- *WhoAm 92*
Smith, Sharon Jean 1951- *WhoAmW 93*
Smith, Sharon Kay 1954- *WhoWrEP 92*
Smith, Sharon Patricia 1948- *WhoE 93*
Smith, Sharron Williams 1941- *WhoAmW 93, WhoE 93*
Smith, Shawn A. *Law&B 92*
Smith, Sheila Bowman 1953- *WhoAmW 93*
Smith, Sheila M. 1957- *St&PR 93*
Smith, Shelagh Alison 1949- *WhoAmW 93*
Smith, Sheldon Evard 1930- *St&PR 93*
Smith, Sheldon L. 1942- *St&PR 93*
Smith, Shelly Gerald, Jr. 1949- *WhoSSW 93*
Smith, Sherman Allen 1920- *WhoAm 92*
Smith, Sherri Davis 1955- *St&PR 93*
Smith, Sherwood 1951- *ScF&FL 92*
Smith, Sherwood Draughon 1925- *WhoAm 92*
Smith, Sherwood Hubbard, Jr. 1934- *St&PR 93, WhoAm 92, WhoSSW 93*
Smith, Sheryl L. 1947- *WhoWrEP 92*
Smith, Shirley 1929- *WhoAm 92*
Smith, Shirley A. 1939- *WhoAmW 93*
Smith, Shirley B. 1941- *St&PR 93*
Smith, Shirley K. 1934- *WhoAmW 93*
Smith, Shirley Mae 1923- *WhoWrEP 92*
Smith, Shirley O'Bryan 1949- *WhoWrEP 92*
Smith, Sidney 1915- *BioIn 17*
Smith, Sidney Oslin, Jr. 1923- *WhoAm 92, WhoSSW 93*
Smith, Sidney Rufus, Jr. 1931- *WhoAm 92*
Smith, Simon Harcourt Nowell- 1909- *BioIn 17*
Smith, Sonja Irene 1967- *WhoAmW 93*
Smith, Soren Friis 1950- *WhoWor 93*
Smith, Spencer *Law&B 92*
Smith, Spencer Bailey 1927- *WhoAm 92*
Smith, Stacey Ellen 1958- *WhoE 93*
Smith, Stan Vladimir 1946- *WhoAm 92, WhoEmL 93*
Smith, Standish Harshaw 1931- *WhoE 93*
Smith, Stanford 1919- *WhoSSW 93*
Smith, Stanford Lee 1935- *WhoSSW 93*
Smith, Stanford Sidney 1923- *WhoAm 92*
Smith, Stanley Desmond *WhoScE 91-1*
Smith, Stanley H. 1920- *ConAu 138*
Smith, Stanley O'Neil, Sr. 1941- *WhoAm 92*
Smith, Stanley Roger 1946- *WhoAm 92*
Smith, Stanton Kinnie, Jr. 1931- *St&PR 93, WhoAm 92*
Smith, Stephanie A. *ScF&FL 92*
Smith, Stephanie Zaharoudis 1958- *WhoAmW 93*
Smith, Stephen *Law&B 92*
Smith, Stephen Alexander 1957- *St&PR 93, WhoAm 92*
Smith, Stephen Charles 1951- *WhoSSW 93*
Smith, Stephen Charles 1955- *WhoE 93*
Smith, Stephen E. 1927-1990 *BioIn 17*
Smith, Stephen F. 1940- *WhoIns 93*
Smith, Stephen Grant 1949- *WhoAm 92*
Smith, Stephen Kevin *WhoScE 91-1*
Smith, Stephen Lewis 1943- *St&PR 93*
Smith, Stephen Manly 1952- *WhoSSW 93*
Smith, Stephen R. *Law&B 92*
Smith, Stephen Ross 1938- *WhoE 93*
Smith, Stephenson Percy 1840-1922 *IntDcAn*
Smith, Sterling T. 1918- *St&PR 93*
Smith, Steve *BioIn 17*
Smith, Steven 1945- *WhoCanL 92*
Smith, Steven Alden 1941- *St&PR 93, WhoAm 92*
Smith, Steven D. 1941- *WhoIns 93*
Smith, Steven D. 1953- *St&PR 93*
Smith, Steven F. 1948- *St&PR 93*
Smith, Steven G(arry) 1953- *ConAu 139*
Smith, Steven Harold 1954- *WhoSSW 93*
Smith, Steven James 1945- *St&PR 93, WhoAm 92, WhoIns 93*
Smith, Steven Lee 1952- *WhoEmL 93, WhoSSW 93*
Smith, Steven Lee 1958- *WhoEmL 93, WhoSSW 93*
Smith, Steven Sidney 1946- *WhoEmL 93*
Smith, Stevie 1902-1971 *BioIn 17, BritWr S2*
Smith, Stewart Edward 1937- *WhoE 93*
Smith, Stewart Gregory 1953- *WhoE 93*
Smith, Stuart A. 1941- *WhoAm 92*
Smith, Stuart H. B. 1945- *St&PR 93*
Smith, Stuart Lyon 1938- *WhoAm 92*
Smith, Stuart Seaborne 1930- *WhoAm 92*
Smith, Stuff 1909-1967 *BioIn 17*
Smith, Sue Frances 1940- *WhoAm 92, WhoWrEP 92*
Smith, Sumner M. *St&PR 93*
Smith, Survilla Marie 1933- *WhoE 93*
Smith, Susan 1950- *ScF&FL 92*
Smith, Susan Arlene 1957- *WhoAmW 93*
Smith, Susan Converse 1956- *WhoAmW 93*
Smith, Susan Daniels d1989 *BioIn 17*
Smith, Susan Finnegan 1954- *WhoAmW 93*
Smith, Susan Kimsey 1947- *WhoAmW 93*
Smith, Susan L. *Law&B 92*
Smith, Susan Lynn 1958- *WhoSSW 93*
Smith, Susan M. 1942- *ConAu 137*
Smith, Susan Papa 1952- *WhoAmW 93*
Smith, Susan Ross 1945- *WhoWrEP 92*
Smith, Susan Sumner *AmWomPl*
Smith, Susanna Schaeffer 1966- *WhoE 93*
Smith, Susanne H. 1933- *St&PR 93*
Smith, Susie Sanderson 1961- *WhoSSW 93*
Smith, Suzanne Bates 1960- *WhoAmW 93*
Smith, Sybil *BioIn 17*
Smith, Sydney 1771-1845 *BioIn 17*
Smith, Sydney G. 1938- *St&PR 93*
Smith, Sylvia Jo 1950- *WhoAmW 93*
Smith, T. Arthur 1923- *WhoSSW 93*
Smith, T.D. *WhoScE 91-1*
Smith, T. Ian M. *Law&B 92*
Smith, T.J., III 1930- *St&PR 93*
Smith, T. Kent 1956- *WhoSSW 93*
Smith, Tad Randolph 1928- *WhoAm 92, WhoSSW 93, WhoWor 93*
Smith, Taylor 1953- *WhoAm 92, WhoSSW 93*
Smith, Ted D. *Law&B 92*
Smith, Ted Jay, III 1945- *WhoSSW 93, WhoWor 93*
Smith, Terence A. 1934- *WhoScE 91-1*
Smith, Terence Fitzgerald 1938- *WhoAm 92*
Smith, Terence Michael Frederick *WhoScE 91-1*
Smith, Terrence John 1931- *St&PR 93*
Smith, Terrence Lore 1942-1988 *ScF&FL 92*
Smith, Terry Edward 1940- *WhoE 93*
Smith, Tevis Clyde 1908-1984 *ScF&FL 92*
Smith, Thelma Marie 1936- *WhoAmW 93*
Smith, Thelma Tina Harriette 1938- *WhoAmW 93, WhoSSW 93*
Smith, Theodore Floyd 1931- *St&PR 93*
Smith, Theodore Goodwin 1934- *WhoAm 92*
Smith, Theresa Catherine Sullivan 1924- *WhoWor 93*
Smith, Thomas Arthur 1954- *WhoSSW 93*
Smith, Thomas Clair 1925- *WhoE 93, WhoWor 93*
Smith, Thomas Clayton 1927- *WhoAm 92*
Smith, Thomas E. 1947- *St&PR 93*
Smith, Thomas Earle 1910-1980 *BioIn 17*
Smith, Thomas Edward 1951- *WhoSSW 93*
Smith, Thomas Eugene 1930- *WhoAm 92*
Smith, Thomas F. 1934- *St&PR 93*
Smith, Thomas Franklin 1947- *WhoSSW 93*
Smith, Thomas Fred 1939- *WhoWor 93*
Smith, Thomas G. 1938- *ScF&FL 92*
Smith, Thomas Gregory 1959- *WhoEmL 93*
Smith, Thomas H. 1948- *St&PR 93*
Smith, Thomas Hunter 1939- *WhoSSW 93*
Smith, Thomas N. 1956- *St&PR 93*
Smith, Thomas R. 1909- *St&PR 93*
Smith, Thomas Ray 1949- *St&PR 93*
Smith, Thomas Shore 1924- *WhoAm 92*
Smith, Thomas W. *Law&B 92*
Smith, Thomas Walter 1955- *WhoE 93*
Smith, Thomas Winston 1935- *WhoAm 92*
Smith, Thomas Woodward 1936- *WhoAm 92*
Smith, Thor L. 1920- *WhoAm 92*
Smith, Thornton E. 1923- *St&PR 93*
Smith, Tim L. 1924-1990? *ScF&FL 92*
Smith, Timmy *BioIn 17*
Smith, Timothy Andre 1937- *WhoSSW 93*
Smith, Timothy Lawrence 1924- *WhoAm 92*
Smith, Timothy P. *Law&B 92*
Smith, Timothy Randolph 1945- *WhoSSW 93*
Smith, Timothy Treadwell 1768-1803 *BioIn 17*
Smith, Todd Malcolm 1961- *WhoSSW 93*
Smith, Tom d1870 *BioIn 17*
Smith, Tom d1893 *BioIn 17*
Smith, Tom Calvin 1942- *WhoSSW 93*
Smith, Tom E. *BioIn 17*
Smith, Tom E. 1941- *St&PR 93*
Smith, Tom Eugene 1941- *WhoAm 92*
Smith, Tom Eugene 1942- *WhoSSW 93*
Smith, Tom H. 1938- *WhoSSW 93*
Smith, Tom W. 1935- *St&PR 93*
Smith, Tommie *BioIn 17*
Smith, Toni Colette 1952- *WhoAmW 93*
Smith, Tony *MiSFD 9*
Smith, Tony S. d1991 *BioIn 17*
Smith, Toukie *BioIn 17*
Smith, Travis Edward 1931- *WhoWor 93*
Smith, Trevor Dudley- *ScF&FL 92*
Smith, Troy Alvin 1922- *WhoWor 93*
Smith, Troy N., Sr. 1922- *St&PR 93*
Smith, Tyler *BioIn 17*
Smith, V. Kerry 1945- *WhoAm 92*
Smith, V. La Monte 1938- *WhoWrEP 92*
Smith, Valor C. 1919- *St&PR 93*
Smith, Van *BioIn 17*
Smith, Van P. 1928- *St&PR 93*
Smith, Vangy Edith 1937- *WhoAmW 93, WhoWor 93*
Smith, Verity Carlisle 1922- *St&PR 93*
Smith, Vernon J. 1929- *St&PR 93*
Smith, Vernon Soruix 1938- *WhoSSW 93*
Smith, Veronica Latta 1925- *WhoAm 92, WhoWor 93*
Smith, Vicki Lynn 1954- *WhoAmW 93*
Smith, Victor Earle 1914- *WhoAm 92*
Smith, Victor L. 1930- *St&PR 93*
Smith, Victoria F. *Law&B 92*
Smith, Vilma J. 1927- *St&PR 93*
Smith, Vin 1944- *WhoWor 93*
Smith, Vincent DaCosta 1929- *WhoAm 92*
Smith, Virgil C., Jr. *AfrAmBi [port]*
Smith, Virginia Brown 1954- *WhoAmW 93*
Smith, Virginia Dodd 1911- *BioIn 17, WhoAm 92, WhoAmW 93*
Smith, Virginia Eleanore 1940- *WhoE 93*
Smith, Virginia S. *Law&B 92*
Smith, Vme 1929- *WhoAmW 93*
Smith, W. Clement 1954- *St&PR 93*
Smith, W. Douglass 1936- *WhoAm 92*
Smith, W.F. *Law&B 92*
Smith, W. Griswold 1921- *St&PR 93*
Smith, W. J., Mrs. *AmWomPl*
Smith, W. Kirk 1938- *St&PR 93*
Smith, W. Richard 1932- *St&PR 93*
Smith, W. Scott, Jr. 1924- *St&PR 93*
Smith, Waldo Gregorius 1911- *WhoWor 93*
Smith, Wallace Bunnell 1929- *WhoAm 92*
Smith, Wallace H. 1936- *St&PR 93*
Smith, Walter Arnold 1943- *WhoE 93*
Smith, Walter B., Jr. 1915- *WhoIns 93*
Smith, Walter Bedell 1895-1961 *BioIn 17, ColdWar 1 [port], HarEnMi*
Smith, Walter Douglas 1918- *WhoAm 92*
Smith, Walter H. 1929- *St&PR 93*
Smith, Walter Hall 1920- *WhoAm 92*
Smith, Walter J. 1917- *ScF&FL 92*
Smith, Walter Joseph, Jr. 1936- *WhoE 93*
Smith, Walter Julius, Jr. 1911- *WhoE 93*
Smith, Walter L. 1957- *St&PR 93*
Smith, Walter S., Jr. 1940- *WhoSSW 93*
Smith, Walter Tilford 1907- *WhoAm 92*
Smith, Walter Wellesley 1905-1982 *BioIn 17*
Smith, Walter Wulfing 1948- *St&PR 93*
Smith, Wanda VanHoy 1926- *BioIn 17*
Smith, Ward *ConAu 40NR, WhoWrEP 92*
Smith, Ward 1930- *St&PR 93, WhoAm 92*
Smith, Warren Allen 1921- *St&PR 93, WhoWor 93*
Smith, Warren F. *St&PR 93*
Smith, Warren James 1922- *WhoAm 92*
Smith, Warren L. 1924- *WhoAm 92, WhoE 93*
Smith, Warren W. 1948- *St&PR 93*
Smith, Warwick Leslie 1954- *WhoAsAP 91*
Smith, Watson 1897- *WhoAm 92*
Smith, Watson B., Jr. 1931- *St&PR 93*
Smith, Wayland 1880-1972 *ScF&FL 92*
Smith, Wayman Flynn 1940- *St&PR 93*
Smith, Wayne Calvin 1935- *WhoAm 92*
Smith, Wayne D. 1944- *St&PR 93*
Smith, Wayne David *Law&B 92*
Smith, Wayne H. 1948- *St&PR 93*
Smith, Wayne Henry 1941- *St&PR 93*
Smith, Wayne L. 1936- *WhoAm 92*
Smith, Wayne L. 1937- *St&PR 93*
Smith, Wayne O. *St&PR 93*
Smith, Wayne T. 1943- *St&PR 93*
Smith, Wayne T. 1946- *WhoSSW 93*
Smith, Wendell M. 1935- *St&PR 93*
Smith, Wendell Murray 1935- *WhoAm 92*
Smith, Wendy 1956- *ConAu 138*
Smith, Wesley Omar 1943- *WhoSSW 93*
Smith, Wilber G. d1992 *NewYTBS 92 [port]*
Smith, Wilber G. 1928- *St&PR 93*
Smith, Wilbur *St&PR 93*
Smith, Wilbur A. *BioIn 17*
Smith, Wilbur Cowan 1914- *WhoWor 93*
Smith, Wilbur S. 1911-1990 *BioIn 17*
Smith, Wilbur Stevenson 1911- *WhoWrEP 92*
Smith, Wilburn Jackson, Jr. 1921- *WhoAm 92*
Smith, Wilda M(axine) 1924- *ConAu 137*
Smith, Wilfred Irvin 1919- *WhoAm 92*
Smith, Will *BioIn 17*
Smith, William *WhoScE 91-1*
Smith, William 1762-1840 *OxCSupC*
Smith, William A. d1991 *BioIn 17*
Smith, William A. 1948- *WhoAm 92*
Smith, William A., III 1927- *St&PR 93*
Smith, William Adams, Jr. 1929- *WhoSSW 93*
Smith, William Allen 1940- *WhoSSW 93*
Smith, William Ashley *Law&B 92*
Smith, William B. 1936- *St&PR 93*
Smith, William Burton 1927- *WhoAm 92, WhoSSW 93*
Smith, William Charles 1930- *WhoAm 92*
Smith, William Curtis 1946- *WhoSSW 93*
Smith, William D. *Law&B 92*
Smith, William Dee 1933- *WhoAm 92*
Smith, William E. 1912- *St&PR 93*
Smith, William Earl 1951- *WhoAm 92*
Smith, William Edgar, Jr. 1940- *St&PR 93*
Smith, William Edgett d1992 *BioIn 17, NewYTBS 92*
Smith, William Ewem 1941- *WhoWor 93*
Smith, William Ewen *WhoScE 91-1*
Smith, William Francis, Jr. 1935- *WhoAm 92*
Smith, William French *BioIn 17*
Smith, William Gardner 1927-1974 *BioIn 17*
Smith, William Henry 1833-1896 *JrnUS*
Smith, William Henry, Jr. 1942- *WhoSSW 93*
Smith, William Henry Preston 1924- *WhoAm 92*
Smith, William Hulse 1939- *WhoAm 92*
Smith, William J. *Law&B 92*
Smith, William Jay 1918- *BioIn 17, MajAI [port], WhoAm 92, WhoWrEP 92*
Smith, William Kennedy *BioIn 17*
Smith, William Kennerly *Law&B 92*
Smith, William Kevin 1951- *WhoE 93*
Smith, William L. 1928- *St&PR 93*
Smith, William Lester 1940- *WhoSSW 93*
Smith, William Lewis 1925- *WhoAm 92*
Smith, William Maurice 1929- *St&PR 93*
Smith, William Milton 1918- *WhoAm 92*
Smith, William O(verton) 1926- *Baker 92*
Smith, William Permar 1920- *St&PR 93*
Smith, William R. 1929- *St&PR 93*
Smith, William Randolph 1928- *WhoAm 92*
Smith, William Randolph 1948- *WhoAm 92, WhoSSW 93*
Smith, William Ray 1925- *WhoWor 93*
Smith, William Robert 1916- *St&PR 93*
Smith, William Robertson 1846-1894 *IntDcAn*
Smith, William Roy 1920- *WhoAm 92*
Smith, William Sidney 1764-1840 *HarEnMi*
Smith, William Stevens 1773-1837 *BioIn 17*
Smith, William U. 1940- *St&PR 93*
Smith, William W. 1922- *St&PR 93*
Smith, William Walker 1940- *WhoSSW 93*
Smith, William Young 1925- *WhoAm 92*
Smith, Willie 1897-1973 *Baker 92*
Smith, Willie Tesreau, Jr. 1920- *WhoSSW 93*
Smith, Willis Allen 1919- *WhoAm 92*
Smith, Wilma Janice 1926- *WhoWrEP 92*
Smith, Wilson Earl 1949- *WhoSSW 93*
Smith, Winifred 1879- *AmWomPl*
Smith, Winthrop Hiram, Jr. 1949- *WhoAm 92*
Smith, Wm. Hovey 1941- *WhoWrEP 92*
Smith, Wofford Kreth d1990 *BioIn 17*
Smith, Woodrow D. *Law&B 92*
Smith, Wrede H. 1921- *St&PR 93*
Smith, Yvonne Carolyn 1923- *WhoAmW 93*
Smith, Z.Z. *WhoWrEP 92*
Smith, Zachary Alden 1953- *WhoEmL 93*
Smith, Zachary Taylor, II 1923- *WhoAm 92*
Smith-Alexander, Melanie Sue 1959- *WhoAmW 93, WhoWor 93*
Smithart-Weitzman, Debra L. 1954- *St&PR 93*
Smith Brindle, Reginald 1917- *Baker 92*
Smithburg, William D. 1938- *St&PR 93*
Smithburg, William Dean 1938- *WhoAm 92*
Smith-Dorrien, Horace Lockwood 1858-1930 *HarEnMi*
Smithee, Alan 1969- *MiSFD 9*
Smithee, Jeannette P. 1946- *BioIn 17*
Smither, Howard E(lbert) 1925- *Baker 92*
Smither, Howard Elbert 1925- *WhoAm 92*
Smitherman, Carole Catlin *AfrAmBi*
Smitherman, Gustavus Scott 1921- *WhoAm 92*
Smithers, Donald Lee 1937- *WhoSSW 93*
Smithers, Peter Henry Berry Otway 1913- *WhoWor 93*
Smithers, Wayne Donovan 1943- *St&PR 93*
Smithey, Jeffery D. 1960- *St&PR 93*

Smithey, Jerry de Roy 1919- *St&PR 93*
Smithey, Sarah Elizabeth 1932- *St&PR 93*
Smith Family *BioIn 17*
Smithfield, David Alan 1945- *St&PR 93*
Smithfield, William Ronald 1942- *St&PR 93*
Smith-Grayton, Patricia Karen *Law&B 92*
Smith-Hefner, Nancy Joan 1952- *WhoE 93*
Smith-Hunter, Susan Harriet 1939- *WhoAmW 93*
Smithmier, Mary Louise 1950- *WhoAmW 93*
Smith-Pierce, Patricia A. 1939- *WhoWor 93*
Smith-Reichert, Sue-Ellen 1954- *WhoSSW 93*
Smith-Silvetti, Kimberly A. 1957- *St&PR 93*
Smithson, Alison Margaret 1928- *WhoWor 93*
Smithson, Evelyn Lord d1992 *BioIn 17, NewYTBS 92*
Smithson, John W. 1946- *WhoIns 93*
Smithson, John Wynne 1946- *St&PR 93*
Smithson, Lowell Lee 1930- *WhoWor 93*
Smithson, Peter Denham 1923- *WhoWor 93*
Smithson, Richard Joseph 1923- *St&PR 93*
Smithson, Susan Mary 1952- *WhoAmW 93*
Smithson, Thomas Alan 1928- *WhoWor 93*
Smith-Taylor, Melanie Kathleen 1963- *WhoAmW 93*
Smith-Townsend, Barbara Elizabeth 1950- *WhoAmW 93*
Smith-Vaniz, William Reid 1925- *WhoAm 92*
Smith-Vaniz, Wm. Reid 1925- *St&PR 93*
Smith-Wade-El, Rita Rorate 1948- *WhoAmW 93*
Smithwick, Carolyn Dale 1946- *WhoAmW 93*
Smithwick, Carolyn Frances *AmWomPl*
Smithwick, Fred, Jr. 1934- *WhoWor 93*
Smithwick, J. Jerry 1944- *St&PR 93*
Smith-Young, Anne Victoria 1947- *WhoE 93*
Smitley, Barbara Anne 1956- *WhoAmW 93*
Smitley, Christopher Kane 1952- *WhoAm 92*
Smits, Edward John 1933- *WhoE 93*
Smits, Helen Lida 1936- *WhoAm 92, WhoAmW 93*
Smits, Jimmy *WhoAm 92*
Smits, Jimmy 1955- *HolBB [port]*
Smits, Lieven Lode Maria 1964- *WhoWor 93*
Smits, Marc Peter 1949- *WhoWor 93*
Smits, Robert L. 1943- *St&PR 93*
Smitson, Harrison Adam, Jr. 1933- *St&PR 93*
Smits van Waesberghe, Jos(eph Maria Antonius Franciscus) 1901-1986 *Baker 92*
Smitten, Richard 1940- *ConAu 136*
Smittle, Burrell Joe 1934- *WhoSSW 93*
Smiy, Paul R. 1923- *St&PR 93*
Smiy, William Charles 1927- *St&PR 93*
Smoak, Gary Alan 1939- *WhoSSW 93*
Smoak, Joseph F. 1936- *St&PR 93*
Smoak, Neil A. 1946- *St&PR 93*
Smoak, Samuel D. 1933- *St&PR 93*
Smock, Arthur Reseau, Jr. 1920- *WhoE 93*
Smock, James Arthur 1938- *St&PR 93*
Smock, Joseph B. *St&PR 93*
Smock, Raymond William 1941- *WhoAm 92*
Smock, Roger P. 1942- *St&PR 93*
Smockhoffmann, Sharon Lynne 1941- *WhoAmW 93*
Smodish, Michael Paul 1945- *WhoSSW 93*
Smogolski, Henry Richard 1931- *St&PR 93*
Smoke, Richard 1944- *WhoAm 92, WhoE 93*
Smoke, Richard Edwin 1945- *WhoWor 93*
Smoke, Stephen L. 1949- *ScF&FL 92*
Smoker, Constance M. *Law&B 92*
Smoker, Richard E. *WhoIns 93*
Smokler, Carol Shalita 1946- *WhoAmW 93*
Smokovitis, Athanassios A. 1935- *WhoWor 93*
Smola, Josef 1931- *WhoScE 91-4*
Smolan, Sandy *MiSFD 9*
Smolander, Aino 1959- *WhoScE 91-4*
Smolander, Heikki Kalevi 1949- *WhoScE 91-4*
Smolenoi *OxDcByz*
Smolenski, Mary Catherine 1950- *WhoAmW 93*
Smolenski, Zygmunt 1929- *WhoScE 91-4*
Smolensky, Eugene 1932- *WhoAm 92*
Smolensky, Stepan (Vasilievich) 1848-1909 *Baker 92*
Smoler, Harry 1911-1991 *BioIn 17*
Smolev, Terence Elliot 1944- *WhoE 93*
Smoliar, Burton B. *Law&B 92*
Smolik, Ellis F. 1919- *St&PR 93*
Smolik, Mark Andrew *Law&B 92*
Smolin, Bernard 1916- *St&PR 93*
Smolinski, Edward Albert 1928- *WhoAm 92*
Smoljak, Ladislav 1931- *DrEEuF*
Smolker, Jennifer A. *Law&B 92*
Smolla, Rodney Alan 1953- *WhoAm 92*
Smollett, Tobias George 1721-1771 *BioIn 17*
Smolley, Laurence Arnood 1950- *WhoSSW 93*
Smolowitz, Ira Ephraim 1941- *WhoAm 92*
Smoltczyk, Ulrich 1928- *WhoScE 91-3*
Smoluchowski, Roman 1910- *WhoAm 92*
Smook, John T. 1927- *WhoSSW 93*
Smook, Malcolm Andrew 1924- *WhoAm 92*
Smoot, George Fitzgerald, III 1945- *WhoAm 92*
Smoot, Hazel Lampkin 1916- *WhoAmW 93, WhoWor 93*
Smoot, Jeanne Johannessen 1943- *WhoSSW 93*
Smoot, Joseph Grady 1932- *WhoWor 93*
Smoot, Leon Douglas 1934- *WhoAm 92*
Smoot, Leslie Allen 1953- *WhoSSW 93*
Smoot, Marianna Hancock 1949- *WhoAmW 93*
Smoot, Oliver Reed, Jr. 1940- *WhoAm 92*
Smoot, Thomas William 1933- *WhoSSW 93*
Smoot, Wendell M., Jr. 1921- *St&PR 93*
Smoot, Wendell McMeans, Jr. 1921- *WhoAm 92*
Smorodinski, Yacob Abramovich 1917- *WhoWor 93*
Smorol, Albert Edward, Jr. 1940- *WhoAm 92*
Smotherman, Scott Ferrell 1963- *WhoSSW 93*
Smothers, Dick 1939- *WhoAm 92*
Smothers, Ella *BioIn 17*
Smothers, James Floyd 1955- *WhoSSW 93*
Smothers, Jimmy 1933- *WhoSSW 93*
Smothers, Tom 1937- *WhoAm 92*
Smothers, W.D. 1948- *St&PR 93*
Smothers, William Edgar, Jr. 1928- *WhoAm 92*
Smotrich, David Isadore 1933- *WhoAm 92*
Smoulder, Blair Thomas 1942- *St&PR 93*
Smouse, Hervey Russell *WhoAm 92*
Smoyer, William P. 1942- *St&PR 93*
Smrtnik, David K. *Law&B 92*
Smucker, Barbara 1915- *WhoCanL 92*
Smucker, Barbara (Claassen) 1915- *DcChlFi, MajAI [port], WhoAm 92*
Smucker, Paul H. 1917- *St&PR 93*
Smuckler, Jack Dennis 1946- *WhoAm 92*
Smuckler, Ralph Herbert 1926- *WhoAm 92*
Smuda, Hubert Bernard 1956- *WhoWor 93*
Smuglewicz, Franciszek 1745-1807 *PolBiDi*
Smuin, Michael 1938- *WhoAm 92*
Smukler, Barbara Quinn 1942- *WhoAmW 93*
Smulders, Charles 1863-1934 *Baker 92*
Smulewicz, Jan Jacob d1992 *NewYTBS 92*
Smull, Cynthia Ann 1944- *WhoAmW 93*
Smullen, Harold Arthur, Jr. 1954- *WhoE 93*
Smullen, James Dennis 1916- *WhoAm 92*
Smullin, Louis Dijour 1916- *WhoAm 92*
Smulowitz, William Joseph 1929- *St&PR 93*
Smulyan, Jeffrey *WhoAm 92*
Smurfit, Michael William Joseph 1936- *WhoAm 92*
Smusz, Deborah Ann 1957- *WhoAmW 93*
Smutny, Joan Franklin *WhoAm 92*
Smutny, Peter J. 1935- *St&PR 93*
Smuts, Barbara B. *BioIn 17*
Smuts, Jan Christiaan 1870-1950 *HarEnMi*
Smuts, Jan Christian 1870-1950 *DcTwHis*
Smy, Jack Rayment *WhoScE 91-1*
Smyczek, Karel 1950- *DrEEuF*
Smyer, Michael Anthony 1950- *WhoE 93*
Smyer, Myrna Ruth 1946- *WhoAmW 93*
Smyer, Sidney William, Jr. 1928- *St&PR 93*
Smyntek, John Eugene, Jr. 1950- *WhoAm 92*
Smyser, Adam A. 1920- *St&PR 93*
Smyser, Adam Albert 1920- *WhoAm 92*
Smyslov, V.V. 1921- *BioIn 17*
Smyslov, Vasilii Vasil'evich 1921- *BioIn 17*
Smyth, Alexander 1765-1830 *HarEnMi*
Smyth, Bernard John 1915- *WhoAm 92*
Smyth, Charles Phelps 1895-1990 *BioIn 17*
Smyth, Craig Hugh 1915- *WhoAm 92, WhoWor 93*
Smyth, David 1929- *WhoE 93, WhoWor 93*
Smyth, David John 1936- *WhoAm 92, WhoSSW 93, WhoWor 93*
Smyth, Donald Morgan 1930- *WhoAm 92*
Smyth, Ethel 1858-1944 *IntDcOp, OxDcOp*
Smyth, Ethel (Mary) 1858-1944 *Baker 92, BioIn 17*
Smyth, Glen Miller 1929- *WhoAm 92*
Smyth, James P. 1944- *St&PR 93*
Smyth, Jeffrey J. 1940- *St&PR 93*
Smyth, Joel Douglas 1941- *WhoAm 92*
Smyth, John Crocket *WhoScE 91-1*
Smyth, John Fletcher *WhoScE 91-1*
Smyth, John Fletcher 1945- *WhoWor 93*
Smyth, John M. 1915- *St&PR 93*
Smyth, Joseph Patrick 1933- *WhoAm 92*
Smyth, Joseph Vincent 1919- *WhoAm 92*
Smyth, Judalon *BioIn 17*
Smyth, Peter Hayes 1952- *WhoE 93*
Smyth, Reginald 1917- *WhoAm 92*
Smyth, Richard Andrew 1933- *WhoSSW 93*
Smyth, Robert K. 1927- *St&PR 93*
Smyth, Rosina K. *AmWomPl*
Smyth, Susan Ruth 1946- *WhoAmW 93*
Smyth, Theodore Hilton 1915- *WhoWor 93*
Smythe, Colin 1958- *WhoWor 93*
Smythe, John *WhoSSW 93*
Smythe, Joseph Denis 1947- *WhoSSW 93*
Smythe, Kym Corscadden 1963- *WhoE 93*
Smythe, Marianne Koral 1942- *WhoAm 92*
Smythe, Reggie 1917- *WhoAm 92*
Smythe, Robert C. *St&PR 93*
Smythe, Robert O. 1921- *St&PR 93*
Smythe, Sheila Mary 1932- *WhoAmW 93, WhoE 93*
Smythe, William Rodman 1930- *WhoAm 92*
Smythe-Haith, Mabel Murphy 1918- *WhoAm 92*
Snaith, Martin Somerville *WhoScE 91-1*
Snape, John William *WhoScE 91-1*
Snape, Royden Eric 1922- *WhoWor 93*
Snape, William John, Jr. 1943- *WhoAm 92*
Snaper, Alvin Allyn 1929- *St&PR 93*
Snapp, Bryan A. *Law&B 92*
Snapp, Elizabeth 1937- *WhoAm 92, WhoAmW 93, WhoSSW 93*
Snapp, Harry Franklin 1930- *WhoSSW 93*
Snapp, James A. 1935- *St&PR 93*
Snapp, Robert Bruce, Jr. 1928- *St&PR 93*
Snapp, Roy Baker 1916- *WhoAm 92*
Snapp, William A. *Law&B 92*
Snapper, Ernst 1913- *WhoAm 92, WhoE 93*
Snare, Carl Lawrence, Jr. 1936- *WhoWor 93*
Snarey, John Robert 1948- *WhoSSW 93*
Snarr, Steven W. *Law&B 92*
Snatzke, Gunther 1928- *WhoScE 91-3*
Snavely, Richard Mellinger 1931- *WhoE 93*
Snavely, William Pennington 1920- *WhoAm 92, WhoWor 93*
Snavely, William Pennington, Jr. 1948- *WhoWor 93*
Snead, Edwin DeSteiguer 1929- *St&PR 93*
Snead, George Murrell, Jr. 1922- *WhoAm 92*
Snead, John L. Shaw 1912- *St&PR 93*
Snead, Kathleen Marie *Law&B 92*
Snead, Michael James 1927- *WhoIns 93*
Snead, Norman Bailey 1939- *BiDAMSp 1989*
Snead, Richard Thomas 1951- *St&PR 93, WhoAm 92*
Snead, Robert H. 1922- *St&PR 93*
Snead, Samuel Jackson 1912- *WhoAm 92*
Snead, William G. *Law&B 92*
Sneade, Barbara Herbert 1947- *WhoSSW 93*
Snearly, Sandra Jo 1954- *WhoAmW 93*
Sneath, Peter Henry Andrews *WhoScE 91-1*
Sneath, William Scott 1926- *St&PR 93*
Snedaker, Catherine Raupagh *WhoAmW 93*
Snedaker, Dianne *WhoAm 92*
Snedden, James Douglas 1925- *WhoAm 92*
Snedden, Louis Lyle 1913- *St&PR 93, WhoAm 92*
Sneddon, Ian Naismith 1919- *WhoWor 93*
Snedeker, Clifford Eugene, Jr. 1939- *WhoSSW 93*
Snedeker, Don E. *Law&B 92*
Snedeker, James Phyfe 1948- *WhoIns 93*
Snedeker, John Christian 1927- *WhoSSW 93*
Snedeker, John Haggner 1925- *WhoAm 92*
Snedeker, Robert D. 1943- *WhoSSW 93*
Snedeker, Robert Dunbar 1943- *St&PR 93*
Sneden, George Kenneth 1932- *St&PR 93*
Snediker, Ellen 1930- *St&PR 93*
Snediker, Robert R. 1927- *St&PR 93*
Snee, Charles Edwards, III *Law&B 92*
Sneed, Bob 1942- *St&PR 93*
Sneed, Brenda Darlene *Law&B 92*
Sneed, George Lovell 1940- *WhoSSW 93*
Sneed, Harry Marsh 1940- *WhoWor 93*
Sneed, Joseph Donald 1938- *WhoAm 92*
Sneed, Marie Eleanor Wilkey 1915- *WhoWor 93*
Sneed, Michael Michele 1943- *WhoAm 92*
Sneed, Paula *BioIn 17*
Sneed, Paula Ann 1947- *WhoAmW 93*
Sneed, Richard C. *Law&B 92*
Sneeringer, Stephen Geddes *Law&B 92*
Sneeringer, Stephen Geddes 1949- *WhoEmL 93*
Snegur, Mircha Ivanovich 1940- *WhoWor 93*
Sneh, Moshe 1909-1972 *PolBiDi*
Sneider, David Abbott *Law&B 92*
Sneider, Joseph G. 1927- *St&PR 93*
Sneider, Martin Karl 1942- *St&PR 93*
Sneirson, Gregg Abner 1953- *WhoE 93*
Sneirson, William B. *Law&B 92*
Snel, Joseph-Francois 1793-1861 *Baker 92*
Snelbecker, Glenn Eugene 1931- *WhoE 93*
Snelgrove, Brent E. 1948- *St&PR 93*
Snell, Christopher Ray 1943- *St&PR 93*
Snell, Corinne Marie 1961- *WhoE 93*
Snell, Daniel Clair 1947- *WhoSSW 93*
Snell, Edmund 1889- *ScF&FL 92*
Snell, Esmond Emerson 1914- *WhoAm 92*
Snell, George D. 1909- *St&PR 93*
Snell, George Davis 1903- *WhoAm 92, WhoE 93, WhoWor 93*
Snell, Gordon *ScF&FL 92*
Snell, Jack Eastlake 1935- *WhoAm 92*
Snell, James Laurie 1925- *WhoAm 92*
Snell, John Raymond 1912- *WhoAm 92*
Snell, John T. 1947- *St&PR 93*
Snell, John Thomas 1947- *WhoE 93*
Snell, Keith 1946- *WhoWor 93*
Snell, Michael D. 1952- *St&PR 93*
Snell, Mina Sloane *AmWomPl*
Snell, Peter *BioIn 17*
Snell, Peter 1941- *ConTFT 10*
Snell, Richard 1930- *St&PR 93, WhoAm 92*
Snell, Richard Saxon 1925- *WhoAm 92*
Snell, Robert L. S. 1932- *St&PR 93*
Snell, Stephen Pedersen 1936- *St&PR 93*
Snell, Thaddeus Stevens, III 1919- *WhoAm 92*
Snell, Timothy J. *Law&B 92*
Snell, V.H. 1931- *St&PR 93*
Snell, William Joel 1946- *WhoSSW 93*
Sneller, Erin O'Shea 1962- *WhoAmW 93*
Sneller, Lee James 1940- *St&PR 93*
Sneller, Sherry *MiSFD 9*
Snelling, Anne Morris 1935- *St&PR 93*
Snelling, Charles D. 1931- *St&PR 93*
Snelling, George Arthur 1929- *St&PR 93, WhoAm 92*
Snelling, Henry Hunt 1817-1897 *JrnUS*
Snelling, Lonie Eugene, Jr. 1937- *WhoSSW 93*
Snelling, Richard *BioIn 17*
Snelling, Richard Kelly 1931- *St&PR 93*
Snelling, Robert O., Sr. 1932- *St&PR 93*
Snelling, William Lee 1931- *WhoWor 93*
Snelling, William Rodman 1931- *WhoWor 93*
Snellings, John *ScF&FL 92*
Snelson, Keith R. 1928- *St&PR 93*
Snelson, Kenneth 1927- *BioIn 17*
Snelson, Kenneth Duane 1927- *WhoAm 92*
Snelson, Robert Luke *WhoSSW 93*
Snelson, Roy 1927- *WhoAm 92*
Sneppen, Otto 1935- *WhoScE 91-2*
Snethlage, Maria Emilia 1868-1929 *IntDcAn*
Snetsinger, David Clarence 1930- *WhoAm 92*
Snetzer, Michael Alan 1940- *St&PR 93, WhoAm 92, WhoSSW 93*
Snetzler, Johann 1710-1785 *Baker 92*
Sneva, Thomas Edsol 1948- *WhoAm 92*
Sniadecki, Jan 1756-1830 *PolBiDi*
Sniadecki, Jedrzej 1768-1838 *PolBiDi*
Snibbe, Patricia Miscall 1932- *WhoE 93, WhoWor 93*
Snibbe, Richard W. 1916- *WhoAm 92*
Snibbe, Robert McCawley 1913- *WhoSSW 93*
Snider, Basil 1927- *St&PR 93*
Snider, Clifton Mark 1947- *WhoWrEP 92*
Snider, Cynthia Deniston 1947- *WhoAmW 93, WhoSSW 93*
Snider, Dana E. *Law&B 92*
Snider, Donald Lee 1939- *WhoAm 92*
Snider, Drew 1944- *St&PR 93*

Snider, Edward Malcolm 1933- *WhoAm 92*
Snider, Eliot I. 1921- *St&PR 93*
Snider, Elizabeth Leigh *Law&B 92*
Snider, Gordon Lloyd 1922- *WhoAm 92*
Snider, Harlan Tanner 1926- *WhoAm 92*
Snider, Harold Wayne 1923- *WhoAm 92*
Snider, James Harry 1958- *WhoE 93*
Snider, James Rhodes 1931- *WhoSSW 93*
Snider, Jay T. *WhoAm 92*
Snider, Joel 1945- *WhoSSW 93*
Snider, John Joseph 1928- *WhoAm 92*
Snider, L. Britt 1945- *WhoAm 92*
Snider, Marie Anna 1927- *WhoAmW 93, WhoWor 93*
Snider, Martin S. 1956- *St&PR 93*
Snider, Michael Robert 1953- *St&PR 93*
Snider, R. Larry 1932- *St&PR 93*
Snider, Robert F. 1931- *WhoAm 92*
Snider, Robert Larry 1932- *WhoAm 92*
Snider, Ronald Edward, Jr. 1955- *St&PR 93*
Snider, Ruth *WhoWrEP 92*
Snider, Ruth Atkinson 1930- *WhoSSW 93*
Snider, Scott Forrest *Law&B 92*
Snider, Skott *MiSFD 9*
Snider, William Alan 1967- *WhoE 93*
Snider, William D. 1941- *St&PR 93*
Sniderman, Allan David 1941- *WhoAm 92*
Sniderman, Marvin 1923- *WhoE 93*
Sniegon, Karol 1927- *WhoScE 91-4*
Sniffen, Michael Joseph 1949- *WhoE 93*
Sniffin, John Harrison 1942- *WhoAm 92*
Snijders, C.H.A. 1960- *WhoScE 91-3*
Sninchak, Faye Rita 1947- *WhoE 93*
Snipes, Barry E. *St&PR 93*
Snipes, Candace Leigh 1949- *WhoAmW 93*
Snipes, James Vance 1943- *St&PR 93*
Snipes, Marian *BioIn 17*
Snipes, Wesley *BioIn 17, WhoAm 92*
Snipes, Wesley 1962- *ConBlB 3 [port], News 93-1 [port]*
Snipes, Wesley 1963?- *ConTFT 10*
Snith, Lars Ake 1962- *WhoWor 93*
Snitow, Charles 1907- *WhoE 93*
Snitzer, Elias 1925- *WhoAm 92*
Snitzer, Isadore 1921- *St&PR 93*
Snively, David Frederick *Law&B 92*
Snively, Stephen Wayne 1949- *WhoSSW 93*
Snively, William Daniel, Jr. 1911- *WhoAm 92*
Sno, William *ScF&FL 92*
Snoddon, Larry E. 1945- *WhoAm 92*
Snoddy, Charles Edison, Jr. 1923- *WhoE 93, WhoWor 93*
Snoddy, James Ernest 1932- *WhoAm 92*
Snodgrass, Ann A. 1958- *WhoWrEP 92*
Snodgrass, Billie Kay 1947- *WhoWrEP 92*
Snodgrass, Faye Birdwell 1941- *WhoSSW 93*
Snodgrass, Jeanne Ellen 1930- *WhoE 93*
Snodgrass, John J. 1920-1990 *BioIn 17*
Snodgrass, Linda Lee 1950- *WhoWrEP 92*
Snodgrass, Melinda M. 1951- *ScF&FL 92*
Snodgrass, Quentin Curtius *MajAI*
Snodgrass, Richard 1940- *ScF&FL 92*
Snodgrass, Richard W. 1942- *St&PR 93*
Snodgrass, Robert William 1921- *St&PR 93*
Snodgrass, Sara E. 1942- *WhoAmW 93, WhoSSW 93*
Snodgrass, Thomas Jefferson *MajAI*
Snodgrass, Tod John 1945- *WhoWrEP 92*
Snodgrass, W.D. 1926- *BioIn 17, WhoAm 92, WhoWrEP 92*
Snodgrass, William Albert 1933- *WhoIns 93*
Snodgrass, William De Witt 1926- *BioIn 17*
Snodgres, Elizabeth Ann 1948- *WhoSSW 93*
Snoeck, Jacques 1928- *WhoScE 91-2*
Snoeckx, Luc H.E.H. 1947- *WhoScE 91-3*
Snoeys, Raymond A.J. 1936- *WhoScE 91-2*
Snogerup, Sven 1929- *WhoScE 91-4*
Snoke, George R. 1922- *St&PR 93*
Snook, Herbert Edgar 1945- *WhoWrEP 92*
Snook, John McClure 1917- *WhoWor 93*
Snook, Lon Fredrick 1951- *St&PR 93*
Snook, Peter *St&PR 93*
Snook, Quinton 1925- *WhoWor 93*
Snook, Thomas James 1961- *WhoSSW 93*
Snooks, Graeme Donald 1944- *WhoWor 93*
Snoozy, Robert Sherrill 1946- *St&PR 93*
Snopkowski, Daniel M. 1952- *St&PR 93*
Snopkowski, Richard Raymond 1942- *WhoE 93*
Snorf, Lowell Delford, Jr. 1919- *WhoIns 93*
Snorrason, H. *WhoScE 91-4*
Snortland, Howard Jerome 1912- *WhoAm 92*
Snow, Amy Eileen 1949- *WhoAmW 93*
Snow, Barbara Ann 1940- *WhoAmW 93*
Snow, Bonnie 1952- *WhoWrEP 92*
Snow, Bonnie Jean 1952- *WhoAmW 93*
Snow, Bradley 1953- *ScF&FL 92*
Snow, C.P. 1905-1980 *BioIn 17, ScF&FL 92*
Snow, Carolyn Sue 1939- *WhoAmW 93*
Snow, Charles Percy 1905-1980 *BioIn 17*
Snow, Claude Ray 1936- *St&PR 93*
Snow, Clyde *BioIn 17*
Snow, Dean Richard 1940- *WhoE 93*
Snow, Donald 1951- *ConAu 138*
Snow, Dwight L. 1933- *St&PR 93*
Snow, E. Ned 1930- *St&PR 93*
Snow, Edgar Parks 1905-1971 *JrnUS*
Snow, Edgar Parks 1905-1972 *ConAu 38NR*
Snow, Edward Leon 1931- *WhoE 93*
Snow, Elizabeth Jean 1943- *WhoAmW 93*
Snow, Frederick M. *Law&B 92*
Snow, George *ScF&FL 92*
Snow, George Abraham 1926- *WhoAm 92*
Snow, George K. 1933- *St&PR 93*
Snow, George L. 1921- *St&PR 93*
Snow, Hank 1914- *Baker 92*
Snow, Ida *AmWomPl*
Snow, Jack 1907-1956 *ScF&FL 92*
Snow, James Byron, Jr. 1932- *WhoAm 92, WhoE 93*
Snow, James Henry 1934- *WhoAsAP 91*
Snow, John D. 1954- *WhoAm 92*
Snow, John William 1939- *St&PR 93, WhoAm 92, WhoSSW 93*
Snow, Johnnie Park 1942- *WhoSSW 93*
Snow, Joseph H., III *Law&B 92*
Snow, Judith Rohletter 1948- *WhoAmW 93*
Snow, Karl Nelson, Jr. 1930- *WhoAm 92*
Snow, Keith Ronald *WhoScE 91-1*
Snow, Laura E. V. *AmWomPl*
Snow, Lloyd Dale 1947- *WhoSSW 93*
Snow, Lucy *WhoCanL 92*
Snow, Marina Sexton 1937- *WhoAmW 93*
Snow, Mary C. *Law&B 92*
Snow, Nancy Elizabeth 1962- *WhoAmW 93*
Snow, Randy *BioIn 17*
Snow, Richard F. 1939- *St&PR 93*
Snow, Richard F(olger) 1947- *DcAmChF 1960*
Snow, Richard Robert 1952- *WhoSSW 93*
Snow, Robert B. 1917- *St&PR 93*
Snow, Robert Brian 1953- *WhoE 93*
Snow, Robert Lawrence 1949- *WhoWrEP 92*
Snow, Robert W. 1931- *St&PR 93*
Snow, Samuel J. 1950- *St&PR 93*
Snow, Sue *BioIn 17*
Snow, Theodore Peck, Jr. 1947- *WhoAm 92*
Snow, William Cullum 1929- *St&PR 93*
Snow, William Hayden 1926- *St&PR 93, WhoAm 92*
Snow, Zachary *Law&B 92*
Snowday, H. Terry, Jr. 1935- *St&PR 93*
Snowden, Bernice Rives 1923- *WhoAmW 93*
Snowden, Bertha Jeanne 1948- *WhoAmW 93*
Snowden, Charles Jeffry 1772-1855 *BioIn 17*
Snowden, Frank Martin, Jr. 1911- *WhoAm 92*
Snowden, Guy B. 1945- *St&PR 93*
Snowden, Guy Bernhard 1945- *WhoAm 92*
Snowden, Isaac 1764-1835 *BioIn 17*
Snowden, Lawrence Fontaine 1921- *WhoAm 92*
Snowden, Lillian Ruth Johnson 1941- *WhoSSW 93*
Snowden, Michael Starke 1939- *WhoWor 93*
Snowden, Nancy L. *Law&B 92*
Snowden, Nathaniel Randolph 1770-1850 *BioIn 17*
Snowden, Philip 1864-1937 *BioIn 17, DcTwHis*
Snowden, Robert G. 1917- *St&PR 93*
Snowden, Samuel Finley 1767-1845 *BioIn 17*
Snowdon, Earl of 1930- *BioIn 17*
Snowdon, Anthony 1930- *WhoWor 93*
Snowdon, W. Latimer, Jr. 1936- *St&PR 93*
Snowdon, Warren Edward 1950- *WhoAsAP 91*
Snowe, Olympia J. *BioIn 17*
Snowe, Olympia J. 1947- *CngDr 91, WhoAm 92, WhoAmW 93*
Snowling, Margaret Jean *WhoScE 91-1*
Snoy, Bernard Baudouin 1945- *WhoWor 93*
Snukal, Sherman 1946- *WhoCanL 92*
Snycerz, Jan d1545 *PolBiDi*
Snydacker, William Fackert 1945- *St&PR 93*
Snydal, James Matthew 1949- *WhoWrEP 92*
Snyde, David Edward 1944- *St&PR 93*
Snyder, Agnes *BioIn 17*
Snyder, Alan Carhart 1946- *WhoAm 92*
Snyder, Allegra Fuller 1927- *WhoAm 92, WhoAmW 93*
Snyder, Arnold Lee, Jr. 1937- *WhoE 93*
Snyder, Arthur 1925- *St&PR 93, WhoAm 92, WhoWor 93*
Snyder, Arthur, III 1955- *St&PR 93*
Snyder, Benjamin Norman *Law&B 92*
Snyder, Bernadette McCarver 1930- *ConAu 37NR*
Snyder, Bernard *Law&B 92*
Snyder, Betsy Roberts 1950- *St&PR 93*
Snyder, Beverly Ann 1941- *WhoSSW 93*
Snyder, Bill Joseph 1938- *WhoSSW 93*
Snyder, Bruce Franklin 1938- *St&PR 93*
Snyder, C. Robert 1937- *WhoIns 93*
Snyder, Carl W., Jr. 1928- *St&PR 93*
Snyder, Carolyn Ann 1942- *WhoAmW 93*
Snyder, Charles Aubrey 1941- *WhoAm 92*
Snyder, Charles J. 1915- *St&PR 93*
Snyder, Charles Royce 1924- *WhoAm 92*
Snyder, Charles Thomas 1938- *WhoAm 92*
Snyder, Christopher Spencer *Law&B 92*
Snyder, Clair A. 1921- *St&PR 93*
Snyder, Clair Allison 1921- *WhoAm 92*
Snyder, Clark L. *Law&B 92*
Snyder, Claude Robert 1937- *WhoAm 92*
Snyder, Colleen K. 1954- *ScF&FL 92*
Snyder, David *BioIn 17*
Snyder, Deborah *BioIn 17*
Snyder, Dennis Chrisman 1940- *St&PR 93*
Snyder, Diane Carsillo 1960- *WhoSSW 93*
Snyder, Diann Layne 1952- *WhoAmW 93*
Snyder, Dick Gene 1936- *St&PR 93*
Snyder, Dominique *BioIn 17*
Snyder, Donald Benjamin 1935- *WhoE 93*
Snyder, Donald Edward 1928- *WhoAm 92*
Snyder, Donna Lynn *Law&B 92*
Snyder, E. Russell 1927-1990 *BioIn 17*
Snyder, Edwin Arthur 1932- *St&PR 93*
Snyder, Eugene V. *ScF&FL 92*
Snyder, Frank *Law&B 92*
Snyder, Frank Ronald, II 1939- *St&PR 93*
Snyder, Franklin Cooper 1915-1990 *BioIn 17*
Snyder, Franklin F. d1992 *NewYTBS 92*
Snyder, Franklin Farison 1910- *WhoAm 92*
Snyder, Gary *BioIn 17*
Snyder, Gary 1930- *MagSAmL [port]*
Snyder, Gary Dean 1960- *WhoE 93*
Snyder, Gary Sherman 1930- *WhoAm 92, WhoWrEP 92*
Snyder, Gene 1943- *ScF&FL 92*
Snyder, George Edward 1934- *WhoAm 92, WhoWor 93*
Snyder, George W. 1942- *St&PR 93*
Snyder, Gerald 1944- *St&PR 93*
Snyder, Giles D.H. *Law&B 92*
Snyder, Giles D.H. 1931- *St&PR 93, WhoAm 92*
Snyder, Ginger R. 1951- *WhoAmW 93*
Snyder, H.L. *Law&B 92*
Snyder, H. Ralph *Law&B 92*
Snyder, Harry M. *BioIn 17*
Snyder, Henry Leonard 1929- *WhoAm 92*
Snyder, Hugh Robin 1936- *St&PR 93*
Snyder, Irvin Stanley 1931- *WhoAm 92*
Snyder, Irving George, Jr. 1937- *St&PR 93, WhoAm 92*
Snyder, Jack O. 1942- *WhoAm 92*
Snyder, Jack Ralph 1940- *WhoAm 92*
Snyder, James *BioIn 17*
Snyder, James A. *Law&B 92*
Snyder, James Donald 1937- *WhoWrEP 92*
Snyder, James F. 1944- *St&PR 93*
Snyder, James M. 1940- *St&PR 93*
Snyder, James Milton 1946- *WhoSSW 93*
Snyder, Jane Peters 1925- *WhoAmW 93, WhoE 93*
Snyder, Jeanne Anne 1945- *WhoAm 92*
Snyder, Jed Cobb 1955- *WhoE 93, WhoEmL 93, WhoWor 93*
Snyder, Jeffrey C. 1955- *St&PR 93*
Snyder, Jo Anna W. 1961- *WhoAmW 93*
Snyder, Joan 1940- *WhoAm 92*
Snyder, John 1956- *BioIn 17*
Snyder, John B. *Law&B 92*
Snyder, John Bennett 1929- *St&PR 93*
Snyder, John C. *St&PR 93*
Snyder, John Joseph 1908- *WhoWor 93*
Snyder, John Joseph 1925- *WhoAm 92, WhoSSW 93*
Snyder, John Lindsey 1933- *WhoAm 92*
Snyder, John Mendenhall 1909- *WhoE 93*
Snyder, John W. 1958- *St&PR 93*
Snyder, Joseph H. 1920-1991 *BioIn 17*
Snyder, Joseph John 1946- *WhoEmL 93, WhoSSW 93, WhoWor 93*
Snyder, Joseph Leo 1957- *WhoSSW 93*
Snyder, Joy Irving *Law&B 92*
Snyder, Judith Beverly 1947- *WhoE 93*
Snyder, Jules 1937- *WhoE 93*
Snyder, Kathleen Ann 1949- *WhoAmW 93*
Snyder, Kathryn *AmWomPl*
Snyder, Kathryn Dee 1956- *St&PR 93*
Snyder, Kathy Munson 1962- *WhoAmW 93*
Snyder, Lawrence Clement 1932- *WhoE 93*
Snyder, Leonard Michael 1948- *St&PR 93*
Snyder, Lewis Emil 1939- *WhoAm 92*
Snyder, Lisa Anne 1966- *WhoAmW 93*
Snyder, Loretta Marie 1943- *WhoAmW 93*
Snyder, Louis Leo 1907- *WhoAm 92, WhoWor 93*
Snyder, Lury Domingo 1964- *WhoSSW 93*
Snyder, Marcia K. 1955- *St&PR 93*
Snyder, Mari C. *Law&B 92*
Snyder, Maria Lynne 1962- *WhoAmW 93*
Snyder, Marian H. 1942- *WhoAmW 93*
Snyder, Marion Gene 1928- *WhoAm 92*
Snyder, Mark Jeffrey 1947- *WhoE 93*
Snyder, Marsha Whinston 1952- *WhoAmW 93*
Snyder, Martha Jane 1953- *WhoE 93, WhoEmL 93*
Snyder, Marvin *Law&B 92*
Snyder, Marvin 1940- *WhoAm 92*
Snyder, Mary Ellen 1952- *WhoAmW 93*
Snyder, Mary W. *Law&B 92*
Snyder, Michael B. *Law&B 92*
Snyder, Michele Manne 1952- *St&PR 93*
Snyder, Midori *ScF&FL 92*
Snyder, Mitch *BioIn 17*
Snyder, Nancy Ellen 1935- *WhoWrEP 92*
Snyder, Nathan 1934- *St&PR 93, WhoAm 92*
Snyder, Oliver P. 1927- *St&PR 93*
Snyder, Pamela Sue Gordon 1958- *WhoAmW 93*
Snyder, Patricia M. *Law&B 92*
Snyder, Patricia Marie 1952- *WhoAmW 93*
Snyder, Peter Larsen 1952- *WhoAm 92*
Snyder, Ralph Sheldon 1922- *WhoAm 92*
Snyder, Richard A. 1940- *St&PR 93*
Snyder, Richard E. *BioIn 17*
Snyder, Richard E. 1933- *St&PR 93*
Snyder, Richard Elliot 1933- *WhoAm 92*
Snyder, Richard G. 1932- *St&PR 93*
Snyder, Richard Joseph 1939- *WhoAm 92*
Snyder, Richard L. 1931- *St&PR 93*
Snyder, Richard Lee 1940- *WhoAm 92*
Snyder, Richard Lynne *WhoWrEP 92*
Snyder, Richard W. *Law&B 92*
Snyder, Robert B. 1944- *St&PR 93*
Snyder, Robert C. 1933- *WhoSSW 93*
Snyder, Robert Harvey 1918- *St&PR 93*
Snyder, Robert J. 1949- *St&PR 93*
Snyder, Robert Martin 1912- *WhoAm 92, WhoWor 93*
Snyder, Robert Martin 1940- *St&PR 93*
Snyder, Robert Orin 1951- *WhoE 93*
Snyder, Robert Raboin 1946- *WhoAm 92*
Snyder, Ronald Edward *Law&B 92*
Snyder, Ross 1902-1992 *BioIn 17*
Snyder, Sam A. *Law&B 92*
Snyder, Sam A. 1930- *WhoAm 92*
Snyder, Scott Edward 1963- *WhoE 93*
Snyder, Scott William 1946- *WhoAm 92, WhoSSW 93*
Snyder, Sheryl G. *Law&B 92*
Snyder, Simon 1759-1819 *BioIn 17*
Snyder, Solomon H. 1938- *BioIn 17*
Snyder, Solomon Halbert 1938- *WhoAm 92*
Snyder, Sonya Lynn 1960- *WhoAmW 93*
Snyder, Stanley Paul 1934- *St&PR 93*
Snyder, Stephen F. 1938- *St&PR 93*
Snyder, Steven Eliot 1952- *WhoE 93*
Snyder, Stuart I. 1940- *St&PR 93*
Snyder, Susan Brooke 1934- *WhoAm 92, WhoAmW 93, WhoWrEP 92*
Snyder, Terrence B. 1951- *St&PR 93*
Snyder, Thoma Mees van'tHoff 1916- *WhoWor 93*
Snyder, Thomas D. 1949- *St&PR 93*
Snyder, Thomas Daniel 1925- *WhoSSW 93*
Snyder, Thomas R. *St&PR 93*
Snyder, Troxell K. *Law&B 92*
Snyder, Virginia Ann *WhoSSW 93*
Snyder, Virginia Lea 1957- *WhoAmW 93*
Snyder, W.P., III 1918- *St&PR 93*
Snyder, Wesley Warren 1935- *WhoSSW 93*
Snyder, Willard A. 1936- *St&PR 93*
Snyder, Willard B. 1940- *St&PR 93*
Snyder, Willard Breidenthal 1940- *WhoWor 93*
Snyder, William B. 1929- *St&PR 93*
Snyder, William Burton 1929- *WhoAm 92, WhoIns 93*
Snyder, William D. 1959- *WhoAm 92, WhoSSW 93*
Snyder, William Fortune 1941- *WhoE 93*
Snyder, William H. 1946- *St&PR 93*
Snyder, William L. 1935- *St&PR 93*
Snyder, William M. *Law&B 92*
Snyder, William Penn, III 1918- *WhoAm 92*

Snyder, William Russell 1926- *St&PR 93, WhoAm 92*
Snyder, William T. *WhoSSW 93*
Snyder, Zilpha K. 1927- *ScF&FL 92*
Snyder, Zilpha Keatley 1927- *ConAu 38NR, DcAmChF 1960, MajAI [port], WhoWrEP 92*
Snyder Garrett, Lori Gayle 1961- *WhoSSW 93*
Snyderman, Barbara Bloch 1932- *WhoAmW 93*
Snyderman, Nancy *BioIn 17*
Snyderman, Reuven Kenneth 1922- *WhoAm 92*
Snyderman, Selma Eleanore 1916- *WhoAmW 93*
Snyder-Spear, Catherine Gail 1960- *WhoAmW 93*
So, Louisa Lee 1947- *WhoE 93*
So, Moonsup 1931- *WhoUN 92*
Soames, James Victor *WhoScE 91-1*
Soane, B.D. *WhoScE 91-1*
Soane, Brennan Derry *WhoScE 91-1*
Soane, John 1753-1837 *BioIn 17*
Soare, Warren Gordon 1947- *WhoE 93*
Soares, Cecelia Jenkins 1943- *WhoAmW 93*
Soares, Eusebio Lopes 1918- *WhoWor 93*
Soares, Gregory Louis 1951- *WhoE 93*
Soares, Laila A. *Law&B 92*
Soares, Mario *BioIn 17*
Soares, Mario Alberto Nobre Lopes 1924- *WhoWor 93*
Soares De Gouveia, Artur *WhoScE 91-3*
Soares Ribeiro, Carlos 1926- *WhoScE 91-3*
Sobalvarro, J. Roberto 1927- *St&PR 93*
Sobba, John W. *Law&B 92*
Sobchack, Vivian Carol 1940- *ScF&FL 92*
Sobchak, Anatoliy Aleksandrovich 1937- *WhoWor 93*
Sobchak, Anatoly *BioIn 17*
Sobchak, Anatoly A. 1937- *CurBio 92 [port]*
Sobczak, Eric James *Law&B 92*
Sobczak, Howard John *Law&B 92*
Sobczak, Mark Leslie 1955- *WhoE 93*
Sobczyk, Kazimierz 1939- *WhoScE 91-4*
Sobczyk, Lucjan 1927- *WhoScE 91-4*
Sobczyk, Tadeusz J. 1944- *WhoScE 91-4*
Sobczynska-Konczak, Zofia 1930- *WhoScE 91-4*
Sobeck, James Robert 1954- *WhoSSW 93*
Sobecki, John Francis 1948- *WhoE 93*
Sobecki, Mark S. *Law&B 92*
Sobel, Alan 1928- *WhoAm 92*
Sobel, Arthur H. *Law&B 92*
Sobel, Burton Elias 1937- *WhoAm 92*
Sobel, Erwin 1938- *WhoWor 93*
Sobel, Howard Bernard 1929- *WhoAm 92*
Sobel, Irwin Philip 1901-1991 *BioIn 17, ScF&FL 92*
Sobel, Jael Sabina 1935- *WhoE 93*
Sobel, Joan Lasker *BioIn 17*
Sobel, Joseph Peter 1945- *WhoE 93*
Sobel, Kenneth Mark 1954- *WhoE 93*
Sobel, Lester Albert 1919- *WhoWrEP 92*
Sobel, Mark Esar 1949- *WhoE 93*
Sobel, Mark S. 1956- *MiSFD 9*
Sobel, Melvin 1926- *St&PR 93*
Sobel, Rochelle M. *Law&B 92*
Sobel, Stanton 1933- *St&PR 93*
Sobel, Walter Howard 1913- *WhoAm 92*
Soben, Robert Sidney 1947- *WhoSSW 93*
Sober, Debra E. 1953- *WhoAmW 93*
Soberman, Glenn Barry 1952- *WhoE 93*
Soberon, Guillermo 1925- *WhoAm 92*
Soberon, Presentacion Zablan 1935- *WhoAmW 93*
Soberon-Ferrer, Horacio 1954- *WhoWor 93*
Sobers, Edward K. 1922-1988 *BioIn 17*
Sobers, Garfield 1936- *BioIn 17*
Sobey, David F. *St&PR 93*
Sobey, David F. 1931- *WhoAm 92, WhoE 93*
Sobey, Donald Creighton Rae *WhoAm 92*
Sobey, Edwin J. C. 1948- *WhoAm 92*
Sobey, Paul D. 1958- *St&PR 93*
Sobieska, Maria Casimira 1640-1716 *PolBiDi*
Sobieska, Maria Clementina 1702-1735 *PolBiDi*
Sobieski, Carol 1939-1990 *BioIn 17*
Sobieski, J. Thomas 1941- *St&PR 93*
Sobieski, James Louis 1936- *St&PR 93*
Sobieski, Jan, III 1629-1696 *PolBiDi*
Sobieski, Jaroslaw 1934- *WhoAm 92, WhoSSW 93*
Sobiloff, Myer Nathaniel 1907- *WhoAm 92*
Sobin, Anthony 1944- *WhoWrEP 92*
Sobin, Carole *Law&B 92*
Sobin, Gustaf 1935- *ConAu 38NR*
Sobin, Julian Melvin 1920- *WhoAm 92*
Sobin, Leslie Howard 1934- *WhoE 93*
Sobin, Louise *Law&B 92*
Sobin, Michael B. 1941- *St&PR 93*
Sobin, Morris 1913- *WhoAm 92*
Sobina, Donald Eugene 1943- *St&PR 93*
Sobinov, Leonid 1872-1934 *OxDcOp*
Sobinov, Leonid (Vitalievich) 1872-1934 *Baker 92*
Sobkoviak, Kenneth R. 1944- *St&PR 93*
Sobkow, RoseAnne 1938- *WhoAmW 93*
Sobkowicz, Hanna Maria 1931- *WhoAm 92, WhoAmW 93*
Sobkowicz, Henryk 1928- *PolBiDi*
Sobkowski, Jerzy 1929- *WhoScE 91-4*
Sobkowski, Shawn 1956- *WhoE 93*
Sobkowski, Stanislaw Zbigniew 1925- *WhoScE 91-4*
Soble, David S. 1943- *St&PR 93*
Soble, Mae Stein *AmWomPl*
Sobleskie, Patricia Angela 1947- *WhoWrEP 92*
Sobnosky, Mary T. *Law&B 92*
Sobocinski, Ryszard Aleksander 1931- *WhoScE 91-4*
Sobol, Donald J. 1924- *ConAu 38NR, DcAmChF 1960, MajAI [port], ScF&FL 92, SmATA 73 [port]*
Sobol, Harold 1930- *WhoAm 92*
Sobol, Judith Ellen 1946- *WhoAm 92*
Sobol, Lawrence Raymond *Law&B 92*
Sobol, Lawrence Raymond 1950- *WhoAm 92*
Sobol, Louis 1920-1992 *BioIn 17, NewYTBS 92*
Sobol, Michael Richard 1946- *St&PR 93*
Sobol, Thomas 1932- *WhoE 93*
Sobol, Tom 1932- *BioIn 17*
Soboleski, Leon 1946- *St&PR 93*
Sobolev, Mikhail Arkadievich 1937- *WhoWor 93*
Sobolev, Vladimir Andreevich 1949- *WhoWor 93*
Sobolewski, Edward 1804-1872 *Baker 92*
Sobolewski, Edward 1808-1872 *PolBiDi*
Sobolewski, Paul 1816-1884 *PolBiDi*
Sobolewski, Timothy R. 1951- *St&PR 93*
Sobolewski, Timothy Richard 1951- *WhoE 93*
Sobolik, Craig Terry 1949- *WhoWrEP 92*
Sobong, Loreto Calibo 1931- *WhoSSW 93*
Sobotik, Mark *St&PR 93*
Sobotka, Gabrielle Pessl d1991 *BioIn 17*
Sobotka, P. 1928- *WhoScE 91-4*
Sobotka, Zdenek 1926- *WhoScE 91-4*
Sobral, J.D. Torres 1942- *WhoScE 91-3*
Sobralske, Barbara Nila 1949- *WhoAmW 93*
Sobre, Judith Berg 1941- *ConAu 139*
Sobrero, Enrico *WhoScE 91-3*
Sobrie, Herman *Law&B 92*
Sobrinho, Jose Pinto Ferreira 1954- *WhoWor 93*
Sobrino, Jon *BioIn 17*
Sobukwe, Robert Mangaliso 1924-1978 *BioIn 17*
Sobyak, Lawrence Edward 1937- *St&PR 93*
Socarides, Charles William 1922- *WhoE 93*
Socci, Patrick J. 1948- *St&PR 93*
Socci, Robert A. *Law&B 92*
Soch, Henry John 1948- *WhoE 93*
Socha, Jack A. *Law&B 92*
Socha, Theresa Marie 1948- *WhoAmW 93*
So Chau Yim-Ping, Hon. 1927- *WhoAsAP 91*
Sochen, June 1937- *WhoAm 92, WhoAmW 93*
Sochet, Mary Allen 1938- *WhoE 93*
Socie, Darrell Frederick 1948- *WhoAm 92*
Sockett, Hugh Talbot 1937- *WhoSSW 93*
Sockman, Ralph Washington 1889-1970 *BioIn 17*
Sockol, Craig Stewart 1950- *St&PR 93*
Sockwell, Joel Clinton 1938- *St&PR 93*
Sockwell, Oliver R., Jr. 1943- *WhoAm 92*
Socol, Myrna *WhoAmW 93*
Socolofsky, Iris Kay 1952- *WhoEmL 93*
Socolofsky, Jon E. 1946- *St&PR 93*
Socolofsky, Jon Edward 1946- *WhoAm 92*
Socolow, Arthur Abraham 1921- *WhoAm 92, WhoE 93*
Socolow, Elizabeth A. 1940- *WhoWrEP 92*
Socolow, Robert Harry 1937- *WhoAm 92*
Socolow, Sanford 1928- *St&PR 93*
Socor, Matei 1908-1980 *Baker 92*
Socrate, Carlo 1889-1967 *BioIn 17*
Socrates 469BC-399BC *OxDcByz*
Socufka, Frantisek *BioIn 17*
Soczynska, Urszula 1933- *WhoScE 91-4*
Sodahl, Eiliv *WhoScE 91-4*
Sodak, John Joseph 1964- *WhoE 93*
Sodal, Ingvar Edmund 1934- *WhoAm 92*
Sodano, Angelo Cardinal 1927- *WhoWor 93*
Sodano, Pasquale 1950- *WhoWor 93*
Sodaro, Craig 1948- *ConAu 40NR*
Sodaro, Edward Richard 1947- *WhoE 93*
Sodaro, Jennifer Prager 1951- *WhoAmW 93*
Sodd, Vincent Joseph 1934- *WhoAm 92*
Sode, Lizabeth G. *St&PR 93*
Sodeman, Thomas Michael 1941- *WhoAm 92*
Sodeman, William Anthony, Sr. 1906- *WhoSSW 93*
Soden, Paul A. *Law&B 92*
Soden, Paul A. 1944- *St&PR 93*
Soden, Paul Anthony 1944- *WhoAm 92*
Soder, Per-Osten 1928- *WhoScE 91-4*
Soderberg, B.W. 1931- *St&PR 93*
Soderberg, Bo Sigfrid 1939- *WhoSSW 93, WhoWor 93*
Soderberg, Dale LeRoy 1929- *WhoE 93*
Soderberg, Erik A. O. Rson 1926- *WhoWor 93*
Soderberg, Harold J. 1928- *St&PR 93*
Soderbergh, Ragnhild 1933- *WhoWor 93*
Soderbergh, Steven *BioIn 17*
Soderbergh, Steven 1963- *MiSFD 9*
Soderbergh, Steven Andrew 1963- *WhoAm 92*
Soderblom, Ulf 1930- *Baker 92*
Soderini, Agostin fl. 16th cent.-17th cent. *Baker 92*
Soderlind, Carl Robert 1933- *St&PR 93*
Soderlind, Olof 1926- *WhoScE 91-4*
Soderlind, Ragnar 1945- *Baker 92*
Soderlind, Sterling Eugene 1926- *WhoAm 92*
Soderlund, Gustav Frederic 1881-1972 *Baker 92*
Soderlund, Jens Emil 1961- *WhoWor 93*
Soderlund, Robert C. 1928- *St&PR 93*
Soderlund, Stephen Charles 1944- *St&PR 93*
Soderman, (Johan) August 1832-1876 *Baker 92*
Soderman, D. *WhoScE 91-1*
Soderman, Erik 1939- *WhoScE 91-4*
Soderman, William A. d1980 *BioIn 17*
Sodero, Cesare 1886-1947 *Baker 92*
Soderquist, Donald G. 1934- *St&PR 93*
Soderquist, Donald G. 1935- *WhoSSW 93*
Soderstrom, Christian Emanuel 1938- *WhoE 93*
Soderstrom, Elisabeth 1927- *IntDcOp, OxDcOp*
Soderstrom, Hans Tson 1945- *WhoWor 93*
Soderstrom, Jan Roland 1961- *WhoWor 93*
Soderstrom (-Olow), (Anna) Elisabeth 1927- *Baker 92*
Soderstrom, Rolf 1932- *St&PR 93*
Soderstrom, Torsten 1945- *WhoScE 91-4*
Sodhi, Mankuram 1934- *WhoAsAP 91*
Sodi, Ranuccio 1953- *WhoWor 93*
Soding, Paul H. 1933- *WhoScE 91-3*
Sodja, Steven Paul 1962- *WhoSSW 93*
Sodnom, Dumaagiyn 1933- *WhoAsAP 91*
Sodnom, Namsrai 1923- *WhoWor 93*
Soe, Olga *NewYTBS 92 [port]*
Soebadio, Haryati 1928- *WhoAsAP 91*
Soechtig, Jacqueline Elizabeth 1949- *WhoAmW 93*
Soedarman, Soesilo 1928- *WhoAsAP 91*
Soeder, Bernhard 1959- *WhoWor 93*
Soeder, Carl J. 1933- *WhoScE 91-3*
Soederstrom, Elisabeth Anna 1927- *WhoAm 92, WhoWor 93*
Soedjatmoko *BioIn 17*
Soegaard, Karen 1953- *WhoScE 91-2*
Soegiarto, Lt.-Gen 1936- *WhoAsAP 91*
Soeharto 1921- *BioIn 17, CurBio 92 [port], WhoWor 93*
Soeharto, Gen. 1921- *WhoAsAP 91*
Soeharto, Tommy *BioIn 17*
Soehngen, Jane Marie 1957- *WhoAmW 93*
Soehnlein, Rainer 1941- *MiSFD 9*
Soekarno 1901-1970 *BioIn 17*
Soelter, Robert R. 1926- *WhoAm 92*
Soenksen, Patricia Ann 1952- *WhoAmW 93*
Soennichsen, Jean Elizabeth 1926- *WhoAmW 93*
Soens, Lawrence D. 1926- *WhoAm 92*
Soerensen, Bent 1924- *WhoScE 91-2*
Soerensen, Erik *St&PR 93*
Soerensson, Per Henrik 1947- *WhoAm 92*
Soergel, Konrad Hermann 1929- *WhoAm 92*
Soergel, Richard William 1938- *St&PR 93*
Soergel, Volker H.A. 1931- *WhoScE 91-3*
Soers, Erik *WhoScE 91-2*
Soesbe, Douglas *ScF&FL 92*
Soetanto, Kawan 1951- *WhoWor 93*
Soeteber, Ellen 1950- *WhoAm 92*
Soetenhorst-Lohman, Jacquelien 1933- *WhoWor 93*
Sofaer, Abraham David 1938- *WhoAm 92*
Sofer, Barbara *BioIn 17*
Sofer, Michael 1954- *St&PR 93*
Soffa, Albert 1920- *St&PR 93*
Soffel, Andrew J. 1930- *St&PR 93*
Soffer, Alfred 1922- *WhoAm 92, WhoWrEP 92*
Soffer, Jacques *WhoScE 91-2*
Soffer, Morton L. 1933- *St&PR 93*
Soffer, Robert M. 1947- *St&PR 93*
Soffer, Sheldon 1927- *WhoAm 92*
Soffing, Dietmar *Law&B 92*
Soffredini, Alfredo 1854-1923 *Baker 92*
Soffronoff, John Charles 1947- *St&PR 93*
Soffronoff, Pierce 1949- *WhoE 93*
Sofia, Theodore, Jr. 1927- *St&PR 93*
Sofianos, Leo 1941- *St&PR 93*
Sofonea, Liviu 1932- *WhoScE 91-4*
Sofronitzky, Vladimir (Vladimirovich) 1901-1961 *Baker 92*
Softness, Donald Gabriel *WhoAm 92*
Softness, John 1930- *WhoAm 92*
Sogbesan-Benson, Anthony Olu 1957- *WhoE 93*
Sogg, Wilton Sherman 1935- *WhoAm 92*
Sogin, Harold Hyman 1920- *WhoAm 92*
Soglin, Paul R. 1945- *WhoAm 92*
Soglo, Nicephore *WhoWor 93*
Soglo, Nicephore 1934- *WhoAfr*
Sognefest, Peter William 1941- *WhoAm 92*
Soh, Eric You Keng 1954- *WhoWor 93*
Sohal, Naresh (Kumar) 1939- *Baker 92*
Sohappy, David d1991 *BioIn 17*
Sohl, Charles E. *Law&B 92*
Sohl, Gerald A. *ScF&FL 92*
Sohl, Jerry 1913- *ScF&FL 92, WhoWrEP 92*
Sohlenius, Gunnar H. 1935- *WhoWor 93*
Sohlenius, Gunnar Hugo 1935- *WhoScE 91-4*
Sohlman, Michael 1944- *WhoWor 93*
Sohm, Jacque Edward 1938- *St&PR 93*
Sohm, Jim *WhoAm 92*
Sohm, Lawrence Richard 1942- *St&PR 93*
Sohmer, Bernard 1929- *WhoAm 92*
Sohmer, Steve *ScF&FL 92*
Sohn, Bertha Schooler 1915- *WhoE 93*
Sohn, David L. *Law&B 92*
Sohn, David Youngwhan 1942- *WhoE 93*
Sohn, Howard A. 1929- *St&PR 93*
Sohn, Israel Gregory 1911- *WhoE 93*
Sohn, Jeanne *WhoE 93*
Sohn, Louis Bruno 1914- *WhoAm 92*
Sohn, Ruth Southard d1992 *NewYTBS 92*
Sohn, Stephen 1941- *St&PR 93, WhoE 93*
Sohn-Bush, Janet Terese 1955- *WhoAmW 93*
Sohnen, Theodore 1943- *St&PR 93*
Sohnen-Moe, Cherie Marilyn 1956- *WhoAmW 93*
Sohngen, Oskar 1900-1983 *Baker 92*
Soibelman, Yan Semenovich 1956- *WhoWor 93*
Soiefer, Alan J. *Law&B 92*
Soifer, Jack 1940- *WhoWor 93*
Soifer, Lawrence M. *Law&B 92*
Soifer, Lawrence M. 1927- *St&PR 93*
Soifer, Leonard *St&PR 93*
Soiffer, Bill *BioIn 17*
Soika, Helmut Emil 1941- *WhoAm 92*
Soike, Kenneth Fieroe 1927- *WhoSSW 93*
Soileau, Dorothy Joanna Jumonville 1943- *WhoSSW 93*
Soileau, Louis Claudmire, III 1919- *WhoAm 92*
Soileau, Marion Joseph 1944- *WhoAm 92, WhoSSW 93*
Soisson, Jean-Pierre 1934- *BioIn 17*
Soja, Claire Elaine 1946- *WhoE 93*
Soja, Joseph Frank 1942- *St&PR 93*
Sojka, Gary Allan 1940- *WhoAm 92*
Sojka, Sandra Kay 1942- *WhoAmW 93*
Sojo, M. *Law&B 92*
Sojo, Vicente Emilio 1887-1974 *Baker 92*
Sojourner Truth d1883 *BioIn 17*
Sok, Robert M. 1946- *St&PR 93*
Sokach, Thomas Joseph 1947- *WhoSSW 93*
Sokal, Michael Mark 1945- *WhoE 93*
Sokal, Robert Reuven 1926- *WhoAm 92*
Sokalski, Debra Ann 1959- *WhoAmW 93*
Sokalski, Henryk Jerzy 1936- *WhoUN 92*
Sokalsky, Pyotr 1832-1887 *OxDcOp*
Sokalsky, Pyotr (Petrovich) 1832-1887 *Baker 92*
Sokmensuer, Adil 1928- *WhoAm 92*
Sokol, Barnett Jerome 1942- *WhoWor 93*
Sokol, Barry Steven 1951- *St&PR 93*
Sokol, Eli 1912- *St&PR 93*
Sokol, Elsie 1925- *St&PR 93*
Sokol, Gerald J. *St&PR 93*
Sokol, Hilda Weyl 1928- *WhoAmW 93*
Sokol, Mae Sandra 1951- *WhoE 93*
Sokol, Robert James 1941- *WhoAm 92*
Sokol, Si 1927- *St&PR 93*
Sokol, Sidney 1913-1990 *BioIn 17*
Sokol, Yuri 1937- *WhoWor 93*
Sokola, Milos 1913-1976 *Baker 92*
Sokolic, Josip 1930- *WhoScE 91-4*
Sokolichin, Alexander Alexandrovich 1965- *WhoWor 93*
Sokolnikoff, Nicholas *WhoWrEP 92*
Sokol'nikov, Grigorii IAkovlevich 1888-1939 *BioIn 17*
Sokolnikov, Nicholas S. 1928- *WhoSSW 93*
Sokolof, Phil *BioIn 17*
Sokolof, Phil 1922- *WhoAm 92*

Sokoloff, Edward A. *Law&B 92*
Sokoloff, Louis 1921- *WhoAm 92, WhoE 93*
Sokoloff, Nicolai 1886-1965 *Baker 92*
Sokolofski, Edward George 1945- *St&PR 93*
Sokolov, B.M. 1889-1930 *IntDcAn*
Sokolov, Jacque J. 1954- *St&PR 93*
Sokolov, Jacque Jenning 1954- *WhoWor 93*
Sokolov, Nikolai Alexandrovich 1859-1922 *Baker 92*
Sokolov, Richard S. *Law&B 92*
Sokolov, Yuri Mikhailovich 1932- *WhoWor 93*
Sokolove Weinstein, Ruth Ann 1940- *WhoAmW 93*
Sokolow, Al 1928- *St&PR 93*
Sokolow, Anna 1915- *BioIn 17*
Sokolow, Asa D. d1992 *NewYTBS 92*
Sokolow, Asa D. 1919- *WhoAm 92*
Sokolow, Kenneth 1955- *WhoE 93*
Sokolow, Lloyd Bruce 1949- *WhoE 93*
Sokolow, Maurice 1911- *WhoAm 92*
Sokolow, Melvin L. d1992 *BioIn 17, NewYTBS 92 [port]*
Sokolow, Stephen B. 1941- *St&PR 93*
Sokolower, Lester 1931- *St&PR 93*
Sokolowski, Aleksander 1932- *WhoScE 91-4*
Sokolowski, Linda Robinson 1943- *WhoE 93*
Sokolowski, Marek 1927- *WhoWor 93*
Sokolowski, Marek A. 1927- *WhoScE 91-4*
Sokolowski, Peter Daniel 1928- *St&PR 93*
Sokolowski, Stefan Andrzej 1950- *WhoWor 93*
Sokolski, Thomas John 1959- *WhoSSW 93*
Sokol'skii, Nikolai Pavlovich Smirnov- *BioIn 17*
Sokolsky, George E. 1893-1962 *JrnUS*
Sokolsky, Robert Lawrence 1928- *WhoAm 92*
Sokrates c. 380-c. 439 *OxDcByz*
Sokulski, Florette *BioIn 17*
Sokurov, Aleksandr 1951- *DrEEuF*
Sol, Alisson Augusto Souza 1968- *WhoWor 93*
Sola, Janet Elaine 1935- *WhoAmW 93*
Solal, Annie Cohen- *BioIn 17*
Solamito, C.C. *WhoScE 91-4*
Solan, Peter 1929- *DrEEuF*
Solana, Fernando Morales 1931- *WhoAm 92*
Solana, Rafael 1915- *DcMexL*
Solana Madariaga, Javier 1942- *WhoWor 93*
Solana Morales, Fernando 1931- *WhoWor 93*
Solanas, Fernando E. 1936- *MiSFD 9*
Solanas, Valerie *BioIn 17*
Solanch, Larry S. 1947- *WhoE 93*
Soland, Norman R. *Law&B 92*
Soland, Norman R. 1940- *St&PR 93*
Soland, Richard Martin 1940- *WhoE 93*
Solandt, Omond McKillop 1909- *WhoAm 92*
Solanki, Madhavsinh 1927- *WhoAsAP 91, WhoWor 93*
Solano, Francisco Ignacio c. 1720-1800 *Baker 92*
Solano, Gustavo *HispAmA*
Solano, Paul Leonard 1943- *WhoE 93*
Solano, Ronald Edward 1948- *WhoE 93*
Solanto, Mary Victoria 1951- *WhoE 93*
Solar, Richard L. 1939- *St&PR 93*
Solar, Richard Leon 1939- *WhoAm 92*
Solares, Andres Jose 1946- *WhoE 93, WhoSSW 93, WhoWor 93*
Solares, Enrique 1910- *Baker 92*
Solares, Ignacio 1945- *DcMexL, SpAmA*
Solarez, Abbie C. *MiSFD 9*
Solari, Joseph G., Jr. 1945- *St&PR 93*
Solari, Pietro Jose-Luis 1958- *WhoWor 93*
Solari, Robert M. 1951- *St&PR 93*
Solari Vicente, Andres Humberto 1945- *WhoWor 93*
Solarte, Tristan 1924- *SpAmA*
Solarz, Jerzy A. 1934- *WhoScE 91-4*
Solarz, Stephen J. *BioIn 17*
Solarz, Stephen J. 1940- *CngDr 91*
Solarz, Stephen Joshua 1940- *WhoAm 92, WhoE 93*
Solaski, Paul Edward 1922- *WhoSSW 93*
Solaun, Mauricio 1935- *ConAu 138*
Solberg, Daniel M. 1953- *St&PR 93*
Solberg, Elizabeth Transou 1939- *WhoAm 92, WhoAmW 93*
Solberg, James Burton 1953- *St&PR 93*
Solberg, James Joseph 1942- *WhoAm 92*
Solberg, Jan Ketil 1946- *WhoScE 91-4*
Solberg, Jeffrey M. 1952- *St&PR 93*
Solberg, Jon J. *Law&B 92*
Solberg, Kjell Oddvar 1931- *WhoScE 91-4*
Solberg, Mary Kathryn *Law&B 92*
Solberg, Morten Edward 1935- *BioIn 17*
Solberg, Myron 1931- *WhoAm 92*
Solberg, Nellie Florence Coad *WhoAm 92*
Solberg, Norman Robert 1939- *WhoAm 92*
Solberg, Ronald Louis 1953- *WhoAm 92*
Solberg, Ruell Floyd, Jr. 1939- *WhoSSW 93*
Solberg, Winton Udell 1922- *WhoAm 92*
Solbert, Peter Omar Abernathy 1919- *WhoE 93*
Solbiati, Vittorio *BioIn 17*
Solbraa, Knut 1934- *WhoScE 91-4*
Solbrig, Ingeborg Hildegard 1923- *WhoAm 92, WhoWor 93*
Soldan, Patricia Paz *Law&B 92*
Soldano, Louis P. *Law&B 92*
Soldat, Marie 1863-1955 *Baker 92*
Soldati, Francisco d1991 *BioIn 17*
Soldati, Mario 1906- *ScF&FL 92*
Soldatos, G. Eugene 1918- *St&PR 93*
Soldek, Jerzy Kazimierz 1931- *WhoScE 91-4*
Soldini, Silvio 1958- *MiSFD 9*
Soldner, Paul Edmund *WhoAm 92*
Soldo, Beth Jean 1948- *WhoEmL 93*
Soldo, John J. 1945- *WhoWrEP 92*
Soldon, Norbert Carroll 1932- *WhoE 93*
Soldoveri, Jane A. *Law&B 92*
Soldwedel, Kenneth J. 1947- *St&PR 93*
Soldwish, Janet Guenther 1940- *WhoAmW 93*
Sole, Alfred 1943- *MiSFD 9*
Sole, Antoinette Rampinelli d1991 *BioIn 17*
Sole, Charles Woodrow 1914- *WhoSSW 93*
Sole, Deborah Reitter 1958- *WhoSSW 93*
Sole, Patrick Felix 1960- *WhoWor 93*
Solecki, Albert J. 1940- *St&PR 93*
Solecki, R. Stefan 1917- *WhoAm 92*
Soled, Howard 1932- *St&PR 93*
Soledad, Miguel Doria 1953- *WhoWor 93*
Solender, Arthur Michael 1928- *St&PR 93*
Solender, Elsie 1928- *St&PR 93*
Solender, Mike 1928- *St&PR 93*
Solender, Robert Lawrence 1923- *St&PR 93, WhoAm 92*
Solender, Sanford 1914- *WhoAm 92*
Solender, Stephen L. 1951- *St&PR 93*
Solensky, Edward, Jr. *Law&B 92*
Soler, Arthur R. 1944- *WhoE 93*
Soler, Dianna *Law&B 92*
Soler, Dona K. 1921- *WhoWrEP 92*
Soler, Francisco Gabilando d1990 *BioIn 17*
Soler, Josep 1935- *Baker 92*
Soler (Ramos), Antonio (Francisco Javier Jose) 1729?-1783 *Baker 92*
Soler, Ronald Andrew 1949- *WhoSSW 93*
Soler, Terrell Diane *WhoAmW 93, WhoE 93, WhoWor 93*
Soler, Vicente 1954- *WhoScE 91-3*
Soler, Vincent Emile, Jr. 1936- *St&PR 93*
Solera, Temistocle 1815-1878 *IntDcOp, OxDcOp*
Soler Andres, Antonio 1939- *WhoScE 91-3*
Soleri, Paolo 1919- *WhoAm 92, WhoWor 93*
Soler Puig, Jose 1916- *SpAmA*
Soler-Roig, Miguel 1961- *WhoWor 93*
Soler-Sala, Victor 1933- *WhoUN 92*
Solerti, Angelo 1865-1907 *Baker 92*
Soles, Ada Leigh 1937- *WhoAmW 93*
Soles, Alfred J. 1950- *St&PR 93*
Soles, James Ralph 1935- *WhoE 93*
Soles, W. Roger 1920- *WhoIns 93*
Soles, William Roger 1920- *St&PR 93, WhoAm 92, WhoSSW 93*
Soletsky, Albert 1937- *WhoE 93*
Solferino, Thomas Philip *Law&B 92*
Solfisburg, Roy J. *BioIn 17*
Solfisburg, Roy J., III 1943- *St&PR 93*
Solfisburg, Roy John, III 1943- *WhoAm 92*
Solganik, Marvin 1930- *WhoAm 92*
Solganik, Marvin Joseph 1930- *St&PR 93*
Solh, Takieddine al- 1909-1988 *DcTwHis*
Solheim, Audrey Helene 1945- *WhoAmW 93*
Solheim, Karen Diane 1951- *WhoAmW 93*
Solheim, Wilhelm Gerhard, II 1924- *WhoAm 92*
Solidum, Emilio Solidum 1936- *WhoWor 93*
Solidum, James 1925- *WhoWor 93*
Solie, Jean-Pierre 1755-1812 *OxDcOp*
Solik, Imrich 1934- *WhoScE 91-4*
Soliman, Anwar 1938- *WhoAm 92*
Soliman, Patricia Brehaut 1937- *WhoAm 92*
Solinas, Mario *WhoScE 91-3*
Solinga, Steven *Law&B 92*
Solinger, David Morris 1906- *WhoAm 92*
Solinger, Martha *Law&B 92*
Solino, Ronald W. *Law&B 92*
Solis, Alfredo 1946- *WhoSSW 93*
Solis, Catherine Duque *ScF&FL 92*
Solis, Faustina 1923- *NotHsAW 93*
Solis, Javier *Law&B 92*
Solis, Javier 1946- *St&PR 93*
Solis, Jose A. *Law&B 92*
Solis, Jose Angel, Jr. *Law&B 92*
Solis, Juan Diaz de 1470-1516 *Expl 93*
Solis, Ruth Elizabeth 1935- *WhoAmW 93*
Solish, Jonathan Craig 1949- *WhoAm 92*
Solis Palma, Manuel *DcCPCAm*
Soliz, Joseph Guy 1954- *WhoAm 92, WhoSSW 93*
Soljacic, Ivo 1935- *WhoScE 91-4*
Soll, Larry 1942- *St&PR 93, WhoAm 92*
Soll, Richard Sigmund 1948- *WhoSSW 93*
Solladie, Guy Jean 1939- *WhoScE 91-2*
Sollano, Rosemarie 1962- *WhoAmW 93*
Sollars, E. Roe 1947- *St&PR 93*
Sollars, Eileen F. *Law&B 92*
Sollazo, Jerry Jon 1953- *WhoIns 93*
Sollberger, Harvey (Dene) 1938- *Baker 92*
Sollenberger, Harold Myers 1941- *WhoAm 92*
Sollenberger, Howard Edwin 1917- *WhoAm 92*
Sollenberger, Judith Katrina 1901- *AmWomPl*
Sollenberger, Robert Neil 1929- *WhoE 93*
Sollender, Joel D. 1924- *St&PR 93*
Sollender, Joel David 1926- *WhoAm 92*
Sollers, Joseph S. 1927- *St&PR 93*
Sollers, Philippe 1936- *BioIn 17*
Sollertinsky, Ivan (Ivanovich) 1902-1944 *Baker 92*
Solley, Larry W. *St&PR 93*
Solley, Michael William 1957- *WhoSSW 93*
Sollid, Faye 1913- *WhoAmW 93, WhoSSW 93, WhoWor 93*
Sollins, Irving V. d1991 *BioIn 17*
Sollins, Susan *WhoE 93*
Sollitt, Charles Kevin 1943- *WhoAm 92*
Sollman, George H. *St&PR 93*
Sollon, Phillip Benedict 1952- *WhoE 93*
Sollov, Jacques 1935- *WhoWrEP 92*
Solloway, Bram 1950- *St&PR 93*
Solloway, C. Robert 1935- *WhoAm 92*
Solloway, Charles Robert 1935- *St&PR 93*
Solloway, Erwin 1924- *St&PR 93*
Solls, Cynthia Fay 1958- *WhoSSW 93*
Solls, Mark A. *St&PR 93*
Solman, Joseph 1909- *BioIn 17, WhoAm 92*
Solmon, Vicki R. *Law&B 92*
Solms, Jurg 1925- *WhoScE 91-4*
Solmssen, Peter 1931- *WhoAm 92*
Solmundson, David L. 1941- *St&PR 93*
Solnceva, Julija 1901-1989 *DrEEuF*
Solnit, Albert Jay 1919- *WhoAm 92*
Solo, Alan Jere 1933- *WhoAm 92, WhoE 93*
Solo, Robert A(lexander) 1916- *ConAu 37NR*
Solo, Robert Alexander 1916- *WhoAm 92*
Solochek, Harold 1934- *WhoIns 93*
Solochek, Marc R. 1946- *St&PR 93*
Solodar, Donald Jay 1942- *St&PR 93*
Solodar, Todd E. *Law&B 92*
Soloff, Louis Alexander 1904- *WhoAm 92*
Sologub, Fedor 1863-1927 *ScF&FL 92*
Sologuren, Javier 1921- *SpAmA*
Soloman, Sol *St&PR 93*
Solomey, Nickolas 1961- *WhoWor 93*
Solomita, Anthony Francis 1935- *St&PR 93*
Solomon d544 *OxDcByz*
Solomon 1902-1988 *Baker 92*
Solomon, King of Israel *BioIn 17*
Solomon, A. Malama 1951- *WhoAmW 93*
Solomon, Andrew 1963- *BioIn 17*
Solomon, Andrew Wallace 1963- *WhoWor 93*
Solomon, Anthony Joseph 1932- *WhoAm 92, WhoE 93*
Solomon, Arthur Charles 1947- *St&PR 93, WhoAm 92*
Solomon, Arthur Herman 1934- *St&PR 93*
Solomon, Arthur Kaskel 1912- *WhoAm 92*
Solomon, Barbara Hochster 1936- *WhoE 93*
Solomon, Barbara Miller d1992 *NewYTBS 92*
Solomon, Barbara Stauffacher *BioIn 17*
Solomon, Barry 1949- *St&PR 93*
Solomon, Barry A. *Law&B 92*
Solomon, Bender d1992 *BioIn 17*
Solomon, Bernard 1923- *St&PR 93*
Solomon, Beth J. *Law&B 92*
Solomon, Bettina Schonfeld *Law&B 92*
Solomon, Betty Jeanne *BioIn 17*
Solomon, Carl *St&PR 93*
Solomon, Charles Francis 1932- *WhoSSW 93*
Solomon, Cynthia Ann 1954- *WhoAmW 93*
Solomon, David Eugene 1931- *St&PR 93, WhoAm 92*
Solomon, David Harris 1923- *WhoAm 92*
Solomon, Douglas H. *Law&B 92*
Solomon, Edward A. 1948- *St&PR 93*
Solomon, Edward L., III 1955- *St&PR 93*
Solomon, Elaine R. 1921- *St&PR 93*
Solomon, Elise S. *Law&B 92*
Solomon, George Freeman 1931- *WhoAm 92*
Solomon, George J. 1927- *St&PR 93*
Solomon, George M. 1940- *WhoAm 92*
Solomon, Gerald 1931- *St&PR 93*
Solomon, Gerald B.H. 1930- *CngDr 91*
Solomon, Gerald Brooks Hunt 1930- *WhoAm 92, WhoE 93*
Solomon, Geri Ellen 1957- *WhoAmW 93*
Solomon, Henry 1926- *WhoAm 92*
Solomon, Howard 1927- *St&PR 93, WhoAm 92*
Solomon, Ionel 1929- *WhoWor 93*
Solomon, Irvin D. 1946- *WhoSSW 93*
Solomon, Izler 1910-1987 *Baker 92*
Solomon, Jack, Jr. 1928- *St&PR 93*
Solomon, Jack Avrum 1928- *WhoAm 92*
Solomon, James D. 1934- *WhoSSW 93*
Solomon, Jean-Pierre 1950- *WhoWor 93*
Solomon, Jeffrey David *Law&B 92*
Solomon, Jeffrey Jonathan *St&PR 93*
Solomon, Jerrold M. 1951- *St&PR 93*
Solomon, Jerry L. 1917- *St&PR 93*
Solomon, Jerry Lawrence 1954- *WhoE 93*
Solomon, Jesse Robert 1909-1991 *BioIn 17*
Solomon, Jimmy Lloyd 1941- *WhoSSW 93*
Solomon, Joel Martin 1932- *WhoAm 92, WhoE 93*
Solomon, John *Law&B 92*
Solomon, Joseph 1904- *WhoAm 92*
Solomon, Judith Anne 1943- *WhoSSW 93*
Solomon, Larry 1933- *St&PR 93*
Solomon, Liviu Edmond 1927- *WhoScE 91-2*
Solomon, Louis *WhoScE 91-1*
Solomon, Louise 1946- *WhoAmW 93*
Solomon, Martin M. 1950- *WhoE 93*
Solomon, Maynard (Elliott) 1930- *Baker 92, WhoAm 92*
Solomon, Michael L. *Law&B 92*
Solomon, Paul *BioIn 17*
Solomon, Paul Robert 1948- *WhoE 93*
Solomon, Phyllis Linda 1945- *WhoAmW 93*
Solomon, Richard Allan 1917- *WhoAm 92*
Solomon, Richard Harvey 1937- *WhoAm 92*
Solomon, Richard Hugh 1934- *WhoAm 92*
Solomon, Richard Lester 1918- *WhoAm 92, WhoE 93*
Solomon, Risa Greenberg 1948- *WhoAmW 93, WhoSSW 93*
Solomon, Robert 1921- *WhoAm 92*
Solomon, Robert B. 1930- *BioIn 17*
Solomon, Robert Charles 1942- *WhoAm 92*
Solomon, Robert Douglas 1917- *WhoSSW 93*
Solomon, Robert Harris 1938- *WhoAm 92*
Solomon, Robert L. 1945- *St&PR 93*
Solomon, Robert O. 1937- *St&PR 93*
Solomon, Ron *BioIn 17*
Solomon, Russ *BioIn 17*
Solomon, Samuel 1925- *WhoAm 92*
Solomon, Saul 1918- *St&PR 93*
Solomon, Saul A. *Law&B 92*
Solomon, Selina *AmWomPl*
Solomon, Seymour 1924- *WhoE 93*
Solomon, Sheilah Marguerite 1931- *WhoUN 92*
Solomon, Solomon Sidney 1936- *WhoAm 92, WhoSSW 93*
Solomon, Susan 1956- *BioIn 17, WhoAm 92, WhoAmW 93*
Solomon, Susan Carol 1959- *WhoAmW 93*
Solomon, Syd 1917- *WhoAm 92*
Solomon, Vita Petrosky 1916- *WhoAm 92*
Solomon, William Backus, Jr. *Law&B 92*
Solomon, William Evan 1955- *WhoSSW 93*
Solomon, William R. 1950- *St&PR 93*
Solomon, William Tarver 1942- *St&PR 93, WhoAm 92*
Solomon, Yonty 1938- *WhoWor 93*
Solomon, Zachary Leon 1934- *WhoAm 92*
Solomon ben Isaac 1040-1105 *BioIn 17*
Solomons, Adolphus Simeon 1826-1910 *BioIn 17*
Solomons, Ella Kopp *Law&B 92*
Solomons, Gerald Lionel *WhoScE 91-1*
Solomons, Gus, Jr. *WhoAm 92*
Solomons, Mark Elliott 1946- *WhoE 93*
Solomons, Theodore Seixas *BioIn 17*
Solomon-Schwartz, Phyllis 1937- *WhoE 93*
Solomonson, Charles D. *WhoAm 92*
Solon, Carol Lynn 1938- *WhoAmW 93*
Solon, Daniel Peter 1931- *WhoWor 93*
Solon, John Thomas 1938- *St&PR 93*
Solon, Samuel 1953- *St&PR 93*
Solonche, Joel R. 1946- *WhoWrEP 92*
Solondz, Todd *MiSFD 9*
Solorow, Karen W. 1954- *WhoAmW 93*
Solorzano, Carlos 1922- *DcMexL*
Solorzano, Jorge *Law&B 92*

Solot, Robert J. 1939- *St&PR 93*
Solotaroff, Ted 1928- *WhoWrEP 92*
Solotruk, Ronald J. 1952- *St&PR 93*
Soloukhin, Vladimir Alekseevich 1924- *BioIn 17*
Solov, Zachary 1923- *WhoAm 92*
Solove, Steven Daniel 1951- *St&PR 93*
Soloveitchik, Joseph Dov 1903- *BioIn 17, JeAmHC*
Solov'ev, Aleksandr Artemovich 1948- *WhoWor 93*
Solov'ev, Sergej 1944- *DrEEuF*
Soloviev, Nikolai (Feopemptovich) 1846-1916 *Baker 92*
Soloviev-Sedoy, Vasili (Pavlovich) 1907-1979 *Baker 92*
Solow, B. 1934- *WhoScE 91-2*
Solow, Martin X. 1920-1991 *BioIn 17*
Solow, Robert B. 1916- *St&PR 93*
Solow, Robert M. *BioIn 17*
Solow, Robert Merton 1924- *WhoAm 92, WhoE 93, WhoWor 93*
Solow, Sidney *St&PR 93*
Soloway, Albert Herman 1925- *WhoAm 92*
Soloway, Jay N. *Law&B 92*
Soloway, Roger David 1935- *WhoSSW 93*
Soloway, Rose Ann Gould 1949- *WhoAmW 93*
Soloway, Saul 1916- *WhoE 93*
Solska, Irena 1878-1958 *PolBiDi*
Solski, Bill Peter 1943- *WhoAm 92*
Solski, Ludwik 1855-1954 *PolBiDi*
Solso, Theodore Mathew 1947- *St&PR 93*
Solstrand, Ragnvald H. 1942- *WhoScE 91-4*
Solsvig, Curtis Gerhardt, III 1954- *WhoE 93*
Solt, Andrew 1947- *MiSFD 9*
Solt, Andrew P. 1916-1990 *BioIn 17*
Solt, George Stefan *WhoScE 91-1*
Solt, Janos Gabor 1942- *WhoScE 91-4*
Solt, Leo Frank 1921- *WhoAm 92*
Solt, Paul Ervin 1929- *WhoE 93*
Solt, Walter John 1944- *St&PR 93*
Soltan, Valeriu 1951- *WhoWor 93*
Soltanoff, Jack 1915- *WhoE 93, WhoWor 93*
Solter, Aletha Lucia 1945- *WhoWrEP 92*
Soltero, Eugene A. 1943- *St&PR 93*
Soltero, Nona M. *Law&B 92*
Soltesz, Istvan *WhoScE 91-4*
Solti, Georg 1912- *Baker 92, IntDcOp [port], OxDcOp, WhoAm 92, WhoWor 93*
Soltis, Robert Alan 1955- *WhoEmL 93, WhoWor 93*
Soltis, William Thomas 1935- *St&PR 93*
Soltman, Ronald P. *Law&B 92*
Soltys, Adam 1890-1968 *Baker 92, PolBiDi*
Soltys, Michael Joseph 1959- *WhoE 93*
Soltys, Mieczyslaw 1863-1929 *Baker 92, PolBiDi*
Soltz, Judith E. *Law&B 92*
Soltzberg, Leonard Jay 1944- *WhoE 93*
Soltz-Szots, Josef *WhoScE 91-4*
Solum, James Maurice 1951- *WhoWor 93*
Solum, John Henry 1935- *WhoE 93, WhoWor 93*
Solum, Ola 1943- *MiSFD 9*
Solursh, Lionel Paul 1936- *WhoSSW 93*
Solway, David 1941- *WhoCanL 92*
Solway, Gordon R. 1936- *WhoAm 92*
Solway, Gordon Ridley 1936- *St&PR 93*
Solwitz, Sharon Dee 1945- *WhoWrEP 92*
Solymar, George G. 1939- *St&PR 93*
Solymos, Rezso 1929- *WhoScE 91-4*
Solymosi, Frigyes 1931- *WhoScE 91-4*
Solymosi, Peter 1945- *WhoScE 91-4*
Solymossy, Joseph Martin 1945- *WhoSSW 93*
Solymosy, Edmond Sigmond Albert 1937- *WhoAm 92*
Solz, Adam von Trott zu 1909-1944 *BioIn 17*
Solzhenitsyn, Aleksandr 1918- *BioIn 17, ColdWar 2 [port], MagSWL [port], WorLitC [port]*
Solzhenitsyn, Aleksandr I(sayevich) 1918- *ConAu 40NR*
Solzhenitsyn, Alexander 1918- *WhoAm 92, WhoWor 93*
Solzhenitsyn, Alexander 1919- *DcTwHis*
Som, Mihir Kumar 1943- *WhoWor 93*
Soma, Jeffrey A. 1949- *St&PR 93*
Soma, Rose Smeraldi 1940- *WhoAmW 93*
Somach, Abraham B. *St&PR 93*
Somach, S. Dennis 1952- *WhoE 93, WhoWor 93*
Somadasa, Hettiwatte 1937- *WhoWor 93*
Somain, Jean-Francois 1943- *WhoCanL 92*
Soman, Shirley Camper *WhoAmW 93, WhoE 93*
Somani, Arun Kumar 1951- *WhoWor 93*
Somare, Michael 1936- *WhoAsAP 91*
Somare, Michael Thomas 1936- *WhoWor 93*
Somary, Johannes 1935- *Baker 92*
Somary, Johannes Felix 1935- *WhoE 93*
Somasundaran, Ponisseril 1939- *WhoAm 92, WhoE 93*
Somavia, Juan Octavio 1941- *WhoUN 92*
Somberg, James S. 1937- *St&PR 93*
Sombre, Robert Magnus de 1915-1991 *BioIn 17*
Sombroek, Wim G. 1934- *WhoScE 91-3*
Sombroek, Wim Gerard 1934- *WhoWor 93*
Somcynsky, Jean-Francois *WhoCanL 92*
Somdahl, Stacy 1945- *St&PR 93*
Some, Marvin Lester 1927- *St&PR 93*
Someda, Carlo G. 1941- *WhoScE 91-3*
Somek, Branko 1931- *WhoScE 91-4*
Somelofske, Robert Joseph 1947- *WhoIns 93*
Someple *AmWomPl*
Somer, (Ruth) Hilde 1922-1979 *Baker 92*
Somer, John 1936- *ScF&FL 92*
Somer, Tarik G. 1927- *WhoScE 91-4*
Somerall, Leon Hanks 1919- *St&PR 93*
Somerfield, Neil 1953- *WhoWrEP 92*
Somerhalder, John William, II 1956- *St&PR 93*
Somerlott, Robert 1928- *BioIn 17, ScF&FL 92*
Somero, George Nicholls 1940- *WhoAm 92*
Somers, Andrew B. *Law&B 92*
Somers, Anne Ramsay 1913- *WhoAm 92, WhoAmW 93*
Somers, Antoinette Nadezhda 1947- *WhoAm 92*
Somers, Armonia 1914- *SpAmA*
Somers, Armonia 1920- *BioIn 17*
Somers, Carin A. 1934-1990 *BioIn 17*
Somers, Clifford Louis 1940- *WhoSSW 93, WhoWor 93*
Somers, Dan Michael 1951- *WhoE 93*
Somers, Dean Albert 1945- *St&PR 93*
Somers, Donald Louis 1931- *St&PR 93*
Somers, Edward W. *Law&B 92*
Somers, George Fredrick 1914- *WhoAm 92, WhoE 93*
Somers, Hans Peter 1922- *WhoAm 92*
Somers, Harold Milton 1915- *WhoAm 92*
Somers, Harry 1925- *OxDcOp*
Somers, Harry Stewart 1925- *Baker 92*
Somers, Herman Hendrik 1921- *WhoWor 93*
Somers, Herman Miles 1911-1991 *BioIn 17*
Somers, Jane 1919- *BioIn 17*
Somers, John A. 1944- *WhoIns 93*
Somers, John Arthur 1944- *St&PR 93, WhoAm 92*
Somers, Karl Brent 1948- *WhoAm 92*
Somers, Margaret Lee 1941- *WhoWrEP 92*
Somers, Marion *WhoAmW 93, WhoE 93*
Somers, Paul C. *Law&B 92*
Somers, Paul Preston, Jr. 1942- *WhoWrEP 92*
Somers, Robert Vance 1937- *WhoSSW 93*
Somers, Suzanne *BioIn 17*
Somers, Suzanne 1946- *ConAu 139*
Somers, William L. *Law&B 92*
Somerset, David *DcChlFi*
Somerset, Harold Richard 1935- *WhoAm 92*
Somerson, Paul *ScF&FL 92*
Somervell, Arthur 1863-1937 *Baker 92*
Somervell, Brehon Burke 1892-1955 *HarEnMi*
Somervill, Cynthia B. *Law&B 92*
Somerville, A.J., Jr. 1929- *St&PR 93*
Somerville, David W. *St&PR 93*
Somerville, Edith Anna OEnone 1858-1949 *BioIn 17*
Somerville, Hernan Guillermo 1941- *WhoWor 93*
Somerville, (James) Hugh (Miller) 1922-1992 *ConAu 137*
Somerville, James D. *St&PR 93*
Somerville, James Fownes 1882-1949 *HarEnMi*
Somerville, Margaret Anne Ganley 1942- *WhoAmW 93*
Somerville, Mason Harold 1941- *WhoAm 92*
Somerville, Robert Eugene *WhoAm 92*
Somerville, Romaine Stec 1930- *WhoAm 92*
Somerville, Theodore E. *Law&B 92*
Somerville, Theodore E. 1940- *St&PR 93*
Somerville, Theodore Elkin 1940- *WhoAm 92*
Somerville, Walter Raleigh, Jr. 1930- *WhoE 93*
Somerville, Warren Thomas 1942- *WhoE 93*
Somerville, William J. D. 1933- *St&PR 93*
Somerwitz, Herbert Saul *Law&B 92*
Somes, Charles J. *Law&B 92*
Somes, Daniel E. 1935- *WhoAm 92*
Somes, Daniel Earl 1935- *St&PR 93*
Somfai, Laszlo 1934- *Baker 92*
Somis, Francesco Lorenzo 1663-1736 *See* Somis, Giovanni Battista 1686-1763 *Baker 92*
Somis, Giovanni Battista 1686-1763 *Baker 92*
Somis, Lorenzo Giovanni 1688-1775 *Baker 92*
Somit, Albert 1919- *WhoAm 92*
Somjen, George Gustav 1929- *WhoAm 92*
Somlyo, Andrew Paul 1930- *WhoAm 92, WhoSSW 93*
Somma, Donna *Law&B 92*
Somma, Henry Jeremiah 1921- *St&PR 93*
Somma, Herman Robert 1925- *St&PR 93*
Sommer, Alfred 1942- *WhoAm 92*
Sommer, Alphonse Adam, Jr. 1924- *WhoAm 92*
Sommer, Clifford G. *Law&B 92*
Sommer, Elke *BioIn 17*
Sommer, Elke 1941- *WhoAm 92*
Sommer, Ernest L. d1990 *BioIn 17*
Sommer, Ernest W. 1947- *WhoScE 91-4*
Sommer, Erwin 1936- *WhoScE 91-3*
Sommer, Evelyn M. *Law&B 92*
Sommer, Frederick 1905- *BioIn 17*
Sommer, Gert 1941- *WhoScE 91-3*
Sommer, Hans 1837-1922 *Baker 92*
Sommer, Harvey Robert 1922- *St&PR 93*
Sommer, Heiner 1932- *WhoScE 91-3*
Sommer, Heinrich 1928- *WhoScE 91-3*
Sommer, Hermann 1936- *WhoScE 91-4*
Sommer, Howard E. 1918- *St&PR 93*
Sommer, Howard Ellsworth 1918- *WhoAm 92*
Sommer, Jean 1937- *WhoScE 91-2*
Sommer, John A., Jr. 1933- *St&PR 93*
Sommer, Josef 1934- *ConTFT 10*
Sommer, Joseph T. 1941- *St&PR 93*
Sommer, Karl-Heinz 1933- *WhoWor 93*
Sommer, Kathleen Ruth 1947- *WhoAmW 93, WhoSSW 93*
Sommer, Larry 1940- *St&PR 93*
Sommer, Maria E. 1921- *WhoSSW 93*
Sommer, Miriam Goldstein 1929- *WhoE 93*
Sommer, Richard 1934- *WhoCanL 92*
Sommer, Richard Samuel 1941- *St&PR 93*
Sommer, Robert *BioIn 17*
Sommer, Robert Eugene 1918- *St&PR 93*
Sommer, Robert George 1959- *WhoAm 92*
Sommer, Sandra Reading 1947- *WhoSSW 93*
Sommer, Scott 1951- *BioIn 17*
Sommer, Shirley Zila 1958- *WhoAmW 93*
Sommer, Siegfried Dieter 1938- *WhoWor 93*
Sommer, Steve *BioIn 17*
Sommer, Steven P. *Law&B 92*
Sommer, Theo 1930- *WhoWor 93*
Sommer, Theodore Levon 1920- *St&PR 93*
Sommer, Vladimir 1921- *Baker 92*
Sommer-Bodenburg, Angela *BioIn 17*
Sommer-Bodenburg, Angela 1948- *ScF&FL 92*
Sommerfeld, Gretchen *Law&B 92*
Sommerfeld, Helen Ray 1955- *WhoAmW 93*
Sommerfeld, Jude Thomas 1936- *WhoSSW 93*
Sommerfeld, Nicholas Ulrich 1926- *WhoAm 92*
Sommerfeld, Raynard Matthias 1933- *WhoAm 92*
Sommerfeldt, John Robert 1933- *WhoAm 92, WhoSSW 93*
Sommerfeldt, Oistein 1919- *Baker 92*
Sommerfelt, Gary John *Law&B 92*
Sommerfelt, Soren Christian 1916- *WhoAm 92*
Sommerhalder, John E. 1934- *St&PR 93*
Sommerlad, Robert Edward 1937- *WhoAm 92*
Sommers, Albert Trumbull 1919- *WhoAm 92*
Sommers, Beverly *ScF&FL 92*
Sommers, Bill *St&PR 93*
Sommers, Gene R. *Law&B 92*
Sommers, Herbert Myron 1925- *WhoAm 92*
Sommers, Lawrence Allan *Law&B 92*
Sommers, Lawrence Melvin 1919- *WhoAm 92*
Sommers, Patrick Charles 1947- *St&PR 93*
Sommers, Robert Thomas 1926- *WhoAm 92*
Sommers, Sally M. *Law&B 92*
Sommers, Sandra Jean *Law&B 92*
Sommers, Shari Catherine 1950- *WhoAmW 93*
Sommers, Stephen *MiSFD 9*
Sommers, Tish d1985 *BioIn 17*
Sommers, William E. 1944- *St&PR 93*
Sommers, William J. 1945- *St&PR 93*
Sommers, William John, Jr. *Law&B 92*
Sommers, William Paul 1933- *WhoAm 92*
Sommerschild, Hilchen 1926- *WhoScE 91-4*
Sommerville, C(harles) John 1938- *ConAu 137*
Sommerville, Frank 1952- *WhoWor 93*
Sommerville, Ian *WhoScE 91-1*
Sommerville, Paul B. *Law&B 92*
Sommese, Andrew John 1948- *WhoAm 92*
Somnolet, Michel 1940- *St&PR 93*
Somnolet, Michel Pierre 1940- *WhoAm 92, WhoWor 93*
Somodi, Edward M. 1957- *St&PR 93*
Somogi, Judith 1937-1988 *Baker 92*
Somogy, Aimery 1897-1991 *BioIn 17*
Somogy, Milivoj von 1928- *WhoWor 93*
Somogyi, Endre 1922- *WhoScE 91-4*
Somogyi, J. *WhoScE 91-4*
Somogyi, Jozsef 1916- *WhoWor 93*
Somogyi, Laszlo 1908- *Baker 92*
Somogyi, Pal A. 1940- *WhoScE 91-4*
Somogyi-McPherson, Jeanette Rosemary 1960- *WhoAmW 93*
Somogyl, Arpad *WhoScE 91-3*
Somolinos, Juan 1938- *WhoWor 93*
Somorjai, Gabor Arpad 1935- *WhoAm 92*
Somorowski, Czeslaw 1930- *WhoScE 91-4*
Somosvari, Zsolt 1941- *WhoScE 91-4*
Somoza, Anastasio 1896-1956 *BioIn 17* *See Also* Somoza family *DcTwHis*
Somoza, Anastasio 1925-1980 *BioIn 17*
Somoza, Luis d1967 *See* Somoza family *DcTwHis*
Somoza Debayle, Anastasio 1925-1980 *ColdWar 2 [port], DcCPCAm*
Somoza Debayle, Luis 1922-1967 *DcCPCAm*
Somoza family *DcTwHis*
Somoza Garcia, Anastasio 1896-1956 *DcCPCAm*
Somoza Portocarrero, Anastasio *DcCPCAm*
Somrock, J.D. 1942- *St&PR 93*
Somrock, John Douglas 1942- *WhoAm 92*
Somtow, S.P. *ScF&FL 92*
Son, Chang Hyun 1957- *WhoSSW 93*
Son, Ki Sub 1928- *WhoWor 93*
Son, Masayoshi *BioIn 17*
Son, Mun Shig 1950- *WhoE 93*
Sona, Alberto 1934- *WhoScE 91-3*
Son Chu-Whan 1940- *WhoAsAP 91*
Sondag, Bonnie T. *Law&B 92*
Sondakh, Widyawati Deborah 1945- *WhoWor 93*
Sonder, Edward 1928- *WhoSSW 93*
Sonderby, Susan Pierson 1947- *WhoAmW 93*
Sonderegger, Theo Brown 1925- *WhoAm 92*
Sondergeld, Donald Ray 1930- *WhoAm 92*
Sonderman, Andrew Justin *Law&B 92*
Sondermann, H. *WhoScE 91-3*
Sonders, Mark *ScF&FL 92*
Sondheim, Henry Leon 1920- *WhoSSW 93*
Sondheim, Herbert 1927- *St&PR 93*
Sondheim, Stephen *BioIn 17*
Sondheim, Stephen 1930- *ConMus 8 [port], OxDcOp*
Sondheim, Stephen (Joshua) 1930- *Baker 92, WhoAm 92, WhoE 93, WhoWor 93*
Sondheimer, Joseph 1918- *St&PR 93*
Sondhi, Jay *Law&B 92*
Sondhi, Vir K. 1929- *St&PR 93*
Sondles, R. Dan 1947- *St&PR 93*
Sondock, Ruby Kless 1926- *WhoAmW 93, WhoWor 93*
Sone, Bruce H. 1940- *St&PR 93*
Sone, Toshio 1935- *WhoWor 93*
Sonea, Sorin I. 1920- *WhoAm 92*
Sonel, Ahmet 1931- *WhoScE 91-4*
Sonenberg, Jack 1925- *WhoAm 92*
Sonenberg, Martin 1920- *WhoAm 92, WhoE 93*
Sonenberg, Maya 1960- *WhoWrEP 92*
Sonenberg, Suzy Dalton 1943- *WhoE 93*
Sonenschein, David Walter 1941- *WhoWrEP 92*
Sonenshein, Nathan 1915- *WhoAm 92*
Sonenstein, David M. *Law&B 92*
Sones, Charles Gaylon 1922- *WhoAm 92*
Sonesson, Mats *WhoScE 91-4*
Sonett, Charles Philip 1924- *WhoAm 92*
Sonfield, Robert Leon, Jr. 1931- *WhoAm 92*
Song, Jong Hwan 1944- *WhoUN 92*
Song, Renming 1963- *WhoSSW 93*
Song, Suk Man 1945- *WhoWor 93*
Song, Yuan-Qing 1924- *WhoWor 93*
Songa, Tullio 1926- *WhoScE 91-3*
Song Defu 1946- *WhoAsAP 91*
Song Doo Ho, Dr. 1930- *WhoAsAP 91*
Songer, Elena Margarita 1954- *WhoE 93*
Songer, Gregory Alan 1957- *WhoSSW 93*
Songer, H.S. 1940- *WhoIns 93*
Songer, Marcia Jeannette 1936- *WhoAmW 93*
Song Hanliang 1934- *WhoAsAP 91*

Song Hyun Sup 1938- *WhoAsAP 91*
Song Jian 1932- *WhoAsAP 91, WhoWor 93*
Song Keda 1928- *WhoAsAP 91*
Song Ong, Roxanne Kay 1953- *WhoAmW 93*
Song Ping 1917- *WhoAsAP 91, WhoWor 93*
Song Qingling 1892-1981 *DcTwHis*
Song Renqiong 1904- *WhoWor 93*
Songsiridej, Vanee 1949- *WhoAmW 93*
Songster, John Hugh 1934- *WhoE 93*
Songster, Thomas B. *BioIn 17*
Sonheim, Richard C. 1930- *St&PR 93*
Soni, Jennifer Sue Rose 1948- *WhoAmW 93*
Soni, Kusum Kapila 1930- *WhoAmW 93*
Sonia 1907- *BioIn 17*
Sonic Youth *ConMus 9 [port]*
Son Joo-Hang 1935- *WhoAsAP 91*
Sonju, David Andrew 1951- *St&PR 93*
Sonju, Norm Arnold 1938- *WhoAm 92*
Sonkin, Jack 1926- *St&PR 93*
Sonkin, Michelle Anne Eisemann 1952- *WhoAmW 93*
Sonkin, Paul Edward 1932- *St&PR 93*
Sonko, Andre 1944- *WhoWor 93*
Sonkoly, Carl A. 1959- *St&PR 93*
Sonkowsky, Robert Paul 1931- *WhoAm 92*
Sonksen, Peter H. 1936- *WhoScE 91-1*
Sonksen, Peter Henri 1936- *WhoWor 93*
Sonna, Linda Gail 1950- *WhoAmW 93*
Sonnabend, Ileana *BioIn 17*
Sonnabend, Lawrence C. 1943- *St&PR 93*
Sonnabend, Paul *St&PR 93*
Sonnabend, Peter J. *Law&B 92*
Sonnabend, Peter J. 1954- *St&PR 93*
Sonnabend, Roger P. 1925- *St&PR 93*
Sonnabend, Roger Philip 1925- *WhoAm 92*
Sonnabend, Stephanie 1953- *St&PR 93*
Sonnabend, Stephen *St&PR 93*
Sonne, Finn 1946- *WhoWor 93*
Sonne, Maggie Lee 1958- *WhoAmW 93*
Sonneborn, Henry, III 1918- *WhoAm 92*
Sonneborn, Marcene Schnell 1954- *WhoE 93*
Sonneborn, Richard F. 1918- *St&PR 93*
Sonneck, Oscar G(eorge) T(heodore) 1873-1928 *Baker 92*
Sonneck, Oscar George Theodore 1873-1928 *BioIn 17*
Sonnecken, Edwin Herbert 1916- *WhoAm 92*
Sonnedecker, Glenn Allen 1917- *WhoAm 92*
Sonneman, Eve 1946- *WhoAm 92*
Sonnemann, George 1926- *WhoE 93*
Sonnemann, Harry 1924- *WhoAm 92*
Sonnenberg, Alan 1951- *St&PR 93*
Sonnenberg, Andrea *Law&B 92*
Sonnenberg, Ben *BioIn 17*
Sonnenberg, Ben 1936- *ConAu 139, WhoAm 92, WhoWrEP 92*
Sonnenberg, Benjamin 1901-1978 *BioIn 17*
Sonnenberg, Hardy 1939- *WhoAm 92*
Sonnenberg, Nadja Salerno- *BioIn 17*
Sonnenblick, Carol Anne *WhoE 93*
Sonnenblick, Edmund H. 1932- *WhoWrEP 92*
Sonnenblick, Harvey Irwin 1936- *WhoE 93*
Sonnenborn, Monroe R. *Law&B 92*
Sonnenfeld, Barry *BioIn 17, MiSFD 9*
Sonnenfeld, Gerald 1949- *WhoSSW 93*
Sonnenfeld, Jeffrey Alan 1954- *WhoAm 92*
Sonnenfeld, Marion 1928- *WhoAm 92, WhoE 93*
Sonnenfeld, Michael J. 1956- *St&PR 93*
Sonnenfeldt, Helmut 1926- *WhoAm 92*
Sonnenfeldt, Richard Wolfgang 1923- *WhoAm 92*
Sonnenmark, Laura A. 1958- *SmATA 73 [port]*
Sonnenschein, Adam 1938- *WhoAm 92*
Sonnenschein, Hugo Freund 1940- *WhoAm 92*
Sonnenschein, Ralph Robert 1923- *WhoAm 92*
Sonnentag, Richard H. 1940- *WhoAm 92*
Sonnerup, Anna *BioIn 17*
Sonneveld, C. 1954- *WhoScE 91-3*
Sonni Ali Ber d1492 *HarEnMi*
Sonnichsen, C. L. 1901- *ConAu 39NR*
Sonnichsen, Dorothy Griffith 1942- *St&PR 93*
Sonnichsen, George Carl 1941- *WhoE 93*
Sonnichsen, Harold Marvin 1912- *WhoE 93*
Sonnie, Elena J. 1966- *WhoAmW 93*
Sonnier, Beverly Onezime 1957- *WhoSSW 93*
Sonnier, David Joseph 1939- *WhoSSW 93*
Sonnier, David W. 1959- *St&PR 93*
Sonnier, Suzie 1954- *St&PR 93*
Sonninen, Ahti 1914-1984 *Baker 92*
Sonnino, Carlo Benvenuto 1904- *WhoAm 92*
Sonnleithner *Baker 92*
Sonnleithner, Christoph 1734-1786 *Baker 92*
Sonnleithner, Ignaz 1770-1831 *Baker 92*
Sonnleithner, Joseph 1766-1835 *Baker 92*
Sonnleithner, Leopold von 1797-1873 *Baker 92*
Sonntag, Hans Guenther 1938- *WhoWor 93*
Sonntag, Linda 1950- *ScF&FL 92*
Sonntag, Linda D. *St&PR 93*
Sonntag, Lynn Evelyn *Law&B 92*
Sonntag, Martin Hans 1957- *WhoWor 93*
Sonntagbauer, Hans 1946- *WhoWor 93*
Sono, Kazuaki 1934- *WhoUN 92*
Sonoda, Hiroyuki 1942- *WhoAsAP 91*
Sonoda, Roxana Aki 1962- *WhoWor 93*
Sonogashira, Kenkichi 1931- *WhoWor 93*
Sons, Linda Ruth 1939- *WhoAmW 93*
Sons, Raymond W(illiam) 1926- *ConAu 136*
Sons, Raymond William 1926- *WhoAm 92*
Son Sann 1911- *WhoAsAP 91, WhoWor 93*
Son Sen 1930- *WhoAsAP 91, WhoWor 93*
Sonsino, C.M. 1946- *WhoScE 91-3*
Sonsino, Victor *Law&B 92*
Sonsteby, Kristi Lee 1958- *WhoAmW 93*
Sonstelie, Richard Robert 1945- *St&PR 93, WhoAm 92*
Sonstroem, Jed P. *Law&B 92*
Sontag, David Burt 1934- *WhoWor 93*
Sontag, Frederick Burnett 1942- *St&PR 93*
Sontag, Frederick Earl 1924- *WhoAm 92*
Sontag, Henriette 1806-1854 *Baker 92, IntDcOp, OxDcOp*
Sontag, James Mitchell 1939- *WhoAm 92*
Sontag, John d1893 *BioIn 17*
Sontag, John G. 1948- *St&PR 93*
Sontag, Peter Michael 1943- *WhoE 93*
Sontag, R.F. 1950- *St&PR 93*
Sontag, Sheldon 1938- *St&PR 93*
Sontag, Susan *MiSFD 9, NewYTBS 92 [port], WhoAm 92, WhoAmW 93*
Sontag, Susan 1933- *AmWrS3, BioIn 17, CurBio 92 [port], JeAmFiW*
Sontheimer, James Albert 1926- *St&PR 93*
Sontheimer, Robert Max 1941- *St&PR 93*
Sontvedt, Terje 1939- *WhoScE 91-4*
Sonzogni, Louis A. *Law&B 92*
Sonzogno, Edoardo 1836-1920 *Baker 92, OxDcOp*
Sonzogno, Giulio Cesare 1906-1976 *Baker 92*
Sonzogno, Renzo 1877-1920 *See* Sonzogno, Edoardo 1836-1920 *Baker 92*
Sonzogno, Riccardo 1871-1915 *See* Sonzogno, Edoardo 1836-1920 *Baker 92*
Soo, Shao Lee 1922- *WhoAm 92, WhoWor 93*
Sood, Mary 1960- *WhoAmW 93*
Sooder, Karl Michael 1943- *St&PR 93*
Soodhalter, Deborah Ann 1948- *WhoAmW 93*
SooHoo, Tony Glen 1965- *WhoE 93*
Soomro, Akbar Haider 1947- *WhoWor 93*
Soomro, Khuda Dino 1950- *WhoWor 93*
Soomro, Mahfooz Ahmed 1953- *WhoWor 93*
Soon, Tay Eng 1940- *WhoAsAP 91*
Soong, James Chu Yul 1942- *WhoWor 93*
Soong, Mayling *BioIn 17*
Soong, T.V. 1894-1971 *DcTwHis*
Soong, Zosan Sam *Law&B 92*
Sooprayen, Paul Henry 1941- *WhoWor 93*
Soos, Imre 1935- *WhoUN 92*
Soos, James Francis 1942- *WhoSSW 93*
Soos, Pal 1928- *WhoScE 91-4*
Soos, Richard A., Jr. 1955- *WhoWrEP 92*
Soot, Fritz 1878-1965 *Baker 92, OxDcOp*
Sooy, Charles Dalmage 1908- *St&PR 93*
Sooy, William Ray 1951- *WhoSSW 93*
Sopena (Ibanez), Federico 1917- *Baker 92*
Soper, Alexander Coburn 1904- *WhoAm 92*
Soper, David Bryan *Law&B 92*
Soper, Holly Spencer 1958- *WhoSSW 93*
Soper, James Herbert 1916- *WhoAm 92*
Soper, Quentin Francis 1919- *WhoAm 92*
Soper, Richard Graves 1950- *WhoSSW 93*
Soper, Roberta Mae 1948- *WhoAmW 93*
Soper, Thomas, III 1949- *St&PR 93*
Sophia *OxDcByz*
Sophia c. 530-c. 600 *OxDcByz*
Sophia Alekseevna, Regent of Russia *BioIn 17*
Sophia Palaiologina 1450?-1503 *OxDcByz*
Sophocles c. 496BC-c. 406BC *MagSWL [port], OxDcByz*
Sophonpanich, Chali 1961- *WhoWor 93*
Sophonpanich, Charnwut 1965- *WhoWor 93*
Sophronios c. 560-638 *OxDcByz*
Sophronius, Eusebius Hieronymus d419? *BioIn 17*
Sopkin, George 1914- *WhoAm 92*
Sopkin, Henry 1903-1988 *Baker 92*
Sopko, M.D. 1939- *St&PR 93*
Sopko, Michael D. 1939- *WhoAm 92, WhoWor 93*
Soponski, Charles R. 1942- *St&PR 93*
Sopov, Dimitar *WhoScE 91-4*
Soppelsa, George Nicholas 1939- *WhoE 93*
Sopranos, O.J. 1935- *St&PR 93*
Sopranos, Orpheus Javaras 1935- *WhoAm 92*
Soproni, Jozsef 1930- *Baker 92*
Sopwith, Thomas 1803-1879 *BioIn 17*
Sor, (Joseph) Fernando (Macari) 1778-1839 *Baker 92*
Sora, Constantin 1924- *WhoScE 91-4*
Sora, Sebastian Antony 1943- *WhoE 93, WhoWor 93*
Sorabji, Cornelia 1866-1954 *AmWomPl*
Sorabji, Kaikhosru Shapurji 1892-1988 *Baker 92*
Soran, Robert L. 1943- *WhoSSW 93*
Sorano, Victor Hugo 1948- *WhoWor 93*
Sorauf, Linda Marie 1957- *WhoAmW 93*
Sorba, Antoine 1933- *WhoScE 91-2*
Sorba, Francois X. *Law&B 92*
Sorbanelli, Patricia Lowney 1963- *WhoAmW 93*
Sorber, Charles Arthur 1939- *WhoAm 92*
Sorby, Donald Lloyd 1933- *WhoAm 92*
Sordahl, Louis A. 1936- *WhoSSW 93*
Sordellini, Rita Jane 1936- *WhoSSW 93*
Sorden, Hetty Lovejoy *AmWomPl*
Sordi, Alberto 1919- *IntDcF 2-3*
Sordi, Alberto 1920- *MiSFD 9*
Sordill, Patricia Anne 1954- *WhoAmW 93, WhoE 93*
Sordillo, Willie 1951- *WhoE 93*
Sordoni, Andrew J., III 1943- *St&PR 93, WhoAm 92*
Soref, Dror *MiSFD 9*
Soref, Richard Allan 1936- *WhoE 93*
Soregaroli, Arthur E. 1933- *St&PR 93*
Soregeloos, Keith Raymond 1952- *WhoE 93*
Soreide, Nancy Niblett 1942- *WhoAmW 93*
Soreide, Tore H. 1948- *WhoScE 91-4*
Sorel, Claudette Marguerite *WhoAm 92, WhoAmW 93*
Sorel, Edward 1929- *BioIn 17, WhoAm 92*
Sorel, Elizabeth d1991 *BioIn 17*
Sorel, Georges 1847-1922 *BioIn 17*
Sorel-Cameron, James (Robert) 1948- *ConAu 136*
Sorell, Carole Suzanne 1940- *WhoAmW 93*
Sorell, Kitty Julia 1937- *WhoAmW 93*
SoRelle, Ruth Doyle 1948- *WhoSSW 93*
Soremark, Rune 1925- *WhoWor 93*
Soremark, Rune S.A. 1926- *WhoScE 91-4*
Soren, David *ScF&FL 92*
Soren, David 1946- *WhoAm 92*
Soren, Howard 1930- *St&PR 93*
Sorensen, A.K. *Law&B 92*
Sorensen, Allan C. 1938- *St&PR 93*
Sorensen, Allan Chresten 1938- *WhoAm 92*
Sorensen, Andrew Aaron 1938- *WhoAm 92*
Sorensen, Anne Elder 1956- *WhoAmW 93*
Sorensen, Bengt Algot 1927- *WhoWor 93*
Sorensen, Bent Erik 1941- *WhoScE 91-2*
Sorensen, Borge 1931- *WhoScE 91-2*
Sorensen, Borge 1942- *WhoWor 93*
Sorensen, Burton Erhard 1929- *WhoAm 92*
Sorensen, Cary V. *Law&B 92*
Sorensen, David Allen 1953- *WhoWrEP 92*
Sorensen, Debra Lynnette 1954- *WhoAmW 93*
Sorensen, Elizabeth Julia 1934- *WhoAmW 93*
Sorensen, Erik 1944- *WhoAm 92*
Sorensen, Geir Moe 1944- *WhoUN 92*
Sorensen, Gillian Martin 1941- *WhoAm 92*
Sorensen, Hans Christian *WhoScE 91-2*
Sorensen, Hans Christian 1942- *WhoScE 91-2*
Sorensen, Henning 1926- *WhoScE 91-2*
Sorensen, Henrik Smith 1947- *WhoWor 93*
Sorensen, Ian *ScF&FL 92*
Sorensen, J. Nygaard 1956- *WhoScE 91-2*
Sorensen, Jacki Faye 1942- *WhoAm 92, WhoAmW 93, WhoSSW 93*
Sorensen, Jan-Eirik 1941- *WhoUN 92*
Sorensen, Jorgen Philip 1938- *WhoWor 93*
Sorensen, Leif Boge 1928- *WhoAm 92*
Sorensen, Meredith Jean 1940- *WhoAmW 93, WhoE 93*
Sorensen, Niels Kristian 1940- *WhoScE 91-2*
Sorensen, Nina M. *Law&B 92*
Sorensen, Palle 1933- *WhoScE 91-2*
Sorensen, R.H. 1928- *St&PR 93*
Sorensen, Raymond Andrew 1931- *WhoE 93*
Sorensen, Robert C. 1923- *WhoAm 92, WhoWor 93*
Sorensen, Robert Holm 1921- *St&PR 93, WhoAm 92*
Sorensen, Roy A. 1957- *ConAu 139*
Sorensen, Sheila 1947- *WhoAmW 93*
Sorensen, Soren 1920- *Baker 92*
Sorensen, Soren Peter 1924- *St&PR 93*
Sorensen, Stephen H. 1950- *St&PR 93*
Sorensen, Stephen J. *Law&B 92*
Sorensen, Stuart L. 1948- *St&PR 93*
Sorensen, Susan Krieger 1951- *WhoAmW 93*
Sorensen, Svend Otto 1916- *BioIn 17*
Sorensen, Theodore Chaikin 1928- *WhoAm 92*
Sorensen, Thomas Chaikin 1926- *WhoAm 92*
Sorensen, Torben 1927- *WhoScE 91-2*
Sorensen, Virginia 1912- *DcAmChF 1960*
Sorensen, Virginia 1912-1991 *ConAu 139, MajAI [port], SmATA 72, -15AS [port]*
Sorensen, Virginia Eggertsen 1912-1991 *BioIn 17*
Sorensen, William Stephen *Law&B 92*
Sorensen-Ristinmaa, Stacey 1961- *WhoWor 93*
Sorenson, Brice K. 1940- *St&PR 93*
Sorenson, C.J. *St&PR 93*
Sorenson, Christine *WhoWrEP 92*
Sorenson, Dean Philip 1939- *WhoAm 92*
Sorenson, Erik Denison *BioIn 17*
Sorenson, Grace *AmWomPl*
Sorenson, Jane *BioIn 17*
Sorenson, Mary Louise 1950- *WhoEmL 93*
Sorenson, Patricia Ann 1955- *WhoAmW 93*
Sorenson, Paul Victor 1955- *St&PR 93*
Sorenson, Ralph Z. 1933- *St&PR 93*
Sorenson, Sandra Louise 1948- *WhoEmL 93*
Sorenson, Sharon O. 1943- *WhoWrEP 92*
Sorenson, Torsten 1908- *Baker 92*
Sorenson, Villy 1929- *ScF&FL 92*
Soresina, Alberto 1911- *Baker 92*
Sorestad, Glen 1937- *WhoCanL 92, WhoWrEP 92*
Sorett, Stephen M. *Law&B 92*
Sorg, Francis Joseph, Jr. 1922- *St&PR 93*
Sorg, Gilbert B. 1926- *St&PR 93*
Sorg, Gilbert Bruce 1926- *WhoAm 92*
Sorge, Anthony R. *Law&B 92*
Sorge, Georg Andreas 1703-1778 *Baker 92*
Sorge, Reinhard Johannes 1892-1916 *DcLB 118*
Sorge, Richard 1895-1944 *BioIn 17*
Sorgenfrei, Mal Edward 1939- *St&PR 93*
Sorgenti, Harold A. *BioIn 17*
Sorgenti, Harold Andrew 1934- *St&PR 93, WhoAm 92, WhoE 93*
Soriaga, Manuel Ponce 1949- *WhoSSW 93*
Soriamo, Amanda M. 1960- *St&PR 93*
Soriani, Paolo Ezio 1921- *WhoWor 93*
Soriano, Alberto 1915- *Baker 92*
Soriano, Beverly Ann 1952- *WhoE 93*
Soriano, Francesco 1548?-1621 *Baker 92*
Soriano, Gonzalo 1913-1972 *Baker 92*
Soriano, Osvaldo 1943- *SpAmA*
Soriano, Rene Ykalina 1945- *WhoWor 93*
Soriano Fuertes y Piqueras, Mariano 1817-1880 *Baker 92*
Soria-Olmedo, Andres 1954- *WhoWor 93*
Sorin, Carlos 1944- *MiSFD 9*
Sorio, Cesare 1936- *WhoE 93*
Sorkin, Aaron *BioIn 17*
Sorkin, Alan Lowell 1941- *WhoAm 92*
Sorkin, Barbara C. 1956- *WhoAmW 93*
Sorkin, Bernard R. *Law&B 92*
Sorkin, Mary Ann 1952- *St&PR 93*
Sorkin, Steven Arthur 1937- *St&PR 93*
Sorknes, Suzanne S. *Law&B 92*
Sorknes, Suzanne Smith 1950- *St&PR 93*
Sorkoram, Paul Ollie 1937- *St&PR 93*
Sorkow, Eli 1923- *WhoSSW 93*
Sorman, Steven Robert 1948- *WhoAm 92*
Sormani, Charles Robert 1938- *WhoAm 92, WhoIns 93*
Sormann, Alfred (Richard Gotthilf) 1861-1913 *Baker 92*
Sornborger, William Edward 1926- *St&PR 93*
Sornicle, D. *WhoScE 91-2*
Sornstein, Anne 1915- *St&PR 93*
Soro (Barriga), Enrique 1884-1954 *Baker 92*
Sorobay, Roman Taras 1958- *WhoE 93*
Sorochen, Frank 1946- *St&PR 93*
Soroka, James W. *Law&B 92*
Soroka, John Michael 1956- *WhoE 93*

Sorokin, Alexander Sergeevich 1944- *WhoUN 92*
Sorokin, Jack E. *Law&B 92*
Sorokin, Peter Pitirimovich 1931- *WhoAm 92*
Soroko, Anna Maria Fell *Law&B 92*
Soron, J.E. *St&PR 93*
Soros, George *BioIn 17*
Soros, Istvan 1935- *WhoScE 91-4*
Sorouri, Parviz 1929- *WhoE 93*
Sorrel, Eugene C. 1943- *St&PR 93*
Sorrel, William Edwin 1913- *WhoAm 92*
Sorrell, Daniel J., Jr. 1942- *St&PR 93*
Sorrell, Furman Yates 1938- *WhoAm 92*
Sorrell, Gary Lee 1943- *WhoWor 93*
Sorrell, J(ohn) E(dward) 1954- *ConAu 137*
Sorrell, Martin S. *BioIn 17*
Sorrell, Martin Stuart 1945- *WhoAm 92*
Sorrells, Rick D. 1955- *WhoSSW 93*
Sorrells, Robert Taliaferro 1932- *WhoWrEP 92*
Sorrells, Russell Bazemore, III 1938- *WhoSSW 93*
Sorrels, James E. 1933- *St&PR 93*
Sorrels, John Paul 1950- *WhoSSW 93*
Sorrels, Roy *ScF&FL 92*
Sorrentino, Charles Alan 1944- *St&PR 93, WhoSSW 93*
Sorrentino, Charles L. 1928- *St&PR 93*
Sorrentino, Dario Rosario 1957- *WhoWor 93*
Sorrentino, Dominick Ralph 1940- *WhoSSW 93*
Sorrentino, Gilbert 1929- *BioIn 17, WhoAm 92, WhoWrEP 92*
Sorrentino, John Anthony 1948- *WhoE 93*
Sorrentino, Renate Maria 1942- *WhoAmW 93, WhoWor 93*
Sorrow, Jerry W. 1945- *St&PR 93*
Sorrow, Ronald Thomas 1946- *St&PR 93*
Sorrows, Howard Earle 1918- *WhoE 93*
Sorsa, Kalevi 1930- *WhoWor 93*
Sorsby, J. Larry 1955- *St&PR 93*
Sorsby, James Larry 1955- *WhoAm 92*
Sorsoleil, Lori Marie 1962- *WhoWrEP 92*
Sorstokke, Ellen Kathleen 1954- *WhoAmW 93, WhoWor 93*
Sorstokke, Susan Eileen 1955- *WhoAmW 93, WhoEmL 93, WhoWor 93*
Sorstrom, Stein Erik 1951- *WhoScE 91-4*
Sorteni, Paolo 1933- *WhoWor 93*
Sorter, Bruce Wilbur 1931- *WhoE 93*
Sorter, George Hans 1927- *WhoAm 92, WhoWor 93*
Sortland, Paul Allan 1953- *WhoEmL 93*
Sortor, Harold Edward 1925- *WhoAm 92*
Sortore, Timothy 1956- *St&PR 93*
Sortwell, Christopher T. 1957- *St&PR 93*
Sorvaag, Jim L. *Law&B 92*
Sorvino, Paul *WhoAm 92*
Sorvoja, Markku 1955- *WhoWor 93*
Sosa, Alonzo Hernandez 1941- *WhoSSW 93*
Sosa, Ernest 1940- *WhoE 93*
Sosa, Francisco 1848-1925 *DcMexL*
Sosa, Horacio Alejandro 1954- *WhoE 93*
Sosa, Lionel 1939- *HispAmA [port]*
Sosa, Roberto 1930- *SpAmA*
Sosabowski, Stanislaw 1893-1967 *PolBiDi*
Sosa Branger, Juan Andres 1956- *WhoWor 93*
Sosa-Riddell, Adaljiza 1937- *NotHsAW 93 [port]*
SOS Band *SoulM*
Soshnick, Julian *Law&B 92*
Soshnick, Julian 1932- *St&PR 93*
Soshnik, Joseph 1920- *St&PR 93, WhoAm 92*
Soshnik, Robert Mark *Law&B 92*
Sosin, Sidney 1924- *St&PR 93, WhoAm 92*
Sosinski, David Alan *Law&B 92*
Soskel, Norman Terry 1948- *WhoSSW 93*
Soskin, David Howell 1942- *WhoAm 92*
Sosland, Morton Irvin 1925- *St&PR 93*
Sosland, Neil N. 1930- *St&PR 93*
Soslow, Arnold 1938- *WhoE 93*
Sosman, Frederic P., III 1938- *St&PR 93*
Sosman, Herbert 1932- *St&PR 93*
Sosna, Robert William 1941- *WhoIns 93*
Sosna, Sharon 1950- *ScF&FL 92*
Sosnick, Stephen Howard 1930- *WhoAm 92*
Sosnkowski, Kazimierz 1885-1970 *PolBiDi*
Sosnoski, Donald Raymond 1942- *St&PR 93*
Sosnow, Lawrence Ira 1935- *WhoAm 92*
Sosnow, Peter Lewis 1951- *WhoE 93*
Sosnowska, Izabela 1939- *WhoScE 91-4*
Sosnowski, Andrzej Maciej 1952- *WhoWor 93*
Sosnowski, Blaze H. *Law&B 92*
Sosnowski, Michael Lawrence 1947- *WhoAm 92*
Soss, Neal M. 1949- *St&PR 93*
Soss, Neal Martin 1949- *WhoAm 92*
Sossaman, James J. 1932- *WhoAm 92*
Sossei, Fran *BioIn 17*
Sossenheimer, Heinz 1924- *WhoScE 91-3*
Sossong, Anthony Terrance 1934- *St&PR 93*
Sostchen, Cindy 1957- *WhoWrEP 92*
Sostilio, Robert Francis 1942- *WhoE 93*
Sotelo, Constantino *WhoScE 91-2*
Sotelo, Jose 1948- *WhoUN 92*
Sotelo, Julio E. 1950- *WhoWor 93*
Sotelo Borgen, Enrique *DcCPCAm*
Soter, George Nicholas 1924- *WhoAm 92*
Soteras, Solon C. 1922- *St&PR 93*
Soteriades, Michael Cosmas 1923- *WhoE 93*
Sotheby, William 1757-1833 *BioIn 17*
Sothern, Winifred *AmWomPl*
Sotherton, Nicolas William 1954- *WhoScE 91-1*
Sotin, Hans 1939- *Baker 92, OxDcOp*
Sotir, Thomas Alfred 1936- *WhoAm 92*
Sotirakis, Dimitri 1935- *MiSFD 9*
Sotirakos, Iannis 1962- *WhoWor 93*
Sotirhos, Michael 1928- *WhoAm 92, WhoWor 93*
Sotiriadis, Sotirios E. 1929- *WhoScE 91-3*
Sotirios of Toronto, Bishop 1936- *WhoAm 92*
Sotiriou, Sam *BioIn 17*
Sotiropoulos, Blasios 1930- *WhoScE 91-3*
Sotiropoulos, George H. 1939- *WhoScE 91-3*
Sotirov, Kukn K. 1944- *WhoUN 92*
Sotnick, David Adam 1963- *St&PR 93*
Soto, Aida R. 1931- *HispAmA*
Soto, Elaine 1947- *WhoE 93*
Soto, Frederick Earl, Jr. 1954- *WhoSSW 93*
Soto, Gary *BioIn 17*
Soto, Gary 1952- *Au&Arts 10 [port], HispAmA [port], WhoAm 92*
Soto, Hernando de *BioIn 17*
Soto, Hernando de c. 1500-1542 *BioIn 17*
Soto, Jesus-Rafael 1923- *WhoWor 93*
Soto, Jesus Raphael *BioIn 17*
Soto, Jock 1965- *WhoAm 92*
Soto, Jorge 1947- *HispAmA*
Soto, Juan *BioIn 17*
Soto, Juan d1871 *BioIn 17*
Soto, Luis *MiSFD 9*
Soto, Pedro Juan 1928- *SpAmA*
Soto, Rosana De *NotHsAW 93*
Soto, Shirlene Ann 1947- *NotHsAW 93*
Soto de Langa, Francisco 1534-1619 *Baker 92*
Sotomayor, Arturo 1913- *DcMexL*
Sotomayor, Daniel d1992 *BioIn 17, NewYTBS 92*
Sotomayor, Javier *BioIn 17*
Sotomayor, Marta 1939- *NotHsAW 93 [port]*
Sotomora-von Ahn, Ricardo Federico 1947- *WhoWor 93*
Sotos, Hercules P. 1933- *St&PR 93*
Sotos, Jim *MiSFD 9*
Sotos, Timothy S. 1948- *St&PR 93*
Soto Vargas, Claudio Wesley 1948- *WhoWor 93*
Sotskov, Yuri Nazarovich 1948- *WhoWor 93*
Sott, Herbert 1920- *WhoAm 92*
Sottak, Barry Jean 1941- *WhoAm 92*
Sottile, Benjamin J. 1937- *St&PR 93*
Sottile, Benjamin Joseph 1937- *WhoAm 92*
Sottile, James 1913- *St&PR 93, WhoAm 92*
Sottile, John H. 1947- *St&PR 93*
Sotton, M. *WhoScE 91-2*
Sottorf, Gerd Kenvyn 1921- *WhoWor 93*
Sottosanti, Vincent William 1936- *St&PR 93, WhoAm 92*
Sottsass, Ettore 1917- *BioIn 17*
Souaid, George Joseph 1928- *St&PR 93*
Souaid, Robert George 1955- *St&PR 93*
Soubies, Albert 1846-1918 *Baker 92*
Soubiran, Julien J. d1992 *BioIn 17*
Soubise, Benjamin de Rohan, Duke of c. 1589-1642 *HarEnMi*
Soubise, Charles de Rohan, Prince of 1715-1787 *HarEnMi*
Soubliere, Jean-Pierre 1947- *St&PR 93*
Soubre, Etienne-Joseph 1813-1871 *Baker 92*
Soucacos, Panayotis 1941- *WhoScE 91-3*
Souccar, Thierry Gerard 1955- *WhoWor 93*
Soucek, Branko 1930- *WhoScE 91-4*
Souch, K.W. 1931- *WhoScE 91-1*
Souci, Robert D. San *ScF&FL 92*
Soucie, Gary Arnold 1937- *WhoAm 92*
Soucy, Barbara Marie 1949- *WhoWrEP 92*
Soucy, Irene Laura 1948- *St&PR 93*
Soucy, Kevin Albert 1955- *St&PR 93, WhoE 93*
Soucy, Paul L. 1957- *St&PR 93*
Soucy, Robert Guy 1928- *WhoAm 92*
Souder, Charles 1948- *St&PR 93*
Souder, Dorothea Selina 1956- *WhoAmW 93*
Souder, Frances M. *St&PR 93*
Souder, Harvey *St&PR 93*
Souder, Mark Stephen 1956- *WhoWrEP 92*
Souder, Robert R. 1940- *WhoAm 92*
Souder, Robert Raymond 1940- *St&PR 93*
Souder, Stephen Meredith 1943- *St&PR 93*
Souder, W. Granger *Law&B 92*
Souders, Bruce Chester 1920- *WhoSSW 93, WhoWor 93*
Souders, Ronald L. *Law&B 92*
Souders, Thomas Lee 1946- *St&PR 93*
Souders, William Franklin 1928- *St&PR 93*
Soudine, Alexandre Vladimirovich 1940- *WhoUN 92*
Soudovtsev, Vladimir Antonovich 1943- *WhoUN 92*
Souers, Marjorie Elaine 1936- *WhoAmW 93*
Souers, Paul Eric *Law&B 92*
Souerwine, Andrew Harry 1924- *WhoE 93*
Souez, Ina d1992 *NewYTBS 92 [port]*
Souez, Ina 1908- *OxDcOp*
Sougy, Jean Marcel Andre 1927- *WhoScE 91-2*
Souhaitty, Jean-Jacques fl. 17th cent.- *Baker 92*
Souham, Gerard 1928- *WhoAm 92, WhoE 93*
Souhami, Mark 1935- *WhoWor 93*
Souhami, Robert Leon *WhoScE 91-1*
Souhan, George G. 1929- *St&PR 93*
Souillard, Georges Jules 1923- *WhoScE 91-2*
Soukiassian, Patrick Gilles 1944- *WhoWor 93*
Soukup, Jane Klinkner 1958- *WhoAmW 93*
Soukup, Jaroslav 1946- *DrEEuF*
Soukupova, Vera 1932- *Baker 92*
Soul, Tom 1951- *St&PR 93*
Soula, G. 1931- *WhoScE 91-2*
Soulages, Pierre 1919- *WhoWor 93*
Soulairac, Andre Alphonse 1913- *WhoScE 91-2*
Soulal, M.J. *WhoScE 91-1*
Soulas, Guy 1945- *WhoScE 91-2*
Soul Clan *SoulM*
Soule, Charles Everett, Sr. 1934- *St&PR 93*
Soule, David Conder 1946- *WhoE 93*
Soule, Dorothy Fisher 1923- *WhoAm 92*
Soule, Edward Lawrence 1929- *WhoAm 92*
Soule, Gardner Bosworth 1913- *WhoAm 92*
Soule, James C. 1942- *St&PR 93*
Soule, Jeffrey Lyn 1953- *WhoE 93*
Soule, John Dutcher 1920- *WhoAm 92*
Soule, Phillip E. 1950- *St&PR 93, WhoIns 93*
Soule, Sallie Thompson 1928- *WhoAmW 93*
Soule, Sandra W(olf) 1946- *ConAu 137*
Souleau, Charles Arnaud 1938- *WhoScE 91-2*
Soules, Alonso, Jr. 1933- *St&PR 93*
Soules, Roberta Jean 1948- *WhoAmW 93*
Soulieres, Robert 1950- *WhoCanL 92*
Soul II Soul *SoulM*
Soulillou, Jean Paul 1944- *WhoScE 91-2*
Souliotis, Barbara Anne 1942- *WhoAmW 93*
Souliotis, Elena 1943- *Baker 92*
Souliotis, George *Law&B 92*
Souljah, Sister
See Public Enemy *News 92*
Soul Machine *SoulM*
Soulsby, Lord *WhoScE 91-1*
Soulsby, Jeffrey L. 1949- *St&PR 93*
Soulsby, Micheal Edward 1941- *WhoSSW 93*
Soult, Launcelot Espy, Jr. 1928- *St&PR 93*
Soult, Nicolas-Jean de Dieu 1769-1851 *BioIn 17, HarEnMi*
Soultanopoulos, Constantine 1930- *WhoScE 91-3*
Soumah, Amara 1947- *WhoUN 92*
Soumoy, Vincent Albert 1964- *WhoWor 93*
Soupault, Philippe 1897-1990 *BioIn 17*
Souphanouvong 1902- *WhoAsAP 91*
Souphanouvong, Tiao 1902- *DcTwHis*
Souquet, Pierre 1935- *WhoScE 91-2*
Sourac, Ladislav 1927- *WhoScE 91-4*
Sourbes, I. 1957- *WhoScE 91-2*
Sourbrine, Richard Don, II 1965- *WhoEmL 93*
Sourek, Otakar 1883-1956 *Baker 92*
Sourell, Heinz 1949- *WhoScE 91-3*
Soures, John M. 1943- *WhoE 93*
Souria, Robert Selim 1942- *WhoUN 92*
Sourian, Peter 1933- *WhoWrEP 92*
Souriau, Jean-Marie 1922- *WhoScE 91-2*
Souris, Andre 1899-1970 *Baker 92*
Souris, Jane K. *Law&B 92*
Sourkes, Theodore Lionel 1919- *WhoAm 92*
Sourniadin, Bob *Law&B 92*
Souroujon d'Alcala, Ben S. 1927- *WhoWor 93*
Sours, James Kingsley 1925- *WhoAm 92*
Sousa, Augustine Pedro, Jr. 1949- *WhoE 93*
Sousa, Barbara Anne *Law&B 92*
Sousa, Consuelo Maria 1931- *WhoAmW 93*
Sousa, Irene Helen 1948- *WhoE 93*
Sousa, Joan Ann 1949- *WhoE 93*
Sousa, Joao Arnaldo Rodrigues 1938- *WhoWor 93*
Sousa, John Philip 1854-1932 *Baker 92, GayN, OxDcOp*
Sousa, Lorraine Christine 1959- *WhoAmW 93*
Sousa, Louis R. 1953- *St&PR 93*
Sousa, Terry 1943- *St&PR 93*
Sousa Dias, M.T.F.S.N. 1940- *WhoScE 91-3*
Sousa-Pinto, Alexandre A. 1936- *WhoScE 91-3*
Sousberghe, Leon de 1903- *IntDcAn*
Souser, Roslyn Coskery 1939- *WhoE 93*
Soustelle, Jacques 1912-1990 *BioIn 17, IntDcAn*
Soustelle, Michel Marcel Philippe 1937- *WhoWor 93*
Souster, Raymond 1921- *BioIn 17, WhoCanL 92*
Souster, Tim(othy Andrew James) 1943- *Baker 92*
Soutar, Charles Frederick 1936- *St&PR 93*
Soutar, Geoffrey Norman 1948- *WhoWor 93*
Soutar, Ian A. *St&PR 93*
Soutas-Little, Robert William 1933- *WhoAm 92*
Soutendijk, Dirk R. *Law&B 92*
Soutendijk, Dirk R. 1938- *St&PR 93*
Soutendijk, Dirk Rutger 1938- *WhoAm 92*
Souter, David 1939- *OxCSupC [port]*
Souter, David H. *NewYTBS 92 [port]*
Souter, David H. 1939- *BioIn 17*
Souter, David Hackett 1939- *CngDr 91, WhoAm 92, WhoE 93*
Souter, Robert Taylor 1909- *WhoAm 92*
South, Clark *ConAu 37NR*
South, Dudley Pritchett, Jr. 1926- *St&PR 93*
South, Frank Edwin 1924- *WhoAm 92*
South, Furman, III 1921- *St&PR 93*
South, Galen R. *Law&B 92*
South, Hugh Miles 1947- *WhoE 93*
South, Joe 1940- *SoulM*
South, Mary Ann 1933- *WhoAmW 93*
South, Pamela Dawn 1948- *WhoAm 92*
South, Patricia Gail 1960- *WhoAmW 93*
South, Richard C. 1925- *St&PR 93*
South, William Preston 1943- *St&PR 93*
Southall, Ivan 1921- *BioIn 17*
Southall, Ivan (Francis) 1921- *ChlFicS, DcChlFi, MajAI [port], WhoAm 92*
Southall, James Cocke 1828-1897 *JrnUS*
Southall, Leslie Roy 1945- *WhoSSW 93*
Southall, Maycie Katherine 1895- *BioIn 17*
Southall, Spalding 1912- *WhoIns 93*
Southall, Sylvia Lennette 1960- *WhoAmW 93*
Southam, Chester Milton 1919- *WhoE 93*
Southam, Gordon Hamilton 1916- *WhoAm 92*
Southard, David E. 1948- *St&PR 93*
Southard, David Gordon 1941- *WhoE 93*
Southard, Frank A. 1907-1989 *BioIn 17*
Southard, Jeffrey Scott *Law&B 92*
Southard, Paul Raymond 1948- *WhoE 93*
Southard, Rupert Barron, Jr. 1923- *WhoAm 92*
Southard, Ruth Kephart 1946- *WhoAmW 93*
Southard, Steven J. 1940- *St&PR 93*
Southcombe, Colin *WhoScE 91-1*
Souther, George Parks 1939- *St&PR 93*
Southerland, Betty Jo 1944- *WhoAmW 93*
Southerland, Louis Feno, Jr. 1906- *WhoAm 92*
Southerland, S. Duane 1949- *WhoAm 92*
Southerland, Sydney Duane 1949- *St&PR 93*
Southern, Arlen Duane 1933- *WhoE 93*
Southern, Byron Scott 1946- *St&PR 93*
Southern, Edwin Mellor *WhoScE 91-1*
Southern, Eileen 1920- *Baker 92, WhoAm 92, WhoAmW 93*
Southern, Hugh 1932- *WhoAm 92*
Southern, Jeri 1926-1991 *BioIn 17*
Southern, John Robert *WhoScE 91-1*
Southern, Lloyd James Franklin 1935- *WhoSSW 93*
Southern, Neta Snook d1991 *BioIn 17*
Southern, Robert Allen 1930- *WhoAm 92*
Southern, Robert E. *St&PR 93*
Southern, Ronald *BioIn 17*

Southern, Ronald Donald 1930- *St&PR 93, WhoAm 92, WhoWor 93*
Southern, Tony Ervin 1957- *WhoSSW 93*
Southey, Caroline Anne Bowles 1786?-1854 *DcLB 116 [port]*
Southey, Robert 1774-1843 *BioIn 17*
Southgate, David Alfred Thomas *WhoScE 91-1*
Southgate, Marie Therese 1928- *WhoAmW 93*
Southgate, Martha *BioIn 17*
Southgate, Richard W. 1929- *WhoAm 92*
Southmayd, Peter Brown 1940- *WhoSSW 93*
Southon, Edward Henry *Law&B 92*
Southwell, Gilbert L., III *Law&B 92*
Southwell, P.L. 1927- *St&PR 93*
Southwell, Paul *DcCPCAm*
Southwell, Richard V. 1946- *St&PR 93*
Southwell, W. Wood 1955- *St&PR 93*
Southwell, William Joseph 1914- *WhoE 93*
Southwick, Arthur Frederick 1924- *WhoAm 92*
Southwick, Billy L. 1925- *St&PR 93*
Southwick, Charles Henry 1928- *WhoAm 92*
Southwick, Harry Webb 1918- *WhoAm 92*
Southwick, Kathryn Louise 1959- *WhoAmW 93*
Southwick, Paul 1920- *WhoAm 92*
Southwick, Philip Lee 1916- *WhoAm 92*
Southwick, Stephen William *Law&B 92*
Southwood, David John *WhoScE 91-1*
Southwood, John Eugene *WhoAm 92*
Southwood, John Eugene 1929- *St&PR 93*
Southwood, T. Richard E. *WhoScE 91-1*
Southworth, Anne *WhoWrEP 92*
Southworth, E.D.E.N. 1819-1899 *BioIn 17*
Southworth, Emma Dorothy Eliza Nevitte 1819-1899 *BioIn 17*
Southworth, Hamilton 1907- *WhoE 93*
Southworth, Horton Coe 1926- *WhoE 93*
Southworth, John David *Law&B 92*
Southworth, John David 1945- *St&PR 93*
Southworth, John Franklin, Jr. 1949- *WhoSSW 93*
Southworth, John Hayward 1927- *St&PR 93*
Southworth, Miles F. 1935- *WhoWrEP 92*
Southworth, William Dixon 1918- *WhoAm 92, WhoWor 93*
Soutis, Constantinos 1958- *WhoWor 93*
Souto, Carlos D. 1938- *WhoScE 91-3*
Souto Alabarce, Arturo 1930- *DcMexL*
Soutos, Nicolaos 1932- *WhoWor 93*
Soutter, Thomas D. *Law&B 92*
Soutter, Thomas D. 1934- *WhoAm 92*
Soutter, Thomas Douglas 1934- *St&PR 93*
Souvanna Phouma, Prince 1901-1984 *DcTwHis*
Souvannavong, Oudara 1952- *WhoScE 91-2*
Souvarine, Boris *BioIn 17*
Souveroff, Vernon William, Jr. 1934- *WhoAm 92*
Souyris, F. 1932- *WhoScE 91-2*
Souza, Alvaro da Silva e 1932- *WhoWor 93*
Souza, Arthur P. 1947- *St&PR 93*
Souza, Donald R. 1940- *St&PR 93*
Souza, Dudley de *ScF&FL 92*
Souza, Ernest 1893-1963 *BioIn 17*
Souza, Everett J. 1945- *WhoIns 93*
Souza, Ken *BioIn 17*
Souza, Marcio 1946- *ScF&FL 92*
Souza, Matthew F. 1957- *St&PR 93*
Souza, Ronald J. 1936- *St&PR 93*
Souza, Ronald Joseph 1936- *WhoAm 92*
Souza, William J. *Law&B 92*
Souza-Strong, Lynne Allison 1959- *WhoAmW 93*
Souzay, Gerard 1918- *Baker 92, OxDcOp*
Sova, Vasile 1930- *WhoScE 91-4*
Sovde-Pennell, Barbara Ann 1955- *WhoSSW 93*
Sovereign, Kenneth Lester 1919- *St&PR 93*
Sovern, Michael Ira 1931- *WhoAm 92, WhoE 93, WhoWor 93*
S/O Vethamuthu, David 1932- *WhoAsAP 91*
Sovey, L. Terrell, Jr. 1931- *WhoAm 92, WhoSSW 93*
Sovey, Terrell *St&PR 93*
Sovey, William Pierre 1933- *WhoAm 92*
Sovie, Margaret Doe 1934- *WhoAm 92, WhoAmW 93*
Soviero, Diana Barbara 1946- *WhoAm 92*
Sovik, Edward Anders 1918- *WhoAm 92*
Sovik, William E., Jr. 1944- *St&PR 93*
Sow, Abdourahmane 1942- *WhoUN 92*
Sow, Daouda 1933- *WhoAfr*
Sow, Thierno Faty 1941- *MiSFD 9*
Sowa, Kazimierz Zbigniew 1942- *WhoWor 93*
Sowa, Randolph 1956- *St&PR 93*
Sowada, Alphonse Augustus 1933- *WhoAm 92*
Sowande, Fela 1905-1987 *Baker 92*
Soward, Andrew Michael *WhoScE 91-1*
Soward, Clifford A. *Law&B 92*
Sowards, Ann Phelps 1933- *St&PR 93*
Sowards, Patricia Lutie 1952- *WhoAmW 93*
Sowden, Roy *BioIn 17*
Sowden, William B., III 1944- *St&PR 93*
Sowder, Ann Laverne 1953- *St&PR 93*
Sowder, Donald Dillard 1937- *WhoSSW 93*
Sowder, Douglas A. 1948- *St&PR 93*
Sowder, Fred Allen 1940- *WhoWor 93*
Sowder, Robert Robertson 1928- *St&PR 93, WhoAm 92, WhoWor 93*
Sowder, Tony R. 1920- *St&PR 93*
Sowecke, Timothy M. *St&PR 93*
Sowell, Carol Ann 1946- *WhoWrEP 92*
Sowell, David (Lee) 1952- *ConAu 139*
Sowell, David S. *St&PR 93*
Sowell, Elizabeth Lee Sledge 1938- *WhoSSW 93*
Sowell, Frances Key 1945- *WhoAmW 93*
Sowell, James Edwin 1948- *WhoAm 92*
Sowell, Jeff 1954- *St&PR 93*
Sowell, Katye Marie Oliver 1934- *WhoSSW 93*
Sowell, Mayme Gust 1934- *WhoSSW 93*
Sowell, Michael Robert 1948- *WhoSSW 93*
Sowell, Sam C. 1933- *St&PR 93*
Sowell, Thomas 1930- *BioIn 17, WhoAm 92*
Sowell, W. R. 1920- *WhoSSW 93, WhoWor 93*
Sower, Victor Edmund 1946- *WhoSSW 93*
Sowerby, Leo 1895-1968 *Baker 92*
Sowerby, Ronald E. 1943- *St&PR 93*
Sowers, Anita Ann 1959- *WhoEmL 93*
Sowers, David F. 1934- *St&PR 93*
Sowers, Donald 1949- *St&PR 93*
Sowers, George F. 1921- *St&PR 93*
Sowers, George Frederick 1921- *WhoAm 92*
Sowers, Robert 1923-1990 *BioIn 17*
Sowers, Wesley H. 1905- *St&PR 93*
Sowers, Wesley Hoyt 1905- *WhoAm 92*
Sowers, William Armand 1923- *WhoAm 92*
Sowersby, Lewann 1939- *St&PR 93*
Sowinski, Andrzej 1919- *WhoScE 91-4*
Sowinski, Andrzej 1922- *WhoWor 93*
Sowinski, William A., Jr. *Law&B 92*
Sowinski, Wojciech 1803-1880 *PolBiDi*
Sowinski, Wojciech (Albert) c. 1803-1880 *Baker 92*
Sowko, Victoria Ann 1969- *WhoAmW 93*
Sowle, Donald Edgar 1915- *WhoAm 92*
Sowles, Beth A. 1960- *WhoAmW 93*
Sowles, John Dean 1921- *St&PR 93*
Sowman, Harold Gene 1923- *WhoAm 92*
Sowokinos, Frank F. 1936- *St&PR 93*
Sowter, Nita *SmATA 69*
Sowton, M. *WhoScE 91-1*
Sox, Harold Carleton, Jr. 1939- *WhoAm 92*
Sox, Jonathan Whitfield *Law&B 92*
Soyak, Yusuf Edip 1951- *WhoWor 93*
Soyars, Melindalee T. 1965- *WhoAmW 93*
Soyer, Alexis 1809-1858 *BioIn 17*
Soyer, David 1923- *WhoAm 92*
Soyer, Isaac 1907-1981 *BioIn 17*
Soyer, Jacques 1938- *WhoScE 91-2*
Soyer, Moses 1899-1974 *BioIn 17*
Soyer, Raphael 1899-1987 *BioIn 17*
Soyer, Roger 1939- *IntDcOp*
Soyer, Roger (Julien Jacques) 1939- *Baker 92*
Soyfer, Jura 1912-1939 *DcLB 124 [port]*
Soyinka, Akinwande Oluwole *BioIn 17*
Soyinka, Oluwole 1934- *DcTwHis*
Soyinka, Wole *BioIn 17*
Soyinka, Wole 1934- *ConAu 39NR, ConBlB 4 [port], DcLB 125 [port], IntLitE, WhoWor 93, WorLitC [port]*
Soyka, Ellen *BioIn 17*
Soyke, Peter W. *Law&B 92*
Soylemez, Sezer M. 1941- *St&PR 93*
Soysa, Widanelage Harshadeva 1947- *WhoWor 93*
Soysal, Adnan 1963- *WhoWor 93*
Soysal, Atac 1937- *WhoScE 91-4*
Soysal, Sule Fatma 1944- *WhoUN 92*
Soyupak, Selcuk 1947- *WhoScE 91-4*
Sozanski, Jerzy 1929- *WhoScE 91-4*
Sozen, Mete Avni 1930- *WhoAm 92*
Sozen, Mustafa Engin 1946- *WhoScE 91-4*
Sozomenos 5th cent.- *OxDcByz*
Spaak, Paul-Henri 1899-1972 *DcTwHis*
Spaan, Jos A.E. 1945- *WhoScE 91-3*
Spaan, Willy Josephus 1954- *WhoWor 93*
Spaar, D. *WhoScE 91-3*
Spaar, Kenneth L. 1933- *St&PR 93*
Spaar, Lisa Russ 1956- *WhoWrEP 92*
Spaatz, Carl 1891-1974 *BioIn 17*
Space, Theodore Maxwell 1938- *WhoE 93, WhoWor 93*
Spacek, Sissy *BioIn 17*
Spacek, Sissy 1949- *HolBB [port], IntDcF 2-3 [port], WhoAm 92, WhoAmW 93*
Spacey, Kevin *BioIn 17*
Spacey, Kevin 1959- *WhoAm 92*
Spach, Gerard 1930- *WhoScE 91-2*
Spach, Jule Christian 1923- *WhoAm 92, WhoSSW 93*
Spach, Madison Stockton 1926- *WhoAm 92*
Spacht, David B. 1959- *St&PR 93*
Spacie, Anne 1945- *WhoAmW 93*
Spack, Carol Jane *Law&B 92*
Spackman, G. Brett 1950- *St&PR 93*
Spackman, Thomas James 1937- *WhoAm 92*
Spackman, W.M. 1905-1990 *BioIn 17*
Spackman, William Mode 1905-1990 *BioIn 17*
Spacks, Barry *BioIn 17*
Spacks, Patricia Meyer 1929- *WhoAm 92*
Spacone, Andrew Carl *Law&B 92*
Spada, Andrew Thomas 1962- *WhoWor 93*
Spada, Marietta 1943- *St&PR 93*
Spadacene, Joseph C. *Law&B 92*
Spadafora, Hugo *DcCPCAm*
Spadafora, Jo-Una *Law&B 92*
Spadafora, John A. 1943- *St&PR 93*
Spadafora, Joseph William 1954- *WhoSSW 93*
Spadafora, Robert William 1932- *St&PR 93*
Spadaro, Joseph A. 1950- *St&PR 93*
Spadavecchia, Antonio (Emmanuilovich) 1907-1988 *Baker 92*
Spader, James *BioIn 17*
Spader, James 1960- *WhoAm 92*
Spadone, Charles Dubois *St&PR 93*
Spadone, John C. *St&PR 93*
Spadorcia, Doreen *Law&B 92*
Spady, Elma K. *Law&B 92*
Spaeder, Roger Campbell 1943- *WhoAm 92, WhoE 93*
Spaeh, Winfried Heinrich 1930- *WhoWor 93*
Spaepen, Frans August 1948- *WhoAm 92*
Spaepen, Gustaaf J.F.L. 1935- *WhoScE 91-2*
Spaet, Theodore H. d1992 *NewYTBS 92*
Spaeth, Anthony Parry 1955- *WhoWor 93*
Spaeth, Carl B. 1907-1991 *BioIn 17*
Spaeth, Edmund Benjamin, Jr. 1920- *WhoAm 92*
Spaeth, George Link 1932- *WhoAm 92*
Spaeth, James Thomas 1943- *WhoE 93*
Spaeth, Johann-Martin 1937- *WhoScE 91-3*
Spaeth, Karl Henry *Law&B 92*
Spaeth, Karl Henry 1929- *St&PR 93, WhoAm 92*
Spaeth, Mary Shepard 1957- *WhoAmW 93*
Spaeth, Michael E. 1941- *St&PR 93*
Spaeth, Nicholas John 1950- *WhoAm 92*
Spaeth, Otto Lucian, Jr. 1934- *WhoE 93*
Spaeth, Sigmund 1885-1965 *Baker 92*
Spafford, Michael Charles 1935- *WhoAm 92*
Spafford, Ray P. 1943- *St&PR 93*
Spagna, Arnold Joseph 1952- *WhoE 93*
Spagna, Joseph Vincenzo d1990 *BioIn 17*
Spagna, Louis Anthony 1937- *St&PR 93*
Spagna, Richard Leo 1956- *WhoE 93*
Spagnardi, Ronald L. 1943- *St&PR 93*
Spagnardi, Ronald Lee 1943- *WhoAm 92*
Spagnesi, M. *WhoScE 91-3*
Spagnoletti, Fred L. 1941- *St&PR 93*
Spagnoli, Gina Gail 1954- *WhoE 93*
Spagnoli, Nick R. 1936- *St&PR 93*
Spagnuola, Francis Michael 1940- *WhoE 93*
Spahl, Gary Michael 1960- *WhoWrEP 92*
Spahn, Charles DeForest 1943- *St&PR 93*
Spahn, James Francis 1957- *WhoSSW 93*
Spahn, Mary Attea 1929- *WhoAm 92*
Spahn, Moe C. d1991 *BioIn 17*
Spahn, Priscilla Talcott 1934- *WhoAmW 93*
Spahn, Warren 1921- *BioIn 17*
Spahn-Langguth, Hildegard J. 1955- *WhoScE 91-3*
Spahr, D. Lorraine 1925- *St&PR 93*
Spahr, Frederick Thomas 1939- *WhoAm 92*
Spahr, Gregory Gene 1955- *WhoE 93*
Spahr, Philip M. 1951- *St&PR 93*
Spahr, Robert N. 1938- *St&PR 93*
Spaid, Joseph Snyder 1906- *WhoAm 92*
Spain, Barbara Wortham 1934- *WhoAmW 93*
Spain, Cecil 1935- *St&PR 93*
Spain, Charles H., Jr. *Law&B 92*
Spain, James Dorris, Jr. 1929- *WhoAm 92*
Spain, James William 1926- *WhoAm 92*
Spain, Jayne Baker *WhoWor 93*
Spain, Nettie Edwards 1918- *WhoAmW 93, WhoSSW 93, WhoWor 93*
Spain, Pamela Ruth *Law&B 92*
Spain, Patrick J. 1952- *St&PR 93*
Spain, Thomas B. *WhoSSW 93*
Spain, William James, Jr. 1927- *St&PR 93*
Spainhour, Elizabeth Anne Stroupe 1944- *WhoSSW 93*
Spainhour, Ralph Alexander, III 1947- *WhoSSW 93*
Spainhour, Sterling Ashley *Law&B 92*
Spainhour, Tremaine Howard 1924- *WhoAm 92*
Spainhower, Paul J. 1927- *St&PR 93*
Spak, Gale Tenen 1946- *WhoE 93*
Spak, Lorin Mitchell 1941- *St&PR 93, WhoAm 92*
Spake, Karen Jo 1943- *WhoAmW 93*
Spake, Ned Bernarr 1933- *WhoAm 92*
Spake, Reuben Michael 1957- *WhoSSW 93*
Spalding, Albert 1888-1953 *Baker 92*
Spalding, Catherine *Law&B 92*
Spalding, D. Brian *WhoScE 91-1*
Spalding, Daniel L. 1953- *St&PR 93*
Spalding, Donald E. 1930- *St&PR 93*
Spalding, E. Susan 1965- *WhoSSW 93*
Spalding, Henry A. 1899- *WhoWor 93*
Spalding, James H. *Law&B 92*
Spalding, James Stuart 1934- *WhoAm 92*
Spalding, Julian 1947- *WhoWor 93*
Spalding, Leonard A., III *Law&B 92*
Spalding, (Billups) Phinizy 1930- *ConAu 39NR*
Spalding, Robert George 1923- *WhoE 93*
Spalding, Steven L. *Law&B 92*
Spalding, Timothy J. 1955- *St&PR 93*
Spalitta, Salvadore V. *Law&B 92*
Spallholz, Julian Ernest 1943- *WhoSSW 93*
Spallina, James Peter 1919- *St&PR 93*
Spallone, Henry J. *WhoAm 92*
Spalteholz, Robert William 1945- *St&PR 93, WhoE 93*
Spampinato, Arline C. *St&PR 93*
Spanbauer, Tom *BioIn 17*
Spandorf, Lily Gabriella *WhoE 93*
Spandorfer, Merle Sue 1934- *WhoAm 92, WhoAmW 93*
Spanfeller, James J(ohn) 1930- *MajAI [port]*
Spanfeller, Jim *MajAI*
Spanfelner, Robert Bruce 1939- *WhoIns 93*
Spang, J. Maurice, Jr. 1940- *St&PR 93*
Spang, Mark W. 1948- *St&PR 93*
Spangenberg, Brenda Lois 1944- *WhoAmW 93*
Spangenberg, Dorothy Breslin 1931- *WhoWor 93*
Spangenberg, Edward Brindley 1935- *St&PR 93*
Spangenberg, Hans-Joachim 1932- *WhoScE 91-3*
Spangenberg, Heinrich 1861-1925 *Baker 92*
Spangenberg, Karl A. 1947- *St&PR 93*
Spangle, Clarence W. 1925- *St&PR 93*
Spangler, Arnold E. 1948- *St&PR 93*
Spangler, Arnold Eugene 1948- *WhoAm 92*
Spangler, Arthur Stephenson, Jr. 1949- *WhoE 93, WhoWor 93*
Spangler, C. Gregory 1940- *St&PR 93*
Spangler, Clarence John 1924- *St&PR 93*
Spangler, Clemmie Dixon, Jr. 1932- *WhoAm 92, WhoSSW 93*
Spangler, Daisy Kirchoff 1913- *WhoWor 93*
Spangler, David B. 1938- *St&PR 93*
Spangler, David Robert 1940- *WhoAm 92*
Spangler, David Sheridan 1948- *WhoEmL 93, WhoWor 93*
Spangler, Dennis Lee 1947- *WhoSSW 93*
Spangler, Harrison E. 1879-1965 *PolPar*
Spangler, Harrison Earl 1879-1965 *BioIn 17*
Spangler, J.L. *St&PR 93*
Spangler, Larry G. *MiSFD 9*
Spangler, Miller Brant 1923- *WhoE 93*
Spangler, Otto Maurice 1936- *WhoSSW 93*
Spangler, Ronald Leroy 1937- *WhoE 93, WhoWor 93*
Spangler, Scott Michael 1938- *St&PR 93, WhoAm 92*
Spangler, Susan E. *Law&B 92*
Spangler, William C. 1930- *St&PR 93*
Spani, Hina 1896-1969 *Baker 92*
Spaniardi, Richard J. 1936- *WhoIns 93*
Spanidou, Irini *BioIn 17*
Spanier, Arthur 1889-1944 *BioIn 17*
Spanier, Arthur Melvin 1948- *WhoSSW 93*
Spanier, David 1932- *ConAu 39NR*
Spanier, Graham Basil 1948- *WhoAm 92*
Spanier, "Muggsy" 1906-1967 *Baker 92*
Spanier, Muriel 1928- *WhoWrEP 92*
Spanier, Richard Frederick 1940- *St&PR 93*
Spanio, Francesco *WhoScE 91-3*

Spanlol, Joseph Frederick, Jr. 1925- *WhoAm 92*
Spankuch, Dietrich Hartwin 1936- *WhoWor 93*
Spann, Allen Troy 1944- *St&PR 93*
Spann, George William 1946- *WhoAm 92, WhoSSW 93*
Spann, Gloria Carter 1926-1990 *BioIn 17*
Spann, Harold Glen 1927- *WhoSSW 93*
Spann, Katharine Doyle *WhoWor 93*
Spann, Laura Nason 1947- *WhoSSW 93*
Spann, Meno H. 1903-1991 *ConAu 136*
Spann, Milton Graham, Jr. 1942- *WhoSSW 93*
Spann, Stephen *Law&B 92*
Spann, Stephen Allison 1941- *WhoWor 93*
Spanninger, Beth Anne *Law&B 92*
Spannuth, Kay Louise 1957- *WhoAmW 93*
Spano, Charles A., Jr. 1948- *ScF&FL 92*
Spano, Ellen *Law&B 92*
Spano, John Joseph 1919- *WhoE 93*
Spano, Paolo 1952- *WhoWor 93*
Spano, Rina Gangemi 1948- *WhoE 93*
Spano, Vincent *BioIn 17*
Spanos, Alexander Gus 1923- *WhoAm 92*
Spanos, Dean A. 1950- *WhoAm 92*
Spanos, Elias 1948- *WhoE 93*
Spanos, Olympia Critikou *Law&B 92*
Spanovich, Milan 1929- *St&PR 93, WhoAm 92*
Spar, Edward Joel 1939- *St&PR 93, WhoAm 92*
Spar, Warren Hal 1953- *WhoWor 93*
Sparacio, Annmarie *WhoE 93*
Sparacio, John J. 1925- *St&PR 93*
Sparano, Diane Madeline 1966- *WhoAmW 93*
Sparano, Vin(cent) T(homas) 1934- *WhoWrEP 92*
Sparano, Vincent Thomas 1934- *WhoAm 92*
Sparatore, Fabio 1928- *WhoScE 91-3*
Sparatore, Maria Anna 1964- *WhoAmW 93*
Sparberg, Esther B. 1922- *WhoAm 92*
Sparberg, Marshall Stuart 1936- *WhoAm 92*
Sparby, Neal 1936- *St&PR 93*
Sparck, J.V. *WhoScE 91-2*
Sparck Jones, Karen *WhoScE 91-1*
Sparer, Laurie A. *ScF&FL 92*
Sparer, William J. *Law&B 92*
Sparger, Rex *ScF&FL 92*
Sparis, Panagiotis 1945- *WhoScE 91-3*
Spark, Michelle 1951- *WhoE 93*
Spark, Muriel *BioIn 17*
Spark, Muriel 1918- *MagSWL [port], ScF&FL 92, ShSCr 10 [port]*
Spark, Muriel Sarah *WhoAm 92, WhoWor 93*
Sparker, William Holbrook 1925- *St&PR 93*
Sparkes, Ivan G(eorge) 1930- *ConAu 38NR*
Sparkes, John Richard *WhoScE 91-1*
Sparkman, Alexa Fay 1955- *WhoSSW 93*
Sparkman, Brandon Buster 1929- *WhoAm 92*
Sparkman, Dennis Raymond 1954- *WhoSSW 93*
Sparkman, Ernest Lee 1958- *WhoSSW 93*
Sparkman, Glenda Kathleen 1941- *WhoAmW 93, WhoSSW 93*
Sparkman, John 1899-1985 *PolPar*
Sparkman, Robert Satterfield 1912- *WhoAm 92*
Sparkowski, Edward Frank 1955- *WhoE 93*
Sparkrock, Fred *ScF&FL 92*
Sparks, Asa Howard 1937- *WhoSSW 93*
Sparks, Beatrice 1918- *ScF&FL 92*
Sparks, Bertel Milas 1918- *WhoAm 92*
Sparks, Billy Schley 1923- *WhoWor 93*
Sparks, Bradley E. 1946- *St&PR 93*
Sparks, David Glen 1948- *WhoIns 93*
Sparks, David Stanley 1922- *WhoAm 92*
Sparks, Earl Edwin 1920- *WhoAm 92*
Sparks, Edgar C. 1931- *St&PR 93*
Sparks, Grant Todd 1960- *WhoSSW 93*
Sparks, Greg E. 1967- *WhoSSW 93*
Sparks, Harvey Vise, Jr. 1938- *WhoAm 92*
Sparks, Hugh Cullen 1946- *WhoSSW 93*
Sparks, Jack D. 1922- *St&PR 93*
Sparks, James D. 1928- *St&PR 93*
Sparks, John Edward 1930- *WhoAm 92*
Sparks, Kenneth Dale 1937- *WhoSSW 93*
Sparks, Kenneth George 1935- *St&PR 93*
Sparks, Laura Jean 1962- *WhoE 93*
Sparks, Lawrence John 1942- *St&PR 93*
Sparks, Marshall F. 1940- *St&PR 93*
Sparks, Mary Ruth 1942- *WhoAmW 93*
Sparks, Maureen Anne 1954- *WhoAmW 93*
Sparks, Meredith Pleasant *WhoWor 93*
Sparks, (Theo) Merrill 1922- *WhoWrEP 92*
Sparks, Michael Blythe 1960- *WhoSSW 93*
Sparks, Michael W. 1947- *St&PR 93*
Sparks, Morgan 1916- *WhoAm 92*
Sparks, O.C. *Law&B 92*
Sparks, Richard B. 1946- *St&PR 93*
Sparks, Richard T. 1935- *St&PR 93*
Sparks, Robert Dean 1932- *WhoAm 92*
Sparks, Robert Hutchen 1929- *St&PR 93*
Sparks, Robert William 1925- *WhoAm 92*
Sparks, Ronald Wayne 1955- *WhoSSW 93*
Sparks, Sheila L. *Law&B 92*
Sparks, Sherman Paul 1909- *WhoSSW 93*
Sparks, Shirley Nichols 1933- *WhoAmW 93*
Sparks, Teresa 1952- *MiSFD 9*
Sparks, W.A., Jr. 1935- *St&PR 93*
Sparks, Walter Chappel 1918- *WhoAm 92*
Sparks, William J.A. *Law&B 92*
Sparks, Willis Breazeal, III 1934- *WhoSSW 93*
Sparks-MacDiarmada Rua, Casandra Sessa *WhoE 93*
Sparler, Daniel 1917- *St&PR 93*
Sparling, Mary Christine 1928- *WhoAm 92*
Sparling, Mary Lee 1934- *WhoAmW 93*
Sparling, Peter David 1951- *WhoAm 92*
Sparling, Winston Bruce 1919- *St&PR 93*
Sparnaay, Harry 1944- *Baker 92*
Sparr, Daniel Beattie 1931- *WhoAm 92*
Sparre, Pierre-Francois 1927- *WhoScE 91-4*
Sparrgrove, Dewain A. 1941- *WhoIns 93*
Sparrman, Anders 1748-1820 *IntDcAn*
Sparrow, Barbara Jane 1935- *WhoAmW 93*
Sparrow, David Arnold 1947- *WhoSSW 93*
Sparrow, Dorothy Talmadge 1943- *WhoAmW 93*
Sparrow, Ephraim Maurice 1928- *WhoAm 92*
Sparrow, Herbert George, III 1936- *WhoAm 92, WhoWor 93*
Sparrow, Jimmy *BioIn 17*
Sparrow, John Austin 1956- *WhoWor 93*
Sparrow, Minnie Shepherd *AmWomPl*
Sparrow, R.W. *WhoScE 91-1*
Sparrow, Rodney G. 1948- *St&PR 93*
Sparrow, Susanna *ScF&FL 92*
Sparrow, William Holliday 1943- *St&PR 93*
Sparshott, Francis Edward 1926- *WhoAm 92, WhoCanL 92, WhoWrEP 92*
Sparso, Henning Hempel 1929- *WhoAm 92*
Spartac, Nicolai Nicolaevich 1940- *WhoUN 92*
Spartacus d71BC *HarEnMi*
Sparvoli, Elio 1930- *WhoScE 91-3*
Spash, Clive Laurence 1962- *WhoWor 93*
Spasov, Alexandre Yankov 1934- *WhoScE 91-4*
Spasov, Ivan 1934- *Baker 92*
Spasowski, Romuald 1920- *PolBiDi*
Spasowski, Wladyslaw 1877-1941 *PolBiDi*
Spass, Stan 1929- *St&PR 93*
Spasser, Frank B. 1929- *St&PR 93*
Spassky, Boris Vasilyevich 1937- *BioIn 17*
Spat, Andras 1940- *WhoScE 91-4*
Spatafora, Denise *BioIn 17*
Spatafore, Anthony R. 1952- *WhoEmL 93*
Spatafore, Tim *BioIn 17*
Spataro, Alan C., Sr. *St&PR 93*
Spataro, Alan C., Jr. *St&PR 93*
Spataro, Francis Cajetan 1936- *WhoE 93*
Spataro, Giovanni c. 1458-1541 *Baker 92*
Spataro, Mario 1931- *WhoWor 93*
Spater-Zimmerman, Susan *WhoE 93*
Spath, Thomas F. 1933- *St&PR 93*
Spatola, Adriano 1941-1988 *DcLB 128 [port]*
Spatschek, Karl Heinz 1943- *WhoWor 93*
Spatt, Arthur D. 1925- *WhoAm 92*
Spatt, Michael David 1957- *St&PR 93*
Spatt, Robert Edward 1956- *WhoAm 92, WhoE 93, WhoEmL 93*
Spatta, Carolyn Davis 1935- *WhoAmW 93*
Spatz, Donald Dean 1944- *St&PR 93*
Spatz, Hanns-Christof 1936- *WhoScE 91-3*
Spatz, Hugo David 1913- *WhoSSW 93*
Spatz, Joanne *Law&B 92*
Spatz, Lois Settler 1940- *WhoAmW 93*
Spatz, Martin W. 1931- *St&PR 93*
Spatz, Neal J. 1934- *St&PR 93*
Spatz, Ronald M. 1949- *WhoWrEP 92*
Spatz, Walter Bates 1921- *St&PR 93*
Spaugh, Gerald G. 1953- *St&PR 93*
Spaulding, Asa T. d1990 *BioIn 17*
Spaulding, Douglas *ConTFT 10*
Spaulding, Frank Henry 1932- *WhoAm 92*
Spaulding, Jacqueline Susan 1955- *WhoSSW 93*
Spaulding, Karla Rae 1954- *WhoSSW 93*
Spaulding, Malcolm L. *WhoE 93*
Spaulding, Margaret A. *AmWomPl*
Spaulding, Richard W. 1949- *WhoIns 93*
Spaulding, Robert Mark 1929- *WhoAm 92*
Spaulding, Romeo Orlando 1940- *WhoE 93*
Spaulding, Seth Joseph 1928- *WhoE 93*
Spaulding, Thomas B. *Law&B 92*
Spaulding, William Rowe 1915- *WhoE 93, WhoWor 93*
Spaw, June 1925- *WhoWrEP 92*
Spaziani, JoAnn 1952- *WhoAmW 93*
Spaziani, Maria Luisa 1924- *DcLB 128 [port]*
Spazier, Johann Gottlieb Karl 1761-1805 *Baker 92*
Spazzapan, Federico Mirko 1953- *WhoWor 93*
Speak, Charles E. *Law&B 92*
Speake, Bob C. 1930- *St&PR 93*
Speaker, John E. 1931- *St&PR 93*
Speaker, Mark Daniel *Law&B 92*
Speaker, Richard L. 1920- *WhoSSW 93*
Speaker, Tris 1888-1958 *BioIn 17*
Speakes, Larry 1939- *JrnUS*
Speakes, Larry (Melvin) 1939- *ConAu 137, WhoAm 92*
Speakman, Kenneth Riley 1937- *WhoSSW 93*
Speakman, Willard A., III 1938- *St&PR 93*
Speaks, Donald Wesley 1921- *St&PR 93*
Speaks, John Robert *St&PR 93*
Speaks, John Thomas, Jr. 1945- *WhoSSW 93*
Speaks, Joseph A. *St&PR 93*
Speaks, Oley 1874-1948 *Baker 92*
Speaks, Stephen Patrick 1950- *St&PR 93*
Spear, Alice Rideout 1943- *WhoAmW 93*
Spear, Alison *BioIn 17*
Spear, Amy R. *St&PR 93*
Spear, Cecil C., Jr. 1935- *St&PR 93*
Spear, Charles Michael 1942- *St&PR 93*
Spear, Harvey M. 1922- *WhoAm 92*
Spear, Herb 1940- *St&PR 93*
Spear, Jonathan L. *Law&B 92*
Spear, Kathleen Kelly *Law&B 92*
Spear, Kenneth Ray 1949- *St&PR 93*
Spear, Laurinda *BioIn 17*
Spear, Lloyd C. 1940- *St&PR 93*
Spear, Louis L. 1915- *St&PR 93*
Spear, Paul William 1908- *WhoE 93*
Spear, Richard Edmund 1940- *WhoAm 92*
Spear, Robert Bruce 1931- *St&PR 93*
Spear, Robert Clinton 1939- *WhoAm 92*
Spear, Robert D. 1945- *St&PR 93*
Spear, Ruth *WhoE 93*
Spear, Steven C. 1947- *St&PR 93*
Spear, Walter Eric *WhoScE 91-1*
Spearbecker, Kim La Rae 1957- *WhoWrEP 92*
Speare, Dorothy 1898-1951 *AmWomPl*
Speare, Elizabeth George 1908- *BioIn 17, DcAmChF 1960, MajAI [port], WhoAm 92, WhoAmW 93*
Speare, Florence Lewis 1886-1965 *AmWomPl*
Speares, Scott Bruce, III 1960- *WhoSSW 93*
Spearing, Anthony Colin 1936- *WhoAm 92*
Spearing, Judith 1922- *ScF&FL 92*
Spearman, Donald R. *Law&B 92*
Spearman, Jerry C. 1943- *St&PR 93*
Spearman, Leonard H. O., Sr. 1929- *WhoAm 92, WhoWor 93*
Spearman, Leonard H. O., Jr. *AfrAmBi [port]*
Spearman, Lionel 1964- *WhoSSW 93*
Spearman, Maxie Ann 1942- *WhoAmW 93, WhoSSW 93, WhoWor 93*
Spearman, Thomas David 1937- *WhoScE 91-3, WhoWor 93*
Spear-Obermiller, Mary Patricia 1954- *WhoAmW 93*
Spears, Alexander White, III 1932- *St&PR 93, WhoAm 92*
Spears, C.S. 1930- *St&PR 93*
Spears, Carleton Blaise 1958- *WhoSSW 93, WhoWor 93*
Spears, Clarence Wiley 1894-1964 *BiDAMSp 1989*
Spears, Colin John *WhoScE 91-1*
Spears, David Alan *WhoScE 91-1*
Spears, Diane C. *Law&B 92*
Spears, Franklin Scott 1931- *WhoAm 92*
Spears, Heather 1934- *ScF&FL 92*
Spears, Howard Calvin Knox 1925- *WhoE 93*
Spears, Jae *WhoAmW 93, WhoSSW 93*
Spears, Jerome Jennings 1943- *WhoE 93*
Spears, Jerry Mack 1942- *WhoSSW 93*
Spears, John Douglas 1948- *St&PR 93*
Spears, Kermit *ScF&FL 92*
Spears, Marian Caddy 1921- *WhoAm 92*
Spears, Mary Carol 1940- *WhoAmW 93*
Spears, Monroe Kirk 1916- *WhoWrEP 92*
Spears, Paul Edward 1924- *St&PR 93*
Spears, R. Warren 1926- *WhoE 93*
Spears, Ralph Warren 1926- *St&PR 93*
Spears, Richard R. *Law&B 92*
Spears, Richard W. 1936- *WhoAm 92*
Spears, Sally 1938- *WhoAm 92*
Spears, Sandra Lee 1950- *WhoSSW 93*
Spears, William Martin 1955- *WhoSSW 93*
Speas, Charles Stuart 1944- *WhoWor 93*
Speas, John Kelly 1946- *St&PR 93*
Speas, R. Dixon 1916- *St&PR 93*
Speas, Raymond Aaron 1925- *WhoAm 92*
Speas, Robert Dixon 1916- *WhoAm 92, WhoWor 93*
Speca, Bruce Robert 1956- *St&PR 93*
Specer, Thomas Frederick 1943- *St&PR 93*
Spechalske, Frank Herman 1923- *WhoSSW 93*
Specht, Charles Alfred 1914- *WhoAm 92*
Specht, Donald W.J. 1939- *St&PR 93*
Specht, Gordon Dean 1927- *WhoE 93*
Specht, Lawrence H. 1931- *St&PR 93*
Specht, Lois Darlene 1931- *WhoAmW 93*
Specht, Steven Michael 1959- *WhoE 93*
Specht, Susan Jean 1954- *WhoAmW 93*
Specht, William A., Jr. 1931- *St&PR 93*
Specht, William A., III *St&PR 93*
Speciale, Charles J. *Law&B 92*
Speciale, Richard 1945- *WhoAm 92*
Specian, Robert David 1950- *WhoSSW 93*
Speck, David George 1945- *WhoSSW 93*
Speck, Frank G. 1881-1950 *IntDcAn*
Speck, J. Craig 1947- *St&PR 93*
Speck, Jochen 1930- *WhoScE 91-3*
Speck, Kathleen Marie 1957- *St&PR 93*
Speck, Lawrence W. *BioIn 17*
Speck, Marvin Luther 1913- *WhoAm 92*
Speck, Richard 1941-1991 *BioIn 17*
Speck, Ross V. 1927- *WhoE 93*
Speck, Samuel Wallace, Jr. 1937- *WhoAm 92*
Specker, Alex James 1955- *WhoE 93*
Specker, J. David 1943- *WhoE 93*
Speckman, John Goyert 1947- *WhoSSW 93*
Speckman, John Thomas 1945- *WhoIns 93*
Speckman, Mark Christopher 1948- *St&PR 93*
Specter, Arlen *BioIn 17*
Specter, Arlen 1930- *CngDr 91, WhoAm 92, WhoE 93*
Spector, Abraham 1926- *WhoAm 92*
Spector, Adam Keith 1963- *WhoE 93*
Spector, Alan J. *Law&B 92*
Spector, Barbara Holmes 1927- *WhoAmW 93*
Spector, Bruce Darwin 1953- *WhoE 93*
Spector, Cecile Cyrul *WhoE 93*
Spector, Craig 1958- *ScF&FL 92*
Spector, Daniel Earl 1942- *WhoSSW 93*
Spector, David M. 1946- *WhoAm 92*
Spector, Dorothy J. 1918- *St&PR 93*
Spector, Earl Melvin 1939- *St&PR 93*
Spector, Eleanor Ruth 1943- *WhoAm 92, WhoAmW 93*
Spector, Gershon Jerry 1937- *WhoAm 92*
Spector, Harold Norman 1935- *WhoAm 92*
Spector, Harvey M. 1938- *WhoE 93*
Spector, Johanna Lichtenberg *WhoAm 92, WhoAmW 93*
Spector, Joseph Robert 1923- *WhoAm 92*
Spector, Judith Ann 1958- *WhoE 93*
Spector, Karen 1951- *WhoAmW 93*
Spector, Larry *BioIn 17*
Spector, Louis 1918- *WhoAm 92*
Spector, Marshall 1936- *WhoAm 92*
Spector, Martin W. *Law&B 92*
Spector, Martin Wolf 1938- *St&PR 93*
Spector, Melbourne Louis 1918- *WhoAm 92*
Spector, Michael Jay 1940- *WhoAm 92*
Spector, Norman *BioIn 17*
Spector, Paul R. *Law&B 92*
Spector, Phil *BioIn 17*
Spector, Phil 1940- *SoulM, WhoAm 92*
Spector, Reynold 1940- *WhoE 93*
Spector, Robert Donald 1922- *ScF&FL 92, WhoWrEP 92*
Spector, Ronnie *SoulM*
Spector, Ronnie 1943- *BioIn 17*
Spector, Roy Geoffrey *WhoScE 91-1*
Spector, Russell 1957- *St&PR 93*
Spector, Stanley 1924- *WhoAm 92*
Spector, Stephen 1946- *ConAu 138*
Spector, Thomas 1944- *WhoSSW 93*
Spector, Warren *ScF&FL 92*
Spector-Zacks, Rosalind 1950- *St&PR 93*
Spectre, Jay d1992 *NewYTBS 92*
Spectre, Jay 1929- *WhoAm 92*
Spedale, Robert Joseph 1949- *St&PR 93*
Spedden, Sewell Lee, Jr. 1938- *St&PR 93*

Spedding *ScF&FL 92*
Spedding, Alan *WhoScE 91-1*
Spedding, Colin Raymond William *WhoScE 91-1*
Spedding, Peter Lee *WhoScE 91-1*
Spedicato, Emilio Giuseppe 1945- *WhoWor 93*
Spee, B.M. *WhoScE 91-3*
Spee, Maximilian von 1861-1914 *HarEnMi*
Speece, Jack Howard 1947- *WhoE 93*
Speece, Richard Eugene 1933- *WhoAm 92*
Speed, Billie Cheney 1927- *WhoAm 92*
Speed, Edwin Maurice 1918- *WhoSSW 93*
Speed, John Sackett 1927- *WhoAm 92*
Speed, Leland Rhymes 1932- *St&PR 93*
Speed, Lillian Castillo *NotHsAW 93*
Speed, Mary Waletta 1954- *WhoAmW 93*
Speed, Nell 1878-1913 *BioIn 17*
Speegle, Christopher F. *Law&B 92*
Speelman, H. *WhoScE 91-3*
Speelman, Irving A. 1919- *St&PR 93*
Speelman, Irving Arnold 1919- *WhoE 93*
Speelman, Joseph F. *Law&B 92*
Speer, Albert 1905-1981 *ConAu 40NR, DcTwHis*
Speer, Allen Paul, III 1951- *WhoSSW 93, WhoWrEP 92*
Speer, Betty Jean 1931- *WhoWrEP 92*
Speer, Dana S. *Law&B 92*
Speer, Daniel 1636-1707 *Baker 92*
Speer, David Gordon 1913- *WhoSSW 93*
Speer, David James 1927- *WhoAm 92*
Speer, Flora *ScF&FL 92*
Speer, G. William 1940- *St&PR 93*
Speer, Garry Wayne 1957- *WhoWrEP 92*
Speer, Jack Atkeson 1941- *WhoAm 92*
Speer, Jack Bristol 1915-1989 *ScF&FL 92*
Speer, Laurel 1940- *WhoWrEP 92*
Speer, Raymond M. *Law&B 92*
Speer, Robert L. 1931- *St&PR 93*
Speer, Roy M. 1932- *ConEn, St&PR 93, WhoSSW 93*
Speer, Thomas M. 1934- *St&PR 93*
Speer, William Thomas, Jr. 1936- *WhoAm 92*
Speers, Charles R. 1907-1991 *BioIn 17*
Speers, J. Alvin 1930- *WhoWrEP 92*
Speers, J. Kent 1949- *St&PR 93*
Speers, Roland Root, II 1933- *WhoAm 92*
Speert, Arnold 1945- *WhoAm 92*
Speet, Kirtland Paul, II 1963- *WhoWor 93*
Speets, Jan Arien 1943- *WhoUN 92*
Speght, Rachel 1597-c. 1630 *DcLB 126*
Spehner, Jean-Claude 1935- *WhoScE 91-2*
Speicher, Betsy Mary Elizabeth 1948- *WhoAmW 93*
Speicher, Edwin W. 1931- *St&PR 93*
Speicher, Edwin Waller 1931- *WhoE 93*
Speicher, Franklin S., Jr. 1918- *St&PR 93*
Speicher, JoAnne *BioIn 17*
Speicher, Mary Elizabeth 1949- *WhoAmW 93*
Speicher, Rita L. 1954- *WhoWrEP 92*
Speicher, Scott d1991 *BioIn 17*
Speicher, William C. 1937- *St&PR 93*
Speicher, William Clayton 1937- *WhoAm 92*
Speidel, Benjamin Burtlin, IV 1953- *St&PR 93*
Speidel, David Harold 1938- *WhoAm 92*
Speidel, Hans 1897-1984 *BioIn 17*
Speidel, Hans 1897-1987 *HarEnMi*
Speidel, John Joseph 1937- *WhoAm 92*
Speidel, Richard Eli 1933- *WhoAm 92*
Speidel, Volker *WhoScE 91-3*
Speidel, Wilhelm 1826-1899 *Baker 92*
Speier, Hans 1905-1990 *BioIn 17*
Speier, Hermine 1898-1989 *BioIn 17*
Speier, John L. 1918- *WhoAm 92*
Speier, Karen Rinardo 1947- *WhoAmW 93*
Speierer, Gert-W. 1941- *WhoScE 91-3*
Speierl, Charles Frank, Jr. 1945- *WhoE 93*
Speight, James Glassford 1940- *WhoAm 92*
Speight, Jeanette Aline 1946- *WhoE 93*
Speiller-Morris, Joyce 1945- *WhoSSW 93*
Speir, Marcia Ann 1935- *WhoAmW 93*
Speir, Martha Ann 1946- *WhoAmW 93*
Speir, Susan *BioIn 17*
Speirs, Derek James 1933- *WhoAm 92*
Speirs, Joseph A. 1952- *St&PR 93*
Speirs, Patricia Lynn 1965- *WhoAmW 93*
Speirs, Ronald Lamont *WhoScE 91-1*
Speiser, Ambros P. 1922- *WhoScE 91-4*
Speiser, Ambros Paul 1922- *WhoWor 93*
Speiser, E. Pat 1937- *St&PR 93*
Speiser, Lawrence 1923-1991 *BioIn 17*
Speiser, Robert Douglas 1953- *St&PR 93*
Speitel, Gerald E. 1930- *St&PR 93*
Speitel, Gerald Eugene 1930- *WhoAm 92*
Speizer, Mark Adler 1943- *St&PR 93, WhoIns 93*
Spejewski, Eugene Henry 1938- *WhoAm 92*
Speke, John Hanning 1827-1864 *Expl 93 [port]*
Spekreijse, H. 1940- *WhoScE 91-3*
Spelber, Leonard George 1925- *St&PR 93*
Spelfogel, Evan J. 1936- *WhoWor 93*
Spelfogel, Scott D. *Law&B 92*
Spelke, Richard A. 1941- *St&PR 93*
Spelker, Amy Causing 1962- *WhoAmW 93*
Spelker, Arnold William 1934- *WhoE 93*
Spell, Belenda Kesler 1958- *WhoSSW 93*
Spell, Ernest D. 1941- *St&PR 93*
Spellacy, William Nelson 1934- *WhoSSW 93*
Speller, David Charles Endersby *WhoScE 91-1*
Speller, John Arthur Leslie 1936- *St&PR 93*
Speller, William Thomas 1940- *WhoSSW 93*
Spelleri, Richard J. *St&PR 93*
Spelling, Aaron *BioIn 17*
Spelling, Aaron 1923- *WhoAm 92*
Spelling, Aaron 1928- *St&PR 93*
Spellings, James M., Jr. *Law&B 92*
Spelliscy, Peter T. 1944- *St&PR 93*
Spellman, Benny *SoulM*
Spellman, Elizabeth May 1933- *WhoAmW 93*
Spellman, Eugene P. 1930-1991 *BioIn 17*
Spellman, Francis 1889-1967 *ColdWar 1 [port]*
Spellman, George Geneser, Sr. 1920- *WhoAm 92, WhoWor 93*
Spellman, Gladys Noon 1918-1988 *BioIn 17*
Spellman, John William, Jr. 1925- *WhoSSW 93*
Spellman, Robert R. 1948- *St&PR 93*
Spellman, Warren Kean 1956- *WhoSSW 93*
Spelman, Brenda Gates *ScF&FL 92*
Spelman, Dick 1931- *ScF&FL 92*
Spelman, Mary *ScF&FL 92*
Spelman, Nancy Latting 1945- *WhoAmW 93*
Spelman, Philip Ohel 1923- *WhoWrEP 92*
Spelman, Timothy (Mather) 1891-1970 *Baker 92*
Spelsberg, Thomas Coonan 1940- *WhoAm 92*
Spelts, Dorothy T. 1922- *St&PR 93*
Spelts, Richard E., Jr. 1919- *St&PR 93*
Spelts, Richard John 1939- *WhoAm 92, WhoWor 93*
Speltz, George Henry 1912- *WhoAm 92*
Speltz, Stephen Eugene 1933- *St&PR 93*
Spence, A. Michael 1943- *WhoAm 92*
Spence, Alastair Andrew *WhoScE 91-1*
Spence, Arthur G. *Law&B 92*
Spence, Barbara Harrington Earnshaw 1921- *WhoAmW 93*
Spence, Bradley Antone 1960- *St&PR 93*
Spence, Brenda Sue 1942- *WhoSSW 93*
Spence, Catherine Helen 1825-1910 *ScF&FL 92*
Spence, Clark Christian 1923- *WhoAm 92*
Spence, David Allan *WhoScE 91-1*
Spence, Donald Pond 1926- *WhoE 93*
Spence, Doralyne *AmWomPl*
Spence, Elaine Keenan 1960- *BioIn 17*
Spence, Eleanor (Rachel) 1927?- *DcChlFi*
Spence, Eulalie *AmWomPl*
Spence, Eulalie 1894-1981 *BioIn 17*
Spence, Floyd 1928- *CngDr 91*
Spence, Floyd Davidson 1928- *WhoAm 92, WhoSSW 93*
Spence, Frank Richard 1935- *WhoSSW 93*
Spence, Gerald Leonard 1929- *WhoAm 92, WhoWrEP 92*
Spence, Glen Oscar 1927- *WhoAm 92*
Spence, Greggory Keith *Law&B 92*
Spence, Gusty *BioIn 17*
Spence, Guy W. 1939- *WhoSSW 93*
Spence, Harry Metcalfe 1905- *WhoAm 92*
Spence, James Robert, Jr. 1936- *WhoAm 92*
Spence, Janet Blake Conley 1915- *WhoAmW 93, WhoE 93*
Spence, Janet Taylor 1923- *BioIn 17*
Spence, John *WhoScE 91-1*
Spence, John Daniel 1915- *WhoAm 92*
Spence, John William 1940- *WhoSSW 93*
Spence, Jonathan D. *BioIn 17*
Spence, Jonathan Dermot 1936- *WhoAm 92*
Spence, Margaret 1944- *WhoAmW 93*
Spence, Mary C. *AmWomPl*
Spence, Mary Lee 1927- *WhoAmW 93*
Spence, Michael *MiSFD 9*
Spence, Michele *ScF&FL 92*
Spence, Norman Thomas 1934- *St&PR 93*
Spence, Paul Herbert 1923- *WhoAm 92*
Spence, R. *WhoScE 91-1*
Spence, Ralph Beckett 1901-1990 *BioIn 17*
Spence, Richard Dee 1925- *St&PR 93, WhoAm 92*
Spence, Robert Dean 1917- *WhoAm 92*
Spence, Robert James 1947- *WhoE 93*
Spence, Robert John Summerford *WhoScE 91-1*
Spence, Robert Leroy 1931- *WhoAm 92*
Spence, Ronald G. 1940- *St&PR 93*
Spence, Sandra 1941- *WhoAm 92*
Spence, Stan Clynton *BioIn 17*
Spence, Stevan Thomas 1947- *St&PR 93*
Spence, Steve *BioIn 17*
Spence, Susan Bateman 1947- *WhoAmW 93, WhoSSW 93*
Spence, Thomas J. *Law&B 92*
Spence, William Guthrie 1846-1926 *DcTwHis*
Spence, William Rayburn 1942- *St&PR 93*
Spenceley, G.D. *WhoScE 91-1*
Spencer, Earl 1924-1992 *NewYTBS 92 [port]*
Spencer, A.J.M. *WhoScE 91-1*
Spencer, Alan *MiSFD 9*
Spencer, Alan H. 1937- *St&PR 93, WhoIns 93*
Spencer, Allison Darrow 1961- *WhoAmW 93*
Spencer, Anna Garlin 1851-1932 *BioIn 17*
Spencer, Anna Lou 1939- *WhoSSW 93*
Spencer, Anne 1882-1975 *EncAACR*
Spencer, Baldwin *DcCPCAm*
Spencer, Baldwin 1860-1929 *IntDcAn*
Spencer, Brian *WhoScE 91-1*
Spencer, C. Stanley 1946- *St&PR 93*
Spencer, Carlton Wentworth 1906- *St&PR 93*
Spencer, Caroline M. 1932- *WhoAm 92*
Spencer, Christopher Peter *WhoScE 91-1*
Spencer, Dan S., Jr. 1930- *St&PR 93*
Spencer, Dana Richard 1940- *WhoSSW 93*
Spencer, Daniel P. 1948- *WhoIns 93*
Spencer, David Gelvin, Jr. 1953- *WhoWor 93*
Spencer, David James 1943- *WhoAm 92*
Spencer, David Robert 1942- *WhoE 93*
Spencer, Deborah Joyce 1950- *WhoAmW 93*
Spencer, Derek Wardle 1934- *WhoAm 92*
Spencer, Diane Brown *WhoAmW 93*
Spencer, Dick, III 1921- *WhoWrEP 92*
Spencer, Domina Eberle 1920- *WhoAmW 93, WhoE 93*
Spencer, Donald Clayton 1912- *WhoAm 92*
Spencer, Donald P. *Law&B 92*
Spencer, Donald Spurgeon 1945- *WhoAm 92, WhoE 93*
Spencer, Dwain Frank 1934- *WhoAm 92*
Spencer, Edgar Winston 1931- *WhoSSW 93*
Spencer, Edson White 1926- *WhoAm 92*
Spencer, Edward Francis Dudley 1945- *WhoSSW 93*
Spencer, Edward John 1924-1992 *BioIn 17*
Spencer, Eleanor P. d1992 *NewYTBS 92*
Spencer, Elizabeth *BioIn 17*
Spencer, Elizabeth 1921- *WhoAm 92, WhoAmW 93*
Spencer, Elizabeth Ann 1954- *WhoSSW 93*
Spencer, Emile-Alexis-Xavier 1859-1921 *Baker 92*
Spencer, Eric W. 1930- *WhoE 93*
Spencer, Foster Lewis 1932- *WhoAm 92*
Spencer, Frances Pemberton *AmWomPl*
Spencer, Francis Montgomery James 1943- *WhoSSW 93, WhoWor 93*
Spencer, Frank 1941- *ConAu 139*
Spencer, Frederick Gilman 1925- *WhoAm 92*
Spencer, Greg *BioIn 17*
Spencer, Gregory S. *Law&B 92*
Spencer, Guy J., Jr. 1933- *WhoSSW 93*
Spencer, Harold Edwin 1920- *WhoE 93*
Spencer, Harry Chadwick 1905- *WhoAm 92*
Spencer, Harry Irving, Jr. 1925- *WhoAm 92*
Spencer, Henry Benning 1940- *St&PR 93, WhoAm 92*
Spencer, Herbert 1820-1903 *IntDcAn*
Spencer, Ivan Carlton 1914- *WhoAm 92*
Spencer, Ivan K. 1936- *St&PR 93*
Spencer, J. Greg *Law&B 92*
Spencer, J. Jeffers *Law&B 92*
Spencer, James Darrell *Law&B 92*
Spencer, James LaFayette 1932- *WhoAm 92*
Spencer, James M. 1949- *St&PR 93*
Spencer, James R. *WhoAm 92, WhoSSW 93*
Spencer, James Richardson *WhoWrEP 92*
Spencer, Jane *MiSFD 9*
Spencer, Janet Marie 1955- *WhoSSW 93*
Spencer, Jean W. *WhoWrEP 92*
Spencer, John *BioIn 17*
Spencer, John 1944- *ScF&FL 92*
Spencer, John Andrew 1948- *St&PR 93*
Spencer, John C. 1788-1855 *OxCSupC*
Spencer, John Eaton d1812? *BioIn 17*
Spencer, John Hedley 1933- *WhoAm 92*
Spencer, John Henri 1929- *WhoAm 92*
Spencer, John Lionel *WhoScE 91-1*
Spencer, John Richard 1923- *WhoAm 92*
Spencer, John S. *WhoAm 92*
Spencer, Joyce Ann 1942- *WhoE 93*
Spencer, Judy Shifflett 1947- *WhoAmW 93*
Spencer, Julian Kaj 1946- *St&PR 93*
Spencer, Kara Lynn 1962- *WhoAmW 93*
Spencer, Kathelen V. *St&PR 93*
Spencer, Kathleen 1947- *ScF&FL 92*
Spencer, Kenneth W. 1935- *St&PR 93*
Spencer, Lawrence Jerome, III 1963- *WhoSSW 93*
Spencer, Leonard G. *MajAI*
Spencer, Lewis Douglas 1917- *WhoAm 92*
Spencer, Lilian White *AmWomPl*
Spencer, Lloyd M. 1940- *St&PR 93*
Spencer, Lyman G. *Law&B 92*
Spencer, Mark Morris 1956- *WhoWrEP 92*
Spencer, Mary Eileen 1923- *WhoAm 92*
Spencer, Mary Miller 1924- *WhoAmW 93*
Spencer, Max R. 1921-1990 *BioIn 17*
Spencer, Max R. 1924- *St&PR 93*
Spencer, Melvin Joe 1923- *WhoAm 92*
Spencer, Michael 1936-1990 *BioIn 17*
Spencer, Michael J. *St&PR 93*
Spencer, Milton Harry 1926- *WhoAm 92*
Spencer, Murlin Bertrand 1909- *WhoAm 92*
Spencer, Ollie d1991 *BioIn 17*
Spencer, Ouida J. 1956- *St&PR 93*
Spencer, Patricia Louise 1943- *WhoE 93*
Spencer, Paul Samuel John *WhoScE 91-1*
Spencer, Prince 1917- *BioIn 17*
Spencer, Raine 1929- *BioIn 17*
Spencer, Rebecca Elaine Emily 1919- *WhoAmW 93*
Spencer, Reid C. 1930- *St&PR 93*
Spencer, Richard Henry 1926- *St&PR 93*
Spencer, Richard Paul 1929- *WhoAm 92, WhoE 93*
Spencer, Richard Thomas, III 1936- *WhoSSW 93*
Spencer, Robert C. 1920- *WhoAm 92*
Spencer, Robert Lee 1932- *BiDAMSp 1989*
Spencer, Samuel 1910- *WhoAm 92*
Spencer, Samuel C. 1937- *St&PR 93*
Spencer, Samuel Reid, Jr. 1919- *WhoAm 92, WhoSSW 93*
Spencer, Scott 1945- *ScF&FL 92, WhoAm 92*
Spencer, Sherwood Fredrick 1928- *WhoE 93*
Spencer, Stanley 1891-1959 *BioIn 17*
Spencer, Susan 20th cent.- *JrnUS*
Spencer, Susan Elizabeth 1954- *WhoE 93*
Spencer, Thomas Halsey 1932- *WhoWor 93*
Spencer, Thomas Watson 1929- *St&PR 93*
Spencer, Tracie *BioIn 17*
Spencer, Tricia Jane 1952- *WhoAmW 93*
Spencer, Vaino Hassan 1920- *WhoAm 92*
Spencer, Victor Vance 1924- *St&PR 93*
Spencer, W. E. 1937- *WhoSSW 93*
Spencer, Walter A., Jr. 1950- *St&PR 93*
Spencer, Walter Eugene 1937- *St&PR 93*
Spencer, Wayne Dennis 1940- *St&PR 93*
Spencer, William A. 1922- *WhoAm 92*
Spencer, William Alva 1947- *St&PR 93*
Spencer, William Courtney 1919- *WhoAm 92*
Spencer, William Franklin, Sr. 1923- *WhoAm 92*
Spencer, William H. 1940- *St&PR 93*
Spencer, William Micajah, III 1920- *St&PR 93, WhoAm 92*
Spencer-Churchill, Charles James 1955- *BioIn 17*
Spencer-Green, George Thomas 1946- *WhoE 93*
Spencer Smith, David *WhoScE 91-1*
Spender, Barry *BioIn 17*
Spender, John A. 1862-1942 *BioIn 17*
Spender, John Michael 1935- *WhoAsAP 91*
Spender, Stephen 1909- *BioIn 17, BritWr S2*
Spender, Stephen K. 1909- *WhoWor 93*
Spendiarov, Alexander (Afanasii) 1871-1928 *Baker 92*
Spener, Friedrich 1939- *WhoScE 91-3*
Spengler, Dan M. 1941- *WhoAm 92*
Spengler, John Edward 1933- *St&PR 93*
Spengler, Joseph John 1902-1991 *BioIn 17*
Spengler, Silas 1930- *St&PR 93*
Spenny, Louise Virginia 1937- *WhoAmW 93*
Spenser, Edmund c. 1552-1599 *MagSWL [port], WorLitC [port]*
Spenser, Ian Daniel 1924- *WhoAm 92*
Spera, Johnna Sorg *Law&B 92*
Spera, Peter Joseph 1946- *WhoSSW 93*
Sperakis, Nicholas George 1943- *WhoAm 92, WhoE 93*
Sperandio, Glen Joseph 1918- *WhoAm 92*
Speranza, Ernest V. 1946- *St&PR 93*

Speranza, George Phillip 1924- WhoSSW 93
Speranza, Leo S. 1936- St&PR 93
Speranza, Paul S. Law&B 92
Speranzella, Charles Joseph, Jr. Law&B 92
Speratti Pinero, Emma Susana 1919- DcMexL
Sperber, Daniel 1930- WhoAm 92, WhoE 93, WhoWor 93
Sperber, James 1929- WhoE 93
Sperber, Jerome M. Law&B 92
Sperber, Manes 1905-1984 BioIn 17
Sperber, Martin 1931- WhoAm 92
Sperber, Matthew Arnold 1938- WhoSSW 93
Sperber, Perry 1931- St&PR 93
Sperber, Robert Irwin 1929- WhoE 93
Sperber, Wendie Jo BioIn 17
Sperber, William H. 1933- St&PR 93
Sperelakis, Nicholas 1930- WhoAm 92, WhoWor 93
Sperger, John M. 1950- St&PR 93
Sperlich, Diether 1929- WhoScE 91-3
Sperlich, Harold Keith 1929- WhoAm 92
Sperling, Alan M. Law&B 92
Sperling, Allan George 1942- WhoAm 92, WhoE 93
Sperling, Andrew Nathan Law&B 92
Sperling, Dan 1949- BioIn 17
Sperling, Daniel Lee 1949- WhoE 93
Sperling, Elliot Harris 1951- WhoAm 92
Sperling, George WhoAm 92
Sperling, George Elmer, Jr. 1915- WhoAm 92
Sperling, George Joseph 1945- St&PR 93
Sperling, Godfrey, Jr. 1915- WhoAm 92
Sperling, Lee Todd Law&B 92
Sperling, Louis J. Law&B 92
Sperling, Mindy Toby 1954- WhoE 93
Sperling, Robert B. Law&B 92
Spero, Donald J. Law&B 92
Spero, Joan E. 1944- St&PR 93
Spero, Joan Edelman 1944- WhoAm 92, WhoAmW 93
Spero, Leslie Wayne 1926- WhoAm 92, WhoWor 93
Spero, Mitchell E. 1958- WhoSSW 93
Spero, Stanley L. 1919- St&PR 93
Spero, Stanley Leonard 1919- WhoAm 92, WhoWor 93
Sperontes 1705-1750 Baker 92
Sperr, Martin 1944- DcLB 124 [port]
Sperrazza, Augustine J. 1941- St&PR 93
Sperrazza, Barbara 1949- St&PR 93
Sperry, Ann Elizabeth 1954- WhoSSW 93
Sperry, Armstrong W. 1897-1976 MajAI [port]
Sperry, Elwood G. 1926- St&PR 93
Sperry, James Edward 1936- WhoAm 92
Sperry, John Reginald 1924- WhoAm 92
Sperry, Michael Winton 1946- St&PR 93, WhoAm 92
Sperry, Paul 1934- Baker 92
Sperry, Ralph A. 1944- ScF&FL 92
Sperry, Roger Wolcott 1913- WhoAm 92, WhoWor 93, WhoWrEP 92
Sperry, Ronald Earl 1942- St&PR 93
Sperry, Victoria B. 1943- WhoAmW 93
Sperry, Warren M. 1900-1990 BioIn 17
Sperry, William Elliott 1930- St&PR 93
Spertell, Alayne 1934- WhoE 93
Sperti, George Speri 1900-1991 BioIn 17
Spertus, Philip 1934- St&PR 93
Sperzel, George Edward 1951- St&PR 93
Spessard, John Emory 1931- WhoSSW 93
Spessivtseva, Olga 1895-1991 AnObit 1991, BioIn 17
Speth, Gerald Lennus 1934- WhoWor 93
Speth, James Gustave 1942- WhoAm 92
Speth, Josef 1938- WhoScE 91-3
Spetrino, Russell John 1926- St&PR 93, WhoAm 92
Spett, Kenneth Mark 1952- St&PR 93
Spetter, Barry Herbert 1947- WhoE 93
Spetzler, Hartmut A. W. 1939- WhoAm 92
Spetzler, Robert F. 1944- BioIn 17
Spevacek, Jennifer Jeanene 1961- WhoE 93
Spevack, Marvin 1927- WhoAm 92
Spevak, Irving Bertram 1917- WhoE 93
Spevak, Teryl A. 1951- WhoWrEP 92
Spewack, Bella 1899-1990 BioIn 17
Spewack, Bella Cohen 1899- AmWomPl
Speyer, Edward 1839-1934 See Speyer, Wilhelm 1790-1878 Baker 92
Speyer, Jason Lee 1938- WhoAm 92
Speyer, Jerry I. BioIn 17
Speyer, Jerry I. 1940- St&PR 93
Speyer, Leonora von Stosch 1872-1956 AmWomPl
Speyer, Sharon S. Law&B 92
Speyer, Wilhelm 1790-1878 Baker 92
Speyrer, Jude 1929- WhoAm 92, WhoSSW 93
Speziale, A. John 1916- WhoAm 92
Speziale, Charles Gregory 1948- WhoSSW 93
Speziale, John Albert 1922- WhoAm 92
Spezio, Carl P. 1945- St&PR 93
Spezzano, Roy D. 1944- St&PR 93
Spezzano, Sheila St&PR 93
Spezzano, Vincent Edward 1926- WhoAm 92, WhoE 93
Sphar, Gail Ellen 1946- WhoAmW 93
Sphar, Joe Dee 1941- St&PR 93
Sphar, Lisa Ann 1967- WhoE 93
Sphar, Raymond Leslie, Jr. 1934- WhoE 93
Spheeris, Andrew Miltiades 1916- St&PR 93
Spheeris, Penelope BioIn 17
Spheeris, Penelope 1945- MiSFD 9, WhoAm 92
Sphire, Raymond Daniel 1927- WhoAm 92
Sphon, Richard J. 1937- St&PR 93
Sphrantzes, George 1401-1477? OxDcByz
Spialek, Hans 1894-1983 Baker 92
Spice, Dennis Dean 1950- WhoEmL 93
Spice, John Overstreet 1931- St&PR 93
Spicer, Anthony J. 1929- St&PR 93
Spicer, Carol Inglis 1907- WhoAmW 93
Spicer, Debra A. Law&B 92
Spicer, Dorothy ScF&FL 92
Spicer, Dorothy Gladys AmWomPl
Spicer, Edward Holland 1906-1983 BioIn 17, IntDcAn
Spicer, Eric 1962- WhoWor 93
Spicer, Erik John 1926- WhoAm 92
Spicer, Haden 1923- BioIn 17
Spicer, Harold Reginald WhoScE 91-1
Spicer, Holt Vandercook 1928- WhoAm 92
Spicer, Jack 1925-1965 ConLC 72 [port]
Spicer, Keith BioIn 17
Spicer, Laura Katherine 1963- WhoAmW 93
Spicer, Marcella H. 1920- WhoWrEP 92
Spicer, Mary Ann Law&B 92
Spicer, Michael 1943- ScF&FL 92
Spicer, Philip M. 1937- St&PR 93
Spicer, Robert J. 1936- WhoIns 93
Spicer, Ross H. 1926- St&PR 93
Spicer, Stella Rochelle 1961- WhoAmW 93
Spicer, Virden Gerome, Jr. 1959- WhoSSW 93
Spicer, William Ambrose 1866-1952 BioIn 17
Spicer, William Edward, III 1929- WhoAm 92
Spicer, Wm. V. 1932- St&PR 93
Spicer-Brooks, Marianna Chase 1951- WhoE 93
Spicher, Julia ConAu 139
Spicher, Ulrich 1947- WhoScE 91-3
Spicka, Richard 1936- St&PR 93
Spicker, Max 1858-1912 Baker 92
Spickerman, William Reed 1925- WhoSSW 93
Spickert, Charles P. 1954- St&PR 93
Spicola, James R. 1930-1991 BioIn 17
Spicola, Joseph G., Jr. Law&B 92
Spidel, John W. 1937- St&PR 93
Spiegel, Allen D. 1927- WhoE 93
Spiegel, Allen D(avid) 1927- ConAu 139
Spiegel, Ann Law&B 92
Spiegel, Arthur Henry, III 1939- WhoAm 92
Spiegel, Barry J. St&PR 93, WhoIns 93
Spiegel, Bernard Herbert 1924- St&PR 93
Spiegel, Burton 1944- St&PR 93
Spiegel, Evelyn Sclufer 1924- WhoAmW 93
Spiegel, Francis H. 1935- St&PR 93
Spiegel, Francis Herman, Jr. 1935- WhoAm 92
Spiegel, Frederick Michael 1939- St&PR 93
Spiegel, Gary Mitchel Law&B 92
Spiegel, George 1924- St&PR 93
Spiegel, Hart Hunter 1918- WhoAm 92
Spiegel, Herbert 1914- WhoAm 92, WhoWor 93
Spiegel, Jayson Leslie 1959- WhoE 93, WhoEmL 93, WhoWor 93
Spiegel, John E. 1929- St&PR 93
Spiegel, John P. 1911-1991 BioIn 17
Spiegel, John William 1941- St&PR 93, WhoAm 92
Spiegel, Joseph 1928- St&PR 93
Spiegel, Kathleen Marie 1948- WhoAmW 93
Spiegel, Kathleen Muriel 1949- WhoAmW 93
Spiegel, Laurie 1945- Baker 92
Spiegel, Lawrence Howard 1942- WhoAm 92
Spiegel, Leo 1924- St&PR 93
Spiegel, Marilyn Harriet 1935- WhoAmW 93
Spiegel, Melvin 1925- WhoAm 92
Spiegel, Modie Joseph 1901-1990 BioIn 17
Spiegel, Phil 1917- St&PR 93
Spiegel, Rene 1943- WhoWor 93
Spiegel, S. Arthur 1920- WhoAm 92
Spiegel, Scott MiSFD 9
Spiegel, Sharon Baron 1946- WhoAmW 93
Spiegel, Stanley 1925- WhoE 93
Spiegel, Steven Law&B 92
Spiegel, Susan 1953- WhoAm 92
Spiegel, Wolfgang 1944- WhoWor 93
Spiegelberg, Eldora Haskell 1915- WhoAmW 93
Spiegelberg, Herbert 1904-1990 BioIn 17
Spiegelhalder, Eric A. 1910- St&PR 93
Spiegelman, Art 1948- Au&Arts 10 [port], WhoAm 92
Spiegelman, James Michael 1958- WhoE 93
Spiegelman, Joel (Warren) 1933- Baker 92
Spiegelman, Robert Law&B 92
Spiegler, Morris BioIn 17
Spiekerman, James Frederick 1933- WhoAm 92
Spiekhout, Ronald L. 1939- St&PR 93
Spielberg, Julie Law&B 92
Spielberg, Peter 1929- WhoWrEP 92
Spielberg, Steven NewYTBS 92 [port]
Spielberg, Steven 1947- BioIn 17, ConTFT 10, MiSFD 9, ScF&FL 92, WhoAm 92
Spieler, Francis Joseph 1943- WhoWrEP 92
Spielfogel, Kenneth Law&B 92
Spielhagen, Frances Rose 1946- WhoAmW 93
Spielholtz, Gerald I. 1937- WhoE 93
Spielman, Andrew Ian 1950- WhoWor 93
Spielman, Barbara Helen New 1929- WhoSSW 93
Spielman, Chris 1965- WhoAm 92
Spielman, David Vernon 1929- WhoSSW 93
Spielman, Edgar E., III Law&B 92
Spielman, Patrick E. 1936- WhoWrEP 92
Spielman, Richard Saul 1946- WhoE 93
Spielman, Robert M. Law&B 92
Spielmann, Gunter WhoScE 91-4
Spielmann, Solveig Bjorke 1943- WhoE 93
Spielvogel, Carl St&PR 93
Spielvogel, Carl 1928- WhoAm 92, WhoE 93
Spielvogel, Sidney Meyer 1925- WhoAm 92
Spier, Anthony Samuel 1944- WhoAm 92
Spier, Guy Selmar 1966- WhoWor 93
Spier, Jerome Bertram 1928- St&PR 93, WhoAm 92
Spier, Juliann Ruppel 1962- WhoSSW 93
Spier, Leslie 1893-1961 IntDcAn
Spier, Luise Emma 1928- WhoAmW 93
Spier, Peggy A. Law&B 92
Spier, Peter (Edward) 1927- MajAI [port]
Spier, Raymond Eric WhoScE 91-1
Spierer, Lisa BioIn 17
Spiering, Frank 1946- ScF&FL 92
Spiering, Maria Susanna O. Law&B 92
Spiering, Nancy Jean 1958- WhoAmW 93, WhoEmL 93
Spierings, Walter Christianus 1956- WhoWor 93
Spiero, Francois 1964- WhoWor 93
Spiers, D.M. WhoScE 91-1
Spiers, Ronald Ian 1925- WhoAm 92, WhoUN 92
Spiers, William Kesler, Jr. 1957- WhoSSW 93
Spiertz, J.H.J. 1941- WhoScE 91-3
Spies, Claudio 1925- Baker 92, WhoAm 92
Spies, Dennis J. 1941- WhoSSW 93
Spies, Hermine 1857-1893 Baker 92
Spies, Jacob John 1931- WhoSSW 93, WhoWor 93
Spies, Leo 1899-1965 Baker 92
Spies, Peter Paul 1939- WhoScE 91-3
Spies, Philip T. 1946- St&PR 93
Spies, Phyllis Bova 1949- WhoAmW 93
Spies, Robert J. St&PR 93
Spies, Robert M. Law&B 92
Spies, Tom A. 1935- St&PR 93
Spies, Wayne Thomas 1953- WhoE 93
Spiess, Ernst 1930- WhoScE 91-4
Spiess, Fred Noel 1919- WhoAm 92
Spiess, Gary A. Law&B 92
Spiess, Gary A. 1940- St&PR 93
Spiess, Hans Wolfgang 1942- WhoScE 91-3, WhoWor 93
Spiess, Heinz 1920- WhoWor 93
Spiess, Joachim WhoScE 91-3
Spiess, John Edward 1920- St&PR 93
Spiess, Meinrad 1683-1761 Baker 92
Spiess, Priscilla Joice 1926- St&PR 93
Spiess, Robert Clayton 1921- WhoWrEP 92
Spiewak, Gerald Jack 1926- St&PR 93
Spiewak, Michael I. 1951- St&PR 93
Spiewak, Philip d1991 BioIn 17
Spiewak, Robert Louis 1922- St&PR 93
Spiewakowski, Eugeniusz Ryszard 1928- WhoScE 91-4
Spiezio, James Mark 1948- St&PR 93
Spigai, Daniel J. 1933- St&PR 93
Spigarelli, James L. 1941- St&PR 93
Spigel, Lynn ScF&FL 92
Spigler, Linda Jo 1947- WhoAmW 93
Spignesi, Stephen 1953- ScF&FL 92
Spike, Marvin St&PR 93
Spiker, Elliott Cedric 1946- WhoSSW 93
Spiker, Joan E. 1945- WhoAmW 93
Spiker, William T. 1947- St&PR 93
Spikerman, Richard C. 1940- St&PR 93, WhoAm 92
Spikes, Dolores R. WhoAmW 93, WhoSSW 93
Spikes-Wilson, Susan Law&B 92
Spikings, Barry Peter 1939- WhoAm 92
Spikol, Art 1936- WhoAm 92
Spikowski, William Michael 1950- WhoSSW 93
Spilchen, William St&PR 93
Spilhaus, Athelstan 1911- WhoAm 92
Spilhaus, Karl Henry 1946- WhoAm 92, WhoE 93
Spiliotopoulos, Epaminonas 1925- WhoWor 93
Spilka, Frantisek 1887-1960 Baker 92
Spilka, Karen Eileen Law&B 92
Spilka, Leonard S. 1945- St&PR 93
Spilka, Mark 1925- WhoAm 92, WhoWrEP 92
Spilker, H. Larry Law&B 92
Spilker, James Julius, Jr. 1933- St&PR 93
Spill, Frank 1938- St&PR 93
Spillane, Brian B. 1936- St&PR 93
Spillane, Mary Catherine 1956- WhoEmL 93
Spillane, Mickey WhoWrEP 92
Spillane, Mickey 1918- BioIn 17, WhoAm 92
Spillane, Robert Thomas 1942- St&PR 93
Spillane, Stephen Andrew 1955- WhoE 93
Spillane, Todd L. Law&B 92
Spillard, E.J. 1939- St&PR 93
Spillard, Ernest John 1939- WhoAm 92
Spillard, Sarah V. AmWomPl
Spillecke, Frank Heinz 1953- WhoWor 93
Spiller, Callie Cline, Jr. 1944- WhoAm 92
Spiller, Eberhard Adolf 1933- WhoAm 92
Spiller, Ellen Brubaker 1932- WhoSSW 93
Spiller, Henry Alfred LaGrandeur 1954- WhoE 93
Spiller, Jeanette M. 1952- St&PR 93
Spiller, Monica Alton 1938- WhoAmW 93
Spiller, Scott L. Law&B 92
Spiller, Scott L. 1951- St&PR 93
Spiller, Warren Logan 1947- St&PR 93
Spillers, Helen Hyatt 1927- WhoAmW 93
Spillers, Karen Erks 1960- St&PR 93
Spillers, William Russell 1934- WhoAm 92
Spillman, Gordon E. 1947- St&PR 93
Spillman, Jane Shadel 1942- WhoAm 92
Spillman, John Henry 1940- St&PR 93
Spillman, Marjorie Rose WhoAmW 93, WhoE 93
Spillman, Ray A. Law&B 92
Spillmann, Kurt Robert 1937- WhoWor 93
Spillsbury, Julian ScF&FL 92
Spilman, Charles B. 1951- St&PR 93
Spilman, Harry 1954- BioIn 17
Spilman, Raymond 1911- WhoAm 92, WhoE 93
Spilman, Richard Stuart 1946- WhoSSW 93
Spilman, Robert Henkel 1927- St&PR 93, WhoAm 92, WhoSSW 93
Spilman, Timothy Frank 1961- WhoWor 93
Spilner, Maggie L. 1952- WhoE 93
Spina, Anthony WhoAm 92
Spina, Anthony Ferdinand 1937- WhoWor 93
Spina, David Anthony 1942- St&PR 93
Spina, Dennis J. 1944- St&PR 93
Spina, Greye La ScF&FL 92
Spina, P. WhoScE 91-3
Spinaci, Sergio 1951- WhoUN 92
Spinadel, Erico Alfredo 1929- WhoWor 93
Spinadel, Vera Winitzky de 1929- WhoWor 93
Spinal Tap ConMus 8 [port]
Spina-Naranjo, Carolyn R. 1954- WhoAmW 93
Spinar, Donald E. 1948- St&PR 93
Spinas, Otmar 1962- WhoWor 93
Spincic, Wesley James 1945- WhoSSW 93, WhoWor 93
Spindel, Robert Charles 1944- WhoAm 92
Spindel, William 1922- WhoAm 92
Spinden, Herbert Joseph 1879-1967 IntDcAn
Spindle, Eva Louise 1931- WhoAmW 93
Spindler, Evelyn Blanchard BioIn 17
Spindler, Fritz 1817-1905 Baker 92
Spindler, George Dearborn 1920- WhoAm 92
Spindler, George S. Law&B 92, WhoAm 92

Spindler, George S. 1938- St&PR 93
Spindler, Harry Keeler 1929- WhoE 93
Spindler, James W. 1939- St&PR 93
Spindler, John Frederick 1929- WhoAm 92
Spindler, Judith Tarleton 1932- WhoSSW 93
Spindler, Klaus-Dieter 1942- WhoScE 91-3
Spindler, Melvin 1930- St&PR 93
Spindler, Michael H. BioIn 17
Spindler, Paul 1931- WhoAm 92
Spindler, Suzanne Joan 1946- WhoAmW 93, WhoSSW 93
Spinella, Joseph Carl 1925- St&PR 93
Spinelli, Frank 1930- St&PR 93
Spinelli, Jerry 1941- BioIn 17, MajAI [port], SmATA 71 [port], WhoAm 92
Spinelli, Luca Carlo 1955- WhoWor 93
Spinelli, Melissa Ball 1964- WhoAmW 93
Spinelli, Nicola 1865-1909 Baker 92
Spinelli, Vincent John 1947- WhoE 93
Spinetti, Donald A. 1931- St&PR 93
Spingarn, Arthur Barnett 1878-1971 EncAACR
Spingarn, Clifford Leroy 1912- WhoE 93, WhoWor 93
Spingarn, Howard S. d1990 BioIn 17
Spingarn, Joel Elias 1875-1939 BioIn 17
Spingarn, Richard Alan 1951- WhoE 93
Spingern, Lawrence Perreira 1917- WhoWrEP 92
Spink, Frank Henry, Jr. 1935- WhoE 93
Spink, Ian (Walter Alfred) 1932- Baker 92
Spink, Lynn BioIn 17
Spinka, Penina Keen 1945- SmATA 72 [port]
Spinks, David Wayne 1952- WhoEmL 93, WhoWor 93
Spinks, John Lee 1924- WhoAm 92
Spinks, Michael 1956- BiDAMSp 1989, WhoAm 92
Spinks, Nelda Hughes 1928- WhoSSW 93
Spinks, Paul 1922- WhoAm 92
Spinnato, John Michael Law&B 92
Spinner, Allan L. 1930- St&PR 93
Spinner, Bob 1932-1990 Baker 92
Spinner, Carol Johnson 1945- WhoAmW 93
Spinner, Ernest 1944- St&PR 93
Spinner, Leopold 1906-1980 Baker 92
Spinner, Stephanie 1943- ScF&FL 92
Spinner, Werner 1948- St&PR 93
Spinners SoulM
Spinney, Caroll BioIn 17
Spinola, Frank M. St&PR 93
Spinoza, Benedictus de 1632-1677 BioIn 17
Spinrad, Bernard Israel 1924- WhoAm 92
Spinrad, Hyron 1934- WhoAm 92
Spinrad, Norman BioIn 17
Spinrad, Norman 1940- ScF&FL 92
Spinrad, Richard William 1954- WhoSSW 93
Spinrad, Robert Joseph 1932- WhoAm 92
Spiotta, Raymond Herman 1927- WhoAm 92
Spiotto, Ann H. Law&B 92
Spira, Henry BioIn 17
Spira, Israel d1989 BioIn 17
Spira, Joel Solon 1927- St&PR 93
Spira, Melvin 1925- WhoAm 92
Spira, Robert Alan 1932- WhoWor 93
Spira, Robert M. Law&B 92
Spira, Robert S. 1949- WhoE 93
Spirakis, Paul 1955- WhoScE 91-3
Spirakis, Paul George 1955- WhoWor 93
Spire, Hazel Jean 1950- WhoWrEP 92
Spire, Nancy Woodson 1917- WhoAmW 93
Spirer, Herbert Fred 1925- WhoE 93
Spirer, June Dale 1943- WhoAmW 93
Spirer, Kenneth S. Law&B 92
Spirer, Peter Richman 1931- St&PR 93
Spires, Elizabeth 1952- DcLB 120 [port], SmATA 71 [port], WhoWrEP 92
Spires, R. Keith 1939- St&PR 93
Spires, Robert Cecil 1936- WhoAm 92
Spires, Roberta Lynn 1952- WhoAmW 93
Spirgel, Christine Marie 1963- WhoAmW 93
Spiridakis, Tony WhoAm 92
Spiridonova, Mariya Aleksandrovna 1884-1941 BioIn 17
Spirito, Anthony 1953- WhoE 93
Spirn, Michele Sobel 1943- WhoAmW 93
Spiro, Benjamin Paul 1917- WhoAm 92
Spiro, Donald W. St&PR 93, WhoAm 92
Spiro, Gyorgy 1946- BioIn 17
Spiro, Herbert John 1924- WhoAm 92, WhoWor 93
Spiro, Howard Marget 1924- WhoAm 92
Spiro, Jody Donna 1952- WhoE 93
Spiro, Lionel 1939- St&PR 93
Spiro, Melford Elliot 1920- WhoAm 92
Spiro, Robert Gunter 1929- WhoAm 92, WhoE 93
Spiro, Robert Harry, Jr. 1920- WhoAm 92
Spiro, Samuel 1885-1960 BioIn 17
Spiro, Thomas George 1935- WhoAm 92, WhoE 93
Spiro, Walter Anselm 1923- WhoAm 92
Spiroiu, Constantin Niculae 1936- WhoWor 93
Spiros, Andrew Law&B 92
Spirtos, Nicholas George 1950- WhoWor 93
Spisak, Cora Belle 1948- WhoAmW 93
Spisak, Michal 1914-1965 Baker 92
Spisak, Richard Warren, Jr. 1952- WhoSSW 93
Spisak, Sara Louise 1966- WhoAmW 93
Spitaleri, Vito John 1945- WhoSSW 93
Spitalny, Evelyn Klein d1990 BioIn 17
Spitalny, Frank Jay 1929- WhoIns 93
Spitalny, Gloria Diane 1946- WhoAmW 93
Spitalny, Phil(ip) 1889-1970 Baker 92
Spiteller, Gerhard 1931- WhoScE 91-3
Spitler, Denise Ann 1954- St&PR 93
Spitler, Nancy McAlpin 1957- WhoAmW 93
Spitler, Richard W. 1950- St&PR 93
Spitsberg, Vitaly Lev 1938- WhoE 93
Spitsbergen, Dorothy May 1932- WhoAmW 93
Spitsbergen, James C. 1926- WhoE 93
Spitta, (Julius August) Philipp 1841-1894 Baker 92
Spitter, The WhoWrEP 92
Spittle, John Barrie 1944- WhoWor 93
Spittler, Jayne Zenaty 1948- WhoAmW 93
Spitz, Arnold Law&B 92
Spitz, Arnold A. 1914- St&PR 93
Spitz, Arnoldt John 1929- St&PR 93
Spitz, Barbara Salomon 1926- WhoAm 92, WhoAmW 93
Spitz, Charles Alfred 1945- WhoE 93
Spitz, Charles Thomas, Jr. 1921- WhoAm 92
Spitz, Edward A. d1990 BioIn 17
Spitz, Erich 1931- WhoScE 91-2
Spitz, Francois 1932- WhoScE 91-2
Spitz, Herman Heinrich 1925- WhoE 93
Spitz, Hugo Max 1927- WhoSSW 93
Spitz, Jeff Glen 1956- St&PR 93
Spitz, Lewis William 1922- WhoAm 92
Spitz, Mark BioIn 17
Spitz, Robert Irving 1942- WhoE 93
Spitz, Seymour James, Jr. 1921- WhoAm 92
Spitzberg, Irving Joseph, Jr. 1942- WhoAm 92
Spitzberg, Jerrold 1939- St&PR 93
Spitzberg, Larry A. 1944- WhoSSW 93
Spitze, Robert George Frederick 1922- WhoAm 92
Spitzer, Adrian 1927- WhoAm 92
Spitzer, Alexander 1946- St&PR 93
Spitzer, Cary Redford 1937- WhoAm 92, WhoSSW 93
Spitzer, Charles Anthony Law&B 92
Spitzer, David William 1951- WhoE 93
Spitzer, Eric Randolph 1943- WhoE 93
Spitzer, Jack J. 1917- WhoAm 92
Spitzer, John Brumback 1918- WhoAm 92
Spitzer, John J. 1927- WhoAm 92
Spitzer, Josef 1943- WhoScE 91-4
Spitzer, Judy A. 1931- WhoAmW 93
Spitzer, Laura BioIn 17
Spitzer, Lyman, Jr. 1914- WhoAm 92
Spitzer, M. James 1911- St&PR 93
Spitzer, Morton E. 1937- St&PR 93
Spitzer, Neil BioIn 17
Spitzer, Nicholas Canaday 1942- WhoAm 92
Spitzer, Peter George 1956- WhoEmL 93
Spitzer, Robert 1927-1990 BioIn 17
Spitzer, Robert Ralph 1922- WhoAm 92
Spitzer, Scott L. Law&B 92
Spitzer, Scott L. 1951- St&PR 93
Spitzer, Serge BioIn 17
Spitzer, William George 1927- WhoAm 92
Spitzmuller (-Harmersbach), Alexander, Freiherr von 1894-1962 Baker 92
Spitznagel, John Keith 1923- WhoAm 92
Spitznagel, John Keith 1951- WhoSSW 93
Spitznagel, Ronald Joseph 1939- WhoSSW 93
Spitznass, Richard B. 1936- St&PR 93
Spivack, Charlotte 1926- ScF&FL 92
Spivack, Charlotte Ruth 1926- WhoE 93
Spivack, Ellen Sue 1937- WhoWrEP 92
Spivack, Gordon Bernard 1929- WhoAm 92
Spivack, Harvey Marvin 1948- WhoSSW 93
Spivack, Herbert Lenard St&PR 93
Spivack, Joseph 1948- St&PR 93
Spivack, Kathleen 1938- WhoWrEP 92
Spivacke, Harold 1904-1977 Baker 92, BioIn 17
Spivak, Alberto 1936- WhoWor 93
Spivak, Alvin A. 1927- WhoAm 92
Spivak, Charlie 1905-1982 Baker 92
Spivak, Helayne BioIn 17, St&PR 93, WhoAm 92, WhoAmW 93
Spivak, Jacque R. 1929- WhoAmW 93
Spivak, Jerry Lepow 1938- WhoE 93
Spivak, Jonathan M. 1928- WhoAm 92, WhoWor 93
Spivak, Lawrence E. 1906- JrnUS
Spivak, Lawrence Edmund 1900- WhoAm 92
Spivak, Melvin Ezra 1937- WhoWrEP 92
Spivak, Stanley 1940- St&PR 93
Spivak, Steven Mark 1942- WhoE 93
Spivakov, Vladimir 1944- Baker 92
Spivakovsky, Tossy 1907- Baker 92
Spivey, Bruce E. 1934- WhoAm 92
Spivey, Edward Carlyle 1932- St&PR 93
Spivey, Gerald Homer 1937- St&PR 93
Spivey, Nigel ConAu 139
Spivey, Nigel Jonathon 1958- ConAu 139
Spivey, Rex J. Law&B 92
Spivey, Robert Atwood 1931- WhoSSW 93
Spivey, Robert P. 1941- St&PR 93
Spivey, Robert Peterson 1948- WhoSSW 93
Spivey, Sarah E. 1943- WhoSSW 93
Spivey, Shell St&PR 93
Spivey, Suzan Brooks Nisbet 1932- WhoSSW 93
Spivey, Ted Ray 1927- WhoAm 92
Spivy, Samuel Oscar Johnson 1952- WhoWor 93
Spiwak, J. Tracey Law&B 92
Spizer, David Bruce 1955- WhoSSW 93
Spizzirri, Richard Dominic 1933- WhoAm 92
Splain, Charles 1964- St&PR 93
Splain, Francis J., Jr. 1955- WhoIns 93
Splaine, Nancy W. 1959- St&PR 93
Splane, Helen Burnham AmWomPl
Splane, Richard Beverley 1916- WhoAm 92
Splaver, Sarah WhoAmW 93, WhoSSW 93
Splete, Allen Peterjohn 1938- WhoAm 92, WhoE 93
Splete, Marilyn Detweiler 1942- WhoAmW 93
Spletinckx, Christian Adelin 1944- WhoWor 93
Spliethoff, William Ludwig 1926- WhoAm 92
Splinter, Betty Ann M. 1946- St&PR 93
Splinter, William Eldon 1925- WhoAm 92
Splitstone, George Dale 1925- WhoAm 92
Splitt, Frank George 1930- WhoAm 92
Splittstoesser, Walter Emil 1937- WhoAm 92
Splude, John W. 1945- St&PR 93, WhoAm 92
Spochart, Richard L. 1947- St&PR 93
Spock, Benjamin 1903- BioIn 17, NewYTBS 92 [port]
Spock, Benjamin M. 1903- PolPar
Spock, Benjamin McLane 1903- WhoAm 92, WhoWor 93
Spodak, Michael Kenneth 1944- WhoAm 92
Spodark, Edwina 1954- WhoSSW 93
Spodek, Bernard 1931- WhoAm 92
Spodick, David Howard 1927- WhoE 93
Spodick, Pearl Blegen 1927- WhoE 93
Spoegler, Christina Marie 1950- WhoAmW 93
Spoehr, Alexander 1913- WhoAm 92
Spoehr, Alexander 1913-1992 ConAu 139
Spoelstra, Beth E. 1961- WhoE 93
Spoelstra, Thomas A. 1955- St&PR 93
Spoering, Judell 1955- WhoAmW 93
Spoerner, Thomas Willis 1951- WhoSSW 93
Spoerri, Daniel 1930- BioIn 17
Spofford, Charles Merville 1902-1991 BioIn 17
Spofford, Harriet Elizabeth Prescott 1835-1921 AmWomPl
Spofford, Harriet Prescott 1835-1921 ScF&FL 92
Spofford, Robert Houston 1941- WhoAm 92
Spofford, Sally Hyslop 1929- WhoAmW 93, WhoE 93, WhoWor 93
Spofford, William B. 1921- WhoAm 92
Spohler, John 1928- St&PR 93
Spohn, Beatrice Evelyn 1907- WhoAmW 93
Spohn, David 1948- SmATA 72 [port]
Spohn, Herbert Emil 1923- WhoAm 92
Spohn, William Gideon, Jr. 1923- WhoE 93
Spohr, Arnold Theodore 1927- WhoAm 92
Spohr, Louis 1784-1859 Baker 92, OxDcOp
Spohr, Ludewig 1784-1859 IntDcOp
Spohr, P. WhoScE 91-3
Spokane, Earle Jay 1937- WhoAm 92
Spokony, Lawrence 1961- WhoE 93
Spokowski, David C. 1952- St&PR 93
Spolan, Harmon S. 1935- St&PR 93
Spolan, Harmon Samuel 1935- WhoAm 92
Spolan, Suzanne 1963- WhoAmW 93
Spolane, David A. 1954- St&PR 93
Spolestra, Sierk F. 1946- WhoScE 91-3
Spollen, James P. 1932- St&PR 93
Spolton, Roger L. WhoScE 91-1
Spoltoree, Janet Dee 1955- WhoAmW 93
Spolum, Robert N. 1931- St&PR 93
Sponberg, R.T. Law&B 92
Sponemann, Jurgen 1931- WhoScE 91-3
Spong, Douglas Kevin 1959- St&PR 93
Spong, John Shelby BioIn 17
Spong, John Shelby 1931- WhoAm 92
Spong, Richard C. 1942- St&PR 93
Spong, William Belser, Jr. 1920- WhoAm 92
Sponholz, Joseph G. 1944- St&PR 93
Sponholz, Joseph Gerald 1944- WhoAm 92
Sponseller, Mary Ann 1955- St&PR 93, WhoSSW 93
Sponseller, Robert W. 1933- St&PR 93
Sponsler, George Curtis, III 1927- WhoAm 92
Sponsler, James R. 1934- St&PR 93
Spontini, Gaspare 1774-1851 IntDcOp, OxDcOp
Spontini, Gaspare (Luigi Pacifico) 1774-1851 Baker 92
Spoo, Robert Edward 1957- WhoSSW 93
Spoon, Alan G. 1951- St&PR 93
Spoon, Alan Gary 1951- WhoAm 92
Spoon, Bruce P. Law&B 92
Spoonauer, John W. 1948- WhoIns 93
Spooner, Bernard Myrick 1934- WhoSSW 93
Spooner, Elaine Margaret 1952- WhoAmW 93
Spooner, Forrest Allen 1941- St&PR 93
Spooner, J.B. 1932- WhoScE 91-1
Spooner, Janice Sue 1946- WhoAmW 93
Spooner, Larry Walter 1939- St&PR 93
Spooner, Linda Greer 1950- WhoAm 92
Spooner, Mark Jordan 1945- WhoAm 92
Spooner, Nancy L. 1954- St&PR 93
Spooner, Neil John Curwen 1960- WhoWor 93
Spooner, Richard 1944- St&PR 93
Spooner, Robert Bruce 1920- WhoE 93
Spoonhour, James Michael 1946- WhoSSW 93
Spoor, Daniel Richard 1956- St&PR 93
Spoor, John Edward 1935- WhoE 93
Spoor, Roger BioIn 17
Spoor, Thomas Richard 1934- WhoAm 92
Spoor, William WhoScE 91-1
Spoor, William Howard 1923- St&PR 93, WhoAm 92
Spoorenberg, Erna 1926- Baker 92
Spoorenberg, P.M. 1959- WhoScE 91-3
Sporck, Charles E. BioIn 17
Sporck, Charles E. 1927- St&PR 93, WhoAm 92
Sporck, Georges 1870-1943 Baker 92
Spore, Gerald Arthur 1932- St&PR 93
Spores, Ronald Marvin 1931- WhoAm 92
Sporkin, Stanley 1932- CngDr 91, WhoAm 92
Sporleder, Audrey Law&B 92
Sporleder, Dale E. 1940- St&PR 93
Sporleder, Dale Ernest Law&B 92
Sporleder, James G. Law&B 92
Sporn, Judith Beryl 1951- WhoAmW 93
Sporn, Lee Stuart Law&B 92
Sporn, Stanley R. 1928- St&PR 93
Sporn, Stanley Robert 1928- WhoAm 92
Spors, Karen E. Law&B 92
Sport, Haywood M. 1937- St&PR 93
Sporton, T.M. WhoScE 91-1
Sposato, Anthony J. 1927- St&PR 93
Sposato, Charles Gabriel, Jr. 1927- WhoAm 92
Sposato, Paul A. 1952- St&PR 93
Spota, Luis 1925- DcMexL
Spoto, Angelo Peter, Jr. 1933- WhoSSW 93
Spoto, Donald 1941- WhoAm 92
Spottiswoode, Roger MiSFD 9
Spotts, Bonnie Walp 1960- WhoWrEP 92
Spotts, George R. 1922- St&PR 93
Spottswood, Curran 1943- St&PR 93
Spoturno, Francesco Giuseppe 1874-1934 BioIn 17
Spotz, James D. 1946- St&PR 93
Spowart, Jay R. 1955- St&PR 93
Spraberry, Carol Ann 1945- WhoSSW 93
Spracker, Marilyn S. Law&B 92
Spracklen, Charles Timothy WhoScE 91-1
Spradley, A. John 1853-1940 BioIn 17
Spradlin, G. D. MiSFD 9
Spradlin, Joseph Edgar 1941- WhoE 93
Spraetz, Kenneth M. 1937- St&PR 93
Sprafkin, Robert Peter 1940- WhoE 93
Spragens, Thomas Arthur 1917- WhoAm 92
Spragens, William Clark 1925- WhoSSW 93

Spragg, Howard E. 1917-1991 *BioIn 17*
Spraggins, Alethia Lucille 1938- *WhoAmW 93*
Spraggins, James Carleton *WhoSSW 93*
Spraggins, Thomas Wayne 1937- *St&PR 93*
Sprague, Alan Peter 1942- *WhoSSW 93*
Sprague, Alice *ScF&FL 92*
Sprague, B. Allan 1946- *WhoWor 93*
Sprague, Brenda Lee 1953- *WhoWrEP 92*
Sprague, Charles Cameron 1916- *WhoAm 92*
Sprague, Claire 1926- *ScF&FL 92*
Sprague, Clifford G. 1943- *St&PR 93*
Sprague, Clifton Albert Furlow 1896-1955 *HarEnMi*
Sprague, David Wayne 1958- *WhoE 93*
Sprague, Donald L. 1932- *St&PR 93*
Sprague, E. Sue *Law&B 92*
Sprague, Edward Auchincloss 1932- *WhoAm 92*
Sprague, Forrest Raymond 1929- *St&PR 93*
Sprague, Gretchen (Burnham) 1926- *DcAmChF 1960*
Sprague, James B. 1942- *WhoSSW 93*
Sprague, James C. 1946- *St&PR 93*
Sprague, James Darrell 1933- *WhoSSW 93*
Sprague, James Mather 1916- *WhoAm 92*
Sprague, Jerry Ronald 1948- *WhoSSW 93*
Sprague, John Louis 1930- *St&PR 93, WhoAm 92*
Sprague, Mary L. *WhoIns 93*
Sprague, Milton Alan 1914- *WhoAm 92*
Sprague, Norman Frederick, Jr. 1914- *WhoAm 92, WhoWor 93*
Sprague, Peter Julian 1939- *WhoAm 92*
Sprague, Raymond 1947- *WhoSSW 93*
Sprague, Robert Chapman 1900-1991 *BioIn 17*
Sprague, Robert Walter *Law&B 92*
Sprague, Sharon *BioIn 17*
Sprague, Susan Marie 1949- *WhoAmW 93*
Sprague, Thomas Lamison 1894-1972 *HarEnMi*
Sprague, Vance Glover, Jr. 1941- *WhoWor 93*
Sprague, W.W., Jr. 1926- *St&PR 93*
Sprague, William D. *Law&B 92*
Sprague, William Douglas 1941- *WhoAm 92*
Sprague, William E. 1923- *WhoAm 92*
Sprague, William Leigh 1938- *WhoWrEP 92*
Sprague, William Wallace 1913- *WhoAm 92*
Sprague, William Wallace, Jr. 1926- *WhoAm 92, WhoSSW 93*
Spraker, Harold Stephen 1929- *WhoSSW 93*
Sprang, Milton LeRoy 1944- *WhoAm 92*
Spranger, Hanno W. 1935- *St&PR 93*
Spranger, Jurgen 1931- *WhoScE 91-3*
Sprangers, John C. *Law&B 92*
Spransy, Joseph W. *Law&B 92*
Spratford, Kenneth Michael 1951- *St&PR 93*
Spratlan, Lewis 1940- *Baker 92*
Spratlin, Rebecca W. 1955- *St&PR 93*
Spratt, John Arthur 1954- *WhoSSW 93*
Spratt, John M., Jr. 1942- *CngDr 91*
Spratt, John McKee, Jr. 1942- *WhoAm 92, WhoSSW 93*
Spratt, Lalla Lee 1912- *St&PR 93*
Spratt, Mercedes 1957- *WhoAmW 93*
Spratt, Robert Leonard 1951- *WhoE 93*
Sprawka, Gregory 1950- *St&PR 93*
Spray, J. Russell 1947- *St&PR 93*
Spray, Paul 1921- *WhoAm 92, WhoSSW 93, WhoWor 93*
Sprayregen, Joel Jay 1934- *WhoAm 92*
Spreadbury, Ray *WhoScE 91-1*
Spreafico, Federico 1940- *WhoScE 91-3*
Sprecher, David A. 1930- *WhoAm 92*
Sprecher, Gustav Ewald 1922- *WhoWor 93*
Sprecher, Rose *St&PR 93*
Sprecher, William Gunther 1924- *WhoE 93, WhoWor 93*
Sprechman, J.R. *ScF&FL 92*
Spreckley, Colin *BioIn 17*
Spreen, Dieter 1947- *WhoWor 93*
Spreen, Wesley Eugene 1947- *WhoWor 93*
Spreiregen, Paul David 1931- *WhoAm 92*
Spreiter, John Robert 1921- *WhoAm 92*
Spreng, Manfred P.J. 1936- *WhoScE 91-3*
Sprengeler, Donald A. 1940- *St&PR 93*
Sprenger, Charles Everett 1955- *St&PR 93*
Sprenger, Gordon M. 1937- *WhoAm 92*
Sprenger, Thomas Robert 1931- *WhoSSW 93*
Sprengle, E. Carl 1930- *St&PR 93*
Sprengler-Ruppenthal, Anneliese Brunhilde 1923- *WhoWor 93*
Sprenkle, Case Middleton 1934- *WhoAm 92*
Sprent, Janet Irene *WhoScE 91-1*
Spresser, Mark A. 1950- *St&PR 93*
Sprieser, John R. 1947- *St&PR 93*
Spriestersbach, Duane Caryl 1916- *WhoAm 92*
Spriet, Jan A.J.L. 1950- *WhoScE 91-2*
Spriggs, Dillard P. 1926- *St&PR 93*
Spriggs, Everett Lee 1930- *WhoWor 93*
Spriggs, James A. 1934- *St&PR 93*
Spriggs, Richard Moore 1931- *WhoAm 92*
Spriggs, Robert Paul 1932- *St&PR 93*
Spring, Agnes Wright 1894- *AmWomPl*
Spring, Arthur Thomas 1935- *WhoAm 92*
Spring, Bernard Polmer 1927- *WhoAm 92*
Spring, David J. 1944- *WhoScE 91-1*
Spring, Dean William 1951- *WhoE 93*
Spring, Dee 1934- *WhoAmW 93*
Spring, Dick 1950- *WhoWor 93*
Spring, Gary Stephen 1953- *WhoSSW 93*
Spring, John Benham 1936- *WhoAm 92*
Spring, L. John *BioIn 17*
Spring, Michael 1941- *WhoAm 92*
Spring, Molly A. 1963- *WhoAmW 93*
Spring, Raymond Lewis 1932- *WhoAm 92*
Spring, Robert Harry *Law&B 92*
Spring, Samuel Newton 1927- *St&PR 93*
Spring, Stanley Lloyde 1942- *WhoSSW 93, WhoWor 93*
Springborn, Robert C. 1929- *St&PR 93*
Springer, Alfred *WhoScE 91-4*
Springer, Anthony *BioIn 17*
Springer, Bessie Wreford *AmWomPl*
Springer, Carol *WhoAmW 93*
Springer, Carolyn Mae 1959- *WhoE 93*
Springer, Charles Edward 1928- *WhoAm 92*
Springer, Clyde H. *St&PR 93*
Springer, Colby H. 1947- *St&PR 93*
Springer, Denis E. 1946- *St&PR 93*
Springer, Douglas D. 1950- *St&PR 93*
Springer, Douglas Hyde 1927- *WhoAm 92*
Springer, Edwin Kent 1912- *WhoAm 92*
Springer, Fleta Campbell *AmWomPl*
Springer, Fred Charles *Law&B 92*
Springer, George Stephen 1933- *WhoAm 92*
Springer, Gerard K. *St&PR 93*
Springer, Gustav *BioIn 17*
Springer, Hugh *DcCPCAm*
Springer, Hugh Worreil 1913- *WhoWor 93*
Springer, James T. 1951- *St&PR 93*
Springer, Jeffrey Alan 1950- *WhoWor 93*
Springer, Jeffrey R. 1944- *St&PR 93*
Springer, Jerry M. 1932- *St&PR 93, WhoAm 92*
Springer, John Kelley 1931- *WhoAm 92*
Springer, John Shipman 1916- *WhoAm 92*
Springer, Jorn 1957- *WhoWor 93*
Springer, Karl *BioIn 17*
Springer, Karl Josef 1935- *St&PR 93, WhoAm 92*
Springer, Katherine Curtis 1943- *WhoUN 92*
Springer, Kenneth S. 1953- *St&PR 93*
Springer, Margaret Ann 1941- *WhoWrEP 92*
Springer, Marilyn *ScF&FL 92*
Springer, Max 1877-1954 *Baker 92*
Springer, Michael Louis 1938- *WhoAm 92*
Springer, Nancy *BioIn 17*
Springer, Nancy 1948- *ScF&FL 92*
Springer, Nancy Connor 1948- *WhoWrEP 92*
Springer, Nathaniel E., Jr. 1928- *St&PR 93*
Springer, Neil A. 1938- *St&PR 93*
Springer, Neil Allen 1938- *WhoAm 92*
Springer, Nesha Bass 1930-1990 *BioIn 17*
Springer, Paul D. *Law&B 92*
Springer, Paul D. 1942- *St&PR 93*
Springer, Paul David 1942- *WhoAm 92*
Springer, Robert *St&PR 93*
Springer, Robert Coleman, III 1945- *WhoE 93*
Springer, Robert Dale 1933- *WhoAm 92*
Springer, Sally Pearl 1947- *WhoWor 93*
Springer, Stanley G. 1927- *WhoAm 92*
Springer, Timothy Alan 1948- *WhoE 93*
Springer, Wayne Gilbert 1951- *WhoEmL 93, WhoSSW 93*
Springer, William H. 1929- *WhoAm 92*
Springer, William Henry 1929- *St&PR 93*
Springett, Brian Edward 1936- *WhoE 93*
Springfield, Dan R., III 1951- *St&PR 93*
Springfield, James F. *Law&B 92*
Springfield, James F. 1929- *St&PR 93*
Springfield, James Francis 1929- *WhoAm 92*
Springfield, Rick 1949- *ConMus 9 [port]*
Springford, Michael *WhoScE 91-1*
Springford, Michael 1936- *WhoWor 93*
Springle, Franklin Lee 1944- *WhoSSW 93*
Springman, Paul W. 1951- *WhoIns 93*
Springmann, Douglas Mandel, Jr. 1941- *WhoSSW 93*
Springmier, Robert Samuel 1928- *St&PR 93*
Springob, H. Karl 1930- *WhoE 93*
Springorum, D. *WhoScE 91-3*
Spring Rice, Cecil 1859-1918 *BioIn 17*
Springs, Darryl M. *Law&B 92*
Springstead, Ralph E. 1925- *St&PR 93*
Springsteen, Bruce *BioIn 17, NewYTBS 92*
Springsteen, Bruce 1949- *Baker 92, CurBio 92 [port], WhoAm 92*
Springsteen, Evan James *BioIn 17*
Springsteen, George Stoney, Jr. 1923- *WhoAm 92*
Springsteen, R.G. (Bud) 1904-1989 *MiSFD 9N*
Springstein, Karl-August Hermann 1918- *WhoWor 93*
Springston, Dan *BioIn 17*
Springston, James Raymond 1947- *WhoE 93*
Sprinkel, Beryl Wayne 1923- *WhoAm 92*
Sprinkle, Edward 1923- *BiDAMSp 1989*
Sprinkle, Myriam Goldsmith 1933- *St&PR 93*
Sprinkle, Robert Marshall 1936- *WhoE 93*
Sprinkle, Robert Shields, III 1935- *St&PR 93*
Sprinson, David Benjamin 1910- *WhoAm 92*
Sprinthall, Norman Arthur 1931- *WhoAm 92*
Sprinzak, Ehud 1940- *ConAu 139*
Sprinzen, Scott 1956- *St&PR 93*
Sprissler, Gregory Paul 1907-1990 *BioIn 17*
Sprizzo, John Emilio 1934- *WhoAm 92, WhoE 93*
Sproat, Brian Stephen 1951- *WhoScE 91-3*
Sproat, John Gerald 1921- *WhoAm 92*
Sproge, Ralf Harold 1928- *St&PR 93*
Sproger, Charles Edmund 1933- *WhoAm 92*
Sprole, Frank Arnott 1918- *WhoAm 92*
Sprole, Jonathan K. *Law&B 92*
Sprole, Robert R., II 1937- *St&PR 93*
Sprong, Gerald R. 1933- *St&PR 93*
Sprongl, Norbert 1892-1983 *Baker 92*
Spross, Charles Gilbert 1874-1961 *Baker 92*
Spross, Werner *WhoScE 91-3*
Sprott, David Arthur 1930- *WhoAm 92*
Sprott, J.M. 1925- *St&PR 93*
Sprott, Richard Lawrence 1940- *WhoAm 92*
Sproul, A. Erskine *St&PR 93*
Sproul, Barbara Chamberlain 1945- *WhoAmW 93*
Sproul, Elmer C. 1921- *St&PR 93*
Sproul, Gayle C. *Law&B 92*
Sproul, Gordon Duane 1944- *WhoSSW 93*
Sproul, John Allan 1924- *St&PR 93, WhoAm 92*
Sproul, Loretta Ann Schroeder 1938- *WhoSSW 93*
Sproul, Otis Jennings 1930- *WhoAm 92*
Sproul, Philip Tate 1915- *WhoE 93*
Sproul, William Cameron 1870-1928 *BioIn 17*
Sproule, J.R. *Law&B 92*
Sproule, Robert Harvey *Law&B 92*
Sproull, Edward I., Jr. 1926- *St&PR 93, WhoAm 92*
Sproull, James E. 1924- *St&PR 93*
Sproull, Nancy May *Law&B 92*
Sproull, Robert Lamb 1918- *WhoAm 92*
Sproull, Wayne Treber 1906- *WhoWor 93*
Sprouls, Joseph W. *Law&B 92*
Sprouse, Charline Higgins 1942- *WhoAmW 93*
Sprouse, Gary L. 1938- *St&PR 93*
Sprouse, James Dean 1949- *WhoSSW 93*
Sprouse, James Marshall 1923- *WhoAm 92, WhoSSW 93*
Sprouse, John A. 1908- *St&PR 93*
Sprouse, John Alwyn 1908- *WhoAm 92*
Sprouse, Robt. A., II 1935- *St&PR 93*
Sprouse, Walter Clayton, Jr. 1948- *WhoSSW 93*
Sprow, Frank Barker 1939- *WhoAm 92*
Sprow, Howard Thomas 1919- *WhoAm 92*
Sprowl, Charles Riggs 1910- *WhoAm 92*
Sprowl, David Charles 1940- *WhoSSW 93*
Sprowls, Robert Wayne 1946- *WhoAm 92*
Spruance, Raymond Ames 1886-1969 *HarEnMi*
Spruce, Everett Franklin 1908- *WhoAm 92*
Spruce, Richard 1817-1893 *Expl 93*
Spruch, Grace Marmor 1926- *WhoAmW 93*
Sprugel, George, Jr. 1919- *WhoAm 92*
Spruill, Howard Vernon 1919- *WhoWor 93*
Spruill, Joseph E., Jr. 1931- *WhoSSW 93*
Spruill, Joseph E., III *Law&B 92*
Spruill, Louise Elam 1918- *WhoAmW 93*
Spruill, Norman Louis 1933- *St&PR 93, WhoIns 93*
Spruill, Steven G. 1946- *ScF&FL 92*
Spruit, Joseph N. 1924- *St&PR 93*
Sprung, Donald W. L. 1934- *WhoAm 92*
Sprung, John B. *Law&B 92*
Sprunt, Eve Silver 1951- *WhoAmW 93*
Spruyt, Michael J. 1933- *St&PR 93*
Spry, Christopher John Farley *WhoScE 91-1*
Spry, Robin 1939- *MiSFD 9*
Spry, Stephen Charles 1948- *WhoSSW 93*
Spude, John Frederick 1957- *St&PR 93*
Spudic, Thomas Joseph 1946- *WhoE 93*
Spudich, James A. 1942- *WhoAm 92*
Spuehler, Donald Roy 1934- *WhoAm 92*
Spuhler, James Norman 1917- *WhoAm 92*
Spulber, Nicolas 1915- *WhoAm 92*
Spuller, Thomas M. *WhoIns 93*
Spungin, Gardner Mawney 1935- *WhoAm 92*
Spungin, Joel D. 1937- *St&PR 93, WhoAm 92*
Spunt, Shepard Armin 1931- *WhoE 93, WhoWor 93*
Spur, Gunter 1928- *WhoScE 91-3*
Spurck, Fredric C. 1947- *St&PR 93*
Spurgeon, Dennis Ray 1943- *St&PR 93*
Spurgeon, Dickie Allen 1936- *WhoWrEP 92*
Spurgeon, Edward Dutcher 1939- *WhoAm 92*
Spurgeon, Kenneth McKenzie 1925- *St&PR 93*
Spurgin, Sally De Witt 1952- *WhoSSW 93*
Spurlin, E. Eugene 1932- *St&PR 93*
Spurling, David E. *Law&B 92*
Spurling, Everett Gordon, Jr. 1923- *WhoAm 92*
Spurlock, Cynthia Marie 1953- *WhoAmW 93*
Spurlock, Delbert L., Jr. 1941- *WhoAm 92*
Spurlock, Dorothy Ann 1957- *WhoAmW 93*
Spurlock, Dwight Ross 1932- *St&PR 93*
Spurlock, Holly B. 1925- *St&PR 93*
Spurlock, Ted Lee 1938- *St&PR 93, WhoAm 92*
Spurlock Dahlke, Rhonda 1959- *WhoAmW 93*
Spurny, Frantisek 1942- *WhoScE 91-4*
Spurny, Zdenek 1929- *WhoScE 91-4*
Spurr, Charles Lewis 1913- *WhoAm 92*
Spurr, John H., Jr. 1946- *St&PR 93*
Spurr, Stephen H. 1918-1990 *BioIn 17*
Spurrier, James I. 1922-1984 *BioIn 17*
Spurrier, John Frederick 1959- *WhoSSW 93*
Spurrier, Junior J. 1922-1984 *BioIn 17*
Spurrier, Robert Lewis, Jr. 1944- *WhoSSW 93*
Spychaj, Tadeusz Jozef 1946- *WhoWor 93*
Spyer, Geoffrey *WhoScE 91-1*
Spyer, Kenneth Michael *WhoScE 91-1*
Spyers-Duran, Peter 1932- *WhoAm 92*
Spykman, E(lizabeth) C(hoate) 1896-1965 *DcAmChF 1960*
Spyri, Johanna (Heusser) 1827-1901 *ConAu 137, MajAI [port]*
Spyridon fl. 4th cent.- *OxDcByz*
Spyridonakes, John fl. c. 1195-1201 *OxDcByz*
Spyropoulos, G.S. *WhoScE 91-3*
Spyropoulos, Siegi 1940- *WhoWor 93*
Spyrou, George Andrew Rankin 1949- *WhoWor 93*
Spyrou, Spyros 1954- *WhoWor 93*
Squadere, Frank *St&PR 93*
Squadra, John Harley 1932- *WhoE 93*
Squadron, Howard Maurice 1926- *WhoAm 92*
Squanto d1622 *BioIn 17*
Squarci, P. *WhoScE 91-3*
Squarcialupi, Antonio 1416-1480 *Baker 92*
Squarcy, Charlotte Van Horne 1947- *WhoAmW 93*
Squartini, Francesco 1927- *WhoScE 91-3*
Squasoni, Douglas Wade 1964- *WhoE 93*
Squatrito-Chaltin, Geraldine Donna 1953- *WhoSSW 93*
Squazzo, Mildred Katherine *WhoAmW 93, WhoE 93*
Squeri, Doris A. *Law&B 92*
Squeri, Therese V. *Law&B 92*
Squibb, Edward Robinson *BioIn 17*
Squibb, Samuel Dexter 1931- *WhoAm 92, WhoSSW 93*
Squibbs, Gerald G. 1935- *St&PR 93*
Squibob 1823-1861 *BioIn 17*
Squier, David L. 1945- *St&PR 93*
Squier, David Louis 1945- *WhoAm 92*
Squier, E.G., Mrs. 1836-1914 *BioIn 17*
Squier, Ephraim George 1821-1888 *IntDcAn*
Squier, Florence Miriam 1836-1914 *BioIn 17*
Squier, George Owen 1865-1934 *BioIn 17*

Squier, Jack Leslie 1927- WhoAm 92
Squier, Leslie Hamilton 1917- WhoAm 92
Squier, Robert 1934- PolPar
Squier, Robert Dave 1934- WhoAm 92
Squier, Thomas K. BioIn 17
Squier, Thomas Keith 1948- WhoSSW 93
Squier, Zadoc d1789 BioIn 17
Squiers, Carol 1948- WhoE 93
Squiers, Jay D. Law&B 92
Squillace, Sandra Carswell 1968- WhoAmW 93
Squillante, F. Donald 1935- St&PR 93
Squillaro, Jerome C. Law&B 92
Squire, Alexander 1917- WhoAm 92, WhoSSW 93
Squire, Anne Marguerite 1920- WhoAm 92
Squire, Chris 1948- See Yes ConMus 8
Squire, J.C. 1884-1958 ScF&FL 92
Squire, James Robert 1922- WhoAm 92
Squire, John Michael WhoScE 91-1
Squire, Laurie Rubin 1953- WhoAmW 93, WhoE 93
Squire, Molly Ann WhoAmW 93, WhoWor 93
Squire, Robert W. 1931- St&PR 93
Squire, Rose Elizabeth 1861-1938 BioIn 17
Squire, Russel Nelson 1908- WhoWor 93
Squire, W(illiam) Barclay 1855-1927 Baker 92
Squire, Walter Charles 1945- WhoE 93, WhoWor 93
Squires, Arthur Morton 1916- WhoAm 92
Squires, Beulah Greene AmWomPl
Squires, Edith Lombard 1884-1939 AmWomPl
Squires, Euan James WhoScE 91-1
Squires, George 1947- St&PR 93
Squires, James Radcliffe 1917- WhoAm 92
Squires, James Ralph 1940- WhoSSW 93
Squires, James Robert 1922- WhoWrEP 92
Squires, John Henry 1946- WhoEmL 93
Squires, Lawrence S. Law&B 92
Squires, Patricia Eileen Coleman 1927- WhoE 93
Squires, Patrick 1914-1990 BioIn 17
Squires, (James) Radcliffe 1917- WhoWrEP 92
Squires, Richard Felt 1933- WhoE 93, WhoWor 93
Squires, Roy A. 1920-1988 ScF&FL 92
Squires, Scott WhoAm 92
Squires, Therese Mary Brendan WhoScE 91-1
Squires, Vernon T. Law&B 92
Squires, W. Kenneth 1939- St&PR 93
Squires, William Randolph, III 1947- WhoWor 93
Squirrel, Alan ScF&FL 92
Squitieri, Victor Carmine 1923- St&PR 93
Squyres, Janet Truitt 1961- WhoSSW 93
Squyres, Veronica 1959- WhoSSW 93
Sraffa, Piero 1898-1983 BioIn 17
Sragow, Daniel E. Law&B 92
Sramek, B.B. 1933- St&PR 93
Sramek, Hevka 1936- St&PR 93
Sramek, Vladimir 1923- Baker 92
Srbljanovic, Predrag WhoScE 91-4
Srdanovic, Velimia 1941- WhoUN 92
Srdoc, Dusan 1929- WhoScE 91-4
Srebnik, Herbert Harry 1923- WhoAm 92
Srebocan, Vjekoslav 1927- WhoScE 91-4
Srebotnjak, Alojz 1931- Baker 92
Sredy, Janet 1954- WhoE 93
Sreebny, Daniel 1955- WhoE 93
Sreebny, Leo M. 1922- WhoAm 92
Sreedhar, Vijay WhoE 93
Sreedharan, Arangil 1923- WhoAsAP 91
Sreenan-Auger, Melaney Kay 1955- WhoAmW 93, WhoSSW 93
Sreenivasa Prasad, V. 1949- WhoAsAP 91
Srenger, Zeljko 1922- WhoScE 91-4
Srere, Benson M. 1928- St&PR 93, WhoAm 92
Srere, David Benson 1958- WhoE 93
Srere, Linda Jean 1955- WhoAm 92, WhoAmW 93
Sridjak, Ksenija Jorgic WhoScE 91-4
Srigley, William R. 1941- St&PR 93
Srimushnam, Vittal G. 1951- St&PR 93
Srinidhi, Bin 1952- WhoE 93
Srinivas, M.N. 1916- IntDcAn
Srinivasan, Arul Malar 1953- WhoWor 93
Srinivasan, Mandayam Paramekanthi 1940- WhoE 93
Srinivasan, Mandyam Veerambudi 1948- WhoWor 93
Srinivasan, Narayanan 1955- WhoWor 93
Srinivasan, Venkataraman 1944- WhoAm 92
Srinivasan-Rao, Triveni St&PR 93
Srivastava, Bhakt Chand 1934- WhoUN 92
Srivastava, Ramesh Kumar 1931- WhoUN 92, WhoWor 93
Srivastava, Satya Deo 1934- WhoUN 92
Srivastava, Satya Prakash 1943- WhoWor 93
Srnec, Susan Lee 1942- WhoAmW 93
Srnka, Jiri 1907-1982 Baker 92
Sroda, George 1911- WhoWrEP 92
Sroge, Maxwell Harold 1927- St&PR 93, WhoAm 92
Sroka, Francis T. 1915- St&PR 93
Sroka, Frank John Law&B 92
Sroka, John Walter 1946- WhoAm 92
Srole, Leo 1908- WhoAm 92
Srom, Karel 1904-1981 Baker 92
Srouji, Maurice Nakhleh 1928- WhoE 93
Srour, Joseph Ralph 1941- WhoAm 92, WhoWor 93
S.-Rozsa, Katalin 1930- WhoScE 91-4
Srubas, Robert Charles 1953- St&PR 93, WhoE 93
Srull, Thomas K. BioIn 17
Srybnik, Louis David 1924- St&PR 93
Srybnik, Simon 1918- St&PR 93
Srygley, Fletcher Douglas 1938- WhoSSW 93
Srygley, Sara Krentzman 1916-1991 BioIn 17
Ssali, Jaberi Bidandi 1937- WhoAfr
Ssekandi, Francis Muzingu 1940- WhoUN 92
Ssemogerere, Paul WhoWor 93
Ssemogerere, Paulo Kawanga 1932- WhoAfr
Ssentumbwe, William BioIn 17
S. Subramaniam, Dato' 1944- WhoAsAP 91
Staab, Diane D. Law&B 92
Staab, Gary Richard 1949- St&PR 93
Staab, Heinz A. 1926- WhoWor 93
Staab, Heinz August 1926- WhoScE 91-3
Staab, Thomas R. 1942- St&PR 93
Staab, Thomas Robert 1942- WhoAm 92
Staab, Walter Edward 1933- WhoAm 92
Staak, Michael 1933- WhoScE 91-3
Staake, Bob BioIn 17
Staal, Dennis R. 1948- St&PR 93
Staal, Flossie Wong- BioIn 17
Staaland, Hans 1938- WhoScE 91-4
Staalner, Claus 1960- WhoSSW 93
Staar, Rene 1951- WhoWor 93
Staar, Richard F(elix) 1923- ConAu 38NR
Staar, Richard Felix 1923- WhoAm 92
Staas, John A. St&PR 93
Staats, Dean Roy 1924- WhoAm 92
Staats, Elmer Boyd 1914- WhoAm 92
Staats, Frank George 1957- WhoSSW 93
Staats, Marilyn Dorn 1939- ConAu 139
Staats, Norman L. 1926- St&PR 93
Staats, Norman Lansing 1926- WhoAm 92
Staats, Thomas Elwyn WhoSSW 93
Staats, William Austin 1938- WhoWor 93
Staba, Emil John 1928- WhoAm 92
Stabbetorp, Hans WhoScE 91-4
Stabej, Rudolph John 1952- WhoEmL 93
Stabenau, James Raymond 1930- WhoAm 92, WhoWor 93
Stabenau, M. Catherine 1948- WhoE 93
Stabenau, Walter Frank 1942- WhoE 93
Stabenow, Dana 1952- ScF&FL 92
Stabenow, Deborah Ann 1950- WhoAmW 93
Staber, Dorothee Beatrice 1961- WhoSSW 93
Stabile, Benedict Louis 1927- WhoAm 92
Stabile, Mariano 1885-1968 OxDcOp
Stabile, Mariano 1888-1968 Baker 92, IntDcOp
Stabile, Rose Towne WhoAmW 93, WhoWor 93
Stabile, Susan 1960- WhoAmW 93
Stabinger, Mathias c. 1750-c. 1815 Baker 92, OxDcOp
Stableford, Brian M. 1948- ScF&FL 92
Stablein, Bruno 1895-1978 Baker 92
Stablein, Marilyn Estelle 1946- WhoWrEP 92
Stabler, Donald Billman 1908- WhoAm 92
Stabler, Gerhard F. 1949- Baker 92
Stabler, John Roberts 1932- WhoSSW 93
Stabler, Laird A. St&PR 93
Stabler, Lewis Vastine, Jr. 1936- WhoAm 92
Stabler, Robert Eugene 1936- WhoSSW 93
Stabler, William L. 1925- St&PR 93
Stabosz, Thomas F. 1942- St&PR 93
Staby, Jack Bradford 1926- WhoE 93
Stacey, A.G. WhoScE 91-1
Stacey, C.P. 1906-1989 BioIn 17
Stacey, Carol Ann WhoIns 93
Stacey, Charles Perry 1906-1989 BioIn 17
Stacey, D. Russell Law&B 92
Stacey, Gary 1951- WhoSSW 93
Stacey, Kathleen Mary 1951- WhoAmW 93
Stacey, Kenneth Arthur WhoScE 91-1
Stacey, Margaret 1922- ConAu 38NR
Stacey, Norma Elaine 1925- WhoSSW 93
Stacey, Patrick 1963- WhoSSW 93
Stacey, Roger Foy 1942- WhoE 93
Stacey, Terence Edward WhoScE 91-1
Stacey, Truman 1916- WhoSSW 93
Stach, Claude WhoScE 91-2
Stach, Hans WhoScE 91-3
Stach, Mark Alan Law&B 92
Stachel, Gunter Max Albert 1922- WhoWor 93
Stachel, Hans-Dietrich 1928- WhoScE 91-3, WhoWor 93
Stachel, John Jay 1928- WhoAm 92
Stachel, Kenneth Joseph Law&B 92
Stacher, Alois 1925- WhoScE 91-4
Stacher, Georg 1939- WhoScE 91-4
Stachiw, Mark A. Law&B 92
Stachler, Robert G. 1929- WhoAm 92
Stacho, Zoltan Aladar 1930- WhoAm 92
Stachofsky, Robert G. 1937- St&PR 93
Stachowiak, Henryk 1933- WhoScE 91-4
Stachowiak, Sharon Ann Law&B 92
Stachowicz, Michal 1768-1825 PolBiDi
Stachowski, Marek 1936- Baker 92
Stachowski, William T. 1949- WhoE 93
Staciokas, Leon Joseph 1928- St&PR 93
Stack, Angela Johann 1946- WhoAmW 93
Stack, Beatriz de Greiff 1939- WhoWor 93
Stack, Denis G. Law&B 92
Stack, Edward William 1935- WhoAm 92, WhoE 93
Stack, Elaine M. Law&B 92
Stack, George Joseph WhoAm 92
Stack, J. William, Jr. 1918- WhoAm 92
Stack, Karl 1946- WhoAsAP 91
Stack, Mary Judith 1947- WhoAmW 93
Stack, Maurice Daniel 1917- WhoAm 92
Stack, Norman C. d1992 NewYTBS 92
Stack, Paul Francis 1946- WhoWor 93
Stack, Philip Wayne 1946- St&PR 93
Stack, Raymond John, Jr. 1936- St&PR 93
Stack, Robert BioIn 17
Stack, Robert Douglas 1956- WhoE 93, WhoEmL 93
Stack, Robert Langford 1919- WhoAm 92
Stack, Stephen S. 1934- St&PR 93, WhoAm 92
Stack, William J. Law&B 92
Stackelberg, Olaf Patrick von 1932- WhoAm 92
Stackelberg, Peter Georg Johan 1946- WhoWor 93
Stackhouse, David Lee 1963- WhoSSW 93
Stackhouse, Marion St&PR 93
Stackhouse, Richard Gilbert 1929- WhoAm 92
Stackhouse, Roger B. St&PR 93
Stackhouse, Ruby 1947- BioIn 17
Stackpole, Kerry Clifford 1955- WhoE 93
Stackpole, Michael 1957- ScF&FL 92
Stackpole, Robert J. 1938- St&PR 93
Stacom, Matthew John 1918- St&PR 93
Stacy, Bill Wayne 1938- WhoAm 92
Stacy, Carl J. 1929- WhoSSW 93
Stacy, Charles Brecknock 1924- WhoAm 92
Stacy, Delores WhoWrEP 92
Stacy, Donald ConAu 37NR
Stacy, Gardner W. 1921- WhoAm 92
Stacy, Hollis 1954- BiDAMSp 1989
Stacy, Jan 1948-1989 ScF&FL 92
Stacy, Jane Cooper 1938- WhoAmW 93
Stacy, Joseph L., Mrs. AmWomPl
Stacy, Pauline French 1915- WhoWrEP 92
Stacy, Richard A. 1942- WhoAm 92
Stacy, Ryder ScF&FL 92
Stacy, T. Don 1934- WhoAm 92
Stacy, Thomas 1938- Baker 92
Staddon, John Eric Rayner WhoAm 92
Stade, Frederica von Baker 92, IntDcOp
Stade, Frederica von 1945- OxDcOp
Stade, George Gustav WhoAm 92
Stadel, Manfred Peter 1950- WhoWor 93
Stadelbauer, Jorg 1944- WhoScE 91-3
Stadelman, Peter B. 1931- St&PR 93
Stadelman, Russell Carl 1913- St&PR 93
Stadelman, William Ralph 1919- WhoAm 92
Staden, Johann 1581?-1634? Baker 92
Staden, Sigmund Theophil 1607?-1655? Baker 92, OxDcOp
Stader, Maria 1911- Baker 92
Stadie, Klaus B. 1929- WhoScE 91-2
Stadil, Thor 1944- WhoWor 93
Stading, Donald Charles 1935- St&PR 93
Stading, Donald R. 1941- St&PR 93
Stading, Donald Robert Law&B 92
Stadlbauer, Harald Stefan 1963- WhoWor 93
Stadler, Anton (Paul) 1753-1812 Baker 92
Stadler, Craig Robert 1953- WhoAm 92
Stadler, Donald Arthur 1943- WhoSSW 93
Stadler, Gerald P. St&PR 93
Stadler, Harald Alfred 1954- WhoWor 93
Stadler, Johann 1755-1804 See Stadler, Anton (Paul) 1753-1812 Baker 92
Stadler, Martin F. 1942- WhoAm 92
Stadler, Maximilian 1748-1833 Baker 92
Stadler, Peter 1925- WhoWor 93
Stadler, Rudolf 1953- WhoWor 93
Stadlin, Walter Olaf 1929- WhoAm 92
Stadlmair, Hans 1929- Baker 92
Stadlman, Rebecca Murphy 1952- WhoAmW 93
Stadlmayr, Johann c. 1575-1648 Baker 92
Stadnicki, Stanley Walter, Jr. 1943- WhoE 93
Stadnik, Thomas J. Law&B 92
Stadnyk, Vladimir Yaroslav 1952- St&PR 93
Stadter, Philip Austin 1936- WhoAm 92, WhoWrEP 92
Stadter, Richard Perry 1932- WhoAm 92
Stadtfeld, Alexandre 1826-1853 Baker 92
Stadtler, Beatrice Horwitz 1921- WhoAm 92, WhoWrEP 92
Stadtman, Earl Reece 1919- WhoAm 92
Stadtman, Thressa Campbell 1920- WhoAm 92
Stadtman, Verne August 1926- WhoAm 92
Stadtman, Walter E. 1923- St&PR 93
Stadtmueller, Joseph Peter 1942- WhoAm 92
Staeb, Rick W. 1951- St&PR 93
Staebler, Neil O. 1905- PolPar
Staebler, Sally W. Law&B 92
Staebler, Tom 1943- St&PR 93
Staedel, August Wilhelm 1938- WhoWor 93
Staedtler, Richard Edward 1944- St&PR 93
Staehelin, Lucas Andrew 1939- WhoAm 92
Staehely, David Merle 1947- St&PR 93
Staehle, Robert L. 1955- WhoAm 92
Staehle, Sandra J. Law&B 92
Stael, Madame de 1766-1817 BioIn 17
Stael, Germaine de 1766-1817 DcLB 119 [port]
Stael, Nicolas de 1914-1955 BioIn 17
Staelens, Peter John 1940- St&PR 93
Stael-Holstein, Anne Louise Germaine 1766-1817 BioIn 17
Staelin, David Hudson 1938- WhoAm 92
Staelin, Richard 1939- WhoAm 92
Staempfli, Edward 1908- Baker 92
Staempfli, George William 1910- WhoAm 92
Stafast, Herbert 1947- WhoWor 93
Staff, Donald Albert 1935- WhoE 93
Staff, Joel V. 1944- St&PR 93
Staff, La Vada Falkner 1924- WhoWrEP 92
Staff, Leopold 1878-1957 PolBiDi
Staff, Robert James, Jr. 1946- WhoWor 93
Staffansson, Lars-Ingvar 1924- WhoScE 91-4
Staffel, Rudolf 1911- BioIn 17
Staffelbach, Andre 1939- WhoSSW 93
Staffier, Pamela Moorman 1942- WhoE 93
Staffieri, Nicholas J. Law&B 92
Staffopoulos, William Peter 1948- WhoWor 93
Stafford, Arthur Charles 1947- WhoWor 93
Stafford, Barbara Rose 1949- WhoAmW 93
Stafford, Byron Donald 1946- WhoWrEP 92
Stafford, C. Richard 1935- St&PR 93
Stafford, Carlene Roussel 1952- WhoAmW 93
Stafford, Donald Gene 1930- WhoSSW 93
Stafford, Donnie V. St&PR 93
Stafford, Douglas Lewis 1952- WhoSSW 93
Stafford, Drucille Hutchinson 1938- WhoE 93
Stafford, Emily-Mae 1934- WhoAmW 93
Stafford, Ernest Kay, Jr. 1946- St&PR 93
Stafford, Frank Peter, Jr. 1940- WhoAm 92
Stafford, Frederick E. 1942- WhoE 93
Stafford, Godfrey Harry 1920- WhoWor 93
Stafford, J. Francis 1932- WhoAm 92
Stafford, J.V. 1946- WhoScE 91-1
Stafford, James Polk, Jr. 1918- WhoSSW 93
Stafford, Jan 1951- WhoWrEP 92
Stafford, Jane R. Law&B 92
Stafford, Jean 1915-1979 AmWomWr 92, BioIn 17
Stafford, Jennifer Leigh WhoAmW 93
Stafford, Jeremy James Boanson 1943- WhoWor 93
Stafford, Jo WhoAm 92
Stafford, Jo 1920- BioIn 17
Stafford, Joel Lindsey 1946- WhoSSW 93
Stafford, John M. 1936- WhoAm 92

Stafford, John Rogers 1937- *St&PR 93, WhoAm 92*
Stafford, John Warner 1932- *St&PR 93*
Stafford, Josephine Howard 1921- *WhoAmW 93*
Stafford, Kathleen L. *Law&B 92*
Stafford, Keith David *WhoScE 91-1*
Stafford, Marilyn *WhoWrEP 92*
Stafford, Martin Douglas 1933- *WhoUN 92*
Stafford, Mary Ellen 1933- *WhoE 93*
Stafford, Nancy *BioIn 17*
Stafford, P. Gorden *Law&B 92*
Stafford, P. Gordon 1934- *St&PR 93*
Stafford, Paul Gordon 1934- *WhoAm 92*
Stafford, Rebecca 1936- *WhoAm 92*
Stafford, Robert Mc Kinley, Jr. 1952- *WhoWrEP 92*
Stafford, Robert Neil 1940- *St&PR 93*
Stafford, Robert Theodore 1913- *WhoAm 92*
Stafford, Russell Bennett 1936- *WhoWrEP 92*
Stafford, Stephen Thomas *MiSFD 9*
Stafford, Susan Buchanan 1948- *WhoE 93*
Stafford, Thomas *Law&B 92*
Stafford, Thomas P. 1930- *BioIn 17*
Stafford, Thomas Patten 1930- *WhoAm 92*
Stafford, Will Elbert 1935- *WhoSSW 93*
Stafford, William Edgar 1914- *BioIn 17, WhoAm 92, WhoWrEP 92*
Stafford, William Talmadge 1924- *WhoWrEP 92*
Stafford-Clark, Max 1941- *BioIn 17*
Stafford-Mallis, Valerie 1955- *WhoAmW 93*
Staffrude, Paul R. 1953- *St&PR 93*
Stafleu, Frans A. 1921- *WhoScE 91-3*
Stage, Ginger Rooks 1946- *WhoAmW 93*
Stage, Thomas Benton 1926- *WhoAm 92*
Stagen, Mary-Patricia Healy 1955- *WhoAmW 93*
Stager, Alan N. 1949- *St&PR 93*
Stager, Donald K. *WhoAm 92*
Stager, Lawrence E. 1943- *WhoAm 92*
Stager, Nancy Huntington 1960- *WhoAmW 93*
Stager, Paul *Law&B 92*
Stager, William Harry 1953- *WhoSSW 93*
Stagg, Amos Alonzo *BioIn 17*
Stagg, Evelyn Wheeler 1916- *WhoAmW 93*
Stagg, Katherine *AmWomPl*
Stagg, Louis Charles 1933- *WhoAm 92, WhoSSW 93*
Stagg, Nancy *Law&B 92*
Stagg, Paul Lynwood 1942- *WhoE 93*
Stagg, Tom 1923- *WhoAm 92*
Staggers, Harley O. 1907-1991 *BioIn 17*
Staggers, Harley O., Jr. 1951- *CngDr 91, WhoAm 92, WhoSSW 93*
Staggers, William A. Fort 1956- *St&PR 93*
Staggs, Gary L. 1953- *St&PR 93*
Stagliano, Domenico 1936- *WhoUN 92*
Stagliano, Vito Alexander 1942- *WhoE 93*
Staglin, Garen Kent 1944- *St&PR 93, WhoAm 92*
Stagmer, Holly J. 1951- *St&PR 93*
Stagnaro-Green, Doreen *Law&B 92*
Stagner, John Irvin, III 1944- *WhoSSW 93*
Stagno, Roberto 1840-1897 *Baker 92, OxDcOp*
Stagno-Bellincioni, Bianca 1888-1980 *OxDcOp*
Stahl, Andre J.C. 1932- *WhoScE 91-2*
Stahl, Armin Mueller- *BioIn 17*
Stahl, Arnulf N.F. 1924- *WhoScE 91-3*
Stahl, Barbara J. 1930- *WhoAmW 93, WhoE 93*
Stahl, Ben 1910-1987 *ScF&FL 92*
Stahl, Chester Wesley 1926- *St&PR 93*
Stahl, David 1949- *WhoSSW 93*
Stahl, David Bohus, Sr. 1935- *St&PR 93*
Stahl, David Edward 1934- *WhoAm 92*
Stahl, David G. 1926- *WhoE 93*
Stahl, Deborah Ann 1950- *WhoAmW 93*
Stahl, Edward T. 1947- *St&PR 93*
Stahl, Eric Steven *MiSFD 9*
Stahl, Frank Ludwig 1920- *WhoAm 92*
Stahl, Fred F. 1937- *St&PR 93*
Stahl, G.E. 1926- *St&PR 93*
Stahl, Gerold 1926- *WhoWor 93*
Stahl, Glenn W. 1913- *St&PR 93*
Stahl, Henry George 1902- *WhoAm 92*
Stahl, Hilda 1938- *ConAu 40NR*
Stahl, Jack Leland 1934- *WhoAm 92*
Stahl, Joel S. 1918- *St&PR 93*
Stahl, John M. 1886-1950 *MiSFD 9N*
Stahl, Kenneth L. 1947- *St&PR 93*
Stahl, Laddie L. 1921- *WhoAm 92*
Stahl, Leroy Lee 1928- *St&PR 93*
Stahl, Lesley R. 1941- *BioIn 17, JrnUS, WhoAm 92, WhoAmW 93, WhoE 93*
Stahl, Marc P. 1935- *St&PR 93*
Stahl, Michelle Akers- *BioIn 17*
Stahl, Norman 1931- *ScF&FL 92*
Stahl, Oscar Glenn 1910- *WhoAm 92*
Stahl, Philip Anthony 1946- *WhoWor 93*
Stahl, Philip Damien 1941- *WhoAm 92*
Stahl, Phyllis A. 1956- *St&PR 93*
Stahl, Ray Emerson 1917- *WhoSSW 93*
Stahl, Richard Alan 1929- *St&PR 93*
Stahl, Richard G. C. 1934- *WhoAm 92*
Stahl, Robert 1927- *St&PR 93*
Stahl, Robert Alan 1942- *WhoE 93*
Stahl, Ronald Albert 1946- *St&PR 93*
Stahl, Roy 1952- *St&PR 93*
Stahl, Roy Howard *Law&B 92*
Stahl, Ruthanne 1939- *WhoAmW 93*
Stahl, Sandra Michelle 1962- *St&PR 93*
Stahl, Ulf 1944- *WhoScE 91-3*
Stahl, Yvette Jan 1957- *St&PR 93*
Stahlberg, Ronald H. 1936- *St&PR 93*
Stahle, Donald Winslow 1935- *St&PR 93*
Stahle, Jan 1924- *WhoScE 91-4*
Stahler, Charles *WhoWrEP 92*
Stahler, Gerald Jay 1952- *WhoE 93*
Stahlin, Jacob von 1709-1785 *Baker 92*
Stahlin, Paul V. 1952- *St&PR 93*
Stahlman, G.M. 1938- *St&PR 93*
Stahlman, Mildred Thornton 1922- *WhoAm 92*
Stahlman, Sylvia 1933- *Baker 92*
Stahman, Robert W. *Law&B 92*
Stahmann, Robert F. 1939- *WhoAm 92*
Stahmer, Robert T. 1924- *St&PR 93*
Stahr, Curtis Brent *WhoWor 93*
Stahr, Elvis Jacob, Jr. 1916- *WhoAm 92*
Stahr, Karl 1945- *WhoWor 93*
Staiano, Edward F. 1936- *WhoAm 92*
Staiano, Edward Frank 1936- *St&PR 93*
Staiano, Salvatore George 1950- *St&PR 93*
Staib, Cheryl Marie 1962- *WhoAmW 93*
Staicar, Thomas E. *ScF&FL 92*
Staicar, Tom 1946- *ScF&FL 92*
Staico, Kathy *BioIn 17*
Staig, Laurence *ScF&FL 92*
Staiger, Nancy Lee 1953- *WhoSSW 93*
Staiger, Ralph Conrad 1917- *WhoAm 92*
Staijen, J.E. *WhoScE 91-3*
Stailey, Robert V. 1947- *St&PR 93*
Stainback, George d1992 *NewYTBS 92*
Stainback, John Philip 1948- *WhoWor 93*
Staine, Ross 1924- *WhoAm 92*
Stainer, Jacob 1617?-1683 *Baker 92*
Stainer, John 1840-1901 *Baker 92*
Staines, B.W. *WhoScE 91-1*
Staines, David McKenzie 1946- *WhoAm 92*
Staines, Michael L. 1949- *St&PR 93*
Staines, Morgan L. *Law&B 92*
Staines, Norman Allyn *WhoScE 91-1*
Staines, Phyllis 1962- *WhoAmW 93*
Staines, Trevor *ConAu 37NR*
Stainlein, Louis Charles Georges Corneille de 1819-1867 *Baker 92*
Stainov, Petko 1896-1977 *Baker 92*
Stainrook, Harry Richard 1937- *WhoAm 92*
Stains, Scott Frank *Law&B 92*
Stainton, David Murray *Law&B 92*
Stair, Frederick Rogers 1918- *WhoAm 92, WhoSSW 93*
Stair, Gobin 1912- *WhoAm 92*
Stair, Jeffrey Carlton *Law&B 92*
Stair, Patty 1869-1926 *Baker 92*
Stair, Randel Nelson 1950- *St&PR 93*
Stairs, Denis Winfield 1939- *WhoAm 92*
Stajer, Geza 1936- *WhoScE 91-4*
Stajkov, Ljudmil 1937- *DrEEuF*
Stakemann, Georg 1920- *WhoScE 91-2*
Staker, Robert Jackson 1925- *WhoAm 92, WhoSSW 93*
Stakgold, Ivar 1925- *WhoAm 92*
Stakosch, Maurice 1825-1887 *OxDcOp*
Staland, Bertil 1913- *WhoWor 93*
Stalberg, Zachary 1947- *St&PR 93, WhoAm 92, WhoE 93*
Stalcup, Joe Alan 1931- *WhoAm 92*
Stalder, Charles 1943- *St&PR 93*
Stalder, Ruedi 1940- *St&PR 93*
Staley, Allen Percival Green 1935- *WhoAm 92*
Staley, Augustus Eugene, III 1928- *WhoAm 92*
Staley, Charles Earl 1927- *WhoE 93*
Staley, Charles Ralls 1938- *WhoAm 92*
Staley, Clyde D. 1937- *St&PR 93*
Staley, Dawn *BioIn 17*
Staley, Delbert C. 1924- *St&PR 93, WhoAm 92, WhoE 93*
Staley, Frederick Seton 1942- *WhoE 93*
Staley, Henry Mueller 1932- *WhoAm 92*
Staley, James Dephro 1949- *St&PR 93*
Staley, John Charles 1941- *WhoAm 92*
Staley, Louise Wilma 1944- *WhoAmW 93*
Staley, Patricia Len *Law&B 92*
Staley, Paul R. 1929- *St&PR 93*
Staley, Robert W. 1935- *WhoAm 92*
Staley, Robert Wayne 1935- *St&PR 93*
Staley, Robin Cheryl 1954- *St&PR 93*
Staley, Rosemary Ann 1946- *WhoAmW 93*
Staley, Sheila Jean 1954- *WhoAmW 93*
Stalin, Josef 1879-1953 *HarEnMi*
Stalin, Josef Vissarionovich 1879-1953 *DcTwHis*
Stalin, Joseph 1879-1953 *BioIn 17, ColdWar 2 [port]*
Stalinski, B. *WhoScE 91-4*
Stalinski, Zbigniew 1923- *WhoScE 91-4*
Stalker, Clara Inglis *AmWomPl*
Stalker, Dianne Sylvia 1951- *WhoAmW 93*
Stalker, Duncan d1991 *BioIn 17*
Stalker, Jacqueline D'Aoust 1933- *WhoAmW 93, WhoWor 93*
Stalker, Robert E. 1951- *WhoIns 93*
Stalker, Suzy Wooster 1948- *WhoAmW 93*
Stalkup, Fred Irving, Jr. 1936- *WhoAm 92*
Stall, Alan David 1951- *WhoEmL 93, WhoWor 93*
Stallard, Carl Eldon 1929- *St&PR 93*
Stallard, Gerald L. 1946- *St&PR 93*
Stallard, Glenn E. 1922- *St&PR 93*
Stallard, John *WhoScE 91-1*
Stallard, Troy Francis 1944- *St&PR 93*
Stallcup, William Blackburn, Jr. 1920- *WhoAm 92*
Stalle, George Etienne 1952- *WhoSSW 93*
Stalling, Gustav H., III 1930- *St&PR 93*
Stallings, Charles Henry 1941- *St&PR 93, WhoAm 92*
Stallings, Frank, Jr. 1954- *WhoEmL 93, WhoSSW 93, WhoWor 93*
Stallings, Gene Clifton 1935- *WhoAm 92*
Stallings, James H. 1892-1990 *BioIn 17*
Stallings, Jo Alessi 1934- *St&PR 93*
Stallings, Larry Joseph 1941- *St&PR 93*
Stallings, Lisa Rawl 1958- *WhoAmW 93*
Stallings, Norman 1914- *WhoAm 92*
Stallings, Patricia L. *BioIn 17*
Stallings, Richard H. 1940- *CngDr 91*
Stallings, Richard Howard 1940- *WhoAm 92*
Stallings, Robert Lee, Jr. 1933- *WhoSSW 93*
Stallings, Ronald Denis 1943- *WhoAm 92*
Stallkamp, James Hubert 1936- *St&PR 93*
Stallman, Alvin 1929- *St&PR 93*
Stallman, David C. 1929- *St&PR 93*
Stallman, Donald Lee 1930- *WhoE 93*
Stallman, Robert 1930-1980 *ScF&FL 92*
Stallmeyer, James Edward 1926- *WhoAm 92*
Stallone, Sylvester *BioIn 17*
Stallone, Sylvester 1946- *HolBB [port], IntDcF 2-3, MiSFD 9*
Stallone, Sylvester Enzio 1946- *WhoAm 92*
Stallsmith, William Paul, Jr. *Law&B 92*
Stallworthy, Jon Howie 1935- *WhoWrEP 92*
Stalmack, Lawrence S. 1948- *St&PR 93*
Stalmans, Willy L.R. 1942- *WhoScE 91-2*
Stalnaker, Armand *BioIn 17*
Stalnaker, Armand C. 1916- *St&PR 93*
Stalnaker, Armand Carl 1916- *WhoAm 92*
Stalnaker, John Hulbert 1918- *WhoWor 93*
Stalnaker, John Marshall 1903-1990 *BioIn 17*
Stalnaker, Judith Ann 1942- *WhoAmW 93*
Stalnecker, Mark E. 1951- *St&PR 93*
Stalnecker, Mark Eric 1951- *WhoAm 92*
Staloff, Arnold Fred 1944- *WhoAm 92*
Stalsberg, Helge 1932- *WhoScE 91-4*
Staluppi, John *BioIn 17*
Stalvey, Dorrance 1930- *Baker 92*
Stalvey, Troy Leevon, Sr. 1939- *WhoSSW 93*
Stalzer, David 1914- *WhoWrEP 92*
Stalzer, Richard Francis 1936- *WhoE 93*
Stalzer, Robert Joseph 1942- *St&PR 93*
Stam, David Harry 1935- *WhoAm 92*
Stam, Henk 1922- *Baker 92*
Stam, Jeffrey Hendrik 1954- *St&PR 93*
Sta Maria, Manuel Olivar 1947- *WhoWor 93*
Stamas, Stephen 1931- *WhoAm 92*
Stamas, Theodore Stephen 1960- *WhoE 93*
Stamatakis, Carol Marie 1960- *WhoAmW 93*
Stamatis, Lynne Baker 1958- *WhoAmW 93*
Stamatovic, Aleksandar 1940- *WhoScE 91-4*
Stamats, Peter Owen 1929- *St&PR 93*
Stamaty, Camille (-Marie) 1811-1870 *Baker 92*
Stambaugh, Armstrong A., Jr. 1920- *WhoAm 92*
Stambaugh, Charles Lee 1945- *St&PR 93*
Stambaugh, E.B. *ScF&FL 92*
Stambaugh, John Edgar 1940- *WhoE 93, WhoWor 93*
Stambaugh, Larry G. 1947- *WhoWor 93*
Stambaugh, Mervil Ronald 1939- *WhoE 93*
Stambaugh, Perry Allen 1960- *WhoWrEP 92*
Stambaugh, Phillip Francis 1944- *WhoE 93*
Stamberg, Arthur Jay 1934- *St&PR 93*
Stamberg, Susan 1938- *BioIn 17*
Stamberg, Susan Levitt 1938- *WhoAm 92, WhoE 93*
Stambler, Irwin 1924- *WhoWrEP 92*
Stambler, Peter Lane 1944- *WhoWrEP 92*
Stambolian, George *BioIn 17*
Stambolian, George 1938-1991 *ConAu 136*
Stamboliisky, Alexander 1879-1923 *DcTwHis*
Stambone, Lisa Marie 1964- *WhoE 93*
Stamelman, Richard Howard 1942- *WhoAm 92*
Stamenkovic, Hrista 1917- *WhoWor 93*
Stamenkovic, Miomir 1928- *DrEEuF*
Stamenkovic, Svetomir 1948- *WhoScE 91-4*
Stamenkovic, Tomislav *WhoScE 91-4*
Stamer, Hans 1925- *WhoScE 91-3*
Stamer, Howard 1929- *St&PR 93*
Stamey, Sara 1953- *ScF&FL 92*
Stamey, Thomas A. 1928- *WhoAm 92*
Stamiris, Eleni *WhoUN 92*
Stamison, Peter George 1942- *St&PR 93*
Stamitz *Baker 92*
Stamitz, Anton 1750?-1789? *Baker 92*
Stamitz, Carl 1745?-1801 *Baker 92*
Stamitz, Johann (Wenzel Anton) 1717-1757 *Baker 92*
Stamler, Jeremiah 1919- *WhoAm 92*
Stamm, Alan 1931- *WhoAm 92*
Stamm, Andre Michel 1946- *WhoScE 91-2*
Stamm, Charles H. 1938- *WhoIns 93*
Stamm, Manfred 1949- *WhoWor 93*
Stamm, Robert Calvin 1925- *WhoSSW 93*
Stamm, Robert J. 1921- *St&PR 93*
Stamm, Robert Jenne 1921- *WhoAm 92*
Stamm, Rudolf 1909-1991 *BioIn 17*
Stamm, Walter 1924- *WhoWor 93*
Stammel, Thomas S. *Law&B 92*
Stammer, Roger Wilbert 1938- *St&PR 93*
Stammler, Albrecht 1918- *WhoScE 91-3*
Stamnes, Jakob Johan 1943- *WhoWor 93*
Stamnes, Knut Henrik 1943- *WhoWor 93*
Stamoolis, Gus 1940- *St&PR 93*
Stamos, John *BioIn 17, WhoAm 92*
Stamos, John James 1924- *WhoAm 92*
Stamos, Theodoros 1922- *WhoAm 92*
Stamp, Duane M. *Law&B 92*
Stamp, Frederick Pfarr, Jr. 1934- *WhoAm 92*
Stamp, Frederick Pfarr, Jr. 1945- *WhoSSW 93*
Stamp, John McConnel *WhoScE 91-1*
Stamp, Neal Roger 1918- *WhoAm 92*
Stamp, Terence 1938- *IntDcF 2-3 [port]*
Stamp, Terence 1939- *MiSFD 9*
Stamp, Terence Henry 1938- *WhoWor 93*
Stamper, Eugene 1928- *WhoE 93*
Stamper, J.B. 1947- *ScF&FL 92*
Stamper, James Harris 1938- *WhoSSW 93*
Stamper, James Walter 1932- *St&PR 93*
Stamper, Joe Allen 1914- *WhoAm 92*
Stamper, Lori 1959- *WhoWrEP 92*
Stamper, Malcolm T. 1925- *St&PR 93*
Stamper, Malcolm Theodore 1925- *WhoAm 92*
Stamper, Russell W., Sr. *AfrAmBi [port]*
Stamperius, Pieter C. 1941- *WhoScE 91-3*
Stampfl, Rudolf Alois 1926- *WhoAm 92*
Stampfli, Peter 1937- *BioIn 17*
Stampiglia, Silvio 1664-1725 *OxDcOp*
Stampley, Norris Lochlen 1920- *WhoAm 92*
Stampley, Robert K. 1943- *St&PR 93*
Stampone, Frederick Albert 1956- *St&PR 93, WhoAm 92*
Stampone, John Richard, Sr. 1918- *WhoE 93*
Stampp, Kenneth Milton 1912- *WhoAm 92*
Stampp, Sara Katherine 1945- *WhoAmW 93*
Stamps, Barry Kenneth 1945- *WhoWor 93*
Stamps, E. Roe, IV 1946- *St&PR 93*
Stamps, George Moreland 1924- *WhoWor 93*
Stamps, Thomas Paty 1952- *WhoEmL 93, WhoSSW 93, WhoWor 93*
Stan, Gheorghe 1933- *WhoScE 91-4*
Stan, Patricia 1952- *WhoEmL 93*
Stan, Sabina 1942- *WhoScE 91-4*
Stana, Regis Richard 1941- *WhoSSW 93*
Stanaland, Sandra Lee 1946- *WhoAmW 93, WhoEmL 93*
Stanaland, William Whit, Jr. 1930- *WhoSSW 93, WhoWor 93*
Stanard, Dennis Michael 1946- *WhoSSW 93*
Stanard, Mary Newton 1865-1929 *ScF&FL 92*
Stanaszek, Walter F. 1940- *WhoSSW 93*
Stanat, Donald F. 1937- *WhoAm 92*

Stanat, Ruth Ellen 1947- WhoAmW 93
Stanaway, Anne 1931- WhoAmW 93, WhoE 93
Stanaway, Loretta Susan 1954- WhoAmW 93
Stanbery, Henry 1803-1881 OxCSupC
Stanbridge, Roger P. 1941- St&PR 93
Stanbury, H. Norman 1911- St&PR 93
Stanbury, John Bruton 1915- WhoAm 92
Stanbury, Robert Douglas George 1929- WhoAm 92
Stancati, Joseph A. Law&B 92
Stancavage, Gerald 1953- St&PR 93
Stancel, Charles John 1935- St&PR 93
Stancell, Arnold BioIn 17
Stanchak, John Edward 1951- WhoAm 92
Stanchev, P.L. 1949- WhoScE 91-4
Stanchich, Maria Estella 1939- WhoAmW 93
Stancil, John Luther 1946- WhoSSW 93
Stancill, James McNeill 1932- WhoAm 92
Stanciu, Ionel 1929- WhoScE 91-4
Stanciu, Virgil V. 1932- St&PR 93
Stanco, J. 1938- WhoScE 91-4
Stanculescu, Victor Atanasie 1928- WhoWor 93
Stanczak, Julian 1928- WhoAm 92
Stanczak, Stephen P. Law&B 92
Standa, Jerzy 1924- WhoScE 91-4
Standaert, Frank George 1929- WhoAm 92
Standaert, James V. 1938- WhoIns 93
Standaert, James Victor 1938- St&PR 93
Standage, Simon 1941- Baker 92
Standard, James Noel 1940- WhoAm 92
Standard, Jess 1854-1935 BioIn 17
Standard, Kenneth G. Law&B 92
Standberry, Herman Lee 1945- WhoWor 93
Standbridge, Peter Thomas 1934- WhoAm 92
Standefer, Mark C. Law&B 92
Standel, Richard Reynold, Jr. Law&B 92
Standel, Richard Reynold, Jr. 1936- St&PR 93, WhoAm 92
Standen, Craig C. BioIn 17
Standen, Michael Alan 1937- St&PR 93
Standen, Nika BioIn 17
Stander, Joseph William 1928- WhoAm 92
Stander, Nancy Lucas 1945- WhoSSW 93
Stander, Richard Wright 1922- WhoAm 92
Stander, Siegfried BioIn 17
Stander, Stephen F. Law&B 92
Stander, Stephen F. 1943- St&PR 93
Standford, Patric 1939- Baker 92
Standfuss, Johann dc. 1759 OxDcOp
Standifer, Noah Orval 1950- WhoSSW 93
Standiford, Les 1945- ScF&FL 92
Standiford, Sally Newman 1941- WhoAmW 93
Standig, Rosetta 1925- St&PR 93
Standing, Guy 1948- WhoUN 92
Standing, Sue 1952- WhoWrEP 92
Standing Bear, Zugguelgeres Galafach 1941- WhoSSW 93, WhoWor 93
Standish, Craig Peter 1953- WhoWrEP 92
Standish, J. Spencer 1925- St&PR 93
Standish, John Spencer 1925- WhoAm 92, WhoE 93
Standish, Linda S. 1952- St&PR 93
Standish, Roberta BioIn 17
Standish, Samuel Miles 1923- WhoAm 92
Standish, Victor J. 1936- St&PR 93
Standish, William Lloyd 1930- WhoAm 92, WhoE 93, WhoWor 93
Standley, Richard Albert, Jr. 1926- WhoE 93
Standley, Thomas R. Law&B 92
Standley, William Harrison 1872-1963 HarEnMi
Standridge, George M. 1937- St&PR 93
Standridge, Kim Diane 1957- WhoEmL 93
Standring, James Douglas 1951- WhoWor 93
Standring, Lesley ScF&FL 92
Stanek, Alan Edward 1939- WhoAm 92
Stanek, Lou Willett BioIn 17
Stanek, Steven Robert 1957- WhoSSW 93
Stanfield, Andrew William 1927- BiDAMSp 1989
Stanfield, Elizabeth Poplin 1930- WhoSSW 93
Stanfield, F. Thomas 1943- St&PR 93
Stanfield, John Richard 1931- St&PR 93
Stanfield, Paul W. 1946- St&PR 93
Stanfield, Peter Robert WhoScE 91-1
Stanfield, Peter Robert 1944- WhoWor 93
Stanfield, Robert Everett 1934- WhoE 93
Stanfield, Steven W. 1950- St&PR 93
Stanfill, Dennis C. 1927- St&PR 93
Stanfill, Dennis Carothers 1927- WhoAm 92
Stanford, Charles L. Law&B 92
Stanford, Charles Villiers 1852-1924 Baker 92, OxDcOp
Stanford, Dennis Joe 1943- WhoAm 92
Stanford, Donald Elwin 1913- WhoAm 92, WhoWrEP 92
Stanford, Gwendolyn Caldwell 1925- WhoAmW 93, WhoSSW 93
Stanford, Henry King 1916- WhoAm 92
Stanford, James M. St&PR 93
Stanford, John Henry 1938- AfrAmBi [port]
Stanford, Joseph Stephen 1934- WhoAm 92
Stanford, Kimberley Alice 1954- WhoAmW 93
Stanford, Leland 1824-1893 BioIn 17, GayN
Stanford, Lynn d1991 BioIn 17
Stanford, Melvin Joseph 1932- WhoAm 92
Stanford, Muriel ScF&FL 92
Stanford, Paul Law&B 92
Stanford, Paul 1942- St&PR 93
Stanford, Richard Alexander 1943- WhoSSW 93
Stanford, Rose Mary 1942- WhoAmW 93
Stanford, Thomas H. Law&B 92
Stanford, Thomas Welton 1832-1918 BioIn 17
Stang, Christopher Brian Law&B 92
Stang, Ivan 1949- ScF&FL 92
Stang, John H. 1944- St&PR 93
Stang, Richard 1925- WhoWrEP 92
Stang, Rolf Kristian 1939- WhoE 93
Stanga, Mark V. Law&B 92
Stange, Deborah Louise 1962- WhoSSW 93
Stange, Dennis Earle 1952- WhoEmL 93
Stange, Lionel Alvin 1935- WhoSSW 93
Stange, Luise M.C. 1926- WhoScE 91-3
Stange, Richard Thomas Law&B 92
Stange, Richard Thomas 1947- St&PR 93
Stange, Wanda Jean 1950- WhoAmW 93
Stangeland, Roger E. 1929- St&PR 93
Stangeland, Roger Earl 1929- WhoAm 92
Stangeland, Tor Oscar 1929- WhoAm 92
Stanger, Ila 1940- WhoAm 92, WhoWrEP 92
Stanger, John W. 1923- St&PR 93
Stanger, John William 1923- WhoAm 92
Stanger, Paul Norman 1944- St&PR 93
Stanger, Robert Henry 1937- WhoE 93
Stanger, Wesley A., Jr. 1909- St&PR 93
Stangerup, Henrik 1937- ScF&FL 92
Stanghellini, Cecilia 1953- WhoScE 91-3
Stangl, Jean BioIn 17
Stangl, (Mary) Jean 1928- ConAu 136
Stangl, Peter 1936- WhoAm 92
Stangle, James F. 1948- St&PR 93
Stangler, Ferdinand Karl Ludwig 1928- WhoScE 91-4
Stangler, Kevin John 1948- St&PR 93
Stanglin, Deborah Ann Law&B 92
Stango, Joseph, Jr. 1960- WhoE 93
Stanhagen, William H. 1928- St&PR 93
Stanhope, Hester 1776-1839 Expl 93 [port]
Stanhope, Hester Lucy 1776-1839 BioIn 17
Stanhope, Philip Dormer 1694-1773 BioIn 17
Stanhope, Russell C. d1989 BioIn 17
Stania, Peter Richard 1943- WhoWor 93
Staniar, Burton B. 1942- St&PR 93, WhoAm 92
Staniar, Linda B. 1948- St&PR 93
Staniar, Linda Burton 1948- WhoAmW 93, WhoE 93
Stanich, Stephen E. 1952- St&PR 93
Stanig, Gerald Joseph 1944- WhoE 93
Stanisci, Thomas William 1928- WhoE 93
Stanish, Jean Marie 1947- WhoAmW 93
Stanislao, Joseph 1928- WhoAm 92
Stanislav, Josef 1897-1971 Baker 92
Stanislavsky, Konstantin 1863-1938 BioIn 17, IntDcOp, OxDcOp
Stanislavsky, Konstantin (Sergeievich) 1863-1938 Baker 92
Stanislaw, Richard K. 1949- St&PR 93
Stanislawczyk, Piotr WhoScE 91-4
Staniszewski, Andrzej Marek 1952- WhoWor 93
Staniszewski, Bogumil Edward 1924- WhoScE 91-4
Stanitz, Christopher Law&B 92
Stanivukovic, Dragutin D. 1946- WhoScE 91-4
Stank, Gerald J. 1947- St&PR 93
Stanka, H.P. 1934- WhoScE 91-3
Stanke, Howard Joseph 1948- St&PR 93
Stankey, Suzanne M. 1951- WhoAm 92, WhoAmW 93
Stankiewicz, Andrzej 1942- WhoScE 91-4
Stankiewicz, Jolanta 1946- WhoWor 93
Stankiewicz, Raymond 1932- WhoE 93
Stankiewicz, Roman 1943- WhoWor 93
Stankiewicz, Wladyslaw Jozef 1922- WhoAm 92
Stanklus, Gary L. 1946- St&PR 93
Stanko, Elizabeth Anne 1950- ConAu 38NR
Stanko, Kevin M. Law&B 92
Stanko, Richard E. 1957- St&PR 93
Stanko, Robert M. 1957- St&PR 93
Stanko, Robert Michael 1957- WhoE 93
Stankov, Krassimir Angelov 1950- WhoWor 93
Stankovic, Aleksandar M. 1960- WhoE 93
Stankovic, Snezana WhoScE 91-4
Stankovich, Evgeny 1942- Baker 92
Stankowski, Jan WhoScE 91-4
Stankus-Saulaitis, Marija Edita 1941- WhoE 93
Stanky, Edward Raymond 1916- BiDAMSp 1989
Stankye, C.M., Jr. 1933- St&PR 93
Stanland, Jackson E. Law&B 92
Stanleigh, Lyle B. 1946- St&PR 93
Stanley, Arthur Jehu, Jr. 1901- WhoAm 92
Stanley, Barbara Keyes 1946- WhoSSW 93
Stanley, Bob 1932- WhoAm 92
Stanley, Brian C. St&PR 93
Stanley, C. Maxwell 1904-1984 BioIn 17
Stanley, Carl M. 1935- St&PR 93
Stanley, Charles J. 1943- WhoWrEP 92
Stanley, Claude Maxwell 1904-1984 BioIn 17
Stanley, Clifford W. 1946- St&PR 93
Stanley, Colin 1952- ScF&FL 92
Stanley, Daniel Jean 1934- WhoAm 92
Stanley, David 1935- St&PR 93
Stanley, David 1944- ConAu 39NR
Stanley, David H. Law&B 92
Stanley, Dean Peter 1935- St&PR 93
Stanley, Diane ChlBIID [port]
Stanley, Diane 1943- SmATA 15AS [port]
Stanley, Douglas Oliver 1964- WhoSSW 93
Stanley, E. Richard 1944- WhoE 93
Stanley, Edmund A., Jr. 1924- St&PR 93
Stanley, Edmund Allport, Jr. 1924- WhoAm 92
Stanley, Edward Alexander 1929- WhoAm 92, WhoWor 93
Stanley, Elizabeth 1951- WhoAmW 93
Stanley, Elizabeth Colelli 1942- WhoAmW 93
Stanley, Ellen May 1921- WhoAm 92
Stanley, Fay 1925-1990 BioIn 17
Stanley, Forrest F. Law&B 92
Stanley, Furman K., Jr. 1942- St&PR 93
Stanley, George 1934- WhoCanL 92
Stanley, George Edward 1942- ConAu 39NR
Stanley, George Geoffrey 1953- WhoSSW 93
Stanley, Harriett Lari 1950- WhoAmW 93, WhoE 93
Stanley, Harry Eugene 1941- WhoAm 92, WhoWor 93
Stanley, Henry M. 1841-1904 BioIn 17
Stanley, Henry Morton 1841-1904 Expl 93 [port]
Stanley, Howard Cromwell Law&B 92
Stanley, Hugh Monroe, Jr. 1944- WhoAm 92
Stanley, Ian Malcolm WhoScE 91-1
Stanley, J. Wayne 1946- St&PR 93
Stanley, James Alan 1952- St&PR 93
Stanley, James Gordon 1925- WhoSSW 93
Stanley, James Paul 1915- WhoAm 92
Stanley, James R. Law&B 92
Stanley, James R. 1931- St&PR 93
Stanley, James Richard 1931- WhoAm 92
Stanley, Joel Francis 1934- WhoWor 93
Stanley, John 1712-1786 Baker 92
Stanley, John 1940- ScF&FL 92
Stanley, John Alfred 1937- WhoAm 92
Stanley, John D. Law&B 92
Stanley, John Maxwell 1936- St&PR 93
Stanley, John W. 1940- WhoWrEP 92
Stanley, John Walker 1906- St&PR 93
Stanley, Julian C. BioIn 17
Stanley, Julian Cecil, Jr. 1918- WhoAm 92, WhoE 93
Stanley, Justin Armstrong 1911- WhoAm 92
Stanley, Karen 1951- WhoAmW 93
Stanley, Karlyn Dana Law&B 92
Stanley, Kendra Eunice 1936- WhoAmW 93
Stanley, LaNett Lorraine 1962- WhoAmW 93
Stanley, Lawrence 1947- St&PR 93
Stanley, Louise 1915-1982 SweetSg C [port]
Stanley, M. Lizzie AmWomPl
Stanley, Malchan Craig 1948- WhoEmL 93
Stanley, Margaret BioIn 17
Stanley, Margaret King 1929- WhoAmW 93
Stanley, Mari R. Law&B 92
Stanley, Marilyn Vieira 1938- WhoAmW 93
Stanley, Mark James 1955- WhoE 93
Stanley, Marlyse Reed 1934- WhoWor 93
Stanley, Martha M. Burgess 1879- AmWomPl
Stanley, Mary Frances 1938- WhoAmW 93
Stanley, P.I. WhoScE 91-1
Stanley, Pamela Mary 1947- WhoAmW 93
Stanley, Patricia H. ConAu 138, WhoSSW 93
Stanley, Patricia Mary 1948- WhoAmW 93
Stanley, Paul MiSFD 9
Stanley, Paula Helen 1952- WhoSSW 93
Stanley, Peter Ian 1946- WhoScE 91-1
Stanley, Peter William 1940- WhoAm 92
Stanley, Ralph 1927- WhoAm 92
Stanley, Ralph W. BioIn 17
Stanley, Richard MiSFD 9
Stanley, Richard Eugene 1947- St&PR 93
Stanley, Richard H. 1932- St&PR 93
Stanley, Richard Holt 1932- WhoAm 92
Stanley, Robert L. St&PR 93
Stanley, Robert Warren 1941- WhoAm 92
Stanley, Roderic Kenneth 1941- WhoSSW 93
Stanley, Ron 1947- St&PR 93
Stanley, Russel M. Law&B 92
Stanley, Scott, Jr. 1938- WhoAm 92
Stanley, Sherry Law&B 92
Stanley, Sherry A. 1955- WhoAmW 93
Stanley, Sheryl Lynn 1952- WhoAmW 93
Stanley, Sonya Faith Stephenson 1965- WhoAmW 93
Stanley, Steven Mitchell 1941- WhoAm 92
Stanley, Terence Eric WhoScE 91-1
Stanley, Terry L. 1951- St&PR 93
Stanley, Thomas Bahnson, Jr. 1927- WhoAm 92
Stanley, Timothy David Law&B 92
Stanley, Timothy Wadsworth 1927- WhoAm 92, WhoWor 93
Stanley, Warren S. 1948- WhoIns 93
Stanley, William, Jr. 1919- WhoAm 92
Stanley, William D. Law&B 92
Stanley, William Eugene 1844-1910 BioIn 17
Stanley, William R. St&PR 93
Stanley, Wilmer Austin 1907- St&PR 93
Stanley, Winnifred Claire 1909- BioIn 17
Stanley Gilbert, Janice Gail 1940- St&PR 93
Stanley-Smith, Lisa Ann 1965- WhoAmW 93
Stanly, Jack d1990 BioIn 17
Stann, Robert 1938- WhoIns 93
Stannard, Carl Roy, Jr. 1935- WhoE 93
Stannard, Daphne Evon 1963- WhoWor 93
Stannard, Derek C. 1927- St&PR 93
Stannard, Frank Russell 1931- WhoWor 93
Stannard, Richard L. St&PR 93
Stannard, Russell ScF&FL 92
Stanner, W.E.H. 1906-1981 IntDcAn
Stanners, Jerry K. 1935- St&PR 93
Stanny, Gary 1953- WhoEmL 93, WhoWor 93
Stano, Rosemary C. Law&B 92
Stanoch, Mark Joseph 1952- St&PR 93
Stanojev, Edward Charles, Jr. 1953- St&PR 93
Stanojev, John Edward 1951- WhoE 93
Stanojevic, Dragoljub 1925- WhoScE 91-4
Stanovnik, Branko 1938- WhoWor 93
Stans, Maurice Hubert 1908- WhoAm 92
Stansberry, Carolyn Dannelly 1946- WhoSSW 93
Stansberry, Domenic Joseph 1952- WhoWrEP 92
Stansberry, James Wesley 1927- WhoAm 92
Stansberry, Warren H. St&PR 93
Stansbury, John P. Law&B 92
Stansbury, Philip Roger 1931- WhoAm 92
Stansell, James Lewis 1953- WhoWor 93
Stansfield, George Hodgson Law&B 92
Stansfield, J. Malcolm WhoScE 91-1
Stansfield, Lisa BioIn 17
Stansfield, Lisa 1966- ConMus 9 [port]
Stansgate, Viscountess 1897-1991 AnObit 1991
Stansky, Peter 1932- ScF&FL 92
Stansky, Peter David Lyman 1932- WhoAm 92
Stanton, Alexander 1953- WhoAm 92
Stanton, Aloysius F. 1940- St&PR 93
Stanton, Barbara Hadley 1935- WhoE 93
Stanton, Bernard Freeland 1925- WhoE 93
Stanton, Blair Hughes- 1902-1981 BioIn 17
Stanton, Bruce Alston 1966- WhoSSW 93
Stanton, Bruce Elliot Law&B 92
Stanton, Carey 1923-1987 BioIn 17
Stanton, Charles G. d1992 BioIn 17
Stanton, David Bert 1941- St&PR 93
Stanton, Donald S. 1932- St&PR 93

Stanton, Donald Sheldon 1932- *WhoAm 92*
Stanton, Edward M. 1921- *WhoAm 92*
Stanton, Edwin M. 1814-1869 *OxCSupC, PolPar*
Stanton, Edwin McMasters 1814-1869 *BioIn 17*
Stanton, Elizabeth Cady 1815-1902 *AmWomWr 92, BioIn 17, GayN, PolPar*
Stanton, Frank 1908- *St&PR 93, WhoAm 92*
Stanton, Frank 1929- *WhoAm 92*
Stanton, Frank L. 1857-1927 *JrnUS*
Stanton, Frederick Perry 1814-1894 *BioIn 17*
Stanton, Gardner Kimmel 1942- *WhoSSW 93*
Stanton, George Duwe 1949- *WhoSSW 93*
Stanton, Gerald E. 1922- *WhoAm 92*
Stanton, Gregory Howard 1946- *WhoE 93*
Stanton, Harry Dean 1926- *IntDcF 2-3, WhoAm 92*
Stanton, James Adkins 1941- *WhoAm 92*
Stanton, James E. 1945- *St&PR 93*
Stanton, Jane Graham 1922- *WhoAmW 93*
Stanton, Janice B. *Law&B 92*
Stanton, Jeanne Frances 1920- *WhoAmW 93, WhoWor 93*
Stanton, Jimmy Royce 1938- *WhoSSW 93*
Stanton, John Jeffrey 1956- *WhoSSW 93*
Stanton, John M. *St&PR 93*
Stanton, John P. 1936- *St&PR 93*
Stanton, John Pinckney 1936- *WhoWor 93*
Stanton, Joseph Robert 1920- *WhoE 93*
Stanton, Ken *ScF&FL 92*
Stanton, Kevin Joseph *Law&B 92*
Stanton, Louis Lee 1927- *WhoAm 92*
Stanton, Mary 1947- *ScF&FL 92*
Stanton, Mary McSherry 1946- *WhoAmW 93*
Stanton, Maura 1946- *DcLB 120 [port], WhoWrEP 92*
Stanton, Patricia *Law&B 92*
Stanton, Peter W. 1938- *St&PR 93*
Stanton, Priscilla Anne 1953- *WhoWrEP 92*
Stanton, Robert Alan 1946- *WhoE 93*
Stanton, Robert J. 1940- *St&PR 93*
Stanton, Robert James, Jr. 1931- *WhoAm 92*
Stanton, Robert John 1913- *WhoAm 92, WhoSSW 93*
Stanton, Robert M. *Law&B 92*
Stanton, Roger D. 1938- *WhoAm 92*
Stanton, Sara Lee 1930- *WhoAmW 93*
Stanton, Sherri C. *Law&B 92*
Stanton, Sylvia Doucet 1935- *WhoSSW 93*
Stanton, Thomas Cousar 1929- *WhoAm 92*
Stanton, Thomas Joyce, Jr. 1928- *St&PR 93*
Stanton, Thomas L., Jr. *Law&B 92*
Stanton, Thomas Mitchell 1922- *WhoAm 92*
Stanton, Thomas R. *Law&B 92*
Stanton, Vance *ConAu 39NR*
Stanton, Victoria M. 1960- *St&PR 93*
Stanton, Vincent A. 1926- *St&PR 93*
Stanton, Virginia May 1957- *WhoAmW 93*
Stanton, Walter O. 1914- *St&PR 93*
Stanton, Walter Oliver 1914- *WhoWor 93*
Stanton, William Edward 1961- *WhoSSW 93*
Stanton, William John, Jr. 1919- *WhoAm 92, WhoWor 93*
Stanton, William K. 1942- *St&PR 93*
Stanton-Cotter, Mary Elizabeth *Law&B 92*
Stanwick, Kathy Ann 1950- *WhoAmW 93*
Stanwick, Tad 1916- *WhoAm 92*
Stanwood, Brooks *ScF&FL 92*
Stanwyck, Barbara *BioIn 17*
Stanwyck, Barbara 1907-1990 *IntDcF 2-3 [port], SweetSg D [port]*
Stanzione, Daniel C. 1945- *St&PR 93*
Stanzione, Kaydon Al 1956- *WhoE 93*
Stanzler, Jeff *MiSFD 9*
Stap, Donald L. 1949- *WhoWrEP 92*
Stapells, Richard Bredin 1925- *St&PR 93*
Stapen, Candyce Homnick 1951- *WhoAmW 93*
Staph, Jack A. *Law&B 92*
Staph, Jack Alan 1945- *St&PR 93*
Staphidakes fl. c. 1320- *OxDcByz*
Stapier, Michael J. 1935- *St&PR 93*
Staple, Peter D. *Law&B 92*
Stapledon, Agnes 1894?-1983? *ScF&FL 92*
Stapledon, Michael *ScF&FL 92*
Stapledon, Olaf 1886-1950 *BioIn 17, ScF&FL 92*
Stapler, Richard Nathanial, Jr. *Law&B 92*
Staples, Brent *BioIn 17*
Staples, Charles O. 1937- *St&PR 93*
Staples, Eugene Leo 1926- *WhoAm 92*
Staples, John Albert 1942- *WhoE 93*
Staples, Katherine Eugenia 1947- *WhoSSW 93*
Staples, Mark Andrew 1954- *WhoE 93*
Staples, Mavis *SoulM*
Staples, O. Sherwin 1908- *WhoAm 92*
Staples, Peter 1947- *WhoAsAP 91*
Staples, Richard Bruce 1963- *WhoE 93*
Staples, Richard Farnsworth 1919- *WhoAm 92*
Staples, Robert Edward 1931- *WhoE 93*
Staples, Robert Taylor 1931- *St&PR 93*
Staples, Suzanne Fisher 1945- *SmATA 70*
Staple Singers *SoulM*
Stapleton, Charles M. 1939- *WhoIns 93*
Stapleton, Claudia Ann 1947- *WhoAmW 93, WhoSSW 93*
Stapleton, Darwin Heilman 1947- *WhoE 93*
Stapleton, Harvey James 1934- *WhoAm 92*
Stapleton, J.P. 1945- *St&PR 93*
Stapleton, James Alford 1916- *St&PR 93*
Stapleton, James Francis 1932- *WhoAm 92*
Stapleton, James Hall 1931- *WhoAm 92*
Stapleton, Jean *BioIn 17, WhoAm 92, WhoAmW 93*
Stapleton, John Owen 1951- *WhoSSW 93*
Stapleton, Katharine Laurence 1911- *WhoAm 92, WhoWrEP 92*
Stapleton, Kathleen Mary 1938- *St&PR 93*
Stapleton, Larry *St&PR 93*
Stapleton, Margaret M. 1936- *St&PR 93*
Stapleton, Marilyn S. 1950- *WhoAmW 93*
Stapleton, Maureen 1925- *WhoAm 92, WhoAmW 93*
Stapleton, P.G. *WhoScE 91-1*
Stapleton, Paul J. d1991 *BioIn 17*
Stapleton, R.R. *WhoScE 91-1*
Stapleton, Raymond D. 1939- *St&PR 93*
Stapleton, Thomas David 1912- *WhoE 93, WhoWor 93*
Stapleton, Thomas F. 1939- *St&PR 93*
Stapleton, Thomas M. 1956- *St&PR 93*
Stapleton, Walter King 1934- *WhoAm 92, WhoE 93*
Stapley, Edward Olley 1927- *WhoE 93*
Stapley, Virginia Johnson 1951- *WhoSSW 93*
Stapp, Bruce B. 1933- *St&PR 93*
Stapp, Carol Buchalter 1946- *WhoE 93*
Stapp, Emilie Blackmore *AmWomPl*
Stapp, John Barr 1962- *St&PR 93*
Stapp, John Paul *BioIn 17*
Stapp, John Paul 1910- *WhoAm 92*
Stapp, Mary E. 1909- *St&PR 93*
Stapp, Olivia 1940- *Baker 92*
Stapp, Olivia Brewer 1940- *WhoAm 92*
Stapp, Peter J. *Law&B 92*
Stapp, Steven Jay *Law&B 92*
Stapp, William Francis 1945- *WhoAm 92*
Staprans, Armand 1931- *WhoAm 92*
Staquet, Maurice J. 1930- *WhoScE 91-2*
Star, Anne Marie 1947- *WhoAmW 93*
Star, Richard William 1934- *St&PR 93*
Starbird, Kaye 1916- *ConAu 38NR, MajAI [port]*
Starcevic, Joseph F. *Law&B 92*
Starck, Ann Roach 1942- *WhoSSW 93*
Starck, Louis P. 1923- *St&PR 93*
Starck, Patricia Lee 1938- *WhoAmW 93*
Starck, Philippe 1949- *BioIn 17*
Starcke, Carl Nicolai 1858-1926 *IntDcAn*
Starczewski, Felix 1868-1945 *Baker 92*
Stare, Fredrick John *BioIn 17*
Stare, Fredrick John 1910- *WhoAm 92, WhoWor 93*
Starer, David 1955- *WhoE 93*
Starer, Robert 1924- *Baker 92, WhoAm 92*
Starfield, Barbara Helen 1932- *WhoAm 92, WhoAmW 93*
Stargell, Willie 1941- *WhoAm 92*
Stargell, Wilver Dornel 1941- *WhoAm 92*
Starger, Andrew *Law&B 92*
Staring, Graydon Shaw 1923- *WhoAm 92*
Starita, Joseph 1922- *St&PR 93*
Stark, Agnes Louise 1929- *WhoAmW 93*
Stark, Albert 1897-1968 *BiDAMSp 1989*
Stark, Amy Louise 1954- *WhoAmW 93*
Stark, Arthur Alan 1935- *St&PR 93*
Stark, Bruce Gunsten 1933- *WhoAm 92*
Stark, Charles Arthur 1961- *WhoSSW 93*
Stark, Charles Werner 1948- *WhoE 93*
Stark, Cruce 1942- *ConAu 137*
Stark, Daniel *Law&B 92*
Stark, Daniel Ernest 1927- *St&PR 93*
Stark, David Callum Carmichael 1927- *WhoAm 92*
Stark, David Charles 1936- *WhoAm 92*
Stark, David Keith 1937- *St&PR 93*
Stark, Dennis Edwin 1937- *WhoAm 92*
Stark, Donald Gerald 1926- *St&PR 93, WhoAm 92*
Stark, Douglas George 1952- *WhoSSW 93*
Stark, Edward J. 1938- *St&PR 93*
Stark, Edward Joseph 1938- *WhoAm 92*
Stark, Eliot Richard 1952- *St&PR 93*
Stark, Ervin 1922- *WhoScE 91-4*
Stark, Fortney H. *BioIn 17*
Stark, Fortney Hillman 1931- *WhoAm 92*
Stark, Fortney Pete 1931- *CngDr 91*
Stark, Fran *BioIn 17*
Stark, Frances Brice d1992 *NewYTBS 92*
Stark, Francis C., Jr. 1919- *WhoAm 92, WhoE 93*
Stark, Frederic Remy 1947- *WhoE 93*
Stark, George Robert 1933- *WhoScE 91-1*
Stark, Graham 1922- *QDrFCA 92 [port]*
Stark, Guenther 1938- *WhoScE 91-3*
Stark, H. Allan *Law&B 92*
Stark, H. James 1940- *St&PR 93*
Stark, Harold R. 1880-1972 *BioIn 17*
Stark, Harold Walter 1932- *St&PR 93*
Stark, J.E. *WhoScE 91-1*
Stark, J.W.B. 1939- *WhoScE 91-3*
Stark, Jaroslav Frantisek 1934- *WhoWor 93*
Stark, Joan Scism 1937- *WhoAm 92, WhoAmW 93*
Stark, John D. 1944- *St&PR 93*
Stark, John Edwin 1916- *WhoAm 92*
Stark, Jonathan *BioIn 17*
Stark, Joshua *ConAu 39NR*
Stark, Karen *WhoAm 92*
Stark, Martin Alan 1956- *WhoE 93*
Stark, Marvin 1921- *St&PR 93*
Stark, Marvin L. 1937- *St&PR 93*
Stark, Mary Barbara 1920- *WhoAmW 93*
Stark, Maurice Gene 1935- *St&PR 93, WhoAm 92*
Stark, Michael *Law&B 92*
Stark, Nathan Julius 1920- *WhoAm 92*
Stark, Nathene Lynne 1953- *WhoSSW 93*
Stark, Nellie May 1933- *WhoAmW 93*
Stark, Otakar 1925- *WhoScE 91-4*
Stark, Patricia Ann 1937- *WhoAmW 93, WhoWor 93*
Stark, Paul Calvert Hollister 1959- *WhoE 93*
Stark, Pete *BioIn 17*
Stark, Philip Herald 1936- *St&PR 93*
Stark, Ray *WhoAm 92*
Stark, Richard *BioIn 17*
Stark, Richard Boies 1915- *WhoAm 92*
Stark, Richard Clinton 1948- *WhoE 93*
Stark, Robert *Law&B 92*
Stark, Robert 1847-1922 *Baker 92*
Stark, Robert Alfred 1934- *St&PR 93*
Stark, Robert Martin 1930- *WhoAm 92*
Stark, Rohn 1959- *WhoAm 92*
Stark, Ron *Law&B 92*
Stark, Ruth Daryl 1942- *WhoUN 92*
Stark, S. Daniel, Jr. 1953- *WhoWor 93*
Stark, Stanley 1948- *St&PR 93, WhoE 93*
Stark, Steven 1943- *WhoE 93*
Stark, Temple C. 1946- *St&PR 93*
Stark, Temple Cunningham 1946- *WhoIns 93*
Stark, Theodore E., Jr. 1930- *St&PR 93*
Stark, W.P., Jr. 1927- *St&PR 93*
Stark, Werner E. 1921- *St&PR 93*
Stark, William Richard 1945- *WhoSSW 93*
Stark-Adamec, Cannie 1945- *WhoAm 92*
Starke, Catherine Juanita 1913- *WhoE 93*
Starke, Edgar Arlin, Jr. 1936- *WhoAm 92*
Starke, Gunter 1921- *WhoScE 91-3*
Starke, Hortensia L. *WhoAsAP 91*
Starke, Linda *WhoWrEP 92*
Starkel, Leszek 1931- *WhoScE 91-4*
Starken, George Mathew 1934- *WhoE 93*
Starker, Janos 1924- *Baker 92*
Starkes, Darnell, Jr. 1955- *WhoE 93*
Starkey, David 1952- *ScF&FL 92*
Starkey, Douglas E. *Law&B 92*
Starkey, Elizabeth Carmella 1947- *WhoSSW 93*
Starkey, James H. 1940- *St&PR 93*
Starkey, James Henry, III 1940- *WhoAm 92*
Starkey, Janet Voigt 1953- *WhoSSW 93*
Starkey, Lee *BioIn 17*
Starkey, Mary Beth 1956- *WhoAmW 93*
Starkey, Naomi *ScF&FL 92*
Starkey, Patrick E. 1933- *St&PR 93*
Starkey, Richard 1940- *Baker 92, WhoWor 93*
Starkey, Richard L. 1952- *St&PR 93*
Starkey, Russell B., Jr. 1942- *St&PR 93*
Starkey, Russell Bruce, Jr. 1942- *WhoSSW 93*
Starkey, William E. 1935- *St&PR 93*
Starkey, William Edward 1935- *WhoAm 92*
Starkhammar, Lars F. 1937- *WhoScE 91-4*
Starkie, Walter Fitzwilliam 1894-1976 *BioIn 17*
Starklint, Jan Faber 1945- *WhoWor 93*
Starkoff, Bernard J. 1917-1991 *BioIn 17*
Starkov, Andrey Viktorovich 1961- *WhoWor 93*
Starks, Charles Wiley 1954- *WhoSSW 93*
Starks, Christopher *ScF&FL 92*
Starks, Fred William 1921- *WhoAm 92*
Starks, Richard 1947- *ScF&FL 92*
Starks, Richard W. *St&PR 93*
Starks, William Edward 1965- *WhoE 93*
Starkweather, Charles Woodruff 1938- *WhoE 93*
Starlin, Jim 1950- *ScF&FL 92*
Starling, H. Ray, Jr. *Law&B 92*
Starling, James Lyne 1930- *WhoAm 92*
Starling, Larry Eugene 1954- *WhoSSW 93*
Starling, Lynn 1891- *AmWomPl*
Starling, Maud *AmWomPl*
Starling, Thomas *WhoWrEP 92*
Starlinger, Peter 1931- *WhoScE 91-3*
Starmann, George H., III 1943- *St&PR 93*
Starmann, Richard G. 1945- *St&PR 93*
Starn, Douglas 1961- *WhoAm 92*
Starn, Mike P. 1961- *WhoAm 92*
St-Arnaud, C. 1933- *St&PR 93*
Starner, Bradley W. 1964- *St&PR 93*
Starner, Craig Leslie 1934- *WhoSSW 93*
Starner, William Stuart 1953- *St&PR 93*
Starnes, Earl Maxwell 1926- *WhoAm 92*
Starnes, Edward Clinton 1950- *WhoE 93, WhoEmL 93*
Starnes, John 1918- *WhoCanL 92*
Starnes, Kenneth Deen 1942- *WhoSSW 93*
Starnes, William Herbert, Jr. 1934- *WhoAm 92, WhoSSW 93*
Starns, Douglas Lee 1955- *WhoSSW 93*
Starns, Larry D. *Law&B 92*
Starobin, Herman 1921- *WhoE 93*
Starobin, Naomi 1927- *WhoAmW 93*
Starodubtsev, Vasily *BioIn 17*
Starokadomsky, Mikhail 1901-1954 *Baker 92*
Staroselsky, Naum *BioIn 17*
Starosolszky, Odon 1931- *WhoScE 91-4*
Starowicz, Wieslaw 1947- *WhoScE 91-4*
Starr, Alice Jean Mendell 1949- *WhoSSW 93*
Starr, Arnold 1932- *WhoAm 92*
Starr, Augusta M. *AmWomPl*
Starr, Barbara Schaap 1935- *WhoE 93*
Starr, Bart 1934- *BioIn 17, WhoAm 92*
Starr, Belle 1848-1889 *BioIn 17*
Starr, Bill *ScF&FL 92*
Starr, Bob *BioIn 17*
Starr, Carol L. *Law&B 92*
Starr, Chauncey 1912- *WhoAm 92*
Starr, Chester 1914- *WhoWrEP 92*
Starr, Chester G. 1914- *WhoAm 92*
Starr, David 1922- *WhoAm 92, WhoE 93*
Starr, David Evan 1962- *WhoWor 93*
Starr, Duane Edwin 1942- *St&PR 93*
Starr, Edwin 1942- *SoulM*
Starr, Frances Louise 1927- *WhoAmW 93*
Starr, Frank O. 1922- *St&PR 93*
Starr, Frederick 1858-1933 *IntDcAn*
Starr, Frederick Brown 1932- *WhoAm 92*
Starr, Gary 1955- *St&PR 93*
Starr, Harold Page 1932- *WhoE 93*
Starr, Harry A. d1990 *BioIn 17*
Starr, Harvey 1946- *WhoAm 92, WhoSSW 93*
Starr, Helen *AmWomPl*
Starr, Henry d1992 *NewYTBS 92 [port]*
Starr, Henry 1873-1921 *BioIn 17*
Starr, Heriwentha Mae Faggs 1932- *BiDAMSp 1989*
Starr, Ila Mae 1917- *WhoAmW 93*
Starr, Isidore 1911- *WhoAm 92*
Starr, James A. d1990 *BioIn 17*
Starr, Jamie *SoulM*
Starr, Jan *WhoWrEP 92*
Starr, Janice Desocio 1959- *WhoE 93*
Starr, John C. 1939- *WhoAm 92*
Starr, John Robert 1927- *WhoAm 92, WhoSSW 93*
Starr, John Thornton, Jr. 1939- *WhoWor 93*
Starr, Jonathan Andrew 1951- *St&PR 93*
Starr, Joyce Ives 1932- *WhoE 93*
Starr, Kay 1922- *BioIn 17*
Starr, Kenneth W. 1946- *BioIn 17*
Starr, Leon 1937- *St&PR 93, WhoAm 92*
Starr, M. Philip 1945- *St&PR 93*
Starr, Malcolm White 1943- *St&PR 93*
Starr, Mark T. *Law&B 92*
Starr, Martin Kenneth 1927- *WhoAm 92*
Starr, Maurice Kenneth 1922- *WhoAm 92*
Starr, Michael Robert 1954- *WhoScE 91-4*
Starr, Nancy Hamburger 1958- *WhoAmW 93*
Starr, Norbert T. *Law&B 92*
Starr, Paul Elliot 1949- *WhoAm 92*
Starr, Richard Cawthon 1924- *WhoAm 92*
Starr, Richard M. *Law&B 92*
Starr, Richard William 1920- *WhoAm 92*
Starr, Rick 1947- *WhoAm 92*
Starr, Ringo *BioIn 17*
Starr, "Ringo" 1940- *Baker 92, MiSFD 9, WhoAm 92, WhoWor 93*
Starr, Robert M. 1928- *St&PR 93*
Starr, Robert Morton 1928- *WhoAm 92*
Starr, Roger W. 1946- *St&PR 93*
Starr, Roland *ScF&FL 92*
Starr, Ross Marc 1945- *WhoAm 92*
Starr, Shelley Marie 1954- *WhoAm 92*
Starr, Stephen Frederick 1940- *WhoAm 92*

Starr, Steven Dawson 1944- *WhoAm 92*
Starr, Tama 1946- *St&PR 93*
Starr, V. Hale 1936- *WhoAm 92*
Starr, Walter Douglas, Jr. 1944- *WhoAm 92*
Starr, Wanda Mae 1942- *WhoAmW 93*
Starr, Warren David 1939- *WhoWor 93*
Starr, William J. 1923- *WhoWrEP 92*
Starratt, Patricia Elizabeth 1943- *WhoAmW 93*
Starrenburg, Johan A. 1951- *St&PR 93*
Starrett, Jack 1936-1989 *MiSFD 9N*
Starrett, Lucinda 1957- *WhoAmW 93*
Starrett, Pamela Elizabeth 1962- *WhoAmW 93*
Starrett, Vincent 1886-1974 *ScF&FL 92*
Starrock, Volker 1941- *WhoWor 93*
Starron, Robert Edward 1935- *St&PR 93*
Starrs, Arthur F. *Law&B 92*
Starr-White, Debi *WhoWrEP 92*
Starry, Donn Albert 1925- *WhoAm 92*
Starsen, Melle 1952- *BioIn 17*
Starsick, Joseph J., Jr. *Law&B 92*
Start, Joanne E. *St&PR 93*
Startup, Charles Harry 1914- *WhoAm 92*
Startzman, Shirley Kayleen 1946- *WhoAmW 93*
Staruszkiewicz, Andrzej 1940- *WhoScE 91-4*
Staryk, Steven 1932- *Baker 92*
Staryk, Steven S. 1932- *WhoAm 92*
Starzak, Michael Edward 1942- *WhoWrEP 92*
Starzecka, Aleksandra 1930- *WhoScE 91-4*
Starzecki, Wlodzimierz *WhoScE 91-4*
Starzer, Josef 1726?-1787 *Baker 92*
Starzinger, Vincent Evans 1929- *WhoAm 92*
Starzl, Thomas E. 1926- *BioIn 17*
Starzl, Thomas Earl 1926- *WhoAm 92*
Starzmann, Eleanor Gloria 1947- *WhoE 93*
Starzycki, Stanislaw 1923- *WhoScE 91-4*
Starzyk, Jerzy Roman 1942- *WhoWor 93*
Starzyk, Richard Alan 1964- *WhoE 93*
Starzynski, Stefan 1893-1943 *PolBiDi*
Stasack, Edward Armen 1929- *WhoAm 92*
Stasch, Julia M. *BioIn 17*
Stasey, Michael J. 1946- *St&PR 93*
Stasheff, Christopher 1944- *ScF&FL 92*
Stashower, Daniel 1960- *ScF&FL 92*
Stashower, David L. 1929- *St&PR 93*
Stashower, Michael 1926- *St&PR 93*
Stashower, Michael David 1926- *WhoAm 92*
Stasicka, Zofia Danuta 1933- *WhoScE 91-4*
Stasik, Walter William 1946- *St&PR 93*
Stasiowski, Peter Charles 1968- *WhoSSW 93*
Staskiel, James *Law&B 92*
Staskiewicz, Bernard Alexander 1924- *WhoE 93*
Stasny, Ludwig 1823-1883 *Baker 92*
Stasov, Vladimir 1824-1906 *OxDcOp*
Stasov, Vladimir (Vasilievich) 1824-1906 *Baker 92*
Stassen, Flemming 1959- *WhoWor 93*
Stassen, John Henry 1943- *WhoAm 92*
Stassi, Pete *BioIn 17*
Stasson, Debra M. *Law&B 92*
Stastny, Vladimir 1952- *WhoWor 93*
Stasz, Peter J. 1947- *St&PR 93*
Staszak, Lucille *ScF&FL 92*
Staszak, William C. *Law&B 92*
Staszesky, Francis Myron 1918- *WhoAm 92, WhoE 93*
Staszewski, Harry 1954- *WhoE 93*
Staszewski, Zygmunt 1932- *WhoScE 91-4*
Staszic, Stanislaw *BioIn 17*
Staszic, Stanislaw 1755-1826 *PolBiDi*
Staszkiewicz, Robert A. *St&PR 93*
Stata, Ray 1934- *St&PR 93*
Stateham, B.R. *ScF&FL 92*
Staten, Marcea Bland *Law&B 92*
States, John P. *Law&B 92*
Statezny, Judith Mary 1946- *WhoWrEP 92*
Stath, Peggy *BioIn 17*
Statham, Oliver John Henry 1941- *WhoScE 91-1*
Statham, Peter B. 1936- *St&PR 93*
Stathis, Nicholas John 1924- *WhoE 93, WhoWor 93*
Stathoplos, Demmie *BioIn 17*
Statkowski, Roman 1860-1925 *Baker 92, PolBiDi*
Statler, Betty Jean 1947- *WhoAmW 93*
Statler, Irving Carl 1923- *WhoAm 92*
Statler, Oliver Hadley 1915- *WhoAm 92*
Statler Brothers, The *ConMus 8 [port]*
Staton, Candi 1943- *SoulM*
Staton, Johanna Bilbo 1939- *WhoWrEP 92*
Staton, John C. 1903-1990 *BioIn 17*
Staton, Mary *ScF&FL 92*
Staton, Robert E. *Law&B 92*
Staton, Robert Emmett 1946- *St&PR 93*
Staton-Reinstein, Rebecca Eugenia 1940- *WhoAmW 93*
Statter, Edward F. 1934- *St&PR 93*
Stattler, Wojciech Korneli 1800-1875 *PolBiDi*
Statton, Philip James 1944- *St&PR 93*
Statton, Thomas M. 1948- *St&PR 93*
Statucki, W. Gary 1939- *St&PR 93*
Statuto, Carol M. 1949- *WhoAmW 93*
Staub, August William 1931- *WhoAm 92*
Staub, E. Brian 1927- *WhoIns 93*
Staub, Edie Laughman 1957- *St&PR 93*
Staub, Howard Randall d1991 *BioIn 17*
Staub, Jacob Joseph 1951- *WhoE 93*
Staub, Michael Joseph 1952- *St&PR 93*
Staub, Molly Belle 1937- *WhoWrEP 92*
Staub, Randy Craig 1947- *St&PR 93*
Staub, Ray 1931- *St&PR 93*
Staub, Ronald J. 1930- *St&PR 93*
Staub, Travis Edwin 1933- *St&PR 93*
Staub, W. Arthur 1923- *WhoAm 92*
Staubach, John Francis 1925- *St&PR 93*
Staubach, Roger 1942- *BioIn 17*
Staubach, Roger Thomas 1942- *WhoAm 92*
Stauber, Donald Joseph *Law&B 92*
Stauber, Patricia Marron Van Deusen 1923- *WhoAmW 93*
Stauber, Ronald J. 1940- *St&PR 93*
Staubitz, Arthur F. *Law&B 92*
Staubitz, Arthur Frederick 1939- *St&PR 93, WhoAm 92*
Staubley, Steven Richard 1966- *WhoSSW 93*
Staubus, George Joseph 1926- *WhoAm 92*
Stauch, Victor Daniel 1932- *St&PR 93*
Staude, Eberhard R.F. 1933- *WhoScE 91-3*
Staudenmaier, Mary Louise 1938- *WhoAmW 93*
Stauder, Jack Richard 1939- *WhoE 93*
Stauder, William Vincent 1922- *WhoAm 92*
Stauderman, Albert P(hilip) 1910- *ConAu 39NR*
Stauderman, Bruce Ford 1919- *WhoAm 92*
Staudhammer, John 1932- *WhoSSW 93*
Staudigl, Gisela d1929
See Staudigl, Joseph, II 1850-1916 *Baker 92*
Staudigl, Joseph, I 1807-1861 *Baker 92*
Staudigl, Joseph, II 1850-1916 *Baker 92*
Staudinger, Michael C. *ScF&FL 92*
Staudt, Chr. *WhoScE 91-3*
Staudt, F.J. 1940- *WhoScE 91-3*
Staudt, Gunter 1926- *WhoScE 91-3*
Staudt, John Eugene 1948- *St&PR 93*
Staudte, Wolfgang 1906-1984 *DrEEuF*
Stauer, Helen Grothe 1913- *WhoAmW 93*
Stauff, Michael F. 1950- *St&PR 93*
Stauffacher, C.F., Jr. 1921- *St&PR 93*
Stauffacher, Charles B. 1916- *WhoAm 92*
Stauffacher, David George 1931- *St&PR 93*
Stauffenberg, Franz-Ludwig Schenk von 1938- *BioIn 17*
Stauffenberg, Klaus Philip Schenk von 1907-1944 *HarEnMi*
Stauffenberg, Klaus Philipp Schenk von 1907-1944 *BioIn 17*
Stauffer, Charles Henry 1913- *WhoAm 92, WhoWor 93*
Stauffer, Delmar J. *WhoAm 92*
Stauffer, Dietrich 1943- *WhoScE 91-3*
Stauffer, Dorothy Hubbell 1905- *WhoWrEP 92*
Stauffer, Douglas Andrew 1931- *WhoE 93*
Stauffer, Hans P. 1932- *WhoScE 91-4*
Stauffer, Jerry *Law&B 92*
Stauffer, Joanne Rogan 1956- *WhoAmW 93*
Stauffer, John H. 1928- *St&PR 93*
Stauffer, Kent T. *Law&B 92*
Stauffer, Louise Lee 1915- *WhoAmW 93*
Stauffer, Robert Allen 1920- *WhoAm 92*
Stauffer, Ronald Eugene 1949- *WhoE 93, WhoWor 93*
Stauffer, Sarah Ann 1915- *WhoAm 92*
Stauffer, Shelby Alvina 1958- *St&PR 93*
Stauffer, Stanley Howard 1920- *WhoAm 92*
Stauffer, Thomas George 1932- *St&PR 93, WhoAm 92*
Stauffer, Thomas Michael 1941- *WhoAm 92, WhoSSW 93*
Stauffer, William Albert 1930- *WhoAm 92*
Stauffer, Zane Richard 1932- *St&PR 93*
Stauffer-Cole, Patricia Irene 1957- *WhoEmL 93*
Staulcup, James M., Jr. *Law&B 92*
Staun, Henning 1933- *WhoScE 91-2*
Staunch, G. Richard 1943- *St&PR 93*
Staunstrup, Jorgen 1952- *WhoWor 93*
Staunton, Hugh Patrick 1937- *WhoWor 93*
Staunton, Marshall A. *St&PR 93*
Staunton, Schuyler *MajAI*
Staunton, Ted *WhoCanL 92*
Staupers, Mabel 1898- *EncAACR*
Staupitz, Johann von d1524 *BioIn 17*
Staurakios d800 *OxDcByz*
Staus, Frank A. 1915- *St&PR 93*
Stauss, Hans Josef 1956- *WhoWor 93*
Stautner, Ernie 1925- *BioIn 17*
Stavchansky, Salomon 1947- *WhoSSW 93*
Stave, Carl Edward 1942- *WhoE 93*
Staveley, Henry Scowcroft 1920- *WhoWor 93*
Stavely, Richard W. *Law&B 92*
Stavely, Richard William 1927- *St&PR 93*
Stavenhagen, Bernhard 1862-1914 *Baker 92*
Stavenhagen, Joseph 1930- *St&PR 93*
Stavenhagen, Lutz 1940-1992 *BioIn 17*
Staver, Leroy Baldwin 1908- *WhoAm 92*
Stavert, Alexander Bruce 1940- *WhoAm 92*
Stavert, John L. *Law&B 92*
Staves, Marion C. *Law&B 92*
Staves, Susan 1942- *WhoAm 92*
Stavig, Mark Luther 1935- *WhoAm 92*
Stavinoha, Edward Lane 1945- *WhoSSW 93*
Stavinoha, Marcus J. 1933- *St&PR 93*
Stavis, Morton d1992 *NewYTBS 92 [port]*
Stavisky, Serge d1934 *DcTwHis*
Stavisky, Serge Alexandre 1886-1934 *BioIn 17*
Stavitsky, Abram Benjamin 1919- *WhoAm 92*
Stavitsky, Bruce Jaime *Law&B 92*
Stavola, John Joseph 1929- *WhoWor 93*
Stavola, Patricia *Law&B 92*
Stavrakos, Sotirios 1955- *WhoWor 93*
Stavridis, Jack 1949- *WhoE 93*
Stavrinos, George *BioIn 17*
Stavropoulos, D. John 1933- *St&PR 93*
Stavropoulos, Dionysos John 1933- *WhoAm 92, WhoWor 93*
Stavropoulos, George 1920-1990 *BioIn 17*
Stavropoulos, Nickolas 1958- *St&PR 93*
Stavropoulos, Rose Mary Grant *WhoAmW 93*
Stavropoulos, Thomas C. *Law&B 92*
Stavropoulos, William S. 1939- *St&PR 93, WhoAm 92*
Stavrou, Nikolaos Athanasios 1935- *WhoAm 92*
Staw, Barry Martin 1945- *WhoAm 92*
Stawarska, Renata Elisabeth 1948- *WhoWor 93*
Stawell, William Foster 1815-1889 *BioIn 17*
Stawinski, T. *WhoScE 91-4*
Stay, Barbara 1926- *WhoAmW 93*
Stayduhar, John J. 1935- *St&PR 93*
Stayin, Randolph John 1942- *WhoE 93*
Stayman, Samuel M. 1909- *WhoAm 92*
Stayner, Richard M. 1941- *WhoScE 91-1*
Stayner, Richard Mildmay *WhoScE 91-1*
Staynes, Barry W. *WhoScE 91-1*
Stayton, Gracia *AmWomPl*
Stayton, Janet *WhoE 93*
Stayton, William Ralph 1933- *WhoE 93*
Staz, John Michael 1938- *St&PR 93*
Staz, Robert K. 1935- *St&PR 93*
Stazoni, Ray *St&PR 93*
Stchur, John *ScF&FL 92*
Stea, David 1936- *WhoAm 92, WhoWor 93*
Stead, Bette Ann 1935- *WhoSSW 93*
Stead, C.K. 1932- *ScF&FL 92*
Stead, Christina 1902-1983 *BioIn 17, IntLitE, ScF&FL 92*
Stead, Christina (Ellen) 1902-1983 *ConAu 40NR*
Stead, Edward B. *Law&B 92*
Stead, Eugene Anson, Jr. 1908- *WhoAm 92*
Stead, Ivan Ward 1928- *St&PR 93*
Stead, James Joseph, Jr. 1930- *WhoAm 92, WhoWor 93*
Stead, Jerre L. *BioIn 17*
Stead, Jerre L. 1943- *WhoAm 92*
Stead, Robert J.C. 1880-1959 *BioIn 17*
Stead, William Thomas 1849-1912 *TwCLC 48 [port]*
Stead, William White 1919- *WhoAm 92*
Steadham, Charles Victor, Jr. 1944- *WhoSSW 93*
Steadle, John M. 1932- *St&PR 93*
Steadman, Charles *Law&B 92*
Steadman, Charles Walters 1914- *WhoAm 92, WhoWor 93*
Steadman, David Rosslyn Ayton 1937- *WhoAm 92*
Steadman, David Wilton 1936- *WhoAm 92*
Steadman, Douglas 1926- *WhoSSW 93*
Steadman, Jack W. 1928- *WhoAm 92*
Steadman, James Andrew *WhoScE 91-1*
Steadman, John Marcellus, III 1918- *WhoAm 92, WhoWrEP 92*
Steadman, John Montague 1930- *WhoAm 92*
Steadman, Lydia Duff 1934- *WhoAmW 93*
Steadman, Mark S. 1930- *WhoWrEP 92*
Steadman, Mark Sidney 1930- *WhoSSW 93*
Steadman, Ralph *BioIn 17*
Steadman, Richard Cooke 1932- *WhoAm 92*
Steadman, Robert Kempton 1943- *WhoWor 93*
Steadman, Sue Ann 1931- *St&PR 93*
Steagall, Henry Bascom, II 1922- *WhoSSW 93*
Steakley, John 1951- *ScF&FL 92*
Steakley, Marvin L. *St&PR 93*
Steakley, Zollie Coffer, Jr. 1908- *WhoAm 92*
Stealey, James Francis 1948- *St&PR 93*
Stealey, John W., Sr. *St&PR 93*
Stealey, Patricia Ann Terrill 1942- *WhoSSW 93*
Steane, James H., II 1944- *St&PR 93*
Stear, Edwin Byron 1932- *WhoAm 92*
Stearley, Mildred Sutcliffe Volandt 1905- *WhoAmW 93, WhoSSW 93*
Stearley, Robert Jay 1929- *WhoAm 92*
Stearn, Carl W. 1933- *St&PR 93*
Stearn, Jess *ScF&FL 92*
Stearns, Albert *ScF&FL 92*
Stearns, Clifford B. 1941- *CngDr 91*
Stearns, Clifford Bundy 1941- *WhoAm 92, WhoSSW 93*
Stearns, Frank Warren 1949- *WhoSSW 93*
Stearns, Frederic William 1943- *WhoSSW 93*
Stearns, James Gerry 1922- *WhoAm 92*
Stearns, John H. 1934- *St&PR 93, WhoIns 93*
Stearns, Jon Rod 1958- *WhoWrEP 92*
Stearns, Kendall 1915-1991 *BioIn 17*
Stearns, Linda *WhoAm 92*
Stearns, Lloyd Worthington 1910- *WhoWor 93*
Stearns, Mark Edison 1949- *WhoWor 93*
Stearns, Mark S. 1934- *St&PR 93*
Stearns, Milton S., Jr. 1923- *St&PR 93*
Stearns, Milton Sprague, Jr. 1923- *WhoAm 92*
Stearns, Pamela 1935- *ScF&FL 92*
Stearns, Peter Nathaniel 1936- *WhoAm 92, WhoE 93*
Stearns, Peter Ogden 1937- *WhoAm 92*
Stearns, Robert B. 1952- *St&PR 93*
Stearns, Robert Leland 1947- *WhoAm 92*
Stearns, Robert Paul 1937- *St&PR 93*
Stearns, Stewart Warren 1947- *WhoSSW 93*
Stearns, Wanda June 1948- *WhoAmW 93*
Stearns, William Allen 1937- *WhoAm 92*
Stebbing, Nowell 1941- *WhoWor 93*
Stebbings, Robert Yeo 1942- *WhoE 93*
Stebbins, Charles Fleming 1939- *WhoSSW 93*
Stebbins, Donald R. *Law&B 92*
Stebbins, Esther Signe 1947- *WhoWrEP 92*
Stebbins, George C(oles) 1846-1945 *Baker 92*
Stebbins, George Ledyard 1906- *WhoAm 92*
Stebbins, Gregory Kellogg 1951- *WhoEmL 93, WhoWor 93*
Stebbins, Henry Blanchard 1951- *WhoEmL 93*
Stebbins, Kathleen Brown 1905-1962 *BioIn 17*
Stebbins, Leroy Joseph 1945- *WhoSSW 93*
Stebbins, Lou Hirsch 1930- *WhoSSW 93*
Stebbins, Richard Henderson 1938- *WhoSSW 93, WhoWor 93*
Stebbins, Robert Alan 1938- *WhoAm 92*
Stebbins, Sheryl Beth 1953- *WhoAmW 93*
Stebbins, Stuart John 1916- *St&PR 93*
Stebbins, Theodore Ellis, Jr. 1938- *WhoAm 92*
Stebbins, Theodore Leon 1941- *St&PR 93*
Stebbins, William Cooper 1929- *WhoAm 92*
Stebel, S.L. 1924- *ScF&FL 92*
Steber, Eleanor *BioIn 17*
Steber, Eleanor 1914-1990 *Baker 92, OxDcOp*
Steber, Eleanor 1916-1990 *IntDcOp [port]*
Steblay, Ralph E. 1921- *St&PR 93*
Steblay, Raymond William 1922- *WhoE 93*
Stebleton, Brian C. 1942- *St&PR 93*
Stec, John Z. 1925- *St&PR 93*
Stec, John Zygment 1925- *WhoAm 92*
Stec, Wojciech Jacek 1940- *WhoWor 93*
Stecco, Sergio 1943- *WhoScE 91-3*
Stecher, Cheryl Chadurgian 1950- *WhoAmW 93*
Stecher, Donald A. *St&PR 93*
Stecher, Kenneth William 1946- *St&PR 93*
Stecher, Rodney L. 1951- *St&PR 93*
Stechert, Robert B. *Law&B 92*

Steciuk, George L. 1942- *WhoIns 93*
Steck, Carol R. 1954- *WhoWrEP 92*
Steck, Theodore Lyle 1939- *WhoAm 92*
Steckbeck, Mark D. *Law&B 92*
Steckel, Barbara Jean 1939- *WhoAm 92*
Steckel, James W. 1927- *St&PR 93*
Steckel, Richard J. 1936- *WhoAm 92*
Steckelberg, Jean Marie 1959- *WhoAmW 93*
Stecker, Carl S. 1916- *WhoIns 93*
Stecker, Elinor Horwitz 1928- *WhoE 93*
Stecker, Floyd William 1942- *WhoE 93*
Stecker, Karel 1861-1918 *Baker 92*
Steckhan, Rainer B. 1935- *WhoUN 92*
Stecklein, Leonard F. 1946- *St&PR 93*
Steckler, Arthur 1921-1985 *BioIn 17*
Steckler, Henry I. *Law&B 92*
Steckler, Joseph Leo 1933- *WhoSSW 93*
Steckler, Judith J. *Law&B 92*
Steckler, Larry 1933- *WhoAm 92, WhoWrEP 92*
Steckler, Laura Hope 1952- *WhoSSW 93*
Steckler, Lawrence 1933- *St&PR 93*
Steckler, Patricia 1951- *WhoE 93*
Steckler, Philip M., Jr. *BioIn 17*
Steckler, Phyllis Betty *WhoAm 92, WhoAmW 93*
Steckler, Ray Dennis *MiSFD 9*
Steckler, William Elwood 1913- *WhoAm 92*
Steckling, Adrienne *WhoAm 92, WhoAmW 93*
Steckman, Walter Gerald 1940- *St&PR 93*
Steckmest, Lawrence D. *Law&B 92*
Stedham, Austin W. 1928- *St&PR 93*
Stedingh, R.W. 1944- *WhoCanL 92*
Stedman, Adelaide *AmWomPl*
Stedman, Edmund Clarence 1833-1908 *GayN, JrnUS*
Stedman, Graham 1956- *WhoWor 93*
Stedman, John 1919-1990 *BioIn 17*
Stedman, Myrtle *BioIn 17*
Stedman, Myrtle 1885-1938 *SweetSg A*
Stedman, Richard Ralph 1936- *WhoAm 92*
Stedman, Robert William 1941- *WhoAm 92*
Stedron, Bohumir 1905-1982 *Baker 92*
Stedron, Milos 1942- *Baker 92*
Stedron, Vladimir 1900-1982 *Baker 92*
Stedronsky, Frank 1935- *St&PR 93*
Steed, Ethel Laverna Williams 1920- *WhoSSW 93*
Steed, Howard Drew, Jr. 1954- *WhoSSW 93*
Steed, James Larry 1939- *WhoSSW 93*
Steed, Michael John Peter 1944- *WhoWor 93*
Steed, Neville *ScF&FL 92*
Steed, Thomas Warwick, III *Law&B 92*
Steede, David W. 1943- *St&PR 93*
Steedle, Joseph Richard 1952- *WhoSSW 93*
Steedly, James E., Jr. 1938- *St&PR 93*
Steedman, Donald L. 1945- *St&PR 93*
Steedman, Doria Lynne Silberberg *WhoAm 92, WhoAmW 93*
Steedman, Ian *BioIn 17*
Steeg, James Howe 1950- *WhoE 93*
Steeg, Melba Law 1923- *WhoWor 93*
Steeg, Moise S., Jr. 1916- *WhoWor 93*
Steeg, Theodore 1868-1950 *BioIn 17*
Steege, Deborah Anderson 1946- *WhoAmW 93*
Steeger, Henry 1903-1990 *BioIn 17*
Steeger, William Paul 1945- *WhoSSW 93*
Steegmann, Albert Theodore, Jr. 1936- *WhoAm 92*
Steegmuller, Francis 1906- *BioIn 17, WhoAm 92*
Steel, Abbey *BioIn 17*
Steel, Alan Richard 1945- *WhoAm 92*
Steel, Byron 1906- *BioIn 17*
Steel, C. Eugene 1934- *St&PR 93*
Steel, (Charles) Christopher 1939- *Baker 92*
Steel, Christopher Michael *WhoScE 91-1*
Steel, Danielle *BioIn 17*
Steel, Danielle Fernande 1947- *WhoAm 92, WhoAmW 93, WhoWrEP 92*
Steel, Dawn *BioIn 17, WhoAm 92, WhoAmW 93*
Steel, Evelyn Agnes *AmWomPl*
Steel, Geoffrey A. 1926- *St&PR 93*
Steel, George Gordon *WhoScE 91-1*
Steel, Howard Haldeman 1921- *WhoAm 92*
Steel, Joan E. 1953- *St&PR 93*
Steel, Joan Elizabeth 1953- *WhoAm 92, WhoIns 93*
Steel, Mark Florimond Joseph 1958- *WhoWor 93*
Steel, Robert Howard 1928- *WhoAm 92*
Steel, Roger K. 1937- *St&PR 93*
Steel, Ronald *BioIn 17*
Steel, Ronald Lewis 1931- *WhoAm 92*
Steel, Sam *Law&B 92*
Steel, Scott Allan 1950- *WhoSSW 93*
Steel, Shirley Ann 1957- *WhoWor 93*
Steel, William Howard 1920- *WhoWor 93*
Steelbaugh, Larry *ScF&FL 92*
Steele, A(rchibald) T(rojan) 1903-1992 *ConAu 137*
Steele, Addison E. *ScF&FL 92*
Steele, Alfred Nu 1901-1959 *BioIn 17*
Steele, Allen 1958- *ConAu 136, ScF&FL 92*
Steele, Ana Mercedes 1939- *WhoAmW 93*
Steele, Anthony *WhoScE 91-1*
Steele, Archibald T. 1903-1992 *BioIn 17*
Steele, Asa Manchester *AmWomPl*
Steele, Barbara 1938?- *BioIn 17*
Steele, Betty Louise 1920- *WhoAm 92*
Steele, Beverly Louise 1944- *WhoAmW 93*
Steele, Bill F. 1928- *St&PR 93*
Steele, Brian Charles Hilton *WhoScE 91-1*
Steele, Carolyn Skinner 1928- *St&PR 93*
Steele, Charles Glen 1925- *WhoAm 92*
Steele, Charles Kenzie 1914-1980 *EncAACR*
Steele, Cheryl Ann 1955- *WhoAmW 93*
Steele, Connie Wiseman 1944- *WhoSSW 93*
Steele, Curtis *ScF&FL 92*
Steele, David 1960-
See English Beat, The *ConMus 9*
See Also Fine Young Cannibals *SoulM*
Steele, David Gentry 1941- *WhoSSW 93*
Steele, Davis Tillou 1923- *WhoSSW 93*
Steele, Denise Ann *Law&B 92*
Steele, Denny Wayne 1943- *St&PR 93*
Steele, Donald Ernest 1923- *St&PR 93*
Steele, Donald F. 1938- *St&PR 93*
Steele, Earl Larsen 1923- *WhoAm 92*
Steele, Elizabeth M. *Law&B 92*
Steele, Elizabeth Meyer 1952- *WhoAmW 93*
Steele, Ernest Clyde 1925- *WhoAm 92*
Steele, Fletcher 1885-1971 *BioIn 17*
Steele, Fletcher 1952- *St&PR 93*
Steele, Frank Channel 1938- *WhoAm 92*
Steele, Frank Pettus 1935- *WhoWrEP 92*
Steele, Frederic R. 1953- *St&PR 93*
Steele, G.E. *WhoScE 91-1*
Steele, George Peabody 1924- *WhoE 93, WhoWor 93*
Steele, Gregory William *Law&B 92*
Steele, Harold B. 1922- *WhoAm 92*
Steele, Howard Loucks 1929- *WhoE 93, WhoWor 93*
Steele, Ilene Ulmer *Law&B 92*
Steele, Jack 1942- *WhoSSW 93*
Steele, Jacqueline Beth *Law&B 92*
Steele, James B. *BioIn 17, WhoAm 92*
Steele, James Lewis, Jr. 1954- *WhoSSW 93*
Steele, John 1953- *St&PR 93*
Steele, John D. 1923- *WhoIns 93*
Steele, John F. 1924- *St&PR 93*
Steele, John Hyslop 1926- *WhoAm 92*
Steele, John Lawrence 1917- *WhoAm 92*
Steele, John W., III *Law&B 92*
Steele, Joseph Raymond 1932- *St&PR 93*
Steele, Joseph Richard 1953- *WhoE 93*
Steele, Karen Kiarsis 1942- *WhoAmW 93*
Steele, Kenneth Franklin, Jr. 1944- *WhoAm 92, WhoSSW 93*
Steele, Kurt D. *Law&B 92*
Steele, Larry D. 1945- *St&PR 93*
Steele, Lendell Eugene 1928- *WhoAm 92*
Steele, Lewis McKinnie 1911- *St&PR 93*
Steele, Linda *ScF&FL 92*
Steele, Marilyn May 1931- *WhoSSW 93*
Steele, Marla Judith 1957- *WhoAmW 93*
Steele, Mary *DcChlFi*
Steele, Mary M. 1936- *WhoAmW 93*
Steele, Mary Q. 1922-1992 *ScF&FL 92*
Steele, Mary Q(uintard Govan) 1922- *DcAmChF 1960, MajAI [port]*
Steele, Mary Q(uintard Govan) 1922-1992 *ConAu 139, SmATA 72*
Steele, Matthew R. 1956- *St&PR 93*
Steele, Oliver 1928- *WhoAm 92*
Steele, Patrick Scott 1949- *St&PR 93, WhoAm 92*
Steele, Paula Laird 1952- *WhoAmW 93*
Steele, Philip T. *St&PR 93*
Steele, R.C. *WhoScE 91-1*
Steele, Raymond *WhoScE 91-1*
Steele, Reed F. *Law&B 92*
Steele, Reg N. 1945- *St&PR 93*
Steele, Rhea Lynn 1958- *WhoAmW 93*
Steele, Richard *BioIn 17*
Steele, Richard 1672-1729 *BioIn 17*
Steele, Richard Charles 1928- *WhoScE 91-1*
Steele, Richard Lewis 1929- *WhoSSW 93*
Steele, Robert *BioIn 17*
Steele, Robert Bainum, Jr. 1937- *WhoWrEP 92*
Steele, Robert Carl 1953- *St&PR 93*
Steele, Robert Edward 1954- *St&PR 93, WhoIns 93*
Steele, Robert P. *Law&B 92*
Steele, Robert Steven 1946- *WhoE 93*
Steele, Rose Marie 1949- *WhoAmW 93*
Steele, Ruth Smith 1941- *WhoAmW 93, WhoSSW 93*
Steele, Samuel McDowell 1939- *WhoSSW 93*
Steele, Samuel S. 1916- *St&PR 93*
Steele, Sandra Elaine Noel 1939- *WhoAmW 93*
Steele, Shelby *BioIn 17, WhoAm 92*
Steele, Stuart James *WhoScE 91-1*
Steele, Thomas A., III 1940- *St&PR 93*
Steele, Thomas P. *Law&B 92*
Steele, Timothy (Reid) 1948- *DcLB 120 [port], WhoWrEP 92*
Steele, Valerie (Fahnestock) 1955- *ConAu 138*
Steele, Vernon H. 1925- *St&PR 93*
Steele, Virginia Whitsitt 1955- *WhoSSW 93*
Steele, W. Perrin 1924- *St&PR 93*
Steele, Warren B. 1962- *St&PR 93*
Steele, William O(wen) 1917-1979 *MajAI [port]*
Steele-Herman, Lisa Michelle 1964- *WhoAmW 93*
Steele Oates, Valerie Anne 1968- *WhoSSW 93*
Steeley, Charles B. 1931- *St&PR 93*
Steelman, Bennett Loften 1954- *WhoSSW 93*
Steelman, Charles William 1941- *St&PR 93*
Steelman, J.D., Jr. *Law&B 92*
Steelman, John Knight 1952- *WhoSSW 93*
Steelman, John S. 1946- *St&PR 93*
Steelman, Sara Gerling 1946- *WhoAmW 93*
Steelman-Bragato, Susan Jean 1957- *WhoWor 93*
Steels, Paul Stanislas Justin 1945- *WhoScE 91-2*
Steelsmith, Shari 1962- *SmATA 72*
Steen, A.B. 1929- *St&PR 93*
Steen, Bertil 1938- *WhoScE 91-4*
Steen, Carlton Duane 1932- *WhoAm 92*
Steen, Carol J. 1943- *WhoE 93*
Steen, Donald E. 1946- *St&PR 93*
Steen, Gordon E., Jr. 1941- *St&PR 93*
Steen, Henrikus 1938- *WhoScE 91-3*
Steen, John Thomas, Jr. 1949- *WhoAm 92, WhoEmL 93, WhoSSW 93*
Steen, Lias J. *Law&B 92*
Steen, Lowell Harrison 1923- *WhoAm 92*
Steen, Lynn Arthur 1941- *BioIn 17*
Steen, Melvin C. d1992 *NewYTBS 92 [port]*
Steen, Norman Frank 1933- *WhoAm 92*
Steen, Paul Joseph 1932- *WhoAm 92*
Steen, Sara Jayne 1949- *ScF&FL 92*
Steen, Wesley Wilson 1946- *WhoSSW 93, WhoWor 93*
Steen, William Maxwell *WhoScE 91-1*
Steen, William T. *Law&B 92*
Steenbeke, James Henry, Jr. 1939- *St&PR 93*
Steenblik, Joseph F. 1904- *St&PR 93*
Steenburg, Thomas Nelson *Law&B 92*
Steenburgen, Mary *BioIn 17*
Steenburgen, Mary 1953- *WhoAm 92, WhoAmW 93*
Steene, Karl Michael 1948- *WhoSSW 93*
Steeneck, Lee R. 1948- *WhoIns 93*
Steeneck, Lee Robert 1948- *St&PR 93*
Steeneck, Regina Aultice *WhoAmW 93*
Steenhagen, Robert Lewis 1922- *WhoAm 92*
Steenhoek, Preston John 1940- *WhoAm 92*
Steenkolk, Tony J. *Law&B 92*
Steenland, Douglas *Law&B 92*
Steen-McIntyre, Virginia Carol 1936- *WhoAmW 93*
Steeno, Omer Pieter 1936- *WhoScE 91-2*
Steensland, Odd 1931- *WhoScE 91-4*
Steensland, Ronald Paul 1946- *WhoAm 92, WhoSSW 93*
Steensma, Robert Charles 1930- *WhoAm 92*
Steenson, Delos Vernal 1934- *St&PR 93*
Steenson, Michael Steven 1961- *WhoSSW 93*
Steeples, Douglas Wayne 1935- *WhoAm 92*
Steeples, James Duane 1949- *St&PR 93*
Steer, Alfred Gilbert, Jr. 1913- *WhoAm 92*
Steer, Anne Eileen 1951- *WhoE 93*
Steer, Helen Vane 1926- *WhoAmW 93, WhoSSW 93*
Steer, Martin William 1942- *WhoScE 91-3*
Steere, Allen Caruthers, Jr. 1943- *WhoAm 92*
Steere, Bruce 1918- *St&PR 93*
Steere, Terry 1949- *St&PR 93*
Steere, William C. 1936- *St&PR 93*
Steere, William Campbell, Jr. 1936- *WhoAm 92*
Steers, Newton Ivan, Jr. 1917- *WhoAm 92*
Steers, Philip Lawrence, III 1948- *WhoWor 93*
Stees, Timothy Lynn 1957- *WhoSSW 93*
Steese, Ruth Junia 1907- *WhoAmW 93*
Steesy, Walter Wesley 1940- *WhoE 93*
Steetle, David Ross 1930- *St&PR 93*
Steeves, Edna Leake 1909- *WhoAmW 93*
Steeves, Harrison R. 1881-1981 *ScF&FL 92*
Steeves, Lynne Mary 1922- *WhoE 93*
Steeves, Mark Aaron 1958- *WhoAm 92*
Steeves, Paula Jean 1965- *WhoAmW 93*
Steeves, Robert Francis 1938- *WhoE 93*
Stefan, Joseph *WhoAm 92*
Stefan, Joseph P. 1953- *St&PR 93*
Stefan, Klaus *WhoScE 91-4*
Stefan, Paul 1879-1943 *Baker 92*
Stefan, Paul 1929- *St&PR 93*
Stefan, Steve A. 1937- *WhoAm 92*
Stefancik, Ladislav 1929- *WhoScE 91-4*
Stefanelli, Joseph James 1921- *WhoAm 92*
Stefanelli, Renato 1932- *WhoScE 91-3*
Stefan-Grunfeldt, Paul 1879-1943 *Baker 92*
Stefani, Giovanni 1946- *WhoScE 91-3*
Stefani, Jan 1746-1829 *Baker 92, PolBiDi*
Stefani, Jozef 1800-1867 *Baker 92*
Stefaniak, Jaroslaw Eryk 1929- *WhoScE 91-4*
Stefaniak, Norbert John 1921- *WhoAm 92*
Stefaniak, Ojcumila 1922- *WhoScE 91-4*
Stefanic, David W. 1950- *St&PR 93*
Stefanick, Patti Ann 1957- *WhoAmW 93*
Stefanides, Dean 1955- *WhoAm 92*
Stefanik, Janet Ruth 1938- *WhoAmW 93*
Stefanis, Nico George 1951- *WhoWor 93*
Stefaniuk, Robert Michael 1955- *St&PR 93*
Stefanko, Robert Allen 1943- *St&PR 93, WhoAm 92*
Stefanko, Stanislaw Z. 1923- *WhoScE 91-3*
Stefan Lazarevic c. 1373-1427 *OxDcByz*
Stefan Nemanja d1199? *OxDcByz*
Stefano, Anthony De *ScF&FL 92*
Stefano, George B. 1945- *WhoE 93*
Stefano, Joseph William 1922- *WhoAm 92*
Stefano, R.L. 1923- *St&PR 93*
Stefano, Ross William 1955- *WhoAm 92*
Stefan of Novgorod *OxDcByz*
Stefanov, Boris 1935- *WhoScE 91-4*
Stefanov, John 1952- *St&PR 93*
Stefanovic, Milutin 1924- *WhoScE 91-4*
Stefanovic, Petar 1924- *WhoScE 91-4*
Stefanovits, Paul 1920- *WhoScE 91-4*
Stefanowicz, A. Richard 1939- *St&PR 93*
Stefanowicz, John F. *Law&B 92*
Stefans, Vikki Ann 1957- *WhoSSW 93*
Stefanschi, Sergiu 1941- *WhoAm 92*
Stefanski, Walenty 1813-1877 *PolBiDi*
Stefansson, Fjolnir 1930- *Baker 92*
Stefansson, Olafur E. 1922- *WhoScE 91-4*
Stefansson, Vilhjalmur 1879-1962 *BioIn 17, Expl 93, IntDcAn*
Stefan the First-Crowned c. 1165-1227 *OxDcByz*
Stefan Uros, I d1277 *OxDcByz*
Stefan Uros, V d1371 *OxDcByz*
Stefan Uros Decanski, III d1331 *OxDcByz*
Stefan Uros Dusan, IV d1355 *OxDcByz*
Stefan Uros Milutin, II d1321 *OxDcByz*
Stefany, Bruce R. 1949- *St&PR 93*
Steffan, Frederick V. *Law&B 92*
Steffan, Frederick V. 1948- *St&PR 93*
Steffan, Joseph *BioIn 17*
Steffan, Joseph Anton 1726?-1797 *Baker 92*
Steffan, Wallace Allan 1934- *WhoAm 92*
Steffani, Agostino 1654-1728 *Baker 92, OxDcOp*
Steffek, Hanny 1927- *Baker 92*
Steffek, Marvin C. 1930- *St&PR 93*
Steffen, Chr. *WhoScE 91-4*
Steffen, Christopher James 1942- *St&PR 93*
Steffen, David Joseph 1938- *St&PR 93*
Steffen, Elizabeth Allen *WhoAmW 93*
Steffen, James Richard 1962- *WhoSSW 93*
Steffen, Jan A. 1936- *WhoScE 91-4*
Steffen, Jurg 1942- *WhoWor 93*
Steffen, Patrick Mathew 1949- *St&PR 93*
Steffen, Tina Marie 1958- *WhoAmW 93*
Steffen, Walter Peter 1886-1937 *BiDAMSp 1989*
Steffen, Wolfgang 1923- *Baker 92*
Steffenhagen, Ronald Albert 1923- *WhoSSW 93*
Steffens, Dorothy R. 1921- *WhoAm 92*
Steffens, Franz Eugen Aloys 1933- *WhoWor 93*
Steffens, John L. 1941- *St&PR 93*
Steffens, Lincoln 1866-1936 *GayN, JrnUS*
Steffens, Robert S. 1946- *St&PR 93*
Steffensen, D. David, Jr. *Law&B 92*
Steffensen, Dwight A. 1943- *St&PR 93*
Steffenson, Gary G. 1948- *St&PR 93*

Steffes, Arnold M., Jr. 1931- *St&PR 93*
Steffes, Dale William 1933- *WhoWor 93*
Steffes, Larry R. *Law&B 92*
Steffey, Eugene Paul 1942- *WhoAm 92*
Steffey, Lela 1928- *WhoAmW 93*
Steffey, Stewart H., Jr. *WhoIns 93*
Steffien, A.T. *St&PR 93*
Steffien, E.J. *St&PR 93*
Steffy, John Richard 1924- *WhoAm 92*
Stefoff, James E. 1928- *St&PR 93*
Steg, Adolphe 1925- *WhoScE 91-2*
Steg, James Louis 1922- *WhoAm 92*
Steg, Leo 1922- *WhoAm 92*
Stegall, Danny James 1955- *WhoWor 93*
Stegall, Diana Marie 1966- *WhoSSW 93*
Stegall, Laurette 1956- *WhoAmW 93*
Stegall, Pauline M. 1923- *WhoWrEP 92*
Stegall, Rodney B. 1933- *St&PR 93*
Stege, George Henry 1947- *St&PR 93*
Stegeland, Garry *Law&B 92*
Stegeman, Thomas Albert 1948- *WhoE 93*
Stegeman, William H. 1914- *WhoWrEP 92*
Stegemann, Otto *St&PR 93*
Stegemeier, Richard J. 1928- *St&PR 93*
Stegemeier, Richard Joseph 1928- *WhoAm 92*
Stegemeyer, Horst 1931- *WhoScE 91-3*
Stegemier, Edward J. 1939- *St&PR 93*
Stegemoeller, Susan Warner 1956- *WhoEmL 93*
Stegemoller, Donald L. 1938- *St&PR 93*
Stegena, Lajos 1921- *WhoScE 91-4*
Stegenga, Dawn Ann 1940- *WhoAmW 93*
Stegenga, Preston Jay 1924- *WhoAm 92*
Stegens, Ron *BioIn 17*
Steger, Catherine B. *Law&B 92*
Steger, Charles William 1947- *WhoAm 92*
Steger, Evan Evans, III 1937- *WhoAm 92*
Steger, Joseph A. *WhoAm 92*
Steger, Meritt Homer 1906- *WhoAm 92*
Steger, Ron E. 1945- *St&PR 93*
Steger, Susan Z. *Law&B 92*
Steger, Will 1944- *Expl 93 [port]*
Steger, William Merritt 1920- *WhoAm 92*
Steggall, Charles 1826-1905 *Baker 92*
Steggall, Reginald 1867-1938 *See* Steggall, Charles 1826-1905 *Baker 92*
Steggall, Stuart Norris 1937- *St&PR 93*
Steggerda, J.J. 1929- *WhoScE 91-3*
Steggles, John Charles 1919- *WhoAm 92*
Steglich, Frank 1941- *WhoScE 91-3, WhoWor 93*
Steglich, Rudolf 1886-1976 *Baker 92*
Stegmaier, Anne Marie 1951- *WhoE 93*
Stegman, Bryan W. *Law&B 92*
Stegman, Gary L. 1949- *St&PR 93*
Stegmann, Carl David 1751-1826 *Baker 92*
Stegmann, Eugene C. 1931- *St&PR 93*
Stegmann, Franz Josef 1930- *WhoWor 93*
Stegmann, Thomas Joseph 1946- *WhoWor 93*
Stegmayer, Ferdinand 1803-1863 *Baker 92*
Stegmayer, Joseph H. 1951- *St&PR 93*
Stegmayer, Joseph Henry 1951- *WhoAm 92*
Stegmayer, Matthaus 1771-1820 *Baker 92*
Stegner, Douglas Dewitt 1928- *St&PR 93*
Stegner, Stuart Page 1937- *WhoWrEP 92*
Stegner, Wallace Earle 1909- *BioIn 17, WhoAm 92, WhoWrEP 92*
Stehelin, Dominique 1943- *WhoScE 91-2*
Stehle, Adelina 1860-1945 *Baker 92*
Stehle, Edward Raymond 1942- *WhoE 93*
Stehle, J. Gustav Eduard 1839-1915 *Baker 92*
Stehle, Sophie 1838-1921 *Baker 92, OxDcOp*
Stehle-Garbin, Adelina 1861?-1945 *OxDcOp*
Stehli, Francis Greenough 1924- *WhoAm 92*
Stehli, Georgiana *BioIn 17*
Stehlik, Stephen N. 1957- *St&PR 93*
Stehlin, John Sebastian, Jr. 1923- *WhoAm 92*
Stehling, Kurt Richard 1919- *WhoAm 92*
Stehm, John 1938- *St&PR 93*
Stehman, Burnell Ray 1931- *St&PR 93*
Stehman, Jacques 1912-1975 *Baker 92*
Stehno, Joseph John 1947- *WhoE 93*
Stehr, Rolf 1956- *WhoScE 91-3*
Steib, Gail Therese 1958- *WhoSSW 93*
Steibelt, Daniel 1765-1823 *Baker 92, OxDcOp*
Steider, Kenneth Waldean 1926- *WhoWor 93*
Steidl, Gabriele 1963- *WhoWor 93*
Steidry, Fritz 1883-1968 *OxDcOp*
Steier, Arthur A. 1953- *St&PR 93*
Steier, Rodney Dean 1949- *WhoWrEP 92*
Steierwald, Gerd 1929- *WhoScE 91-3*
Steifel, Herbert d1992 *NewYTBS 92*
Steifel, S. Gray, Jr. 1938- *St&PR 93*
Steig, Jeanne *BioIn 17*
Steig, William 1907- *BioIn 17, DcAmChF 1960, MajAI [port], SmATA 70 [port], WhoAm 92*
Steigbigel, Roy Theodore 1941- *WhoAm 92*
Steigelman, Steven L. 1941- *St&PR 93*
Steiger, Bettie Alexander 1934- *WhoAmW 93*
Steiger, Brad 1936- *ScF&FL 92*
Steiger, Dale Arlen 1928- *WhoE 93, WhoWor 93*
Steiger, Fred Harold 1929- *WhoE 93*
Steiger, Heidi Schwarzbauer 1953- *WhoE 93*
Steiger, Janet Dempsey 1939- *WhoAm 92, WhoAmW 93*
Steiger, Mark Neil 1950- *WhoSSW 93*
Steiger, Paul Ernest 1942- *WhoAm 92*
Steiger, Rand 1957- *Baker 92*
Steiger, Renee Lynn 1958- *WhoAmW 93*
Steiger, Robert D. *Law&B 92*
Steiger, Rod 1925- *ConTFT 10, IntDcF 2-3, WhoAm 92*
Steigerwald, Carl Jacob, II 1939- *St&PR 93*
Steigerwald, Louis John, III 1953- *St&PR 93*
Steigerwald, Robert Joseph 1939- *St&PR 93*
Steigerwaldt, Donna Wolf 1929- *WhoAm 92, WhoAmW 93*
Steigerwalt, William J. 1939- *WhoIns 93*
Steigleder *Baker 92*
Steigleder, Adam 1561-1633 *Baker 92*
Steigleder, Gerd-Klaus 1925- *WhoScE 91-3*
Steigleder, Johann Ulrich 1593-1635 *Baker 92*
Steigleder, Utz d1581 *Baker 92*
Steil, George Kenneth, Sr. 1924- *WhoAm 92*
Steil, Gordon E. 1920- *St&PR 93*
Steil, Robert A. 1925- *St&PR 93*
Stein, Abbe Pomerance *Law&B 92*
Stein, Alan *Law&B 92*
Stein, Alan L. 1948- *WhoE 93*
Stein, Alfred Joseph 1933- *St&PR 93*
Stein, Allyn 1946- *St&PR 93*
Stein, Alvin Maurice 1924- *WhoAm 92*
Stein, Amy *BioIn 17, Law&B 92*
Stein, Arnold 1915- *WhoAm 92*
Stein, Arthur William 1953- *WhoAm 92*
Stein, Aurel 1862-1943 *Expl 93 [port]*
Stein, Baker *ScF&FL 92*
Stein, Belle Weiss 1923- *WhoAmW 93*
Stein, Benjamin 1944- *ScF&FL 92*
Stein, Bennett Mueller 1931- *WhoAm 92*
Stein, Bernard 1913- *St&PR 93, WhoAm 92*
Stein, Bernard Alvin 1923- *WhoAm 92*
Stein, Bob 1920- *St&PR 93*
Stein, Bruce *Law&B 92*
Stein, Bruno 1930- *WhoE 93*
Stein, Carey M. *Law&B 92*
Stein, Carey M. 1947- *St&PR 93*
Stein, Carl 1943- *WhoAm 92*
Stein, Carroll Vincent 1947- *St&PR 93*
Stein, Charles 1912- *WhoAm 92*
Stein, Cheryl Denise 1953- *WhoAmW 93*
Stein, Christine K. 1946- *St&PR 93*
Stein, Clarence Samuel 1882-1975 *BioIn 17*
Stein, Clifford H. *Law&B 92*
Stein, Dale Franklin 1935- *WhoAm 92*
Stein, Daniel Stephen 1947- *WhoSSW 93*
Stein, David F. 1940- *St&PR 93*
Stein, David Fred 1940- *WhoAm 92*
Stein, David Lewis 1937- *WhoCanL 92*
Stein, David S. *Law&B 92*
Stein, Donald Gerald 1939- *WhoAm 92*
Stein, Donald Gilbert 1941- *St&PR 93*
Stein, Donald Jay 1931- *St&PR 93*
Stein, Donald L. 1934- *St&PR 93*
Stein, Douglas J. 1947- *St&PR 93*
Stein, Duffy 1927- *ScF&FL 92*
Stein, Edith 1891-1942 *BioIn 17, PolBiDi*
Stein, Edward B. 1917- *St&PR 93*
Stein, Edward Dalton *WhoWrEP 92*
Stein, Edward E. 1937- *St&PR 93*
Stein, Edward William 1928- *St&PR 93*
Stein, Ellen Cohen 1947- *WhoE 93*
Stein, Ellen Gail 1951- *WhoEmL 93*
Stein, Elliot H. 1918- *St&PR 93, WhoAm 92*
Stein, Elliott Jonathan *Law&B 92*
Stein, Eric 1913- *WhoAm 92*
Stein, Eric Sedwick 1930- *WhoSSW 93*
Stein, Ernest D. *WhoAm 92*
Stein, Erwin 1885-1958 *Baker 92*
Stein, Fritz 1879-1961 *Baker 92*
Stein, Gary M. *St&PR 93*
Stein, George Henry 1934- *WhoAm 92, WhoWrEP 92*
Stein, Gerald 1937- *St&PR 93*
Stein, Gertrude 1874-1946 *AmWomPl, AmWomWr 92, BioIn 17, TwCLC 48 [port], WorLitC [port]*
Stein, Gilbert Taylor 1928- *St&PR 93*
Stein, Hans Nikolaus 1929- *WhoScE 91-3*
Stein, Herbert 1910- *St&PR 93*
Stein, Herbert 1915?-1989? *ScF&FL 92*
Stein, Herbert 1916- *BioIn 17, WhoAm 92*
Stein, Herman David 1917- *WhoAm 92, WhoWrEP 92*
Stein, Horst 1928- *OxDcOp*
Stein, Horst (Walter) 1928- *Baker 92*
Stein, Howard 1926- *WhoAm 92*
Stein, Howard M. 1926- *St&PR 93*
Stein, Howard S. 1939- *WhoAm 92*
Stein, Ira C. *Law&B 92*
Stein, Irvin 1906- *WhoAm 92*
Stein, Irving N. *Law&B 92*
Stein, Irwin M. *Law&B 92*
Stein, Israel A. *Law&B 92*
Stein, Jack A. *Law&B 92*
Stein, Jacob 1960- *WhoE 93*
Stein, Jacqlyn D. *Law&B 92*
Stein, James C. 1943- *St&PR 93*
Stein, Janet Lee 1946- *WhoAmW 93, WhoE 93*
Stein, Jay M. 1946- *WhoAm 92*
Stein, Jean *BioIn 17*
Stein, Jeff *MiSFD 9*
Stein, Jeff 1947- *St&PR 93*
Stein, Jeff M. 1940- *St&PR 93*
Stein, Johann (Georg) Andreas 1728-1792 *Baker 92*
Stein, Josef Dieter 1934- *St&PR 93*
Stein, Joseph *WhoAm 92*
Stein, Joseph 1912- *WhoWrEP 92*
Stein, Joseph F. d1990 *BioIn 17*
Stein, Julia A. 1946- *WhoWrEP 92*
Stein, Ken *MiSFD 9*
Stein, Kevin 1965- *ScF&FL 92*
Stein, Larry I. *Law&B 92*
Stein, Leon 1910- *Baker 92*
Stein, Leon 1912-1990 *BioIn 17*
Stein, Leonard 1916- *Baker 92*
Stein, Leslie *Law&B 92*
Stein, Leslie Reicin *Law&B 92*
Stein, Lewis *Law&B 92*
Stein, Lewis 1937- *St&PR 93*
Stein, Linda *BioIn 17*
Stein, Linda Ann 1955- *WhoWrEP 92*
Stein, Lotte C. 1926- *WhoSSW 93*
Stein, Louis 1917- *ConAu 138*
Stein, M. Luisa 1926- *WhoScE 91-3*
Stein, Marjorie G. *Law&B 92*
Stein, Mark Andrew 1958- *WhoE 93*
Stein, Mark Rodger 1943- *WhoSSW 93*
Stein, Marsha E. 1948- *WhoE 93*
Stein, Martin Alexander 1951- *WhoE 93*
Stein, Martin E. 1922- *St&PR 93*
Stein, Marvin 1923- *WhoAm 92*
Stein, Mary Katherine 1944- *WhoAmW 93*
Stein, Maureen K. *Law&B 92*
Stein, Melvin A. 1932- *WhoE 93*
Stein, Melvin H. 1943- *St&PR 93*
Stein, Michael A. 1938- *St&PR 93*
Stein, Michael David 1942- *WhoE 93*
Stein, Michael Jeffrey *Law&B 92*
Stein, Milton Michael 1936- *St&PR 93, WhoE 93, WhoWor 93*
Stein, Murray 1943- *ScF&FL 92*
Stein, Murray Walter 1943- *WhoWrEP 92*
Stein, Myron 1925- *WhoAm 92*
Stein, Nannette (Maria Anna) 1769-1835 *See* Streicher, Johann Andreas 1761-1833 *Baker 92*
Stein, Neil A. 1950- *St&PR 93*
Stein, Otto Ludwig 1925- *WhoAm 92*
Stein, Paul A. 1937- *St&PR 93*
Stein, Paul Arthur 1937- *WhoE 93, WhoWor 93*
Stein, Paul David 1934- *WhoAm 92*
Stein, Paula Jean Anne Barton 1929- *WhoAmW 93, WhoWor 93*
Stein, Peter C. *Law&B 92*
Stein, Philip 1930- *St&PR 93*
Stein, Ralph Michael 1943- *WhoE 93*
Stein, Richard Alan 1959- *St&PR 93*
Stein, Richard Arno 1945- *St&PR 93*
Stein, Richard George 1916-1990 *BioIn 17*
Stein, Richard Heinrich 1882-1942 *Baker 92*
Stein, Richard James 1930- *WhoE 93*
Stein, Richard Jay 1946- *WhoE 93*
Stein, Richard M. 1948- *St&PR 93*
Stein, Richard P. 1925- *St&PR 93*
Stein, Richard Paul 1925- *WhoAm 92*
Stein, Richard Stephen 1925- *WhoAm 92*
Stein, Robert *Law&B 92*
Stein, Robert 1939- *WhoAm 92, WhoWor 93*
Stein, Robert Alan 1930- *WhoAm 92*
Stein, Robert Benjamin 1950- *WhoEmL 93*
Stein, Robert de R. 1949- *St&PR 93*
Stein, Robert Elihu 1939- *WhoE 93*
Stein, Robert William 1949- *WhoAm 92*
Stein, Roberta Katchen 1941- *WhoWrEP 92*
Stein, Roger Richard 1942- *WhoSSW 93*
Stein, Ron 1951- *BioIn 17*
Stein, Ronald A. *Law&B 92*
Stein, Ronald Jay 1930- *WhoAm 92*
Stein, Ronald Marc 1951- *WhoSSW 93*
Stein, Rosemary *Law&B 92*
Stein, Sandra Lou 1942- *WhoAmW 93*
Stein, Seymour 1928- *WhoAm 92*
Stein, Sheldon I. 1953- *St&PR 93*
Stein, Sidney J. 1921- *St&PR 93*
Stein, Sol 1926- *WhoAm 92, WhoWor 93*
Stein, Stanley 1922- *WhoAm 92*
Stein, Stanley R. *Law&B 92*
Stein, Stanley Richard 1942- *WhoAm 92*
Stein, Stephen *WhoScE 91-1*
Stein, Steven 1948- *St&PR 93*
Stein, Steven Andrew 1960- *WhoE 93*
Stein, Steven B. 1948- *St&PR 93*
Stein, Steven Hal 1956- *WhoE 93*
Stein, Susan 1951- *WhoAmW 93*
Stein, Susan Alyson 1956- *WhoE 93*
Stein, Tobie Sabrina 1957- *WhoAmW 93*
Stein, Tony 1921-1945 *BioIn 17*
Stein, Vicki d1990 *BioIn 17*
Stein, William E. 1938- *WhoAm 92*
Stein, William J. *Law&B 92*
Stein, William Warner 1921- *WhoAm 92*
Stein, Wolfgang 1927- *WhoScE 91-3*
Steinacker, Ronald Alan 1940- *St&PR 93*
Steinau, Leslie 1943- *WhoE 93*
Steinbach, Alice *BioIn 17*
Steinbach, Beryl J. *Law&B 92*
Steinbach, Fritz 1855-1916 *Baker 92*
Steinbach, Jorg 1935- *WhoScE 91-3*
Steinbach, Karel 1894-1990 *BioIn 17*
Steinbach, Konrad K. 1937- *WhoScE 91-4*
Steinbach, L. Rawls 1953- *St&PR 93*
Steinbach, Meredith Lynn 1949- *WhoWrEP 92*
Steinbacher, John Adam 1925- *WhoWor 93*
Steinbauer, Mark Leo 1959- *WhoSSW 93*
Steinbauer, Othmar 1895-1962 *Baker 92*
Steinbaugh, Robert P. 1927- *WhoAm 92, WhoWor 93*
Steinbeck, John 1902-1968 *BioIn 17, ConLC 75 [port], MagSAmL [port], ScF&FL 92, ShSCr 11 [port], WorLitC [port]*
Steinbeck, John 1946-1991 *BioIn 17*
Steinbereithner, Karl 1920- *WhoScE 91-4*
Steinberg, Alvin M. 1921- *St&PR 93*
Steinberg, Andrew B. *Law&B 92*
Steinberg, Andrew David 1957- *WhoE 93*
Steinberg, Arthur Gerald 1912- *WhoAm 92*
Steinberg, Barry Charles 1952- *St&PR 93*
Steinberg, Bernard D. 1924- *St&PR 93, WhoAm 92*
Steinberg, Bernhard Evanbar 1900- *WhoWrEP 92*
Steinberg, Burt 1945- *St&PR 93, WhoAm 92*
Steinberg, Carl *WhoCanL 92*
Steinberg, Charles 1943- *St&PR 93*
Steinberg, Charles Allan 1934- *WhoAm 92*
Steinberg, Daniel 1922- *WhoAm 92*
Steinberg, Darrell *Law&B 92*
Steinberg, David 1942- *MiSFD 9, WhoAm 92*
Steinberg, David 1944- *WhoWrEP 92*
Steinberg, David Joel 1937- *WhoAm 92*
Steinberg, David Joseph 1934- *St&PR 93*
Steinberg, Deborah F. 1955- *St&PR 93*
Steinberg, Ellis Philip 1920-1991 *BioIn 17*
Steinberg, Eugene Barry 1953- *WhoSSW 93*
Steinberg, Gayfryd *BioIn 17*
Steinberg, Gilbert 1931- *St&PR 93*
Steinberg, Hank Jay 1958- *WhoSSW 93*
Steinberg, Harold d1991 *BioIn 17*
Steinberg, Harold S. *Law&B 92*
Steinberg, Harvey Laurance *Law&B 92*
Steinberg, Herbert Joseph 1929- *WhoE 93*
Steinberg, Herman Joseph 1911- *St&PR 93*
Steinberg, Howard E. *Law&B 92*
Steinberg, Howard E. 1944- *WhoAm 92*
Steinberg, Irwin Ira 1926- *St&PR 93*
Steinberg, Jack 1915- *WhoWor 93*
Steinberg, James M. *Law&B 92*
Steinberg, Janet Eckstein 1932- *WhoAmW 93*
Steinberg, Jill 1962- *St&PR 93*
Steinberg, Joel *BioIn 17*
Steinberg, John D. *Law&B 92*
Steinberg, Jonathan *BioIn 17*
Steinberg, Joseph 1920- *WhoE 93*
Steinberg, Joseph S. 1944- *St&PR 93*
Steinberg, Joseph Saul 1944- *WhoAm 92*
Steinberg, Laurence 1952- *WhoE 93*
Steinberg, Lawrence E. 1935- *St&PR 93*
Steinberg, Lawrence Edward 1935- *WhoAm 92*
Steinberg, Lawrence William 1942- *St&PR 93*
Steinberg, Leigh *BioIn 17*
Steinberg, Leo 1920- *WhoAm 92, WhoE 93*
Steinberg, Lisa d1987 *BioIn 17*
Steinberg, Malcolm Saul 1930- *WhoE 93*
Steinberg, Mark Stephen 1941- *WhoSSW 93*

Steinberg, Marshall 1932- *St&PR 93, WhoAm 92*
Steinberg, Maximilian (Osseievich) 1883-1946 *Baker 92*
Steinberg, Melvin Allen 1933- *WhoAm 92, WhoE 93, WhoWor 93*
Steinberg, Meyer 1924- *WhoAm 92*
Steinberg, Michael *MiSFD 9*
Steinberg, Michael 1928- *Baker 92, WhoAm 92*
Steinberg, Michael Alan 1952- *WhoE 93*
Steinberg, Michael Ward 1952- *WhoAm 92*
Steinberg, Milton 1903-1950 *JeAmHC*
Steinberg, Morris Albert 1920- *WhoAm 92*
Steinberg, Morton 1928- *St&PR 93*
Steinberg, Neil 1960- *ConAu 139*
Steinberg, Paul Jay 1948- *WhoE 93*
Steinberg, Pinchas 1945- *Baker 92*
Steinberg, Richard Maurice 1928- *St&PR 93*
Steinberg, Robert Alan 1946- *WhoSSW 93*
Steinberg, Robert M. 1942- *St&PR 93, WhoIns 93*
Steinberg, Rolf *WhoScE 91-3*
Steinberg, S. Ty 1928- *St&PR 93*
Steinberg, Saul 1914- *BioIn 17, WhoAm 92*
Steinberg, Saul 1939- *St&PR 93*
Steinberg, Saul P. *BioIn 17*
Steinberg, Saul Phillip 1939- *WhoAm 92, WhoE 93*
Steinberg, Selwyn F. 1934- *St&PR 93*
Steinberg, Sherwin L. 1936- *St&PR 93*
Steinberg, Stephen Cobbett d1991 *BioIn 17*
Steinberg, Steve Leslie 1950- *St&PR 93*
Steinberg, Terry I. 1955- *St&PR 93*
Steinberg, Warren Linnington 1924- *WhoWor 93*
Steinberg, William 1899-1978 *Baker 92*
Steinberg, Ze'ev (Wolfgang) 1918- *Baker 92*
Steinberg, Ziggy *MiSFD 9*
Steinberger, Jack 1921- *WhoAm 92, WhoWor 93*
Steinberger, Jeffrey Wayne 1947- *WhoEmL 93*
Steinberger, Mark N. *Law&B 92*
Steinberger, Richard L. 1939- *St&PR 93*
Steinberger, Richard Lynn 1939- *WhoAm 92*
Steinberg-Oren, Susan Lynne 1959- *WhoAmW 93*
Steinbock, A.P. *Law&B 92*
Steinbock, John T. 1937- *WhoAm 92*
Steinbock, Mark A. *Law&B 92*
Steinborn, Ernst Otto Heinrich 1932- *WhoScE 91-3*
Steinborn, Otto H. 1932- *WhoWor 93*
Steinbrecher, Hank *BioIn 17*
Steinbrecht, Rudolf Alexander 1937- *WhoWor 93*
Steinbrecker, John E. 1950- *St&PR 93*
Steinbreder, H. John *BioIn 17*
Steinbrenner, Carl A. *Law&B 92*
Steinbrenner, George E. 1947- *St&PR 93*
Steinbrenner, George M. 1930- *BioIn 17*
Steinbrenner, George M., III 1930- *St&PR 93*
Steinbrenner, George Michael, III 1930- *WhoAm 92, WhoE 93*
Steinbrick, Mark Gerard 1958- *WhoE 93*
Steinbrink, Jerold C. 1953- *WhoWrEP 92*
Steinbronn, Richard Eugene 1941- *WhoAm 92*
Steinbrook, Richard Alan 1951- *WhoE 93*
Steinbruckner, Bruno Friedrich 1941- *WhoAm 92*
Steinbrueck, Charles E. *BioIn 17*
Steinbruegge, Robert Wallace 1947- *St&PR 93*
Steinbugler, Kathryn *Law&B 92*
Steindl, Josef 1912- *BioIn 17*
Steindler, Walter G. 1927- *WhoE 93*
Steindorf, Gerhard 1929- *WhoWor 93*
Steine, Vicki Marlene 1960- *WhoSSW 93*
Steineger, Margaret Leisy 1926- *WhoAmW 93*
Steinem, Gloria *BioIn 17*
Steinem, Gloria 1934- *PolPar, WhoAm 92, WhoAmW 93*
Steinen, Karl von den 1855-1929 *Expl 93, IntDcAn*
Steiner, Abram A. 1920- *WhoScE 91-3*
Steiner, Adolf Martin 1937- *WhoScE 91-3, WhoWor 93*
Steiner, Alan Burton 1941- *St&PR 93*
Steiner, Andrea Lynne 1964- *WhoE 93*
Steiner, Barbara 1934- *ScF&FL 92*
Steiner, Barbara Annette 1934- *WhoWrEP 92*
Steiner, Barry H(oward) 1942- *ConAu 137*
Steiner, Charles L. 1936- *St&PR 93*
Steiner, Cindy Lee 1947- *WhoAmW 93*
Steiner, Clarence H. 1958- *St&PR 93*
Steiner, Donald Frederick 1930- *WhoAm 92*
Steiner, Edward L. 1944- *St&PR 93*
Steiner, Emma 1850-1928 *Baker 92*
Steiner, Erich Ernst 1919- *WhoAm 92*
Steiner, Ferenc 1932- *WhoScE 91-4*
Steiner, Frederick 1949- *ConAu 39NR*
Steiner, Frederick Karl, Jr. 1927- *WhoAm 92*
Steiner, George 1929- *BioIn 17, WhoAm 92, WhoWor 93*
Steiner, George 1947- *WhoWor 93*
Steiner, Gilbert Yale 1924- *WhoAm 92*
Steiner, Gloria Litwin 1922- *WhoAmW 93*
Steiner, Hans-Georg 1928- *WhoWor 93*
Steiner, Hans Jorg 1937- *WhoScE 91-4*
Steiner, Henry Jacob 1930- *WhoAm 92*
Steiner, Herbert Max 1927- *WhoAm 92*
Steiner, Ismat A. 1941- *WhoUN 92*
Steiner, Jeffrey Josef 1937- *WhoAm 92*
Steiner, John Victor 1944- *WhoSSW 93*
Steiner, Joyce *BioIn 17*
Steiner, Jules Nicolas 1832-1902 *BioIn 17*
Steiner, Karl B. 1932- *WhoScE 91-4*
Steiner, Kenneth Donald 1936- *WhoAm 92*
Steiner, Lawrence Frederick 1947- *St&PR 93*
Steiner, Lee Nathan 1922- *WhoAm 92*
Steiner, Mark H. 1952- *St&PR 93*
Steiner, Max(imilian Raoul Walter) 1888-1971 *Baker 92*
Steiner, Merrilee *ScF&FL 92*
Steiner, Michael 1945- *WhoE 93*
Steiner, Michael Steven 1950- *WhoE 93*
Steiner, Patricia Jean *Law&B 92*
Steiner, Paul *ConAu 37NR, WhoE 93*
Steiner, Paul 1913- *WhoAm 92*
Steiner, Paul A. 1929- *WhoIns 93*
Steiner, Paul Andrew 1929- *St&PR 93*
Steiner, Peter Otto 1922- *WhoAm 92*
Steiner, Pierre 1943- *WhoWor 93*
Steiner, R.L. 1926- *St&PR 93*
Steiner, Ray G. 1931- *WhoAm 92*
Steiner, Raymond George 1931- *St&PR 93*
Steiner, Richard Russell 1923- *WhoAm 92*
Steiner, Robert Frank 1926- *WhoAm 92, WhoE 93*
Steiner, Robert Lisle 1921- *WhoAm 92*
Steiner, Roger Jacob 1924- *WhoE 93*
Steiner, Rudolf 1861-1925 *BioIn 17*
Steiner, Rudolf 1938- *WhoScE 91-3*
Steiner, Shari Yvonne 1941- *WhoAmW 93*
Steiner, Stan(ley) 1925-1987 *ConAu 39NR*
Steiner, Stuart 1937- *WhoAm 92*
Steiner, Thomas A. 1936- *St&PR 93*
Steiner, Timothy J. 1946- *WhoScE 91-1*
Steiner, Wilfred Alfred, Jr. 1940- *WhoAm 92*
Steinert, Alan, Jr. 1936- *St&PR 93, WhoAm 92*
Steinert, Alexander Lang 1900-1982 *Baker 92*
Steines, S. John 1947- *St&PR 93*
Steinetz, Bernard George, Jr. 1927- *WhoE 93*
Steinfals, Christian Werner 1933- *WhoAm 92*
Steinfeld, J.J. *WhoCanL 92*
Steinfeld, Jake *BioIn 17*
Steinfeld, Jeffrey Irwin 1940- *WhoAm 92, WhoE 93*
Steinfeld, Manfred 1924- *St&PR 93, WhoAm 92*
Steinfeld, Thomas Albert 1917- *WhoAm 92*
Steinfels, Margaret O'Brien 1941- *WhoAm 92, WhoAmW 93*
Steinfield, Carl F. 1931- *St&PR 93*
Steinfink, Hugo 1924- *WhoAm 92*
Steinfort, Charles Roy 1921- *WhoAm 92*
Steinfort, Robert E. 1918- *St&PR 93*
Steinfort, Rosemary G. 1917- *St&PR 93*
Steingarten, Karen Ann 1948- *WhoAmW 93, WhoSSW 93*
Steingass, David Herbert 1940- *WhoWrEP 92*
Steingraber, Fred George 1938- *St&PR 93*
Steingraber, Frederick George 1938- *WhoAm 92*
Steingraber, Kathleen Marie 1940- *WhoAmW 93*
Steingruber, Ilona 1912-1962 *Baker 92*
Steinhagen, Frederick Houston 1948- *St&PR 93*
Steinhardt, David *St&PR 93*
Steinhardt, Henry 1920- *WhoAm 92*
Steinhardt, Herschel S. 1910- *ConAu 40NR*
Steinhardt, J. Michael 1942- *WhoIns 93*
Steinhardt, Jerry P. 1951- *St&PR 93*
Steinhardt, Milton 1909- *Baker 92*
Steinhardt, Nancy Shatzman 1954- *WhoE 93*
Steinhardt, Paul C. *Law&B 92*
Steinhardt, Paul F. 1958- *WhoWor 93*
Steinhardt, Paul Joseph 1952- *WhoAm 92*
Steinhardt, Ralph Gustav, Jr. 1918- *WhoAm 92*
Steinhardt, Robert F. *St&PR 93*
Steinhart, Albert B. 1930- *St&PR 93*
Steinhart, Albert Benny 1930- *WhoAm 92*
Steinhart, Ashley 1943- *WhoAm 92*
Steinhart, Barry M. 1952- *St&PR 93*
Steinhart, Gary 1955- *St&PR 93*
Steinhart, Hans 1940- *WhoScE 91-3*
Steinhart, Kathy Sue 1952- *WhoAmW 93*
Steinhart, Ronald G. 1940- *WhoSSW 93*
Steinhart, Ronald Glen 1940- *St&PR 93*
Steinhauer, F. Chuck 1952- *St&PR 93*
Steinhauer, Gillian 1938- *WhoAmW 93, WhoE 93, WhoWor 93*
Steinhauer, Kurt Gerard 1949- *WhoIns 93*
Steinhauer, LuAnn 1934- *WhoAmW 93*
Steinhauer, W.R. 1941- *St&PR 93*
Steinhauer, Wayne 1956- *St&PR 93*
Steinhauer, William J. 1955- *St&PR 93*
Steinhaus, Carolyn Pinkerton 1950- *WhoAmW 93*
Steinhaus, Hugo 1887-1972 *PolBiDi*
Steinhaus, John Edward 1917- *WhoAm 92*
Steinhausen, Detlef 1944- *WhoScE 91-3*
Steinhausen, Theodore Behn, Jr. 1942- *WhoE 93*
Steinhauser, Emil W. 1926- *WhoScE 91-3*
Steinhauser, Hugo 1929- *WhoScE 91-3*
Steinhauser, J. Chris 1959- *St&PR 93*
Steinhauser, Janice Maureen 1935- *WhoAmW 93*
Steinhauser, John 1958- *St&PR 93*
Steinhauser, John W. 1924- *St&PR 93*
Steinhauser, Peter *WhoScE 91-4*
Steinhauser, Sheldon Eli 1930- *WhoWor 93*
Steinhausler, Friedrich 1946- *WhoScE 91-4*
Steinheider, James Henry 1949- *WhoAm 92*
Steinheiser, Sylvia Ellen *Law&B 92*
Steinherz, Laurel Judith 1947- *WhoAmW 93*
Steinhilber, Helmut 1942- *WhoScE 91-3*
Steinhoff, David A. 1954- *St&PR 93*
Steinhoff, Edward 1934- *St&PR 93*
Steinhoff, Harold William 1919- *WhoAm 92*
Steinhoff, Monika 1941- *BioIn 17*
Steinhoff, Wendy Jean 1964- *WhoSSW 93*
Steinhoff, William R. 1914- *ScF&FL 92*
Steinhoff, William Richard 1914- *WhoAm 92, WhoWrEP 92*
Steinhorn, Irwin Harry 1940- *WhoAm 92, WhoWor 93*
Steinhouse, Carl Lewis 1931- *WhoAm 92*
Steinhouse, Clarence Leroy 1920- *St&PR 93*
Steinhouse, Clarence Leroy, III 1950- *St&PR 93*
Steinhouse, James Welch 1956- *St&PR 93*
Steinhouse, John Thomas 1953- *St&PR 93*
Steinhouse, Lurene Richardson 1921- *St&PR 93*
Steinhurst, William 1947- *WhoE 93*
Steinig, Stephen N. *WhoIns 93*
Steinig, Stephen N. 1945- *St&PR 93*
Steinig, Stephen Nelson 1945- *WhoAm 92*
Steininger, Fritz F. 1939- *WhoScE 91-4*
Steininger, Richard *St&PR 93*
Steinitz, Bernard *BioIn 17*
Steinitz, (Charles) Paul (Joseph) 1909-1988 *Baker 92*
Steinitz, Wilhelm 1836-1900 *BioIn 17*
Steinkamp, John L. *Law&B 92*
Steinke, Richard A. 1940- *St&PR 93*
Steinkrass, John Edwin 1946- *St&PR 93*
Steinkraus, Warren E. *BioIn 17*
Steinlage, Paul Nicholas 1941- *St&PR 93, WhoIns 93*
Steinlage, William S. 1946- *St&PR 93*
Steinle, John G. d1990 *BioIn 17*
Steinle, Paul Michael 1939- *WhoAm 92*
Steinle, Russell Joseph 1950- *WhoE 93*
Steinle, Wolfgang Josef 1953- *WhoWor 93*
Steinman, Alexander 1926- *St&PR 93*
Steinman, Gary David 1941- *WhoE 93*
Steinman, Kathryn G. *Law&B 92*
Steinman, Lisa Malinowski 1950- *WhoAmW 93, WhoWrEP 92*
Steinman, Peter E. *Law&B 92*
Steinman, Richard H. d1992 *NewYTBS 92*
Steinman, Richard H. 1945- *St&PR 93*
Steinman, Robert Cleeton 1931- *WhoAm 92*
Steinman, Sandra 1944- *WhoAmW 93*
Steinman, Shirley P. 1938- *WhoIns 93*
Steinmanis, Karl S. *Law&B 92*
Steinmann, Daniel *MiSFD 9*
Steinmann, Derick Otis 1943- *WhoE 93*
Steinmetz, Alfred George *Law&B 92*
Steinmetz, Charles Proteus 1865-1923 *GayN*
Steinmetz, David Curtis 1936- *WhoAm 92*
Steinmetz, G. *WhoScE 91-2*
Steinmetz, Helmuth 1955- *WhoWor 93*
Steinmetz, John Charles 1947- *WhoWor 93*
Steinmetz, Leon *ConAu 136*
Steinmetz, Michael 1947- *WhoWor 93*
Steinmetz, Paula *BioIn 17*
Steinmetz, Philip Rolf 1927- *WhoE 93*
Steinmetz, Richard Bird, Jr. 1929- *WhoAm 92*
Steinmetz, Richard C., Jr. *Law&B 92*
Steinmetz, S.R. 1862-1940 *IntDcAn*
Steinmetz, William F. 1917- *St&PR 93*
Steinmetz, William Richard 1948- *St&PR 93*
Steinmeyer, Charles Henry 1941- *WhoE 93*
Steinmiller, Frank Neal 1931- *St&PR 93*
Steinmiller, John F. *WhoAm 92*
Steinnes, Eiliv 1938- *WhoScE 91-4*
Steinpress, Boris (Solomonovich) 1908-1986 *Baker 92*
Steinrauf, Jean Hamilton 1938- *WhoAmW 93*
Steinruck, Charles Francis, Jr. 1908- *WhoAm 92*
Stein-Sapir, Leonard R. 1938- *St&PR 93*
Steinthal, A. John, Jr. 1936- *St&PR 93*
Steinthal, Nicholas 1931- *St&PR 93*
Steinthal, Thomas Michael 1968- *WhoE 93*
Steinvall, K. Ove. J. 1944- *WhoScE 91-4*
Steinvall, Kurt Ove 1944- *WhoWor 93*
Steinwandel, A. Charles 1941- *St&PR 93*
Steinway, Albert 1840-1877 *Baker 92*
Steinway, Charles 1829-1865 *Baker 92*
Steinway, Heinrich Engelhard 1797-1871 *Baker 92*
Steinway, Henry *Baker 92*
Steinway, Henry 1830-1865 *Baker 92*
Steinway, (Christian Friedrich) Theodore 1825-1889 *Baker 92*
Steinway, Theodore E. d1957 *Baker 92*
Steinway, William 1835-1896 *Baker 92*
Steinway, William 1836-1896 *GayN*
Steinway & Sons *Baker 92*
Steinweg *Baker 92*
Steiny, John Olerich 1922- *St&PR 93*
Steir, Pat 1940- *BioIn 17*
Steir, Pat Iris 1940- *WhoAm 92, WhoE 93*
Steitieh, Khaled Nayef 1936- *WhoWor 93*
Steitz, Edward d1990 *BioIn 17*
Steitz, Joan Argetsinger 1941- *WhoAm 92, WhoAmW 93*
Steitz, William N. 1933- *St&PR 93*
Stek, Robert Joseph 1948- *WhoE 93*
Steketee, J. 1932- *WhoScE 91-3*
Steketee, Richard Walton 1924- *St&PR 93*
Stekke, Leon 1904-1970 *Baker 92*
Stekly, Karel 1903-1987 *DrEEuF*
Stelben, Robert Patrick 1942- *WhoAm 92*
Stelck, Charles Richard 1917- *WhoAm 92*
Stelian, Judith 1937- *St&PR 93*
Stelios, Jean J. *St&PR 93*
Stell, Gerald 1927- *WhoWor 93*
Stell, Philip Michael *WhoScE 91-1*
Stell, Rodney D. 1947- *St&PR 93*
Stella, Albert A.M. 1942- *WhoWrEP 92*
Stella, Antonietta 1929- *Baker 92*
Stella, Carl C. 1938- *St&PR 93*
Stella, Clara 1920- *WhoScE 91-3*
Stella, Concetta Amelia 1940- *WhoAmW 93*
Stella, Daniel Francis 1943- *WhoWor 93*
Stella, Frank Daniel 1919- *St&PR 93*
Stella, Frank Dante 1919- *WhoAm 92*
Stella, Frank Philip 1936- *WhoAm 92*
Stella, Jeffrey *St&PR 93*
Stella, John Anthony 1938- *WhoAm 92*
Stella, Joseph 1877-1946 *BioIn 17*
Stella, Rachel *BioIn 17*
Stellar, Eliot 1919- *WhoAm 92*
Stellar, Frederick William 1952- *WhoE 93*
Stellato, Louis Eugene *Law&B 92*
Stellburg, Vernon Paul 1942- *WhoSSW 93*
Stelle, Kellogg Sheffield 1948- *WhoWor 93*
Steller, Arthur Wayne 1947- *WhoAm 92, WhoEmL 93, WhoSSW 93*
Steller, Kazimierz J. 1925- *WhoScE 91-4*
Steller, L.A. 1935- *St&PR 93*
Steller, Mitchell Edward 1948- *WhoAm 92*
Stelling, J.G. 1931- *WhoScE 91-3*
Stellinger, Thomas S. 1948- *St&PR 93*
Stellingwerf, Frank D. *Law&B 92*
Stellingwerf, Steve(n Lee) 1962- *ConAu 138*
Stellman, Martin *MiSFD 9*
Stellman, Samuel David 1918- *WhoAm 92*
Stello, Patricia Anne 1949- *WhoAmW 93*
Stello, Victor *BioIn 17*
Stellwag, George William 1921- *WhoIns 93*

Stellwagen, Robert Harwood 1941- *WhoAm 92*
Stellwagen, Walter R. 1929- *St&PR 93*
Stelly, Noelie Marie *WhoSSW 93*
Stelmak, Dalton Roy 1941- *WhoE 93*
Stelow, Alice M. 1905- *St&PR 93*
Stelpstra, William John 1934- *WhoE 93*
Stelting-Schultz, Kathleen M. 1942- *St&PR 93*
Steltmann, Harry Frederick 1943- *St&PR 93*
Stelzel, Walter Tell 1940- *St&PR 93*
Stelzel, Walter Tell, Jr. 1940- *WhoAm 92*
Stelzer, Glenn Irving 1927- *WhoWor 93*
Stelzer, Irwin Mark 1932- *WhoE 93, WhoWor 93*
Stelzer, John Friedrich 1928- *WhoWor 93*
Stelzer, Pat *WhoSSW 93*
Stelzle, Jacob Charles *BiDAMSp 1989*
Stelzner, Edward H. 1931- *St&PR 93*
Stem, Carl Herbert 1935- *WhoAm 92*
Stemberg, Thomas G. 1949- *ConEn, St&PR 93*
Stemberg, Thomas George 1949- *WhoAm 92*
Stemberg, Tom *BioIn 17*
Stembridge, Melodie Weeks 1949- *WhoAmW 93*
Stembridge, Vernie Albert 1924- *WhoAm 92*
Stemen, Nancy Marie 1932- *WhoAmW 93*
Stemen, Sue Ellen *Law&B 92*
Stemme, Fred George 1939- *WhoWrEP 92*
Stemmer, Wayne J. 1942- *St&PR 93*
Stemmler, Edward Joseph 1929- *WhoAm 92, WhoE 93*
Stemmler, Guin 1929- *St&PR 93*
Stempel, Alan R. *Law&B 92*
Stempel, Edward 1926- *WhoE 93*
Stempel, Ernest Edward 1916- *St&PR 93, WhoAm 92, WhoIns 93, WhoWor 93*
Stempel, Guido Hermann, III 1928- *WhoAm 92*
Stempel, Robert C. *BioIn 17*
Stempel, Robert C. 1933- *WhoAm 92*
Stempel, Susan de *BioIn 17*
Stemper, Frank 1951- *Baker 92*
Stemper, William Herman, Jr. *WhoAm 92, WhoWor 93*
Stemple, Jane *ScF&FL 92*
Stempler, Allan Ivan 1942- *WhoE 93*
Stempler, Jack Leon 1920- *WhoAm 92*
Stempler, Stanley *Law&B 92*
Stemprok, Miroslav 1933- *WhoScE 91-4*
Stemwedel, John Albert *Law&B 92*
Sten, Christopher (W.) 1944- *ConAu 137*
Sten, Christopher Willie 1944- *WhoE 93*
Sten, Matti *WhoScE 91-4*
Stenback, Guy Olof 1924- *WhoWor 93*
Stenback, Par O. 1941- *WhoUN 92*
Stenback, S. Lynn *Law&B 92*
Stenbeck, Merrill *BioIn 17*
Stenberg, Abraham B. 1935- *St&PR 93*
Stenberg, Carl Waldamer, III 1943- *WhoAm 92*
Stenberg, Donald B. 1948- *WhoAm 92*
Stenberg, Jordan 1947- *Baker 92*
Stenberg, Ragnar Herman 1945- *WhoWor 93*
Stenberg, Rolf Bernhard 1953- *WhoWor 93*
Stenbit, John Paul 1940- *WhoAm 92*
Stenborg, Carl 1752-1813 *Baker 92*
Stenchever, Morton Albert 1931- *WhoAm 92*
Stendahl 1913-1991 *BioIn 17*
Stendahl, Allen Jon 1946- *WhoIns 93*
Stendahl, Krister 1921- *WhoAm 92*
Stendahl, Ulf Herman 1936- *WhoWor 93*
Stendal, Henrik 1948- *WhoScE 91-2*
Stendel, David 1927- *St&PR 93*
Stendhal 1783-1842 *Baker 92, DcLB 119 [port], MagSWL [port], OxDcOp, WorLitC [port]*
Stene, Jon 1935- *WhoWor 93*
Stenehjem, Leland Manford 1918- *WhoAm 92*
Steneman, Shep 1945- *ScF&FL 92*
Stener, Sven Bertil Charles 1920- *WhoScE 91-4*
Steneroth, Erik Robert 1923- *WhoScE 91-4*
Stenerud, Jan *BioIn 17*
Stenerud, Jan 1942- *BiDAMSp 1989*
Stenestad, Erik 1933- *WhoScE 91-2*
Stenflo, Jan Olof 1942- *WhoScE 91-4*
Stenflo, Lennart 1939- *WhoScE 91-4*
Stengel, Casey *BioIn 17*
Stengel, Eberhard Friedrich Otto 1936- *WhoWor 93*
Stengel, James Lowell 1926- *St&PR 93*
Stengel, Jerome 1936- *St&PR 93*
Stengel, John J. 1936- *St&PR 93*
Stengel, Renato 1940- *WhoScE 91-3*
Stengel, Richard 1955- *ConAu 136*
Stengel, Robert Frank 1938- *WhoAm 92*
Stengel, Robert H. *St&PR 93*
Stenger, Georgia *AmWomPl*
Stenger, James W. *St&PR 93*
Stenger, John A. 1935- *St&PR 93*
Stenger, John Robert 1926- *WhoE 93*
Stenger, Karl Ludwig 1951- *WhoSSW 93*
Stenger, William 1942- *WhoSSW 93*
Stenham, Robin Henry *WhoScE 91-1*
Stenhammar, Olof *BioIn 17*
Stenhammar, Per Ulrik 1828-1875 *Baker 92*
Stenhammar, Wilhelm 1871-1927 *Baker 92, OxDcOp*
Stenholm, Anne *WhoWrEP 92*
Stenholm, Charles W. 1938- *CngDr 91, WhoAm 92, WhoSSW 93*
Stenholm, Charles Walter 1938- *NewYTBS 92 [port]*
Stenholm, Stig Torsten 1939- *WhoScE 91-4*
Stenhouse, D. Scott *Law&B 92*
Stenhouse, Henry Merritt *BioIn 17*
Stenius, Marianne Inger 1951- *WhoWor 93*
Stenius, Per J. 1938- *WhoScE 91-4*
Stenius, Vilma 1946- *WhoScE 91-4*
Stenkvist, Bjorn Gunnar 1934- *WhoWor 93*
Stenlake, Rodney Lee 1957- *WhoE 93, WhoEmL 93*
Stenlund, Bengt G.V. 1939- *WhoScE 91-4*
Stenlund, Bengt Gustav Verner 1939- *WhoWor 93*
Stenmark, Jean Kerr 1922- *WhoAmW 93*
Stenmayer, Janet Lee *Law&B 92*
Stenner, Jerome M. 1919- *St&PR 93*
Stennes, Herbert J. 1932- *St&PR 93*
Stennett, William Mitchell 1948- *WhoSSW 93*
Stenning, Keith *WhoScE 91-1*
Stennis, John C. 1901- *PolPar*
Stennis, John Cornelius 1901- *WhoAm 92*
Stennis, Tom *Law&B 92*
Stenquist, Donald Ray 1929- *St&PR 93*
Stenram, Unne 1926- *WhoWor 93*
Stensland, Craig W. *Law&B 92*
Stensland, Jill Rebecca 1960- *WhoAmW 93*
Stensland, Linda L. *WhoAmW 93*
Stenson, Frederick 1951- *WhoCanL 92*
Stenson, Richard Marshall 1935- *St&PR 93*
Stenstrom, Guy Otis, Jr. 1919- *WhoSSW 93*
Stenstrom, Tore 1936- *WhoScE 91-4*
Stent, Gunther Siegmund 1924- *WhoAm 92, WhoWrEP 92*
Stentz, Jon W. *Law&B 92*
Stenzel, Alvin Milton, Jr. 1951- *St&PR 93*
Stenzel, H.G. *ScF&FL 92*
Stenzel, Jacob Charles 1867-1919 *BiDAMSp 1989*
Stenzel, Kurt Hodgson 1932- *WhoAm 92*
Stenzel, Larry G. 1949- *WhoWrEP 92*
Stenzel, Robert A. *Law&B 92*
Stenzel, William A. 1923- *St&PR 93, WhoAm 92*
Stenzl, Jurg (Thomas) 1942- *Baker 92*
Steodle, Laurence J. 1947- *St&PR 93*
Steorts, Nancy Harvey 1936- *WhoAm 92, WhoAmW 93*
Step, Eugene L. 1929- *St&PR 93*
Step, Eugene Lee 1929- *WhoAm 92*
Stepakoff, Mark H. *Law&B 92*
Stepan, Alfred C. 1936- *WhoWor 93*
Stepan, F. Quinn 1937- *St&PR 93*
Stepan, Frank Quinn 1937- *WhoAm 92*
Stepan, Jan 1913- *WhoScE 91-4*
Stepan, Vaclav 1889-1944 *Baker 92*
Stepan, Walter 1939- *St&PR 93*
Stepanek, Anton G. 1924- *St&PR 93*
Stepanek, Jan 1937- *WhoWor 93*
Stepanek, Michael John, Jr. *Law&B 92*
Stepaniak, Kurt E. *Law&B 92*
Stepanian, Aro (Levoni) 1897-1966 *Baker 92*
Stepanian, Ira 1936- *St&PR 93, WhoAm 92*
Stepanik, Dennis S. 1944- *St&PR 93*
Stepanov, Lev 1908- *Baker 92*
Stepanov, Sergei Alexandrovich 1941- *WhoWor 93*
Stepanova, Elena 1891-1978 *OxDcOp*
Stepanovich, Pamela Hopkins 1944- *WhoSSW 93*
Stepanski, Anthony Francis 1942- *St&PR 93*
Stephan, Alexander F. 1946- *WhoAm 92, WhoSSW 93*
Stephan, Allan L. 1942- *St&PR 93*
Stephan, Dan S. *St&PR 93*
Stephan, Dan Sanders 1936- *St&PR 93*
Stephan, Eberhart O. 1926- *WhoScE 91-3*
Stephan, Edmund A. 1911- *St&PR 93*
Stephan, Edmund Anton 1911- *WhoAm 92*
Stephan, Edward Clark 1907-1990 *BioIn 17*
Stephan, Edwin Bernard 1937- *St&PR 93*
Stephan, George Peter 1933- *St&PR 93, WhoAm 92*
Stephan, Hans-Joachim 1945- *WhoScE 91-3*
Stephan, John Jason 1941- *WhoAm 92*
Stephan, Joseph Ibrahim 1961- *WhoSSW 93*
Stephan, Karl 1930- *WhoScE 91-3*
Stephan, Naomi Irene 1938- *WhoAmW 93*
Stephan, Richard C. 1940- *St&PR 93*
Stephan, Rita F. 1937- *St&PR 93*
Stephan, Robert A. 1932- *St&PR 93*
Stephan, Robert Conrad 1952- *WhoE 93*
Stephan, Robert M. 1942- *St&PR 93*
Stephan, Robert Taft 1933- *WhoAm 92*
Stephan, Rudi 1887-1915 *Baker 92*
Stephan, Rudolf 1925- *Baker 92*
Stephan, Steven P. *Law&B 92*
Stephanescu, George 1843-1925 *Baker 92*
Stephani, Hermann 1877-1960 *Baker 92*
Stephani, Michael James 1944- *St&PR 93*
Stephanick, Carol Ann 1952- *WhoAmW 93*
Stephanie, Princess of Monaco *BioIn 17*
Stephanie, Gottlieb 1741-1800 *OxDcOp*
Stephanis, Basil C. 1948- *WhoScE 91-3*
Stephanites, Conrad R. 1940- *St&PR 93*
Stephano, Stephen L. 1953- *St&PR 93*
Stephanopoulos, George Robert 1961- *NewYTBS 92 [port]*
Stephanopoulos, Gregory 1950- *WhoAm 92*
Stephans, William W.T. 1942- *St&PR 93*
Stephans, William Walter Thomas 1942- *WhoAm 92*
Stephansson, Ove *WhoScE 91-4*
Stephany, M. *WhoScE 91-3*
Stephen *OxDcByz*
Stephen, David 1910- *ScF&FL 92*
Stephen, Donald Alexander 1935- *St&PR 93, WhoAm 92*
Stephen, John Erle 1918- *WhoAm 92*
Stephen, Kenneth William *WhoScE 91-1*
Stephen, Martin 1949- *ScF&FL 92*
Stephen, Michael Anthony 1929- *WhoAm 92*
Stephen, Norman Scott 1941- *WhoIns 93*
Stephen, Patrice 1927- *St&PR 93*
Stephen, Paul Roderick 1957- *St&PR 93*
Stephen, Richard Joseph 1945- *WhoWor 93*
Stephen of Alexandria 550?-c. 619 *OxDcByz*
Stephen of Byzantium fl. c. 528-535 *OxDcByz*
Stephen of Sougdaia c. 700-c. 787 *OxDcByz*
Stephen of Taron *OxDcByz*
Stephens, Adele 1949- *WhoWrEP 92*
Stephens, Aleta Anne 1959- *WhoAmW 93*
Stephens, Alexander H. 1812-1883 *PolPar*
Stephens, Alice Barber 1858-1932 *BioIn 17*
Stephens, Allison Anne *Law&B 92*
Stephens, Barry L. 1939- *St&PR 93*
Stephens, Bart Nelson 1922- *WhoAm 92*
Stephens, Bobby Gene 1935- *WhoAm 92*
Stephens, Bobby W. 1944- *St&PR 93*
Stephens, Bobby Wayne 1944- *WhoAm 92*
Stephens, Brad 1951- *WhoAm 92*
Stephens, Bruce 1924- *St&PR 93*
Stephens, Brynne 1958- *ScF&FL 92*
Stephens, C. Michael 1949- *WhoSSW 93*
Stephens, Calvin Weldon 1948- *WhoSSW 93*
Stephens, Catherine 1794-1882 *Baker 92, OxDcOp*
Stephens, Christopher *BioIn 17*
Stephens, Christopher David *WhoScE 91-1*
Stephens, Christopher P. *WhoWrEP 92*
Stephens, Christopher P. 1943- *ScF&FL 92*
Stephens, Clive Beddoe *St&PR 93*
Stephens, Deborah Lynn 1952- *WhoAmW 93*
Stephens, Denny 1932- *WhoAm 92*
Stephens, Donald Joseph 1918- *WhoAm 92*
Stephens, Donald Richards 1938- *WhoAm 92*
Stephens, Douglas Kimble 1939- *WhoSSW 93*
Stephens, Edgar R. 1924-1990 *BioIn 17*
Stephens, Edward B. 1947- *St&PR 93*
Stephens, Edward Carl 1924- *WhoAm 92, WhoE 93, WhoWrEP 92*
Stephens, Elizabeth D. 1955- *St&PR 93*
Stephens, Elton B. 1911- *St&PR 93*
Stephens, Elton Bryson 1911- *WhoAm 92*
Stephens, Frances Carter 1952- *WhoSSW 93*
Stephens, Frank Pearson 1944- *WhoSSW 93*
Stephens, Franklin Wilson 1940- *WhoAm 92*
Stephens, Frederick Howard, Jr. 1931- *St&PR 93*
Stephens, Gay 1951- *WhoAmW 93*
Stephens, George Edward, Jr. 1936- *WhoAm 92*
Stephens, George Robert 1929- *WhoE 93*
Stephens, Gerald D. 1932- *WhoIns 93*
Stephens, Gerald Dean 1932- *St&PR 93*
Stephens, Gertrude W. 1910- *St&PR 93*
Stephens, Gertrude Whaley 1910- *WhoAmW 93*
Stephens, Glenn Arthur 1926- *WhoWrEP 92*
Stephens, Helen 1918- *BioIn 17*
Stephens, Henrietta *ScF&FL 92*
Stephens, Howard L. 1919- *BioIn 17*
Stephens, J. Hall 1925- *ScF&FL 92*
Stephens, J.T. 1923- *St&PR 93*
Stephens, Jack Thomas, Jr. 1947- *WhoAm 92, WhoSSW 93*
Stephens, James 1825-1901 *BioIn 17*
Stephens, James 1882-1950 *ScF&FL 92*
Stephens, James M. 1946- *WhoAm 92*
Stephens, James Page, III 1954- *WhoSSW 93*
Stephens, James T. 1939- *WhoAm 92*
Stephens, Jay B. 1946- *WhoAm 92*
Stephens, Jerry Wayne 1949- *WhoAm 92*
Stephens, John David 1954- *St&PR 93*
Stephens, John (Elliott) 1929- *Baker 92*
Stephens, John F. 1916- *St&PR 93*
Stephens, John F., Jr. *Law&B 92*
Stephens, John Frank 1949- *WhoAm 92, WhoE 93*
Stephens, John Joseph 1928- *St&PR 93*
Stephens, John Lloyd *BioIn 17*
Stephens, John Lloyd 1805-1852 *IntDcAn*
Stephens, John P. 1941- *St&PR 93*
Stephens, John S. 1943- *St&PR 93*
Stephens, John Samuel 1938- *WhoSSW 93*
Stephens, Kenneth G. *WhoScE 91-1*
Stephens, Kenneth Snowden 1932- *WhoUN 92, WhoWor 93*
Stephens, Larry R. *Law&B 92*
Stephens, Lawrence James 1940- *WhoE 93*
Stephens, Lawrence Keith *Law&B 92*
Stephens, Leona *AmWomPl*
Stephens, Lester Dow 1933- *WhoSSW 93*
Stephens, Lester John 1943- *St&PR 93*
Stephens, Lester John, Jr. 1943- *WhoAm 92*
Stephens, Lewis Phillip 1945- *WhoSSW 93*
Stephens, Lynn Miles 1955- *WhoSSW 93*
Stephens, Madelyn Anne 1953- *WhoAmW 93*
Stephens, Margaret 1958- *WhoWrEP 92*
Stephens, Martha Foster 1961- *WhoAm 92*
Stephens, Martha T. 1937- *WhoWrEP 92*
Stephens, Mary Elizabeth 1949- *WhoAmW 93*
Stephens, Mary June 1948- *WhoSSW 93*
Stephens, Milton E. 1927- *St&PR 93*
Stephens, Mitchell 1949- *ConAu 136*
Stephens, Nan Bagby *AmWomPl*
Stephens, Nancy V. *Law&B 92*
Stephens, Nelson K. *Law&B 92*
Stephens, Norval Blair, Jr. 1928- *WhoAm 92*
Stephens, O. David *Law&B 92*
Stephens, Olin James, II 1908- *WhoAm 92*
Stephens, Pamela Mitchell 1955- *WhoAmW 93*
Stephens, Patricia Ann 1945- *WhoAmW 93*
Stephens, Patricia Anne 1954- *WhoWor 93*
Stephens, Paul Alfred 1921- *WhoWor 93*
Stephens, Paul Andrew, Jr. 1950- *WhoSSW 93*
Stephens, Perry Lee 1928- *WhoSSW 93*
Stephens, Randall H. *Law&B 92*
Stephens, Reed *WhoWrEP 92*
Stephens, Rehema *BioIn 17*
Stephens, Richard Bernard 1934- *St&PR 93, WhoAm 92*
Stephens, Richard Harry 1945- *WhoE 93*
Stephens, Robert 1931- *WhoWor 93*
Stephens, Robert Allan 1937- *WhoAm 92, WhoE 93*
Stephens, Robert David 1949- *WhoSSW 93*
Stephens, Robert F. 1927- *WhoAm 92, WhoSSW 93*
Stephens, Robert F. 1948- *St&PR 93*
Stephens, Robert Floyd 1948- *WhoAm 92*
Stephens, Robert J. 1917- *St&PR 93*
Stephens, Robert Louis, Jr. 1940- *AfrAmBi [port], WhoAm 92*
Stephens, Robert Newton 1945- *St&PR 93*
Stephens, Robert Oren 1928- *WhoSSW 93*
Stephens, Robert W. 1939- *St&PR 93*
Stephens, Robert William, Jr. 1948- *WhoSSW 93*
Stephens, Ronald Carlyle 1941- *WhoSSW 93*

Stephens, Samuel Everett 1960- *WhoSSW 93*
Stephens, Sheryl Lynne 1949- *WhoAmW 93, WhoEmL 93, WhoWor 93*
Stephens, Sidney Dee 1945- *WhoSSW 93*
Stephens, Stanley Graham 1929- *WhoAm 92*
Stephens, Stephen Owen *WhoSSW 93*
Stephens, Thomas B. 1944- *St&PR 93*
Stephens, Thomas M. 1931- *WhoWrEP 92*
Stephens, Thomas Mack 1951- *WhoE 93*
Stephens, Thomas Maron 1931- *WhoAm 92*
Stephens, W.R. 1907-1991 *BioIn 17*
Stephens, Wheeler Ralph 1926- *St&PR 93*
Stephens, William Harold, III *Law&B 92*
Stephens, William Harold, III 1949- *St&PR 93*
Stephens, William Henry 1948- *WhoE 93*
Stephens, William Leonard 1929- *WhoAm 92*
Stephens, William Mark 1952- *WhoAm 92*
Stephens, William Richard 1932- *WhoAm 92*
Stephens, William Ronald 1944- *WhoWrEP 92*
Stephens, William T. 1922- *St&PR 93*
Stephens, William Theodore 1922- *WhoAm 92, WhoWor 93*
Stephens, William Thomas *WhoAm 92*
Stephens, Wilton Robert 1907-1991 *BioIn 17*
Stephens, Woodford Cefis 1913- *WhoAm 92*
Stephens, Wray M. 1948- *St&PR 93*
Stephen Sabaites 725?-807 *OxDcByz*
Stephensen-Payne, Phil 1952- *ScF&FL 92*
Stephenson, Alan Clements 1944- *WhoAm 92*
Stephenson, Andrew M. 1946- *ScF&FL 92*
Stephenson, Ann *AmWomPl*
Stephenson, Anthony 1937- *WhoWrEP 92*
Stephenson, Arthur Emmet, Jr. 1945- *St&PR 93, WhoAm 92, WhoWor 93*
Stephenson, Bette M. 1924- *WhoAmW 93*
Stephenson, Blair Y. 1947- *WhoSSW 93*
Stephenson, Bryan W. 1950- *St&PR 93*
Stephenson, Calvin P. 1924- *St&PR 93*
Stephenson, Cora Bennett *AmWomPl*
Stephenson, Cyndeé Anne 1948- *WhoE 93*
Stephenson, Daisy D. *AmWomPl*
Stephenson, David Merrill 1963- *WhoE 93*
Stephenson, Donald Grier, Jr. 1942- *WhoE 93*
Stephenson, Donnan 1919- *WhoAm 92*
Stephenson, Dorothy Belcher 1930- *St&PR 93*
Stephenson, Douglas E. *Law&B 92*
Stephenson, Elizabeth Weiss 1927- *WhoAm 92*
Stephenson, Frank B. *St&PR 93*
Stephenson, G. Warren 1944- *WhoSSW 93*
Stephenson, Gary 1944- *St&PR 93*
Stephenson, Geoffrey *WhoScE 91-1*
Stephenson, George 1781-1848 *BioIn 17*
Stephenson, George M. *St&PR 93*
Stephenson, Gordon 1908- *BioIn 17*
Stephenson, Gregory 1947- *ScF&FL 92*
Stephenson, H. Howard 1929- *St&PR 93*
Stephenson, Harold F. 1915- *WhoAm 92*
Stephenson, Helga *BioIn 17*
Stephenson, Herman Howard 1929- *WhoAm 92*
Stephenson, Hugh Edward, Jr. 1922- *WhoAm 92*
Stephenson, Irene Hamlen 1923- *WhoAmW 93, WhoWor 93*
Stephenson, J. Phil, Jr. 1941- *St&PR 93*
Stephenson, Jack V. 1932- *St&PR 93*
Stephenson, James Edward 1933- *WhoWor 93*
Stephenson, James Gordon *Law&B 92*
Stephenson, James M., Jr. 1936- *St&PR 93*
Stephenson, James W. *Law&B 92*
Stephenson, Jan Lynn 1951- *WhoAm 92, WhoAmW 93*
Stephenson, John *WhoScE 91-1*
Stephenson, John B. *St&PR 93*
Stephenson, John Robert *WhoScE 91-1*
Stephenson, Joseph E. 1933- *St&PR 93, WhoAm 92*
Stephenson, Junius Winfield 1922- *St&PR 93*
Stephenson, Kathryn Lyle 1912- *WhoWrEP 92*
Stephenson, Kent R. *Law&B 92*
Stephenson, Kent R. 1949- *St&PR 93*
Stephenson, Lani Sue 1948- *WhoAmW 93*
Stephenson, Linda Jean 1952- *WhoAmW 93*
Stephenson, Lisa G. 1955- *WhoAmW 93*
Stephenson, Lois Carpenter 1929- *WhoSSW 93*
Stephenson, Louise Scott 1921- *St&PR 93*
Stephenson, Lynne *ScF&FL 92*
Stephenson, Maureen 1927- *ConAu 38NR*
Stephenson, Michael James 1945- *St&PR 93*
Stephenson, Neal 1959- *ScF&FL 92*
Stephenson, Nelson L. 1952- *St&PR 93*
Stephenson, Norman Leslie 1942- *WhoSSW 93*
Stephenson, Phil 1941- *St&PR 93*
Stephenson, R.H., III 1922- *St&PR 93*
Stephenson, R. Lee *Law&B 92*
Stephenson, Richard Ismert 1937- *WhoWor 93*
Stephenson, Richard Keith 1925- *St&PR 93*
Stephenson, Robert M. 1948- *WhoAm 92*
Stephenson, Robert T. *Law&B 92*
Stephenson, Ronald Bart 1947- *WhoSSW 93*
Stephenson, Roscoe Bolar, Jr. 1922- *WhoAm 92, WhoSSW 93*
Stephenson, Russell L. 1915- *St&PR 93*
Stephenson, Sallie 1944- *WhoSSW 93*
Stephenson, Samuel Edward, Jr. 1926- *WhoAm 92, WhoSSW 93*
Stephenson, Shelby 1938- *WhoWrEP 92*
Stephenson, Thomas *WhoScE 91-1*
Stephenson, Toni Edwards 1945- *WhoAm 92, WhoWor 93*
Stephenson, William 1902-1989 *BioIn 17*
Stephenson, William B. 1933- *WhoIns 93*
Stephenson, William E. 1942- *St&PR 93*
Stephen the Persian *OxDcByz*
Stephen the Younger c. 713-764 *OxDcByz*
Stephney, Bill
See Public Enemy *News 92*
Stepien, Kazimierz S. 1940- *WhoScE 91-4*
Stepinac, Aloysius 1898-1960 *DcTwHis*
Stepinski, Marian 1935- *WhoScE 91-4*
Stepka, Stephen Anthony 1959- *WhoSSW 93*
Stepka, William 1917- *WhoSSW 93*
Stepkoski, Robert John 1933- *WhoSSW 93*
Stepler, Paul Stoneham 1949- *St&PR 93*
Stepner, Laraine E. Adler 1943- *WhoAmW 93*
Stepney, Philip Harold Robert 1947- *WhoAm 92*
Stepnick, Arlene Alice *WhoAmW 93*
Stepniczka, Heinrich E. 1940- *WhoWor 93*
Stepniewski, Marian 1935- *WhoScE 91-4*
Stepnowski, Edmund Joseph 1930- *WhoSSW 93*
Steponavicius, Julijonas d1991 *BioIn 17*
Stepp, George Allan, Jr. 1922- *WhoWor 93*
Stepp, James Michael 1944- *WhoAm 92*
Stepp, John R. 1941- *WhoAm 92*
Stepp, Marc *AfrAmBi*
Stepp, Patricia Joy 1940- *WhoAmW 93*
Steppe, Donald Joseph 1942- *St&PR 93*
Steppler, Howard Alvey 1918- *WhoAm 92*
Stepro, B.J. 1929- *St&PR 93*
Steps, B. Jill *Law&B 92*
Stepter, Paula F. *Law&B 92*
Stepto, Michele 1946- *BioIn 17*
Stepto, Robert Charles 1920- *WhoAm 92*
Stepto, Robert Frederick Thomas 1937- *WhoWor 93*
Steptoe, Andrew P.A. *WhoScE 91-1*
Steptoe, John 1950-1989 *BioIn 17, BlkAuII 92, ChlBIID [port]*
Steptoe, John (Lewis) 1950-1989 *MajAI [port]*
Steptoe, Lydia *AmWomPl*
Steptoe, Roger (Guy) 1953- *Baker 92*
Stepton, Rick 1942- *WhoE 93*
Ster, John W. 1937- *St&PR 93*
Sterba, Frantisek 1932- *WhoScE 91-4*
Sterba, Gunther 1922- *WhoScE 91-3*
Sterba, Hubert W. 1945- *WhoScE 91-4*
Sterba, Oldrich 1930- *WhoScE 91-4*
Sterbak, Jana *BioIn 17*
Sterban, Richard *BioIn 17*
Sterban, Richard Anthony 1943- *WhoAm 92*
Sterbenz, Henry William, Jr. 1943- *WhoSSW 93*
Stergiadis, George Char. 1927- *WhoScE 91-3*
Stergios, Jerry 1917- *St&PR 93*
Stergiou, E. James 1949- *WhoIns 93*
Sterkel, Alice V. *Law&B 92*
Sterkel, Johann Franz Xaver 1750-1817 *Baker 92*
Sterling, Ada 1870-1939 *AmWomPl*
Sterling, Alida Baker 1955- *WhoAmW 93*
Sterling, Antoinette 1850-1904 *Baker 92*
Sterling, Arthur MacLean 1938- *WhoSSW 93*
Sterling, Bruce *BioIn 17*
Sterling, Bruce 1954- *ConLC 72 [port], ScF&FL 92*
Sterling, Carlos Marquez 1899-1991 *BioIn 17*
Sterling, Charles 1901-1991 *BioIn 17*
Sterling, David L. 1929- *ConAu 139*
Sterling, Donald Justus, Jr. 1927- *WhoAm 92*
Sterling, Donald R. 1936- *St&PR 93*
Sterling, Donald T. *WhoAm 92*
Sterling, Dorothy 1913- *MajAI [port]*
Sterling, Dorothy Anne 1963- *WhoAmW 93*
Sterling, Edythe d1962 *SweetSg A*
Sterling, Ford 1880-1939 *QDrFCA 92 [port]*
Sterling, Frank 1945- *St&PR 93*
Sterling, Gary Campbell 1941- *WhoWrEP 92*
Sterling, Harry, Jr. 1943- *St&PR 93*
Sterling, Ivan Charles 1956- *WhoWor 93*
Sterling, Jack 1915-1990 *BioIn 17*
Sterling, John 1806-1844 *DcLB 116 [port]*
Sterling, John C. *Law&B 92*
Sterling, John Robert 1945- *St&PR 93*
Sterling, Keir Brooks 1934- *WhoAm 92*
Sterling, Kenneth 1920- *WhoAm 92*
Sterling, Michael John Howard *WhoScE 91-1*
Sterling, Philip 1907-1989 *BioIn 17*
Sterling, Rand E. *Law&B 92*
Sterling, Raymond Leslie 1949- *WhoAm 92*
Sterling, Reay 1932- *St&PR 93*
Sterling, Robert H. *St&PR 93*
Sterling, Robert Lee, Jr. 1933- *WhoE 93*
Sterling, Sara Hawks *AmWomPl*
Sterling, Scott E. *Law&B 92*
Sterling, Shirley Frampton 1920- *WhoSSW 93*
Sterling, Suzanne K. *Law&B 92*
Sterling, Thomas William, III 1947- *St&PR 93*
Sterling, William F. *Law&B 92*
Sterling of Plaistow, Baron 1934- *WhoWor 93*
Stermac, Anthony George 1921- *WhoAm 92*
Sterman, Betsy 1927- *ScF&FL 92*
Sterman, Samuel 1918- *ScF&FL 92*
Stermer, Dugald Robert 1936- *WhoAm 92, WhoWor 93*
Stermer-Ogle, Anita June 1951- *WhoAmW 93*
Stern, Aaron 1918- *WhoWrEP 92*
Stern, Abraham Jacob 1769-1842 *PolBiDi*
Stern, Alan I. 1934- *St&PR 93*
Stern, Alan Isaac 1948- *WhoE 93*
Stern, Alfred K. 1897-1986 *BioIn 17*
Stern, Alfred Phillip 1933- *WhoAm 92*
Stern, Allan D.R. 1932- *St&PR 93*
Stern, Andrew R. *Law&B 92*
Stern, Ann C. *Law&B 92*
Stern, Ann C. 1952- *St&PR 93*
Stern, Ann Kay 1962- *WhoAmW 93*
Stern, Annie Ward 1944- *WhoE 93*
Stern, Arthur C. d1992 *NewYTBS 92 [port]*
Stern, Arthur Cecil 1909-1992 *BioIn 17*
Stern, Arthur Charles 1957- *WhoWrEP 92*
Stern, Arthur O. *Law&B 92*
Stern, Arthur O. 1938- *St&PR 93*
Stern, Arthur Ogden 1938- *WhoE 93*
Stern, Arthur Paul 1925- *St&PR 93, WhoAm 92, WhoWor 93*
Stern, Authur Cecil 1909-1992 *CurBio 92N*
Stern, Barry John 1940- *St&PR 93*
Stern, Bernhard J. 1894-1956 *IntDcAn*
Stern, Bruce E. *Law&B 92*
Stern, C. Elizabeth Espin 1961- *WhoEmL 93*
Stern, Carl Leonard 1937- *WhoAm 92*
Stern, Carolyn H. *AmWomPl*
Stern, Celia Ellen 1954- *WhoE 93*
Stern, Charles 1920- *St&PR 93, WhoAm 92*
Stern, Charles Bertram 1915- *St&PR 93*
Stern, Charles M. 1943- *WhoAm 92*
Stern, Chester Martin 1923- *St&PR 93*
Stern, Claudia d1990 *BioIn 17*
Stern, Curt 1902-1981 *BioIn 17*
Stern, Daniel *BioIn 17*
Stern, Daniel 1805-1876 *BioIn 17*
Stern, Daniel 1928- *WhoAm 92*
Stern, Daniel Alan 1944- *WhoAm 92*
Stern, Daniel N. 1934- *ConAu 136*
Stern, David *BioIn 17*
Stern, David 1949- *ConAu 138*
Stern, David 1958- *ScF&FL 92*
Stern, David Harold 1935- *WhoWor 93*
Stern, David Joel 1942- *WhoAm 92*
Stern, Dennis M. *Law&B 92*
Stern, Dennis M. 1941- *St&PR 93*
Stern, Dennis M. 1947- *WhoAm 92*
Stern, Douglas Donald 1939- *WhoSSW 93*
Stern, Edgar B., Jr. 1922- *St&PR 93*
Stern, Edith Rosenwald 1895-1980 *JeAmHC*
Stern, Edward Abraham 1930- *WhoAm 92*
Stern, Edward Lee 1935- *WhoSSW 93*
Stern, Edward R. 1914- *St&PR 93*
Stern, Elisabeth G. 1890-1954 *BioIn 17*
Stern, Elizabeth Vera Loeb 1893-1991 *BioIn 17*
Stern, Elliott *Law&B 92*
Stern, Eric Petru 1941- *WhoWor 93*
Stern, Ernest 1920- *St&PR 93*
Stern, Ernest 1928- *WhoAm 92*
Stern, Eugene B. *Law&B 92*
Stern, Frank 1928- *WhoAm 92*
Stern, Fritz Richard 1926- *WhoAm 92*
Stern, Gail Frieda 1950- *WhoAm 92*
Stern, Gary Hilton 1944- *St&PR 93*
Stern, Gary Peter 1943- *St&PR 93*
Stern, Geoffrey 1942- *WhoAm 92*
Stern, Geoffrey Adlai 1955- *WhoAm 92*
Stern, George 1924- *St&PR 93*
Stern, Gerald *BioIn 17*
Stern, Gerald Daniel 1933- *WhoAm 92*
Stern, Gerald Joseph 1925- *WhoAm 92*
Stern, Gerald M. *Law&B 92*
Stern, Gerald M. 1937- *St&PR 93, WhoAm 92*
Stern, Grace Mary 1925- *WhoAmW 93*
Stern, Guy 1922- *WhoAm 92*
Stern, H.J. *WhoScE 91-1*
Stern, Hans L. 1929- *St&PR 93*
Stern, Harold *St&PR 93*
Stern, Harris I. 1928- *St&PR 93*
Stern, Harvey 1946- *WhoE 93*
Stern, Harvey B. 1939- *St&PR 93*
Stern, Henry L. 1924- *St&PR 93*
Stern, Henry Louis 1924- *WhoAm 92*
Stern, Henry M. d1991 *BioIn 17*
Stern, Herbert A. *Law&B 92*
Stern, Herbert B. 1937- *St&PR 93*
Stern, Herbert Jay 1936- *WhoAm 92*
Stern, Howard *BioIn 17*
Stern, Howard S. 1931- *St&PR 93*
Stern, Isaac 1920- *Baker 92, WhoAm 92, WhoWor 93*
Stern, J(oseph) P(eter Maria) 1920-1991 *ConAu 136*
Stern, James A. 1950- *St&PR 93*
Stern, James Andrew 1950- *WhoAm 92*
Stern, Jan Peter 1926- *WhoAm 92*
Stern, Jeffrey 1950- *St&PR 93*
Stern, Jerome H. 1929- *WhoIns 93*
Stern, Joel A. *Law&B 92*
Stern, Joel Mark 1941- *WhoAm 92*
Stern, John 1926- *WhoE 93*
Stern, John Peter 1944- *WhoWor 93*
Stern, Jonathan H. 1944- *St&PR 93*
Stern, Jonathan Michael 1959- *WhoE 93*
Stern, Joseph Aaron 1927- *WhoAm 92*
Stern, Joseph Smith, Jr. 1918- *WhoAm 92*
Stern, Julian N. 1924- *St&PR 93*
Stern, Julius 1820-1883 *Baker 92*
Stern, Kalika Evelyn 1941- *WhoE 93*
Stern, Kate Macomber 1952- *WhoE 93*
Stern, Laurence Robert *Law&B 92*
Stern, Lawrence N. 1942- *WhoAm 92*
Stern, Leni *BioIn 17*
Stern, Leo(pold Lawrence) 1862-1904 *Baker 92*
Stern, Leon M. 1930- *St&PR 93*
Stern, Leonard *BioIn 17*
Stern, Leonard B. 1923- *MiSFD 9*
Stern, Leonard Bernard 1923- *WhoAm 92*
Stern, Leonard Norman 1938- *WhoAm 92*
Stern, Louis William 1935- *WhoAm 92*
Stern, Louise 1921- *WhoAmW 93, WhoE 93*
Stern, Madeleine Bettina 1912- *BioIn 17, WhoAm 92, WhoWrEP 92*
Stern, Marc Irwin 1944- *WhoAm 92, WhoWor 93*
Stern, Marianne 1950- *WhoE 93, WhoWor 93*
Stern, Martha Dodd 1908-1990 *BioIn 17*
Stern, Marvin 1916- *WhoAm 92*
Stern, Marvin 1923- *WhoAm 92*
Stern, Michael 1910- *WhoWor 93*
Stern, Michael D. 1949- *St&PR 93*
Stern, Michael Lawrence 1948- *WhoE 93, WhoEmL 93*
Stern, Milton d1989 *BioIn 17*
Stern, Milton 1927- *WhoAm 92*
Stern, Milton H. d1992 *NewYTBS 92 [port]*
Stern, Milton H. 1924- *WhoAm 92*
Stern, Miriam Pauline 1946- *WhoAmW 93*
Stern, Mortimer Phillip 1926- *WhoAm 92*
Stern, Nancy Ann 1944- *WhoAmW 93*
Stern, Nancy Fortgang 1944- *WhoAmW 93*
Stern, Neal M. 1951- *St&PR 93, WhoIns 93*
Stern, Ned *St&PR 93*
Stern, Nicholas Herbert *WhoScE 91-1*
Stern, Noah *MiSFD 9*
Stern, Paul George 1938- *WhoAm 92*
Stern, Paula 1945- *WhoAm 92, WhoAmW 93*
Stern, Philip M. *BioIn 17*
Stern, Philip M. 1926-1992 *NewYTBS 92 [port]*
Stern, Philip M(aurice) 1926-1992 *ConAu 137*

Stern, Philip Maurice 1926- *WhoWrEP 92*
Stern, Philip Van Doren 1900-1984 *ScF&FL 92*
Stern, Ralph B. *St&PR 93*
Stern, Richard *Law&B 92*
Stern, Richard David 1936- *WhoAm 92*
Stern, Richard G. 1928- *JeAmFiW*
Stern, Richard Gustave 1928- *WhoAm 92, WhoWrEP 92*
Stern, Richard H. 1950- *St&PR 93*
Stern, Richard James 1922- *WhoAm 92*
Stern, Richard L. *Law&B 92*
Stern, Richard Martin 1915- *ConAu 40NR, WhoWrEP 92*
Stern, Richard Moritz 1933- *WhoUN 92*
Stern, Robert *Law&B 92*
Stern, Robert 1932- *WhoE 93*
Stern, Robert A.M. 1939- *BioIn 17*
Stern, Robert Alan *Law&B 92*
Stern, Robert Arthur Morton 1939- *WhoAm 92*
Stern, Robert D. 1929- *St&PR 93, WhoAm 92*
Stern, Robert E. *Law&B 92*
Stern, Robert Louis 1908- *WhoAm 92*
Stern, Robert Morris 1937- *WhoAm 92*
Stern, Ronald A. *Law&B 92*
Stern, Roslyne Paige 1926- *WhoAm 92, WhoAmW 93*
Stern, Russell T., Jr. 1927- *St&PR 93*
Stern, Ruth 1929- *WhoAmW 93*
Stern, Samuel Alan 1929- *WhoAm 92*
Stern, Sandor 1936- *MiSFD 9*
Stern, Sandra *Law&B 92*
Stern, Sandra 1937- *St&PR 93*
Stern, Sheila (Frances) 1922- *ConAu 136*
Stern, Steve 1947- *ScF&FL 92*
Stern, Steven A. 1943- *St&PR 93*
Stern, Steven David *Law&B 92*
Stern, Steven Hilliard 1937- *MiSFD 9*
Stern, Steven L. *ScF&FL 92*
Stern, Stewart 1922- *BioIn 17*
Stern, Stuart *ScF&FL 92*
Stern, T. Noel 1913- *WhoAm 92*
Stern, Walter Eugene 1920- *WhoAm 92*
Stern, Walter P. 1928- *St&PR 93*
Stern, Walter Phillips 1928- *WhoAm 92, WhoE 93*
Stern, Walter S. 1925- *St&PR 93*
Stern, Warren Charles 1944- *St&PR 93*
Stern, Wayne Brian 1948- *WhoSSW 93*
Stern, William Louis 1926- *WhoAm 92*
Stern, Wilma 1940- *ConAu 138*
Sternad, Gary E. 1953- *St&PR 93*
Sternal, Sandra Gaunt 1946- *WhoAmW 93*
Sternbach, Harvey 1924- *St&PR 93*
Sternbach, Richard M. *ScF&FL 92*
Sternbach, Rick 1951- *ScF&FL 92*
Sternbach, Sidney M., Jr. 1909- *St&PR 93*
Sternberg, Alan Lee *Law&B 92*
Sternberg, Cecilia 1908-1983 *ConAu 39NR*
Sternberg, Charles H. 1850-1943 *BioIn 17*
Sternberg, Christina *BioIn 17*
Sternberg, Constantin 1852-1924 *Baker 92*
Sternberg, Daniel Arie 1913- *WhoAm 92*
Sternberg, David Edward 1946- *WhoWor 93*
Sternberg, Eldon R. *Law&B 92*
Sternberg, Erich Walter 1891-1974 *Baker 92*
Sternberg, Harry d1991 *BioIn 17*
Sternberg, Harry 1904- *WhoAm 92*
Sternberg, Helene 1962- *WhoAmW 93*
Sternberg, James C. 1927- *St&PR 93*
Sternberg, Jonathan *Law&B 92*
Sternberg, Jonathan 1919- *Baker 92*
Sternberg, Judi Ann 1941- *WhoE 93*
Sternberg, Marvin Edward 1934- *St&PR 93*
Sternberg, Michael Joseph Ezra *WhoScE 91-1*
Sternberg, Paul 1918- *WhoAm 92*
Sternberg, Paul J. 1933- *St&PR 93, WhoAm 92*
Sternberg, Phyllis 1960- *WhoE 93*
Sternberg, Richard Ira 1948- *WhoE 93*
Sternberg, Robert 1913-1991 *BioIn 17*
Sternberg, Ronald I. *St&PR 93*
Sternberg, Seymour 1943- *WhoAm 92, WhoIns 93*
Sternberger, Ludwig Amadeus 1921- *WhoAm 92*
Sternberger, Stephen Jeffrey 1949- *St&PR 93*
Sterne, Bobbie Lynn 1919- *WhoAmW 93*
Sterne, Joseph Robert Livingston 1928- *WhoAm 92*
Sterne, Laurence 1713-1768 *MagSWL [port], WorLitC [port]*
Sterne, Lawrence Jon 1949- *WhoE 93*
Sterne, Michael Lyon 1936- *WhoAm 92*
Sternefeld, Daniel 1905-1986 *Baker 92*
Sterner, Frank Maurice 1935- *St&PR 93, WhoAm 92*
Sterner, Gene Edward 1940- *St&PR 93*
Sterner, James Hervi 1904- *WhoAm 92*
Sterner, John 1912- *St&PR 93*
Sterner, Judy Murtz 1953- *WhoAmW 93*
Sterner, Michael Edmund 1928- *WhoAm 92*
Sternfeld, F(riedrich) W(ilhelm) 1914- *Baker 92*
Sternfeld, Leon 1913- *WhoE 93*
Sternfeld, Marc Howard 1947- *WhoE 93*
Sternfeld, Sue *BioIn 17*
Sternfelt, Linda Anne 1962- *WhoAmW 93*
Sternfield, Scott Frederic 1940- *St&PR 93*
Sternglass, Lila M. 1934- *WhoAm 92*
Sterngold, James Sheldon 1954- *WhoWor 93*
Sternhagen, Frances 1930- *WhoAm 92*
Sternheim, (William Adolf) Carl 1878-1942 *DcLB 118 [port]*
Sternheimer, Mark Aiden 1929- *St&PR 93*
Sterni, John 1938- *St&PR 93*
Sternlicht, Beno *WhoAm 92*
Sternlicht, Sanford 1931- *WhoAm 92*
Sternlieb, Barry F. 1947- *WhoWrEP 92*
Sternlieb, Lynne R. *Law&B 92*
Sternlight, Peter Donn 1928- *WhoAm 92*
Sterns, Harvey Nelson 1924- *WhoE 93*
Sterns, Joel Henry 1934- *WhoAm 92*
Sternson, Larry Allen 1946- *WhoE 93*
Sterpone, L. *WhoScE 91-3*
Sterrer, Neil E. 1945- *WhoE 93*
Sterrett, James Edward 1931- *St&PR 93*
Sterrett, Joel A. *Law&B 92*
Sterrett, Joel A. 1936- *St&PR 93*
Sterrett, Malcolm McCurdy Burdett 1942- *WhoAm 92*
Sterrett, Robert W., Jr. *Law&B 92*
Sterrett, Samuel Black 1922- *WhoWor 93*
Stertz, Kurt N. *Law&B 92*
Sterud, Eugene LeRoy 1933- *WhoAm 92*
Sterzer, Fred 1929- *WhoAm 92*
Sterzin, Donald M. d1992 *NewYTBS 92*
Sterzinsky, Georg Maximilian 1936- *WhoWor 93*
Stesney, Linda A. *Law&B 92*
Stessel, Jerry H. 1937- *St&PR 93*
Steth, Raymond 1917- *BioIn 17*
Stethatos, Niketas 1005?-c. 1090 *OxDcByz*
Stetler, C. Joseph 1917- *WhoAm 92*
Stetler, Harrison Crawford 1940- *WhoSSW 93*
Stetler, Larry D. 1934- *St&PR 93*
Stetler, Russell Dearnley, Jr. 1945- *WhoAm 92, WhoWrEP 92*
Stetson, Augusta E. 1842?-1928 *BioIn 17*
Stetson, Daniel Everett 1956- *WhoAm 92*
Stetson, Eugene William, III 1951- *WhoE 93, WhoWor 93*
Stetson, John B., IV 1936- *St&PR 93*
Stetson, John Batterson, IV 1936- *WhoAm 92*
Stetson, John Benjamin Blank 1927- *WhoAm 92, WhoWor 93*
Stetson, John Charles 1920- *WhoAm 92, WhoWor 93*
Stetson, Kathryn T. 1956- *WhoAmW 93*
Stetson, Richard Brian 1928- *St&PR 93*
Stetson, William Wallace 1941- *St&PR 93*
Stette, Gunnar R. 1936- *WhoScE 91-4*
Stette, Gunnar Rolf 1936- *WhoWor 93*
Stetten, DeWitt 1909-1990 *BioIn 17*
Stetten, George *ScF&FL 92*
Stetten, Nancy Zufall 1954- *WhoAmW 93*
Stetter, Hans Joerg 1930- *WhoWor 93*
Stetter, Karl O. 1941- *WhoScE 91-3*
Stettheimer, Florine 1871-1944 *BioIn 17*
Stettinius, Wallace 1933- *St&PR 93, WhoAm 92, WhoSSW 93*
Stettler, Carla Rice 1947- *WhoAmW 93, WhoEmL 93*
Stettler, John Everett 1942- *WhoSSW 93*
Stettner, Enid Ballinger 1933- *WhoE 93*
Stettner, Irving 1922- *ConAu 37NR*
Stettner, Jerald W. 1952- *WhoSSW 93*
Stetz, Frederick W. 1927- *St&PR 93*
Stetzer, Leah Manning *Law&B 92*
Stetzner, Leah Manning 1948- *WhoAm 92*
Steuart, James 1712-1780 *BioIn 17*
Steuart, Sybil Jean 1954- *WhoAmW 93*
Steuben, Baron von 1730-1794 *BioIn 17*
Steuben, Friedrich Wilhelm von 1730-1794 *HarEnMi*
Steuben, Norton Leslie 1936- *WhoAm 92*
Steudel, Ralf 1937- *WhoScE 91-3*
Steudler, Theresa Marie 1962- *WhoAmW 93*
Steuer, Erwin 1928- *St&PR 93*
Steuer, Richard Marc 1948- *WhoAm 92, WhoE 93*
Steuer, Sharon 1959- *BioIn 17*
Steuerle, C. Eugene 1946- *WhoAm 92*
Steuerlein, Johann 1546-1613 *Baker 92*
Steuerman, Walter 1926- *St&PR 93*
Steuermann, Edward 1892-1964 *Baker 92*
Steuert, D. Michael 1948- *St&PR 93*
Steuert, Douglas Michael 1948- *WhoAm 92*
Steuerwald, David A. 1940- *St&PR 93*
Steurer, Joseph Frederick 1936- *St&PR 93*
Steurer, Stephen Joseph 1944- *WhoE 93*
Steusloff, Hartwig U. 1937- *WhoScE 91-3*
Steussy, Martha J. *ScF&FL 92*
Steussy, Marti 1955- *ScF&FL 92*
Stevanato, Roberto 1946- *WhoWor 93*
Stevelink, Walter 1935- *WhoScE 91-3*
Stevely, William Stewart *WhoScE 91-1*
Steven, Sue Elizabeth 1953- *WhoAmW 93*
Steven, William P. 1908-1991 *BioIn 17*
Stevenin, Jean-Francois 1944- *MiSFD 9*
Stevens, A(rthur) Wilber, Jr. 1921- *WhoWrEP 92*
Stevens, Alan Douglas 1926- *WhoAm 92*
Stevens, Albert David 1942- *WhoE 93*
Stevens, Allyssa Elizabeth 1961- *WhoE 93*
Stevens, Andrew 1955- *MiSFD 9, WhoAm 92*
Stevens, Andrew L. 1936- *WhoWrEP 92*
Stevens, Andy *ConAu 39NR*
Stevens, Art *MiSFD 9*
Stevens, Art 1935- *WhoAm 92*
Stevens, Arthur J. *Law&B 92*
Stevens, Arthur J. 1934- *St&PR 93*
Stevens, Arthur Wilber, Jr. 1921- *WhoAm 92*
Stevens, Barbara Constance 1924- *WhoWrEP 92*
Stevens, Beatrice M. *AmWomPl*
Stevens, Benjamin 1915- *St&PR 93*
Stevens, Bernard (George) 1916-1983 *Baker 92*
Stevens, Brenda Anita 1949- *WhoAmW 93*
Stevens, Brooks 1911- *WhoWor 93*
Stevens, Bruce Russell 1952- *WhoSSW 93*
Stevens, Bryna *BioIn 17*
Stevens, Bryna 1924- *ConAu 136*
Stevens, C. Glenn 1941- *WhoWor 93*
Stevens, C(lysle) J(ulius) 1927- *WhoWrEP 92*
Stevens, Carl *WhoWrEP 92*
Stevens, Carol M. *Law&B 92*
Stevens, Caroline D. *AmWomPl*
Stevens, Charles David 1912- *WhoSSW 93*
Stevens, Charles F. 1934- *WhoAm 92*
Stevens, Charles Harry 1923- *St&PR 93*
Stevens, Charles W. *St&PR 93*
Stevens, Charles W. 1955- *ConAu 136*
Stevens, Chester Leo, Jr. 1947- *WhoSSW 93*
Stevens, Christine Hyde 1926- *WhoWrEP 92*
Stevens, Christopher Andrew 1958- *WhoWor 93*
Stevens, Clark V. 1933- *St&PR 93*
Stevens, Clark Valentine 1933- *WhoWor 93*
Stevens, Connie 1938- *WhoAm 92*
Stevens, Courtney McKay 1944- *WhoAmW 93*
Stevens, Craig S. *Law&B 92*
Stevens, Craig Stewart 1947- *St&PR 93*
Stevens, Cynthia Brown 1948- *WhoAmW 93*
Stevens, Dana J. *AmWomPl*
Stevens, Daniel David Dean 1935- *WhoE 93*
Stevens, Daniel Josephus 1946- *WhoE 93*
Stevens, David *MiSFD 9*
Stevens, David 1926- *WhoAm 92*
Stevens, David L. 1942- *St&PR 93*
Stevens, David Michael 1941- *WhoSSW 93*
Stevens, Debra Rolquin 1954- *WhoAmW 93*
Stevens, Denis (William) 1922- *Baker 92, WhoAm 92*
Stevens, Dennis Max 1944- *WhoSSW 93*
Stevens, Don Eldon 1957- *WhoSSW 93*
Stevens, Donald King 1920- *WhoSSW 93, WhoWor 93*
Stevens, Donald Vernet, Jr. 1921- *WhoE 93*
Stevens, Doris Loraine 1912- *WhoAmW 93*
Stevens, Duane Arthur 1948- *St&PR 93*
Stevens, Dwight Marlyn 1933- *WhoAm 92*
Stevens, Earl Patrick 1925- *WhoSSW 93*
Stevens, Edmund 1910-1992 *BioIn 17*
Stevens, Edmund W. 1910-1992 *NewYTBS 92*
Stevens, Edmund William 1910-1992 *ConAu 137, CurBio 92N*
Stevens, Elisabeth 1929- *WhoWrEP 92*
Stevens, Elisabeth Goss 1929- *WhoAm 92, WhoAmW 93, WhoE 93*
Stevens, Elizabeth *AmWomPl*
Stevens, Elizabeth 1950- *WhoSSW 93*
Stevens, Elizabeth Ellen 1943- *WhoAmW 93*
Stevens, Elizabeth M. *AmWomPl*
Stevens, Elliot Leslie 1948- *WhoAm 92*
Stevens, Eugene Steve 1938- *WhoE 93*
Stevens, Eva B. *Law&B 92*
Stevens, Ford Woods, Jr. 1942- *WhoE 93*
Stevens, Forrest Wayne 1928- *St&PR 93*
Stevens, Frank 1941- *WhoE 93*
Stevens, G.H. 1937- *WhoScE 91-2*
Stevens, Garfield Reeves- *ScF&FL 92*
Stevens, Gary P. 1951- *St&PR 93*
Stevens, George 1904-1975 *MiSFD 9N*
Stevens, George, Jr. 1932- *MiSFD 9, WhoAm 92*
Stevens, George Richard 1932- *WhoAm 92*
Stevens, Gerald F. 1938-1990 *BioIn 17*
Stevens, Gladstone Taylor, Jr. 1930- *WhoAm 92*
Stevens, Glen Roy *St&PR 93*
Stevens, Glenn Howard *Law&B 92*
Stevens, Gordon 1945- *ScF&FL 92*
Stevens, Gordon Sefton *Law&B 92*
Stevens, Halsey 1908-1989 *Baker 92*
Stevens, Harold A. 1907-1990 *BioIn 17*
Stevens, Harold Ray 1936- *WhoE 93*
Stevens, Helen Jean 1934- *WhoAmW 93*
Stevens, Henry 1819-1886 *BioIn 17*
Stevens, Holly *BioIn 17*
Stevens, Holly d1992 *NewYTBS 92*
Stevens, Holly 1924- *WhoWrEP 92*
Stevens, Holly 1924-1992 *ConAu 137*
Stevens, Howard L. *Law&B 92*
Stevens, Inger 1934?-1970 *BioIn 17*
Stevens, Isaac H. *St&PR 93, WhoE 93*
Stevens, J. Paul 1942- *WhoWor 93*
Stevens, James Hervey, Jr. 1944- *WhoWor 93*
Stevens, James J., Sr. 1935- *St&PR 93*
Stevens, James J., Jr. 1955- *St&PR 93*
Stevens, James M. 1947- *WhoSSW 93*
Stevens, James Regis, Jr. *Law&B 92*
Stevens, James Robley 1934- *St&PR 93*
Stevens, James Walter 1932- *WhoE 93*
Stevens, James William 1936- *St&PR 93, WhoAm 92*
Stevens, Jeanine Robinson 1958- *WhoSSW 93*
Stevens, Jeffrey L. 1948- *St&PR 93*
Stevens, Jeffrey N. *Law&B 92*
Stevens, John Christopher 1918- *WhoAm 92*
Stevens, John (Edgar) 1921- *Baker 92*
Stevens, John Flournoy 1914- *WhoSSW 93*
Stevens, John Frederick *Law&B 92*
Stevens, John Michael 1940- *St&PR 93*
Stevens, John P. *Law&B 92*
Stevens, John P. 1897?-1976 *BioIn 17*
Stevens, John P. 1929- *St&PR 93*
Stevens, John Paul *BioIn 17*
Stevens, John Paul 1920- *CngDr 91, OxCSupC [port], WhoAm 92, WhoE 93*
Stevens, John R. 1940- *St&PR 93*
Stevens, Jonathan A. 1951- *St&PR 93*
Stevens, Joseph Charles 1929- *WhoAm 92*
Stevens, Joseph Edward, Jr. 1928- *WhoAm 92*
Stevens, Joseph John, Jr. 1949- *WhoE 93*
Stevens, Judith Reeves- *ScF&FL 92*
Stevens, Judy Silver 1951- *WhoAmW 93*
Stevens, Karen *Law&B 92*
Stevens, Kathleen 1936- *ConAu 39NR*
Stevens, Kenneth Noble 1924- *WhoAm 92*
Stevens, Larry *BioIn 17*
Stevens, Leonard A. *BioIn 17*
Stevens, Leota Mae 1921- *WhoAmW 93*
Stevens, Leslie 1924- *MiSFD 9*
Stevens, Lisa *BioIn 17*
Stevens, Lisa Gay 1952- *WhoAmW 93*
Stevens, Lydia Hastings 1918- *WhoAmW 93*
Stevens, Malcolm F.G. *WhoScE 91-1*
Stevens, Malcolm Peter 1934- *WhoE 93*
Stevens, Margaret Talbott *AmWomPl*
Stevens, Marilyn Ruth 1943- *St&PR 93, WhoAmW 93*
Stevens, Marion Louise Wall 1939- *WhoAmW 93*
Stevens, Mark *WhoWrEP 92*
Stevens, Mark 1947- *St&PR 93, WhoAm 92*
Stevens, Mark J. *Law&B 92*
Stevens, Mark Kemble 1952- *WhoSSW 93*
Stevens, Mark L. 1941- *St&PR 93*
Stevens, Mark Paul 1951- *WhoE 93*
Stevens, Mark Whitney 1951- *WhoAm 92*
Stevens, Marre Dangar 1943- *WhoAmW 93*
Stevens, Martin 1927- *WhoAm 92*
Stevens, May 1924- *WhoAm 92*
Stevens, Michael Paul *Law&B 92*
Stevens, Michelle Louise 1954- *WhoAmW 93*
Stevens, Milton Lewis, Jr. 1942- *WhoAm 92*
Stevens, Morton 1929-1991 *BioIn 17*
Stevens, P.J.B. *St&PR 93*
Stevens, Patricia Ann 1946- *WhoAmW 93*
Stevens, Paul Achiel 1956- *WhoWor 93*
Stevens, Paul Edward 1916- *WhoAm 92*
Stevens, Paul I. 1915- *St&PR 93*
Stevens, Paul Irving 1915- *WhoAm 92*
Stevens, Paul K. 1946- *St&PR 93*
Stevens, Perry G. 1931- *WhoIns 93*
Stevens, Peter 1927- *WhoCanL 92*
Stevens, Peter B. 1937- *St&PR 93*
Stevens, Peter N. *Law&B 92*

Stevens, Philip Ashworth 1934- *St&PR 93*
Stevens, Philip L. 1940- *St&PR 93*
Stevens, Phyliss Elizabeth 1953- *WhoAmW 93*
Stevens, Prescott Allen 1922- *WhoWor 93*
Stevens, R.A. 1928- *St&PR 93*
Stevens, R.L. *WhoWrEP 92*
Stevens, Raymond D., Jr. 1927- *St&PR 93*
Stevens, Raymond Donald, Jr. 1927- *WhoAm 92*
Stevens, Richard J. *Law&B 92*
Stevens, Richard John Samuel 1757-1837 *Baker 92*
Stevens, Richard Paul 1944- *WhoE 93*
Stevens, Richard S. 1912- *WhoScE 91-1*
Stevens, Richard St. John 1943- *WhoWor 93*
Stevens, Richard Yates 1948- *WhoEmL 93, WhoSSW 93*
Stevens, Rick D. 1950- *WhoSSW 93*
Stevens, Rise 1913- *Baker 92, IntDcOp, OxDcOp*
Stevens, Robert Bocking 1933- *WhoAm 92*
Stevens, Robert David 1921- *WhoAm 92*
Stevens, Robert Edward 1957- *WhoWor 93*
Stevens, Robert Edwin 1927- *WhoAm 92*
Stevens, Robert Evan 1943- *WhoAm 92*
Stevens, Robert James 1947- *WhoScE 91-1*
Stevens, Robert Jay 1945- *WhoAm 92, WhoWrEP 92*
Stevens, Robert L. 1947- *St&PR 93*
Stevens, Robert T. 1899-1983 *BioIn 17*
Stevens, Roger Lacey 1910- *WhoAm 92, WhoE 93*
Stevens, Roger R. *Law&B 92*
Stevens, Roger R. 1949- *St&PR 93*
Stevens, Ron A. 1945- *WhoAm 92*
Stevens, Rosemary *BioIn 17*
Stevens, Rosemary Anne *WhoAm 92, WhoAmW 93*
Stevens, Roy W. 1924- *WhoAm 92*
Stevens, Sally Wallace 1949- *WhoSSW 93*
Stevens, Sayre 1925- *WhoAm 92*
Stevens, Serita (Deborah) 1949- *SmATA 70 [port], WhoAmW 93*
Stevens, Shane 1951- *WhoE 93*
Stevens, Shira *SmATA 70*
Stevens, Sinclair McKnight 1927- *WhoAm 92*
Stevens, Sophie S. *AmWomPl*
Stevens, Stanley Allen 1957- *WhoSSW 93*
Stevens, Stella *BioIn 17*
Stevens, Stella 1936- *SweetSg D [port]*
Stevens, Stella 1938- *MiSFD 9*
Stevens, Stephen Edward *WhoWor 93*
Stevens, Susan Gregg 1945- *WhoSSW 93*
Stevens, Suzanne *WhoWrEP 92*
Stevens, Suzannne H. 1938- *ConAu 136*
Stevens, Ted *BioIn 17*
Stevens, Ted 1923- *CngDr 91*
Stevens, Ted 1945- *St&PR 93*
Stevens, Thaddeus 1792-1868 *EncAACR [port], PolPar*
Stevens, Thelma d1990 *BioIn 17*
Stevens, Theodore Fulton 1923- *WhoAm 92*
Stevens, Thomas *BioIn 17*
Stevens, Thomas L. 1930- *WhoIns 93*
Stevens, Tina Wagner 1957- *WhoAmW 93*
Stevens, W.F. 1941- *WhoScE 91-3*
Stevens, W. Tris *WhoIns 93*
Stevens, Wallace 1879-1955 *BioIn 17, MagSAmL [port], PoeCrit 6 [port], TwCLC 45 [port], WorLitC [port]*
Stevens, Walter Joseph 1944- *WhoE 93*
Stevens, Walter S. *Law&B 92*
Stevens, Warren 1919- *WhoAm 92*
Stevens, Wendell Claire 1931- *WhoAm 92*
Stevens, Whitney 1926- *BioIn 17*
Stevens, Wilbur Hunt 1918- *WhoWor 93*
Stevens, Willem Frans Casimir 1938- *WhoWor 93*
Stevens, William Dollard 1918- *WhoAm 92*
Stevens, William J. 1948- *St&PR 93*
Stevens, William John 1915- *WhoSSW 93, WhoWor 93*
Stevens, William Kenneth 1917- *WhoAm 92*
Stevens, William R. 1951- *St&PR 93*
Stevens, Win *BioIn 17*
Stevens-Haynes, Gale *WhoAmW 93*
Stevens-Kelly, Marjorie E. *Law&B 92*
Stevenson, A. Brockie 1919- *WhoAm 92, WhoE 93*
Stevenson, Adlai 1900-1965 *ColdWar 1 [port]*
Stevenson, Adlai E. 1835-1914 *PolPar*
Stevenson, Adlai E. 1900-1965 *BioIn 17*
Stevenson, Adlai E., II 1900-1965 *PolPar*
Stevenson, Adlai E., III 1930- *PolPar*
Stevenson, Adlai Ewing 1835-1914 *BioIn 17*
Stevenson, Adlai Ewing 1900-1965 *DcTwHis*
Stevenson, Adlai Ewing, III 1930- *WhoAm 92*
Stevenson, Alan B. 1943- *St&PR 93*
Stevenson, Alexandra *BioIn 17*
Stevenson, Andrew *WhoScE 91-1*
Stevenson, Andrew 1784-1857 *PolPar*
Stevenson, Andrew K. 1947- *BioIn 17*
Stevenson, Anne 1933- *BioIn 17*
Stevenson, Archibald Robert 1937- *WhoAm 92*
Stevenson, Augusta *AmWomPl*
Stevenson, Ben 1936- *WhoAm 92*
Stevenson, Bernard A. *Law&B 92*
Stevenson, Bernard A. 1952- *St&PR 93*
Stevenson, Bruce *ScF&FL 92*
Stevenson, C. Scott *Law&B 92*
Stevenson, Charles Arthur 1942- *WhoE 93*
Stevenson, Charles Rae 1936- *WhoUN 92*
Stevenson, Christine Wetherill *AmWomPl*
Stevenson, Coke R. 1888-1975 *BioIn 17*
Stevenson, Dave Carl 1951- *St&PR 93*
Stevenson, David G. *Law&B 92*
Stevenson, David L. *Law&B 92*
Stevenson, David R. *Law&B 92*
Stevenson, David R. 1949- *St&PR 93*
Stevenson, Deborah Lynne 1963- *WhoAmW 93*
Stevenson, Denise L. 1946- *WhoEmL 93*
Stevenson, Dennis Elliott 1943- *WhoSSW 93*
Stevenson, Derek *WhoScE 91-1*
Stevenson, Dewie O. 1926- *St&PR 93*
Stevenson, Donald J. *Law&B 92*
Stevenson, Donald Williams 1912- *St&PR 93*
Stevenson, Douglas 1953- *WhoWrEP 92*
Stevenson, Drew 1947- *BioIn 17, ScF&FL 92*
Stevenson, Dwight Eshelman 1906- *WhoWrEP 92*
Stevenson, E. 1943- *ScF&FL 92*
Stevenson, Earl, Jr. 1921- *WhoWor 93*
Stevenson, Edward Ward 1926- *WhoSSW 93*
Stevenson, Elizabeth 1919- *WhoAm 92*
Stevenson, Eric Van Cortlandt 1926- *WhoAm 92*
Stevenson, Ernest Vail 1922- *WhoAm 92*
Stevenson, Fern *AmWomPl*
Stevenson, Florence *ScF&FL 92*
Stevenson, Frances Grace 1921- *WhoAmW 93*
Stevenson, Frances Kellogg *WhoAmW 93, WhoWor 93*
Stevenson, Frank John 1938- *St&PR 93*
Stevenson, George Franklin 1922- *WhoAm 92*
Stevenson, George Telford *WhoScE 91-1*
Stevenson, Grace 1900-1992 *BioIn 17*
Stevenson, Grace Hope 1904- *WhoAmW 93*
Stevenson, Gratton A. 1917-1991 *BioIn 17*
Stevenson, Harold William 1924- *WhoAm 92*
Stevenson, Henry Miller 1914- *WhoAm 92*
Stevenson, Henry S. 1924- *St&PR 93*
Stevenson, Howard Higginbotham 1941- *WhoAm 92*
Stevenson, Ian 1918- *WhoAm 92*
Stevenson, Irone Edmund, Jr. 1930- *WhoE 93*
Stevenson, Jack Lovett 1928- *WhoSSW 93*
Stevenson, James *MajAI [port]*
Stevenson, James 1929- *BioIn 17, SmATA 71 [port]*
Stevenson, James Donald, Jr. *Law&B 92*
Stevenson, James Harold 1933- *WhoAm 92*
Stevenson, James R. 1940- *St&PR 93*
Stevenson, Jennifer Anne 1946- *WhoAm 92*
Stevenson, Jo Ann C. 1942- *WhoAmW 93*
Stevenson, JoAnne 1935- *WhoSSW 93*
Stevenson, John *ScF&FL 92*
Stevenson, John Edward 1952- *WhoWrEP 92*
Stevenson, John Franklin *Law&B 92*
Stevenson, John Landee 1927- *WhoAm 92*
Stevenson, John Reese 1921- *WhoAm 92, WhoWor 93*
Stevenson, John S. 1950- *St&PR 93*
Stevenson, Josiah, IV 1935- *WhoE 93*
Stevenson, Judy G. 1937- *St&PR 93*
Stevenson, Justin Jason, III 1941- *WhoAm 92*
Stevenson, Kenneth Lee 1939- *WhoAm 92*
Stevenson, Laura C. 1946- *ScF&FL 92*
Stevenson, Mabel B. *AmWomPl*
Stevenson, Margaretta *AmWomPl*
Stevenson, Marilyn Esther 1933- *WhoAmW 93*
Stevenson, Mary Huff 1945- *WhoAmW 93*
Stevenson, Matilda Coxe 1849-1915 *IntDcAn*
Stevenson, McLean 1929- *BioIn 17*
Stevenson, Milton F., Jr. 1955- *St&PR 93*
Stevenson, Parker *BioIn 17*
Stevenson, Patricia Louise 1945- *WhoAmW 93*
Stevenson, Paul E. 1928- *St&PR 93*
Stevenson, Paul Michael 1954- *WhoSSW 93*
Stevenson, Peggy Lee Denise 1958- *WhoAmW 93*
Stevenson, Philip Davis 1936- *WhoAm 92*
Stevenson, Richard M. *Law&B 92*
Stevenson, Robert 1905-1986 *MiSFD 9N*
Stevenson, Robert 1951- *St&PR 93*
Stevenson, Robert B. *Law&B 92*
Stevenson, Robert Edwin 1926- *WhoAm 92*
Stevenson, Robert H. 1942- *St&PR 93*
Stevenson, Robert Louis 1850-1894 *BioIn 17, MagSWL [port], ScF&FL 92, ShSCr 11 [port], WorLitC [port]*
Stevenson, Robert Louis 1941- *WhoSSW 93*
Stevenson, Robert Louis 1952- *WhoE 93*
Stevenson, Robert Louis (Balfour) 1850-1894 *MajAI [port]*
Stevenson, Robert (Murrell) 1916- *Baker 92, WhoAm 92, WhoWor 93*
Stevenson, Robert W. 1939- *St&PR 93*
Stevenson, Robin *ScF&FL 92*
Stevenson, Ronald 1928- *Baker 92*
Stevenson, Ronald J. 1951- *St&PR 93*
Stevenson, Ruth Carter 1923- *WhoAm 92*
Stevenson, Thomas Herbert 1951- *WhoEmL 93, WhoWor 93*
Stevenson, Walker Woods d1992 *BioIn 17*
Stevenson, Warren Howard 1938- *WhoAm 92*
Stevenson, William *SoulM*
Stevenson, William Alexander 1934- *WhoAm 92*
Stevenson, William B. 1952- *St&PR 93*
Stevenson, William Booth, II 1952- *WhoE 93*
Stevenson, William Edward 1938- *WhoSSW 93*
Stevenson, William Henri 1924- *WhoAm 92, WhoWrEP 92*
Stevenson, William (Henri) 1925- *DcChlFi*
Stevenson, William John, III 1948- *St&PR 93*
Stevenson, William T. 1928- *St&PR 93*
Stevenson Ledet, Debra Sue 1958- *WhoSSW 93*
Stevenson-Yang, Anne Kittredge 1959- *WhoAmW 93*
Stevens-Ratchford, Regena *BioIn 17*
Steventon, Robert Wesley 1948- *WhoSSW 93*
Stever, David *ScF&FL 92*
Stever, Horton Guyford 1916- *WhoAm 92, WhoWor 93*
Stever, Jill Andrea 1965- *WhoAmW 93*
Stever, Margo Taft 1950- *WhoWrEP 92*
Steverink, Antonius T.G. 1944- *WhoScE 91-3*
Stevermer, C. J. *ConAu 136*
Stevermer, Caroline *ScF&FL 92*
Stevermer, Caroline 1955- *ConAu 136*
Steves, Edward G. 1952- *St&PR 93*
Steves, Marshall T. 1923- *St&PR 93*
Steves, William Arthur 1946- *St&PR 93*
Stevinson, Stanley Raymond *Law&B 92*
Stevovich, Andrew Vlastimir 1948- *WhoE 93*
Steward, Ann *AmWomPl*
Steward, Anthony Paul *WhoScE 91-1*
Steward, Carlos Warren 1950- *WhoEmL 93, WhoSSW 93*
Steward, Charles Robert 1935- *WhoWor 93*
Steward, D.E. 1936- *WhoWrEP 92*
Steward, H. Leighton 1934- *WhoAm 92, WhoSSW 93*
Steward, Hal David 1918- *WhoWrEP 92*
Steward, Hugh Leighton 1934- *St&PR 93*
Steward, Jane A. *BioIn 17*
Steward, Julian H. 1902-1972 *IntDcAn*
Steward, Michael W. *WhoScE 91-1*
Steward, Nanncy Jean 1953- *WhoWrEP 92*
Steward, Oswald 1948- *WhoAm 92*
Steward, Patricia Ann Rupert 1945- *WhoAmW 93*
Steward, Vernon Rudston Whitefoord 1931- *WhoUN 92*
Steward, Weldon Cecil 1934- *WhoAm 92*
Steward, William Henry 1847-1935 *BioIn 17*
Stewart, Agnes 1897-1990? *BioIn 17*
Stewart, Alan *MiSFD 9, ScF&FL 92*
Stewart, Alan R. 1954- *St&PR 93*
Stewart, Albert Clifton 1919- *WhoE 93*
Stewart, Albert Elisha 1927- *WhoAm 92*
Stewart, Alec Thompson 1925- *WhoAm 92*
Stewart, Alex *ScF&FL 92*
Stewart, Alexander c. 1737-1794 *HarEnMi*
Stewart, Alexander Doig 1926- *WhoAm 92*
Stewart, Alexander Peter 1821-1908 *BioIn 17*
Stewart, Allyson Lee 1961- *WhoWor 93*
Stewart, Alva Ware 1931- *WhoSSW 93*
Stewart, Amy Watson *Law&B 92*
Stewart, Andrew 1938- *WhoAm 92*
Stewart, Anita *BioIn 17*
Stewart, Ann Hamilton *Law&B 92*
Stewart, Ann Harleman *WhoWrEP 92*
Stewart, Anna Bird *AmWomPl*
Stewart, Anne M. 1951- *St&PR 93*
Stewart, Anthony J. *Law&B 92*
Stewart, Arlene Jean Golden 1943- *WhoE 93*
Stewart, Arthur Anthony *Law&B 92*
Stewart, Arthur Irving, III 1958- *WhoE 93, WhoEmL 93*
Stewart, B.F. *Law&B 92*
Stewart, Barbara D. 1943- *WhoIns 93*
Stewart, Barbara Elizabeth 1923- *WhoAmW 93*
Stewart, Barbara Lynn *Law&B 92*
Stewart, Barbara Yost 1932- *WhoAmW 93, WhoE 93*
Stewart, Bennett McVey 1912-1988 *BioIn 17*
Stewart, Billy d1970 *SoulM*
Stewart, Billy 1937- *BioIn 17*
Stewart, Bingham C. 1905- *St&PR 93*
Stewart, Bonnie Louise 1952- *WhoE 93*
Stewart, Buddy 1921-1950 *BioIn 17*
Stewart, Burton Gloyden, Jr. 1933- *St&PR 93, WhoAm 92*
Stewart, Byran James 1956- *WhoWor 93*
Stewart, Calvin *BioIn 17*
Stewart, Cameron Leigh 1950- *WhoAm 92*
Stewart, Carleton M. 1921- *WhoAm 92*
Stewart, Carol Ann 1940- *WhoE 93*
Stewart, Carol Johnson 1949- *WhoAmW 93*
Stewart, Charles 1778-1869 *HarEnMi*
Stewart, Charles A. *Law&B 92*
Stewart, Charles Arthur *Law&B 92*
Stewart, Charles C. 1925- *St&PR 93*
Stewart, Charles Edward, Jr. 1916- *WhoAm 92*
Stewart, Charles Evan 1952- *WhoAm 92*
Stewart, Charles Everett 1935- *St&PR 93*
Stewart, Charles Haines 1958- *WhoE 93*
Stewart, Charles Henry 1929- *St&PR 93*
Stewart, Charles Henry, Jr. 1929- *WhoSSW 93*
Stewart, Charles Leslie 1919- *WhoAm 92*
Stewart, Charles Wayne 1955- *WhoSSW 93*
Stewart, Charles Wesley *Law&B 92*
Stewart, Chere Lynn 1955- *WhoWrEP 92*
Stewart, Cherie Anita 1945- *WhoAmW 93, WhoSSW 93*
Stewart, Christine Ruth 1959- *WhoAmW 93*
Stewart, Christine Susan 1941- *WhoAmW 93*
Stewart, Colin Samuel *WhoScE 91-1*
Stewart, Connie Sue 1951- *WhoSSW 93*
Stewart, Cornelius James, II 1925- *St&PR 93, WhoAm 92, WhoSSW 93*
Stewart, Cornelius Van Leuven 1936- *WhoAm 92*
Stewart, Cynthia Anne 1952- *WhoSSW 93*
Stewart, D.L. 1942- *BioIn 17*
Stewart, Daniel Robert 1938- *WhoAm 92*
Stewart, Dave *BioIn 17*
Stewart, David E. *Law&B 92*
Stewart, David Edward 1945- *St&PR 93*
Stewart, David Hugh 1926- *WhoAm 92*
Stewart, David Lane 1960- *WhoSSW 93*
Stewart, David Marshall 1916- *WhoAm 92*
Stewart, David Wayne 1951- *WhoEmL 93, WhoWor 93*
Stewart, Dawn Marie 1964- *WhoSSW 93*
Stewart, Deborah Fisher 1952- *WhoSSW 93*
Stewart, Deborah Ruth 1954- *WhoAmW 93*
Stewart, Deirdre O'Brien *Law&B 92*
Stewart, Desmond 1924-1981 *ScF&FL 92*
Stewart, Diana *ScF&FL 92*
Stewart, Diane Basnett 1955- *WhoAmW 93*
Stewart, Diane Carol 1953- *WhoE 93*
Stewart, Dolores Ann 1947- *WhoAmW 93*
Stewart, Don M. 1937- *St&PR 93, WhoIns 93*
Stewart, Donald A. 1946- *WhoIns 93*
Stewart, Donald Bruce *WhoAm 92*
Stewart, Donald C. 1930- *WhoWrEP 92*
Stewart, Donald James 1952- *St&PR 93*
Stewart, Donald Ogden 1894-1980 *BioIn 17*
Stewart, Donna Ludwig 1945- *WhoSSW 93*
Stewart, Dorathy Anne 1937- *WhoSSW 93*
Stewart, Doris Mae 1927- *WhoAmW 93, WhoE 93*
Stewart, Douglas A. 1940- *St&PR 93*

Stewart, Douglas Day MiSFD 9
Stewart, Duncan James 1939- St&PR 93, WhoAm 92
Stewart, Earl d1990 BioIn 17
Stewart, Earl Douglas 1940- St&PR 93
Stewart, Edgar Allen 1909- WhoAm 92
Stewart, Eileen Rose 1942- WhoAmW 93
Stewart, Elaine Thelma 1952- WhoAmW 93
Stewart, Eleanor SweetSg C [port]
Stewart, Elinore Pruitt 1878- BioIn 17
Stewart, Elizabeth 1943- WhoAmW 93
Stewart, Elke ScF&FL 92
Stewart, Ellen AmWomPl
Stewart, Ellen Smith 1945- WhoAmW 93
Stewart, Elmer B. 1951- St&PR 93
Stewart, Eugene Lawrence 1920- WhoAm 92, WhoE 93
Stewart, Frank B., Jr. St&PR 93
Stewart, Frank Maurice 1939- WhoAm 92
Stewart, George 1848-1906 BioIn 17
Stewart, George H. 1931- St&PR 93
Stewart, George Hudson 1925- WhoSSW 93
Stewart, George O. M. 1935- St&PR 93
Stewart, George R. 1895-1980 ScF&FL 92
Stewart, George Ray 1944- WhoAm 92, WhoSSW 93
Stewart, George Richard 1933- WhoSSW 93
Stewart, George Russell WhoScE 91-1
Stewart, George Taylor 1924- St&PR 93, WhoAm 92
Stewart, Gilbert Wright 1940- WhoAm 92
Stewart, Grace WhoAmW 93
Stewart, Gregory 1958- WhoSSW 93
Stewart, Gregory K. 1956- St&PR 93
Stewart, Guthrie John Law&B 92
Stewart, Guy Harry 1924- WhoAm 92
Stewart, Gwyneth G. Law&B 92
Stewart, Harold Brown 1921- WhoAm 92
Stewart, Harold Leroy 1899- WhoAm 92, WhoE 93
Stewart, Harris Bates, Jr. 1922- WhoAm 92
Stewart, Harry Eaton 1951- WhoE 93
Stewart, Heather Kellerhals- ScF&FL 92
Stewart, Helen G. 1948- St&PR 93
Stewart, Homer Joseph 1915- WhoAm 92
Stewart, Hugh Natheniel 1944- WhoWor 93
Stewart, Humphrey John 1856-1932 Baker 92
Stewart, Iain Alastair 1961- WhoWor 93
Stewart, Ian (Nicholas) 1945- ConAu 139
Stewart, Ireland J. 1934- St&PR 93
Stewart, Iris Parsons 1926- St&PR 93, WhoAm 92
Stewart, Irvin 1899-1990 BioIn 17
Stewart, Isaac Daniel, Jr. 1932- WhoAm 92, WhoWor 93
Stewart, J.I.M. 1906- BioIn 17
Stewart, J.W.B. WhoScE 91-2
Stewart, Jack 1926- WhoE 93
Stewart, James BioIn 17
Stewart, James d1991 BioIn 17
Stewart, James 1908- IntDcF 2-3 [port]
Stewart, James 1912- St&PR 93
Stewart, James Alexander Carson WhoScE 91-1
Stewart, James B. BioIn 17
Stewart, James Brewer 1940- WhoAm 92
Stewart, James Charles, II 1952- WhoSSW 93
Stewart, James E. BioIn 17
Stewart, James F. C. 1946- St&PR 93
Stewart, James Gathings 1942- St&PR 93, WhoAm 92
Stewart, James Kevin 1942- WhoAm 92
Stewart, James M. 1943- WhoAm 92
Stewart, James Maitland 1908- WhoAm 92, WhoWor 93
Stewart, James Montgomery 1939- St&PR 93, WhoAm 92
Stewart, James Stuart d1990 BioIn 17
Stewart, Jane AmWomPl
Stewart, Jane Agnes AmWomPl
Stewart, Janet 1939- ScF&FL 92
Stewart, Janet E. Law&B 92
Stewart, Jason BioIn 17
Stewart, Jean Catherine 1948- WhoAmW 93, WhoEmL 93
Stewart, Jeannie Calder 1913- WhoE 93
Stewart, Jeff 1939- WhoWor 93
Stewart, Jefferson Davis, III Law&B 92
Stewart, Jim 1930- SoulM
Stewart, Jim 1948- WhoCanL 92
Stewart, Jimmy BioIn 17
Stewart, JoAnn BioIn 17
Stewart, JoAnne 1944- WhoAmW 93
Stewart, Jody Ann 1940- WhoAmW 93
Stewart, Joe J. 1938- St&PR 93, WhoSSW 93
Stewart, John BioIn 17, MiSFD 9
Stewart, John 1933- ConAu 37NR
Stewart, John C. 1930-1991 BioIn 17
Stewart, John Cameron 1943- WhoE 93, WhoWor 93
Stewart, John D. 1915- St&PR 93
Stewart, John Daugherty 1915- WhoAm 92
Stewart, John H., Jr. 1929- St&PR 93
Stewart, John Harger WhoAm 92
Stewart, John Innes Mackintosh 1906- BioIn 17
Stewart, John K. 1905- St&PR 93
Stewart, John Lincoln 1917- WhoAm 92
Stewart, John O. Law&B 92
Stewart, John R. Law&B 92
Stewart, John T., III 1936- St&PR 93
Stewart, John W. WhoAm 92
Stewart, John Wray Black 1936- WhoAm 92
Stewart, Joseph Law&B 92
Stewart, Joseph Allen 1949- WhoE 93
Stewart, Joseph Lester 1915- WhoAm 92
Stewart, Joseph M. 1942- St&PR 93
Stewart, Joseph Melvin 1942- WhoAm 92
Stewart, Joseph Richard Law&B 92
Stewart, Joseph Todd 1963- WhoAm 92
Stewart, Joseph Turner, Jr. 1929- St&PR 93, WhoAm 92, WhoWor 93
Stewart, Joy L. 1948- St&PR 93
Stewart, June Gary 1931- WhoWrEP 92
Stewart, Karl A. Law&B 92
Stewart, Kate 1951- WhoSSW 93
Stewart, Katherine L. Law&B 92
Stewart, Kay Lorraine 1962- WhoAmW 93
Stewart, Kenneth Stanley Law&B 92
Stewart, Kenneth Wilson 1935- WhoSSW 93
Stewart, Kent Kallam 1934- WhoAm 92
Stewart, Kerry ScF&FL 92
Stewart, Kim Kristine 1952- WhoAmW 93
Stewart, Kirk T. 1957- WhoAm 92
Stewart, Larry MiSFD 9
Stewart, Lee M. 1945- St&PR 93
Stewart, Leon Otto 1929- WhoAm 92
Stewart, Lever Law&B 92
Stewart, Lewis Moore 1935- WhoSSW 93
Stewart, Lila AmWomPl
Stewart, Linda ScF&FL 92
Stewart, Linda Berenfield 1942- WhoAmW 93
Stewart, Linda Joan 1938- WhoAmW 93
Stewart, Linda Lee 1941- WhoAmW 93
Stewart, Lindsay D. Law&B 92
Stewart, Lynne Ellen 1953- WhoAmW 93
Stewart, Madonna Jean 1957- WhoSSW 93
Stewart, Margaret Jensen 1950- WhoEmL 93
Stewart, Margaret McBride 1927- WhoAm 92, WhoAmW 93
Stewart, Maria Ann 1967- WhoAmW 93
Stewart, Marjorie C. WhoAmW 93
Stewart, Marjorie May 1941- WhoAmW 93
Stewart, Mark Carroll 1947- WhoAm 92
Stewart, Mark Thomas 1948- WhoE 93, WhoEmL 93, WhoWor 93
Stewart, Martha BioIn 17
Stewart, Martha c. 1942- News 92 [port]
Stewart, Martha Kostyra WhoAmW 93
Stewart, Martha LeAnn 1961- WhoAmW 93
Stewart, Marva LaVern 1952- WhoAmW 93
Stewart, Marvin Lewis 1953- WhoE 93
Stewart, Mary d1943 AmWomPl
Stewart, Mary 1916- ScF&FL 92
Stewart, Mary Elinore Pruitt 1878- BioIn 17
Stewart, Mary Florence Elinor 1916- WhoAm 92, WhoWrEP 92
Stewart, Mary L. DeCampli- BioIn 17
Stewart, Maurice Laverne 1929- WhoAm 92
Stewart, Maxwell S. d1990 BioIn 17
Stewart, Melbourne George, Jr. 1927- WhoAm 92
Stewart, Melville Yorke 1935- WhoWor 93
Stewart, Michael 1906-1990 BioIn 17
Stewart, Michael 1933- ScF&FL 92
Stewart, Michael 1945- ConAu 138, ScF&FL 92
Stewart, Michael Duane 1947- WhoSSW 93
Stewart, Michael Ian 1955- WhoSSW 93
Stewart, Michael J. Law&B 92
Stewart, Michael McFadden 1938- WhoSSW 93
Stewart, Moses BioIn 17
Stewart, N.J. Law&B 92
Stewart, Neil 1912- ScF&FL 92
Stewart, Neville 1932- St&PR 93
Stewart, Norman B. 1935- BiDAMSp 1989
Stewart, Norman J. 1948- St&PR 93, WhoAm 92
Stewart, Norman L. 1942- St&PR 93
Stewart, Norman Lawrence 1942- WhoAm 92
Stewart, Ora Marie 1927- WhoAmW 93
Stewart, Pangle 1915- St&PR 93
Stewart, Patrice Lafferty 1933- WhoAmW 93
Stewart, Patricia Ann 1953- WhoAmW 93
Stewart, Patricia Carry 1928- WhoAm 92, WhoAmW 93
Stewart, Paul Anthony, II 1952- WhoWor 93
Stewart, Paul James, Jr. 1929- WhoE 93
Stewart, Paul Richard 1934- St&PR 93
Stewart, Payne 1957- WhoAm 92
Stewart, Peggy 1923- SweetSg C [port]
Stewart, Peter A.M. WhoScE 91-1
Stewart, Peter Beaufort 1923- WhoAm 92
Stewart, Peter Pauls 1920- WhoWor 93
Stewart, Potter 1915-1985 BioIn 17, OxCSupC [port]
Stewart, Priscilla Ann Mabie 1926- WhoSSW 93
Stewart, R.J. 1948- ScF&FL 92
Stewart, Ralph P. 1940- St&PR 93
Stewart, Ramona 1922- ScF&FL 92
Stewart, Randall 1896-1964 BioIn 17
Stewart, Reginald 1900-1984 Baker 92
Stewart, Renice Ann 1947- WhoAmW 93, WhoEmL 93
Stewart, Rex William 1907-1967 BioIn 17
Stewart, Richard Alfred 1945- WhoAm 92
Stewart, Richard Burleson 1940- WhoAm 92
Stewart, Richard C., II Law&B 92
Stewart, Richard D. Law&B 92
Stewart, Richard Douglas 1949- WhoSSW 93
Stewart, Richard E. 1933- WhoIns 93
Stewart, Richard Edwin 1933- WhoAm 92, WhoWor 93
Stewart, Richard R. Law&B 92
Stewart, Richard R. 1930- St&PR 93
Stewart, Richard W. 1943- St&PR 93
Stewart, Robert Alan 1943- WhoE 93
Stewart, Robert Andrew 1928- WhoAm 92
Stewart, Robert B. BioIn 17
Stewart, Robert C. 1932- St&PR 93
Stewart, Robert D., Jr. Law&B 92
Stewart, Robert Forrest, Jr. 1943- WhoAm 92
Stewart, Robert G. 1956- St&PR 93
Stewart, Robert Gordon 1931- WhoAm 92
Stewart, Robert H., III 1925- St&PR 93
Stewart, Robert Lee 1942- WhoAm 92
Stewart, Robert Morrison 1922- St&PR 93
Stewart, Robert N. 1917- St&PR 93
Stewart, Robert (Prescott) 1825-1894 Baker 92
Stewart, Robert William 1923- WhoAm 92
Stewart, Rod BioIn 17
Stewart, Roderick David 1945- WhoAm 92
Stewart, Roger Harold 1940- WhoSSW 93
Stewart, Roger John WhoScE 91-1
Stewart, Ronald Vernon 1949- St&PR 93
Stewart, Rosalind Landis 1941- WhoAmW 93
Stewart, Ross 1924- WhoAm 92
Stewart, Ruth Ann 1942- BlkAull 92, WhoAm 92
Stewart, Ruth Carol 1928- WhoAmW 93
Stewart, Ruth F. 1928- WhoSSW 93
Stewart, S. Jay 1938- WhoAm 92
Stewart, Sally Beal 1955- WhoAmW 93
Stewart, Sam 1915- WhoAm 92
Stewart, Samuel B. 1908- WhoAm 92
Stewart, Samuel Robert 1766-1802 BioIn 17
Stewart, Sandra Itzel 1964- WhoAmW 93
Stewart, Sandy Brown 1938- WhoE 93, WhoWor 93
Stewart, Sharon Diane 1951- WhoWrEP 92
Stewart, Shirley Anne 1957- WhoE 93
Stewart, Stephen Thompson 1954- St&PR 93
Stewart, Stewart 1942- WhoSSW 93
Stewart, Sue Stern 1942- WhoAmW 93
Stewart, Suzan M. Law&B 92
Stewart, Suzanne Florence 1939- WhoAmW 93
Stewart, Teresa Marie 1957- WhoE 93
Stewart, Terry C. St&PR 93
Stewart, Thomas 1928- OxDcOp
Stewart, Thomas Francis, III 1953- WhoSSW 93
Stewart, Thomas (James) 1928- Baker 92
Stewart, Thomas James, Jr. 1928- WhoAm 92
Stewart, Thomas Penney 1927- WhoAm 92
Stewart, Thomas Wilson 1926- WhoSSW 93
Stewart, Trevor Richard 1946- WhoAm 92
Stewart, Virginia Haken 1941- WhoAmW 93
Stewart, Vivian Frances 1946- WhoAmW 93
Stewart, Walter J. CngDr 91
Stewart, Wanda Lee 1946- WhoE 93
Stewart, Warren Earl 1924- WhoAm 92
Stewart, William B. d1991 BioIn 17
Stewart, William C. 1929- St&PR 93
Stewart, William Charles 1955- WhoSSW 93
Stewart, William Clayton 1928- St&PR 93
Stewart, William Clayton, Jr. Law&B 92
Stewart, William Glen 1941- St&PR 93
Stewart, William H. 1942- St&PR 93
Stewart, William McCausland 1900-1989 BioIn 17
Stewart, William Mitton 1859-1913 BioIn 17
Stewart, William R. St&PR 93
Stewart, William Robert 1941- WhoE 93
Stewart, Winburn Earl 1917- St&PR 93
Stewart, Zeph 1921- WhoAm 92
Stewart-Clarke, John Ernest 1928- WhoWor 93
Stewart-Frank, Jean Hood 1956- WhoAmW 93
Stewart of Fulham, Robert Michael Maitland Stewart 1906-1990 BioIn 17
Stewart-Pinkham, Sandra Morral 1942- WhoAmW 93
Stewartt, Michael BioIn 17
Steyaart, James L. 1940- St&PR 93
Steyer, Roy Henry 1918- WhoAm 92
Steyermark, Paul R. Law&B 92
Steytler, Alan L. S. 1947- St&PR 93
St-Germain, Andre 1944- WhoCanL 92
Sthapit, Sanu Ratna 1945- WhoWor 93
Stibal, Marcia Raye 1948- WhoEmL 93
Stibel, Gary Marshall 1946- WhoE 93
Stibich, Donald Clinton 1931- St&PR 93
Stibilj, Milan 1929- Baker 92
Stibitz, George Robert 1904- WhoAm 92
Stibolt, Carl Bradford 1957- WhoWor 93
Stice, Bob G. 1947- WhoSSW 93
Stice, Dwayne Lee 1956- WhoSSW 93
Stice, James Edward 1928- WhoAm 92
Stich, George N. Law&B 92
Stich, Hans Franz 1927- WhoAm 92
Stich, Johann Wenzel 1746-1803 Baker 92
Stich, June Jeacoma 1939- WhoE 93
Stich, Michael BioIn 17
Stich, Otto 1927- WhoWor 93
Stich, Sally 1950- BioIn 17
Sticher, Hans 1934- WhoScE 91-4
Stichman, Robert W. 1948- St&PR 93
Stich-Randall, Teresa 1927- Baker 92, IntDcOp, OxDcOp
Sticht, J. Paul 1917- St&PR 93, WhoAm 92
Stichweh, Rudolf 1951- WhoWor 93
Stick, Alyce Cushing 1944- WhoAmW 93, WhoE 93
Stick, Thomas Howard Fitchett 1938- WhoE 93
Stickel, Fred A. 1921- St&PR 93
Stickel, Frederick A. 1921- WhoAm 92
Stickel, Tom C. 1949- St&PR 93
Stickeler, Carl Ann Louise 1930- WhoAmW 93
Stickelman, Timothy Gerard Law&B 92
Stickgold, Bob 1945- ScF&FL 92
Stickle, Charles Edward 1941- WhoWrEP 92
Stickler, Alfons Maria Cardinal 1910- WhoWor 93
Stickler, Daniel Lee 1938- WhoAm 92, WhoSSW 93
Stickler, David Bruce 1941- WhoE 93
Stickler, Fred Charles 1931- WhoAm 92
Stickler, Gunnar Brynolf 1925- WhoAm 92
Stickler, Peter Bleier 1952- St&PR 93
Stickler, Sam d1992 NewYTBS 92
Stickles, Wayne Arthur 1945- St&PR 93
Stickley, Dan C., Jr. 1931- St&PR 93
Stickley, Walter J., Jr. Law&B 92
Stickney, Jessica 1929- WhoAmW 93
Stickney, John Moore 1926- WhoWor 93
Stickney, Trumbull 1874-1904 GayN
Stickney, Walt Christopher 1944- WhoWrEP 92
Stidham, Betty Lou BioIn 17
Stidham, David Gordon 1938- WhoSSW 93
Stidham, Shaler, Jr. 1941- WhoAm 92, WhoSSW 93
Stidman, Edith Janet Scales 1922- WhoAmW 93
Stidworthy, John BioIn 17
Stieb, Dave BioIn 17
Stieb, David Andrew 1957- BiDAMSp 1989, WhoAm 92
Stieb, Ronald Peter 1939- St&PR 93
Stiebel, Gerald Gustave 1944- WhoAm 92
Stieber, Charles J. Law&B 92
Stieber, Sharon Jewel 1953- WhoE 93
Stieber, Tamar 1955- WhoAmW 93
Stiedry, Fritz 1883-1968 Baker 92
Stief, Louis John 1933- WhoAm 92
Stiefel, Beat Law&B 92
Stiefel, Charles W. Law&B 92
Stiefel, Edward Ira 1942- WhoE 93

Stiefel, Janice J. 1936- WhoWrEP 92
Stiefel, John T. d1990 BioIn 17
Stiefel, Roger H. 1949- St&PR 93
Stiefel, Susan Carol 1945- WhoAmW 93
Stieff, James W. 1952- St&PR 93
Stieff, Rodney Gilbert 1925- St&PR 93
Stieg, Lewis F. 1909-1990 BioIn 17
Stiegel, Henry William 1729-1785 BioIn 17
Stiegler, Herbert 1926- WhoScE 91-3
Stiegler, Karl Drago 1919- WhoWor 93
Stiegler, Marc ScF&FL 92
Stiegler, Paul W., Jr. 1939- St&PR 93
Stiegler, Theodore Donald 1934- WhoSSW 93
Stieglitz, Alfred 1864-1946 BioIn 17, GayN, JeAmHC
Stieglitz, Julius 1867-1937 BioIn 17
Stieglitz, Leonard 1929- St&PR 93
Stieglitz, Perry Jesse 1920- WhoE 93
Stieglitz, Robert J. 1935- St&PR 93
Stiehl Baker 92
Stiehl, Carl (Karl) Johann Christian 1826-1911 Baker 92
Stiehl, Heinrich (Franz Daniel) 1829-1886 Baker 92
Stiehl, Johann Dietrich 1800-1873 Baker 92
Stiehl, Ruth Rasco 1939- WhoAmW 93
Stiehl, William D. 1925- WhoAm 92
Stiehm, E. Richard 1933- WhoAm 92
Stiehm, Judith Hicks 1935- WhoAm 92
Stiekema, Willem J. 1950- WhoScE 91-3
Stieler, Kathryn Lee 1956- St&PR 93
Stielow, Frederick Joseph 1946- WhoE 93
Stienmier, Saundra Kay Young 1938- WhoAmW 93
Stiens, Richard J. 1945- St&PR 93
Stiens, Scott Robert 1965- WhoWor 93
Stienstra, Albert Jan 1943- WhoWor 93
Stiepan, James L. Law&B 92
Stier, Mary Parks 1956- St&PR 93
Stierhoff, Harold F. 1933- St&PR 93
Stierle, Edward d1991 BioIn 17
Stierle, Wolf F. 1937- St&PR 93
Stierlin, H.R. WhoScE 91-4
Stiernstedt, Jan 1925- WhoScE 91-4
Stiers, David Ogden 1942- WhoAm 92
Stierwalt, Brian K. Law&B 92
Stievater, James Edward 1934- St&PR 93
Stieve, Edwin Mark 1950- WhoSSW 93
Stieve, Hennig 1930- WhoScE 91-3
Stifel, Laurence Davis 1930- WhoE 93
Stiff, John Sterling 1921- WhoAm 92
Stiff, Robert Martin 1931- WhoAm 92, WhoWrEP 92
Stiffey, James P. 1953- St&PR 93
Stiffler, David B. 1948- St&PR 93
Stiffler, Jack Justin 1934- St&PR 93, WhoAm 92, WhoE 93
Stifler, William Curtis, III 1941- WhoAm 92
Stiftel, Bruce 1954- WhoSSW 93
Stifter, Francis J. 1930- St&PR 93
Stigall, Ray 1932- St&PR 93
Stigebrandt, Anders G. 1942- WhoScE 91-4
Stigelli, Giorgio 1815-1868 Baker 92
Stigers, Curtis BioIn 17
Stigge, Merlin L. 1939- St&PR 93
Stigler, George 1911-1991 AnObit 1991
Stigler, George J(oseph) 1911-1991 ConAu 136, CurBio 92N
Stigler, George Joseph 1911-1991 BioIn 17
Stigler, Stephen Mack 1941- WhoAm 92
Stigliani, Linda A. Law&B 92
Stiglic, Bruno WhoScE 91-4
Stiglic, Bruno 1931- WhoScE 91-4
Stiglic, France 1919- DrEEuF
Stiglich, Jaime M. 1945- WhoUN 92
Stiglitz, Beatrice 1945- WhoSSW 93
Stiglitz, Douglas E. 1953- St&PR 93
Stiglitz, Joseph Eugene 1943- WhoAm 92
Stiglitz, Martin Richard 1920- WhoE 93, WhoWor 93
Stignani, Ebe 1903-1974 OxDcOp
Stignani, Ebe 1903-1975 IntDcOp
Stignani, Ebe 1904-1974 Baker 92
Stignani, Ebe 1907-1974 BioIn 17
Stigwood, Robert BioIn 17
Stigwood, Robert 1934- ScF&FL 92
Stigwood, Robert Colin 1934- WhoAm 92, WhoE 93
Stikeleather, Roger C. St&PR 93
Stikkelman, Robertus Martinus 1959- WhoWor 93
Stilbes, Constantine OxDcByz
Stile, Alice Eleanor 1945- WhoAmW 93
Stiles, Alvin Barber 1909- WhoE 93
Stiles, Curtis F. 1942- St&PR 93
Stiles, Donald George 1926- St&PR 93
Stiles, Ezra 1727-1795 BioIn 17
Stiles, G. E. R. 1932- St&PR 93, WhoAm 92
Stiles, Geoffrey BioIn 17
Stiles, Jane E. Law&B 92
Stiles, John Barry 1951- St&PR 93
Stiles, John S. 1913- St&PR 93
Stiles, John Stephen 1913- WhoAm 92
Stiles, Kaye Chelette 1949- WhoAmW 93
Stiles, Kevin Patrick 1949- WhoAm 92
Stiles, Kurt Edward 1963- WhoE 93
Stiles, Lynn Feibel, Jr. 1942- WhoE 93
Stiles, Martha Bennett DcAmChF 1960, WhoWrEP 92
Stiles, Mary Ann 1944- WhoAmW 93
Stiles, Patricia M. 1955- St&PR 93
Stiles, Phillip John 1934- WhoAm 92
Stiles, Robert B. Law&B 92
Stiles, Stephen Lee 1946- St&PR 93
Stiles, Stuart L. 1915- St&PR 93
Stiles, Thomas B. 1940- St&PR 93
Stiles, Thomas Beveridge, II 1940- WhoAm 92
Stiles, Thomas Edward 1934- St&PR 93, WhoAm 92
Stiles, William Larkin d1908 BioIn 17
Stilgenbauer, Nancy Kieffer 1934- WhoAmW 93
Stilgoe, John R. 1949- WhoAm 92
Stilianov, Ganu 1926- WhoScE 91-4
Stilicho d408 OxDcByz
Stilicho, Flavius c. 355-408 HarEnMi
Still, Bayrd 1906- WhoAm 92
Still, Charles Henry 1942- WhoAm 92
Still, Charles Neal 1929- WhoSSW 93
Still, Chris BioIn 17
Still, Eugene Fontaine, II 1937- WhoSSW 93, WhoWor 93
Still, James 1906- ConAu 17AS [port]
Still, John C., III 1952- WhoE 93
Still, John Taylor, III 1947- St&PR 93
Still, Mary Jane 1940- WhoSSW 93, WhoWor 93
Still, Ray 1920- WhoAm 92
Still, Robert 1910-1971 Baker 92
Still, Stephen Allen 1919- WhoAm 92
Still, Steve Law&B 92
Still, William Clark, Jr. 1946- WhoAm 92
Still, William Grant 1895-1978 Baker 92, EncAACR, OxDcOp
Stille, Dexter L. 1951- St&PR 93
Stille, Marvin A. 1941- St&PR 93
Stille, Wolfgang 1935- WhoScE 91-3
Stillebroer, Carel Marinus 1937- WhoWor 93
Stiller, Ben BioIn 17
Stiller, H. WhoScE 91-3
Stiller, Jerry WhoAm 92
Stiller, Mauritz 1883-1928 MiSFD 9N
Stiller, Robert P. BioIn 17
Stiller, Shale David 1935- WhoAm 92
Stiller, Sharon Paula 1951- WhoEmL 93
Stilley, Frank Wood 1954- St&PR 93
Stilley, Walter A., III 1930- St&PR 93
Stilling, Johann Heinrich Jung- 1740-1817 BioIn 17
Stillinger, Frank Henry 1934- WhoAm 92
Stillinger, Jack Clifford 1931- WhoAm 92
Stillings, Irene Cordiner 1918- WhoE 93
Stillitano, Charles V. Law&B 92
Stillman, Anne Walker 1951- WhoEmL 93
Stillman, Chris J. 1934- WhoScE 91-3
Stillman, Elinor Hadley 1938- WhoAmW 93
Stillman, G. Patrick 1940- St&PR 93
Stillman, Joyce L. 1943- WhoE 93
Stillman, Larry B. 1941- St&PR 93
Stillman, Lucille Terese WhoE 93
Stillman, Mitya 1892-1936 Baker 92
Stillman, Noam ConAu 136
Stillman, Norman A(rthur) 1945- ConAu 136
Stillman, Norman Arthur 1945- WhoE 93
Stillman, Paul O. 1933- WhoIns 93
Stillman, Paul Oster 1933- St&PR 93
Stillman, Richard Henry 1940- St&PR 93
Stillman, Robert D. 1929- St&PR 93
Stillman, Ron ScF&FL 92
Stillman, Thomas P. Law&B 92
Stillman, Whit BioIn 17, MiSFD 9
Stillman, William ScF&FL 92
Stillman, William Everett 1952- WhoWrEP 92
Stillman, William M., Jr. 1939- St&PR 93
Stillman-Kelley, Edgar Baker 92
Stillmun, John F. Law&B 92
Stillo Lyons, Debra Marie 1956- WhoAmW 93
Stillson, Richard Thomas 1942- WhoUN 92
Stillwaggon, James George 1920- WhoE 93
Stillwagon, James R. St&PR 93
Stillwagon, Wesley William 1940- WhoE 93, WhoWor 93
Stillwell, George Keith 1918- WhoAm 92
Stillwell, James Paul 1931- WhoAm 92
Stillwell, James Todd 1965- WhoSSW 93
Stillwell, Kathy Elizabeth Law&B 92
Stillwell, Mary Kathryn 1944- WhoWrEP 92
Stillwell, Richard Newhall 1935- WhoE 93
Stillwell, Roger George 1939- WhoE 93
Stilson, Charles B. 1880-1932 ScF&FL 92
Stilson, Eileen Claire Law&B 92
Stilson, Suzanne L. St&PR 93
Stilson, Walter Leslie 1908- WhoWor 93
Stiltner, Gary L. 1940- St&PR 93
Stilwell, Betty L. Law&B 92
Stilwell, Dan D. Law&B 92
Stilwell, Frank Barton, III 1957- WhoAm 92
Stilwell, Frank C. 1857?-1882 BioIn 17
Stilwell, James Edward 1947- St&PR 93
Stilwell, John Albert WhoScE 91-1
Stilwell, Joseph 1883-1946 ColdWar 1 [port]
Stilwell, Joseph Warren 1883-1946 BioIn 17, DcTwHis, HarEnMi
Stilwell, Laura Jean Libbey AmWomPl
Stilwell, Richard (Dale) 1942- Baker 92, WhoAm 92
Stilwell, Richard G. BioIn 17
Stilwell, Richard William 1936- St&PR 93
Stilwell, Ronald E. 1948- St&PR 93
Stilwell, Ronald Edward 1948- WhoE 93
Stim, Stephen George Law&B 92
Stimac, Gary Allen 1951- St&PR 93
Stimler, Michael Kevin 1959- WhoE 93
Stimmel, Andrea Katz 1954- WhoAmW 93
Stimmel, Barry 1939- WhoAm 92
Stimmel, David Craig 1954- WhoSSW 93
Stimmer, Herbert 1922- WhoScE 91-4
Stimpert, Michael Alan 1944- St&PR 93, WhoAm 92
Stimpson, Catharine Roslyn 1936- WhoAm 92, WhoAmW 93
Stimpson, J. R. 1949- St&PR 93
Stimpson, James Wilbert, Sr. 1934- WhoAm 92
Stimpson, John Hallowell 1926- WhoAm 92
Stimson, David C. Law&B 92
Stimson, Dorothy 1890-1988 BioIn 17
Stimson, Frederick Sparks 1919- WhoAm 92
Stimson, Gerald Vivian WhoScE 91-1
Stimson, Henry L. 1867-1950 ColdWar 1 [port], PolPar
Stimson, Henry Lewis 1867-1950 BioIn 17, DcTwHis
Stimson, Janice A. 1956- St&PR 93
Stimson, Richard W. Law&B 92
Stimson, Robbe Pierce 1948- ConAu 136
Stimson, Robert Frederick 1939- WhoWor 93
Stimson, W.H. WhoScE 91-1
Stinchcomb, Carl J. 1938- St&PR 93
Stinchcomb, Eleanor AmWomPl
Stinchcomb, James Delwin WhoSSW 93
Stinchcomb, Sheri Ann 1964- WhoAmW 93
Stinchecum, Amanda Mayer 1941- ConAu 139
Stinchfield, Dean James 1963- WhoWor 93
Stinchfield, Frank E. d1992 NewYTBS 92
Stinchfield, John Edward Law&B 92
Stinchfield, John Edward 1947- St&PR 93
Stine, Claire L. 1928- WhoIns 93
Stine, Darrell W. 1938- St&PR 93
Stine, David P. 1952- St&PR 93
Stine, Earle John, Jr. 1932- WhoSSW 93
Stine, G. Harry 1928- BioIn 17, ScF&FL 92
Stine, George Harry 1928- BioIn 17, WhoAm 92
Stine, H. William 1946- ScF&FL 92
Stine, Jack William 1924- St&PR 93
Stine, John Law&B 92
Stine, Joseph Evans 1937- St&PR 93
Stine, Jovial Bob ScF&FL 92
Stine, Larry Wayne 1941- St&PR 93
Stine, Megan 1950- ScF&FL 92
Stine, Philip Andrew 1944- WhoSSW 93
Stine, R.L. 1943- ScF&FL 92
Stine, R(obert) L(awrence) 1943- WhoWrEP 92
Stine, Steven T. Law&B 92
Stinecipher, LeAnne 1965- WhoAmW 93
Stinecipher, Mary Margaret 1940- WhoAmW 93
Stinehart, Roger Ray 1945- WhoAm 92, WhoWor 93
Stiner, Carl Wade 1936- WhoAm 92
Stiner, Frederic Matthew, Jr. 1946- WhoE 93
Stines, Fred, Jr. 1925- WhoAm 92
Stines, Meredith C. 1954- St&PR 93
Stinespring, William F. 1901-1991 BioIn 17
Sting BioIn 17
Sting 1951- Baker 92, WhoAm 92, WhoWor 93
Stingel, Donald Eugene 1920- WhoAm 92
Stingel, Russell E. 1930- St&PR 93
Stingelin, Valentin 1933- WhoAm 92
Stinger, William W. 1946- St&PR 93
Stingl, Georg 1948- WhoWor 93
Stingl, Manfred 1939- WhoScE 91-3
Stingle, Sandra Fromer 1946- WhoAmW 93
Stini, William Arthur 1930- WhoAm 92
Stinnett, Charles Edgar, Jr. 1934- St&PR 93
Stinnett, Hester Ann 1956- WhoAmW 93
Stinnett, J. Daniel Law&B 92
Stinnett, John Clay 1951- WhoAm 92
Stinnett, Lee Houston 1939- WhoAm 92
Stinnett, Mark Allan 1955- WhoSSW 93
Stinnett, Wayne D., Jr. 1951- St&PR 93
Stinnett, Wayne Deward, Jr. 1951- WhoAm 92
Stinson, Aviva Jochebed 1933- WhoAmW 93
Stinson, Charles B. 1930- St&PR 93
Stinson, Clara Gottier 1910- WhoWrEP 92
Stinson, David Leo 1957- WhoWrEP 92
Stinson, Deane Brian 1930- WhoWor 93
Stinson, Edward Brad 1938- WhoAm 92
Stinson, George A. 1915- St&PR 93
Stinson, George Arthur 1915- WhoAm 92
Stinson, J. Michael 1943- WhoWor 93
Stinson, Joe 1838-1902 BioIn 17
Stinson, Katherine 1891-1977 BioIn 17
Stinson, Katherine Anne 1949- WhoE 93
Stinson, Kathy 1952- WhoCanL 92
Stinson, L. Trent Law&B 92
Stinson, Louis, Jr. 1943- St&PR 93
Stinson, Nancy Ann Petrits 1959- WhoAmW 93
Stinson, Peter Andrew 1961- WhoE 93
Stinson, Richard James 1929- WhoAm 92
Stinson, Robert C. Law&B 92
Stinson, Robert C. 1946- St&PR 93
Stinson, Robert Charles 1946- WhoAm 92
Stinson, Stanley Thomas 1961- WhoSSW 93
Stinson, Steven Arthur 1946- WhoSSW 93
Stinson, Terry L. Law&B 92
Stinson, William W. 1933- WhoAm 92, WhoWor 93
Stinson, William Wade 1933- St&PR 93
Stinton Family BioIn 17
Stipa, Sergio 1929- WhoScE 91-3
Stipanovic, Robert Douglas 1939- WhoSSW 93
Stipanuk, Martha Harney 1948- WhoE 93
Stipe, John Ryburn 1930- WhoSSW 93
Stipetic, Joan D. 1935- WhoAmW 93
Stipetic, Vladimir M. 1928- WhoScE 91-4
Stipetic, Werner 1942- WhoWor 93
Stipick, Deborah J. Law&B 92
Stipkovits, Laszlo 1938- WhoScE 91-4
Stipp, John Edgar 1914- WhoAm 92
Stipp, Scott Lee 1951- St&PR 93
Stippler, A. David Law&B 92
Stirbois, Jean-Pierre 1945-1988 BioIn 17
Stirbu, C. WhoScE 91-4
Stirbu-Teofanescu, Constantin 1944- WhoScE 91-4
Stirdivant, Michael T. WhoAm 92
Stires, David Warfield 1933- WhoAm 92
Stiritz, William P. 1934- WhoAm 92, WhoWor 93
Stiritz, William Paul 1934- St&PR 93
Stirk, John J. Law&B 92
Stirling, Alexa BiDAMSp 1989
Stirling, Charles James Matthew 1930- WhoWor 93
Stirling, Dale Alexander 1956- WhoWrEP 92
Stirling, David 1915-1990 BioIn 17
Stirling, Douglas Bleecker, Jr. 1959- WhoSSW 93
Stirling, Edwin Murdoch 1940- WhoSSW 93
Stirling, Elizabeth 1819-1895 Baker 92
Stirling, Geoffrey William 1925- WhoAm 92
Stirling, James 1926-1992 NewYTBS 92 [port]
Stirling, James H. St&PR 93
Stirling, James Paulman 1941- WhoAm 92
Stirling, Linda 1921- SweetSg C [port]
Stirling, Roger Ludington 1951- WhoWor 93
Stirling, S.M. 1953- ScF&FL 92
Stirm, Eugene Robert 1945- WhoWor 93
Stirm, Robert Paul 1923- WhoAm 92
Stirn, Jack Joseph 1927- St&PR 93
Stirnemann, S.A. WhoWrEP 92
Stirrat, William Albert 1919- WhoE 93
Stirsman, William E. 1946- St&PR 93
Stirton, David Kirk 1949- WhoSSW 93
Stishan, Peter Michael 1949- WhoE 93
Stishov, Sergei Michaelovich 1937- WhoWor 93
Stiska, John C. 1942- WhoAm 92
Stitely, Louise AmWomPl
Stites, C. Thomas 1942- WhoAm 92
Stites, Samuel H. 1948- St&PR 93
Stith, Forrest C. 1934- WhoAm 92
Stith, Gladys Wheeler 1942- WhoAmW 93
Stith, John E. 1947- ScF&FL 92
Stith, John E(dward) 1947- ConAu 40NR
Stith, Richard Taylor, Jr. 1919- WhoAm 92

Stith, Sandra Murdock 1948- WhoSSW 93
Stith, Steve Lee 1955- St&PR 93
Stitsworth, Karen Elizabeth Law&B 92
Stitt, Donald Meredith 1940- WhoE 93
Stitt, Gerald Earl 1932- St&PR 93
Stitt, John Brenneman 1947- WhoSSW 93
Stitt, Pauline George 1909- WhoAmW 93
Stitt, Richard Payne 1926- St&PR 93
Stitt, Robert Sharp 1927-1991 BioIn 17
Stitt, "Sonny" 1924-1982 Baker 92
Stitt, Susan 1942- WhoE 93
Stitz, John J. 1956- St&PR 93
Stitzer, Raymond D. d1991 BioIn 17
Stitzinger, Ernest Lester 1940- WhoSSW 93
Stivala, Michael Joseph 1966- WhoE 93
Stiven, Alan Ernest 1935- WhoAm 92
Stivender, David BioIn 17
Stivender, Donald Lewis 1932- WhoAm 92, WhoWor 93
Stivens, Dal 1911- ScF&FL 92
Stiver, William Earl 1921- WhoE 93, WhoWor 93
Stivers, Donald DeWitt 1955- WhoSSW 93
Stivers, Jan BioIn 17
Stivers, Roger Neil 1936- St&PR 93
Stivers, William Charles 1938- St&PR 93, WhoAm 92
Stivison, David Vaughn 1946- WhoE 93, WhoEmL 93, WhoWor 93
Stivori, Francesco c. 1550-1605 Baker 92
Stix, John 1920- MiSFD 9
Stix, Thomas Howard 1924- WhoAm 92
Stjernswaro, Jan Erik Eyvino 1936- WhoUN 92
St-Laurent, Claude Law&B 92
Stob, Martin 1926- WhoAm 92
Stobaeus, Johann 1580-1646 Baker 92
Stobaios fl. 4th cent.-5th cent. OxDcByz
Stobaugh, Clay Edward 1957- WhoAm 92
Stobaugh, Robert Blair 1927- WhoAm 92
Stobb, Margaret Anne 1937- WhoAmW 93
Stobbe, Victor John 1941- St&PR 93
Stobbs, Chuck 1929- BioIn 17
Stobbs, Emmett Eugene, Jr. 1946- WhoE 93
Stobbs, William Michael WhoScE 91-1
Stober, Matthaeus M.C. 1927- WhoScE 91-3
Stober, Richard Paul 1942- WhoE 93
Stober, William John, II 1933- WhoAm 92
Stobie, Robert Stewart 1941- WhoScE 91-1
Stobo, John David 1941- WhoAm 92
Stock, Ann Marie 1957- WhoE 93
Stock, Carl William 1945- WhoSSW 93
Stock, Catherine BioIn 17
Stock, Daniel Michael Law&B 92
Stock, David (Frederick) 1939- Baker 92
Stock, Dorothy C. 1926- St&PR 93
Stock, Eleanor Bang AmWomPl
Stock, Elliot d1911 BioIn 17
Stock, Francis E. 1936- St&PR 93
Stock, Frederick 1872-1942 Baker 92
Stock, Gloriann J. 1948- St&PR 93
Stock, Gregg Francis 1925- WhoAm 92
Stock, Jan H. 1931- WhoScE 91-3
Stock, Jeffry Benton 1946- WhoE 93
Stock, Larry 1896-1984 Baker 92
Stock, Leon Milo 1930- WhoAm 92
Stock, Leroy A. 1942- St&PR 93
Stock, Leroy A., Jr. 1942- WhoIns 93
Stock, Margot Therese 1936- WhoAmW 93, WhoSSW 93
Stock, Michael John WhoScE 91-1
Stock, Micheal Zacharia 1959- St&PR 93
Stock, Norman 1940- WhoWrEP 92
Stock, Otto F., Jr. Law&B 92
Stock, Otto F., Jr. 1935- St&PR 93
Stock, Peggy Ann 1936- WhoAmW 93
Stock, Rodney Clifford 1929- WhoWor 93
Stock, Simon S., Jr. 1927- St&PR 93
Stock, Stuart H. ScF&FL 92
Stock, Timothy Francis Law&B 92
Stock, Tony BioIn 17
Stockamp, Robert L. 1943- St&PR 93
Stockard, Alan Ray 1949- WhoSSW 93
Stockard, James Alfred 1935- WhoAm 92
Stockard, Olivia Tate 1946- WhoAmW 93
Stockbridge, Dorothy 1896- AmWomPl
Stockbridge, Grant ScF&FL 92
Stockdale, G.W. WhoScE 91-1
Stockdale, Harold James 1931- WhoAm 92
Stockdale, James Bond 1923- NewYTBS 92, WhoAm 92
Stockdell, Richard Price 1951- WhoSSW 93
Stockel, H. Henrietta 1938- ConAu 139
Stockel, Ivar Howard 1927- WhoSSW 93
Stockell, Albert W., III 1945- WhoSSW 93
Stocker, Arthur Frederick 1914- WhoAm 92
Stocker, Beatrice 1909- WhoAmW 93
Stocker, David BioIn 17
Stocker, Edgar Josef 1949- WhoWor 93
Stocker, Erich Franz 1946- WhoE 93
Stocker, Harold Sydney 1916- WhoSSW 93
Stocker, John Edward 1924- WhoSSW 93
Stocker, John M., Jr. Law&B 92
Stocker, John R. Law&B 92
Stocker, Jule E. 1906- St&PR 93
Stocker, Jule Elias 1906- WhoAm 92
Stocker, Kurt P. 1934- St&PR 93
Stocker, Marc Bernard 1961- WhoAm 92
Stocker, Mary Todd 1954- St&PR 93
Stocker, Peter Moseley WhoScE 91-1
Stocker, Ronald John 1934- St&PR 93
Stocker, Stella Prince AmWomPl
Stockert, Thomas R. 1941- St&PR 93
Stockham, Thomas Greenway, Jr. 1933- WhoAm 92
Stockhausen Baker 92
Stockhausen, Franz 1789-1868 Baker 92
Stockhausen, Franz 1839-1926 Baker 92
Stockhausen, Julius (Christian) 1826-1906 Baker 92
Stockhausen, Karlheinz 1928- Baker 92, IntDcOp, OxDcOp, WhoWor 93
Stockhausen, Margarethe 1803-1877 Baker 92
Stockhoff, Walter William 1876-1968 Baker 92
Stockholm, Charles M. 1933- St&PR 93
Stockholm, Donald Dean 1925- St&PR 93
Stockhouse, Janis BioIn 17
Stocking, B. WhoScE 91-1
Stocking, Frank A. Law&B 92
Stocking, George Ward, Jr. 1928- WhoAm 92
Stocking, Helen AmWomPl
Stocking, Marion Kingston 1922- WhoWrEP 92
Stockinger, Hannes 1955- WhoWor 93
Stockinger, Leopold 1919- WhoScE 91-4
Stockinger, Richard C. 1958- St&PR 93
Stocklan, Martin B. 1941- St&PR 93
Stocklin, Alma Katherine 1926- WhoAmW 93
Stocklin, Gerhard L. 1930- WhoScE 91-3
Stockmal, Henry F., Jr. 1942- WhoE 93
Stockman, David Alan 1946- BioIn 17
Stockman, David Allen 1946- WhoAm 92
Stockman, Gerald Richard 1935- WhoE 93
Stockman, Gordon 1929- St&PR 93
Stockman, Kenneth B. 1940- St&PR 93
Stockman, Richard Owen 1930- St&PR 93
Stockman, Ronald Jaudon 1941- WhoSSW 93
Stockmann, (Christine) Doris 1929- Baker 92
Stockmann, Erich 1926- Baker 92
Stockmann, Hans-Jurgen 1945- WhoScE 91-3
Stockmann, Kurt Joachim Wolfgang 1939- WhoWor 93
Stockmar, Jurgen WhoScE 91-4
Stockmar, Ted P. 1921- WhoAm 92
Stockmayer, Walter Hugo 1914- WhoAm 92, WhoE 93
Stockmeyer, C. B., Jr. 1939- St&PR 93
Stockmeyer, Paul Kelly 1943- WhoSSW 93
Stockmeyer, Rolf-Peter 1956- WhoWor 93
Stockner, Robert David 1958- WhoEmL 93, WhoSSW 93
Stocks, David Charles WhoScE 91-1
Stocks, Elizabeth Lunn 1936- WhoAmW 93
Stocks, Gerald Richard 1932- WhoWor 93
Stocks, Kenneth Duane 1934- St&PR 93, WhoAm 92
Stocks, Rundell Kingsley 1925- WhoWor 93
Stocks, Susan Jennifer 1963- WhoAmW 93
Stocks, William L., III 1955- St&PR 93
Stockschlaeder, Marcus Andreas 1960- WhoWor 93
Stockton, Anderson Berrian 1943- WhoAm 92, WhoWor 93
Stockton, David Knapp 1941- WhoAm 92
Stockton, Dora H. AmWomPl
Stockton, Eddy R. 1957- WhoSSW 93
Stockton, Francis R. ScF&FL 92
Stockton, Francis Richard 1834-1902 ConAu 137, MajAI [port]
Stockton, Frank R. ConAu 137, MajAI
Stockton, Frank R. 1834-1902 GayN, ScF&FL 92, TwCLC 47 [port]
Stockton, James Alexander Law&B 92
Stockton, John 1962- WhoAm 92
Stockton, John B. Law&B 92
Stockton, John B. 1946- WhoAm 92
Stockton, Judy Ann 1942- WhoAmW 93
Stockton, Kenton L. 1928- St&PR 93
Stockton, Lucius Horatio 1768-1835 BioIn 17
Stockton, Pamela Law&B 92
Stockton, Phillip Winston 1941- St&PR 93
Stockton, Port 1854-1881 BioIn 17
Stockton, Ralph Madison, Jr. 1927- WhoAm 92
Stockton, Robert Field 1795-1866 HarEnMi
Stockton, Robert Louis 1932- WhoSSW 93
Stockton, Scott 1954- WhoE 93
Stockton, Stephen F. 1947- St&PR 93
Stockton, Thomas B. 1930- WhoAm 92
Stockwell, Dean 1935- BioIn 17
Stockwell, Dean 1936- WhoAm 92
Stockwell, Erma M. AmWomPl
Stockwell, Ernest Farnham, Jr. 1923- WhoAm 92
Stockwell, George L. Law&B 92
Stockwell, George Lewis 1928- St&PR 93
Stockwell, John MiSFD 9
Stockwell, John Robert 1937- WhoSSW 93
Stockwell, Joseph M. Law&B 92
Stockwell, Oliver Perkins 1907- WhoAm 92, WhoSSW 93
Stockwell, Peter Bernard 1940- WhoWor 93
Stockwell, Richard E. 1917- WhoAm 92
Stockwell, Robert WhoScE 91-1
Stockwell, Robert Paul 1925- WhoAm 92
Stockwell, Shelley Lessin 1945- WhoWrEP 92
Stockwell, Sherwood Beach 1926- WhoAm 92
Stockwin, James Arthur Ainscow 1935- WhoWor 93
Stoclet, Jean-Claude 1933- WhoScE 91-2
Stoddard, Alexandra BioIn 17
Stoddard, Althene S. AmWomPl
Stoddard, Anne Glen 1880- AmWomPl
Stoddard, Brandon 1937- WhoAm 92
Stoddard, Charles Hatch 1912- WhoAm 92
Stoddard, Charles Warren 1843-1909 BioIn 17, GayN
Stoddard, Donald B. 1951- WhoIns 93
Stoddard, Douglas Paul 1945- WhoSSW 93
Stoddard, Elizabeth 1823-1902 BioIn 17
Stoddard, Ellwyn R. 1927- WhoAm 92, WhoSSW 93
Stoddard, Ellwyn R(eed) 1927- ConAu 38NR
Stoddard, Forrest Shaffer 1944- WhoE 93
Stoddard, Frances Ellen 1941- WhoWrEP 92
Stoddard, George Earl 1917- WhoAm 92
Stoddard, Laurence Ralph, Jr. 1936- WhoAm 92
Stoddard, Philip Hendrick 1929- WhoE 93
Stoddard, Richard Ethridge 1950- WhoAm 92
Stoddard, Richard Russell 1948- WhoSSW 93
Stoddard, Roger Eliot 1935- WhoAm 92
Stoddard, Sandol 1927- WhoAmW 93
Stoddard, Solomon 1643-1729 BioIn 17
Stoddard, Stephen Davidson 1925- WhoAm 92
Stoddard, W. Randall 1948- St&PR 93
Stoddard, William Bert, Jr. 1926- WhoE 93, WhoWor 93
Stoddard-Fitzgerald, Cynthia L. Law&B 92
Stoddart, Alfred 1941- St&PR 93
Stoddart, George A. 1933- St&PR 93
Stoddart, George Anderson 1933- WhoAm 92
Stoddart, J.L. WhoScE 91-1
Stoddart, James Fraser WhoScE 91-1
Stoddart, Kenneth R. 1926- St&PR 93
Stodder, John Wesley 1923- St&PR 93
Stoddert, Sandra Smith 1942- WhoE 93
Stodghill, William Wardell 1927- WhoIns 93
Stodnick, Gregory John 1942- St&PR 93
Stodola, Gerald William 1951- St&PR 93
Stodola, Randall Joseph 1953- St&PR 93
Stodolnik, Ludmila 1937- WhoWor 93
Stoeber, F. WhoScE 91-2
Stoeber, John d1988 BioIn 17
Stoeckel, Carl 1858-1925 Baker 92
Stoeckel, Gustave J(acob) 1819-1907 Baker 92
Stoecker, David Thomas 1939- WhoAm 92
Stoecker, Leo Joseph 1919- WhoAm 92
Stoecker, Steven O. 1948- St&PR 93
Stoeckl, Ernst G. 1944- St&PR 93
Stoeckl, Shelley Joan 1951- WhoAmW 93
Stoeckle, M. L. 1931- St&PR 93
Stoeckley, John Bolton 1943- St&PR 93
Stoefen, Gary E. 1939- St&PR 93, WhoIns 93
Stoeffhaas, Jerry MiSFD 9
Stoeffhaas, W. H. St&PR 93
Stoehr, Charles Michael 1946- St&PR 93, WhoAm 92
Stoehr, Ingo Roland 1956- WhoSSW 93
Stoehr, James Harkness 1929- St&PR 93
Stoelting-Richert, Wilfried 1942- WhoWor 93
Stoeltje, Beverly June 1940- WhoAmW 93
Stoemenos, John 1934- WhoScE 91-3
Stoemmer, Peter Erasmus 1951- WhoWor 93
Stoery, Lauren A. Law&B 92
Stoesen, Alexander Rudolph 1932- WhoSSW 93
Stoessel, Albert (Frederic) 1894-1943 Baker 92
Stoesser, Rudolf G. 1938- WhoScE 91-3
Stoesser, Susan Alice 1947- WhoAmW 93
Stoett, Herman Pieter 1930- WhoAm 92
Stoetzel, Berthold 1938- WhoWor 93
Stoetzner, Eric W. d1990 BioIn 17
Stoev, Stoytcho 1931- WhoScE 91-4
Stoeving, (Carl Heinrich) Paul 1861-1948 Baker 92
Stoewer, H. 1940- WhoScE 91-3
Stoewsand, Gilbert Saari 1932- WhoE 93
Stofer, Kathryn Tamara 1948- WhoAmW 93
Stofer, Wolfgang 1944- St&PR 93
Stoff, Joshua 1958- ConAu 136
Stoffa, James Victor 1942- WhoAm 92
Stoffel, Klaus Peter 1957- WhoE 93, WhoEmL 93, WhoWor 93
Stoffel, Wilhelm 1928- WhoWor 93
Stoffel-Rosales, Michele Lynn 1962- WhoAmW 93
Stoffer, Christiane M. Law&B 92
Stoffer, James Myron, Jr. 1952- WhoAm 92
Stofferson, Terry Lee 1957- WhoEmL 93
Stoffregen-Harwell, Teresa Anne Law&B 92
Stofko, Karl Peter 1938- WhoE 93
Stogner, Jennifer Dawn 1961- WhoAmW 93
Stogner, William Louis 1957- WhoSSW 93
Stogorsky, Alexander 1910- Baker 92
Stohl, Stephen A. 1945- St&PR 93
Stohler, Michael D. 1942- St&PR 93
Stohlquist, Roger Harold 1925- St&PR 93
Stohr, Richard 1874-1967 Baker 92
Stohr, Walter Benjamin 1928- WhoWor 93
Stoia, Viorel G. 1924- WhoWor 93
Stoiber, Thomas J. 1952- St&PR 93
Stoica, Susana 1946- WhoWor 93
Stoicescu, Liviu 1933- WhoScE 91-4
Stoicheff, Boris Peter 1924- WhoAm 92
Stoicovy, Monica Rose 1939- WhoAmW 93
Stoik, John Lentis 1920- St&PR 93, WhoAm 92
Stoike, Lyla Bell BioIn 17
Stoikes, Mary Eloise 1960- WhoAmW 93
Stoin, Elena 1915- Baker 92
Stoin, Vassil 1880-1938 Baker 92
Stoitcheff, Krassimir 1955- WhoWor 93
Stojanov, Georgi 1936- DrEEuF
Stojanov, Luchezar Nedelchev 1954- WhoWor 93
Stojanov, Todor 1930- DrEEuF
Stojanovic, Peter Lazar 1877-1957 Baker 92
Stojilkovic, Stanko Stamen 1950- WhoE 93
Stojowski, Sigismund 1869-1946 Baker 92
Stojowski, Zygmunt 1869-1946 PolBiDi
Stokeld, Michael P. Law&B 92
Stokely, Craig Ranford 1945- St&PR 93
Stokely, Elizabeth Susan Law&B 92
Stokely, Freddie BioIn 17
Stokely, Hugh Lawson 1933- WhoAm 92
Stokely, John Edwin 1952- St&PR 93
Stokely, Mary Curry 1950- WhoE 93
Stoker, Abraham ScF&FL 92
Stoker, Bram 1847-1912 BioIn 17, ScF&FL 92, WorLitC [port]
Stoker, Dennis J. 1928- WhoScE 91-1
Stoker, Eugene Edgar Law&B 92
Stoker, James Johnston, Jr. d1992 NewYTBS 92
Stoker, James Rienewerf 1935- St&PR 93, WhoAm 92
Stoker, John ScF&FL 92
Stoker, Michael George Parke 1918- WhoWor 93
Stoker, Richard 1938- Baker 92
Stoker, Warren Cady 1912- WhoAm 92
Stokes, Adrian Victor 1945- WhoWor 93
Stokes, Angela Rochelle Law&B 92
Stokes, Anthony BioIn 17
Stokes, Arch Yow 1946- WhoWor 93
Stokes, Arnold Paul 1932- WhoAm 92
Stokes, B. R. 1924- WhoAm 92
Stokes, Barbara S. Law&B 92
Stokes, Barrie Balzli Law&B 92
Stokes, Becky BioIn 17
Stokes, Carl 1927- AfrAmBi
Stokes, Carl B. 1927- EncAACR
Stokes, Carl Burton 1927- WhoAm 92
Stokes, Charles Junius 1922- WhoAm 92, WhoWor 93
Stokes, Charles Shannon 1941- WhoE 93
Stokes, Coleman ScF&FL 92
Stokes, Colin J. 1940- WhoScE 91-1

Stokes, Colleen Shelley 1955- *WhoAmW 93*
Stokes, Cynthia Louise *Law&B 92*
Stokes, David Kershaw, Jr. 1927- *WhoSSW 93*
Stokes, Donald Elkinton 1927- *WhoAm 92*
Stokes, Donald Gresham 1914- *WhoAm 92*
Stokes, Eric (Norman) 1930- *Baker 92*
Stokes, George Gabriel 1819-1903 *BioIn 17*
Stokes, Gordon Arthur 1929- *WhoWor 93*
Stokes, James Randall 1948- *WhoSSW 93*
Stokes, James Sewell 1944- *WhoAm 92*
Stokes, John Dennis 1946- *WhoEmL 93*
Stokes, John Emmett 1947- *St&PR 93*
Stokes, John F.G. 1875-1960 *IntDcAn*
Stokes, John Lemacks, II 1908- *WhoAm 92*
Stokes, Joseph C., Jr. 1947- *St&PR 93*
Stokes, Joseph Clement, Jr. 1947- *WhoAm 92*
Stokes, Joseph Franklin 1934- *WhoSSW 93*
Stokes, Linda K. *Law&B 92*
Stokes, Linda Kay 1948- *St&PR 93*
Stokes, Louis *BioIn 17*
Stokes, Louis 1925- *AfrAmBi [port], CngDr 91, ConBlB 3 [port], WhoAm 92*
Stokes, Louise *BioIn 17, BlkAmWO*
Stokes, Mack Marion Boyd 1911- *WhoAm 92*
Stokes, Manning Lee 1911-1976 *ScF&FL 92*
Stokes, Patrick 1942- *St&PR 93*
Stokes, Patrick T. *BioIn 17*
Stokes, Patrick T. 1942- *WhoAm 92*
Stokes, Paul Allen 1927- *WhoAm 92*
Stokes, Penelope June 1950- *WhoWrEP 92*
Stokes, Robert Allan 1942- *WhoAm 92*
Stokes, Robert M. *Law&B 92*
Stokes, Robert Stephen 1936- *WhoSSW 93*
Stokes, Rose Harriet Pastor 1879-1933 *BioIn 17*
Stokes, Rose Pastor Wieslander 1879-1933 *AmWomPl*
Stokes, Sara Margaret 1945- *WhoAmW 93*
Stokes, Terry 1943- *WhoWrEP 92*
Stokes, Theodore Frederick 1938- *St&PR 93*
Stokes, Theresa Emma 1943- *WhoWor 93*
Stokes, Thomas Elder, III 1949- *WhoSSW 93*
Stokes, Thomas F. 1948- *WhoIns 93*
Stokes, Thomas L., Jr. 1898-1958 *JrnUS*
Stokes, William Finley, Jr. 1938- *WhoSSW 93*
Stokes, William Forest 1931- *WhoWrEP 92*
Stokes, William P., Jr. 1941- *St&PR 93*
Stokes, William Roy, Jr. 1955- *WhoSSW 93*
Stokesbury, James L(awton) 1934- *ConAu 38NR*
Stokesbury, Leon 1945- *DcLB 120 [port], WhoWrEP 92*
Stokes Elias, Janice Elaine 1952- *WhoAmW 93*
Stokey, Bobby Neal 1944- *WhoSSW 93*
Stokke, Julie A. 1963- *St&PR 93*
Stokke, Milo B. 1926- *St&PR 93*
Stokowski, Leopold 1882-1977 *BioIn 17, PolBiDi*
Stokowski, Leopold (Anthony) 1882-1977 *Baker 92*
Stokstad, Marilyn Jane 1929- *WhoAm 92*
Stokvis, Jack Raphael 1944- *WhoAm 92*
Stolar, Henry S. *Law&B 92*
Stolar, Henry S. 1939- *St&PR 93*
Stolar, Henry Samuel 1939- *WhoAm 92*
Stolar, Kathleen S. *Law&B 92*
Stolar, Paul Louis 1940- *WhoSSW 93*
Stolarik, M. Mark 1943- *WhoAm 92*
Stolarik, Michael G. 1951- *St&PR 93*
Stolarz, Stanislaw 1922- *WhoScE 91-4*
Stolber, Dean Charles 1944- *St&PR 93*
Stolberg, Christian, Graf von 1748-1821 *BioIn 17*
Stolberg, Friedrich Leopold, Graf von 1750-1819 *BioIn 17*
Stolberg, Irving J. 1936- *WhoAm 92*
Stolbov, Bruce *ScF&FL 92*
Stolen, Olav 1931- *WhoScE 91-2*
Stoler, Mark *Law&B 92*
Stolfi, Robert Louis 1938- *WhoE 93*
Stoliarsky, Piotr (Solomonovich) 1871-1944 *Baker 92*
Stolier, Louis 1907- *St&PR 93*
Stoline, Anne Marie 1961- *WhoE 93*
Stolk, Gloria 1918-1979 *SpAmA*
Stolk, Jan Hendrik 1946- *WhoScE 91-3*
Stoll, Barbara J. *WhoAmW 93*
Stoll, Bobbi 1932- *WhoAmW 93*
Stoll, Charles Buckner 1923- *WhoAm 92*
Stoll, Clifford *BioIn 17*
Stoll, Clifford 1950- *ConAu 136*
Stoll, Howard Lester, Jr. 1928- *WhoAm 92*
Stoll, Lillian *AmWomPl*
Stoll, Myron S. *Law&B 92*
Stoll, Neal Richard 1948- *WhoAm 92, WhoEmL 93*
Stoll, Richard Edmund 1927- *St&PR 93, WhoAm 92*
Stoll, Richard Giles 1946- *WhoAm 92*
Stoll, Roger Gerhard 1942- *St&PR 93*
Stoll, Roy M. 1934- *St&PR 93*
Stoll, Victoria Ann 1960- *WhoAmW 93*
Stoll, Wilhelm 1923- *WhoAm 92*
Stoll, William F., Jr. *Law&B 92*
Stollenwerk, James Henry 1930- *St&PR 93*
Stollenwerk, John Joseph 1940- *St&PR 93*
Stoller, Claude 1921- *WhoAm 92*
Stoller, Ezra 1915- *WhoAm 92*
Stoller, Gary 1953- *St&PR 93*
Stoller, Herbert E. 1942- *St&PR 93*
Stoller, Jacob 1920- *St&PR 93*
Stoller, Madeline C. *Law&B 92*
Stoller, Michael Jay 1931- *WhoAm 92*
Stoller, Mike 1933- *BioIn 17*
See Also Leiber & Stoller *SoulM*
Stoller, Robert J. *BioIn 17*
Stoller, Stuart Paul 1955- *St&PR 93*
Stollerman, Gene Howard 1920- *WhoAm 92*
Stollerman, Ray 1931- *WhoAm 92*
Stollery, David Paul 1954- *WhoE 93*
Stollery, J. W. 1937- *St&PR 93*
Stollery, John Leslie *WhoScE 91-1*
Stollery, Robert 1924- *WhoAm 92*
Stolley, Alexander 1922- *WhoAm 92*
Stolley, Paul David 1937- *WhoAm 92*
Stolley, Richard B. *NewYTBS 92 [port]*
Stolley, Richard Brockway 1928- *WhoAm 92*
Stollman, Israel 1923- *WhoAm 92*
Stollman, Ulla 1946- *WhoScE 91-4*
Stollnitz, Fred 1939- *WhoE 93*
Stolmeier, Robert C. 1944- *St&PR 93*
Stolnitz, George Joseph 1920- *WhoAm 92*
Stoloff, Carolyn 1927- *WhoWrEP 92*
Stoloff, Carolyn Ruth 1947- *WhoAmW 93*
Stoloff, Norman Stanley 1934- *WhoE 93*
Stolojan, Theodore Dumitru 1943- *WhoWor 93*
Stolovy, Alexander 1926- *WhoE 93*
Stolow, David M. *Law&B 92*
Stolp, Lauren Elbert 1921- *WhoAm 92*
Stolp, Loren P. *Law&B 92*
Stolpe, Antoni 1851-1872 *Baker 92*
Stolpe, Norman Dean 1946- *WhoE 93*
Stolper, Aleksandr 1907-1979 *DrEEuF*
Stolper, Carolyn Louise 1953- *WhoAmW 93*
Stolper, Joseph V. d1990 *BioIn 17*
Stolper, Pinchas Aryeh 1931- *WhoAm 92*
Stolper, Wolfgang Friedrich 1912- *WhoAm 92*
Stolt, Bengt 1923- *WhoWor 93*
Stolte, Dieter 1934- *WhoWor 93*
Stolte, Larry Gene 1945- *St&PR 93*
Stoltenberg, Gerhard 1928- *WhoWor 93*
Stoltenberg, Thorvald 1931- *WhoWor 93*
Stoltz, Deane H. 1929- *St&PR 93*
Stoltz, Eric 1961- *WhoAm 92*
Stoltz, Jean-Francois 1942- *WhoScE 91-2*
Stoltz, Jon T. 1946- *St&PR 93*
Stoltz, Rosine 1815-1903 *Baker 92, OxDcOp*
Stoltzer, Thomas c. 1480-1526 *Baker 92*
Stoltzfus, (Mary) Louise 1952- *ConAu 138*
Stoltzfus, Victor Ezra 1934- *WhoAm 92*
Stoltzman, Richard (Leslie) 1942- *Baker 92, WhoAm 92*
Stoltzmann, William A. *Law&B 92*
Stoltzmann, William A. 1948- *WhoIns 93*
Stolusky, Warren Gerald *Law&B 92*
Stolwijk, Jan Adrianus Jozef 1927- *WhoAm 92*
Stolypin, Petr Arkad'evich 1862-1911 *BioIn 17*
Stolz, Alan J. 1931- *WhoE 93*
Stolz, Benjamin Armond 1934- *WhoAm 92*
Stolz, Francesca 1827- *OxDcOp*
See Also Ricci, Federico 1809-1877 *OxDcOp*
Stolz, Irving H. 1903-1990 *BioIn 17*
Stolz, Joel M. 1940- *St&PR 93*
Stolz, John William 1931- *St&PR 93*
Stolz, Ludmilla 1827- *OxDcOp*
See Also Ricci, Federico 1809-1877 *OxDcOp*
Stolz, Mary 1920- *ScF&FL 92*
Stolz, Mary Slattery 1920- *DcAmChF 1960, DcAmChF 1985, MajAI [port], SmATA 71 [port]*
Stolz, Richard *BioIn 17*
Stolz, Robert 1880-1975 *OxDcOp*
Stolz, Robert (Elisabeth) 1880-1975 *Baker 92*
Stolz, Teresa 1834-1902 *Baker 92, IntDcOp, OxDcOp*
Stolz, Walter Sargent 1938- *WhoAm 92*
Stolzberg, Mark Elliott 1944- *WhoE 93*
Stolze, Gerhard 1926-1979 *Baker 92, OxDcOp*
Stolzel, Gottfried Heinrich 1690-1749 *Baker 92*
Stolzenberg, Pearl 1946- *WhoAmW 93*
Stolzer, Leo William 1934- *WhoAm 92*
Stolzer, Paul E. *Law&B 92*
Stolzman, Alison A. *Law&B 92*
Stolzmann, Wlodzimierz Maciej 1940- *WhoScE 91-4*
Stolzova, Teresina 1834-1902 *Baker 92*
Stomberg, Rolf S.O. 1933- *WhoScE 91-4*
Stombler, Milton Philip 1939- *WhoSSW 93*
Stommel, Henry M. d1992 *NewYTBS 92*
Stommel, Henry M. 1920-1992 *BioIn 17*
Stone, Alan 1928- *St&PR 93, WhoAm 92*
Stone, Alan James 1944- *WhoAm 92*
Stone, Alan Jay 1942- *WhoAm 92*
Stone, Alan John 1940- *WhoE 93*
Stone, Albert Leo, Jr. 1943- *WhoSSW 93*
Stone, Albert Mordecai 1913- *WhoE 93*
Stone, Alexander James 1923- *WhoIns 93*
Stone, Alfred E. *Law&B 92*
Stone, Alfred Ward 1925- *WhoE 93*
Stone, Alison Jo. 1964- *WhoWrEP 92*
Stone, Allan Barry 1932- *WhoAm 92*
Stone, Alma 1908- *ScF&FL 92*
Stone, Amy Elizabeth 1960- *WhoAmW 93*
Stone, Andrew *ScF&FL 92*
Stone, Andrew Grover 1942- *WhoE 93*
Stone, Andrew L. 1902- *MiSFD 9*
Stone, Andrew L. 1915- *St&PR 93*
Stone, Andy *ScF&FL 92*
Stone, Ann *BioIn 17*
Stone, Ann Elizabeth 1952- *WhoAmW 93*
Stone, Anne *Law&B 92*
Stone, Anthony Oliver 1962- *WhoWor 93*
Stone, Anthony Van Wezel 1947- *WhoSSW 93*
Stone, Arthur Harold 1916- *WhoAm 92*
Stone, Arthur Joseph 1929- *WhoE 93*
Stone, Arthur R. 1945- *St&PR 93*
Stone, Barbara Suzanne 1951- *WhoAmW 93*
Stone, Barrett 1941- *SoulM*
Stone, Ben M. 1914- *St&PR 93*
Stone, Bob *BioIn 17*
Stone, Bonnie Carol 1945- *WhoAmW 93*
Stone, Bonnie Mae Domrose 1941- *WhoAmW 93*
Stone, Bradley H. 1946- *St&PR 93*
Stone, Bruce W. *Law&B 92*
Stone, Burgess W. *Law&B 92*
Stone, Carl 1953- *Baker 92*
Stone, Caroline Fleming 1936- *WhoAmW 93*
Stone, Catherine Louise 1956- *WhoAmW 93*
Stone, Cathy *BioIn 17*
Stone, Charlotte *ScF&FL 92*
Stone, Chuck *BioIn 17*
Stone, Claudia Elizabeth *Law&B 92*
Stone, Clifton *Law&B 92*
Stone, Clive Graham 1936- *WhoWor 93*
Stone, Curtis J., Jr. 1930- *St&PR 93*
Stone, Cynthia Hutchinson 1940- *WhoAmW 93*
Stone, Cynthia Marie Beavers 1952- *WhoAmW 93*
Stone, Dan Gilbert 1958- *WhoE 93*
Stone, Daniel B. 1943- *St&PR 93*
Stone, Daniel Hunter 1938- *WhoAm 92*
Stone, David 1770-1818 *BioIn 17*
Stone, David B. 1927- *St&PR 93*
Stone, David Barnes 1927- *WhoAm 92*
Stone, David Deaderick 1932- *WhoAm 92*
Stone, David E. *Law&B 92*
Stone, David Karl 1922- *WhoSSW 93*
Stone, David Kendall 1942- *St&PR 93, WhoAm 92, WhoE 93*
Stone, David L. 1942- *St&PR 93*
Stone, David Shelton 1942- *St&PR 93*
Stone, Deanne Cohn 1939- *WhoAmW 93*
Stone, Deborah Lee 1950- *WhoAmW 93*
Stone, Debra F. *Law&B 92*
Stone, Diane Mary *WhoE 93*
Stone, Donald Crawford 1903- *WhoAm 92*
Stone, Donald Raymond 1938- *WhoAm 92*
Stone, Donald Wayne 1931- *St&PR 93*
Stone, Doris Venning 1922- *WhoAmW 93*
Stone, Dorothea Elaine 1947- *WhoAmW 93*
Stone, Douglas H. 1941- *St&PR 93*
Stone, Edmund Crispen, III 1942- *WhoAm 92*
Stone, Edward C. *BioIn 17*
Stone, Edward Carroll 1936- *WhoAm 92*
Stone, Edward Durell, Jr. 1932- *WhoAm 92*
Stone, Edward Harris, II 1933- *WhoAm 92*
Stone, Edward Luke 1937- *WhoE 93*
Stone, Elaine Murray 1922- *ConAu 38NR*
Stone, Elizabeth Caecilia 1949- *WhoAmW 93*
Stone, Elizabeth Campbell 1957- *WhoEmL 93*
Stone, Elizabeth Wenger 1918- *WhoAm 92, WhoAmW 93, WhoWor 93*
Stone, Elna *ScF&FL 92*
Stone, Emily C. d1991 *BioIn 17*
Stone, Errol M. *Law&B 92*
Stone, Ezra Chaim 1917- *WhoAm 92*
Stone, Frances 1923- *WhoE 93*
Stone, Francis Gordon Albert *WhoScE 91-1*
Stone, Frank Andrews 1929- *WhoE 93*
Stone, Franz Theodore 1907- *WhoAm 92, WhoWor 93*
Stone, Fred A. 1916- *St&PR 93*
Stone, Fred Michael 1943- *WhoAm 92*
Stone, Frederic Scott 1959- *WhoE 93*
Stone, Frederick Anderson 1943- *St&PR 93*
Stone, Frederick H. 1921- *St&PR 93*
Stone, Frederick Joseph 1949- *WhoE 93*
Stone, Ganga *BioIn 17*
Stone, Garold L. 1956- *St&PR 93*
Stone, Gary H. 1953- *St&PR 93*
Stone, Gary L. *Law&B 92*
Stone, Gary Leon 1941- *St&PR 93, WhoAm 92*
Stone, Gene d1991 *BioIn 17*
Stone, Geoffrey Richard 1946- *WhoAm 92*
Stone, George *ScF&FL 92*
Stone, George E. 1934- *St&PR 93*
Stone, George L. 1934- *St&PR 93, WhoIns 93*
Stone, George Milton 1929- *St&PR 93*
Stone, Gerald Paul 1918- *WhoAm 92*
Stone, Grace Zaring 1891-1991 *AnObit 1991, BioIn 17, ConLC 70*
Stone, Graham 1926- *ScF&FL 92*
Stone, Harlan Fiske 1872-1946 *OxCSupC*
Stone, Harold Stuart 1938- *WhoAm 92*
Stone, Harriett Abramson 1941- *St&PR 93*
Stone, Harry 1926- *ScF&FL 92*
Stone, Harry H. 1917- *WhoAm 92*
Stone, Harvey H. 1942- *WhoE 93*
Stone, Henry *SoulM*
Stone, Henry E. 1922- *WhoAm 92*
Stone, Henry P. 1933- *St&PR 93*
Stone, Herbert S. 1817-1915 *GayN*
Stone, Howard Francis 1931- *WhoAm 92*
Stone, Howard Lawrence 1941- *WhoWor 93*
Stone, Hubert Dean 1924- *WhoSSW 93, WhoWor 93*
Stone, I.F. 1907-1989 *BioIn 17*
Stone, I(sidor) F(einstein) 1907-1989 *ConAu 40NR*
Stone, Idella Purnell 1901-1982 *ScF&FL 92*
Stone, Ileane Gertrude 1933- *WhoAmW 93*
Stone, Irving 1903-1989 *BioIn 17*
Stone, Irving I. 1909- *St&PR 93, WhoAm 92*
Stone, Isidor Feinstein 1907-1989 *BioIn 17, JrnUS*
Stone, Isobel 1891?-1969? *ScF&FL 92*
Stone, Jacqueline Smith 1940- *WhoAmW 93*
Stone, James Conley 1931- *WhoAm 92*
Stone, James Edward, Jr. *Law&B 92*
Stone, James H. 1922- *St&PR 93*
Stone, James Howard 1939- *WhoWor 93*
Stone, James J. 1947- *WhoAm 92*
Stone, James Lester 1940- *WhoE 93*
Stone, James Robert 1948- *WhoWor 93*
Stone, James Thomas 1948- *St&PR 93*
Stone, James William 1917- *St&PR 93*
Stone, Jane *AmWomPl*
Stone, Jane Buffington 1942- *WhoAmW 93*
Stone, Janice *BioIn 17*
Stone, Jeffrey Charles *WhoScE 91-1*
Stone, Jennifer 1933- *WhoWrEP 92*
Stone, Jennings Edward 1942- *WhoSSW 93*
Stone, Jeremy Judah 1935- *WhoAm 92*
Stone, Jeri 1954- *WhoEmL 93*
Stone, Jerome Carl, Jr. 1963- *WhoE 93*
Stone, Jerome H. 1913- *St&PR 93*
Stone, Jerry Broadwell 1923- *WhoSSW 93*
Stone, Jesse 1901- *SoulM*
Stone, Jim *AfrAmBi [port]*
Stone, Joan Elizabeth *WhoWrEP 92*
Stone, Joe Allan 1948- *WhoAm 92*
Stone, Joe Thomas 1941- *WhoE 93*
Stone, Joel 1931- *ConAu 138*
Stone, John 1936- *BioIn 17, WhoWrEP 92*
Stone, John McWilliams, Jr. 1927- *St&PR 93, WhoAm 92*
Stone, John Owen 1929- *WhoAsAP 91*
Stone, John R. 1938- *St&PR 93*
Stone, John T. 1933- *St&PR 93*
Stone, John Timothy, Jr. 1933- *WhoWor 93*

Stone, Jonathon Thomas 1905-1955 *BiDAMSp 1989*
Stone, Joseph 1920- *WhoAm 92*
Stone, Joseph E. 1961- *St&PR 93*
Stone, Josephine Rector 1936- *ScF&FL 92*
Stone, Julie Lynn 1959- *WhoWrEP 92*
Stone, Karen Rasmussen 1948- *WhoAmW 93*
Stone, Kenneth A. 1929- *St&PR 93*
Stone, Kenneth Michael 1942- *WhoWrEP 92*
Stone, Kurt 1911-1989 *Baker 92*
Stone, L. Mark 1957- *WhoE 93*
Stone, Larry R. 1935- *St&PR 93*
Stone, Laurence M. 1925- *St&PR 93*
Stone, Lawrence *BioIn 17*
Stone, Lawrence 1919- *WhoAm 92*
Stone, Lawrence Maurice 1931- *WhoAm 92*
Stone, Leon 1914- *St&PR 93, WhoAm 92*
Stone, Leslie F. 1905-1991 *ScF&FL 92*
Stone, Lewis 1879-1953 *BioIn 17*
Stone, Lewis Bart 1938- *WhoAm 92*
Stone, Lewis M. 1927- *St&PR 93*
Stone, Linda D. 1947- *WhoE 93*
Stone, Linda Ellen 1955- *WhoAmW 93*
Stone, Lisa Jane 1944- *WhoAmW 93*
Stone, Lloyd Evan 1962- *St&PR 93*
Stone, Lucius Harold 1940- *WhoAm 92*
Stone, Lucy 1818-1893 *PolPar*
Stone, Marguerite Beverley 1916- *WhoAm 92*
Stone, Marie Kirchner *WhoWrEP 92*
Stone, Marjorie E. *Law&B 92*
Stone, Mark William *Law&B 92*
Stone, Martha Jane 1919- *WhoSSW 93*
Stone, Martin 1928- *St&PR 93*
Stone, Marvin Jules 1937- *WhoAm 92, WhoSSW 93, WhoWor 93*
Stone, Marvin Lawrence 1924- *WhoAm 92*
Stone, Mary Irene *AmWomPl*
Stone, Mary Overstreet 1924- *WhoSSW 93*
Stone, Mary R. 1953- *St&PR 93*
Stone, Mary Ruth 1942- *WhoSSW 93*
Stone, Melissa Kay 1956- *WhoSSW 93*
Stone, Melissa Middleton 1948- *WhoE 93*
Stone, Melville Elijah 1848-1929 *JrnUS*
Stone, Merlin 1931- *ConAu 39NR*
Stone, Mervyn *WhoScE 91-1*
Stone, Michael H. *Law&B 92*
Stone, Michael Omarr 1937- *WhoSSW 93*
Stone, Michael P. W. 1925- *WhoAm 92, WhoE 93*
Stone, Michael Reeves 1958- *St&PR 93, WhoSSW 93*
Stone, Michael Robert 1951- *WhoWrEP 92*
Stone, Mike *ScF&FL 92*
Stone, Mildred Mary-Anne *WhoAmW 93*
Stone, Morris Denor 1902- *WhoE 93*
Stone, Nelson 1923- *St&PR 93*
Stone, Norman *MiSFD 9*
Stone, Norman Michael 1949- *WhoWor 93*
Stone, Oliver *BioIn 17*
Stone, Oliver 1946- *ConLC 73 [port], MiSFD 9, WhoAm 92*
Stone, Pamela Anne 1965- *WhoE 93*
Stone, Patricia 1952- *WhoCanL 92*
Stone, Paul *ScF&FL 92*
Stone, Peter 1930- *BioIn 17, WhoAm 92, WhoE 93*
Stone, Peter G. *Law&B 92*
Stone, Peter George 1937- *St&PR 93, WhoAm 92*
Stone, Peter Howard 1948- *WhoE 93*
Stone, Philip Avery 1893-1967 *BioIn 17*
Stone, Ralph Kenny 1952- *WhoEmL 93*
Stone, Ralph Upson 1958- *WhoE 93*
Stone, Randolph Noel 1946- *WhoAm 92*
Stone, Raymond E. *Law&B 92*
Stone, Raymond William 1945- *WhoSSW 93*
Stone, Richard 1913-1991 *AnObit 1991*
Stone, Richard 1940- *ScF&FL 92*
Stone, Richard B. 1928- *WhoAm 92, WhoWor 93*
Stone, Richard D. *Law&B 92*
Stone, Richard E. 1937- *WhoIns 93*
Stone, Richard Lee 1963- *WhoWor 93*
Stone, Richard Nicholas 1913- *WhoWor 93*
Stone, Robert 1937- *BioIn 17, MagSAmL [port], NewYTBS 92 [port]*
Stone, Robert Alan 1935- *WhoAm 92*
Stone, Robert Anthony 1937- *WhoAm 92, WhoWrEP 92*
Stone, Robert B. 1930- *WhoAm 92*
Stone, Robert Delmar 1922- *WhoE 93*
Stone, Robert F. *BioIn 17*
Stone, Robert G., Jr. 1923- *St&PR 93*
Stone, Robert L. *Law&B 92*
Stone, Robert N. *Law&B 92*
Stone, Robert Ryrie 1943- *WhoAm 92*
Stone, Robert S. *Law&B 92*
Stone, Robert Sidney 1923- *WhoSSW 93*
Stone, Roger *BioIn 17*
Stone, Roger W. *BioIn 17*
Stone, Roger Warren 1935- *St&PR 93, WhoAm 92, WhoWor 93*
Stone, Ronald F. 1945- *WhoIns 93*
Stone, Ronald H. 1939- *ConAu 40NR*
Stone, Rosetta *MajAI*
Stone, Royce M. 1935- *St&PR 93*
Stone, Ruby R. 1924- *WhoAmW 93*
Stone, Russell A. 1944- *WhoAm 92*
Stone, Ruth 1915- *BioIn 17*
Stone, Scott C(linton) S(tuart) 1932- *ConAu 40NR*
Stone, Selma B. *AmWomPl*
Stone, Sharon *BioIn 17*
Stone, Sharon 1958- *WhoAmW 93*
Stone, Sharon R. *Law&B 92*
Stone, Shepard 1908-1990 *BioIn 17*
Stone, Sly *SoulM*
Stone, Sly 1944- *ConMus 8 [port]*
Stone, Stephen A. 1917- *St&PR 93*
Stone, Steve 1947- *BioIn 17*
Stone, Steven F. *Law&B 92*
Stone, Steven Michael 1947- *WhoAm 92*
Stone, Susan Foster 1954- *WhoAmW 93*
Stone, Susan Gail 1957- *WhoWrEP 92*
Stone, Susan Ridgaway 1950- *WhoAmW 93*
Stone, Sylvia Iris 1928- *WhoAm 92*
Stone, Theodore C. *BioIn 17*
Stone, Thomas Edward 1939- *WhoAm 92*
Stone, Thomas Richardson 1939- *WhoE 93*
Stone, Thomas S. 1909- *WhoAm 92*
Stone, Todd Alan 1961- *WhoSSW 93*
Stone, Trevor W. *WhoScE 91-1*
Stone, W. Clement 1902- *St&PR 93, WhoIns 93*
Stone, Walter Arthur 1940- *WhoSSW 93*
Stone, Walter B. 1941- *St&PR 93*
Stone, Warren N. *Law&B 92*
Stone, Warren R. *St&PR 93*
Stone, Wendy E. *Law&B 92*
Stone, Willard 1916-1985 *BioIn 17*
Stone, Willard John 1913- *WhoAm 92*
Stone, William A. 1936- *St&PR 93*
Stone, William Alexis 1846-1920 *BioIn 17*
Stone, William Edward 1945- *WhoAm 92*
Stone, William Harold 1924- *WhoAm 92*
Stone, William Ross 1947- *WhoEmL 93*
Stone, William Samuel 1923- *WhoSSW 93*
Stone, Williard Everard 1910- *WhoAm 92*
Stone, Zachary 1949- *BioIn 17*
Stoneback, Thomas 1950- *St&PR 93*
Stoneback, W. Keith 1953- *St&PR 93*
Stone-Blackburn, Susan 1941- *ScF&FL 92*
Stonebraker, Barbara J. 1944- *St&PR 93*
Stoneburner, Craig B. 1946- *St&PR 93*
Stoneburner, Rand Lawson 1949- *WhoUN 92*
Stonecipher, David Allen 1941- *St&PR 93*
Stonecipher, Harland C. 1938- *St&PR 93*
Stonecipher, Harry C. *WhoAm 92*
Stonecipher, Harry C. 1936- *St&PR 93*
Stoneham, Edward Bryant 1946- *WhoEmL 93*
Stoneham, Marshall 1940- *WhoWor 93*
Stonehill, Robert Berrell 1921- *WhoAm 92*
Stonehill, Robert Michael 1949- *WhoAm 92*
Stonehill, Susan L. *Law&B 92*
Stonehill, Susan Louise 1957- *WhoAmW 93*
Stonehouse, James Adam 1937- *WhoWor 93*
Stoneking, Johanna Marie Aucremanne 1953- *WhoSSW 93*
Stoneking, Lillian Stanford 1951- *WhoAmW 93*
Stoneley, Robert *WhoScE 91-1*
Stoneman, Douglas Grayson 1931- *WhoAm 92*
Stoneman, James Curtis, Jr. 1954- *WhoSSW 93*
Stoneman, Samuel Sidney 1911- *WhoAm 92*
Stoneman, William, III 1927- *WhoAm 92*
Stoneman, William Hambly, III 1944- *WhoAm 92*
Stoner, Anna Louisa Wellington *BioIn 17*
Stoner, Douglas E. *Law&B 92*
Stoner, Fredric A. 1931- *St&PR 93*
Stoner, Graham Alexander 1929- *WhoSSW 93*
Stoner, James Lloyd 1920- *WhoAm 92*
Stoner, Jeffrey Wayne 1953- *WhoE 93*
Stoner, John David 1935- *St&PR 93*
Stoner, John Richard 1958- *WhoAm 92*
Stoner, Leonard Dudley 1950- *WhoEmL 93, WhoWor 93*
Stoner, Richard Burkett 1920- *St&PR 93, WhoAm 92*
Stoner, Richard Burkett, Jr. 1946- *St&PR 93*
Stoner, Robert Franklin 1933- *St&PR 93*
Stoner, Roy Frederick *WhoScE 91-1*
Stoner, Samuel G. *ScF&FL 92*
Stoner, Sherri *BioIn 17*
Stoner, Susan Dee 1959- *WhoAmW 93*
Stoner, Thomas H. 1935- *WhoAm 92*
Stoner, Virgil Ray 1923- *St&PR 93*
Stones, (Cyril) Anthony 1934- *SmATA 72 [port]*
Stonesifer, Richard James 1922- *WhoAm 92*
Stoney, Janice D. 1940- *St&PR 93, WhoAm 92*
Stong, Mabel Ruth 1905- *AmWomPl*
Stong, Stephen J. 1953- *St&PR 93*
St-Onge, Denis Alderic 1929- *WhoAm 92*
Stonich, Timothy W. 1947- *St&PR 93*
Stonich, Timothy Whitman 1947- *WhoAm 92*
Stonier, Tom 1927- *WhoE 93*
Stonitch, William Jon 1951- *WhoWor 93*
Stonner, Dean Franklin *Law&B 92*
Stonnington, Henry Herbert 1927- *WhoSSW 93*
Stonor, Oliver *ScF&FL 92*
Stoodley, Dale G. *Law&B 92*
Stoodley, Dale G. 1939- *St&PR 93*
Stoodley, Richard John *WhoScE 91-1*
Stoodt, Barbara Dern 1934- *WhoAmW 93, WhoSSW 93*
Stooges, Three, The *QDrFCA 92 [port]*
Stookesberry, James J. 1940- *St&PR 93*
Stookey, George Kenneth 1935- *WhoAm 92*
Stookey, John Hoyt 1930- *St&PR 93, WhoAm 92*
Stookey, Laurence Hull 1937- *WhoAm 92*
Stookey, Noel Paul 1937- *WhoAm 92*
Stooksberry, Stanley Dwight 1934- *St&PR 93*
Stooksbury, Walter Elbert 1940- *WhoAm 92*
Stoolmiller, Allen Charles 1940- *WhoE 93*
Stoop, Johann J. *St&PR 93*
Stoop, Norma Mc Lain 1910- *WhoWrEP 92*
Stoop, Norma McLain 1910- *WhoAmW 93, WhoWor 93*
Stoopler, Mark Benjamin 1950- *WhoE 93*
Stoops, Alice Parry *AmWomPl*
Stoops, Denzel D. 1946- *St&PR 93*
Stoops, Georges J. 1937- *WhoScE 91-2*
Stoops, Lewis Emmor 1944- *WhoSSW 93*
Stopczyk, Mariusz J. 1935- *WhoScE 91-4*
Stopes, Marie Charlotte Carmichael 1880-1958 *BioIn 17*
Stophel, Sonya Whitlow 1967- *WhoSSW 93*
Stopherd, John Raymond 1945- *WhoE 93*
Stoppani, Andres Oscar Manuel 1915- *WhoWor 93*
Stoppard, Tom *BioIn 17*
Stoppard, Tom 1937- *ConAu 39NR, MagSWL [port], MiSFD 9, WhoAm 92, WhoWor 93, WorLitC [port]*
Stoppford, Michael J. 1953- *WhoUN 92*
Stopsky, David C. *Law&B 92*
Stor, Carl 1814-1889 *Baker 92*
Storaasli, Olaf Oliver 1943- *WhoSSW 93*
Storace *Baker 92*
Storace, Anna Selina 1765-1817 *BioIn 17*
Storace, Nancy 1765-1817 *Baker 92, BioIn 17, IntDcOp [port], OxDcOp*
Storace, Stephen c. 1725-c. 1781 *Baker 92*
Storace, Stephen 1762-1796 *OxDcOp*
Storace, Stephen (John Seymour) 1762-1796 *Baker 92*
Storandt, Martha 1938- *WhoAm 92, WhoAmW 93*
Storaro, Vittorio 1940- *WhoAm 92, WhoWor 93*
Storb, Ursula Beate 1936- *WhoAmW 93*
Storch, Arthur 1925- *WhoAm 92*
Storch, Barbara Jean 1942- *WhoSSW 93*
Storch, Joel Abraham 1949- *WhoE 93*
Storch, M. Anton 1813-1888 *Baker 92*
Storch, Marcie Y. *Law&B 92*
Storch, Margaret 1941- *ConAu 137*
Storch, Margaret Mary Bryce 1941- *WhoAmW 93, WhoE 93*
Storch, Volker 1943- *WhoScE 91-3*
Storchio, Rosina 1876-1945 *Baker 92, IntDcOp, OxDcOp*
Storchschnabel, Georg 1932- *WhoWor 93*
Storck, Alain 1949- *WhoScE 91-2*
Storck, Herb E. 1954- *St&PR 93*
Storck, Herbert Evan 1954- *WhoE 93, WhoEmL 93*
Storck, Karl G(ustav) L(udwig) 1873-1920 *Baker 92*
Stordahl, Larry D. 1942- *St&PR 93*
Storer, Donald E. 1939- *WhoAm 92, WhoE 93*
Storer, Donald Edgar 1939- *St&PR 93*
Storer, John 1858-1930 *Baker 92*
Storer, Larry D. 1945- *WhoSSW 93*
Storer, Morris Brewster 1904- *WhoAm 92*
Storer, Norman William 1930- *WhoAm 92*
Storer, Robert L. 1923- *St&PR 93*
Storer, Roy 1928- *WhoWor 93*
Storey, Alice *ScF&FL 92*
Storey, Anthony 1928- *ScF&FL 92*
Storey, Benjamin M., Jr. 1915- *St&PR 93*
Storey, Beverly Lu 1953- *WhoSSW 93*
Storey, Brit Allan 1941- *WhoAm 92*
Storey, Charles Porter 1922- *WhoAm 92*
Storey, Colin *WhoScE 91-1*
Storey, David 1933- *BioIn 17*
Storey, David John *WhoScE 91-1*
Storey, David Malcolm 1933- *WhoWor 93*
Storey, Frank H. 1933- *St&PR 93*
Storey, James Moorfield 1931- *WhoAm 92*
Storey, James Roger 1941- *WhoE 93*
Storey, John *WhoScE 91-1*
Storey, John 1947- *WhoWor 93*
Storey, June 1918- *SweetSg C [port]*
Storey, Kenneth Bruce 1949- *WhoAm 92*
Storey, M. John 1943- *St&PR 93*
Storey, Margaret 1926- *ScF&FL 92*
Storey, Moorfield 1845-1929 *EncAACR*
Storey, R.M.J. *WhoScE 91-1*
Storey, Rob 1936- *WhoAsAP 91*
Storey, Thomas J. 1922- *St&PR 93*
Storey, Veda Catherine 1956- *WhoAmW 93*
Storey, Will Miller 1931- *St&PR 93*
Storey, Woodrow Wilson 1912- *WhoAm 92*
Storie, Kyle G. *Law&B 92*
Storin, Matthew Victor 1942- *WhoAm 92, WhoE 93*
Storing, Paul Edward 1929- *WhoAm 92*
Stork, Donald Arthur 1939- *WhoAm 92*
Stork, Dylan *BioIn 17*
Stork, Gerald *St&PR 93*
Stork, Gilbert Josse 1921- *WhoAm 92*
Stork, Karl 1935- *St&PR 93*
Storke, William Frederick Joseph 1922- *WhoAm 92*
Storla, Richard *BioIn 17*
Storm, Christopher *ConAu 39NR*
Storm, Esben *MiSFD 9*
Storm, Gale 1922- *SweetSg D [port]*
Storm, Howard *MiSFD 9*
Storm, Hyemeyohsts 1935- *ScF&FL 92*
Storm, Jane Lauer *Law&B 92*
Storm, June Gleason 1918- *St&PR 93*
Storm, Nicolaas Gerard *Law&B 92*
Storm, William J. 1925- *St&PR 93*
Storme, Marcel Leon 1930- *WhoWor 93*
Stormer, Georg 1939- *WhoWor 93*
Stormer, Horst Ludwig 1949- *WhoAm 92*
Stormer, John Charles, Jr. 1941- *WhoAm 92*
Stormer, Kent Allen *Law&B 92*
Stormes, Ben F. 1922- *St&PR 93*
Stormont, Jonathan 1955- *WhoE 93*
Stormont, Richard Mansfield 1936- *WhoAm 92, WhoSSW 93*
Storms, Clifford B. *Law&B 92*
Storms, Clifford Beekman 1932- *St&PR 93, WhoAm 92, WhoWor 93*
Storms, Harrison A., Jr. d1992 *NewYTBS 92 [port]*
Storms, Harrison A(llen), Jr. 1915-1992 *CurBio 92N*
Storms, Kevin Patrick 1954- *St&PR 93*
Storms, Lowell Hanson 1928- *WhoAm 92*
Storms, Robert J. 1952- *St&PR 93*
Storms, Stephanie A. *Law&B 92*
Storni, Alfonsina 1892-1938 *BioIn 17*
Storoschuk, Stephen *ScF&FL 92*
Storr, Catherine 1913- *ScF&FL 92*
Storr, Hans George 1931- *St&PR 93*
Storr, John Frederick 1915- *WhoWrEP 92*
Storr, Robert *BioIn 17*
Storr, Robert 1949- *WhoAm 92*
Storrs, Eleanor Emerett 1926- *WhoAm 92*
Storrs, James Hollister 1944- *WhoE 93*
Storrs, Norman B. 1934- *St&PR 93*
Storrs, Thomas Irwin 1918- *WhoAm 92*
Storrs, Val B. 1931- *St&PR 93*
Storry, Junis Oliver 1920- *WhoAm 92*
Storseth, Jeannie Pearce 1948- *WhoAmW 93*
Storseth, Marjorie *St&PR 93*
Storseth, S. L. 1927- *St&PR 93*
Storstrom, Helge 1935- *WhoScE 91-4*
Stortz, John Dixon 1935- *WhoAm 92*
Stortz, Thomas C. *Law&B 92*
Story, Anne Winthrop 1914- *WhoE 93*
Story, Anthony d1991 *BioIn 17*
Story, Benjamin Sprague, III 1945- *St&PR 93*
Story, Bruce Allen 1952- *WhoSSW 93*
Story, Carol M. 1947- *WhoAmW 93, WhoE 93*
Story, Charles S. 1946- *St&PR 93*
Story, David Frederick 1940- *WhoWor 93*
Story, Donny R. *St&PR 93*
Story, Elliott Lemuel 1821-1886 *BioIn 17*
Story, George Morley 1927- *WhoAm 92, WhoWrEP 92*
Story, Gertrude 1929- *WhoCanL 92*
Story, Jack Trevor 1917-1991 *AnObit 1991, ConAu 136, ScF&FL 92*
Story, James Clinton 1939- *WhoAm 92*
Story, Jim Lewis 1931- *WhoAm 92*
Story, John Townsend 1940- *St&PR 93*
Story, Joseph 1779-1845 *OxCSupC [port]*

Story, Joseph A. Law&B 92
Story, Leslie J. 1939- St&PR 93
Story, Liz 1956- Baker 92
Story, Mark MiSFD 9
Story, Mona Dee 1945- WhoAmW 93
Story, Richard P. 1952- St&PR 93
Stos, Jerzy 1941- WhoScE 91-4
Stosz, Sandra L. BioIn 17
Stosz, Sandra Leigh 1960- WhoAmW 93
Stothard, David W. 1948- St&PR 93
Stothard, James Vincent 1943- St&PR 93
Stothers, John B. 1931- WhoAm 92
Stotland, Ezra 1924- WhoAm 92
Stotlar, Cynthia Byrd 1953- WhoAmW 93, WhoEmL 93
Stotler, Alicemarie H. 1942- WhoAm 92, WhoAmW 93
Stotler, John L. Law&B 92
Stotler, John Leonard 1938- St&PR 93, WhoAm 92
Stotser, George Raymond 1935- WhoAm 92
Stotsky, Janet Gale 1959- WhoAmW 93
Stott, A.N.B. WhoScE 91-1
Stott, Barbara Paxton 1925- WhoAmW 93
Stott, Brian 1941- WhoAm 92
Stott, Donald B. 1939- St&PR 93
Stott, Donald Bishop 1939- WhoE 93
Stott, Dorothy M. BioIn 17
Stott, Grady Bernell 1921- WhoAm 92
Stott, Jill Ann 1959- WhoE 93
Stott, John R. W. 1921- ConAu 40NR
Stott, K.G. 1928- WhoScE 91-1
Stott, Kathleen AmWomPl
Stott, Mary Roelofs 1918- WhoWrEP 92
Stott, Nancy Netzel Law&B 92
Stott, Paul Edwin 1948- WhoE 93
Stott, Richard Keith 1943- WhoWor 93
Stott, Stephen L. 1942- WhoScE 91-1
Stott, Thomas Edward, Jr. 1923- WhoAm 92
Stott, William Ross, Jr. 1935- WhoAm 92
Stotter, David W. 1904- WhoAm 92
Stotter, Harry Shelton 1928- WhoAm 92
Stotter, Lawrence Henry 1929- WhoAm 92
Stottlemyer, David Lee 1935- WhoAm 92
Stottlemyre, Melvin Leon, Sr. 1941- BiDAMSp 1989
Stotts, J. Bradley 1962- St&PR 93
Stotts, Paul Alan 1943- St&PR 93
Stotz, Carl E. d1992 BioIn 17, NewYTBS 92
Stotzas d545 OxDcByz
Stotzer, Beatriz Olvera 1950- NotHsAW 93
Stotzfus, Ben Frank 1927- WhoWrEP 92
Stoudemire, Sterling A. d1992 NewYTBS 92
Stoudemire, Sterling A. 1902-1992 BioIn 17
Stoudemire, Sterling A(ubrey) 1902-1992 ConAu 137
Stoudenmire, Dallas 1845-1882 BioIn 17
Stouder, Leo Benjamin, Jr. 1956- WhoSSW 93
Stoudt, Daniel G. 1946- St&PR 93
Stoudt, H. Craig 1955- St&PR 93
Stoudt, Marilyn Ann 1934- WhoAmW 93
Stoudt, Richard Mayo 1929- St&PR 93
Stoudt, Thomas Henry 1922- WhoE 93
Stoufer, Ruth Hendrix 1916- WhoAmW 93
Stouffer, Edith J. AmWomPl
Stouffer, Larry Lee 1942- St&PR 93
Stouffer, Mark MiSFD 9
Stouffer, Nancy Kathleen 1951- WhoE 93
Stough, Patricia Marie 1950- WhoAmW 93
Stoughton, Beverly Foss 1932- WhoWrEP 92
Stoughton, David H. Law&B 92
Stoughton, Richard Baker 1923- WhoAm 92
Stoughton, Richard E. 1920- St&PR 93
Stoughton, Richard P. ScF&FL 92
Stoughton, W. Vickery 1946- WhoAm 92
Stoumen, Louis Clyde 1917-1991 BioIn 17
Stoup, Arthur Harry 1925- WhoAm 92, WhoWor 93
Stout, Alan (Burrage) 1932- Baker 92
Stout, Alan C. 1947- St&PR 93
Stout, Amy 1960- ScF&FL 92
Stout, Andrew Varick 1902-1991 BioIn 17
Stout, Anthony Carder 1939- WhoWor 93
Stout, Arthur Wendel, III 1949- WhoSSW 93
Stout, Bill A. 1932- WhoAm 92
Stout, Carter Louis 1960- WhoSSW 93
Stout, D. R. 1937- St&PR 93
Stout, David 1942- ConAu 136
Stout, Dennis Lee 1948- WhoAm 92
Stout, Don B. 1936- St&PR 93
Stout, Donald E. Law&B 92
Stout, Donald Everett 1926- St&PR 93, WhoWor 93
Stout, Donald Roy 1938- WhoSSW 93
Stout, Douglas Richard 1945- WhoE 93
Stout, Edward Irvin 1939- WhoWor 93
Stout, Elisabeth R. 1950- St&PR 93
Stout, Francis Joseph 1926- WhoE 93
Stout, Gene Edwin 1933- St&PR 93
Stout, Glenn 1958- ConAu 138
Stout, Glenn Emanuel 1920- WhoAm 92
Stout, Gregory Stansbury 1915- WhoAm 92
Stout, James C. 1936- St&PR 93
Stout, Janis P. 1939- ConAu 139
Stout, Jerry W. 1951- St&PR 93
Stout, John Frederick 1925- St&PR 93
Stout, John Thomas, Jr. 1954- St&PR 93
Stout, John Wilson 1942- WhoE 93
Stout, Joseph Norman 1957- WhoSSW 93
Stout, Josephine Singerman WhoSSW 93
Stout, Juanita Kidd 1919- WhoAmW 93
Stout, Kate 1949- WhoWrEP 92
Stout, Kenneth John WhoScE 91-1
Stout, Landon Clarke, Jr. 1933- WhoSSW 93
Stout, Linda BioIn 17
Stout, Lonnie James, II 1947- St&PR 93, WhoAm 92
Stout, Madalyn Joanne 1954- WhoWrEP 92
Stout, Marguerite Annette WhoAmW 93
Stout, Mark Robert 1962- WhoE 93
Stout, Michael W. St&PR 93
Stout, Mike ScF&FL 92
Stout, N.L. Sunny 1950- WhoWor 93
Stout, Nancy 1942- ConAu 137
Stout, Rex 1886-1975 ScF&FL 92
Stout, Richard A. 1927- WhoIns 93
Stout, Robert L. St&PR 93
Stout, Robert William WhoScE 91-1
Stout, Samuel Darrel 1943- WhoAm 92
Stout, Thomas Calvin 1939- St&PR 93
Stout, Thomas James 1964- WhoWrEP 92
Stout, Tim 1946- ScF&FL 92
Stout, Travis BioIn 17
Stout, Virgil Loomis 1921- WhoAm 92
Stout, William Jewell 1914- WhoAm 92
Stout, William M. 1941- St&PR 93
Stoutamore, James B. 1931- St&PR 93
Stoute, Marguerite Allyn 1949- WhoEmL 93
Stoutenbeek, Christiaan Peter 1947- WhoWor 93
Stoutenburg, Adrien 1916-1982 ScF&FL 92
Stoutenburgh, Robert Dean 1944- WhoSSW 93
Stout-Pierce, Susan 1954- WhoAmW 93
Stout-Powell, Brenda Lee 1960- WhoAmW 93
Stoutt, Lavity 1929- DcCPCAm
Stoutz, Edmond de 1920- Baker 92
Stovall, Allen D. 1937- WhoAm 92
Stovall, David Calvin 1941- WhoSSW 93
Stovall, David D. 1956- St&PR 93
Stovall, David Dwight 1956- WhoSSW 93
Stovall, Doris Grace 1934- WhoAmW 93
Stovall, Floyd 1896- ScF&FL 92
Stovall, Geleta H. Law&B 92
Stovall, James Truman, III 1937- WhoUN 92
Stovall, Jerry 1936- WhoAm 92
Stovall, Jerry C. 1936- WhoIns 93
Stovall, Robert H. BioIn 17
Stovall, Robert Henry 1926- WhoAm 92
Stove, D. C. ConAu 136
Stove, David (Charles) 1927- ConAu 136
Stoveken, James Edwin, Jr. 1939- St&PR 93
Stover, A. ScF&FL 92
Stover, Barbara M. St&PR 93
Stover, Brian Allan 1947- WhoSSW 93
Stover, Carl Frederick 1930- WhoAm 92, WhoE 93
Stover, David Frank 1941- WhoAm 92
Stover, F. Gary 1945- St&PR 93
Stover, Glenn A. Law&B 92
Stover, Gordon Rishel, Jr. 1948- WhoSSW 93
Stover, Harry M. 1926- WhoAm 92
Stover, Harry Manning 1926- St&PR 93
Stover, James Howard 1911- WhoAm 92
Stover, James Michael Law&B 92
Stover, James Robert 1927- St&PR 93
Stover, John Ford 1912- WhoAm 92
Stover, John Raymond Law&B 92
Stover, Joseph G. Law&B 92
Stover, Larry K. 1946- St&PR 93
Stover, Leon 1929- ScF&FL 92
Stover, Leon Eugene 1929- WhoAm 92
Stover, Martha Ellen Law&B 92
Stover, Matthew Joseph 1955- St&PR 93, WhoAm 92, WhoE 93
Stover, Paula LeFan 1941- WhoAmW 93
Stover, Phil Sheridan, Jr. 1926- WhoAm 92
Stover, Richard Louis 1942- St&PR 93
Stover, W. Robert 1921- St&PR 93
Stover, Wendy Smith 1945- WhoAm 92
Stover, William R. 1922- St&PR 93, WhoIns 93
Stover, William Reitzel 1906- WhoSSW 93
Stover, William Ruffner 1922- WhoAm 92
Stow, Clara AmWomPl
Stow, Edith 1875- AmWomPl
Stow, Randolph 1935- BioIn 17, IntLitE, ScF&FL 92
Stow, (Julian) Randolph 1935- DcChlFi
Stoward, P.J. WhoScE 91-1
Stowasser, Friedrich 1928- WhoWor 93
Stowe, Allen Howard 1937- St&PR 93
Stowe, David Henry 1910- WhoAm 92
Stowe, David Henry, Jr. 1936- St&PR 93, WhoAm 92, WhoWor 93
Stowe, David Metz 1919- WhoAm 92
Stowe, Harriet Beecher 1811-1896 BioIn 17, MagSAmL [port], WorLitC [port]
Stowe, Harriet (Elizabeth) Beecher 1811-1896 MajAI [port]
Stowe, Hugh A. Law&B 92
Stowe, Jacqueline 1936- WhoSSW 93
Stowe, John V. Law&B 92
Stowe, Leland 1899- BioIn 17, JrnUS, WhoAm 92
Stowe, Nonnie St&PR 93
Stowe, Nonnie 1934- WhoIns 93
Stowe, Pauline Malovrh 1927- WhoAmW 93
Stowe, Robert Lee, III 1954- WhoSSW 93
Stowe, William S. Law&B 92
Stowell, Calvin S. 1950- St&PR 93
Stowell, Christopher R. 1966- WhoAm 92
Stowell, Frank Arthur WhoScE 91-1
Stowell, Harold Hilton 1956- WhoSSW 93
Stowell, Jett E. 1942- St&PR 93
Stowell, Kent 1939- WhoAm 92
Stowell, Robert Eugene 1914- WhoAm 92
Stowell, Robert John Law&B 92
Stowell, Samuel C. 1929- St&PR 93
Stowens, Daniel 1919- WhoE 93
Stowers, Carlton Eugene 1942- WhoAm 92
Stowers, Freddie d1918 BioIn 17
Stowers, James Evans, Jr. 1924- WhoAm 92
Stowers, John Marcus 1919- WhoWor 93
Stowers, Judy Marie 1944- WhoAmW 93
Stowes, Patricia Anne 1948- WhoAmW 93, WhoEmL 93, WhoSSW 93, WhoWor 93
Stoy, C. Volkmar 1924- WhoScE 91-4
Stoyak, Debra A. 1957- St&PR 93
Stoyan, Dietrich Kurt 1940- WhoWor 93
Stoyanoff, David J. Law&B 92
Stoyanov, Pencho 1931- Baker 92
Stoyanov, Veselin 1902-1969 Baker 92
Stoychev, Mitko 1929- WhoScE 91-4
Stoychkov, Jordan 1931- WhoScE 91-4
Stoyko, William N. 1946- St&PR 93
Stoyko, William Nelson Law&B 92
Stoykovich, Christine Anne 1949- WhoAmW 93
Stoynoff, R. D. 1946- St&PR 93
Straat, Kent Leon 1934- WhoE 93
Straat, Patricia Ann 1936- WhoAmW 93
Straatsma, Bradley Ralph 1927- WhoAm 92
Straayer, Carole Kathleen 1934- WhoAmW 93
Strabo c. 63BC-c. 21AD OxDcByz
Straboromanos, Manuel c. 1070- OxDcByz
Straburzynski, Gerard WhoScE 91-4
Straburzynski, Gerard Stanislaw 1930- WhoScE 91-4
Stracciari, Riccardo 1875-1955 Baker 92, IntDcOp, OxDcOp
Stracer, Slavomir d1990 BioIn 17
Strach, Michael William 1930- St&PR 93
Strachan, Alan James WhoScE 91-1
Strachan, David E. 1947- WhoAm 92
Strachan, Donald M. 1923- WhoAm 92
Strachan, Edna Higgins AmWomPl
Strachan, Graham 1938- WhoE 93
Strachan, Harry L., III Law&B 92
Strachan, Ian ScF&FL 92
Strachan, Ian 1938- ChlFicS
Strachan, James 1828-1893 BioIn 17
Strachan, Jane Ann 1950- WhoAmW 93
Strachan, Leroy BioIn 17
Strachan, Lynn Ann Wilson 1957- WhoSSW 93
Strachan, Patricia Harting 1948- WhoWrEP 92
Strachan, Stuart Raeburn Law&B 92
Strachan, Winifred DcCPCAm
Stracher, Alfred 1930- WhoAm 92
Stracher, Dorothy Altman 1934- WhoE 93
Strachey, Barbara 1912- ScF&FL 92
Strachey, Lytton 1880-1932 BritWr S2, DcLB DS10
Strachman, Howard Lewis 1944- St&PR 93
Strack, Ann Marie 1968- WhoAmW 93
Strack, Harold Arthur 1923- WhoAm 92, WhoWor 93
Strack, Lilian Holmes 1886- AmWomPl
Strack, William Richard 1936- St&PR 93
Stracke, Kenneth J. 1928- St&PR 93
Stracke, Win 1908-1991 BioIn 17
Straczynski, J. Michael 1954- ScF&FL 92
Strada, Anna Maria fl. 18th cent.- Baker 92
Strada, Christina Bryson WhoAmW 93
Strada del Po, Anna fl. 1720-1740 OxDcOp
Strada del Po, Anna Maria fl. 18th cent.- Baker 92
Stradal, August 1860-1930 Baker 92
Stradella, Alessandro 1639-1682 Baker 92
Stradella, Alessandro 1644-1682 OxDcOp
Strader, Haywood 1935- St&PR 93
Strader, Theodore J. 1953- St&PR 93
Stradiot, James E. 1959- St&PR 93
Stradivari, Antonio 1644-1737 Baker 92
Stradivari, Francesco 1671-1743 Baker 92
Stradivari, Omobono 1679-1742 Baker 92
Stradivarius, Antonio 1644-1737 Baker 92
Stradley, Carolyn J. 1946- ConEn
Stradley, David Cowan 1922- WhoAm 92
Stradley, William Jackson 1939- WhoAm 92, WhoWor 93
Stradley, William Lamar 1940- WhoSSW 93
Stradling, Richard Anthony WhoScE 91-1
Stradwick, John Conway 1930- St&PR 93
Straede, Christen Andersen 1952- WhoWor 93
Straesser, Joep 1934- Baker 92
Straeter, Jane L. 1919- WhoWor 93
Straetker, Diane Mogannam 1960- WhoAmW 93
Straetz, Donald Frederick 1938- WhoE 93
Straetz, Robert P. 1921- St&PR 93, WhoAm 92
Straffon, Ralph Atwood 1928- WhoAm 92
Strafford, Kenneth Norman WhoScE 91-1
Strafford, William Francis 1943- St&PR 93
Strahan, Bradley R. 1937- WhoWrEP 92
Strahan, Julia Celestine 1938- WhoAmW 93
Strahan, Linda Carol 1945- WhoE 93
Strahan, Randall (W.) 1954- ConAu 136
Strahan, Ronald 1922- WhoWor 93
Strahilevitz, Meir 1935- WhoWor 93
Strahilov, D. WhoScE 91-4
Strahl-Bolstorff, Donna Myrtle 1940- WhoAmW 93
Strahle, Warren Charles 1938- WhoAm 92
Strahler, Arthur N(ewell) 1918- ConAu 139
Strahler, Violet Ruth 1918- WhoWor 93
Strahm, Samuel Edward 1936- WhoAm 92
Strahs, Martin Paul St&PR 93
Straight, Beatrice Whitney 1918- WhoAm 92, WhoE 93
Straight, Clio Edwin d1991 BioIn 17
Straight, William Goddard 1937- WhoSSW 93
Strain, David L. 1921- St&PR 93
Strain, Denise O'Brien Law&B 92
Strain, Douglas C. 1919- St&PR 93
Strain, Gladys Witt 1934- WhoE 93
Strain, James Ellsworth 1923- WhoAm 92
Strain, Jennifer M.H. Law&B 92
Strain, John J. 1939- St&PR 93
Strain, Lee O. 1938- St&PR 93
Strain, Lucille Brewton WhoE 93
Strain, Richard Allen 1942- St&PR 93
Strain, Robert W. 1924- WhoIns 93
Strain, Ronald Reid 1935- St&PR 93
Strait, Bradley Justus 1932- WhoAm 92
Strait, Charles McIver 1931- St&PR 93
Strait, George 1952- WhoAm 92
Strait, Gregory Mark 1950- St&PR 93
Strait, Peggy Tang 1933- WhoE 93
Strait, Ralph d1992 NewYTBS 92
Strait, Rick E. 1947- St&PR 93
Strait, William Henry Law&B 92
Straiton, Archie Waugh 1907- WhoAm 92
Straiton, John S(eal) 1922- ConAu 136
Straitz, John Frederick 1946- St&PR 93
Straka, Angeline C. Law&B 92
Straka, Herbert Karl 1920- WhoWor 93
Straka, Laszlo 1934- St&PR 93
Straka, Laszlo Richard 1934- WhoAm 92, WhoWor 93
Straka, Randolph J. 1952- St&PR 93
Strakacz, Sylwin George 1892-1973 PolBiDi
Strake, D. A. 1940- St&PR 93
Straker, Edward Albert, Sr. 1937- St&PR 93
Straker, J. W. 1921- St&PR 93
Straker, Philip ScF&FL 92
Strakosch, Ferdinando d1902 OxDcOp
Strakosch, Katherine Wenton 1933- WhoAmW 93
Strakosch, Maurice 1825-1887 Baker 92
Strakosch, Max 1834-1852 OxDcOp
Strakosch, Max 1835-1892 See Strakosch, Maurice 1825-1887 Baker 92
Stralem, Pierre 1909- WhoAm 92
Straley, Ruth A. Stewart 1949- WhoAmW 93

Straling, Phillip Francis 1933- *WhoAm 92*
Stram, Hank Louis 1923- *WhoAm 92*
Strambini, Giovanni B. 1944- *WhoScE 91-3*
Stramignoni, Aldo 1923- *WhoScE 91-3*
Stranahan, Robert Paul, Jr. 1929- *WhoAm 92*
Stranberg, Wynne Lee 1948- *WhoAmW 93*
Strand, Beverly M. 1949- *WhoEmL 93*
Strand, C. Torsten 1939- *WhoScE 91-4*
Strand, Charles G. 1947- *St&PR 93*
Strand, Curt Robert 1920- *WhoAm 92*
Strand, David Axel 1935- *WhoAm 92*
Strand, Eloise Brown 1929- *AfrAmBi [port]*
Strand, Gerald C. 1938- *St&PR 93*
Strand, Marion Delores 1927- *WhoAmW 93*
Strand, Mark 1934- *BioIn 17, ConAu 40NR, ConLC 71 [port], WhoAm 92, WhoWrEP 92*
Strand, Paul 1890-1976 *BioIn 17*
Strand, Ray Walter 1924- *St&PR 93*
Strand, Rebecca *BioIn 17*
Strand, Richard A. 1935- *St&PR 93*
Strand, Roger Gordon 1934- *WhoAm 92*
Strand, Sven-Erik 1946- *WhoScE 91-4*
Strand, Ted Raymond, Jr. 1945- *WhoWor 93*
Strand, William Keith 1931- *St&PR 93*
Strandberg, Keith William 1957- *WhoWrEP 92*
Strandberg, Kyell *WhoScE 91-4*
Strandberg, Malcom Woodrow Pershing 1919- *WhoAm 92*
Strandberg, Newton Dwight 1921- *WhoSSW 93*
Strandberg, Sven Ake 1927- *WhoWor 93*
Strandberg, Victor Hugo 1935- *WhoSSW 93*
Stranddorf, Peter *WhoScE 91-2*
Strandenes, Siri Pettersen 1949- *WhoWor 93*
Strandgaard, Helmuth 1927- *WhoScE 91-2*
Strandjord, Mary Jeannine 1945- *St&PR 93, WhoAm 92*
Strandjord, Paul Edphil 1931- *WhoAm 92*
Strandman, Benkt Ivar 1936- *WhoWor 93*
Strandness, Donald Eugene, Jr. 1928- *WhoAm 92*
Strandwitz, Norman C. 1933- *St&PR 93*
Strane, Susan 1944- *ConAu 136*
Straney, Gerald R. 1946- *WhoSSW 93*
Strang, Allen L. *Law&B 92*
Strang, Allen Louis 1951- *St&PR 93*
Strang, Charles D. 1921- *St&PR 93*
Strang, Charles Daniel 1921- *WhoAm 92*
Strang, Emily *AmWomPl*
Strang, George Ellis 1939- *St&PR 93*
Strang, Gerald 1908-1983 *Baker 92*
Strang, Gunnar d1992 *NewYTBS 92 [port]*
Strang, Gunnar 1906-1992 *BioIn 17*
Strang, John Lawrence 1951- *WhoE 93*
Strang, Leonard Birnie *WhoScE 91-1*
Strang, Marian Boundy 1918- *WhoAm 92*
Strang, Richard N. 1929- *St&PR 93*
Strang, Ruth Hancock 1923- *WhoAm 92*
Strang, Sandra Lee 1936- *WhoAmW 93*
Strang, Stephen Edward 1951- *WhoAm 92*
Strang, William Gilbert 1934- *WhoAm 92*
Strange, Curtis *BioIn 17*
Strange, Curtis Northrop 1955- *BiDAMSp 1989, WhoAm 92*
Strange, Donald Ernest 1944- *WhoAm 92*
Strange, Douglas Hart McKoy 1929- *WhoSSW 93*
Strange, Glenn 1899-1973 *BioIn 17*
Strange, J. Leland 1941- *WhoAm 92*
Strange, James Leland 1941- *St&PR 93*
Strange, Joanna Gleed *AmWomPl*
Strange, John H. *WhoScE 91-1*
Strange, John Robert 1950- *WhoSSW 93*
Strange, Michael *AmWomPl*
Strange, Peter Stanton 1949- *WhoAm 92*
Strange, Randall S. *Law&B 92*
Strange, Theresa Margaret 1964- *WhoWor 93*
Strange, William Bryan, III *Law&B 92*
Strangfeld, James E. 1946- *St&PR 93*
Strangi, Thomas Carl 1957- *St&PR 93*
Strangis, Joel Stephen 1948- *WhoSSW 93*
Strangway, David William 1934- *WhoAm 92*
Stranka, Erwin 1935- *DrEEuF*
Strano, Richard August 1943- *WhoAm 92*
Stransky, Annette Cecelia 1948- *WhoAmW 93*
Stransky, Josef 1872-1936 *Baker 92*
Stransky, Minnie Block 1912- *WhoAmW 93*
Stranz, Paul Michael 1959- *WhoSSW 93*
Strapp, Paul E. *Law&B 92*
Straram, Walther 1876-1933 *Baker 92*
Strasberg, Andy *BioIn 17*
Strasberg, Daoma *ScF&FL 92*
Strasberg, Jeffrey H. 1957- *St&PR 93*
Strasberg, Susan 1938- *WhoAm 92*
Strasburger, Joseph Julius 1913- *WhoAm 92*
Strasen, Kenneth Richard 1945- *St&PR 93*
Strasfogel, Ian 1940- *WhoAm 92*
Strasfogel, Ignace 1909- *WhoAm 92*
Strasheim, Gene A. 1940- *St&PR 93*
Strasma, John Drinan 1932- *WhoAm 92*
Strasma, Norman Edward 1932- *St&PR 93*
Strass, John J. 1956- *St&PR 93*
Strassberg, Merri *St&PR 93*
Strassberg, Stanley 1932- *St&PR 93*
Strassburg, Robert 1915- *Baker 92*
Strassburger, Gustav Alfred 1939- *WhoSSW 93*
Strassburger, John 1960- *WhoSSW 93*
Strassen, Volker 1936- *WhoWor 93*
Strasser, Bruce Elliott 1925- *St&PR 93*
Strasser, David J. *Law&B 92*
Strasser, Elmer E. 1912- *St&PR 93*
Strasser, Ewald 1867-1933 *Baker 92*
Strasser, Gabor 1929- *WhoAm 92*
Strasser, Harold A. 1907- *St&PR 93*
Strasser, Jack C. 1934- *WhoSSW 93*
Strasser, Joel A. 1938- *WhoE 93*
Strasser, Louis A. 1934- *St&PR 93*
Strasser, Peter R. 1938- *St&PR 93*
Strasser, Reto J. 1943- *WhoScE 91-4*
Strasser, Richard J., Jr. 1947- *St&PR 93*
Strasser, Richard Joseph, Jr. 1947- *WhoAm 92*
Strasser, Robin 1945- *ConTFT 10, WhoAm 92*
Strasser, Rose Louise 1907- *WhoAmW 93*
Strasser, Steven Frederick 1946- *WhoAm 92*
Strasser, Todd 1950- *DcAmChF 1985, MajAI [port], ScF&FL 92, SmATA 71 [port], WhoWrEP 92*
Strasser, William Carl, Jr. 1930- *WhoAm 92*
Strasser-King, Victor Esehwanu 1942- *WhoWor 93*
Strassl, Hubert *ScF&FL 92*
Strassler, Gerald N. 1927- *St&PR 93*
Strassler, Marc *Law&B 92*
Strassman, John Michael 1953- *St&PR 93*
Strassmann, W. Paul 1926- *WhoAm 92*
Strassmeyer, Amy *Law&B 92*
Strassmeyer, Mary 1929- *WhoAm 92*
Strassner, Laurence M. 1941- *St&PR 93*
Strasz, Witold 1955- *WhoWor 93*
Straszheim, Donald Henry 1941- *WhoAm 92*
Stratakis, Anastasia 1938- *Baker 92*
Stratas, Teresa *BioIn 17*
Stratas, Teresa 1938- *Baker 92, IntDcOp, OxDcOp, WhoAm 92, WhoWor 93*
Strate, Robert A. 1944- *St&PR 93*
Strategier, Herman 1912-1988 *Baker 92*
Strategopoulos, Alexios fl. 13th cent.- *OxDcByz*
Stratemeier, Edward H. *Law&B 92*
Stratemeyer, Edward 1862-1930 *BioIn 17*
Stratemeyer, Edward L. 1862-1930 *MajAI [port], ScF&FL 92*
Stratemeyer, George Edward 1890-1969 *HarEnMi*
Stratford, Lauren *BioIn 17*
Stratford, Philip 1927- *WhoCanL 92*
Stratford, Ray Paul 1925- *WhoAm 92*
Strathern, Fiona Lamont 1947- *WhoAmW 93*
Strathman, Charles O. *Law&B 92*
Strathmeyer, Michael 1953- *St&PR 93*
Stratiev, A.V. 1929- *WhoScE 91-4*
Stratis, George 1947- *WhoE 93*
Stratman, John W. *Law&B 92*
Stratman, Joseph Lee 1924- *WhoAm 92*
Stratman, Orlando John 1951- *St&PR 93*
Stratmann, Gayle G. *Law&B 92*
Straton, John Charles, Jr. 1932- *WhoAm 92*
Stratoudakis, James Peter 1949- *WhoE 93*
Stratt, Randy Allen 1956- *St&PR 93*
Strattan, Byron Doan 1930- *St&PR 93*
Strattan, Charles Edward 1945- *WhoSSW 93*
Stratten, Dorothy 1960-1980 *BioIn 17*
Strattner, Lawrence J. *St&PR 93*
Stratton, Allan 1951- *WhoCanL 92*
Stratton, Anna Reese *AmWomPl*
Stratton, Cedric 1931- *WhoSSW 93*
Stratton, Charles Abner 1916- *WhoSSW 93*
Stratton, Charles Lynn 1944- *St&PR 93*
Stratton, Elizabeth Macy 1958- *WhoE 93*
Stratton, Frederick Prescott, Jr. 1939- *St&PR 93*
Stratton, George (Robert) 1897-1954 *Baker 92*
Stratton, Gregory Alexander 1946- *WhoAm 92*
Stratton, James W. 1936- *St&PR 93*
Stratton, Jane L. *Law&B 92*
Stratton, John E. 1929- *St&PR 93*
Stratton, Julius Adams 1901- *WhoAm 92*
Stratton, Lewis Palmer 1937- *WhoSSW 93*
Stratton, Lois Jean 1927- *WhoAmW 93*
Stratton, Mariann 1945- *WhoAmW 93*
Stratton, Monica *ScF&FL 92*
Stratton, Monty Eugene *Law&B 92*
Stratton, Richard Allen 1931- *WhoE 93*
Stratton, Robert 1928- *WhoAm 92*
Stratton, Rodney Patrick *WhoScE 91-1*
Stratton, Samuel S. *BioIn 17*
Stratton, Stephen Samuel 1840-1906 *Baker 92*
Stratton, Thomas Oliver 1930- *WhoAm 92*
Stratton, Thomas William 1946- *WhoWrEP 92*
Stratton, Walter Love 1926- *WhoAm 92*
Stratton, William G. 1914- *BioIn 17*
Stratton, William Grant 1914- *St&PR 93*
Stratton, William R. 1934- *St&PR 93*
Stratton, William Richard 1934- *WhoAm 92*
Stratton-Crooke, Thomas Edward 1933- *WhoAm 92*
Stratton-Porter, Gene 1863-1924 *BioIn 17, MajAI [port]*
Stratton-Porter, Gene(va Grace) 1863-1924 *ConAu 137*
Straty, Stephen M. 1955- *St&PR 93*
Straub, Carl C., Jr. *Law&B 92*
Straub, Chester J. 1937- *St&PR 93*
Straub, Chester John 1937- *WhoAm 92*
Straub, Donald A. 1933- *St&PR 93*
Straub, Frank G. 1932- *St&PR 93*
Straub, Gerard Donald 1945- *St&PR 93*
Straub, Gerhard Herbert 1936- *WhoWor 93*
Straub, Herbert J. 1927- *St&PR 93*
Straub, Jean-Marie 1933- *MiSFD 9*
Straub, Jennifer 1959- *St&PR 93*
Straub, John W. 1926- *St&PR 93*
Straub, Melvin J. 1930- *St&PR 93*
Straub, Peter *BioIn 17*
Straub, Peter 1943- *ScF&FL 92*
Straub, Peter Francis 1943- *WhoAm 92, WhoWrEP 92*
Straub, Peter Thornton 1939- *WhoAm 92*
Straub, Ralph W. 1927- *WhoScE 91-4*
Straub, Sylvia Ann 1938- *WhoE 93*
Straub, Terrence D. 1945- *St&PR 93*
Straub, William D. 1932- *St&PR 93*
Straub, Willy *WhoScE 91-4*
Straube, Harald 1926- *WhoScE 91-4*
Straube, Karl 1873-1950 *Baker 92*
Straube, Win *St&PR 93*
Straubing, Charles Robert 1921- *St&PR 93*
Strauch, Charles S. 1935- *St&PR 93*
Strauch, Dennis G. *St&PR 93*
Strauch, Dieter 1928- *WhoScE 91-3*
Strauch, Dieter 1940- *WhoScE 91-3*
Strauch, Friedrich 1935- *WhoScE 91-3*
Strauch, Gerald Otto 1932- *WhoAm 92*
Strauch, Karl 1922- *WhoAm 92*
Strauch, Katina *ScF&FL 92*
Strauch, Lisa H. *Law&B 92*
Strauch, Patricia *St&PR 93*
Strauch, Ralph E. 1937- *WhoWrEP 92*
Strauch, Richard George 1934- *WhoAm 92*
Strauch, Roger A. *St&PR 93*
Straughan, Brian *WhoScE 91-1*
Straughan, Brian Penrose *WhoScE 91-1*
Straughan, Carol Annette 1935- *WhoAmW 93*
Straughn, Claire Valencia Lee 1953- *WhoAmW 93*
Straumanis, John Janis, Jr. 1935- *WhoAm 92*
Straumann, Heinrich 1902-1991 *BioIn 17*
Straus, Austin Guy 1939- *WhoWrEP 92*
Straus, David Conrad 1947- *WhoSSW 93*
Straus, David J. 1923- *St&PR 93*
Straus, Dennis *WhoWrEP 92*
Straus, Dennis 1940?- *ScF&FL 92*
Straus, Donald Blun 1916- *WhoAm 92*
Straus, Helen Lorna Puttkammer 1933- *WhoAmW 93*
Straus, Helen Sachs 1895-1990 *BioIn 17*
Straus, Irving Lehman 1921- *WhoAm 92*
Straus, Isidor 1845-1912 *JeAmHC*
Straus, Joseph Pennington 1911- *WhoAm 92*
Straus, Kenneth Hollister 1925- *WhoAm 92*
Straus, Kim 1946- *St&PR 93*
Straus, Nathan 1848-1931 *BioIn 17, JeAmHC*
Straus, Oscar 1870-1954 *Baker 92, OxDcOp*
Straus, Oscar S. 1914- *St&PR 93*
Straus, Oscar S., II 1914- *WhoAm 92, WhoWor 93*
Straus, Oscar Solomon 1850-1926 *JeAmHC*
Straus, Peter *St&PR 93*
Straus, R. Peter 1923- *WhoAm 92*
Straus, Reuben 1907-1991 *BioIn 17*
Straus, Robert 1923- *WhoAm 92*
Straus, Roger W., Jr. 1917- *WhoAm 92*
Straus, Thomas James *Law&B 92*
Strausbaugh, Melvin Roy 1936- *WhoE 93*
Strausborger, David Edwin 1948- *St&PR 93*
Strausburg, William Wayne 1939- *St&PR 93*
Strauser, Charles Wayne 1953- *St&PR 93*
Strauser, Robert Wayne 1943- *WhoAm 92, WhoSSW 93, WhoWor 93*
Strausman, Jack E. *Law&B 92*
Strauss *Baker 92*
Strauss, Abby F. *Law&B 92*
Strauss, Albert 1864-1929 *BioIn 17*
Strauss, Albrecht Benno 1921- *WhoAm 92*
Strauss, Alfred C. 1932- *St&PR 93*
Strauss, Andrew Alexander 1953- *St&PR 93*
Strauss, Andrew W. 1965- *St&PR 93*
Strauss, Annette 1924- *WhoAmW 93*
Strauss, Botho 1944- *BioIn 17, DcLB 124 [port]*
Strauss, Bruno 1926- *St&PR 93*
Strauss, Carol Kahn 1944- *WhoAmW 93, WhoE 93*
Strauss, Catherine B. 1947- *St&PR 93*
Strauss, Charles A. 1935- *WhoIns 93*
Strauss, Charles Bernhard 1943- *St&PR 93*
Strauss, Christoph c. 1577-1631 *Baker 92*
Strauss, Christopher 1943- *St&PR 93*
Strauss, Claude Levi- *BioIn 17*
Strauss, David Levi 1953- *WhoWrEP 92*
Strauss, David Sheldon 1932- *St&PR 93*
Strauss, Diane Carol Wheeler 1943- *WhoSSW 93*
Strauss, Dorothy Brandfon *WhoE 93, WhoWor 93*
Strauss, Eduard 1835-1916 *Baker 92*
Strauss, Eduard (Leopold Maria) 1910-1969 *Baker 92*
Strauss, Edward Robert 1942- *WhoE 93*
Strauss, Elaine Rae 1926- *WhoAmW 93*
Strauss, Elliott Bowman 1903- *WhoAm 92*
Strauss, Elton 1948- *WhoE 93*
Strauss, Erwin S. 1943- *ScF&FL 92*
Strauss, Eugene Milton 1919- *St&PR 93*
Strauss, Eva Williams 1953- *WhoAmW 93*
Strauss, Frank 1935- *WhoE 93*
Strauss, Franz Josef 1915-1988 *ColdWar 1 [port], DcTwHis*
Strauss, Franz (Joseph) 1822-1905 *Baker 92*
Strauss, Harlee Sue 1950- *WhoAmW 93*
Strauss, Harold L. 1930- *WhoAm 92*
Strauss, Herbert Arthur 1918- *WhoE 93*
Strauss, Herbert Leopold 1936- *WhoAm 92*
Strauss, Jack S. 1900- *St&PR 93*
Strauss, Jeanne H. 1928- *WhoSSW 93, WhoWor 93*
Strauss, Jerome Frank, III 1947- *WhoE 93*
Strauss, Jerome Manfred 1934- *WhoAm 92*
Strauss, Johann, I 1804-1849 *OxDcOp*
Strauss, Johann, (II) 1825-1899 *OxDcOp*
Strauss, Johann (Baptist) 1804-1849 *Baker 92*
Strauss, Johann (Baptist) 1825-1899 *Baker 92*
Strauss, Johann (Maria Eduard) 1866-1939 *Baker 92*
Strauss, John 1913- *WhoAm 92*
Strauss, John Steinert 1926- *WhoAm 92*
Strauss, Jon Calvert 1940- *WhoAm 92*
Strauss, Jonathan *Law&B 92*
Strauss, Jonathan 1954- *St&PR 93*
Strauss, Jose 1930- *WhoAm 92*
Strauss, Josef 1827-1870 *Baker 92*
Strauss, Justin J. 1933- *St&PR 93*
Strauss, Karen Adelson 1954- *WhoAmW 93*
Strauss, Lawrence Victor 1942- *WhoAm 92*
Strauss, Levi 1829-1902 *BioIn 17*
Strauss, Mary Ann 1928- *WhoAmW 93*
Strauss, Michael E. 1912- *WhoSSW 93*
Strauss, Michael Ernest 1943- *St&PR 93*
Strauss, Michael Sherman *Law&B 92*
Strauss, Monika Maria 1943- *WhoAmW 93*
Strauss, Monty Joseph 1945- *WhoSSW 93*
Strauss, Norman, Jr. 1937- *St&PR 93*
Strauss, Peter 1947- *WhoAm 92*
Strauss, Peter Lester 1940- *WhoAm 92*
Strauss, Phyllis R. 1943- *WhoAmW 93*
Strauss, Raymond Bernard 1930- *WhoE 93, WhoWor 93*
Strauss, Richard *BioIn 17*
Strauss, Richard 1864-1949 *BioIn 17, IntDcOp [port], OxDcOp*
Strauss, Richard (Georg) 1864-1949 *Baker 92*
Strauss, Richard H. 1935- *St&PR 93*
Strauss, Rita *AmWomPl*

Strauss, Robert C. 1941- St&PR 93, WhoAm 92
Strauss, Robert Philip WhoAm 92
Strauss, Robert Phillip 1944- WhoE 93
Strauss, Robert S. BioIn 17
Strauss, Robert S. 1918- CurBio 92 [port], PolPar
Strauss, Robert Schwarz 1918- WhoAm 92, WhoWor 93
Strauss, Roberta Joanne 1943- WhoAmW 93
Strauss, Simon David 1911- WhoAm 92
Strauss, Stanley Carroll 1935- St&PR 93
Strauss, Stanley Robert 1915- WhoAm 92
Strauss, Steven Brian Law&B 92
Strauss, Ulrich Paul 1920- WhoAm 92, WhoE 93
Strauss, Victoria ScF&FL 92
Strauss, Walter Adolf 1923- WhoAm 92
Strauss, William BioIn 17
Strauss, William David 1949- St&PR 93
Straussner, Joel Harvey 1947- WhoE 93
Strausz-Hupe, Robert 1903- WhoAm 92
Strautmanis, Edvins 1933-1992 NewYTBS 92
Stravinski, Steven John 1945- St&PR 93
Stravinsky, Feodor (Ignatievich) 1843-1902 Baker 92
Stravinsky, Fyodor 1843-1902 OxDcOp
Stravinsky, Igor 1882-1971 BioIn 17, IntDcOp, OxDcOp
Stravinsky, Igor (Feodorovich) 1882-1971 Baker 92
Stravinsky, Sviatoslav Soulima 1910- Baker 92
Straw, Ann L. Law&B 92
Straw, Erwin T. 1929- St&PR 93
Straw, Lawrence Joseph, Jr. 1945- WhoWor 93
Straw, Martyn William 1953- WhoAm 92
Straw, Ralph L., Jr. Law&B 92
Straw, Syd WhoAm 92
Strawberry, Darryl BioIn 17
Strawberry, Darryl 1962- WhoAm 92
Strawbridge, Francis Reeves, III 1937- St&PR 93, WhoAm 92
Strawbridge, Herbert Edward 1918- St&PR 93
Strawbridge, Peter S. 1938- St&PR 93, WhoAm 92
Strawbridge, Steven Lowry 1943- St&PR 93, WhoAm 92
Strawderman, Dennis Lowell Law&B 92
Strawderman, Virginia 1949- WhoAmW 93
Strawhim, Samuel 1841?-1869 BioIn 17
Strawitz, Peter Bernard, III 1962- WhoSSW 93
Strawn, Frances Freeland 1946- WhoAmW 93, WhoWor 93
Strawn, Harry Culp 1918- WhoAm 92
Strawn, James R. Law&B 92
Strawn, Judy C. 1950- WhoAmW 93, WhoEmL 93
Strawn, Lois Kathleen Bailey 1954- WhoAmW 93
Strawn, Louis F. Law&B 92
Strawn, Marvin I. Law&B 92
Strawn-Hamilton, Frank 1934- WhoAm 92
Strawser, Robert Dale 1924- St&PR 93
Strawther, William W., Jr. 1926- St&PR 93
Strayer, Charles A. 1947- St&PR 93
Strayer, E. Ward MajAI
Strayhorn, Billy 1915-1967 Baker 92
Strayhorn, Earl E. 1918- AfrAmBi
Strayhorn, Martha Jane 1939- WhoAmW 93
Strayhorn, Ralph Nichols, Jr. 1923- WhoAm 92
Strayton, Robert Gerard 1935- WhoAm 92
Strazdon, Maureen Elaine 1948- WhoAmW 93
Strazzella, James Anthony 1939- WhoE 93
Strcic, Petar 1936- WhoWor 93
Stream, Arnold Crager 1918- WhoAm 92
Stream, Jay Wilson 1921- WhoAm 92
Strean, Bernard M. 1910- WhoAm 92, WhoWor 93
Strean, Richard Lockey 1939- WhoWor 93
Strear, Joseph D. 1933- WhoAm 92
Streat, Michael WhoScE 91-1
Streater, Raymond Frederick WhoScE 91-1
Streatfeild, David Anthony 1945- St&PR 93
Streatfeild, (Mary) Noel 1897-1986 MajAI [port]
Streatfeild, Richard Alexander 1866-1919 Baker 92
Streatfield, Eric, Mrs. AmWomPl
Streator, Edward James 1930- WhoAm 92
Streb, Alan Joseph 1932- WhoAm 92
Streb, Elizabeth BioIn 17
Streb, Jack Martin 1931- WhoE 93
Streb, Joseph Edward 1931- St&PR 93
Strebeigh, Barbara 1902- WhoAmW 93
Strebelle, Jacques 1940- WhoUN 92
Streblow, James Bruce 1951- St&PR 93
Strecansky, James Frank 1940- St&PR 93
Streck, Ludwig A. 1945- St&PR 93
Strecker, A. M. 1943- St&PR 93
Strecker, David Eugene 1950- WhoSSW 93
Strecker, Ian 1939- St&PR 93, WhoAm 92
Strecker, Ignatius J. 1917- WhoAm 92
Strecker, Ludwig 1853-1943 See Schott, Anton 1846-1913 Baker 92
Strecker, Ludwig 1883-1978 See Schott, Anton 1846-1913 Baker 92
Strecker, Richard L. 1944- St&PR 93
Strecker, Willy 1884-1958 See Schott, Anton 1846-1913 Baker 92
Stred, Kristin H. Law&B 92
Streeb, Gordon Lee 1935- WhoAm 92, WhoWor 93
Streed, Donna 1923- St&PR 93
Streef, Willem 1933- WhoWor 93
Streelman, Peter H. 1940- St&PR 93
Streep, Meryl BioIn 17
Streep, Meryl 1949- HolBB [port], IntDcF 2-3 [port], WhoAm 92, WhoAmW 93, WhoWor 93
Street, Brian Frederick 1927- WhoWor 93
Street, Dana Morris 1910- WhoAm 92
Street, David Hargett 1943- St&PR 93, WhoAm 92, WhoWor 93
Street, Deborra Lynn 1953- WhoSSW 93
Street, Emmet 1923-1964 BioIn 17
Street, Erica Catherine Law&B 92
Street, Gary D. Law&B 92
Street, Gordon Parkhurst, Jr. 1938- St&PR 93
Street, J.C. 1906-1989 BioIn 17
Street, Jabez Curry 1906-1989 BioIn 17
Street, James Richard 1937- St&PR 93
Street, James Stewart 1934- WhoE 93
Street, John Charles 1930- WhoAm 92
Street, Julia Montgomery 1898- WhoWrEP 92
Street, Patricia Lynn 1940- WhoAmW 93, WhoE 93, WhoWor 93
Street, Robert 1920- WhoWor 93
Street, Robert Lynnwood 1934- WhoAm 92
Street, Ronald E. 1950- WhoE 93
Street, Ross Howard 1945- WhoWor 93
Street, Steven Charles St&PR 93
Street, Tison 1943- Baker 92
Street, William May 1938- St&PR 93, WhoAm 92, WhoSSW 93
Street, William Sherman 1904- WhoAm 92
Streeten, Paul BioIn 17
Streeten, Paul Patrick 1917- WhoE 93
Streeter, Anne Paul 1926- WhoAmW 93
Streeter, Bernard Albra, Jr. 1935- WhoE 93
Streeter, Charles M. 1939- St&PR 93
Streeter, David Louis 1941- St&PR 93
Streeter, George William 1947- St&PR 93
Streeter, Henry Schofield 1920- WhoAm 92
Streeter, John Willis 1947- WhoEmL 93
Streeter, Minette 1942- WhoAmW 93
Streeter, Myron 1926- St&PR 93
Streeter, Richard Edward 1934- WhoAm 92
Streeter, Ruth Cheney 1895-1990 BioIn 17
Streeter, Sam Wilson 1937- WhoSSW 93
Streeter, Tal 1934- WhoAm 92
Streeter, Tom Law&B 92
Streeter, William J. Law&B 92
Streeter, William J. 1938- St&PR 93
Streeter, William Joseph 1938- WhoWor 93
Streetman, Ben Garland 1939- WhoAm 92
Streetman, John William, III 1941- WhoAm 92
Streetman, Nancy Katherine 1933- WhoAmW 93
Streeton, Jacqui 1943- WhoSSW 93
Streets, William Carl Law&B 92
Streett, Alexander Graham 1939- WhoAm 92
Streett, Donald Howard 1934- St&PR 93
Streett, William Bernard 1932- WhoAm 92
Strehblow, Hans-Henning Steffen 1939- WhoWor 93
Strehle, Alice M. AmWomPl
Strehle, Glenn Preston 1936- WhoE 93
Strehler, Giorgio 1921- BioIn 17, IntDcOp, OxDcOp
Streib, Dan 1928- ScF&FL 92
Streibich, Harold Cecil 1928- WhoAm 92
Streich, Peter Wakely 1931- St&PR 93
Streich, Rita 1920-1987 Baker 92, IntDcOp, OxDcOp
Streicher, James Franklin 1940- WhoAm 92, WhoWor 93
Streicher, Johann Andreas 1761-1833 Baker 92
Streicher, Johann Baptist 1796-1871 See Streicher, Johann Andreas 1761-1833 Baker 92
Streicher, Julius 1885-1946 DcTwHis
Streicher, Sharon A. Law&B 92
Streicher, Theodor 1874-1940 See Streicher, Johann Andreas 1761-1833 Baker 92
Streichler, Jerry 1929- WhoAm 92
Streicker, Richard Daniel Law&B 92
Streiff, Thomas F. 1958- WhoIns 93
Streisand, Barbra BioIn 17
Streisand, Barbra 1942- Baker 92, CurBio 92 [port], IntDcF 2-3 [port], MiSFD 9, News 92 [port]
Streisand, Barbra Joan 1942- WhoAm 92, WhoAmW 93
Streisinger, Cory Law&B 92
Streit, Allan Lee 1950- WhoE 93
Streit, Bruno 1948- WhoScE 91-3
Streit, Frances Norris 1918- WhoE 93
Streit, Ludwig P. 1938- WhoWor 93
Streith, Jacques 1933- WhoScE 91-2
Streitwieser, Andrew, Jr. 1927- WhoAm 92
Streitwieser, Franz Xaver 1939- WhoWor 93
Strejc, Vladimir 1921- WhoScE 91-4
Strek, Fryderyk 1926- WhoScE 91-4
Streletzky, Kathryn D. 1957- WhoEmL 93
Strelezki, Anton 1849-1911? Baker 92
Strelioff, Wayne BioIn 17
Strelitz, Steven L. Law&B 92
Strelka, Joseph Peter 1927- WhoE 93
Strelkoff, Joseph J. Law&B 92
Streller, Richard 1943- St&PR 93
Strelnikov, Nikolai 1888-1939 Baker 92
Strelzer, Martin 1925- WhoAm 92
Strelzoff, Alan 1937- St&PR 93
Strem, Michael E. 1936- St&PR 93
Stremlau, Michael W. WhoIns 93
Stremler, Ferrel G. 1933- WhoAm 92
Stremsterfer, John G. 1947- St&PR 93
Stren, Patti 1949- WhoCanL 92
Streng, William Paul 1937- WhoAm 92
Strenge, Billy BioIn 17
Strening, William Robert Law&B 92
Strenio, Andrew John, Jr. 1952- WhoAm 92
Strenko, Dolores BioIn 17
Strenkowski, Edward Albert Law&B 92
Strens, Jules 1892-1971 Baker 92
Strepponi, Giuseppina BioIn 17
Strepponi, Giuseppina 1815-1897 Baker 92, IntDcOp, OxDcOp
Stresemann, Gustav 1878-1929 DcTwHis
Stresemann, Walter Carl Gustav 1955- WhoWor 93
Stresemann, Wolfgang 1904- Baker 92
Stresov, Alexander 1935- WhoWor 93
Stretch, John Joseph 1935- WhoAm 92
Stretch, Maureen Law&B 92
Stretch, Thomas G. 1939- St&PR 93
Strete, Craig 1950- ScF&FL 92
Stretton, Barbara (Humphrey) 1936- ConAu 39NR
Stretton, J.M. WhoScE 91-1
Stretton, Ross WhoAm 92
Streufert, Victor C. 1957- St&PR 93
Streuli, Konrad Law&B 92
Streun-Leatherman, Merrilee Arafaith 1942- WhoAmW 93
Strevell, Robert Stuart 1945- St&PR 93
Strevinsky, Christine Maria 1932- WhoWrEP 92
Streydio, J.M. 1939- WhoScE 91-2
Striano, John A. 1942- WhoE 93
Strianse, Sabbat J. 1913-1991 BioIn 17
Stribling, Cherry Davis 1930- St&PR 93
Strichard, Diana J. Law&B 92
Strick, Joseph 1923- MiSFD 9, WhoAm 92
Strick, Philip 1939- ScF&FL 92
Strick, Sadie Elaine 1929- WhoAmW 93
Stricker, Augie E. 1929- St&PR 93
Stricker, Dana R. Law&B 92
Stricker, George BioIn 17
Stricker, Herbert 1931- WhoScE 91-3
Stricker, Irwin J. 1932- St&PR 93
Stricker, James Albert 1940- WhoSSW 93
Stricker, Jed M. Law&B 92
Stricker, Pamela 1951- St&PR 93
Strickland, A.J., III 1928- St&PR 93
Strickland, A.W. 1940- ScF&FL 92
Strickland, Anita Maurine 1923- WhoSSW 93
Strickland, Arvarh Eunice 1930- WhoAm 92
Strickland, B. L. 1940- St&PR 93
Strickland, Billy Jack 1940- WhoSSW 93
Strickland, Bonnie R. 1936- BioIn 17
Strickland, Bonnie Ruth 1936- WhoAm 92
Strickland, Brad 1947- ScF&FL 92
Strickland, Carl Donald 1935- WhoSSW 93
Strickland, Carol A. 1949- St&PR 93
Strickland, Carol Colclough 1946- WhoE 93
Strickland, Charles Everett 1930- WhoSSW 93
Strickland, Charles William 1942- WhoSSW 93
Strickland, Daniel Michael 1944- WhoWor 93
Strickland, David Gordon 1946- St&PR 93
Strickland, David J., III Law&B 92
Strickland, David Miles 1948- St&PR 93
Strickland, Elroy Law&B 92
Strickland, Frank Dallas 1946- WhoSSW 93
Strickland, George Thomas, Jr. 1934- WhoAm 92
Strickland, Hugh Alfred 1931- WhoAm 92
Strickland, James Allan 1924- St&PR 93
Strickland, James Mell, Jr. 1929- St&PR 93
Strickland, Jeffrey 1958- St&PR 93
Strickland, Jills 1965- WhoAmW 93
Strickland, John David 1956- WhoWrEP 92
Strickland, John E. Law&B 92
Strickland, Judy Evelyn 1947- WhoWrEP 92
Strickland, Karen Louise 1960- WhoAmW 93
Strickland, Lily (Teresa) 1887-1958 Baker 92
Strickland, Mary Opal 1933- St&PR 93
Strickland, Nellie B. 1932- WhoAm 92
Strickland, Normalie 1938- WhoAmW 93
Strickland, Robert 1927- St&PR 93, WhoAm 92, WhoSSW 93
Strickland, Robert Louis 1931- St&PR 93, WhoAm 92, WhoSSW 93, WhoWor 93
Strickland, Ruth G. d1987 BioIn 17
Strickland, Samuel 1804-1867 BioIn 17
Strickland, Samuel Ray 1950- St&PR 93
Strickland, Stephen Parks 1933- WhoE 93
Strickland, Ted L. 1932- WhoAm 92
Strickland, Thomas Joseph 1932- WhoAm 92, WhoSSW 93, WhoWor 93
Strickland, Vernon Brantley 1925- St&PR 93
Strickland, William 1914- Baker 92
Strickland, William Bradley 1947- WhoWrEP 92
Strickland, William Murray Edouard 1956- WhoSSW 93
Strickland, William R. 1914-1991 BioIn 17
Strickler, Daniel B. 1897-1992 NewYTBS 92
Strickler, Howard Martin 1950- WhoSSW 93
Strickler, Ivan K. 1921- WhoAm 92
Strickler, Joan Carole 1935- WhoAmW 93
Stricklin, Carl Spencer 1917- WhoE 93
Stricklin, James Thomas, II 1947- WhoSSW 93
Stricklin, Robert Curtis 1943- St&PR 93
Strickling, Lawrence E. Law&B 92
Strickman, Arthur Edwin 1924- St&PR 93, WhoAm 92
Strickman, Stephen E. 1938- St&PR 93
Stricoff, R. Scott 1949- St&PR 93
Strid, Arne 1943- WhoScE 91-2
Stride, Richard J. 1927- St&PR 93
Strider, Marjorie Virginia WhoAm 92, WhoE 93
Stridh, Bengt Erik 1957- WhoWor 93
Stridsberg, Albert Borden 1929- WhoE 93
Striebe, William F., Jr. Law&B 92
Strieber, Whitley 1945- DcAmChF 1985, ScF&FL 92
Strieck, Johanna Renate 1936- WhoUN 92
Strieder, John William 1901- WhoAm 92
Striefsky, Linda Ann 1952- WhoAmW 93
Striegel, Jeffery A. 1958- WhoE 93
Striegel, Judith Marie 1943- WhoAmW 93
Striegel, Lawrence William 1957- WhoE 93
Striegel, Peggy Simsarian 1941- WhoAmW 93
Striegler, Kurt 1886-1958 Baker 92
Strier, Murray Paul 1923- WhoE 93
Strieter, Frederick John 1934- WhoSSW 93
Strietzel, Catherine Joanne 1961- WhoAmW 93
Strife, Mary Louise 1959- WhoAmW 93
Striffler, David Frank 1922- WhoAm 92
Striffler, Eugene, Jr. Law&B 92
Striggio, Alessandro c. 1540-1592 Baker 92
Striggio, Alessandro 1573?-1630 IntDcOp See Also Striggio, Alessandro c. 1540-1592 Baker 92
Striggio, Alessandro, I c. 1540-1592 OxDcOp
Striggio, Alessandro, II 1573?-1630 OxDcOp

Stright, I. Leonard 1916- *WhoAm 92*
Stright, Melanie Jean 1954- *WhoAmW 93*
Strigl, Dennis Francis 1946- *St&PR 93*
Strigle, Richard Bush 1939- *ScF&FL 92*
Strijdom, Johannes Gerhardus 1893-1958 *DcTwHis*
Strike, Donald Peter 1936- *WhoE 93*
Strike, George L. 1930- *St&PR 93*
Striker, Cecil Leopold 1932- *WhoAm 92*
Striker, Gary E. 1934- *WhoAm 92*
Striker, Sandra Darlene *WhoAmW 93*
Striker, Susan 1942- *BioIn 17*
Striker, Susan Joan Glaser 1942- *WhoAmW 93*
Strimas, John P. *St&PR 93*
Strimbu, Victor, Jr. 1932- *WhoAm 92*
Strimer, Joseph 1881-1962 *Baker 92*
Strimling, W. E. 1926- *St&PR 93*
Strindberg, August 1849-1912 *BioIn 17, MagSWL [port], TwCLC 47, WorLitC [port]*
Strine, Linda Hull 1953- *WhoE 93*
Striner, Herbert Edward 1922- *WhoAm 92*
String, John F. 1946- *WhoAm 92*
Stringa, Luigi 1939- *WhoWor 93*
Stringer, Arthur 1874-1950 *ScF&FL 92*
Stringer, Arthur John Arbuthnott 1874-1950 *BioIn 17*
Stringer, C. Vivian *AfrAmBi [port]*
Stringer, Christopher John 1944- *St&PR 93*
Stringer, David Walter 1961- *St&PR 93*
Stringer, Edward Charles 1935- *WhoAm 92*
Stringer, Howard 1942- *St&PR 93, WhoWor 93*
Stringer, Jonathan A. *Law&B 92*
Stringer, Kenneth N. *Law&B 92*
Stringer, Kenneth Robert 1943- *WhoSSW 93*
Stringer, Loren Frank 1925- *WhoAm 92*
Stringer, Mary Evelyn 1921- *WhoAm 92*
Stringer, Michael Frederick 1950- *WhoScE 91-1*
Stringer, Michael R. 1943- *St&PR 93*
Stringfellow, Dale A. 1944- *St&PR 93*
Stringfellow, Gerald B. 1942- *WhoAm 92*
Stringfellow, Tom Lynn 1953- *WhoSSW 93*
Stringfellow, Vivian H. 1935- *St&PR 93*
Stringfellow, William George 1952- *WhoSSW 93*
Stringfield, Charles David 1939- *WhoAm 92, WhoSSW 93*
Stringfield, Hezz, Jr. 1921- *WhoAm 92*
Stringfield, Lamar (Edwin) 1897-1959 *Baker 92*
Stringham, Edwin John 1890-1974 *Baker 92*
Stringham, Jack F., II *Law&B 92*
Stringham, Jack Fred, II 1946- *St&PR 93, WhoAm 92*
Stringham, Joseph Strong 1939- *WhoAm 92*
Stringham, Luther Winters 1915- *WhoAm 92*
Strintzis, Michael G. 1944- *WhoScE 91-3*
Strintzis, Michael Gerassimos 1944- *WhoWor 93*
Stripling, Byron *BioIn 17*
Stripling, William R. 1955- *WhoSSW 93*
Stripp, Alan 1924- *BioIn 17*
Strippelhoff, Carl Daniel 1960- *St&PR 93*
Strisik, Paul 1918- *BioIn 17, WhoAm 92*
Strisower, Suzanne 1956- *WhoAmW 93*
Stritch, Clifford Francis, Jr. 1947- *St&PR 93*
Stritch, Elaine 1926- *WhoAm 92*
Strite, L. Gerald 1949- *St&PR 93*
Strite, Lewis Edgar 1920- *St&PR 93*
Strittmater, Victoria Moulton 1954- *WhoE 93*
Strittmatter, Cornelius Frederick, IV 1926- *WhoSSW 93*
Strittmatter, Peter Albert 1939- *WhoAm 92*
Stritzinger, John Louis 1955- *WhoE 93*
Strizic, Mark 1928- *WhoWor 93*
Strnat, Karl Josef 1929- *WhoAm 92*
Strnisa, Fred 1941- *WhoE 93*
Strobach, Nettina Louise *AmWomPl*
Strobaugh, Terence P. *Law&B 92*
Strobbe, R.P. 1929- *WhoScE 91-2*
Strobel, Bartlomiej 1591-1650 *PolBiDi*
Strobel, David Allen 1942- *WhoAm 92*
Strobel, Heinrich 1898-1970 *Baker 92*
Strobel, Lisa Mae 1966- *WhoAmW 93*
Strobel, Martin J. *Law&B 92*
Strobel, Martin Jack 1940- *St&PR 93, WhoAm 92*
Strobel, Otto 1895-1953 *Baker 92*
Strobel, Richard Charles 1963- *WhoE 93*
Strobel, Shirley Holcomb 1929- *WhoAmW 93*
Strober, Samuel 1940- *WhoAm 92*
Strober, Stanley Allen *Law&B 92*
Strobl, Enrique Antonio 1939- *WhoWor 93*
Strobl, Frederick T. 1949- *St&PR 93*
Strobl, Greg F. *Law&B 92*
Strobl, Reiner Maria 1942- *WhoWor 93*
Stroble, David Carroll 1943- *St&PR 93*
Stroble, Francis Anthony 1930- *St&PR 93, WhoAm 92*
Strock, Don 1950- *BioIn 17*
Strock, Herbert Leonard 1918- *WhoAm 92*
Strock, Ian Randal 1966- *WhoWrEP 92*
Strock, James Martin 1956- *WhoAm 92*
Strock Family *BioIn 17*
Strode, Ralph fl. 1358-1400 *BioIn 17*
Strode, Steven Wayne 1949- *WhoSSW 93*
Strode, William 1603-1645 *DcLB 126*
Strode, William Hall, III 1937- *WhoAm 92*
Strodel, Robert Carl 1930- *WhoAm 92*
Stroe, Aurel 1932- *Baker 92*
Stroebel, John S. *Law&B 92*
Stroebel, Richard H. 1929- *St&PR 93*
Stroecker, William G. 1920- *St&PR 93*
Stroeher, Roy Edgar 1929- *St&PR 93*
Stroesenreuther, George Dale 1954- *St&PR 93, WhoAm 92, WhoWor 93*
Stroessner, Alfredo 1912- *DcTwHis*
Stroetmann, Clemens *WhoScE 91-3*
Stroetmann, Karl Antonius 1944- *WhoWor 93*
Stroetz, Edward William, Jr. *Law&B 92*
Stroganova, Nina *BioIn 17*
Strogoff, Alfred 1928- *WhoAm 92*
Stroh, John H. *Law&B 92*
Stroh, John W. *St&PR 93*
Stroh, Oscar Henry 1908- *WhoWor 93*
Stroh, Peter Wetherill 1927- *WhoAm 92*
Strohal, Petar 1932- *WhoUN 92*
Strohan, James Michael 1946- *St&PR 93, WhoAm 92*
Strohbehn, John Walter 1936- *WhoAm 92*
Strohecker, Albert J. *Law&B 92*
Strohecker, Carol 1954- *WhoAmW 93*
Strohecker, Ethel 1913- *St&PR 93*
Strohecker, H. Ross 1913- *St&PR 93*
Strohl, James A. 1937- *St&PR 93, WhoAm 92*
Strohl, Lowell K. 1937- *St&PR 93*
Strohl, Pierre *WhoScE 91-2*
Strohl, Tom Ashley 1954- *WhoE 93*
Strohlein, Stephen Santo 1953- *WhoE 93*
Strohm, David L. 1951- *St&PR 93*
Strohm, Michael D. 1951- *St&PR 93*
Strohm, Paul Holzworth, Jr. 1938- *WhoAm 92*
Strohm, Reinhard 1942- *Baker 92*
Strohm, Robert Dean 1945- *WhoE 93*
Strohm, Thomas Gregory 1949- *St&PR 93*
Strohmenger, Thomas Charles *Law&B 92*
Strohmeyer, John 1924- *WhoAm 92*
Stroik, Denise Louise 1962- *WhoAmW 93*
Stroik, E. R. 1928- *St&PR 93*
Stroka, Albert A. *Law&B 92*
Stroke, George Wilhelm 1924- *WhoWor 93*
Stroke, Hinko Henry 1927- *WhoAm 92*
Strolin, Maryann 1943- *WhoIns 93*
Strom, Earl *BioIn 17*
Strom, Frederick W. 1939- *St&PR 93*
Strom, Goran 1950- *WhoScE 91-4*
Strom, Gordon H. 1914-1989 *BioIn 17*
Strom, Grace Sax 1928- *WhoAmW 93*
Strom, James A. *Law&B 92*
Strom, Lyle Elmer 1925- *WhoAm 92*
Strom, Mark Adams 1961- *WhoSSW 93*
Strom, Milton Gary 1942- *WhoAm 92*
Strom, Richard *Law&B 92*
Strom, Richard Gordon 1944- *WhoScE 91-3*
Strom, Sten Torbjorn 1944- *WhoWor 93*
Strom, Steven Russell 1963- *WhoSSW 93*
Strom, Terry Barton 1941- *WhoE 93*
Stroman, Carolyn A. 1945- *WhoE 93*
StrOmback, Ulf Gustaf 1946- *WhoWor 93*
Stromberg, Arthur Harold 1928- *WhoAm 92*
Stromberg, Gregory 1948- *St&PR 93, WhoWor 93*
Stromberg, Jarl-Ove 1936- *WhoScE 91-4*
Stromberg, Kirk Lester 1937- *WhoWor 93*
Stromberg, Patricia Roberts 1932- *WhoAmW 93*
Stromberg, Roland Nelson 1916- *WhoAm 92*
Stromberger, Theodore Leo 1905- *WhoWrEP 92*
Strombom, Cathy Jean 1949- *WhoAmW 93*
Strombom, David Glen 1951- *WhoEmL 93*
Strome, C. Bowman, Jr. *Law&B 92*
Strome, Charles Bowman, Jr. *Law&B 92*
Strome, Charles Bowman, Jr. 1928- *St&PR 93, WhoAm 92*
Strome, Stephen 1945- *St&PR 93, WhoAm 92*
Stromgaard, Peter 1951- *WhoScE 91-2*
Stromgren, Mats E.V. 1945- *WhoScE 91-4*
Stromholm, Stig Fredrik 1931- *WhoWor 93*
Stromme, Lu Ann Joy 1958- *WhoAmW 93*
Strommer, Anne Elizabeth Rivard 1940- *WhoAmW 93*
Strom-Paikin, Joyce Elizabeth 1946- *WhoSSW 93, WhoWrEP 92*
Stromsness, John E. 1932- *St&PR 93*
Stronach, Frank *St&PR 93, WhoAm 92, WhoE 93*
Stronberg, Michael David 1942- *St&PR 93*
Stronczer, John J. 1937- *St&PR 93*
Strone, Michael J. *Law&B 92*
Strong, Andrew *BioIn 17*
Strong, Anna Louise 1885-1970 *JrnUS*
Strong, Barbara *BioIn 17*
Strong, Benjamin 1872-1928 *BioIn 17*
Strong, Bethany J. 1906- *WhoWrEP 92*
Strong, C. W., Jr. 1929- *St&PR 93*
Strong, Charles *ConAu 39NR*
Strong, Charmaine Recker 1952- *WhoE 93*
Strong, David F. 1944- *WhoAm 92*
Strong, Donald Russell 1931-1990 *BioIn 17*
Strong, Dorothy B. d1991 *BioIn 17*
Strong, Earl Poe 1910- *WhoWor 93*
Strong, Edward W. 1901-1990 *BioIn 17*
Strong, Elizabeth May 1940- *WhoE 93*
Strong, Elliot Wilson 1930- *WhoE 93*
Strong, Eric Q. 1954- *WhoSSW 93*
Strong, Frank P., Jr. *St&PR 93*
Strong, Gary Eugene 1944- *WhoAm 92*
Strong, George Gordon, Jr. 1947- *St&PR 93, WhoEmL 93*
Strong, George J. 1952- *St&PR 93*
Strong, George Templeton 1856-1948 *Baker 92*
Strong, Grace Cooke *AmWomPl*
Strong, Harry M. 1918- *St&PR 93*
Strong, Henry 1923- *WhoAm 92*
Strong, James Walter 1941- *WhoSSW 93*
Strong, Janet Konhaus *WhoWrEP 92*
Strong, John 1905-1992 *BioIn 17*
Strong, John D. d1992 *NewYTBS 92 [port]*
Strong, John D. 1936- *WhoIns 93*
Strong, John David 1936- *St&PR 93, WhoAm 92*
Strong, John F. *Law&B 92*
Strong, John S. 1956- *ConAu 138*
Strong, John William 1935- *WhoAm 92*
Strong, Jonathan 1944- *ConGAN*
Strong, Josiah 1847-1916 *BioIn 17*
Strong, Julia Helen 1954- *WhoSSW 93*
Strong, Ken 1906-1979 *BioIn 17*
Strong, Kimberly R. *Law&B 92*
Strong, Lawrence Franklin 1940- *St&PR 93*
Strong, Leslie Walker 1953- *WhoE 93*
Strong, Maurice *NewYTBS 92*
Strong, Maurice 1929- *News 93-1 [port]*
Strong, Maurice F. *BioIn 17*
Strong, Maurice Frederick 1929- *WhoUN 92*
Strong, Mervyn Stuart 1924- *WhoAm 92*
Strong, Michael Blundell 1942- *WhoWor 93*
Strong, Pamela Kay 1950- *WhoAmW 93*
Strong, Patricia Arlene 1949- *WhoAmW 93*
Strong, Patricia L. *Law&B 92*
Strong, Robert George 1916- *WhoWor 93*
Strong, Robert S. 1949- *St&PR 93, WhoAm 92*
Strong, Robert Thomas 1936- *WhoE 93*
Strong, Roy Colin 1935- *WhoWor 93*
Strong, Susan Clancey 1939- *WhoAmW 93*
Strong, Virginia Rose 1942- *WhoSSW 93*
Strong, Warren Robert 1933- *WhoAm 92*
Strong, William 1808-1895 *OxCSupC [port]*
Strong, William Duncan 1899-1962 *IntDcAn*
Strong, William L., III 1932- *St&PR 93, WhoAm 92*
Strong, William O., III *Law&B 92*
Stronge, William Bernard 1944- *WhoSSW 93*
Stronge, William James, Jr. 1937- *WhoWor 93*
Strongin, Barbara 1935- *WhoE 93*
Strongin, Theodore 1918- *WhoAm 92*
Stronski, Victor 1932- *WhoAm 92*
Stroo, James C. *Law&B 92*
Stroock, Daniel Wyler 1940- *WhoAm 92*
Stroock, Mark Edwin, II 1922- *WhoAm 92, WhoWor 93*
Stroock, Thomas Frank 1925- *WhoAm 92, WhoWor 93*
Strople, Peter W. 1942- *St&PR 93*
Stroppa, Marco 1959- *WhoWor 93*
Strosahl, William Austin 1910- *WhoAm 92*
Strosberg, Arthur Donny 1945- *WhoWor 93*
Stroschein, Sharon Marie 1944- *WhoAmW 93*
Stroscio, Michael Anthony 1949- *WhoAm 92*
Strosnider, Lloyd N. 1936- *St&PR 93*
Stross, Jeoffrey Knight 1941- *WhoAm 92*
Strossen, Nadine 1950- *BioIn 17, WhoAm 92, WhoAmW 93*
Strossman, Marion Rae 1884- *AmWomPl*
Strote, Joel Richard 1939- *WhoAm 92*
Strother, Dora Dougherty 1921- *WhoAmW 93*
Strother, James French 1938- *WhoAm 92*
Strother, James M. *Law&B 92*
Strother, Lester James 1925- *WhoWrEP 92*
Strother, Pat *ScF&FL 92*
Strother, Sheryl Dianne 1959- *WhoAmW 93*
Strother, Tillie 1908- *WhoAmW 93*
Stroth Gernot, Hans Walter 1949- *WhoWor 93*
Strothman, James Edward 1939- *WhoAm 92*
Strothman, Lloyd F. *Law&B 92*
Strothman, Wendy Jo 1950- *WhoAm 92*
Strotman, Stanley W. 1922- *St&PR 93*
Strotmann, Heinrich 1938- *WhoScE 91-3*
Strotz, Robert H. 1922- *St&PR 93*
Strotzka, Hans 1917- *WhoScE 91-4*
Stroud, Carole Sherman 1942- *WhoAmW 93*
Stroud, Carter J. *Law&B 92*
Stroud, D. Michael *Law&B 92*
Stroud, Debra Sue 1954- *WhoAmW 93*
Stroud, Drew McCord 1944- *WhoWrEP 92*
Stroud, Frank Berry 1930- *WhoSSW 93*
Stroud, J. B., Jr. 1944- *WhoSSW 93*
Stroud, James C. 1938- *St&PR 93*
Stroud, James Stanley 1915- *WhoAm 92*
Stroud, Joe Hinton 1936- *St&PR 93, WhoAm 92*
Stroud, John Fred, Jr. 1931- *WhoAm 92*
Stroud, Junius Brutus, III 1929- *WhoSSW 93*
Stroud, Karen 1956- *WhoIns 93*
Stroud, Matthew David 1950- *WhoSSW 93*
Stroud, Patricia Tyson 1932- *ConAu 138, WhoE 93*
Stroud, Penny 1948- *WhoAmW 93*
Stroud, Richard Hamilton 1918- *WhoAm 92*
Stroud, Robert Edward 1934- *WhoAm 92*
Stroud, Robert Malone 1931- *WhoSSW 93*
Stroud, Sally Dawley 1947- *WhoSSW 93*
Stroud, William A. 1920- *St&PR 93*
Stroud, William Harvey 1942- *WhoAm 92*
Strougal, Patricia Greganti 1939- *WhoSSW 93*
Stroughter, Janice M. *Law&B 92*
Stroup, Alice 1943- *WhoE 93*
Stroup, David Richard 1954- *WhoSSW 93*
Stroup, Elizabeth Faye 1939- *WhoAmW 93*
Stroup, Kala Mays *WhoAmW 93*
Stroup, Kenneth Ephriam, Jr. *Law&B 92*
Stroup, Larry Dale 1942- *St&PR 93*
Stroup, Richard Lyndell 1943- *WhoAm 92*
Stroup, Rolland Eugene 1943- *WhoE 93*
Stroup, Sheila Tierney 1943- *WhoAmW 93*
Stroup, Stanley S. *Law&B 92*
Stroup, Stanley S. 1944- *St&PR 93*
Stroup, Stanley Stephenson 1944- *WhoAm 92*
Stroup, Thomas Allen 1954- *WhoE 93*
Stroupe, Henry Smith 1914- *WhoAm 92*
Stroupe, William Edward 1943- *WhoSSW 93, WhoWrEP 92*
Strouse, Charles (Louis) 1928- *Baker 92*
Strouse, Jean *BioIn 17*
Strouse, John Irvin 1946- *WhoE 93*
Strouse, Joseph George 1945- *St&PR 93*
Strouse, Richard B. d1991 *BioIn 17*
Stroustrup, Bjarne *BioIn 17*
Strout, Linda J. *Law&B 92*
Strout, Richard L. 1898-1990 *JrnUS*
Strout, Richard Lee 1898-1990 *BioIn 17*
Strout, Sewall Cushing, Jr. 1923- *WhoAm 92*
Strout, Steven Brian 1957- *WhoSSW 93*
Strover, Russell G. 1937- *St&PR 93*
Stroy, Gary H. 1942- *St&PR 93*
Stroyd, Arthur Heister 1945- *WhoAm 92*
Strozzi, Barbara 1619- *BioIn 17*
Strozzi, Giulio 1583-1652 *OxDcOp*
Strozzi, Piero c. 1550-1609? *Baker 92*
Strub, Armin A. 1937- *WhoWor 93*
Strub, Christopher Michael 1959- *WhoSSW 93*
Strubbe, Thomas R. 1940- *WhoAm 92*
Strube, Gustav 1867-1953 *Baker 92*
Strube, Roger H. 1942- *St&PR 93*
Strubel, Ella Doyle 1940- *WhoAm 92*
Strubel, Richard Perry 1939- *WhoAm 92*

Strubelt, Wendelin *WhoScE 91-3*
Struble, Daniel O. 1940- *St&PR 93*
Struble, Daniel Otterbein 1940- *WhoAm 92*
Struble, Thelma Pauline 1934- *WhoAmW 93*
Struchkov, Yuri Timofeevich 1926- *WhoWor 93*
Struck, Bernhard 1888-1971 *IntDcAn*
Struck, David Carl 1937- *St&PR 93*
Struck, Herman 1887-1954 *BioIn 17*
Struck, John Seward 1952- *WhoWor 93*
Struck, Nolan 1940- *BioIn 17*
Struck, Norma Johansen 1929- *WhoAmW 93, WhoE 93*
Struck, Robert Frederick 1932- *WhoSSW 93*
Struckhoff, Eugene Charles 1920- *WhoE 93*
Struckmeyer, Frederick Christian, Jr. 1912- *WhoAm 92*
Strudler, Robert J. 1942- *St&PR 93*
Strudwick, Dorothy J. 1918- *WhoWrEP 92*
Strudwick, Karen Ann Drew 1959- *WhoAmW 93*
Strudwick, Nora Zeller 1933- *WhoAmW 93*
Struebing, Robert Virgil 1919- *WhoAm 92*
Struecker, Gerhard 1954- *WhoWor 93*
Struelens, Michel Maurice Joseph Georges 1928- *WhoAm 92*
Struff, Richard 1935- *WhoScE 91-3*
Strug, Andrzej 1871-1937 *PolBiDi*
Strugatskii, Arkadii Natanovich *BioIn 17*
Strugatskii, Boris Natanovich *BioIn 17*
Strugatsky, Arkady 1925-1991 *ScF&FL 92*
Strugatsky, Boris 1933- *ScF&FL 92*
Strugatz, Peter 1955- *St&PR 93*
Struggles, John E. 1913- *St&PR 93*
Struggles, John Edward 1913- *WhoAm 92*
Strugnell, John *BioIn 17*
Struhar, Linda Marie 1957- *WhoAmW 93*
Struik, Leendert C.E. 1941- *WhoScE 91-3*
Strukelj, Mark Steven *Law&B 92*
Strukoff, Rudolf Stephen 1935- *WhoWor 93*
Strul, Gene M. 1927- *WhoSSW 93*
Strull, Gene 1929- *WhoAm 92*
Strull, Steven H. *St&PR 93*
Strull, Wm. 1916- *St&PR 93*
Strum, Brian J. 1939- *WhoAm 92*
Strum, Jay Gerson 1938- *WhoAm 92*
Strum, Judy May 1938- *WhoAmW 93*
Strum, Marvin Kent 1943- *WhoAm 92*
Strumia, Franco 1939- *WhoScE 91-3*
Strumillo, Czeslaw 1930- *WhoScE 91-4, WhoWor 93*
Strumingher, Laura Sharon 1945- *WhoAm 92*
Struminsky, Vladimir Vasilievich 1914- *WhoWor 93*
Strunck, Stephen S. *Law&B 92*
Strunecka, Anna 1944- *WhoScE 91-4*
Strungk, Delphin 1600?-1694? *Baker 92*
Strungk, Nicolaus Adam 1640?-1700 *Baker 92, OxDcOp*
Strunk, Betsy Ann Whitenight 1942- *WhoAmW 93*
Strunk, Carl A. 1938- *St&PR 93*
Strunk, Gary Arnold 1940- *St&PR 93*
Strunk, Michael Joseph 1949- *St&PR 93*
Strunk, (William) Oliver 1901-1980 *Baker 92*
Strunk, Orlo C. *WhoWrEP 92*
Strunk, Orlo Christopher, Jr. 1925- *WhoAm 92*
Strunk, Robert Keen, II 1951- *WhoE 93*
Strunkov, Sergey Petrovitch 1942- *WhoWor 93*
Strunsky, Frances *AmWomPl*
Strunsky, Robert d1991 *BioIn 17*
Strunz, Jorge *BioIn 17*
Strupp, Cory N. *Law&B 92*
Strupp, Hans Hermann 1921- *WhoAm 92, WhoSSW 93*
Strupp, Jacqueline Virginia 1963- *WhoAmW 93*
Strupp, Janet Kaye 1947- *WhoAmW 93*
Struppa, Daniele Carlo 1955- *WhoWor 93*
Strus, Jozef 1510-1568 *PolBiDi*
Strusick, Jozef 1510-1568 *PolBiDi*
Struss, David H. *Law&B 92*
Struthers, Archibald Gold 1928- *St&PR 93*
Struthers, Betsy 1951- *WhoCanL 92*
Struthers, Nancy Jane 1942- *WhoAmW 93*
Strutner, Raymond James 1934- *St&PR 93*
Strutt, David *Law&B 92*
Strutton, Bill 1918- *ScF&FL 92*
Strutton, Rebeca *AmWomPl*
Strutton, Robert James 1948- *WhoWor 93*
Strutton, William H. *ScF&FL 92*
Strutz, George Arthur 1932- *St&PR 93, WhoAm 92*
Struve, A. Wolfgang D. 1924- *WhoScE 91-3*
Struve, Guy Miller 1943- *WhoAm 92, WhoWor 93*
Struyk, Raymond Jay 1944- *WhoAm 92*
Struyk, Robert John 1932- *WhoAm 92*
Struyker-Boudier, H.A.J. 1950- *WhoScE 91-3*
Struyker-Boudier, Harry Alexander Jozef 1950- *WhoWor 93*
Struzak, Ryszard G. 1933- *WhoScE 91-4, WhoUN 92*
Struzinski, Allan David 1954- *St&PR 93*
Struzyna, Dieter G. *Law&B 92*
Strychalski, Irene Dorothea 1948- *WhoAmW 93*
Stryckers, Jos M.T. 1921- *WhoScE 91-2*
Stryckmans, Pierre A.A.M. 1932- *WhoScE 91-2*
Stryer, Lubert 1938- *WhoAm 92*
Strygler, Bernardo 1959- *WhoWor 93*
Strygler, Harry Sam 1918- *St&PR 93*
Stryjenska, Zofia 1894-1982 *PolBiDi*
Stryjenski, Karol 1887-1932 *PolBiDi*
Stryker, Allan Kent 1946- *WhoE 93*
Stryker, Charles William 1947- *WhoAm 92*
Stryker, Daniel *ScF&FL 92*
Stryker, Derek Jan 1940- *St&PR 93*
Stryker, Hal *ScF&FL 92*
Stryker, James William 1946- *WhoAm 92*
Stryker, Maria Halsey *AmWomPl*
Stryker, Steven C. 1944- *St&PR 93*
Stryker, Steven Charles 1944- *WhoAm 92*
Stryker, Timothy Dewey 1952- *WhoE 93*
Stryker, Timothy James 1954- *WhoSSW 93*
Stryker-Rodda, Kenn 1903-1990 *BioIn 17*
Strykowski, Waclaw Kazimierz 1942- *WhoWor 93*
Strykowski, Wladyslaw 1944- *WhoScE 91-4*
Stryphnos, Michael fl. c. 1190-1203 *OxDcByz*
Strysik, John *MiSFD 9*
Strzalko, Jan Dominik 1943- *WhoWor 93*
Strzalkowski, Adam 1923- *WhoScE 91-4*
Strzelczyk, Edmund Zygmunt 1930- *WhoScE 91-4*
Strzelec, M.E. 1945- *St&PR 93*
Strzelecka-Golaszewska, Hanna 1935- *WhoScE 91-4*
Strzelecki, Edward Leopold 1929- *WhoWor 93*
Strzelecki, Pawel Edmund 1797-1873 *PolBiDi*
Strzelecki, Tadeusz Waclaw 1929- *WhoScE 91-4*
Strzembosz, Adam Justyn 1930- *WhoWor 93*
Strzeminski, Wladyslaw 1893-1952 *PolBiDi*
Strzezek, Jerzy 1939- *WhoScE 91-4*
Stuanes, Arne Oddvar 1946- *WhoScE 91-4*
Stuart, Alesia Knight 1957- *WhoSSW 93*
Stuart, Alex R. *ScF&FL 92*
Stuart, Alice Melissa 1957- *WhoAmW 93, WhoE 93, WhoEmL 93, WhoWor 93*
Stuart, Anne *ScF&FL 92*
Stuart, Anne Elizabeth 1956- *WhoAmW 93, WhoWrEP 92*
Stuart, Arabella c. 1575-1615 *BioIn 17*
Stuart, Barbara *AmWomPl*
Stuart, Barbara Lawlor 1951- *WhoE 93*
Stuart, Brian *MiSFD 9*
Stuart, Bruce D. *Law&B 92*
Stuart, Bruce L. 1938- *St&PR 93*
Stuart, Carol d1989 *BioIn 17*
Stuart, Carole 1941- *St&PR 93*
Stuart, Charles *BioIn 17*
Stuart, Charles 1924- *ScF&FL 92*
Stuart, Colleen Murray 1945- *WhoAmW 93*
Stuart, D. Riley 1927- *St&PR 93*
Stuart, Dabney 1937- *BioIn 17, WhoAm 92, WhoWrEP 92*
Stuart, Deborah Ann 1960- *WhoSSW 93*
Stuart, Derald Archie 1925- *WhoAm 92*
Stuart, Diana *WhoWrEP 92*
Stuart, Donald *ScF&FL 92*
Stuart, Donald E. 1925- *St&PR 93*
Stuart, Donald James 1955- *WhoE 93*
Stuart, Dorothy Mae 1933- *WhoAmW 93*
Stuart, Douglas Earl 1938- *WhoE 93*
Stuart, Edwin J. 1936- *St&PR 93*
Stuart, Edwin Jay 1936- *WhoWor 93*
Stuart, Edwin Sydney 1853-1937 *BioIn 17*
Stuart, Errett d1991 *BioIn 17*
Stuart, Eve Lynne 1942- *WhoE 93*
Stuart, Francis M. 1902- *ScF&FL 92*
Stuart, Gary M. 1940- *St&PR 93*
Stuart, Gary Miller 1940- *WhoAm 92*
Stuart, Gerard William, Jr. 1939- *WhoWor 93*
Stuart, Harold C. 1912- *St&PR 93*
Stuart, Harold Cutliff 1912- *WhoAm 92*
Stuart, Ian 1922-1987 *BioIn 17*
Stuart, James 1917- *WhoAm 92*
Stuart, James Ewell Brown 1833-1864 *HarEnMi*
Stuart, James Fortier 1928- *WhoAm 92*
Stuart, Jane Elizabeth 1947- *WhoAmW 93*
Stuart, Jesse 1907-1984 *BioIn 17*
Stuart, (Hilton) Jesse 1907- *DcAmChF 1960*
Stuart, Joan Martha 1945- *WhoAmW 93*
Stuart, John *WhoScE 91-1*
Stuart, John 1713-1792 *BioIn 17*
Stuart, John James, Jr. 1939- *St&PR 93*
Stuart, John Leighton 1876-1962 *BioIn 17*
Stuart, John M. 1927- *WhoAm 92*
Stuart, John Malcolm 1946- *WhoAm 92*
Stuart, John McDouall 1815-1866 *Expl 93 [port]*
Stuart, John McHugh, Jr. 1916- *WhoAm 92*
Stuart, John Trevor *WhoScE 91-1*
Stuart, John William *Law&B 92*
Stuart, Kenneth James 1905- *WhoAm 92*
Stuart, Kiel 1951- *WhoE 93, WhoWrEP 92*
Stuart, L.T. *ScF&FL 92*
Stuart, Larry Gayle 1947- *WhoSSW 93*
Stuart, Laura Jean 1961- *WhoE 93*
Stuart, Lawrence David, Jr. 1944- *WhoAm 92*
Stuart, Leonard A. 1942- *St&PR 93*
Stuart, Leslie 1864-1928 *Baker 92*
Stuart, Lyle 1922- *WhoAm 92*
Stuart, Marian Ruth 1930- *WhoE 93*
Stuart, Marie Jean 1943- *WhoAmW 93*
Stuart, Marjorie Louise 1926- *WhoE 93*
Stuart, Mark Franklin 1953- *WhoE 93*
Stuart, Marty 1958- *ConMus 9 [port]*
Stuart, Mary *WhoAm 92*
Stuart, Mary M. *Law&B 92*
Stuart, Mel 1928- *MiSFD 9*
Stuart, Moses 1780-1852 *BioIn 17*
Stuart, Muriel 1903-1991 *BioIn 17*
Stuart, Norton A. 1935- *St&PR 93*
Stuart, Peter Chadbourne 1940- *WhoWrEP 92*
Stuart, Reginald (Charles) 1943- *ConAu 38NR*
Stuart, Rick *ScF&FL 92*
Stuart, Robert 1785-1848 *See* Hunt, Wilson Price 1782-1842 & Stuart, Robert 1785-1848 *Expl 93*
Stuart, Robert 1921- *St&PR 93, WhoAm 92*
Stuart, Robert Crampton 1938- *WhoAm 92*
Stuart, Robert Douglas, Jr. 1916- *WhoAm 92*
Stuart, Ruth McEnery 1849?-1917 *AmWomPl*
Stuart, Sally Elizabeth 1940- *WhoWrEP 92*
Stuart, Sandra Joyce 1950- *WhoAmW 93, WhoEmL 93, WhoWor 93*
Stuart, Sarah Payne 1952- *ConAu 136*
Stuart, Sidney *ConAu 39NR*
Stuart, Thomas Joseph 1935- *WhoAm 92*
Stuart, Thomas R. 1944- *St&PR 93*
Stuart, Virginia Elaine 1953- *WhoWrEP 92*
Stuart, Virginia Emilie 1931- *WhoAmW 93*
Stuart, W.J. 1899-1980 *ScF&FL 92*
Stuart, Walter Bynum 1922- *St&PR 93*
Stuart, Walter Bynum, III 1922- *WhoAm 92*
Stuart, Walter Bynum, IV 1946- *WhoAm 92, WhoWor 93*
Stuart, William Corwin 1920- *WhoAm 92*
Stuart, William J. 1951- *St&PR 93*
Stubb, A. Henrik 1946- *WhoScE 91-4*
Stubban, Patricia Denise 1957- *WhoAmW 93*
Stubbe, JoAnne *WhoAm 92*
Stubben, Dolus Jane 1951- *WhoEmL 93*
Stubberud, Allen Roger 1934- *WhoAm 92*
Stubbins, Hugh A., Jr. 1912- *WhoAm 92*
Stubbins, Sara Louise 1947- *WhoAmW 93*
Stubblebine, D.J. *St&PR 93*
Stubblebine, Donald J(ames) 1925- *ConAu 139*
Stubblefield, Austin Peay 1926- *St&PR 93*
Stubblefield, David E. 1937- *St&PR 93*
Stubblefield, Dewey Austin 1937- *St&PR 93*
Stubblefield, Frank M., Jr. *St&PR 93*
Stubblefield, Hal S. 1932- *St&PR 93*
Stubblefield, Karen Holt McIntosh 1965- *WhoAmW 93*
Stubblefield, P.K. 1914- *St&PR 93*
Stubblefield, Page Kindred 1914- *WhoAm 92*
Stubblefield, Robert LeRoy 1918- *WhoSSW 93*
Stubblefield, Terry Wayne 1952- *WhoSSW 93*
Stubblefield, Travis Elton 1935- *WhoSSW 93*
Stubblefield, William *Law&B 92*
Stubbs, Alice *AmWomPl*
Stubbs, Daniel Gaie 1940- *WhoWor 93*
Stubbs, David Allen *WhoScE 91-1*
Stubbs, Donald Francis 1930- *St&PR 93*
Stubbs, Glenn R. 1947- *St&PR 93*
Stubbs, Harry Clement *ScF&FL 92*
Stubbs, Harry Clement 1922- *BioIn 17*
Stubbs, J. Eugene 1939- *St&PR 93*
Stubbs, James Carlton 1924- *WhoAm 92*
Stubbs, Jan Didra 1937- *WhoAmW 93, WhoWor 93*
Stubbs, John Caldwell 1936- *WhoSSW 93*
Stubbs, John Heath- *ScF&FL 92*
Stubbs, Kendon Lee 1938- *WhoAm 92*
Stubbs, Linwood L., Jr. 1956- *St&PR 93*
Stubbs, Michael Geoffrey 1936- *WhoUN 92*
Stubbs, Robert R. 1948- *St&PR 93*
Stubbs, Robert Ramsay *Law&B 92*
Stubbs, Steven Howard 1938- *St&PR 93*
Stubbs, Wallace G. 1942- *St&PR 93*
Stubbs, Walter Roscoe 1858-1929 *BioIn 17*
Stubbs, William Benjamin, III 1961- *WhoSSW 93*
Stuber, Alan Lynn 1953- *WhoSSW 93*
Stuber, Charles William 1931- *WhoAm 92*
Stuber, James William 1947- *St&PR 93*
Stuber, Marilyn Martha Cook 1930- *WhoSSW 93*
Stuber, Walter Douglas 1949- *WhoWor 93*
Stubert, Harald Gunnar 1948- *WhoWor 93*
Stubits, Joseph Stephen 1943- *St&PR 93*
Stubler, Daniel J. *St&PR 93*
Stuchlik, Leon 1931- *WhoScE 91-4*
Stuchlik, Ludwig 1935- *St&PR 93*
Stuchtey, Rolf W. 1940- *WhoScE 91-3*
Stuck, David T. 1924- *St&PR 93*
Stuck, Franz von 1863-1928 *BioIn 17*
Stuck, Jean-Baptiste 1680-1755 *Baker 92*
Stuck, Mary Frances 1949- *WhoAmW 93*
Stuck, Roger Dean 1924- *WhoWor 93*
Stucke, Kenneth Joseph 1948- *St&PR 93*
Stuckelman, Robert 1932- *St&PR 93*
Stuckeman, H. Campbell 1914- *St&PR 93*
Stuckeman, Herman Campbell 1914- *WhoAm 92*
Stucken, Frank Van Der *Baker 92*
Stuckenberg, Fritz 1881-1944 *BioIn 17*
Stuckenschmidt, Hans Heinz 1901-1988 *Baker 92*
Stucker, Dina Lee 1932- *WhoAmW 93*
Stucker, Gilles A. E. 1947- *St&PR 93*
Stucker, Paul E. 1926- *St&PR 93*
Stucker, Robert Joseph 1945- *WhoAm 92*
Stuckey, Ray David 1959- *St&PR 93*
Stuckey, Scott Sherwood 1956- *WhoAm 92*
Stuckey, Walter Jackson 1927- *WhoAm 92, WhoSSW 93*
Stuckey, Wilson Maurice, Jr. 1961- *WhoSSW 93*
Stuckgold, Grete 1895-1977 *Baker 92*
Stuckgold, Jacques 1877-1953 *Baker 92*
Stucki, Jorg Werner 1942- *WhoWor 93*
Stuckman, Bruce Edward 1959- *WhoSSW 93*
Stuckwisch, Clarence George 1916- *WhoAm 92*
Stucky, James B. 1945- *St&PR 93*
Stucky, Marvin Wayne 1932- *St&PR 93*
Stucky, Naomi R. 1922- *SmATA 72 [port]*
Stucky, Steven (Edward) 1949- *Baker 92, WhoAm 92*
Stuczynska, Jadwiga Maria 1922- *WhoScE 91-4*
Studds, Gerry E. 1937- *CngDr 91*
Studds, Gerry Eastman 1937- *WhoAm 92, WhoE 93*
Stude, Everett Wilson, Jr. 1939- *WhoAm 92*
Studebaker, Blair R. *Law&B 92*
Studebaker, Bonnie A. 1942- *St&PR 93*
Studebaker, Donald *ScF&FL 92*
Studebaker, Irving Glen 1931- *WhoWor 93*
Studebaker, Joseph Elizah, III 1956- *WhoWrEP 92*
Studebaker, Merton Leland 1913-1982 *BioIn 17*
Studebaker, Michael John 1949- *WhoWrEP 92*
Studebaker, William Vern 1947- *WhoWrEP 92*
Studeman, William Oliver 1940- *WhoAm 92*
Studen, Greg E. *Law&B 92*
Studen, Joyce 1946- *St&PR 93*
Student, Kurt 1890-1978 *BioIn 17, HarEnMi*
Student, Menachem 1948- *BioIn 17*
Studer, Cheryl *BioIn 17*
Studer, Cheryl 1955- *Baker 92, CurBio 92 [port], OxDcOp, WhoAm 92*
Studer, Constance Elaine 1942- *WhoWrEP 92*
Studer, Gregory N. 1947- *St&PR 93*
Studer, Richard T. 1927- *St&PR 93*
Studer, Robert *St&PR 93*

Studer, William Allen 1939- WhoAm 92
Studer, William Joseph 1936- WhoAm 92
Studer-Johnson, Marian Kaye 1954- WhoWrEP 92
Studier, Eugene Herbert 1940- WhoAm 92
Studier, Frederick William 1936- WhoAm 92
Studley, David William Law&B 92
Studley, Karen O. Law&B 92
Studley, Marcia Ann 1958- WhoAmW 93
Studley, Michael H. Law&B 92
Studley, Michael H. 1946- St&PR 93
Studner, Michael S. 1936- St&PR 93
Studness, Charles Michael 1935- WhoE 93, WhoWor 93
Studniarski, Kazimierz 1923- WhoScE 91-4
Studnicki, Peter 1946- St&PR 93
Studnicki, Robert J. 1941- St&PR 93
Studzinski, Edward Alfred 1949- St&PR 93
Studzinski, Tadeusz 1935- WhoScE 91-4
Studzinski, William, Jr. Law&B 92
Stueart, Robert D. WhoAm 92
Stuebe, John Walter 1949- St&PR 93
Stueber, Gustav 1909- WhoWor 93
Stuebgen, William J. 1947- St&PR 93
Stuebing, Bradley Ford Law&B 92
Stuebner, James Cloyd 1931- WhoWor 93
Stueck, Maurita Estes 1922- WhoAmW 93
Stuecker, Phillip James 1951- St&PR 93
Stueflotten, Steinar Olav 1949- WhoWor 93
Stuehrenberg, Paul Frederick 1947- WhoAm 92
Stuehrk, Christine M. Law&B 92
Stueland, Dean Theodore 1950- WhoAm 92
Stuenkel, Wayne E. 1953- WhoIns 93
Stuermer, Michael 1938- WhoWor 93
Stuessi, Edgar 1945- WhoScE 91-4
Stuessy, Tod Falor 1943- WhoAm 92
Stuessy, W.B. 1941- St&PR 93
Stuewe, Paul 1943- WhoCanL 92
Stuewer, Roger H. BioIn 17
Stufflebean, John Howard 1918- WhoAm 92
Stufft, Maynard Ray 1939- St&PR 93
Stuhl, Friedrich J. 1937- WhoScE 91-3
Stuhl, Harold Maxwell 1934- St&PR 93, WhoAm 92
Stuhl, Oskar Paul 1949- WhoWor 93
Stuhl, Robert C. St&PR 93
Stuhldreher, Justin M. Law&B 92
Stuhlfire, Thomas Albert 1935- St&PR 93
Stuhlinger, Ernst 1913- WhoAm 92
Stuhlmacher, Peter Otto Johannes 1932- WhoWor 93
Stuhlmacher, Rae K. Law&B 92
Stuhlman, Daniel D. 1950- WhoWrEP 92
Stuhlreyer, Paul Augustus, III 1952- WhoAm 92
Stuhr, David Paul 1938- WhoAm 92
Stuhr, Edward Phillip 1905- WhoAm 92
Stuhr, Walter M. 1932- WhoAm 92
Stuiver, Minze 1929- WhoAm 92
Stukel, James Joseph 1937- WhoAm 92
Stukenbroeker, Berthold Karl-Heinz 1945- WhoWor 93
Stukey, Virginia Margaret WhoE 93
Stulak, John N. 1946- St&PR 93
Stular, Pavel 1922- WhoScE 91-4
Stulberg, Leslie Ann Law&B 92
Stulberg, Neal Howard 1954- WhoAm 92
Stull, Donald LeRoy 1937- WhoAm 92, WhoWor 93
Stull, Frank Walter 1935- WhoE 93
Stull, G. Alan 1933- WhoAm 92, WhoE 93
Stull, James L. 1948- St&PR 93
Stull, Lonnie N. 1939- St&PR 93
Stull, Richard J., II BioIn 17
Stulpnagel, Karl Heinrich von 1886-1944 BioIn 17
Stults, Keith M. 1964- St&PR 93
Stults, Theodore McConnell, II 1937- St&PR 93
Stults, Walter Black 1921- WhoAm 92
Stultz, John Anthony 1963- WhoE 93
Stultz, John L. 1930- St&PR 93
Stultz, Newell Maynard 1933- WhoAm 92
Stultz, Richard Thomas 1944- St&PR 93
Stultz, Stanley H. 1931- St&PR 93
Stultz, Thomas Joseph 1951- WhoSSW 93
Stum, Kenneth Eugene 1939- St&PR 93
Stumbaugh, Kurt John 1957- WhoE 93
Stumbo, Bella BioIn 17
Stumbo, Helen Luce 1947- WhoAmW 93
Stumbo, W. Keith St&PR 93
Stumbras, Jerome M. 1933- St&PR 93
Stumfoll, Lisa Marie 1963- WhoAmW 93
Stumler, David James 1954- St&PR 93
Stumm, Werner 1924- WhoScE 91-4, WhoWor 93
Stump, Bob 1927- CngDr 91, WhoAm 92
Stump, C. Jeffrey 1956- St&PR 93
Stump, Charles H. 1925- St&PR 93
Stump, Gail Alden 1951- WhoWrEP 92
Stump, Greg BioIn 17
Stump, Jane 1936- ScF&FL 92
Stump, John Edward 1934- WhoAm 92
Stump, John Sutton 1929- WhoAm 92
Stump, R.J. Law&B 92
Stump, Richard Carl 1952- WhoE 93
Stump, Roger Vincent 1946- St&PR 93
Stump, Sam BioIn 17
Stump, Troy Elwood 1954- WhoAm 92
Stump, Weldon Frederick 1915- St&PR 93
Stumpe, Dorothy May 1918- WhoAmW 93
Stumpe, Rainer Wolfgang 1947- WhoWor 93
Stumpe, Warren Robert 1925- St&PR 93, WhoAm 92
Stumpers, Frans Louis 1911- WhoWor 93
Stumpf, (Friedrich) Carl 1848-1936 Baker 92
Stumpf, Carolyn Joan 1940- WhoAmW 93, WhoE 93
Stumpf, Christof 1924- WhoScE 91-4
Stumpf, George Charles, Jr. 1950- WhoSSW 93
Stumpf, Helmut 1934- WhoScE 91-3
Stumpf, John Anthony 1952- St&PR 93
Stumpf, Joseph George 1938- WhoAm 92
Stumpf, Mark Howard 1947- WhoAm 92
Stumpf, Paul Karl 1919- WhoAm 92
Stumpf, Richard H. Law&B 92
Stumpf, Samuel Enoch 1918- WhoAm 92
Stumpf, Waldo Edmund 1942- WhoWor 93
Stumpf, Walter J., Jr. Law&B 92
Stumpff, Robert Thomas 1945- WhoE 93
Stumpfl, Eugen Friedrich 1931- WhoScE 91-4
Stumpo, Betty Louise 1966- WhoAmW 93
Stumpo, Carmine De Rogatis 1963- WhoWrEP 92
Stundza, Thomas John 1948- WhoAm 92
Stunkard, Albert James 1922- WhoAm 92
Stunkard, Horace W. 1889-1989 BioIn 17
Stunke, Eva 1913-1988 BioIn 17
Stuntz, Joseph Hartmann 1793-1859 Baker 92
Stuntz, Linda Gillespie 1954- WhoAm 92, WhoAmW 93
Stup, Janet Anita 1945- WhoAmW 93
Stupak, Ellen Mary 1948- WhoAmW 93
Stupfel, Maurice A. 1923- WhoScE 91-2
Stupin, Susan Lee 1954- WhoE 93, WhoEmL 93, WhoWor 93
Stupka, Frantisek 1879-1965 Baker 92
Stupka, Richard Cyril 1948- WhoWor 93
Stupnicka, Ewa 1931- WhoScE 91-4
Stupnicki, Jacek 1934- WhoScE 91-4
Stupnicki, Romuald 1932- WhoScE 91-4
Stupp, Edward Henry 1932- WhoE 93
Stupp, George W. 1942- St&PR 93
Stupp, Robert P. 1930- St&PR 93
Stupple, Donna-Marie Kathleen 1945- WhoWrEP 92
Stur, Margarete Wabnig 1958- WhoAmW 93
Stur, Otto B. 1926- WhoScE 91-4
Sturbaum, Barbara Ann 1936- WhoAmW 93
Sturdee, David William 1945- WhoWor 93
Sturdevant, Eugene J. 1930- WhoE 93
Sturdevant, George A. 1935- St&PR 93
Sturdevant, Richard G. 1937- St&PR 93
Sturdevant, Wayne Alan 1946- WhoSSW 93
Sturdivant, Frederick David 1937- WhoWrEP 92
Sturdivant, Linda Lee 1949- WhoE 93
Sturdivant, Thomas Carlock 1933- WhoSSW 93
Sturdy, Denise M. Law&B 92
Sturdy, Raymond O., Jr. Law&B 92
Sture-Vasa, Mary MajAI
Sturge, Michael Dudley 1931- WhoAm 92, WhoE 93
Sturgeon, Anna Louise 1951- WhoAmW 93
Sturgeon, Charles E. 1928- St&PR 93
Sturgeon, Charles Edwin 1928- WhoAm 92
Sturgeon, John A. 1940- St&PR 93
Sturgeon, Nicholas d1454 Baker 92
Sturgeon, Robert Stanley 1932- WhoSSW 93
Sturgeon, Theodore 1918-1985 BioIn 17, ScF&FL 92
Sturges, Hollister, III 1939- WhoAm 92
Sturges, Jeffrey Robert 1947- St&PR 93
Sturges, John d1992 NewYTBS 92 [port]
Sturges, John 1911- MiSFD 9
Sturges, John Eliot 1910- WhoAm 92
Sturges, John Siebrand 1939- WhoAm 92
Sturges, Preston BioIn 17
Sturges, Preston 1898-1959 MiSFD 9N, TwCLC 48 [port]
Sturges, Robert S(tuart) 1953- ConAu 138
Sturges, Sherry Lynn 1946- WhoAmW 93, WhoWor 93
Sturges, Wilton, III 1935- WhoAm 92
Sturgess, John Harry 1936- WhoAm 92
Sturgess, Thomas W. 1950- St&PR 93
Sturgill, Monnette Nairn 1948- WhoSSW 93
Sturgis, Bruce Thomas 1959- St&PR 93
Sturgis, Lawrence J. 1937- St&PR 93
Sturgis, Rebecca Forbes AmWomPl
Sturgis, Robert Shaw 1922- WhoAm 92
Sturgis, Somers Hayes 1904-1991 BioIn 17
Sturgis, Susanna J. ScF&FL 92
Sturgis, Thomas D. 1934- St&PR 93
Sturgis, William Beaufort 1934- St&PR 93
Sturley, Michael F. 1955- WhoAm 92
Sturm, Carolyn Parnell 1944- WhoSSW 93
Sturm, Douglas Earl 1929- WhoE 93
Sturm, Frank Conrad 1930- St&PR 93
Sturm, Fred Gillette 1925- WhoAm 92
Sturm, Glen Mark 1956- St&PR 93
Sturm, James Lester 1940-1990 BioIn 17
Sturm, Michael Richard 1930- St&PR 93
Sturm, Omer O. 1922- St&PR 93
Sturm, Robert K. 1937- St&PR 93
Sturm, Sandra 1947- St&PR 93
Sturman, Jonathan Mark 1943- St&PR 93
Sturman, Joseph Benjamin 1937- St&PR 93
Sturman, Joseph Howard 1931- WhoAm 92
Sturman, Robert Harries 1923- WhoAm 92, WhoWor 93
Sturmer, Boris Vladimirovich 1849-1917 BioIn 17
Sturmer, Bruno 1892-1958 Baker 92
Sturmey, Peter WhoScE 91-1
Sturner, Fred 1932- WhoE 93
Sturner, Michael 1962- St&PR 93
Sturnick, Judith Ann 1939- WhoAmW 93
Sturridge, Charles 1951- MiSFD 9
Sturrock, Peter Andrew 1924- WhoAm 92
Sturrock, Thomas Tracy 1921- WhoAm 92
Stursa, Jan 1956- WhoScE 91-4
Stursa, Jarmil 1933- WhoScE 91-4
Stursberg, Carl W. 1920-1991 BioIn 17
Sturt, Brian A. 1933- WhoScE 91-4
Sturt, Charles 1795-1869 Expl 93 [port]
Sturtevant, Brereton 1921- WhoAm 92
Sturtevant, Craig Mitchell Law&B 92
Sturtevant, Donald L. St&PR 93
Sturtevant, Jill M. Law&B 92
Sturtevant, Julian Munson 1908- WhoAm 92
Sturtevant, Richard Pearce 1943- WhoE 93
Sturtevant, Thomas C., Jr. Law&B 92
Sturtevant, William Curtis 1926- WhoAm 92
Sturtz, Donald Lee 1933- WhoAm 92, WhoE 93
Sturtz, George Stephen 1924- WhoE 93
Sturtz, Ronald M. 1930- WhoAm 92
Sturtz, W.B. 1951- St&PR 93
Sturtz-Davis, Shirley Zampelli 1937- WhoE 93
Sturzenegger, Otto 1926- WhoAm 92
Sturzenegger, Otto 1926-1990 BioIn 17
Sturzenegger, (Hans) Richard 1905-1976 Baker 92
Stusek, Anton 1932- WhoWor 93
Stusnick, Eric 1939- WhoSSW 93
Stusnick, Madeline Seidelle 1943- WhoAmW 93
Stussy, Jan 1921-1990 BioIn 17
Stute, Leona Irene 1938- WhoAmW 93
Stuter, Janice Cesolini 1946- WhoAmW 93
Stutman, Leonard Jay 1928- WhoE 93
Stutman, Perry J. 1929- St&PR 93
Stutrud, D.M. 1947- St&PR 93
Stutschewsky, Joachim 1892-1982 Baker 92
Stutt, William C. 1927- St&PR 93
Stutt, William Chapman 1927- WhoAm 92
Stuttering John BioIn 17
Stutts, David Y. 1959- St&PR 93
Stutts, Terrell E. 1929- St&PR 93
Stutz, Bruce 1950- ConAu 139
Stutz, Eugene Lee 1938- WhoSSW 93
Stutz, George L. 1921- St&PR 93
Stutz, Peter L. 1940- WhoScE 91-4
Stutz, Rolf 1949- St&PR 93
Stutz, Stanley J. 1920-1975 BiDAMSp 1989
Stutzman, Anita 1934- St&PR 93
Stutzman, Byron William 1938- WhoE 93
Stutzman, Esther Friesner- ScF&FL 92
Stutzman, Frederic M. 1949- St&PR 93
Stutzman, Linford L. 1950- ConAu 139
Stutzman, Rebecca Lynn 1953- WhoAmW 93
Stutzman, Thomas Chase, Sr. 1950- WhoWor 93
Stutzman, Warren Lee 1941- WhoAm 92, WhoSSW 93
Stuven, Susan Knauf 1945- WhoE 93
Stuver, Francis Edward 1912- WhoAm 92
Stuvinski, B. C. 1953- WhoEmL 93
Stuwe, Hein P. 1930- WhoScE 91-4
Stuy, Timothy Ogden 1962- WhoE 93
Stuzin, Charles Law&B 92
Stuzin, Charles Bryan 1942- St&PR 93, WhoAm 92
Stwalley, William Calvin 1942- WhoAm 92
Stwosz, Wit 1438-1533 PolBiDi
Styan, John Louis 1923- WhoAm 92
Styblo, Karel WhoScE 91-2
Stycos, Joseph Mayone 1927- WhoAm 92
Styczen, Krystyn Antoni 1947- WhoWor 93
Styczynski, Lyn Eileen 1950- WhoAmW 93
Stydahar, Joe 1912-1977 BioIn 17
Styer, J. Franklin 1900- BioIn 17
Styers, Ronald Evan 1952- WhoSSW 93
Styka, Jan 1858-1925 PolBiDi
Styka, Tadeusz 1889-1958 PolBiDi
Styles, Beverly 1923- WhoAmW 93, WhoWor 93
Styles, Deborah Merritt 1939- WhoAmW 93
Styles, John Henry 1937- St&PR 93
Styles, Margretta Madden 1930- WhoAm 92, WhoAmW 93
Styles, Richard Geoffrey Pentland 1930- WhoAm 92
Styles, Teresa Jo 1950- WhoAmW 93, WhoWrEP 92
Stylianides, Dimitrious 1929- WhoScE 91-3
Stylianos, Andrew John 1956- ConAu 138
Stylianou, Yerolemos 1935- WhoScE 91-4
Stylistics SoulM
Styne, Jule 1905- Baker 92, WhoAm 92
Stynes, Barbara Bilello 1951- WhoAmW 93
Stynes, Stanley Kenneth 1932- WhoAm 92
Stypinski, Anthony 1937- St&PR 93
Styppeiotes OxDcByz
Styrikovich, Mikhail Adolfovich 1902- WhoWor 93
Styron, Charles Woodrow, Sr. 1913- WhoSSW 93
Styron, Rose Burgunder 1928- WhoAmW 93
Styron, William 1925- BioIn 17, WhoAm 92, WhoE 93, WhoWor 93, WhoWrEP 92
Stys, Rudolph Donald 1935- St&PR 93
Styskal, Richard A. d1990 BioIn 17
Styslinger, Lee Joseph, Jr. 1933- St&PR 93, WhoAm 92, WhoWor 93
Su, Dongzhuang 1932- WhoWor 93
Su, Helen Chien-fan 1922- WhoAm 92, WhoSSW 93, WhoWor 93
Su, Huang 1934- WhoWor 93
Su, Jen-Houne Hannsen 1954- WhoE 93
Su, Judy Ya Hwa Lin 1938- WhoAmW 93
Su, Kendall Ling-Chiao 1926- WhoAm 92
Su, Nan-Yao 1951- WhoSSW 93
Su, Qi 1947- WhoWor 93
Su, Sandra 1946- WhoAmW 93
Su, Stephen Y. H. 1938- WhoAm 92
Su, Teddy Tsauh-An 1935- WhoE 93
Su, Tzu-Jeng 1956- WhoSSW 93
Su, Yucai 1963- WhoWor 93
Suadlenak, Loree Dean 1931- St&PR 93
Suard, Pierre Henri Andre 1934- WhoWor 93
Suares, Jean-Claude 1942- ScF&FL 92
Suarez, Carlos Enrique 1936- WhoWor 93
Suarez, Dennis Lee 1948- WhoSSW 93
Suarez, Eduardo BioIn 17
Suarez, Eduardo 1952- WhoWor 93
Suarez, George Michael 1955- WhoSSW 93
Suarez, James A. 1944- St&PR 93
Suarez, Jose Edison 1962- WhoWor 93
Suarez, Joseph Peter Law&B 92
Suarez, Michael Anthony 1948- WhoEmL 93
Suarez, Robert 1928- HispAmA [port]
Suarez, Roberto WhoAm 92, WhoSSW 93
Suarez, Roberto J. 1928- St&PR 93
Suarez, Xavier L. 1949- HispAmA [port]
Suarez, Xavier Louis 1949- WhoAm 92, WhoSSW 93
Suarez-Fernandez, Guillermo 1929- WhoScE 91-3
Suarez Gonzalez, Adolfo 1932- WhoWor 93
Suarez-Murias, Marguerite C. 1921- WhoAm 92
Suazo Cordova, Roberto 1927- DcCPCAm
Suba, Antonio Ronquillo 1927- WhoAm 92
Suba, Steven Antonio 1957- WhoSSW 93
Subach, Albert John 1943- St&PR 93
Subach, James Alan 1948- WhoWor 93
Subak, John T. Law&B 92
Subak, John Thomas 1929- St&PR 93, WhoAm 92

Subak-Sharpe, Genell Jackson *WhoAmW 93*
Subak-Sharpe, Gerald Emil 1925- *WhoAm 92*
Subak-Sharpe, J.H. *WhoScE 91-1*
Subbiah, Nat 1932- *WhoWor 93*
Subbotin, Igor Yakov 1950- *WhoWor 93*
Suber, Donald Byron 1935- *St&PR 93*
Suber, Margaret Adele 1917- *WhoSSW 93*
Suber, Tommie Lee 1947- *WhoWor 93*
Subercaseaux, Benjamin 1902-1973 *SpAmA*
Suberlak, Raymond John *Law&B 92*
Subhas Chandra Bose 1897-1945 *BioIn 17*
Subiela, Eliseo 1944- *MiSFD 9*
Subin, Bertram W. 1930-1991 *BioIn 17*
Subira (Puig), Jose 1882-1980 *Baker 92*
Subirana, Juan A. 1936- *WhoScE 91-3*
Subirana, Juan Antonio 1936- *WhoWor 93*
Subkowsky, Elizabeth 1949- *WhoAmW 93*
Subler, Edward Pierre 1927- *WhoAm 92*
Sublett, Bobby Jones 1931- *WhoSSW 93*
Sublett, Carl Cecil 1919- *WhoAm 92*
Sublett, Edward Ray *Law&B 92*
Sublett, Henry Lee, Jr. 1926- *WhoAm 92*
Subono, Blacius 1954- *Baker 92*
Subotai c. 1172-1245 *HarEnMi*
Subotnick, Morton 1933- *Baker 92*
Subotowicz, Mieczyslaw 1924- *WhoScE 91-4*
Subotowicz, Wieslaw 1935- *WhoScE 91-4*
Subotsky, Milt *ConTFT 10*
Subotsky, Milton 1921-1991 *ConTFT 10, ScF&FL 92*
Subowo, Yohanes 1960- *Baker 92*
Subrahmanyam, Devaguptapu 1932- *WhoUN 92*
Subramaniam, Chidambaram 1910- *WhoAsAP 91*
Subramaniam, Shivan S. 1949- *WhoIns 93*
Subramaniam, Shivan Sivaswamy 1949- *St&PR 93, WhoAm 92*
Subramanian, Eswar 1957- *St&PR 93*
Subramanian, P.N. Ganapathi 1938- *WhoUN 92*
Subramanian, R. Shankar 1947- *WhoE 93*
Subramanian, Veerappan Sellappan 1950- *WhoAm 92*
Subramanyam, Madakasira 1949- *WhoE 93*
Subramanyam, Mark 1949- *St&PR 93*
Substad Lokensgard-Schimmelpfennig, Kathryn Ann 1941- *WhoAmW 93*
Subtelny, Joanne *BioIn 17*
Subuh, Pak 1901-1987 *BioIn 17*
Succuso, Peter James 1950- *WhoAm 92*
Sucena Paiva, Jose Pedro 1943- *WhoWor 93*
Such, Peter 1939- *WhoCanL 92*
Suchanek, Leonard Joseph 1937- *WhoAm 92*
Sucharitkul, Somtow *BioIn 17*
Sucharitkul, Somtow 1952- *ScF&FL 92*
Sucharow, Lawrence Alan 1949- *WhoE 93*
Suchek, Valentin Irineu 1945- *WhoWor 93*
Sucher, Cynthia Clayton Crumb 1943- *WhoAmW 93*
Sucher, Josef 1843-1908 *Baker 92*
Sucher, Rosa 1847-1927 *OxDcOp*
Sucher, Rosa 1849-1927 *Baker 92*
Suchet, Louis Gabriel 1770-1826 *HarEnMi*
Suchik, Martin 1945- *St&PR 93*
Suchil, Sally *Law&B 92*
Suchil, Sally 1951- *St&PR 93*
Suchinda Kraprayoon *BioIn 17*
Suchla, David F. 1947- *St&PR 93*
Suchlicki, Jaime 1939- *WhoSSW 93*
Suchman, Charles Lustig 1930- *St&PR 93*
Suchman, Jaroslav 1942- *WhoUN 92*
Suchocka, Hanna 1946- *WhoWor 93*
Suchocki, Andrzej 1953- *WhoWor 93*
Suchodolski, January 1797-1875 *PolBiDi*
Suchodolski, Ronald Eugene 1946- *WhoAm 92*
Suchodolski, Stanley Edward, Jr. 1949- *WhoE 93*
Suchoff, Benjamin 1918- *Baker 92*
Suchomel, James M. 1950- *St&PR 93*
Suchomel, Jeffrey Raymond 1956- *WhoWor 93*
Suchon, Eugen 1908- *Baker 92, OxDcOp*
Suchy, Frantisek 1891-1973 *Baker 92*
Suchy, Frantisek 1902-1977 *Baker 92*
Suchy, Jiri Jan 1931- *WhoWor 93*
Suchy, Kurt 1926- *WhoScE 91-3, WhoWor 93*
Suchy, Susanne N. 1945- *WhoAmW 93*
Sucich, Diana Catherine 1948- *WhoE 93*
Suckert, Curzio 1898-1957 *BioIn 17*
Suckiel, Ellen Kappy 1943- *WhoAm 92*
Suckley, Margaret L. d1991 *BioIn 17*
Suckling, Colin James *WhoScE 91-1*
Suckling, John 1609-1641? *DcLB 126 [port]*
Suckling, John 1609-1642 *BioIn 17*
Suckling, Nigel *ScF&FL 92*
Suckling, Norman 1904- *Baker 92*
Suckling, Robert John 1944- *WhoAsAP 91*
Suckon, Deborah R. *St&PR 93*
Suckow, Ruth 1892-1960 *AmWomPl, BioIn 17*
Sucksdorff, Christian G. 1928- *WhoScE 91-4*
Suczek, Alexander 1928- *St&PR 93*
Sud, Veena Cabreros- *BioIn 17*
Suda, Stanislav 1865-1931 *Baker 92*
Sudak, Howard Stanley 1932- *WhoAm 92*
Sudak, Janice 1958- *WhoAmW 93*
Sudan, Nalin Kumar 1951- *WhoE 93*
Sudan, Ravindra Nath 1931- *WhoAm 92*
Sudanowicz, Elaine Marie 1956- *WhoAmW 93*
Sudarkasa, Niara 1938- *ConBlB 4 [port], WhoAmW 93*
Sudarshan, George 1931- *WhoAm 92*
Sudarsky, Jerry M. 1918- *WhoAm 92*
Sudarsky, Michael 1924- *St&PR 93*
Sudarsono, Budi Santoso 1936- *WhoUN 92*
Sudbery, Anthony 1943- *WhoWor 93*
Sudbery, Rodie 1943- *ScF&FL 92*
Sudbury, Charles Steven 1954- *WhoSSW 93*
Sudbury, David Marshall *Law&B 92*
Sudbury, David Marshall 1945- *St&PR 93, WhoAm 92*
Sudbury, John Dean 1925- *WhoAm 92*
Suddath, John Frank 1935- *WhoSSW 93*
Sudderth, Robert Jamison, Jr. 1942- *St&PR 93*
Suddick, Patrick Joseph 1923- *WhoAm 92*
Suddick, Richard Phillips 1934- *WhoAm 92*
Suddock, Frances Suter Thorson 1914- *WhoAmW 93*
Sudds, Richard Huyette, Jr. 1927- *WhoAm 92*
Sudds, William 1843-1920 *Baker 92*
Sudduth, Dan D. *St&PR 93*
Sudduth, William McLean 1945- *WhoSSW 93*
Sudek, Josef 1896-1976 *BioIn 17*
Sudermann, Hermann 1857-1928 *DcLB 118 [port]*
Sudharmono 1927- *WhoWor 93*
Sudharmono, Lt. Gen. *WhoAsAP 91*
Sudhoff, Juergen H. 1935- *WhoWor 93*
Sudhoff, Robert J. 1955- *St&PR 93*
Sudikoff, J.P. *BioIn 17*
Sudler, Louis C. d1992 *NewYTBS 92*
Sudler, Louis Courtenay 1903- *WhoAm 92*
Sudnick, Edward L. 1939- *St&PR 93*
Sudo, Ryotaro 1933- *WhoAsAP 91*
Sudo, Seiichi 1949- *WhoWor 93*
Sudol, Michael C., Jr. *Law&B 92*
Sudol, Walter E. *Law&B 92*
Sudol, Walter Edward 1942- *St&PR 93*
Sudomo 1926- *WhoAsAP 91*
Sudrajat, Edi *BioIn 17*
Sudweeks, Earl Max 1933- *WhoSSW 93*
Sudweeks, Walter Bentley 1940- *WhoAm 92*
Sue, Alan Kwai Keong 1946- *WhoEmL 93, WhoWor 93*
Sue, Eugene 1804-1857 *DcLB 119 [port]*
Sue, Herbert John *Law&B 92*
Sue, L.J. *St&PR 93*
Suebsaeng, Apinya 1951- *St&PR 93*
Suedekum, Ron N. 1952- *St&PR 93*
Suedfeld, Peter 1935- *WhoAm 92*
Suehs, Derrick Jourdain 1954- *WhoEmL 93*
Suelflow, August Robert 1922- *WhoAm 92*
Sueltenfuss, Elizabeth Anne 1921- *WhoAm 92, WhoAmW 93, WhoSSW 93*
Sueltenfuss, Gene A. 1955- *St&PR 93*
Suelter, Len G. 1935- *St&PR 93*
Suen, Ching Yee 1942- *WhoAm 92*
Suen, James Yee 1940- *WhoAm 92*
Suenens, Leo Joseph Cardinal 1904- *WhoWor 93*
Suenholz, Herman H. 1924- *St&PR 93*
Suenholz, Herman Harry 1924- *WhoAm 92*
Suer, Marvin David 1923- *WhoAm 92*
Sues, Alan *BioIn 17*
Suess, Duane A. 1955- *St&PR 93*
Suess, James Francis 1950- *WhoWor 93*
Suess, Michael J. 1933- *WhoUN 92*
Suesse, Dana 1911-1987 *Baker 92*
Suetaka, Kamezo 1884-1955 *HarEnMi*
Suetaka, Tohru 1929- *WhoWor 93*
Sue-Ting-Len, Barbara 1942- *WhoAmW 93*
Suetonius Paulinus, Gaius fl. 41-69 *HarEnMi*
Suey, David P. 1932- *St&PR 93*
Suffling, Mark *ScF&FL 92*
Suffolk, Countess of 1681-1767 *BioIn 17*
Suffredini, Kathleen Deery 1951- *WhoAmW 93*
Suffren Saint-Tropez, Pierre Andre de 1729-1788 *HarEnMi*
Sufian, Harris Ian *Law&B 92*
Sufrin, Erica Marie 1944- *WhoAmW 93, WhoE 93*
Sufrin, Howard Leon 1930- *St&PR 93*
Sufrin, Janice Richman 1941- *WhoAmW 93*
Sufrin, Joseph H. 1935- *St&PR 93*
Suga, Hiroshi 1930- *WhoWor 93*
Suga, Nelson 1942- *WhoWor 93*
Suga, Yoichi 1935- *WhoWor 93*
Suga, Yusuke *BioIn 17*
Sugano, Etsuko 1942- *WhoAsAP 91*
Sugano, Hisamitsu 1928- *WhoAsAP 91*
Sugano, Shigeru 1924- *WhoWor 93*
Suganuma, Masahisa 1927- *WhoWor 93*
Sugar, Andrew *ScF&FL 92*
Sugar, Bert Randolph 1937- *WhoWrEP 92*
Sugar, Jack 1929- *WhoE 93*
Sugar, Lawrence D. 1945- *St&PR 93*
Sugar, Michael Alan 1954- *St&PR 93*
Sugar, Peter Frigyes 1919- *WhoAm 92*
Sugar, Rezso 1919-1988 *Baker 92*
Sugar, Sandra Lee 1942- *WhoAmW 93*
Sugarman, Alan William 1924- *WhoAm 92*
Sugarman, Bahira 1945- *WhoAmW 93*
Sugarman, Burt 1938- *WhoAm 92*
Sugarman, Charles Jules 1949- *WhoSSW 93*
Sugarman, David *WhoScE 91-1*
Sugarman, George *BioIn 17*
Sugarman, George 1912- *WhoAm 92*
Sugarman, Jay *BioIn 17*
Sugarman, Joan 1917- *BioIn 17*
Sugarman, Jule M. 1927- *WhoAm 92*
Sugarman, Leonard *St&PR 93*
Sugarman, Nathan 1917-1990 *BioIn 17*
Sugarman, Paul Ronald 1931- *WhoAm 92*
Sugarman, Richard H. *Law&B 92*
Sugarman, Robert Gary 1939- *WhoAm 92*
Sugarman, Robert Jay 1938- *WhoAm 92*
Sugarman, Samuel Louis 1927- *WhoAm 92*
Sugarman, Stuart *Law&B 92*
Sugarman, Suzi Loewenstern 1944- *WhoAm 92*
Sugavanam, Ananthanarayanan 1946- *WhoSSW 93*
Sugavanam, Balasubramanyan 1938- *WhoUN 92*
Sugawara, Hideaki 1945- *WhoWor 93*
Sugawara, Isamu 1949- *WhoWor 93*
Sugawara, Kijuro 1926- *WhoAsAP 91*
Sugaya, Eiichi 1929- *WhoWor 93*
Sugden, David Edward *WhoScE 91-1*
Sugden, George W. 1924- *St&PR 93*
Sugden, John Kennedy *WhoScE 91-1*
Sugden, Richard Lee 1959- *WhoEmL 93*
Sugden, Robert *WhoScE 91-1*
Sugendran, Vadivelan 1949- *WhoWor 93*
Sugerman, Abraham Arthur 1929- *WhoAm 92*
Sugerman, Andrew *MiSFD 9*
Sugerman, Danny 1954- *ConAu 137*
Sugerman, Lewis 1927- *St&PR 93*
Sugeta, Shigeaki 1933- *WhoWor 93*
Sugg, B. Alan *WhoSSW 93*
Sugg, John Logan 1914- *WhoAm 92*
Sugg, Michael Ned 1950- *WhoSSW 93*
Sugg, Phyllis Taylor 1951- *WhoSSW 93*
Sugg, Robert Perkins 1916- *WhoAm 92*
Suggett, A. *WhoScE 91-1*
Suggia, Guilhermina 1888-1950 *Baker 92*
Suggs, Alvin *Law&B 92*
Suggs, Carroll W. 1938- *St&PR 93, WhoSSW 93*
Suggs, Marion Jack 1924- *WhoAm 92*
Suggs, Shelly 1966- *St&PR 93*
Suggs, Susan Gordy 1951- *WhoSSW 93*
Suggs, Welch *ScF&FL 92*
Sughrue, Karen Marie 1951- *WhoAmW 93*
Sugihara, Gohsuke 1936- *WhoWor 93*
Sugihara, Hikoichi 1919- *WhoWor 93*
Sugihara, Kenzi 1940- *WhoAm 92*
Sugihara, Thomas Tamotsu 1924- *WhoAm 92*
Sugiki, Shigemi 1936- *WhoWor 93*
Sugimoto, L.A. *Law&B 92*
Sugintas, Nora Maria 1956- *WhoAmW 93*
Sugioka, Kenneth 1920- *WhoAm 92*
Sugita, Kimio 1941- *WhoWor 93*
Sugiura, Masahiro 1936- *WhoWor 93*
Sugiura, Nariaki 1935- *WhoWor 93*
Sugiura, Seiken 1934- *WhoAsAP 91*
Sugiyama, Hajime 1880-1945 *HarEnMi*
Sugiyama, Hiroshi 1956- *WhoWor 93*
Sugiyama, Kazunori 1950- *WhoE 93*
Sugiyama, Meiko 1934- *WhoWor 93*
Sugiyama, Norio 1930- *WhoAsAP 91*
Sugiyama, Toku Mary 1921- *WhoE 93*
Suglia, Anthony F. 1926- *WhoAm 92*
Suglia, Patrick Vincent 1962- *WhoE 93*
Sugrim, Charles 1960- *WhoWor 93*
Sugrue, Francis J. d1990 *BioIn 17*
Sugrue, Terrance B. 1939- *St&PR 93*
Suh, Byungse 1941- *WhoE 93*
Suh, Gina *BioIn 17*
Suh, Ki-Won 1930- *WhoWor 93*
Suh, Nam Pyo 1936- *WhoAm 92*
Suhag, Sunil 1958- *St&PR 93*
Suharto 1921- *BioIn 17, WhoWor 93*
Suharto, Raden 1921- *DcTwHis*
Suh Chung Hwa 1934- *WhoAsAP 91*
Suh Chung Won 1944- *WhoAsAP 91*
Suher, Thomas R. *Law&B 92*
Suh Jung-Hwa 1940- *WhoAsAP 91*
Suhl, Yuri (Menachem) 1908-1986 *ConAu 38NR, MajAI [port]*
Suhler, John Stuart 1943- *WhoAm 92*
Suhler, Kenneth Charles 1930- *WhoSSW 93*
Suhm, Raymond Walter 1941- *WhoSSW 93*
Suhocki, Donald James 1950- *WhoE 93*
Suhor, Yvonne *BioIn 17*
Suhowatsky, Stephen J. 1939- *St&PR 93*
Suhowatsky, Stephen Joseph 1939- *WhoAm 92*
Suhr, Gregory Kelley 1947- *WhoSSW 93*
Suhr, Heinrich P. d1990 *BioIn 17*
Suhr, J. Nicholas 1942- *WhoE 93, WhoWor 93*
Suhr, L. Gene 1934- *St&PR 93*
Suhr, Meredith L. 1943- *St&PR 93*
Suhr, Paul Heinrich *Law&B 92*
Suhr, Peter John 1927- *St&PR 93*
Suhrbier, Klaus Rudolf 1930- *WhoWor 93*
Suhre, Joanne Osman 1944- *St&PR 93*
Suhre, Walter A., Jr. *Law&B 92*
Suhre, Walter Anthony, Jr. 1933- *St&PR 93, WhoAm 92*
Suhrheinrich, Richard Fred 1936- *WhoAm 92*
Suhrholm, Ole 1932- *WhoWor 93*
Suh Sang-Mok 1948- *WhoAsAP 91*
Suhubi, Erdogan Suleyman 1934- *WhoScE 91-4*
Suhud, Kharis *WhoAsAP 91*
Sui, Frank 1962- *WhoE 93*
Suinn, Richard Michael 1933- *WhoAm 92*
Suisman, Edward d1991 *BioIn 17*
Suisman, Michael 1928- *St&PR 93*
Suissa, Daniele J. 1940- *MiSFD 9*
Suissa, Mireille Renee 1942- *WhoAmW 93*
Suit, John McCeney, II 1944- *St&PR 93*
Suiter, John William 1926- *WhoWor 93*
Suiter, Roger Norman 1939- *WhoSSW 93*
Suiter, Sheary Sue 1951- *WhoWrEP 92*
Suitner, Otmar 1922- *Baker 92, OxDcOp, WhoWor 93*
Suits, Bernard Herbert 1925- *WhoAm 92, WhoWrEP 92*
Suits, Chauncey Guy 1905-1991 *BioIn 17*
Suits, Daniel Burbidge 1918- *WhoAm 92*
Suits, Janice Crye 1947- *WhoAmW 93*
Suits, Valerie Faye 1957- *WhoAmW 93*
Suitt, Thomas Howard 1926- *St&PR 93, WhoAm 92*
Suizzo-Morris, Karen A. *Law&B 92*
Sujack, Edwin Thomas 1927- *WhoAm 92*
Sujak, John J. 1946- *St&PR 93*
Sujan, Mita 1953- *WhoE 93*
Sujarit, Bum Soon Park 1951- *WhoSSW 93*
Sujkowski, Ziemowid 1933- *WhoScE 91-4*
Sujo, Clara Diament *WhoAm 92*
Su Juxian d1991 *BioIn 17*
Suk, Jin Hong 1937- *WhoE 93*
Suk, Josef 1929- *WhoWor 93*
Suk, Josef, I 1874-1935 *Baker 92*
Suk, Josef, II 1929- *Baker 92*
Suk, Julie *ConAu 38NR*
Suk, Vasa 1861-1933 *Baker 92*
Suk, Vojtech 1879-1967 *IntDcAn*
Sukam, Osu Bin Haji 1949- *WhoAsAP 91*
Sukandar, Dadang 1936- *WhoUN 92*
Sukarno 1901-1970 *BioIn 17*
Sukarno, Achmad 1901-1970 *DcTwHis*
Sukarno, Bung 1901-1970 *ColdWar 2 [port]*
Sukegawa, Toshiya 1930- *Baker 92*
Sukel, Arthur 1937- *St&PR 93, WhoAm 92*
Sukenick, Ronald *BioIn 17*
Sukenick, Ronald 1932- *JeAmFiW*
Sukert, Bruce Steven 1960- *WhoSSW 93*
Sukerta, Pande Made 1953- *Baker 92*
Suket, Judith Ann 1942- *WhoAmW 93*
Sukhodrev, Victor M. 1932- *WhoUN 92*
Sukhomlinov, Vladimir Aleksandrovich 1848-1926 *BioIn 17*
Sukina'a, John Forman 1954- *WhoAsAP 91*
Suk Joon Kyu 1934- *WhoAsAP 91*
Suknaski, Andrew 1942- *WhoCanL 92*
Suko, Anna Guest 1933- *WhoAmW 93*
Sukow, Russell L. 1943- *St&PR 93*
Sukrau, Janis Lee *Law&B 92*
Sukriket, Parichote 1946- *WhoWor 93*
Sukselainen, Juhani *WhoScE 91-4*
Suksin, Vasilij 1929-1974 *DrEEuF*

Sukul, P.N. 1932- *WhoAsAP 91*
Sukun, Kamil Mehmet 1948- *WhoWor 93*
Sulaiman Bin Haji Daud, Dato' Raja Ariffin Bin Raja 1941- *WhoAsAP 91*
Sulavik, Stephen Blaise 1930- *WhoAm 92*
Sulcer, Frederick Durham 1932- *WhoAm 92*
Sulcer, James R. 1928- *WhoIns 93*
Sulcz, Ferenc 1921- *WhoScE 91-4*
Sule, Sandor *WhoScE 91-4*
Sule, Yusuf Maitama (Alhaji) 1929- *WhoAfr*
Suleik, Mercedes Balota 1940- *WhoWor 93*
Suleiman, I 1494-1566 *HarEnMi*
Suleiman, I, Sultan of the Turks 1495-1566 *BioIn 17*
Suleiman, II 1494-1566 *HarEnMi*
Suleimanov, Naim *BioIn 17*
Suleimenov, Tuleutai 1941- *WhoWor 93*
Sulek, Stjepan 1914-1986 *Baker 92*
Suleman, Farid 1951- *St&PR 93*
Sulentic, Jack William 1947- *WhoSSW 93*
Suleri, Sara 1953- *ConAu 136*
Suleski, James 1953- *WhoIns 93*
Suleski, Scott D. 1959- *St&PR 93*
Suleyman, I, Sultan of the Turks 1495-1566 *BioIn 17*
Suleyman Celebi 1377?-1411 *OxDcByz*
Suleyman Ibn Kutulmus d1086 *OxDcByz*
Suleymanoglu, Naim *BioIn 17*
Suleyman Pasha d1357 *OxDcByz*
Sulfaro, Joyce A. 1948- *WhoSSW 93*
Sulfaro, Susan K. *Law&B 92*
Sulg, Madis 1943- *St&PR 93, WhoAm 92, WhoWor 93*
Sulger, Francis Xavier 1942- *WhoAm 92*
Suliburk, William P. 1947- *St&PR 93*
Sulica, Andrei 1938- *WhoScE 91-4*
Sulick, Peter, Jr. 1950- *WhoAm 92*
Sulick, Robert John 1947- *WhoWor 93*
Sulieman, Omer Elhag M. 1940- *WhoUN 92*
Sulik, Edwin 1957- *WhoSSW 93, WhoWor 93*
Sulimirski, Witold Stanislaw 1933- *St&PR 93, WhoAm 92*
Sulinowski, Stanislaw *WhoScE 91-4*
Suliotis, Elena 1943- *WhoWor 93*
Sulivan, Jean 1913-1980 *BioIn 17*
Sulkava, Seppo A. 1931- *WhoScE 91-4*
Sulkes, Carol F. 1953- *St&PR 93*
Sulkin, Howard Allen 1941- *WhoAm 92*
Sulkin, Sidney 1918- *WhoAm 92, WhoWrEP 92*
Sulla, Lucius Cornelius 138BC-78BC *HarEnMi*
Sullavan, Margaret 1911-1960 *IntDcF 2-3 [port]*
Sullebarger, John Thompson 1957- *WhoSSW 93*
Sullenbarger, Daniel James *Law&B 92*
Sullenberger, Debra Marie 1956- *WhoAmW 93*
Sullender, J.E. 1930- *St&PR 93*
Suller, Debra Jane 1948- *WhoAmW 93*
Sullerot, Evelyne 1924- *BioIn 17*
Sullini, Roberto 1943- *WhoScE 91-3*
Sullins, Thomas Neal *Law&B 92*
Sullivan, Adele Woodhouse *WhoAm 92*
Sullivan, Alan 1868-1947 *BioIn 17*
Sullivan, Allen R. 1941- *WhoSSW 93*
Sullivan, Allen Trousdale 1927- *WhoAm 92*
Sullivan, Andrew *BioIn 17, NewYTBS 92 [port]*
Sullivan, Andrew Richard 1956- *WhoE 93*
Sullivan, Anne Dorothy Hevner 1929- *WhoE 93*
Sullivan, Anne Elizabeth 1942- *WhoAm 92*
Sullivan, Arnold C. 1935- *WhoAm 92*
Sullivan, Arthur 1842-1900 *BioIn 17, OxDcOp*
Sullivan, Arthur Philip 1943- *WhoE 93*
Sullivan, Arthur (Seymour) 1842-1900 *Baker 92*
Sullivan, Austin P., Jr. 1940- *St&PR 93*
Sullivan, Austin Padraic, Jr. 1940- *WhoAm 92*
Sullivan, Barbara Ann 1952- *WhoAmW 93*
Sullivan, Barbara Boyle 1937- *WhoAm 92*
Sullivan, Barry 1949- *WhoEmL 93*
Sullivan, Barry M. 1945- *St&PR 93*
Sullivan, Barry Michael 1945- *WhoAm 92*
Sullivan, Ben Frank, Jr. 1919- *WhoSSW 93*
Sullivan, Benjamin Joseph 1918- *St&PR 93*
Sullivan, Bernice Dekko 1927- *St&PR 93*
Sullivan, Bolton 1896-1990 *BioIn 17*
Sullivan, Bonnie Alice *Law&B 92*
Sullivan, Brendan V. *BioIn 17*
Sullivan, Brian 1924- *WhoAm 92*
Sullivan, C.W., III 1944- *ScF&FL 92*
Sullivan, C(harles) W(illiam) III 1944- *ConAu 139*
Sullivan, Carol Fischer 1954- *WhoAmW 93*
Sullivan, Carol M. Nestor 1954- *WhoAmW 93*
Sullivan, Charles 1933- *WhoAm 92, WhoE 93*
Sullivan, Charles Irving 1918- *WhoE 93*
Sullivan, Charles J. 1939- *St&PR 93*
Sullivan, Charles William, III 1944- *WhoSSW 93*
Sullivan, Charlotte Thomas 1963- *WhoAmW 93*
Sullivan, Chris T. *St&PR 93*
Sullivan, Christine Calliontzis 1961- *WhoAmW 93*
Sullivan, Claire Ferguson 1937- *WhoAmW 93, WhoWor 93*
Sullivan, Colleen 1950-1991 *BioIn 17*
Sullivan, Connie Castleberry 1934- *WhoAmW 93, WhoWor 93*
Sullivan, Cornelius F., Jr. *Law&B 92*
Sullivan, Cornelius G. *Law&B 92*
Sullivan, Cornelius Wayne 1943- *WhoAm 92*
Sullivan, Daniel A. 1951- *St&PR 93*
Sullivan, Daniel A., Jr. *Law&B 92*
Sullivan, Daniel Edmond 1946- *WhoSSW 93*
Sullivan, Daniel F. 1935- *St&PR 93*
Sullivan, Daniel Joseph 1935- *WhoAm 92*
Sullivan, Daniel Joseph 1949- *WhoE 93*
Sullivan, Daniel Richard 1951- *WhoE 93*
Sullivan, Daniel W. *Law&B 92*
Sullivan, Danny *BioIn 17*
Sullivan, David Ignatius 1951- *St&PR 93*
Sullivan, David J., Jr. 1931- *St&PR 93*
Sullivan, Denis Francis, Jr. 1944- *WhoE 93*
Sullivan, Dennis F. 1943- *WhoAm 92*
Sullivan, Dennis Francis 1943- *St&PR 93*
Sullivan, Dennis J., Jr. 1932- *St&PR 93*
Sullivan, Dennis James, Jr. 1932- *WhoAm 92*
Sullivan, Dennis K. *Law&B 92*
Sullivan, Dennis Kelly *Law&B 92*
Sullivan, Dennis W. 1938 *St&PR 93, WhoAm 92*
Sullivan, Dolores P. 1925- *WhoAmW 93*
Sullivan, Donald 1930- *WhoAm 92*
Sullivan, Donald G. 1941- *St&PR 93*
Sullivan, Dorothy Louise 1938- *WhoE 93*
Sullivan, Dorothy Rona 1941- *WhoE 93*
Sullivan, E. D. S. 1918- *ScF&FL 92*
Sullivan, Earl Iseman 1923- *WhoSSW 93*
Sullivan, Ed 1902-1974 *BioIn 17*
Sullivan, Edmund 1941- *BioIn 17*
Sullivan, Edmund Joseph 1951- *WhoE 93*
Sullivan, Edward Cuyler 1906- *WhoAm 92*
Sullivan, Edward J. 1929- *St&PR 93*
Sullivan, Edward Joseph 1915- *WhoWor 93*
Sullivan, Edward L., Jr. *Law&B 92*
Sullivan, Edward M. 1947- *St&PR 93*
Sullivan, Edward Myles 1948- *WhoSSW 93*
Sullivan, Eleanor *BioIn 17*
Sullivan, Eleanor 1928-1991 *ScF&FL 92*
Sullivan, Eleanor (Regis) 1928-1991 *ConAu 139*
Sullivan, Elizabeth Ann 1962- *WhoAmW 93*
Sullivan, Elizabeth Higgins 1874- *AmWomPl*
Sullivan, Ellen F. 1956- *St&PR 93*
Sullivan, Eugene John Joseph 1920- *WhoAm 92*
Sullivan, Eugene Joseph 1943- *WhoAm 92*
Sullivan, Eugene R. 1941- *CngDr 91*
Sullivan, Eugene Raymond 1941- *WhoAm 92*
Sullivan, Faith 1933- *ScF&FL 92*
Sullivan, Francis Charles 1927- *WhoAm 92*
Sullivan, Francis Edward 1941- *WhoAm 92*
Sullivan, Frank 1892-1976 *JrnUS*
Sullivan, Fred G. *MiSFD 9*
Sullivan, Fred R. 1914- *St&PR 93*
Sullivan, Frederick William 1928- *St&PR 93, WhoAm 92*
Sullivan, Garrett 1945- *St&PR 93*
Sullivan, Gary J. *Law&B 92*
Sullivan, George Anerson *WhoWor 93*
Sullivan, George D. *Law&B 92*
Sullivan, George Edmund 1932- *WhoAm 92*
Sullivan, George Edward 1927- *WhoAm 92*
Sullivan, George Murray 1922- *WhoAm 92, WhoWor 93*
Sullivan, Gerald Clayton 1930- *St&PR 93*
Sullivan, Gladys Ann 1931- *WhoWrEP 92*
Sullivan, Glen J. *Law&B 92*
Sullivan, Gordon R. 1937- *WhoAm 92*
Sullivan, Gordon Russell 1937- *CmdGen 1991 [port]*
Sullivan, Gregory A. 1948- *St&PR 93*
Sullivan, Gregory Francis 1940- *WhoE 93*
Sullivan, Harold E., III 1959- *St&PR 93*
Sullivan, Harry Truman 1952- *WhoSSW 93*
Sullivan, Harry Ward, Jr. *Law&B 92*
Sullivan, Haywood Cooper 1930- *WhoAm 92*
Sullivan, Hugh D. 1958- *St&PR 93*
Sullivan, J. Langdon 1903- *St&PR 93*
Sullivan, J. Langdon, Mrs. *WhoE 93, WhoWor 93*
Sullivan, J. Timothy *Law&B 92*
Sullivan, Jack 1946- *ScF&FL 92*
Sullivan, James Ash 1946- *WhoE 93*
Sullivan, James Benjamin 1941- *WhoSSW 93*
Sullivan, James Bernard *Law&B 92*
Sullivan, James C. 1934- *St&PR 93*
Sullivan, James Dwight 1942- *St&PR 93*
Sullivan, James Edward 1928- *WhoWrEP 92*
Sullivan, James F. 1926- *St&PR 93*
Sullivan, James F.X. *Law&B 92*
Sullivan, James Francis 1930- *WhoAm 92*
Sullivan, James Hall 1918- *WhoAm 92*
Sullivan, James Kirk 1935- *WhoAm 92, WhoWor 93*
Sullivan, James Lenox 1910- *WhoAm 92*
Sullivan, James Leo 1925- *WhoAm 92*
Sullivan, James Norman 1937- *St&PR 93*
Sullivan, James Thomas 1939- *WhoAm 92*
Sullivan, Janet Wright 1926- *WhoWrEP 92*
Sullivan, Jay Michael 1936- *WhoAm 92*
Sullivan, Jeffrey 1949- *St&PR 93*
Sullivan, Jeremiah Stephen 1920- *WhoAm 92*
Sullivan, Jerry Ford 1944- *St&PR 93*
Sullivan, Jerry Stephen 1945- *WhoSSW 93*
Sullivan, Jerry Warner 1942- *WhoSSW 93*
Sullivan, Jill M. *Law&B 92*
Sullivan, Jim 1939- *WhoAm 92*
Sullivan, Joe Malcolm 1938- *WhoSSW 93*
Sullivan, John *BioIn 17*
Sullivan, John 1740-1795 *HarEnMi*
Sullivan, John 1920- *St&PR 93*
Sullivan, John B. *Law&B 92*
Sullivan, John Donahue *Law&B 92*
Sullivan, John Fox 1943- *WhoAm 92*
Sullivan, John Gerard 1941- *WhoE 93*
Sullivan, John Greenfelder 1936- *WhoSSW 93*
Sullivan, John Henry 1935- *St&PR 93*
Sullivan, John J. *Law&B 92*
Sullivan, John Joseph 1920- *WhoAm 92*
Sullivan, John L. *Law&B 92*
Sullivan, John L. 1858-1918 *GayN*
Sullivan, John Louis, Jr. 1928- *WhoAm 92*
Sullivan, John Magruder, II 1959- *WhoWor 93*
Sullivan, John Mark 1935- *St&PR 93, WhoAm 92*
Sullivan, John Patrick 1930- *WhoWrEP 92*
Sullivan, John Paul 1926- *St&PR 93*
Sullivan, John van Buren d1992 *BioIn 17, NewYTBS 92*
Sullivan, Joseph B. 1922- *WhoAm 92*
Sullivan, Joseph Edward 1934- *St&PR 93*
Sullivan, Joseph Michael 1939- *St&PR 93*
Sullivan, Joseph Peter 1939- *WhoE 93, WhoIns 93*
Sullivan, Julie *Law&B 92*
Sullivan, Justin L. 1939- *St&PR 93*
Sullivan, Katherine M. *Law&B 92*
Sullivan, Kathleen *BioIn 17*
Sullivan, Kathryn Ann 1954- *WhoAmW 93*
Sullivan, Kathryn D. 1951- *WhoAmW 93*
Sullivan, Kathryn Jean 1942- *WhoAsAP 91*
Sullivan, Kathryn Meara 1942- *WhoAmW 93*
Sullivan, Kevin 1955- *MiSFD 9*
Sullivan, Kevin J. 1953- *WhoIns 93*
Sullivan, Kevin M. *Law&B 92*
Sullivan, Kevin Michael 1964- *WhoE 93*
Sullivan, Kevin P. *Law&B 92*
Sullivan, Kevin Patrick 1953- *WhoEmL 93*
Sullivan, Kevin T. *Law&B 92*
Sullivan, Larry *BioIn 17*
Sullivan, Larry E. 1944- *ConAu 136*
Sullivan, Larry Michael 1948- *WhoWrEP 92*
Sullivan, Laura P. *Law&B 92*
Sullivan, Laura P. 1947- *St&PR 93*
Sullivan, Laura Patricia 1947- *WhoAmW 93*
Sullivan, Lauraine D. *Law&B 92*
Sullivan, Lee 1925- *St&PR 93*
Sullivan, Leon H. 1922- *ConBlB 3 [port]*
Sullivan, Leon Howard 1922- *WhoAm 92*
Sullivan, Leonor K. 1902-1988 *BioIn 17*
Sullivan, Linda Ann 1961- *WhoAmW 93*
Sullivan, Louis 1856-1924 *GayN*
Sullivan, Louis W. *BioIn 17*
Sullivan, Louis W. 1933- *AfrAmBi [port], CngDr 91*
Sullivan, Louis Wade 1933- *WhoAm 92, WhoE 93, WhoWor 93*
Sullivan, Marcia M. 1952- *St&PR 93*
Sullivan, Margaret Ann 1941- *WhoAmW 93*
Sullivan, Margaret M. *Law&B 92*
Sullivan, Margaret Mary 1957- *WhoAmW 93*
Sullivan, Margaret Murphy 1944- *WhoSSW 93*
Sullivan, Marie Celeste 1929- *WhoAm 92*
Sullivan, Marilyn Bobette 1931- *WhoAmW 93*
Sullivan, Marilyn Dill 1939- *St&PR 93*
Sullivan, Mark Francis *Law&B 92*
Sullivan, Mark P. 1956- *St&PR 93*
Sullivan, Mary Ann 1954- *BioIn 17*
Sullivan, Mary Jane Leahy 1939- *WhoAmW 93*
Sullivan, Mary L. *Law&B 92*
Sullivan, Mary Margaret 1952- *WhoAmW 93*
Sullivan, Mary Rose 1931- *WhoAm 92*
Sullivan, Mary W. 1907- *ScF&FL 92*
Sullivan, Maude J. *AmWomPl*
Sullivan, Maureen *BioIn 17, Law&B 92*
Sullivan, Maureen Patricia 1946- *WhoAmW 93*
Sullivan, Maureen W. *Law&B 92*
Sullivan, Maxine 1911-1987 *BioIn 17*
Sullivan, May Miller 1899- *BioIn 17*
Sullivan, Mel Ann Britton 1965- *WhoSSW 93*
Sullivan, Melinda Knisley *Law&B 92*
Sullivan, Michael Aloysius 1939- *WhoSSW 93*
Sullivan, Michael C. 1940- *St&PR 93*
Sullivan, Michael David 1938- *WhoAm 92, WhoSSW 93*
Sullivan, Michael Dennis 1939- *St&PR 93*
Sullivan, Michael F. 1935- *St&PR 93*
Sullivan, Michael J. 1950- *St&PR 93*
Sullivan, Michael John 1939- *WhoAm 92, WhoWor 93*
Sullivan, Michael Lee 1945- *St&PR 93, WhoSSW 93*
Sullivan, Michael M. *Law&B 92*
Sullivan, Michael Maurice 1942- *WhoAm 92*
Sullivan, Michael P. *Law&B 92*
Sullivan, Michael P. 1948- *St&PR 93*
Sullivan, Michael Patrick 1933- *WhoAm 92*
Sullivan, Michael Patrick 1934- *St&PR 93, WhoAm 92*
Sullivan, Michael R. 1949- *St&PR 93*
Sullivan, Mike *ScF&FL 92*
Sullivan, Mortimer Allen, Jr. 1930- *WhoAm 92*
Sullivan, Nancy Jean 1957- *WhoSSW 93*
Sullivan, Neil Maxwell 1942- *WhoSSW 93*
Sullivan, Neil Samuel 1942- *WhoWor 93*
Sullivan, Nell Inklebarger 1932- *WhoAmW 93*
Sullivan, Nicholas G. 1927- *WhoAm 92*
Sullivan, Nick *BioIn 17*
Sullivan, P(atricia) Lance 1950- *WhoWrEP 92*
Sullivan, Patricia Ann 1953- *WhoAmW 93*
Sullivan, Patricia Ann 1956- *WhoAmW 93*
Sullivan, Patricia Clare 1928- *WhoAm 92*
Sullivan, Patricia W. 1936- *WhoWor 93*
Sullivan, Patrick *WhoAm 92*
Sullivan, Patrick J. 1948- *St&PR 93*
Sullivan, Patrick James 1943- *WhoWor 93*
Sullivan, Paul A., Jr. 1934- *St&PR 93*
Sullivan, Paul E. *Law&B 92*
Sullivan, Paul Joseph 1947- *WhoE 93*
Sullivan, Paul Richard 1940- *St&PR 93*
Sullivan, Paul William 1939- *WhoSSW 93*
Sullivan, Peggy Anne 1929- *WhoAmW 93*
Sullivan, Penelope Dietz 1939- *WhoAmW 93*
Sullivan, Philip G. 1932- *St&PR 93*
Sullivan, Philis Evon 1954- *WhoAmW 93*
Sullivan, Ralph M. 1936- *St&PR 93*
Sullivan, Ralph Michael 1934- *WhoE 93*
Sullivan, Richard C. 1928- *St&PR 93*
Sullivan, Richard Cyril 1928- *WhoAm 92*
Sullivan, Richard John 1949- *WhoAm 92, WhoE 93*
Sullivan, Richard P. 1933- *St&PR 93*
Sullivan, Richard T. 1955- *St&PR 93*
Sullivan, Robert Bryan 1960- *WhoSSW 93*
Sullivan, Robert C. *Law&B 92*
Sullivan, Robert Edward 1936- *WhoAm 92*
Sullivan, Robert Emmet, Jr. 1955- *WhoWor 93*
Sullivan, Robert J. *Law&B 92*
Sullivan, Robert J. 1949- *WhoIns 93*
Sullivan, Robert Martin 1953- *WhoE 93*
Sullivan, Robert W. *Law&B 92*
Sullivan, Robert Welles *Law&B 92*
Sullivan, Roger John 1921- *St&PR 93*

Sullivan, Roger Joseph 1947- WhoE 93
Sullivan, Roger Winthrop 1929- WhoAm 92
Sullivan, Ronald Dee 1939- WhoSSW 93
Sullivan, Ronald Frederick 1930- WhoAm 92
Sullivan, Ronald Lee 1946- WhoSSW 93
Sullivan, Rosemary 1947- WhoCanL 92
Sullivan, Sandra Carol 1950- WhoAmW 93
Sullivan, Sandra Jones 1948- WhoEmL 93
Sullivan, Sandra LaRae 1937- WhoAmW 93
Sullivan, Sarah Louise 1954- WhoAmW 93
Sullivan, Sean Mei WhoWrEP 92
Sullivan, Selby William 1934- WhoAm 92
Sullivan, Sheila 1927- ScF&FL 92
Sullivan, Stephen Gene 1947- WhoE 93
Sullivan, Stephen Kelly 1961- WhoE 93
Sullivan, Stephen Norman 1947- WhoWor 93
Sullivan, Stephen Wentworth 1946- WhoAm 92
Sullivan, Steven R. Law&B 92
Sullivan, Sullins Grenfell 1912- WhoE 93
Sullivan, Teresa Ann 1949- WhoAm 92, WhoAmW 93, WhoSSW 93
Sullivan, Terrance Charles 1950- WhoEmL 93
Sullivan, Terrence M. 1938- St&PR 93
Sullivan, Thomas 1940- ScF&FL 92
Sullivan, Thomas C. 1937- St&PR 93
Sullivan, Thomas Christopher 1937- WhoAm 92
Sullivan, Thomas J. 1935- St&PR 93
Sullivan, Thomas John 1935- WhoAm 92
Sullivan, Thomas M. 1913-1991 BioIn 17
Sullivan, Thomas M. 1942- St&PR 93
Sullivan, Thomas Patrick 1930- WhoAm 92
Sullivan, Tim 1948- ScF&FL 92
Sullivan, Timothy Allen 1955- WhoSSW 93
Sullivan, Timothy Burns 1940- St&PR 93
Sullivan, Timothy Daniel 1863-1913 BioIn 17
Sullivan, Timothy G. Law&B 92
Sullivan, Timothy Jackson 1944- WhoAm 92, WhoSSW 93
Sullivan, Timothy Patrick 1942- St&PR 93
Sullivan, Timothy Patrick 1958- WhoEmL 93
Sullivan, Tom ScF&FL 92
Sullivan, Tom 1947- BioIn 17
Sullivan, Toni J. WhoAmW 93
Sullivan, Ulric R. Law&B 92
Sullivan, Walter 1918- JrnUS
Sullivan, Walter Francis 1928- WhoAm 92, WhoSSW 93
Sullivan, Walter Laurence 1924- WhoAm 92, WhoSSW 93
Sullivan, Walter Seager 1918- WhoAm 92, WhoWrEP 92
Sullivan, William BioIn 17, Law&B 92
Sullivan, William A. Law&B 92
Sullivan, William Alan 1951- St&PR 93
Sullivan, William Arnett 1942- WhoSSW 93
Sullivan, William Butler 1934- St&PR 93
Sullivan, William Courtney 1928- WhoAm 92
Sullivan, William Hallisey, Jr. 1915- WhoAm 92, WhoE 93
Sullivan, William James 1930- WhoAm 92
Sullivan, William Joseph 1931- WhoWrEP 92
Sullivan, William Laurence 1872-1935 BioIn 17
Sullivan, William Patrick 1952- WhoE 93
Sulloway, Frank Jones 1947- WhoAm 92
Sullwold, Corliss Kay 1946- WhoAmW 93
Sully, Cary William 1945- WhoSSW 93
Sulman, D.A. 1953- St&PR 93
Sulman, Douglas Anthony Law&B 92
Sulonen, Martti Seppo 1922- WhoScE 91-4
Sulovic, Vojin 1923- WhoScE 91-4
Sult, Jeffery Scot 1956- WhoE 93
Sultan, Daniel Isom 1885-1947 HarEnMi
Sultan, Donald K. 1951- BioIn 17
Sultan, Donald Keith 1951- WhoAm 92
Sultan, Fath'Ali Tipu 1753-1799 BioIn 17
Sultan, Grete 1906- Baker 92
Sultan, Leslie Harris 1959- WhoSSW 93
Sultan, Stanley 1928- WhoWrEP 92
Sultan, Terrie BioIn 17
Sultan, Terrie Frances 1952- WhoAm 92
Sultana, Najma 1948- WhoAmW 93
Sultan bin Muhammad Al-Qasimi, Sheikh 1939- WhoWor 93
Sultan Ibn Abdulaziz, Prince 1924- WhoWor 93
Sultan Mahmood Iskandar Al-Haj Ibni Al-M, His Royal Highness 1932- WhoAsAP 91
Sultanof, Jeffrey Brad 1954- WhoE 93, WhoEmL 93, WhoWor 93
Sulte, Benjamin 1841-1923 BioIn 17
Sultzbaugh, C. Tom 1917- St&PR 93
Sultzer, Barnet Martin 1929- WhoE 93
Sulvetta, Anthony J. 1939- St&PR 93
Sulyk, Stephen 1924- WhoAm 92, WhoE 93
Sulzbach, Christi Rocovich Law&B 92
Sulzberger, Arthur Hays 1891-1968 DcLB 127 [port], JrnUS
Sulzberger, Arthur O., Jr. BioIn 17
Sulzberger, Arthur Ochs NewYTBS 92 [port]
Sulzberger, Arthur Ochs 1926- BioIn 17, DcLB 127 [port], St&PR 93
Sulzberger, Arthur Ochs, Sr. 1926- WhoAm 92, WhoE 93
Sulzberger, Arthur Ochs, Jr. 1951- WhoAm 92, WhoE 93
Sulzberger, Cyrus Leo 1912- WhoAm 92
Sulzberger, Iphigene Ochs 1892-1990 BioIn 17
Sulzberger, Suzanne 1903-1990 BioIn 17
Sulzer, David Louis 1956- WhoE 93
Sulzer, Julius Salomon 1834-1891 Baker 92
Sulzer, Salomon 1804-1890 Baker 92
Sum, Joan M. Law&B 92
Suma, Margaret Ann Law&B 92
Sumac, Yma 1927- Baker 92
Sumanasekera, Deepthi Upul 1959- WhoWor 93
Sumanatilake, Piyadigamage Saranapala 1932- WhoWor 93
Sumanth, David Jonnakoty 1946- WhoAm 92, WhoSSW 93
Sumari, O. WhoScE 91-4
Sumarlin, Johannes Baptista 1932- WhoAsAP 91
Sumas, James 1933- St&PR 93
Sumera, Lepo 1950- Baker 92
Sumerau, Dorothy Lehman AmWomPl
Sumi, Hiroshi 1954- WhoAsAP 91
Sumichrast, Jozef 1948- WhoAm 92
Sumida, Gerald Aquinas 1944- WhoWor 93
Sumida, Kevin P.H. 1954- WhoEmL 93, WhoWor 93
Sumiga, John Heinrich WhoScE 91-1
Sumihiro, Gary K. Law&B 92
Sumin, Vladimir Iosifovich 1946- WhoWor 93
Suminski, Jeanne G. Law&B 92
Suminski, Richard Law&B 92
Sumintapura, Nasrudin 1938- WhoAsAP 91
Sumita, Yoichi 1924- WhoWor 93
Sumlin, Hubert BioIn 17
Sumlin, Margaret Brown 1950- WhoAmW 93
Sumlin, Roger Lewis 1942- WhoSSW 93
Summa, John F. 1932-1991 BioIn 17
Summanen, Paula Anneli 1952- WhoWor 93
Summer, Alexander, Jr. 1938- St&PR 93
Summer, Charles Edgar 1923- WhoAm 92
Summer, Donna 1948- SoulM, WhoAm 92
Summer, Joel Sherwood Law&B 92
Summer, Kenneth 1944- St&PR 93
Summer, Lloyd Langston, Jr. 1923- St&PR 93
Summer, Mark c. 1958- See Turtle Island String Quartet ConMus 9
Summer, Robert Jesse 1941- WhoSSW 93
Summer, V.C. 1920- St&PR 93
Summerall, Charles Pelot 1867-1955 CmdGen 1991 [port], HarEnMi
Summerall, Pat BioIn 17
Summerall, Pat 1931- WhoAm 92
Summerfield, Arthur WhoScE 91-1
Summerfield, Arthur E. 1899-1972 PolPar
Summerfield, Arthur Ellsworth 1899-1972 BioIn 17
Summerfield, Arthur Quentin WhoScE 91-1
Summerfield, Geoffrey 1931- ScF&FL 92
Summerfield, Herbert Gibson, Jr. 1940- WhoAm 92
Summerfield, Joanne 1940- WhoAmW 93
Summerfield, John Robert 1917- WhoAm 92
Summerfield, Martin 1916- WhoAm 92
Summerfield, Rodney John WhoScE 91-1
Summerfield, Thomas Warren 1947- St&PR 93
Summerford, Ben Long 1924- WhoAm 92
Summerford, Harold C. 1936- St&PR 93
Summerford, R. Michael 1948- St&PR 93
Summerhayes, Martha 1846-1911 BioIn 17
Summerhays, Charles Callis 1932- St&PR 93
Summerlin, Glenn Wood 1934- St&PR 93
Summerlin, Ralph Mitchell 1958- WhoSSW 93
Summerlin, Roy C. 1923- St&PR 93
Summerlin, Sam 1928- WhoWrEP 92
Summerlin, Vernon Shelley 1943- WhoSSW 93
Summerour, Darlene Ann 1951- WhoAmW 93
Summers, Alfred Lawrence, Jr. 1950- WhoEmL 93
Summers, Anita Arrow 1925- WhoAm 92
Summers, Anne BioIn 17
Summers, Anne Fairhurst 1945- WhoAmW 93, WhoE 93
Summers, Anthony J. 1953- WhoWrEP 92
Summers, Bessie Eva 1937- WhoAmW 93
Summers, Carol 1925- WhoAm 92
Summers, Clyde Wilson 1918- WhoAm 92
Summers, Dale Edwards 1949- WhoE 93, WhoEmL 93
Summers, Dan Law&B 92
Summers, David P. St&PR 93
Summers, Dennis ScF&FL 92
Summers, Dorothy H. St&PR 93
Summers, Edward Lee 1937- WhoAm 92
Summers, Ernest Law&B 92
Summers, Frank William 1933- WhoAm 92
Summers, George Donald 1927- WhoSSW 93
Summers, Glenda Jeanne 1956- WhoSSW 93
Summers, Hardy 1933- WhoAm 92, WhoSSW 93
Summers, Harold B. 1930- St&PR 93
Summers, Hugh Bloomer, Jr. 1921- WhoSSW 93
Summers, Ian 1939- ScF&FL 92
Summers, James Irvin 1921- WhoAm 92
Summers, James Richard 1962- WhoWor 93
Summers, Janie I. WhoAmW 93
Summers, Jeremy MiSFD 9
Summers, Joseph Frank 1914- WhoSSW 93, WhoWor 93
Summers, Joseph Holmes 1920- WhoE 93
Summers, Joseph W. 1930- AfrAmBi
Summers, Lawrence Henry 1954- WhoUN 92
Summers, Lorraine Dey Schaeffer 1946- WhoAm 92
Summers, Mark Steven 1947- WhoSSW 93
Summers, Martin BioIn 17
Summers, Mary Ellen 1949- St&PR 93
Summers, Max Duane 1938- WhoAm 92
Summers, Max Duanne 1938- WhoSSW 93
Summers, Merna WhoCanL 92
Summers, Montague 1880-1948 ScF&FL 92
Summers, Patsy Williams 1940- WhoSSW 93
Summers, Peter 1916- WhoAm 92, WhoWor 93
Summers, Robert 1922- WhoAm 92
Summers, Robert Samuel 1933- WhoAm 92, WhoWrEP 92
Summers, Robert Taylor 1946- WhoSSW 93
Summers, Rosalie Eve 1938- WhoAmW 93
Summers, Stephanie Horanszki 1944- WhoSSW 93
Summers, Stuart G. Law&B 92
Summers, Terry J. 1942- St&PR 93
Summers, William Cofield 1939- WhoAm 92
Summers, William E., III AfrAmBi
Summers, William Lawrence 1942- WhoAm 92, WhoSSW 93
Summers, Wilma Poos 1937- WhoE 93
Summersby, Edmund Kirkwood 1931- St&PR 93
Summersby, Kay 1908?-1975 BioIn 17
Summerscales, William 1921- WhoE 93
Summersell, Charles Grayson 1908- WhoWrEP 92
Summersell, Frances Sharpley WhoAmW 93, WhoSSW 93, WhoWor 93
Summerskill, Edith 1901-1980 BioIn 17
Summerskill, John d1990 BioIn 17
Summerskill, Shirley Catherine W. 1931- WhoWor 93
Summerson, John 1904-1992 NewYTBS 92 [port]
Summerton, Jeffrey Edward 1954- WhoE 93
Summertree, Katonah 1938- WhoAm 92
Summerville, David WhoE 93
Summerville, James 1947- WhoWrEP 92
Summerville, Jane Schneider 1942- WhoAmW 93
Summerville, Jessiephine W. Law&B 92
Summerville, Katie Mae 1936- WhoAmW 93
Summerville, Slim 1892-1946 BioIn 17, QDrFCA 92 [port]
Summey, Melissa Billings 1967- WhoAmW 93
Summey, Steven Michael 1946- WhoEmL 93, WhoSSW 93, WhoWor 93
Summit, Roger Kent 1930- WhoAm 92
Summitt, Pat Head BioIn 17
Summitt, Robert 1935- WhoAm 92
Summitt, Robert Layman 1932- WhoAm 92, WhoSSW 93
Summitt, Robert Murray 1924- WhoAm 92
Summons, Susan P. WhoAmW 93
Summons-McGuire, Agatha Bryna 1951- WhoE 93
Summy, Greg Edwards Law&B 92
Summy-Long, Joan Yvette 1943- WhoAmW 93
Sumner, Billy Taylor 1923- WhoAm 92
Sumner, Bonnie BioIn 17
Sumner, Charles 1811-1874 BioIn 17, EncAACR [port], PolPar
Sumner, Claire AmWomPl
Sumner, Daniel Alan 1950- WhoAm 92
Sumner, David St&PR 93
Sumner, David George 1949- WhoE 93
Sumner, Edward Donald 1925- WhoSSW 93
Sumner, Edwin Vose 1797-1863 HarEnMi
Sumner, Eric Eden 1924- WhoAm 92
Sumner, Gordon BioIn 17
Sumner, Gordon Heyward 1945- WhoSSW 93
Sumner, Gordon Matthew Baker 92
Sumner, Gordon Matthew 1951- WhoWor 93
Sumner, Jason M. 1951- St&PR 93
Sumner, Jessie 1898- BioIn 17
Sumner, John Philip WhoScE 91-1
Sumner, Mary Janice 1939- WhoAmW 93
Sumner, Randall Clay 1949- St&PR 93
Sumner, Sheron Keel 1941- WhoSSW 93
Sumner, Stephen I. 1941- WhoWrEP 92
Sumner, Stephen Isaac WhoE 93
Sumner, William Graham 1840-1910 GayN
Sumner, William Marvin 1928- WhoAm 92
Sumner, William Thomas 1954- WhoE 93
Sumners, William Glenn, Jr. 1928- WhoWor 93
Sumney, Jerry Lee 1955- WhoSSW 93
Sumney, Roland L. 1933- St&PR 93, WhoIns 93
Sumnicht, June E. 1936- St&PR 93
Sumpter, James Hardee, III 1950- WhoEmL 93, WhoSSW 93
Sumpter, Jerry Lee 1942- WhoWor 93
Sumption, Jonathan (Philip Chadwick) 1948- ConAu 136
Sumrall, Lester Frank 1913- WhoAm 92
Sumrall, Lois Anne Richard 1935- WhoAmW 93
Sumrall, Oliphant Malcolm 1932- St&PR 93
Sumrell, Gene 1919- WhoSSW 93, WhoWor 93
Sumser, John Raymond 1954- WhoE 93
Sumsion, Robert J. St&PR 93
Sumsion, Steven R. Law&B 92
Sumter, Thomas 1734-1832 HarEnMi
Sumulong, Francisco S. 1918- WhoAsAP 91
Sumwalt, Robert Llewellyn, Jr. 1927- WhoSSW 93
Sun, Benedict Ching-San 1934- WhoE 93
Sun, Chieh 1943- St&PR 93
Sun, Christopher I-Chum 1953- WhoWor 93
Sun, Congting 1962- WhoE 93
Sun, Cossette Tsung-hung Wu 1937- WhoAm 92
Sun, Dean T. 1962- WhoSSW 93
Sun, Emily M. WhoE 93
Sun, Hun H. 1925- WhoAm 92
Sun, Li-jen 1900-1990 BioIn 17
Sun, Li-Teh 1939- WhoWor 93
Sun, May BioIn 17
Sun, Osman 1934- WhoScE 91-4
Sun, Richard Alan 1950- St&PR 93
Sun, Sadi 1922- WhoScE 91-4
Sun, Shan Li 1945- WhoWor 93
Sun, Shirley BioIn 17, MiSFD 9
Sun, Wan Gui 1963- WhoWor 93
Sun, Wen-yih 1945- WhoAm 92
Sun, Yat-sen 1866-1925 BioIn 17
Sunada, Shigetami 1917- WhoAsAP 91
Sunaga, Toru 1950- WhoAsAP 91
Sunagawa, Masakatsu 1943- WhoWor 93
Sunakawa, Sigenobu 1925- WhoWor 93
Sunao, Kaneko 1946- WhoWor 93
Sunbeck, Deborah Teresa 1953- WhoE 93
Sunberg, Phyllis Mary 1939- WhoAmW 93
Sun Ch'uan-feng 1884-1935 HarEnMi
Sund, Eldon Harold 1930- WhoSSW 93
Sund, Eric O. 1941- St&PR 93
Sund, Horst 1926- WhoScE 91-3
Sund, Jeffrey O. 1940- WhoAm 92
Sund, Jerome Louis 1943- St&PR 93
Sundance Kid 1861?-1908 BioIn 17

Sundaram, T. R. 1937- *WhoE 93*
Sundararaj, N. 1944- *WhoAsAP 91*
Sundararajan, Srinivasan 1940- *WhoWor 93*
Sundararaman, Narasimhan 1937- *WhoUN 92*
Sundaresan, Mosur Kalyanaraman 1929- *WhoAm 92*
Sundarrajan, Raj Mathchan 1956- *WhoE 93*
Sunday, Billy 1862-1935 *BioIn 17, GayN*
Sunday, Jeffery H. *Law&B 92*
Sunday, Nancy Lee 1935- *WhoAmW 93*
Sundberg, Alan Carl 1933- *WhoAm 92, WhoSSW 93*
Sundberg, Carl-Erik Wilhelm 1943- *WhoAm 92*
Sundberg, Edward August 1947- *WhoEmL 93*
Sundberg, Frederick Michael 1942- *St&PR 93*
Sundberg, James Howard 1951- *BiDAMSp 1989*
Sundberg, Johan E.F. 1936- *WhoScE 91-4*
Sundberg, Mark William 1957- *WhoE 93*
Sundberg, N. *WhoScE 91-4*
Sundberg, Norma Jean 1933- *WhoWrEP 92*
Sundberg, Ove 1933- *WhoWor 93*
Sundberg, R. Dorothy 1915- *WhoAm 92*
Sundberg, Richard 1927- *St&PR 93*
Sundberg, Richard Jay 1938- *WhoAm 92, WhoSSW 93*
Sundberg, Sven Victor 1942- *WhoScE 91-4*
Sundblad, Lars K.M. 1921- *WhoScE 91-4*
Sundborg, Ake O.F. 1921- *WhoScE 91-4*
Sundby, Harold C., Jr. 1942- *St&PR 93*
Sunde, Rob *BioIn 17*
Sundeen, John E. 1936- *St&PR 93*
Sundel, Martin 1940- *WhoAm 92*
Sundelius (Sandtvig), Marie 1884-1958 *Baker 92*
Sundell, Bjorn *WhoScE 91-4*
Sundell, Duane J. 1931- *St&PR 93*
Sundelof-Asbrand, Karin *AmWomPl*
Sundem, Gary Lewis 1944- *WhoWor 93*
Sunder, Shyam 1944- *WhoE 93*
Sunderhaft, Eugene R. 1948- *St&PR 93*
Sunderhauf, Karen Heather 1955- *WhoAmW 93*
Sunderland, Craig Gordon *Law&B 92*
Sunderland, Harry David 1935- *St&PR 93*
Sunderland, Jacklyn Giles 1937- *WhoAmW 93*
Sunderland, James P. 1928- *St&PR 93*
Sunderland, John 1943- *WhoWor 93*
Sunderland, Kent W. 1958- *St&PR 93*
Sunderland, Louise A. *Law&B 92*
Sunderland, Paul 1896- *WhoAm 92*
Sunderland, Ray, Jr. 1913- *WhoAm 92*
Sunderland, Riley 1917- *WhoSSW 93*
Sunderland, Robert 1921- *St&PR 93, WhoAm 92*
Sunderland, Thomas Elbert 1907-1991 *BioIn 17*
Sunderman, Deborah Ann 1955- *WhoAmW 93, WhoWor 93*
Sunderman, Duane Neuman 1928- *St&PR 93, WhoAm 92*
Sunderman, Frederick William 1898- *WhoAm 92*
Sunderman, Martha-Lee 1934- *WhoWor 93*
Sunderman, Robert E. *Law&B 92*
Sundermann, Jurgen 1938- *WhoScE 91-3*
Sundermann, Justus Daniel 1934- *WhoAm 92, WhoSSW 93*
Sundgaard, Arnold Olaf 1909- *WhoWor 93*
Sundgren-Schneevoigt, Sigrid Ingeborg 1878-1953 *Baker 92*
Sundheim, Nancy Straus *Law&B 92*
Sundholm, Franciska 1937- *WhoScE 91-4*
Sundholm, Goran 1936- *WhoScE 91-4*
Sundin, Lennart Karl 1935- *St&PR 93*
Sundin, Stephen R. 1949- *St&PR 93*
Sundius, Robert Edwin 1930- *St&PR 93*
Sundkler, Bengt 1909- *IntDcAn*
Sundler, Frank E.G. 1943- *WhoScE 91-4*
Sundler, Frank Eskil Georg 1943- *WhoWor 93*
Sundlun, Bruce George 1920- *WhoAm 92, WhoE 93*
Sundnes, Gunnar 1926- *WhoScE 91-4, WhoWor 93*
Sundown, Will *ScF&FL 92*
Sundquist, Dean Allan 1960- *St&PR 93*
Sundquist, Don 1936- *CngDr 91*
Sundquist, Donald Kenneth 1936- *WhoAm 92, WhoSSW 93*
Sundquist, Helge Erik 1930- *WhoWor 93*
Sundquist, James Lloyd 1915- *WhoAm 92*
Sundquist, Jorma J. 1936- *WhoScE 91-4*
Sundquist, Leah Renata 1963- *WhoAmW 93*
Sundqvist, Christer 1943- *WhoScE 91-4*
Sundqvist, Hilding 1934- *WhoScE 91-4*
Sundsbro, S. *WhoScE 91-4*
Sundseth, Christopher Carl 1954- *WhoE 93*
Sundstrom, Alan C. 1934- *St&PR 93*
Sundstrom, Cedric *MiSFD 9*
Sundstrom, Charles 1930- *St&PR 93*
Sundstrom, V. Glenn 1928- *St&PR 93*
Sundt, Eilert Lund 1817-1875 *IntDcAn*
Sundt, H. Wilson 1932- *St&PR 93*
Sundt, Harry Wilson 1932- *WhoAm 92, WhoWor 93*
Sundt, Robert Stout 1926- *St&PR 93, WhoAm 92*
Sundt, Thoralf M., Jr. 1930-1992 *NewYTBS 92*
Sundt, Thoralf Mauritz, Jr. 1930- *WhoAm 92*
Sundue, Judith *St&PR 93*
Suneli, Kari L.J. 1950- *WhoScE 91-4*
Sunell, Robert John 1929- *WhoAm 92*
Sunenshine, Harry S. 1945- *St&PR 93*
Suneson, Scott *St&PR 93*
Sunesson, Fanny *BioIn 17*
Sung, Chi Wai Raymond 1953- *WhoWor 93*
Sung, Dae Dong 1945- *WhoWor 93*
Sung, Dean 1954- *St&PR 93*
Sung, Eva May 1962- *WhoAmW 93*
Sung, Kihong 1933- *St&PR 93*
Sung, Nak-Ho 1940- *WhoAm 92*
Sung, Peter 1940- *WhoAsAP 91*
Sung, Tak Ki *Law&B 92*
Sung, Yuan-Ming 1930- *WhoWrEP 92*
Sung, Yun-Chen *WhoAm 92*
Sung Che-yuen 1885-1940 *HarEnMi*
Suni, Juha 1964- *WhoScE 91-4*
Sunil Dutt 1929- *WhoAsAP 91*
Sun Jiadong *BioIn 17*
Sun Jiazheng 1944- *WhoAsAP 91*
Sunjic, Vitomir 1939- *WhoScE 91-4*
Sunka, Pavel 1936- *WhoScE 91-4*
Sunkel, Robert Jacob 1926- *St&PR 93*
Sunko, Dionis E. 1922- *WhoScE 91-4*
Sunley, Emil McKee 1942- *WhoAm 92*
Sunley, Raymond L. 1944- *WhoWor 93*
Sunley, Robert M. 1917- *WhoE 93*
Sunlight *ScF&FL 92*
Sunmonu, Hassan 1941- *WhoAfr*
Sunmonu, Hassan Adebayo 1941- *WhoUN 92*
Sunnyland Slim *BioIn 17*
Sunol (y Baulenas), Gregoria Maria 1879-1946 *Baker 92*
Sun Qi 1930- *WhoAsAP 91*
Sun Ra 1914- *Baker 92*
Sun Ra 1915- *WhoAm 92*
Sun Ra Le Sony'r Ra *WhoAm 92*
Sunshine, Eugene Samuel 1950- *WhoAm 92, WhoWor 93*
Sunshine, Kenneth H. 1961- *WhoSSW 93*
Sunshine, Nancy Jean 1935- *WhoE 93*
Sunstein, Emily W. 1924- *ScF&FL 92*
Sunter, William Robert, Jr. 1958- *WhoSSW 93*
Sun Tongchuan 1941- *WhoAsAP 91*
Sun Tzu fl. c. 500BC- *HarEnMi*
Sununu, John *BioIn 17*
Sununu, John H. 1939- *WhoAm 92, WhoE 93*
Sun Weiben 1929- *WhoAsAP 91*
Sun Wengsheng 1942- *WhoAsAP 91*
Sunyer, Joaquin 1874?-1956 *BioIn 17*
Sun Yixian 1866-1925 *DcTwHis*
Suojanen, Deborah Kindler *Law&B 92*
Suojanen, Waino W. 1920- *WhoAm 92*
Suojanen, Wayne William 1950- *WhoEmL 93, WhoWor 93*
Suokas, Jouko *WhoScE 91-4*
Suolahti, Heikki 1920-1936 *Baker 92*
Suomala, Richard Michael 1947- *St&PR 93*
Suomi, Heikki Ilmari 1944- *WhoWor 93*
Suomi, Verner Edward 1915- *WhoAm 92*
Suoninen, Eero Juhani 1929- *WhoScE 91-4, WhoWor 93*
Suonio, Vaino K. 1926- *WhoScE 91-4*
Suotmaa, Juha Olavi 1963- *WhoWor 93*
Suozzo, Frank Vincent 1928- *WhoAm 92, WhoIns 93*
Sup, Stuart Allen 1943- *WhoE 93, WhoWor 93*
Supa, Nathaniel 1947- *WhoAsAP 91*
Super, Donald E. 1910- *WhoAm 92, WhoSSW 93*
Super, John Thomas 1962- *WhoSSW 93*
Super, Robert Henry 1914- *WhoAm 92*
Super D. J. Dmitry 1965- *See* Deee-Lite *ConMus 9*
Supervia, Conchita 1895-1936 *Baker 92, IntDcOp, OxDcOp*
Supey, Robert Andrew 1941- *St&PR 93*
Supicic, Ivo 1928- *Baker 92*
Supinit, Vijit 1941- *WhoWor 93*
Supino, David J. 1933- *St&PR 93*
Supiro, Lester D. d1991 *BioIn 17*
Suppan, Wolfgang 1933- *Baker 92*
Suppe, Francis J. 1940- *St&PR 93, WhoIns 93*
Suppe, Franz 1819-1895 *OxDcOp*
Suppe, Franz (von) 1819-1895 *Baker 92*
Supper, Erich 1939- *WhoUN 92*
Suppes, Patrick 1922- *WhoAm 92*
Supple, Diane Marie 1956- *WhoAmW 93*
Supple, Jerome H. 1936- *WhoAm 92, WhoSSW 93*
Supple, Sharon A. 1962- *St&PR 93*
Supplee, Henderson 1903-1992 *BioIn 17*
Supplee, Henderson, Jr. d1992 *NewYTBS 92*
Supplee, James E. 1946- *St&PR 93*
Supplee, Sarah *BioIn 17*
Supree, Burt d1992 *NewYTBS 92*
Supree, Burt(on) 1941-1992 *ConAu 137, SmATA 73*
Supree, Burton 1941-1992 *BioIn 17*
Supremes *SoulM*
Suprenant, Thomas Terry 1942- *WhoAm 92*
Supriano, Susan Jean 1938- *WhoAmW 93*
Suprono, Constance Louise 1941- *WhoAmW 93*
Suput, Ray Radoslav 1922- *WhoAm 92*
Suqi, Mahmud M. 1940- *WhoUN 92*
Suquia Goicoechea, Angel Cardinal 1916- *WhoWor 93*
Sur, Dusan 1934- *WhoScE 91-4*
Sur, Serge *WhoUN 92*
Suraci, Charles Xavier, Jr. 1933- *WhoAm 92*
Suraci, Henry A. 1932- *St&PR 93*
Suraci, Richard R. 1949- *WhoE 93*
Surak, John Godfrey 1948- *WhoSSW 93*
Suranyi-Unger, Theodore, Jr. 1930- *WhoAm 92*
Surarerks, Vanpen 1939- *WhoWor 93*
Suratno, Nano 1944- *Baker 92*
Suratt, Paul Michael 1944- *WhoAm 92*
Suraweera, Francis 1945- *WhoWor 93*
Surbeck, Leighton Homer 1902- *WhoAm 92, WhoWor 93*
Surber, David Francis 1940- *WhoSSW 93, WhoWor 93*
Surber, Eugene Lynn 1938- *WhoSSW 93*
Surdam, John L. 1916- *St&PR 93*
Surdam, Robert McClellan 1917- *WhoAm 92*
Surdez, Marjorie Chase *AmWomPl*
Surdick, Robert F. 1934- *St&PR 93*
Surdin, Morris 1914-1979 *Baker 92*
Surdoval, Donald James 1932- *WhoAm 92*
Surdoval, Lawrence Anthony, Jr. 1930- *WhoE 93*
Sureau, Claude 1927- *WhoScE 91-2*
Surenas fl. c. 54BC-53BC *HarEnMi*
Surette, Thomas Whitney 1861-1941 *Baker 92*
Surewicz, Wlodzimierz 1918- *WhoScE 91-4*
Surfin, Ronald Kent *Law&B 92*
Surgenor, Daniel Delaney 1945- *St&PR 93*
Surgenor, Keith S. 1947- *St&PR 93*
Surgi, Marion Rene 1956- *WhoWor 93*
Surgyk, Marian *WhoScE 91-4*
Surh, Dae Suk 1945- *WhoWor 93*
Suria, Amin Mohammed 1942- *WhoWor 93*
Suriano, Deborah Lynn 1968- *WhoAmW 93*
Suriano, Francesco *Baker 92*
Surikova, Alla 1940- *DrEEuF*
Surinach, Carlos 1915- *Baker 92*
Suris, Yuri Borisovich 1963- *WhoWor 93*
Surjaatmadja, Jim Basuki 1945- *WhoSSW 93*
Surkin, Elliot Mark 1942- *WhoAm 92*
Surkin, Martin 1920- *St&PR 93*
Surks, Martin I. 1934- *WhoAm 92*
Surlaker, Samir Manohar 1953- *WhoWor 93*
Surma, Ronald F. 1936- *St&PR 93*
Surman, Owen Stanley 1943- *WhoE 93, WhoWor 93*
Surman, William Robert 1926- *WhoAm 92*
Surmeli, Suphi 1931- *WhoE 93*
Surmonte, Hugo N. 1908- *St&PR 93*
Surnamer, Shulamith *WhoWrEP 92*
Suro, Dario 1917- *WhoAm 92, WhoWor 93*
Surowiec, Stanley Albert 1943- *St&PR 93*
Surpin, Jo 1954- *WhoAmW 93*
Surplus, Robert W. 1923- *WhoSSW 93*
Surprenant, Edith Martha *WhoAmW 93*
Surprenant, H. George 1939- *WhoIns 93*
Surprise, Juanee 1944- *WhoAmW 93*
Surratt, April Gibson 1964- *WhoAmW 93*
Surratt, H. Lloyd 1929- *St&PR 93*
Surratt, John Harrison 1844-1916 *BioIn 17*
Surratt, Mary E. *BioIn 17*
Surrey, Henry Howard, Earl of 1517?-1547 *BioIn 17*
Surrey, Milt 1922- *WhoAm 92*
Surrey, Philip Henry 1910- *WhoAm 92*
Surridge, Nigel Anthony 1960- *WhoWor 93*
Surridge, Robert C., III *Law&B 92*
Surridge, Stephen Zehring 1940- *WhoAm 92*
Sursa, Charles David 1925- *WhoAm 92*
Sursa, David 1925- *St&PR 93*
Surtees, Robert E. 1933- *St&PR 93*
Surucu, Gulerman 1941- *WhoScE 91-4*
Surugue, Bernard Michel 1946- *WhoUN 92*
Surving, Natalie Ann Bacon 1938- *WhoE 93*
Sury, Earl 1937- *St&PR 93*
Sury, Jiri *WhoScE 91-4*
Suryaatmadja, Amelia Juliana 1962- *WhoAmW 93*
Suryanarayanan, Ramanathan 1939- *WhoScE 91-2*
Suryavanshi, O. P. S. 1961- *WhoWor 93*
Suryavarman, I c. 980-1050 *HarEnMi*
Suryavarman, II c. 1085-1150 *HarEnMi*
Suryawanshi, Narsing 1952- *WhoAsAP 91*
Surzynski, Jozef 1851-1919 *Baker 92*
Surzynski, Mieczyslaw 1866-1924 *See* Surzynski, Jozef 1851-1919 *Baker 92*
Surzynski, Stefan 1855-1919 *See* Surzynski, Jozef 1851-1919 *Baker 92*
Susa, Conrad 1935- *Baker 92, WhoAm 92*
Susalla, Anne A. 1934- *WhoAmW 93*
Susann, Jacqueline 1918-1974 *ScF&FL 92*
Susann, Jacqueline 1921-1974 *BioIn 17*
Susann, Philip William 1943- *WhoE 93*
Susanne, Charles 1943- *WhoScE 91-2*
Susanszky, Janos 1923- *WhoScE 91-4*
Susato, Johannes de 1448-1506 *Baker 92*
Susato, Tylman c. 1500-c. 1562 *Baker 92*
Susco, Michael J. 1943- *St&PR 93*
Susen, John William *Law&B 92*
Susens, Millicent Milanovich *WhoAmW 93*
Susens, Stephanie *Law&B 92*
Sushak, Frank R. (Rick) *Law&B 92*
Susic, Goran 1958- *WhoScE 91-4*
Susic, Milenko 1925- *WhoScE 91-4*
Susie, Sharon Kay 1951- *WhoAmW 93*
Susin, Alfredo 1928- *WhoWor 93*
Suske, Joe E. 1931- *St&PR 93*
Suski, Sherrie Leigh 1960- *WhoAmW 93*
Suski, Wojciech 1936- *WhoScE 91-4*
Suski, Zbigniew W. 1931- *WhoScE 91-4*
Suskie, Linda Anne 1953- *WhoE 93*
Suskin, Douglas Sidney 1920- *St&PR 93*
Suskind, Dennis A. 1942- *WhoAm 92*
Suskind, Patrick 1949- *ScF&FL 92*
Suskind, Raymond Robert 1913- *WhoAm 92*
Suskind, Sigmund Richard 1926- *WhoAm 92*
Susko, Carol Lynne 1955- *WhoAmW 93*
Suslak, Howard Robinson 1920- *WhoAm 92*
Suslak, Howard Robinson 1922- *St&PR 93*
Suslov, Mikhail 1902-1982 *ColdWar 2 [port]*
Susman, Ellen P. 1946- *WhoAmW 93*
Susman, Gerald I. 1941- *ConAu 139*
Susman, Karen Hantze 1942- *BiDAMSp 1989*
Susman, Mary Beth 1947- *WhoAmW 93*
Susman, Millard 1934- *WhoAm 92*
Susman, Morton Lee 1934- *WhoAm 92*
Susman, Stephen Daily 1941- *WhoAm 92*
Susman, Thomas Michael 1943- *WhoAm 92*
Susnjara, Kenneth John 1947- *St&PR 93*
Suson, David V. *Law&B 92*
Suss, Lester J. 1913- *St&PR 93*
Sussel, Jean-Jacques *WhoScE 91-2*
Sussen, Daniel Charles 1928- *St&PR 93*
Sussenbach, John Samuel 1938- *WhoScE 91-3*
Sussenguth, Edward Henry 1932- *WhoAm 92*
Susser, Danielle F. *Law&B 92*
Susser, Mervyn Wilfred 1921- *WhoAm 92*
Sussex, Alan D. 1934- *WhoScE 91-1*
Sussex, James Neil 1917- *WhoAm 92*
Sussex, Lucy 1957- *ScF&FL 92*
Susskind, Charles *WhoAm 92*
Susskind, Harriet *WhoWrEP 92*
Susskind, Herbert 1929- *WhoAm 92, WhoE 93*
Susskind, J. Wallace 1924- *St&PR 93*
Susskind, Jacob Louis 1933- *WhoE 93*
Susskind, Lawrence Elliott 1947- *WhoAm 92*
Susskind, Teresa Gabriel 1921- *WhoAm 92*
Susskind, (Jan) Walter 1913-1980 *Baker 92*
Sussler, Betsy Ruth 1952- *WhoWrEP 92*
Sussman, Andrew David 1951- *St&PR 93*
Sussman, Barry 1934- *WhoAm 92*
Sussman, Barry 1939- *St&PR 93*
Sussman, David A. *Law&B 92*
Sussman, Deborah Evelyn 1931- *WhoAmW 93*
Sussman, George David 1943- *WhoE 93*

Sussman, Gerald 1927- *WhoE 93*
Sussman, Gerald 1934- *St&PR 93, WhoAm 92*
Sussman, Harry 1912- *St&PR 93*
Sussman, Harvey A. *Law&B 92*
Sussman, Herbert L. 1937- *ScF&FL 92*
Sussman, I. Harvey 1939- *St&PR 93*
Sussman, Ida A. *St&PR 93*
Sussman, Jeremy D. *Law&B 92*
Sussman, Leonard Richard 1920- *WhoAm 92, WhoE 93*
Sussman, Martin Victor *WhoAm 92*
Sussman, Marvin Lawrence 1948- *WhoSSW 93*
Sussman, Marvin S. 1947- *St&PR 93*
Sussman, Neil A. *Law&B 92*
Sussman, Norma J. *St&PR 93*
Sussman, Ocie Jones 1935- *WhoWrEP 92*
Sussman, Pamela Jane Babich 1962- *WhoAmW 93*
Sussman, Raquel Rotman 1921- *WhoAmW 93*
Sussman, Robert J. *Law&B 92*
Sussman, Stephen P. 1945- *St&PR 93*
Sussman, Susan *WhoWrEP 92*
Sussman, Susan Kamsky 1951- *WhoE 93*
Sussmayr, Franz Xaver 1766-1803 *Baker 92, OxDcOp*
Sussmuth, Rita 1937- *WhoWor 93*
Sussmuth, Roland Franzberth 1934- *WhoScE 91-3*
Sussna, Edward 1926- *WhoAm 92*
Sussna, Marshall 1935- *St&PR 93*
Sussna, Robert Earl 1939- *WhoE 93*
Sustarsic, Janez 1943- *WhoScE 91-4*
Sustendal, Diane Marie 1944- *WhoE 93*
Suster, Gerald 1951- *ScF&FL 92*
Susulic, Velibor 1933- *WhoScE 91-4*
Suszczynski, Louise Veronica 1940- *WhoE 93*
Suszka, Boleslaw Michal 1925- *WhoScE 91-4*
Suszko, William A. 1948- *St&PR 93*
Suszynska, Maria 1940- *WhoWor 93*
Suta, Aurel 1924- *WhoScE 91-4*
Suta, D. Deborah 1946- *WhoE 93*
Suta, Victoria 1925- *WhoScE 91-4*
Sutabutr, Harit 1936- *WhoWor 93*
Sutalo, Jozo *WhoScE 91-4*
Sutanto 1954- *Baker 92*
Sutcliff, Rosemary 1920- *ConAu 37NR, MajAI [port]*
Sutcliff, Rosemary 1920-1992 *Au&Arts 10 [port], BioIn 17, ConAu 139, ScF&FL 92, SmATA 73*
Sutcliff, Walter G. *Law&B 92*
Sutcliffe, Candace L. *Law&B 92*
Sutcliffe, Charles Martin Sydenham *WhoScE 91-1*
Sutcliffe, Charles Martin Sydenham 1948- *WhoWor 93*
Sutcliffe, Eric 1909- *WhoAm 92, WhoWor 93*
Sutcliffe, Halliwell *ScF&FL 92*
Sutcliffe, James Helme 1929- *WhoWor 93*
Sutcliffe, Leslie Howard *WhoScE 91-1*
Sutcliffe, Marion Shea 1918- *WhoE 93*
Sutcliffe, Peter John Christopher *WhoScE 91-1*
Sutcliffe, Sonia *BioIn 17*
Suter, Albert Edward 1935- *St&PR 93*
Suter, Bruce H. 1921- *St&PR 93, WhoIns 93*
Suter, Daniel Blosser 1920- *WhoSSW 93*
Suter, David L. *Law&B 92*
Suter, David Thomas 1927- *St&PR 93*
Suter, George August 1934- *WhoSSW 93, WhoWor 93*
Suter, Hermann 1870-1926 *Baker 92*
Suter, Jon Michael 1941- *ScF&FL 92*
Suter, Keith Douglas 1948- *WhoUN 92*
Suter, P.F. 1930- *WhoScE 91-4*
Suter, Peter 1930- *WhoScE 91-4*
Suter, Robert 1919- *Baker 92*
Suter, Ronald Eugene *Law&B 92*
Suter, Stuart R. *Law&B 92*
Suter, Suzanne *Law&B 92, St&PR 93*
Suter, Ulrich Werner 1944- *WhoWor 93*
Suter, William Kent 1937- *WhoAm 92*
Sutera, Salvatore Philip 1933- *WhoAm 92*
Sutermeister, Heinrich 1910- *Baker 92, OxDcOp*
Suteu, Eronim 1926- *WhoScE 91-4*
Sutey, John Lucas 1946- *WhoSSW 93*
Sutfin, John S. 1939- *St&PR 93*
Suthaus, Ludwig 1906-1971 *OxDcOp*
Suthaus, (Heinrich) Ludwig 1906-1971 *Baker 92*
Sutherland, Alan Roy 1944- *WhoAm 92*
Sutherland, Andrew Victor, II 1966- *WhoE 93*
Sutherland, Audrey 1921- *BioIn 17*
Sutherland, Barbara L. 1954- *WhoIns 93*
Sutherland, Bruce Taylor 1930- *St&PR 93*
Sutherland, Charles A. 1951- *St&PR 93*
Sutherland, Donald 1934- *BioIn 17, IntDcF 2-3*
Sutherland, Donald 1935- *WhoAm 92, WhoWor 93*
Sutherland, Donald Eugene 1947- *WhoSSW 93*
Sutherland, Donald Gray 1929- *WhoAm 92*
Sutherland, Donald James 1931- *St&PR 93, WhoAm 92*
Sutherland, Duncan Ian *Law&B 92*
Sutherland, Edward 1895-1974 *MiSFD 9N*
Sutherland, Efua 1924- *BlkAuII 92*
Sutherland, Efua (Theodora Morgue) 1924- *DcLB 117 [port]*
Sutherland, Elizabeth 1930- *St&PR 93*
Sutherland, Evelyn Greenleaf 1855-1908 *AmWomPl*
Sutherland, Francis A. 1940- *WhoIns 93*
Sutherland, Francis A., Jr. *Law&B 92*
Sutherland, Fraser 1946- *WhoCanL 92*
Sutherland, Fredric P. 1938-1991 *BioIn 17*
Sutherland, Gail Russell 1923- *WhoAm 92*
Sutherland, Gary Edward 1941- *St&PR 93*
Sutherland, George 1862-1942 *OxCSupC [port]*
Sutherland, George H. *Law&B 92*
Sutherland, George Leslie 1922- *WhoAm 92, WhoE 93, WhoWor 93*
Sutherland, Gregg David 1959- *WhoE 93*
Sutherland, Gwyn Ray 1953- *WhoSSW 93*
Sutherland, Hal *MiSFD 9*
Sutherland, Hoge T. *Law&B 92*
Sutherland, Ian Oxley *WhoScE 91-1*
Sutherland, Jack L. 1943- *St&PR 93*
Sutherland, Joan 1926- *Baker 92, BioIn 17, IntDcOp, OxDcOp, WhoAm 92, WhoWor 93*
Sutherland, Joe Allen 1934- *WhoAm 92*
Sutherland, John Beattie 1932- *WhoAm 92*
Sutherland, John M., Jr. 1923- *St&PR 93*
Sutherland, Jon *ScF&FL 92*
Sutherland, Judith L. *ScF&FL 92*
Sutherland, Kiefer *BioIn 17*
Sutherland, Kiefer 1967- *WhoAm 92*
Sutherland, Larry 1951- *WhoAsAP 91*
Sutherland, Lewis Frederick 1952- *St&PR 93, WhoAm 92*
Sutherland, Lynn Sparks 1958- *WhoSSW 93*
Sutherland, M. Robert *Law&B 92*
Sutherland, Malcolm Livingston *Law&B 92*
Sutherland, Malcolm Read, Jr. 1916- *WhoAm 92*
Sutherland, Margaret 1897-1984 *BioIn 17*
Sutherland, Margaret (Ada) 1897-1984 *Baker 92*
Sutherland, Monika Lea 1955- *WhoAmW 93*
Sutherland, Norman Stuart *WhoScE 91-1*
Sutherland, Peter 1956- *St&PR 93*
Sutherland, Ralph M. 1943- *St&PR 93*
Sutherland, Raymond Carter 1917- *WhoAm 92, WhoWrEP 92*
Sutherland, Raymond E. 1937- *St&PR 93*
Sutherland, Richard K. 1893-1966 *BioIn 17*
Sutherland, Robert Alec 1945- *WhoE 93*
Sutherland, Robert D. 1937- *WhoWrEP 92*
Sutherland, Robert John 1943- *WhoWor 93*
Sutherland, Robert L. 1916- *WhoAm 92*
Sutherland, Ronald 1933- *WhoCanL 92*
Sutherland, Roydon Godfrey 1941- *WhoUN 92*
Sutherland, Scott McKellan 1951- *WhoE 93*
Sutherland, Stanley E. *Law&B 92*
Sutherland, Stewart Ross 1941- *WhoWor 93*
Sutherland, Thomas Lee, Jr. 1938- *WhoAm 92*
Sutherland, Thomas M. *BioIn 17*
Sutherland, William Owen Sheppard 1921- *WhoAm 92, WhoWrEP 92*
Sutherland, William Paul 1941- *WhoAm 92*
Sutherland-Brown, Malcolm Corsan 1917- *WhoAm 92*
Sutherlin, Henry D. 1943- *St&PR 93*
Sutherlund, David Arvid 1929- *WhoAm 92, WhoWor 93*
Suthimai, Nicole Marie 1936- *WhoUN 92*
Suthren, Victor J. H. 1942- *WhoAm 92*
Sutic, Dragoljub 1919- *WhoScE 91-4*
Sutin, Lawrence 1951- *ScF&FL 92*
Sutin, Norman *WhoAm 92*
Sutinen, Sirkka Anneli 1951- *WhoScE 91-4*
Sutis, Robert W. *Law&B 92*
Sutka, Jozsef 1936- *WhoScE 91-4*
Sutliff, Toni Marie *Law&B 92*
Sutlin, Vivian *WhoAmW 93, WhoWor 93*
Sutman, Francis Xavier 1927- *WhoAm 92*
Sutnar, Ladislav 1897-1976 *BioIn 17*
Sutnick, Alton Ivan 1928- *WhoAm 92, WhoE 93*
Sutowski, Thor *BioIn 17*
Sutowski, Thor Brian 1945- *WhoAm 92, WhoSSW 93*
Sutphen, Harold Amerman, Jr. 1926- *WhoAm 92*
Sutphen, Richard 1937- *ScF&FL 92*
Sutphin, James Hoynes 1932- *WhoE 93*
Sutphin, Lester Insley, Jr. 1956- *WhoSSW 93*
Sutphin, Winfield Blair d1990 *BioIn 17*
Sutresna, Nana S. 1933- *WhoWor 93*
Sutresna, Nana Sastradidjaja 1933- *WhoUN 92*
Sutrisno, Try 1935- *WhoAsAP 91*
Sutro, Alfred 1863-1933 *BioIn 17*
Sutro, Frederick Charles, Jr. 1920- *St&PR 93*
Sutro, John Alfred 1905- *WhoAm 92*
Sutro, Ottilie 1872-1970
See Sutro, Rose Laura 1870-1957 *Baker 92*
Sutro, Rose Laura 1870-1957 *Baker 92*
Suttell, Paul Allyn 1949- *WhoE 93*
Sutter, Blanche M. 1946- *St&PR 93*
Sutter, Brent 1962- *BioIn 17*
Sutter, Brian *WhoAm 92*
Sutter, Brian 1956- *BioIn 17*
Sutter, Charles William *Law&B 92*
Sutter, Dale Merle 1934- *St&PR 93*
Sutter, Darryl *WhoAm 92*
Sutter, Darryl 1958- *BioIn 17*
Sutter, David L. 1953- *St&PR 93*
Sutter, Duane 1960- *BioIn 17*
Sutter, Elaine Joyce 1932- *WhoAmW 93*
Sutter, Emily May Geeseman 1939- *WhoSSW 93*
Sutter, Gary M. *Law&B 92*
Sutter, Harvey Mack 1906- *WhoWor 93*
Sutter, James Francis 1937- *WhoAm 92*
Sutter, James Stewart 1940- *WhoE 93*
Sutter, Jay Laurence 1927- *WhoE 93*
Sutter, John Ben 1953- *WhoSSW 93*
Sutter, Joseph F. 1921- *WhoAm 92*
Sutter, June H. 1917- *St&PR 93*
Sutter, Martin Paul 1955- *WhoWor 93*
Sutter, Morley Carman 1933- *WhoAm 92*
Sutter, Rich *BioIn 17*
Sutter, Richard *Law&B 92*
Sutter, Richard Anthony 1909- *WhoAm 92*
Sutter, Ron *BioIn 17*
Sutter, William Franklin 1938- *St&PR 93, WhoAm 92*
Sutter, William P., Jr. 1957- *St&PR 93*
Sutter, William Paul 1924- *WhoAm 92*
Sutterby, Larry Quentin 1950- *WhoWor 93*
Suttin, Joan S. *Law&B 92*
Suttinger, Mary Catherine 1945- *WhoAmW 93*
Suttle, Dorwin Wallace 1906- *WhoAm 92, WhoSSW 93*
Suttle, Jimmie Ray 1932- *WhoAm 92*
Suttle, Patricia L. *Law&B 92*
Suttles, David Clyde 1948- *WhoEmL 93*
Suttles, Larry 1950- *St&PR 93*
Suttles, Shirley Janet 1922- *WhoWrEP 92*
Suttles, William Maurrelle 1920- *WhoAm 92, WhoSSW 93*
Sutton, Ann Theresa 1951- *WhoAmW 93*
Sutton, Barrett Boulware 1927- *WhoAm 92*
Sutton, Berrien Daniel 1926- *WhoAm 92*
Sutton, Beverly Jewell 1932- *WhoSSW 93*
Sutton, Bill 1944- *WhoAsAP 91*
Sutton, Brian Charles *WhoScE 91-1*
Sutton, Charles Franklin 1944- *WhoIns 93*
Sutton, Charles Richard 1927- *WhoAm 92*
Sutton, Charles Samuel 1913- *WhoSSW 93*
Sutton, Connie Jane 1951- *WhoAmW 93*
Sutton, Constance Rita 1926- *WhoE 93*
Sutton, Dana Ferrin 1942- *WhoAm 92*
Sutton, Daniel 1951- *St&PR 93*
Sutton, Dave *BioIn 17*
Sutton, David 1947- *ScF&FL 92*
Sutton, David Leroy 1926- *WhoSSW 93*
Sutton, Denys 1917-1991 *BioIn 17*
Sutton, Derek H. 1937- *WhoScE 91-1*
Sutton, Dolores *WhoAm 92*
Sutton, Don *BioIn 17*
Sutton, Donald Howard 1945- *WhoAm 92*
Sutton, Donald Raymond 1926- *St&PR 93*
Sutton, Dorothy Moseley 1938- *WhoWrEP 92*
Sutton, Eugene Wilson 1948- *WhoE 93*
Sutton, Eve(lyn Mary Breakell) 1906- *DcChlFi*
Sutton, Francis Xavier 1917- *WhoAm 92*
Sutton, Frank T. 1946- *St&PR 93*
Sutton, Frederick Isler, Jr. 1916- *WhoWor 93*
Sutton, Gary William *Law&B 92*
Sutton, Gary William 1944- *WhoE 93*
Sutton, George Douglas 1949- *St&PR 93*
Sutton, George Walter 1927- *WhoAm 92*
Sutton, Gerald Winfred 1943- *St&PR 93*
Sutton, Grady 1908- *QDrFCA 92 [port]*
Sutton, H. Spence, III 1955- *WhoE 93*
Sutton, Harry Eldon 1927- *WhoAm 92*
Sutton, Henry *WhoWrEP 92*
Sutton, Henry 1935- *ScF&FL 92*
Sutton, Hirst 1911- *WhoSSW 93*
Sutton, Homer Bates 1949- *WhoSSW 93*
Sutton, Horace 1919-1991 *BioIn 17*
Sutton, Howard George 1950- *St&PR 93*
Sutton, James Andrew 1934- *St&PR 93, WhoAm 92*
Sutton, James Kenneth 1936- *St&PR 93*
Sutton, Jean Miller 1948- *WhoAmW 93*
Sutton, Jeff 1913-1979 *ScF&FL 92*
Sutton, Jim 1941- *WhoAsAP 91*
Sutton, John *WhoScE 91-1*
Sutton, John E. 1947- *St&PR 93*
Sutton, John Ewing 1950- *WhoSSW 93, WhoWor 93*
Sutton, John F., Jr. 1918- *WhoAm 92*
Sutton, John Matthias Dobson 1932- *WhoWor 93*
Sutton, John Paul 1934- *WhoAm 92*
Sutton, John Schuhmann, Jr. 1931- *WhoSSW 93*
Sutton, Jonathan Fairbairn 1954- *WhoE 93*
Sutton, Jonathan Stone 1944- *WhoAm 92*
Sutton, Joseph Thomas 1922- *WhoAm 92*
Sutton, Judith Bailey 1941- *WhoWrEP 92*
Sutton, Julia Sumberg 1928- *WhoAm 92*
Sutton, Kathy Ballard 1954- *WhoSSW 93*
Sutton, Kelso Furbush 1939- *St&PR 93, WhoAm 92*
Sutton, Lee 1916-1978 *ScF&FL 92*
Sutton, Leonard von Bibra 1914- *WhoWor 93*
Sutton, Lester Earl 1937- *WhoAm 92*
Sutton, Marcella French 1946- *WhoAmW 93*
Sutton, Marchita Lynn Bartlett 1948- *WhoAmW 93*
Sutton, Michael 1927- *WhoWor 93*
Sutton, Nancy d1990 *BioIn 17*
Sutton, Norma *Law&B 92*
Sutton, Pat Lipsky 1941- *WhoAm 92*
Sutton, Percy F. 1920- *AfrAmBi*
Sutton, Peter Alfred 1934- *WhoAm 92*
Sutton, Peter Campbell 1949- *WhoAm 92*
Sutton, Peter Morgan 1932- *WhoScE 91-1*
Sutton, Pierre 1943- *BioIn 17*
Sutton, R.S. *Law&B 92*
Sutton, Randy J. *Law&B 92*
Sutton, Ray Sandy *Law&B 92*
Sutton, Ray Sandy 1937- *St&PR 93*
Sutton, Richard Lauder 1935- *WhoAm 92*
Sutton, Ronald Gene 1941- *St&PR 93*
Sutton, Roy Wallace, III *Law&B 92*
Sutton, T. (Thomas) Michael *Law&B 92*
Sutton, Thomas 1532-1611 *BioIn 17*
Sutton, Thomas C. 1942- *WhoIns 93*
Sutton, Thomas Carl 1921- *St&PR 93, WhoAm 92*
Sutton, Vida Ravenscroft 1880- *AmWomPl*
Sutton, Walter 1916- *WhoAm 92*
Sutton, William D. *Law&B 92*
Sutton, William E. 1846-1874 *BioIn 17*
Sutton, William James, III 1930- *WhoSSW 93*
Sutton, William Joseph 1945- *WhoE 93*
Sutton, William M. *Law&B 92*
Sutton, William Michael 1940- *St&PR 93*
Sutton, Willis Anderson, Jr. 1917- *WhoAm 92*
Sutton-Finley, Nancy 1962- *WhoAmW 93*
Sutton-Straus, Joan M. 1932- *WhoAm 92*
Suuberg, Eric Michael 1951- *WhoE 93*
Suu Kyi *BioIn 17*
Suu Kyi, Aung San 1945- *ConHero 2 [port], News 92 [port]*
Suurmond, Dirk 1926- *WhoWor 93*
Suva, Suzanne 1947- *WhoAmW 93*
Suvachittanont, Sirikalaya 1951- *WhoWor 93*
Suvakovic, Vojislav 1925- *WhoScE 91-4*
Suvanto, Matti Olavi 1942- *WhoScE 91-4*
Suver, James Donald 1931- *WhoSSW 93*
Suver, Jami Kay *Law&B 92*
Suvin, Darko 1930- *BioIn 17, ScF&FL 92*
Suvin, Darko (Ronald) 1932- *ConAu 38NR*
Suvorov, Alexander Vasilievich 1729-1800 *HarEnMi*
Suwa, Joji 1953- *St&PR 93*
Suwak, Lawrence M. 1940- *St&PR 93*
Suwansathien, Bhasna 1936- *WhoWor 93*
Suwardi, Aloysius 1951- *Baker 92*
Suwinski, Jan H. 1941- *St&PR 93*
Suy, Eric 1933- *WhoWor 93*
Suydam, Eunice M. *St&PR 93*
Suydam, Peter R. 1945- *WhoWor 93*
Suyematsu, Toshiro 1918- *WhoAm 92*
Suyetsugu, Grace Tamiko 1957- *WhoEmL 93*
Suzen, Bertan 1944- *WhoScE 91-4*
Suziedelis, Vytautas A. 1930- *WhoAm 92*
Suzin, Jacek 1947- *WhoScE 91-4*
Suzuki, Akira 1930- *WhoWor 93*
Suzuki, Daisetz Teitaro 1870-1966 *BioIn 17*

Suzuki, Gengo 1904- *WhoSSW 93, WhoWor 93*
Suzuki, Hakushin 1934- *WhoWor 93*
Suzuki, Hidetaro 1937- *WhoAm 92*
Suzuki, Hisashi 1912- *IntDcAn*
Suzuki, Hisashi 1940- *WhoAsAP 91*
Suzuki, Howard Kazuro 1927- *WhoAm 92*
Suzuki, Isamu 1930- *WhoAm 92*
Suzuki, Itoko 1940- *WhoUN 92*
Suzuki, Kantaro 1867-1948 *DcTwHis*
Suzuki, Kantaro 1868-1948 *HarEnMi*
Suzuki, Kazumi 1929- *WhoAsAP 91*
Suzuki, Kazunobu 1936- *WhoWor 93*
Suzuki, Kazuo 1920- *WhoWor 93*
Suzuki, Kei 1920- *WhoWor 93*
Suzuki, Keiji 1897-1967 *HarEnMi*
Suzuki, Kikuko 1935- *WhoAsAP 91*
Suzuki, Kunihiko 1932- *WhoAm 92*
Suzuki, Masaichi James 1935- *WhoSSW 93*
Suzuki, Michio 1926- *WhoAm 92*
Suzuki, Muneo 1948- *WhoAsAP 91*
Suzuki, Noriyuki 1923- *WhoAm 92*
Suzuki, Peter M. *Law&B 92*
Suzuki, Seigo 1910- *WhoAsAP 91*
Suzuki, Shin'ichi 1898- *Baker 92*
Suzuki, Shuichi 1924- *WhoWor 93*
Suzuki, Shunichi 1953- *WhoAsAP 91*
Suzuki, Soroku 1865-1940 *HarEnMi*
Suzuki, Sosaku 1891-1945 *HarEnMi*
Suzuki, Steven S. 1948- *St&PR 93*
Suzuki, Taira 1918- *WhoWor 93*
Suzuki, Takashi 1967- *WhoSSW 93*
Suzuki, Takuma 1938- *St&PR 93*
Suzuki, Takuya 1935- *St&PR 93*
Suzuki, Teibin 1925- *WhoAsAP 91*
Suzuki, Tetsuya 1942- *WhoWor 93*
Suzuki, Toshio 1926- *WhoWor 93*
Suzuki, Tsuneo 1941- *WhoAsAP 91*
Suzuki, Yasuo 1928- *WhoWor 93*
Suzuki, Yukikazu 1954- *Baker 92*
Suzuki, Zenko 1911- *WhoWor 93*
Suzukida, Michael 1944- *St&PR 93*
Suzuki Zenko 1911- *DcTwHis*
Suzumura, Kotaro 1944- *WhoWor 93*
Svaasand, Lars Othar 1938- *WhoWor 93*
Svadlenak, Jean Hayden 1955- *WhoAm 92*
Svadlenak, Loree Dean 1931- *St&PR 93*
Svahn, John Alfred 1943- *WhoAm 92, WhoWor 93*
Svahn, Karl-Erik S. 1942- *WhoUN 92*
Svaiter, Nami Fux 1958- *WhoWor 93*
Svanberg, Olof 1941- *WhoScE 91-4*
Svanberg, Sune Roland 1943- *WhoWor 93*
Svanda, Peter L. 1934- *St&PR 93*
Svane, Christian 1933- *WhoScE 91-2*
Svanholm, Poul Johan 1933- *WhoWor 93*
Svanholm, Set 1904-1964 *IntDcOp, OxDcOp*
Svanholm, Set (Karl Viktor) 1904-1964 *Baker 92*
Svanstrom, Leif O.E. 1943- *WhoScE 91-4*
Svara, Danilo 1902-1981 *Baker 92*
Svare, A.O. 1927- *St&PR 93*
Svare, Ivar 1931- *WhoScE 91-4*
Svarney, Patricia Barnes- *BioIn 17*
Svec, Charles H. 1941- *St&PR 93*
Svec, Harry John 1918- *WhoAm 92*
Svec, Janice Lynn 1948- *WhoAmW 93*
Svec, Sandra Jean 1947- *WhoAmW 93*
Sved, Sandor 1904-1979 *Baker 92*
Sveda, Michael 1912- *WhoAm 92, WhoWor 93*
Svedberg, Bjorn Magnus Ivar 1937- *WhoWor 93*
Svedlow, Andrew Jay 1955- *WhoE 93*
Svedmyr, Nils L.V. 1927- *WhoScE 91-4*
Svee, Gary Duane 1943- *WhoAm 92*
Sveen, Donald Earl 1932- *St&PR 93*
Svehag, Sven-Erik 1932- *WhoScE 91-2*
Svehla, Gyula I.P. 1929- *WhoScE 91-3*
Svehla, John John 1946- *WhoWrEP 92*
Svehlak, Jane Elizabeth 1963- *WhoAmW 93*
Svehlik, Zdenek Jan *WhoScE 91-1*
Sveinbjornsson, Sveinbjorn 1847-1927 *Baker 92*
Sveinson, E. Glen *Law&B 92*
Sveinsson, Atli Heimir 1938- *Baker 92*
Sveinsson, Johannes 1912- *WhoWor 93*
Svejcer, Mihail 1920- *DrEEuF*
Svejda, Peter 1940- *WhoScE 91-3*
Svelto, Orazio 1936- *WhoScE 91-3*
Svelto, Vito 1934- *WhoScE 91-3*
Svelto, Vito Antonio 1934- *WhoWor 93*
Svend, Otto S. 1916- *BioIn 17*
Svendsbye, Lloyd August 1930- *WhoAm 92*
Svendsen, Hanne Marie 1933- *ScF&FL 92*
Svendsen, Ib Arne 1937- *WhoE 93*
Svendsen, Johan (Severin) 1840-1911 *Baker 92*
Svendsen, John Sverre 1937- *WhoUN 92*
Svendsen, Joyce Rose 1948- *WhoAmW 93*
Svendsen, Linda 1954- *ConAu 139*
Svendsen, Louise Averill 1915- *WhoAm 92*
Svendsen, Sven B. 1921- *St&PR 93*
Svennerholm, Lars 1925- *WhoScE 91-4*
Svennilson, Peter Haqvin Erland 1961- *WhoWor 93*
Svenson, Bo 1941- *WhoAm 92*
Svenson, Charles Oscar 1939- *WhoAm 92, WhoWor 93*
Svensson, Bengt E.Y. 1935- *WhoScE 91-4*
Svensson, Hans 1935- *WhoScE 91-4*
Svensson, Ingemar 1939- *WhoScE 91-4*
Svensson, Lars Erik Oscar 1947- *WhoWor 93*
Svensson, Nils B. 1927- *WhoScE 91-4*
Svensson, Nils-Eric 1923- *WhoScE 91-4*
Svensson, Paul Edward 1953- *WhoE 93*
Svensson, Rune 1935- *WhoWor 93*
Svensson, Sven Hakan 1942- *WhoWor 93*
Svensson, Sven-Ingvar 1932- *St&PR 93*
Sverdlik, Irv *Law&B 92*
Sverdlik, Irving 1919- *St&PR 93*
Sverdrup-Jensen, Sten 1946- *WhoScE 91-2*
Svernlov, Magnus Jan 1963- *WhoWor 93*
Svestka, Jaromir 1937- *WhoScE 91-4*
Svetlanov, Evgeny (Feodorovich) 1928- *Baker 92*
Svetlanova, Nina *BioIn 17*
Svetlova, Marina 1922- *WhoAm 92, WhoAmW 93*
Svevo, Italo 1861-1928 *BioIn 17*
Svezia, Vera Tisheff 1937- *WhoAmW 93*
Sviatopolk-Mirskii, Peter *BioIn 17*
Sviben, Marijan 1932- *WhoScE 91-4*
Svikla, Alius Julius 1947- *WhoE 93*
Svilar, Daniel P. 1930- *St&PR 93*
Sviridov, Georgi (Vasilevich) 1915- *Baker 92*
Sviridyuk, Georgii Antolevich 1952- *WhoWor 93*
Svistun, Leonid 1938- *WhoAm 92*
Svjatoslav d972 *OxDcByz*
Svoboda, Elizabeth Jane 1944- *WhoAmW 93*
Svoboda, Glenn Richard 1930- *St&PR 93*
Svoboda, Jerry Joseph 1951- *WhoE 93*
Svoboda, Jiri 1945- *DrEEuF*
Svoboda, Joanne Dzitko 1948- *WhoEmL 93*
Svoboda, Josef 1920- *IntDcOp, OxDcOp, WhoWor 93*
Svoboda, Katerina Pavla 1948- *WhoWor 93*
Svoboda, Ludovik 1895-1979 *DcTwHis*
Svoboda, Miroslav *WhoScE 91-4*
Svoboda, Richard Alan 1956- *WhoAm 92*
Svoboda, Tomas 1939- *Baker 92*
Svokos, Steve G. 1934- *St&PR 93*
Svoronos, Spyros Artchariyavivit 1954- *WhoSSW 93*
Svrcek, Leonard Edward Jr. 1954- *St&PR 93*
Svrluga, Richard Charles 1949- *WhoWor 93*
Swaab, Dick Frans 1944- *WhoScE 91-3*
Swaay, Henri van 1919- *WhoWor 93*
Swacker, Frank Warren 1922- *WhoSSW 93*
Swackhamer, E.W. *MiSFD 9*
Swaddling, David Curtis *St&PR 93*
Swader, Claude W., Jr. 1931- *St&PR 93*
Swadesh, Morris 1909-1967 *IntDcAn*
Swadling, Ross Douglas 1943- *WhoWor 93*
Swados, Elizabeth *BioIn 17*
Swados, Elizabeth A. 1951- *WhoAm 92, WhoAmW 93*
Swados, Harvey 1920-1972 *JeAmFiW*
Swados, Lincoln *BioIn 17*
Swaffield, John Arthur *WhoScE 91-1*
Swafford, Barbara Brown *Law&B 92*
Swafford, Douglas Richard, Sr. 1951- *WhoSSW 93*
Swafford, Earl L. 1943- *St&PR 93*
Swager, Eugene Calvin 1924- *WhoAm 92*
Swager, James R. 1943- *St&PR 93*
Swaggart, Jimmy Lee *BioIn 17*
Swaggart, Paul E. 1941- *St&PR 93*
Swahn, Sven 1933- *ScF&FL 92*
Swaim, Alice Mackenzie 1911- *WhoE 93, WhoWrEP 92*
Swaim, Bob 1943- *MiSFD 9*
Swaim, Charles Hall 1939- *WhoAm 92*
Swaim, David Dee 1947- *WhoAm 92*
Swaim, David W. 1956- *St&PR 93*
Swaim, James C. 1952- *St&PR 93*
Swaim, Joan (Hewatt) 1934- *ConAu 138*
Swaim, Joe Terry 1937- *St&PR 93*
Swaim, Joseph Carter, Jr. 1934- *WhoAm 92*
Swaim, Lawrence Eugene 1920- *WhoSSW 93*
Swaim, Lloyd B. 1936- *St&PR 93*
Swaim, Mary Lou *WhoSSW 93*
Swaim, Wilborn Sink 1916- *St&PR 93*
Swaiman, Kenneth Fred 1931- *WhoAm 92, WhoWor 93*
Swain, Anna Canada 1889- *AmWomPl*
Swain, Corinne Rockwell *AmWomPl*
Swain, Daniel Mack 1939- *St&PR 93*
Swain, Diane Scott 1946- *WhoAmW 93*
Swain, Donald Christie 1931- *WhoAm 92, WhoSSW 93*
Swain, Dwight V. 1915-1992 *ScF&FL 92*
Swain, Dwight V(reeland) 1915- *ConAu 37NR*
Swain, E.G. 1861-1938 *ScF&FL 92*
Swain, Edward Parsons, Jr. 1935- *WhoAm 92*
Swain, Elizabeth Anne 1941- *WhoAmW 93*
Swain, Elizabeth Curtis *Law&B 92*
Swain, James C. 1933- *St&PR 93*
Swain, Joe Oliver 1931- *St&PR 93*
Swain, Joseph P(eter) 1955- *ConAu 136*
Swain, Kathryn Watkins 1932- *WhoAmW 93*
Swain, Kenneth Robert 1943- *WhoE 93*
Swain, Mack 1876-1935 *QDrFCA 92 [port]*
Swain, Madeleine Traube 1938- *WhoE 93*
Swain, Philip Raymond 1929- *WhoE 93*
Swain, Robert 1940- *WhoAm 92*
Swain, Robert J. 1934- *St&PR 93*
Swain, Robert O. d1991 *BioIn 17*
Swain, Roger 1924- *St&PR 93*
Swain, Scott C. 1946- *St&PR 93*
Swain, Stephen James 1949- *WhoE 93*
Swain, Susan Elaine 1950- *WhoAmW 93*
Swain, Thomas R. 1945- *St&PR 93*
Swain, Virginia 1899-1984? *ScF&FL 92*
Swain, Virginia Mary 1943- *WhoE 93*
Swain, William A. 1937- *St&PR 93*
Swain, William Grant 1923- *WhoAm 92*
Swain-Baronofsky, Emaline Mae 1949- *WhoAmW 93*
Swaine, John Joseph 1932- *WhoAsAP 91*
Swaisgood, Harold Everett 1936- *WhoAm 92*
Swakon, Doreen Heather Downer 1953- *WhoSSW 93*
Swales, John Douglas *WhoScE 91-1*
Swales, Thomas J. d1991 *BioIn 17*
Swales, William Edward 1925- *St&PR 93, WhoAm 92*
Swalin, Richard Arthur 1929- *WhoAm 92*
Swaller, Katherine C. *Law&B 92*
Swalley, Robert Farrell 1930- *WhoWor 93*
Swallom, Daniel Warren 1946- *WhoE 93*
Swallow, R. Philip B. *Law&B 92*
Swallow, Steve *BioIn 17*
Swalm, Priscilla L. *Law&B 92*
Swalm, Thomas Sterling 1931- *WhoAm 92, WhoWor 93*
Swaminathan, G. 1931- *WhoAsAP 91*
Swaminathan, Jagdish 1928- *WhoWor 93*
Swaminathan, Jayanta Mootatamby 1941- *WhoWor 93*
Swaminathan, Monkombu Sambasivan 1925- *WhoWor 93*
Swamy, Srikanta M. N. 1935- *WhoAm 92*
Swamy, Subramaniam 1939- *WhoAsAP 91*
Swan, Alfred (Julius) 1890-1970 *Baker 92*
Swan, Anthony Victor *WhoScE 91-1*
Swan, Barbara 1922- *WhoAm 92*
Swan, Barbara J. *Law&B 92*
Swan, Carl Wayne 1925- *St&PR 93*
Swan, Charles E. 1935- *WhoE 93*
Swan, Christopher 1946- *ScF&FL 92*
Swan, Cynthia J. *Law&B 92*
Swan, Frances Adele 1919- *WhoWrEP 92*
Swan, George Steven *WhoAm 92, WhoSSW 93, WhoWor 93*
Swan, Gerald F. *Law&B 92*
Swan, Gladys 1934- *ConAu 39NR, WhoWrEP 92*
Swan, James Ellery 1937- *WhoE 93*
Swan, John 1935- *DcCPCAm*
Swan, John Charles 1945- *WhoE 93*
Swan, John William David 1935- *WhoWor 93*
Swan, Joyce Ann 1964- *WhoAmW 93*
Swan, Kenneth Carl 1912- *WhoAm 92*
Swan, Kenneth G. 1934- *WhoAm 92*
Swan, Mabel M. *AmWomPl*
Swan, Madonna 1928- *BioIn 17*
Swan, Mark E. 1871- *ScF&FL 92*
Swan, Martha Louise 1912- *WhoAmW 93, WhoWrEP 92*
Swan, Peer Alden 1944- *St&PR 93*
Swan, Peter Alfred 1945- *WhoSSW 93*
Swan, Peter Lawrence 1944- *WhoWor 93*
Swan, Phyllis *BioIn 17*
Swan, Ralph Edward 1946- *WhoE 93*
Swan, Richard Gordon 1933- *WhoAm 92*
Swan, Rita *BioIn 17*
Swan, Robert C. *Law&B 92*
Swan, Roberta J. 1942- *St&PR 93*
Swan, Stuart Bulkley 1957- *St&PR 93*
Swan, Susan 1945- *WhoCanL 92*
Swan, Thor 1903-1978 *ScF&FL 92*
Swan, Timothy 1758-1842 *Baker 92*
Swan, Walter *BioIn 17*
Swan, Yvette Victoria 1945- *WhoUN 92*
Swanbeck, Gunnar Pontus Emanuel 1934- *WhoWor 93*
Swanbeck, Jan 1948- *ScF&FL 92*
Swanberg, Edmund Raymond 1921- *WhoAm 92*
Swanberg, Ingrid 1947- *WhoWrEP 92*
Swanberg, W.A. 1907- *BioIn 17*
Swanberg, W(illiam) A(ndrew) 1907-1992 *ConAu 139*
Swanberg, William A. d1992 *NewYTBS 92 [port]*
Swanberg, William Andrew 1907- *WhoAm 92*
Swanek, Richard E. *St&PR 93*
Swanepoel, Pieter Andries 1948- *WhoWor 93*
Swaney, Arlene *BioIn 17*
Swaney, Cynthia Ann 1959- *WhoAmW 93*
Swang, John *BioIn 17*
Swang, Ronald Axel 1950- *WhoSSW 93*
Swanger, David 1940- *WhoWrEP 92*
Swanger, Russel S., Jr. *Law&B 92*
Swanger, Sterling Orville 1922- *WhoAm 92*
Swanger, William Earl, III 1954- *WhoE 93*
Swango, Billy Joe 1928- *St&PR 93*
Swanick, Brian Herbert *WhoScE 91-1*
Swanick, Patrick Joseph 1957- *WhoE 93*
Swank, Annette Marie 1953- *WhoAmW 93*
Swank, Emory Coblentz 1922- *WhoAm 92*
Swank, Richard Bruce 1931- *St&PR 93*
Swank, Robert Roy, Jr. 1939- *WhoAm 92*
Swank, Roy Laver 1909- *WhoAm 92, WhoWor 93*
Swank, Scott Trego 1941- *WhoE 93*
Swank, Thaddeus W. 1925- *St&PR 93*
Swanke, Albert Homer 1909- *WhoAm 92*
Swankin, David Arnold 1934- *WhoAm 92*
Swann, Brian 1940- *WhoAm 92, WhoWrEP 92*
Swann, Frederick (Lewis) 1931- *Baker 92, WhoAm 92*
Swann, Harold 1942- *WhoAm 92*
Swann, Harold S. 1942- *St&PR 93, WhoIns 93*
Swann, Ingo 1933- *ScF&FL 92*
Swann, Jerre Bailey 1939- *WhoAm 92*
Swann, John William 1937- *St&PR 93*
Swann, Lois 1944- *WhoWrEP 92*
Swann, Lucy Renate 1916- *WhoAmW 93*
Swann, Lynn Curtis 1952- *WhoAm 92*
Swann, Madeline Bruce 1951- *WhoE 93*
Swann, Michael 1920-1990 *BioIn 17*
Swann, Roberta 1947- *WhoWrEP 92*
Swann, Roberta Shiela 1948- *WhoAmW 93*
Swann, Thomas Burnett 1928-1976 *ScF&FL 92*
Swansen, Samuel Theodore 1937- *WhoAm 92*
Swanson, Anne Barrett 1948- *WhoAmW 93*
Swanson, Armour 1932- *St&PR 93*
Swanson, Arnold Arthur 1923- *WhoSSW 93*
Swanson, August George 1925- *WhoAm 92*
Swanson, Austin Delain 1930- *WhoE 93*
Swanson, Bernet Steven 1921- *WhoAm 92*
Swanson, Carl H. 1942- *St&PR 93*
Swanson, Charles Andrew 1929- *WhoAm 92*
Swanson, Charles Howard 1935- *WhoSSW 93*
Swanson, Charles Otto, II 1931- *St&PR 93*
Swanson, Charles Richard 1953- *WhoWor 93*
Swanson, Charles Sanford 1949- *WhoSSW 93*
Swanson, Dale Charles 1927- *St&PR 93*
Swanson, Dane Craig 1955- *WhoE 93*
Swanson, Darlene Marie Carlson 1925- *WhoAmW 93*
Swanson, David Dean 1951- *St&PR 93*
Swanson, David H. *St&PR 93*
Swanson, David Heath 1942- *WhoAm 92*
Swanson, David Warren 1932- *WhoAm 92*
Swanson, Dean Edward 1949- *WhoE 93*
Swanson, Denise Elaine 1957- *WhoAmW 93*
Swanson, Don Richard 1924- *WhoAm 92*
Swanson, Don Wallace 1934- *St&PR 93*
Swanson, Donald Alan 1938- *WhoAm 92*
Swanson, Donald D. 1959- *St&PR 93*
Swanson, Donald Frederick 1927- *WhoAm 92*
Swanson, Donald Lee 1947- *St&PR 93*
Swanson, Douglas E. 1938- *St&PR 93*
Swanson, Dwain V. 1934- *WhoAm 92*
Swanson, Edward Benjamin 1953- *St&PR 93*
Swanson, Edwin Leroy 1938- *St&PR 93*
Swanson, Eleanora 1916- *WhoWrEP 92*
Swanson, Esther Marie 1954- *St&PR 93*
Swanson, Francine G. *Law&B 92*
Swanson, Gayle Ruff 1944- *WhoSSW 93*
Swanson, Gerald R. 1937- *St&PR 93*
Swanson, Gladys Irene 1922- *WhoWrEP 92*

Swanson, Gloria 1898-1983 *BioIn 17*
Swanson, Gloria 1899-1983 *IntDcF 2-3 [port]*
Swanson, Guy Edwin 1922- *WhoAm 92*
Swanson, H.N. d1991 *BioIn 17*
Swanson, Harry Frederick 1931- *WhoE 93*
Swanson, Hilmer Irvin *BioIn 17*
Swanson, Howard 1907-1978 *Baker 92*
Swanson, Howard 1909-1978 *BioIn 17*
Swanson, James T. 1949- *St&PR 93*
Swanson, Jill S. 1959- *St&PR 93*
Swanson, Judith A(nn) 1957- *ConAu 139*
Swanson, Judith Ann 1957- *WhoE 93*
Swanson, Karin 1942- *WhoAmW 93*
Swanson, Larry Williams 1945- *WhoAm 92*
Swanson, Laurence Albert 1941- *WhoWrEP 92*
Swanson, Lawrence W. 1904-1990 *BioIn 17*
Swanson, Lloyd Oscar 1913- *WhoAm 92*
Swanson, Logan *ScF&FL 92*
Swanson, Lowell N. 1926- *St&PR 93*
Swanson, Lucia D. *Law&B 92*
Swanson, Marvin F. 1935- *WhoIns 93*
Swanson, Mary Linda 1959- *WhoAmW 93*
Swanson, Murray L. 1941- *St&PR 93*
Swanson, Murray Luverne 1941- *WhoAm 92*
Swanson, Nathan Anthony 1958- *WhoSSW 93*
Swanson, Norma Frances 1923- *WhoE 93*
Swanson, Patricia K. 1940- *WhoAm 92*
Swanson, Peggy Eubanks 1936- *WhoSSW 93*
Swanson, Phillip Dean 1932- *WhoAm 92*
Swanson, Ray 1937- *BioIn 17*
Swanson, Raynold A. 1920- *WhoWor 93*
Swanson, Reuel Clarion 1938- *St&PR 93*
Swanson, Richard D. *Law&B 92*
Swanson, Robert A. 1947- *WhoAm 92*
Swanson, Robert Draper 1915- *WhoAm 92*
Swanson, Robert J. 1949- *St&PR 93*
Swanson, Robert Killen 1932- *WhoAm 92*
Swanson, Roy Arthur 1925- *WhoAm 92, WhoWor 93, WhoWrEP 92*
Swanson, Rune E. 1919- *WhoAm 92*
Swanson, Stephen Olney 1932- *WhoWrEP 92*
Swanson, Sue A. *Law&B 92*
Swanson, Thomas A. *Law&B 92*
Swanson, Thomas Richard 1954- *WhoEmL 93, WhoWor 93*
Swanson, Thomas Willard 1943- *WhoAm 92*
Swanson, Wallace Martin 1941- *WhoAm 92*
Swanson, Walter J. *St&PR 93*
Swanson, Walter Loring *Law&B 92*
Swanson, Wyman Peter 1942- *St&PR 93*
Swanston, Harry M. 1947- *St&PR 93*
Swanston, Thomas Robinson 1931- *St&PR 93*
Swanstrom, John Oakley 1937- *St&PR 93*
Swanstrom, Thomas Evan 1939- *WhoAm 92*
Swant, David E. 1950- *St&PR 93*
Swantak, Judy L. 1955- *St&PR 93*
Swantek, John Edward, III 1947- *WhoE 93, WhoWrEP 92*
Swantko, Karen Marlene 1952- *WhoAmW 93*
Swanton, John Reed 1873-1958 *BioIn 17, IntDcAn*
Swanton, Robert 1957- *St&PR 93*
Swanton, Virginia Lee 1933- *WhoAmW 93*
Swanwick, Betty 1915-1989 *BioIn 17*
Swanwick, Michael 1950- *ScF&FL 92*
Swanzey, Robert Joseph 1935- *St&PR 93, WhoAm 92*
Sward, Edward Lawrence, Jr. 1933- *WhoSSW 93*
Sward, Robert 1933- *WhoCanL 92*
Sward, Robert S. 1933- *WhoWrEP 92*
Sware, Richard Michael, Jr. 1952- *WhoE 93*
Swarowsky, Hans 1899-1975 *Baker 92*
Swart, Michael 1941- *WhoAm 92*
Swart, Vernon D., Jr. 1955- *St&PR 93*
Swarthout, Gladys 1900-1969 *Baker 92*
Swarthout, Glendon d1992 *NewYTBS 92*
Swarthout, Glendon 1918- *MagSAmL [port]*
Swarthout, Glendon (Fred) 1918- *DcAmChF 1960, WhoWrEP 92*
Swarthout, Glendon (Fred) 1918-1992 *ConAu 139*
Swarthout, Kathryn 1919- *DcAmChF 1960*
Swartley, David Warren 1950- *WhoWrEP 92*
Swartout, Steven H. *Law&B 92*
Swarts, James Law *Law&B 92*
Swarts, Richard R. 1938- *St&PR 93*
Swartwood, T. Marshall 1933- *St&PR 93*
Swartwout, Joseph Rodolph 1925- *WhoAm 92, WhoWor 93*
Swartz, Allen 1924- *St&PR 93*
Swartz, Benjamin Kinsell, Jr. 1931- *WhoAm 92*
Swartz, Beth Ames 1936- *BioIn 17*
Swartz, Burton Eugene 1934- *WhoWrEP 92*
Swartz, Carl Axel Richard 1945- *WhoWor 93*
Swartz, Christian LeFevre 1915- *WhoSSW 93*
Swartz, Dan R. 1951- *St&PR 93*
Swartz, Dennis Alan 1949- *St&PR 93*
Swartz, Donald Everett 1916- *WhoAm 92*
Swartz, Donald Percy 1921- *WhoAm 92*
Swartz, Duane E. 1942- *St&PR 93*
Swartz, Glenn I. 1940- *St&PR 93*
Swartz, Gordon E. *Law&B 92*
Swartz, Harvie *BioIn 17*
Swartz, Jack Ernest 1931- *St&PR 93*
Swartz, Jeffrey L. 1954- *St&PR 93*
Swartz, Jesse Karl 1953- *St&PR 93*
Swartz, John Michael 1936- *St&PR 93, WhoAm 92*
Swartz, Jon D(avid) 1934- *ConAu 39NR*
Swartz, Jon David 1934- *WhoAm 92*
Swartz, Laura C. *AmWomPl*
Swartz, Leonard S. 1932- *St&PR 93*
Swartz, Malcolm Gilbert 1931- *WhoAm 92*
Swartz, Margaret Warren *Law&B 92*
Swartz, Margaret Z. 1950- *St&PR 93*
Swartz, Morton Norman 1923- *WhoAm 92*
Swartz, Renee Becker 1935- *WhoAmW 93*
Swartz, Robert Mark 1952- *St&PR 93, WhoSSW 93*
Swartz, Roslyn Holt 1940- *WhoAmW 93*
Swartz, Stephen *MiSFD 9*
Swartz, Stephen Arthur 1941- *St&PR 93, WhoAm 92*
Swartz, Steven S. *Law&B 92*
Swartz, Thomas B. 1932- *St&PR 93*
Swartz, William H. 1944- *St&PR 93*
Swartz, William John 1934- *WhoAm 92*
Swartz, William Michael 1946- *WhoE 93*
Swartzbaugh, Marc L. 1937- *WhoAm 92*
Swartz-Buckley, Rita Bryna 1955- *WhoAmW 93*
Swartzell, Ann Garling 1955- *WhoAmW 93*
Swartzendruber, Dale 1925- *WhoAm 92*
Swartzendruber, Harlan L. 1922- *St&PR 93*
Swartzlander, Earl Eugene, Jr. 1945- *WhoAm 92*
Swartzwelder, John Joseph 1949- *WhoWor 93*
Swarvar, Larry Carl 1949- *WhoSSW 93*
Swarz, Sahl 1912- *WhoAm 92*
Swatek, Frank Edward 1929- *WhoAm 92*
Swaters, Cherie Lynn Butler 1954- *WhoAmW 93*
Swaty, Franz *WhoScE 91-4*
Swatzell, Marilyn Louise 1942- *WhoAmW 93*
Swatzky, George Albert 1942- *WhoWor 93*
Swavely, Michael S. *BioIn 17*
Swaybill, Roger E. 1943-1991 *BioIn 17*
Swayne, Giles (Oliver Cairnes) 1946- *Baker 92*
Swayne, Keith Dauer 1940- *St&PR 93*
Swayne, Lawrence Calvin 1953- *WhoE 93*
Swayne, Noah Haynes 1804-1884 *OxCSupC [port]*
Swayne, Thompson M. *BioIn 17*
Swayne, Thompson M. 1951- *St&PR 93*
Swayze, John Cameron, Sr. 1906- *WhoAm 92*
Swayze, Patrick *BioIn 17*
Swayze, Patrick 1952?- *HolBB [port]*
Swayze, Patrick 1954- *WhoAm 92*
Swazee, Ruth *ScF&FL 92*
Swazey, Judith Pound 1939- *WhoAm 92, WhoAmW 93*
Sweaney, Robert Eugene *Law&B 92*
Swearengen, Mark T. 1912- *St&PR 93*
Swearer, Donald Keeney 1934- *WhoAm 92*
Swearer, Howard R. 1932-1991 *BioIn 17*
Swearingen, John Eldred 1918- *WhoAm 92*
Swearingen, Judson Sterling 1907- *WhoAm 92, WhoWor 93*
Swearingen, Lawson L., Jr. *WhoSSW 93*
Swearingen, Mary Addie 1906- *WhoWor 93*
Swearingen, Wayne E. 1924- *St&PR 93*
Swearingen, Wilba Shaw 1939- *WhoSSW 93*
Sweasy, Joyce Elizabeth 1948- *WhoAmW 93*
Sweat, Keith *BioIn 17*
Sweat, Robert Warren 1946- *WhoSSW 93*
Sweat, Yvonne Johnson 1954- *WhoAmW 93*
Sweatman, Alan Travers *Law&B 92*
Sweatman, Alan Travers 1946- *St&PR 93*
Sweatt, James Nelson 1960- *WhoSSW 93*
Sweatt, Millard E. *Law&B 92*
Sweatt, William David 1947- *St&PR 93*
Sweazey, George E. d1992 *NewYTBS 92*
Sweazey, George E. 1905-1992 *BioIn 17*
Swech, Stephen T. *St&PR 93*
Sweda, Gerald J. 1942- *St&PR 93*
Swedback, James Miller 1935- *St&PR 93*
Swedberg, Richard 1948- *ConAu 139*
Swedberg, Robert Mitchell 1950- *WhoAm 92, WhoSSW 93*
Swede, George 1940- *BioIn 17, WhoCanL 92*
Swedjemark, Gun Astri 1930- *WhoScE 91-4*
Swedlund, Peggy *BioIn 17*
Sweed, Phyllis 1931- *St&PR 93*
Sweedler, Barry Martin 1937- *WhoAm 92*
Sweelinck, Dirck Janszoon Sweelinck 1591?-1652
See Sweelinck, Jan Pieterszoon 1562-1621 *Baker 92*
Sweelinck, Jan Pieterszoon 1562-1621 *Baker 92*
Sweely, Linda Ann 1960- *WhoAmW 93*
Sweem, Leslie Lynn 1960- *St&PR 93*
Sween, R.D. 1940- *ScF&FL 92*
Sweeney, Anita Marie 1956- *WhoAmW 93*
Sweeney, Anne *BioIn 17*
Sweeney, Anthony John 1929- *St&PR 93*
Sweeney, Arthur Hamilton, Jr. 1920- *WhoAm 92*
Sweeney, Asher William 1920- *WhoAm 92*
Sweeney, Bob *MiSFD 9*
Sweeney, Carol J. *Law&B 92*
Sweeney, Clayton Anthony 1931- *St&PR 93, WhoAm 92*
Sweeney, D.B. *BioIn 17*
Sweeney, Daniel Thomas 1929- *WhoAm 92*
Sweeney, David Brian 1941- *WhoAm 92*
Sweeney, David Michael *Law&B 92*
Sweeney, David Michael 1948- *St&PR 93*
Sweeney, Deborah Leah 1945- *WhoAmW 93*
Sweeney, Deryl Leon 1951- *WhoSSW 93*
Sweeney, Eamon Charles 1942- *WhoScE 91-3*
Sweeney, Edward J. 1931- *St&PR 93*
Sweeney, Francis W. 1916- *BioIn 17*
Sweeney, Frank B. 1938- *St&PR 93*
Sweeney, Frank Bernard *Law&B 92*
Sweeney, Frank J. *Law&B 92*
Sweeney, George Bernard 1933- *WhoWor 93*
Sweeney, Gerald P. 1928- *WhoScE 91-3*
Sweeney, James Edward William 1933- *WhoSSW 93*
Sweeney, James F., Jr. 1922- *St&PR 93*
Sweeney, James L. 1951- *St&PR 93*
Sweeney, James Lawrence 1951- *WhoIns 93*
Sweeney, James Patrick 1952- *WhoAm 92, WhoWor 93*
Sweeney, James Raymond 1928- *WhoAm 92*
Sweeney, Janet Casale 1961- *WhoAmW 93*
Sweeney, Jean M. *Law&B 92*
Sweeney, Jim *BioIn 17*
Sweeney, John Dean 1948- *St&PR 93*
Sweeney, John J. *Law&B 92*
Sweeney, John Vincent, Jr. 1944- *WhoWor 93*
Sweeney, Joseph F. 1931- *St&PR 93*
Sweeney, Joyce 1955- *BioIn 17, ScF&FL 92*
Sweeney, Kathy A. 1949- *WhoAmW 93*
Sweeney, Kevin M. 1929- *St&PR 93*
Sweeney, Lawrence E. 1942- *St&PR 93*
Sweeney, Liam Patrick *Law&B 92*
Sweeney, Linda *ScF&FL 92*
Sweeney, Linda 1934- *St&PR 93*
Sweeney, Lucy Graham *WhoAmW 93*
Sweeney, Mark O. 1942- *St&PR 93*
Sweeney, Mark Owen 1942- *WhoAm 92*
Sweeney, Mary Ann 1945- *WhoAmW 93*
Sweeney, Mary Francis 1938- *WhoAmW 93*
Sweeney, Mary Louise 1936- *WhoAmW 93*
Sweeney, Michael 1950- *WhoAm 92*
Sweeney, Michael Andrew 1948- *WhoE 93*
Sweeney, Michael G. 1938- *St&PR 93*
Sweeney, Michael T. *Law&B 92*
Sweeney, Michael William 1962- *WhoE 93*
Sweeney, Ned Francis 1955- *WhoE 93*
Sweeney, Patricia *Law&B 92*
Sweeney, Patrick D. *Law&B 92*
Sweeney, Paul R. 1942- *St&PR 93*
Sweeney, Randall James *St&PR 93*
Sweeney, Richard James 1944- *WhoAm 92*
Sweeney, Robert *BioIn 17*
Sweeney, Robert E. 1932- *St&PR 93*
Sweeney, Robert H. 1929- *St&PR 93*
Sweeney, Robert Joseph, Jr. 1927- *WhoAm 92*
Sweeney, Roger Damien 1942- *St&PR 93*
Sweeney, Rosemarie 1950- *WhoAmW 93*
Sweeney, Sharon Ann *Law&B 92*
Sweeney, Stanley Dale 1942- *WhoSSW 93*
Sweeney, Stender Edward 1939- *St&PR 93, WhoAm 92*
Sweeney, Stephen Joseph 1928- *St&PR 93, WhoAm 92*
Sweeney, Stephen Michael 1936- *St&PR 93*
Sweeney, Susan Elizabeth 1958- *WhoE 93*
Sweeney, Susan Margaret 1963- *WhoAmW 93*
Sweeney, Susan W. *St&PR 93*
Sweeney, Thomas Joseph, Jr. 1923- *WhoAm 92*
Sweeney, Timothy A. *Law&B 92*
Sweeney, Vonny Hilton 1947- *WhoWor 93*
Sweeney, William Edward 1933- *St&PR 93, WhoIns 93*
Sweeney, William S. 1944- *St&PR 93*
Sweeny, Bradley Patterson 1940- *WhoE 93*
Sweeny, Kenneth S. 1948- *WhoE 93*
Sweeny, Paul Vincent J. *Law&B 92*
Sweeny, Robert Joseph 1931- *WhoE 93*
Sweeny, Stephen Jude 1943- *WhoE 93*
Sweeper, Deann Kay 1954- *WhoE 93*
Sweeris, Charles L. *Law&B 92*
Sweet, Bernard 1923- *St&PR 93*
Sweet, Blanche 1896-1986 *IntDcF 2-3 [port], SweetSg A [port]*
Sweet, Bradley Carl *Law&B 92*
Sweet, Charles Wheeler 1943- *St&PR 93, WhoAm 92*
Sweet, Cody *WhoAm 92*
Sweet, Cynthia Kay 1949- *WhoAmW 93*
Sweet, Daniel Philip 1955- *WhoSSW 93*
Sweet, Donald C. 1944- *St&PR 93*
Sweet, Donald Nelson 1953- *St&PR 93*
Sweet, Eileen Smith *WhoAmW 93*
Sweet, Harold 1929- *St&PR 93*
Sweet, James Brooks 1934- *WhoSSW 93*
Sweet, James R. 1898-1991 *BioIn 17*
Sweet, John R. 1946- *St&PR 93*
Sweet, Judith M. *BioIn 17*
Sweet, Judy *WhoAmW 93*
Sweet, Lawrence Lester 1938- *WhoAm 92*
Sweet, Lewis Taber, Jr. 1932- *WhoAm 92*
Sweet, Matthew *BioIn 17*
Sweet, Matthew 1964- *ConMus 9 [port]*
Sweet, Melinda *BioIn 17*
Sweet, Melinda M. *Law&B 92*
Sweet, Neale E. 1943- *St&PR 93*
Sweet, Norbert H. 1930- *St&PR 93*
Sweet, O. Robin 1952- *ConAu 139*
Sweet, Ossian Hayes 1895-1960 *EncAACR*
Sweet, Ozzie 1918- *BioIn 17*
Sweet, Patrick Henry 1938- *St&PR 93*
Sweet, Rachel *BioIn 17*
Sweet, Robert *BioIn 17*
Sweet, Robert D. 1937- *St&PR 93*
Sweet, Robert T. 1938- *St&PR 93*
Sweet, Robert W., Jr. 1937- *WhoAm 92*
Sweet, Robert Workman 1922- *WhoAm 92, WhoE 93*
Sweet, Stedman Glenn 1936- *St&PR 93*
Sweet, Steve Mark 1952- *WhoAm 92*
Sweetbaum, Henry Alan 1937- *WhoWor 93*
Sweetgall, Roy L. *Law&B 92*
Sweeting, Charles Harvard *WhoE 93*
Sweeting, Linda Marie 1941- *WhoAmW 93*
Sweeting, Martin Nicholas *WhoScE 91-1*
Sweet Inspirations *SoulM*
Sweetman, Beverly Yarroll 1939- *WhoAmW 93*
Sweetman, Brian Jack 1936- *WhoAm 92*
Sweetman, Don R. *WhoScE 91-1*
Sweetman, Jack 1940- *WhoE 93*
Sweetman, James Edward, Jr. 1937- *St&PR 93*
Sweetnam, James 1952- *St&PR 93*
Sweetnam, Richard J. *Law&B 92*
Sweetnam, William F., Jr. *Law&B 92*
Sweetser, Anne Thompson 1948- *WhoAmW 93*
Sweetser, Peter J. 1946- *St&PR 93*
Sweetser, Richard Stuart 1950- *WhoE 93*
Sweetser, Susan W. 1958- *WhoAmW 93*
Sweetser, Wesley 1919- *ScF&FL 92*
Sweezy, Paul M. 1910- *BioIn 17*
Sweezy, Paul Marlor 1910- *WhoAm 92*
Sweigart, Anne Brossman 1914- *St&PR 93*
Sweigart, Frederick Charles 1952- *St&PR 93*
Sweinberg, Barbara Luisa 1939- *WhoSSW 93*
Sweitzer, James M. 1947- *St&PR 93, WhoIns 93*
Swell, Lila 1936- *WhoE 93*
Swenarton, June *AmWomPl*

Swencicki, Robert Edward 1935- *St&PR 93*
Swencki, Steven J. 1943- *St&PR 93*
Swendrowski, John 1948- *St&PR 93*
Swendsen, Robert Haakon 1943- *WhoE 93*
Sweney, Michael K. 1955- *St&PR 93*
Swenka, Arthur J. 1937- *St&PR 93*
Swenka, Arthur John 1937- *WhoAm 92*
Swennen, R.L.A. 1955- *WhoScE 91-2*
Swensen, Clifford Henrik, Jr. 1926- *WhoAm 92*
Swensen, Grace Hartman 1931- *WhoAmW 93*
Swensen, Mary Jean Hamilton 1910- *WhoWor 93*
Swenson, Barbara Joan 1931- *WhoAmW 93*
Swenson, Betty Howliston 1923- *WhoSSW 93*
Swenson, Charis M. 1952- *St&PR 93*
Swenson, Charles *MiSFD 9*
Swenson, Courtland Sevander 1936- *WhoAm 92*
Swenson, Craig S. 1946- *St&PR 93*
Swenson, Edward 1939- *St&PR 93*
Swenson, Eric David 1954- *WhoE 93*
Swenson, Eric Pierson 1918- *WhoAm 92*
Swenson, Gary A. *Law&B 92*
Swenson, Gary L. 1937- *St&PR 93*
Swenson, George Warner, Jr. 1922- *WhoAm 92*
Swenson, Grace Stageberg *WhoWrEP 92*
Swenson, Gregory S. *Law&B 92*
Swenson, Harold Francis 1915- *WhoWor 93*
Swenson, Houston Lamar *Law&B 92*
Swenson, James Reed 1933- *WhoAm 92*
Swenson, James Warren 1932- *St&PR 93*
Swenson, Jill Dianne 1958- *WhoSSW 93*
Swenson, Karen 1936- *WhoAm 92, WhoWrEP 92*
Swenson, Kenneth C. d1991 *BioIn 17*
Swenson, Kurt McFarland 1945- *St&PR 93*
Swenson, Lawrence Paul 1931- *St&PR 93*
Swenson, Leland H. 1947- *St&PR 93*
Swenson, Lloyd A. 1924- *St&PR 93*
Swenson, May 1919-1989 *BioIn 17*
Swenson, Orvar 1909- *WhoAm 92*
Swenson, Ronald J. 1930- *St&PR 93*
Swenson, Ruth Wildman 1924- *WhoAmW 93*
Swensson, Earl Simcox 1930- *WhoAm 92*
Swepston, Jack Herbert 1928- *WhoSSW 93*
Swepston, Lee St. Clair 1947- *WhoUN 92*
Swerdlove, Dorothy Louise 1928- *WhoAm 92*
Swerdlow, Amy 1923- *WhoAmW 93*
Swerdlow, David *BioIn 17*
Swerdlow, Martin Abraham 1923- *WhoAm 92*
Swerdlow, Max *BioIn 17*
Swerdlow, Stanley d1991 *BioIn 17*
Swerdzewski, Frank 1947- *WhoSSW 93*
Swergold, Marcelle Miriam 1927- *WhoAmW 93, WhoE 93*
Swerhun, Walter William 1936- *St&PR 93*
Swerling, Jack Bruce 1946- *WhoSSW 93, WhoWor 93*
Swerling, Jo, Jr. 1931- *MiSFD 9*
Swerling, Peter 1929- *WhoAm 92*
Swert, Jules de 1843-1891 *Baker 92*
Swert, Robert Edward 1926- *St&PR 93*
Swetland, Kenneth L. 1937- *WhoE 93*
Swetlik, William Philip 1950- *WhoEmL 93, WhoWor 93*
Swetman, Glenn Robert 1936- *WhoSSW 93, WhoWor 93*
Swetman, R.E. 1938- *St&PR 93*
Swetnam, Monte Newton 1936- *St&PR 93, WhoAm 92*
Swetnam, Susan H. *BioIn 17*
Swets, John Arthur 1928- *BioIn 17, WhoAm 92*
Swets, Paul William 1941- *WhoWrEP 92*
Swett, Albert Hersey 1923- *WhoAm 92*
Swett, Daniel Robert 1936- *WhoAm 92*
Swett, Dick 1957- *CngDr 91*
Swett, James E. 1920- *BioIn 17*
Swett, Jeremy F. *Law&B 92*
Swett, Richard Nelson 1957- *WhoAm 92, WhoE 93*
Swett, Robert E. 1928- *WhoIns 93*
Swett, Stephen Frederick, Jr. 1935- *WhoE 93*
Swetz, Frank Joseph 1937- *WhoE 93*
Swetz, Ken *BioIn 17*
Swetz, Ken J. 1942- *St&PR 93*
Swezey, Robert William 1943- *WhoSSW 93*
Swiatek, W. Jay *Law&B 92*
Swiatkowski, Cheryl L. 1951- *St&PR 93*
Swiatocha, John *Law&B 92*
Swick, James Robert 1950- *WhoE 93*
Swick, Larry Marvin 1932- *WhoWor 93*
Swick, Norman H. 1949- *St&PR 93*
Swick, Thomas *BioIn 17*
Swick, Thomas 1952- *ConAu 138*
Swicklik, Mary Lou Marquardt 1927- *WhoAmW 93*
Swicord, Earl L. 1930- *St&PR 93*
Swid, David d1991 *BioIn 17*
Swid, Nan *BioIn 17*
Swid, Stephen Claar 1940- *WhoAm 92*
Swiden, Ladell Ray 1938- *WhoAm 92*
Swider, Wojciech *WhoScE 91-4*
Swiderski, Karen Alexandra 1955- *WhoUN 92*
Swidler, Joseph Charles 1907- *WhoAm 92*
Swidler, Thomas Alan 1936- *St&PR 93*
Swiech, Robert A. *Law&B 92*
Swiecicki, Martin 1934- *WhoE 93*
Swientek, Francis Martin 1944- *WhoE 93*
Swierczewski, Gerard *WhoScE 91-2*
Swierk, Alan Edward 1945- *St&PR 93*
Swierkiewicz, Akos 1946- *WhoIns 93*
Swierniak, Andrzej Piotr 1950- *WhoWor 93*
Swiers, Richard Howard 1929- *St&PR 93*
Swierzawski, Tadeusz Jerzy 1925- *WhoE 93*
Swietek, Richard Michael 1962- *WhoE 93*
Swieten, Gottfried, Baron van 1733-1803 *Baker 92*
Swietering, Johannes Wilhelmus 1944- *WhoUN 92*
Swietliczko, Irena 1923- *WhoScE 91-4*
Swietlikowski, Marian Josef 1929- *WhoScE 91-3*
Swiezynski, K.M. 1922- *WhoScE 91-4*
Swift, Al 1935- *CngDr 91, WhoAm 92*
Swift, Aubrey Earl 1933- *St&PR 93*
Swift, Calvin Thomas 1937- *WhoAm 92*
Swift, Carolyn J.A. *Law&B 92*
Swift, David 1919- *MiSFD 9*
Swift, David L. *Law&B 92*
Swift, David L. 1936- *St&PR 93, WhoAm 92*
Swift, Dolores Monica Marcinkevich 1936- *WhoAm 92*
Swift, E.J. 1827-1887 *BioIn 17*
Swift, E. Kent, Jr. 1924- *St&PR 93*
Swift, Edward Foster 1923- *St&PR 93*
Swift, Edward Foster, III 1923- *WhoAm 92*
Swift, Eliza Morgan *AmWomPl*
Swift, Elizabeth *WhoWrEP 92*
Swift, Evangeline Wilson 1939- *WhoAm 92, WhoAmW 93*
Swift, Frank Meador 1911- *WhoAm 92*
Swift, George P., Jr. 1919- *St&PR 93*
Swift, Graham 1939- *WhoE 93*
Swift, Graham 1949- *BioIn 17*
Swift, Humphrey H. 1915- *St&PR 93*
Swift, Innis Palmer 1882-1953 *HarEnMi*
Swift, Isaac d1991 *BioIn 17*
Swift, Isabel Davidson *WhoAm 92*
Swift, James *Law&B 92*
Swift, James P. *Law&B 92*
Swift, James William 1945- *WhoAm 92*
Swift, Jane Maria 1965- *WhoAmW 93, WhoE 93*
Swift, Janet Margaret Bronson 1947- *WhoAmW 93*
Swift, Jill Anne 1959- *WhoAmW 93*
Swift, John Douglas *WhoScE 91-1*
Swift, John F. 1959- *St&PR 93*
Swift, John Francis 1935- *WhoAm 92*
Swift, John Staples, III 1952- *St&PR 93*
Swift, Jonathan 1667-1745 *BioIn 17, MagSWL [port], WorLitC [port]*
Swift, Kenneth Rod 1930- *St&PR 93*
Swift, Malcolm S. *Law&B 92*
Swift, Margaret 1939- *BioIn 17*
Swift, Mary Howard Davidson 1926- *WhoWrEP 92*
Swift, Mathews Dismuke 1947- *St&PR 93*
Swift, Mettje *BioIn 17*
Swift, Michael Ronald 1935- *WhoAm 92*
Swift, Patricia Condon 1948- *WhoAmW 93*
Swift, Paul 1942- *WhoE 93*
Swift, Peter J. *Law&B 92*
Swift, Rebecca *ScF&FL 92*
Swift, Richard 1927- *Baker 92*
Swift, Robert Frederic 1940- *WhoE 93*
Swift, Robert L. *St&PR 93*
Swift, Sally C. *Law&B 92*
Swift, Simon Timothy 1960- *WhoWor 93*
Swift, Stephen J. 1943- *CngDr 91*
Swift, Stephen Jensen 1943- *WhoAm 92*
Swift, Virgil Neil 1928- *St&PR 93*
Swift, Wayne Bradley 1927- *WhoE 93*
Swift, William Charles 1931- *WhoIns 93*
Swift, William Porter 1914- *WhoE 93*
Swift, Yolanda V. *Law&B 92*
Swig, Richard L. 1925- *WhoAm 92*
Swig, Roselyne Chroman 1930- *WhoAm 92*
Swigar, Mary Eva 1940- *WhoAmW 93*
Swigart, Rob 1941- *ScF&FL 92, WhoWrEP 92*
Swigart, Theodore Earl 1895- *WhoAm 92*
Swiger, Elinor Porter 1927- *WhoAmW 93*
Swiger, Elizabeth Davis 1926- *WhoAmW 93*
Swigert, James Mack 1907- *WhoAm 92*
Swigger, Kathleen Mary 1947- *WhoAmW 93*
Swiggett, Hal 1921- *WhoSSW 93*
Swiggett, Robert Lewis 1921- *St&PR 93*
Swihart, Fred Jacob 1919- *WhoWor 93*
Swihart, Harry E. 1951- *St&PR 93*
Swihart, John Marion 1923- *WhoAm 92*
Swihart, Lynne Andrews 1961- *WhoWor 93*
Swikard, Janet L. 1949- *St&PR 93*
Swilik, Robert Charles 1934- *St&PR 93*
Swiller, Randolph Jacob 1946- *WhoSSW 93*
Swilling, Jack 1830-1878 *BioIn 17*
Swilling, Ken *BioIn 17*
Swilling, Pat 1964- *WhoAm 92*
Swim, Jesse Rogene 1945- *WhoSSW 93*
Swimm, Richard Michael 1953- *St&PR 93*
Swimmer, Betsy Ross 1943- *WhoAmW 93*
Swimmer, Gerald E. *Law&B 92*
Swimmer, Saul *MiSFD 9*
Swims, Melanie Parnell 1965- *WhoSSW 93*
Swinarski, Konrad 1929-1975 *PolBiDi*
Swinburn, Charles 1942- *WhoAm 92*
Swinburne, Algernon 1837-1909 *WorLitC [port]*
Swinburne, Algernon Charles 1837-1909 *BioIn 17, MagSWL [port]*
Swinburne, Herbert Hillhouse 1912- *WhoAm 92*
Swinburne, T.R. *WhoScE 91-1*
Swindell, Archie Calhoun, Jr. 1936- *WhoAm 92*
Swindell, Brennon Ray 1933- *St&PR 93*
Swindell, Calvin M. 1923- *St&PR 93*
Swindell, R. David d1991 *BioIn 17*
Swindells, David W. 1936- *St&PR 93, WhoAm 92*
Swindells, Ralph 1934- *WhoScE 91-1*
Swindells, Robert E. 1939- *ScF&FL 92*
Swindells, Robert (Edward) 1939- *ChlFicS, MajAI [port]*
Swindells, William 1930- *St&PR 93*
Swindells, William, Jr. 1930- *WhoAm 92*
Swindle, Jonathan Cameron 1942- *St&PR 93*
Swindle, Orson George, III 1937- *NewYTBS 92 [port]*
Swindle, Robert Ian 1949- *WhoScE 91-1*
Swindler, Kathryn Elizabeth 1947- *WhoAmW 93*
Swindler, Sherry Horton 1957- *WhoSSW 93*
Swindoll, Charles R. *BioIn 17*
Swinea, Robert Wayne 1950- *WhoWrEP 92*
Swinehart, Marcia J. *Law&B 92*
Swinehart, Robert Dane 1937- *St&PR 93*
Swinerton, William Arthur 1917- *WhoAm 92*
Swiney, Willie Lee 1948- *WhoE 93*
Swinfen, Ann *ScF&FL 92*
Swinford, Ann Elizabeth 1958- *WhoAmW 93*
Swinford, John Walker 1909- *WhoSSW 93*
Swing, Bruce H. 1941- *St&PR 93*
Swing, Elizabeth Sherman 1927- *WhoE 93*
Swing, John Temple 1929- *St&PR 93, WhoAm 92*
Swing, Joseph May 1894-1984 *HarEnMi*
Swing, Peter Gram 1922- *WhoAm 92*
Swing, Ross G. *Law&B 92*
Swing, William Edwin 1936- *WhoAm 92*
Swing, William Lacy 1934- *WhoAm 92, WhoWor 93*
Swingen, Daniel Lock 1960- *St&PR 93*
Swingen, Lowell James 1929- *St&PR 93*
Swinger, Denise Ann 1958- *WhoAmW 93*
Swingle, Loren Carl *Law&B 92*
Swingle, Richard Steven 1945- *St&PR 93*
Swingley, Sheryl Ann 1951- *WhoAmW 93*
Swink, Ann 1945- *WhoAmW 93*
Swink, David Blair 1944- *WhoSSW 93*
Swink, John L. d1991 *BioIn 17*
Swinnerton-Dyer, Peter Francis 1927- *WhoWor 93*
Swinney, Harry Leonard 1939- *WhoAm 92*
Swinney, Richard *Law&B 92*
Swinsky, Bruce Clayton 1946- *St&PR 93*
Swinstead, Philip *WhoScE 91-1*
Swint, Diane Mary 1948- *WhoAmW 93*
Swint, Thomas Lloyd 1933- *St&PR 93*
Swinton, Phyllis McNeal *AmWomPl*
Swinton, R. Timothy 1946- *St&PR 93*
Swintosky, Joseph Vincent 1921- *WhoAm 92*
Swire, Edith Wypler 1943- *WhoAmW 93*
Swire, Lawrence J. *Law&B 92*
Swire, Willard 1910-1991 *BioIn 17*
Swirling, Deborah V. *Law&B 92*
Swirnoff, Brad *MiSFD 9*
Swirsky, Benjamin *WhoAm 92*
Swirsky, Judith Perlman 1928- *WhoAmW 93*
Swisher, Gerald John *Law&B 92*
Swisher, Glenda Regina 1964- *WhoSSW 93*
Swisher, Lloyd K. *St&PR 93*
Swisher, Randall Scott 1947- *WhoE 93*
Swisher, Ronald Dale 1936- *WhoAm 92*
Swisher, Samuel D. *Law&B 92*
Swisher, Thane 1956- *St&PR 93*
Swisher, Thane Allison 1956- *WhoAm 92*
Swisshelm, Jane Grey 1815-1884 *JrnUS*
Swistak, Irena 1964- *WhoAmW 93*
Swistel, Alexander Julian 1949- *WhoE 93*
Swit, Loretta 1937- *WhoAm 92*
Switaj, Carmen Marie 1948- *WhoAmW 93*
Swithin, Antony *ScF&FL 92*
Switka, Romuald 1933- *WhoScE 91-4*
Switlik, Richard 1918- *St&PR 93*
Switten, Margaret Louise *WhoAmW 93*
Switz, Donald MacLean 1937- *WhoSSW 93*
Switz, Elise Hurd 1942- *WhoSSW 93*
Switz, Mary Ann 1944- *WhoAmW 93*
Switz, Robert E. 1946- *St&PR 93*
Switz, Thomas Richard 1957- *WhoE 93*
Switzer, Barry *BioIn 17*
Switzer, David A. 1947- *St&PR 93*
Switzer, Frank C. 1959- *St&PR 93*
Switzer, Hugh Kent 1938- *St&PR 93*
Switzer, Janet 1932- *WhoAmW 93*
Switzer, Kathrine *BioIn 17*
Switzer, Larry K. 1943- *St&PR 93*
Switzer, Lisle J. 1929- *St&PR 93*
Switzer, Michael *MiSFD 9*
Switzer, Michael H. *Law&B 92*
Switzer, Robert L. *Law&B 92*
Switzer, Robert Lee 1940- *WhoAm 92*
Switzer, Ronald H. 1938- *St&PR 93*
Switzer, Thomas W. 1945- *St&PR 93*
Switzer, Vernon J. 1930- *St&PR 93*
Switzer, William Lynn 1948- *St&PR 93*
Switzer, William Paul 1927- *WhoAm 92*
Switzler, William Franklin 1819-1906 *JrnUS*
Swoap, David Bruce 1937- *WhoAm 92*
Swoboda, Henry 1897-1990 *Baker 92*
Swoboda, James John 1948- *WhoAm 92*
Swoboda, Ralph S. 1948- *St&PR 93*
Swoboda, Ralph Sande 1948- *WhoAm 92*
Swoboda, Richard Allan 1943- *WhoE 93*
Swoboda, Wolfgang *WhoScE 91-4*
Swofford, Donald Anthony 1947- *WhoAm 92*
Swoger, Peggy Ann *BioIn 17*
Swogger, Kurt W. 1950- *St&PR 93*
Swokin, Kala 1943- *WhoAsAP 91*
Swomley, James Anthony 1929- *WhoAm 92*
Swon, Cassandra Ann *St&PR 93*
Swon, James Ellis 1946- *St&PR 93*
Swonger, Alvin Kent 1943- *WhoAm 92*
Swope, Charles Evans 1930- *WhoAm 92, WhoWor 93*
Swope, David M. *Law&B 92*
Swope, Donald Downey 1926- *WhoAm 92*
Swope, George Wendell 1916- *WhoWor 93*
Swope, Herbert Bayard 1882-1958 *JrnUS*
Swope, Hunter 1927- *St&PR 93*
Swope, Jeffrey Peyton 1945- *WhoAm 92*
Swope, John Franklin 1938- *St&PR 93, WhoAm 92, WhoIns 93*
Swope, John Peter 1935- *WhoE 93*
Swope, Joseph John 1958- *WhoWrEP 92*
Swope, Marjory Mason 1940- *WhoE 93*
Swope, R. Hain *Law&B 92*
Swope, Samuel David 1949- *St&PR 93*
Swope, William Richards 1920- *WhoSSW 93*
Sword, Christopher Patrick 1928- *WhoAm 92*
Sword, Donald Graham *Law&B 92*
Sword, Ian P. 1942- *WhoScE 91-1*
Swords, Charles Raymond 1935- *St&PR 93*
Swords, Gary A. 1947- *St&PR 93, WhoIns 93*
Swords, Maurice J. 1929- *St&PR 93*
Swormstedt, J.R. 1934- *St&PR 93*
Swortzel, Douglas Scott 1962- *WhoE 93*
Swortzell, Nancy Foell 1930- *WhoAmW 93*
Swoyer, Vincent Harry 1932- *St&PR 93*
Swycaffer, Jefferson P. 1956- *ScF&FL 92*
Swycaffer, Ruth Helen *ScF&FL 92*
Swyers, John 1952- *WhoSSW 93*
Swygert, H. Patrick 1943- *WhoAm 92, WhoE 93*
Swynghedauw, Bernard 1935- *WhoScE 91-2*
Swystun, W.M. *Law&B 92*
Swystun-Rives, Bohdana Alexandra 1925- *WhoWor 93*
Sy, Francisco Santos 1949- *WhoSSW 93, WhoWor 93*
Sy, Henry *BioIn 17*
Sy, Mame Balla 1946- *WhoUN 92*
Syahruddin, Saodah Batin Akuan 1939- *WhoUN 92*
Syak, Harry A. 1935- *St&PR 93*

Sybenga, John Robert 1947- WhoEmL 93
Syberberg, Hans Jurgen 1935- BioIn 17, MiSFD 9
Syberg, Franz (Adolf) 1904-1955 Baker 92
Sybesma, Christiaan 1928- WhoScE 91-2
Sybesma, Watse 1929- WhoScE 91-3
Sybilla 1963- BioIn 17
Syblik, Detlev Adolf 1943- WhoWor 93
Sybrandt, John L. 1938- St&PR 93
Syc, Allan Ronald Law&B 92
Sych, Roman 1931- WhoScE 91-4
Sychra, Antonin 1918-1969 Baker 92
Sychterz, Teresa Anne 1952- WhoE 93
Sycip, George Edwin 1956- St&PR 93
SyCip, Washington 1921- WhoWor 93
Sycks, Richard A. 1931- St&PR 93
Syde, Harvey 1927- St&PR 93
Sydeman, William (Jay) 1928- Baker 92
Sydenham, Thomas 1624-1689 BioIn 17
Sydney, Algernon 1622-1683 BioIn 17
Sydney, Allan William 1928- St&PR 93
Sydney, Boone Kenton, Jr. Law&B 92
Sydney, Cynthia ConAu 40NR
Sydney, Doris S. 1934- WhoAmW 93
Sydney, Sydelle Marian 1935- St&PR 93
Sydnor, Ashby Kendall, Jr. 1943- St&PR 93
Sydnor, Charles F. 1958- St&PR 93
Sydnor, E. Starke Law&B 92
Sydnor, Edythe Lois 1920- WhoE 93, WhoWor 93
Sydnor, John Terry 1928- St&PR 93
Sydnor, Rebecca BioIn 17
Sydor, Daniel J. 1939- St&PR 93
Sydor, Edward J. 1923- St&PR 93
Sydow, Erik von WhoScE 91-4
Sydow, Max von IntDcF 2-3
Sydow, Max von 1929- BioIn 17
Syed, Ibrahim Bijli 1939- WhoWor 93
Syed, Mahmood Ahmad 1939- WhoWor 93
Syed, Sabiha H. 1939- WhoUN 92
Syed Putra, Ibni Al-Marhum Syed Hassan Jamalullail 1920- WhoWor 93
Syer, Warren Bertram 1923- WhoAm 92
Syers, John Keith WhoScE 91-1
Sygietynski, Tadeusz 1896-1955 Baker 92, PolBiDi
Syiek, Joseph Alexander 1951- WhoEmL 93
Sykala, U. ScF&FL 92
Sykes, Alan O'Neil 1925- WhoSSW 93
Sykes, Alfred Geoffrey WhoScE 91-1
Sykes, Brian Douglas 1943- WhoAm 92
Sykes, Dana Burdett Law&B 92
Sykes, David B. 1918- St&PR 93
Sykes, David Edmund WhoScE 91-1
Sykes, David Terrence 1937- WhoAm 92
Sykes, Donald Joseph 1936- WhoE 93
Sykes, Eric 1923- QDrFCA 92 [port]
Sykes, Gresham M'Cready 1922- WhoAm 92
Sykes, J.J.W. 1948- WhoScE 91-1
Sykes, James (Andrews) 1908-1985 Baker 92
Sykes, John Michael WhoScE 91-1
Sykes, Joseph Stuart 1923- St&PR 93
Sykes, Judith L. Law&B 92
Sykes, Kimberly Anne 1968- WhoSSW 93
Sykes, Lynn Ray 1937- WhoAm 92
Sykes, Melvin Julius 1924- WhoAm 92
Sykes, Percy 1867-1945 Expl 93
Sykes, Peter 1939- MiSFD 9
Sykes, R.B. WhoScE 91-1
Sykes, Richard M. 1940- St&PR 93
Sykes, Robert F. 1924- St&PR 93
Sykes, Robert H. 1927- WhoWrEP 92
Sykes, Robert Leonard WhoScE 91-1
Sykes, Roy Arnold, Jr. 1948- St&PR 93
Sykes, S.C. 1943- ScF&FL 92
Sykes, William Maltby 1911- WhoAm 92
Sykora, Donald D. 1930- St&PR 93, WhoAm 92
Sykora, Harold James 1939- WhoAm 92
Sykora, Ondrej 1951- WhoWor 93
Sykora, Richard J. 1940- St&PR 93
Sykut, Kazimierz Wojciech 1923- WhoScE 91-4
Sylbert, Paul MiSFD 9
Sylbing, Garth 1945- WhoScE 91-3
Sylk, Harry Stanley 1903- WhoAm 92
Sylk, Leonard Allen 1941- WhoE 93
Syll, Erik 1930- WhoWor 93
Sylla, Mady Oury 1932- WhoUN 92
Sylla, Richard Eugene 1940- WhoE 93
Sylva, John R. 1948- St&PR 93
Sylvan, Sanford BioIn 17
Sylvest, Harold Maynard, Jr. 1941- St&PR 93
Sylvester 1947-1988 Baker 92
Sylvester, George Howard 1927- WhoAm 92
Sylvester, Janet 1950- WhoWrEP 92
Sylvester, John 1935- St&PR 93
Sylvester, John Vance, IV 1954- WhoE 93
Sylvester, Josuah 1562?-1618 DcLB 121 [port]
Sylvester, Leonard 1933- St&PR 93
Sylvester, Lynda Joann 1950- WhoE 93
Sylvester, Nancy Katherine 1947- WhoAmW 93
Sylvester, Sandra M. 1942- WhoAmW 93
Sylvestre, Jean Guy 1918- WhoAm 92
Sylvestre, Louis DcCPCAm
Sylvestri, Mario Frank 1948- WhoEmL 93
Sylvia, B. Ralph 1940- St&PR 93
Sylvia, Joseph L. 1945- St&PR 93
Symanski, Robert Anthony 1946- WhoAm 92
Symansky, Gary K. 1950- St&PR 93
Symansky, Steven Alan 1951- WhoUN 92
Syme, Daniel Bailey 1946- WhoE 93, WhoEmL 93
Syme, Robert P. 1934- St&PR 93
Syme, Ronald 1903-1989 BioIn 17
Syme, Sherman Leonard 1932- WhoAm 92
Symeon d1429 OxDcByz
Symeon, II d1098 OxDcByz
Symeon Logothete fl. 10th cent.- OxDcByz
Symeon Magistros, Pseudo- OxDcByz
Symeon Metaphrastes dc. 1000 OxDcByz
Symeon of Blachernai OxDcByz
Symeon of Bulgaria 863?-927 OxDcByz
Symeon of Emesa OxDcByz
Symeon of Mytilene OxDcByz
Symeon of Mytilene 764-843 See David of Mytilene 716-783? OxDcByz
Symeon, Pseudo- OxDcByz
Symeon the Fool OxDcByz
Symeon the Stylite the Elder c. 389-459 OxDcByz [port]
Symeon the Stylite the Younger 521-592 OxDcByz
Symeon the Theologian 949?-1022 OxDcByz
Symeon Uros dc. 1369 OxDcByz
Symes, Garry Stuart 1954- WhoWor 93
Symes, Mike ScF&FL 92
Symington, Fife BioIn 17
Symington, Fife 1945- WhoAm 92
Symington, James McKim d1992 NewYTBS 92
Symington, Stuart 1901-1989 PolPar
Symm, Robert Edwin 1957- WhoSSW 93
Symmachus d514 OxDcByz
Symmachus c. 345-c. 402 OxDcByz
Symmank, D. G. 1933- WhoSSW 93
Symmers, William Garth 1910- WhoAm 92
Symmes, Daniel Leslie 1949- WhoEmL 93, WhoWor 93
Symmes, Lee Richardson 1941- WhoAm 92
Symmes, Robert 1919-1988 BioIn 17
Symmes, William Daniel 1938- WhoWor 93
Symmonds, Richard Earl 1922- WhoAm 92
Symms, Steve 1938- CngDr 91
Symms, Steve D. 1938- WhoAm 92
Symoens, Jean-Jacques A. 1927- WhoScE 91-2
Symon, James Gordon 1928- WhoAm 92
Symon, Lindsay 1929- WhoScE 91-1
Symon, Peter Dudley 1922- WhoAsAP 91
Symon, Robert J. 1931- St&PR 93
Symonds, Alexandra d1992 NewYTBS 92 [port]
Symonds, Alexandra 1918-1992 BioIn 17
Symonds, Arlene R. 1932- St&PR 93
Symonds, Carl Joseph 1920- St&PR 93
Symonds, Edwin Malcolm WhoScE 91-1
Symonds, Francis C. 1926-1990 BioIn 17
Symonds, Johnnie Pirkle 1900- WhoWor 93
Symonds, Norman 1920- Baker 92
Symonds, Paul Southworth 1916- WhoAm 92
Symonides, Ewa Luiza 1944- WhoScE 91-4
Symonides, Janusz Ignacy 1938- WhoUN 92
Symons, A.P. WhoIns 93
Symons, Adelaide Bangs AmWomPl
Symons, Allene 1944- ScF&FL 92
Symons, Arthur 1865-1945 BioIn 17
Symons, Edward Leonard, Jr. 1941- WhoAm 92
Symons, Geraldine 1909- ScF&FL 92
Symons, Irving Joseph 1907- St&PR 93
Symons, J. Keith 1932- WhoAm 92, WhoSSW 93
Symons, James Martin 1931- WhoAm 92
Symons, James Martin 1937- WhoAm 92
Symons, Julian 1912- BioIn 17, DcLB Y92 [port], ScF&FL 92
Symons, Julian Gustave 1912- WhoAm 92
Symons, Leslie John WhoScE 91-1
Symons, Louise Q. Law&B 92
Symons, Martyn Christian 1925- WhoWor 93
Symons, Martyn Christian Raymond WhoScE 91-1
Symons, Norman J. BioIn 17
Symons, Robert Spencer 1925- WhoAm 92
Symons, Stuart ConAu 39NR
Symons, Thomas H. B. 1929- WhoAm 92
Symons, Timothy James McNeil 1951- WhoAm 92
Symons, Walter Vaughan 1930- St&PR 93
Syms, Helen Maksym 1918- WhoAmW 93
Syms, Sy 1926- St&PR 93
Syms, Sylvia 1917-1992 BioIn 17, NewYTBS 92 [port]
Synadenos OxDcByz
Synal, Bogdan Jan 1928- WhoScE 91-4
Synan, Edward Aloysius, Jr. 1918- WhoAm 92
Synan, Regis J. 1954- St&PR 93
Synar, Michael Lynn 1950- WhoAm 92, WhoSSW 93
Synar, Mike 1950- CngDr 91
Synder, Vince E. St&PR 93
Synes, Robert d1990 BioIn 17
Synesios c. 370-c. 413 OxDcByz
Synge, J.M. 1871-1909 BioIn 17
Synge, John Lighton 1897- WhoAm 92
Synge, John Millington 1871-1909 BioIn 17, MagSWL [port]
Synge, Richard Laurence Millington 1914- WhoWor 93
Synge, Ursula 1930-1981? ScF&FL 92
Synk, James Arthur 1934- WhoAm 92
Synn, Ilhi 1939- WhoWor 93
Synnett, Robert John 1958- St&PR 93
Synnevag, Gry WhoScE 91-4
Synnott, Aidan Brendan Mars 1954- WhoWor 93
Synnott, Marcia Graham 1939- WhoAmW 93
Synnott, Paul A., Jr. 1939- WhoIns 93
Synnott, William Raymond 1929- St&PR 93, WhoAm 92
Synodinos, John Anthony 1934- WhoAm 92
Synowiec, Ewa (Krystyna) 1942- Baker 92
Syozi, Itiro 1920- WhoWor 93
Syozo, Kubo 1941- WhoWor 93
Sype, Minnie 1869-1956 BioIn 17
Sypek, Joseph Paul 1954- WhoE 93
Sypert, George Walter 1941- WhoAm 92
Sypherd, Paul Starr 1936- WhoAm 92
Syphers, Mary Frances 1912- WhoAmW 93
Sy-Quenel, Claude-Germaine 1944- WhoWor 93
Syquia, Enrique Pineda 1930- WhoWor 93
Syracuse, Ross Michael 1950- WhoE 93
Syrbe, M. WhoScE 91-3
Syred, Celia (Mary) 1911- DcChlFi
Syred, Nicholas WhoScE 91-1
Syreeta SoulM
Syrek, Richard William 1947- St&PR 93, WhoE 93
Syrell, Linda Anne 1939- WhoAmW 93
Syrett, Netta AmWomPl
Syrett, Philip Joseph WhoScE 91-1
Syrgiannes c. 1290-1334 OxDcByz
Syrjala-Qvist, Liisa 1938- WhoScE 91-4
Syrjamaki, Jaakko A. 1933- WhoScE 91-4
Syrkin, Marie 1899-1989 JeAmHC
Syrnick, Mark Stephen Law&B 92
Syrnyk, Irene M. Law&B 92
Syrogianis Camara, Jean 1934- WhoUN 92
Syron, M. Bernard 1936- St&PR 93
Syron, Richard F. 1943- St&PR 93
Syron, Richard Francis 1943- WhoAm 92
Syropoulos, John fl. 12th cent.- OxDcByz
Syropoulos, Sylvester c. 1400-c. 1453 OxDcByz
Syros, Constantin 1929- WhoScE 91-3
Syrstad, Ola 1922- WhoScE 91-4
Syse, Glenna Marie Lowes WhoAm 92
Syse, Jan BioIn 17
Syskin, Sergei Aleksandrovich 1948- WhoWor 93
Syslak, Morten 1961- WhoWor 93
Sysoev, Igor Nickolaevich 1944- WhoUN 92
Sytsema, Gerald D. 1938- St&PR 93
Sytsma, Frederick Ray 1939- St&PR 93
Syukur, Slamet Abdul 1935- Baker 92
Syvertsen, Edwin T., Jr. 1923- St&PR 93
Syvertsen, Ryder 1941- ScF&FL 92
Syvertson, Clarence Alfred 1926- WhoAm 92
Sywak, Myron 1925- WhoE 93
Sywolski, Robert John 1938- St&PR 93
Syz, Hans 1894-1991 BioIn 17
Szabad, George Michael 1917- WhoAm 92
Szabadi, Elemer WhoScE 91-1
Szabadi, Elemer 1939- WhoWor 93
Szabados, Bela Antal 1867-1936 Baker 92
Szabadvary, Ferenc 1923- WhoScE 91-4
Szabadvary, Laszlo 1931- WhoScE 91-4
Szabatura, Michael Raymond 1956- WhoE 93
Szabelski, Boleslaw 1896-1979 Baker 92, PolBiDi
Szablak, Laura Rosemary 1957- WhoAmW 93
Szablya, Helen Mary 1934- WhoAmW 93
Szablya, John Francis 1924- WhoAm 92
Szabo, Albert 1925- WhoAm 92
Szabo, Andras 1936- WhoScE 91-4
Szabo, Barna Aladar 1935- WhoAm 92
Szabo, Daniel 1933- WhoAm 92
Szabo, Denis 1929- WhoAm 92
Szabo, Denise Zarotney 1953- WhoE 93
Szabo, Ernest J. Law&B 92
Szabo, Ferenc 1902-1969 Baker 92
Szabo, Ferenc 1926- WhoScE 91-4
Szabo, Frank Charles 1952- St&PR 93
Szabo, Gabor 1927- WhoScE 91-4
Szabo, Gyorgy 1939- WhoScE 91-4
Szabo, Ildiko 1946- WhoScE 91-4
Szabo, Imre 1934- WhoScE 91-4
Szabo, Istvan 1938- DrEEuF, MiSFD 9, WhoWor 93
Szabo, Ivan d1858 BioIn 17
Szabo, Joseph George 1950- WhoE 93
Szabo, L. WhoScE 91-4
Szabo, Laszlo 1949- WhoScE 91-4
Szabo, Laszlo Ferenc 1931- WhoScE 91-4
Szabo, Magda 1917- BioIn 17, WhoWor 93
Szabo, Rudy BioIn 17
Szabo, Shari Ann 1962- WhoAmW 93
Szabo, Zoltan 1929- WhoScE 91-4
Szabolcs, Ingrid Helena 1936- WhoUN 92
Szabolcsi, Bence 1899-1973 Baker 92
Szabolcsi, Miklos 1921- WhoWor 93
Szafarczyk, Maciej 1931- WhoWor 93
Szafer, Wladyslaw 1886-1970 PolBiDi
Szafranek, Ryszard Cz. 1927- WhoScE 91-4
Szafranski, John George 1935- St&PR 93
Szafranski, Przemyslaw 1925- WhoScE 91-4
Szajna, Jozef 1922- WhoWor 93
Szajowski, Krzysztof Jozef 1950- WhoWor 93
Szak, Dona Law&B 92
Szakolczai, Jozsef 1936- WhoScE 91-4
Szala, Jozef 1938- WhoScE 91-4
Szalai, Gyula 1945- WhoScE 91-4
Szalay-Marzso, Laszlo 1929- WhoScE 91-4
Szalkay, John Harro 1932- WhoE 93
Szalkowski, Mary Bernadette 1951- WhoAmW 93
Szalkowski, Zbigniew 1924- WhoScE 91-4
Szaller, James Francis 1945- WhoWor 93
Szaloczy, Balint 1934- WhoScE 91-4
Szaloki, Sandor 1933- WhoScE 91-4
Szalonek, Witold (Jozef) 1927- Baker 92
Szalowski, Antoni 1907-1973 Baker 92
Szalowski, Bonifacy 1867-1923 PolBiDi
Szamatowicz, Marian 1935- WhoScE 91-4
Szamek, Pierre Ervin WhoWor 93
Szamotul, Waclaw z c. 1524-c. 1560 Baker 92
Szander, Dinah L. Law&B 92
Szaniszlo, Mihaly 1941- WhoScE 91-4
Szantay, Csaba 1928- WhoScE 91-4
Szanti, Richard J. 1939- St&PR 93
Szanto, Alexander 1899-1972 BioIn 17
Szanto, Andras 1931- WhoScE 91-4
Szanto, Ferenc 1925- WhoScE 91-4
Szanto, George 1940- WhoAm 92, WhoCanL 92
Szanto, Ivan Gabor Law&B 92
Szanto, Theodor 1877-1934 Baker 92
Szanton, Peter Loeb 1930- WhoE 93
Szapocznik, Jose 1947- WhoSSW 93
Szapocznikow, Alina 1926-1973 PolBiDi
Szarabajka, Keith BioIn 17
Szarek, Jan Jozef 1936- WhoScE 91-4
Szarek, Stanislaw Jerzy 1953- WhoAm 92
Szarek, Walter Anthony 1938- WhoAm 92
Szarka, J. Tivadar 1934- WhoScE 91-4
Szarka, Sandor I. 1937- St&PR 93
Szarka, Zoltan 1927- WhoScE 91-4
Szarkowicz, Ed Law&B 92
Szarkowski, Jan W. 1924- WhoScE 91-4
Szarkowski, John BioIn 17
Szarkowski, Thaddeus John BioIn 17
Szarkowski, Thaddeus John 1925- WhoAm 92
Szarleta, Ellen Jean 1959- WhoAmW 93
Szaro, Richard Stanley 1942- St&PR 93
Szarvas, Ferenc 1930- WhoScE 91-4
Szarzynski, Stanislaus Sylvestre c. 1650-c. 1700 PolBiDi
Szasz, Andras Istvan 1947- WhoWor 93
Szasz, Gabor 1927- WhoScE 91-4
Szasz, Gyorgy 1927- WhoScE 91-4
Szasz, Ilma WhoScE 91-4
Szasz, Suzy BioIn 17
Szasz, Thomas Stephen 1920- WhoAm 92
Szasz, Tibor 1923- WhoScE 91-4
Szasz, Tibor 1948- Baker 92
Szatala, Odon 1924- WhoScE 91-4
Szathmary, Ivan K. 1936- St&PR 93
Szathmary, Louis Istvan, II 1919- WhoWor 93
Szatkowski, Thomas S. Law&B 92

T

Taaffe, George A., Jr. *Law&B 92*
Taaffe, James Griffith 1932- *WhoAm 92*
Taaffe, Philip 1955- *BioIn 17*
Taagepera, Rein 1933- *WhoAm 92*
Taalab, Farid Mostafa 1935- *WhoUN 92*
Taam, Ronald Everett 1948- *WhoAm 92*
Taapken, Albertus 1916- *St&PR 93*
Taav, Michael *MiSFD 9*
Tabacchi, Raphael 1940- *WhoScE 91-4*
Tabachnick, Kenneth Eliot 1955- *WhoE 93*
Tabachnick, Milton 1922- *WhoE 93*
Tabachnick, Stephen Ely 1944- *WhoSSW 93*
Tabachnik, Michel 1942- *Baker 92*
Taback, Harry 1945- *St&PR 93*
Tabai, Ieremia 1950- *WhoWor 93*
Tabai, Ieremia T. 1950- *WhoAsAP 91*
Tabak, Israel 1904-1991 *BioIn 17*
Tabak, S. Charles 1932- *St&PR 93*
Tabakaucoro, Adi Tamari Finau *WhoAsAP 91*
Tabakin, Burnley M. 1926- *St&PR 93*
Tabakin, Gary Alan 1955- *St&PR 93*
Tabakin, Mark H. 1946- *St&PR 93*
Tabakoglu, Gaser 1954-1991 *BioIn 17*
Tabakov, Mikhail 1877-1956 *Baker 92*
Taban, Paride *BioIn 17*
Tabandera, Kathlynn Rosemary 1960- *WhoAmW 93*
Taban lo Liyong 1939- *DcLB 125 [port]*
Tabano, Luis L. 1941- *St&PR 93*
Tabaqchali, Soad *WhoScE 91-1*
Tabari, Al- 839-923 *OxDcByz*
Tabart, John E. 1949- *St&PR 93*
Tabas, Daniel M. 1923- *St&PR 93*
Tabata, Yoneho 1928- *WhoWor 93*
Tabata, Yukio 1948- *WhoEmL 93, WhoWor 93*
Tabatabai, Kia 1951- *WhoUN 92*
Tabatabai, Mahmood 1938- *WhoE 93*
Tabatabai, Zuzu 1947- *WhoUN 92*
Tabatchnick, Meryl S. 1950- *WhoAmW 93*
Tabatoni, Pierre 1923- *WhoWor 93*
Tabatt, Bunny *BioIn 17*
Tabatznik, Bernard 1927- *WhoAm 92*
Tabau, Robert Louis 1928- *WhoWor 93*
Tabb, Kelli Benston *Law&B 92*
Tabbert, Rondi Jo 1953- *WhoAmW 93*
Tabell, Anthony 1931- *WhoAm 92*
Taben, Stanley 1932- *WhoIns 93*
Taber, Carol A. *WhoAm 92, WhoAmW 93*
Taber, Charles Russell 1928- *WhoSSW 93*
Taber, Douglass Fleming 1948- *WhoE 93*
Taber, Gladys Leona Bagg 1899-1980 *AmWomPl*
Taber, James Lester 1921- *St&PR 93*
Taber, Janet Marie *Law&B 92*
Taber, Jean Anne 1952- *WhoAmW 93*
Taber, Margaret Ruth 1935- *WhoAm 92*
Taber, Michael Dennis *Law&B 92*
Taber, Peter *BioIn 17*
Taber, Robert Clinton 1917- *WhoAm 92*
Taber, Thomas E. *Law&B 92*
Tabet, Sylvio *MiSFD 9*
Tabibzadeh, Iraj 1932- *WhoUN 92*
Tabickman, Maurice Louis 1944- *St&PR 93*
Tabin, Janet Hale 1946- *WhoWrEP 92*
Tabin, Julius 1919- *WhoAm 92*
Tabio, Martha S. 1948- *St&PR 93*
Tablada, Jose Juan 1871-1945 *DcMexL*
Tabler, Joseph *ScF&FL 92*
Tabler, Kenneth Alfred 1958- *WhoE 93*
Tabler, Shirley May 1936- *WhoAmW 93*
Tabler, William Benjamin 1914- *WhoAm 92, WhoWor 93*
Tabner, Mary Frances 1918- *WhoAmW 93, WhoE 93, WhoWor 93*
Taboada, John 1943- *HispAmA*
Tabone, Vincent 1913- *WhoWor 93*
Tabor, Charles Gordon 1925- *WhoSSW 93*
Tabor, Curtis Harold, Jr. 1936- *WhoSSW 93*
Tabor, David *WhoScE 91-1*
Tabor, Doris Dee 1918- *WhoAm 92*
Tabor, Franklin Claire 1919- *WhoWrEP 92*
Tabor, Gladys Leona Bagg 1899-1980 *AmWomPl*
Tabor, Herbert 1918- *WhoAm 92*
Tabor, John Kaye 1921- *WhoAm 92*
Tabor, Jon Kenneth 1933- *St&PR 93*
Tabor, Margaret *ScF&FL 92*
Tabor, Marvin, Jr. 1938- *WhoSSW 93*
Tabor, Mary Leeba 1946- *WhoE 93*
Tabor, Samuel Lynn 1945- *WhoSSW 93*
Tabor, Sandra L. 1954- *St&PR 93*
Tabora, Cristina 1944- *St&PR 93*
Taborda, Carlos A. 1942- *St&PR 93*
Tabori, Kristoffer 1955?- *ConTFT 10*
Tabori, Paul 1908-1974 *ScF&FL 92*
Taborsak, Dragutin 1925- *WhoScE 91-4*
Taborsky, C. Jeanne 1947- *WhoAmW 93*
Tabouis, Genevieve R. 1892-1985 *BioIn 17*
Tabourot, Jehan *Baker 92*
Tabrisky, Phyllis Page 1930- *WhoAmW 93*
Tabrizi, Gholam-Reza Sabri- *BioIn 17*
Tabuchi, Kazuo 1940- *WhoWor 93*
Tabuchi, Kunji 1930- *WhoAsAP 91*
Tabuchi, Mamoru *BioIn 17*
Tabuchi, Mamoru 1924- *WhoAm 92*
Tabuchi, Tetsuya 1925- *WhoAsAP 91*
Tabuenca, Concepcion 1930- *WhoScE 91-3*
Tabuenca, M.C. 1930- *WhoScE 91-3*
Tabuteau, Marcel 1887-1966 *Baker 92*
Tacchella, Jean-Charles 1925- *MiSFD 9*
Tacchinardi, Guido 1840-1917 *See* Tacchinardi, Nicola 1772-1859 *Baker 92*
Tacchinardi, Nicola 1772-1859 *Baker 92, OxDcOp*
Tacchino, Gabriel 1934- *Baker 92*
Tacey, Ronald William 1949- *St&PR 93*
Tacha, Deanell Reece 1946- *WhoAm 92, WhoAmW 93*
Tachau, Carla *Law&B 92*
Tache, Jacques *Law&B 92*
Tache, Joseph Charles 1820-1894 *BioIn 17*
Tacheny, J.R. 1932- *St&PR 93*
Tacher, Georges 1934- *WhoScE 91-2*
Tacher, Mary G. *Law&B 92*
Tachezi, Herbert 1930- *Baker 92*
Tachibana, Akitomo 1951- *WhoWor 93*
Tachibana, Koichiro 1861-1929 *HarEnMi*
Tachick, Robert Daniel 1948- *St&PR 93*
Tachikawa, Masami *St&PR 93*
Tachikawa, Tetsusaburo 1924- *WhoWor 93*
Tachiki, Hiroshi 1931- *WhoAsAP 91*
Tachiwaki, Tokumatsu 1938- *WhoWor 93*
Tachmindji, Alexander John 1928- *WhoAm 92, WhoWor 93*
Tack, H. *WhoScE 91-3*
Tacka, David W. 1953- *St&PR 93*
Tackaberry, Robert R. 1939- *St&PR 93*
Tackel, Ira S. 1954- *WhoE 93*
Tacker, Edgar Carroll 1935- *WhoAm 92*
Tacker, Martha McClelland 1943- *WhoAmW 93*
Tackett, Ben Dahlman, Jr. 1962- *WhoSSW 93*
Tackett, Gayle Enslow 1956- *WhoAmW 93*
Tackett, Keith M. *Law&B 92*
Tackett, Natalie Jane *WhoAmW 93*
Tacki, Bernadette Susan 1913- *WhoAmW 93*
Tackovich, Jo Ann 1938- *WhoAmW 93*
Tacla, Jorge *BioIn 17*
Taconis, Kryn 1918-1979 *BioIn 17*
Tacticos, George *Law&B 92*
Tada, Joni Eareckson *BioIn 17*
Tadano, Kota 1934- *St&PR 93*
Tadda, Thomas A. 1941- *St&PR 93*
Taddei, Armando 1926- *St&PR 93*
Taddei, Ferdinando 1936- *WhoScE 91-3*
Taddei, Giuseppe *WhoAm 92*
Taddei, Giuseppe 1916- *Baker 92, OxDcOp*
Taddei, Italo 1922- *WhoScE 91-3*
Taddei, Mirian Hunter 1930- *St&PR 93*
Taddeo, Angelo A. 1927- *WhoIns 93*
Taddesse, Samuel 1944- *WhoWor 93*
Taddie, Daniel Lawrence 1949- *WhoSSW 93*
Tade, Darrell Lynn 1963- *WhoSSW 93*
Tade, George Thomas 1923- *WhoAm 92*
Tade, JeanMarie B. *Law&B 92*
Tadema, Lawrence Alma- 1836-1912 *BioIn 17*
Tadic, Dubravko 1934- *WhoScE 91-4*
Tadic, Radoljub 1934- *WhoScE 91-4*
Tadie, Andrew A. *ScF&FL 92*
Tadikonda, Sivakumara Sarma Kedara 1960- *WhoSSW 93*
Tadio, Samuel William 1937- *WhoE 93*
Tadjo, Veronique 1955- *BlkAull 92*
Tadolini, Eugenia 1809-1851? *Baker 92*
Tadolini, Eugenia 1809-1872 *OxDcOp*
Tadolini, Giovanni 1785-1872 *Baker 92, OxDcOp*
Tadry, Raymond Stephen 1934- *St&PR 93*
Tae Joon Park 1929- *WhoAsAP 91*
Taenzer, Hans J. 1932- *St&PR 93*
Taeschler, Debra Ann 1953- *WhoE 93*
Taetle, Joseph L. *Law&B 92*
Taets, James E. 1955- *St&PR 93*
Taetzsch, Lynne 1941- *WhoSSW 93*
Taeuber, Conrad 1906- *WhoAm 92*
Taeuber, Irene B. 1906-1974 *BioIn 17*
Taeusch, Carl F. *Law&B 92*
Taeyaerts, Frederick J. 1939- *St&PR 93*
Tafares, Robert Edmond 1941- *WhoE 93*
Tafari Makonnen 1891-1975 *BioIn 17*
Tafel, Edgar 1912- *WhoAm 92*
Tafel, Kenneth B. 1941- *St&PR 93*
Tafelski, Michael Dennis 1949- *WhoWor 93*
Tafelski, Thomas A. 1939- *St&PR 93*
Taffanel, (Claude-) Paul 1844-1908 *Baker 92*
Taffe, Horace Oliver 1952- *WhoWor 93*
Taffel, Abram 1906- *WhoE 93*
Taffet, Edward D. *Law&B 92*
Taffet, Elizabeth Rose 1934- *WhoAmW 93*
Taffet, Mary Dresser 1958- *WhoAmW 93*
Taflove, Allen 1949- *WhoAm 92*
Tafolla, Carmen 1951- *NotHsAW 93*
Tafoya, Arthur N. 1933- *WhoAm 92*
Tafoya, Cathy Jo 1953- *WhoWrEP 92*
Tafoya, Roman L. 1945- *St&PR 93*
Taft, Charles Kirkland 1928- *WhoE 93*
Taft, Claudia L. *Law&B 92*
Taft, David Dakin 1938- *WhoAm 92*
Taft, Grace Ellis *AmWomPl*
Taft, Harold E. 1922-1991 *BioIn 17*
Taft, Helen Herron 1861-1943 *BioIn 17*
Taft, Henry Waters 1926-1991 *BioIn 17*
Taft, James W. 1945- *St&PR 93*
Taft, Jessie 1882-1961 *BioIn 17*
Taft, Lorado 1860-1936 *GayN*
Taft, Martin C. 1942- *WhoIns 93*
Taft, Nathaniel Belmont 1919- *WhoE 93, WhoWor 93*
Taft, Richard George 1913- *WhoAm 92*
Taft, Robert, Jr. 1917- *PolPar, WhoAm 92*
Taft, Robert A. 1889-1953 *BioIn 17, ColdWar 1 [port], PolPar*
Taft, Seth Chase 1922- *WhoAm 92*
Taft, Sheldon Ashley 1937- *WhoAm 92*
Taft, William H. 1857-1930 *BioIn 17*
Taft, William H. 1915-1991 *BioIn 17*
Taft, William Howard *DcCPCAm*
Taft, William Howard 1857-1930 *OxCSupC [port], PolPar*
Taft, William Howard 1915- *WhoAm 92*
Taft, William Howard, IV 1945- *WhoAm 92, WhoWor 93*
Taft, William Wilson 1932- *WhoAm 92*
Tafur, Pero c. 1410-c. 1484 *OxDcByz*
Tafuri, Nancy *ChlBIID [port]*
Tafuri, Nancy 1946- *MajAI [port]*
Tafuri, Spencer Andrew 1952- *WhoWor 93*
Tag, Christian Gotthilf 1735-1811 *Baker 92*
Tagagi, Takeshi 1925- *WhoWor 93*
Tagarao, Mario L. 1932- *WhoAsAP 91*
Tagaris *OxDcByz*
Tagaris, Paul Palaiologos c. 1340-c. 1394 *OxDcByz*
Tagatz, George Elmo 1935- *WhoAm 92*
Tagawa, Kunio 1929- *WhoWor 93*
Tagawa, Seiichi 1918- *WhoAsAP 91*
Tageno d1190 *OxDcByz*
Tager, Jack 1936- *WhoAm 92*
Tager, William Samuel *Law&B 92*
Tager, William Samuel 1928- *St&PR 93*
Tagg, Adrian Geoffrey *WhoScE 91-1*
Tagg, Janet Melodini 1953- *WhoE 93*
Taggart, Ann G. 1913- *WhoAmW 93*
Taggart, Austin Dale, II 1952- *WhoSSW 93*
Taggart, David Peter 1954- *WhoE 93, WhoEmL 93*
Taggart, Ganson Powers 1918- *WhoAm 92, WhoWor 93*
Taggart, Jennifer Tracy 1968- *WhoAmW 93*
Taggart, John C. *Law&B 92*
Taggart, John P(aul) 1942- *WhoWrEP 92*
Taggart, Leslie Davidson 1910-1991 *BioIn 17*

Taggart, Philip W. 1930- *St&PR 93*
Taggart, Robert Alexander, Jr. 1946- *WhoE 93*
Taggart, Robert Burdett 1943- *WhoWor 93*
Taggart, Sondra 1934- *WhoAmW 93*
Taggart, Thomas 1856-1929 *BioIn 17, PolPar*
Taggie, Benjamin Fredrick 1938- *WhoAm 92*
Tagiuri, Renato 1919- *WhoWrEP 92*
Tagle, Tessa Martinez 1947- *NotHsAW 93*
Taglia, R. Victor *St&PR 93*
Tagliabue, Carlo 1898-1978 *Baker 92*
Tagliabue, John 1923- *WhoWrEP 92*
Tagliabue, Paul *BioIn 17*
Tagliabue, Paul 1940- *CurBio 92 [port]*
Tagliabue, Paul John 1940- *WhoAm 92, WhoE 93*
Tagliaferri, Lee Gene 1931- *WhoE 93, WhoWor 93*
Tagliaferri, Mark Lee 1963- *WhoWor 93*
Tagliaferro, John Anthony 1944- *WhoAm 92*
Tagliaferro, Magda 1893-1986 *Baker 92*
Tagliafico, Joseph 1821-1900 *OxDcOp*
Tagliafico, (Dieudonne) Joseph 1821-1900 *Baker 92*
Tagliapietra, Gino 1887-1954 *Baker 92*
Tagliapietra, Giovanni 1846-1921 *Baker 92*
Tagliarini, Patricia Rose 1952- *WhoAmW 93*
Tagliarino, Scott Alan 1953- *WhoAm 92*
Tagliavini, Ferruccio 1913- *Baker 92, IntDcOp*
Tagliavini, Feruccio 1913- *OxDcOp*
Tagliavini, Luigi Ferdinando 1929- *Baker 92*
Taglichsbeck, Thomas 1799-1867 *Baker 92*
Taglieri, Richard James 1939- *WhoE 93*
Taglieri, Ron H. *Law&B 92*
Tagnani, Giovanni 1943- *WhoUN 92*
Tagore, Rabindranath 1861-1941 *BioIn 17, DcTwHis*
Tagore, Surindro Mohun 1840-1914 *Baker 92*
Taguchi, Kazuo 1930- *WhoWor 93*
Taguchi, Kenji 1930- *WhoAsAP 91*
Taguchi, Minoru 1931- *WhoWor 93*
Taguchi, Tadao 1929- *St&PR 93*
Taguchi, Yoshitaka 1933- *WhoAm 92*
Tague, Barry Elwert 1938- *WhoAm 92, WhoE 93*
Tague, Charles F. 1924- *St&PR 93*
Tague, Charles Francis 1924- *WhoAm 92*
Taha, Karen T(erry) 1942- *SmATA 71 [port]*
Taha Husayn 1889-1973 *BioIn 17*
Tahan, William Nicholas 1924- *St&PR 93*
Tahara, Eiichi 1936- *WhoWor 93*
Tahara, Ken-Ichi 1939- *WhoWor 93*
Taheri, Amir 1942- *ConAu 136*
Tahiliani, Radhakrishnan Hariram 1930- *WhoAsAP 91*
Tahilramani, Sham Atmaram 1945- *WhoWor 93*
Tahir, Bassam Mahmoud 1962- *WhoWor 93*
Tahir, Mary Elizabeth 1933- *WhoAmW 93, WhoSSW 93*
Tahir, Thabit 1928- *WhoWor 93*
Tahourdin, Barbara Ker *ScF&FL 92*
Tai, Chen-To 1915- *WhoAm 92*
Tai, Chin-wah 1952- *WhoAsAP 91*
Tai, Chong-Soo Stephen 1940- *WhoSSW 93*
Tai, Christopher Chee-Cheng *Law&B 92*
Tai, Douglas Leung-Tak 1940- *WhoSSW 93*
Tai, Heng-Ming 1957- *WhoSSW 93*
Tai, Julia Chow 1935- *WhoAmW 93*
Taibleson, Mitchell Herbert 1929- *WhoAm 92*
Taib Mahmud, Pattinggi Haji Abdul 1936- *WhoAsAP 91*
Taibo, Paco Ignacio, II 1949- *SpAmA*
Taich, Arlene Vicki 1943- *WhoAmW 93*
Taicher, Robert *MiSFD 9*
Taiclet, Lynne Marie 1959- *WhoAmW 93*
Taieb, Essayem 1935- *WhoUN 92*
Taigue, Richard J. *Law&B 92*
Taikeff, Stanley 1940- *WhoE 93*
Tai Li 1895-1946 *HarEnMi*
Tailleferre, Germaine 1892-1983 *BioIn 17*
Tailleferre, (Marcelle) Germaine 1892-1983 *Baker 92*
Taillefesse, (Marcelle) Germaine 1892-1983 *Baker 92*
Taillet, Joseph 1922- *WhoScE 91-2*
Taillibert, Rene Roger 1926- *WhoWor 93*
Tailliez, Roger 1938- *WhoScE 91-2*
Taillon, Roger deBoucherville 1946- *St&PR 93*
Taimuty, Samuel Isaac 1917- *WhoWor 93*
Taine, Jean 1949- *WhoScE 91-2*
Taira, Eric M. *Law&B 92*
Taira, Frances Snow 1935- *WhoAmW 93*
Taira, Kiyomori 1118-1181 *HarEnMi*
Taira, Masakado d940 *HarEnMi*
Taira, Munemori 1147-1185 *HarEnMi*
Taishin *WhoWrEP 92*
Taishoff, Lawrence B. 1933- *St&PR 93*
Taishoff, Lawrence Bruce 1933- *WhoAm 92, WhoWor 93*
Tait, Alan Anderson 1934- *WhoUN 92*
Tait, Andrew *WhoScE 91-1*
Tait, Elizabeth Joyce *WhoScE 91-1*
Tait, Elizabeth Leeds 1906- *WhoWrEP 92*
Tait, George B. *ScF&FL 92*
Tait, Irene Grayson 1918- *WhoWrEP 92*
Tait, J.W. 1915- *St&PR 93*
Tait, John Charles 1945- *WhoAm 92*
Tait, John Edwin 1932- *St&PR 93*
Tait, Nancy Louise 1947- *St&PR 93*
Tait, Stewart R. 1945- *St&PR 93*
Tait, Thomas Harrison 1932- *WhoAm 92*
Tait, Thomas Smith 1882-1954 *BioIn 17*
T'ai-Tsu 927-976 *HarEnMi*
T'ai-Tsu 1328-1398 *HarEnMi*
Taitt, Branford 1938- *DcCPCAm*
Taitt, Earl Paul 1956- *WhoE 93*
Taitt, Sam 1946- *WhoWor 93*
Taittinger, Pierre Charles 1887-1965 *BioIn 17*
Tajcevic, Marko 1900-1984 *Baker 92*
Tajem Anak Miri, Daniel 1936- *WhoAsAP 91*
Tajima, Arthur Hiroyuki 1933- *WhoWor 93*
Tajima, Hajime 1947- *WhoWor 93*
Tajima, Mikio 1934- *WhoUN 92*
Tajima, Renee *MiSFD 9*
Tajima, Takashi 1935- *WhoWor 93*
Tajima, Tatsuya 1923- *WhoWor 93*
Tajnafoi, Jozsef 1930- *WhoScE 91-4*
Tajo, Italo 1915- *Baker 92, IntDcOp, OxDcOp*
Takac, Jeffrey Scott 1965- *WhoSSW 93*
Takacs, Andrew J. 1933- *St&PR 93*
Takacs, Istvan 1928- *WhoScE 91-4*
Takacs, Jeno 1902- *Baker 92*
Takacs, Lajos 1924- *WhoScE 91-4*
Takacs, Michael Joseph 1940- *WhoE 93*
Takacs, Tibor 1954- *MiSFD 9*
Takada, Kenzo *BioIn 17*
Takafuji, June H. *Law&B 92*
Takagi, Haruo 1949- *WhoWor 93*
Takagi, Hideaki 1950- *WhoWor 93*
Takagi, Kentaro 1909- *WhoAsAP 91*
Takagi, Masaaki 1929- *WhoAsAP 91*
Takagi, Seizo 1933- *St&PR 93*
Takagi, Shigeo 1932- *WhoWor 93*
Takagi, Shinji 1953- *WhoWor 93*
Takagi, Shinjiro 1935- *WhoWor 93*
Takagi, Sokichi 1893- *HarEnMi*
Takagi, Takeo 1892-1944 *HarEnMi*
Takagi, Takio 1930- *WhoWor 93*
Takagi, Toroku 1904- *Baker 92*
Takahara, Atsushi 1955- *WhoWor 93*
Takahara, Paul Osamu 1937- *WhoWor 93*
Takahashi, Aki 1944- *Baker 92*
Takahashi, Beth Ann 1939- *WhoAmW 93*
Takahashi, Chikuzan 1910- *BioIn 17*
Takahashi, Fumiki 1929- *WhoWor 93*
Takahashi, Ibo 1888-1947 *HarEnMi*
Takahashi, Ichiro 1926- *WhoAsAP 91*
Takahashi, Iichiro 1922- *WhoWor 93*
Takahashi, Kazuhiro 1959- *WhoWor 93*
Takahashi, Keiichi 1931- *WhoWor 93*
Takahashi, Kiyotaka 1920- *WhoAsAP 91*
Takahashi, Mary Chiyeko 1909- *WhoAmW 93*
Takahashi, Masayoshi 1926- *WhoWor 93*
Takahashi, Masayuki 1942- *WhoWor 93*
Takahashi, Megumi 1929- *WhoWor 93*
Takahashi, Moto-o 1941- *WhoWor 93*
Takahashi, Patrick Kenji 1940- *WhoAm 92*
Takahashi, S. *WhoUN 92*
Takahashi, Sechiko 1942- *WhoWor 93*
Takahashi, Shotaro 1920- *WhoWor 93*
Takahashi, Teney Kunio 1938- *St&PR 93*
Takahashi, Tsutomu 1935- *WhoWor 93*
Takahashi, Yasuhiro 1946- *St&PR 93*
Takahashi, Yasuo 1925- *WhoE 93*
Takahashi, Yasushi 1956- *WhoWor 93*
Takahashi, Yoichi 1933- *WhoWor 93*
Takahashi, Yuji 1938- *Baker 92*
Takahashi, Yuzo 1948- *WhoWor 93*
Takahata, Masato 1937- *WhoWor 93*
Takai, Kazunobu 1940- *WhoAsAP 91*
Takaishi, Masahiro 1929- *WhoWor 93*
Takaki, Ryuji 1940- *WhoWor 93*
Takaki, Yoshiaki 1945- *WhoAsAP 91*
Takakuwa, Eimatsu 1919- *WhoAsAP 91*
Takakuwa, Yasuo 1929- *WhoWor 93*
Takal, Peter 1905- *WhoAm 92*
Takala, Jukka Antero 1953- *WhoWor 93*
Takala, Jukka Sakari 1946- *WhoUN 92*
Takamine, Hideko *BioIn 17*
Takamine, Hideko 1924- *IntDcF 2-3 [port]*
Takamori, Akira 1928- *WhoWor 93*
Takamori, Yoichiro 1930- *WhoWor 93*
Takamura, Kotaro 1883-1956 *BioIn 17*
Takanaka, Chiei 1952- *WhoWor 93*
Takano, Masaharu 1935- *WhoAm 92*
Takano, Shizuo d1992 *BioIn 17*
Takano, Shizuo 1923-1992 *NewYTBS 92*
Takano, Tatsuya 1937- *WhoWor 93*
Takarabe, Takeshi 1867-1949 *HarEnMi*
Takas, Vassili N. 1951- *WhoWor 93*
Takasaki, Etsuji 1929- *WhoWor 93*
Takasaki, Yoshitaka 1938- *WhoWor 93*
Takasaki, Yuko 1948- *WhoAsAP 91*
Takase, Fumiko 1927- *WhoWor 93*
Takase, Tamotsu 1932- *WhoUN 92*
Takashi, Ogawa 1915- *WhoWor 93*
Takashima, Nobuyuki 1927- *WhoWor 93*
Takashima, Shoji 1931- *WhoWor 93*
Takasugi, Nao 1922- *WhoAm 92*
Takasugi, Robert Mitsuhiro 1930- *WhoAm 92*
Takata, Marcel Ray 1923- *St&PR 93*
Takata, Richard T. 1949- *St&PR 93*
Takata, Saburo 1913- *Baker 92*
Takata, Shin-ichi 1920- *Baker 92*
Takata, Yoshinori 1940- *WhoWor 93*
Takatori, Osamu 1926- *WhoAsAP 91*
Takatori, Takehiko 1938- *WhoWor 93*
Takatsuki, Kiyoshi 1930- *WhoWor 93*
Takaya, Akio 1939- *St&PR 93*
Takayama, Akira *WhoAm 92*
Takayama, Fujio *St&PR 93*
Takayama, Masayoshi *BioIn 17*
Takayama, Tomohiro 1937- *WhoWor 93*
Takayanagi, Hiromu 1928- *WhoWor 93*
Takayanagi, Kenjiro *BioIn 17*
Takayanagi, Motowo 1920- *WhoWor 93*
Takazawa, Robert S., Jr. 1951- *St&PR 93*
Takazawa, Torao 1926- *WhoAsAP 91*
Takebe, Bun J. 1920- *WhoAsAP 91*
Takebe, Hiraku 1934- *WhoWor 93*
Takebe, Tsutomu 1941- *WhoAsAP 91*
Takebe, Tsuyoshi 1929- *WhoWor 93*
Takeda, Katsuyori 1546-1582 *HarEnMi*
Takeda, Koichi 1958- *WhoWor 93*
Takeda, Shingen 1521-1573 *HarEnMi*
Takeda, Sueo 1915- *WhoWor 93*
Takeda, Tsuneo 1925- *WhoWor 93*
Takeda, Yasuhiro 1940- *WhoWor 93*
Takeda, Yoshimi 1933- *Baker 92*
Takeda, Yoshiyuki 1933- *WhoWor 93*
Takefman, Earl *St&PR 93*
Takehara, Dan E. 1922- *St&PR 93*
Takei, George 1939- *ScF&FL 92*
Takei, Toshihisa 1931- *WhoWor 93*
Takemitsu, Toru 1930- *Baker 92, BioIn 17*
Takemoto, James H. *Law&B 92*
Takemoto, Kiichi 1930- *WhoWor 93*
Takemura, Masayoshi 1934- *WhoAsAP 91*
Takemura, Michael Francis 1961- *WhoWor 93*
Takemura, Yasuko 1933- *WhoAsAP 91*
Takemura, Yukio 1930- *WhoAsAP 91*
Taken, Mark A. *Law&B 92*
Taken, Richard Lee 1944- *St&PR 93*
Takenaka, Tadashi 1946- *WhoWor 93*
Takenouchi, Osamu 1925- *WhoWor 93*
Takeoka, Shinji 1963- *WhoWor 93*
Takeoka, Tsuneyuki 1944- *WhoWor 93*
Takes Enemy, Jonathan *BioIn 17*
Takeshi, Baba *WhoWor 93*
Takeshi, Fukuda 1943- *WhoWor 93*
Takeshima, Yoichi 1952- *WhoWor 93*
Takeshita, Kikuo 1933- *WhoWor 93*
Takeshita, Noboru 1924- *WhoAsAP 91, WhoWor 93*
Takeshita, Toru 1931- *WhoWor 93*
Taketomo, Yasuhiko 1921- *WhoE 93*
Takeuchi, Akikazu 1953- *WhoWor 93*
Takeuchi, Katsuhiko 1938- *WhoAsAP 91*
Takeuchi, Ken'ichi 1938- *WhoWor 93*
Takeuchi, Masao 1941- *WhoWor 93*
Takeuchi, Nozomu 1931- *WhoWor 93*
Takeuchi, Takeshi 1922- *WhoAsAP 91*
Takeuchi, Toyohide 1954- *WhoWor 93*
Takeyama, Yasuo 1923- *WhoWor 93*
Takeyama, Yutaka 1913- *WhoAsAP 91*
Takhar, Harinder S. 1951- *St&PR 93*
Taki *BioIn 17*
Taki, A. Amir 1932- *St&PR 93*
Takiguchi, Genji 1928- *WhoE 93*
Takino, Masuichi 1905- *WhoWor 93*
Takita, Natsuki 1931- *WhoWor 93*
Takita, Yojiro *MiSFD 9*
Takizawa, Akira 1927- *WhoWor 93*
Takizawa, Nobuhiko 1937- *WhoWor 93*
Takizawa, Takehisa 1931- *WhoWor 93*
Takken, H.J. 1936- *WhoScE 91-3*
Takman, Bertil Herbert 1921- *WhoE 93*
Tako, Anthony *St&PR 93*
Tako, Masakuni 1947- *WhoWor 93*
Takooshian, Harold 1949- *WhoE 93*
Takovskij, Andrej 1932-1986 *DrEEuF*
Taksdal, Gudmund 1928- *WhoScE 91-4*
Taktakishvili, Otar 1924- *OxDcOp*
Taktakishvili, Otar (Vasilievich) 1924-1989 *Baker 92*
Taktakishvili, Shalva 1900-1965 *OxDcOp*
Taktakishvili, Shalva (Mikhailovich) 1900-1965 *Baker 92*
Taku, Koji 1904- *Baker 92*
Takulja, M. *WhoScE 91-3*
Takuma, Takeo 1940- *St&PR 93, WhoAm 92*
Takyi, Isaac Kwame *WhoE 93*
Tal, Israel 1924- *HarEnMi*
Tal, Jacob 1945- *WhoSSW 93*
Tal, Josef 1910- *Baker 92, OxDcOp, WhoWor 93*
Tal, Mikhail 1936-1992 *BioIn 17, NewYTBS 92*
Tala, Eero Otto 1931- *WhoWor 93*
Tala, Eero Otto Juhani 1931- *WhoScE 91-4*
Talagrand, Jacques 1909-1988 *BioIn 17*
Talal, Marilynn Carole Glick *WhoWrEP 92*
Talalay, Kathryn Marguerite 1949- *WhoAmW 93*
Talalay, Paul 1923- *WhoAm 92*
Talalay, Rachel *MiSFD 9*
Talalov, Sergei Vladimirovich 1958- *WhoWor 93*
Talamo, Barbara Lisann 1939- *WhoE 93*
Talamo, Sal 1941- *St&PR 93*
Talan, Jamie Lynn 1956- *WhoE 93, WhoWrEP 92*
Talan, Len *MiSFD 9*
Talankin, Igor' 1927- *DrEEuF*
Talanti, Seppo Ilmari 1926- *WhoScE 91-4*
Talarchek, Gary Mark 1951- *WhoSSW 93*
Talari Manohar 1954- *WhoAsAP 91*
Talas, Margarita 1929- *WhoScE 91-4*
Talbert, Charles Harold 1934- *WhoSSW 93*
Talbert, Frances Suzanne *WhoSSW 93*
Talbert, James Lewis 1931- *WhoAm 92*
Talbert, John Berry, Jr. 1939- *St&PR 93*
Talbert, Leslie D. 1937- *St&PR 93*
Talbert, Luther Marcus 1926- *WhoAm 92*
Talbert, Marc 1953- *BioIn 17, ConAu 136*
Talbert, Melvin George 1934- *WhoAm 92*
Talbert, Roy, Jr. 1943- *WhoSSW 93*
Talbot, Bernard 1937- *WhoAm 92, WhoE 93*
Talbot, Bob *BioIn 17*
Talbot, Christopher J. 1940- *WhoScE 91-4*
Talbot, Christopher John 1940- *WhoWor 93*
Talbot, Deborah L. *BioIn 17*
Talbot, Donald Roy 1931- *WhoAm 92*
Talbot, Emile Joseph 1941- *WhoAm 92*
Talbot, Frank *BioIn 17*
Talbot, Frank Hamilton 1930- *WhoAm 92, WhoE 93, WhoWor 93*
Talbot, Gladys *AmWomPl*
Talbot, Hannah Lincoln *AmWomPl*
Talbot, Helen *SweetSg C*
Talbot, Henry J. d1863 *BioIn 17*
Talbot, Howard 1865-1928 *Baker 92*
Talbot, Howard Chase, Jr. 1925- *WhoAm 92*
Talbot, James Adam 1937- *WhoSSW 93*
Talbot, James S. *Law&B 92*
Talbot, James Thomas 1935- *WhoAm 92*
Talbot, Jim d1896 *BioIn 17*
Talbot, John J. 1956- *St&PR 93*
Talbot, Jonathan 1939- *WhoE 93*
Talbot, Joseph Chanel 1949- *WhoE 93*
Talbot, Lee Merriam 1930- *WhoAm 92*
Talbot, Marion 1858-1947 *BioIn 17*
Talbot, Matthew 1865-1952 *BioIn 17*
Talbot, Matthew J. 1937- *WhoAm 92*
Talbot, Michael 1953-1992 *BioIn 17, ConAu 137, ScF&FL 92*
Talbot, Norman 1936- *ScF&FL 92*
Talbot, Pamela 1946- *WhoAm 92*
Talbot, Patricia *Law&B 92*
Talbot, Phillips 1915- *WhoAm 92, WhoE 93*
Talbot, Prue *WhoAm 92*
Talbot, R.S. *WhoScE 91-1*
Talbot, Richard Burritt 1933- *WhoAm 92*
Talbot, Susan Anderson 1930- *WhoAmW 93*
Talbott, Audrey Sharpe 1918- *St&PR 93*
Talbott, Frank, III 1929- *WhoAm 92*
Talbott, George Robert 1925- *WhoWor 93*
Talbott, Gloria *SweetSg D*
Talbott, Gloria 1932?- *BioIn 17*
Talbott, John Harold 1902-1990 *BioIn 17*
Talbott, John Wallace 1937- *WhoSSW 93*
Talbott, Karen Lee 1947- *WhoAmW 93*
Talbott, Mark *BioIn 17*
Talbott, Martha Wild 1951- *WhoSSW 93*
Talbott, Mary Ann Britt 1945- *WhoAmW 93, WhoSSW 93*
Talbott, Nelson S. 1920- *St&PR 93*
Talbott, Richard Berner 1959- *WhoSSW 93*
Talcott, Ann Ward 1945- *WhoAmW 93*
Talcott, Jane Victoria 1944- *WhoAm 92, WhoAmW 93*
Talcott, Joel *Law&B 92*
Talcott, Mary White Rowlandson c. 1637-1710? *BioIn 17*
Talekar, Narayan Sarjerao 1940- *WhoWor 93*
Talen, Bruce L. *Law&B 92*
Talenti, Pier F. 1925- *St&PR 93*
Talerico, James A. *Law&B 92*

Talero, Luis Alberto 1926- St&PR 93
Talese, Gay BioIn 17
Talese, Gay 1932- WhoAm 92, WhoWor 93, WhoWrEP 92
Talese, Nan Ahearn 1933- WhoAm 92, WhoAmW 93
Talesnick, Ellen Stacey 1966- WhoAmW 93
Talesnick, Stanley 1927- WhoWor 93
Talge, Henry Stephen 1937- St&PR 93
Talhouni, Bassam Tawfic 1957- WhoWor 93
Taliaferro, Elizabeth Ann 1953- WhoEmL 93
Taliaferro, Gary Day 1940- WhoSSW 93
Taliaferro, James Hubert, Jr. 1924- WhoE 93
Taliaferro, John 1768-1852 BioIn 17
Taliaferro, Lilton Roosevelt, Jr. Law&B 92
Taliani, Corrado 1930- WhoUN 92
Taliani, Marietta L. d1990 BioIn 17
Talich, Vaclav 1883-1961 Baker 92, OxDcOp
Talingdan, Arsenio Preza 1930- WhoE 93
Talintyre, Terence David WhoScE 91-1
Talion, Robert W. St&PR 93
Talisayon, Vivien Millan 1945- WhoWor 93
Taljedal, Inge-Bert V. 1942- WhoScE 91-4
Talkington, Robert Van 1929- WhoAm 92
Talkner, Peter Wolfgang WhoWor 93
Talkovsky, Steven H. Law&B 92
Talkowski, Ted 1933- St&PR 93
Tall, Ali Badara 1936- WhoUN 92
Tall, Deborah 1951- WhoWrEP 92
Tall, Franklin David 1944- WhoAm 92
Tall, Stephen 1908-1981 ScF&FL 92
Tallackson, Harvey 1925- St&PR 93
Tallackson, Jeffrey S. 1943- St&PR 93
Tallackson, Jeffrey Stephen Law&B 92
Tallackson, Jeffrey Stephen 1943- WhoAm 92
Talladay, Jennie AmWomPl
Tallal, Paula 1947- WhoAm 92
Tallant, David, Jr. 1931- WhoAm 92, WhoWor 93
Tallarico, Anthony ScF&FL 92
Tallarico, Tony ScF&FL 92
Tallawy, Mervat 1937- WhoUN 92
Tallchief, Maria 1925- WhoAm 92, WhoAmW 93
Tallent, Marc Andrew 1954- WhoE 93
Tallent, Robert Glenn 1954- WhoSSW 93
Tallent, Stephen Edison 1937- WhoAm 92
Tallent, Wanda Leatherman 1935- WhoAmW 93
Tallent, William Hugh 1928- WhoAm 92
Tallet, Stephanie C. Law&B 92
Talleur, John Joseph 1925- WhoAm 92
Talley, Bob Eugene 1935- St&PR 93
Talley, Bonnie Eileen 1928- WhoAmW 93
Talley, Carol Lee 1937- WhoAm 92, WhoAmW 93
Talley, Charles Richmond 1925- WhoAm 92
Talley, Dan R. 1951- WhoE 93
Talley, David Charles 1954- WhoSSW 93
Talley, Eugene Alton 1911- WhoE 93
Talley, James Arthur 1942- St&PR 93
Talley, Jody Elizabeth 1958- WhoAmW 93, WhoEmL 93, WhoSSW 93, WhoWor 93
Talley, John St&PR 93
Talley, John S. Law&B 92
Talley, Joseph Eugene 1949- WhoSSW 93
Talley, Marion 1906-1983 Baker 92
Talley, Nancy White 1959- WhoAmW 93
Talley, Richard Bates 1947- WhoWor 93
Talley, Richard Sterling 1951- WhoSSW 93
Talley, Richard Woodrow 1941- WhoSSW 93
Talley, Robert Cochran 1936- WhoAm 92
Talley, Robert M. Law&B 92
Talley, Robert Morrell 1924- WhoAm 92
Talley, Steven ScF&FL 92
Talley, Truman Macdonald 1925- WhoAm 92
Talley, Warren Dennis Rick 1934- WhoAm 92
Talley, William Giles, Jr. 1939- St&PR 93, WhoSSW 93
Talley, William R., Jr. 1955- St&PR 93
Talley, Wilson Kinter 1935- WhoWor 93
Talley-Morris, Neva Bennett 1909- WhoAm 92, WhoWor 93
Tallgren, John H. 1929- St&PR 93
Tallgren, Leif Johan Gustav 1928- WhoWor 93
Tallgren, R. 1935- St&PR 93
Tallichet, Jan Bowen 1936- WhoSSW 93
Tallichet, Leon Edgar 1925- WhoAm 92
Tallichet, Margaret d1991 BioIn 17
Tallie, Diana Lee 1955- WhoAmW 93
Tallini, Fiory Anthony 1962- WhoE 93
Tallis, Alan Louis 1946- WhoAm 92
Tallis, Cedric d1991 BioIn 17
Tallis, Raymond Courtney WhoScE 91-1
Tallis, Robyn ScF&FL 92
Tallis, Thomas c. 1505-1585 Baker 92
Tallman, Daniel Culler 1925- St&PR 93
Tallman, Francine Rose 1966- WhoAmW 93
Tallman, Gerald Morris 1931- St&PR 93
Tallman, Jane Darrow AmWomPl
Tallman, Johanna Eleonore 1914- WhoAm 92, WhoWor 93
Tallman, John F. 1947- St&PR 93
Tallman, John Wallace 1935- WhoSSW 93
Tallman, Mariana M. Bisbee AmWomPl
Tallman, Patricia BioIn 17
Tallman, Robert O. 1935- St&PR 93
Tallman, Samuel Vose, Jr. 1947- St&PR 93
Tallman, Steven Charles 1955- St&PR 93
Tallman, Thomas Abel 1951- WhoIns 93
Tallmer, Margot 1925- WhoAm 92, WhoAmW 93
Tallon, Guy 1922- WhoScE 91-2
Tallon, Robert M., Jr. 1946- WhoAm 92
Tallon, Robert M. Robin, Jr. 1946- WhoSSW 93
Tallon, Robin 1946- CngDr 91
Tallon, Stephen William 1942- St&PR 93
Tallon, Wesley Carlisle 1950- WhoSSW 93
Tallone, Eugene F. 1939- St&PR 93
Tally, Lura Self 1921- WhoAmW 93, WhoSSW 93
Tally, Ted 1952- ConTFT 10
Tallyn, Robert Douglas 1939- St&PR 93
Tallys, Thomas c. 1505-1585 Baker 92
Talma, Louise J. 1906- BioIn 17
Talma, Louise (Juliette) 1906- Baker 92
Talmadge, Constance 1898-1973 QDrFCA 92 [port]
Talmadge, Eugene 1884-1946 PolPar
Talmadge, Jeffrey D. 1953- WhoWrEP 92
Talmadge, John Mills 1946- WhoSSW 93
Talmadge, Mary Christine 1940- WhoAmW 93, WhoWor 93
Talmadge, Naomi 1932- WhoAmW 93
Talmadge, Norma 1897-1957 IntDcF 2-3
Talmadge, Richard 1892-1981 BioIn 17
Talmadge-Bickmore, Deborah ScF&FL 92
Talmage, Archibald A. d1990 BioIn 17
Talmage, David Wilson 1919- WhoAm 92
Talmage, Kenneth Kellogg 1946- WhoWor 93
Talmage, Oliver Arthur 1923- St&PR 93
Talmage, Ralph William 1948- St&PR 93
Talmage, William Howard Law&B 92
Talmi, Yoav 1943- Baker 92, WhoAm 92, WhoWor 93
Talner, Norman Stanley 1925- WhoAm 92
Talpalar, Jose 1925- St&PR 93
Talreja, Ramesh Ramchand 1946- WhoWor 93
Talsania, Bharat Himatlal 1948- WhoWor 93
Taltabull, Cristofor 1888-1964 Baker 92
Talton, Chester Lovelle 1941- WhoAm 92
Talton, David H. Law&B 92
Talton, Karen Bryant 1955- WhoAmW 93
Talts, Juri Johan 1936- WhoScE 91-4
Talty, Don 1911- BioIn 17
Talty, Lorraine Caguioa 1957- WhoEmL 93
Talucci, Samuel James 1929- WhoAm 92
Talukdar, Mohammed Ishaq 1941- WhoUN 92
Talvacchia, John L. 1950- St&PR 93
Talvela, Martti 1935-1989 IntDcOp, OxDcOp
Talvela, Martti (Olavi) 1935-1989 Baker 92
Talvi, Ilkka Ilari 1948- WhoAm 92
Talvinto, Tapani WhoScE 91-4
Talvitie, Antti P. 1941- WhoScE 91-4
Talvitie, Jouko J. 1932- WhoScE 91-4
Talwani, Manik 1933- WhoAm 92
Talwar, Devki Nandan 1949- WhoE 93
Talwar, Vinod K. 1953- St&PR 93
Talys, Thomas c. 1505-1585 Baker 92
Talyzin, Nikolai BioIn 17
Talz, F.J. 1944- St&PR 93
Tam, Alfred Yat-Cheung 1953- WhoWor 93
Tam, B.K. St&PR 93
Tam, Bit-Shun 1951- WhoWor 93
Tam, Christopher K. W. 1939- WhoSSW 93
Tam, Colin Shiutung 1948- WhoWor 93
Tam, Jane Kwok Ping 1965- WhoAmW 93
Tam, Maria Wai-chu 1945- WhoAsAP 91
Tam, Marilyn H. BioIn 17
Tam, Reuben 1916-1991 BioIn 17
Tam, Rosanna Yick-ming 1952- WhoAsAP 91
Tam, S.C. St&PR 93
Tam, Samson Chi-Leung 1954- WhoWor 93
Tamagna, Frank M. 1910-1991 BioIn 17
Tamagni, John Searle 1935- St&PR 93, WhoAm 92
Tamagno, Francesco 1850-1905 Baker 92, IntDcOp [port], OxDcOp
Tamaka, Nobuyuki 1936- St&PR 93
Tamaki, Eiichi 1934- WhoAsAP 91
Tamaki, Norio 1940- WhoWor 93
Tamano, Mamintal Abdul Jabar 1928- WhoAsAP 91
Tamanoi, Hisashi 1927- WhoWor 93
Tamanyan, Gagik Juli 1953- WhoWor 93
Tamaoki, Bun-Ichi 1925- WhoWor 93
Tamar, Erika 1934- BioIn 17
Tamara, Florenz d1946 BioIn 17
T'amara of Georgia c. 1156-1207? OxDcByz
Tamarelli, A. Wayne 1941- St&PR 93
Tamarelli, Alan Wayne 1941- WhoAm 92, WhoE 93
Tamaru, Hideharu BioIn 17
Tamaru, Kenzi 1923- WhoWor 93
Tamas, Ferenc 1928- WhoScE 91-4
Tamas, Gyula 1941- WhoScE 91-4
Tamashiro, Hiko 1949- WhoUN 92
Tamasi, Michael 1961- St&PR 93
Tamasi, Raymond Valentino 1942- WhoE 93
Tamasson, Verna 1932- WhoWrEP 92
Tamassy, Istvan 1924- WhoScE 91-4
Tamassy, Lajos 1923- WhoScE 91-4
Tamayo, Augusto MiSFD 9
Tamayo, Luis Alejandro Law&B 92
Tamayo, Raymond Thomas 1953- St&PR 93
Tamayo, Reve WhoWrEP 92
Tamayo, Rufino 1899-1991 AnObit 1991, BioIn 17, News 92
Tamba, Maurizio 1942- WhoScE 91-3
Tamber, Selma d1991 BioIn 17
Tamberg, Eino 1930- Baker 92
Tamberlick, Enrico 1820-1889 IntDcOp
Tamberlik, Enrico 1820-1889 Baker 92, OxDcOp
Tambi, Brian 1943- St&PR 93
Tambiah, Stanley Jeyarajah 1929- WhoAm 92
Tambling, Grant Ernest John 1943- WhoAsAP 91
Tamblyn, Ken C. 1943- St&PR 93
Tamblyn, Wayne I. 1932- St&PR 93
Tambo, Oliver BioIn 17
Tambo, Oliver Reginald 1917- WhoAfr
Tamboli, Frances Faye 1951- WhoAmW 93
Tamborlane, Rebecca L. 1966- St&PR 93
Tambourin, P. WhoScE 91-2
Tambrallo, Laura Jeanne 1959- WhoAmW 93
Tambs, Lewis Arthur 1927- WhoAm 92, WhoWor 93
Tambuev, Georgi Stefanov 1933- WhoWor 93
Tamburello, Tony d1992 NewYTBS 92
Tamburini, Antonio 1800-1876 Baker 92, OxDcOp
Tamburlaine 1336-1405 BioIn 17
Tamburo, Vincent A. 1934- St&PR 93
Tamburri, Anthony Julian 1949- ConAu 138
Tamburrino, Ronnie Michael Law&B 92
Tamburro, Harold C. St&PR 93
Tamburro, Kathleen O'Connell WhoAmW 93
Tambuzi, Jitu WhoWrEP 92
Tamen, Harriet 1947- WhoAmW 93
Tamen, Miguel Benard Da Costa 1960- WhoWor 93
Tamerlane 1336-1405 BioIn 17, HarEnMi
Tames, Richard BioIn 17
Tamimi, Abdulrahman Ibrahim 1949- WhoWor 93
Tamir, Theodor 1927- WhoAm 92, WhoE 93
Tamiran, David 1951- WhoE 93, WhoWrEP 92
Tamirat Layne WhoWor 93
Tamiso, Robert M. 1965- WhoE 93
Tamkevicius, Sigitas BioIn 17
Tamkin, David 1906-1975 Baker 92
Tamkin, Lewis Donald 1932- WhoSSW 93
Tamkin, S. Jerome 1926- WhoAm 92
Tamlyn, Pete ScF&FL 92
Tamm, Christoph 1923- WhoScE 91-4
Tamm, Eleanor Ruth 1921- WhoAmW 93
Tamm, Igor 1922- WhoAm 92, WhoE 93
Tamm, Mary Anne DeCamp 1949- WhoE 93
Tammann, Gustav Andreas 1932- WhoScE 91-4
Tammany, D. Timothy Law&B 92
Tammeus, William David 1945- ConAu 136, WhoAm 92
Tamminen, Pekka 1949- WhoScE 91-4
Tamminga, Frederick W. 1935- ScF&FL 92
Tamminga, Frederick William 1934- BioIn 17
Tamminga, Seerp 1942- WhoScE 91-3
Tammirinne, Markku 1941- WhoScE 91-4
Tammisto, Arto Tapani 1932- WhoScE 91-4
Tammivuori, Juhani Tapio 1941- WhoWor 93
Tammuz, Benjamin 1919-1989 BioIn 17
Tamon, Jiro 1878-1934 HarEnMi
Tamondong-Helin, Susan Daet 1957- WhoAmW 93, WhoEmL 93
Tamoney, Thomas H., Jr. Law&B 92
Tampa, Harry MiSFD 9
Tamparong, Casimiro Roy, Jr. 1926- WhoWor 93
Tampion, John WhoScE 91-1
Tamposi, Elizabeth Marian 1955- WhoAm 92, WhoAmW 93
Tampow, Don 1942- St&PR 93
Tamres, Milton 1922- WhoAm 92
Tams SoulM
Tams, D.E. 1942- WhoScE 91-1
Tamsberg, William Templeton 1945- St&PR 93
Tamsitt, James Ray 1928- WhoSSW 93
Tamte, Roger R. Law&B 92
Tamulevich, Janet A. 1948- St&PR 93
Tamulevich, Joan Frances 1940- WhoE 93
Tamulevich, Kevin Paul 1949- St&PR 93
Tamura, Hajime 1924- WhoAm 92, WhoAsAP 91
Tamura, Hideaki 1932- WhoAsAP 91
Tamura, Hideo 1923- WhoWor 93
Tamura, Hiroyuki 1940- WhoWor 93
Tamura, Imao 1923- WhoWor 93
Tamura, Kenji 1933- WhoWor 93
Tamura, Rui 1953- WhoWor 93
Tamura, Saburo 1927- WhoWor 93
Tamura Iyozo 1854-1903 HarEnMi
Tamuramaro, Sakanoue fl. 780-806 HarEnMi
Tam Yiu-Chung 1949- WhoAsAP 91
Tan, Abdusakur M. 1950- WhoAsAP 91
Tan, Ali 1946- WhoScE 91-4
Tan, Allen Li 1947- WhoWor 93
Tan, Amy BioIn 17
Tan, Amy 1952- AmWomWr 92, Au&Arts 9 [port], ConAu 136, CurBio 92 [port]
Tan, Amy Ruth 1952- WhoAm 92
Tan, Arjun 1943- WhoAm 92, WhoSSW 93, WhoWor 93
Tan, Ben 1952- WhoWor 93
Tan, Bienvenido Alejandro, Jr. 1923- WhoWor 93
Tan, Chai Tiam 1943- WhoWor 93
Tan, Charlotte T. C. 1923- WhoAmW 93
Tan, Eng Meng 1926- WhoAm 92
Tan, Evelyn Loriega WhoWor 93
Tan, Fred d1990 BioIn 17
Tan, John K. 1934- WhoWor 93
Tan, Kong Yam 1955- WhoWor 93
Tan, Manuel C. St&PR 93
Tan, Margaret Leng 1945- Baker 92
Tan, Melvyn 1956- Baker 92
Tan, Meng Han 1966- WhoWor 93
Tan, Steven W. Law&B 92
Tan, Teresa Law&B 92
Tan, Terry R. 1942- St&PR 93
Tan, Tjiauw-Ling 1935- WhoE 93, WhoWor 93
Tan, Wai H. d1990 BioIn 17
Tan, Xiao-Jiang 1955- WhoWor 93
Tan, Yew-oo 1945- WhoWor 93
Tan, Yew Seng 1950- WhoWor 93
Tan, Yoke San 1955- WhoWor 93
Tana, Patti 1945- WhoWrEP 92
Tanabe, Hiroo 1925- WhoAsAP 91
Tanabe, Hisao 1883-1984 Baker 92
Tanabe, Kunio 1913- WhoAsAP 91
Tanabe, Makoto 1922- WhoAsAP 91
Tanabe, Masahiko 1930- WhoWor 93
Tanabe, Tetsuo 1929- WhoAsAP 91
Tanabe, Yo 1950- WhoWor 93
Tanabu, Masami 1934- WhoAsAP 91
Tanada, Lorenzo d1992 NewYTBS 92
Tanada, Lorenzo 1898-1992 BioIn 17
Tanada, Wigberto Ebarle 1934- WhoAsAP 91
Tanaka, Chisato 1924- WhoWor 93
Tanaka, Giichi 1863-1929 HarEnMi
Tanaka, Hiroshi 1939- WhoWor 93
Tanaka, Hitoshi 1939- St&PR 93
Tanaka, Janet M. Cullen 1936- WhoWrEP 92
Tanaka, Jeannie E. 1942- WhoAmW 93
Tanaka, John 1924- WhoE 93
Tanaka, Junji 1929- WhoWor 93
Tanaka, Kinuyo 1909-1977 IntDcF 2-3
Tanaka, Kouichi Robert 1926- WhoAm 92
Tanaka, Kyoshi 1943- WhoWor 93
Tanaka, Leila Chiyako 1954- WhoEmL 93
Tanaka, Masami 1917- WhoAsAP 91
Tanaka, Masao 1947- St&PR 93
Tanaka, Mitsuyoshi 1944- WhoE 93
Tanaka, Nobuyoshi 1934- WhoWor 93
Tanaka, Nobuyuki 1936- St&PR 93
Tanaka, Osamu 1936- WhoWor 93
Tanaka, Raizo 1892-1969 HarEnMi
Tanaka, Richard I. 1928- St&PR 93, WhoAm 92, WhoWor 93
Tanaka, Ryukichi 1893- HarEnMi
Tanaka, Shigetoshi 1929- WhoWor 93

Tanaka, Shin'ichi 1893- *HarEnMi*
Tanaka, Shizuichi 1887-1945 *HarEnMi*
Tanaka, Shoichi 1933- *WhoAsAP 91*
Tanaka, Shusei 1940- *WhoAsAP 91*
Tanaka, Stanley Katsuki 1932- *WhoWor 93*
Tanaka, Takeo 1937- *WhoAm 92*
Tanaka, Thomas H. *Law&B 92*
Tanaka, Tomoyasu *WhoWor 93*
Tanaka, Toshijiro 1944- *WhoWor 93*
Tanaka, Toshimitsu 1930- *Baker 92*
Tanaka, Tsunetoshi 1925- *WhoAsAP 91*
Tanaka Kakuei 1918- *DcTwHis*
Tanami, Taneaki 1932- *WhoAsAP 91*
Tanana, Frank Daryl 1953- *BiDAMSp 1989*
Tanao, Avusi 1948- *WhoAsAP 91*
Tanarro, Fernando Manuel 1933- *WhoWor 93*
Tanase, Dinu 1946- *DrEEuF*
Tanasescu, Florin-Teodor 1932- *WhoScE 91-4*
Tanasescu, Gino *MiSFD 9*
Tanchev, Stoyan Stoychev 1932- *WhoScE 91-4*
Tan-Chi, Ernesto Fu, Jr. 1947- *WhoWor 93*
Tancred d1112 *HarEnMi*
Tancred d1194 *HarEnMi*
Tancred c. 1075-c. 1112 *OxDcByz*
Tancredi, Laurence R(ichard) 1940- *ConAu 39NR*
Tancredi, Laurence Richard 1940- *WhoAm 92*
Tancred of Lecce d1194 *OxDcByz*
Tancrell, Roger Henry 1935- *WhoAm 92*
Tand, Barbara Lucile 1942- *St&PR 93*
Tand, David 1923- *St&PR 93*
Tandberg, Olof G. 1932- *WhoScE 91-4*
Tandler, Bernard 1933- *WhoAm 92*
Tandlich, Steve Eric 1952- *St&PR 93*
Tandon, Sanjiv 1946- *St&PR 93*
Tandon, Sirjang Lal 1941- *WhoAm 92*
Tandori, Karoly 1925- *WhoScE 91-4*
Tandowsky, Ralph Myron 1929- *St&PR 93*
Tandy, Charles David 1918-1978 *BioIn 17*
Tandy, Jessica *BioIn 17*
Tandy, Jessica 1909- *WhoAm 92, WhoAmW 93, WhoE 93*
Tane, Irwin R. 1923- *St&PR 93*
Taneda, Makoto 1945- *WhoAsAP 91*
Tanen, Norman *BioIn 17*
Tanenbaum, Alvin d1991 *BioIn 17*
Tanenbaum, Andrew Stuart 1944- *WhoWor 93*
Tanenbaum, Basil Samuel 1934- *WhoAm 92*
Tanenbaum, Bernard Jerome, Jr. 1934- *WhoAm 92*
Tanenbaum, Jill Nancy 1954- *WhoE 93*
Tanenbaum, Marc H. 1925-1992 *NewYTBS 92 [port]*
Tanenbaum, Marc Herman 1925- *WhoAm 92*
Tanenbaum, Morris 1928- *St&PR 93*
Tanenbaum, Myron 1955- *WhoSSW 93*
Tanenbaum, Sidney 1925-1986 *BiDAMSp 1989*
Tanenbaum, Stuart William 1924- *WhoE 93*
Tanenbaum, Susan G. *WhoAmW 93*
Taner, Dogan 1930- *WhoScE 91-4*
Tanev, Alexander 1928- *Baker 92*
Taney, Charles R. 1946- *St&PR 93*
Taney, J. Charles *WhoAm 92, WhoE 93*
Taney, Roger Brooke 1777-1864 *OxCSupC [port]*
Taneyev, Alexander (Sergeievich) 1850-1918 *Baker 92*
Taneyev, Sergei (Ivanovich) 1856-1915 *Baker 92*
Taneyev, Sergey 1856-1919 *OxDcOp*
Tanford, Charles 1921- *WhoAm 92*
Tang, A.K. *Law&B 92*
Tang, Albert Kwok *WhoE 93*
Tang, Denny D. *WhoAm 92*
Tang, Esther Don 1917- *WhoAmW 93, WhoWor 93*
Tang, Frances Young d1992 *BioIn 17, NewYTBS 92*
Tang, James Yue-Tak 1941- *St&PR 93*
Tang, Jennifer Karyee 1970- *WhoAmW 93*
Tang, Jordan Jien-Nan 1931- *WhoSSW 93*
Tang, Kenneth Y. *St&PR 93*
Tang, Peixiong 1958- *WhoWor 93*
Tang, Thomas 1922- *WhoAm 92*
Tang, Thomas Li-Ping 1949- *WhoSSW 93*
Tang, Tom T. 1931- *St&PR 93*
Tang, Tom Y.C. 1918- *St&PR 93*
Tang, Victor 1942- *ConAu 138*
Tang, Wilson Hon-chung 1943- *WhoAm 92*
Tang, Yu-Sun 1922- *WhoE 93*
Tangco, Ambrosio Flores 1912- *WhoWor 93*
Tangco, Marcelo V. 1893-1987 *IntDcAn*
Tangen, Cheryl Crandall *Law&B 92*
Tangen, Roy Allan 1947- *WhoE 93*
Tang Guan Seng 1947- *WhoAsAP 91*
Tangie, Carol Irene 1965- *WhoAmW 93*
Tangney, Eugene M. 1928- *St&PR 93*
Tangney, Eugene Michael 1928- *WhoAm 92*
Tangney, Joseph G. 1944- *St&PR 93, WhoAm 92*
Tangney, Michael J. 1945- *St&PR 93*
Tango, Egisto 1873-1951 *Baker 92*
Tangonan, Naomi Gaac 1947- *WhoWor 93*
Tangora, Albert L. 1937- *St&PR 93*
Tanguay, Anita Walburga 1936- *WhoAmW 93, WhoE 93*
Tanguay, Eva 1878-1947 *BioIn 17*
Tanguay, George R. 1932- *WhoSSW 93*
Tanguay, Marcel M. 1940- *St&PR 93*
Tanguy, Brian A. *St&PR 93*
Tanguy, Charles Reed 1921- *WhoAm 92*
Tanguy, Edward Earley 1934- *WhoSSW 93*
Tanguy, Henri Jean 1930- *WhoWor 93*
Tanham, George Kilpatrick 1922- *WhoAm 92*
Tan Hock Lye, David 1951- *WhoWor 93*
Tani, Andrew Emmanuel B. 1955- *WhoWor 93*
Tani, Shohei 1942- *WhoWor 93*
Tani, Tateki 1837-1911 *HarEnMi*
Tani, Yoichi 1926- *WhoAsAP 91*
Taniewska-Osinska, Stefania 1923- *WhoScE 91-4*
Tanigaki, Sada Kazu 1945- *WhoAsAP 91*
Tanigawa, Kanzo 1920- *WhoAsAP 91*
Tanigawara, Yusuke 1956- *WhoWor 93*
Taniguchi, Alan Yamato 1922- *WhoAm 92*
Taniguchi, Isao 1947- *WhoWor 93*
Taniguchi, Izumi 1926- *WhoAm 92*
Taniguchi, Naoyuki 1941- *WhoWor 93*
Taniguchi, Tadatsugu 1948- *WhoWor 93*
Taniguchi, Tokuso 1915- *WhoWor 93*
Taniguchi, Yoshiteru 1952- *WhoWor 93*
Tanihata, Takashi 1947- *WhoAsAP 91*
Tanikawa, Kazuo 1930- *WhoAsAP 91*
Tanikawa, Shuntaro 1931- *BioIn 17*
Tanila, Asko Vilhelm 1951- *WhoScE 91-4*
Tanila, Juhani *WhoScE 91-4*
Tanimoto, George 1926- *WhoWor 93*
Tanimoto, Takashi 1928- *WhoAsAP 91*
Tanimura, Keisuke 1932- *WhoAsAP 91*
Taningco, Cora Marie De Guzman 1959- *WhoE 93*
Tanis, James Robert 1928- *WhoAm 92*
Tanis, John J. 1926- *St&PR 93*
Tanis, John Jacob 1926- *WhoAm 92*
Tanis, Kim Robert 1948- *WhoSSW 93*
Tanis, Norman Earl 1929- *WhoAm 92, WhoWor 93*
Tanishita, Ichimatsu 1906- *WhoWor 93*
Taniuchi, Kiyoshi 1926- *WhoWor 93*
Tanjuatco, Emigdio S., Jr. 1945- *WhoAsAP 91*
Tanjung, Akbar 1945- *WhoAsAP 91*
Tanjutco, Paul Saldana 1946- *WhoWor 93*
Tank, Patrick Wayne 1950- *WhoSSW 93*
Tank, Turan 1933- *WhoScE 91-4*
Tankard, Elaine Fuller 1947- *WhoWrEP 92*
Tankard, James William, Jr. 1941- *WhoSSW 93*
Tankard, Judith B. 1942- *WhoAmW 93*
Tan Keng Yam, Tony 1940- *WhoAsAP 91*
Tankenoff, Gary L. 1934- *St&PR 93*
Tankersley, Anita Gayle 1949- *WhoSSW 93*
Tankersley, Daniel *Law&B 92*
Tankersley, George Jackson 1921- *WhoAm 92*
Tankersley, James I. 1942- *St&PR 93*
Tankersley, M.B. 1933- *St&PR 93*
Tankersley, N. Frank 1940- *St&PR 93*
Tankin, Richard Samuel 1924- *WhoAm 92*
Tanko, Calvin James 1941- *St&PR 93*
Tankoos, Sandra Maxine 1936- *WhoAmW 93, WhoE 93, WhoWor 93*
Tann, Georgia *BioIn 17*
Tannatt, Michael B. *Law&B 92*
Tanne, Sol 1923- *St&PR 93*
Tannebaum, Edward Jay 1948- *St&PR 93*
Tannebaum, Samuel Hugo 1933- *WhoSSW 93, WhoWor 93*
Tanneberger, S. *WhoScE 91-3*
Tannebring, Bill 1937- *MiSFD 9*
Tannehill, Jayne *ScF&FL 92*
Tannehill, John C. 1943- *WhoAm 92*
Tannehill, Kenneth L. 1917- *St&PR 93*
Tannehill, Norman Bruce, Jr. 1950- *WhoE 93*
Tannehill, Robert E. *Law&B 92*
Tannehill, Steven James 1956- *St&PR 93*
Tannen, Jack *BioIn 17*
Tannen, Jack 1907-1991 *ConAu 136*
Tannen, Mary 1943- *ScF&FL 92*
Tannen, Terrel *MiSFD 9*
Tannen, William *MiSFD 9*
Tannenbaum, Anne Marsha *Law&B 92*
Tannenbaum, Bernice Salpeter *WhoAm 92*
Tannenbaum, Gary Kenneth *Law&B 92*
Tannenbaum, Harvey 1923- *WhoE 93*
Tannenbaum, Jerome S. 1950- *St&PR 93*
Tannenbaum, John O. 1946- *WhoAm 92*
Tannenbaum, Judith Nettie 1947- *WhoWrEP 92*
Tannenbaum, Leonard H. 1933- *St&PR 93*
Tannenbaum, Nathan d1991 *BioIn 17*
Tannenbaum, Richard J. *Law&B 92*
Tannenbaum, Samuel Victor 1942- *WhoSSW 93*
Tannenbaum, Sanford *Law&B 92*
Tannenbaum, Steven Robert 1937- *WhoAm 92, WhoE 93*
Tannenbaum, Ted M. 1947- *St&PR 93*
Tannenberg, David 1728-1804 *Baker 92*
Tannenberg, Dieter E. A. 1932- *WhoAm 92, WhoWor 93*
Tannenwald, Leslie Keiter 1949- *WhoAmW 93*
Tannenwald, Theodore, Jr. 1916- *CngDr 91, WhoAm 92*
Tanner, Alain *BioIn 17*
Tanner, Alain 1929- *MiSFD 9*
Tanner, Benjamin Tucker 1835-1923 *EncAACR*
Tanner, Brian Keith *WhoScE 91-1*
Tanner, Champ Bean 1920-1990 *BioIn 17*
Tanner, Courtenay Tyler 1948- *WhoAmW 93*
Tanner, Daniel 1926- *WhoAm 92, WhoWor 93*
Tanner, Dee Boshard 1913- *WhoWor 93*
Tanner, Frederick C., Jr. 1917- *St&PR 93*
Tanner, George 1924- *BioIn 17*
Tanner, H. Max 1926- *St&PR 93*
Tanner, Harold 1932- *WhoAm 92*
Tanner, Hazel Marie 1946- *WhoAmW 93*
Tanner, Helen Hornbeck 1916- *WhoAm 92, WhoAmW 93*
Tanner, Henry Ossawa 1859-1937 *BioIn 17, GayN*
Tanner, Jack Edward 1919- *WhoAm 92*
Tanner, Jack Gene 1940- *WhoSSW 93*
Tanner, Jerry Joseph 1948- *St&PR 93*
Tanner, Jimmie Eugene 1933- *WhoAm 92*
Tanner, John *WhoWrEP 92*
Tanner, John Douglas, Jr. 1943- *WhoWor 93*
Tanner, John S. 1944- *CngDr 91, WhoAm 92, WhoSSW 93*
Tanner, John S. 1950- *ConAu 138*
Tanner, L. Gene 1932- *St&PR 93*
Tanner, Laurel Nan 1929- *WhoAm 92, WhoWor 93*
Tanner, Laurence Aram 1946- *WhoE 93*
Tanner, Lynn 1953- *WhoAmW 93, WhoWor 93*
Tanner, Mack *ScF&FL 92*
Tanner, Martha M. 1934- *St&PR 93*
Tanner, Mary Catherine 1951- *St&PR 93*
Tanner, Mauri Uuno Ensio 1930- *WhoWor 93*
Tanner, Michael A. *Law&B 92*
Tanner, Nolen Kyle 1956- *WhoWor 93*
Tanner, Obert C. 1904- *St&PR 93*
Tanner, Ray U. 1931- *St&PR 93*
Tanner, Richard Stephen 1940- *St&PR 93*
Tanner, Robert Hugh 1915- *WhoSSW 93*
Tanner, Robert Stanley 1928- *St&PR 93*
Tanner, Stephen B. 1953- *St&PR 93*
Tanner, Steve Alan *Law&B 92*
Tanner, Terry Finley 1926- *St&PR 93*
Tanner, Tony 1935- *ScF&FL 92*
Tanner, Tyler *BioIn 17*
Tanner, Vasco Myron 1892-1989 *BioIn 17*
Tanner, Vernon W. 1934- *St&PR 93*
Tanner, Virginia 1881- *AmWomPl*
Tanner, Walter Rhett 1938- *WhoAm 92*
Tanner, William Francis, Jr. 1917- *WhoSSW 93*
Tanner, William George 1939- *St&PR 93*
Tanney, Allen D. 1911-1990 *BioIn 17*
Tannhauser, Der c. 1205-c. 1270 *Baker 92*
Tannian, Francis Xavier 1933- *WhoAm 92*
Tannir, Safwan Mahmoud 1949- *WhoWor 93*
Tannis, Hudson *DcCPCAm*
Tannura, Nicholas Donald 1960- *WhoAm 92*
Tanny, Gerald Brian 1945- *St&PR 93*
Tanoos, Ann 1940- *WhoAmW 93*
Tanos, Bela 1925- *WhoScE 91-4*
Tanous, Helene Mary 1939- *WhoSSW 93*
Tanouye, Elyse Toshie 1955- *WhoWrEP 92*
Tanphaichitr, Kongsak 1946- *WhoEmL 93*
Tanquary, Fred T. 1943- *St&PR 93*
Tanselle, Donald William 1924- *St&PR 93*
Tanselle, George Thomas 1934- *WhoAm 92*
Tan Seng Giaw Tan Chun Tin, Dr. 1942- *WhoAsAP 91*
Tansey, Joseph A. *St&PR 93*
Tansill, Frederick Riker 1914- *WhoAm 92*
Tansill, Mel 1954- *WhoWrEP 92*
Tanskanen, Antli 1946- *WhoScE 91-4*
Tanskanen, Pekka J. 1936- *WhoScE 91-4*
Tanski, Czeslaw 1863-1942 *PolBiDi*
Tanski, James Michael 1946- *WhoEmL 93*
Tanski, Ronald J. *Law&B 92*
Tanski, Sharon Wirkus *Law&B 92*
Tansman, Aleksander 1897-1986 *PolBiDi*
Tansman, Alexandre 1897-1986 *Baker 92, BioIn 17*
Tansor, Robert Henry 1935- *WhoAm 92*
Tans'ur, William 1700-1783 *Baker 92*
Tantam, Digby *WhoScE 91-1*
Tantari, Mark Richard *Law&B 92*
Tantia Topi c. 1810-1859 *HarEnMi*
Tantillo, James Michael 1938- *St&PR 93*
Tantillo, John 1951- *WhoE 93*
Tantillo, Joseph George, Jr. 1952- *WhoE 93*
Tantillo, Thomas Joseph 1923- *St&PR 93*
Tantisunthorn, Udorn *WhoAsAP 91*
Tanumafili, Malietoa, II 1913- *WhoAsAP 91*
Tanur, Judith Mark 1935- *WhoAmW 93*
Tan-Wilson, Anna Li 1946- *WhoAmW 93*
Tanwir, Rehana *WhoUN 92*
Tanzer, Arnold 1871-1937 *BioIn 17*
Tanzer, Kim Michele 1955- *WhoSSW 93*
Tanzer, Lester 1929- *WhoAm 92*
Tanzer, Martin E. 1933- *St&PR 93*
Tanzer, William 1700-1783 *Baker 92*
Tanzi, Anthony 1948- *WhoE 93*
Tanzi, Vito 1935- *WhoE 93, WhoUN 92*
Tanzini, Franco 1953- *WhoWor 93*
Tanzmann, Virginia Ward 1945- *WhoAmW 93*
Tanzola, Anthony James 1939- *St&PR 93*
Tanzola, Frank John 1931- *St&PR 93*
Tao, James F. *Law&B 92*
Tao, Jeffrey Kin-Cheung 1948- *WhoUN 92*
Tao, Kar-Ling James 1941- *WhoWor 93*
Tao, Wen 1935- *WhoWor 93*
Taofinu'u, Pio Cardinal 1923- *WhoAm 92, WhoWor 93*
Taoras, Bronius K. *Law&B 92*
Tao Siju 1935- *WhoAsAP 91*
Taozhu, Xu 1936- *WhoWor 93*
Tapak, Martin 1926- *DrEEuF*
Tape, Gerald Frederick 1915- *WhoAm 92*
Tapella, Gary L. 1943- *St&PR 93*
Tapella, Gary Louis 1943- *WhoAm 92, WhoE 93*
Tapellini, Donna Lynn 1955- *WhoWrEP 92*
Taper, Geri 1929- *WhoE 93*
Tapia, Luis 1950- *HispAmA*
Tapia, Richard Alfred 1939- *WhoAm 92, WhoSSW 93*
Tapia de Castellanos, Esther 1842-1897 *DcMexL*
Tapie, Bernard *BioIn 17*
Tapies, Antoni 1923- *BioIn 17, ModArCr 3 [port]*
Tapineng, Felix 1952- *WhoAsAP 91*
Tapio, Eeva 1927- *WhoScE 91-4, WhoWor 93*
Taplett, Lloyd Melvin 1924- *WhoAm 92, WhoWor 93*
Taplett, Lynn Craven *WhoAmW 93*
Tapley, Byron Dean 1933- *WhoAm 92, WhoSSW 93*
Tapley, David A. 1931- *St&PR 93*
Tapley, Donald Fraser 1927- *WhoAm 92*
Tapley, Earl Mays 1913- *WhoSSW 93*
Tapley, James Leroy 1923- *WhoAm 92*
Tapley, John Mark 1929- *St&PR 93*
Tapley, Lance E. 1944- *WhoWrEP 92*
Tapley, Lance Edwin 1944- *WhoE 93*
Taplin, David M.R. 1939- *WhoScE 91-3*
Taplin, Frank E., Jr. 1915- *WhoAm 92*
Taplin, Jonathan Trumbull 1947- *WhoAm 92*
Taplin, Martin W. *BioIn 17*
Taplitz, Daniel *MiSFD 9*
Tapp, Helen Preston 1954- *WhoAmW 93*
Tapp, John Cecil 1940- *WhoSSW 93, WhoWor 93*
Tapp, Kathy Kennedy 1949- *ConAu 39NR, ScF&FL 92*
Tapp, Lawrence G. 1937- *WhoAm 92*
Tapp, Linda Marie Dennison 1965- *WhoE 93*
Tapp, M.D. *WhoScE 91-1*
Tapp, Ronald Gene 1941- *WhoWor 93*
Tapp, Tommy Von 1943- *WhoSSW 93*
Tapp, William F., Jr. 1927- *St&PR 93*
Tappan, Lewis 1788-1873 *BioIn 17, EncAACR*
Tappan, Ronald P. 1934- *St&PR 93*
Tappan, Sandra Hazen 1940- *WhoAmW 93, WhoE 93, WhoWor 93*
Tappan, Steven G. 1952- *St&PR 93*
Tappata, Heber Nazareno, Jr. 1950- *WhoWor 93*
Tappe, Albert Anthony 1928- *WhoAm 92, WhoE 93*

Tappeiner, Gerhard 1947- *WhoWor 93*
Tappen, Mary Lou *WhoE 93*
Tapper, Bertha Feiring 1859-1915 *See* Tapper, Thomas 1864-1958 *Baker 92*
Tapper, David Alfred 1928- *WhoE 93*
Tapper, Jack W. *Law&B 92*
Tapper, Joan Judith 1947- *WhoAm 92, WhoWrEP 92*
Tapper, Stephen Charles 1946- *WhoScE 91-1*
Tapper, Thomas 1864-1958 *Baker 92*
Tappert, Wilhelm 1830-1907 *Baker 92*
Tappin, Anthony Gerald 1925- *St&PR 93*
Tapply, William George 1940- *WhoWrEP 92*
Tappolet, Willy 1890-1981 *Baker 92*
Taprogge, Rainer H. 1937- *WhoScE 91-3*
Tapscott, Cathy Jane 1945- *WhoAmW 93*
Tapscott, Robert Carl 1951- *St&PR 93*
Tapsell, Peter 1930- *WhoAsAP 91*
Taqi, Ali 1943- *WhoUN 92*
Taquet, Philippe *WhoScE 91-2*
Taquet, Philippe 1940- *WhoScE 91-2*
Taquey, Charles Henri *WhoAm 92*
Taquey, Charles Henri 1912- *WhoWrEP 92*
Tar, Zoltan John 1941- *WhoUN 92*
Tara 1921- *WhoWor 93*
Taraba, Tibor *WhoE 93*
Tarabar, Salim 1940- *WhoScE 91-4*
Tarabick, Lyn Everda 1953- *WhoAmW 93*
Tarabilda, James 1948- *ScF&FL 92*
Taraborelli, David A. 1936- *St&PR 93*
Tarachow, Michael 1954- *WhoWrEP 92*
Taradash, Daniel 1913- *BioIn 17, MiSFD 9*
Taradash, Meryl 1953- *WhoE 93*
Tarafdar, Enayet Ullah 1935- *WhoWor 93*
Taragano, Jose 1954- *WhoWor 93*
Taragano, Martin 1959- *ConAu 139*
Taraila, Drita Stambolli 1945- *WhoAmW 93*
Tarakhovsky, Alexander 1955- *WhoWor 93*
Tarallo, Angelo N. *Law&B 92*
Tarallo, Angelo N. 1940- *St&PR 93*
Tarallo, Angelo Nicholas 1940- *WhoAm 92*
Tarallo, Barry Joseph *WhoE 93*
Taran, Leonardo 1933- *WhoAm 92*
Taran, Richard Bruce 1942- *WhoSSW 93*
Tarangioli, Edward G. *Law&B 92*
Taranik, James Vladimir 1940- *WhoAm 92*
Taranovsky, Kiril 1911- *WhoAm 92*
Taranow, Gerda *WhoE 93*
Taranta, Angelo Visca 1927- *WhoAm 92*
Tarantino, Louis Gerald 1934- *WhoE 93, WhoWor 93*
Tarantino, Quentin *MiSFD 9*
Tarantino, Quentin 1963- *NewYTBS 92 [port]*
Tarantino, Robert Vincent 1943- *St&PR 93*
Tarantino, Rocco J. 1933- *St&PR 93*
Taranto, Joseph Victor 1949- *WhoIns 93*
Taranto, Maria Antoinette 1941- *WhoE 93*
Taranto, Thomas M. *Law&B 92*
Tarantola, Albert 1949- *WhoWor 93*
Taranu, Cornel 1934- *Baker 92*
Tarapata, Peter 1919- *WhoAm 92*
Taras, David J. *Law&B 92*
Taras, John 1919- *WhoAm 92*
Taras, Paul 1941- *WhoAm 92*
Taras, Raymond (C.) 1946- *ConAu 139*
Tarascio, Vincent Joseph 1930- *WhoSSW 93*
Tarasenko, Felix Petrovich 1932- *WhoWor 93*
Tarasios c. 730-806 *OxDcByz*
Tarasoff, Koozma John 1932- *WhoWrEP 92*
Tarasovic, Nicholas J. 1952- *St&PR 93*
Tarassov, Nikolai Konstantinovitch 1923- *WhoUN 92*
Tarassuk, Leonid d1990 *BioIn 17*
Tarasyev, Alexander Michailovich 1959- *WhoWor 93*
Taraszka, Anthony John 1935- *St&PR 93*
Taraszkiewicz, Czeslaw 1930- *WhoScE 91-4*
Taraszkiewicz, Franciszek 1923- *WhoScE 91-4*
Taraszkiewicz, Waldemar 1936- *WhoWor 93*
Taratoot, Louis J. 1923- *St&PR 93*
Taravan, Christine *Law&B 92*
Taravella, Christopher A. *Law&B 92*
Tarawallie, Mohamed Sheku 1939- *WhoAfr*
Taraz, Ramin *St&PR 93*
Tarbell, Dean Stanley 1913- *WhoAm 92*
Tarbell, Ida M. 1857-1944 *GayN, JrnUS, PolPar*
Tarbell, James 1949- *WhoWrEP 92*
Tarbell, Roberta K. 1944- *ConAu 139*
Tarbell, Roberta Kupfrian 1944- *WhoE 93*
Tarbell, Stanley Martin 1960- *St&PR 93*
Tarbet, Ted N. 1953- *St&PR 93*
Tarbox, Frank Kolbe 1923- *St&PR 93, WhoAm 92*
Tarbox, Gurdon Lucius, Jr. 1927- *WhoSSW 93*
Tarbox, Judith Ann 1945- *WhoE 93*
Tarbox, Katharine Riggs 1948- *WhoAmW 93*
Tarbox, Richard J. 1920- *St&PR 93*
Tarbutton, Lloyd Tilghman 1932- *WhoAm 92*
Tarchaneiotes *OxDcByz*
Tarchaneiotes, Michael Doukas Glabas *OxDcByz*
Tarchi, Angelo c. 1755-1814 *Baker 92*
Tarchi, Angelo c. 1760-1814 *OxDcOp*
Tarcov, Edith H. 1919-1990 *BioIn 17*
Tardat, Claude 1949- *ConAu 136*
Tarde, Gerard 1956- *St&PR 93*
Tardieu, Andre Pierre Gabriel Amedee 1876-1945 *BioIn 17*
Tardieu, Catherine 1922- *WhoScE 91-2*
Tardif, Monique Bernatchez 1936- *WhoAmW 93*
Tardif, Richard C. 1944- *St&PR 93*
Tardio, Robert F. 1929- *St&PR 93*
Tarditi, Giovanni 1857-1935 *Baker 92*
Tarditi, Orazio 1602-1677 *Baker 92*
Tardivel, Jules-Paul 1851-1905 *BioIn 17, ScF&FL 92*
Tardivo, Giuseppe 1948- *WhoWor 93*
Tardos, Bela 1910-1966 *Baker 92*
Tardy, Daniel Louis 1934- *WhoWor 93*
Tardy, Vicky *BioIn 17*
Tardy, Yves 1939- *WhoScE 91-2*
Tarella, Douglas Francis 1952- *WhoE 93*
Tarello, John Alexander 1931- *St&PR 93*
Taren, James Arthur 1924- *WhoAm 92*
Taresvuori, Alpo Juhanni 1949- *WhoWor 93*
Targ, William 1907- *WhoAm 92*
Targe, Francois Henri Rene Allain- 1832-1902 *BioIn 17*
Targoff, Michael B. 1944- *St&PR 93*
Targoff, Michael Bart *Law&B 92*
Targoff, Michael Bart 1944- *WhoAm 92*
Targon, Lenny M. *St&PR 93*
Targowski, Andrew Stanislaw 1937- *WhoWor 93*
Tariang, Jerlie E. 1922- *WhoAsAP 91*
Tarica, James Allan 1940- *St&PR 93*
Tarics, Camille Nielson *Law&B 92*
Tarik ibn Ziyad fl. 711-712 *HarEnMi*
Tarila, B. Sophia 1938- *WhoWrEP 92*
Tarino, Gary Edward *Law&B 92*
Tario, Francisco *DcMexL*
Tario, Francisco 1911-1977 *SpAmA*
Tario, James Richard *Law&B 92*
Tariol-Bauge, Anne 1872-1944 *Baker 92*
Tarisio, Luigi c. 1795-1854 *Baker 92*
Tarjan, Ivan 1930- *WhoScE 91-4*
Tarjan, Robert Endre 1948- *WhoAm 92*
Tarjan, Robert Wegg 1943- *WhoAm 92*
Tarjanne, Pekka *WhoScE 91-4*
Tarjanne, Pekka 1937- *WhoUN 92*
Tarkanian, Jerry 1930- *BioIn 17, WhoAm 92*
Tarkenton, Fran 1940- *BioIn 17*
Tarkenton, Francis A. 1940- *BioIn 17*
Tarkenton, Francis Asbury 1940- *WhoAm 92*
Tarkhanov, Nikolai Nikolaevic 1956- *WhoWor 93*
Tarkington, Booth 1869-1946 *BioIn 17, GayN*
Tarkington, Lizbeth Bridwell 1947- *St&PR 93*
Tarkington, Lloyd James 1939- *WhoWor 93*
Tarkka, Jaakko Toivo 1938- *WhoWor 93*
Tarkovsky, Andrei *BioIn 17*
Tarkovsky, Andrei 1932-1986 *ConLC 75 [port], MiSFD 9N*
Tarkowska, Anna 1931- *WhoScE 91-4*
Tarkowski, Czeslaw 1926- *WhoScE 91-4*
Tarlau, Milton 1910-1991 *BioIn 17*
Tarleton, Banastre 1754-1833 *HarEnMi*
Tarleton, Bennett 1943- *WhoSSW 93*
Tarleton, K.Γ. 1940- *St&PR 93*
Tarleton, Larry Wilson 1943- *WhoSSW 93*
Tarlock, A(nthony) Dan 1940- *ConAu 37NR*
Tarlov, Alvin Richard 1929- *WhoAm 92*
Tarlow, Elyana *Law&B 92*
Tarlow, Eric K. *Law&B 92*
Tarlow, Lawrence E. 1924- *St&PR 93*
Tarlow, Richard N. 1923- *St&PR 93*
Tarlow, Rose *BioIn 17*
Tarlton, Curt Stoddard 1932- *St&PR 93*
Tarlton, Peter W. 1940- *St&PR 93*
Tarman, Charles William 1923- *St&PR 93*
Tarman, Paul Bernard *St&PR 93*
Tarmashirin fl. 1320-1330 *HarEnMi*
Tarn, Nathaniel 1928- *ConAu 16AS [port], WhoAm 92, WhoWrEP 92*
Tarn, Tzyh-Jong 1937- *WhoAm 92*
Tarnawski, Maciej 1955- *WhoWor 93*
Tarnay, Dennis B. 1952- *St&PR 93*
Tarnecki, Remigiusz Leszek 1933- *WhoWor 93*
Tarney, Robert E. 1931- *WhoE 93*
Tarnoff, Peter 1937- *WhoAm 92*
Tarnopol, Michael L. 1936- *WhoAm 92*
Tarnopol, Nat 1931- *BioIn 17*
Tarnopolsky, Walter Surma 1932- *WhoAm 92*
Tarnoski, Lori *Law&B 92*
Tarnoski, Lori M. 1940- *WhoAm 92, WhoAmW 93*
Tarnow, Robert Laurence 1924- *St&PR 93*
Tarnow, William M. *Law&B 92*
Tarnowski, George *Law&B 92*
Taroni, Tony Christopher 1942- *St&PR 93*
Taronites *OxDcByz*
Taronji, Jaime 1944- *St&PR 93*
Taronji, Jaime, Jr. *Law&B 92*
Taronji, Jaime, Jr. 1944- *WhoAm 92*
Taronov, Gleb (Pavlovich) 1904- *Baker 92*
Taroy, Morten 1951- *WhoWor 93*
Tarp, Finn 1951- *WhoWor 93*
Tarp, Svend Erik 1908- *Baker 92*
Tarpey, Kenneth J. 1952- *St&PR 93*
Tarpey, Marie Veronica 1924- *WhoAmW 93*
Tarpirian, Gregory 1956- *St&PR 93*
Tarpley, Brenda Mae 1944- *WhoAm 92, WhoAmW 93*
Tarpley, Fred Anderson *WhoWrEP 92*
Tarpley, James Douglas 1946- *WhoEmL 93, WhoSSW 93, WhoWor 93*
Tarpley, James Merrell 1934- *St&PR 93, WhoAm 92*
Tarpley, Michael J. *Law&B 92*
Tarpley, Robert W. 1940- *St&PR 93*
Tarpley, Timothy Norman 1943- *St&PR 93*
Tarpley, William Beverly, Jr. 1917- *WhoE 93*
Tarplin, Marv *SoulM*
Tarpy, Martin L. 1913- *St&PR 93*
Tarpy, Martin Lyster 1913- *WhoE 93*
Tarquini, Achille 1928- *WhoWor 93*
Tarquini, Tarquinia 1883-1976 *See* Zandonai, Riccardo 1883-1944 *OxDcOp*
Tarquinio, Cris J. 1958- *St&PR 93*
Tarquinius *OxDcOp*
Tarr, Charles Edwin 1940- *WhoAm 92, WhoWor 93*
Tarr, Curtis W. 1924- *WhoAm 92, WhoWrEP 92*
Tarr, Curtis William 1924- *St&PR 93*
Tarr, David William 1931- *WhoAm 92*
Tarr, Edward H(ankins) 1936- *Baker 92*
Tarr, G. Alan 1946- *WhoE 93*
Tarr, Joel A(rthur) 1934- *ConAu 38NR*
Tarr, Joel Arthur 1934- *WhoAm 92, WhoE 93, WhoWrEP 92*
Tarr, Judith *BioIn 17*
Tarr, Judith 1955- *ScF&FL 92*
Tarr, Kathleen Rose Ross 1949- *WhoAmW 93*
Tarr, Kenneth J. 1945- *WhoE 93*
Tarr, Linda *Law&B 92*
Tarr, Linda Haas 1948- *WhoSSW 93*
Tarr, Murray 1928- *St&PR 93*
Tarr, Paul C., III 1933- *WhoIns 93*
Tarr, Paul Cresson, III 1933- *St&PR 93*
Tarr, Robert J., Jr. 1943- *St&PR 93*
Tarr, Robert Joseph, Jr. 1943- *WhoAm 92*
Tarradellas, Joseph 1942- *WhoScE 91-4*
Tarrance, Vernon Lance, Jr. 1940- *WhoAm 92*
Tarrant, Desmond 1924- *ScF&FL 92*
Tarrant, Doris M. 1927- *St&PR 93*
Tarrant, Eddie Faye Battee 1942- *WhoAmW 93, WhoSSW 93, WhoWor 93*
Tarrant, James Richard 1936- *WhoWor 93*
Tarrant, Kathleen McGrath 1954- *St&PR 93*
Tarrant, Mae Cross 1923- *WhoWrEP 92*
Tarrant, Patrick Vivion 1943- *WhoScE 91-3*
Tarrant, Richard John 1945- *WhoAm 92*
Tarrant, Ronald W. 1937- *St&PR 93*
Tarrant, Thomas N. *Law&B 92*
Tarrants, William Eugene 1927- *WhoAm 92*
Tarrasch, Siegbert 1862-1934 *BioIn 17*
Tarrega (y Eixea), Francisco 1852-1909 *Baker 92*
Tarreto, Leonard Robert 1954- *St&PR 93*
Tarro, Giulio 1938- *WhoWor 93*
Tarry, Ellen 1906- *BioIn 17, BlkAull 92, SmATA 16AS [port]*
Tarry, Patricia 1928- *WhoAmW 93*
Tarsem *BioIn 17*
Tarshis, Lorie *BioIn 17*
Tarski, Alfred 1901-1983 *PolBiDi*
Tarson, Herbert Harvey 1910- *WhoAm 92*
Tart, Brian J. 1944- *WhoAm 92*
Tart, M.B. 1955- *St&PR 93*
Tartabull, Danilo Mora 1962- *WhoAm 92*
Tartabull, Danny 1962- *WhoAm 92*
Tartaglia, Anthony Philip 1932- *WhoE 93*
Tartaglia, Paul Edward 1944- *WhoE 93*
Tartar, Clarissa R. 1963- *WhoAmW 93*
Tartara, Guido 1938- *WhoScE 91-3*
Tartarini, Alessandro 1937- *WhoScE 91-3*
Tarte, Bernard J., Jr. 1948- *St&PR 93*
Tarte, Rodrigo 1936- *WhoWor 93*
Tartell, Robert Morris 1926- *WhoE 93, WhoWor 93*
Tarter, Barbara Jane 1946- *WhoE 93*
Tarter, Curtis Bruce 1939- *WhoAm 92*
Tarter, Fred Barry 1943- *WhoAm 92, WhoE 93*
Tarter, Jill Cornell 1944- *BioIn 17*
Tarter, Robert Richmond 1948- *St&PR 93*
Tartikoff, Brandon *BioIn 17, NewYTBS 92 [port]*
Tartikoff, Brandon 1949- *ConTFT 10, WhoAm 92*
Tartikoff, Peter Allen 1941- *St&PR 93*
Tartikoff, William M. *Law&B 92*
Tartini, Giuseppe 1692-1770 *Baker 92*
Tarto, Joe 1902-1986 *BioIn 17*
Tartt, Blake 1929- *WhoAm 92*
Tartt, Tyrone Chris *Law&B 92*
Taruc, Luis 1913- *DcTwHis*
Tarui, Seiichiro 1927- *WhoWor 93*
Tarullo, Jules John 1950- *WhoSSW 93*
Tarun, Robert Walter 1949- *WhoAm 92*
Tarver, David Joe 1951- *WhoSSW 93*
Tarver, David Paul 1951- *WhoWrEP 92*
Tarver, Jackson Williams 1917- *WhoAm 92*
Tarver, Michael Keith 1941- *WhoAm 92*
Tarvin, William Lester 1942- *WhoWor 93*
Tarzan, Deloris Lehman *ScF&FL 92*
Tarzi, Farouk Y. 1943- *WhoUN 92*
Tarzik, Jack 1946- *WhoWrEP 92*
Tarzwell, Clarence Matthew 1907- *WhoAm 92, WhoE 93, WhoWor 93*
Tas, Hugo A.W. 1940- *WhoScE 91-2*
Tasa, Kendall Sherwood 1947- *WhoSSW 93*
Tasche, Boris 1959- *WhoWor 93*
Tasco, Frank J. 1927- *St&PR 93*
Tasco, Frank John 1927- *WhoAm 92*
Tash, Martin E. 1941- *St&PR 93*
Tash, Martin Elias 1941- *WhoAm 92*
Tash, Max *MiSFD 9*
Tash, Stuart Barry 1949- *WhoE 93*
Tashan *BioIn 17*
Tashima, Atsushi Wallace 1934- *WhoAm 92*
Tashima, Irland Lee 1948- *St&PR 93*
Tashiro, Paul Yukio 1933- *WhoSSW 93*
Tashiro, Takahide 1929- *WhoWor 93*
Tashiro, Yukio 1916- *WhoAsAP 91*
Tashjian, Julia Zakarian 1938- *WhoAm 92, WhoAmW 93*
Tashlick, Irving 1928- *WhoE 93*
Tashlin, Frank 1913-1972 *MiSFD 9N*
Tashman, C. Mildred 1929- *WhoAmW 93*
Tashman, Myles R. *Law&B 92*
Tashman, Philip N. 1924- *St&PR 93*
Tashnek, Arthur Bernard 1925- *WhoSSW 93*
Tasic, Maria Barbara *Law&B 92*
Tasiopoulos, Nancy Joy 1946- *St&PR 93*
Tasker, John 1942- *St&PR 93*
Tasker, John Baker 1933- *WhoAm 92*
Tasker, Steve *BioIn 17*
Taskin, (Emile-) Alexandre 1853-1897 *Baker 92*
Taskin, Henri-Joseph 1779-1852 *See* Taskin, Pascal (-Joseph) 1723-1793 *Baker 92*
Taskin, Osman 1937- *WhoScE 91-4*
Taskin, Pascal (-Joseph) 1723-1793 *Baker 92*
Taskin, Pascal-Joseph 1750-1829 *See* Taskin, Pascal (-Joseph) 1723-1793 *Baker 92*
Taskinen, Pentti Juhani 1932- *WhoScE 91-4*
Taslim, Mohammad Ali 1951- *WhoWor 93*
Tasman, Abel Janszoon 1603-1659 *Expl 93*
Tasovac, Maryann 1957- *WhoAmW 93*
Tass, Nadia *MiSFD 9*
Tassani, Sally Marie 1948- *WhoAmW 93*
Tasse, Roger 1931- *WhoAm 92*
Tasseli, D. Van *ScF&FL 92*
Tassell-Getman, Terri Louanne 1956- *WhoAmW 93*
Tassello, Ronald J. 1957- *St&PR 93*
Tassie, Lindsay James 1930- *WhoWor 93*
Tassin, Becky La Grange 1956- *WhoSSW 93*
Tassin, Maurice Francis, Jr. 1940- *WhoSSW 93*
Tassin, Raymond Jean 1926- *WhoSSW 93*
Tassinari, Audrey Knight 1938- *St&PR 93*
Tassinari, Pia 1903-1990 *See* Tagliavini, Feruccio 1913- *OxDcOp*

Tassinari, Pia 1909- Baker 92
Tassinari, R. Peter Law&B 92
Tassinari, Silvio John 1922- WhoE 93
Tassios, P. Theodossius 1930- WhoScE 91-3
Tassis, Thomas R. 1946- St&PR 93
Tasso, Pierre Charif 1959- WhoWor 93
Tasso, Richard Michael 1925- St&PR 93
Tasso, Torquato 1544-1595 OxDcOp
Tassone, Bruce Anthony 1960- WhoE 93
Tassone, Gelsomina 1944- WhoAmW 93, WhoE 93
Tassone, Joseph V. Law&B 92
Tassopoulos, Stanton Kerry Law&B 92
Tassotti, Teresa 1957- WhoEmL 93
Tastan, Baki 1949- WhoScE 91-4
Taswell, Howard Filmore 1928- WhoAm 92
Tasy, Stephen P. Law&B 92
Tat, Peter Kiet 1947- WhoSSW 93
Tata, Anthony D. 1927- St&PR 93
Tata, Giovanni 1954- WhoWor 93
Tata, J.R.D. BioIn 17
Tata, Jahangir Ratanji Dadabhai 1904- See Tata family DcTwHis
Tata, Jamshed Rustom WhoScE 91-1
Tata family DcTwHis
Tatanene Manata 1946- WhoWor 93
Tatarczuk, Anthony J. 1947- St&PR 93
Tatarian, Hrach Roger 1916- WhoAm 92
Tatarinov, Leonid Petrovich 1926- WhoWor 93
Tatarinov, Yaroslav Vsevolodovich 1950- WhoWor 93
Tatarkiewicz, Krzysztof 1923- WhoScE 91-4
Tatarkiewicz, Wladyslaw 1886-1980 PolBiDi
Tataru, Emil 1937- WhoScE 91-4
Tatchell, Gerald Mark WhoScE 91-1
Tate, Allen 1899-1979 BioIn 17
Tate, Anne Wilson 1947- WhoAmW 93
Tate, Arthur William 1940- St&PR 93
Tate, Austin WhoScE 91-1
Tate, Barbara Louise 1921- WhoAmW 93
Tate, Carl Bob Starr 1932- WhoWrEP 92
Tate, David Henry 1929- WhoWor 93
Tate, David Kirk Law&B 92
Tate, Doris d1992 NewYTBS 92
Tate, Eleanora Elaine 1948- BlkAuII 92
Tate, Ellienne Todd 1940- WhoAmW 93
Tate, Ernest D. 1926- St&PR 93
Tate, Evelyn Ruth 1914- WhoAmW 93
Tate, Florence Louise 1931- WhoAmW 93
Tate, Fran M. 1929- WhoAmW 93
Tate, Frederick George 1925- WhoAm 92
Tate, Gene M. 1948- St&PR 93
Tate, Geoff See Queensryche ConMus 8
Tate, George Tony 1930- WhoSSW 93
Tate, Geraldine Williams 1954- WhoAmW 93
Tate, Grover Cleveland, Jr. 1922- WhoWrEP 92
Tate, Guy Morris, III 1944- St&PR 93
Tate, Harold Simmons, Jr. 1930- WhoAm 92
Tate, Howard 1943- SoulM
Tate, James 1943- WhoWrEP 92
Tate, James Donald 1951- St&PR 93
Tate, James Fletcher 1922- St&PR 93
Tate, Jeffrey 1943- Baker 92, WhoWor 93
Tate, Jeffrey S. 1957- WhoIns 93
Tate, Jo Anne 1949- WhoAmW 93
Tate, Jo Osborne WhoAmW 93, WhoE 93
Tate, John E. Law&B 92
Tate, John E. 1919- St&PR 93
Tate, Ken BioIn 17
Tate, Lawrence K. 1942- St&PR 93
Tate, Loretta Clara 1948- WhoE 93
Tate, Manford Ben 1916- WhoWor 93
Tate, Manley Sidney 1919- WhoSSW 93
Tate, Maybird Constance 1893-1947 BioIn 17
Tate, Michael Carter 1945- WhoAsAP 91
Tate, Michele L. Law&B 92
Tate, Paul 1954- WhoAm 92
Tate, Paul Hamilton 1951- St&PR 93, WhoAm 92
Tate, Peter ScF&FL 92
Tate, Peter J. 1946- St&PR 93
Tate, Phyllis (Margaret Duncan) 1911-1987 Baker 92
Tate, Richard ScF&FL 92
Tate, Robert J. Law&B 92
Tate, Robert L. 1924- St&PR 93
Tate, Sharon Sue 1949- WhoSSW 93
Tate, Sheila Burke 1942- WhoAm 92, WhoAmW 93, WhoE 93
Tate, Sherman E. 1945- St&PR 93
Tate, Shirley Ann 1943- WhoSSW 93
Tate, Stonewall Shepherd 1917- WhoAm 92
Tate, Thaddeus Wilbur, Jr. 1924- WhoAm 92, WhoSSW 93
Tatebe, Hiroko 1950- St&PR 93
Tateishi, Kazuo 1930- WhoUN 92
Tatekawa, Yoshitsugu 1880-1945 HarEnMi
Tatelbaum, Brenda Loew 1951- WhoWrEP 92
Tatelbaum, Shelley Grod 1950- WhoE 93
Tate-Nadeau, Alicia Ann 1964- WhoAmW 93
Tatera, James Frank 1946- WhoSSW 93
Taterka, Harvey B. 1931-1990 BioIn 17
Tateyama, Ichiro 1952- WhoWor 93
Tatgenhorst, Robert 1918- WhoAm 92
Tatham, Arthur Sydney WhoScE 91-1
Tatham, Charles Heathcote 1937- St&PR 93
Tatham, David 1932- ConAu 138
Tatham, David Frederic 1932- WhoAm 92
Tatham, Julie Campbell 1908- WhoAmW 93, WhoWor 93
Tatham, Marcel Andre Armand WhoScE 91-1
Tatham, Robert Haines 1943- WhoSSW 93
Tati, Jacques 1908-1982 MiSFD 9N, QDrFCA 92 [port]
Tatic, Budislav 1926- WhoScE 91-4
Tatikios fl. 1057-1099 OxDcByz
Tatistcheff, Alexis B. d1990 BioIn 17
Tatlin, Vladimir 1885-1953 ModArCr 3 [port]
Tatlock, Anne M. 1939- St&PR 93, WhoAm 92, WhoAmW 93
Tatlow, John Colin 1923- WhoWor 93
Tatlow, Marilyn Rose 1940- WhoWrEP 92
Tatlow, Michael Q. Law&B 92
Tatlow, Richard H., IV 1939- St&PR 93
Tatman, Richard W. 1943- St&PR 93
Tatoian, Phillip E. Law&B 92
Tatom, James Francis 1927- St&PR 93
Tatom, Kenneth Duke 1949- WhoSSW 93
Tatooles, Constantine John 1936- WhoAm 92
Tatos, Alexandru 1937-1990 DrEEuF
Tatoul, Warren Panosian 1932- WhoSSW 93
Tatrai, Gyorgy F.R. 1946- WhoScE 91-4
Tatro, Dwight W. 1950- St&PR 93
Tatro, Paul E. 1938- St&PR 93
Tatro, Peter Richard 1936- St&PR 93
Tatroe, Ruth AmWomPl
Tatrow, Lisa Gail 1960- WhoSSW 93
Tatsis, George Peter 1958- WhoSSW 93
Tatsumi, Naobumi 1845-1907 HarEnMi
Tatsumi, Takayuki 1955- WhoWor 93
Tatsuta, Kuniaki 1940- WhoWor 93
Tatsuta, Yoshinori 1951- WhoUN 92
Tatta, John Louis 1920- WhoAm 92
Tattan, Gertrude Casey 1899- WhoAmW 93
Tattembach, Cristian DcCPCAm
Tatter, Jordan Bradley 1937- St&PR 93
Tattersall, Alan Peter 1943- St&PR 93
Tattersall, Jill 1931- ScF&FL 92
Tattersall, Robert WhoScE 91-1
Tattersall, Robert Booth 1943- WhoWor 93
Tattersall, Viva AmWomPl
Tattersall, William James 1932- WhoAm 92
Tattersfield, Anne Elizabeth WhoScE 91-1
Tatti, Jacopo d'Antonio 1486-1570 BioIn 17
Tatum, Art 1910-1956 BioIn 17
Tatum, Art(hur) 1910-1956 Baker 92
Tatum, Beverly Daniel 1954- WhoAmW 93
Tatum, David 1953- St&PR 93
Tatum, David Rowe 1956- WhoSSW 93
Tatum, Deborah Elaine 1952- WhoAmW 93
Tatum, Donn Benjamin 1913- WhoAm 92
Tatum, Frank M., Jr. 1919- St&PR 93
Tatum, Grace Martinez 1960- NotHsAW 93
Tatum, H. Michael 1928- St&PR 93
Tatum, Hassoun BioIn 17
Tatum, Joe F. 1925- St&PR 93
Tatum, John Allen, Jr. 1936- St&PR 93
Tatum, John M. 1943- St&PR 93
Tatum, John Merl, Jr. 1951- St&PR 93
Tatum, Mary Lee d1991 BioIn 17
Tatum, Rita 1948- WhoAm 92
Tatum, Roger P. 1941- St&PR 93
Tatum, Stephen R. Law&B 92
Tatum, Thomas Walter 1937- St&PR 93
Tatyrek, Alfred Frank 1930- WhoE 93, WhoWor 93
Tatz, Paul H. 1935- St&PR 93
Tatzates fl. 8th cent.- OxDcByz
Taub, Catherine E. Law&B 92
Taub, Edward 1931- WhoSSW 93
Taub, Henry 1927- WhoAm 92
Taub, Jesse J. 1927- WhoAm 92
Taub, Kathy Sperling Law&B 92
Taub, Larry Steven 1952- WhoE 93
Taub, Melvin S. Law&B 92
Taub, Richard Paul 1937- WhoAm 92
Taub, Robert Allan 1923- WhoAm 92
Taub, Roy N. 1948- St&PR 93
Taub, Susan Jane 1956- WhoAmW 93
Taube, Adam A.S. 1932- WhoWor 93
Taube, Henry 1915- WhoAm 92, WhoWor 93
Taube, Lester S. 1920- WhoWrEP 92
Taube, Nicholas 1944- WhoIns 93
Taube, Thomas N. 1928- St&PR 93
Taubeneck, Ted D. 1926- St&PR 93
Taubenfeld, Harry Samuel 1929- WhoE 93
Tauber, Alfred Imre 1947- WhoAm 92
Tauber, David Mark 1959- WhoE 93
Tauber, Gregory John 1951- WhoE 93
Tauber, Henrik WhoScE 91-2
Tauber, Jack d1991 BioIn 17
Tauber, Joel David 1935- WhoAm 92
Tauber, Laura Jeanne 1958- WhoAmW 93
Tauber, Maurice Falcolm 1908-1980 BioIn 17
Tauber, Orner J., Jr. 1914- WhoAm 92
Tauber, Richard 1891-1948 Baker 92, IntDcOp
Tauber, Richard 1892-1948 BioIn 17, OxDcOp
Tauber, Ronald Steven 1944- WhoAm 92
Tauber, Thomas Ernst 1939- St&PR 93
Taubert, Frederick Wayne 1933- WhoAm 92
Taubert, (Carl Gottfried) Wilhelm 1811-1891 Baker 92
Taubin, Robin Livingston Law&B 92
Taubitz, Fredricka 1944- WhoAm 92, WhoWor 93
Taubman, A. Alfred BioIn 17, NewYTBS 92 [port]
Taubman, A. Alfred 1925- WhoAm 92
Taubman, Howard 1907- Baker 92
Taubman, Jane Andelman 1942- WhoAmW 93
Taubman, Joseph 1928- WhoSSW 93
Taubman, Martin Arnold 1940- WhoAm 92, WhoE 93
Taubman, Paul James 1939- WhoAm 92
Taubman, Robert S. 1953- WhoAm 92
Taubman, William Chase 1941- WhoAm 92
Taubmann, Otto 1859-1929 Baker 92
Taubner, Valentine J., III 1966- St&PR 93
Tauby, Diana Marie 1965- WhoAmW 93
Tauc, Jan 1922- WhoAm 92
Tauc, Ladislav 1926- WhoScE 91-2
Taucher, Curt 1885-1954 Baker 92
Tauchert, Patricia Annette Law&B 92
Tauchert, Theodore Richmond WhoAm 92, WhoSSW 93
Tauchid, Mohamad 1934- WhoUN 92
Taudou, Antoine (-Antonin-Barthelemy) 1846-1925 Baker 92
Tauer, John Anthony 1941- St&PR 93
Tauer, Paul E. 1941- WhoAm 92
Tauerbach, Sebastian d1553 PolBiDi
Taufa'ahau Tupou, IV, King of Tonga 1918- BioIn 17
Taufen, Lester J. Law&B 92
Taufiq, Farook 1940- WhoWor 93
Taugner, Gabriele 1931- WhoWor 93
Taujoo, Moussa 1945- WhoUN 92
Tauke, Beverly Hubble 1949- WhoWrEP 92
Tauke, Dale B. Law&B 92
Tauke, Regina Voelker 1938- WhoAmW 93, WhoE 93
Taulbee, Carl D. 1928- St&PR 93
Taulbee, John E. 1934- St&PR 93
Taulet, Francisco de Paula Rius y 1833-1889 BioIn 17
Tauman, Harvey Stephen 1941- St&PR 93
Taunton, Kathryn Jayne 1953- WhoAmW 93, WhoEmL 93, WhoWor 93
Taunton, Roma Lee WhoAmW 93
Taureau, Edgard 1948- St&PR 93
Taurel, Sidney A. 1949- St&PR 93
Taurel, Sidney Afriat 1949- WhoAm 92
Tauriainen, Juhani WhoScE 91-4
Tauriello, Antonio 1931- Baker 92
Tauro, Joseph Louis 1931- WhoAm 92, WhoE 93
Taurog, Norman 1899-1981 MiSFD 9N
Taus, Robert Leo 1938- WhoSSW 93
Tausch, Franz (Wilhelm) 1762-1817 Baker 92
Tausch, Gerry Margaret 1930- WhoWrEP 92
Tausch, Gilbert H. 1926- St&PR 93
Tausch, Julius 1827-1895 Baker 92
Tausch, Susan Diane 1955- WhoWrEP 92
Tausch, William Joseph 1930- St&PR 93
Tausche, Charles Anthony Law&B 92
Tauscher, Bernhard 1943- WhoScE 91-3
Tauscher, John Walter 1929- WhoAm 92
Tauscher, Walter M. 1939- WhoScE 91-4
Tausig, Aloys 1820-1885 See Tausig, Carl 1841-1871 Baker 92
Tausig, Carl 1841-1871 Baker 92
Tausik, David MiSFD 9
Tausinga, Job Dudley 1948- WhoAsAP 91
Tausinger, Jan 1921-1980 Baker 92
Tausk, Victor 1879-1919 BioIn 17
Taussig, Andrew Richard 1951- St&PR 93
Taussig, Eric A. Law&B 92
Taussig, Joseph Knefler, Jr. 1920- WhoAm 92
Taussky, Olga 1906- WhoAmW 93
Tautenhahn, Ulrich Michael 1951- WhoWor 93
Tauts, Ants 1936- WhoWor 93
Tautu, Petre 1927- WhoScE 91-3
Tauwitz, Eduard 1812-1894 Baker 92
Tauzin, W. J. 1943- CngDr 91
Tauzin, Wilbert J., II 1943- WhoAm 92, WhoSSW 93
Tauzovic, Branka 1946- WhoWor 93
Tavard, George H(enry) 1922- ConAu 37NR
Tavares SoulM
Tavares, Albert d1992 NewYTBS 92
Tavares, Antonio Raposo 1598-1659 Expl 93
Tavares, Hekel 1896-1969 Baker 92
Tavares, Joan Christine 1941- WhoAmW 93
Tavares, Joe F. 1952- St&PR 93
Tavares, Morton 1823-1900 BioIn 17
Tavares, Robert F. Law&B 92
Tavares, Robert F. 1936- St&PR 93
Tavares Sanchez, Manuel Enrique 1951- WhoWor 93
Tavassoli, Ali-Asghar 1944- WhoWor 93
Taveggia, Thomas Charles 1943- WhoAm 92
Tavel, Mark Kivey 1945- St&PR 93, WhoAm 92
Tavel, Morton Allen 1939- WhoAm 92
Tavel, Ronald 1968- WhoWrEP 92
Tavenas, Francois 1942- WhoAm 92
Tavener, John (Kenneth) 1944- Baker 92
Tavenner, R. Gaines Law&B 92
Tavens, Albert L. 1927- St&PR 93
Tavens, Lester 1931- St&PR 93
Taveras, Juan Manuel 1919- WhoAm 92
Taveras-Guzman, Juan Aristides 1936- WhoWor 93
Taverna, Darice Marie 1951- WhoAmW 93
Taverne, Dick 1928- St&PR 93
Taverner, John c. 1490-1545 Baker 92
Tavernier, Bertrand BioIn 17
Tavernier, Bertrand 1941- MiSFD 9
Tavernier, Bertrand Rene Maurice 1941- WhoWor 93
Tavernier, Hubert R. WhoWor 93
Taviani, Paolo 1931- MiSFD 9
Taviani, Vittorio 1929- MiSFD 9
Tavitian, Armand WhoScE 91-2
Tavkhelidze, Ilia 1955- WhoWor 93
Tavkov, Georgi Atanassov 1931- WhoScE 91-4
Tavlin, Michael J. 1946- St&PR 93
Tavoularis, Dean 1932- ConTFT 10
Tavris, Carol BioIn 17
Tavrow, Richard Lawrence 1935- St&PR 93, WhoAm 92
Taw, Dudley Joseph 1916- WhoAm 92
Tawa, Nicholas E. 1923- ConAu 136
Tawa, Nicholas Edward, Jr. 1956- WhoE 93
Tawara, Takashi 1925- WhoAsAP 91
Tawaststjerna, Erik (Werner) 1916- Baker 92
Tawfik, Ezzat Sarwat 1938- WhoScE 91-3
Tawfik, Sayed d1990 BioIn 17
Tawfiq al-Hakim 1898-1987 BioIn 17
Tawgin, John Shawn BioIn 17
Tawil, Henry 1942- St&PR 93
Tawil, Joseph E. 1913- WhoAm 92
Tawil, Moise 1934- St&PR 93
Tawney, Kenneth Eugene Law&B 92
Tawney, Lenore BioIn 17
Tawney, Richard Henry 1880-1962 DcTwHis
Tawpash, Christine McCauley 1959- WhoSSW 93
Tawpash, William Robert 1962- WhoSSW 93
Tax, L.J.W.M. 1937- WhoScE 91-3
Tax, Richard Loren 1945- WhoE 93
Tax, Sol 1907- BioIn 17, IntDcAn
Taxe, Howard A. 1953- St&PR 93
Taxerman, Alan R. Law&B 92
Taxis, Gloria Thurn und BioIn 17
Taxis, Johannes Thurn und BioIn 17
Tay, C.N. ScF&FL 92
Tay, Cephas Yao 1929- WhoWor 93
Tay, Kim Hui 1963- WhoSSW 93
Tay, Michael T. 1955- St&PR 93
Taya, Maaouya Ould Sid Ahmed 1943- WhoWor 93
Taya, Maawiya Ould Sid'Ahmed 1943- WhoAfr
Taya, Teizo 1945- WhoWor 93
Tayback, Vic 1929?-1990 BioIn 17
Tayler, Alan B. WhoScE 91-1
Tayler, David Leonard 1937- St&PR 93
Tayler, Irene ConAu 136
Tayler, John James 1797-1869 BioIn 17
Tayler, Roger John WhoScE 91-1
Taylert, Gertrude Ermatinger AmWomPl
Tayloe, David Thomas 1925- WhoSSW 93

Tayloe, Edward Dickinson, II 1942- *WhoSSW 93*
Tayloe, Margaret Howell 1926- *WhoAmW 93*
Taylor, A.J.P. 1906-1990 *BioIn 17*
Taylor, Abram D. d1991 *BioIn 17*
Taylor, Al 1949- *ScF&FL 92*
Taylor, Alan John Percivale 1906-1990 *BioIn 17*
Taylor, Alan R(os) 1926-1992 *ConAu 139*
Taylor, Alexander Clark *Law&B 92*
Taylor, Alexander Douglas 1931- *WhoWrEP 92*
Taylor, Alfred Hendricks, Jr. 1930- *WhoAm 92*
Taylor, Allan R. 1932- *St&PR 93*
Taylor, Allan Richard 1932- *BioIn 17, WhoAm 92*
Taylor, Allan Ross 1931- *WhoAm 92*
Taylor, Allegra 1940- *ConAu 136*
Taylor, Alton Lee 1936- *WhoSSW 93*
Taylor, Andrew (John Robert) 1951- *SmATA 70 [port]*
Taylor, Angus 1945- *ScF&FL 92*
Taylor, Anita Dopico 1940- *WhoAmW 93*
Taylor, Ann Louise 1937- *WhoAmW 93*
Taylor, Ann Siegrist 1953- *WhoAmW 93*
Taylor, Anna Diggs 1932- *WhoAm 92, WhoAmW 93*
Taylor, Anne *Law&B 92*
Taylor, Annie Royle 1855- *Expl 93*
Taylor, Anthony *WhoScE 91-1*
Taylor, Anthony George *WhoScE 91-1*
Taylor, Arthur G. *Law&B 92*
Taylor, Arthur H. 1960- *St&PR 93*
Taylor, Arthur Robert 1935- *WhoAm 92*
Taylor, Aubrey Elmo 1933- *WhoWor 93*
Taylor, Austin Randall 1954- *WhoSSW 93*
Taylor, Barbara Alden 1943- *WhoE 93*
Taylor, Barbara Ann 1944- *WhoE 93*
Taylor, Barbara Ann 1950- *WhoAmW 93*
Taylor, Barbara Anne *Law&B 92*
Taylor, Barbara Grace 1942- *WhoSSW 93*
Taylor, Barbara Jo Anne Harris 1936- *WhoAm 92, WhoAmW 93, WhoE 93, WhoWor 93*
Taylor, Barbara Luther *WhoSSW 93*
Taylor, Barbara Q. 1940- *St&PR 93*
Taylor, Barry 1945- *WhoE 93*
Taylor, Barry L. 1948- *WhoE 93*
Taylor, Barry Norman 1936- *WhoAm 92*
Taylor, Barry W. *Law&B 92*
Taylor, Bayard 1825-1878 *JrnUS*
Taylor, Baz *MiSFD 9*
Taylor, Becky Sue 1953- *WhoAmW 93*
Taylor, Benson Langdon 1954- *WhoWor 93*
Taylor, Bernard *BioIn 17*
Taylor, Bernard 1936- *ScF&FL 92*
Taylor, Bernard D. *St&PR 93*
Taylor, Bernard J., II 1925- *St&PR 93, WhoAm 92*
Taylor, Bert Leston 1866-1921 *JrnUS*
Taylor, Bettie *BioIn 17*
Taylor, Betty Jo 1933- *WhoAmW 93*
Taylor, Bev 1924- *St&PR 93*
Taylor, Beverly White 1947- *WhoSSW 93*
Taylor, Bill *BioIn 17*
Taylor, "Billy" 1921- *Baker 92, BioIn 17*
Taylor, Brian D. 1941- *St&PR 93*
Taylor, Brian James 1948- *WhoAm 92*
Taylor, Brian S. *Law&B 92*
Taylor, Brian William 1942- *WhoAm 92*
Taylor, Brien *BioIn 17*
Taylor, Bron Raymond 1955- *ConAu 138*
Taylor, Bruce *WhoCanL 92, WhoWrEP 92*
Taylor, Bruce Raymond 1945- *WhoE 93*
Taylor, Burton 1943-1991 *BioIn 17*
Taylor, Byron David 1943- *WhoSSW 93*
Taylor, Byron L. 1930- *St&PR 93*
Taylor, C. Harold d1992 *NewYTBS 92*
Taylor, C. Harold 1908-1992 *BioIn 17*
Taylor, Carl Ernest 1916- *WhoAm 92*
Taylor, Carl Larsen 1937- *WhoAm 92*
Taylor, Carol A. *Law&B 92*
Taylor, Carol Atkinson *BioIn 17*
Taylor, Carol J. 1942- *St&PR 93*
Taylor, Carole Ann 1958- *WhoAmW 93*
Taylor, Carole Jan Hudson 1949- *WhoAmW 93*
Taylor, Carson William 1942- *WhoAm 92*
Taylor, Catherine A. *Law&B 92*
Taylor, Cecil *BioIn 17*
Taylor, Cecil 1929?- *ConMus 9 [port]*
Taylor, Cecil (Percival) 1933- *Baker 92, WhoAm 92*
Taylor, Cedric *WhoScE 91-1*
Taylor, Celianna I. *WhoAm 92, WhoWor 93*
Taylor, Charles 1931- *BioIn 17*
Taylor, Charles 1948?- *CurBio 92 [port], WhoAfr*
Taylor, Charles Bruce 1949- *WhoWrEP 92*
Taylor, Charles D. 1938- *ScF&FL 92*
Taylor, Charles D(oonan) 1938- *ConAu 37NR*
Taylor, Charles Durwood 1946- *WhoEmL 93*
Taylor, Charles Edward *Law&B 92*
Taylor, Charles F. 1946- *St&PR 93*
Taylor, Charles F., Jr. 1948- *St&PR 93*
Taylor, Charles G. d1990 *BioIn 17*
Taylor, Charles George 1917- *WhoE 93*
Taylor, Charles H. 1846-1921 *JrnUS*
Taylor, Charles H. 1941- *CngDr 91, WhoAm 92, WhoSSW 93*
Taylor, Charles Henry 1928- *WhoAm 92*
Taylor, Charles Otto 1965- *WhoSSW 93*
Taylor, Charles R. 1941- *St&PR 93*
Taylor, Charles Richard 1939- *WhoAm 92*
Taylor, Charley *BioIn 17*
Taylor, Chris J. 1950-1979 *BiDAMSp 1989*
Taylor, Christie Crews 1952- *WhoSSW 93*
Taylor, Christopher Joseph 1950- *St&PR 93*
Taylor, Clarence Albert, Jr. 1950- *WhoSSW 93*
Taylor, Claude I. *St&PR 93*
Taylor, Claude I. 1925- *WhoAm 92*
Taylor, Claudia Ann 1946- *WhoAmW 93*
Taylor, Clifford 1923-1987 *Baker 92*
Taylor, Clyde Calvin, Jr. 1936- *WhoAm 92*
Taylor, Conciere Marlana 1950- *WhoWrEP 92*
Taylor, Cora 1936- *ScF&FL 92, WhoCanL 92*
Taylor, Cora Howarth Stewart 1868-1910 *BioIn 17*
Taylor, Cora Lorraine 1936- *BioIn 17, DcChlFi*
Taylor, Cynthia Roberts 1958- *WhoAmW 93*
Taylor, Cyril 1935- *WhoAm 92*
Taylor, Cyril J. H. 1935- *St&PR 93*
Taylor, D. Edgar 1958- *WhoSSW 93*
Taylor, D.H.C. 1938- *WhoScE 91-1*
Taylor, D.I. *WhoScE 91-1*
Taylor, D.J. *WhoScE 91-1*
Taylor, Dallas *BioIn 17*
Taylor, Dalmas Arnold 1933- *WhoAm 92*
Taylor, Dan *BioIn 17*
Taylor, Dan F. *St&PR 93*
Taylor, Dana M., Jr. *Law&B 92*
Taylor, Daniel J. 1906- *St&PR 93*
Taylor, Darl Coder 1913- *WhoAm 92*
Taylor, David 1934- *BioIn 17*
Taylor, David 1956- *WhoScE 91-3*
Taylor, David Alexander Harrison 1927- *WhoWor 93*
Taylor, David Brooke 1942- *WhoAm 92, WhoE 93, WhoWor 93*
Taylor, David Charles *WhoScE 91-1*
Taylor, David Cobb 1939- *WhoE 93*
Taylor, David George 1929- *WhoAm 92*
Taylor, David George Pendleton 1933- *WhoWor 93*
Taylor, David J. 1946- *WhoScE 91-1*
Taylor, David John 1943- *WhoE 93*
Taylor, David Kerr 1928- *WhoE 93*
Taylor, David Marshall 1927- *WhoScE 91-3*
Taylor, David Mathieson *WhoScE 91-1*
Taylor, David Peter 1934- *WhoUN 92*
Taylor, David R. 1946- *St&PR 93*
Taylor, David Wyatt Aiken 1925- *WhoAm 92*
Taylor, Deborah Lynn 1953- *WhoAmW 93*
Taylor, Debra Anne 1964- *WhoAmW 93*
Taylor, Deems 1885-1966 *OxDcOp*
Taylor, (Joseph) Deems 1885-1966 *Baker 92*
Taylor, Delores *ConAu 138*
Taylor, Dennis Lee, Sr. 1946- *WhoSSW 93*
Taylor, Derek *ScF&FL 92*
Taylor, Derek 1939- *WhoScE 91-1*
Taylor, Dermot Brownrigg 1915- *WhoAm 92*
Taylor, Doboy d1871 *BioIn 17*
Taylor, Domini 1929- *ScF&FL 92*
Taylor, Don 1920- *MiSFD 9*
Taylor, Don L. 1932- *St&PR 93*
Taylor, Donald Adams 1943- *WhoE 93*
Taylor, Donald Arthur 1923- *WhoAm 92*
Taylor, Donald D. 1932- *St&PR 93*
Taylor, Donald M. 1932- *St&PR 93*
Taylor, Donna Bloyd 1958- *WhoAmW 93*
Taylor, Doris Denice 1955- *WhoAmW 93*
Taylor, Dorothy Elizabeth 1961- *WhoAmW 93*
Taylor, Dorothy Harlow 1932- *St&PR 93*
Taylor, Dorothy Harris 1931- *WhoAmW 93, WhoE 93, WhoWor 93*
Taylor, Dorothy Jean 1950- *WhoWrEP 92*
Taylor, Douglas John *Law&B 92*
Taylor, Douglas L. *Law&B 92*
Taylor, Douglas Niall 1957- *WhoE 93*
Taylor, Duncan Paul 1949- *WhoE 93*
Taylor, E. Douglas 1941- *WhoAm 92*
Taylor, Edith *AmWomPl*
Taylor, Edmund Dryer 1920- *St&PR 93*
Taylor, Edmund Frederick 1960- *WhoE 93*
Taylor, Edna Jane 1934- *WhoAmW 93, WhoWor 93*
Taylor, Edward 1642-1729 *BioIn 17*
Taylor, Edward Curtis 1923- *WhoAm 92*
Taylor, Edward S. 1903-1991 *BioIn 17*
Taylor, Edward Stewart 1911- *WhoAm 92*
Taylor, Eldon Donivan 1929- *WhoAm 92*
Taylor, Elisabeth Coler 1942- *WhoAmW 93*
Taylor, Elisabeth D. *ScF&FL 92*
Taylor, Elisabeth Russell *ScF&FL 92*
Taylor, Elizabeth 1912-1975 *BioIn 17*
Taylor, Elizabeth 1932- *BioIn 17, IntDcF 2-3 [port], WhoAm 92, WhoAmW 93, WhoWor 93*
Taylor, Elizabeth Jane 1941- *WhoSSW 93*
Taylor, Ellen Borden Broadhurst 1913- *WhoAmW 93, WhoSSW 93, WhoWor 93*
Taylor, Elmer Louis, Jr. 1926- *St&PR 93*
Taylor, Ernest Lee 1949- *WhoSSW 93*
Taylor, Estelle Wormley 1924- *WhoAm 92*
Taylor, Ethel Mary Luevenia 1927- *WhoAmW 93*
Taylor, Eva Marietta *WhoWor 93*
Taylor, Foster Jay 1923- *WhoAm 92*
Taylor, Frank E. 1936- *WhoScE 91-1*
Taylor, Frank Eugene 1923- *WhoSSW 93*
Taylor, Frank Gordon 1940- *St&PR 93*
Taylor, Franklin 1843-1919 *Baker 92*
Taylor, Fred J. 1929- *St&PR 93*
Taylor, Frederick B. 1941- *St&PR 93*
Taylor, Frederick William, Jr. 1933- *WhoWor 93*
Taylor, Frederick Winslow 1856-1915 *BioIn 17*
Taylor, Fredric William *WhoScE 91-1*
Taylor, Frieda D. 1936- *WhoIns 93*
Taylor, G.J. 1944- *ScF&FL 92*
Taylor, Gail Richardson 1949- *WhoEmL 93*
Taylor, Gary *BioIn 17*
Taylor, Gary G. *Law&B 92*
Taylor, Gary G. 1946- *St&PR 93*
Taylor, Gary Lynn 1940- *WhoSSW 93*
Taylor, Gary R. *Law&B 92*
Taylor, Gayland Wayne 1958- *WhoEmL 93*
Taylor, Gayle Rogers 1964- *WhoAmW 93*
Taylor, Gene 1953- *CngDr 91, WhoAm 92, WhoSSW 93*
Taylor, Geoff *ScF&FL 92*
Taylor, George 1904- *WhoWor 93*
Taylor, George Allen 1906- *WhoAm 92*
Taylor, George F. 1932- *St&PR 93*
Taylor, George Frederick 1928- *WhoAm 92*
Taylor, George H. 1943- *St&PR 93*
Taylor, George Kimbrough, Jr. 1939- *WhoAm 92*
Taylor, George S. *Law&B 92*
Taylor, George Simpson 1940- *St&PR 93*
Taylor, George William 1934- *WhoWor 93*
Taylor, Gerald L. 1935- *WhoAm 92*
Taylor, Gerald R. 1940- *St&PR 93*
Taylor, Gladstone Van 1929- *WhoWor 93*
Taylor, Glenhall E. 1925- *WhoAm 92*
Taylor, Gloria J. 1955- *WhoAmW 93*
Taylor, Grace Elizabeth Woodall 1926- *WhoAmW 93*
Taylor, Graham Roy *WhoScE 91-1*
Taylor, Greg *Law&B 92*
Taylor, Gregory *Law&B 92, WhoAm 92*
Taylor, Gregory Lee 1951- *St&PR 93*
Taylor, Grover Durwood 1937- *WhoSSW 93*
Taylor, Guy E. 1914- *St&PR 93*
Taylor, Guy Watson 1919- *WhoAm 92*
Taylor, Harold 1914- *WhoAm 92*
Taylor, Harold Allen, Jr. 1936- *WhoE 93, WhoWor 93*
Taylor, Harold Evans 1939- *WhoE 93*
Taylor, Harry Danner 1944- *St&PR 93*
Taylor, Harry William 1925- *WhoAm 92*
Taylor, Hays *BioIn 17*
Taylor, Helen Louise 1908- *AmWomPl*
Taylor, Henry 1942- *BioIn 17*
Taylor, Henry L. 1952- *St&PR 93*
Taylor, Henry Merle, Jr. 1928- *WhoSSW 93*
Taylor, Henry Roth 1940- *WhoE 93*
Taylor, Henry Splawn 1942- *WhoAm 92, WhoWrEP 92*
Taylor, Herbert H. 1920- *St&PR 93*
Taylor, Herbert John 1893-1978 *BioIn 17*
Taylor, Hershel L. 1914- *St&PR 93*
Taylor, Hobart, Jr. 1920-1981 *EncAACR*
Taylor, Hollis 1935- *St&PR 93*
Taylor, Howard Francis 1939- *WhoAm 92*
Taylor, Howard R. 1923- *St&PR 93*
Taylor, Hubert C. 1937-1991 *BioIn 17*
Taylor, Hugh M. 1944- *WhoAm 92*
Taylor, Hugh Pettingill, Jr. 1932- *WhoAm 92*
Taylor, Hugh Ringland 1947- *WhoWor 93*
Taylor, Humphrey John Fausitt 1934- *WhoE 93*
Taylor, Ian Keith 1943- *WhoWor 93*
Taylor, Ida Scott *AmWomPl*
Taylor, Ira Mooney 1935- *WhoSSW 93*
Taylor, Irving *WhoScE 91-1*
Taylor, Irving J. 1919- *St&PR 93*
Taylor, Isidore-Justin-Severin 1789-1879 *BioIn 17*
Taylor, J. Allyn 1907- *St&PR 93*
Taylor, J. F. Reeh 1924- *St&PR 93*
Taylor, Jack Arthur 1935- *WhoSSW 93*
Taylor, Jackson, Jr. 1938- *WhoSSW 93*
Taylor, Jacqueline Self 1935- *WhoAmW 93*
Taylor, James, Jr. 1942- *WhoAm 92*
Taylor, James Allan *WhoScE 91-1*
Taylor, James B. 1938- *St&PR 93*
Taylor, James C. 1938- *WhoWor 93*
Taylor, James Clagett, Jr. 1935- *WhoSSW 93*
Taylor, James D., Jr. 1910- *St&PR 93*
Taylor, James Daniel 1928- *WhoSSW 93*
Taylor, James Daniel 1941- *WhoE 93*
Taylor, James E. *Law&B 92*
Taylor, James F., Jr. 1944- *WhoAm 92*
Taylor, James Felton 1961- *WhoSSW 93*
Taylor, James Francis 1951- *WhoSSW 93*
Taylor, James Harry, II 1951- *WhoWor 93*
Taylor, James Herbert 1916- *WhoAm 92*
Taylor, James Hugh *Law&B 92*
Taylor, James Hugh 1940- *WhoE 93*
Taylor, James Hutchings 1930- *WhoAm 92*
Taylor, James I. *WhoIns 93*
Taylor, James I. 1939- *St&PR 93*
Taylor, James Irwin 1938- *WhoSSW 93*
Taylor, James John 1940- *WhoSSW 93*
Taylor, James Marion, II 1926- *St&PR 93*
Taylor, James Marshall 1929- *WhoAm 92*
Taylor, James Robert, III 1950- *WhoWrEP 92*
Taylor, James (Vernon) 1948- *Baker 92, WhoAm 92*
Taylor, James W. 1918- *St&PR 93*
Taylor, James Wagner 1925- *St&PR 93*
Taylor, Jane Frances *Law&B 92*
Taylor, Janelle 1944- *ScF&FL 92*
Taylor, Janelle Diane Williams 1944- *WhoAm 92, WhoSSW 93*
Taylor, Jayne *ConAu 139*
Taylor, Jean *St&PR 93*
Taylor, Jeffrey W. *BioIn 17*
Taylor, Jenny 1949- *ScF&FL 92*
Taylor, Jeremy F. 1952- *ConAu 137*
Taylor, Jeri 1946?- *ScF&FL 92*
Taylor, Jerry Duncan 1938- *WhoSSW 93*
Taylor, Jerry Lynn 1947- *WhoAmW 93*
Taylor, Jesse, Jr. *Law&B 92*
Taylor, Jim *WhoScE 91-1*
Taylor, Jim 1852-1875 *BioIn 17*
Taylor, Jim 1935- *BioIn 17*
Taylor, Jimmie Wilkes 1934- *WhoAm 92*
Taylor, Joan *SweetSg D*
Taylor, Joan Leslie *BioIn 17*
Taylor, Joanne Carol 1945- *WhoAmW 93*
Taylor, Job, III 1942- *WhoAm 92*
Taylor, Jocelyn Mary 1931- *WhoAm 92, WhoAmW 93*
Taylor, Joe Clinton 1942- *WhoAm 92*
Taylor, John 1577?-1653 *DcLB 121 [port]*
Taylor, John 1770-1832 *BioIn 17*
Taylor, John A. *Law&B 92*
Taylor, John Andrew 1953- *WhoE 93*
Taylor, John Chestnut, III 1928- *WhoAm 92*
Taylor, John Clayton *WhoScE 91-1*
Taylor, John Earl 1935- *WhoSSW 93*
Taylor, John Gerald *WhoScE 91-1*
Taylor, John H(ilton) 1958- *ConAu 138*
Taylor, John Jackson 1931- *WhoAm 92*
Taylor, John Joseph 1922- *WhoAm 92*
Taylor, John Lee, Jr. 1954- *WhoAm 92*
Taylor, John Lockhart 1927- *WhoAm 92*
Taylor, John Michael 1943- *WhoScE 91-1*
Taylor, John N. *St&PR 93*
Taylor, John R. *Law&B 92*
Taylor, John Randolph 1929- *WhoAm 92*
Taylor, John Richard 1945- *WhoWor 93*
Taylor, John Robert *SmATA 70*
Taylor, John Robert 1952- *WhoWrEP 92*
Taylor, John Russell 1935- *ConAu 37NR, WhoWor 93*
Taylor, John W. 1784-1854 *PolPar*
Taylor, John Wilkinson 1906- *WhoAm 92, WhoWor 93*
Taylor, John William Ransom 1922- *WhoWor 93*
Taylor, Johnnie 1938- *SoulM*
Taylor, Jonathan Francis 1935- *WhoAm 92*
Taylor, Joseph Hooton, Jr. 1941- *WhoAm 92*
Taylor, Joseph William 1953- *WhoSSW 93*
Taylor, Joyce G. *BioIn 17*
Taylor, Joycelynn W. 1931- *St&PR 93*
Taylor, Jud 1940- *MiSFD 9*
Taylor, Judith Anne 1937- *WhoAmW 93, WhoE 93*

Taylor, Judy 1932- *BioIn 17*
Taylor, Judy 1935- *BioIn 17*
Taylor, Julia W. *WhoAm 92, WhoAmW 93*
Taylor, Julia Yvonne 1955- *WhoAmW 93*
Taylor, Julian Howard 1943- *WhoAm 92*
Taylor, Karen Sue 1942- *WhoSSW 93*
Taylor, Katharine *AmWomPl*
Taylor, Katharine Haviland 1888- *AmWomPl*
Taylor, Kathleen Christine 1942- *WhoAm 92*
Taylor, Kathleen Mary 1964- *WhoAmW 93*
Taylor, Kathleen P. *Law&B 92*
Taylor, Kathryn Evans 1929- *WhoAmW 93*
Taylor, Kathy Lane 1951- *WhoSSW 93*
Taylor, Keith 1946- *ScF&FL 92*
Taylor, Keith 1952- *WhoWrEP 92*
Taylor, Keith Breden 1924- *WhoAm 92*
Taylor, Keith David Anthony *WhoScE 91-1*
Taylor, Keith William *WhoScE 91-1*
Taylor, Kendra Clair 1963- *WhoE 93*
Taylor, Kendrick Jay 1914- *WhoWor 93*
Taylor, Kenneth Boivin 1935- *WhoSSW 93*
Taylor, Kenneth D. *BioIn 17*
Taylor, Kenneth Douglas 1942- *WhoE 93*
Taylor, Kenneth Doyle 1949- *WhoE 93*
Taylor, Kenneth Grant 1936- *WhoAm 92, WhoSSW 93*
Taylor, Kenneth John W. 1939- *WhoAm 92*
Taylor, Kenneth M., Jr. *Law&B 92*
Taylor, Kenneth Macdonald 1947- *WhoWor 93*
Taylor, Kenneth Nathaniel *BioIn 17*
Taylor, Kenneth Nathaniel 1917- *WhoAm 92*
Taylor, Kenneth R. 1929- *St&PR 93*
Taylor, Kent 1907-1987 *BioIn 17*
Taylor, Kent Gregory 1941- *WhoE 93*
Taylor, (Paul) Kent 1940- *WhoWrEP 92*
Taylor, Kristin Clark *AfrAmBi, BioIn 17*
Taylor, Kristin Clark 1959- *WhoAmW 93, WhoEmL 93*
Taylor, L. *WhoScE 91-1*
Taylor, L.A. 1939- *ScF&FL 92*
Taylor, L. Kay 1939- *WhoAmW 93*
Taylor, Lance *BioIn 17*
Taylor, Lance Jerome 1940- *WhoAm 92*
Taylor, Larissa J(uliet) 1952- *ConAu 138*
Taylor, Larry Phillip 1948- *WhoSSW 93, WhoWor 93*
Taylor, Laura Marie *WhoSSW 93*
Taylor, Laurette 1884-1946 *AmWomPl*
Taylor, Lauriston Sale 1902- *WhoAm 92*
Taylor, Lawrence *BioIn 17*
Taylor, Lawrence 1959- *WhoAm 92*
Taylor, Lawrence Jay d1991 *BioIn 17*
Taylor, Leah Cathy *Law&B 92*
Taylor, Leigh Herbert 1941- *WhoAm 92*
Taylor, Leila *AmWomPl*
Taylor, Leonard Bernard 1955- *WhoE 93*
Taylor, Leonard M. *Law&B 92*
Taylor, Leonard Stuart 1928- *WhoAm 92*
Taylor, Lesli Ann 1953- *WhoAmW 93*
Taylor, Leslie G. 1922- *St&PR 93*
Taylor, Leslie George 1922- *WhoWor 93*
Taylor, Lili *BioIn 17*
Taylor, Linda Marianne 1948- *WhoAmW 93, WhoSSW 93*
Taylor, Linda Rathbun 1946- *WhoAmW 93*
Taylor, Linda Scott *Law&B 92*
Taylor, Lindsay David, Jr. 1945- *WhoAm 92*
Taylor, Lisa 1933-1991 *BioIn 17*
Taylor, Lisa 1959- *ScF&FL 92*
Taylor, Lottie *BioIn 17*
Taylor, Louis *Law&B 92*
Taylor, Louise Todd 1939- *WhoSSW 93*
Taylor, Lowell 1958- *WhoE 93*
Taylor, Lucille Ann 1949- *WhoSSW 93*
Taylor, Lucy 1950?- *ScF&FL 92*
Taylor, Lyle Dewey 1934- *WhoAm 92*
Taylor, Marcella Bernadette 1933- *WhoAmW 93*
Taylor, Margaret Alexander 1926- *WhoAmW 93*
Taylor, Margaret Lee 1949- *WhoAmW 93*
Taylor, Margaret Smith 1788-1852 *BioIn 17*
Taylor, Margaret Turner 1944- *WhoAmW 93, WhoE 93*
Taylor, Margaret Uhrich 1952- *WhoEmL 93*
Taylor, Margaret W. 1920- *WhoAmW 93, WhoWor 93*
Taylor, Marian Celia 1948- *WhoAmW 93*
Taylor, Marilyn *BioIn 17*
Taylor, Mark Alan 1955- *WhoWor 93*
Taylor, Mark Alan 1959- *WhoWor 93*
Taylor, Mark David 1964- *WhoSSW 93*
Taylor, Mark Douglas 1951- *WhoAm 92*
Taylor, Marsha Lu 1956- *WhoAmW 93*
Taylor, Martha Sue 1947- *WhoAmW 93*
Taylor, Martin John *WhoScE 91-1*
Taylor, Marvin H. *Law&B 92*
Taylor, Marvin P. 1921- *St&PR 93*
Taylor, Mary Ann 1937- *WhoAmW 93*
Taylor, Mary Beth *Law&B 92*
Taylor, Mary D. 1936- *WhoAmW 93, WhoWor 93*
Taylor, Mary Elizabeth 1933- *WhoAmW 93*
Taylor, Mary G. *AmWomPl*
Taylor, Mary Kathryn 1963- *WhoAmW 93*
Taylor, Mary Lou *BioIn 17*
Taylor, Maryann Courtney 1948- *WhoE 93*
Taylor, Maurice D. 1927- *St&PR 93*
Taylor, Maurice Derrick 1927- *WhoAm 92*
Taylor, Maxwell 1945- *WhoScE 91-3*
Taylor, Maxwell D. 1901-1987 *BioIn 17, ColdWar 1 [port]*
Taylor, Maxwell Davenport 1901-1987 *CmdGen 1991 [port], HarEnMi*
Taylor, Melisa Bell 1960- *St&PR 93*
Taylor, Merle E. 1939- *St&PR 93*
Taylor, Merrily Ellen 1945- *WhoAm 92*
Taylor, Meshach *WhoAm 92*
Taylor, Meshach 1947?- *ConBlB 4 [port]*
Taylor, Michael *BioIn 17*
Taylor, Michael Alan 1940- *WhoAm 92*
Taylor, Michael Graeme *WhoScE 91-1*
Taylor, Michael L. 1944- *St&PR 93*
Taylor, Michelle M. 1945- *WhoAmW 93*
Taylor, Michelle Witteman *BioIn 17*
Taylor, Mick *BioIn 17*
Taylor, Mildred D. *DcAmChF 1960, DcAmChF 1985, WhoAm 92*
Taylor, Mildred D. 1943- *Au&Arts 10 [port], BlkAuII 92, MajAI [port], SmATA 70 [port]*
Taylor, Mildred Juanita 1947- *WhoAmW 93*
Taylor, Millard Benjamin 1913- *WhoAm 92*
Taylor, Mimi Veres 1929- *WhoAmW 93*
Taylor, Morris 1956- *WhoWrEP 92*
Taylor, Morris Anthony 1922- *WhoWor 93*
Taylor, Nancy Allene 1950- *WhoAm 92*
Taylor, Nancy M. *Law&B 92*
Taylor, Nathaniel W. 1786-1858 *BioIn 17*
Taylor, Nellie Rosilla *AmWomPl*
Taylor, Nicholas C. 1937- *St&PR 93*
Taylor, Noel C. 1924- *WhoAm 92, WhoSSW 93*
Taylor, Norman Floyd 1932- *WhoAm 92*
Taylor, Norman William 1923- *WhoAm 92*
Taylor, Norton Warren 1922- *St&PR 93*
Taylor, Oliver B. 1931- *St&PR 93*
Taylor, P(hilip) A. M. 1920- *ConAu 136*
Taylor, Pamela Lynn 1954- *WhoAmW 93*
Taylor, Pat Ellis 1941- *BioIn 17*
Taylor, Patricia Elsie 1929- *WhoE 93*
Taylor, Patricia Jane 1946- *WhoAmW 93*
Taylor, Patrick *BioIn 17*
Taylor, Patrick Joseph Donald 1962- *WhoSSW 93*
Taylor, Patrick Robinson 1927- *WhoSSW 93*
Taylor, Paul d1992 *NewYTBS 92*
Taylor, Paul 1930- *BioIn 17, News 92 [port], -92-3 [port], WhoAm 92, WhoWor 93*
Taylor, Paul 1958- *WhoE 93*
Taylor, Paul Albert 1943- *WhoAm 92*
Taylor, Paul Daniel 1939- *WhoAm 92, WhoWor 93*
Taylor, Paul Dennis *Law&B 92*
Taylor, Paul Franklin 1946- *WhoSSW 93*
Taylor, Paul Graham 1962- *St&PR 93*
Taylor, Paul Howard 1916- *WhoE 93*
Taylor, Paul J. 1946- *WhoWrEP 92*
Taylor, Paul Michael *WhoScE 91-1*
Taylor, Pauline Elizabeth 1948- *St&PR 93*
Taylor, Perry L., Jr. *Law&B 92*
Taylor, Peter 1917- *ConLC 71 [port], ShSCr 10 [port]*
Taylor, Peter Hillsman 1917- *BioIn 17, WhoWrEP 92*
Taylor, Peter James 1947- *WhoWor 93*
Taylor, Peter Matthew Hillsman 1917- *WhoAm 92*
Taylor, Peter van Voorhees 1934- *WhoWor 93*
Taylor, Peter William Edward 1917- *WhoWor 93*
Taylor, Peyton Troy, Jr. 1941- *WhoAm 92*
Taylor, Phil *BioIn 17*
Taylor, Philip Liddon 1937- *WhoAm 92*
Taylor, Philip R. 1946- *St&PR 93*
Taylor, Phyllis Johnstone 1933- *WhoAmW 93*
Taylor, R.G. *ScF&FL 92*
Taylor, R. Jeffrey 1949- *WhoSSW 93*
Taylor, R.L., II 1941- *St&PR 93*
Taylor, R. Lee, II 1941- *WhoAm 92*
Taylor, Ralph C. 1941- *St&PR 93*
Taylor, Ralph Orien, Jr. 1919- *WhoWor 93*
Taylor, Ramona G. 1930- *St&PR 93*
Taylor, Ramona Garrett 1930- *WhoAm 92*
Taylor, Raynor 1747-1825 *Baker 92*
Taylor, Reese Hale, Jr. 1928- *WhoAm 92*
Taylor, Reeves Ramsey 1929- *WhoSSW 93*
Taylor, Reginald Keith *Law&B 92*
Taylor, Renee 1945- *MiSFD 9*
Taylor, Rhoda Evans 1936- *WhoE 93*
Taylor, Richard 1826-1879 *HarEnMi*
Taylor, Richard 1919- *WhoAm 92, WhoWrEP 92*
Taylor, Richard Bertrom 1951- *WhoSSW 93*
Taylor, Richard Breckinridge 1930- *St&PR 93*
Taylor, Richard Dean 1935- *WhoWor 93*
Taylor, Richard Edward 1929- *BioIn 17, WhoAm 92*
Taylor, Richard Edward 1930- *WhoWor 93*
Taylor, Richard Fred, Jr. 1933- *WhoAm 92, WhoWor 93*
Taylor, Richard James *Law&B 92*
Taylor, Richard K(night) 1933- *ConAu 39NR*
Taylor, Richard L. 1944- *St&PR 93*
Taylor, Richard Powell 1928- *WhoAm 92, WhoE 93, WhoWor 93*
Taylor, Richard S(helley) 1912- *ConAu 38NR*
Taylor, Richard Trelore 1917- *WhoAm 92*
Taylor, Richard W. 1926- *St&PR 93*
Taylor, Richard William 1926- *WhoAm 92*
Taylor, Richard Wirth 1923- *WhoAm 92*
Taylor, Rick Joseph 1956- *WhoEmL 93*
Taylor, Robbins 1925- *St&PR 93*
Taylor, Robbins 1956- *St&PR 93*
Taylor, Robert *MiSFD 9*
Taylor, Robert 1911-1969 *BioIn 17, IntDcF 2-3*
Taylor, Robert A. *Law&B 92*
Taylor, Robert Bannatyne *WhoScE 91-1*
Taylor, Robert Brown 1936- *WhoAm 92*
Taylor, Robert Clark *Law&B 92*
Taylor, Robert D. *St&PR 93*
Taylor, Robert Edward 1931- *WhoSSW 93*
Taylor, Robert G. 1943- *St&PR 93*
Taylor, Robert K. 1928- *St&PR 93*
Taylor, Robert L. 1949- *St&PR 93*
Taylor, Robert Lee 1944- *WhoAm 92*
Taylor, Robert Lewis 1912- *WhoWrEP 92*
Taylor, Robert Lewis 1934- *WhoSSW 93*
Taylor, Robert Lewis 1939- *WhoAm 92*
Taylor, Robert Louis *Law&B 92*
Taylor, Robert Love, Jr. 1941- *WhoWrEP 92*
Taylor, Robert M. 1942- *St&PR 93*
Taylor, Robert Mark 1960- *WhoSSW 93*
Taylor, Robert Morgan 1941- *WhoAm 92*
Taylor, Robert Pendleton 1951- *WhoSSW 93*
Taylor, Robert Sundling 1925- *WhoAm 92*
Taylor, Robert T. d1992 *BioIn 17, NewYTBS 92*
Taylor, Robert U. 1941- *ConTFT 10*
Taylor, Robert Wayne 1946- *WhoE 93*
Taylor, Robert William 1929- *WhoAm 92*
Taylor, Robert William 1932- *WhoAm 92*
Taylor, Robin *WhoScE 91-1*
Taylor, Robin 1951- *WhoWor 93*
Taylor, Rod 1930- *WhoAm 92*
Taylor, Roderick *MiSFD 9*
Taylor, Roger *ScF&FL 92*
Taylor, Roger Conant 1931- *WhoAm 92*
Taylor, Roger K. 1948- *St&PR 93*
Taylor, Romey A. 1934- *St&PR 93*
Taylor, Ronald *Law&B 92*
Taylor, Ronald L. *St&PR 93*
Taylor, Ronald Lloyd *Law&B 92*
Taylor, Ronald Wentworth *WhoScE 91-1*
Taylor, Rosemary *WhoAmW 93, WhoE 93*
Taylor, Ross Jenkins *WhoScE 91-1*
Taylor, Roy G. 1918- *WhoWrEP 92*
Taylor, Roy Lewis 1932- *WhoAm 92*
Taylor, Royston James 1946- *WhoScE 91-1*
Taylor, Samuel A. L., Jr. 1935- *St&PR 93*
Taylor, Samuel Albert 1912- *WhoAm 92*
Taylor, Samuel Edwin 1941- *WhoSSW 93*
Taylor, Samuel J. 1939- *St&PR 93*
Taylor, Samuel James 1929- *WhoAm 92*
Taylor, Scott *BioIn 17*
Taylor, Scott Maxfield 1953- *St&PR 93, WhoEmL 93*
Taylor, Shahane Richardson, Jr. 1928- *WhoSSW 93, WhoWor 93*
Taylor, Sheila Ortiz 1939- *ScF&FL 92*
Taylor, Sherril Wightman 1924- *WhoAm 92*
Taylor, Stanford E. 1927- *St&PR 93*
Taylor, Stanley Gabriel 1942- *WhoUN 92*
Taylor, Stephen Craig 1954- *WhoE 93*
Taylor, Stephen John 1954- *WhoSSW 93*
Taylor, Steve *BioIn 17*
Taylor, Steve Henry 1947- *WhoAm 92*
Taylor, Steven B. 1943- *St&PR 93*
Taylor, Steven James 1946- *WhoSSW 93*
Taylor, Stuart Symington 1913- *WhoAm 92*
Taylor, Susan Elizabeth 1966- *WhoAmW 93*
Taylor, Susan Kay 1962- *WhoAmW 93*
Taylor, Susan Merril 1947- *WhoEmL 93*
Taylor, Susanne 1953- *WhoAmW 93*
Taylor, Sybil 1933- *ScF&FL 92*
Taylor, Sydney (Brenner) 1904-1978 *MajAI [port]*
Taylor, Sylvia Pindle *WhoAmW 93*
Taylor, T(homas) F(is) 1913- *ConAu 136*
Taylor, Tad Michael *Law&B 92*
Taylor, Ted *SoulM*
Taylor, Ted 1934-1987 *BioIn 17*
Taylor, Telford 1908- *BioIn 17, WhoAm 92, WhoWrEP 92*
Taylor, Terrie Lynn 1962- *WhoAmW 93*
Taylor, Theadoll Peace 1938- *WhoWor 93*
Taylor, Theodore 1921- *ConAu 38NR, DcAmChF 1960, MajAI [port]*
Taylor, Theodore Brewster 1925- *WhoAm 92*
Taylor, Theodore Langhans *WhoWrEP 92*
Taylor, Theodore Langhans 1921- *WhoAm 92*
Taylor, Thomas A. 1942- *St&PR 93*
Taylor, Thomas Alexander, III 1930- *WhoAm 92, WhoSSW 93*
Taylor, Thomas Alfred 1942- *WhoIns 93*
Taylor, Thomas E. *Law&B 92*
Taylor, Thomas Edward *Law&B 92*
Taylor, Thomas Edward 1946- *St&PR 93*
Taylor, Thomas Franklin 1951- *St&PR 93*
Taylor, Thomas Fuller 1937- *WhoWor 93*
Taylor, Thomas H., Jr. 1935- *St&PR 93*
Taylor, Thomas Hewitt, Jr. 1935- *WhoAm 92*
Taylor, Thomas Hudson, Jr. 1920- *WhoSSW 93, WhoWor 93*
Taylor, Thomas L. *St&PR 93*
Taylor, Thomas Perry 1958- *St&PR 93*
Taylor, Thomas Roger 1945- *WhoWor 93*
Taylor, Tim d1992 *NewYTBS 92*
Taylor, Timothy Gilbert 1951- *WhoSSW 93*
Taylor, Timothy Lee 1960- *WhoSSW 93*
Taylor, Van Aaron 1956- *WhoE 93*
Taylor, Vernon F., III 1947- *St&PR 93*
Taylor, Volney 1939- *St&PR 93, WhoAm 92, WhoE 93*
Taylor, Walker C. *Law&B 92*
Taylor, Warren Fredrick 1925- *St&PR 93*
Taylor, Warren Justin 1921- *WhoE 93*
Taylor, Watson Robbins 1925- *St&PR 93*
Taylor, Watson Robbins, Jr. 1956- *WhoSSW 93*
Taylor, Wayne F. *Law&B 92*
Taylor, Wayne F. 1943- *St&PR 93*
Taylor, Wayne Fletcher 1943- *WhoAm 92*
Taylor, William *BioIn 17, DcChlFi, WhoAm 92*
Taylor, William d1992 *NewYTBS 92 [port]*
Taylor, William 1939- *St&PR 93, WhoAm 92*
Taylor, William A., Jr. 1931- *St&PR 93*
Taylor, William Al 1938- *WhoSSW 93, WhoWor 93*
Taylor, William Brooks, II 1910- *WhoAm 92*
Taylor, William Davis 1908- *St&PR 93, WhoAm 92*
Taylor, William Desmond 1877-1922 *BioIn 17, MiSFD 9N*
Taylor, William Douglas 1948- *WhoSSW 93*
Taylor, William E. *Law&B 92*
Taylor, William Edward 1921- *BioIn 17*
Taylor, William F. *Law&B 92*
Taylor, William J. 1951- *St&PR 93*
Taylor, William James 1948- *WhoAm 92*
Taylor, William Jape 1924- *WhoAm 92*
Taylor, William Jesse, Jr. 1933- *WhoAm 92, WhoWor 93*
Taylor, William M. 1944- *St&PR 93*
Taylor, William Menke, Jr. 1946- *WhoEmL 93*
Taylor, William Michael 1944- *WhoAm 92*
Taylor, William O. 1932- *St&PR 93*
Taylor, William Osgood 1932- *WhoAm 92, WhoE 93*
Taylor, William R(obert) 1922- *ConAu 138*
Taylor, William Randolph 1895-1990 *BioIn 17*
Taylor, William S. 1938- *St&PR 93*
Taylor, William W. 1951- *St&PR 93*
Taylor, Wilma Best 1953- *St&PR 93*
Taylor, Wilson H. *WhoAm 92*
Taylor, Wilson H. 1943- *St&PR 93*
Taylor, Winfield d1992 *BioIn 17*

Taylor, Yvette E. *Law&B 92*
Taylor, Zachary 1784-1850 *BioIn 17, HarEnMi, PolPar*
Taylor, Zachary L. 1954- *St&PR 93*
Taylor-Clarke, Anna-Marie 1960- *WhoAmW 93*
Taylor Claud, Andrea 1952- *WhoAmW 93*
Taylor-Hunt, Mary Bernis Buchanan 1904- *WhoAmW 93*
Taylor-Ide, Daniel Carl 1945- *WhoSSW 93*
Taylor-Little, Carol Joyce 1941- *WhoAmW 93*
Taylor-Papadimitriou, Joyce 1932- *WhoScE 91-1*
Taylor-Payne, Mary Lee 1931- *WhoSSW 93*
Taylor Smith, Denzil *WhoScE 91-1*
Taymor, Julie *BioIn 17*
Tayoun, Gaby Barbar 1958- *WhoWor 93*
Tazawa, Kichiro 1918- *WhoAsAP 91*
Tazawa, Tomoharu 1932- *WhoAsAP 91*
Tazewell, Calvert Walke 1917- *WhoWor 93*
Tazi-Mokha, Abdelali 1948- *WhoUN 92*
Tazi Riffi, Abdelkhalek 1939- *WhoUN 92*
Tazkarji, Mohd Mounir 1936- *WhoWor 93*
Tazzari, S. *WhoScE 91-3*
Tchaban, Anatoli Sergey 1941- *WhoUN 92*
Tchaikovsky, Boris (Alexandrovich) 1925- *Baker 92*
Tchaikovsky, Modest 1850-1916 *Baker 92*
Tchaikovsky, Peter Ilich 1840-1893 *BioIn 17*
Tchaikovsky, Piotr Ilyich 1840-1893 *Baker 92, IntDcOp [port]*
Tchaikovsky, Pyotr 1840-1893 *OxDcOp*
Tchaikowsky, Andre 1935-1982 *Baker 92*
Tchakarov, Emil 1948- *Baker 92*
Tchalykh, Leonid Alexander 1946- *WhoUN 92*
Tchamitchian, Philippe 1957- *WhoWor 93*
Tcheknavorian-Asenbauer, Archalus 1936- *WhoUN 92*
Tchelistcheff, Victor 1929- *WhoSSW 93*
Tcherepnin, Alexander (Nikolaievich) 1899-1977 *Baker 92*
Tcherepnin, Ivan (Alexandrovich) 1943- *Baker 92*
Tcherepnin, Nikolai (Nikolaievich) 1873-1945 *Baker 92*
Tcherepnin, Serge (Alexandrovich) 1941- *Baker 92*
Tcherkassky, Marianna Alexsavena 1952- *WhoAm 92, WhoAmW 93*
Tcherneshoff, Lyndon Mark 1956- *WhoSSW 93*
Tchernykhov, Jacob 1889-1951 *BioIn 17*
Tchertkoff, Victor 1919- *WhoE 93*
Tchesnokov, Pavel 1877-1944 *Baker 92*
Tchibota-Souamy, Roger 1944- *WhoUN 92*
Tchibozo, Guy 1960- *WhoWor 93*
Tchicaya, Felix 1931-1988 *BioIn 17*
Tchicaya-Thystere, Jean Pierre 1936- *WhoAfr*
Tchicaya U Tam'si 1931-1988 *BioIn 17*
Tchinnis, John F. *St&PR 93*
Tchobanoglous, George 1935- *WhoAm 92*
Tcholakov, Neofit 1934- *WhoScE 91-4*
Tchon, Wallace Edward 1944- *St&PR 93*
Tchoryk, Robert Charles 1956- *WhoEmL 93, WhoSSW 93, WhoWor 93*
Tchorzewski, Ronald J. 1950- *St&PR 93*
Tchuruk, Serge *St&PR 93*
Tea, Charles Lewis, Jr. 1934- *St&PR 93*
Tea, Traves *ScF&FL 92*
Tea Banh *WhoWor 93*
Teach, Carole A. 1944- *St&PR 93*
Teacher, Anonymous c. 870- *OxDcByz*
Teacher, Rebecca 1948- *ScF&FL 92*
Teachers College Library *ScF&FL 92*
Teachey, Jerold Cannell 1946- *WhoSSW 93*
Teachey, Teresa Jolley 1948- *WhoAmW 93*
Teachworth, E. Anne 1937- *WhoSSW 93*
Teaf, Howard M. 1903-1991 *BioIn 17*
Teaford, John Harry 1947- *St&PR 93*
Teagan, J. Gerard 1947- *St&PR 93*
Teagan, John Gerard 1947- *WhoAm 92*
Teagan, Mark Tilden 1945- *WhoWrEP 92*
Teagan, Robert *Law&B 92*
Teagan, Robert L. *Law&B 92*
Teagarden, Jack *BioIn 17*
Teagarden, Jack 1905-1964 *Baker 92*
Teague, Baden Chapman 1944- *WhoAsAP 91*
Teague, Barry Elvin 1944- *WhoAm 92*
Teague, Bernard George 1938- *WhoWor 93*
Teague, Bernice Rita 1957- *WhoE 93*
Teague, Bruce T. 1953- *St&PR 93*
Teague, Bruce Williams 1947- *WhoEmL 93*
Teague, Burton William 1912- *WhoWrEP 92*
Teague, Frances 1949- *ConAu 139*
Teague, Frances Nicol 1949- *WhoSSW 93*
Teague, Henry H. 1936- *St&PR 93*
Teague, Hyman Faris 1916- *WhoAm 92*
Teague, Joel R. 1939- *WhoIns 93*
Teague, Larry Gene 1954- *WhoAm 92*
Teague, Lavette Cox, Jr. 1934- *WhoWor 93*
Teague, Lewis 1941- *MiSFD 9*
Teague, Mark 1963- *BioIn 17*
Teague, Mark (Christopher) 1963- *ConAu 136*
Teague, Mary Elizabeth 1928- *WhoAmW 93*
Teague, Michael Allen 1946- *WhoWor 93*
Teague, Olin E. *BioIn 17*
Teague, P. Martin *Law&B 92*
Teague, Peyton Clark 1915- *WhoAm 92, WhoSSW 93*
Teague, Richard A. *BioIn 17*
Teague, Robert 1929- *ScF&FL 92*
Teague, S.W., Jr. 1927- *St&PR 93*
Teague, Sam Fuller 1918- *WhoAm 92, WhoSSW 93*
Teague, Wayne 1927- *WhoAm 92, WhoSSW 93*
Teague-Jones, Reginald 1889-1988 *BioIn 17*
Teakle, Neil William 1949- *WhoWor 93*
Teal, Charles Robert *Law&B 92*
Teal, Cindy *BioIn 17*
Teal, Elizabeth Jenrette 1962- *WhoAmW 93*
Teal, Ernest David 1946- *St&PR 93*
Teal, Gilbert Earle 1912- *WhoWor 93*
Teal, Gordon Kidd 1907- *WhoAm 92, WhoWor 93*
Teal, Ramona P. 1937- *WhoSSW 93*
Teale, Sarah *ScF&FL 92*
Teale, William Herbert 1947- *WhoSSW 93*
Teall, Robert Wayne 1941- *St&PR 93*
Teaney, Carol Ruth 1950- *WhoAmW 93*
Teaney, Dale Thorpe 1933- *WhoE 93*
Teaney, Myron Rex, II 1943- *St&PR 93*
Teannaki, Teatao *WhoWor 93*
Tear, Robert 1939- *Baker 92, OxDcOp*
Teare, C.A. *St&PR 93*
Teare, George William, Jr. 1930- *St&PR 93*
Teare, Gregory L. 1954- *St&PR 93*
Teare, Iwan Dale 1931- *WhoAm 92*
Teare, Scott William 1961- *WhoWor 93*
Tearle, Conway 1878-1938 *BioIn 17*
Tearney, Michael Gautier 1942- *WhoSSW 93*
Teas, Diann Dishongh 1941- *WhoSSW 93*
Teas, John Frederick 1934- *WhoSSW 93*
Teas, Kathie B. 1955- *St&PR 93*
Teasdale, Graham Michael *WhoScE 91-1*
Teasdale, Leslie Malcolm 1935- *WhoScE 91-1*
Teasdale, Russell E. *Law&B 92*
Teasdale, Russell Edward 1931- *St&PR 93*
Teasdale, Sara 1884-1933 *AmWomPl*
Teasdale, Thomas Hennings 1933- *WhoAm 92*
Tease, James Edward 1939- *WhoAm 92*
Teasley, Harry E., Jr. 1937- *St&PR 93*
Teasley, Larkin 1936- *St&PR 93, WhoIns 93*
Teasley, Merrily Austin 1943- *WhoSSW 93*
Teat, Teri L. 1955- *WhoAm 92*
Teater, Richard M. 1948- *St&PR 93*
Teates, Charles David 1936- *WhoAm 92*
Teather, Derek *WhoScE 91-1*
Teator, Robert Hemingway 1948- *WhoE 93*
Teaze, Kathryn d1991 *BioIn 17*
Tebaldi, Renata 1922- *Baker 92, IntDcOp [port], OxDcOp, WhoAm 92*
Tebaldini, Giovanni 1864-1952 *Baker 92*
Tebault, James Curtis 1951- *WhoSSW 93*
Tebay, James Elwood 1930- *WhoAm 92*
Tebbe, Horst 1940- *St&PR 93*
Tebbe, Joachim 1947- *WhoScE 91-3*
Tebbe, Karl-Friedrich 1941- *WhoWor 93*
Tebbel, John 1912- *WhoAm 92, WhoWrEP 92*
Tebbit, Norman *BioIn 17*
Tebbit, Norman 1931- *ConAu 138*
Tebbs, C.J. *WhoScE 91-1*
Tebby, John Caesar *WhoScE 91-1*
Tebeau, Oliver Wendell 1864-1918 *BiDAMSp 1989*
Tebedo, MaryAnne 1936- *WhoAmW 93*
Teblum, Gary Ira 1955- *WhoEmL 93*
Tebo-Messina, Margaret 1941- *WhoSSW 93*
Teboul, Albert 1936- *WhoWor 93*
Tec, Leon 1919- *WhoE 93*
Tecce, Giorgio *WhoScE 91-3*
Tecco, Betsy Dru 1960- *WhoWrEP 92*
Tecco, Romuald Gilbert Louis Joseph 1941- *WhoAm 92*
Techine, Andre 1943- *MiSFD 9*
Tecklenburg, Helga Anna 1954- *WhoWor 93*
Tecklenburg, John Christian, II *Law&B 92*
Tecklin, Stacy E. *Law&B 92*
Teck Wu, Lawrence Wong 1955- *WhoWor 93*
Teclaff, Ludwik Andrzej 1918- *WhoAm 92*
Tecle, Tesfai 1944- *WhoUN 92*
Tecoz, Henri Francois 1919- *WhoWor 93*
Tecumseh 1768-1813 *BioIn 17, HarEnMi*
Tedaldi, Jacopo fl. c. 1453- *OxDcByz*
Tedd, Michael David *WhoScE 91-1*
Tedder, Arthur William 1890-1967 *DcTwHis*
Tedder, Arthur Williams 1890-1967 *HarEnMi*
Tedder, Dewey Ray 1937- *St&PR 93*
Tedder, J. *WhoScE 91-1*
Tedder, Richard S. *WhoScE 91-1*
Tedder, S. Russell 1935- *St&PR 93*
Teder, Ants 1936- *WhoScE 91-4*
Teders, Ella Grove 1931- *WhoSSW 93*
Tedeschi, Arthur C. *St&PR 93*
Tedeschi, Frederick C. *Law&B 92*
Tedeschi, John Alfred 1931- *WhoAm 92*
Tedeschi, Michael A. 1946- *St&PR 93*
Tedeschi, Pasquale *WhoScE 91-3*
Tedeschi, Robert James 1921- *WhoE 93*
Tedesco, Anne Cavolo 1951- *WhoAmW 93, WhoE 93*
Tedesco, Francis Joseph 1944- *WhoAm 92, WhoSSW 93*
Tedesco, Giovanni 1929- *WhoUN 92*
Tedesco, Ignaz (Amadeus) 1817-1882 *Baker 92*
Tedesco, Lisa Ann 1950- *WhoE 93*
Tedesco, Lucie M.A. *Law&B 92*
Tedesco, Mario Castelnuovo- 1895-1968 *BioIn 17*
Tedesco, Saverio P. *Law&B 92*
Tedesco, Susan Mary 1954- *WhoAmW 93*
Tedesko, Anton 1903- *WhoAm 92, WhoE 93*
Tedford, Dwain d1992 *NewYTBS 92*
Tedford, Jack Nowlan, III 1943- *WhoWor 93*
Tedford, William G. *ScF&FL 92*
Tedford, William Howard, Jr. 1936- *WhoAm 92*
Tedford, William L. 1939- *St&PR 93*
Tedjeske, James J. *Law&B 92*
Tedla, Addis *WhoAfr*
Tedlock, Dennis 1939- *WhoAm 92*
Tedman, Carol S. *Law&B 92*
Tedor, Michael L. 1950- *WhoE 93*
Tedros, Theodore Zaki 1910- *WhoSSW 93, WhoWor 93*
Tedrow, Eugene Leroy 1950- *St&PR 93*
Tedrow, John Charles Fremont 1917- *WhoAm 92*
Tee, Dudley E.H. *WhoScE 91-1*
Teece, David J(ohn) 1948- *ConAu 138*
Teed, C. Cason 1941- *WhoAmW 93*
Teed, Cason 1941- *WhoWrEP 92*
Teed, Jack Hamilton *ScF&FL 92*
Teed, Roy (Norman) 1928- *Baker 92*
Teedyuscung 1700-1775 *BioIn 17*
Teegarden, James W. 1936- *St&PR 93*
Teegarden, Kenneth Leroy 1921- *WhoAm 92*
Teegen, Evelyn Irene Hoopes 1931- *WhoAm 92, WhoAmW 93, WhoWor 93*
Teeger, John L. 1943- *St&PR 93*
Teeguarden, Dennis Earl 1931- *WhoAm 92*
Teehan, Thomas J. 1943- *WhoScE 91-3*
Teehan, Thomas R. *Law&B 92*
Teehankee, Claudio d1989 *BioIn 17*
Teel, Bertha L. 1918- *St&PR 93*
Teel, Dale 1925- *WhoAm 92*
Teel, Edwin Alfred 1911- *St&PR 93*
Teel, Mary Jo *Law&B 92*
Teel, Theodore Trevanian, Jr. 1928- *WhoSSW 93*
Teele, Gerald Allen 1944- *St&PR 93*
Teeling, Joseph E. 1955- *St&PR 93*
Teely, Peter *WhoWor 93*
Teem, John McCorkle 1925- *WhoAm 92*
Teem, Paul Lloyd, Jr. 1948- *WhoEmL 93, WhoSSW 93, WhoWor 93*
Teem, William Milton, IV 1959- *WhoSSW 93*
Teepen, Thomas Henry 1935- *WhoAm 92*
Teeple, Fiona Diane 1943- *WhoAm 92*
Teeple, Howard Merle 1911- *WhoWor 93, WhoWrEP 92*
Teeple, Richard Duane *Law&B 92*
Teeple, Richard Duane 1942- *St&PR 93, WhoAm 92*
Teeples, C.A., Mrs. fl. 1879-1880 *BioIn 17*
Teer, Barbara Ann *AfrAmBi*
Teer, Harold Benton, Jr. 1945- *WhoSSW 93*
Teer, Kay Stoltz 1947- *WhoAmW 93*
Teer, Kees 1925- *WhoScE 91-3*
Teerlink, Richard F. *St&PR 93*
Teerman, John H. 1948- *St&PR 93*
Tees, Richard Chisholm 1940- *WhoAm 92*
Teesdale, Thomas Joseph 1949- *St&PR 93*
Teeter, Dwight Leland, Jr. 1935- *WhoAm 92*
Teeter, James Herring 1927- *WhoE 93*
Teeter, Karl van Duyn 1929- *WhoAm 92*
Teeter, Robert *BioIn 17*
Teeter, Robert G. *Law&B 92*
Teeter, Ruth S. 1916- *St&PR 93*
Teeters, Bruce William 1945- *St&PR 93*
Teeters, Elsie Barbara 1918- *WhoAmW 93*
Teeters, James M. 1947- *St&PR 93*
Teeters, Nancy H. 1930- *St&PR 93*
Teeters, Nancy Hays 1930- *BioIn 17, WhoAm 92, WhoAmW 93*
Teeters, Susan Marie 1960- *WhoAmW 93*
Teets, Charles Edward 1947- *St&PR 93*
Teets, Frank David 1936- *St&PR 93*
Teets, John W. 1933- *St&PR 93*
Teets, John William 1933- *WhoAm 92*
Teevan, Richard Collier 1919- *WhoAm 92, WhoE 93*
Teffeteller, Gordon Lamar 1931- *WhoSSW 93*
Tefft, Melvin 1932- *WhoAm 92*
Tefft, Phillip W. 1917- *St&PR 93*
Tegarden, LoRetta Tudor 1940- *WhoSSW 93*
Tegeler, Christine L. 1952- *WhoAmW 93*
Tegeler, Dorothy 1950- *WhoWrEP 92*
Tegeler, Erich 1947- *WhoWor 93*
Tegeris, Andrew Stanley 1929- *WhoAm 92*
Tegeris, John Steven 1963- *WhoSSW 93*
Tegethoff, Linda Ann 1945- *WhoAmW 93*
Tegetthoff, Wilhelm von 1827-1871 *HarEnMi*
Teggers, Aert 1637-1689 *BioIn 17*
Teghtmeyer, Edward Lee 1943- *St&PR 93*
Tegmeyer, Marlene M. 1932- *St&PR 93*
Tegner, Bruce 1928-1985 *BioIn 17*
Tegtmeier, Patricia Mae Read 1937- *WhoWrEP 92*
Tegze, Miklos 1926- *WhoScE 91-4*
Tehrani, Julliette S. 1946- *St&PR 93*
Tei, Takuri 1924- *WhoWor 93*
Teia d552 *OxDcByz*
Teich, Daniel B. 1947- *St&PR 93*
Teich, Erwin Richard 1923- *St&PR 93*
Teich, Irwin 1937- *St&PR 93*
Teich, Malvin Carl 1939- *WhoAm 92*
Teich, Mildred Brody 1920- *WhoAmW 93*
Teich, Richard E. 1942- *St&PR 93*
Teich, Susan F. *Law&B 92*
Teichen, Karl-Theodor 1930- *WhoScE 91-3*
Teicher, Arthur Mace 1946- *WhoE 93*
Teicher, Martin *Law&B 92*
Teicher, Martin Hersch 1951- *WhoE 93*
Teicher, Morton Irving 1920- *WhoAm 92, WhoSSW 93*
Teichert, Curt 1905- *WhoAm 92*
Teichgraeber, Richard Koenig 1928- *St&PR 93*
Teichgraeber, Thomas G. *Law&B 92*
Teichler, Ulrich Christian 1942- *WhoWor 93*
Teichman, Carl F. 1956- *St&PR 93*
Teichman, Evelyn 1929- *WhoAmW 93*
Teichmuller, Robert 1863-1939 *Baker 92*
Teichner, Bruce A. *Law&B 92*
Teichner, Lester 1944- *WhoAm 92*
Teichner, S.J. 1923- *WhoScE 91-2*
Teig, Gerald Carlyle 1947- *St&PR 93*
Teig, Marlowe G. 1938- *St&PR 93*
Teigen, Philip Martin 1941- *WhoAm 92*
Teigland, Stanley M. *Law&B 92*
Teikari, Veikko Olavi 1943- *WhoScE 91-4*
Teike, Carl (Albert Hermann) 1864-1922 *Baker 92*
Teilhard de Chardin, Pierre *BioIn 17*
Teiling, Bernard 1942- *WhoWor 93*
Teillac, Jean 1920- *WhoWor 93*
Teininger, Mark *Law&B 92*
Teirstein, Alvin Stanley 1927- *WhoE 93*
Teisler, David A. 1953- *WhoWrEP 92*
Teismann, Kevin P. 1945- *St&PR 93*
Teison, Herbert J. 1927- *WhoWrEP 92*
Teisseyre, Roman Marian 1929- *WhoScE 91-4*
Teissier, Bernard Henri 1945- *WhoWor 93*
Teit, James 1864-1922 *BioIn 17*
Teitel, Jeffrey H. *Law&B 92*
Teitel, Jeffrey Hale 1943- *WhoE 93*
Teitel, Simon 1928- *WhoE 93*
Teitelbaum, Aaron 1946- *WhoE 93*
Teitelbaum, Balega Ruth 1964- *WhoAmW 93*
Teitelbaum, David d1990 *BioIn 17*
Teitelbaum, Gene *BioIn 17*
Teitelbaum, Irving 1939- *St&PR 93, WhoAm 92*
Teitelbaum, Joel *JeAmHC*
Teitelbaum, Miguel 1934- *WhoWor 93*
Teitelbaum, Naftali 1934- *St&PR 93*
Teitelbaum, Philip 1928- *WhoAm 92*

Teitelbaum, Seymour 1927- WhoE 93
Teitelbaum, Sheldon ScF&FL 92
Teitelbaum, Steven Lazarus 1938- WhoAm 92
Teitell, Conrad Laurence 1932- WhoAm 92
Teitgen, Pierre-Henri 1908- BioIn 17
Teitler, Ronald Fred 1943- WhoE 93
Teitsworth, Robert Allan 1930- St&PR 93
Teittinen, Pentti J. 1927- WhoScE 91-4
Teitz, Michael B. 1935- WhoAm 92
Teiwes, William Manfred 1941- St&PR 93
Teixeira, Arthur Alves 1944- WhoSSW 93
Teixeira, Cathy Ann 1956- WhoAmW 93
Teixeira, Fernando Manuel Da Silva 1948- WhoWor 93
Teixeira, Jose 1944- WhoScE 91-2
Teixeira, Jose Mendes 1944- WhoWor 93
Teixeira, MaryAnn C. 1948- WhoAmW 93
Teixeira, Pedro de 1587-1641 Expl 93
Teixeira da Cruz, Antonio 1935- WhoWor 93
Teixeira de Oliveira, Carlos Alberto 1951- WhoWor 93
Teixeira-Dias, Jose J.C. 1944- WhoScE 91-3
Teixido, Raul 1943- SpAmA
Teixier, Annie Mireille J. 1937- WhoWor 93
Tejada, Francisco 1942- WhoSSW 93
Tejas, Vernon BioIn 17
Tejchman, Andrzej 1933- WhoScE 91-4
Tejeda de Tamez, Altair 1926- DcMexL
Tejedor, Carlos 1949- WhoWor 93
Tejera, Diego Vicente 1941- WhoWor 93
Tejo, Fernando 1952- WhoWor 93
Tek, Arthur D. 1949- St&PR 93
Tekahionwake Johnson, Pauline 1861-1913 BioIn 17
Te Kamp, W.G.B. WhoScE 91-3
Te Kanawa, Kiri 1944- Baker 92, OxDcOp, WhoAm 92, WhoWor 93
Te Kanawa, Kiri Janette 1944- IntDcOp [port]
Tekeliev, Alexander 1942- Baker 92
Tekelioglu, Meral 1936- WhoScE 91-4, WhoWor 93
Tekere, Edgar Ziganai 1937- WhoAfr
Tekeres, Miklos 1936- WhoScE 91-4
Tekin, Mehmet Aytug 1949- WhoScE 91-4
Tekin, Robert William 1935- St&PR 93
Tekinel, Osman 1936- WhoScE 91-4
Teklehaimanot, Awash 1942- WhoUN 92
Teklits, Joseph A. Law&B 92
Tekoah, Yosef 1925-1991 BioIn 17
Tekulve, Kenton Charles 1947- BiDAMSp 1989
Telahun, Hailu 1935- WhoUN 92
Telegdi, Valentine Louis 1922- WhoAm 92, WhoWor 93
Telegdy, Gyula 1935- WhoScE 91-4
Teleki, Jane King 1943- WhoSSW 93
Teleki, Pal 1879-1941 DcTwHis
Telemann, Georg Michael 1748-1831 Baker 92
Telemann, Georg Philipp 1681-1767 Baker 92, IntDcOp [port], OxDcOp
Telemaque, Eleanor Wong 1933- WhoWrEP 92
Telepchak, M.J. 1947- St&PR 93
Telerig OxDcByz
Telesca, Francis Eugene 1921- WhoAm 92
Telesca, Michael Anthony 1929- WhoAm 92
Telesca, Thomas Louis 1936- St&PR 93
Telesco, Patricia Gaynor 1946- WhoSSW 93
Telescope, Tom MajAI
Telese, Renee Norine 1953- WhoAmW 93
Telesetsky, Walter 1938- WhoE 93, WhoWor 93
Teletzke, Gary Francis 1956- WhoSSW 93
Televantos, John Yiannakis 1952- WhoSSW 93
Telewski, Frank William 1955- WhoAm 92
Telfair, Oscar Matthew, III Law&B 92
Telfer, Gordon H. Law&B 92
Telfer, James Stuart 1932- WhoAm 92
Telford, Ira Rockwood 1907- WhoAm 92
Telford, Mary E. AmWomPl
Telford, Robert ScF&FL 92
Telge, Susan Law&B 92
Telionis, Demetri Pyrros 1941- WhoSSW 93
Telitz, Gary Lee 1947- St&PR 93
Telkes, Bela 1935- WhoScE 91-4
Tell, A. Charles 1937- WhoAm 92
Tell, Bjorn V. 1918- WhoScE 91-4
Tell, William Kirn, Jr. 1934- St&PR 93, WhoAm 92
Tella, Alfred ScF&FL 92
Telleen, John Martin 1922- WhoAm 92
Telleen, Philip R. Law&B 92
Tellefsen, Gerald 1938- WhoE 93
Tellefsen, Thomas (Dyke Acland) 1823-1874 Baker 92
Tellem, Susan Mary 1945- WhoAm 92
Tellep, Daniel Michael 1931- St&PR 93, WhoAm 92
Teller, Aaron Joseph 1921- WhoAm 92
Teller, Alvin N. 1944- St&PR 93
Teller, Alvin Norman 1944- WhoAm 92, WhoWor 93
Teller, David Norton 1936- WhoAm 92
Teller, Davida Young 1938- WhoAmW 93
Teller, Edward 1908- BioIn 17, ColdWar 1 [port], WhoAm 92
Teller, Gayl Florene 1946- WhoWrEP 92
Teller, Jeff 1950- St&PR 93
Teller, Rosalind Elaine 1946- WhoAmW 93
Teller, Sonia Ruth 1938- WhoSSW 93
Teller, Stan 1924- St&PR 93
Teller, Walter M. 1928- WhoScE 91-3
Telleria, Anthony F. 1938- WhoWor 93
Telles, Lygia Fagundes 1923- ScF&FL 92
Telles, Rick BioIn 17
Tellesbo, Marsha Louise 1948- WhoAmW 93
Tellez, Carlos Nunez d1990 BioIn 17
Tellez, Debra S. Law&B 92
Tellez, George Henry 1951- WhoSSW 93
Tellez, Hernando 1908-1966 SpAmA
Tellez, Laura Elsa 1955- WhoAmW 93
Tellez Rendon, Maria Nestora 1828-1890 DcMexL
Tellier, Henri 1918- WhoAm 92
Tellier, Paul M. 1939- WhoAm 92
Tellier, Richard Davis 1942- WhoAm 92
Telling, Edward Riggs 1919- St&PR 93, WhoAm 92
Tello, Donna 1955- WhoAmW 93, WhoWor 93
Tello, Julio Cesar 1880-1947 IntDcAn
Tellor, M.D. 1951- St&PR 93
Telma, Robert Joseph 1946- St&PR 93
Telmanyi, Emil 1892-1988 Baker 92
Telmer, Frederick H. 1937- St&PR 93
Telmer, Frederick Harold 1937- WhoAm 92, WhoE 93
Telmosse, Robert Dennis 1941- WhoAm 92
Telnack, John J. 1937- WhoAm 92
Telotte, J.P. 1949- ScF&FL 92
Telotte, Jay Paul 1949- WhoSSW 93
Telpner, Joel Stephan Law&B 92
Telser, Lester Greenspan 1931- WhoWrEP 92
Telsey, Leon G. 1907-1991 BioIn 17
Telshaw, H.L., Jr. 1925- St&PR 93
Teltscher, Herry Otto WhoE 93
Telva, Marian 1897-1962 Baker 92
Tem, Melanie ScF&FL 92
Tem, Steve Rasnic 1950- ScF&FL 92
Tema-Lyn, Laurie 1951- WhoAmW 93
Temam, Roger M. 1940- WhoWor 93
Temanel, Billy Estoque 1958- WhoWor 93
Tembeck, John P. d1991 BioIn 17
Tembo, George Sande 1956- WhoUN 92
Tembo, John Zenas Ungapake 1932- WhoAfr
Temby, Fred C. St&PR 93
Temelkoff, Vonda Lee 1937- WhoAmW 93
Temerlin, Liener 1928- St&PR 93, WhoAm 92
Temes, Gabor Charles 1929- WhoAm 92
Temeyer, Kevin Bruce 1951- WhoSSW 93
Temianka, Henri 1906- Baker 92, WhoAm 92
Temianka, Henri 1906-1992 NewYTBS 92 [port]
Temin, Davia B. 1952- St&PR 93
Temin, Davia Beth 1952- WhoAmW 93
Temin, Howard Martin 1934- WhoAm 92, WhoWor 93
Temin, Michael Lehman 1933- WhoAm 92
Temirkanov, Yuri 1938- Baker 92
Temirkanov, Yuri Khatuevich 1938- WhoWor 93
Temiz, Kasif 1938- WhoScE 91-4
Temkin, Aaron 1929- WhoE 93
Temkin, Karen Katz 1963- WhoE 93
Temkin, Richard Joel 1945- WhoE 93
Temkin, Robert Harvey 1943- WhoAm 92, WhoE 93
Temkin, Samuel 1936- WhoE 93
Temkin, Steven Mark 1957- St&PR 93
Temko, Allan 1924- ConAu 136
Temko, Allan Bernard 1924- WhoAm 92
Temko, Florence ConAu 37NR
Temko, Jerrold H. Law&B 92
Temko, Spartak W. 1925- WhoWor 93
Temko, Stanley Leonard 1920- WhoAm 92
Temlyakov, Vladimir Nikolaevich 1953- WhoWor 93
Temme, Leonard A. BioIn 17
Temmen, Robert P. 1925- St&PR 93
Temmer, Stephen F. d1992 NewYTBS 92
Temo, Anthony 1950- WhoAsAP 91
Tempel, Jean C. WhoAm 92
Tempel, Thomas Robert 1939- WhoAm 92
Tempelis, Constantine Harry 1927- WhoAm 92
Tempels, Placide 1906- IntDcAn
Temperley, Harold William Vazeille 1879-1939 BioIn 17
Temperley, Judith Kantack 1936- WhoAmW 93
Temperley, Nicholas 1932- Baker 92
Tempero, Kenneth Floyd 1939- St&PR 93, WhoAm 92
Temperton, Rod SoulM
Tempest, David Walker WhoScE 91-1
Tempest, John ScF&FL 92
Tempest, Mark Jacquot Law&B 92
Tempest, William R. Law&B 92
Tempesta, Michele S. 1946- WhoE 93
Temple, Annette Kendrick WhoAmW 93
Temple, Arthur 1920- WhoSSW 93
Temple, Bobby Louis 1930- WhoSSW 93
Temple, Byron BioIn 17
Temple, Charles Adams 1947- WhoE 93
Temple, David Jonathan WhoScE 91-1
Temple, Donald 1933- WhoAm 92
Temple, Donald Edward 1946- WhoE 93, WhoEmL 93
Temple, Gordon J. 1952- WhoScE 91-1
Temple, Howard Lynn 1913- WhoWor 93
Temple, John F. 1940- St&PR 93
Temple, John Tempest WhoScE 91-1
Temple, Joseph G., Jr. 1929- St&PR 93
Temple, Joseph George, Jr. 1929- WhoAm 92
Temple, Julien 1953- MiSFD 9
Temple, Larry Eugene 1935- WhoAm 92
Temple, Leah ScF&FL 92
Temple, Paul N., Jr. 1923- St&PR 93
Temple, Paul Nathaniel 1923- WhoWor 93
Temple, Penelope Denver WhoWrEP 92
Temple, Phillip Aaron 1940- WhoAm 92
Temple, Robert 1941- WhoAm 92
Temple, Robert (Kyle Grenville) 1945- ConAu 40NR
Temple, Robert Winfield 1934- WhoSSW 93
Temple, Robin ScF&FL 92
Temple, Shirley 1928- BioIn 17, IntDcF 2-3 [port]
Temple, Stephen David 1954- St&PR 93
Temple, Wayne Calhoun 1924- WhoAm 92
Temple, Wick 1937- WhoAm 92
Temple, William 1628-1699 BioIn 17
Temple, William 1881-1944 DcTwHis
Temple, William F. 1914-1989 ScF&FL 92
Temple, William Norman 1932- St&PR 93, WhoSSW 93
Templeman, Andrew Burgess WhoScE 91-1
Templeman, Conny MiSFD 9
Templeman, Kristine Hofgren 1947- WhoWrEP 92
Templeman, Marie Louise 1952- WhoSSW 93
Templer, Charles E. 1945- St&PR 93
Templer, David Allen 1942- WhoSSW 93
Templer, Gerald 1898-1979 DcTwHis
Templer, Jeffrey Arnold 1947- St&PR 93
Temples, Dent L., Jr. 1946- St&PR 93
Temples, Dent Larkin, Jr. 1946- WhoAm 92
Templeton, Alan Robert 1947- WhoAm 92
Templeton, Alec (Andrew) 1909-1963 Baker 92
Templeton, Allan WhoScE 91-1
Templeton, Benjamin John 1936- WhoAm 92
Templeton, Carson Howard 1917- WhoAm 92
Templeton, Charles 1915- ScF&FL 92
Templeton, Charles B. 1915- WhoCanL 92
Templeton, Darrel Lloyd 1943- St&PR 93
Templeton, Fiona Anne 1951- WhoWrEP 92
Templeton, Garry Lewis 1956- BiDAMSp 1989
Templeton, Gordon Huffine 1940- WhoSSW 93
Templeton, Harvey Maxwell, III Law&B 92
Templeton, Herminie AmWomPl
Templeton, Ian Malcolm 1929- WhoAm 92
Templeton, John 1802-1886 Baker 92
Templeton, John Marks 1912- WhoAm 92
Templeton, John Marks, Jr. 1940- St&PR 93, WhoWor 93
Templeton, Randall Keith 1957- WhoSSW 93
Templeton, Richard Allan 1922- St&PR 93
Templeton, Robert Clark 1929-1991 BioIn 17
Templeton, Robert Earl 1931- WhoAm 92
Templin, Howard Paul 1932- St&PR 93
Templin, John Leon, Jr. 1940- WhoE 93
Templin, Kenneth Elwood 1927- WhoAm 92
Templin, Mildred Clara 1913- WhoAmW 93
Tempone, Joanne Westwood 1959- WhoAmW 93
Temptations SoulM
Temske, Arthur John, Jr. 1935- St&PR 93
Temu, Peter Eliezer 1936- WhoUN 92
Tenayuca, Emma 1916- NotHsAW 93
Ten Boom, Corrie BioIn 17
ten Boom, Corrie 1892-1983 ConHero 2 [port]
Ten Bosch, Jacobus Johannes 1935- WhoWor 93
Tenbrook, Abraham 1765-1841 BioIn 17
Tenbrook, Don M. 1932- St&PR 93
Ten Bruggencate, Gerrit 1934- WhoScE 91-3
Ten Cate, Arnold Richard 1933- WhoAm 92
Tencer, Steven Charles 1961- St&PR 93
Tench, Ray Terrance 1947- WhoSSW 93
Tenchev, Ivan Ivanov 1930- WhoScE 91-4
Tencin, Claudine Alexandrine Guerin de 1682-1749 BioIn 17
Tencza, Zenon C. Law&B 92
Tendler, David 1938- WhoAm 92
Tenducci, Giusti Ferdinando c. 1735-c. 1790 OxDcOp
Tenducci, Giusto Ferdinando c. 1735-1790 Baker 92
Tendzin, Osel 1943-1990 BioIn 17
Teneback, Anders Helmer 1946- St&PR 93
Tenebaum, Henry Abraham 1951- WhoSSW 93
Tenenbaum, Bernard Hirsh 1954- WhoE 93
Tenenbaum, Harvey 1933- St&PR 93
Tenenbaum, Jeffrey Mark 1945- WhoE 93
Tenenbaum, Lee J. Law&B 92
Tenenbaum, Louis 1922- WhoAm 92
Tenenbaum, Michael 1913- WhoAm 92
Tener, John Kinley 1863-1946 BioIn 17
Tener, Robert L. 1924- WhoWrEP 92
Tenerelli, L. Donald 1948- St&PR 93
Tenery, Cecile A. Law&B 92
Tenety, Dennis Richard 1950- WhoWrEP 92
Ten Eyck, Charles Scott 1948- St&PR 93
TenEyck, Gregory Alden 1957- WhoE 93
Teng, Hsiao-p'ing 1904- BioIn 17
Teng, Lilly C. Law&B 92
Teng, Weizao 1917- WhoWor 93
Teng, Zhidong 1960- WhoWor 93
Tengbom, Anders 1911- WhoWor 93
Tengbom, Mildred 1921- ConAu 39NR
Tengdin, Robert C. 1930- St&PR 93
Tenges, Robert Eugene 1942- St&PR 93
Tenges, Tom Alan 1949- WhoE 93
Tenggren, Gustaf 1896-1970 BioIn 17
Tengroth, Bjorn M. 1931- WhoScE 91-4
Tengzelius, Jan WhoScE 91-4
Tengzelius, Jan 1949- WhoScE 91-4
Tengzelius, Jan Robert 1949- WhoScE 91-4
Ten Hag, B.A. 1941- WhoScE 91-3
Ten Haken, Richard Ervin 1934- WhoWor 93
Tenham, Martijn 1938- WhoUN 92
Ten Hoopen, Carl A., Jr. 1927- St&PR 93
Ten Hoor, Foppe 1927- WhoScE 91-3
Ten Houte De Lange, S.M. 1944- WhoScE 91-3
Tenhundfeld, A.H., Jr. 1947- St&PR 93
Tenhundfelt, Albert H., Jr. 1947- WhoAm 92
Teninga, Walter Henry 1928- WhoAm 92
Tenison, Renee BioIn 17
Tenison, Robert B. 1924- St&PR 93
Tenkiller, Louis WhoWrEP 92
Tenn, William 1920- BioIn 17
Tennant, Andy MiSFD 9
Tennant, Billy M. Law&B 92
Tennant, Diane Bakke 1946- WhoAmW 93
Tennant, Don 1922- WhoAm 92
Tennant, Emma 1937- BioIn 17, ScF&FL 92
Tennant, Emma (Christina) 1937- ConAu 38NR
Tennant, Forest BioIn 17
Tennant, Frances O. Law&B 92
Tennant, Geraldine B. 1922- WhoAmW 93
Tennant, Hazel M. Bennett 1907- WhoAmW 93
Tennant, John Randall 1940- WhoAm 92
Tennant, Kylie 1912-1988 BioIn 17, DcChlFi
Tennant, May Edith Abraham 1869-1940 BioIn 17
Tennant, Otto Addison 1918- WhoAm 92
Tennant, Stephen 1906-1987 BioIn 17
Tennant, Veronica 1947- WhoAm 92
Tennant, William J. 1947- St&PR 93
Tennant, William Jon 1947- WhoAm 92
Tenne, Arie 1938- WhoUN 92

Tennekes, Hendrik 1936- *WhoScE 91-3*
Tennen, Howard 1948- *ConAu 138*
Tennen, Ken 1949- *WhoEmL 93*
Tennen, Leslie Irwin 1952- *WhoWor 93*
Tennenbaum, Michael Ernest 1935- *St&PR 93, WhoAm 92*
Tennenhouse, Donald L. 1940- *St&PR 93*
Tennenhouse, K.M. *Law&B 92*
Tennent, Frank Dewey 1926- *St&PR 93*
Tenner, Edward Harvey 1944- *WhoE 93*
Tennert, Charles W. 1938- *St&PR 93*
Tenneshaw, S. M. *MajAI*
Tennet, Elizabeth *WhoAsAP 91*
Tenney, Charles H., II *WhoAm 92*
Tenney, Charles Henry 1911- *WhoAm 92, WhoE 93*
Tenney, Dudley Bradstreet 1918- *WhoAm 92*
Tenney, Frank Putnam 1937- *WhoE 93*
Tenney, George W. *Law&B 92*
Tenney, James (Carl) 1934- *Baker 92*
Tenney, Kevin S. *MiSFD 9*
Tenney, Reginald I. *Law&B 92*
Tenney, Stephen Marsh 1922- *WhoAm 92*
Tenney, Tom Fred 1933- *WhoSSW 93*
Tenney, Vivian Allison 1913-1990 *BioIn 17*
Tenniel, John 1820-1914 *BioIn 17, MajAI [port]*
Tennies, Winston L. 1940- *St&PR 93*
Tennill, William Robert 1927- *St&PR 93*
Tennille, Ben *Law&B 92*
Tennison, Gary D. 1953- *St&PR 93*
Tennov, Dorothy 1928- *WhoAmW 93*
Tennstedt, Klaus 1926- *Baker 92, WhoAm 92, WhoWor 93*
Tenny, Morton *St&PR 93*
Tennyson, Alfred 1809-1892 *BioIn 17, MagSWL [port], WorLitC [port]*
Tennyson, Alfred, Lord 1809-1892 *PoeCrit 6 [port]*
Tennyson, Jean 1905-1991 *BioIn 17*
Tennyson, Wilmat 1927- *WhoAm 92*
Tenold, Robert Gordon 1942- *St&PR 93*
Tenopyr, Mary Louise Welsh 1929- *WhoAmW 93, WhoE 93, WhoWor 93*
Tenora, Frantisek 1930- *WhoScE 91-4*
Tenovuo, Jorma 1949- *WhoScE 91-4*
Tenpas, Kathleen Mason 1952- *WhoWrEP 92*
Tenpas, Kevin S. 1957- *St&PR 93*
Tenpas, Paul H. *Law&B 92*
Tenschert, Roland 1894-1970 *Baker 92*
Tent, Lothar 1928- *WhoScE 91-3*
Tenuta, Jean Louise 1958- *WhoAmW 93, WhoWrEP 92*
Tenuta, Luigia 1954- *WhoEmL 93, WhoWor 93*
Tenyak, Carol L. *Law&B 92*
Tenyi, Jeno 1932- *WhoScE 91-4*
Tenzel, Richard Ruvin 1929- *WhoAm 92*
Tenzer, Gail 1945- *WhoAmW 93*
Tenzer, Michael L. 1930- *St&PR 93, WhoAm 92*
Tenzer, Rudolf Kurt 1920- *WhoE 93*
Tenzing Norgay 1914-1986 *BioIn 17*
Tenzin Gyatso 1935- *WhoWor 93*
Tenzyk, Michael J. 1938- *St&PR 93*
Teo, Patrick Chong Nghee 1947- *WhoWor 93*
Teodorescu, Al. Mihai 1941- *WhoScE 91-4*
Teodorescu, Georgeta 1949- *WhoScE 91-4*
Teodorini, Elena 1857-1926 *Baker 92*
Teodoru, Constantin V. 1915-1991 *BioIn 17*
Teodosije c. 1246-c. 1328 *OxDcByz*
Teoh, George Min-Loke 1941- *WhoSSW 93*
Teoh Teik Huat *WhoAsAP 91*
Teoli, Ida 1955- *St&PR 93*
Teoli, William A. *Law&B 92*
Tepas, Gary L. 1942- *St&PR 93*
TePaske, John J(ay) 1929- *ConAu 40NR*
Tepaske, John Jay 1929- *WhoSSW 93*
Tepe, Ann Silcott 1946- *WhoAmW 93*
Tepe, John B., Jr. *Law&B 92*
Tephly, Thomas Robert 1936- *WhoAm 92*
Teplick, Ellen 1949- *WhoWrEP 92*
Teplow, Theodore H. 1928- *St&PR 93*
Teplow, Theodore Herzl 1928- *WhoAm 92*
Teply, Karleen Ingrid 1944- *WhoE 93*
Teply, Lester J. 1920- *WhoE 93*
TePoel, Donna Lee Fuller 1942- *WhoAmW 93*
Tepper, Amanda 1963- *WhoAmW 93*
Tepper, Blossom Weiss 1921- *WhoE 93*
Tepper, Frederick 1934- *St&PR 93*
Tepper, Harold Max 1930- *St&PR 93*
Tepper, Lisa Dickson 1960- *WhoAmW 93*
Tepper, Sheri S. 1929- *ConAu 137, ScF&FL 92*
Tepperman, Emile C. *ScF&FL 92*
Tepperman, Fred 1934- *WhoAm 92*
Tepperman, Helen Murphy 1917- *WhoAmW 93*
Te Puea Herangi 1883-1952 *DcTwHis*
Terabe, Shigeru 1940- *WhoWor 93*
Terada, Yoshinaga 1919- *WhoWor 93*
Teramae, Iwao 1926- *WhoAsAP 91*
Teramoto, Akira, Sr. *St&PR 93*
Teramura, Alan Hiroshi 1948- *WhoE 93*
Teran, Ana-Zully 1954- *WhoAmW 93*
Teranchi, Erik Iraj 1945- *St&PR 93*
Te Rangi Hiroa c. 1877-1951 *IntDcAn*
Terao, Shinji 1938- *WhoWor 93*
Terao, Toshio 1930- *WhoWor 93*
Ter-Arutunian, Rouben 1920-1992 *NewYTBS 92 [port]*
Terasaki, Akihisa 1936- *WhoAsAP 91*
Terasaki, Gwen Harold d1990 *BioIn 17*
Terasaki, Masao 1932- *WhoWor 93*
Terasawa, Jun 1947- *WhoWor 93*
Terasawa, Mititaka 1937- *WhoWor 93*
Terasawa, Yoshia 1931- *WhoUN 92*
Teraskiewicz, Edward Arnold 1946- *WhoE 93*
Terasmae, Jaan 1926- *WhoAm 92*
Terauchi, Hikaru 1942- *WhoWor 93*
Terauchi, Hisaichi 1879-1946 *HarEnMi*
Terauchi, Makakata 1852-1919 *HarEnMi*
Terayama, Hiroshi 1922- *WhoWor 93*
Terbancea, M. *WhoScE 91-4*
Ter Beek, Aurelus Louis Relus 1944- *WhoWor 93*
Terbell, Thomas Green, Jr. 1938- *WhoWor 93*
Terbizan, Donna Jean 1953- *WhoAmW 93*
ter Borg, Richard A. *Law&B 92*
Terborgh, Bert 1945- *WhoAm 92*
Terborg-Penn, Rosalyn Marian 1941- *WhoAmW 93*
Tereka, Sylvia 1958- *WhoUN 92*
Terelak, Henryk *WhoScE 91-4*
Terent'eva, L.N. 1910-1982 *IntDcAn*
Terenyi, Ede 1935- *Baker 92*
Terenzio, Joseph Vincent 1918- *WhoAm 92*
Terenzio, Peter Bernard 1916- *WhoAm 92*
Teresa, Mother 1910- *BioIn 17, WhoWor 93*
Teresa, Vincent d1990 *BioIn 17*
Teresa Benedicta, of the Cross 1891-1942 *BioIn 17*
Teresa, of Avila, Saint 1515-1582 *BioIn 17*
Tereshchenko, Sergey *WhoWor 93*
Tereshin, Vladimir Ivanovich 1928- *BioIn 17*
Tereshkin, N.I. 1913-1986 *IntDcAn*
Tereshkova, Valentina 1937- *BioIn 17*
Tereshkova, Valentina Vladimirovna 1937- *Expl 93*
Teresi, Joseph 1941- *WhoAm 92, WhoWor 93*
Teresiak, Zdzislaw 1925- *WhoScE 91-4*
Terestman, Nettie *WhoAmW 93*
Teretean, Teodor-Stefan 1942- *WhoScE 91-4*
Terez, Angela 1965- *WhoSSW 93*
Terfera, Raymond Anthony 1929- *WhoAm 92*
Terfloth, Klaus 1929- *WhoWor 93*
Ter Haar, Johan Willem 1951- *WhoWor 93*
Terhes, Joyce Lyons 1940- *WhoE 93*
Terho, Erkki O. 1944- *WhoScE 91-4*
ter Horst, Enrique Embden 1948- *WhoUN 92*
Ter Horst, Gerrit Johannes 1955- *WhoWor 93*
terHorst, Jerald Franklin 1922- *WhoAm 92*
Ter Horst, Katie d1992 *BioIn 17*
Terhorst, Paul *BioIn 17*
Terhorst, Paul Byrne 1914- *WhoAm 92*
Terhune, Albert Payson 1872-1942 *ConAu 136, MajAI [port]*
Terhune, Anice 1873-1964 *Baker 92*
Terhune, Anice Morris Stocton *AmWomPl*
Terhune, Anne B. *Law&B 92*
Terhune, Jane Howell 1932- *WhoAmW 93*
Terhune, Stanley Banks 1925- *St&PR 93*
Teringo, James Kennedy, Jr. *Law&B 92*
Terjesen, Terje 1942- *WhoScE 91-4*
Terkel, Louis 1912- *BioIn 17*
Terkel, Studs *NewYTBS 92 [port]*
Terkel, Studs 1912- *BioIn 17, WhoAm 92*
Terkel, Studs Louis 1912- *WhoWrEP 92*
Terkel, Susan N(eiburg) 1948- *ConAu 38NR*
Terkel, Susan Neiburg 1948- *WhoAm 92*
ter Keurs, Henk E. D. J. 1942- *WhoAm 92*
Terkhorn, Henry K. 1930- *WhoAm 92*
Terkhorn, Robert Eugene 1936- *St&PR 93*
Terkla, Louis Gabriel 1925- *WhoAm 92*
Terlaky, Tamas 1955- *WhoWor 93*
Terlizzi, Garth J. 1949- *St&PR 93*
Terlouw, Jan 1931- *ScF&FL 92*
Terman, Allen Roy 1941- *WhoSSW 93*
Terman, Douglas 1933- *ConAu 136, ScF&FL 92*
Terman, Lewis Madison 1935- *WhoAm 92*
Terman, Michael 1943- *WhoE 93*
Termeer, Henri Adrianus 1946- *St&PR 93*
Termeer, Louis Petrus 1951- *WhoWor 93*
Termes Carrero, Rafael 1918- *WhoWor 93*
ter Meulen, Alice Geraldine Baltina 1952- *WhoAmW 93*
Ter Meulen, Volker 1933- *WhoScE 91-3*
Ter-Minassian-Saraga, Lisbeth 1922- *WhoScE 91-2*
Terminello, Dominic Joseph *Law&B 92*
Termini, Roseann Bridget 1953- *WhoAm 92*
Ternan, Ellen Lawless 1839-1914 *BioIn 17*
Ternberg, Jessie Lamoin 1924- *WhoAm 92, WhoAmW 93*
Ternbo, Gosta Verner Ingemar 1927- *WhoWor 93*
Ternero Rodriguez, Miguel 1953- *WhoWor 93*
Ternes, Alan Paul 1931- *WhoAm 92*
Ternina, Milka 1863-1941 *Baker 92, OxDcOp*
Ternyik, Stephen 1960- *WhoWor 93*
Te Ronde, Allan William 1941- *St&PR 93*
Terpak, John B. 1912- *St&PR 93*
Terpening, Debera J. 1960- *St&PR 93*
Ter-Petrosyan, Levon *WhoWor 93*
Terpil, Frank *BioIn 17*
Terpinski, Eva Antonina 1946- *WhoAmW 93*
Terplan, Zeno 1921- *WhoScE 91-4*
Terpo, Andras 1925- *WhoScE 91-4*
Ter-Pogossian, Michel M. 1925- *WhoAm 92*
Terpstra, Catharinus 1933- *WhoScE 91-3*
Terpstra, Jean M. *Law&B 92*
Terr, Lenore Cagen 1936- *WhoAmW 93*
Terr, Vivian A. *Law&B 92*
Terra, Daniel J. 1911- *St&PR 93*
Terra, Daniel James 1911- *WhoAm 92*
Terra, John *ScF&FL 92*
Terra, Nelcindo Nascimento 1939- *WhoWor 93*
Terrabugio, Giuseppe 1842-1933 *Baker 92*
Terracciano, Anthony P. *BioIn 17*
Terracciano, Anthony Patrick 1938- *WhoAm 92*
Terracina, Roy David 1946- *WhoAm 92*
Terracina, Stephen Joseph 1956- *WhoSSW 93*
Terradellas, Domingo (Miguel Bernabe) 1713?-1751 *Baker 92*
Terraglia, Victor, Sr. 1936- *St&PR 93*
Terragni, Giuseppe 1904-1943 *BioIn 17*
Terragno, Paul James 1938- *WhoAm 92*
Terraine, John Alfred 1921- *WhoWor 93*
Terral, Thomas Forrest 1942- *St&PR 93*
Terramano, Joseph Daniel 1952- *WhoWor 93*
Terrana, Benedetto 1946- *WhoWor 93*
Terrana, Beth *BioIn 17*
Terrana, Judith Anne Hahn 1942- *WhoAmW 93*
Terranova, Elaine 1939- *ConAu 139*
Terranova, James M. *Law&B 92*
Terranova, Patrick *Law&B 92*
Terranova, Paul 1919- *St&PR 93*
Terras, Audrey Anne 1942- *WhoAmW 93*
Terras, Rita 1927- *WhoAmW 93*
Terras, Victor 1921- *WhoAm 92*
Terrassa, Juan A. 1948- *WhoIns 93*
Terrasse, Claude (Antoine) 1867-1923 *Baker 92*
Terrazas, Francisco de 1525?-1600 *DcMexL*
Terreault, R. Charles 1935- *WhoAm 92*
Terrebonne, Annie Marie 1932- *WhoAmW 93, WhoWor 93*
Terrel, Ronald Lee 1936- *WhoAm 92*
Terrell, Charles Leroy 1941- *St&PR 93*
Terrell, Charles Richard 1943- *WhoE 93*
Terrell, Charles William 1927- *WhoAm 92*
Terrell, David Lawrence 1935- *WhoSSW 93*
Terrell, Dorothy *BioIn 17*
Terrell, Edgar A., Jr. 1920- *St&PR 93*
Terrell, Edward P. 1936- *St&PR 93*
Terrell, Howard Bruce 1952- *WhoWor 93*
Terrell, James 1923- *WhoAm 92*
Terrell, James Franklin, Jr. 1920- *St&PR 93*
Terrell, John Upton 1900-1988 *BioIn 17*
Terrell, Leonetta Eloise 1956- *WhoSSW 93*
Terrell, Linda Diana 1947- *WhoSSW 93*
Terrell, Mary Church 1863-1954 *BioIn 17, EncAACR*
Terrell, Norman Edwards 1933- *WhoAm 92*
Terrell, Robert Herberton 1857-1925 *EncAACR*
Terrell, Tammi 1947-1970 *SoulM*
Terrell, W. Glenn 1920- *WhoAm 92*
Terrell, William Pace 1937- *St&PR 93*
Terrenato, Luciano 1939- *WhoWor 93*
Terrenzi, John Thomas 1946- *St&PR 93*
Terreri, Edward C. *Law&B 92*
Terreri, Peter R. *St&PR 93*
Terretta, Paul 1916- *St&PR 93*
Terribas, Jaume 1935- *WhoWor 93*
Terribile, Charles L. *Law&B 92*
Terrier, Gilbert Leon 1952- *WhoUN 92*
Terrific, Ted *ScF&FL 92*
Terrile, Stephen Alan *Law&B 92*
Terrill, Burdett Henry 1947- *WhoSSW 93*
Terrill, Clair Elman 1910- *WhoAm 92*
Terrill, Edward Berkshire, Jr. 1912- *St&PR 93*
Terrill, James E. 1944- *WhoAm 92*
Terrill, Richard D. *Law&B 92*
Terrill, Richard Dean 1954- *St&PR 93*
Terrill, Robert Carl 1927- *WhoAm 92*
Terrill, Ross Gladwin *WhoAm 92, WhoWrEP 92*
Terrio, Francis C. *Law&B 92*
Terris, Albert 1916- *WhoE 93*
Terris, John James 1939- *WhoAsAP 91*
Terris, Lillian Dick 1914- *WhoAmW 93*
Terris, Martin Frederick 1946- *WhoSSW 93*
Terris, Milton 1915- *WhoAm 92*
Terris, Norma d1989 *BioIn 17*
Terris, Susan 1937- *WhoWrEP 92*
Terris, Virginia Rinaldy 1917- *WhoWrEP 92*
Terris, William 1937- *St&PR 93, WhoWor 93*
Terroir, Patrick 1948- *WhoWor 93*
Terrone, Maria 1951- *WhoAmW 93*
Terry, Addison, Jr. *Law&B 92*
Terry, Alfred Howe 1827-1890 *BioIn 17*
Terry, Brian R. 1961- *WhoE 93*
Terry, Bridget *ScF&FL 92*
Terry, Charles P. 1935- *St&PR 93*
Terry, Charles Sanford 1864-1936 *Baker 92*
Terry, Clark 1920- *Baker 92, WhoAm 92*
Terry, Clifford Lewis 1937- *WhoAm 92*
Terry, David Smith 1823-1889 *OxCSupC*
Terry, Dolores G. *Law&B 92*
Terry, Doris Ann 1935- *WhoAmW 93*
Terry, Edward Davis 1927- *WhoSSW 93*
Terry, Eleanor Foster 1942- *WhoAmW 93*
Terry, Elizabeth Hays 1935- *WhoE 93*
Terry, Eugene 1934- *St&PR 93*
Terry, Frank R. 1928- *WhoAm 92*
Terry, Frank Reilly 1928- *St&PR 93*
Terry, Frederick Arthur, Jr. 1932- *WhoAm 92*
Terry, Frederick H. 1944- *WhoE 93*
Terry, Gary A. 1935- *WhoAm 92*
Terry, Glen Charles 1945- *WhoSSW 93*
Terry, H.P. Baldwin d1991 *BioIn 17*
Terry, Inci Incikaya 1932- *WhoAmW 93*
Terry, James M. 1931- *St&PR 93*
Terry, Jay Dean 1931- *WhoSSW 93*
Terry, Jo Ann *BioIn 17, BlkAmWO [port]*
Terry, John Alfred 1933- *WhoAm 92*
Terry, John Hart 1924- *WhoAm 92*
Terry, John Joseph 1937- *WhoAm 92, WhoWor 93*
Terry, John Timothy 1933- *WhoAm 92*
Terry, Kay Adell 1939- *WhoAmW 93*
Terry, Kibrel S. 1938- *St&PR 93*
Terry, Lawrence 1899-1991 *BioIn 17*
Terry, Leon Cass 1940- *WhoAm 92*
Terry, Marshall Northway, Jr. 1931- *WhoAm 92*
Terry, Mary Sue 1947- *WhoAm 92, WhoAmW 93, WhoSSW 93*
Terry, Megan 1932- *WhoAm 92*
Terry, Melissa *BioIn 17*
Terry, Michael Durham 1946- *St&PR 93*
Terry, Michael Joseph 1957- *WhoEmL 93*
Terry, Michael Patrick 1940- *St&PR 93*
Terry, Nicole 1934- *St&PR 93*
Terry, Percy 1919- *St&PR 93*
Terry, Philip John *WhoScE 91-1*
Terry, R(ichard) R(unciman) 1865-1938 *Baker 92*
Terry, Randall *BioIn 17*
Terry, Randall B., Jr. 1934- *St&PR 93*
Terry, Richard Allan 1920- *WhoAm 92*
Terry, Richard Edward 1937- *St&PR 93, WhoAm 92*
Terry, Richard Frank 1949- *WhoWor 93*
Terry, Richmond Bohler 1934- *WhoAm 92*
Terry, Ricky Don 1957- *WhoSSW 93*
Terry, Robert B. *Law&B 92*
Terry, Robert Davis 1924- *WhoAm 92*
Terry, Robert Meredith 1939- *WhoSSW 93*
Terry, Roger Harold 1925- *WhoWor 93*
Terry, Ronald A. 1930- *St&PR 93*
Terry, Ronald Anderson 1930- *WhoSSW 93*
Terry, Ruth 1919- *SweetSg C [port]*
Terry, Sarah Meiklejohn 1937- *WhoE 93*
Terry, Sherrie Lynn 1957- *WhoAmW 93*
Terry, Sonny 1911-1986 *Baker 92*
Terry, Stephen C. 1942- *St&PR 93*
Terry, Steven Craig 1950- *WhoSSW 93*
Terry, Tai C. *Law&B 92*
Terry, Taylor Rankin 1914- *WhoSSW 93*
Terry, Thomas *ConTFT 10*

Terry, Thomas E. Law&B 92
Terry, Thomas E. 1937- St&PR 93
Terry, Thomas Edward 1937- WhoAm 92
Terry, Walter 1924-1991 AnObit 1991
Terry, Walter Bliss d1991 BioIn 17
Terry, William Burks, Jr. Law&B 92
Terry, William E. 1933- WhoAm 92
Terry, William F. 1941- St&PR 93
Terry, William Hutchinson 1951- WhoEmL 93, WhoSSW 93
Terry, Wyllys 1908-1991 BioIn 17
Terry-Thomas 1911-1990 BioIn 17, ConTFT 10, IntDcF 2-3 [port], QDrFCA 92 [port]
Terschak, Adolf 1832-1901 Baker 92
ter Schegget, Gysbertus Hendricus 1927- WhoWor 93
Terschluse, Marilyn Ann 1956- WhoWrEP 92
Tersenov, Savva Auzaam 1924- WhoWor 93
Tersteeg, Beth BioIn 17
Terstriep, Matthew E. 1952- St&PR 93
Tertea, Igor 1928- WhoScE 91-4
Tertis, Lionel 1876-1975 Baker 92
Terumi, Saito 1943- WhoWor 93
Teruo, Yasui 1929- WhoWor 93
Teruoka, Itsuko 1928- WhoWor 93
Tervani, Irma 1887-1936 Baker 92
See Also Ackte, Aino 1876-1944 OxDcOp
Tervel OxDcByz
Tervo, Malcolm 1949- BioIn 17
Tervo, Sonja BioIn 17
Tervo, Timo Martti 1950- WhoWor 93
Terwilleger, Ken B. Law&B 92
Terwilliger, Cynthia Lou 1955- WhoAmW 93
Terwilliger, Dennis Thomas 1948- St&PR 93
Terwilliger, George James, III 1950- WhoAm 92
Terwilliger, Kent M. 1924-1989 BioIn 17
Terwilliger, Robert Elwin 1917-1991 BioIn 17
Terzakis, Dimitri 1938- Baker 92
Terzakis, John Anthony 1935- WhoE 93
Terzi, Mario 1936- WhoScE 91-3
Terzi, Nice 1936- WhoScE 91-3
Terzian, Kristi BioIn 17
Terzian, Philip Henry 1950- WhoE 93
Terzian, Pierre 1948- ConAu 136
Terzian, Richard H. 1937- St&PR 93
Terzian, Yervant 1939- WhoAm 92
Terziani, Eugenio 1824-1889 Baker 92
Terzuolo, Carlo WhoScE 91-3
Tesar, Delbert 1935- WhoAm 92
Tesar, Milo Benjamin 1920- WhoAm 92
Tesarek, Dennis George 1935- WhoSSW 93
Tesche, Manfred 1934- WhoScE 91-3
Teschemacher, Hansjorg 1938- WhoScE 91-3
Teschemacher, Margarete 1903-1959 OxDcOp
Tescher, John P. 1938- St&PR 93
Teschner, Richard Rewa 1908- WhoAm 92
Teschner, Thomas Martin 1956- St&PR 93
Tesei, Alberto 1944- WhoScE 91-3
TeSelle, Eugene Arthur, Jr. 1931- WhoSSW 93
Te Selle, Grace H. 1928- WhoWrEP 92
Tesh, John BioIn 17
Tesh, Ruby Nifong 1917- WhoWrEP 92
Tesh, Samuel Lee, III 1937- WhoSSW 93
Teshigahara, Hiroshi 1927- MiSFD 9
Teshigawara, Saburo BioIn 17
Teshoian, Nishan 1941- WhoAm 92
Tesich, Steve 1942- BioIn 17, WhoAm 92
Tesio, Vittorio 1940- WhoWor 93
Tesi-Tramontini, Vittoria 1700-1775 Baker 92, OxDcOp
Teske, Gerald Peter 1934- St&PR 93
Teske, Richard Henry 1939- WhoAm 92
Tesla, Nikola 1856-1943 GayN
Tesler, Lawrence Gordon 1945- St&PR 93
Teslik, Sarah Anna Ball 1953- WhoE 93
Tesone, Judy 1943- WhoAmW 93
Tesoriere, Silvan A. d1991 BioIn 17
Tesoriero, Albert 1939- St&PR 93
Tesoriero, Anthony Ronald 1943- St&PR 93
Tesoriero, John d1991 BioIn 17
Tesoriero, John S. 1953- WhoE 93
Tesoriero, Lisa Monica 1958- St&PR 93
Tesoro, Giuliana Cavaglieri 1921- WhoAmW 93
Tesovic, Zarko 1936- WhoScE 91-4
Tesreau, Charles Monroe 1889-1946 BiDAMSp 1989
Tess, Giulia 1889-1976 Baker 92, OxDcOp
Tessa, Marian Lorraine 1950- WhoE 93, WhoWor 93
Tessa, Paul 1938- WhoAfr
Tessari, Luigi 1931- WhoScE 91-3
Tessarini, Carlo c. 1690-c. 1766 Baker 92
Tessarotto, Massimo 1946- WhoScE 91-3
Tesscorolo, Giulia 1889-1976 Baker 92
Tessel, Carla Joy 1959- WhoAmW 93
Tessen, Gail Eileen 1937- WhoAmW 93
Tessier, Andre 1886-1931 Baker 92
Tessier, Charles fl. 16th cent.- Baker 92
Tessier, Gaston 1887-1960 BioIn 17
Tessier, Jean-Michel 1941- St&PR 93, WhoAm 92
Tessier, Thomas 1947- ScF&FL 92
Tessitore, Joseph St&PR 93
Tessler, Arthur Ned 1927- WhoE 93
Tessler, Ellen Louise 1949- WhoAmW 93
Tessler, Lisa Beth 1957- WhoE 93
Tessler, Mark A(rnold) 1941- ConAu 37NR
Tessler, Martin Melvyn 1937- WhoE 93
Tessler, Stephanie 1940- ScF&FL 92
Tessler, Stephanie Gordon BioIn 17
Tessman, Irwin 1929- WhoAm 92
Tessmann, Gunther 1884-1969 IntDcAn
Testa, Andreas Lodewyk Franciscus Maria 1942- WhoWor 93
Testa, Bernard J. 1941- WhoScE 91-4
Testa, Douglas 1944- St&PR 93
Testa, Jack Anthony 1927- St&PR 93
Testa, Michael Harold 1939- WhoAm 92
Testa, Nicholas Michael 1940- St&PR 93
Testa, Richard J. 1939- St&PR 93
Testa, Stephen Michael 1951- WhoWor 93
Testa-Egan, Frances Ann 1956- WhoAmW 93
Testanero, Nick 1950- St&PR 93
Testaverde, Vincent Frank 1963- BiDAMSp 1989
Tester, Leonard Wayne 1933- WhoE 93
Tester, Sylvia Root 1939- BioIn 17
Tester, William John 1950- WhoE 93
Testerman, Jean Leighton 1923- WhoWrEP 92
Testore, Carlo Giuseppe c. 1660-c. 1720 Baker 92
Testori, Carlo Giovanni 1714-1782 Baker 92
Testori, Giovanni 1923-1993 DcLB 128 [port]
Testut, Richard Stanton 1910- St&PR 93
Testwuide, Thomas R. 1945- St&PR 93
Tetart, C. WhoScE 91-2
Tetelman, Alice Fran 1941- WhoE 93
Tetenman, Alison 1964- WhoEmL 93
Tetens, Arnold R. 1937- St&PR 93
Tetenyi, Pal Gabor 1929- WhoScE 91-4
Teter, John S. 1930- St&PR 93
Teteris, Nicholas John 1929- WhoAm 92
Tether, Anthony John 1941- WhoWor 93
Tether, Ivan Joseph Law&B 92
Teti, Alfred L. 1935- WhoSSW 93
Teti, Maria Anna 1954- WhoWor 93
Tetiwa, Werner Law&B 92
Tetley, Arthur Russell 1930- WhoWrEP 92
Tetley, Glen 1926- WhoAm 92
Tetlow, Edwin BioIn 17
Tetlow, Edwin 1905- WhoAm 92, WhoWrEP 92
Tetmajer, Kazimierz Przerwa 1865-1940 PolBiDi
Tetmajer, Wlodzimierz 1861-1923 PolBiDi
Tetrazzini, Elvira OxDcOp
Tetrazzini, Eva 1862-1938 Baker 92, OxDcOp
Tetrazzini, Luisa 1871-1940 Baker 92, BioIn 17, IntDcOp [port], OxDcOp
Tetreault, Richard J. Law&B 92
Tetreault, Wilfred F. 1927- WhoWrEP 92
Tetrick, Elbert Lain 1923- WhoAm 92
Tetrick, Roberta Gail 1949- WhoAmW 93
Tetrick, William M. 1915- St&PR 93
Tetro, John M. 1946- St&PR 93
Tetsu, Yozo 1935- St&PR 93
Tetzeli, Frederick Edward 1930- WhoAm 92
Tetzlaff, Charles David 1954- St&PR 93
Tetzlaff, David BioIn 17
Tetzner, Ruth 1917- WhoWor 93
Teu, Sanfjord Brogdyne, III 1943- St&PR 93
Teuber, Hans-Joachim 1918- WhoScE 91-3
Teuber, Michael 1937- WhoScE 91-3
Teubner, Ferdinand C. 1921- St&PR 93
Teubner, Ferdinand Cary, Jr. 1921- WhoAm 92
Teufel, Dolores Enid Arlene 1921- WhoWrEP 92
Teufel, Partricia Ann 1950- WhoE 93
Teugels, Jozef Lodewyk 1939- WhoWor 93
Teunissen, John J. 1933- ScF&FL 92
Teuscher, Eberhard 1934- WhoWor 93
Teuscher, George William 1908- WhoAm 92
Teutsch, David Alan 1950- WhoE 93
Teutsch, Jonathan 1961- WhoE 93
Teutsch, Miriam Law&B 92
Teutsch, Robert E. 1944- St&PR 93
Teutsch, Robert Eugene Law&B 92
Tevault, David Earl 1948- WhoE 93
Tevebaugh, Charles Richard 1935- St&PR 93
Teveit, Brenton L. St&PR 93
Teverbaugh, Kerry Dean 1954- WhoWor 93
Teves, Margarito B. 1943- WhoAsAP 91
Tevis, G. Phillip 1942- St&PR 93
Tevis, George Phillip 1942- WhoSSW 93
Tevis, Gregory C. Law&B 92
Tevis, Walter 1928-1984 ScF&FL 92
Tevlin, Michael F. 1953- WhoWrEP 92
Tevrizian, Dickran M., Jr. 1940- WhoAm 92
Tevy, Marcel 1926- WhoWor 93
Tew, E. James, Jr. 1933- WhoSSW 93, WhoWor 93
Tew, Jannette Riggs 1945- WhoAmW 93
Tew, Ryan M. Law&B 92
TeWalt, Louise Varney 1915- WhoAmW 93
Tewari, Kirti Prakash 1943- WhoWor 93
Tewari, Prayag Dutta 1935- WhoWor 93
Teweles, Claude ScF&FL 92
Tewell, Joseph Robert, Jr. 1934- WhoAm 92, WhoSSW 93
Tewi, Thea WhoAm 92, WhoE 93
Tewinkle, Randall V. Law&B 92
Tewkesbury, Alan Matthew, Jr. Law&B 92
Tewkesbury, Edward P. Law&B 92
Tewkesbury, Joan 1937- MiSFD 9
Tewkesbury, Joan F. 1936- WhoAm 92
Tewksbury, Bob BioIn 17
Tewksbury, Edwin d1904 BioIn 17
Tewksbury, Jim d1888 BioIn 17
Tewksbury, John Walter Beardsley 1878-1968 BiDAMSp 1989
Tewksbury, Peter 1924- MiSFD 9
Tews, Thomas D. Law&B 92
Tews, William L. 1936- St&PR 93
Tex, Joe 1933-1982 SoulM
Texas Tornados, The ConMus 8 [port]
Texter, Elmer Clinton, Jr. 1923- WhoAm 92
Textor, Robert Bayard 1923- WhoAm 92
Tey, Wei-Ming 1952- WhoWor 93
Teyber Baker 92
Teyber, Anton 1754-1822 Baker 92
Teyber, Elisabeth 1744?-1816 Baker 92
Teyber, Franz 1756-1810 Baker 92
Teyber, Matthaus c. 1711-1785 Baker 92
Teyber, Therese 1760?-1830 Baker 92
Teymour, Aly I. 1920- WhoUN 92
Teyssie, Philippe 1928- WhoScE 91-2
Teyte, Maggie 1888-1976 Baker 92, IntDcOp, OxDcOp
Tezak, Paul 1954- St&PR 93
Tezcan, Semih Salih 1933- WhoScE 91-4
Tezel, Ahmet 1943- WhoE 93
Tezza, Angel 1951- WhoWor 93
Thabard, F. WhoScE 91-2
Thacher, Angela BlkAmWO
Thacher, Barbara Burrall 1943- WhoAmW 93
Thacher, Mollie Day AmWomPl
Thacher, Russell 1919-1990 BioIn 17
Thacker, James Douglas 1949- WhoE 93
Thacker, John WhoScE 91-1
Thacker, John E. 1944- St&PR 93
Thacker, Michael M. 1936- St&PR 93
Thacker, Shannon Stephen 1956- WhoSSW 93
Thacker, Ted Allan 1948- St&PR 93
Thackeray, Jonathan E. 1936- WhoAm 92
Thackeray, William Makepeace 1811-1863 MagSWL [port], ScF&FL 92, WorLitC [port]
Thackery, Anne ScF&FL 92
Thackery, Bud 1903-1990 BioIn 17
Thackery, Ronald Law&B 92
Thackray, Arnold Wilfrid 1939- WhoAm 92, WhoE 93
Thackray, James Carden 1924- St&PR 93
Thackray, Richard Irving 1927- WhoAm 92
Thackston, Edward Lee 1937- WhoSSW 93
Thackston, Tom 1937- St&PR 93
Thaddeus, Michael 1967- WhoWor 93
Thaddeus, Patrick 1932- WhoAm 92
Thaden, Edward Carl 1922- WhoAm 92
Thadewaldt, Hermann 1827-1909 Baker 92
Thadhani, Suresh 1939- St&PR 93
Thagard, Greg Bruce 1951- St&PR 93
Thagard, Norman E. 1943- WhoAm 92
Thaha, Mohamed Nizam Mohamed WhoWor 93
Thai, Paul BioIn 17
Thai, Van-Can 1944- WhoUN 92
Thais, Luis Alberto 1942- WhoUN 92
Thakker, Ashok 1947- WhoSSW 93
Thakor, Haren Bhaskerrao 1938- WhoAm 92
Thakral, R.P. 1949- St&PR 93
Thakur, Arvind 1941- WhoWor 93
Thakur, Chandresh P. 1935- WhoAsAP 91
Thakur, Jagatpal Singh 1923- WhoAsAP 91
Thakur, Ramesh Chandra 1948- WhoWor 93
Thakur, Rameshwar WhoAsAP 91
Thakur, Surendra Singh 1954- WhoAsAP 91
Thal, Herbert Ludwig, Jr. 1932- WhoAm 92
Thal, Herbert Van ScF&FL 92
Thal, Russell K. 1934- St&PR 93
Thalacker, Arbie Otto 1907- St&PR 93
Thalacker, Arbie Robert 1935- WhoAm 92, WhoWor 93
Thalacker, Weldon A. 1933- St&PR 93
Thalberg, Irving Grant 1899-1936 BioIn 17
Thalberg, Sigismond (Fortune Francois) 1812-1871 Baker 92
Thalden, Barry R. 1942- WhoAm 92, WhoWor 93
Thalelaios OxDcByz
Thalen, D.C.P. 1943- WhoScE 91-3
Thalenfeld, David 1919- St&PR 93
Thaler, Alice Marie 1955- WhoAmW 93
Thaler, Donald Bruce 1947- St&PR 93
Thaler, Martin S. 1932- WhoAm 92
Thaler, Otto Felix 1923- WhoAm 92
Thaler, Richard H. 1945- WhoAm 92
Thaler, Richard Winston, Jr. 1951- WhoE 93, WhoWor 93
Thaler, Shmuel 1958- SmATA 72 [port]
Thaler, Wendell L. 1934- St&PR 93
Thalheim, David T. 1954- St&PR 93
Thalheim, Jay Richard 1922- WhoE 93, WhoWor 93
Thalheimer, Louis B. 1944- WhoAm 92, WhoE 93
Thalheimer, Richard Hastings 1940- St&PR 93
Thall, Burnett M. 1922- St&PR 93
Thall, Burnett Murray 1922- WhoAm 92
Thall, Sheila 1926- St&PR 93
Thallemer, John D. Law&B 92
Thaller, George Erwin 1947- WhoWor 93
Thaller, Karl E. 1936- WhoE 93
Thaller, Thomas Victor 1941- St&PR 93
Thalmann, Alfred 1940- WhoScE 91-3
Thalmann, Daniel 1946- WhoWor 93
Thalmann, Joan Louise 1952- WhoAmW 93, WhoEmL 93
Thalwitz, Wilfried P. 1932- WhoUN 92
Tham, Hilary WhoWrEP 92
Tham, Seong Chee 1932- WhoWor 93
Tham, Yee Kiong 1955- WhoWor 93
Thaman, Michael Edwards 1949- St&PR 93, WhoAm 92
Thambi Durai, M. 1947- WhoAsAP 91
Thamelt, Wolfgang 1938- WhoWor 93
Thames, J.A. 1935- St&PR 93
Thamm, Erik Gerhardt 1950- St&PR 93
Thamm, Jochen Walter 1952- WhoWor 93
Thampi, Mohan Varghese 1960- WhoEmL 93, WhoSSW 93, WhoWor 93
Thanassoulopoulos, Constantine C. 1933- WhoScE 91-3
Thane, Elswyth 1900-1984 ScF&FL 92
Thanepohn, Donald A. 1925- St&PR 93
Thang, Ming Nguy 1929- WhoScE 91-2
Thangkabalu, K.V. 1950- WhoAsAP 91
Thani, Hamad Bin Khalifa Al 1949- WhoWor 93
Thani, Khalifa bin Hamad Al 1932- WhoWor 93
Thannhauser, Isaac 1774- BioIn 17
Thant, U 1909-1974 ColdWar 2 [port], DcTwHis
Thapa, Govinda Bahadur 1948- WhoWor 93
Thapa, Minto Jung 1945- WhoUN 92
Thapar, Valmik 1952- ConAu 139
Thar, Ferdinand August 1940- WhoAm 92
Tharin, Frank 1910-1990 BioIn 17
Tharney, Leonard John 1929- WhoE 93
Tharoor, Shashi 1956- ConLC 70 [port]
Tharp, Benjamin Carroll, Jr. 1919- WhoAm 92
Tharp, David Minton 1948- WhoEmL 93, WhoSSW 93, WhoWor 93
Tharp, Joseph B. 1934- St&PR 93
Tharp, Karen Ann 1944- WhoAmW 93
Tharp, Marye Charlese 1947- WhoSSW 93
Tharp, Roland George 1930- WhoAm 92
Tharp, Twyla BioIn 17
Tharp, Twyla 1941- WhoAm 92, WhoAmW 93, WhoE 93
Tharp, Twyla 1942- News 92 [port]
Tharpe, Frazier Eugene 1941- WhoAm 92
Thas, Joseph Adolphe Francois 1944- WhoWor 93
Thatcher, Barbara Cone 1942- WhoAmW 93
Thatcher, Blythe Darlyn 1947- WhoWrEP 92
Thatcher, Connie Sue 1940- WhoAmW 93
Thatcher, Donald d1990 BioIn 17

Thatcher, Everett W. d1992 NewYTBS 92
Thatcher, Everett W. 1904-1992 BioIn 17
Thatcher, J.R. 1940- St&PR 93
Thatcher, Kristine Marie 1950- WhoAmW 93
Thatcher, Margaret BioIn 17
Thatcher, Margaret 1925- ColdWar 1 [port]
Thatcher, Margaret Hilda 1925- DcTwHis, WhoWor 93
Thatcher, Paul Rexford, Sr. 1935- St&PR 93
Thatcher, Sanford Gray 1943- WhoAm 92
Thau, Claude 1948- St&PR 93
Thau, William Albert, Jr. 1940- WhoAm 92, WhoSSW 93
Thauer, Peter E. 1939- St&PR 93
Thaulow, Haakon 1944- WhoScE 91-4
Thaung, Raymond Saw 1940- WhoWor 93
Thaut Family BioIn 17
Thavarajah, Maniccam 1950- WhoWor 93
Thaw, Barbara Cooley 1958- St&PR 93
Thaw, Murray Charles 1915- St&PR 93
Thaw, Robert M. 1953- St&PR 93
Thaw, Wayne Howard 1957- St&PR 93
Thawerbhoy, Nazim G. 1947- St&PR 93
Thawka, Mao d1991 BioIn 17
Thaxter, Celia Laighton 1835-1894 BioIn 17
Thaxter, Phyllis 1921- BioIn 17
Thaxton, Linda Nell 1945- WhoWrEP 92
Thaxton, Mary Lynwood 1944- WhoSSW 93
Thayer, A. Bronson 1939- St&PR 93
Thayer, Alexander Wheelock 1817-1897 Baker 92
Thayer, Artemas Bronson 1939- WhoSSW 93
Thayer, Carlyle Alan 1945- WhoWor 93
Thayer, Edna Louise 1936- WhoAmW 93, WhoWor 93
Thayer, Edwin Cabot 1935- WhoAm 92
Thayer, Ernest Lawrence 1863-1940 BioIn 17
Thayer, (Whitney) Eugene 1838-1889 Baker 92
Thayer, Gerald Campbell 1943- St&PR 93, WhoAm 92
Thayer, Graydon Allan 1931- St&PR 93
Thayer, James Bradley 1831-1902 OxCSupC
Thayer, James Norris 1926- WhoAm 92
Thayer, Jane 1904- WhoAm 92, WhoAmW 93, WhoWor 93
Thayer, John E. 1923-1990 BioIn 17
Thayer, Larry A. St&PR 93
Thayer, Lee BioIn 17
Thayer, Lee 1927- WhoAm 92
Thayer, Marjorie 1908-1992 BioIn 17
Thayer, Nancy 1943- ScF&FL 92
Thayer, Nelson S.T. d1990 BioIn 17
Thayer, Nina Nichols 1945- WhoAmW 93
Thayer, Paul William 1927- WhoSSW 93
Thayer, Richard E. St&PR 93
Thayer, Robert E. 1931- St&PR 93
Thayer, Robert Louayn, Jr. 1960- WhoAm 92
Thayer, Russell, III 1922- WhoAm 92
Thayer, Scott David Law&B 92
Thayer, Stephen C. 1939- St&PR 93
Thayer, Stuart Wallace 1924- St&PR 93
Thayer, Stuart Wilson Walker 1926- WhoAm 92
Thayer, Tiffany 1902-1959 ScF&FL 92
Thayer, Walter Stephen, III 1946- WhoAm 92
Thayer, William S. 1948- WhoE 93
Thayne, Emma Lou Warner 1924- WhoWrEP 92
Thayne, Richard Grant 1930- WhoWor 93
The, Victor 1942- WhoWor 93
Theall, Donald Francis 1928- WhoAm 92
Theander, Olof 1924- WhoScE 91-4
Theberge, Jean-Yves 1937- WhoCanL 92
Theberge, Pierre Georges 1942- WhoAm 92
Thebom, Blanche 1918- Baker 92, OxDcOp
Thecla, of Iconium, Saint BioIn 17
Thede, John C. Law&B 92
Thedinger, Robert Scott 1949- St&PR 93
Thee, Susan M. Law&B 92
Thee, William N., Jr. Law&B 92
Theede, Hans Johannes 1934- WhoWor 93
Theen, John Frederick 1952- St&PR 93
Theen, Rolf Heinz-Wilhelm 1937- WhoAm 92
Theenhaus, R. WhoScE 91-3
Theesfeld, Harold L. 1935- St&PR 93
Theeuwes, Felix 1937- St&PR 93
Theibert, Philip Reed 1952- WhoWrEP 92
Theil, Henri 1924- WhoAm 92
Theil, Johann 1646-1724? Baker 92
Theile, Konstantin Leo Albert 1951- WhoWor 93
Theiler, Carol Alice 1951- WhoAmW 93
Theiller, George J. 1950- St&PR 93
Theimer, Roland R. 1941- WhoScE 91-3
Thein, Edmund 1934- WhoWor 93
Thein, Jack Lee 1945- St&PR 93
Thein, Peter Joseph, Jr. 1938- St&PR 93
Theis, Adolf 1933- WhoWor 93
Theis, Bernard Regis 1957- WhoE 93
Theis, Francis William 1920- WhoAm 92
Theis, Frank Gordon 1911- WhoAm 92
Theis, Henry E. 1933- St&PR 93
Theis, James F. 1924- WhoIns 93
Theis, Nancy Elizabeth 1948- WhoE 93
Theis, Paul Anthony 1923- WhoE 93
Theis, Robert J. 1924- WhoAm 92
Theis, Steven Thomas 1959- WhoE 93, WhoEmL 93, WhoWor 93
Theis, Stuart H. Law&B 92
Theis, Werner R. 1926- WhoScE 91-3, WhoWor 93
Theis, Willi Hans Paul 1941- WhoUN 92
Theisen, Clifford Richard 1951- St&PR 93
Theisen, Edwin M. 1930- St&PR 93
Theisen, Edwin Mathew 1930- WhoAm 92
Theisen, George I. 1926- St&PR 93, WhoSSW 93
Theisen, Lee Scott 1943- WhoAm 92
Theisen, Virgil J. 1942- St&PR 93
Theiss, Louis Leonard, Jr. 1925- WhoE 93
Theiss, Walter Otto Law&B 92
Thek, Paul 1933-1988 BioIn 17
Thekkekara, Jack 1949- St&PR 93
Thekla OxDcByz
Thelan, Anne Marguerite 1959- WhoAmW 93
Thelen, John F. 1949- WhoIns 93
Thelen, John Frederick Law&B 92
Thelen, John Frederick 1949- St&PR 93
Thelen, Max 1957- St&PR 93
Thelen, Max, Jr. 1919- WhoAm 92
Thelen, Robert Frederick 1950- WhoSSW 93
Thelen, Robert L. 1938- St&PR 93
Thelian, John 1941- St&PR 93
Thelian, Lorraine 1948- WhoAmW 93
Thelin, John Robert 1947- WhoSSW 93
Thellier, Michel 1933- WhoScE 91-2
Thellman, Fred 1933- St&PR 93
Thelman, John Patrick 1942- WhoE 93
Thelwall, John 1764-1834 BioIn 17
Themal, Henry Gunther 1926- St&PR 93
Themann, Hermann 1927- WhoScE 91-3
Themelis, Nickolas John WhoAm 92
Themerson, Stefan 1910-1988 BioIn 17, ScF&FL 92
Themistios c. 317-c. 388 OxDcByz
Themistocles c. 514BC-c. 449BC HarEnMi
Themstrup, Bendt WhoIns 93
Themstrup, Bendt 1941- St&PR 93
Then, George J. 1942- St&PR 93
Thenabadu, Pujitha Nihal 1941- WhoWor 93
Thenen, Shirley Warnock 1935- WhoAmW 93
Theobald, Edward Robert 1947- WhoEmL 93, WhoWor 93
Theobald, Forrest D. Law&B 92
Theobald, Francois Roland 1942- WhoWor 93
Theobald, Greg Law&B 92
Theobald, Harold L., Jr. 1961- WhoSSW 93
Theobald, Jean-Gerard 1937- WhoScE 91-2
Theobald, Jurgen Peter 1933- WhoScE 91-3
Theobald, Michael Francis WhoScE 91-1
Theobald, Robert 1929- WhoWrEP 92
Theobald, Robert Alfred 1884-1957 HarEnMi
Theobald, Thomas Charles 1937- St&PR 93, WhoAm 92
Theobald, William Louis 1936- WhoAm 92
Theocaris, Pericles S. 1921- WhoScE 91-3
Theodahad d536 OxDcByz
Theodamus 1896-1970 ScF&FL 92
Theodoli, Fillipo M. BioIn 17
Theodoli-Braschi, Giovanni Angelo 1942- WhoWor 93
Theodora dc. 867 OxDcByz
Theodora d1056 OxDcByz
Theodora c. 497-548 OxDcByz
Theodoracopulos, Taki BioIn 17
Theodorakis, Mikis 1925- Baker 92, WhoWor 93
Theodora of Arta dc. 1270 OxDcByz
Theodora of Thessalonike c. 812-892 OxDcByz
Theodore OxDcByz
Theodore d636 OxDcByz
Theodore, Ares Nicholas 1933- WhoWor 93
Theodore, Brother ScF&FL 92
Theodore, Chris P. BioIn 17
Theodore, Eustace D. 1941- WhoAm 92, WhoE 93
Theodore, Gregory George 1954- WhoSSW 93
Theodore, Jasmina A. Law&B 92
Theodore, Louis 1934- WhoE 93
Theodore, Nick Andrew 1928- WhoAm 92, WhoSSW 93
Theodore, Rene 1940- DcCPCAm
Theodore, Samuel S. 1952- WhoE 93
Theodore Abu-Qurra c. 74-?-c. 820 OxDcByz
Theodoredis, Roger Emmanuel Law&B 92
Theodore Graptos c. 775-c. 841 OxDcByz
Theodore Komnenos Doukas c. 1180-c. 1253 OxDcByz
Theodore Laskaris, I c. 1174-1221 OxDcByz
Theodore Laskaris, II 1221-1258 OxDcByz
Theodore Lector dc. 527 OxDcByz
Theodore of Alania fl. 13th cent.- OxDcByz
Theodore of Dekapolis fl. 10th cent.- OxDcByz
Theodore of Edessa OxDcByz
Theodore of Kyzikos fl. 10th cent.- OxDcByz
Theodore of Mopsuestia c. 350-c. 428 OxDcByz
Theodore of Raithou fl. 7th cent.- OxDcByz
Theodore of Smyrna dc. 1112 OxDcByz
Theodore of Stoudios 759-826 OxDcByz
Theodore of Sykeon d613 OxDcByz
Theodore Palaiologos, I 135-?-1407 OxDcByz
Theodore Palaiologos, II c. 1395-1448 OxDcByz
Theodores, Thomas Law&B 92
Theodore Scholastikos fl. 6th cent.- OxDcByz
Theodorescu, Radu Amza Serban 1933- WhoAm 92
Theodorescu, Razvan 1939- WhoWor 93
Theodore Stratelates OxDcByz
Theodore Svetoslav OxDcByz
Theodore Synkellos fl. 7th cent.- OxDcByz
Theodore Teron OxDcByz
Theodoret of Cyrrhus c. 393-c. 466 OxDcByz
Theodoric the Great c. 454-526 OxDcByz
Theodoric the Great, I c. 454-526 HarEnMi
Theodorokanos OxDcByz
Theodoropoulos, George 1935- WhoScE 91-3
Theodorou, Jerry 1959- WhoE 93
Theodorou, Nikolaos 1929- WhoScE 91-3
Theodorsson, Pall 1928- WhoScE 91-4
Theodosios OxDcByz
Theodosios 583?-602 OxDcByz
Theodosios, I 347?-395 OxDcByz
Theodosios, II 401-450 OxDcByz
Theodosios, III dc. 754 OxDcByz
Theodosios Boradiotes OxDcByz
Theodosios of Pecera OxDcByz
Theodosios of Turnovo c. 1300-1363 OxDcByz
Theodosios the Deacon OxDcByz
Theodosios the Koinobiarches d529 OxDcByz
Theodosios the Monk fl. 9th cent.- OxDcByz
Theodosis, Dimitri 1945- BioIn 17
Theodosius d376 HarEnMi
Theodosius, His Beatitude Metropolitan 1933- WhoAm 92
Theodosius Flavius the Great, I c. 346-395 HarEnMi
Theodosius the Elder dc. 375 OxDcByz
Theodotos Kassiteras, I OxDcByz
Theodotus fl. 8th cent.- OxDcByz
Theognostos OxDcByz
Theognostos fl. 9th cent.- OxDcByz
Theohari-Apostolidi, Theodora 1947- WhoWor 93
Theoharides, Theoharis Constantin 1950- WhoWor 93
Theoktiste of Lesbos OxDcByz
Theoktistos d855 OxDcByz
Theoktistos the Stoudite fl. 14th cent.- OxDcByz
Theoleptos c. 1250-1322 OxDcByz
Theologitis, John Michael 1956- WhoWor 93
Theon, John Speridon 1934- WhoAm 92
Theon of Alexandria fl. c. 360-380 OxDcByz
Theophanes dc. 947 OxDcByz
Theophanes fl. c. 1100- OxDcByz
Theophanes Graptos c. 778-845 OxDcByz
Theophanes Kerameus OxDcByz
Theophanes of Byzantium fl. 6th cent.- OxDcByz
Theophanes of Medeia OxDcByz
Theophanes of Sicily fl. 9th cent.- OxDcByz
Theophanes the Confessor c. 760-817? OxDcByz
Theophanes The Greek fl. 1378-1405 OxDcByz
Theophano c. 940-c. 976 OxDcByz
Theophanous, Andrew Charles 1946- WhoAsAP 91
Theophilos 812?-842 OxDcByz
Theophilos fl. 6th cent.- OxDcByz
Theophilos of Edessa c. 695-785 OxDcByz
Theophilos Protospatharios OxDcByz
Theophilos the Indian dc. 364 OxDcByz
Theophilus, Bimal David Madhukar 1960- WhoWor 93
Theophobos d840? OxDcByz
Theophylaktos 917- OxDcByz
Theophylaktos c. 1050-c. 1126 OxDcByz
Theorell, (Per Gunnar) Toeres 1942- ConAu 139
Theorell, (Per Gunnar) Tores ConAu 139
Theoret, France 1942- WhoCanL 92
Theorianos fl. 12th cent.- OxDcByz
Theotokopoulos, Domenikos 1541-1614 BioIn 17
Therburg, Rolf-Dieter 1955- WhoScE 91-3
Theremin, Leon 1896- Baker 92
Therese, de Lisieux, Saint 1873-1897 BioIn 17
Theriault, Adrien WhoCanL 92
Theriault, Marlene Lynn 1943- WhoSSW 93
Theriault, Neyle Colquitt 1931- WhoSSW 93
Theriault, Normand Adrien 1938- WhoE 93
Theriault, Omer Courtland 1922- St&PR 93
Theriault, Yves d1983 WhoCanL 92
Theriault, Yves 1915-1983 BioIn 17
Therio, Adrien 1925- WhoCanL 92, WhoWrEP 92
Therios, Ioannis 1944- WhoScE 91-3
Theris, Andrea 1962- St&PR 93
Thermansen, Peter H. 1955- St&PR 93
Thern, Karoly 1817-1886 Baker 92
Thern, Lajos 1848-1920 See Thern, Karoly 1817-1886 Baker 92
Thern, Vilmos 1847-1911 See Thern, Karoly 1817-1886 Baker 92
Thernstrom, Melanie 1964- BioIn 17
Thernstrom, Stephan Albert 1934- WhoAm 92, WhoE 93, WhoWrEP 92
Theros, Elias George 1919- WhoAm 92
Theroux, Alexander 1939- BioIn 17
Theroux, Dennis Robert 1951- WhoE 93
Theroux, Eugene 1938- WhoAm 92
Theroux, Paul BioIn 17
Theroux, Paul 1941- ScF&FL 92
Theroux, Paul Edward 1941- WhoAm 92, WhoWor 93
Therre, John Patrick 1951- St&PR 93
Therrien, Francois Xavier, Jr. 1928- WhoWor 93
Therrien, Rene A. 1945- St&PR 93
Therrien, Robert Wilfrid 1929- St&PR 93
Therrien, Wally C. 1950- WhoE 93
Thervil, Walner Jacques 1953- WhoSSW 93
Thesen, Arne 1943- WhoAm 92
Thesen, Sharon 1946- BioIn 17, WhoCanL 92
Thesiger, Wilfred 1910- BioIn 17, Expl 93
Thesing, Michael 1955- St&PR 93
Thesman, Jean ScF&FL 92
Thessin, Mark Gregory Law&B 92
Thestrup, Ole Emil 1943- WhoWor 93
Theuer, Paul John 1936- St&PR 93
Theuer, Richard C. 1939- St&PR 93
Theuerkauf, Barbara Leigh 1963- WhoAmW 93
Theuninck, Donald W. 1947- St&PR 93
Theunissen, Lydia Marie 1959- WhoSSW 93
Theurer, Byron W. 1939- WhoWor 93
Theurer, Gary L. St&PR 93
Theuretzbacher, Norbert WhoScE 91-4
Theus, Lucius 1922- AfrAmBi
Theuws, Jacques A. 1914- IntDcAn
Thevenet, Patricia Confrey 1924- WhoAmW 93
Thevenet, Rene 1926- WhoWor 93
Thevenin, Marc 1938- WhoScE 91-2
Thevenote, William J. 1934- St&PR 93
Thews, Joe-Dietrich 1930- WhoScE 91-3
Thews, Marvin Emory, Jr. 1946- WhoSSW 93
Thexton, Peter Mason 1928- WhoE 93
Theydon, John ScF&FL 92
Theye, Terry L. St&PR 93
Theys, M. WhoScE 91-1
Theys, Michel Hubert 1934- WhoScE 91-2
Thiam, Habib 1933- WhoAfr, WhoWor 93
Thiandoum, Hyacinthe Cardinal 1921- WhoWor 93
Thibadeau, Eugene Francis 1933- WhoE 93
Thibaud, Jacques 1880-1953 Baker 92
Thibaudeau, Colleen 1925- WhoCanL 92
Thibaudeau, May Murphy 1908- BioIn 17, WhoAmW 93
Thibaudet, Jean-Yves 1961- Baker 92
Thibault, Catherine 1942- WhoScE 91-2, WhoWor 93
Thibault, Genevieve 1902-1975 Baker 92

Thibault, Harry G. *Law&B 92*
Thibault, Jacques Anatole 1844-1924 *BioIn 17*
Thibault, Joseph Laurent 1944- *WhoAm 92*
Thibault, L. *Law&B 92*
Thibault, Robert Paul *Law&B 92*
Thibault, Ronald Martin 1943- *St&PR 93*
Thibault, Stanley M. 1944- *St&PR 93*
Thibaut, IV 1201-1253 *Baker 92*
Thibaut, Anton Friedrich Justus 1772-1840 *Baker 92*
Thibaut, Howard Woodrow 1938- *St&PR 93*
Thibblin, Alf N.F. 1949- *WhoScE 91-4*
Thibeau, Michel 1939- *WhoScE 91-2*
Thibeault, Dale Wilkins 1938- *WhoAmW 93*
Thibeault, George Walter 1941- *WhoE 93*
Thibeault, Jack Claude 1946- *WhoE 93*
Thibert, Roger Joseph 1929- *WhoAm 92*
Thibodeau, David M. *BioIn 17*
Thibodeau, David Michael 1940- *St&PR 93*
Thibodeau, Gary A. 1938- *WhoAm 92*
Thibodeau, Paul E. 1946- *St&PR 93*
Thibodeaux, Eileen Nehiley 1959- *WhoSSW 93*
Thibodeaux, Elizabeth Cancienne 1960- *WhoAmW 93*
Thibodeaux, Julius P. 1929- *St&PR 93*
Thibodeaux, Michael Jared *Law&B 92*
Thibos, Charles Ray 1947- *St&PR 93*
Thibout, Eric 1942- *WhoScE 91-2*
Thickins, Graeme Richard 1946- *WhoEmL 93*
Thickstun, Steve 1948- *St&PR 93*
Thickstun, Timothy Lee 1950- *St&PR 93*
Thiebaud, Jean-Marie Andre Marcel 1944- *WhoWor 93*
Thiebaud, Wayne 1920- *BioIn 17, WhoAm 92*
Thiebaut, Luc 1946- *WhoScE 91-2*
Thiebauth, Bruce Edward 1947- *WhoEmL 93*
Thiede, James F. 1938- *St&PR 93*
Thiede, Janet Lynn 1958- *WhoAmW 93*
Thiede, Jorn 1941- *WhoScE 91-3*
Thiel, Douglas J. 1942- *St&PR 93*
Thiel, Frank Anthony 1928- *St&PR 93, WhoIns 93*
Thiel, Gregory Robert 1939- *St&PR 93*
Thiel, Heinz-Jurgen 1949- *WhoScE 91-3*
Thiel, John E. 1951- *WhoE 93*
Thiel, Kathryn E. *Law&B 92*
Thiel, Philip 1920- *WhoAm 92*
Thiel, Rebecca Baldwin 1947- *WhoAmW 93*
Thiel, Wilbert A. 1937- *St&PR 93*
Thiele, Alan R. *Law&B 92*
Thiele, Carlton H. d1991 *BioIn 17*
Thiele, Colin 1920- *ChlLR 27 [port], DcChlFi*
Thiele, Colin (Milton) 1920- *MajAI [port], SmATA 72 [port]*
Thiele, Edward Earl 1940- *St&PR 93*
Thiele, Gerhard 1935- *WhoScE 91-3*
Thiele, Gloria Day 1931- *WhoAmW 93*
Thiele, Herbert William Albert 1953- *WhoEmL 93, WhoSSW 93, WhoWor 93*
Thiele, Howard Nellis, Jr. 1930- *WhoAm 92*
Thiele, Irma Edna 1918- *WhoAmW 93*
Thiele, Norma Jean 1930- *WhoAmW 93*
Thiele, Paul Frederick 1914- *St&PR 93, WhoAm 92*
Thiele, Robert Edward, Jr. 1948- *WhoE 93*
Thiele, Robert Wilhelm 1932- *WhoUN 92*
Thiele, Terry V. *Law&B 92*
Thiele, William Edward 1942- *St&PR 93*
Thielemann, Carrie Lou 1956- *WhoWor 93*
Thielen, Benedict 1902-1965 *BioIn 17*
Thielen, Claire Marie 1957- *WhoAmW 93*
Thielen, Cynthia *WhoAmW 93*
Thielen, Gerd 1942- *WhoScE 91-3*
Thielen, Peter Gerrit 1924- *WhoWor 93*
Thielheim, Klaus Oswald 1932- *WhoScE 91-3, WhoWor 93*
Thielman, Ann 1959- *WhoSSW 93*
Thielman, Jeff(rey D.) 1963- *ConAu 139*
Thielman, William Albert 1915- *St&PR 93*
Thielmann, Jeannine Henderson 1956- *WhoAmW 93*
Thielmann, Johann Adolf 1765-1824 *HarEnMi*
Thielsch, Deborah L. *St&PR 93*
Thielsch, Helmut John 1922- *WhoAm 92*
Thieman, Alice Anne 1941- *WhoAmW 93*
Thieman, Ralph 1932- *St&PR 93*
Thieman, Ronald George 1947- *St&PR 93*
Thiemann, Charles Lee 1937- *WhoAm 92*
Thiemann, Friedrich 1940- *WhoWor 93*
Thiemann, Jeffrey J. 1957- *St&PR 93*
Thiemann, Kevin Barry 1957- *WhoEmL 93*
Thiemann, Paul Peter 1927- *WhoAm 92*
Thiemann, Ronald Frank 1946- *WhoAm 92*
Thiemann, Walter K. 1926- *WhoScE 91-3*
Thieme, Allan Roy 1937- *St&PR 93*
Thieme, Beth L. 1955- *St&PR 93*
Thieme, Fredrick Patton 1914-1989 *BioIn 17*
Thieme, G. *WhoScE 91-3*
Thieme, Jerzy Krzysztof 1947- *WhoWor 93*
Thien Ah Koon, Andre *WhoAsAP 91*
Thienen, Marcel van 1922- *Baker 92*
Thier, Hans-Peter 1937- *WhoScE 91-3*
Thier, Herbert David 1932- *WhoAm 92*
Thier, J. Jay 1952- *St&PR 93*
Thier, Norman S. 1930- *St&PR 93*
Thier, Samuel Osiah 1937- *WhoAm 92, WhoE 93*
Thierauf, Robert J. 1933- *WhoWor 93*
Thierfelder, Jorg 1955- *WhoWor 93*
Thierfelder, Stefan 1933- *WhoScE 91-3*
Thierfelder, William Richard, III *WhoE 93*
Thieriot, Charles H. 1914- *St&PR 93*
Thieriot, Richard Tobin 1942- *WhoAm 92*
Thierry, J. *WhoScE 91-3*
Thierry, John Adams 1913- *WhoAm 92*
Thierry, Mikolaj Henryk 1920- *WhoScE 91-4*
Thierry, Robert Charles 1938- *WhoWor 93*
Thiers, Adolphe 1797-1877 *BioIn 17*
Thiers, Eugene Andres 1941- *WhoWor 93*
Thiers, G. *WhoScE 91-2*
Thierwechter, Lester Valentine, Jr. 1953- *WhoE 93*
Thiery, Jean Paul 1947- *WhoScE 91-2*
Thiery, Michel 1924- *WhoScE 91-2, WhoWor 93*
Thies, Austin Cole 1921- *WhoAm 92*
Thies, Frank R. 1929- *St&PR 93*
Thies, Richard Henry 1941- *St&PR 93*
Thies, Roger Elliot 1933- *WhoSSW 93*
Thiesenhusen, William Charles 1936- *WhoAm 92*
Thiesing, John E. 1938- *St&PR 93*
Thiess, Gregory G. *Law&B 92*
Thiess, Kenneth C. *Law&B 92*
Thiessen, Cherie *WhoCanL 92*
Thiessen, Delbert Duane 1932- *WhoAm 92*
Thiessen, G.G. 1938- *St&PR 93*
Thiessen, Gordon George 1938- *WhoAm 92*
Thiessen, J. Grant 1947- *ScF&FL 92*
Thiessen, Tiffani-Amber *BioIn 17*
Thiessen, William Ernest 1934- *WhoSSW 93*
Thieu, Nguyen Van 1923- *BioIn 17, DcTwHis*
Thigpen, Alton Hill 1927- *WhoAm 92*
Thigpen, Annette 1963- *WhoAmW 93*
Thigpen, Bobby *BioIn 17*
Thigpen, E. Eugene *Law&B 92*
Thigpen, Edward Eugene *Law&B 92*
Thigpen, James Tate 1944- *WhoWor 93*
Thigpen, James W. 1937- *St&PR 93*
Thigpen, Jill 1959- *St&PR 93*
Thigpen, Morris Lee, Sr. 1939- *WhoSSW 93*
Thigpen, Peter Lee 1939- *St&PR 93*
Thigpen, Richard Elton, Jr. 1930- *WhoAm 92, WhoSSW 93*
Thigpen, Robert Thomas 1963- *WhoAm 92*
Thilander, Holger O.I. 1922- *WhoScE 91-4*
Thill, Andre 1924- *WhoScE 91-2*
Thill, Georges 1897-1984 *Baker 92, IntDcOp, OxDcOp*
Thill, James Francis 1939- *St&PR 93*
Thill, John Peter 1912- *St&PR 93*
Thill-DaDaBo, Mary Kay 1954- *WhoAmW 93*
Thilly, Claude Hector 1937- *WhoScE 91-2*
Thilman, Johannes Paul 1906-1973 *Baker 92*
Thilo, Susan Lynn 1953- *WhoAmW 93*
Thim, Dennis d1992 *NewYTBS 92*
Thimann, Kenneth Vivian 1904- *WhoAm 92*
Thimbleby, Harold William *WhoScE 91-1*
Thimm, Alfred Louis 1923- *WhoAm 92, WhoE 93*
Thimm, Ronald G. 1955- *St&PR 93*
Thiong'o, Ngugi wa 1938- *BioIn 17*
Thiounn, Prasith 1930- *WhoWor 93*
Thiriet, Maurice 1906-1972 *Baker 92*
Thirkell, Gary J. 1944- *St&PR 93*
Thirkell, Thomas James 1960- *St&PR 93*
Thirring, Walter E. 1927- *WhoScE 91-4*
Thirring, Walter Eduard 1927- *WhoWor 93*
Thirugnana Sambanthar, Vettivelu 1934- *WhoWor 93*
Thiry, Medard 1947- *WhoScE 91-2*
Thiry, Paul 1904- *WhoAm 92, WhoWor 93*
Thissen, Wil Antonius Helena 1949- *WhoWor 93*
Thistlewood, David John 1944- *WhoWor 93*
Thivend, Pierre 1939- *WhoScE 91-2*
Thivolet, J. *WhoScE 91-2*
Thliveris, Elizabeth Hope 1939- *WhoWrEP 92*
Tho, Nguyen Huu 1910- *DcTwHis*
Thobo-Carlsen, John 1943- *WhoWor 93*
Thoburn, Helen *AmWomPl*
Thoday, Alan G. 1933- *St&PR 93*
Thode, Edward Frederick 1921- *WhoAm 92*
Thoden Van Velzen, Syo K. 1934- *WhoScE 91-3*
Thodos, Constantine N. 1926- *St&PR 93*
Thody, Philip 1928- *ScF&FL 92*
Thoemke, Kris Walter 1951- *WhoSSW 93*
Thoemke, Lorrie *BioIn 17*
Thoene, Carl Louis 1927- *St&PR 93*
Thoenen, Hans 1928- *WhoScE 91-3*
Thoenes, Wolfgang Carl 1929- *WhoScE 91-3*
Thoeni, Mary Irene 1950- *WhoAmW 93*
Thoet, Carolyn D. 1943- *St&PR 93*
Thoet, Felicity *ScF&FL 92*
Thofner, Jeffrey *Law&B 92*
Thoft-Christensen, Palle 1936- *WhoScE 91-2*
Thoinan, Ernest 1827-1894 *Baker 92*
Thokar, Greg 1955- *ScF&FL 92*
Thoke, Ann Elisabeth 1952- *St&PR 93*
Thole, Mary Elizabeth 1950- *WhoAmW 93*
Thole, Rodney G. 1939- *St&PR 93*
Tholen, A.R. 1938- *WhoScE 91-2*
Tholey, James Michael 1952- *St&PR 93*
Tholey, Paul Nikolaus 1937- *WhoWor 93*
Tholle, Anders 1931- *WhoUN 92*
Tholstrom, Kendell V. 1945- *St&PR 93*
Thom, Clifford 1948- *St&PR 93*
Thom, Douglas A. 1939- *St&PR 93*
Thom, Douglas Andrew 1939- *WhoAm 92*
Thom, James Alexander 1933- *WhoWrEP 92*
Thom, Joseph M. 1919- *WhoAm 92*
Thom, Paul 1941- *ConAu 139*
Thom, Randy 1951- *WhoAm 92*
Thom, Richard David 1944- *WhoAm 92*
Thom, Robert 1929-1979 *ScF&FL 92*
Thoma, Carl D. *St&PR 93*
Thoma, Carl Dee 1948- *WhoAm 92*
Thoma, Edward W. 1945- *St&PR 93*
Thoma, Elmar Herbert 1926- *WhoWor 93*
Thoma, Manfred H.F. 1929- *WhoScE 91-3*
Thoma, Manfred Hubert 1929- *WhoWor 93*
Thoma, Richard William 1921- *WhoSSW 93*
Thoma, Stephen Joseph 1953- *WhoSSW 93*
Thoma, Susan Jane 1951- *WhoAmW 93*
Thoma, Therese 1845-1921 *See* Vogl, Heinrich 1845-1900 *Baker 92* *See Also* Vogl, Heinrich 1845-1900 *OxDcOp*
Thomadakis, Panagiotis Evangelos 1941- *WhoWor 93*
Thomais of Lesbos 10th cent.?- *OxDcByz*
Thomalske, R.E. Gunther 1925- *WhoWor 93*
Thoman, George M. 1926- *St&PR 93*
Thoman, Henry Nixon 1957- *St&PR 93, WhoAm 92*
Thoman, Istvan 1862-1940 *Baker 92*
Thoman, James M. 1955- *WhoE 93*
Thoman, Joseph Karol, Jr. 1947- *WhoE 93*
Thoman, Maria 1899-1948 *See* Thoman, Istvan 1862-1940 *Baker 92*
Thoman, Mark 1935- *WhoAm 92*
Thoman, Mark Edward 1936- *WhoAm 92*
Thoman, Valerie 1878-1948 *See* Thoman, Istvan 1862-1940 *Baker 92*
Thomann, J. Donald 1931- *WhoE 93*
Thomarios, Paul Nick 1947- *St&PR 93*
Thomas *OxDcByz*
Thomas, A. *WhoScE 91-1*
Thomas, A.D. *WhoScE 91-1*
Thomas, A.G. *WhoScE 91-1*
Thomas, A.T. 1927- *WhoScE 91-1*
Thomas, Adrian Wesley 1939- *WhoSSW 93*
Thomas, Alan Richard 1942- *WhoAm 92*
Thomas, Albert 1878-1932 *BioIn 17*
Thomas, Alice Holmes 1965- *WhoAmW 93*
Thomas, Allen Lloyd 1939- *WhoAm 92, WhoE 93, WhoWor 93*
Thomas, Ambroise 1811-1896 *IntDcOp [port], OxDcOp*
Thomas, (Charles Louis) Ambroise 1811-1896 *Baker 92*
Thomas, Andrea Kojm *Law&B 92*
Thomas, Andrew Houston 1935- *WhoE 93*
Thomas, Andrew J., Jr. *Law&B 92*
Thomas, Anika D. 1976- *BioIn 17*
Thomas, Ann Bolton 1935- *WhoAmW 93*
Thomas, Ann Emery 1924- *WhoE 93*
Thomas, Ann Van Wynen 1919- *WhoAm 92*
Thomas, Anna 1948- *MiSFD 9*
Thomas, Anthony 1947- *St&PR 93*
Thomas, Anthony William 1949- *WhoWor 93*
Thomas, Antony *MiSFD 9*
Thomas, Archibald Johns, III 1952- *WhoSSW 93, WhoWor 93*
Thomas, Armand Cecil 1939- *WhoWor 93*
Thomas, Arthur Ellis 1938- *St&PR 93*
Thomas, Arthur Goring 1850-1892 *Baker 92, OxDcOp*
Thomas, Arthur L. 1947- *St&PR 93*
Thomas, Arthur Lawrence 1931- *WhoAm 92*
Thomas, Arthur Lawrence 1952- *WhoWrEP 92*
Thomas, Audrey Callahan *BioIn 17*
Thomas, Audrey Grace 1935- *WhoCanL 92*
Thomas, Augusta Read 1964- *Baker 92*
Thomas, Bailey Alfred *WhoAm 92*
Thomas, Barbara Siebel *BioIn 17*
Thomas, Barbara Singer 1946- *WhoAm 92, WhoAmW 93*
Thomas, Barbara Susan 1949- *WhoAmW 93*
Thomas, Barbara Yvonne 1953- *WhoE 93*
Thomas, Barlett L. *Law&B 92*
Thomas, Barry 1942- *WhoScE 91-1*
Thomas, Benjamin E. *Law&B 92*
Thomas, Bernard Alain 1941- *WhoUN 92*
Thomas, Bertha Sophia 1959- *WhoEmL 93*
Thomas, Beth Eileen Wood 1916- *WhoAm 92*
Thomas, Betty *AmWomPl, MiSFD 9, WhoAm 92*
Thomas, Beverly Phyllis 1938- *WhoWrEP 92*
Thomas, Bide L. 1935- *St&PR 93*
Thomas, Bide Lakin 1935- *WhoAm 92*
Thomas, Bill *BioIn 17, ScF&FL 92*
Thomas, Billy 1920- *WhoWor 93*
Thomas, Billy Joe 1942- *WhoAm 92*
Thomas, Billy Marshall 1940- *WhoAm 92*
Thomas, Bransby William John *WhoScE 91-1*
Thomas, Brantley D., Jr. 1933- *St&PR 93*
Thomas, Brenda E. 1957- *WhoAmW 93, WhoEmL 93*
Thomas, Brian 1955- *WhoE 93*
Thomas, Brian G. 1934- *St&PR 93*
Thomas, Brook 1947- *ConAu 139*
Thomas, Brooks 1931- *WhoAm 92*
Thomas, Brunhilde S. 1911- *St&PR 93*
Thomas, C. A., Mrs. *AmWomPl*
Thomas, C.S. 1939- *St&PR 93*
Thomas, Calvert 1916- *WhoAm 92*
Thomas, Cameron *BioIn 17*
Thomas, Carl O. *Law&B 92*
Thomas, Carla 1942- *SoulM*
Thomas, Carlos 1931- *WhoScE 91-3*
Thomas, Carmen Adele 1934- *WhoSSW 93*
Thomas, Carol Taylor 1952- *WhoAmW 93*
Thomas, Carol Todd 1952- *WhoEmL 93*
Thomas, Charles *BioIn 17*
Thomas, Charles Brosius 1935- *St&PR 93*
Thomas, Charles F. *WhoAm 92*
Thomas, Charles Howard, II 1934- *WhoAm 92*
Thomas, Cheri Autumn 1959- *WhoSSW 93*
Thomas, Chester Wiley 1940- *WhoSSW 93*
Thomas, Chris *BioIn 17*
Thomas, Christian Gottfried 1748-1806 *Baker 92*
Thomas, Christina Joan 1940- *WhoWrEP 92*
Thomas, Christopher R. 1948- *St&PR 93*
Thomas, Christopher Robert 1948- *WhoAm 92*
Thomas, Christopher Yancey, III 1923- *WhoAm 92*
Thomas, Clara 1919- *WhoCanL 92*
Thomas, Clara Mc Candless 1919- *WhoWrEP 92*
Thomas, Clara McCandless 1919- *WhoAm 92, WhoAmW 93*
Thomas, Clarence *BioIn 17*
Thomas, Clarence 1948- *AfrAmBi, CngDr 91, CurBio 92 [port], News 92 [port], OxCSupC [port], WhoAm 92, WhoE 93*
Thomas, Claudewell Sidney 1932- *WhoAm 92*
Thomas, Clinton C. d1990 *BioIn 17*
Thomas, Clinton Lavurn, Jr. 1943- *WhoSSW 93*
Thomas, Colin Gordon, Jr. 1918- *WhoAm 92*

Thomas, Craig 1933- CngDr 91, WhoAm 92
Thomas, Craig 1942- ScF&FL 92
Thomas, Curtis H. Law&B 92
Thomas, Cynthia Gail 1956- WhoAmW 93
Thomas, Cyrus H. 1925- St&PR 93
Thomas, D.E. WhoScE 91-2
Thomas, D.M. BioIn 17
Thomas, D.M. 1935- ScF&FL 92
Thomas, Dale 1951- WhoSSW 93
Thomas, Dale John 1940- WhoE 93
Thomas, Daniel B. WhoWrEP 92
Thomas, Daniel Foley 1950- WhoAm 92
Thomas, Daniel Holcombe 1906- WhoAm 92
Thomas, Danny 1912-1991 AnObit 1991, BioIn 17
Thomas, Darlene Marie 1957- WhoAmW 93
Thomas, Dave MiSFD 9
Thomas, Dave 1932- News 93-2 [port]
Thomas, David BioIn 17
Thomas, David A. Law&B 92
Thomas, David A. 1958- St&PR 93
Thomas, David A., Jr. 1936- St&PR 93
Thomas, David Ansell 1917- WhoAm 92, WhoWor 93
Thomas, David Brynmor WhoScE 91-1
Thomas, David Burton 1943- WhoWor 93
Thomas, David Earl, III 1945- St&PR 93
Thomas, David Eirian Lewis WhoScE 91-1
Thomas, David Hurst 1945- WhoAm 92
Thomas, David John 1924- WhoWor 93
Thomas, David John 1962- WhoWor 93
Thomas, David Joseph 1955- WhoWrEP 92
Thomas, David Lee 1962- WhoWor 93
Thomas, David (Lionel Mercer) 1943- Baker 92
Thomas, David Lloyd 1942- WhoSSW 93
Thomas, David Northcutt 1934- WhoSSW 93
Thomas, David Phillip 1918- WhoAm 92
Thomas, David Raymond 1946- WhoSSW 93
Thomas, David Robert 1954- WhoE 93, WhoEmL 93, WhoWor 93
Thomas, David Trevillyan 1921- WhoE 93
Thomas, Davis 1928- WhoAm 92
Thomas, (Charles) Davis 1928- WhoWrEP 92
Thomas, Dawn C. BlkAull 92
Thomas, Debi BioIn 17
Thomas, Debi 1967- AfrAmBi
Thomas, Deborah Allen 1943- WhoAmW 93
Thomas, Debra Janine BiDAMSp 1989
Thomas, Demetria Lucille 1963- WhoAmW 93
Thomas, Dennis D. Law&B 92
Thomas, Dennis R. WhoIns 93
Thomas, Diane E. Law&B 92
Thomas, Donald Charles 1935- WhoAm 92
Thomas, Donald Earl, Jr. 1951- WhoAm 92
Thomas, Donald James 1944- WhoE 93
Thomas, Donna ScF&FL 92
Thomas, Dorothy Jean 1931- WhoSSW 93
Thomas, Dorothy Swaine 1899-1977 BioIn 17
Thomas, Dudley Jerome 1940- WhoE 93
Thomas, Dwight 1944- ScF&FL 92
Thomas, Dwight Elwood, Jr. 1945- WhoSSW 93
Thomas, Dwight Rembert 1944- WhoSSW 93
Thomas, Dylan 1914-1953 BioIn 17, MagSWL [port], TwCLC 45 [port], WorLitC [port]
Thomas, E. Donnall BioIn 17
Thomas, Eapen 1939- WhoAm 92
Thomas, Edith Matilda 1854-1925 AmWomPl
Thomas, Edward 1878-1917 BioIn 17
Thomas, Edward Donnall 1920- WhoAm 92, WhoWor 93
Thomas, Edward Francis, Jr. 1937- WhoAm 92
Thomas, Edward John 1937- WhoWor 93
Thomas, Edward Llewellyn- ScF&FL 92
Thomas, Edward M. ScF&FL 92
Thomas, Elizabeth Ann WhoAmW 93
Thomas, Elizabeth Marshall 1931- ScF&FL 92
Thomas, Ella Gertrude Clanton 1848-1889 BioIn 17
Thomas, Eric BioIn 17
Thomas, Eric Jackson WhoScE 91-1
Thomas, Eric James WhoScE 91-1
Thomas, Ernest Henry BioIn 17
Thomas, Esther Merlene 1945- WhoAmW 93, WhoWor 93
Thomas, Eugene Anthony 1930- St&PR 93
Thomas, Eugene C. 1931- WhoAm 92
Thomas, Eugene Ritter 1954- WhoSSW 93
Thomas, Evelyn F. 1922- WhoWrEP 92
Thomas, F(ranklin) Richard 1940- WhoWrEP 92
Thomas, Fillmore 1916- St&PR 93
Thomas, Florence Kathleen 1945- WhoAmW 93
Thomas, Francis 1912-1977 ScF&FL 92
Thomas, Francois Pierre 1957- WhoWor 93
Thomas, Frank BioIn 17
Thomas, Frank Edward 1968- WhoAm 92
Thomas, Frank Howard 1929- St&PR 93
Thomas, Frank Joseph 1943- St&PR 93
Thomas, Frank Joseph 1950- WhoE 93
Thomas, Frank Joseph, Jr. 1929- BiDAMSp 1989
Thomas, Franklin Augustine 1934- WhoAm 92
Thomas, Fred 1932- WhoScE 91-3
Thomas, Frederick William 1806-1866 JrnUS
Thomas, Garnett Jett 1920- WhoSSW 93, WhoWor 93
Thomas, Garth Johnson 1916- WhoAm 92
Thomas, Gary BioIn 17
Thomas, Gary L. 1937- WhoE 93
Thomas, Gary Lynn 1942- WhoAm 92, WhoE 93
Thomas, Gary Wayne 1953- WhoSSW 93, WhoWor 93
Thomas, Gene Allen 1935- WhoSSW 93
Thomas, Geoffrey C. WhoAm 92
Thomas, George Henry 1816-1870 BioIn 17, HarEnMi
Thomas, George Leicester, III 1934- St&PR 93
Thomas, George Martin 1941- WhoSSW 93
Thomas, George S. Law&B 92
Thomas, George Stanley 1942- St&PR 93
Thomas, Georgie A. WhoAm 92, WhoAmW 93
Thomas, Gerald 1920- MiSFD 9
Thomas, Gerald Everett 1935- St&PR 93
Thomas, Geraldine P. 1951- WhoAmW 93
Thomas, Gerard 1925- St&PR 93
Thomas, Gerard P. 1930- St&PR 93
Thomas, Gertrude Ida 1889- AmWomPl
Thomas, Gilda M. Law&B 92
Thomas, Gordon 1933- ConAu 40NR
Thomas, Gordon W. Law&B 92
Thomas, Gregory C. Law&B 92
Thomas, Gregory C. 1947- St&PR 93
Thomas, Gregory E. 1949- WhoWrEP 92
Thomas, Gustav Adolf 1842-1870 Baker 92
Thomas, H. Emerson 1902- St&PR 93
Thomas, H. Gregory 1907-1990 BioIn 17
Thomas, H. Suzanne Law&B 92
Thomas, Hans Guenter 1937- WhoScE 91-3
Thomas, Hans Michael 1920- WhoWor 93
Thomas, Harold Allen, Jr. 1913- WhoAm 92
Thomas, Harold Edward 1954- WhoSSW 93, WhoWor 93
Thomas, Harold Stephen 1943- WhoE 93
Thomas, Harry Dorrett 1944- WhoE 93
Thomas, Hazel Foster 1923- WhoWrEP 92
Thomas, Heck 1850-1912 BioIn 17
Thomas, Helen 1877-1967 BioIn 17
Thomas, Helen A. 1920- WhoAm 92, WhoAmW 93
Thomas, Henri 1912- WhoWor 93
Thomas, Hilary Bryn 1943- WhoAmW 93, WhoE 93, WhoWor 93
Thomas, Howard Christopher WhoScE 91-1
Thomas, Hugh 1931- WhoWor 93
Thomas, Ian St&PR 93
Thomas, Ian Leslie Maurice 1937- WhoAm 92
Thomas, Ianthe 1951- BlkAull 92
Thomas, Irma BioIn 17, SoulM
Thomas, Irma Gail 1956- WhoAmW 93
Thomas, Isaiah 1750-1831 BioIn 17, JrnUS
Thomas, Isiah BioIn 17
Thomas, Isiah Lord 1961- WhoAm 92
Thomas, Isiah Lord, III 1961- AfrAmBi
Thomas, J. Darrell 1960- WhoE 93
Thomas, J. Earl 1918- WhoAm 92
Thomas, J.M. WhoScE 91-1
Thomas, J. Mikesell 1951- WhoAm 92
Thomas, Jack Anthony 1940- WhoSSW 93
Thomas, Jack Boyd 1944- St&PR 93
Thomas, Jack H. 1941- St&PR 93, WhoAm 92
Thomas, Jack Robert 1937- St&PR 93
Thomas, Jackie L. 1941- St&PR 93
Thomas, Jacqueline Marie 1952- WhoAm 92
Thomas, James BioIn 17
Thomas, James Alphaeus Emanuel 1929- WhoUN 92
Thomas, James Bert, Jr. 1935- WhoAm 92
Thomas, James Brown 1922- WhoIns 93
Thomas, James Edward 1944- WhoE 93, WhoWor 93
Thomas, James Edward, Jr. 1950- WhoWor 93
Thomas, James Naughton 1934- WhoSSW 93
Thomas, James Raymond 1947- WhoSSW 93
Thomas, James S., Jr. Law&B 92
Thomas, James W. St&PR 93
Thomas, Jane Resh 1936- ScF&FL 92
Thomas, Jay BioIn 17
Thomas, Jean E. St&PR 93
Thomas, Jean-Jacques Robert 1948- WhoSSW 93, WhoWor 93
Thomas, Jeanette M. Law&B 92
Thomas, Jeanette Mae 1946- WhoAmW 93, WhoEmL 93
Thomas, Jeffrey B. Law&B 92
Thomas, Jennie 1952- WhoEmL 93
Thomas, Jeremy Ambler WhoScE 91-1
Thomas, Jerry R. BioIn 17
Thomas, Jess 1927- OxDcOp, WhoAm 92
Thomas, Jess (Floyd) 1927- Baker 92
Thomas, Jesse James 1933- WhoWrEP 92
Thomas, Jimmy Linn 1941- St&PR 93
Thomas, Jimmy Lynn 1941- WhoAm 92, WhoSSW 93
Thomas, Joab Langston 1933- WhoAm 92, WhoE 93
Thomas, Joe Carroll 1931- WhoAm 92
Thomas, John 1826-1913 Baker 92
Thomas, John Bowman 1925- WhoAm 92
Thomas, John C. 1928- St&PR 93
Thomas, John Charles 1891-1960 Baker 92
Thomas, John Charles 1950- St&PR 93, WhoAm 92
Thomas, John Charles 1959- WhoSSW 93
Thomas, John Clayton 1944- ConAu 139
Thomas, John Cox, Jr. 1927- WhoAm 92
Thomas, John Curtis 1941- BiDAMSp 1989
Thomas, John David 1935- WhoSSW 93
Thomas, John David 1951- WhoEmL 93, WhoWor 93
Thomas, John E. Law&B 92
Thomas, John Earl 1943- WhoAm 92
Thomas, John Edward 1947- WhoAm 92
Thomas, John Edwin 1931- WhoAm 92, WhoSSW 93
Thomas, John G. MiSFD 9
Thomas, John Hansford, Jr. 1909- WhoSSW 93
Thomas, John Howard 1941- WhoAm 92
Thomas, John Jacob 1869-1952 BioIn 17
Thomas, John Kerry 1934- WhoAm 92
Thomas, John L. BioIn 17
Thomas, John Lovell 1926- WhoAm 92
Thomas, John Mark Law&B 92
Thomas, John Melvin 1933- WhoAm 92, WhoWor 93
Thomas, John Oswald 1944- WhoScE 91-4
Thomas, John R. 1917- St&PR 93
Thomas, John Richard Law&B 92
Thomas, John Richard 1921- WhoAm 92
Thomas, John Robert 1939- WhoE 93
Thomas, John Rogers 1829-1896 Baker 92
Thomas, John Russell WhoScE 91-1
Thomas, John Thieme 1935- St&PR 93, WhoAm 92
Thomas, John Wesley 1932- WhoE 93
Thomas, John Willard, Jr. 1927- St&PR 93
Thomas, John William 1937- WhoAm 92
Thomas, Jon Roger 1946- WhoAm 92
Thomas, Jonathan Wesley 1963- WhoE 93
Thomas, Jose Honore 1946- WhoWor 93
Thomas, Joseph Allan Law&B 92
Thomas, Joseph Allan 1929- WhoAm 92
Thomas, Joseph Fleshman 1915- WhoAm 92
Thomas, Joseph R. Law&B 92
Thomas, Joseph R. 1935- WhoAm 92
Thomas, Joseph Winand 1940- WhoSSW 93
Thomas, Joyce Augusta 1946- WhoE 93
Thomas, Joyce Carol BioIn 17
Thomas, Joyce Carol 1938- BlkAull 92, MajAI [port], ScF&FL 92, WhoWrEP 92
Thomas, Juanita M. Law&B 92
Thomas, Judith A. Waugh 1940- WhoE 93
Thomas, Judith Becker 1943- St&PR 93
Thomas, Judith E. St&PR 93
Thomas, K.V. 1946- WhoAsAP 91
Thomas, Kate AmWomPl
Thomas, Kelly S. Law&B 92
Thomas, Kenneth Alfred, Jr. 1946- WhoE 93
Thomas, Kenneth Glyndwr 1944- St&PR 93, WhoAm 92
Thomas, Kevin E. 1951- WhoWor 93
Thomas, Kurt BioIn 17
Thomas, (Georg Hugo) Kurt 1904-1973 Baker 92
Thomas, L.B. 1936- St&PR 93
Thomas, Lance WhoScE 91-1
Thomas, Langley C. 1953- St&PR 93
Thomas, Laura Marlene 1936- WhoAmW 93, WhoWor 93
Thomas, Laurence 1949- BioIn 17
Thomas, Laurence W. 1927- WhoWrEP 92
Thomas, Lawrason Dale 1934- WhoAm 92
Thomas, Lawrence E. 1942- WhoAm 92
Thomas, Lawrence Eugene 1931- WhoAm 92
Thomas, Lawrence R. 1935- St&PR 93
Thomas, Lee B., Jr. 1926- St&PR 93
Thomas, Lee W. 1926- WhoE 93
Thomas, Leo J. 1936- WhoAm 92
Thomas, Leona Marlene 1933- WhoAmW 93, WhoWor 93
Thomas, Lera Millard 1900- BioIn 17
Thomas, Lewis 1913- BioIn 17, ConAu 38NR, WhoAm 92
Thomas, Lewis Jones, Jr. 1930- WhoAm 92
Thomas, Lida Larrimore Turner 1897- AmWomPl
Thomas, Linda J. Law&B 92
Thomas, Lindsay 1943- WhoAm 92
Thomas, Lisa Neufeld 1947- WhoAmW 93
Thomas, Liz BioIn 17
Thomas, Llewellyn Hilleth 1903- WhoAm 92
Thomas, Louise d1991 BioIn 17
Thomas, Lowell 1892-1981 BioIn 17, JrnUS
Thomas, Lowell, Jr. 1923- WhoAm 92
Thomas, Lowell Phillip 1933- WhoSSW 93
Thomas, Lowell S., Jr. 1931- St&PR 93
Thomas, Loyd A. 1933- St&PR 93
Thomas, Ludwig Karl 1933- WhoWor 93
Thomas, Lydia Waters 1944- WhoAmW 93
Thomas, Lyn Carey WhoScE 91-1
Thomas, M. Donald 1926- WhoAm 92
Thomas, M. Sava B. Law&B 92
Thomas, Mabel R. d1992 NewYTBS 92
Thomas, Mable 1957- WhoAmW 93
Thomas, Mack 1952- St&PR 93
Thomas, Mack L. Law&B 92
Thomas, Malayilmelathethil 1932- WhoSSW 93
Thomas, Margaret G. Law&B 92
Thomas, Margaret Jean 1943- WhoAm 92, WhoAmW 93
Thomas, Marie Giannella 1962- WhoAmW 93
Thomas, Marjorie L. Law&B 92
Thomas, Mark E. Law&B 92
Thomas, Mark Ellis 1955- WhoWrEP 92
Thomas, Mark Stanton 1931- WhoAm 92
Thomas, Mark U. Law&B 92
Thomas, Marlo BioIn 17
Thomas, Marlo 1938- ConTFT 10
Thomas, Marlo 1943- WhoAm 92, WhoAmW 93
Thomas, Marsha McKeon 1951- WhoAmW 93
Thomas, Martha Wetterhall 1949- WhoAmW 93
Thomas, Martin 1913-1985 ScF&FL 92
Thomas, Martin David 1947- WhoScE 91-1
Thomas, Martin Vincent 1950- WhoWor 93
Thomas, Martyn 1948- WhoWor 93
Thomas, Mary BioIn 17
Thomas, Mary Corbin 1958- WhoSSW 93
Thomas, Mary E. 1929- St&PR 93
Thomas, Mary Elizabeth 1962- WhoE 93
Thomas, Mary Jane WhoAmW 93
Thomas, Mary Louise 1927- WhoWrEP 92
Thomas, Mary M. 1946- St&PR 93
Thomas, Mary Martin 1961- WhoEmL 93
Thomas, Matthew Henderson, Jr. 1948- WhoWrEP 92
Thomas, Michael A. 1949- St&PR 93
Thomas, Michael Allan 1957- WhoSSW 93
Thomas, Michael David 1957- WhoWor 93
Thomas, Michael Duane 1948- WhoSSW 93
Thomas, Michael G. Law&B 92
Thomas, Michael M(ackenzie) 1936- ConAu 139
Thomas, Michael Ridley 1948- WhoE 93
Thomas, Michael Tilson 1944- Baker 92, WhoAm 92, WhoWor 93
Thomas, Michele Karin 1948- WhoSSW 93
Thomas, Michele Y. ScF&FL 92
Thomas, Mildred 1930- St&PR 93
Thomas, Miriam AmWomPl
Thomas, Mitchell, Jr. 1936- WhoAm 92
Thomas, Nadine 1952- WhoAmW 93
Thomas, Nanette S. Law&B 92

Thomas, Nate 1957- *AfrAmBi [port]*
Thomas, Nick *BioIn 17*
Thomas, Norman *BioIn 17*
Thomas, Norman 1884-1968 *BioIn 17, JrnUS*
Thomas, Norman Carl 1932- *WhoWrEP 92*
Thomas, Norman M. 1884-1968 *PolPar*
Thomas, Norman Percy d1989 *BioIn 17*
Thomas, Norwood Anderson, Jr. 1932- *St&PR 93*
Thomas, Oomman 1950- *WhoSSW 93*
Thomas, Orville C. 1915- *WhoAm 92*
Thomas, Owen Clark 1922- *WhoAm 92*
Thomas, Pamela Mary 1937- *WhoUN 92*
Thomas, Pascal Joseph 1958- *WhoWor 93*
Thomas, Patricia Anne 1927- *WhoAmW 93*
Thomas, Patrick F. 1954- *St&PR 93*
Thomas, Patrick H. 1942- *St&PR 93*
Thomas, Patrick Herbert 1942- *WhoSSW 93*
Thomas, Patrick Robert Maxwell 1943- *WhoE 93*
Thomas, Paul Emery 1927- *WhoAm 92*
Thomas, Paul G. 1955- *St&PR 93*
Thomas, Paul Irving 1906- *WhoAm 92*
Thomas, Payne Edward Lloyd 1919- *WhoAm 92*
Thomas, Peter *BioIn 17, ScF&FL 92*
Thomas, Peter Charles 1947- *WhoSSW 93*
Thomas, Peter D. 1928- *WhoWrEP 92*
Thomas, Peter David *WhoScE 91-1*
Thomas, Peter Kynaston *WhoScE 91-1*
Thomas, Peter M. 1950- *St&PR 93, WhoAm 92*
Thomas, Philip Robinson 1934- *WhoWor 93*
Thomas, Philip Stanley 1928- *WhoAm 92*
Thomas, Piri 1928- *BioIn 17, HispAmA*
Thomas, Pullolickal Eapen 1928- *WhoSSW 93*
Thomas, R. David *BioIn 17*
Thomas, R. David 1932- *WhoAm 92*
Thomas, R.S. 1913- *BioIn 17*
Thomas, Ralph 1915- *MiSFD 9*
Thomas, Ralph C., III 1949- *WhoE 93*
Thomas, Ralph Edward 1928- *St&PR 93*
Thomas, Ralph L. *MiSFD 9*
Thomas, Ralph Upton 1942- *WhoSSW 93*
Thomas, Rand T. 1950- *St&PR 93*
Thomas, Raymond Elliott *WhoScE 91-1*
Thomas, Raymond Jean 1923- *WhoWor 93*
Thomas, Raymond V. *St&PR 93*
Thomas, Reba Tucker 1935- *WhoSSW 93*
Thomas, Rene Paul-Emile 1928- *WhoWor 93*
Thomas, Rhonda Robbins 1958- *WhoSSW 93*
Thomas, Richard 1951- *WhoAm 92*
Thomas, Richard Clark 1937-1991 *BioIn 17*
Thomas, Richard E. *St&PR 93*
Thomas, Richard Emery 1929- *WhoE 93, WhoWor 93*
Thomas, Richard L. 1931- *St&PR 93*
Thomas, Richard Lee 1931- *WhoAm 92*
Thomas, Richard P. *Law&B 92*
Thomas, Richard Stephen 1949- *WhoEmL 93*
Thomas, Richard Van 1932- *WhoAm 92*
Thomas, Richard Warren, Jr. 1947- *WhoSSW 93*
Thomas, Robert *WhoScE 91-1*
Thomas, Robert Chanler Bryant 1951- *WhoE 93*
Thomas, Robert D. 1933- *St&PR 93*
Thomas, Robert Dean 1933- *WhoAm 92*
Thomas, Robert Dickinson 1945- *WhoAm 92, WhoWrEP 92*
Thomas, Robert Eggleston 1914- *WhoAm 92*
Thomas, Robert Joseph *Law&B 92*
Thomas, Robert Lee 1938- *WhoSSW 93*
Thomas, Robert Lindsay 1943- *CngDr 91, WhoSSW 93*
Thomas, Robert Lloyd 1941- *WhoSSW 93, WhoWor 93*
Thomas, Robert Murray 1921- *WhoAm 92*
Thomas, Robert P. *Law&B 92*
Thomas, Robert Ray 1926- *WhoSSW 93*
Thomas, Robert Stanley 1947- *St&PR 93*
Thomas, Robert W. *Law&B 92*
Thomas, Robert W. 1921- *St&PR 93*
Thomas, Robert Walton 1935- *WhoAm 92*
Thomas, Robert Wilburn 1937- *WhoAm 92*
Thomas, Roger Christopher *WhoScE 91-1*
Thomas, Roger Geraint 1945- *WhoWor 93*
Thomas, Roger Humphrey 1942- *St&PR 93*
Thomas, Roger Meriwether 1930- *WhoAm 92*
Thomas, Roger Warren 1937- *WhoAm 92*
Thomas, Ronald O. *Law&B 92*
Thomas, Ronald Stuart 1913- *BioIn 17*
Thomas, Rose 1952- *St&PR 93*
Thomas, Rose Lorraine Crossett 1921- *WhoAmW 93*
Thomas, Ross Elmore 1926- *WhoAm 92*
Thomas, Roy Allen 1874-1959 *BiDAMSp 1989*
Thomas, Roy Weldon 1929- *St&PR 93*
Thomas, Rudolph J. d1990 *BioIn 17*
Thomas, Rufus 1917- *SoulM*
Thomas, Russ 1924-1991 *BioIn 17*
Thomas, Russell Alvin 1939- *St&PR 93*
Thomas, Ruth *BioIn 17, ChlFicS*
Thomas (Sabater), Juan Maria 1896-1966 *Baker 92*
Thomas, Sally Smith 1938- *St&PR 93*
Thomas, Samuel 1951- *St&PR 93*
Thomas, Samuel Dee 1930- *WhoE 93*
Thomas, Sandra Paul 1940- *WhoSSW 93*
Thomas, Sarah Beth 1957- *WhoAmW 93*
Thomas, Scott E. 1953- *WhoAm 92*
Thomas, Segun 1954- *WhoSSW 93*
Thomas, Sheryl Elaine 1950- *WhoEmL 93*
Thomas, Shirley *WhoAmW 93*
Thomas, Sidney 1915- *WhoAm 92*
Thomas, Smitty 1950- *St&PR 93*
Thomas, Stacy Paul *Law&B 92*
Thomas, Stephen C. 1948- *St&PR 93*
Thomas, Stephen Paul 1938- *WhoAm 92*
Thomas, Steven *Law&B 92*
Thomas, Steven E. *Law&B 92*
Thomas, Stuart Denis 1938- *WhoAm 92, WhoE 93*
Thomas, Susan 1956- *WhoAmW 93*
Thomas, Susan Barnes *WhoE 93*
Thomas, Susan Manning 1960- *WhoAmW 93*
Thomas, Suzanne Ward 1954- *WhoAmW 93*
Thomas, Tamara Byrd 1940- *WhoAmW 93*
Thomas, Ted d1992 *NewYTBS 92*
Thomas, Ted LaRue 1935- *WhoSSW 93*
Thomas, Terence Haydn *WhoScE 91-1*
Thomas, Terry *ConTFT 10*
Thomas, Thalia Ann 1935- *WhoE 93*
Thomas, Theodore (Christian Friedrich) 1835-1905 *Baker 92*
Thomas, Theodore L. 1920- *ScF&FL 92*
Thomas, Thomas 1829-1913
See Thomas, John 1826-1913 *Baker 92*
Thomas, Thomas A. 1919- *WhoAm 92*
Thomas, Thomas Darrah 1932- *WhoAm 92*
Thomas, Thomas T. 1948- *ScF&FL 92*
Thomas, Thurman *BioIn 17*
Thomas, Thurman 1966- *News 93-1 [port], WhoAm 92*
Thomas, Timothy R. *Law&B 92*
Thomas, Tom 1932- *WhoE 93*
Thomas, Tracy Richard 1934- *St&PR 93*
Thomas, Troy *BioIn 17*
Thomas, Tudor Henry *WhoScE 91-1*
Thomas, Violeta de los Angeles 1949- *WhoAmW 93, WhoEmL 93, WhoWor 93*
Thomas, Virginia Lamp *BioIn 17*
Thomas, W. Bruce 1926- *St&PR 93*
Thomas, W. Dennis 1943- *WhoAm 92*
Thomas, W.I. 1863-1947 *IntDcAn*
Thomas, W. John *WhoScE 91-1*
Thomas, Walter B. *St&PR 93*
Thomas, Warren G. 1921- *St&PR 93*
Thomas, Warren Hafford 1933- *WhoAm 92*
Thomas, Wayne D. 1949- *St&PR 93*
Thomas, Wayne Lee 1945- *WhoAm 92*
Thomas, Wendy *BioIn 17*
Thomas, Wendy Catherine 1950- *WhoE 93*
Thomas, Wilfrid 1904-1991 *AnObit 1991*
Thomas, Wilkin E., Jr. *Law&B 92*
Thomas, William A. 1928- *St&PR 93*
Thomas, William B. *St&PR 93*
Thomas, William Bruce 1926- *WhoAm 92*
Thomas, William Charles 1926- *WhoAm 92*
Thomas, William Griffith 1939- *WhoAm 92*
Thomas, William Harry 1949- *WhoSSW 93*
Thomas, William Holland 1805-1893 *BioIn 17*
Thomas, William J. *Law&B 92*
Thomas, William Keith *WhoScE 91-1*
Thomas, William Kernahan 1911- *WhoAm 92*
Thomas, William LeRoy 1920- *WhoAm 92*
Thomas, William Leslie 1951- *WhoSSW 93*
Thomas, William M. 1941- *CngDr 91*
Thomas, William M. 1943- *St&PR 93*
Thomas, William M., Jr. *Law&B 92*
Thomas, William Marshall 1941- *WhoAm 92*
Thomas, William T. 1935- *St&PR 93*
Thomas, Wright M. 1935- *WhoAm 92*
Thomas, Yvonne Shirey 1938- *WhoAmW 93*
Thomas Aquinas *OxDcByz*
Thomas Aquinas, Saint 1224?-1274 *Baker 92*
Thomas, Aquinas, Saint 1225?-1274 *BioIn 17*
Thomasen, Ole 1934- *WhoWor 93*
Thomashow, Stanley Melvin 1943- *St&PR 93*
Thomasius, Harald 1929- *WhoScE 91-3*
Thomas Magistros c. 1275-c. 1347 *OxDcByz*
Thomas Morosini 1170?-1211 *OxDcByz*
Thomason, Caroline Wasson *AmWomPl*
Thomason, Don L. 1939- *St&PR 93*
Thomason, Harry *BioIn 17, WhoAm 92*
Thomason, Harry 1940?- *ConTFT 10*
Thomason, James Bruce 1952- *WhoSSW 93*
Thomason, Karin Joyce 1950- *WhoAmW 93*
Thomason, Ken 1954- *St&PR 93*
Thomason, Linda Bloodworth- *BioIn 17*
Thomason, Robert Wayne 1952- *WhoWor 93*
Thomason, Ron K. *Law&B 92*
Thomason, Sally Palmer 1934- *WhoSSW 93*
Thomas-Orr, Betty Jo 1937- *WhoAmW 93*
Thomas Palaiologos 1409-1465 *OxDcByz*
Thomas-Phillips, Linda 1940- *St&PR 93*
Thomas Preljubovic d1384 *OxDcByz*
Thomas-Roman, Delsey Ivette 1954- *WhoE 93*
Thomas-San-Galli, Wolfgang Alexander 1874-1918 *Baker 92*
Thomassen, Carsten 1948- *WhoWor 93*
Thomassen, Jacques J. 1945- *WhoWor 93*
Thomassen, Tore *Law&B 92*
Thomasson, Bjorn Henrik 1931- *WhoScE 91-4*
Thomasson, Dan King 1933- *WhoAm 92, WhoE 93*
Thomasson, Phil 1930- *WhoSSW 93*
Thomasson, Samuel M., III *Law&B 92*
Thomas the Archdeacon c. 1200-1268 *OxDcByz*
Thomas the Slav c. 760-823 *OxDcByz*
Thomas Topp, Margaret Ann 1951- *WhoAmW 93*
Thombs, Lori Ann 1958- *WhoSSW 93*
Thomchick, Gerard M. 1955- *St&PR 93*
Thome, Clement R. *Law&B 92*
Thome, Francis 1850-1909 *Baker 92*
Thome, James J. 1955- *St&PR 93*
Thome, John R. 1943- *St&PR 93*
Thomes, Howard M. 1941- *St&PR 93*
Thomey, Tedd 1920- *ScF&FL 92*
Thomford, Arline Gesine 1932- *WhoWrEP 92*
Thomford, Neil Roger 1931- *WhoAm 92*
Thomi, Lois Joy 1927- *WhoAmW 93, WhoWor 93*
Thominet, Maurice J. 1928- *WhoAm 92*
Thomka-Gazdik, Julian 1918- *WhoE 93*
Thomlinson, Ralph 1925- *WhoAm 92*
Thomlison, Ray J. 1943- *WhoAm 92*
Thomm, Michael Wolfgang 1951- *WhoWor 93*
Thommessen, Olav Anton 1946- *Baker 92*
Thomopoulos, Christos 1927- *WhoScE 91-3*
Thomopulos, Gregs G. 1942- *St&PR 93, WhoAm 92*
Thompkins, Jennifer Eley 1952- *WhoAmW 93*
Thompkins, Stephen R. 1944- *St&PR 93*
Thompson, A. Frederick 1941- *St&PR 93*
Thompson, Alan Eric 1924- *WhoWor 93*
Thompson, Alden Lloyd 1943- *WhoAm 92*
Thompson, Alice Callender *AmWomPl*
Thompson, Alice Roxana 1940- *WhoAmW 93*
Thompson, Allen Joseph 1937- *WhoSSW 93*
Thompson, Allyn *ScF&FL 92*
Thompson, Almose Alphonse 1942- *WhoSSW 93*
Thompson, Alta E. *AmWomPl*
Thompson, Anna-Christina 1937- *WhoE 93*
Thompson, Anna Sue 1930- *WhoSSW 93*
Thompson, Anne Elise 1934- *WhoAm 92, WhoAmW 93*
Thompson, Anne Marie 1920- *WhoAmW 93*
Thompson, Annie Figueroa 1941- *WhoAm 92*
Thompson, Annie Laura 1937- *WhoAmW 93, WhoSSW 93*
Thompson, Ansel Frederick, Jr. 1941- *WhoAm 92*
Thompson, Anthony Arthur Richard 1932- *WhoWor 93*
Thompson, Anthony Richard 1931- *WhoAm 92*
Thompson, Anthony Wayne 1940- *WhoAm 92*
Thompson, Arthur Raymond 1938- *WhoSSW 93*
Thompson, Baird McKee 1950- *St&PR 93*
Thompson, Barbara Giles 1956- *WhoAmW 93*
Thompson, Barbara Ling 1939- *WhoSSW 93*
Thompson, Barbara Storck 1924- *WhoAm 92*
Thompson, Barnaby 1961- *MiSFD 9*
Thompson, Barry B. *WhoSSW 93*
Thompson, Belinda 1955- *WhoAmW 93*
Thompson, Ben 1842-1884 *BioIn 17*
Thompson, Benjamin 1918- *BioIn 17*
Thompson, Bernadine L. 1936- *WhoSSW 93*
Thompson, Bert Allen 1930- *WhoAm 92*
Thompson, Bert Martin 1928- *WhoIns 93*
Thompson, Bertha Boya 1917- *WhoAmW 93*
Thompson, Betsy Otter 1936- *WhoWrEP 92*
Thompson, Bette Lee 1935- *WhoWrEP 92*
Thompson, Bill M. 1932- *WhoAm 92, WhoSSW 93*
Thompson, Bina 1949- *St&PR 93*
Thompson, Bjorn J. 1934- *St&PR 93, WhoAm 92*
Thompson, Blair H. 1925- *St&PR 93*
Thompson, Blanche Jennings 1887- *AmWomPl*
Thompson, Bobby Jack 1930- *WhoAm 92*
Thompson, Bobby Joe 1950- *WhoSSW 93*
Thompson, Boyd 1921- *WhoAm 92*
Thompson, Bradbury 1911- *WhoAm 92, WhoWor 93*
Thompson, Brandi Lee 1965- *WhoSSW 93*
Thompson, Brett *MiSFD 9*
Thompson, Brett F. 1949- *St&PR 93*
Thompson, Brian John 1932- *WhoAm 92, WhoE 93*
Thompson, Bruce Edward, Jr. 1949- *WhoAm 92, WhoEmL 93*
Thompson, Bruce H. *Law&B 92*
Thompson, Bryan Earnest 1922- *St&PR 93*
Thompson, C.H., Jr. 1927- *St&PR 93*
Thompson, Carla Jo Horn 1951- *WhoSSW 93*
Thompson, Carol Lewis 1918- *WhoAm 92, WhoWrEP 92*
Thompson, Carol Lufkin 1941- *WhoAmW 93*
Thompson, Carole Rapp 1935- *WhoUN 92*
Thompson, Carolyn Wynelle 1939- *WhoAmW 93*
Thompson, Carson R. 1939- *St&PR 93, WhoAm 92*
Thompson, Caryn Elizabeth 1954- *WhoAmW 93*
Thompson, Catherine B. *Law&B 92*
Thompson, Charles *BioIn 17*
Thompson, Charles Edwin 1938- *WhoAm 92*
Thompson, Charles Glover 1928- *WhoSSW 93*
Thompson, Charles I. 1950- *St&PR 93*
Thompson, Charles Murray 1942- *WhoAm 92*
Thompson, Charles Otis 1942- *WhoSSW 93*
Thompson, Charles R. 1949- *St&PR 93*
Thompson, Charles Ray 1943- *WhoSSW 93*
Thompson, Charles Wesley 1925- *WhoSSW 93*
Thompson, Charlotte *AmWomPl*
Thompson, Cheryl L. 1950- *St&PR 93*
Thompson, Chester C. 1921- *St&PR 93*
Thompson, Chic *BioIn 17*
Thompson, Chris D. *Law&B 92*
Thompson, Chris R. 1940- *St&PR 93*
Thompson, Christopher *WhoScE 91-1*
Thompson, Clarence Miles 1929- *St&PR 93*
Thompson, Clarence Miles, Jr. 1929- *WhoAm 92*
Thompson, Cleon F., Jr. *WhoAm 92*
Thompson, Cliff F. 1934- *WhoAm 92*
Thompson, Clifton C. 1939- *WhoAm 92*
Thompson, Craig Snover 1932- *WhoAm 92*
Thompson, Curl *DcCPCAm*
Thompson, D.J. 1933- *WhoScE 91-1*
Thompson, Dale Gilbert, Jr. 1951- *WhoSSW 93*
Thompson, Dale Willard, Jr. 1938- *WhoAm 92*
Thompson, Daniel Emerson 1947- *WhoWor 93*
Thompson, Daniel Joseph 1940- *St&PR 93*
Thompson, Danny Charles 1956- *WhoSSW 93*
Thompson, Darrell Theodore 1929- *St&PR 93*

Thompson, David *BioIn 17*
Thompson, David 1770-1857 *BioIn 17, Expl 93, IntDcAn*
Thompson, David A. *Law&B 92*
Thompson, David A. 1941- *St&PR 93*
Thompson, David Alfred 1929- *WhoAm 92*
Thompson, David Allen 1941- *WhoAm 92*
Thompson, David Anthony 1939- *WhoAm 92*
Thompson, David B. *WhoAm 92, WhoSSW 93*
Thompson, David Duvall 1922- *WhoAm 92*
Thompson, David E. 1955- *WhoSSW 93*
Thompson, David George 1948- *WhoWor 93*
Thompson, David Henry 1933- *WhoUN 92*
Thompson, David James 1945- *WhoWrEP 92*
Thompson, David Jerome 1937- *WhoAm 92*
Thompson, David K. *Law&B 92*
Thompson, David L. 1953- *St&PR 93*
Thompson, David Martin *Law&B 92*
Thompson, David N. 1950- *WhoIns 93*
Thompson, David R. 1955- *St&PR 93*
Thompson, David Renwick *WhoAm 92*
Thompson, David Ross *Law&B 92*
Thompson, David W. 1954- *ConEn*
Thompson, David Walker 1954- *WhoAm 92*
Thompson, David William 1914- *WhoAm 92, WhoWor 93*
Thompson, Dayle Ann 1954- *WhoAmW 93*
Thompson, Deal, Mrs. *AmWomPl*
Thompson, Debbie *BioIn 17, BlkAmWO [port]*
Thompson, Deborah Colussy 1954- *WhoWrEP 92*
Thompson, Dennis 1948- *See* MC5, The *ConMus 9*
Thompson, Dennis Frank 1940- *WhoAm 92*
Thompson, Dennis Peters 1937- *WhoAm 92*
Thompson, Dennis Roy 1939- *WhoWor 93*
Thompson, Diane *ScF&FL 92*
Thompson, Diane E. 1944- *St&PR 93*
Thompson, Diane Paige 1940- *WhoSSW 93*
Thompson, Dianne Lynn 1959- *WhoAmW 93*
Thompson, Didi Castle 1918- *WhoAmW 93, WhoWor 93*
Thompson, Diedra *St&PR 93*
Thompson, Don *Law&B 92*
Thompson, Don 1935- *ScF&FL 92*
Thompson, Don Clinton 1933- *St&PR 93*
Thompson, Donald *ScF&FL 92*
Thompson, Donald Charles 1930- *WhoAm 92*
Thompson, Donald Edward 1930- *St&PR 93*
Thompson, Donna Marie 1956- *WhoAmW 93*
Thompson, Donna Northam 1964- *WhoAmW 93*
Thompson, Dorothy *BioIn 17*
Thompson, Dorothy 1893-1961 *JrnUS*
Thompson, Dorothy 1923- *BioIn 17*
Thompson, Dorothy Brown 1896- *WhoAmW 93, WhoWor 93*
Thompson, Dorothy Denise 1953- *WhoAmW 93*
Thompson, Dorothy Mae 1932- *WhoAmW 93*
Thompson, Douglas Carl 1940- *WhoE 93*
Thompson, Duane *SweetSg B*
Thompson, Dwight Alan 1955- *WhoEmL 93*
Thompson, E.P. 1924- *BioIn 17, ScF&FL 92*
Thompson, Earl Albert 1938- *WhoAm 92*
Thompson, Earl Ryan 1939- *St&PR 93, WhoE 93*
Thompson, Edmund Andy, III 1949- *WhoE 93*
Thompson, Edward Francis 1938- *St&PR 93, WhoAm 92*
Thompson, Edward George 1936- *St&PR 93*
Thompson, Edward Kramer *BioIn 17*
Thompson, Edward Kramer 1907- *WhoAm 92*
Thompson, Edward P. *St&PR 93*
Thompson, Edward Palmer 1924- *BioIn 17*
Thompson, Edward Thorwald 1928- *WhoAm 92, WhoWrEP 92*
Thompson, Edwin R. 1949- *St&PR 93*
Thompson, Eileen (Panowski) 1920- *DcAmChF 1960*
Thompson, Elbert Orson 1910- *WhoWor 93*
Thompson, Eldon D. 1934- *St&PR 93*
Thompson, Eldon Dale 1934- *WhoAm 92*
Thompson, Eleanor Dumont 1935- *WhoAmW 93*
Thompson, Elizabeth Jane 1927- *WhoAmW 93*
Thompson, Ellen Keith 1947- *WhoAmW 93*
Thompson, Ellen Kubacki 1950- *WhoE 93*
Thompson, Eloise Bibb *AmWomPl*
Thompson, Emma *BioIn 17*
Thompson, Emma 1959- *News 93-2 [port]*
Thompson, Ernest 1950- *MiSFD 9*
Thompson, Ernest B. 1936- *St&PR 93*
Thompson, Ernest L. 1938- *St&PR 93*
Thompson, Ernest Thorne 1897- *WhoAm 92*
Thompson, Eugene A. *ScF&FL 92*
Thompson, Eugene George 1948- *WhoIns 93*
Thompson, Ezra Enwood 1916- *St&PR 93*
Thompson, Flora 1877-1947 *BioIn 17*
Thompson, Francesca Morosani *BioIn 17*
Thompson, Frank Edward 1943- *WhoSSW 93*
Thompson, Frank H., Jr. 1926- *ScF&FL 92*
Thompson, Frank Joseph 1944- *WhoAm 92*
Thompson, Frank Walden 1932- *WhoWor 93*
Thompson, Fred *Law&B 92*
Thompson, Fred Clayton 1928- *St&PR 93, WhoAm 92*
Thompson, Fred T. 1940- *St&PR 93*
Thompson, Frederick Dyer *Law&B 92*
Thompson, G. Allen 1927- *WhoAm 92*
Thompson, G. Gaye 1945- *WhoAmW 93*
Thompson, G.R. 1937- *ScF&FL 92*
Thompson, Gary 1951- *ScF&FL 92*
Thompson, Gary Allen 1951- *WhoWrEP 92*
Thompson, Gary Harold 1940- *St&PR 93*
Thompson, Gary S. 1944- *St&PR 93*
Thompson, Gary William 1947- *St&PR 93*
Thompson, Gene 1924- *ScF&FL 92*
Thompson, Geneva Florence 1915- *WhoAmW 93*
Thompson, Geoffrey A. 1940- *St&PR 93*
Thompson, George Albert 1919- *WhoAm 92*
Thompson, George Clifford 1920- *WhoAm 92*
Thompson, George Francis 1939- *St&PR 93*
Thompson, George Lee 1933- *WhoAm 92, WhoE 93, WhoWor 93*
Thompson, George Leroy 1952- *WhoSSW 93*
Thompson, George S. *ScF&FL 92*
Thompson, George Selden 1929-1989 *ConAu 37NR, MajAI [port], SmATA 73 [port]*
Thompson, Gerald E. 1947- *WhoAm 92*
Thompson, Gerald Luther 1923- *WhoAm 92, WhoWrEP 92*
Thompson, Geraldine Jean 1931- *WhoAmW 93*
Thompson, Gerard F. *Law&B 92*
Thompson, Glenn Hiram, Jr. 1936- *WhoE 93*
Thompson, Glenn Judean 1936- *WhoAm 92*
Thompson, Gordon, Jr. 1929- *WhoAm 92*
Thompson, Gordon William 1940- *WhoAm 92*
Thompson, Graham 1951- *WhoScE 91-1*
Thompson, Guy Bryan 1940- *WhoAm 92*
Thompson, Guy Thomas 1942- *WhoSSW 93*
Thompson, H. Neill 1942- *St&PR 93*
Thompson, Harlan 1894-1987 *ScF&FL 92*
Thompson, Harold Jerome 1947- *WhoSSW 93*
Thompson, Harrison R. *ScF&FL 92*
Thompson, Harry *MiSFD 9*
Thompson, Harry R. 1929- *WhoAm 92*
Thompson, Helen Louise 1918- *St&PR 93*
Thompson, Henrietta Spotts 1920- *WhoAmW 93*
Thompson, Henry L. 1935- *St&PR 93*
Thompson, Henry L., Jr. 1915- *St&PR 93*
Thompson, Herbert Joseph 1881-1937 *BiDAMSp 1989*
Thompson, Herbert Stanley 1932- *WhoAm 92*
Thompson, Herbert W. 1947- *St&PR 93*
Thompson, Herbert Walter 1915- *WhoE 93*
Thompson, Holland 1840-1888? *BioIn 17*
Thompson, Howard *ScF&FL 92*
Thompson, Howard Elliott 1934- *WhoAm 92*
Thompson, Hugh Currie 1906- *WhoAm 92*
Thompson, Hugh Lee 1934- *WhoAm 92*
Thompson, Hunter S. *BioIn 17*
Thompson, Hunter S. 1939- *News 92 [port]*
Thompson, Hunter Stockton 1939- *WhoAm 92, WhoWrEP 92*
Thompson, Ian David *St&PR 93*
Thompson, Inga *BioIn 17*
Thompson, Irene Loy 1950- *WhoAmW 93*
Thompson, J.A. 1934- *St&PR 93*
Thompson, J. Andy 1943- *WhoAm 92*
Thompson, J. Edward *Law&B 92*
Thompson, J. Lee 1914- *MiSFD 9*
Thompson, J. Stark 1941- *WhoAm 92*
Thompson, Jack Edward 1924- *WhoAm 92*
Thompson, Jack Lyle 1947- *WhoE 93*
Thompson, Jacqueline 1945- *ConAu 38NR, WhoWrEP 92*
Thompson, Jacqueline Kay 1954- *WhoAmW 93*
Thompson, James 1931- *WhoAm 92, WhoSSW 93*
Thompson, James B. 1929- *WhoSSW 93*
Thompson, James Bernard *BioIn 17*
Thompson, James Bruce 1937- *WhoAm 92*
Thompson, James Burleigh, Jr. 1921- *WhoAm 92*
Thompson, James C. 1939- *St&PR 93*
Thompson, James Charles 1928- *WhoAm 92*
Thompson, James Clark 1939- *WhoAm 92*
Thompson, James Dan 1935- *St&PR 93*
Thompson, James Daniel, Sr. 1930- *WhoSSW 93*
Thompson, James David 1945- *WhoAm 92, WhoIns 93*
Thompson, James Edward 1941- *WhoAm 92*
Thompson, James Gordon 1934- *St&PR 93*
Thompson, James Harry 1925- *WhoAm 92*
Thompson, James Howard 1934- *WhoAm 92*
Thompson, James Jarrard 1944- *WhoSSW 93*
Thompson, James Kirk 1953- *St&PR 93*
Thompson, James M. 1938- *WhoSSW 93*
Thompson, James Mace 1941- *St&PR 93*
Thompson, James N. 1931- *St&PR 93*
Thompson, James P. *Law&B 92*
Thompson, James Patrick 1946- *St&PR 93*
Thompson, James R. *Law&B 92*
Thompson, James R. 1906- *St&PR 93*
Thompson, James Richard *Law&B 92*
Thompson, James Richard 1933- *WhoSSW 93*
Thompson, James Richard 1951- *WhoSSW 93*
Thompson, James Robert 1936- *WhoAm 92*
Thompson, James S., III 1947- *St&PR 93*
Thompson, James William 1939- *St&PR 93, WhoAm 92*
Thompson, Jan *BioIn 17*
Thompson, Jane F. 1937- *WhoAmW 93*
Thompson, Jane J. 1951- *St&PR 93*
Thompson, Jane Johnson 1951- *WhoAmW 93*
Thompson, Janet Kim 1954- *WhoAmW 93*
Thompson, Jayne C. 1959- *St&PR 93*
Thompson, Jean 1950- *ConAu 136*
Thompson, Jean Alford 1937- *WhoAmW 93*
Thompson, Jean Blake 1919- *St&PR 93*
Thompson, Jean Margaret 1945- *WhoAmW 93*
Thompson, Jean Marie 1962- *WhoAmW 93*
Thompson, Jean Tanner 1929- *WhoAm 92*
Thompson, Jeanne Coombs 1949- *St&PR 93*
Thompson, Jennifer Anne 1939- *WhoWor 93*
Thompson, Jenny *WhoAmW 93*
Thompson, Jere William 1932- *BioIn 17, WhoAm 92*
Thompson, Jerry A. 1934- *St&PR 93*
Thompson, Jesse Eldon 1919- *WhoAm 92*
Thompson, Jewel Taylor 1935- *WhoE 93*
Thompson, Jim *BioIn 17*
Thompson, Jim L. 1942- *WhoSSW 93*
Thompson, Joan Kathryn 1956- *WhoAmW 93, WhoWor 93*
Thompson, Joe C. d1961 *BioIn 17*
Thompson, Joe O. 1915- *St&PR 93*
Thompson, John *BioIn 17*
Thompson, John 1922- *WhoWor 93*
Thompson, John 1941- *WhoAm 92*
Thompson, John A. *Law&B 92*
Thompson, John Albert, Jr. 1942- *WhoSSW 93*
Thompson, John Archibald 1934- *WhoAm 92*
Thompson, John C. 1926- *St&PR 93*
Thompson, John D. *Law&B 92*
Thompson, John D. d1992 *NewYTBS 92*
Thompson, John Daniel 1927- *WhoAm 92*
Thompson, John Douglas 1934- *St&PR 93, WhoAm 92, WhoWor 93*
Thompson, John E. *St&PR 93*
Thompson, John E., Jr. 1923- *St&PR 93*
Thompson, John Eric Sidney 1898-1975 *IntDcAn*
Thompson, John Frederick, Jr. 1951- *St&PR 93*
Thompson, John G. 1940- *St&PR 93*
Thompson, John Griggs *WhoScE 91-1*
Thompson, John H. 1933- *St&PR 93*
Thompson, John Henry 1938- *St&PR 93*
Thompson, John Jeffrey 1938- *WhoWor 93*
Thompson, John L. *WhoScE 91-1*
Thompson, John L. 1943- *St&PR 93*
Thompson, John Lester 1926- *WhoAm 92*
Thompson, John More 1938- *WhoAm 92*
Thompson, John P. 1925- *BioIn 17, WhoAm 92*
Thompson, John Richard 1946- *WhoSSW 93*
Thompson, John Robert 1947- *St&PR 93*
Thompson, John Robert 1955- *WhoE 93*
Thompson, John Theodore 1917- *WhoAm 92*
Thompson, John W. 1926- *St&PR 93*
Thompson, John Warburton *WhoScE 91-1*
Thompson, John Winter 1867-1951 *Baker 92*
Thompson, Joseph B. 1937- *WhoE 93*
Thompson, Joseph F. 1944- *St&PR 93*
Thompson, Joseph V. 1942- *St&PR 93*
Thompson, Joyce 1948- *ScF&FL 92*
Thompson, Joyce Elizabeth 1951- *WhoAmW 93*
Thompson, Joyce Lurine 1931- *WhoAmW 93*
Thompson, Judith 1954- *WhoCanL 92*
Thompson, Judith Ann 1954- *WhoAmW 93*
Thompson, Judith Kastrup 1933- *WhoAmW 93, WhoWor 93*
Thompson, Julia Ann 1943- *WhoAmW 93*
Thompson, Julian F. 1927- *Au&Arts 9 [port], ScF&FL 92*
Thompson, Julian F(rancis) 1927- *MajAI [port]*
Thompson, Karen *BioIn 17*
Thompson, Karen Elaine 1958- *WhoAmW 93*
Thompson, Karin Elorriaga 1962- *WhoAmW 93*
Thompson, Kate Vernon d1927 *AmWomPl*
Thompson, Kathleen Marie 1954- *WhoAmW 93*
Thompson, Kathy M. 1947- *St&PR 93*
Thompson, Kay 1912- *MajAI [port]*
Thompson, Kay Francis *WhoE 93*
Thompson, Kelly Ann 1954- *WhoSSW 93*
Thompson, Kenneth 1930- *WhoUN 92*
Thompson, Kenneth A. 1936- *St&PR 93*
Thompson, Kenneth Alfred *WhoScE 91-1*
Thompson, Kenneth Winfred 1921- *WhoAm 92*
Thompson, Kent *WhoCanL 92*
Thompson, Kevin d1991 *BioIn 17*
Thompson, Kirk 1953- *St&PR 93*
Thompson, Lance Eric 1956- *St&PR 93*
Thompson, Larry Angelo 1944- *WhoAm 92, WhoWor 93*
Thompson, Larry Dean 1945- *WhoAm 92*
Thompson, Larry Eugene *Law&B 92*
Thompson, Larry Flack 1944- *WhoAm 92*
Thompson, Larry James 1952- *WhoE 93*
Thompson, Laura Ann 1950- *WhoAmW 93*
Thompson, Laura Maud 1905- *IntDcAn*
Thompson, LaVerne Elizabeth Thomas 1945- *WhoAmW 93, WhoWor 93*
Thompson, Lawrance Roger 1906-1973 *BioIn 17*
Thompson, Lawrence Franklin, Jr. 1941- *WhoWor 93*
Thompson, Lee Bennett 1902- *WhoAm 92*
Thompson, LeRoy, Jr. 1913- *WhoSSW 93, WhoWor 93*
Thompson, Leslie Melvin 1936- *WhoAm 92*
Thompson, Lester Eugene 1938- *St&PR 93*
Thompson, Lilian Spencer *AmWomPl*
Thompson, Lillian Bennet 1883- *AmWomPl*
Thompson, Lillian Hurlburt 1947- *WhoAmW 93*
Thompson, Lillian Willean 1950- *WhoAmW 93*
Thompson, Lincoln, Jr. 1928- *St&PR 93*
Thompson, Lindsay 1923- *BioIn 17*
Thompson, Linwood 1952- *St&PR 93*
Thompson, Lisa Carol 1967- *WhoAmW 93*
Thompson, Llewellyn E., Jr. 1904-1972 *ColdWar 1 [port]*
Thompson, Lloyd A(rthur) 1932- *ConAu 137*
Thompson, Lohren Matthew 1926- *WhoAm 92*

Thompson, Lois Jean Heidke Ore 1933- *WhoAmW 93, WhoWor 93*
Thompson, Lola May 1931- *WhoAmW 93*
Thompson, Loran Tyson 1947- *WhoE 93*
Thompson, Loring Moore 1918- *WhoAm 92*
Thompson, Lotus *SweetSg B*
Thompson, Lou Ann 1953- *WhoWrEP 92*
Thompson, Louis F. 1923-1990 *BioIn 17*
Thompson, Louis Milton 1914- *WhoAm 92*
Thompson, Louise Saari 1943- *WhoWrEP 92*
Thompson, Lutis Pryor 1916-1989 *BiDAMSp 1989*
Thompson, Lynn Poucher 1922- *WhoE 93*
Thompson, Lynne Charles 1944- *WhoSSW 93*
Thompson, Mack Eugene 1921- *WhoAm 92*
Thompson, Maggie *ScF&FL 92*
Thompson, Malcolm Francis 1921- *WhoWor 93*
Thompson, Maravene Kennedy *AmWomPl*
Thompson, Margaret M. 1921- *WhoAm 92*
Thompson, Marguerite 1887-1968 *BioIn 17*
Thompson, Marguerite Myrtle Graming 1912- *WhoAmW 93, WhoSSW 93*
Thompson, Mari Hildenbrand 1951- *WhoAmW 93*
Thompson, Marian Lynn Greene 1951- *WhoSSW 93*
Thompson, Marie C. McGuire- *BioIn 17*
Thompson, Mark A. 1952- *St&PR 93*
Thompson, Mark B., III *Law&B 92*
Thompson, Mark L. 1945- *ConAu 137*
Thompson, Marshall *BioIn 17*
Thompson, Marshall 1925-1992 *BioIn 17, NewYTBS 92*
Thompson, Martha Godfrey 1900- *WhoAmW 93*
Thompson, Martha Kay 1936- *WhoAmW 93*
Thompson, Martha Ruth *WhoAmW 93*
Thompson, Martin Christian 1938- *WhoAm 92*
Thompson, Mary Catherine 1942- *WhoAmW 93*
Thompson, Mary Eileen 1928- *WhoAmW 93*
Thompson, Mary Helen 1948- *WhoAmW 93*
Thompson, Mary Koleta 1938- *WhoAmW 93, WhoSSW 93*
Thompson, Maureen F. *Law&B 92*
Thompson, Melinda Lucy 1958- *WhoSSW 93*
Thompson, Melissa Ann 1950- *WhoEmL 93*
Thompson, Mercedes Arisso 1938- *WhoAmW 93*
Thompson, Michael *Law&B 92*
Thompson, Michael David 1929- *WhoAm 92*
Thompson, Michael William 1963- *WhoE 93*
Thompson, Mickey *BioIn 17*
Thompson, Milton Orville 1926- *WhoAm 92*
Thompson, Morley P. 1927- *St&PR 93*
Thompson, Morley Punshon 1927- *WhoAm 92*
Thompson, Morris Lee 1946- *WhoAm 92*
Thompson, Mozelle Willmont 1954- *WhoE 93*
Thompson, Mychal *BioIn 17*
Thompson, Myron H. *WhoAm 92*
Thompson, N. David 1934- *WhoAm 92, WhoIns 93*
Thompson, Nancy Jean 1954- *WhoAmW 93*
Thompson, Nancy Lynn 1956- *WhoSSW 93*
Thompson, Natalie A. 1960- *WhoAmW 93*
Thompson, Neal Philip 1936- *WhoSSW 93*
Thompson, Neil E. 1932- *St&PR 93*
Thompson, Norma Jean 1935- *WhoAmW 93*
Thompson, Norman Winslow 1932- *WhoAm 92*
Thompson, Orval N. 1914- *St&PR 93*
Thompson, Orval Nathan 1914- *WhoWor 93*
Thompson, Oscar 1887-1945 *Baker 92*
Thompson, Oscar William, III 1955- *WhoSSW 93*
Thompson, Ott, II 1924- *St&PR 93*
Thompson, P.A. *WhoScE 91-1*
Thompson, Patricia Eileen 1945- *WhoAmW 93*
Thompson, Paul 1935- *ScF&FL 92*
Thompson, Paul B. 1951- *ScF&FL 92*
Thompson, Paul Banks 1951- *WhoSSW 93*
Thompson, Paul Harold 1938- *WhoAm 92*
Thompson, Paul Mark *Law&B 92*
Thompson, Paul Michael 1935- *WhoAm 92*
Thompson, Paul (Richard) 1935- *ConAu 38NR*
Thompson, Pauline Jane T. 1931- *WhoWrEP 92*
Thompson, Peter Campbell 1933- *St&PR 93*
Thompson, Peter Lindsay 1941- *WhoWor 93*
Thompson, Philip Andrew 1928- *WhoAm 92*
Thompson, Phillip Wayne 1949- *St&PR 93*
Thompson, Phyllis E. 1943- *WhoAmW 93*
Thompson, Phyllis Hoge 1926- *WhoWrEP 92*
Thompson, R.C. *Law&B 92*
Thompson, R.N. *WhoScE 91-1*
Thompson, R.S. *St&PR 93*
Thompson, Ralph Gordon 1934- *WhoAm 92, WhoSSW 93*
Thompson, Ralph LaSalle 1927- *St&PR 93*
Thompson, Ralph Luther 1943- *WhoSSW 93*
Thompson, Ralph Newell 1918- *WhoAm 92*
Thompson, Randall 1899-1984 *Baker 92, BioIn 17*
Thompson, Randall L. *Law&B 92*
Thompson, Ray Fern 1936- *St&PR 93*
Thompson, Raymond D. *Law&B 92*
Thompson, Raymond H. 1941- *ScF&FL 92*
Thompson, Rebecca *WhoWrEP 92*
Thompson, Rebecca Lynn 1949- *WhoAmW 93*
Thompson, Renold Durant 1926- *St&PR 93, WhoAm 92*
Thompson, Reyna *BioIn 17*
Thompson, Richard A. *Law&B 92*
Thompson, Richard Arlen 1930- *WhoSSW 93*
Thompson, Richard C. *WhoAm 92*
Thompson, Richard Frederick 1930- *WhoAm 92*
Thompson, Richard Ives 1947- *St&PR 93*
Thompson, Richard L. *WhoAm 92*
Thompson, Richard Leon 1944- *WhoAm 92, WhoE 93*
Thompson, Richard Stephen 1931- *WhoAm 92*
Thompson, Richard Victor, Jr. 1951- *WhoSSW 93*
Thompson, Rob *MiSFD 9*
Thompson, Robert A. *Law&B 92*
Thompson, Robert A. 1952- *St&PR 93*
Thompson, Robert C. 1937- *MiSFD 9*
Thompson, Robert Charles 1936- *WhoSSW 93*
Thompson, Robert Charles 1942- *WhoAm 92*
Thompson, Robert Clay 1949- *WhoE 93*
Thompson, Robert Clifton *Law&B 92*
Thompson, Robert E. 1921- *ScF&FL 92*
Thompson, Robert Earl 1947- *WhoSSW 93*
Thompson, Robert Elliott 1921- *WhoAm 92*
Thompson, Robert Eugene 1942- *St&PR 93*
Thompson, Robert F. 1926- *St&PR 93*
Thompson, Robert H. 1929- *WhoIns 93*
Thompson, Robert Howard 1929- *St&PR 93*
Thompson, Robert J. *BioIn 17*
Thompson, Robert J. 1940- *St&PR 93*
Thompson, Robert L., Jr. *Law&B 92*
Thompson, Robert L., Jr. 1937- *St&PR 93*
Thompson, Robert L., Jr. 1944- *WhoAm 92*
Thompson, Robert Lee 1945- *WhoAm 92*
Thompson, Robert M. 1928- *St&PR 93*
Thompson, Robert M. 1932- *WhoIns 93*
Thompson, Robert McBroom 1928- *WhoAm 92*
Thompson, Robert Thomas 1930- *WhoAm 92, WhoWor 93*
Thompson, Robert Thomas, Jr. 1951- *WhoEmL 93*
Thompson, Robert W. 1939- *St&PR 93*
Thompson, Roberta Ann 1946- *WhoAmW 93*
Thompson, Roby Calvin, Jr. 1934- *WhoAm 92*
Thompson, Rocky *BioIn 17*
Thompson, Roger Kennedy 1929- *St&PR 93*
Thompson, Ronald Edward 1931- *WhoAm 92*
Thompson, Ronald F. *Law&B 92*
Thompson, Ronald Russell 1942- *WhoE 93*
Thompson, Ronald Wesley 1937- *WhoSSW 93*
Thompson, Roy S., Jr. 1917- *St&PR 93, WhoIns 93*
Thompson, Rufus E. 1943- *WhoAm 92*
Thompson, Ruth 1887-1970 *BioIn 17*
Thompson, Ruth Cowen 1958- *WhoAmW 93*
Thompson, Ruth Plumly 1893-1976 *BioIn 17*
Thompson, Sada Carolyn 1929- *WhoAm 92*
Thompson, Sally Ann 1943- *WhoAmW 93*
Thompson, Sally Engstrom 1940- *WhoAm 92, WhoAmW 93*
Thompson, Sally Gail 1938- *WhoAmW 93*
Thompson, Sandra Jean 1943- *WhoWrEP 92*
Thompson, Sandra Romaine 1938- *WhoAmW 93, WhoE 93, WhoWor 93*
Thompson, Scot Bycroft *St&PR 93*
Thompson, Scott Gallatin 1944- *St&PR 93, WhoIns 93*
Thompson, Shirley N. *Law&B 92*
Thompson, Smith 1768-1843 *BioIn 17, OxCSupC [port]*
Thompson, Stephen Arthur 1934- *WhoAm 92*
Thompson, Stephen M. 1935- *St&PR 93*
Thompson, Stephen R. *Law&B 92*
Thompson, Steven Allen 1953- *WhoAm 92*
Thompson, Stuart James 1951- *St&PR 93*
Thompson, Sue Byrd *AmWomPl*
Thompson, Sue Ellen 1948- *WhoWrEP 92*
Thompson, Susan Arnetas Conklin 1956- *WhoWrEP 92*
Thompson, Susan Ball 1950- *WhoAmW 93*
Thompson, Susan D. *Law&B 92*
Thompson, Susan Jane 1950- *WhoAmW 93*
Thompson, Terence William 1952- *WhoEmL 93*
Thompson, Teressa Ann 1959- *WhoSSW 93*
Thompson, Terrance Michael 1947- *St&PR 93*
Thompson, Terry A. *Law&B 92*
Thompson, Terry W. 1950- *St&PR 93*
Thompson, Texas Billy 1845?-1888? *BioIn 17*
Thompson, Theodore Kvale 1944- *WhoAm 92*
Thompson, Theodore Robert 1943- *WhoAm 92*
Thompson, Theodosia Jessup *AmWomPl*
Thompson, Thomas A. d1991 *BioIn 17*
Thompson, Thomas C. 1938- *St&PR 93*
Thompson, Thomas Dwight 1945- *WhoWrEP 92*
Thompson, Thomas Henry 1924- *WhoAm 92*
Thompson, Thomas Martin 1943- *WhoAm 92*
Thompson, Thomas Phillips 1843-1933 *BioIn 17*
Thompson, Thomas Sanford 1916- *WhoAm 92*
Thompson, Thomas Wright d1990 *BioIn 17*
Thompson, Tina Lewis Chryar 1929- *WhoAmW 93*
Thompson, Todd William 1949- *WhoE 93*
Thompson, Tommy *BioIn 17*
Thompson, Tommy George 1941- *WhoAm 92*
Thompson, Tommy R. 1952- *St&PR 93*
Thompson, Tyler 1915- *WhoAm 92*
Thompson, V.M. *ScF&FL 92*
Thompson, Vance, Mrs. *AmWomPl*
Thompson, Venita Brant 1936- *WhoSSW 93*
Thompson, Verona Cooper 1932- *St&PR 93*
Thompson, Victor Alexander 1912- *WhoAm 92*
Thompson, Victor Montgomery, Jr. 1924- *WhoAm 92*
Thompson, W.R. 1955- *ScF&FL 92*
Thompson, W. Reid 1924- *St&PR 93, WhoAm 92*
Thompson, Wade Francis Bruce 1940- *WhoAm 92, WhoWor 93*
Thompson, Walter David, Jr. 1952- *WhoSSW 93*
Thompson, Walter Earl, Jr. 1946- *WhoSSW 93*
Thompson, Wayne E. 1948- *St&PR 93*
Thompson, Wayne Edwin 1927- *WhoAm 92*
Thompson, Wayne Wray 1945- *WhoE 93, WhoWor 93*
Thompson, Wesley D. 1926- *St&PR 93*
Thompson, Wesley Duncan 1926- *WhoAm 92*
Thompson, Wesley Ernest 1939- *St&PR 93*
Thompson, Will L(amartine) 1847-1909 *Baker 92*
Thompson, William *WhoScE 91-1*
Thompson, William 1736-1781 *HarEnMi*
Thompson, William, Jr. 1936- *WhoAm 92, WhoE 93*
Thompson, William Benbow, Jr. 1923- *WhoWor 93*
Thompson, William Bonner, Jr. 1956- *St&PR 93*
Thompson, William C. 1938- *St&PR 93*
Thompson, William Cannon, Jr. 1938- *WhoAm 92*
Thompson, William D. *St&PR 93*
Thompson, William David 1921- *WhoAm 92*
Thompson, William David 1929- *WhoAm 92*
Thompson, William Francis 1947- *St&PR 93*
Thompson, William Grant 1925- *WhoE 93*
Thompson, William Grant 1943- *St&PR 93*
Thompson, William H. 1867-1944 *PolPar*
Thompson, William Irwin 1938- *ScF&FL 92, WhoAm 92, WhoWrEP 92*
Thompson, William Joseph 1934- *St&PR 93*
Thompson, William Keith 1950- *WhoSSW 93*
Thompson, William M. *Law&B 92*
Thompson, William Moreau 1943- *WhoAm 92*
Thompson, William Neil 1920- *WhoAm 92*
Thompson, William Reid 1924- *WhoAm 92*
Thompson, William Robert 1958- *WhoSSW 93*
Thompson, William Scott *Law&B 92*
Thompson, William Taliaferro, Jr. 1913- *WhoAm 92, WhoWor 93*
Thompson, Wilmer Leigh 1938- *WhoAm 92*
Thompson, Winfred Lee 1945- *WhoAm 92, WhoSSW 93*
Thompson, Winston 1940- *WhoWor 93*
Thompson, Wynelle Doggett 1914- *WhoAmW 93*
Thompson, Yaakov 1954- *WhoE 93*
Thompson, Zilla 1964- *WhoAmW 93*
Thompson-Jurich, Susan Kaye 1953- *WhoAmW 93*
Thompson-Moraga, Gary A. *ScF&FL 92*
Thompson-Stroble, Colette Mary Houle 1947- *WhoAmW 93*
Thompson-Wells, Diane Janelle 1950- *WhoAmW 93*
Thoms, David Moore 1948- *WhoEmL 93*
Thoms, Robert A. 1926- *St&PR 93*
Thomsen, Brian *ScF&FL 92*
Thomsen, Carl A. 1945- *St&PR 93*
Thomsen, Charles B. 1932- *St&PR 93*
Thomsen, Charles Burton 1932- *WhoAm 92*
Thomsen, Christian Jurgensen 1788-1865 *IntDcAn*
Thomsen, D.U. 1925- *WhoScE 91-2*
Thomsen, Donald Laurence, Jr. 1921- *WhoAm 92, WhoE 93*
Thomsen, Gailyn Dean 1936- *St&PR 93*
Thomsen, Ian 1956- *St&PR 93*
Thomsen, James M. 1955- *WhoE 93*
Thomsen, Jens Segelcke 1942- *WhoWor 93*
Thomsen, John Frederick *Law&B 92*
Thomsen, Marcia Rozen 1958- *WhoAmW 93*
Thomsen, Mary Joan Margaret 1934- *WhoAmW 93*
Thomsen, Moritz *BioIn 17*
Thomsen, Pamela Dee 1948- *WhoAmW 93*
Thomsen, Peter Karl 1942- *St&PR 93*
Thomsen, Thomas Richard 1935- *WhoAm 92*
Thomsen, William Howard, Jr. 1946- *St&PR 93*
Thomsen, Willy Frolund *WhoScE 91-2*
Thomson, Albert W. 1915- *St&PR 93*
Thomson, Alexander Bennett, Jr. 1954- *WhoE 93, WhoEmL 93*
Thomson, Andrew James *WhoScE 91-1*
Thomson, Angus William 1948- *WhoE 93*
Thomson, Barbara Jeanne 1929- *WhoAmW 93*
Thomson, Basil Henry, Jr. 1945- *WhoSSW 93*
Thomson, Bobby 1923- *BioIn 17*
Thomson, Bruce John *WhoScE 91-1*
Thomson, Bryden 1928- *Baker 92*
Thomson, Bryden 1928-1991 *BioIn 17*
Thomson, Cesar 1857-1931 *Baker 92*
Thomson, Cheryl Ann 1950- *WhoAmW 93*
Thomson, Chris *MiSFD 9, WhoWrEP 92*
Thomson, Christine Campbell 1897-1985 *ScF&FL 92*
Thomson, Colin 1937- *WhoScE 91-1*
Thomson, Dale Cairns 1923- *WhoAm 92*
Thomson, David 1941- *ScF&FL 92*

Thornton, William H. *Law&B 92*
Thornton, William James, Jr. 1919- *WhoAm 92*
Thornton, William Lewis 1923- *WhoSSW 93, WhoWor 93*
Thornton, William P., Jr. *Law&B 92*
Thornton, Winfred L. 1928- *St&PR 93*
Thornton, Winfred Lamotte 1923- *WhoSSW 93*
Thornton, Winfred Lamotte 1928- *WhoAm 92*
Thornwell, Allison, Jr. *St&PR 93*
Thoros, I *OxDcByz*
Thorp, Albert 1955- *St&PR 93*
Thorp, Annie Longfellow *AmWomPl*
Thorp, Barbara Curit 1937- *St&PR 93*
Thorp, Benjamin A., III 1938- *WhoAm 92*
Thorp, Charles Philip 1949- *WhoWor 93*
Thorp, Eric C. *Law&B 92*
Thorp, Grace Fish 1923- *WhoAmW 93*
Thorp, Ian *WhoScE 91-1*
Thorp, James Shelby 1937- *WhoAm 92*
Thorp, Josephine *AmWomPl*
Thorp, Willard 1899-1990 *BioIn 17*
Thorp, Willard L. d1992 *NewYTBS 92 [port]*
Thorp, Willard L(ong) 1899-1992 *CurBio 92N*
Thorp, Willard Long 1899-1992 *BioIn 17, ConAu 137*
Thorpe, Betsy Tucker 1956- *WhoAmW 93*
Thorpe, Calvin E. 1938- *WhoWor 93*
Thorpe, Cynthia Ann 1952- *WhoAmW 93*
Thorpe, Donald Elving 1936- *WhoAm 92*
Thorpe, Donna Lorine 1944- *St&PR 93*
Thorpe, Fred d1899 *ScF&FL 92*
Thorpe, Geoffrey L. *Law&B 92*
Thorpe, J. Trevor 1932- *WhoAsAP 91*
Thorpe, James 1915- *WhoAm 92, WhoWrEP 92*
Thorpe, James, III 1942- *WhoAm 92, WhoE 93*
Thorpe, James A. 1929- *St&PR 93*
Thorpe, James Alfred 1929- *WhoAm 92*
Thorpe, Janet Claire *Law&B 92*
Thorpe, Janet Claire 1953- *St&PR 93*
Thorpe, Jeremy 1929- *BioIn 17*
Thorpe, Jerry 1930- *MiSFD 9*
Thorpe, Jim 1888-1953 *BioIn 17, ConHero 2 [port]*
Thorpe, John A. 1934- *St&PR 93*
Thorpe, Joseph B. 1930- *St&PR 93*
Thorpe, Marjorie Ruth 1941- *WhoUN 92*
Thorpe, Merle, Jr. 1917- *WhoAm 92*
Thorpe, Michael 1932- *ScF&FL 92*
Thorpe, Norman R. *Law&B 92*
Thorpe, Richard 1896-1991 *AnObit 1991, BioIn 17, MiSFD 9N*
Thorpe, Robin Christopher 1948- *WhoScE 91-1*
Thorpe, Samuel Josiah 1942- *WhoUN 92*
Thorpe, Stephen J. 1944- *WhoWrEP 92*
Thorpe-Bates, Peggy 1914-1989 *BioIn 17*
Thorpe Davie, Cedric 1913-1983 *Baker 92*
Thorrington, Peter 1945- *St&PR 93*
Thorsen, Donald R. *Law&B 92*
Thorsen, Glen M. 1954- *St&PR 93*
Thorsen, Karen *MiSFD 9*
Thorsen, Nancy Dain 1944- *WhoAmW 93, WhoWor 93*
Thorsen, Pearl Jenny 1948- *WhoAmW 93*
Thorsen, Roy T. 1930- *St&PR 93*
Thorsen, Thomas Oliver 1931- *WhoAm 92*
Thorshaug, Niels Peter *WhoScE 91-4*
Thorshov, Roy Norman 1905- *WhoAm 92*
Thorsoe, Flemming 1938- *WhoScE 91-2*
Thorson, Connie Capers 1940- *WhoAmW 93*
Thorson, James Donald 1933- *St&PR 93*
Thorson, James L. 1934- *ScF&FL 92*
Thorson, John Martin, Jr. 1929- *WhoAm 92*
Thorson, Linda Christine 1952- *WhoAmW 93*
Thorson, Marcelyn Marie 1927- *WhoSSW 93*
Thorson, Milton Z. 1902- *St&PR 93*
Thorson, Oswald Hagen 1912- *WhoAm 92*
Thorson, Robert Mark 1951- *WhoWrEP 92*
Thorson, Steve 1945- *St&PR 93*
Thorson, Stuart J. 1946- *WhoAm 92*
Thorson, Thomas Bertel 1917- *WhoAm 92*
Thorstad, Bruce 1946- *WhoWrEP 92*
Thorstad, Linda E. 1954- *St&PR 93*
Thorsteinsson, Birger 1950- *WhoWor 93*
Thorsteinsson, Raymond 1921- *WhoAm 92*
Thorstenberg, Laurence 1925- *WhoAm 92*
Thorup, David M. 1935- *WhoUN 92*
Thostrup, Nils 1936- *WhoWor 93*
Thouless, David James 1934- *WhoAm 92*
Thoulon, J.M. 1937- *WhoScE 91-2*
Thow, George Bruce 1930- *WhoAm 92*
Thoyer, Judith Reinhardt 1940- *WhoAmW 93*
Thrailkill, Francis Marie 1937- *WhoAmW 93*
Thrale, Hester 1741-1821 *BioIn 17*
Thrall, Arthur Alvin 1926- *WhoAm 92*
Thrall, Debra *ScF&FL 92*
Thrall, Donald Stuart 1918- *WhoAm 92, WhoWor 93*
Thrall, Richard Cameron, Jr. 1929- *WhoE 93*
Thrall, Robert McDowell 1914- *WhoAm 92*
Thrane, Waldemar 1790-1828 *Baker 92*
Thrapp, Gary J. 1949- *St&PR 93*
Thrash, Edsel E. 1925- *WhoAm 92*
Thrash, James Lee 1949- *St&PR 93*
Thrash, John Curtis, Jr. 1925- *WhoSSW 93*
Thrash, Patricia Ann 1929- *WhoAm 92*
Thrash, Purvis James, Sr. 1927- *St&PR 93, WhoAm 92*
Thrash, Robert M. 1929- *WhoUN 92*
Thrash, Roy, Jr. *Law&B 92*
Thrasher, Dianne Elizabeth 1945- *WhoAmW 93*
Thrasher, Hugh 1941- *St&PR 93*
Thrasher, Hugh Matthew 1944- *WhoWor 93*
Thrasher, James Parker 1932- *WhoWor 93*
Thrasher, John M. 1952- *St&PR 93*
Thrasher, Kenneth 1949- *St&PR 93*
Thrasher, Paul McNeel, III 1950- *WhoE 93*
Thrasher, Penelope Ann 1954- *WhoAmW 93*
Thrasher, Randell Hue 1955- *WhoEmL 93*
Thrasybulus d388BC *BioIn 17*
Threadcraft, Hal Law, III 1952- *WhoEmL 93, WhoSSW 93*
Threadgill, Henry 1944- *ConMus 9 [port]*
Threadgill, Mae Ellen 1938- *WhoAmW 93*
Threadgill, Walter Leonard 1945- *St&PR 93*
Threadgold, Michael Andrew 1950- *WhoAm 92*
Threatt, Ned Leon, Sr. 1922- *WhoAm 92*
Thredgold, Jeff K. 1951- *St&PR 93*
Threefoot, Sam Abraham 1921- *WhoAm 92*
Three Stooges, The *IntDcF 2-3 [port]*
Threet, Jack Curtis 1928- *WhoAm 92*
Threinen, David T. 1934- *St&PR 93*
Threlkeld, Dennis John 1942- *St&PR 93*
Threlkeld, Richard Davis 1937- *WhoAm 92*
Thresher, John James 1929- *WhoScE 91-4*
Thrift, Julianne S. *WhoAmW 93*
Thrift, Syd, Jr. *BioIn 17*
Thring, Frank 1926- *BioIn 17*
Throckmorton, Joan Helen 1931- *WhoAm 92*
Throckmorton, John Ford 1941- *St&PR 93*
Throckmorton, Katherine M. *Law&B 92*
Throckmorton, Melissa Leigh 1966- *WhoSSW 93*
Throckmorton, Peter 1928-1990 *BioIn 17*
Throckmorton, Robert Bentley 1915- *WhoAm 92*
Throckmorton, William Robert, Sr. 1923- *WhoE 93*
Throdahl, Monte Corden 1919- *WhoAm 92*
Throgmorton, Richard Leon 1940- *St&PR 93*
Throndsen, Jahn 1936- *WhoScE 91-4*
Throne, Marilyn Elizabeth 1939- *WhoAmW 93, WhoWrEP 92*
Throner, Guy Charles, Jr. 1919- *WhoAm 92*
Thropay, John Paul 1949- *WhoEmL 93*
Thrower, Ellen *WhoAmW 93*
Thrower, Ellen E. 1947- *WhoIns 93*
Thrower, Frederick Mitchell, III 1968- *WhoE 93*
Thrower, James Arthur 1936- *WhoWor 93*
Thrower, Joey *BioIn 17*
Thrower, Keith Leonard 1944- *St&PR 93*
Thrower, Norman Joseph William 1919- *WhoAm 92*
Thrower, William Hicks *Law&B 92*
Thrubis, Anthony P. *Law&B 92*
Thrune, Elaine *BioIn 17*
Thrush, Brian Arthur *WhoScE 91-1*
Thrush, Murl E. d1990 *BioIn 17*
Ththill, William Edgar 1934- *St&PR 93*
Thucydides *BioIn 17, HarEnMi, OxDcByz*
Thue, Anniken 1944- *WhoWor 93*
Thue-Hansen, Vidar 1944- *WhoScE 91-4, WhoWor 93*
Thueme, William Harold 1945- *WhoWor 93*
Thuering, George Lewis 1919- *WhoAm 92*
Thuesen, Gerald Jorgen 1938- *WhoAm 92, WhoSSW 93*
Thuille, Ludwig (Wilhelm Andreas Maria) 1861-1907 *Baker 92*
Thul, Frederick W., Jr. 1948- *St&PR 93*
Thul, Lawrence A. 1957- *St&PR 93*
Thul, Nicholas R. 1950- *St&PR 93*
Thulean, Donald Myron 1929- *WhoAm 92*
Thulin, Ingrid 1929- *BioIn 17, IntDcF 2-3 [port]*
Thulin, Walter Willis 1929- *WhoAm 92*
Thull, Roger 1941- *WhoScE 91-3*
Thullen, George 1936- *WhoUN 92*
Thulstrup, Erik Waaben 1941- *WhoE 93*
Thum, Marcella *DcAmChF 1960*
Thum, Melvin Joseph 1932- *St&PR 93*
Thumann, Albert 1942- *ConAu 139, WhoAm 92*
Thumann, Rolf Gunther 1949- *WhoUN 92*
Thumb, Norbert *WhoScE 91-4*
Thumma, Samuel Anderson 1962- *WhoE 93*
Thummel, Moritz August von 1738-1817 *BioIn 17*
Thummel, Vera Current *BioIn 17*
Thummler, Fritz Ernst 1924- *WhoScE 91-3*
Thums, Charles William 1945- *WhoWor 93*
Thun, Matteo 1952- *BioIn 17*
Thun, Susanne *BioIn 17*
Thunborg, Anders Ingemar 1934- *WhoWor 93*
Thundal, Bjorn G. 1940- *WhoScE 91-4*
Thundal, Bjorn Gustaf 1940- *WhoWor 93*
Thunder, James Michael *Law&B 92*
Thunders, Johnny 1952-1991 *AnObit 1991*
Thunders, Johnny 1954-1991 *BioIn 17*
Thune, Michael 1956- *WhoWor 93*
Thungon, P.K. 1946- *WhoAsAP 91*
Thunman, Nils Ronald 1932- *WhoAm 92, WhoE 93*
Thunquest, Marilyn Matilda 1935- *WhoAmW 93*
Thuot, Pierre Joseph 1955- *WhoSSW 93*
Thurber, Albert W. 1937- *St&PR 93*
Thurber, Cleveland, Jr. 1925- *WhoAm 92*
Thurber, Davis P. 1925- *St&PR 93*
Thurber, Davis Peabody 1925- *WhoAm 92*
Thurber, Donald MacDonald Dickinson 1918- *WhoAm 92, WhoWor 93*
Thurber, James 1894-1961 *BioIn 17*
Thurber, James (Grover) 1894-1961 *ConAu 39NR, JrnUS, MajAI [port]*
Thurber, Jeannette Meyers 1850-1946 *BioIn 17*
Thurber, John Alexander 1939- *WhoAm 92*
Thurber, Peter Palms 1928- *WhoAm 92*
Thurber, Robert E. 1940- *St&PR 93*
Thurber, Robert Eugene 1932- *WhoAm 92, WhoSSW 93*
Thurber, William Bartlett 1930- *WhoE 93*
Thureau, Lani Carole 1948- *WhoE 93*
Thuren, Hjalmar Lauritz 1873-1912 *Baker 92*
Thurer, Richard Jerome 1936- *WhoSSW 93*
Thuriaux, Michel Camille 1939- *WhoUN 92*
Thurlbeck, William Michael 1929- *WhoAm 92*
Thurlo, Aimee *ScF&FL 92*
Thurlow, David 1932- *ScF&FL 92*
Thurm, Gil 1947- *WhoE 93*
Thurman, Addison Eugene, Jr. 1943- *WhoSSW 93*
Thurman, Andrew Edward 1954- *WhoEmL 93, WhoWor 93*
Thurman, David Michael 1947- *St&PR 93*
Thurman, Howard 1900-1981 *ConBlB 3 [port]*
Thurman, Jerry W. 1947- *St&PR 93*
Thurman, Karen 1951- *WhoAmW 93*
Thurman, Kay Ellen *Law&B 92*
Thurman, Mark 1948- *BioIn 17, WhoCanL 92*
Thurman, Maxwell *BioIn 17*
Thurman, Maxwell R. 1931- *WhoAm 92*
Thurman, Oliver 1935- *St&PR 93*
Thurman, Ralph H. 1949- *St&PR 93*
Thurman, Ralph Holloway 1949- *WhoAm 92, WhoWor 93*
Thurman, Richard Keith *WhoSSW 93*
Thurman, Samuel David 1913- *WhoAm 92*
Thurman, Uma 1970- *ConTFT 10*
Thurman, William Gentry 1928- *WhoAm 92*
Thurman, William Lee 1928- *WhoWor 93*
Thurmann, Hollis 1946- *WhoWrEP 92*
Thurmann-Moe, Torkild *WhoScE 91-4*
Thurmeier, Edward F. 1948- *St&PR 93*
Thurmer, Stefan M.W. 1950- *WhoScE 91-3*
Thurmond, Charles J. 1910- *St&PR 93*
Thurmond, George Murat 1930- *WhoSSW 93*
Thurmond, Gerald P. *Law&B 92*
Thurmond, Jimmie Victor, Jr. 1934- *St&PR 93*
Thurmond, John Peter 1955- *WhoSSW 93*
Thurmond, Strom 1902- *CngDr 91, CurBio 92 [port], PolPar, WhoAm 92, WhoSSW 93*
Thurmond, Vera Belinda *WhoSSW 93*
Thurn, Clark *Law&B 92*
Thurn, Heinrich Matthias 1567-1640 *HarEnMi*
Thurn, Max d1991 *BioIn 17*
Thurner, Frederic Eugene de 1785-1827 *Baker 92*
Thurn und Taxis, Gloria *BioIn 17*
Thurn und Taxis, Johannes, Furst von *BioIn 17*
Thurn-Valsassina, Maximilian, Graf von d1991 *BioIn 17*
Thurnwald, Richard 1869-1954 *IntDcAn*
Thurow, Donna J. 1935- *WhoAmW 93*
Thurow, Lester C. *BioIn 17*
Thurow, Lester Carl 1938- *WhoAm 92*
Thurrott, Hope Elizabeth *Law&B 92*
Thursby, Emma (Cecilia) 1845-1931 *Baker 92*
Thursby, Gene Robert 1939- *WhoSSW 93*
Thursby, Peter Michael 1945- *WhoWor 93*
Thursby, W. Gerald *Law&B 92*
Thurston, Alice Janet 1916- *WhoAm 92*
Thurston, Althea Cooms *AmWomPl*
Thurston, Bob 1944- *St&PR 93*
Thurston, Charles R. 1933- *St&PR 93*
Thurston, Charles W. 1960- *St&PR 93*
Thurston, Charlie A. 1939- *St&PR 93*
Thurston, Christopher F. *WhoScE 91-1*
Thurston, David E. 1957- *WhoAm 92, WhoE 93*
Thurston, Donald Allen 1930- *WhoAm 92*
Thurston, Fred Stone 1931- *St&PR 93*
Thurston, George Butte 1924- *WhoAm 92*
Thurston, Harry 1950- *WhoCanL 92*
Thurston, Jarvis A. 1914- *BioIn 17*
Thurston, John A. 1951- *St&PR 93*
Thurston, Julian *BioIn 17*
Thurston, Patricia Ann 1951- *WhoAmW 93*
Thurston, Robert 1936- *ScF&FL 92*
Thurston, Robert N. 1932- *St&PR 93*
Thurston, Russell Charles 1939- *St&PR 93*
Thurston, William Paul 1946- *WhoAm 92*
Thurston, William R. 1921- *WhoAm 92*
Thurstone, Thelma Gwinn 1897- *BioIn 17*
Thursz, Daniel 1929- *WhoAm 92*
Thursz, Frederic Matys 1930-1992 *NewYTBS 92*
Thurtle, Dorothy 1890- *BioIn 17*
Thuruthickara, John Chandy 1955- *WhoE 93*
Thutmose, III d1449BC *HarEnMi*
Thutmose, IV, King of Egypt c. 1420BC-1411BC *BioIn 17*
Thwaites, Alfred *WhoScE 91-1*
Thwe, Myo *WhoUN 92*
Thwing, R.C. 1921- *St&PR 93*
Thyagarajan, G. *WhoScE 91-1*
Thyberg, Bertil 1919- *WhoScE 91-4*
Thyberg, Kenneth Robert 1948- *St&PR 93*
Thybo, Hans 1954- *WhoScE 91-2*
Thybo, Leif 1922- *Baker 92*
Thyen, Herbert Edward 1912- *St&PR 93*
Thyen, James Conrad 1943- *St&PR 93*
Thyen, Ronald Joseph 1937- *St&PR 93*
Thyfault, Michel Daniel 1947- *St&PR 93*
Thygerson, Alton L(uie) 1940- *ConAu 39NR*
Thygerson, Kenneth J. 1945- *St&PR 93*
Thygerson, Kenneth James 1945- *WhoAm 92*
Thyll, Szilard 1934- *WhoScE 91-4*
Thym, Jurgen 1943- *WhoE 93*
Thynn, Alexander 1932- *ScF&FL 92*
Thyret, Kathryn Margaret *Law&B 92*
Thys, Henri 1941- *WhoScE 91-2*
Thys, Jean-Regnier 1929- *WhoWor 93*
Thys, Thierry N. 1931- *St&PR 93*
Thysen, Benjamin 1932- *WhoE 93*
Thyssen-Bornemisza, Francesca *BioIn 17*
Thyssen-Bornemisza, Hans Heinrich *NewYTBS 92 [port]*
Thys Van Den Audenaerde, Dirk F.E. 1934- *WhoScE 91-2*
Tiago de Oliveira, Jose 1928- *WhoWor 93*
Tiainen, Tuomo Johannes 1947- *WhoScE 91-4*
Tian, Feng 1940- *WhoWor 93*
Tian, Guo Dong 1937- *WhoWor 93*
Tian, Jie 1960- *WhoWor 93*
Tiangco, Elito 1940- *WhoE 93*
Tian Han 1898-1968 *BioIn 17*
Tian Jiyun 1920- *WhoAsAP 91*
Tian Jiyun 1929- *WhoWor 93*
Tianming, Wu 1939- *MiSFD 9*
Tiano, J. Richard *Law&B 92*
Tiano, J. Richard 1944- *St&PR 93*
Tiano, Piero 1947- *WhoScE 91-3*
Tiant, Luis 1940- *HispAmA*

Tiant, Luis Clemente Vega, Jr. 1940- *BiDAMSp 1989*
Tiarks, Stephen T. *Law&B 92*
Tibaldi, Antonio *MiSFD 9*
Tibaldi, Pellegrino 1527-1596 *BioIn 17*
Tibaldi Chiesa, Maria 1896-1968 *Baker 92*
Tibbalds, Francis Eric 1941- *WhoWor 93*
Tibbals, David Lester 1945- *WhoSSW 93*
Tibbals, Dawn Marie 1967- *WhoAmW 93*
Tibben, Engelbertus 1947- *WhoWor 93*
Tibbet, Lawrence 1896-1960 *Baker 92*
Tibbets, Robin Frank 1924- *WhoWor 93*
Tibbett, Lawrence 1896-1960 *Baker 92, IntDcOp [port], OxDcOp*
Tibbetts, Dennis Oliver 1941- *WhoWor 93*
Tibbetts, George C. 1925- *St&PR 93*
Tibbetts, Larry Newton 1934- *WhoAm 92*
Tibbetts, Steve *BioIn 17*
Tibbits, George (Richard) 1933- *Baker 92*
Tibbitts, J. Brett *Law&B 92*
Tibbitts, Kent D. 1937- *WhoWor 93*
Tibbitts, Samuel John 1924- *WhoAm 92*
Tibbitts, Theodore William 1929- *WhoAm 92*
Tibbs, Donald Fredrick 1966- *WhoSSW 93*
Tibbs, Edward A. 1940- *AfrAmBi [port]*
Tibbs, Martha Jane Pullen 1932- *WhoSSW 93*
Tibbs, Vicki Lee 1954- *WhoAmW 93*
Tibby, M.A. *WhoScE 91-1*
Tibell, Anders Gunnar 1930- *WhoWor 93*
Tiberg, Hugo Georg 1929- *WhoWor 93*
Tiberghien, Albert 1915- *WhoWor 93*
Tibergien, Mark C. 1952- *St&PR 93*
Tiberii, Dorothy Anne 1954- *WhoAmW 93*
Tiberios, I d582 *OxDcByz*
Tiberios, II d706 *OxDcByz*
Tiberi-Smolenski, Sandra Josephine 1964- *WhoAmW 93*
Tiberius, Dennis E. 1944- *St&PR 93*
Tiberius Claudius Nero Caesar 42BC-37AD *HarEnMi*
Tibler, Lee Walter 1952- *WhoSSW 93*
Tibo, Gilles *BioIn 17*
Tibo, Gilles 1951- *ConAu 136*
Tiburzi, Bonnie 1948- *BioIn 17, ConAu 136*
Tiby, Ottavio 1891-1955 *Baker 92*
Tice, Carol Hoff 1931- *WhoAmW 93*
Tice, Charles L. 1934- *St&PR 93*
Tice, David Allan 1952- *WhoSSW 93, WhoWor 93*
Tice, George Andrew 1938- *WhoAm 92, WhoE 93*
Tice, Kirk Clifford 1954- *WhoE 93*
Tice, Linwood Franklin 1909- *WhoAm 92*
Tice, Mark Randolph 1941- *St&PR 93*
Tice, Patricia Kaye 1953- *WhoAmW 93*
Tice, Raphael Dean 1927- *WhoAm 92*
Tice, Thomas Robert 1948- *WhoSSW 93*
Ticer, Patricia *WhoSSW 93*
Ticer, Terri Jean 1955- *WhoAmW 93*
Tichacek, Josef Aloys 1807-1886 *Baker 92*
Tichatschek, Joseph 1807-1886 *Baker 92, OxDcOp*
Tichauer, Klaus Max 1930- *WhoWor 93*
Tichauer, Ricardo 1942- *WhoUN 92*
Tichenor, Arthur G. 1913- *St&PR 93*
Tichenor, Donald Keith 1937- *WhoAm 92*
Tichenor, Fred Cooper, Jr. 1932- *WhoSSW 93, WhoWor 93*
Tichenor, McHenry Taylor 1955- *BioIn 17*
Tichi, Cecelia 1942- *WhoSSW 93*
Tichler, Rosemarie 1939- *WhoAm 92*
Tichnor, Alan Jerome 1924- *WhoAm 92*
Ticho, Harold Klein 1921- *WhoAm 92*
Tichy, Gottfried 1942- *WhoScE 91-4*
Tichy, Paul 1913- *St&PR 93*
Tichy, Robert Franz 1957- *WhoWor 93*
Tichy, Susan Elizabeth 1952- *WhoWrEP 92*
Tick, Daniel J. *Law&B 92*
Tickell, Renee Oriana Haynes *ConAu 139*
Tickett, Deborah L. 1951- *WhoAmW 93*
Tickle, Ian James *WhoScE 91-1*
Tickle, John D. 1942- *St&PR 93*
Tickle, Phyllis Alexander 1934- *WhoSSW 93, WhoWrEP 92*
Tickle, Samuel Milton 1933- *WhoSSW 93*
Tickner, John J. *Law&B 92*
Tickner, Judith Ann 1937- *WhoE 93*
Tickner, Robert Edward 1951- *WhoAsAP 91*
Ticknor, Arthur W. 1934- *St&PR 93*
Ticknor, Benjamin Holt, II 1909-1979 *BiDAMSp 1989*
Ticknor, Howard Malcolm 1936- *St&PR 93*
Ticotin, Rachel 1958- *ConTFT 10*
Tidball, Charles Stanley 1928- *WhoAm 92*
Tidball, E.C. *Law&B 92*
Tidball, M. Elizabeth Peters 1929- *WhoAm 92, WhoAmW 93*
Tidball, Robert N. 1939- *St&PR 93*
Tidd, Cynthia Ann 1956- *WhoWrEP 92*
Tidd, Kathy J. *Law&B 92*
Tidd, Mark James *Law&B 92*
Tidd, Ronald Robert 1953- *WhoE 93*
Tiddens, Mark E. 1951- *St&PR 93*
Tideman, Henk 1942- *WhoWor 93*
Tidemann, Even 1946- *WhoScE 91-4*
Tidman, Derek Albert 1930- *WhoAm 92*
Tidmarsh, David *BioIn 17*
Tidmarsh, David Harry *WhoScE 91-1*
Tidmarsh, Karen MacAusland 1949- *WhoE 93*
Tidor, Manfred 1932- *St&PR 93*
Tidrick, Larry James 1939- *St&PR 93*
Tidwell, Ardis M. 1932- *St&PR 93*
Tidwell, Enid Eugenie 1944- *WhoAmW 93*
Tidwell, George Ernest 1931- *WhoAm 92*
Tidwell, Linda Darnell 1953- *WhoAmW 93*
Tidwell, Moody R. 1939- *WhoAm 92, WhoE 93*
Tidwell, Moody R., III 1939- *CngDr 91*
Tidwell, Robert 1934- *St&PR 93*
Tidwell, Stanley Charles 1943- *WhoSSW 93*
Tidwell, Thomas Tinsley 1939- *WhoAm 92*
Tidwell, W.T. 1937- *St&PR 93*
Tidyman, Ernest 1928-1984 *ScF&FL 92*
Tieck, Ludwig 1773-1853 *BioIn 17*
Tieck, William Arthur 1908- *WhoE 93*
Tiecke, Richard William 1917- *WhoAm 92*
Tiede, Tom Robert 1937- *WhoAm 92, WhoWor 93*
Tiedeck, Michael Thomas 1951- *St&PR 93*
Tiedeken, Kathleen Helen 1945- *WhoAmW 93*
Tiedeman, David Valentine 1919- *WhoAm 92*
Tiedeman, Donald Louis 1936- *WhoE 93*
Tiedeman, Edward D. *Law&B 92*
Tiedeman, Edward D. 1944- *St&PR 93*
Tiedemann, Albert William, Jr. 1924- *WhoSSW 93, WhoWor 93*
Tiedemann, Heinz 1923- *WhoWor 93*
Tiedemann, Klaus Martin 1938- *WhoWor 93*
Tiedemann, Margaret Mary 1920- *St&PR 93*
Tiedemann, Ruth Elizabeth Fulton 1935- *WhoAmW 93*
Tiedemann, Waldemar 1937- *St&PR 93*
Tiedemann, William Harold 1943- *WhoAm 92*
Tieder, Barbara Ann 1960- *WhoAmW 93*
Tiedge-Lafranier, Jeanne Marie 1960- *WhoAm 92*
Tiedman, Richard *ScF&FL 92*
Tiedt, Iris McClellan *WhoAmW 93*
Tiefel, Virginia May 1926- *WhoAm 92*
Tiefel, William Reginald 1934- *St&PR 93, WhoAm 92*
Tiefenbach, E.J. 1941- *St&PR 93*
Tiefenbrun, Susan 1943- *WhoE 93*
Tiefenthal, Marguerite Aurand 1919- *WhoAmW 93*
Tieffenbrucker, Gaspar *Baker 92*
Tieger, Jeff *St&PR 93*
Tieger, Samuel 1934- *WhoWor 93*
Tiegerman, Bernard *Law&B 92*
Tiegs, Cheryl *BioIn 17, WhoAm 92, WhoAmW 93*
Tiehsen, Otto 1817-1849 *Baker 92*
Tielemans, Louis 1947- *WhoScE 91-2*
Tielens, Steven Robert 1953- *WhoSSW 93*
Tielke, James Clemens 1931- *WhoAm 92*
Tielkemeier, Esther *AmWomPl*
Tieman, Nathan 1943- *St&PR 93*
Tieman, Suzannah Bliss 1943- *WhoAmW 93*
Tiemann, Jerome Johnson 1932- *WhoAm 92*
Tiemann, Karl-Heinz 1940- *WhoScE 91-3*
Tiemann, Norbert Theodore 1924- *WhoAm 92*
Tiemeyer, Richard Wayne 1935- *WhoSSW 93*
Tien, Chang L. 1935- *BioIn 17*
Tien, Chang Lin 1935- *WhoAm 92, WhoWor 93*
Tien, H. Ti 1928- *WhoAm 92*
Tien, James Pei-chun 1947- *WhoAsAP 91*
Tien, John K. 1940-1992 *BioIn 17*
Tien, John Kai 1940- *WhoSSW 93*
Tien, Ping King 1919- *WhoAm 92*
Tienari, Martti J. 1935- *WhoScE 91-4*
Tienari, Pekka J. 1931- *WhoScE 91-4*
Tiencken, John H., Jr. *Law&B 92*
Tienda, Marta *WhoAmW 93*
Tienghi, Amelia 1955- *WhoWor 93*
Tienken, Arthur T. 1922- *WhoAm 92*
Tiensch, Charles John 1941- *St&PR 93*
Tiensuu, Jukka 1948- *Baker 92*
Tiensuu, Roland *BioIn 17*
Tiepel, Robert E.C.H. 1938- *WhoScE 91-3*
Tierling, Kenneth Shane 1961- *WhoSSW 93*
Tiernan, Bernadette Brunhuber 1951- *WhoE 93*
Tiernan, Charles W. d1990 *BioIn 17*
Tiernan, John F. 1944- *St&PR 93*
Tierney, A. Eleanor 1929- *WhoAmW 93*
Tierney, Anita Rachel 1946- *WhoE 93*
Tierney, Brian Patrick 1957- *WhoAm 92*
Tierney, David Bernard 1949- *St&PR 93*
Tierney, Don *BioIn 17*
Tierney, Gene 1920-1991 *AnObit 1991, BioIn 17, IntDcF 2-3*
Tierney, George *St&PR 93*
Tierney, Harry (Austin) 1890-1965 *Baker 92*
Tierney, James Edward 1947- *WhoAm 92, WhoE 93*
Tierney, James T. 1942- *St&PR 93*
Tierney, John Mark 1924- *WhoE 93*
Tierney, John Patrick 1931- *St&PR 93, WhoAm 92*
Tierney, John William 1923- *WhoAm 92*
Tierney, Kevin J. *Law&B 92*
Tierney, Kevin Joseph 1951- *St&PR 93, WhoAm 92*
Tierney, Madeleine Hood 1937- *WhoE 93*
Tierney, Michael E. *Law&B 92*
Tierney, Michael John 1947- *WhoSSW 93*
Tierney, Michael Peter 1947- *St&PR 93*
Tierney, Patrick John 1945- *WhoAm 92*
Tierney, Paul E., Jr. 1943- *WhoSSW 93*
Tierney, Richard 1936- *ScF&FL 92*
Tierney, Thomas F. 1934- *St&PR 93*
Tierney, William Gerard 1953- *WhoE 93*
Tierno, Philip Mario, Jr. 1943- *WhoE 93*
Tiernon, Carlos H. 1930- *St&PR 93*
Tiernon, Carlos Herschel 1930- *WhoAm 92*
Tiersky, Terri S. 1959- *WhoAmW 93*
Tiersot, (Jean-Baptiste-Elisee-) Julien 1857-1936 *Baker 92*
Tiesler, Ekkehard 1934- *WhoScE 91-3*
Tiessen, (Richard Gustav) Heinz 1887-1971 *Baker 92*
Tietgens, Edward R. 1938- *St&PR 93*
Tietjen, Heinz 1881-1967 *Baker 92, OxDcOp*
Tietjen, James 1933- *WhoAm 92*
Tietjen, John H. *BioIn 17*
Tietjen, John Henry 1940- *WhoAm 92*
Tietjens, Eunice Hammond 1884-1944 *AmWomPl*
Tietjens, Therese 1831-1877 *OxDcOp*
Tietjens, Therese (Carolina Johanna Alexandra) 1831-1877 *Baker 92, IntDcOp*
Tietke, Wilhelm 1938- *WhoSSW 93, WhoWor 93*
Tietz, Adrienne Teissier 1946- *St&PR 93*
Tietz, Jean Paul 1938- *St&PR 93*
Tietz, Michael F. *Law&B 92*
Tietz, Norbert Wolfgang 1926- *WhoAm 92*
Tietz, Reinhard 1928- *WhoWor 93*
Tietze, Fred Byron *Law&B 92*
Tietze, Lutz Friedjan 1942- *WhoWor 93*
Tiezzi, Enzo On. 1938- *WhoScE 91-3*
Tiffany, Arthur L. V. 1933- *St&PR 93*
Tiffany, C. Hunton 1939- *St&PR 93*
Tiffany, Dorte Frikke 1959- *WhoWor 93*
Tiffany, Esther Brown 1858- *AmWomPl*
Tiffany, Louis Comfort 1848-1933 *BioIn 17, GayN*
Tiffany, William Swart 1943- *WhoSSW 93*
Tiffen, Ira A. 1951- *St&PR 93*
Tiffen, Nathan 1925- *St&PR 93*
Tiffen, Steven D. 1960- *St&PR 93*
Tiffin, Jay H. 1928- *St&PR 93*
Tiffin, Joseph 1905-1989 *BioIn 17*
Tifft, Ellen *WhoWrEP 92*
Tift, Leigh Ann *Law&B 92*
Tift, Mary Louise 1913- *WhoAm 92, WhoAmW 93*
Tigani, Bruce William 1956- *WhoE 93, WhoWor 93*
Tigar, Michael Edward 1941- *WhoAm 92, WhoWor 93*
Tigay, Alan Merrill 1947- *WhoAm 92*
Tiger, Ira Paul 1936- *WhoAm 92*
Tiger, Lionel 1937- *WhoAm 92*
Tiger, Madeline Joan 1934- *WhoWrEP 92*
Tiger, Virginia 1940- *ScF&FL 92*
Tigerman, Stanley 1930- *BioIn 17, WhoAm 92*
Tigerstedt, P.M.A. 1936- *WhoScE 91-4*
Tigges, John 1932- *ScF&FL 92*
Tigges, John Thomas 1932- *WhoWrEP 92*
Tigges, Kenneth Edwin 1927- *WhoAm 92*
Tigges, Timothy John 1956- *WhoE 93*
Tighe, Anne Hodgdon 1941- *St&PR 93*
Tighe, Barbara Ellen 1953- *WhoAmW 93*
Tighe, Gary 1948- *St&PR 93*
Tighe, James *St&PR 93*
Tighe, James C. 1950- *WhoAm 92*
Tighe, John Richard *WhoScE 91-1*
Tighe, Joseph J. 1944- *St&PR 93*
Tighe, Michael J. 1931- *St&PR 93*
Tighe, Thomas James Gasson, Jr. 1946- *WhoE 93*
Tighe-Moore, Barbara Jeanne 1961- *WhoEmL 93, WhoWor 93*
Tight, Dexter C. 1924- *St&PR 93*
Tight, Dexter Corwin 1924- *WhoAm 92*
Tiglath-Pileser fl. 1120BC-1093BC *HarEnMi*
Tiglath-Pileser, III fl. 745BC-727BC *HarEnMi*
Tignanelli, James A. *Law&B 92*
Tignol, Jean-Pierre Eliane 1954- *WhoWor 93*
Tignor, Beth *ScF&FL 92*
Tigranes c. 140BC-55BC *HarEnMi*
Tigranian, Armen (Tigran) 1879-1950 *Baker 92*
Tigyi, Andrew 1924- *WhoScE 91-4*
Tigyi, Jozsef 1926- *WhoScE 91-4*
Tihany, Adam D. 1948?- *BioIn 17*
Tihany, Leslie Charles 1911- *WhoAm 92*
Tiihonen, Lawrence H. d1990 *BioIn 17*
Tiistola, David Walter *Law&B 92*
Tijardovic, Ivo 1895-1976 *Baker 92*
Tijdeman, Hendrik 1939- *WhoScE 91-3*
Tikaram, Tanita 1970- *ConMus 9 [port]*
Tikhomirov, Vasily 1876-1956 *BioIn 17*
Tikka, Kari (Juhani) 1946- *Baker 92*
Tikkanen, Esa *BioIn 17*
Tikkanen, George D. 1934- *St&PR 93*
Tikotsky, Evgeni (Karlovich) 1893-1970 *Baker 92*
Tiktin, Carl 1930- *WhoWrEP 92*
Tilak Bal Gangadhar 1856-1920 *DcTwHis*
Tilanus, C. Bernhard 1936- *WhoScE 91-3*
Tilbian, Lorna Mona 1957- *WhoWor 93*
Tilbury, Rodney Neil 1960- *WhoWor 93*
Tilbury, Roger Graydon 1925- *WhoAm 92*
Tilden, Bill 1893-1953 *BioIn 17*
Tilden, Charles R. 1953- *St&PR 93*
Tilden, Rebecca R. *Law&B 92*
Tilden, Samuel J. 1814-1886 *PolPar*
Tildesley, Alice L. *AmWomPl*
Tildesley, Arthur H. d1990 *BioIn 17*
Tiley, Sharon Kay 1952- *WhoWrEP 92*
Tilg, Howard A. 1914- *St&PR 93*
Tilger, Justine Tharp 1931- *WhoAmW 93*
Tilghman, Bill 1854-1924 *BioIn 17*
Tilghman, Michelle Lynn 1957- *WhoAmW 93*
Tilghman, Richard Albert, Jr. 1945- *St&PR 93*
Tilghman, Richard Carmichael, Jr. 1947- *WhoAm 92*
Tilghman, Richard Granville 1940- *St&PR 93, WhoAm 92, WhoSSW 93*
Tilghman, Richard Henry 1949- *WhoAm 92*
Tilghman, Shirley Marie *WhoAm 92*
Tilghman, Thomas Slocum 1946- *WhoE 93*
Till, Beatriz Maria 1952- *WhoAmW 93*
Till, D. Allen 1951- *St&PR 93*
Till, Emmett *BioIn 17*
Till, Emmett Louis 1941-1955 *EncAACR*
Till, Eric 1929- *MiSFD 9*
Till, Frances Deleon 1941- *WhoSSW 93*
Till, George G. 1929- *St&PR 93*
Till, James Edgar 1931- *WhoAm 92*
Till, James Paul 1949- *WhoSSW 93*
Till, Johann Christian 1762-1844 *Baker 92*
Till, Larry Percy 1944- *St&PR 93*
Till, Paul H. 1929- *St&PR 93*
Tillack, Robert Charles 1952- *WhoE 93*
Tillack, Thomas Warner 1937- *WhoAm 92*
Tillage, Granville Christian 1936- *St&PR 93*
Tillander, Thomas 1938- *St&PR 93*
Tillar, Thomas Cato, Jr. 1947- *WhoSSW 93*
Tillberg, Bjorn Tomas 1944- *WhoWor 93*
Tille, James Eugene 1951- *WhoSSW 93*
Tillema, Hendrik Freerk 1870-1952 *IntDcAn*
Tiller, Carl W. 1915-1991 *BioIn 17*
Tiller, Kathleen Blanche 1925- *WhoAmW 93*
Tiller, Randy G. 1948- *WhoSSW 93*
Tiller, Ronald Roy 1947- *St&PR 93*
Tillery, Bill W. 1938- *WhoAm 92*
Tillery, Dwight 1948- *WhoAm 92*
Tilles, Gilbert d1990 *BioIn 17*
Tilles, Nurit 1952- *Baker 92*
Tilleskjor, Darrell Erwin 1936- *St&PR 93*
Tillet, Leslie d1992 *NewYTBS 92*
Tillett, Benjamin 1860-1943 *DcTwHis*
Tillett, Dorothy Stockbridge *AmWomPl*
Tilley, Anne M. *Law&B 92*
Tilley, C. Ronald 1935- *WhoAm 92*
Tilley, Carolyn Bittner 1947- *WhoAm 92*
Tilley, David Reginald *WhoScE 91-1*
Tilley, David Wayne 1949- *WhoSSW 93*
Tilley, Frank William 1945- *WhoSSW 93*
Tilley, James Michael 1945- *WhoWor 93*
Tilley, Norwood Carlton, Jr. *WhoAm 92, WhoSSW 93*
Tilley, Patrick 1928- *ScF&FL 92*

Tilley, Rice Matthews, Jr. 1936- WhoWor 93
Tilley, Richard John David WhoScE 91-1
Tilley, Robert J. ScF&FL 92
Tilley, Stephen George 1943- WhoE 93
Tilley, T. Bruce 1927- St&PR 93
Tilley, Terrence William 1947- WhoSSW 93
Tilley, Thomas G. 1946- St&PR 93
Tillich, Paul 1886-1965 BioIn 17
Tillim, Steven Marc 1966- St&PR 93
Tillinghast, Charles C. 1936- St&PR 93
Tillinghast, Charles Carpenter, Jr. 1911- WhoAm 92
Tillinghast, Charles Carpenter, III 1936- WhoAm 92
Tillinghast, David Rollhaus 1930- WhoAm 92
Tillinghast, Jimmy Lee 1944- WhoSSW 93
Tillinghast, John A. 1927- St&PR 93
Tillinghast, John Avery 1927- WhoAm 92
Tillinghast, Meta Ione WhoAmW 93
Tillinghast, Richard Williford 1940- WhoWrEP 92
Tillinghast, Walter C. 1929- St&PR 93
Tillis, Alan Casal 1939- WhoE 93
Tillis, Barry I. Law&B 92
Tillis, David Roger 1955- WhoSSW 93
Tillis, Joy Wellington 1949- WhoAmW 93
Tillis, Mel 1932- Baker 92
Tillis, Melvin 1932- WhoAm 92
Tillis, Pam BioIn 17
Tillis, Pam 1957- ConMus 8 [port]
Tillis, Randy E. 1957- St&PR 93
Tillistrand, John Anthony 1956- WhoE 93
Tillman, Benjamin R. 1847-1918 PolPar
Tillman, Douglas L. Law&B 92
Tillman, Eugene C. AfrAmBi [port]
Tillman, Glenn Monroe 1955- WhoSSW 93
Tillman, H. Robert Law&B 92
Tillman, Katherine Davis AmWomPl
Tillman, Kay Heidt 1945- WhoAmW 93, WhoSSW 93, WhoWor 93
Tillman, Kayla Linn 1962- WhoWrEP 92
Tillman, Kenneth A. 1944- St&PR 93
Tillman, Lauralee A. 1951- WhoIns 93
Tillman, Massie Monroe 1937- WhoAm 92
Tillman, Nancy Norton 1954- WhoAmW 93
Tillman, Raymond St&PR 93
Tillman, Rollie, Jr. 1933- WhoAm 92, WhoSSW 93
Tillman, Vickie A. 1951- St&PR 93
Tillmann, Ulrike Luise 1962- WhoWor 93
Tillmanns, Ekkehart 1941- WhoWor 93
Tillon, Charles 1897- BioIn 17
Tillotson, Brian Jay 1959- WhoSSW 93
Tillotson, Edith Sanford AmWomPl
Tillotson, Frank Lee 1941- WhoAm 92
Tillotson, Henry Barber 1921- St&PR 93
Tillotson, Karin Ruth Myers 1942- WhoE 93
Tillotson, Kenneth Malcolm WhoScE 91-1
Tills, Donald 1934- WhoWor 93
Tillson, Albert H., Jr. 1948- ConAu 139
Tillson, Albert Holmes, Jr. 1948- WhoSSW 93
Tillson, James F. Law&B 92
Tillson, Linda Lou 1951- WhoAmW 93
Tilly, G.P. WhoScE 91-1
Tilly, Johan Tserclaes 1559-1632 HarEnMi
Tilly, Leslie A. Law&B 92
Tilly, Louise Audino 1930- WhoAmW 93
Tilly, Nancy 1935- BioIn 17
Tillyard, Aelfrida 1883- ScF&FL 92
Tillyard, H(enry) J(ulius) W(etenhall) 1881-1968 Baker 92
Tillyard, Helen Virginia 1954- WhoE 93
Tilman, Alfred 1848-1895 Baker 92
Tilmant, Theophile (Alexandre) 1799-1878 Baker 92
Tilney, Colin 1933- Baker 92
Tilney, William Stephen 1939- WhoAm 92, WhoSSW 93
Tilscher, Hans WhoScE 91-4
Tilson, Dorothy Ruth 1918- WhoE 93
Tilson, Hugh Arval, Jr. 1946- WhoSSW 93
Tilson, Hugh Hanna 1940- WhoAm 92
Tilson, John Quillin 1911- WhoAm 92
Tilson, M. David 1941- WhoE 93
Tilson, Marion W. Law&B 92
Tilson, Philip A. 1930- St&PR 93
Tilstra, Sally Ann 1958- WhoAmW 93
Tilton, Bernice Sheppard WhoAmW 93
Tilton, David Lloyd 1926- WhoAm 92
Tilton, George Robert 1923- WhoAm 92
Tilton, James Floyd 1937- WhoAm 92
Tilton, John Elvin 1939- WhoAm 92
Tilton, Kathleen Joan 1953- WhoAmW 93
Tilton, Kenneth Lee 1940- St&PR 93
Tilton, Lois 1946- ScF&FL 92
Tilton, Michael J. St&PR 93
Tilton, Rafael 1929- WhoWrEP 92
Tilton, Tanya Tylene 1960- WhoEmL 93
Tilton, Webster, Jr. 1922- WhoE 93
Tily, Stephen Bromley, III 1937- WhoE 93
Tilzer, James A. 1939- St&PR 93
Tilzer, Max 1939- WhoScE 91-3
Timakata, Frederick Karlemuana 1936- WhoWor 93
Timar, John J. Law&B 92
Timar, Sandor 1930- WhoWor 93
Timar, Tibor 1953- WhoWor 93
Timberg, Robert K. Law&B 92
Timberg, Sigmund 1911- WhoAm 92
Timberlake, Charles Edward 1935- WhoAm 92
Timberlake, Daphne Diane 1962- WhoAmW 93
Timberlake, Stephen Grant 1958- WhoSSW 93
Timberlake, Thomas Howard 1916- WhoAm 92
Timberlake, William Edward 1948- WhoSSW 93
Timberman, David G. 1955- ConAu 139
Timbers, Mary-Ellen Moran Law&B 92
Timbers, Michael J. 1941- St&PR 93
Timbers, Michael James 1941- WhoAm 92
Timbers, Stephen B. 1944- St&PR 93
Timbers, William Homer 1915- WhoAm 92, WhoE 93
Timbury, M.C. WhoScE 91-1
Timby, Elmer K. d1992 NewYTBS 92
Time SoulM
Timerbaev, Roland Makhmoutovich 1927- WhoUN 92
Timerman, Jacobo 1923- BioIn 17
Timet, Dubravko 1924- WhoScE 91-4
Timikata, Fred 1936- WhoAsAP 91
Timken, Suzanne BioIn 17
Timken, William Robert, Jr. 1938- St&PR 93
Timko, Christine 1956- WhoAmW 93
Timko, Francis Martin Michael 1944- WhoE 93
Timko, Judit J. 1931- WhoScE 91-4
Timko, Karen Lisa Law&B 92
Timko, Michael J. Law&B 92
Timlen, Thomas M. 1928-1991 BioIn 17
Timlen, Thomas M., Jr. 1928- St&PR 93
Timlen, Thomas Michael 1928- WhoAm 92
Timlett, Peter Valentine 1933- ScF&FL 92
Timlin, James Clifford 1927- WhoAm 92
Timlin, William M. 1892-1943 ScF&FL 92
Timm, Henry Christian 1811-1892 Baker 92
Timm, Jerry Roger 1942- St&PR 93
Timm, John C. Law&B 92
Timm, Maynard L. Law&B 92
Timm, Patricia Jo 1955- WhoAmW 93
Timm, Ralph Fulton 1921- WhoAm 92
Timm, Tammy Marie 1959- St&PR 93
Timm, Terry L. 1948- WhoIns 93
Timm, William 1930- St&PR 93
Timma, M.C. St&PR 93
Timme, Kathryn Pearl 1934- WhoAmW 93
Timmel, Timothy L. Law&B 92
Timmer, Barbara 1946- WhoAm 92, WhoAmW 93
Timmer, Charles Peter 1941- WhoAm 92
Timmer, Diane Leah 1956- WhoAmW 93
Timmerhaus, Klaus Dieter 1924- WhoAm 92
Timmerman, Dora Mae 1931- WhoAmW 93
Timmerman, George Bell, Jr. 1912- WhoAm 92, WhoWor 93
Timmerman, Hendrik 1937- WhoScE 91-3, WhoWor 93
Timmerman, John H. 1945- ScF&FL 92
Timmerman, Leon Bernard 1924- WhoE 93
Timmerman, Robert Wilson 1944- WhoE 93
Timmerman, Timothy Neal Law&B 92
Timmermans, Ferdinand 1891-1967 Baker 92
Timmermans, J.A. WhoScE 91-2
Timmers, Jacob 1938- St&PR 93
Timmes, Charles J. d1990 BioIn 17
Timmes, G.D. ScF&FL 92
Timmes, Graeme de ScF&FL 92
Timmes, Joseph J. 1914-1990 BioIn 17
Timmins, Bob BioIn 17
Timmins, Edward Patrick 1955- WhoEmL 93
Timmins, John Michael 1937- St&PR 93
Timmins, John Thomas 1931- St&PR 93
Timmins, Lois Fahs 1914- WhoWrEP 92
Timmins, Margo BioIn 17
Timmins, Michael Joseph 1953- St&PR 93
Timmins, Patrick Anthony 1932- St&PR 93
Timmins, Robert Nelson d1990 BioIn 17
Timmons, Andrea Carroll 1945- WhoAmW 93
Timmons, Charles McDonald 1926- WhoIns 93
Timmons, Charles McDonald, Jr. 1950- WhoIns 93
Timmons, Debra B. Law&B 92
Timmons, Earl L. 1937- WhoAm 92
Timmons, Edwin O'Neal 1928- WhoAm 92
Timmons, Francis Donald, Jr. 1956- WhoSSW 93
Timmons, Gerald Dean 1931- WhoAm 92
Timmons, Glen Robert 1939- St&PR 93
Timmons, Gordon David 1919- WhoSSW 93
Timmons, Joseph Dean 1948- WhoAm 92
Timmons, Leon Robert Law&B 92
Timmons, Madelon Aylwin 1934- WhoAmW 93
Timmons, Richard Brendan 1938- WhoAm 92
Timmons, S. Diane Law&B 92
Timmons, Thomas Joseph 1948- WhoSSW 93
Timmons, William D. 1927- St&PR 93
Timmons, William E. 1924- St&PR 93
Timmons, William Evan 1930- WhoAm 92
Timmons, William R., Jr. 1924- St&PR 93, WhoIns 93
Timmons, William Richardson, III 1951- WhoIns 93
Timmreck, Thomas C. 1946- WhoEmL 93, WhoWor 93
Timms, Alan R. St&PR 93
Timms, Donald 1927- St&PR 93
Timms, G.D. ScF&FL 92
Timms, Graeme de ScF&FL 92
Timms, Kevin P.K. Law&B 92
Timms, Leonard Joseph, Jr. 1936- St&PR 93, WhoAm 92, WhoSSW 93
Timms, Lorna Margaret WhoScE 91-1
Timms, Peter Rowland 1942- WhoAm 92
Timms, Rex A. 1932- St&PR 93
Timofeyev, Yermak 1540?-1585? Expl 93
Timon, Clay Scott 1943- St&PR 93
Timon, Lawrence Joseph 1927- St&PR 93
Timon, Vivian 1937- WhoScE 91-3
Timoney, Alice AmWomPl
Timoney, John Henry 1933- St&PR 93
Timoney, Peter Joseph 1941- WhoAm 92
Timoney, Richard Ferrer 1921- WhoScE 91-3
Timoney, Seamus G. 1926- WhoScE 91-3
Timoshenko, Semen Konstantinovich 1895-1970 HarEnMi
Timotheos Ailouros d477 OxDcByz
Timotheos of Gaza fl. c. 491-518 OxDcByz
Timotheos Salophakialos OxDcByz
Timothy, Bishop 1928- WhoAm 92
Timothy, Benjamin Franklin 1771-1807 BioIn 17
Timothy, David H. 1928- WhoAm 92
Timothy, Peter c. 1725-1782 JrnUS
Timothy, Raymond Joseph 1932- WhoAm 92
Timothy, Robert Keller 1918- WhoAm 92
Timour, John Arnold 1926- WhoAm 92
Timpa, Judy Dommert 1943- WhoSSW 93
Timpane, Philip Michael 1934- WhoAm 92, WhoE 93
Timpano, Anne 1950- WhoAm 92, WhoSSW 93
Timpany, Robert Daniel 1919- WhoSSW 93, WhoWor 93
Timperlake, Edward Thomas 1946- WhoAm 92
Timperley, Rosemary 1920-1988 ScF&FL 92
Timpka, Toomas 1957- WhoWor 93
Timpone, Ray 1946- St&PR 93
Timpson, Adele Wood d1991 BioIn 17
Timpson, Dierdre 1965?- BioIn 17
Timpson, Sarah L. 1938- WhoUN 92
Tims, Jodi Lynn 1958- WhoE 93
Tims, Robert Austin 1942- WhoSSW 93
Timson, Karen Sue 1959- WhoAmW 93
Timson, Keith 1945- ScF&FL 92
Timte, Lawrence D. Law&B 92
Timucin, Muharrem 1941- WhoScE 91-4
Timur 1336-1405 OxDcByz
Timurlenk 1336-1405 BioIn 17
Timur, the Great 1336-1405 BioIn 17
Timyan, Steve J. 1955- St&PR 93
Tinari, Anthony Philip Law&B 92
Tinari, Frank Dale 1943- WhoE 93
Tinaut, Diego 1923- WhoScE 91-3
Tinayre, Yves (Jean) 1891-1972 Baker 92
Tinbergen, Jan 1903- BioIn 17, WhoAm 92, WhoWor 93
Tinbergen, Niko 1907-1988 BioIn 17
Tinbergen, Nikolaas 1907-1988 IntDcAn
Tincelin, Edouard 1920- WhoScE 91-2
Tincher, Barbara Jean 1963- WhoAmW 93
Tincher, Charlotte Leggitt 1943- WhoSSW 93
Tinctoris, Johannes c. 1435-c. 1511 Baker 92
Tindal, Ralph Lawrence 1940- WhoAm 92
Tindale, Norman B. 1900- DcChlFi
Tindall, Carolyn V. Christian 1957- WhoSSW 93
Tindall, George Brown 1921- WhoAm 92
Tindall, George Taylor 1928- WhoAm 92
Tindall, Gillian BioIn 17
Tindall, Jill Denise 1958- WhoAmW 93
Tindall, Robert E. 1932- St&PR 93
Tindall, Robert Emmett 1934- WhoWor 93
Tindall, Suzie Cunningham 1944- WhoAmW 93
Tindall, Victor Ronald WhoScE 91-1
Tindell, William Norman 1921- WhoSSW 93
Tinder, Frank C. 1957- St&PR 93
Tinder, John Daniel 1950- WhoAm 92
Tinder, John Everett 1939- St&PR 93
Tinder, Sue 1953- WhoWrEP 92
Tinder, Susan Denise 1956- WhoAmW 93
Tinder, Wallace Winfrey, Jr. 1925- St&PR 93
Tindle, Christopher Thomas 1943- WhoWor 93
Tindoy, Cresente Rojas 1951- WhoWor 93
Tine, Armand 1960- WhoWor 93
Tine, Guido 1927- WhoScE 91-3
Tine, Michael P. 1945- St&PR 93, WhoAm 92
Tine, Robert ScF&FL 92
Tinebra, Carl Peter 1934- WhoAm 92
Tinel, Edgar (Pierre Joseph) 1854-1912 Baker 92
Tiner, Billy Don 1950- WhoSSW 93
Tiner, Carolyn BioIn 17
Tiner, Corey BioIn 17
Tiner, Donna Townsend 1947- WhoAmW 93
Tiner, John Hudson 1944- ConAu 40NR
Tiner, Stanley Ray 1942- WhoAm 92
Ting, Albert Chia 1950- WhoAm 92
Ting, Chung-Yu 1939- WhoWor 93
Ting, James H. St&PR 93
Ting, K.H. BioIn 17
Ting, Kenneth W. 1942- St&PR 93
Ting, Kwun-Lon 1948- WhoSSW 93
Ting, Ling 1904-1986 BioIn 17
Ting, Robert Yen-ying 1942- WhoSSW 93
Ting, S.C.C. 1936- BioIn 17
Ting, Samuel Chao-chung 1936- BioIn 17, WhoAm 92, WhoE 93, WhoWor 93
Tinga, Dante O. 1939- WhoAsAP 91
Ting Chew Peh, Dr. 1943- WhoAsAP 91
Tingelhoff, Henry Michael 1940- BiDAMSp 1989
Tingelstad, Jon Bunde 1935- WhoAm 92, WhoSSW 93
Tinger, Richard M. 1945- St&PR 93
Tinggom, Peter WhoAsAP 91
Tinggren, Carl Jurgen 1958- St&PR 93
Tinghitella, Stephen 1915- WhoAm 92, WhoWrEP 92
Tingir, Raffi Nurhan 1954- WhoE 93
Tingle, Aubrey James 1943- WhoAm 92
Tingle, James O'Malley 1928- WhoAm 92
Tingleff, John Burnier 1935- St&PR 93
Tingleff, Thomas Alan 1946- WhoAm 92
Tingley, Charles E. 1939- St&PR 93
Tingley, Charles Elbert 1939- WhoE 93
Tingley, Floyd Warren 1933- WhoAm 92, WhoSSW 93
Tingley, Kenneth Elliott 1932- St&PR 93
Ting Ling Kiew 1920- WhoAsAP 91
Tinguely, Jean 1925-1991 AnObit 1991, BioIn 17
Tinic, Seha Mehmet 1941- WhoAm 92
Tinkelman, Joseph 1924- WhoE 93
Tinker, Debra Ann 1951- WhoAmW 93
Tinker, Grant A. 1926- WhoAm 92
Tinker, Harold Burnham 1939- WhoAm 92
Tinker, John S. Law&B 92
Tinker, Mark MiSFD 9
Tinker, P.B. 1930- WhoScE 91-1
Tinker, Richard William 1929- St&PR 93
Tinkham, David R. 1955- St&PR 93
Tinkham, Michael 1928- WhoAm 92
Tinkham, Nancy Lynn 1961- WhoAmW 93
Tinkler, David Knox Law&B 92
Tinkler, Jack Donald 1936- WhoAm 92
Tinkoff, Florence 1937- St&PR 93
Tinkoff, Jay 1956- St&PR 93
Tinling, Teddy BioIn 17
Tinlot, Robert WhoScE 91-2
Tinmouth, William W. Law&B 92
Tinne, Alexine 1835-1869 Expl 93 [port]
Tinnell, (Marvin) Al(len) 1949- WhoWrEP 92
Tinney, J.F. 1937- St&PR 93
Tinney, M.E. 1944- St&PR 93
Tinney, Marian D. AmWomPl
Tinney, William Frank 1921- WhoAm 92
Tinnila, Aulis Tapio 1931- WhoScE 91-4
Tinnin, Glenna Smith AmWomPl
Tinnon, Susan Curtis Hughes 1952- WhoSSW 93
Tinoco, Cesar Ortiz 1915-1991 BioIn 17
Tinoco, Ignacio, Jr. 1930- WhoAm 92
Tinoco, Janet Kay 1960- WhoSSW 93

Tinoco, Judith Marshall 1959- *WhoAmW 93*
Tinsley, Adrian 1937- *WhoAm 92*
Tinsley, Barbara Vaughn *Law&B 92*
Tinsley, Donna Melissa 1965- *WhoSSW 93*
Tinsley, Edward 1833-1866 *BioIn 17*
Tinsley, Eleanor Whilden 1926- *WhoAmW 93*
Tinsley, Harry Lee, III 1947- *WhoSSW 93*
Tinsley, Jackson Bennett 1934- *St&PR 93, WhoAm 92, WhoSSW 93*
Tinsley, Pauline 1928- *OxDcOp*
Tinsley, Pauline (Cecilia) 1928- *Baker 92*
Tinsley, Peter A. 1939- *WhoE 93*
Tinsley, Robert 1949- *St&PR 93*
Tinsley, Walton Eugene 1921- *WhoAm 92*
Tinsley, William 1831-1902 *BioIn 17*
Tinsman, Margaret Neir 1936- *WhoAmW 93*
Tinsman, Sue *St&PR 93*
Tinstman, Carl C. 1945- *WhoUN 92*
Tinstman, Dale 1919- *St&PR 93*
Tinstman, Dale Clinton 1919- *WhoAm 92*
Tinsworth, Steven Howard 1945- *WhoSSW 93*
Tintes, Philip H. 1945- *St&PR 93*
Tintner, Adeline R. 1912- *ScF&FL 92*
Tintner, Georg *BioIn 17*
Tinyes, Kelly Ann *BioIn 17*
Tinz, Bernhard Harald 1945- *WhoWor 93*
Tiollais, Pierre J.R. 1934- *WhoScE 91-2*
Tiomkin, Dimitri 1894-1979 *Baker 92*
Tiona, Jim 1934- *St&PR 93*
Tiongco, Dionisio Ciria Cruz 1910- *WhoWor 93*
Tipe, David 1948- *WhoCanL 92*
Tipirneni, Tirumala Rao 1948- *WhoWor 93*
Tipo, Maria (Luisa) 1931- *Baker 92*
Tippenhauer, Carl Harry 1934- *WhoUN 92*
Tippens, Jack Kelvin 1939- *WhoSSW 93*
Tipper, Kenneth C. d1991 *BioIn 17*
Tippet, Clark *BioIn 17*
Tippet, Clark d1992 *NewYTBS 92*
Tippet, Karl Mathie 1928- *WhoAm 92*
Tippets, Dennis Wilcock 1938- *St&PR 93, WhoAm 92*
Tippets, Dianne Barkley 1939- *St&PR 93*
Tippets, Linda 1943- *BioIn 17*
Tippett, Bryan Keith 1957- *WhoE 93*
Tippett, Helen 1933- *WhoWor 93*
Tippett, James Sterling 1885-1956 *BioIn 17*
Tippett, Kenneth Guy Martin *WhoScE 91-1*
Tippett, Michael 1905- *IntDcOp, OxDcOp*
Tippett, Michael (Kemp) 1905- *Baker 92, WhoWor 93*
Tippett, Patricia *WhoScE 91-1*
Tippett, Virginia Monroe 1901- *WhoWrEP 92*
Tippett, Willis Paul, Jr. 1932- *WhoAm 92*
Tippette, Giles 1934- *ConAu 37NR*
Tippie, Henry B. 1927- *St&PR 93, WhoAm 92*
Tipping, Edward William *WhoScE 91-1*
Tipping, Marla *Law&B 92*
Tipping, William Malcolm 1931- *WhoAm 92, WhoSSW 93*
Tippins, J. Rankin *Law&B 92*
Tippins, Timothy Michael 1949- *WhoAm 92*
Tippit, John Harlow 1916- *WhoAm 92*
Tipple, Marilyn May 1943- *WhoAmW 93*
Tippo, Oswald 1911- *WhoAm 92*
Tippoo Sahibi 1753-1799 *BioIn 17*
Tipson, Lynn Baird 1943- *WhoAm 92*
Tipsword, Jean Ann 1961- *WhoAmW 93*
Tipton, Bernard J. 1943- *St&PR 93*
Tipton, Billy 1914-1989 *Baker 92*
Tipton, Carl Belt 1957- *St&PR 93*
Tipton, Carl William 1935- *WhoAm 92*
Tipton, Carolyn Louise 1950- *WhoWrEP 92*
Tipton, Clyde Raymond, Jr. 1921- *WhoAm 92*
Tipton, Donald Lloyd 1931- *St&PR 93*
Tipton, Donna Florine 1960- *WhoSSW 93*
Tipton, Gary Lee 1941- *WhoWor 93*
Tipton, Hiram Gardner *Law&B 92*
Tipton, Hiram Gardner 1943- *St&PR 93*
Tipton, James McCall 1948- *WhoSSW 93*
Tipton, James W. 1943- *St&PR 93*
Tipton, Jennifer *BioIn 17*
Tipton, Jennifer 1937- *WhoAm 92, WhoAmW 93*
Tipton, Keith Francis 1938- *WhoScE 91-3*
Tipton, Kenneth Warren 1932- *WhoSSW 93*
Tipton, Marilyn Oglesby 1944- *WhoAmW 93*
Tipton, Mary Davison 1947- *WhoAmW 93*
Tipton, Paul S. *WhoAm 92*
Tipton, Richard D. *Law&B 92*
Tipton, Steven Michael 1956- *WhoSSW 93*
Tipton, Stuart G. 1910-1981 *EncABHB 8 [port]*
Tipton, Thomas J. 1926- *St&PR 93*
Tipton, Thomas Wesley 1952- *WhoE 93*
Tiptree, James 1916-1987 *BioIn 17*
Tiptree, James, Jr. 1915-1987 *ScF&FL 92*
Tipu, Ioan d1991 *BioIn 17*
Tipu Sultan, Fath Ali 1753-1799 *BioIn 17*
Tirabasso, Annette Marie 1965- *WhoAmW 93*
Tirado, Romualdo *HispAmA*
Tirado Lopez, Victor *DcCPCAm*
Tirador, Licurgo P. 1931- *WhoAsAP 91*
Tiraky, Piyus 1929- *WhoAsAP 91*
Tirana, Bardyl Rifat 1937- *WhoAm 92*
Tirao, Juan Alfredo 1942- *WhoWor 93*
Tirard, Pierre Emmanuel 1827-1893 *BioIn 17*
Tiras, Herbert Gerald 1924- *WhoWor 93*
Tircuit, Stacie Denyse 1965- *WhoAmW 93*
Tirelli, Maria Del Carmen S. 1919- *WhoAmW 93*
Tirelli, Umberto *BioIn 17*
Tirer, Samuel 1950- *WhoE 93*
Tirey, Norman L. 1930- *St&PR 93*
Tiria, Kumari Sushila 1956- *WhoAsAP 91*
Tiriac, Ion *BioIn 17*
Tiridates the Great *OxDcByz*
Tirikatene-Sullivan, Whetu 1932- *WhoAsAP 91*
Tirindelli, Pier Adolfo 1858-1937 *Baker 92*
Tirino, Philip Joseph 1940- *WhoE 93*
Tiritakene, Eruera Tihema 1895-1967 *DcTwHis*
Tirkel, Anatol Zygmunt 1949- *WhoWor 93*
Tirnauer, Lawrence Theodore 1933- *WhoE 93*
Tirol, David B. 1933- *WhoAsAP 91*
Tirone, Elizabeth R. *Law&B 92*
Tirone, Robert J. 1945- *WhoE 93*
Tirpitz, Alfred von 1849-1930 *BioIn 17, DcTwHis, HarEnMi*
Tirrell, Bruce Kevin 1964- *WhoE 93*
Tirrell, Janet Anthony 1938- *WhoAmW 93*
Tirrell, John Albert 1934- *WhoAm 92*
Tirrell, Peg Harriet 1924- *WhoE 93*
Tirrito, Joe 1964- *BioIn 17*
Tirro, Frank Pascale 1935- *WhoAm 92*
Tirro, S. *WhoScE 91-3*
Tirro, Sebastiano 1941- *WhoScE 91-3*
Tirschwell, Kathy Ann 1961- *WhoAmW 93*
Tirtoff, Romain de 1892-1990 *BioIn 17*
Tirva, Algis A. *Law&B 92*
Tiryakian, Edward Ashod 1929- *WhoAm 92*
Tisch, Andrew Herbert 1949- *St&PR 93, WhoAm 92*
Tisch, James S. 1953- *WhoAm 92*
Tisch, Johannes Hermann 1929- *WhoWor 93*
Tisch, Jonathan M. *BioIn 17*
Tisch, Jonathan Mark 1953- *WhoAm 92*
Tisch, Laurence A. *BioIn 17*
Tisch, Laurence A. 1923- *St&PR 93*
Tisch, Laurence Alan 1923- *WhoAm 92, WhoE 93, WhoWor 93*
Tisch, Preston Robert 1926- *BioIn 17, St&PR 93, WhoAm 92*
Tisch, Richard G. *Law&B 92*
Tisch, Ronald Irwin 1944- *WhoAm 92*
Tisch, Sayde d1990 *BioIn 17*
Tischer, Carolyn Lois 1943- *WhoE 93*
Tischer, Donald 1944- *St&PR 93*
Tischhauser, Franz 1921- *Baker 92*
Tischler, Gary Lowell 1935- *WhoAm 92*
Tischler, Hans 1915- *Baker 92*
Tischler, Herbert 1924- *WhoAm 92*
Tischler, Louis 1915- *St&PR 93*
Tischler, Monte Maurice 1931- *WhoWrEP 92*
Tischman, Michael Bernard 1937- *WhoAm 92*
Tischner, Marian 1936- *WhoWor 93*
Tiscornia, Lester Clinton 1910- *WhoAm 92*
Tisdale, Bruce R. 1948- *St&PR 93*
Tisdale, Douglas Michael 1949- *WhoEmL 93*
Tisdale, John Robert 1932- *WhoE 93*
Tisdale, Kathryn Eads Hoss 1945- *WhoAmW 93*
Tisdale, Patrick David *WhoSSW 93*
Tisdale, Robert Clayton 1958- *WhoSSW 93*
Tisdale, Sallie *BioIn 17*
Tisdale, Stuart Williams 1928- *St&PR 93, WhoAm 92*
Tisdel, Donald L. 1934- *St&PR 93*
Tise, Larry Edward 1942- *WhoAm 92*
Tisei, Virginia M. *Law&B 92*
Tishby, Isaiah d1992 *NewYTBS 92*
Tishby, Isaiah 1908-1992 *BioIn 17*
Tishchenko, Boris (Ivanovich) 1939- *Baker 92*
Tishkoff, Jane Michelle *Law&B 92*
Tishler, Louis B., Jr. 1933- *St&PR 93*
Tishler, Max 1907-1989 *BioIn 17*
Tishler, Sidney 1937- *WhoE 93*
Tishler, William Henry 1936- *WhoAm 92*
Tishman, Alan V. 1917- *St&PR 93*
Tishman, Henry 1931- *St&PR 93*
Tishman, John L. 1926- *WhoAm 92*
Tishman, Robert V. 1916- *WhoAm 92*
Tishok, John M. *Law&B 92*
Tisinger, Catherine Anne 1936- *WhoAm 92, WhoE 93*
Tisnado, Rodo 1940- *WhoWor 93*
Tisne, Antoine 1932- *Baker 92*
Tiso, Josef 1887-1947 *DcTwHis*
Tiso, Jozef 1887-1947 *BioIn 17*
Tison, Benjamin T., III 1930- *St&PR 93*
Tison-Braun, Micheline Lucie 1913- *WhoAm 92*
Tisquantum d1622 *BioIn 17*
Tisser, Doron Moshe 1955- *WhoEmL 93, WhoWor 93*
Tisser, Eli 1951- *St&PR 93*
Tisseyre-Berry, Monique 1935- *WhoScE 91-2*
Tissot, Rene 1927- *WhoScE 91-4*
Tissue, John W. *Law&B 92*
Tissut, Michel 1938- *WhoScE 91-2*
Tisza, Istvan 1861-1918 *BioIn 17*
Tisza, Miklos 1949- *WhoScE 91-4*
Tita *BioIn 17*
Titas, Francis G. *Law&B 92*
Titchell, Haskell C. 1927- *St&PR 93*
Titchener, Edward Bradford 1867-1927 *BioIn 17*
Titchmarsh, Alan *BioIn 17*
Titcomb, Bonnie L. *WhoAmW 93*
Titcomb, Caldwell 1926- *WhoAm 92*
Titcomb, Woodbury C. 1923- *St&PR 93*
Titcomb, Woodbury Cole 1923- *WhoAm 92*
Tite, Michael Stanley *WhoScE 91-1*
Titelman, Carol *ScF&FL 92*
Titelman, Russ 1944- *WhoE 93, WhoWor 93*
Titelouze, Jean c. 1562-1633 *Baker 92*
Titera, Dalibor 1955- *WhoScE 91-4*
Tith, Naranhkiri 1933- *WhoUN 92*
Tither, W. Thomas, Jr. *Law&B 92*
Titialii, Jacinta Eleina *Law&B 92*
Titian c. 1488-1576 *BioIn 17*
Titiev, Mischa 1901-1978 *IntDcAn*
Titl, Anton Emil 1809-1882 *Baker 92*
Titland, Martin Nils 1938- *WhoAm 92*
Title, Elise *ScF&FL 92*
Titley, Nigel Roy 1955- *WhoWor 93*
Titlow, Larry Wayne 1945- *WhoSSW 93*
Titmarsh, M.A. *ScF&FL 92*
Tito, Diego Quispe *BioIn 17*
Tito, Josip 1892-1980 *DcTwHis*
Tito, Josip Broz 1892-1980 *BioIn 17, ColdWar 2 [port]*
Tito, Kostag *St&PR 93*
Tito, Maureen Louise 1946- *WhoAmW 93*
Tito, Richard Joseph 1947- *St&PR 93*
Titon, Jeff Todd 1943- *ConAu 37NR, WhoE 93*
Titone, Joseph P. *Law&B 92*
Titone, Vito Joseph 1929- *WhoAm 92*
Titov, Alexei Nikolaievich 1769-1827 *Baker 92*
Titov, Alexey 1769-1827 *OxDcOp*
Titov, Gherman Stepanovich 1935- *BioIn 17*
Titov, Nikolai Alexeievich 1800-1875 *Baker 92*
Titov, Sergei Nikolaievich 1770-1825 *Baker 92*
Titov, Sergey 1770-1825 *OxDcOp*
Titov, Sergey Sergeyevich 1952- *WhoWor 93*
Titov, Vladimir 1947- *BioIn 17*
Titowsky, Bernie *BioIn 17*
Titrud, Blake K. *Law&B 92*
Titsworth, Judson 1845-1919 *BioIn 17*
Titta, Ruffo Cafiero *Baker 92*
Titterington, Donald Michael *WhoScE 91-1*
Titterington, Donald Michael 1945- *WhoWor 93*
Titterton, Charles Frederick 1941- *St&PR 93*
Tittle, Carole Jean 1959- *WhoAmW 93*
Tittle, Y.A. 1926- *BioIn 17*
Tittle, Yelberton Abraham 1926- *BioIn 17*
Tittmann, Bernhard Rainer 1935- *WhoAm 92*
Titulaer, Urbaan M. 1941- *WhoScE 91-4*
Titus dc. 378 *OxDcByz*
Titus, Emperor of Rome 40-81 *BioIn 17*
Titus, Alan (Wilkowski) 1945- *Baker 92*
Titus, Alice Cestandina 1950- *WhoAmW 93*
Titus, Arthur Leroy 1944- *St&PR 93, WhoAm 92*
Titus, Barbara *WhoAm 92*
Titus, Bertha Smith *AmWomPl*
Titus, Charles Otis 1927- *WhoE 93*
Titus, Christina M. *Law&B 92*
Titus, Christina Maria 1950- *St&PR 93*
Titus, Curtis Vest 1933- *WhoE 93*
Titus, David Anson 1934- *WhoAm 92*
Titus, Hiram 1947- *Baker 92*
Titus, Jack L. 1926- *WhoAm 92*
Titus, James Fairbanks, Jr. 1961- *St&PR 93*
Titus, James Paul 1933- *WhoE 93*
Titus, John Joseph 1945- *WhoE 93*
Titus, John Samuel 1940- *St&PR 93*
Titus, Lowell Dean 1926- *St&PR 93*
Titus, Robert Wayne 1947- *WhoE 93*
Titus, Susan Feldt 1944- *WhoAmW 93*
Titus-Dillon, Pauline Yvonne 1938- *WhoE 93*
Titze, Ingo Roland 1941- *WhoAm 92*
Tiu, Carlos 1938- *WhoWor 93*
Tiu, Rudy Dy 1959- *WhoWor 93*
Tiueco, Aria 1958- *WhoWor 93*
Tiuri, Martti E. 1925- *WhoScE 91-4*
Tiwana, Omar *Law&B 92*
Tiwari, Surendra Nath 1936- *WhoSSW 93*
Tixier, Maurice Pierre 1913- *WhoSSW 93*
Tixier-Vignancour, Jean-Louis 1907-1989 *BioIn 17*
Tizard, Catherine Anne 1931- *WhoAsAP 91, WhoWor 93*
Tizard, Robert James 1924- *WhoAsAP 91*
Tizes, Reuben 1930- *WhoE 93*
Tiziano Vecelli c. 1488-1576 *BioIn 17*
Tizoc *WhoWrEP 92*
Tizol, Juan 1900-1984 *Baker 92*
Tizyakov, Alexander *BioIn 17*
Tizzio, Thomas R. 1938- *St&PR 93, WhoIns 93*
Tizzio, Thomas Ralph 1938- *WhoAm 92*
Tjalve, Hans 1942- *WhoScE 91-4*
Tjeknavorian, Loris-Zare 1937- *WhoWor 93*
Tjelmeland, M. Katherine 1937- *St&PR 93*
Tjoflat, Gerald Bard 1929- *WhoAm 92*
Tkac, Debora *BioIn 17*
Tkacenko, Michael Helii 1955- *WhoWor 93*
Tkach, Walter Robert 1917-1989 *BioIn 17*
Tkachenko, Victor Alexandrovich 1939- *WhoWor 93*
Tkachev, Vladimir Gennadjevich 1963- *WhoWor 93*
Tkacs, Anne C. *Law&B 92*
Tkaczynski, Tadeusz Marian 1925- *WhoWor 93*
Tkatch, Nancy Paluck 1958- *WhoAmW 93*
Tkatchenko, Igor B. 1939- *WhoScE 91-2*
Tkocz, Jan 1939- *WhoScE 91-4*
T'Lan, K.S. *ScF&FL 92*
Tlass, Mustafa 1932- *HarEnMi*
Tlass, Mustafa Abdul-Kader 1932- *WhoWor 93*
Tloome, Dan d1992 *NewYTBS 92*
'T Mannetje, Leendert 1933- *WhoScE 91-3*
Toadvin-Bester, Josephine Vesella 1926- *WhoAmW 93*
Toal, James Francis 1932- *WhoAm 92*
Toal, Jean Hoefer 1943- *WhoAm 92, WhoAmW 93, WhoSSW 93*
Toal, Philip Owen 1957- *WhoSSW 93*
Toan, Charles S. 1919- *St&PR 93*
Toase, Mary *WhoScE 91-1*
Tobach, Ethel 1921- *WhoAmW 93*
Toback, James 1944- *MiSFD 9*
Tobaining, Ereman 1937- *WhoAsAP 91*
Tobani, Theodore Moses 1855-1933 *Baker 92*
Tobe, John E. 1940- *WhoAm 92*
Tobe, Stephen Solomon 1944- *WhoAm 92*
Tobe, Susan Bring 1949- *WhoEmL 93*
Tobel, Paul Von 1940- *St&PR 93*
Tobena, Adolf 1950- *WhoWor 93*
Tober, Barbara D. 1934- *WhoAmW 93*
Tober, Lester Victor 1916- *St&PR 93, WhoAm 92*
Tober, Stephen Lloyd 1949- *WhoAm 92*
Tobey, Alton Stanley 1914- *WhoAm 92*
Tobey, Bruce H. *Law&B 92*
Tobey, Carl Wadsworth 1923- *WhoAm 92*
Tobey, Edward David 1939- *St&PR 93*
Tobey, Gene 1945- *BioIn 17*
Tobey, Hamlin G. d1991 *BioIn 17*
Tobey, Joel N. 1929- *WhoIns 93*
Tobey, Joel Nye 1929- *St&PR 93*
Tobey, Michael B. 1950- *St&PR 93*
Tobey, Rebecca *BioIn 17*
Tobey, Robert F. 1945- *St&PR 93*
Tobey, Timothy A. 1949- *St&PR 93*
Tobia, Annette M. *Law&B 92*
Tobia, Sergio B. 1939- *WhoIns 93*
Tobia, Stephen Francis, Jr. 1955- *WhoAm 92*
Tobias, Andrew Previn 1947- *WhoAm 92, WhoWrEP 92*
Tobias, Audrey Faye 1958- *WhoAmW 93*
Tobias, Beth Ann 1959- *WhoAmW 93*
Tobias, Carolyn J. *St&PR 93*

Tobias, Charles Harrison, Jr. 1921- *WhoAm 92*
Tobias, Charles William 1920- *WhoAm 92*
Tobias, Daniel Ross 1963- *WhoSSW 93*
Tobias, Deborah J. 1964- *WhoAmW 93*
Tobias, Donald E. 1928- *St&PR 93*
Tobias, Jeffrey Stewart 1946- *WhoWor 93*
Tobias, John L. M. 1921- *St&PR 93*
Tobias, Judy *WhoAmW 93, WhoE 93*
Tobias, Julius 1915- *WhoAm 92, WhoE 93*
Tobias, Kal 1946- *WhoE 93*
Tobias, Kevin Richard 1964- *WhoE 93*
Tobias, Lester Lee 1946- *WhoE 93, WhoEmL 93, WhoWor 93*
Tobias, Michael 1947?- *ScF&FL 92*
Tobias, Paul D. 1951- *St&PR 93*
Tobias, Paul Henry 1930- *WhoAm 92*
Tobias, Randall L. 1942- *WhoAm 92*
Tobias, Robert Max 1943- *WhoAm 92*
Tobias, Ronald Benjamin 1946- *WhoWrEP 92*
Tobias, Rudolf 1873-1918 *Baker 92*
Tobias, Sara *ScF&FL 92*
Tobias, Sheila 1935- *WhoAmW 93*
Tobiasen, Carl G. 1955- *St&PR 93*
Tobiason, Peter John *Law&B 92*
Tobiasz, Robert Brian 1945- *WhoAm 92*
Tobin, Alexander 1927- *WhoE 93*
Tobin, Bentley 1924- *WhoAm 92*
Tobin, Bertha Irene *AmWomPl*
Tobin, Calvin Jay 1927- *WhoAm 92, WhoWor 93*
Tobin, Carol R. 1948- *WhoAmW 93*
Tobin, Craig Daniel 1954- *WhoWor 93*
Tobin, David R. *Law&B 92*
Tobin, Dennis Michael 1948- *WhoEmL 93, WhoWor 93*
Tobin, Donal B. *Law&B 92*
Tobin, Donal B. 1941- *St&PR 93*
Tobin, Donald 1939- *St&PR 93*
Tobin, Donna Mae 1945- *WhoAmW 93*
Tobin, Elizabeth Carroll 1962- *WhoAmW 93*
Tobin, Gregory B. *Law&B 92*
Tobin, James 1918- *WhoAm 92, WhoE 93, WhoWor 93*
Tobin, James M. *Law&B 92*
Tobin, James Michael 1948- *WhoAm 92*
Tobin, James R. 1944- *St&PR 93*
Tobin, James Robert 1944- *WhoAm 92*
Tobin, John Everard 1923- *WhoAm 92, WhoWor 93*
Tobin, John Henry, Jr. 1930- *St&PR 93*
Tobin, Kathleen T. *Law&B 92*
Tobin, Lois Moore 1928- *WhoE 93*
Tobin, Mark Gerard 1960- *WhoWor 93*
Tobin, Mary Jane 1931- *PolPar*
Tobin, Michael E. *Law&B 92*
Tobin, Michael Edward 1926- *WhoAm 92*
Tobin, Myles Lloyd *Law&B 92*
Tobin, Nancy Ruth 1943- *WhoAmW 93, WhoE 93*
Tobin, Peter J. 1944- *St&PR 93, WhoAm 92*
Tobin, Richard D. *BioIn 17*
Tobin, Richard George 1943- *WhoE 93*
Tobin, Richard J. 1934- *WhoAm 92*
Tobin, Richard J. 1946- *ConAu 137*
Tobin, Robert G. 1938- *St&PR 93*
Tobin, Roger Lee 1940- *WhoE 93*
Tobin, Shirley Ann 1953- *WhoSSW 93*
Tobin, Steven Michael 1940- *St&PR 93*
Tobin, Thomas M. *Law&B 92*
Tobin, Thomas M. 1943- *WhoIns 93*
Tobin, Thomas Vincent 1926- *WhoE 93*
Tobin, William Joseph 1944- *St&PR 93*
Tobin, William Thomas 1931- *St&PR 93, WhoAm 92*
Tobis, Jerome Sanford 1915- *WhoAm 92*
Tobita, Shigeo 1927- *WhoWor 93*
Tobiyama, Kazuo 1925- *WhoWor 93*
Tobkin, Christine Anderson 1952- *WhoAm 92*
Tobler, D. Lee 1933- *St&PR 93, WhoAm 92*
Tobler, Heinz R. 1935- *WhoScE 91-4*
Tobler, Waldo Rudolph 1930- *WhoAm 92*
Tobolowsky, Stephen *MiSFD 9*
Toboroff, Leonard *St&PR 93*
Tobriner, M.W. 1939- *St&PR 93*
Toburen, Karen Ruth 1945- *WhoAmW 93*
Toburen, Lawrence Richter 1915- *WhoAm 92, WhoWor 93*
Toby, Jackson 1925- *WhoAm 92*
Tocchet, Rick *BioIn 17*
Tocchi, Gian-Luca 1901- *Baker 92*
Tocchini-Valentini, Glauco *WhoScE 91-3*
Tocci, Cynthia Malzenski 1953- *WhoAmW 93*
Tocci, Dennis *Law&B 92*
Tocco *OxDcByz*
Tocco, Dominick Joseph 1930- *WhoE 93*
Tocco, James 1943- *Baker 92, WhoAm 92*
Toce, Dominic R. 1931- *St&PR 93*
Toce, Thomas Clifford 1956- *WhoE 93*
Toch, Ernst 1887-1964 *Baker 92*
Tochigi, Yoshitada 1935- *WhoWor 93*
Tochman, Casper 1797-1882 *PolBiDi*
Tochner, Joan May 1941- *WhoSSW 93*
Tochner, Max 1938- *WhoSSW 93*
Tochowicz, Stanislaw 1923- *WhoScE 91-4*
Tochtermann, Werner Kurt 1934- *WhoScE 91-3*
Tocker, Edwin *Law&B 92*
Tocklin, Adrian Martha 1951- *St&PR 93, WhoAm 92, WhoAmW 93, WhoEmL 93, WhoIns 93*
Tocqueville, Alexis de *BioIn 17*
Tocqueville, Alexis de 1805-1859 *PolPar*
Toczek, Peter Martin 1931- *St&PR 93*
Toczko, Kazimierz 1928- *WhoScE 91-4*
Toczyska, Stefania 1943- *Baker 92*
Tod, April 1948- *WhoWor 93*
Tod, G. Robert 1939- *WhoAm 92*
Toda, Keishi 1933- *St&PR 93*
Toda, Kikuo 1924- *WhoAsAP 91*
Toda, Kunikazu 1925- *WhoWor 93*
Toda, Kunio 1915- *Baker 92*
Toda, Shusaku 1938- *St&PR 93*
Toda, Tadasumi 1946- *WhoWor 93*
Todar Malla d1589 *HarEnMi*
Todaro, George Joseph 1937- *WhoAm 92*
Todaro, Joan Philippa 1957- *WhoAmW 93*
Todaro, Laura Jean 1956- *WhoEmL 93*
Todaro, Ralph 1950- *St&PR 93*
Todd, Adrian Christopher *WhoScE 91-1*
Todd, Alexander Robertus 1907- *WhoAm 92, WhoWor 93*
Todd, Anderson 1921- *WhoAm 92*
Todd, Bruce *WhoSSW 93*
Todd, Casey *ScF&FL 92*
Todd, Cherie Clemens 1950- *WhoSSW 93*
Todd, Christina Adrian Tamburo 1943- *WhoE 93*
Todd, David Arnold, II 1932- *St&PR 93*
Todd, David Fenton Michie 1915- *WhoAm 92*
Todd, David G. 1942- *St&PR 93*
Todd, Deborah J. 1951- *WhoAmW 93, WhoEmL 93, WhoWor 93*
Todd, Edward Francis, Jr. 1956- *WhoE 93*
Todd, Eleanor Schley 1911-1990 *BioIn 17*
Todd, Elizabeth *WhoWrEP 92*
Todd, Elizabeth Grace 1926-1990 *BioIn 17*
Todd, Eric Campbell *WhoScE 91-1*
Todd, Furney A. 1921-1991 *BioIn 17*
Todd, Gilbert H. 1927- *St&PR 93*
Todd, Glenn Daniel 1952- *WhoSSW 93*
Todd, Glenn William 1927- *WhoAm 92*
Todd, Grant Edward 1939- *St&PR 93*
Todd, Harold Bicknell, Jr. 1941- *WhoAm 92*
Todd, Harold Wade 1938- *WhoAm 92*
Todd, Harry Williams 1922- *St&PR 93, WhoAm 92*
Todd, Helen L. *AmWomPl*
Todd, Henry C. 1913- *St&PR 93*
Todd, Howell Eric 1959- *WhoSSW 93*
Todd, Imo Kellam 1943- *WhoAmW 93*
Todd, J. C. 1943- *WhoAm 92*
Todd, J. Donald 1933- *St&PR 93*
Todd, James A., Jr. 1928- *St&PR 93*
Todd, James Averill, Jr. 1928- *WhoAm 92*
Todd, James Dale 1943- *WhoAm 92, WhoSSW 93*
Todd, James Marion 1929- *WhoSSW 93*
Todd, James Stiles 1931- *WhoAm 92*
Todd, James William 1946- *St&PR 93*
Todd, Jessie A. 1946- *WhoEmL 93*
Todd, John 1911- *WhoAm 92*
Todd, John Calhoun 1937- *WhoSSW 93*
Todd, John Dickerson, Jr. 1912- *WhoAm 92*
Todd, John Douglas *WhoScE 91-1*
Todd, John Duncan 1914- *St&PR 93*
Todd, John Franklin *Law&B 92*
Todd, John Joseph 1927- *WhoAm 92*
Todd, John Odell 1902- *WhoWor 93*
Todd, John William 1949- *WhoSSW 93*
Todd, Joyce Anderson 1940- *WhoAmW 93*
Todd, Judith Kay 1948- *WhoSSW 93*
Todd, Kenneth S., Jr. 1936- *WhoAm 92*
Todd, Lewis Paul 1906-1990 *BioIn 17*
Todd, Linda Marie 1948- *WhoAmW 93*
Todd, Lisa Anderson 1942- *WhoAmW 93*
Todd, Louise *ConAu 136*
Todd, M.J. *WhoScE 91-1*
Todd, Mabel Loomis 1856-1932 *BioIn 17*
Todd, Malcolm Clifford 1913- *WhoAm 92*
Todd, Malcolm F. W. *St&PR 93*
Todd, Margaret Louise 1919- *WhoAmW 93*
Todd, Mary Van Lennup Ives 1849- *AmWomPl*
Todd, Norma Jean Ross 1920- *WhoE 93*
Todd, Norma Lee 1961- *WhoAmW 93*
Todd, Paterson Arnold 1927- *WhoAm 92*
Todd, Patricia Anne 1957- *WhoAmW 93*
Todd, R. Campbell 1927- *St&PR 93*
Todd, Richard Henry 1906- *WhoE 93, WhoWor 93*
Todd, Robert H. O. 1962- *St&PR 93*
Todd, Robert Lee 1953- *WhoWor 93*
Todd, Robert Royce 1937- *St&PR 93*
Todd, Ron *WhoIns 93*
Todd, Ruthven 1914-1978 *ScF&FL 92*
Todd, Samuel Richard, Jr. 1940- *WhoWrEP 92*
Todd, Sereno Edwards 1820-1898 *JrnUS*
Todd, Shirley Ann 1935- *WhoSSW 93*
Todd, Stephen K. *Law&B 92*
Todd, Steven O. *Law&B 92*
Todd, Susan Marie 1946- *WhoSSW 93*
Todd, Susan Pogue 1960- *WhoAmW 93*
Todd, T.W. 1928- *St&PR 93*
Todd, Thelma d1935 *BioIn 17*
Todd, Thelma 1905-1935 *QDrFCA 92 [port]*
Todd, Thomas 1765-1826 *OxCSupC [port]*
Todd, Thomas Abbott 1928- *WhoAm 92*
Todd, Virgil Holcomb 1921- *WhoAm 92*
Todd, Walker F. *Law&B 92*
Todd, Webb 1929- *St&PR 93*
Todd, William Burton 1919- *WhoAm 92, WhoWrEP 92*
Todd, William Joseph 1948- *WhoSSW 93*
Todd, William Russell 1928- *WhoAm 92*
Todd, Zane Grey 1924- *St&PR 93, WhoAm 92, WhoWor 93*
Todd Copley, Judith Ann 1950- *WhoEmL 93*
Todd Goodson, Deanna Arlene 1942- *WhoAmW 93*
Toddington, Janet *Law&B 92*
Todd of Trumpington, Baron 1907- *WhoAm 92, WhoWor 93*
Todea, Alexandru Cardinal 1912- *WhoWor 93*
Todeschini, Claudio Edmondo Gianfranco 1937- *WhoUN 92*
Todesco, Jay D. *Law&B 92*
Todhunter, Emily *BioIn 17*
Todi, Luisa 1753-1833 *Baker 92*
Todleben, Franz Eduard Ivanovich 1818-1884 *HarEnMi*
Todman, Terence A. 1926- *WhoAm 92, WhoWor 93*
Todman, Terence A., Jr. *Law&B 92*
Todnem, Odd Ragnvald 1922- *WhoWor 93*
Todoroff, Davis Steven 1958- *WhoE 93*
Todorov, Dobromir Todorov 1948- *WhoWor 93*
Todorov, Ivan Todorov 1933- *WhoScE 91-4*
Todorov, Pavel Georgiev 1931- *WhoWor 93*
Todorov, S. *WhoScE 91-4*
Todorov, Stanko 1920- *WhoWor 93*
Todorov, Todor 1932- *WhoScE 91-4*
Todorov, Tzvetan 1939- *BioIn 17, ScF&FL 92*
Todorovic, Radmilo Antonije 1927- *WhoWor 93*
Todorovskij, Petr 1925- *DrEEuF*
Todreas, Neil Emmanuel 1935- *WhoAm 92*
Todreas, Timothy Michael 1961- *WhoE 93*
Todryk, Alan A. 1946- *St&PR 93*
Todsen, Dana Rognar 1947- *WhoEmL 93*
Todt, Malcolm S. 1945- *WhoAm 92*
Todt, Malcolm Spenker 1945- *St&PR 93*
Todtman, Estie *BioIn 17*
Toduta, Sigismund 1908- *Baker 92*
Toebosch, Louis 1916- *Baker 92*
Toedtman, James Smith 1941- *WhoAm 92*
Toegemann, Alfred C. 1928- *WhoIns 93*
Toegemann, Alfred Conrad 1928- *St&PR 93*
Toelle, John C. *Law&B 92*
Toenjes, Wayne Arthur 1950- *St&PR 93*
Toennies, Alfred W. *Law&B 92*
Toenniessen, Gary Herbert 1944- *WhoE 93*
Toensing, Victoria *BioIn 17*
Toensing, Victoria 1941- *WhoAm 92, WhoAmW 93*
Toepel, Mike 1944- *St&PR 93*
Toepel, Steven E. *St&PR 93*
Toepfer, Robert Adolph 1920- *WhoAm 92*
Toepfer, Susan Jill 1948- *WhoAmW 93*
Toepffer, Christian 1941- *WhoScE 91-3*
Toepke, Utz Peter 1940- *WhoAm 92*
Toepker, Anne M. 1943- *St&PR 93*
Toepp, Alta M. *AmWomPl*
Toepperwein, Adolp P. 1869-1962 *BioIn 17*
Toerber, C.C. 1949- *St&PR 93*
Toerber, Charlotte C. *Law&B 92*
Toesca *Baker 92*
Toesca de Castellamonte 1735?-1800 *Baker 92*
Toeschi *Baker 92*
Toeschi, Alessandro c. 1700-1758 *Baker 92*
Toeschi, Carl Joseph 1731?-1788 *Baker 92*
Toeschi, Johann Christoph 1735?-1800 *Baker 92*
Toeschi, Karl Theodor 1768-1843 *Baker 92*
Toews, B. *Law&B 92*
Tofani, Loretta A. 1953- *WhoAm 92*
Tofel, Jennings 1891-1959 *BioIn 17*
Tofel, Karen *BioIn 17*
Tofel, Richard *Law&B 92*
Toffel, Alvin Eugene 1935- *WhoAm 92*
Toffler, Alvin *BioIn 17*
Toffler, Alvin 1928- *WhoAm 92, WhoWrEP 92*
Toffler, Barbara Ley 1941- *WhoAmW 93, WhoE 93*
Toffolo, Luigi J. 1929- *St&PR 93*
Tofft, Alfred 1865-1931 *Baker 92*
Tofias, Allan 1930- *WhoE 93, WhoWor 93*
Toft, Jurgen Herbert 1943- *WhoWor 93*
Toft, Pam Cheney 1959- *WhoAmW 93*
Toft, Richard Paul 1936- *St&PR 93*
Toft, S.C. 1931- *WhoScE 91-2*
Tofte, Arthur 1902-1980 *ScF&FL 92*
Tofteland, Curt L. 1952- *WhoSSW 93*
Toftner, Richard Orville 1935- *WhoAm 92*
Toftness, Cecil Gillman 1920- *WhoWor 93*
Tofts, Catherine c. 1685-1756 *OxDcOp*
Togafau, Malaetasi Mauga 1946- *WhoAm 92*
Toganivalu, William Brown 1928- *WhoAsAP 91*
Togi, Suenobu 1932- *Baker 92*
Toglhofer, Wolfgang 1959- *WhoWor 93*
Togliatti, Palmiro 1893-1964 *DcTwHis*
Tognazzi, Ugo 1922-1990 *BioIn 17*
Togni, Camillo 1922- *Baker 92*
Tognino, Alexander *Law&B 92*
Tognino, John Nicholas 1938- *WhoAm 92*
Tognoni, Gianni 1941- *WhoScE 91-3*
Togo, Heihachiro 1848-1934 *HarEnMi*
Togo, Yukiyasu *BioIn 17*
Togo, Yukiyasu 1924- *WhoAm 92*
Togores, Josep de 1893-1970 *BioIn 17*
Togrol, Ergun 1933- *WhoScE 91-4*
Toguchi, Tamako 1937- *WhoAsAP 91*
Togut, Torin Dana 1951- *WhoSSW 93*
Tohgi, Hideo 1937- *WhoWor 93*
Tohme, Georges 1932- *WhoUN 92*
Toi, Masami 1921- *WhoWor 93*
Toida, Saburo 1918- *WhoAsAP 91*
Toigo-D'Angeli, Miriam d1990 *BioIn 17*
Toimitusjohtaja, Olof Enbom 1920- *WhoWor 93*
Toivanen, Auli 1938- *WhoScE 91-4*
Toivanen, Paavo 1937- *WhoScE 91-4*
Toivanen, Paavo Uuras 1937- *WhoWor 93*
Toivo ja Toivo, Herman Andimba 1924- *WhoAfr*
Toivola, Yrjo Ilmari 1927- *WhoWor 93*
Toivonen, Hannu Juhani 1947- *WhoScE 91-4*
Toivonen, Hannu Tapio 1952- *WhoWor 93*
Tojio, Melanie *BioIn 17*
Tojo, Hideki 1884-1948 *HarEnMi*
Tojo, Kakuji 1947- *WhoWor 93*
Tojo Hideki 1884-1948 *DcTwHis*
Tokai, Kisaburo 1948- *WhoAsAP 91*
Tokar, Bette Lewis 1935- *WhoE 93*
Tokar, Daniel 1937- *St&PR 93*
Tokar, Edward Thomas 1947- *WhoAm 92*
Tokarev, S.A. 1899-1985 *IntDcAn*
Tokarski, Mieczyslaw 1920- *WhoScE 91-4*
Tokarzewski, Ludomir 1921- *WhoScE 91-4*
Tokatyan, Armand 1896-1960 *Baker 92*
Tokdemir, Faruk 1950- *WhoScE 91-4*
Toke, Laszlo 1933- *WhoScE 91-4*
Toker, Franklin K. 1944- *WhoAm 92*
Tokes, Laszlo *BioIn 17*
Tokioka, Franklin M. 1936- *WhoIns 93*
Tokioka, Franklin Makoto 1936- *St&PR 93*
Tokizaki, Yuji 1940- *WhoAsAP 91*
Toklas, Alice B. *BioIn 17*
Toko, Kiyoshi 1953- *WhoWor 93*
Tokofsky, Jerry Herbert 1936- *WhoAm 92*
Tokoly, Mary Andree 1940- *WhoAmW 93*
Tokoro, Masaaki 1929- *WhoWor 93*
Tokos, Sylvia Juriga 1940- *WhoE 93*
Tokowitz, Harold I. 1929- *St&PR 93*
Tokuda, Torao 1938- *WhoAsAP 91*
Tokugawa, Hidetada 1579-1632 *HarEnMi*
Tokugawa, Ieyasu 1542-1616 *HarEnMi*
Tokumaru, Katsumi 1931- *WhoWor 93*
Tokumitsu, Yoshito 1936- *St&PR 93*
Tokuo, Miyamoto 1938- *WhoWor 93*
Tokyo Rose *BioIn 17*
Tol, Peter J. 1935- *WhoIns 93*
Tolan, Alfred Norman 1928- *St&PR 93*
Tolan, David Joseph 1933- *St&PR 93, WhoAm 92*
Tolan, James Francis 1934- *WhoAm 92*
Tolan, Stephanie S. 1942- *DcAmChF 1985*
Toland, Clyde William 1947- *WhoEmL 93*
Toland, John *BioIn 17*
Toland, John 1670-1722 *BioIn 17*
Toland, John Francis *WhoScE 91-1*

Toland, John Willard 1912- *WhoAm 92, WhoWor 93, WhoWrEP 92*
Toland, Joy E. 1965- *WhoAmW 93*
Toland, Marguerite 1958- *WhoAmW 93*
Toland, Peter Christopher 1942- *WhoE 93*
Tolar, Billy Joe 1948- *WhoSSW 93*
Tolar, Carroll T. 1929- *St&PR 93, WhoAm 92*
Tolar, Thomas Ray, Jr. 1948- *St&PR 93*
Tolay, Ulvi 1939- *WhoScE 91-4*
Tolba, Mostafa Kamal 1922- *WhoUN 92*
Tolbecque *Baker 92*
Tolbecque, August-Joseph 1801-1869 *Baker 92*
Tolbecque, Auguste 1830-1919 *Baker 92*
Tolbecque, Charles-Joseph 1806-1835 *Baker 92*
Tolbecque, Isidore-Joseph 1794-1871 *Baker 92*
Tolbecque, Jean-Baptiste-Joseph 1797-1869 *Baker 92*
Tolbert, Bert Mills 1921- *WhoAm 92*
Tolbert, Charles Madden 1922- *WhoAm 92*
Tolbert, Charles Ray 1936- *WhoSSW 93*
Tolbert, Cledith Cassidy 1922- *WhoWrEP 92*
Tolbert, James R. 1935- *St&PR 93*
Tolbert, James R., III 1935- *WhoAm 92*
Tolbert, John T. 1913- *St&PR 93*
Tolbert, John Taylor 1913- *WhoSSW 93*
Tolbert, Mary Ann 1947- *WhoAmW 93*
Tolbert, Nathan Edward 1919- *WhoAm 92*
Tolbert, Richard Martin 1939- *WhoAm 92*
Tolbert, William R. 1942- *St&PR 93*
Tolces, Stephen B. 1934- *St&PR 93*
Tolchenkov, Dmitry Leonidovich 1937- *WhoUN 92*
Tolchin, Martin 1928- *WhoAm 92, WhoWrEP 92*
Tolchin, Susan Jane 1941- *WhoAmW 93*
Toldra, Eduardo 1895-1962 *Baker 92*
Toldra, Fidel 1958- *WhoScE 91-3*
Toledano, Adolfo *WhoScE 91-3*
Toledano, Ben C. 1932- *BioIn 17*
Toledano, John O. H. 1931- *St&PR 93*
Toledano, Ralph de 1916- *WhoAm 92, WhoWrEP 92*
Toledano, Raul G. 1939- *WhoSSW 93*
Toledo, Bridget Marie 1959- *WhoAm 92*
Toledo, Isabel 1963?- *NotHsAW 93*
Toledo, Leila Josephine 1933- *WhoAmW 93*
Toledo, Sergio 1956- *MiSFD 9*
Toledo-Pereyra, Luis Horacio 1943- *WhoWor 93, WhoWrEP 92*
Toleman, Mark Anthony 1957- *WhoWor 93*
Tolentino, V. Bruce J. 1953- *WhoWor 93*
Toler, Ann Patrick 1948- *WhoAmW 93*
Toler, James E. 1931- *St&PR 93*
Toler, James Larkin 1935- *WhoAm 92*
Toler, Melissa Ann 1953- *WhoEmL 93*
Toler, Ray Edward 1942- *WhoSSW 93*
Toler-Million, Darla Layne 1960- *WhoAmW 93*
Tolerton, Robert H. 1926- *St&PR 93*
Toles, Cynthia *Law&B 92*
Toles, Cynthia A. 1951- *St&PR 93*
Toles, Edward Bernard 1909- *WhoAm 92*
Toles, Thomas Gregory 1951- *WhoAm 92, WhoE 93*
Toles, Tom 1951- *BioIn 17*
Toles-Kendall, Lolita 1949- *WhoE 93*
Tolete-Velcek, Francisca Agatep 1943- *WhoAmW 93*
Tolev, Ivan Todorov 1920- *WhoScE 91-4*
Tolford, George K. 1938- *St&PR 93*
Tolg, Gunther 1929- *WhoScE 91-3*
Tolia, Bhupendra Manilal 1936- *WhoE 93*
Tolic, Aleksandar 1935- *WhoScE 91-4*
Tolin, Donald Lee 1953- *WhoWor 93*
Toliver, Maxwell Doel 1959- *WhoE 93*
Tolkien, Christopher 1924- *ScF&FL 92*
Tolkien, J.R.R. 1892-1973 *BioIn 17, BritWr S2, MagSWL [port], ScF&FL 92, WorLitC [port]*
Tolkien, J(ohn) R(onald) R(euel) 1892-1973 *Au&Arts 10 [port], MajAI [port]*
Tolkien, John Ronald Reuel 1892-1973 *BioIn 17*
Tolkin, Michael *MiSFD 9, NewYTBS 92 [port]*
Tolkin, Michael 1950- *ConAu 137*
Tolkowsky, Marcel d1991 *BioIn 17*
Toll, Alexander Robert 1954- *WhoE 93*
Toll, Bruce E. 1943- *St&PR 93*
Toll, Bruce Elliot 1943- *WhoAm 92*
Toll, Daniel Roger 1927- *St&PR 93, WhoAm 92*
Toll, Gordon L. 1947- *St&PR 93*
Toll, Jack Benjamin 1925- *WhoAm 92*
Toll, Jeffrey *Law&B 92*
Toll, John Sampson 1923- *WhoAm 92, WhoWor 93*
Toll, Maynard Joy, Jr. 1942- *WhoAm 92*
Toll, Richard Jay 1954- *WhoE 93*
Toll, Robert Irwin 1940- *St&PR 93, WhoAm 92*
Toll, Roberta Darlene 1944- *WhoAmW 93*
Toll, Sheldon Samuel 1940- *WhoAm 92*
Tollan, Arne 1938- *WhoScE 91-4*
Tolland, W.R. *SmATA 73*
Toll-Crossman, Jacqueline Joy 1947- *WhoAmW 93*
Tolle, Dennis B. *Law&B 92*
Tolle, Donald James 1918- *WhoAm 92*
Tolle, Henning 1932- *WhoScE 91-3*
Tolle, Norman L. *Law&B 92*
Tollefsen, Adrianne L. *Law&B 92*
Tollefsen, Carl H(enry) 1882-1963 *Baker 92*
Tollefson, Daniel H. *Law&B 92*
Tollefson, Steve K. 1960- *St&PR 93*
Tollenaere, J.P. 1938- *WhoScE 91-2*
Tollenaere, Lawrence R. 1922- *St&PR 93*
Tollenaere, Lawrence Robert 1922- *WhoAm 92*
Toller, Ernst 1893-1939 *BioIn 17, DcLB 124 [port]*
Toller, William R. 1930- *St&PR 93*
Toller, William Robert 1930- *WhoAm 92, WhoE 93*
Tolles, Bryant Franklin, Jr. 1939- *WhoAm 92*
Tolles, Denise Dinkelacker *Law&B 92*
Tolles, E. Leroy 1922- *WhoAm 92*
Tolles, Martha *WhoWrEP 92*
Tolles, Robert Erving 1927- *WhoE 93*
Tolles, Walter Edwin 1916- *WhoAm 92*
Tolleson, Evangeline W. *WhoWrEP 92*
Tollestrup, Alvin Virgil 1924- *WhoAm 92*
Tollet, Elizabeth 1694-1754 *BioIn 17*
Tollett, Brenda Lynne *Law&B 92*
Tollett, Leland Edward 1937- *WhoAm 92, WhoSSW 93*
Tolley, Aubrey Granville 1924- *WhoAm 92*
Tolley, Edward Donald 1950- *WhoSSW 93*
Tolley, Gary Maurice 1935- *WhoSSW 93, WhoWor 93*
Tolley, James Little 1930- *WhoAm 92*
Tolley, Jerry Russell 1942- *WhoAm 92*
Tolley, Michael J. *ScF&FL 92*
Tolley, Tresa Gail 1946- *WhoWrEP 92*
Tolley, William Pearson 1900- *WhoAm 92*
Tolliver, Don L. 1938- *WhoAm 92*
Tolliver, Dorothy Olivia *WhoAmW 93*
Tolliver, Edith Catherine 1925- *WhoAmW 93*
Tolliver, Harold J. 1919- *St&PR 93*
Tolliver, Norris L. *St&PR 93*
Tolly, David Hayes 1950- *St&PR 93*
Tolman, Frits P. 1939- *WhoScE 91-3*
Tolman, Gareth W. 1938- *WhoIns 93*
Tolman, Gareth Wells 1938- *St&PR 93*
Tolman, K. Wade 1948- *St&PR 93*
Tolman, Kimberly S. *Law&B 92*
Tolman, Leland Locke d1991 *BioIn 17*
Tolman, Prescott A. d1990 *BioIn 17*
Tolmie, David McEachern 1955- *WhoE 93*
Tolmie, Donald McEachern 1928- *WhoAm 92*
Tolmie, John Alexander *Law&B 92*
Tolmie, Kenneth Donald 1941- *WhoAm 92*
Tolnay, Thomas *ScF&FL 92*
Tolnay, Tom *ScF&FL 92*
Tolo, Kare Johan 1927- *WhoWor 93*
Toloff, Michael G. 1954- *St&PR 93*
Tolone, Thomas Allen 1952- *St&PR 93*
Tolonen, James Robert 1949- *St&PR 93*
Tolonen, Jouko (Paavo Kalervo) 1912-1986 *Baker 92*
Tolor, Alexander 1928- *WhoAm 92*
Tolpa, John Michael 1944- *St&PR 93*
Tolpin, Larry *BioIn 17*
Tolpin, Thomas Willard *Law&B 92*
Tolsdorf, Frank Frederick 1936- *St&PR 93*
Tolsma, Dennis Dwayne 1939- *WhoAm 92*
Tolson, Jay Henry 1935- *St&PR 93, WhoAm 92*
Tolson, Jennifer Gale *Law&B 92*
Tolson, John F. 1943- *St&PR 93*
Tolson, John Franklin, Jr. *Law&B 92*
Tolson, John J. 1915-1991 *BioIn 17*
Tolson, John J. 1948- *WhoAm 92*
Tolson, Lance S. *Law&B 92*
Tolson, Melvin Beaunorus *BioIn 17*
Tolson, Melvin Beaunorus 1898-1966 *EncAACR*
Tolstaia, Sof'ia Andreevna Bers 1844-1919 *BioIn 17*
Tolstaia, Tat'iana 1951- *BioIn 17*
Tolstoguzov, Vladimir Borisovich 1937- *WhoWor 93*
Tolstoi, Aleksei 1882-1945 *ScF&FL 92*
Tolstoi-Miloslavskii, Nikolai *ScF&FL 92*
Tolstoshev, Paul *St&PR 93*
Tolstov, S.P. 1907-1976 *IntDcAn*
Tolstoy, Alexey *ScF&FL 92*
Tolstoy, Dmitri 1923- *Baker 92*
Tolstoy, Ivan 1923- *BioIn 17, WhoWor 93*
Tolstoy, Leo 1828-1910 *BioIn 17, MagSWL [port], WorLitC [port]*
Tolstoy, Lev 1828-1910 *OxDcOp*
Tolstoy, Nikolai 1935- *ScF&FL 92*
Tolstoy, Sophie Andreevna 1844-1919 *BioIn 17*
Tolstrup, Karl *WhoScE 91-2*
Tolstrup, Rex W. 1939- *St&PR 93*
Tolstrup, Tor 1938- *WhoWor 93*
Tolstykh, Valery Dmitrievich 1943- *WhoUN 92*
Tolton, Stephen P. 1946- *St&PR 93*
Tolun, Aslihan 1949- *WhoScE 91-4*
Tolun, Mehmet R. 1960- *WhoScE 91-4*
Tolun, Rasit 1921- *WhoScE 91-4*
Toly, Elena Lujan *WhoAmW 93*
Tolzmann, Don Heinrich 1945- *ConAu 38NR*
Tom, Creighton Harvey 1944- *WhoWrEP 92*
Tom, James Robert 1939- *WhoSSW 93*
Tom, Jean Carter 1938- *WhoAmW 93*
Tom, Lawrence 1950- *WhoEmL 93, WhoWor 93*
Tom, Margaret M. *Law&B 92*
Tom, Merle H. *Law&B 92*
Tom, Susan E. *Law&B 92*
Toma, Albert H., III *Law&B 92*
Toma, Bernard 1937- *WhoScE 91-2*
Toma, Jeanne Broemmelsick 1950- *WhoAmW 93*
Toma, Maiava Iulai 1940- *WhoAsAP 91*
Tomain, Robert F. 1941- *St&PR 93*
Tomaino, Joseph Carmine 1948- *WhoWor 93*
Tomaino, Joseph Roy *Law&B 92*
Tomaino, Michael Thomas 1937- *WhoAm 92*
Tomaino, William N. 1954- *St&PR 93*
Tomajko, Charles Anthony 1955- *WhoSSW 93*
Tomajko, Kathy Gillespie 1948- *WhoSSW 93*
Tomal, Dan *BioIn 17*
Tomal, Jonathan *BioIn 17*
Tomalia, Donald Andrew 1938- *WhoAm 92*
Tomalin, Ruth *ScF&FL 92*
Toman, Donald Joseph 1934- *WhoE 93*
Toman, M.D. 1949- *ScF&FL 92*
Toman, Mary Ann 1954- *WhoAm 92, WhoAmW 93*
Toman, Michael J. *WhoIns 93*
Toman, Richard J. *Law&B 92*
Tomar, Russell Herman 1937- *WhoAm 92*
Tomarin, Harry P. 1916- *St&PR 93*
Tomarin, Seymour Aaron 1948- *St&PR 93*
Tomas, Jerold F. V. *WhoAm 92*
Tomas, Mark R. *Law&B 92*
Tomas, Xavier 1948- *WhoScE 91-3*
Tomaschek, Wenzel Johann 1774-1850 *Baker 92*
Tomasek, Frantisek 1899-1992 *NewYTBS 92 [port]*
Tomasek, Jaroslav 1896-1970 *Baker 92*
Tomasek, Robert Dennis 1928- *WhoAm 92*
Tomasek, Vaclav 1774-1850 *OxDcOp*
Tomaselli, Ivan 1951- *WhoWor 93*
Tomaselli, Sylvana 1957- *ConAu 137*
Tomasetta, Lou *BioIn 17*
Tomasetta, Louis R. *St&PR 93*
Tomasetti, Perry Joseph 1963- *WhoSSW 93*
Tomasetti, Robert J. *Law&B 92*
Tomash, Erwin 1921- *WhoAm 92*
Tomashefsky, Michael 1953- *St&PR 93*
Tomasi, Gioacchino Lanza *BioIn 17*
Tomasi, Henri 1901-1978 *OxDcOp*
Tomasi, Henri (Fredien) 1901-1971 *Baker 92*
Tomasi, Thomas B. 1927- *WhoAm 92, WhoE 93*
Tomasi, Thomas E(dward) 1955- *ConAu 139*
Tomasi di Lampedusa, Giuseppe 1896-1957 *BioIn 17*
Tomasik, Piotr 1937- *WhoScE 91-4*
Tomasini, Alois (Basil Nikolaus) (Luigi) 1779-1858
See Tomasini, Alois Luigi 1741-1808 *Baker 92*
Tomasini, Alois Luigi 1741-1808 *Baker 92*
Tomasini, Anton (Edmund) 1775-1824
See Tomasini, Alois Luigi 1741-1808 *Baker 92*
Tomasini, Wallace John 1926- *WhoAm 92*
Tomasko, Mark Daniel 1948- *St&PR 93, WhoAm 92*
Tomassi, Stephen J. *Law&B 92*
Tomassini, Lawrence Anthony 1945- *WhoAm 92*
Tomassini, Luciano 1935- *WhoWor 93*
Tomasson, Helgi *BioIn 17*
Tomasson, Helgi 1942- *WhoAm 92*
Tomasson, Jonas 1946- *Baker 92*
Tomasson, Thorsteinn *WhoScE 91-4*
Tomasson, Tomas Armann 1929- *WhoWor 93*
Tomasulo, Virginia Merrills 1919- *WhoAm 92*
Tomasuolo, Vincent Anthony 1958- *WhoE 93*
Tomasz, Jeno 1935- *WhoScE 91-4*
Tomaszek, Thomas Richard 1952- *WhoE 93*
Tomaszeski, Josephine Gallas 1919- *WhoAmW 93*
Tomaszewicz, Elizabeth Eleonora 1946- *WhoAmW 93*
Tomaszewski, Carlos Alberto 1930- *St&PR 93*
Tomaszewski, John Joseph *Law&B 92*
Tomaszewski, Maciej Ryszard 1941- *WhoWor 93*
Tomaszunas, Stanislaw 1927- *WhoScE 91-4, WhoWor 93*
Tomatis, Lorenzo 1929- *WhoScE 91-2*
Tomatis, Roberto 1940- *WhoScE 91-3*
Tomazi, George Donald 1935- *WhoWor 93*
Tomazinis, Anthony Rodoflos 1929- *WhoAm 92*
Tomb, David A(lan) 1944- *ConAu 40NR*
Tomb, Myron Hay 1947- *WhoE 93*
Tomba, Alberto *BioIn 17*
Tomba, Alberto 1966- *News 92 [port], -92-3 [port]*
Tombaugh, Clyde 1906- *BioIn 17*
Tombaugh, Clyde William 1906- *WhoAm 92*
Tombelle, Fernand de la *Baker 92*
Tomberlin, W.J. 1944- *St&PR 93*
Tombet, Andre 1927- *WhoWor 93*
Tomblin, Frederick L. 1926- *St&PR 93*
Tomblin, Kelly Ann *Law&B 92*
Tomblinson, James Edmond 1927- *WhoAm 92*
Tombol, Terez 1925- *WhoScE 91-4*
Tombolini, Robert Dominick 1961- *St&PR 93*
Tombrello, Thomas Anthony, Jr. 1936- *WhoAm 92*
Tombros, Peter G. 1942- *St&PR 93*
Tombros, Peter George 1942- *WhoAm 92*
Tombs, Francis Leonard *WhoScE 91-1*
Tomcala, Maryjane 1937- *WhoAmW 93*
Tomchik, Paul W. 1947- *St&PR 93*
Tomcik, David J. *Law&B 92*
Tomcsanyi, Pal 1924- *WhoScE 91-4*
Tomczak, Catherine Marie 1959- *WhoAmW 93*
Tomczak, Robert F. 1935- *St&PR 93*
Tom Dieck, Heindirk 1939- *WhoScE 91-3*
Tome, Philip 1782-1855 *BioIn 17*
Tomei, Donny *BioIn 17*
Tomek, William G. 1932- *BioIn 17*
Tomek, William Goodrich 1932- *WhoAm 92, WhoE 93*
Tomeny, Lynne Johnson *Law&B 92*
Tomera, John Frank 1952- *WhoE 93*
Tomes, Henry 1932- *BioIn 17*
Tomes, Margaret Otey *AmWomPl*
Tomes, Margot 1917-1991 *BioIn 17*
Tomes, Margot (Ladd) 1917-1991 *MajAI [port], SmATA 69, -70 [port]*
Tomfohrde, Heinn Frederic, III 1933- *St&PR 93*
Tomfool *MajAI*
Tomhave, Beverly Korstad 1947- *WhoAmW 93*
Tomialojc, Ludwik 1939- *WhoScE 91-4*
Tomic, Biljana Jelesije 1940- *WhoWor 93*
Tomic, Charlotte Frenkel 1949- *WhoAmW 93*
Tomich, John Allen *Law&B 92*
Tomich, Nancy Ellen 1945- *WhoWrEP 92*
Tomich, Peter 1893-1941 *BioIn 17*
Tomick, David *BioIn 17*
Tomic Romero, Radomiro 1914- *WhoUN 92*
Tomida, Masayuki 1956- *WhoWor 93*
Tomilin, Victor 1908-1941 *Baker 92*
Tomino, Yoshiyuki *ScF&FL 92*
Tominovich, A. Robert 1935- *St&PR 93*
Tomioka, Hideo 1941- *WhoWor 93*
Tomioka, Kiyoshi 1948- *WhoWor 93*
Tomioka, Sadatoshi 1897-1970 *HarEnMi*
Tomislav fl. 10th cent.- *OxDcByz*
Tomita, Akira 1940- *WhoWor 93*
Tomita, Etsuji 1942- *WhoWor 93*
Tomita, Tamlyn *BioIn 17, ConTFT 10*
Tomiyama, Akira 1945- *WhoWor 93*
Tomiyasu, Kiyo 1919- *WhoAm 92*
Tomiyasu, Yoshikazu Eishin 1938- *WhoWor 93*
Tomizawa, Yoshimi *Law&B 92*
Tomizuka, Mitsuo 1929- *WhoAsAP 91*
Tomka, Ondrej 1928- *WhoScE 91-4*
Tomka, Peter 1956- *WhoUN 92*
Tomkiel, Judith Irene 1949- *WhoAmW 93, WhoWrEP 92*
Tomkiewicz, Joseph A. *Law&B 92*

Tomkiewicz, Stanislaw 1925- *WhoScE 91-2*
Tomkin, Michael 1948- *St&PR 93*
Tomkins *Baker 92*
Tomkins, Alexander C., Jr. 1933- *St&PR 93*
Tomkins, Calvin 1925- *BioIn 17, WhoAm 92, WhoWrEP 92*
Tomkins, Cyril Robert *WhoScE 91-1*
Tomkins, David 1940- *St&PR 93*
Tomkins, Frank Sargent 1915- *WhoAm 92*
Tomkins, Giles 1587?-1688? *Baker 92*
Tomkins, Joanne Kark 1953- *WhoAmW 93*
Tomkins, John 1586-1638 *Baker 92*
Tomkins, Julia M. Hunter Manchee *ScF&FL 92*
Tomkins, Nathaniel 1599-1681 *Baker 92*
Tomkins, Robert fl. 17th cent.- *Baker 92*
Tomkins, Silvan Samuel 1911-1991 *BioIn 17*
Tomkins, Thomas 1572-1656? *Baker 92*
Tomko, Jozef Cardinal 1924- *WhoAm 92, WhoWor 93*
Tomko, Robert P. 1940- *St&PR 93*
Tomko, Ronald Thomas 1966- *WhoE 93*
Tomlan, Michael A. 1947- *ConAu 137*
Tomlin, Donald Reid 1933- *WhoE 93*
Tomlin, Eugene B. 1933- *St&PR 93*
Tomlin, Judson Eugene, Jr. *Law&B 92*
Tomlin, Lily 1939- *QDrFCA 92 [port], WhoAm 92, WhoAmW 93*
Tomlin, Richard A. *Law&B 92*
Tomlin, Robert Michael 1945- *St&PR 93*
Tomlinson, A. Robert, III 1934- *St&PR 93*
Tomlinson, Alexander Cooper 1922- *WhoAm 92*
Tomlinson, Ann Watts 1950- *WhoSSW 93*
Tomlinson, Bill *WhoAm 92*
Tomlinson, Bill E. *WhoSSW 93*
Tomlinson, Brian Lee 1958- *WhoWor 93*
Tomlinson, Charles Wesley, Jr. 1947- *WhoAm 92*
Tomlinson, David 1917- *QDrFCA 92 [port]*
Tomlinson, David Charles *Law&B 92*
Tomlinson, David Ellis *Law&B 92*
Tomlinson, David R. 1928- *St&PR 93*
Tomlinson, David Richard *WhoScE 91-1*
Tomlinson, George Herbert 1912- *WhoAm 92*
Tomlinson, Gerald (Arthur) 1933- *WhoWrEP 92*
Tomlinson, Geraldine Ann 1931- *WhoAmW 93*
Tomlinson, Gus 1933- *WhoAm 92*
Tomlinson, H.M. 1873-1958 *BioIn 17*
Tomlinson, Henry Major 1873-1958 *BioIn 17*
Tomlinson, J. Richard 1930- *WhoAm 92, WhoWor 93*
Tomlinson, James F. 1925- *St&PR 93*
Tomlinson, James Francis 1925- *WhoAm 92*
Tomlinson, Janet Fox 1944- *WhoWrEP 92*
Tomlinson, Jeff *BioIn 17*
Tomlinson, John 1946- *OxDcOp*
Tomlinson, John P., III 1950- *St&PR 93*
Tomlinson, John Randolph 1931- *WhoAm 92*
Tomlinson, John (Rowland) 1946- *Baker 92*
Tomlinson, Joseph Ernest 1939- *WhoAm 92*
Tomlinson, Kenneth Y. 1944- *St&PR 93, WhoAm 92, WhoE 93*
Tomlinson, Leland E. *Law&B 92*
Tomlinson, Martin *WhoScE 91-1*
Tomlinson, Mary Burns *Law&B 92*
Tomlinson, Milton Ambrose 1906- *WhoAm 92*
Tomlinson, Richard Allan 1932- *WhoWor 93*
Tomlinson, Robert J. *Law&B 92*
Tomlinson, Robert John 1936- *St&PR 93*
Tomlinson, Rolfe Cartwright *WhoScE 91-1*
Tomlinson, Stephen *WhoScE 91-1*
Tomlinson, Stephenson Anthony 1950- *WhoWor 93*
Tomlinson, Warren Leon 1930- *WhoAm 92*
Tomlinson, William Holmes 1922- *WhoSSW 93*
Tomlinson-Keasey, Carol Ann 1942- *WhoAm 92, WhoAmW 93*
Tomljanovich, Esther M. 1931- *WhoAmW 93*
Tommasi, Giulio 1941- *WhoScE 91-3*
Tommasi, Michel 1928- *WhoScE 91-2*
Tommasini, Vincenzo 1878-1950 *Baker 92*
Tomme, Alan W. *Law&B 92*
Tomme, John Carlin 1930- *WhoWrEP 92*
Tommeraasen, Miles 1923- *WhoAm 92*
Tommerdahl, James B. 1926- *St&PR 93*
Tomner, Sigvard *WhoScE 91-4*
Tomney, David K. *Law&B 92*
Tomoe fl. 12th cent.- *BioIn 17*
Tom, of Finland 1920-1991 *BioIn 17*
Tomola, James D. *Law&B 92*
Tomolo, Michael L. *Law&B 92*
Tomonaga, Susumu 1939- *WhoWor 93*
Tomonto, James Robert 1932- *WhoSSW 93*
Tomosugi, Yoshimasa 1942- *WhoWor 93*
Tomotani, Koji 1947- *Baker 92*
Tomov, Valentin T. 1935- *WhoScE 91-4*
Tomowa-Sintow, Anna 1941- *Baker 92, OxDcOp*
Tompa, Kalman 1934- *WhoScE 91-4*
Tompkins, A. Kathleen Kelly 1903- *WhoAmW 93*
Tompkins, Curtis Johnston 1942- *WhoAm 92, WhoWor 93*
Tompkins, Daniel Reuben 1931- *WhoAm 92, WhoE 93*
Tompkins, Doug *BioIn 17*
Tompkins, Edward Eugene 1936- *St&PR 93*
Tompkins, Francine Maria 1947- *WhoE 93*
Tompkins, J. Richard 1938- *St&PR 93*
Tompkins, James Arthur 1946- *WhoAm 92*
Tompkins, James Haviland 1923- *St&PR 93*
Tompkins, Jane P(arry) 1940- *ConAu 39NR*
Tompkins, Joseph Buford, Jr. 1950- *WhoAm 92*
Tompkins, Julia M. *ScF&FL 92*
Tompkins, Juliet Wilbor 1871- *AmWomPl*
Tompkins, Keith R. 1942- *St&PR 93*
Tompkins, Molly *BioIn 17*
Tompkins, Ralph Joel 1919- *WhoWrEP 92*
Tompkins, Richard Weller, Jr. 1934- *WhoAm 92*
Tompkins, Robert 1944- *ScF&FL 92*
Tompkins, Robert Charles 1924- *WhoE 93*
Tompkins, Robert George 1923- *WhoAm 92*
Tompkins, Ronald K. 1934- *WhoAm 92*
Tompkins, Seldon T. 1943- *St&PR 93*
Tompkins, Stephen Stern 1938- *WhoSSW 93*
Tompkins, Susie *BioIn 17*
Tompkins, Walker A. 1909-1988 *ScF&FL 92*
Tomppo, Erkki Olavi 1947- *WhoScE 91-4*
Tompsett, Kenneth Roger 1946- *WhoScE 91-1*
Tompsett, Michael Francis 1939- *WhoAm 92*
Tompsett, Ralph 1913- *WhoAm 92*
Tompson, Marian Leonard 1929- *WhoAm 92*
Toms, Bonnie Bayer 1954- *WhoEmL 93*
Toms, Carlton Ralph 1937- *St&PR 93*
Toms, Curtis, Jr. 1943- *St&PR 93*
Toms, David John 1953- *WhoWor 93*
Toms, Herbert Logan, Jr. *Law&B 92*
Toms, Kathleen Moore 1943- *WhoAmW 93*
Tomsett, Janet Moffat 1943- *WhoAmW 93*
Tomshinsky, Ida 1953- *WhoSSW 93*
Tomsic, Joseph Andrew Michael 1949- *WhoEmL 93, WhoWor 93*
Tomsick, Richard D. *Law&B 92*
Tomski, Lech 1942- *WhoScE 91-4*
Tomson, Michael 1954- *See* Cooper, Joel 1953- & Tomson, Michael 1954- *ConEn*
Tomsovic, Edward Joseph 1922- *WhoAm 92*
Tomter, Gary Lynn 1950- *St&PR 93*
Tomu, Sosu 1951- *WhoAsAP 91*
Tomur Dawamat 1928- *WhoAsAP 91*
Ton, Dao-Rong 1940- *WhoWor 93*
Tona, Andrew Joseph 1951- *St&PR 93*
Tona, Pedro Maria *WhoAfr*
Tondello, Giuseppe 1938- *WhoScE 91-3*
Tonder, Olav 1926- *WhoScE 91-4*
Tondering, Claus 1953- *WhoWor 93*
Tondeur, Daniel 1939- *WhoScE 91-2*
Tondeur, Philippe Maurice 1932- *WhoAm 92*
Tondro, Helle S. *Law&B 92*
Tone, Kaoru 1931- *WhoWor 93*
Tone, Kenneth Edward 1930- *WhoAm 92*
Tone, Mark Burton *Law&B 92*
Tone, Philip Willis 1923- *WhoAm 92*
Tone, Theobald Wolfe 1763-1798 *BioIn 17*
Tone, Yasunao 1935- *Baker 92*
Tonegawa, Susumu 1939- *WhoAm 92, WhoWor 93*
Tonellato, Umberto R. 1935- *WhoScE 91-3*
Tonelli, Kathleen Eloise 1929- *WhoAmW 93*
Tonello-Stuart, Enrica Maria *WhoAm 92, WhoWor 93*
Tonelson, Jack Martin 1930- *St&PR 93, WhoAm 92*
Toner, David C. *Law&B 92*
Toner, Edward Joseph 1921- *St&PR 93*
Toney, Anthony 1913- *WhoAm 92*
Toney, Creola Sarah 1920- *WhoWor 93*
Toney, Danny Michael 1957- *WhoSSW 93*
Toney, Frederick Arthur 1887-1953 *BiDAMSp 1989*
Toney, Kelly Lynne Smith 1959- *WhoSSW 93*
Toney, Oscar, Jr. 1939- *SoulM*
Toney, Robert L. 1934- *AfrAmBi [port]*
Tong, Fu 1936- *WhoWor 93*
Tong, Gary 1942- *BioIn 17*
Tong, Hing 1922- *WhoAm 92*
Tong, Howell *WhoScE 91-1*
Tong, Mary Powderly 1924- *WhoE 93*
Tong, Penelope Wat *Law&B 92*
Tong, Theody Mongaya 1955- *WhoWor 93*
Tong, Winton 1927- *WhoAm 92*
Tong, Yit Chow 1948- *WhoWor 93*
Tongate, Darrel Edwin 1943- *WhoSSW 93*
Tongiorgi, Marco 1934- *WhoScE 91-3*
Tongue, Paul Graham 1932- *St&PR 93, WhoAm 92*
Tongue, William Walter 1915- *WhoAm 92*
Tong-Yoo, Boonlue 1941- *WhoWor 93*
Tonha, Pedro Maria *WhoWor 93*
Toni, Alceo 1884-1969 *Baker 92*
Toni, B.S. *Law&B 92*
Toni, Bernard S. 1943- *St&PR 93*
Toni, Eugene Joseph 1949- *WhoE 93*
Tonick, Illene 1951- *WhoAmW 93*
Tonielli, Richard B. 1939- *St&PR 93*
Tonino, Robert Henry Anthony 1944- *St&PR 93*
Toniolo, Lucio *WhoScE 91-3*
Tonjum, Stein 1941- *WhoScE 91-4*
Tonk, Robert 1947- *St&PR 93*
Tonkin, Dean G. 1940- *St&PR 93*
Tonkin, Elizabeth Smoot *Law&B 92*
Tonkin, Heather *BioIn 17*
Tonkin, Humphrey 1939- *ConAu 38NR*
Tonkin, Humphrey Richard 1939- *WhoAm 92, WhoE 93, WhoWor 93*
Tonkin, John Paul 1926- *WhoWor 93*
Tonkin, Leo Sampson 1937- *WhoAm 92*
Tonkin, Mary McGrath *Law&B 92*
Tonkin, Peter 1950- *ScF&FL 92*
Tonkin, Richard *WhoScE 91-1*
Tonkin, Terry Michael 1942- *St&PR 93*
Tonkovic, Kruno 1911- *WhoScE 91-4*
Tonkovich, Eugene J. 1940- *St&PR 93*
Tonkovich, Robert Steven 1945- *St&PR 93*
Tonks, Robert Stanley *WhoAm 92*
Tonkyn, Richard George 1927- *St&PR 93, WhoAm 92*
Tonn, Colleen E. *Law&B 92*
Tonn, Melissa Dawn 1959- *WhoSSW 93*
Tonn, Victor Lux 1943- *WhoE 93*
Tonna, Arthur J. 1927- *St&PR 93*
Tonna, Edgar Anthony 1928- *WhoAm 92*
Tonnard, Victor E.J. 1929- *WhoScE 91-2*
Tonndorf, Juergen 1914-1989 *BioIn 17*
Tonne, Tore 1948- *WhoWor 93*
Tonnemaker, Frank Clayton 1928- *BiDAMSp 1989*
Tonnesen, Mark K. 1951- *St&PR 93*
Tonnessen, Bruce Hunter 1948- *St&PR 93*
Tonning, Gerard 1860-1940 *Baker 92*
Tonolini, Franco 1934- *WhoScE 91-3*
Tonomura, A. 1942- *BioIn 17*
Tonomura, Akira 1942- *BioIn 17*
Tonra, Joan E. 1946- *St&PR 93*
Tonshoff, Hans Kurt 1934- *WhoScE 91-3*
Tonsing, Carol E. *WhoWrEP 92*
Tonso, Arnaldo *WhoScE 91-3*
Tonso, Cheryl Jackson 1934- *WhoAmW 93*
Tonti, Rita Rose 1943- *WhoWrEP 92*
Tontti, Mikko Antero 1947- *WhoScE 91-4*
Tonty, Henri de 1650?-1704 *Expl 93*
Tontz, Jay Logan 1938- *WhoAm 92*
Tontz, Robert L. 1917- *WhoAm 92*
Tonutti, Manfred *WhoWor 93*
Tony, Janine Alexandra 1967- *WhoAmW 93*
Too, Ng Pock 1945- *WhoAsAP 91*
Toochin, Joseph Efim 1935- *WhoUN 92*
Tood, Troy W. 1928- *St&PR 93*
Toogood, Granville Newbold 1943- *WhoE 93*
Tooher, James Marshall 1931- *St&PR 93*
Toohey, Brian Frederick 1944- *WhoAm 92*
Toohey, Edward Joseph 1930- *St&PR 93, WhoE 93, WhoWor 93*
Toohey, Janice E. *Law&B 92*
Toohey, Philip S. *Law&B 92*
Toohey, Richard 1929- *St&PR 93*
Toohig, Michael Francis 1924- *St&PR 93*
Toohy, Nora Jane *Law&B 92*
Tooker, Carl E. 1947- *St&PR 93*
Tooker, Elisabeth Jane 1927- *WhoAmW 93, WhoE 93*
Tooker, Eric Sumner *Law&B 92*
Tooker, Gary Lamarr 1939- *WhoAm 92*
Tooker, Gertrude Fulton *AmWomPl*
Tooker, Mary Hull *Law&B 92*
Tooker, Richard 1902-1988 *ScF&FL 92*
Tookes, James Nelson 1934- *WhoSSW 93*
Tookey, Robert C. 1925- *WhoIns 93*
Tool, Dennis Casler 1948- *WhoWrEP 92*
Tool, Marc R. *BioIn 17*
Toolan, Dennis Michael 1946- *St&PR 93, WhoAm 92*
Toolan, Helene Wallace d1992 *NewYTBS 92*
Toolan, John Thomas *Law&B 92*
Toolan, Michael J. *Law&B 92*
Toole, Albert J. 1937- *St&PR 93*
Toole, Allan H. 1920- *WhoAm 92*
Toole, Cynthia *Law&B 92*
Toole, Daniel A. *Law&B 92*
Toole, David G. 1942- *St&PR 93*
Toole, David George 1942- *WhoAm 92*
Toole, Edward D. *Law&B 92*
Toole, Eileen Marie 1940- *WhoE 93*
Toole, James Francis 1925- *WhoAm 92, WhoSSW 93, WhoWor 93*
Toole, John Edward 1934- *WhoE 93*
Toole, John Kennedy 1937-1969 *BioIn 17*
Toole, Lee K. 1936- *WhoAm 92*
Toole, Rex *ConAu 40NR*
Toole, Richard H. *Law&B 92*
Toole, Wm. K., II 1926- *St&PR 93*
Tooley, Lowell James 1923- *WhoE 93*
Tooley, Nola Sue 1940- *WhoAmW 93*
Tooley, Terry Lee 1948- *St&PR 93, WhoEmL 93*
Tooley, William H. d1992 *NewYTBS 92*
Toombs, Frederick C. *St&PR 93*
Toombs, Jane Ellen 1926- *WhoWrEP 92*
Toombs, Jane Jenke 1926- *ScF&FL 92*
Toombs, John 1927- *ScF&FL 92*
Toombs, Kenneth Eldridge 1928- *WhoAm 92*
Toombs, Margaret Stutts 1948- *WhoAmW 93*
Toombs, Robert A. 1810-1885 *PolPar*
Toombs, Russ William 1951- *WhoE 93, WhoEmL 93, WhoWor 93*
Toomer, Anthony 1768?- *BioIn 17*
Toomer, Cynthia Yvonne 1947- *WhoE 93*
Toomer, Jean 1894-1967 *AmWrS3, BioIn 17, EncAACR*
Toomey, Beverly Guella 1940- *WhoAmW 93*
Toomey, David Charles 1938- *WhoAm 92*
Toomey, Gary Kenneth 1955- *WhoWor 93*
Toomey, Jean Ann 1957- *WhoSSW 93*
Toomey, Jeanne Elizabeth *WhoWrEP 92*
Toomey, Jeanne Elizabeth 1921- *WhoE 93*
Toomey, John Boyne 1924- *St&PR 93*
Toomey, John Edward 1952- *St&PR 93*
Toomey, Kent E. 1935- *St&PR 93*
Toomey, Kent Edward 1935- *WhoAm 92, WhoSSW 93*
Toomey, Laura Carolyn 1929- *WhoE 93*
Toomey, Priscilla R. 1946- *St&PR 93*
Toomey, Regis 1898-1991 *AnObit 1991, BioIn 17*
Toomey, Richard *Law&B 92*
Toomey, Richard A., Jr. *Law&B 92*
Toomey, Stephen J. 1959- *St&PR 93*
Toomey, T. Murray 1923- *St&PR 93*
Toomey, Thomas Murray 1923- *WhoAm 92*
Toomre, Alar 1937- *WhoAm 92*
Toon, Malcolm 1916- *WhoAm 92*
Toon, Steven Bates 1948- *St&PR 93*
Toone, Elam Cooksey, Jr. 1908- *WhoAm 92*
Toone, Frederick Lavern 1936- *WhoSSW 93*
Tooney, Nancy Marion 1939- *WhoAmW 93*
Toop, R. Scott *Law&B 92*
Toor, Harold O. d1991 *BioIn 17*
Toor, Herbert Lawrence 1927- *WhoAm 92*
Toos, A.J. *WhoWrEP 92*
Toot, Joseph F., Jr. 1935- *WhoAm 92*
Toot, Joseph Frederick, Jr. 1935- *St&PR 93*
Toote, Gloria E. A. *WhoAm 92, WhoAmW 93*
Tooth, Alwyn Stanley *WhoScE 91-1*
Toothaker, Ronald Wayne 1940- *St&PR 93*
Tootle, Milton, Jr. *Law&B 92*
Tootle, Milton, Jr. 1943- *St&PR 93*
Tooze, John 1938- *WhoScE 91-3*
Top, Franklin Henry, Jr. 1936- *WhoAm 92*
Top, Siden 1950- *WhoWor 93*
Topa, Edward F. 1941- *WhoIns 93*
Topakoglu, Huseyin Cavit 1925- *WhoSSW 93*
Topas, George 1924- *BioIn 17*
Topaz, Muriel 1932- *WhoE 93*
Topaz, William N. 1947- *WhoEmL 93*
Topazio, Virgil William 1915- *WhoAm 92*
Topcik, Barry 1924- *WhoE 93*
Topden, Karma 1941- *WhoAsAP 91*
Topel, David Glen 1937- *WhoAm 92*
Topel, Eugene *Law&B 92*
Topelius, Kathleen E. 1948- *WhoAmW 93*

Topencharov, Vladimir 1933- *WhoScE 91-4*
Toperzer, Thomas Raymond 1939- *WhoAm 92, WhoSSW 93*
Topete y Carballo, Juan Bautista 1821-1885 *HarEnMi*
Topf, Barbara May 1944- *WhoE 93*
Topf, Michael David 1942- *WhoE 93*
Topfer, Johann Gottlob 1791-1870 *Baker 92*
Topfer, Morton Louis 1936- *St&PR 93, WhoAm 92*
Topham, Douglas William *WhoWor 93*
Topham, Murray Herbert 1937- *St&PR 93*
Topham, Neil *St&PR 93*
Topham, Neville *WhoScE 91-1*
Topham, Renee Ann 1964- *WhoAmW 93*
Topham, Verl Reed 1934- *St&PR 93, WhoAm 92*
Topholm, Ib Le Roy 1935- *WhoWor 93*
Topi, Gian Carlo 1925- *WhoScE 91-3*
Topinka, Judy Baar 1944- *WhoAmW 93*
Topitsch, Ernst 1919- *ConAu 136*
Topjon, Gary Malcolm 1940- *St&PR 93*
Topkins, Katharine 1927- *WhoWrEP 92*
Topley, Christopher Gordon *WhoScE 91-1*
Toplin, Ellen 1952- *WhoAmW 93*
Topliss, Harry, Jr. 1923- *WhoAm 92*
Toplovich, P. Ann 1955- *WhoAm 92*
Topmese, Cahit 1945- *WhoScE 91-4*
Topodas, Jonathan Michael *Law&B 92*
Topol 1935- *IntDcF 2-3 [port]*
Topol, Allan 1941- *ScF&FL 92*
Topol, B.H. *ScF&FL 92*
Topol, Chaim 1935- *WhoWor 93*
Topol, Edward 1938- *ConAu 139*
Topol, Eric Jeffrey 1954- *WhoAm 92*
Topol, Martin Theodore 1952- *WhoE 93*
Topol, Robert Martin 1925- *St&PR 93, WhoAm 92*
Topol, Sidney 1924- *WhoAm 92*
Topolosky, Gary Paul *Law&B 92*
Topolosky, Sanford 1924- *St&PR 93*
Topolski, Feliks 1907- *PolBiDi*
Topolski, Jerzy 1928- *WhoWor 93*
Topor, Tom *MiSFD 9*
Toporcer, Specs 1899-1989 *BioIn 17*
Toporoff, Ralph *MiSFD 9*
Topp, Arnold 1887- *BioIn 17*
Topp, Elliott 1930- *St&PR 93*
Topp, George Clarke 1937- *WhoAm 92*
Topp, Robert George 1937- *St&PR 93*
Toppan, Clara Anna Raab 1910- *WhoAmW 93*
Toppel, Milton 1919- *WhoAm 92*
Topper, Barbara MacNeal Blake 1942- *WhoE 93*
Topper, Burt 1928- *MiSFD 9*
Topper, Hertha 1924- *Baker 92*
Topper, John Abram, Jr. 1943- *WhoE 93*
Topper, Joseph Ray 1928- *WhoAm 92*
Topper, Leonard 1929- *WhoE 93*
Topper, Paul Quinn 1925- *WhoSSW 93*
Topper, Philip D., Sr. 1942- *St&PR 93*
Toppeta, Barbara S. *Law&B 92*
Toppeta, William J. *Law&B 92*
Topping, B.H.V. *WhoScE 91-1*
Topping, Brian B. 1934- *St&PR 93*
Topping, John Carruthers, Jr. 1943- *WhoE 93, WhoWor 93*
Topping, John Thomas 1934- *St&PR 93*
Topping, Mary Ann *AmWomPl*
Topping, Melissa Stutsman d1992 *BioIn 17, NewYTBS 92*
Topping, Norman Hawkins 1908- *BioIn 17, WhoAm 92*
Topping, Peter 1916- *WhoAm 92*
Topping, Seymour 1921- *WhoAm 92*
Topping, Thomas Edwin 1933- *St&PR 93*
Topping, Thomas Stirling Reid 1947- *WhoUN 92*
Topps, John Herbert *WhoScE 91-1*
Toprakcioglu, Christo 1954- *WhoWor 93*
Topsacalian, Harutiun 1961- *WhoE 93*
Topsch, Wilhelm 1941- *WhoWor 93*
Topsoe, Henrik 1944- *WhoScE 91-2*
Topuz, Ahmet 1949- *WhoScE 91-4*
Tora, Apisai Vuniyayawa 1934- *WhoAsAP 91*
Toradze, Alexander (David) 1952- *Baker 92*
Toradze, David (Alexandrovich) 1922-1983 *Baker 92*
Toral, Raul 1958- *WhoWor 93*
Toran, Daniel James 1948- *WhoAm 92*
Toran, Dante R. 1921- *St&PR 93*
Torano, Maria Elena 1938- *NotHsAW 93*
Torashima, Kazuo 1928- *WhoAsAP 91*
Torbert, Alice Coyle *AmWomPl*
Torbert, Carl A., Jr. 1935- *St&PR 93*
Torbert, Clement Clay, Jr. 1929- *WhoAm 92*
Torbert, Frank Duke 1936- *WhoSSW 93*
Torbet, Sylvia Lily 1930- *WhoSSW 93*
Torborg, Jeffrey Allen 1941- *WhoAm 92*
Torchi, Luigi 1858-1920 *Baker 92*
Torchiana, Donald Thornhill 1923- *WhoWrEP 92*
Torchinsky, Benjamin B. 1926- *St&PR 93*
Torcivia, Benedict J. 1929- *St&PR 93*
Torcivia, Joseph Arthur 1959- *WhoAm 92*
Torcivia, Santo Joseph 1949- *St&PR 93*
Torczyner, Joshua 1910-1990 *BioIn 17*
Torday, Ursula *ScF&FL 92*
Tordiff, Hazel Midgley 1920- *WhoAmW 93*
Tordjman, Jean Daniel 1944- *WhoE 93*
Tordoff, Harrison Bruce 1923- *WhoAm 92*
Tordoir, Peter Paul 1952- *St&PR 93*
Torell, Jeff Warren 1947- *WhoSSW 93*
Torell, John *BioIn 17*
Torell, John Raymond, III 1939- *St&PR 93*
Torelli, Gasparo dc. 1613 *Baker 92*
Torelli, Giacomo 1608-1678 *OxDcOp*
Torelli, Giuseppe 1658-1709 *Baker 92*
Torelli, Helen *Law&B 92*
Torello, Judy S. 1940- *WhoAm 92, WhoAmW 93*
Toremalm, Nils Gunnar 1923- *WhoScE 91-4*
Toren, Mark 1950- *WhoE 93*
Toren, Robert 1915- *WhoWor 93*
Torey, Donald C. *Law&B 92*
Torfason, Kristjan Gudmundur 1953- *WhoWor 93*
Torg, Joseph Steven 1934- *WhoAm 92*
Torge, Wolfgang 1931- *WhoScE 91-3*
Torgelson, David J. *Law&B 92*
Torgersen, Donald B. 1939- *St&PR 93*
Torgersen, Paul Ernest 1931- *WhoAm 92*
Torgersen, Torwald Harold 1929- *WhoAm 92*
Torgerson, Arthur Dennis 1929- *St&PR 93*
Torgerson, James Paul 1952- *WhoAm 92*
Torgerson, Larry Keith 1935- *WhoWor 93*
Torgerson, Paul E. 1947- *St&PR 93*
Torgerson, W.T. *Law&B 92*
Torgerson, William T. 1944- *St&PR 93*
Torgeson, Earl 1924-1990 *BioIn 17*
Torgeson, Roy *ScF&FL 92*
Torgeson, Steven Wayne 1947- *WhoSSW 93*
Torgo, W. *WhoScE 91-3*
Torgov, Morley 1927- *WhoCanL 92*
Torgovnick, Marianna De Marco 1949- *WhoSSW 93*
Torgow, Eugene N. 1925- *WhoAm 92*
Torgrimson, Darvin A. 1935- *St&PR 93*
Torgunrud, Fred A. *WhoScE 91-4*
Torgusen, Robert Guy 1935- *St&PR 93*
Toribara, Taft Yutaka 1917- *WhoAm 92*
Torii, Kazuo 1937- *WhoAsAP 91*
Torii, Shinichiro *BioIn 17*
Torii, Shuko 1930- *WhoWor 93*
Torii, Sigeru 1932- *WhoWor 93*
Torii, Tetsuya 1918- *WhoWor 93*
Torikai, Kinichi 1925- *WhoWor 93*
Torin, Jan M. 1936- *WhoScE 91-4*
Torino, Thomas Michael 1947- *WhoE 93*
Torinus, John B., Jr. 1937- *St&PR 93*
Torisky, Donald David 1938- *St&PR 93*
Toriumi, Koshiro 1949- *WhoWor 93*
Torjussen, Trygve 1885-1977 *Baker 92*
Torkan, Akbar *WhoWor 93*
Torkanowksy, Werner 1926-1992 *NewYTBS 92*
Torkanowsky, David *BioIn 17*
Torkanowsky, Werner 1926- *Baker 92*
Torke, Michael *BioIn 17*
Torke, Michael 1961- *Baker 92*
Torkelson, Dean J. 1944- *St&PR 93*
Torkelson, Lucile Emma 1915- *WhoAmW 93*
Torkildson, Patricia A. *Law&B 92*
Torlegard, Kennert 1937- *WhoScE 91-4*
Torley, John Frederic 1911- *St&PR 93, WhoAm 92*
Torlonia, Giovanni *BioIn 17*
Torma, Michael Joseph 1942- *WhoAm 92*
Tormala, Pertti Olavi 1945- *WhoScE 91-4*
Torme, Mel 1925- *BioIn 17*
Torme, Mel(vin Howard) 1925- *Baker 92*
Torme, Melvin 1925- *WhoAm 92*
Tormey, Douglass Cole 1938- *WhoAm 92*
Tormey, John J., III *Law&B 92*
Tormey, Randolph T. *Law&B 92*
Tormey, Randolph T. 1953- *St&PR 93*
Tormey, Terrence O'Brien 1954- *St&PR 93, WhoE 93*
Torn, Lawrence 1926- *WhoE 93*
Torn, Lawrence J. 1926- *St&PR 93*
Torn, Rip 1931- *MiSFD 9, WhoAm 92*
Tornabene, Russell C. 1923- *WhoAm 92*
Tornabene, Thomas Guy 1937- *WhoAm 92*
Tornatore, Giuseppe 1956- *MiSFD 9*
Tornatore, James P. 1945- *St&PR 93*
Tornatore, Joe *MiSFD 9*
Tornberg, Edward Wilmer 1934- *St&PR 93*
Tornberg, Eva 1948- *WhoScE 91-4*
Tornblom, Alvin R. 1928- *WhoWor 93*
Torne, Bengt (Axel) von 1891-1967 *Baker 92*
Torneden, Connie Jean 1955- *WhoAmW 93*
Torner, Eduardo Martinez 1888-1955 *Baker 92*
Tornese, Judith M. 1942- *WhoAmW 93*
Tornetta, Frank Joseph 1916- *WhoE 93*
Torney-Purta, Judith Vollmar 1937- *WhoE 93*
Tornikios *OxDcByz*
Tornikios, Euthymios dc. 1222 *OxDcByz*
Tornikios, George *OxDcByz*
Tornikios, George 111-?-1156? *OxDcByz*
Tornikios, Leo dc. 1047 *OxDcByz*
Torning, Jacob L. 1936- *WhoScE 91-2*
Torno, Tim Dale 1957- *St&PR 93*
Tornow, Kathleen Ann 1966- *WhoAmW 93*
Tornquist, Perry Lee 1938- *St&PR 93*
Tornudd, Elin Maria 1924- *WhoScE 91-4*
Toro, Alfonso de 1950- *WhoWor 93*
Toro, Amalia Maria 1920- *WhoAmW 93*
Toro, Carlos H. 1943- *St&PR 93*
Toro, Frank Louis 1928- *St&PR 93*
Toro, Gustavo 1935- *WhoUN 92*
Torok, Arthur F. 1928- *St&PR 93*
Torok, Bela 1925- *WhoScE 91-4*
Torok, Ibolya 1937- *WhoScE 91-4*
Torok, Margaret Louise 1922- *WhoAmW 93*
Toron, Armand S. 1930- *St&PR 93*
Toronto, Ellen Leslie Kaylor 1944- *WhoAmW 93*
Toropin, Youri Vasilyevich 1951- *WhoUN 92*
T'oros, I *OxDcByz*
T'oros, II *OxDcByz*
Torosian, George 1936- *WhoE 93*
Torosian, Jeanne Wylie 1913- *WhoWrEP 92*
Torp, Jan 1950- *WhoScE 91-2*
Torp, Susan Joan 1954- *WhoAmW 93*
Torphy, Thomas Emmett *Law&B 92*
Torpy, Kathleen Ann 1950- *WhoE 93*
Torquato, Salvatore 1954- *WhoSSW 93*
Torr, Graham R. 1953- *WhoScE 91-1*
Torralba, Marcelino 1931- *WhoScE 91-3*
Torrance, A.A. 1946- *WhoScE 91-3*
Torrance, E. Paul 1915- *ConAu 40NR*
Torrance, Ellis Paul 1915- *WhoAm 92*
Torrance, George William 1835-1907 *Baker 92*
Torrance, Gregory Scott 1946- *St&PR 93*
Torrance, Kenneth Eric 1940- *WhoE 93*
Torrance, Walter F., Jr. *Law&B 92*
Torrance, Walter F., Jr. 1927- *St&PR 93*
Torras, Carme 1956- *WhoScE 91-3*
Torras, Joseph Hill 1924- *St&PR 93*
Torras y Bages, Jose 1846-1916 *BioIn 17*
Torre, Aldo Stella 1963- *WhoWor 93*
Torre, Douglas Paul 1919- *WhoAm 92*
Torre, Giovanni 1936- *WhoScE 91-3*
Torre, Joseph Paul 1940- *WhoAm 92*
Torre, Susana 1944- *BioIn 17*
Torreano, John 1941- *BioIn 17*
Torrebella, Joaquin Antonio 1959- *WhoWor 93*
Torre-Cervigon, Miguel 1939- *WhoScE 91-3*
Torrefranca, Fausto 1883-1955 *Baker 92*
Torrella, Carlos Rudolph 1943- *WhoAm 92*
Torrence, David J. *St&PR 93*
Torrence, Ernest 1878-1933 *BioIn 17*
Torrence, Gwen *WhoAmW 93*
Torrence, Helen H. *AmWomPl*
Torrence, Margaret Ann 1946- *WhoWor 93*
Torrence, Richard 1936- *WhoAm 92*
Torrens, Frank J. 1928- *St&PR 93*
Torrens, Mary-Elizabeth *Law&B 92*
Torrens, Robert 1780-1864 *BioIn 17*
Torrenzano, Richard *WhoAm 92, WhoEmL 93*
Torrenzano, Richard 1950- *St&PR 93*
Torres, Alvair Silveira, Jr. 1963- *WhoWor 93*
Torres, Anthony R. 1959- *St&PR 93*
Torres, Art 1941- *HispAmA*
Torres, Celia G. 1936- *NotHsAW 93 [port]*
Torres, Christine Marie 1962- *WhoAmW 93*
Torres, Cynthia Ann 1958- *WhoAmW 93, WhoWor 93*
Torres, David 1934- *WhoSSW 93*
Torres, Denice M. 1959- *WhoAmW 93*
Torres, Edwin *BioIn 17*
Torres, Eleanor *BioIn 17*
Torres, Elizabeth 1950- *WhoWrEP 92*
Torres, Ernest C. 1941- *HispAmA, WhoAm 92*
Torres, Esteban Edward 1930- *CngDr 91, HispAmA [port], WhoAm 92*
Torres, Fernando 1924- *WhoAm 92*
Torres, Gabe *MiSFD 9*
Torres, Gerald 1952- *HispAmA*
Torres, Guido Adolfo 1938- *WhoWor 93*
Torres, Hector d1990 *BioIn 17*
Torres, Hector Norberto 1935- *WhoWor 93*
Torres, Israel 1934- *WhoSSW 93, WhoWor 93*
Torres, Jane Allen 1947- *WhoSSW 93*
Torres, Jorge Horacio 1945- *WhoWor 93*
Torres, Jose Luis 1936- *HispAmA [port]*
Torres, Liz *BioIn 17*
Torres, Luis Vaez de d1613? *Expl 93*
Torres, Manuel 1963- *WhoE 93*
Torres, Maria de los Angeles 1955- *NotHsAW 93*
Torres, Marta Gloria *DcCPCAm*
Torres, Omar 1945- *HispAmA*
Torres, Pedro Luis 1947- *WhoE 93*
Torres, Sixto E. 1944- *WhoSSW 93*
Torres, Teodoro 1891-1944 *DcMexL*
Torres, Vera Trinchero 1938- *St&PR 93*
Torresam, Janine *WhoScE 91-2*
Torres-Aybar, Francisco Gualberto 1934- *WhoWor 93*
Torres-Blasini, Gladys 20th cent.- *HispAmA*
Torres Bodet, Jaime 1902-1974 *BioIn 17, DcMexL*
Torres Darias, Nestor Vicente 1958- *WhoWor 93*
Torrese, Dante Michael 1949- *WhoE 93*
Torresella, Fanny 1856-1914 *OxDcOp*
Torres-Metzgar, Joseph V. 1933- *DcLB 122*
Torres-Nadal, Jorge Rafael 1933- *WhoSSW 93*
Torres Oliver, Juan Fremiot 1925- *WhoAm 92*
Torres Pereira, Artur 1924- *WhoScE 91-3*
Torres-Santos, Raymond 1958- *Baker 92*
Torres-Ullauri, Maria Isabel *WhoAmW 93*
Torretto, Lisa Michele *Law&B 92*
Torrey, David L. 1931- *St&PR 93*
Torrey, David Leonard 1931- *WhoAm 92*
Torrey, David Stewart *Law&B 92*
Torrey, E. Fuller *BioIn 17*
Torrey, Edwin Fuller *BioIn 17*
Torrey, John Gordon 1921- *WhoAm 92*
Torrey, Richard Frank 1926- *WhoAm 92*
Torrey, Suzanne K. *Law&B 92*
Torrey, William Arthur 1934- *WhoAm 92*
Torri, Julio 1889-1970 *DcMexL*
Torri, Pietro c. 1650-1737 *Baker 92*
Torriani-Gorini, Annamaria 1918- *WhoAm 92*
Torricella, Roland A. 1924- *St&PR 93*
Torricelli, Robert G. 1951- *CngDr 91, WhoAm 92, WhoE 93*
Torriente, Christobal 1895-c. 1938 *BiDAMSp 1989*
Torrieri, Joan Maria 1950- *WhoAmW 93*
Torrigiani, Giorgio 1933- *WhoUN 92*
Torrijos, Delia Espiritu 1938- *WhoUN 92*
Torrijos Herrera, Moises d1990 *BioIn 17*
Torrijos Herrera, Omar 1929-1981 *BioIn 17, DcCPCAm*
Torrington, Arthur Edward 1940- *WhoE 93*
Torrington, Arthur Herbert, Earl of 1647-1716 *HarEnMi*
Torrington, Fredrick Herbert 1837-1917 *Baker 92*
Torrini, Cinzia Th 1954- *MiSFD 9*
Torrito, Richard *Law&B 92*
Torronen, Kari *WhoScE 91-4*
Torruella, Juan R. 1933- *HispAmA, WhoAm 92, WhoE 93*
Torruella, Trish Moylan *NotHsAW 93*
Torshen, Jerome Harold 1929- *WhoWor 93*
Torske, Tore 1931- *WhoScE 91-4*
Torsney, Cheryl Beth 1955- *WhoSSW 93*
Torsney, Jack Russell, Jr. 1946- *WhoSSW 93*
Torson, Victor J. 1930- *St&PR 93*
Torssell, Krister 1938- *WhoScE 91-4*
Torstensson, Hakan O. 1947- *WhoScE 91-4*
Torstensson, Lennart 1603-1651 *HarEnMi*
Torsun, Imad S. *WhoScE 91-1*
Torsvan, Traven *BioIn 17*
Tort, Cesar 1929- *Baker 92*
Tort, F. *Law&B 92*
Tortel, Maxime M. 1937- *WhoUN 92*
Tortelier, Paul 1914-1990 *Baker 92, BioIn 17*
Tortelier, Yan Pascal 1947- *Baker 92*
Torti, Henry J. 1925- *St&PR 93*
Torto, Raymond Gerald 1941- *WhoE 93*
Tortolano, J. Vincent *Law&B 92*
Tortopidis, Antonios 1946- *WhoWor 93*
Tortora, William 1956- *St&PR 93*
Tortorella, Albert James 1942- *WhoAm 92*
Tortorella, Robert Anthony 1939- *WhoE 93*
Tortorelli, Ann Eichorn *WhoE 93*
Tortorelli, Louis Joseph 1959- *WhoSSW 93*
Tortorello, Laurie Anne 1965- *WhoAmW 93*
Tortorello, Nicholas John 1948- *WhoE 93*
Tortorello, Robert J. *Law&B 92*

Tortorello, Robert Joseph 1949- *St&PR 93*
Tortoric, B.K. *WhoWrEP 92*
Tortorice, Michael J. 1945- *St&PR 93*
Tortorici, Frank Charles 1963- *WhoE 93*
Tortorici, John 1942- *St&PR 93*
Tortorici, Linda Reese 1947- *St&PR 93*
Tortorici, Peter 1949- *BioIn 17*
Tortosa, Juan Miguel *WhoScE 91-3*
Tortu, Christian *BioIn 17*
Tortuero Cosialls, Francisco 1931- *WhoScE 91-3*
Toru, Matsunaga 1929- *WhoWor 93*
Torud, Yngve 1940- *WhoWor 93*
Torvela, Matias 1928- *WhoScE 91-4*
Torvik, Ansgar 1925- *WhoScE 91-4*
Torvill, Jayne *BioIn 17*
Tory, Avraham *BioIn 17*
Tory, John A. *BioIn 17*
Torza, John 1944- *St&PR 93*
Tosar Errecart, Hector 1923- *Baker 92*
Tosatti, Vieri 1920- *Baker 92*
Toscani, Carol Cullison 1940- *WhoAmW 93*
Toscani, Dominic Paul 1928- *St&PR 93*
Toscanini, Arturo 1867-1957 *Baker 92, BioIn 17, IntDcOp [port], OxDcOp*
Toscanini, Wally 1900-1991 *BioIn 17*
Toscano, Carmen 1910-1988 *DcMexL*
Toscano, Eamon F. 1946- *St&PR 93*
Toscano, Filippo-Maria 1942- *WhoE 93*
Toscano, James Vincent 1937- *WhoAm 92*
Toscano, Salvatore Mauro 1947- *WhoWor 93*
Tosch, Gilbert B. 1939- *WhoIns 93*
Tosches, Nick *NewYTBS 92 [port]*
Toschi, Paolo 1893-1974 *IntDcAn*
Toschi, Romano *WhoScE 91-3*
Tosco, Federico 1941- *WhoScE 91-3*
Toselli, Enrico 1883-1926 *Baker 92*
Tosh, Juanita Prillaman 1930- *WhoAmW 93*
Toshima, Kazunobu 1960- *WhoWor 93*
Toshima, Naoki 1939- *WhoWor 93*
Toshiyuki, Yanase 1921- *WhoWor 93*
Tosi, Giuseppe fl. 1677-1693 *OxDcOp*
Tosi, Laurence A., Jr. 1935- *St&PR 93*
Tosi, Mario 1932- *WhoScE 91-3*
Tosi, Oscar I. 1929- *WhoAm 92*
Tosi, Pier Francesco c. 1653-1732 *Baker 92*
Tosi, Piero Francesco 1653?-1732 *OxDcOp*
Tosics, Ivan 1952- *ConAu 138*
Tossberg, Frederick B. *St&PR 93*
Tosser, A.J. 1940- *WhoScE 91-2*
Tossizza, Evangelos Averoff- 1910-1990 *BioIn 17*
Tosswill, T.M. Stephen 1949- *WhoWor 93*
Tostado, Maria Elena 1940- *WhoAmW 93*
Tosteson, Daniel Charles 1925- *WhoAm 92*
Tosteson, Heather 1950- *WhoWrEP 92*
Tosti, (Francesco) Paolo 1846-1916 *Baker 92*
Tosti, Robert *St&PR 93*
Tosto, Dawn Fitzpatrick 1958- *WhoAmW 93*
Tosun, Oguz 1949- *WhoScE 91-4*
Tosunlar, Akif Zafer 1950- *WhoWor 93*
Tota, Frank Peter 1938- *WhoSSW 93*
Totaram, Sanadhya *BioIn 17*
Totaro, David J. 1947- *St&PR 93*
Totaro, James M. 1956- *St&PR 93*
Totawatte, Don Shelton 1929- *WhoWor 93*
Totenberg, Nina *BioIn 17*
Totenberg, Nina 1944- *News 92 [port], WhoE 93*
Totenberg, Roman 1911- *Baker 92, WhoAm 92*
Toter, Benjamin 1940- *St&PR 93*
Toter, Kimberly Mrowiec 1956- *WhoAmW 93, WhoEmL 93, WhoWor 93*
Toth, A.G. *WhoScE 91-1*
Toth, Anne Patten 1947- *WhoAmW 93*
Toth, Bela Lajos 1925- *WhoScE 91-4*
Toth, Christina Ann 1947- *WhoAmW 93*
Toth, Danny Andrew 1946- *WhoSSW 93*
Toth, David G. 1959- *St&PR 93*
Toth, Elizabeth Levay *WhoAmW 93*
Toth, Gary P. *Law&B 92*
Toth, Imre Gerhard 1937- *WhoE 93*
Toth, Istvan 1945- *WhoScE 91-4*
Toth, Janos 1937- *WhoScE 91-4*
Toth, Jill Sutherland 1957- *WhoAmW 93*
Toth, Jozsef 1932- *WhoScE 91-4*
Toth, Kalman 1942- *WhoScE 91-4*
Toth, Laszlo 1939- *WhoScE 91-4*
Toth, Laura Anne 1949- *WhoAmW 93*
Toth, Paolo 1941- *WhoWor 93*
Toth, Richard J. 1952- *St&PR 93*
Toth, Robert Charles 1928- *WhoAm 92*
Toth, Robert J. *Law&B 92*
Toth, Robert W. *St&PR 93*
Toth, Stephen J. 1949- *St&PR 93*
Toth, Stephen Michael 1946- *WhoSSW 93*
Toth, Susan Erickson Allen 1940- *WhoWrEP 92*
Toth, Tibor 1942- *WhoScE 91-4*
Toth, Tibor 1954- *WhoUN 92*
Toth, William J. 1936- *St&PR 93*
Tothill, Francis David 1936- *WhoWor 93*
Toth-Martinez, Bela L. 1931- *WhoScE 91-4*
Tothmeresz, Bela 1960- *WhoScE 91-4*
Toth-Zsiga, Istvan 1924- *WhoScE 91-4*
Totila c. 511-552 *OxDcByz*
Totino, Nino 1961- *WhoWor 93*
Totlis, Gust John 1939- *WhoAm 92*
Totman, Conrad 1934- *ConAu 38NR*
Totman, Conrad Davis 1934- *WhoAm 92*
Totman, Patrick Steven 1944- *St&PR 93, WhoAm 92*
Toton, Thomas M. 1961- *St&PR 93*
Totsuka, Shinya 1940- *WhoAsAP 91*
Tott, K. *WhoScE 91-4*
Totta, Paul Anthony 1930- *WhoE 93*
Totten, Albert S. *Law&B 92*
Totten, Dwight L. 1944- *St&PR 93*
Totten, George Oakley, III 1922- *WhoAm 92*
Totten, Mary Anne 1946- *WhoAmW 93*
Totten, Robert 1937- *MiSFD 9*
Totter, John Randolph 1914- *WhoAm 92*
Tottey, Robert Leslie 1945- *WhoE 93*
Tottola, Leone d1831 *OxDcOp*
Totu, Ioan d1992 *BioIn 17*
Toub, Allan Howard 1929- *WhoE 93*
Toubon, Jacques 1941- *BioIn 17*
Touborg, Margaret Earley Bowers 1941- *WhoAmW 93, WhoE 93*
Touby, Kathleen Anita 1943- *WhoSSW 93*
Touby, Michael Brian 1966- *WhoSSW 93*
Touchard, Jacques Jean Henry 1921- *WhoWor 93*
Touchet, Donovan B. 1949- *St&PR 93*
Touchett, John Louis 1933- *St&PR 93*
Touchon, Robert Charles 1939- *WhoAm 92*
Touchstone, Billie L. *WhoWrEP 92*
Touchton, John Thomas 1938- *WhoSSW 93*
Tougas, Gerald 1933- *WhoCanL 92*
Tougas, Roger C. 1936- *St&PR 93*
Touger, Jerold Steven 1945- *WhoE 93*
Touger, Judy B. 1942- *St&PR 93*
Tough, "Dave" 1908-1948 *Baker 92*
Tough, Jack C. 1949- *St&PR 93*
Touhill, Blanche Marie 1931- *WhoAm 92, WhoAmW 93*
Toujas, L.J. 1939- *WhoScE 91-2*
Toukan, Abdullah Baha-Uddin 1951- *WhoWor 93*
Toulin, Dimitry V. 1956- *WhoWor 93*
Toullec, Rene 1940- *WhoScE 91-2*
Toulmin, Peter Noyes 1927- *St&PR 93*
Toulmin, Priestley, III 1930- *WhoAm 92*
Toulmin, Stephen Edelston *BioIn 17*
Toulmin, Stephen Edelston 1922- *WhoAm 92*
Toulmin-Rothe, Ann *BioIn 17*
Toulmouche, Frederic (Michel) 1850-1909 *Baker 92*
Toulouse, Robert Bartell 1918- *WhoAm 92*
Toulouse-Lautrec, Henri de 1864-1901 *BioIn 17*
Toulson, Shirley 1924- *ConAu 38NR*
Touma, Habib Hassan 1934- *Baker 92*
Toumey, Hubert John *WhoAm 92*
Tounens, Orelie-Antoine de 1825-1878 *BioIn 17*
Toungate, Zachariah *BioIn 17*
Toupin, Arthur Venon 1921- *St&PR 93*
Toupin, Harold Ovid 1927- *WhoAm 92*
Touponce, William F. 1948- *ScF&FL 92*
Toups, John M. 1926- *St&PR 93*
Tour, Robert Louis 1918- *WhoWor 93*
Touraine, Jean-Louis Didier 1945- *WhoScE 91-2*
Touraine Cordier, Agnes Marie 1955- *WhoWor 93*
Tourand, Guy Gilbert Joseph 1929- *WhoScE 91-2*
Tourangeau, David Matthew 1939- *St&PR 93, WhoAm 92*
Tourangeau, (Marie Jeannine) Huguette 1938- *Baker 92*
Tourassis, Vassilios Dimitrios 1958- *WhoWor 93*
Toure, Ahmed Sekou 1922-1984 *DcTwHis*
Toure, Amadou Toumani *WhoWor 93*
Toure, Amadou Toumany 1943- *WhoAfr*
Toure, Amara 1945- *WhoUN 92*
Toure, Mamoudou 1928- *WhoUN 92*
Toure, Mohamed Alousseni *WhoWor 93*
Tourel, Jennie 1899-1973 *OxDcOp*
Tourel, Jennie 1900-1973 *Baker 92, IntDcOp*
Tourette, Aileen La *ScF&FL 92*
Touretz, William 1915- *St&PR 93*
Touretzky, Simeon Jacob 1929- *St&PR 93*
Tourigny, Christine 1943- *WhoAmW 93*
Tourin, Richard Harold 1922- *WhoE 93*
Tourino, Ralph Gene 1941- *WhoAm 92*
Tourjee, Eben 1834-1891 *Baker 92*
Tourlentes, Thomas Theodore 1922- *WhoAm 92*
Tournade, Linda Diane 1950- *WhoAmW 93*
Tournas, Methodios 1946- *WhoAm 92*
Tournemire, Charles (Arnould) 1870-1939 *Baker 92*
Tourneur, Jacques 1904-1977 *MiSFD 9N*
Tourneur, Maurice 1876-1961 *MiSFD 9N*
Tourney, Leonard D. 1942- *ScF&FL 92*
Tournier, Jean-Pierre 1943- *WhoWor 93*
Tournier, Michel *BioIn 17*
Tournier, Michel 1924- *WhoWor 93*
Tournillon, Nicholas Brady 1933- *St&PR 93, WhoAm 92*
Touro, Judah 1765-1854 *BioIn 17*
Tourou, Jean Fernand 1937- *WhoUN 92*
Tourrette, Jacqueline La *ScF&FL 92*
Tours, Barthelemy 1797-1864 *See* Tours, Berthold 1838-1897 *Baker 92*
Tours, Berthold 1838-1897 *Baker 92*
Tours, Frank E(dward) 1877-1963 *Baker 92*
Tour-Sarkissian, Tania *Law&B 92*
Tourte, Francois (Xavier) 1747-1835 *Baker 92*
Tourtelier, Michel Francois 1937- *WhoWor 93*
Tourtellot, Robert C. 1939- *St&PR 93*
Tourtellotte, Charles Dee 1931- *WhoAm 92*
Tourtellotte, Wallace William 1924- *WhoAm 92*
Touscany, William J. 1918- *St&PR 93*
Tous de Torres, Luz M. 1944- *WhoSSW 93*
Touse, James L. *Law&B 92*
Tousey, Richard 1908- *WhoAm 92*
Tousignant, Jacques 1948- *St&PR 93*
Touslee, Robert D. *Law&B 92*
Tousley, Rebecca Perkins 1926- *WhoAmW 93*
Toussaint, Allen 1938- *SoulM*
Toussaint, Allen Richard 1938- *WhoAm 92*
Toussaint, Cheryl *BlkAmWO*
Toussaint, Frederick John 1936- *St&PR 93*
Toussaint, Jeanne Isabella 1964- *WhoAmW 93*
Toussaint, Manuel 1890-1955 *DcMexL*
Toussaint, Pierre *BioIn 17*
Toussaint Louverture 1743?-1803 *BioIn 17*
Tousset, Jean 1930- *WhoScE 91-2*
Touster, Saul 1925- *WhoAm 92*
Tout, Charles *IntDcAn*
Toutenburg, Helge Willi Richard 1943- *WhoWor 93*
Toutz, James Otto 1932- *St&PR 93*
Touyz, Stephen William 1950- *WhoWor 93*
Touzani, Rachid 1955- *WhoWor 93*
Tovar, Carole L. 1940- *WhoAmW 93*
Tovar, Juan 1941- *DcMexL*
Tovar, Manuel 1947- *WhoWor 93*
Tovar, Pantaleon 1828-1876 *DcMexL*
Tove, Per-Arne 1924- *WhoScE 91-4*
Tove, Shirley Ruth 1925- *WhoSSW 93*
Tovey, Donald (Francis) 1875-1940 *Baker 92*
Tovey, Michael John *WhoScE 91-1*
Tovey, Mike d1893 *BioIn 17*
Tovish, Harold 1921- *WhoAm 92*
Tovua, Paul 1947- *WhoAsAP 91*
Tow, Leonard 1928- *St&PR 93, WhoAm 92*
Towar, Jeanne C. *St&PR 93*
Towarnicki, John A. 1946- *St&PR 93*
Towarnicki, Stanley J. 1940- *St&PR 93*
Towbin, Abraham Robert 1935- *WhoAm 92*
Towbin, Belmont 1910- *St&PR 93*
Towe, Harry Lancaster 1898-1991 *BioIn 17*
Towe, Kenneth McCarn 1935- *WhoE 93*
Towe, Rolf Harvy 1938- *St&PR 93*
Towell, Ronald John *Law&B 92*
Towell, S. Gilmer *Law&B 92*
Towell, S. Gilmer 1928- *St&PR 93*
Towell, Thomas 1941- *St&PR 93*
Towell, Timothy Lathrop 1934- *WhoE 93*
Towell, William Earnest 1916- *WhoAm 92*
Tower, Alton G., Jr. 1927- *WhoSSW 93*
Tower, Burton Harry 1909- *WhoWor 93*
Tower, Diana *ScF&FL 92*
Tower, Ensley Anthony 1938- *St&PR 93*
Tower, H.L. 1932- *St&PR 93*
Tower, Harker *ScF&FL 92*
Tower, Horace Linwood, III 1932- *WhoAm 92, WhoE 93*
Tower, James 1945- *St&PR 93*
Tower, Joan *BioIn 17*
Tower, Joan (Peabody) 1938- *Baker 92, WhoAm 92, WhoAmW 93*
Tower, John *BioIn 17, DcCPCAm*
Tower, John 1925-1991 *AnObit 1991*
Tower, John G. 1925-1991 *PolPar*
Tower, Roni Beth 1943- *WhoAmW 93, WhoE 93*
Tower, Russell B., Mrs. *AmWomPl*
Tower, Thomas N. 1942- *St&PR 93*
Towerly, William 1870?-1887 *BioIn 17*
Towers, Bernard Leonard 1922- *WhoAm 92*
Towers, David Anthony *WhoScE 91-1*
Towers, Dwight R. 1934- *St&PR 93*
Towers, John 1921- *St&PR 93*
Towers, John Henry 1885-1955 *BioIn 17*
Towers, Marsha Carol 1945- *WhoAmW 93*
Towers, Robert, Jr. 1923- *WhoAm 92*
Towers, T. Gordon 1919- *WhoAm 92*
Towery, Curtis Kent 1954- *WhoEmL 93, WhoSSW 93, WhoWor 93*
Towey, Anne Patricia 1945- *WhoE 93*
Towey, Edward Andrew 1945- *St&PR 93*
Towey, Jim *BioIn 17*
Towey, Marie Elizabeth 1934- *WhoWor 93*
Towfighi, Parviz S. 1933- *WhoUN 92*
Towiicz, Micky 1958- *WhoE 93*
Towill, Denis R. *WhoScE 91-1*
Towle, Dorothy *AmWomPl*
Towle, George Makepeace 1841-1893 *JrnUS*
Towle, Laird Charles 1933- *WhoAm 92, WhoE 93*
Towle, Leland Hill 1931- *WhoAm 92*
Towle, Louise Marie 1956- *WhoAmW 93*
Towler, John S. 1948- *St&PR 93*
Towler, Ralph S. *Law&B 92*
Towles, Donald Blackburn 1927- *St&PR 93, WhoAm 92*
Towles, Stokley Porter 1935- *St&PR 93, WhoAm 92*
Towles-Moore, Stacy Maria 1958- *AfrAmBi [port]*
Towlson, Ivan 1967- *ScF&FL 92*
Town, A. Hays *BioIn 17*
Town, Donald 1927- *WhoIns 93*
Town, Harold 1924-1990 *BioIn 17*
Town, Ithiel 1784-1844 *BioIn 17*
Town, Joe R. 1943- *St&PR 93*
Town, William Geoffrey 1943- *WhoWor 93*
Towne, Addie L. *AmWomPl*
Towne, Anthony 1928-1980 *ScF&FL 92*
Towne, Benjamin 1740-1793 *JrnUS*
Towne, Edward S. 1933- *St&PR 93*
Towne, Kathleen Dugan 1947- *WhoAmW 93*
Towne, Mary 1934- *ScF&FL 92*
Towne, Richard Peale 1935- *St&PR 93*
Towne, Robert *WhoAm 92*
Towne, Robert 1936- *BioIn 17, MiSFD 9*
Towne, Ross C. 1944- *WhoAm 92, WhoSSW 93*
Towne, William Bruce 1944- *St&PR 93*
Towner, George Rutherford 1933- *WhoWrEP 92*
Towner, Lawrence William d1992 *NewYTBS 92*
Towner, Naomi Whiting 1940- *WhoAmW 93*
Townes, Bobby Joe 1932- *WhoSSW 93*
Townes, Charles Hard 1915- *WhoAm 92, WhoWor 93*
Townes, Philip Leonard 1927- *WhoAm 92*
Townes, Stephen Douglas 1952- *St&PR 93*
Townesend, Frances Eliza Hodgson Burnett 1849-1924 *BioIn 17*
Townhill, Philip Arthur *WhoScE 91-1*
Townley, A. C. 1880-1959 *PolPar*
Townley, John Mark 1932- *WhoAm 92, WhoWrEP 92*
Townley, Jon *WhoAm 92*
Townley, Lawrence Earl 1933- *St&PR 93*
Townley, Linda Rose 1947- *WhoAmW 93*
Townley, Preston 1939- *WhoAm 92*
Townley, Shirley Vallacchi 1929- *WhoAmW 93*
Towns, Donald Lionel 1935- *WhoE 93*
Towns, Edolphus 1934- *BioIn 17, CngDr 91, WhoAm 92, WhoE 93*
Towns, Jeanne R. *BioIn 17*
Towns, Kathryn Louise 1923- *WhoAmW 93, WhoE 93*
Towns, Robert Forrest 1938- *WhoSSW 93*
Towns, Spec d1991 *BioIn 17*
Townsel, A. Sylviane 1943- *WhoE 93*
Townsend, Alair Ane 1942- *WhoAmW 93, WhoE 93*
Townsend, Andrea Lilly 1958- *WhoAmW 93*
Townsend, Anna Stofflet 1899- *WhoAmW 93*
Townsend, Anne *AmWomPl*
Townsend, Barbara Jean 1960- *WhoAmW 93*
Townsend, Blanch *AmWomPl*
Townsend, Bonnie Shook 1942- *WhoAmW 93*
Townsend, Bud *MiSFD 9*
Townsend, Charles Coe 1917- *WhoAm 92*

Townsend, Charles Edward 1932- *WhoAm 92*
Townsend, Cheryl Ann 1957- *WhoWrEP 92*
Townsend, Christopher Gordon *Law&B 92*
Townsend, Colin Richard 1949- *WhoWor 93*
Townsend, David D. 1927- *St&PR 93*
Townsend, David Dallam 1927- *WhoSSW 93*
Townsend, David Lee 1954- *St&PR 93*
Townsend, Douglas 1921- *Baker 92*
Townsend, Earl Cunningham, Jr. 1914- *WhoAm 92, WhoWor 93*
Townsend, Edward Allen 1942- *WhoAm 92*
Townsend, Francis E. 1867-1960 *PolPar*
Townsend, Francis Everett 1867-1960 *DcTwHis*
Townsend, Frank Marion 1914- *WhoAm 92, WhoSSW 93, WhoWor 93*
Townsend, George Alfred 1841-1914 *JrnUS*
Townsend, George P. *ScF&FL 92*
Townsend, Harold Guyon, Jr. 1924- *WhoAm 92, WhoWor 93*
Townsend, Herbert Earl 1938- *WhoE 93*
Townsend, Irene Fogleman 1932- *WhoAmW 93, WhoE 93, WhoSSW 93, WhoWor 93*
Townsend, James Courtland 1938- *WhoSSW 93*
Townsend, James Douglas 1959- *WhoEmL 93, WhoWor 93*
Townsend, James Roger 1932- *WhoAm 92*
Townsend, James Willis 1936- *WhoSSW 93*
Townsend, Jane Kaltenbach 1922- *WhoAm 92, WhoAmW 93*
Townsend, Janis Barbara Lubawsky 1946- *WhoE 93*
Townsend, Jeremy Noble 1957- *WhoE 93*
Townsend, Jerry L. 1947- *St&PR 93*
Townsend, John *ScF&FL 92*
Townsend, John Ford 1936- *WhoAm 92*
Townsend, John Marshall 1941- *WhoE 93*
Townsend, John Rowe *BioIn 17*
Townsend, John Rowe 1922- *ChlFicS, MajAI [port], ScF&FL 92*
Townsend, John William 1949- *WhoSSW 93*
Townsend, John William, Jr. 1924- *WhoAm 92*
Townsend, Johnny Tim 1961- *WhoSSW 93*
Townsend, Kathleen *BioIn 17*
Townsend, Larry 1935- *ConAu 136*
Townsend, LeRoy B. 1933- *WhoAm 92*
Townsend, Lloyd M. *St&PR 93*
Townsend, Lonny Eugene *Law&B 92*
Townsend, M. Wilbur 1912- *WhoAm 92*
Townsend, Margaret *AmWomPl*
Townsend, Margaret Elizabeth 1947- *WhoSSW 93*
Townsend, Marjorie Rhodes 1930- *WhoAm 92, WhoE 93*
Townsend, Mark Russell *Law&B 92*
Townsend, Maurice Karlen 1926- *WhoAm 92, WhoWor 93*
Townsend, Melvin C. 1927- *St&PR 93*
Townsend, Merton L. 1934- *St&PR 93*
Townsend, Merton LeRoy 1934- *WhoAm 92*
Townsend, Miles Averill 1935- *WhoAm 92, WhoSSW 93*
Townsend, P. Coleman, Jr. 1945- *St&PR 93*
Townsend, Pat *MiSFD 9*
Townsend, Paul Brorstrom 1919- *St&PR 93*
Townsend, Peter *WhoScE 91-1*
Townsend, Peter David *WhoScE 91-1*
Townsend, Philip W., Jr. 1949- *WhoE 93*
Townsend, Phinn William 1927- *St&PR 93*
Townsend, Preston Coleman 1945- *WhoAm 92*
Townsend, Ralph N. 1931- *St&PR 93*
Townsend, Rhonda Joyce 1960- *WhoAmW 93*
Townsend, Richard K 1939- *WhoIns 93*
Townsend, Richard Kennard 1939- *St&PR 93*
Townsend, Robert *BioIn 17, WhoAm 92*
Townsend, Robert 1957- *ConBlB 4 [port], MiSFD 9*
Townsend, Robert Glenn, Jr. 1929- *WhoSSW 93*
Townsend, Robert L., Jr. *Law&B 92*
Townsend, Ronald *BioIn 17*
Townsend, Ruth 1935- *WhoE 93*
Townsend, Shuron Keith *Law&B 92*
Townsend, Sue *BioIn 17*
Townsend, Sue 1946- *ConTFT 10*
Townsend, Terry 1920- *WhoAmW 93, WhoE 93, WhoWor 93*
Townsend, Teryl Archer 1938- *WhoE 93*
Townsend, Thatcher L., Jr. 1932- *St&PR 93*
Townsend, Theodore Peter 1937- *WhoAm 92*
Townsend, Thomas Gerald 1941- *WhoSSW 93*
Townsend, Thomas P., Jr. 1937- *St&PR 93*
Townsend, Thomas Perkins 1917- *WhoAm 92*
Townsend, Tom *ScF&FL 92*
Townsend, Tom David 1952- *WhoSSW 93*
Townsend, Willa A. *AmWomPl*
Townsend, Willard Saxby 1897-1957 *EncAACR*
Townshend, Alan *WhoScE 91-1*
Townshend, Aurelian c. 1583-c. 1651 *DcLB 121*
Townshend, Charles Vere Ferrers 1861-1924 *HarEnMi*
Townshend, J.R.G. *WhoScE 91-1*
Townshend, Pete(r Dennis Blandford) 1945- *Baker 92*
Townshend, Peter 1945- *WhoAm 92*
Townsley, Carla Rae 1953- *WhoAmW 93*
Townsley, John *ScF&FL 92*
Townsley, Michael K. 1945- *WhoE 93*
Townson, Hazel 1928- *ChlFicS*
Towsend, Terry 1920- *St&PR 93*
Towsley, John E. 1950- *St&PR 93*
Towson, Sheldon K., Jr. 1927- *St&PR 93*
Toxvaerd, Soren 1942- *WhoWor 93*
Toy, Arthur Dock Fon 1915- *WhoAm 92*
Toy, Atala Dorothy 1941- *WhoE 93*
Toy, Claudia L. *Law&B 92*
Toy, Herbert John, Jr. 1936- *WhoE 93*
Toy, Jane *AmWomPl*
Toy, Malcolm Delano 1934- *WhoWor 93*
Toy, Peter F. 1949- *St&PR 93*
Toy, Peter Francis 1949- *WhoIns 93*
Toy, Theresa Maureen 1947- *WhoAmW 93*
Toy, Wing N. 1926-1990 *BioIn 17*
Toya, Yoshiyuki 1927- *WhoAsAP 91*
Toyad, Leo Michael 1950- *WhoAsAP 91*
Toyama, Keisuke 1935- *WhoWor 93*
Toyama, Yuzo 1931- *Baker 92*
Toye, D.E. *Law&B 92*
Toye, (John) Francis 1883-1964 *Baker 92*
Toye, (Edward) Geoffrey 1889-1942 *Baker 92*
Toye, Richard Charles 1958- *WhoE 93*
Toye, Robert Vernon *BioIn 17*
Toye, Wendy 1917- *WhoWor 93*
Toye, William 1926- *WhoCanL 92*
Toyka, Klaus V. 1945- *WhoScE 91-3*
Toyne, Dorothy Jean 1932- *WhoAmW 93*
Toynton, Ian *MiSFD 9*
Toyoda, Eiji 1913- *WhoAm 92, WhoWor 93*
Toyoda, Shoichiro 1925- *WhoWor 93*
Toyoda, Soemu 1885-1957 *HarEnMi*
Toyoda, Tadashi 1949- *WhoWor 93*
Toyoda, Tatsuro 1929- *WhoWor 93*
Toyomura, Dennis Takeshi 1926- *WhoAm 92, WhoWor 93*
Toyotomi, Hideyoshi c. 1536-1598 *HarEnMi*
Toyozawa, Yutaka 1926- *WhoWor 93*
Toyser, Francine 1946- *WhoAmW 93*
Tozawa, Kenji 1949- *WhoWor 93*
Tozawa, Yasuhisa 1923- *WhoWor 93*
Tozawa, Yoshio 1952- *WhoWor 93*
Tozer, A.W. 1897-1963 *BioIn 17*
Tozer, Aiden Wilson 1897-1963 *BioIn 17*
Tozer, Forrest Leigh 1922- *WhoAm 92*
Tozer, George Knowlton 1926- *WhoAm 92*
Tozer, Theodore William 1957- *WhoEmL 93, WhoWor 93*
Tozer, W. James, Jr. 1941- *WhoAm 92*
Tozer, William T. 1934- *WhoIns 93*
Tozer, William Thomas 1934- *St&PR 93*
Tozzer, Alfred Marston 1877-1954 *IntDcAn*
Tozzer, Charles Phillip 1953- *WhoWor 93*
Tozzi, Giorgio 1923- *Baker 92, IntDcOp*
Tozzi, Richard R. 1941- *St&PR 93*
Traavik, Ingemar Terje 1943- *WhoWor 93*
Traba, Marta *BioIn 17*
Traba, Marta 1928-1983 *SpAmA*
Trabaci, Giovanni Maria c. 1575-1647 *Baker 92*
Trabal, Jose Francisco 1941- *WhoSSW 93*
Trabaris, Kevin Edward *Law&B 92*
Trabka, Jan Jakub 1931- *WhoScE 91-4*
Trabucco, John Edward *Law&B 92*
Trabucco, John Edward 1946- *St&PR 93*
Tracey, Christine *Law&B 92*
Tracey, Edward John 1931- *WhoAm 92*
Tracey, Jay Walter, Jr. 1925- *WhoAm 92*
Tracey, Joseph P. 1941- *St&PR 93*
Tracey, William J. *Law&B 92*
Trachevski, Lisa Ann 1956- *WhoAmW 93*
Trachimovsky, S.B. *Law&B 92*
Trachlieva-Koitcheva, Mariana 1937- *WhoScE 91-4*
Trachsel, William H. *Law&B 92*
Trachsel, William Henry 1943- *St&PR 93, WhoAm 92*
Trachta, Pamela Lochhead 1943- *WhoAmW 93*
Trachte, K.R. *Law&B 92*
Trachtenberg, Edward Norman 1927- *WhoE 93*
Trachtenberg, Lawrence 1956- *St&PR 93*
Trachtenberg, Marvin Lawrence 1939- *WhoAm 92*
Trachtenberg, Matthew J. 1953- *St&PR 93, WhoAm 92, WhoE 93, WhoEmL 93, WhoWor 93*
Trachtenberg, Robert I. 1940- *St&PR 93*
Trachtenberg, Stephen Joel 1937- *WhoAm 92, WhoE 93, WhoWor 93*
Trachter, Gary Dennis 1948- *WhoE 93*
Trachtman, Arnold Sheldon 1930- *WhoAm 92*
Trachtman, Michael Glenn 1949- *WhoE 93*
Traci, Donald Philip 1927- *WhoAm 92*
Trackman, Jay Harold 1929- *WhoE 93*
Tract, Harold M. 1926- *WhoAm 92*
Tract, Harold M. 1926-1991 *BioIn 17*
Tract, Marc Mitchell 1959- *WhoWor 93*
Tracton, Linda Jo 1956- *WhoAmW 93*
Tracy, Allen W. 1943- *St&PR 93*
Tracy, Allen Wayne 1943- *WhoAm 92*
Tracy, Aloise 1914- *WhoSSW 93*
Tracy, Ann B. 1941- *ScF&FL 92*
Tracy, Barbara Marie 1945- *WhoAmW 93, WhoSSW 93*
Tracy, Boyd Allen *Law&B 92*
Tracy, Carley Dean 1923- *WhoAmW 93*
Tracy, Daniel Keith *Law&B 92*
Tracy, Daniel LeRoy 1946- *WhoSSW 93*
Tracy, Dennie Matisoff 1932- *WhoAmW 93*
Tracy, Don 1905-1976 *ScF&FL 92*
Tracy, Edward *BioIn 17*
Tracy, Emily Anne Miller 1947- *WhoAmW 93*
Tracy, Eugene Arthur 1927- *St&PR 93, WhoAm 92*
Tracy, Harry 1874-1902 *BioIn 17*
Tracy, Harry Arnold, Jr. 1949- *WhoSSW 93*
Tracy, Helen Y. *Law&B 92*
Tracy, Hugh (Travers) 1903-1977 *Baker 92*
Tracy, James Donald 1938- *WhoAm 92, WhoWrEP 92*
Tracy, Jean C. 1930- *St&PR 93*
Tracy, Joseph Igoe 1954- *WhoE 93*
Tracy, Leland *ConAu 40NR*
Tracy, Lisa *WhoAmW 93*
Tracy, Louis 1863-1928 *ScF&FL 92*
Tracy, Michael *BioIn 17*
Tracy, Michael Cameron 1952- *WhoAm 92*
Tracy, Philip R. 1942- *St&PR 93, WhoSSW 93*
Tracy, Richard E. 1934- *WhoSSW 93*
Tracy, Robert Edward 1928- *WhoAm 92*
Tracy, Sharon Kaye 1943- *WhoAmW 93*
Tracy, Spencer 1900-1967 *BioIn 17, IntDcF 2-3 [port]*
Tracy, Stephen V(ictor) 1941- *WhoWrEP 92*
Tracy, Stephen Victor 1941- *WhoAm 92*
Tracy, Thomas Kit 1938- *WhoAm 92*
Tracy, Thomas Michael *Law&B 92*
Tracy, Thomas Miles 1936- *WhoAm 92*
Tracy, William 1917-1967 & Sawyer, Joe 1901-1982 *QDrFCA 92 [port]*
Tracy, William B. 1943- *WhoIns 93*
Tracy, William Edward, Jr. 1947- *WhoSSW 93*
Tracz, Marian 1943- *WhoScE 91-4*
Tracz, William Joseph 1950- *WhoE 93*
Traczyk, Wladyslaw Zygmunt 1928- *WhoScE 91-4, WhoWor 93*
Traczyk, Zdzislawa 1930- *WhoScE 91-4*
Trader, Herbert Frederick 1937- *WhoAm 92*
Trader, Joseph Edgar 1946- *WhoAm 92*
Tradewell, Tanya Phillips 1967- *WhoAmW 93*
Trado, Charles Diamond 1932- *St&PR 93*
Traeger, Charles H., III *Law&B 92*
Traeger, Charles Henry, III 1942- *WhoAm 92*
Traeger, Donna Jean 1956- *WhoAmW 93*
Traeger, Faye M. 1950- *St&PR 93*
Traeger, Jules E.C. 1920- *WhoScE 91-2*
Traeger, Norman Lewis 1939- *St&PR 93*
Traenkle, Jeffrey William 1934- *St&PR 93*
Traetta, Filippo 1777-1854 *Baker 92*
Traetta, Tommaso 1727-1779 *Baker 92, OxDcOp*
Trafalis, Theodoros Vassilios 1959- *WhoWor 93*
Trafficante, Santos *DcCPCAm*
Trafford, Katherine *BioIn 17*
Traficant, James A., Jr. 1941- *CngDr 91, WhoAm 92*
Traficante, Daniel Dominick 1933- *WhoWor 93*
Traficonte, John Carmen *Law&B 92*
Trafton, George 1896-1971 *BioIn 17*
Trafton, Jack R. 1948- *St&PR 93*
Tragakiss, Michael J. 1932- *St&PR 93*
Tragarz, Nancy D. 1943- *St&PR 93*
Trager, David G. 1937- *WhoAm 92*
Trager, Gary Alan 1950- *WhoWor 93*
Trager, George E. fl. 1889-1892 *BioIn 17*
Trager, Neil Jay 1939- *St&PR 93*
Trager, Philip 1935- *WhoAm 92*
Trager, Tamas 1933- *WhoScE 91-4*
Trager, William 1910- *WhoAm 92*
Trageser, Debra Anne 1961- *WhoE 93*
Trageser, Raymond Mattern, Jr. 1934- *WhoE 93*
Tragesser, Charles W. 1938- *St&PR 93*
Tragl, K.H. *WhoScE 91-4*
Trago, Jose 1856-1934 *Baker 92*
Tragos, George Euripedes 1949- *WhoWor 93*
Trahan, Claude *Law&B 92*
Trahan, Ellen Vauneil 1941- *WhoAmW 93*
Trahan, Loralice Anne 1955- *WhoSSW 93*
Trahan, Robert Andre 1954- *St&PR 93*
Trahern, Joseph Baxter, Jr. 1937- *WhoAm 92*
Traherne, Michael *ConAu 38NR*
Traicoff, George 1932- *WhoAm 92*
Traicoff, Sandra M. 1944- *WhoAm 92*
Trail, Jack R. 1931- *St&PR 93*
Trail, Margaret Ann 1941- *WhoAmW 93*
Traill, Catharine Parr Strickland 1802-1899 *BioIn 17*
Trailor, Colette B. 1940- *WhoAmW 93*
Trails, Mayette *WhoWrEP 92*
Train, David 1935- *St&PR 93*
Train, Harry Depue, II 1927- *WhoAm 92*
Train, John 1928- *WhoAm 92, WhoWrEP 92*
Train, Russell Errol 1920- *WhoAm 92, WhoWor 93*
Traina, Albert Salvatore 1927- *WhoAm 92*
Traina, Paul Joseph 1934- *WhoSSW 93*
Traina, Richard Paul 1937- *WhoAm 92*
Trainer, Ellen Mccart 1922- *St&PR 93*
Trainer, John Patrick 1943- *WhoAsAP 91*
Trainer, Lorraine *BioIn 17*
Trainer, Orvel Leroy 1925- *WhoWrEP 92*
Trainer, Raymond Edward 1947- *St&PR 93*
Trainer, William Francis 1939- *St&PR 93*
Trainor, Bernard Edmund 1928- *WhoAm 92, WhoE 93*
Trainor, Bernard Michael 1954- *St&PR 93*
Trainor, Charles J. 1937- *St&PR 93*
Trainor, Howard Edgar 1943- *St&PR 93*
Trainor, James J. *Law&B 92*
Trainor, Jean Ann, Sr. 1938- *WhoE 93*
Trainor, Joseph *ScF&FL 92*
Trainor, Lillian 1936- *WhoAmW 93, WhoE 93*
Trainor, Patricia H. *Law&B 92*
Trainor, Richard *ConAu 40NR*
Trainor, Richard H. *WhoScE 91-1*
Trainor, Robert James *Law&B 92*
Trainor, Sandy *ScF&FL 92*
Trainor, Starr *ScF&FL 92*
Traisman, Howard Sevin 1923- *WhoAm 92*
Traisman, Kenneth Neil 1958- *WhoEmL 93*
Traister, Robert Edwin 1937- *WhoAm 92*
Trajan 53-117 *HarEnMi*
Trajan, Emperor of Rome 53-117 *BioIn 17*
Trajtenberg, Mario 1936- *WhoUN 92*
Trakas, Deno 1952- *WhoWrEP 92*
Trakhtman, Vladimir Yurievich 1932- *WhoWor 93*
Trakofler, Carl J. 1936- *St&PR 93*
Trakseli, John Joseph 1945- *St&PR 93*
Tralins, Bob *ConAu 40NR*
Tralins, Robert 1926- *ScF&FL 92*
Tralins, Robert S. *ConAu 40NR*
Tralins, S(andor) Robert 1926- *ConAu 40NR*
Trallo, Ralph A. 1945- *St&PR 93*
Tramaglini, Salvatore L., Jr. 1941- *St&PR 93*
Tramaloni, Dennis P. *Law&B 92*
Tramantano, Robert S. *Law&B 92*
Trambitsky, Victor (Nikolaievich) 1895-1970 *Baker 92*
Trambley, Estela Portillo 1936- *HispAmA*
Trambley, Estela Potillo *NotHsAW 93*
Trambouze, Pierre J. 1930- *WhoScE 91-2*
Tramburg, Robert Steven 1947- *St&PR 93*
Tramel, Gregory Lee 1960- *WhoSSW 93*
Tramel, Thomas Milton 1959- *WhoSSW 93*
Tramiel, Sam 1950- *St&PR 93, WhoAm 92*
Trammell, Alan Stuart 1958- *BiDAMSp 1989, WhoAm 92*
Trammell, Daniel Boyd 1960- *WhoSSW 93*
Trammell, Dennis C. 1940- *St&PR 93*
Trammell, Dennis L. 1947- *St&PR 93*
Trammell, Dennis LaFrance *Law&B 92*

Trammell, Herbert Eugene 1927- *WhoAm 92*
Trammell, Martha J. *Law&B 92*
Trammell, Mary Jacqueline Watson 1952- *WhoAmW 93*
Trammell, Nevin Compton, Jr. 1937- *WhoSSW 93*
Trammell, Terry *BioIn 17*
Trammer, Monte Irvin 1951- *WhoE 93*
Tramont, Jean-Claude 1934- *MiSFD 9*
Tramontana, C.J. *ScF&FL 92*
Tramontano, Anthony Richard 1933- *St&PR 93*
Trampler, Walter 1915- *Baker 92*
Tramposch, William Joseph 1948- *WhoAm 92*
Tramuto, James Arnold 1948- *St&PR 93, WhoAm 92*
Tran, Alan B. *Law&B 92*
Tran, Alan R., Jr. 1945- *St&PR 93*
Tran, Dinh-Khiem 1937- *WhoScE 91-2*
Tran, Dung Phuoc 1949- *WhoE 93*
Tran, Henry Bang Q. 1952- *WhoEmL 93, WhoSSW 93*
Tran, Jean-Marie 1962- *WhoWor 93*
Tran, John Kim-Son Tan 1945- *WhoE 93, WhoWor 93*
Tran, Long Trieu 1956- *WhoEmL 93, WhoSSW 93, WhoWor 93*
Tran, Quang Hai 1944- *WhoWor 93*
Tran, Qui-Phiet 1937- *WhoSSW 93*
Tran, Tim 1950- *St&PR 93*
Tran, Toan Vu 1956- *WhoSSW 93*
Tran, Van Khe 1921- *Baker 92*
Tran, Van Tho 1942- *WhoWor 93*
Tranbarger, Ossie Elmo 1914- *WhoWrEP 92*
Tranchell, Peter (Andrew) 1922- *Baker 92*
Tranchitella, Vincent Edward 1938- *WhoE 93*
Trancik, Dusan 1946- *DrEEuF*
Tran-Cong, Ton 1953- *WhoWor 93*
Trandem, Donald J. *St&PR 93*
Tranelli, Kathleen Frensky *Law&B 92*
Tranfaglia, Christina Marie 1962- *WhoAmW 93*
Tranfield, David Ronald *WhoScE 91-1*
Tranggono, Retno Iswari 1939- *WhoWor 93*
Trani, Eugene Paul 1939- *WhoAm 92, WhoSSW 93*
Tranin, Amy Strauss 1959- *WhoAmW 93*
Trank, Burgess N., Jr. *Law&B 92*
Trank, Douglas Monty 1944- *WhoAm 92*
Trankmann, Gert Joachim 1935- *WhoScE 91-3*
Tranopolsky, Rafael 1922- *WhoWrEP 92*
Tranquada, Robert Ernest 1930- *WhoAm 92*
Tranquard, Aymond 1932- *WhoScE 91-2*
Tranquillini, Walter *WhoScE 91-4*
Transou, Lynda Lew 1949- *WhoAmW 93*
Transtromer, Tomas 1931- *BioIn 17, ConAu 17AS [port]*
Trant, Gerald Ion 1928- *WhoUN 92*
Trant, Thomas K. 1951- *St&PR 93*
Tranthim-Fryer, David John 1956- *WhoWor 93*
Tran-Viet, Tu 1949- *WhoWor 93*
Traore, Alioune 1947- *WhoUN 92*
Traore, Moussa *BioIn 17*
Traore Moussa 1936- *WhoAfr*
Trap, M. *WhoWrEP 92*
Trapane, Ruth 1945- *WhoAmW 93*
Trapasso, Patricia M. 1932- *St&PR 93*
Trapesnikov, Nikolai Nikolaevitch 1928- *WhoWor 93*
Trapido, Harold 1916-1991 *BioIn 17*
Trapnell, Britt *WhoIns 93*
Trapnell, Joan P. 1946- *WhoIns 93*
Trapold, Milton Alvin 1936- *WhoAm 92*
Trapolin, Frank Winter 1913- *WhoSSW 93, WhoWor 93*
Trapolino, Louis N. *St&PR 93*
Trapp, Edward Philip 1923- *WhoSSW 93*
Trapp, Ernst Joachim 1935- *WhoWor 93*
Trapp, Frank Anderson 1922- *WhoAm 92*
Trapp, George Joseph 1947- *St&PR 93*
Trapp, Gerald Bernard 1932- *WhoAm 92*
Trapp, Larry *BioIn 17*
Trapp, Marvin D. 1929- *St&PR 93*
Trapp, (Hermann Emil Alfred) Max 1887-1971 *Baker 92*
Trapp, Peter Jarl Rudolf 1945- *WhoE 93*
Trapp, Peter Paul 1944- *St&PR 93*
Trappe, James Martin 1931- *WhoAm 92*
Trapp-Fleenor, Kathryn Anne 1957- *WhoAmW 93*
Trappl, Robert 1939- *WhoScE 91-4*
Trasatti, Sergio 1937- *WhoScE 91-3*
Trasher, Virginia Snow 1936- *WhoE 93*
Trask, Betty M. 1928- *WhoE 93, WhoWor 93*
Trask, Betty May 1928- *WhoWrEP 92*
Trask, Blair Dwayne 1933- *St&PR 93*
Trask, George W., Jr. 1947- *St&PR 93*
Trask, James L. 1932- *WhoIns 93*
Trask, Jonathan *ScF&FL 92*
Trask, Kate Nichols 1853-1922 *AmWomPl*
Trask, Robert B. 1946- *St&PR 93*
Traskos, Richard M. *St&PR 93*
Trason, Ann *BioIn 17*
Trastotenojo, Moeljono S. 1934- *WhoWor 93*
Traub, Bennett *Law&B 92*
Traub, Joseph Frederick 1932- *WhoAm 92*
Traub, Judy 1940- *WhoAmW 93*
Traub, Marvin S. *BioIn 17*
Traub, Marvin S. 1925- *St&PR 93*
Traub, Peter 1935- *WhoScE 91-3*
Traub, Richard Kenneth 1950- *WhoAm 92, WhoE 93, WhoWor 93*
Traub, Robert S. 1916- *WhoE 93*
Traub, Sophie C. *Law&B 92*
Traube, Ruy *ConAu 40NR*
Traubee, Jacques d1990 *BioIn 17*
Traubel, Helen 1899-1972 *IntDcOp, OxDcOp*
Traubel, Helen (Francesca) 1899-1972 *Baker 92*
Traubenheim, Jens *WhoScE 91-3*
Trauberg, Leonid 1902-1990 *DrEEuF*
Trauboth, Heinz H. 1931- *WhoScE 91-3*
Traudt, Mary B. 1930- *WhoAmW 93*
Traue, Harald C. 1950- *WhoScE 91-3*
Trauger, Donald Byron 1920- *WhoAm 92*
Traughber, Sam Hendley 1935- *WhoSSW 93*
Traugott, Elizabeth Closs 1939- *WhoAm 92, WhoWrEP 92*
Traugott, Rohner 1906- *Baker 92*
Traum, Jerome S. 1935- *WhoAm 92*
Traum, Richard Scot 1940- *WhoE 93*
Traunmuller, Hartmut Roland 1944- *WhoWor 93*
Traurig, Robert Henry 1925- *WhoAm 92*
Trausch, Arthur Nicholas, III *Law&B 92*
Trausch, Paul Joseph 1941- *WhoAm 92*
Trauscht, Donald Charles 1933- *St&PR 93*
Traut, Donald L. *Law&B 92*
Traut, Donald L., Sr. 1932- *WhoIns 93*
Traut, Donald Louis 1932- *St&PR 93*
Traut, Horst 1932- *WhoScE 91-3*
Traut, John D. 1926- *St&PR 93*
Trauth, Eileen Moore 1951- *WhoAmW 93*
Trautlein, Donald Henry 1926- *St&PR 93*
Trautlein, Eugene Charles *Law&B 92*
Trautman, Andrzej M. 1933- *WhoScE 91-4*
Trautman, Donald W. 1936- *WhoAm 92*
Trautman, Stephen M. *Law&B 92*
Trautmann, Dean C. 1950- *St&PR 93*
Trautmann, Les d1992 *NewYTBS 92 [port]*
Trautmann, Les 1918-1992 *BioIn 17*
Trautmann, Norbert Gunter 1939- *WhoWor 93*
Trautmann, Thomas Roger 1940- *WhoAm 92*
Trautner, Thomas A. *WhoScE 91-3*
Trautwein, Alfred Xaver 1940- *WhoScE 91-3*
Trautwein, Betty Boldwin 1947- *St&PR 93*
Trautwein, Friedrich (Adolf) 1888-1956 *Baker 92*
Trautwein, George William 1927- *WhoAm 92*
Trautwein, James William 1935- *St&PR 93*
Trautz, Otto Rudolf 1899-1990 *BioIn 17*
Travaglini, A.F. 1923- *St&PR 93*
Travaille, Hubert Duane *Law&B 92*
Travaille, Hubert Duane 1939- *St&PR 93*
Travanti, Daniel John *WhoAm 92*
Travassos, Luiz Rodolpho R.G. 1938- *WhoWor 93*
Travassos Dias, J.A. *WhoScE 91-3*
Travelstead, Chester Coleman 1911- *WhoAm 92*
Traven, B. *BioIn 17*
Traven, B. 1882-1969 *ScF&FL 92*
Traven, B. 1890-1969 *DcMexL*
Traver, Harry J. 1947- *St&PR 93*
Traver, Mary I. *Law&B 92*
Traver, Noel Allen 1959- *WhoWor 93*
Traver, Phyllis Anne 1952- *WhoAmW 93*
Traver, Robert 1903-1991 *BioIn 17*
Traver, Robert William, Sr. 1930- *WhoE 93, WhoWor 93*
Travers, Bernard F., III *Law&B 92*
Travers, George F. 1928- *St&PR 93*
Travers, John c. 1703-1758 *Baker 92*
Travers, Maureen Kelliher 1954- *St&PR 93*
Travers, Oliver Slater, Jr. 1926- *St&PR 93*
Travers, P.L. 1906- *ScF&FL 92*
Travers, P(amela) L(yndon) 1899- *MajAI [port]*
Travers, Paul J(oseph) 1951- *ConAu 138*
Travers, Peter *WhoScE 91-1*
Travers, Scott Andrew 1961- *WhoE 93, WhoEmL 93, WhoWor 93*
Travers, Stephen W. *Law&B 92*
Traversa, Halyna M. *Law&B 92*
Traverse, Alfred 1925- *WhoAm 92, WhoE 93*
Travierso, Tina Marie 1966- *WhoAmW 93*
Travilla, Bill d1990 *BioIn 17*
Travillian-Vonesh, Ami Lynn 1961- *WhoSSW 93*
Travino, Jesus Salvador *MiSFD 9*
Travis, Andrew D. *Law&B 92*
Travis, Andrew D. 1944- *St&PR 93*
Travis, Andrew David 1944- *WhoAm 92*
Travis, Arlene Carey 1935- *WhoAmW 93*
Travis, Artie Lee 1956- *WhoSSW 93*
Travis, Buck *DcAmChF 1960*
Travis, Cecil 1913- *BioIn 17*
Travis, Cecil Howell 1913- *BiDAMSp 1989*
Travis, Dempsey Jerome 1920- *WhoAm 92*
Travis, Dianne *Law&B 92*
Travis, Edward T. 1936- *St&PR 93*
Travis, Eugene C. 1920- *St&PR 93*
Travis, Harold 1929- *St&PR 93*
Travis, Jack Beryl 1944- *St&PR 93*
Travis, James Leslie 1923- *WhoSSW 93*
Travis, Jon Tyler 1958- *WhoSSW 93*
Travis, Lawrence Allan 1942- *WhoWor 93*
Travis, Mark W. *MiSFD 9*
Travis, Marlene O. *WhoWor 93*
Travis, Martin Bice 1917- *WhoAm 92*
Travis, Merle (Robert) 1917-1983 *Baker 92*
Travis, Nancy *BioIn 17*
Travis, Nancy 1936- *WhoAmW 93, WhoSSW 93*
Travis, R(osemarie) L. *WhoWrEP 92*
Travis, Randy *BioIn 17*
Travis, Randy 1959- *Baker 92, ConMus 9 [port]*
Travis, Randy Bruce 1959- *WhoAm 92*
Travis, Roy (Elihu) 1922- *Baker 92*
Travis, Susan Kathryn 1940- *WhoAmW 93*
Travis, T.J. 1944- *St&PR 93*
Travis, Vance Kenneth 1926- *WhoAm 92*
Travis, W. Vance 1947- *WhoSSW 93*
Travis, William Barret 1809-1836 *HarEnMi*
Travis Copess, Joyce Marie 1947- *WhoAmW 93*
Travisono, Anthony P. *BioIn 17*
Traviss, Donald Parthen 1944- *St&PR 93*
Travitzky, Virginia Anne 1958- *WhoAmW 93*
Travolta, John *BioIn 17*
Travolta, John 1954- *HolBB [port], IntDcF 2-3 [port], WhoAm 92*
Travous, Louise *AmWomPl*
Traw, William L. 1937- *St&PR 93*
Trawick, Jack Durward 1932- *St&PR 93*
Trawick, LaVergne 1947- *WhoE 93*
Trawick, Leonard M. 1933- *ConAu 137*
Trawinski, David Lee 1959- *WhoE 93*
Traxel, Josef 1916-1975 *Baker 92*
Traxler, Bob 1931- *CngDr 91, WhoAm 92*
Traxler, Eva Maria 1955- *WhoAmW 93*
Traxler, Vieri 1928- *WhoUN 92*
Traylor, Angelika 1942- *WhoSSW 93*
Traylor, Barbara Carlton 1942- *WhoSSW 93*
Traylor, Bill 1854-1947 *BioIn 17*
Traylor, Claire Guthrie 1931- *WhoAmW 93*
Traylor, Joan Sadler *WhoSSW 93*
Traylor, John L. *Law&B 92*
Traylor, Mary Rose 1940- *WhoAmW 93*
Traylor, Orba Forest 1910- *WhoAm 92*
Traylor, Richard Kent 1946- *WhoSSW 93*
Traylor, Wendell Douglas 1959- *WhoSSW 93*
Traylor, William Robert 1921- *WhoWor 93*
Traynelis-Yurek, Elaine Ann 1933- *WhoSSW 93*
Traynham, James Gibson 1925- *WhoAm 92*
Traynham, Wayne O. *Law&B 92*
Traynor, Barbara Mary 1935- *WhoAmW 93*
Traynor, Carl M. *Law&B 92*
Traynor, Gerald Stevens *St&PR 93*
Traynor, Harry Sheehy 1911- *WhoAm 92*
Traynor, J. Michael 1934- *WhoAm 92*
Traynor, James Edmund 1949- *St&PR 93*
Traynor, Michael H. 1940- *St&PR 93*
Traynor, Stephanie M. Wozasek *Law&B 92*
Traynor, Steven P. *Law&B 92*
Traywick, Joseph B. 1945- *St&PR 93*
Trbovich, Mike 1921- *St&PR 93*
Trbovich, Robert 1937- *St&PR 93*
Trbovich, Tom *MiSFD 9*
Trdat the Great *OxDcByz*
Treacy, James Joseph, Jr. 1958- *WhoE 93*
Treacy, Philip *BioIn 17*
Treacy, Richard F., Jr. *Law&B 92*
Treacy, Richard F., Jr. 1945- *St&PR 93*
Treacy, Sandra Joanne Pratt 1934- *WhoAmW 93, WhoWor 93*
Treadgold, Donald Warren 1922- *WhoAm 92*
Treado, Paul A. *BioIn 17*
Treadway, Clifford John 1948- *WhoSSW 93*
Treadway, Douglas Morse 1942- *WhoAm 92*
Treadway, Elizabeth 1946- *WhoAmW 93*
Treadway, James Curran *Law&B 92*
Treadway, James Curran 1943- *WhoAm 92*
Treadway, Stephen J. 1947- *St&PR 93*
Treadway, Susan Marie 1951- *WhoSSW 93, WhoWor 93*
Treadwell, Barry Lincoln 1942- *St&PR 93*
Treadwell, Carlene Rollins 1955- *WhoE 93*
Treadwell, George Edward, Jr. 1941- *WhoSSW 93*
Treadwell, Hugh Wilson 1921- *WhoAm 92*
Treadwell, Kenneth Myron 1923- *WhoE 93*
Treadwell, May L. *AmWomPl*
Treadwell, Sophie 1891?-1970 *AmWomPl*
Treanor, Charles Edward 1924- *WhoAm 92*
Treanor, Harold J. 1900-1991 *BioIn 17*
Treanor, Robert V. 1948- *St&PR 93*
Treas, Judith 1947- *WhoAm 92*
Trease, Geoffrey 1909- *BioIn 17*
Trease, (Robert) Geoffrey 1909- *ConAu 38NR, MajAI [port]*
Treash, Leonard W., Jr. *Law&B 92*
Treasure, John Albert Penberthy 1924- *WhoAm 92*
Treat, Asher Eugene 1907- *WhoE 93*
Treat, James J. 1942- *WhoSSW 93*
Treat, John Elting 1946- *WhoAm 92*
Treat, Lawrence 1903- *WhoAm 92, WhoWrEP 92*
Treat, Sharon Anglin 1956- *WhoAmW 93*
Trebat, Alan G. *Law&B 92*
Trebek, Alex *BioIn 17*
Trebek, Alex 1940- *WhoAm 92*
Trebelli, Zelia 1838-1892 *Baker 92, OxDcOp*
Treber, Gayle Renne 1949- *WhoAmW 93*
Trebilcock, Charles Edward 1926- *St&PR 93*
Trebilcock, Dorothy Warner 1926- *WhoWrEP 92*
Trebilcott, James Joseph 1917- *WhoAm 92*
Trebino, Stephen G. 1953- *St&PR 93*
Trebitsch-Lincoln, Ignatius Timothy 1879-1943 *BioIn 17*
Treble, John G. *WhoScE 91-1*
Trebor, Robert *ScF&FL 92*
Trebour, Burton Charles 1942- *St&PR 93*
Trebst, Achim 1929- *WhoScE 91-3*
Trecartin, James A. *Law&B 92*
Trecat, Jacques Georges 1940- *WhoScE 91-2*
Treccagnoli, Philip David 1958- *WhoE 93*
Trecek, Sallie L. 1944- *WhoSSW 93*
Trechak, Richard B. 1945- *St&PR 93*
Treciokas, Charles John, Jr. *Law&B 92*
Treckelo, Richard M. 1926- *WhoAm 92*
Trecker, Janice Law 1941- *WhoWrEP 92*
Trecker, Stan Matthew 1944- *WhoE 93*
Treco-Jones, Sheryl Lynn 1948- *WhoAmW 93*
Tredell, Nicolas *ScF&FL 92*
Tredennick, Wm. T. 1906- *St&PR 93*
Tredinnick, Frank A., Jr. 1921- *St&PR 93*
Tredway, John Thomas 1935- *WhoAm 92*
Tredwen, Ray 1923-1990 *BioIn 17*
Tree, David L. *WhoAm 92*
Tree, Dorothy 1909-1992 *BioIn 17*
Tree, Marietta *BioIn 17*
Tree, Marietta 1917-1991 *AnObit 1991*
Tree, Michael 1934- *WhoAm 92*
Treece, Corina Renee 1963- *WhoSSW 93*
Treece, Henry 1912-1966 *MajAI [port]*
Treece, James Lyle 1925- *WhoWor 93*
Treece, Patricia 1938- *WhoWrEP 92*
Treece, Roger A. *Law&B 92*
Treen, David Conner 1928- *WhoSSW 93*
Trees, George S. 1916- *St&PR 93*
Trees, John Simmons 1932- *WhoAm 92*
Trefan, Laszlo 1937- *WhoScE 91-4*
Trefethen, Florence 1921- *WhoWrEP 92*
Treffert, Darold Allen 1933- *WhoAm 92*
Treffinger, James William *Law&B 92*
Treffinger, William M. 1946- *St&PR 93*
Trefftzs, Kenneth Lewis 1911- *St&PR 93*
Trefil, James S. 1938- *WhoAm 92*
Trefousse, Hans Louis 1921- *WhoE 93*
Trefts, Albert S. 1929- *WhoWor 93*
Trefts, Byron Lee 1938- *WhoE 93*
Trefusis, Violet Keppel 1894-1972 *BioIn 17*
Trefz, Harlin J. 1943- *St&PR 93*
Trefz, Linda Marie 1959- *WhoE 93*
Trefz, Richard V. 1942- *St&PR 93*
Tregebov, Rhea 1953- *WhoCanL 92*
Tregenza, Norman Hughson 1937- *WhoE 93*

Treger, Charles 1935- *Baker 92*
Tregian, Francis 1574-1619 *Baker 92*
Tregilgas, Alan Jeffrey 1949- *St&PR 93*
Treglown, Jeremy Dickinson 1946- *WhoWor 93*
Tregoe, Benjamin Bainbridge 1927- *WhoAm 92*
Tregre, Louis Severin d1991 *BioIn 17*
Tregubovic, Viktor 1935- *DrEEuF*
Treguer, Paul J. 1942- *WhoScE 91-2*
Tregurtha, Paul Richard 1935- *St&PR 93, WhoAm 92*
Treharne, Bryceson 1879-1948 *Baker 92*
Treharne, George David 1943- *WhoSSW 93*
Treharne, K.J. *WhoScE 91-1*
Treharne, Kenneth John 1939-1989 *BioIn 17*
Trehel, Michel 1940- *WhoScE 91-2*
Trehen, Paul 1936- *WhoScE 91-2*
Treher, Elizabeth Noah 1947- *WhoE 93*
Treherne, J.E. *BioIn 17, WhoScE 91-1*
Treherne, John Edwin *BioIn 17*
Treiber, Hubert 1942- *WhoWor 93*
Treiber, Robert W. d1990 *BioIn 17*
Treibick, Richard 1935- *St&PR 93*
Treible, Kirk 1941- *WhoSSW 93*
Treichel, Jeanie Nieri 1931- *WhoAmW 93*
Treichelt, Timothy N. *Law&B 92*
Treichler, Francis Norman 1928- *WhoE 93*
Treichler, Rachel 1951- *WhoE 93*
Treichler, Ray 1907- *WhoE 93*
Treiger, Irwin Louis 1934- *WhoAm 92*
Treigle, Norman 1927-1975 *Baker 92, IntDcOp, OxDcOp*
Treilhou, John Paul 1942- *WhoScE 91-2*
Treiman, Sam Bard 1925- *WhoAm 92, WhoE 93*
Treimer, Wilbert M. 1911- *St&PR 93*
Treinavicz, Kathryn Mary 1957- *WhoEmL 93*
Treinen, David C. 1939- *St&PR 93*
Treinen, Sylvester William 1917- *WhoAm 92*
Treinen, Thomas F. *St&PR 93*
Treinish, Nathan J. *Law&B 92*
Treinkman, Leonard 1928- *St&PR 93*
Treint, Albert 1889-1971 *BioIn 17*
Treirat, Eduard 1912- *WhoE 93*
Treisman, Anne *BioIn 17*
Treisner, George Henry, Jr. 1936- *WhoE 93*
Treister, George Marvin 1923- *WhoAm 92*
Treister, Kenneth 1930- *WhoAm 92*
Treistman, Steven N. 1945- *WhoE 93*
Treit, Sandor 1921- *WhoScE 91-4*
Treitel, David Henry 1954- *St&PR 93*
Treitel, G(uenter) H(einz) 1928- *ConAu 139*
Treitel, Jonathan 1959- *ConLC 70 [port]*
Treitel, Rudolf 1938- *St&PR 93*
Treitler, Leo 1931- *Baker 92*
Trejbal, Zdenek 1938- *WhoScE 91-4*
Trejo, Blanca Lydia 1906-1970 *DcMexL*
Trejo, Ernesto 1950-1991 *DcLB 122 [port]*
Trela, James Edward 1943- *WhoE 93*
Treland, Linda R. *Law&B 92*
Trelawny, Edward John 1792-1881 *BioIn 17, DcLB 116 [port]*
Trelease, Allen William 1928- *WhoAm 92*
Treleaven, John Waterloo 1922- *WhoWrEP 92*
Treleaven, P.C. *WhoScE 91-1*
Treleaven, Phillips Albert 1928- *WhoAm 92*
Trelford, Donald Gilchrist 1937- *WhoWor 93*
Trella, Christine Joy 1945- *WhoAmW 93, WhoSSW 93*
Trella, M. *WhoScE 91-2*
Trelstad, Robert Laurence 1940- *WhoE 93*
Tremaglio, Angelo F. 1926- *St&PR 93*
Tremaglio, Caesar D. 1929- *St&PR 93*
Tremaglio, Neil L. 1924- *St&PR 93*
Tremain, Edward W. H. 1935- *St&PR 93*
Tremain, Kenneth D. *Law&B 92*
Tremaine, B.G., Jr. 1922- *St&PR 93*
Tremaine, Burton G. d1991 *BioIn 17*
Tremaine, Kit 1907- *BioIn 17, ConAu 139*
Tremaine, Scott Duncan 1950- *WhoAm 92*
Tremallo, Mark Van Bael *Law&B 92*
Tremayne, Bertram William, Jr. 1914- *WhoAm 92*
Tremayne, Peter 1943- *ScF&FL 92*
Tremayne, William H. 1935- *St&PR 93*
Trembaczowski, Jan 1920- *WhoScE 91-4*
Trembath, Peter H. *Law&B 92*
Trembath, Peter H. 1952- *St&PR 93*
Trembecki, Stanislaw August 1722-1812 *PolBiDi*
Tremblay, Andre Gabriel 1937- *WhoAm 92*
Tremblay, Bill 1940- *WhoWrEP 92*
Tremblay, Charles N. 1930- *St&PR 93*
Tremblay, Ermenegildo 1932- *WhoScE 91-3*
Tremblay, Francois-Joseph le Clerc du 1577-1638 *BioIn 17*
Tremblay, George (Amedee) 1911-1982 *Baker 92*
Tremblay, Gilles 1932- *Baker 92*
Tremblay, Julie *Law&B 92*
Tremblay, Marc Adelard 1922- *WhoAm 92*
Tremblay, Marcel J. 1941- *St&PR 93*
Tremblay, Michel 1942- *BioIn 17, WhoCanL 92*
Tremblay, Renald 1943- *WhoCanL 92*
Tremblay, Rodrigue 1939- *WhoAm 92*
Tremblay, William Andrew 1940- *WhoWrEP 92*
Tremble, Edward C. 1913- *St&PR 93*
Tremble, Rita Mae 1916- *St&PR 93*
Trembley, Helen Rebecca 1962- *WhoE 93*
Trembly, Bruce Eldon 1963- *WhoSSW 93*
Trembly, Dennis Michael 1947- *WhoAm 92*
Trembly, Randall M. 1946- *WhoAm 92*
Tremeau, Marcel 1936- *WhoUN 92*
Tremeaud, Jean-Francois 1943- *WhoUN 92*
Tremel, Gerard Thomas 1956- *WhoE 93*
Tremier, Wilbert M. 1911- *WhoIns 93*
Tremillon, Bernard L. 1930- *WhoScE 91-2*
Tremiti, Joseph F. *Law&B 92*
Treml, Raymond Francis 1940- *St&PR 93*
Treml, Vladimir Guy 1929- *WhoAm 92*
Tremmel, Robert Arnold 1948- *WhoWrEP 92*
Tremonte Spigonardo, Ada Mary 1959- *WhoAmW 93*
Tremoulis, James L. *St&PR 93*
Tremper, Kimberly Ann 1963- *WhoAmW 93*
Trempus, Thomas R. *Law&B 92*
Trenary, Jill *BioIn 17*
Trenberth, Kevin Edward 1944- *WhoAm 92*
Trench, William Frederick 1931- *WhoAm 92, WhoSSW 93*
Trenchard, Hugh Montague 1873-1956 *DcTwHis, HarEnMi*
Trenchard-Smith, Brian 1946- *MiSFD 9*
Trenda, Regis J. *Law&B 92*
Trendelenburg, Ullrich Georg 1922- *WhoScE 91-3*
Trendov, Oscar 1920- *St&PR 93*
Trenery, Gladys Gordon *ScF&FL 92*
Trenev, Georgy Simeonov 1946- *WhoWor 93*
Trenk, Lawrence Ira 1954- *WhoE 93*
Trenker, Luis 1893-1990 *BioIn 17*
Trenkler, Gotz *WhoScE 91-3*
Trenkmann, Richard S. 1942- *St&PR 93*
Trennepohl, Gary Lee 1946- *WhoAm 92*
Trenner, Nelson Richards, Jr. 1948- *WhoE 93*
Trenner, Robert Allen, Jr. 1943- *St&PR 93*
Trent, Barbara *MiSFD 9*
Trent, Bertram James 1918- *WhoE 93*
Trent, Darrell M. 1938- *St&PR 93, WhoAm 92*
Trent, James Alfred 1946- *WhoE 93*
Trent, John d1983 *MiSFD 9N*
Trent, John Thomas, Jr. 1954- *WhoSSW 93*
Trent, Richard Lee 1937- *WhoE 93*
Trent, Richard O. 1920- *WhoIns 93*
Trent, Robert Harold 1933- *WhoAm 92, WhoSSW 93*
Trent, Rose Marie 1943- *WhoAmW 93*
Trent, Sarah 1902-1991 *BioIn 17*
Trent, William B., Jr. *Law&B 92*
Trent, William Bret, Jr. 1947- *St&PR 93*
Trent, William Johnson, Jr. 1910- *EncAACR*
Trentacosta, John F. 1952- *St&PR 93*
Trentalance, Albert Enrique 1935- *WhoSSW 93*
Trento, Vittorio 1761-1833 *Baker 92*
Trepal, George *BioIn 17*
Trepanier, Richard J. *Law&B 92*
Trepanier, Robert *BioIn 17*
Trepanowski, Judith Mary 1948- *WhoAmW 93*
Trepel, Jeffrey Mark *Law&B 92*
Trepka, William James 1933- *WhoSSW 93*
Trepo, Christian G. 1943- *WhoScE 91-2*
Trepov, Aleksandr Fyodorovich 1862-1928 *BioIn 17*
Trepp, Gian 1947- *WhoWor 93*
Trepp, L. Ronald 1938- *St&PR 93*
Trepp, Leo 1913- *ConAu 40NR*
Trepp, Robert Martin *Law&B 92*
Trepper, Leyb 1904-1981 *PolBiDi*
Treppler, Irene Esther 1926- *WhoAmW 93*
Treppunti, Philip J. 1930- *St&PR 93*
Treptow, Gunther 1907-1981 *OxDcOp*
Treptow, Gunther (Otto Walther) 1907-1981 *Baker 92*
Trerotola, Joseph d1992 *BioIn 17, NewYTBS 92*
Tresalti, Emilio 1935- *WhoWor 93*
Treschitta, Domenick Phillip 1941- *St&PR 93*
Trescott, Harold Charles 1938- *WhoIns 93*
Trescott, Paul Barton 1925- *WhoWrEP 92*
Tresedder, Connie Jean 1963- *WhoAmW 93*
Treseder, Terry W. 1956- *BioIn 17*
Tresh, Tom 1937- *BioIn 17*
Tresmontan, Olympia Davis 1925- *WhoAmW 93*
Tresnowski, Bernard Richard 1932- *WhoAm 92*
Trespacz, Karen Lynn *Law&B 92*
Tress, Mitchell 1942- *St&PR 93*
Tressaud, Alain R. 1943- *WhoScE 91-2*
Tresselt, Alvin 1916- *MajAI [port]*
Tressler, Clyde L. 1937- *St&PR 93*
Tressler, Josef Snyder 1918- *WhoAm 92*
Trestman, Frank D. 1934- *St&PR 93, WhoAm 92*
Tresvant, Ralph *BioIn 17, SoulM*
Tretheway, Catherine M. *Law&B 92*
Trethowan, Ian 1922-1990 *BioIn 17*
Tretin, Jeffrey Jay *Law&B 92*
Tretler, Donald C. 1936- *WhoIns 93*
Trettel, Charles R. 1946- *St&PR 93*
Tretter, James Ray 1933- *St&PR 93, WhoAm 92, WhoE 93*
Tretter, Steven Alan 1940- *WhoE 93*
Tretter, Vincent Joseph, Jr. 1940- *WhoSSW 93*
Tretyakov, Viktor (Viktorovich) 1946- *Baker 92*
Tretyakov, Vitaly *BioIn 17*
Treu, Daniel Gottlob 1695-1749 *Baker 92*
Treu, Dennis L. 1947- *St&PR 93*
Treude, Sandra Sue Hall 1939- *WhoSSW 93*
Treuer, Robert *BioIn 17*
Treuhaft, Robert 1912- *BioIn 17*
Treuhold, Charles Richard 1930- *St&PR 93, WhoAm 92*
Treumann, William Borgen 1916- *WhoAm 92*
Treurnicht, Andries 1921- *News 92 [port]*
Treurnicht, Andries Petrus 1921- *WhoWor 93*
Treusch, J. *WhoScE 91-3*
Treutel, Lucile Veronica *WhoWrEP 92*
Trevan, Michael David *WhoScE 91-1*
Trevanian, Michael, of Erewhon 1909- *BioIn 17*
Trevarrow, David *St&PR 93*
Trevarthen, Donald Scott *Law&B 92*
Trevarthen-Jordan, John *BioIn 17*
Treveiler, A.R. 1927- *St&PR 93*
Trevelyan, Julia *ScF&FL 92*
Treventi, Carol H. 1952- *St&PR 93*
Treves, Frederick 1853-1923 *BioIn 17*
Treves, Peter G. d1992 *NewYTBS 92*
Treves, Samuel Blain 1925- *WhoAm 92*
Treves, Umberto 1914- *St&PR 93*
Trevethin and Oaksey, Geoffrey Lawrence, Baron 1880-1971 *BioIn 17*
Treville, Yvonne de 1881-1954 *Baker 92*
Trevillian, Paul Raymond 1946- *WhoWor 93*
Trevillian, Wallace Dabney 1918- *WhoAm 92, WhoSSW 93*
Trevillion, Dale *MiSFD 9*
Trevino, Armando Lozano 1941- *St&PR 93*
Trevino, Elizabeth B(orton) de 1904- *MajAI [port]*
Trevino, Elizabeth Borton (De) 1904- *DcAmChF 1960*
Trevino, Jesse 1946- *HispAmA*
Trevino, Jesus *WhoScE 91-3*
Trevino, Jesus Salvador *HispAmA*
Trevino, Lee *BioIn 17*
Trevino, Lee 1939- *HispAmA [port]*
Trevino, Lee 1945- *WhoIns 93*
Trevino, Lee Buck 1939- *WhoAm 92*
Trevino, Margarita Christela 1943- *WhoSSW 93*
Trevino, Mario M. 1958- *WhoSSW 93*
Trevino, Rudy 1945- *HispAmA*
Trevino Diaz, Josue 1959- *WhoWor 93*
Trevisan, Carey Ralph, Jr. 1948- *WhoE 93*
Trevisan, Nello R. 1947- *St&PR 93*
Trevisan, Rolfe D. *Law&B 92*
Trevisani, Edmund Thomas, Jr. 1949- *WhoE 93*
Trevisi, Massimo 1925- *WhoScE 91-3*
Trevits, Michael Anthony 1953- *WhoE 93*
Trevor, Alexander B. 1945- *St&PR 93*
Trevor, Alexander Bruen 1945- *WhoAm 92*
Trevor, Bronson 1910- *WhoE 93, WhoWor 93*
Trevor, Claire 1909?- *IntDcF 2-3*
Trevor, Claire 1912- *SweetSg D [port]*
Trevor, Dan *ScF&FL 92*
Trevor, Elleston 1920- *ScF&FL 92*
Trevor, Kirk David Niell 1952- *WhoAm 92, WhoWor 93*
Trevor, Leigh Barry 1934- *WhoAm 92*
Trevor, Meriol 1919- *ScF&FL 92*
Trevor, William *ConAu 37NR*
Trevor, William 1928- *BioIn 17, ConLC 71 [port], ScF&FL 92, WhoWor 93*
Trevor-Roper, Hugh Redwald 1914- *WhoWor 93*
Trevors, Ellen P. *Law&B 92*
Trevvett, James D. 1940- *St&PR 93*
Trew, Marion Elizabeth *WhoScE 91-1*
Trewhella, Raymond M. 1935- *St&PR 93*
Trewhella, Stephen W. 1926- *St&PR 93*
Trewin, John E. 1946- *St&PR 93*
Trexler, C. Deforrest *Law&B 92*
Trexler, Edgar Ray 1937- *WhoAm 92*
Treybig, Edwina Hall 1949- *WhoAmW 93*
Treybig, James G. 1940- *St&PR 93, WhoAm 92*
Treybig, Leon Bruce 1931- *WhoSSW 93*
Treyz, Joseph Henry 1926- *WhoAm 92*
Trezek, George James 1937- *WhoAm 92*
Trezevant, John Gray 1923-1991 *BioIn 17*
Trezise, Philip Harold 1912- *WhoAm 92*
Trezza, Alphonse Fiore 1920- *WhoAm 92*
Trezza, William Robert 1946- *St&PR 93*
Trgovcevic, Zeljko 1939- *WhoScE 91-4*
Trial *Baker 92*
Trial, Antoine 1737-1795 *Baker 92, OxDcOp*
Trial, Armand-Emmanuel 1771-1803 *Baker 92, OxDcOp*
Trial, Jean-Claude 1732-1771 *Baker 92, OxDcOp*
Trial, Marie-Jeanne 1746-1818 *Baker 92*
Triana, Raymond F. *Law&B 92*
Triano, Michael Anthony 1960- *St&PR 93*
Triano, Nicholas D. 1931- *St&PR 93*
Triano, Nicholas P., III *Law&B 92*
Triantafyllou, Michael Stafanos 1951- *WhoE 93*
Triantaphilides, Constantin 1951- *WhoSSW 93*
Triantaphyllidis, Constantinos Demetrios 1940- *WhoWor 93*
Triantis, Frixos A. 1940- *WhoScE 91-3*
Triarhou, Lazaros Constantinos 1957- *WhoWor 93*
Trias, Jose Enrique 1944- *WhoAm 92*
Trias-Monge, Jose 1920- *WhoAm 92*
Tribble, B. Jodie 1932- *WhoAmW 93*
Tribble, Jack L. *Law&B 92*
Tribble, John Atwood 1945- *WhoE 93*
Tribble, Margaret R. *Law&B 92*
Tribble, Pamela Ann Whitmire 1957- *WhoSSW 93*
Tribe, Laurence H. *BioIn 17*
Tribe, Laurence Henry 1941- *WhoAm 92, WhoE 93*
Tribe Called Quest, A *ConMus 8 [port]*
Tribigild dc. 400 *OxDcByz*
Trible, Clayton J., Jr. 1949- *St&PR 93*
Tribler, Willis R. 1934- *WhoIns 93*
Tribonian c. 500-542? *OxDcByz*
Tribou, William H., III *Law&B 92*
Tribull, Christoph 1941- *St&PR 93*
Tribuno, Carlo 1928- *WhoScE 91-3*
Tribus, Myron 1921- *St&PR 93, WhoAm 92*
Tribush, Brenda *BioIn 17*
Tricarico, James A., Jr. 1952- *WhoAm 92*
Tricarico, Janice 1942- *WhoAmW 93*
Tricart, Jean Leon Francois 1920- *WhoScE 91-2*
Trice, Donal W. 1948- *St&PR 93*
Trice, Judith Andrea *Law&B 92*
Trice, Martin Louis 1957- *WhoE 93*
Trice, William H. 1933- *St&PR 93*
Trice, William Henry 1933- *WhoAm 92*
Trice, Wilson R. *Law&B 92*
Triche, Arthur, Jr. 1961- *WhoSSW 93*
Trick, Thomas Lee 1947- *WhoSSW 93*
Trick, Timothy Noel 1939- *WhoAm 92*
Tricker, Roy *BioIn 17*
Trickey, F. David *Law&B 92*
Trickey, Samuel Baldwin 1940- *WhoSSW 93*
Tricoles, Gus Peter 1931- *WhoAm 92*
Tricules, Homer George 1931- *WhoE 93*
Tridente, Giuseppe 1939- *WhoWor 93*
Trider, Robert 1935- *St&PR 93*
Tridle, David R. 1950- *WhoAm 92*
Tridle, David Russeel 1950- *St&PR 93*
Tridot, Gabriel 1924- *WhoScE 91-2*
Triebwasser, Sol 1921- *WhoAm 92*
Trieff, Richard P. 1940- *St&PR 93*
Triem, Eve 1902- *WhoWrEP 92*
Trier, Jerry Steven 1933- *WhoAm 92*
Trieschmann, Gerald Robert, Jr. *Law&B 92*
Trieweiler, Terry Nicholas 1948- *WhoAm 92*
Triffin, Nicholas 1942- *WhoAm 92*
Triffin, Robert 1911- *WhoAm 92*
Triffler, Fay L. *Law&B 92*
Trifoli-Cunniff, Laura Catherine 1958- *WhoAmW 93*
Trifon, David Arthur 1944- *WhoSSW 93*
Trifonidis, Beverly Ann 1947- *WhoAm 92, WhoAmW 93*

Trifonov, IUrii Valentinovich 1925-1981 *BioIn 17*
Triftshauser, Werner 1938- *WhoWor 93*
Triftshouser, Werner Carl 1934- *St&PR 93*
Trifunovic, Vitomir 1916- *Baker 92*
Trigari, Giancarlo 1945- *WhoWor 93*
Trigere, Pauline 1912- *WhoAm 92, WhoAmW 93*
Trigg, Donald Clark *Law&B 92*
Trigg, George L. 1925- *ConAu 139*
Trigg, Harold L. 1924-1990 *BioIn 17*
Trigg, Hastings S., Jr. *Law&B 92*
Trigg, Jack Walden, Jr. 1932- *WhoSSW 93*
Trigg, Karen Ann 1947- *WhoAmW 93*
Trigg, Paul R., Jr. 1913- *St&PR 93*
Trigg, Paul Reginald, Jr. 1913- *WhoAm 92*
Trigg, Roger Hugh 1941- *WhoWor 93*
Trigger, Bruce Graham 1937- *WhoAm 92*
Triggiani, Leonard Vincent 1930- *WhoAm 92*
Triggle, David John 1935- *WhoAm 92*
Triggs, Jonna F. 1950- *WhoAmW 93*
Triggs, Tony D. 1946- *ConAu 138, SmATA 70 [port]*
Trigoboff, Daniel Howard 1953- *WhoE 93*
Trigoso, Miguel P.S. 1924- *WhoScE 91-3*
Trigub, Roald Michailovich 1936- *WhoWor 93*
Trikaminas, Peter A. 1943- *WhoIns 93*
Trikilis, E.M. 1916- *St&PR 93*
Trikilis, Emmanuel Mitchell 1916- *WhoAm 92*
Trikilis, Ted N. 1944- *St&PR 93*
Triklinios, Demetrios fl. c. 1300-1325 *OxDcByz*
Trikonis, Gus *MiSFD 9*
Trillas Ruiz, Enrique 1940- *WhoScE 91-3*
Trilli, James Victor 1950- *WhoE 93*
Trillin, Calvin *BioIn 17*
Trillin, Calvin Marshall 1935- *WhoAm 92, WhoWrEP 92*
Trilling, Diana *BioIn 17*
Trilling, Diana 1905- *WhoAm 92*
Trilling, George Henry 1930- *WhoAm 92*
Trilling, Leon 1924- *WhoAm 92*
Trilling, Lionel 1905-1975 *AmWrS3, BioIn 17, JeAmFiW, JeAmHC*
Trilling, Morton 1929- *St&PR 93*
Trimarchi, Eugene James 1922- *St&PR 93*
Trimarco, Vincent N. 1906-1991 *BioIn 17*
Trimble, Bernard Henry 1930- *WhoE 93*
Trimble, Betty *ScF&FL 92*
Trimble, Bjo 1933- *ScF&FL 92*
Trimble, Blake William *Law&B 92*
Trimble, Dale Lee 1954- *WhoSSW 93*
Trimble, Edward Geoffrey *WhoScE 91-1*
Trimble, Eric Cameron *Law&B 92*
Trimble, George Robert *WhoE 93*
Trimble, George Simpson 1915- *WhoAm 92*
Trimble, James E. 1957- *St&PR 93*
Trimble, James Whitman 1925- *St&PR 93*
Trimble, Jessie 1873- *AmWomPl*
Trimble, Joyce Ann 1947- *St&PR 93*
Trimble, Karen E. *Law&B 92*
Trimble, Kathleen Goette 1950- *WhoAmW 93*
Trimble, Lester (Albert) 1920-1986 *Baker 92*
Trimble, Louis 1917-1988 *ScF&FL 92*
Trimble, Marian Alice Eddy 1933- *WhoAm 92*
Trimble, Marian Eddy 1933- *St&PR 93*
Trimble, Mark Ray 1951- *St&PR 93*
Trimble, Michael Anthony 1942- *St&PR 93*
Trimble, P. Joseph *Law&B 92*
Trimble, P. Joseph 1930- *St&PR 93*
Trimble, Paul Joseph 1930- *WhoAm 92*
Trimble, Preston Albert 1930- *WhoAm 92*
Trimble, Richard Wade 1948- *St&PR 93*
Trimble, Robert 1776-1828 *OxCSupC [port]*
Trimble, Robert Bogue 1943- *WhoE 93*
Trimble, Thomas D. *Law&B 92*
Trimble, Thomas J. *Law&B 92*
Trimble, Thomas J. 1931- *St&PR 93*
Trimble, Thomas James 1931- *WhoAm 92*
Trimble, Vance H. 1913- *JrnUS*
Trimble, Vance Henry 1913- *WhoAm 92*
Trimble, Wanda Jean 1947- *WhoSSW 93*
Trimble, William Cattell, Jr. 1935- *WhoAm 92*
Trimbur, William 1951- *St&PR 93*
Trimm, David Lawrence 1937- *WhoWor 93*
Trimm, Kathleen A. 1932- *St&PR 93*
Trimmer, Brenda Kay 1955- *WhoSSW 93*
Trimmer, Harold Sharp, Jr. 1938- *WhoAm 92*
Trimmer, Larry Lee 1936- *WhoAm 92*
Trimmier, Roscoe, Jr. 1944- *WhoWor 93*
Trimpey, Jack *ConAu 139*
Trimpey, John P. 1941- *ConAu 139*
Trimpin, (Gerhard) 1951- *Baker 92*
Trinajstic, Nenad 1936- *WhoScE 91-4*
Trinchero, Louis 1936- *St&PR 93, WhoAm 92*
Trinci, Anthony Peter Joseph *WhoScE 91-1*
Trinder, Rachel Bandele 1955- *WhoEmL 93*
Trinder, Tommy 1909-1989 *QDrFCA 92 [port]*
Tringale, Anthony Rosario 1942- *WhoSSW 93*
Tringali, John Cameron 1964- *WhoSSW 93*
Tringas, James J. *BioIn 17*
Tringham, Neal 1966- *ScF&FL 92*
Trinh, Pierre Vo Thanh d1991 *BioIn 17*
Trinh, Quang Binh 1944- *St&PR 93*
Trinh, T. Minh-Ha 1952- *BioIn 17*
Trinh Van Can, Joseph Marie 1921-1990 *BioIn 17*
Trinh Xuan Lang 1927- *WhoUN 92*
Trinidad, Albert Andrew James 1963- *WhoWor 93*
Trinidad, David Allen 1953- *WhoWrEP 92*
Trinidad, Joveliano S., Jr. *Law&B 92*
Trinidad, Kellie Allen 1963- *WhoAmW 93*
Trinkaus, John Philip 1918- *WhoAm 92*
Trinker, Steven T. *Law&B 92*
Trinkle, David Alexander 1964- *WhoE 93*
Trinkle, Robert P. *Law&B 92*
Trinks, Hauke 1943- *WhoScE 91-3*
Trinque, James *St&PR 93*
Trinquier, Jacques *WhoScE 91-2*
Trintignant, Jean-Louis 1930- *IntDcF 2-3 [port], WhoWor 93*
Trintignant, Nadine 1934- *MiSFD 9*
Trintis, Basilios Anthony 1940- *St&PR 93*
Triola, Tony J. 1947- *St&PR 93*
Triolo, Pamela *Law&B 92*
Triolo, Peter 1927- *WhoAm 92*
Triolo, Sandra Patricia 1938- *St&PR 93*
Tripathi, Chandrika Prasad 1922- *WhoAsAP 91*
Tripathi, Gaya-Charan 1939- *WhoWor 93*
Tripathi, Ramesh Chandra 1936- *WhoAm 92*
Tripathi, Vijay Kumar 1943- *WhoWor 93*
Triphiodoros *OxDcByz*
Triplehorn, Charles A. 1927- *WhoAm 92*
Triplett, Arlene Ann 1942- *WhoAm 92*
Triplett, Beth Ann 1959- *WhoAmW 93*
Triplett, Gary Joe *Law&B 92*
Triplett, Rufus Morgan 1946- *WhoSSW 93*
Triplett, Thomas McIntyre 1940- *WhoAm 92*
Triplett, William Carryl 1915- *WhoSSW 93*
Triplett, William E., III 1953- *St&PR 93*
Tripodi, Daniel 1939- *WhoE 93*
Tripodi, Louis Anthony 1930- *St&PR 93*
Tripodi, Richard F. 1945- *St&PR 93*
Tripodi, Tony 1932- *WhoE 93*
Tripoli, Joseph S. *Law&B 92*
Tripp, Beth Holmes 1946- *WhoAmW 93*
Tripp, David L. 1941- *St&PR 93*
Tripp, Frederick Gerald 1936- *WhoE 93*
Tripp, Granger 1922-1991 *BioIn 17*
Tripp, H. Frank *Law&B 92*
Tripp, Linda Lynn 1946- *WhoSSW 93*
Tripp, Montie Udell 1946- *St&PR 93*
Tripp, Paul 1916- *WhoAm 92*
Tripp, Randy L. 1956- *St&PR 93*
Tripp, Susan Gerwe 1945- *WhoE 93*
Tripp, Thomas Neal 1942- *WhoWor 93*
Trippe, Charles T., Jr. 1950- *St&PR 93*
Trippe, Hillery Bolt *Law&B 92*
Trippe, Juan T. 1899-1981 *EncABHB 8 [port]*
Trippe, Kenneth Alvin Battershill 1933- *WhoAm 92, WhoSSW 93*
Trippett, Peter 1934- *St&PR 93*
Trippi, Charley 1922- *BioIn 17*
Tripplet, Sharlie *WhoAmW 93*
Tripplin, Theodore 1813-1881 *PolBiDi*
Tris, Mary S. *Law&B 92*
Trischetta, Elaine Anne 1951- *WhoAmW 93*
Trischler, W. Ronald 1936- *St&PR 93*
Trisco, Robert Frederick 1929- *WhoAm 92, WhoE 93*
Trish, Rita Kathryn 1921- *WhoE 93*
Triska, Jan Francis 1922- *WhoAm 92*
Triska, Pavel *WhoScE 91-4*
Trisko, S. Carol 1945- *WhoAmW 93*
Trisko, Tracy Seaver 1950- *WhoSSW 93*
Trisler, Henry Franklin, Jr. 1937- *WhoWrEP 92*
Trissel, Sandra Lynne 1941- *WhoAmW 93*
Trissl, Hans-Wilhelm 1941- *WhoWor 93*
Trist, E.L. 1909- *BioIn 17*
Trist, Elizabeth House d1828 *BioIn 17*
Trist, Eric Lansdown 1909- *BioIn 17*
Trist, Nicholas Philip 1800-1874 *BioIn 17*
Tristan, Flora 1803-1844 *BioIn 17*
Tristan de Escamilla, Luis 1586?-1624 *BioIn 17*
Tristano, "Lennie" 1919-1978 *Baker 92*
Tristan y Moscozo, Flore Celestine Therese Henriette 1803-1844 *BioIn 17*
Tristine, Martin P. 1944- *St&PR 93*
Tritch, Martha *AmWomPl*
Trites, Donald George 1941- *WhoE 93*
Tritonius, Petrus c. 1465-c. 1525 *Baker 92*
Tritsch, Robert Grant 1926- *St&PR 93*
Tritsis, Antonis 1937-1992 *BioIn 17*
Tritt, Clyde Edward 1920- *WhoAm 92*
Tritthart, Helmut A. 1940- *WhoScE 91-4*
Trittipo, Jane Knecht 1933- *WhoAmW 93*
Tritto, Giacomo 1733-1824 *Baker 92*
Tritton, David W. 1950- *St&PR 93*
Tritton, Thomas Richard 1947- *WhoE 93*
Trivelpiece, Alvin William 1931- *WhoAm 92*
Trivison, Donna Rae 1951- *WhoAmW 93*
Trivoli, George William 1934- *WhoSSW 93*
Trkal, Viktor 1929- *WhoScE 91-4*
Trkulja, Milan 1932- *WhoUN 92*
Trnecek, Hanus 1858-1914 *Baker 92*
Trnka, Jiri 1912-1969 *MajAI [port]*
Troallic, Jean Pierre 1945- *WhoWor 93*
Troast, John G. 1931- *St&PR 93*
Troast, Paul L., Jr. 1921- *St&PR 93*
Troast, William C. 1904- *St&PR 93*
Troccoli, Rosario 1933- *WhoScE 91-3*
Trochak, Stephanie Ellen 1953- *WhoAmW 93*
Trochimczuk, Witold M. 1932- *WhoScE 91-4*
Trochoulias, Timoleon 1937- *WhoWor 93*
Trodahl, Harry Joseph 1941- *WhoWor 93*
Trodlier, Linda Esther 1950- *WhoSSW 93*
Troeger, Curtis Ralph 1931- *St&PR 93, WhoAm 92*
Troell, Jan 1931- *MiSFD 9*
Troelstra, Arne 1935- *WhoAm 92*
Troemel, Jean Wagner-Willhite 1921- *WhoAmW 93*
Troen, Philip 1925- *WhoAm 92, WhoE 93*
Troester, Carl A. *BioIn 17*
Troester, Carl Augustus, Jr. 1916- *WhoAm 92*
Trofatter, Kenneth Frank 1951- *WhoSSW 93*
Troffkin, Howard J. *Law&B 92*
Trofimov, Eugene 1951- *WhoWor 93*
Trogan, John Frederick 1937- *St&PR 93*
Trogden, Zelbie 1936- *St&PR 93*
Trogdon, Dewey Leonard 1932- *St&PR 93*
Trogdon, Dewey Leonard, Jr. 1932- *WhoAm 92, WhoSSW 93*
Trogdon, Wendell Ward 1929- *WhoAm 92*
Trogdon, William *BioIn 17*
Trogdon, William Lewis 1939- *WhoAm 92*
Troge, Andreas *WhoScE 91-3*
Troglita, John dc. 552 *OxDcByz*
Trohan, Walter 1903- *WhoAm 92, WhoWor 93*
Trohatos, Peter John 1924- *St&PR 93*
Troiani, Elisa Adelaide 1938- *WhoAmW 93*
Troiani, Maryann Victoria 1958- *WhoAmW 93*
Troiano, Carl E. 1952- *St&PR 93*
Troiano, Gabriele John 1941- *St&PR 93*
Troiano, Lawrence *St&PR 93*
Troiano, Paul Francis 1937- *St&PR 93*
Troidi, Richard John 1944- *St&PR 93*
Troidl, Richard John 1944- *WhoAm 92*
Troike, Robert L. *Law&B 92*
Troilo, Arthur, III 1953- *WhoE 93*
Troilo, Joseph Carmen 1934- *St&PR 93*
Trois, Charles *BioIn 17*
Troise, Fred 1937- *WhoWrEP 92*
Troise, Fred L. 1937- *St&PR 93*
Troise, Michelle 1950- *WhoAmW 93*
Troisi, Lawrence Anthony 1952- *St&PR 93*
Troisi, Massimo 1953- *MiSFD 9*
Troitskaia, E.E. *BioIn 17*
Troitskaia, Elena Evgen'evna *BioIn 17*
Troitskii, V.S. 1913- *BioIn 17*
Troitskii, Vsevolod Sergeevich 1913- *BioIn 17*
Troitsky, Artemy *BioIn 17*
Troitsky, Artemy 1955- *ConAu 136*
Trojahn, Manfred 1949- *Baker 92*
Trojan, Robert 1939- *St&PR 93*
Trojan, Stanislav 1934- *WhoScE 91-4*
Trojan, Vaclav 1907-1983 *Baker 92*
Trojanowski, Henryk Marian 1924- *WhoScE 91-4*
Trojanowski, Leonard E. *Law&B 92*
Trojanowski, Wojciech Jan 1935- *WhoScE 91-4*
Trolander, Hardy Wilcox 1921- *WhoAm 92*
Trolinger, James Davis 1940- *WhoAm 92*
Trolio, Andrew Edmond 1929- *St&PR 93*
Trolio, William Michael 1947- *WhoE 93*
Troll, Christian Michael 1954- *WhoE 93*
Troll, John R. *Law&B 92*
Troll, Lillian Ellman 1915- *WhoAmW 93*
Trollat, Philippe *WhoScE 91-2*
Trolldenier, Gunter 1932- *WhoScE 91-3*
Troller, David Edward *Law&B 92*
Troller, Fred 1930- *WhoAm 92*
Trollope, Anthony 1815-1882 *BioIn 17, MagSWL [port], WorLitC [port]*
Tromanhauser, Roger Karl 1936- *St&PR 93*
Trombetta, Jolene Michele 1962- *WhoAmW 93*
Trombetta, R. Nick 1925- *St&PR 93*
Trombetti, Ascanio 1544?-1590 *Baker 92*
Trombino, Raymond David 1949- *WhoE 93*
Trombino, Robert W. d1990 *BioIn 17*
Trombino, Roger A. 1939- *WhoAm 92*
Trombka, Candace Conley 1956- *WhoAmW 93*
Trombley, Fitterer *WhoAmW 93*
Trombley, William Holden 1929- *WhoAm 92*
Trombly, Preston (Andrew) 1945- *Baker 92*
Trombold, Walter S. 1910- *St&PR 93*
Tromboncino, Bartolomeo c. 1470-c. 1535 *Baker 92*
Trombski, Marek Stanislaw 1937- *WhoScE 91-4*
Tromel, Martin Gerhard 1934- *WhoScE 91-3*
Tromlitz, Johann Georg 1725-1805 *Baker 92*
Trommer, Joseph Abraham 1925- *St&PR 93*
Trommer, Wolfgang E. 1943- *WhoScE 91-3*
Tromp, Cornelis van 1629-1691 *HarEnMi*
Tromp, Maarten Harpertzoon van 1597-1653 *HarEnMi*
Tromp, S.W. *WhoScE 91-3*
Trompeter, Richard Simon 1946- *WhoWor 93*
Tron, Barrie Rene 1959- *WhoAm 92*
Tronche, Philippe *ScF&FL 92*
Tronchet *WhoScE 91-2*
Tronchet, Jean M.J. 1934- *WhoScE 91-4*
Troncin, James Edward 1934- *St&PR 93*
Troncone, Reginald C. 1932- *St&PR 93*
Troncoso, Antonio 1938- *WhoScE 91-3*
Troncoso, Ignacio R. 1946- *St&PR 93*
Trone, Kerstin M. 1942- *WhoUN 92*
Troner, William Alan *Law&B 92*
Trongone, Richard James 1953- *WhoE 93*
Tronolone, Carmine *Law&B 92*
Tronolone, William 1936- *WhoE 93*
Tronsmo, Arne 1947- *WhoScE 91-4*
Tronson, Keith Frederick 1943- *WhoAm 92*
Trook, Jackie Lee 1942- *St&PR 93, WhoAm 92*
Trop, Sandra *WhoAmW 93*
Tropa, Ataban 1940- *WhoAsAP 91*
Troparevsky, Alejandro 1936- *WhoWor 93*
Tropeano, Elio 1953- *St&PR 93*
Tropia, Marc C. *MiSFD 9*
Tropia, Tano *MiSFD 9*
Tropiano, Marie Joyce 1942- *WhoAmW 93*
Tropp, James B. 1956- *St&PR 93*
Tropp, Janis Ellen 1956- *WhoAmW 93*
Tropp, Lawrence B. *St&PR 93*
Tropp, Louise Constance Velardi 1942- *WhoAmW 93*
Tropp, Martin 1945- *ScF&FL 92*
Troppenberg, Ulderico di *ScF&FL 92*
Trosch, Joel S. 1939- *St&PR 93*
Trosclair, Carlton James *Law&B 92*
Troshkin, Olec Valentinovich 1955- *WhoWor 93*
Trosin, Walter R. 1933- *St&PR 93*
Trosino, Vincent Joseph 1940- *St&PR 93, WhoAm 92*
Troske, L. A. 1931- *WhoAm 92, WhoIns 93*
Trosley, Beverly Dawson 1941- *WhoAmW 93*
Tross, Evangeline Wyche *Law&B 92*
Trost, Barry Martin 1941- *WhoAm 92*
Trost, Carlisle Albert Herman 1930- *WhoAm 92*
Trost, Donald Craig 1951- *WhoE 93*
Trost, Eileen Bannon 1951- *WhoAm 92*
Trost, F. J., Jr. 1937- *WhoSSW 93*
Trost, J. Ronald 1932- *WhoAm 92*
Trost, Steven R. *Law&B 92*
Trostel, Michael Frederick 1931- *WhoAm 92*
Trostel, Otto Paul 1944- *St&PR 93*
Trosten, Leonard Morse 1932- *WhoAm 92*
Trostmann, Erik 1929- *WhoScE 91-2*
Trotenberg, Andrea *BioIn 17*
Trotere, Henry 1855-1912 *Baker 92*
Trotmann, Julia *WhoAmW 93*
Trotot, Pierre M. 1942- *WhoScE 91-2*
Trotot, Pierre Marcel 1942- *WhoWor 93*
Trotsky, Leon 1879-1940 *BioIn 17, ColdWar 2 [port], DcTwHis, HarEnMi*

Trott, Annie Frances Roberts 1930- WhoSSW 93
Trott, John E. 1944- St&PR 93
Trott, John Stephen Law&B 92
Trott, Klaus-Rudiger WhoScE 91-1
Trott, Ralph E. St&PR 93
Trott, Sabert Scott, II 1941- St&PR 93, WhoAm 92
Trott, Stephen Spangler 1939- WhoAm 92
Trott, Thomas G. Law&B 92
Trott, Trevor Law&B 92
Trott, William Macnider 1946- WhoSSW 93
Trotta, Anna Marie 1937- WhoWrEP 92
Trotta, Carmen St&PR 93
Trotta, George Benedict 1930- St&PR 93, WhoIns 93
Trotta, Liz BioIn 17
Trotta, Marcia Marie 1949- WhoAmW 93, WhoE 93
Trotte, Gennaro E. 1932- St&PR 93
Trotter, Cameron BioIn 17
Trotter, Caroline Cook 1951- WhoAmW 93
Trotter, Catharine 1679-1749 BioIn 17
Trotter, Debra Mills 1953- WhoAmW 93
Trotter, Desmond DcCPCAm
Trotter, Donald Wayne 1939- WhoSSW 93
Trotter, Donne E. 1950- AfrAmBi [port]
Trotter, Frederick Thomas 1926- WhoAm 92
Trotter, Henry 1855-1912 Baker 92
Trotter, Ide Peebles 1932- WhoSSW 93
Trotter, John A. 1943- St&PR 93
Trotter, John J. 1935- St&PR 93
Trotter, Johnny Ray 1950- WhoWor 93
Trotter, Lawrence Robert Law&B 92
Trotter, Lorry Simmons 1952- WhoSSW 93
Trotter, (William) Monroe 1872-1934 EncAACR
Trotter, Nancy Louisa 1934- WhoAmW 93
Trotter, Robert Lawrence 1954- BioIn 17
Trotter, Ronald Ramsay 1927- WhoWor 93
Trotter, Thomas Bates, Sr. 1947- WhoSSW 93
Trotter, William C. 1934- St&PR 93
Trotter-Stewart, Ava Marie 1958- WhoE 93
Trottier, Bryan John 1956- WhoAm 92
Trottier, J.P. 1943- WhoScE 91-2
Trottier, Maurice Edmond 1917- WhoWrEP 92
Trottier, Michel 1952- St&PR 93
Trottier, Nelson Phillippe 1950- WhoAm 92
Trott zu Solz, Adam von 1909-1944 BioIn 17
Troubetzkoy, Amelie Rives Chanler 1863-1945 AmWomPl
Troubetzkoy, Dorothy Ulrich WhoWrEP 92
Troubridge, Ernest Charles Thomas 1862-1926 HarEnMi
Trouillot, Ertha Pascal- BioIn 17
Troup, Daniel J. 1946- St&PR 93
Troup, Diana Claire 1942- WhoAm 92
Troup, Frank W. 1921- St&PR 93
Troup, James S. 1945- St&PR 93
Troup, Thomas James 1923- WhoAm 92
Troupe, Joseph E. 1945- St&PR 93
Troupe, Lee Wayne 1946- WhoSSW 93
Troupe, Terry Lee 1947- St&PR 93, WhoAm 92
Troupe, Tom 1928- BioIn 17
Troupp, Henry Eugen 1932- WhoScE 91-4
Trousdale, Gary MiSFD 9
Trousdale, Jean Baker 1933- WhoAmW 93
Trousdale, Marion Stelling 1929- WhoE 93
Trout, Charles Hathaway 1935- WhoAm 92
Trout, Ethel Wendell AmWomPl
Trout, G. Malcolm 1896-1990 BioIn 17
Trout, George Malcolm 1896-1990 BioIn 17
Trout, Kenneth H. 1948- St&PR 93
Trout, Kilgore ScF&FL 92, WhoWrEP 92
Trout, Maurice Elmore 1917- WhoAm 92
Trout, Monroe Eugene 1931- St&PR 93, WhoAm 92, WhoWor 93
Trout, Paul Howard 1915-1972 BiDAMSp 1989
Trout, Ralph Wilbur 1922- WhoSSW 93
Troutman, Conaught M. 1955- WhoIns 93
Troutman, Conaught Marie 1955- St&PR 93
Troutman, E. Mac 1915- WhoAm 92, WhoE 93
Troutman, Edward L. 1943- St&PR 93
Troutman, Gerald Stevenson 1933- WhoAm 92
Troutman, James Voight 1946- St&PR 93
Troutman, Robert Battey 1918-1991 BioIn 17
Troutman, Ronald R. 1940- WhoAm 92
Troutman, W. Wilson 1954- St&PR 93
Troutner, Leonard P. 1951- St&PR 93
Troutt, William Earl 1949- WhoAm 92
Troutwine-Braun, Charlotte Temperley 1906- WhoAmW 93, WhoWor 93
Trova, Ernest Tino 1927- WhoAm 92
Trovato, Anthony John 1947- St&PR 93
Trovato, Frank Douglas 1948- St&PR 93
Trovato, Joseph Law&B 92
Trover, Ellen Lloyd 1947- WhoWor 93
Trovero, Leonard J. St&PR 93
Trovoada, Miguel WhoWor 93
Trovoada, Miguel 1937- WhoAfr
Trow, Jo Anne Johnson 1931- WhoAmW 93
Trowbridge, Alexander Buel, Jr. 1929- WhoAm 92
Trowbridge, C. Robertson 1932- WhoAm 92
Trowbridge, Calvin D., III Law&B 92
Trowbridge, Charles L. St&PR 93
Trowbridge, David Cole Law&B 92
Trowbridge, Edward K. 1928- WhoIns 93
Trowbridge, Edward Kenneth 1928- St&PR 93, WhoAm 92
Trowbridge, John Parks 1947- WhoEmL 93, WhoSSW 93, WhoWor 93
Trowbridge, Marjorie AmWomPl
Trowbridge, Martin E. 1925- St&PR 93
Trowbridge, Thomas, Jr. 1938- WhoAm 92
Trowbridge, Vicki Jane 1950- WhoAmW 93
Trowbridge, William L. 1941- WhoWrEP 92
Trowell, Michael ScF&FL 92
Trower, E. Dale Law&B 92
Troxclair, Debra Ann 1953- WhoAmW 93
Troxel, Donald Eugene 1934- WhoE 93
Troxel, Sylvia Ortiz 1958- WhoAmW 93
Troxell, Gregory A. Law&B 92
Troxell, Lucy Davis 1932- WhoAmW 93
Troxell, Richard Harold 1934- WhoSSW 93
Troxell, William James 1957- WhoE 93
Troy, B. Theodore 1932- WhoAm 92
Troy, Doris SoulM
Troy, Frank James, Sr. Law&B 92
Troy, James Michael 1955- St&PR 93
Troy, John F. Law&B 92
Troy, John J. 1945- St&PR 93
Troy, Joseph Freed 1938- WhoAm 92
Troy, Kathleen Elizabeth Law&B 92
Troy, Mary Delphine 1948- WhoWrEP 92
Troy, Michael A. 1950- St&PR 93
Troy, Nancy J. 1952- ConAu 37NR
Troy, Patricia Humphreys 1946- WhoAmW 93
Troy, Richard H. Law&B 92
Troy, Ronald Anthony 1952- WhoSSW 93
Troy, Steven M. 1948- St&PR 93
Troy, Timothy John Law&B 92
Troy, William C. 1938- St&PR 93
Troyan, George William 1932- St&PR 93
Troyan, John Anthony, III 1968- WhoE 93
Troyanek, Richard L. 1932- St&PR 93
Troyanos, Tatiana 1938- Baker 92, IntDcOp, OxDcOp, WhoAm 92
Troyat, Henri 1911- BioIn 17, CurBio 92 [port]
Troyer, Alvah Forrest 1929- WhoAm 92
Troyer, John Robert 1928- WhoAm 92
Troyer, Lisa Lynn 1964- WhoAmW 93
Troyer, Steven Alan Law&B 92
Troyer, Thomas Alfred 1933- WhoAm 92, WhoE 93
Troyna, Barry 1951- ConAu 40NR
Troyon, Francis 1933- WhoScE 91-4
Trozzi, Mark A. 1945- St&PR 93
Trozzolo, Anthony Marion 1930- WhoAm 92, WhoWor 93
Trpis, Milan 1930- WhoAm 92
Truan, George 1944- HispAmA
Truax, Barry 1947- Baker 92
Truax, James Francis 1948- WhoSSW 93
Truax, Mary A. Law&B 92
Truax, Robert Charles 1936- WhoSSW 93
Truax, William Howard, II 1947- WhoSSW 93
Trub, Aaron D. 1935- St&PR 93
Trub, Richard Gibson 1930- St&PR 93
Trubek, Josephine S. Law&B 92
Trubek, Josephine Susan 1942- WhoAm 92
Trubestein, Gustav Klaus 1939- WhoWor 93
Trubin, John 1917- WhoAm 92
Trubow, Susan Elizabeth 1949- WhoAmW 93
Trubshaw, J.D. WhoScE 91-1
Truby, Charles L. 1928- St&PR 93
Truby, John Louis 1933- WhoAm 92
Truce, William Everett 1917- WhoAm 92
Truchas Master, The fl. 1790-1830 HispAmA
Truck, James L. 1945- St&PR 93
Truckenbrodt, Charles David 1939- St&PR 93
Trucks, Virgil Oliver 1919- BiDAMSp 1989
Trucksess, A. William St&PR 93
Trucksess, H.A., III 1949- St&PR 93
Trucksis, Theresa A. 1924- WhoAmW 93
Trudeau, Arthur Gilbert 1902-1991 BioIn 17
Trudeau, G.B. 1948- BioIn 17
Trudeau, Garry 1948- Au&Arts 10 [port]
Trudeau, Garry B. 1948- BioIn 17, WhoAm 92, WhoE 93, WhoWrEP 92
Trudeau, Jane Pauley BioIn 17
Trudeau, Patricia Margaret 1931- WhoWrEP 92
Trudeau, Paul R. Law&B 92
Trudeau, Pierre Elliott BioIn 17
Trudeau, Pierre Elliott 1919- DcTwHis, WhoAm 92, WhoE 93, WhoWor 93
Trudel, A.F. 1949- St&PR 93
Trudel, Marc J. WhoAm 92
Trudell, Sharon WhoWrEP 92
Trudic, Bozidar 1911- Baker 92
Trudinger, John Philip 1943- St&PR 93
Trudnak, Stephen Joseph 1947- WhoSSW 93
Trudo, Jerry Norman 1944- St&PR 93
True, Charles Wesley, Jr. 1916- WhoSSW 93
True, Claudia 1948- WhoAmW 93, WhoEmL 93
True, Edward Keene 1915- WhoAm 92
True, Emma Jane Vaughan AmWomPl
True, Graham WhoScE 91-1
True, Henry Alfonso, Jr. 1915- WhoAm 92, WhoWor 93
True, Jean Durland 1915- WhoAmW 93, WhoWor 93
True, June Audrey 1927- WhoWrEP 92
True, Louis Poole, Jr. 1943- WhoAm 92
True, Mary E. AmWomPl
True, Michael (D.) 1933- ConAu 37NR
True, Roy Joe 1938- WhoAm 92, WhoWor 93
True, S.M., Jr. WhoIns 93
True, Wendell Cleon 1934- St&PR 93, WhoAm 92, WhoWor 93
Trueb, Kurt 1926- St&PR 93
Trueb, Lucien Felix 1934- WhoWor 93
Trueba, Eugenio 1921- DcMexL
Trueba, Fernando 1955- MiSFD 9, WhoWor 93
Truebenbach, Paul R. Law&B 92
Trueblood, Alan Stubbs 1917- WhoAm 92
Trueblood, Carol d1991 BioIn 17
Trueblood, David Elton 1900- WhoAm 92
Trueblood, Elton 1900- BioIn 17
Trueblood, Gene E. 1951- St&PR 93
Trueblood, Harry A., Jr. 1925- St&PR 93
Trueblood, Harry Albert, Jr. 1925- WhoAm 92
Trueblood, Paul Graham 1905- WhoAm 92, WhoWor 93
Trueeb, Ernst 1924- WhoScE 91-4
Trueheart, William C. 1918-1992 NewYTBS 92
Trueheart, William E. 1942- WhoAm 92
Truehill, Marshall, Jr. 1948- WhoSSW 93
Truelle, Jean-Luc 1939- WhoScE 91-2
Truelove, C. Keith 1949- St&PR 93
Truelove, Randall J. 1948- St&PR 93
Truelson, Roy Willfred Law&B 92
Trueman, Fred 1932- BioIn 17
Trueman, Ian Christopher WhoScE 91-1
Trueman, Stephen G. Law&B 92
Trueman, Terry Earl 1947- WhoWrEP 92
Trueman, Walter 1928- WhoAm 92
Trueman, William Peter Main 1934- WhoAm 92
Truemper, John James, Jr. 1924- WhoAm 92
Truemper, Walter E. 1918-1944 BioIn 17
Trueschler, Bernard C. 1923- St&PR 93
Truesdale, Carole Law&B 92
Truesdale, Dave ScF&FL 92
Truesdale, Geoffrey Ashworth 1927- WhoWor 93
Truesdale, Gerald Lynn 1949- WhoSSW 93
Truesdale, John Cushman 1921- WhoAm 92
Truesdell, Carolyn Gilmour 1939- WhoAmW 93
Truesdell, Clifford Ambrose, III 1919- WhoAm 92, WhoWrEP 92
Truesdell, James E., Jr. 1930- St&PR 93
Truesdell, James Leslie 1949- St&PR 93
Truesdell, Jerry William 1940- St&PR 93
Truesdell, Lillian W. 1917- St&PR 93
Truesdell, Wesley E. 1927- St&PR 93
Truesdell, Wesley Edwin 1927- WhoAm 92
Truett, Bob 1932- WhoAm 92
Truett, Casey 1944- WhoSSW 93
Truett, Cecily St&PR 93
Truett, George Washington 1867-1944 BioIn 17
Truett, Harold Joseph, III 1946- WhoEmL 93
Truett, Lila Flory 1947- WhoSSW 93
Truettner, W. James 1931- St&PR 93
Truex, Dorothy Adine 1915- WhoAm 92
Truex, Frances Beach 1938- WhoSSW 93
Truex, Max d1991 BioIn 17
Truffaut, Francois 1932-1984 BioIn 17, MiSFD 9N
Truffelman, Joanne 1943- WhoAmW 93
Truglio, Dominick Joseph 1947- St&PR 93
Trugman, Ina F. Law&B 92
Truhlar, Donald Gene 1944- WhoAm 92
Truhlsen, Stanley Marshall 1920- WhoAm 92
Truhn, Friedrich Hieronymus 1811-1886 Baker 92
Truillier-Lacombe, Joseph-Patrice 1807-1863 BioIn 17
Truinet Baker 92
Truitt, Anne 1921- News 93-1 [port]
Truitt, Bruce Evin 1950- WhoSSW 93
Truitt, David Charles 1951- WhoE 93
Truitt, Gary Law&B 92
Truitt, Gary Arthur 1947- WhoE 93
Truitt, James W. 1937- St&PR 93
Truitt, Jean Marie 1964- WhoAmW 93
Truitt, Phyllis Lynn 1945- WhoAmW 93
Truitt, Richard Hunt 1932- WhoAm 92
Truitt, Robert Ralph, Jr. 1948- WhoEmL 93, WhoSSW 93
Truitt, Suzanne 1943- WhoAmW 93
Truitt, Thomas Hulen 1935- WhoAm 92
Truitt, Ulysses 1936- WhoSSW 93
Trujillo, Jackie BioIn 17
Trujillo, Paul Edward 1952- WhoWrEP 92
Trujillo, Rafael 1891-1961 DcCPCAm, DcTwHis
Trujillo, Veda Arlene Spriggs 1924- St&PR 93
Trujillo Herrera, Rafael 1897- HispAmA
Trujillo Molina, Rafael Leonidas 1891-1961 BioIn 17, ColdWar 2 [port]
Trujillo-Ventura, Arturo 1963- WhoWor 93
Trukenbrod, William Sellery 1939- WhoAm 92
Trull, Michael John Law&B 92
Trull, Steven Gregory 1952- St&PR 93
Trulove, Harry David 1927- WhoSSW 93
TruLuck, James Paul, Jr. 1933- WhoSSW 93
Truluck, Phillip Nelson 1947- WhoE 93
Truly, Ethel Rawle Law&B 92
Truly, Richard BioIn 17
Truman, Aubrey WhoScE 91-1
Truman, Benjamin Cummings 1835-1916 JrnUS
Truman, Bess Wallace 1885-1982 BioIn 17
Truman, David Bicknell 1913- BioIn 17
Truman, Gary Tucker 1950- WhoSSW 93, WhoWor 93
Truman, Harry S PolPar
Truman, Harry S. 1884-1972 BioIn 17, ColdWar 1 [port], ConHero 2 [port], DcTwHis
Truman, John Lee 1944- WhoUN 92
Truman, Margaret 1924- BioIn 17, WhoAm 92, WhoAmW 93
Truman, Ruth C. Law&B 92
Trumble, Melvin J. 1940- St&PR 93
Trumble, Robert Roy 1940- WhoAm 92
Trumble, Thomas E. 1953- St&PR 93
Trumbo, Cynthia L. 1955- WhoAmW 93, WhoSSW 93
Trumbo, Dalton 1905-1976 BioIn 17
Trumbo, George William 1926- AfrAmBi
Trumbo, Steven Robert Law&B 92
Trumbore, Conrad Noble 1931- WhoE 93
Trumbower, Frank S. St&PR 93
Trumbull, Annie Eliot 1857- AmWomPl
Trumbull, Douglas WhoAm 92
Trumbull, Douglas 1942- ConTFT 10, MiSFD 9
Trumbull, George Vincent Law&B 92
Trumbull, Jane T. AmWomPl
Trumbull, Jonathan, Jr. 1740-1809 PolPar
Trumbull, Lyman 1813-1896 PolPar
Trumbull, Richard 1916- WhoAm 92
Trumbull, Robert 1912- WhoAm 92
Trumbull, Robert 1912-1992 ConAu 139, NewYTBS 92 [port]
Trumka, Richard Louis 1949- WhoAm 92
Trumley, Richard L. St&PR 93
Trump, Becky Ann 1955- WhoAmW 93, WhoE 93
Trump, Benjamin Franklin 1932- WhoAm 92
Trump, Donald J. BioIn 17
Trump, Donald John 1946- WhoAm 92, WhoE 93
Trump, Douglas P. Law&B 92
Trump, Ivana BioIn 17, NewYTBS 92 [port]
Trumpeldor, Josef 1880-1920 BioIn 17
Trumper, Joachim E. 1933- WhoScE 91-3
Trumpy, Ernst 1927- WhoScE 91-4
Trumpy, R.C. 1928- St&PR 93

Trumpy, Robert Theodore, Jr. 1945- *BiDAMSp 1989*
Trumpy, Stefano 1945- *WhoScE 91-3*
Truncellito, Gene *Law&B 92*
Trundle, W. Scott 1939- *St&PR 93*
Trundle, Winfield Scott 1939- *WhoAm 92*
Trungpa, Chogyam 1939-1987 *BioIn 17*
Trunk, Richard 1879-1968 *Baker 92*
Trunnell, Thomas Newton 1942- *WhoSSW 93*
Trunzo, Claire Elaine *Law&B 92*
Trunzo, Vincent Eugene 1944- *WhoSSW 93*
Truog, Dean-Daniel Wesley 1938- *WhoE 93*
Truog, W. Randle 1912- *St&PR 93*
Truog, William R. 1945- *St&PR 93*
Truong, Thanh-Dam 1949- *ConAu 136*
Truono, Eugene Joseph, Jr. *Law&B 92*
Truper, Hans G. 1936- *WhoScE 91-3*
Truppa, Michael R. 1944- *St&PR 93*
Truran, James Wellington, Jr. 1940- *WhoAm 92*
Truran, William R. 1951- *WhoE 93, WhoWor 93*
Truscott, Gerry 1955- *ScF&FL 92*
Truscott, Lucian King 1895-1965 *BioIn 17*
Truscott, Lucian King, Jr. 1895-1965 *HarEnMi*
Truscott, Terence George *WhoScE 91-1*
Truscott, William Harold 1946- *WhoSSW 93*
Trusculescu, Marin 1926- *WhoScE 91-4*
Trusdell, Laurence Michael *Law&B 92*
Trusheim, H. Edwin 1927- *WhoAm 92*
Truskey, Jeffrey J. *Law&B 92*
Truskolaska, Agnieszka 1755-c. 1820 *PolBiDi*
Truskowski, John B. 1945- *St&PR 93*
Truskowski, John Budd 1945- *WhoWor 93*
Trusler, James R. 1944- *St&PR 93*
Trusler, Suzanne Small 1949- *WhoAmW 93*
Truslove, Tom Elsworth *WhoScE 91-1*
Truslow, Henry A. 1913-1991 *BioIn 17*
Truslow, Robert Gurdon 1936- *St&PR 93*
Truss, Jan 1925- *DcChlFi, WhoCanL 92*
Truss, John Kenneth 1947- *WhoWor 93*
Trussell, Charles Tait 1925- *WhoAm 92*
Trusselle, Gar DeLano 1946- *WhoE 93*
Trussler, Phyllis Ann 1936- *WhoAmW 93*
Trusso, Gregory M. *Law&B 92*
Trustman, Benjamin Arthur 1902- *WhoAm 92*
Trustrum, Leslie Bernard *WhoScE 91-1*
Trusty, Kerri *BioIn 17*
Trusty, Roy Lee 1924- *WhoAm 92*
Trusty, Thomas F. 1931- *WhoIns 93*
Truswell, Derek Paul 1943- *St&PR 93*
Truszczynski, Marian Janusz 1929- *WhoScE 91-4*
Truszkowska, Mary Angela 1825-1899 *PolBiDi*
Truszkowski, Wojciech 1921- *WhoScE 91-4*
Truta, Joseph M. 1920- *St&PR 93*
Truta, Marianne Patricia 1951- *WhoAmW 93*
Truter, Mary Rosaleen *WhoScE 91-1*
Truth, Sojourner d1883 *BioIn 17*
Truth, Sojourner 1797?-1883 *AmWomWr 92*
Truthan, Charles Edwin 1955- *WhoWor 93*
Trutovsky, Vasili (Fyodorovich) c. 1740-1810 *Baker 92*
Trutt, William J. 1937- *WhoIns 93*
Trutter, John Thomas 1920- *St&PR 93, WhoAm 92, WhoWor 93*
Trux, Walter Rudolf 1928- *WhoWor 93*
Truxal, John Groff 1924- *WhoAm 92*
Truxtun, Thomas 1755-1822 *HarEnMi*
Truzinski, Charles G. 1934- *St&PR 93*
Truzzi, Marcello 1935- *ScF&FL 92*
Trybula, Walter Joseph 1940- *WhoSSW 93*
Trybus, Janice R. *Law&B 92*
Trygg, I.A. 1925- *St&PR 93*
Trygg, Steve Lennart 1947- *WhoAm 92*
Tryggvason, Eysteinn 1924- *WhoScE 91-4*
Trygstad, Lawrence Benson 1937- *WhoAm 92*
Tryhane, Gerald Aubrey Lisle 1929- *St&PR 93*
Tryhane, Gerald H. L. 1952- *St&PR 93*
Trynin, Nathan Kalman 1930- *St&PR 93*
Tryon, Edward Polk 1940- *WhoAm 92*
Tryon, Georgiana Shick 1945- *WhoE 93*
Tryon, Katey 1949- *St&PR 93*
Tryon, Leslie *BioIn 17*
Tryon, Richard R. 1932- *St&PR 93*
Tryon, Thomas *BioIn 17*
Tryon, Thomas 1926-1991 *AnObit 1991, ConTFT 10, ScF&FL 92*
Tryon, Warren Willard 1944- *WhoE 93*
Tryon, William 1729-1788 *BioIn 17, HarEnMi*
Tryon, William S. 1931- *St&PR 93*
Tryphiodoros *OxDcByz*
Trythall, (Harry) Gil(bert) 1930- *Baker 92*
Trythall, Harry Gilbert 1930- *WhoAm 92*
Trythall, Richard 1939- *Baker 92*
Trythall, Willoughby Agar 1937- *St&PR 93*
Trytsman-Gray, Linda Teresa 1961- *WhoWor 93*
Trytten, Don F. 1943- *St&PR 93*
Trzasko, Joseph Anthony 1946- *WhoEmL 93, WhoWor 93*
Trzaskus, Edward A. 1947- *St&PR 93*
Trzebiatowski, Gregory L. 1937- *WhoAm 92*
Trzebiatowski, Rajmund 1932- *WhoScE 91-4*
Trzebicka, Barbara Grabianowska 1927- *WhoWor 93*
Trzebinski, Andrzej 1922-1943 *PolBiDi*
Trzeciak, Leonard Peter 1945- *WhoWor 93*
Trzesniowski, Wieslaw *WhoScE 91-4*
Trzeszczynski, Jerzy 1934- *WhoScE 91-4*
Trznadel, Frank Dwight 1942- *St&PR 93*
Trznadel, Frank Dwight, Jr. 1942- *WhoAm 92*
Tsagarakis, Evaggelos Emman 1965- *WhoWor 93*
Tsagas, Grigorios Fotios 1935- *WhoWor 93*
Tsagas, Nicolaos 1938- *WhoScE 91-3*
Tsai, Gerald, Jr. *BioIn 17*
Tsai, Gerald, Jr. 1928- *St&PR 93*
Tsai, James Tarng 1943- *WhoSSW 93*
Tsai, King-Young 1953- *WhoWor 93*
Tsai, Mavis 1954- *WhoAmW 93*
Tsai, Tong-Ching 1934- *WhoE 93*
Tsai, Wen-Ying 1928- *WhoAm 92*
Ts'ai, Yuan-P'ei 1868-1940 *BioIn 17*
Ts'ai O 1882-1916 *HarEnMi*
Tsakanikas, Konstantinos T. 1933- *St&PR 93*
Tsakas, Spyros Christos 1941- *WhoWor 93*
Tsakiridis, Christos L. 1941- *St&PR 93*
Tsakiris, Constantine Haralambos 1954- *WhoWor 93*
Tsaloumas, Dimitris 1921- *BioIn 17*
Tsamblak *OxDcByz*
Tsamis, Donna Robin 1957- *WhoAmW 93*
Tsanev, Roumen Georgiev 1922- *WhoScE 91-4*
Tsang, Carl T. 1947- *St&PR 93*
Tsang, Eric *ScF&FL 92*
Tsang, Jon York 1955- *WhoSSW 93*
Tsang, King-Long 1949- *WhoWor 93*
Tsang, Leung 1950- *WhoAm 92*
Tsang, Philip 1956- *WhoWor 93*
Tsang, Philip Chung-Tak 1949- *St&PR 93*
Tsangaris, John Michael 1933- *WhoScE 91-3*
Tsantiris, Susan B. *Law&B 92*
Tsao, Jeffrey Y. *BioIn 17*
Tsao, Tsung Chen d1991 *BioIn 17*
Ts'ao, Yu 1910- *BioIn 17*
Ts'ao K'un 1862-1928 *HarEnMi*
Tsao Kwang-Yung, Peter 1933- *WhoAsAP 91*
Ts'ao Ts'ao 155-220 *HarEnMi*
Tsapogas, Makis J. 1926- *WhoAm 92*
Tsatsaronis, George 1949- *WhoSSW 93*
Tsavliris, Nicolas Alexander 1946- *WhoWor 93*
Tschacbasov, Nahum 1899-1984 *BioIn 17*
Tschantz, Bruce Allen 1938- *WhoAm 92*
Tschappat, Douglas Wilson 1927- *St&PR 93, WhoAm 92*
Tscharnuter, Werner M. 1945- *WhoScE 91-3*
Tschechowa, Olga 1896-1980 *IntDcF 2-3 [port]*
Tschemmernegg, Ferdinand 1939- *WhoScE 91-4*
Tscherny, George 1924- *WhoAm 92*
Tscheuschner, Ralf Dietrich 1956- *WhoWor 93*
Tschinkel, Sheila Lerner 1940- *WhoAm 92, WhoAmW 93*
Tschirch, (Friedrich) Wilhelm 1818-1892 *Baker 92*
Tschirhart, Paul Michael *Law&B 92*
Tschoepe, Thomas 1915- *WhoAm 92, WhoSSW 93*
Tschudi, Burkhard *Baker 92*
Tschudi, Burkhard 1702-1773 *See* Broadwood & Sons *Baker 92*
Tschudi, Theo 1941- *WhoScE 91-3*
Tschumy, Freda Coffing 1939- *WhoAmW 93*
Tse, Bernard Kapang 1948- *WhoAm 92*
Tse, Daniel Chi-wai 1934- *WhoAsAP 91*
Tse, Edmund Sze-Wing 1938- *St&PR 93, WhoWor 93*
Tse, George Kam Chuen 1944- *WhoWor 93*
Tse, Mary Mo-Yung 1949- *WhoE 93*
Tse, Ronald Siu-man 1935- *WhoWor 93*
Tse, Stephen Y. N. 1931- *St&PR 93*
Tse, Stephen Yung Nien 1931- *WhoAm 92*
Tse, Tsun-Him 1948- *WhoWor 93*
Tsechkovski, Mark Stanislav 1937- *WhoUN 92*
Tseckares, Charles Nicholas 1936- *WhoAm 92*
Tsedenbal, Yumjagiyn 1916-1991 *BioIn 17*
Tsekanovskii, Eduard Ruvimovich 1937- *WhoWor 93*
Tsekos, Ioannes 1936- *WhoScE 91-3*
Tselentis, Raissa Panayi *WhoAmW 93*
Tselikas, Emmanuel 1930- *WhoScE 91-3*
Tseng, Amelie Fan-in 1963- *WhoE 93*
Tseng, Ampere An-Pei 1946- *WhoWor 93*
Tseng, Evelina Meichih 1938- *WhoSSW 93*
Tseng, Howard Shih Chang 1935- *WhoSSW 93, WhoWor 93*
Tseng, Jack H. N. 1950- *St&PR 93*
Tseng, Joan Liu 1939- *WhoAmW 93*
Tseng, Kadin 1946- *WhoE 93*
Tseng, Linda 1936- *WhoE 93*
Tseng, Michael Tsung 1944- *WhoSSW 93*
Tseng, Tien-Jiunn 1938- *WhoWor 93*
Tseng, Vivian Sung-Yung *Law&B 92*
Tseng Kuo-feng 1811-1872 *HarEnMi*
Tseng Kwang-Shun 1924- *WhoAsAP 91*
Tsering, Dago 1941- *WhoAsAP 91*
Tsering, Dawa 1935- *WhoWor 93*
Tsering, Lyonpo Dawa 1935- *WhoAsAP 91*
Tsernoglou, Demetrius 1935- *WhoScE 91-3*
Tseu, Joseph Kum Kwong 1935- *WhoWor 93*
Tsevdos, Estelle J. *Law&B 92*
Tsfasman, Alexander 1906-1971 *Baker 92*
Tsfasman, Michael Anatolievich 1954- *WhoWor 93*
Tshabalala, Headman d1991 *BioIn 17*
Tshabalala, Thembeka Ruth 1942- *WhoUN 92*
Tshisekedi, Etienne *WhoWor 93*
Tshombe, Moise-Kapenda 1919-1969 *ColdWar 2 [port]*
Tshombe, Moise Kapenda 1920-1969 *DcTwHis*
Tshudy, Thomas Paul *Law&B 92*
Tsiang Yien-Si 1915- *WhoAsAP 91*
Tsiapalis, Chris Milton 1938- *WhoScE 91-3*
Tsiapera, Maria 1935- *WhoAm 92*
Tsien, Billie *BioIn 17*
Tsien, Frederick R. *Law&B 92*
Tsiganos, Constantine P. 1935- *WhoScE 91-3*
Tsigdinos, Karl Andrew 1954- *WhoWor 93*
Tsikalas, MaryBeth Vetock 1958- *WhoAmW 93*
Tsikata, Kojo *WhoAfr*
Tsikis, Stefanos 1953- *WhoWor 93*
Tsikrikas, Thomas 1936- *WhoWor 93*
Tsin, Andrew Tsang Cheung 1950- *WhoSSW 93*
Tsingas, Erotokritos P. 1926- *WhoScE 91-3*
Tsintsadze, Sulkhan 1925- *Baker 92*
Tsiolkovskii, Konstantin 1857-1935 *BioIn 17*, *ScF&FL 92*
Tsipis, Constantinos A. 1942- *WhoScE 91-3*
Tsipouridis, Constantinos 1942- *WhoScE 91-3*
Tsirigotis, M. Kathryn B. *Law&B 92*
Tsirimokos, Thomas Xenophon *Law&B 92*
Tsirpanlis, Constantine N. 1935- *WhoAm 92*
Tsivian, Yuri 1950- *BioIn 17*
Tsividis, Yannis P. 1946- *WhoAm 92*
Tsivin, Vladimir 1949- *BioIn 17*
Tsivitse, Peter J. 1930- *St&PR 93*
Tso, Kerrin Ilaina *Law&B 92*
Ts'o, Paul On-Pong 1929- *WhoAm 92, WhoWor 93*
Tso, Tien Chioh 1917- *WhoAm 92*
Tsogas, Miltiadis 1951- *WhoScE 91-3*
Tsoi, Viktor d1990 *BioIn 17*
Tsolakidis, Stefanos Konstantinos 1950- *WhoWor 93*
Tsolas, Orestes E. 1933- *WhoScE 91-3*
Tsolis, Alexandros K. 1935- *WhoScE 91-3*
Tsongas, Paul *BioIn 17*
Tsongas, Paul E. 1941- *NewYTBS 92 [port]*
Tsongas, Paul Efthemios 1941- *WhoAm 92*
Tsontakis, George 1951- *Baker 92*
Tsotetsi, Michael Nkhahle 1938- *WhoAfr*
Tsotsoros, Stathis 1949- *WhoEmL 93, WhoWor 93*
Tso Tsung-t'ang 1812-1885 *HarEnMi*
Tsou, Tang 1918- *WhoAm 92*
Tsoucalas, Nicholas 1926- *CngDr 91, WhoAm 92, WhoE 93*
Tsoulfanidis, Nicholas 1938- *WhoAm 92*
Tsoungas, Petros Georgios 1953- *WhoWor 93*
Tsoupaki, Calliope 1963- *Baker 92*
Tsoutrelis, Charalambos 1933- *WhoScE 91-3*
Tsoutsos, Andreas G. 1927- *WhoWor 93*
Tsouyopoulos, Georges 1930- *Baker 92*
Tsuang, Ming Tso 1931- *WhoAm 92*
Tsuboi, Kozo 1843-1898 *HarEnMi*
Tsuboi, Shogoro 1863-1913 *IntDcAn*
Tsubouchi, Daniel T. 1955- *St&PR 93*
Tsuchihashi, Atsuhide 1926- *WhoWor 93*
Tsuchihashi, Yuitsu 1891- *HarEnMi*
Tsuchikura, Tamotsu 1922- *WhoWor 93*
Tsuchiya, Masaharu 1928- *WhoWor 93*
Tsuchiya, Mitsuharu 1848-1920 *HarEnMi*
Tsuchiya, Suma 1924- *WhoWor 93*
Tsuchiya, Takumi 1923- *WhoAm 92*
Tsuchiya, Yoshihiko 1926- *WhoAsAP 91, WhoWor 93*
Tsuchiya, Yutaka 1942- *WhoWor 93*
Tsuda, Kyosuke 1907- *WhoWor 93*
Tsuda, Takao 1940- *WhoWor 93*
Tsuda, Ume 1864-1929 *BioIn 17*
Tsudia, Robert E. 1942- *St&PR 93*
Tsue, John Masaichi 1949- *WhoWor 93*
Tsuge, Shin 1939- *WhoWor 93*
Tsui, Benjamin Ming Wah 1948- *WhoSSW 93*
Tsui, Chia-Chi 1953- *WhoE 93*
Tsui, Hark *MiSFD 9*
Tsui, Lap-Chee 1950- *WhoAm 92, WhoE 93*
Tsuida, Maye 1941- *St&PR 93*
Tsuji, Daiichi 1926- *WhoAsAP 91*
Tsuji, Haruo 1933- *WhoWor 93*
Tsuji, Kazuhiko 1924- *WhoAsAP 91*
Tsuji, Shinichi *ConAu 138*
Tsuji, Shoichi 1895-1987 *Baker 92*
Tsuji, Tadakazu 1927- *WhoWor 93*
Tsuji, Tatsuo 1949- *WhoWor 93*
Tsujimoto, Trude A. *Law&B 92*
Tsujimoto, Trude A. 1953- *St&PR 93*
Tsujimura, Koichi 1922- *WhoWor 93*
Tsujita, Yoshihisa 1936- *St&PR 93*
Tsukada, Taiho 1745-1832 *BioIn 17*
Tsukahara, Shunpei 1947- *WhoAsAP 91*
Tsukamoto, Naoki 1940- *WhoWor 93*
Tsukamoto, Saburo 1927- *WhoAsAP 91*
Tsukasa, Yoko 1934- *IntDcF 2-3*
Tsukatani, Akihiro 1919- *Baker 92*
Tsukerman, Slava *MiSFD 9*
Tsukerman, Vladislav 1939- *WhoWor 93*
Tsukuda, Takuji 1942- *St&PR 93*
Tsumura, Takashi 1936- *WhoWor 93*
Tsunehiro, Ohgita Tsunmehiro 1923- *WhoWor 93*
Tsunematsu, Hiroshi 1940- *WhoAsAP 91*
Tsunematsu, Katsuyasu 1933- *WhoAsAP 91*
Tsung, Christine Chai-yi 1948- *WhoAmW 93*
Tsuno, Hisanori 1933- *WhoWor 93*
Tsunoda, Giichi 1937- *WhoAsAP 91*
Tsurtani, Taketsugu 1935- *WhoAm 92*
Tsuru, Shigeto 1912- *BioIn 17*
Tsurumi, Shunsuke 1922- *ConAu 138*
Tsuruno, Shiro 1946- *WhoWor 93*
Tsuruoka, Hiroshi 1932- *WhoAsAP 91*
Tsuruta, Kuniaki 1936- *St&PR 93*
Tsuruta, Yutaka 1936- *WhoWor 93*
Tsuruya, Hiroichi 1949- *WhoWor 93*
Tsushima, Rikio 1946- *WhoWor 93*
Tsushima, Takakatsu 1925- *WhoAsAP 91*
Tsushima, Yuji 1930- *WhoAsAP 91*
Tsushima, Yuko 1947- *WhoWor 93*
Tsusue, Akio 1928- *WhoWor 93*
Tsutakawa, George 1910- *BioIn 17*
Tsutani, Motohiro 1935- *WhoWor 93*
Tsutsui, Nobutaka 1944- *WhoAsAP 91*
Tsutsui, Yasutaka 1934- *ScF&FL 92*
Tsutsumi, Hisao 1949- *WhoWor 93*
Tsutsumi, Kinzoh 1944- *WhoWor 93*
Tsutsumi, Seiji *BioIn 17*
Tsutsumi, Yoshiaki *WhoWor 93*
Tsuzuki, Hideko 1943- *WhoWor 93*
Tsuzuki, Sadatoshi 1940- *WhoWor 93*
TSvetaeva, Marina Ivanovana 1892-1941 *BioIn 17*
Tsvetanov, Tsvetan 1931-1982 *Baker 92*
Tsvetkov, Petko 1924- *WhoScE 91-4*
Tsyganov, Shamil Irekovich 1963- *WhoWor 93*
Tsypin, George *BioIn 17*
Tsypin, George 1954- *ConTFT 10*
Tsyplenkov, Vladimir Sergeevich 1941- *WhoUN 92*
Tu, Elsie 1913- *WhoAsAP 91*
Tu, Feng-Sheng 1937- *WhoWor 93*
Tu, Hailing 1946- *WhoWor 93*
Tu, Jenn-Hwa 1954- *WhoWor 93*
Tu, Loring Wuliang 1952- *WhoE 93*
Tu, Wei-Ming 1940- *WhoAm 92*
Tu, Yueh-sheng 1887-1951 *BioIn 17*
Tua, Teresina 1867-1955 *Baker 92*
Tuaillon, Jean-Louis *WhoScE 91-2*

Tuakli-Williams, Juliette 1950- *WhoE 93*
Tuan, Debbie Fu-Tai 1930- *WhoAmW 93*
Tuan, Paul 1944- *St&PR 93*
Tuan, San Fu 1932- *WhoAm 92*
Tuan, Yi-Fu 1930- *ConAu 37NR*
Tuan Ch'i-jui 1865-1936 *HarEnMi*
Tuba, I. Stephen 1932- *St&PR 93*
Tubb, Allen R. *Law&B 92*
Tubb, Carrie 1876-1976 *Baker 92*
Tubb, E.C. 1919- *ScF&FL 92*
Tubb, Ernest (Dale) 1914-1984 *Baker 92*
Tubb, James Clarence *WhoAm 92*
Tubb, Joe Curtis 1947- *WhoSSW 93*
Tubb, Quenton *Law&B 92*
Tubbesing, Robert V. *St&PR 93*
Tubbs, Alan R. *BioIn 17*
Tubbs, Billy 1935- *BiDAMSp 1989*
Tubbs, David Eugene 1948- *WhoSSW 93*
Tubbs, Gerald Patrick 1949- *WhoE 93*
Tubbs, Joan Rose 1943- *WhoAmW 93*
Tubbs, Linda Marie 1947- *St&PR 93*
Tubbs, Richard Holmes, Jr. 1946- *St&PR 93*
Tubbs, Robert J., II *Law&B 92*
Tubbs, William Johnston 1938- *WhoE 93*
Tubby, I. M. *MajAI*
Tubby, Roger Wellington 1910-1991 *BioIn 17*
Tuberville, W.P. *St&PR 93*
Tubesing, Richard Lee 1937- *WhoSSW 93*
Tubin, Eduard 1905-1982 *Baker 92*
Tubis, Seymour 1919- *WhoAm 92*
Tublin, Ira Nathan 1929- *WhoE 93*
Tubman, Harriet 1815?-1913 *BioIn 17*
Tubman, William C. 1932- *St&PR 93*
Tubman, William Charles *Law&B 92*
Tubman, William Charles 1932- *WhoAm 92*
Tubman, William Vacanarat Shadrach 1895-1971 *DcTwHis*
Tuburan, Isidra Bombeo 1955- *WhoWor 93*
Tucceri, Clive Knowles 1953- *WhoAmW 93, WhoE 93, WhoEmL 93, WhoWor 93*
Tucceri, Ellen Lee 1945- *WhoWor 93*
Tucci, Albert William 1938- *WhoE 93*
Tucci, Daniel Patrick 1943- *St&PR 93, WhoAm 92*
Tucci, Edmond R. 1933- *WhoE 93*
Tucci, Gabriella 1929- *Baker 92*
Tucci, Gerald F. 1926- *St&PR 93*
Tucci, Gerald Frank 1926- *WhoE 93*
Tucci, Jacqueline 1935- *WhoAmW 93*
Tucci, Mark Anthony 1950- *WhoE 93*
Tucci, Robert, II 1954- *St&PR 93*
Tucci, Robert S. 1952- *WhoAm 92*
Tucci, Tony 1935- *St&PR 93*
Tuccillo, Anthony J. 1938- *St&PR 93*
Tucek, Jan c. 1743-1783 *OxDcOp*
Tucek, Josef *WhoScE 91-4*
Tucek, Stanislav 1932- *WhoScE 91-4*
Tucek, Vincenc 1773-c. 1821 *OxDcOp*
Tuchais, Edmond 1940- *WhoScE 91-2*
Tuchi, Ben Joseph 1936- *WhoSSW 93*
Tuchinsky, Joseph Benjamin *Law&B 92*
Tuchman, Avraham 1935- *WhoAm 92*
Tuchman, Barbara W. 1912-1989 *JeAmHC*
Tuchman, Barbara Wertheim *BioIn 17*
Tuchman, Kenneth I. 1950- *WhoAm 92*
Tuchman, Martin 1941- *St&PR 93*
Tuchman, Maurice 1936- *WhoAm 92*
Tuchman, Maurice Simon 1936- *WhoE 93*
Tuchman, Steven Leslie 1946- *WhoEmL 93*
Tuchmann, Philipp 1810-1883 *BioIn 17*
Tuchner, Michael 1934- *MiSFD 9*
Tucholke, Brian Edward 1946- *WhoE 93*
Tuck, Alan W. 1948- *St&PR 93*
Tuck, April Elizabeth 1956- *WhoAmW 93*
Tuck, Brian *WhoScE 91-1*
Tuck, Dennis R. 1943- *St&PR 93*
Tuck, Donald H. 1922- *ScF&FL 92*
Tuck, Edward Hallam 1927- *WhoAm 92*
Tuck, Grayson Edwin 1927- *WhoAm 92*
Tuck, Hugh Macauley 1945- *St&PR 93*
Tuck, John Chatfield 1945- *WhoAm 92*
Tuck, Lily 1938- *ConAu 139, ConLC 70 [port]*
Tuck, Lynne 1938- *WhoAmW 93*
Tuck, Marcus Jonathan 1961- *WhoWor 93*
Tuck, Mary Beth 1930- *WhoSSW 93*
Tuck, Michael R. 1941- *St&PR 93*
Tuck, Murray 1920- *WhoE 93*
Tuck, N. Barton 1938- *St&PR 93*
Tuck, Robert Mell 1921- *St&PR 93*
Tuck, Russell R., Jr. 1934- *WhoAm 92*
Tucker, Alan Curtiss 1943- *WhoAm 92*
Tucker, Alan David 1936- *WhoAm 92*
Tucker, Alan J. 1946- *St&PR 93*
Tucker, Albert William 1905- *WhoE 93*
Tucker, Allen Brown, Jr. 1942- *WhoAm 92*
Tucker, Allen Phillip 1936- *St&PR 93*
Tucker, Althea Sprague *AmWomPl*
Tucker, Ann Manning 1957- *WhoAmW 93*
Tucker, Anne Wilkes 1945- *WhoAm 92*
Tucker, Anthony 1924- *WhoWor 93*
Tucker, Arthur Farrar 1948- *St&PR 93*
Tucker, Arthur V. 1949- *St&PR 93*
Tucker, Arthur Wilson 1914- *BioIn 17*
Tucker, Aubrey Stephen 1945- *WhoWor 93*
Tucker, Barbara Ann 1939- *WhoAmW 93*
Tucker, Bernice Gallup *AmWomPl*
Tucker, Beverly Sowers 1936- *WhoAmW 93*
Tucker, Billy Bob 1928- *WhoAm 92*
Tucker, Bob *ScF&FL 92*
Tucker, Bob 1914- *BioIn 17*
Tucker, Bowen Hayward *Law&B 92*
Tucker, Brian H. *Law&B 92*
Tucker, Carll 1951- *St&PR 93*
Tucker, Carroll M. 1927- *WhoIns 93*
Tucker, Carter Harrison *Law&B 92*
Tucker, Charles Christopher 1950- *WhoWrEP 92*
Tucker, Charles Ray 1950- *WhoSSW 93*
Tucker, Christopher Sloan 1963- *WhoE 93*
Tucker, D. Weston 1938- *St&PR 93*
Tucker, Dale D. 1940- *St&PR 93*
Tucker, Deborah Diane 1952- *WhoAmW 93*
Tucker, Deborah M. 1952- *St&PR 93*
Tucker, Don E. *Law&B 92*
Tucker, Don Eugene 1928- *St&PR 93, WhoAm 92*
Tucker, Donald M. *Law&B 92*
Tucker, Donald M. 1922- *St&PR 93*
Tucker, Donna Frances 1958- *WhoAmW 93*
Tucker, E. Carolyn 1949- *WhoSSW 93*
Tucker, Edward Llewellyn 1921- *WhoSSW 93*
Tucker, Edwin Earl 1926- *WhoSSW 93*
Tucker, Ellis E. 1931-1990 *BioIn 17*
Tucker, Frances Laughridge 1916- *WhoAmW 93*
Tucker, Frank T. 1949- *St&PR 93*
Tucker, Frederick Thomas 1940- *WhoAm 92*
Tucker, Gail Susan 1945- *WhoAmW 93*
Tucker, Gardiner Luttrell 1925- *WhoAm 92*
Tucker, Garland Scott, III 1947- *St&PR 93, WhoE 93*
Tucker, Gary C. *Law&B 92*
Tucker, Gary Francis 1936- *St&PR 93*
Tucker, Gary Jay 1934- *WhoAm 92*
Tucker, Gene Milton 1935- *WhoSSW 93*
Tucker, Geoffrey Thomas *WhoScE 91-1*
Tucker, George 1775-1861 *ScF&FL 92*
Tucker, George Maxwell, Sr. 1950- *WhoEmL 93*
Tucker, George Mckinney, Jr. 1934- *St&PR 93*
Tucker, Glenn Gorham 1928- *WhoSSW 93*
Tucker, Gordon Michael 1955- *St&PR 93*
Tucker, H. Richard 1936- *WhoAm 92*
Tucker, Hal Beall 1928- *WhoAm 92*
Tucker, Harlan Winthrop 1923- *WhoSSW 93*
Tucker, Harvey Michael 1938- *WhoAm 92*
Tucker, Helen W. 1926- *WhoWrEP 92*
Tucker, Henry *DcCPCAm*
Tucker, Herbert J. 1934- *St&PR 93*
Tucker, Irving Francis 1933- *WhoSSW 93*
Tucker, Jalie Ann 1954- *WhoAmW 93*
Tucker, James 1929- *ScF&FL 92*
Tucker, James Arthur 1959- *WhoE 93*
Tucker, James E. 1943- *St&PR 93*
Tucker, James L. *Law&B 92*
Tucker, James Lanny *Law&B 92*
Tucker, Janet L. *Law&B 92*
Tucker, Janet Lynn 1957- *WhoAmW 93*
Tucker, Jay Scott 1957- *St&PR 93*
Tucker, Jeffrey A. *Law&B 92*
Tucker, Jeffrey Allen 1947- *St&PR 93*
Tucker, Jeffrey Thomas 1955- *WhoSSW 93*
Tucker, Jess 1913- *St&PR 93*
Tucker, Jim Guy 1943- *WhoAm 92*
Tucker, Jim Guy, Jr. 1943- *WhoSSW 93*
Tucker, Jo-Von *BioIn 17*
Tucker, Jo Von 1937- *WhoE 93*
Tucker, John Avery 1924- *WhoE 93*
Tucker, John Barry *WhoScE 91-1*
Tucker, John Joseph 1940- *WhoAm 92*
Tucker, John Pierce, Jr. 1943- *WhoSSW 93*
Tucker, John Randolph 1812-1883 *BioIn 17*
Tucker, Joseph 1920- *WhoE 93*
Tucker, Judith Lynne 1963- *WhoE 93*
Tucker, K. Gregory *Law&B 92*
Tucker, Katherine Virginia 1946- *WhoAmW 93*
Tucker, Kay Hartman 1957- *WhoWrEP 92*
Tucker, Keith A. 1945- *St&PR 93, WhoAm 92*
Tucker, Kenneth Howard 1953- *WhoSSW 93*
Tucker, Kevin *Law&B 92*
Tucker, Laura Megan *Law&B 92*
Tucker, Laura R. *Law&B 92*
Tucker, Laurey Dan 1936- *WhoAm 92*
Tucker, Lemuel 1938-1991 *BioIn 17*
Tucker, Louis Leonard 1927- *WhoAm 92*
Tucker, Louise Emery 1876- *AmWomPl*
Tucker, Marcia 1940- *WhoAm 92*
Tucker, Marcus Othello 1934- *WhoWor 93*
Tucker, Marie Ila 1922- *WhoAmW 93*
Tucker, Martin 1928- *WhoWrEP 92*
Tucker, Melvin Jay 1931- *WhoWrEP 92*
Tucker, Michael *BioIn 17, WhoAm 92*
Tucker, Michael J. 1948- *St&PR 93*
Tucker, Morrison G. 1911- *St&PR 93*
Tucker, Morrison Graham 1911- *WhoAm 92, WhoSSW 93*
Tucker, Nancy Meredith 1946- *WhoWrEP 92*
Tucker, Neil Thomas 1949- *WhoSSW 93*
Tucker, Nicholas J. 1951- *St&PR 93*
Tucker, Nimrod Holt, III 1947- *WhoSSW 93*
Tucker, Norman 1910-1978 *OxDcOp*
Tucker, Paul Andrew 1939- *St&PR 93*
Tucker, Paul Hayes 1950- *BioIn 17*
Tucker, Paul William 1921- *WhoAm 92*
Tucker, Phyllis Anita 1952- *WhoSSW 93*
Tucker, Randolph Wadsworth 1949- *WhoAm 92*
Tucker, Ray Moss *WhoAm 92*
Tucker, Raymond William, Jr. 1951- *WhoE 93*
Tucker, Richard 1913-1975 *Baker 92, IntDcOp, OxDcOp*
Tucker, Richard Frank 1926- *WhoAm 92*
Tucker, Richard Lee 1935- *WhoAm 92*
Tucker, Richard Lee 1940- *St&PR 93, WhoAm 92*
Tucker, Robert A. 1926- *St&PR 93*
Tucker, Robert D. 1933- *St&PR 93*
Tucker, Robert Dennard 1933- *WhoAm 92*
Tucker, Robert Macom 1959- *WhoSSW 93*
Tucker, Robert Warren 1924- *WhoAm 92*
Tucker, Rodney Stuart 1948- *WhoWor 93*
Tucker, Ronald Edward 1955- *WhoE 93*
Tucker, Rosina C. 1881-1987 *EncAACR*
Tucker, Royster M., Jr. 1931- *St&PR 93*
Tucker, Ruth A(nne) 1945- *ConAu 40NR*
Tucker, Ruth Wilkinson *AmWomPl*
Tucker, S. *WhoScE 91-1*
Tucker, Shirley Elizabeth 1936- *WhoSSW 93*
Tucker, Shirley Lois Cotter 1927- *WhoAm 92*
Tucker, Skip 1947- *St&PR 93*
Tucker, Sophie 1884-1966 *Baker 92*
Tucker, Spencer Coakley 1937- *WhoSSW 93*
Tucker, Stefan Franklin 1938- *WhoAm 92*
Tucker, Tanya Denise 1958- *WhoAm 92*
Tucker, Terry Lee 1953- *WhoSSW 93*
Tucker, Thomas J. *Law&B 92*
Tucker, Thomas James 1929- *St&PR 93, WhoAm 92*
Tucker, Thomas S., Jr. 1948- *St&PR 93*
Tucker, Tom *BioIn 17*
Tucker, Tommy 1934-1982 *SoulM*
Tucker, Tracy J. 1948- *St&PR 93*
Tucker, W. Lee 1934- *St&PR 93*
Tucker, Walter 1924- *AfrAmBi [port]*
Tucker, Watson Billopp 1940- *WhoAm 92*
Tucker, William *BioIn 17*
Tucker, William Edward 1932- *WhoAm 92, WhoSSW 93*
Tucker, William Handley 1952- *WhoSSW 93*
Tucker, William Jewett 1839-1926 *BioIn 17*
Tucker, William Vincent 1934- *WhoAm 92*
Tucker, Willis Carleton 1907- *WhoAm 92*
Tucker, Wilson 1914- *BioIn 17, ScF&FL 92*
Tuckerman, Donald M. 1930- *WhoAm 92*
Tuckerman, Joseph 1778-1840 *BioIn 17*
Tuckerman, Samuel Parkman 1819-1890 *Baker 92*
Tucker-Pickens, Mary Olive 1947- *WhoWrEP 92*
Tuckett, Rhona Bennett 1947- *WhoAmW 93*
Tuckey, Bruce M. 1957- *St&PR 93*
Tuckey, John S. 1921-1987 *ScF&FL 92*
Tuckey, William 1708-1781 *Baker 92*
Tuckey, Wilson 1935- *WhoAsAP 91*
Tuckman, Bruce Wayne 1938- *WhoAm 92*
Tuckman, Howard Paul 1941- *WhoAm 92*
Tuckwell, Barry (Emmanuel) 1931- *Baker 92, WhoAm 92*
Tuczek-Ehrenburg, Leopoldine 1821-1883 *OxDcOp*
Tudisco, Jasper Thomas 1917- *WhoE 93*
Tudjman, Franjo *WhoWor 93*
Tudor, Andrew 1942- *ScF&FL 92*
Tudor, Antony 1909-1987 *BioIn 17*
Tudor, David (Eugene) 1926- *Baker 92*
Tudor, Edward C. 1920- *St&PR 93*
Tudor, Eugeniu 1937- *WhoScE 91-4*
Tudor, Jim Patrick 1946- *WhoSSW 93, WhoWrEP 92*
Tudor, John 1954- *BioIn 17*
Tudor, John Colin 1941- *WhoWor 93*
Tudor, Margaret Beaufort 1443-1509 *BioIn 17*
Tudor, Robert Beall, Jr. 1935- *St&PR 93*
Tudor, Tasha 1915- *MajAI [port], SmATA 69 [port]*
Tudoran, Ionel 1913- *Baker 92*
Tudryn, Joyce Marie 1959- *WhoE 93*
Tudway, Thomas c. 1650-1726 *Baker 92*
Tuell, Jack Marvin 1923- *WhoAm 92*
Tuemmler, William Bruce 1927- *WhoAm 92*
Tuempel, Christian Ludwig 1937- *WhoWor 93*
Tuerff, James Rodrick 1941- *St&PR 93, WhoAm 92, WhoIns 93, WhoSSW 93*
Tuerk, Hanne 1951- *SmATA 71*
Tuerk, James R. 1953- *St&PR 93*
Tuerk, Richard Carl 1941- *WhoSSW 93*
Tuers, La Verne *AmWomPl*
Tueting, William Francis 1942- *WhoAm 92*
Tufail, Amer 1964- *WhoWor 93*
Tufano, Manuela 1957- *WhoAmW 93*
Tufariello, Joseph James 1935- *WhoAm 92*
Tufaro, Judith Boettger 1939- *WhoE 93*
Tufekcioglu, Zeki 1935- *WhoScE 91-4*
Tufeld, Howard L. 1935- *St&PR 93*
Tuffen, Michael James 1940- *WhoWor 93*
Tuffey, Thomas J. 1946- *St&PR 93*
Tuffin, Christina G. *Law&B 92*
Tuffley, Francis Douglas 1946- *WhoEmL 93*
Tufnel, Nigel 1948-
See Spinal Tap *ConMus 8*
Tufnell, Richard John *WhoScE 91-1*
Tuft, Jerold H. 1929- *St&PR 93*
Tuft, Mary Ann 1934- *WhoAm 92*
Tufte, Edward *NewYTBS 92 [port]*
Tufte, Edward R. 1942- *BioIn 17*
Tufte, Edward Rolf 1942- *WhoAm 92, WhoWrEP 92*
Tufte, Marilyn Jean 1939- *WhoAmW 93*
Tufte, Obert Norman 1932- *WhoAm 92*
Tufton, Jane Lee 1949- *WhoAmW 93*
Tufts, Bert *St&PR 93*
Tufts, David d1990 *BioIn 17*
Tufts, David Albert, Jr. 1945- *WhoAm 92, WhoE 93*
Tufts, Donald Winston 1933- *WhoAm 92*
Tufts, Donna Lee 1948- *WhoE 93*
Tufts, Eleanor *BioIn 17*
Tufts, Eleanor (May) 1927-1991 *ConAu 136*
Tufts, John 1689-1750 *Baker 92*
Tufts, John Wheeler 1825-1908 *Baker 92*
Tufts, Marie Dreuil *Law&B 92*
Tufts, Warren G. 1917- *St&PR 93*
Tufty, Harold Guilford 1922- *WhoE 93*
Tu Fu 712-770 *MagSWL [port]*
Tugendhat, Christopher 1937- *St&PR 93*
Tugendhat, Fritz *BioIn 17*
Tuggle, Francis Douglas 1943- *WhoAm 92*
Tuggle, Ralph E. 1937- *St&PR 93*
Tuggle, Richard 1948- *MiSFD 9*
Tuggle, Richard (Allan) 1948- *ConAu 139*
Tuggle, Richard Brittain d1990 *BioIn 17*
Tughan, V.D. *WhoScE 91-1*
Tughrul Beg c. 993-1063 *OxDcByz*
Tugman, John Charles 1949- *St&PR 93*
Tugman, Stuart Grady 1937- *St&PR 93*
Tugsavul, Aysen 1938- *WhoScE 91-4*
Tugwell, Rexford G. 1891-1979 *PolPar*
Tuhanuku, Joses 1948- *WhoAsAP 91*
Tuholski, Elizabeth Murray 1956- *WhoAmW 93*
Tuholsky, Bruce 1940- *St&PR 93*
Tuhy, Philip Radmir 1930- *WhoE 93*
Tuinebreijer, Willem Eduard 1945- *WhoWor 93*
Tuinstra, Robert Jacob 1925- *St&PR 93*
Tu'ipelehake, Fatafehi 1922- *WhoAsAP 91, WhoWor 93*
Tuita, Siosaia Aleamotu'a Laufilitonga 1920- *WhoAsAP 91, WhoWor 93*
Tuite, James R. *Law&B 92*
Tuite, Michael Leon 1943- *WhoWor 93*
Tuitt, Ron S. 1958- *WhoWrEP 92*
Tujak-Weiss, Monica Cari 1966- *WhoAmW 93*
Tuke, Anthony Favill 1920- *St&PR 93*
Tukey, Brad R. 1946- *St&PR 93*
Tukey, David Davenport 1953- *WhoSSW 93*
Tukey, Harold Bradford, Jr. 1934- *WhoAm 92*
Tukey, John Wilder 1915- *WhoAm 92*
Tukey, Loren Davenport 1921- *WhoAm 92*
Tukhachevsky, Mikhail Nikolaevich 1893-1937 *HarEnMi*

Tukiainen, Jouko *WhoScE 91-4*
Tuksar, Stanislav 1945- *Baker 92*
Tulalamba, Danai 1936- *WhoWor 93*
Tulchin, Stanley *WhoAm 92*
Tuleja, Thaddeus V. 1944- *ScF&FL 92*
Tuley, B.B. 1936- *St&PR 93*
Tuley, John L. 1922- *St&PR 93*
Tuley, Richard William 1942- *St&PR 93*
Tuley, Thomas W. 1940- *St&PR 93*
Tuley, Thomas Wayne 1940- *WhoAm 92*
Tulin, John Alexander 1947- *WhoAm 92*
Tulindberg, Erik (Eriksson) 1761-1814 *Baker 92*
Tuliszka, Edmund 1920- *WhoScE 91-4*
Tull, Donald Stanley 1924- *WhoAm 92*
Tull, Jewel Bothwell *AmWomPl*
Tull, Renee Martin 1950- *WhoAmW 93*
Tull, Robert Lewis 1926- *St&PR 93*
Tull, Theresa Anne 1936- *WhoAm 92, WhoAmW 93*
Tull, William G. 1928- *St&PR 93*
Tull, Willis Clayton, Jr. 1931- *WhoE 93*
Tullar, Beverly Ann 1955- *WhoAmW 93*
Tullar, Dudley 1932- *St&PR 93*
Tulledge, Robert Eugene 1929- *St&PR 93*
Tuller, Harry L. *WhoE 93*
Tuller, Raimund 1932- *WhoScE 91-3*
Tuller, S. Mark *Law&B 92*
Tuller, Tammy Elaine *Law&B 92*
Tulley, Francis Mark *WhoScE 91-1*
Tulley, James Joseph 1950- *St&PR 93*
Tulley, Monica Elaine 1953- *WhoAmW 93*
Tullio, Douglas J. 1943- *St&PR 93*
Tullio-Altan, Carlo 1916- *IntDcAn*
Tullis, Bill 1953- *WhoSSW 93*
Tullis, Edward Lewis 1917- *WhoAm 92*
Tullis, James Luther Lyman 1947- *WhoAm 92, WhoE 93*
Tullis, John Ledbetter 1911- *WhoAm 92*
Tullman, Arthur S. 1917- *St&PR 93*
Tullman, Glen Edward 1959- *St&PR 93*
Tullman, Howard A. 1945- *St&PR 93*
Tullman, John J. 1904-1990 *BioIn 17*
Tullner, Donna Anita 1954- *WhoAmW 93*
Tulloch, George S. 1932- *St&PR 93*
Tulloch, George S., Jr. *Law&B 92*
Tulloch, George Sherlock, Jr. 1932- *WhoAm 92*
Tulloch, John 1942- *ScF&FL 92*
Tulloch, John R. 1947- *St&PR 93*
Tulloch, Peter 1943- *WhoUN 92*
Tulloch, Renee La Couture *BioIn 17*
Tulloch, Rodney William 1939- *WhoSSW 93*
Tulloch, William W. 1954- *St&PR 93*
Tulloch, William W., Jr. 1930- *St&PR 93*
Tullock, Joyce *ScF&FL 92*
Tullos, Hugh Simpson 1935- *WhoAm 92*
Tullos, John Baxter 1915- *St&PR 93, WhoAm 92*
Tulloss, Michael Byron *Law&B 92*
Tully, Albert Julian 1911- *WhoAm 92*
Tully, Alice 1902- *Baker 92, BioIn 17*
Tully, Andrew Frederick, Jr. 1914- *WhoWrEP 92*
Tully, Chris *Law&B 92*
Tully, Christopher Carl 1913- *WhoSSW 93*
Tully, D.P. 1932- *St&PR 93*
Tully, Daniel Patrick 1932- *WhoAm 92, WhoWor 93*
Tully, Darrow 1932- *St&PR 93, WhoAm 92*
Tully, James H., Jr. *Law&B 92*
Tully, James K. 1921- *St&PR 93*
Tully, Jane Williams 1946- *WhoAmW 93*
Tully, John 1923- *ScF&FL 92*
Tully, John F. *Law&B 92*
Tully, Judd 1947- *WhoE 93*
Tully, Kathryn Croft 1918- *WhoAmW 93*
Tully, (William) Mark 1935- *ConAu 136*
Tully, May *AmWomPl*
Tully, Paul d1992 *NewYTBS 92 [port]*
Tully, Paul C. 1917- *St&PR 93*
Tully, Richard Lowden 1911- *WhoAm 92*
Tully, Robert Gerard 1955- *WhoEmL 93*
Tully, Suzan M. 1944- *St&PR 93*
Tully, Thomas Alois 1940- *St&PR 93, WhoAm 92*
Tully, William P. 1940- *WhoAm 92*
Tulman, Daniel Jay 1950- *WhoSSW 93*
Tulman, Lorraine Johnson 1950- *WhoE 93*
Tulou, Jean-Louis 1786-1865 *Baker 92*
Tulp, Gaye G.K. 1947- *WhoAmW 93*
Tulsa Jack 1862?-1895 *BioIn 17*
Tulsky, Alex Sol 1911- *WhoAm 92*
Tulsky, Fredric Neal 1950- *WhoAm 92, WhoE 93*
Tultolsky, Bruce *St&PR 93*
Tulving, Endel 1927- *WhoAm 92*
Tuma, Franz 1704-1774 *Baker 92*
Tuman, E. William 1942- *St&PR 93*
Tuman, Myron C(hester) 1946- *ConAu 139*
Tumarkin, Joel Ellis 1934- *WhoE 93*
Tumbelston, Peter *BioIn 17*
Tumberlinson, Travis D. 1949- *WhoSSW 93*
Tumbler, Joseph M. 1949- *WhoAm 92*
Tumbleson, Treva Rose 1927- *WhoAmW 93*
Tumi, Christian Wiyghan Cardinal 1930- *WhoWor 93*
Tuminello, S.J. *BioIn 17*
Tuminello, William Joseph 1920- *WhoWor 93*
Tummala, Rao Ramamohana 1942- *WhoAm 92*
Tummers, John Pierre *Law&B 92*
Tumminelli, Susan Jean 1959- *WhoAmW 93*
Tumminello, Anthony Paul *Law&B 92*
Tumminello, Lee Mosier *Law&B 92*
Tumminello, Stephen C. 1936- *St&PR 93*
Tumminello, Stephen Charles 1936- *WhoAm 92*
Tumminello, Ted *Law&B 92*
Tumpane, John D. 1922- *WhoWrEP 92*
Tumpel, Herbert *WhoScE 91-4*
Tumsavas, Zeynal 1966- *WhoScE 91-4*
Tumulty, Joseph P. 1879-1954 *PolPar*
Tumwine, Elly 1954- *WhoAfr*
Tun, Maung Myint Thein 1950- *WhoWor 93*
Tunakan, Seniha 1908- *IntDcAn*
Tunbo, Frances G. *DcAmChF 1985*
Tunbridge, William Michael Gregg 1940- *WhoWor 93*
Tuncer, Ahmet 1929- *WhoScE 91-4*
Tuncer, Ali Ugur 1941- *WhoUN 92*
Tunder, Franz 1614-1667 *Baker 92*
Tundermann, John Hayes 1940- *St&PR 93*
Tundo, Pietro Rosario 1945- *WhoWor 93*
Tune, Tommy *BioIn 17*
Tune, Tommy 1939- *WhoAm 92, WhoE 93*
Tunell, Kevin *BioIn 17*
Tung, David Hsi Hsin 1923- *WhoAm 92*
Tung, Fong-Chung 1915- *WhoWor 93*
Tung, Gea *Law&B 92*
Tung, Ko-Yung 1947- *WhoAm 92, WhoWor 93*
Tung, Lian Shen 1953- *WhoWor 93*
Tung, Ling *BioIn 17*
Tung, Po-Nan 1949- *WhoE 93*
Tung, Rosalie Lam 1948- *WhoAmW 93*
Tung, Sandy *MiSFD 9*
Tung, Shih-Ping 1953- *WhoWor 93*
Tung, Theodore H. 1934- *St&PR 93*
Tung, Theodore Hschum 1934- *WhoAm 92*
Tung Fu-hsiang 1839-1908 *HarEnMi*
Tungsvik, Mary Elizabeth 1932- *WhoAmW 93*
Tunheim, Jerald Arden 1940- *WhoAm 92*
Tunick, Bonnie I. *Law&B 92*
Tunick, Richard David 1946- *St&PR 93*
Tuning, William 1935-1982 *ScF&FL 92*
Tunis, Edwin (Burdett) 1897-1973 *MajAI [port]*
Tunis, Elliot Charles *Law&B 92*
Tunis, John R(oberts) 1889-1975 *DcAmChF 1960, MajAI [port]*
Tunison, James H. 1938- *St&PR 93*
Tunkelo, Eino *WhoScE 91-4*
Tunkieicz, Mary Ursula 1937- *WhoAmW 93*
Tunley, David (Evatt) 1930- *Baker 92*
Tunley, Roul 1912- *WhoAm 92*
Tunnell, Clida Diane 1946- *WhoAmW 93, WhoEmL 93, WhoWor 93*
Tunnell, Daniel Robinson 1948- *WhoE 93*
Tunnell, Ella J. *AmWomPl*
Tunnell, Emlen 1925-1975 *BioIn 17*
Tunnell, Kenneth Welch 1929- *St&PR 93*
Tunnell, Michael O. *ScF&FL 92*
Tunnell, T.R. *Law&B 92*
Tunnell, William Newton, Jr. 1945- *WhoSSW 93*
Tunner, William Henry 1906-1983 *HarEnMi*
Tunney, Francis R. 1947- *St&PR 93*
Tunney, Francis R., Jr. *Law&B 92*
Tunney, Francis Richard, Jr. 1947- *WhoAm 92*
Tunney, Gene 1898-1978 *BioIn 17*
Tunney, John Varick 1934- *WhoAm 92*
Tunnicliffe, C.F. 1901-1979 *BioIn 17*
Tunnicliffe, Charles Frederick 1901-1979 *BioIn 17*
Tunnicliffe, William Warren 1922- *WhoE 93, WhoWor 93*
Tunno, Robert 1946- *St&PR 93*
Tunon, Modaldo Antonio 1950- *WhoWor 93*
Tun Tin *WhoWor 93*
Tuohy, John Edward *Law&B 92*
Tuohy, Patricia C. *Law&B 92*
Tuohy, William 1926- *WhoAm 92*
Tuomilehto, Jaakko 1946- *WhoScE 91-4*
Tuominen, Francis William 1943- *WhoAm 92*
Tuomisto, Jouko Juhani 1939- *WhoScE 91-4*
Tuori, Charles Raymond 1948- *WhoSSW 93*
Tuorto, Andrew John 1946- *St&PR 93*
Tupamaki, Paavo Artturi 1920- *WhoScE 91-4*
Tupas, Maria Isabel 1964- *WhoAmW 93*
Tupas, Niel D. 1932- *WhoAsAP 91*
Tupkov, Dimiter 1929- *Baker 92*
Tupler, Harriet 1935- *WhoAmW 93*
Tupman, Jane *AmWomPl*
Tupou, Taufa'ahau, IV 1918- *WhoAsAP 91, WhoWor 93*
Tupouto'a, Crown Prince 1948- *WhoAsAP 91*
Tupouto'a, Prince 1948- *WhoWor 93*
Tupper, Charles John 1920- *WhoAm 92*
Tupper, David Edward 1955- *WhoE 93*
Tupper, Edith Sessions *AmWomPl*
Tupper, Loretta d1990 *BioIn 17*
Tur, Mario Rodolfo, Jr. 1950- *WhoSSW 93*
Tura, Tessi *WhoWrEP 92*
Turabi, Hassan al- *BioIn 17, NewYTBS 92 [port]*
Turaj, Frank 1934- *WhoAm 92, WhoWor 93*
Turakainen, Paavo Kalevi 1942- *WhoScE 91-4*
Turan, Edward G. *Law&B 92*
Turanciol, Nihat O. 1934- *St&PR 93*
Turano, Emanuel Nicolas 1917- *WhoAm 92*
Turanski, Anita Marlene 1951- *WhoWor 93*
Turay, Abdul Rahnman 1938- *WhoWor 93*
Turbak, Edward F. 1961- *St&PR 93*
Turbak, Stephen Albin *Law&B 92*
Turbanisch, Gerhard Otmar 1956- *WhoWor 93*
Turbay, Diana d1991 *BioIn 17*
Turbayne, Colin Murray 1916- *WhoAm 92*
Turberg, Phillip A. 1928- *St&PR 93*
Turbervill, Edith Picton- 1872-1960 *BioIn 17*
Turbeville, Deborah 1937- *BioIn 17*
Turbeville, Gus 1923- *WhoAm 92*
Turbeville, James Clyde 1932- *St&PR 93*
Turbeville, Robert Morris 1951- *WhoE 93*
Turbeville, William Jackson, Jr. 1915- *WhoAm 92*
Turbide, David Andrew 1949- *WhoE 93*
Turbidy, John Berry 1928- *WhoAm 92*
Turbiville, J.F. 1928- *St&PR 93*
Turbiville, John F. *Law&B 92*
Turbyfill, John R. 1931- *St&PR 93*
Turbyfill, John Ray 1931- *WhoAm 92*
Turchaninov, Piotr (Ivanovich) 1779-1856 *Baker 92*
Turchi, Guido 1916- *Baker 92*
Turchi, Richard A. 1934- *WhoSSW 93*
Turchyn, William, Jr. 1945- *WhoWor 93*
Turcios Lima, Luis Augusto *DcCPCAm*
Turck, Joseph Neil 1944- *St&PR 93*
Turco, Aldo 1922- *WhoScE 91-3*
Turco, Alfred A. *Law&B 92*
Turco, Alfred John 1929- *St&PR 93*
Turco, Charlene Mary *WhoAmW 93*
Turco, Lewis Putnam 1934- *WhoAm 92, WhoE 93, WhoWrEP 92*
Turco, Richard Peter 1943- *WhoAm 92*
Turcot, Marguerite Hogan 1934- *WhoAmW 93, WhoSSW 93, WhoWor 93*
Turcott, Robert G. *Law&B 92*
Turcott, Robert George 1944- *St&PR 93*
Turcotte, Donald Lawson 1932- *WhoAm 92*
Turcotte, Jean-Claude 1936- *WhoAm 92*
Turcotte, Jeremiah George 1933- *WhoAm 92*
Turcotte, Joe C. 1960- *St&PR 93*
Turcotte, Martine *Law&B 92*
Turcotte, Martine 1960- *St&PR 93*
Turcotte, Thomas E. *Law&B 92*
Turcq, Dominique Florimond 1950- *WhoWor 93*
Turczynowicz, Roman 1813-1882 *PolBiDi*
Turczyn-Toles, Doreen Marie 1958- *WhoAmW 93, WhoEmL 93, WhoWor 93*
Ture, Norman Bernard 1923- *WhoAm 92*
Tureaud, Alexander Pierre 1899-1972 *EncAACR [port]*
Tureck, Rosalyn 1914- *Baker 92, WhoAm 92, WhoAmW 93*
Tureen, Phyllis 1932- *WhoE 93*
Turek, Leslie *ScF&FL 92*
Turekian, Karl Karekin 1927- *WhoAm 92*
Turel, Joan Marie *WhoAmW 93*
Turenne, Henri de la Tour d'Auvergne, Viscount of 1611-1675 *HarEnMi*
Turesky, Samuel 1916- *WhoE 93*
Turesky, Stanley F. 1927- *WhoE 93*
Turetaev, Isabek Djolshibekovich 1956- *WhoWor 93*
Turetsky, Judith 1944- *WhoAmW 93*
Turetsky, Samuel Harvey 1946- *St&PR 93*
Turgenev, Ivan 1818-1883 *MagSWL [port], NinCLC 37 [port], OxDcOp, ScF&FL 92, WorLitC [port]*
Turgeon, Alfred Joseph 1943- *WhoAm 92*
Turgeon, Edgar Lynn 1920- *WhoE 93*
Turgeon, Guy 1942- *St&PR 93, WhoAm 92*
Turgeon, Leo 1928- *St&PR 93*
Turgot, Anne Robert Jacques 1727-1781 *BioIn 17*
Turi, A. Edward *Law&B 92*
Turi, Andrew Steven 1951- *St&PR 93*
Turiace, Eleanor Marie 1939- *WhoAmW 93*
Turiano, Vincent Charles 1950- *St&PR 93*
Turiel, Maurizio 1948- *WhoWor 93*
Turillo, Michael Joseph, Jr. 1947- *WhoAm 92, WhoE 93, WhoEmL 93, WhoWor 93*
Turin, George Lewis 1930- *WhoAm 92*
Turina, Marko 1937- *WhoScE 91-4*
Turina, Marko Ivan 1937- *WhoWor 93*
Turina (y Perez), Joaquin 1882-1949 *Baker 92*
Turing, Alan Mathison 1912-1954 *BioIn 17*
Turini, Francesco c. 1589-1656 *See* Turini, Gregorio c. 1560-c. 1600 *Baker 92*
Turini, Gregorio c. 1560-c. 1600 *Baker 92*
Turini, Ronald (Walter) 1934- *Baker 92*
Turino, Gerard Michael 1924- *WhoAm 92, WhoE 93*
Turinsky, Paul Josef 1944- *WhoAm 92*
Turits, Philip D. 1933- *St&PR 93*
Turk, Austin Theodore 1934- *WhoAm 92*
Turk, Daniel Gottlob 1750-1813 *Baker 92*
Turk, H.C. 1958- *ScF&FL 92*
Turk, Herman 1924- *WhoAm 92*
Turk, Jack L. 1931- *St&PR 93*
Turk, James Clinton 1923- *WhoAm 92, WhoSSW 93*
Turk, James Clinton, Jr. 1956- *WhoEmL 93, WhoSSW 93*
Turk, Jessie Rose 1920- *WhoAmW 93, WhoE 93*
Turk, John Leslie *WhoScE 91-1*
Turk, Joseph E. 1943- *St&PR 93*
Turk, Kenneth L. 1908-1991 *BioIn 17*
Turk, Milan J. 1938- *St&PR 93*
Turk, Milan Joseph 1938- *WhoAm 92*
Turk, Roman *WhoScE 91-4*
Turk, Rudy Henry 1927- *WhoAm 92*
Turk, S. Maynard 1925- *WhoAm 92*
Turk, Stanley Martin 1934- *WhoAm 92*
Turk, Thomas Liebig 1936- *WhoSSW 93*
Turkal, Mark James 1952- *St&PR 93*
Turkaly, Louis G. 1945- *St&PR 93*
Turkel, Harris A. 1945- *St&PR 93*
Turkel, Jonathan D. *Law&B 92*
Turkel, Pauline *ConAu 37NR*
Turkel, Stanley 1925- *WhoAm 92*
Turkevich, Anthony Leonid 1916- *WhoAm 92*
Turkevich, John 1907- *WhoE 93*
Turki, Fawzi Gasem 1951- *WhoWor 93*
Turkiewicz, Jan Andrzej 1934- *WhoScE 91-4*
Turkiewicz, Sophia *MiSFD 9*
Turkin, Marshall William 1926- *WhoAm 92*
Turkington, Donald James 1938- *WhoWor 93*
Turkington, Gregg McPatrick 1967- *WhoWrEP 92*
Turkmen, Mehmet Faik 1965- *WhoWor 93*
Turko, John Walter 1944- *St&PR 93, WhoE 93*
Turko, Rose-Marie 1951- *MiSFD 9*
Turkoglu, Kazim 1926- *WhoScE 91-4*
Turkoly-Joczik, Robert Louis 1931- *WhoE 93*
Turkovic, Michael James 1932- *St&PR 93*
Turkovich, Carolyn Wells 1946- *WhoSSW 93*
Turkow, Zygmunt 1896-1970 *PolBiDi*
Turleau, Catherine *WhoScE 91-2*
Turley, Betty Hood McLain 1937- *WhoAmW 93*
Turley, Brian Christian 1936- *St&PR 93*
Turley, Craig *BioIn 17*
Turley, Gerald H. 1931- *ConAu 136*
Turley, James Anthony, Jr. 1918- *WhoAm 92*
Turley, John N. 1945- *St&PR 93*
Turley, Joseph Francis 1925- *WhoAm 92*
Turley, Keith L. 1923- *St&PR 93*
Turley, Mark William 1954- *St&PR 93*
Turley, Michael Roy 1945- *WhoAm 92*
Turley, Richard L. *Law&B 92*
Turley, Robert Walters 1939- *St&PR 93*
Turley, Sharon *Law&B 92*
Turley, Stewart 1934- *St&PR 93, WhoAm 92, WhoSSW 93*
Turley, William Harrison 1930- *St&PR 93*
Turley, Windle 1939- *WhoAm 92*
Turlington, Christy *BioIn 17*

Turlington, Phyllis Nibe 1944- *WhoSSW 93*
Turman, George 1928- *WhoAm 92*
Turman, Glynn *BioIn 17*
Turman, John *ScF&FL 92*
Turman, Lawrence 1926- *ConTFT 10, MiSFD 9*
Turman, Michael H. 1948- *St&PR 93*
Turmel, Antoine 1918- *St&PR 93*
Turmel, Jean 1944- *St&PR 93*
Turmel, Jean Bernard 1944- *WhoAm 92*
Turmelle, Michael Conrad 1959- *St&PR 93*
Turnage, Fred Douglas 1920- *WhoAm 92*
Turnage, Janet James 1939- *WhoAmW 93, WhoSSW 93*
Turnage, Jean A. 1926- *WhoAm 92*
Turnage, Mark-Anthony 1960- *Baker 92*
Turnage, Mark Antony 1960- *OxDcOp*
Turnage, Martha Allen 1922- *WhoAmW 93*
Turnage, Wayne J. d1990 *BioIn 17*
Turnage-Ferber, Jacqueline Kay 1965- *WhoAmW 93*
Turnbaugh, Douglas Blair 1934- *WhoAm 92*
Turnbole, Kathleen McCombe 1951- *WhoAmW 93*
Turnbough, David R. *St&PR 93*
Turnbow, Cornelia Kirby 1943- *WhoSSW 93*
Turnbow, Penelope *Law&B 92*
Turnbow, Walter 1924- *St&PR 93*
Turnbull, Adam Michael Gordon 1935- *WhoAm 92*
Turnbull, Andrew 1921-1970 *BioIn 17*
Turnbull, Ann 1943- *ScF&FL 92*
Turnbull, Ann Patterson 1947- *WhoAm 92*
Turnbull, Benjamin H. 1938- *St&PR 93*
Turnbull, Charles Vincent 1933- *WhoAm 92*
Turnbull, David 1915- *WhoAm 92*
Turnbull, Derek *BioIn 17*
Turnbull, Douglass Matthew *WhoScE 91-1*
Turnbull, Fred Gerdes 1931- *WhoAm 92*
Turnbull, G. Keith 1935- *St&PR 93*
Turnbull, Gerry *ScF&FL 92*
Turnbull, Gordon Keith 1935- *WhoAm 92*
Turnbull, Joanne Emily 1949- *WhoAmW 93*
Turnbull, John Cameron 1923- *WhoAm 92*
Turnbull, John Neil 1940- *WhoAm 92, WhoWor 93*
Turnbull, Kathryn Elizabeth 1944- *WhoWor 93*
Turnbull, Kenneth W. *WhoAm 92*
Turnbull, Margaret *AmWomPl*
Turnbull, Norman A. 1949- *St&PR 93*
Turnbull, P.W. *WhoScE 91-1*
Turnbull, R. Gary 1947- *St&PR 93*
Turnbull, Robert G. *Law&B 92*
Turnbull, Robert Scott 1929- *St&PR 93, WhoAm 92*
Turnbull, Vernona Harmsen 1916- *WhoAmW 93*
Turnbull, William, Jr. 1935- *WhoAm 92*
Turnbull, William D. d1991 *BioIn 17*
Turndorf, Herman 1930- *WhoAm 92*
Turner, Alan Burrows *WhoScE 91-1*
Turner, Albert Joseph, Jr. 1938- *WhoSSW 93*
Turner, Alberta T. 1919- *WhoWrEP 92*
Turner, Alfred L. 1944- *WhoSSW 93*
Turner, Alix Breillat 1965- *WhoWor 93*
Turner, Allen 1955- *WhoSSW 93*
Turner, Almon Richard 1932- *WhoAm 92*
Turner, Alvis Greely 1929- *WhoSSW 93*
Turner, Amos 1926- *St&PR 93*
Turner, Andrew Ollen 1954- *WhoSSW 93*
Turner, Ann *MiSFD 9*
Turner, Ann W. 1945- *ScF&FL 92*
Turner, Annabel *AmWomPl*
Turner, Annabelle *AmWomPl*
Turner, Anthony Peter Francis *WhoScE 91-1*
Turner, Arlin 1909-1980 *BioIn 17*
Turner, Arnella K. 1917- *ConAu 138*
Turner, Arthur Campbell 1918- *WhoAm 92*
Turner, Arthur Edward 1931- *WhoAm 92*
Turner, Ben d1873 *BioIn 17*
Turner, Benjamin Sterling 1825-1894 *BioIn 17*
Turner, Bernice Hilburn 1937- *WhoAmW 93, WhoWor 93*
Turner, Big Joe 1911-1985 *BioIn 17*
Turner, Billie B. 1930- *St&PR 93, WhoAm 92*
Turner, Billie Lee 1925- *WhoAm 92*
Turner, Bonese Collins *WhoAmW 93*
Turner, Brenda *BioIn 17*
Turner, Bulldog 1919- *BioIn 17*
Turner, Burnett Coburn 1902- *WhoAm 92*
Turner, C. Phillip 1940- *St&PR 93*
Turner, Cal, Sr. 1915- *St&PR 93*
Turner, Cal, Jr. 1940- *St&PR 93*
Turner, Caren Zeldie 1957- *WhoE 93*
Turner, Carl Jeane 1933- *WhoSSW 93, WhoWor 93*
Turner, Carl Joseph 1931- *St&PR 93*
Turner, Carmen E. *BioIn 17*
Turner, Carmen E. d1992 *NewYTBS 92*
Turner, Caroline *WhoAmW 93*
Turner, Carolyn Ann 1949- *WhoWrEP 92*
Turner, Cathy *WhoAmW 93*
Turner, Charles Carre 1944- *WhoAm 92*
Turner, Charles Dean 1938- *St&PR 93*
Turner, Charles Hamilton 1936- *WhoAm 92*
Turner, Charles R. 1938- *St&PR 93*
Turner, Clive *MiSFD 9*
Turner, Clorinda Matto de 1852-1909 *BioIn 17*
Turner, Clyde 1919- *BioIn 17*
Turner, Cornelius P. d1990 *BioIn 17*
Turner, Curtis L. 1939- *St&PR 93*
Turner, Curtis Morton 1924-1970 *BioIn 17*
Turner, D.W. *WhoScE 91-1*
Turner, Daniel L. 1947- *St&PR 93*
Turner, Daniel Shelton 1945- *WhoSSW 93*
Turner, Daniel W. *Law&B 92*
Turner, Darwin T. 1931-1991 *BioIn 17*
Turner, David Kay 1942- *St&PR 93*
Turner, David Louis 1933- *WhoUN 92*
Turner, David Lowery 1936- *WhoSSW 93*
Turner, David Reuben 1915- *WhoAm 92*
Turner, David Robert *WhoScE 91-1*
Turner, David Robert 1939- *WhoWor 93*
Turner, Debbye *BioIn 17*
Turner, Dee Stone 1934- *WhoAmW 93*
Turner, Denise Y. *Law&B 92*
Turner, Dennis I. *Law&B 92*
Turner, Dennis M. J. *St&PR 93*
Turner, Dennis Roy 1947- *St&PR 93*
Turner, Don L. 1953- *St&PR 93*
Turner, Donald Frank 1921- *WhoAm 92*
Turner, Donald M. 1947- *St&PR 93*
Turner, Donald R. 1938- *WhoIns 93*
Turner, Dorothy Bremer *WhoAmW 93*
Turner, E. Deane 1928- *WhoAm 92*
Turner, E. Victoria 1946- *WhoAmW 93*
Turner, Edith Litton 1919- *St&PR 93*
Turner, Edward T., Jr. 1925- *St&PR 93*
Turner, Edwin Arnold, Jr. 1937- *WhoE 93*
Turner, Eldridge John, Jr. 1947- *WhoSSW 93*
Turner, Eleana Clyde 1949- *WhoAmW 93*
Turner, Elizabeth Adams Noble 1931- *WhoAm 92, WhoAmW 93, WhoSSW 93*
Turner, Elvie, Jr. 1929- *WhoAm 92*
Turner, Eric Vernon *Law&B 92*
Turner, Eugene Andrew 1928- *WhoAm 92*
Turner, Eugene Lauderdale, Jr. 1918- *St&PR 93*
Turner, Eva 1892-1990 *Baker 92, BioIn 17, IntDcOp [port], OxDcOp*
Turner, Evan Hopkins 1927- *WhoAm 92*
Turner, F. Cort 1926- *St&PR 93*
Turner, Frances Bernadette 1903- *WhoAmW 93*
Turner, Francis A. 1896-1991 *BioIn 17*
Turner, Francis Joseph (Michael) 1929- *WhoWrEP 92*
Turner, Frank K. 1939- *St&PR 93*
Turner, Frank Miller 1944- *WhoAm 92*
Turner, Franklin Delton 1933- *WhoAm 92*
Turner, Franklin Lippitt, Jr. 1955- *WhoSSW 93*
Turner, Fred L. 1933- *St&PR 93, WhoAm 92*
Turner, Frederic Scott 1955- *WhoSSW 93*
Turner, Frederick 1943- *BioIn 17, ScF&FL 92*
Turner, Frederick Cortez 1926- *St&PR 93*
Turner, Frederick Jackson 1861-1932 *GayN*
Turner, Genevieve *AmWomPl*
Turner, Geoffrey *WhoScE 91-1*
Turner, George 1916- *ScF&FL 92*
Turner, George B. 1899-1963 *BioIn 17*
Turner, George D. *Law&B 92*
Turner, George E. 1925- *ScF&FL 92*
Turner, George Pearce 1915- *WhoAm 92*
Turner, Gerald Phillip 1930- *WhoAm 92*
Turner, Gerald Rufus 1950- *WhoSSW 93*
Turner, Ges 1946- *St&PR 93*
Turner, Girard Hart 1943- *WhoSSW 93*
Turner, Glennette Tilley 1933- *BlkAuII 92, SmATA 71 [port]*
Turner, Gloria Louise 1951- *WhoAmW 93*
Turner, Gloria Townsend Burke 1938- *WhoAmW 93, WhoWor 93*
Turner, Godfrey 1913-1948 *Baker 92*
Turner, H. *WhoScE 91-4*
Turner, H. Allen 1952- *St&PR 93*
Turner, Hans W. *St&PR 93*
Turner, Harold, Jr. 1952- *St&PR 93*
Turner, Harold Edward 1921- *WhoAm 92*
Turner, Harold W. 1949- *St&PR 93*
Turner, Harry Edward 1927- *WhoAm 92*
Turner, Harry M. 1903- *St&PR 93*
Turner, Harry Woodruff 1939- *WhoE 93*
Turner, Heather Ann 1965- *WhoE 93*
Turner, Helen Lee 1950- *WhoAmW 93*
Turner, Henry A., Jr. 1919- *WhoAm 92*
Turner, Henry Brown 1936- *WhoAm 92, WhoWor 93*
Turner, Henry McNeal 1834-1915 *BioIn 17, EncAACR [port]*
Turner, Herbert David 1923- *WhoE 93*
Turner, Hester Hill 1917- *WhoAm 92*
Turner, Howard Sinclair 1911- *WhoAm 92*
Turner, Ike *BioIn 17*
Turner, Ike 1931- *Baker 92, SoulM*
Turner, Iris Evelyn 1927- *WhoWrEP 92*
Turner, J.P., Jr. 1924- *St&PR 93*
Turner, Jack *BioIn 17*
Turner, Jack 1947- *WhoSSW 93*
Turner, Jack Henry 1934- *WhoAm 92*
Turner, James 1909-1975 *ScF&FL 92*
Turner, James 1945- *ScF&FL 92*
Turner, James Charles Robin *WhoScE 91-1*
Turner, James Eric 1960- *WhoSSW 93*
Turner, James G. 1938- *St&PR 93*
Turner, James Johnson *WhoScE 91-1*
Turner, James Milton 1840-1915 *BioIn 17, EncAACR*
Turner, James R. 1928- *St&PR 93*
Turner, James T. 1938- *CngDr 91*
Turner, James Taft 1931- *WhoAm 92*
Turner, James Thomas 1938- *WhoAm 92, WhoE 93*
Turner, Janet Sullivan 1935- *WhoAmW 93, WhoE 93*
Turner, Janine *BioIn 17*
Turner, Janine 1962- *News 93-2 [port]*
Turner, Janine 1963?- *ConTFT 10*
Turner, Jean-Rae 1920- *WhoWrEP 92*
Turner, Jean Riggsbee 1946- *WhoAmW 93*
Turner, Jerome 1942- *WhoAm 92, WhoSSW 93*
Turner, Jesse *BioIn 17*
Turner, Joe 1907-1990 *Baker 92, BioIn 17*
Turner, Joe 1911-1985 *BioIn 17*
Turner, John Andrew 1949- *WhoE 93, WhoWor 93*
Turner, John Bunyan 1916- *WhoSSW 93*
Turner, John Christopher 1928- *WhoWor 93*
Turner, John D. 1946- *St&PR 93*
Turner, John G. 1939- *WhoIns 93*
Turner, John Gosney 1939- *St&PR 93, WhoAm 92*
Turner, John J. 1949- *St&PR 93*
Turner, John L. 1924- *St&PR 93*
Turner, John Napier 1929- *WhoWor 93*
Turner, John R. 1947- *WhoScE 91-1*
Turner, John Richard George *WhoScE 91-1*
Turner, John Sidney, Jr. 1930- *WhoAm 92, WhoWor 93*
Turner, John W. 1923- *St&PR 93*
Turner, Jon B. 1950- *St&PR 93*
Turner, Jonathan Andrew 1947- *WhoWor 93*
Turner, Joseph Ellis 1939- *AfrAmBi [port]*
Turner, Joseph Vernon 1911-1985 *Baker 92*
Turner, Judith Ann 1952- *WhoAmW 93*
Turner, Justin Leroy 1915- *WhoSSW 93*
Turner, Karel L. *Law&B 92*
Turner, Karen Elaine 1953- *WhoAmW 93*
Turner, Karen M. 1954- *WhoAmW 93*
Turner, Kathleen *BioIn 17*
Turner, Kathleen 1954- *HolBB [port], IntDcF 2-3 [port], WhoAm 92, WhoAmW 93*
Turner, Kathleen J. 1952- *ConAu 138*
Turner, Keena 1958- *BioIn 17*
Turner, Keith E. 1949- *St&PR 93*
Turner, Ken 1954- *St&PR 93, WhoAm 92*
Turner, Kenneth *BioIn 17*
Turner, Kenneth John *WhoScE 91-1*
Turner, Kim *BlkAmWO*
Turner, L.F. *WhoScE 91-1*
Turner, Lana 1920- *IntDcF 2-3 [port], WhoAm 92*
Turner, Lawrence Anthony 1927- *St&PR 93*
Turner, Lawrence Oliver, Jr. 1940- *St&PR 93*
Turner, Lee S., Jr. 1926- *WhoAm 92, WhoSSW 93*
Turner, Leonard 1921- *St&PR 93*
Turner, Lester Liggett 1925- *St&PR 93*
Turner, Letitia Rhodes 1923- *WhoAmW 93*
Turner, Lewis Thomas 1947- *WhoE 93*
Turner, Lida Larrimore *AmWomPl*
Turner, Lillian Ann 1961- *WhoSSW 93*
Turner, Lisa Hill 1959- *WhoAmW 93*
Turner, Lisa Joyce 1959- *WhoAmW 93*
Turner, Lisa Phillips 1951- *WhoAmW 93, WhoSSW 93*
Turner, Lorenzo Dow 1895-1972 *BioIn 17*
Turner, Lori A. 1957- *St&PR 93*
Turner, Lowell 1947- *ConAu 138*
Turner, Loyd Leonard 1917- *St&PR 93, WhoAm 92, WhoSSW 93*
Turner, Lynne Alison 1941- *WhoAm 92*
Turner, M.J.B. 1937- *WhoScE 91-1*
Turner, Malcolm Elijah, Jr. 1929- *WhoAm 92, WhoSSW 93*
Turner, Marguerite Rose Cowles 1941- *WhoSSW 93, WhoWor 93*
Turner, Marshall *BioIn 17*
Turner, Marshall Chittenden, Jr. 1941- *WhoAm 92*
Turner, Marshall Ross 1941- *St&PR 93*
Turner, Marta Dawn 1954- *WhoAmW 93*
Turner, Martha Fuller 1940- *WhoAmW 93*
Turner, Marvin Wentz 1959- *WhoSSW 93*
Turner, Mary Lee 1945- *WhoAm 92, WhoAmW 93*
Turner, Mary Louise 1954- *WhoAmW 93, WhoSSW 93*
Turner, Maurice T. *BioIn 17*
Turner, Michael Griswold 1925- *WhoAm 92*
Turner, Michael James *WhoScE 91-1*
Turner, Myron 1935- *WhoCanL 92*
Turner, Nancy Delane 1956- *WhoSSW 93*
Turner, Nancy Elizabeth 1955- *WhoAmW 93*
Turner, Nat 1800?-1831 *BioIn 17*
Turner, Natalie A. *WhoAmW 93*
Turner, Norman Huntington 1939- *WhoE 93*
Turner, Pamela Jayne *BioIn 17*
Turner, Patricia Busby Whitney 1923- *WhoAmW 93*
Turner, Paul *WhoScE 91-1*
Turner, Paul S. *Law&B 92*
Turner, Peggy Ann 1951- *WhoAmW 93*
Turner, Pete 1934- *BioIn 17*
Turner, Peter *BioIn 17*
Turner, Peter Merick 1931- *St&PR 93*
Turner, Peter Merrick 1931- *WhoAm 92*
Turner, Philip Michael 1948- *WhoAm 92*
Turner, R.E. 1921- *St&PR 93*
Turner, R. Gerald *BioIn 17*
Turner, Ralph Herbert 1919- *WhoAm 92*
Turner, Randall Mead 1949- *WhoSSW 93*
Turner, Raymond *WhoScE 91-1*
Turner, Raymond Joseph 1929- *WhoAm 92*
Turner, Richard *ScF&FL 92*
Turner, Richard W. *St&PR 93*
Turner, Richmond Kelly 1885-1961 *BioIn 17, HarEnMi*
Turner, Rick *BioIn 17*
Turner, Rita Annette 1964- *WhoAmW 93*
Turner, Robert Carlton 1952- *WhoSSW 93, WhoWor 93*
Turner, Robert (Comrie) 1920- *Baker 92, WhoAm 92*
Turner, Robert Edward 1926- *WhoAm 92*
Turner, Robert Edward 1938- *St&PR 93, WhoAm 92*
Turner, Robert Foster 1944- *WhoAm 92*
Turner, Robert Gerald 1945- *WhoAm 92, WhoSSW 93*
Turner, Robert H. 1952- *St&PR 93*
Turner, Robert Hal 1948- *WhoE 93*
Turner, Robert Kerry *WhoScE 91-1*
Turner, Robert Lee 1941- *BioIn 17*
Turner, Robert Spilman 1952- *WhoSSW 93*
Turner, Roderick L. 1931- *St&PR 93, WhoAm 92*
Turner, Roger C. *Law&B 92*
Turner, Ronald D. V. 1936- *St&PR 93*
Turner, Ronald Gary 1936- *St&PR 93*
Turner, Ross J. 1930- *St&PR 93*
Turner, Ross James 1930- *WhoAm 92, WhoE 93*
Turner, Ruth Weed 1925- *WhoAmW 93*
Turner, Sandra 1945- *ScF&FL 92*
Turner, Scott Conners 1957- *St&PR 93*
Turner, Sharon Lou Willson 1946- *WhoAmW 93*
Turner, Sherrod E. 1939- *St&PR 93, WhoIns 93*
Turner, Stansfield 1923- *WhoAm 92*
Turner, Stephen M. *Law&B 92*
Turner, Stephen M. 1939- *St&PR 93*
Turner, Stephen Miller 1939- *WhoAm 92*
Turner, Steven M. *Law&B 92*
Turner, Stuart *St&PR 93*
Turner, Suzanne A. 1952- *St&PR 93, WhoIns 93*
Turner, Ted 1938- *BioIn 17, WhoAm 92*
Turner, Thomas Creagher 1924- *WhoSSW 93*
Turner, Thomas Edward 1948- *WhoE 93*
Turner, Thomas Gerald 1930- *St&PR 93*
Turner, Thomas Marshall 1951- *WhoE 93, WhoEmL 93, WhoWor 93*
Turner, Thomas W. 1925- *St&PR 93*
Turner, Thomas W. 1946- *WhoAm 92*
Turner, Tina *BioIn 17*
Turner, Tina 1939- *Baker 92, SoulM, WhoAm 92*
Turner, Tom 1942- *ConAu 136*
Turner, Vickery *ScF&FL 92*

Turner, Virginia 1946- *St&PR 93*
Turner, W(alter) J(ames Redfern) 1889-1946 *Baker 92*
Turner, W. Keith *Law&B 92*
Turner, Wallace L. 1921- *WhoAm 92*
Turner, Walter Emery 1927- *St&PR 93*
Turner, Wayne Connelly 1942- *WhoAm 92, WhoSSW 93*
Turner, Weld Winston 1931- *WhoE 93*
Turner, William 1651-1740 *Baker 92*
Turner, William Cochrane 1929- *St&PR 93, WhoAm 92*
Turner, William Donald 1904- *WhoE 93*
Turner, William Ervin, III 1948- *St&PR 93*
Turner, William Hutchins 1940- *WhoAm 92*
Turner, William Ian MacKenzie, Jr. 1929- *WhoAm 92*
Turner, William J. 1944- *WhoAm 92*
Turner, William Joseph 1957- *WhoSSW 93*
Turner, William Kay 1933- *WhoAm 92*
Turner, William R. 1943- *St&PR 93*
Turner, William Russell 1911- *WhoE 93*
Turner, William Wilson 1916- *WhoAm 92*
Turner-Smith, Alan Robert *WhoScE 91-1*
Turner-Warwick, Margaret 1924- *WhoWor 93*
Turnes, George Keeler 1947- *WhoE 93*
Turney, Emma Lee Preslar 1928- *WhoWor 93*
Turney, Ray *ScF&FL 92*
Turney-High, Harry Holbert 1899-1982 *IntDcAn*
Turnheim, Palmer 1921- *WhoAm 92*
Turnhout, Gerard de (van) c. 1520-1580 *Baker 92*
Turnhout, Jan-Jacob van c. 1545-c. 1618 *See* Turnhout, Gerard de (van) c. 1520-1580 *Baker 92*
Turnik *WhoWrEP 92*
Turnipseed, Patsy Ruth 1935- *St&PR 93*
Turnipseed, Sara Sadler *Law&B 92*
Turnipseed, Tina Marie 1958- *WhoSSW 93*
Turnley, David C. 1953- *BioIn 17*
Turnley, David Carl 1955- *WhoAm 92*
Turnley, Peter 1953- *BioIn 17*
Turnovsky, Martin 1928- *Baker 92*
Turnovsky, Stephen John 1941- *WhoAm 92*
Turnow, Rolland 1929- *St&PR 93*
Turnquist, Mark Alan 1949- *WhoE 93*
Turnquist, Paul Kenneth 1935- *WhoAm 92*
Turo, Jan 1943- *WhoWor 93*
Turock, Betty Jane *WhoAm 92, WhoAmW 93*
Turock, Jane Parsick 1947- *WhoAmW 93, WhoEmL 93*
Turofsky, Charles Sheldon 1942- *WhoE 93*
Turok, Paul (Harris) 1929- *Baker 92, WhoAm 92*
Turow, Joseph Gregory 1950- *WhoE 93*
Turow, Scott *BioIn 17*
Turow, Scott 1949- *ConAu 40NR*
Turow, Scott F. 1949- *WhoAm 92*
Turowski, Janusz 1927- *WhoScE 91-4*
Turpen, Michael Craig 1949- *WhoAm 92*
Turpin, Anita Jane 1954- *WhoSSW 93*
Turpin, Ben 1868-1940 *QDrFCA 92 [port]*
Turpin, Ben 1869-1940 *BioIn 17*
Turpin, Dick d1990 *BioIn 17*
Turpin, Edmund Hart 1835-1907 *Baker 92*
Turpin, John Timothy 1945- *WhoWor 93*
Turpin, Michel 1936- *WhoScE 91-2*
Turpin, Miles J. *St&PR 93*
Turpin, Rebecca Vernon 1949- *WhoAmW 93*
Turpin, William H. 1929- *St&PR 93*
Turpit, William J. *Law&B 92*
Turrell, George Charles 1931- *WhoWor 93*
Turrell, James 1943- *BioIn 17*
Turrell, James Archie 1943- *WhoAm 92*
Turrell, Julia Brown *BioIn 17*
Turrell, Richard H. 1925- *St&PR 93*
Turrell, Richard Horton, Sr. 1925- *WhoAm 92, WhoE 93, WhoWor 93*
Turrens, Julio Francisco 1953- *WhoSSW 93*
Turrentine, Haywood Lynwood 1945- *WhoE 93*
Turrentine, Robert E. 1927- *St&PR 93*
Turrentine, Stanley William 1934- *WhoAm 92*
Turriff, Lowell *BioIn 17*
Turrin, Joseph Egidio 1947- *WhoEmL 93*
Turrini, Peter 1944- *DcLB 124 [port]*
Turriziani, Vincent Michael 1956- *WhoE 93*
Turro, Nicholas John 1938- *WhoAm 92*
Tursi, Carl T. *Law&B 92*
Tursi, Carl Thomas 1941- *St&PR 93*
Tursi, Francis d1991 *NewYTBS 92*
Tursi, Francis 1922-1991 *BioIn 17*
Turski, Lechoslaw 1955- *WhoWor 93*
Turski, Lukasz Andrzej 1943- *WhoWor 93*
Turski, Wladyslaw Marek 1938- *WhoScE 91-4, WhoWor 93*
Turski, Zbigniew 1908-1979 *Baker 92, PolBiDi*
Turso, Vito Anthony 1948- *WhoE 93*
Tursun Beg dc. 1499 *OxDcByz*
Turtell, Neal Timothy 1949- *WhoE 93*
Turteltaub, Jon *MiSFD 9*
Turtledove, Harry 1949- *ScF&FL 92*
Turtle Island String Quartet *ConMus 9 [port]*
Turtola, Risto Pekka 1934- *WhoWor 93*
Turturro, John 1957?- *BioIn 17, MiSFD 9, WhoAm 92*
Turunen, Denise Ellen 1958- *WhoSSW 93*
Turunen, Markus Johannes 1947- *WhoWor 93*
Turvey, Samuel A. *Law&B 92*
Turvey, Samuel A. d1991 *BioIn 17*
Turzo, Joseph A. *St&PR 93*
Tusa, Joseph, Jr. 1942- *St&PR 93, WhoAm 92*
Tusa, Tricia 1960- *SmATA 72*
Tusa, Wayne Kenenth 1951- *WhoE 93*
Tuschak, Robert 1927- *WhoScE 91-4*
Tuseo, Norbert Joseph John 1950- *WhoEmL 93, WhoSSW 93, WhoWor 93*
Tusher, Thomas William 1941- *St&PR 93*
Tushingham, Douglas 1914- *WhoAm 92*
Tusiani, Joseph 1924- *WhoWrEP 92*
Tusing, James C. 1926- *WhoSSW 93*
Tusken, Roger Anthony 1929- *WhoAm 92*
Tuskey, Lawrence Michael *Law&B 92*
Tusler, Robert Leon 1920- *Baker 92*
Tusman, Elana *BioIn 17*
Tusman, Janna *BioIn 17*
Tusman, Vladimir *BioIn 17*
Tusquets, Esther 1936- *BioIn 17*
Tusquets, Oscar *BioIn 17*
Tusseau, Dominique A.P. 1953- *WhoScE 91-2*
Tussie, Diana Alicia 1948- *WhoWor 93*
Tussman, Malka Heifetz 1893-1987 *JeAmHC*
Tusuz, Mehmet Ali 1948- *WhoScE 91-4*
Tuszynski, Daniel J., Jr. 1947- *WhoSSW 93, WhoWor 93*
Tutag, Robert S. 1941- *St&PR 93*
Tutankhamen, King of Egypt *BioIn 17*
Tutcher, Larry Clifford 1945- *WhoSSW 93, WhoWor 93*
Tutein, David Warren 1937- *WhoE 93*
Tutelman, Jacki Deena 1954- *WhoAmW 93*
Tuten, John C., Jr. 1943- *St&PR 93*
Tuten, Nancy Lewis 1960- *WhoSSW 93*
Tuthill, Allen *WhoIns 93*
Tuthill, Allen Floyd 1961- *St&PR 93*
Tuthill, Burnet Corwin 1888-1982 *Baker 92*
Tuthill, David F. *Law&B 92*
Tuthill, James G. 1926- *St&PR 93*
Tuthill, James Gates, Jr. 1953- *St&PR 93*
Tuthill, James P. *Law&B 92*
Tuthill, John Wills 1910- *WhoAm 92*
Tuthill, Oliver W. 1906- *St&PR 93*
Tuthill, Robert E. 1928- *St&PR 93*
Tuthill, Theresa Ann 1962- *WhoAmW 93*
Tuthill, Walter Warren 1941- *WhoAm 92*
Tutin, Dorothy 1930- *WhoWor 93*
Tutino, Barbara Jean 1958- *WhoAmW 93*
Tutino, Rosalie Jacqueline 1937- *WhoAmW 93, WhoE 93*
Tutins, Antons 1933- *WhoWor 93*
Tutko, Robert Joseph 1955- *WhoSSW 93*
Tutkun, Ertac 1941- *WhoScE 91-4*
Tutle, Danny C. 1959- *WhoSSW 93*
Tutle, Edward George 1927- *WhoSSW 93*
Tutolo, Leonard J. 1931- *St&PR 93*
Tutrone, Joseph A. 1951- *St&PR 93*
Tutsch, Hans Emanuel 1918- *WhoE 93*
Tutschke, Wolfgang 1934- *WhoWor 93*
Tutt, Carolyn Helms 1941- *WhoSSW 93*
Tutt, Charles Leaming, Jr. 1911- *WhoAm 92, WhoWor 93*
Tutt, Gloria J. Rutherford 1945- *WhoAmW 93, WhoSSW 93*
Tutt, J. Michael 1942- *WhoSSW 93*
Tutt, Nancy Jean *WhoAmW 93*
Tutt, Russell Thayer 1913- *WhoAm 92, WhoWor 93*
Tutt, William Bullard 1941- *St&PR 93*
Tuttle, Brian John 1950- *St&PR 93*
Tuttle, Charles W. 1948- *St&PR 93*
Tuttle, Clifford Horace, Jr. 1930- *St&PR 93*
Tuttle, David Bauman 1948- *WhoE 93, WhoEmL 93, WhoWor 93*
Tuttle, Don Wesley 1960- *WhoSSW 93*
Tuttle, Donna Frame 1947- *WhoAm 92*
Tuttle, Dorothy Edith Lorne *WhoAmW 93*
Tuttle, Douglas Freeman 1950- *WhoE 93*
Tuttle, Edward E. 1907- *St&PR 93*
Tuttle, Edwin E. 1927- *St&PR 93*
Tuttle, Edwin Ellsworth 1927- *WhoAm 92*
Tuttle, Elbert Parr 1897- *EncAACR, WhoAm 92, WhoSSW 93*
Tuttle, Frank James 1941- *St&PR 93, WhoAm 92*
Tuttle, Gedney 1926- *St&PR 93*
Tuttle, George Palliser 1933- *WhoE 93*
Tuttle, Harold Douglas 1951- *WhoE 93*
Tuttle, Helen *AmWomPl*
Tuttle, James C. *Law&B 92*
Tuttle, Jerome E. *St&PR 93*
Tuttle, Jerry Owen 1934- *WhoAm 92*
Tuttle, Jon d1991 *BioIn 17*
Tuttle, Judith Aurre 1942- *WhoWrEP 92*
Tuttle, Laura Shive 1962- *WhoAmW 93*
Tuttle, Lisa 1952- *ScF&FL 92*
Tuttle, Mark Gerald 1947- *St&PR 93*
Tuttle, Merlin D. *BioIn 17*
Tuttle, Merlin D. 1941- *CurBio 92 [port], WhoSSW 93*
Tuttle, Paul *BioIn 17*
Tuttle, Richard James 1941- *WhoSSW 93*
Tuttle, Robert D. 1925- *St&PR 93, WhoAm 92*
Tuttle, Roger R. 1946- *St&PR 93*
Tuttle, Seale W. *Law&B 92*
Tuttle, Stephen P. *Law&B 92*
Tuttle, Toni Brodax 1952- *WhoEmL 93*
Tuttle, William Gilbert Townsend, Jr. 1935- *WhoAm 92*
Tuttle, William Julian 1912- *WhoWor 93*
Tuttle, William McCullough, Jr. 1937- *WhoAm 92*
Tuttle, William R. 1939- *St&PR 93*
Tuttle, Wylie F. L. 1922- *St&PR 93*
Tuttleton, James Wesley 1934- *WhoAm 92*
Tutton, Betty Jane 1924- *WhoAmW 93*
Tutton, James Wilfred 1939- *St&PR 93*
Tutton, Roger Headley 1931- *WhoSSW 93*
Tutton, S.J. *WhoScE 91-1*
Tutu, Desmond *BioIn 17*
Tutu, Desmond Mpilo 1931- *DcTwHis, WhoAfr, WhoWor 93*
Tutun, Edward H. 1924- *WhoAm 92*
Tutundjian, Joseph Michel 1948- *WhoWor 93*
Tutunjian, John Peter 1936- *WhoE 93*
Tutuola, Amos *BioIn 17*
Tutuola, Amos 1920- *DcLB 125 [port], WhoWor 93*
Tutwiler, Julia Strudwick 1841-1916 *BioIn 17*
Tutwiler, Margaret 1950- *News 92 [port]*
Tutwiler, Margaret Ann 1958- *WhoE 93*
Tutwiler, Margaret D. *BioIn 17*
Tutwiler, Margaret DeBardeleben 1950- *WhoAm 92, WhoAmW 93*
Tuukkanen, Kalervo 1909-1979 *Baker 92*
Tuuliranta, Mikko Jaakko 1949- *WhoWor 93*
Tuunainen, Pekka *WhoScE 91-4*
Tuuri, Matti *WhoScE 91-4*
Tu Wen-hsiu d1873 *HarEnMi*
Tuwim, Julian 1894-1953 *PolBiDi*
Tuxbury, William F. 1942- *St&PR 93*
Tuxen, Anders Morch 1930- *WhoWor 93*
Tuxen, Erik (Oluf) 1902-1957 *Baker 92*
Tuxen Falbe, Christian 1791-1849 *BioIn 17*
Tuya, Theodore F. 1948- *WhoAsAP 91*
Tuyl, Rosealtha Van *ScF&FL 92*
Tuyl, Zaara Van *ScF&FL 92*
Tuzcu, Onder 1943- *WhoScE 91-4*
Tuzla, Kemal 1943- *WhoAm 92*
Tuznik, Franciszek Stanislaw 1945- *WhoWor 93*
Tuzon, Domingo A. 1923- *WhoAsAP 91*
Tuzzio, Margaret 1962- *WhoAmW 93*
Tvbulczuk, Jerzy Roman 1937- *WhoScE 91-4*
Tveitt, (Nils) Geirr 1908-1981 *Baker 92*
Tvergaard, Viggo 1943- *WhoScE 91-2*
Tvrdon, Jiri 1942- *WhoScE 91-4*
Twa, Craighton Oliver 1937- *WhoAm 92*
Twa, Inez Louisa Arbuthnot 1905- *WhoAmW 93*
Twaddell, Hannah Wilcox 1961- *WhoAmW 93*
Twaddle, Andrew Christian 1938- *WhoAm 92*
Twain, David 1929-1991 *BioIn 17*
Twain, Mark *DcLB Y92 [port], MajAI*
Twain, Mark 1835-1910 *BioIn 17, GayN, MagSAmL [port], ScF&FL 92, TwCLC 48 [port], WorLitC [port]*
Twamley, John Paul 1940- *St&PR 93*
Twardowicz, Stanley Jan 1917- *WhoAm 92*
Twardowski, Romuald 1930- *Baker 92, PolBiDi*
Twardowski, Tomasz Jan 1949- *WhoWor 93*
Twardy, John Philip 1951- *WhoE 93*
Twardy, Stanley Albert, Jr. 1951- *WhoAm 92*
Twardzik, Timothy F. *BioIn 17*
Twardzik, Timothy F. 1959- *St&PR 93*
Tway, Eileen d1990 *BioIn 17*
Tway, Patricia 1931- *WhoWrEP 92*
Tweddle, Jennifer Lynne 1963- *WhoAmW 93*
Twedt, Bonnie Jean 1947- *WhoAmW 93*
Tweed, Barrymore, Mrs. *AmWomPl*
Tweed, John Christopher *Law&B 92*
Tweed, John Louis 1947- *WhoEmL 93*
Tweed, Katharine W. *AmWomPl*
Tweed, Thomas A. 1954- *ConAu 137*
Tweed, Thomas F. 1890-1940 *ScF&FL 92*
Tweed, William M. 1823-1878 *PolPar*
Tweed, William Marcy 1823-1878 *BioIn 17*
Tweedel, Ronald W. *Law&B 92*
Tweedie, Jill 1936- *BioIn 17*
Tweedley, John M., Jr. 1945- *St&PR 93*
Tweedsmuir, Baron *ScF&FL 92*
Tweedsmuir, John Buchan, Baron 1875-1940 *BioIn 17*
Tweedue, Terry Stewart 1945- *St&PR 93*
Tweedy, David Alan 1953- *WhoE 93*
Tweedy, Donald (Nichols) 1890-1948 *Baker 92*
Tweedy, John R. 1929- *St&PR 93*
Tweedy, Rackham *WhoWrEP 92*
Tweedy, Robert Hugh 1928- *WhoAm 92*
Tweedy, Robert James 1942- *St&PR 93*
Tweedy, Timothy Thaddeus 1964- *WhoE 93*
Tweel, Nicholas J. 1916- *WhoE 93*
Tweel, Phillip C. 1958- *WhoSSW 93*
Tweito, Eleanor Marie 1909- *WhoAmW 93*
Twells, Thomas R. 1934- *St&PR 93*
Twenhafel, Bruce David 1951- *WhoSSW 93*
Twersky, Victor 1923- *WhoAm 92*
Twichell, Chase 1950- *WhoWrEP 92*
Twidale, Charles Rowland 1930- *WhoWor 93*
Twiddy, Norman David *WhoScE 91-1*
Twidell, John W. *WhoScE 91-1*
Twietmeyer, Don Henry 1954- *WhoE 93, WhoEmL 93*
Twiford, H. Hunter, III 1949- *WhoSSW 93*
Twigg, Arlena *BioIn 17*
Twigg, Rebecca *WhoAmW 93*
Twigg, Theresa Anne *Law&B 92*
Twigger, Anthony John 1939- *WhoUN 92*
Twiggs, David Emanuel 1790-1862 *BioIn 17, HarEnMi*
Twigg-Smith, Thurston 1921- *St&PR 93, WhoAm 92*
Twiggy 1949- *WhoAm 92*
Twin, Peter John *WhoScE 91-1*
Twiname, John Dean 1931- *WhoAm 92*
Twine, E.H. *Law&B 92*
Twinem, Carita Rademacher *Law&B 92*
Twining, Nathan Farragut 1897-1982 *HarEnMi*
Twisdale, Harold Winfred 1933- *WhoAm 92, WhoSSW 93*
Twiss, Page Charles 1929- *WhoAm 92*
Twiss, Robert Hamilton, Jr. 1934- *WhoAm 92*
Twiss, Robert Manning 1948- *WhoEmL 93*
Twiss, Stephen R. *Law&B 92*
Twiss, Wesley R. *St&PR 93*
Twisselman, Roger P. *Law&B 92*
Twiste, Walter Leroy 1945- *St&PR 93, WhoE 93*
Twist-Rudolph, Donna Joy 1955- *WhoE 93*
Twitchell, David *BioIn 17*
Twitchell, E. Eugene 1932- *St&PR 93*
Twitchell, Ervin Eugene *Law&B 92*
Twitchell, Ginger *BioIn 17*
Twitchell, H. Mead 1927- *St&PR 93*
Twitchell, James 1942- *WhoSSW 93*
Twitchell, James B. 1943- *ScF&FL 92*
Twitchell, Karen A. 1955- *St&PR 93*
Twitchell, Paul 1908-1971 *ScF&FL 92*
Twitchell, Paul Francis, Jr. 1960- *WhoE 93*
Twitchell, Robyn d1986 *BioIn 17*
Twitchett, Denis Crispin 1925- *WhoAm 92*
Twitty, Conway 1933- *Baker 92*
Twitty, H. R. 1941- *WhoSSW 93*
Twitty, James Watson 1916- *WhoAm 92*
Twitty, William Bradley 1920- *WhoWrEP 92*
Twohy, David *MiSFD 9*
Twombly, Angus *BioIn 17*
Twombly, Carol 1959- *BioIn 17*
Twombly, Cy 1929- *BioIn 17*
Twombly, Gray 1905-1992 *BioIn 17*
Twombly, Gray Huntington d1992 *NewYTBS 92*
Two Men, a Drum Machine & a Trumpet *SoulM*
Twomey, Janet Louise Wilkov 1952- *WhoAmW 93*
Twomey, John A. *Law&B 92*
Twomey, John J. 1934- *WhoIns 93*
Twomey, John Joseph 1934- *St&PR 93*
Twomey, Joseph G. *Law&B 92*
Twomey, Joseph Gerald 1926- *WhoAm 92*

Twomey, Mary Regina 1941- *WhoAmW 93, WhoE 93*
Twomey, Robert Denis 1947- *St&PR 93*
Twomey, Thomas Aloysius, Jr. 1945- *WhoE 93*
Twomey, Thomas N. *Law&B 92*
Twomey, William P. 1942- *St&PR 93*
Twomey, William Peter 1942- *WhoAm 92*
Twomlow, Stephen John 1960- *WhoScE 91-1*
Twyford, Vivien Jennifer 1942- *WhoWor 93*
Ty, Mario S. 1927- *WhoAsAP 91*
Tyabji, Hatim A. 1945- *St&PR 93*
Tyabji, Hatim Ahredi 1945- *WhoAm 92*
Tyacke, Steven W. *Law&B 92*
Tyagi, Shanti 1920- *WhoAsAP 91*
Tyau, Gaylore Choy Yen 1934- *WhoAmW 93*
Tyburczy, Edward 1949- *St&PR 93*
Tyc-Dumont, Suzanne *WhoScE 91-2*
Tyce, Francis Anthony 1917- *WhoAm 92*
Tychowski, Christopher Roman 1937- *WhoWor 93*
Tyczka, Sabina Maria 1923- *WhoScE 91-4*
Tydings, Joseph Davies 1928- *WhoAm 92*
Tydings, Millard E. 1890-1961 *BioIn 17, PolPar*
Tye, Christopher c. 1505-c. 1572 *Baker 92*
Tye, George W. 1946- *WhoIns 93*
Tye, Henry, Jr. 1962- *WhoWrEP 92*
Tye, Michael W. *Law&B 92*
Tye, R. Dowell 1949- *St&PR 93*
Tyer, Travis Earl 1930- *WhoAm 92*
Tyerman, David M. 1906- *St&PR 93*
Tyers, Geddes Owen 1935- *WhoAm 92*
Tyers, Kathleen *ScF&FL 92*
Tyers, Kathy 1952- *ScF&FL 92, WhoWrEP 92*
Tyes, John fl. 15th cent.- *Baker 92*
Tygrett, Howard Volney, Jr. 1940- *WhoAm 92*
Tygstrup, Niels 1926- *WhoScE 91-2, WhoWor 93*
Tyink, Frans G.J. 1955- *WhoScE 91-3*
Tykeson, Donald Erwin 1927- *WhoAm 92*
Tykocinski, Judith S. *Law&B 92*
Tyksinski, Marin J. *Law&B 92*
Tyl, Noel Jan 1936- *WhoAm 92*
Tyle, Robert M. 1937- *St&PR 93*
Tylec, Gail Louise 1960- *WhoAmW 93*
Tylee, Claire Margaret 1946- *WhoWor 93*
Tylen, Ulf 1938- *WhoScE 91-4*
Tyler, Alton Thomas 1921- *St&PR 93*
Tyler, Anne 1941- *BioIn 17, MagSAmL [port], WhoAm 92, WhoAmW 93, WhoWrEP 92*
Tyler, Bennet 1783-1858 *BioIn 17*
Tyler, Carl Walter, Jr. 1933- *WhoAm 92*
Tyler, Craig Alan 1962- *WhoSSW 93*
Tyler, David Earl 1928- *WhoAm 92*
Tyler, Donald Stephen 1946- *WhoAm 92*
Tyler, H. Richard 1927- *WhoAm 92*
Tyler, Harold Russell, Jr. 1922- *WhoAm 92*
Tyler, J.E.A. *ScF&FL 92*
Tyler, James B. 1938- *St&PR 93*
Tyler, James (Henry) 1940- *Baker 92*
Tyler, Jean 1933- *BioIn 17*
Tyler, Jesse d1900 *BioIn 17*
Tyler, Jo Cynthia Stanley 1952- *WhoSSW 93*
Tyler, Joanna Armiger 1943- *WhoE 93*
Tyler, John 1790-1862 *BioIn 17, OxCSupC, PolPar*
Tyler, John Randolph, Jr. 1934- *WhoAm 92*
Tyler, Joseph E. 1950- *St&PR 93*
Tyler, Julia Gardiner 1820-1889 *BioIn 17*
Tyler, Kenneth Scott, Jr. 1940- *St&PR 93*
Tyler, Leona Elizabeth 1906- *BioIn 17*
Tyler, Letitia Christian 1790-1842 *BioIn 17*
Tyler, Linda *ConAu 136*
Tyler, Linda Sue 1947- *WhoAmW 93*
Tyler, Linda W(agner) 1952- *ConAu 136*
Tyler, Linda Wagner *BioIn 17*
Tyler, Lloyd John 1924- *WhoAm 92*
Tyler, Loretta T. 1943- *WhoSSW 93*
Tyler, Manley d1986 *BioIn 17*
Tyler, Paul I. *Law&B 92*
Tyler, R. Michael 1947- *St&PR 93*
Tyler, Ralph Winfred 1902- *BioIn 17*
Tyler, Richard *BioIn 17*
Tyler, Richard Willis 1917- *WhoSSW 93*
Tyler, Robert L. 1922- *WhoWrEP 92*
Tyler, Robert L. 1935- *St&PR 93*
Tyler, Robert Norton 1921- *St&PR 93*
Tyler, Ronnie Curtis 1941- *WhoAm 92*
Tyler, Scott *BioIn 17*
Tyler, Sidney F., Jr. 1932- *St&PR 93*
Tyler, Thomas Lee 1933- *St&PR 93*
Tyler, Tom 1903-1954 *BioIn 17*
Tyler, Tony *ScF&FL 92*
Tyler, Vicki 1952- *BioIn 17*
Tyler, Wendell Avery 1955- *BiDAMSp 1989*
Tyler, William Bernard 1940- *WhoWor 93*
Tyler, William D. d1991 *BioIn 17*
Tyler, William Ed 1952- *WhoAm 92*
Tyler, William Howard, Jr. 1932- *WhoAm 92, WhoWor 93*
Tyler, William King 1944- *St&PR 93, WhoAm 92*
Tyler, Winston F. *Law&B 92*
Tylikowski, Andrzej Feliks 1942- *WhoScE 91-4*
Tylke, Keith B. 1956- *St&PR 93*
Tylor, E.B. 1832-1917 *IntDcAn*
Tymes *SoulM*
Tyminski, Jerzy *WhoScE 91-4*
Tyminski, Stanislaw *BioIn 17*
Tymn, Gregory Anthony 1949- *St&PR 93*
Tymn, Marshall B. 1937- *ScF&FL 92*
Tymon, Leo F., Jr. 1942- *WhoAm 92*
Tymon, Leo Francis, Jr. 1942- *St&PR 93*
Tymon, Marylyn A. 1936- *WhoIns 93*
Tynan, John Patrick 1945- *St&PR 93*
Tynan, Kathleen *BioIn 17*
Tynan, Kenneth 1927-1980 *BioIn 17*
Tynan, Laurie Francine 1951- *WhoE 93*
Tynan, Michael John *WhoScE 91-1*
Tynan, Patricia Tynan 1927- *St&PR 93*
Tynan, Tracy *MiSFD 9*
Tyndall, David Gordon 1919- *WhoAm 92*
Tyndall, James B. 1950- *St&PR 93*
Tyndall, Marshall Clay, Jr. 1943- *WhoAm 92*
Tynecka, Zofia Helena 1925- *WhoWor 93*
Tyner, David N. *Law&B 92*
Tyner, George S. 1916- *WhoAm 92*
Tyner, (Alfred) McCoy 1938- *Baker 92*
Tyner, Neal Edward 1930- *St&PR 93, WhoAm 92, WhoIns 93*
Tyner, Rob 1944-1991 *BioIn 17*
See Also MC5, The *ConMus 9*
Tyner, Rob c. 1945-1991 *News 92*
Tyner, Wallace Edward 1945- *WhoAm 92*
Tynes, Bayard Shields 1929- *WhoSSW 93*
Tynes, William Donnie 1953- *St&PR 93*
Tyng, Anne Griswold 1920- *WhoAm 92, WhoAmW 93*
Type, David *WhoCanL 92*
Typermass, Arthur G. 1937- *St&PR 93, WhoAm 92*
Typhoid Mary d1938 *BioIn 17*
Typp, W. fl. 15th cent.- *Baker 92*
Tyranny, "Blue" Gene 1945- *Baker 92*
Tyre, Milton S. *St&PR 93*
Tyre, Norman Ronald 1910- *WhoAm 92*
Tyree, Alan Dean 1929- *WhoAm 92*
Tyree, Darlene Rae 1953- *WhoAmW 93*
Tyree, Earl Garland 1921- *WhoWor 93*
Tyree, Lewis, Jr. 1922- *WhoAm 92, WhoWor 93*
Tyree, Melvin Thomas 1946- *WhoE 93*
Tyrer, John Lloyd 1928- *WhoAm 92*
Tyrie, James Campbell 1938- *St&PR 93*
Tyring, Nels A. 1931- *St&PR 93*
Tyring, Nels Andrew 1931- *WhoE 93*
Tyrka, Eugeniusz *WhoScE 91-4*
Tyrkiel, Eugeniusz F. 1919- *WhoScE 91-4*
Tyrl, Paul 1951- *WhoEmL 93*
Tyrnauer, Isaac M. Z. 1949- *St&PR 93*
Tyro, Gustaw 1927- *WhoScE 91-4*
Tyroler, Herman Alfred *WhoAm 92*
Tyrone, Earl of 1540?-1616 *BioIn 17*
Tyrone, Hugh O'Neill, Earl of c. 1545-1616 *HarEnMi*
Tyrone, James C. 1954- *St&PR 93*
Tyrrel, Richard B. *St&PR 93*
Tyrrel, Robert E., Jr. *St&PR 93*
Tyrrel, Thomas B. *St&PR 93*
Tyrrell, Albert Ray 1919- *WhoE 93, WhoWor 93*
Tyrrell, Calvin E. *WhoWrEP 92*
Tyrrell, D.A.J. *WhoScE 91-1*
Tyrrell, Eleanore Day 1938- *WhoAmW 93*
Tyrrell, George 1861-1909 *BioIn 17*
Tyrrell, James 1931- *St&PR 93*
Tyrrell, Joseph C. *Law&B 92*
Tyrrell, Joseph Patrick 1925- *WhoAm 92*
Tyrrell, Margot 1948- *ScF&FL 92*
Tyrrell, Michael Anthony *Law&B 92*
Tyrrell, Peter J. *Law&B 92*
Tyrrell, R. Emmett *BioIn 17*
Tyrrell, R.J. *WhoScE 91-1*
Tyrrell, Terry *BioIn 17*
Tyrrell, Thomas Neal *BioIn 17*
Tyrrell, Thomas Neil 1945- *St&PR 93, WhoAm 92*
Tyrwhitt-Wilson, Gerald Hugh *Baker 92*
Tysall, John Robert 1938- *St&PR 93, WhoAm 92*
Tyser, Wallace C., Jr. *Law&B 92*
Tysiac, Lawrence Leon 1953- *St&PR 93*
Tyson, Alan (Walker) 1926- *Baker 92*
Tyson, Andre *BioIn 17*
Tyson, Charlotte Rose 1954- *WhoAmW 93*
Tyson, Cicely *WhoAm 92, WhoAmW 93*
Tyson, Cynthia Haldenby 1937- *WhoAmW 93*
Tyson, Don 1930- *St&PR 93*
Tyson, Donald John 1930- *WhoAm 92, WhoSSW 93*
Tyson, Graham 1923- *St&PR 93*
Tyson, H. Michael 1938- *St&PR 93, WhoAm 92*
Tyson, Harry James 1945- *WhoAm 92*
Tyson, Helen Flynn 1913- *WhoAmW 93*
Tyson, J. Aubrey 1870-1930 *ScF&FL 92*
Tyson, Jeff 1948- *St&PR 93*
Tyson, John C. 1951- *WhoAm 92*
Tyson, John E. 1942- *St&PR 93*
Tyson, John Jeanes 1947- *WhoSSW 93*
Tyson, John Marsh 1953- *WhoSSW 93*
Tyson, Joseph B(lake) 1928- *ConAu 38NR*
Tyson, Joseph Blake 1928- *WhoSSW 93*
Tyson, Julian Fell 1949- *WhoE 93*
Tyson, Kenneth Robert Thomas 1936- *WhoAm 92*
Tyson, Luther E. 1922- *St&PR 93*
Tyson, Mary 1909- *WhoAmW 93, WhoE 93*
Tyson, Michael Gerald 1966- *BiDAMSp 1989*
Tyson, Mike *BioIn 17*
Tyson, Nancy Jane 1949- *WhoSSW 93*
Tyson, Nathan N. 1914- *St&PR 93*
Tyson, Patti Birge *WhoAm 92, WhoAmW 93*
Tyson, R.G. *WhoScE 91-1*
Tyson, Thomas Edgar *Law&B 92*
Tyszkiewicz, Beata 1938- *IntDcF 2-3*
Tyszkowa Tyszka, Maria 1932- *WhoWor 93*
Tytaneck, Robert W. 1949- *St&PR 93*
Tytanic, Christopher Alan *Law&B 92*
Tytel, Judith E. *Law&B 92*
Tytell, John 1939- *WhoAm 92, WhoWrEP 92*
Tytler, Linda Jean 1947- *WhoAmW 93*
Tyus, Shirley *BioIn 17*
Tyus, Wyomia 1945- *AfrAmBi, BioIn 17, BlkAmWO [port]*
Tyzack, Margaret *WhoAmW 93*
Tyzack, Margaret 1931- *ConTFT 10*
Tzachas dc. 1093 *OxDcByz*
Tzadua, Paulos Cardinal 1921- *WhoAm 92, WhoWor 93*
Tzafestas, Spyros Georgiou 1939- *WhoScE 91-3*
Tzagournis, Manuel *WhoAm 92*
Tzallas, Niove 1938- *WhoWor 93*
Tzamblakon *OxDcByz*
Tzanakakis, John-Minos E. 1927- *WhoScE 91-3*
Tzanakos, George Stefanos 1940- *WhoWor 93*
Tzannetakis, Tzannis 1927- *WhoWor 93*
Tzara, Tristan 1896-1963 *BioIn 17*
Tzaribashev, K.N. 1935- *WhoScE 91-4*
Tzartos, Socrates 1945- *WhoScE 91-3*
Tzeng, Kenneth Kai-Ming 1937- *WhoE 93*
Tzeng, Nian-Feng 1956- *WhoSSW 93*
Tzeng, Wen-Bih 1953- *WhoWor 93*
Tzetzes, John c. 1110-1180? *OxDcByz*
Tzidon, E. Avid *St&PR 93*
Tzikandeles *OxDcByz*
Tzimas, Nicholas Achilles 1928- *WhoAm 92*
Tzimet, Naftali *WhoWrEP 92*
Tzimopoulos, Nicholas D. 1941- *WhoE 93*
Tzipine, Georges 1907- *Baker 92*
Tzitsikas, Helene 1926- *WhoAmW 93*
Tzivanidis, George 1932- *WhoScE 91-3*
Tzonkov, Stojan 1939- *WhoScE 91-4*
Tzou, Horn-Sen 1952- *WhoSSW 93*
Tz'u-hsi, Empress dowager of China 1835-1908 *BioIn 17*
Tzybin, Vladimir 1877-1949 *Baker 92*

U

U, Ko Ko 1929- *WhoUN 92*
Uba, Jude Ebere 1960- *WhoSSW 93, WhoWor 93*
Ubben, Donald Thomas 1946- *WhoE 93*
Ubell, Earl 1926- *WhoAm 92, WhoWrEP 92*
Ubell, Robert Neil 1938- *WhoAm 92, WhoWrEP 92*
Uber *Baker 92*
Uber, Alexander 1783-1824 *Baker 92*
Uber, Christian Benjamin 1746-1812 *Baker 92*
Uber, Christian Friedrich Hermann 1781-1822 *Baker 92*
Uber, John William 1955- *WhoE 93*
Uberall, Herbert Michael Stefan 1931- *WhoAm 92*
Uberla, Karl K. 1935- *WhoScE 91-3*
Uberman, Ryszard 1937- *WhoScE 91-4*
Uberoi, Mahinder Singh 1924- *WhoAm 92, WhoWor 93*
Ubertalle, Antonio 1927- *WhoScE 91-3*
Uberti, Antonio 1697-1783 *Baker 92*
Ubertini, Lucio *WhoScE 91-3*
Ubico, Arturo *DcCPCAm*
Ubico y Castaneda, Jorge 1878-1946 *DcCPCAm*
Ubl, Walter William 1941- *St&PR 93*
Ubuka, Toshihiko 1934- *WhoWor 93*
Uby, Bjorn Olof 1939- *WhoWor 93*
Ubysz, Ignacy 1921- *WhoScE 91-4*
Ucang, Cicil Bungabong 1965- *WhoWor 93*
Uccellini, Louis William 1949- *WhoE 93*
Uccellini, Marco c. 1603-1680 *Baker 92*
Uccello, Vincenza Agatha 1921- *WhoAm 92*
Ucci, Donald Richard 1948- *WhoEmL 93*
Uchida, Hisashi *St&PR 93*
Uchida, Irene Ayako 1917- *WhoAm 92*
Uchida, Katsuhisa 1938- *WhoWor 93*
Uchida, Mitsuko *BioIn 17*
Uchida, Mitsuko 1948- *Baker 92*
Uchida, Naoya 1939- *WhoWor 93*
Uchida, Prentiss Susumu 1940- *WhoSSW 93, WhoWor 93*
Uchida, Shigeo 1941- *WhoWor 93*
Uchida, Takahiro 1929- *WhoWor 93*
Uchida, Takeo 1940- *WhoUN 92*
Uchida, Yoshiko *BioIn 17*
Uchida, Yoshiko d1992 *NewYTBS 92*
Uchida, Yoshiko 1921-1992 *ConAu 139, MajAI [port], SmATA 72*
Uchikura, Douglas E. *Law&B 92*
Uchill, Ida Libert 1917- *WhoWrEP 92*
Uchimoto, Dennis Den 1945- *St&PR 93*
Uchimoto, William W. 1955- *St&PR 93*
Uchimura, Glenn George 1952- *WhoWor 93*
Uchimura, Kanzo 1861-1930 *BioIn 17*
Uchitelle, Benjamin *Law&B 92*
Uchitelle, Louis 1932- *WhoAm 92*
Uchiyama, Michiaki 1924- *WhoWor 93*
Ucisik, A. Hikmet 1945- *WhoScE 91-4*
Ucko, Barbara 1945- *ConAu 136*
Ucko, David Alan 1948- *WhoAm 92*
Ucros, Juan C. *Law&B 92*
Udagawa, Kiyoshi 1934- *St&PR 93*
Udall, Calvin Hunt 1923- *WhoAm 92*
Udall, Morris K. *BioIn 17*
Udall, Morris K. 1922- *CngDr 91, PolPar*
Udall, Morris King 1922- *WhoAm 92*
Udall, Norma *BioIn 17*
Udall, Tom 1948- *WhoAm 92*
Udasin, Seth Lawrence 1956- *St&PR 93*
Udavchak, Raymond M. 1933- *WhoIns 93*
Udbye, Martin Andreas 1820-1889 *Baker 92*
Udcoff, George J. 1946- *St&PR 93*
Udcoff, George Joseph 1946- *WhoAm 92*
Uddenberg, A. Keith 1915- *St&PR 93*
Uddenberg, Thomas W. 1936- *St&PR 93*
Ude, Wayne Richard 1946- *WhoWrEP 92*
Udel, George 1930- *WhoE 93*
Udell, Daniel Erling 1935- *WhoE 93*
Udell, Howard Robert *Law&B 92*
Udell, Jon G(erald) 1935- *ConAu 37NR*
Udell, Richard *Law&B 92*
Udell, Richard 1932- *St&PR 93, WhoAm 92*
Udell, William Nathan 1921- *WhoSSW 93*
Uden, Peter Christopher 1939- *WhoE 93*
Udenfriend, Sidney 1918- *WhoAm 92*
Udevitz, Norman 1929- *WhoAm 92*
Uding, George 1932- *St&PR 93*
Udink, John Ray 1947- *St&PR 93*
Udo, Aart A.J. 1939- *WhoUN 92*
Udoh, Emmanuel Eyikojoka 1959- *WhoWor 93*
Udo-Inyang, Philip Denis 1960- *WhoE 93*
Udolf, Roy 1926- *WhoE 93*
Udouj, Richard John 1936- *St&PR 93*
Udovich, William Richard 1938- *St&PR 93*
Udovitch, Abraham Labe 1933- *WhoWrEP 92*
Udow, Henry A. 1957- *St&PR 93*
Udrys, A.T. *Law&B 92*
Udvardy, John Warren *WhoE 93*
Udvar-Hazy, Steven F. 1946- *WhoAm 92*
Udvarhelyi, George Bela 1920- *WhoAm 92*
Udwadia, Firdaus Erach 1947- *WhoEmL 93, WhoWor 93*
Udwin, Gerald Edward *BioIn 17*
Udy, Lex Lynn 1933- *St&PR 93*
Udziela, Seweryn 1857-1937 *IntDcAn*
Ueberhorst, Reinhard Ernst 1948- *WhoWor 93*
Ueberroth, John 1943- *WhoAm 92*
Ueberroth, Peter *BioIn 17*
Ueberroth, Peter Victor 1937- *WhoAm 92*
Uebleis, Andreas Michael 1963- *WhoWor 93*
Uechi, Gordon *Law&B 92*
Uecker, Bob 1935- *WhoAm 92*
Uecker, Raymond Louis, Jr. 1941- *WhoAm 92*
Ueda, Einosuke 1933- *WhoWor 93*
Ueda, Kazuo 1949- *WhoWor 93*
Ueda, Kenichi 1927- *WhoWor 93*
Ueda, Kenkichi 1875-1962 *HarEnMi*
Ueda, Koichiro 1927- *WhoAsAP 91*
Ueda, Masao 1918- *WhoWor 93*
Ueda, Minoru 1929- *St&PR 93*
Ueda, Risei 1930- *WhoAsAP 91*
Ueda, Takeshi 1941- *WhoWor 93*
Ueda, Takumi 1938- *WhoAsAP 91*
Ueda, Tetsu 1928- *WhoAsAP 91*
Ueda, Tsutomu *ScF&FL 92*
Uehara, Kazuma 1916- *WhoWor 93*
Uehara, Kosuke 1932- *WhoAsAP 91*
Uehara, Yusaku 1856-1933 *HarEnMi*
Uehlein, Edward Carl, Jr. 1941- *WhoE 93*
Uehlin, Stephen L. 1947- *St&PR 93*
Uehling, Barbara Staner 1932- *WhoAm 92, WhoAmW 93, WhoWor 93*
Uehling, Gordon Alexander, Jr. 1939- *St&PR 93*
Uehling, James Harvey Tomb 1935- *WhoE 93*
Uehling, Robert Henry *Law&B 92*
Uehlinger, John Clark 1929- *WhoAm 92*
Uek, Robert William 1941- *WhoE 93*
Uekusa, Yoshiteru 1939- *WhoAsAP 91*
Ueland, Brenda *BioIn 17*
Ueland, Sigurd, Jr. 1937- *St&PR 93, WhoAm 92*
Uelsmann, Jerry 1934- *BioIn 17*
Uelsmann, Jerry Norman 1934- *WhoAm 92*
Ueltschi, Albert L. 1917- *St&PR 93*
Uematsu, Debra Faye 1964- *WhoAmW 93*
Uematsu, Kunihiko 1931- *WhoScE 91-2*
Uemoto, Karen Toshie 1942- *St&PR 93, WhoAm 92*
Uemura, Ken Takashi 1948- *St&PR 93*
Uemura, Sakae 1941- *WhoWor 93*
Uemura, Teruki 1944- *WhoWor 93*
Ueno, Akira 1929- *WhoWor 93*
Ueno, Itaru 1930- *WhoWor 93*
Ueno, Kenichi 1931- *WhoAsAP 91*
Ueno, Masao 1937- *WhoWor 93*
Ueno, Susumu 1946- *WhoWor 93*
Ueno, Tomiko F. 1930- *WhoWor 93*
Ueno, Yubun 1927- *WhoAsAP 91*
Uesugi, Akisada 1454-1510 *HarEnMi*
Uesugi, Kagekatsu 1555-1623 *HarEnMi*
Uesugi, Kenshin 1530-1578 *HarEnMi*
Uesugi, Mitsuhiro 1942- *WhoAsAP 91*
Uesugi, Norizane d1455 *HarEnMi*
Ufema, Joy *BioIn 17*
Uffelman, Malcolm Rucj 1935- *St&PR 93, WhoAm 92*
Uffen, Robert James 1923- *WhoAm 92, WhoWor 93*
Uffner, Gary Harold 1954- *St&PR 93*
Uffner, Michael S. 1945- *WhoE 93, WhoWor 93*
Ufford, Charles Wilbur, Jr. 1931- *WhoAm 92*
Ufford, Kimberly 1954- *St&PR 93*
Ufheil, John Lloyd 1933- *St&PR 93*
Ugaki, Matome 1890-1945 *BioIn 17, HarEnMi*
Ugalde, Delphine 1829-1910 *Baker 92, OxDcOp*
Ugalde, Marguerite 1862-1940 *OxDcOp*
Ugarchinski, Bogdan Vassilev 1943- *WhoScE 91-4*
Ugarte, Floro M(anuel) 1884-1975 *Baker 92*
Ugarte, Jorge *St&PR 93*
Ugarte, Miguel F. *Law&B 92*
Uggams, Leslie 1943- *WhoAm 92*
Ugglas, Wargaretha af 1939- *WhoWor 93*
Ughamadu, Cyprian Ozomenam 1956- *WhoWor 93*
Ughetta, William C. *Law&B 92*
Ughetta, William C. 1933- *St&PR 93*
Ughetta, William C. 1954- *WhoAm 92*
Ughetta, William Casper 1933- *WhoAm 92*
Ughi, Uto 1944- *Baker 92*
Ugland, Steven L. *Law&B 92*
Uglanov, Aleksei Vladimirovich 1948- *WhoWor 93*
Ugljesa *OxDcByz*
Ugolina da Orvieto c. 1380-1457 *Baker 92*
Ugolini, Alberto 1929- *WhoScE 91-3*
Ugolini, Richard P. *St&PR 93*
Ugolini, Vincenzo c. 1580-1638 *Baker 92*
Ugolino di Francesco Urbevetano c. 1380-1457 *Baker 92*
Ugolyn, Victor 1947- *St&PR 93*
Ugresic, Dubravka 1949- *ConAu 136*
Ugrin, Bela 1928- *WhoAm 92, WhoWor 93*
Ugrinsky, Alexej *ScF&FL 92*
Ugwu, David Egbo 1950- *WhoWor 93*
Ugwu, Martin Cornelius 1956- *WhoSSW 93*
Uhde, Fritz von 1848-1911 *BioIn 17*
Uhde, George Irvin 1912- *WhoAm 92*
Uhde, Hermann 1914-1965 *Baker 92, OxDcOp*
Uhde, Thomas Whitley *WhoE 93*
Uher, Lorna *WhoCanL 92*
Uher, Stefan 1930- *DrEEuF*
Uhl, Alfred 1909- *Baker 92*
Uhl, Donald P. 1936- *St&PR 93*
Uhl, Fritz 1928- *Baker 92*
Uhl, George David 1934- *St&PR 93, WhoAm 92*
Uhl, Scott Mark 1950- *WhoE 93*
Uhl, William J. *Law&B 92*
Uhland, Johann Ludwig 1787-1862 *BioIn 17*
Uhle, Donald Earl, Jr. 1951- *WhoSSW 93*
Uhle, George 1898-1985 *BioIn 17*
Uhle, Max 1856-1944 *IntDcAn*
Uhlen, Gotfred M. 1923- *WhoScE 91-4*
Uhlenbeck, C.C. 1866-1951 *IntDcAn*
Uhlenbeck, George Eugene 1900-1988 *BioIn 17*
Uhlenbeck, Karen Keskulla 1942- *WhoAm 92, WhoAmW 93*
Uhlenbrauck, Keith 1946- *St&PR 93*
Uhlenburg, Donald G. 1934- *St&PR 93*
Uhlenhuth, Eberhard Henry 1927- *WhoAm 92*
Uhler, Francis Morey 1902-1990 *BioIn 17*
Uhler, Walter Charles 1948- *WhoE 93, WhoEmL 93, WhoWor 93*
Uhlig, Barney Uve 1939- *St&PR 93*
Uhlig, D. *WhoScE 91-3*
Uhlig, Egon 1929- *WhoWor 93*
Uhlig, Gotram 1928- *WhoScE 91-3*
Uhlig, Gregory Edward 1955- *WhoSSW 93*
Uhlig, John Richard 1941- *WhoE 93*
Uhlig, Max 1937- *BioIn 17*
Uhlig, Theodor 1822-1853 *Baker 92*
Uhlin, Bernt Eric 1950- *WhoScE 91-4*
Uhling, Terry T. *Law&B 92*
Uhlir, Arthur, Jr. 1926- *WhoAm 92*
Uhlir, Frank Allen 1952- *WhoSSW 93*
Uhlir, Gladys Ann 1934- *WhoAmW 93*
Uhlir, Golby Cleigh 1932- *WhoWor 93*
Uhliu, Hans-Erik *WhoScE 91-4*
Uhlmann, Frederick Godfrey 1929- *WhoAm 92*
Uhlmann, Paul, Jr. 1920- *St&PR 93*
Uhlmann, Paul, III 1950- *St&PR 93*
Uhlmann, R.H. 1916- *St&PR 93*
Uhlmann, Richard Frederick 1898-1989 *BioIn 17*
Uhr, Stanley A. 1946- *St&PR 93*
Uhrich, Carole J. 1943- *St&PR 93*

Uhrich, Richard Beckley 1932- *WhoAm 92*
Uhrig, Robert Eugene 1928- *WhoAm 92, WhoSSW 93*
Uhrik, Steven Brian 1949- *WhoEmL 93*
Uhrman, Celia 1927- *WhoE 93*
Uhrman, Esther 1921- *ScF&FL 92, WhoE 93, WhoWrEP 92*
Uhrman, Gary H. 1935- *St&PR 93*
Uhrman, Hal *St&PR 93*
Uhry, Alfred 1936- *ConTFT 10*
Uhry, Alfred Fox 1936- *WhoAm 92*
Uhry, Edmond 1874-1954 *BioIn 17*
Uhrynuk, Gregory Michael *Law&B 92*
Uible, Frank R., Jr. *Law&B 92*
Uicker, Jospeh Bernard 1940- *St&PR 93*
Uicker, Theresa A. 1962- *WhoAmW 93*
Uihlein, Stephen Ellis 1953- *St&PR 93*
Uilenberg, Gerrit 1929- *WhoScE 91-2*
Uilkema, Gayle Burns 1938- *WhoAmW 93*
Uitermark, Helen Joan 1941- *WhoAmW 93*
Uitti, Karl David 1933- *WhoAm 92, WhoWrEP 92*
Ujejski, Kornel 1823-1897 *PolBiDi*
Ujfalussy, Jozsef 1920- *Baker 92*
Ujhely, Richard J. 1941- *St&PR 93*
Ujhidy, Aurel 1927- *WhoScE 91-4*
Ujihara, Kosaku 1947- *WhoWor 93*
Ujj, Bela 1873-1942 *Baker 92*
Ujma, Janina Helena 1929- *WhoScE 91-4*
Ukaegbu, Alfred Onyeohuhu 1941- *WhoUN 92*
Ukai, Clara A.M. *Law&B 92*
Ukeiwe, Dick 1928- *WhoAsAP 91*
Ukeles, Mierle Laderman *BioIn 17*
Ukena, Paul d1991 *BioIn 17*
Ukhueduan, Michael Edd 1962- *WhoE 93*
Ukita, Hideie 1574-c. 1665 *HarEnMi*
Ukita, Naoie 1530-1582 *HarEnMi*
Ukkonen, Esko J. 1950- *WhoScE 91-4*
Ukropina, James Robert 1937- *St&PR 93, WhoAm 92*
Ulaby, Fawwaz Tayssir 1943- *WhoAm 92*
Ulak, Dennis M. *Law&B 92*
Ulam, Adam B. 1922- *WhoAm 92*
Ulam, Stanislaw M. *BioIn 17*
Ulan, Martin Sylvester 1912- *WhoE 93*
Ulan, Michael Kenneth 1946- *WhoE 93*
Ulanov, Ann Belford 1938- *ConAu 38NR, WhoAmW 93*
Ulanov, Barry 1918- *ConAu 38NR, WhoAm 92, WhoWrEP 92*
Ulanova, Galina 1910- *BioIn 17*
Ulanowicz, Robert Edward 1943- *WhoE 93*
Ulansey, Vivienne K. 1922- *WhoAmW 93*
Ulanski, Jacek Pawel 1949- *WhoWor 93*
Ulate Blanco, Otilio *DcCPCAm*
Ulbrecht, Jaromir Josef 1928- *WhoAm 92, WhoWor 93*
Ulbrich, Fred, Jr. 1930- *St&PR 93*
Ulbrich, Maximilian c. 1741-1814 *Baker 92*
Ulbrich, Richard J. 1934- *St&PR 93*
Ulbrich, Scott Carl 1954- *WhoAm 92*
Ulbrich, Volker R. *Law&B 92*
Ulbricht, John 1926- *WhoAm 92*
Ulbricht, Robert E. *Law&B 92*
Ulbricht, Robert E. 1930- *St&PR 93*
Ulbricht, Walter 1893-1973 *ColdWar 2 [port], DcTwHis*
Ulchaker, Stanley Louis 1938- *WhoAm 92*
Uldal, Lise *WhoScE 91-2*
Ulehla, Ivan 1921- *WhoScE 91-4*
Ulene, Art *BioIn 17*
Ulerich, William Keener 1910- *St&PR 93, WhoAm 92, WhoWor 93*
Ulery, Byron Wayne 1940- *St&PR 93*
Ulery, Shari L. *Law&B 92*
Ulery, Shari Lee 1953- *WhoAmW 93*
Ulevich, Neal Hirsh 1946- *WhoAm 92*
Ulf, Franklin E. 1931- *St&PR 93*
Ulfelder, Howard 1911-1990 *BioIn 17*
Ulfilas c. 311-382? *OxDcByz*
Ulfrstad, Marius Moaritz 1890-1968 *Baker 92*
Ulfstrand, Staffan 1933- *WhoScE 91-4*
Ulfung, Ragnar 1927- *OxDcOp*
Ulfung, Ragnar (Sigurd) 1927- *Baker 92*
Ulfvarson, Anders Y.J. 1943- *WhoScE 91-4*
Ulfvarson, Ulf O. 1931- *WhoScE 91-4*
Ulfves, Bjorn Olav 1929- *WhoWor 93*
Ulguray, Metin 1940- *WhoWor 93*
Ul'ianinskii, Nikolai IUr'evich 1872-1937 *BioIn 17*
Ulibarri, Sabine 1919- *HispAmA [port]*
Ulichny, Barbara L. 1947- *WhoAmW 93*
Ulicny, Luke *Law&B 92*
Ulin, Peter A. 1930- *WhoE 93*
Ulin, Robert Charles 1951- *WhoE 93*
Ulinski, Susan Elizabeth 1952- *St&PR 93*
Uliss, Barbara Turk 1947- *WhoAmW 93*
Ulisse, Peter James 1944- *WhoWrEP 92*
Ulke, Asim 1940- *WhoE 93*
Ulke, Helmut *WhoScE 91-3*
Ulku, Dincer 1940- *WhoScE 91-4*
Ulla, Noemi 1933- *WhoWor 93*
Ullah, Atta 1952- *WhoWor 93*
Ullah, Nemat 1952- *WhoWor 93*
Ulland, Grete Ek *WhoScE 91-4*
Ullberg, Kent 1945- *BioIn 17*
Ullberg, Kent Jean 1945- *WhoAm 92*
Ulle, Albin Edward 1938- *St&PR 93*
Ulleberg, Tore *Law&B 92*
Ulleland, Magnus Gustav 1929- *WhoWor 93*
Ullendorff, Edward 1920- *ConAu 40NR*
Ullenius, C.I. Christina 1943- *WhoScE 91-4*
Ullensvang, Leon P. 1933- *St&PR 93*
Ullery, Donald E., Jr. 1935- *St&PR 93*
Ullestad, Merwin Allan 1949- *WhoSSW 93*
Ullian, Joseph Silbert 1930- *WhoAm 92*
Ullman, Edwin Fisher 1930- *WhoAm 92*
Ullman, Harlan Kenneth 1941- *WhoE 93*
Ullman, Jeffrey David 1942- *WhoAm 92*
Ullman, Joan Connelly 1929- *WhoAm 92*
Ullman, Leo Solomon 1939- *WhoAm 92*
Ullman, Louis Jay 1931- *St&PR 93, WhoAm 92*
Ullman, Marie 1914- *WhoAmW 93, WhoWor 93*
Ullman, Myron E. 1946- *St&PR 93*
Ullman, Myron Edward, III 1946- *WhoAm 92*
Ullman, Nelly Szabo 1925- *WhoAmW 93*
Ullman, Richard Henry 1933- *WhoAm 92*
Ullman, Sharon Lee 1960- *WhoAmW 93*
Ullman, Sydney 1910-1990 *BioIn 17*
Ullman, Tracey *BioIn 17*
Ullman, Tracey 1959- *WhoAm 92, WhoAmW 93*
Ullmann, Agnes *WhoScE 91-2*
Ullmann, Alex d1992 *NewYTBS 92*
Ullmann, Gerald W., Jr. 1961- *St&PR 93*
Ullmann, Klaus 1937- *St&PR 93*
Ullmann, Liv *BioIn 17*
Ullmann, Liv 1938- *WhoAm 92, WhoWor 93*
Ullmann, Liv 1939- *IntDcF 2-3 [port], MiSFD 9*
Ullmann, Margaret 1882- *AmWomPl*
Ullmann, Michael H. *Law&B 92*
Ullmann, Owen *BioIn 17*
Ullmann, Uwe 1939- *WhoScE 91-3*
Ullmann, Viktor 1898-1944 *Baker 92*
Ullmann, Wilmer R. *Law&B 92*
Ullmark, Hans 1946- *WhoAm 92*
Ullmer, John 1932- *WhoSSW 93*
Ulloa, Francisco Noguerol de 16th cent.- *BioIn 17*
Ulloa Elias, Manuel d1992 *NewYTBS 92*
Ulloa Ulloa, Miguel 1951- *WhoWor 93*
Ullrich, Axel *WhoScE 91-3*
Ullrich, Bruce 1938- *WhoWor 93*
Ullrich, John Frederick 1940- *St&PR 93, WhoAm 92*
Ullrich, Karl J. 1925- *WhoScE 91-3*
Ullrich, Robert Albert 1939- *WhoAm 92*
Ullrich, Volker 1939- *WhoScE 91-3*
Ullring, Sven *WhoScE 91-4*
Ullring, Sven Bang 1935- *WhoWor 93*
Ullstein, Hans L. 1930- *St&PR 93*
Ullstrom, Galen F. *Law&B 92*
Ulm, Ernest H. 1916- *St&PR 93*
Ulman, Cynthia M. 1954- *WhoAmW 93*
Ulman, Louis Jay 1946- *WhoAm 92*
Ulmer, Alfred Conrad 1916- *WhoAm 92*
Ulmer, Anne Close 1940- *WhoAmW 93*
Ulmer, Edgar G. 1904-1972 *MiSFD 9N*
Ulmer, Evonne Gail 1947- *WhoEmL 93*
Ulmer, Flo Rene 1955- *WhoAmW 93*
Ulmer, Gordon I. 1932- *St&PR 93*
Ulmer, Gregory L(eland) 1944- *ConAu 136*
Ulmer, John R. *Law&B 92*
Ulmer, Laura J. *Law&B 92*
Ulmer, Melville Jack 1911- *WhoAm 92*
Ulmer, Melville Paul 1943- *WhoAm 92*
Ulmer, Nancy Clemens 1937- *WhoSSW 93*
Ulmer, Peter Eugen 1933- *WhoWor 93*
Ulmer, Shirley Sidney 1923- *WhoAm 92, WhoWor 93*
Ulmer, Walter F., Jr. 1929- *WhoAm 92*
Ulmer, Wolfgang T. 1924- *WhoScE 91-3*
Ulmschneider, Peter H. 1938- *WhoScE 91-3*
Ulon, Robert Joseph 1935- *St&PR 93*
Ulosevich, Steven Nils 1947- *WhoWor 93*
Ulph, Alistair Mitchell *WhoScE 91-1*
Ulpios *OxDcByz*
Ulrich, Alfred Daniel, III 1961- *WhoSSW 93*
Ulrich, Ann Carol 1952- *WhoWrEP 92*
Ulrich, Bernhard 1926- *WhoScE 91-3*
Ulrich, Carolyn Ann 1964- *WhoAmW 93*
Ulrich, Carolyn F. 1880-1969 *BioIn 17*
Ulrich, David Mark 1956- *St&PR 93*
Ulrich, Donald R. d1990 *BioIn 17*
Ulrich, Donna M. 1944- *St&PR 93*
Ulrich, Finn 1944- *WhoUN 92*
Ulrich, George Henry 1947- *WhoE 93*
Ulrich, Gladys Marjorie 1932- *WhoAmW 93*
Ulrich, Harold Charles, Jr. 1929- *St&PR 93*
Ulrich, Henri 1925- *WhoAm 92*
Ulrich, Homer 1906- *Baker 92*
Ulrich, Hugo 1827-1872 *Baker 92*
Ulrich, Laurel *BioIn 17*
Ulrich, Laurel Thatcher 1938- *WhoAm 92, WhoAmW 93, WhoE 93*
Ulrich, Lawrence P. 1947- *St&PR 93*
Ulrich, Max Marsh 1925- *WhoAm 92*
Ulrich, Norbert M. 1922- *St&PR 93*
Ulrich, Paul Graham 1938- *WhoAm 92, WhoWor 93*
Ulrich, Peter Henry 1922- *WhoAm 92*
Ulrich, Reinhard 1935- *WhoWor 93*
Ulrich, Richard William 1950- *St&PR 93, WhoSSW 93*
Ulrich, Robert Gardner *Law&B 92*
Ulrich, Robert Gardner 1935- *St&PR 93, WhoAm 92*
Ulrich, Robert Gene 1941- *WhoAm 92*
Ulrich, Theodore Albert 1943- *WhoAm 92, WhoE 93*
Ulrich, Werner *Law&B 92*
Ulrich, Werner 1931- *WhoAm 92*
Ulrich, Wesley A. 1950- *St&PR 93*
Ulsamer, Andrew George 1941- *WhoAm 92*
Ulseth, George Walter 1918- *WhoIns 93*
Ulsh, Keith A. 1961- *St&PR 93*
Ulster, Harley *St&PR 93*
Ultan, Lloyd 1938- *WhoE 93*
Ultmann, John Ernest 1925- *WhoAm 92*
Uludag, Nevzat 1929- *WhoScE 91-4*
Ulufa'alu, Bartholomew 1945- *WhoAsAP 91*
Ulug, Erkin 1942- *WhoScE 91-4*
Ulusoy, A. Gunduz 1947- *WhoScE 91-4*
Ulvang, Vegard *BioIn 17*
Ulveling, Ralph Adrian 1902-1980 *BioIn 17*
Ulverstad, Larry 1941- *St&PR 93*
Ulvila, Jacob Walter 1950- *WhoSSW 93*
Ulvonas, Staffan 1928- *WhoScE 91-4*
Ulyatt, J.M. *WhoScE 91-1*
Ulybyshev, Alexander Dmitrievich *Baker 92*
Um, Dong-Suk 1934- *WhoWor 93*
Um, Gregory S. 1948- *St&PR 93*
Umadevi c. 1150-1218 *HarEnMi*
Umakoshi, Keisuke 1960- *WhoWor 93*
Uman, Martin Allan 1936- *WhoAm 92*
Uman, Myron F. 1939- *WhoE 93*
Umano, Motohide 1951- *WhoWor 93*
Umans, Al R. 1927- *St&PR 93*
Umans, Alvin Robert 1927- *WhoAm 92*
Umans-Gough, Terry A. *Law&B 92*
Umanskii, Yan Lazarevitch 1945- *WhoWor 93*
Umansky, Raphael D. *Law&B 92*
Umansky, Raphael Douglas 1950- *WhoSSW 93*
'Umar d863 *OxDcByz*
'Umar c. 592-644 *OxDcByz*
'Umar, II 682?-720 *OxDcByz*
Umarov, Khasan Galsanovich 1950- *WhoWor 93*
Umaru, Alhaji 1858-1934 *IntDcAn*
Umbach, Clayton August, Jr. 1930- *St&PR 93*
Umbach, D.K. 1953- *St&PR 93*
Umbach, Eberhard 1948- *WhoWor 93*
Umba di Lutete, Jean Theodore 1939- *WhoAfr*
Umbdenstock, Judy Jean 1952- *WhoEmL 93, WhoWor 93*
Umberfield, Sherry Ann 1954- *St&PR 93*
Umbhau, Jurgen 1943- *St&PR 93*
Umbreit, Gerald Ross 1930- *WhoE 93*
Umbreit, Wayne William 1913- *WhoAm 92, WhoE 93*
Umeda, James O. *Law&B 92*
Umeda, Judy *Law&B 92*
Umeda, Tomio 1953- *WhoWor 93*
Umeki, Shigenobu 1951- *WhoWor 93*
Umemura, Hiroshi 1944- *WhoWor 93*
Umemura, Kyoji 1959- *WhoWor 93*
Umen, Samuel d1990 *BioIn 17*
Umenai, Takusei 1941- *WhoUN 92*
Umetani, Shin-ichi 1955- *WhoWor 93*
Umezawa, Hiroomi 1924- *WhoAm 92*
Umezawa, Yoshio 1944- *WhoWor 93*
Umezu, Yoshijiro 1882-1949 *HarEnMi*
Umhoefer, Lois 1936- *St&PR 93*
Umhoefer, Paul 1935- *St&PR 93*
Umhoefer, Sharon Ann *Law&B 92*
Umhoefer, Theodore E. 1950- *St&PR 93*
Uminski, Tadeusz 1930- *WhoScE 91-4*
Um Kalthoum 1898-1975 *Baker 92*
Umland, Jean Blanchard 1924- *WhoSSW 93*
Umland, Pauline Sawyer 1903- *WhoAmW 93*
Umlauf, Carl Ignaz Franz 1824-1902 *Baker 92*
Umlauf, Ignaz 1746-1796 *Baker 92*
Umlauf, Michael 1781-1842 *Baker 92*
Umlauff, Ignaz 1746-1796 *OxDcOp*
Umlauff, Michael 1781-1842 *OxDcOp*
Ummel-Olson, Carolyn Lockwood 1947- *WhoAmW 93*
Umminger, Bruce Lynn 1941- *WhoAm 92*
Umont, Frank 1918-1991 *BioIn 17*
Umphenour, Jillian Darrelyn 1957- *WhoWrEP 92*
Umphlett, Archie Watford, Jr. *Law&B 92*
Umphred, William James 1928- *St&PR 93*
Umphrey, Kirk A. 1955- *St&PR 93*
Umphry, Debbie K. 1967- *WhoAmW 93*
Umpierre, Luz Maria 1947- *BioIn 17*
Umpire Medina, Juan Silvio 1949- *WhoWor 93*
Umpleby, Stuart Anspach 1944- *WhoWor 93*
Umpujh, Supaluck *BioIn 17*
Umscheid, Rod *BioIn 17*
Umthun, Steven Henry 1955- *St&PR 93*
Umthun, Virgil Louis 1930- *St&PR 93*
Umur Beg 1309-1348 *OxDcByz*
Un *WhoWrEP 92*
Unagi, David 1959- *WhoAsAP 91*
Unakar, Nalin Jayantilal 1935- *WhoAm 92*
Unal, Esin 1942- *WhoScE 91-4*
Unal, Mehmet 1943- *WhoScE 91-4*
Unamuno, Miguel de 1864-1936 *BioIn 17, ShScr 11 [port]*
Unan, Coskun 1936- *WhoScE 91-4*
Unanue, Emil Raphael 1934- *WhoAm 92*
Unanue, Manuel de Dios *BioIn 17*
Unbehauen, Heinz-Dietrich 1935- *WhoScE 91-3*
Unbehauen, Rolf 1930- *WhoScE 91-3*
Unberant, Donald E. 1932- *St&PR 93*
Uncapher, Mark Elson 1926- *St&PR 93*
Uncapher, Mark Elson 1953- *WhoE 93*
Unckel, Kurt *IntDcAn*
Uncle Gus *MajAI, SmATA 69*
Uncles, Reginald James 1947- *WhoScE 91-1*
Uncle Shelby *MajAI*
Underberg, Alan J. 1929- *WhoAm 92*
Underberg, Charlene Marie 1947- *WhoAmW 93*
Underberg, Mark A. 1955- *St&PR 93*
Underberg, Mark Alan 1955- *WhoAm 92*
Underberg, Neil 1928- *WhoAm 92*
Underberg, Rita Posner 1926- *WhoE 93*
Underberg, Sharon E. *Law&B 92*
Underdown, David Edward 1925- *WhoAm 92*
Underhill, Allan Edward *WhoScE 91-1*
Underhill, Anne Barbara 1920- *WhoAm 92, WhoAmW 93*
Underhill, Evelyn 1875-1941 *BioIn 17*
Underhill, Jack Arthur 1932- *WhoE 93*
Underhill, Jacob Berry, III 1926- *WhoAm 92*
Underhill, James Felton 1955- *St&PR 93*
Underhill, Linn *BioIn 17*
Underhill, Nancy Dudley 1938- *WhoWor 93*
Underhill, Phil Eugene 1945- *St&PR 93*
Underhill, Robert Louis 1953- *St&PR 93*
Underhill, Ruth 1883?-1984 *IntDcAn*
Underhill, Ruth Murray 1884-1984 *ConAu 39NR*
Underkofler, James R. 1923- *St&PR 93*
Underman, Rik 1947- *St&PR 93*
Underweiser, Irwin Philip 1929- *WhoAm 92, WhoE 93, WhoWor 93*
Underwood, Alfred H., Jr. 1930- *WhoSSW 93*
Underwood, Arthur Louis, Jr. 1924- *WhoAm 92*
Underwood, Barbara Ann *WhoE 93*
Underwood, Benjamin Hayes 1942- *WhoSSW 93*
Underwood, Bernard Edward 1925- *WhoAm 92*
Underwood, (Mary) Betty (Anderson) 1921- *DcAmChF 1960*
Underwood, Beverly H. 1963- *WhoAmW 93*
Underwood, Blair *BioIn 17, WhoAm 92*
Underwood, Brenda S. 1948- *WhoAmW 93, WhoE 93*
Underwood, Brian C. *Law&B 92*
Underwood, Cecil H. 1922- *WhoAm 92*
Underwood, Charles Brannon 1936- *WhoSSW 93*
Underwood, Christopher Patrick *WhoScE 91-1*
Underwood, Darlene Joyce 1949- *WhoAmW 93*
Underwood, David W. 1946- *St&PR 93*
Underwood, Edward Douglas 1926- *WhoSSW 93*
Underwood, Ellen Franklin 1955- *WhoAmW 93*
Underwood, George 1947- *BioIn 17*
Underwood, George C., II *St&PR 93*
Underwood, Harry Burnham, II 1943- *St&PR 93, WhoAm 92*
Underwood, Harvey Cockrell *WhoSSW 93*
Underwood, Helen 1914- *ConAu 139*

Underwood, James 1951- *Baker 92*
Underwood, James C.E. *WhoScE 91-1*
Underwood, James Martin 1909- *WhoAm 92*
Underwood, Jane Hainline Hammons 1931- *WhoAm 92*
Underwood, Jeffery S(cott) 1954- *ConAu 137*
Underwood, Joanna DeHaven 1940- *WhoAm 92*
Underwood, Lisa Claudine Witherow 1966- *WhoSSW 93*
Underwood, Marylyn Joyce 1939- *WhoSSW 93, WhoWrEP 92*
Underwood, McLean Rodney 1951- *WhoWor 93*
Underwood, Oscar W. 1862-1929 *PolPar*
Underwood, Paul 1940- *WhoAm 92*
Underwood, Paul Benjamin 1934- *WhoAm 92*
Underwood, Peter 1923- *ScF&FL 92*
Underwood, Ralph Edward 1947- *WhoEmL 93*
Underwood, Randy S. *Law&B 92*
Underwood, Richard Allan 1933- *WhoSSW 93*
Underwood, Robert K. 1917- *St&PR 93*
Underwood, Rodney *BioIn 17*
Underwood, Ron *MiSFD 9*
Underwood, Ronald Nelson 1959- *WhoSSW 93*
Underwood, Sheila Marie 1952- *WhoAmW 93*
Underwood, T. Bryan, Jr. *Law&B 92*
Underwood, Thomas Carroll *Law&B 92*
Underwood, Thomas Carroll 1936- *St&PR 93*
Underwood, Thomas Clayton, III 1955- *WhoSSW 93*
Underwood, Tim 1948- *ScF&FL 92*
Underwood, Vernon O., Jr. 1940- *WhoAm 92*
Underwood, Virgie Dunman 1951- *WhoAmW 93*
Underwood, Virginia H. *Law&B 92*
Undisputed Truth *SoulM*
Undlin, Charles Thomas 1928- *WhoAm 92*
Undset, Sigrid 1882-1949 *BioIn 17, WorLitC [port]*
Undurraga, Jose Andres 1929- *WhoWor 93*
Unestam, Torgny K.G. 1931- *WhoScE 91-4*
Unetich, Robert M. 1946- *St&PR 93*
Unfried, Stephen Mitchell 1943- *St&PR 93, WhoAm 92*
Unfried, W. Thomas 1926- *St&PR 93*
Ung, Chinary 1942- *Baker 92*
Ung, Eugene 1954- *WhoWor 93*
Ungar, Andrew 1961- *St&PR 93*
Ungar, Carole Wilson 1933- *WhoAmW 93*
Ungar, Emanuel 1933- *St&PR 93*
Ungar, Eric Edward 1926- *WhoAm 92*
Ungar, Irwin Allan 1934- *WhoAm 92*
Ungar, Jay *BioIn 17*
Ungar, Jonas *WhoScE 91-4*
Ungar, Manya Shayon 1928- *WhoAm 92*
Ungaro, Emanuel *BioIn 17*
Ungaro, Emanuel Matteotti 1933- *WhoWor 93*
Ungaro, Joan *WhoWrEP 92*
Ungaro, Joseph Michael 1930- *WhoAm 92*
Ungemach, Frank Schneider *Law&B 92*
Ungemach, Fritz Rupert 1947- *WhoScE 91-3*
Ungemach, Harald *WhoScE 91-3*
Ungemah, Donald W. *Law&B 92*
Ungemuth, Michel-Pierre 1943- *WhoWor 93*
Unger, A. Leslie 1943- *St&PR 93*
Unger, Adrienne P. *Law&B 92*
Unger, Andras 1949- *WhoScE 91-4*
Unger, Arthur Charles 1943- *St&PR 93*
Unger, Barbara 1932- *ConAu 40NR*
Unger, Barbara Frankel 1932- *WhoAmW 93*
Unger, Burton 1939- *WhoWrEP 92*
Unger, Caroline 1803-1877 *Baker 92, OxDcOp*
Unger, David 1934- *St&PR 93*
Unger, Donna Jean 1951- *WhoE 93*
Unger, Douglas Arthur 1952- *WhoWrEP 92*
Unger, Emerson V. 1946- *St&PR 93*
Unger, Frederick Branson 1940- *St&PR 93*
Unger, Friederike Helene 1741?-1813 *BioIn 17*
Unger, Georg 1837-1887 *Baker 92, OxDcOp*
Unger, Gerald Franz 1950- *St&PR 93*
Unger, Gerhard 1916- *Baker 92*
Unger, Gladys Buchanan 1885-1940 *AmWomPl*
Unger, Hans-Georg 1926- *WhoScE 91-3*
Unger, Heinz 1895-1965 *Baker 92*
Unger, (Gustav) Hermann 1886-1958 *Baker 92*
Unger, Howard Albert 1944- *WhoAm 92, WhoE 93, WhoWor 93*
Unger, Irwin 1927- *WhoAm 92*
Unger, James Joseph 1948- *WhoAm 92*
Unger, Jim *BioIn 17*
Unger, Larry D. 1948- *St&PR 93*
Unger, Marcel N. *Law&B 92*
Unger, Marianne Louise 1957- *WhoAmW 93*
Unger, Mary Ann *WhoE 93*
Unger, (Ernst) Max 1883-1959 *Baker 92*
Unger, Paul A. 1914- *St&PR 93, WhoWor 93*
Unger, Paul R. 1902- *St&PR 93*
Unger, Paul Walter 1931- *WhoAm 92*
Unger, Peter K(enneth) 1942- *ConAu 136*
Unger, Peter Kenneth 1942- *WhoAm 92, WhoE 93*
Unger, Rhoda Kesler 1939- *WhoAmW 93, WhoE 93*
Unger, Richard Watson 1942- *WhoAm 92*
Unger, Robert Martin 1954- *WhoE 93*
Unger, Ronald Lawrence 1930- *WhoAm 92*
Unger, Sharon Louise 1942- *WhoE 93*
Unger, Sonja Franz 1921- *St&PR 93*
Unger, Stefan Howard 1944- *WhoAm 92*
Unger, Stephen Herbert 1931- *WhoAm 92*
Unger, Thomas William 1945- *St&PR 93*
Unger, Walter Scott 1928- *St&PR 93*
Ungerbuehler, Richard Arthur 1941- *St&PR 93*
Ungerer, Jean Tomi 1931- *WhoWrEP 92*
Ungerer, (Jean) Thomas 1931- *MajAI [port]*
Ungerer, Tomi *MajAI*
Ungerland, Thomas J. *Law&B 92*
Ungerman, Robert T. 1943- *St&PR 93*
Ungers, Oswald M. 1926- *WhoAm 92*
Unger-Smith, David Lloyd 1951- *WhoE 93*
Ungewickell, Ernst *WhoScE 91-3*
Unggah Ak Embas, Douglas *WhoAsAP 91*
Unglesby, Lewis O. 1949- *WhoSSW 93*
Ungo, Guillermo 1931- *DcCPCAm*
Ungo, Guillermo Manuel *BioIn 17*
Ungstrup, Eigil 1927- *WhoScE 91-2*
Ungthavorn, Suchin 1936- *WhoWor 93*
Unholz, Stefan Paul 1953- *WhoWor 93*
Uniack, Ann Gerber 1941- *WhoAmW 93*
Uniacke, Keith *St&PR 93*
Unico, Renato M. 1939- *WhoAsAP 91*
Uniman, Diane Young *Law&B 92*
Unimuke, Venessa Dale 1955- *WhoAmW 93*
Uninsky, Alexander 1910-1972 *Baker 92*
Union, Marvin Louis *Law&B 92*
Unipan, John T. 1943- *St&PR 93, WhoAm 92*
Unis, Richard L. 1928- *WhoAm 92*
Unitas, John Constantine 1933- *WhoAm 92*
Unitas, Johnny 1933- *BioIn 17*
Univer, Scott M. *Law&B 92*
Unkefer, Duane 1937- *ScF&FL 92*
Unkefer, Ronald A. 1944- *St&PR 93*
Unkel, Kurt *IntDcAn*
Unklesbay, Athel Glyde 1914- *WhoAm 92*
Unkovic, Slobodan 1938- *WhoWor 93*
Unluata, Umit 1945- *WhoScE 91-4*
Unnikrishnan, K.P. 1936- *WhoAsAP 91*
Unnithan, Sindhu Syamasundaran 1957- *WhoSSW 93*
Uno, Hisashi 1935- *WhoUN 92*
Uno, Kozo 1897-1977 *BioIn 17*
Uno, Michael Toshiyuki *MiSFD 9*
Uno, Sosuke *BioIn 17*
Uno, Sosuke 1922- *WhoAsAP 91*
Uno, Sousuke 1922- *WhoWor 93*
Unrue, Bill 1959- *St&PR 93*
Unrue, Darlene Harbour 1938- *ConAu 139*
Unrug, Jozef 1884-1973 *PolBiDi*
Unrug, Wojciech Jerzy 1951- *WhoWor 93*
Unruh, Elizabeth Lee 1943- *WhoAm 92*
Unruh, Fritz von 1885-1970 *DcLB 118 [port]*
Unruh, James A. 1941- *St&PR 93*
Unruh, James Arlen 1941- *WhoAm 92, WhoE 93*
Unruh, Jesse M. 1922- *PolPar*
Unruh, Nancy Jo 1955- *WhoAmW 93*
Unruh, Robert John 1946- *St&PR 93*
Unruh, V. Paul 1948- *St&PR 93*
Unruh, William G. 1945- *WhoAm 92*
Unseld, Westley Sissel 1946- *WhoAm 92*
Unsell, Eva *AmWomPl*
Unsell, Lloyd Neal 1922- *WhoAm 92*
Unser, Al 1939- *WhoAm 92*
Unser, Bobby 1934- *WhoAm 92*
Unser, Guenther 1936- *WhoWor 93*
Unsoeld, Jolene 1931- *BioIn 17, CngDr 91, WhoAm 92, WhoAmW 93*
Unsold, Eberhard 1940- *WhoScE 91-3*
Unsworth, Anthony *WhoScE 91-1*
Unsworth, M. *WhoScE 91-1*
Unsworth, Michael *ScF&FL 92*
Unsworth, Richard Preston 1927- *WhoAm 92*
Unsworth, Walt(er) 1928- *ConAu 38NR*
Untener, David J. *Law&B 92*
Untener, Kenneth E. 1937- *WhoAm 92*
Unterberg, Hannelore 1940- *DrEEuF*
Unterberg, Thomas I. 1931- *St&PR 93*
Unterberger, Betty Miller 1923- *WhoAm 92, WhoAmW 93, WhoWrEP 92*
Unterbrink, L.V. *St&PR 93*
Unterhalt, Bernard 1933- *WhoScE 91-3*
Unterkoefler, Ernest L. 1917- *WhoAm 92*
Unterman, Eugene Rex 1953- *WhoEmL 93*
Untermeyer, Bryna Ivens 1909-1985 *BioIn 17*
Untermeyer, Charles G. 1946- *WhoAm 92*
Untermeyer, Salle Podos 1938- *WhoAmW 93*
Untermeyer, Walter, Jr. 1924- *WhoE 93*
Unterreiner, Bernard *WhoIns 93*
Unterreiner, Ronald J. 1945- *St&PR 93*
Untersee, Philip A. 1934- *St&PR 93*
Unterweiser, Carl Henry *Law&B 92*
Unthank, G. Wix 1923- *WhoAm 92*
Unthank, Tessa *WhoAm 92*
Unver, Erdal Ali 1953- *WhoE 93*
Unverfehrt, Carl A. 1954- *St&PR 93*
Unverzagt, Georgia Lyons *AmWomPl*
Unverzagt, John Gerald 1939- *WhoSSW 93*
Unwerth, Ellen von 1954- *BioIn 17*
Unwin, Nora Spicer 1907-1982 *BioIn 17*
Unwin, Rodney T. *WhoScE 91-1*
Unwin, Stephen Forman 1927- *WhoWor 93*
Unwin, Thomas Fisher 1848-1935 *BioIn 17*
Unz, Richard Frederick 1935- *WhoAm 92*
Unzner-Fischer, Christa 1948- *BioIn 17*
Unzueta, Silvia Maria 1948- *WhoAmW 93, WhoSSW 93*
Uosaki, Katsuji 1942- *WhoWor 93*
Uosaki, Kohei 1947- *WhoWor 93*
Uosukainen, Hely Marjatta 1950- *WhoScE 91-4*
Uotila, Urho Antti Kalevi 1923- *WhoAm 92*
Uotinen, Jorma *BioIn 17*
Uozumi, Hirohide 1940- *WhoAsAP 91*
Upadhaya, Yog Prasad *WhoAsAP 91*
Upadhya, Shail Kumar 1935- *WhoUN 92*
Upadhyay, Ishwar Prasad 1939- *WhoWor 93*
Upadhyay, Shatrughna Prasad 1933- *WhoUN 92*
Upadhyay, Yog Prasad 1927- *WhoWor 93*
Upadhyay, Yogendra Nath 1938- *WhoE 93, WhoWor 93*
Upadhyaya, Shrinivasa Kumbhashi 1950- *WhoEmL 93*
Upadrashta, Kameswara Rao *WhoWor 93*
Upagupta *BioIn 17*
Upatnieks, Juris 1936- *WhoAm 92*
Upbin, Hal J. 1939- *St&PR 93*
Upbin, Hal Jay 1939- *WhoAm 92*
Upbin, Shari *WhoAm 92, WhoAmW 93*
Upcher, David L. *Law&B 92*
Upchurch, Boyd *ScF&FL 92*
Upchurch, Phil *SoulM*
Upchurch, Phil 1941- *BioIn 17*
Upchurch, Samuel E., Jr. *Law&B 92*
Upchurch, Samuel E., Jr. 1952- *WhoAm 92*
Upchurch, Samuel Earl, Jr. 1952- *St&PR 93*
Upchurch Fee, Elizabeth Ann *Law&B 92*
Updegraff, Fred M. 1934- *St&PR 93*
Updegraff, Jan Peter 1943- *St&PR 93*
Updike, Helen Hill 1941- *WhoAm 92*
Updike, John *BioIn 17*
Updike, John 1932- *ConLC 70 [port], MagSAmL [port], ScF&FL 92, WorLitC [port]*
Updike, John Hoyer 1932- *WhoAm 92, WhoE 93, WhoWor 93, WhoWrEP 92*
Updike, Malon S. 1951- *St&PR 93*
Updike, Robert Stanley 1940- *St&PR 93*
Upendra, Parvathaneni 1936 *WhoAsAP 91*
Upfield, James E. 1920- *St&PR 93*
Upgaard, E. Terence *St&PR 93*
Upgren, Arthur Reinhold, Jr. 1933- *WhoAm 92*
Uphill, Sandra Ann *Law&B 92*
Uphoff, James Kent 1937- *WhoAm 92*
Uphoff, Joseph Anthony, Jr. 1950- *WhoWrEP 92*
Uphoff, Russell L. 1920- *St&PR 93*
Uphold, Marge Broadwater 1948- *WhoAmW 93*
Upmeyer, Arnold J.J. 1938- *WhoWor 93*
Upp, James R. 1932- *St&PR 93*
Uppal, Khushdil 1942- *WhoWor 93*
Uppaluri, Subbarao V. 1949- *St&PR 93*
Uppenkamp, Glenn Charles 1956- *St&PR 93*
Upper, Dennis 1942- *WhoE 93*
Uppercu, Inglis Moore 1875-1944 *EncABHB 8 [port]*
Uppman, Jean Seward 1922- *ConAu 136*
Uppman, Theodor 1920- *Baker 92, WhoAm 92*
Uppmann, Theodor 1920- *OxDcOp*
Upright, Blanche *AmWomPl*
Upright, Diane Warner *WhoAmW 93*
Upshaw, Dawn *BioIn 17*
Upshaw, Dawn 1960- *Baker 92, ConMus 9 [port], WhoAm 92, WhoAmW 93*
Upshaw, Gene *BioIn 17*
Upshaw, Harry Stephan 1926- *WhoAm 92*
Upshaw, Lynn Benjamin 1947- *St&PR 93*
Upshaw, Martha G. 1936- *St&PR 93*
Upshaw, Vic 1940-1990 *BioIn 17*
Upshaw-McClenny, Louise Adams 1953- *WhoAmW 93*
Upshur, Carole Christofk 1948- *WhoEmL 93*
Upson, Annie Valentino 1953- *WhoAmW 93*
Upson, Donald V. 1934- *WhoAm 92*
Upson, Jeannine Martin 1942- *WhoE 93*
Upson, Stuart Barnard 1925- *WhoAm 92, WhoE 93*
Upson, Thomas Fisher 1941- *WhoE 93*
Upthegrove, Daniel E. 1953- *WhoWor 93*
Upton, Arthur Canfield 1923- *WhoAm 92*
Upton, Brian Geoffrey Johnson *WhoScE 91-1*
Upton, Charles Stanley 1947- *WhoE 93*
Upton, Edward F. 1950- *St&PR 93*
Upton, Emory 1839-1881 *HarEnMi*
Upton, Frederick S. 1953- *CngDr 91*
Upton, Frederick Stephen 1953- *WhoAm 92*
Upton, George P(utnam) 1834-1919 *Baker 92*
Upton, George Putnam 1834-1919 *JrnUS*
Upton, Graham John Gilbert 1944- *WhoWor 93*
Upton, Howard B., Jr. 1922- *WhoAm 92*
Upton, Larry Dewayne 1949- *WhoE 93*
Upton, Lee 1953- *WhoWrEP 92*
Upton, Mark *ScF&FL 92*
Upton, Mark 1957- *St&PR 93*
Upton, Mark R. 1957- *WhoAm 92*
Upton, Martin *WhoScE 91-1*
Upton, Mary Davis 1942- *WhoAmW 93*
Upton, Minnie Leona *AmWomPl*
Upton, Patrick K. 1944- *WhoScE 91-3*
Upton, Patti *BioIn 17*
Upton, Peter Dodds 1936- *WhoE 93*
Upton, Richard F. 1914- *WhoAm 92*
Upton, Richard Thomas 1931- *WhoAm 92*
Upton, Robert J. 1934- *WhoWrEP 92*
Upton, Simon David 1958- *WhoAsAP 91*
Upton, Stephen E. 1924- *St&PR 93*
Upton, Susan Hollis 1950- *WhoAmW 93*
Upton, Wade E. 1945- *St&PR 93*
Upton, William Treat 1870-1961 *Baker 92*
Upward, Allen 1863-1926 *BioIn 17, ScF&FL 92*
Urai Bin Datuk Hakim Abang Haji Mohideen, Setia Negara Abang Haji Ahmad 1933- *WhoAsAP 91*
Uranga, Jose N. *Law&B 92*
Urano, Yasuoki 1941- *WhoAsAP 91*
Uranschek, Rainer *WhoScE 91-4*
Uras, Ivo *WhoScE 91-3*
Uras, Tevfik Gungor 1933- *WhoWor 93*
Urash, Robert N. M. 1923- *St&PR 93*
Urato, Barbra Casale 1941- *WhoAmW 93*
Urbach, Efraim Elimelech 1912-1991 *BioIn 17*
Urbach, Frederick 1922- *WhoAm 92*
Urbach, Frederick Lewis 1938- *WhoAm 92*
Urbach, Herman B. 1923- *WhoE 93*
Urbach, Otto 1871-1927 *Baker 92*
Urban, II c. 1035-1099 *OxDcByz*
Urban, V c. 1310-1370 *OxDcByz*
Urban, Andras 1945- *WhoScE 91-4*
Urban, Carlyle Woodrow 1914- *WhoAm 92*
Urban, Cathleen Andrea 1947- *WhoE 93*
Urban, Erin Mary 1948- *WhoE 93*
Urban, Frank J. 1937- *St&PR 93*
Urban, Gilbert William 1928- *WhoAm 92*
Urban, Heinrich 1837-1901 *Baker 92*
Urban, Heinz 1928- *WhoScE 91-3*
Urban, Henry Zeller 1920- *WhoAm 92*
Urban, James Arthur 1927- *WhoAm 92*
Urban, Jerome 1914-1991 *BioIn 17*
Urban, John S. 1933- *St&PR 93*
Urban, Joseph 1872-1933 *IntDcOp*
Urban, L. *WhoScE 91-4*
Urban, Laszlo Andrew 1951- *WhoSSW 93*
Urban, Matt *BioIn 17*
Urban, Miroslawa 1939- *WhoScE 91-4*
Urban, Scott H. *ScF&FL 92*
Urban, Sharon Kay *WhoAmW 93*
Urban, Stanley B. 1928- *St&PR 93*
Urban, Theodore W. 1950- *St&PR 93*
Urban, Theodore Walter *Law&B 92*

Urban, Thomas N. 1934- *St&PR 93, WhoAm 92*
Urban, Timothy Lou 1956- *WhoSSW 93*
Urban, Zdenek 1923- *WhoScE 91-4*
Urbanczyk, Grzegorz Waldemar 1928- *WhoScE 91-4*
Urbanek, Adam J. 1928- *WhoScE 91-4*
Urbanek, Fred Francis 1935- *St&PR 93*
Urbanek, Guenther Ernst 1933- *WhoWor 93*
Urbani, Valentino fl. 1690-1719 *OxDcOp*
Urbaniak, George Carl 1947- *WhoWrEP 92*
Urbaniak, James Randolph 1936- *WhoAm 92*
Urbanick, Burton Alfred 1929- *St&PR 93*
Urbanik, Thomas, II 1946- *WhoSSW 93*
Urbanner, Erich 1936- *Baker 92*
Urbano, Michael John *Law&B 92*
Urbanowski, A. *WhoScE 91-4*
Urbanowski, Alojzy 1933- *WhoScE 91-4*
Urbanowski, Frank 1936- *WhoAm 92*
Urbanski, James F. 1927- *St&PR 93*
Urbantke, Hugh Edmund 1922- *WhoAm 92*
Urbel, David A. 1941- *St&PR 93*
Urben, Fredrick E. 1941- *St&PR 93*
Urbigkit, Walter C., Jr. 1927- *WhoAm 92*
Urbina, Nicasio 1958- *WhoSSW 93*
Urbina, Susana Patricia 1946- *WhoAmW 93*
Urbom, Donna Lynne 1951- *WhoAmW 93*
Urbom, Warren Keith 1925- *WhoAm 92*
Urbsys, Juozas 1896-1991 *BioIn 17*
Urch, David Selway 1933- *WhoWor 93*
Urch, George E. 1930- *WhoE 93*
Urciolo, John Raphael, II 1947- *WhoE 93*
Urciuoli, J. Arthur 1937- *WhoAm 92, WhoWor 93*
Urcuyo, Francisco *DcCPCAm*
Urda, Michael William 1954- *St&PR 93*
Urdahl, Nils 1934- *WhoScE 91-4*
Urdan, James Alan 1931- *WhoAm 92*
Urdaneta, Andres de 1508-1568 *Expl 93*
Urdaneta, Maria-Luisa 1931- *HispAmA*
Urdang, Alexandra 1956- *WhoAm 92*
Urdang, Laurence 1927- *ConAu 40NR, WhoAm 92*
Ure, Jean 1924- *ScF&FL 92*
Ure, Jean 1943- *ChlFicS, MajAI [port]*
Ure, Jim 1939- *BioIn 17*
Ureel, Patricia Lois 1923- *WhoAmW 93*
Ureles, Jeff *MiSFD 9*
Uren, Thomas 1921- *WhoAsAP 91*
Urena-Alexiades, Jose Luis 1949- *WhoEmL 93, WhoWor 93*
Urena de Henriquez, Salome 1850-1897 *BioIn 17*
Urenovitch, Joseph Victor 1937- *St&PR 93*
Uresti, Herminia Magdalena 1939- *WhoAmW 93*
Urey, Dawn Rochelle 1962- *WhoSSW 93*
Urey, Jon Russell 1956- *WhoSSW 93*
Urfey, Thomas d' 1653-1723 *Baker 92*
Urfirer, Michael J. 1959- *St&PR 93*
Urhan, Chretien 1790-1845 *Baker 92*
Uri, George Wolfsohn 1920- *WhoAm 92*
Uri, Pierre 1911-1992 *NewYTBS 92*
Uri, Pierre (Emmanuel) 1911-1992 *ConAu 138*
Uriarte, Eustaquio de 1863-1900 *Baker 92*
Uribe, Eduardo 1959- *WhoWor 93*
Uribe, Javier Miguel 1941- *WhoSSW 93*
Uribe, Jennie Ann 1958- *WhoAmW 93*
Uribe-Holguin, Guillermo 1880-1971 *Baker 92*
Uribe Rugeles, Diego Ivan 1959- *WhoWor 93*
Uribe-Valle, Jose 1957- *WhoWor 93*
Uricchio, William Andrew 1924- *WhoE 93*
Urich, Jean 1849-1939 *Baker 92*
Urich, Klaus 1926- *WhoScE 91-3*
Urich, Robert *WhoAm 92*
Uricheck, Maryanne 1960- *WhoE 93*
Uricho, Robert, Jr. 1915- *St&PR 93*
Urick, Kevin 1952- *ScF&FL 92*
Urick, Lisa G. *Law&B 92*
Urie, Caroline Foulke *AmWomPl*
Urie, John James 1920- *WhoAm 92, WhoE 93*
Urio, Francesco Antonio c. 1631-c. 1719 *Baker 92*
Urion, David Kimball 1954- *WhoE 93, WhoWor 93*
Urion, Melinda 1953- *WhoIns 93*
Urioste, Frank J. *WhoAm 92*
Urioste, Pat L. *WhoWrEP 92*
Uris, Dorothy d1992 *NewYTBS 92 [port]*
Uris, Dorothy 1909-1992 *BioIn 17*
Uris, Leon 1924- *BioIn 17, JeAmFiW, WhoAm 92, WhoWrEP 92*
Uris, Leon (Marcus) 1924- *ConAu 40NR*
Urist, Carl H. *Law&B 92*
Urist, Joseph J. 1934- *St&PR 93*
Urist, Marshall Raymond 1914- *WhoAm 92*
Urista-Heredia, Alberto Baltazar 1947- *WhoAm 92*
Uritani, Ikuzo 1919- *WhoWor 93*
Uriu, Sotokichi 1857-1937 *HarEnMi*
Uriu, Stanley A. 1933- *WhoSSW 93*
Urkowitz, Harry 1921- *WhoAm 92*
Urkowitz, Michael 1943- *St&PR 93, WhoAm 92*
Urland, Alice Irene 1934- *St&PR 93*
Urland, Robert S. 1941- *St&PR 93*
Urlaub, Charles Joseph 1956- *WhoE 93*
Urli, Natko B. 1937- *WhoScE 91-4*
Urlus, Jacques 1867-1935 *Baker 92, OxDcOp*
Urman, Huseyin K. 1921- *WhoScE 91-4*
Urmer, Diane Hedda 1934- *WhoAmW 93*
Urness, Kent D. 1948- *WhoIns 93*
Urofsky, Melvin Irving 1939- *WhoAm 92, WhoSSW 93, WhoWrEP 92*
Uronen, Paavo 1938- *WhoScE 91-4*
Uros, V *OxDcByz*
Urpo, Seppo *WhoScE 91-4*
Urquhardt, MacGregor *ScF&FL 92*
Urquhart, Alexander Edwards *WhoScE 91-1*
Urquhart, Alexander W. 1924- *St&PR 93*
Urquhart, Andrew Willard 1939- *WhoAm 92*
Urquhart, Brian E. 1919- *WhoUN 92*
Urquhart, Colin 1940- *ConAu 37NR*
Urquhart, Elizabeth *AmWomPl*
Urquhart, Fred 1912- *ScF&FL 92*
Urquhart, George MacDonald *WhoScE 91-1*
Urquhart, Irene *AmWomPl*
Urquhart, J.D. *WhoScE 91-1*
Urquhart, J. Duncan 1953- *St&PR 93*
Urquhart, Jane 1949- *ScF&FL 92, WhoCanL 92*
Urquhart, Jennifer Mack 1947- *St&PR 93*
Urquhart, John 1934- *St&PR 93, WhoAm 92*
Urquhart, John Alexander 1928- *St&PR 93, WhoAm 92*
Urquhart, Margaret M. 1949- *St&PR 93*
Urquhart, Sally Ann 1946- *WhoAmW 93, WhoSSW 93*
Urquhart, Stephen E. 1949- *WhoE 93, WhoWor 93*
Urquhart, Tony 1934- *WhoAm 92*
Urquhart, William Johnson 1952- *WhoSSW 93*
Urquilla, Pedro Ramon 1939- *HispAmA*
Urquiza, Concha 1910-1945 *DcMexL*
Urquizo, Francisco L. 1891- *DcMexL*
Urrea, Teresa 1873-1906 *NotHsAW 93*
Urreda, Johannes fl. 15th cent.- *Baker 92*
Urrelo-Guerra, Rafael 1946- *WhoWor 93*
Urreta, Alicia 1935-1986 *Baker 92*
Urrutia, Juan Pablo *DcCPCAm*
Urrutia, Manuel *DcCPCAm*
Urrutia-Blondel, Jorge 1903-1981 *Baker 92*
Urry, Dan Wesley 1935- *WhoAm 92, WhoSSW 93*
Urry, Grant Wayne 1926- *WhoAm 92*
Urry, John Richard *WhoScE 91-1*
Ursache, Victorin 1912- *WhoAm 92*
Urschel, Joe Richard 1913- *St&PR 93*
Ursell, Fritz Joseph *WhoScE 91-1*
Ursell, Geoffrey 1943- *WhoCanL 92*
Ursi, Corrado Cardinal 1908- *WhoAm 92, WhoWor 93*
Ursiak, David Allen 1952- *WhoE 93*
Ursianu, Malvina 1927- *DrEEuF*
Ursic, Josip 1923- *WhoScE 91-4*
Ursic, Srebrenka 1947- *WhoWor 93*
Ursin, Holger Thormvald 1934- *WhoWor 93*
Ursini, Edilio 1929- *St&PR 93*
Ursini, James 1947- *ScF&FL 92*
Ursino, Joseph *St&PR 93*
Urso, Camilla 1842-1902 *Baker 92, BioIn 17*
Urso, Frank P. *Law&B 92*
Urso, Josette Marie 1959- *WhoE 93*
Urso, Paul 1925- *WhoSSW 93*
Urspruch, Anton 1850-1907 *Baker 92*
Ursprung, Alex William 1952- *WhoE 93*
Ursprung, Heinrich Peter Klaus 1932- *WhoScE 91-4*
Ursprung, Otto 1879-1960 *Baker 92*
Ursrey, Lawton Randall 1940- *WhoSSW 93*
Urstadt, Charles Deane 1959- *WhoE 93*
Urstadt, Charles J. 1928- *St&PR 93*
Ursu, Ioan 1928- *WhoScE 91-4*
Ursu, John Joseph *Law&B 92*
Ursula 1921- *BioIn 17*
Ursuleac, Viorica 1894-1985 *Baker 92, OxDcOp*
Urteaga Cabrera, Luis 1940- *SpAmA*
Uruburu, Federico 1934- *WhoScE 91-3*
Urueta, Margarita 1913?- *DcMexL*
Urumov, Alexander Ivanov 1944- *WhoScE 91-4*
Urusemal, Joseph 1952- *WhoAsAP 91*
Uruska, Irmina 1926- *WhoScE 91-4*
Urwich-Ferry, Johann *BioIn 17*
Urwin, Derek William *WhoScE 91-1*
Ury, Joan Louise 1944- *WhoE 93*
Ury, Perry S. 1925- *WhoAm 92*
Urysohn, Pavel Samuilovic 1898-1924 *BioIn 17*
Uryu, Toshiyuki 1939- *WhoWor 93*
Usamah Ibn Munqidh 1095-1188 *OxDcByz*
Usami, Yuko *Law&B 92*
Usandizaga, Jose Maria 1887-1915 *Baker 92*
Uschuk, Pamela Marie 1948- *WhoWrEP 92*
Uscian, Paula M. *Law&B 92*
Usdan, James M. *St&PR 93*
Usdan, James Morris 1949- *WhoSSW 93*
Usdin, Gene Leonard 1922- *WhoAm 92*
Useem, Ruth Hill 1915- *WhoAm 92*
Uselton, James Clayton 1939- *St&PR 93, WhoAm 92*
Uselton, Kenneth Wayne 1943- *St&PR 93*
Usher, Assouan Arsene 1930- *WhoAfr*
Usher, Bobby Clyde 1935- *St&PR 93, WhoAm 92*
Usher, Elizabeth Reuter *WhoAm 92*
Usher, F. Barrie 1942- *St&PR 93*
Usher, Frank E. 1946- *WhoSSW 93*
Usher, Gray 1903- *ScF&FL 92*
Usher, Jeffrey R. *Law&B 92*
Usher, John Richard *WhoScE 91-1*
Usher, Juan Oscar 1928- *WhoWor 93*
Usher, Leonard Gray 1907- *WhoAm 92*
Usher, Richard S. *Law&B 92*
Usher, Shaun 1937- *ScF&FL 92*
Usher, Thomas J. *NewYTBS 92 [port]*
Usher-Jones, Brian Ernest 1946- *St&PR 93*
Usherwood, Peter Norman Russell *WhoScE 91-1*
Ushewokunze, Herbert 1934- *WhoAfr*
Ushijima, John Takeji 1924- *WhoAm 92*
Ushijima, Mitsuru 1887-1945 *HarEnMi*
Ushiogi, Morikazu 1934- *WhoWor 93*
Ushiroku, Jun 1884- *HarEnMi*
Ushkow, Charmaine Marie 1955- *WhoAmW 93*
Usigli, Rodolfo 1905-1979 *DcMexL*
Usiglio, Emilio 1841-1910 *Baker 92*
Usignol, Laurence J. *Law&B 92*
Usilton, R. David *St&PR 93*
Usina, Joseph Timothy 1955- *St&PR 93*
Usinger, Martha Putnam 1912- *WhoAmW 93, WhoWor 93*
Usiskin, Charles *St&PR 93*
Uslan, Michael Elliot 1951- *WhoWor 93*
Uslar-Pietri, Arturo 1906- *SpAmA*
Usmanbas, Ilhan 1921- *Baker 92*
Uson, Rafael *WhoWor 93*
Uson Lacal, Rafael 1926- *WhoScE 91-3*
Usoskin, Michael Neil 1956- *St&PR 93*
Usoskin, Robert N. 1920- *St&PR 93*
Uspensky, Victor Alexandrovich 1879-1949 *Baker 92*
Usrey, Euleta Gustava 1956- *WhoWrEP 92*
Usrey, Martin William 1911- *St&PR 93*
Usry, George Howard 1938- *St&PR 93*
Usry, Jana Privette 1943- *WhoAmW 93*
Usry, Milton Franklin 1931- *WhoAm 92*
Ussachevsky, Vladimir (Alexis) 1911-1990 *Baker 92*
Usseglio-Tomasset, Luciano *WhoScE 91-3*
Usselmann, Pierre 1940- *WhoScE 91-2*
Ussery, Albert Travis 1928- *WhoAm 92*
Ussery, Luanne 1938- *WhoAm 92*
Ussery, Richard W. 1947- *St&PR 93*
Ussher, Jane M. 1961- *ConAu 139*
Ussler-Trumbull, Christine 1954- *WhoE 93*
Ustaran, Juan Ignacio 1955- *WhoWor 93*
Ustian, Daniel C. 1950- *St&PR 93*
Ustinov, Dmitry Fedorovich 1908-1984 *ColdWar 2 [port]*
Ustinov, Peter *BioIn 17*
Ustinov, Peter 1921- *IntDcF 2-3, MiSFD 9, ScF&FL 92*
Ustinov, Peter Alexander 1921- *WhoAm 92, WhoWor 93*
Uston, Ken *BioIn 17*
Ustun, Ali 1961- *WhoScE 91-4*
Ustvolskaya, Galina (Ivanovna) 1919- *Baker 92*
Usui, Hideo 1939- *WhoAsAP 91*
Usui, Leslie Raymond 1946- *WhoEmL 93, WhoWor 93*
Usuki, Satoshi 1944- *WhoWor 93*
Usunov, P. *WhoScE 91-4*
Utada, Beth Brown 1953- *WhoWrEP 92*
Utama Syed Ahmad Al-Haj Bin Syed, Tuan Yang Terutama Tun Seri Mahmud Shahabudin 1925- *WhoAsAP 91*
U Tam'si, Tchicaya Gerard-Felix 1931-1988 *BioIn 17*
Utaski, J.R. 1939- *St&PR 93*
Utay, Joe Martin 1956- *WhoSSW 93*
Utay, Joseph 1887-1977 *BiDAMSp 1989*
Utechin, Nicholas *ScF&FL 92*
Uteem, Cassam 1941- *WhoWor 93*
Utendal, Alexander c. 1535-1581 *Baker 92*
Uter, Lawrence A. *Law&B 92*
Utermohlen, Herbert Georg 1948- *WhoE 93*
Utesch, Dorothy Marie 1923- *WhoAmW 93*
Uteusz, Zygmunt 1930- *WhoScE 91-4*
Uth, Michael R. *Law&B 92*
U Than, Sein 1946- *WhoUN 92*
'Uthman c. 569-656 *OxDcByz*
Uthoff, Loren H., Jr. *Law&B 92*
Utiger, Robert David 1931- *WhoAm 92, WhoWrEP 92*
Utkin, Ilya 1955- *BioIn 17*
Utku, Senol 1931- *WhoAm 92, WhoSSW 93*
Utlaut, William Frederick 1922- *WhoAm 92*
Utlee, (J.) Maarten 1949- *ConAu 37NR*
Utley, Clarence W. 1941- *St&PR 93*
Utley, Clifton Garrick 1939- *WhoAm 92*
Utley, F. Knowlton 1935- *WhoE 93*
Utley, Garrick *BioIn 17*
Utley, James Henry Paul *WhoScE 91-1*
Utley, John Eddy 1941- *WhoAm 92*
Utley, Mark S. *Law&B 92*
Utley, Steven 1948- *ScF&FL 92*
Utley, W. David *Law&B 92*
Utne, Eric *BioIn 17*
Utne, Vera Bergaas *WhoScE 91-4*
Utnik, David Alan 1960- *WhoSSW 93*
Uto, Shokichi 1929- *WhoWor 93*
Utreja, Lajpat Rai 1944- *WhoSSW 93*
Utriainen, Sirpa Anneli 1950- *WhoUN 92*
Utrillo, Maurice 1883-1955 *BioIn 17*
Utroska, William Robert 1946- *WhoAm 92*
Utsu, Tokuji 1928- *WhoWor 93*
Utsumi, Hidoe 1922- *WhoAsAP 91*
Utsunomiya, Mayumi 1949- *WhoAsAP 91*
Utsunomiya, Tokuma 1905- *WhoAsAP 91*
Utt, Glenn S., Jr. 1926- *WhoAm 92*
Uttal, William Reichenstein 1931- *WhoAm 92*
Uttaro, Angela E. 1959- *St&PR 93*
Uttaro, Ralph A. *Law&B 92*
Utter, Charles W. 1917- *St&PR 93*
Utter, Charles Wilbar 1917- *WhoE 93*
Utter, George H. 1922- *St&PR 93*
Utter, Helen *St&PR 93*
Utter, Howard M. 1909- *St&PR 93*
Utter, Nicholas Charles 1948- *St&PR 93*
Utter, Robert French 1930- *WhoAm 92*
Utter, Virgil S., Jr. 1925- *ScF&FL 92*
Utterback, Denise Suzanne 1954- *WhoAmW 93*
Utterback, Edith Gwynne *AmWomPl*
Utterback, James E. *Law&B 92*
Utterback, Joe 1944- *WhoE 93*
Utterback, Ron 1947- *St&PR 93*
Utterback, Will Hay, Jr. 1947- *WhoSSW 93*
Utting, John Edward 1932- *WhoWor 93*
Uttini, Francesco Antonio Baldassare 1723-1795 *Baker 92*
Utton, Michael *WhoScE 91-1*
Utyosov, Leonid 1895-1982 *Baker 92*
Utz, Carolyn Glover 1913- *WhoWor 93*
Utz, Joanne-Marie *WhoAmW 93*
Utz, John Philip 1922- *WhoAm 92*
Utz, Sarah Winifred 1921- *WhoAmW 93*
Utzinger, David Ray 1947- *St&PR 93*
Uusitalo, Anne Aino Mirjami 1956- *WhoScE 91-4*
Uusitalo, Arto J. 1935- *WhoScE 91-4*
Uusvaara, Olli Antero 1936- *WhoScE 91-4*
Uva, Anthony N. *Law&B 92*
Uva, Kenneth J. 1949- *WhoE 93*
Uveges, George 1948- *St&PR 93*
Uvena, Frank John 1934- *WhoAm 92*
Uwihanganye, Jean-Bosco 1946- *WhoUN 92*
Uwujaren, Gilbert Patrick 1945- *WhoE 93*
Uy, Antonio J. 1934- *WhoUN 92*
Uy, Enrico Dy 1955- *WhoWor 93*
Uy, Eufrocinio Velasco 1960- *WhoWor 93*
Uy, Felipe Ratunil 1942- *WhoE 93*
Uyeda, Ken T. 1943- *St&PR 93*
Uyeda, Seiya 1929- *WhoAm 92, WhoWor 93*
Uyehara, Stanley *Law&B 92*
Uyemura, Dennis G. *St&PR 93*
Uyenco, Elizabeth 1953- *WhoAmW 93*
Uyenishi, Roy I. 1932- *St&PR 93*
Uyesato, Daniel E. *Law&B 92*
Uygur, Vural 1929- *St&PR 93*
Uylings, H.B.M. 1947- *WhoScE 91-3*
Uys, Errol Lincoln 1943- *ConAu 136*
Uys, Jamie 1921- *MiSFD 9*
Uysal, Huseyin 1932- *WhoScE 91-4*
Uyterhoeven, Hugo Emil Robert 1931- *WhoAm 92*
Uyttenbroeck, Frans Joseph 1921- *WhoWor 93*
Uyttenbroeck, Frans L.J.M.A. 1921- *WhoScE 91-2*
Uyttenbroeck, Jozef L.F.M. 1933- *WhoScE 91-2*
Uytterhoeven, Jan B. 1931- *WhoScE 91-2*

Uz, Johann Peter 1720-1796 *BioIn 17*
Uzan, Bernard Franck 1944- *WhoAm 92, WhoE 93*
Uzarewicz, Arkadiusz 1928- *WhoScE 91-4*
Uzawa, Hirofumi 1928- *BioIn 17, WhoWor 93*
Uze, Irving 1918- *WhoSSW 93*
Uzes, duchesse d' 1847-1933 *BioIn 17*
Uzi, Ralph R. 1933- *St&PR 93*
Uziak, Stanislaw 1926- *WhoScE 91-4*
Uzieblo, Lidia 1923- *WhoScE 91-4*
Uzielli, Philip Albert 1931- *St&PR 93, WhoAm 92*
Uzman, Betty Geren 1922- *WhoAm 92*
Uzmanski, Arkadiusz 1936- *WhoUN 92*
Uzun, Abdurrahman 1946- *WhoScE 91-4*
Uzun, Gungor 1941- *WhoScE 91-4*
Uzun Hasan c. 1420-c. 1478 *HarEnMi*
Uzunov, Dimcho Yonkov 1947- *WhoWor 93*
Uzzell, Allen H. *Law&B 92*
Uzzell, David L. *WhoScE 91-1*
Uzzell, John Douglas 1937- *WhoSSW 93*

V

V. K. Sellappan 1936- *WhoAsAP 91*
V., Octavio I. Romano- 1932- *BioIn 17*
Vaadia, Boaz 1951- *WhoE 93*
Vaage, Roald *WhoScE 91-4*
Vaananen, Jouko Antero 1950- *WhoWor 93*
Vaaranen, Vesa *WhoScE 91-4*
Vaarsi, Mart *Law&B 92*
Vaasjoki, Matti 1946- *WhoScE 91-4*
Vabalas, Raimondas 1937- *DrEEuF*
Vacca, A. *WhoScE 91-3*
Vacca, John Joseph, Jr. 1922- *WhoAm 92*
Vaccai, Nicola 1790-1848 *Baker 92, OxDcOp*
Vaccare, Carmel John 1950- *WhoSSW 93*
Vaccariello, Paula Ann 1967- *WhoSSW 93*
Vaccaro, Brenda 1939- *WhoAm 92*
Vaccaro, Christopher Mark 1959- *WhoWor 93*
Vaccaro, Dennis Earle 1949- *St&PR 93*
Vaccaro, Louis Charles 1930- *WhoAm 92*
Vaccaro, Maria Angelica *ScF&FL 92*
Vaccaro, Martha Walsh 1930- *WhoE 93*
Vaccaro, Nicholas Carmine 1942- *WhoE 93*
Vaccaro, Ralph Francis 1919- *WhoAm 92*
Vaccaro, Richard Francis 1949- *WhoE 93*
Vaccaro, Roberto *WhoScE 91-3*
Vacco, Dennis C. 1952- *WhoAm 92*
Vacco, Roger Pasquale 1944- *WhoAm 92*
Vacek, Jaroslav *WhoScE 91-4*
Vacek, Karel 1930- *WhoScE 91-4*
Vacek, Milos 1928- *Baker 92*
Vacek, Vaclav 1929- *WhoScE 91-4*
Vacelet, Jean 1935- *WhoScE 91-2*
Vach, Ferdinand 1860-1939 *Baker 92*
Vache, Warren Webster 1914- *WhoWrEP 92*
Vacher, Rene 1943- *WhoScE 91-2*
Vacher-Morris, Elizabeth Michele 1963- *WhoAmW 93, WhoSSW 93*
Vachher, Prehlad Singh 1933- *WhoWor 93*
Vachiery, Victor Luc 1934- *WhoScE 91-2*
Vachon, Annmarie 1966- *WhoAmW 93*
Vachon, Brian 1941- *St&PR 93*
Vachon, Christiane *Law&B 92*
Vachon, John 1914-1975 *BioIn 17*
Vachon, Louis-Albert Cardinal 1912- *WhoAm 92, WhoWor 93*
Vachon, Marilyn Ann 1924- *WhoAm 92*
Vachon, Myra Kathleen 1939- *WhoAmW 93*
Vachon, Pierre 1731-1803 *Baker 92*
Vachon, Reginald Irenee 1937- *WhoSSW 93*
Vachon, Rogatien Rosaire 1945- *WhoAm 92*
Vachon, Russell Bertrand 1945- *WhoAm 92*
Vachon, Serge Jean 1939- *WhoAm 92*
Vachss, Andi *Law&B 92*
Vachss, Andrew Henry 1942- *WhoWrEP 92*
Vachtsevanos, George 1938- *WhoScE 91-3*
Vacic, Aleksandar M. 1936- *WhoUN 92, WhoWor 93*
Vacik, James Paul 1931- *WhoSSW 93*
Vackar *Baker 92*
Vackar, Dalibor Cyril 1906-1984 *Baker 92*
Vackar, Tomas 1945-1963 *Baker 92*
Vackar, Vaclay 1881-1954 *Baker 92*
Vacketta, Carl Lee 1941- *WhoAm 92*
Vadakin, Charles Edward, II 1941- *St&PR 93*
Vadas, Erno 1899-1962 *BioIn 17*
Vadasdi, Karoly 1942- *WhoScE 91-4*
Vadasy, Patricia Frances 1949- *WhoAmW 93*
Vadasz, Denes 1944- *WhoScE 91-4*
Vadasz, Kalman 1939- *St&PR 93*
Vadasz, Laszlo 1927- *WhoScE 91-4*
Vade, Jean-Joseph 1719-1757 *Baker 92*
Vadehra, Dave Kumar 1941- *WhoE 93, WhoWor 93*
Vadgama, Pankaj *WhoScE 91-1*
Vadgama, Virji Karabhai 1924- *WhoWor 93*
Vadi, Sylvia *Law&B 92*
Vadim, Roger 1928- *MiSFD 9*
Vadim, Roger Plemiannikov 1928- *WhoWor 93*
Vadlamudi, Sri Krishna 1927- *WhoE 93*
Vadlejch, Jan 1944- *WhoWor 93*
Vadman, David R. *St&PR 93*
Vadnais, Alfred William 1935- *WhoAm 92*
Vadot, Jean 1933- *WhoScE 91-2*
Vadovicky, Paul J. 1952- *St&PR 93*
Vadus, Gloria A. *WhoAmW 93, WhoE 93, WhoWor 93*
Vaea, Baron *WhoWor 93*
Vaerman, J.P. 1937- *WhoScE 91-2*
Vaerno, Oscar 1930- *WhoUN 92*
Vaes, Gilbert M. 1932- *WhoScE 91-2*
Vaet, Jacobus c. 1529-1567 *Baker 92*
Vaeth, George Bernard 1928- *St&PR 93*
Vafaie, Foad 1949- *WhoSSW 93*
Vafiades, Markos d1992 *NewYTBS 92*
Vafiadis, Markos 1906-1992 *BioIn 17*
Vagell, Peter Michael 1948- *St&PR 93*
Vagelos, P. Roy *BioIn 17*
Vagelos, P. Roy 1929- *St&PR 93*
Vagelos, Pindaros Roy 1929- *WhoAm 92, WhoE 93, WhoWor 93*
Vagenakis, Apostolos G. 1938- *WhoScE 91-3*
Vaget, Hans Rudolf 1938- *WhoAm 92*
Vaghela, Shanker Sinh 1940- *WhoAsAP 91*
Vagley, Robert Everett 1940- *WhoAm 92*
Vagliano, Alexander Marino 1927- *WhoAm 92*
Vaglio-Laurin, Roberto 1929- *WhoAm 92*
Vagnini, Kenneth L. 1947- *St&PR 93*
Vago, Clara Ivanne 1940- *WhoScE 91-4*
Vago, Constantin 1921- *WhoScE 91-2, WhoWor 93*
Vago, Istvan 1924- *WhoScE 91-4*
Vago, Pierre 1910- *WhoWor 93*
Vagstad, Donald W. *Law&B 92*
Vagts, Detlev Frederick 1929- *WhoAm 92*
Vague, Jean Marie 1911- *WhoWor 93*
Vague, Vera 1904-1974 *QDrFCA 92 [port]*
Vahaviolos, Sotirios John 1946- *St&PR 93, WhoAm 92*
Vaheri, Antti I. 1938- *WhoScE 91-4*
Vahey, Daniel A. 1945- *St&PR 93*
Vahey, Harry Martin 1936- *WhoE 93*
Vahi, Tiit 1947- *WhoWor 93*
Vahl, Richard James 1940- *WhoSSW 93*
Vahlquist, Bo Anders 1947- *WhoScE 91-4*
Vahlsing, Erwin William, Jr. 1956- *St&PR 93*
Vahlun, Svend 1932- *WhoScE 91-2*
Vahram fl. 13th cent.- *OxDcByz*
Vahsholtz, Robert John 1935- *WhoAm 92*
Vaiao, Leiataua Ala'Ilima 1921- *WhoAsAP 91*
Vaidman, Anna 1948- *WhoE 93*
Vaidya, Ashok W. *WhoScE 91-1*
Vaidya, Bijaya Kumar 1949- *WhoWor 93*
Vaidya, Kirit Rameshchandra 1937- *WhoE 93, WhoWor 93*
Vaidya, Vic 1935- *St&PR 93*
Vaikhman, Elia A. 1949- *WhoSSW 93*
Vail, Charles Daniel 1936- *WhoAm 92*
Vail, Charles Rowe 1915- *WhoAm 92*
Vail, Charles S. *Law&B 92*
Vail, Chris M. *Law&B 92*
Vail, Dennis 1951- *St&PR 93*
Vail, Donald E. 1933- *WhoSSW 93*
Vail, Eleanor *St&PR 93*
Vail, Elizabeth Moore 1964- *WhoSSW 93*
Vail, Frederick Scott 1944- *WhoSSW 93*
Vail, George A. 1933- *St&PR 93*
Vail, Iris Jennings 1928- *WhoAmW 93, WhoWor 93*
Vail, James L. 1937- *St&PR 93*
Vail, John Randolph *WhoScE 91-1*
Vail, Lucinda Covert- *BioIn 17*
Vail, Mary S. *Law&B 92*
Vail, Patricia *Law&B 92*
Vail, Richard C. 1930- *St&PR 93*
Vail, Richard T. 1938- *WhoE 93*
Vail, Steve 1950- *St&PR 93*
Vail, Thomas V. H. 1926- *St&PR 93*
Vail, Van Horn 1934- *WhoAm 92, WhoE 93*
Vail, Warren Hetherington, Jr. 1931- *St&PR 93*
Vaill, Edward Everett *Law&B 92*
Vaill, Timothy L. 1941- *St&PR 93*
Vaillancourt, Daniel Gilbert 1947- *WhoWrEP 92*
Vaillancourt, Donald Charles 1943- *St&PR 93*
Vaillancourt, Jean-Guy 1937- *WhoAm 92*
Vailland, Roger 1907-1965 *BioIn 17*
Vaillant, Edouard 1840-1915 *BioIn 17*
Vaillant, George C. 1901-1945 *IntDcAn*
Vaillant, George Eman 1934- *WhoAm 92*
Vaillant, Janet G. 1937- *ConAu 136*
Vaillant, Jean-Marie 1927- *WhoScE 91-2*
Vaillaud, Pierre *St&PR 93*
Vaina, Lucia Maria 1946- *WhoAmW 93*
Vainberg, Moisei 1919- *Baker 92*
Vainikko, Gennadi 1938- *WhoWor 93*
Vainio, Harri U. 1947- *WhoScE 91-2, -91-4*
Vainio, Harri Volevi 1947- *WhoUN 92*
Vainio, Yrjo Erkki 1933- *WhoWor 93*
Vainisi, William A. *Law&B 92*
Vainius-Norman, Monika 1954- *WhoE 93*
Vainos, Nikolaos Athanasios 1960- *WhoWor 93*
Vainshtein, Boris Konstantinovich 1921- *WhoWor 93*
Vainstein, Rose 1920- *WhoAm 92*
Vaio, Bruce A. 1960- *St&PR 93*
Vaira, Peter Francis 1937- *WhoAm 92*
Vairo, Philip Dominic 1933- *WhoAm 92*
Vairo, Robert John 1930- *WhoAm 92*
Vaishnavi, Vijay Kumar 1948- *WhoSSW 93*
Vaitkus, V. Anthony 1932- *St&PR 93*
Vaitukaitis, Judith Louise 1940- *WhoAmW 93*
Vajda, Gyorgy 1927- *WhoScE 91-4*
Vajda, Janos 1949- *Baker 92*
Vajeeprasee Thongsak, Thomas 1935- *WhoE 93*
Vajk, Hugo 1928- *WhoAm 92, WhoWor 93*
Vajpayee, Atal Beharl 1926- *WhoAsAP 91*
Vajrathon-Childers, Mallica 1936- *WhoUN 92*
Vakarelski, Khristo Tomov 1896-1979 *IntDcAn*
Vakatora, Tomasi Rayalu 1926- *WhoAsAP 91*
Vakiener, Bruce Alfred 1940- *St&PR 93*
Vakil, Hassan Charharsough 1934- *WhoE 93*
Vakis, N. *WhoScE 91-4*
Vakkilainen, Pertti 1945- *WhoScE 91-4*
Vaky, Viron Peter 1925- *WhoAm 92*
Valaas, John R. 1944- *St&PR 93*
Valachovic, Anton 1939- *WhoScE 91-4*
Valade, Robert C. 1926- *St&PR 93*
Valades, Edmundo 1915- *DcMexL*
Valadez, Susana *BioIn 17*
Valadon, Luc Guy 1932- *WhoWor 93*
Valadon, Suzanne 1865-1938 *BioIn 17*
Valaika, George A. 1943- *St&PR 93*
Valalas, Dimitri 1920- *WhoScE 91-3*
Valance, Edward H. *Law&B 92*
Valaskovic, David William 1961- *WhoWor 93*
Valasquez, Joseph Louis 1955- *WhoEmL 93, WhoSSW 93, WhoWor 93*
Valauri, Susan Rogers 1954- *WhoAmW 93*
Valavanis, Timothy Angelos 1959- *WhoWor 93*
Val Baker, Denys *ScF&FL 92*
Valberg, Leslie Stephen 1930- *WhoAm 92*
Valbuena-Briones, Angel Julian 1928- *WhoAm 92*
Valcana, Theony 1936- *WhoScE 91-3*
Valcarcel, Edgar 1932- *Baker 92*
Valcarcel, Luis E. 1891-1987 *IntDcAn*
Valcarcel, Marta Iris 1931- *WhoAm 92*
Valcarcel, Teodoro 1900-1942 *Baker 92*
Valcarcel Cases, Miguel 1946- *WhoScE 91-3*
Valcavi, Umberto 1928- *WhoScE 91-3, WhoWor 93*
Valcic, Susan Joan 1956- *WhoAmW 93*
Valcourt, Bernard *BioIn 17*
Valcourt, Bernard 1952- *WhoAm 92*
Valcroze, Jacques Doniol- 1920-1989 *BioIn 17*
Valdcmarin, Livio 1944- *WhoWor 93*
Valdemi, Maria 1947- *ScF&FL 92*
Valdengo, Giuseppe 1914- *Baker 92, OxDcOp*
Valderrabano, Enrique Enriquez de *Baker 92*
Valderrama, Carlos 1887-1950 *Baker 92*
Valderrama, Pamela Griffith *Law&B 92*
Valdes, Carlos 1928- *DcMexL*
Valdes, Gina 1943- *DcLB 122*
Valdes, James J. 20th cent.- *HispAmA [port]*
Valdes, Karen W. 1945- *WhoAm 92, WhoAmW 93*
Valdes, Maximiano *WhoAm 92*
Valdes, Nelson P. 1945- *ConAu 38NR*
Valdes, Octaviano 1901- *DcMexL*

Valdes-Dapena, Marie Agnes 1921- WhoAm 92, WhoAmW 93
Valdes Leal, Juan de 1622-1690 BioIn 17
Valdes-Lora, Mario Enrique Law&B 92
Valdespino, Henry, Jr. Law&B 92
Valdesuso, Maria 1965- WhoAmW 93
Valdes-Valle, Nancy Barba 1938- WhoAmW 93
Valdez, Abelardo Lopez 1942- HispAmA
Valdez, Carlos J. 1953- St&PR 93
Valdez, Elmer Romulo Galangco 1953- WhoWor 93
Valdez, Eppie Enrique 1930- St&PR 93
Valdez, Estanislao V. 1932- WhoAsAP 91
Valdez, James Law&B 92
Valdez, Jenny Wayland BioIn 17
Valdez, Luis 1940- HispAmA [port], MiSFD 9
Valdez, Luis Miguel 1940- DcLB 122 [port]
Valdez, Manuel A. 1946- WhoSSW 93
Valdez, Maria del Rosario 1955- WhoSSW 93
Valdez, Michele M. Law&B 92
Valdich, Luis Alfonso 1967- WhoSSW 93
Valdiguie, Pierre M. 1935- WhoScE 91-2
Valdimarsson, Grimur Thor 1949- WhoScE 91-4
Valdimarsson, Helgi 1936- WhoScE 91-4
Valdivia, Jose F., Jr. 1932- St&PR 93
Valdivia, Pedro de 1497-1553 HarEnMi
Valdivia, Pedro de 1500?-1553 Expl 93 [port]
Valdiviez, Robert Joseph 1952- St&PR 93
Valdman, Albert 1931- WhoAm 92
Valdonio, Giulio Cesare 1937- WhoWor 93
Valdre, Ugo 1926- WhoScE 91-3
Valdrighi, Luigi Francesco 1827-1899 Baker 92
Valduga, Patrizia 1953- DcLB 128 [port]
Vale, Brenda 1949- ScF&FL 92
Vale, Catharine H. Law&B 92
Vale, Collier BioIn 17
Vale, James W. 1916- St&PR 93
Vale, John S. Law&B 92
Vale, Norman BioIn 17
Vale, Norman 1930- St&PR 93, WhoAm 92
Vale, Rena 1898-1983 ScF&FL 92
Vale, Ronald D. 1959- WhoAm 92
Vale, Sara Elizabeth 1945- WhoAmW 93
Vale, Stephen E. Law&B 92
Vale, Virginia 1921- SweetSg C [port]
Valeani, Bernard Marie 1945- WhoWor 93
Valeds-Zacky, Dolores 1947- WhoAmW 93
Valega, Thomas Michael 1937- WhoE 93
Valek, Albert 1925- WhoScE 91-4
Valek, Jiri 1923- Baker 92
Valembois, Pierre 1937- WhoScE 91-2
Valen, (Olav) Fartein 1887-1952 Baker 92
Valencia, Antonio Maria 1902-1952 Baker 92
Valencia, Catalina Law&B 92
Valencia, Guillermo 1927- St&PR 93
Valencia, Luis Gerardo 1944- WhoWor 93
Valencia, Rodolfo G. 1942- WhoAsAP 91
Valencia, Rogelio Pasco 1939- WhoWor 93
Valenciano, Randal Grant Bolosan 1958- WhoEmL 93, WhoWor 93
Valens c. 328-378 OxDcByz
Valens, Amy 1946- ConAu 138, SmATA 70 [port]
Valens, Evans Gladstone 1920- WhoAm 92
Valensi, Paul Elie 1953- WhoWor 93
Valenstein, Elliot Spiro 1923- WhoAm 92
Valenstein, Karen BioIn 17
Valenstein, Suzanne Gebhart 1928- WhoAm 92
Valent, Leander R. Law&B 92
Valenta, Jaroslav 1927- WhoScE 91-4
Valenta, Zdenek 1927- WhoAm 92
Valente, Antonio fl. 16th cent.- Baker 92
Valente, Benita 1934- Baker 92
Valente, Giorgio Baker 92
Valente, Jose Angel 1929- BioIn 17
Valente, Louis P. 1930- St&PR 93
Valente, Louis Patrick 1930- WhoAm 92
Valente, Nicola 1881-1946 See Valente, Vincenzo 1855-1921 Baker 92
Valente, Vincenzo 1855-1921 Baker 92
Valenti, Carl M. WhoE 93
Valenti, Carl Michael 1938- St&PR 93
Valenti, Chi Chi BioIn 17
Valenti, Dan 1951- WhoWrEP 92
Valenti, Fernando 1926-1990 Baker 92, BioIn 17
Valenti, Jack BioIn 17
Valenti, Jack Joseph 1921- WhoAm 92
Valenti, JoAnn Myer 1945- WhoSSW 93
Valenti, Peter Carl 1943- WhoSSW 93
Valenti, Rita 1948- WhoAmW 93
Valenti, Robert M. 1939- St&PR 93
Valenti, Salvatore 1925- WhoScE 91-3
Valenti, Samuel 1946- St&PR 93
Valentim, Marta 1958- WhoWor 93
Valentin, Erich 1906- Baker 92
Valentine, Al 1931- St&PR 93
Valentine, Alan Darrell 1958- WhoAm 92
Valentine, Andrew Jackson Law&B 92
Valentine, Beatriz Ferrer 1957- WhoAmW 93
Valentine, Bill Terry 1932- WhoSSW 93
Valentine, Brunhilde E. 1929- St&PR 93
Valentine, Carol Ann 1942- WhoAmW 93
Valentine, De Wain 1936- WhoAm 92
Valentine, DeWain 1936- BioIn 17
Valentine, Douglas 1949- ConAu 139
Valentine, Foy Dan 1923- WhoAm 92
Valentine, George Edward 1942- WhoE 93
Valentine, George H. Law&B 92
Valentine, H. Jeffrey 1945- WhoAm 92
Valentine, Herman Edward 1937- St&PR 93
Valentine, I. T., Jr. 1926- WhoAm 92
Valentine, I. Tim, Jr. 1926- WhoSSW 93
Valentine, James C. Law&B 92
Valentine, James Stuart Law&B 92
Valentine, James William 1926- WhoAm 92
Valentine, Jean BioIn 17
Valentine, John Phillip 1923- WhoSSW 93
Valentine, John William Law&B 92
Valentine, Johnny SmATA 72 [port]
Valentine, Judith L. 1938- St&PR 93
Valentine, Mark ScF&FL 92
Valentine, Nelson 1960- BioIn 17
Valentine, Patrick Michel 1946- WhoSSW 93
Valentine, Peggy Ann 1950- WhoAmW 93
Valentine, Ralph Schuyler 1932- WhoAm 92
Valentine, Robert John 1950- WhoSSW 93
Valentine, Robert John Bobby 1950- WhoAm 92
Valentine, Steven Richards 1956- WhoAm 92
Valentine, Theresa A. Law&B 92
Valentine, Thomas James 1942- WhoWor 93
Valentine, Tim 1926- CngDr 91
Valentine, Valerie 1942- WhoAmW 93
Valentine, William Edson 1937- WhoAm 92
Valentine, William Newton 1917- WhoAm 92
Valentine-Thon, Elizabeth Anne 1948- WhoWor 93
Valentini, Caterina OxDcOp
Valentini, Caterina 1722-1808 See Mingotti, Angelo c. 1700-c. 1767 OxDcOp
Valentini, David BioIn 17
Valentini, Giovanni 1582-1649 Baker 92
Valentini, Giuseppe c. 1680-c. 1759 Baker 92
Valentini, Jose Esteban 1950- WhoWor 93
Valentini, Pier (Pietro) Francesco c. 1570-1654 Baker 92
Valentinian, I 321-375 OxDcByz
Valentinian, II 371-392 OxDcByz
Valentinian, III 419-455 OxDcByz
Valentini Terrani, Lucia 1946- OxDcOp
Valentini-Terrani, Lucia 1948- Baker 92
Valentino BioIn 17
Valentino 1932- WhoWor 93
Valentino, Flora WhoScE 91-3
Valentino, Frank 1907-1991 BioIn 17
Valentino, Harry 1944- St&PR 93
Valentino, Henri-Justin-Armand-Joseph 1785-1865 Baker 92
Valentino, John 1940- St&PR 93
Valentino, Mario 1927-1991 BioIn 17
Valentino, Rudolph 1895-1926 BioIn 17, IntDcF 2-3 [port]
Valentino, Tina 1959- WhoWrEP 92
Valentinos SoulM
Valentinos Arsakuni d645 OxDcByz
Valentinuzzi, Max Eugene 1932- WhoWor 93
Valenza, Anji ScF&FL 92
Valenza, Antoinette Josephine 1923- WhoE 93
Valenza, Elaine Dawn 1938- St&PR 93
Valenza, S.W. 1935- St&PR 93
Valenzuela, Fernando BioIn 17
Valenzuela, Fernando 1960- HispAmA, WhoAm 92
Valenzuela, Gary 1957- St&PR 93
Valenzuela, Gaspar Rodolfo 1933- HispAmA
Valenzuela, Jaime Galvez 1940- WhoWor 93
Valenzuela, Jesus E. 1856-1911 DcMexL
Valenzuela, Julio Samuel 1948- WhoAm 92
Valenzuela, Luisa 1938- BioIn 17, SpAmA
Valenzuela, Manuel Anthony, Jr. 1955- WhoWor 93
Valenzuela, Nelson Alexander 1946- WhoUN 92
Valenzuela, Pablo Detarso 1941- St&PR 93
Valera Zerpa, Maria Virginia 1945- WhoWor 93
Valeri, Diego 1887-1976 DcLB 128 [port]
Valeri, Martin 1917- St&PR 93
Valerian, W. A. St&PR 93
Valeriani, Richard 1932- BioIn 17
Valeriani, Richard Gerard 1932- WhoAm 92
Valerio, Dennis C. 1947- St&PR 93
Valerio, Louis J. 1949- St&PR 93
Valerio, Mark Luke 1954- WhoE 93
Valerio, Martha Medlar 1946- WhoAmW 93
Valerio, Michael Anthony 1953- WhoAm 92
Valerius, Adrianus c. 1575-1625 Baker 92
Valerius, M. Mark 1929- St&PR 93
Valery, Paul 1871-1945 BioIn 17
Valesano, Robert D. 1929- St&PR 93
Valesio, Paolo 1939- WhoAm 92
Valeskie-Hamner, Gail Yvonne 1953- WhoAmW 93
Valet, Eugene H. Law&B 92
Valeton, Ida 1922- WhoScE 91-3
Valette, Jean Paul 1937- WhoE 93
Valette, Rebecca Marianne 1938- WhoAm 92, WhoAmW 93
Valeur-Jensen, Margaret Eline Law&B 92
Val Falcon, Jesus 1958- WhoScE 91-3
Valfre, Franco 1933- WhoWor 93
Valgardson, W.D. 1939- BioIn 17
Valgardson, W(illiam) D(empsey) 1939- ConAu 38NR
Valgardson, William Dempsey 1939- WhoCanL 92
Valgemae, Mardi 1935- WhoE 93
Vali, Ferenc Albert 1905-1984 ConAu 37NR
Valiaho, Hannu Sakari 1938- WhoScE 91-4, WhoWor 93
Valiant, Leslie Gabriel 1949- WhoAm 92
Valice, Debra Diane 1956- St&PR 93
Valicenti, Mitchel J. 1909- St&PR 93
Valicenti, Mitchel Joseph 1909- WhoAm 92
Valiente, Gabriel Alejandro 1963- WhoWor 93
Valiga, Theresa M. 1949- WhoAmW 93
Valimanas R, Ramon 1948- WhoWor 93
Valimont, Anastasia Mary 1920- WhoE 93
Valin, Jonathan Louis 1948- ConAu 38NR
Valincour, Jean Baptiste Henri du Trousset de 1653-1730 BioIn 17
Valines, A. Irene 1958- WhoEmL 93
Valiquette, Amy L. 1941- St&PR 93
Valiquette, E. Charlene 1951- St&PR 93
Valiquette, Evelyn Charlene 1951- WhoAm 92
Valiullah, Raoof 1945- WhoAsAP 91
Valiunas, Joseph d1992 BioIn 17
Valiunas, Joseph Kestutis d1992 NewYTBS 92
Valk, Elizabeth 1950- WhoAm 92, WhoAmW 93
Valk, Henry Snowden 1929- WhoAm 92, WhoSSW 93
Valk, Jerome E. 1935- St&PR 93
Valk, Robert Earl 1914- WhoAm 92, WhoWor 93
Valkan, Constance Law&B 92
Valkare, Gunnar 1943- Baker 92
Valkovic, Vladivoj WhoUN 92
Valkovic, Vlado 1939- WhoScE 91-4
Valla, Pierre 1947- St&PR 93
Valla, Thomas John 1933- St&PR 93
Valladares, Armando 1937- DcCPCAm
Valladares, Ysidro 1927- WhoScE 91-3
Vallan, Ronald Louis 1946- St&PR 93
Vallance, David Michael WhoScE 91-1
Vallance, Elizabeth (Mary) 1945- ConAu 40NR
Vallance-Jones, Alister 1924- WhoAm 92
Vallandigham, Clement L. 1820-1871 PolPar
Vallano, Richard David 1931- WhoIns 93
Vallarino, Joaquin J., Jr. 1921- St&PR 93
Vallarta, Ray 1927- St&PR 93
Vallas, Leon 1879-1956 Baker 92
Vallasciani, Vicente Roberto 1940- WhoWor 93
Vallat, Xavier 1891-1972 BioIn 17
Vallbo, Ake B. 1933- WhoScE 91-4
Vallbona, Carlos 1927- HispAmA, WhoAm 92
Vallbona, Rima De 1931- WhoWrEP 92
Vallbona, Rima-Gretel Rothe 1931- WhoAmW 93
Valle, Juan 1838-1864? DcMexL
Valle, Juvencio 1900- SpAmA
Valle, Rafael Heliodoro 1891-1959 DcMexL
Valle, Victor Manuel 1950- DcLB 122 [port]
Valle-Aguiluz, Jorge Enrique 1957- WhoWor 93
Valle-Arizpe, Artemio de 1888-1961 DcMexL
Vallecorsa, Joseph A., Jr. Law&B 92
Valle de Paz, Edgardo del Baker 92
Vallee, Bert Lester 1919- WhoAm 92
Vallee, Jacques Fabrice 1939- WhoWor 93
Vallee, Jacques Laurent 1939- St&PR 93
Vallee, Robert 1922- WhoScE 91-2
Vallee, Rudy 1901-1986 Baker 92
Vallegio, Giuseppe Eugenio 1949- WhoWor 93
Vallejo, Antonio Buero 1916- BioIn 17
Vallejo, Armando 1949- DcLB 122 [port]
Vallejo, Boris 1941- ScF&FL 92
Vallejo, Cesar 1892-1938 SpAmA
Vallejo, Doris ScF&FL 92
Vallejo, Estella Law&B 92
Vallem, Bradley S. 1953- St&PR 93
Vallentine, Josephine 1946- WhoAsAP 91
Vallentyne, Mary Ellen 1933- WhoAmW 93
Vallerand, Francois 1943- WhoScE 91-2
Vallerand, Jean 1915- Baker 92
Vallerand, Philippe Georges 1954- WhoWor 93
Valleria, Alwina 1848-1925 Baker 92
Valle-Riestra, Jose Maria 1859-1925 Baker 92
Valleron, Alain-Jacques WhoScE 91-2
Vallery, Janet Alane 1948- WhoAmW 93, WhoWor 93
Valles, Jean Paul 1936- St&PR 93, WhoAm 92
Valles, Jose-Lorenzo 1958- WhoWor 93
Valles, Jules 1832-1885 DcLB 123 [port]
Valles, Jules Louis Joseph 1832-1885 BioIn 17
Valles, Michel 1941- WhoScE 91-2
Vallet, Georges 1921- WhoScE 91-2
Vallet, Nicolas c. 1583-c. 1642 Baker 92
Valleton, Jean-Marc 1954- WhoWor 93
Vallett, Walter Irving, Jr. 1923- St&PR 93
Valletti, Cesare 1922- Baker 92, IntDcOp
Valley, George Edward, Jr. 1913- WhoAm 92
Valley, John Richard 1919- WhoSSW 93
Vallhonrat, Javier 1953- BioIn 17
Valli, Alida 1921- IntDcF 2-3 [port]
Valli, Frankie 1937- WhoAm 92
Valli, Louis A. 1932- St&PR 93
Valli, Peter Constantine 1927- St&PR 93
Valliani, Aziz Amirali 1953- St&PR 93
Vallianos, Fred 1935- WhoSSW 93
Vallier Pino, Pedro WhoScE 91-3
Valli Muthusamy WhoAsAP 91
Vallin, Ivar WhoScE 91-4
Vallin, Ninon 1886-1961 IntDcOp, OxDcOp
Vallio, Gwendolyn Marie 1936- WhoAmW 93
Valli-Steliotes, Lida Andrea 1959- WhoAmW 93
Vallo, Joseph A. Law&B 92
Vallon, Delphine Denise 1967- WhoWor 93
Vallone, Gerard Frank 1942- WhoE 93
Vallone, Norman J. 1949- St&PR 93
Vallone, Pam 1953- St&PR 93
Vallort, Ronald Peter 1942- St&PR 93
Vallotti, Francesco Antonio 1697-1780 Baker 92
Vallotton, Michel 1933- WhoScE 91-4
Valls, Pedro M. d1992 BioIn 17
Valls, Pedro Manuel d1992 NewYTBS 92
Valmassoi, Nancy M. Law&B 92
Valmont, Alejo Carpentier y ScF&FL 92
Valmore, Marceline Desbordes- 1786-1859 BioIn 17
Valois, Denis Gabriel 1956- WhoWor 93
Valois, Gaetane Law&B 92
Valois, Georges 1878-1945 BioIn 17
Valois, Robert Arthur 1938- WhoSSW 93
Valone, Thomas Francis 1951- WhoWrEP 92
Valoon, Patricia Louise 1936- WhoAmW 93
Valore, Kenneth Joseph 1941- St&PR 93, WhoAm 92
Valore, Richard Howard 1931- St&PR 93
Valov, Vesko Marinov 1950- WhoWor 93
Valrie, Georgia Mae 1949- WhoAmW 93
Valsamakis, Emmanuel Anthony 1933- WhoE 93
Valsamidis, Nicholas 1943- WhoUN 92
Valsamis, Marius Peter 1932- WhoE 93
Valsgard, Sverre 1945- WhoScE 91-4
Valsik, Jindrich Antonin 1903-1977 IntDcAn
Valtanen, Hannu WhoScE 91-4
Valtanen, Jukka 1931- WhoScE 91-4
Valtasaari, Jukka Robert 1940- WhoWor 93
Valtat, Louis 1869-1952 BioIn 17
Valtcev, Vladimir 1934- WhoScE 91-4
Valterova, Alena BioIn 17
Valtin, Donald Edward 1936- St&PR 93
Valtman, Edmund 1914- WhoE 93
Valtonen, Jukka Ossi Tapani 1934- WhoScE 91-4

Van Dam, Roeland H. 1949- *WhoScE 91-3*
Van Dam, Wils 1941- *St&PR 93*
Vandament, William Eugene 1931- *WhoAm 92*
Vandamme, Dominique Joseph Rene 1770-1830 *HarEnMi*
Vandamme, Erick J. 1943- *WhoScE 91-2*
Vandamme, Fernand Jozef 1943- *WhoWor 93*
Van Damme, H. *WhoScE 91-2*
Van Damme, Johannes Martinus G. 1937- *WhoWor 93*
Van Damme, Jos M.M. 1952- *WhoScE 91-3*
Van Damme, Joseph 1940- *Baker 92*
Van Damme, Paul J. 1950- *St&PR 93*
Van Dantzig, R. 1937- *WhoScE 91-3*
Vandaveer, Vicki V. 1944- *WhoAmW 93*
Vandeberg, James L. *Law&B 92*
VandeBerg, John Lee 1947- *WhoSSW 93*
Van De Braak, N.J. 1947- *WhoScE 91-3*
van de Bunt, Dirk W. *Law&B 92*
Van Deburg, William L. 1948- *ConAu 139*
Vandecandelaere, Gaston 1941- *WhoScE 91-2*
VanDeCasteele, Michael John 1953- *WhoSSW 93*
Van De Geijn, S.C. 1944- *WhoScE 91-3*
Van De Graaf, Jacobus J. 1938- *WhoIns 93*
Van De Graaf, Jacobus John 1938- *St&PR 93*
Vandegrift, Alexander Archer 1887-1973 *HarEnMi*
Vandegrift, Alfred Eugene 1937- *WhoAm 92*
Vandegrift, Donald P. 1960- *WhoIns 93*
Vandegrift, Donald Paul, Jr. *Law&B 92*
Vandegrift, John Raymond 1928- *WhoE 93*
Vandegrift, Vaughn 1946- *WhoE 93*
Vande Hey, James Michael 1916- *WhoAm 92*
Van De Kaa, Dirk Jan 1933- *WhoScE 91-3, WhoWor 93*
Van de Kamp, John 1936- *BioIn 17*
Van de Kamp, John Kalar 1936- *WhoAm 92*
Van de Kasteele, J. C. W. 1946- *WhoWor 93*
VandeKieft, Ruth Marguerite 1925- *WhoE 93*
Vandel, Diana Geis 1947- *WhoAmW 93*
Van Delden, Lex *Baker 92*
van de Leuv, John Henri 1926- *WhoSSW 93*
Van Delft, Antonius M.L. 1939- *WhoScE 91-3*
Vande Linde, Vernon David 1942- *WhoAm 92*
Vandell, Deborah Lowe 1949- *WhoAmW 93, WhoEmL 93*
Vandell, Kerry Dean 1947- *WhoAm 92*
Van De Loo, Jurgen C.W. 1932- *WhoScE 91-3*
Van de Maele, Albert Camille Louis 1914- *WhoAm 92*
Van Demark, Robert Eugene 1913- *WhoAm 92, WhoWor 93*
Vandemark, Robert Goodyear 1921- *WhoAm 92*
Van Demark, Ruth Elaine 1944- *WhoAmW 93*
Van De Mieroop, Marc 1956- *ConAu 139*
Van de Moortel, Arie 1918-1976 *Baker 92*
Van Den Abeele, Jan Hendrik Albyn 1951- *WhoWor 93*
Van den Akker, Johannes Archibald 1904- *WhoWor 93*
Van Den Assum, Baudouin *Law&B 92*
van den Assum, Laetitia 1950- *WhoUN 92*
Van Den Audenaerde, D. Thys *WhoScE 91-2*
Vandenberg, Arthur 1884-1951 *ColdWar 1 [port]*
Vandenberg, Arthur H. 1884-1951 *PolPar*
Vandenberg, Arthur Hendrick 1884-1951 *DcTwHis*
Vandenberg, Donald A. *St&PR 93*
Vandenberg, Edwin J. 1918- *BioIn 17*
Van Den Berg, G.A. 1945- *WhoScE 91-3*
Van Den Berg, H.C. 1936- *WhoScE 91-3*
Van den Berg, Jan Hendrik 1914- *WhoWor 93*
Vanden Berg, Les D. 1948- *St&PR 93*
Van Den Berg, Margrietus Max Johannes 1946- *WhoWor 93*
Vanden Berg, Michael Russell *Law&B 92*
Vandenberg, Patricia Clasina 1948- *WhoAmW 93*
Vandenberg, Peter, Jr. 1955- *St&PR 93*
Vandenberg, Roger A. 1947- *St&PR 93*
Vandenberg, Russell Clayton 1933- *St&PR 93*
Vandenberg, Thomas E. *Law&B 92*
Vandenberg, Thomas Fairbanks 1941- *WhoWrEP 92*
van den Berg, Wilhelmus Albertus 1937- *WhoWor 93*
Van Den Bergh, Govaert Carolus Joannes J 1926- *WhoWor 93*
Vandenbergh, John Garry 1935- *WhoSSW 93*
van den Bergh, Sidney 1929- *WhoAm 92*
Van Den Berghe, Herman 1933- *WhoScE 91-2*
Van den Berghe, Pierre L. *BioIn 17*
van den Berghe, Pierre Louis 1933- *WhoAm 92*
Vanden Berghe, Remy Alphonse 1947- *WhoWor 93*
van den Blink, Nelson Mooers 1934- *St&PR 93*
Van den Bogaert, Harmen Meyndertsz *BioIn 17*
Van Den Boom, A.J.W. 1943- *WhoScE 91-3*
Van Den Boom, Esperanza 1953- *WhoAmW 93*
Van den Boorn-Coclet, Henriette 1866-1945 *Baker 92*
Vandenborre, Hugo 1944- *WhoScE 91-2*
Van den Borren, Charles (-Jean-Eugene) 1874-1966 *Baker 92*
VandenBos, Gary Roger 1943- *WhoAm 92*
Van Den Bos, Jan 1936- *WhoScE 91-3*
Vanden Bosch, Henry *St&PR 93*
Vanden Bout, Paul Adrian 1939- *WhoAm 92*
Van Den Brink, Cornelis 1932- *WhoWor 93*
Van Den Broek, P. *WhoScE 91-1*
Vandenbroucke, Jan P. 1950- *WhoScE 91-3, WhoWor 93*
van den Brul, Caroline 1954- *WhoWor 93*
VanDenburg, Arland Franklin 1920- *St&PR 93*
Vandenburg, Edith P. 1923- *St&PR 93*
Vandenburg, Hoyt Sanford 1899-1954 *HarEnMi*
Vandenburg, Mary Lou 1943- *WhoE 93*
VanDenburgh, Howard F. *Law&B 92*
Vandenbyvang, P. *WhoScE 91-2*
Vandendriessche, Gaston Roger 1924- *WhoScE 91-2*
Vanden Driessche-Oedenkoven, Therese 1925- *WhoScE 91-2*
Vandendris, Michel F.R. 1947- *WhoScE 91-2*
Van den Eeden, Jean-Baptiste *Baker 92*
Van Den Ende, Joost 1925- *WhoScE 91-3*
van den Essen, Arno Richardus 1951- *WhoWor 93*
van den Haag, Ernest 1914- *WhoE 93*
Van Den Hende, Jan H. 1934- *WhoScE 91-3*
Van Den Herik, Hendrik Jacob 1947- *WhoWor 93*
Van Den Herrewegen, Marc 1944- *WhoScE 91-2*
Van Den Heuvel, Edward Peter Jacobus 1940- *WhoScE 91-3*
Van Den Heuvel, W.M.C. 1928- *WhoScE 91-3*
Vanden Hogen, Debra Janine Thomas 1967- *BiDAMSp 1989*
Van Den Hout, M.A. 1955- *WhoScE 91-3*
Van Den Houten, Hans 1940- *St&PR 93*
Vandenhouten, Kevin Joseph 1963- *St&PR 93*
Van Den Meersschaut, C. *WhoScE 91-2*
van den Muyzenberg, Laurens 1933- *WhoWor 93*
Van Den Noort, P.C. 1935- *WhoScE 91-3*
van-den-Noort, Stanley 1930- *WhoAm 92*
Van de North, John Bernard, Jr. 1945- *WhoAm 92*
Vandenplas, Paul E.M. 1931- *WhoScE 91-2*
Vandenplas-Holper, Christiane 1942- *WhoScE 91-2*
Van Den Sande, Paul 1935- *WhoScE 91-2*
Van Den Schrieck, Henry-George 1925- *WhoScE 91-2*
Vandepitte, Daniel C.C. 1922- *WhoScE 91-2*
Van De Poel, Alphonsius C.M. 1934- *WhoScE 91-3*
Van De Poll, K.W. 1942- *WhoScE 91-3*
Van de Putte, Leticia 1954- *WhoAmW 93*
Vandeputte, Michel Charles 1930- *WhoScE 91-2*
Van Der Aa, H.A. 1935- *WhoScE 91-3*
Van Der Avoird, Ad 1943- *WhoScE 91-3*
Van Der Avoird, Adrianus Wilhelmus 1947- *WhoWor 93*
Vanderbaan, Russell H. 1950- *St&PR 93*
Vanderbeck, Barbara Ann *Law&B 92*
Van Der Beek, M.A. 1932- *WhoScE 91-3*
vanderBeek, Tony Martinus 1967- *WhoE 93*
Van Der Beken, Andre M.L. 1939- *WhoScE 91-2*
Vanderberg, James Leonard 1943- *St&PR 93*
Vanderberry, James Greer *Law&B 92*
Vanderberry, James Greer 1932- *St&PR 93*
Vanderbilt, Alfred Gwynne, Jr. 1949- *WhoE 93*
Vanderbilt, Arthur T., II 1950- *WhoE 93, WhoEmL 93*
Vanderbilt, Cornelius 1794-1877 *BioIn 17*
Vanderbilt, George Washington 1862-1914 *GayN*
Vanderbilt, Gloria Morgan 1924- *WhoAmW 93*
Vanderbilt, Hugh Bedford 1921- *St&PR 93*
Vanderbilt, Hugh Bedford, Sr. 1921- *WhoAm 92*
Vanderbilt, Kermit 1925- *WhoAm 92*
Vanderbilt, Oliver DeG 1914- *St&PR 93*
Vanderbilt, Oliver Degray 1914- *WhoAm 92*
Van Der Borg, Heiko H. 1925- *WhoScE 91-3*
Vanderbrook, Don *BioIn 17*
Van Derbur, Gwendolyn Olinger *BioIn 17*
Van Derbur, Marilyn *BioIn 17*
Vanderburg, Kathleen 1951- *WhoAmW 93*
Vanderburg, Paul Stacey 1941- *WhoWor 93*
Van Der Burg, W.J. 1950- *WhoScE 91-3*
Vanderbylt, Whiteford *WhoWrEP 92*
Vander Clay, Steven Dennis *Law&B 92*
Vander Clute, Howard Edmund, Jr. 1929- *WhoAm 92*
Vander Clute, Norman Roland 1932- *WhoAm 92*
Van Der Does, Emanuel 1928- *WhoScE 91-3*
Vanderdonckt, Jean Marie 1965- *WhoWor 93*
Vander Dussen, Neil Richard 1931- *WhoE 93*
Van der Duyn Schouten, Frank Anthonie 1949- *WhoWor 93*
Van der Eb, Henry Gerard 1918- *WhoAm 92*
Vander Eecken, Henri 1920- *WhoScE 91-2*
Vander Els, Betty 1936- *BioIn 17*
Vanderflugt, Gary Daryl 1948- *St&PR 93*
Van der Geest, Berber 1938- *BioIn 17*
Vandergeten, Jean-Pierre 1954- *WhoScE 91-2*
Vander Goot, Mary Elizabeth 1947- *WhoAmW 93*
Van Der Graaff, Nicolaas A. 1945- *WhoScE 91-3*
Van Der Greef, J. *WhoScE 91-3*
Vandergriendt, Pieter S. *St&PR 93*
Vandergriff, Jerry Dodson 1943- *WhoWor 93*
Vandergrift, Mary 1901-1991 *BioIn 17*
Vander Haegen, Eleanor Marie 1941- *WhoAmW 93*
Van Der Haegen, Herman 1929- *WhoScE 91-2*
Vanderhaeghe, Guy 1951- *WhoCanL 92*
Vanderhaeghe, Hubert Jean Henri 1921- *WhoScE 91-2*
Van der Hamen y Leon, Juan c. 1596-c. 1632 *BioIn 17*
Vanderhei, George Lloyd 1921- *St&PR 93*
Vander Heide, G. Peter 1947- *WhoEmL 93*
Vanderheiden, Richard Thomas 1947- *WhoWor 93*
Van Der Heul, R.O. *WhoScE 91-3*
Vander Heyden, W. H. 1936- *St&PR 93*
Vanderhill, Charles Warren 1937- *WhoAm 92*
Van Derhoef, Gwendolyn Renee 1952- *St&PR 93*
Vanderhoef, Larry Neil 1941- *WhoAm 92*
Vanderhoef, Peter C. 1940- *St&PR 93*
Vanderhoef, Victoria Lee 1961- *WhoAmW 93*
Van Der Hoek, J.A. 1932- *WhoScE 91-3*
Van Der Honing, Y. 1941- *WhoScE 91-3*
Vanderhoof, Irwin T. 1927- *St&PR 93*
Vanderhoof, Irwin Thomas 1927- *WhoAm 92*
Vanderhoof-Forschner, Karen MacNeil 1951- *WhoE 93*
Van der Horst, Anthon *Baker 92*
Vander Horst, Donald J. 1924- *St&PR 93*
Van Der Horst, Ellen G. 1956- *St&PR 93*
Vanderhost, Leonette Louise 1924- *WhoE 93*
Van Der Hulst, Jan Mathijs 1948- *WhoWor 93*
Vander Jagt, Guy 1931- *CngDr 91, WhoAm 92*
Van Der Jagt, Martin 1944- *WhoScE 91-3*
Van Der Kaay, Hugo Jan 1929- *WhoScE 91-3*
Van Der Kamp, Jan Willem 1944- *WhoScE 91-3*
Van Der Kelen, Gustaaf Petrus 1928- *WhoScE 91-2*
van der Kelen, Luc M. J. 1948- *WhoWor 93*
van der Kloet, Hendrik 1935- *WhoUN 92*
Vanderkloot, William *MiSFD 9*
Vander Kolk, Kenneth Jay 1928- *WhoAm 92*
Van Der Koogh, Peter D. 1935- *WhoScE 91-3*
Van Der Korst, Jan K. 1931- *WhoScE 91-3*
van der Kroef, Justus Maria 1925- *WhoAm 92*
Vanderlaan, Alice D. *AmWomPl*
van der Laan, Gerrit *WhoWor 93*
Van Der Laan, H. *WhoScE 91-3*
Van der Laan, Hans 1904-1991 *BioIn 17*
van der Laan, Paul 1952- *WhoWor 93*
Van Der Laan, Piet C.T. 1935- *WhoScE 91-3*
VanderLaan, Robert D. 1952- *WhoWor 93*
Van Der Land, Jacob 1935- *WhoScE 91-3*
van der Leun, Jan Cornelis 1928- *WhoWor 93*
Vander Linde, Albert 1929- *WhoE 93*
Vanderlinde, Derek E. 1946- *St&PR 93*
Van Der Linde, Hans 1948- *WhoScE 91-3*
Van Der Linde, J. *WhoScE 91-3*
Vanderlinde, Raymond Edward 1924- *WhoAm 92*
Van der Linden, Cornelis 1839-1918 *Baker 92*
Van Der Linden, Frans P.G.M. 1932- *WhoScE 91-3*
Van Der Linden, H.J.L.J. 1940- *WhoScE 91-3*
Vander Linden, Michel Marie 1927- *WhoWor 93*
Vanderlip, Caroline *BioIn 17*
Vanderlip, Elin 1919- *WhoAm 92*
Vanderlip, Nancy Lynn *Law&B 92*
Vanderlippe, Richard Hampton 1932- *St&PR 93*
Vanderlyn, John 1775-1852 *BioIn 17*
Van Der Maarel, Eddy 1934- *WhoScE 91-4*
Vandermaesbrugge, Max 1933- *Baker 92*
Van Der Maesen, Laurentius Josephus Gerardus 1944- *WhoScE 91-3*
van der Marck, Jan 1929- *WhoAm 92*
Vandermark, Ed J. *Law&B 92*
Vandermause, Richard Lee 1948- *St&PR 93*
Vandermay, Jack 1942- *St&PR 93*
Vandermay, Joyce A. 1939- *St&PR 93*
Vandermay, William J. 1938- *St&PR 93*
Van Der Mee, Cornelis Victor 1953- *WhoWor 93*
Vander Meer, C.L.J. 1944- *WhoScE 91-3*
Van Der Meer, D. *WhoScE 91-3*
Vandermeer, H.W.A. 1930- *St&PR 93*
Van der Meer, Jan 1632-1675 *BioIn 17*
van der Meer, Jan 1950- *WhoWor 93*
VanderMeer, Jeff *ScF&FL 92*
Vander Meer, John Samuel 1914- *BiDAMSp 1989*
van der Meer, Simon 1925- *WhoWor 93*
Van Der Meij, Govert Pieter 1951- *WhoWor 93*
Van Der Meij, P.H. *WhoScE 91-3*
van der Mensbrugghe, Emmanuel Michel 1957- *WhoUN 92*
van der Merwe, Nikolaas Johannes 1940- *WhoAm 92*
Van Der Meulen, Barry 1937- *St&PR 93*
Vander Meulen, Conrad 1925- *St&PR 93*
Van der Meulen, Daan 1894-1989 *BioIn 17*
Van Der Meulen, Joseph Pierre 1929- *WhoAm 92, WhoWor 93*
Vanderminden, Henry J. W., Jr. 1896- *St&PR 93*
Vanderminden, Henry J. W., III 1925- *St&PR 93*
Vanderminden, Robert D. 1927- *St&PR 93*
Van Der Molen, H.J. *WhoScE 91-3*
Vander Molen, Robert L. 1947- *WhoWrEP 92*
Vandermotten, Christian 1944- *WhoScE 91-2*
Vander Myde, Paul Arthur 1937- *St&PR 93, WhoAm 92*
Van Der Nat, Mattheus 1951- *WhoWor 93*
Vandernoot, Andre 1927- *Baker 92*
Vander Noot, Norman Carey 1935- *WhoE 93*
Van Dernoot, Richard Norman 1945- *St&PR 93*
Vanderpan, Mary L. *Law&B 92*
Van Der Panne, Wessel Willem Hendrik Wouter 1944- *WhoWor 93*
Van Der Plas, Henk C. 1929- *WhoScE 91-3*
Van Der Plas, Leendert 1928- *WhoScE 91-3*
van der Plas, Rob(ert) 1938- *ConAu 138*
Van Der Ploeg, Frederick 1956- *WhoWor 93*

Van Mierlo, Hans Johannes Gysbertus Andreas 1953- *WhoWor 93*
Van Miert, Adelbert S.J.P.A.M. 1937- *WhoScE 91-3*
Van Miltenburg, Cornelis M. 1935- *St&PR 93*
Van Moffaert, Myriam Marcelle 1943- *WhoWor 93*
Van Mol, Louis John, Jr. 1943- *WhoAm 92*
Van Mols, Brian 1931- *WhoAm 92*
Van Montagu, Marc C.E. 1933- *WhoScE 91-2*
Van Mourik, Dan 1948- *WhoWrEP 92*
Van Mourik, Jan A. 1943- *WhoScE 91-3*
Van Munching, Leo d1990 *BioIn 17*
Van Mynen, Ronald 1937- *St&PR 93*
Vann, Bobb 1939- *WhoE 93*
Vann, Clifton B. 1939- *St&PR 93*
Vann, Danny 1953- *BioIn 17*
Vann, Frank Simms 1947- *St&PR 93*
Vann, Gerald 1906- *ScF&FL 92*
Vann, James A., Jr. 1931- *St&PR 93*
Vann, James Murdock 1928- *St&PR 93*
Vann, John Daniel, III 1935- *WhoE 93*
Vann, Joseph Mc Alpin 1937- *WhoE 93*
Vann, Robert 1879-1940 *EncAACR*
Vann, Robert L. 1879-1940 *JrnUS*
Vann, Thomas Phillips 1939- *St&PR 93*
Van Name, Frederick Warren, III 1946- *WhoE 93*
Van Name, Richard Bradley 1953- *WhoSSW 93*
Vannas, Salme Fredrika 1918- *WhoScE 91-4*
Vannasse, Dana Edward 1935- *WhoE 93*
Vannatta, Dennis 1946- *ConAu 138*
Van Nederynen, David Scott 1960- *WhoSSW 93*
Van Nelson, Nicholas Lloyd 1942- *WhoAm 92*
Vanneman, Edgar, Jr. 1919- *WhoAm 92*
Vannerberg, Nils-Gosta 1930- *WhoScE 91-4*
Van Nes, Florus 1945- *WhoWor 93*
Van Ness, C. Charles 1920- *St&PR 93*
Van Ness, Cheryl Deborah 1957- *WhoAmW 93*
Van Ness, James Edward 1926- *WhoAm 92*
Van Ness, John Ralph 1939- *WhoAm 92, WhoE 93*
Van Ness, Lottye Gray 1925- *WhoSSW 93*
Van Ness, Patricia Catheline 1951- *WhoAmW 93*
Van Ness, Paul Duffield 1932- *WhoE 93*
Vanneste, Alex Maurice Simon 1946- *WhoWor 93*
Van Niekerk, Hendrik Albertus 1759-1833 *BioIn 17*
Van Nieuwenhuizen, Gerrit H. 1946- *WhoScE 91-3*
van Nievelt, M. C. Augustus 1928- *WhoE 93*
Vanni-Marcoux *Baker 92*
Vannini, Enrico 1914- *WhoScE 91-3*
Vannman, Lars E. 1937- *St&PR 93*
Van Noord, Andrew 1922- *St&PR 93*
Van Noorden, Anna *AmWomPl*
van Noordwijk, Jacobus 1920- *WhoWor 93*
Van Norden, Langdon 1915- *WhoAm 92*
Van Norman, Daniel L. *St&PR 93*
Van Norman, Etta C. *AmWomPl*
Van Norman, Willis Roger 1938- *WhoWor 93*
Van Norstrand, R. E. 1937- *WhoAm 92*
Van Nort, Alan Delos 1943- *WhoSSW 93*
Van Nortwick, Barbara Louise 1940- *WhoAmW 93*
Van Nortwick, Terry Biehl 1948- *WhoWrEP 92*
Van Nortwick, Thomas H. 1949- *WhoE 93*
Van Nostern, Julie *Law&B 92*
Van Nostrand, Catharine Marie Herr 1937- *WhoAmW 93*
Van Nostrand, M. Abbott 1911- *St&PR 93*
Van Nostrand, Morris Abbott, Jr. 1911- *WhoAm 92*
Van Nostrand, Richard K. d1991 *BioIn 17*
Van Noy, Christine Ann 1948- *WhoAmW 93*
Van Noy, Loran 1942- *St&PR 93*
Vannoy, Robert Glenn, III 1956- *St&PR 93*
Van Noy, Terry W. 1947- *WhoIns 93*
Van Noy, Terry Willard 1947- *St&PR 93*
Vannucchi, Guido *WhoScE 91-3*
Vannucci, Giorgio 1931- *St&PR 93*
Vannucci, Osvaldo I. 1945- *St&PR 93*
Vannuccini, Luigi 1828-1911 *Baker 92*
van Nuffel, Jeannette Therese W. 1932- *WhoAmW 93*
Van Obberghen, E. *WhoScE 91-2*
Van Oeveren, Edward Lanier 1954- *WhoSSW 93*
Vanoff, Nick d1991 *BioIn 17*
Vanoff, Nick 1930?-1991 *ConTFT 10*
van Ogtrop, Kristin *DcLB Y92 [port]*
Vanoni, Vito August 1904- *WhoAm 92*
Van Onsem, Jan Gustaaf 1924- *WhoScE 91-2*
Van Oordt, Robert Ferdinand Willem 1936- *WhoWor 93*
Van Oorschot, Rolf Dieter 1930- *WhoScE 91-3*
Van Oosten, H.J. *WhoScE 91-3*
Van Oosterom, A.T. 1940- *WhoScE 91-3*
Van Oosterom, Adriaan 1942- *WhoScE 91-3*
Van Oostrum, Kees 1954- *MiSFD 9*
Van Ooteghem, Marc Michel Martin 1927- *WhoScE 91-2, WhoWor 93*
van Ootmarsum, Harry Robert 1941- *WhoWor 93*
Van Opdenbosch, Emmanuel 1949- *WhoScE 91-2*
Van Oppen, Peter Henry 1952- *St&PR 93*
Van Orden, Herbert George 1912- *St&PR 93*
Van Orden, Mary *AmWomPl*
Van Orden, William *BioIn 17*
Van Orman, Chandler L. 1941- *WhoAm 92*
Van Orman, Jeanne 1939- *WhoAmW 93, WhoE 93*
Van Ornum, Harry Delbert 1946- *St&PR 93*
Vanorsdale, David William, Jr. 1965- *WhoE 93*
Van Os, Adrian G. 1946- *WhoScE 91-3*
Van Os, Willem A.A. 1930- *WhoScE 91-3*
Van Oss, Richard *WhoScE 91-1*
Van Osselaer, Paul J.E. 1954- *WhoScE 91-2*
Van Otterloo, Willem *Baker 92*
van Oudenhover, Frank J. M. 1935- *St&PR 93*
Vanourek, Robert A. 1942- *St&PR 93*
Vanover, Boyd Russell 1950- *WhoSSW 93*
van Over, Raymond 1934- *ScF&FL 92*
Van Overstraeten, Roger J. 1937- *WhoScE 91-2*
Van Pamel, Duane 1943- *St&PR 93*
Van Patten, Dick Vincent 1928- *WhoAm 92*
Van Patten, George F. 1953- *WhoWrEP 92*
Van Patten, James Jeffers 1925- *WhoSSW 93, WhoWor 93*
Van Patten, Joyce Benignia *WhoAm 92*
Vanpatten, Robert M. 1945- *St&PR 93*
Van Patten, Vance Scott *Law&B 92*
Van Peebles, Mario *BioIn 17, MiSFD 9*
Van Peebles, Melvin 1932- *BioIn 17, MiSFD 9*
Van Pel, Aline 1948- *WhoScE 91-2*
VanPelt, Arnold Francis, Jr. 1924- *WhoSSW 93*
Van Pelt, Brad Allan 1951- *BiDAMSp 1989*
Van Pelt, Frances Evelyn 1937- *WhoAmW 93*
Van Pelt, J. 1946- *WhoScE 91-3*
Van Pelt, Jack Franklin 1938- *St&PR 93*
Van Pelt, Janet Ruth 1948- *WhoAmW 93*
Van Pelt, John Robert 1896-1991 *BioIn 17*
Van Pelt, Robert Irving 1931- *WhoWor 93*
van Pelt, Robert-Jan 1955- *ConAu 139*
Van Pelt, Thomas E. 1939- *St&PR 93*
Van Peski, Aart Cornelis Hendrik 1939- *WhoWor 93*
Van Peteghem, Carlos H.M. 1946- *WhoScE 91-2*
Van Philips, Theo Lucien 1937- *WhoWor 93*
Van Poole, Thomas Bennett 1921- *WhoAm 92*
Van Poppel, Todd *BioIn 17*
Van Poucke, L.C. 1937- *WhoScE 91-2*
Van Poznak, Alan 1927- *WhoE 93*
van Praag, Eric 1946- *WhoUN 92*
Van Praag, Herman Meir 1929- *WhoAm 92*
Vanpraet, G.J.M. 1933- *WhoScE 91-2*
Van Put, August Jan 1935- *WhoWor 93*
Vanquickenborne, Luc Georges 1938- *WhoScE 91-2*
Van Raalte, Albert *Baker 92*
van Raalte, John A. 1938- *WhoAm 92*
Van Raalte, Polly Ann 1951- *WhoE 93, WhoEmL 93*
Van Raaphorst, J.G. 1935- *WhoScE 91-3*
Van Raden, David Frederick 1949- *St&PR 93*
Van Ravenswaay, Charles *BioIn 17*
Van Reck, Jack 1941- *WhoScE 91-2*
Van Ree, Jan W. 1971- *WhoScE 91-3*
Van Reeken, Anton John 1938- *WhoWor 93*
Van Rees, Cornelius S. 1929- *WhoAm 92*
Van Reet, Gustaaf 1945- *WhoScE 91-2*
Van Reeth, George *BioIn 17*
Van Reeuwijk, L.P. 1941- *WhoScE 91-3*
Van Regenmortel, Marc Hubert Victor 1934- *WhoScE 91-2*
vanReken, Mary K. 1947- *WhoAmW 93, WhoSSW 93*
van Remoortere, Francois Petrus 1943- *WhoAm 92*
Van Rensselaer, Stephen 1764-1839 *HarEnMi*
Van Rensselaer, Stephen 1905- *WhoAm 92*
Van Renterghem, R.E.C. 1947- *WhoScE 91-2*
Van Riel, Michel Joannes 1948- *WhoWor 93*
Van Riet, Frank M. *Law&B 92*
Van Rijsbergen, Cornelis Joost *WhoScE 91-1*
Van Riper, Jeffrey L. 1956- *St&PR 93*
Van Riper, Paul Kent 1938- *WhoAm 92*
Van Riper, Paul P. *BioIn 17*
Van Riper, Paul Pritchard 1916- *WhoAm 92*
Van Riper, Robert Austin 1921- *WhoE 93*
Van Risseghem, Georges Leon Marie 1930- *WhoScE 91-2*
Van Rjndt, Philippe 1950- *ScF&FL 92*
van Roden, Donald 1924- *St&PR 93*
Van Roekel, Anthony F. 1938- *WhoAm 92*
Van Roijen, Jan Herman 1905-1991 *BioIn 17*
Van Roijen, Robert Dudley 1939- *St&PR 93*
Van Rompay, Paul V. 1937- *WhoScE 91-2*
Van Rompay, Paul Venantius 1937- *WhoWor 93*
Van Rompuy, Paul Frans 1940- *WhoWor 93*
van Roosbroeck, Willy Werner 1913- *WhoWor 93*
Van Roost, Christiaan 1957- *WhoScE 91-2*
Van Rooy, Anton(ius Maria Josephus) 1870-1932 *Baker 92*
van Rooy, Jean-Pierre 1934- *WhoAm 92*
Van Rooyen, Edward Van 1952- *St&PR 93*
Van Rooyen, Philip 1923- *St&PR 93*
Van Rooyen, Rene 1944- *WhoUN 92*
van Rosendaal, John Cornelius Gerard Mar 1962- *WhoE 93*
Van Rosmalen, Jan W.G. 1920- *WhoWor 93*
Van Rossum, G.M.J.M. 1952- *WhoScE 91-3*
Van Rossum, Gerard J. *WhoScE 91-3*
Van Royen, Oliver Henri Aurel 1930- *WhoWor 93*
van Runkle, Theadora *ConTFT 10*
van ryn, Ted Mattheus 1948- *WhoE 93*
Van Ryssel, Ernst 1948- *WhoScE 91-3*
Van Saarloos, Wim 1955- *WhoWor 93*
Van Sande, Marc Henry 1927- *WhoWor 93*
Van Sandick, Leonard Hendrik Willem 1933- *WhoWor 93*
Vansandt, James Albert 1951- *WhoSSW 93*
Van Sant, Gus *BioIn 17, MiSFD 9*
Van Sant, Gus 1952- *CurBio 92 [port], News 92 [port]*
VanSant, Joanne Frances 1924- *WhoAmW 93*
Van Sant, Robert M. 1922- *St&PR 93*
Van Sant, Robert William 1938- *St&PR 93, WhoAm 92, WhoSSW 93*
Van Sante, Frans Joseph 1921- *WhoScE 91-3*
Van Saun, Richard W. 1937- *St&PR 93*
Van Schaack, Eric 1931- *WhoAm 92*
Van Schaften, Andre 1940- *St&PR 93*
Van Schaick, Anthony Gerard 1945- *St&PR 93, WhoAm 92*
Vanschaick, Francis G. 1942- *St&PR 93*
Van Schaik, G. *WhoScE 91-3*
Van Schaik, Gerard 1930- *WhoWor 93*
Van Schaik, Robert J. 1927- *WhoUN 92*
Van Schendel, Michel 1929- *WhoCanL 92*
Van Schilfgaarde, Jan 1929- *WhoAm 92*
Van Schoik, Milton L. 1928- *St&PR 93*
Van Schoonenberg, Robert G. *Law&B 92*
Van Schoonenberg, Robert G. 1946- *St&PR 93, WhoAm 92, WhoEmL 93*
van Schooneveld, Cornelis Hendrik 1921- *WhoWor 93*
Van Schothorst, Michiel 1938- *WhoScE 91-4*
Van Schuyver, Connie Jo 1951- *WhoAmW 93*
Van Schyndel, Mitzi Dorton 1954- *WhoSSW 93*
Van Sciver, Warner 1939- *St&PR 93*
Van Scotter, Donald Eugene 1930- *WhoWrEP 92*
Van Scoyk, Mark Lynn *Law&B 92*
Van Scoyk, Susie Kosan 1953- *WhoAmW 93*
Van Scyoc, Sydney J. 1939- *ScF&FL 92*
Vanselow, Neal Arthur 1932- *WhoAm 92, WhoSSW 93*
Van Seters, John 1935- *ConAu 38NR, WhoAm 92, WhoWrEP 92*
Van Seters, Virginia Ann 1947- *WhoWor 93*
Van Shelton, Ricky 1952- *WhoAm 92*
Van Sickel, Edward Lincoln 1929- *St&PR 93*
Van Sickels, Martin J. 1942- *St&PR 93*
Van Sickle, Barbara Ann 1932- *WhoAmW 93*
Vansickle, Barbara Jean 1948- *WhoAmW 93*
Van Sickle, Bruce Marion 1917- *WhoAm 92*
Vansickle, Charles D. 1941- *St&PR 93*
Van Sickle, David Clark 1934- *WhoAm 92*
Van Sickle, Donald Ritchie 1932- *St&PR 93*
Van Sickle, John Babcock 1936- *WhoWrEP 92*
Van Sickle, Paul B. 1939- *St&PR 93*
Van Sickle, V.A. 1892- *ScF&FL 92*
Vansina, Leopold Servilus 1932- *WhoWor 93*
Van Sinderen, Alfred White 1924- *WhoAm 92*
Van Singel, Willard J. 1918- *St&PR 93*
Vansittart, Peter 1920- *ScF&FL 92, WhoAm 92*
Van Slingerlandt, William H. *Law&B 92*
Van Sloan, Edward 1882-1964 *BioIn 17*
Van Slobig, Robert Charles 1942- *St&PR 93*
Van Slooten, Ronald Henry Joseph 1937- *WhoE 93*
Vanslot, Lowell S. 1942- *St&PR 93*
van Sloten, Dirk Hendrick 1949- *WhoUN 92*
Van Sloun, Leon H. 1926- *St&PR 93*
Van Slyck, Nicholas 1922-1983 *Baker 92*
Van Slyke, Andrew James 1960- *WhoAm 92*
Van Slyke, Andy 1960- *News 92 [port]*
Van Slyke, Leonard DuBose, Jr. 1944- *WhoSSW 93, WhoWor 93*
Van Slyke, Richard Maurice 1937- *WhoE 93*
Van Soest, Louis J.M. 1947- *WhoScE 91-3*
Van Soest, Robert David 1927- *St&PR 93*
van Soest, Walter Maria Alfons Denis 1950- *WhoWor 93*
Van Son, Levinus George 1934- *WhoE 93*
Van Spanckeren, Kathryn 1945- *WhoWrEP 92*
Vansplinter, Michael Dennis 1939- *WhoE 93*
Van Staalduinen, C.J. *WhoScE 91-3*
Van Stavoren, William David 1936- *WhoAm 92*
Van Stee, Donn C. 1927- *St&PR 93*
Van Stee, Scott A. 1959- *St&PR 93*
Van Steekelenburg, N.A.M. 1941- *WhoScE 91-3*
Vansteelandt, R.J. *Law&B 92*
Vansteelandt, Rene J. 1938- *St&PR 93*
Van Steelant, Priscilla *BioIn 17*
Van Steenberge, Kevin Paul 1957- *St&PR 93*
Van Steenberge, Vickie 1928- *St&PR 93*
Van Steenbergen, Guido H.J. 1937- *WhoScE 91-2*
Vansteenberghe, Alice d1991 *BioIn 17*
Van Steenberghe, Daniel 1947- *WhoScE 91-2*
Van Steenburgh, Barbara Jean 1927- *WhoWrEP 92*
Van Steenkiste, Dwight P. 1951- *St&PR 93*
Vansteenkiste, Johan Filip 1957- *WhoWor 93*
Van Steenkiste, Julian Charles 1924- *St&PR 93*
Vansteenkiste, Sandra Patricia 1962- *WhoAmW 93*
Van Steensel-Moll, Henriette A. 1955- *WhoScE 91-3*
Van Steenwyk, Elizabeth (Ann) 1928- *ConAu 40NR*
Van Steirteghem, Andre 1940- *WhoScE 91-2*
Van Stekelenburg, Mark 1951- *St&PR 93*
Van Stockum, Hilda 1908- *DcAmChF 1960*
Vanstone, Amanda Eloise 1952- *WhoAsAP 91*
Van Stone, Jack 1930- *St&PR 93*
Van Straten, Clyde Kenneth 1935- *St&PR 93*
van Straten, Florence W(ilhelmina) 1913-1992 *ConAu 137*
van Stratum, Rob 1952- *WhoWor 93*
Vanstrom, Marilyn June 1924- *WhoAmW 93*
Vanstry, Robert Francis 1950- *St&PR 93*
van Swol, Noel Warren 1941- *WhoE 93, WhoWor 93*
Van Syckle, William 1942- *WhoIns 93*

van Tamelen, Eugene Earle 1925- WhoAm 92
Van Tassel, D. 1939- ScF&FL 92
Van Tassel, Gary Winthrop 1951- WhoE 93, WhoWor 93
Van Tassel, James H. BioIn 17
Van Tassel, James Henry 1929- WhoAm 92
Van Tassel, Kate AmWomPl
Van Tassel, Katrina 1921- WhoWrEP 92
Van Tassel, Kurt Detrick Law&B 92
Van Tassell, Robert E. 1935- St&PR 93
Van Tatenhove, James M. 1929- WhoAm 92
Vanterpool, Hugo Felix 1944- WhoWor 93
Van Thal, Herbert 1904-1983 ScF&FL 92
van't Hoff, Winfried C. J. 1928- WhoAm 92
Van Tieghem, David 1955- Baker 92
van Tienhoven, Ari 1922- WhoE 93
Van Til, William 1911- WhoAm 92
Van Toller, Steve WhoScE 91-1
Van Tomme, Emmanuel Rene Marie Jean 1964- WhoWor 93
Van Tongeren, Steven A. 1959- St&PR 93
Van Tongeren, Steven Petrus 1957- WhoWor 93
Van Toorn, Peter 1944- WhoCanL 92
Vantrappen, Gaston R.A. 1927- WhoScE 91-2
Vantrappen, Gaston Robert 1927- WhoWor 93
Van Triet, Adrianus J. 1926- WhoScE 91-3
Van't Riet, Klaas 1945- WhoWor 93
Van Trump, James Edmond 1943- WhoE 93
Van Trump, Jessalyn 1887-1939 SweetSg A
Van Trump, Joseph W. 1933- St&PR 93
Van Tunen, Arjen J. 1959- WhoScE 91-3
Van Tuyl, Jaap M. 1950- WhoScE 91-3
Van Tuyl, Kathryn Ursula Leach 1909- WhoAmW 93
Van Tuyl, Rosealtha ScF&FL 92
Van Tuyl, Zaara 1901-1989 ScF&FL 92
van Tuyll, Jaap G.H.C. 1945- WhoWor 93
Van't Veer, Frans 1929- WhoScE 91-2
Van Twembeke, Urbain Leon 1928- WhoScE 91-2
Van Uitert, LeGrand Gerard 1922- WhoAm 92
Van Ummersen, Claire Ann 1935- WhoAm 92, WhoAmW 93, WhoE 93
van Urk, J. Blan 1902- WhoAm 92
Van Vactor, David 1906- Baker 92
Van Vaerenbergh, Emmanuel 1949- WhoScE 91-2
Van Valen, Leigh Maiorana 1935- WhoAm 92
Van Valin, Clyde Emory 1929- WhoAm 92
Van Valkenburg, James Edward Law&B 92
Van Valkenburg, Mac Elwyn 1921- WhoAm 92
Van Valkenburgh, Faith AmWomPl
Van Valkenburgh, Holly 1936- WhoAmW 93
Van Varick, H.L. 1939- St&PR 93
Van Vechten, Carl 1880-1964 Baker 92
Van Vechten, Frederick Rust 1916-1991 BioIn 17
Van Veen, Frederick Thomas 1930- St&PR 93
Van Veen, Johannes A. 1949- WhoScE 91-3
Van Veghel, Lawrence Adrian 1947- WhoWrEP 92
Van Velde, Bram 1895-1981 BioIn 17
Van Velzer, Verna Jean 1929- WhoAmW 93
Van Vinkenroye du Waysaeck, Fedia Maurice Gilles 1932- WhoWor 93
Van Vleck, Jacob 1751-1831 Baker 92
Van Vleck, James 1930- St&PR 93, WhoAm 92
Van Vleck, Pamela Kay 1951- WhoAmW 93
Van Vleet, K. Troy 1952- St&PR 93
Van Vleet, Susan Ellen Bash 1946- WhoAmW 93
Van Vleet, W.B. 1924- St&PR 93
Van Vleet, William Benjamin 1924- WhoAm 92
Van Vliet, C.B. WhoScE 91-3
Van Vliet, Carolyne Marina 1929- WhoAm 92
Van Vliet, Claire 1933- WhoAm 92
Van Vloten-Doting, L. WhoScE 91-3
Van Vloten-Doting, L. 1942- WhoScE 91-3
Van Vogt, A.E. 1912- BioIn 17, ScF&FL 92
Van Vogt, Alfred Elton 1912- BioIn 17, WhoAm 92
Van Volkenburgh, Derek Law&B 92
Van Voorhis, Dale W. 1941- St&PR 93
Van Voorhis, Jane Leslie 1962- WhoAmW 93
Van Voorhis, John Albright 1939- St&PR 93
Van Voorhis, William M. 1949- St&PR 93
Van Vorst, Charles Brian 1943- WhoAm 92
Van Vranken, J. Frederick, Jr. 1935- St&PR 93
Van Vranken, John Frederick, Jr. 1935- WhoAm 92
Van Vranken, Michael H. 1940- St&PR 93
Van Vugt, Frits 1948- WhoScE 91-3
Van Vuure, Willem 1942- WhoScE 91-3
van Wachem, L.C. St&PR 93
Van Wachem, Lodewijk Christiaan 1931- WhoAm 92, WhoSSW 93, WhoWor 93
van Waegeningh, Hubert Gerlof 1935- WhoWor 93
Van Waes, J. WhoScE 91-2
Van Wagenen, Paul G. BioIn 17
Van Wagenen, Paul G. 1946- St&PR 93
Vanwagenen, Sterling MiSFD 9
Van Wageninge, Robert 1953- WhoE 93
Van Wageningen, Henry J. Law&B 92
Van Wagner, Bruce 1925- St&PR 93, WhoAm 92
Van Wagner, Ellen 1942- WhoAmW 93
Van Wagtendonk, Willem Johan 1910-1990 BioIn 17
Vanwalle, Dirk Michel 1947- WhoWor 93
Van Walleghen, Michael J(ospeh) 1938- WhoWrEP 92
Van Wambeke, Etienne J.G.L. 1947- WhoScE 91-2
Van Waning, Willem Ernst 1948- WhoWor 93
Van Wart, Alice 1948- ConAu 137
Van Weel, P.A. 1951- WhoScE 91-3
Van Weert, Gezinus 1933- WhoWor 93
van Weezendonk, Jaap Joris 1946- WhoWor 93
van Wel, Peter Willem 1946- St&PR 93
Van Went, J.L. 1942- WhoScE 91-3
Van Werkhooven, Anthony John 1945- St&PR 93
Van Wert, Ken BioIn 17
Van Wert, Paul H. 1920- St&PR 93
Van Westerhout, Nicola 1857-1898 Baker 92
van Wezel, Ru 1936- WhoWor 93
Van Wie, Virginia Putnam 1909- BiDAMSp 1989
Van Wijk, Nicolaas 1880-1941 BioIn 17
Van Wijngaarden, Marjolein WhoScE 91-3
Van Wijnsberghe, Johan E. Law&B 92
Van Winden, C.M.M. 1946- WhoScE 91-3
van Winden, Francesco Adrianus 1946- WhoWor 93
Van Wing, Joseph 1884-1979 IntDcAn
van Winkelen, Barbara WhoE 93
Vanwinkle, Cheryl Lyn Hamlin 1955- WhoAmW 93
Van Winkle, Edgar Walling 1913- WhoWor 93
Van Winkle, Joseph ScF&FL 92
Van Winkle, Monica F. 1892-1985 ScF&FL 92
Van Winkle, Neil Law&B 92
Van Winkle, Richard A. 1913- St&PR 93
Van Winkle, Robby BioIn 17
van Wissen, Gerardus Wilhelmus Johannes Maria 1941- WhoWor 93
Van Wittkamper, Gerry Law&B 92
Van Witzenburg, Willem 1938- WhoWor 93
Van Woerden, P. WhoScE 91-3
Van Woerkom, Dorothy O'Brien 1924- WhoWrEP 92
Van Woert, James Winston 1943- WhoE 93
Van Wormer, Laura Eleanor 1955- WhoWrEP 92
Vanwormhout, Marc C. 1933- WhoScE 91-2
Van Wyck, D. Law&B 92
Van Wyck, George Richard 1928- WhoAm 92
Van Wyck, Kenneth Paul Law&B 92
Van Wye, David Rodman 1947- WhoE 93
Van Wyk, Arnold Baker 92
Van Wyk, Brooke 1941- St&PR 93
Van Wyk, Helen 1930- WhoE 93
Van Wyk, James Lavern 1932- St&PR 93
Van Wyk, Judson John 1921- WhoAm 92
Van Wyk, Marinus 1909- St&PR 93
Van Wyk, Roger L. 1931- St&PR 93
Van Wylen, Gordon John 1920- WhoAm 92
Van Young, Oscar 1906- WhoAm 92
Van Yperen, Cathy 1952- St&PR 93
van Ypersele de Strihou, Charles 1933- WhoWor 93
Vanyur, John Martin 1956- WhoE 93
Van Zandt, Claudia Anne-Margaret 1952- WhoAmW 93
Van Zandt, J. Parker 1894-1990 BioIn 17
Van Zandt, Jeffrey R. 1942- St&PR 93
van Zandt, Jennie
See Van Zandt, Marie 1858-1919 Baker 92
Van Zandt, Lonnie Lee 1937- WhoAm 92
Van Zandt, Marie 1858-1919 Baker 92
Van Zandt, Roland 1918-1991 BioIn 17
Van Zandt, Tina Louise 1960- WhoE 93
Van Zandt, William Chamblee 1939- St&PR 93
Van Zandwijk, Nico 1944- WhoScE 91-3
Van Zant, Carlos Ray 1939- St&PR 93
Van Zant, Ronnie 1949-1977
See Lynyrd Skynyrd ConMus 9
Van Zante, Shirley Mae WhoAm 92
Van Zanten, Arnold 1912- St&PR 93
Van Zanten, Cornelie 1855-1946 Baker 92
Van Zanten, Frank Veldhuyzen 1932- WhoAm 92
Van Zeeland, Albert A. 1945- WhoScE 91-3
Van Zeggeren, W.A. 1931- WhoScE 91-3
Van Zele, Eric 1948- St&PR 93
van Zeller, Claude ScF&FL 92
Van Zelst, Theodore W. 1923- St&PR 93
Van Zelst, Theodore William 1923- WhoAm 92
Vanzetti, Bartolomeo 1888-1927 BioIn 17
Van Zeyl, John Joseph Law&B 92
Van Zijl, Cornelis Henricus W. 1925- WhoScE 91-3
Van Zijl, Deborah Gupton 1958- St&PR 93
Van Zijl, Willem Jacobus 1932- WhoWor 93
Van Zile, John R. Law&B 92
Van Zile, Philip Taylor, III 1945- WhoE 93
Vanzina, Carlo 1952- MiSFD 9
Vanzo, Alain 1928- OxDcOp
Van Zoeren, Charles Andrew 1931- St&PR 93
Van Zoeren, Joan Carol 1931- St&PR 93
Van Zoeren, John Burr 1926- St&PR 93
Van Zutphen, Lambertus Bert F.M. 1941- WhoWor 93
van Zuylen van Nyevelt, Emmanuel 1934- WhoWor 93
Van Zwieten, Pieter Adriaan 1937- WhoScE 91-3
van Zyl, Jacobus Lodewyk 1936- WhoAm 92
Van Zyle, Jon 1942- BioIn 17
Vapaatalo, Heikki Ilmari 1939- WhoScE 91-4
Vapaavuori, Elina Margareta 1948- WhoScE 91-4
Vapaavuori, Matti J. 1928- WhoScE 91-4
Vapaavuori, O. WhoScE 91-4
Vaporciyan, Harutun 1929- St&PR 93
Vappi, C. Vincent 1926- St&PR 93
Vaquero Nazabal, C. WhoScE 91-3
Vaquero Sanchez, Antonio 1938- WhoWor 93
Vara, Timothy J. Law&B 92
Varacalli, Joseph A. 1961- St&PR 93
Varadaraj, G. 1936- WhoAsAP 91
Varadi, Janos 1920- WhoScE 91-4
Varady, Andrew Stephen Law&B 92
Varady, Jozef 1939- WhoScE 91-4
Varady, Julia 1941- Baker 92, IntDcOp, OxDcOp
Varady, Tamas 1945- WhoScE 91-4
Varagic, Vladislav 1921- WhoScE 91-4
Varagona, Alan Joseph 1956- WhoSSW 93
Varalli, E.R. 1931- St&PR 93
Varallo, Deborah Garr 1952- WhoAmW 93
Varallyay, Gyorgy 1935- WhoScE 91-4
Varandas, Antonio Joaquim de Campos 1947- WhoScE 91-3, WhoWor 93
Varas, Barbara Guadalupe 1953- WhoE 93
Varbanov, Varban 1942- WhoScE 91-4
Varchmin, Thomas Edward 1947- WhoAm 92
Varcho, Raymond Andrew Law&B 92
Varda, Agnes 1926- WhoWor 93
Varda, Agnes 1928- MiSFD 9
Vardabasso, Arturo V. 1929- WhoScE 91-3
Vardaman, James K. 1861-1930 PolPar
Vardaman, James Kimble 1894-1972 BioIn 17
Vardan Vardapet 120-?-1271 OxDcByz
Vardaro, Joseph E. 1949- St&PR 93
Vardeman, Jan Michael 1936- St&PR 93
Vardeman, Robert E. 1947- ScF&FL 92
Vardi, Emanuel 1917- Baker 92
Vardon, James Lewes 1941- St&PR 93, WhoAm 92
Varduca, Aurel 1944- WhoScE 91-4
Vardy, Agnes Huszar 1951- WhoWrEP 92
Vardy, Alan Edward WhoScE 91-1
Vardy, Peter 1930- St&PR 93
Vare, Edwin H.
See Vare Brothers PolPar
Vare, George A.
See Vare Brothers PolPar
Vare, Glenna Collett 1903-1989 BioIn 17
Vare, William S.
See Vare Brothers PolPar
Vare Brothers PolPar
Varel, Joan Elizabeth 1947- WhoAmW 93
Varela, Frank J. Law&B 92
Varela, Jaime A. Law&B 92
Varela, Jose F. Law&B 92
Varela, Maria BioIn 17
Varella, Frank John 1950- WhoSSW 93
Varellas, Sandra Motte 1946- WhoAm 92, WhoAmW 93
Varenne, Andre Georges 1926- WhoScE 91-2, WhoWor 93
Vareschi, Susan Luigs 1951- WhoAmW 93
Varesco, Giambattista fl. 1775-1783 OxDcOp
Varese, Edgard (Victor Achille Charles) 1883-1965 Baker 92
Varesi, Elena Boccabadati 1854-1920 OxDcOp
Varesi, Felice 1813-1889 Baker 92, OxDcOp
Varesi, Gilda AmWomPl
Varet, Jacques L. 1944- WhoScE 91-2
Varet, Michael A. 1942- WhoE 93
Varey, Nicolas Calvert 1940- WhoScE 91-1
Varg, Paul Albert 1912- WhoAm 92
Varga, Dezso 1939- WhoScE 91-4
Varga, Emil 1921- WhoScE 91-4
Varga, Ferenc 1929- WhoScE 91-4
Varga, Frances Andrea Irma 1956- WhoAmW 93
Varga, Istvan 1933- WhoScE 91-4
Varga, Janos 1927- WhoWor 93
Varga, Janos 1928- WhoScE 91-4
Varga, Laszlo 1931- WhoScE 91-4
Varga, Louis Stephen, Jr. 1947- WhoSSW 93
Varga, Ludenia Elizabeth 1922- WhoAmW 93
Varga, Margit 1908- BioIn 17
Varga, Margit 1923- WhoScE 91-4
Varga, Mary Ann K. Law&B 92
Varga, Ovidiu 1913- Baker 92
Varga, Paul Mihail 1928- WhoScE 91-4
Varga, Thomas 1935- WhoScE 91-4, WhoWor 93
Varga, Tibor 1921- Baker 92
Vargaftig, Boris 1937- WhoScE 91-2
Vargas, Adolfo M. d1990 BioIn 17
Vargas, Azael DcCPCAm
Vargas, Eduardo 1944- St&PR 93, WhoAm 92, WhoWor 93
Vargas, Getulio 1883-1954 DcTwHis
Vargas, Hernan 1957- St&PR 93
Vargas, Joe Flores 1940- WhoSSW 93
Vargas, Josephine 1946- WhoE 93
Vargas, Laura Dennison 1945- WhoWrEP 92
Vargas, Luis de 1505-1557 BioIn 17
Vargas, Luis Fernandez 1912- WhoWor 93
Vargas, Manuel 1952- SpAmA
Vargas, Maria Josefina 1956- WhoAmW 93
Vargas, Pedro 1904-1989 Baker 92
Vargas, Pedro de BioIn 17
Vargas, Virgilio Barco BioIn 17
Vargas-Hernandez, Jose Guadalupe 1951- WhoWor 93
Vargas Llosa, Mario 1936- BioIn 17, MagSWL [port], SpAmA, WhoWor 93
Vargas Martinez, Ubaldo 1913- DcMexL
Vargas-Zapata, Ruben Antonio 1940- WhoWor 93
Vargess, Gabe Shawn Law&B 92
Vargha, Endre D. 1939- St&PR 93
Vargo, Deborah Jean Law&B 92
Vargo, George Francis, Jr. 1942- St&PR 93
Vargo, Katharine Sperko 1951- WhoSSW 93
Vargo, Ricky Craig 1954- WhoSSW 93
Vargo, Robert M. Law&B 92
Varhama, Timo Ilmari 1948- WhoWor 93
Varhol, James Andrew 1955- St&PR 93
Varholy, John Robert Law&B 92
Vari, George BioIn 17
Varia, Mahesh Amratlal 1943- WhoSSW 93
Varian, Hal Ronald 1947- WhoAm 92
Varian, John W. St&PR 93
Varilly, Joseph C. 1952- WhoWor 93
Varin, Edward C. H. 1957- St&PR 93
Varin, Roger Robert 1925- WhoSSW 93
Varju, Dezso 1932- WhoScE 91-3
Varju, Dezsoe 1932- WhoWor 93
Varkados, Nicholas G. 1933- WhoUN 92
Varkonyi, Bela 1878-1947 Baker 92
Varkonyi, Zoltan 1912-1979 DrEEuF
Varl, Bojan 1920- WhoScE 91-4
Varlamov, Alexander Egorovich 1801-1848 Baker 92
Varlamov, Vladimir Valentinovich 1957- WhoWor 93
Varley, Andrew 1934- St&PR 93
Varley, Herbert Paul 1931- WhoAm 92
Varley, John 1947- BioIn 17, ScF&FL 92
Varley, John Herbert 1947- WhoWrEP 92

Vaughn, Garold Forrest 1919- WhoSSW 93, WhoWor 93
Vaughn, Gerald E. 1942- St&PR 93
Vaughn, Hippo 1888-1966 BioIn 17
Vaughn, Howard F. 1928- St&PR 93
Vaughn, Jackie, III 1930- AfrAmBi [port]
Vaughn, James Eldon 1925- WhoSSW 93, WhoWor 93
Vaughn, James Lloyd 1934- WhoE 93
Vaughn, James Michael 1939- WhoWrEP 92
Vaughn, James T. 1925- WhoE 93
Vaughn, John Carroll 1948- WhoSSW 93
Vaughn, John Rolland 1938- WhoAm 92
Vaughn, John V. 1909- St&PR 93
Vaughn, John Vernon 1909- WhoAm 92, WhoWor 93
Vaughn, Karen Iversen 1944- WhoAm 92
Vaughn, Kenneth W. 1910-1991 BioIn 17
Vaughn, Lisa Dawn 1961- WhoWor 93
Vaughn, Mary M. 1941- St&PR 93
Vaughn, Maurice Samuel BioIn 17
Vaughn, Michael Edward Law&B 92
Vaughn, Michael Ladd 1946- WhoAm 92
Vaughn, Mo BioIn 17
Vaughn, Paul Wilbur, Jr. 1938- WhoSSW 93
Vaughn, Phoebe Juanita 1939- WhoWrEP 92
Vaughn, Richard Van W. 1929- St&PR 93
Vaughn, Robert 1932- BioIn 17, WhoAm 92
Vaughn, Robert Donald 1925- WhoWor 93
Vaughn, Robert Lockard 1922- WhoAm 92
Vaughn, Ronald H. 1936- St&PR 93
Vaughn, Rosella Harris 1934- WhoE 93
Vaughn, Rufus Mahlon 1924- WhoAm 92
Vaughn, Steve C. Law&B 92
Vaughn, Stuart F. 1935- St&PR 93
Vaughn, William H. 1935- St&PR 93
Vaughn, William John 1931- WhoSSW 93
Vaughn, William Preston 1933- WhoAm 92
Vaughn, William T. 1947- St&PR 93
Vaughn, William Weaver 1930- WhoAm 92
Vaughn-Carrington, Debra Miller 1951- WhoEmL 93
Vaught, Bette Jenne 1924- WhoAmW 93
Vaught, Darrel Mandel 1943- WhoSSW 93
Vaught, Donald Ray 1938- St&PR 93
Vaught, Dorothy B. 1939- WhoSSW 93
Vaught, Jeffry Lynn 1950- WhoE 93
Vaught, Kevin S. Law&B 92
Vaught, Lawrence Calvin, Jr. 1952- WhoSSW 93
Vaught, Wilma L. 1930- WhoAm 92
Vaul, Francis Michael 1957- WhoE 93
Vaupel, Michael Christian 1936- St&PR 93
Vaupel, Peter W. 1943- WhoScE 91-3
Vaupen, Burton 1930- WhoAm 92
Vause, Edwin Hamilton 1923- WhoAm 92
Vaussy, Pierre 1941- WhoScE 91-2
Vautin, William C. St&PR 93
Vautor, Thomas c. 1590- Baker 92
Vautour, Paul J. Law&B 92
Vautour, Roland Rene 1929- WhoAm 92
Vaux, Dora Louise 1922- WhoAmW 93, WhoWor 93
Vaux, Henry James 1912- WhoAm 92
Vaux, Richard 1940- WhoE 93
Vaux, Brougham and, Baron 1778-1868 BioIn 17
Vavala, Domenic Anthony 1925- WhoAm 92, WhoWor 93
Vavasour, Robert Shanley Law&B 92
Vavilov, Andrey Mikhailovitch 1936- WhoUN 92
Vavoudis, Arthur Plato 1959- WhoWrEP 92
Vavra, Otakar 1911- DrEEuF
Vavra, R.J. 1950- St&PR 93
Vavrin, Elizabeth Ann 1954- WhoAmW 93
Vavrin, Petr 1937- WhoScE 91-4
Vawter, Gordon Fuller 1923-1990 BioIn 17
Vawter, Robert Roy, Jr. 1943- WhoAm 92, WhoSSW 93
Vawter, William Snyder 1931- WhoWor 93
Vax, John Joseph 1929- St&PR 93
Vayle, Valerie ConAu 39NR
Vayrynen, Paavo Matti 1946- WhoWor 93
Vaysse, Nicole WhoScE 91-2
Vaz, Daniel E. 1951- St&PR 93
Vaz, Francisco 1945- WhoScE 91-3
Vaz, Joseph 1958- WhoE 93
Vaz, Mark Cotta ScF&FL 92
Vaz, Nuno Artur 1951- WhoWor 93
Vazdauteanu, Vlad F. 1920- WhoScE 91-4
Vazirani, Suresh Hassanand 1950- WhoWor 93
Vaziri, Fakhri Fay 1929- WhoE 93
Vazov, Janus 1927- DrEEuF
Vaz Portugal, Apolinario J.B.C. 1930- WhoScE 91-3
Vazquez, Alfonso J. 1939- WhoScE 91-3
Vazquez, Carlos Manuel, Jr. 1963- WhoSSW 93
Vazquez, Gilbert Falcon 1952- WhoAm 92
Vazquez, Hector I. d1992 NewYTBS 92 [port]
Vazquez, Jorge A. 1943- WhoUN 92
Vazquez, Jorge Adalberto 1886-1959 DcMexL
Vazquez, Jose Antonio 1936- WhoE 93
Vazquez, Louie 1934- WhoSSW 93
Vazquez, Mariza Law&B 92
Vazquez, Oscar 1950- WhoWor 93
Vazquez-Cuervo, Alfonso 1955- WhoSSW 93
Vazquez-Vaamonde, Alfonso J. 1939- WhoScE 91-3
Vazsonyi, Andrew 1916- WhoAm 92
Vazsonyi, Balint 1936- Baker 92
Vazza, Diane J. 1957- St&PR 93
Vazzana, Anthony 1922- Baker 92
Vazzano, Andrew Anthony 1948- St&PR 93
Veach, James Jeffers Law&B 92
Veach, James Lewis Law&B 92
Veach, Stephen Read 1943- WhoE 93
Veach, Wayne 1946- St&PR 93
Veaco, Kristina Law&B 92
Veal, Rex R. 1956- WhoEmL 93, WhoSSW 93
Veal, Steven L. 1958- St&PR 93
Veale, Angela M. 1948- WhoAmW 93
Veale, Bob 1935- BioIn 17
Veale, Erwin Olin 1930- St&PR 93
Veale, John Edmond 1954- WhoEmL 93, WhoWor 93
Veale, Tinkham, II 1914- WhoAm 92
Vearil, James Wilson 1955- WhoSSW 93
Veasey, Arthur H. 1949- St&PR 93
Veasey, Diane BioIn 17
Veasey, E. Norman 1933- St&PR 93
Veasey, Josephine 1930- Baker 92, OxDcOp
Veasey, W. Samuel 1961- St&PR 93
Veatch, John William 1923- WhoWor 93
Veatch, Julian Lamar, Jr. 1949- WhoSSW 93
Veatch, Kathleen A. 1948- St&PR 93
Veatch, Robert Marlin 1939- WhoAm 92
Veater, Lee Beth 1965- WhoSSW 93
Veazey, Carl R. 1927- St&PR 93
Veazey, John Hobson 1901- WhoSSW 93, WhoWor 93
Veazey, Mary Virginia 1943- WhoWrEP 92
Veazey, Patricia Lynn 1956- WhoAmW 93
Veazey-Watson, Chrystal L. Law&B 92
Veazie, Adella F. AmWomPl
Veber, Francis 1937- MiSFD 9
Veblen, Thomas Clayton 1929- WhoE 93, WhoWor 93
Veblen, Thorstein 1857-1929 BioIn 17, GayN, IntDcAn
Vecbastiks, Cynthia Susan Law&B 92
Vecchi, Horatio 1550?-1605 Baker 92
Vecchi, Orfeo c. 1550-1604? Baker 92
Vecchia, Eugene F. 1925- St&PR 93
Vecchiarelli, Panfilo Guido 1937- WhoE 93
Vecchierini, Francoise 1942- WhoScE 91-2
Vecchio, Anthony Joseph 1955- WhoAm 92
Vecchio, Robert Peter 1950- WhoAm 92
Vecchio Family 18th cent.-19th cent. BioIn 17
Vecchione, Alfred Thomas BioIn 17
Vecchione, John E. 1915- St&PR 93
Vecchione, Joseph John 1937- WhoAm 92
Vecci, Raymond Joseph 1943- WhoAm 92
Vecelli, Tiziano c. 1488-1576 BioIn 17
Vecellio, Leo 1915- St&PR 93
Vecellio, Leo Arthur, Jr. 1946- WhoAm 92
Vecht, Aron WhoScE 91-1
Vecker, Lawrence 1929- St&PR 93
Vecoli, Rudolph John 1927- WhoAm 92, WhoWrEP 92
Vecsey, George Spencer 1939- WhoAm 92
Vecsey, Jeno 1909-1966 Baker 92
Vecsey, Marian Edith Graham 1939- WhoAmW 93
Vedamuthu, Ebenezer Rajkumar 1932- WhoSSW 93
Vedder, Alexander Madison 1831-1870 BioIn 17
Vedder, Byron Charles 1910- WhoAm 92
Veder, Slava J. WhoAm 92
Vederman, Ron Keith 1950- WhoE 93
Vedernikov, Alexander 1927- Baker 92, OxDcOp
Vedra, Joseph John 1946- St&PR 93
Vedral, Joyce L. BioIn 17
Vedrenne, Gilbert WhoScE 91-2
Vedres, Istvan 1927- WhoScE 91-4
Vedrine, Jacques C.R. 1938- WhoScE 91-2
Vedros, Jamsel Joseph 1948- St&PR 93
Vedros, Julian Barry 1934- St&PR 93
Vedros, Neylan Anthony 1929- WhoAm 92
Vedung, Evert Oskar 1938- WhoWor 93
Vee, Tommy 1951- WhoEmL 93
Veech, Alex B., III 1949- St&PR 93
Veeck, Bill BioIn 17
Veeck, Mike BioIn 17
Veeck, Richard Irvin 1947- St&PR 93
Veeder, Nancy Walker 1937- WhoAmW 93
Veeder, William 1940- ScF&FL 92
Veelenturf, John 1928- St&PR 93
Veen, Egbert 1954- WhoWor 93
Veen, John P. 1928- St&PR 93
Veen, W.J. WhoScE 91-3
Veenker, Claude Harold 1919- WhoAm 92
Veenstra, F.A. 1948- WhoScE 91-3
Veenstra, Mark Allen 1956- WhoSSW 93
Veerhoff, Carlos 1926- Baker 92
Veerjee, Rudy 1958- St&PR 93
Veerkamp, Mark A. 1957- St&PR 93
Veerkamp, Paul Jan 1959- WhoWor 93
Vega, Ana Lydia 1946- SpAmA
Vega, Angela M. 1936- WhoUN 92
Vega, Antonio M. 1959- St&PR 93
Vega, Aurelio de la 1925- Baker 92
Vega, Benjamin Urbizo 1916- WhoWor 93
Vega, Beth Susan 1950- WhoAmW 93
Vega, Bridgette Law&B 92
Vega, Carlos 1898-1966 Baker 92
Vega, Ed BioIn 17
Vega, Ed 1936- HispAmA [port]
Vega, Edward J. 1947- St&PR 93
Vega, Garcilaso de la 1539-1616 BioIn 17
Vega, Isela MiSFD 9
Vega, J. William 1931- WhoAm 92
Vega, Jose Luis 1948- SpAmA
Vega, Julio de la 1924- SpAmA
Vega, Marta Moreno BioIn 17
Vega, Marylois Purdy 1914- WhoAm 92
Vega, Milo C. St&PR 93
Vega, Suzanne BioIn 17
Vega, Suzanne 1960- Baker 92
Vega Carpio, Lope de 1562-1635 MagSWL [port]
Vegega, Carlos S. 1921- WhoUN 92
Vegeto, Antonio 1928- WhoScE 91-3
Vegetti, Ernesto ScF&FL 92
Vegezzi Ruscalla, Giovenale 1799-1884 IntDcAn
Veggeberg, Kurt William 1953- WhoSSW 93
Vegh, Sandor (Alexandre) 1912- Baker 92
Vegliante, Robert A. Law&B 92
Vegotsky, Allen 1931- WhoSSW 93
VeHaun, Marshall Jerry 1943- WhoSSW 93
Vehh, Gabriel B. St&PR 93
Vehlewald, Steven John 1956- St&PR 93
Veidenheimer, Malcolm Charles 1928- WhoAm 92
Veidt, Conrad 1893-1943 IntDcF 2-3 [port]
Veiga, Carlos Alberto Wahnon de Carvalho WhoWor 93
Veiga, Carlos Alberto Wahnon de Carvalho 1950- WhoAfr
Veiga Simao, J. WhoScE 91-3
Veigel, Jon Michael 1938- WhoSSW 93
Veigelt, Lori Ann 1966- WhoAmW 93
Veihmeyer, Carol Anne 1957- WhoAmW 93
Veijalainen, Jari Antti 1954- WhoWor 93
Veil, Fred W. Law&B 92
Veil, Simone 1927- BioIn 17
Veillette, Michael R. Law&B 92
Veillette, Robert E. Law&B 92
Veilleux, Gerard 1942- WhoAm 92, WhoE 93
Veilleux, Kimberley Anne 1958- WhoE 93
Veilleux, Patricia Law&B 92
Veilleux, Ronald B. 1941- St&PR 93
Veinott, Cyril George 1905- WhoAm 92
Veinus, Abraham 1916- Baker 92
Veira, Stanford Maurice 1915- WhoSSW 93
Veistola, Jukka Pellervo 1946- WhoWor 93
Veisz, Otto Balint 1955- WhoScE 91-4
Veit, Bruce Clinton 1942- WhoSSW 93
Veit, Fritz 1907- WhoAm 92, WhoWor 93
Veit, Herman C. 1934- St&PR 93
Veit, Wenzel Heinrich 1806-1864 Baker 92
Veit, Werner 1929- St&PR 93, WhoAm 92
Veit, William R. 1941- St&PR 93
Veitch, Boyer Lewis 1930- St&PR 93, WhoE 93, WhoWor 93
Veitch, Patrick Lee 1944- WhoWor 93
Veitch, Stephen William 1927- WhoAm 92
Veitenheimer, Michael Joseph 1956- St&PR 93
Veith, Edwin Thomas 1931- WhoAm 92
Veith, Ilza 1915- WhoAm 92
Veith, Mary Roth 1931- WhoAmW 93
Veith, Michael 1944- WhoWor 93
Veith, Richard St&PR 93
Veith, Richard Lee 1940- WhoAm 92
Veitia, D.J. 1943- St&PR 93
Veitz, Mary Frances 1941- WhoAmW 93
Veizer, Jan 1941- WhoAm 92, WhoScE 91-3
Vejar, Mike MiSFD 9
Vejtasa, S.W. 1914- BioIn 17
Vejtasa, Stanley Winfield 1914- BioIn 17
Vejvanovsky, Pavel Josef c. 1633-1693 Baker 92
Vekas, Mary Kelly 1961- St&PR 93
Vekeny, Henrik 1927- WhoScE 91-4
Vekert, Charles Thomas 1948- WhoEmL 93
Vekony, Edward D. 1931- St&PR 93
Vela, Arqueles 1899- DcMexL
Vela, Filemon B. 1935- HispAmA, WhoSSW 93
Vela, Lloyd A. 1933- St&PR 93
Vela, Pamela Leonel 1967- WhoAmW 93
Velarde, Guillermo 1928- WhoScE 91-3
Velarde, Manuel Garcia 1941- WhoScE 91-3, WhoWor 93
Velardo, Joseph Thomas 1923- WhoAm 92, WhoWor 93
Velasco, Alberto 1946- WhoWor 93
Velasco, Antonio Palomino de Castro 1655-1726 BioIn 17
Velasco, J.A. 1954- St&PR 93
Velasco, Joseph Eugene 1931- WhoSSW 93
Velasco, Kathy Lynn 1956- WhoWrEP 92
Velasco, Raymond L. ScF&FL 92
Velasco, Victor Ramon 1952- WhoWor 93
Velasco-Llanos, Santiago 1915- Baker 92
Velasco Mackenzie, Jorge 1949- SpAmA
Velasco Maidana, Jose Maria 1899- Baker 92
Velasco-Mills, John Anthony 1945- WhoE 93
Velasco Negueruela, Arturo 1944- WhoWor 93
Velasquez, Ana Maria 1947- WhoWor 93
Velasquez, Andrea Lee 1960- WhoSSW 93
Velasquez, Osvaldo 1920- WhoUN 92
Velasquez, Ricardo Elias 1943- WhoWor 93
Velasquez, Susan Margaret 1946- WhoAmW 93
Velasquez Perez, Jose R. 1949- WhoWor 93
Velasquez-Trevino, Gloria 1949- DcLB 122 [port]
Velastegui, Jose Ramiro 1943- WhoWor 93
Velayati, Ali Akbar 1945- WhoWor 93
Velayo, Alfred Allan 1948- WhoWor 93
Velazquez, Anabel 1958- WhoAmW 93
Velazquez, Diego 1599-1660 BioIn 17
Velazquez, Diego Rodriguez de Silva fl. 17th cent.- DcAmChF 1960
Velazquez, Fidel 1900- DcCPCAm
Velazquez, Higinio 1926- Baker 92
Velazquez, Nydia WhoAmW 93
Velazquez, Nydia Margarita 1953- NotHsAW 93 [port]
Velcek, Damir 1944- WhoE 93
Velcev, Ilja 1947- DrEEuF
Velchev, Velcho Ivanov 1928- WhoScE 91-4
Velde, Bram van 1895-1981 BioIn 17
Velde, John Ernest, Jr. 1917- WhoAm 92, WhoWor 93
Velde, Vivian Vande ScF&FL 92
Veldeman, R. WhoScE 91-2
Velder, Eli 1925- WhoE 93
Veldkamp, Gerald W. 1937- St&PR 93
Veldman, Donald John 1931- WhoAm 92
Velella, Benjamin J. Law&B 92
Veler, Richard P. 1936- ScF&FL 92
Veley, Charles 1943- ScF&FL 92
Veley, Hugh J. 1926- St&PR 93
Velez, Deborah Aguiar- BioIn 17
Velez, Eileen McLellan de 1955- WhoAmW 93
Velez, George Law&B 92
Velez, Glen BioIn 17
Velez, Lisa 1967?- NotHsAW 93
Velez, Lupe 1908-1944 HispAmA, QDrFCA 92 [port]
Velez, Lupe 1909-1944 BioIn 17
Velez, Miguel 1949- WhoE 93
Velez Munoz, Ricardo WhoScE 91-3
Velgakis, Michael John 1948- WhoWor 93
Velgouse, Michael 1940- St&PR 93
Velicer, Leland Frank 1939- WhoAm 92
Velick, Sidney Frederick 1913- WhoAm 92
Velickovic, Gmitar 1921- WhoScE 91-4
Velie, Lester 1907- WhoAm 92
Veligdan, Robert George 1949- WhoE 93
Velimirovic, Milos 1922- Baker 92
Velimirovic, Milos M. 1922- WhoAm 92
Velimirovic, Zdravko 1930- DrEEuF
Velinov, Ivan WhoScE 91-4

Veliotes, Nicholas Alexander 1928- *WhoAm 92*
Velis, Andrea *BioIn 17*
Veljkovic, Branko 1925- *WhoScE 91-4*
Veljkovic, Veljko 1947- *WhoScE 91-4*
Velk, Robert James 1938- *WhoWor 93*
Vella, Charles 1930- *WhoWor 93*
Vella, Charles V. 1930- *WhoUN 92*
Velle, Weiert 1925- *WhoScE 91-4*
Velle, Weiert Martin 1925- *WhoWor 93*
Vellekoop, Pieter 1947- *WhoWor 93*
Vellenga, Kathleen Osborne 1938- *WhoAmW 93*
Velling, Pirkko Marjatta 1949- *WhoScE 91-4*
Vellis, Clark *Law&B 92*
Velluti, Giovanni Battista 1780-1861 *OxDcOp*
Velluti, Giovanni Battista 1781-1861 *Baker 92*
Velmans, Loet Abraham 1923- *WhoAm 92*
Velona, Franco *WhoScE 91-3*
Veloso, Alberto S. 1929- *WhoAsAP 91*
Veloso, Caetano *NewYTBS 92 [port]*
Veloso, Jacinto Soares 1937- *WhoAfr*
Velotta, Michael J. *Law&B 92*
Velten, Carl 1862-c. 1935 *IntDcAn*
Velten, Kathleen Ann 1950- *WhoWrEP 92*
Veltman, C.A. 1929- *St&PR 93*
Veltman, Warren A. *St&PR 93*
Veltmann, Christopher P. 1954- *St&PR 93*
Veltze, Michel Victor 1939- *WhoUN 92*
Velvelettes *SoulM*
Velz, John William 1930- *WhoAm 92, WhoSSW 93*
Velzel, Christiaan Hendrik Frans 1938- *WhoWor 93*
Velzy, Charles O. 1930- *WhoAm 92*
Velzy, Richard James 1931- *WhoSSW 93*
Ven, Victor Linovich 1944- *WhoWor 93*
Vena, Dennis J. *Law&B 92*
Vena, H. Dante 1930- *WhoE 93*
Venable, Charles H. 1932- *St&PR 93, WhoIns 93*
Venable, Phillip W. *St&PR 93*
Venables, Hubert d1980 *ScF&FL 92*
Venables, John A. *WhoScE 91-1*
Venables, John Anthony 1936- *WhoWor 93*
Venables, John D. 1963- *St&PR 93*
Venables, Joseph *BioIn 17*
Venables, Peter Henry *WhoScE 91-1*
Venables, R.K. *WhoScE 91-1*
Venables, Thomas Russell 1955- *St&PR 93*
Venaleck, Howard Joseph 1940- *St&PR 93*
Vencil, Cornelia C. *AmWomPl*
Vendela *BioIn 17*
Vendeland, Gail A. *Law&B 92*
Venderbos, D.J. 1941- *WhoScE 91-3*
Venderhoof, Lina May 1938- *St&PR 93*
Vendetti, Randall Peter 1953- *WhoE 93*
Vendeuvre, Jean-Luc *WhoScE 91-2*
Venditto, James Joseph 1951- *WhoSSW 93*
Vendler, Helen Hennessy *BioIn 17*
Vendler, Helen Hennessy 1933- *WhoAm 92, WhoWrEP 92*
Vendrig, J.C. 1929- *WhoScE 91-2*
Venegas, Daniel *HispAmA*
Venegas, Emilio J. 1928- *St&PR 93*
Venegas de Henestrosa, Luis c. 1510-c. 1557 *Baker 92*
Veneman, Ann M. 1949- *WhoAmW 93*
Veneman, Dirk J. *Law&B 92*
Veneman, Gerard E. 1920- *St&PR 93*
Veneman, Gerard Earl 1920- *WhoAm 92*
Venerable Bede 673-735 *BioIn 17*
Veness, Tim *BioIn 17*
Venet, Louis d1992 *NewYTBS 92*
Venet, Louis 1914-1992 *BioIn 17*
Venet, Michelle *WhoWrEP 92*
Venetiaan, Roland R. *WhoWor 93*
Venetianer, Aniko 1941- *WhoScE 91-4*
Venetianer, Stephen *Law&B 92*
Venetis, Nicholas G. 1950- *St&PR 93*
Veneto, A. Joseph 1941- *WhoE 93*
Venetsanopoulos, Anastasios Nicolaos 1941- *WhoAm 92*
Venezia, Joyce Ann 1960- *WhoAmW 93*
Venezia, Morris *St&PR 93*
Veneziani, Bruno 1941- *WhoWor 93*
Veneziano, Patricia Joan Morse 1931- *WhoAmW 93*
Venezky, Richard Lawrence 1938- *WhoAm 92, WhoWrEP 92*
Vengen, Frances d1990 *BioIn 17*
Vengerov, Vladimir 1920- *DrEEuF*
Vengerova, Isabelle 1877-1956 *Baker 92*
Vengren, Laurette Y. *St&PR 93*
Vengren, Robert W. 1951- *St&PR 93*
Vengren, Walter J. 1931- *St&PR 93*
Veniaminov, I.E. 1797-1879 *IntDcAn*
Venice, Frank Paul 1940- *St&PR 93*
Venick, Robert B. 1947- *St&PR 93*
Venick, Robert Benjamin *WhoAm 92*
Venick, Shelley J. *Law&B 92*
Veninga, James Frank 1944- *WhoWrEP 92*
Veninga, Louise Ann 1948- *WhoAmW 93, WhoEmL 93, WhoWor 93*
Veninga, Robert Louis 1941- *WhoWrEP 92*
Venino, Thomas M. 1928- *St&PR 93*
Venishnick, Joseph Karel *Law&B 92*
Venison, Alfred *ConAu 40NR*
Venissat, Wade Louis, Jr. 1944- *WhoSSW 93*
Venit, Mark Louis 1948- *WhoE 93*
Venitt, Stanley 1939- *WhoScE 91-1*
Veniukov, Mikhail Ivanovich 1832-1901 *BioIn 17*
Venizelos, Eleutherios 1864-1936 *DcTwHis*
Venkata, Subrahmanyam Saraswati 1942- *WhoAm 92*
Venkataraman, Balakrishnan 1945- *St&PR 93*
Venkataraman, Krishnaswamy 1935- *WhoUN 92, WhoWor 93*
Venkataraman, Ramaswamy 1910- *WhoAsAP 91, WhoWor 93*
Venkataramanayya, Iyyanki 1890-1979 *BioIn 17*
Venkatesan, P.R.S. 1950- *WhoAsAP 91*
Venkatesan, Sharon Lynne 1946- *WhoE 93*
Venn, George Andrew 1943- *WhoWrEP 92*
Venn, John Jeffrey 1949- *WhoSSW 93*
Vennamo, Pekka 1944- *WhoWor 93*
Vennat, Michel 1941- *WhoAm 92, WhoE 93*
Venne, Pierrette 1945- *WhoAmW 93*
Venne, Vernon F. *Law&B 92*
Vennel, Charles Reed 1933- *St&PR 93*
Vennemann, Jerome A. *Law&B 92*
Venner, George A. 1929- *St&PR 93*
Venning, Michael Charles 1948- *WhoWor 93*
Vennings, Hugh 1905-1984 *ScF&FL 92*
Vennstrom, Bjorn R. 1948- *WhoScE 91-4, WhoWor 93*
Venokur, Sherri *Law&B 92*
Venolia, Janet 1928- *WhoAmW 93*
Venora, Daniel P. *Law&B 92*
Venrick, Naomi B. 1938- *St&PR 93*
Vensel, Clarence R. 1939- *St&PR 93*
Vent, Richard H. 1941- *St&PR 93*
Ventantonio, James B. *Law&B 92*
Venter, Josiah B. 1945- *St&PR 93*
Venter, Petrus Frans 1954- *WhoWor 93*
Venters, Archie *ScF&FL 92*
Venters, Carl Vernon, Jr. 1933- *WhoAm 92*
Ventimiglia, Katharine Jane Garver 1949- *WhoAmW 93*
Ventline, Joseph S. 1944- *St&PR 93*
Vento, Bruce F. 1940- *CngDr 91*
Vento, Bruce Frank 1940- *WhoAm 92*
Vento, Ivo de 1544-1575 *Baker 92*
Vento, Richard Patrick 1948- *St&PR 93*
Ventola, Dean Samuel 1958- *WhoE 93*
Ventosa, Antonio 1954- *WhoWor 93*
Ventour, Michelle Marie 1954- *WhoAmW 93*
Ventre, Francis Thomas 1937- *WhoAm 92*
Ventre, John, Jr. 1914- *St&PR 93*
Ventre, Martin A. 1945- *St&PR 93*
Ventrella, Joseph A. 1948- *St&PR 93*
Ventres, Judith Martin 1943- *WhoWor 93*
Ventres, Romeo J. 1924- *St&PR 93*
Ventres, Romeo John 1924- *WhoAm 92, WhoE 93*
Ventresca, Louis N. 1944- *St&PR 93*
Ventress, William T., Jr. 1956- *St&PR 93*
Ventriglia, P. Francesco 1942- *WhoWor 93*
Ventrone, Arthur R. 1947- *St&PR 93*
Ventrone, Giuseppe 1927- *WhoScE 91-3*
Ventrudo, Kevin James 1959- *WhoAm 92*
Ventry, Catherine Valerie 1949- *WhoAmW 93, WhoE 93, WhoWor 93*
Ventry, Paul Guerin 1934- *WhoE 93, WhoWor 93*
Ventsov, Yurij Georgievich 1963- *WhoWor 93*
Ventura, Anthony F. 1927- *WhoIns 93*
Ventura, Anthony P. 1927- *WhoE 93*
Ventura, Bruce *Law&B 92*
Ventura, Carol L. *Law&B 92*
Ventura, Charlie d1992 *NewYTBS 92*
Ventura, Charlie 1916-1992 *BioIn 17*
Ventura, Jules C. 1925- *St&PR 93*
Ventura, Michael *MiSFD 9*
Ventura, Piero *BioIn 17*
Ventura, Piero (Luigi) 1937- *ConAu 39NR, MajAI [port]*
Ventura, Ray(mond) 1908-1979 *Baker 92*
Ventura, Robin *BioIn 17*
Ventura, Salvatore *BioIn 17*
Venturi, Robert *BioIn 17*
Venturi, Robert 1925- *WhoAm 92, WhoE 93*
Venturini, Martin John 1948- *St&PR 93*
Venturo, Betty Lou *ScF&FL 92*
Venuti, Dennis P. *Law&B 92*
Venuti, Dennis P. 1943- *St&PR 93*
Venuti, "Joe" 1898-1978 *Baker 92*
Venuti, Lawrence M. 1953- *WhoWrEP 92*
Venuti, Michael H. 1940- *St&PR 93*
Venuti, Steven 1956- *St&PR 93*
Venuto, Kenneth Joseph 1952- *WhoSSW 93*
Venuto, Michael Francis 1946- *WhoE 93*
Venuto, T. 1954- *St&PR 93*
Venza, Jac 1926- *WhoAm 92*
Venzano, Luigi 1814-1878 *Baker 92*
Veon, Dorothy Helene 1924- *WhoAmW 93, WhoWor 93*
Veon, Gregory Richard 1952- *WhoAm 92*
Vepraskas, Nancy Murphy 1950- *WhoAmW 93*
Veprik, Alexander (Moiseievich) 1899-1958 *Baker 92*
Veprintsev, Boris N. 1928-1990 *BioIn 17*
Ver, Antonio Agbayani, Jr. 1959- *WhoWor 93*
Vera, Agustin 1889-1946 *DcMexL*
Vera, Gerardo *MiSFD 9*
Vera, Onelia *Law&B 92*
Vera, Pedro Jorge 1914- *SpAmA*
Vera, Roslyn 1932- *WhoAmW 93*
Veraart, J.J.M. *WhoScE 91-3*
Verachtert, Hubert 1932- *WhoScE 91-2*
Veracini, Antonio 1659-1733 *Baker 92*
Veracini, Francesco Maria 1690-1768 *Baker 92*
Vera Garcia, Rafael 1939- *WhoWor 93*
Verage, Thomas Joseph 1941- *St&PR 93*
Veraguth, Peter Conradin 1924- *WhoWor 93*
Veraldi, Lewis *BioIn 17*
Verances, Senen Joel Afinidad 1955- *WhoWor 93*
Verano, Anthony Frank 1931- *WhoAm 92*
Verano-Yap, Lorna L. 1951- *WhoAsAP 91*
Verardi, Peter Louis 1945- *St&PR 93*
Veraverbeke, Noel Daniel Cornelius 1946- *WhoWor 93*
Verazi, Mattia c. 1725-1794 *OxDcOp*
Verb, M. L. *ConAu 136*
Verba, Sidney 1932- *WhoAm 92, WhoE 93*
Ver Becke, W. Edwin 1913- *WhoWrEP 92*
Verbeeck, Franki Arthur 1959- *WhoWor 93*
Verbeke, Karen Lynn 1958- *WhoAmW 93*
Verbelen, Robert Jan 1911-1990 *BioIn 17*
Verberk, W.H.J. *WhoScE 91-3*
Verbesselt, August 1919- *Baker 92*
Verbeure, Andre Frans Maria 1940- *WhoScE 91-2*
Verbeure, Frans Etienne 1942- *WhoScE 91-2*
Verbick, Louis A. 1942- *St&PR 93*
Verbist, F. *WhoScE 91-2*
Verbitsky, Bernardo 1907-1979 *SpAmA*
Verbofsky, Howard I. *Law&B 92*
Verboom, Gerrit Klaas 1941- *WhoWor 93*
Verboon, Hans 1951- *St&PR 93*
Verbrugge, Betty Lou 1927- *WhoWor 93*
Verbrugge, Jean-Claude C. 1945- *WhoScE 91-2*
Verbruggen, Renaat William 1960- *WhoWor 93*
Verbrugghen, Henri 1873-1934 *Baker 92*
Verbryke, Louis Eugene 1926- *St&PR 93*
Verbunt, F. *WhoScE 91-3*
Verburg, Edwin Arnold 1945- *WhoE 93, WhoWor 93*
Verby, Jane Crawford 1923- *WhoWrEP 92*
Vercaemer, Claude *WhoScE 91-1*
Vercauteren, Guy Alice 1946- *WhoWor 93*
Vercauteren, Michel E.M. 1937- *WhoScE 91-2*
Verciglio, Tina Maria 1955- *WhoAmW 93*
Vercingetorix dc. 45BC *HarEnMi*
Vercoe, Barry 1937- *Baker 92*
Vercoe, Elizabeth 1941- *Baker 92*
Vercollone, Richard Walter *Law&B 92*
Vercollone, Richard Walter 1947- *St&PR 93*
Vercors 1902-1991 *AnObit 1991, BioIn 17, ScF&FL 92*
Vercueil, Jacques 1941- *WhoUN 92*
Vercz, Carol Ann 1946- *WhoWrEP 92*
Verdaguer, Jacinto 1845-1902 *BioIn 17*
Verde, Campo *ScF&FL 92*
Verdeaux *WhoScE 91-2*
Verdecia-Arza, Carlos Enrique *Law&B 92*
Verdejo, Joseph J. 1943- *St&PR 93*
Verdelot, Philippe c. 1470-1552? *Baker 92*
Verdenius, Jacob Geert 1934- *WhoScE 91-4*
Verderber, Joseph Anthony 1938- *WhoAm 92*
Verdesca, Arthur Salvatore 1930- *WhoE 93*
Verdeyen, Guido 1938- *WhoWor 93*
Verdi, Alfred Joseph *Law&B 92*
Verdi, Giuseppe 1813-1901 *BioIn 17, IntDcOp [port], OxDcOp*
Verdi, Giuseppe (Fortunino Francesco) 1813-1901 *Baker 92*
Verdi, Nejat Hasan 1913- *WhoWor 93*
Verdi, Philip Paul 1940- *WhoAm 92*
Verdi, Robert William 1946- *WhoAm 92*
Verdier, G.P.-J. 1943- *WhoScE 91-2*
Verdier, Peter Howard 1931- *WhoE 93*
Verdier, Philippe Maurice 1912- *WhoAm 92*
Verdina, Ben J. *St&PR 93*
Verdon, Dorothy *ConAu 40NR*
Verdon, Gwen 1925- *WhoAm 92*
Verdon, John Joseph, Jr. 1939- *WhoE 93*
Verdon, Joseph Michael 1941- *WhoE 93*
Verdon, William P. *Law&B 92*
Verdonck, Cornelis 1563-1625 *Baker 92*
Verdone, Carlo 1950- *MiSFD 9*
Verdone, Mario 1917- *WhoWor 93*
Verdonk, George Wessel 1946- *WhoWor 93*
Verdonk, Rene Emmeric Constance 1946- *WhoScE 91-2*
Verdoorn, Robert J. 1934- *WhoIns 93*
Verdoorn, Robert James 1934- *St&PR 93*
Verdu, Jacques 1942- *WhoScE 91-2*
Verdugo Alonso, Miguel Angel 1954- *WhoWor 93*
Verduin, Claire Leone 1932- *WhoAmW 93, WhoWor 93*
Verduin, Jacob 1913- *WhoAm 92*
Verduin, Nicholas 1931- *St&PR 93*
Vere, Clementine Duchene de 1864-1954 *Baker 92*
Vere, Cora Eliza 1919- *WhoAmW 93, WhoWrEP 92*
Vere, V.C. de *ScF&FL 92*
Vereb, Michael Joseph 1931- *WhoE 93*
Verebey, Karl Geza 1938- *WhoE 93*
Vered, Ilana 1939- *Baker 92*
Vered, Ruth 1940- *WhoAmW 93*
Vereecken, J. 1942- *WhoScE 91-2*
Vereen, Barbara B. 1938- *St&PR 93*
Vereen, Ben 1946- *ConBlB 4 [port], WhoAm 92*
Vereen, Ben(jamin Augustus) 1946- *Baker 92*
Vereen, D.G. 1939- *St&PR 93*
Vereen, Eugene M. 1920- *St&PR 93*
Vereen, Harvey Bunn 1945- *St&PR 93*
Vereen, Robert Charles 1924- *WhoAm 92*
Vereen, William Coachman, Jr. 1913- *WhoAm 92*
Vereen, William Jerome 1940- *St&PR 93, WhoAm 92, WhoWor 93*
Vereerstraeten, P.J.C. 1932- *WhoScE 91-2*
Vere-Hodge, Conrad *ScF&FL 92*
Vereketis, Constantin Kimon 1908- *WhoWor 93*
Verelst, Gilbert E. 1946- *WhoWor 93*
Veremans, Renaat 1894-1969 *Baker 92*
Veres, Alojz 1930- *WhoScE 91-4*
Veres, Arpad 1926- *WhoScE 91-4*
Veress, Laszlo 1928- *WhoScE 91-4*
Veress, Sandor 1907- *Baker 92*
Veretennikov, Alexander 1953- *WhoWor 93*
Veretti, Antonio 1900-1978 *Baker 92*
Verevka, Grigori 1895-1964 *Baker 92*
Verevkina, Antonina Nikolaevna *BioIn 17*
Verey, David 1950- *WhoWor 93*
Vergados, J.D. 1937- *WhoScE 91-3*
Vergados, John Ioannis Demetrios 1937- *WhoWor 93*
Vergakis, Ron 1948- *St&PR 93*
Vergamini, Thomas P. *Law&B 92*
Vergaretti, Cecelia *Law&B 92*
Vergari, Edward Louis 1947- *St&PR 93*
Verga Sheggi, Annamaria 1929- *WhoWor 93*
Vergason, E. Michael *BioIn 17*
Vergau, Hans-Joachim 1935- *WhoUN 92*
Verge, George David 1942- *St&PR 93*
Verge, Pierre 1936- *WhoAm 92*
Verge, Roger 1930- *BioIn 17*
Verge, S. James 1951- *St&PR 93*
Verge, William John 1934- *St&PR 93*
Verger, Fernand 1929- *WhoScE 91-2*
Verger, Morris David 1915- *WhoAm 92*
Verger, Robert 1944- *WhoScE 91-2*
Vergeront, Susan Bowers 1945- *WhoAmW 93*
Verges, Marianne Murphree 1939- *WhoAmW 93*
Vergets, Paul *Law&B 92*
Vergez, Johnny 1906-1991 *BioIn 17*
Vergil *BioIn 17, ClMLC 9, OxDcByz*
Vergil 70BC-19BC *MagSWL [port]*
Vergin, Heinz A. 1935- *WhoUN 92*
Vergis, Anastasios Stylianos 1957- *WhoWor 93*
Verglas, Antoine 1961- *BioIn 17*
Vergnani, L.J. 1939- *St&PR 93*
Vergnaud, Jean-Pierre *WhoScE 91-2*
Vergne-Marini, Pedro Juan 1942- *WhoAm 92*
Vergnes, F. *WhoScE 91-2*
Vergnes, Michel N. 1932- *WhoScE 91-2*
Vergnet, Edmond-Alphonse-Jean 1850-1904 *Baker 92*

Vergon, James F. 1948- *St&PR 93*
Vergoni, Paul R. 1947- *St&PR 93*
Vergouwen, H.J.J. *WhoScE 91-3*
Verhaar, Boudewyn Johannes 1937- *WhoWor 93*
Verhaegen, Georges M.A. 1937- *WhoScE 91-2*
Verhaegen, Lode August 1925- *WhoScE 91-2*
Verhaegen, Thierry J. *Law&B 92*
Verhage, David James 1950- *St&PR 93*
Verhage, Frans 1927- *WhoScE 91-3*
Verhage, Paul Alan 1938- *St&PR 93*
Ver Hagen, Jan Karol 1937- *St&PR 93, WhoAm 92*
Verhagen, Timothy J. *Law&B 92*
Verhagen, Timothy James 1946- *St&PR 93*
Verhalen, Robert Donald 1935- *WhoAm 92*
Verhasselt, Andre Francois 1940- *WhoWor 93*
Verhasselt, Yola L.G. 1937- *WhoScE 91-2*
Verhegge, Ruth Decker 1944- *WhoSSW 93*
Verheij, Richard H. *Law&B 92*
Verhelst, H.A.M. *WhoScE 91-3*
Verhelst, Werner D.E. 1957- *WhoScE 91-2*
Verhesen, Anna Maria Hubertina 1932- *WhoAmW 93*
Verheulen, Robert J. *Law&B 92*
Verheulpen-Heymans, Nicole 1946- *WhoScE 91-2*
Verheyden, Claude 1939- *WhoScE 91-2*
Verheyden, Clement Marcel 1949- *WhoScE 91-2*
Verheyden, Edward 1878-1959 *Baker 92*
Verheyen, Dirk 1957- *ConAu 139*
Verheyen, Egon 1936- *WhoAm 92*
Verheyen, Marcel Mathieu 1951- *WhoWor 93*
Verhines, Jack 1932- *St&PR 93*
Verhoef, Hans Paul d1990 *BioIn 17*
Verhoeff, Caroline *AmWomPl*
Verhoeff, J. *WhoScE 91-3*
Verhoeff, Koenraad 1931- *WhoScE 91-3*
Verhoeff, Theo J. M. L. 1949- *St&PR 93*
Verhoek, Susan Elizabeth 1942- *WhoAmW 93*
Ver Hoeve, Raymond Warren 1925- *St&PR 93*
Verhoeven, Guido 1945- *WhoScE 91-2*
Verhoeven, Michael 1938- *MiSFD 9*
Verhoeven, Paul *BioIn 17*
Verhoeven, Paul 1938- *MiSFD 9*
Verhoeven, Philippe Edgard 1958- *WhoWor 93*
Verhoeven, Wilhelmus Franciscus J. 1947- *WhoWor 93*
Verhoff, C.A. *St&PR 93*
Verhoogen, John 1912- *WhoAm 92*
Verhoyen, Michel N.J. 1933- *WhoScE 91-2*
Verhulst, Johannes 1816-1891 *Baker 92*
Veri, Giuliano *WhoScE 91-3*
Verie, Christian 1935- *WhoScE 91-2*
Verina dc. 484 *OxDcByz*
Verini, Gregory A. 1952- *St&PR 93*
Verinis, James *BioIn 17*
Verink, Ellis Daniel, Jr. 1920- *WhoAm 92*
Verite, R. *WhoScE 91-2*
Verity, Brian Clifton 1933- *WhoUN 92*
Verity, George Luther 1914- *WhoAm 92*
Verity, James Edward 1947- *WhoEmL 93*
Verity, Maurice Anthony 1931- *WhoAm 92*
Verity, Simon *BioIn 17*
Verjus, J.P. 1943- *WhoScE 91-2*
Verkaart, Isabelle McDonough 1915- *WhoSSW 93*
Verkaik, A.P. *WhoScE 91-3*
Verkerk, Gerard C. 1943- *St&PR 93*
Verklin, David *BioIn 17*
Verkuil, Paul Robert 1939- *WhoAm 92*
Verlaan, Paul 1955- *WhoScE 91-3*
Verlaine, Paul 1844-1896 *MagSWL [port]*
Verlander, W. Ashley 1920- *St&PR 93*
Verlanic, Kenneth Joseph 1953- *St&PR 93*
Verleger, Philip King 1918- *WhoAm 92*
Verlet, Pierre 1908-1987 *BioIn 17*
Verlich, Jean Elaine 1950- *WhoAmW 93*
Verlinden, Marleen 1953- *WhoWor 93*
Verma, Ashok Nath 1921- *WhoAsAP 91*
Verma, Kapil 1928- *WhoAsAP 91*
Verma, Ram Sagar 1946- *WhoE 93*
Verma, S.D. 1908- *BioIn 17*
Verma, Usha 1933- *WhoAsAP 91*
Verma, Veena 1941- *WhoAsAP 91*
Verma, Virendra 1916- *WhoAsAP 91*
Vermaat, Arend Jan 1939- *WhoWor 93*
Vermagen, Frank Simon 1938- *WhoUN 92*
Vermedahl, Joe Erik 1943- *St&PR 93*
Vermeer, Jan 1632-1675 *BioIn 17*
Vermeer, Johannes 1632-1675 *BioIn 17*
Vermeer, Marianne 1957- *WhoAmW 93*
Vermeer, Maureen Dorothy 1945- *WhoAmW 93, WhoE 93*
Vermeer, Richard Douglas 1938- *WhoAm 92*
Vermeersch, Jeannette Thorez- 1910- *BioIn 17*
Vermeersch, Pierre M. 1938- *WhoScE 91-2*
Vermehren, Poul Henrik 1932- *WhoScE 91-2*
Vermes, Laszlo 1936- *WhoScE 91-4*
Vermes, Pal 1942- *WhoScE 91-4*
Vermes, Sheldon A. *St&PR 93*
Vermette, Raymond Edward 1942- *WhoAm 92*
Vermeule, Cornelius Clarkson, III 1925- *WhoAm 92*
Vermeule, Emily Townsend 1928- *WhoAm 92, WhoAmW 93*
Vermeulen, Carl William 1939- *WhoSSW 93*
Vermeulen, Martine *BioIn 17*
Vermeulen, Matthijs 1888-1967 *Baker 92*
Vermeylen, G. *WhoScE 91-2*
Vermeylen, Roland Karel 1945- *WhoWor 93*
Vermie, Craig D. *Law&B 92*
Vermillion, Mark Edward, Sr. 1957- *WhoSSW 93*
Vermillion, Richard D. 1920- *St&PR 93*
Vermillion, Stephen Dorsey, III 1960- *WhoE 93*
Vermillion, William C. 1945- *St&PR 93*
Vermillion-Radford, Kathy Ann 1961- *WhoAmW 93*
Vermilya, Claire (Szala) 1919- *WhoWrEP 92*
Vermilya, Dale Nelson 1959- *WhoEmL 93*
Vermilye, Henry Rowland 1936- *St&PR 93*
Vermilye, Jocelyn Alice 1916- *WhoAmW 93*
Vermilye, Kate Jordan *AmWomPl*
Vermilye, Peter Hoagland 1920- *WhoAm 92*
Vermund, Sten Halvor 1954- *WhoE 93*
Vermylen, Debra Mae Singleton 1955- *WhoAmW 93*
Vermylen, Paul A. 1919- *St&PR 93*
Vermylen, Paul A., Jr. 1946- *St&PR 93*
Vermylen, Paul Anthony, Jr. 1946- *WhoAm 92*
Vermylen, Robert Arthur 1954- *St&PR 93*
Verna, Barbara 1942- *WhoAmW 93*
Verna, Louis F. 1943- *St&PR 93*
Verna, Mario 1937- *WhoE 93*
Verna, Peter J., Jr. 1926- *St&PR 93*
Vernadskii, Vladimir Ivanovich 1863-1945 *BioIn 17*
Vernam, Glenn R. 1896-1980 *ScF&FL 92*
Vernamonti, Karen L. 1960- *St&PR 93*
Vernarelli, Michael Joseph 1948- *WhoE 93*
Vernberg, Frank John 1925- *WhoAm 92*
Verne *Baker 92*
Verne, Adela 1877-1952 *Baker 92*
Verne, Jean Jules- *ScF&FL 92*
Verne, Jules 1828-1905 *BioIn 17, DcLB 123 [port], MagSWL [port], ScF&FL 92*
Verne, Jules (Gabriel) 1828-1905 *MajAI [port]*
Verne, Mathilde 1865-1936 *Baker 92*
Verne, Maxine H. *Law&B 92*
Verne, Maxine H. 1955- *WhoIns 93*
Verne Bredt, Alice 1868-1958 *Baker 92*
Verner, Douglas H. *Law&B 92*
Verner, Gerald 1896-1980 *ScF&FL 92*
Verner, James Melton 1915- *WhoAm 92*
Verner, Jules L. 1925- *St&PR 93*
Vernerder, Gloria Jean 1930- *WhoAmW 93*
Verner-Loehr, Dean G. 1952- *St&PR 93*
Vernes, Alain Jean-Michel 1940- *WhoScE 91-2*
Vernet, Jean-Pierre 1930- *WhoScE 91-4*
Vernet, Philippe Paul Emile 1939- *WhoScE 91-2*
Verneuil, Henri 1920- *MiSFD 9*
Verneuil, Raoul de 1899- *Baker 92*
Vernex, Jean-Claude 1940- *WhoWor 93*
Verney, James C. 1952- *St&PR 93*
Verney, Richard Greville 1946- *St&PR 93, WhoE 93*
Verni, Ralph Francis 1943- *St&PR 93, WhoAm 92*
Vernick, Ruth 1934- *St&PR 93*
Vernicos-Eugenides, Nicolas Michel 1920- *WhoWor 93*
Vernier, Christine Ann 1945- *WhoAmW 93*
Vernier, D. Paul, Jr. 1951- *WhoAm 92*
Vernier, Pierre Jacques 1929- *WhoScE 91-2*
Vernier, Richard 1929- *WhoAm 92*
Verniero, Robert 1926- *St&PR 93*
Vernin, J. 1946- *WhoScE 91-2*
Vernon, Andrew Anthony 1948- *WhoSSW 93*
Vernon, Ashley *Baker 92*
Vernon, Brian Elliot 1953- *St&PR 93*
Vernon, Carl Atlee, Jr. 1926- *WhoAm 92*
Vernon, Charles Robertson 1926- *WhoSSW 93*
Vernon, Dai d1992 *NewYTBS 92*
Vernon, David Harvey 1925- *WhoWrEP 92*
Vernon, Ethel Joslin 1890-1964 *BioIn 17*
Vernon, Geoffrey P. 1941- *St&PR 93*
Vernon, Gerald B. 1941- *St&PR 93*
Vernon, Harriet Dorothy 1914- *WhoWrEP 92*
Vernon, Howard 1914- *BioIn 17*
Vernon, Jack Allen 1922- *WhoAm 92*
Vernon, John 1943- *ScF&FL 92*
Vernon, John Philip *Law&B 92*
Vernon, Kara Lon 1958- *WhoAmW 93*
Vernon, Lacy Sinkford 1931- *St&PR 93*
Vernon, Lawrence Gordon 1937- *WhoWor 93*
Vernon, Lillian *BioIn 17, St&PR 93*
Vernon, Lillian 1927- *WhoAm 92, WhoAmW 93*
Vernon, Mary 1942- *WhoAmW 93*
Vernon, McCay 1928- *WhoE 93*
Vernon, Merry Ann *Law&B 92*
Vernon, Raymond 1913- *ConAu 40NR, WhoAm 92, WhoWrEP 92*
Vernon, Richard G. 1943- *WhoScE 91-1*
Vernon, Robert *BioIn 17*
Vernon, Shirley Jane 1930- *WhoAm 92*
Vernon, Sidney 1906- *WhoWrEP 92*
Vernon, Thomas Martin, Jr. 1939- *WhoAm 92*
Vernon, Virginia Fox-Brooks 1894- *AmWomPl*
Vernon, Walter Ray, Jr. *Law&B 92*
Vernon, Weston, III 1931- *WhoAm 92, WhoE 93*
Vernon, William *ScF&FL 92*
Vernon, William F., Jr. 1931- *St&PR 93*
Vernone, Michael Jerome 1962- *WhoSSW 93*
Vernon-Wortzel, Heidi 1938- *WhoAmW 93*
Vernot, Gertrude W. 1941- *WhoSSW 93*
Vero, Jozsef 1933- *WhoScE 91-4*
Veroiu, Mircea 1941- *DrEEuF*
Veron, Earl E. 1922-1990 *BioIn 17*
Veron, J. *WhoScE 91-2*
Veron, J. Michael 1950- *WhoSSW 93*
Veron, James D. 1930- *St&PR 93*
Veron, Louis 1798-1867 *OxDcOp*
Veron, Philippe 1939- *WhoScE 91-2*
Verona, Pasquale A. 1936- *St&PR 93*
Verona, Stephen F. 1940- *MiSFD 9*
Veronesi, Judith M. 1946- *St&PR 93*
Veronesi, Karen Tropp 1954- *WhoAmW 93*
Veronesi, Umberto 1925- *WhoScE 91-3*
Veronis, John James *WhoAm 92*
Veronis, Peter 1923- *WhoAm 92*
Verosub, Kenneth Lee 1944- *WhoAm 92*
Verpillot, Earl A. d1990 *BioIn 17*
Verplaetse, Alfons Remi Emiel 1930- *WhoWor 93*
Verplanck, William Samuel 1916- *WhoAm 92*
Verplanke, Anna Louise 1935- *WhoAmW 93*
Verpoorte, Robert 1946- *WhoWor 93*
Verral, Charles Spain 1904-1990 *BioIn 17, ConAu 37NR*
Verrall, John (Weedon) 1908- *Baker 92*
Verran, Robert S. 1932- *St&PR 93*
Verrant, James J. 1938- *St&PR 93*
Verrazzano, Giovanni da 1485-1528 *Expl 93 [port]*
Verrecchia, Alfred J. 1943- *St&PR 93, WhoAm 92*
Verrecchio, Roseann *Law&B 92*
Verrecchio, Roseann B. *Law&B 92*
Verret, Jean-Luc 1945- *WhoScE 91-2*
Verret, Joseph Marc 1953- *WhoE 93*
Verret, Stephen K. 1953- *St&PR 93*
Verrett, Shirley *BioIn 17*
Verrett, Shirley 1931- *Baker 92, IntDcOp [port], OxDcOp, WhoWor 93*
Verrette, James Francis 1956- *WhoE 93*
Verrette, Joyce 1939- *ScF&FL 92*
Verrette, Louise Madeleine 1949- *WhoWrEP 92*
Verrico, Ernest Joseph 1955- *WhoAm 92*
Verrier, John J. 1935- *St&PR 93*
Verrier, Paul Jonathan *WhoScE 91-1*
Verrier-Skutt, Anne *WhoWrEP 92*
Verrill, A. Hyatt 1871-1954 *ScF&FL 92*
Verrill, Charles Owen, Jr. 1937- *WhoAm 92, WhoE 93, WhoWor 93*
Verrill, Dana C. 1950- *St&PR 93*
Verrill, David C. 1943- *St&PR 93*
Verrill, F. Glenn 1923- *WhoAm 92*
Verrill, K.E. *WhoScE 91-1*
Verrill, Ralph T. *Law&B 92*
Verrill, Richard George, Jr. 1958- *WhoSSW 93*
Verrill, Ted Wright *Law&B 92*
Verron, Robert 1935?-1984 *ScF&FL 92*
Versacci, Alfred C. 1942- *St&PR 93*
Versace, Gianni 1946- *BioIn 17, WhoAm 92, WhoWor 93*
Versace, Pasquale *WhoScE 91-3*
Versalie, Robert M. 1931- *St&PR 93*
Verschoor, Curtis Carl 1931- *WhoAm 92*
Verschoor, Gerd *BioIn 17*
Verseau, Dominique *ScF&FL 92*
Vershbow, Arthur 1922- *St&PR 93*
Versluis, Arthur 1959- *ScF&FL 92*
Versluis, Johannes Willem 1935- *WhoWor 93*
Ver Snyder, Francis Louis 1925- *WhoAm 92*
Verson, Karol Ruth 1939- *WhoAmW 93*
Verspille, Marie Ann 1955- *WhoSSW 93*
Versprille, Adrian 1934- *WhoScE 91-3*
Verst, Paul Thomas 1957- *St&PR 93*
Verst, William G. 1931- *St&PR 93*
VerStandig, John David 1947- *WhoAm 92*
Verstappen, Frans T.J. 1946- *WhoScE 91-3*
Verstappen, Herman Th. 1925- *WhoScE 91-3*
Ver Steeg, Clarence Lester 1922- *WhoAm 92, WhoWor 93, WhoWrEP 92*
Versteeg, Jean Dorothy 1921- *WhoAmW 93*
VerSteeg, Jennie Elizabeth 1963- *WhoAmW 93*
Verstegen, Deborah A. 1946- *WhoAmW 93, WhoSSW 93*
Verster, Anneke 1947- *WhoUN 92*
Verstovsky, Alexei (Nikolaievich) 1799-1862 *Baker 92*
Verstraete, Marc 1925- *WhoScE 91-2, WhoWor 93*
Verstraete, Willy 1946- *WhoScE 91-2*
Verstraeten, Jean-J.-G. 1930- *WhoScE 91-2*
Verstringhe, Marc Emile Sidonie 1934- *WhoWor 93*
Vert, Michel Rene 1942- *WhoScE 91-2*
Vert, Paul 1933- *WhoScE 91-2*
Vertes, James A. *St&PR 93*
Vertes, Victor 1927- *WhoAm 92*
Vertlieb, Steve 1945- *WhoWrEP 92*
Vertopoulos, Stefanos *St&PR 93*
Vertov, Dziga 1896-1954 *MiSFD 9N*
Vertovsky, Alexey 1799-1862 *OxDcOp*
Vertreace, Martha Modena 1945- *WhoWrEP 92*
Verts, Lita Jeanne 1935- *WhoAmW 93*
Vertua, Rodolfo 1932- *WhoScE 91-3, WhoWor 93*
Vertucci, Frank L. 1914- *St&PR 93*
Veru, Theodore *WhoAm 92*
Vervack, Jimmy C. 1944- *WhoIns 93*
Verveen, A.A. 1930- *WhoScE 91-3*
Vervier, Jean F. 1934- *WhoScE 91-2*
Verville, Anne-Lee 1945- *WhoE 93*
Verville, Elizabeth Giavani 1940- *WhoAm 92, WhoAmW 93*
Verville, Jeanne M. *Law&B 92*
Verville, Sarah A. *Law&B 92*
Verwey, Anton Abraham Klaas 1947- *WhoUN 92*
Verweyen, Hans Jurgen 1936- *WhoWor 93*
Verwoerd, C.D.A. 1936- *WhoScE 91-3*
Verwoerd, Hendrik Frensch 1901-1966 *DcTwHis*
Verwoerdt, Adriaan 1927- *WhoAm 92*
Verwys, David Allen 1948- *St&PR 93*
Verwys, Phillip Marvin 1952- *St&PR 93*
Verzar, Christine Beatrice 1940- *WhoAmW 93*
Verzelloni, Franco 1934- *WhoUN 92*
Vesak, Norbert 1936-1990 *BioIn 17*
Vesci, Dennis J. 1947- *St&PR 93*
Vesco, John A. *Law&B 92*
Vesco, Robert L. *BioIn 17*
Vescovi, Selvi 1930- *St&PR 93*
Vescovo, Giorgio 1941- *St&PR 93*
Veselinovic, Vesimir 1924- *WhoScE 91-4*
Veselits, Charles Francis 1930- *St&PR 93*
Vesell, Elliot Saul 1933- *WhoE 93*
Veselov, Alexander Petrovich 1955- *WhoWor 93*
Vesely, Alexander 1926- *WhoAm 92*
Vesely, Donald V. 1929- *St&PR 93*
Vesely, Kenneth Donald 1936- *St&PR 93*
Vesely, Vladimir 1933- *WhoScE 91-4*
Vesey, A. *BioIn 17*
Vesey, Denmark c. 1767-1822 *BioIn 17*
Vesey, Gary Lee 1928- *St&PR 93*
Vesey, Robert A. 1948- *St&PR 93*
Veski, Erik 1952- *WhoE 93*
Vesler, Igor 1949- *WhoE 93*
Ve Sota, Bruno 1922-1976 *BioIn 17*
Vespa, Ned Angelo 1942- *WhoAm 92*
Vespa, William David 1960- *WhoSSW 93*
Vespasiano, da Bisticci 1421-1498 *BioIn 17*
Vespasianus, Titus Flavius 9-79 *HarEnMi*
Vespasianus, Titus Flavius Sabinus 40-81 *BioIn 17*
Vesper, Gerald Wallace 1932- *WhoAm 92*

Vesper, Karl Hampton 1932- WhoAm 92
Vesperi, Maria Davoren 1951- WhoAmW 93
Vespo, Jo Ellen 1956- WhoE 93
Vespoli, Leila L. Law&B 92
Vespucci, Amerigo 1451-1512 BioIn 17, Expl 93 [port]
Vesque von Puttlingen, Johann 1803-1883 Baker 92
Vess, George Edward, Jr. 1957- WhoSSW 93
Vessenes, Katherine 1949- St&PR 93, WhoAmW 93
Vesser, Carolyn 1934- ScF&FL 92
Vessey, Iris 1940- WhoAmW 93
Vessey, Martin Paterson WhoScE 91-1
Vessiere, Roger 1926- WhoScE 91-2
Vessot, Robert Frederick Charles 1930- WhoAm 92
Vest, Barbara E. Law&B 92
Vest, Charles Marstiller 1941- WhoAm 92, WhoE 93, WhoWor 93
Vest, Frank Harris, Jr. 1936- WhoAm 92
Vest, Gary Wilson 1955- WhoSSW 93
Vest, George Graham 1930- WhoAm 92
Vest, George Southall 1918- WhoAm 92
Vest, Herb D. 1944- St&PR 93
Vest, Hyrum Grant, Jr. 1935- WhoAm 92
Vest, Jon Phillip 1949- St&PR 93
Vest, Marvin Lewis 1906- WhoAm 92
Vest, Randy Johnson 1949- St&PR 93
Vest, Robert Wilson 1930- WhoAm 92
Vestal, Bonita Klahn 1945- WhoAmW 93
Vestal, James Edward 1955- WhoWor 93
Vestal, Jeanne Marie Goodspeed 1930- WhoAm 92
Vestal, John H. Law&B 92
Vestal, John Harrison 1951- WhoSSW 93
Vestal, Lucian LaRoe 1925- WhoAm 92
Vestal, Tommy Ray 1939- WhoWor 93
Vestberg, Mauritz Vilhelm 1951- WhoScE 91-4
Vesterberg, Olof A.Y. 1937- WhoScE 91-4
Vestergaard, Bent Faber WhoScE 91-2
Vestergaard, Hans Peter Skafte 1940- WhoScE 91-2
Vestmar, Brigel Johannes Ahlmann 1937- WhoWor 93
Vestris, Lucia Elizabeth 1797-1856 OxDcOp
Veszely, Gyula 1938- WhoScE 91-4
Vet, Charles V. De ScF&FL 92
Vetere, Colleen Marie 1957- WhoSSW 93
Vetere, Eduardo 1945- WhoUN 92
Vetere, Robert Louis Law&B 92
Veters, Frederick Law&B 92
Vetesi, Ferenc 1935- WhoScE 91-4
Veth, Pieter Johannes 1814-1895 IntDcAn
Veth, Stephen R. 1948- St&PR 93
Vethers, Alexander BioIn 17
Vetlutsky, Vitaly Nikolaevich 1937- WhoWor 93
Vetog, Edwin Joseph 1921- St&PR 93, WhoAm 92
Vetrano, Anthony Philip 1946- St&PR 93
Vetrano Tiberge, J. Bea 1956- WhoAmW 93
Vetri, Peter Joseph 1955- St&PR 93
Vetro, Walter J. d1990 BioIn 17
Vette, John Lyle, III 1937- St&PR 93
Vette, John R. 1935- St&PR 93
Vetter, Betty McGee 1924- WhoAm 92, WhoE 93
Vetter, Charles Richard 1927- St&PR 93
Vetter, Cyril Edward BioIn 17
Vetter, Edward Oswald 1920- WhoSSW 93
Vetter, Emily Durso 1950- WhoAmW 93
Vetter, Frank William 1936- St&PR 93
Vetter, Gerhard 1933- WhoScE 91-3
Vetter, Heinz 1924- WhoScE 91-3
Vetter, Herbert 1920- WhoAm 92
Vetter, J.E. 1940- WhoScE 91-3
Vetter, James George, Jr. 1934- WhoAm 92, WhoSSW 93
Vetter, James L. 1933- WhoAm 92
Vetter, Michael 1943- Baker 92
Vetter, Pamela Jane 1948- WhoAmW 93
Vetter, Philip L. 1954- St&PR 93
Vetter, Richard H. Law&B 92
Vetter, Walther 1891-1967 Baker 92
Vetter, William Law&B 92
Vettorazzi, Gaston 1928- WhoWor 93
Vettore, Luciano A. 1936- WhoScE 91-3
Vetulani, Jerzy 1936- WhoScE 91-4
Veuhoff, Heinz 1933- WhoWrEP 92
Veum, Jonathan Roger 1963- WhoE 93
Veuve, Michael L. 1948- St&PR 93
Veverica, Henry William 1927- St&PR 93
Veverka, George F. 1927- St&PR 93
Veverka, Ruth Tonry 1918- WhoAmW 93
Vevers, Tony 1926- WhoE 93
Vevier, Charles 1924- WhoAm 92
Vevoda, Ernest 1927- St&PR 93
Vey, Edward L. 1942- St&PR 93
Vey, Mary M. Law&B 92
Veyre, Annie WhoScE 91-2
Veyron-Lacroix, Robert 1922-1991 Baker 92, BioIn 17
Veysey, Arthur Ernest 1914- WhoAm 92
Veysey, Michael C. Law&B 92
Vez, Alexandre 1933- WhoScE 91-4
Vezeau, Jeannette Eva 1913- WhoAm 92
Vezel, Mikhail Ivanovich 1934- WhoUN 92
Vezer, Rudolph R. Law&B 92
Vezeridis, Michael Panagiotis 1943- WhoE 93, WhoWor 93
Vezhinov, Pavel ConAu 37NR
Vezina, George Robert 1935- WhoAm 92
Vezina, Monique WhoAmW 93, WhoE 93
Vezina, Monique 1935- WhoAm 92
Vezina, Raynald 1947- St&PR 93
Vezinhet, A. WhoScE 91-2
Veziroglu, Turhan Nejat 1924- WhoAm 92
Vezzoli, Gianalberto 1943- WhoScE 91-3
Vezzuto, Lucy Ann 1950- WhoAmW 93
Vgenopoulos, Constantinos George 1941- WhoWor 93
Via, Dennis Martin 1952- WhoIns 93
Via, Michael M. 1957- St&PR 93
Viacava, Lillian D. WhoAmW 93, WhoE 93
Viadana, Lodovico c. 1560-1627 Baker 92
Viaene, Jozef 1928- WhoScE 91-2
Viaene, W. 1940- WhoScE 91-2
Viaggio, Sergio Geronimo 1945- WhoUN 92
Vial, Debra Lynn 1965- WhoSSW 93
Vial, Leslie A. Law&B 92
Vial, Paula Boulet 1953- WhoAmW 93
Vial, Timothy Joseph 1959- WhoSSW 93
Viala, Alain R.G. 1928- WhoScE 91-2
Viala, Jean Jacques 1926- WhoScE 91-2
Viall, Paul G., Jr. 1946- St&PR 93
Vial Larrain, Juan de Dios 1924- WhoWor 93
Vialle, Karen WhoAm 92, WhoAmW 93
Vialpando, Joan Frances 1927- WhoAmW 93
Vian, Boris 1920-1959 ScF&FL 92
Vian, Felice 1933- WhoScE 91-3
Viana, Fructuoso 1896-1976 Baker 92
Vianello, Elio 1929- WhoScE 91-3
Vianello-Chiodo, Marco 1932- WhoUN 92
Vianesi, Auguste 1837-1908 OxDcOp
Vianesi, Auguste-Charles-Leonard-Francois 1837-1908 Baker 92
Viani, James L. 1932- WhoAm 92
Vianna, Eduardo Pereira 1961- WhoWor 93
Vianna, Fructuoso 1896-1976 Baker 92
Vianna da Motta, Jose 1868-1948 Baker 92
Viano, David Charles 1946- WhoAm 92
Viar, Betty Ann 1924- WhoAmW 93
Viardo, Vladimir BioIn 17
Viardot, Louise 1841-1918 OxDcOp
Viardot, Louise (Pauline Marie) Heritte 1841-1918
See Viardot-Garcia, (Michelle Fedinande) Pauline 1821-1910 Baker 92
Viardot, Paul 1857-1941 OxDcOp
Viardot, Paul (Louis Joachim) 1857-1941
See Viardot-Garcia, (Michelle Fedinande) Pauline 1821-1910 Baker 92
Viardot, Pauline 1821-1910 IntDcOp, OxDcOp
Viardot, Pauline Garcia 1821-1910 BioIn 17
Viardot-Garcia, (Michelle Fedinande) Pauline 1821-1910 Baker 92
Viart, Guy Pascal 1957- WhoEmL 93, WhoWor 93
Viault, Birdsall Scrymser 1932- WhoSSW 93
Viault, Sarah Underhill 1938- WhoAmW 93
Vibber, Lee ScF&FL 92
Vibe, Kjeld 1927- WhoWor 93
Viby-Mogensen, Jorgen 1938- WhoScE 91-2
Vicari, Clement Joseph Law&B 92
Vicari, Giuseppe 1929- WhoScE 91-3
Vicario, Giovanni Bruno 1932- WhoScE 91-3
Vicariot, Jean 1933- WhoScE 91-2
Vicars, Peter N. 1947- St&PR 93
Vicars, Richard John 1940- St&PR 93, WhoAm 92
Vicary, Thomas C. 1941- St&PR 93
Viccajee, Victor Framje 1903- WhoWor 93
Viccaro, Patrick Joseph Law&B 92
Viccellio, Nancy Blair 1914- WhoSSW 93
Vicchio, Stephen (John) 1950- ConAu 138
Vice, Fannie Collins AmWomPl
Vice, LaVonna Lee 1952- WhoAmW 93, WhoE 93, WhoWor 93
Vicens, Josefina 1911-1988 SpAmA
Vicens, Josefina 1915- DcMexL
Vicente, Esteban BioIn 17
Vicente Soler, Jose 1943- WhoScE 91-3, WhoWor 93
Vicentino, Nicola 1511-1575? Baker 92
Vichev, Nedelcho Nedelchev 1948- WhoWor 93
Vichich, Jon Joseph Law&B 92
Vichinsky, Renee BioIn 17
Vicinanza, Francesco WhoScE 91-3
Vick, Alfred 1925- St&PR 93
Vick, Edward Hoge, Jr. 1944- WhoAm 92
Vick, Frances Brannen 1935- WhoSSW 93
Vick, G. Etheridge 1947- St&PR 93
Vick, Gerald Keith 1930- WhoE 93
Vick, James Albert 1945- WhoAm 92
Vick, John Braxton, Jr. 1952- WhoAm 92
Vick, Katherine Novak 1951- WhoAmW 93
Vick, Marie 1922- WhoAm 92
Vick, Robert Louis 1946- St&PR 93
Vick, William Edward, Jr. 1958- WhoWrEP 92
Vicker, Ray 1917- WhoAm 92, WhoWor 93, WhoWrEP 92
Vickerman, John Charles WhoScE 91-1
Vickerman, John Clifford 1937- WhoE 93
Vickerman, Keith WhoScE 91-1
Vickerman, Keith 1933- WhoWor 93
Vickers, Arthur E. Law&B 92
Vickers, Charles Geoffrey 1894-1982 BioIn 17
Vickers, David Leroy 1942- St&PR 93
Vickers, Donat Osmond 1931- WhoUN 92
Vickers, Edward Davin 1945- WhoWrEP 92
Vickers, Geoffrey 1894-1982 BioIn 17
Vickers, Jacquelyn Pridgen 1932- WhoSSW 93
Vickers, James Hudson 1930- WhoAm 92, WhoWor 93
Vickers, Janeen WhoAmW 93
Vickers, Jeffrey P. 1952- St&PR 93
Vickers, Jon 1926- BioIn 17, IntDcOp, OxDcOp
Vickers, Jon(athan Stewart) 1926- Baker 92
Vickers, Julie Estelle 1960- WhoSSW 93
Vickers, Katherine Monica 1935- WhoAmW 93
Vickers, Marilyn Anne 1945- WhoSSW 93
Vickers, Roger Spencer 1937- WhoAm 92
Vickers, Rollin C. 1926- St&PR 93
Vickers, Thomas Joseph 1939- WhoSSW 93
Vickers, Thomas Wesley 1945- WhoSSW 93
Vickers, Tirey Kenneth 1915- WhoE 93
Vickers, Yvette 1936- BioIn 17
Vickerstaff, Robert Percy 1935- WhoIns 93
Vickery, Brice Elwood 1928- WhoE 93
Vickery, Eugene Livingstone 1913- WhoWor 93
Vickery, Glenn Wheeler 1938- WhoSSW 93
Vickery, Harold Kirby, Jr. 1941- WhoWor 93
Vickery, J. WhoScE 91-1
Vickery, James A. 1931- WhoIns 93
Vickery, James Alexander 1931- St&PR 93
Vickery, James Larry 1946- WhoSSW 93
Vickery, Jim Dale 1951- WhoWrEP 92
Vickery, Millie Margaret 1920- WhoWor 93
Vickery, Raymond Ezekiel, Jr. 1942- WhoSSW 93
Vickery, Robert F. 1952- St&PR 93
Vickland, Arthur Ferdinand, Jr. 1918- WhoSSW 93
Vickland, John R. Law&B 92
Vicklund, John H. 1946- St&PR 93
Vickrey, David H. Law&B 92
Vickrey, R. Duke Law&B 92
Vickrey, Robert Remsen 1926- WhoAm 92
Vickrey, Roy L. 1937- St&PR 93
Vickroy, Virgil Vester, Jr. 1931- WhoSSW 93
Vickruck, Tracey L. 1958- St&PR 93
Vicks, Dwight E., Jr. 1933- St&PR 93
Vico, Giambattista 1668-1744 BioIn 17
Vico, Giovanni Battista 1668-1744 BioIn 17
Vico, Paul 1946- WhoE 93
Vicsek, Tamas 1948- WhoScE 91-4, WhoWor 93
Victor, A. Paul 1938- WhoAm 92
Victor, Charlene d1991 BioIn 17
Victor, Cindy ScF&FL 92
Victor, Daniel J. Law&B 92
Victor, James Stuart, III 1961- WhoE 93
Victor, Katherine 1928- BioIn 17
Victor, Marlyn A. Law&B 92
Victor, Martin d1990 BioIn 17
Victor, Michael T. 1961- St&PR 93
Victor, Richard Michael 1929- WhoAm 92
Victor, Robert E. 1929- St&PR 93
Victor, Robert Eugene 1929- WhoAm 92
Victor, Ronald Joseph, Jr. 1964- WhoE 93
Victor, Royall 1916-1992 BioIn 17
Victor, Royall, Jr. d1992 NewYTBS 92 [port]
Victor, Steve ScF&FL 92
Victor, William W. 1924- St&PR 93
Victor, William Weir 1924- WhoAm 92
Victor Emanuel, III 1869-1947 DcTwHis
Victor Emmanuel, Prince of Savoy 1937- BioIn 17
Victoria, Empress 1840-1901 BioIn 17
Victoria, Queen of Great Britain 1819-1901 BioIn 17
Victoria, Tomas Luis de 1548-1611 Baker 92
Victori-Companys, Lluis 1935- WhoScE 91-3
Victorin, His Eminence The Most Reverend 1912- WhoAm 92
Victorin, Steven Robert 1961- WhoE 93
Victorio d1880 BioIn 17
Victoroff, Jeffrey Ivan ScF&FL 92
Victorov, Serge Vasiliy 1941- WhoWor 93
Victor-Perrin, Claude 1764-1841 HarEnMi
Victorson, Michael Bruce 1954- WhoSSW 93
Victor Tonnensis dc. 567 OxDcByz
Victor Vitensis fl. 5th cent.- OxDcByz
Victory, A. Michael 1934- St&PR 93
Victory, Gerard 1921- Baker 92
Victory, Pedro J. 1928- WhoScE 91-3
Vicuna, Cecilia 1948- SpAmA
Viczian, Istvan 1940- WhoScE 91-4
Vidacek, Stjepan 1927- WhoScE 91-4
Vidakovic, Mirko 1924- WhoScE 91-4
Vidakovic, Velibor 1932- WhoWor 93
Vidal, Alain M. 1944- WhoScE 91-2
Vidal, Bernard Marie Raymond 1943- WhoWor 93
Vidal, Eduardo R. 1957- WhoE 93
Vidal, Eugene ScF&FL 92
Vidal, Eugene L. 1895-1969 EncABHB 8 [port]
Vidal, Evalena Sharp 1927- WhoE 93
Vidal, Gore 1925- BioIn 17, ConGAN, ConLC 72 [port], MagSAmL [port], ScF&FL 92, WhoAm 92, WhoWrEP 92
Vidal, Harriette ScF&FL 92
Vidal, Jacques Georges 1928- WhoWor 93
Vidal, Jean-Louis 1941- WhoScE 91-2
Vidal, John A. 1919- St&PR 93
Vidal, Joseph Bernard 1859-1924
See Vidal, Paul (Antonin) 1863-1931 Baker 92
Vidal, K.J. 1943- St&PR 93
Vidal, Louis-Antoine 1820-1891 Baker 92
Vidal, Paul (Antonin) 1863-1931 Baker 92
Vidal, Pierre 1937- WhoScE 91-2
Vidal, Ricardo Cardinal 1931- WhoWor 93
Vidali, Roberto 1953- WhoWor 93
Vidalie, Henri 1936- WhoWor 93
Vidalin, K.E. 1947- St&PR 93
Vidalis, Orestis Efthimios 1917- WhoWor 93
Vidal Santaella, Irma NotHsAW 93
Vidal Serin, Antonio Ramon 1921- WhoWor 93
Vidano, Carlo 1923- WhoScE 91-3
Vidaver, Anne Marie 1938- WhoAmW 93
Videan, Ann Narcisian 1959- WhoAmW 93
Videla, Juan A. Law&B 92
Videla del Mazo, Jose Maria 1936- WhoWor 93
Videnov, Nikola Borisov 1924- WhoScE 91-4
Viderman, Linda Jean 1957- WhoAmW 93, WhoEmL 93, WhoSSW 93, WhoWor 93
Videro, Finn 1906-1987 Baker 92
Videtti, Linda K. 1965- WhoAmW 93
Vidic, Jeffrey Jon 1957- WhoSSW 93
Vidler, Alec 1899-1991 AnObit 1991
Vidler, Alexander Roper 1899-1991 BioIn 17
Vidmar, John P. 1952- St&PR 93
Vidon, Dominique Jean-Marie 1939- WhoScE 91-2
Vidor, Charles 1900-1959 MiSFD 9N
Vidor, King 1894-1982 MiSFD 9N
Vidor, King 1895-1982 BioIn 17
Vidossi, Giuseppe 1878-1969 IntDcAn
Vidrine, Malcolm Francis 1949- WhoSSW 93
Vidu, Ion 1863-1931 Baker 92
Vidybida, Alexander Konstantin 1949- WhoWor 93
Vie, Richard C. 1937- St&PR 93
Vie, Richard Carl 1937- WhoAm 92
Viebrock, Michael Eugene Law&B 92
Vieceli, John A. Law&B 92
Viechnicki, Dennis John 1940- WhoE 93
Viegas, Domingos Xavier 1950- WhoScE 91-3
Viegas, Juliana Laura Bruna 1945- WhoWor 93
Viegas, Leonardo Mayerhofer 1940- WhoWor 93
Viegas, Louis Paul 1940- WhoE 93

Viehbock, Franz P. 1923- *WhoScE 91-4*
Viehe, Heinz Gunter 1929- *WhoScE 91-2*
Viehe, John S. 1937- *St&PR 93*
Viehe, Karl William 1943- *WhoWor 93*
Viehl, Steven L. 1951- *St&PR 93*
Viehman, John W. 1929- *St&PR 93*
Viehman, Russel R. 1928- *St&PR 93*
Vieillard, Jean 1922- *WhoScE 91-2*
Vieira, Alberto De Lima 1934- *WhoWor 93*
Vieira, Carlos Jose 1937- *WhoWor 93*
Vieira, David Gueiros 1929- *WhoWor 93*
Vieira, Joao Bernardo 1939- *WhoAfr, WhoWor 93*
Vieira, Meredith *BioIn 17*
Vieira, Michael John 1953- *WhoWrEP 92*
Vieira, N.J. 1934- *St&PR 93*
Vieira, Sher Janet 1962- *WhoE 93*
Vieira-Da-Silva, Jorge 1929- *WhoScE 91-2*
Vieira da Silva, Maria Helena 1908-1992 *BioIn 17, CurBio 92N, NewYTBS 92 [port]*
Vieira de Mello, Sergio 1948- *WhoUN 92*
Viele, George Brookins 1932- *WhoAm 92, WhoSSW 93*
Vielmo, Paolo 1943- *WhoScE 91-3*
Viemeister, Tucker *BioIn 17*
Viener, John D. 1939- *WhoAm 92, WhoWor 93*
Viener, Michael 1941- *WhoSSW 93*
Vienken, Joerg Hans 1948- *WhoWor 93*
Vienot, Jean-Charles A. 1930- *WhoScE 91-2*
Viens, John Michael 1957- *St&PR 93*
Viens, Kenneth P. 1951- *St&PR 93*
Viens, Nancy Fitz-Gerald 1932- *WhoWrEP 92*
Viera, David John 1943- *WhoSSW 93*
Viera, James J. 1940- *St&PR 93*
Viera, James Joseph 1940- *WhoAm 92*
Viera, John Joseph 1932- *St&PR 93, WhoAm 92*
Vierck, Charles John, Jr. 1936- *WhoAm 92*
Vierdanck, Johann c. 1605-c. 1646 *Baker 92*
Viereck, George Sylvester 1884-1962 *ScF&FL 92*
Viereck, Peter 1916- *WhoAm 92, WhoE 93, WhoWrEP 92*
Viereck, Phillip R. 1925- *DcAmChF 1960*
Vieregg, James Robert 1950- *St&PR 93*
Vierk, Lois V 1951- *Baker 92*
Vierkant, Robert 1945- *St&PR 93*
Vierling, Georg 1820-1901 *Baker 92*
Vierling, Johann Gottfried 1750-1813 *Baker 92*
Viermetz, Kurt F. 1939- *WhoAm 92*
Vierne, Louis 1870-1937 *Baker 92*
Vierno, George R. d1990 *BioIn 17*
Vierra, Fred Arnold *BioIn 17*
Viertel, Janet d1992 *NewYTBS 92 [port]*
Viertel, Joseph 1915- *St&PR 93*
Viertel, Thomas *BioIn 17*
Viertel, Thomas M. 1941- *St&PR 93*
Viertl, Reinhard Karl Wolfgang 1946- *WhoWor 93*
Vieru, Anatol 1926- *Baker 92*
Vieser, Richard W. 1927- *St&PR 93*
Vieser, Richard William 1927- *WhoE 93*
Viessman, Warren, Jr. 1930- *WhoAm 92*
Viest, Ivan Miroslav 1922- *WhoAm 92*
Vietata, Taniela 1937- *WhoAsAP 91*
Vieth, G. Duane 1923- *WhoAm 92*
Vieth, George W., Jr. *Law&B 92*
Vieth, George W., Jr. 1955- *St&PR 93*
Vieth, John C. 1942- *St&PR 93*
Vieth, Wolf Randolph 1934- *WhoAm 92*
Vieth, Xenia *Law&B 92*
Vietinghoff-Scheel, Boris 1829-1901 *Baker 92*
Vietor, Harold Duane 1931- *WhoAm 92*
Viets, Hermann 1943- *WhoAm 92, WhoE 93*
Viets, Margaret Ann 1950- *WhoWor 93*
Viets, Robert O. 1943- *WhoAm 92*
Viets, Robert Oscar 1943- *St&PR 93*
Viets, Roger 1738-1811 *BioIn 17*
Viets, William C. *Law&B 92*
Vietti, Teresa Jane 1927- *WhoAm 92*
Vietto, Lorenzo 1958- *WhoScE 91-3*
Vieuille, Felix 1872-1953 *Baker 92, OxDcOp*
Vieuxtemps, (Jules-Joseph-) Ernest 1832-1896
See Vieuxtemps, Henri 1820-1881 *Baker 92*
Vieuxtemps, Henri 1820-1881 *Baker 92*
Vieuxtemps, (Jean-Joseph-) Lucien 1828-1901
See Vieuxtemps, Henri 1820-1881 *Baker 92*
Vig, Peter R. 1940- *St&PR 93*
Vig, Pradeep Kumar 1954- *WhoSSW 93*
Vig, Vernon Edward 1937- *WhoAm 92*
Vigano, Salvatore 1769-1821 *Baker 92*
Vigarie, Andre 1921- *WhoScE 91-2*
Vigdor, Irving 1929- *St&PR 93*
Vigdor, Martin George 1939- *WhoE 93*
Vige, Hans 1956- *BioIn 17*
Vigee-Lebrun, Louise-Elisabeth 1755-1842 *BioIn 17*
Vigen, Kathryn L. Voss 1934- *WhoAmW 93*
Vigerie, Emmanuel d'Astier de la 1900-1969 *BioIn 17*
Vigerstad, Alice Emily Frost 1907- *WhoAmW 93*
Vigfusson, Johannes Orn 1945- *WhoWor 93*
Viggiano, Victor A. 1925- *St&PR 93*
Vigh, Albert 1920- *WhoScE 91-4*
Vigh, Laszlo *WhoScE 91-4*
Vigier, Francois Claude Denis 1931- *WhoAm 92*
Vigier, Marc-Noel 1935- *WhoWor 93*
Vigil, Charles S. 1912- *WhoAm 92*
Vigil, Frederico *BioIn 17*
Vigil, Jose Maria 1829-1909 *DcMexL*
Vigil, Kathleen Rolfe 1964- *WhoAmW 93*
Vigil, Patricia Lorraine 1952- *WhoAmW 93*
Vigil, Ricardo 1943- *WhoUN 92*
Vigilante, Joseph Louis 1925- *WhoAm 92*
Vigil-Giron, Rebecca D. 1954- *WhoAmW 93*
Vigilius c. 500-555 *OxDcByz*
Vigil-Pinon, Evangelina 1949- *DcLB 122 [port], NotHsAW 93*
Vigini, Raul Alberto 1958- *WhoWor 93*
Vigliante, Mary 1946- *ScF&FL 92*
Vigliatore, Leonard James 1954- *WhoE 93*
Viglienzone, James 1953- *St&PR 93*
Viglione, Anthony 1943- *St&PR 93*
Viglione-Borghese, Domenico 1877-1957 *Baker 92, OxDcOp*
Vigmo, Josef 1922- *WhoWor 93*
Vigna, Angelo Albert 1941- *St&PR 93*
Vigna, Cheryl E. *Law&B 92*
Vigna Guidi, Guido 1942- *WhoScE 91-3*
Vignancour, Jean-Louis Tixier- 1907-1989 *BioIn 17*
Vignas, Francisco 1863-1933 *Baker 92*
Vignat, Jean-Pierre 1940- *WhoWor 93*
Vigne, Daniel 1942- *MiSFD 9*
Vigneault, Gilles 1928- *WhoCanL 92*
Vigneault, Lucien *St&PR 93*
Vigneaux, Michel *WhoScE 91-2*
Vignelles, Roger 1936- *WhoScE 91-2*
Vignelli, Massimo 1931- *WhoAm 92*
Vigneresse, Jean-Louis 1946- *WhoScE 91-2*
Vigneron, Claude Jean 1941- *WhoScE 91-2*
Vignier, Michel Robert 1948- *WhoWor 93*
Vignocchi, Anthony Joseph 1948- *WhoSSW 93*
Vignola, Chad Alexander 1958- *WhoE 93*
Vignolo, Biagio N. 1947- *St&PR 93*
Vignolo, Biagio Nickolas, Jr. 1947- *WhoAm 92*
Vignolo, Roger 1937- *St&PR 93*
Vignon, Bernard 1942- *WhoScE 91-2*
Vignone, Ronald John 1941- *WhoAm 92*
Vignos, Janice A. *St&PR 93*
Vignos, Lawrence R. *St&PR 93*
Vigny, Alfred (Victor) de 1797-1863 *DcLB 119 [port]*
Vigo, Jean 1905-1934 *MiSFD 9N*
Vigoda, Abe 1921- *WhoAm 92*
Vigon, Larry *BioIn 17*
Vigtel, Gudmund 1925- *WhoAm 92, WhoSSW 93*
Vigue, James F. 1949- *St&PR 93*
Vigus, Frank Edward *Law&B 92*
Vihavainen, Tuija Talvikki 1941- *WhoScE 91-4*
Vihko, Reijo Kalevi 1939- *WhoScE 91-4*
Viirlaid, Arved 1922- *WhoCanL 92*
Viitanen, Jari Heikki Antero 1957- *WhoScE 91-4*
Viitasaari, M.A. 1932- *WhoScE 91-4*
Vijande Vazquez, Manuel 1951- *WhoScE 91-3*
Vijayan, O.V. *ScF&FL 92*
Vijh, Ashok Kumar 1938- *WhoAm 92*
Vik, Gretchen N. *BioIn 17*
Vik, Stanley Merle 1941- *St&PR 93*
Vik, Torbjorn J. *WhoScE 91-4*
Vikal, Ram Chanda 1916- *WhoAsAP 91*
Vikander, Richard A. 1927- *St&PR 93*
Viken, Linda Lea Margaret 1945- *WhoAmW 93*
Viker, Dacques 1965- *WhoSSW 93*
Vikis-Freibergs, Vaira 1937- *WhoAm 92, WhoAmW 93*
Viklund, William Edwin 1940- *St&PR 93, WhoAm 92*
Vikner, David Walter 1944- *WhoE 93*
Viktil, Martin 1944- *WhoWor 93*
Viktorovitch, Pierre 1947- *WhoScE 91-2*
Vila, Adis Maria 1953- *WhoAm 92, WhoAmW 93*
Vila, Camilo 1947- *MiSFD 9*
Vila, Herminio Portell d1992 *NewYTBS 92*
Vila, Herminio Portell 1901-1992 *BioIn 17*
Vila, Pedro Alberto 1517-1582 *Baker 92*
Vila, Richard E. *Law&B 92*
Vila, Robert Joseph 1946- *WhoAm 92*
Vilain, Georges 1933- *WhoUN 92*
Vilalta, Maruxa 1932- *DcMexL*
Vilar, Antonio 1944- *St&PR 93*
Vilar, Jean 1912-1971 *BioIn 17*
Vilar, Rui Mario C.S. 1951- *WhoScE 91-3*
Vilardel, F. *WhoScE 91-4*
Vilardell, Francisco *WhoScE 91-3*
Vilardo, Veronica 1962- *WhoAmW 93*
Vilarino, Idea 1920- *SpAmA*
Vilas, Faith Van Valkenburgh *AmWomPl*
Vilas-Boas, Luis *WhoScE 91-3*
Vilback, (Alfonse Charles) Renaud de 1829-1884 *Baker 92*
Vilboa (Villebois), Konstantin 1817-1882 *Baker 92*
Vilcek, Jan Tomas 1933- *WhoAm 92*
Vilche, Jorge Roberto 1946- *WhoWor 93*
Vilches, Antonio Ricardo 1946- *WhoWor 93*
Vilches-O'Bourke, Octavio Augusto 1923- *WhoSSW 93*
Vilchez, Victoria Anne 1955- *WhoWor 93*
Vilchinsky, Edward P. 1930- *St&PR 93*
Vilela, Marcio Garcia 1939- *WhoWor 93*
Vilela Mendes, Rui 1938- *WhoScE 91-3*
Vilen, Erik Olavi 1933- *St&PR 93*
Vilenius, M.J. 1948- *WhoScE 91-4*
Viles, Daniel F. 1912- *St&PR 93*
Vilet C, Jordi 1950- *WhoWor 93*
Viley, Wylla Jamison *AmWomPl*
Vilhar, Franz 1852-1928 *Baker 92*
Vilhjalmsson, Hjalmar 1937- *WhoScE 91-4*
Vilhjalmsson, Thorsteinn 1940- *WhoWor 93*
Vilicic, Damir 1948- *WhoScE 91-4*
Vilim, George *BioIn 17*
Vilim, Nancy Catherine 1952- *WhoAmW 93*
Viljanen, Juha Heikki 1953- *WhoWor 93*
Viljoen, Gerrit Van Niekerk 1926- *WhoAfr*
Villa, David N. *Law&B 92*
Villa, Francisco *DcCPCAm*
Villa, Francisco 1877-1923 *DcTwHis*
Villa, Juan Francisco 1941- *WhoE 93*
Villa, Mario *BioIn 17*
Villa, Pancho 1878-1923 *BioIn 17*
Villa, Ricardo 1873-1935 *Baker 92*
Villa, Rita C. 1954- *St&PR 93*
Villa, Russell Steven 1957- *St&PR 93*
Villaareal, Sarah Jane 1961- *St&PR 93*
Villablanca, Jaime Rolando 1929- *WhoAm 92*
Villada Alzate, Oscar de Jesus 1946- *WhoWor 93*
Villadsen, Villads 1945- *WhoWor 93*
Villafana, Manuel A. *BioIn 17*
Villaflor, Adelina C. 1946- *St&PR 93*
Villafranca, Joseph J. 1944- *WhoAm 92*
Villagomez, Ramon Garrido 1949- *WhoAm 92*
Villagonzalo, Amparo De la Cerna 1939- *WhoAmW 93*
Villagra, Nelson 1937- *IntDcF 2-3 [port]*
Villain, Jacques 1934- *WhoScE 91-3*
Villa-Komaroff, Lydia 1947- *WhoAmW 93*
Villalba, Alfonso J. *Law&B 92*
Villalba Munoz, Luis 1872-1921 *Baker 92*
Villalobos, Debra Ruth 1952- *WhoAmW 93*
Villa-Lobos, Heitor *BioIn 17*
Villa-Lobos, Heitor 1887-1959 *Baker 92, IntDcOp, OxDcOp*
Villalobos, Joaquin 1951- *DcCPCAm*
Villalobos, Reynaldo *MiSFD 9*
Villalobos, Sergio *Law&B 92*
Villalobos Padilla, Francisco 1921- *WhoAm 92*
Villalobos Rivera, Sergio Fernando 1930- *WhoWor 93*
Villalon, Dalisay Manuel 1941- *WhoAmW 93*
Villalon, Silvia Duran 1941- *WhoAmW 93*
Villalpando, Catalina Vasquez *WhoAm 92, WhoAmW 93*
Villalpando, Catalina Vasquez 1940- *HispAmA*
Villalpando, Waldo *WhoUN 92*
Villamil, Richard J. 1942- *WhoE 93*
Villani, Frank John 1921- *WhoE 93*
Villani, G. Joseph 1937- *St&PR 93*
Villani, Jim 1948- *ScF&FL 92, WhoWrEP 92*
Villani, Nick P. 1937- *St&PR 93*
Villani, Paolo *WhoScE 91-3*
Villani, Stelio 1929- *WhoScE 91-3*
Villano, William N. 1943- *St&PR 93*
Villanova, Melissa Hope 1922- *WhoAm 92*
Villanova, Robert Allan, Sr. 1945- *WhoWor 93*
Villante, Umberto *WhoScE 91-3*
Villanti, Anthony V., Jr. 1943- *St&PR 93*
Villanueva, Alma Luz 1944- *DcLB 122 [port], NotHsAW 93*
Villanueva, Angelino Z. *Law&B 92*
Villanueva, Asdrubal d1991 *BioIn 17*
Villanueva, Carmen 1940- *WhoWor 93*
Villanueva, Dario 1950- *WhoWor 93*
Villanueva, Delano Segundo 1944- *WhoUN 92*
Villanueva, Eugenio 1949- *WhoWor 93*
Villanueva, Julio R. *WhoScE 91-3*
Villanueva, Luciana Marcella 1963- *WhoAmW 93, WhoSSW 93*
Villanueva Canadas, Enrique 1940- *WhoScE 91-3*
Villar, Cecilia Y. 1960- *WhoE 93*
Villar, Isabel Elsa 1948- *WhoE 93*
Villar, James Walter 1930- *WhoAm 92*
Villar, Manuel Carbonell 1856-1928
See Ferni, Vincenzina 1853-1926 *OxDcOp*
Villar, Rogelio del 1875-1937 *Baker 92*
Villard, Dimitri Serrano 1943- *St&PR 93*
Villard, Henry 1835-1900 *BioIn 17, JrnUS*
Villard, Katharine Neilley 1938- *WhoAmW 93*
Villard, Oswald Garrison 1872-1949 *BioIn 17, EncAACR, JrnUS*
Villareal, Cornelio T. 1903- *WhoAsAP 91*
Villarejos, Miguel O. *St&PR 93*
Villari, Robert 1932- *WhoE 93*
Villarini, Pedro 1933- *HispAmA*
Villa Rojas, Alfonso 1906- *IntDcAn*
Villarosa, Clara *BioIn 17*
Villarosa, Linda *BioIn 17*
Villar-Palasi, Carlos 1928- *WhoAm 92, WhoSSW 93*
Villarreal, Carlos Castaneda 1924- *WhoAm 92, WhoWor 93*
Villarreal, Ernesto 1948- *WhoUN 92*
Villarreal, G. Claude 1930- *St&PR 93*
Villarreal, Homero Atenogenes 1946- *WhoAm 92*
Villarreal, Irma *Law&B 92*
Villarreal, Irma 1958- *St&PR 93*
Villarreal, Jesse M. *Law&B 92*
Villarreal, Jesse M. 1939- *St&PR 93*
Villarreal, Joaquin Alfonso 1952- *WhoSSW 93*
Villarreal Garcia, Juliet *NotHsAW 93*
Villarrubia, Jan (Martha) 1948- *WhoWrEP 92*
Villars, Claude Louis Hector 1653-1734 *HarEnMi*
Villars, Elizabeth *ConAu 39NR*
Villars, Felix Marc Hermann 1921- *WhoAm 92*
Villasenor, Eduardo 1896- *DcMexL*
Villasenor, Gervasio Gallardo *ScF&FL 92*
Villasenor, Victor *BioIn 17*
Villasenor, Victor 1940- *HispAmA [port]*
Villasenor Family *BioIn 17*
Villate, Jaime Enrique 1959- *WhoWor 93*
Villati, Leopoldo di 1702-1752 *OxDcOp*
Villaurrutia, Xavier 1903-1950 *DcMexL, SpAmA*
Villavaso, Stephen Donald 1949- *WhoAm 92*
Villax, Ivan Joao 1925- *WhoWor 93*
Villeda Morales, Ramon 1908-1971 *DcCPCAm*
Villedieu, Madame de d1683 *BioIn 17*
Villee, Claude Alvin, Jr. 1917- *WhoAm 92*
Villegas, Oscar 1943- *DcMexL*
Villegas de Magnon, Leonor 1876-1955 *DcLB 122 [port]*
Villehardouin, Geoffrey c. 1152-1212? *OxDcByz*
Villela, Carlos Rocha 1956- *WhoWor 93*
Villela, J.O. 1941- *St&PR 93*
Villella, David Russell 1952- *St&PR 93*
Villella, Edward *BioIn 17*
Villella, Edward Joseph 1936- *WhoAm 92, WhoSSW 93, WhoWor 93*
Villella, Joseph F., Jr. *Law&B 92*
Villemaire, Roland 1937- *St&PR 93*
Villemonteix, Jean-Claude 1957- *WhoE 93*
Villeneuve, Jeannette 1937- *St&PR 93*
Villeneuve, Jocelyne Marie 1941- *WhoWrEP 92*
Villeneuve, Laurence 1952- *WhoWor 93*
Villeneuve, Pierre Charles Jean Baptiste Silvestre de 1763-1806 *HarEnMi*
Villeneuve, Ronald 1940- *St&PR 93*
Villeneuve De Janti, Philippe 1944- *WhoScE 91-2*
Villereal, Gary Lynn 1949- *WhoE 93*
Villermain-Lecolier, Gerard 1945- *WhoScE 91-2*
Villermaux, Jacques 1935- *WhoScE 91-2*
Villeroi, Francois de Neufville, Duke of 1644-1730 *HarEnMi*
Villers, Arthur 1934- *WhoScE 91-2*
Villers, Philippe 1935- *WhoAm 92*
Villette, Marie-Therese 1744-1837
See Laruette, Jean-Louis 1731-1792 *OxDcOp*
Villforth, John Carl 1930- *WhoAm 92*

Villiers, Alan 1903- *DcChlFi*
Villiers, Margot *ScF&FL 92*
Villiers de L'Isle Adam, Auguste, Comte de 1838-1889 *ScF&FL 92*
Villiers de l'Isle-Adam, Jean-Marie Mathias Philippe-Auguste, Comte de 1838-1889 *DcLB 123 [port]*
Villiger, Kaspar 1941- *WhoWor 93*
Villimal, J. Antonio *WhoAm 92*
Villinski, Paul Stephen 1960- *WhoE 93*
Villion, Jean-Francois *St&PR 93*
Villoch, Kelly Carney 1950- *WhoAmW 93*
Villodas, Steven *St&PR 93*
Villoing, Alexander 1804-1878 *Baker 92*
Villoing, Vasili 1850-1922 *Baker 92*
Villon, François 1431- *BioIn 17*
Villon, Jacques 1875-1963 *BioIn 17*
Villoteau, Guillaume-Andre 1759-1839 *Baker 92*
Villwock, Wolfgang H. 1930- *WhoScE 91-3*
Vilmos, Cserveny 1951- *WhoUN 92*
Vilnrotter, Victor Alpar 1944- *WhoWor 93*
Viloski, Benjamin J. *Law&B 92*
Vilott, Rhondi *ScF&FL 92*
Vilott-Salsitz, Rhondi *ScF&FL 92*
Vilsack, Gladys Brace *AmWomPl*
Vilsack, Robert D. *Law&B 92*
Vilter, Richard William 1911- *WhoAm 92*
Vina (Manteola), Facundo de la 1876-1952 *Baker 92*
Vinacke, W. Edgar 1917- *WhoWrEP 92*
Vinarub, Murray E. 1934- *St&PR 93*
Vinas, David 1929- *SpAmA*
Vinas, Sara Lahr *Law&B 92*
Vinaver, Michel 1927- *BioIn 17*
Vinay, Ramon 1912- *Baker 92, IntDcOp, OxDcOp*
Vinayagamoorthy, Manickavasagar 1958- *WhoSSW 93*
Vince, Murray *Law&B 92*
Vince, Terry *BioIn 17*
Vince, Terry 1929- *St&PR 93, WhoAm 92*
Vincel, Donald George 1940- *St&PR 93*
Vincelette, Muril D. 1931- *St&PR 93*
Vincelli, Mary Nicholas 1927- *WhoSSW 93*
Vincendon, Guy *WhoScE 91-2*
Vincens, Louis-Francois 1939- *WhoWor 93*
Vincent, Alexandre-Joseph Hydulphe 1797-1868 *Baker 92*
Vincent, Andre 1931- *WhoScE 91-2*
Vincent, Anthony M. 1946- *St&PR 93*
Vincent, Brad L. 1950- *St&PR 93*
Vincent, Bruce Havird 1947- *WhoSSW 93*
Vincent, Burton J. 1925- *St&PR 93*
Vincent, Charles Eagar, Jr. 1940- *WhoAm 92*
Vincent, Charles M. 1938- *St&PR 93*
Vincent, Clark Edward 1923- *WhoAm 92*
Vincent, Colin Angus *WhoScE 91-1*
Vincent, David Paul 1943- *St&PR 93*
Vincent, David Ridgely 1941- *WhoAm 92, WhoWor 93*
Vincent, E. Duke 1932- *St&PR 93*
Vincent, Edward 1920- *WhoAm 92*
Vincent, Edward 1934- *WhoAm 92*
Vincent, Ewart Albert *WhoScE 91-1*
Vincent, Fay *BioIn 17*
Vincent, Fay 1938- *WhoE 93*
Vincent, Francis T., Jr. *BioIn 17*
Vincent, Francis Thomas, Jr. 1938- *WhoAm 92, WhoE 93*
Vincent, Frederick Michael 1948- *WhoEmL 93, WhoWor 93*
Vincent, Gabrielle *BioIn 17, MajAI [port]*
Vincent, Hal Wellman 1927- *WhoAm 92*
Vincent, Harl 1893-1968 *ScF&FL 92*
Vincent, Heinrich Joseph 1819-1901 *Baker 92*
Vincent, Helen *WhoWrEP 92*
Vincent, James L. 1939- *BioIn 17*
Vincent, James Louis 1939- *St&PR 93, WhoAm 92, WhoWor 93*
Vincent, James Noah 1939- *WhoSSW 93*
Vincent, James Sidney 1935- *WhoE 93*
Vincent, Jean-Didier 1935- *WhoScE 91-2*
Vincent, Jeffrey R. 1952- *St&PR 93*
Vincent, John *ScF&FL 92*
Vincent, John 1902-1977 *Baker 92*
Vincent, John D. 1934- *St&PR 93*
Vincent, Johnny *SoulM*
Vincent, Julie 1922- *WhoWor 93*
Vincent, Kenneth Claude 1940- *WhoSSW 93*
Vincent, Kirk F. *Law&B 92*
Vincent, Lloyd Drexell 1924- *WhoAm 92, WhoSSW 93*
Vincent, Louis E. *Law&B 92*
Vincent, M. 1949- *WhoAsAP 91*
Vincent, Marjorie Judith *BioIn 17*
Vincent, Mary Lillian Carter 1931- *WhoE 93*
Vincent, Michael Thor *WhoE 93*
Vincent, Musette T. *Law&B 92*
Vincent, Nicholas *Law&B 92*
Vincent, Nigel Bruce *WhoScE 91-1*
Vincent, Norman Fuller 1930- *WhoAm 92, WhoSSW 93*
Vincent, Norman L. 1933- *WhoAm 92*
Vincent, R.J. 1943-1990 *BioIn 17*
Vincent, Rabiah 1952- *WhoAmW 93, WhoWor 93*
Vincent, Raymond 1928- *St&PR 93*
Vincent, Raymond John 1943-1990 *BioIn 17*
Vincent, Richard *WhoScE 91-1*
Vincent, Robert Victor *Law&B 92*
Vincent, Rodney Keith *Law&B 92*
Vincent, Roger Bracher 1945- *St&PR 93*
Vincent, Ronald 1960- *St&PR 93*
Vincent, Scott Garrison 1958- *WhoE 93*
Vincent, Sharidan Dee Ann 1965- *WhoAmW 93*
Vincent, Susan Gailey *Law&B 92*
Vincent, Susan Gailey 1957- *St&PR 93, WhoIns 93*
Vincent, Thomas James 1934- *WhoAm 92*
Vincent, William R. *SmATA 73*
Vincenti, Francesco 1952- *WhoUN 92*
Vincenti, John Richard 1946- *WhoE 93*
Vincenti, Walter Guido 1917- *WhoAm 92*
Vincenti, William Gene 1934- *WhoE 93*
Vincenti Mareri, Ippolito 1935- *WhoWor 93*
Vincentini, Deanna Lee 1939- *WhoAmW 93*
Vincenzi, Harry 1950- *WhoE 93*
Vincenzini, Pietro 1939- *WhoScE 91-3*
Vinchon, Bertrand 1930- *WhoScE 91-2*
Vinci, Frank J. *Law&B 92*
Vinci, Gerald F. *Law&B 92*
Vinci, John Nicholas 1937- *WhoAm 92*
Vinci, Leonardo c. 1690-1730 *Baker 92, OxDcOp*
Vinci, Leonardo da 1452-1519 *BioIn 17*
Vinci, Pietro c. 1535-c. 1584 *Baker 92*
Vinciguerra, Jean-Louis 1944- *WhoAm 92*
Vinciguerra, Ralph D. 1951- *St&PR 93*
Vinciguerra, Salvatore J. 1938- *St&PR 93*
Vinckier, Andre Gustaaf 1931- *WhoScE 91-2*
Vincola, Lyman David 1941- *St&PR 93*
Vincoli, Jeffrey Wayne 1959- *WhoSSW 93*
Vincze, Imre 1926-1969 *Baker 92*
Vinczeffy, Imre 1923- *WhoScE 91-4*
Vine, Allyn Collins 1914- *WhoAm 92*
Vine, Barbara 1930- *BioIn 17, WhoAmW 93*
Vine, David 1927- *St&PR 93*
Vine, Dorothy Goldberg 1943- *St&PR 93*
Vine, Frederick John *WhoScE 91-1*
Vine, Janet Diana 1937- *WhoWrEP 92*
Vine, P. A. L. 1927- *WhoWor 93*
Vineburgh, James Hollander 1943- *WhoAm 92*
Vinella, Ray 1933- *BioIn 17*
Vinen, William Frank *WhoScE 91-1*
Vinen, William Frank 1930- *WhoWor 93*
Viner, Arthur William 1922- *St&PR 93*
Viner, Donald Lee 1930- *WhoSSW 93*
Vines, Carolyn Marie Wadkins 1934- *WhoAmW 93*
Vines, Charles Jerry 1937- *WhoAm 92*
Vines, Ellsworth 1911- *BioIn 17*
Vines, Kimberly Gee *Law&B 92*
Vines, Martha Timberlake 1951- *WhoSSW 93*
Vines, Pamela Lynn Dyson 1955- *WhoAmW 93, WhoEmL 93, WhoWor 93*
Vines, Ricardo 1875-1943 *Baker 92*
Vineyard, Daniel E. *Law&B 92*
Vineyard, Michael Gene 1944- *St&PR 93*
Vineyard, Phyllis Smith 1924- *St&PR 93*
Vineyard, Susan Kay 1938- *WhoAmW 93*
Vinge, Joan D. 1948- *BioIn 17, ScF&FL 92*
Vinge, Vernor 1944- *ScF&FL 92*
Vingerhoets, Jan W.A. 1942- *WhoUN 92*
Vingo, James Ray 1938- *St&PR 93, WhoAm 92*
Vingoe, Francis James 1931- *WhoWor 93*
Vingsbo, Olof B. 1931- *WhoScE 91-4*
Vinha, Matti Uolevi 1947- *WhoWor 93*
Vinh Mau, Robert 1931- *WhoWor 93*
Vinicoff, Eric *ScF&FL 92*
Vinik, Hymie Ronald 1932- *WhoAm 92*
Vinik, Jeffrey *WhoAm 92*
Vining, Elizabeth Gray 1902- *MajAI [port], WhoAm 92*
Vining, Elizabeth Janet Gray 1902- *DcAmChF 1960*
Vining, Glen W., Jr. 1939- *St&PR 93*
Vining, John Kie 1953- *WhoSSW 93*
Vining, John Wiley 1942- *St&PR 93*
Vining, Jon R. 1939- *St&PR 93*
Vining, Joseph 1938- *WhoAm 92*
Vining, Kent M. 1947- *St&PR 93*
Vining, Mark A. *Law&B 92*
Vining, Michael Paul 1949- *WhoE 93*
Vining, Peggy Sue 1929- *WhoWrEP 92*
Vining, Robert Luke, Jr. 1931- *WhoAm 92*
Vinje, Annette E. *AmWomPl*
Vink, Frans 1918- *WhoWor 93*
Vinke, James Paul 1940- *St&PR 93*
Vinkler, Peter 1941- *WhoScE 91-4*
Vinocur, M. Richard 1934- *WhoAm 92*
Vinocur, Peter A. *Law&B 92*
Vinogradov, G.V. *BioIn 17*
Vinogradov, Georgii Vladimirovich *BioIn 17*
Vinogradsky, Alexander 1855-1912 *Baker 92*
Vinokour, Jan L. *Law&B 92*
Vinokurov, Javier Esteban *Law&B 92*
Vinsant, George O'Neal 1951- *WhoSSW 93*
Vinsavich, Stephen M. *Law&B 92*
Vinson, B. Finley 1914- *St&PR 93*
Vinson, Bernard L. 1919- *WhoE 93*
Vinson, C. Roger 1940- *WhoAm 92*
Vinson, Craig Olin 1950- *WhoSSW 93*
Vinson, David Allen 1958- *WhoSSW 93*
Vinson, David Berwick 1917- *WhoSSW 93*
Vinson, Eddie 1917-1988 *Baker 92*
Vinson, Frederick Moore 1890-1953 *OxCSupC [port]*
Vinson, Gavin Paul *WhoScE 91-1*
Vinson, James A. 1945- *WhoAm 92*
Vinson, James Anthony 1945- *St&PR 93*
Vinson, James Spangler 1941- *WhoAm 92*
Vinson, Lance C. *Law&B 92*
Vinson, Leila Terry Walker 1928- *WhoAmW 93*
Vinson, Maribel 1911-1961 *BioIn 17*
Vinson, Phyllis Tucker *AfrAmBi [port]*
Vinson, Rex *ScF&FL 92*
Vinson, S. Bradleigh 1938- *WhoSSW 93*
Vinson, Shirley Mae 1959- *WhoAmW 93*
Vinson, Thomas Glenn 1923- *St&PR 93*
Vinson, William Lloyd 1959- *WhoE 93*
Vinson, William T. *Law&B 92, WhoAm 92*
Vint, Gregory L. *Law&B 92*
Vint, Jesse *MiSFD 9*
Vint, Karalee 1943- *St&PR 93*
Vint, Richard C. *Law&B 92*
Vint, Robert J. 1934- *St&PR 93*
Vintem, Antonio Feliciano Bento 1945- *WhoWor 93*
Vinten, Gerald 1948- *WhoWor 93*
Vinter, Michael 1927- *ScF&FL 92*
Vintiadis, Polyvios Constantine 1935- *St&PR 93*
Vinton, Alfred M. *BioIn 17*
Vinton, Bobby *WhoAm 92*
Vinton, Iris *AmWomPl*
Vinton, Victoria *SweetSg C [port]*
Vinton, Will *MiSFD 9*
Vinue, Ricardo Juan Lorenzo 1935- *WhoWor 93*
Vinuesa, Julio Hector 1947- *WhoWor 93*
Vinyard, John Wesley 1945- *WhoSSW 93*
Vinz, Mark 1942- *WhoWrEP 92*
Viola, Alfonso *Baker 92*
Viola, Alfred 1928- *WhoE 93*
Viola, Francesco *Baker 92*
Viola, Frank 1960- *BioIn 17*
Viola, Frank John, Jr. 1960- *WhoAm 92*
Viola, Herman Joseph 1938- *WhoAm 92*
Viola, James Stephen *Law&B 92*
Viola, P. Anselm 1738-1798 *Baker 92*
Viola, Robert Allen 1943- *St&PR 93*
Viola, Roger Keith *Law&B 92*
Viola, Ronald James 1943- *St&PR 93*
Viola, Vincent James 1953- *WhoSSW 93*
Violante, Joseph Anthony 1950- *WhoEmL 93*
Violante, Marcela Fernandez *MiSFD 9*
Violant i Simorra, Ramon 1903-1956 *IntDcAn*
Viole, Rudolf 1825-1867 *Baker 92*
Violenus, Agnes A. *WhoE 93*
Violet, Timothy C. *Law&B 92*
Violet, Ultra *ConAu 136*
Violet, Woodrow Wilson, Jr. 1937- *WhoWor 93*
Violette, Daniel Markus 1951- *St&PR 93*
Violette, Diane Marie 1958- *WhoAmW 93*
Violi, Giuseppe 1921- *WhoScE 91-3*
Violi, Paul Randolph 1944- *WhoWrEP 92*
Vionnet, Madeleine 1876-1975 *BioIn 17*
Vioque, Agustin 1923- *WhoScE 91-3*
Vior, Constantin 1930- *WhoScE 91-4*
Viorst, Judith 1931- *MajAI [port], SmATA 70 [port]*
Viorst, Judith Stahl 1931- *WhoAm 92, WhoWrEP 92*
Viorst, Milton 1930- *WhoAm 92, WhoWrEP 92*
Viosky, George Thomas 1935- *St&PR 93*
Viotta, Henri 1848-1933 *OxDcOp*
Viotta, Henri(cus Anastasius) 1848-1933 *Baker 92*
Viotta, Johannes Josephus 1814-1859 *Baker 92*
Viotti, Giovanni Battista 1755-1824 *Baker 92*
Vipont, Charles *ConAu 38NR, MajAI*
Vipont, Elfrida *ConAu 38NR, MajAI*
Vipperman, Joseph H. 1940- *St&PR 93, WhoAm 92*
Vipperman, Ramona *Law&B 92*
Virag, Ronald 1938- *WhoWor 93*
Viramontes, Arnold 1948- *St&PR 93*
Viramontes, Helena Maria 1954- *AmWomWr 92, DcLB 122 [port], NotHsAW 93*
Virapoulle, Jean-Paul 1944- *WhoAsAP 91*
Virapoulle, Louis 1934- *WhoAsAP 91*
Virato, Swami 1938- *WhoWrEP 92*
Viravaidhya, Mechai *BioIn 17*
Virchenko, Yuri Petrovich 1949- *WhoWor 93*
Virchow, Rudolf Ludwig Karl 1821-1902 *BioIn 17*
Virdee, Pritpal Singh 1959- *St&PR 93*
Virdi, Kuldeep Singh *WhoScE 91-1*
Virdon, William Charles 1931- *BiDAMSp 1989*
Virdung, Sebastian c. 1465- *Baker 92*
Virelli, Louis James, Jr. *Law&B 92*
Virenque, Christian 1939- *WhoScE 91-2*
Virg, Leo *ScF&FL 92*
Virgalitte, Anthony David 1949- *St&PR 93*
Virgil *BioIn 17*
Virgin Mary *BioIn 17*
Virgo, John Michael 1943- *WhoAm 92*
Virgo, Julie Anne Carroll 1944- *WhoAm 92*
Virgo, Katherine Sue 1959- *WhoAmW 93*
Virgo, Sean 1940- *WhoCanL 92*
Virieux, Jean-Michel 1939- *WhoScE 91-4*
Virizlay, Mihaly 1931- *Baker 92*
Virkus, Kenneth Juri 1933- *WhoWor 93*
Virmani, Sant Singh 1940- *WhoWor 93*
Virnicchi, Tommaso 1954- *WhoWor 93*
Virnig, Jerry T. 1932- *St&PR 93*
Virolainen, Erkki 1938- *WhoScE 91-4*
Virosztek, Attila 1958- *WhoWor 93*
Virri, Esko Kalevi 1929- *WhoScE 91-4*
Virshup, Edward Marc 1945- *St&PR 93*
Virta, Juhani 1935- *WhoScE 91-4*
Virtanen, Ismo T. 1949- *WhoScE 91-4*
Virtanen, Keijo Tapio 1947- *WhoWor 93*
Virtanen, Pekka. V. 1929- *WhoScE 91-4*
Virtanen, Pentti Olavi Ilmari 1931- *WhoScE 91-4*
Virtanen, Simo K. 1925- *WhoScE 91-4*
Virtue, Judson E. *Law&B 92*
Virtue, Richard L. 1921- *WhoSSW 93*
Virtue, Stephen Linn 1953- *WhoSSW 93*
Virzi, Richard A. 1927- *St&PR 93*
Visaggio, Peter 1955- *St&PR 93*
Visca, Arturo Sergio 1917- *WhoWor 93*
Viscarra Monje, Humberto 1898-1971 *Baker 92*
Visceglia, Diego R. 1943- *St&PR 93*
Visceglia, Frank 1914- *St&PR 93*
Visceglia, Frank D. d1991 *BioIn 17*
Visceglia, Vincent 1905- *St&PR 93*
Viscelli, Therese Rauth 1955- *WhoAmW 93*
Vischer, Daniel L. 1932- *WhoScE 91-4*
Vischer, Harold Harry 1914- *WhoAm 92*
Viscio, Donald P. 1934- *St&PR 93*
Visclosky, Peter J. 1949- *CngDr 91*
Visclosky, Peter John 1949- *WhoAm 92*
Visco, Ferdinand Joseph 1941- *WhoE 93*
Visco, Giuseppe 1927- *WhoWor 93*
Visco, Susan Josephine 1938- *WhoAmW 93*
Visconti, Angelo 1951- *WhoScE 91-3*
Visconti (di Modrone), Luchino 1906-1976 *Baker 92*
Visconti, Joan Marie 1935- *WhoE 93*
Visconti, Julius Arthur 1931- *St&PR 93*
Visconti, Luchino 1906-1976 *ConAu 39NR, IntDcOp, MiSFD 9N, OxDcOp*
Visconti, Richard A. *Law&B 92*
Viscontini, Max 1913- *WhoWor 93*
Viscott, David S. 1938- *BioIn 17*
Viscount Weir, William Kenneth James 1933- *WhoWor 93*
Viscusi, Anthony 1932- *St&PR 93*
Viscusi, W. Kip 1949- *ConAu 138*
Viscusi, William G. Kip 1949- *WhoSSW 93*
Vise, Harry 1921- *St&PR 93*
Visedo, Javier 1961- *St&PR 93*
Visee, Robert de c. 1650-c. 1725 *Baker 92*
Visek, Willard James 1922- *WhoAm 92*
Visentin, Roberto 1937- *WhoScE 91-3*
Visetti, Alberto Antonio 1846-1928 *Baker 92*
Visher, Emily Browning 1918- *WhoAmW 93*
Vishnevskaya, Galina 1926- *IntDcOp, OxDcOp*
Vishnevskaya, Galina (Pavlovna) 1926- *Baker 92, WhoAm 92*
Vishniac, Ethan Tecumseh 1955- *WhoSSW 93*
Vishniac, Roman *BioIn 17*
Vishnisky, Morris Irving 1941- *WhoWrEP 92*
Visich, Marian, Jr. 1930- *WhoAm 92*
Visintin, Arnaldo 1954- *WhoSSW 93*
Viskanta, Raymond 1931- *WhoAm 92*

Viski, Janos 1906-1961 *Baker 92*
Viskum, Kaj 1938- *WhoWor 93*
Vislocky, Joseph M. 1943- *St&PR 93*
Vislosky, George, Jr. 1933- *St&PR 93*
Vislykh, Victor Alexander 1945- *WhoUN 92*
Visneaskus, Daniel Joseph 1943- *WhoAm 92*
Visocki, Nancy Gayle 1952- *WhoAmW 93*
Visone, Albert Michael 1946- *St&PR 93*
Visotsky, Harold Meryle 1924- *WhoAm 92*
Visotzky, Burton L. 1951- *ConAu 138*
Visscher, Pieter Bernard 1945- *WhoSSW 93*
Visscher, William Lightfoot 1842-1921 *JrnUS*
Visschers, Raoul Guillaume 1930- *WhoWor 93*
Visser, Greg D. 1957- *St&PR 93*
Visser, H.K.A. 1930- *WhoScE 91-3*
Visser, John Evert 1920- *WhoAm 92*
Vissers, Christian F. *Law&B 92*
Vissers, Toon H. 1943- *WhoUN 92*
Vissicchio, Andrew John, Jr. 1941- *WhoSSW 93*
Vissol, Thierry-Louis 1951- *WhoWor 93*
Viste, Arlen Ellard 1936- *WhoWor 93*
Visuri, Osmo Olavi 1927- *WhoScE 91-4*
Viswanathan, Chand Ram 1929- *WhoAm 92*
Viswanathan, Gauri 1950- *WhoE 93*
Viswanathan, Ramaswamy 1949- *WhoEmL 93, WhoWor 93*
Vitagliano, Kenneth John 1954- *WhoE 93*
Vitagliano, Vincent J. 1927- *WhoSSW 93*
Vital, Claude Bernard 1932- *WhoWor 93*
Vitale, Alberto Aldo 1933- *WhoAm 92*
Vitale, Anne T. *Law&B 92*
Vitale, Branko 1932- *WhoScE 91-4*
Vitale, Dale T. *Law&B 92*
Vitale, David 1946- *St&PR 93*
Vitale, Dick *BioIn 17*
Vitale, Edoardo 1872-1937 *OxDcOp*
Vitale, Ettore 1936- *BioIn 17*
Vitale, Francis X. 1944- *St&PR 93*
Vitale, Frederick R. 1941- *WhoE 93*
Vitale, Gerald Lee 1950- *WhoEmL 93*
Vitale, Henry Rico Edward 1966- *WhoSSW 93*
Vitale, Louis 1902- *St&PR 93*
Vitale, Magda 1939- *WhoE 93*
Vitale, Patricia Frances 1959- *WhoAmW 93*
Vitale, Riccardo 1903- *OxDcOp*
Vitale, Rosanna 1952- *WhoSSW 93*
Vitale, Ruth A. 1952- *St&PR 93*
Vitale, Salvatore John, Jr. 1939- *St&PR 93*
Vitale, Tamaam 1948- *WhoE 93*
Vitale-Salajanu, Annette Louise 1957- *WhoAmW 93*
Vitali, Filippo c. 1590-1653? *Baker 92, OxDcOp*
Vitali, Giovanni Battista 1632-1692 *Baker 92*
Vitalian dc. 520 *OxDcByz*
Vitaliano, Charles Joseph 1910- *WhoAm 92*
Vitalini, Alberico 1921- *Baker 92*
Vitalis, George 1895-1959 *Baker 92*
Vitalis, Gyorgy 1929- *WhoScE 91-4*
Vitalos, Robert Francis 1947- *WhoWrEP 92*
Vitamante, Robert J. 1945- *St&PR 93*
Vitanidis, Gheorghe 1929- *DrEEuF*
Vitanov, Todor Donchev 1926- *WhoScE 91-4*
Vitantonio, Louis A. 1943- *St&PR 93*
Vitanza, Carlo 1947- *WhoScE 91-4*
Vitanza, Lorraine Lucy Istre 1938- *WhoSSW 93*
Vitarelli, Robert Francis 1940- *WhoE 93*
Vitek, Jan 1928- *WhoWor 93*
Vitek, Karen Ann 1956- *WhoAmW 93*
Vitek, Kenn E. 1926- *St&PR 93*
Vitek, Vaclav 1940- *WhoAm 92*
Vitek, Vojtech *WhoScE 91-4*
Vitelli, Alessandro 1963- *WhoWor 93*
Vitelli, James Thomas *Law&B 92*
Vitello, Guy *Law&B 92*
Vitello, Robert Blair 1958- *WhoSSW 93*
Vitello, Stanley John 1944- *WhoE 93*
Viteo, Penelope Rhude *Law&B 92*
Viterbi, Andrew J. *St&PR 93*
Viterbi, Andrew James 1935- *WhoAm 92*
Vitez, Antoine 1930-1990 *BioIn 17*
Vithoontien, Mana 1934- *WhoWor 93*
Vitiello, Justin 1941- *ConAu 139, WhoWrEP 92*
Vitiello, Mario James 1952- *WhoIns 93*
Vitiello, Pierre 1940- *WhoScE 91-2*
Vitiges dc. 542 *OxDcByz*
Vititoe, William P. 1938- *St&PR 93*
Vititoe, William Paul 1938- *WhoAm 92*
Vitkowsky, Vincent Joseph 1955- *WhoE 93, WhoEmL 93, WhoWor 93*
Vito, Steven M. 1954- *St&PR 93*
Vito, Vincenzo Bianco *WhoScE 91-3*
Vitola, Jack Joseph 1931- *St&PR 93*
Vitole, Nicholas M. 1937- *St&PR 93*
Vitolins, Jekab 1898- *Baker 92*
Vitolo, Arlene Gayle 1945- *St&PR 93*
Vitolo, Michael J. *Law&B 92*
Vitolo, Ralph S. *Law&B 92*
Vitols, Reinhards *WhoScE 91-1*
Vitoratos, Evagelos G. 1954- *WhoScE 91-3*
Vitoratos, Evagelos Geras 1954- *WhoWor 93*
Vitriaco, Philippus de 1291-1361 *Baker 92*
Vitro, Frank Thomas, Jr. 1941- *WhoSSW 93*
Vitry, Philippe de 1291-1361 *Baker 92*
Vitsut, Ullar *Law&B 92*
Vitt, David Aaron 1938- *WhoAm 92*
Vitt, David Arron 1938- *St&PR 93*
Vitt, Sam B. 1926- *St&PR 93, WhoAm 92, WhoE 93, WhoWor 93*
Vitt, Sam Bradshaw 1926- *WhoWrEP 92*
Vittadini, Adrienne *BioIn 17, WhoAm 92, WhoAmW 93*
Vittadini, Franco 1884-1948 *Baker 92*
Vittadini, Gian Luigi Maria *BioIn 17*
Vittands, Jekabs Paulis 1936- *St&PR 93*
Vittas, Harilaos 1941- *WhoUN 92*
Vittek, Jozef 1934- *WhoE 93*
Vitter, Jeffrey Scott 1955- *WhoAm 92*
Vittetoe, Marie Clare 1927- *WhoAmW 93, WhoSSW 93*
Vitti, Louis Peter 1940- *WhoE 93*
Vitti, Monica 1931- *BioIn 17, IntDcF 2-3 [port]*
Vittitow, Chester Allen, Jr. 1931- *WhoSSW 93*
Vittitow, Mary L(ou) 1937- *ConAu 139*
Vitt-Maucher, Gisela Maria 1934- *WhoAm 92*
Vittone, Bernard John 1951- *WhoE 93*
Vittor, Kenneth M. 1949- *St&PR 93*
Vittor, Kenneth Mark *Law&B 92*
Vittore, Nicholas A. 1935- *St&PR 93*
Vittori, Darlene Marie 1966- *WhoAmW 93*
Vittori, Francois 1941- *WhoWor 93*
Vittori, Loreto 1600?-1670 *Baker 92, OxDcOp*
Vittoria, Alessandro 1525-1608 *BioIn 17*
Vittoria, Joseph V. 1935- *WhoAm 92*
Vittorini, Carlo 1929- *St&PR 93, WhoAm 92*
Vittorio, Salvatore Anthony 1952- *WhoE 93*
Vittrup Christensen, Jorgen 1929- *WhoScE 91-2*
Vittu, Christian 1916- *WhoScE 91-2*
Vittu, Michel 1948- *WhoScE 91-2*
Vitu, Christian 1945- *WhoScE 91-2*
Vitug, Mylene Virginia Gonzales 1963- *WhoWor 93*
Vitulli, William Francis 1936- *WhoSSW 93*
Vitulli, William Joseph 1918- *St&PR 93*
Vitz, Carl 1883-1981 *BioIn 17*
Vitz, Robert C. 1938- *ConAu 136*
Vivaldi, Antonio 1678-1741 *IntDcOp [port], OxDcOp*
Vivaldi, Antonio (Lucio) 1678-1741 *Baker 92*
Vivaldi, Giovanni Battista c. 1655-1736 See Vivaldi, Antonio (Lucio) 1678-1741 *Baker 92*
Vivanco, Luis Felipe 1907-1975 *BioIn 17*
Vivante, Arturo 1923- *WhoWrEP 92*
Vivas, Julie *ChlBIID [port]*
Vive, Kurt 1935- *WhoScE 91-2*
Viveiros, Sharon Sumie 1959- *WhoAmW 93*
Vivell, Colestin 1846-1923 *Baker 92*
Vivelo, Jackie *BioIn 17*
Vivelo, Jackie 1943- *ScF&FL 92*
Vivelo, Jacqueline *ScF&FL 92*
Vivelo, Jacqueline Jean 1943- *WhoE 93, WhoWor 93*
Vivera, Arsenio Bondoc 1931- *WhoE 93*
Vives, Amadeo 1871-1932 *Baker 92*
Vivian, Daisy *WhoWrEP 92*
Vivian, E. Charles 1882-1947 *ScF&FL 92*
Vivian, Herbert 1865- *ScF&FL 92*
Vivian, James Robert 1946- *WhoE 93*
Vivian, Jean A. *Law&B 92*
Vivian, Johnson Edward 1913- *WhoAm 92*
Vivian, Joyce 1951- *St&PR 93*
Vivian, Kaye 1947- *WhoWrEP 92*
Vivian, Linda Bradt 1945- *WhoAmW 93*
Vivian, Peter Edward *Law&B 92*
Viviani, Cesare 1947- *DcLB 128 [port]*
Viviani, Gary Lee 1955- *WhoWor 93*
Viviani, Rene Raphael 1863-1925 *BioIn 17*
Viviano, Bartholomew J. d1990 *BioIn 17*
Viviano, Catherine 1899-1992 *BioIn 17, NewYTBS 92*
Viviano, Joseph P. 1938- *St&PR 93*
Viviano, Sam Joseph 1953- *WhoAm 92*
Vivier, Albert-Joseph 1816-1903 *Baker 92*
Vivier, Claude 1948-1983 *Baker 92*
Vivier, Eugene (-Leon) 1817-1900 *Baker 92*
Viviers, Lyn *ScF&FL 92*
Vivinis, Bernard 1948- *WhoScE 91-2*
Vivo, Paquita 20th cent.- *HispAmA*
Vivona, Daniel Nicholas 1924- *WhoWor 93*
Vivona, Franco M. 1944- *WhoScE 91-3*
Vivona, John Anthony 1952- *WhoE 93*
Vivona, Thomas R. 1934- *St&PR 93*
Vivoni, Armando 1924- *St&PR 93*
Vix, Carol A. *Law&B 92*
Vix, Genevieve 1879-1939 *Baker 92*
Vixen, Richard M. *ScF&FL 92*
Vizard, Frank Joseph 1955- *WhoAm 92, WhoE 93*
Vizas, Robert J. *Law&B 92*
Vizdak, Karoly 1950- *WhoScE 91-4*
Vizenor, Gerald Robert 1934- *BioIn 17*
Vizetelly, Henry 1820-1894 *BioIn 17*
Vizinczey, Stephen 1933- *WhoCanL 92*
Vizkelety, Tibor L. 1929- *WhoScE 91-4*
Vizner, Nikola 1945- *WhoE 93*
Vizoukis, Steven P. 1956- *St&PR 93*
Vizy, Kalman Nicholas 1940- *WhoE 93*
Vizza, Robert Francis 1933- *WhoAm 92*
Vizzi, Carl J. *St&PR 93*
Vizzier, Etta Yvonne 1946- *WhoAmW 93*
Vlaar, Nicolaas Jacob 1933- *WhoWor 93*
Vlach, Jeffrey Allen 1953- *WhoWor 93*
Vlach, Jiri 1922- *WhoAm 92*
Vlach, Milan 1936- *WhoScE 91-4*
Vlachakis, George 1956- *WhoWor 93*
Vlachopoulos, Evangelos 1949- *WhoScE 91-3, WhoWor 93*
Vlachos, Dimitris 1935- *WhoScE 91-3*
Vlachos, Nicholas Spyro 1943- *WhoSSW 93*
Vlacich, Nino M. 1949- *St&PR 93*
Vlacil, Frantisek 1924- *DrEEuF*
Vlacq, Adrian 1600?-1667 *BioIn 17*
Vlad, Roman 1919- *Baker 92*
Vlad, Viorel George 1946- *WhoE 93*
Vladavsky, Lyubov 1957- *WhoAmW 93*
Vlad Dracul, II, Prince of Wallachia 1431-1476 *BioIn 17*
Vladeck, Bruce Charney 1949- *WhoAm 92*
Vladigerov, Alexander 1933- *Baker 92*
Vladigerov, Pantcho 1899-1978 *Baker 92*
Vladimir c. 1110-1153 *OxDcByz*
Vladimir, I d1015 *OxDcByz*
Vladimir Monomach 1053-1125 *OxDcByz*
Vladimir of Russia, Grand Duke 1917- *NewYTBS 92 [port]*
Vladimirtsov, B.IA. 1884-1931 *IntDcAn*
Vladislav Jagello, III 1424-1444 *OxDcByz*
Vladutiu, Adrian O. 1940- *WhoE 93*
Vladutiu, Georgirene Dietrich 1944- *WhoE 93*
Vlaemynck, Maria *BioIn 17*
Vlahokosta, Frideriki V. *WhoWor 93*
Vlahos, Darlene M. *Law&B 92*
Vlaminck, Maurice de 1876-1958 *BioIn 17*
Vlaovic, Milan Stephen 1936- *WhoE 93*
Vlasak, Walter Raymond 1938- *WhoWor 93*
Vlasek, Mary C. *AmWomPl*
Vlases, George C. 1936- *WhoAm 92*
Vlasic, R.J. *St&PR 93*
Vlasic, Robert Joseph 1926- *WhoAm 92, WhoWor 93*
Vlasich, James A(nthony) 1944- *ConAu 137*
Vlasnik, Lincoln A. 1914- *St&PR 93*
Vlasopolos, Anca 1948- *WhoWrEP 92*
Vlasov, Vladimir 1946- *WhoWor 93*
Vlasov, Vladimir (Alexandrovich) 1903-1986 *Baker 92*
Vlassak, Karel F.R. 1934- *WhoScE 91-2*
Vlassopoulos, Nicholas Ch. 1935- *WhoWor 93*
Vlastimir fl. 9th cent.- *OxDcByz*
Vlastos, Antonios E. 1931- *WhoScE 91-4*
Vlastos, Gregory 1907-1991 *BioIn 17*
Vlavianos, John G. 1933- *WhoE 93, WhoWor 93*
Vlazny, John George 1937- *WhoAm 92*
Vlcanov, Rangel 1928- *DrEEuF*
Vlcek, Donald Joseph, Jr. 1949- *WhoWor 93*
Vlcek, Ernst *ScF&FL 92*
Vlcek, Jan Benes 1943- *WhoAm 92*
Vliet, Gary Clark 1933- *WhoAm 92*
Vliet, R.G. 1929- *BioIn 17*
Vliet, Rollin Dale 1914- *WhoAm 92*
Vliet, Walter C. *Law&B 92*
Vlietinck, Arnold Jozef 1941- *WhoScE 91-2, WhoWor 93*
Vlijmen, Jan van 1935- *Baker 92*
Vlugt, Hans Rene Pieter Cornelis 1935- *WhoWor 93*
Vnuk, John Andrew 1934- *St&PR 93*
Vo, Nguyen Giap 1912- *BioIn 17*
Voaden, Graham d1992 *BioIn 17*
Voaden, Herman 1903- *WhoCanL 92*
Voake, Richard Charles 1940- *WhoWor 93*
Vocatura, David Michael 1963- *St&PR 93*
Voce, Joan A. Cifonelli 1936- *WhoAmW 93*
Vo Chi Cong 1913- *WhoWor 93*
Vo Chi Cong 1914- *WhoAsAP 91*
Vochis, Charles George 1943- *St&PR 93*
Vocht, Michelle Elise 1956- *WhoWor 93*
Voci, Frank Anthony 1936- *St&PR 93*
Vocia, Phoenix 1956- *WhoE 93*
Vocke, Louis J. 1924- *St&PR 93*
Vockel, Richard L. 1920- *St&PR 93*
Vockerodt, Gottfried 1665-1727 *Baker 92*
Vockner, Josef 1842-1906 *Baker 92*
Vodak, James W. 1943- *St&PR 93*
Vodden, Lisa A. 1966- *St&PR 93*
Voderberg, Kurt Ernest 1921- *St&PR 93*
Vodovnik, Raymond Frank *Law&B 92*
Vodovnik, Raymond Frank 1935- *St&PR 93*
Vodusek, Valens 1912- *Baker 92*
Vodyanoy, Vitaly Jacob 1941- *WhoSSW 93, WhoWor 93*
Voecks, Daniel Michael 1934- *St&PR 93*
Voegelein, Glenn E. 1912- *St&PR 93*
Voegeli, Victor Jacque 1934- *WhoAm 92*
Voegelin, C.F. 1906-1986 *IntDcAn*
Voegelin, Erminie Wheeler *IntDcAn*
Voegelin, Erminie Wheeler- 1903-1988 *BioIn 17*
Voeks, Dean W. 1942- *St&PR 93*
Voelkel, Harold J. *St&PR 93*
Voelker, Christopher *BioIn 17*
Voelker, Dorothy E. *Law&B 92*
Voelker, John 1903-1991 *AnObit 1991*
Voelker, John Donaldson 1903-1991 *BioIn 17*
Voelker, Larry 1933- *St&PR 93, WhoAm 92*
Voell, Richard Allen 1933- *WhoAm 92*
Voellmicke, John L. *Law&B 92*
Voelpel, Lawrence W. 1950- *St&PR 93*
Voelpel, Mark S. *Law&B 92*
Voelte, Donald R. 1952- *WhoSSW 93*
Voelter, Wolfgang 1936- *WhoWor 93*
Voermans, Jan A.M. 1943- *WhoScE 91-3*
Voet, Martin A. *Law&B 92*
Voet, Paul C. 1946- *St&PR 93, WhoAm 92*
Voetmann, Jan 1941- *WhoScE 91-2*
Vogae, Bernard *WhoAsAP 91*
Vogan, David Nicholas 1951- *WhoSSW 93*
Vogan, Sara *BioIn 17*
Vogan, Sara 1947- *WhoWrEP 92*
Vogds, Daniel E. 1948- *St&PR 93*
Vogel, Adolf 1897-1969 *Baker 92*
Vogel, Alfred 1927- *St&PR 93*
Vogel, Anna Kirwan- *ScF&FL 92*
Vogel, Arthur Anton 1924- *WhoAm 92*
Vogel, Brenda *BioIn 17*
Vogel, Bruce Sandor 1937- *WhoE 93*
Vogel, Carole Garbuny 1951- *ConAu 138, SmATA 70 [port]*
Vogel, Cedric Wakelee 1946- *WhoWor 93*
Vogel, Charles A., Jr. 1925- *WhoAm 92*
Vogel, Charles Donald *Law&B 92*
Vogel, Charles Louis Adolphe 1808-1892 *Baker 92*
Vogel, Charles Orville 1948- *WhoE 93*
Vogel, Claus 1933- *WhoWor 93*
Vogel, Daniel James 1960- *St&PR 93*
Vogel, David Jay 1947- *WhoAm 92*
Vogel, Donald Sears *WhoAm 92*
Vogel, Donald Stanley 1917- *WhoAm 92, WhoWrEP 92*
Vogel, (Johannes) Emil (Eduard Bernhard) 1859-1908 *Baker 92*
Vogel, Eugene L. 1931- *WhoAm 92*
Vogel, Eugenio Emilio 1946- *WhoWor 93*
Vogel, Ezra F. 1930- *WhoAm 92*
Vogel, Frank 1929- *DrEEuF*
Vogel, Frederick Wilmont Blanton *Law&B 92*
Vogel, Friedrich 1925- *WhoScE 91-3*
Vogel, Friedrich Wilhelm Ferdinand 1807-1892 *Baker 92*
Vogel, George Becker 1926- *St&PR 93*
Vogel, Gerald Leon 1952- *St&PR 93*
Vogel, Gerhard Hans 1927- *WhoWor 93*
Vogel, H. Victoria *WhoAmW 93, WhoE 93, WhoWor 93*
Vogel, Hans-Jochen 1926- *WhoWor 93*
Vogel, Harold Ray 1936- *St&PR 93*
Vogel, Henry Elliott 1925- *WhoAm 92*
Vogel, Henry James 1920- *WhoAm 92, WhoWor 93*
Vogel, Herman L. 1923- *St&PR 93*
Vogel, Hermann Carl 1841-1907 *BioIn 17*
Vogel, Howard H. 1949- *WhoAm 92*
Vogel, Howard Stanley 1934- *WhoE 93, WhoWor 93*
Vogel, Irene Susan *WhoAmW 93*
Vogel, J. Vann *Law&B 92*
Vogel, Jaroslav 1894-1970 *Baker 92*
Vogel, Johann Christoph 1756?-1788 *Baker 92*
Vogel, John M. *Law&B 92*
Vogel, John Walter 1948- *WhoE 93, WhoEmL 93*
Vogel, Joseph Otto 1936- *WhoAm 92*

Vogel, Judith Ann 1943- *WhoAmW 93*
Vogel, Julius 1924- *WhoAm 92*
Vogel, June Elaine 1940- *St&PR 93*
Vogel, Karen Jean 1958- *WhoAmW 93*
Vogel, Klaus 1931- *WhoScE 91-3*
Vogel, Leonard Bernard 1924- *St&PR 93*
Vogel, Linda I. *Law&B 92*
Vogel, Malvina Graff 1932- *WhoAmW 93*
Vogel, Marilyn B. *Law&B 92*
Vogel, Marion Lack *WhoSSW 93*
Vogel, Michael J. *BioIn 17*
Vogel, Michael N. 1947- *WhoE 93*
Vogel, Michael W. 1962- *St&PR 93*
Vogel, Orville Alvin 1907-1991 *BioIn 17*
Vogel, Paul Mark 1968- *WhoWrEP 92*
Vogel, Peter *WhoScE 91-4*
Vogel, Pierre 1944- *WhoWor 93*
Vogel, Rainer 1938- *WhoUN 92*
Vogel, Richard A. *Law&B 92*
Vogel, Richard Hunter 1930- *WhoAm 92*
Vogel, Robert 1918- *WhoAm 92*
Vogel, Robert 1919- *WhoWor 93*
Vogel, Robert Alan 1943- *WhoE 93*
Vogel, Robert Henry 1946- *St&PR 93*
Vogel, Robert Lee 1934- *WhoAm 92*
Vogel, Robert P. *Law&B 92*
Vogel, Theodore John *Law&B 92*
Vogel, Valorie Lynn 1961- *WhoAmW 93*
Vogel, Virgil *BioIn 17*
Vogel, Virgil W. *MiSFD 9*
Vogel, Virginia Reynolds 1946- *WhoE 93*
Vogel, Willa Hope 1929- *WhoAmW 93*
Vogel, Wladimir (Rudolfovich) 1896-1984 *Baker 92*
Vogel, Zygmunt 1764-1826 *PolBiDi*
Vogelbacker, John Jeffrey 1947- *St&PR 93*
Vogelberger, Peter John, Jr. 1932- *St&PR 93*
Vogele, Allan W. *Law&B 92*
Vogeleis, Martin 1861-1930 *Baker 92*
Vogeler, Wilfried 1930- *WhoWor 93*
Vogelgesang, Sandra Louise 1942- *WhoAmW 93*
Vogelhuber, William W. 1933- *St&PR 93*
Vogelhut, Farrel *Law&B 92*
Vogellehner, Dieter 1937- *WhoScE 91-3*
Vogelman, Joseph Herbert 1920- *WhoAm 92*
Vogelman, Richard P. *Law&B 92*
Vogelpohl, Alfons F.B. 1932- *WhoScE 91-3*
Vogelsang, Carl Richard 1946- *St&PR 93*
Vogelsang, Peter Rockwell *Law&B 92*
Vogelsgesang, Wolfgang Maria 1932- *WhoWor 93*
Vogelsinger, Hubert *BioIn 17*
Vogelstein, John L. 1934- *St&PR 93*
Vogel von Falckenstein, Ernst Eduard 1797-1885 *HarEnMi*
Vogelweide, Walther von der c. 1170-c. 1230 *Baker 92*
Vogelzang, A. Randall *Law&B 92*
Vogelzang, Jeanne Marie 1950- *WhoAmW 93*
Voggel, Gerhard 1935- *St&PR 93*
Vogian, Peter John 1931- *St&PR 93*
Vogl, George 1912- *WhoWor 93*
Vogl, Gero 1941- *WhoScE 91-4*
Vogl, Heinrich 1845-1900 *Baker 92, OxDcOp*
Vogl, Johann Michael 1768-1840 *Baker 92*
Vogl, Kathryn St. Vincent *Law&B 92*
Vogl, Otto 1927- *WhoAm 92*
Vogler, Donald Charles 1924- *St&PR 93*
Vogler, Frederick Wright 1931- *WhoAm 92*
Vogler, Georg Joseph 1749-1814 *Baker 92*
Vogler, Harry William 1925- *St&PR 93*
Vogler, Rudiger 1942- *IntDcF 2-3*
Vogler, Theresa Mary 1957- *WhoE 93*
Vogrich, Max (Wilhelm Karl) 1852-1916 *Baker 92*
Vogt, A.E. van *ScF&FL 92*
Vogt, Augustus Stephen 1861-1926 *Baker 92*
Vogt, Erich Wolfgang 1929- *WhoAm 92*
Vogt, Evon Zartman, Jr. 1918- *WhoAm 92, WhoWrEP 92*
Vogt, Ferd August 1935- *St&PR 93*
Vogt, Frank H. 1954- *St&PR 93*
Vogt, Gerard Robert 1942- *St&PR 93*
Vogt, Gregory Max 1949- *ConAu 137*
Vogt, Gustave 1781-1870 *Baker 92*
Vogt, Hans 1911- *Baker 92*
Vogt, Hartmut 1923- *WhoWor 93*
Vogt, Helmut F.T. 1931- *WhoScE 91-3*
Vogt, Jean-Jacques *WhoScE 91-2*
Vogt, Jim *BioIn 17*
Vogt, Johann 1823-1888 *Baker 92*
Vogt, John Henry 1918- *WhoAm 92*
Vogt, Peter Karl Hermann 1930- *WhoScE 91-3*
Vogt, R. Eric *Law&B 92*
Vogt, Robert Lawrence 1942- *WhoE 93*
Vogt, Rochus E. 1929- *St&PR 93*
Vogt, Rochus Eugen 1929- *WhoAm 92*
Vogt, Ronald Charles 1942- *St&PR 93*
Vogt, Sara *BioIn 17*
Vogt, Sue 1953- *WhoE 93*
Vogt, Theodore J. 1949- *St&PR 93*
Vogt, William 1902- *BioIn 17*
Vogt, William Handley 1940- *St&PR 93*
Vogtle, Fritz 1939- *WhoScE 91-3*
Vogtli, K. *WhoScE 91-4*
Vogtmann, Hartmut 1942- *WhoScE 91-3*
Vogtsberger, Martin Henry 1947- *St&PR 93*
Vogus, Danny Lee *Law&B 92*
Vohor, Serge *WhoWor 93*
Vohra, Ranbir 1928- *WhoAm 92*
Vohra, Sudy L. 1936- *St&PR 93*
Vohs, James Arthur 1928- *WhoAm 92*
Voicu, Ion 1925- *Baker 92*
Voiculescu, Dan Dumitru 1946- *WhoWor 93*
Voiculescu, Vlad *WhoScE 91-4*
Voight, Elizabeth Anne 1944- *WhoAmW 93*
Voight, Jerry D. 1937- *WhoE 93*
Voight, Jon 1938- *IntDcF 2-3, WhoAm 92*
Voight, Phyllis J. 1955- *WhoAmW 93*
Voight, Robert J. 1949- *St&PR 93*
Voignac, Laurent 1960- *WhoWor 93*
Voigt, Cynthia 1942- *ConAu 37NR, -40NR, DcAmChF 1960, DcAmChF 1985, MajAI [port], ScF&FL 92, WhoAm 92, WhoAmW 93, WhoWrEP 92*
Voigt, Ellen Bryant 1943- *DcLB 120 [port], WhoWrEP 92*
Voigt, Hans-Dieter 1941- *WhoWor 93*
Voigt, Harry Holmes 1931- *WhoAm 92*
Voigt, Heinz W.M. 1924- *WhoScE 91-3*
Voigt, Henriette 1808-1839 *Baker 92*
Voigt, Herbert Frederick 1952- *WhoE 93*
Voigt, Howard Francis *Law&B 92*
Voigt, Johann Georg Hermann 1769-1811 *Baker 92*
Voigt, John Jacob 1942- *WhoE 93*
Voigt, Klaus Friedrich 1934- *WhoScE 91-3, WhoUN 92*
Voigt, Paul Warren 1940- *WhoAm 92*
Voigt, Robert D. 1951- *St&PR 93*
Voils, Georgia Elizabeth 1947- *WhoWrEP 92*
Voina, Alexander Andrejevich 1954- *WhoWor 93*
Voinovich, George V. 1936- *WhoAm 92*
Voinovich, Vladimir 1932- *BioIn 17, ScF&FL 92*
Voipio, Aarno *WhoScE 91-4*
Voisin, Guy Andre 1920- *WhoScE 91-2*
Voisin, Henry Georges 1929- *WhoWor 93*
Voisin, Marcel 1935- *WhoWor 93*
Voisin, Roger (Louis) 1918- *Baker 92*
Voisin, Russell L. 1932- *St&PR 93*
Voisin, William R. 1935- *St&PR 93*
Voisinet, James Raymond 1931- *St&PR 93, WhoAm 92, WhoWor 93*
Voislav, Stefan dc. 1043 *OxDcByz*
Voissem, Marvin C. *St&PR 93*
Voit, Franz Johann, Jr. 1932- *WhoWor 93*
Voitech, George d1073? *OxDcByz*
Voith, Charles J. 1922- *St&PR 93*
Voith, Marton 1934- *WhoScE 91-4*
Voitle, Robert Allen 1938- *WhoAm 92*
Voity, Maurice Joseph 1944- *WhoSSW 93*
Vojdani, Simon 1951- *St&PR 93*
Vojnovic, B. 1951- *WhoScE 91-1*
Vojtas, Peter 1951- *WhoWor 93*
Vokac, David Roland 1940- *WhoWrEP 92*
Voketaitis, Arnold Mathew 1930- *WhoAm 92*
Vola, Louis d1990 *BioIn 17*
Vola, M.J.J.M. *WhoScE 91-3*
Volavola, Mosese *WhoAsAP 91*
Volbach, Fritz 1861-1940 *Baker 92*
Volberg, Herman William 1925- *WhoWor 93*
Volcker, Paul A. *BioIn 17*
Volcker, Paul A. 1927- *WhoAm 92, WhoWor 93*
Volckhausen, Grace Lyu- *BioIn 17*
Volckhausen, William A. 1937- *St&PR 93*
Volckhausen, William Alexander 1937- *WhoAm 92*
Volckmar, Wilhelm (Adam Valentin) 1812-1887 *Baker 92*
Vold, Raymond S. 1933- *St&PR 93*
Volding, M.J. 1923- *St&PR 93*
Voldman, Steven Howard 1957- *WhoE 93, WhoEmL 93, WhoWor 93*
Voldrich, Lubos 1927- *WhoScE 91-4*
Voldseth, Beverly Ann 1935- *WhoWrEP 92*
Voldseth, John Eric 1949- *St&PR 93*
Voldstad, John *BioIn 17*
Volejnicek, David *Law&B 92*
Volek, Frantisek *WhoScE 91-4*
Volek, Jaroslav 1923- *Baker 92*
Volgenau, Douglas 1937- *WhoAm 92*
Volgenau, Stephen 1959- *St&PR 93*
Volger, Georg Joseph 1749-1814 *OxDcOp*
Volger, H.C. 1932- *WhoScE 91-1*
Volgy, Thomas John 1946- *WhoAm 92*
Volicer, Ladislav 1935- *WhoE 93*
Volk, Christine Suzanne 1969- *WhoE 93*
Volk, Eugene J. *Law&B 92*
Volk, Eugene John 1931- *St&PR 93, WhoIns 93*
Volk, Harold D. *Law&B 92*
Volk, Harry J. 1905- *WhoAm 92*
Volk, Heinrich J. 1936- *WhoScE 91-3*
Volk, Jan *WhoAm 92*
Volk, John Louis 1943- *St&PR 93*
Volk, Kenneth H. 1922- *WhoAm 92*
Volk, Martin *Law&B 92*
Volk, Matthias 1943- *WhoWor 93*
Volk, Norman Hans 1935- *WhoE 93*
Volk, Peter 1949- *St&PR 93*
Volk, Thomas W. *Law&B 92*
Volk, Wesley Aaron 1924- *WhoSSW 93*
Volkart, Edmund Howell 1919- *WhoWrEP 92*
Volkart, Judith H. *Law&B 92*
Volkening, Robert d1992 *BioIn 17*
Volkening-Quarternik, Debra Lynn 1962- *WhoAmW 93*
Volkenstein, Mikhail Vladimirovich 1912- *WhoWor 93*
Volker, Beverly *ScF&FL 92*
Volker, Dale Martin 1940- *WhoE 93*
Volker, Dorothy E. *Law&B 92*
Volker, Franz 1899-1965 *Baker 92*
Volkering, Mary Joe 1936- *WhoAmW 93*
Volkert, Franz (Joseph) 1767-1845 *Baker 92*
Volkhardt, John Malcolm 1917- *WhoAm 92*
Volkle, Hansruedi 1946- *WhoScE 91-4*
Volkman, Alvin 1926- *WhoSSW 93*
Volkman, David J. 1945- *WhoE 93*
Volkman, P.E., Jr. 1931- *St&PR 93*
Volkmann, Daniel George, Jr. 1924- *WhoAm 92*
Volkmann, Frances Cooper 1935- *WhoAm 92, WhoAmW 93*
Volkmann, John 1906-1990 *BioIn 17*
Volkmann, Ludwig 1870-1947 *See* Breitkopf & Hartel *Baker 92*
Volkmann, (Friedrich) Robert 1815-1883 *Baker 92*
Volkmann, Wilhelm 1837-1896 *See* Breitkopf & Hartel *Baker 92*
Volkmer, Burkhard 1966- *WhoWor 93*
Volkmer, Harold L. 1931- *CngDr 91, WhoAm 92*
Volkoff, George Michael 1914- *WhoAm 92*
Volkoff, Vladimir 1932- *BioIn 17*
Volkonsky, Andrei (Mikhailovich) 1933- *Baker 92*
Volkov, Dmitryi 1957- *WhoWor 93*
Volkov, Evgenii Alekseevich 1926- *WhoWor 93*
Volkov, F.K. 1847-1918 *IntDcAn*
Volkov, Felix Mihailovich 1932- *WhoWor 93*
Volkov, Feodor (Grigorievich) 1729-1763 *Baker 92*
Volkov, Igor Michailovich 1945- *WhoUN 92*
Volkwein, Edward Arthur 1941- *WhoAm 92*
Voll, John Obert 1936- *WhoAm 92, WhoWor 93*
Voll, Richard A. *Law&B 92*
Voll, Robert R. 1928- *St&PR 93*
Voll, Sarah Potts 1942- *WhoE 93*
Voll, William H., Jr. 1950- *St&PR 93*
Voll, William Holland 1925- *St&PR 93*
Volla, Steven L. 1946- *St&PR 93*
Volland, Carol Tascher 1935- *WhoAmW 93*
Volland, Richard K. 1938- *St&PR 93*
Volland, Robert S. 1941- *St&PR 93*
Volland, Robert Stephen 1941- *WhoAm 92*
Volland, Stephen James *Law&B 92*
Vollant, Florent *BioIn 17*
Vollaro, Frank T. 1943- *St&PR 93*
Vollaro, John D. 1944- *St&PR 93*
Vollbrecht, Edward Alan 1941- *WhoE 93*
Volldal, Olav 1950- *WhoWor 93*
Volle, Robert Leon 1930- *WhoAm 92*
Vollebergh, Jos J. A. 1925- *WhoWor 93*
Vollen, Robert Jay 1940- *WhoAm 92*
Vollenweider, Andreas 1953- *Baker 92*
Vollenweider, Emmett J. 1956- *St&PR 93*
Vollenweider, Richard Albert 1922- *WhoAm 92*
Vollenweider, Richard Henry 1942- *St&PR 93*
Vollerthun, Georg 1876-1945 *Baker 92*
Volles, Warren K. *Law&B 92*
Vollhardt, Dieter 1951- *WhoWor 93*
Vollintine, Larry Reed *Law&B 92*
Vollkommer, John James *Law&B 92*
Vollman, Thomas J. 1951- *St&PR 93*
Vollman, William T. 1959- *ScF&FL 92*
Vollmann, John Jacob, Jr. 1938- *WhoE 93, WhoSSW 93*
Vollmar, Elizabeth Ellen *Law&B 92*
Vollmar, Gary Lee 1951- *St&PR 93*
Vollmar, Georg Heinrich von 1850-1922 *BioIn 17*
Vollmar, John Raymond 1929- *WhoAm 92*
Vollmar, Olive *BioIn 17*
Vollmer, Denise Kay 1957- *WhoAmW 93*
Vollmer, Gerhard 1943- *WhoScE 91-3*
Vollmer, Gunter 1940- *WhoWor 93*
Vollmer, James 1924- *WhoAm 92, WhoWor 93*
Vollmer, Lula 1898-1955 *AmWomPl*
Vollmer, Richard Henry 1931- *St&PR 93*
Vollmer, Richard Wade 1926- *WhoAm 92*
Vollmershausen, Dennis W. 1943- *St&PR 93*
Vollrath, Walter J., III 1955- *St&PR 93*
Vollstedt, Steve 1951- *St&PR 93*
Vollum, Robert Boone 1933- *WhoE 93, WhoWor 93*
Volman, David Herschel 1916- *WhoAm 92*
Volney, Taylor 1939- *WhoAm 92*
Volny, Peter Ivan 1946- *St&PR 93*
Volodarskii, Alexander Ilich 1938- *WhoWor 93*
Volodin, Igor Nikolaevich 1937- *WhoWor 93*
Volonte, Gian Maria 1933- *IntDcF 2-3 [port]*
Voloshin, Arkady 1946- *WhoE 93*
Voloshinov, Victor 1905-1960 *Baker 92*
Volovic, Robert C. 1936- *St&PR 93*
Volovnik, Patricia Ann 1947- *WhoE 93*
Volpano, Linda B. *Law&B 92*
Volpe, Angelo Anthony 1938- *WhoAm 92, WhoSSW 93*
Volpe, Arnold (David) 1869-1940 *Baker 92*
Volpe, Edmond Loris 1922- *WhoAm 92*
Volpe, Erminio Peter 1927- *WhoAm 92*
Volpe, Ignatius D. d1992 *NewYTBS 92*
Volpe, John 1908- *PolPar*
Volpe, Joseph *WhoAm 92*
Volpe, Joseph B., Jr. 1931- *St&PR 93*
Volpe, Joseph John 1938- *WhoAm 92*
Volpe, Judith Ann 1955- *WhoE 93*
Volpe, Kenneth Ralph 1945- *WhoE 93*
Volpe, Peter Anthony 1936- *WhoAm 92*
Volpe, Ralph C. 1924- *St&PR 93*
Volpe, Ralph Pasquale 1936- *WhoE 93*
Volpe, Robert 1926- *WhoAm 92, WhoE 93, WhoWor 93*
Volpe, Thomas J. 1935- *WhoAm 92*
Volpe, Thomas James 1935- *St&PR 93*
Volpi, Luigi 1937- *WhoScE 91-3*
Volpi, Walter M. *Law&B 92*
Volpi, Walter Mark 1946- *WhoAm 92*
Volpp, Louis Donovan 1929- *WhoAm 92*
Vol'Skiy, Vladimir Ivanovich 1950- *WhoWor 93*
Volsky, Arkady *BioIn 17*
Volsky, Paula *ScF&FL 92*
Volta, Ezio *WhoScE 91-3*
Voltaire 1694-1778 *BioIn 17, MagSWL [port], OxDcOp, ScF&FL 92, WorLitC [port]*
Voltmer, Aileen Marie 1968- *WhoAmW 93*
Voltmer, John G. 1941- *St&PR 93*
Volturo, Carolyn Lanora 1938- *WhoAmW 93*
Voltz, David L. *Law&B 92*
Voltz, David L. 1953- *St&PR 93*
Voltz, Gunnar Charles 1945- *St&PR 93*
Voltz, Jeanne Appleton *WhoAmW 93, WhoSSW 93*
Voltz, Ramon John 1938- *WhoE 93*
Voltz, Sterling Ernest 1921- *WhoWor 93*
Voltz, William 1938-1984 *ScF&FL 92*
Voluck, Allan S. *WhoE 93*
Volwiler, Ernest H. d1992 *NewYTBS 92*
Volz, Annabelle Wekar 1926- *WhoAmW 93*
Volz, Charles Harvie, Jr. 1925- *WhoAm 92*
Volz, Heinrich Jakob 1928- *WhoWor 93*
Volz, Joan *Law&B 92*
Volz, John Phillip 1935- *WhoAm 92*
Volz, Marlin Milton 1917- *WhoAm 92, WhoWor 93*
Volz, Robert George 1932- *WhoAm 92*
Volz, William Harry 1946- *WhoAm 92*
Vomacka, Boleslav 1887-1965 *Baker 92*
Vomacka, David H. 1943- *St&PR 93*
vom Baur, Francis Trowbridge 1908- *WhoAm 92, WhoWor 93*
Vom Stein, Heinz-Dieter 1934- *WhoScE 91-3*
Vona, Joseph *St&PR 93*
Vonach, Herbert 1931- *WhoScE 91-4*
Vonach, Herbert Karl 1931- *WhoWor 93*
Vona Evans, Gail Margaret 1954- *WhoE 93*
Von Ah, Joseph F. 1928- *WhoScE 91-4*
von Ahrens, C. *St&PR 93*
von Almedingen, Martha *ScF&FL 92*
Von Anhalt, Frederic *BioIn 17*
Vonarburg, Elisabeth 1947- *ScF&FL 92*
von Arnauld de la Periere, Angelique 1940- *WhoAmW 93*
Von Arnim, Bettina 1785-1859 *BioIn 17*

Von Arnim, Hans-Jurgen 1889-1962 *BioIn 17*
von Arnim, Ruprecht P. 1938- *WhoUN 92*
von Arx, Dolph William 1934- *St&PR 93, WhoAm 92, WhoWor 93*
von Arx, Jeffrey Paul 1947- *WhoE 93*
Von Auw, Ivan 1903-1991 *BioIn 17*
Von Auwers, Arthur 1838-1915 *BioIn 17*
Von Baer, Karl Ernst 1792-1876 *BioIn 17*
Von Balthasar, Hans Urs 1905-1988 *BioIn 17*
Von Bargen, Donna Marie 1951- *WhoAmW 93*
von Bauer, Eric Ernst 1942- *St&PR 93*
Von Baumgarten, Rudolf J. 1922- *WhoScE 91-3*
Von Baumgart-Psayla, Romeo Leopold 1916- *WhoE 93*
Von Behr, Amalie *AmWomPl*
Von Behr, Hans d1990 *BioIn 17*
Von Behren, Linda Marie 1948- *WhoAmW 93*
Von Behren, Ruth Lechner 1933- *WhoAmW 93*
von Below, Joachim Ruediger 1952- *WhoWor 93*
Von Bennigsen-Foerder, Rudolf 1926-1989 *BioIn 17*
Vonberg, D.D. *WhoScE 91-1*
Von Berg, Horst Rudiger 1941- *St&PR 93, WhoE 93*
von Bernuth, Carl 1944- *St&PR 93*
Von Bernuth, Carl W. *Law&B 92, WhoAm 92*
Von Bernuth, Gotz 1935- *WhoScE 91-3*
Von Bethmann-Hollweg, Theobald 1856-1921 *BioIn 17*
Von Bismarck, Wilhelm 1935- *WhoScE 91-3*
Von Blanckenburg, Christian Friedrich 1744-1796 *BioIn 17*
Von Blanckenhagen, Peter Heinrich 1909-1990 *BioIn 17*
Von Blomberg, Werner 1878-1946 *BioIn 17*
Von Blon, Franz 1861-1945 *Baker 92*
Von Blon, Philip 1921- *St&PR 93*
Von Brandenstein, Patrizia *BioIn 17, WhoAm 92*
Von Brauchitsch, Walter 1881-1948 *BioIn 17*
Von Braun, Wernher 1912-1977 *BioIn 17*
Von Braunmuhl, Hermann 1937- *WhoScE 91-3*
von Braunmuhl, Joachim W.G. 1940- *WhoUN 92*
von Breitenbuch, Bernd Melchior 1936- *WhoWor 93*
von Brock, A. Raymond 1922- *WhoAm 92*
Von Bulow, Claus *BioIn 17*
Von Bulow, Hans 1830-1894 *BioIn 17*
Von Bulow, Martha *BioIn 17*
Von Bulow, Vicco 1930- *WhoScE 91-3*
von Bun, Friedrich Otto 1925- *WhoE 93*
Von Bunau, Gunther 1930- *WhoScE 91-3, WhoWor 93*
Von Buttlar, Haro R.F.W. 1926- *WhoScE 91-3*
Voncanon, Robert Dale 1933- *St&PR 93*
Von Chamisso, Adelbert 1781-1838 *BioIn 17*
Von Clausewitz, Karl 1780-1831 *BioIn 17*
von Collani, Gernot Ulrich 1942- *WhoWor 93*
Von Culin, Raymond Pearson 1913- *St&PR 93*
Vondale, James Philip *Law&B 92*
Vonderach, Stephen H. 1934- *St&PR 93*
Vondercrone, C. Stephens, Jr. *Law&B 92*
von der Esch, Hans Ulrik 1928- *WhoWor 93*
VonderHaar, William Purcell 1930- *WhoAm 92*
Von der Heide, John G. d1991 *BioIn 17*
von der Heyden, Ingolf Karl Mueller 1936- *WhoAm 92*
Von Der Heyden, Karl M. 1936- *St&PR 93*
von der Heydt, James Arnold 1919- *WhoAm 92*
von der Lieth, Dion 1943- *St&PR 93*
Von der Lippe, Edward Joseph 1934- *WhoAm 92*
Von Der Luhe, Oskar Friedrich Harald 1954- *WhoWor 93*
Von Der Mark, Klaus *WhoScE 91-3*
von der Mehden, Fred Robert 1927- *WhoSSW 93*
Vonderohe, Alan Paul 1947- *WhoAm 92*
von der Osten, Harold R. 1929- *St&PR 93*
Von Der Osten, Wolf Dietrich Rudolf 1934- *WhoScE 91-3*
Von Der Portern, Peter G. 1946- *St&PR 93*
Von Der Recke, Dieter Baron *WhoScE 91-3*
Von Dettre, Gabe *MiSFD 9*
VonDeylen, Robert W. 1952- *St&PR 93*
von Dohlen, Robert John 1928- *WhoAm 92*
von Dohnanyi, Christoph 1929- *WhoAm 92, WhoWor 93*
Vondrasek, Frank Charles 1928- *St&PR 93*
Vondrasek, Frank Charles, Jr. 1928- *WhoAm 92*
Von Drehle, Ramon Arnold 1930- *St&PR 93, WhoAm 92*
von Dreusch, Karen A. *Law&B 92*
Vondrich, Yari Vaclav 1931- *St&PR 93*
von Droste zu Hulshoff, Bernd 1938- *WhoUN 92*
Von Dungen, Emil 1945- *St&PR 93*
Vondy, David Ray 1927- *WhoWrEP 92*
Von Ebner-Eschenbach, Marie 1830-1916 *BioIn 17*
Von Eckardt, Wolf 1918- *WhoAm 92*
Von Eiff, August Wilhelm 1921- *WhoScE 91-3*
Von Engelhardt, Wolfgang 1932- *WhoScE 91-3*
Von Ense, Rahel Varnhagen 1771-1833 *BioIn 17*
Von Eschen, Kenneth B. 1948- *St&PR 93*
Von Eschen, Robert Leroy 1936- *WhoSSW 93*
Von Euler, Curt 1918- *WhoScE 91-4*
Von Eye, Rochelle Kay 1949- *WhoAmW 93*
Von Faber, Hans 1927- *WhoScE 91-3*
Von Faber-Castell, Anton-Wolfgang *BioIn 17*
Von Faber-Castell, Mary Elizabeth *BioIn 17*
von Ferstel, Marilou McCarthy 1937- *WhoAm 92*
Von Flotow, Andreas Hubertus 1955- *WhoE 93*
Von Forell, Kenneth J., Jr. 1949- *St&PR 93*
von Franz, Marie-Luise *ScF&FL 92*
Von Fricker, Udo 1936- *WhoScE 91-3*
von Furstenberg, Betsy 1931- *WhoAm 92*
Von Furstenberg, Diane *BioIn 17*
Von Furstenberg, Diane Simone Michelle 1946- *WhoAm 92, WhoAmW 93*
von Furstenberg, George Michael 1941- *WhoAm 92*
Von Furstenberg, Tatiana *BioIn 17*
Von Gehlen, Kurt 1927- *WhoScE 91-3*
Von Geramb, Heinrich Victor 1938- *WhoScE 91-3*
Vongerichten, Jean-Georges *BioIn 17*
Von Gerstenberg, Heinrich Wilhelm 1737-1823 *BioIn 17*
Von Gierke, Gerhart 1922- *WhoScE 91-3*
Von Gierke, Henning Edgar 1917- *WhoAm 92*
Vongkhamsao, Saly d1991 *BioIn 17*
von Glahn, William Giles *Law&B 92*
Von Glasersfeld, Ernst C. 1917- *WhoE 93*
Von Goethe, Johann Wolfgang 1749-1832 *BioIn 17*
Von Gorres, Joseph 1776-1848 *BioIn 17*
Von Graevenitz, Alexander 1932- *WhoScE 91-4*
Von Graevenitz, Alexander Wilhelm Carlo 1932- *WhoWor 93*
Von Gruben, Brian Gerard 1948- *St&PR 93*
von Grumbkow, Jasper 1945- *WhoWor 93*
Vongsathorn, Xan 1929- *WhoUN 92*
Von Gunden, Kenneth 1946- *ScF&FL 92*
Von Gunderode, Karoline 1780-1806 *BioIn 17*
von Haartman, Harry Ulf 1942- *WhoWor 93*
Von Habsburg-Lothringen, Otto *BioIn 17*
Von Hagen, Peter Albrecht, Jr. c. 1779-1837
See Van Hagen, Peter Albrecht, Sr. 1755-1803 *Baker 92*
von Hake, Margaret Joan 1933- *WhoE 93*
von Harbou, Thea *ScF&FL 92*
von Harz, James Lyons 1915- *WhoAm 92*
von Hassel, George A. 1929- *St&PR 93, WhoIns 93*
Von Hassel, William R. 1929- *St&PR 93*
Von Hassell, Ulrich 1881-1944 *BioIn 17*
Von Hayek, Friedrich A. 1899-1992 *BioIn 17*
von Heimburg, Roger Lyle 1931- *WhoWor 93*
Von Hentig, Wolf-Uwe 1928- *WhoScE 91-3*
Von Herkomer, Hubert 1849-1914 *BioIn 17*
Von Herzen, Richard Pierre 1930- *WhoAm 92*
Von Hess, Jovak *WhoWrEP 92*
Vonheyn, William A. 1922- *St&PR 93*
Von Hilsheimer, George Edwin, III 1934- *WhoSSW 93, WhoWor 93*
Von Hindenburg, Paul 1847-1934 *BioIn 17*
Von Hippel, Frank Niels 1937- *WhoAm 92*
von Hippel, Peter Hans 1931- *WhoAm 92*
Von Hippel, Theodor Gottlieb 1741-1796 *BioIn 17*
von Hoelle, John Jacob 1940- *WhoE 93*
Von Hoelscher, Russel 1942- *WhoWrEP 92*
von Hoffman, Nicholas 1929- *WhoAm 92, WhoE 93*
Von Hofsten, Bengt 1928- *WhoScE 91-4*
Von Holden, Martin Harvey 1942- *WhoAm 92, WhoE 93*
Von Holstein, Friedrich 1837-1909 *BioIn 17*
Von Houwald, Ernst 1778-1845 *BioIn 17*
Von Hoyningen-Huene, Jurgen 1936- *WhoScE 91-3*
Von Ilberg, Christoph 1935- *WhoScE 91-3*
Von Jawlensky, Alexej c. 1864-1941 *BioIn 17*
Vonk, Cornelis 1940- *WhoScE 91-3*
Vonk, F.P.M. *WhoScE 91-3*
Vonk, Gerrit Rokus 1962- *WhoWor 93*
Vonk, Hans 1942- *Baker 92*
VonKaenel, James F. *Law&B 92*
von Kann, Clifton Ferdinand 1915- *WhoAm 92*
Von Karajan, Herbert *BioIn 17*
Vonkeman, Hendrik 1935- *WhoWor 93*
Von Kersting, Lynn *BioIn 17*
von Keviczky, Colman Stephen 1909- *WhoE 93*
Von Kiderlen-Waechter, Alfred 1852-1912 *BioIn 17*
Von Kleist, Ewald 1881-1954 *BioIn 17*
Von Kleist, Ewald Christian 1715-1759 *BioIn 17*
Von Kleist, Heinrich 1777-1811 *BioIn 17*
Von Kleist, Sabine Freifrau 1933- *WhoScE 91-3*
Von Kleist-Retzow, Ruth 1867-1945 *BioIn 17*
von Klemperer, Klemens 1916- *WhoAm 92*
Von Klitzing, Klaus 1943- *WhoScE 91-3*
Von Kluge, Gunther 1882-1944 *BioIn 17*
Von Kohorn, Ralph 1919- *St&PR 93*
von Kohorn, Ralph Steven 1919- *WhoWor 93*
Von Kotzebue, August 1761-1819 *BioIn 17*
Von Krudener, Juliane 1764-1824 *BioIn 17*
Von Kuenheim, Eberhard *WhoScE 91-3*
von Kuenheim, Eberhard 1928- *WhoWor 93*
von Kunes, Karen Zdenka Jessica 1949- *WhoE 93*
von Kutzleben, Siegfried Edwin 1920- *WhoE 93, WhoWor 93*
von Lang, Frederick William 1929- *WhoAm 92*
Von la Roche, Sophie 1731-1807 *BioIn 17*
Von Laue, Theodore Herman 1916- *WhoAm 92, WhoWrEP 92*
Von Laun, Wolfram *Law&B 92*
Von Lehman, John I. 1952- *St&PR 93*
von Leitis, Gregorij Hirt 1944- *WhoWor 93*
von Liebig, William J. 1923- *St&PR 93*
Von Linne, Carl 1707-1778 *BioIn 17*
von Linsowe, Marina Dorothy 1952- *WhoAmW 93*
Von Loewenich, C.H. Volker 1937- *WhoScE 91-3*
von Lucius, Wulf D. 1938- *WhoWor 93*
Von Lukowicz, Mathias 1939- *WhoScE 91-3*
von Maack, Wolfgang 1940- *St&PR 93*
von Malapert, Robert *Law&B 92*
Von Malmborg, Lars *WhoScE 91-4*
Von Malmborg, Lars 1938- *WhoScE 91-4*
Von Manstein, Erich 1887-1973 *BioIn 17*
Von Manteuffel, Hasso 1897-1978 *BioIn 17*
Von Martinez, Marianne 1744-1812 *BioIn 17*
von Maur, J.R. 1919- *St&PR 93*
von Mehren, Arthur Taylor 1922- *WhoAm 92*
von Mehren, Robert Brandt 1922- *WhoAm 92*
von Mering, Otto Oswald 1922- *WhoAm 92, WhoWor 93*
Von Meyenburg, Kaspar 1941- *WhoScE 91-4*
Von Milloss, Aurel 1906-1988 *BioIn 17*
von Minckwitz, Bernhard 1944- *WhoAm 92*
Von Moltke, Freya *BioIn 17*
Von Moos, Ludwig 1910-1990 *BioIn 17*
Von Morpurgo, Henry 1909- *WhoWrEP 92*
Von Muller, Erik *BioIn 17*
Von Muralt, Alex 1903-1990 *BioIn 17*
von Muralt, Jurgen 1935- *WhoUN 92*
Vonnegut, Kurt 1922- *BioIn 17, ScF&FL 92*
Vonnegut, Kurt, Jr. 1922- *MagSAmL [port], WhoAm 92, WhoE 93, WhoWor 93, WhoWrEP 92, WorLitC [port]*
Von Nell-Breuning, Oswald 1890-1991 *BioIn 17*
Von Neumann, John 1903-1957 *BioIn 17*
Von Niebelschutz, Wolf *ScF&FL 92*
von Noorden, Gunter Konstantin 1928- *WhoAm 92*
Von Oerthel, Irmgard 1934- *BioIn 17*
Von Oertzen, Wolfram 1939- *WhoScE 91-3*
Von Ohain, Hans *BioIn 17*
von Ohain, Hans Joachim 1911- *WhoAm 92*
Von Ohlen, H. Bernt *Law&B 92*
von Palko, David Michael 1953- *WhoSSW 93*
Von Paradis, Maria Theresia 1759-1824 *BioIn 17*
Von Paris, George H. 1924- *St&PR 93*
Von Passenheim, John Burr 1964- *WhoWor 93*
Von Paulus, Friedrich 1890-1957 *BioIn 17*
von Paulus, Mary 1947- *St&PR 93*
von Pfetten-Arnbach, Karl Berthold 1934- *WhoWor 93*
Von Platen, August 1796-1835 *BioIn 17*
Von Praunheim, Rosa 1942- *MiSFD 9*
von Prittwitz und Gaffron, Joachim Bernhard Herman 1929- *WhoWor 93*
von Raffler-Engel, Walburga 1920- *WhoAm 92, WhoAmW 93, WhoSSW 93, WhoWor 93*
Von Reichenau, Walter 1884-1942 *BioIn 17*
von Renteln, Michael 1942- *WhoWor 93*
von Rezzori (d'Arezzo), Gregor *ConAu 136*
Von Rezzori, Gregor *BioIn 17*
von Rhein, John Richard 1945- *WhoAm 92*
Von Ringelheim, Paul Helmut *WhoAm 92*
Von Rohr, Jerry S. 1945- *St&PR 93*
von Rosen, Rudiger *WhoWor 93*
Von Rosen, Ulric Eugene 1944- *St&PR 93*
von Rosenberg, Arthur James 1936- *St&PR 93*
Von Rosenstiel, Martha Elizabeth 1950- *WhoE 93*
Von Rundstedt, Karl Rudolf Gerd 1875-1953 *BioIn 17*
von Sandor, Robert 1929- *WhoWor 93*
von Schack, Wesley W. 1944- *St&PR 93, WhoAm 92*
Von Schellendorf, Ingeborg Bronsart 1840-1913 *BioIn 17*
Von Schlegel, August Wilhelm 1767-1845 *BioIn 17*
Von Schlegel, Dorothea Mendelssohn 1763-1839 *BioIn 17*
Von Schlegel, Friedrich 1772-1829 *BioIn 17*
Von Schlegell, David 1920- *WhoAm 92*
von Schlegell, David 1920-1992 *NewYTBS 92 [port]*
Von Schleussner, Anna Rikarda 1933- *WhoUN 92*
von Schmidt, Katherine Barnes Hornbogen 1928- *WhoAmW 93*
Von Schroeder, Janet M. *AmWomPl*
von Schuller-Goetzburg, Viktorin Wolfgan 1924- *WhoWor 93*
von Schulthess, Dieter C.A. 1937- *WhoWor 93*
Von Seebach, Michael H. 1937- *St&PR 93*
Von Segebaden, Gustaf 1927- *WhoScE 91-4*
von Segesser, Ludwig Karl 1952- *WhoWor 93*
von Seldeneck, Judith Metcalfe 1940- *WhoAm 92, WhoAmW 93*
Von Senger und Etterlin, Frido 1891-1963 *BioIn 17*
von Spakovsky, Hans Anatol *Law&B 92*
von Sponeck, Hans Cristof 1939- *WhoUN 92*
Von Stade, Frederica *BioIn 17*
Von Stade, Frederica 1945- *Baker 92, IntDcOp, WhoAm 92, WhoAmW 93*
Von Stauffenberg, Franz-Ludwig Schenk 1938- *BioIn 17*
Von Stauffenberg, Klaus Philipp Schenk 1907-1944 *BioIn 17*
Von Stauptiz, Johann d1524 *BioIn 17*
von Stein, Johann Heinrich 1937- *WhoWor 93*
Von Sternberg, Josef 1894-1969 *MiSFD 9N*
Von Stroheim, Erich 1885-1957 *BioIn 17, MiSFD 9N*
Von Stuck, Franz 1863-1928 *BioIn 17*
Von Stulpnagel, Karl Heinrich 1886-1944 *BioIn 17*
Von Sydow, Erik 1930- *WhoScE 91-4*
Von Sydow, Max 1929- *BioIn 17, IntDcF 2-3 [port], MiSFD 9, WhoAm 92, WhoWor 93*
Von Tavel, Hans Christoph 1935- *WhoWor 93*

Von Tersch, Lawrence Wayne 1923- *WhoAm 92*
Von Thummel, Moritz August 1738-1817 *BioIn 17*
Von Thury, Thomas *Law&B 92*
Von Tilzer, Harry 1872-1946 *Baker 92*
Von Tirpitz, Alfred 1849-1930 *BioIn 17*
von Trapp, George Edward 1948- *St&PR 93*
von Trapp, Johannes Georg 1939- *St&PR 93*
von Trier, Lars 1956- *MiSFD 9*
Von Troschke, Baron Jurgen H.P.C. 1941- *WhoScE 91-3*
von Trotta, Margarethe 1942- *MiSFD 9*
Von Trott zu Solz, Adam 1909-1944 *BioIn 17*
von Tungeln, George Robert 1931- *WhoAm 92*
von Turk, Philipp *Law&B 92*
Von Uhde, Fritz 1848-1911 *BioIn 17*
Von Unwerth, Ellen 1954- *BioIn 17*
Von Urff, Charles A. 1934- *St&PR 93*
Von Vollmar, Georg Heinrich 1850-1922 *BioIn 17*
Von Wacker, Alexander *WhoWrEP 92*
Von Wald, Richard B. *Law&B 92, WhoAm 92*
von Watzdorf, Wolf *Law&B 92*
Von Weissenberg, Kim J.A. 1941- *WhoScE 91-4*
Von Weizsacker, Richard 1920- *WhoWor 93*
von Werner, Konrad Herbert 1943- *WhoWor 93*
von Westerholt, Hartwig *Law&B 92*
Von Wiesenthal, Peter d1990 *BioIn 17*
von Winckler, Beverly Ann Purnell 1935- *WhoAmW 93*
Von Witzleben, Erwin Job 1881-1944 *BioIn 17*
von Wolfersdorf, Lothar 1934- *WhoWor 93*
von Wolfsberg, Christian-Alexander 1958- *WhoWor 93*
Von Wright, Ferdinand 1822-1906 *BioIn 17*
Von Wright, Georg Henrik 1916- *WhoWor 93*
von Wyss, Marc R. 1931- *St&PR 93*
von Wyss, Marc Robert 1931- *WhoAm 92*
von Zedlitz, Hans Albrecht, Baron 1955- *WhoWor 93*
von Zerneck, Peter d1992 *NewYTBS 92*
von Ziegesar, Franz 1924- *St&PR 93*
Von Zur Muhlen, Alexander Meinhard 1936- *WhoWor 93*
Voog, Mary McGuire *Law&B 92*
Voogd, Anthonie Maarten *Law&B 92*
Vook, Frederick Ludwig 1931- *WhoAm 92*
Vook, Richard Werner 1929- *WhoE 93*
Voorburg, Jacobus H. 1929- *WhoScE 91-3*
Voorhees, Arthur B. 1921-1992 *BioIn 17*
Voorhees, Chad *BioIn 17*
Voorhees, Donald 1903-1989 *Baker 92*
Voorhees, Ellen Marie 1958- *WhoAmW 93*
Voorhees, James Dayton, Jr. 1917- *WhoAm 92*
Voorhees, John H. 1936- *AfrAmBi*
Voorhees, John James *WhoAm 92*
Voorhees, John Schenck 1923- *WhoAm 92*
Voorhees, Lee R., Jr. 1937- *WhoAm 92*
Voorhees, Lillian Welch *AmWomPl*
Voorhees, Michael R. *Law&B 92*
Voorhees, Richard 1916- *ScF&FL 92*
Voorhees, Richard Lesley 1941- *WhoAm 92, WhoSSW 93*
Voorhees, Steven C. 1954- *St&PR 93*
Voorhees, Vernon W., II 1942- *WhoIns 93*
Voorhees, William Wolverton, Jr. 1946- *WhoE 93*
Voorheis, Marion Marascio 1946- *WhoAmW 93*
Voorheis, T.S. 1914- *St&PR 93*
Voorhess, Mary Louise 1926- *WhoAmW 93*
Voorhies, Barbara *WhoAmW 93*
Voorhies, Lark *BioIn 17*
Voormolen, Alexander (Nicolas) 1895-1980 *Baker 92*
Voorn, Barry N. *Law&B 92*
Voorn, Joop (Josephus Hermanus Maria) 1932- *Baker 92*
Voorneveld, Richard Burke 1949- *WhoSSW 93*
Voorsanger, Bartholomew 1937- *WhoAm 92, WhoWor 93*
Voorsanger, Elkan Cohen 1889-1963 *BioIn 17*
Voortman, Hermanus 1940- *WhoWor 93*
Voortman, John J. 1931- *WhoAm 92*
Voos, James 1955- *St&PR 93*
Voos, William John 1930- *WhoAm 92*
Vopelius, Gottfried 1635-1715 *Baker 92*
Vopnford, Barbara L. 1952- *St&PR 93*
Vopnford, David Thor, Sr. 1942- *St&PR 93*
Vora, Ashok 1947- *WhoAm 92*
Vora, Hasmukh Jayantilal 1953- *WhoWor 93*
Vora, Motilal 1928- *WhoAsAP 91*
Vora, S.B. 1946- *St&PR 93*
Voracek, Jaroslav 1934- *WhoScE 91-4*
Vorachek, Mitzi M. 1944- *WhoSSW 93*
Vorbach, Renee R. 1946- *WhoWrEP 92*
Vorbrich, Lynn Karl 1939- *St&PR 93, WhoAm 92*
Vor Broker, Robert Stuart 1946- *St&PR 93*
Vorchheimer, Norman 1935- *WhoE 93*
Vorderman, Anton David 1953- *WhoWor 93*
Vore, Mary Edith 1947- *WhoAmW 93*
Voreis, Marilyn Louise 1941- *WhoWor 93*
Vorenberg, James 1928- *WhoAm 92*
Vorenkamp, Johannes 1928- *WhoScE 91-3*
Vorhaus, William G. d1991 *BioIn 17*
Vorhees, John H. 1936- *WhoAm 92*
Vorhies, Mahlon Wesley 1937- *WhoAm 92*
Vorhoff, Gilbert Harold 1919- *St&PR 93*
Vorholt, Jeffrey Joseph 1953- *WhoAm 92*
Voris, D. Thomas 1940- *St&PR 93*
Voris, William 1924- *WhoAm 92, WhoWor 93*
Vorisek, Jan Vaclav *Baker 92*
Vorisek, Richard J. d1989 *BioIn 17*
Vorlicek, Vaclav 1930- *DrEEuF*
Vorlova, Slava 1894-1973 *Baker 92*
Vorma, Atso *WhoScE 91-4*
Vornholt, John 1951- *ScF&FL 92*
Vornle, Paul 1929- *St&PR 93*
Vornle von Haagenfels, John P. 1958- *WhoE 93*
Vorob'ev, N.I. 1895-1967 *IntDcAn*
Vorobyev, Yakov 1766?-1809 *See* Petrov, Osip 1806-1878 *OxDcOp*
Vorobyeva, Anna 1816-1901 *See* Petrov, Osip 1806-1878 *OxDcOp*
Voron, Barbara Joanne 1951- *St&PR 93*
Voronjec, Dimitrije 1936- *WhoScE 91-4*
Vorontsov, Yuliy M. 1929- *WhoUN 92*
Vorontzoff, Alexis Nicolas 1927- *WhoWor 93*
Voros, Gerald John 1930- *WhoAm 92*
Voros, Joseph Paul 1961- *WhoE 93*
Voros, Laszlo 1934- *WhoScE 91-4*
Voroshilov, Kliment Efremovich 1881-1969 *ColdWar 2 [port]*
Vorosmarti, James 1935- *WhoE 93*
Voross, Lajos 1940- *WhoScE 91-4*
Vorozhtsov, Evgenii Vasil'evich 1946- *WhoWor 93*
Vorpahl, Debra Lynn 1963- *WhoAmW 93*
Vorpahl, George Steven *Law&B 92*
Vorren, Tore O. 1944- *WhoScE 91-4*
Vorris, Dimitrios P. 1966- *WhoWor 93*
Vorsanger, Fred S. 1928- *WhoAm 92*
Vorse, Mary Heaton 1874-1966 *BioIn 17*
Vorse, Mary Marvin Heaton 1874-1966 *AmWomPl*
Vorselman, Torsten Gerrit 1942- *WhoWor 93*
Vorster, Balthazar Johannes 1915-1983 *DcTwHis*
Vorys, Arthur I. 1923- *WhoIns 93*
Vorys, Arthur Isaiah 1923- *WhoAm 92*
Vos, Alvin Paul 1943- *WhoE 93*
Vos, C.J. *WhoScE 91-3*
Vos, Ch.J. *WhoScE 91-3*
Vos, Frank 1919- *WhoAm 92*
Vos, H. *WhoScE 91-3*
Vos, Hubert Daniel 1933- *St&PR 93, WhoAm 92*
Vos, Ida 1931- *ConAu 137, SmATA 69 [port]*
Vos, Luk de 1949- *ScF&FL 92*
Vos, Thomas J. 1947- *St&PR 93*
Vosbeck, Robert Randall 1930- *WhoAm 92*
Vosbein, Eleanor Edna 1935- *WhoSSW 93*
Vosburgh, Frederick George 1904- *WhoAm 92*
Vosburgh, Maude Batchelder *AmWomPl*
Vosburgh, Victoria Lynn 1965- *WhoAmW 93*
Voschinin, Nikolai Mihailovitch 1930- *WhoUN 92*
Vose, Robert Churchill, Jr. 1911- *WhoAm 92*
Vos-Fitzsimmons, Nancy Ellen 1954- *WhoE 93*
Voshall, Roy Edward 1933- *WhoE 93*
Voskresensky, K. *WhoScE 91-1*
Voskresensky, Konstantin Ilich 1937- *WhoUN 92*
Vosler, David M. 1951- *St&PR 93*
Voso, Deborah Elizabeth 1950- *WhoAmW 93, WhoEmL 93*
Vosotas, Paula J. 1942- *St&PR 93*
Vosotas, Peter L. 1941- *St&PR 93*
Vosper, Robert Gordon 1913- *WhoAm 92*
Voss, Charles 1815-1882 *Baker 92*
Voss, Christopher Arnold *WhoScE 91-1*
Voss, Claus Manfred 1932- *WhoWor 93*
Voss, Edward William, Jr. 1933- *WhoAm 92*
Voss, Edwin Price 1936- *St&PR 93*
Voss, F. Gwyn 1939- *St&PR 93*
Voss, Friedrich 1930- *Baker 92*
Voss, Harlan F. 1925- *St&PR 93*
Voss, Harry F. 1937- *St&PR 93*
Voss, Heinrich 1944- *WhoWor 93*
Voss, Hilda H. 1910-1990 *BioIn 17*
Voss, Howard G. *BioIn 17*
Voss, Jack D. 1921- *St&PR 93*
Voss, Jack Donald 1921- *WhoAm 92*
Voss, James E. *Law&B 92*
Voss, James Frederick 1930- *WhoAm 92*
Voss, James Leo 1934- *WhoAm 92*
Voss, Jeffrey M. 1958- *St&PR 93*
Voss, Jerrold Richard 1932- *WhoAm 92*
Voss, Johann Heinrich 1751-1826 *BioIn 17*
Voss, John 1917- *WhoAm 92*
Voss, Jurgen 1936- *WhoScE 91-3*
Voss, Katherine Evelyn 1957- *WhoAmW 93*
Voss, Kurt *MiSFD 9*
Voss, M. William 1921-1991 *BioIn 17*
Voss, Marilyn Elizabeth Price 1936- *WhoAmW 93*
Voss, Mary Ann 1942- *St&PR 93*
Voss, Ned Aus 1936- *St&PR 93*
Voss, Omer Gerald 1916- *WhoAm 92*
Voss, Palle 1949- *WhoScE 91-2*
Voss, Paul Joseph 1943- *WhoE 93*
Voss, Ralph F. 1943- *ConAu 137*
Voss, Richard K. 1947- *St&PR 93*
Voss, Robert K. 1949- *WhoAm 92*
Voss, Theodore Robert *Law&B 92*
Voss, Thomas Gorman 1938- *WhoSSW 93*
Voss, Werner 1949- *WhoWor 93*
Voss, Werner Konrad Karl 1935- *WhoWor 93*
Voss, Wilber C. *St&PR 93*
Voss, William Charles 1937- *St&PR 93, WhoAm 92*
Voss, William R. 1951- *WhoAm 92*
Voss Bark, Conrad 1913- *ScF&FL 92*
Vossberg, Carl A., III 1948- *St&PR 93*
Vossberg, Carl August 1918- *St&PR 93*
Vosseler, Heidi d1992 *BioIn 17, NewYTBS 92*
Vossenaar, Rene 1945- *WhoUN 92*
Vossius, Gerhard 1926- *WhoScE 91-3*
Vossius, Isaac 1618-1689 *Baker 92*
Vossler, Charlotte Emilie 1938- *WhoAmW 93*
Vossler, John Albert 1925- *WhoE 93*
Vossler, Mathilde A. *AmWomPl*
Vossoughi, Shapour 1945- *WhoWor 93*
Vosteen, W.E. 1952- *St&PR 93*
Vosti, Stephen Anthony 1955- *WhoE 93*
Vostradovsky, Jiri 1933- *WhoScE 91-4*
Vostrak, Zbynek 1920-1985 *Baker 92*
Voszka, Rudolf 1928- *WhoScE 91-4*
Votano, Paul Anthony 1929- *WhoWrEP 92*
Votapek, Ralph 1939- *Baker 92*
Votaw, Carmen Delgado 20th cent.- *HispAmA [port]*
Votaw, Charles Lesley 1929- *WhoAm 92*
Vote, C. Robert *Law&B 92*
Votel, Richard H. 1940- *St&PR 93*
Voth, Alden H. 1926- *WhoWor 93*
Voth, Donald J. *St&PR 93*
Votto, Antonino 1896-1985 *Baker 92, OxDcOp*
Vought, Kenneth Dean 1926- *St&PR 93*
Voulgaris, Nicholas 1933- *WhoScE 91-3*
Voulgaropoulos, Anastasios Nicolaos 1946- *WhoWor 93*
Voulkos, Peter 1924- *BioIn 17, WhoAm 92*
Voultsos-Vourtzis, Pericles 1910- *WhoAm 92*
Voultsos-Vourtzis, Pericles, Count 1910- *WhoWor 93*
Vounas, Ronald R. 1936- *WhoIns 93*
Vourdas, Apostolos 1954- *WhoWor 93*
Vournakis, John Nicholas 1939- *WhoE 93*
Vournas, John 1944- *WhoScE 91-3*
Vouros, James G. *Law&B 92*
Voute, William J. *BioIn 17*
Voute, William J. d1992 *NewYTBS 92 [port]*
Voutilainen, Pertti *WhoScE 91-4*
Voutsas, Alexander Matthew 1923- *WhoWor 93*
Vovan, Lou 1929- *WhoScE 91-2*
Vo Van Kiet 1922- *WhoWor 93*
Voves, Joseph Anthony 1922- *St&PR 93*
Vowell, Daniel Owen 1946- *WhoSSW 93*
Vowell, Jeff D. 1952- *WhoE 93*
Vowell, Susan Sibley 1963- *WhoAmW 93*
Vowels, Gary B. d1992 *NewYTBS 92*
Vowles, Richard Beckman 1917- *WhoAm 92*
Voyager, Alyn 1950- *WhoE 93, WhoWor 93*
Voyer, Thomas G. *St&PR 93*
Voyles, Gale Stanley Fegert 1951- *WhoEmL 93*
Voyles, J. Bruce 1953- *WhoWrEP 92*
Voyles, James K. *Law&B 92*
Voyles, James Wesley 1931- *St&PR 93*
Voysey, Peter D. *Law&B 92*
Voyt, Thomas M. *St&PR 93*
Voytko, James Emery 1933- *WhoE 93*
Voytovich, Anna M. *Law&B 92*
Voytovich, Debrah M. *Law&B 92*
Vozick, David 1940- *St&PR 93*
Voznesenskii, Andrei 1933- *BioIn 17*
Voznesensky, Andrei 1933- *WhoWor 93*
Voznesensky, Andrei (Andreivich) 1933- *ConAu 37NR*
Vrablik, Edward Robert 1932- *WhoAm 92*
Vraciu, Alexander *BioIn 17*
Vradenburg, George, III *WhoAm 92*
Vradenburg, George, III 1943- *St&PR 93*
Vradenburgh, Merry Christine 1963- *WhoWrEP 92*
Vrahotes, Peter *Law&B 92*
Vrana, Debora Shawn 1963- *WhoAmW 93*
Vrana, Maulfrey Adele Stewart 1933- *WhoWrEP 92*
Vrana, Verlon Kenneth 1925- *WhoAm 92*
Vrancea, Cecilia Anitta 1953- *WhoAmW 93*
Vranceanu, Alexandru Viorel 1927- *WhoScE 91-4*
Vranek, Johannes O. 1926- *WhoWor 93*
Vranich, Joseph 1945- *ConAu 138*
Vranitzky, Franz 1937- *WhoWor 93*
Vranken, Jaap 1897-1956 *Baker 92*
Vranken, Joseph 1870-1948 *See* Vranken, Jaap 1897-1956 *Baker 92*
Vratsinas, Gus Michael 1944- *St&PR 93*
Vray, Bernard 1945- *WhoScE 91-2*
Vrbancic, John Emerick 1955- *WhoEmL 93, WhoWor 93*
Vredenberg, W.J. 1937- *WhoScE 91-3*
Vredenbregt, Jeffrey Carl 1953- *St&PR 93*
Vredenburg, Max 1904-1976 *Baker 92*
Vredevoe, Donna Lou 1938- *WhoAm 92*
Vree, Ben 1954- *WhoWor 93*
Vreeken, Johannes 1929- *WhoWor 93*
Vreeland, Frederick 1927- *WhoAm 92, WhoWor 93*
Vreeland, Herb *WhoIns 93*
Vreeland, Herbert Henry 1948- *St&PR 93*
Vreeland, Russell Glenn 1960- *WhoE 93, WhoEmL 93*
Vrensen, Gys F.J.M. 1941- *WhoScE 91-3*
Vretblad, Viktor Patrik 1876-1953 *Baker 92*
Vrettakos, Nikiforos 1912-1991 *BioIn 17*
Vreuls, Victor (Jean Leonard) 1876-1944 *Baker 92*
Vriend, Jan 1938- *Baker 92*
Vrieslander, Otto 1880-1950 *Baker 92*
Vrieze, David J. 1945- *St&PR 93*
Vris, Thomas W. 1951- *WhoE 93*
Vrla, Libbie M. 1932- *St&PR 93*
Vrogaard, Rikard 1945- *WhoWor 93*
Vroklage, B.A.G. 1897-1951 *IntDcAn*
Vroman, Barbara Fitz *WhoWrEP 92*
Vroman, Karen Lyn 1963- *WhoAmW 93*
Vroman, Susan Berkowitz 1946- *WhoAmW 93*
Vronsky, Vitya 1909- *Baker 92*
Vroom, Meto J. 1929- *WhoScE 91-3*
Vroom, Victor Harold 1932- *WhoAm 92*
Vrooman, Erwin Ray 1943- *St&PR 93*
Vroons, Frans 1911-1983 *Baker 92*
Vroye, Thedore-Joseph *Baker 92*
Vrsansky, Carla J. *Law&B 92*
Vrtiak, Otto Jaroslav 1924- *WhoScE 91-4*
Vryonis, Speros, Jr. 1928- *WhoAm 92*
Vsevolod 1030-1093 *OxDcByz*
Vu, Jean-Pierre 1934- *WhoWor 93*
Vu, Tom *BioIn 17*
Vuagnat, Marc 1922- *WhoScE 91-4*
Vuataz, Roger 1898-1988 *Baker 92*
Vucanovich, Barbara F. *BioIn 17*
Vucanovich, Barbara F. 1921- *CngDr 91*
Vucanovich, Barbara Farrell 1921- *WhoAm 92, WhoAmW 93*
Vucelic, Dusan 1938- *WhoScE 91-4*
Vucenich, Momchilo 1945- *St&PR 93*
Vucinic-Superina, Alice 1930- *WhoScE 91-4*
Vuckovic, Vladan 1928- *WhoScE 91-4*
Vuckovic, Vojislav 1910-1942 *Baker 92*
Vuckovich, Carol Yetso 1940- *WhoAmW 93, WhoE 93*
Vuckovich, Dragomir Michael 1927- *WhoAm 92*
Vugteveen, Verna Aardema 1911- *ConAu 39NR*
Vugts, Hans F. 1941- *WhoScE 91-3*
Vuillaume, Claude 1772-1834 *See* Vuillaume, Jean-Baptiste 1798-1875 *Baker 92*
Vuillaume, Jean-Baptiste 1798-1875 *Baker 92*
Vuillaume, Nicolas-Francois 1802-1876 *See* Vuillaume, Jean-Baptiste 1798-1875 *Baker 92*

Vuillaume, Sebastien 1835-1875 *See* Vuillaume, Jean-Baptiste 1798-1875 *Baker 92*
Vuillemin, Jean-Claude 1954- *WhoE 93*
Vuillemot, Patricia Maretta 1953- *WhoAmW 93*
Vuillequez, Jean J. d1991 *BioIn 17*
Vuillermoz, Emile 1878-1960 *Baker 92*
Vuillermoz, Jean 1906-1940 *Baker 92*
Vuillet, Didier 1953- *St&PR 93*
Vuilleumier, Francois 1938- *WhoAm 92*
Vuitton, Henry-Louis 1911- *WhoAm 92*
Vujovich, Christine M. 1951- *WhoAmW 93*
Vukadinovic, Sreto 1924- *WhoScE 91-4*
Vukasin d1371 *OxDcByz*
Vukasin, John Peter, Jr. 1928- *WhoAm 92*
Vukdragovic, Mihailo 1900-1986 *Baker 92*
Vukhac, Dung 1944- *St&PR 93*
Vukmir, Branko 1927- *WhoWor 93*
Vukotic, Dusan 1927- *DrEEuF*
Vukovic, Drago Vuko 1934- *WhoWor 93*
Vukovich, Bill d1990 *BioIn 17*
Vukovich, Robert A. *St&PR 93*
Vukovich, Robert Anthony 1943- *WhoAm 92*
Vukovich, Sheryl Jan 1952- *WhoAmW 93*
Vuksic, Nelly 1939- *NotHsAW 93 [port]*
Vukson, John Thomas 1954- *St&PR 93*
Vuksta, Charles E., Jr. *Law&B 92*
Vulcanoff, Linda 1953- *St&PR 93*
Vulchanov, Nikolai Lyubomirov 1948- *WhoWor 93*
Vulchev, Todor Yordanov 1922- *WhoWor 93*
Vuletic, Dusanka 1931- *WhoScE 91-4*
Vulgamore, Melvin L. 1935- *WhoAm 92*
Vulis, Dimitri Lvovich 1964- *WhoE 93, WhoEmL 93*
Vulpius, Melchior c. 1570-1615? *Baker 92*
Vultaggio, Bill *St&PR 93*
Vumbacco, Joseph V. *Law&B 92*
Vumbacco, Joseph Vincent 1945- *St&PR 93*
Vumbaco, Brenda J. 1941- *WhoAmW 93*
Vunibobo, Berenado 1932- *WhoAsAP 91*
Vuokila, Yrjo Ilmari 1924- *WhoScE 91-4*
Vuole, Marie d1990 *BioIn 17*
Vuolo, Timothy John 1960- *St&PR 93*
Vuong, Lynette Dryer 1938- *WhoWrEP 92*
Vuong, Lynette Dyer 1938- *BioIn 17*
Vuono, Carl E. 1934- *WhoAm 92*
Vuono, Carl Edward 1934- *CmdGen 1991 [port]*
Vuorela, Lauri A. 1913- *WhoScE 91-4, WhoWor 93*
Vuori, Hannu V. 1941- *WhoScE 91-2*
Vuori, Hannu Veikki 1941- *WhoUN 92*
Vuoria, Pekka 1924- *WhoScE 91-4*
Vuorinen, A.P.U. 1932- *WhoScE 91-4*
Vuorinen, Jouko Juhani 1937- *WhoScE 91-4*
Vuorinen, Martti Juhani 1947- *WhoScE 91-4*
Vuorinen, Matti Keijo 1948- *WhoWor 93*
Vuorinen, Riitta Helena 1942- *WhoWor 93*
Vuorinen Ruppi, Sakari Antero 1948- *WhoWor 93*
Vuorio, Eero Ilkka 1948- *WhoScE 91-4*
Vurgaropulos, Fotini 1961- *WhoE 93*
Vuurde, Jim W.L. Van 1945- *WhoScE 91-3*
Vuust, Jens *WhoScE 91-2*
Vuylsteke, Jacques P. 1922- *WhoScE 91-2*
Vuylsteke, Susan A. 1958- *WhoAmW 93*
V. Wysocki, Klaus 1925- *WhoWor 93*
Vyas, Chand B. 1944- *St&PR 93*
Vyas, Dilip S. 1948- *St&PR 93*
Vyas, Girish Narmadashankar 1933- *WhoAm 92*
Vyas, Udaykumar Dayalal 1940- *WhoSSW 93*
Vyatkin, Alexey Konstantinovich 1946- *WhoWor 93*
Vycpalek, Ladislav 1882-1969 *Baker 92*
Vydra, Frank N. *Law&B 92*
Vye, John Quentin 1942- *St&PR 93, WhoAm 92*
Vygotskii, L.S. 1896-1934 *BioIn 17*
Vygotskii, Lev Semenovich 1896-1934 *BioIn 17*
Vykukal, Eugene Lawrence 1929- *WhoAm 92*
Vyncke, W.A. 1935- *WhoScE 91-2*
Vyner, Leslie *AmWomPl*
Vysata, Olga Malvina 1941- *WhoAmW 93*
Vyse, Brian 1930- *WhoScE 91-1*
Vyse, Michael *ScF&FL 92*
Vyse, Stuart Arthur 1950- *WhoE 93*
Vyshinskii, Andrei IAnuar'evich 1883-1954 *BioIn 17*
Vyshinsky, Andrei 1883-1954 *ColdWar 2 [port]*
Vyshinsky, Andrey Yanuarievich 1883-1955 *DcTwHis*
Vyshinsky, Andrey Yanuaryevich 1883-1954 *BioIn 17*
Vyslouzil, Jiri 1924- *Baker 92*
Vyvyan, Jennifer 1925-1974 *OxDcOp*
Vyvyan, Jennifer (Brigit) 1925-1974 *Baker 92*

W

W., Bill 1895-1971 *BioIn 17*
Waag, C. Michael 1944- *WhoSSW 93*
Waag, Susan S. *Law&B 92*
Waagaard, Knut *WhoScE 91-4*
Waagbo, Rune 1959- *WhoScE 91-4*
Waaland, Irving Theodore 1927- *WhoAm 92*
Waaland, Pamela Kaye 1951- *WhoAmW 93, WhoSSW 93*
Waaler, Bjarne Arentz 1925- *WhoWor 93*
Waart, Edo de 1941- *Baker 92, BioIn 17*
Waart, Hendrikus Aloysius Petrus de 1863-1931 *Baker 92*
Wabeck, Charles John 1938- *WhoE 93*
Waber, Bernard 1924- *ConAu 38NR, MajAI [port]*
Waber, Harry Edward 1911- *WhoWor 93*
Wabitsch, K. Rudolf 1945- *WhoUN 92*
Wabler, Robert Charles, II 1948- *WhoAm 92, WhoEmL 93, WhoWor 93*
Wabnitz, Hans Werner 1942- *WhoWor 93*
Wach, Piotr 1944- *WhoScE 91-4*
Wach, Roger 1929- *St&PR 93*
Wacha, Frank Albert, Jr. 1950- *WhoSSW 93*
Wachal, David E. 1939- *WhoAm 92*
Wachal, Robert Stanley 1929- *WhoAm 92*
Wachberger, Michael *WhoScE 91-4*
Wachenfeld, William Thomas 1926- *WhoAm 92*
Wachi, Takaji 1891- *HarEnMi*
Wachman, Harold Yehuda 1927- *WhoAm 92*
Wachman, Marvin 1917- *WhoAm 92, WhoWor 93*
Wachner, Brian Gary 1945- *St&PR 93*
Wachner, Linda J. *NewYTBS 92 [port]*
Wachner, Linda Joy 1946- *BioIn 17, WhoAm 92, WhoAmW 93*
Wachs, Alan Leonard 1959- *WhoSSW 93*
Wachs, David V. *WhoAm 92*
Wachs, David V. 1926- *St&PR 93*
Wachs, Jay S. 1930- *St&PR 93*
Wachs, John J. *St&PR 93*
Wachs, Martin 1941- *WhoAm 92*
Wachs, Mitchell *Law&B 92*
Wachs, Paul Etienne Victor 1851-1915 *Baker 92*
Wachs, Robert M. 1923- *St&PR 93*
Wachs, Saul Philip 1931- *WhoE 93*
Wachsberg, Orin *MiSFD 9*
Wachsberger, Clyde *BioIn 17*
Wachsberger, Ken 1949- *WhoWrEP 92*
Wachsberger, Ken(neth) 1949- *ConAu 138*
Wachsberger, Patrick Daniel 1951- *St&PR 93*
Wachsler, Robert Alan 1934- *WhoAm 92*
Wachsman, Harvey Frederick 1936- *WhoAm 92, WhoWor 93*
Wachsmann, Daniel *MiSFD 9*
Wachsmann, Klaus P(hilipp) 1907-1984 *Baker 92*
Wachstein, Joan Martha 1941- *WhoAmW 93, WhoE 93*
Wachtel, David Edward 1962- *WhoAm 92*
Wachtel, Eli 1951- *WhoAm 92*
Wachtel, Harry H. 1917- *WhoAm 92*
Wachtel, Theodor 1823-1893 *Baker 92, OxDcOp*
Wachter, Dieter R. 1944- *St&PR 93*
Wachter, Eberhard d1992 *NewYTBS 92*
Wachter, Eberhard 1929- *IntDcOp*
Wachter, Eberhard 1929-1992 *BioIn 17*
Wachter, George Charles 1951- *St&PR 93*
Wachter, Helmut 1929- *WhoScE 91-4*
Wachter, Joseph Edward 1933- *St&PR 93*
Wachter, Kenneth W. 1947- *ConAu 139*
Wachter, Mark F. *Law&B 92*
Wachter, Oralee *BioIn 17*
Wachter, Paul J. 1931- *St&PR 93*
Wachter, Paul Sidney 1946- *St&PR 93*
Wachter, Susan Melinda 1943- *WhoE 93*
Wachter, William B. 1946- *St&PR 93*
Wachterman, Richard 1947- *St&PR 93*
Wachterman, Richard Michael *Law&B 92*
Wachtler, Sol 1930- *WhoAm 92*
Wachtman, John Bryan, Jr. 1928- *WhoAm 92*
Wachtmeister, Axel Raoul 1865-1947 *Baker 92*
Wachtmeister, Wilhelm H. F. 1923- *WhoAm 92*
Wac'Inyanpi, Oyate 1932- *WhoWor 93*
Wack, Gina Maria 1959- *WhoSSW 93*
Wack, Henry Paul 1934- *WhoE 93*
Wack, Mary Frances 1954- *WhoAmW 93*
Wackenheim, Auguste 1925- *WhoScE 91-2*
Wackenhut, George R. 1919- *St&PR 93*
Wackenhut, George Russell 1919- *WhoAm 92*
Wackenhut, Richard Russell 1947- *St&PR 93, WhoAm 92, WhoSSW 93*
Wackenhut, Ruth J. 1922- *St&PR 93*
Wackenhut, Ruth Johann Bell 1922- *WhoAmW 93*
Wackenroder, Wilhelm Heinrich 1773-1798 *BioIn 17*
Wacker, Daniel James *Law&B 92*
Wacker, Diane Williams 1959- *WhoSSW 93*
Wacker, Frederick G. 1918- *St&PR 93*
Wacker, Frederick G., III 1960- *St&PR 93*
Wacker, Frederick Glade, Jr. 1918- *WhoAm 92, WhoWor 93*
Wacker, Hansjorg 1939- *WhoScE 91-4*
Wacker, Margaret Morrissey 1951- *WhoEmL 93*
Wacker, Phyllis Ullmont Gee 1935- *WhoAmW 93*
Wacker, Richard Allen *Law&B 92*
Wacker, Warren Ernest Clyde 1924- *WhoAm 92, WhoWor 93*
Wackerbarth, E.S. *Law&B 92*
Wackerbauer, Karl 1931- *WhoScE 91-3*
Wackerle, Frederick William 1939- *WhoAm 92*
Wackerlin, Tess Rose 1956- *WhoAmW 93*
Wacks, Jonathan 1948- *MiSFD 9*
Waclawski, Eugene 1959- *WhoScE 91-1*
Wada, Akiyoshi 1929- *WhoWor 93*
Wada, Ben Tsutom 1955- *WhoWor 93*
Wada, Eitaro 1939- *WhoWor 93*
Wada, Harry Nobuyoshi 1919- *WhoAm 92*
Wada, Kazuhito 1924- *WhoAsAP 91*
Wada, Kazuo *BioIn 17*
Wada, Mitchell Michio 1963- *St&PR 93*
Wada, Ryusaburo 1943- *St&PR 93*
Wada, Sadami Chris 1932- *WhoAm 92*
Wada, Sadao 1925- *WhoAsAP 91*
Wada, Shizou 1926- *WhoAsAP 91*
Wada, Takao 1930- *WhoWor 93*
Wada, Takayoshi 1919- *WhoAsAP 91*
Wadas, Andrzej 1954- *WhoWor 93*
Waddell, Alfred Moore, Jr. 1939- *WhoAm 92*
Waddell, Bonnie Carlene 1944- *WhoSSW 93*
Waddell, Clyde C., Jr. 1942- *WhoAm 92*
Waddell, Harry Lee 1912- *WhoAm 92*
Waddell, Helen Jane 1889-1965 *BioIn 17*
Waddell, Howard Ernest 1943- *WhoSSW 93*
Waddell, Jimmy Carroll 1946- *St&PR 93*
Waddell, John Comer 1937- *St&PR 93*
Waddell, John L., Jr. 1943- *WhoSSW 93*
Waddell, Jonathan H. 1941- *WhoSSW 93*
Waddell, Kenneth Gary 1962- *WhoSSW 93*
Waddell, Leila *AmWomPl*
Waddell, Lisa Bird 1960- *St&PR 93*
Waddell, M. Keith 1957- *St&PR 93*
Waddell, Malcolm 1952- *St&PR 93*
Waddell, Martin *ScF&FL 92*
Waddell, Martin 1941- *ChlFicS, SmATA 15AS [port]*
Waddell, Oliver Wendell 1930- *St&PR 93*
Waddell, Phillip Dean 1948- *WhoSSW 93*
Waddell, Robert Earnest 1938- *WhoSSW 93*
Waddell, Robert Fowler 1926- *St&PR 93*
Waddell, William Joseph 1929- *WhoAm 92*
Waddell, William L. 1931- *St&PR 93*
Wadden, Marie 1955- *ConAu 139*
Wadden, Richard Albert 1936- *WhoAm 92*
Wadden, Thomas Antony 1952- *WhoE 93, WhoWor 93*
Waddill, Graham Walker 1927- *St&PR 93*
Waddilove, David 1910-1991 *AnObit 1991*
Wadding, Luke 1588-1657 *BioIn 17*
Waddingham, John *BioIn 17*
Waddingham, John Alfred 1915- *WhoAm 92*
Waddington, David 1929- *WhoWor 93*
Waddington, David James *WhoScE 91-1*
Waddington, F.B. *WhoScE 91-1*
Waddington, Henry G. 1922- *St&PR 93*
Waddington, Miriam 1917- *WhoCanL 92*
Waddington, Raymond Bruce, Jr. 1935- *WhoAm 92*
Waddington, William Henry 1826-1894 *BioIn 17*
Waddle, Floyd Robert 1942- *WhoSSW 93*
Waddle, James E. 1949- *St&PR 93*
Waddle, Jeffrey R. *WhoWrEP 92*
Waddle, Jerry M. 1931- *St&PR 93*
Waddle, John Frederick 1927- *WhoAm 92, WhoWor 93*
Waddle, Roberta Snowbarger 1943- *WhoAmW 93*
Waddleton, Beverly Lynne 1952- *WhoSSW 93*
Wadds, Jean Casselman 1920- *WhoAm 92*
Wade, Abdoulaye *BioIn 17*
Wade, Abdoulaye 1927- *WhoAfr*
Wade, Barbara *WhoScE 91-1*
Wade, Ben Frank 1935- *WhoAm 92*
Wade, Benjamin F. 1800-1878 *PolPar*
Wade, Bill 1931- *St&PR 93*
Wade, Brenda Ann *Law&B 92*
Wade, Bryan 1950- *WhoCanL 92*
Wade, Byron 1947- *St&PR 93*
Wade, Byron L. *Law&B 92*
Wade, Carole *St&PR 93*
Wade, Carolyn R. *Law&B 92*
Wade, Charles Byrd, Jr. 1915- *WhoAm 92*
Wade, Charles D. 1946- *St&PR 93*
Wade, Cheryl Marie 1948- *WhoWrEP 92*
Wade, Craig *BioIn 17*
Wade, Darby J. *Law&B 92*
Wade, Donald L. 1934- *WhoIns 93*
Wade, Dudley Freeman 1918- *St&PR 93*
Wade, Dwight Robert 1907- *WhoSSW 93*
Wade, Edwin Lee 1932- *St&PR 93, WhoAm 92, WhoWor 93*
Wade, Elizabeth *ScF&FL 92*
Wade, Elmo B. 1925- *St&PR 93*
Wade, Eva Jean 1945- *WhoAmW 93*
Wade, Frederick *DcCPCAm*
Wade, George Joseph 1938- *WhoAm 92*
Wade, George Sinclair 1926- *St&PR 93*
Wade, Glen 1921- *WhoAm 92*
Wade, Harry Randolph 1938- *St&PR 93*
Wade, Helene Hopper *Law&B 92*
Wade, Hubert Claude 1936- *St&PR 93*
Wade, James A. 1937- *WhoAm 92*
Wade, James Michael 1943- *WhoAm 92*
Wade, James O'Shea 1940- *WhoAm 92*
Wade, Jarrel Blake 1943- *WhoAm 92*
Wade, Jeptha H. 1924- *St&PR 93*
Wade, Jeptha Homer, III 1924- *WhoAm 92*
Wade, Jimmie L. 1954- *St&PR 93*
Wade, John Graham *WhoScE 91-1*
Wade, John Stevens *WhoWrEP 92*
Wade, John Webster 1911- *WhoWor 93*
Wade, John Webster, Jr. *Law&B 92*
Wade, Joseph Augustine 1796-1845 *Baker 92*
Wade, Kenneth *WhoScE 91-1*
Wade, Leigh 1897-1991 *BioIn 17*
Wade, Leila A. *AmWomPl*
Wade, Malcolm Smith 1923- *WhoSSW 93*
Wade, Margaret Gaston 1948- *WhoSSW 93*
Wade, Marion *BioIn 17*
Wade, Mary Hazelton Blanchard 1860-1936 *AmWomPl*
Wade, Mary McKnight 1949- *WhoAmW 93*
Wade, Michael Daniel 1961- *WhoSSW 93*
Wade, Michael Gerard *Law&B 92*
Wade, Michael James 1954- *St&PR 93*
Wade, Michael John 1949- *WhoAm 92*
Wade, Michael R. A. 1945- *St&PR 93*
Wade, Neil M. 1936- *WhoScE 91-1*
Wade, Nicholas Michael Landon 1942- *WhoAm 92*
Wade, Ormand Joseph 1939- *St&PR 93*
Wade, Patricia Lynne 1950- *WhoAmW 93*
Wade, Rebecca Haygood 1946- *WhoAmW 93, WhoWor 93*
Wade, Richard Conant 1945- *WhoSSW 93*
Wade, Robert Glenn 1933- *WhoWor 93*
Wade, Robert Hirsch Beard 1916- *WhoAm 92*
Wade, Robert Patrick 1947- *St&PR 93*
Wade, Robert Paul 1936- *WhoAm 92*
Wade, Rodger Grant 1945- *WhoWor 93*
Wade, Roger C. 1941- *St&PR 93*
Wade, Ronald J. 1936- *St&PR 93*
Wade, Seth 1928- *WhoWrEP 92*
Wade, Sidney 1951- *ConAu 136*
Wade, Steven R. *St&PR 93*
Wade, Susie Ann 1955- *WhoAmW 93*

Wade, Suzanne 1938- *WhoWor 93*
Wade, Theodore Everett, Jr. 1936- *WhoWrEP 92*
Wade, Thomas Edward 1943- *WhoAm 92, WhoSSW 93*
Wade, Thomas W. *ScF&FL 92*
Wade, Timothy Andrew 1958- *WhoWrEP 92*
Wade, Tom *ScF&FL 92*
Wade, Tom W. 1933- *St&PR 93*
Wade, Tom Wilton, Jr. 1933- *WhoSSW 93*
Wade, Victor Nigel *WhoScE 91-1*
Wade, Virginia 1945- *WhoWor 93*
Wadekin, Karl-Eugen 1921- *WhoWor 93*
Wadell, Goran 1941- *WhoScE 91-4*
Wadelski, Leslie Anthony 1947- *WhoSSW 93*
Wadelton, Maggie-Owen 1890-1972 *ScF&FL 92*
Wadensten, Ted S. 1931- *St&PR 93*
Wadhams, Lester John *WhoScE 91-1*
Wadhams, Neva Mc Farland *AmWomPl*
Wadhams, Peter *WhoScE 91-1*
Wadhwa, Anil K. 1964- *St&PR 93*
Wadhwa, Gulshan R. 1931- *St&PR 93*
Wadhwa, Manohar H. *Law&B 92*
Wadiyar, Srikanta Dapta Narasimharaja 1953- *WhoAsAP 91*
Wadkins, Jerry Lanston 1949- *BiDAMSp 1989*
Wadkins, Lanny *BioIn 17*
Wadkins, Lanny 1949- *WhoAm 92*
Wadleigh, Michael *MiSFD 9*
Wadleigh, Richard Stanley 1944- *WhoE 93*
Wadler, Arnold L. *Law&B 92*
Wadler, Arnold L. 1943- *St&PR 93, WhoAm 92*
Wadler, Sanford *St&PR 93*
Wadley, M. Richard *WhoWor 93*
Wadley, M. Richard 1942- *WhoAm 92*
Wadley, Susan Snow 1943- *WhoAmW 93*
Wadlington, Cuba 1943- *St&PR 93*
Wadlington, Linda Denise 1955- *WhoAmW 93*
Wadlington, Walter James 1931- *WhoAm 92*
Wadlington, Warwick Paul 1938- *WhoAm 92, WhoSSW 93*
Wadlow, Joan Krueger 1932- *WhoAm 92, WhoAmW 93*
Wadman, Bruce William 1931- *St&PR 93*
Wadman, Walter John 1935- *WhoAm 92*
Wadman, Wesley Woodrow 1937- *St&PR 93*
Wadsworth, Beverley B. *BioIn 17*
Wadsworth, Brenton H. 1929- *St&PR 93*
Wadsworth, Charles Anthony *Law&B 92*
Wadsworth, Charles (William) 1929- *Baker 92, WhoAm 92*
Wadsworth, David A. *Law&B 92*
Wadsworth, David A. 1949- *St&PR 93*
Wadsworth, Douglas J. *Law&B 92*
Wadsworth, Dyer Seymour *Law&B 92*
Wadsworth, Dyer Seymour 1936- *St&PR 93, WhoAm 92, WhoWor 93*
Wadsworth, Euleta *AmWomPl*
Wadsworth, Frank Whittemore 1919- *WhoAm 92*
Wadsworth, Frederick John 1933- *St&PR 93*
Wadsworth, Homer Clark 1913- *WhoAm 92*
Wadsworth, James Marshall 1939- *WhoAm 92*
Wadsworth, John Spencer, Jr. 1939- *WhoAm 92*
Wadsworth, Maurice Arden 1929- *St&PR 93*
Wadsworth, Michael Robert *Law&B 92*
Wadsworth, Philip Richard *Law&B 92*
Wadsworth, Robert Arthur 1949- *St&PR 93*
Wadsworth, Robert David 1942- *St&PR 93, WhoAm 92*
Wadsworth, Robert Woodman 1913-1990 *BioIn 17*
Wadsworth, Virginia W. *Law&B 92*
Wadsworth, William Whitney 1934- *St&PR 93*
Wadya, Hubert 1953- *St&PR 93*
Waechter, Alfred von Kiderlen- 1852-1912 *BioIn 17*
Waechter, Antoine 1949- *BioIn 17*
Waechter, Arthur Joseph, Jr. 1913- *WhoAm 92*
Waechter, Eberhard 1929- *Baker 92*
Waechter, Eberhard 1929-1992 *OxDcOp*
Waechter, Eleanor 1939- *WhoAmW 93*
Waechter, F.B., Jr. 1957- *St&PR 93*
Waechter, Ralph Watson *Law&B 92*
Waechter, Thomas Charles *Law&B 92*
Waedt, Carl F. *ScF&FL 92*
Waefelghem, Louis van 1840-1908 *Baker 92*
Waegelein, Robert A. 1960- *St&PR 93*
Waeger, Robert W. 1946- *St&PR 93*
Waehner, Ralph Livingston 1935- *WhoAm 92, WhoE 93*
Waelde, Gail Patricia 1953- *WhoE 93*
Waelput, Hendrik 1845-1885 *Baker 92*
Waelrant, Hubert 1516?-1595 *Baker 92*
Waelsch, Salome 1907- *BioIn 17*
Waelsch, Salome Gluecksohn 1907- *WhoAm 92, WhoAmW 93*
Waelti-Walters, Jennifer 1942- *ConAu 136, ScF&FL 92*
Waena, Nathaniel 1945- *WhoAsAP 91*
Waern-Bugge, Peder 1932- *WhoScE 91-4*
Waes, Guido 1936- *WhoScE 91-2*
Waesberghe, Jos Smits van *Baker 92*
Waesche, Richard Henley Woodward 1930- *WhoSSW 93*
Waetjen, Herman Charles 1929- *WhoAm 92*
Waetjen, Walter Bernhard 1920- *WhoAm 92*
Wafta, Nabil T. 1945- *WhoUN 92*
Waganheim, Arthur Brian 1959- *WhoEmL 93*
Wagar, James Lee 1934- *St&PR 93, WhoAm 92*
Wagar, W. Warren 1932- *ScF&FL 92*
Wageman, James Carter 1935- *WhoE 93*
Wageman, Thomas J. *WhoAm 92*
Wagemann, Hans G. 1935- *WhoScE 91-3*
Wagemans, Peter Jan 1952- *Baker 92*
Wagenaar, Bernard 1894-1971 *Baker 92*
Wagenaar, Johan 1862-1941 *Baker 92*
Wagener, Donna Lynn 1959- *WhoWor 93*
Wagener, Dorothy Spencer 1949- *WhoAmW 93*
Wagener, Hans C. 1933- *WhoUN 92*
Wagener, Hans-Wilfried 1934- *WhoScE 91-3*
Wagener, Hobart D. 1921- *WhoAm 92*
Wagener, James Wilbur 1930- *WhoAm 92, WhoSSW 93*
Wagener, Jean-Pierre 1935- *WhoScE 91-3*
Wagener, Klaus P.E. 1930- *WhoScE 91-3*
Wagener, Klaus Paul 1930- *WhoWor 93*
Wagenet, Robert Jeffrey 1950- *WhoAm 92*
Wagenfeld, Wilhelm 1900- *BioIn 17*
Wagenfuehrer, Carl Mitchell 1947- *WhoE 93*
Wagenknecht, Edward 1900- *BioIn 17, ScF&FL 92, WhoAm 92*
Wagenmakers, Hendrick 1936- *WhoUN 92*
Wagenmakers, Patricia S. 1958- *WhoScE 91-3*
Wagenmann, William David, Jr. 1943- *St&PR 93*
Wagensberg, Jorge 1948- *WhoWor 93*
Wagenseil, Georg Christoph 1715-1777 *Baker 92, OxDcOp*
Wagenseil, Johann Christoph 1633-1708 *Baker 92*
Wager, James Joseph 1937- *St&PR 93*
Wager, Jonathan Field 1937- *WhoWor 93*
Wager, Patricia London *Law&B 92*
Wager, Richard Kenneth 1939- *WhoAm 92*
Wager, Ross Gaylord 1939- *St&PR 93*
Wager, Walter 1924- *ScF&FL 92*
Wager, Walter Herman 1924- *WhoAm 92*
Wagers, Patricia A. *Law&B 92*
Wagers, Robert Shelby 1943- *WhoAm 92*
Wages, Raymond B. 1932- *St&PR 93*
Wages, Terry W. 1944- *St&PR 93*
Waggener, Anna Thompson 1954- *WhoAmW 93*
Waggener, Ronald Edgar 1926- *WhoAm 92*
Waggener, Susan Lee 1951- *WhoAm 92, WhoAmW 93*
Waggett, Jean M. *Law&B 92*
Waggoner, D.E. 1935- *St&PR 93*
Waggoner, Diana *ScF&FL 92*
Waggoner, James Norman 1925- *WhoAm 92*
Waggoner, James Virgil 1927- *St&PR 93, WhoAm 92*
Waggoner, John K. *Law&B 92*
Waggoner, John M. *Law&B 92*
Waggoner, Lawrence William 1937- *WhoAm 92*
Waggoner, Leland Tate 1916- *WhoAm 92, WhoIns 93*
Waggoner, Lyle *BioIn 17*
Waggoner, Paul Edward 1923- *WhoAm 92*
Waggoner, Paulette Amburgey 1945- *WhoAmW 93*
Waggoner, Raymond Walter 1901- *WhoAm 92*
Waggoner, Richard M. 1948- *St&PR 93, WhoAm 92*
Waggoner, Samuel Lee 1930- *St&PR 93*
Waggoner, Thomas C. 1944- *St&PR 93*
Waggoner, Thomas Jefferson, III 1934- *St&PR 93*
Waggoner, Timothy Edward 1964- *WhoWrEP 92*
Waggoner, William Albert 1936- *St&PR 93*
Waggoner, William Johnson 1928- *WhoSSW 93*
Waghalter, Ignatz 1882-1949 *Baker 92*
Wagley, Charles 1913-1991 *BioIn 17*
Wagley, Charles (Walter) 1913-1991 *ConAu 136*
Wagley, Charles William 1913- *IntDcAn*
Wagley, John Raible 1931- *WhoE 93*
Wagman, David S. 1951- *WhoAm 92*
Wagman, Frederick Herbert 1912- *WhoAm 92*
Wagman, Gerald Howard 1926- *WhoE 93*
Wagman, John F. 1955- *St&PR 93*
Wagman, Robert John 1942- *WhoAm 92*
Wagner, Alan Cyril 1931- *WhoAm 92, WhoE 93*
Wagner, Albert Charles 1932- *St&PR 93*
Wagner, Aleksander Andrzej 1935- *WhoScE 91-4*
Wagner, Allan Ray 1934- *WhoAm 92, WhoE 93*
Wagner, Ann Dorothy 1950- *WhoEmL 93*
Wagner, Arne D. *Law&B 92*
Wagner, Arthur Lockwood 1853-1905 *HarEnMi*
Wagner, Arthur Ward, Jr. 1930- *WhoAm 92, WhoSSW 93*
Wagner, Audrey Adele 1958- *WhoAmW 93*
Wagner, Barbara Christy 1937- *WhoWrEP 92*
Wagner, Barbara J. *Law&B 92*
Wagner, Barry J. *Law&B 92*
Wagner, Barry J. 1940- *St&PR 93*
Wagner, Bart Jay 1937- *St&PR 93*
Wagner, Bernard Meyer 1928- *WhoAm 92*
Wagner, Bernhard Rupert 1951- *WhoWor 93*
Wagner, Bertram 1937- *St&PR 93*
Wagner, Bruce Stanley 1943- *St&PR 93, WhoAm 92*
Wagner, Burton Allan 1941- *WhoAm 92*
Wagner, Carl J. 1933- *St&PR 93*
Wagner, Carol Kilbourne 1933- *WhoAmW 93*
Wagner, Carruth John 1916- *WhoAm 92*
Wagner, Catherine 1953- *WhoAmW 93*
Wagner, Cecilia Louise 1958- *WhoE 93*
Wagner, Charlene Brook *WhoAmW 93, WhoSSW 93, WhoWor 93*
Wagner, Charles Abraham 1901- *WhoWrEP 92*
Wagner, Charles Leonard 1925- *WhoAm 92*
Wagner, Christian Joergen 1960- *WhoWor 93*
Wagner, Christian Nikolaus Johann 1927- *WhoAm 92*
Wagner, Christina Breuer 1954- *WhoAm 92, WhoAmW 93*
Wagner, Christopher Allen *Law&B 92*
Wagner, Clark L. *Law&B 92*
Wagner, Clark Leslie 1932- *St&PR 93*
Wagner, Constance Z. *Law&B 92*
Wagner, Cosima 1837-1930 *Baker 92, OxDcOp*
Wagner, Curtis Lee, Jr. 1928- *WhoAm 92*
Wagner, Cynthia Kaye 1957- *WhoAmW 93*
Wagner, Cyril, Jr. 1935- *WhoSSW 93*
Wagner, Cyrus Edward 1955- *WhoSSW 93*
Wagner, Dan *BioIn 17*
Wagner, David *Law&B 92*
Wagner, David 1950- *WhoE 93*
Wagner, David J. 1952- *WhoAm 92*
Wagner, David J. 1954- *St&PR 93*
Wagner, Dennis Larry 1940- *WhoE 93*
Wagner, Donald Bert 1930- *WhoAm 92, WhoSSW 93*
Wagner, Donald Roger 1926- *WhoSSW 93*
Wagner, Donna *WhoAmW 93*
Wagner, Douglas W.E. 1938- *WhoWrEP 92*
Wagner, Durrett 1929- *WhoAm 92*
Wagner, E. *WhoScE 91-3*
Wagner, Edward Kurt 1936- *WhoAm 92*
Wagner, Edwin Eric 1930- *WhoSSW 93*
Wagner, Eliot *Law&B 92*
Wagner, Elmar 1937- *WhoUN 92*
Wagner, Elmer Lenhart 1931- *St&PR 93*
Wagner, Eric Armin 1941- *WhoWor 93*
Wagner, Eric Gerhardt 1931- *WhoE 93*
Wagner, Eric M. *Law&B 92*
Wagner, Eugene *Law&B 92*
Wagner, Florence Signaigo 1919- *WhoAmW 93*
Wagner, Frank Stevens 1925- *WhoSSW 93*
Wagner, Fred John, Jr. 1929- *WhoSSW 93*
Wagner, Frederick Balthas, Jr. 1916- *WhoAm 92*
Wagner, Frederick Reese 1928- *WhoAm 92*
Wagner, Frederick William 1933- *WhoAm 92*
Wagner, Friedelind 1918-1991 *AnObit 1991, BioIn 17*
Wagner, Friedrich 1943- *WhoScE 91-3*
Wagner, G.A. *WhoScE 91-3*
Wagner, G. Keith 1929- *St&PR 93*
Wagner, Gail Ann 1950- *WhoAmW 93*
Wagner, Gary Wayne 1946- *WhoSSW 93*
Wagner, Georg Gottfried 1698-1756 *Baker 92*
Wagner, George Francis Adolf 1941- *WhoAm 92*
Wagner, George Hoyt 1914- *WhoSSW 93*
Wagner, George Phillip 1946- *St&PR 93*
Wagner, Gerhard 1933-1990 *BioIn 17*
Wagner, Gerrit Anthonie Alexander 1862-1892 *Baker 92*
Wagner, Gilbert Keith 1929- *WhoIns 93*
Wagner, Gottfried 1943- *WhoScE 91-3*
Wagner, Gustav Alfred 1918- *WhoWor 93*
Wagner, Harbart J. 1937- *St&PR 93*
Wagner, Harold A. 1935- *St&PR 93, WhoAm 92*
Wagner, Harvey Alan 1941- *St&PR 93*
Wagner, Harvey Arthur 1905- *WhoAm 92*
Wagner, Harvey E. *St&PR 93*
Wagner, Heinrich Leopold 1747-1779 *BioIn 17*
Wagner, Heinz Georg 1928- *WhoScE 91-3, WhoWor 93*
Wagner, Helen Adeene 1931- *WhoAmW 93*
Wagner, Henry Carrh, III 1942- *WhoSSW 93*
Wagner, Henry George 1917- *WhoAm 92*
Wagner, Henry Nicholas, Jr. 1927- *WhoAm 92*
Wagner, Herman Leon 1921- *WhoE 93*
Wagner, Honus 1874-1955 *BioIn 17*
Wagner, Howard Andrew 1960- *WhoSSW 93*
Wagner, I.J. 1915- *St&PR 93*
Wagner, J(osef) F(ranz) 1856-1908 *Baker 92*
Wagner, Jack *BioIn 17, ScF&FL 92*
Wagner, Jack Andrew, Jr. 1949- *WhoSSW 93*
Wagner, Jacqueline Letourneau 1947- *WhoAmW 93*
Wagner, James D. 1930- *St&PR 93*
Wagner, James R. 1958- *St&PR 93*
Wagner, James W. d1992 *BioIn 17, NewYTBS 92*
Wagner, Jane *DcAmChF 1960, ScF&FL 92*
Wagner, Jane 1935- *MiSFD 9*
Wagner, Jeffrey Widness *Law&B 92*
Wagner, Johanna 1826-1894 *Baker 92, OxDcOp*
Wagner, John 1955- *WhoWrEP 92*
Wagner, John A. 1930- *St&PR 93*
Wagner, John Daniel 1942- *WhoSSW 93*
Wagner, John Edward, Sr. 1931- *St&PR 93*
Wagner, John G. 1924- *St&PR 93*
Wagner, John Garnet 1921- *WhoAm 92*
Wagner, John Philip 1940- *WhoSSW 93*
Wagner, John Robert *Law&B 92*
Wagner, John Victor 1947- *WhoIns 93*
Wagner, Joseph Edward 1938- *WhoAm 92*
Wagner, Joseph Frederick 1900-1974 *Baker 92*
Wagner, Judith A. *St&PR 93*
Wagner, Judith B. 1943- *St&PR 93*
Wagner, Judith Buck 1943- *WhoAm 92, WhoAmW 93*
Wagner, Julia Anne 1924- *WhoAm 92*
Wagner, Karen B. 1956- *St&PR 93*
Wagner, Karl Edward 1945- *ScF&FL 92*
Wagner, Karl Jakob 1772-1822 *Baker 92*
Wagner, Kathleen Ann 1947- *WhoAmW 93*
Wagner, Keith *Law&B 92*
Wagner, Keith Anthony 1932- *WhoAm 92*
Wagner, Kenneth C. 1928- *St&PR 93*
Wagner, Kenneth John 1951- *St&PR 93*
Wagner, Klaus 1943- *WhoUN 92*
Wagner, Linda R. *Law&B 92*
Wagner, Linda Stralka 1945- *WhoAmW 93*
Wagner, Lindsay 1949- *HolBB [port]*
Wagner, Lindsay J. 1949- *WhoAm 92*
Wagner, Louis Carson, Jr. 1932- *WhoAm 92*
Wagner, Louise Hemingway Benton 1937- *WhoAm 92, WhoWor 93*
Wagner, Louise Natale d1992 *NewYTBS 92*
Wagner, Lynn Edward 1941- *WhoSSW 93, WhoWor 93*
Wagner, Marcia Claire 1943- *WhoAmW 93*
Wagner, Margaret Louise 1947- *WhoAmW 93*
Wagner, Mark Todd 1953- *WhoE 93*
Wagner, Martin S. *Law&B 92*

Wagner, Mary Kathryn 1932- *WhoAmW 93*
Wagner, Mary M. 1946- *BioIn 17*
Wagner, Maryanne 1946- *St&PR 93*
Wagner, Maryfrances Cusumano 1947- *WhoWrEP 92*
Wagner, Michael D. *Law&B 92*
Wagner, Michael D. 1948- *WhoIns 93*
Wagner, Michael Duane 1948- *WhoEmL 93*
Wagner, Morton Jules 1925- *St&PR 93*
Wagner, Nancy Lynn 1955- *WhoAmW 93*
Wagner, Natalie Z. *AmWomPl*
Wagner, Norbert 1935- *St&PR 93, WhoE 93*
Wagner, Norman Ernest 1935- *WhoAm 92*
Wagner, Norman Paul 1924- *St&PR 93, WhoAm 92*
Wagner, Paul Anthony, Jr. 1947- *WhoEmL 93*
Wagner, Peggy Talbot 1930- *WhoSSW 93*
Wagner, Peter Ewing 1929- *WhoAm 92, WhoE 93*
Wagner, Peter (Joseph) 1865-1931 *Baker 92*
Wagner, Phillip 1946- *WhoCanL 92*
Wagner, Ralph B. 1933- *WhoAm 92*
Wagner, Ralph H. 1943- *St&PR 93*
Wagner, Raymond C. 1926- *St&PR 93*
Wagner, Richard 1813-1883 *BioIn 17, IntDcOp [port], OxDcOp*
Wagner, Richard 1927- *WhoAm 92, WhoWor 93*
Wagner, Richard B. *Law&B 92*
Wagner, Richard Charles 1931- *St&PR 93, WhoIns 93*
Wagner, Richard Eric 1951- *WhoAm 92*
Wagner, Richard H. *Law&B 92*
Wagner, (Wilhelm) Richard 1813-1883 *Baker 92*
Wagner, Robert *BioIn 17*
Wagner, Robert 1910-1991 *AnObit 1991*
Wagner, Robert 1930- *IntDcF 2-3, WhoAm 92*
Wagner, Robert B. 1961- *St&PR 93*
Wagner, Robert C. 1927- *St&PR 93*
Wagner, Robert Earl 1921- *WhoAm 92, WhoSSW 93*
Wagner, Robert F., Sr. 1877-1953 *PolPar*
Wagner, Robert F., Jr. 1910-1991 *PolPar*
Wagner, Robert Ferdinand 1910-1991 *BioIn 17*
Wagner, Robert Jules *Law&B 92*
Wagner, Robert K. 1931- *St&PR 93*
Wagner, Robert L. 1932- *St&PR 93*
Wagner, Robert Owen 1935- *WhoAm 92*
Wagner, Robert Roderick 1923- *WhoAm 92, WhoSSW 93*
Wagner, Robert Rutherford *Law&B 92*
Wagner, Robert S. 1908- *St&PR 93*
Wagner, Robert Scott 1956- *WhoSSW 93*
Wagner, Robert Todd 1932- *WhoAm 92*
Wagner, Robert Wayne 1956- *WhoSSW 93*
Wagner, Robin L. 1959- *WhoE 93*
Wagner, Robin M. Halpern *Law&B 92*
Wagner, Robin S. *ScF&FL 92*
Wagner, Robin Samuel Anton 1933- *WhoAm 92, WhoE 93*
Wagner, Roger d1992 *NewYTBS 92*
Wagner, Roger (Francis) 1914- *Baker 92*
Wagner, Ronald Francis Vincent 1952- *WhoE 93*
Wagner, Ronald H. 1936- *St&PR 93*
Wagner, Roy 1938- *WhoAm 92*
Wagner, Rudolf Georg 1941- *WhoWor 93*
Wagner, Sharon 1936- *ScF&FL 92*
Wagner, Shirley Ann 1942- *WhoAmW 93*
Wagner, Siegfried 1869-1930 *OxDcOp*
Wagner, Siegfried (Helferich Richard) 1869-1930 *Baker 92*
Wagner, Siegfried R. 1924- *WhoScE 91-3*
Wagner, Sieglinde 1921- *Baker 92*
Wagner, Sigurd *WhoAm 92*
Wagner, Stephen Anthony 1953- *WhoAm 92*
Wagner, Stephen Evon 1951- *WhoIns 93*
Wagner, Stephen H. *Law&B 92*
Wagner, Sterling Robacker 1904- *WhoE 93*
Wagner, Sue Ellen 1940- *WhoAm 92, WhoAmW 93*
Wagner, Susan Jane *WhoAmW 93, WhoE 93*
Wagner, Susan Marie 1953- *WhoAmW 93*
Wagner, Sylvia R. 1949- *St&PR 93*
Wagner, Terrence J. 1946- *St&PR 93*
Wagner, Thomas Edward 1956- *WhoSSW 93*
Wagner, Thomas J. *Law&B 92*
Wagner, Thomas John 1938- *St&PR 93, WhoAm 92*
Wagner, Thomas Joseph 1939- *WhoAm 92*
Wagner, Thomas R. *Law&B 92*
Wagner, Timothy W. 1942- *St&PR 93*
Wagner, Ulrich *WhoScE 91-3*
Wagner, Virgil D. 1935- *St&PR 93*
Wagner, W.C. *WhoScE 91-4*
Wagner, Wanda Faye 1956- *WhoAmW 93*
Wagner, Warren Herbert, Jr. 1920- *WhoAm 92*
Wagner, Wayne Elwell 1938- *WhoE 93*
Wagner, Wieland 1917-1966 *Baker 92, OxDcOp*
Wagner, Wieland Adolf Gottfried 1917-1966 *IntDcOp*
Wagner, William Burdette 1941- *WhoAm 92*
Wagner, William Charles 1932- *WhoAm 92*
Wagner, William Gerard 1936- *WhoAm 92*
Wagner, William Michael 1949- *WhoSSW 93*
Wagner, William O. 1931- *St&PR 93*
Wagner, William Sherwood 1928- *WhoSSW 93*
Wagner, Wolfgang 1919- *IntDcOp, OxDcOp*
Wagner, Wolfgang 1940- *WhoScE 91-3*
Wagner, Wolfgang (Manfred Martin) 1919- *Baker 92*
Wagner Aloia, Victoria Ann 1961- *St&PR 93*
Wagner-Findeisen, Anne M. *Law&B 92*
Wagner-Jacobsen, Carolyn Frieda 1945- *WhoAmW 93*
Wagner-Mann, Colette Carol 1952- *WhoAmW 93*
Wagner-Regeny, Rudolf 1903-1969 *Baker 92, OxDcOp*
Wagner-Stevens, Tina Marie 1957- *WhoWrEP 92*
Wagner-Westbrook, Bonnie Joan 1953- *WhoAmW 93*
Wagniere, Georges Henry 1933- *WhoScE 91-4*
Wagoner, Dale Eugene 1936- *WhoSSW 93*
Wagoner, David Eugene 1949- *WhoSSW 93*
Wagoner, David Everett 1928- *WhoAm 92*
Wagoner, David Russell 1926- *WhoAm 92, WhoWrEP 92*
Wagoner, F. Nan Todd *Law&B 92*
Wagoner, George Frederick 1953- *WhoSSW 93*
Wagoner, J.L. Clifford *St&PR 93*
Wagoner, Porter 1927- *Baker 92, WhoAm 92*
Wagoner, Ralph Howard 1938- *WhoAm 92*
Wagoner, Randy 1951- *St&PR 93*
Wagoner, Richard K. 1937- *St&PR 93*
Wagoner, Richard Kenneth 1937- *WhoAm 92*
Wagoner, Robert Vernon 1938- *WhoAm 92*
Wagoner, W. Ray 1935- *St&PR 93*
Wagoner, William Douglas 1947- *WhoEmL 93, WhoWor 93*
Wagoner, William Hampton 1927- *WhoAm 92*
Wagonseller, James Myrl 1920- *WhoAm 92*
Wagstaff, Blanche Shoemaker 1888- *AmWomPl*
Wagstaff, Lula Virginia 1935- *WhoSSW 93*
Wagstaff, Marguerite Falkenburg d1990 *BioIn 17*
Wagstaff, Marilyn Rose 1950- *WhoAmW 93*
Wagstaff, Mark Cleland 1959- *WhoE 93*
Wagstaff, Thomas Walton 1946- *St&PR 93*
Wah, Fred 1939- *WhoCanL 92*
Wahba, Grace *WhoAm 92, WhoAmW 93*
Wahby, Victor Samuel 1945- *WhoE 93*
Wahdan, Mohammed Helmy 1933- *WhoUN 92*
Waheed Aziz, Abdul 1968- *WhoWor 93*
Wahid, Jawid 1953- *St&PR 93*
Wahid, Shanaz Ansari 1958- *WhoWor 93*
Wahl, Albert J. 1908- *St&PR 93*
Wahl, C. Richard 1937- *St&PR 93*
Wahl, Eberhard W. 1914-1990 *BioIn 17*
Wahl, Floyd Michael 1931- *WhoAm 92*
Wahl, Georg F.H. 1938- *WhoScE 91-3*
Wahl, Howard Wayne 1935- *WhoAm 92*
Wahl, Jacques Henri 1932- *St&PR 93, WhoAm 92*
Wahl, Jan (Boyer) 1933- *ConAu 38NR, MajAI [port], SmATA 73 [port], WhoAm 92*
Wahl, Joan Constance 1921- *WhoAmW 93*
Wahl, John Robert *Law&B 92*
Wahl, Keith Andrew 1959- *WhoE 93*
Wahl, Margaret Derby 1911- *St&PR 93*
Wahl, Martha Stoessel 1916- *WhoAmW 93, WhoWor 93*
Wahl, Paul 1922- *WhoAm 92, WhoWor 93*
Wahl, Philippe 1930- *WhoScE 91-2*
Wahl, Raymond 1948- *St&PR 93*
Wahl, Roger A. 1948- *St&PR 93*
Wahl, Rosalie E. 1924- *WhoAm 92, WhoAmW 93*
Wahl, Sharon Marie 1945- *WhoAmW 93, WhoE 93*
Wahl, Steven Alan 1953- *WhoE 93*
Wahl, Timothy S. *Law&B 92*
Wahl, William Bryan 1963- *WhoEmL 93, WhoSSW 93, WhoWor 93*
Wahl, William Joseph, Jr. 1947- *WhoE 93*
Wahlback, Bengt Magnus 1943- *WhoWor 93*
Wahlberg, Allen H. 1933- *St&PR 93*
Wahlberg, Allen Henry 1933- *WhoAm 92, WhoE 93*
Wahlberg, Donnie 1969- *BioIn 17*
Wahlberg, Jan Erik 1945- *WhoUN 92*
Wahlberg, Mark *BioIn 17*
Wahlberg, Marky Mark *NewYTBS 92 [port]*
Wahlberg, Philip Lawrence 1924- *WhoAm 92*
Wahlberg, Rune 1910- *Baker 92*
Wahlberg, Stanley L. 1936- *St&PR 93*
Wahlberg, Thomas Bertil 1943- *WhoWor 93*
Wahle, F(rederick) Keith 1947- *WhoWrEP 92*
Wahle, Ingrid E. *Law&B 92*
Wahlen, Edwin Alfred 1919- *WhoAm 92*
Wahlen, Edwin Alfred, Jr. 1947- *WhoSSW 93*
Wahlert, Robert Henry 1939- *St&PR 93*
Wahlgren, Carl Mats 1952- *WhoScE 91-4*
Wahlgren, Erick 1911- *WhoWrEP 92*
Wahlgren, Gordon J. 1949- *St&PR 93*
Wahlgren, Lars-Eric Malcolm 1929- *WhoUN 92*
Wahlgren, Otto Gosta 1927- *WhoScE 91-4*
Wahli, Walter 1946- *WhoScE 91-4*
Wahli, Walter Arthur 1946- *WhoWor 93*
Wahlig, Michael J. *Law&B 92*
Wahlin, Anders C.E. 1944- *WhoScE 91-4*
Wahlke, John Charles 1917- *WhoAm 92*
Wahlman, Mark M. 1948- *St&PR 93*
Wahlmeier, Mark Anthony 1955- *St&PR 93*
Wahloo, Per 1926-1975 *ScF&FL 92*
Wahlquist, Jack R. 1933- *WhoIns 93*
Wahlquist, Jack Rainard 1933- *St&PR 93*
Wahlquist, John T. 1899- *BioIn 17*
Wahlqvist, Lars *WhoScE 91-4*
Wahls, Shirley 1941- *BioIn 17*
Wahlstrom, Bjorn 1944- *WhoScE 91-4*
Wahlstrom, Bjorn Gosta 1944- *WhoWor 93*
Wahlstrom, Goran 1933- *WhoScE 91-4*
Wahlstrom, Mary Jean Jones 1947- *WhoSSW 93*
Wahlstrom, Paul Burr 1947- *WhoSSW 93*
Wahman, Thomas Walter 1938- *WhoE 93*
Wahn, Robert 1954- *St&PR 93*
Wahnon, Judith Mascarenhas 1943- *WhoAmW 93*
Wahrahaftig, Paul *WhoE 93*
Wahren, Douglas 1934- *WhoScE 91-4*
Wahren, John 1937- *WhoScE 91-4*
Wahrendorf, Jurgen 1948- *WhoScE 91-3*
Wahrman, Tirza S. *Law&B 92*
Wai, Logan L. 1947- *St&PR 93*
Wai, Samuel Siu Ming 1953- *WhoAm 92*
Waiblinger, Wilhelm Friedrich 1804-1830 *BioIn 17*
Waid, Allen G. 1946- *St&PR 93*
Waid, Jim 1942- *BioIn 17*
Waid, Mary Joan 1939- *BioIn 17*
Waid, Richard File 1928- *St&PR 93*
Waid, Stephen Hamilton 1948- *WhoWrEP 92*
Waide, Michael J. 1947- *St&PR 93*
Waigand, Ann Hutchinson 1954- *WhoWrEP 92*
Waigel, Theodor *BioIn 17*
Waigel, Theodor 1939- *WhoWor 93*
Waignein, Andre Pierre 1942- *WhoWor 93*
Waihee, John David, III 1946- *WhoAm 92, WhoWor 93*
Wailand, Adele R. 1949- *St&PR 93*
Wailand, Adele Rosen 1949- *WhoAmW 93*
Wailly, (Louis Auguste) Paul (Warnier) de 1854-1933 *Baker 92*
Waim, Jim Yer 1954- *WhoAsAP 91*
Wain, Alan P. *Law&B 92*
Wain, John *BioIn 17*
Wain, John James 1950- *St&PR 93*
Wainberg, Alan 1937- *WhoAm 92*
Wainberg, Jacob M. 1906- *St&PR 93*
Waine, Charles Richard 1931- *WhoSSW 93*
Wainer, Herbert Alan 1941- *St&PR 93*
Wainer, Larry Alan *Law&B 92*
Wainer, Laurie Beth 1962- *WhoSSW 93*
Wainer, Stanley A. 1926- *St&PR 93*
Wainer, Stanley Allen 1926- *WhoAm 92*
Wainerdi, Richard Elliott 1931- *WhoAm 92, WhoSSW 93*
Wainess, Marcia Watson 1949- *WhoAmW 93, WhoEmL 93, WhoWor 93*
Wainger, Allen Jay 1953- *WhoE 93*
Wainick, Daniel 1929- *St&PR 93*
Wainwright, Alfred 1907-1991 *AnObit 1991*
Wainwright, Alice Cutts d1991 *BioIn 17*
Wainwright, Carroll Livingston, Jr. 1925- *WhoAm 92*
Wainwright, Charles Anthony 1933- *WhoAm 92*
Wainwright, Hilda Alexander 1925- *WhoAmW 93*
Wainwright, J.A. 1946- *WhoCanL 92*
Wainwright, J. Kenneth, Jr. *Law&B 92*
Wainwright, Jonathan Mayhew 1883-1953 *BioIn 17*
Wainwright, Jonathan Mayhew, IV 1883-1953 *HarEnMi*
Wainwright, Paul Edward Blech 1917- *WhoAm 92*
Wainwright, Raymond Parr 1943- *WhoScE 91-1*
Wainwright, Rupert *MiSFD 9*
Wainwright, Stephen A. 1931- *WhoAm 92*
Wainwright, Stuyvesant, II 1921- *WhoAm 92*
Wainzo, Ainde Kanauko 1948- *WhoAsAP 91*
Wais de Badgen, Irene Rut 1957- *WhoWor 93*
Waisman, Jerry 1934- *WhoE 93*
Waisman, Morris 1911- *WhoSSW 93*
Waisman, Taina 1912-1990 *BioIn 17*
Waissel, Matthaus c. 1537-1602 *Baker 92*
Waisselius, Matthaus c. 1537-1602 *Baker 92*
Wait, Carol Grace Cox 1942- *WhoAm 92, WhoE 93*
Wait, Charles E. 1950- *St&PR 93*
Wait, Charles Valentine 1951- *WhoE 93, WhoEmL 93, WhoWor 93*
Wait, Dash 1853-1895 *BioIn 17*
Wait, George William 1958- *WhoSSW 93*
Wait, James Richard 1924- *WhoAm 92*
Waite, Arthur Edward 1857-1942 *BioIn 17*
Waite, Betty June 1926- *WhoAmW 93*
Waite, Charles Morrison 1932- *WhoAm 92*
Waite, Clark Greene 1932- *St&PR 93*
Waite, Daniel Elmer 1926- *WhoAm 92*
Waite, Darvin Danny *WhoWor 93*
Waite, David William 1942- *WhoSSW 93*
Waite, Dennis Vernon 1938- *WhoAm 92*
Waite, Edward J., III *Law&B 92*
Waite, Ian Angus 1962- *WhoWor 93*
Waite, Ian Mowbray *WhoScE 91-1*
Waite, James Arthur *WhoScE 91-1*
Waite, James Lewis 1947- *St&PR 93*
Waite, Jocelyn K. *Law&B 92*
Waite, Judith Gail 1947- *St&PR 93*
Waite, Kenneth J. 1948- *St&PR 93*
Waite, Kyle 1935- *St&PR 93*
Waite, Lawrence Wesley 1951- *WhoWor 93*
Waite, Lena *BioIn 17*
Waite, Louis E. 1926- *St&PR 93*
Waite, Morrison Remick 1816-1888 *OxCSupC [port]*
Waite, Nancy C. *Law&B 92*
Waite, Norman, Jr. 1936- *WhoAm 92*
Waite, P.B. 1922- *BioIn 17*
Waite, P.J. *WhoScE 91-1*
Waite, Peter Arthur 1951- *WhoE 93*
Waite, Peter Busby 1922- *BioIn 17*
Waite, Ralph *BioIn 17*
Waite, Ralph 1928- *MiSFD 9*
Waite, Ralph 1929- *WhoAm 92*
Waite, Robert George Leeson 1919- *WhoAm 92, WhoWrEP 92*
Waite, Stephen Holden 1936- *WhoAm 92*
Waite, Terry *BioIn 17*
Waite, Terry 1939- *ConHero 2 [port]*
Waite, Thomas A. *Law&B 92*
Waite, William 1936- *WhoScE 91-1, WhoWor 93*
Waiter, Joseph J. 1951- *St&PR 93*
Waiter, Serge-Albert 1930- *WhoAm 92*
Waites, Candy Yaghjian 1943- *WhoAmW 93*
Waites, Elizabeth Angeline 1939- *WhoAmW 93*
Waites, Geoffrey Malcolm Hasting 1928- *WhoUN 92*
Waites, John Nigel Michael 1960- *WhoWor 93*
Waites, William Ernest 1934- *WhoSSW 93*
Waites, William Michael *WhoScE 91-1*
Waithe, Fitz Steven 1966- *WhoE 93*
Waiting, Graham Roger 1954- *St&PR 93*
Waitkavicz, Tana Gehret 1957- *WhoAmW 93*
Waits, Bruce Edwin *Law&B 92*
Waits, Freddie d1989 *BioIn 17*
Waits, James A. *Law&B 92*
Waits, Pamela Cherie 1956- *WhoAmW 93*

Waits, Thomas Alan 1949- *WhoAm 92*
Waits, Tom 1949- *Baker 92, BioIn 17*
Waitz, Grete 1953- *BioIn 17*
Waitzkin, Howard B. 1945- *WhoAm 92*
Waitzkin, Stella Pumpkin 1920- *WhoE 93*
Waiwood, Michael *Law&B 92*
Waixel, Vivian 1946- *WhoE 93*
Wajda, Andrzej 1926- *DrEEuF, MiSFD 9, PolBiDi, WhoWor 93*
Wajda, Eligiusz 1951- *WhoWor 93*
Wajenberg, Arnold Sherman 1929- *WhoAm 92*
Wajenberg, Earl 1953- *ScF&FL 92*
Wajgt, Andrzej Maciej 1942- *WhoWor 93*
Wajnert, T.C. *St&PR 93*
Wajnert, Thomas C. 1943- *WhoAm 92*
Waka, Lukas 1943- *WhoAsAP 91*
Wakabayashi, Jiro 1928- *WhoWor 93*
Wakabayashi, Shin 1929- *WhoWor 93*
Wakae, Masami 1934- *WhoWor 93*
Wakaizumi, Kei 1930- *WhoWor 93*
Wakamatu, Nobuyuki 1949- *WhoWor 93*
Wakao, Noriaki 1930- *WhoWor 93*
Wakao, Shinjiro 1923- *WhoWor 93*
Wakasugi, Hiroshi 1935- *Baker 92*
Wake, David B. 1964- *ScF&FL 92*
Wake, David Burton 1936- *WhoAm 92*
Wake, Graeme Charles 1943- *WhoWor 93*
Wake, Marvalee Hendricks 1939- *WhoAm 92, WhoAmW 93*
Wake, Robert Alan *WhoE 93*
Wake, Thomas H. 1905- *St&PR 93*
Wakeen, Teresa Ann *Law&B 92*
Wakefield, Allan Gale 1941- *St&PR 93*
Wakefield, Benton McMillin, Jr. 1920- *WhoAm 92*
Wakefield, Dan *BioIn 17*
Wakefield, Dan 1932- *WhoAm 92, WhoWrEP 92*
Wakefield, David Anthony 1946- *WhoWor 93*
Wakefield, H. Russell 1888-1964 *ScF&FL 92*
Wakefield, Janet Ruth 1926- *WhoAmW 93, WhoE 93*
Wakefield, John Frederick 1952- *WhoSSW 93*
Wakefield, John Joseph, Jr. 1952- *WhoSSW 93*
Wakefield, Kim Stoeckle 1953- *WhoWrEP 92*
Wakefield, Lyman E., Jr. 1911- *St&PR 93*
Wakefield, Meri Kelline 1962- *WhoWrEP 92*
Wakefield, Patricia A. 1942- *St&PR 93*
Wakefield, Penny *BioIn 17*
Wakefield, Richard G. 1942- *St&PR 93*
Wakefield, Roger Emerson 1948- *WhoE 93*
Wakefield, Samuel Norris 1938- *WhoAm 92*
Wakefield, Stanley M. 1948- *St&PR 93*
Wakefield, Tom 1935- *ScF&FL 92*
Wakefield, Tommie Wayne *Law&B 92*
Wakeham, Helmut Richard Rae 1916- *WhoAm 92*
Wakeham, John 1932- *WhoWor 93*
Wakeham, William Arnot *WhoScE 91-1*
Wakeley, John Halbert 1932- *WhoSSW 93*
Wakelin, James H. 1911-1990 *BioIn 17*
Wakelin, Joan *BioIn 17*
Wakeling, Anthony *WhoScE 91-1*
Wakeling, David 1956- *See* English Beat, The *ConMus 9*
Wakely, James K. 1949- *St&PR 93*
Wakeman, Antoinette Prudence Van Hoesen *AmWomPl*
Wakeman, Fred Joseph 1928- *St&PR 93, WhoAm 92*
Wakeman, Frederic Evans, Jr. 1937- *WhoAm 92*
Wakeman, Mary Lalley 1955- *WhoSSW 93*
Wakeman, Olivia Van Horn *WhoE 93*
Wakeman, Rick 1949- *WhoAm 92*
See Also Yes *ConMus 8*
Wakeman, Sherwood G. *Law&B 92*
Waki, Kunio 1943- *WhoUN 92*
Wakil, Abdul 1945- *WhoAsAP 91 WhoWor 93*
Wakil, Idris Abdul 1925- *WhoAfr*
Wakil, Salih Jawad 1927- *WhoAm 92*
Wakin, Edward 1927- *WhoWrEP 92*
Wakjer, Roderick S. *St&PR 93*
Wakley, James Turner 1921- *WhoAm 92*
Waknine, Samuel 1959- *WhoWor 93*
Wako, S. Amos 1945- *WhoAfr*
Wakoski, Diane 1937- *WhoAm 92, WhoWrEP 92*
Waksal, Samuel D. *St&PR 93*
Waksman, Byron Halsted 1919- *WhoAm 92*
Waksmundzki, Andrzej 1910- *WhoScE 91-4*
Wakuri, Hidekazu 1934- *WhoWor 93*
Walacinski, Adam 1928- *Baker 92*
Walas, Chris *MiSFD 9*
Walasiewicz, Stanislawa 1911-1980 *PolBiDi*
Walaszek, Edward Joseph 1927- *WhoAm 92*
Walaszek, Slawoj 1928- *WhoScE 91-4*
Walatka, Pamela Portugal 1942- *WhoWrEP 92*
Walberg, Betty 1921-1990 *BioIn 17*
Walberg, Fred 1921- *WhoScE 91-4*
Walberg, Herbert John 1937- *WhoAm 92, WhoWor 93*
Walbert, Florence Catherine 1929- *WhoAmW 93*
Walbert, Thomas D. *Law&B 92*
Walbolt, Sylvia H. 1941- *WhoAm 92*
Walborn, Earl J. 1943- *St&PR 93*
Walborsky, Harry M. 1923- *WhoAm 92*
Walbran, John W. *Law&B 92*
Walbrecher, William C. *St&PR 93*
Walbrick, J.M. 1941- *St&PR 93*
Walbridge, John T. 1950- *St&PR 93*
Walbridge, John T., Jr. 1925- *St&PR 93*
Walbridge, Willard E. 1913- *St&PR 93*
Walbridge, Willard Eugene 1913- *WhoAm 92*
Walbridge, William C. 1933- *St&PR 93*
Walbridge, William Mark 1957- *WhoE 93*
Walbrook, Anton 1896-1967 *IntDcF 2-3 [port]*
Walburg, James Brenner 1953- *St&PR 93*
Walcamp, Marie 1894-1936 *SweetSg A [port]*
Walch, Peter Sanborn 1940- *WhoAm 92*
Walch, Resa Ellenburg 1957- *WhoAmW 93*
Walcha, Helmut 1907-1991 *BioIn 17*
Walcha, (Arthur Emil) Helmut 1907- *Baker 92*
Walcher, Alan Ernest 1949- *WhoWor 93*
Walcher, Dwain Newton 1915- *WhoWor 93*
Walcher, Thomas 1941- *WhoScE 91-3*
Walcher, Wilhelm 1910- *WhoWor 93*
Walcker, Eberhard 1850-1927 *See* Walcker, Eberhard Friedrich 1794-1872 *Baker 92*
Walcker, Eberhard Friedrich 1794-1872 *Baker 92*
Walcker, Friedrich 1829-1895 *See* Walcker, Eberhard Friedrich 1794-1872 *Baker 92*
Walcker, Heinrich 1828-1903 *See* Walcker, Eberhard Friedrich 1794-1872 *Baker 92*
Walcker, Johann Eberhard 1756-1843 *See* Walcker, Eberhard Friedrich 1794-1872 *Baker 92*
Walcker, Karl 1845-1908 *See* Walcker, Eberhard Friedrich 1794-1872 *Baker 92*
Walcker, Oscar 1869-1948 *See* Walcker, Eberhard Friedrich 1794-1872 *Baker 92*
Walcker, Paul 1846-1928 *See* Walcker, Eberhard Friedrich 1794-1872 *Baker 92*
Walcker-Mayer, Werner 1923- *See* Walcker, Eberhard Friedrich 1794-1872 *Baker 92*
Walcott, Charles Doolittle 1850-1927 *BioIn 17*
Walcott, Delbert Lee 1930- *St&PR 93, WhoSSW 93*
Walcott, Derek *BioIn 17*
Walcott, Derek 1930- *DcLB Y92 [port], IntLitE, MagSWL [port], NewYTBS 92 [port]*
Walcott, Derek (Alton) 1930- *DcLB 117 [port], WhoAm 92, WhoWor 93*
Walcott, Frank 1916- *DcCPCAm*
Walcott, James W. 1944- *St&PR 93*
Walcott, Peter W. *Law&B 92*
Walczak, Karl *St&PR 93*
Walczak, Ryszard Tadeusz 1943- *WhoScE 91-4*
Walczak, Stanislaw 1942- *WhoWor 93*
Walczak, Wlodzimierz 1937- *WhoScE 91-4*
Walczak, Zbigniew Kazimierz 1932- *WhoSSW 93, WhoWor 93*
Walczewski, Jacek 1931- *WhoScE 91-4*
Walczuk, Peter P. 1949- *St&PR 93*
Wald, Barbara Ann 1935- *WhoE 93*
Wald, Bernard Joseph 1932- *WhoAm 92, WhoE 93, WhoWor 93*
Wald, Donna Gene 1947- *WhoAm 92*
Wald, Elfriede *WhoWrEP 92*
Wald, Francine Joy Weintraub 1938- *WhoAmW 93, WhoE 93*
Wald, George 1906- *WhoAm 92, WhoWor 93*
Wald, Ignacy 1923- *WhoScE 91-4*
Wald, Jeff 1944- *St&PR 93*
Wald, John R. *Law&B 92*
Wald, Lillian 1867-1940 *JeAmHC*
Wald, Lillian D. 1867-1940 *BioIn 17, WomChHR [port]*
Wald, Malvin *BioIn 17*
Wald, Marlena Malmstedt 1950- *WhoSSW 93*
Wald, Martin 1934- *WhoAm 92*
Wald, Mary S. 1943- *WhoAmW 93, WhoE 93*
Wald, Max 1889-1954 *Baker 92*
Wald, Michael 1911- *St&PR 93*
Wald, Nicholas John *WhoScE 91-1*
Wald, Niel 1925- *WhoAm 92*
Wald, Patricia McGowan 1928- *CngDr 91, WhoAm 92, WhoAmW 93, WhoE 93*
Wald, Richard Charles *WhoAm 92*
Wald, Sandra L. *Law&B 92*
Wald, Sylvia 1915- *WhoAm 92, WhoAmW 93*
Wald, William G. 1927- *St&PR 93*
Waldau, Helen Frances 1925- *WhoAmW 93, WhoE 93*
Waldbauer, Gilbert Peter 1928- *WhoAm 92*
Waldbaum, Jane Cohn 1940- *WhoAmW 93*
Waldbillig, Charles Craig 1926- *St&PR 93*
Waldbillig, Gerald William 1905- *WhoE 93*
Waldeck, Dennis J. 1940- *St&PR 93*
Waldeck, John Walter, Jr. 1949- *WhoEmL 93*
Waldeck, Kenneth Theodore 1942- *WhoSSW 93*
Waldeck, Kenneth Theodore, Jr. 1942- *St&PR 93*
Waldeck, Steve P. 1951- *St&PR 93*
Waldecker, Sondra Kay 1948- *WhoAmW 93*
Waldeck-Rousseau, Pierre Marie Rene Ernest 1846-1904 *BioIn 17*
Walden, Alfred S. 1941- *St&PR 93*
Walden, Alyssa *Law&B 92*
Walden, Amelia Elizabeth *WhoAm 92*
Walden, Betty Martindale *WhoAmW 93*
Walden, Daniel 1922- *WhoAm 92*
Walden, Elda Jannae 1942- *WhoSSW 93*
Walden, Henryk 1917- *WhoScE 91-4*
Walden, James William 1936- *WhoWor 93*
Walden, Joseph Lawrence 1956- *WhoEmL 93, WhoSSW 93*
Walden, Lars Johan 1930- *WhoScE 91-4*
Walden, Lea Ann 1964- *WhoWrEP 92*
Walden, Linda L. *Law&B 92*
Walden, Marion Patrick 1939- *St&PR 93*
Walden, Mark *ScF&FL 92*
Walden, Narada Michael 1952- *SoulM*
Walden, Nelson Ewing 1924- *St&PR 93*
Walden, Noel Harry 1925- *WhoWor 93*
Walden, Phil 1940- *SoulM*
Walden, Philip Michael 1940- *WhoAm 92*
Walden, Robert 1943- *WhoAm 92*
Walden, Robert Wyndham 1844-1905 *BiDAMSp 1989*
Walden, Royce B. 1928- *St&PR 93*
Walden, Stanley Eugene 1932- *WhoAm 92*
Walden, Sue Cole 1947- *WhoAmW 93*
Walden, Thomas, III 1940- *St&PR 93*
Walden, Thomas Alfred 1949- *WhoSSW 93*
Waldenfels, Hans 1931- *WhoWor 93*
Waldenstrom, Martin M. 1948- *St&PR 93*
Walder, Jeannette M. *Law&B 92*
Waldera, Wanda Frances 1952- *WhoAmW 93*
Waldera, Wayne Eugene 1930- *WhoAm 92*
Waldersee, Alfred von 1832-1904 *HarEnMi*
Waldfogel, Morton Sumner 1922- *St&PR 93, WhoAm 92*
Waldfogel, Peter Douglas 1951- *St&PR 93*
Waldhart, Thomas E. 1956- *St&PR 93*
Waldhauer, Fred Donald 1927- *WhoAm 92*
Waldhausen, John Anton 1929- *WhoAm 92*
Waldhauser, Cathy H. 1949- *St&PR 93*
Waldhauser, Cathy Howard 1949- *WhoAm 92, WhoAmW 93*
Waldheger, Martha Jane *Law&B 92*
Waldheim, Kurt *BioIn 17*
Waldheim, Kurt 1918- *DcTwHis, WhoWor 93*
Waldhof, Sharka Eva *Law&B 92*
Waldichuk, Michael 1929-1991 *BioIn 17*
Waldie, Brian *WhoScE 91-1*
Waldinger, Martin Harris 1938- *St&PR 93*
Waldman, Anne 1945- *ConAu 17AS [port]*
Waldman, Anne Lesley 1945- *WhoAm 92, WhoWrEP 92*
Waldman, Barry Jerome 1940- *St&PR 93*
Waldman, David Stuart *Law&B 92*
Waldman, Frank 1919-1990 *ScF&FL 92*
Waldman, Frederic 1903- *Baker 92*
Waldman, Grant Austin *MiSFD 9*
Waldman, Hal K. *Law&B 92*
Waldman, Harry 1942- *St&PR 93*
Waldman, Jay Carl 1944- *WhoE 93*
Waldman, Kenneth Robert 1947- *WhoSSW 93*
Waldman, Martin Jay 1934- *St&PR 93*
Waldman, Maryo *St&PR 93*
Waldman, Myron Richard 1940- *WhoE 93*
Waldman, Paul 1936- *WhoE 93*
Waldman, Robert Allan *Law&B 92*
Waldman, Robert Hart 1938- *WhoAm 92*
Waldman, Robert James 1960- *WhoWor 93*
Waldman, Saul Joseph 1931- *St&PR 93*
Waldman, Stanley *St&PR 93*
Waldmann, Herman *WhoScE 91-1*
Waldmann, Herman 1945- *WhoWor 93*
Waldmann, Maria 1842-1920 *Baker 92, OxDcOp*
Waldmann, Robert 1960- *WhoWor 93*
Waldmann, Thomas Alexander 1930- *WhoAm 92, WhoE 93*
Waldmeier, Max Robert 1912- *WhoScE 91-4*
Waldmeir, Peter Nielsen 1931- *WhoAm 92*
Waldner, Flavio A. 1937- *WhoWor 93*
Waldner, Lulu de *BioIn 17*
Waldo, Dorothy *AmWomPl*
Waldo, Dwight 1913- *WhoAm 92*
Waldo, Edith H. *AmWomPl*
Waldo, Edna La Moore 1893- *AmWomPl*
Waldo, Edward H. *ScF&FL 92*
Waldo, Joseph Thomas 1950- *WhoEmL 93*
Waldo, Kurt Richard *Law&B 92*
Waldo, Robert Carl, Jr. 1954- *WhoE 93*
Waldo, Robert Leland 1923- *WhoAm 92*
Waldo, Suzanne Tracey 1953- *WhoE 93*
Waldo, Willard H. 1912- *St&PR 93*
Waldoch, Donna Mae 1951- *WhoAmW 93*
Waldoff, Milton 1931- *St&PR 93*
Waldoks, Phillip Harry 1952- *St&PR 93*
Waldon, Alton 1936- *BioIn 17*
Waldon, Grace Roberta 1941- *WhoAmW 93*
Waldorf, Douglas L., Jr. *Law&B 92*
Waldorf, James A. 1938- *St&PR 93*
Waldrep, Alvis Kent, Jr. 1954- *WhoSSW 93*
Waldrep, Marvin L. *Law&B 92*
Waldrep, Phil 1960- *WhoWrEP 92*
Waldron, Agnes d1991 *BioIn 17*
Waldron, Anthony James 1924- *WhoE 93*
Waldron, Charles Andrew 1922- *WhoSSW 93*
Waldron, Charles F. 1920- *St&PR 93*
Waldron, Ellis Leigh 1915- *WhoAm 92*
Waldron, Eric L. *St&PR 93*
Waldron, Georgia *AmWomPl*
Waldron, Ingrid Lore 1939- *WhoAmW 93*
Waldron, James 1958- *St&PR 93*
Waldron, Joan Mary 1954- *WhoAmW 93*
Waldron, Margaret Ann 1927- *WhoAmW 93*
Waldron, Marion *AmWomPl*
Waldron, Reuben Howard 1920- *St&PR 93*
Waldron, Richard Glenn *Law&B 92*
Waldron, Robert James 1928- *WhoE 93*
Waldron, Robert Leroy, II 1936- *WhoSSW 93*
Waldron, Sharon Elaine 1941- *WhoE 93*
Waldron, Theodore Charles 1946- *WhoEmL 93*
Waldron, Tom *BioIn 17*
Waldrop, Bernard Keith 1932- *WhoAm 92*
Waldrop, Charles Wesley 1933- *WhoSSW 93*
Waldrop, Francis Neil 1926- *WhoAm 92*
Waldrop, Gideon W(illiam) 1919- *Baker 92*
Waldrop, Gideon William 1919- *WhoAm 92*
Waldrop, Heidi *BioIn 17*
Waldrop, Howard 1946- *ScF&FL 92*
Waldrop, Milton Jeffrey 1962- *WhoSSW 93*
Waldrop, Richard Edward 1952- *St&PR 93*
Waldrop, Richard J. 1943- *St&PR 93*
Waldrop, Robert Louis 1937- *St&PR 93*
Waldrop, Rosmarie 1935- *ConAu 39NR*
Waldrop, Rosmariex 1935- *WhoWrEP 92*
Waldrop, S.M. 1930- *St&PR 93*
Waldschmidt, Paul Edward 1920- *WhoAm 92*
Waldsmith, Dinah Leigh 1958- *WhoE 93*
Waldstein, Ferdinand Ernst Joseph Gabriel 1762-1823 *Baker 92*
Waldstein, Sheldon Saul 1924- *WhoAm 92*
Waldteufel, (Charles-) Emile 1837-1915 *Baker 92*
Walduck, Robert Philip *WhoScE 91-1*
Waldvogel, Albert 1941- *WhoScE 91-4*
Wale, Stuart John *WhoScE 91-1*
Walek, Thomas A. 1957- *WhoAm 92*

Walen, Harry Leonard 1915- *WhoAm 92, WhoWor 93*
Walendowski, George Jerry 1947- *WhoEmL 93*
Walenkamp, G.H.I.M. 1947- *WhoScE 91-3*
Walenta, Kurt 1927- *WhoScE 91-3*
Walentia, John R. 1947- *St&PR 93*
Walentynowicz, Anna 1929- *PolBiDi*
Wales, Amy *AmWomPl*
Wales, Arthur Paul d1991 *BioIn 17*
Wales, Gwynne Huntington 1933- *WhoAm 92*
Wales, Harold Webster 1928- *WhoAm 92*
Wales, Hugh Gregory 1910- *WhoAm 92, WhoWor 93*
Wales, M. Elizabeth 1932- *WhoAmW 93*
Wales, Richard P. 1933- *St&PR 93*
Wales, Thomas Cody *Law&B 92*
Wales, Walter D. 1933- *WhoAm 92*
Walesa, Lech 1943- *BioIn 17, ColdWar 2 [port], DcTwHis, PolBiDi, WhoWor 93*
Walesby, John Robert, Sr. 1931- *WhoSSW 93*
Walewski, Alex Joseph 1949- *St&PR 93*
Walewski, Bogdan *BioIn 17*
Waley-Cohen, Bernard 1914-1991 *AnObit 1991, BioIn 17*
Walf, Knut Willibrord 1936- *WhoWor 93*
Walford, Brian G. *St&PR 93*
Walford, James 1913- *BioIn 17*
Walford, Roy L. *BioIn 17*
Walford, Thomas Leonard Howard 1955- *WhoWor 93*
Walfred, Hugo Anderson 1925- *WhoAm 92*
Walgran, Craig Chance 1953- *WhoE 93*
Walgrave, Carmen Rojean 1934- *WhoAmW 93*
Walgreen, Charles R., III 1935- *St&PR 93*
Walgreen, Charles Rudolph, III 1935- *WhoAm 92*
Walhout, Justine Simon 1930- *WhoAmW 93*
Wali, Kameshwar 1927- *WhoAm 92*
Wali, Mohan Kishen 1937- *WhoAm 92, WhoWor 93*
Walia, Jasjit Singh 1934- *WhoSSW 93*
Walicki, Andrzej Stanislaw 1930- *WhoAm 92*
Waligorski, Andrzej 1908-1974 *IntDcAn*
Waligorski, Michael Patrick Russell 1945- *WhoWor 93*
Waligorski, Stanislaw 1934- *WhoWor 93*
Waligurski, Raymond J. 1940- *St&PR 93*
Walinder, Gunnar O.S. 1926- *WhoScE 91-4*
Walinsky, Adam 1937- *WhoWor 93*
Walinsky, Louis Joseph 1908- *WhoAm 92*
Walinsky, Michael David 1945- *WhoE 93*
Walinsky, Paul 1940- *WhoE 93*
Waliser, Beverly Kay 1956- *WhoAmW 93*
Walish, Geralyn Rose 1956- *WhoE 93*
Waliszewski, John S. 1946- *St&PR 93*
Waliszewski, Zygmunt 1897-1936 *PolBiDi*
Walize, Reuben Thompson, III 1950- *WhoWor 93*
Walk, Donald W. *Law&B 92*
Walk, Mary Anne *BioIn 17*
Walk, Richard David 1920- *WhoAm 92, WhoWor 93*
Walk, Robert Allen 1948- *St&PR 93*
Walk, Rochelle Friedman *Law&B 92*
Walk, Ronald Douglas 1943- *WhoAm 92*
Walke, Bernhard H. 1940- *WhoScE 91-3*
Walke, Debra Dee 1965- *WhoAmW 93*
Walke, Julia Annette 1908- *WhoWrEP 92*
Walke, Raymond J. 1936- *WhoIns 93*
Walken, Christopher *BioIn 17, NewYTBS 92 [port]*
Walken, Christopher 1943- *WhoAm 92*
Walkenhorst, Stewart R. 1953- *St&PR 93*
Walker, A. David 1918- *St&PR 93*
Walker, A. Harris *Law&B 92*
Walker, A. Harris 1935- *St&PR 93*
Walker, A. Maceo 1909- *WhoIns 93*
Walker, Alan 1930- *Baker 92*
Walker, Alan Christopher *WhoScE 91-1*
Walker, Alberta 1878- *AmWomPl*
Walker, Alexander 1818-1893 *JrnUS*
Walker, Alice 1944- *AmWomWr 92, AmWrS3, BioIn 17, BlkAuII 92, EncAACR, MagSAmL [port], ScF&FL 92*
Walker, Alice Johnstone 1871- *AmWomPl*
Walker, Alice Malsenior 1944- *AfrAmBi, WhoAm 92, WhoAmW 93, WhoWrEP 92*
Walker, Alicia Ramirez 1963- *WhoAmW 93*
Walker, Allen Crane *Law&B 92*
Walker, Allen Michael 1951- *WhoSSW 93*
Walker, Amelia H. *AmWomPl*
Walker, Andrew Charles *WhoScE 91-1*
Walker, Andrew Morris 1921- *WhoWor 93*
Walker, Anita Billet 1946- *WhoAmW 93*
Walker, Anita L. 1936- *St&PR 93*
Walker, Anne Core 1945- *WhoAmW 93*
Walker, Anthony Blair 1956- *WhoSSW 93*
Walker, Arthur Carleton 1943- *WhoE 93*
Walker, Arthur Lonzo 1926- *WhoSSW 93*
Walker, Audley Lawson 1935- *WhoWor 93*
Walker, B.J. 1919- *St&PR 93*
Walker, Baker 1942- *St&PR 93*
Walker, Barbara Hills 1946- *WhoE 93*
Walker, Barbara Humphrey 1962- *WhoAmW 93*
Walker, Barbara (Jeanne) K(erlin) 1921- *ConAu 38NR*
Walker, Benton LeRoy 1939- *WhoSSW 93*
Walker, Bert H. 1923- *St&PR 93*
Walker, Bertha E. *Law&B 92*
Walker, Betsy Ellen 1953- *St&PR 93, WhoAm 92*
Walker, Billie Rae 1944- *WhoAmW 93*
Walker, Billy J. 1931- *WhoAm 92*
Walker, Billy Kenneth 1946- *WhoSSW 93*
Walker, Brenda Louise Jolitz 1950- *WhoAmW 93*
Walker, Brenda Sue 1958- *WhoAmW 93*
Walker, Brian David *Law&B 92*
Walker, Brian John *WhoScE 91-1*
Walker, Bridgett 1958- *St&PR 93*
Walker, Brigitte Maria 1934- *WhoSSW 93, WhoWor 93*
Walker, Brooks, Jr. 1928- *St&PR 93*
Walker, Bruce Edward 1926- *WhoAm 92*
Walker, C. Eugene 1939- *WhoSSW 93*
Walker, C.J., Madame 1867-1919 *BioIn 17*
Walker, Carol Ellen Burton 1934- *WhoSSW 93*
Walker, Carolyn Smith 1946- *WhoSSW 93*
Walker, Carrie Kathryn 1964- *WhoAmW 93*
Walker, Catherine *BioIn 17*
Walker, Catherine L. 1954- *St&PR 93*
Walker, Catherine Louise *Law&B 92*
Walker, Cedric Frank 1950- *WhoSSW 93*
Walker, Celine Foster *WhoUN 92*
Walker, Charlene Ann 1948- *WhoAmW 93*
Walker, Charles Allen 1914- *WhoAm 92*
Walker, Charles Anthony *Law&B 92*
Walker, Charles Arthur 1944- *St&PR 93*
Walker, Charles B. 1939- *St&PR 93, WhoSSW 93*
Walker, Charles D. *BioIn 17*
Walker, Charles Leland 1926- *St&PR 93, WhoAm 92*
Walker, Charles Montgomery 1915- *WhoAm 92*
Walker, Charles Norman 1923- *WhoAm 92*
Walker, Charles R., III 1930- *WhoAm 92*
Walker, Charles Urmston 1931- *WhoAm 92*
Walker, Charles W. *AfrAmBi*
Walker, Charlotte Zoe 1935- *WhoE 93*
Walker, Charls Edward 1923- *WhoAm 92*
Walker, Cheryl Ann 1947- *WhoAmW 93*
Walker, Chris *BioIn 17*
Walker, Chris L. 1957- *WhoIns 93*
Walker, Clarence 1951- *WhoE 93*
Walker, Clarence W. 1887-1959 *BiDAMSp 1989*
Walker, Clarence Wesley 1931- *WhoAm 92*
Walker, Clinton *Law&B 92*
Walker, Colin David 1955- *WhoWor 93*
Walker, Colleen *WhoAmW 93*
Walker, Cora *BioIn 17*
Walker, Craig H. *Law&B 92*
Walker, Craig James 1940- *St&PR 93*
Walker, Craig Michael 1947- *WhoE 93*
Walker, D.A. 1946- *St&PR 93*
Walker, Dale N. 1952- *St&PR 93*
Walker, Dale Rush 1943- *WhoAm 92*
Walker, Daniel 1922- *PolPar*
Walker, Daniel Joshua, Jr. 1915- *WhoSSW 93*
Walker, Darcell *Law&B 92*
Walker, David 1911-1992 *ScF&FL 92*
Walker, David Alan *WhoScE 91-1*
Walker, David Ellis, Jr. 1938- *WhoSSW 93*
Walker, David G. 1926- *BioIn 17*
Walker, David Harry 1911- *WhoCanL 92*
Walker, David Harry 1911-1992 *ConAu 137, SmATA 71*
Walker, David M. 1958- *St&PR 93*
Walker, David Michael 1951- *WhoAm 92, WhoEmL 93*
Walker, David Rudger 1929- *WhoAm 92*
Walker, David Todd *Law&B 92*
Walker, David Todd 1937- *St&PR 93*
Walker, Dean Craig *Law&B 92*
Walker, Debra May 1956- *WhoAmW 93*
Walker, Dennis William, III 1948- *WhoSSW 93*
Walker, Deryck George *WhoScE 91-1*
Walker, Diann 1949- *WhoAmW 93*
Walker, Dilworth 1918-1990 *BioIn 17*
Walker, Doak 1927- *BioIn 17*
Walker, Don T. 1942- *St&PR 93*
Walker, Donald Ezzell 1921- *WhoAm 92*
Walker, Donald L. *Law&B 92*
Walker, Donald P. *Law&B 92*
Walker, Donna McAuley 1947- *WhoAmW 93*
Walker, Dorian *MiSFD 9*
Walker, Douglas Dunning 1940- *WhoAm 92*
Walker, Duard Lee 1921- *WhoAm 92*
Walker, E. Cardon 1916- *St&PR 93*
Walker, Earl E. 1921- *WhoAm 92*
Walker, Eben T. 1948- *St&PR 93*
Walker, Edward K. *Law&B 92*
Walker, Edward Keith, Jr. 1933- *WhoAm 92*
Walker, Edward S., Jr. 1940- *WhoAm 92, WhoWor 93*
Walker, Edyth 1867-1950 *Baker 92*
Walker, Elaine Virginia 1957- *WhoAmW 93*
Walker, Elizabeth 1909-1990 *BioIn 17*
Walker, Elizabeth Troy *Law&B 92*
Walker, Eljana M. du Vall 1924- *WhoWor 93*
Walker, Elkanah 1805-1877 *BioIn 17*
Walker, Elva Mae Dawson 1914- *WhoWor 93*
Walker, Elvin F. 1935- *St&PR 93*
Walker, Eric Arthur 1910- *WhoAm 92*
Walker, Ernest 1870-1949 *Baker 92*
Walker, Ernest Winfield 1917- *WhoAm 92*
Walker, Evelyn *WhoAmW 93, WhoSSW 93, WhoWor 93*
Walker, F. Ann 1940- *WhoAmW 93*
Walker, Florence Ann 1939- *WhoSSW 93*
Walker, Floyd Lee 1919- *WhoAm 92*
Walker, Francis Charles 1926- *WhoSSW 93*
Walker, Francis G. 1928- *St&PR 93*
Walker, Francis Gene 1928- *WhoAm 92*
Walker, Francis Roach 1944- *WhoSSW 93*
Walker, Frank 1907-1962 *Baker 92*
Walker, Frank Banghart 1931- *WhoAm 92, WhoWor 93*
Walker, Frank C. 1886-1959 *PolPar*
Walker, Frank Comerford 1886-1959 *BioIn 17*
Walker, Frank D. 1934- *St&PR 93*
Walker, Frank Dilling 1934- *WhoAm 92*
Walker, Frank Robinson 1899-1976 *HarEnMi*
Walker, Fred Elmer 1931- *WhoAm 92*
Walker, Fred R. 1933- *St&PR 93*
Walker, Fred Wyeth 1942- *WhoWrEP 92*
Walker, Frederic Rockwell 1933- *WhoSSW 93*
Walker, Frederick *WhoScE 91-1*
Walker, Gabriel F. 1950- *St&PR 93*
Walker, Gail Flanagan 1946- *WhoAmW 93*
Walker, Gary Chitwood 1946- *WhoSSW 93*
Walker, Gary Lee 1941- *St&PR 93*
Walker, Gay Hunner Parsons 1939- *WhoAm 92*
Walker, Gayle Jean 1947- *WhoAmW 93*
Walker, Geoffrey S. *Law&B 92*
Walker, George *BioIn 17*
Walker, George d1690 *BioIn 17*
Walker, George 1873-1911 *BioIn 17*
Walker, George A. 1929- *St&PR 93*
Walker, George Allen 1929- *WhoAm 92*
Walker, George F. 1927- *St&PR 93*
Walker, George F. 1947- *WhoCanL 92*
Walker, George Herbert, III 1931- *WhoAm 92*
Walker, George Kontz 1938- *WhoAm 92, WhoSSW 93, WhoWor 93*
Walker, George P. *Law&B 92*
Walker, George R. 1915- *St&PR 93*
Walker, George Robert 1915- *WhoIns 93*
Walker, George (Theophilus) 1922- *Baker 92*
Walker, George Theophilus, Jr. 1922- *WhoAm 92, WhoE 93*
Walker, Gerald T. 1940- *St&PR 93, WhoIns 93*
Walker, Gerald Wayne 1946- *WhoSSW 93*
Walker, Giles 1946- *MiSFD 9*
Walker, Gladys Lorraine 1927- *WhoWrEP 92*
Walker, Glen Dale 1934- *WhoSSW 93*
Walker, Gordon Arlon 1928- *St&PR 93*
Walker, Gordon Arthur Hunter 1936- *WhoAm 92*
Walker, Gordon Davies 1944- *WhoAm 92*
Walker, Greg A. *Law&B 92*
Walker, Gurnsey, Mrs. *AmWomPl*
Walker, Gus A. 1899- *St&PR 93, WhoAm 92*
Walker, Harold Blake 1904- *WhoAm 92*
Walker, Harold D. 1947- *St&PR 93*
Walker, Harold Osmonde 1928- *WhoAm 92*
Walker, Harold T. *Law&B 92*
Walker, Harriet K. *AmWomPl*
Walker, Harry Grey 1924- *WhoAm 92*
Walker, Harry Webster, II 1921- *WhoSSW 93*
Walker, Hay 1931- *St&PR 93*
Walker, Helen 1893- *AmWomPl*
Walker, Henry A., Jr. 1922- *St&PR 93*
Walker, Henry Alexander, Jr. 1922- *WhoAm 92*
Walker, Henry Gary 1921- *WhoSSW 93*
Walker, Henry Gilbert 1947- *WhoAm 92*
Walker, Herbert Leslie, Jr. 1918- *WhoAm 92*
Walker, Herbert S. 1924- *WhoUN 92*
Walker, Herschel *BioIn 17*
Walker, Herschel 1962- *WhoAm 92*
Walker, Hillman P. *Law&B 92*
Walker, Howard Allen 1932- *St&PR 93*
Walker, Howard Kent 1935- *WhoAm 92, WhoWor 93*
Walker, Howard Oldham 1923- *St&PR 93*
Walker, Hugh 1941- *ScF&FL 92*
Walker, I.M. *ScF&FL 92*
Walker, Ian *WhoScE 91-1*
Walker, Ian 1951-1990 *BioIn 17*
Walker, Ian James 1950- *WhoWor 93*
Walker, Inez Nathaniel 1911-1990 *BioIn 17*
Walker, Irma 1921- *ScF&FL 92*
Walker, Jack Leroy 1925- *WhoAm 92*
Walker, James 1944- *BiDAMSp 1989*
Walker, James, Jr. *Law&B 92*
Walker, James Alvin, Jr. 1946- *St&PR 93*
Walker, James Arthur 1948- *WhoEmL 93*
Walker, James Cornelius 1953- *WhoSSW 93*
Walker, James E. *WhoSSW 93*
Walker, James Elliot Cabot 1926- *WhoAm 92*
Walker, James George 1958- *WhoE 93*
Walker, James J. 1881-1946 *PolPar*
Walker, James Kenneth 1936- *WhoAm 92*
Walker, James Marion 1945- *WhoAm 92*
Walker, James Mitchell *Law&B 92*
Walker, James Roy 1937- *WhoAm 92*
Walker, James Silas 1933- *WhoAm 92*
Walker, James W., Jr. 1927- *St&PR 93*
Walker, James Willard 1943- *WhoAm 92*
Walker, James William, Jr. 1927- *WhoAm 92*
Walker, James William, III *Law&B 92*
Walker, Jane Ann *WhoE 93*
Walker, Jeanne Murray 1944- *WhoAmW 93, WhoWrEP 92*
Walker, Jeff *BioIn 17*
Walker, Jeff 1943- *BioIn 17*
Walker, Jeffrey A. *Law&B 92*
Walker, Jerald Carter 1938- *WhoAm 92*
Walker, Jewett Lynius 1930- *WhoSSW 93, WhoWor 93*
Walker, Jim *BioIn 17*
Walker, Joe 1850?-1898 *BioIn 17*
Walker, Joe Louis *BioIn 17*
Walker, Joe Robert 1932- *St&PR 93*
Walker, John *WhoScE 91-1*
Walker, John 1939- *BioIn 17*
Walker, John Alfred 1950- *WhoE 93*
Walker, John Andrew 1939- *WhoAm 92*
Walker, John Denley 1921- *WhoAm 92*
Walker, John E. 1938- *WhoIns 93*
Walker, John Ernst 1938- *St&PR 93, WhoAm 92*
Walker, John M. 1909-1990 *BioIn 17*
Walker, John Mark 1955- *WhoSSW 93*
Walker, John Mercer, Jr. 1940- *WhoAm 92*
Walker, John Michael 1942- *WhoWor 93*
Walker, John Neal 1930- *WhoAm 92*
Walker, Johnny Del 1947- *WhoSSW 93*
Walker, Jonathan Lee 1948- *WhoEmL 93*
Walker, Joseph 1922- *WhoAm 92*
Walker, Joseph P. 1946- *St&PR 93*
Walker, Joseph Reddeford 1798-1876 *Expl 93*
Walker, Judith M. *Law&B 92*
Walker, Julian Wilson, Jr. 1934- *St&PR 93*
Walker, Junior 1942- See Walker, Junior, & the Allstars *SoulM*
Walker, Junior, & the Allstars *SoulM*
Walker, K. Grahame 1937- *WhoAm 92*
Walker, K.L. *WhoScE 91-1*
Walker, Karen Lynette *WhoAmW 93*
Walker, Keith Grahame 1937- *St&PR 93*
Walker, Kenneth *BioIn 17*
Walker, Kenneth A. 1949- *St&PR 93*
Walker, Kenneth Adley 1949- *WhoE 93*
Walker, Kenneth Edward 1956- *WhoSSW 93*
Walker, Kenneth Henry 1940- *WhoAm 92*
Walker, Kenneth Lloyd 1952- *WhoSSW 93*
Walker, Kenny *BioIn 17*

Walker, Kim Bishton 1955- *WhoAm 92*
Walker, L.G., Jr. 1931- *WhoSSW 93*
Walker, Lannon 1936- *WhoAm 92, WhoWor 93*
Walker, Larry B. 1941- *St&PR 93*
Walker, Larry J. 1952- *St&PR 93*
Walker, Larry Moore 1935- *WhoSSW 93*
Walker, Laura Sewell 1937- *WhoAmW 93*
Walker, Leland Jasper 1923- *WhoAm 92*
Walker, Leland Max 1940- *St&PR 93*
Walker, Leola H. *ScF&FL 92*
Walker, Leroy Tashreau 1918- *WhoAm 92, WhoWor 93*
Walker, Leslie 1953?- *ConAu 139*
Walker, Leslie D. 1930- *St&PR 93*
Walker, Leslie Gresson *WhoScE 91-1*
Walker, Lewis 1855-1934 *GayN*
Walker, Lillie M. *AmWomPl*
Walker, Lillie Nolting *AmWomPl*
Walker, Linda Doty 1953- *St&PR 93*
Walker, Linda Farrell *Law&B 92*
Walker, Linda Lee *Law&B 92*
Walker, Lisa J. 1945- *WhoE 93*
Walker, Lisa Renee 1965- *WhoAmW 93*
Walker, Lois Virginia 1929- *WhoWrEP 92*
Walker, Loren Haines 1936- *WhoAm 92*
Walker, Lorene 1911- *WhoAmW 93*
Walker, Loretta *BioIn 17*
Walker, Lou Ann *BioIn 17*
Walker, Lou Ann 1952- *WhoWrEP 92*
Walker, Lucille Yost 1933- *WhoE 93*
Walker, Lydia Le Baron *AmWomPl*
Walker, M. Lucius, Jr. 1936- *WhoAm 92*
Walker, Mabel *BlkAmWO*
Walker, Madame C.J. 1867-1919 *EncAACR*
Walker, Maggie Lena *BioIn 17*
Walker, Malcolm Mickey 1937- *St&PR 93*
Walker, Mallory 1939- *WhoAm 92*
Walker, Mallory Elton 1935- *WhoAm 92*
Walker, Marcia Beth 1948- *WhoAmW 93*
Walker, Marcy *BioIn 17*
Walker, Margaret *EncAACR*
Walker, Margaret 1915- *BioIn 17*
Walker, Marilyn Jane 1932- *WhoAmW 93*
Walker, Mark Edward 1958- *St&PR 93*
Walker, Mark J. 1947- *St&PR 93*
Walker, Mark S. *Law&B 92*
Walker, Marshall 1941- *St&PR 93*
Walker, Martin *WhoScE 91-1*
Walker, Martin Alan 1947- *WhoE 93*
Walker, Martin D. 1932- *WhoAm 92*
Walker, Martin Dean 1932- *St&PR 93*
Walker, Marvin Edwin 1957- *WhoSSW 93*
Walker, Mary Alexander 1927- *BioIn 17, ScF&FL 92*
Walker, Mary Ann 1953- *WhoAm 92, WhoAmW 93*
Walker, Mary L. 1948- *WhoAm 92, WhoAmW 93*
Walker, Mary Molter 1959- *WhoAmW 93*
Walker, Mary Trueheart *Law&B 92*
Walker, Max N. 1936- *St&PR 93*
Walker, Maynard Bartram 1930- *St&PR 93*
Walker, Melvin Duane 1954- *WhoE 93*
Walker, Michael Claude 1940- *WhoAm 92*
Walker, Michael R. *St&PR 93*
Walker, Mildred Lucile 1923- *WhoAmW 93*
Walker, Mollie Cullom *AmWomPl*
Walker, Mort *BioIn 17*
Walker, Mort 1923- *WhoAm 92*
Walker, Myron Dow *Law&B 92*
Walker, Nancy 1922- *MiSFD 9*
Walker, Nancy 1922-1992 *BioIn 17, CurBio 92N, NewYTBS 92 [port], News 92, -92-3*
Walker, Nancy A. 1942- *ConAu 136, ScF&FL 92*
Walker, Norman S. 1925- *St&PR 93*
Walker, P. Michael *Law&B 92*
Walker, Pamela 1948- *WhoWrEP 92*
Walker, Pamela Drexel 1943- *WhoWor 93*
Walker, Patric *BioIn 17*
Walker, Patricia Ann 1938- *WhoAmW 93*
Walker, Patricia Boleyn *Law&B 92*
Walker, Paul *ScF&FL 92*
Walker, Paul 1921- *ScF&FL 92*
Walker, Paul Anthony *WhoScE 91-1*
Walker, Paul Dean 1937- *WhoSSW 93*
Walker, Paul G. *Law&B 92*
Walker, Peggy Jean 1940- *WhoAmW 93*
Walker, Peter *BioIn 17, MiSFD 9*
Walker, Peter Graham 1957- *WhoWor 93*
Walker, Peter S. 1941- *WhoScE 91-1*
Walker, Philip C. 1944- *St&PR 93*
Walker, Philip Chamberlain, II 1944- *WhoAm 92*
Walker, Philip M. *Law&B 92*
Walker, Philip Mitchell 1943- *St&PR 93*
Walker, Philip Smith 1933- *WhoAm 92*
Walker, Phillip M. *Law&B 92*
Walker, Priscilla Bowman 1949- *WhoAmW 93*
Walker, R.C. *Law&B 92*
Walker, Ralph P. 1914- *St&PR 93*
Walker, Ralph Waldo 1928- *WhoWor 93*
Walker, Ramsey R. *St&PR 93*
Walker, Ray Starkey 1912- *St&PR 93*
Walker, Reddick Russell, Jr. 1964- *WhoSSW 93*
Walker, Richard, Jr. 1948- *WhoSSW 93*
Walker, Richard A. *Law&B 92*
Walker, Richard H. 1950- *St&PR 93*
Walker, Richard Harold 1928- *WhoAm 92*
Walker, Richard Louis 1922- *WhoAm 92*
Walker, Richard N. 1931- *St&PR 93*
Walker, Richard Willard 1946- *WhoE 93*
Walker, Robert *MiSFD 9, WhoScE 91-1*
Walker, Robert 1918-1951 *IntDcF 2-3 [port]*
Walker, Robert 1946- *Baker 92*
Walker, Robert Allan 1944- *WhoSSW 93*
Walker, Robert C. *Law&B 92*
Walker, Robert Dixon, III 1936- *WhoAm 92*
Walker, Robert H. 1947- *St&PR 93*
Walker, Robert Harris 1924- *WhoAm 92, WhoWor 93*
Walker, Robert Hugh 1935- *WhoAm 92*
Walker, Robert J. *Law&B 92*
Walker, Robert J. 1801-1869 *PolPar*
Walker, Robert James *WhoScE 91-1*
Walker, Robert John 1801-1869 *BioIn 17*
Walker, Robert Lewis *Law&B 92*
Walker, Robert Luke *Law&B 92*
Walker, Robert Mowbray 1929- *WhoAm 92*
Walker, Robert Ross 1954- *WhoEmL 93*
Walker, Robert S. 1942- *CngDr 91*
Walker, Robert Smith 1942- *WhoAm 92, WhoE 93*
Walker, Robert W. 1948- *BioIn 17, ScF&FL 92*
Walker, Robert Wayne 1948- *WhoWrEP 92*
Walker, Robert Zabriski, Jr. 1952- *WhoSSW 93*
Walker, Roger Geoffrey 1939- *WhoAm 92*
Walker, Roger Raymond 1935- *St&PR 93*
Walker, Ronald *WhoScE 91-1*
Walker, Ronald Alexander 1940- *WhoWor 93*
Walker, Ronald C. *WhoAm 92*
Walker, Ronald Edward 1935- *WhoAm 92*
Walker, Ronald Eugene 1942- *St&PR 93*
Walker, Ronald F. 1938- *WhoAm 92, WhoIns 93*
Walker, Ronald Frederick 1938- *St&PR 93*
Walker, Ronald G(ary) 1945- *ConAu 39NR*
Walker, Ronald Hugh 1937- *WhoAm 92, WhoWor 93*
Walker, Ronald M. 1938- *St&PR 93*
Walker, Ronald R. 1934- *WhoE 93, WhoWor 93*
Walker, Russell Edward 1958- *St&PR 93*
Walker, Ruth Ann 1954- *WhoAmW 93*
Walker, Sally Barbara 1921- *WhoAmW 93*
Walker, Sally Jo 1946- *WhoWrEP 92*
Walker, Samuel Craig, Jr. 1924- *St&PR 93*
Walker, Samuel S. d1992 *NewYTBS 92*
Walker, Sandra 1946- *WhoAm 92*
Walker, Sandra Lynne 1968- *WhoAmW 93*
Walker, Sarah 1943- *Baker 92, OxDcOp*
Walker, Sarah Breedlove 1867-1919 *BioIn 17*
Walker, Sebastian *BioIn 17*
Walker, Sebastian 1942-1991 *AnObit 1991*
Walker, Sherri 1953- *St&PR 93*
Walker, Sherry D. 1960- *WhoAmW 93*
Walker, Sonja Caprice 1964- *WhoAmW 93*
Walker, Stanley 1935- *St&PR 93*
Walker, Stanley M. *Law&B 92*
Walker, Stanley P. 1955- *WhoAm 92, WhoE 93, WhoEmL 93, WhoSSW 93, WhoWor 93*
Walker, Steven C. 1949- *St&PR 93*
Walker, Steven G. 1949- *St&PR 93*
Walker, Steven R. *Law&B 92*
Walker, Sue Brannan *WhoWrEP 92*
Walker, Susan *Law&B 92*
Walker, Susan Hull 1962- *WhoAmW 93*
Walker, Suzanne Lenore 1960- *WhoAmW 93*
Walker, T.E.H. *WhoScE 91-1*
Walker, T.G. 1936- *WhoScE 91-1*
Walker, Ted A. 1955- *St&PR 93*
Walker, Tennyson A. 1927- *St&PR 93, WhoAm 92*
Walker, Theodore Delbert 1933- *WhoAm 92*
Walker, Thomas F. *BioIn 17*
Walker, Thomas H., Jr. 1950- *St&PR 93*
Walker, Thomas J. 1920- *St&PR 93*
Walker, Thomas N. 1946- *St&PR 93*
Walker, Timothy 1802-1856 *BioIn 17*
Walker, Timothy Blake 1940- *WhoAm 92*
Walker, Timothy Craig 1945- *St&PR 93, WhoE 93*
Walker, Todd R. *Law&B 92*
Walker, Vaughan *WhoScE 91-1*
Walker, Vaughn R. 1944- *WhoAm 92*
Walker, Vincent Henry 1915- *WhoAm 92*
Walker, Waldo Sylvester 1931- *WhoAm 92*
Walker, Wallace Earl 1944- *WhoE 93*
Walker, Walter G. 1911- *St&PR 93*
Walker, Walton Harris 1889-1950 *HarEnMi*
Walker, Warren Franklin, Jr. 1918- *WhoE 93*
Walker, Warren S(tanley) 1921- *ConAu 38NR*
Walker, Warren Stanley 1921- *WhoAm 92*
Walker, Watson H. 1918-1990 *BioIn 17*
Walker, Wayne R. *Law&B 92*
Walker, Wendy Joy 1949- *WhoAm 92*
Walker, Wesley M. 1915- *WhoAm 92*
Walker, Wilbert Lee 1925- *WhoWrEP 92*
Walker, Willard Brewer 1926- *WhoAm 92*
Walker, Willard T. 1933- *St&PR 93*
Walker, William Baker 1942- *St&PR 93*
Walker, William Bond 1930- *WhoAm 92*
Walker, William Easton 1945- *WhoAm 92*
Walker, William Frank 1939- *St&PR 93*
Walker, William Graham 1935- *WhoAm 92, WhoWor 93*
Walker, William H., III 1940- *St&PR 93*
Walker, William John 1930- *WhoE 93*
Walker, William L. 1956- *St&PR 93*
Walker, William Laurens 1937- *WhoAm 92*
Walker, William Oliver, Jr. 1930- *WhoSSW 93*
Walker, William Ray 1923- *WhoAm 92*
Walker, William Ross 1934- *WhoAm 92*
Walker, William Tidd, Jr. 1931- *WhoAm 92*
Walker, William Warner 1958- *WhoAm 92*
Walker, Williston 1860-1922 *BioIn 17*
Walker, Winston Wakefield 1943- *St&PR 93*
Walker, Winston Wakefield, Jr. 1943- *WhoSSW 93*
Walker, Woodrow Wilson 1919- *WhoSSW 93, WhoWor 93*
Walker, Wyatt Tee 1929- *EncAACR*
Walker de Felix, Judith 1943- *WhoAmW 93*
Walkerdine, Ken Martin 1946- *St&PR 93*
Walker-Jacks, Maryellen *Law&B 92*
Walker-Lee, Robin A. *Law&B 92*
Walker-Nixon, Donna Lou 1953- *WhoSSW 93*
Walkham, Walter 1921- *ScF&FL 92*
Walkington, Ethlyn Lindley 1895- *WhoWrEP 92*
Walklet, John James, Jr. 1922- *WhoAm 92*
Walkley, Barbara A. 1945- *St&PR 93*
Walkley, Barbara Ann 1945- *WhoAmW 93*
Walkley, Nancy L. *Law&B 92*
Walkovitz, D. Neil 1944- *St&PR 93*
Walkow, Gary *MiSFD 9*
Walkowicz, Chris J. 1943- *WhoWrEP 92*
Walkowitz, Abraham 1878-1965 *BioIn 17*
Walkowski, Kevin Michael 1964- *WhoE 93, WhoWor 93*
Walktendonk, Jim *BioIn 17*
Walkup, Bruce 1914- *WhoAm 92*
Walkup, David C. 1944- *St&PR 93*
Walkup, Glenn Frederick 1928- *St&PR 93*
Walkup, John Frank 1941- *WhoAm 92*
Walkus, Bernard Ryszard 1922- *WhoScE 91-4*
Walkush, Margaret Ann 1963- *WhoAmW 93*
Wall, Arthur Edward Patrick 1925- *WhoSSW 93*
Wall, Barbara Wartelle *Law&B 92*
Wall, Barron Stephen 1951- *WhoIns 93*
Wall, Bennett Harrison 1914- *WhoAm 92*
Wall, Betty Jane 1936- *WhoAmW 93*
Wall, Beverly Fishell 1958- *St&PR 93*
Wall, Brian Arthur 1931- *WhoAm 92*
Wall, Brian Raymond 1940- *WhoWor 93*
Wall, C.G. *WhoScE 91-1*
Wall, Carolyn *BioIn 17*
Wall, Carroll Edward 1942- *WhoAm 92*
Wall, Charles R. *Law&B 92*
Wall, Charles R. 1945- *St&PR 93*
Wall, Charles Terence Clegg 1936- *WhoWor 93*
Wall, Diane Eve 1944- *WhoAmW 93, WhoSSW 93*
Wall, Dieter Karl 1932- *WhoScE 91-3*
Wall, Edward E. *Law&B 92*
Wall, Edward Millard 1929- *WhoWor 93*
Wall, Erving Henry, Jr. 1934- *WhoE 93*
Wall, Fletcher H., Jr. 1925- *St&PR 93*
Wall, Fred G. 1934- *St&PR 93*
Wall, Fred Graham 1934- *WhoAm 92*
Wall, Frederick Theodore 1912- *WhoAm 92*
Wall, Garrett Buckner, III 1932- *St&PR 93*
Wall, Glennie Murray 1931- *WhoAmW 93*
Wall, Howard Elden 1929- *St&PR 93, WhoAm 92*
Wall, Howard Milton, Jr. 1945- *St&PR 93*
Wall, Isabelle Louise Wood 1909- *WhoWrEP 92*
Wall, J. Brent 1947- *St&PR 93*
Wall, Jacqueline Remondet 1958- *WhoSSW 93*
Wall, James Edward 1947- *St&PR 93, WhoAm 92*
Wall, James McKendree 1928- *WhoAm 92*
Wall, Janet Ilene 1951- *WhoAmW 93*
Wall, Jeff 1946- *BioIn 17*
Wall, Jennie *AmWomPl*
Wall, Jeremy George Lynton 1936- *WhoUN 92*
Wall, Jerry Leon 1942- *WhoSSW 93, WhoWor 93*
Wall, Jerry S. 1926- *WhoWrEP 92*
Wall, John Edmund 1926- *St&PR 93*
Wall, John F., III *Law&B 92*
Wall, John Murray 1930- *St&PR 93*
Wall, John Patrick 1928- *St&PR 93*
Wall, John W. *ScF&FL 92*
Wall, John Winthrop 1924- *St&PR 93*
Wall, Joseph Frazier 1920- *WhoAm 92*
Wall, Jozef 1752-1798 *PolBiDi*
Wall, Katharine Adelle 1944- *WhoSSW 93*
Wall, Kathleen H. *Law&B 92*
Wall, Kathleen Mavourneen 1944- *WhoAmW 93*
Wall, M. Danny *WhoAm 92, WhoSSW 93*
Wall, Max 1908-1990 *BioIn 17*
Wall, Mervyn 1908- *ScF&FL 92*
Wall, Michael A. *St&PR 93*
Wall, Morton J. *St&PR 93*
Wall, O. Edward 1934- *St&PR 93, WhoAm 92*
Wall, Patrick David *WhoScE 91-1*
Wall, Richard J., Jr. *Law&B 92*
Wall, Richard M. *Law&B 92*
Wall, Robert E. *St&PR 93*
Wall, Robert Emmet 1937- *WhoAm 92, WhoWrEP 92*
Wall, Robert H. 1928- *WhoIns 93*
Wall, Robert Joseph 1932- *St&PR 93*
Wall, Robert Wilson, Jr. 1916- *WhoAm 92*
Wall, Shari *BioIn 17*
Wall, Sigrid H. *St&PR 93*
Wall, Silda Alice *Law&B 92*
Wall, Sonja Eloise 1938- *WhoAmW 93, WhoWor 93*
Wall, Stephen E. 1942- *St&PR 93*
Wall, Timothy Lee 1950- *WhoE 93*
Wall, Tina Michele 1966- *WhoAmW 93*
Wall, Toby Douglas *WhoScE 91-1*
Wall, Vernon Antonio 1959- *WhoSSW 93*
Wall, William *ScF&FL 92*
Wall, William E. 1928- *St&PR 93*
Wall, William Lloyd 1946- *St&PR 93*
Wallace, Agnes *AmWomPl*
Wallace, Alfred C. 1935- *St&PR 93*
Wallace, Alfred Leon 1931- *WhoWrEP 92*
Wallace, Alfred Russel 1823-1913 *BioIn 17*
Wallace, Alfred Russell 1823-1913 *Expl 93 [port]*
Wallace, Aliceanne 1925- *WhoSSW 93*
Wallace, Andrew Grover 1935- *WhoAm 92*
Wallace, Anthony F.C. 1923- *BioIn 17*
Wallace, Anthony Francis Clarke 1923- *WhoAm 92*
Wallace, Arthur 1939- *St&PR 93*
Wallace, Arthur, Jr. 1939- *WhoAm 92*
Wallace, Barbara J. 1944- *WhoE 93*
Wallace, Bertha M. *AmWomPl*
Wallace, Betty Ann Woolard 1954- *WhoAmW 93*
Wallace, Betty Frances Abernathy 1926- *WhoWrEP 92*
Wallace, Betty Jean 1927- *WhoAmW 93, WhoSSW 93, WhoWor 93*
Wallace, Betty Kaye 1951- *WhoAmW 93*
Wallace, Betty Louise Dollar 1935- *WhoAmW 93*
Wallace, Bonnie Ann *BioIn 17*
Wallace, Bonnie Ann 1951- *WhoAmW 93, WhoWor 93*
Wallace, Brian S. 1946- *St&PR 93*
Wallace, Bronwen d1989 *WhoCanL 92*
Wallace, Bruce Jay 1947- *St&PR 93*
Wallace, Carol Ann 1962- *WhoE 93*
Wallace, Carol McD. 1955- *ScF&FL 92*
Wallace, Catherine *BioIn 17*

Wallace, Charles Leslie 1945- *WhoAm 92*
Wallace, Christopher 1947- *WhoAm 92*
Wallace, Claire 1956- *ConAu 138*
Wallace, Clifford Noble, III 1947- *WhoSSW 93*
Wallace, Constance Wolyniec 1954- *WhoAmW 93*
Wallace, Craig Kesting 1928- *WhoAm 92, WhoUN 92*
Wallace, Cynthia Jones *Law&B 92*
Wallace, Darrell R. 1951- *St&PR 93*
Wallace, David Alexander 1917- *WhoAm 92*
Wallace, David Alexander Ross *WhoScE 91-1*
Wallace, David Alexander Ross 1933- *WhoWor 93*
Wallace, David Foster *BioIn 17*
Wallace, David Foster 1962- *ScF&FL 92*
Wallace, David Francis 1923- *St&PR 93*
Wallace, David Gilman 1944- *St&PR 93*
Wallace, David Harold 1936- *St&PR 93*
Wallace, David James *WhoScE 91-1*
Wallace, David James 1945- *WhoWor 93*
Wallace, David Rains 1945- *ScF&FL 92*
Wallace, David W. 1924- *St&PR 93*
Wallace, David William 1924- *WhoAm 92, WhoE 93*
Wallace, Deborah 1945- *ConAu 138*
Wallace, DeWitt 1889-1981 *BioIn 17*
Wallace, Don *BioIn 17*
Wallace, Don, Jr. 1932- *WhoAm 92*
Wallace, Donald D. 1947- *St&PR 93*
Wallace, Donald Graham 1965- *WhoSSW 93*
Wallace, Donald John, III 1941- *WhoSSW 93*
Wallace, Donald Querk 1931- *WhoAm 92*
Wallace, Dwane L. 1911-1989 *BioIn 17*
Wallace, Edgar 1875-1932 *ScF&FL 92*
Wallace, Eileen S. *WhoAmW 93*
Wallace, Elizabeth Ann 1939- *WhoAmW 93*
Wallace, Elizabeth Mary 1954- *WhoAmW 93*
Wallace, Emma B. *AmWomPl*
Wallace, Emma Gary *AmWomPl*
Wallace, Ernest N. 1931- *St&PR 93*
Wallace, F. Blake 1933- *WhoAm 92*
Wallace, Fitzhugh Lee, Jr. 1928- *St&PR 93*
Wallace, Florence Magill *AmWomPl*
Wallace, Floyd 1921- *St&PR 93*
Wallace, Fran *BioIn 17*
Wallace, Gail Penman 1950- *WhoAmW 93*
Wallace, George C. 1919- *PolPar*
Wallace, George C., Jr. 1951- *WhoAm 92, WhoSSW 93*
Wallace, George Corley 1919- *BioIn 17, DcTwHis, WhoAm 92*
Wallace, George F. 1938- *WhoE 93*
Wallace, George Francis 1954- *WhoE 93*
Wallace, Gerald L. 1900-1990 *BioIn 17*
Wallace, Gladys Baldwin 1923- *WhoSSW 93*
Wallace, Gordon 1909- *WhoWrEP 92*
Wallace, Gregory Louis *Law&B 92*
Wallace, Gwendolyn 1926- *St&PR 93*
Wallace, Harold James, Jr. 1930- *WhoAm 92*
Wallace, Harold Lew 1932- *WhoAm 92*
Wallace, Helen Margaret 1913- *WhoAmW 93*
Wallace, Henry A. 1888-1965 *ColdWar 1 [port], PolPar*
Wallace, Henry Agard 1888-1965 *BioIn 17, DcTwHis*
Wallace, Henry Cantwell 1866-1924 *BioIn 17*
Wallace, Herbert William 1930- *WhoAm 92*
Wallace, Ian 1912- *ScF&FL 92*
Wallace, Ian 1919- *OxDcOp*
Wallace, Ian 1950- *ConAu 38NR, MajAI [port], WhoCanL 92*
Wallace, Irving 1914- *St&PR 93*
Wallace, Irving 1916-1990 *BioIn 17, ScF&FL 92*
Wallace, J. Clifford 1928- *WhoAm 92*
Wallace, James *ScF&FL 92*
Wallace, James 1947- *ConAu 138*
Wallace, James 1962- *BioIn 17*
Wallace, James Martin 1939- *WhoAm 92*
Wallace, James Michael 1958- *WhoE 93*
Wallace, James Oldham 1917- *WhoSSW 93*
Wallace, James P. 1928- *WhoSSW 93*
Wallace, James Wendell 1930- *WhoAm 92*
Wallace, Jane *BioIn 17*
Wallace, Jane House 1926- *WhoAmW 93, WhoE 93*
Wallace, Janet B. *St&PR 93*
Wallace, Jay S. 1931- *St&PR 93*
Wallace, Jean 1923-1990 *BioIn 17*
Wallace, Jean Ann 1953- *WhoSSW 93*
Wallace, Jeannette Owens 1934- *WhoAmW 93*
Wallace, Jeffrey J. *Law&B 92*
Wallace, Jesse Wyatt 1925- *WhoAm 92, WhoWor 93*
Wallace, Jim *ScF&FL 92*
Wallace, Joan S. 1930- *WhoAm 92, WhoWor 93*
Wallace, Jody Marie 1954- *WhoWrEP 92*
Wallace, John Anthony 1946- *WhoAm 92*
Wallace, John Clements 1920- *St&PR 93*
Wallace, John D. *Law&B 92*
Wallace, John Douglas 1951- *WhoE 93*
Wallace, John Duncan 1933- *St&PR 93, WhoAm 92*
Wallace, John Edwin 1913- *WhoAm 92*
Wallace, John Hall *Law&B 92*
Wallace, John Kennard 1903- *WhoAm 92*
Wallace, John Loys 1941- *St&PR 93, WhoAm 92*
Wallace, John Malcolm 1928- *WhoAm 92*
Wallace, John Melvin 1942- *St&PR 93*
Wallace, John Powell 1923- *St&PR 93*
Wallace, John R. 1913- *WhoAm 92*
Wallace, John W. *BioIn 17*
Wallace, John William 1815-1884 *OxCSupC*
Wallace, Joyce *BioIn 17*
Wallace, Keith 1945- *WhoWor 93*
Wallace, Keith G. 1926- *St&PR 93*
Wallace, Kenneth Donald 1918- *WhoAm 92, WhoWor 93*
Wallace, Kirk 1944- *St&PR 93*
Wallace, Leigh Allen, Jr. 1927- *WhoAm 92*
Wallace, Len 1940- *St&PR 93*
Wallace, Leora 1935- *WhoAmW 93*
Wallace, Lew 1827-1905 *GayN*
Wallace, Lew Gerald 1946- *WhoWrEP 92*
Wallace, Lisa A. *Law&B 92*
Wallace, Malcolm Vincent Timothy 1915- *WhoAm 92*
Wallace, Marcia *Law&B 92*
Wallace, Mark Edward 1955- *WhoE 93*
Wallace, Mark I. 1956- *WhoE 93*
Wallace, Mark McColough *Law&B 92*
Wallace, Martha Redfield 1927-1989 *BioIn 17*
Wallace, Mary Elaine *WhoAm 92, WhoSSW 93*
Wallace, Mary Hardwick 1924- *WhoWrEP 92*
Wallace, Mary Katherine 1959- *WhoSSW 93*
Wallace, Matthew Walker 1924- *St&PR 93, WhoWor 93*
Wallace, Maude Orita *AmWomPl*
Wallace, Michael J. d1991 *BioIn 17*
Wallace, Michael John 1948- *St&PR 93*
Wallace, Michele *BioIn 17*
Wallace, Mike 1918- *BioIn 17, ConTFT 10, JrnUS, WhoAm 92, WhoE 93*
Wallace, Milton J. 1935- *St&PR 93*
Wallace, Minor Gordon, Jr. 1936- *WhoSSW 93*
Wallace, Miriam Loder *AmWomPl*
Wallace, Mona Sue 1937- *St&PR 93*
Wallace, Myron *ConTFT 10*
Wallace, Pamela 1949- *ScF&FL 92*
Wallace, Pat 1929- *ScF&FL 92*
Wallace, Patricia *ScF&FL 92*
Wallace, Patrick Francis 1948- *WhoWor 93*
Wallace, Paul Harvey 1944- *WhoWor 93*
Wallace, Paul Joseph 1946- *St&PR 93*
Wallace, Paul Vincent, Jr. 1934- *WhoSSW 93*
Wallace, Paula Yvette 1965- *WhoSSW 93*
Wallace, Philip Russell 1915- *WhoAm 92*
Wallace, Phyllis Ann *WhoAm 92*
Wallace, Ralph *WhoE 93*
Wallace, Ralph Howes 1916- *WhoAm 92*
Wallace, Raymond Howard, Jr. 1936- *WhoE 93*
Wallace, Raymond Paul d1991 *BioIn 17*
Wallace, Richard 1957- *WhoAm 92*
Wallace, Richard Christopher, Jr. 1931- *WhoAm 92*
Wallace, Richard J. *Law&B 92*
Wallace, Richard John 1946- *WhoSSW 93*
Wallace, Rick *MiSFD 9*
Wallace, Roanne 1949- *WhoAmW 93, WhoSSW 93, WhoWor 93*
Wallace, Robert 1932- *WhoWrEP 92*
Wallace, Robert 1943- *WhoCanL 92*
Wallace, Robert A. *Law&B 92*
Wallace, Robert Bruce 1931- *WhoAm 92*
Wallace, Robert Earl 1916- *WhoAm 92*
Wallace, Robert Fergus 1934- *WhoAm 92*
Wallace, Robert G. *Law&B 92*
Wallace, Robert Glenn 1926- *St&PR 93, WhoAm 92*
Wallace, Robert H. 1932- *St&PR 93*
Wallace, Robert Henry 1930- *WhoWor 93*
Wallace, Robert J. *Law&B 92*
Wallace, Robert Keith 1938- *WhoSSW 93*
Wallace, Robert Kimball 1944- *WhoSSW 93*
Wallace, Rodney Sanford 1924- *St&PR 93*
Wallace, Ron *WhoE 93*
Wallace, Ronald Derek 1943- *WhoE 93*
Wallace, Ronald K. 1935- *St&PR 93*
Wallace, Ronald Lynn 1945- *WhoWrEP 92*
Wallace, Ronald W. 1945- *WhoWrEP 92*
Wallace, Ronald Wesley 1934- *St&PR 93*
Wallace, Rusty *BioIn 17*
Wallace, Ruth E. 1965- *WhoE 93*
Wallace, Samuel Taylor 1943- *WhoAm 92*
Wallace, Sandy *WhoSSW 93*
Wallace, Sara A. *AmWomPl*
Wallace, Sippie 1898-1986 *BioIn 17*
Wallace, Spencer Miller, Jr. 1923- *WhoAm 92*
Wallace, Stephen *MiSFD 9*
Wallace, Stephen Philip 1962- *WhoWor 93*
Wallace, Steven Charles 1953- *WhoWor 93*
Wallace, Ted 1948- *WhoAm 92*
Wallace, Thomas A. 1949- *WhoIns 93*
Wallace, Thomas C(hristopher) 1933- *WhoWrEP 92*
Wallace, Thomas Christopher 1933- *WhoAm 92*
Wallace, Thomas Edward, Jr. 1948- *WhoE 93*
Wallace, Thomas Llewellyn, Jr. 1952- *WhoSSW 93*
Wallace, Thomas Patrick 1935- *WhoAm 92*
Wallace, Thomas R. 1954- *WhoAm 92*
Wallace, Tommy Lee *MiSFD 9*
Wallace, Vincent 1812-1865 *IntDcOp, OxDcOp*
Wallace, (William) Vincent 1812-1865 *Baker 92*
Wallace, Volney *St&PR 93*
Wallace, W.R. 1923- *St&PR 93*
Wallace, Walter C. 1924- *WhoAm 92*
Wallace, Walter L. 1927- *WhoAm 92*
Wallace, William c. 1270-1305 *HarEnMi*
Wallace, William 1768-1816 *BioIn 17*
Wallace, William 1860-1940 *Baker 92*
Wallace, William 1891-1976 *BioIn 17*
Wallace, William, III 1926- *WhoAm 92*
Wallace, William, IV 1954- *WhoSSW 93*
Wallace, William Alan 1935- *WhoAm 92*
Wallace, William Angus *WhoScE 91-1*
Wallace, William Augustine 1918- *WhoAm 92*
Wallace, William B. 1929- *St&PR 93*
Wallace, William C. 1941- *WhoAm 92*
Wallace, William Edward 1917- *WhoAm 92*
Wallace, William Frederick Matthew *WhoScE 91-1*
Wallace, William Hall 1933- *WhoAm 92*
Wallace, William L. 1934- *St&PR 93*
Wallace, William Laurie 1934- *WhoAm 92*
Wallace, William Ray 1923- *WhoSSW 93*
Wallace, William Sheldon 1915- *WhoE 93*
Wallace, Wilton Lawrence 1949- *WhoAm 92*
Wallace, Wm. Dean 1946- *St&PR 93*
Wallace-Crabbe, Chris *BioIn 17*
Wallace-Hadrill, Andrew (Frederic) 1951- *ConAu 40NR*
Wallace-Johnson, Isaac T.A. 1895-1965 *DcTwHis*
Wallace-Whitfield, Cecil 1930-1990 *DcCPCAm*
Wallach, Allan Henry 1927- *WhoAm 92*
Wallach, Anne Jackson *WhoAm 92, WhoAmW 93*
Wallach, Barbara Price 1946- *WhoAmW 93*
Wallach, Carla Charlotta 1930- *WhoWrEP 92*
Wallach, Cathy Lee 1955- *WhoAmW 93*
Wallach, David Lee 1940- *WhoE 93*
Wallach, Edward Eliot 1933- *WhoAm 92*
Wallach, Eli 1915- *BioIn 17, IntDcF 2-3 [port], WhoAm 92*
Wallach, Evan Jonathan 1949- *WhoWor 93*
Wallach, Frederick K. *Law&B 92*
Wallach, Hans 1904- *WhoAm 92*
Wallach, Hans Gert Peter 1938- *WhoE 93*
Wallach, Ira 1913- *WhoAm 92, WhoWrEP 92*
Wallach, Ira D. 1909- *St&PR 93*
Wallach, Ira David 1909- *WhoAm 92*
Wallach, Ira M. *Law&B 92*
Wallach, Jack S. *Law&B 92*
Wallach, Jacques Burton 1926- *WhoE 93*
Wallach, Janet 1942- *ConAu 38NR*
Wallach, Janet Lee 1942- *WhoE 93*
Wallach, Jean M. 1945- *WhoScE 91-2*
Wallach, John P. 1943- *ConAu 139*
Wallach, John Paul 1943- *WhoE 93*
Wallach, John Sidney 1939- *WhoAm 92*
Wallach, Kenneth Arnold *Law&B 92*
Wallach, Magdalena Falkenberg *WhoAmW 93*
Wallach, Michael N. *Law&B 92*
Wallach, Philip C. 1912- *St&PR 93*
Wallach, Philip Charles 1912- *WhoAm 92, WhoWor 93*
Wallach, Robert Charles 1935- *WhoAm 92*
Wallach, Ronald Michael 1937- *St&PR 93*
Wallach, Stanley 1928- *WhoSSW 93*
Wallach, Susan Silverman 1956- *WhoAm 92*
Wallach, Timothy Charles 1957- *WhoAm 92*
Wallach, Walter D. *St&PR 93*
Wallack-Roselli, Rina Evelyn 1949- *WhoAmW 93*
Wallance, Don 1909-1990 *BioIn 17*
Wall-Angelides, Phyllis 1957- *WhoAmW 93*
Wallant, Edward Lewis 1926-1962 *BioIn 17, JeAmFiW*
Wallard, Andrew John 1945- *WhoScE 91-1*
Wallaschek, Richard 1860-1917 *Baker 92*
Wallat, Hans 1929- *Baker 92*
Wallbank, Allan Robert *WhoAsAP 91*
Wallberg, Heinz 1923- *Baker 92*
Wallbillich, John J. *Law&B 92*
Wallbridge, Lewis C. 1943- *St&PR 93*
Wallbridge, Malcolm George Hugh *WhoScE 91-1*
Walle, Baudouin van de 1901-1988 *BioIn 17*
Walle, Gerald Yvon 1953- *WhoE 93*
Walle, James P. *Law&B 92*
Walleigh, Robert Shuler 1915- *WhoAm 92*
Wallek, Lee 1908- *WhoWrEP 92*
Wallek-Walewski, Boleslaw 1885-1944 *Baker 92*
Wallen, Lina Hambali 1952- *WhoAmW 93*
Wallen, Vera S. 1941- *WhoAmW 93*
Wallenberg, Louis *Law&B 92*
Wallenberg, Peter *BioIn 17*
Wallenberg, Peter 1926- *St&PR 93, WhoWor 93*
Wallenberg, Raoul *BioIn 17*
Wallenberg, Raoul 1912-1945? *ConHero 2 [port]*
Wallenberg, Richard *Law&B 92*
Wallenborn, Janice Rae 1938- *WhoAmW 93*
Wallenborn, White McKenzie 1929- *WhoSSW 93*
Wallenburg, Henk C.S. 1938- *WhoScE 91-3*
Wallenda, Angel *BioIn 17*
Wallender, Michael Todd 1950- *WhoE 93*
Wallenfels, Helmut *Law&B 92*
Wallenstein, Albert Eusebius von 1583-1634 *HarEnMi*
Wallenstein, Alfred 1898-1983 *Baker 92*
Wallenstein, Barry *DcLB Y92*
Wallenstein, James Harry 1942- *WhoAm 92, WhoSSW 93*
Wallenstein, Martin 1843-1896 *Baker 92*
Wallentinus, Inger 1942- *WhoScE 91-4*
Waller, Aaron Bret, III 1935- *WhoAm 92*
Waller, Alan Vernon 1944- *WhoWor 93*
Waller, Bob D. 1928- *St&PR 93*
Waller, Calvin Agustine Hoffman 1937- *AfrAmBi*
Waller, Charlotte Reid 1936- *WhoSSW 93*
Waller, Christine Anne 1962- *WhoSSW 93*
Waller, David Barclay 1948- *St&PR 93*
Waller, Diane Elisabeth *Law&B 92*
Waller, Edmund 1606-1687 *DcLB 126 [port]*
Waller, Edmund Meredith, Jr. 1931- *WhoWor 93*
Waller, "Fats" 1904-1943 *Baker 92*
Waller, Gary F. 1944- *WhoWrEP 92*
Waller, Gary Fredric 1944- *WhoAm 92*
Waller, Gregory A. 1950- *ScF&FL 92*
Waller, Hans Dierck 1926- *WhoScE 91-3*
Waller, Harold Myron 1940- *WhoAm 92*
Waller, Heinz Peter Barthold 1935- *WhoScE 91-3*
Waller, Jerome Howard 1935- *WhoSSW 93*
Waller, John Henry 1923- *WhoWor 93*
Waller, John Louis 1944- *WhoSSW 93*
Waller, John Oscar 1916- *WhoAm 92*
Waller, Jonathan C. *Law&B 92*
Waller, Kurt V. 1940- *WhoScE 91-4*
Waller, Larry Gene 1948- *WhoWor 93*
Waller, Leslie 1923- *ScF&FL 92*
Waller, Louise *ScF&FL 92*
Waller, Marie Tuttle 1923- *WhoAmW 93*
Waller, Michael R. 1953- *St&PR 93*
Waller, Paul H., Jr. 1933- *St&PR 93*
Waller, Robert A. 1928- *St&PR 93*
Waller, Robert Alfred 1931- *WhoSSW 93*
Waller, Robert Bradford, Jr. 1960- *WhoE 93*
Waller, Robert Edward *Law&B 92*
Waller, Robert Edward 1936- *St&PR 93*
Waller, Robert Rex 1937- *WhoAm 92*
Waller, Rodney L. *St&PR 93*
Waller, Seth 1933- *St&PR 93*

Waller, Susan (Stewart) 1948- *ConAu 139*
Waller, Suzan Janiece 1952- *WhoAmW 93*
Waller, Terry Lee 1948- *WhoSSW 93*
Waller, Wilhelmine Kirby 1914- *WhoAm 92*
Waller, William c. 1597-1668 *HarEnMi*
Waller, Wilma Ruth 1921- *WhoAmW 93*
Wallerstedt, Robert W. 1928- *St&PR 93*
Wallerstedt-Wehrle, Joanna Katherine 1944- *WhoWrEP 92*
Wallerstein, Anton 1813-1892 *Baker 92*
Wallerstein, David B. 1905- *St&PR 93, WhoAm 92*
Wallerstein, George 1930- *WhoAm 92*
Wallerstein, Harry 1906- *WhoE 93*
Wallerstein, James S. 1910-1990 *ScF&FL 92*
Wallerstein, James Scheuer 1910-1990 *BioIn 17*
Wallerstein, Lawrence Bernard 1919- *St&PR 93*
Wallerstein, Leibert Benet 1922- *WhoE 93*
Wallerstein, Lothar 1882-1949 *Baker 92, IntDcOp, OxDcOp*
Wallerstein, Ralph Oliver 1922- *WhoAm 92*
Wallerstein, Robert Solomon 1921- *WhoAm 92*
Wallerstein, Seth Michael 1960- *WhoE 93*
Wallerstein, Sheldon M. 1931- *WhoE 93*
Walles, Bjorn S. 1936- *WhoScE 91-4*
Walles, James A. 1933- *St&PR 93*
Wallestad, Philip Weston 1922- *WhoWor 93*
Walley, Byron 1951- *WhoAm 92*
Walley, Craig D. *Law&B 92*
Walley, Craig D. 1943- *St&PR 93*
Walley, David G. 1945- *ConAu 37NR*
Walley, Fawazi 1958- *WhoWor 93*
Walley, James Marvin, Jr. 1947- *WhoSSW 93*
Walley, John Charles *Law&B 92*
Wallfesh, Henry Maurice 1937- *WhoAm 92*
Wallfisch, Raphael 1953- *Baker 92*
Wallgren, Anita L. 1954- *St&PR 93*
Wallgren, L. Henrik 1928- *WhoScE 91-4*
Wallhauser, George Marvin 1900- *WhoAm 92*
Wallich, Henry Christopher 1914-1988 *BioIn 17*
Wallick, Robert Daniel 1926- *WhoAm 92*
Wallick, Robin C. 1958- *St&PR 93*
Wallick, Rollin Herbert 1929- *WhoSSW 93*
Wallie, William Jack 1940- *WhoE 93*
Wallin, Ake Herman Olof 1917- *WhoWor 93*
Wallin, Bengt Gunnar 1936- *WhoWor 93*
Wallin, Daniel Guy 1927- *WhoAm 92*
Wallin, Daniel Neil 1947- *St&PR 93*
Wallin, David Allen 1945- *St&PR 93*
Wallin, Douglas Dean 1964- *WhoSSW 93*
Wallin, Franklin Whittelsey 1925- *WhoAm 92*
Wallin, Frederick E. 1943- *WhoE 93*
Wallin, Jack Robb 1915- *WhoAm 92*
Wallin, John David 1932- *WhoSSW 93*
Wallin, Judith Kerstin 1938- *WhoE 93*
Wallin, Leland Dean 1942- *WhoE 93*
Wallin, Louann Velo 1947- *St&PR 93*
Wallin, Nils Lennart 1924- *WhoWor 93*
Wallin, Norman Elroy 1914- *St&PR 93*
Wallin, Robert M. 1923- *St&PR 93*
Wallin, Thomas N. *Law&B 92*
Wallin, Winston Roger 1926- *St&PR 93, WhoAm 92*
Walling, B. Haven, Jr. *Law&B 92*
Walling, Cheves T. 1916- *WhoAm 92, WhoE 93*
Walling, Dana McNeil 1950- *WhoWrEP 92*
Walling, Douglas Dean 1934- *WhoSSW 93*
Walling, J.C. *WhoScE 91-1*
Walling, John Daniel, III 1937- *WhoSSW 93*
Walling, Linda Lucas 1939- *WhoSSW 93*
Walling, Michael Louis 1944- *WhoAm 92*
Walling, Stephen C. *Law&B 92*
Walling, William 1926- *ScF&FL 92*
Walling, William A. *ScF&FL 92*
Walling, William Russell 1959- *WhoSSW 93*
Wallinger, George Arthur 1930- *St&PR 93*
Wallinger, Karl *BioIn 17*
Wallinger, Ralph Scott 1939- *St&PR 93*
Wallingford, Anne 1949- *WhoAmW 93*
Wallingford, Donald Hale 1919- *WhoSSW 93*
Wallington, Peter Thomas *WhoScE 91-1*
Wallis, Adrian Fredrick 1940- *WhoWor 93*
Wallis, Bernard Joseph 1910- *St&PR 93*
Wallis, Carlton Lamar 1915- *WhoAm 92*
Wallis, David Ian *WhoScE 91-1*
Wallis, Diana Lynn 1946- *WhoAm 92*
Wallis, Douglas John *Law&B 92*
Wallis, Edward B. *Law&B 92*
Wallis, G. McDonald *ScF&FL 92*
Wallis, George C. 1871-1956 *ScF&FL 92*
Wallis, Graham Blair 1936- *WhoAm 92*
Wallis, H. Dann 1930- *St&PR 93*
Wallis, Jack R. 1935- *St&PR 93*
Wallis, James Rees 1948- *St&PR 93*
Wallis, James Stephen 1951- *WhoE 93*
Wallis, Jim *BioIn 17*
Wallis, Kenneth D. *Law&B 92*
Wallis, Kenneth Frank *WhoScE 91-1*
Wallis, Kenneth Frank 1938- *WhoWor 93*
Wallis, Kent *BioIn 17*
Wallis, Lila Amdurska 1921- *WhoE 93*
Wallis, Maria Fisher 1959- *WhoAmW 93*
Wallis, Martha Hyer *BioIn 17*
Wallis, Melissa Myers 1960- *WhoAmW 93*
Wallis, Michael 1945- *ConAu 139*
Wallis, Redmond 1933- *ScF&FL 92*
Wallis, Richard Fisher 1924- *WhoAm 92, WhoWor 93*
Wallis, Robert 1900- *BioIn 17*
Wallis, Robert Brian 1956- *St&PR 93*
Wallis, Robert Joe 1938- *WhoSSW 93*
Wallis, Robert Ray 1927- *WhoAm 92*
Wallis, Samuel 1728-1795 *Expl 93*
Wallis, Sandra Rhodes 1945- *WhoE 93*
Wallis, William Budge 1940- *St&PR 93*
Wallis, William George 1946- *WhoWrEP 92*
Wallis, William Robert 1931- *WhoE 93*
Wallis, Wilson Allen 1912- *WhoAm 92, WhoE 93*
Walliser, Christoph Thomas 1568-1648 *Baker 92*
Walliser, Otto H. 1928- *WhoScE 91-3*
Wallison, Frieda K. 1943- *WhoAm 92, WhoAmW 93, WhoE 93*
Wallison, Peter J. 1941- *WhoAm 92*
Wallman, Charles Stephen 1953- *WhoWor 93*
Wallman, David Thees 1949- *St&PR 93, WhoIns 93*
Wallman, Dwillis Gwan *WhoSSW 93*
Wallman, George 1917- *WhoAm 92*
Wallman, Raymond Louis 1953- *WhoE 93*
Wallmann, Jeffrey M. 1941- *ScF&FL 92*
Wallmann, Jeffrey Miner 1941- *WhoWor 93*
Wallmann, Johannes Christian 1930- *WhoWor 93*
Wallmann, Margherita 1904- *IntDcOp*
Wallmark, J. Torkel 1919- *WhoScE 91-4*
Wallnau, Carl N., Jr. 1920- *St&PR 93*
Wallner, Felix *WhoScE 91-4*
Wallner, Franz 1937- *WhoWor 93*
Wallner, John C. 1945- *MajAI [port]*
Wallner, Mary Jane 1946- *WhoAmW 93*
Wallner, Peter M. 1949- *WhoIns 93*
Wallnoefer, Peter F. 1945- *WhoScE 91-4*
Wallnofer, Adolf 1854-1946 *Baker 92*
Wallock, Terrance *Law&B 92*
Walloe, Lars 1938- *WhoScE 91-4*
Wallop, Douglass 1920-1985 *ScF&FL 92*
Wallop, Malcolm 1933- *CngDr 91, WhoAm 92*
Wallot, Jean-Pierre 1935- *WhoAm 92, WhoE 93, WhoWrEP 92*
Wallraff, Barbara Jean 1953- *WhoAm 92*
Wallrapp, Lynn *ScF&FL 92*
Walls, Betty L. Webb 1932- *WhoAmW 93*
Walls, Carmage 1908- *WhoAm 92, WhoWor 93*
Walls, Carmage Lee, Jr. 1962- *WhoSSW 93*
Walls, Charles Grey 1946- *WhoSSW 93*
Walls, Charlotte A. *Law&B 92*
Walls, Clyde Wayne 1939- *St&PR 93*
Walls, Daniel Frank 1942- *WhoWor 93*
Walls, Donald W. *St&PR 93*
Walls, Dwayne Estes 1932- *WhoAm 92, WhoWrEP 92*
Walls, Edward Franklin 1929- *WhoSSW 93*
Walls, Gary Lee 1949- *WhoSSW 93*
Walls, George R. *Law&B 92*
Walls, George Rodney 1945- *WhoAm 92*
Walls, Gloria Jeanne Wilson 1963- *WhoAmW 93*
Walls, Janetta S. *Law&B 92*
Walls, Jeanne M. 1956- *St&PR 93*
Walls, John William 1927- *St&PR 93*
Walls, Josiah Thomas 1842-1905 *BioIn 17*
Walls, Martha Ann Williams 1927- *WhoAm 92, WhoWor 93*
Walls, Melinda Ford *Law&B 92*
Walls, Patricia Rae 1936- *WhoWrEP 92*
Walls, Robert *St&PR 93*
Walls, Robert C. 1950- *St&PR 93*
Walls, Stephen Roderick 1947- *WhoWor 93*
Walls, Tom 1883-1949
See Lynn, Ralph 1881-1962 & Walls, Tom 1883-1949 *QDrFCA 92*
Walls, William J. *Law&B 92*
Wallsgrove, Roger Martin *WhoScE 91-1*
Wallskog, Alan George 1940- *St&PR 93*
Wallston, Barbara Strudler *BioIn 17*
Wallwork, John Anthony *WhoScE 91-1*
Wallwork, William Wilson, III 1961- *St&PR 93*
Wally, Josef 1939- *St&PR 93*
Wally, Walter Edward 1929- *St&PR 93*
Walman, Jerome 1937- *WhoE 93, WhoWor 93*
Walmer, Edwin Fitch 1930- *WhoAm 92*
Walmer, James L. 1948- *WhoEmL 93*
Walmisley, Thomas Attwood 1814-1856 *Baker 92*
Walmisley, Thomas Forbes 1783-1866 *Baker 92*
Walmsley, David George *WhoScE 91-1*
Walmsley, David George 1938- *WhoWor 93*
Walmsley, Dorothy Brush *AmWomPl*
Walmsley, Tom 1948- *WhoCanL 92*
Waln, Mabel *AmWomPl*
Waln, William *BioIn 17*
Walner, Robert J. *Law&B 92*
Walner, Robert Joel 1946- *WhoAm 92*
Walnes, Jack Robert 1947- *St&PR 93*
Walode, Scott 1958- *St&PR 93*
Walotsky, Ron B. 1943- *WhoSSW 93*
Walp, Robert M. 1927- *St&PR 93*
Walpin, Gerald 1931- *WhoAm 92, WhoWor 93*
Walpole, Charles E. 1938- *St&PR 93*
Walpole, Forrest 1941- *St&PR 93*
Walpole, Forrest T. *Law&B 92*
Walpole, Horace 1717-1797 *BioIn 17*
Walpole, Richard K. *St&PR 93*
Walpole, Robert 1676-1745 *BioIn 17*
Walpole, Robert D. 1953- *WhoAm 92*
Walrath, Patricia A. 1941- *WhoAmW 93*
Walrath, Robert E. *Law&B 92*
Walrave, Michel *WhoScE 91-2*
Walraven, Pieter Louis 1930- *WhoScE 91-3*
Walrod, David James 1946- *St&PR 93, WhoAm 92*
Walrond, Errol Ricardo 1936- *WhoWor 93*
Walsby, Anthony Edward *WhoScE 91-1*
Walschot, Leopold Gustave 1936- *WhoWor 93*
Walsdorf, John J. *ScF&FL 92*
Walseman, Kathryn Bingle 1964- *WhoSSW 93*
Walser, Charlotte Gwen 1965- *WhoSSW 93*
Walser, Donald 1940- *St&PR 93*
Walser, John T., Jr. 1939- *St&PR 93*
Walser, Mackenzie 1924- *WhoAm 92*
Walser, Martin 1927- *DcLB 124 [port], WhoWor 93*
Walser, Robert 1878-1956 *BioIn 17*
Walser, Robert Dean 1955- *St&PR 93*
Walser, William Duke 1918- *St&PR 93*
Walseth, Daniel G. *Law&B 92*
Walsh, Abigail Margaret 1935- *WhoWrEP 92*
Walsh, Ann 1942- *BioIn 17*
Walsh, Anna Charlene 1951- *WhoAmW 93*
Walsh, Anne Huddleston 1949- *St&PR 93*
Walsh, Annmarie Hauck 1938- *WhoAm 92*
Walsh, Anthony Francis 1930- *WhoSSW 93*
Walsh, Anthony Peter 1951- *WhoAm 92*
Walsh, Arthur William 1945- *St&PR 93*
Walsh, Barbara Fallon- *BioIn 17*
Walsh, Basil Francis 1934- *WhoSSW 93*
Walsh, Betty Jane 1931- *St&PR 93*
Walsh, Brian J. *Law&B 92*
Walsh, Brian James *Law&B 92*
Walsh, Catherine 1812?-1889 *BioIn 17*
Walsh, Chad 1914-1991 *BioIn 17, ScF&FL 92*
Walsh, Charles Richard 1939- *WhoAm 92, WhoE 93*
Walsh, Christine *Law&B 92*
Walsh, Cornelius Stephen 1907- *WhoAm 92*
Walsh, Craig Wilkinson 1949- *WhoWor 93*
Walsh, D. Terry 1959- *WhoSSW 93*
Walsh, Daniel A. *Law&B 92*
Walsh, Daniel Francis 1937- *WhoAm 92*
Walsh, David G. 1950- *St&PR 93*
Walsh, David James 1936- *St&PR 93*
Walsh, David L. *Law&B 92*
Walsh, Deleon d1990 *BioIn 17*
Walsh, Denny Jay 1935- *WhoAm 92*
Walsh, Dermot 1931- *WhoScE 91-3*
Walsh, Desmond 1954- *WhoCanL 92*
Walsh, Diane 1950- *WhoAmW 93*
Walsh, Don 1931- *WhoAm 92*
Walsh, Donald F. *WhoIns 93*
Walsh, Donald Francis 1932- *St&PR 93*
Walsh, Donald James 1949- *WhoWrEP 92*
Walsh, Donald P. *Law&B 92*
Walsh, Donald Peter 1930- *St&PR 93*
Walsh, Donnie *WhoAm 92*
Walsh, Doris Montague Huntley *WhoWrEP 92*
Walsh, E. Stephen 1942- *St&PR 93*
Walsh, Edward Joseph 1932- *St&PR 93, WhoAm 92*
Walsh, Edward M. 1939- *WhoScE 91-3*
Walsh, Edward Nelson 1925- *WhoE 93*
Walsh, Edward Patrick 1937- *WhoAm 92*
Walsh, Eileen Cecile 1914- *WhoWrEP 92*
Walsh, Eileen M. *Law&B 92*
Walsh, Eleanor Lucille 1962- *WhoAmW 93*
Walsh, Ellen Stoll *ChlBIID [port]*
Walsh, F. Howard 1913- *WhoAm 92*
Walsh, Fiona Marie 1963- *WhoWor 93*
Walsh, Gary William *Law&B 92*
Walsh, Geoffrey *BioIn 17*
Walsh, George 1889-1981 *BioIn 17*
Walsh, George William 1923- *WhoAm 92*
Walsh, George William 1931- *WhoWrEP 92*
Walsh, Gordon R. 1944- *St&PR 93*
Walsh, Helen Horning *AmWomPl*
Walsh, Henry A., Jr. 1943- *St&PR 93*
Walsh, Holly Ann 1963- *WhoE 93*
Walsh, Hugh Sleight 1810-1877 *BioIn 17*
Walsh, J. Richard *Law&B 92*
Walsh, James d1991 *BioIn 17*
Walsh, James A. 1906-1991 *BioIn 17*
Walsh, James Fred, III *Law&B 92*
Walsh, James Hamilton 1947- *WhoEmL 93, WhoSSW 93*
Walsh, James J. 1927- *WhoScE 91-3*
Walsh, James Jerome 1924- *WhoAm 92*
Walsh, James Louis 1909- *WhoAm 92*
Walsh, James Michael 1947- *St&PR 93, WhoEmL 93*
Walsh, James P. 1913- *St&PR 93*
Walsh, James Patrick 1936- *WhoSSW 93*
Walsh, James Patrick 1954- *St&PR 93*
Walsh, James Patrick, Jr. 1910- *WhoAm 92, WhoWor 93*
Walsh, James Paul 1917- *WhoE 93*
Walsh, James T. 1947- *CngDr 91*
Walsh, James Thomas 1947- *WhoAm 92, WhoE 93*
Walsh, James William 1923- *St&PR 93*
Walsh, Jane Ellen McCann 1941- *WhoWor 93*
Walsh, Jeanne 1924- *WhoAmW 93*
Walsh, Jeannette 1944- *St&PR 93*
Walsh, Jeni Lee 1944- *WhoE 93*
Walsh, Jeremiah Edward, Jr. 1937- *WhoAm 92*
Walsh, Jill Paton *ScF&FL 92, SmATA 72*
Walsh, Jill Paton 1937- *ChlFicS*
Walsh, Joan Eileen *WhoScE 91-1*
Walsh, John *BioIn 17*
Walsh, John c. 1666-1736 *Baker 92*
Walsh, John 1709-1766
See Walsh, John c. 1666-1736 *Baker 92*
Walsh, John 1937- *BioIn 17, WhoAm 92, WhoWor 93*
Walsh, John A., Jr. *Law&B 92*
Walsh, John Breffni 1927- *WhoAm 92*
Walsh, John Bronson 1927- *WhoE 93*
Walsh, John Charles 1924- *WhoAm 92*
Walsh, John E., Jr. 1927- *WhoAm 92*
Walsh, John Evangelist 1927- *ScF&FL 92*
Walsh, John Flewellen 1928- *WhoE 93*
Walsh, John Harley 1938- *WhoAm 92*
Walsh, John Joseph 1924- *WhoAm 92*
Walsh, John P. *Law&B 92*
Walsh, John Robert 1930- *St&PR 93, WhoAm 92*
Walsh, Joseph A. 1962- *St&PR 93*
Walsh, Joseph Edward, Jr. *Law&B 92*
Walsh, Joseph Fidler 1947- *WhoAm 92*
Walsh, Joseph Michael 1943- *St&PR 93, WhoAm 92*
Walsh, Joseph Thomas 1930- *WhoAm 92*
Walsh, Joseph Thomas, III *Law&B 92*
Walsh, Joy 1935- *WhoWrEP 92*
Walsh, Judith B. *Law&B 92*
Walsh, Julia Montgomery 1923- *WhoAm 92, WhoAmW 93*
Walsh, Katherine *AmWomPl*
Walsh, Katherine Herald 1944- *WhoAmW 93*
Walsh, Kathleen Huberta 1929- *St&PR 93*
Walsh, Keith Keeler 1952- *WhoE 93*
Walsh, Kevin E. *Law&B 92*
Walsh, Kevin Kane 1950- *WhoE 93*
Walsh, Kevin M. *Law&B 92*
Walsh, Kevin M. 1950- *St&PR 93*
Walsh, Kevin Matthew *Law&B 92*
Walsh, Lawrence A. 1930- *St&PR 93*
Walsh, Lawrence E. *BioIn 17*
Walsh, Lawrence Edward 1912- *WhoAm 92, WhoWor 93*
Walsh, Leo M., Jr. 1932- *WhoIns 93*
Walsh, Leo Marcellus 1931- *WhoAm 92*
Walsh, Loren Melford 1927- *WhoAm 92, WhoWrEP 92*
Walsh, Lynne Brandner 1959- *WhoAmW 93*
Walsh, M.C. *WhoScE 91-3*
Walsh, Marianne Lyda 1942- *WhoE 93*

Walsh, Marie Leclerc 1928- *WhoAmW 93, WhoWor 93*
Walsh, Marie Therese 1935- *WhoAm 92*
Walsh, Martha Condon 1968- *WhoAmW 93*
Walsh, Martin R. 1952- *WhoAm 92*
Walsh, Martin Raymond 1952- *St&PR 93*
Walsh, Martin T. *Law&B 92*
Walsh, Mary Ann 1944- *WhoAmW 93*
Walsh, Mary D. Fleming 1913- *WhoAmW 93, WhoSSW 93, WhoWor 93*
Walsh, Mary Williams 1955- *ConAu 136*
Walsh, Mason 1912- *WhoAm 92*
Walsh, Mason, Jr. 1935- *St&PR 93*
Walsh, Matthew Myles, Jr. *St&PR 93*
Walsh, Maurice David, Jr. 1924- *WhoAm 92*
Walsh, Michael F. *St&PR 93*
Walsh, Michael F. 1946- *WhoIns 93*
Walsh, Michael Francis 1956- *WhoAm 92*
Walsh, Michael H. *BioIn 17*
Walsh, Michael H. 1942- *NewYTBS 92 [port]*
Walsh, Michael Harries 1942- *WhoAm 92, WhoSSW 93*
Walsh, Michael J. 1932- *WhoAm 92*
Walsh, Michael Joseph, Jr. 1939- *St&PR 93*
Walsh, Michiyo Shiota 1953- *WhoE 93*
Walsh, Mike 1955- *WhoWrEP 92*
Walsh, Morgan S. *Law&B 92*
Walsh, Patrick Craig 1938- *WhoAm 92*
Walsh, Patrick D. *Law&B 92*
Walsh, Patrick F. *Law&B 92*
Walsh, Patrick W. 1939- *St&PR 93*
Walsh, Paul F. 1949- *St&PR 93*
Walsh, Peter Alexander 1935- *WhoAsAP 91*
Walsh, Peter Joseph 1929- *WhoAm 92, WhoE 93*
Walsh, Philip Cornelius 1921- *St&PR 93, WhoAm 92*
Walsh, Philip Joseph, III 1951- *WhoSSW 93*
Walsh, R.F. 1930- *St&PR 93*
Walsh, Raoul *HispAmA*
Walsh, Raoul 1887-1980 *MiSFD 9N*
Walsh, Raymond J. 1949- *St&PR 93*
Walsh, Raymond Michael 1939- *WhoAm 92*
Walsh, Richard F. d1992 *NewYTBS 92*
Walsh, Richard George 1930- *WhoAm 92*
Walsh, Richard Troy 1935- *St&PR 93, WhoAm 92*
Walsh, Robb *ScF&FL 92*
Walsh, Robert 1784-1859 *JrnUS*
Walsh, Robert A. *Law&B 92*
Walsh, Robert C. 1938- *St&PR 93*
Walsh, Robert Charles 1938- *WhoAm 92*
Walsh, Rodger John 1924- *St&PR 93, WhoAm 92*
Walsh, Rodolfo 1927-1977 *SpAmA*
Walsh, Ronald E. *Law&B 92*
Walsh, Semmes Guest 1926- *WhoAm 92*
Walsh, Stephen F. 1954- *St&PR 93*
Walsh, Susan Linda 1957- *WhoE 93*
Walsh, Tammy Turner *Law&B 92*
Walsh, Thomas Charles 1940- *WhoAm 92*
Walsh, Thomas G. 1942- *WhoIns 93*
Walsh, Thomas Gerard 1942- *St&PR 93, WhoAm 92*
Walsh, Thomas J. 1859-1933 *PolPar*
Walsh, Thomas Joseph 1931- *WhoAm 92, WhoE 93, WhoWor 93*
Walsh, Thomas K. 1946- *St&PR 93*
Walsh, Tony 1947- *WhoSSW 93*
Walsh, Vincent J., Jr. *Law&B 92*
Walsh, Walter J. 1929- *WhoIns 93*
Walsh, Walter Joseph 1929- *St&PR 93*
Walsh, William 1931- *WhoAm 92*
Walsh, William A. 1932- *St&PR 93*
Walsh, William Albert 1933- *WhoAm 92*
Walsh, William Bertalan 1920- *WhoAm 92*
Walsh, William Desmond 1930- *St&PR 93, WhoAm 92*
Walsh, William Egan 1948- *St&PR 93*
Walsh, William F. 1938- *St&PR 93*
Walsh, William I. d1990 *BioIn 17*
Walsh, William Joseph, Jr. 1942- *WhoIns 93*
Walsh, William Joseph, III 1945- *St&PR 93*
Walsh, William Marshall 1936-1990 *BioIn 17*
Walsh, William P. *Law&B 92*
Walsham, Bruce Taylor 1936- *WhoWor 93*
Walsh-McGehee, Martha Bosse *WhoE 93, WhoWor 93*
Walsh-O'Brien, Maura *Law&B 92*
Walska, Ganna 1887-1984 *PolBiDi*
Walske, Max Carl, Jr. 1922- *WhoAm 92*
Walstad, Dennis Carlton 1942- *St&PR 93*
Walstam, Rune E. 1923- *WhoScE 91-4*
Walsten, Michael *BioIn 17*
Walster, Elaine Hatfield *ConAu 38NR*
Walston, Carl Frederick 1939- *WhoAm 92*
Walston, James Patrick 1949- *WhoWor 93*
Walston, Ray 1918?- *ConTFT 10*
Walston, Ray 1924- *WhoAm 92*
Walston, Roderick Eugene 1935- *WhoAm 92, WhoWor 93*
Walsworth, James Frank 1927- *St&PR 93*
Walsworth, Ronald Lee 1935- *WhoAm 92*
Walsworth, Virgil Ray 1943- *WhoSSW 93*
Walt, Alexander Jeffrey 1923- *WhoAm 92*
Walt, Cathy Lynn 1957- *WhoE 93*
Walt, Dick K. 1935- *WhoAm 92, WhoWrEP 92*
Walt, Harold Richard 1923- *WhoAm 92*
Walt, Martin 1926- *WhoAm 92*
Waltari, Lauri Juhani 1939- *WhoScE 91-4*
Waltari, Mika 1908-1979 *ScF&FL 92*
Waltemeyer, Robert Victor 1934- *St&PR 93, WhoAm 92*
Walter, Alfred Anthony 1932- *St&PR 93*
Walter, Arnold (Maria) 1902-1973 *Baker 92*
Walter, Barbara Louise 1949- *WhoAmW 93*
Walter, Brad *Law&B 92*
Walter, Bruce V. 1958- *St&PR 93*
Walter, Bruno 1876-1962 *Baker 92, IntDcOp [port], OxDcOp*
Walter, Carl W. d1992 *NewYTBS 92*
Walter, Carl W. 1905-1992 *BioIn 17*
Walter, Carolyn Ambler 1945- *WhoE 93*
Walter, Chrysandra Lou 1947- *WhoAmW 93*
Walter, David Edgar 1953- *Baker 92*
Walter, Dennis John 1944- *St&PR 93*
Walter, Donald Ellsworth 1936- *WhoSSW 93*
Walter, Dorothy C. *ScF&FL 92*
Walter, Elizabeth *ConAu 38NR, ScF&FL 92*
Walter, Elizabeth Mitchell 1936- *WhoAmW 93, WhoSSW 93*
Walter, Elizabeth Thomas 1958- *WhoAmW 93*
Walter, Eric G. 1964- *WhoE 93*
Walter, Eric P. 1950- *WhoScE 91-2*
Walter, Filip Neriusz 1810-1847 *PolBiDi*
Walter, Frances V. 1923- *SmATA 71 [port]*
Walter, Frank Sherman 1926- *WhoAm 92*
Walter, Franklin B. 1929- *WhoAm 92*
Walter, Frans 1932- *WhoScE 91-3*
Walter, Franz Robert 1947- *WhoWor 93*
Walter, Fried 1907- *Baker 92*
Walter, G. *WhoScE 91-2*
Walter, Gary James *Law&B 92*
Walter, Gary Steven 1949- *WhoSSW 93*
Walter, Georg A. 1875-1952 *Baker 92*
Walter, George 1928- *DcCPCAm*
Walter, Gerhild 1936- *St&PR 93*
Walter, Helen Joy 1938- *WhoAmW 93*
Walter, Henry Alexander 1912- *WhoE 93*
Walter, Howard J., Jr. *Law&B 92*
Walter, (Johann) Ignaz (Joseph) 1755-1822 *Baker 92*
Walter, Ingo 1940- *WhoAm 92*
Walter, J. Jackson 1940- *WhoAm 92, WhoE 93*
Walter, J.W. 1922- *St&PR 93*
Walter, James W. *BioIn 17*
Walter, James W. 1922- *WhoSSW 93*
Walter, Janet Theresa 1967- *WhoAmW 93*
Walter, Jessica 1944- *WhoAm 92*
Walter, Johann(es) 1496-1570 *Baker 92*
Walter, John Douglas *WhoScE 91-1*
Walter, John Fenner 1934- *WhoE 93*
Walter, John Fitler 1943- *WhoE 93*
Walter, John Grant 1932- *St&PR 93*
Walter, John R. 1947- *St&PR 93*
Walter, John Robert 1947- *WhoAm 92*
Walter, Karl 1862-1929 *Baker 92*
Walter, Kenneth D. 1929- *St&PR 93*
Walter, Kenneth Gaines 1932- *WhoE 93*
Walter, Kerry D. 1951- *St&PR 93*
Walter, Kimbra D. *Law&B 92*
Walter, Kurt 1925- *St&PR 93*
Walter, Lloyd Guy, Jr. 1934- *WhoSSW 93*
Walter, Mark R. *Law&B 92*
Walter, Martin J. *Law&B 92*
Walter, Michael Charles 1956- *WhoEmL 93*
Walter, Mildred 1922- *BlkAuII 92*
Walter, Mildred Pitts 1922- *ConAu 138, DcAmChF 1985, MajAI [port], SmATA 69 [port]*
Walter, Nancy Keesee 1945- *WhoSSW 93*
Walter, Nina Willis 1900- *AmWomPl*
Walter, Patricia A. 1937- *St&PR 93*
Walter, Paul 1933- *WhoScE 91-4*
Walter, Paul F. 1935- *St&PR 93*
Walter, Paul Josef 1935- *WhoScE 91-2*
Walter, Paul W. d1992 *NewYTBS 92*
Walter, Philipp J., Jr. 1936- *WhoAm 92*
Walter, Richard Lawrence 1933- *WhoAm 92*
Walter, Robert C. 1918- *St&PR 93*
Walter, Robert E. *Law&B 92*
Walter, Robert Irving 1920- *WhoAm 92*
Walter, Robert John 1948- *WhoWor 93*
Walter, Robert L. 1928- *St&PR 93*
Walter, Robert M. *Law&B 92*
Walter, Scott James 1963- *WhoSSW 93*
Walter, Stephen 1912- *St&PR 93*
Walter, Stephen Bunch 1942- *WhoSSW 93*
Walter, Thomas 1696-1725 *Baker 92*
Walter, Thomas G. *Law&B 92*
Walter, Thomas G. 1941- *St&PR 93*
Walter, Timothy Harold 1957- *WhoE 93*
Walter, Villiam Christian *MajAI*
Walter, Virginia Lee 1937- *WhoAm 92*
Walter, William Arnold, Jr. 1922- *WhoAm 92*
Walter, William B. 1935- *WhoSSW 93*
Walter, William E. *Law&B 92*
Walter, William Paul 1925- *WhoWor 93*
Walter, Wolfgang Ludwig 1927- *WhoWor 93*
Walterhouse, George Francis 1937- *St&PR 93*
Walters, A.A. 1926- *BioIn 17*
Walters, Alan Arthur 1926- *BioIn 17, WhoWor 93*
Walters, Alexander 1858-1917 *EncAACR*
Walters, Allan N. 1944- *WhoE 93*
Walters, Andrew Schrack *BioIn 17*
Walters, Anita Duke 1944- *WhoAmW 93*
Walters, Barbara *NewYTBS 92 [port]*
Walters, Barbara 1931- *BioIn 17, JrnUS, WhoAm 92, WhoAmW 93, WhoWor 93*
Walters, Bette J. 1946- *St&PR 93*
Walters, Bette Jean *Law&B 92*
Walters, Bette Jean 1946- *WhoAm 92*
Walters, Bradford Blair 1952- *WhoSSW 93*
Walters, Bryan James 1968- *WhoSSW 93*
Walters, Bucky 1909-1991 *BioIn 17*
Walters, C. Thomas 1934- *St&PR 93*
Walters, Charles 1911-1982 *MiSFD 9N*
Walters, Charles D. *St&PR 93*
Walters, Charles Joseph 1945- *WhoE 93*
Walters, Curt *BioIn 17*
Walters, Dan Francis 1949- *WhoSSW 93*
Walters, David 1951- *WhoAm 92, WhoSSW 93*
Walters, David D. 1932- *St&PR 93*
Walters, David McLean 1917- *WhoAm 92, WhoWor 93*
Walters, Dennis 1928- *BioIn 17*
Walters, Dianne Pendergrass 1948- *WhoAmW 93*
Walters, Donald E. *Law&B 92*
Walters, Donald E. 1934-1990 *BioIn 17*
Walters, Donald Lee 1937- *WhoE 93*
Walters, Doris Lavonne 1931- *WhoAmW 93*
Walters, Douglas Bruce 1942- *WhoSSW 93*
Walters, Edwin K. 1951- *St&PR 93*
Walters, Elizabeth Ogg d1992 *BioIn 17, NewYTBS 92*
Walters, Ernest Edward 1927- *WhoE 93*
Walters, Everett 1915- *WhoAm 92*
Walters, Fan Zhang 1961- *WhoAmW 93*
Walters, Floyd G. 1926- *St&PR 93*
Walters, Fred Ashmore *Law&B 92*
Walters, Glen Robert 1943- *WhoAm 92*
Walters, Harry N. 1936- *WhoAm 92*
Walters, Harry T. *Law&B 92*
Walters, Heather MacLean *WhoE 93*
Walters, Hugh 1910- *ScF&FL 92*
Walters, J. Donald 1926- *WhoWor 93*
Walters, James Lee 1944- *WhoSSW 93*
Walters, James Leland *Law&B 92*
Walters, James Michael 1947- *WhoE 93*
Walters, Jay B. 1946- *St&PR 93*
Walters, Jefferson Brooks 1922- *WhoWor 93*
Walters, Jennifer Waelti *ConAu 136, ScF&FL 92*
Walters, Jerry Willard 1936- *WhoE 93*
Walters, Jess 1906- *OxDcOp*
Walters, Jesse Chandler 1956- *WhoE 93*
Walters, Jesse Marvin 1940- *St&PR 93, WhoAm 92*
Walters, Joanne-Theresa 1942- *WhoAmW 93*
Walters, Joe A. 1920- *St&PR 93*
Walters, John Edward 1925- *St&PR 93*
Walters, John Sherwood 1917- *WhoAm 92*
Walters, Johnnie McKeiver 1919- *WhoAm 92*
Walters, Judith Richmond 1944- *WhoAm 92, WhoAmW 93*
Walters, Kenn David 1957- *WhoWor 93*
Walters, Kenneth *WhoScE 91-1*
Walters, Kenneth 1934- *WhoWor 93*
Walters, Lawrence Charles 1948- *WhoAm 92*
Walters, Lawrence James 1948- *WhoE 93*
Walters, Leonard M. 1922- *St&PR 93*
Walters, Louis M. *St&PR 93*
Walters, Luana 1912- *SweetSg C [port]*
Walters, Marc Anton 1952- *WhoE 93*
Walters, Martha Bernadine 1947- *WhoEmL 93*
Walters, Mary Dawson 1923- *WhoWrEP 92*
Walters, Michael W. 1946- *WhoAm 92*
Walters, Milt Kirkland 1940- *St&PR 93*
Walters, Milton James 1942- *WhoAm 92*
Walters, Nancy Lu 1938- *WhoAmW 93*
Walters, Norman Edward 1941- *WhoSSW 93*
Walters, Patricia Diane 1961- *WhoAmW 93*
Walters, R.R. *ScF&FL 92*
Walters, Ralph E. *St&PR 93*
Walters, Ratus William 1932- *St&PR 93*
Walters, Raymond, Jr. 1912- *WhoAm 92, WhoWrEP 92*
Walters, Raymond L. 1949- *St&PR 93*
Walters, Rebecca Ellis 1955- *WhoSSW 93*
Walters, Rebecca Russell Yarborough 1951- *WhoAmW 93*
Walters, Robert Willis 1953- *WhoSSW 93*
Walters, Roland Evans 1943- *WhoSSW 93*
Walters, Ronald *ConAu 139*
Walters, Ronald E. *St&PR 93*
Walters, Ronald Ogden 1939- *St&PR 93, WhoAm 92*
Walters, Ronald W. *BioIn 17*
Walters, Shirley 1925- *WhoAsAP 91*
Walters, Thomas Joseph 1930- *WhoE 93*
Walters, Thorley 1913-1991 *AnObit 1991, ConTFT 10*
Walters, Timothy Edward 1949- *WhoE 93*
Walters, Tyler *WhoAm 92*
Walters, Vernon Anthony 1917- *WhoAm 92*
Walters, Wilfred Nelson, Jr. 1942- *WhoSSW 93*
Walters, William Armand 1944- *St&PR 93*
Walters, William Ben 1938- *WhoE 93*
Walters, William Lee 1946- *WhoSSW 93*
Walters, William LeRoy 1932- *WhoAm 92*
Walters, Zelia Margaret *AmWomPl*
Waltersdorf, John Galt 1954- *St&PR 93*
Waltersdorf, John Maurice 1926- *St&PR 93*
Waltersdorf, Margaret Stott 1929- *St&PR 93*
Waltershausen, Hermann Wolfgang Sartorius, Freiherr von 1882-1954 *Baker 92*
Walters-Lucy, Jean 1941- *WhoWrEP 92*
Walthall, Gary David 1942- *St&PR 93*
Walthall, Henry B. 1878-1936 *IntDcF 2-3 [port]*
Walthall, Lee Wade 1953- *WhoAm 92*
Walther, Daniel 1940- *ScF&FL 92*
Walther, Gary D. *St&PR 93*
Walther, Gregory Louis 1954- *WhoWor 93*
Walther, Herbert 1935- *WhoScE 91-3*
Walther, Joachim-Ulrich 1948- *WhoWor 93*
Walther, Johann Gottfried 1684-1748 *Baker 92*
Walther, Johann Jakob c. 1650-1717 *Baker 92*
Walther, John H. 1935- *St&PR 93*
Walther, John Henry 1935- *WhoAm 92*
Walther, Joseph Edward 1912- *WhoAm 92*
Walther, Manfred Odo 1938- *WhoWor 93*
Walther, Ralph 1951- *St&PR 93*
Walther, Roger O. 1936- *WhoAm 92*
Walther, Thomas Evans 1938- *St&PR 93*
Walther, Zerita 1927- *WhoAmW 93*
Walthers, B.J. 1919- *St&PR 93*
Walthers, J. Philip 1948- *St&PR 93*
Walther von der Vogelweide *Baker 92*
Walthew, Richard Henry 1872-1951 *Baker 92*
Walti, James Randall *Law&B 92*
Walti, Kenneth John 1947- *St&PR 93*
Waltien, Albert A. 1942- *St&PR 93*
Waltking, Arthur Ernest 1937- *WhoE 93*
Waltman, Lynne Marie 1952- *WhoSSW 93*
Waltner, G.H. 1918- *St&PR 93*
Walton, Alan *WhoScE 91-4*
Walton, Alan George 1936- *St&PR 93, WhoAm 92*
Walton, Alice *BioIn 17*
Walton, Alice L. 1949- *WhoAmW 93*
Walton, Amanda Loretta 1941- *WhoAmW 93, WhoE 93*
Walton, Anthony John 1934- *WhoWor 93*
Walton, Bessie Reed *AmWomPl*
Walton, Bill 1952- *WhoAm 92*
Walton, Bobbi Smith 1949- *ConAu 137*
Walton, Brian James *WhoScE 91-1*
Walton, Bryce 1918-1988 *ScF&FL 92*
Walton, Carol 1965- *WhoAmW 93*
Walton, Charles D. *AfrAmBi [port]*
Walton, Charles Michael 1941- *WhoAm 92*

Walton, Chelle Koster 1954- *WhoWrEP 92*
Walton, Chester Lee, Jr. 1926- *WhoSSW 93*
Walton, Clarence 1915- *WhoAm 92, WhoWrEP 92*
Walton, Clyde Cameron 1925- *WhoWrEP 92*
Walton, Conrad Gordon, Sr. 1928- *WhoSSW 93*
Walton, Dan Thomas 1956- *WhoSSW 93*
Walton, Daniel 1941- *St&PR 93*
Walton, Danna M. *Law&B 92*
Walton, Darwin McBeth 1926- *BlkAuII 92*
Walton, David Lee, Jr. 1953- *WhoSSW 93*
Walton, David W.H. *WhoScE 91-1*
Walton, DeWitt T., Jr. 1937- *WhoSSW 93*
Walton, Douglas N(eil) 1942- *ConAu 40NR*
Walton, Eileen Rowan *Law&B 92*
Walton, Elbert Arthur, Jr. 1942- *AfrAmBi*
Walton, Emma Lee 1874- *AmWomPl*
Walton, Ernest Thomas Sinton 1903- *WhoWor 93*
Walton, Evangeline 1907- *ScF&FL 92*
Walton, Ewart Kendall *WhoScE 91-1*
Walton, Francis Ray 1910- *WhoAm 92*
Walton, Frank E. 1909- *WhoWrEP 92*
Walton, Frank Emulous 1909- *WhoAm 92*
Walton, Frank H. 1933- *St&PR 93*
Walton, Fred *MiSFD 9*
Walton, Georgina Jones *AmWomPl*
Walton, Gerald Wayne 1934- *WhoAm 92, WhoSSW 93*
Walton, Harold Vincent 1921- *WhoAm 92*
Walton, Ian S. 1954- *St&PR 93*
Walton, Isaac 1593-1683 *BioIn 17*
Walton, Izaak 1593-1683 *BioIn 17*
Walton, J.H. 1933- *St&PR 93*
Walton, James M. 1930- *WhoAm 92, WhoWor 93*
Walton, Joan 1939- *WhoAm 92*
Walton, John Brooks *BioIn 17*
Walton, John E. 1944- *St&PR 93*
Walton, John H. 1939- *St&PR 93, WhoIns 93*
Walton, John Nicholas 1922- *BioIn 17*
Walton, Jon D. *Law&B 92*
Walton, Jon David 1942- *WhoAm 92*
Walton, Jonathan Taylor 1930- *St&PR 93, WhoAm 92*
Walton, Joseph A. 1935- *St&PR 93*
Walton, Joseph Carroll 1955- *WhoEmL 93*
Walton, Joseph M. 1926- *St&PR 93*
Walton, Keith John 1946- *WhoUN 92*
Walton, Kendall L(ewis) 1939- *ConAu 136*
Walton, Kenneth C. *WhoScE 91-1*
Walton, Kenneth Wayne 1954- *WhoSSW 93*
Walton, Mark Alan 1955- *WhoE 93*
Walton, Matt Savage 1915- *WhoAm 92*
Walton, Merrick C. *Law&B 92*
Walton, Morgan Lauck, III 1932- *WhoAm 92*
Walton, Paul Talmage 1914- *St&PR 93*
Walton, Philip W. 1940- *WhoScE 91-3*
Walton, Rhondetta Goble *Law&B 92*
Walton, Richard 1962- *WhoWor 93*
Walton, Richard E. *Law&B 92*
Walton, Richard Eugene 1931- *WhoAm 92, WhoWrEP 92*
Walton, Rob *BioIn 17*
Walton, Robert A. *BioIn 17*
Walton, Robert Cutler 1932- *WhoWor 93*
Walton, Robert Martin 1964- *WhoE 93*
Walton, Robert Owen 1927- *WhoAm 92*
Walton, Robert Pierce *Law&B 92*
Walton, Robert Wheeler 1919- *WhoAm 92*
Walton, Rodney Earl 1947- *WhoEmL 93*
Walton, Roland Jerome 1934- *St&PR 93*
Walton, Ronald Elwood 1932- *WhoSSW 93*
Walton, S. Robson 1945- *WhoAm 92*
Walton, Sam *BioIn 17*
Walton, Sam 1918- *CurBio 92 [port]*
Walton, Sam 1918-1992 *CurBio 92N, NewYTBS 92 [port], News 93-1*
Walton, Scott *BioIn 17*
Walton, Sean M. *St&PR 93*
Walton, Stanley Anthony, III 1939- *WhoAm 92*
Walton, Tony 1934- *WhoAm 92*
Walton, Virginia 1908-1992 *BioIn 17*
Walton, William 1902-1983 *IntDcOp, OxDcOp*
Walton, William B. 1945- *St&PR 93*
Walton, William (Turner) 1902-1983 *Baker 92*
Waltrip, Burroughs Allen 1928- *WhoSSW 93*
Waltrip, Darrell *BioIn 17*
Waltrip, Darrell Lee 1947- *WhoAm 92*
Waltrip, Robert L. 1931- *WhoAm 92*
Waltrip, Robert Lynn 1931- *St&PR 93*
Walts, Charles F. 1948- *St&PR 93*
Walts, Jack C. 1919- *St&PR 93*
Walts, Robert Warren 1921- *WhoWrEP 92*
Waltz, Debora J. *Law&B 92*
Waltz, Gerald Donn 1939- *St&PR 93, WhoAm 92*
Waltz, Gustavus dc. 1759 *Baker 92*
Waltz, Gustavus fl. 1732-1759 *OxDcOp*
Waltz, Jon Richard 1929- *WhoAm 92, WhoWrEP 92*
Waltz, Joseph McKendree 1931- *WhoAm 92, WhoE 93, WhoWor 93*
Waltz, Kenneth Neal 1924- *WhoAm 92*
Waltz, Mark Edward 1932- *WhoE 93*
Waltz, Thomas M. 1933- *St&PR 93*
Waltzer, Joel 1943- *St&PR 93*
Waluk, Stanley Peter 1943- *WhoE 93, WhoWor 93*
Walvin, James 1942- *ConAu 37NR*
Walvoord, Edgar A. 1936- *St&PR 93, WhoIns 93*
Walvoord, Ellen Molleston 1939- *St&PR 93*
Walvoord, John Flipse 1910- *WhoAm 92*
Walwer, Frank Kurt 1930- *WhoAm 92, WhoSSW 93*
Walworth, Arthur 1903- *WhoAm 92*
Walworth, Charles Arthur 1931- *WhoAm 92*
Walworth, Edward Zinsser 1945- *WhoE 93*
Walworth, Reuben Hyde 1788-1867 *OxCSupC*
Walworth, Reubena Hyde 1867-1898 *AmWomPl*
Walwyn, Fulke 1910-1991 *AnObit 1991*
Walz, Barbra d1990 *BioIn 17*
Walz, Felix H. 1948- *WhoScE 91-4*
Walz, Guido Johannes 1959- *WhoWor 93*
Walz, James Eric 1951- *St&PR 93*
Walz, Jay 1907-1991 *BioIn 17*
Walz, Robert DeHaven 1944- *WhoWor 93*
Walz, Tommy 1945- *WhoWrEP 92*
Walz, William R. *Law&B 92*
Walzak, Edward J. 1945- *St&PR 93*
Walzak, Myron Paul, Jr. 1930- *WhoAm 92*
Walzel, Leopold Matthias 1902-1970 *Baker 92*
Walzer, Ann Werlin 1945- *WhoE 93*
Walzer, Emily *BioIn 17*
Walzer, Gerald 1940- *WhoUN 92*
Walzer, Judith Borodovko 1935- *WhoAm 92*
Walzer, Michael *BioIn 17*
Walzer, William Charles 1912- *WhoAm 92*
Walzer, William G. *St&PR 93*
Walzog, Nancy Lee 1963- *WhoAmW 93*
Wamaling, Mark Hunter 1959- *WhoWrEP 92*
Wambach, Emile 1854-1924 *Baker 92*
Wambaugh, Joseph *BioIn 17*
Wambaugh, Joseph 1937- *WhoAm 92*
Wamble, Clara 1947- *St&PR 93*
Wambles, Lynda England 1937- *WhoAmW 93*
Wambold, Ali E. 1954- *St&PR 93*
Wamboldt, Donald G. 1932- *St&PR 93*
Wamboldt, Donald George 1932- *WhoAm 92, WhoIns 93*
Wambolt, Ronald Ralph 1934- *St&PR 93, WhoAm 92*
Wambsganss, Richard E. 1940- *St&PR 93*
Wambuzi, Samuel William Wako 1931- *WhoWor 93*
Wamer, Gary L. *Law&B 92*
Wamester, William David 1945- *WhoE 93*
Wampler, Barbara Bedford 1932- *WhoWor 93*
Wampler, Bernard Campbell 1931- *St&PR 93*
Wampler, Charles Edwin 1908- *WhoAm 92*
Wampler, Donald Eugene 1935- *WhoE 93*
Wampler, John Edward 1944- *WhoSSW 93*
Wampler, John M. 1955- *St&PR 93*
Wampler, Jon R. 1951- *WhoSSW 93*
Wampler, Lloyd Charles 1920- *WhoAm 92*
Wampler, Thornton Garland 1925- *St&PR 93*
Wampold, Babette Levy 1934- *WhoAmW 93*
Wampold, Charles Henry, Jr. 1925- *WhoAm 92*
Wamser, Christian Albert 1913- *WhoE 93*
Wamsley, Donna Ailene 1949- *WhoAmW 93*
Wan, Bonnie B. *Law&B 92*
Wan, Chin Chin Yip 1945- *WhoWor 93*
Wan, Frederic Yui-Ming 1936- *WhoAm 92*
Wan, Lawrence A. *St&PR 93*
Wan, Paul A. 1945- *St&PR 93*
Wan, Peter Janssen 1943- *WhoSSW 93*
Wan, Shao-Hong 1946- *WhoE 93*
Wanamaker, Ellen Ponce 1956- *WhoAmW 93*
Wanamaker, John Lawrence *Law&B 92*
Wanamaker, Robert Joseph 1924- *WhoAm 92*
Wanamaker, Sam 1919- *MiSFD 9, WhoAm 92*
Wanat, Stanley Frank 1939- *WhoE 93*
Wanczek, Karl Peter 1940- *WhoScE 91-3*
Wand, Gunter 1912- *Baker 92*
Wand, Ian Christopher *WhoScE 91-1*
Wand, Richard Walton 1939- *St&PR 93, WhoAm 92*
Wandasiewicz, Stefania 1948- *WhoE 93*
Wandel, William Robert 1951- *WhoE 93*
Wanden, Stig 1940- *WhoWor 93*
Wander, Elyse Gay 1948- *St&PR 93, WhoAm 92*
Wander, Herbert Stanton 1935- *WhoAm 92*
Wander, Joseph Day 1941- *WhoSSW 93*
Wander, Philip 1922- *WhoAm 92*
Wander, Philip 1923- *St&PR 93*
Wanderlingh, Franco *WhoScE 91-3*
Wanderman, Susan Mae *Law&B 92*
Wanderman, Susan Mae 1947- *WhoEmL 93*
Wanders, Hans W. 1925- *St&PR 93*
Wanders, Hans Walter 1925- *WhoAm 92*
Wandersman, Lois Pall 1950- *WhoSSW 93*
Wandler, Leslie Roy 1945- *St&PR 93, WhoAm 92*
Wandmacher, Cornelius 1911- *WhoAm 92*
Wandrasz, Janusz Wladyslaw 1941- *WhoScE 91-4*
Wandrei, Donald 1908-1987 *ScF&FL 92*
Wandschneider, John Frederick 1943- *St&PR 93*
Wandycz, Piotr Stefan 1923- *WhoAm 92*
Wandzel, Leszek 1954- *WhoWor 93*
Wane, Marc P. *Law&B 92*
Wanek, Jerrold 1958- *WhoEmL 93*
Wanek, William Charles 1932- *WhoAm 92*
Wanenmacher, Kathleen Murphy 1944- *WhoAmW 93, WhoSSW 93*
Wanfalt, Donald G. 1943- *St&PR 93*
Wang, Ai-Nung 1952- *WhoWor 93*
Wang, An *BioIn 17*
Wang, Arthur Woods 1918- *WhoAm 92, WhoWrEP 92*
Wang, Biao 1963- *WhoWor 93*
Wang, Bo-Ying 1937- *WhoWor 93*
Wang, Bosco Shang 1947- *WhoE 93*
Wang, Chang Yi 1951- *WhoEmL 93*
Wang, Chao-Cheng 1938- *WhoAm 92*
Wang, Chao Tsung 1912- *WhoWor 93*
Wang, Chao-Ying 1956- *WhoAmW 93*
Wang, Chao Yong 1964- *St&PR 93*
Wang, Charles B. 1944- *St&PR 93, WhoAm 92*
Wang, Chen Chi 1932- *WhoWor 93*
Wang, Chi-ming 1933- *WhoWor 93*
Wang, Chi-Sun 1942- *WhoSSW 93*
Wang, Chia-Gee 1936- *St&PR 93*
Wang, Chia Ping *WhoAm 92, WhoE 93, WhoWor 93*
Wang, Chien-shien *BioIn 17*
Wang, Chuan-Lun 1922- *WhoWor 93*
Wang, Dahong 1919- *WhoWor 93*
Wang, Daniel I-Chyau 1936- *WhoAm 92*
Wang, David I. J. 1932- *WhoAm 92*
Wang, Deren 1933- *WhoWor 93*
Wang, Dian Y. *Law&B 92*
Wang, Dong 1936- *WhoWor 93*
Wang, Dou Wen 1950- *WhoWor 93*
Wang, Eddy An Di 1923- *WhoWor 93*
Wang, Edwin James 1962- *WhoE 93*
Wang, Fan-hsi 1907- *BioIn 17*
Wang, Fusheng 1945- *WhoSSW 93*
Wang, Gung H. 1909- *WhoWor 93*
Wang, Haihong 1964- *WhoWor 93*
Wang, Herbert Fan 1946- *WhoAm 92*
Wang, Hsueh-Hwa 1923- *WhoE 93*
Wang, James Chia-Fang 1926- *WhoAm 92*
Wang, James Chuo 1936- *WhoAm 92, WhoE 93*
Wang, Jaw-Kai 1932- *WhoAm 92*
Wang, Jerry H. 1937- *WhoAm 92*
Wang, Ji-Tao 1918- *WhoWor 93*
Wang, Ji Zu 1922- *WhoWor 93*
Wang, Jia-yuan 1932- *WhoWor 93*
Wang, Jian 1968- *BioIn 17*
Wang, Jin-Ling 1943- *WhoWor 93*
Wang, John Cheng Hwai 1934- *WhoAm 92*
Wang, Josephine L. Fen 1948- *WhoAmW 93, WhoWor 93*
Wang, Jui Hsin 1921- *WhoAm 92*
Wang, Julie Caroline 1947- *WhoAm 92*
Wang, Junde *WhoWor 93*
Wang, Jyhpyng 1958- *WhoWor 93*
Wang, Knut W. 1937- *WhoWor 93*
Wang, Kuk-Kei Kenneth 1947- *WhoWor 93*
Wang, L. Edwin 1919- *WhoAm 92*
Wang, Leon Ru-Liang 1932- *WhoSSW 93*
Wang, Li-Ying Hilary 1961- *WhoAmW 93*
Wang, Liang-guo 1945- *WhoWor 93*
Wang, Lin 1929- *WhoWor 93*
Wang, Ming-Hsien Kenneth 1920- *WhoSSW 93*
Wang, Ming-tao 1900-1991 *BioIn 17*
Wang, Peter *Law&B 92, MiSFD 9*
Wang, Peter Zhenming 1940- *WhoWor 93*
Wang, Ruqing 1941- *WhoWor 93*
Wang, Sam Shu-Yi 1936- *WhoSSW 93*
Wang, Sheng Fu 1925- *WhoWor 93*
Wang, Shih C. 1910- *WhoAm 92*
Wang, Shih-Ho 1944- *WhoAm 92*
Wang, Shiqian Steven 1942- *WhoWor 93*
Wang, Shu-Rong 1939- *WhoWor 93*
Wang, Shu-sen 1916-1989 *BioIn 17*
Wang, Shu-Tang 1933- *WhoWor 93*
Wang, Shuanglong 1964- *WhoWor 93*
Wang, Sing-wu 1920- *WhoWor 93*
Wang, Song-Gui 1940- *WhoWor 93*
Wang, Stanley *Law&B 92*
Wang, Steve *MiSFD 9*
Wang, Su Sun 1934- *WhoAm 92*
Wang, Sue Hwa 1948- *WhoAmW 93, WhoWor 93*
Wang, Susan S. 1951- *St&PR 93*
Wang, Taylor Gunjin 1940- *WhoAm 92*
Wang, Ting Fu 1933- *WhoWor 93*
Wang, Tong 1937- *WhoSSW 93*
Wang, Trevor Leon *WhoScE 91-1*
Wang, Tso-Ren 1943- *WhoWor 93*
Wang, Vera *BioIn 17*
Wang, Victor Michael 1965- *St&PR 93*
Wang, Wayne 1949- *MiSFD 9*
Wang, William Kai-Sheng 1946- *WhoAm 92*
Wang, William Shi-Yuan 1933- *WhoAm 92*
Wang, Wuying 1928- *WhoWor 93*
Wang, Xiaoji 1961- *WhoWor 93*
Wang, XiaoLu 1954- *WhoE 93*
Wang, Ya Ko 1956- *WhoWor 93*
Wang, Yan 1953- *WhoSSW 93*
Wang, Ying-Luo 1930- *WhoWor 93*
Wang, Yong Cheng 1939- *WhoWor 93*
Wang, Yu 1963- *WhoWor 93*
Wang, Zeke 1942- *WhoWor 93*
Wang, Zhao Zhong 1946- *WhoWor 93*
Wang, Zheng-Xian 1917- *WhoWor 93*
Wang, Zhicheng 1933- *WhoWor 93*
Wang, Zhijiang 1930- *WhoWor 93*
Wang, Zhong-Han 1913- *WhoWor 93*
Wangaard, Arthur Carl, Jr. 1927- *St&PR 93*
Wangaard, Clark F. 1950- *St&PR 93*
Wang Aiqun *BioIn 17*
Wangberg, Mark Thomas 1952- *WhoWrEP 92*
Wangbichler, Robert James 1938- *St&PR 93*
Wang Bingqian 1925- *WhoAsAP 91, WhoWor 93*
Wang Chaowen 1931- *WhoAsAP 91*
Wang Chen d1449 *HarEnMi*
Wang Chengbin 1928- *WhoAsAP 91*
Wang Chien-Shien 1938- *WhoAsAP 91, WhoWor 93*
Wang Chou-Ming 1920- *WhoAsAP 91*
Wangchuck, Jigme Singye 1955- *WhoWor 93*
Wangchuck, Sonam Chhoden 1953- *WhoAsAP 91, WhoWor 93*
Wangchuk, Druk Gyalpo Jigme Singye 1955- *WhoAsAP 91*
Wang Dan 1968- *WhoAsAP 91*
Wang Dongxing 1916- *BioIn 17*
Wangel, Lance Heywood 1960- *WhoE 93*
Wangemann, Otto 1848-1914 *Baker 92*
Wangenheim, Alice *AmWomPl*
Wangenheim, Karl-Hartmut Freiherr 1924- *WhoScE 91-3*
Wangenheim, Volker 1928- *Baker 92*
Wangenheins, Alice *AmWomPl*
Wangensteen, Stephen Lightner 1933- *WhoSSW 93*
Wanger, Beatrice *AmWomPl*
Wanger, Oliver Winston 1940- *WhoAm 92*
Wangerin, Matthew *BioIn 17*
Wangerin, Walter *BioIn 17*
Wangerin, Walter, Jr. 1944- *ScF&FL 92*
Wangermann, Jochen Rolf 1939- *WhoWor 93*
Wangermee, Robert 1920- *Baker 92*
Wang Fang *WhoWor 93*
Wang Fang 1920- *WhoAsAP 91*
Wang Hai 1925- *WhoAsAP 91*
Wang Hanbin 1926- *WhoAsAP 91*
Wang Hongwen 1934?-1992 *NewYTBS 92 [port]*
Wang Jialiu 1929- *WhoAsAP 91*
Wang Jingwei 1883-1944 *DcTwHis*
Wang Juntao *BioIn 17*
Wang Kai Yuen, Dr. 1947- *WhoAsAP 91*
Wangler, William C. 1929- *WhoIns 93*

Wangler, William Clarence 1929- St&PR 93, WhoAm 92
Wanglie, Helga d1991 BioIn 17
Wang Luolin WhoAsAP 91
Wang Maolin 1934- WhoAsAP 91
Wang Meng BioIn 17
Wang Meng 1934- WhoAsAP 91
Wang Ming 1904?-1974 BioIn 17
Wang Qun 1926- WhoAsAP 91
Wang Renzhi 1933- WhoAsAP 91
Wang Renzhong d1992 NewYTBS 92
Wang Renzhong 1917- WhoAsAP 91
Wang Renzhong 1917-1992 BioIn 17
Wang Ruilin 1929- WhoAsAP 91
Wang Senhao 1932- WhoAsAP 91
Wangsgard, Robert Louis 1915- WhoAm 92
Wang Shusen 1916-1989 BioIn 17
Wang Tao 1932- WhoAsAP 91
Wang Xuezhen 1927- WhoAsAP 91
Wang Yani BioIn 17
Wang Yongzhi 1932- BioIn 17
Wang Youcai 1966- WhoAsAP 91
Wang Yuefeng 1932- WhoAsAP 91
Wang Yun-ch'u 1154-1214 HarEnMi
Wang Zhaoguo 1940- WhoAsAP 91
Wang Zhen 1908- WhoWor 93
Wang Zhen 1909- WhoAsAP 91
Wang Zhenguo BioIn 17
Wang Zhiren BioIn 17
Wang Zhongyu 1933- WhoAsAP 91
Wanhill, Russell James Hugh 1943- WhoWor 93
Wanhill, Stephen Robert Charles WhoScE 91-1
Waniak, Donna Marie Law&B 92
Waniek, Marilyn Nelson 1946- BioIn 17, DcLB 120 [port], WhoAmW 93, WhoWrEP 92
Waniewski, Eugene C. 1946- St&PR 93
Waniurski, Jozef 1942- WhoWor 93
Wanjau, Paul Kahuho 1962- WhoWor 93
Wanjik, Paul 1952- WhoAsAP 91
Wank, Gerald Sidney 1925- WhoAm 92
Wankat, Phillip Charles 1944- WhoAm 92
Wanke, Klaus 1933- WhoWor 93
Wankel, Charles Bernhard 1948- WhoE 93
Wankmiller, James J. 1954- St&PR 93
Wankowicz, Melchior 1892-1974 PolBiDi
Wankowicz, Walenty 1799-1842 PolBiDi
Wanless, John d1712? Baker 92
Wanless, Thomas d1721
See Wanless, John d1712? Baker 92
Wanley, Humphrey 1672-1726 BioIn 17
Wan Li 1916- WhoAsAP 91
Wan Li 1917- WhoWor 93
Wann, David L. 1949- WhoWrEP 92
Wann, Garry S. Law&B 92
Wannall, Walter Raymond, III 1944- WhoE 93
Wannan, Bill 1915- ScF&FL 92
Wannan, William F. ScF&FL 92
Wannenmacher, Johannes c. 1485-1551 Baker 92
Wanner, James Alan Law&B 92
Wanner, James E. 1930- St&PR 93
Wanninen, Erkki Verner 1925- WhoScE 91-4
Wannop, William Bryan 1937- WhoUN 92
Wanrooy, Willem Frederik 1925- WhoWrEP 92
Wan Runnan BioIn 17
Wansel, Dexter SoulM
Wanser, David Ray 1947- WhoSSW 93
Wan Shaofen 1931- WhoAsAP 91
Wanski, Jan 1762-1800 PolBiDi
Wansley, William Dunn 1962- WhoSSW 93
Wanthal, Theodore Ray 1937- St&PR 93
Wantland, Karen Lee 1970- WhoAmW 93
Wantland, William Charles 1934- WhoAm 92
Wantuck, Karen E. 1940- WhoSSW 93
Wantz, George Edward 1923- WhoE 93
Wan Ullok, Stephen Timothy 1938- WhoAsAP 91
Wanvig, James Louis 1921- WhoAm 92
Wan-yen A-ku-ta c. 1069-1123 HarEnMi
Wanzer, Mary Kathryn 1942- WhoAmW 93
Wapato, S. Timothy 1935- WhoAm 92
Wapenaar, K.E.D. 1955- WhoScE 91-3
Wapenaar, Willem P. 1941- WhoScE 91-3
Wapenhans, Willi Adolf 1931- WhoAm 92
Waplennik, Carl Francis 1926- WhoAm 92
Wapler, Vincent 1947- WhoWor 93
Waples, David Lloyd 1941- WhoSSW 93
Waples, Douglas 1893-1978 BioIn 17
Waples, John Christopher 1940- St&PR 93
Wapnarski, Robert David 1952- WhoSSW 93
Wapner, Beth M. Law&B 92
Wapner, Joseph A. 1919- WhoAm 92
Wapner, Seymour 1917- WhoAm 92
Wappaus, Herbert Edward 1939- St&PR 93
War SoulM
War, Thomas L. 1914- St&PR 93
Warady, Timothy S. 1948- St&PR 93
Warakomski, Alphonse Walter Joseph, Jr. 1943- WhoWor 93
Waranch, Seeman WhoIns 93
Warantz, Elisa Law&B 92
Wara-Wasowski, Janusz Bogumil 1935- WhoScE 91-4
Warbel, Samuel 1930- St&PR 93
Warbinton, Douglas L. 1952- St&PR 93
Warbritton, Scott 1951- St&PR 93
Warburg, Bettina 1900-1990 BioIn 17
Warburg, Edward M. M. 1908-1992 NewYTBS 92 [port]
Warburg, Eric M. 1900-1990 BioIn 17
Warburg, Paul M. 1868-1932 BioIn 17
Warburton, Elizabeth A.M. 1938- WhoUN 92
Warburton, Irvine Eugene 1911-1982 BiDAMSp 1989
Warburton, Peter 1813-1889 Expl 93
Warburton, Ralph Joseph 1935- WhoAm 92, WhoSSW 93, WhoWor 93
Warburton, Samuel 1943- St&PR 93
Warburton, William 1698-1779 BioIn 17
Warch, George W. 1912- WhoIns 93
Warch, Richard 1939- WhoAm 92
Warchalowski, Andrzej 1927- WhoScE 91-4
Warchol, Kenneth J. 1943- WhoE 93
Warcup, Howard J. 1932- St&PR 93
Warczak, James E. Law&B 92
Ward, A.S. WhoScE 91-1
Ward, Aileen 1919- BioIn 17
Ward, Alan S. 1931- WhoAm 92
Ward, Alex 1944- WhoAm 92
Ward, Andrew 1946- BioIn 17
Ward, Anita Lucine 1938- WhoAmW 93
Ward, Annette Persis AmWomPl
Ward, Anthony L. 1939- St&PR 93
Ward, Anthony Thomas 1941- WhoE 93
Ward, Artemas 1727-1800 HarEnMi
Ward, Arthur Henry ScF&FL 92
Ward, Arthur Sarsfield ScF&FL 92
Ward, B. ScF&FL 92
Ward, Barbara Conner 1940- WhoAmW 93
Ward, Bennie Franklin Leon 1948- WhoSSW 93
Ward, Bill 1948-
See Black Sabbath ConMus 9
Ward, Billy, & the Dominoes SoulM
Ward, Bruce E. 1947- St&PR 93
Ward, C. Daniel Law&B 92
Ward, Calvin Eugene 1944- WhoSSW 93
Ward, Carolyn Nancy 1956- WhoAmW 93
Ward, Charles Philip 1937- WhoWor 93
Ward, Charles W.R. WhoScE 91-1
Ward, Charlotte Berkley Reed 1929- WhoSSW 93
Ward, Chester Lawrence 1932- WhoAm 92
Ward, Claude 1930- St&PR 93
Ward, Cynthia Ruth 1960- WhoAmW 93
Ward, D.A. Law&B 92
Ward, Daniel Patrick 1918- WhoAm 92
Ward, Daniel Thomas 1942- WhoAm 92, WhoWor 93
Ward, Dave 1931- St&PR 93
Ward, Dave Lee 1929- WhoSSW 93
Ward, David 1922-1983 Baker 92, OxDcOp
Ward, David 1938- WhoAm 92
Ward, David Allen 1933- WhoAm 92
Ward, David Pearce 1953- WhoSSW 93
Ward, David S. 1945- MiSFD 9
Ward, David Schad 1947- WhoAm 92
Ward, Debora Elliott 1954- WhoE 93
Ward, Deborah C. Law&B 92
Ward, Declan 1951- WhoScE 91-3
Ward, Denise Yvonne 1952- WhoAmW 93
Ward, Donald Butler 1919- WhoAm 92
Ward, Doris Elizabeth 1935- WhoE 93
Ward, Douglas Alfred 1945- WhoE 93
Ward, E. D. MajAI, ScF&FL 92, SmATA 70
Ward, Ed MajAI
Ward, Edgar W. d1991 BioIn 17
Ward, Edith Miller 1911- WhoAmW 93
Ward, Edward ScF&FL 92
Ward, Edward, Jr. 1950- St&PR 93
Ward, Elizabeth Stuart Phelps 1844-1911 AmWomPl, BioIn 17
Ward, Erica Anne 1950- WhoAm 92, WhoAmW 93
Ward, Eugene W. Law&B 92
Ward, Ferdinand BioIn 17
Ward, Frank Jay 1934- St&PR 93, WhoAm 92
Ward, Frederick Townsend 1831-1862 BioIn 17
Ward, G. William 1931- St&PR 93
Ward, Gail Marie 1948- WhoAmW 93
Ward, Galen E. Law&B 92
Ward, Gene d1992 BioIn 17, NewYTBS 92
Ward, Geoffrey Champion 1940- WhoAm 92, WhoWrEP 92
Ward, George B. P., Jr. 1935- St&PR 93
Ward, George Truman 1927- WhoSSW 93
Ward, Glenyse 1949- BioIn 17
Ward, Gordon Roy 1938- WhoWor 93
Ward, Grace Anne 1951- WhoSSW 93
Ward, Harold ScF&FL 92
Ward, Harry Merrill 1929- WhoSSW 93
Ward, Harry Orrin 1954- WhoSSW 93
Ward, Harry Pfeffer 1933- WhoAm 92
Ward, Haskell George 1940- WhoE 93
Ward, Helen 1916- BioIn 17
Ward, Helen 1962- SmATA 72 [port]
Ward, Henry Alfred 1946- WhoSSW 93
Ward, Herman Matthew 1914- ConAu 39NR
Ward, Hiley Henry WhoWrEP 92
Ward, Hiley Henry 1929- WhoAm 92, WhoWrEP 92
Ward, Hiram Hamilton 1923- WhoAm 92, WhoSSW 93
Ward, Horace Taliaferro 1927- AfrAmBi, WhoAm 92
Ward, Humphry, Mrs. 1851-1920 BioIn 17
Ward, Ian MacMillan WhoScE 91-1
Ward, Irene 1895-1980 BioIn 17
Ward, J. Dexter 1948- St&PR 93
Ward, J. Richard 1933- St&PR 93
Ward, J.T. WhoScE 91-1
Ward, Jack Francis 1921- WhoWor 93
Ward, Jackie M. WhoAm 92
Ward, James Arthur, III 1941- WhoSSW 93
Ward, James J., Jr. Law&B 92
Ward, James M. 1951- ScF&FL 92
Ward, James V. 1928- WhoSSW 93
Ward, Jamye Boone Law&B 92
Ward, Jane BioIn 17
Ward, Jane Pamela 1948- WhoAmW 93
Ward, Janet Lynn 1955- WhoAmW 93, WhoSSW 93
Ward, Janice Kathryn St&PR 93
Ward, Jasper Dudley, III 1921- WhoAm 92
Ward, Jay d1989 BioIn 17
Ward, Jeanine Ann 1966- WhoSSW 93
Ward, Jeanine Elizabeth 1952- WhoAmW 93
Ward, Jeanne Patricia 1945- WhoAmW 93
Ward, Jeannette Poole 1932- WhoAmW 93
Ward, Jeffrey W. Law&B 92
Ward, Jennifer C. 1944- WhoAmW 93
Ward, Jennifer Margaret WhoScE 91-1
Ward, Jerry Leroy 1945- WhoAm 92
Ward, Joan Gaye WhoAmW 93
Ward, John 1571?-1638? Baker 92
Ward, John Brooks 1946- St&PR 93
Ward, John C. 1963- BlkAuII 92
Ward, John D. 1945- St&PR 93
Ward, John Ellsworth 1930- St&PR 93
Ward, John F. 1958- WhoAm 92
Ward, John J.B. 1944- WhoScE 91-1
Ward, John LeRoy 1949- WhoE 93
Ward, John M(ilton) 1917- Baker 92
Ward, John Milton 1917- WhoAm 92
Ward, John Montgomery 1860-1925 BioIn 17
Ward, John Orson 1942- WhoAm 92
Ward, John P. Law&B 92
Ward, John Paul 1930- WhoAm 92
Ward, John Quincy Adams 1830-1910 GayN
Ward, John Robert 1923- WhoAm 92
Ward, John S. 1916- St&PR 93
Ward, John Thomas 1925- WhoE 93
Ward, John W. Law&B 92
Ward, John Wesley 1925- WhoAm 92, WhoWor 93
Ward, John Whiteley 1943- WhoE 93
Ward, Joseph A. 1934- St&PR 93
Ward, Joseph George 1856-1930 DcTwHis
Ward, Joseph Jorgenson 1946- WhoAm 92
Ward, Joseph Simeon 1925- WhoAm 92, WhoSSW 93
Ward, Joshua J. Law&B 92
Ward, Judith Ann 1946- WhoSSW 93
Ward, Judith Linda Burton 1953- WhoAmW 93
Ward, Judy Kitchen 1940- WhoAmW 93
Ward, Karen Stafford 1944- WhoAmW 93
Ward, Karin 1936- St&PR 93
Ward, (John Stephen) Keith 1938- ConAu 37NR
Ward, Ken 1949- ConAu 136
Ward, Kenneth Gray 1946- St&PR 93
Ward, Kevin L. Law&B 92
Ward, L.E. 1944- WhoWrEP 92
Ward, L. Taylor, III Law&B 92
Ward, Larry Law&B 92
Ward, Lena Kay WhoScE 91-1
Ward, Leonard George 1930- WhoSSW 93
Ward, Leslie Allyson 1946- WhoAm 92, WhoAmW 93
Ward, Lester Frank 1841-1913 GayN
Ward, Lester Lowe, Jr. 1930- WhoAm 92
Ward, Linda Elaine 1949- WhoAmW 93
Ward, Llewellyn Orcutt, III 1930- WhoAm 92, WhoSSW 93, WhoWor 93
Ward, Lloyd Arthur 1927- St&PR 93
Ward, Loretta Jean 1939- WhoAmW 93
Ward, Louis Emmerson 1918- WhoAm 92
Ward, Louis L. 1919- St&PR 93
Ward, Louis Larrick 1920- WhoAm 92
Ward, Lucile Ahrens AmWomPl
Ward, Lynd 1905-1985 ScF&FL 92
Ward, Lynd (Kendall) 1905-1985 MajAI [port]
Ward, Marcus L. 1812-1884 PolPar
Ward, Marcus Lawrence 1812-1884 BioIn 17
Ward, Maria Frances 1949- WhoAmW 93
Ward, Marilyn Kay 1961- WhoAmW 93
Ward, Marion Haggard 1924- WhoAm 92
Ward, Mark Lee, Sr. 1958- WhoWrEP 92
Ward, Marvin Martin 1914- WhoSSW 93
Ward, Mary Augusta Arnold 1851-1920 BioIn 17
Ward, Mary E. Law&B 92
Ward, Mary Patsel 1957- WhoSSW 93
Ward, Matthew BioIn 17
Ward, Maureen St&PR 93
Ward, Maxwell Colin Bernard 1949- WhoWor 93
Ward, McLain BioIn 17
Ward, Michael L. Law&B 92
Ward, Michael V. Law&B 92
Ward, Michelle Annette 1961- WhoAmW 93
Ward, Milton Hawkins 1932- St&PR 93
Ward, Muriel AmWomPl
Ward, Nancy Joan 1939- WhoWrEP 92
Ward, Nelson 1941- St&PR 93
Ward, Nicholas Anthony 1936- WhoUN 92
Ward, Nicholas Donnell 1941- WhoAm 92
Ward, Nick MiSFD 9
Ward, Norman BioIn 17
Ward, Norman 1918- WhoCanL 92
Ward, Oliver O. 1935- St&PR 93
Ward, Paul Hutchins 1928- WhoAm 92
Ward, Penny L. 1961- WhoWrEP 92
Ward, Peter Allan 1934- WhoAm 92
Ward, Peter Matthew 1951- WhoWor 93
Ward, Peter Minton 1924- WhoAm 92
Ward, Philip Stewart 1944- St&PR 93
Ward, Phillip Wayne 1935- WhoSSW 93
Ward, Rachel 1957- WhoAmW 93
Ward, Renee Janet 1964- WhoAmW 93
Ward, Richard 1943- WhoUN 92
Ward, Richard Heron 1910-1969 ScF&FL 92
Ward, Richard Hurley 1939- WhoWor 93
Ward, Richard James 1932- WhoSSW 93
Ward, Richard James 1936- WhoScE 91-1
Ward, Richard Joseph 1921- WhoAm 92
Ward, Richard S. Law&B 92
Ward, Richard S. 1940- St&PR 93, WhoAm 92
Ward, Richard Storer 1920- WhoAm 92
Ward, Richard Vance, Jr. 1929- WhoAm 92
Ward, Robert 1917- IntDcOp, WhoAm 92
Ward, Robert Allen 1940- WhoAm 92
Ward, Robert Earle Law&B 92
Ward, Robert Edward 1916- WhoAm 92
Ward, Robert (Eugene) 1917- Baker 92
Ward, Robert Franklin 1949- WhoAm 92
Ward, Robert James 1926- St&PR 93
Ward, Robert Joseph 1926- WhoAm 92, WhoE 93
Ward, Robert Ross 1943- WhoWrEP 92
Ward, Robertson, Jr. 1922- WhoAm 92
Ward, Rodman, Jr. 1934- WhoAm 92
Ward, Roger BioIn 17
Ward, Roger Barry 1954- WhoAm 92
Ward, Roger Coursen 1922- WhoAm 92
Ward, Roscoe Fredrick 1930- WhoAm 92
Ward, Roy Charles WhoScE 91-1
Ward, Russell 1924- WhoE 93
Ward, S. Joseph 1928- St&PR 93
Ward, Samuel Augustus 1848-1903 Baker 92
Ward, Sela BioIn 17
Ward, Seth Crawford 1961- WhoE 93
Ward, Sharon Lynne 1942- WhoAmW 93
Ward, Sidney Charles 1929- WhoSSW 93
Ward, Simon 1941- WhoWor 93
Ward, Susan Bayer 1944- WhoWrEP 92
Ward, Susan Marie 1954- WhoAmW 93
Ward, Suzanne Mary 1956- WhoAmW 93
Ward, Sylvan Donald 1909- WhoAm 92
Ward, Teresa JoAnne 1960- WhoE 93
Ward, Thomas E. Law&B 92
Ward, Thomas Francis 1934- St&PR 93, WhoE 93
Ward, Thomas Francis 1961- WhoSSW 93

Ward, Thomas Jerome 1936- *St&PR 93, WhoAm 92*
Ward, Thomas Joseph 1948- *WhoE 93*
Ward, Thomas Julian 1930- *WhoE 93*
Ward, Thomas Leon 1930- *WhoAm 92*
Ward, Thomas Michael *Law&B 92*
Ward, Thomas P. 1931- *St&PR 93*
Ward, Thomas Richard 1940- *St&PR 93*
Ward, Thomas W. 1934- *St&PR 93*
Ward, Timothy 1938- *WhoAsAP 91*
Ward, Tom *MajAI*
Ward, Vincent 1956- *MiSFD 9*
Ward, Virginia Lee 1944- *WhoAmW 93*
Ward, W. Dixon *BioIn 17*
Ward, Wallace Dixon 1924- *WhoAm 92*
Ward, Walter Bernard, Jr. 1927- *St&PR 93*
Ward, William Binnington 1917- *WhoAm 92*
Ward, William C. 1961- *St&PR 93*
Ward, William David 1943- *St&PR 93*
Ward, William E. *WhoSSW 93*
Ward, William Forrest, Jr. 1945- *St&PR 93*
Ward, William Francis 1951- *WhoEmL 93*
Ward, William Francis, Jr. 1928- *WhoAm 92*
Ward, William Herbert 1931- *St&PR 93*
Ward, William I., Jr. *Law&B 92*
Ward, William Joseph 1928- *WhoSSW 93*
Ward, William L. *Law&B 92*
Ward, William L. 1936- *WhoIns 93*
Ward, William P. *St&PR 93*
Ward, William Quincy 1924- *WhoSSW 93*
Ward, William R., Jr. 1928- *St&PR 93*
Ward, William Reed 1918- *WhoAm 92*
Ward, William Weaver 1924- *WhoE 93*
Ward, Windsor Earl 1939- *St&PR 93*
Ward, Winifred Duncan *AmWomPl*
Ward, Wm. Michael 1957- *WhoWrEP 92*
Ward, Yvette Hennig 1910- *WhoAm 92*
Warda, Mark 1952- *WhoSSW 93, WhoWrEP 92*
Warde, Beatrice *ScF&FL 92*
Warde, George Andres 1921- *WhoAm 92*
Warde, Margaret *AmWomPl*
Warde, Shirley *AmWomPl*
Warde, William F. *ConAu 139*
Wardell, Charles Willard Bennett, III 1945- *St&PR 93, WhoAm 92*
Wardell, Christine A. *Law&B 92*
Wardell, David *Law&B 92*
Wardell, J. William 1938- *WhoAm 92*
Wardell, James Lewis 1939- *WhoWor 93*
Wardell, Joe Russell, Jr. 1929- *WhoAm 92, WhoE 93*
Wardell, John Watson 1929- *WhoWor 93*
Wardell, Richard N. *Law&B 92*
Wardell, Ricky Ray 1949- *WhoSSW 93*
Wardell, Weston B., Jr. *Law&B 92*
Wardell, William Michael 1938- *WhoAm 92*
Warden, Gary Russell 1950- *WhoE 93, WhoWor 93*
Warden, Hays R. 1942- *St&PR 93*
Warden, Herbert Edgar 1920- *WhoAm 92*
Warden, Jack 1920- *WhoAm 92*
Warden, James Bryce 1937- *St&PR 93*
Warden, John L. 1941- *WhoAm 92, WhoWor 93*
Warden, Michael L. 1950- *St&PR 93*
Warden, Richard Dana 1931- *WhoAm 92*
Warden, William R. 1958- *St&PR 93*
Warder, Charles A. 1933- *St&PR 93*
Warder, Lee Oran 1949- *St&PR 93*
Warder, Richard Currey, Jr. 1936- *WhoAm 92*
Ward-Jackson, Adrian *BioIn 17*
Ward-Jackson, Adrian 1950-1991 *AnObit 1991*
Wardlaw, Alastair Connell *WhoScE 91-1*
Wardlaw, Andrew Bowie, Jr. 1944- *WhoE 93*
Wardlaw, Anita Louise *WhoWrEP 92*
Wardlaw, Frank Harper 1913-1989 *BioIn 17*
Wardlaw, Jack 1907- *WhoIns 93, WhoSSW 93*
Wardlaw, John Waller, Sr. 1907- *WhoSSW 93*
Wardle, Charles Edward 1944- *WhoSSW 93*
Wardle, John Carruthers 1944- *WhoWor 93*
Wardle, Ralph 1909-1988 *BioIn 17*
Wardley, George P. *Law&B 92*
Wardlow, Anne *Law&B 92*
Wardman, Ervin 1865-1923 *JrnUS*
Wardman, Gordon *ScF&FL 92*
Wardman, Gordon 1948- *ConAu 136*
Wardman, Peter 1943- *WhoScE 91-1*
Ward-McLemore, Ethel 1908- *WhoAmW 93, WhoSSW 93, WhoWor 93*
Ward of North Tyneside, Baroness 1895-1980 *BioIn 17*
Wardojo 1933- *WhoAsAP 91*
Wardrop, John Glen *BioIn 17*
Wardrop, Terrence *Law&B 92*
Wardrop, Terrence H. 1944- *St&PR 93*
Wardropper, Bruce Wear 1919- *WhoAm 92*
Wardropper, Ian (Bruce) 1951- *ConAu 137, WhoAm 92*
Ward-Shaw, Sheila Theresa 1951- *WhoAmW 93*
Ward-Steinman, David 1936- *Baker 92, WhoAm 92*
Ward-Steinman, Irving 1905- *WhoSSW 93*
Ward Thompson, Catharine J. *WhoScE 91-1*
Wardwell, Allen 1935- *WhoAm 92*
Wardwell, George J. *Law&B 92*
Wardwell, William Francis 1944- *St&PR 93*
Wardynski, Edmund *St&PR 93*
Wardynski, Raymond Francis 1921- *St&PR 93*
Wardzinski, Georgean M. 1954- *St&PR 93*
Wardzinski, Stephen T. *Law&B 92*
Ware, Abbot K. 1914- *St&PR 93*
Ware, Alice Holdship *AmWomPl*
Ware, Alton Douglas 1943- *St&PR 93*
Ware, Andre *BioIn 17*
Ware, Betty Fletcher 1932- *WhoSSW 93*
Ware, Brendan John 1932- *WhoAm 92*
Ware, Carl 1943- *WhoAm 92*
Ware, Caroline *BioIn 17*
Ware, Clyde 1936- *MiSFD 9*
Ware, D. Clifton 1937- *WhoAm 92*
Ware, Dyahanne *Law&B 92*
Ware, E. Frank 1944- *St&PR 93*
Ware, Edward Winslow 1919- *St&PR 93*
Ware, Elizabeth Fisher 1915- *WhoAmW 93, WhoSSW 93*
Ware, Eugene Fitch 1841-1911 *BioIn 17*
Ware, Guilford Dudley 1925- *St&PR 93*
Ware, Harriet 1877-1962 *Baker 92*
Ware, Henry 1764-1845 *BioIn 17*
Ware, James Edwin 1925- *WhoAm 92*
Ware, James Gareth 1929- *WhoSSW 93*
Ware, James T. 1926- *WhoSSW 93*
Ware, John David 1947- *WhoSSW 93*
Ware, John Rosswork 1922- *WhoAm 92*
Ware, Joyce *BioIn 17*
Ware, LaVern Willette 1958- *WhoAmW 93*
Ware, Leon *SoulM*
Ware, Leon (Vernon) 1909- *DcAmChF 1960*
Ware, Malcolm *ScF&FL 92*
Ware, Marcus John 1904- *WhoAm 92*
Ware, Margaret Isabel Rose 1915- *WhoAmW 93*
Ware, Mary Catherine 1945- *WhoAmW 93*
Ware, Mitchell 1933- *WhoAm 92*
Ware, Pamela R. 1963- *WhoAmW 93*
Ware, Paul A. 1946- *St&PR 93*
Ware, Paul W. 1946- *St&PR 93*
Ware, Pearl Cunningham 1939- *WhoAmW 93*
Ware, Randolph Wayne 1951- *WhoSSW 93*
Ware, Richard Anderson 1919- *WhoAm 92*
Ware, Robert 1958- *WhoE 93*
Ware, Roger B. 1934- *St&PR 93*
Ware, Sandra Cole 1935- *WhoE 93*
Ware, Susan 1962- *WhoAmW 93*
Ware, Thaddeus Van 1935- *WhoAm 92*
Ware, Willis Howard 1920- *WhoAm 92*
Ware-Campbell, Louise *WhoWrEP 92*
Wareham, A.B. 1943- *St&PR 93*
Wareham, James L. 1939- *St&PR 93, WhoAm 92, WhoSSW 93*
Wareing, Lavere Hansen 1924- *St&PR 93*
Wareing, Peter Staub 1951- *St&PR 93*
Waren, Allan David 1935- *WhoWor 93*
Waren, Jack L. 1936- *St&PR 93*
Waren, Stanley A. 1919- *WhoAm 92*
Warfel, Daniel L. 1947- *St&PR 93*
Warfield, Dale E. 1943- *St&PR 93*
Warfield, Edwin, III 1924- *St&PR 93*
Warfield, Gerald Alexander 1940- *WhoAm 92*
Warfield, John Nelson 1925- *WhoAm 92*
Warfield, Mark R. *Law&B 92*
Warfield, Marsha 1955- *BioIn 17*
Warfield, Paul *BioIn 17*
Warfield, Sandra 1929- *Baker 92*
Warfield, Wallis 1896-1986 *BioIn 17*
Warfield, Wayne *ScF&FL 92*
Warfield, William (Caesar) 1920- *Baker 92, WhoAm 92*
Warfield, William H. d1992 *NewYTBS 92*
Warfield, William H. 1937- *St&PR 93*
Warga, David 1932- *WhoE 93*
Warga, Jack 1922- *WhoAm 92, WhoE 93*
Wargnier, Regis *MiSFD 9*
Wargo, Chris A. 1948- *St&PR 93*
Wargo, Elmer *Law&B 92*
Warhanek, Hans 1926- *WhoScE 91-4*
Warheit, Israel Albert 1912-1973 *BioIn 17*
Warhol, Andy 1927-1987 *MiSFD 9N*
Warhol, Andy 1928?-1987 *BioIn 17*
Warhola, Andrew 1927-1987 *MiSFD 9N*
Warhover, Stephen H. 1944- *St&PR 93*
Warhover, Stephen Hunt 1944- *WhoAm 92*
Waricha, Jean *ScF&FL 92*
Warin, J.W. *WhoScE 91-1*
Warin, Oliver N. 1931- *St&PR 93*
Waring, Anthony John 1938- *WhoWor 93*
Waring, Charles Douglas 1923- *St&PR 93*
Waring, Fred(eric Malcolm) 1900-1984 *Baker 92*
Waring, Glenn Howell 1948- *St&PR 93*
Waring, J. Waties 1880-1968 *EncAACR*
Waring, John Alfred 1913- *WhoSSW 93, WhoWor 93*
Waring, Mowton LeCompte 1906-1990 *BioIn 17*
Waring, Richard Babcock 1955- *WhoWrEP 92*
Waring, Thomas A. 1947- *St&PR 93*
Waring, Walter Weyler 1917- *WhoAm 92*
Waring, William Michael 1945- *WhoSSW 93*
Waring, William Winburn 1923- *WhoAm 92*
Warioba, Joseph Sinde 1940- *WhoAfr, WhoWor 93*
Waris, Michael, Jr. 1921- *WhoAm 92*
Wark, Allen W. *Law&B 92*
Wark, Robert Rodger 1924- *WhoAm 92*
Wark, Thomas Edison 1934- *WhoAm 92*
Warkany, Josef d1992 *NewYTBS 92*
Warley, Deas H. *St&PR 93*
Warlich, Reinhold von 1877-1939 *Baker 92*
Warlick, Chris *BioIn 17*
Warlick, Robert Patterson 1924- *WhoAm 92*
Warlick, Roger Kinney 1930- *WhoAm 92*
Warlimont, Walther 1895- *BioIn 17*
Warlitner, Todd Jeffrey 1962- *WhoSSW 93*
Warlock, Peter *Baker 92*
Warlow, Charles P. *WhoScE 91-1*
Warm, Stephen F. *St&PR 93*
Warman, C. Dale 1929- *WhoAm 92*
Warman, E.A. 1935- *WhoScE 91-1*
Warmath, John T., Jr. 1929- *WhoIns 93*
Warmath, John Thomas, Jr. 1929- *St&PR 93, WhoAm 92*
Warmbold, David A. *Law&B 92*
Warmbrand, Martin Joseph 1926- *WhoE 93*
Warmbrod, James Robert 1929- *WhoAm 92*
Warmenhoven, Daniel John 1950- *WhoAm 92*
Warmerdam, Cornelius *BioIn 17*
Warmington, Robert Vernon *WhoScE 91-1*
Warmus, Carolyn *BioIn 17*
Warmuth, Walter Heinz 1948- *WhoWor 93*
Warn, Emily 1953- *WhoWrEP 92*
Warn, Grace Helen 1922- *WhoAmW 93*
Warn, Michael Thurston 1952- *St&PR 93*
Warnath, Charles F. *BioIn 17*
Warnath, Maxine Ammer 1928- *WhoAmW 93*
Warncke, Esbern 1939- *WhoWor 93*
Warne, David W. 1940- *St&PR 93*
Warne, Richard Arthur 1932- *St&PR 93*
Warne, Ronson Joseph 1930- *WhoWor 93*
Warne, V.B. 1948- *WhoScE 91-1*
Warne, William Elmo 1905- *WhoAm 92, WhoWor 93*
Warnecke, Hans-Jurgen 1934- *WhoScE 91-3*
Warnecke, Richard 1953- *St&PR 93*
Warneke, Lothar 1936- *DrEEuF*
Warnement, Pamela Pearson *Law&B 92*
Warnemunde, Bradley L. 1933- *St&PR 93*
Warnemunde, Bradley Lee 1933- *WhoAm 92, WhoWor 93*
Warner, Adolphe Joseph 1917- *WhoE 93*
Warner, Alfred *WhoScE 91-3*
Warner, Alice Sizer 1929- *WhoAmW 93, WhoE 93*
Warner, Anne *AmWomPl*
Warner, Anne R. *WhoAmW 93*
Warner, Bonny *BioIn 17*
Warner, Bradford Arnold 1910- *WhoAm 92*
Warner, Brainard H. 1959- *St&PR 93*
Warner, Bruce E. 1912- *St&PR 93*
Warner, Cari *BioIn 17*
Warner, Carolyn *BioIn 17*
Warner, Cecil Randolph, Jr. 1929- *St&PR 93, WhoAm 92, WhoSSW 93*
Warner, Charles Dudley 1829-1900 *BioIn 17*
Warner, Charles S. *WhoUN 92*
Warner, Charles Schoen 1963- *St&PR 93*
Warner, Christine Louisette *WhoScE 91-1*
Warner, Christopher J. *Law&B 92*
Warner, Colin Bertram *WhoAm 92*
Warner, Dale *BioIn 17*
Warner, David 1941- *WhoWor 93*
Warner, David K. 1950- *St&PR 93*
Warner, Dean G. 1920- *St&PR 93*
Warner, Dennis Allan 1940- *WhoAm 92*
Warner, Don Lee 1934- *WhoAm 92*
Warner, Donald Francis 1931- *WhoAm 92, WhoE 93, WhoWor 93*
Warner, Donna Sikes 1939- *WhoAmW 93*
Warner, Dorothy Ann 1960- *WhoAmW 93*
Warner, Douglas *BioIn 17*
Warner, Douglas Alexander, III 1946- *WhoAm 92, WhoE 93*
Warner, Edward P. *BioIn 17*
Warner, Edward P. 1894-1958 *EncABHB 8 [port]*
Warner, Ellen E. Kenyon *AmWomPl*
Warner, Frederick Edward *WhoScE 91-1*
Warner, George Edward *Law&B 92*
Warner, Gerald 1926- *St&PR 93*
Warner, Gerald Truscott *WhoScE 91-1*
Warner, Gertrude Chandler *AmWomPl*
Warner, Gertrude Chandler 1890-1979 *SmATA 73*
Warner, Glen W. 1940- *St&PR 93*
Warner, Gregory S. *Law&B 92*
Warner, Guy Edward, Jr. 1919- *St&PR 93*
Warner, H.B. 1876-1958 *BioIn 17*
Warner, Harold Clay, Jr. 1939- *WhoAm 92*
Warner, Harry B. 1916-1991 *BioIn 17*
Warner, Harry Hathaway 1935- *WhoAm 92*
Warner, Harry Waldo 1874-1945 *Baker 92*
Warner, J. Paul *Law&B 92*
Warner, Jack, Jr. 1916- *WhoAm 92*
Warner, Jack L. 1892-1978 *BioIn 17*
Warner, James Alan *BioIn 17*
Warner, James Daniel 1924- *WhoAm 92*
Warner, James J. 1942- *St&PR 93*
Warner, Janet Claire 1964- *WhoAmW 93*
Warner, Jerry A. 1947- *St&PR 93*
Warner, John 1942- *St&PR 93*
Warner, John Andrew 1924- *WhoAm 92*
Warner, John Edward 1936- *WhoAm 92*
Warner, John Hilliard, Jr. 1941- *WhoAm 92*
Warner, John W. 1927- *CngDr 91*
Warner, John William 1927- *WhoAm 92, WhoSSW 93*
Warner, John William 1936- *WhoAm 92*
Warner, Jonathan W., Sr. 1917- *St&PR 93*
Warner, Joseph Patrick 1937- *WhoSSW 93*
Warner, Judith Kay 1940- *WhoAmW 93*
Warner, Julie *BioIn 17, ConTFT 10*
Warner, Kenneth E. 1947- *WhoAm 92*
Warner, Kenneth Wilson, Jr. 1928- *WhoAm 92*
Warner, Laverne 1941- *WhoSSW 93*
Warner, Lawrence Askew 1933- *St&PR 93*
Warner, Lee Marlene 1942- *WhoSSW 93*
Warner, Malcolm-Jamal *BioIn 17*
Warner, Malcolm-Jamal 1970- *ConTFT 10, WhoAm 92*
Warner, Martin 1940- *ConAu 137*
Warner, Matt 1864-1938 *BioIn 17*
Warner, Michael *ScF&FL 92*
Warner, Mignon *ScF&FL 92*
Warner, Miner Hill 1942- *WhoAm 92*
Warner, Nelson Alfred 1940- *WhoSSW 93*
Warner, Olin Levi 1844-1896 *GayN*
Warner, Peter David 1942- *WhoAm 92*
Warner, Philip 1914- *ConAu 40NR*
Warner, R.D. *ScF&FL 92*
Warner, Rachel 1952- *WhoAmW 93*
Warner, Ralph E. *BioIn 17*
Warner, Rawleigh, Jr. 1921- *WhoAm 92*
Warner, Reginald E. *ScF&FL 92*
Warner, Rex 1905-1986 *ScF&FL 92*
Warner, Richard David 1943- *WhoAm 92*
Warner, Richard Patrick 1951- *WhoSSW 93*
Warner, Richard Vance 1929- *St&PR 93*
Warner, Robert d1992 *NewYTBS 92*
Warner, Robert 1912-1992 *BioIn 17*
Warner, Robert Anio 1966- *WhoE 93*
Warner, Robert Mark 1927- *WhoAm 92*
Warner, Robert S. 1907- *WhoAm 92*
Warner, Rollin Miles, Jr. 1930- *WhoWor 93*
Warner, Ronald Douglass 1946- *WhoSSW 93*
Warner, Russell Stuart 1924- *St&PR 93*
Warner, Sam Bass, Jr. 1928- *ConAu 39NR*
Warner, Sandy *BioIn 17*
Warner, Seth L. 1927- *WhoAm 92, WhoSSW 93*
Warner, Sharon Oard 1952- *ConAu 138*
Warner, Sidney R. 1935- *St&PR 93*
Warner, Sidney Taylor 1934- *St&PR 93*
Warner, Susan 1940- *WhoAmW 93*
Warner, Susan F. *Law&B 92*
Warner, Susan Marie 1959- *WhoAmW 93*
Warner, Sylvia Ashton- 1908-1984 *BioIn 17*
Warner, Sylvia Townsend 1893-1978 *BioIn 17, ScF&FL 92*

Warner, Theodore Kugler, Jr. 1909- *WhoAm 92*
Warner, Thomas S. 1949- *St&PR 93*
Warner, Tucker H. 1932- *St&PR 93*
Warner, W. David 1931- *WhoE 93*
Warner, W. Lloyd 1898-1970 *IntDcAn*
Warner, Wellman Joel 1897-1990 *BioIn 17*
Warner, William Diaz 1929- *WhoAm 92*
Warner, William Eaton 1954- *WhoWrEP 92*
Warner, William H. 1944- *St&PR 93*
Warner, William Hamer 1929- *WhoAm 92*
Warner, William S. 1924- *St&PR 93*
Warner, Willis Lee 1930- *WhoWor 93*
Warner, Wilson Keith 1930- *WhoWor 93*
Warneryd, Karl-Erik 1927- *WhoWor 93*
Warnes, Anthony Michael *WhoScE 91-1*
Warnick, John Peter 1946- *St&PR 93*
Warnick, Jordan Edward 1942- *WhoE 93*
Warnick, Kenneth L. 1944- *St&PR 93*
Warnick, Pegg 1953- *WhoAmW 93*
Warnke, Mark R. *Law&B 92*
Warnke, Paul C. 1920- *ColdWar 1 [port]*
Warnke, Paul Culliton 1920- *WhoAm 92*
Warnke, Thomas 1943- *WhoIns 93*
Warnken, Douglas Richard 1930- *WhoAm 92*
Warnken, Virginia Muriel Thompson 1927- *WhoAmW 93*
Warnock, Benny Wyman 1943- *WhoSSW 93*
Warnock, Curt L. *Law&B 92*
Warnock, Curtlon Lee 1954- *WhoWor 93*
Warnock, Fred William 1940- *St&PR 93*
Warnock, Inez Elizabeth 1934- *St&PR 93*
Warnock, John Edward 1932- *WhoAm 92*
Warnock, John Edward 1940- *St&PR 93*
Warnock, John William 1951- *WhoSSW 93*
Warnock, Lowell Wayne *Law&B 92*
Warnock, Paul Franklin 1942- *St&PR 93*
Warnots, Henri 1832-1893 *Baker 92*
Warns, Raymond H. 1920- *WhoAm 92*
Waronka, Joseph Martin 1941- *St&PR 93*
Warp, Harold 1903- *St&PR 93*
Warr, Angela Faye 1964- *WhoAmW 93*
Warr, Don R. 1936- *St&PR 93*
Warr, Otis Sumter, Jr. 1914- *WhoSSW 93*
Warr, Peter Bryan *WhoScE 91-1*
Warr, Wendy Anne 1945- *WhoWor 93*
Warrack, Guy (Douglas Hamilton) 1900-1986 *Baker 92*
Warrack, John (Hamilton) 1928- *Baker 92*
Warrack, Maria Perini 1931- *WhoE 93*
Warrell, Lincoln A. 1931- *St&PR 93*
Warren, Adrienne Rochelle 1957- *WhoAmW 93*
Warren, Alan 1952- *ScF&FL 92*
Warren, Albert 1920- *WhoAm 92, WhoE 93, WhoWor 93*
Warren, Alvin Clifford, Jr. 1944- *WhoAm 92*
Warren, Andrea Jean 1946- *WhoWrEP 92*
Warren, Andrew *WhoScE 91-1*
Warren, Anthony C. 1941- *St&PR 93*
Warren, Anthony J. 1945- *St&PR 93*
Warren, Barbara Jones 1944- *WhoAmW 93*
Warren, Barbara Kathleen 1943- *WhoAmW 93*
Warren, Barbara Leonard 1943- *WhoWrEP 92*
Warren, Bernhardt Chaffer 1948- *St&PR 93*
Warren, Bill 1943- *ScF&FL 92*
Warren, Blossom J. *St&PR 93*
Warren, Caleb Thomas 1950- *WhoE 93*
Warren, Cathy *BioIn 17*
Warren, Chad *ScF&FL 92*
Warren, Charles 1868-1954 *OxCSupC*
Warren, Charles David 1944- *WhoAm 92*
Warren, Charles Edward, Jr. 1947- *WhoSSW 93*
Warren, Charles L. *Law&B 92*
Warren, Charles M. 1912-1990 *BioIn 17*
Warren, Charles Marquis 1917-1990 *MiSFD 9N*
Warren, Charles Robert 1948- *St&PR 93*
Warren, Cheryl Ott 1956- *WhoAmW 93*
Warren, Clifford Martin *Law&B 92*
Warren, Craig Bishop 1939- *WhoAm 92*
Warren, D. Elayne 1949- *WhoAmW 93*
Warren, David B. 1937- *BioIn 17*
Warren, David Boardman 1937- *WhoAm 92*
Warren, David Chipley 1954- *WhoSSW 93*
Warren, David Grant *WhoAm 92*
Warren, David H.D. *WhoScE 91-1*
Warren, David Hardy 1943- *WhoAm 92*
Warren, David Hugh Diggory *WhoScE 91-1*
Warren, David Liles 1943- *WhoAm 92*
Warren, David Stephen 1949- *WhoSSW 93*
Warren, Dennis R. 1943- *St&PR 93*
Warren, Deryn *MiSFD 9*
Warren, Diane *BioIn 17*
Warren, Doane Herring 1924- *St&PR 93*
Warren, Donald William 1935- *WhoAm 92*
Warren, Doris Isabelle *WhoAmW 93*
Warren, Douglas B. *Law&B 92*
Warren, Douglas Edgar 1955- *WhoSSW 93*
Warren, Earl 1891-1974 *DcTwHis, OxCSupC [port], PolPar*
Warren, Eda Anne 1948- *WhoAmW 93*
Warren, Edna *AmWomPl*
Warren, Edus Houston, Jr. 1923- *WhoAm 92*
Warren, Elgine *AmWomPl*
Warren, Elinor Remick 1900-1991 *Baker 92, BioIn 17*
Warren, Elizabeth M. *Law&B 92*
Warren, Elwood Gene 1929- *WhoSSW 93*
Warren, Evelina Marie 1963- *WhoAmW 93*
Warren, F. Michael P. 1935- *St&PR 93*
Warren, Felix 1852-1937 *BioIn 17*
Warren, Fletcher d1992 *NewYTBS 92*
Warren, Fletcher 1895-1992 *BioIn 17*
Warren, Fletcher 1896-1992 *CurBio 92N*
Warren, Frederick J. 1939- *St&PR 93*
Warren, George 1934- *ScF&FL 92*
Warren, George Frederick 1913- *WhoAm 92*
Warren, George Garry 1948- *WhoSSW 93*
Warren, George Lewis 1940- *WhoSSW 93*
Warren, George William 1828-1902 *Baker 92*
Warren, Gerald Edward 1924- *WhoAm 92*
Warren, Gerald Lee 1930- *WhoAm 92*
Warren, Gladys Evelyn *AmWomPl*
Warren, Graham Barry 1948- *WhoScE 91-1*
Warren, H. David 1937- *St&PR 93*
Warren, Harry 1893-1981 *Baker 92*
Warren, Harry Verney 1904- *WhoAm 92*
Warren, Henry L. 1940- *St&PR 93*
Warren, Ira Marshall 1950- *St&PR 93*
Warren, Irene Jacobson 1954- *WhoSSW 93*
Warren, J. Benedict 1930- *WhoAm 92*
Warren, Jack d1991 *BioIn 17*
Warren, Jack Hamilton 1921- *WhoAm 92*
Warren, Jack Keith 1934- *St&PR 93*
Warren, James C. *St&PR 93*
Warren, James Caldwell 1930- *WhoAm 92*
Warren, James Edward 1931- *St&PR 93*
Warren, James Edward, Jr. 1908- *WhoWrEP 92*
Warren, James Ronald 1925- *WhoAm 92*
Warren, James V. 1915-1990 *BioIn 17*
Warren, Jesse Francis 1944- *WhoE 93*
Warren, Joan Leigh 1957- *WhoAmW 93*
Warren, Joe G., Jr. 1945- *St&PR 93*
Warren, John Charles 1945- *St&PR 93*
Warren, John Crain *Law&B 92*
Warren, John H., III 1948- *St&PR 93*
Warren, John Hertz, III 1946- *WhoSSW 93*
Warren, John M. 1944- *St&PR 93*
Warren, John Robin 1937- *WhoWor 93*
Warren, (William) John 1937- *ConAu 138*
Warren, Johnny Wilmer 1946- *WhoWrEP 92*
Warren, Jonathan Turner 1950- *WhoE 93*
Warren, Katherine Brehme 1909-1991 *BioIn 17*
Warren, Katherine Virginia 1948- *WhoAmW 93*
Warren, Kathleen Janine 1942- *WhoWrEP 92*
Warren, Kelcy L. 1955- *St&PR 93*
Warren, Kelcy Lee 1955- *WhoAm 92*
Warren, Kenneth S. 1929- *WhoAm 92*
Warren, Larkin *BioIn 17*
Warren, Leann *BioIn 17*
Warren, Leonard 1911-1960 *Baker 92, IntDcOp, OxDcOp*
Warren, Lesley Ann *BioIn 17, WhoAm 92*
Warren, Lisbeth A. *Law&B 92*
Warren, M. Robert 1921- *St&PR 93*
Warren, Margaret Townsend 1943- *WhoAmW 93*
Warren, Marie Josephine *AmWomPl*
Warren, Mark 1938- *MiSFD 9*
Warren, Mark Lyell 1943- *WhoUN 92*
Warren, Mary Alice 1931- *WhoSSW 93*
Warren, Michael 1946- *WhoAm 92*
Warren, Mildred Elberta 1944- *WhoAmW 93*
Warren, Nagueyalti 1947- *WhoSSW 93*
Warren, Naomi White *AfrAmBi*
Warren, Nina Otero *NotHsAW 93*
Warren, Norman O., Jr. 1962- *St&PR 93*
Warren, Patricia J. 1950- *WhoAmW 93*
Warren, Patricia Nell 1936- *ScF&FL 92*
Warren, Peter 1943- *WhoE 93*
Warren, Peter Gigstad 1958- *WhoSSW 93*
Warren, Peter T. 1937- *WhoScE 91-1*
Warren, Raymond (Henry Charles) 1928- *Baker 92*
Warren, Raymond McLeod, Jr. 1931- *WhoSSW 93*
Warren, Richard Ernest 1942- *WhoSSW 93*
Warren, Richard Glenn *Law&B 92*
Warren, Richard Henry 1859-1933 *Baker 92*
Warren, Richard K. 1920- *St&PR 93*
Warren, Richard Kearney 1920- *WhoAm 92*
Warren, Richard M. 1925- *WhoAm 92*
Warren, Richard Wayne 1935- *WhoWor 93*
Warren, Robert A. 1922- *WhoAm 92*
Warren, Robert C. 1918- *St&PR 93*
Warren, Robert Carlton 1918- *WhoAm 92*
Warren, Robert J. 1946- *St&PR 93*
Warren, Robert Kenneth 1948- *WhoSSW 93*
Warren, Robert Penn 1905-1989 *BioIn 17, MagSAmL [port], WorLitC [port]*
Warren, Robin K. *Law&B 92*
Warren, Roger Frederick 1941- *St&PR 93, WhoAm 92*
Warren, Ronald L. 1940- *St&PR 93*
Warren, Rose *AmWomPl*
Warren, Rupert 1908- *St&PR 93*
Warren, Russell Glen 1942- *WhoAm 92*
Warren, Russell James 1938- *WhoWor 93*
Warren, Sally Marie 1958- *WhoAmW 93*
Warren, Samuel Prowse 1841-1915 *Baker 92*
Warren, Sandra K. 1944- *ConAu 138*
Warren, Stephen Charles 1939- *WhoScE 91-1*
Warren, Steve 1952- *BioIn 17*
Warren, Steven A. *Law&B 92*
Warren, Susan Lee 1950- *WhoAmW 93*
Warren, Theodore Ray 1947- *St&PR 93*
Warren, Thomas S. 1903- *St&PR 93*
Warren, Tony Edwin 1952- *WhoSSW 93*
Warren, Val *ScF&FL 92*
Warren, W. Louise 1952- *WhoAmW 93*
Warren, Wendy Kaye 1957- *WhoAmW 93*
Warren, Wilfred Lewis 1929- *WhoWor 93*
Warren, William B. *ScF&FL 92*
Warren, William Bradford 1934- *WhoAm 92*
Warren, William Clements 1909- *WhoAm 92, WhoE 93, WhoWor 93*
Warren, William D. *St&PR 93*
Warren, William D. 1936- *WhoIns 93*
Warren, William David 1924- *WhoAm 92*
Warren, William Gerald 1930- *WhoAm 92*
Warren, William Herbert 1924- *WhoAm 92*
Warren, William Kermit 1941- *WhoSSW 93*
Warren, William M. *Law&B 92*
Warren, William Michael 1947- *St&PR 93*
Warren, William Michael, Jr. 1947- *WhoAm 92*
Warren, William Robinson 1931- *WhoAm 92*
Warren, William Stanford 1955- *St&PR 93*
Warren, William Walter, III *Law&B 92*
Warrender, Glenda Kay 1949- *WhoSSW 93*
Warrener, Richard Carlton 1944- *St&PR 93*
Warrens, Oakley 1935- *St&PR 93*
Warrick, Donald D. 1940- *WhoWor 93*
Warrick, James C. 1938- *St&PR 93*
Warrick, James Craig 1938- *WhoAm 92*
Warrick, James Gordon 1953- *WhoWrEP 92*
Warrick, Meta Vaux 1877-1968 *BioIn 17*
Warrick, Mildred Lorine 1917- *WhoAmW 93, WhoWor 93*
Warrick, Pamela Dianne 1958- *WhoAmW 93*
Warrick, Patricia S. 1925- *ScF&FL 92*
Warrick, Royce *Law&B 92*
Warrick, Stuart C., Jr. 1937- *St&PR 93*
Warrick, William W. *WhoAm 92*
Warrick, William Wiley 1940- *St&PR 93*
Warrick, Woodward A. 1922- *St&PR 93*
Warrillow, James K. *St&PR 93*
Warrilow, Clive 1938- *St&PR 93*
Warriner, Frederic 1916-1992 *NewYTBS 92 [port]*
Warriner, Joseph B. 1934- *WhoIns 93*
Warriner, Richard Bascomb, III 1947- *WhoSSW 93*
Warrington, Clayton Linwood, Jr. 1936- *WhoAm 92*
Warrington, Frank J. 1943- *St&PR 93*
Warrington, Freda *ScF&FL 92*
Warrington, Joan P. *Law&B 92*
Warrington, John Wesley 1914- *WhoAm 92*
Warrington, Willard Glade 1920- *WhoAm 92*
Warriss, Ben 1909-
See Jewel, Jimmy 1909- & Warriss, Ben 1909- *QDrFCA 92*
Warrol, Hans I. 1926- *WhoScE 91-4*
Warsavage, Jeanette Nancy 1938- *WhoAmW 93*
Warsaw, Ernest E. 1920- *St&PR 93*
Warsaw, Irene 1908- *WhoWrEP 92*
Warsaw, Stanley 1922- *St&PR 93*
Warsawer, Harold Newton *WhoE 93*
Warschauer, Murray H. *Law&B 92*
Warschausky, Judith Sue 1957- *WhoAmW 93*
Warsen, Jennifer *BioIn 17*
Warsh, Lewis David 1944- *WhoE 93*
Warshauer, Marshall A. 1930- *St&PR 93*
Warshaw, Allen Charles 1948- *WhoEmL 93*
Warshaw, Bruce J. 1947- *St&PR 93*
Warshaw, Jean *Law&B 92*
Warshaw, Joseph Bennett 1936- *WhoAm 92*
Warshaw, Larry *Law&B 92*
Warshaw, Leon J. 1917- *WhoAm 92, WhoIns 93*
Warshaw, Martin Richard 1924- *WhoAm 92*
Warshaw, Max 1913- *BioIn 17*
Warshaw, Stanley 1929- *WhoWrEP 92*
Warshaw, Stanley Irving 1931- *WhoAm 92*
Warshawsky, Stanford S. 1937- *St&PR 93*
Warshof, Richard Stephen 1948- *St&PR 93*
Warshofsky, Isaac *ConAu 39NR, MajAI*
Warsi, Shoaib 1956- *WhoWor 93*
Warsick-Rinzivillo, Mary Katrina 1956- *WhoSSW 93*
Warso, Barbara *Law&B 92*
Warson, Henry 1916- *WhoWor 93*
Warson, Toby Gene 1937- *WhoAm 92*
Warstadt, Gary Michael 1959- *WhoE 93*
Wartegg, Ernst Hesse- 1854-1918 *BioIn 17*
Wartel, Atale Therese Annette 1814-1865 *Baker 92*
Wartel, Pierre-Francois 1806-1882 *Baker 92*
Wartel, Roger 1932- *WhoScE 91-2*
Wartel, Stanislas 1939- *WhoScE 91-2*
Wartels, Nat 1902-1990 *BioIn 17*
Wartena, Lambertus 1923- *WhoScE 91-3*
Wartenbee, D.R. 1949- *St&PR 93*
Wartenberg, Hubert 1930- *WhoScE 91-3*
Warter, Gregg D. 1954- *St&PR 93*
Wartes, Burleigh d1991 *BioIn 17*
Wartgow, Diane Beirl 1942- *WhoAmW 93*
Warth, James Arthur 1942- *WhoE 93*
Warth, Robert Douglas 1921- *WhoAm 92*
Warthin, Thomas Angell 1909- *WhoAm 92*
Wartick, Ronald D. 1942- *WhoIns 93*
Wartik, Thomas 1921- *WhoAm 92*
Wartiovaara, Jorma J. 1938- *WhoScE 91-4*
Wartluft, David Jonathan 1938- *WhoAm 92, WhoWor 93, WhoWrEP 92*
Wartman, Carl H. *Law&B 92*
Wartman, Carl H. 1952- *St&PR 93*
Wartman, R. Christopher *Law&B 92*
Wartman, Rebecca Hensley 1957- *WhoSSW 93*
Wartofsky, Victor 1931- *ScF&FL 92*
Warton, Joseph 1722-1800 *BioIn 17*
Warton, Thomas 1728-1790 *BioIn 17*
Wartski, Maureen (Ann Crane) 1940- *DcAmChF 1960*
Warung, Price 1855-1911 *TwCLC 45 [port]*
Warwick, Benjamin Troy 1962- *WhoSSW 93*
Warwick, Dee Dee *SoulM*
Warwick, Dionne *BioIn 17*
Warwick, Dionne 1940- *SoulM*
Warwick, Dionne 1941- *WhoAmW 93*
Warwick(e), (Marie) Dionne 1941- *Baker 92*
Warwick, John Benjamin 1948- *WhoWor 93*
Warwick, John Petersen 1926- *WhoAm 92*
Warwick, John S. 1930- *St&PR 93*
Warwick, Kevin *WhoScE 91-1*
Warwick, Richard Neville, Earl of 1428-1471 *HarEnMi*
Warwick, Robert Alan *Law&B 92*
Warwick, William James 1934- *St&PR 93*
Warwick, William O. 1932- *St&PR 93*
Warye, Richard Jonathan 1929- *WhoE 93*
Warynski, Ludwik 1856-1889 *PolBiDi*
Warzak, Lavera A. 1926- *St&PR 93*
Warzala, Richard S. 1953- *St&PR 93*
Warzecha, Antoni Tadeusz 1929- *WhoWor 93*
Warzecha, Gene *Law&B 92*
Warzel, Ronald J. 1933- *St&PR 93*
Warzeski, Mary Joan 1930- *WhoAmW 93*
Was, Don *BioIn 17*
Wasag, Tadeusz 1926- *WhoScE 91-4*
Wasan, Darsh Tilakchand 1938- *WhoAm 92, WhoWor 93*
Wasatonic, John J. *Law&B 92*

Wasby, Stephen L(ewis) 1937- ConAu 139
Wascher, Rick R. Law&B 92
Wascou, Ellen Fern 1950- WhoAmW 93
Wasden, H.D. Law&B 92
Waser, Peter Gaudenz 1918- WhoScE 91-4
Waserman, David B. 1960- St&PR 93
Wasey, Jane d1992 NewYTBS 92
Wash, James R. 1930- St&PR 93
Washawanny, William J. 1954- St&PR 93
Washbourne, James WhoScE 91-1
Washbrook, E.H. 1937- St&PR 93
Washburn, A. Michael 1940- WhoE 93
Washburn, Abbott McConnell 1915- WhoAm 92
Washburn, Berk W. Law&B 92
Washburn, Bryant 1889-1963 BioIn 17
Washburn, Caryl Anne 1943- WhoSSW 93
Washburn, David Thacher 1930- WhoAm 92
Washburn, Donald Arthur 1944- St&PR 93, WhoAm 92
Washburn, H.B. 1946- St&PR 93
Washburn, Harriet Louise 1946- WhoAmW 93
Washburn, Henry Bradford, Jr. 1910- WhoAm 92
Washburn, Jack d1992 NewYTBS 92
Washburn, Jack 1927-1992 BioIn 17
Washburn, Jan 1926- BioIn 17
Washburn, John C. 1930- St&PR 93
Washburn, John H. Law&B 92
Washburn, John L. 1937- WhoUN 92
Washburn, John Merrow, Jr. 1927- St&PR 93
Washburn, Margaret Floy 1871-1939 BioIn 17
Washburn, Mark ScF&FL 92
Washburn, Mildred Baer AmWomPl
Washburn, Ramona Kemp 1932- WhoAmW 93, WhoSSW 93
Washburn, Robert 1928- Baker 92
Washburn, Robert Brooks 1928- WhoAm 92
Washburn, Robert Douglas 1935- St&PR 93
Washburn, Stan 1943- WhoAm 92
Washburn, Stewart Alexander 1923- WhoE 93
Washburn, Stewart Putnam 1929- St&PR 93, WhoE 93
Washburn, Thomas D. Law&B 92
Washburn, Thomas Dale 1947- St&PR 93
Washburn, Wilcomb Edward 1925- WhoAm 92, WhoWrEP 92
Washburne, Norman F. 1927-1991 BioIn 17
Washco, Christopher John 1957- WhoE 93
Washic, Thomas Eugene 1950- WhoE 93
Washington, Alvin C. St&PR 93
Washington, Barbara Jean Wright 1946- WhoAmW 93
Washington, Bennetta 1918-1991 BioIn 17
Washington, Booker T. 1856-1915 BioIn 17, ConBlB 4 [port], ConHero 2 [port], GayN, PolPar
Washington, Booker Taliaferro 1856-1915 EncAACR [port]
Washington, Bushrod 1762-1829 BioIn 17, OxCSupC [port]
Washington, Charles Joseph 1938- St&PR 93
Washington, Clarence Edward, Jr. 1953- WhoE 93, WhoEmL 93
Washington, Cleo AfrAmBi [port]
Washington, Clotee Woodruff 1947- WhoEmL 93
Washington, Craig 1941- BioIn 17
Washington, Craig A. 1941- CngDr 91, WhoAm 92, WhoSSW 93
Washington, Craig Anthony AfrAmBi [port]
Washington, Deborah Reynolds Law&B 92
Washington, Dennis BioIn 17
Washington, Denzel BioIn 17, NewYTBS 92 [port], WhoAm 92
Washington, Denzel 1954- CurBio 92 [port], News 93-2 [port]
Washington, Dinah 1924-1963 Baker 92
Washington, Donald W. Law&B 92
Washington, Fanny Norton Smith BioIn 17
Washington, Forrester 1887-1963 EncAACR
Washington, Gary 1953- WhoE 93
Washington, George 1732-1799 BioIn 17, CmdGen 1991 [port], HarEnMi, OxCSupC, PolPar
Washington, Gregory Keith 1952- WhoEmL 93
Washington, Grover, Jr. 1943- SoulM, WhoAm 92
Washington, Harold BioIn 17
Washington, Harold 1922-1987 AfrAmBi, PolPar
Washington, James MacKnight 1938- WhoSSW 93
Washington, James Winston, Jr. 1909- WhoAm 92
Washington, John M. G. 1948- St&PR 93
Washington, Justine Gloria-Mae 1941- WhoE 93
Washington, Keith BioIn 17
Washington, Linda Little 1950- WhoAmW 93
Washington, Margaret James Murray BioIn 17
Washington, Martha 1731-1802 BioIn 17
Washington, Mary Ball 1708-1789 BioIn 17
Washington, Napoleon, Jr. 1948- WhoEmL 93, WhoWor 93
Washington, Olivia A. Davidson BioIn 17
Washington, Pauletta BioIn 17
Washington, Reginald Louis 1949- WhoWor 93
Washington, Robert Orlanda 1935- WhoAm 92
Washington, Ruth BioIn 17
Washington, Ruth V. BioIn 17
Washington, Sandra Yvonne 1949- WhoAmW 93
Washington, Tia Denise 1955- WhoE 93
Washington, Tom F. 1949- WhoWrEP 92
Washington, Valdemar Luther 1952- WhoEmL 93
Washington, Valora 1953- WhoAmW 93
Washington, Vivian Edwards 1914- WhoAmW 93
Washington, Walter 1923- WhoAm 92, WhoSSW 93
Washington, Walter Edward 1915- AfrAmBi, WhoAm 92
Washington, Wanda Patrice Law&B 92
Washington, Warren Morton 1936- WhoAm 92
Washington, William 1752-1810 HarEnMi
Washington, Willis WhoWrEP 92
Washington, Wilma J. 1949- WhoAmW 93
Washko, John A. 1951- St&PR 93
Washlow, Robert J. 1944- St&PR 93
Washlow, Robert Jacob 1944- WhoAm 92
Washo, Gabriel A. 1944- St&PR 93
Washow, Lawrence E. 1953- St&PR 93
Washow, Paula Burnette 1948- WhoAmW 93, WhoEmL 93, WhoWor 93
Wasiak, Stan d1992 NewYTBS 92
Wasick, Mary Ann 1946- WhoAmW 93
Wasicki, James C. 1942- St&PR 93
Wasiele, Harry W., Jr. 1926- WhoAm 92, WhoE 93
Wasieleski, David Thomas 1968- WhoWrEP 92
Wasieleski, John Charles 1947- St&PR 93
Wasielewski, Wilhelm Joseph von 1822-1896 Baker 92
Wasik, Boguslaw Wincenty 1938- WhoWor 93
Wasik, John Francis 1957- WhoAm 92
Wasik, Robert A. 1938- St&PR 93
Wasik, Vincent A. 1944- WhoAm 92
Wasilewska, Wanda 1905-1964 PolBiDi
Wasilewski, Edward John 1950- St&PR 93
Wasilewski, Gail BioIn 17
Wasilewski, Vincent Thomas 1922- WhoAm 92
Wasiluk, Wiktor 1924- WhoScE 91-4
Wasiolek, Edward 1924- WhoAm 92
Wasiolek, Suzanne J. 1955- WhoSSW 93
Wasitodiningrat, K.R.T. 1909- Baker 92
Wasiutynski, Wojciech Joseph 1910- WhoE 93
Waskel, Shirley Ann 1935- WhoAmW 93
Waskiewich, Gregory E. Law&B 92
Waskin, Alan Law&B 92
Wasko-Flood, Sandra Jean 1943- WhoAmW 93
Waskom, Michael A. 1940- St&PR 93
Waskow, Arthur Ocean 1933- WhoAm 92
Waskowiak, David A. Law&B 92
Waslien, Carol Irene 1940- WhoAmW 93
Wasmer, Carmenia Ann 1934- WhoAmW 93, WhoE 93
Wasmund, Suzanne 1936- WhoAmW 93
Wasmus, J.F. BioIn 17
Wasmuth, Carl E., Jr. Law&B 92
Wasmuth, Carl Erwin 1916- WhoAm 92
Wasmuth, Edmund M. 1927- St&PR 93
Wasney, Cynthia Star Law&B 92
Wasoff, Lois F. Law&B 92
Wason, Robert A., IV Law&B 92
Wason, Robert Wesley 1945- WhoE 93
Wason, Sandys 1870?- ScF&FL 92
Wasowski, Andrzej 1935- WhoScE 91-4
Wasp, Deidra Lynn Law&B 92
Wasp, Edmund J. Law&B 92
Waspe, Robert A. 1952- St&PR 93
Wass, Douglas (William Gretton) 1923- ConAu 138
Wass, Hannelore Lina 1926- WhoAm 92, WhoAmW 93
Wass, Herbert Franklin 1932- St&PR 93
Wass, Wallace Milton 1929- WhoAm 92
Wass-Brewer, Carol Napier 1945- WhoAmW 93, WhoSSW 93
Wasselin, Jean O. 1935- WhoUN 92
Wassell, Stephen Robert 1963- WhoSSW 93, WhoWor 93
Wassell, William John 1934- WhoE 93
Wassen, S. Henry 1908- IntDcAn
Wassenaar, Carolyn Mae 1951- WhoAmW 93
Wassenaer, Unico Wilhelm van 1692-1766 Baker 92
Wassenich, Linda Pilcher 1943- WhoSSW 93
Wasser, Alan Charles 1948- WhoE 93
Wasser, Henry 1919- WhoAm 92, WhoWor 93
Wasser, Lawrence Jay 1948- WhoSSW 93
Wasser, Margaret ScF&FL 92
Wasser, Marilyn J. Law&B 92
Wasser, Sidney 1929- St&PR 93
Wasser, Steven A. 1952- St&PR 93
Wasserburg, Gerald Joseph 1927- WhoAm 92
Wasser Edelstein, Vicki 1963- WhoAmW 93
Wasserlein, John H. 1941- St&PR 93
Wasserlein, John Henry 1941- WhoAm 92
Wasserman, Albert 1921- WhoAm 92
Wasserman, Albert Julian 1928- WhoSSW 93
Wasserman, Andrew 1955- St&PR 93
Wasserman, Arnold BioIn 17
Wasserman, Arnold Saul 1934- WhoAm 92
Wasserman, Barry Lee 1935- WhoAm 92
Wasserman, Bernard 1925- WhoE 93
Wasserman, Bert W. WhoAm 92
Wasserman, Bronna L. Law&B 92
Wasserman, Charles 1929- WhoE 93
Wasserman, Dale 1917- WhoAm 92
Wasserman, David Sherman 1942- St&PR 93
Wasserman, Debra WhoWrEP 92
Wasserman, Edel 1932- WhoAm 92
Wasserman, Edward Arnold 1946- WhoAm 92
Wasserman, Elyse Sheri 1957- WhoAmW 93
Wasserman, Eugene M. 1931- WhoE 93
Wasserman, Evan H. Law&B 92
Wasserman, Harvey S. 1943- St&PR 93
Wasserman, Herbert 1916- St&PR 93
Wasserman, J. Donald 1930- St&PR 93
Wasserman, Jeffrey Andrew 1946- WhoE 93
Wasserman, Jerry 1931- St&PR 93
Wasserman, Karen Boling 1944- WhoSSW 93
Wasserman, Krystyna 1937- WhoE 93
Wasserman, Kurt Jonah 1921- St&PR 93
Wasserman, Lawrence Alan 1942- St&PR 93
Wasserman, Lee S. Law&B 92
Wasserman, Leonard M. 1931- St&PR 93
Wasserman, Lew R. 1913- BioIn 17, St&PR 93, WhoAm 92
Wasserman, Lori Drucker 1956- WhoAmW 93
Wasserman, Louis Robert 1910- WhoAm 92
Wasserman, Manuele D. 1950- WhoE 93
Wasserman, Marlie Parker 1947- WhoAm 92, WhoAmW 93
Wasserman, Martin Allan 1941- WhoAm 92
Wasserman, Myron Beau 1947- WhoE 93
Wasserman, Paul 1924- WhoAm 92
Wasserman, Peter J. Law&B 92
Wasserman, Robert Harold 1926- WhoAm 92
Wasserman, Sheldon d1992 NewYTBS 92
Wasserman, Sheldon 1940-1992 BioIn 17, ConAu 137
Wasserman, Susan Valesky 1956- WhoAmW 93
Wasserman, Sy St&PR 93
Wasserman, Walter Leonard 1936- WhoE 93
Wasserman, Zelda Rakowitz 1935- WhoE 93
Wasserman-Arthur, Lorraine Jean 1938- St&PR 93
Wassermann, E.F. 1937- WhoScE 91-3
Wassermann, Heinrich Joseph 1791-1838 Baker 92
Wassermann, Herbert Edward 1936- WhoE 93
Wassermann, Jack 1929- ScF&FL 92
Wasserstein, Bernard Mano Julius 1948- WhoAm 92
Wasserstein, Bruce BioIn 17
Wasserstein, Bruce 1947- WhoAm 92
Wasserstein, Jeffrey Alan Law&B 92
Wasserstein, Wendy BioIn 17
Wasserstein, Wendy 1950- NewYTBS 92 [port], WhoAm 92, WhoAmW 93, WhoE 93
Wasserstrum, Harriet Sue 1948- St&PR 93
Wasshausen, Dieter Carl 1938- WhoAm 92
Wasshausen, Wolfgang 1943- WhoScE 91-3
Wassil, Michael J. 1951- St&PR 93
Wassinger, Marion St&PR 93
Wassipaul, Friedrich 1926- WhoScE 91-4
Wassle, Heinz WhoScE 91-3
Wassler, Alfred Richard 1944- St&PR 93, WhoAm 92
Wassman, James A. 1941- St&PR 93
Wassmuth, Rudolf G.H. 1928- WhoScE 91-3
Wassner, Steven Joel 1946- WhoAm 92
Wassom, Allan Wayne 1933- St&PR 93
Wasson, Barbara Hickam 1918- WhoAmW 93, WhoWor 93
Wasson, Christina 1964- WhoAmW 93
Wasson, Gordon McKenzie Law&B 92
Wasson, John Calvin 1931- St&PR 93, WhoAm 92
Wasson, John Russell 1941- WhoSSW 93
Wasson, R.G. 1945- St&PR 93
Wasson, R. Gordon 1898-1986 BioIn 17, IntDcAn
Wasson, Samuel Brown 1936- St&PR 93
Wasson, Samuel C., Jr. 1939- St&PR 93
Wasson, Steven D. 1950- St&PR 93
Wasson, Tamela Jo 1963- WhoSSW 93
Wassong, Dan Karol 1930- St&PR 93
Wassung, Charlotte AmWomPl
Wastberg, Olle M. 1945- WhoWor 93
Wastenson, Leif E.V. 1936- WhoScE 91-4
Wasti, Syed Tanvir 1941- WhoScE 91-4
Wasunna, Ambrose Eric Onyango 1938- WhoUN 92
Wasylyk, John Stanley 1942- WhoE 93
Wasylynchuk, L.G. 1940- St&PR 93
Waszczyszyn, Zenon Wlodzimierz 1935- WhoScE 91-4
Waszkiewicz, Joan E. 1927- St&PR 93
Waszkiewicz, John Chester, Jr. 1927- St&PR 93
Waszkiewicz, John Chester, III 1953- St&PR 93
Wat, Aleksander 1900-1967 PolBiDi, ScF&FL 92
Watanabe, Akeo 1919-1990 Baker 92
Watanabe, August Masaru 1941- WhoAm 92
Watanabe, Eiichi 1918- WhoAsAP 91
Watanabe, Eimi 1947- WhoUN 92
Watanabe, Eric Katsuji 1951- WhoWor 93
Watanabe, Gary T. 1947- St&PR 93
Watanabe, Gary Yoichi 1945- St&PR 93
Watanabe, Hajime 1929- WhoWor 93
Watanabe, Hideo 1934- WhoAsAP 91
Watanabe, Ichiro 1931- WhoAsAP 91
Watanabe, Kathleen Naomi 1956- WhoAmW 93
Watanabe, Kazo 1926- WhoAsAP 91
Watanabe, Kazumi BioIn 17
Watanabe, Kazutami 1932- WhoWor 93
Watanabe, Ken-ichi 1942- WhoWor 93
Watanabe, Koichi 1938- WhoWor 93
Watanabe, Kouichi 1942- WhoWor 93
Watanabe, Kozo 1932- WhoAsAP 91, WhoWor 93
Watanabe, Mamoru 1933- WhoAm 92
Watanabe, Michio 1923- WhoAsAP 91, WhoWor 93
Watanabe, Richard Megumi 1962- WhoWor 93
Watanabe, Roy Noboru 1947- WhoEmL 93
Watanabe, Ruth Taiko 1916- WhoAm 92, WhoAmW 93, WhoE 93, WhoWor 93
Watanabe, Ryojiro 1936- WhoWor 93
Watanabe, Sachiko WhoWrEP 92
Watanabe, Shigeo 1928- MajAI [port]
Watanabe, Shiro 1929- WhoAsAP 91
Watanabe, Shoichi 1930- WhoAsAP 91
Watanabe, Shoji 1927- WhoWor 93
Watanabe, Takashi 1926- WhoWor 93
Watanabe, Takenobu 1938- WhoWor 93
Watanabe, Toshiharu 1924- WhoWor 93
Watanabe, Tsuneo 1926- WhoWor 93
Watanabe, Yoichi 1954- WhoSSW 93
Watanabe, Yoko 1953- WhoAm 92
Watanabe, Yoshihisa 1931- WhoWor 93
Watanabe, Yoshihito 1953- WhoWor 93
Watanabe, Yukio 1925- WhoAsAP 91
Watanjar, Mohammad Aslam WhoWor 93
Watanuki, Haruko Law&B 92
Watanuki, Joji 1931- WhoWor 93
Watanuki, Tamisuke 1927- WhoAsAP 91
Watase, Kenmei 1925- WhoAsAP 91
Watbridge, D.J. WhoScE 91-1
Watchorn, C.L.F. 1945- WhoIns 93
Watchorn, William E. 1943- St&PR 93
Watchorn, William Ernest 1943- WhoAm 92

Waterbrook, Keith Jennings 1946- *WhoAm 92*
Waterbury, James M. *Law&B 92*
Waterbury, Robert Douglas, Jr. 1962- *WhoSSW 93*
Waterer, Bonnie Clausing 1940- *WhoAmW 93*
Waterfield, Bob 1920-1983 *BioIn 17*
Waterfield, Harry Lee, II 1943- *St&PR 93, WhoIns 93*
Waterfield, Michael Derek 1941- *WhoWor 93*
Waterfield, Robin 1952- *ScF&FL 92*
Waterfill, Dorothy Jane 1957- *WhoAmW 93, WhoSSW 93*
Waterfill, Karen *BioIn 17*
Waterford, Van *WhoWrEP 92*
Waterhouse, Ernest Lewis, III 1952- *WhoSSW 93*
Waterhouse, James 1842-1922 *BioIn 17*
Waterhouse, John William 1849-1917 *BioIn 17*
Waterhouse, Keith *BioIn 17*
Waterhouse, Keith (Spencer) 1929- *ConAu 38NR*
Waterhouse, Mona Elisabeth 1942- *WhoAmW 93*
Waterhouse, Richard V. 1924- *BioIn 17*
Waterhouse, Stephen Lee 1943- *WhoE 93, WhoWor 93*
Waterloo, Claudia 1952- *WhoAm 92*
Waterloo, Stanley 1846-1913 *ScF&FL 92*
Waterlot, Michel 1937- *WhoScE 91-2*
Waterlow, Simon Gordon 1941- *St&PR 93, WhoAm 92*
Waterman, Asa 1940- *St&PR 93*
Waterman, Carolyn Sue 1941- *WhoAmW 93*
Waterman, Daniel 1927- *WhoAm 92, WhoE 93*
Waterman, Esther 1960- *WhoAmW 93*
Waterman, John *BioIn 17*
Waterman, John Thomas 1918- *WhoAm 92*
Waterman, Joseph Francis 1951- *St&PR 93*
Waterman, Michael Alan *Law&B 92*
Waterman, Michael Spencer 1942- *WhoAm 92*
Waterman, Mignon Redfield 1944- *WhoAmW 93*
Waterman, Peter George *WhoScE 91-1*
Waterman, Richard Gordon *Law&B 92*
Waterman, Thomas Chadbourne 1937- *WhoAm 92*
Waterman, Thomas Talbot 1885-1936 *IntDcAn*
Waters, Aaron C. 1905-1991 *BioIn 17*
Waters, Allan L. 1957- *St&PR 93*
Waters, Benny 1902- *BioIn 17*
Waters, Bernard J. *St&PR 93*
Waters, Betty Lou 1943- *WhoAmW 93, WhoSSW 93*
Waters, Brenda Joyce 1950- *WhoAmW 93*
Waters, Brian *St&PR 93*
Waters, Brian Kent 1939- *WhoSSW 93*
Waters, Carol Weir 1942- *WhoSSW 93*
Waters, Chocolate 1949- *WhoWrEP 92*
Waters, David M. 1942- *St&PR 93*
Waters, David Rogers 1932- *St&PR 93, WhoAm 92*
Waters, Donald Henry 1937- *WhoWor 93*
Waters, Donald Joseph 1952- *WhoAm 92*
Waters, Donald Samuel B. 1916- *St&PR 93*
Waters, Donovan W. 1928- *WhoAm 92*
Waters, Edward N(eighbor) 1906-1991 *Baker 92*
Waters, Edward Neighbor 1906-1991 *BioIn 17*
Waters, Edward Sarsfield 1930- *WhoWor 93*
Waters, Elizabeth Ann *Law&B 92*
Waters, Ellen Maureen 1938- *WhoAmW 93*
Waters, Ethel 1896-1977 *Baker 92, BioIn 17*
Waters, Frances Roffey 1914- *WhoAmW 93*
Waters, George B. 1920- *St&PR 93*
Waters, George Bausch 1920- *WhoAm 92*
Waters, George Wilbur 1916- *WhoAm 92*
Waters, Gregory Alan 1967- *WhoSSW 93*
Waters, Gregory Leo 1948- *WhoE 93*
Waters, H. Franklin 1932- *WhoAm 92, WhoSSW 93*
Waters, Helen Eugenia 1917- *WhoWrEP 92*
Waters, Howard Richard *WhoScE 91-1*
Waters, James Logan 1925- *St&PR 93, WhoAm 92*
Waters, Jean Beth 1947- *WhoSSW 93*
Waters, John 1946- *BioIn 17, ConTFT 10, MiSFD 9, WhoAm 92, WhoE 93*
Waters, John B. 1929- *WhoSSW 93*
Waters, John Robert *WhoScE 91-1*
Waters, John W. 1936- *WhoSSW 93*
Waters, Karl R. 1952- *St&PR 93*
Waters, Laughlin Edward 1914- *WhoAm 92*
Waters, Louis Albert 1938- *St&PR 93*
Waters, Maxine *AfrAmBi [port], BioIn 17*
Waters, Maxine 1938- *CngDr 91, ConBlB 3 [port], CurBio 92 [port], WhoAm 92, WhoAmW 93*
Waters, Michael 1949- *DcLB 120 [port], WhoWrEP 92*
Waters, Michael Robert 1955- *WhoE 93*
Waters, Muddy 1915-1983 *Baker 92, BioIn 17*
Waters, Norman Edward *WhoScE 91-1*
Waters, Pat *BioIn 17*
Waters, Reita Olita Clifton 1930- *WhoWrEP 92*
Waters, Richard 1926- *St&PR 93, WhoAm 92*
Waters, Richard George 1936- *St&PR 93*
Waters, Robert Craig 1956- *WhoSSW 93*
Waters, Rodney Lewis 1936- *WhoWor 93*
Waters, Roger *BioIn 17*
Waters, Rollie Odell 1942- *WhoSSW 93*
Waters, Ronald Thomas *WhoScE 91-1*
Waters, Shirley B. 1921- *St&PR 93*
Waters, Stanley *BioIn 17*
Waters, Stephen Monroe, III 1963- *WhoSSW 93*
Waters, Sylvia *WhoAm 92*
Waters, T.A. 1938- *ScF&FL 92*
Waters, Timothy Doyle *Law&B 92*
Waters, Todd Vern 1947- *WhoWor 93*
Waters, Tom d1881 *BioIn 17*
Waters, Walter Kenneth, Jr. 1927- *WhoSSW 93*
Waters, William Alfred 1912- *WhoSSW 93*
Waters, William F. *Law&B 92*
Waters, William Francis 1932- *WhoAm 92*
Waters, William V. 1934- *St&PR 93*
Waters, Willie Anthony *BioIn 17*
Waters, Willie Anthony 1951- *WhoAm 92*
Waterson, Carolyn Marie 1961- *WhoAmW 93*
Waterson, Jane M. *Law&B 92*
Waterson, Michael John 1950- *WhoWor 93*
Waters-Savant, Marc Edward 1966- *WhoE 93*
Waterston, R.M. 1947- *WhoScE 91-1*
Waterston, Sam 1940- *ConTFT 10*
Waterston, Samuel Atkinson 1940- *WhoAm 92*
Waterstone, Mary M. *Law&B 92*
Waterton, Betty 1923- *WhoCanL 92*
Waterton, Eric 1943- *WhoAm 92*
Waterwash, James Samuel 1938- *St&PR 93*
Watford, George Franklin 1921- *St&PR 93*
Watford, Jamie Denise 1955- *WhoAmW 93*
Watford, Patti Eileen 1961- *WhoAmW 93*
Wathan, Herbert Harold 1926- *WhoSSW 93*
Wathelet, Melchior 1949- *WhoWor 93*
Wathen, Daniel Everett 1939- *WhoAm 92*
Wathen, Thomas W. 1929- *St&PR 93*
Wathes, Christopher Michael *WhoScE 91-1*
Wathey, Claude 1926- *BioIn 17, DcCPCAm*
Wa Thiong'o, James 1938- *BioIn 17*
Wathne, Carl Norman 1930- *WhoE 93*
Watkin, David 1925- *WhoAm 92*
Watkin, Lawrence Edward 1901-1981 *ScF&FL 92*
Watkin, Nancy K. *Law&B 92*
Watkins, A.H. *ScF&FL 92*
Watkins, Amelia T.C. *Law&B 92*
Watkins, Amy J. *Law&B 92*
Watkins, Bettyjane 1954- *WhoAmW 93*
Watkins, Bill *St&PR 93*
Watkins, Birge Swift 1949- *WhoAm 92*
Watkins, Brian d1990 *BioIn 17*
Watkins, Carlton Gunter 1919- *WhoAm 92*
Watkins, Carol Ann *Law&B 92*
Watkins, Cathy Collins 1952- *WhoAmW 93*
Watkins, Charles Booker, Jr. 1942- *WhoAm 92*
Watkins, Christopher J. *Law&B 92*
Watkins, Clifton Edward, Jr. 1954- *WhoSSW 93*
Watkins, Cynthia Ann 1951- *WhoAmW 93*
Watkins, Daniel Joseph 1923- *WhoAm 92*
Watkins, David 1966- *WhoE 93*
Watkins, David J., II 1959- *St&PR 93*
Watkins, Dean A. 1922- *St&PR 93*
Watkins, Dean Allen 1922- *WhoAm 92*
Watkins, Diana *ScF&FL 92*
Watkins, Don L. 1952- *St&PR 93*
Watkins, Eugene Leonard 1918- *WhoE 93*
Watkins, Evan Scott 1961- *WhoWrEP 92*
Watkins, F. Scott 1946- *St&PR 93*
Watkins, Felix Scott 1946- *WhoEmL 93*
Watkins, Floyd C. 1920- *WhoSSW 93*
Watkins, Frances Ellen 1825-1911 *BioIn 17*
Watkins, Frederick D. 1915- *WhoIns 93*
Watkins, George Daniels 1924- *WhoAm 92*
Watkins, Gilbert Kim 1952- *WhoE 93*
Watkins, Grace Gregory 1874- *AmWomPl*
Watkins, Graham *ScF&FL 92*
Watkins, Hays T. 1926- *St&PR 93*
Watkins, Hays Thomas 1926- *WhoAm 92*
Watkins, Helen *BioIn 17*
Watkins, Henry Grady, III 1959- *WhoSSW 93*
Watkins, Ivor *ScF&FL 92*
Watkins, James B. *Law&B 92*
Watkins, James D. *BioIn 17*
Watkins, James D. 1927- *CngDr 91*
Watkins, James D. 1947- *St&PR 93*
Watkins, James David 1927- *WhoAm 92, WhoE 93, WhoWor 93*
Watkins, James David 1947- *WhoAm 92*
Watkins, Jeffrey Clifton *WhoScE 91-1*
Watkins, Jerry W. *Law&B 92*
Watkins, Jerry West 1931- *St&PR 93, WhoAm 92*
Watkins, Joe 1947- *St&PR 93*
Watkins, John C. A. 1912- *St&PR 93*
Watkins, John Chester Anderson 1912- *WhoAm 92*
Watkins, John F. 1925- *St&PR 93*
Watkins, John Francis 1925- *WhoAm 92*
Watkins, John G(oodrich) 1913- *ConAu 38NR*
Watkins, John Goodrich 1913- *WhoAm 92*
Watkins, John W. 1944- *St&PR 93*
Watkins, John W., Jr. 1938- *WhoIns 93*
Watkins, Julia M. 1941- *WhoAmW 93*
Watkins, Karen G. *Law&B 92*
Watkins, Karen J. 1947- *WhoAmW 93*
Watkins, Katherine K. *Law&B 92*
Watkins, Kathleen Blake *BioIn 17*
Watkins, Leslie *ScF&FL 92*
Watkins, Lewis Boone 1945- *WhoSSW 93*
Watkins, Linda Theresa 1947- *WhoAmW 93*
Watkins, Liz Leid 1943- *WhoSSW 93*
Watkins, Lloyd Irion 1928- *WhoAm 92*
Watkins, Louise Ward *AmWomPl*
Watkins, Luevenia 1934- *AfrAmBi*
Watkins, Lura Woodside *AmWomPl*
Watkins, Maurine Dallas 1900-1968 *AmWomPl*
Watkins, Michael 1947- *BioIn 17*
Watkins, Neil B. 1947- *WhoIns 93*
Watkins, Norma Lea 1923- *St&PR 93*
Watkins, Oliver Timberlake 1928- *WhoE 93*
Watkins, Paul Lindsay 1947- *WhoWor 93*
Watkins, Peter 1934- *BioIn 17*
Watkins, Peter 1935- *MiSFD 9*
Watkins, Peyton Cottrell *Law&B 92*
Watkins, Ray 1931- *WhoScE 91-1*
Watkins, Richard F. *St&PR 93*
Watkins, Richard M. 1948- *St&PR 93*
Watkins, Robert Fred 1927- *WhoWor 93*
Watkins, Robert Todd, Sr. 1929- *St&PR 93, WhoAm 92*
Watkins, Robert Wayne 1949- *WhoE 93*
Watkins, Roland H. W. 1932- *St&PR 93*
Watkins, Scott D. 1949- *St&PR 93*
Watkins, Stephen Edward 1922- *WhoAm 92*
Watkins, Steven F. 1940- *WhoSSW 93*
Watkins, Ted *NewYTBS 92*
Watkins, Theresa R. *Law&B 92*
Watkins, Trevor *WhoScE 91-1*
Watkins, Vincent Gates 1945- *WhoWor 93*
Watkins, W. Hale *Law&B 92*
Watkins, Wallace Holmes 1936- *St&PR 93*
Watkins, Wendell Lynn 1932- *St&PR 93*
Watkins, Wesley Lee 1953- *WhoSSW 93*
Watkins, William, Jr. 1932- *St&PR 93*
Watkins, William Henry 1929- *WhoSSW 93*
Watkins, William John 1942- *ScF&FL 92, WhoWrEP 92*
Watkins, William Jon *ScF&FL 92*
Watkins, William Law 1910- *WhoAm 92*
Watkins, William Shepard 1950- *WhoWor 93*
Watkins, Yoko Kawashima *DcAmChF 1985*
Watkinson, Carolyn 1949- *Baker 92*
Watkinson, D. James *Law&B 92*
Watkinson, John Ronald 1950- *WhoWor 93*
Watkinson, Patricia Grieve 1946- *WhoAm 92*
Watkinson, Thomas Guy 1931- *St&PR 93*
Watkins-Pitchford, D.J. 1905-1990 *BioIn 17*
Watkins-Pitchford, Denys James 1905-1990 *ConAu 38NR*
Watlack, Linda Ann 1959- *WhoAmW 93*
Watland, Ross T. *Law&B 92*
Watley, Jody *BioIn 17*
Watley, Jody 1959- *SoulM*
Watley, Jody c. 1960- *ConMus 9 [port]*
Watley, Martha Jones 1936- *WhoAmW 93*
Watling, James *BioIn 17*
Watling, Roy 1938- *WhoScE 91-1*
Watlington, Deborah Kaye 1958- *WhoAmW 93*
Watlington, John Francis, Jr. 1911- *WhoAm 92*
Watlington, Phillip B. 1944- *St&PR 93*
Watlington-Cox, Adrian Denise 1954- *WhoAmW 93, WhoE 93*
Watman, Carolyn Prescott 1944- *WhoAmW 93*
Watman, William A. 1949- *St&PR 93*
Watmough, David 1926- *WhoCanL 92*
Watney, John 1915- *ScF&FL 92*
Watney-Klass, Lynne Mountford 1953- *WhoWor 93*
Watral, David Michael 1948- *WhoE 93*
Watrel, Warren George 1935- *WhoE 93*
Watrelot, Antoine-Andre 1952- *WhoWor 93*
Watrous, P.J. 1933- *St&PR 93*
Watrous, Philip Jordan 1933- *WhoE 93*
Watrous, Robert Thomas 1952- *WhoE 93*
Watrous, Ronald Eugene *Law&B 92*
Watrous, William Russell 1939- *WhoAm 92*
Watsa, V. Prem 1950- *St&PR 93*
Watsky, Morris J. *Law&B 92*
Watson, Abbie I. 1905- *WhoWor 93*
Watson, Ada Louise Mitchell 1951- *WhoAmW 93*
Watson, Adam *WhoScE 91-1*
Watson, Alan Andrew *WhoScE 91-1*
Watson, Alan E. 1956- *St&PR 93*
Watson, Alan Eugene *WhoIns 93*
Watson, Aldren A(uld) 1917- *ConAu 39NR*
Watson, Alexander Fletcher 1939- *WhoAm 92, WhoUN 92*
Watson, Alice Evelyn *AmWomPl*
Watson, Allen C. 1917- *St&PR 93*
Watson, Alonzo Wallace, Jr. 1922- *WhoAm 92*
Watson, Andrew Graham *Law&B 92*
Watson, Andrew Samuel 1920- *WhoAm 92*
Watson, Andy *ScF&FL 92*
Watson, Annah Walker Robinson 1848- *AmWomPl*
Watson, Arthur A. *BioIn 17*
Watson, Arthur Dennis 1950- *WhoAm 92, WhoEmL 93*
Watson, Arthur Richard 1915- *WhoE 93*
Watson, Barry Lee 1963- *WhoSSW 93*
Watson, Beatrice Sigmund 1925- *WhoAmW 93*
Watson, Ben Charles 1944- *WhoAm 92*
Watson, Bernard Charles *WhoAm 92, WhoE 93*
Watson, Beverly Ann 1948- *WhoAmW 93*
Watson, Bobby *BioIn 17*
Watson, Bonnie Jane *Law&B 92*
Watson, Bruce W. 1926- *St&PR 93*
Watson, Camille C. *AmWomPl*
Watson, Carol 1957- *WhoAmW 93*
Watson, Caroline N. *Law&B 92*
Watson, Carolyn Barrett- *BioIn 17*
Watson, Catherine Elaine 1944- *WhoAm 92, WhoAmW 93*
Watson, Charlotte Bushnell 1943- *WhoE 93*
Watson, Christopher S. 1946- *St&PR 93*
Watson, Claire 1924-1986 *Baker 92*
Watson, Claire 1927-1986 *OxDcOp*
Watson, Clarissa Alden *WhoE 93*
Watson, Clyde 1947- *BioIn 17, ConAu 39NR, MajAI [port]*
Watson, Craig R. *Law&B 92*
Watson, Cynthia 1957- *ConAu 137*
Watson, David 1943- *St&PR 93*
Watson, David Goulding 1929- *WhoSSW 93*
Watson, David John 1960- *WhoEmL 93*
Watson, David Lee 1946- *WhoSSW 93*
Watson, David Mathew 1956- *WhoSSW 93*
Watson, Denise Sander 1960- *WhoAmW 93*
Watson, Dennis Rahiim 1953- *AfrAmBi [port]*
Watson, Dennis Wallace 1914- *WhoAm 92*
Watson, Denton L. *BioIn 17*
Watson, Diane E. *AfrAmBi [port]*
Watson, Diane Edith 1933- *WhoAmW 93*
Watson, Diane Gardner 1958- *WhoAmW 93*
Watson, Doc 1923- *WhoAm 92*
Watson, Donald Ralph 1937- *WhoAm 92, WhoWrEP 92*
Watson, Donald S. 1960- *St&PR 93*
Watson, Dorothy Park *Law&B 92*
Watson, Douglas 1916- *St&PR 93*

Watson, Douglas Hugh *WhoScE 91-1*
Watson, Edward Donald 1932- *WhoE 93*
Watson, Edward L. 1934- *WhoAm 92*
Watson, (Lois) Elaine 1921- *WhoWrEP 92*
Watson, Elbert 1926- *St&PR 93*
Watson, Elena M. 1958- *ScF&FL 92*
Watson, Elizabeth Louise 1968- *WhoAmW 93*
Watson, Elizabeth M. *BioIn 17*
Watson, Elizabeth Marion 1949- *WhoAm 92, WhoSSW 93*
Watson, Ellen I. 1948- *WhoAmW 93*
Watson, Eric Robert 1962- *WhoSSW 93*
Watson, Evelyn *AmWomPl*
Watson, Evelyn Egner 1928- *WhoAmW 93*
Watson, Felicia 1962- *WhoAmW 93*
Watson, Fletcher D. 1922- *St&PR 93*
Watson, Forrest Albert 1951- *WhoEmL 93, WhoSSW 93*
Watson, Forrest I. 1926- *St&PR 93*
Watson, Frank D. *BioIn 17*
Watson, G. *WhoScE 91-3*
Watson, G. Dennis *Law&B 92*
Watson, Gary Hunter 1951- *WhoSSW 93*
Watson, Gavin Laird 1946- *WhoWor 93*
Watson, Gene D. *Law&B 92*
Watson, George Alistair *WhoScE 91-1*
Watson, George Elder, III 1931- *WhoE 93*
Watson, George Henry, Jr. 1936- *WhoAm 92, WhoWor 93*
Watson, George T. 1925- *AfrAmBi [port]*
Watson, George William 1926- *WhoAm 92*
Watson, George William 1947- *WhoAm 92*
Watson, Georgia Brown *WhoAmW 93*
Watson, Glegg *BioIn 17*
Watson, Grace E. *Law&B 92*
Watson, H. Knox, III 1951- *St&PR 93*
Watson, Harlan Leroy 1944- *WhoAm 92*
Watson, Harold George 1931- *WhoAm 92*
Watson, Hathaway, III *Law&B 92*
Watson, Helen Richter 1926- *WhoAmW 93*
Watson, Henry Crocker Marriott 1835- *ScF&FL 92*
Watson, Ian 1943- *ScF&FL 92*
Watson, Ian C. 1950- *St&PR 93*
Watson, Ian James *WhoScE 91-1*
Watson, J. R. 1934- *ConAu 39NR*
Watson, J. Robert 1926- *St&PR 93*
Watson, J. Warren 1923- *AfrAmBi*
Watson, J. Wreford 1915-1990 *BioIn 17*
Watson, Jack d1890 *BioIn 17*
Watson, Jack B. *St&PR 93*
Watson, Jack Crozier 1928- *WhoAm 92, WhoSSW 93*
Watson, Jack H., Jr. 1938- *WhoAm 92*
Watson, Jacqueline J. *Law&B 92*
Watson, James D. d1992 *NewYTBS 92 [port]*
Watson, James D. 1928- *BioIn 17*
Watson, James Dewey 1928- *WhoAm 92, WhoWor 93*
Watson, James E. 1863-1948 *PolPar*
Watson, James Elwyn, Jr. 1938- *WhoSSW 93*
Watson, James F. *Law&B 92*
Watson, James L. 1922- *CngDr 91*
Watson, James Lopez 1922- *WhoAm 92, WhoE 93*
Watson, James Patrick *WhoScE 91-1*
Watson, James R. *Law&B 92*
Watson, James R. 1920- *St&PR 93*
Watson, James Ray, Jr. 1935- *WhoSSW 93*
Watson, James Wreford 1915-1990 *BioIn 17*
Watson, Jane Werner 1915- *ScF&FL 92*
Watson, Jean Louise 1943- *WhoAmW 93*
Watson, Jean S. *Law&B 92*
Watson, Jennifer 1949- *WhoWor 93*
Watson, Jeremy Filmer 1941- *WhoWor 93*
Watson, Jerome Richard 1938- *WhoAm 92*
Watson, Jerry Carroll 1943- *WhoE 93, WhoSSW 93, WhoWor 93*
Watson, Jerry Franklin 1936- *WhoSSW 93*
Watson, Jim Albert 1939- *WhoSSW 93*
Watson, John *MiSFD 9, WhoScE 91-1*
Watson, John 1947- *MiSFD 9*
Watson, John C. 1932- *WhoIns 93*
Watson, John D. 1937- *St&PR 93*
Watson, John E. 1927- *St&PR 93*
Watson, John Edward 1949- *WhoWor 93*
Watson, John H. *ScF&FL 92*
Watson, John H. 1940- *St&PR 93*
Watson, John Kevin 1956- *WhoSSW 93*
Watson, John King, Jr. 1926- *WhoAm 92*
Watson, John Lawrence, III 1932- *St&PR 93, WhoAm 92*
Watson, John Michael *Law&B 92*
Watson, John R. 1922- *WhoAm 92*
Watson, John S. *AfrAmBi [port]*
Watson, Johnny 1935- *SoulM*
Watson, Joy Ann 1963- *WhoAmW 93*
Watson, Joyce Ann 1946- *WhoWor 93*
Watson, Julia *ScF&FL 92*
Watson, Julian 1918- *WhoAm 92*
Watson, Karen *BioIn 17*
Watson, Kate J. 1936- *WhoAmW 93*
Watson, Katharine Johnson 1942- *WhoAm 92, WhoAmW 93, WhoE 93*
Watson, Keith Dewey 1957- *St&PR 93*
Watson, Keith Stuart 1942- *WhoAm 92*
Watson, Kenneth 1908-1991 *AnObit 1991*
Watson, Kenneth Harrison *St&PR 93*
Watson, Kenneth Marshall 1921- *WhoAm 92*
Watson, Kerr Francis 1944- *WhoSSW 93*
Watson, Kurt Douglas 1952- *St&PR 93*
Watson, Larry Paul 1948- *St&PR 93*
Watson, Laura Humphreys 1954- *WhoSSW 93*
Watson, Leo 1898-1950 *BioIn 17*
Watson, Leonard James 1930- *WhoSSW 93*
Watson, Linda R. 1943- *St&PR 93*
Watson, Louis H. 1938- *St&PR 93*
Watson, M. Douglas, Jr. 1946- *St&PR 93*
Watson, M.I. *St&PR 93*
Watson, Malcolm John *WhoScE 91-1*
Watson, Marilyn Fern 1934- *WhoWrEP 92*
Watson, Mark Christopher 1968- *WhoE 93*
Watson, Marsha Jean 1957- *WhoWrEP 92*
Watson, Mary Ann 1944- *WhoAmW 93*
Watson, Maryanne Mitchell 1948- *WhoAmW 93, WhoSSW 93*
Watson, Max P. 1945- *St&PR 93*
Watson, Newton Frank *WhoScE 91-1*
Watson, Noelle 1958- *ScF&FL 92*
Watson, P. *WhoScE 91-1*
Watson, Pamela Marie 1946- *WhoAmW 93*
Watson, Patricia L. 1939- *WhoAmW 93*
Watson, Patrick 1929- *ScF&FL 92*
Watson, Patty Jo 1932- *WhoAm 92*
Watson, Paul 1942- *MiSFD 9*
Watson, Paul L. *Law&B 92*
Watson, Paula D. 1945- *WhoAm 92*
Watson, Peter Anthony *WhoScE 91-1*
Watson, Peter J. *Law&B 92*
Watson, Phil 1914-1991 *BioIn 17*
Watson, Phillip *St&PR 93*
Watson, R. Caird d1990 *BioIn 17*
Watson, R.J.A. *Law&B 92*
Watson, Ralph Edward 1948- *WhoWor 93*
Watson, Ralph Evans 1940- *WhoE 93*
Watson, Raymond Leslie 1926- *WhoAm 92*
Watson, Richard Allan 1931- *WhoAm 92, WhoWrEP 92*
Watson, Richard F. *MajAI*
Watson, Richard Jesse *ChlBIID [port]*
Watson, Richard Jesse 1951- *BioIn 17*
Watson, Richard L., Jr. 1914- *WhoSSW 93*
Watson, Richard Paul 1937- *St&PR 93*
Watson, Robert 1947- *ScF&FL 92*
Watson, Robert Carrall 1944- *WhoAm 92*
Watson, Robert Jay 1949- *WhoE 93*
Watson, Robert Jones 1929- *WhoE 93*
Watson, Robert K. 1932- *WhoIns 93*
Watson, Robert N., Jr. 1942- *St&PR 93*
Watson, Robert R. 1963- *WhoWrEP 92*
Watson, Robert Tanner 1922- *WhoAm 92*
Watson, Robert William 1949- *St&PR 93*
Watson, Robert Winthrop 1925- *WhoAm 92, WhoWrEP 92*
Watson, Roger Elton 1944- *WhoSSW 93*
Watson, Roger H. 1941- *St&PR 93*
Watson, Roland L. 1927- *St&PR 93*
Watson, Ronald Dean *Law&B 92*
Watson, Roosevelt d1990 *BioIn 17*
Watson, Royce Andrew 1932- *WhoE 93*
Watson, Sally (Lou) 1924- *DcAmChF 1960*
Watson, Sergio da Veiga 1934- *WhoWor 93*
Watson, Sharon Gitin 1943- *WhoAm 92*
Watson, Sheila 1909- *WhoCanL 92*
Watson, Simon *ScF&FL 92*
Watson, Solomon B., IV *Law&B 92*
Watson, Solomon Brown, IV 1944- *St&PR 93, WhoAm 92*
Watson, Stanley Ellis 1957- *WhoWor 93*
Watson, Stella Marie 1953- *WhoAmW 93*
Watson, Stephen E. *WhoAm 92*
Watson, Stephen Roger *WhoScE 91-1*
Watson, Sterl Arthur, Jr. 1942- *WhoAm 92*
Watson, Steven Christopher 1949- *WhoE 93*
Watson, Steven Edward 1952- *WhoSSW 93*
Watson, Stewart Charles 1922- *WhoAm 92*
Watson, Stuart D. 1916- *St&PR 93*
Watson, Sue Carter 1933- *WhoAmW 93*
Watson, Susan 1938- *ConTFT 10*
Watson, T. E., Mrs. *AmWomPl*
Watson, Thomas Allan, Jr. 1950- *WhoSSW 93*
Watson, Thomas Campbell 1931- *WhoAm 92*
Watson, Thomas Craig, Jr. 1941- *WhoSSW 93*
Watson, Thomas J. 1914- *BioIn 17*
Watson, Thomas J., Jr. 1914- *WhoAm 92*
Watson, Thomas J(ohn), Jr. 1914- *ConAu 138*
Watson, Thomas Sturges 1949- *WhoAm 92*
Watson, Tom 1856-1922 *PolPar*
Watson, Tony J. *Law&B 92*
Watson, W.A. *WhoScE 91-1*
Watson, Wallace Bailey *Law&B 92*
Watson, Wallace Robert 1943- *WhoSSW 93*
Watson, Warren Edward 1925- *WhoE 93*
Watson, Wendy (McLeod) 1942- *ConAu 39NR, MajAI*
Watson, Wilfred 1911- *WhoCanL 92*
Watson, William A. J. 1933- *WhoAm 92*
Watson, William Calvin, Jr. 1938- *WhoE 93*
Watson, William E. d1992 *NewYTBS 92*
Watson, William G. 1949- *St&PR 93*
Watson, William George 1934- *WhoWor 93*
Watson, William Hughes 1950- *WhoWor 93*
Watson, William V. 1939- *St&PR 93*
Watson, William W. 1899-1992 *NewYTBS 92 [port]*
Watson-Jones, Virginia 1936- *WhoAmW 93*
Watt, Andrew J. 1916- *WhoAm 92*
Watt, Arthur Dwight, Jr. 1955- *WhoSSW 93*
Watt, Barbara Ann 1939- *St&PR 93*
Watt, Beth 1943- *WhoSSW 93*
Watt, Charles Vance 1934- *WhoE 93, WhoWor 93*
Watt, David Edwin *WhoScE 91-1*
Watt, Dean Day 1917- *WhoAm 92*
Watt, Donald 1938- *ScF&FL 92*
Watt, Douglas 1914- *WhoAm 92*
Watt, E. Blake *Law&B 92*
Watt, Gary Wayne 1947- *St&PR 93*
Watt, Ian Pierre 1917- *WhoAm 92*
Watt, James 1736-1819 *BioIn 17*
Watt, James Gaius 1938- *WhoAm 92*
Watt, James Walker 1936- *St&PR 93*
Watt, Janice Lynn 1960- *WhoAmW 93*
Watt, John H. 1927- *St&PR 93, WhoAm 92*
Watt, John Reid 1914- *WhoSSW 93*
Watt, Joseph *WhoSSW 93*
Watt, Kenneth Edmund Ferguson 1929- *WhoAm 92*
Watt, Leslie Allen 1913- *St&PR 93*
Watt, Robert 1774-1819 *BioIn 17*
Watt, Robert Douglas 1945- *WhoAm 92*
Watt, Ronald Wilfred 1946- *WhoAm 92*
Watt, Ronald William 1943- *WhoWor 93*
Watt, Stuart George 1934- *WhoAm 92*
Watt, Stuart L. *Law&B 92*
Watt, Thomas Christian 1936- *St&PR 93*
Watt, Thomas Joseph 1939- *St&PR 93*
Watt, Tim 1939- *St&PR 93*
Watt, Tom 1935- *WhoAm 92*
Watt, William Buell 1919- *WhoE 93*
Watt, William G. 1934- *St&PR 93*
Watt, William George 1934- *WhoIns 93*
Watt, William John 1943- *WhoAm 92*
Watt, William Joseph 1925- *WhoAm 92, WhoSSW 93*
Wattanapongsiri, Anuwat *WhoAsAP 91*
Wattel, Harold Louis 1921- *WhoAm 92, WhoE 93*
Wattelet, Benny J. 1936- *St&PR 93*
Wattenbarger, James Lorenzo 1922- *WhoSSW 93*
Wattenberg, Albert 1917- *WhoAm 92*
Wattenberg, Ben J. 1933- *JrnUS, WhoAm 92, WhoWrEP 92*
Wattenberg, Carl August, Jr. *Law&B 92*
Wattenberg, Carl August, Jr. 1938- *St&PR 93*
Wattenberg, Frank Arvey 1943- *WhoE 93*
Wattenberger, Joyce H. 1923- *WhoSSW 93*
Wattenmaker, Richard Joel 1941- *WhoAm 92, WhoE 93*
Watterich, Andrea 1942- *WhoScE 91-4*
Watters, Barbara *ScF&FL 92*
Watters, Bud 1923- *WhoWrEP 92*
Watters, Charles Kenneth 1929- *St&PR 93*
Watters, Christopher Deffner 1939- *WhoE 93*
Watters, Cynthia Ellen 1944- *WhoAmW 93*
Watters, David J. 1931- *WhoAm 92*
Watters, Earl G., Sr. 1915- *St&PR 93*
Watters, Ethel Reed 1899- *WhoAmW 93*
Watters, Lu(cius Carl) 1911- *Baker 92*
Watters, Patricia Anne 1948- *WhoAmW 93*
Watterson, Bill *BioIn 17*
Watterson, Bill 1958- *Au&Arts 9, WhoAm 92*
Watterson, Henry 1840-1921 *JrnUS*
Watterson, Susan Joan 1953- *WhoAmW 93*
Watt-Evans, Lawrence 1954- *ScF&FL 92*
Wattez, Edouard Adrien 1941- *WhoUN 92*
Wattis, Janice L. *Law&B 92*
Wattles, Joshua Scadron *Law&B 92*
Wattleton, Alyce Faye 1943- *AfrAmBi, WhoAm 92, WhoAmW 93*
Wattleton, Faye *BioIn 17*
Wattre, Pierre 1937- *WhoScE 91-2*
Watts, Alan 1915-1973 *BioIn 17*
Watts, Alan Wilson 1915-1973 *BioIn 17*
Watts, Andre 1946- *Baker 92, WhoAm 92*
Watts, Andrew W. *Law&B 92*
Watts, Anne *BioIn 17*
Watts, Anthony Lee 1947- *WhoEmL 93, WhoSSW 93*
Watts, Charles DeWitt 1917- *WhoAm 92*
Watts, Charles H., II 1926- *St&PR 93*
Watts, Charles Henry, II 1926- *WhoAm 92*
Watts, Charlie *BioIn 17*
Watts, Clark 1938- *WhoAm 92*
Watts, Claudius Elmer, III 1936- *WhoAm 92, WhoSSW 93*
Watts, Daniel Thomas 1916- *WhoAm 92*
Watts, Dave Henry 1932- *St&PR 93, WhoAm 92*
Watts, David Eide 1921- *WhoAm 92*
Watts, David H. 1938- *St&PR 93*
Watts, David L. 1943- *St&PR 93*
Watts, Derryck Albert *WhoScE 91-1*
Watts, Dey Wadsworth 1923- *WhoAm 92*
Watts, Dick 1933- *St&PR 93*
Watts, Don Sandford 1951- *WhoSSW 93*
Watts, Donald Walter 1934- *WhoWor 93*
Watts, Donald Wayne *Law&B 92*
Watts, Emily Stipes 1936- *WhoAm 92*
Watts, Ernest Francis 1937- *WhoAm 92*
Watts, George W(illiam) 1952- *ConAu 139*
Watts, Glenn Ellis 1920- *WhoAm 92*
Watts, Glenn Richard 1929- *St&PR 93*
Watts, Harold H. 1906- *ScF&FL 92*
Watts, Harold Ross 1944- *WhoAm 92*
Watts, Harold Wesley 1932- *WhoAm 92*
Watts, Heather 1953- *WhoAm 92, WhoAmW 93*
Watts, Helen *ScF&FL 92*
Watts, Helen (Josephine) 1927- *Baker 92*
Watts, Helena Roselle 1921- *WhoAmW 93, WhoSSW 93, WhoWor 93*
Watts, Henry Miller, Jr. 1904- *WhoAm 92*
Watts, Howard L., Mrs. *AmWomPl*
Watts, Hugh M. 1926- *St&PR 93*
Watts, Irene N. 1931- *WhoCanL 92*
Watts, Isaac 1674-1748 *BioIn 17*
Watts, James Foster, Jr. 1936- *St&PR 93*
Watts, James Thomas, Jr. 1945- *WhoSSW 93*
Watts, Jeffrey Alan 1950- *St&PR 93*
Watts, John 1937- *ScF&FL 92*
Watts, John (Everett) 1930-1982 *Baker 92*
Watts, John M., Jr. 1941- *WhoWrEP 92*
Watts, John Mccleave 1933- *St&PR 93, WhoAm 92*
Watts, John Morton, Jr. 1941- *WhoE 93*
Watts, John R. 1926- *St&PR 93*
Watts, John Walter *WhoScE 91-1*
Watts, Katherine 1949- *WhoAmW 93*
Watts, Kathleen C. *Law&B 92*
Watts, Kellie Joan 1958- *WhoAmW 93*
Watts, Linda Sizer 1957- *WhoAmW 93*
Watts, Malcolm Stuart McNeal 1915- *WhoAm 92*
Watts, Mary Ann 1927- *WhoE 93*
Watts, Mary Stanberry 1868-1958 *AmWomPl*
Watts, Michael P. 1937- *St&PR 93*
Watts, Nancy Ashford 1941- *WhoAmW 93*
Watts, Oliver Edward 1939- *WhoAm 92*
Watts, Pamela Rae 1952- *WhoAmW 93*
Watts, Patsy Jeanne 1943- *WhoAmW 93, WhoWor 93*
Watts, Ralph Charles 1944- *St&PR 93*
Watts, Richard Eugene 1956- *WhoSSW 93*
Watts, Robert Glenn 1933- *WhoSSW 93*
Watts, Roger H. *Law&B 92*
Watts, Ronald Lester 1934- *WhoAm 92*
Watts, Ross Leslie 1942- *WhoE 93*
Watts, Roy *MiSFD 9*
Watts, Sara Casey 1948- *WhoSSW 93*
Watts, Sewell S., III 1932- *St&PR 93*
Watts, Stacy Chyla 1963- *WhoE 93*
Watts, Steven C. 1951- *St&PR 93*
Watts, Susanna Kaye 1951- *WhoAmW 93*
Watts, Thomas Lee 1938- *WhoAm 92*
Watts, W. *WhoScE 91-3*
Watts, Wendy Burch 1955- *St&PR 93*
Watts, Wilford David, Jr. 1945- *WhoSSW 93*
Watts, William David 1938- *WhoSSW 93*

Watts, William E. 1952- St&PR 93
Watts, William Edward 1952- WhoAm 92
Watts, William Park 1916- WhoSSW 93
Watts, Wintter (Haynes) 1884-1962 Baker 92
Watts-Jackson, Genelle R. Law&B 92
Watts-Russell, David O'Reilly 1944- WhoWor 93
Watwood, Melanie Ann 1961- WhoAmW 93
Waty, Jean Clement 1937- WhoWor 93
Watz, James Hartman 1942- WhoAm 92
Watz, Martin Charles 1938- WhoWor 93
Watzke, Rudolf 1892-1972 Baker 92
Watzlawick, Helmut Leo 1938- WhoUN 92
Wauchope, Dorothy Thomson 1912- WhoAmW 93
Wauchope, Keith L. 1941- WhoAm 92, WhoWor 93
Waud, Roger Neil 1938- WhoAm 92
Wauer, William 1866-1962 BioIn 17
Waugh, A.B. Law&B 92
Waugh, A. Bruce 1949- St&PR 93
Waugh, Ann BioIn 17
Waugh, Auberon BioIn 17
Waugh, Carol-Lynn Rossel 1947- ScF&FL 92
Waugh, Carolyn Sue 1960- WhoAmW 93
Waugh, Carrie Jane Holland 1938- WhoAmW 93
Waugh, Charles G. 1943- ScF&FL 92
Waugh, Constance E. AmWomPl
Waugh, Denis BioIn 17
Waugh, Douglas Oliver William 1918- WhoAm 92
Waugh, Evelyn 1903-1966 BioIn 17, MagSWL [port], WorLitC [port]
Waugh, Frederick J. 1861- ScF&FL 92
Waugh, George St&PR 93
Waugh, Harriet 1944- ScF&FL 92
Waugh, James Stephen 1947- St&PR 93
Waugh, Jennie Suiter 1930- WhoAmW 93
Waugh, Jenny-Lynn 1968- ScF&FL 92
Waugh, John David 1932- WhoAm 92
Waugh, John Stewart 1929- WhoAm 92
Waugh, Richard Earl 1947- WhoE 93
Waugh, Richard W. 1943- WhoIns 93
Waugh, Robert James 1934- WhoAm 92
Waugh, Theodore Rogers 1926- WhoAm 92
Waughtal, Perry McAllister 1935- St&PR 93
Wauhop, Iles W. 1934- WhoIns 93
Wauquier, Albert 1940- WhoWor 93
Waurishuk, James M., Jr. 1954- WhoE 93
Wauters, Luc 1926- St&PR 93
Wauters, Luc Victor 1926- WhoWor 93
Wautier, Jean Luc 1942- WhoWor 93
Wauwai, John 1936- WhoAsAP 91
Wavell, Archibald Percival 1883-1950 DcTwHis, HarEnMi
Wawelberg, Hipolit 1843-1901 PolBiDi
Wawrose, Frederick Eugene 1929- WhoE 93
Wawryn, Krzysztof Waldemar 1952- WhoWor 93
Wawrzaszek, Zbigniew WhoScE 91-4
Wawrzynczak, Stefan 1932- WhoScE 91-4
Wawrzyniak, Stephen David 1949- St&PR 93
Wax, Bernard 1930- WhoAm 92
Wax, David 1939- St&PR 93
Wax, David M. WhoSSW 93
Wax, Edward L. 1937- WhoE 93
Wax, George Louis 1928- WhoSSW 93
Wax, Michael Jay 1957- WhoE 93
Wax, Nadine Virginia 1927- St&PR 93, WhoAmW 93
Wax, Robert P. Law&B 92
Wax, Rosalie 1911- BioIn 17
Wax, Stanley H. 1941- St&PR 93
Wax, Wendy A. 1963- SmATA 73
Wax, William Edward 1956- WhoAm 92
Waxberg, Myron Law&B 92
Waxberg, Myron D. 1933- St&PR 93
Waxenberg, Alan M. 1935- WhoAm 92, WhoE 93
Waxenberg, Susan A. Law&B 92
Waxlax, Lorne Rudolph 1933- St&PR 93
Waxler, Robert Phillip 1944- WhoE 93
Waxman, Al 1935- MiSFD 9
Waxman, Albert S. St&PR 93
Waxman, Albert Samuel 1935- WhoAm 92
Waxman, Armond 1938- St&PR 93
Waxman, Avrom S. 1930- St&PR 93
Waxman, David 1918- WhoAm 92
Waxman, Franz 1906-1967 Baker 92
Waxman, Henry A. 1939- CngDr 91, CurBio 92 [port]
Waxman, Henry Alan 1945- WhoE 93
Waxman, Henry Arnold 1939- WhoAm 92
Waxman, Herbert J. 1913- WhoWrEP 92
Waxman, Herbert Sumner 1936- WhoE 93
Waxman, Keoni MiSFD 9
Waxman, Melvin 1934- St&PR 93
Waxman, Ronald 1933- WhoAm 92
Waxman, Shelley C. Law&B 92
Waxman, Stephen George 1945- WhoAm 92
Way, Alva Otis, III 1929- St&PR 93
Way, Carol Jane 1940- WhoAmW 93
Way, Carole Lindley 1946- WhoAmW 93
Way, Charles D. 1953- St&PR 93
Way, Edward Leong 1916- WhoAm 92
Way, George 1950- BioIn 17
Way, Jacob Edson, III 1947- WhoAm 92
Way, James Leong 1926- WhoSSW 93
Way, John H. ScF&FL 92
Way, Kenneth L. 1939- WhoAm 92
Way, Paul H. 1937- St&PR 93
Way, Peter 1936- ScF&FL 92
Way, Richard D. 1941- St&PR 93
Way, Thomas John 1941- WhoSSW 93
Way, Walter Lee 1931- WhoAm 92
Way, Wilson Spencer 1910- WhoSSW 93
Wayans, Damon 1961?- ConTFT 10
Wayans, Keenen BioIn 17
Wayans, Keenen Ivory WhoAm 92
Wayans, Keenen Ivory 1958?- ConTFT 10, MiSFD 9
Waybourn, Marilu M. 1931- WhoWrEP 92
Waybright, George Warren St&PR 93
Waybright, Horace H. 1926- St&PR 93
Waybur, David C. d1945 BioIn 17
Wayburn, Edgar BioIn 17
Wayburn, Peggy BioIn 17
Wayditch, Gabriel 1888-1969 Baker 92
Waygood, Ernest Roy 1918- WhoAm 92
Waylan, C.J. 1941- St&PR 93
Waylan, Cecil Jerome 1941- WhoAm 92
Waylan, Mildred WhoWrEP 92
Wayland, Adelaide Schmidt AmWomPl
Wayland, Clive Philip 1952- WhoWor 93
Wayland, David M. 1943- St&PR 93
Wayland, James Harold 1909- WhoAm 92
Wayland, L. C. Newton 1909- WhoWor 93
Wayland, Newton Hart 1940- WhoAm 92
Wayland, Russell Gibson, Jr. 1913- WhoAm 92
Wayland, William F. 1935- St&PR 93
Wayland, William Francis 1935- WhoAm 92
Wayman, Clarence Marvin 1930- WhoAm 92
Wayman, David Anthony 1950- WhoWor 93
Wayman, Donald Paul 1957- WhoE 93
Wayman, Morris 1915- WhoAm 92
Wayman, Patrick Arthur 1927- WhoScE 91-3, WhoWor 93
Wayman, Richard E. 1934- St&PR 93
Wayman, Robert Paul 1945- WhoAm 92
Wayman, Russell 1945- St&PR 93
Wayman, Tom 1945- WhoCanL 92
Wayman, W. Russell Law&B 92
Waymire, Gary Wendell 1945- St&PR 93
Waymire, Jimmy D. 1944- St&PR 93
Waymouth, Charity 1915- WhoAm 92
Waymouth, John Francis 1926- WhoAm 92
Waymouth, Victoria BioIn 17
Wayne, Anthony 1745-1796 CmdGen 1991 [port], HarEnMi
Wayne, Bill Tom 1946- WhoSSW 93
Wayne, Bobbie Joan 1947- WhoE 93
Wayne, Burt BioIn 17
Wayne, Carol 1945?-1985 BioIn 17
Wayne, Charles M. ScF&FL 92
Wayne, Hal WhoWrEP 92
Wayne, Herbert Monteith 1932- St&PR 93
Wayne, James Moore 1790-1867 OxCSupC
Wayne, Jane O. 1938- WhoWrEP 92
Wayne, Jerry Kramer 1933- WhoSSW 93
Wayne, John 1907-1979 BioIn 17, IntDcF 2-3 [port], MiSFD 9N
Wayne, Johnny BioIn 17
Wayne, Lowell Grant 1918- WhoAm 92
Wayne, Matt ScF&FL 92
Wayne, Naunton 1901-1970 See Radford, Basil 1897-1952 & Wayne, Naunton 1901-1970 QDrFCA 92
Wayne, Norman Murray 1941- St&PR 93
Wayne, Priscilla AmWomPl
Wayne, Robert Andrew 1938- WhoWor 93
Wayne, Valerie 1945- ConAu 137
Wayne, Victor Samuel 1953- WhoWor 93
Wayner, Peter Charles, Jr. 1934- WhoE 93
Waynik, Cyril 1928- WhoE 93
Wayrick, Isobel 1937- St&PR 93
Ways, John A. 1942- St&PR 93
Wayte, Alan 1936- WhoAm 92
Waytena, Gary Albert 1942- St&PR 93
Waytula, Anthony J. 1944- St&PR 93, WhoIns 93
Wazeter, Francis X. 1925- St&PR 93
Waziri, Mary Hronik 1941- WhoAmW 93
Wazontek, Stella Catherine 1961- WhoAmW 93
Wazyk, Adam 1905-1982 PolBiDi
Wazzan, Ahmed Rassem Frank 1935- WhoAm 92
Wdowiak, John S. 1963- WhoE 93
Weaber, John F. Law&B 92
Weadon, William Randolph 1926- St&PR 93
Weagraff, John Duane 1928- WhoAm 92
Weaire, Denis L. 1942- WhoScE 91-3
Weakland, Rembert G. 1927- BioIn 17, WhoAm 92
Weakley, Clare George, Jr. 1928- WhoSSW 93, WhoWor 93
Weaks, Mary Louise 1961- ConAu 136, WhoAmW 93
Weaks, Nathan E. 1956- St&PR 93
Weale, Mary Jo 1924- WhoSSW 93
Wean, Blanche McNeely 1901- WhoAmW 93
Wean, Raymond John, Jr. 1921- St&PR 93
Wear, James Otto 1937- WhoSSW 93
Wear, Judith Ann 1944- WhoAmW 93
Wear, Kenneth Willard 1932- WhoSSW 93
Weare, Ashley 1927- St&PR 93
Weare, T. John 1943- WhoScE 91-1
Wearing, Betsy May 1932- WhoWor 93
Wearly, William Levi 1915- WhoAm 92
Wearn, Jonathan Richard 1943- WhoWor 93
Wearn, Wilson Cannon 1919- WhoAm 92
Weart, William G. d1992 BioIn 17
Weary, Billy Ray, Jr. 1944- AfrAmBi
Weary, Danel Croft 1927- St&PR 93
Weary, Dolphus BioIn 17
Weary, Marianne 1929- St&PR 93
Weary, Ogdred MajAI, SmATA 70
Weary, Peyton Edwin 1930- WhoAm 92
Weary, Thomas Squires 1925- WhoE 93
Weathall, Tom WhoSSW 93
Weatherald, Keith Baynes Law&B 92
Weatherall, Buc 1939- St&PR 93
Weatherall, David John WhoScE 91-1
Weatherall, James M. 1956- St&PR 93
Weatherall, Jim d1992 NewYTBS 92
Weatherbee, Artemus Edwin 1918- WhoAm 92
Weatherbee, Carl 1916- WhoWor 93
Weatherbee, Donald Emery 1932- WhoAm 92
Weatherbee, Ellen Gene Elliott 1939- WhoAmW 93
Weatherby, Gregg L. 1950- WhoWrEP 92
Weatherby, M. Madge 1922- WhoSSW 93
Weatherby, Roger K. Law&B 92
Weatherby, Roy BioIn 17
Weatherby, Susan Moormann 1950- WhoAmW 93
Weatherby, W.J. ScF&FL 92
Weatherby, W(illiam) J(ohn) 1930?-1992 ConAu 139
Weatherby, William J. d1992 NewYTBS 92
Weatherford, James E. 1946- St&PR 93
Weatherford, Jean B. 1947- St&PR 93
Weatherford, Ken M., Jr. 1951- St&PR 93
Weatherford, Mary BioIn 17
Weatherford, Richard L. Law&B 92
Weatherford, Teddy 1903-1945 Baker 92
Weatherford, Willis Duke, Jr. 1916- WhoAm 92
Weatherford-Batman, Mary Virginia WhoAmW 93, WhoSSW 93
Weatherhead, Albert John 1925- St&PR 93
Weatherholtz, Karen D. 1950- St&PR 93
Weatherholtz, Michael Glenn 1957- WhoSSW 93
Weatherill, Anne BioIn 17
Weatherill, John Frederick William 1932- WhoAm 92
Weatherly, Haldon Lee 1933- St&PR 93
Weatherly, John Stephen 1952- St&PR 93
Weatherly, Robert Stone, Jr. 1929- WhoAm 92
Weatherly, Thomas Burdett 1914- WhoAm 92
Weatherred, Thurman W. 1932- St&PR 93
Weathers, Barbara Hiller 1942- WhoSSW 93
Weathers, Brenda 1936- ScF&FL 92
Weathers, Felicia 1937- Baker 92
Weathers, Lawrence Martin 1924- WhoSSW 93
Weathers, Linda Askey 1956- WhoSSW 93
Weathersby, Cecil Jerry 1952- WhoSSW 93
Weathersby, George Byron 1944- St&PR 93, WhoAm 92, WhoWrEP 92
Weathersby, Michael Nelson 1956- WhoSSW 93
Weatherspoon, Clarence BioIn 17
Weatherston, George Douglas, Jr. 1952- WhoSSW 93
Weatherstone, Dennis 1930- BioIn 17, St&PR 93, WhoAm 92
Weatherstone, James W. 1925- WhoIns 93
Weatherup, Samuel Thomas Colin WhoScE 91-1
Weatherup, Wendy Gaines 1952- WhoAmW 93
Weatherwax, David E. 1930- St&PR 93
Weatherwax, David Eugene Law&B 92
Weatherwax, Susan E. Law&B 92
Weaver, Albert Bruce 1917- WhoAm 92
Weaver, Andrew Dudley 1929- St&PR 93
Weaver, Arthur Gordon 1915- WhoAm 92
Weaver, Arthur Lawrence 1936- WhoWor 93
Weaver, Barbara Frances 1927- WhoAm 92, WhoAmW 93
Weaver, Ben 1933- St&PR 93
Weaver, Bill Thomas 1925- WhoWor 93
Weaver, Bradley Miles Law&B 92
Weaver, C. Herschell 1944- WhoSSW 93
Weaver, Carlton Davis 1921- WhoAm 92
Weaver, Carolyn Leslie 1952- WhoE 93
Weaver, Carrie Etta 1935- WhoSSW 93
Weaver, Charles Henry 1914- WhoAm 92
Weaver, Charles Horace 1927- WhoSSW 93
Weaver, Charles Lyndell, Jr. 1945- WhoWor 93
Weaver, Charles Richard 1928- WhoAm 92
Weaver, Charles S. 1932- St&PR 93
Weaver, Charles Stanley 1922- WhoSSW 93
Weaver, Charles Steele 1918- WhoAm 92
Weaver, Clarence Lahr 1904- WhoWrEP 92
Weaver, Connie Marie 1950- WhoAmW 93
Weaver, Craig H. Law&B 92
Weaver, Crystal Dawn 1957- WhoAmW 93
Weaver, David Hugh 1946- WhoAm 92
Weaver, Debra Lynn 1953- WhoAmW 93
Weaver, Debra Stafford Law&B 92
Weaver, Delbert Allen 1931- WhoAm 92
Weaver, Dennis 1924- WhoAm 92
Weaver, Donald Wesley 1933- WhoE 93
Weaver, Donna Rae 1945- WhoAmW 93
Weaver, Earl W. 1908- St&PR 93
Weaver, Edward Myers 1927- St&PR 93
Weaver, Edward T. 1931- WhoAm 92
Weaver, Ella Haith d1991 BioIn 17
Weaver, Ellen Thomas Law&B 92
Weaver, Eric James 1938- WhoE 93
Weaver, Franklin Thomas 1932- WhoAm 92
Weaver, Fritz William 1926- WhoAm 92
Weaver, Geneva A. 1947- WhoAmW 93
Weaver, Genevieve BioIn 17
Weaver, George Daniel 1890-1956 BiDAMSp 1989
Weaver, George F. 1929- St&PR 93
Weaver, George S. 1934- St&PR 93
Weaver, Gertrude ScF&FL 92
Weaver, Gertrude Sophia 1916- WhoAmW 93
Weaver, Gilbert Brewster 1930- WhoSSW 93
Weaver, Gordon Allison 1937- WhoWrEP 92
Weaver, Gustine Nancy Courson 1873-1942 AmWomPl
Weaver, Harriett E. 1908- BioIn 17
Weaver, Howard Cecil 1950- WhoAm 92
Weaver, Jackson J. d1992 NewYTBS 92
Weaver, James B. 1833-1912 GayN, PolPar
Weaver, James P. 1929- St&PR 93
Weaver, Jeanne Moore 1927- WhoSSW 93
Weaver, Jeffrey Lawton 1956- WhoSSW 93
Weaver, Jerry Kent 1941- St&PR 93
Weaver, Joe Law&B 92
Weaver, John Carrier 1915- WhoAm 92
Weaver, John H. 1915- St&PR 93
Weaver, John Lockerbie 1936- WhoAm 92
Weaver, Karen Southworth Law&B 92
Weaver, Kathleen Ann 1957- WhoAmW 93
Weaver, Kennard R. 1940- St&PR 93
Weaver, Kevin L. Law&B 92
Weaver, Lee BioIn 17
Weaver, Lee A. 1932- St&PR 93
Weaver, Lydia ScF&FL 92
Weaver, Lynn Edward 1930- WhoAm 92, WhoSSW 93
Weaver, Marguerite McKinnie 1925- WhoAmW 93, WhoSSW 93, WhoWor 93
Weaver, Marshall Gueringer 1954- WhoSSW 93
Weaver, Michael D. 1961- ScF&FL 92
Weaver, Michael James 1946- WhoWor 93
Weaver, Michele Law&B 92
Weaver, Mollie Little 1934- WhoAmW 93
Weaver, Neal C. 1956- St&PR 93
Weaver, Pamela Ann 1947- WhoAmW 93, WhoEmL 93
Weaver, Paul D. Law&B 92

Weaver, Paul David 1943- *St&PR 93, WhoAm 92*
Weaver, Powell 1890-1951 *Baker 92*
Weaver, R(obert) Kent 1953- *ConAu 138*
Weaver, Richard L., II 1941- *WhoAm 92, WhoWrEP 92*
Weaver, Richard R. 1935- *St&PR 93*
Weaver, Robert 1921- *WhoCanL 92*
Weaver, Robert B. 1939- *St&PR 93*
Weaver, Robert C. 1907- *EncAACR*
Weaver, Robert Clifton 1907- *WhoAm 92*
Weaver, Robert Lamar *BioIn 17*
Weaver, Rose *AmWomPl*
Weaver, Rosetta Loraine 1935- *WhoE 93*
Weaver, Scott James 1958- *WhoWor 93*
Weaver, Sharon Tamargo 1947- *WhoSSW 93*
Weaver, Sigourney *BioIn 17*
Weaver, Sigourney 1949- *ConTFT 10, HolBB [port], IntDcF 2-3 [port], WhoAm 92, WhoAmW 93*
Weaver, Sylvester Laflin, Jr. 1908- *WhoAm 92*
Weaver, Thomas 1929- *WhoWrEP 92*
Weaver, Thomas Raymond *Law&B 92*
Weaver, Tom 1958- *ScF&FL 92*
Weaver, Vicky Lynn 1950- *WhoAmW 93*
Weaver, Virginia Dove *WhoAmW 93*
Weaver, Warren, Jr. 1923- *WhoAm 92*
Weaver, William Bruce 1946- *WhoAm 92*
Weaver, William Charles 1941- *WhoAm 92*
Weaver, William Charles, Jr. 1951- *WhoSSW 93*
Weaver, William Clair, Jr. 1936- *WhoWor 93*
Weaver, William Edward 1931- *St&PR 93*
Weaver, William Merritt, Jr. 1912- *St&PR 93, WhoAm 92*
Weavers, The *ConMus 8 [port]*
Weavil, David C. 1951- *St&PR 93*
Weavil, David Carlton 1951- *WhoAm 92*
Webb, A.C. 1894-1985 *ScF&FL 92*
Webb, A.J. 1947- *WhoScE 91-1*
Webb, Alexander Dwight 1952- *WhoE 93*
Webb, Anthony Allan 1943- *WhoAm 92*
Webb, Arthur Philip 1945- *St&PR 93*
Webb, B.C. 1945- *WhoScE 91-1*
Webb, Barbara *BioIn 17*
Webb, Beatrice Potter 1858-1943 *BioIn 17*
Webb, Benjiman Daniel 1942- *WhoSSW 93*
Webb, Bernice Larson *WhoAmW 93, WhoWrEP 92*
Webb, Bill *Law&B 92*
Webb, Brainard T., Jr. *Law&B 92*
Webb, Brainard Troutman, Jr. 1943- *St&PR 93, WhoAm 92*
Webb, Brian Lockwood 1949- *WhoSSW 93*
Webb, Charles Albert 1917- *WhoAm 92*
Webb, Charles Haizlip, Jr. 1933- *Baker 92, WhoAm 92*
Webb, Charles Harry 1953- *WhoAm 92*
Webb, Charles Henry 1834-1905 *JrnUS*
Webb, Charles Howard 1945- *WhoSSW 93*
Webb, Charles Richard 1919- *WhoAm 92*
Webb, "Chick" (William Henry) 1909-1939 *Baker 92*
Webb, Clarence 1940- *St&PR 93*
Webb, Clifton 1891-1966 *IntDcF 2-3*
Webb, Cyrus E. 1930- *St&PR 93*
Webb, David F. 1930- *St&PR 93*
Webb, David Thomas, Jr. *Law&B 92*
Webb, Don 1960- *ScF&FL 92*
Webb, Donald Arthur 1926- *WhoAm 92*
Webb, Donna Louise 1929- *WhoAmW 93*
Webb, Dorothy Elizabeth 1960- *WhoAmW 93*
Webb, Douglas A. 1942- *St&PR 93*
Webb, Douglas C. *Law&B 92*
Webb, Douglas Chester 1929- *BioIn 17*
Webb, Douglas William 1934- *WhoWor 93*
Webb, Earl 1898-1965 *BioIn 17*
Webb, Edward Timothy 1942- *WhoWor 93*
Webb, Elida d1975 *BioIn 17*
Webb, Elizabeth *Law&B 92*
Webb, Eugene 1938- *WhoAm 92*
Webb, Faye Rappold 1941- *WhoSSW 93*
Webb, Francis Hubert 1927- *WhoE 93*
Webb, Francis Thomas G. 1947- *WhoUN 92*
Webb, Frank McConville 1954- *WhoSSW 93*
Webb, Frank Rush 1851-1934 *Baker 92*
Webb, Freddie N. 1942- *WhoAsAP 91*
Webb, G.A.M. *WhoScE 91-1*
Webb, Gary A. *Law&B 92*
Webb, George Ernest 1952- *WhoSSW 93*
Webb, George H. 1920- *St&PR 93*
Webb, George Henry 1920- *WhoAm 92*
Webb, George James 1803-1887 *Baker 92*
Webb, Gloria O. 1931- *WhoAm 92, WhoSSW 93*
Webb, Grant d1991 *BioIn 17*
Webb, Guy E., Jr. 1931- *WhoIns 93*
Webb, Guy Edmund, Jr. 1931- *WhoAm 92*
Webb, Helen *AmWomPl*
Webb, Helen Parke 1931- *WhoSSW 93*
Webb, Henley Ross *Law&B 92*
Webb, Horace S. 1940- *St&PR 93*
Webb, Howard E. 1940- *St&PR 93*
Webb, Igor Michael 1941- *WhoAm 92*
Webb, Ivan Wayne 1951- *St&PR 93*
Webb, J. David *Law&B 92*
Webb, J.S. 1919- *St&PR 93*
Webb, Jack 1920-1982 *MiSFD 9N*
Webb, Jack M. 1936- *WhoAm 92*
Webb, Jackie *ScF&FL 92*
Webb, James B. 1945- *St&PR 93*
Webb, James David 1936- *WhoSSW 93*
Webb, James E. 1906-1992 *BioIn 17*
Webb, James E(dwin) 1906-1992 *CurBio 92N*
Webb, James Edward 1928- *WhoWrEP 92*
Webb, James Edwin d1992 *NewYTBS 92 [port]*
Webb, James H. *BioIn 17*
Webb, James Okrum, Jr. 1931- *WhoAm 92*
Webb, James Robert 1954- *WhoSSW 93, WhoWor 93*
Webb, James S. 1947- *St&PR 93*
Webb, James Watson 1802-1884 *JrnUS*
Webb, Jean Francis, IV 1937- *WhoIns 93*
Webb, Jean J. 1935- *St&PR 93*
Webb, Jean Kimbrough 1951- *WhoAmW 93*
Webb, Jeffrey G. *St&PR 93*
Webb, Jeffrey Ray 1960- *WhoWor 93*
Webb, Jeffrey Ronald Leslie *WhoScE 91-1*
Webb, Jervis B. 1915- *WhoAm 92*
Webb, Jervis Campbell 1915- *St&PR 93*
Webb, Jessie M. *AmWomPl*
Webb, Jilla Rose 1923- *WhoWor 93*
Webb, Joe Steve 1932- *St&PR 93*
Webb, John 1926- *WhoAm 92, WhoSSW 93*
Webb, John Clayton, Jr. 1937- *WhoSSW 93*
Webb, John G. *Law&B 92*
Webb, John G., III *Law&B 92*
Webb, John G., III 1944- *St&PR 93*
Webb, John Gibbon, III 1944- *WhoE 93*
Webb, John Joshua 1847-1882 *BioIn 17*
Webb, John Peter 1945- *WhoWor 93*
Webb, Julian 1911- *WhoAm 92, WhoWor 93*
Webb, Julie A. *Law&B 92*
Webb, Katharine 1931- *WhoE 93*
Webb, Kaye 1914- *BioIn 17*
Webb, Kenneth 1927- *BioIn 17*
Webb, Lamar Thaxter 1928- *WhoSSW 93*
Webb, Lance 1909- *WhoAm 92*
Webb, Larry A. *St&PR 93*
Webb, Laurent B. *Law&B 92*
Webb, Lenore Lorraine 1952- *WhoAmW 93*
Webb, Leon, Jr. 1943- *St&PR 93*
Webb, Leslie Roy 1935- *WhoWor 93*
Webb, Linda Suzanne 1955- *WhoAmW 93*
Webb, Lucas *ScF&FL 92*
Webb, Lynne McGovern 1951- *WhoAmW 93*
Webb, M. Rodney 1944- *WhoSSW 93*
Webb, Maggie *ScF&FL 92*
Webb, Marcus G.T. 1937- *WhoScE 91-3*
Webb, Margaret *AmWomPl*
Webb, Margot 1934- *BioIn 17*
Webb, Marland O. *Law&B 92*
Webb, Martha Jeanne 1947- *WhoAmW 93*
Webb, Martin E. 1946- *St&PR 93*
Webb, Maurice 1945- *WhoScE 91-1*
Webb, Max A. *Law&B 92*
Webb, Melody 1946- *WhoWrEP 92*
Webb, Michael (Jack) 1953- *ConAu 137*
Webb, Morrison DeSoto *Law&B 92*
Webb, Morrison DeSoto 1947- *WhoAm 92*
Webb, Murrell Lee 1938- *St&PR 93*
Webb, Nigel Rodney Chaney *WhoScE 91-1*
Webb, O. Glenn 1936- *WhoAm 92*
Webb, Orville Lynn 1931- *WhoSSW 93*
Webb, Patricia Holland 1957- *WhoE 93*
Webb, Patricia Ruth Jarvis 1938- *WhoSSW 93*
Webb, Paul D. 1935- *St&PR 93*
Webb, Paul Richard, II *Law&B 92*
Webb, Paula Stephania 1961- *WhoWrEP 92*
Webb, Peter *MiSFD 9*
Webb, Phyllis 1927- *WhoCanL 92*
Webb, R.G. 1926- *St&PR 93*
Webb, Ralph Lee 1934- *WhoAm 92*
Webb, Raymon E. 1919-1989 *BioIn 17*
Webb, Richard C. 1915- *WhoAm 92*
Webb, Richard E. 1931- *St&PR 93*
Webb, Richard Gilbert 1932- *WhoAm 92*
Webb, Richard Olin 1938- *St&PR 93*
Webb, Richard Pierce 1941- *St&PR 93*
Webb, Richard Stephen 1944- *WhoE 93*
Webb, Robert Carroll, Sr. 1947- *WhoSSW 93*
Webb, Robert Kiefer 1922- *WhoAm 92*
Webb, Robert Lee 1926- *WhoAm 92*
Webb, Robert Mark 1953- *WhoE 93*
Webb, Robert P. 1948- *St&PR 93*
Webb, Robert W. *Law&B 92*
Webb, Rodney Scott 1935- *WhoAm 92*
Webb, Roger Paul 1936- *WhoAm 92*
Webb, Roger S. *BioIn 17*
Webb, Roger Stuart 1950- *WhoSSW 93, WhoWor 93*
Webb, Rubin W. 1926- *WhoSSW 93*
Webb, Ryland Edwin 1932- *WhoSSW 93*
Webb, Samuel Blatchley, Jr. 1939- *WhoE 93*
Webb, Sarah Ann 1948- *WhoSSW 93*
Webb, Sharon 1936- *ScF&FL 92*
Webb, Sharon Lynn 1936- *WhoWrEP 92*
Webb, Sidney James 1859-1947 *DcTwHis*
Webb, Spud *BioIn 17*
Webb, Stuart B. A. *St&PR 93*
Webb, Theodore Stratton 1930- *St&PR 93*
Webb, Theodore Stratton, Jr. 1930- *WhoAm 92*
Webb, Thomas C. 1934- *St&PR 93*
Webb, Thomas Crawford 1934- *WhoAm 92*
Webb, Thomas Evan 1932- *WhoAm 92*
Webb, Thomas Irwin, Jr. 1948- *WhoEmL 93, WhoWor 93*
Webb, Todd 1905- *WhoAm 92*
Webb, Veronica *BioIn 17*
Webb, W. Roger 1941- *WhoSSW 93*
Webb, Watt Wetmore 1927- *WhoAm 92*
Webb, Watts Rankin 1922- *WhoAm 92*
Webb, Wellington 1941- *ConBlB 3 [port]*
Webb, Wellington E. *BioIn 17, WhoAm 92*
Webb, William *MiSFD 9*
Webb, William Duncan 1930- *WhoAm 92*
Webb, William Henry 1816-1899 *BioIn 17*
Webb, William Hess 1905- *WhoAm 92, WhoE 93*
Webb, William J. *Law&B 92*
Webb, William John 1922- *WhoAm 92, WhoE 93, WhoWor 93*
Webb, William L., Jr. 1930-1992 *NewYTBS 92*
Webb, William Loyd, Jr. 1925- *WhoAm 92*
Webb, William Thomas 1918- *ScF&FL 92*
Webb, William Y. 1935- *WhoAm 92*
Webb, Wilse Bernard 1920- *WhoSSW 93*
Webb, Yvonne 1954- *St&PR 93*
Webbe, Frank Michael 1947- *WhoSSW 93*
Webbe, Samuel 1740-1816 *Baker 92*
Webbe, Samuel c. 1770-1843 *See* Webbe, Samuel 1740-1816 *Baker 92*
Webbe, Scotson 1917- *St&PR 93*
Webber, Alan J. 1949- *St&PR 93*
Webber, Andrew Lloyd *Baker 92*
Webber, Andrew Lloyd 1948- *BioIn 17*
Webber, Bert *ConAu 39NR*
Webber, Carolyn Forbes 1949- *WhoAmW 93*
Webber, Chris *Law&B 92*
Webber, David Anthony 1929- *WhoAm 92*
Webber, Ebbert T(rue) 1921- *ConAu 39NR*
Webber, Edythe Marie 1954- *WhoEmL 93, WhoWor 93*
Webber, Frederick H. *Law&B 92*
Webber, Gerald A. 1944- *St&PR 93*
Webber, Howard C. *St&PR 93*
Webber, Howard Rodney 1933- *WhoAm 92*
Webber, John A. 1912- *St&PR 93*
Webber, John Bentley 1941- *WhoAm 92, WhoWor 93*
Webber, John Clinton 1943- *WhoSSW 93*
Webber, Judd Lory 1951- *WhoWor 93*
Webber, Julian Lloyd *Baker 92, ScF&FL 92*
Webber, Larry Stanford 1945- *WhoSSW 93*
Webber, Malcolm Scott 1940- *St&PR 93*
Webber, N. Claire *Law&B 92*
Webber, Ralph G. 1923- *St&PR 93*
Webber, Randall M. 1942- *St&PR 93*
Webber, Robert (Eugene) 1933- *ConAu 37NR*
Webber, Robert F. 1946- *St&PR 93*
Webber, Samuel 1759-1810 *BioIn 17*
Webber, William Alexander 1934- *WhoAm 92*
Webberley, Brian J. *BioIn 17*
Webbert, Doreen 1934- *ScF&FL 92*
Webeck, Alfred Stanley 1913- *St&PR 93*
Webel, Richard Karl *WhoAm 92*
Weber, Adelheid Lisa 1934- *WhoAmW 93*
Weber, Alain 1930- *Baker 92*
Weber, Alan Jay 1949- *WhoAm 92*
Weber, Alban 1915- *WhoWor 93*
Weber, Alexander 1921- *St&PR 93*
Weber, Alfred Herman 1906- *WhoAm 92*
Weber, Alois Hughes 1910- *WhoAmW 93, WhoWor 93*
Weber, Aloysia 1759?-1839 *OxDcOp*
Weber, (Maria) Aloysia c. 1760-1839 *See* Weber, Fridolin 1733-1779 *Baker 92*
Weber, Amy L. *AmWomPl*
Weber, Andre-Paul 1939- *WhoWor 93*
Weber, Anthony Clemens 1952- *St&PR 93*
Weber, Anton 1947- *WhoScE 91-4*
Weber, Arnold R. 1929- *WhoAm 92, WhoWor 93*
Weber, Arthur 1926- *WhoAm 92*
Weber, Arthur D. 1898-1983 *BioIn 17*
Weber, Barbara M. 1945- *WhoAmW 93*
Weber, Barrie R. 1940- *St&PR 93*
Weber, Ben 1916-1979 *Baker 92*
Weber, Bernhard Anselm 1764-1821 *Baker 92*
Weber, Bernhard Christian 1712-1758 *Baker 92*
Weber, Beverly Joy 1932- *WhoWrEP 92*
Weber, Brom 1917- *WhoAm 92, WhoWrEP 92*
Weber, Bruce *MiSFD 9*
Weber, Bruce 1942- *SmATA 73, WhoWor 93*
Weber, Bruce Howard 1963- *WhoSSW 93*
Weber, C(larence) A(dam) 1903- *ConAu 37NR*
Weber, Carl Maria, Freiherr von 1786-1826 *IntDcOp [port]*
Weber, Carl Maria von 1786-1826 *OxDcOp*
Weber, Carl Maria (Friedrich Ernst) von 1786-1826 *Baker 92*
Weber, Cary Allen 1962- *WhoSSW 93*
Weber, Charles Edward 1924- *WhoWrEP 92*
Weber, Charles Edward 1930- *WhoAm 92*
Weber, Charles Marie 1814-1881 *BioIn 17*
Weber, Christine Ann 1968- *WhoAmW 93*
Weber, Christine Ruth 1949- *WhoAmW 93*
Weber, Christopher J. *Law&B 92*
Weber, Clarence Adam 1903- *WhoE 93, WhoWor 93*
Weber, Constanze 1762-1842 *OxDcOp*
Weber, (Maria) Constanze 1762-1842 *See* Weber, Fridolin 1733-1779 *Baker 92*
Weber, Daniel R. *St&PR 93*
Weber, David *ScF&FL 92*
Weber, David C. 1936- *St&PR 93*
Weber, David Carter 1924- *WhoAm 92*
Weber, David J. 1940- *WhoSSW 93*
Weber, David Malcolm 1948- *St&PR 93*
Weber, David Paul 1933- *WhoIns 93*
Weber, Deane Fay 1925- *WhoE 93*
Weber, Diane Theresa 1965- *WhoAmW 93*
Weber, Donald Otto 1953- *St&PR 93*
Weber, Donald W. 1936- *St&PR 93*
Weber, Doron 1955- *ConAu 138*
Weber, Douglas Jay 1952- *St&PR 93*
Weber, Edward P., Jr. *Law&B 92*
Weber, Eicke Richard 1949- *WhoWor 93*
Weber, Elizabeth Ann 1950- *WhoWrEP 92*
Weber, Eric 1942- *BioIn 17*
Weber, Ernest Theodore 1938- *WhoAm 92*
Weber, Ernesto Juan 1930- *WhoWor 93*
Weber, Ernst 1901- *WhoAm 92*
Weber, Ernst Juerg 1950- *WhoWor 93*
Weber, Eugen 1925- *WhoAm 92, WhoWor 93*
Weber, Eugene E. 1942- *St&PR 93*
Weber, Everett David 1929- *St&PR 93*
Weber, Fern Alice 1951- *WhoAmW 93*
Weber, Fred J. 1919- *WhoAm 92*
Weber, Frederick Edwin 1924- *WhoWor 93*
Weber, Fridolin 1733-1779 *Baker 92, OxDcOp*
Weber, Friedrich Dionys 1766-1842 *Baker 92*
Weber, Gail E. 1943- *St&PR 93*
Weber, Georg Viktor 1838-1911 *Baker 92*
Weber, George 1922- *WhoAm 92*
Weber, George Richard 1929- *WhoWor 93*
Weber, Gerald W. B. 1951- *St&PR 93*
Weber, Gordon J. 1947- *St&PR 93*
Weber, (Jacob) Gottfried 1779-1839 *Baker 92*
Weber, Guido 1927- *WhoWor 93*
Weber, Gunter 1929- *WhoScE 91-3*
Weber, Gustav 1845-1887 *Baker 92*
Weber, H.-O. *WhoScE 91-3*
Weber, Hans Jurgen 1939- *WhoAm 92, WhoSSW 93*
Weber, Hans-Peter 1941- *WhoWor 93*
Weber, Harald W. 1944- *WhoScE 91-4*
Weber, Harm Allen 1926- *WhoAm 92*
Weber, Heather Wilson 1943- *WhoAmW 93*
Weber, Henry A. 1915- *St&PR 93*
Weber, Herbert G. 1941- *St&PR 93*
Weber, I. 1920- *St&PR 93*

Weber, Jack E., Jr. 1937- St&PR 93
Weber, James Stuart 1947- WhoEmL 93
Weber, Janet M. 1936- WhoAm 92, WhoAmW 93
Weber, Jean MacPhail 1933- WhoAm 92
Weber, Jeffery Allen 1953- St&PR 93
Weber, Jerome Charles 1938- WhoAm 92
Weber, John Bertram 1930- WhoWor 93
Weber, John David Law&B 92
Weber, John Fisher 1956- WhoSSW 93
Weber, John J. 1941- St&PR 93
Weber, John Joseph d1992 NewYTBS 92 [port]
Weber, John Joseph 1919-1992 BioIn 17
Weber, John M. Law&B 92
Weber, John R. 1946- St&PR 93
Weber, Joseph 1920- St&PR 93
Weber, Joseph A., Jr. 1932- St&PR 93
Weber, Joseph H. 1930- WhoAm 92
Weber, Joseph Miroslav 1854-1906 Baker 92
Weber, Josepha 1758?-1819 OxDcOp
Weber, (Maria) Josepha c. 1759-1819 See Weber, Fridolin 1733-1779 Baker 92
Weber, Judith 1938- BioIn 17
Weber, Julian L. 1929- St&PR 93, WhoAm 92
Weber, Karl d1990 BioIn 17
Weber, Karl William 1953- WhoAm 92
Weber, Kathy Kaufman 1961- WhoAmW 93
Weber, Ken(neth J.) 1940- ConAu 39NR
Weber, Lawrence James 1941- St&PR 93
Weber, Lawrence M. St&PR 93
Weber, Leo L. 1929- St&PR 93, WhoAm 92
Weber, Linda Hall 1949- WhoAmW 93
Weber, Lisa B. 1953- BioIn 17
Weber, Lois 1882-1939 MiSFD 9N
Weber, Ludwig 1899-1974 Baker 92, IntDcOp, OxDcOp
Weber, Marcie J. Law&B 92
Weber, Margaret Laura Jane 1933- WhoAmW 93
Weber, Margrit 1924- Baker 92
Weber, Marianne 1870-1954 BioIn 17
Weber, Marilyn Ann Minch 1934- WhoAmW 93, WhoWor 93
Weber, Marlene Elizabeth 1938- WhoAmW 93
Weber, Max 1864-1920 BioIn 17
Weber, Max 1881-1961 BioIn 17
Weber, Max O. 1929- WhoAm 92
Weber, Michael WhoScE 91-1
Weber, Morgan M.W. Law&B 92
Weber, Morton M. 1922- WhoAm 92
Weber, Nancy 1942- ScF&FL 92
Weber, Nancy Jean 1959- WhoAmW 93
Weber, Nelva M. d1990 BioIn 17
Weber, Nicholas Fox 1947- BioIn 17
Weber, Nicholas Noyes 1936- St&PR 93
Weber, Owen 1946- WhoAm 92
Weber, Patricia 1949- WhoSSW 93
Weber, Paul J. 1937- ConAu 137, St&PR 93
Weber, Peggy Ann 1963- WhoAmW 93
Weber, Perry James 1945- St&PR 93
Weber, Peter St&PR 93
Weber, Philip, Jr. 1935- St&PR 93
Weber, Philip Joseph 1909- WhoAm 92
Weber, Philip S. Law&B 92
Weber, R. Christopher 1955- St&PR 93
Weber, Rabbe Johan 1956- WhoWor 93
Weber, Raymond P. Law&B 92
Weber, Richard Earle 1931- WhoE 93
Weber, Richard K. 1934- St&PR 93
Weber, Robert J. 1928- St&PR 93
Weber, Robert J(ohn) 1936- ConAu 139
Weber, Robert Mathias 1939- St&PR 93
Weber, Robert Maxwell 1924- WhoAm 92
Weber, Roberta Barsotti 1944- WhoAmW 93
Weber, Rodney Oscar 1962- WhoWor 93
Weber, Roman 1951- WhoScE 91-3
Weber, Ronald 1934- ScF&FL 92
Weber, Ronald Arthur Gerard 1949- WhoWor 93
Weber, Ronald Gilbert 1916- WhoAm 92
Weber, Rose Minna 1955- WhoAmW 93, WhoE 93
Weber, Roy E. 1938- WhoScE 91-2
Weber, Roy Edwin 1928- WhoAm 92
Weber, Roy P. Law&B 92
Weber, Samuel 1926- WhoAm 92, WhoWrEP 92
Weber, Shirley Anne 1928- WhoWrEP 92
Weber, Sol 1933- WhoWrEP 92
Weber, Sophie 1763-1846 OxDcOp
Weber, (Maria) Sophie 1763-1846 See Weber, Fridolin 1733-1779 Baker 92
Weber, Stephen Kilby Law&B 92
Weber, Stephen Lewis 1942- WhoAm 92
Weber, Stephen Robert 1938- St&PR 93
Weber, Steven Allen 1945- St&PR 93
Weber, Susan 1941- WhoAm 92
Weber, Teddy H. 1939- WhoScE 91-4
Weber, Terrence Emil 1958- WhoE 93
Weber, Thomas Andrew 1944- WhoAm 92
Weber, Thomas William 1930- WhoAm 92
Weber, Vernon William 1949- St&PR 93
Weber, Vin 1952- BioIn 17, CngDr 91, WhoAm 92
Weber, Walter Jacob, Jr. 1934- WhoAm 92
Weber, Warren G. 1938- St&PR 93
Weber, Wendell William 1925- WhoAm 92
Weber, Wilhelm 1859-1918 Baker 92
Weber, William H. 1915- St&PR 93
Weber, William L., Jr. Law&B 92
Weber, William P. 1940- WhoSSW 93
Weber, Wolfgang 1939- WhoScE 91-3
Weber, Wolfgang Hans 1937- WhoScE 91-3
Weber-Kellermann, Ingeborg 1918- IntDcAn
Weberling, Ernest A. 1916- St&PR 93
Weberling, Focko H.E. 1926- WhoScE 91-3
Weberling, Jerry A. 1951- St&PR 93
Weberman, Ben 1923- WhoAm 92
Webern, Anton (Friedrich Wilhelm) von 1883-1945 Baker 92
Webert, G.L. 1942- St&PR 93
Webre, Stephen Andrew 1946- WhoSSW 93
Webster, Alasdair Paine 1934- WhoAsAP 91
Webster, Albert Knickerbocker 1937- WhoAm 92
Webster, Alvin Stanley 1926- WhoSSW 93
Webster, Anthony John Francis WhoScE 91-1
Webster, Barrie J. d1992 BioIn 17
Webster, Beveridge 1908- Baker 92
Webster, Carl M. 1956- WhoIns 93
Webster, Charles Linsley 1930- St&PR 93
Webster, Charles M. 1918- St&PR 93
Webster, Charles William Law&B 92
Webster, Christopher White 1953- WhoEmL 93
Webster, Daniel 1782-1852 BioIn 17, OxCSupC, PolPar
Webster, Daniel J., Jr. 1947- St&PR 93
Webster, Daniel Robert 1945- WhoAm 92
Webster, Darryl Lawrence Law&B 92
Webster, David 1903-1971 OxDcOp
Webster, David Arthur 1937- WhoAm 92
Webster, David Clark 1927- WhoE 93, WhoWor 93
Webster, David Deane 1939- St&PR 93
Webster, David (Lumsden) 1903-1971 Baker 92
Webster, Dean K. 1929- St&PR 93
Webster, Diane Lynn 1954- WhoWrEP 92
Webster, Edward William 1922- WhoAm 92
Webster, Elizabeth 1918- ConAu 40NR
Webster, Elizabeth Carol 1952- WhoSSW 93
Webster, Ernest 1923- ScF&FL 92
Webster, Francis Sinclair, III 1945- St&PR 93
Webster, Frederick Elmer, Jr. 1937- WhoAm 92
Webster, George Arnold WhoScE 91-1
Webster, George Calvin 1924- WhoSSW 93, WhoWrEP 92
Webster, George Drury 1921- WhoAm 92, WhoWor 93
Webster, Guy Noble 1933- St&PR 93
Webster, H.T. BioIn 17
Webster, Harold S. 1935- St&PR 93
Webster, Henry deForest 1927- WhoAm 92, WhoWor 93
Webster, James A. 1952- St&PR 93
Webster, James Colin Eden 1936- WhoAm 92
Webster, James E. 1919- St&PR 93
Webster, James Randolph, Jr. 1931- WhoAm 92
Webster, Janet Brown 1962- WhoSSW 93
Webster, Jani Johe WhoWrEP 92
Webster, Jean 1876-1916 AmWomPl
Webster, Jeanine Cecile 1950- WhoAmW 93
Webster, Jeffrey Leon 1941- WhoWor 93
Webster, Joanne ScF&FL 92
Webster, John WhoScE 91-1
Webster, John 1580?-1634? WorLitC
Webster, John Charles 1944- WhoWor 93
Webster, John Goodwin 1932- WhoAm 92
Webster, John K. 1928- St&PR 93
Webster, John Kimball 1934- WhoAm 92
Webster, John Kingsley Ohl, II 1950- WhoWor 93
Webster, John O. Law&B 92
Webster, Josh 1949- ScF&FL 92
Webster, Kathy Dudley 1955- WhoAmW 93, WhoSSW 93
Webster, Lamont 1928- St&PR 93
Webster, Larry Russell 1930- WhoAm 92
Webster, Lee 1948- WhoWrEP 92
Webster, Lee D. 1923- St&PR 93
Webster, Leslie Tillotson, Jr. 1926- WhoAm 92
Webster, Lillian Brostek 1927- WhoAmW 93
Webster, Lois Shand 1929- WhoAmW 93
Webster, Lyn 1950- ScF&FL 92
Webster, Margaret 1905-1972 BioIn 17
Webster, Mark K. 1954- St&PR 93
Webster, Martyn Robert 1947- WhoWor 93
Webster, Nicholas 1922- MiSFD 9
Webster, Noah 1758-1843 BioIn 17, JrnUS
Webster, Ogden H. Law&B 92
Webster, Pamela J. Law&B 92
Webster, Paul BioIn 17
Webster, Paul T. 1924- St&PR 93
Webster, Peter David 1949- WhoSSW 93, WhoWor 93
Webster, Peter Davies 1940- St&PR 93
Webster, Peter John 1942- WhoE 93
Webster, Philip Jonathan 1939- St&PR 93
Webster, Ralph Leroy 1940- St&PR 93
Webster, Raymond Earl 1948- WhoSSW 93
Webster, Robert Byron 1932- WhoWor 93
Webster, Robert David 1938- WhoAm 92
Webster, Robert L. 1954- St&PR 93
Webster, Ronald 1926- DcCPCAm
Webster, Ronald B. 1942- WhoAm 92
Webster, Ronald David 1949- St&PR 93
Webster, Rosa Lavell 1966- WhoSSW 93
Webster, Sally Beyer 1938- WhoE 93
Webster, Sharon B. 1937- WhoE 93
Webster, Steven Alan 1951- WhoSSW 93
Webster, Stokely 1912- WhoWor 93
Webster, Thomas Glenn 1924- WhoAm 92
Webster, Thomas M. Law&B 92
Webster, Thomas Nathan 1920- St&PR 93
Webster, Victor Alexander 1934- St&PR 93
Webster, Walter D. Law&B 92
Webster, William H. BioIn 17
Webster, William Hedgcock 1924- WhoAm 92
Webster, William John 1927- St&PR 93
Webster, William Lawrence 1953- WhoAm 92
Webster-Eastman, Sarah Elizabeth 1945- WhoSSW 93
Wechman, Robert Joseph 1939- WhoE 93
Wechsberg, Manfred Ingo 1940- WhoWor 93
Wechsler, Alfred Elliot 1934- St&PR 93, WhoAm 92
Wechsler, Arnold 1923- WhoSSW 93
Wechsler, Gil 1942- WhoE 93, WhoWor 93
Wechsler, Henry 1932- WhoAm 92
Wechsler, Herbert 1909- WhoAm 92
Wechsler, Herbert 1920- St&PR 93
Wechsler, Jill 1946- WhoWrEP 92
Wechsler, Judith Glatzer 1940- WhoAmW 93
Wechsler, Mary Heyrman 1948- WhoAmW 93
Wechsler, Raymond H. 1945- St&PR 93
Wechsler, Sergio 1944- WhoWor 93
Wechter, Clari Ann 1953- WhoAmW 93, WhoEmL 93, WhoWor 93
Wechter, David 1956- MiSFD 9
Wechter, Ira Martin 1947- WhoE 93
Wechter, Nell Wise 1913- BioIn 17
Wechter, Nell Wise 1913-1989 ScF&FL 92
Wechter, Norman Robert 1926- WhoWor 93
Wechter, Vivienne Thaul WhoAm 92, WhoE 93
Weck, Kristin Willa 1959- WhoAmW 93
Weck, Thomas L. 1942- BioIn 17
Weckenbrock, James R. 1947- St&PR 93
Weckenmann, Albert A. 1944- WhoScE 91-3
Wecker, Eberhard 1923- WhoScE 91-3
Wecker, Georg Kaspar 1632?-1695 Baker 92
Wecker, Richard A. 1944- St&PR 93
Wecker, Stuart 1944- WhoE 93
Wecker, William A. 1923- WhoE 93
Weckerle, Lawrence Franklin 1954- St&PR 93
Weckerlin, Jean-Baptiste-Theodore 1821-1910 Baker 92
Weckesser, Elden C(hristian) 1910- ConAu 139
Weckesser, Ernest Prosper, Jr. 1933- WhoAm 92
Weckesser, Paul Maurice 1933- WhoE 93
Weckl, Dave BioIn 17
Weckmann, Matthias c. 1619-1674 Baker 92
Weckroth, Johan E. 1924- WhoScE 91-4
Weckstein, Richard Selig 1924- WhoAm 92
Weclew, Robert George 1911- WhoAm 92
Weclew, Thaddeus Victor 1906- WhoAm 92
Weclew, Victor T. 1916- WhoAm 92
Wedaratne, Sumith 1959- WhoWor 93
Wedbush, Edward W. 1932- St&PR 93
Weddel, Shirley Jean 1930- WhoAmW 93
Wedderburn, Kenneth William 1927- WhoWor 93
Weddig, Lee John 1935- WhoAm 92
Weddigen, Gert 1942- WhoScE 91-3
Wedding, Charles Randolph 1934- WhoAm 92
Weddington, Elaine C. BioIn 17
Weddington, Liz Gardner 1932- WhoE 93
Weddington, Sarah Ragle 1945- WhoAm 92
Weddle, Robert Bruce, Jr. 1940- St&PR 93
Weddle, Stephen S. Law&B 92
Weddle, Stephen Shields 1938- St&PR 93, WhoAm 92
Wedeen, Marvin Meyer 1926- WhoE 93
Wedeen, Richard Peter 1934- WhoE 93
Wedeen, Shirley Ullman d1992 BioIn 17, NewYTBS 92
Wedeen, Shirley Ullman 1926-1992 ConAu 137
Wedekind, Carl L., Jr. 1926- St&PR 93
Wedekind, (Benjamin) Frank(lin) 1864-1918 DcLB 118 [port]
Wedel, Millie Redmond 1939- WhoWor 93
Wedel, Paul George 1927- WhoAm 92
Wedel, Stig 1952- WhoWor 93
Wedel, Waldo Rudolph 1908- WhoAm 92
Wedemeyer, Albert BioIn 17
Wedemeyer, Albert Coady 1896-1990 HarEnMi
Wedemeyer, Erich Hans 1927- WhoWor 93
Wedemeyer, Rudolf J. 1929- WhoScE 91-3
Wedepohl, Eric A. Law&B 92
Wedepohl, Leonhard M. 1933- WhoAm 92
Weder, Janet M. 1951- St&PR 93
Weder, Juergen K.P. 1936- WhoScE 91-3
Weder, Juergen Kurt 1936- WhoWor 93
Wedge, Dorothy Ann 1935- WhoAmW 93
Wedge, George Francis, III 1927- WhoWrEP 92
Wedgelock, Colin ScF&FL 92
Wedgeworth, Deborah H. Law&B 92
Wedgeworth, Phillip Wayne 1951- WhoSSW 93
Wedgeworth, Robert BioIn 17
Wedgeworth, Robert 1937- WhoAm 92
Wedgwood, C.V. 1910- BioIn 17
Wedgwood, Cicely Veronica 1910- BioIn 17
Wedgwood, Hensleigh Cecil d1991 BioIn 17
Wedgwood, Jean BioIn 17
Wedgwood, Piers Anthony Weymouth BioIn 17
Wedgwood, Ruth WhoE 93
Wedgwood, William Darwin 1922- St&PR 93
Wedinger, Robert Scott 1957- WhoSSW 93
Wedlake, Gary Douglas 1944- WhoSSW 93
Wedler, Gerd 1929- WhoScE 91-3
Wedow, David Walter 1953- WhoSSW 93
Wedzinski, Wladyslaw Bohdan 1914- WhoScE 91-4
Wedzony, Jozef Tadeudz 1923- WhoScE 91-4
Wee, Raymond 1938- WhoUN 92
Weeber, Dieter Karl 1934- St&PR 93
Weeber, W. S. 1943- WhoAm 92
Weeby, Edward H. Law&B 92
Weed, Cheryl Anne 1947- WhoWrEP 92
Weed, Dorothy d1991 BioIn 17
Weed, Earl D., III Law&B 92
Weed, Edward R. 1940- St&PR 93
Weed, Ithamar Dryden 1914- WhoAm 92
Weed, Joe Keith 1936- St&PR 93
Weed, John A. 1940- St&PR 93
Weed, Maurice James 1912- WhoAm 92
Weed, Thurlow 1797-1882 BioIn 17, JrnUS, PolPar
Weeden, Jeffrey Blane 1956- St&PR 93
Weeden, Maria Howard 1847-1905 BioIn 17
Weeden, Mary Ann 1948- WhoAmW 93
Weeder, Richard Stockton 1936- WhoE 93
Weeditz, Paul Edward 1953- WhoSSW 93
Weedman, Jane Branham ScF&FL 92
Weedn, Trish 1950- WhoAmW 93
Weedon, Alan Charles 1951- WhoAm 92
Weedon, Daniel Reid, Jr. 1919- St&PR 93, WhoAm 92
Weedon, Douglas Lee 1935- St&PR 93
Wee Kim Wee 1915- WhoWor 93
Wee Kim Wee, His Excellency 1915- WhoAsAP 91
Weekley, Dallas A. BioIn 17

Weekley, Frederick Clay, Jr. 1939- WhoAm 92, WhoWor 93
Weekley, Jackie Bell 1956- WhoSSW 93
Weekley, Mary E. 1956- WhoAmW 93
Weekley, Richard J. 1945- WhoWrEP 92
Weekley, Winston Keith 1936- WhoSSW 93
Weekly, James Keith 1933- WhoSSW 93
Weekly, John William 1931- St&PR 93, WhoAm 92
Weeks, Albert Loren 1923- WhoAm 92, WhoWor 93, WhoWrEP 92
Weeks, Ann Armstrong 1935- WhoAmW 93, WhoE 93
Weeks, Arthur Andrew 1914- WhoAm 92
Weeks, Barbara 1913-1954 SweetSg C [port]
Weeks, Bob Lee 1942- WhoSSW 93
Weeks, Brigitte 1943- WhoAm 92, WhoAmW 93
Weeks, Charles, Jr. 1919- WhoSSW 93
Weeks, Charles Richard 1934- St&PR 93
Weeks, Christopher Henry Clark 1950- WhoE 93
Weeks, David Frank 1926- WhoAm 92
Weeks, David I. 1916- WhoIns 93
Weeks, David Leonard 1935- St&PR 93
Weeks, Donna Rita 1935- WhoAmW 93
Weeks, Dorothy W. 1893-1990 BioIn 17
Weeks, Edith M. AmWomPl
Weeks, Francis William 1916- WhoAm 92
Weeks, Fred L. 1920- St&PR 93
Weeks, Frederick Fowler WhoScE 91-1
Weeks, Gary Lynn 1936- WhoAm 92
Weeks, Glen Alan 1951- WhoEmL 93
Weeks, Glen Alden Law&B 92
Weeks, Gwendolen Brannon 1943- WhoAmW 93
Weeks, James W. 1937- St&PR 93
Weeks, Jane Sutherland 1924- WhoWrEP 92
Weeks, Janet Healy 1932- WhoAmW 93
Weeks, Janice Marie 1954- WhoAmW 93
Weeks, John 1949- ScF&FL 92
Weeks, John David 1943- WhoAm 92
Weeks, John Robert 1944- WhoAm 92
Weeks, Lori Ann 1959- St&PR 93
Weeks, Patricia E. Law&B 92
Weeks, Paul Martin 1932- WhoAm 92
Weeks, Richard Ralph 1932- WhoAm 92
Weeks, Robert Andrew 1924- WhoAm 92
Weeks, Robert Gray 1936- WhoAm 92
Weeks, Robert Joe 1929- WhoSSW 93
Weeks, Robert Lewis 1924- WhoWrEP 92
Weeks, Robin Allan 1942- St&PR 93
Weeks, Roland, Jr. 1936- WhoAm 92
Weeks, Ruth Mary AmWomPl, BioIn 17
Weeks, Sinclair, Jr. 1923- St&PR 93
Weeks, Stephen ScF&FL 92
Weeks, Stephen 1948- MiSFD 9
Weeks, Virginia Lynn 1952- WhoAmW 93
Weeks, Walter LeRoy 1923- WhoAm 92
Weeks, Wilford Frank 1929- WhoAm 92
Weeks, William Clayton 1936- St&PR 93
Weeks, William Thomas 1932- WhoE 93
Weelkes, Thomas c. 1575-1623 Baker 92
Weems, Clara C. 1933- WhoE 93
Weems, George S. 1940- St&PR 93
Weems, John Edgar 1932- WhoAm 92
Weems, John Edward 1924- WhoSSW 93, WhoWor 93
Weems, Robert Cicero 1910- WhoAm 92
Weems, Rodger Cary 1952- WhoSSW 93
Weems, Sharon Lea 1941- WhoAmW 93
Weening, Richard W. St&PR 93
Weening, Richard William, Jr. 1945- WhoAm 92
Weepie, Charles Martin 1932- St&PR 93
Weerasinghe, Asoka 1936- WhoCanL 92
Weerbecke, Gaspar van c. 1445-1517 Baker 92
Weerbeke, Gaspar van c. 1445-1517 Baker 92
Weertman, Johannes 1925- WhoAm 92
Weertman, Julia Randall 1926- WhoAm 92, WhoAmW 93
Weese, Benjamin Horace 1929- WhoAm 92
Weese, Cynthia Rogers 1940- WhoAm 92, WhoAmW 93
Weese, Harry Mohr 1915- WhoAm 92
Weese, Samuel H. 1935- WhoIns 93
Weesner, Betty Jean 1926- WhoAmW 93
Weesner, Thomas E. 1929- St&PR 93
Weete, Will H. d1991 BioIn 17
Weetman, Robert Ray 1937- WhoWrEP 92
Wefer, Donald P. Law&B 92
Weg, Carol Ann 1958- WhoAmW 93
Weg, Frank A. 1927- WhoIns 93
Weg, John Gerard 1934- WhoAm 92, WhoWor 93
Wege, Klaus 1931- WhoScE 91-3
Wegeler, Franz Gerhard 1765-1848 Baker 92
Wegelius, Martin 1846-1906 Baker 92
Wegener, Dietrich Burckhardt 1939- WhoScE 91-3
Wegener, Geraldina 1940- WhoUN 92
Wegener, Henning 1936- WhoWor 93
Wegener, Ingo 1950- WhoWor 93
Wegener, Klaus 1940- WhoWor 93
Wegener, Larry Edward 1946- WhoWrEP 92
Wegener, Mark Douglas 1948- WhoEmL 93
Wegener, Paul 1874-1948 IntDcF 2-3 [port]
Wegener, Peter Paul 1917- WhoE 93
Weger, Joseph G. 1931- St&PR 93
Wegert, Mary Magdalene Hardel 1942- WhoAmW 93
Wegge, Leon Louis Francois 1933- WhoAm 92
Wegiel, Glenn Alan 1948- WhoSSW 93
Weglarz, Jan 1947- WhoScE 91-4
Weglarz, M. WhoScE 91-4
Weglarz, Marian Jan 1928- WhoScE 91-4
Weglarz, Terri Marie 1965- WhoWrEP 92
Weglein, Ernst B. Law&B 92
Wegleitner, Karlheinz 1942- WhoScE 91-4
Weglenski, Piotr 1939- WhoScE 91-4
Weglewski, Thomas Gregory Law&B 92
Wegman, Edward Joseph 1943- WhoSSW 93
Wegman, Edwin H. St&PR 93
Wegman, Fred C.M. 1948- WhoScE 91-3
Wegman, Harold Hugh 1916- WhoAm 92
Wegman, Myron Ezra 1908- WhoAm 92
Wegman, Thomas L. St&PR 93
Wegman, William BioIn 17
Wegman, William 1943- CurBio 92 [port]
Wegman, William George 1943- WhoAm 92
Wegmann, Cynthia Anne 1949- WhoSSW 93
Wegmann, George J. 1901- WhoIns 93
Wegmann, Karen 1944- WhoAm 92, WhoAmW 93
Wegmann, Paul Francis 1941- St&PR 93
Wegmann, Raymond J. WhoScE 91-2
Wegmann, Rudolf 1940- WhoWor 93
Wegmiller, Donald Charles 1938- WhoAm 92
Wegner, E. Donald 1929- St&PR 93
Wegner, Gary Alan 1944- WhoAm 92
Wegner, Helmuth Adalbert 1917- WhoAm 92
Wegner, Karl Heinrich 1930- WhoAm 92
Wegner, Laura Christine AmWomPl
Wegner, Ronald A. 1943- St&PR 93
Wegner, Rose-Marie 1924- WhoScE 91-3
Wegner, Susan Dettmann 1947- WhoSSW 93
Wegner, Wilhelm 1932- WhoScE 91-3
Wegrzyn, Jan 1923- WhoScE 91-4
Wegrzyn, Stefan 1925- WhoScE 91-4
Wegscheider, Wolfhard 1950- WhoScE 91-4
Wegwart, Wayne Gordon 1925- WhoSSW 93
Weh, Ludwig 1946- WhoScE 91-3
Wehde, Albert E. Law&B 92
Wehe, David Carl 1949- WhoE 93
Wehe, Diana Joycelyn 1943- WhoAmW 93
Wehe, Fred Gustave 1929- St&PR 93
Wehe, Herbert W. 1928- St&PR 93
Wehe, Homer A. 1931- St&PR 93
Weheba, Abdulsalam Mohamad 1930- WhoWor 93
Wehl, Brandon L. 1953- St&PR 93
Wehl, Glenn Eugene 1926- St&PR 93
Wehle, Gerhard Furchtegott 1884-1973 Baker 92
Wehle, John L. 1916- St&PR 93
Wehle, John L., Jr. 1946- WhoAm 92
Wehle, John Louis 1916- WhoAm 92
Wehle, Karl 1825-1883 Baker 92
Wehling, Ralph Joseph 1914- St&PR 93
Wehling, Robert Louis 1938- WhoAm 92
Wehlitz, Annie Louise WhoWrEP 92
Wehman, Adele WhoAmW 93
Wehman, Robert H. St&PR 93
Wehmeier, Betty BioIn 17
Wehmer, Sally Bell 1934- WhoAmW 93
Wehmeyer, Lillian Biermann 1933- ScF&FL 92
Wehmeyer, Lillian Mabel 1933- WhoAmW 93
Wehner, Alfred Peter 1926- WhoAm 92, WhoWor 93
Wehner, Edward Adam WhoSSW 93
Wehner, Henry Otto, III 1942- WhoSSW 93
Wehner, Rudiger 1940- WhoScE 91-4
Wehner, Theo 1949- WhoWor 93
Wehner, Thomas J. 1950- St&PR 93
Wehr, Allan Gordon 1931- WhoSSW 93
Wehr, Cullie Robert, Jr. 1925- St&PR 93
Wehr, Roberta S. St&PR 93
Wehrberger, Klaus Herbert 1959- WhoWor 93
Wehrenberg, Kim A. Law&B 92
Wehrenberg, Kim Allen 1951- St&PR 93
Wehrer, Charles Siecke 1914- WhoAm 92
Wehrer, Wayne Jesse 1946- WhoSSW 93
Wehrfritz, Bertram Arthur Frederick WhoScE 91-1
Wehrhahn, Allen Long 1959- WhoE 93
Wehrhahn, Rodolfo Francisco 1959- WhoWor 93
Wehring, Bernard William 1937- WhoAm 92
Wehrle, David Michael 1955- St&PR 93
Wehrle, Gary L. 1942- St&PR 93
Wehrle, Henry B., Jr. 1922- St&PR 93
Wehrle, John S. 1952- St&PR 93
Wehrle, Leroy Snyder 1932- WhoAm 92
Wehrle, Martha Gaines 1925- WhoAm 92, WhoAmW 93
Wehrle, Paul L. Law&B 92
Wehrle, Thomas Edward 1934- St&PR 93
Wehrli, Agathe 1938- WhoUN 92
Wehrli, Roger Russell 1947- BiDAMSp 1989
Wehrli, Werner 1892-1944 Baker 92
Wehrlin, Gerald Thomas 1938- St&PR 93
Wehrman, Nancy Beazley 1961- WhoAmW 93
Wehrmann, Ottmar Heinrich 1921- WhoWor 93
Wehrmeyer, Werner 1931- WhoScE 91-3
Wehrschutz, Ferdinand Christian 1961- WhoWor 93
Wehrstein, Karen 1961- ScF&FL 92
Wehry, Earl Luther, Jr. 1941- WhoSSW 93
Wei, Benjamin Min 1930- WhoWor 93
Wei, Ching-Ling 1957- WhoWor 93
Wei, Fu-Shang 1948- WhoE 93
Wei, Gaoyuan 1961- WhoWor 93
Wei, James 1930- WhoAm 92
Wei, Jun Jie 1954- WhoWor 93
Wei, Musheng 1948- WhoWor 93
Wei, Yau-Huei 1952- WhoWor 93
Weiant, Elizabeth Abbott 1913- WhoE 93
Weiant, William Morrow 1938- WhoAm 92
Weibel, Ewald R. 1929- WhoScE 91-4
Weibel, Ewald Rudolf 1929- WhoWor 93
Weibell, Mats Law&B 92
Weible, Deborah Ann 1958- WhoAmW 93
Weible, Robert L. 1938- St&PR 93
Weibull, Peder C.G. 1945- WhoScE 91-4
Weich, Mervyn D. 1938- St&PR 93
Weich, Patricia Gallant 1945- WhoWrEP 92
Wei Ch'ang-hui d1856 HarEnMi
Weichel, Hugo 1937- WhoSSW 93
Weichel, Kenneth 1946- WhoWrEP 92
Weicher, John Charles 1938- WhoAm 92
Weicher, Richard E. Law&B 92
Weichert, Dieter Horst 1932- WhoAm 92
Weichert, Patrick David 1947- WhoSSW 93
Wei Ch'ing d106BC HarEnMi
Weichmann, Louis J. 1842-1902 BioIn 17
Weichsel, Florence King d1990 BioIn 17
Weichsel, Richard Henry 1928- St&PR 93
Weichselberger, Kurt Franz 1929- WhoWor 93
Weick, George Paul 1951- WhoSSW 93
Weick, Paul Charles 1899- WhoAm 92
Weicker, D.E. St&PR 93
Weicker, Lowell P., Jr. BioIn 17
Weicker, Lowell P., Jr. 1931- News 93-1 [port]
Weicker, Lowell Palmer, Jr. 1931- WhoAm 92, WhoE 93, WhoWor 93
Weicker, Reinhold Paul 1944- WhoWor 93
Weickgenant, Peter D. 1928- St&PR 93
Weickmans, Laurent Hubert Jean 1930- WhoScE 91-2
Weida, George A. F. 1936- St&PR 93
Weida, Lewis Dixon 1924- WhoWor 93
Weidberg, Bertrand H. Law&B 92
Weide, William W. 1923- St&PR 93
Weide, William Wolfe 1923- WhoAm 92
Weidel, Herbert Benjamin 1931- St&PR 93
Weidel, Larry 1950- St&PR 93
Weideman, Ryan 1941- ConAu 137
Weidemann, Anton Fredrick 1917- WhoWrEP 92
Weidemann, Celia Jean 1942- WhoAm 92, WhoAmW 93, WhoE 93
Weidemann, Friedrich 1871-1919 Baker 92
Weidemann, Julia Clark 1937- WhoAmW 93, WhoE 93
Weidemann, Rolf WhoScE 91-3
Weidemeyer, Carleton Lloyd 1933- WhoWor 93
Weidenbaum, Murray Lew 1927- WhoAm 92
Weidenbruch, Manfred 1937- WhoScE 91-3
Weidenfeld, Arthur George BioIn 17
Weidenfeld, Edward Lee 1943- WhoAm 92, WhoE 93
Weidenfeld, Sheila Rabb 1943- WhoAmW 93
Weidenhammer, Robert Houston 1937- St&PR 93
Weidenmuller, Hans-Arwed 1933- WhoScE 91-3
Weidenreich, Franz 1873-1948 IntDcAn
Weidensaul, Thomas Craig 1939- WhoAm 92
Weidenthal, Maurice David 1925- WhoAm 92
Weider, Jerome D. 1941- St&PR 93
Weidhorn, Manfred 1931- BioIn 17
Weidig, Adolf 1867-1931 Baker 92
Weidinger, Anton 1767-1852 Baker 92
Weidler, W.F. 1941- St&PR 93
Weidlich, H. Edward, Jr. Law&B 92
Weidlich, Wolfgang 1931- WhoScE 91-3
Weidlinger, Paul 1914- WhoAm 92, WhoE 93
Weidman, Hazel Hitson 1923- WhoAm 92
Weidman, James Edward 1953- WhoE 93
Weidman, Jerome 1913- JeAmFiW, WhoAm 92, WhoWrEP 92
Weidman, John Carl, II 1945- WhoE 93
Weidman, Marsha Claman 1949- St&PR 93
Weidman, William d1992 NewYTBS 92
Weidmann, Eric R. 1949- St&PR 93
Weidmann, Silvio 1921- WhoWor 93
Weidner, Edward William 1921- WhoAm 92
Weidner, James Henry 1940- WhoE 93
Weidner, Marilyn Susan 1960- WhoAmW 93
Weidner, Richard Tilghman 1921- WhoAm 92
Weidner, Roswell Theodore 1911- WhoAm 92
Weidner, Wayne Russell 1942- St&PR 93
Weido, Kevin V. Law&B 92
Weidt, Lucie c. 1876-1940 Baker 92, OxDcOp
Weier, Ulrike 1960- WhoScE 91-3
Weierick, Thomas A. 1953- St&PR 93
Weierman, Robert Joseph 1942- WhoE 93
Weierstall, Richard Paul 1942- WhoAm 92
Weiffenbach, John Frasier 1910-1991 BioIn 17
Weigand, James Gary 1935- St&PR 93, WhoAm 92
Weigand, Kenneth R. Law&B 92
Weigand, Philip Clayton 1937- WhoAm 92
Weigand, William Keith 1937- WhoAm 92
Weigel, Alice M. 1909- WhoWrEP 92
Weigel, C. Philip 1933- St&PR 93
Weigel, Carl E. 1932- St&PR 93
Weigel, Charles A., Jr. Law&B 92
Weigel, Donald A. 1943- St&PR 93
Weigel, Elsie Diven 1948- WhoE 93
Weigel, Eugene (Herbert) 1910- Baker 92
Weigel, Gerald Edward 1943- St&PR 93
Weigel, Hans 1908-1991 BioIn 17
Weigel, John A. 1912- ScF&FL 92
Weigel, Paul Henry 1946- WhoSSW 93
Weigel, Raymond A. 1917- St&PR 93
Weigel, Richard David 1945- WhoSSW 93
Weigel, Teri BioIn 17
Weigel, William F. 1923-1990 BioIn 17
Weigen, Stanley 1931- St&PR 93
Weigend, Guido Gustav 1920- WhoAm 92
Weiger, John George 1933- WhoAm 92
Weigers, Al St&PR 93
Weigert, Alfred 1927- WhoScE 91-3
Weigert, Ludwig Johann 1930- WhoWor 93
Weigert, Peter 1944- WhoScE 91-3
Weight, George Dale 1934- WhoAm 92
Weight, John Philip WhoScE 91-1
Weightman, George d1896 BioIn 17
Weightman, Paul Wesley Harrison WhoScE 91-1
Weigl Baker 92
Weigl, Bruce 1949- DcLB 120 [port]
Weigl, Bruno 1881-1938 Baker 92
Weigl, Joseph 1766-1846 Baker 92, OxDcOp
Weigl, Joseph (Franz) 1740-1820 Baker 92
Weigl, Karl 1881-1949 Baker 92
Weigl, Thaddaus 1776-1844 Baker 92
Weigl, Valery 1894-1982 Baker 92
Weigle, Debbie Kay 1954- WhoSSW 93
Weigle, Marta WhoAmW 93
Weigle, Rebecca A. 1953- WhoAmW 93
Weigle, Richard D. 1912-1992 NewYTBS 92 [port]
Weigle, Richard Daniel 1912- WhoAm 92
Weigle, William Oliver 1927- WhoAm 92
Weigley, Russell Frank 1930- WhoE 93
Weigman, Mary Joanne Law&B 92
Weigmann-Haass, Renate 1937- WhoScE 91-3
Weigold, Calvin C. 1926- St&PR 93
Weihaupt, John George 1930- WhoAm 92

Weiher, Claudine Jackson 1941- *WhoAm 92*
Weihrich, Heinz *WhoAm 92*
Weihs, Carlantonia Leonora 1944- *WhoWor 93*
Weihs, Erika 1917- *WhoE 93*
Weihs, Jerome F. *Law&B 92*
Wei Jianxing 1931- *WhoAsAP 91*
Wei Jinshan 1927- *WhoAsAP 91*
Weik, Charles *WhoE 93*
Weikart, H.N. 1935- *St&PR 93*
Weikart, Lynne Alkire 1943- *WhoE 93*
Weikel, Dana Rose 1943- *WhoWrEP 92*
Weikel, M.K. 1938- *St&PR 93*
Weikel, Robin R. 1953- *St&PR 93*
Weikert, Claire I. *AmWomPl*
Weikert, Ralf 1940- *Baker 92, WhoWor 93*
Weikert, Roy J. 1913- *St&PR 93*
Weikl, Bernd 1942- *IntDcOp*
Weikl, Bernhard 1942- *Baker 92*
Weikle, William Henry 1938- *St&PR 93*
Weiksner, George Bernard 1944- *St&PR 93*
Weiksner, George Bernard, Jr. 1944- *WhoAm 92*
Weil, Albert M. 1907- *St&PR 93*
Weil, Bert 1951- *St&PR 93*
Weil, Cass Sargent 1946- *WhoEmL 93*
Weil, Charles Donald 1944- *St&PR 93*
Weil, Cynthia *SoulM*
Weil, Cynthia 1937- *See* Mann, Barry 1939- & Weil, Cynthia 1937- *SoulM*
Weil, David S. 1925- *St&PR 93, WhoAm 92*
Weil, Donald Wallace 1923- *WhoAm 92*
Weil, Frank A. 1931- *WhoAm 92*
Weil, Gary L. *Law&B 92*
Weil, Gertrude L. 1922- *St&PR 93*
Weil, Gilbert Harry 1912- *WhoAm 92*
Weil, Herman 1905- *WhoAm 92*
Weil, Hermann 1876-1949 *Baker 92*
Weil, Irwin 1928- *WhoAm 92*
Weil, Jack A. 1901- *St&PR 93*
Weil, Jack B. 1929- *St&PR 93*
Weil, Jacques-Henry 1934- *WhoScE 91-2*
Weil, James Beverly 1944- *WhoE 93*
Weil, Jerry *WhoAm 92*
Weil, Jerry P. 1945- *St&PR 93*
Weil, John Ashley 1929- *WhoAm 92*
Weil, John David 1947- *St&PR 93, WhoAm 92*
Weil, John William 1928- *WhoAm 92*
Weil, Julian S. *St&PR 93*
Weil, Kari 1954- *WhoSSW 93*
Weil, Konrad G. 1927- *WhoScE 91-3*
Weil, Kurt H. d1992 *NewYTBS 92*
Weil, Kurt H. 1895-1992 *BioIn 17*
Weil, Laura A. 1957- *St&PR 93*
Weil, Leon Jerome 1927- *WhoAm 92*
Weil, Leonard 1922- *WhoAm 92*
Weil, Lise 1950- *WhoWrEP 92*
Weil, Lisl *WhoE 93*
Weil, Louis Arthur, Jr. 1905- *WhoAm 92*
Weil, Louis Arthur, III 1941- *WhoAm 92*
Weil, Marjorie d1990 *BioIn 17*
Weil, Marvin Lee 1924- *WhoWor 93*
Weil, Max Harry 1927- *WhoAm 92*
Weil, Myron 1918- *WhoAm 92*
Weil, Nancy Hecht 1936- *WhoAmW 93*
Weil, Paul P. 1936- *WhoAm 92*
Weil, Peter Henry 1933- *WhoAm 92*
Weil, Richard A. 1925- *St&PR 93*
Weil, Richard K. 1924- *St&PR 93*
Weil, Roger 1928- *WhoScE 91-4*
Weil, Rolf 1926- *WhoE 93*
Weil, Rolf Alfred 1921- *WhoAm 92*
Weil, Roman Lee 1940- *WhoAm 92*
Weil, Ronald David 1948- *St&PR 93*
Weil, Roswell J. 1916- *St&PR 93*
Weil, Samuel *MiSFD 9*
Weil, Simon Patrick 1955- *WhoWor 93*
Weil, Simone 1909-1943 *BioIn 17*
Weil, Stephen Edward 1928- *WhoAm 92*
Weil, Suzanne S. Fern 1933- *WhoAmW 93*
Weil, Thierry A. 1959- *WhoScE 91-2*
Weil, Thomas Alexander 1930- *WhoAm 92*
Weil, Thomas P. 1932- *WhoSSW 93*
Weil, Timothy Michael 1967- *WhoEmL 93*
Weil, William M. d1990 *BioIn 17*
Weiland, Charles Hankes 1921- *WhoAm 92*
Weiland, Juliette Marie 1944- *WhoE 93*
Weiland, Keith Frederick 1925- *WhoSSW 93*
Weiland, Kurt H. *Law&B 92*
Weiland, Mark 1956- *St&PR 93*
Weiland, Ola R.H. 1946- *WhoScE 91-4*
Weiland, Paul *MiSFD 9*
Weiland, Robert Michael 1948- *St&PR 93*
Weilbacher, William Manning 1928- *WhoAm 92*
Weilbacker, Kristine 1961- *WhoAmW 93*
Weilbaecher, John Gagnet 1948- *WhoSSW 93*
Weilburg, Donald Karl 1936- *WhoE 93*
Weilemann, Peter Robert 1949- *WhoWor 93*
Weilenman, Ferdinand 1941- *WhoScE 91-4*
Weiler, A.R. 1936- *St&PR 93*
Weiler, Barbara Brandt 1937- *WhoAmW 93*
Weiler, Edgar D. 1930- *St&PR 93*
Weiler, Henry Rutter, Jr. 1928- *WhoE 93*
Weiler, Joseph Ashby 1946- *WhoAm 92*
Weiler, Linda *Law&B 92*
Weiler, Michael 1954- *St&PR 93*
Weiler, Michael Reid 1954- *WhoIns 93*
Weiler, Paul Cronin 1939- *WhoAm 92*
Weiler, Richard L. 1945- *WhoIns 93*
Weiler, Robert E. 1932- *St&PR 93*
Weiler, Wolfgang W. 1934- *WhoScE 91-3*
Wei Li-haung 1897- *HarEnMi*
Weiling, Franz Joseph Bernard 1909- *WhoWor 93*
Weill, Alan 1937- *St&PR 93*
Weill, Claudia 1947- *MiSFD 9*
Weill, Georges Gustave 1926- *WhoAm 92, WhoE 93*
Weill, Gilbert 1933- *WhoScE 91-2*
Weill, Gilbert E. 1933- *WhoScE 91-2*
Weill, Hans 1933- *WhoAm 92*
Weill, Jacky *WhoScE 91-2*
Weill, Jacques D. 1929- *WhoScE 91-2*
Weill, Kurt 1900-1950 *IntDcOp [port], OxDcOp*
Weill, Kurt (Julian) 1900-1950 *Baker 92*
Weill, LeAnne 1953- *WhoSSW 93*
Weill, Michael 1914- *WhoWor 93*
Weill, Roger G. d1991 *BioIn 17*
Weill, Sanford I. *BioIn 17*
Weill, Sanford I. 1933- *St&PR 93, WhoAm 92*
Weill, Sheldon Dennis 1943- *St&PR 93*
Weiman, Stephen L. 1958- *St&PR 93*
Weimarck, Anna M.K. 1931- *WhoScE 91-4*
Weimarck, Gunnar 1936- *WhoScE 91-4*
Weimer, Douglas Reid 1953- *WhoE 93*
Weimer, Ferne 1950- *ConAu 137*
Weimer, Gerald A. 1945- *St&PR 93*
Weimer, Paul Kessler 1914- *WhoAm 92*
Weimer, Peter Dwight 1938- *WhoSSW 93, WhoWor 93*
Weimer, Richard P. 1947- *St&PR 93*
Weimer, Robert Jay 1926- *WhoAm 92*
Weimer, Vaughn H. 1953- *St&PR 93*
Weimmer, Karen Hoovestol *Law&B 92*
Wein, Alan Jerome 1941- *WhoAm 92*
Wein, Albert W. 1915-1991 *BioIn 17*
Wein, Bernard J. *St&PR 93*
Wein, Frederick *Law&B 92*
Wein, Len 1948- *ScF&FL 92*
Wein, Leonard N. *ScF&FL 92*
Wein, Robert Michael 1947- *WhoSSW 93*
Weinbach, Arthur F. 1943- *St&PR 93*
Weinbach, Arthur Frederic 1943- *WhoAm 92*
Weinbach, Lawrence Allen 1940- *WhoAm 92*
Weinbaum, Eleanor Perlstein *WhoWrEP 92*
Weinbaum, George 1932- *WhoE 93*
Weinbaum, Martin Paul 1947- *WhoE 93*
Weinbaum, Michael Alan *Law&B 92*
Weinbaum, Robert C. *Law&B 92*
Weinbaum, Stanley G. 1902-1935 *ScF&FL 92*
Weinberg, Adam D. 1954- *WhoAm 92*
Weinberg, Alan M. *Law&B 92*
Weinberg, Alvin Martin 1915- *WhoAm 92*
Weinberg, Anita *AmWomPl*
Weinberg, Barry *St&PR 93*
Weinberg, Bella Hass 1949- *WhoWrEP 92*
Weinberg, Carole Mills d1992 *BioIn 17, NewYTBS 92*
Weinberg, Crispin Bernard 1951- *St&PR 93*
Weinberg, Debbie Pearl *Law&B 92*
Weinberg, Edward 1918- *WhoAm 92*
Weinberg, Edward Herbert 1920- *St&PR 93*
Weinberg, Edward Richard 1963- *WhoSSW 93*
Weinberg, Elbert 1928-1991 *BioIn 17*
Weinberg, Eugene David 1922- *WhoAm 92*
Weinberg, Gary L. 1962- *WhoE 93*
Weinberg, George *ScF&FL 92*
Weinberg, Gerhard Ludwig 1928- *WhoAm 92, WhoWrEP 92*
Weinberg, H. Barbara 1942- *WhoAm 92*
Weinberg, Harold P. 1925- *St&PR 93*
Weinberg, Harry *BioIn 17*
Weinberg, Harry Bernard 1913- *WhoAm 92*
Weinberg, Harvey A. 1937- *WhoAm 92*
Weinberg, Herschel Mayer 1927- *WhoAm 92*
Weinberg, Howard 1949- *St&PR 93*
Weinberg, Irwin Robert 1928- *WhoAm 92*
Weinberg, Jacob 1879-1956 *Baker 92*
Weinberg, James L. 1922- *St&PR 93*
Weinberg, Jane Carol *Law&B 92*
Weinberg, John L. 1925- *St&PR 93*
Weinberg, John Livingston 1925- *WhoAm 92, WhoE 93*
Weinberg, Jonathan David 1967- *WhoWrEP 92*
Weinberg, Kenneth A. 1947- *WhoSSW 93*
Weinberg, Larry *ScF&FL 92*
Weinberg, Lawrence E. *ScF&FL 92*
Weinberg, Leonard Burton 1939- *WhoAm 92*
Weinberg, Lila Shaffer *WhoAm 92, WhoWrEP 92*
Weinberg, Louise *WhoAm 92, WhoSSW 93*
Weinberg, Marc Bernard 1954- *WhoE 93*
Weinberg, Marcy *WhoSSW 93*
Weinberg, Marshall Maslansky 1929- *St&PR 93*
Weinberg, Martin Herbert 1923- *WhoAm 92*
Weinberg, Martin J. 1952- *St&PR 93*
Weinberg, Meyer 1920- *WhoAm 92*
Weinberg, Michael, Jr. 1925- *WhoAm 92*
Weinberg, Mortimer 1922- *St&PR 93*
Weinberg, Norman Louis 1936- *WhoAm 92*
Weinberg, Peter A. *Law&B 92*
Weinberg, Richard A. *Law&B 92*
Weinberg, Richard L. 1922- *St&PR 93*
Weinberg, Robert 1946- *ScF&FL 92*
Weinberg, Robert Allan 1942- *WhoAm 92*
Weinberg, Robert Leonard 1923- *WhoAm 92*
Weinberg, Robert Stephen 1945- *WhoAm 92*
Weinberg, Robert W. 1936- *St&PR 93*
Weinberg, Roger David 1954- *WhoSSW 93*
Weinberg, Samuel 1926- *WhoE 93*
Weinberg, Saul S. d1992 *NewYTBS 92*
Weinberg, Steven 1933- *WhoAm 92, WhoSSW 93, WhoWor 93*
Weinberg, Susan Clare 1959- *WhoWrEP 92*
Weinberg, Sydney Stahl 1938- *WhoAmW 93*
Weinberg, Sylvan Lee 1923- *WhoAm 92*
Weinberg, Ulrich 1958- *WhoWor 93*
Weinberger, Alan D. 1945- *St&PR 93*
Weinberger, Alan David 1945- *WhoAm 92, WhoWor 93*
Weinberger, Arnold 1924- *WhoAm 92*
Weinberger, Caspar 1917- *ColdWar 1 [port]*
Weinberger, Caspar W. *BioIn 17*
Weinberger, Caspar Willard 1917- *WhoAm 92, WhoE 93, WhoWor 93*
Weinberger, Eliot 1949- *ConAu 40NR*
Weinberger, George Martin 1947- *WhoSSW 93*
Weinberger, Harold 1910-1992 *BioIn 17*
Weinberger, Harold Paul 1947- *WhoAm 92*
Weinberger, Jane D. *BioIn 17*
Weinberger, Jaromir 1896-1967 *Baker 92, IntDcOp, OxDcOp*
Weinberger, Leon Joseph 1931- *St&PR 93, WhoAm 92, WhoIns 93*
Weinberger, Leon Judah 1926- *WhoSSW 93*
Weinberger, Leon Walter 1923- *WhoAm 92*
Weinberger, Mildred *AmWomPl*
Weinberger, Miles M. 1938- *WhoAm 92*
Weinberger, Myron Hilmar 1937- *WhoAm 92*
Weinberger, Paul R. 1959- *St&PR 93*
Weinberger, Steven Elliott 1949- *WhoE 93*
Weinblatt, Lisa DeLoria 1950- *WhoAmW 93*
Weinblatt, Seymour Solomon 1922- *WhoE 93*
Weinbrecht, Donna *BioIn 17, WhoAmW 93*
Weinbrenner, Craig Charles 1951- *WhoAm 92*
Weinbrenner, George Ryan 1917- *WhoSSW 93*
Weinbrot, Howard David 1936- *WhoAm 92, WhoWrEP 92*
Weindler, John P. *Law&B 92*
Weindlmayr, Josef 1933- *WhoScE 91-4*
Weindruch, Bruce *BioIn 17*
Weine, Mae *BioIn 17*
Weiner, Abby *Law&B 92*
Weiner, Alan Roy *Law&B 92*
Weiner, Andrew 1949- *ScF&FL 92*
Weiner, Annette B. 1933- *WhoAm 92, WhoAmW 93*
Weiner, Anthony David *BioIn 17*
Weiner, Arnold 1937- *WhoAm 92*
Weiner, Arnold Lawrence 1937- *St&PR 93*
Weiner, Barry M. 1951- *St&PR 93*
Weiner, Benjamin H. 1922- *St&PR 93*
Weiner, Beryl 1918- *St&PR 93*
Weiner, Beth Lisa 1963- *WhoAmW 93*
Weiner, Carl Dorian 1934- *WhoAm 92*
Weiner, Charles 1923- *St&PR 93*
Weiner, Claire Muriel 1951- *WhoAmW 93, WhoE 93, WhoEmL 93, WhoWor 93*
Weiner, David H. d1990 *BioIn 17*
Weiner, David Iver 1952- *St&PR 93*
Weiner, Earl David 1939- *WhoAm 92, WhoE 93, WhoWor 93*
Weiner, Edmund (Simon Christopher) 1950- *ConAu 139*
Weiner, Edward 1941- *WhoE 93*
Weiner, Ellis *BioIn 17*
Weiner, Ellis 1951- *ScF&FL 92*
Weiner, Esther Riza 1938- *WhoAmW 93*
Weiner, Eugene L. 1931- *St&PR 93*
Weiner, Gerry 1933- *WhoAm 92*
Weiner, Gilbert B. *Law&B 92*
Weiner, Hadassah Ruth *Law&B 92*
Weiner, Hal *MiSFD 9*
Weiner, Hannah A. 1928- *WhoWrEP 92*
Weiner, Herbert Berger 1949- *WhoE 93*
Weiner, Herman L. 1914- *St&PR 93*
Weiner, Hollace Ava 1946- *WhoSSW 93*
Weiner, Homer *ScF&FL 92*
Weiner, Howard Lee 1944- *WhoAm 92*
Weiner, Irving Bernard 1933- *WhoAm 92, WhoSSW 93*
Weiner, Irwin M. 1930- *WhoAm 92*
Weiner, Jack H. *Law&B 92*
Weiner, Janet 1930- *WhoSSW 93*
Weiner, Jay H. 1925- *St&PR 93*
Weiner, Jeffrey Stuart 1948- *WhoAm 92*
Weiner, Joel David 1936- *WhoAm 92*
Weiner, Joel S. 1949- *St&PR 93*
Weiner, Jonathan 1943- *WhoE 93*
Weiner, Karen Joan *Law&B 92*
Weiner, Kay Bain 1932- *ConAu 136*
Weiner, Kenneth R. *Law&B 92*
Weiner, Lawrence S. *Law&B 92*
Weiner, Lazar 1897-1982 *Baker 92*
Weiner, Leo 1885-1960 *Baker 92*
Weiner, Leslie J. 1958- *WhoE 93*
Weiner, Leslie Philip 1936- *WhoAm 92*
Weiner, Lynn Joy 1959- *WhoE 93*
Weiner, Marian Murphy 1954- *WhoAmW 93*
Weiner, Martin S. 1938- *St&PR 93*
Weiner, Marvin 1925- *St&PR 93*
Weiner, Max *BioIn 17*
Weiner, Max 1926- *WhoAm 92*
Weiner, Mervyn 1935- *WhoE 93, WhoWor 93*
Weiner, Michael J. 1947- *WhoAm 92*
Weiner, Michael L. *Law&B 92*
Weiner, Morton David 1922- *WhoAm 92*
Weiner, Murray 1934- *WhoE 93*
Weiner, Myron 1931- *WhoAm 92, WhoWrEP 92*
Weiner, Paul 1941- *St&PR 93, WhoAm 92*
Weiner, Richard 1927- *St&PR 93, WhoAm 92*
Weiner, Richard Alan 1952- *WhoE 93*
Weiner, Richard M. 1930- *WhoScE 91-3*
Weiner, Robert E. *Law&B 92*
Weiner, Robert J. 1933- *St&PR 93*
Weiner, Robert Neil 1952- *WhoAm 92*
Weiner, Robert Stephen 1947- *WhoE 93, WhoEmL 93*
Weiner, Roberta Lynne *Law&B 92*
Weiner, Ronald Gary 1945- *WhoWor 93*
Weiner, Sari Donna 1958- *WhoAmW 93*
Weiner, Seymour Sidney 1917- *WhoE 93*
Weiner, Shelley 1949- *ConAu 139*
Weiner, Stephen Arthur 1933- *WhoAm 92*
Weiner, Susan 1946- *WhoSSW 93*
Weiner, Susan Marie 1952- *WhoAmW 93*
Weiner, Susan S. 1946- *WhoAmW 93*
Weiner, Sy 1949- *WhoSSW 93*
Weiner, Thomas Edgar 1949- *St&PR 93*
Weiner, Thomas F. 1953- *St&PR 93*
Weiner, Timothy Emlyn 1956- *WhoAm 92*
Weiner, Walter H. 1930- *St&PR 93*
Weiner, Walter Herman 1930- *WhoAm 92*
Weiner, Warren 1943- *St&PR 93, WhoAm 92*
Weiner-Alexander, Sandra Samuel 1947- *WhoEmL 93*
Weinert, Carl R. 1923- *St&PR 93*
Weinert, Carl Robert 1923- *WhoAm 92*
Weinert, Donald Gregory 1930- *WhoAm 92*
Weinert, Henry M. 1940- *WhoE 93*
Weinert, Kirk William *Law&B 92*
Weinfeld, Lewis Arthur 1943- *St&PR 93*
Weinflash, Jeffrey A. *Law&B 92*
Weinfurter, Erich Brian 1955- *WhoSSW 93*
Weingard, Joseph D. 1945- *St&PR 93*
Weingard, Marvin Allen 1934- *St&PR 93*
Weingarden, Mitchell I. *Law&B 92*
Weingardner, Evelyn Maude *AmWomPl*
Weingart, Carol Jayne 1943- *WhoAmW 93*
Weingarten, Fred W. *BioIn 17*

Weingarten, Hilde *WhoAm 92*
Weingarten, John Louis *BioIn 17*
Weingarten, Kathy 1947- *WhoAmW 93*
Weingarten, Max 1914- *St&PR 93*
Weingarten, Murray 1925- *WhoAm 92*
Weingarten, Robert I. 1941- *St&PR 93, WhoAm 92*
Weingarten, Stephen C. *Law&B 92*
Weingarten, Steven Ellis *Law&B 92*
Weingartner, David Peter 1939- *WhoSSW 93*
Weingartner, Felix 1863-1942 *IntDcOp [port], OxDcOp*
Weingartner, (Paul) Felix 1863-1942 *Baker 92*
Weingartner, Hans Martin 1929- *WhoAm 92*
Weingartner, Jane Ellen 1943- *WhoAmW 93*
Weingartner, Lucile G. *Law&B 92*
Weingartner, Robert 1932- *St&PR 93*
Weingartner, Rudolph Herbert 1927- *WhoAm 92*
Weingeist, Thomas Alan 1940- *WhoAm 92*
Weinglass, Boogie *BioIn 17*
Weinglass, Leonard *BioIn 17*
Weingold, Allan B. 1930- *WhoAm 92*
Weingrow, Howard L. 1922- *WhoAm 92*
Weinhauer, William Gillette 1924- *WhoAm 92*
Weinhaus, Carol L. 1947- *ConAu 137*
Weinheim, Donna Louise 1951- *WhoAmW 93*
Weinheimer, Eric Rudolph *Law&B 92*
Weinhold, John R. 1956- *WhoE 93*
Weinhold, Kurt d1990 *BioIn 17*
Weinhold, Virginia Beamer 1932- *WhoAm 92*
Weinhouse, Sidney 1909- *WhoAm 92*
Weinig, Sheldon 1928- *St&PR 93, WhoAm 92*
Weininger, Robert S. 1950- *WhoE 93*
Weininger, Stephen Joel 1937- *WhoE 93*
Weinkam, John W. 1951- *St&PR 93*
Weinkauf, Mary Louise S. 1938- *WhoWrEP 92*
Weinkauf, Mary Louise Stanley 1938- *WhoAmW 93*
Weinke, Donald C. *Law&B 92*
Weinklam, Walter J. 1915- *St&PR 93*
Weinlig, Christian Ehregott 1743-1813 *Baker 92*
Weinlig, (Christian) Theodor 1780-1842 *Baker 92*
Weinman, Connie G. 1943- *St&PR 93*
Weinman, Joel B. 1937- *WhoE 93*
Weinman, John *WhoScE 91-1*
Weinman, Morris L. 1938- *WhoSSW 93*
Weinman, R.F. *Law&B 92*
Weinman, Richard E. 1934- *St&PR 93*
Weinman, Robert A. 1915- *BioIn 17*
Weinman, Robert Alexander 1915- *WhoAm 92*
Weinman, Serge J. 1928- *WhoScE 91-2*
Weinmann, Bert Millicent Landes 1924- *WhoE 93*
Weinmann, Donald Eugene 1934- *St&PR 93*
Weinmann, John Giffen 1928- *WhoAm 92, WhoE 93, WhoWor 93*
Weinmann, Karl 1873-1929 *Baker 92*
Weinmeister, Arnie 1923- *BioIn 17*
Weinraub, Alan P. 1947- *WhoIns 93*
Weinraub, Michael N. 1943- *St&PR 93*
Weinreb, Efrem 1921- *St&PR 93*
Weinreb, Michael Philip 1939- *WhoE 93*
Weinreb, Sander 1936- *WhoAm 92*
Weinreb, Wolf 1896-1990 *BioIn 17*
Weinreich, Gabriel 1928- *WhoAm 92*
Weinreich, Howard B. *Law&B 92*
Weinreich, Howard B. 1942- *St&PR 93*
Weinrib, Carol Ellen 1949- *WhoE 93*
Weinrib, Sidney 1919- *WhoAm 92*
Weinrich, A(nna) K(atharina) H(ildegard) 1933- *ConAu 37NR*
Weinrich, Brian Erwin 1952- *WhoE 93*
Weinrich, Carl 1904-1991 *Baker 92, BioIn 17*
Weinrich, Marcel 1927- *WhoE 93*
Weinrod, Emanuel 1929- *St&PR 93*
Weinrotter, Klaus 1946- *WhoScE 91-4*
Weins, Leo Matthew 1912- *WhoAm 92*
Weinsaft, Paul Phineas 1908- *WhoE 93*
Weinschel, Alan Jay 1946- *WhoAm 92*
Weinschel, Bruno Oscar 1919- *WhoAm 92, WhoE 93, WhoWor 93*
Weinschelbaum, Emilio 1935- *WhoWor 93*
Weinschenck, Gunther 1926- *WhoScE 91-3*
Weinschenk, Carroll S. 1902-1991 *BioIn 17*
Weinshall, Phyllis Ann 1963- *WhoE 93*
Weinsheimer, William Cyrus 1941- *WhoAm 92*
Weinshenker, Howard L. *Law&B 92*
Weinshienk, Zita Leeson 1933- *WhoAmW 93*
Weinstein, Aaron Meyer 1924- *WhoE 93*
Weinstein, Abraham Hyman 1912- *St&PR 93*
Weinstein, Alan I. 1943- *St&PR 93*
Weinstein, Alexander d1991 *BioIn 17*
Weinstein, Alfred Bernard 1917- *WhoE 93*
Weinstein, Allan M. 1945- *WhoAm 92*
Weinstein, Arnold K. 1937- *WhoE 93*
Weinstein, Arnold Louis 1940- *WhoAm 92*
Weinstein, Barry Dennis 1946- *St&PR 93*
Weinstein, Bernard Allen 1946- *WhoE 93*
Weinstein, Bert I. *Law&B 92*
Weinstein, Beryl J. 1928- *St&PR 93*
Weinstein, Bob *MiSFD 9*
Weinstein, Carol Wendy 1958- *WhoE 93*
Weinstein, David C. *Law&B 92*
Weinstein, David Lee *Law&B 92*
Weinstein, Diane Gilbert 1947- *CngDr 91, WhoAmW 93*
Weinstein, Elliot *ScF&FL 92*
Weinstein, Elliott 1934- *St&PR 93*
Weinstein, George 1924- *St&PR 93*
Weinstein, George William 1935- *WhoAm 92, WhoWor 93*
Weinstein, Grace Wohlner *WhoE 93*
Weinstein, Harel 1945- *WhoE 93*
Weinstein, Harold *Law&B 92*
Weinstein, Harris *WhoAm 92, WhoE 93, WhoWor 93*
Weinstein, Harvey *MiSFD 9*
Weinstein, Herbert 1933- *WhoAm 92, WhoE 93*
Weinstein, Howard 1954- *ScF&FL 92*
Weinstein, I. Bernard 1930- *WhoAm 92*
Weinstein, Ira Phillip 1919- *WhoAm 92*
Weinstein, Irwin Marshall 1926- *WhoAm 92*
Weinstein, Jack B. 1921- *WhoAm 92*
Weinstein, Jay A. 1942- *WhoAm 92*
Weinstein, Jeffrey A. 1951- *St&PR 93*
Weinstein, Jeffrey Allen *Law&B 92*
Weinstein, Jeffrey Allen 1951- *WhoAm 92*
Weinstein, Jerome d1992 *BioIn 17, NewYTBS 92*
Weinstein, Jerome J. 1924- *St&PR 93*
Weinstein, Jerome William 1942- *WhoE 93*
Weinstein, Jerry L. 1936- *St&PR 93, WhoAm 92*
Weinstein, Jim *BioIn 17*
Weinstein, Joel R. 1941- *St&PR 93*
Weinstein, Joyce 1931- *WhoAmW 93*
Weinstein, Larry Philip 1953- *WhoE 93*
Weinstein, Lewis H. 1905- *WhoAm 92, WhoWor 93*
Weinstein, Lewis M. 1940- *St&PR 93*
Weinstein, Louis 1909- *WhoAm 92*
Weinstein, Lucie Ruth 1924- *WhoAmW 93*
Weinstein, Marie Pastore 1940- *WhoAmW 93*
Weinstein, Marion Louis 1944- *WhoSSW 93*
Weinstein, Mark M. *Law&B 92*
Weinstein, Mark Michael 1942- *WhoAm 92*
Weinstein, Martin 1936- *St&PR 93, WhoAm 92*
Weinstein, Marvin M. 1943- *St&PR 93*
Weinstein, Michael Alan 1942- *WhoAm 92*
Weinstein, Michael Joseph 1967- *WhoSSW 93*
Weinstein, Michael Magen 1948- *WhoE 93*
Weinstein, Milton Charles 1949- *WhoAm 92*
Weinstein, Mitchell Ira 1957- *WhoSSW 93*
Weinstein, Nancy Pryce 1944- *WhoAmW 93*
Weinstein, Nina 1951- *SmATA 73 [port]*
Weinstein, Norman 1948- *WhoWrEP 92*
Weinstein, Paul *Law&B 92*
Weinstein, Paul Allen 1933- *WhoE 93*
Weinstein, Paula H. 1945- *ConTFT 10*
Weinstein, Peter M. 1947- *WhoSSW 93*
Weinstein, Philip Meyer 1940- *WhoE 93*
Weinstein, Richard Neal 1948- *WhoSSW 93*
Weinstein, Robert J. 1945- *St&PR 93*
Weinstein, Rocio Aitania 1943- *WhoWrEP 92*
Weinstein, Ronald S. 1938- *WhoAm 92*
Weinstein, Rosalyn Lowe 1951- *WhoAmW 93*
Weinstein, Roy 1927- *WhoAm 92, WhoSSW 93, WhoWor 93*
Weinstein, Ruth Joseph 1933- *WhoAm 92*
Weinstein, Sharon Rae 1943- *WhoAmW 93*
Weinstein, Sharon Schlein 1942- *WhoAmW 93*
Weinstein, Sidney 1920- *WhoAm 92*
Weinstein, Sidney 1922- *WhoAm 92*
Weinstein, Stanley 1929- *WhoAm 92*
Weinstein, Stanley Howard 1948- *St&PR 93*
Weinstein, Stephen Brant 1938- *WhoAm 92*
Weinstein, Steven Matthew *Law&B 92*
Weinstein, Steven Philip 1958- *WhoE 93*
Weinstein, Susan Meg 1955- *WhoAmW 93*
Weinstein, Sydney S. 1955- *WhoE 93*
Weinstein, William Joseph 1917- *WhoWor 93*
Weinstein-Bacal, Stuart Allen 1948- *WhoWor 93*
Weinstock, Anne Marie 1948- *WhoE 93*
Weinstock, Arnold 1924- *WhoWor 93*
Weinstock, Carol Ann 1946- *WhoAmW 93*
Weinstock, David *Law&B 92*
Weinstock, George David 1937- *WhoE 93*
Weinstock, Grace Evangeline 1904- *WhoAmW 93*
Weinstock, Harold 1925- *WhoAm 92*
Weinstock, Herbert 1905-1971 *Baker 92*
Weinstock, Herbert Frank 1913- *WhoAm 92*
Weinstock, Leonard 1935- *WhoAm 92*
Weinstock, Mark Robert 1961- *WhoE 93*
Weinstock, Michael J. *Law&B 92*
Weinstock, Philip D. *Law&B 92*
Weinstock, Robert 1919- *WhoWor 93*
Weinstock, Russell G. 1943- *St&PR 93*
Weinstock, Steven Fred *Law&B 92*
Weinstock, Sylvia *BioIn 17*
Weinstock, Walter Wolfe 1925- *WhoAm 92*
Weintraub, Abner Edward 1954- *WhoSSW 93*
Weintraub, Annette *WhoAmW 93*
Weintraub, Barbara Anne 1960- *WhoAmW 93*
Weintraub, Daniel Ralph 1939- *WhoE 93*
Weintraub, Edward Alan 1947- *St&PR 93*
Weintraub, Eliot Roy 1943- *WhoAm 92*
Weintraub, Eugene d1992 *NewYTBS 92*
Weintraub, Herbert 1933- *St&PR 93*
Weintraub, Hyman L. 1914- *St&PR 93*
Weintraub, Jane Ann 1954- *WhoSSW 93*
Weintraub, Jerry *WhoAm 92*
Weintraub, Joseph 1945- *WhoAm 92, WhoWrEP 92*
Weintraub, Lester 1924- *WhoE 93*
Weintraub, Louis d1991 *BioIn 17*
Weintraub, Mark M. *Law&B 92*
Weintraub, Michael 1938- *St&PR 93*
Weintraub, Michael Ira 1940- *WhoAm 92*
Weintraub, Robert L. *Law&B 92*
Weintraub, Russell Jay 1929- *WhoAm 92*
Weintraub, Ruth G. 1909- *WhoAm 92*
Weintraub, Sam 1927- *WhoWor 93*
Weintraub, Sam, Jr. 1915- *St&PR 93*
Weintraub, Sandra *MiSFD 9*
Weintraub, Sidney 1914-1983 *BioIn 17*
Weintraub, Sidney 1922- *WhoAm 92*
Weintraub, Stan J. 1935- *St&PR 93*
Weintraub, Stanley 1905- *St&PR 93*
Weintraub, Stanley 1929- *BioIn 17, WhoAm 92, WhoWrEP 92*
Weintraub, Thomas E. 1922- *St&PR 93*
Weintraub, William 1926- *ScF&FL 92*
Weintz, Caroline Giles 1952- *WhoE 93*
Weintz, J. Fred, Jr. 1926- *St&PR 93*
Weintz, Walter Louis 1952- *WhoAm 92*
Weinwurm, Rudolf 1835-1911 *Baker 92*
Weinzierl, Max, Ritter von 1841-1898 *Baker 92*
Weinzierl, Peter 1923- *WhoScE 91-4*
Weinzweig, Helen 1915- *WhoCanL 92*
Weinzweig, John (Jacob) 1913- *Baker 92*
Weir, Alexander, Jr. 1922- *WhoAm 92*
Weir, Bruce Spencer 1943- *WhoSSW 93*
Weir, Charles Dudley 1935- *St&PR 93*
Weir, David Stewart 1932- *WhoAm 92*
Weir, David Thomas *Law&B 92*
Weir, David Thomas Henderson *WhoScE 91-1*
Weir, Don Clair 1912- *WhoAm 92*
Weir, Donald George 1934- *WhoScE 91-3*
Weir, Donald MacKay *WhoScE 91-1*
Weir, Elizabeth *AmWomPl*
Weir, Elliott Henry, Jr. 1946- *WhoAm 92*
Weir, Florence Roney 1861-1932 *AmWomPl*
Weir, Gavin 1931- *St&PR 93*
Weir, Gillian (Constance) 1941- *Baker 92, WhoWor 93*
Weir, Henry Sylvester, Jr. 1947- *WhoSSW 93*
Weir, James Robert 1932- *WhoSSW 93*
Weir, Joan 1928- *WhoCanL 92*
Weir, John Marshall 1911-1992 *BioIn 17*
Weir, Judith *BioIn 17*
Weir, Judith 1954- *Baker 92, OxDcOp*
Weir, Judith Bonaventure 1952- *WhoAmW 93*
Weir, Kenneth Wynn 1930- *WhoAm 92*
Weir, Kent Alan 1963- *WhoSSW 93*
Weir, Morton Webster 1934- *WhoAm 92, WhoWor 93*
Weir, Paul Joseph 1923- *St&PR 93, WhoAm 92*
Weir, Peter 1944- *MiSFD 9*
Weir, Peter Frank 1933- *WhoAm 92*
Weir, Peter Lindsay 1944- *WhoAm 92, WhoWor 93*
Weir, Rayner 1930- *St&PR 93*
Weir, Robert Harold *Law&B 92*
Weir, Sean 1956- *St&PR 93*
Weir, Sonja Ann 1934- *WhoAmW 93*
Weir, Stephen James 1940- *WhoAm 92*
Weir, Stephen Lynn 1949- *WhoAm 92*
Weir, Theresa Ann 1954- *WhoWrEP 92*
Weir, Thomas Charles 1933- *WhoAm 92*
Weir, Thomas Edward, Jr. 1949- *WhoE 93*
Weir, Thomas Henry 1934- *St&PR 93*
Weir, Virginia Leigh 1958- *WhoWrEP 92*
Weir, William C. 1937- *St&PR 93*
Weir, William C., III 1937- *WhoAm 92*
Weir, William Wilbur d1990 *BioIn 17*
Weirauch, Kristine R. *Law&B 92*
Weirich, Dieter Karl 1944- *WhoWor 93*
Weirich, Richard D. 1944- *St&PR 93*
Weirich, Steven J. *St&PR 93*
Weirick, William Newton 1952- *WhoSSW 93*
Weirsoe, Steen 1948- *WhoWor 93*
Weis, Al 1938- *BioIn 17*
Weis, Arthur M. 1925- *St&PR 93*
Weis, David H. 1931- *St&PR 93*
Weis, Don 1922- *MiSFD 9*
Weis, (Carl) Flemming 1898-1981 *Baker 92*
Weis, Gary *MiSFD 9*
Weis, Henry B., III 1940- *St&PR 93*
Weis, Janice E. *Law&B 92*
Weis, Jessica 1901-1986 *BioIn 17*
Weis, Judith Shulman 1941- *WhoAmW 93*
Weis, Karel 1862-1944 *Baker 92*
Weis, Konrad M. 1928- *St&PR 93*
Weis, Konrad Max 1928- *WhoAm 92*
Weis, Margaret 1948- *ScF&FL 92*
Weis, Michael Thomas 1945- *St&PR 93*
Weis, Monica Rosemary 1942- *WhoE 93*
Weis, Randall David 1950- *WhoE 93*
Weis, Robert F. 1919- *St&PR 93*
Weis, Serge 1960- *WhoWor 93*
Weis, Sigfried 1916- *St&PR 93, WhoAm 92*
Weis, Walter Robert 1941- *St&PR 93*
Weisbach, Theodore Lowell 1953- *St&PR 93*
Weisbard, James Joseph 1953- *WhoE 93*
Weisbart, Steven Norman 1944- *WhoAm 92*
Weisbaum, Nathaniel 1917- *St&PR 93*
Weisbecker, A.C. *ScF&FL 92*
Weisbecker, Frank D. 1934- *St&PR 93*
Weisbecker, Henry Bezalel 1925- *WhoE 93*
Weisbein, Michael David 1954- *WhoSSW 93*
Weisberg, Alfred Mhyron 1926- *WhoAm 92*
Weisberg, Arthur 1931- *Baker 92*
Weisberg, David Herman 1950- *St&PR 93*
Weisberg, Gerard Maxwell 1925- *WhoWor 93*
Weisberg, Harry M. 1932- *WhoAm 92*
Weisberg, Herbert Frank 1941- *WhoAm 92*
Weisberg, Ira 1949- *St&PR 93*
Weisberg, Jeffrey N. 1957- *St&PR 93*
Weisberg, Jonathan Howard *Law&B 92*
Weisberg, Jonathan Mark 1943- *WhoAm 92*
Weisberg, Joseph Simpson 1937- *WhoE 93*
Weisberg, Lawrence Robert 1943- *WhoAm 92*
Weisberg, Leonard R. 1929- *WhoAm 92*
Weisberg, Lynne Willing 1948- *WhoAmW 93, WhoE 93*
Weisberg, Morris L. 1921- *WhoAm 92*
Weisberg, Pamela L. *Law&B 92*
Weisberg, Ruth *WhoAmW 93*
Weisberg, Ruth Maxine 1956- *WhoAmW 93*
Weisberger, Alan 1961- *St&PR 93*
Weisberger, Barbara 1926- *WhoAm 92*
Weisberger, Edward J. 1942- *St&PR 93*
Weisberger, Joseph Robert 1920- *WhoAm 92*
Weisberger, Mark *Law&B 92*
Weisberrg, Alfred P. 1926- *St&PR 93*
Weisblat, Howard Alan 1935- *St&PR 93*
Weisblatt, Adam 1929- *St&PR 93*
Weisblatt, Alan Joel *Law&B 92*
Weisbord, Vera Buch 1895- *BioIn 17*
Weisbrod, Alain 1936- *WhoScE 91-2*
Weisbrod, Burton Allen 1931- *WhoAm 92, WhoWrEP 92*
Weisbrod, Carl Barry 1944- *WhoE 93*
Weisbrod, Harold 1921- *St&PR 93*
Weisbrod, Roberta Ellen 1943- *WhoE 93*
Weisbrod, Tedra G. *Law&B 92*
Weisbrot, Lucille L. *Law&B 92*
Weisbroth, Steven Harris 1934- *WhoE 93*
Weisbruch, William Douglas 1935- *St&PR 93*

Weisbuch, Robert Alan 1946- *WhoAm 92*
Weisburd, Ellen S. *Law&B 92*
Weisburger, Elizabeth Kreiser 1924- *WhoAm 92, WhoAmW 93, WhoE 93*
Weisburger, John Hans 1921- *WhoAm 92*
Weisburgh, Judith *Law&B 92*
Weisburst, Marsha Jane *Law&B 92*
Weischadle, David Emmanuel 1941- *WhoE 93*
Weischenberg, Peter H. 1938- *St&PR 93*
Weischet, Wolfgang David 1921- *WhoScE 91-3*
Weise, Charles Martin 1926- *WhoAm 92*
Weise, Frank Earl, III 1944- *WhoAm 92*
Weise, Klaus 1934- *WhoScE 91-3, WhoWor 93*
Weise, Len Morris 1958- *WhoSSW 93*
Weise, Richard H. *Law&B 92*
Weise, Richard H. 1935- *St&PR 93*
Weise, Theodore Lewis 1944- *WhoAm 92*
Weise, W. Jeffrey 1942- *WhoE 93*
Weise, Wilhelm *WhoScE 91-3*
Weisel, Kathleen 1950- *WhoAmW 93*
Weisel, Michael L. 1957- *St&PR 93*
Weisel, Rebecca Kathleen 1966- *WhoAmW 93*
Weisel, Walter K. 1940- *St&PR 93*
Weisen, Jean-Henri 1957- *WhoWor 93*
Weisenberger, Scott 1955- *WhoE 93*
Weisenblum, Jaime Paz 1950- *WhoAm 92*
Weisenborn, Gunther 1902-1969 *DcLB 124 [port]*
Weisenburger, Steven *ScF&FL 92*
Weisenburger, Theodore Maurice 1930- *WhoWor 93*
Weisend, C. Frederick 1926- *St&PR 93*
Weisenfeld, Mildred *WhoAmW 93*
Weisenfluh, Frederick Allen 1934- *St&PR 93*
Weisenseel, Charles W. 1933- *St&PR 93*
Weisenseel, Gerald Edward 1938- *WhoSSW 93*
Weisensel, Mary Delbert 1936- *WhoAmW 93*
Weiser, Conrad John 1935- *WhoAm 92*
Weiser, Dan 1933- *WhoSSW 93*
Weiser, Irving 1947- *St&PR 93, WhoAm 92*
Weiser, Jaroslav 1920- *WhoScE 91-4*
Weiser, Jay *Law&B 92*
Weiser, John Wolfgang 1932- *St&PR 93*
Weiser, Mark David 1952- *WhoAm 92*
Weiser, Melvin *ScF&FL 92*
Weiser, Norman Sidney 1919- *WhoAm 92, WhoE 93*
Weiser, Paul D. *Law&B 92*
Weiser, Paul David 1936- *St&PR 93, WhoAm 92*
Weiser, Ralph Raphael 1925- *WhoAm 92*
Weiser, Robert C. 1946- *St&PR 93*
Weiser, Ronald S. 1943- *WhoSSW 93*
Weiser, Sherwood Manuel 1931- *WhoAm 92, WhoSSW 93*
Weiser, Steven F. 1946- *WhoSSW 93*
Weiser, Terry L. 1954- *St&PR 93*
Weiser, Terry Lee 1954- *WhoWor 93*
Weisert, Kathleen Mary 1952- *WhoAmW 93*
Weisert, Kent Albert Frederick 1949- *WhoE 93*
Weisfeld, Lewis Bernard 1929- *St&PR 93*
Weisfeld, Sheldon 1946- *WhoEmL 93*
Weisfeldt, Myron Lee 1940- *WhoAm 92*
Weis-Fogh, Ulla Sivertsen 1936- *WhoScE 91-2*
Weisgall, Hugo 1912- *OxDcOp*
Weisgall, Hugo (David) 1912- *Baker 92, WhoAm 92*
Weisgarber, Elliot 1919- *Baker 92*
Weisgard, Leonard (Joseph) 1916- *MajAI [port]*
Weisgerber, David Wendelin 1938- *WhoAm 92, WhoWrEP 92*
Weisgerber, George Ronald 1933- *St&PR 93*
Weisgerber, Horst 1935- *WhoScE 91-3*
Weisgold, Myra Irene 1939- *WhoE 93*
Weishaar, Ronald E. 1951- *WhoAm 92*
Weishaar, Sandra J. 1947- *WhoAmW 93, WhoEmL 93*
Weishaus, Joel 1939- *WhoWrEP 92*
Weisheit, Lawrence Ernest 1938- *St&PR 93*
Weisiger, Edward Innes 1931- *St&PR 93, WhoAm 92*
Weisiger, Kathleen Wendell 1949- *WhoE 93*
Weisinger, Charles 1942- *WhoSSW 93*
Weisinger, Ronald Jay 1946- *WhoEmL 93, WhoSSW 93, WhoWor 93*
Weiskel, Catherine Lacny 1950- *WhoAm 92*
Weiskerger, Renee Ann 1967- *WhoE 93*
Weiskittel, Barbara Ann 1961- *WhoAmW 93*
Weiskittel, Ralph Joseph 1924- *WhoAm 92*
Weiskrantz, Lawrence *WhoScE 91-1*
Weisl, Edwin Louis, Jr. 1929- *WhoWor 93*
Weisleder, Stanley 1933- *WhoIns 93*
Weislogel, Lee David 1937- *St&PR 93*
Weisman, Abner I. 1907-1990 *BioIn 17*
Weisman, Ann E. 1948- *WhoWrEP 92*
Weisman, Bart Louis 1958- *WhoE 93*
Weisman, Ezra 1940- *St&PR 93*
Weisman, Frederick R. 1913- *BioIn 17*
Weisman, Harlan Frederick 1952- *WhoE 93*
Weisman, Henry *St&PR 93*
Weisman, Irving 1918- *WhoAm 92*
Weisman, Joel 1928- *WhoAm 92*
Weisman, John 1942- *ConAu 40NR, WhoE 93*
Weisman, Jordan K. *ScF&FL 92*
Weisman, Lorenzo David 1945- *St&PR 93, WhoAm 92*
Weisman, Marcia 1918-1991 *BioIn 17*
Weisman, Maxwell Napier 1912- *WhoE 93*
Weisman, Michael Henry 1929- *St&PR 93*
Weisman, Robin *BioIn 17*
Weisman, Roger D. *Law&B 92*
Weisman, Sam *MiSFD 9*
Weisman, Susan 1960- *St&PR 93*
Weismann, Donald Leroy 1914- *WhoAm 92*
Weismann, Julius 1879-1950 *Baker 92*
Weismann, Wilhelm 1900-1980 *Baker 92*
Weismantel, Gregory N. 1940- *St&PR 93*
Weismantle, John Arthur 1942- *St&PR 93*
Weismiller, David R. 1943- *WhoAm 92*
Weismiller, Edward Ronald 1915- *WhoAm 92, WhoWrEP 92*
Weisner, Jeffrey T. 1947- *St&PR 93*
Weisner, Lynnette Brant 1958- *WhoAmW 93*
Weisner, Maurice Franklin 1917- *WhoAm 92*
Weiss *Baker 92*
Weiss 1935- *WhoScE 91-2*
Weiss, Adolph 1891-1971 *Baker 92*
Weiss, Adrienne Joanne 1953- *WhoAmW 93*
Weiss, Alarich 1925- *WhoScE 91-3*
Weiss, Alexander 1944- *WhoSSW 93*
Weiss, Aline Pollitzer d1991 *BioIn 17*
Weiss, Allan Joseph 1932- *WhoAm 92*
Weiss, Allen 1918- *WhoE 93*
Weiss, Allen Charles 1945- *WhoE 93*
Weiss, Alvin Harvey 1928- *WhoAm 92, WhoE 93*
Weiss, Andre 1926- *WhoE 93, WhoWor 93*
Weiss, Andrew Murray 1947- *WhoE 93, WhoWor 93*
Weiss, Ann 1949- *WhoAmW 93, WhoE 93, WhoEmL 93, WhoWor 93*
Weiss, Ann E. 1943- *SmATA 69 [port]*
Weiss, Ann E(dwards) 1943- *MajAI [port]*
Weiss, Anthony Steven 1957- *WhoWor 93*
Weiss, Ardith L. 1947- *WhoSSW 93*
Weiss, Armand Berl 1931- *WhoAm 92, WhoSSW 93, WhoWor 93*
Weiss, Arnold Robert 1932- *WhoSSW 93*
Weiss, Barbara May 1939- *WhoAmW 93*
Weiss, Barry A. *Law&B 92*
Weiss, Bernard 1925- *WhoE 93*
Weiss, Beverly A. 1926- *WhoAmW 93*
Weiss, Beverly Jean 1925- *WhoAmW 93*
Weiss, Bob *WhoAm 92*
Weiss, Brian 1945- *WhoE 93*
Weiss, Carl 1938- *St&PR 93*
Weiss, Charles F. 1939- *St&PR 93*
Weiss, Charles Frederick 1921- *WhoSSW 93*
Weiss, Charles J. *Law&B 92*
Weiss, Charles Manuel 1918- *WhoAm 92*
Weiss, Charles S. 1952- *St&PR 93*
Weiss, Charles Stanard 1952- *WhoAm 92*
Weiss, Clifford L. 1937- *St&PR 93*
Weiss, Dan *St&PR 93*
Weiss, Daniel G. *Law&B 92*
Weiss, Daniel Leigh 1923- *WhoSSW 93*
Weiss, David 1928- *WhoAm 92*
Weiss, David Alan 1953- *WhoE 93*
Weiss, David Raymond 1948- *WhoAm 92*
Weiss, David S. 1943- *St&PR 93*
Weiss, Donald J. 1943- *St&PR 93*
Weiss, Donald Logan 1926- *WhoAm 92*
Weiss, Dudley A. 1912- *St&PR 93*
Weiss, Dudley A. 1912-1991 *BioIn 17*
Weiss, Earle Burton 1932- *WhoAm 92*
Weiss, Edmund Charles, Jr. 1943- *St&PR 93*
Weiss, Edward *Law&B 92*
Weiss, Edward 1929- *St&PR 93, WhoE 93*
Weiss, Edward Craig 1924- *WhoSSW 93*
Weiss, Egon Arthur 1919- *WhoAm 92*
Weiss, Elaine Landsberg *WhoE 93*
Weiss, Elek K. 1926- *St&PR 93*
Weiss, Eli *Law&B 92*
Weiss, Ellen 1953- *ScF&FL 92*
Weiss, Erwin 1924- *St&PR 93*
Weiss, Erwin L. 1926- *WhoScE 91-3*
Weiss, Eugen Franz Josef 1930- *WhoScE 91-3, WhoWor 93*
Weiss, Eve 1930- *WhoE 93*
Weiss, Frank Charles *Law&B 92*
Weiss, Franz 1778-1830 *Baker 92*
Weiss, Fred Geoffrey 1941- *St&PR 93*
Weiss, Gail Ellen 1946- *WhoAm 92, WhoAmW 93*
Weiss, George Arthur 1921- *WhoE 93, WhoWor 93*
Weiss, George David *BioIn 17*
Weiss, George Herbert 1930- *WhoE 93*
Weiss, Gerhard Hans 1926- *WhoAm 92*
Weiss, Gerson 1939- *WhoAm 92*
Weiss, Harald 1929- *WhoScE 91-4*
Weiss, Harlan Lee 1941- *WhoE 93*
Weiss, Harriet 1940- *WhoAmW 93*
Weiss, Harry K. d1990 *BioIn 17*
Weiss, Harvey 1922- *ConAu 38NR, MajAI [port]*
Weiss, Harvey Jerome 1929- *WhoE 93*
Weiss, Harvey Richard 1943- *WhoE 93*
Weiss, Herbert D. 1929- *St&PR 93*
Weiss, Herbert Klemm 1917- *WhoAm 92, WhoWor 93*
Weiss, Hermann 1940- *WhoWor 93*
Weiss, Honnen S. 1929- *St&PR 93*
Weiss, Horst 1937- *WhoScE 91-3*
Weiss, Howard A. *WhoAm 92*
Weiss, Howard Rich 1924- *St&PR 93*
Weiss, Ira Francis 1909- *WhoAm 92*
Weiss, Ira Richard 1947- *WhoSSW 93*
Weiss, Irving 1921- *WhoWrEP 92*
Weiss, Irving I. 1927- *St&PR 93*
Weiss, James Michael 1946- *WhoAm 92*
Weiss, James Moses Aaron 1921- *WhoAm 92, WhoWrEP 92*
Weiss, James Robert 1953- *St&PR 93*
Weiss, James William 1940- *WhoSSW 93*
Weiss, Janet Lois 1946- *WhoE 93*
Weiss, Janet S. 1957- *WhoAmW 93*
Weiss, Jaqueline Shachter *BioIn 17*
Weiss, Jay Michael 1941- *WhoAm 92*
Weiss, Jeffrey G. 1942- *St&PR 93*
Weiss, Jerome P. *Law&B 92*
Weiss, Jerome Paul 1934- *St&PR 93, WhoAm 92*
Weiss, Jerry *Law&B 92*
Weiss, Jess E(dward) 1926- *ConAu 38NR*
Weiss, Jiri 1913- *DrEEuF*
Weiss, Joan Rosenblum 1937- *WhoAmW 93*
Weiss, Joanne Marion 1960- *WhoAmW 93*
Weiss, Joel Alexander *WhoE 93*
Weiss, Joel J. *WhoAm 92*
Weiss, Joel Joseph 1931- *St&PR 93*
Weiss, Johann Adolf Faustinus 1741-1814 *Baker 92*
Weiss, Johann Jacob c. 1662-1754 *Baker 92*
Weiss, Johann Sigismund c. 1689-1737 *Baker 92*
Weiss, John A. *Law&B 92*
Weiss, Jordan P. *Law&B 92*
Weiss, Josef J. 1937- *WhoScE 91-4*
Weiss, Joseph Francis 1940- *WhoE 93*
Weiss, Joseph Franklin 1927- *WhoSSW 93*
Weiss, Joseph Joel 1931- *WhoAm 92*
Weiss, Judith Kelner 1950- *WhoAmW 93*
Weiss, Julien Jalal Eddin *BioIn 17*
Weiss, Kathryn Jana 1955- *WhoAmW 93*
Weiss, Kim Elizabeth 1954- *WhoSSW 93*
Weiss, L. Leonard 1928- *WhoE 93*
Weiss, Lech Jan 1926- *WhoScE 91-4*
Weiss, Leo A. 1918-1991 *BioIn 17*
Weiss, Leon P. 1925- *WhoAm 92*
Weiss, Leonard 1934- *WhoAm 92*
Weiss, Leonard Aaron 1946- *St&PR 93*
Weiss, Leonard D. *St&PR 93*
Weiss, Leonard R. 1927- *St&PR 93*
Weiss, Linda S. *Law&B 92*
Weiss, Lionel Edward 1927- *WhoAm 92*
Weiss, Lois J. *Law&B 92*
Weiss, Louis Alan 1948- *WhoE 93*
Weiss, Louise 1893-1983 *BioIn 17*
Weiss, Mabel Louise 1897- *WhoAmW 93*
Weiss, Margaret R. d1992 *BioIn 17, NewYTBS 92*
Weiss, Margaret R. 1923?-1992 *ConAu 137*
Weiss, Maria Cristina Rodriguez 1949- *WhoAmW 93*
Weiss, Marjorie 1954- *WhoAmW 93*
Weiss, Mark 1960- *St&PR 93*
Weiss, Mark Anschel 1937- *WhoAm 92*
Weiss, Mark Lawrence 1945- *WhoAm 92*
Weiss, Martin Harvey 1939- *WhoAm 92*
Weiss, Marvin 1929- *WhoAm 92, WhoE 93, WhoWor 93*
Weiss, Mary Ethel *AmWomPl*
Weiss, Max Leslie 1933- *WhoAm 92*
Weiss, Max Tibor 1922- *WhoAm 92*
Weiss, Michael Allen 1941- *WhoAm 92*
Weiss, Michael David 1942- *WhoE 93*
Weiss, Monte Eugine *WhoE 93*
Weiss, Morry 1940- *St&PR 93, WhoAm 92*
Weiss, Myrna Grace 1939- *WhoAm 92, WhoAmW 93*
Weiss, Nicki Monica Jane 1954- *WhoAmW 93*
Weiss, Nigel Oscar *WhoScE 91-1*
Weiss, Noel S. 1943- *WhoAm 92*
Weiss, Nora L. 1940- *WhoUN 92*
Weiss, Paul 1901- *BioIn 17, WhoAm 92, WhoWor 93*
Weiss, Paul Thomas 1944- *WhoAm 92*
Weiss, Peter 1916-1982 *DcLB 124 [port]*
Weiss, Pierre 1948- *WhoUN 92*
Weiss, R.A. *WhoScE 91-1*
Weiss, Raymond Otto, Jr. 1952- *WhoE 93*
Weiss, Rhett Louis 1961- *WhoEmL 93, WhoSSW 93, WhoWor 93*
Weiss, Richard 1907-1962 *IntDcAn*
Weiss, Richard J. *WhoScE 91-1*
Weiss, Richard Jerome 1923- *WhoE 93*
Weiss, Richard T. *St&PR 93*
Weiss, Rick *BioIn 17*
Weiss, Rita S. 1935- *WhoAmW 93*
Weiss, Robert A. 1948- *St&PR 93*
Weiss, Robert Alan 1950- *WhoAm 92*
Weiss, Robert Anthony 1940- *WhoScE 91-1*
Weiss, Robert Francis 1924- *WhoAm 92*
Weiss, Robert Franklin 1946- *WhoE 93*
Weiss, Robert G. 1931- *St&PR 93*
Weiss, Robert Howard 1938- *WhoE 93*
Weiss, Robert Jerome 1917- *WhoAm 92*
Weiss, Robert K. *MiSFD 9*
Weiss, Robert M. 1936- *WhoAm 92, WhoE 93*
Weiss, Robert Michael 1940- *WhoE 93*
Weiss, Robert Orr 1926- *WhoAm 92*
Weiss, Robert S. 1946- *St&PR 93*
Weiss, Robert Stephen 1946- *WhoAm 92*
Weiss, Robert William 1942- *WhoSSW 93*
Weiss, Roger Douglas 1951- *WhoAm 92*
Weiss, Roger M. 1930- *St&PR 93*
Weiss, Ronald 1942- *St&PR 93*
Weiss, Ronald Phillip 1947- *WhoE 93, WhoWor 93*
Weiss, Ronald Wencil *Law&B 92*
Weiss, Ronald Whitman 1939- *WhoAm 92*
Weiss, Russell Leonard 1930- *WhoAm 92*
Weiss, Ruth 1928- *WhoWrEP 92*
Weiss, Samuel 1905-1991 *BioIn 17*
Weiss, Samuel Abraham 1923- *WhoE 93*
Weiss, Seymour d1992 *NewYTBS 92 [port]*
Weiss, Seymour 1930- *St&PR 93*
Weiss, Shelley M. *Law&B 92*
Weiss, Shirley F. 1921- *WhoAm 92, WhoAmW 93, WhoSSW 93, WhoWor 93*
Weiss, Sigmund *WhoWrEP 92*
Weiss, Silvius Leopold 1686-1750 *Baker 92*
Weiss, Spencer C. *Law&B 92*
Weiss, Stanford L. 1927- *St&PR 93*
Weiss, Stanley Alan 1926- *WhoAm 92, WhoE 93, WhoWor 93*
Weiss, Stanley C. 1929- *St&PR 93, WhoAm 92*
Weiss, Stanley D. 1910- *EncABHB 8 [port]*
Weiss, Stanley I. 1925- *St&PR 93*
Weiss, Stanley Irwin 1925- *WhoAm 92*
Weiss, Stephen H. *Law&B 92*
Weiss, Stephen Henry 1935- *WhoAm 92*
Weiss, Stephen Joel 1938- *WhoAm 92, WhoE 93*
Weiss, Stephen Z. *Law&B 92*
Weiss, Steven R. *Law&B 92*
Weiss, Steven Reid *Law&B 92*
Weiss, Susan Christine 1944- *WhoAmW 93*
Weiss, Ted 1927- *CngDr 91*
Weiss, Ted 1927-1992 *CurBio 92N, NewYTBS 92 [port]*
Weiss, Theodore Russell 1916- *WhoWrEP 92*
Weiss, Theodore S. 1927- *WhoAm 92, WhoE 93*
Weiss, Thomas Edward 1916- *WhoAm 92*
Weiss, Virgil Wayne 1940- *WhoAm 92*
Weiss, Volker 1930- *WhoAm 92*
Weiss, Walter Stanley 1929- *WhoAm 92*
Weiss, William 1919- *WhoE 93*
Weiss, William C. *Law&B 92*
Weiss, William E. *Law&B 92*
Weiss, William L. 1929- *St&PR 93*
Weiss, William Lee 1929- *WhoAm 92*
Weiss, William Owen *Law&B 92*
Weiss, Wojciech 1875-1950 *PolBiDi*
Weissbach, H. 1932- *St&PR 93*
Weissbach, Herbert 1932- *WhoAm 92, WhoE 93*
Weissbard, Samuel Held 1947- *WhoAm 92, WhoE 93*
Weissberg, Lawrence 1921- *St&PR 93*
Weissberg, Yulia (Lazarevna) 1880-1942 *Baker 92*
Weissbluth, Mitchel 1915-1990 *BioIn 17*
Weissbrod, Ellen *MiSFD 9*
Weisse, Carol Silvia 1961- *WhoAmW 93*

Weisse, Christian Felix 1726-1804 *BioIn 17, OxDcOp*
Weisse, Guenter 1935- *St&PR 93*
Weisse, Hans 1892-1940 *Baker 92*
Weissel, William *St&PR 93*
Weissel, William L. d1992 *BioIn 17, NewYTBS 92*
Weissenback, (Franz) Andreas 1880-1960 *Baker 92*
Weissenberg, Alexis 1929- *WhoWor 93*
Weissenberg, Alexis (Sigismond) 1929- *Baker 92*
Weissenborn, Gunther (Albert Friedrich) 1911- *Baker 92*
Weissenborn, Stanton F. 1925- *St&PR 93*
Weissenburger, Susan Kaye 1946- *WhoWrEP 92*
Weissenfels, Norbert 1926- *WhoScE 91-3*
Weissensee, Friedrich c. 1560-1622 *Baker 92*
Weisser, John Dietmar 1933- *WhoWor 93*
Weisser, Marcia Carole 1934- *WhoAmW 93*
Weisser, Michael *BioIn 17*
Weisser, Sidney 1927- *St&PR 93*
Weisser, William James 1948- *WhoSSW 93*
Weissfeld, Joachim Alexander 1927- *WhoAm 92*
Weissglas, H.G. Peter 1937- *WhoScE 91-4*
Weisshaar, Kenneth R. 1950- *St&PR 93*
Weissheimer, Wendelin 1838-1910 *Baker 92*
Weisskopf, Bernard 1929- *WhoAm 92, WhoWor 93*
Weisskopf, Thomas E. *BioIn 17*
Weisskopf, Victor Frederick *BioIn 17*
Weisskopf, Victor Frederick 1908- *WhoAm 92*
Weissler, Harold Joseph *Law&B 92*
Weisslitz, Edward *Law&B 92*
Weissman, Alan M. 1944- *St&PR 93*
Weissman, Barry Jay 1938- *St&PR 93*
Weissman, Barry Leigh 1948- *WhoWor 93*
Weissman, Craig Louis 1968- *WhoSSW 93*
Weissman, Edward 1927- *St&PR 93*
Weissman, Eugene Yehuda 1931- *WhoAm 92*
Weissman, George 1919- *St&PR 93*
Weissman, Ira J. 1931- *St&PR 93*
Weissman, Jack 1921- *WhoAm 92*
Weissman, Jay B. 1942- *St&PR 93*
Weissman, Jerrold A. 1936- *St&PR 93*
Weissman, Leon 1920- *St&PR 93*
Weissman, Michael Lewis 1934- *WhoAm 92*
Weissman, Norman 1925- *WhoAm 92*
Weissman, Paul I. 1929- *St&PR 93*
Weissman, Paul Marshall 1931- *WhoAm 92*
Weissman, Richard G. *BioIn 17*
Weissman, Robert Evan 1940- *St&PR 93, WhoAm 92, WhoE 93, WhoWor 93*
Weissman, Shirley Sarah 1951- *WhoAmW 93*
Weissman, Steven *Law&B 92*
Weissman, Susan 1938- *WhoE 93*
Weissman, William R. 1940- *WhoAm 92*
Weissmann, Ann B. 1934- *ConAu 139*
Weissmann, Charles 1931- *WhoWor 93*
Weissmann, Gerald 1930- *WhoAm 92*
Weissmann, Heidi Seitelblum 1951- *WhoAmW 93, WhoE 93, WhoEmL 93, WhoWor 93*
Weissmann, John 1910-1980 *Baker 92*
Weissmann, Mariana 1933- *WhoWor 93*
Weissmann, Robin Lee 1953- *WhoAm 92*
Weissmuller, Johnny 1904-1984 *BioIn 17, IntDcF 2-3 [port]*
Weiss-Rosmarin, Trude 1908- *BioIn 17*
Weisstein, Naomi 1939- *BioIn 17*
Weisstein, Ulrich Werner 1925- *WhoAm 92*
Weisstuch, Donald N. 1935- *St&PR 93*
Weist, Dwight d1991 *BioIn 17*
Weist, Robert D., Sr. 1939- *St&PR 93*
Weiswasser, Stephen A. *BioIn 17*
Weiswasser, Stephen Anthony 1940- *St&PR 93, WhoAm 92, WhoE 93*
Weisweiler, Peter 1945- *WhoWor 93*
Weisweiller, Carole *BioIn 17*
Weisweiller, Rudolf Leopold 1922- *WhoWor 93*
Weisz, Alessandro 1955- *WhoWor 93*
Weisz, Carleen Golden 1946- *WhoAmW 93*
Weisz, Helen 1947- *WhoE 93*
Weisz, Ivan Ehrlich 1946- *WhoE 93*
Weisz, Juan Francisco 1946- *WhoWor 93*
Weisz, Louis Max 1941- *St&PR 93*
Weisz, Paul Burg 1919- *WhoAm 92, WhoE 93*
Weisz, William J. 1927- *St&PR 93*
Weisz, William Julius 1927- *WhoAm 92*
Weiszmann, Andrei 1923- *WhoE 93*
Weitekamper, Hans 1934- *St&PR 93*
Weitendorf, Ernst-August 1934- *WhoScE 91-3*
Weith, John Robert 1949- *St&PR 93*
Weithas, William V. 1929- *St&PR 93*
Weithas, William Vincent 1929- *WhoAm 92*
Weithers, John G. 1933- *WhoAm 92*
Weithers, John Gregory 1933- *St&PR 93*
Weithorn, Stanley Stephen 1924- *WhoAm 92*
Weitkamp, Claus Carl Heinrich 1935- *WhoWor 93*
Weitkamp, William George 1934- *WhoAm 92*
Weitlauff, Manfred 1936- *WhoWor 93*
Weitman, Catheryn Julia *WhoSSW 93*
Weitman, Warren P., Jr. 1946- *St&PR 93*
Weitz, Bruce 1943- *WhoAm 92*
Weitz, Frederick William 1929- *St&PR 93, WhoAm 92*
Weitz, John 1923- *WhoAm 92*
Weitz, Leonard 1929- *St&PR 93*
Weitz, Leonard W. *Law&B 92*
Weitz, Martin Mishli 1907- *WhoAm 92*
Weitz, Michael Neal 1939- *St&PR 93*
Weitz, Sue Dee 1948- *WhoAmW 93*
Weitz, Theodore M. *Law&B 92*
Weitz, Wayne Paul 1966- *WhoSSW 93*
Weitzel, J.A. 1945- *St&PR 93*
Weitzel, John F., Jr. 1930- *St&PR 93*
Weitzel, John Patterson 1923- *WhoAm 92*
Weitzel, Lori Louderback 1960- *WhoAmW 93*
Weitzel, Paul Edward, Jr. 1958- *St&PR 93*
Weitzel, Paul J. 1937- *St&PR 93*
Weitzel, Susan K. 1955- *St&PR 93*
Weitzel, William Conrad, Jr. 1935- *WhoAm 92*
Weitzen, Edward H. 1920- *St&PR 93*
Weitzen, Edward H. 1920-1991 *BioIn 17*
Weitzen, Edwin Hylan 1917- *WhoE 93*
Weitzenfeld, Marvin L. 1938- *St&PR 93*
Weitzenhoffer, Aaron Max, Jr. 1939- *WhoE 93, WhoWor 93*
Weitzenhoffer, Frances *BioIn 17*
Weitzer, Bernard 1929- *WhoAm 92*
Weitzman, Arthur Joshua 1933- *WhoAm 92, WhoE 93*
Weitzman, Marilyn 1950- *WhoAmW 93*
Weitzman, Robert Harold 1937- *WhoAm 92*
Weitzman, Sarah Brown 1935- *WhoWrEP 92*
Weitzman, Stuart *BioIn 17*
Weitzmann, Carl Friedrich 1808-1880 *Baker 92*
Weitzner, Bella 1891-1988 *IntDcAn*
Weitzner, Harold 1933- *WhoAm 92*
Weix, Joseph B. 1927- *St&PR 93*
Weixler, Robert Henry, Jr. 1943- *St&PR 93*
Weixlmann, Joseph Norman 1946- *WhoWrEP 92*
Weizmann, Chaim 1874-1952 *BioIn 17*
Weizmann, Chaim Azriel 1874-1952 *DcTwHis*
Weizner, Denise Cecile 1962- *WhoAmW 93*
Weizsacker, Richard von 1920- *WhoWor 93*
Wekerle, Hartmut *WhoScE 91-3*
Wekstein, David Robert 1937- *WhoSSW 93*
Welber, David Alan 1949- *WhoE 93, WhoEmL 93, WhoWor 93*
Welber, Herbert 1935- *St&PR 93*
Welber, Irwin 1924- *WhoAm 92*
Welborn, Doris Ann Albright 1960- *WhoSSW 93*
Welborn, Elizabeth Charles d1990 *BioIn 17*
Welborn, Elsie Elender Jenkins 1937- *WhoAmW 93*
Welborn, Ernest W., Jr. 1922- *St&PR 93*
Welborn, Gordon Lee *Law&B 92*
Welborn, Sarah 1943- *WhoAmW 93*
Welburn, Ron 1944- *WhoWrEP 92*
Welby, Philip *ScF&FL 92*
Welch, Arnold DeMerritt 1908- *WhoAm 92*
Welch, Arthur Stellhorn 1930- *WhoSSW 93*
Welch, Ashley James 1933- *WhoAm 92*
Welch, Bernard Alfred 1908-1991 *BioIn 17*
Welch, Betty Leonora 1961- *WhoEmL 93*
Welch, Bo *WhoAm 92*
Welch, Bob 1956- *BioIn 17*
Welch, Byron Eugene 1928- *WhoAm 92*
Welch, Carol Ann 1938- *WhoAm 92*
Welch, Carol Mae 1947- *WhoAmW 93*
Welch, Charles David 1953- *WhoE 93*
Welch, Charles DeForest 1948- *WhoE 93*
Welch, Charles William, III *Law&B 92*
Welch, Claude Emerson 1906- *WhoAm 92*
Welch, Claude Emerson, Jr. 1939- *WhoAm 92*
Welch, Claude Raymond 1922- *WhoAm 92*
Welch, David C. *WhoAm 92*
Welch, David Otis 1938- *WhoE 93*
Welch, Donald Andrew 1939- *St&PR 93*
Welch, Douglas F. 1957- *St&PR 93*
Welch, Earl E. 1901-1990 *BioIn 17*
Welch, Edward K., II *Law&B 92*
Welch, Edwin Hugh 1944- *WhoAm 92*
Welch, Frank D. *BioIn 17*
Welch, Garth Larry 1937- *WhoAm 92*
Welch, Gerard S., Jr. *Law&B 92*
Welch, Geri Marie 1949- *WhoAmW 93*
Welch, Germaine Burchard 1937- *WhoSSW 93*
Welch, Gita (Bernardo) Honwana 1948- *ConAu 138*
Welch, Harry Scoville 1923- *WhoAm 92*
Welch, James 1940- *BioIn 17*
Welch, James Alexander 1924- *WhoSSW 93*
Welch, James Allen 1950- *St&PR 93*
Welch, James S. *WhoAm 92*
Welch, Jeanie Maxine 1946- *WhoAmW 93, WhoSSW 93*
Welch, Jeffrey Dean 1954- *St&PR 93*
Welch, Jerry 1963- *WhoSSW 93*
Welch, Joan Kathleen 1950- *WhoAmW 93, WhoE 93, WhoEmL 93, WhoWor 93*
Welch, Jody Badger *BioIn 17*
Welch, John F., Jr. *BioIn 17*
Welch, John Francis 1935- *St&PR 93*
Welch, John Francis, Jr. 1935- *WhoAm 92, WhoE 93*
Welch, John R. *Law&B 92*
Welch, John Stanley 1920- *WhoAm 92*
Welch, Joseph Lee 1950- *WhoSSW 93*
Welch, K. M. A. *WhoAm 92*
Welch, Kathleen E(thel) 1951- *ConAu 136*
Welch, Kathleen Elizabeth 1962- *WhoAmW 93*
Welch, Kathryn Haines *St&PR 93*
Welch, Kathy Jane 1952- *WhoAmW 93*
Welch, Katy *BioIn 17*
Welch, Keefer D. 1945- *WhoAm 92*
Welch, L. Dean 1928- *St&PR 93*
Welch, Lance Pat 1964- *WhoSSW 93*
Welch, Lawrence Thomas *Law&B 92*
Welch, Liliane 1937- *WhoCanL 92*
Welch, Linda Ogden 1958- *WhoAmW 93*
Welch, Lloyd Richard 1927- *WhoAm 92*
Welch, Lois Rieser *WhoAmW 93*
Welch, Louie 1918- *WhoAm 92*
Welch, Mary-Scott 1919- *WhoAmW 93, WhoE 93*
Welch, Michael John 1939- *WhoAm 92*
Welch, Michael T. *Law&B 92*
Welch, Michelle L. *Law&B 92*
Welch, Michelle Leslie 1953- *WhoAmW 93*
Welch, Nat *BioIn 17*
Welch, Neal William 1908- *WhoAm 92*
Welch, Noble 1930- *WhoE 93*
Welch, Norman Alphonsus, Jr. 1945- *WhoE 93*
Welch, O. J. 1929- *WhoWor 93*
Welch, Olga Michele 1948- *WhoSSW 93*
Welch, Oliver Wendell 1930- *WhoE 93*
Welch, Patrick Dennis 1963- *St&PR 93*
Welch, Peter Frederick *Law&B 92*
Welch, Philip Burland 1931- *WhoSSW 93*
Welch, Philip David 1954- *WhoWor 93*
Welch, Philip Henry 1849-1889 *JrnUS*
Welch, Priscilla *BioIn 17*
Welch, R. Dewey 1928- *St&PR 93*
Welch, Raquel 1940- *HispAmA, IntDcF 2-3 [port], NotHsAW 93 [port], WhoAm 92*
Welch, Richard Edwin, Jr. 1924- *WhoWrEP 92*
Welch, Robert Bond 1927- *WhoAm 92*
Welch, Robert Gibson 1915- *WhoAm 92*
Welch, Robert Lynn Bob 1956- *WhoAm 92*
Welch, Robert Morrow, Jr. 1927- *WhoAm 92*
Welch, Robert Ray 1957- *WhoSSW 93*
Welch, Robin B. 1940- *St&PR 93*
Welch, Robin I. 1930- *BioIn 17*
Welch, Ronald J. 1945- *WhoAm 92*
Welch, Ronald Jay 1945- *St&PR 93*
Welch, Ross Maynard 1943- *WhoAm 92*
Welch, Sheila J. *Law&B 92*
Welch, Stella Regina *WhoE 93*
Welch, Stephen Anthony 1942- *WhoAm 92*
Welch, Steven K. 1951- *St&PR 93*
Welch, Stuart E. 1945- *St&PR 93*
Welch, Thaddeus 1849-1919 *BioIn 17*
Welch, Theodore Franklyn 1933- *WhoAm 92*
Welch, W. Don *BioIn 17*
Welch, William B. 1922- *St&PR 93*
Welch, William Henry 1929- *WhoAm 92*
Welch, William John 1934- *WhoAm 92*
Welcher, Amy Ogden d1992 *BioIn 17, NewYTBS 92*
Welcher, Dan 1948- *Baker 92*
Welcher, Stephanie Denise 1961- *WhoAmW 93*
Welcher, William Alexander 1947- *WhoE 93*
Welcome, Linda Paar 1949- *WhoE 93*
Welcomme, Robin L. 1938- *WhoScE 91-3*
Welcomme, Robin Leon 1938- *WhoUN 92*
Weld, John 1905- *BioIn 17*
Weld, Jonathan Minot 1941- *WhoAm 92*
Weld, Olive M. *AmWomPl*
Weld, Roger Bowen 1953- *WhoEmL 93, WhoWor 93*
Weld, Tuesday 1943- *IntDcF 2-3 [port]*
Weld, Tuesday Ker 1943- *WhoAm 92, WhoAmW 93*
Weld, William Floyd *BioIn 17*
Weld, William Floyd 1945- *NewYTBS 92 [port], WhoAm 92, WhoE 93, WhoWor 93*
Weld, William George, Jr. 1929- *St&PR 93*
Welden, Alicia Galaz-Vivar 1937- *WhoSSW 93*
Welden, Arthur Luna 1927- *WhoAm 92*
Welden, Daniel William *WhoE 93*
Welden, Mary Clare 1943- *WhoAmW 93*
Welder, Paul E. 1943- *WhoAm 92*
Welder, Thomas 1940- *WhoAmW 93*
Weldon, Casey *BioIn 17*
Weldon, Curt 1947- *CngDr 91*
Weldon, Daniel Patrick 1950- *WhoE 93*
Weldon, David Black 1925- *WhoAm 92*
Weldon, Doris May 1925- *WhoAmW 93*
Weldon, Earl William 1956- *WhoE 93*
Weldon, Elaine Joyce *WhoAmW 93*
Weldon, Fay *BioIn 17*
Weldon, Fay 1931- *ScF&FL 92*
Weldon, George 1906-1963 *Baker 92*
Weldon, Georgina 1837-1914 *Baker 92*
Weldon, H.W., Jr. *BioIn 17*
Weldon, James E. 1934- *St&PR 93*
Weldon, James Ernest 1934- *WhoAm 92*
Weldon, John *ScF&FL 92*
Weldon, John 1676-1736 *OxDcOp*
Weldon, Joseph Patrick 1955- *WhoE 93*
Weldon, Linda Jean 1949- *WhoE 93*
Weldon, Margaret Ann 1957- *WhoAmW 93*
Weldon, Michael 1952- *ScF&FL 92*
Weldon, Norman Ross 1934- *WhoAm 92*
Weldon, Patricia Butler 1922- *St&PR 93*
Weldon, Robert William 1934- *St&PR 93, WhoAm 92, WhoIns 93*
Weldon, Virginia V. 1935- *WhoAm 92, WhoAmW 93*
Weldon, Walter F., Jr. *Law&B 92*
Weldon, Wayne Curtis 1947- *WhoAm 92, WhoE 93*
Weldon, William Forrest 1945- *WhoAm 92*
Weldon, William H. 1932- *St&PR 93*
Weldon-Wilson, Dee Ann *Law&B 92*
Weldrick, Valerie *ScF&FL 92*
Welebir, Andrew John 1951- *WhoSSW 93*
Welensky, Roy 1907- *DcTwHis*
Welensky, Roy 1907-1991 *AnObit 1991, BioIn 17, CurBio 92N*
Welfare, Mary *ScF&FL 92*
Welfer, Thomas, Jr. 1936- *St&PR 93, WhoAm 92*
Welford, George Seymour 1933- *St&PR 93*
Welford, John Mack 1939- *WhoSSW 93*
Welford, Walter Thompson *WhoScE 91-1*
Welge, Donald 1935- *St&PR 93*
Welge, Donald Edward 1935- *WhoAm 92*
Welge, Henry John 1942- *WhoSSW 93*
Welikson, Jeffrey A. *Law&B 92*
Welikson, Jeffrey A. 1957- *St&PR 93*
Welikson, Jeffrey Alan 1957- *WhoAm 92, WhoE 93*
Welin, Karl-Erik 1934-1992 *BioIn 17, NewYTBS 92*
Welin, Karl-Erik (Vilhelm) 1934- *Baker 92*
Welin, Karl Lennart 1941- *WhoWor 93*
Welin, Walter 1908- *WhoWor 93*
Welitsch, Ljuba 1913- *Baker 92, IntDcOp, OxDcOp*
Welk, Lawrence 1903- *Baker 92*
Welk, Lawrence 1903-1992 *BioIn 17, CurBio 92N, NewYTBS 92 [port]*
Welke, James William 1936- *WhoSSW 93*
Welke, Susan Darlene 1961- *WhoAmW 93*
Welker, Jerome L. 1933- *St&PR 93*
Welker, Juanita Margaret 1941- *St&PR 93*
Welker, Wallace Irving 1926- *WhoAm 92*
Welker, William G. 1930- *St&PR 93*
Welkowitz, Joan *WhoAm 92, WhoAmW 93*
Welkowitz, Walter 1926- *WhoAm 92, WhoE 93*
Well, Klaus H. 1940- *WhoScE 91-3*
Welland, James Arthur *Law&B 92*
Wellard, Charles L. 1924- *St&PR 93*
Wellard, James 1909-1987 *ScF&FL 92*
Wellbaum, Edgar Winston 1927- *St&PR 93*

Wellberg, Edward Louis, Jr. 1945- *WhoSSW 93*
Wellborn, Charles Ivey 1941- *WhoWor 93*
Wellbrock, Gladys Bale *ScF&FL 92*
Wellburn, Alan Richard *WhoScE 91-1*
Wellehan, Daniel Joseph, Jr. 1933- *St&PR 93*
Wellek, Albert 1904-1972 *Baker 92*
Wellek, Jeffrey A. 1961- *St&PR 93*
Wellek, Rene *BioIn 17*
Wellek, Richard Lee 1938- *St&PR 93*
Wellemans, Guy F.F.G. 1938- *WhoScE 91-2*
Wellenkotter, Harry W. 1929- *St&PR 93*
Weller, Albert H. 1922- *WhoScE 91-3*
Weller, Alexandra *Law&B 92*
Weller, Berthold Leysaht 1932- *St&PR 93*
Weller, Carl William 1934- *St&PR 93*
Weller, Frank Harlow, Jr. 1938- *WhoAm 92*
Weller, Gunter Ernst 1934- *WhoAm 92*
Weller, Henry Richard 1941- *WhoSSW 93*
Weller, James Patrick 1948- *St&PR 93*
Weller, Janet Louise 1953- *WhoAmW 93*
Weller, Joseph C. 1939- *St&PR 93*
Weller, Karen Anne 1948- *WhoAmW 93*
Weller, Kenneth Roy 1948- *St&PR 93*
Weller, Kevin Blair *Law&B 92*
Weller, M.J. *ScF&FL 92*
Weller, Mark D. *Law&B 92*
Weller, Michael 1942- *WhoAm 92*
Weller, Peter *BioIn 17*
Weller, Peter 1947- *WhoAm 92*
Weller, Ralph Albert 1921- *WhoAm 92*
Weller, Richard Alan *Law&B 92*
Weller, Robert Norman 1939- *WhoAm 92*
Weller, Roy Oliver *WhoScE 91-1*
Weller, Sheila 1945- *WhoWrEP 92*
Weller, Sol William 1918- *WhoAm 92, WhoE 93*
Weller, Stan 1944- *St&PR 93*
Weller, Thomas Huckle 1915- *WhoAm 92, WhoE 93, WhoWor 93*
Weller, Tom *WhoAm 92*
Weller, Walter 1939- *Baker 92, WhoWor 93*
Weller, William Bradford *Law&B 92*
Wellershoff, Dieter 1925- *ConAu 37NR*
Welles, Annette d1991 *BioIn 17*
Welles, Charles Hopkins 1907- *St&PR 93*
Welles, Ernest I. 1925- *WhoE 93*
Welles, Ferne Bingham Malcolm 1921- *WhoAmW 93*
Welles, James Bell, Jr. 1918- *WhoAm 92*
Welles, John Galt 1925- *WhoAm 92*
Welles, Melinda Fassett 1943- *WhoAmW 93, WhoWor 93*
Welles, Orson 1915-1985 *BioIn 17, MiSFD 9N, ScF&FL 92*
Welles, Patricia *ScF&FL 92*
Welles, Paul O'M. 1926- *ScF&FL 92*
Welles, Virginia Chrisman 1954- *WhoE 93*
Wellesley, Arthur 1769-1852 *BioIn 17*
Wellesley, Charles 1816-1855 *BioIn 17*
Wellesz, Egon 1885-1974 *OxDcOp*
Wellesz, Egon (Joseph) 1885-1974 *Baker 92*
Wellfare, Robert Wayne 1933- *WhoSSW 93*
Wellford, Harry Walker 1924- *WhoAm 92*
Wellikoff, Alan Gabriel 1946- *WhoE 93, WhoWrEP 92*
Wellin, Keith Sears 1926- *WhoAm 92*
Welling, Kathryn Marie 1952- *WhoAmW 93*
Welling, Lois *ScF&FL 92*
Welling, Randall Anthony 1955- *WhoSSW 93*
Wellinger, Roger P. 1919- *WhoWor 93*
Wellington, Duke of 1769-1852 *BioIn 17*
Wellington, Arthur Wellesley, Duke of 1769-1852 *HarEnMi*
Wellington, Harry Hillel 1926- *WhoAm 92*
Wellington, James Ellis 1921- *WhoAm 92*
Wellington, Jean Willett *WhoAmW 93*
Wellington, Jeremy James *WhoScE 91-1*
Wellington, John Stanley 1916- *WhoAm 92*
Wellington, Merv 1940- *WhoAsAP 91*
Wellington, Monica *BioIn 17*
Wellington, Monica 1957- *ConAu 136*
Wellington, Peter S. *Law&B 92*
Wellington, Raymond Thomas, Jr. d1992 *NewYTBS 92*
Wellington, Robert Hall 1922- *St&PR 93, WhoAm 92*
Wellington, Roger Dewitt 1927- *St&PR 93*
Wellington, Roger U., Jr. 1941- *St&PR 93*
Wellington, Sheila Wacks 1932- *WhoAm 92*
Wellington, Thomas Dutton 1921- *St&PR 93*
Wellington, William George 1920- *WhoAm 92*
Wellins, Sheldon Gary 1944- *WhoWor 93*
Wellisch, Hans Herbert 1920- *WhoE 93*
Wellish, Corinne Suzanne 1946- *WhoAmW 93*
Welliver, Albertus D. *St&PR 93*
Welliver, Albertus Delmar 1934- *WhoAm 92*
Welliver, Rick E. 1955- *St&PR 93*
Welliver, Warren Dee 1920- *WhoAm 92*
Well-Known Author, A *ScF&FL 92*
Wellman, Anthony Donald Emerson 1955- *WhoE 93*
Wellman, Beth Lucy 1895-1952 *BioIn 17*
Wellman, Carl Pierce 1926- *WhoAm 92*
Wellman, David Allan 1947- *WhoE 93*
Wellman, Donald 1944- *WhoWrEP 92*
Wellman, Howard Stolte 1939- *WhoE 93*
Wellman, Manly Wade 1903-1986 *ScF&FL 92*
Wellman, Mary Margaret 1946- *WhoE 93*
Wellman, Richard Vance 1922- *WhoAm 92*
Wellman, Rita 1890- *AmWomPl*
Wellman, Roy *Law&B 92*
Wellman, Timothy Wayne 1953- *St&PR 93*
Wellman, Wade 1937- *ScF&FL 92*
Wellman, Walter 1858-1934 *JrnUS*
Wellman, William A. 1896-1975 *MiSFD 9N*
Wellman, William Augustus 1896-1975 *BioIn 17*
Wellmer, Friedrich-Wilhelm 1940- *WhoScE 91-3*
Wellner, Alfred M. *BioIn 17*
Wellner, Marcel Nahum 1930- *WhoAm 92*
Wellner, Pierre David 1963- *WhoWor 93*
Wellner, Robert Francis 1928- *WhoE 93*
Wellons, James A. *Law&B 92*
Wellons, Susan Lynn 1956- *WhoAmW 93*
Wells, Alan A. 1924- *WhoScE 91-1*
Wells, Andrew N. *Law&B 92*
Wells, Angus 1943- *ScF&FL 92*
Wells, Ann D. *Law&B 92*
Wells, Anna Mary *AmWomPl*
Wells, Anne Jones 1939- *WhoAmW 93*
Wells, Anne Sharp 1952- *WhoSSW 93*
Wells, Arthur Stanton 1931- *St&PR 93, WhoAm 92*
Wells, Arvin R. 1927- *ScF&FL 92*
Wells, Barbara D. 1944- *WhoSSW 93*
Wells, Barry Leighton 1951- *WhoE 93*
Wells, Basil 1912- *ScF&FL 92*
Wells, Ben Harris 1906- *WhoAm 92*
Wells, Ben K. 1953- *WhoSSW 93*
Wells, Benjamin Gladney 1943- *WhoSSW 93*
Wells, Berri Ann 1963- *WhoAmW 93*
Wells, Betty Ellen 1957- *WhoAmW 93*
Wells, Betty Ruth 1927- *WhoAmW 93, WhoWor 93*
Wells, Brian Scott 1963- *WhoSSW 93*
Wells, Bryan Michael 1943- *WhoE 93*
Wells, Calvin B. 1936- *St&PR 93*
Wells, Carolyn 1869-1942 *AmWomPl*
Wells, Catherine 1952- *ScF&FL 92*
Wells, Cecil Harold, Jr. 1927- *WhoAm 92*
Wells, Charles Joseph 1948- *WhoE 93*
Wells, Charles Lynn *Law&B 92*
Wells, Charles R. 1939- *St&PR 93*
Wells, Charles W. 1934- *St&PR 93*
Wells, Charles William 1934- *WhoAm 92*
Wells, Charlotte Elizabeth *AmWomPl*
Wells, Christine Iva 1950- *WhoAmW 93*
Wells, Clifford Eugene 1927- *St&PR 93*
Wells, Clyde Kirby 1937- *WhoAm 92, WhoE 93*
Wells, Crosby 1922- *St&PR 93*
Wells, Damon, Jr. 1937- *WhoSSW 93, WhoWor 93*
Wells, David Andrew 1948- *WhoSSW 93*
Wells, David F. *BioIn 17*
Wells, David John 1949- *WhoE 93, WhoWor 93*
Wells, David Merlin 1943- *WhoWor 93*
Wells, Deborah Lucille 1957- *WhoAmW 93*
Wells, Donald Smith 1935- *WhoAm 92*
Wells, Donald T. 1931- *St&PR 93*
Wells, Donald Thomas 1931- *WhoSSW 93*
Wells, Donna Jo 1966- *WhoAmW 93*
Wells, Doreen Monica *Law&B 92*
Wells, E.F. *BioIn 17*
Wells, Ed 1900-1986 *BioIn 17*
Wells, Edward Francis *BioIn 17*
Wells, Evelyn M. 1946- *AfrAmBi [port]*
Wells, Everett Clayton, Jr. 1954- *WhoSSW 93*
Wells, Florence *AmWomPl*
Wells, Frank G. 1932- *WhoAm 92*
Wells, Galen Wright *Law&B 92*
Wells, Geoffrey H. 1900- *ScF&FL 92*
Wells, George Douglas 1935- *St&PR 93, WhoAm 92*
Wells, George H. 1944- *St&PR 93*
Wells, George M. 1936- *St&PR 93*
Wells, Gerald Arthur Henry *WhoScE 91-1*
Wells, Gerald W. 1945- *St&PR 93*
Wells, Glenn Albert 1943- *WhoE 93*
Wells, H.G. 1866-1946 *BioIn 17, MagSWL [port], WorLitC [port]*
Wells, H.G. 1886-1946 *ScF&FL 92*
Wells, H. Rickey 1956- *St&PR 93*
Wells, H. Wayne *Law&B 92*
Wells, Harold Nielson *Law&B 92*
Wells, Helen 1910-1986 *ConAu 37NR, MajAI [port]*
Wells, Helen Shea 1917- *WhoAmW 93*
Wells, Henry M., III 1945- *St&PR 93*
Wells, Herbert George 1866-1946 *BioIn 17*
Wells, Herman B. 1902- *WhoAm 92, WhoWor 93*
Wells, Herschel James 1924- *WhoAm 92, WhoWor 93*
Wells, Howard Avery 1909- *St&PR 93*
Wells, Huey Thomas, Jr. 1950- *WhoSSW 93*
Wells, Hugh G. 1933- *St&PR 93*
Wells, Hugh H. 1949- *WhoSSW 93*
Wells, Imogen *BioIn 17*
Wells, J. Eugene M. 1925- *WhoWor 93*
Wells, J. Kendrick, III *Law&B 92*
Wells, Jacqueline 1914- *SweetSg C*
Wells, Jacqueline Erika *Law&B 92*
Wells, James Russell *Law&B 92*
Wells, Jeremy 1945- *WhoSSW 93*
Wells, Jerry Wayne 1950- *WhoSSW 93*
Wells, Joel Freeman 1930- *WhoAm 92, WhoWrEP 92*
Wells, Joel R., Jr. *BioIn 17*
Wells, John 1770-1823 *BioIn 17*
Wells, John A. 1946- *St&PR 93*
Wells, John Andrew 1926- *WhoAm 92*
Wells, John C. 1940- *St&PR 93*
Wells, John C., Jr. 1941- *St&PR 93*
Wells, John Calhoun 1941- *WhoSSW 93*
Wells, John Christopher *WhoScE 91-1*
Wells, John W. 1950- *St&PR 93*
Wells, John West 1907- *WhoAm 92*
Wells, Junior 1934- *BioIn 17*
Wells, Karen Kay 1956- *WhoAmW 93*
Wells, Kitty 1919- *Baker 92, BioIn 17*
Wells, Leonard Nathaniel David, Jr. 1914- *WhoAm 92*
Wells, Linda May 1953- *WhoE 93*
Wells, Lisa Eleanor 1958- *WhoAmW 93*
Wells, Ludmilla Gricenko 1954- *WhoAmW 93*
Wells, Lynn *BioIn 17*
Wells, Mark *BioIn 17, Law&B 92, WhoIns 93*
Wells, Mark Howard 1951- *WhoE 93*
Wells, Marolyn Clark 1949- *WhoSSW 93*
Wells, Mary 1943- *SoulM*
Wells, Mary 1943-1992 *NewYTBS 92 [port], News 93-1*
Wells, Melissa Foelsch 1932- *WhoAm 92, WhoAmW 93*
Wells, Merle William 1918- *ConAu 37NR, WhoWor 93*
Wells, Michael E. *Law&B 92*
Wells, Michael V. 1939- *St&PR 93*
Wells, Michelle Marie 1964- *WhoAmW 93*
Wells, Mitchell E. 1939- *St&PR 93*
Wells, Nancy Marie 1953- *WhoWrEP 92*
Wells, Pamela Tandy 1948- *WhoAmW 93*
Wells, Patricia Ann 1959- *St&PR 93*
Wells, Patricia Bennett 1935- *WhoAmW 93*
Wells, Patricia Lee Kleiber 1946- *WhoWor 93*
Wells, Peter Bernard *WhoScE 91-1*
Wells, Peter Neil Temple *WhoScE 91-1*
Wells, Randall S. 1952- *St&PR 93*
Wells, Raymond 1950- *WhoE 93*
Wells, Reggie *BioIn 17*
Wells, Richard Arthur 1937- *St&PR 93*
Wells, Richard D. *Law&B 92*
Wells, Richard L. *Law&B 92*
Wells, Richard Marshall 1930- *St&PR 93*
Wells, Robert 1929- *ScF&FL 92*
Wells, Robert A. 1930- *St&PR 93*
Wells, Robert C. *Law&B 92*
Wells, Robert Louis 1939- *WhoSSW 93, WhoWor 93*
Wells, Robert Steven 1951- *WhoAm 92*
Wells, Roger 1947- *ConAu 136*
Wells, Rona Lee 1950- *WhoAmW 93, WhoWor 93*
Wells, Ronald Austin 1933- *WhoE 93, WhoWor 93*
Wells, Rosalind Lea 1936- *WhoAmW 93*
Wells, Rosemary 1943- *DcAmChF 1960, DcAmChF 1985, MajAI [port], ScF&FL 92, SmATA 69 [port], WhoAm 92*
Wells, Russel Charles *Law&B 92*
Wells, Samuel d1876 *BioIn 17*
Wells, Samuel Alonzo, Jr. 1936- *WhoAm 92*
Wells, Samuel Fogle, Jr. 1935- *WhoE 93*
Wells, Samuel James *WhoSSW 93*
Wells, Sharon Mooney 1945- *WhoAmW 93*
Wells, Simon *MiSFD 9*
Wells, Simon John 1955- *WhoWor 93*
Wells, Stephen A. 1943- *St&PR 93*
Wells, Steven A. *Law&B 92*
Wells, Stuart P. 1931- *St&PR 93*
Wells, Stuart W., III *ScF&FL 92*
Wells, Theodore Arthur 1907- *St&PR 93*
Wells, Thomas B. 1945- *CngDr 91*
Wells, Toni Lynn 1959- *WhoAmW 93*
Wells, Van L. 1941- *WhoIns 93*
Wells, Victor Hugh, Jr. 1924- *WhoAm 92*
Wells, Warner Lee 1913-1991 *BioIn 17*
Wells, William D. *BioIn 17*
Wells, William Howell 1901?-1991 *BioIn 17*
Wells, William K. *ScF&FL 92*
Wells, William S. *Law&B 92*
Wells-Barnett, Ida B. 1862-1931 *BioIn 17*
Wells-Barnett, Ida Bell 1862-1931 *JrnUS*
Wells-Carr, Elizabeth Antoinette 1930- *WhoAmW 93*
Wells-Davis, Margie Elaine 1944- *AfrAmBi*
Wells-Parker, Nancy Elisabeth 1950- *WhoAmW 93, WhoSSW 93*
Wells-Prines, Vesta Lynn 1950- *WhoAmW 93*
Wells Society *ScF&FL 92*
Wellsted, James 1805-1842 *Expl 93*
Wellstein, Linda M. *Law&B 92*
Wellstone, Paul 1944- *WhoAm 92*
Wellstone, Paul D. 1944- *CngDr 91*
Wellstone, Paul David *BioIn 17*
Wellwarth, George E. 1932- *WhoE 93, WhoWrEP 92*
Welna, Cecilia 1927- *WhoAm 92*
Welnhofer, Robert William 1933- *St&PR 93*
Welnicki, Wieslaw 1927- *WhoScE 91-4*
Welpott, Jack Warren 1923- *WhoAm 92*
Wels, Andrew C. *Law&B 92*
Welsch, David Charles *Law&B 92*
Welsch, Douglas Willim 1950- *St&PR 93*
Welsch, Frank 1941- *WhoSSW 93*
Welsch, Glenn Albert 1915- *WhoAm 92*
Welsch, Jack d1990 *BioIn 17*
Welsch, James Lester 1917- *WhoWor 93*
Welsch, Jerome K. 1953- *St&PR 93*
Welsch, Suzanne Carol 1941- *WhoAmW 93*
Welsch, Walter Nicholas 1924- *St&PR 93*
Welsenseel, Charles W. 1933- *St&PR 93*
Welser-Moest, Franz *BioIn 17*
Welser-Most, Franz 1960- *Baker 92*
Welsh, Alan L. *St&PR 93*
Welsh, Alexis *BioIn 17*
Welsh, Alfred John 1947- *WhoEmL 93*
Welsh, Angela 1953- *St&PR 93*
Welsh, Arthur Craig 1947- *WhoWor 93*
Welsh, Dale Patrick 1953- *St&PR 93*
Welsh, David *Law&B 92*
Welsh, David Malcolm 1942- *St&PR 93*
Welsh, Dennie M. *WhoAm 92*
Welsh, Donald Emory 1943- *WhoAm 92*
Welsh, Edward Cristy 1909-1990 *BioIn 17*
Welsh, Elliott *BioIn 17*
Welsh, Frank 1931- *ScF&FL 92*
Welsh, Greg Jon 1951- *WhoE 93*
Welsh, Harry Edward 1939- *WhoE 93*
Welsh, Hugh H. *Law&B 92*
Welsh, J. Erica 1947- *WhoEmL 93*
Welsh, Judith 1939- *WhoWrEP 92*
Welsh, Judith Schenck 1939- *WhoAmW 93*
Welsh, Kathleen B. *Law&B 92*
Welsh, Ken 1945- *BioIn 17*
Welsh, Matthew Empson 1912- *WhoAm 92*
Welsh, Michael L. 1959- *WhoE 93*
Welsh, N.C. *WhoScE 91-1*
Welsh, Paul 1953- *ScF&FL 92*
Welsh, Paul D., Jr. 1926- *St&PR 93*
Welsh, Peter Corbett 1926- *WhoAm 92*
Welsh, Raymond H. 1931- *St&PR 93*
Welsh, Richard D. *Law&B 92*
Welsh, Richard D. 1931- *WhoIns 93*
Welsh, Richard Donald 1931- *St&PR 93*
Welsh, Rita May 1942- *WhoAmW 93*
Welsh, Robert Edward 1932- *WhoSSW 93*
Welsh, Robert H. 1926- *St&PR 93*
Welsh, Robert J. 1926- *St&PR 93*
Welsh, Robert W. *Law&B 92*
Welsh, Ronald Arthur 1926- *WhoAm 92*
Welsh, Sachiko Ann 1931- *WhoAmW 93*
Welsh, Stanley M. *Law&B 92*
Welsh, Stewart Chalmers 1957- *WhoSSW 93*
Welsh, Suzanne Mary *Law&B 92*
Welsh, Thomas c. 1780-1848 *Baker 92*
Welsh, Thomas J. 1921- *WhoAm 92*
Welsh, Thomas M. 1949- *St&PR 93*
Welsh, Walter Charles *Law&B 92*
Welsh, William E. 1942- *St&PR 93*
Welsh, William F., II 1941- *St&PR 93*
Welsh, Wilmer Hayden 1932- *WhoSSW 93, WhoWor 93*
Welshans, Merle Talmadge 1918- *WhoWor 93*
Welsher, Donald F. 1937- *St&PR 93*
Welshhans, Richard W. 1947- *St&PR 93*
Welshimer, Gwen R. 1935- *WhoAmW 93*

Welshimer, Helen Louise 1901- *AmWomPl*
Welshons, Mark A. *Law&B 92*
Welt, Frank A. 1907-1990 *BioIn 17*
Welt, Henry 1946- *WhoE 93*
Weltch, J.W. 1910- *St&PR 93*
Weltchek, Robert T. 1924-1990 *BioIn 17*
Welte, A. Theodore 1944- *WhoE 93*
Welte, Dietrich Hugo 1935- *WhoScE 91-3, WhoWor 93*
Welte, Edwin 1875-1958
See Welte, Michael 1807-1880 *Baker 92*
Welte, Emil 1841-1923
See Welte, Michael 1807-1880 *Baker 92*
Welte, Grieg *Law&B 92*
Welte, Michael 1807-1880 *Baker 92*
Welte, Noreen McNamara 1946- *WhoAmW 93*
Welte, Wendy Barton *Law&B 92*
Welte, Werner 1948- *WhoWor 93*
Welte, William B., III *Law&B 92*
Welter, Vanessa Marie 1960- *WhoAmW 93*
Welter, William Michael 1946- *WhoAm 92*
Welters, Linda Marie 1949- *WhoE 93*
Weltfish, Gene 1902-1980 *IntDcAn*
Welti, Belinda *Law&B 92*
Welting, Ruth 1949- *Baker 92*
Weltman, David Lee 1933- *WhoAm 92*
Weltman, Mick Gene 1952- *WhoE 93*
Weltner, Betsey 1952- *WhoSSW 93*
Weltner, Charles L. d1992 *NewYTBS 92 [port]*
Weltner, Charles Longstreet 1927- *WhoAm 92*
Weltner, Gary Lee 1944- *St&PR 93*
Weltner, Klaus Volker 1927- *WhoScE 91-3*
Weltner, Peter 1942- *ConGAN*
Weltner, Robert Barry *Law&B 92*
Welton, Charles Ephraim 1947- *WhoEmL 93, WhoWor 93*
Welton, David Goe 1910- *WhoSSW 93*
Welton, Gertrude *AmWomPl*
Welton, Jessica Wheat 1953- *WhoEmL 93*
Welton, Lawrence Jacob *St&PR 93*
Welton, Michael Peter 1957- *WhoEmL 93*
Welton, Robert Breen 1938- *WhoAm 92*
Welty, Eudora *WhoAm 92, WhoAmW 93, WhoWor 93, WhoWrEP 92*
Welty, Eudora 1909- *AmWomWr 92, BioIn 17, MagSAmL [port], WorLitC [port]*
Welty, Joanne *Law&B 92*
Welty, John Donald 1944- *WhoAm 92*
Welty, John R. *Law&B 92*
Welty, John R. 1948- *St&PR 93*
Welty, Robert Vance 1942- *St&PR 93, WhoAm 92*
Welty, Ruth *AmWomPl*
Welty, Stenley R., Jr. 1929- *St&PR 93*
Welty, Steven Philip 1951- *St&PR 93*
Welty, Wayne V. *ScF&FL 92*
Welty, William John 1945- *WhoAm 92*
Weltzien, Heinrich Carl 1928- *WhoScE 91-3*
Welu, James A. 1943- *WhoAm 92, WhoE 93*
Welytok, Walter Steven 1930- *St&PR 93*
Welz, Carl John 1913- *WhoAm 92*
Welzel, Jane *BioIn 17*
Welzenbach, Lanora Frances 1932- *WhoWrEP 92*
Welzig, Werner *WhoScE 91-4*
Wemcken, Christoph Michael 1949- *WhoWor 93*
Wemhaner, Jody 1950- *WhoAmW 93*
Wemmers, Frederick Richard, Jr. 1939- *WhoSSW 93*
Wemple, Andrew P. 1952- *St&PR 93*
Wemple, Donna Wachter 1944- *WhoAmW 93*
Wemple, William 1912- *WhoAm 92*
Wemple-Kinder, Suzanne Fonay 1927- *WhoAmW 93*
Wemyss, Courtney T. 1922- *ScF&FL 92*
Wen, Shih-Liang *WhoAm 92*
Wen, Tien Kuang 1924- *WhoWor 93*
Wenberg, Jordan Hobbs 1951- *WhoSSW 93*
Wenberg, Richard Vincent 1932- *St&PR 93*
Wenck, Edwin O. 1936- *WhoE 93*
Wenck, William Ariste 1947- *WhoE 93*
Wenckus, James R. 1941- *St&PR 93, WhoIns 93*
Wencl, Josef *WhoScE 91-4*
Wenclawiak, Bernd Wilhelm 1951- *WhoWor 93*
Wenda, Elzbieta Maria 1944- *WhoWor 93*
Wendeborn, Richard Donald *WhoAm 92*
Wendel, Albrecht 1943- *WhoScE 91-3*
Wendel, Christopher Mark 1954- *WhoE 93*
Wendel, Eugen 1934- *Baker 92*
Wendel, Francois de 1874-1949 *BioIn 17*
Wendel, Pamela Lois 1960- *WhoAmW 93*
Wendel, Richard Frederick 1930- *WhoAm 92, WhoWor 93*
Wendel, Susan A. *Law&B 92*
Wendel, Wendel R. 1946- *WhoE 93*
Wendel, William Hall 1914-1990 *BioIn 17*
Wendelburg, Norma Ruth 1918- *WhoWor 93*
Wendell, Carolyn 1942- *ScF&FL 92*
Wendell, Charles Warner 1930- *WhoE 93*
Wendell, Karen Ann *Law&B 92*
Wendell, Leilah 1958- *WhoWrEP 92*
Wendell, Marie Ellen 1928- *WhoAmW 93*
Wendell, Matthew Simon 1921- *St&PR 93*
Wendell, Stephen A. 1941- *St&PR 93*
Wendell, Wayne D. 1944- *St&PR 93*
Wendells, David T. *Law&B 92*
Wendelstedt, Harry Hunter, Jr. 1938- *WhoAm 92*
Wendenburg, Carl A. 1945- *St&PR 93*
Wender, Herbert 1937- *St&PR 93*
Wender, Ira Tensard 1927- *WhoAm 92, WhoWor 93*
Wender, Joseph Harris 1944- *WhoAm 92*
Wender, Mieczyslaw B. 1926- *WhoScE 91-4*
Wender, Mieczyslaw Bogumil 1926- *WhoWor 93*
Wender, Phyllis Bellows 1934- *WhoAm 92*
Wenderoff, Dave P. 1961- *St&PR 93*
Wenderoth, Donald Edward *St&PR 93*
Wenders, Wim 1945- *MiSFD 9, WhoWor 93*
Wendi *BioIn 17*
Wendker, Heinrich J. 1938- *WhoScE 91-3*
Wendkos, Paul 1922- *MiSFD 9*
Wendland, Albert 1948- *ScF&FL 92*
Wendland, Erroll 1929- *St&PR 93*
Wendland, Waldemar 1873-1947 *Baker 92*
Wendlandt, Bernd Karl 1942- *WhoWor 93*
Wendlandt, Gary Edward 1950- *St&PR 93*
Wendlandt, H.C. *Law&B 92*
Wendler, Guy H. 1952- *St&PR 93*
Wendling *Baker 92*
Wendling, Dorothea 1736-1811 *Baker 92*
Wendling, Dorothea 1767-1839 *Baker 92*
Wendling, Elisabeth Augusta 1746-1786 *Baker 92*
Wendling, Elisabeth Augusta 1752-1794 *Baker 92*
Wendling, Elizabeth Louise 1949- *WhoAmW 93*
Wendling, Franz (Anton) 1729-1786 *Baker 92*
Wendling, Johann Baptist 1723-1797 *Baker 92*
Wendling, Karl 1750-1834 *Baker 92*
Wendling, Karl 1857-1918 *Baker 92*
Wendon, Mark *Law&B 92*
Wendorf, Denver Fred, Jr. 1924- *WhoAm 92*
Wendorf, Hulen Dee 1916- *WhoAm 92*
Wendorf, Patricia 1928- *ScF&FL 92*
Wendroff, Barnet d1990 *BioIn 17*
Wendroff, Jacob d1991 *BioIn 17*
Wendrow, Sylvia Diann *WhoAmW 93*
Wendt, Albert 1939- *IntLitE*
Wendt, Charles William 1931- *WhoAm 92*
Wendt, E. Allan 1935- *WhoAm 92*
Wendt, Edward George, Jr. 1928- *St&PR 93*
Wendt, Ernst Adolf 1806-1850 *Baker 92*
Wendt, Gary Carl 1942- *WhoAm 92, WhoWor 93*
Wendt, George *BioIn 17*
Wendt, George Robert *WhoAm 92*
Wendt, Henry 1933- *St&PR 93*
Wendt, Henry, III 1933- *WhoAm 92, WhoE 93*
Wendt, Ingrid Darlene 1944- *WhoWrEP 92*
Wendt, Jeffrey Lee *Law&B 92*
Wendt, John 1936- *WhoScE 91-2*
Wendt, John Arthur Frederic, Jr. *WhoWor 93*
Wendt, John Francis 1936- *WhoWor 93*
Wendt, Larry 1946- *Baker 92*
Wendt, Lloyd 1908- *WhoAm 92, WhoWrEP 92*
Wendt, Nina Ullom 1946- *WhoAmW 93*
Wendt, Richard K. 1932- *WhoIns 93*
Wendt, Richard Kurt 1932- *St&PR 93, WhoAm 92*
Wendt, Timothy J. 1961- *St&PR 93*
Wendt, Timothy M. *Law&B 92*
Wendt, William 1865-1946 *BioIn 17*
Wendtland, Mona Bohlmann 1930- *WhoSSW 93*
Wendy *WhoWrEP 92*
Wendy, Johann B. 1928- *St&PR 93*
Wendy & Lisa *SoulM*
Wenger, David K. 1923- *WhoAm 92*
Wenger, Dennis Eugene 1951- *WhoE 93*
Wenger, Dorothy Mae 1917- *WhoAmW 93*
Wenger, Galen Rosenberger 1946- *WhoSSW 93*
Wenger, John Christian 1910- *WhoAm 92*
Wenger, Larry Bruce 1941- *WhoAm 92*
Wenger, Luke Huber 1939- *WhoAm 92*
Wenger, Ronald D. 1948- *St&PR 93*
Wenger, Vicki 1928- *WhoAmW 93, WhoE 93*
Wenger, Virgil E. 1930- *St&PR 93*
Wengerd, Sherman Alexander 1915- *WhoAm 92*
Wengerd, Tim 1945-1989 *BioIn 17*
Wengert, Gloria Herlinda 1948- *WhoAmW 93*
Wengert, Norman Irving 1916- *WhoAm 92*
Wengierski, Thomas Cajetan 1755-1787 *PolBiDi*
Wengler, Wilhelm 1907- *WhoWor 93*
Wenglowski, Gary Martin 1942- *WhoAm 92*
Wenick, Martin Arthur 1939- *WhoE 93*
Wenig, Harold G. 1924- *St&PR 93*
Wenig, Janice K. 1929- *St&PR 93*
Wenig, Mary Moers *WhoAmW 93*
Wenig, Norman H. 1925- *St&PR 93*
Weniger, Nell 1931- *WhoAmW 93*
Weniger, Sidney N. 1920- *St&PR 93*
Weninger, John *Law&B 92*
Wenis, Edward 1919- *WhoE 93*
Wen Jiabao 1943- *WhoAsAP 91*
Wenk, Edward, Jr. 1920- *WhoAm 92*
Wenk, Richard *MiSFD 9, ScF&FL 92*
Wenk, William Bruce 1928- *St&PR 93*
Wenkam, Chiye *Law&B 92*
Wenkel, Ortrun 1942- *Baker 92*
Wenker, Judith Ann *Law&B 92*
Wenker, Judith Ann 1944- *WhoAmW 93*
Wenkle, Sara Jose 1915- *St&PR 93*
Wenkoff, Spas 1928- *Baker 92*
Wenlock, John c. 1425-1471 *HarEnMi*
Wennberg, Brent G. *Law&B 92*
Wennberg, Hans-Erik 1946- *WhoE 93*
Wennemer, Manfred Heinrich 1947- *WhoAm 92*
Wennemer, Robert G. 1952- *St&PR 93*
Wenner, Erwin K. 1955- *St&PR 93*
Wenner, Gene Charles 1931- *WhoAm 92, WhoSSW 93*
Wenner, Heinz-Lothar 1924- *WhoScE 91-3*
Wenner, Herbert Allan 1912- *WhoAm 92*
Wenner, Jann 1946- *News 93-1 [port]*
Wenner, Jann S. *BioIn 17*
Wenner, Jann S. 1946- *WhoWrEP 92*
Wenner, Jann Simon 1946- *WhoAm 92, WhoE 93*
Wenner, Lettie McSpadden 1937- *WhoAmW 93*
Wennerberg, Gunnar 1817-1901 *Baker 92*
Wennerberg, S. *WhoScE 91-4*
Wennerberg, Sigfrid B. 1929- *WhoScE 91-4*
Wennerberg-Reuter, Sara (Margarete Eugenia Euphrosyne)
See Wennerberg, Gunnar 1817-1901 *Baker 92*
Wennerstrom, Jack Albert 1919- *WhoAm 92*
Wenninger, Anja *BioIn 17*
Wenrich, Jay H. 1929- *St&PR 93*
Wenrich, John William 1937- *WhoAm 92, WhoSSW 93*
Wensel, Darrell W. 1934- *St&PR 93*
Wensel, Marvin Max 1934- *St&PR 93*
Wensing, Cornelis J.G. 1938- *WhoScE 91-3*
Wensinger, Arthur Stevens 1926- *WhoAm 92*
Wensley, John Robin Clifton *WhoScE 91-1*
Wensrich, Margaret Fryer 1926- *WhoWrEP 92*
Wenstrand, Donald 1944- *St&PR 93*
Wenstrup, H. Daniel 1934- *St&PR 93 WhoAm 92*
Wente, Carolyn *BioIn 17*
Wente, David O. *Law&B 92*
Wente, Patricia Ann 1954- *St&PR 93*
Wente, Van Arthur 1925- *WhoE 93*
Wenten, Nyoman 1945- *Baker 92*
Wenthe, P.K. 1937- *WhoIns 93*
Wentler, Esther Ruth 1914- *WhoAmW 93*
Wentley, Richard Taylor 1930- *WhoAm 92, WhoWor 93*
Wentorf, Robert Henry 1926- *WhoAm 92*
Wents, Doris Roberta 1944- *WhoAmW 93*
Wentworth, Francis Marston, Jr. *Law&B 92*
Wentworth, John E. 1951- *St&PR 93*
Wentworth, Malinda Ann Nachman *WhoAmW 93, WhoWor 93*
Wentworth, Margaret *AmWomPl*
Wentworth, Margaret H. *AmWomPl*
Wentworth, Marion Jean Craig, Mrs. 1872- *AmWomPl*
Wentworth, Martha 1889-1974 *SweetSg C*
Wentworth, Murray Jackson 1927- *WhoAm 92*
Wentworth, Nathaniel Newcomb, Jr. 1917- *St&PR 93*
Wentworth, Norman R. 1954- *St&PR 93*
Wentworth, Richard Leigh 1930- *WhoAm 92*
Wentworth, Theodore Sumner 1938- *WhoWor 93*
Wentz, Bill M., Jr. 1953- *St&PR 93*
Wentz, Billy Melvin, Jr. 1953- *WhoAm 92*
Wentz, Howard Beck, Jr. 1930- *St&PR 93, WhoAm 92*
Wentz, Jack Lawrence *Law&B 92*
Wentz, Jack Lawrence 1937- *WhoAm 92*
Wentz, Norman Jay 1945- *St&PR 93*
Wentz, Rodney 1943- *St&PR 93*
Wentz, Ronald Elliott 1951- *St&PR 93*
Wentz, Roy A. *Law&B 92*
Wentz, Roy A. 1949- *St&PR 93*
Wentz, Sidney Frederick 1932- *WhoAm 92*
Wentz, W.J. 1902?-1990? *ScF&FL 92*
Wentz, Walter John 1928- *WhoAm 92*
Wentzel, Alan R. 1953- *St&PR 93*
Wentzel, Charles R. *Law&B 92*
Wentzel, Karen Lynn 1949- *WhoAmW 93*
Wentzler, Thomas H. 1947- *WhoSSW 93*
Wenz, Gunther Karl Heinrich 1949- *WhoWor 93*
Wenz, Paul Frederick 1931- *WhoSSW 93*
Wenz, Richard Ernest 1949- *St&PR 93*
Wenz, Werner S. 1926- *WhoScE 91-3*
Wenzek, Eddie *BioIn 17*
Wenzel, David 1950- *ScF&FL 92*
Wenzel, Donald G., Jr. *Law&B 92*
Wenzel, Ernst Ferdinand 1808-1880 *Baker 92*
Wenzel, Evelyn Maklary 1927- *WhoWrEP 92*
Wenzel, Frank K. 1946- *St&PR 93*
Wenzel, Fred H. 1939- *St&PR 93*
Wenzel, Fred W. 1916- *St&PR 93*
Wenzel, Fred William 1916- *WhoAm 92*
Wenzel, Gerhard 1943- *WhoScE 91-3*
Wenzel, James Gottlieb 1926- *WhoAm 92*
Wenzel, Lari Bea 1955- *WhoAmW 93*
Wenzel, Leonard Andrew 1923- *WhoAm 92*
Wenzel, Leopold 1847-1925 *Baker 92*
Wenzel, Lynn 1944- *WhoWrEP 92*
Wenzelburger, Elfriede 1947- *WhoWor 93*
Wenzell, Philip David 1962- *St&PR 93*
Wenzinger, August 1905- *Baker 92*
Wenzl, Helmut Franz Theresia 1934- *WhoScE 91-3*
Wenzler, Edward William 1954- *WhoEmL 93*
Wenzler, William Paul 1929- *WhoAm 92*
Wepierre, Jacques 1932- *WhoScE 91-2*
Wepking, Monica Jean 1956- *WhoAmW 93*
Wepner, Shelley Beth 1951- *WhoE 93*
Weppler, Jay Robert 1943- *WhoE 93*
Weppler, Lawrence G. *Law&B 92*
Weppler, Wilfred W. 1919- *St&PR 93*
Weppner, Eileen Jo 1935- *WhoAmW 93*
Werba, Erik 1918- *Baker 92*
Werba, Gabriel 1930- *WhoAm 92*
Werbel, James David 1949- *WhoSSW 93*
Werber, Clifford Lee *Law&B 92*
Werbitt, Warren 1939- *WhoE 93*
Werblin, David A(braham) 1910-1991 *CurBio 92N*
Werblin, Sonny 1910-1991 *BioIn 17*
Werbow, Stanley Newman 1922- *WhoAm 92*
Werbowski, Michelle Denise 1954- *WhoAmW 93*
Werchick, Jack 1913- *WhoAm 92*
Werckenthien, Charles C. *St&PR 93*
Werckmeister, Andreas 1645-1706 *Baker 92*
Werckmeister, Otto Karl 1934- *WhoAm 92*
Werdehoff, Peggy A. *Law&B 92*
Werdel, Marianne 1967- *WhoAmW 93*
Werden, George W. *Law&B 92*
Werden, Percival Wherrit 1865-1934 *BiDAMSp 1989*
Werder, Felix 1922- *Baker 92*
Werderitsch, Thomas Franklin 1942- *St&PR 93*
Werfel, Franz *BioIn 17*
Werfel, Franz 1890-1945 *DcLB 124 [port]*
Werfelman, William H., Jr. 1953- *WhoE 93*
Werger, Arthur Lawrence 1955- *WhoSSW 93*
Wergley, Albert N. 1947- *St&PR 93*
Werhnyak, Ronald Joseph *Law&B 92*
Werkheiser, Steven Lawrence 1945- *WhoWor 93*
Werkman, Rosemarie Anne 1926- *WhoE 93*
Werkman, Sidney Lee 1927- *WhoAm 92*
Werkstell, Leslie J. 1945- *St&PR 93*
Werle, Joseph 1923- *WhoScE 91-4*
Werle, Lars Johan 1926- *Baker 92, OxDcOp*
Werle, Robert Geary 1944- *WhoSSW 93*
Werlein, Ewing, Jr. 1936- *WhoAm 92, WhoSSW 93, WhoWor 93*

Werler, Paul F. St&PR 93
Werley, Anthony D. 1956- St&PR 93
Werley, Elizabeth Lynn Law&B 92
Werlin, Lewis R. 1933- St&PR 93
Werlin, Mark ScF&FL 92
Werlin, Marvin ScF&FL 92
Werlin, Sidney 1918- St&PR 93
Werlin, Stanley H. 1949- St&PR 93
Werling, Norman Victor 1936- St&PR 93
Werlock, Abby Holmes P(otter) 1942- ConAu 137
Werman, Barry Samuel 1951- WhoSSW 93
Werman, David Sanford 1922- WhoAm 92
Werman, Robert 1929- ConAu 139
Werman, Thomas Ehrlich 1945- WhoAm 92
Wermann, Friedrich Oskar 1840-1906 Baker 92
Werme, Judith Georgette 1950- WhoAm 92
Wermecke, John D. St&PR 93
Wermuth, Lora Dunnam Morgan 1929- WhoAmW 93
Wermuth, Manfred Jakob 1941- WhoWor 93
Wermuth, Mary Louella 1943- WhoAmW 93
Wermuth, Michael Anthony 1946- WhoAm 92
Wermuth, Paul Charles 1925- WhoAm 92
Werneburg, Kenneth Roger 1941- St&PR 93
Werner, Alan Blair 1955- St&PR 93
Werner, Andrew Joseph 1936- WhoE 93
Werner, Anthony C. 1937- WhoUN 92
Werner, Arno 1865-1955 Baker 92
Werner, Aviva Law&B 92
Werner, Burton Kready 1933- WhoIns 93
Werner, Cecelia Marie 1955- WhoAmW 93
Werner, Charles Arthur 1921- WhoWor 93
Werner, Charles George 1909- WhoAm 92
Werner, Christopher O. St&PR 93
Werner, Curtis G. 1964- St&PR 93
Werner, David S. 1948- St&PR 93
Werner, David William 1952- WhoE 93
Werner, Elmer Louis, Jr. 1927- WhoIns 93
Werner, Eric 1901-1988 Baker 92
Werner, Eugene Vernon 1925- WhoSSW 93
Werner, Eyvind ScF&FL 92
Werner, Frank D. 1922- St&PR 93
Werner, Fred H. 1908- WhoWrEP 92
Werner, Fritz WhoAm 92
Werner, George F. 1931- St&PR 93
Werner, Gerhard 1921- WhoAm 92
Werner, Gloria S. 1940- WhoAm 92
Werner, Graham A. 1938- St&PR 93
Werner, Gregor Joseph 1693-1766 Baker 92
Werner, Heinrich 1800-1833 Baker 92
Werner, Helmut 1934- WhoScE 91-3
Werner, Herbert Levy 1908-1991 BioIn 17
Werner, Herman S. 1920- St&PR 93
Werner, Ivar 1923- WhoScE 91-4
Werner, James J. 1934- St&PR 93
Werner, Jeff MiSFD 9
Werner, Jeffrey Brad 1950- WhoSSW 93
Werner, Jeffrey Smith 1945- St&PR 93, WhoAm 92
Werner, Johann Gottlob 1777-1822 Baker 92
Werner, John Bailey 1931- WhoAm 92
Werner, John Ellis 1932- WhoAm 92
Werner, Joseph 1925- WhoE 93
Werner, Jurgen 1940- WhoScE 91-3
Werner, Kenneth D. Law&B 92
Werner, Kenneth H. 1950- St&PR 93
Werner, Lawrence R. 1938- St&PR 93
Werner, Lloyd 1938- BioIn 17
Werner, Mary Ann Law&B 92
Werner, Michael F. 1945- St&PR 93
Werner, Mort 1916-1990 BioIn 17
Werner, Nancy Kay Darlington 1942- WhoAmW 93
Werner, Nat 1907-1991 BioIn 17
Werner, Oskar 1922-1984 IntDcF 2-3 [port]
Werner, Patrice 1937- WhoE 93
Werner, Peter 1947- MiSFD 9
Werner, Peter Johann 1932- WhoWor 93
Werner, R.R. 1928- St&PR 93
Werner, Richard Budd 1931- WhoAm 92
Werner, Richard V. 1948- St&PR 93
Werner, Richard Vincent 1948- WhoAm 92
Werner, Robert Allen 1946- WhoAm 92
Werner, Robert George 1936- WhoE 93
Werner, Robert Joseph 1932- WhoAm 92
Werner, Robert L. 1913- WhoAm 92
Werner, Roger Livingston, Jr. 1950- WhoAm 92
Werner, Roger Livington 1950- BioIn 17
Werner, Ronald Cornelius 1935- WhoE 93
Werner, Ronald G. Law&B 92
Werner, Ronald L. 1945- St&PR 93
Werner, Roy Anthony 1944- WhoWor 93
Werner, S. Mark Law&B 92
Werner, Seth BioIn 17
Werner, Seth Mitchell 1954- WhoAm 92, WhoSSW 93
Werner, Sharon Law&B 92
Werner, Sidney Charles 1909- WhoAm 92
Werner, Stuart Lloyd 1932- WhoE 93, WhoWor 93
Werner, Thomas Carl 1948- St&PR 93
Werner, Tom BioIn 17, WhoAm 92
Werner, Tom G. 1942- St&PR 93
Werner, Warren Winfield 1952- WhoSSW 93, WhoWrEP 92
Werner, Zacharias 1768-1823 BioIn 17
Werner-Jacobsen, Emmy Elisabeth 1929- WhoAm 92
Wernerowski, Krzysztof 1930- WhoScE 91-4
Wernerus, F. WhoScE 91-2
Wernette, Monica M. 1951- WhoUN 92
Wernick, Jack Harry 1923- WhoAm 92
Wernick, Justin 1936- WhoE 93
Wernick, Kenneth A. 1946- St&PR 93
Wernick, Richard (Frank) 1934- Baker 92, WhoAm 92
Wernick, Sandie Margot 1944- WhoAmW 93
Wernick, Saul 1921-1982 ScF&FL 92
Wernick, Stanley 1928- WhoAm 92
Wernick, Stanley S. 1928- St&PR 93
Wernicke, Christian 1959- WhoWor 93
Wernicki, M. Chris 1945- WhoE 93
Wernimont, Cheryl Ann 1944- WhoAmW 93
Wernle, Helen Abigail 1952- WhoWrEP 92
Wernz, Ann Hart Law&B 92
Weron, Aleksander Eugeniusz 1945- WhoWor 93
Werrecore, Matthias Hermann d1574? Baker 92
Werrekoren, Matthias Hermann d1574? Baker 92
Werrenrath, Reinald 1883-1953 Baker 92
Werries, E. Dean 1929- St&PR 93, WhoAm 92, WhoSSW 93
Werry, P.A.Th.J. 1943- WhoScE 91-3
Wersall, Jan O. 1930- WhoScE 91-4
Wersba, Barbara 1932- ConAu 38NR, DcAmChF 1960, MajAI [port]
Wershing, Susan Medler 1938- WhoWrEP 92
Werson, James Byrd 1916- WhoAm 92
Werst, J.J., Jr. 1918- St&PR 93
Wert, Charles Allen 1919- WhoAm 92
Wert, Frank Shadle 1942- WhoSSW 93
Wert, Giaches de 1535-1596 Baker 92
Wert, Harry Emerson 1932- St&PR 93
Wert, Jack Warren 1942- WhoSSW 93
Wert, James Junior 1933- WhoAm 92
Wert, James W. 1946- St&PR 93
Wert, James William 1946- WhoAm 92
Wert, Jonathan Maxwell, II 1939- WhoAm 92, WhoE 93
Wert, Lawrence Joseph 1956- WhoAm 92
Wert, Lucille Mathena 1919- WhoAm 92
Wert, Robert Clifton 1944- WhoE 93
Wert, Robert Joseph 1922-1991 BioIn 17
Wertenbaker, Timberlake ConTFT 10
Werth, Andrew M. 1934- WhoAm 92
Werth, Elizabeth C. 1947- St&PR 93
Werth, Gunter 1938- WhoScE 91-3
Werth, Gunter Heinz 1938- WhoWor 93
Werth, Hans Juergen 1948- WhoWor 93
Werth, Pamela A. 1954- St&PR 93
Werth, Ronald Fred 1936- St&PR 93
Werth, Ronald Paul 1947- St&PR 93
Wertham, Fredric 1895-1981 ScF&FL 92
Werthan, Bernard, Jr. 1931- St&PR 93
Wertheim, Audrey D. 1933- St&PR 93
Wertheim, David Michael Law&B 92
Wertheim, Mary Carole 1939- WhoAmW 93
Wertheim, Mitzi Mallina WhoAm 92
Wertheim, Robert Halley 1922- WhoAm 92
Wertheim, S.J. 1936- WhoScE 91-3
Wertheim, Sally Harris 1931- WhoAmW 93
Wertheimer, David Eliot 1955- WhoSSW 93
Wertheimer, Franc 1927- WhoAm 92, WhoE 93
Wertheimer, Fred 1939- PolPar
Wertheimer, Fredric Michael 1939- WhoAm 92
Wertheimer, Gregory L. 1957- St&PR 93
Wertheimer, Henry 1943- St&PR 93
Wertheimer, Linda BioIn 17, WhoE 93
Wertheimer, Marc Joel 1949- WhoE 93
Wertheimer, Max 1880-1943 BioIn 17
Wertheimer, Merle Law&B 92
Wertheimer, Michael BioIn 17
Wertheimer, Richard James 1936- WhoAm 92
Wertheimer, Robert E. 1928- WhoAm 92
Wertheimer, Sydney Bernard 1914- WhoAm 92
Wertheimer, Thomas 1938- St&PR 93
Werthen, Allan G. 1927- St&PR 93
Wertimer, Sidney 1920- WhoAm 92
Wertjes, Catherine J. Law&B 92
Wertkin, Gerard Charles 1940- WhoAm 92
Wertlieb, Donald Lawrence 1952- WhoE 93
Wertman, Louis 1925- St&PR 93
Wertmueller, Lina 1928- ConAu 39NR
Wertmuller, Lina 1928- MiSFD 9
Wertsman, Vladimir Filip 1929- WhoAm 92
Wertz, Elizabeth Marie 1956- WhoAmW 93
Wertz, Harrison George 1945- St&PR 93
Wertz, Hugh S. 1909-1990 BioIn 17
Wertz, Kathrin 1959- WhoAmW 93
Wertz, Kenneth Dean 1946- WhoAm 92
Wertz, Larry Jean 1946- St&PR 93
Wertz, Richard Lawrence 1947- St&PR 93
Wertz, Spencer K. 1941- WhoAm 92
Wertz, Victor Woodrow 1925-1983 BiDAMSp 1989
Wery, Robert E.O. 1928- WhoScE 91-2
Weryha, Georges Richard 1955- WhoWor 93
Werynski, Andrzej W. 1937- WhoScE 91-4
Werynski, Bronislaw Edward 1931- WhoScE 91-4
Wesberry, James Pickett 1906- WhoAm 92
Wesberry, James Pickett, Jr. 1934- WhoAm 92
Wesbury, Stuart Arnold, Jr. 1933- WhoAm 92
Wesche, Karlhans 1920- WhoScE 91-3
Wesche, Nancy Carol 1954- WhoAmW 93
Weschler, Anita WhoAm 92, WhoE 93
Weschler, Lawrence Michael 1952- WhoAm 92
Weschler, Thomas R. St&PR 93
Wescoe, David B. 1954- St&PR 93
Wescoe, W. Clarke 1920- St&PR 93
Wescoe, William Clarke 1920- WhoAm 92
Wescott, Beatrice 1952- WhoAmW 93
Wescott, Earle 1947- ScF&FL 92
Wescott, Glenway 1901-1987 BioIn 17
Wescott, Paul A. 1931- St&PR 93
Wescott, Roger Williams 1925- WhoAm 92
Wescott, William BioIn 17
Wesel, Charles William 1932- St&PR 93
Wesel, Genevieve Catherine St&PR 93
Wesel, Joseph Henry 1929- St&PR 93
Wesel, Luada E. 1931- St&PR 93
Weseli, Roger William 1932- WhoAm 92
Weselin, Mary Lou 1946- WhoSSW 93
Weseloh, Ronald Mack 1944- WhoE 93
Wesely, Marissa Celeste 1955- WhoAmW 93
Wesely, Yolanda Thereza 1927- WhoE 93
Wesemann, W.O.E. 1931- WhoScE 91-3
Wesemann, Wolfgang 1931- WhoWor 93
Wesembeek, Leon-Philippe-Marie Burbure de Baker 92
Wesenberg, David Gordon 1931- St&PR 93
Wesenberg, John Herman 1927- WhoAm 92
Wesendonck, Mathilde 1828-1902 Baker 92
Wesendonck, Otto 1815-1896 See Wesendonck, Mathilde 1828-1902 Baker 92
Wesener, Barbara Ann 1948- WhoAmW 93
Wesker, Arnold 1932- BioIn 17, WhoWor 93
Weslager, Clinton Alfred 1909- WhoAm 92, WhoE 93, WhoWor 93
Wesler, Oscar 1921- WhoAm 92
Wesley Baker 92
Wesley, Charles 1707-1788 Baker 92, BioIn 17
Wesley, Charles 1757-1834 Baker 92
Wesley, Fred BioIn 17
Wesley, George 1927- St&PR 93
Wesley, J. Michael 1948- St&PR 93
Wesley, James Paul 1921- WhoWor 93
Wesley, James Wyatt, Jr. 1933- WhoAm 92
Wesley, John 1703-1791 Baker 92, BioIn 17
Wesley, John Mercer 1928- WhoAm 92
Wesley, Mary BioIn 17
Wesley, Roy M. 1946- St&PR 93
Wesley, Samuel 1766-1837 Baker 92
Wesley, Samuel Sebastian 1810-1876 Baker 92, BioIn 17
Wesley, Stephen Harrison 1961- WhoSSW 93
Wesley, Valerie Wilson BioIn 17
Wesling, Denise Ann 1959- WhoAmW 93
Wesling, Donald Truman 1939- WhoAm 92, WhoWrEP 92
Wesling, Richard Michael 1932- St&PR 93
Weslow, Norman J. Law&B 92
Weslowski, James J. 1950- St&PR 93
Wesner, John Oliver, Jr. 1916- St&PR 93
Wesnitzer, Corey 1956- St&PR 93
Wesolow, Adam 1923- WhoAm 92
Wesolowski, Adolph John 1916- WhoWor 93
Wesolowski, Andrzej Witold 1942- WhoE 93
Wesolowski, Cindy Lee 1960- WhoE 93
Wesolowski, Gerald F. 1946- St&PR 93
Wesolowski, James J. Law&B 92
Wesolowski, Paul G. 1956- WhoE 93, WhoWrEP 92
Wesolowski, Sigmund Adam 1923- WhoAm 92
Wesolowski, Stefan 1909-1987 PolBiDi
Wesolowski, Sylvia Molenda 1948- WhoE 93
Wesolowski, Zbigniew 1933- WhoScE 91-4
Wesoly, Lorrie Paulette 1954- WhoE 93
Wesoski, M. Nadine 1958- WhoAmW 93
Wespi, Andreas Peter 1947- WhoWor 93
Wess, Theo 1936- WhoScE 91-3
Wessberg, Kenneth d1992 BioIn 17
Wesse, David Joseph 1951- WhoEmL 93, WhoWor 93
Wessel, Henry 1942- WhoAm 92
Wessel, James R. 1940- St&PR 93
Wessel, Joan Strauss 1929- WhoAmW 93
Wessel, Kenneth C. 1928- St&PR 93
Wessel, Kenneth H. 1949- St&PR 93
Wessel, Mark 1894-1973 Baker 92
Wessel, Milton R. 1923-1991 BioIn 17
Wessel, Paul C. 1948- St&PR 93
Wessel, Thomas Mark 1956- WhoE 93
Wesseling, K.H. WhoScE 91-3
Wesselink, David Duwayne 1942- St&PR 93, WhoAm 92
Wessell, David St&PR 93
Wessell, David L. 1942- St&PR 93
Wessell, Nils Y. 1914- WhoSSW 93
Wesselmann, Glenn Allen 1932- WhoAm 92
Wessels, Jan Lucas 1938- St&PR 93
Wessels, Richard H. 1939- St&PR 93
Wessely, Othmar 1922- Baker 92
Wesser, Yvonne Doreen 1935- WhoE 93
Wessex, Martyn ScF&FL 92
Wessing, Armin R.E. 1924- WhoScE 91-3
Wessin y Wessin, Elias 1924- DcCPCAm
Wesslen, Ejda M. 1922- WhoScE 91-4
Wessler, Richard Lee 1936- WhoAm 92
Wessler, Stanford 1917- WhoAm 92, WhoWor 93
Wessling, Donald Moore 1936- WhoAm 92
Wessling, Francis Christopher 1939- WhoSSW 93
Wessman, Harri (Kristian) 1949- Baker 92
Wessner, Deborah Marie 1950- WhoAmW 93
Wessner, Kenneth T. 1922- St&PR 93
Wesson, Bruce F. 1942- St&PR 93
Wesson, Felicia A. Law&B 92
Wesson, Marianne 1948- WhoAmW 93
Wesson, Michael David 1941- WhoSSW 93
Wesson, Robert G. 1920-1991 BioIn 17
Wesson, Robert Michael 1935- WhoE 93
Wesson, William Simpson 1929- WhoAm 92
Wesstrom, Stephen 1949- St&PR 93
West, A. Karen Law&B 92
West, Alan Irving 1948- WhoE 93
West, Alfred Paul 1942- St&PR 93
West, Andrew Collin 1946- WhoUN 92
West, Anthony 1914-1987 ScF&FL 92
West, Anthony Roy WhoScE 91-1
West, Anthony Roy 1947- WhoWor 93
West, Arleigh Burton 1910- WhoAm 92
West, Arnold Bernard Law&B 92
West, Arnold Sumner 1922- WhoAm 92
West, Arthur Graeme 1891-1917 BioIn 17
West, Arthur James, II 1927- WhoAm 92
West, Austin Ward, Jr. 1948- WhoSSW 93
West, B. Kenneth BioIn 17
West, B. Kenneth 1933- St&PR 93
West, Barbara Law&B 92
West, Barbara Ann 1944- WhoAmW 93
West, Bernadette Marie 1951- WhoAmW 93
West, Bernard P. 1945- St&PR 93
West, Billy Gene 1946- WhoWor 93
West, Birdie AmWomPl
West, Bob 1931- WhoAm 92
West, Brian S. Law&B 92
West, Bruce 1951- BioIn 17
West, Byron Kenneth 1933- WhoAm 92
West, C. William Law&B 92
West, Carl ScF&FL 92
West, Carol Catherine 1944- WhoAmW 93, WhoSSW 93
West, Caroline Haigh Law&B 92
West, Carroll Van 1955- WhoSSW 93
West, Chalmer William, Jr. Law&B 92

West, Charles Converse 1921- WhoAm 92
West, Charles H. 1934- WhoAm 92
West, Charles Patrick 1952- WhoSSW 93
West, Chassie L. ScF&FL 92
West, Cheryl Jean 1956- WhoAmW 93
West, Clark Darwin 1918- WhoAm 92
West, Clive E. 1939- WhoScE 91-3
West, Colin 1951- ConAu 136
West, Cornel BioIn 17
West, Dan Carlos 1939- WhoAm 92
West, Darrin Ross 1963- WhoWor 93
West, David Richard Frederick WhoScE 91-1
West, Delouris Jeanne 1943- WhoSSW 93
West, Doe 1951- WhoE 93, WhoEmL 93
West, Don 1906-1992 NewYTBS 92
West, Donald Jack 1922- WhoSSW 93
West, Donald James WhoScE 91-1
West, Donald V. 1930- St&PR 93
West, Donna Rae 1953- WhoAmW 93
West, Dorothy MajAI
West, Dottie 1932- Baker 92
West, Dottie 1932-1991 AnObit 1991, BioIn 17, ConMus 8 [port], News 92
West, Douglas M. Law&B 92
West, Edward St&PR 93
West, Edward Charles 1928- St&PR 93
West, Edward E., Jr. 1927- St&PR 93
West, Elizabeth Fisher 1928- WhoSSW 93
West, Elizabeth Howard 1873-1948 BioIn 17
West, Elizabeth R. 1945- WhoAmW 93
West, Elmer Gordon 1914- WhoAm 92
West, Emma Elise 1876?- AmWomPl
West, Eric Fowler 1923- St&PR 93
West, Ernest Patrick, Jr. 1925- WhoSSW 93
West, Everett Wilson 1930- St&PR 93
West, Felton 1926- WhoAm 92
West, Fowler Claude 1940- WhoAm 92
West, Frederic Hadleigh, Jr. 1956- WhoWor 93
West, Gail Berry 1942- WhoAm 92
West, Gary Wayne 1941- St&PR 93
West, Geoffrey ScF&FL 92
West, George Henry WhoScE 91-1
West, Glenda Murl 1947- WhoAmW 93
West, Glenn, Jr. Law&B 92
West, Glenn Edward 1944- WhoAm 92
West, Gordon Fitzhugh, III 1951- WhoSSW 93
West, Gregory Joseph 1950- St&PR 93
West, Harold E. 1926- St&PR 93
West, Harry Archibald, Jr. 1939- WhoSSW 93
West, Howard Norton 1919- WhoAm 92
West, Howard P., Jr. Law&B 92
West, Hugh Brian 1939- St&PR 93
West, Hugh Sterling 1930- WhoWor 93
West, J. Robinson 1946- WhoAm 92
West, James Harold 1926- WhoAm 92
West, James Joseph 1945- WhoAm 92
West, James Kenneth 1935- St&PR 93
West, James Lionel 1935- WhoWor 93
West, James V. Law&B 92
West, Jean 1935- WhoWrEP 92
West, Jerry BioIn 17
West, Jerry Alan 1938- WhoAm 92
West, Jerry Wayne 1938- St&PR 93
West, Jessamyn d1984 BioIn 17
West, Jessamyn 1902-1984 ScF&FL 92
West, Jo Frances 1947- WhoAmW 93
West, Jodie H. 1960- WhoAmW 93
West, John B. WhoScE 91-1
West, John Burnard 1928- WhoAm 92
West, John C. 1908-1991 BioIn 17
West, John Carl 1922- WhoWor 93
West, John Ebenezer 1863-1929 Baker 92
West, John Henry, III 1954- WhoE 93
West, John Merle 1920- WhoAm 92
West, John S. Law&B 92
West, John Thomas, IV 1946- St&PR 93
West, Joseph W. Law&B 92
West, Karen Elizabeth 1946- St&PR 93
West, Kathleene K. WhoWrEP 92
West, Kenneth Wayne 1950- St&PR 93
West, Laurice Juston 1931- St&PR 93
West, Laurie Law&B 92
West, Lawrence WhoScE 91-1
West, Lee Roy 1929- WhoAm 92, WhoSSW 93
West, Leonard J. 1921- WhoE 93
West, Linda Ann 1953- WhoAmW 93
West, Lindsay ScF&FL 92
West, Lola Tilleux 1940- WhoSSW 93
West, Loretta Marie 1950- WhoAmW 93
West, Louis Jolyon 1924- WhoAm 92
West, Louise Bronson AmWomPl
West, Lu Carole Law&B 92
West, Lucinda Marie Centers 1963- WhoSSW 93
West, Macdonald 1943- WhoWor 93
West, Mae 1892?-1980 AmWomPl, IntDcF 2-3 [port], QDrFCA 92 [port]
West, Marge L. 1928- St&PR 93
West, Marianne V. 1951- WhoAmW 93
West, Marilyn T. Law&B 92
West, Marjorie Edith 1940- WhoAmW 93
West, Mark Irwin 1955- WhoSSW 93
West, Marvin Leon 1934- WhoAm 92, WhoE 93
West, Maryanne WhoE 93
West, Maxine Marilyn 1945- WhoAmW 93
West, Michael Alan 1938- WhoAm 92
West, Michael Gordon 1947- WhoE 93
West, Michael J.H. 1930- WhoScE 91-1
West, Millard Farrar, Jr. 1910- WhoAm 92
West, Morris L. 1916- BioIn 17, ScF&FL 92
West, Morris Langlo 1916- WhoAm 92, WhoWor 93, WhoWrEP 92
West, Myrna Louise 1941- WhoAmW 93
West, Nancy B. AmWomPl
West, Nathanael 1903-1940 BioIn 17, MagSAmL [port]
West, Noah James 1951- WhoSSW 93
West, Olive AmWomPl
West, Owen ScF&FL 92
West, Pamela 1945- ScF&FL 92
West, Patti Jo 1964- WhoAmW 93
West, Paul 1930- BioIn 17, ScF&FL 92
West, Paul J. 1945- St&PR 93
West, Paul Noden 1930- WhoAm 92, WhoWrEP 92
West, Perry Douglas 1947- St&PR 93
West, Peter Christopher WhoScE 91-1
West, Peter Donald 1953- WhoE 93
West, Peter Jonathan Anthony 1955- St&PR 93
West, Philip William 1913- WhoAm 92, WhoSSW 93
West, Phyllis Ann 1940- St&PR 93
West, Ralph Leland 1915- WhoAm 92
West, Rebecca 1892-1983 BioIn 17, ScF&FL 92
West, Rexford Leon 1938- St&PR 93, WhoAm 92
West, Richard 1949- WhoSSW 93
West, Richard C. 1944- ScF&FL 92
West, Richard Gilbert WhoScE 91-1
West, Richard Gilbert 1926- WhoWor 93
West, Richard J. 1939- WhoScE 91-1
West, Richard Luther 1925- WhoAm 92
West, Richard M. 1941- WhoScE 91-3
West, Richard M. 1944- St&PR 93
West, Richard P. 1921- St&PR 93
West, Richard Rollin 1938- WhoAm 92
West, Richard Vincent 1934- WhoAm 92
West, Robert 1925-1991 BioIn 17
West, Robert A. 1934- St&PR 93
West, Robert C. 1920- St&PR 93
West, Robert Cooper 1913- WhoAm 92
West, Robert Culbertson 1928- WhoAm 92
West, Robert H. 1938- St&PR 93
West, Robert Jeremy 1955- WhoWor 93
West, Robert MacLellan 1942- WhoAm 92
West, Robert V., Jr. 1921- St&PR 93
West, Robert Van Osdell, Jr. 1921- WhoAm 92, WhoSSW 93
West, Robert W. 1947- St&PR 93
West, Roger S., III 1949- St&PR 93
West, S.R. 1939- St&PR 93
West, Salli Lou 1939- WhoWrEP 92
West, Samuel Edward 1938- WhoSSW 93
West, Samuel Filmore 1904-1985 BiDAMSp 1989
West, Sandra La Vonne 1947- WhoWrEP 92
West, Sarah Jane 1963- WhoAmW 93
West, Sharon Anne 1944- WhoAmW 93
West, Stephen A. Law&B 92
West, Stephen A. 1935- St&PR 93
West, Stephen Allan 1935- WhoAm 92
West, Stephen Francis 1946- WhoE 93
West, Stephen Owen 1946- St&PR 93, WhoAm 92
West, Stephen R. 1931- St&PR 93
West, Stewart John 1934- WhoAsAP 91
West, Susan Dorothea Weesner 1959- WhoSSW 93
West, T.S. 1927- WhoScE 91-1
West, Terence Douglas 1948- WhoEmL 93, WhoWor 93
West, Thomas Edward 1954- WhoWrEP 92
West, Thomas Lowell, Jr. 1937- St&PR 93
West, Thomas Meade 1940- St&PR 93, WhoAm 92
West, Thomas Summers 1927- WhoScE 91-1
West, Timothy T. Law&B 92
West, Tina BioIn 17
West, Todd K. St&PR 93
West, Tom Harry 1938- WhoSSW 93
West, Uta ScF&FL 92
West, Victoria Sackville- 1892-1962 BioIn 17
West, Wallace 1900-1980 ScF&FL 92
West, Walter B. St&PR 93
West, Walter L. 1943- St&PR 93
West, Walter Lowry 1943- WhoAm 92
West, Warren Henry 1956- WhoE 93
West, Warwick Reed, Jr. 1922- WhoSSW 93
West, Wayne J. 1954- St&PR 93
West, William Beverley, III 1922- WhoAm 92
West, William J. 1945- St&PR 93
West, William Stuart 1927- St&PR 93
West, Wilmer A. 1949- St&PR 93
Westadt, Connie L. Law&B 92
Westall, Karen Katz Law&B 92
Westall, Marta Susan Wolf 1946- WhoEmL 93
Westall, Robert 1929- ScF&FL 92, SmATA 69 [port]
Westall, Robert (Atkinson) 1929- ChlFicS, MajAI [port]
Westbay, Annette AmWomPl
Westberg, John Augustin 1931- WhoWor 93
Westberry, Billy Murry 1926- WhoAm 92
Westberry, Kim M. 1957- St&PR 93
Westbroek, Willem Arie 1946- WhoWor 93
Westbrook, Gayle Robinson Law&B 92
Westbrook, James Edwin 1934- WhoAm 92
Westbrook, Joel Whitsitt, III 1916- WhoAm 92
Westbrook, Karin Luka 1943- St&PR 93
Westbrook, Marianne McIntire 1948- WhoEmL 93
Westbrook, Nicholas Kilmer 1948- WhoE 93
Westbrook, Stephen M. Law&B 92
Westbrook, Susan Elizabeth 1939- WhoAmW 93
Westbrook, W.L. 1939- St&PR 93
Westbrook, William Joseph 1831-1894 Baker 92
Westbrooks, Robert Alan Law&B 92
Westburg, John Edward 1918- WhoWrEP 92
Westbury, G. 1927- WhoScE 91-1
Westbury, Richard G. S. 1926- St&PR 93
Westby, Timothy Scott 1957- WhoSSW 93
Westcott, Brian John 1957- WhoWor 93
Westcott, C.T. ScF&FL 92
Westcott, Elizabeth A. Law&B 92
Westcott, Jeffrey Howard 1956- WhoE 93
Westcott, John Hugh WhoScE 91-1
Westcott, Kathleen Motel 1960- WhoE 93
Westcott, Russell Thrasher 1927- WhoE 93
Westcott, Thompson 1820-1888 JrnUS
West-Eberhard, Mary Jane 1941- WhoAm 92
Westenberger, Friedrich 1925- WhoScE 91-3
Westenborg, Jack A. 1942- St&PR 93
Westenburg, Richard 1932- Baker 92
Westendorf, Douglas Lawrence 1947- St&PR 93
Westenhiser, Gary Robert 1958- WhoSSW 93
Wester, Keith Albert 1940- WhoAm 92
Wester, Neil Charles 1940- St&PR 93
Wester, Nelson Gunnar Law&B 92
Wester, Per Olov 1929- WhoScE 91-4
Westerback, David F. Law&B 92
Westerback, Diane Susan 1956- WhoAmW 93
Westerbeck, David F. 1945- WhoIns 93
Westerbeck, David Francis 1945- St&PR 93, WhoAm 92
Westerbeck, Kenneth Edward 1919- WhoAm 92
Westerberg, Arthur William 1938- WhoAm 92, WhoE 93
Westerberg, Gunnar Olof 1920- WhoWor 93
Westerberg, Stig (Evald Borje) 1918- Baker 92
Westerberg, Verne Edward 1931- WhoAm 92
Westerburg, Louis Richard, Jr. Law&B 92
Westerby, David A. Law&B 92
Westerdahl, John Brian 1954- WhoEmL 93
Westerfield, Carolyn Elizabeth Hess 1933- WhoE 93
Westerfield, Holt Bradford 1928- WhoAm 92
Westerfield, Putney 1930- St&PR 93, WhoAm 92
Westergaard, Peter (Talbot) 1931- Baker 92, WhoAm 92
Westergaard, Richard C. 1944- St&PR 93
Westergaard, Richard C. 1945- WhoAm 92
Westergaard, Svend 1922- Baker 92
Westergaard-Nielsen, Niels Christian 1948- WhoWor 93
Westerhaus, Douglas Bernard 1951- WhoEmL 93
Westerhausen, Matthias 1959- WhoWor 93
Westerheide, Richard J. 1951- St&PR 93
Westerheide, William Joseph, Jr. 1945- WhoSSW 93
Westerhof, Caroline Shaffer 1931- WhoSSW 93
Westerhoff, Harold E. 1915- WhoAm 92
Westerhoff, Heinz 1928- WhoWor 93
Westerhoff, John Henry, III 1933- WhoAm 92
Westerholm, Roger Nils 1953- WhoWor 93
Westerholm, Sune Sigfrid 1941- WhoWor 93
Westerhout, Gart 1927- WhoAm 92
Westerhout, Nicola van Baker 92
Westerhuis, Maurits Willem 1941- WhoWor 93
Westerlinck, Wilfried 1945- Baker 92
Westerlund, Bengt Elis 1921- WhoWor 93
Westerlund, David A. 1950- St&PR 93
Westerlund, Elaine M. 1945- WhoAmW 93
Westerly, Daniel ScF&FL 92
Westerman, Albert Barry 1941- WhoSSW 93
Westerman, George W. 1939- St&PR 93, WhoAm 92
Westerman, Harriet Heaps 1947- WhoAmW 93
Westerman, Jewell G. 1934- WhoE 93
Westerman, Katy Dorothea 1930- WhoAmW 93
Westerman, Mark Lee 1954- St&PR 93
Westerman, Percy F. 1876-1959 ScF&FL 92
Westerman, Robert J. Law&B 92
Westerman, Susan S. 1943- WhoAm 92
Westerman, Sylvia Hewitt WhoAm 92
Westerman, Wm. L. 1931- St&PR 93
Westermann, Anthony J. 1906- St&PR 93
Westermann, David 1920- WhoAm 92
Westermann, Diedrich Hermann 1875-1956 IntDcAn
Westermann, Guenter 1939- St&PR 93
Westermann, Horace Clifford 1922- WhoAm 92
Westermann, Horace Clifford 1922-1981 BioIn 17
Westermann, John Jacob, IV 1952- WhoWrEP 92
Westermann, L.J. WhoScE 91-3
Westermarck, Edvard Alexander 1862-1939 IntDcAn
Westermark, Torbjorn 1923- WhoScE 91-4
Westermark, Torbjorn Erik Gunnar 1923- WhoWor 93
Westermeyer, Michael T. 1949- St&PR 93
Western, Halvor 1944- WhoScE 91-4
Westerterp, Klaas R. 1946- WhoScE 91-3
Westervelt, James 1946- WhoIns 93
Westervelt, James J. 1946- St&PR 93
Westervelt, Peter Jocelyn 1919- WhoAm 92
Westfall, Donald D. Law&B 92
Westfall, Jane Anne 1928- WhoAmW 93
Westfall, Lawrence S. Law&B 92
Westfall, Linda Louise 1954- WhoAmW 93
Westfall, Mary Glenda 1944- WhoWrEP 92
Westfall, Pamela T. Law&B 92
Westfall, Patricia Gay Law&B 92
Westfall, Phillip K. 1943- St&PR 93
Westfall, Richard Samuel 1924- WhoAm 92, WhoWrEP 92
Westfried, Alex Huxley 1919- WhoE 93
Westgate, Lana Laura 1942- WhoAmW 93
Westhafer, J.C. 1932- St&PR 93
Westhead, Paul WhoAm 92
Westheimer, David 1917- WhoWrEP 92
Westheimer, David Kaplan 1917- WhoAm 92
Westheimer, Frank Henry 1912- WhoAm 92, WhoE 93
Westheimer, Gerald 1924- WhoAm 92
Westheimer, Jerome Max, Sr. 1910- WhoWor 93
Westheimer, Julius Milton 1916- WhoAm 92
Westheimer, Karola Ruth Siegel WhoAm 92, WhoAmW 93
Westheimer, Mary Helen 1955- WhoWrEP 92
Westheimer, Ruth BioIn 17
Westheimer, Ruth Welling 1922- WhoAm 92
Westhoff, David John 1942- St&PR 93
Westhoff, Dennis Charles 1942- WhoAm 92
Westhoff, Thomas S. Law&B 92
Westhuiss, Arrien St&PR 93
Westin, Alan Furman 1929- WhoAm 92
Westin, David Lawrence Law&B 92
Westin, Richard A(xel) 1945- ConAu 37NR
Westin, Richard S. 1932- St&PR 93
Westing, Arthur H(erbert) 1928- ConAu 38NR
Westinghouse, George 1846-1914 GayN
Westlake, Abby ScF&FL 92

Westlake, Anthony L. *St&PR 93*
Westlake, Donald E. *BioIn 17*
Westlake, Donald E. 1933- *ScF&FL 92*
Westlake, Donald Edwin 1933- *WhoAm 92*
Westlake, Donald Edwin Edmund 1933- *WhoWrEP 92*
Westlake, Frederick 1840-1898 *Baker 92*
Westlake, James Roger 1928- *WhoSSW 93*
Westlake, Michael 1942- *ScF&FL 92*
Westlake, Robert Elmer, Sr. 1918- *WhoAm 92*
Westlake, Susan E. *Law&B 92*
Westlake, Wayne S. 1947- *St&PR 93*
Westland, Cynthia Lane 1953- *WhoAmW 93*
Westland, Larry *BioIn 17*
West-Lewis, Liz 1956- *WhoAmW 93*
Westley, Dennis J. 1959- *St&PR 93*
Westley, John William 1936- *WhoE 93*
Westling, Jon 1942- *WhoAm 92*
Westling, Snen Hakan 1928- *WhoWor 93*
Westlock, Jeannine Marie 1959- *WhoAmW 93*
Westmacott, Mary *ConAu 37NR*
Westman, Alida Spaans 1944- *WhoAmW 93*
Westman, Barbara *SmATA 70 [port]*
Westman, Carl Edward 1943- *WhoAm 92*
Westman, Daniel P. 1956- *ConAu 139*
Westman, Jack Conrad 1927- *WhoAm 92*
Westman, James Edward 1950- *WhoE 93*
Westman, James R. d1992 *NewYTBS 92*
Westman, James R. 1910-1992 *BioIn 17*
Westman, Kai 1939- *WhoScE 91-4*
Westman, Kathryn L. *Law&B 92*
Westman, Timothy G. *Law&B 92*
Westmeyer, Edward Anthony 1948- *St&PR 93*
Westmeyer, Francis Emery 1949- *St&PR 93*
Westmeyer, Paul Henry Martin 1925- *WhoSSW 93*
Westmore, Michael *BioIn 17*
Westmore, Michael George 1938- *WhoAm 92*
Westmoreland, Barbara Fenn 1940- *WhoAmW 93*
Westmoreland, Carol J. *Law&B 92*
Westmoreland, James Rogers 1952- *WhoSSW 93*
Westmoreland, John William 1932- *WhoUN 92*
Westmoreland, Joyce N. 1938- *St&PR 93*
Westmoreland, O.R. 1948- *St&PR 93*
Westmoreland, R.P. 1936- *St&PR 93*
Westmoreland, Reginald Conway 1926- *WhoSSW 93*
Westmoreland, Samuel Douglass 1944- *WhoE 93*
Westmoreland, William C. *BioIn 17*
Westmoreland, William C. 1914- *ColdWar 1 [port], CmdGen 1991 [port]*
Westmoreland, William Childs 1914- *HarEnMi*
Westmorland, Earl of *Baker 92*
Westmorland, Mildmay Fane, Earl of 1601-1666 *BioIn 17*
Westner, Laureen Marie 1962- *WhoAmW 93*
Westney, John L., Jr. *Law&B 92*
Westoff, Charles Francis 1927- *WhoAm 92*
Weston, Allen *MajAI*
Weston, Arthur Walter 1914- *WhoAm 92*
Weston, Benjamin C. 1954- *St&PR 93*
Weston, Beverly *BioIn 17*
Weston, Blake L. *Law&B 92*
Weston, Brett 1911- *BioIn 17*
Weston, Burns Humphrey 1933- *WhoWor 93*
Weston, C.P. *Law&B 92*
Weston, Carol *BioIn 17*
Weston, Cori C. *Law&B 92*
Weston, Donald Eugene 1935- *St&PR 93*
Weston, Effie Ellsler 1858-1942 *AmWomPl*
Weston, Elisabeth Anne 1947- *WhoE 93*
Weston, Eric *MiSFD 9*
Weston, Francine Evans 1946- *WhoAmW 93, WhoE 93, WhoWor 93*
Weston, Garfield Howard *St&PR 93*
Weston, Gregory M. *Law&B 92*
Weston, Henry Jeffray 1926- *WhoWor 93*
Weston, Janice Leah Colmer 1944- *WhoAmW 93*
Weston, John Frederick 1916- *WhoAm 92*
Weston, Josh S. 1928- *St&PR 93*
Weston, Keith F.C. 1937- *WhoScE 91-1*
Weston, Paul *WhoAm 92*
Weston, Paul Holliday 1944- *St&PR 93*
Weston, Peter 1944- *ScF&FL 92*
Weston, Randy *BioIn 17*
Weston, Randy 1926- *WhoAm 92*
Weston, Richard Henry *WhoScE 91-1*
Weston, Roger Lance 1943- *WhoAm 92*
Weston, Roy F. 1911- *St&PR 93*
Weston, Roy Francis 1911- *WhoAm 92*
Weston, Stanton D. 1930- *St&PR 93*
Weston, Susan B. 1943- *ScF&FL 92, WhoWrEP 92*
Weston, Theodore Brett 1911- *WhoAm 92*
Weston, Thomas 1737-1776 *BioIn 17*
Weston, Willard Galen 1940- *WhoAm 92, WhoWor 93*
Weston, William *WhoScE 91-1*
Weston, William David 1932- *WhoSSW 93*
Weston, William Lee 1938- *WhoAm 92*
Weston, William R. 1947- *WhoIns 93*
Weston-McMillan, Susan Diane 1966- *WhoSSW 93*
Westover, Charles 1939-1990 *BioIn 17*
Westover, Frank Thomas 1938- *St&PR 93*
Westover, Jenny Herr 1965- *WhoAmW 93*
Westover, Karl J. 1933- *St&PR 93*
Westover, Samuel Lee 1955- *WhoAm 92*
Westover Rabe, Colleen Ann 1959- *WhoAmW 93*
Westphal, Anja 1957- *WhoWor 93*
Westphal, Antoinette 1937- *St&PR 93*
Westphal, Bradley Dean *Law&B 92*
Westphal, David W. *Law&B 92*
Westphal, Douglas Herbert 1940- *WhoSSW 93*
Westphal, Gordon Edward 1940- *St&PR 93*
Westphal, Lynne L. *Law&B 92*
Westphal, Michael d1991 *BioIn 17*
Westphal, Paul 1950- *WhoAm 92*
Westphal, Paul Douglas 1950- *BiDAMSp 1989*
Westphal, Rainer John 1935- *St&PR 93*
Westphal, Roger Allen 1946- *WhoSSW 93*
Westphal, Rudolf (Georg Hermann) 1826-1892 *Baker 92*
Westphal, Steven D. 1955- *St&PR 93*
Westphal-Cantrell, Deborah Louise *WhoAmW 93*
Westphalen, Henry, Jr. 1933- *St&PR 93*
Westphalen, Jules 1937- *St&PR 93*
Westphalen, Mary Lynne 1943- *WhoAmW 93*
Westra, Verlyn L. 1936- *St&PR 93*
Westray, William Kenneth 1946- *WhoSSW 93*
Westrick, Elsie Margaret 1910- *WhoWrEP 92*
Westrick, Robert J. 1941- *St&PR 93*
Westrin, Claes-Goran 1929- *WhoScE 91-4*
Westrope, Martha Randolph 1922- *WhoAmW 93, WhoSSW 93*
Westrum, Dexter 1944- *ConAu 139, WhoWrEP 92*
Westrum, Edgar Francis, Jr. 1919- *WhoAm 92*
Westrup, Jack 1904-1975 *OxDcOp*
Westrup, Jack (Allan) 1904-1975 *Baker 92*
Weststeijn, Gerard 1934- *WhoScE 91-3*
Westura, Warren S. 1951- *WhoE 93*
Westwater, James William 1919- *WhoAm 92*
Westwater, Robert Stuart 1920- *St&PR 93*
Westwood, Albert Ronald Clifton 1932- *WhoAm 92*
Westwood, Bryan Percy 1909-1990 *BioIn 17*
Westwood, Chris *ScF&FL 92*
Westwood, Debra Ann 1955- *WhoAmW 93*
Westwood, James Thomas 1939- *WhoSSW 93*
Westwood, Jean 1923- *PolPar*
Westwood, Melvin Neil 1923- *WhoAm 92*
Westwood, Richard E. 1921- *ConAu 137*
Wetanson, Burt *ScF&FL 92*
Wetenhall, John 1957- *ConAu 136*
Wetere, Koro Tainui 1935- *WhoAsAP 91*
Wethe, Christian-Andrew 1942- *WhoE 93*
Wethekam, Marilyn A. *Law&B 92*
Wetherald, Agnes Ethelwyn 1857-1940 *BioIn 17*
Wetherald, David *Law&B 92*
Wetherald, Michele Warholic 1954- *WhoAmW 93*
Wetherbee, Roberta Janis 1948- *WhoAmW 93*
Wethered, Joyce 1901- *BioIn 17*
Wetherell, Alan M. *WhoScE 91-4*
Wetherell, Claire 1919- *WhoAmW 93*
Wetherell, W(alter) D(avid) 1948- *ConAu 138*
Wetherell, Weston B. *Law&B 92*
Wetherhold, Robert Campbell 1951- *WhoE 93*
Wetherill, Alfred 1861-1950 *IntDcAn*
Wetherill, Eikins 1919- *WhoAm 92*
Wetherill, Elkins 1919- *St&PR 93*
Wetherill, George Barrie *WhoScE 91-1*
Wetherill, George West 1925- *WhoAm 92*
Wetherill, Louisa Wade d1945 *BioIn 17*
Wetherill, Phyllis Steiss 1923- *WhoE 93*
Wetherill, Samuel Rogers, III 1945- *WhoWor 93*
Wetherington, James M. 1945- *St&PR 93*
Wethers, Doris Louise 1927- *WhoAmW 93*
Wethington, Charles T., Jr. *WhoAm 92, WhoSSW 93*
Wethington, John Abner, Jr. 1921- *WhoAm 92*
Wethington, R.B. 1944- *St&PR 93*
Wethington, William Orville 1906- *WhoWor 93*
Wethmore, Donald L. 1927- *St&PR 93*
We Three *SoulM*
Wetlaufer, Donald Burton 1925- *WhoAm 92, WhoE 93*
Wetmore, Andrew 1950- *WhoCanL 92*
Wetmore, Claude H. 1862-1944 *ScF&FL 92*
Wetmore, Edward Charles *Law&B 92*
Wetmore, Seth *BioIn 17*
Wetmore, Thomas Trask, III 1925- *WhoAm 92*
Wetmur, James Gerard 1941- *WhoE 93*
Wetreich, William 1953- *St&PR 93*
Wetstein, Gary M. *WhoAm 92*
Wetstone, Howard Jerome 1926- *WhoE 93*
Wettack, F. Sheldon *WhoAm 92*
Wette, Eduard Wilhelm 1925- *WhoWor 93*
Wettenhall, Roger Llewellyn 1931- *WhoWor 93*
Wetter, Carl 1922- *WhoScE 91-3*
Wetter, Edward 1919- *WhoAm 92*
Wetter, Friedrich Cardinal 1928- *WhoWor 93*
Wetter, Larry V. 1933- *St&PR 93*
Wetterau, Theodore C. 1927- *St&PR 93, WhoAm 92*
Wettereau, Richard Bradway 1932- *WhoE 93*
Wetterer, Carolyn Boswell *Law&B 92*
Wettergreen, Richard A. 1943- *WhoIns 93*
Wettergren, Gertrud 1897- *Baker 92*
Wetterhahn, Dawn 1952- *St&PR 93*
Wetterhahn, Karen Elizabeth 1948- *WhoAmW 93, WhoE 93*
Wetterling, Jacob *BioIn 17*
Wetterling, Patricia *BioIn 17*
Wetterwald, Philippe Paul 1952- *WhoWor 93*
Wettig, Patricia *BioIn 17, WhoAm 92, WhoAmW 93*
Wetton, Brian William *WhoScE 91-1*
Wettreich, Daniel *St&PR 93*
Wettstein, Barbara Lipner 1948- *WhoAmW 93*
Wettstein, Diter von 1929- *WhoScE 91-2*
Wettstein, Horst D. 1933- *WhoScE 91-3*
Wettstein, Pierre-Louis 1920- *WhoScE 91-4*
Wettstein, Wieland F. 1949- *St&PR 93*
Wetz, Richard 1875-1935 *Baker 92*
Wetzel, Albert John 1917- *WhoWor 93*
Wetzel, Carroll Robbins 1906- *WhoAm 92*
Wetzel, David L. 1929- *St&PR 93*
Wetzel, Donald C. *St&PR 93*
Wetzel, Edward Thomas 1937- *WhoE 93, WhoWor 93*
Wetzel, Elizabeth 1930- *WhoWrEP 92*
Wetzel, Friedrich Gottlob 1779-1819 *BioIn 17*
Wetzel, Gary Erwin 1938- *St&PR 93*
Wetzel, George T. 1921-1983 *ScF&FL 92*
Wetzel, Gloria Mae Hipps 1941- *WhoE 93*
Wetzel, Harry 1920- *St&PR 93*
Wetzel, Heinz 1935- *WhoAm 92*
Wetzel, James (Richard) 1959- *ConAu 139*
Wetzel, Janice Wood 1931- *WhoE 93*
Wetzel, Justus Hermann 1879-1973 *Baker 92*
Wetzel, Karen J. 1953- *WhoAmW 93*
Wetzel, Karl D. 1948- *St&PR 93*
Wetzel, Klaus Gunter 1932- *WhoScE 91-3*
Wetzel, Robert A. 1937- *St&PR 93*
Wetzel, Robert E. 1937- *St&PR 93*
Wetzel, Robert George 1936- *WhoAm 92*
Wetzel, Roland Herman 1923- *WhoE 93*
Wetzel, Thomas Kelly *Law&B 92*
Wetzler, Hermann (Hans) 1870-1943 *Baker 92*
Wetzler, James Warren 1947- *WhoAm 92*
Wetzler, Monte Edwin 1936- *WhoAm 92*
Weverka, Robert 1926- *ScF&FL 92*
Wevers, Jan D.A. 1945- *WhoScE 91-3*
Wevers, John William 1919- *WhoAm 92*
Weweler, August 1868-1952 *Baker 92*
Wewer, Mildred Elizabeth 1927- *WhoWrEP 92*
Wewer, William Paul 1947- *WhoE 93, WhoWor 93*
Wewerka, Frank W. *Law&B 92*
Wewers, Randy W. *WhoIns 93*
Wex, Bernard 1922-1990 *BioIn 17*
Wexelbaum, Michael 1946- *WhoE 93*
Wexelman, Ronald 1934- *St&PR 93*
Wexler, Anne 1930- *WhoAm 92*
Wexler, David Mark 1938- *WhoE 93*
Wexler, Denis 1931- *WhoScE 91-2*
Wexler, Gene L. *Law&B 92*
Wexler, Ginia Davis 1923- *WhoAm 92*
Wexler, Haskell *BioIn 17*
Wexler, Haskell 1922- *WhoAm 92*
Wexler, Haskell 1926- *MiSFD 9*
Wexler, Herbert I. 1916- *WhoAm 92, WhoWor 93*
Wexler, Howard *MiSFD 9*
Wexler, Howard B. 1951- *WhoIns 93*
Wexler, Jacqueline Grennan 1926- *WhoAm 92, WhoAmW 93*
Wexler, Jerrold d1992 *NewYTBS 92*
Wexler, Jerrold 1924- *WhoAm 92*
Wexler, Jerry 1918- *SoulM*
Wexler, Ken 1954- *St&PR 93*
Wexler, Leonard D. 1924- *WhoE 93*
Wexler, Michael 1944- *WhoE 93*
Wexler, Nancy S. *BioIn 17*
Wexler, Nancy S. 1945- *News 92 [port], -92-3 [port]*
Wexler, Norman 1926- *WhoWrEP 92*
Wexler, Peter John 1936- *WhoAm 92*
Wexler, Philip 1950- *WhoWrEP 92*
Wexler, Phillip M. 1938- *St&PR 93*
Wexler, Robert E. *Law&B 92*
Wexler, Sam O. 1935- *St&PR 93*
Wexler, Tanya *BioIn 17*
Wexner, Leslie H. *BioIn 17*
Wexner, Leslie H. 1937- *St&PR 93*
Wexner, Leslie Herbert 1937- *WhoAm 92*
Wexner, Sondra *Law&B 92*
Wexton, Jane L. *Law&B 92*
Wey, Brenda L. *BioIn 17*
Wey, Ronald R. 1942- *St&PR 93*
Weyand, Alexander Mathias 1892-1982 *BiDAMSp 1989*
Weyand, Frederick Carlton 1916- *CmdGen 1991 [port], St&PR 93, WhoAm 92*
Weybret, Frederick Eugene 1923- *St&PR 93*
Weybret, Martin 1951- *St&PR 93*
Wey Cooke, Sharon Kay 1954- *WhoAmW 93*
Weydert, Marco Marie Pierre 1954- *WhoWor 93*
Weyel, Volker Alfred 1944- *WhoWor 93*
Weyenberg, Donald Richard 1930- *St&PR 93, WhoAm 92*
Weyer, H. *WhoScE 91-3*
Weyer, Heinrich B. 1938- *WhoScE 91-3*
Weyer, Heinz Josef *WhoWor 93*
Weyer, Maurice Constantin- 1881-1964 *BioIn 17*
Weyerer, Siegfried Bernhard 1947- *WhoWor 93*
Weyerhaeuser, George H. 1926- *St&PR 93*
Weyerhaeuser, George Hunt 1926- *WhoAm 92*
Weyers, Helmut Ernst 1932- *WhoUN 92*
Weyforth, Mimi 1944- *WhoAm 92*
Weygand, Maxime 1867-1965 *BioIn 17, DcTwHis, HarEnMi*
Weygandt, John Arkell *Law&B 92*
Weyher, Harry Frederick 1921- *WhoAm 92*
Weyher, Harry Frederick, III 1956- *WhoAm 92*
Weyl, Martin 1940- *WhoWor 93*
Weylandt, Elizabeth Piland *Law&B 92*
Weyler, Walter E. 1939- *St&PR 93*
Weyler, Walter Eugen 1939- *WhoAm 92*
Weyler y Nicolau, Valeriano 1838-1930 *HarEnMi*
Weymann, Albert Conrad, III 1943- *St&PR 93*
Weymar, F. Helmut 1936- *WhoAm 92*
Weymarn, Pavel 1857-1905 *Baker 92*
Weymouth, Viscount *ScF&FL 92*
Weymouth, Lucy C. *Law&B 92*
Weymouth, Marion Z. 1912- *St&PR 93*
Weyn, Suzanne *BioIn 17*
Weyn, Suzanne 1955- *ScF&FL 92*
Weyr, Thomas Hector 1927- *WhoE 93*
Weyrauch, August Heinrich von 1788- *Baker 92*
Weyrauch, Dennis R. *St&PR 93*
Weyrauch, Paul Turney 1941- *WhoAm 92*
Weyrauch, Walter Otto 1919- *WhoAm 92*
Weyrich, Becky Lee *ScF&FL 92*
Weyrich, Paul *BioIn 17*
Weyrich, Paul Michael 1942- *WhoAm 92, WhoWor 93*
Weyrich, Wolf 1941- *WhoScE 91-3*
Weyse, Christoph 1774-1842 *OxDcOp*
Weyse, Christoph Ernst Friedrich 1774-1842 *Baker 92*
Weyssenhoff, Jozef 1860-1932 *PolBiDi*
Wezel, Johann Karl 1747-1819 *BioIn 17*
Wezyk, Stanislaw Henryk 1934- *WhoScE 91-4*
Whale, Arthur Richard 1923- *WhoAm 92*
Whale, James 1896-1957 *MiSFD 9N*
Whalen, Brian B. 1939- *St&PR 93, WhoWor 93*
Whalen, Carol Kupers *WhoAm 92*
Whalen, Charles William, Jr. 1920- *WhoAm 92*
Whalen, David G. 1957- *St&PR 93*
Whalen, Edward E. *Law&B 92*

Whalen, Edward John 1948- *St&PR 93*
Whalen, Edward L. 1936- *ConAu 139*
Whalen, Henry Francis, Jr. 1935- *St&PR 93*
Whalen, James F. 1931- *St&PR 93*
Whalen, James Joseph 1927- *WhoAm 92*
Whalen, James Lawrence 1956- *St&PR 93*
Whalen, Jerome Demaris 1943- *WhoAm 92*
Whalen, Jerome J. 1942- *St&PR 93*
Whalen, John A. 1947- *St&PR 93*
Whalen, John D. 1938- *St&PR 93*
Whalen, John Michael 1945- *WhoE 93*
Whalen, John Sydney 1934- *WhoAm 92*
Whalen, Joseph Philip 1933- *WhoAm 92*
Whalen, Lawrence J. 1944- *CngDr 91*
Whalen, Lucille 1925- *WhoAm 92, WhoAmW 93*
Whalen, Margaret L. 1944- *WhoWor 93*
Whalen, Martin *Law&B 92*
Whalen, Mary Kathryn 1954- *WhoAmW 93*
Whalen, Maureen Therese *Law&B 92*
Whalen, Patricia Therese 1955- *WhoAmW 93*
Whalen, Patrick 1944- *ScF&FL 92*
Whalen, Philip 1923- *ConAu 39NR*
Whalen, Philip Glenn 1923- *WhoAm 92, WhoWrEP 92*
Whalen, Richard James 1935- *WhoAm 92, WhoWrEP 92*
Whalen, Terence T. *Law&B 92*
Whalen, Thomas Douglas 1948- *WhoWrEP 92*
Whalen, Thomas J. 1944- *St&PR 93*
Whalen, Thomas M., III 1934- *WhoE 93*
Whalen, Timothy John 1960- *WhoE 93*
Whaley, Barton *ScF&FL 92*
Whaley, Betti S. d1990 *BioIn 17*
Whaley, Charles Henry, IV 1958- *WhoE 93*
Whaley, Charlotte T. 1925- *WhoWrEP 92*
Whaley, Debra T. 1954- *WhoE 93*
Whaley, Frank *BioIn 17*
Whaley, J. David 1946- *WhoUN 92*
Whaley, James Moore 1928- *WhoSSW 93*
Whaley, Janet 1955- *WhoAmW 93*
Whaley, John A. *Law&B 92*
Whaley, John Alexander 1940- *St&PR 93, WhoAm 92*
Whaley, Keith *WhoScE 91-1*
Whaley, Patricia Mengler *Law&B 92*
Whaley, Paul Arthur 1922- *St&PR 93*
Whaley, Robert D. 1942- *St&PR 93*
Whaley, Ronald L. *St&PR 93*
Whaley, Ross Samuel 1937- *WhoE 93*
Whaley, Steve M. *Law&B 92*
Whaley, Storm Hammond 1916- *WhoAm 92, WhoWor 93*
Whaley, Thomas 1823-1890 *BioIn 17*
Whaley, Thomas Patrick 1923- *WhoWor 93*
Whalley, Edward 1925- *WhoAm 92*
Whalley, George 1915- *BioIn 17*
Whalley, George 1915-1983 *WhoCanL 92*
Whalley, Joyce Irene *BioIn 17*
Whalley, Judy L. 1950- *WhoAm 92*
Whalley, Robert *WhoScE 91-1*
Whalley-Kilmer, Joanne *BioIn 17*
Whallon, Evan Arthur, Jr. 1923- *WhoAm 92*
Whallon, William 1928- *WhoAm 92, WhoWrEP 92*
Wham, David Buffington 1937- *WhoWrEP 92*
Wham, Dorothy Stonecipher 1925- *WhoAmW 93*
Wham, George Sims 1920- *WhoAm 92*
Wham, Tom *ScF&FL 92*
Wham, William Neil 1934- *WhoAm 92*
Whang, Kyu-Young 1951- *WhoWor 93*
Whang, Sung H. 1936- *WhoWor 93*
Whang, Yun Chow 1931- *WhoAm 92*
Whannou, Georges Abiodun 1947- *WhoUN 92*
Whare, Wanda S. *Law&B 92*
Wharff, G. Edward 1940- *St&PR 93*
Wharity, Barry 1946- *St&PR 93*
Wharmby, Margot *BioIn 17*
Wharmby, Tony *MiSFD 9*
Wharram, Paul F. *St&PR 93*
Wharton, Annabel Jane 1944- *WhoAmW 93*
Wharton, Arthur M. *Law&B 92*
Wharton, Beverly Ann 1953- *St&PR 93, WhoAm 92*
Wharton, Charles Benjamin 1926- *WhoAm 92*
Wharton, Charles Ellis 1943- *WhoWor 93*
Wharton, Cliffton Reginald 1926- *EncAACR*
Wharton, Clifton R. *BioIn 17*
Wharton, Clifton R. 1899-1990 *BioIn 17*
Wharton, Clifton R., Jr. 1926- *St&PR 93, WhoIns 93*
Wharton, Clifton Reginald, Jr. 1926- *WhoAm 92, WhoE 93, WhoWrEP 92*
Wharton, David Carrie 1930- *WhoAm 92*
Wharton, Edith 1862-1937 *AmWomWr 92, BioIn 17, GayN, MagSAmL [port], WorLitC [port]*
Wharton, Edith Newbold Jones 1862-1937 *AmWomPl*
Wharton, Garry L. *Law&B 92*
Wharton, Garry Lee 1936- *St&PR 93*
Wharton, Gary Charles 1940- *St&PR 93*
Wharton, Keith 1937- *WhoWor 93*
Wharton, Lennard 1933- *WhoAm 92*
Wharton, Patricia Ann *Law&B 92*
Wharton, Ralph Nathaniel 1932- *WhoE 93, WhoWor 93*
Wharton, Richard Gloor 1932- *St&PR 93*
Wharton, Robert Michael 1943- *WhoE 93*
Wharton, Stuart T. 1943- *WhoScE 91-1*
Wharton, Thomas Heard, Jr. 1930- *WhoAm 92*
Wharton, Thomas William 1943- *St&PR 93*
Wharton, Tilford Girard 1904- *WhoAm 92*
Wharton, William 1926- *ScF&FL 92*
Wharton, William Polk *WhoWor 93*
Whatham, Claude *MiSFD 9*
Whatley, Connie Lynn 1956- *WhoSSW 93*
Whatley, F.R. *WhoScE 91-1*
Whatley, James L. 1946- *St&PR 93*
Whatley, James R. 1926- *St&PR 93*
Whatley, James Wallace 1945- *WhoWrEP 92*
Whatley, Randall Paul 1958- *WhoSSW 93*
Whatley, Robert Southcott 1951- *St&PR 93*
Whatley, Robin Charles *WhoScE 91-1*
Whatmore, D.E. *ScF&FL 92*
Whatmore, George Bernard 1917- *WhoWor 93*
Whatmough, Helen Darlene 1943- *St&PR 93*
Whatmough, J. Jeremy T. 1934- *WhoAm 92*
Whatmough, Jeremy T. 1934- *St&PR 93*
Whayland, William Matthew, III 1957- *WhoE 93*
Whealdon, Everett Whittier 1910- *WhoWrEP 92*
Whealey, Lois Deimel 1932- *WhoAmW 93*
Whealon, John Francis 1921-1991 *BioIn 17*
Whealon, Robert F. 1934- *WhoIns 93*
Whealy, John Fisher 1932- *St&PR 93*
Whear, Paul William 1925- *Baker 92*
Wheary, Eugene C. 1911- *St&PR 93*
Wheat, Alan 1951- *BioIn 17, CngDr 91*
Wheat, Alan Dupree 1951- *WhoAm 92*
Wheat, Francis Millspaugh 1921- *WhoAm 92*
Wheat, James L. 1935- *St&PR 93*
Wheat, Jim *MiSFD 9*
Wheat, Joe Ben 1916- *WhoAm 92*
Wheat, Joe Franklin 1939- *WhoSSW 93*
Wheat, Josiah 1928- *WhoAm 92*
Wheat, Ken *MiSFD 9*
Wheat, Marti Lyn 1956- *WhoWrEP 92*
Wheat, Myron William, Jr. 1924- *WhoSSW 93*
Wheat, Willis J. *St&PR 93*
Wheat, Willis James 1926- *WhoAm 92*
Wheatcroft, John 1925- *BioIn 17*
Wheatcroft, John Stewart 1925- *WhoWrEP 92*
Wheater, Ashley *WhoAm 92*
Wheater, Roger J. 1933- *WhoScE 91-1*
Wheatland, Richard, II 1923- *WhoAm 92*
Wheatley, Barbara Ann 1951- *WhoWor 93*
Wheatley, Bonnie Daniels 1951- *WhoAmW 93*
Wheatley, Charles Nelson, Jr. *Law&B 92*
Wheatley, David *MiSFD 9*
Wheatley, David John *WhoScE 91-1*
Wheatley, Debra Beth 1952- *WhoAmW 93*
Wheatley, Dennis 1897-1977 *BioIn 17, ScF&FL 92*
Wheatley, Edward Warren 1936- *WhoSSW 93*
Wheatley, Gary Francis 1937- *WhoE 93*
Wheatley, George Milholland, Jr. 1937- *St&PR 93*
Wheatley, Hill A. *St&PR 93*
Wheatley, James Edward 1949- *St&PR 93*
Wheatley, John 1869-1930 *BioIn 17*
Wheatley, John E. 1944- *WhoScE 91-1*
Wheatley, Kenneth 1924- *St&PR 93*
Wheatley, Melvin Ernest, Jr. 1915- *WhoAm 92*
Wheatley, Nadia 1949- *DcChlFi*
Wheatley, Phillis 1753-1784 *BioIn 17, WorLitC [port]*
Wheatley, Robert Carroll 1949- *WhoSSW 93*
Wheatley, Robert Ray, III 1934- *WhoSSW 93*
Wheatley, Willard 1915- *DcCPCAm*
Wheatley, William Ogden, Jr. 1944- *WhoAm 92*
Wheatley, William S., Jr. 1939- *St&PR 93*
Wheatly, Ralph S. *Law&B 92*
Wheaton, Bruce R. 1944- *WhoWrEP 92*
Wheaton, Carla Ann 1960- *WhoAmW 93*
Wheaton, David Joe 1940- *WhoAm 92*
Wheaton, Frank H., Jr. 1913- *St&PR 93*
Wheaton, Henry 1785-1848 *OxCSupC*
Wheaton, Scott R. 1929- *St&PR 93*
Wheaton, Wil *BioIn 17*
Wheaton, Wil 1972?- *ConTFT 10*
Wheatstraw, Peetie 1902-1941 *BioIn 17*
Wheble, Jane Elizabeth 1955- *WhoWor 93*
Wheddon, Christopher 1942- *WhoScE 91-1*
Whedon, George Donald 1915- *WhoAm 92*
Whedon, John Ogden d1991 *BioIn 17*
Whedon, Margaret Brunssen *WhoAm 92*
Whedon, Ralph Gibbs 1949- *WhoAm 92*
Wheelan, Susan Alberta 1947- *WhoAmW 93*
Wheeler, Albert Harold 1915- *AfrAmBi*
Wheeler, Albert Lee, III 1954- *WhoSSW 93*
Wheeler, Albin Gray *WhoAm 92*
Wheeler, Andrew Carpenter 1835-1903 *JrnUS*
Wheeler, Anne 1946- *MiSFD 9*
Wheeler, Antony R. 1947- *WhoScE 91-1*
Wheeler, B.E.J. *BioIn 17*
Wheeler, Ben 1854-1884 *BioIn 17*
Wheeler, Bert 1895-1968 & Woolsey, Robert 1889-1938 *QDrFCA 92 [port]*
Wheeler, Bob *BioIn 17*
Wheeler, Bob 1942- *St&PR 93*
Wheeler, Burton 1927- *WhoAm 92*
Wheeler, Burton K. 1882-1975 *BioIn 17, PolPar*
Wheeler, C.C. *WhoScE 91-1*
Wheeler, C. Herbert 1915- *WhoAm 92*
Wheeler, Camille Baudot 1941- *WhoE 93*
Wheeler, Carole Elaine Popuch 1931- *WhoAmW 93*
Wheeler, Carolyn Dew 1946- *WhoAmW 93*
Wheeler, Caron *BioIn 17, SoulM*
Wheeler, Cathy Jo 1954- *WhoAmW 93*
Wheeler, Charles Bertan 1926- *WhoAm 92*
Wheeler, Clarence Joseph, Jr. 1917- *WhoSSW 93, WhoWor 93*
Wheeler, Clayton Eugene, Jr. 1917- *WhoAm 92*
Wheeler, Clyde T. 1942- *St&PR 93*
Wheeler, Courtney Bryan *Law&B 92*
Wheeler, Daniel *BioIn 17*
Wheeler, Daniel Scott 1947- *WhoAm 92, WhoWrEP 92*
Wheeler, David *ScF&FL 92*
Wheeler, David E. *Law&B 92*
Wheeler, David John *WhoScE 91-1*
Wheeler, David Laurie 1934- *WhoAm 92*
Wheeler, David LeRoy 1942- *WhoSSW 93*
Wheeler, David P. 1958- *St&PR 93*
Wheeler, Dennis Earl 1942- *St&PR 93*
Wheeler, Don D. 1932- *St&PR 93*
Wheeler, Don E. *Law&B 92*
Wheeler, Donald Alsop 1931- *WhoE 93*
Wheeler, Donald O. 1938- *St&PR 93*
Wheeler, Donald Owen 1938- *WhoAm 92*
Wheeler, Douglas Michael 1960- *WhoE 93*
Wheeler, Douglas Paul 1942- *WhoAm 92*
Wheeler, Duane E. 1932- *St&PR 93*
Wheeler, Dwight Clark, II 1943- *St&PR 93*
Wheeler, Earl Milton 1939- *WhoSSW 93*
Wheeler, Earl W. 1927- *St&PR 93*
Wheeler, Earle Gilmore 1908-1975 *CmdGen 1991 [port]*
Wheeler, Edward Kendall 1913- *WhoAm 92*
Wheeler, Edward Norwood 1927- *WhoSSW 93*
Wheeler, Edward Stubbs 1927- *WhoE 93*
Wheeler, Ernest Jay 1939- *WhoAm 92*
Wheeler, Gene 1941- *St&PR 93*
Wheeler, George Charles 1923- *WhoE 93*
Wheeler, George E. 1914-1990 *BioIn 17*
Wheeler, George William 1924- *WhoAm 92*
Wheeler, Grant Walton 1941- *St&PR 93*
Wheeler, Harold Alden 1903- *WhoAm 92, WhoWor 93*
Wheeler, Harold Austin, Sr. 1925- *WhoSSW 93*
Wheeler, Harriet Martha 1858- *AmWomPl*
Wheeler, Harry d1925 *BioIn 17*
Wheeler, Harry B. 1937- *St&PR 93*
Wheeler, Henry Clark 1916- *St&PR 93, WhoAm 92*
Wheeler, Hewitt Brownell 1929- *WhoAm 92*
Wheeler, Isabel Crichlow 1929- *WhoAmW 93*
Wheeler, J. Craig 1943- *ScF&FL 92*
Wheeler, Jack Cox 1939- *WhoAm 92*
Wheeler, James Orton 1938- *WhoSSW 93*
Wheeler, Jeanette Norris 1918- *WhoAmW 93*
Wheeler, Jeffrey Allan 1944- *WhoE 93*
Wheeler, Jerry Wayne 1959- *WhoSSW 93*
Wheeler, Joe B. 1941- *WhoSSW 93*
Wheeler, Joe Frank 1955- *WhoSSW 93*
Wheeler, John Archibald 1911- *BioIn 17, WhoAm 92*
Wheeler, John Craig 1943- *WhoAm 92*
Wheeler, John Harvey 1918- *WhoAm 92*
Wheeler, John James 1942- *St&PR 93*
Wheeler, John M. 1956- *St&PR 93*
Wheeler, John Oliver 1924- *WhoAm 92*
Wheeler, John R. *Law&B 92*
Wheeler, John W. 1847-1912 *EncAACR*
Wheeler, John W. 1916-1991 *BioIn 17*
Wheeler, John Watson 1938- *WhoAm 92, WhoSSW 93*
Wheeler, Joseph 1836-1906 *BioIn 17, HarEnMi*
Wheeler, Joseph Coolidge 1926- *WhoUN 92*
Wheeler, Joyce W. 1951- *St&PR 93*
Wheeler, Joyce Wethington *Law&B 92*
Wheeler, Katherine Wells 1940- *WhoAmW 93, WhoE 93, WhoWor 93*
Wheeler, Keith Allen 1950- *St&PR 93*
Wheeler, Kenneth T., Jr. 1940- *WhoSSW 93*
Wheeler, Kenneth William 1929- *WhoAm 92, WhoWor 93*
Wheeler, Ladd 1937- *WhoAm 92*
Wheeler, Larry W. 1946- *St&PR 93*
Wheeler, Leonard 1901- *WhoAm 92*
Wheeler, Lisa Jill *Law&B 92*
Wheeler, Louis O. 1917- *St&PR 93*
Wheeler, Lulu White 1883-1962 *BioIn 17*
Wheeler, Lyle *BioIn 17*
Wheeler, M. Catherine 1942- *WhoAmW 93*
Wheeler, Malcolm Edward 1944- *WhoAm 92*
Wheeler, Margaret Roach- 1942- *BioIn 17*
Wheeler, Marilyn Garnsey 1943- *WhoAmW 93, WhoE 93*
Wheeler, Marshall Ralph 1917- *WhoAm 92*
Wheeler, Martin Bruce 1955- *WhoSSW 93*
Wheeler, Marvin Dwain 1940- *WhoE 93*
Wheeler, Mary Harrison 1938- *WhoE 93*
Wheeler, Michael Burnett 1945- *St&PR 93, WhoAm 92*
Wheeler, Michael Simpson 1942- *WhoAm 92*
Wheeler, Myrna Long 1939- *WhoAmW 93*
Wheeler, Nev *BioIn 17*
Wheeler, Noel S. 1940- *St&PR 93*
Wheeler, Orville Eugene 1932- *WhoAm 92*
Wheeler, Otis Bullard 1921- *WhoAm 92*
Wheeler, Patrick C. *Law&B 92*
Wheeler, Philip D. *Law&B 92*
Wheeler, Porter King 1940- *WhoE 93*
Wheeler, Richard Kenneth 1934- *WhoAm 92*
Wheeler, Richard Warren 1929- *WhoAm 92*
Wheeler, Robert A. 1942- *St&PR 93*
Wheeler, Robert Lee 1944- *WhoSSW 93*
Wheeler, Robert M. *Law&B 92*
Wheeler, Robert Thomas 1955- *WhoSSW 93*
Wheeler, Ron 1954- *ConAu 136*
Wheeler, Ruric E. 1923- *WhoSSW 93*
Wheeler, Sandy *St&PR 93*
Wheeler, Scott *ScF&FL 92*
Wheeler, Sessions Samuel 1911- *WhoAm 92, WhoWor 93*
Wheeler, Susan 1955- *WhoWrEP 92*
Wheeler, Susie Weems 1917- *WhoAmW 93*
Wheeler, Thomas Beardsley 1936- *WhoAm 92*
Wheeler, Thomas Edgar 1946- *WhoAm 92*
Wheeler, Thomas Francis 1937- *WhoWor 93*
Wheeler, Thomas H(utchin) 1947- *ConAu 40NR*
Wheeler, Thomas Hutchin 1947- *WhoAm 92, WhoWrEP 92*
Wheeler, Tom *ConAu 40NR*
Wheeler, Trent H. 1959- *WhoWrEP 92*
Wheeler, V.J. *WhoScE 91-1*
Wheeler, Warren Gage, Jr. 1921- *WhoAm 92*
Wheeler, Wesley Dreer 1933- *WhoE 93*
Wheeler, Willard L. 1932- *St&PR 93*
Wheeler, William A. 1934- *St&PR 93*
Wheeler, William Bryan, III 1940- *WhoSSW 93*
Wheeler, William Crawford 1914- *WhoSSW 93*
Wheeler, William Scott 1952- *WhoE 93*
Wheeler, William Thornton 1911- *WhoAm 92*

Wheeler, Willis Boly 1938- *WhoSSW 93*
Wheeler, Wilmot Fitch, Jr. 1923- *St&PR 93, WhoAm 92*
Wheeler, Zita 1942- *WhoAmW 93*
Wheeler-Nicholson, Malcolm 1890-1968 *ScF&FL 92*
Wheeler-Voegelin, Erminie 1903-1987 *IntDcAn*
Wheeler-Voegelin, Erminie 1903-1988 *BioIn 17*
Wheeless, Robert Allen 1932- *WhoIns 93*
Wheeless, Virginia Eman 1947- *WhoSSW 93*
Wheeling, Robert Franklin 1923- *WhoSSW 93*
Wheeling, Virginia Marie 1935- *WhoAmW 93*
Wheelington, Jimmy Dale *Law&B 92*
Wheeller, Kenneth Peter *WhoScE 91-1*
Wheelock, Arthur Kingsland, Jr. 1943- *WhoAm 92*
Wheelock, Carolyn Minnette 1923- *WhoAmW 93*
Wheelock, Eleazar 1711-1779 *BioIn 17*
Wheelock, Elizabeth Shivers 1932- *WhoSSW 93*
Wheelock, Jaime *DcCPCAm*
Wheelock, John Brian 1952- *WhoSSW 93*
Wheelock, Keith Ward 1933- *WhoE 93*
Wheelock, Major William, Jr. 1936- *WhoAm 92*
Wheelock, Moira Myrl Brewer *WhoSSW 93*
Wheelock, Morgan Dix, Jr. 1938- *WhoAm 92*
Wheelock, William I., Jr. 1947- *St&PR 93*
Wheelon, Albert Dewell 1929- *WhoAm 92*
Wheelwright, Ann 1920- *St&PR 93*
Wheelwright, Betty 1947- *WhoWrEP 92*
Wheelwright, Carolyn Kelley 1939-1989 *BioIn 17*
Wheelwright, E.L. 1921- *BioIn 17*
Wheelwright, Edward Lawrence 1921- *BioIn 17*
Wheelwright, Steven C. 1943- *WhoAm 92*
Whelahan, Yvette Ann 1943- *WhoSSW 93*
Whelan, Daniel P. 1950- *St&PR 93*
Whelan, Elizabeth Ann Murphy 1943- *WhoAm 92*
Whelan, Elizabeth M. *BioIn 17*
Whelan, Francis C. 1907- *WhoAm 92*
Whelan, Geraldine *ScF&FL 92*
Whelan, James F. d1990 *BioIn 17*
Whelan, James P. 1916- *St&PR 93*
Whelan, James Robert 1933- *WhoAm 92, WhoWor 93*
Whelan, John Kenneth 1941- *WhoWor 93*
Whelan, John Michael 1921- *WhoE 93*
Whelan, John William 1922- *WhoAm 92*
Whelan, Joseph L. 1917- *WhoAm 92*
Whelan, Karen M. L. 1947- *St&PR 93, WhoAmW 93*
Whelan, Martin J. 1943- *St&PR 93*
Whelan, Michael 1950- *ScF&FL 92*
Whelan, Michael D. *Law&B 92*
Whelan, Noel 1940- *WhoWor 93*
Whelan, Richard J. 1931- *WhoAm 92*
Whelan, Richard Vincent, Jr. 1933- *WhoAm 92*
Whelan, Robert Louis 1912- *WhoAm 92*
Whelan, Roger Michael 1936- *WhoE 93*
Whelan, Sidney Smith, Jr. 1929- *WhoAm 92*
Whelan, Susan Marren *Law&B 92*
Whelan, Ward Bernard 1949- *St&PR 93*
Whelan, William Joseph 1924- *WhoAm 92*
Whelan-Harrington, Ellen Ann *Law&B 92*
Whelchel, Betty A. *Law&B 92*
Whelchel, E. John *Law&B 92*
Whelchel, Harry J., Jr. 1945- *St&PR 93*
Whelchel, Lucy Beasley 1942- *WhoAmW 93*
Whelchel, Sandra 1944- *WhoWrEP 92*
Whelchel, Susan F. 1951- *St&PR 93*
Whelden, Frederick Howard, Jr. 1931- *St&PR 93*
Whelden, Mark McGill 1950- *WhoE 93*
Wheldon, Graham Herbert 1935- *St&PR 93, WhoWor 93*
Wheldon, Huw 1916-1986 *BioIn 17*
Whelehan, David D. 1942- *WhoIns 93*
Whelehan, Patricia Elizabeth 1947- *WhoAmW 93*
Whelen, Townsend 1877-1961 *BioIn 17*
Wheless, Nicholas Hobson, Jr. 1916- *WhoAm 92*
Wheless, Sherman Eugene 1946- *WhoSSW 93*
Whellan, Floyd 1937- *St&PR 93*
Whelley, Peter Tindale 1954- *WhoE 93*
Wherrett, Brian Spencer *WhoScE 91-1*
Wherrett, Brian Spencer 1946- *WhoWor 93*
Wherry, Stephen R. 1958- *St&PR 93*
Whethamstede, John d1465 *BioIn 17*
Whetsel, Jack Allen 1920- *St&PR 93*
Whettam, Graham (Dudley) 1927- *Baker 92*
Whetten, John Theodore 1935- *WhoAm 92*
Whetten, Lawrence Lester 1932- *WhoAm 92*
Whetzel, Herbert H. 1941- *St&PR 93*
Whetzel, Joshua Clyde, Jr. 1921- *WhoE 93*
Whichard, Willis Padgett 1940- *WhoAm 92, WhoSSW 93*
Whicher, John Templeman *WhoScE 91-1*
Whicher, Stephen E. 1915-1961 *BioIn 17*
Whidden, Ray Harvey 1913- *WhoAm 92*
Whidden, Roger Graham *Law&B 92*
Whidden, Stanley John 1947- *WhoAm 92*
Whiddon, Carol Price 1947- *WhoAmW 93*
Whiddon, Frederick Palmer 1930- *WhoAm 92, WhoSSW 93*
Whiddon, Thomas Gayle 1916- *WhoSSW 93*
Whiffen, James Douglass 1931- *WhoAm 92*
Whigham, Frank Frederick, Jr. 1946- *WhoSSW 93*
Whigham, Joseph Keith 1949- *WhoSSW 93*
Whigham, Mark Anthony 1959- *WhoEmL 93, WhoWor 93*
Whigham, Mary Ellen Flowers 1963- *WhoSSW 93*
Whigham, William Randall 1932- *WhoSSW 93*
Whilden, Richard Douglas Cassan 1933- *St&PR 93*
Whiles, Lillian Castro 1931- *WhoAmW 93*
Whillock, Carl S. 1926- *St&PR 93*
Whillock, Carl Simpson 1926- *WhoAm 92*
Whimpey, Dennis J. d1991 *BioIn 17*
Whimpey, Dennis John 1938- *WhoAm 92*
Whinery, Michael Albert 1951- *WhoSSW 93*
Whinery, Verna 1886- *AmWomPl*
Whinnery, James Elliott 1946- *WhoAm 92*
Whinnery, John Roy 1916- *WhoAm 92*
Whinston, Arthur Lewis 1925- *WhoAm 92*
Whipkey, Stella Dunaway *AmWomPl*
Whipkey-Louden, Harriet Beulah 1932- *WhoAmW 93*
Whipp, Charley Bell 1952- *WhoSSW 93*
Whipp, Richard Thomas Henry *WhoScE 91-1*
Whipper, Lucille Simmons *AfrAmBi*
Whipple, A.B.C. 1918- *BioIn 17*
Whipple, Addison Beecher Colvin 1918- *BioIn 17*
Whipple, Beverly 1941- *WhoE 93*
Whipple, Brent Hanks 1954- *St&PR 93*
Whipple, Charles Lewis 1914-1991 *BioIn 17*
Whipple, David C. 1945- *St&PR 93*
Whipple, Dean 1938- *WhoAm 92*
Whipple, Fred Lawrence 1906- *BioIn 17, WhoAm 92, WhoE 93*
Whipple, James F. *Law&B 92*
Whipple, Janice U. *WhoIns 93*
Whipple, Jeffrey T. *St&PR 93*
Whipple, John L. 1938- *St&PR 93*
Whipple, Katherine Z.W. d1991 *BioIn 17*
Whipple, Kenneth 1934- *WhoAm 92*
Whipple, Taggart d1992 *NewYTBS 92 [port]*
Whipps, Edward Franklin 1936- *WhoAm 92*
Whisenand, James Dudley 1947- *WhoEmL 93, WhoSSW 93, WhoWor 93*
Whisenant, Bert Roy, Jr. 1950- *WhoSSW 93*
Whisenant, Billy *St&PR 93*
Whisenant, J. Douglas 1946- *St&PR 93*
Whisenant, Palmer L. *Law&B 92*
Whisenant, Richard Francis 1937- *St&PR 93*
Whisenant, Thelma *St&PR 93*
Whisenant, W.B. *St&PR 93*
Whisenhunt, Carol Postal 1959- *WhoSSW 93*
Whisenhunt, Donald Wayne 1938- *WhoAm 92*
Whisenhunt, J. Daniel 1943- *St&PR 93*
Whish, Richard Peter 1953- *WhoWor 93*
Whisher, Bradley Edward 1954- *WhoE 93*
Whisker, Robert H. *Law&B 92*
Whisler, James Steven 1954- *St&PR 93, WhoAm 92*
Whisler, Kirk 1951- *WhoWor 93*
Whisler, Walter William 1934- *WhoAm 92*
Whisman, John Michael *Law&B 92*
Whisnand, R.V. 1944- *St&PR 93*
Whisnand, Roy Van Arsdel 1944- *WhoAm 92*
Whisnant, Jack Page 1924- *WhoAm 92*
Whispel, Barbara A. 1949- *St&PR 93*
Whispers *SoulM*
Whistler, James Abbott McNeill 1834-1903 *GayN*
Whistler, James McNeill 1834-1903 *BioIn 17*
Whistler, Kathryn Anne 1948- *WhoAmW 93*
Whistler, Roy Lester 1912- *WhoAm 92*
Whiston, Richard M. *Law&B 92*
Whiston, Richard Michael 1944- *WhoAm 92*
Whitacre, Diane Louise 1953- *WhoAmW 93*
Whitacre, Edward E. 1941- *St&PR 93*
Whitacre, Edward E., Jr. 1941- *WhoAm 92*
Whitacre, John P. 1943- *St&PR 93*
Whitacre, John V. 1933- *St&PR 93*
Whitaker, Albert Duncan 1932- *WhoAm 92, WhoE 93*
Whitaker, Albert E. d1990 *BioIn 17*
Whitaker, Alexandra *ScF&FL 92*
Whitaker, Asa L., Jr. 1941- *WhoSSW 93*
Whitaker, Audie Dale 1949- *WhoEmL 93, WhoWor 93*
Whitaker, Benny *BioIn 17*
Whitaker, Benton F. 1919- *St&PR 93*
Whitaker, Bob *BioIn 17*
Whitaker, Bruce Ezell 1921- *WhoAm 92, WhoWor 93*
Whitaker, Bruce R. 1944- *St&PR 93*
Whitaker, Clem, Sr. 1899-1961 See Whitaker and Baker *PolPar*
Whitaker, Clem, Jr. 1922- *WhoAm 92*
Whitaker, David *Law&B 92*
Whitaker, David 1930-1980 *ScF&FL 92*
Whitaker, David Taylor *Law&B 92*
Whitaker, Dick Sessions 1965- *WhoSSW 93*
Whitaker, Eileen Monaghan 1911- *WhoAm 92, WhoAmW 93*
Whitaker, Elizabeth Diane 1945- *WhoAmW 93*
Whitaker, Evans Parker 1960- *WhoSSW 93*
Whitaker, Forest *BioIn 17*
Whitaker, Gary Robert *Law&B 92*
Whitaker, Gilbert Riley, Jr. 1931- *WhoAm 92*
Whitaker, Isabella A. *Law&B 92*
Whitaker, Jack *BioIn 17*
Whitaker, Jerome *Law&B 92*
Whitaker, Joel 1942- *WhoE 93*
Whitaker, John Carlton 1953- *St&PR 93*
Whitaker, John King 1933- *WhoAm 92*
Whitaker, John Scott 1948- *WhoE 93*
Whitaker, Josephine W. *AmWomPl*
Whitaker, Laura Rothenberg 1948- *WhoAmW 93*
Whitaker, Leroy *Law&B 92*
Whitaker, Leroy 1929- *WhoWor 93*
Whitaker, Lloyd Tait 1934- *St&PR 93*
Whitaker, Louis Rodman 1957- *WhoAm 92*
Whitaker, Louis Rodman, Jr. 1957- *BiDAMSp 1989*
Whitaker, Marvin A. 1922- *St&PR 93*
Whitaker, Meade 1919- *CngDr 91, WhoAm 92*
Whitaker, Michael G. *Law&B 92*
Whitaker, Philip W. *Law&B 92*
Whitaker, Richard Carlton 1949- *WhoSSW 93*
Whitaker, Robert C. 1941- *WhoIns 93*
Whitaker, Roger Anthony *WhoScE 91-1*
Whitaker, Roger Page 1952- *St&PR 93*
Whitaker, Ruth Margaret 1935- *WhoWrEP 92*
Whitaker, Ruth Reed 1936- *WhoAmW 93*
Whitaker, Shirley Ann 1955- *WhoAmW 93*
Whitaker, Susanne Kanis 1947- *WhoAm 92*
Whitaker, Thomas Alexander 1944- *WhoSSW 93*
Whitaker, Thomas Russell 1925- *WhoAm 92*
Whitaker, Wilma Neuman 1937- *WhoAmW 93*
Whitaker and Baker *PolPar*
Whitbeck, Elaine Esther *Law&B 92*
Whitbeck, Frank Lynn, Jr. 1916- *St&PR 93*
Whitbeck, Ruth *AmWomPl*
Whitbourn, John *ScF&FL 92*
Whitbread, Thomas Bacon 1931- *WhoAm 92, WhoWrEP 92*
Whitburn, Gerald 1944- *WhoAm 92*
Whitburn, Merrill Duane 1938- *WhoAm 92*
Whitby, Owen *WhoIns 93*
Whitby, Owen 1942- *WhoE 93*
Whitby, Sharon *ScF&FL 92*
Whitby, Von H. 1948- *St&PR 93*
Whitby-Strevens, Colin 1944- *WhoWor 93*
Whitchurch, Charles R. 1946- *St&PR 93*
Whitcomb, Benjamin Bradford, Jr. 1908- *WhoAm 92*
Whitcomb, James Stuart 1957- *WhoE 93*
Whitcomb, Marion Inez 1927- *WhoAmW 93*
Whitcomb, Mary Burg *ScF&FL 92*
Whitcomb, Michael L. *Law&B 92*
Whitcomb, Mildred *AmWomPl*
Whitcomb, Richard Travis 1921- *WhoAm 92*
Whitcomb, Steven M. 1951- *St&PR 93*
Whitcomb, W. Phillip *Law&B 92*
Whitcomb, Willard Hall 1915- *WhoSSW 93*
Whitcombe, David Niles 1927- *St&PR 93*
Whitcombe, Rick T. *ScF&FL 92*
Whitcraft, Edward C. R. 1914- *WhoAm 92*
Whitcraft, James Richard, Jr. 1947- *WhoWor 93*
White, A. Burton 1927- *WhoE 93*
White, A. Joe 1933- *St&PR 93*
White, Adrian Michael Stephen 1940- *WhoAm 92, WhoE 93*
White, Alan 1924- *ScF&FL 92*
White, Alan 1949- See Yes *ConMus 8*
White, Alan Frederick 1937- *WhoWor 93*
White, Alan Grant Davidson *BioIn 17*
White, Alan Grant Davidson 1938- *WhoWor 93*
White, Alan Jeffrey 1961- *WhoSSW 93*
White, Alan R(ichard) 1922-1992 *ConAu 137*
White, Albert J. *Law&B 92*
White, Albert Joseph 1933- *St&PR 93*
White, Alberta LaVerne 1913- *WhoAmW 93, WhoWor 93*
White, Alfred Earl, Jr. *Law&B 92*
White, Alfred K. *Law&B 92*
White, Alice Virginia 1946- *WhoAmW 93, WhoSSW 93*
White, Alicen *ScF&FL 92*
White, Allen Howard 1948- *WhoSSW 93*
White, Alvin Swauger 1918- *WhoAm 92*
White, Amy Hutchinson 1960- *WhoAmW 93*
White, Andrea J. *Law&B 92*
White, Andrew 1942- *Baker 92*
White, Andrew Stewart 1941- *St&PR 93, WhoIns 93*
White, Ann 1916- *WhoWrEP 92*
White, Ann Elizabeth *Law&B 92*
White, Ann Wells 1927- *WhoSSW 93*
White, Anthony G. 1946- *ScF&FL 92*
White, Anthony Sydney *WhoScE 91-1*
White, Anthony Walker 1936- *WhoAm 92*
White, Ared 1881-1941 *ScF&FL 92*
White, Arthur Clinton 1925- *WhoAm 92*
White, Arthur Joe 1933- *WhoIns 93*
White, Augustus A. 1936- *AfrAmBi [port]*
White, Augustus Aaron, III 1936- *WhoAm 92*
White, B. Ward *Law&B 92*
White, Bailey *BioIn 17*
White, Barbara Buckman 1943- *WhoWrEP 92*
White, Barbara Ehrlich 1936- *ConAu 136, WhoE 93*
White, Barbara Glass *Law&B 92*
White, Barney D. 1951- *St&PR 93*
White, Barry *BioIn 17*
White, Barry 1944- *SoulM*
White, Barry Bennett 1943- *WhoAm 92*
White, Barry David 1943- *St&PR 93*
White, Bernard H. 1947- *St&PR 93*
White, Bernard Henry 1947- *WhoSSW 93*
White, Bernard J. 1944- *St&PR 93*
White, Bertram Milton 1923- *WhoE 93*
White, Betty *BioIn 17*
White, Betty 1922- *WhoAm 92, WhoAmW 93*
White, Betty-Lynn *Law&B 92*
White, Betty Maynard 1922- *WhoSSW 93*
White, Beverly Ingram 1943- *WhoAmW 93*
White, Beverly Jane *Law&B 92*
White, Bill *BioIn 17*
White, Bob *BioIn 17*
White, Bonnie Havana 1926- *WhoE 93*
White, Bonnie Yvonne 1940- *WhoAmW 93, WhoWor 93*
White, Brandon C. 1933- *St&PR 93*
White, Bren Douglas 1957- *WhoE 93*
White, Brenda Hamilton 1940- *WhoAmW 93*
White, Brian Arthur *WhoScE 91-1*
White, Brian Douglas 1956- *WhoSSW 93*
White, Britton, Jr. *Law&B 92*
White, Brooks *Law&B 92*
White, Bruce David 1951- *WhoSSW 93*
White, Bruce Deane 1930- *WhoE 93*
White, Bruce Emerson, Jr. 1961- *WhoSSW 93*
White, Bryan S. *Law&B 92*
White, Burton Leonard 1929- *WhoAm 92*
White, Byron R. 1917- *BioIn 17, WhoAm 92, WhoE 93*
White, Byron Raymond 1917- *CngDr 91, OxCSupC [port]*
White, C.R. *WhoScE 91-1*
White, Carl J. 1935- *St&PR 93*

White, Carl Milton 1903-1983 *BioIn 17*
White, Carol Elaine 1953- *WhoAmW 93*
White, Carrie d1991 *BioIn 17*
White, Carter H. 1916- *St&PR 93*
White, Catharine Boswell 1958- *WhoAmW 93*
White, Catherine Friend 1956- *WhoAmW 93, WhoE 93*
White, Cecile Holmes 1955- *WhoSSW 93*
White, Charles Albert, Jr. 1922- *WhoAm 92*
White, Charles F. 1904-1990 *BioIn 17*
White, Charles F. 1941- *St&PR 93*
White, Charles Luken 1950- *WhoSSW 93*
White, Cheryl Denney *Law&B 92*
White, Christine 1905- *WhoAmW 93, WhoE 93, WhoWor 93*
White, Christopher L. 1953- *St&PR 93*
White, Clair Fox 1949- *WhoSSW 93*
White, Claire Nicolas 1925- *BioIn 17, WhoWrEP 92*
White, Clarence 1944-1973 See Byrds, The *ConMus 8*
White, Clarence Cameron 1880-1960 *Baker 92*
White, Clematis *AmWomPl*
White, Clifford Joseph, III 1956- *WhoAm 92*
White, Craig William 1944- *WhoIns 93*
White, Curtis Keith 1951- *WhoWrEP 92*
White, Cynthia 1932- *WhoWrEP 92*
White, Cynthia Elizabeth 1967- *WhoSSW 93*
White, D. Patton 1962- *WhoSSW 93*
White, Dale Andrew 1958- *WhoWrEP 92*
White, Daniel J. *Law&B 92*
White, Darryl C. *Law&B 92*
White, Daryl Joseph 1947- *St&PR 93, WhoAm 92*
White, David d1990 *BioIn 17*
White, David Alan, Jr. 1942- *St&PR 93*
White, David Ashley *WhoSSW 93*
White, David Calvin 1922- *WhoAm 92*
White, David Cleaveland 1929- *WhoSSW 93*
White, David G. 1947- *St&PR 93*
White, David H. *Law&B 92*
White, David Hywel 1931- *WhoAm 92*
White, David L. *Law&B 92*
White, David L. 1953- *St&PR 93*
White, Dean Tom 1941- *St&PR 93*
White, Delbert Lewis 1941- *WhoSSW 93*
White, Denise L. 1963- *WhoAmW 93*
White, Dennis Allen 1946- *WhoE 93*
White, Dermott J. *Law&B 92*
White, Donald H(oward) 1921- *Baker 92*
White, Donald Hamilton, Jr. 1942- *WhoE 93*
White, Donald Harvey 1931- *WhoAm 92*
White, Donald J. 1938- *WhoIns 93*
White, Donald Keys 1924- *WhoAm 92*
White, Donald Royce Joseph 1926- *St&PR 93*
White, Doris Anne 1924- *WhoAm 92, WhoAmW 93*
White, Dorothy 1923-1990 *BioIn 17*
White, Dorset 1929- *St&PR 93*
White, Douglas James, Jr. 1934- *WhoAm 92*
White, Duane Earl 1955- *St&PR 93*
White, Dwayne K. 1948- *St&PR 93*
White, E.B. 1899-1985 *BioIn 17*
White, E(lwyn) B(rooks) 1899-1985 *ConAu 37NR, DcAmChF 1960, MajAI [port]*
White, Edgar B. 1947- *BlkAuII 92*
White, Edith 1855-1946 *BioIn 17*
White, Edith Mae 1929- *WhoAmW 93*
White, Edmund 1940- *BioIn 17, ConGAN, ScF&FL 92*
White, Edmund Valentine 1940- *WhoAm 92, WhoWrEP 92*
White, Edward A. 1928- *St&PR 93*
White, Edward A. 1935- *St&PR 93*
White, Edward C. 1934- *WhoUN 92*
White, Edward Douglass 1845-1921 *OxCSupC [port]*
White, Eliot Carter 1947- *St&PR 93*
White, Elizabeth 1933- *WhoSSW 93*
White, Elizabeth 1964- *WhoAmW 93*
White, Elizabeth D. 1921- *St&PR 93*
White, Elizabeth E. 1966- *St&PR 93*
White, Ellen Emerson *ScF&FL 92*
White, Elwyn Brooks 1899-1985 *BioIn 17, JrnUS*
White, Eric I. *St&PR 93*
White, Eric Joseph James 1965- *WhoE 93*
White, Eric Walter 1905-1985 *Baker 92*
White, Erskine N., Jr. 1924- *St&PR 93*
White, Erskine Norman, Jr. 1924- *WhoAm 92*
White, Ethel M. 1955- *WhoScE 91-1*
White, Eugene James 1928- *WhoAm 92*
White, Eugene Vaden 1924- *WhoSSW 93*
White, Everett Edison, III 1946- *WhoSSW 93*
White, Everett Lowell 1943- *St&PR 93*
White, F. Clifton 1918- *PolPar*
White, F.M. 1859- *ScF&FL 92*
White, F. William 1938- *St&PR 93*
White, Felix Harold 1884-1945 *Baker 92*
White, Floyd H. 1932- *St&PR 93, WhoIns 93*
White, Francis 1892-1961 *EncABHB 8*
White, Francis Edward 1915- *WhoAm 92*
White, Francis M. 1927- *St&PR 93, WhoAm 92*
White, Francis Vincent 1934- *St&PR 93*
White, Frank, Jr. 1950- *BiDAMSp 1989*
White, Frank, III 1955- *WhoE 93*
White, Fred Rollin, Jr. 1913- *WhoAm 92*
White, Frederick Andrew 1918- *WhoAm 92*
White, Frederick Rollin, Jr. 1913- *St&PR 93*
White, Gage *BioIn 17*
White, Gail *AmWomPl*
White, Garland S. 1928- *St&PR 93*
White, Gary L. 1932- *St&PR 93*
White, Gary M. 1935- *St&PR 93*
White, Gayle Clay 1944- *WhoWor 93*
White, Geneva M. 1958- *WhoAmW 93*
White, George 1872-1953 *BioIn 17, PolPar*
White, George A. 1941- *WhoIns 93*
White, George C. 1919- *WhoIns 93*
White, George Cooke 1935- *WhoAm 92*
White, George Edward 1941- *WhoAm 92, WhoE 93, WhoWor 93*
White, George G., Sr. *Law&B 92*
White, George Henry 1852-1918 *BioIn 17*
White, George L. 1947- *St&PR 93*
White, George M. *BioIn 17*
White, George Malcolm 1920- *WhoAm 92, WhoE 93*
White, George Stephen 1936- *St&PR 93*
White, George Stuart 1835-1912 *HarEnMi*
White, George W. 1931- *WhoAm 92*
White, George Wendell, Jr. 1915- *WhoE 93*
White, Gerald A. 1934- *St&PR 93*
White, Gerald Andrew 1934- *WhoAm 92*
White, Gerald Kent *Law&B 92*
White, Gerard 1939- *WhoScE 91-1*
White, Gilbert 1720-1793 *BioIn 17*
White, Gilbert Fowler 1911- *WhoAm 92*
White, Gill 1936- *ScF&FL 92*
White, Glenn d1992 *NewYTBS 92*
White, Glenn 1949-1992 *BioIn 17*
White, Glenn E. 1926- *St&PR 93*
White, Glenn L. 1941- *St&PR 93*
White, Gloria Constance 1958- *WhoAmW 93*
White, Gloria Waters 1934- *WhoAmW 93, WhoWor 93*
White, Gordon Eliot 1933- *WhoAm 92*
White, Gordon Lindsay 1923- *WhoAm 92, WhoWor 93*
White, Greg Thorp 1961- *WhoSSW 93*
White, Gregory S. 1958- *St&PR 93*
White, H. Blair 1927- *WhoAm 92*
White, H. Katherine *Law&B 92*
White, Harold Tredway, III 1947- *WhoE 93*
White, Harriet Louise Bonifay 1940- *WhoAmW 93*
White, Harrison Colyar 1930- *WhoWrEP 92*
White, Harry Bryant 1938- *St&PR 93*
White, Harry E. *St&PR 93*
White, Harry J. *BioIn 17*
White, Harry Robert 1933- *WhoE 93*
White, Harvey Elliott 1902-1988 *BioIn 17*
White, Harvey P. *St&PR 93*
White, Helen Frances Pearson 1925- *WhoAmW 93*
White, Helen Lyng 1930- *WhoAmW 93*
White, Henry Kirke 1785-1806 *BioIn 17*
White, Herbert C. 1919- *St&PR 93*
White, Herbert S. *BioIn 17*
White, Herbert Spencer 1927- *WhoAm 92*
White, Homer 1917- *WhoAm 92*
White, Horace 1834-1916 *JrnUS*
White, Hugh Clayton 1936- *WhoE 93*
White, Hugh Lawson 1773-1840 *PolPar*
White, Hugh Vernon, Jr. 1933- *WhoAm 92*
White, I.D. 1901-1990 *BioIn 17*
White, I.T. 1951- *St&PR 93*
White, Ian Hugh *WhoScE 91-1*
White, Ian Shaw 1952- *WhoWor 93*
White, Irene 1961- *WhoAmW 93*
White, Isaac Davis 1901-1990 *BioIn 17*
White, J. Coleman 1923- *WhoAm 92*
White, J. Spratt 1941- *St&PR 93*
White, J.V. 1925- *St&PR 93, WhoIns 93*
White, Jack E. *WhoSSW 93*
White, Jack H., Jr. *Law&B 92*
White, Jack L. *Law&B 92*
White, Jack M. 1930- *St&PR 93*
White, Jacqueline I. *Law&B 92*
White, Jaleel *BioIn 17*
White, Jaleel 1976- *News 92 [port], -92-3 [port]*
White, Jameela Adams 1954- *WhoE 93*
White, James 1928- *ScF&FL 92*
White, James 1944- *WhoScE 91-3*
White, James A. 1938- *St&PR 93*
White, James Arthur 1933- *WhoWor 93*
White, James B. 1953- *St&PR 93*
White, James Barr 1941- *WhoAm 92*
White, James Boyd 1938- *WhoAm 92, WhoWrEP 92*
White, James David 1942- *St&PR 93, WhoIns 93*
White, James Edward 1918- *WhoAm 92*
White, James F. d1990 *BioIn 17*
White, James George 1929- *WhoAm 92*
White, James Joseph, II *Law&B 92*
White, James M. 1921- *WhoWrEP 92*
White, James M., III *Law&B 92*
White, James Patrick 1931- *WhoAm 92*
White, James Richard 1948- *WhoEmL 93, WhoSSW 93*
White, James Spratt, IV 1941- *WhoAm 92*
White, James Vaughan 1945- *WhoScE 91-1*
White, James Wilson 1941- *WhoAm 92*
White, Jan 1949- *St&PR 93*
White, Jan E. 1947- *WhoSSW 93*
White, Jan Tuttle 1943- *WhoE 93*
White, Jane 1934-1985 *ScF&FL 92*
White, Jane Millican 1943- *WhoSSW 93*
White, Janet L. 1951- *St&PR 93*
White, Janet Murphree 1946- *WhoAmW 93*
White, Janis G. *Law&B 92*
White, Jean Hamburg 1953- *WhoAmW 93*
White, Jean Tillinghast 1934- *WhoAmW 93*
White, Jeanette 1950- *WhoAmW 93*
White, Jeanne *BioIn 17*
White, Jeff V. 1925- *WhoSSW 93*
White, Jerry Allen 1937- *WhoAm 92*
White, Jerry Glen 1955- *WhoSSW 93*
White, Jesse C., Jr. 1934- *AfrAmBi [port]*
White, Jesse Marc *WhoAm 92*
White, Jessie Braham *AmWomPl*
White, Jimm F. 1944- *WhoAm 92*
White, Joan C. *Law&B 92*
White, Joan Ellen 1945- *WhoWrEP 92*
White, Joe Dan 1939- *St&PR 93*
White, Joe Lloyd 1921- *WhoAm 92*
White, John 1802-1845 *PolPar*
White, John 1855-1902 *Baker 92*
White, John 1924- *ScF&FL 92*
White, John Arnold 1933- *WhoAm 92*
White, John Austin, Jr. 1939- *WhoAm 92*
White, John C. 1925- *PolPar*
White, John Campbell 1932- *St&PR 93*
White, John Charles 1939- *WhoAm 92*
White, John David 1928- *WhoE 93*
White, John David 1931- *WhoAm 92*
White, John Francis 1929- *WhoAm 92*
White, John Glenn, Jr. 1949- *WhoSSW 93*
White, John I. d1992 *NewYTBS 92*
White, John Irwin 1902- *WhoWrEP 92*
White, John J. 1909- *St&PR 93*
White, John Joseph, III 1948- *WhoE 93*
White, John K(enneth) 1952- *ConAu 39NR*
White, John M., Jr. 1955- *St&PR 93*
White, John Marshall 1956- *WhoSSW 93*
White, John Michael 1938- *WhoAm 92*
White, John P. 1937- *St&PR 93, WhoAm 92*
White, John (Reeves) 1924-1984 *Baker 92*
White, John Richard 1930- *St&PR 93*
White, John Simon 1910- *WhoAm 92*
White, John W. 1938- *St&PR 93*
White, John Warren 1939- *WhoWrEP 92*
White, John Wesley, Jr. 1933- *WhoAm 92*
White, John William 1937- *WhoWor 93*
White, John William Loud 1923- *St&PR 93*
White, Jolly Hobart 1928- *St&PR 93*
White, Jon Ewbank Manchip 1924- *BioIn 17*
White, Jon Manchip *WhoWrEP 92*
White, Jon Manchip 1924- *ScF&FL 92*
White, Joseph B. *Law&B 92*
White, Joseph Charles 1922- *WhoAm 92*
White, Joseph Mallie, Jr. 1921- *WhoAm 92*
White, Joseph Murray 1928- *St&PR 93*
White, Joseph Reeves, Jr. 1930- *WhoAm 92*
White, Joy Mieko 1951- *WhoEmL 93*
White, Jude *ScF&FL 92*
White, Julian Darryn 1965- *WhoWor 93*
White, June Miller 1938- *WhoSSW 93*
White, Kande 1950- *WhoWor 93*
White, Karen L. *AfrAmBi [port]*
White, Karen Lorraine 1947- *WhoAmW 93*
White, Karyn *BioIn 17, SoulM*
White, Kate *BioIn 17, WhoAm 92, WhoAmW 93*
White, Kate Alice *AmWomPl*
White, Katharine Sergeant Angell 1892-1977 *BioIn 17*
White, Katherine P. *Law&B 92*
White, Katherine Patricia 1948- *WhoEmL 93*
White, Kathy Mila 1955- *WhoAmW 93*
White, Kenneth Thomas 1947- *WhoSSW 93*
White, Kerr Lachlan 1917- *WhoAm 92*
White, Kevin H. 1929- *PolPar*
White, Kevin P. *Law&B 92*
White, King Solomon 1868-1955 *BiDAMSp 1989*
White, Lana Joyce *WhoSSW 93*
White, Larry D. 1945- *St&PR 93*
White, Larry Keith 1948- *WhoSSW 93*
White, Larry L. 1937- *St&PR 93*
White, Laura Demetry *Law&B 92*
White, Lawrence D. *St&PR 93*
White, Lawrence J. 1943- *WhoAm 92, WhoE 93*
White, Lawrence Keith 1948- *WhoE 93*
White, Lee Calvin 1923- *WhoAm 92*
White, Lee Inman, II 1962- *WhoSSW 93*
White, Leland Jennings 1940- *WhoE 93*
White, Lelia Cayne 1921- *WhoAm 92*
White, Leon 1935- *St&PR 93*
White, Leslie 1967- *WhoSSW 93*
White, Leslie A. 1900-1975 *IntDcAn*
White, Letitia Holliday *Law&B 92*
White, Lianne M. *Law&B 92*
White, Libby Kramer 1934- *WhoAmW 93*
White, Linda Marie 1962- *WhoAmW 93*
White, Linda S. 1940- *WhoAmW 93*
White, Linnea Carol *WhoAmW 93*
White, Lorelei Annette 1962- *WhoWrEP 92*
White, Lorna Louise 1944- *WhoAmW 93*
White, Louis K. 1937- *St&PR 93*
White, Louise V. *Law&B 92*
White, Lowell E., Jr. 1928- *WhoAm 92, WhoSSW 93*
White, Lucy *AmWomPl*
White, Lula C. *AmWomPl*
White, Luther Wesley 1923- *WhoAm 92*
White, Lynn Townsend, III 1941- *WhoE 93*
White, Mahlon T. 1961- *St&PR 93*
White, Margaret Bourke- 1904-1971 *BioIn 17*
White, Margita Eklund 1937- *WhoAm 92*
White, Marie Calderone *WhoAmW 93*
White, Marilyn *BlkAmWO*
White, Marilyn Elaine 1944- *WhoAmW 93*
White, Marjorie Mary 1944- *WhoAmW 93*
White, Mark Arlington 1958- *WhoSSW 93*
White, Martha 1954- *WhoWrEP 92*
White, Martin Christopher 1943- *WhoAm 92*
White, Mary Alice 1920- *ScF&FL 92*
White, Mary Ellen *Law&B 92*
White, Mary Jane 1953- *WhoWrEP 92*
White, Mary Jennie 1936- *WhoWrEP 92*
White, Mary Kay 1954- *WhoAmW 93*
White, Mary Louise 1933- *WhoAmW 93, WhoSSW 93*
White, Mary R. *Law&B 92*
White, Mary Ransford 1941- *St&PR 93*
White, Mary Ruth Wathen 1927- *WhoAmW 93, WhoSSW 93*
White, Matthew 1956- *ScF&FL 92*
White, Maude Valerie 1855-1937 *Baker 92*
White, Maurice *SoulM*
White, Maurice J. *Law&B 92*
White, Maxine L.M. *Law&B 92*
White, Melvin R(obert) 1911- *ConAu 40NR*
White, Merit Penniman 1908- *WhoAm 92, WhoE 93*
White, Michael 1931- *Baker 92*
White, Michael B. *Law&B 92*
White, Michael D. 1948- *WhoIns 93*
White, Michael Harlan 1963- *WhoE 93*
White, Michael J. 1956- *St&PR 93*
White, Michael Joseph *Law&B 92*
White, Michael K. 1938- *St&PR 93, WhoIns 93*
White, Michael R. *AfrAmBi [port]*
White, Michael Reed 1951- *WhoAm 92*
White, Michelle Jo 1945- *WhoAmW 93*
White, Molly Murrell 1933- *WhoAmW 93*
White, Morton Gabriel 1917- *WhoAm 92, WhoWrEP 92*
White, Nancy 1916- *WhoE 93*
White, Nancy Ann 1949- *WhoE 93*
White, Nancy B. *Law&B 92*
White, Nancy Elizabeth 1935- *WhoSSW 93*
White, Nelson Henry 1938- *WhoWrEP 92*
White, Nicholas I. 1950- *St&PR 93*
White, Nicholas J. 1945- *WhoSSW 93*
White, Nicholas John *WhoScE 91-1*
White, Nick J. 1945- *WhoAm 92*
White, Norma Brewer 1940- *WhoAmW 93*
White, Norman Arthur 1922- *WhoWor 93*
White, Norman Lee 1955- *WhoSSW 93*
White, Norris 1944- *St&PR 93*
White, Norval Crawford 1926- *WhoAm 92*
White, O.L. *WhoScE 91-2*

Whitelaw, Nancy Eaton 1933- *WhoWrEP 92*
Whitelaw, Seth Brooks *Law&B 92*
Whitelaw, Stella 1941- *ScF&FL 92*
Whiteleather, Larry W. *Law&B 92*
Whiteley, Benjamin R. 1929- *WhoIns 93*
Whiteley, Benjamin Robert 1929- *St&PR 93, WhoAm 92*
Whiteley, Bessie M. *AmWomPl*
Whiteley, Douglas E. 1946- *St&PR 93*
Whiteley, George d1990 *BioIn 17*
Whiteley, George Andrew *Law&B 92*
Whiteley, Helen R. 1922-1990 *BioIn 17*
Whiteley, Henry Ellen 1945- *WhoWrEP 92*
Whiteley, Richard Clayton 1939- *St&PR 93*
Whiteley, Richard Harold 1947- *WhoWor 93*
Whiteley, Sandra Marie 1943- *WhoAm 92, WhoAmW 93*
Whitely, Julia Farrell *AmWomPl*
Whiteman, Bruce 1952- *WhoCanL 92*
Whiteman, Donald Ray 1941- *St&PR 93*
Whiteman, Douglas E. 1961- *WhoAm 92*
Whiteman, Edward Russell 1938- *WhoAm 92*
Whiteman, Gilbert Lee 1931- *WhoE 93*
Whiteman, Horace Clifton 1925- *WhoAm 92*
Whiteman, Jack William 1914- *St&PR 93*
Whiteman, John F. 1948- *St&PR 93*
Whiteman, John Robert *WhoScE 91-1*
Whiteman, Joseph David *Law&B 92*
Whiteman, Joseph David 1933- *St&PR 93, WhoAm 92*
Whiteman, Paul 1890-1967 *Baker 92*
Whiteman, Richard Frank 1925- *WhoAm 92*
Whiteman, Unison *DcCPCAm*
Whiten, Clifton 1939- *WhoCanL 92*
Whiten, Eva *St&PR 93*
Whitenack, Daniel Patrick 1960- *WhoSSW 93*
Whitener, Jean Veronica *WhoE 93*
Whitener, Lawrence Bruce 1952- *WhoWor 93*
Whitener, William Garnett 1951- *WhoAm 92*
White-Norman, Iona May 1954- *WhoAmW 93*
Whitescarver, Charles Kyle, III 1953- *WhoEmL 93, WhoSSW 93*
Whitescarver, William A. 1930- *St&PR 93*
Whitesel, Candice Gail 1954- *WhoE 93*
Whitesell, Dale Edward 1925- *WhoAm 92*
Whitesell, James Edwin 1909- *WhoSSW 93*
Whitesell, John Edwin 1938- *WhoAm 92*
Whitesell, Lillian Louise 1957- *WhoAmW 93*
Whitesell, Lisa Carol 1962- *WhoSSW 93*
Whitesell, Nancy Jane 1953- *WhoAmW 93*
Whitesell, Terry G. 1939- *St&PR 93*
Whitesell, Terry Gene 1939- *WhoAm 92*
Whiteside, Ann Birdsong 1955- *WhoSSW 93*
Whiteside, Carol Gordon 1942- *WhoAm 92*
Whiteside, Daniel Fowler 1931- *WhoAm 92*
Whiteside, David Powers, Jr. 1950- *WhoSSW 93*
Whiteside, Duncan 1935- *WhoE 93*
Whiteside, Joseph J. 1941- *St&PR 93*
Whiteside, Ralph Talbott 1933- *St&PR 93*
Whiteside, Richard Hartman 1926- *St&PR 93*
Whiteside, William J. d1992 *BioIn 17, NewYTBS 92 [port]*
Whitesides, George McClelland 1939- *WhoAm 92*
Whitesides, Jack Wayne 1945- *St&PR 93*
Whitesides, John Lindsey, Jr. 1943- *WhoSSW 93*
Whitesides, William Lee, Sr. 1931- *WhoSSW 93*
Whitesitt, Linda Marie 1951- *WhoSSW 93*
White-Smith, Richard 1945- *WhoE 93*
Whiteson, Leon 1930- *ScF&FL 92*
Whitestone, Todd A. 1954- *St&PR 93*
White-Thomson, Ian Leonard 1936- *St&PR 93, WhoAm 92*
Whitethorne, Baje 1950- *BioIn 17*
White Thunder, Joanne L. 1956- *WhoAmW 93*
White Wolf, E. Bruce *Law&B 92*
Whitfield, Barrence *BioIn 17*
Whitfield, Bob *BioIn 17*
Whitfield, Charles Richard *WhoScE 91-1*
Whitfield, Debra Burroughs 1955- *WhoAmW 93*
Whitfield, Florence L. *AmWomPl*
Whitfield, Graham Frank 1942- *WhoSSW 93*
Whitfield, Harley *Law&B 92*
Whitfield, Harley A. 1930- *WhoIns 93*
Whitfield, Harry *WhoScE 91-1*
Whitfield, Jack D. 1928- *St&PR 93*
Whitfield, Jack Duane 1928- *WhoAm 92, WhoSSW 93*
Whitfield, James Edward, Jr. 1930- *St&PR 93*
Whitfield, Lynn *BioIn 17, WhoAmW 93*
Whitfield, Mal *BioIn 17*
Whitfield, Marion S., Jr. 1945- *St&PR 93*
Whitfield, Mark *BioIn 17*
Whitfield, Michael 1940- *WhoScE 91-1*
Whitfield, Norman *SoulM*
Whitfield, P.N. *Law&B 92*
Whitfield, Paula Taylor *Law&B 92*
Whitfield, Stephen Jack 1942- *WhoE 93*
Whitfield, William Allan *WhoScE 91-1*
Whitford, George V. 1914- *WhoIns 93*
Whitford, Howard Norman 1938- *St&PR 93*
Whitford, Howard Wayne 1940- *WhoSSW 93*
Whitford, Mary Vaux *AmWomPl*
Whitham, Gerald Beresford 1927- *WhoAm 92*
Whitham, Kenneth 1927- *WhoAm 92*
Whithorne, Emerson 1884-1958 *Baker 92*
Whitin, Richard Courtney, Jr. 1921- *WhoAm 92*
Whiting, Albert Nathaniel 1917- *WhoAm 92*
Whiting, Alfred Frank 1912-1978 *IntDcAn*
Whiting, Allen Suess 1926- *WhoAm 92*
Whiting, Anne Margaret 1941- *WhoE 93*
Whiting, Arthur Battelle 1861-1936 *Baker 92*
Whiting, Arthur Milton 1928- *St&PR 93, WhoAm 92*
Whiting, Charles Goodrich 1842-1922 *JrnUS*
Whiting, David Ashby 1931- *WhoSSW 93*
Whiting, Eleanor Custis *AmWomPl*
Whiting, Eric William John 1948- *WhoUN 92*
Whiting, Estelle Louise *WhoWrEP 92*
Whiting, Evelyn Gray *AmWomPl*
Whiting, George E(lbridge) 1840-1923 *Baker 92*
Whiting, Henry H. *WhoAm 92, WhoSSW 93*
Whiting, John K., IV *Law&B 92*
Whiting, John Randolph 1914- *WhoAm 92*
Whiting, John W.M. 1908- *IntDcAn*
Whiting, Kenneth R. 1927- *St&PR 93*
Whiting, Lisa Lorraine 1959- *WhoAmW 93, WhoEmL 93*
Whiting, Maisie B. *AmWomPl*
Whiting, Margaret 1924- *See* Whiting, Richard 1891-1938 *Baker 92*
Whiting, Margaret Abbott Eaton 1876- *AmWomPl*
Whiting, Martha Countee 1912- *WhoAmW 93*
Whiting, Martin Robert 1967- *WhoWor 93*
Whiting, Michael Francis *WhoScE 91-1*
Whiting, Paul Leo 1943- *St&PR 93*
Whiting, Richard 1891-1938 *Baker 92*
Whiting, Richard Albert 1922- *WhoAm 92*
Whiting, Richard Brooke 1947- *WhoAm 92*
Whiting, Richard Bruce *Law&B 92*
Whiting, Wallace Burton, II 1952- *WhoSSW 93*
Whiting, William E. 1933- *WhoAm 92*
Whitington, G. Luther d1992 *NewYTBS 92*
Whitla, Dean Kay 1925- *WhoE 93*
Whitla, William 1851-1933 *BioIn 17*
Whitlam, Gough 1916- *DcTwHis*
Whitlark, James Stuart 1948- *WhoSSW 93*
Whitlatch, Jo Bell 1943- *WhoAm 92*
Whitley, Arthur Francis 1927- *WhoAm 92*
Whitley, Aubrey Russell, Jr. 1953- *WhoSSW 93*
Whitley, Barbara Ruth 1933- *WhoAmW 93*
Whitley, Carolyn Davis 1933- *WhoAmW 93*
Whitley, Chris *BioIn 17*
Whitley, James Craig 1948- *WhoAm 92*
Whitley, Joe Dally 1950- *WhoAm 92*
Whitley, John Douglas *WhoScE 91-1*
Whitley, John Quention, Jr. 1955- *WhoSSW 93*
Whitley, Juana Lynn 1964- *WhoAmW 93, WhoEmL 93, WhoWor 93*
Whitley, Larry 1940- *St&PR 93*
Whitley, Mary Ann 1951- *BioIn 17, WhoWrEP 92*
Whitley, Michael R. 1943- *St&PR 93*
Whitley, Nancy O'Neil 1932- *WhoAm 92, WhoAmW 93*
Whitley, Ralph Charles 1943- *St&PR 93*
Whitley, Sandra Ann 1951- *WhoE 93*
Whitley, Wilson d1992 *NewYTBS 92*
Whitlock, Albert 1915- *ConTFT 10*
Whitlock, Albert J. *ConTFT 10*
Whitlock, Bennett Clarke, Jr. 1927- *WhoAm 92*
Whitlock, C. William 1942- *WhoAm 92*
Whitlock, Charles Preston 1919- *WhoAm 92*
Whitlock, Darrell Dean 1941- *WhoSSW 93*
Whitlock, David Graham 1924- *WhoAm 92*
Whitlock, Denise 1959- *WhoAmW 93*
Whitlock, Foster Brand 1914-1991 *BioIn 17*
Whitlock, J. William *Law&B 92*
Whitlock, John Joseph 1935- *WhoAm 92*
Whitlock, Kim Christina *Law&B 92*
Whitlock, Margot *AmWomPl*
Whitlock, Meta Webster 1952- *WhoAmW 93*
Whitlock, Orion *WhoIns 93*
Whitlock, Orion Paul 1951- *St&PR 93*
Whitlock, P. Erica *Law&B 92*
Whitlock, Reverdy Robert Hale 1913- *St&PR 93*
Whitlock, William Abel 1929- *WhoAm 92*
Whitlow, Charles Glenn 1954- *WhoE 93*
Whitlow, Donald R. 1932- *WhoAm 92*
Whitlow, Douglas Alan 1947- *WhoSSW 93*
Whitlow, Myra Elaine 1929- *WhoAmW 93*
Whitlow, Pamela A. *Law&B 92*
Whitlow, Woodrow, Jr. 1952- *WhoSSW 93*
Whitman, Alden 1913-1990 *BioIn 17*
Whitman, Ann 1908-1991 *BioIn 17*
Whitman, Ardis Rumsey d1990 *BioIn 17*
Whitman, Barton D. *Law&B 92*
Whitman, Bruce N. 1933- *St&PR 93*
Whitman, Bruce Nairn 1933- *WhoAm 92*
Whitman, Charles David 1938- *WhoSSW 93*
Whitman, Charles Henry 1933- *St&PR 93*
Whitman, Christine Todd *WhoAmW 93*
Whitman, Constance *BioIn 17*
Whitman, Dale Alan 1939- *WhoAm 92*
Whitman, Donna Marie 1961- *WhoAmW 93*
Whitman, Eleanor Wood 1875-1948 *AmWomPl*
Whitman, Helen Herrick 1925- *WhoAmW 93*
Whitman, Hendricks Hallett d1991 *BioIn 17*
Whitman, Homer William, Jr. 1932- *WhoSSW 93*
Whitman, Howard Mitchell 1948- *St&PR 93*
Whitman, Jules Isidore 1923- *WhoAm 92*
Whitman, Kenneth Jay 1947- *WhoEmL 93*
Whitman, Marcus 1802-1847 *BioIn 17*
Whitman, Marina Von Neumann 1935- *WhoAm 92, WhoAmW 93*
Whitman, Martin J. 1924- *St&PR 93*
Whitman, Narcissa Prentiss 1808-1847 *BioIn 17*
Whitman, Paul Beecher *Law&B 92*
Whitman, Reginald Norman 1909- *WhoAm 92, WhoWor 93*
Whitman, Richard L. 1947- *St&PR 93*
Whitman, Robert 1936- *WhoAm 92*
Whitman, Robert Harold 1930- *St&PR 93*
Whitman, Robert Van Duyne 1928- *WhoAm 92*
Whitman, Russell B. *St&PR 93*
Whitman, Ruth 1922- *BioIn 17, WhoAm 92, WhoWrEP 92*
Whitman, Ruth Bourgeois 1946- *WhoAmW 93*
Whitman, Sarah Helen Power 1803-1878 *ScF&FL 92*
Whitman, Sarah Marie 1961- *WhoAmW 93*
Whitman, Sylvia 1961- *BioIn 17*
Whitman, Walt 1819-1892 *BioIn 17, JrnUS, MagSAmL [port], WorLitC [port]*
Whitman, William F. 1940- *St&PR 93*
Whitman, William Tate 1909- *WhoSSW 93*
Whitmer, Melvin Howard 1928- *WhoWrEP 92*
Whitmer, T(homas) Carl 1873-1959 *Baker 92*
Whitmer, William Eward 1933- *WhoSSW 93*
Whitmer, William R. 1933- *St&PR 93*
Whitmer, Yvette Alexandria 1966- *WhoSSW 93*
Whitmire, Donald Boone 1922- *BiDAMSp 1989*
Whitmire, Florence Eileen 1942- *St&PR 93*
Whitmire, Horace Clifton, Jr. 1943- *WhoSSW 93*
Whitmire, John Lee 1924- *WhoSSW 93*
Whitmire, Kathryn Jean 1946- *WhoAmW 93*
Whitmire, Kenneth Neal 1938- *St&PR 93*
Whitmore, Andrew *ScF&FL 92*
Whitmore, Ann Hartley *Law&B 92*
Whitmore, Beatrice Eileen 1935- *WhoAmW 93*
Whitmore, Charles 1949- *ScF&FL 92*
Whitmore, Charles Horace 1914- *WhoAm 92*
Whitmore, Dan C. 1932- *St&PR 93*
Whitmore, Donald Earl, Jr. 1935- *St&PR 93*
Whitmore, Edward Hugh 1926- *WhoAm 92*
Whitmore, Ernest Henry 1958- *WhoSSW 93*
Whitmore, Frank C. 1887-1947 *BioIn 17*
Whitmore, Franklin E. 1935- *St&PR 93*
Whitmore, George 1775-1862 *BioIn 17*
Whitmore, George 1946-1989 *ConGAN*
Whitmore, George Merle, Jr. 1928- *WhoAm 92*
Whitmore, Gordon Francis 1931- *WhoAm 92*
Whitmore, James Allen 1921- *WhoAm 92*
Whitmore, Jon Scott 1945- *WhoAm 92*
Whitmore, Kay Rex 1932- *BioIn 17, St&PR 93, WhoAm 92, WhoE 93, WhoWor 93*
Whitmore, Menandra M. *WhoAmW 93, WhoE 93*
Whitmore, Ralph Ervin, Jr. 1932- *St&PR 93*
Whitmore, Sharp 1918- *WhoAm 92*
Whitmore, William Francis 1917- *WhoAm 92*
Whitmyer, Russell Eliot 1915- *WhoAm 92*
Whitner, Jane Marvin 1935- *WhoAmW 93*
Whitney, Betsey Cushing Roosevelt 1908- *BioIn 17*
Whitney, Carol Marie 1946- *WhoE 93, WhoWor 93*
Whitney, Charles Allen 1929- *WhoAm 92*
Whitney, Chauncey Belden 1842-1873 *BioIn 17*
Whitney, Christopher D. 1944- *St&PR 93*
Whitney, Constance Clein *WhoAmW 93*
Whitney, Cornelius Vanderbilt 1899- *WhoAm 92*
Whitney, Cornelius Vanderbilt 1899-1992 *NewYTBS 92 [port]*
Whitney, Craig Richard 1943- *WhoWor 93*
Whitney, Daniel Eugene 1938- *WhoE 93*
Whitney, David M. *Law&B 92*
Whitney, Dickson Loos 1927- *St&PR 93*
Whitney, E. C., Mrs. *AmWomPl*
Whitney, E.W., III 1947- *St&PR 93*
Whitney, Edward Bonner 1945- *WhoAm 92*
Whitney, Eli 1765-1825 *BioIn 17*
Whitney, Elizabeth Laura 1953- *WhoAmW 93*
Whitney, Elwood d1992 *NewYTBS 92*
Whitney, Fred 1956- *WhoAm 92*
Whitney, George H., Jr. 1927- *St&PR 93*
Whitney, George Ward 1924- *WhoAm 92*
Whitney, Helen *MiSFD 9*
Whitney, Herbert N. 1940- *St&PR 93*
Whitney, J.D. 1940- *WhoWrEP 92*
Whitney, James Saunders 1925- *St&PR 93*
Whitney, Jane 1941- *WhoWor 93*
Whitney, Jay *St&PR 93*
Whitney, Jeffrey Garrett 1941- *St&PR 93*
Whitney, John 1917- *Baker 92*
Whitney, John Clarence 1915- *WhoAm 92*
Whitney, John Hay 1904-1982 *DcLB 127 [port]*
Whitney, Jon R. *St&PR 93*
Whitney, Kayla *WhoWrEP 92*
Whitney, King, Jr. 1925- *St&PR 93*
Whitney, Lester Frank 1928- *WhoE 93*
Whitney, Marlyn Sue 1953- *WhoAmW 93*
Whitney, Mary Ellen *AmWomPl*
Whitney, Marylou *BioIn 17*
Whitney, Michael Anthony 1941- *St&PR 93*
Whitney, Myron, Jr. 1872-1954 *See* Whitney, Myron (William) 1836-1910 *Baker 92*
Whitney, Myron (William) 1836-1910 *Baker 92*
Whitney, Patrick Foster 1951- *WhoAm 92*
Whitney, Philip Mather 1941- *WhoE 93*
Whitney, Phyllis A. 1903- *ScF&FL 92*
Whitney, Phyllis A(yame) 1903- *ConAu 38NR, DcAmChF 1960, MajAI [port]*
Whitney, Phyllis Ayame 1903- *WhoAm 92, WhoAmW 93*
Whitney, Phyllis Burrill 1928- *WhoAmW 93*
Whitney, R. Bruce *Law&B 92*
Whitney, Ralph Royal, Jr. 1934- *St&PR 93, WhoE 93, WhoWor 93*
Whitney, Robert A., Jr. 1935- *WhoAm 92*
Whitney, Robert Avery 1912- *WhoAm 92*

Whitney, Robert L. 1931- *St&PR 93*
Whitney, Robert Stephen 1946- *WhoWor 93*
Whitney, Robert (Sutton) 1904-1986 *Baker 92*
Whitney, Ruth Reinke 1928- *WhoAm 92, WhoAmW 93, WhoWrEP 92*
Whitney, Sam R. *St&PR 93*
Whitney, Sharon *BioIn 17*
Whitney, Thomas Porter 1917- *WhoE 93, WhoWor 93*
Whitney, W. Beaumont, III 1922- *St&PR 93*
Whitney, Wallace French, Jr. 1943- *WhoAm 92*
Whitney, Wayne R. 1945- *St&PR 93*
Whitney, William Chowning 1920- *WhoAm 92*
Whitney, William Elliot, Jr. 1933- *WhoAm 92*
Whitney, William Gordon 1922- *WhoE 93*
Whitney, William J. *Law&B 92*
Whitrow, Robert John *WhoScE 91-1*
Whitsel, Richard Harry 1931- *WhoWor 93*
Whitsel, Robert Malcolm 1929- *St&PR 93, WhoIns 93*
Whitsell, Doris Benner 1923- *WhoAmW 93*
Whitsell, Helen Jo 1938- *St&PR 93, WhoAm 92, WhoAmW 93*
Whitsell, John Crawford, II 1929- *WhoE 93*
Whitsett, Jeffrey Allen 1947- *WhoAm 92*
Whitsitt, Paul K. *Law&B 92*
Whitsitt, Robert James 1956- *WhoAm 92*
Whitsitt, William F. 1945- *St&PR 93*
Whitson, Alice L. *AmWomPl*
Whitson, Barbara Lee 1943- *WhoAmW 93*
Whitson, Betty Jo 1945- *WhoAmW 93*
Whitson, Edward Richard 1944- *WhoE 93*
Whitson, Gwen *Law&B 92*
Whitson, Harold A. 1940- *St&PR 93*
Whitson, James N. 1935- *St&PR 93*
Whitson, James Norfleet, Jr. 1935- *WhoAm 92*
Whitson, Keith Roderick 1943- *St&PR 93*
Whitson, Lish 1942- *WhoWor 93*
Whitson, Robert Edd 1942- *St&PR 93*
Whitson, Rodney Lee 1958- *WhoSSW 93*
Whitson, William Burroughs 1915- *St&PR 93*
Whitson-Fischman, Walter 1924- *WhoWor 93*
Whitt, Alfred B. 1938- *St&PR 93*
Whitt, Dixie Dailey 1939- *WhoAmW 93*
Whitt, Gregory Sidney 1938- *WhoAm 92*
Whitt, John Robert 1946- *St&PR 93*
Whitt, Marcus Calvin 1960- *WhoSSW 93*
Whitt, Phillip Bryant, Sr. 1942- *WhoSSW 93*
Whitt, Richard Ernest 1944- *WhoAm 92*
Whitt, Theresa Marie 1961- *WhoAmW 93*
Whitt, Walter F. 1943- *St&PR 93*
Whittaker, Barry Neil *WhoScE 91-1*
Whittaker, Charles Evans 1901-1973 *OxCSupC [port]*
Whittaker, Douglas Kirkland 1949- *WhoSSW 93*
Whittaker, Hazel Lotze *AmWomPl*
Whittaker, Howard 1922- *Baker 92*
Whittaker, Howard Keith 1963- *WhoSSW 93*
Whittaker, J.K. 1926- *St&PR 93*
Whittaker, Jeanne Evans 1934- *WhoAm 92*
Whittaker, John Brian *WhoScE 91-1*
Whittaker, Johnson C. 1858-1931 *EncAACR*
Whittaker, Judith *Law&B 92*
Whittaker, Mary Frances 1926- *WhoSSW 93*
Whittaker, Peter Anthony 1939- *WhoWor 93*
Whittaker, Richard Pawling 1940- *WhoE 93*
Whittaker, Sheelagh Dillon 1947- *WhoAm 92, WhoAmW 93*
Whittaker, Stephen *MiSFD 9*
Whittaker, Steven Dale 1950- *St&PR 93*
Whittaker, Susan Shumate 1947- *WhoSSW 93*
Whittaker, Victor P. 1919- *WhoScE 91-3*
Whittaker, W(illiam) G(illies) 1876-1944 *Baker 92*
Whittaker, Walter Hugh 1929- *St&PR 93*
Whittaker, Wm David, Jr. 1942- *St&PR 93*
Whittaker, Yolanda *BioIn 17*
Whittal, Arnold (Morgan) 1935- *Baker 92*
Whittall, Gertrude Clarke 1867-1965 *Baker 92*
Whittall, H. Richard 1923- *St&PR 93*
Whittall, Hubert Richard 1923- *WhoAm 92*
Whittelsey, Chick d1990 *BioIn 17*
Whittemore, Colin Trengove *WhoScE 91-1*
Whittemore, Edward Reed, II 1919- *WhoAm 92*
Whittemore, Frank Bowen 1916- *WhoE 93*
Whittemore, Laurence Frederick 1929- *St&PR 93, WhoAm 92*
Whittemore, Marjorie Maas 1947- *WhoAmW 93*
Whittemore, Mattie C. L. *AmWomPl*
Whittemore, Nena Thames 1939- *WhoSSW 93*
Whittemore, William Carlton, III *Law&B 92*
Whitten, Barbara Judith 1941- *WhoAmW 93*
Whitten, Bertwell Kneeland 1941- *WhoAm 92*
Whitten, Charles Alexander, Jr. 1940- *WhoAm 92*
Whitten, David George 1938- *WhoAm 92*
Whitten, Denise *BioIn 17*
Whitten, Dolphus, Jr. 1916- *WhoAm 92*
Whitten, Elton B. 1907-1989 *BioIn 17*
Whitten, Eric Harold Timothy 1927- *WhoAm 92*
Whitten, Guyon Eugene, Jr. 1938- *St&PR 93*
Whitten, Harold Anthony 1912- *WhoSSW 93*
Whitten, Jamie L. *CngDr 91*
Whitten, Jamie L. 1910- *BioIn 17*
Whitten, Jamie Lloyd 1910- *WhoAm 92, WhoSSW 93*
Whitten, Jerry Lynn 1937- *WhoAm 92*
Whitten, Kristian D. *Law&B 92*
Whitten, Les 1928- *ScF&FL 92*
Whitten, Leslie Hunter, Jr. 1928- *WhoAm 92, WhoWrEP 92*
Whitten, Phyllis Ann *Law&B 92*
Whitten, Robert Wesley 1953- *WhoSSW 93*
Whitten, Steven David 1950- *WhoE 93*
Whitten, Susan Elizabeth Smith 1948- *WhoAmW 93*
Whitten, Wesley Kingston 1918- *WhoWor 93*
Whittenberg, Charles 1927-1984 *Baker 92*
Whittenburg, Rosalind Bewley 1938- *WhoAmW 93*
Whittenbury, Roger *WhoScE 91-1*
Whitters, James Payton, III 1939- *WhoAm 92*
Whitters, Joseph Edward 1958- *St&PR 93*
Whittier, E. James 1928- *WhoIns 93*
Whittier, Joan Margaret 1955- *WhoWor 93*
Whittier, John Rensselaer 1919-1990 *BioIn 17*
Whittier, Michael Warren 1943- *WhoSSW 93*
Whittier, Phoebe *AmWomPl*
Whittier, SaraJane 1912- *WhoSSW 93*
Whittingham, Charles Arthur 1930- *WhoAm 92*
Whittingham, Charles Edward 1913- *WhoAm 92*
Whittingham, D.G. *WhoScE 91-1*
Whittingham, Harry Edward, Jr. 1918- *WhoAm 92*
Whittingham, Michael Stanley 1941- *WhoE 93*
Whittingham, Thomas Anthony 1944- *WhoWor 93*
Whittingham, Thomas G. 1928- *St&PR 93*
Whittington, Aven 1917- *WhoAm 92*
Whittington, Bernard Wiley 1920- *WhoAm 92*
Whittington, Constance Victoria 1954- *WhoE 93*
Whittington, Floyd Leon 1909- *WhoAm 92, WhoWor 93*
Whittington, Harrison DeWayne 1931- *WhoE 93*
Whittington, Harry 1915-1989 *ScF&FL 92*
Whittington, Henry *ScF&FL 92*
Whittington, John Jay 1947- *St&PR 93*
Whittington, Robert Bruce 1927- *WhoAm 92*
Whittington, Ronald Frederick 1949- *WhoE 93*
Whittington, Stuart Gordon 1942- *WhoAm 92*
Whittington, Vanessa Elizabeth 1960- *WhoE 93*
Whittington, Vera J. 1929- *St&PR 93*
Whittington, W.J. *WhoScE 91-1*
Whittle, Charles Edward 1938- *St&PR 93*
Whittle, Charles Edward, Jr. 1931- *WhoAm 92*
Whittle, Christopher *BioIn 17*
Whittle, Christopher 1947- *WhoAm 92*
Whittle, David Brian 1953- *WhoE 93*
Whittle, Frank 1907- *WhoAm 92*
Whittle, John J. 1936- *WhoIns 93*
Whittle, John Joseph 1936- *St&PR 93, WhoAm 92*
Whittle, Mack Ira, Jr. 1948- *WhoSSW 93*
Whittle, Paul D. 1946- *St&PR 93*
Whittlesey, Eunice Baird *WhoAmW 93*
Whittlesey, James McDonnell 1943- *WhoSSW 93*
Whittlesey, Jerry Raymond 1934- *WhoSSW 93*
Whittlesey, Judith H. 1942- *WhoE 93*
Whittlesey, Marjorie Tooker 1912- *WhoWrEP 92*
Whittlesey, Robert Hargreaves, II 1945- *St&PR 93*
Whittlesey, Walter Rose 1861-1936 *BioIn 17*
Whitton, Hollis Dale 1925- *St&PR 93*
Whitton, Jeffrey Herschel 1957- *WhoSSW 93*
Whitton, Margaret *BioIn 17*
Whitton, Margaret 1950- *ConTFT 10*
Whitton, Pamela Gail 1956- *St&PR 93*
Whitton, Peggy *ConTFT 10*
Whitton, Walter E. 1911- *St&PR 93*
Whitty, Gerard Charles 1950- *WhoE 93*
Whitty, Larry Joe 1960- *St&PR 93*
Whitty, Lawrence J. 1937- *St&PR 93*
Whitty, Raymond John 1945- *St&PR 93, WhoAm 92*
Whitty, Robin Wallingford *WhoScE 91-1*
Whitty, Thomas J. 1936- *St&PR 93*
Whitwam, David R. 1942- *St&PR 93*
Whitwam, David Ray 1942- *WhoAm 92*
Whitwell, George L. 1940- *St&PR 93*
Whitwell, William Livingston 1936- *WhoSSW 93*
Whitworth, F. Dixon, Jr. 1944- *WhoAm 92*
Whitworth, Hall Baker 1919- *WhoAm 92*
Whitworth, Horace P., Jr. *Law&B 92*
Whitworth, J. Bryan 1938- *St&PR 93*
Whitworth, J. Bryan, Jr. 1938- *WhoAm 92*
Whitworth, Jessamine Sau Wai 1949- *WhoWor 93*
Whitworth, John Harvey, Jr. 1933- *WhoAm 92*
Whitworth, Kathrynne Ann 1939- *WhoAm 92, WhoAmW 93*
Whitworth, Kathy 1939- *BioIn 17*
Whitworth, Randolph Howard 1929- *WhoSSW 93*
Whitworth, Sue Petty 1924- *WhoAmW 93*
Whitworth, William A. 1937- *WhoAm 92, WhoE 93*
Whiz, Walter Raimu 1918- *WhoWrEP 92*
Wholl, Edward R. *Law&B 92*
Whorf, Benjamin Lee 1897-1941 *IntDcAn*
Whorf, Richard 1906-1966 *MiSFD 9N*
Whoriskey, Robert Donald 1929- *WhoAm 92, WhoWor 93*
Whorton, Danna Binder 1905- *WhoSSW 93*
Whorton, M. Donald 1943- *WhoAm 92*
Whritenour, Robert A. 1936- *St&PR 93*
Whybark, David Clay 1935- *WhoSSW 93*
Whybrow, Peter Charles 1939- *WhoAm 92, WhoE 93, WhoWor 93*
Whynot, D.A. 1961- *St&PR 93*
Whynott, Douglas (Vernon) 1950- *ConAu 137*
Whyte, Anne Veronica 1942- *WhoAm 92*
Whyte, Archie James 1936- *WhoIns 93*
Whyte, Bruce Lincoln 1941- *WhoE 93, WhoWor 93*
Whyte, Donald Edward 1918- *St&PR 93*
Whyte, Edna Gardner *BioIn 17*
Whyte, Edna Gardner d1992 *NewYTBS 92*
Whyte, George E. 1937- *St&PR 93*
Whyte, George Kenneth, Jr. 1936- *WhoAm 92*
Whyte, H. Walter *ScF&FL 92*
Whyte, Hamilton 1927-1990 *BioIn 17*
Whyte, James Primrose, Jr. 1921- *WhoAm 92*
Whyte, Malcolm 1933- *BioIn 17*
Whyte, Martin King 1942- *WhoAm 92*
Whyte, Michael *MiSFD 9*
Whyte, Robert Michael 1944- *WhoWor 93*
Whyte, Ron d1989 *BioIn 17*
Whyte, William Foote 1914- *BioIn 17, ConAu 40NR, WhoAm 92*
Whyte, William Hollingsworth 1917- *WhoAm 92, WhoWrEP 92*
Whyte, William R. 1947- *WhoSSW 93*
Whythorne, Thomas 1528-1596 *Baker 92*
Wi, William 1948- *WhoAsAP 91*
Wiaczek, Pamela Paxton 1961- *WhoAmW 93*
Wian, Robert C. d1992 *BioIn 17*
Wianecki, Richard J. *Law&B 92*
Wiart, Robert 1936- *WhoScE 91-2*
Wiater, Stanley 1953- *ScF&FL 92*
Wiatt, James Anthony 1946- *WhoAm 92*
Wibage, Ulf Anders 1958- *WhoWor 93*
Wibald of Stavelot 1098-1158 *OxDcByz*
Wibault, Henri 1937- *WhoWor 93*
Wibbelsman, Robert John 1939- *WhoWor 93*
Wibberenz, Gerd H. 1930- *WhoScE 91-3*
Wibberley, Leonard 1915-1983 *DcAmChF 1960, ScF&FL 92*
Wibell, Lars Bertil 1937- *WhoWor 93*
Wiberg, Donald Martin 1936- *WhoAm 92*
Wiberley, Stephen Edward 1919- *WhoAm 92*
Wibisono, Koento 1930- *WhoWor 93*
Wible, Clarence Edward 1946- *WhoE 93*
Wible, Connie 1943- *WhoAmW 93*
Wible, Robert Thomas 1950- *St&PR 93*
Wibling, Harold C. 1948- *St&PR 93*
Wiborg, James H. 1924- *St&PR 93*
Wiborg, James Hooker 1924- *WhoAm 92*
Wiborg, Mary Hoyt *AmWomPl*
Wich, Gunther 1928- *Baker 92*
Wich, Robert Thomas 1927- *WhoAm 92*
Wichern, Dean William 1942- *WhoAm 92*
Wichinsky, Glenn Ellis 1952- *WhoEmL 93*
Wichman, William C. 1906-1991 *BioIn 17*
Wichmann, Brian A. 1939- *WhoScE 91-1*
Wichmann, H.-Erich 1946- *WhoScE 91-3*
Wichser, Karl 1952- *St&PR 93*
Wichtl, Max 1925- *WhoScE 91-3*
Wick, Arthur D. 1943- *St&PR 93*
Wick, Carter *WhoWrEP 92*
Wick, Chad P. 1942- *St&PR 93*
Wick, David Bruce *Law&B 92*
Wick, Douglas 1917- *St&PR 93*
Wick, Gary Allen 1942- *WhoSSW 93*
Wick, Gian Carlo d1992 *NewYTBS 92 [port]*
Wick, Gian Carlo 1909-1992 *BioIn 17*
Wick, Hilton A. 1920- *St&PR 93*
Wick, Hilton Addison 1920- *WhoAm 92*
Wick, J. Mae Culp *AmWomPl*
Wick, Jeffrey W. 1948- *St&PR 93*
Wick, John G. 1924- *St&PR 93*
Wick, Margaret 1942- *WhoAm 92, WhoAmW 93*
Wick, Michael G. *Law&B 92*
Wick, Paul H. 1936- *WhoSSW 93*
Wick, Randall G. *Law&B 92*
Wick, Richard 1946- *St&PR 93*
Wick, Tamara 1961- *WhoE 93*
Wickard, Frank Oscar 1937- *WhoAm 92*
Wickberg, Jens Erik 1943- *WhoWor 93*
Wicke, Manfred 1933- *WhoScE 91-4*
Wickenburg, Henry 1819-1905 *BioIn 17*
Wickenden, Dan 1913-1989 *BioIn 17*
Wickens, Aryness Joy 1901-1991 *BioIn 17*
Wickens, Donald Lee 1934- *St&PR 93*
Wickens, Mary K. *Law&B 92*
Wickens, Robert G. 1944- *St&PR 93*
Wicker, Danny 1946- *St&PR 93*
Wicker, Elizabeth Ann 1954- *WhoWrEP 92*
Wicker, James Eugene 1935- *WhoSSW 93*
Wicker, James Robert 1954- *WhoSSW 93*
Wicker, Laurie Lois Hamilton 1964- *WhoSSW 93*
Wicker, Marie Peachee 1925- *WhoSSW 93*
Wicker, Nina A. 1927- *WhoWrEP 92*
Wicker, Raymond Blackwell 1934- *WhoSSW 93*
Wicker, Robert Kirk 1939- *WhoE 93*
Wicker, Thomas Grey 1926- *JrnUS, WhoAm 92, WhoE 93*
Wicker, Veronica DiCarlo *WhoAm 92, WhoAmW 93, WhoSSW 93*
Wicker, William Walter 1930- *WhoSSW 93*
Wickers, Rodney William *Law&B 92*
Wickers, Roger T. 1935- *St&PR 93*
Wickersham, Ellen Hancock 1947- *WhoSSW 93*
Wickersham, John *BioIn 17*
Wickersham, John 1951- *St&PR 93*
Wickersham, John Moore 1943- *WhoE 93*
Wickert, William E. 1931- *St&PR 93*
Wickes, David *MiSFD 9*
Wickes, Diana C. 1930- *WhoWrEP 92*
Wickes, Frances Gillespy 1875- *AmWomPl*
Wickes, George 1923- *WhoAm 92, WhoWrEP 92*
Wickes, Henry Gillette, Jr. 1929- *WhoSSW 93*
Wickes, Mary *WhoAm 92*
Wickes, Mary 1912- *QDrFCA 92 [port]*
Wickesberg, Albert Klumb 1921- *WhoAm 92*
Wickesberg, Alfred 1908- *St&PR 93*
Wickesberg, Margaret *St&PR 93*
Wickesberg, Paul *St&PR 93*
Wickett, Ann *BioIn 17*
Wickfield, Eric Nelson 1953- *WhoE 93*
Wickham, Florence 1880-1962 *Baker 92*
Wickham, Gary Alfred 1941- *WhoAm 92*
Wickham, Jody 1956- *WhoAmW 93*
Wickham, John Adams, Jr. 1928- *CmdGen 1991 [port], WhoAm 92*
Wickham, John Ewart Alfred 1927- *WhoWor 93*
Wickham, Kenneth Gregory 1913- *WhoAm 92*
Wickham, Marvin Gary 1942- *WhoSSW 93*
Wickham, Richard James *Law&B 92*
Wickham, Robert B. 1957- *St&PR 93*

Wickham, Robert Dean 1923- WhoE 93
Wicki, Bernhard 1919- MiSFD 9
Wicki, Dieter 1931- WhoWor 93
Wickings, I. WhoScE 91-1
Wickiser, Ralph Lewanda 1910- WhoAm 92
Wickizer, Cindy Louise 1946- WhoAmW 93
Wickizer, Mary A. ScF&FL 92
Wickizer, Mary Alice 1938- WhoAm 92
Wickkiser, Carol Busck 1938- WhoWor 93
Wickland, Carey Bradford 1941- St&PR 93
Wicklander, Philip J. 1938- St&PR 93
Wicklein, John Frederick 1924- WhoAm 92
Wickler, Wolfgang Joachim Herbert 1931- WhoScE 91-3
Wicklife, Jack D. 1939- St&PR 93
Wickliffe, Mary F. AmWomPl
Wickline, David L. 1954- St&PR 93
Wickline, Marian Elizabeth 1915- WhoAmW 93
Wickline, Paul O. Law&B 92
Wicklow, Joseph F. 1941- St&PR 93
Wicklund, Darryl H. 1951- St&PR 93
Wicklund, Kendall Law&B 92
Wicklund, Millie Mae 1936- WhoWrEP 92
Wickman, John Edward 1929- WhoAm 92
Wickman, Kurt 1945- WhoScE 91-4
Wickman, Paul Everett 1912- WhoAm 92
Wickrama, Upali K. 1944- WhoUN 92
Wickramanayake, Sandhya Rukmal Karunarat 1958- WhoE 93
Wickramasinghe, Nalin Chandra WhoScE 91-1
Wickramasinghe, Sunitha Nimal WhoScE 91-1
Wickremasinghe, Tudor Herbert 1937- WhoWor 93
Wicks, (Edward) Allan 1923- Baker 92
Wicks, Sidney 1949- BiDAMSp 1989
Wicks, Wesley D. 1936- WhoAm 92, WhoSSW 93
Wicks, William Withington 1923- St&PR 93, WhoAm 92
Wicksell, Johan Gustaf Knut 1851-1926 BioIn 17
Wicksell, Knut 1851-1926 BioIn 17
Wickser, John Philip 1922- WhoAm 92
Wickser, Josephine Wilhelm AmWomPl
Wickson, Edward James 1920- WhoSSW 93
Wickstead, Anthony William WhoScE 91-1
Wickstead, Anthony William 1947- WhoWor 93
Wickstrom, Andriette Yvonne 1955- WhoAmW 93
Wickstrom, Carl Webster 1944- WhoWor 93
Wickstrom, Gustav 1941- WhoScE 91-4
Wickstrom, Karl Youngert 1935- WhoAm 92
Wickstrom, Lois June 1948- WhoWrEP 92
Wickstrom, Pamela Chase 1942- WhoAmW 93
Wickstrom, Ulf 1947- WhoWor 93
Wickstrum, Barton K. 1913-1991 BioIn 17
Wickware, Jack D. Law&B 92
Wickwire, Emerson MacMillin 1944- WhoAm 92
Wickwire, James D., Jr. WhoIns 93
Widaman, Gregory Alan 1955- WhoWor 93
Widdel, John Earl, Jr. 1936- WhoAm 92
Widdemer, Margaret AmWomPl
Widder, Charles Joseph 1941- WhoIns 93
Widder, Edith Anne 1951- WhoSSW 93
Widder, Kenneth Jon 1953- St&PR 93
Widder, Willard Graves 1924- WhoAm 92
Widders, Sandra L. 1952- St&PR 93
Widdicombe, John Guy WhoScE 91-1
Widdicombe, Richard Palmer 1941- WhoAm 92
Widdis, William J. 1931- St&PR 93
Widdop, Walter 1892-1949 OxDcOp
Widdows, John 1948- WhoScE 91-1
Widdowson, E.J. WhoScE 91-1
Widdrington, P.N.T. 1930- St&PR 93
Widdrington, Peter Nigel Tinling 1930- WhoAm 92, WhoWor 93
Widell, Gary G. Law&B 92
Widell, Gregory Scott 1958- St&PR 93
Widell, Karl Erik 1936- WhoScE 91-2
Wideman, John Edgar BioIn 17
Wideman, John Edgar 1941- MagSAmL [port], WhoAm 92
Widen, Arthur Garland 1951- St&PR 93
Widen, Ingvar 1927- WhoScE 91-4
Widener, Gary Wayne 1946- WhoWor 93
Widener, Hiram Emory, Jr. 1923- WhoAm 92
Widener, James C. 1943- St&PR 93
Widener, James Curtis 1943- WhoAm 92
Widener, Peri Ann 1956- WhoAmW 93
Widener, Susan Dale 1951- St&PR 93
Widenmann, Faye 1948- St&PR 93
Widera, G. E. O. 1938- WhoAm 92
Widerberg, Bo 1930- MiSFD 9
Widerberg, Willard Carl 1920- WhoSSW 93
Widerkehr, Jacques 1759-1823 Baker 92
Wideroe, Tor-Erik 1940- WhoScE 91-4
Wides, Norman A. 1918- St&PR 93
Widforss, Gunnar Mauritz 1879-1934 BioIn 17
Widgery, David 1947-1992 ConAu 139
Widgery, Jeanne-Anna 1920- WhoWrEP 92
Widgoff, Mildred 1924- WhoAm 92, WhoAmW 93, WhoE 93
Widgren, Richard Roy 1942- St&PR 93
Widick, Robert E. 1937- St&PR 93
Widiss, Alan I. 1938- WhoAm 92
Widlar, Robert J. 1937-1991 BioIn 17
Widlocher, Daniel WhoScE 91-2
Widlund, Olof Bertil 1938- WhoAm 92
Widlus, Hannah B. Law&B 92
Widlus, Hannah Beverly 1955- WhoAm 92, WhoAmW 93
Widmaier, Henry Joseph 1945- St&PR 93
Widman, Gary Lee 1936- WhoAm 92
Widman, Judith 1942- WhoAm 92
Widman, Richard Gustave 1922- WhoAm 92
Widman, Sarah Elizabeth 1945- WhoAmW 93, WhoE 93
Widmann, David Nicholas 1949- St&PR 93
Widmann, Erasmus 1572?-1634 Baker 92
Widmann, Joseph Viktor 1842-1911 Baker 92
Widmann, Nancy C. WhoAm 92, WhoAmW 93
Widmann, Roger M. 1939- St&PR 93
Widmann, Roger Maurice 1939- WhoAm 92
Widmar, Russell Charles 1946- St&PR 93
Widmark, Henrik WhoScE 91-4
Widmark, Richard 1914- BioIn 17, IntDcF 2-3, WhoAm 92
Widmayer, Charles Edward d1991 BioIn 17
Widmayer, Francis J. 1929- St&PR 93
Widmayer, Gustav G. 1958- St&PR 93
Widmer, Emmy Louise WhoSSW 93
Widmer, Hans Michael 1933- WhoWor 93
Widmer, James A. 1949- WhoSSW 93
Widmer, Jean 1929- BioIn 17
Widmer, Kemble 1913- WhoAm 92
Widmer, Kingsley 1925- ScF&FL 92
Widmer, Raymond Arthur 1923- WhoAm 92
Widmer, Robert H. 1916- WhoAm 92
Widmer, Robert J. 1940- St&PR 93
Widmer, Wilbur James 1918- WhoE 93
Widmoser, Peter 1935- WhoScE 91-3
Widnall, Sheila Evans 1938- WhoAm 92, WhoAmW 93, WhoE 93
Widner, Ralph Randolph 1930- WhoAm 92
Widner, William Richard 1920- WhoSSW 93
Widom, Benjamin 1927- WhoAm 92
Widom, Chester A. 1940- WhoAm 92
Widor, Charles-Marie 1844-1937 OxDcOp
Widor, Charles-Marie (-Jean-Albert) 1844-1937 Baker 92
Widrig, Richard F. 1952- St&PR 93
Widrow, Bernard 1929- WhoAm 92
Widstrom, Virginia Rose Elder 1939- WhoAmW 93
Widulski, Laura Jean 1961- WhoEmL 93
Widyono, Benny 1936- WhoUN 92
Widy-Wirski, Roslaw Joseph 1944- WhoUN 92
Widzinski, Paul J. Law&B 92
Wie, Yong-Sun 1952- WhoSSW 93
Wiebe, Dallas Eugene 1930- WhoWrEP 92
Wiebe, Donald 1923- WhoE 93
Wiebe, Harvey John Law&B 92
Wiebe, Leonard Irving 1941- WhoAm 92
Wiebe, Rudy 1934- WhoCanL 92
Wiebenga, A.C. Law&B 92
Wiebenson, Dora Louise 1926- WhoAm 92
Wiebers, Herman Augustus 1925- St&PR 93
Wiebes, J.T. WhoScE 91-3
Wiebush, Joseph Roy 1920- WhoSSW 93
Wiecek, William Michael 1938- WhoAm 92
Wiecha, Joseph Augustine 1926- WhoAm 92
Wiechowicz, Stanislaw 1893-1963 Baker 92, PolBiDi
Wiechowski, Seweryn Wieslaw 1935- WhoWor 93
Wieck Baker 92
Wieck, Agnes Burns 1892-1966 BioIn 17
Wieck, Alwin 1821-1885 Baker 92
Wieck, Clara Baker 92
Wieck, (Johann Gottlob) Friedrich 1785-1873 Baker 92
Wieck, Hans-Georg 1928- WhoWor 93
Wieck, James Fredrick 1944- WhoAm 92
Wieck, Marie 1832-1916 Baker 92
Wieckert, Walter Bernard 1934- St&PR 93
Wieckowski, Leonard F. 1939- St&PR 93
Wieczorek, Eberhard 1937- WhoWor 93
Wieczorek, Norbert Georg Walter 1940- WhoWor 93
Wieczorek, Rudolf Hubert Werner 1946- WhoWor 93
Wieczorek, Ulrich Franz Josef 1945- WhoWor 93
Wieczorowski, Kazimierz 1931- WhoScE 91-4
Wieczynski, Frank R. 1939- St&PR 93
Wieczynski, Frank Robert 1939- WhoAm 92
Wieczysty, Artur 1929- WhoScE 91-4
Wied, George Ludwig 1921- WhoWor 93
Wied, Maximilian, Prinz von 1782-1867 BioIn 17
Wiedebein, Gottlob 1779-1854 Baker 92
Wiedefeld, Marcia Fenchak 1964- WhoE 93
Wiedel, William Conrad, Jr. 1959- St&PR 93
Wiedeman, Geoffrey Paul 1917- WhoAm 92
Wiedeman, George H. 1912-1991 BioIn 17
Wiedeman, John Herman 1935- WhoAm 92
Wiedeman, Richard Lawrence 1945- WhoE 93
Wiedemann, Anita Melissa 1960- WhoAmW 93
Wiedemann, Charles Louis 1936- WhoE 93
Wiedemann, Claus Peter 1939- WhoWor 93
Wiedemann, Douglas Henry 1953- WhoE 93
Wiedemann, Ernst Johann 1797-1873 Baker 92
Wiedemann, Frederic Franklin 1923- St&PR 93
Wiedemann, George Stanhope 1944- WhoAm 92
Wiedemann, Joseph R. 1928- WhoIns 93
Wiedemann, Joseph Robert 1928- St&PR 93, WhoAm 92
Wiedemann, Paul 1944- WhoUN 92
Wiedemann, Thomas (E. J.) 1950- ConAu 138
Wieden, Dan BioIn 17
Wiedenhoeft, Ann Marie 1938- WhoAmW 93
Wiedenkeller, Nellie Ann Law&B 92
Wiedenmann, Eric William 1951- St&PR 93
Wiedenmann, Paul W. 1937- St&PR 93
Wiedenmayer, Christopher M. 1941- St&PR 93, WhoAm 92
Wiedenmayer, Gustave E. 1908- St&PR 93
Wiedenroth, Wolfgang 1933- WhoScE 91-3
Wiedepuhl, Christian BioIn 17
Wieder, Bernard R. d1990 BioIn 17
Wieder, Bruce Terrill 1955- WhoE 93
Wieder, Douglas M. 1952- St&PR 93
Wieder, Laurance 1946- WhoWrEP 92
Wieder, Michael D. St&PR 93
Wieder, Thomas Herbert 1948- St&PR 93
Wiederaenders, George A. 1941- St&PR 93
Wiederhold, Hans Dieter 1937- WhoWor 93
Wiederhold, Paul B. 1943- St&PR 93
Wiederhold, Pieter R. 1928- St&PR 93
Wiederhold, Richard Edgar 1949- WhoSSW 93
Wiederholt, Michael 1936- WhoScE 91-3
Wiederhorn, Ken MiSFD 9
Wiederhorn, Sheldon Martin 1933- WhoAm 92
Wiederkehr, Alvin M. 1923- St&PR 93
Wiederspahn, Alvin 1949- St&PR 93
Wiederstein, Franz WhoScE 91-4
Wiedhaup, Koenraad 1938- WhoScE 91-3
Wiedl, Sheila Colleen 1950- WhoEmL 93
Wiedlin, Paul E. 1945- St&PR 93
Wiedman, Wayne Rentchler 1928- WhoAm 92
Wiedmann, Cindy Holley 1961- WhoAmW 93
Wied-Nebbeling, Susanne 1946- WhoWor 93
Wiedow, Carl Paul 1907- WhoAm 92
Wiedrich, Joyce Lorraine 1952- WhoAmW 93
Wieferich, Susan Gates 1947- WhoAmW 93
Wiegand, Bruce 1947- St&PR 93
Wiegand, C. Monroe 1912- WhoAm 92
Wiegand, Craig Loren 1933- WhoSSW 93
Wiegand, Debra Leggett Law&B 92
Wiegand, Donald Arthur 1927- WhoE 93
Wiegand, Frank L., Jr. 1912- St&PR 93
Wiegand, (Josef Anton) Heinrich 1842-1899 Baker 92
Wiegand, Herbert 1941- WhoScE 91-3
Wiegand, James Richard 1928- WhoWor 93
Wiegand, John A. 1926- WhoAm 92
Wiegand, Phillips 1939- St&PR 93
Wiegand, Richard Lee 1942- St&PR 93
Wiegand, Stacie BioIn 17
Wiegand, Sylvia Margaret 1945- WhoAmW 93
Wiegand, Warren 1945- St&PR 93
Wiegel, Robert Louis 1922- WhoAm 92
Wiegenstein, John Gerald 1930- WhoAm 92
Wiegers, George A. 1936- St&PR 93
Wiegers, George Anthony 1936- WhoAm 92
Wiegers, Rolland Lee 1930- WhoIns 93
Wieghart, James Gerard 1933- WhoAm 92
Wiegman, Eugene William 1929- WhoAm 92
Wiegmann, Roger Henry 1934- WhoAm 92
Wiegner, Allen Walter 1947- WhoAm 92
Wiegner, Edward A. 1939- WhoIns 93
Wiegner, Edward Alex 1939- WhoAm 92
Wiegold, James WhoScE 91-1
Wiehen, Michael H. 1932- WhoUN 92
Wiehl, John Jack 1920- WhoE 93
Wiel, Taddeo 1849-1920 Baker 92
Wieland, Christoph Martin 1733-1813 BioIn 17, OxDcOp
Wieland, Ferdinand 1943- WhoAm 92
Wieland, John 1936- St&PR 93
Wieland, Joyce 1931- BioIn 17
Wieland, Katherine Colleen 1953- WhoAmW 93
Wieland, Liza 1960- ConAu 139
Wieland, Paul Otto 1954- WhoSSW 93
Wieland, Robert Richard Law&B 92
Wieland, Robert Richard 1937- St&PR 93, WhoAm 92
Wieland, Timothy E. 1953- St&PR 93
Wieland, William Dean 1948- WhoEmL 93, WhoSSW 93
Wieleba, Joan Law&B 92
Wieleba, Ronald Walter Law&B 92
Wielebinski, Richard 1936- WhoScE 91-3
Wielech, Dennis David 1936- WhoWor 93
Wielen, Roland 1938- WhoScE 91-3
Wielepski, Eugene Carl 1946- St&PR 93
Wieler, Alvin L. 1946- St&PR 93
Wieler, Diana J. 1961- BioIn 17, WhoCanL 92
Wieler, Diana J(ean) 1961- DcChlFi
Wieler, Stephen E. Law&B 92
Wielgosz, Roman WhoScE 91-4
Wielgus, Charles Joseph 1923- WhoAm 92
Wielgus, John Jay 1945- WhoSSW 93
Wielhorsky, Matvei 1794-1866 See Wielhorsky, Mikhail 1788-1856 Baker 92
Wielhorsky, Mikhail 1788-1856 Baker 92
Wiells, Helen ConAu 136
Wiemann, Marion Russell, Jr. 1929- WhoWor 93
Wiemann, Mary O'Loughlin 1947- WhoAmW 93
Wieme, Willem 1941- WhoWor 93
Wiemer, Hermann J. BioIn 17
Wiemer, Robert 1938- MiSFD 9
Wiemer, Robert Anthony 1931- WhoE 93
Wiemer, Robert Ernest 1938- WhoAm 92, WhoWor 93
Wiemers, Deborah Lynn Law&B 92
Wiemerslage, Wayne Leroy Law&B 92
Wiemer-Sumner, Anne-Marie 1938- WhoAmW 93
Wiemken, Andres Martin 1942- WhoScE 91-4
Wien, Noel 1899-1977 EncABHB 8 [port]
Wien, Stuart Lewis 1923- WhoAm 92
Wiencek, Mark A. Law&B 92
Wiencek, Richard J. 1938- St&PR 93
Wiendl, Federico M. 1941- WhoWor 93
Wiene, Robert 1881-1938 MiSFD 9N
Wieneke, Daniel L. Law&B 92
Wieneke, Franz 1927- WhoScE 91-3
Wiener, Annabelle 1922- WhoAmW 93, WhoUN 92, WhoWor 93
Wiener, Arthur Charles 1937- St&PR 93
Wiener, Daniel Eli 1959- St&PR 93
Wiener, Daniel Norman 1921- WhoAm 92
Wiener, Ed 1918-1991 BioIn 17
Wiener, Elliott Maxwell 1935- St&PR 93, WhoAm 92
Wiener, Ferdinand Joseph 1904- WhoWrEP 92
Wiener, Harry 1924- WhoE 93, WhoWor 93
Wiener, Hesh 1946- WhoAm 92, WhoWor 93

Wiener, Jack R. *Law&B 92*
Wiener, Jacques Loeb, Jr. 1934- *WhoAm 92, WhoSSW 93*
Wiener, Jean 1896-1982 *Baker 92*
Wiener, Joel *Law&B 92*
Wiener, Jon 1944- *WhoAm 92*
Wiener, Joseph 1927- *WhoAm 92*
Wiener, Jude 1953- *St&PR 93*
Wiener, Keith 1945- *WhoWor 93*
Wiener, Leo 1862-1939 *BioIn 17*
Wiener, Leonard 1940- *WhoE 93*
Wiener, Malcolm Hewitt 1935- *WhoAm 92*
Wiener, Marvin S. 1925- *WhoAm 92, WhoWrEP 92*
Wiener, Maurice 1942- *St&PR 93*
Wiener, Morton 1920- *WhoE 93*
Wiener, Norbert 1894-1964 *BioIn 17*
Wiener, Norma 1931- *St&PR 93*
Wiener, Norman J. 1919- *WhoAm 92*
Wiener, Otto 1913- *Baker 92*
Wiener, Philip P(aul) 1905-1992 *ConAu 137*
Wiener, Philip Paul 1905-1992 *BioIn 17*
Wiener, Robert Alvin 1918- *WhoAm 92*
Wiener, Sarah d1990 *BioIn 17*
Wiener, Solomon 1915- *WhoE 93, WhoWor 93*
Wiener, Stanley Lewis 1930- *WhoAm 92*
Wiener, Theodore A. 1932- *St&PR 93*
Wiener, Thomas Eli 1940- *WhoAm 92*
Wiener, Valerie 1948- *WhoEmL 93, WhoWor 93*
Wieners, John 1934- *BioIn 17*
Wieniawski, Adam Tadeusz 1879-1950 *Baker 92, PolBiDi*
Wieniawski, Henryk 1835-1880 *Baker 92, PolBiDi*
Wieniawski, Joseph 1837-1912 *PolBiDi*
Wieniawski, Jozef 1837-1912 *Baker 92*
Wieniawski, Witold T. 1926- *WhoScE 91-4*
Wiens, Arthur Nicholai 1926- *WhoAm 92*
Wiens, Gloria Jean 1958- *WhoAmW 93*
Wienshienk, Ralph 1919- *WhoAm 92*
Wieprecht, Friedrich Wilhelm 1802-1872 *Baker 92*
Wiepz, Deborah Wilson 1955- *WhoAmW 93*
Wier, Albert Ernest 1879-1945 *Baker 92*
Wier, Allen 1946- *WhoWrEP 92*
Wier, Dara 1949- *WhoWrEP 92*
Wier, David A. *Law&B 92*
Wier, Ester (Alberti) 1910- *DcAmChF 1960*
Wier, James A. *St&PR 93*
Wier, Jeanne Elizabeth *AmWomPl*
Wier, Patricia Ann 1937- *WhoAm 92, WhoAmW 93*
Wier, Patricia N. 1937- *St&PR 93*
Wier, Richard Royal, Jr. 1941- *WhoAm 92*
Wier, Robert Charles 1928- *St&PR 93*
Wiere, Harry 1908- See Wiere Brothers, The *QDrFCA 92*
Wiere, Herbert 1909- See Wiere Brothers, The *QDrFCA 92*
Wiere, Sylvester 1910-1970 See Wiere Brothers, The *QDrFCA 92*
Wiere Brothers, The *QDrFCA 92 [port]*
Wierenga, Herman K. 1951- *WhoScE 91-3*
Wierman, John Charles 1949- *WhoAm 92, WhoE 93*
Wiernik, Peter Harris 1939- *WhoAm 92, WhoWor 93*
Wiernik, Stan 1947- *St&PR 93*
Wierowski, Henryk Eugeniusz 1923- *WhoScE 91-4*
Wiersbe, Warren Wendell 1929- *WhoAm 92*
Wiersing, Klaus 1943- *WhoUN 92*
Wiersma, Peggy Ann 1956- *WhoAmW 93*
Wiersum, Charles Chester 1940- *St&PR 93*
Wierup, P.J.F. Martin 1943- *WhoScE 91-4*
Wierusz-Kowalski, Alfred 1849-1915 *PolBiDi*
Wierzba, Andrzej 1937- *WhoScE 91-4*
Wierzbicki, Andrzej Piotr 1937- *WhoScE 91-4*
Wierzbicki, Felix Paul 1815-1860 *PolBiDi*
Wierzbicki, Volkmar Erwin 1945- *WhoWor 93*
Wierzchowski, Kazimierz Lech 1929- *WhoScE 91-4*
Wierzynski, Kazimierz 1894-1969 *PolBiDi*
Wies, Winfried 1949- *WhoWor 93*
Wiesbeck, Werner 1942- *WhoWor 93*
Wieschenberg, Klaus 1932- *St&PR 93, WhoWor 93*
Wiese, Allen Franklin 1925- *WhoSSW 93*
Wiese, Dorothy Jean 1940- *WhoAmW 93*
Wiese, James Douglas 1939- *St&PR 93*
Wiese, John Paul 1934- *CngDr 91*
Wiese, Kees 1936- *WhoWor 93*
Wiese, Konrad Artur 1943- *WhoScE 91-3*
Wiese, Kurt 1887-1974 *MajAI [port]*
Wiese, Larry Clevenger *Law&B 92*
Wiese, Michael 1947- *WhoWrEP 92*
Wiese, Otis Lee *BioIn 17*
Wiese, Terry Eugene 1948- *WhoSSW 93*
Wiese, William Allen *Law&B 92*
Wiesebach, Horst *WhoUN 92*
Wiesel, Elie 1928- *BioIn 17, JeAmHC, MagSWL [port], WhoAm 92, WhoE 93, WhoWor 93, WhoWrEP 92*
Wiesel, Elie(zer) 1928- *ConAu 40NR*
Wiesel, Torsten Nils 1924- *WhoAm 92, WhoE 93, WhoWor 93*
Wieseltier, Leon 1952- *WhoWrEP 92*
Wiesemann, Klaus H. 1937- *WhoScE 91-3*
Wiesen, Anne Rhoda 1926- *WhoAmW 93*
Wiesen, David Lipman 1932- *WhoE 93*
Wiesen, Donald Guy 1928- *WhoAm 92*
Wiesen, Irving L. *Law&B 92*
Wiesen, Marvin Arthur 1929- *WhoSSW 93*
Wiesen, Richard A. 1937- *WhoAm 92*
Wiesenack, R. *WhoScE 91-3*
Wiesenberg, Jacqueline Leonardi *WhoAmW 93, WhoWor 93*
Wiesenberg, Jacqueline Leonardi 1928- *WhoE 93*
Wiesenberg, Russel John 1924- *WhoE 93*
Wiesenberg-Bercaw, Gretchen Sue 1961- *WhoAmW 93*
Wiesenfeld, Bess Gazevitz 1915- *WhoAmW 93*
Wiesenfeld, John Richard 1944- *WhoAm 92*
Wiesenfeld, Laurent 1955- *WhoWor 93*
Wiesenfeld, Paul 1942-1990 *BioIn 17*
Wiesengrund-Adorno, Theodor *Baker 92*
Wiesenhahn, David Franklin 1961- *WhoSSW 93*
Wiesenthal, Marc A. 1959- *St&PR 93*
Wiesenthal, Richard Stanley 1929- *St&PR 93*
Wiesenthal, Simon *BioIn 17*
Wiesenthal, Simon 1908- *ConHero 2 [port], WhoWor 93*
Wieser, Charles Edward 1929- *St&PR 93, WhoAm 92*
Wieser, Sharon Teague 1962- *WhoAmW 93*
Wieslander, (Axel Otto) Ingvar 1917-1963 *Baker 92*
Wiesler, James Ballard 1927- *WhoAm 92*
Wiesman, Ronald 1948- *WhoIns 93*
Wiesner, Dallas Charles 1959- *WhoEmL 93, WhoWor 93*
Wiesner, David *ChlBIID [port]*
Wiesner, David 1956- *SmATA 72 [port]*
Wiesner, Donna Rose 1957- *WhoSSW 93*
Wiesner, Douglas Warren 1940- *St&PR 93*
Wiesner, Jerome Bert 1915- *WhoAm 92, WhoE 93*
Wiesner, John J. 1938- *St&PR 93*
Wiesner, John Joseph 1938- *WhoAm 92, WhoSSW 93*
Wiesner, Loren E. 1938- *WhoAm 92*
Wiesner, Robert Joseph 1953- *WhoSSW 93*
Wiesner, Theodora d1992 *NewYTBS 92*
Wiesner, Theodora 1908-1992 *BioIn 17*
Wiess, Edward *Law&B 92*
Wiess, G. Parry 1922- *St&PR 93*
Wiessler, David Albert 1942- *WhoAm 92*
Wiest, Dianne 1948- *WhoAm 92, WhoAmW 93*
Wiest, John Andrew 1946- *WhoSSW 93*
Wiest, Roger V. *Law&B 92*
Wiest, Roger Vaughn 1940- *St&PR 93*
Wietasch, Klaus W. 1933- *WhoScE 91-3*
Wieten, Alida *ScF&FL 92*
Wietfeldt, David Carl 1953- *St&PR 93*
Wieting, Gary Lee 1937- *WhoE 93*
Wietor, Michael George 1937- *WhoSSW 93*
Wiewiorowski, Maciej 1918- *WhoScE 91-4*
Wiezlak, Wlodzimierz 1925- *WhoScE 91-4*
Wigal, Donald Wayne 1933- *WhoE 93*
Wigan, Marcus Ramsay 1941- *WhoWor 93*
Wigand, Arthur F. 1944- *St&PR 93*
Wigdor, Lawrence A. 1941- *St&PR 93*
Wigertz, Ove B. 1934- *WhoScE 91-4*
Wiget, Bernardine d1883 *BioIn 17*
Wigg, Colleen Mary 1960- *WhoAmW 93*
Wigg, Martin Eric 1946- *St&PR 93*
Wiggans, Samuel Claude 1922- *WhoE 93*
Wigger, Diane Bisciotti 1951- *WhoSSW 93*
Wiggers, Albert Johan 1921- *WhoScE 91-3*
Wiggers, Charlotte Suzanne Ward 1943- *WhoAmW 93*
Wiggers, Harold Carl 1910- *WhoSSW 93*
Wigghan, Barrie 1937- *WhoAsAP 91*
Wiggin, Blanton C. 1922- *St&PR 93*
Wiggin, Kate Douglas Smith 1856-1923 *AmWomPl, ConAu 137, MajAI [port]*
Wiggin, Kendall French 1951- *WhoAm 92*
Wiggin, Neal Albert 1930- *WhoWor 93*
Wiggin, Sharon Spooner 1942- *WhoAmW 93*
Wiggin, William F. 1928- *St&PR 93*
Wiggins, A.J. *Law&B 92*
Wiggins, Alan *BioIn 17*
Wiggins, Albert H. 1938- *St&PR 93*
Wiggins, Charles Edward 1927- *WhoAm 92*
Wiggins, Charles Henry, Jr. 1939- *WhoAm 92*
Wiggins, Guy Arthur *WhoE 93*
Wiggins, Henry H. d1990 *BioIn 17*
Wiggins, Ida Silver *WhoAmW 93*
Wiggins, James Bryan 1935- *WhoAm 92, WhoE 93*
Wiggins, James Russell 1903- *JrnUS, WhoAm 92*
Wiggins, James Walter 1949- *WhoSSW 93*
Wiggins, James Wendell 1942- *WhoSSW 93*
Wiggins, Jerome M. 1940- *St&PR 93*
Wiggins, Jerome Meyer 1940- *WhoAm 92*
Wiggins, K. Douglas 1959- *BioIn 17*
Wiggins, Marianne 1947- *ScF&FL 92*
Wiggins, Michael C. 1948- *St&PR 93*
Wiggins, Nancy Bowen 1948- *WhoAmW 93*
Wiggins, Nina Louise 1961- *WhoAmW 93*
Wiggins, Norman Adrian 1924- *WhoAm 92, WhoSSW 93*
Wiggins, Patryc *BioIn 17*
Wiggins, Robert A. 1921- *ScF&FL 92*
Wiggins, Rosalind Zeldina *Law&B 92*
Wiggins, Samuel Paul 1919- *WhoAm 92*
Wiggins, Sarah Woolfolk 1934- *WhoSSW 93*
Wiggins, Stephen F. *St&PR 93*
Wiggins, Timothy J. 1956- *St&PR 93*
Wiggins, Vivian Pinn- *BioIn 17*
Wiggins, Walter James 1925- *St&PR 93*
Wiggins, Walton Wray 1924- *WhoWor 93*
Wiggins, Wanda 1945- *WhoAmW 93*
Wigginton, B. Eliot *BioIn 17*
Wigginton, Eliot *BioIn 17*
Wigginton, Eugene H. 1935- *St&PR 93, WhoAm 92*
Wigginton, James Charles 1949- *WhoEmL 93*
Wigginton, May Wood *AmWomPl*
Wigginton, Wilma *AmWomPl*
Wigglesworth, Frank 1918- *Baker 92*
Wiggs, B. Ryland *Law&B 92*
Wiggs, David H. 1947- *St&PR 93*
Wiggs, David Harold, Jr. 1947- *WhoAm 92*
Wiggs, Eugene Overbey 1928- *WhoAm 92*
Wiggs, Robert Howard 1947- *WhoSSW 93*
Wiggs, Shirley JoAnn 1940- *WhoSSW 93*
Wight, Carol Van Buren *AmWomPl*
Wight, Darlene 1926- *WhoAmW 93, WhoWor 93*
Wight, Doris Teresa 1929- *WhoWrEP 92*
Wight, James Alfred 1916- *WhoWor 93*
Wight, R. Alan 1938- *WhoAm 92*
Wight, Susan K. 1952- *WhoAmW 93*
Wightman, Ann 1958- *WhoAmW 93*
Wightman, Arthur Strong 1922- *WhoAm 92*
Wightman, David Randal 1925- *WhoWor 93*
Wightman, Gerald 1937- *WhoWor 93*
Wightman, Hazel Hotchkiss 1886-1974 *BioIn 17*
Wightman, Linda Leary 1945- *WhoAmW 93*
Wightman, Marian *AmWomPl*
Wigington, Ronald Lee 1932- *WhoAm 92*
Wiginton, Jay Spencer 1941- *WhoSSW 93*
Wigle, James H. *Law&B 92*
Wigle, Richard Lee 1947- *WhoSSW 93*
Wigler, Michael 1947- *WhoAm 92*
Wigler, Paul William 1928- *WhoSSW 93*
Wiglesworth, Michael Bland 1949- *WhoEmL 93, WhoWor 93*
Wigley, Michael Robert 1954- *St&PR 93*
Wigley, Tom Michael Lampe 1940- *WhoWor 93*
Wigley-Morrison, Karen 1950- *WhoSSW 93*
Wigman, James Francis 1935- *St&PR 93*
Wigmore, Barrie Atherton 1941- *WhoAm 92*
Wigmore, W. Mark *Law&B 92*
Wignall, Ernest Carl 1927- *St&PR 93*
Wignall, T.C. 1883-1958 *ScF&FL 92*
Wignell, Edel 1936- *ConAu 137, ScF&FL 92, SmATA 69 [port]*
Wignell, Edna *ScF&FL 92*
Wigner, Eugene Paul 1902- *WhoAm 92, WhoE 93, WhoWor 93*
Wignesan, T. 1933- *WhoWor 93*
Wigodsky, Herman Saul 1915- *St&PR 93*
Wigton, Paul N. 1932- *St&PR 93*
Wigton, Paul Norton 1932- *WhoAm 92*
Wigura, Stanislaw 1901-1932 *PolBiDi*
Wigzell, Hens Lennart Rudolf 1938- *WhoScE 91-4*
Wihan, Hans 1855-1920 *Baker 92*
Wihl, Gunter F. 1943- *WhoScE 91-4*
Wihtol, Joseph 1863-1948 *Baker 92*
Wiig, Elisabeth Hemmersam 1935- *WhoAm 92, WhoAmW 93*
Wiin-Nielsen, Aksel Christopher 1924- *WhoAm 92, WhoScE 91-4*
Wiita, Kathryn Carpenter 1961- *WhoAmW 93*
Wijayaratnas Family *BioIn 17*
Wijdeveld, Wolfgang 1910-1985 *Baker 92*
Wijegoonasekera, Don Piyasena 1932- *WhoWor 93*
Wijeratne, Abhaya 1955- *WhoWor 93*
Wijeratne, Rupa Wijeratne Arachchige 1938- *WhoWor 93*
Wijesekera, Nandadeva 1908- *IntDcAn*
Wijetunga, Dimbiri Banda 1922- *WhoWor 93*
Wijetunge, Dingiri Banda 1922- *WhoAsAP 91*
Wijetunge, Vernon 1920- *WhoWor 93*
Wijeysundera, Nihal Ekanayake 1943- *WhoWor 93*
Wijk, Arnold van *Baker 92*
Wijk, Nicholaas van 1880-1941 *BioIn 17*
Wijnhoven, Jacques 1925- *WhoScE 91-2*
Wijsman, J.A. 1942- *WhoScE 91-3*
Wikander, Lawrence Einar 1915- *WhoAm 92*
Wikant, Duane Edwin 1931- *St&PR 93*
Wike, Andrew 1952- *WhoSSW 93*
Wike, D. Elaine 1954- *WhoEmL 93, WhoSSW 93*
Wike, DeJuana Deniece 1960- *WhoAmW 93*
Wike, James E. 1928- *St&PR 93*
Wike, Walter 1946- *St&PR 93*
Wikenhauser, Charles Joseph 1948- *WhoAm 92*
Wikerd, Paul Hubert 1947- *WhoE 93*
Wiker Moskow, Nancy Eileen 1949- *WhoAmW 93*
Wiklund, Adolf 1879-1950 *Baker 92*
Wiklund, K. Lars C. 1943- *WhoWor 93*
Wiklund, K. Rudolf 1936- *WhoWor 93*
Wiklund, Martin *WhoScE 91-4*
Wikman, Andrew O. 1927- *St&PR 93*
Wikman, Georg Karl 1943- *WhoWor 93*
Wikmanson, Johan 1753-1800 *Baker 92*
Wikoff, Howard Ely 1949- *WhoE 93*
Wiksten, B.F. 1935- *St&PR 93*
Wiksten, Barry Frank 1935- *WhoAm 92*
Wikstrom, Gunnar, Jr. 1936- *WhoAm 92*
Wikstrom, Marten K.F. 1945- *WhoScE 91-4*
Wiktor, Andrzej Hubert 1931- *WhoScE 91-4*
Wikus Pignatti, Erika 1929- *WhoScE 91-3*
Wilamowski, Bogdan M. 1944- *WhoScE 91-4*
Wiland, Phillip A. *BioIn 17*
Wilbanks, Daniel Pinckney 1937- *WhoSSW 93*
Wilbanks, Darrel Jay 1944- *WhoSSW 93*
Wilbanks, J. Cody *Law&B 92*
Wilbanks, Jan Joseph 1928- *WhoAm 92*
Wilbanks, Karen Courtney Kincannon 1945- *WhoSSW 93*
Wilbanks, Robert Smith 1947- *St&PR 93*
Wilbanks-Giatras, Stephanie 1956- *WhoSSW 93*
Wilber, Alix *ScF&FL 92*
Wilber, Charles Grady 1916- *WhoAm 92*
Wilber, Gordon A. 1941- *St&PR 93*
Wilber, Laura Ann 1934- *WhoAm 92*
Wilber, Philip Irving 1927- *St&PR 93, WhoAm 92*
Wilber, Richard A. *ScF&FL 92*
Wilber, Rick 1948- *ScF&FL 92*
Wilber, Robert Edwin 1932- *WhoAm 92*
Wilber, Treya Killam *BioIn 17*
Wilber, William John *WhoScE 91-1*
Wilberger, James Eldridge 1952- *WhoE 93*
Wilbert, Catherine A. *Law&B 92*
Wilbert, Felicia Libo 1959- *WhoWrEP 92*
Wilbert, James Colligan *Law&B 92*
Wilbert, Marlin T. 1930- *St&PR 93*
Wilbor, Garry O. 1940- *St&PR 93*
Wilborn, Richard E. 1945- *St&PR 93*
Wilborn, Thomas Lockart 1930- *WhoE 93*
Wilbourn, Gordon Gene 1933- *St&PR 93*
Wilbourne, Preston Holt 1925- *St&PR 93*
Wilbrecht, Jon Keehn 1942- *St&PR 93*
Wilbur, D. Elliott, Jr. 1929- *St&PR 93*
Wilbur, David E. 1942- *St&PR 93*
Wilbur, E. Packer 1936- *WhoAm 92*
Wilbur, Georgia Delores 1926- *WhoAmW 93*
Wilbur, Helen Hannah Clifford 1878- *AmWomPl*
Wilbur, Henry Miles 1944- *WhoSSW 93*
Wilbur, James Benjamin, III 1924- *WhoAm 92*
Wilbur, James E. *BioIn 17*
Wilbur, John Hearring 1929- *St&PR 93*
Wilbur, Karl Milton 1912- *WhoAm 92*
Wilbur, Leslie Clifford 1924- *WhoAm 92*
Wilbur, Lyman Dwight 1900- *WhoAm 92*
Wilbur, Melissa Ellen 1944- *WhoE 93*

Wilbur, Michael F. 1945- *St&PR 93*
Wilbur, Peter D. *Law&B 92*
Wilbur, Ralph Edwin 1932- *St&PR 93*
Wilbur, Richard 1921- *AmWrS3, BioIn 17, MagSAmL [port]*
Wilbur, Richard Purdy 1921- *WhoAm 92, WhoE 93, WhoWrEP 92*
Wilbur, Richard Sloan 1924- *WhoAm 92*
Wilbur, Robert Lunch 1925- *WhoSSW 93*
Wilbur, William B. 1950- *St&PR 93*
Wilburn, Adolph Yarbrough 1932- *WhoE 93*
Wilburn, Dennis P. 1954- *St&PR 93*
Wilburn, Frances Beth 1959- *WhoSSW 93*
Wilburn, Kathy *BioIn 17*
Wilburn, Mary Nelson 1932- *WhoAmW 93, WhoE 93, WhoWor 93*
Wilburn, Robert Charles 1943- *WhoAm 92*
Wilburn, Tyree G. 1952- *St&PR 93*
Wilburn, Tyree Gary 1952- *WhoAm 92*
Wilburr, Harriette 1891- *AmWomPl*
Wilby, Kathy *BioIn 17*
Wilby, William Langfitt 1944- *WhoAm 92*
Wilbye, John 1574?-c. 1638 *Baker 92*
Wilchek, Meir 1935- *WhoWor 93*
Wilcher, Carol B. 1946- *WhoAmW 93*
Wilcher, LaJuana Sue 1954- *WhoAm 92, WhoAmW 93*
Wilcher, Larry Keith 1950- *WhoAm 92*
Wilcher, Shirley J. 1951- *WhoAmW 93, WhoE 93*
Wilchins, Howard Martin 1945- *WhoE 93*
Wilchins, Sidney A. 1940- *WhoWor 93*
Wilchusky, Bernard Leonard 1932- *WhoE 93*
Wilcken, Michael Alfred *Law&B 92*
Wilckens, Friedrich 1899-1986 *Baker 92*
Wilckens, Hellmut *WhoScE 91-3*
Wilcock, Bill Wayne 1943- *St&PR 93*
Wilcock, David Norman *WhoScE 91-1*
Wilcock, Dennis *WhoScE 91-1*
Wilcock, Donald Frederick 1913- *WhoAm 92*
Wilcock, Gordon Keith *WhoScE 91-1*
Wilcock, James W. 1917- *St&PR 93*
Wilcock, James William 1917- *WhoAm 92*
Wilcock, John *WhoWrEP 92*
Wilcock, William Leslie 1922- *WhoWor 93*
Wilcockson, A. *WhoScE 91-1*
Wilcomes, Ronald Howard *Law&B 92*
Wilcott, Scott J. *Law&B 92*
Wilcott, Scott J. 1938- *St&PR 93*
Wilcox, Allison *BioIn 17*
Wilcox, Barbara Montgomery 1939- *WhoSSW 93*
Wilcox, Bruce Gordon 1947- *WhoAm 92*
Wilcox, Calvin Hayden 1924- *WhoAm 92*
Wilcox, Charlene Deloris 1932- *WhoAmW 93*
Wilcox, Charles Julian 1930- *WhoSSW 93*
Wilcox, Charlotte 1948- *SmATA 72 [port]*
Wilcox, Cheryl Ann 1948- *WhoEmL 93*
Wilcox, Collin M. 1924- *WhoAm 92, WhoWrEP 92*
Wilcox, Constance Grenelle *AmWomPl*
Wilcox, David 1940- *BiDAMSp 1989*
Wilcox, David Albertson 1938- *St&PR 93*
Wilcox, David Cornell 1951- *WhoAm 92*
Wilcox, David Eric 1939- *WhoE 93*
Wilcox, Debra Kay 1955- *WhoEmL 93*
Wilcox, Dina Lynn 1947- *WhoAmW 93*
Wilcox, Don 1908- *ScF&FL 92*
Wilcox, Donald J. 1938-1991 *BioIn 17*
Wilcox, Douglas Warren, Jr. 1965- *WhoSSW 93*
Wilcox, Ella Wheeler 1850?-1919 *AmWomPl*
Wilcox, Gail Patricia Waters 1957- *WhoEmL 93*
Wilcox, Grace *AmWomPl*
Wilcox, Gregory G. 1949- *St&PR 93*
Wilcox, Harry Hammond 1918- *WhoAm 92*
Wilcox, Harry Roger 1936- *St&PR 93*
Wilcox, Harry Wilbur, Jr. 1925- *WhoAm 92*
Wilcox, Harvey John 1937- *WhoAm 92*
Wilcox, Helen (Elizabeth) 1955- *ConAu 136*
Wilcox, Helen L. *AmWomPl*
Wilcox, Herbert 1892-1977 *MiSFD 9N*
Wilcox, Ian 1955- *WhoWor 93*
Wilcox, J.C. *WhoScE 91-1*
Wilcox, Jackson Burton 1918- *WhoWrEP 92*
Wilcox, James *BioIn 17*
Wilcox, James L. *Law&B 92*
Wilcox, James R. 1942- *St&PR 93*
Wilcox, James S. 1946- *St&PR 93*
Wilcox, Jean Marie 1958- *WhoAmW 93*
Wilcox, Jim 1941- *BioIn 17*
Wilcox, John Caven *Law&B 92*
Wilcox, John Caven 1942- *St&PR 93*
Wilcox, John Richard 1939- *WhoE 93*
Wilcox, Kathy Loretta Postell 1961- *WhoAmW 93*
Wilcox, Laird Maurice 1942- *WhoWrEP 92*
Wilcox, Margaret Walker 1918- *WhoAmW 93*
Wilcox, Marion Walter 1922- *WhoAm 92*
Wilcox, Mark Dean 1952- *WhoAm 92, WhoEmL 93, WhoWor 93*
Wilcox, Marsha Ann 1956- *WhoE 93*
Wilcox, Mary Ann 1946- *WhoWrEP 92*
Wilcox, Mary Rose 1949- *NotHsAW 93 [port]*
Wilcox, Maud 1923- *WhoAm 92, WhoAmW 93*
Wilcox, Michael Wing 1941- *WhoAm 92*
Wilcox, Patricia Anne 1932- *WhoWrEP 92*
Wilcox, Paul Horne 1950- *WhoWor 93*
Wilcox, R.I.D. *WhoScE 91-1*
Wilcox, Robert K. 1943- *ScF&FL 92*
Wilcox, Ronald Bruce 1934- *WhoAm 92*
Wilcox, Scott A. 1958- *St&PR 93*
Wilcox, Sharee Leigh 1951- *WhoAmW 93*
Wilcox, Shirley Jean Langdon 1942- *WhoSSW 93*
Wilcox, Tara Leigh 1966- *WhoAmW 93*
Wilcox, Thomas R., III *Law&B 92*
Wilcox, William L., Jr. 1945- *St&PR 93*
Wilcox, William Ross 1935- *WhoAm 92*
Wilcoxen, Joan Heeren 1948- *WhoAmW 93*
Wilcoxon, Henry 1905-1984 *BioIn 17*
Wilcoxson, Carol Ann 1943- *WhoSSW 93*
Wilcoxson, Mozelle Trout 1917- *WhoWor 93*
Wilczek, Elmar Ulrich 1948- *WhoWor 93*
Wilczek, Frank Anthony 1951- *WhoAm 92*
Wilczek, Robert Joseph 1944- *WhoAm 92*
Wilczewski, Melvin Lee 1950- *St&PR 93*
Wilczynski, A. Paul *Law&B 92*
Wilczynski, Donald James 1934- *St&PR 93*
Wilczynski, Janusz S. 1929- *WhoAm 92*
Wilczynski, Ryszard Leslaw 1949- *WhoWor 93*
Wild, Aloysius 1929- *WhoScE 91-3*
Wild, Caroline S. P. *AmWomPl*
Wild, (Robert) David (Fergusson) 1910- *ConAu 139*
Wild, Earl 1915- *Baker 92*
Wild, Hans 1939- *WhoWor 93*
Wild, Hans Jochen 1935- *WhoWor 93*
Wild, James Robert 1945- *WhoSSW 93*
Wild, John Julian 1914- *WhoAm 92, WhoWor 93*
Wild, John Paul 1923- *WhoWor 93*
Wild, Jost 1937- *WhoScE 91-4*
Wild, Nelson Hopkins 1933- *WhoAm 92*
Wild, Ray *WhoScE 91-1*
Wild, Robert Arnold 1946- *WhoSSW 93*
Wild, Robert Keith 1942- *WhoWor 93*
Wild, Robert Lee 1921- *WhoAm 92*
Wild, Stanley *WhoScE 91-1*
Wild, Susan Carole 1953- *WhoAmW 93*
Wild, Urs P. 1936- *WhoScE 91-4*
Wild, Victor Allyn 1946- *WhoEmL 93*
Wild, William Charles, Jr. 1911- *WhoAm 92*
Wildauer, Werner 1934- *St&PR 93*
Wildberger, Jacques 1922- *Baker 92*
Wildbrunn, Helene 1882-1972 *Baker 92*
Wilde, Alan 1929- *WhoWrEP 92*
Wilde, Alexander G. 1948- *WhoIns 93*
Wilde, Carlton D. 1935- *WhoAm 92*
Wilde, Cornel 1915-1989 *BioIn 17, IntDcF 2-3 [port], MiSFD 9N*
Wilde, Daniel Underwood 1937- *WhoAm 92*
Wilde, Darwin John 1944- *St&PR 93*
Wilde, Davis Stewart 1937- *WhoWrEP 92*
Wilde, Donald Raymond 1926- *WhoAm 92*
Wilde, Edwin Frederick 1931- *WhoAm 92, WhoSSW 93*
Wilde, Eva M. *AmWomPl*
Wilde, Fran 1948- *WhoAsAP 91*
Wilde, Garner Lee 1926- *WhoSSW 93*
Wilde, Harold Richard 1945- *WhoAm 92*
Wilde, John 1919- *WhoAm 92*
Wilde, Kelley *ScF&FL 92*
Wilde, Kenneth K. 1933- *WhoUN 92*
Wilde, Larry 1928- *ConAu 40NR, WhoWrEP 92*
Wilde, Nicholas *ChlFicS, ScF&FL 92*
Wilde, Norman Taylor, Jr. 1930- *St&PR 93, WhoAm 92*
Wilde, Oscar 1854-1900 *BioIn 17, MagSWL [port], ScF&FL 92, ShSCr 11 [port], WorLitC [port]*
Wilde, Patricia 1928- *WhoAm 92, WhoAmW 93, WhoE 93*
Wilde, Peter V.D. *Law&B 92*
Wilde, Richard Lawrence 1944- *WhoAm 92*
Wilde, Robert Eugene 1923- *WhoWrEP 92*
Wilde, William Key 1933- *St&PR 93, WhoAm 92*
Wilde, William Lawrence 1936- *WhoWrEP 92*
Wilde, Wilson 1927- *St&PR 93, WhoAm 92, WhoIns 93*
Wildebush, Joseph Frederick 1910- *WhoE 93*
Wildenhain, Ernest D. *Law&B 92*
Wildenhain, Marguerite 1896-1985 *BioIn 17*
Wildenmann, Rudolf 1921- *WhoWor 93*
Wildenthal, Claud Kern 1941- *WhoAm 92, WhoWor 93*
Wilder, Alec 1907-1980 *Baker 92, BioIn 17*
Wilder, Amos Tappan 1940- *WhoE 93*
Wilder, Anne G. d1992 *NewYTBS 92*
Wilder, Billy 1906- *BioIn 17, MiSFD 9, WhoAm 92*
Wilder, Cherry 1930- *ScF&FL 92*
Wilder, Cora Sue 1950- *WhoAmW 93*
Wilder, David Randolph 1929- *WhoAm 92*
Wilder, Douglas *BioIn 17*
Wilder, Duane Edward 1929- *St&PR 93*
Wilder, Eleanor Marie 1950- *WhoAmW 93, WhoEmL 93*
Wilder, Essie Lee 1914- *WhoSSW 93*
Wilder, Gene *BioIn 17*
Wilder, Gene 1934- *QDrFCA 92 [port]*
Wilder, Gene 1935- *IntDcF 2-3 [port], MiSFD 9, WhoAm 92*
Wilder, J. Michael *Law&B 92*
Wilder, Jessie Wilkinson 1871- *AmWomPl*
Wilder, Joe 1920- *BioIn 17*
Wilder, John *MiSFD 9*
Wilder, John Richard *WhoWrEP 92*
Wilder, John Shelton 1921- *WhoAm 92, WhoSSW 93*
Wilder, Kay Maridel 1945- *WhoAmW 93*
Wilder, L. Douglas *BioIn 17*
Wilder, L. Douglas 1931- *ConBlB 3 [port], PolPar*
Wilder, Laura 1867-1957 *ChlFicS*
Wilder, Laura Ingalls 1867-1957 *BioIn 17*
Wilder, Laura (Elizabeth) Ingalls 1867-1957 *ConAu 137, MajAI [port]*
Wilder, Lawrence Douglas *NewYTBS 92 [port]*
Wilder, Lawrence Douglas 1931- *AfrAmBi [port], EncAACR, WhoAm 92, WhoSSW 93, WhoWor 93*
Wilder, Marion *AmWomPl*
Wilder, Michael S. 1941- *WhoIns 93*
Wilder, Michael Stephen *Law&B 92*
Wilder, Myles *ScF&FL 92*
Wilder, Myron F. 1934- *WhoIns 93*
Wilder, Myron Farnham, Jr. 1934- *St&PR 93*
Wilder, Pelham, Jr. 1920- *WhoAm 92*
Wilder, Philip Sawyer, Jr. 1924- *WhoAm 92*
Wilder, Philip van c. 1500-1553 *Baker 92*
Wilder, Richard B. 1943- *St&PR 93*
Wilder, Robert Allen 1944- *WhoSSW 93*
Wilder, Robert David 1948- *WhoAm 92, WhoE 93*
Wilder, Robert George 1920- *St&PR 93, WhoAm 92*
Wilder, Robert O. 1927- *St&PR 93*
Wilder, Robert P. 1863-1938 *BioIn 17*
Wilder, Roland Percival, Jr. 1940- *WhoWor 93*
Wilder, Ronald Lynn 1947- *WhoE 93*
Wilder, Ronald Parker 1941- *WhoAm 92*
Wilder, Stephen M. *BioIn 17*
Wilder, Thornton 1897-1975 *BioIn 17, MagSAmL [port], WorLitC [port]*
Wilder, Thornton (Niven) 1897-1975 *ConAu 40NR*
Wilder, Valerie 1947- *WhoAm 92*
Wilder, Victor 1835-1892 *Baker 92*
Wilder, Wilburetta Micki 1927- *WhoE 93*
Wilder, William Price 1922- *St&PR 93*
Wilderer, Johann Hugo von 1670?-1724? *Baker 92*
Wilderman, Giles H. 1925- *St&PR 93*
Wildermuth, Gordon Lee 1937- *WhoAm 92*
Wildermuth, Karl 1921- *WhoWor 93*
Wildermuth, Kathy Chichester 1947- *WhoAmW 93*
Wildermuth, Mark Edwin 1956- *WhoSSW 93*
Wildermuth, Robert Edward 1929- *St&PR 93*
Wildermuth, Roger Gregory 1944- *St&PR 93*
Wildermuth, Victoria Ann 1953- *WhoSSW 93*
Wilderotter, James Arthur *Law&B 92*
Wilderotter, James Arthur 1944- *WhoAm 92*
Wilderotter, Peter Thomas 1954- *WhoE 93*
Wilderson, Samuel Francis 1946- *WhoE 93*
Wildes, Dudley Joseph 1935- *WhoAm 92*
Wildfang, Martha May 1964- *WhoAmW 93*
Wildfoerster, Christopher Justus 1958- *St&PR 93*
Wildgans, Anton 1881-1932 *DcLB 118 [port]*
Wildgans, Friedrich 1913-1965 *Baker 92*
Wildgen, Mike *BioIn 17*
Wildhack, William August, Jr. 1935- *St&PR 93, WhoAm 92*
Wildi, Otto 1946- *WhoScE 91-4*
Wilding, Chris *WhoScE 91-1*
Wilding, Diane 1942- *WhoAmW 93, WhoSSW 93, WhoWor 93*
Wilding, Dorothy 1893-1976 *BioIn 17*
Wilding, Henry Peter 1922- *St&PR 93*
Wilding, Laurence Paul 1934- *WhoAm 92*
Wilding, Michael 1942- *ConLC 73 [port], ScF&FL 92*
Wilding, Michael 1953- *BioIn 17*
Wilding, Neil *WhoScE 91-1*
Wilding-White, Raymond 1922- *Baker 92*
Wildish, Kat *WhoE 93*
Wildman, Donald C. 1932- *St&PR 93*
Wildman, Eugene 1936- *WhoWrEP 92*
Wildman, Gary Cecil 1942- *WhoAm 92*
Wildman, George Thomas 1935- *WhoE 93*
Wildman, Marian Warner *AmWomPl*
Wildman, Max Edward 1919- *WhoAm 92*
Wildman, Paulette Lee 1946- *WhoAmW 93*
Wildman, R. Joseph 1938- *St&PR 93*
Wildman, Richard W. *Law&B 92*
Wildman, Steven S. 1948- *ConAu 139*
Wildmon, Donald *BioIn 17*
Wildmon, Donald 1938- *CurBio 92 [port]*
Wildpret, Robert Frank 1946- *St&PR 93*
Wildrick, Catherine Ruth 1962- *WhoE 93*
Wildrick, Kenyon Jones 1933- *WhoWor 93*
Wilds, Benjamin James, Jr. 1944- *WhoSSW 93*
Wildsmith, Brian 1930- *MajAI [port], SmATA 69 [port]*
Wildsmith, G. *WhoScE 91-1*
Wildstein, Kenneth B. *Law&B 92*
Wildung, Wendy Jo 1954- *WhoAmW 93*
Wile, Donald Clayton 1931- *St&PR 93*
Wile, Edith B. *ScF&FL 92*
Wile, Joan 1931- *WhoAmW 93*
Wile, Julius 1915- *WhoAm 92*
Wile, Timothy Spaulding 1956- *WhoE 93*
Wilemon, Daniel Huntley 1962- *WhoSSW 93*
Wilen, Israel 1914- *St&PR 93*
Wilen, Joseph M. 1950- *St&PR 93*
Wilen, Samuel Henry 1931- *WhoE 93*
Wilenski, Peter Stephen 1939- *WhoUN 92, WhoWor 93*
Wilensky, Alvin 1921- *St&PR 93, WhoAm 92*
Wilensky, Gail Roggin 1943- *WhoAm 92, WhoAmW 93*
Wilensky, Harold L. 1923- *WhoAm 92*
Wilensky, Ivy Sharyn 1957- *WhoAmW 93*
Wilensky, Julius M. 1916- *WhoAm 92, WhoE 93*
Wilentz, David T. 1894-1988 *PolPar*
Wilentz, Gay (A.) 1950- *ConAu 138*
Wilentz, Robert Nathan 1927- *WhoAm 92*
Wilentz, Robert Sean 1951- *WhoE 93*
Wiler, Edward A. 1927- *St&PR 93*
Wiles, Bill 1941- *St&PR 93*
Wiles, Buster d1990 *BioIn 17*
Wiles, C. David 1942- *St&PR 93*
Wiles, Charles Mark *WhoScE 91-1*
Wiles, Charles Preston 1918- *WhoAm 92*
Wiles, David Kimball 1942- *WhoE 93*
Wiles, David McKeen 1932- *WhoAm 92*
Wiles, Gordon *MiSFD 9*
Wiles, Marilyn McCall 1944- *WhoE 93*
Wiles, Meyer F. d1990 *BioIn 17*
Wiles, Q.T. 1919- *St&PR 93*
Wiles, Richard Chester 1934- *St&PR 93*
Wiles, Russ *St&PR 93*
Wiles, Stuart *BioIn 17*
Wiles, Terry L. *Law&B 92*
Wilets, Lawrence 1927- *WhoAm 92*
Wiley, Barry Holland 1936- *St&PR 93*
Wiley, Basil Leslie *ScF&FL 92*
Wiley, Bonnie Jean *WhoAmW 93*
Wiley, Carl Ross 1930- *St&PR 93, WhoAm 92*
Wiley, Charles Henry 1927- *St&PR 93*
Wiley, David d1813 *BioIn 17*
Wiley, Dayna Ann 1960- *WhoSSW 93*
Wiley, Delphine Donaldson 1928- *WhoAmW 93*
Wiley, Don Craig 1944- *WhoAm 92*
Wiley, Edwin P. 1929- *St&PR 93*
Wiley, Edwin Packard 1929- *WhoAm 92*
Wiley, Elizabeth *ScF&FL 92*
Wiley, Ethan *MiSFD 9*
Wiley, Frank E. *St&PR 93*
Wiley, Gregory Robert 1951- *WhoAm 92*
Wiley, Hannah Christine 1950- *WhoAmW 93*

Wiley, Harvey Washington 1844-1930 *BioIn 17*
Wiley, James Edward 1925- *WhoSSW 93*
Wiley, Jason LaRue, Jr. 1917- *WhoE 93*
Wiley, Jerold Wayne 1944- *WhoSSW 93*
Wiley, John Francis 1954- *WhoSSW 93*
Wiley, John Preston, Jr. 1936- *WhoE 93*
Wiley, Kenneth LeMoyne 1947- *WhoSSW 93*
Wiley, Kerry Lane *BioIn 17*
Wiley, Lee *BioIn 17*
Wiley, Ralph 1952- *ConAu 136*
Wiley, Richard Arthur 1928- *St&PR 93, WhoAm 92*
Wiley, Richard Emerson 1934- *WhoAm 92*
Wiley, Richard Gordon 1937- *WhoAm 92*
Wiley, Richard Haven 1913- *WhoAm 92*
Wiley, Robert Allen 1934- *WhoAm 92*
Wiley, Robert F. 1946- *WhoWrEP 92*
Wiley, Ronald Gordon 1947- *WhoSSW 93*
Wiley, Ronald LeRoy 1936- *WhoAm 92*
Wiley, Sarah King 1871-1909 *AmWomPl*
Wiley, Thomas E. *St&PR 93*
Wiley, Thomas Glen 1928- *WhoAm 92*
Wiley, Timothy L. 1955- *St&PR 93*
Wiley, W. Bradford 1910- *St&PR 93*
Wiley, William R. 1931- *St&PR 93*
Wiley, William Rodney 1931- *WhoAm 92*
Wiley, William T. 1937- *WhoAm 92*
Wilf, Frederic Marshal 1959- *WhoE 93*
Wilfley, Arthur R. 1927- *St&PR 93*
Wilfley, George M. 1924- *St&PR 93*
Wilfley, Michael *Law&B 92*
Wilfong, J. Scott 1950- *St&PR 93*
Wilfong, John Scott 1950- *WhoAm 92*
Wilford, John Noble, Jr. 1933- *WhoAm 92*
Wilford, Pamela Fraser *Law&B 92*
Wilford, Walton Terry 1937- *WhoAm 92*
Wilfried, Grau *WhoAm 92*
Wilgat, Tadeusz 1917- *WhoScE 91-4*
Wilgenbusch, Nancy *WhoAmW 93*
Wilgis, Herbert E., Jr. 1935- *St&PR 93*
Wilgocki, Michal 1947- *WhoWor 93*
Wilgocki, Theresa Ann 1965- *WhoAmW 93*
Wilgus, D.K. 1918-1989 *BioIn 17*
Wilgus, Donald Knight 1918-1989 *BioIn 17*
Wilgus, James L. 1937- *St&PR 93*
Wilgus, Van C. *Law&B 92*
Wilgus, Walter Stephen 1932- *St&PR 93*
Wilhelm, Crown Prince 1882-1951 *HarEnMi*
Wilhelm, II, German Emperor 1859-1941 *BioIn 17*
Wilhelm, Arthur Lee 1946- *St&PR 93*
Wilhelm, Carl F. 1927- *St&PR 93*
Wilhelm, Carl Friedrich 1815-1873 *Baker 92*
Wilhelm, Charles Elliott 1941- *WhoAm 92*
Wilhelm, Charles F. *Law&B 92*
Wilhelm, Donald 1915- *WhoWor 93*
Wilhelm, Gayle Brian 1936- *WhoAm 92*
Wilhelm, Hans Adolf 1919- *WhoWor 93*
Wilhelm, Henry Gilmer 1943- *BioIn 17*
Wilhelm, Jack M. *Law&B 92*
Wilhelm, James Francis 1924- *St&PR 93*
Wilhelm, James K. 1927- *St&PR 93*
Wilhelm, Jim 1954- *WhoE 93*
Wilhelm, Johannes Paul 1926- *WhoWor 93*
Wilhelm, Joseph Lawrence 1909- *WhoAm 92*
Wilhelm, Judy Wayland *BioIn 17*
Wilhelm, Kate *BioIn 17*
Wilhelm, Kate 1928- *ScF&FL 92, WhoAmW 93*
Wilhelm, Kyle M. 1961- *St&PR 93*
Wilhelm, Lambert *ScF&FL 92*
Wilhelm, Linda Rexford 1953- *WhoAmW 93*
Wilhelm, Luther Ray 1939- *WhoSSW 93*
Wilhelm, Max 1928- *WhoScE 91-4*
Wilhelm, Morton 1923- *WhoAm 92*
Wilhelm, Norman D. 1926- *St&PR 93*
Wilhelm, Ralph Vincent, Jr. 1944- *WhoAm 92*
Wilhelm, Richard 1953- *ScF&FL 92*
Wilhelm, Richard A. *Law&B 92*
Wilhelm, Robert Oscar 1918- *WhoAm 92*
Wilhelm, Rolf 1939- *WhoScE 91-3*
Wilhelm, Rudie 1914- *St&PR 93*
Wilhelm, Stephen Paul 1948- *WhoWor 93*
Wilhelm, Vida Meadows 1944- *WhoSSW 93*
Wilhelm, William Jean 1935- *WhoAm 92*
Wilhelmi, Angel Batlas *Law&B 92*
Wilhelmi, Henry Paul 1930- *WhoE 93*
Wilhelmi, Mary Charlotte 1928- *WhoAmW 93*
Wilhelmi, Zdzislaw L. 1921- *WhoScE 91-4*
Wilhelmi, Zdzislaw Ludwik 1921- *WhoWor 93*
Wilhelmina 1880-1962 *DcTwHis*
Wilhelmj, August 1845-1908 *Baker 92*
Wilhelmsen, Harold John 1928- *WhoAm 92*
Wilhelmsen, Lars W. 1932- *WhoScE 91-4*
Wilhelmsson, Lars G. 1955- *WhoScE 91-4*
Wilhem, Guillaume-Louis 1781-1842 *Baker 92*
Wilhite, Clayton Edward 1945- *St&PR 93, WhoAm 92, WhoE 93*
Wilhite, Dixie Terrell *Law&B 92*
Wilhite, Lawrence Howard *Law&B 92*
Wilhite, Sam Yancey 1919- *St&PR 93*
Wilhoit, Henry Rupert, Jr. 1935- *WhoSSW 93*
Wilhoit, Randall Kenneth 1958- *St&PR 93*
Wilinsky, Harriet *WhoAm 92, WhoAmW 93*
Wilk, Andrzej Bronislaw 1940- *WhoScE 91-4*
Wilk, Andrzej Jan 1938- *WhoWor 93*
Wilk, Gerald Michael 1937- *St&PR 93*
Wilk, Ireneusz Stanislaw 1931- *WhoScE 91-4*
Wilk, Johannes F. 1937- *St&PR 93*
Wilk, Leonard Stephen 1927- *WhoE 93*
Wilk, Max 1920- *ConAu 37NR, WhoWrEP 92*
Wilke, Brendt-Michael 1947- *WhoWor 93*
Wilke, Charles Robert 1917- *WhoAm 92*
Wilke, Charles S. 1942- *St&PR 93*
Wilke, Deborah Lee 1949- *WhoAmW 93*
Wilke, F. Ludwig 1931- *WhoScE 91-3*
Wilke, Gunter 1925- *WhoScE 91-3*
Wilke, Gunther *BioIn 17*
Wilke, John M. *Law&B 92*
Wilke, Robert D. 1931- *St&PR 93*
Wilke, William L. 1936- *St&PR 93*
Wilke Montemayor, Joanne Marie 1941- *WhoAmW 93, WhoWor 93*
Wilken, G.A. 1847-1891 *IntDcAn*
Wilken, Iris Evangeline 1965- *WhoSSW 93*
Wilken, Laurence Spencer *Law&B 92*
Wilkening, Laurel Lynn 1944- *WhoAm 92, WhoAmW 93*
Wilkening, William 1932- *St&PR 93*
Wilkens, Christopher William 1947- *WhoE 93*
Wilkens, George Robert 1949- *WhoWrEP 92*
Wilkens, Henry J. 1922- *St&PR 93*
Wilkens, Horst 1939- *WhoScE 91-3*
Wilkens, Jane Rae 1952- *WhoAmW 93*
Wilkens, Klaus 1942- *WhoWor 93*
Wilkens, Leonard Randolph, Jr. 1937- *WhoAm 92*
Wilkens, Robert Allen 1929- *St&PR 93, WhoAm 92*
Wilkens, Robert E. 1929- *St&PR 93*
Wilkens, Steven A. 1957- *WhoWrEP 92*
Wilker, Nachama Laya 1961- *WhoE 93*
Wilkerson, Amy 1962- *WhoAmW 93*
Wilkerson, Brian Scott 1951- *WhoSSW 93*
Wilkerson, Calvin Walter 1934- *St&PR 93*
Wilkerson, Charles Edward 1921- *WhoAm 92*
Wilkerson, David *BioIn 17*
Wilkerson, David Lee 1957- *WhoSSW 93*
Wilkerson, Douglas 1948- *St&PR 93*
Wilkerson, Edward *BioIn 17*
Wilkerson, Floyd Monroe 1932- *WhoAm 92*
Wilkerson, James Edward 1945- *WhoSSW 93, WhoWor 93*
Wilkerson, Leonard Alan 1950- *WhoSSW 93*
Wilkerson, Michael N. 1955- *WhoWrEP 92*
Wilkerson, O.A., III 1935- *St&PR 93*
Wilkerson, Ruth S. 1928- *WhoAmW 93*
Wilkerson, William 1929-1989 *BioIn 17*
Wilkerson, William Holton 1947- *St&PR 93, WhoAm 92, WhoEmL 93*
Wilkerson-Kassel, Tichi *St&PR 93*
Wilkes, Allene Tupper *AmWomPl*
Wilkes, Charles 1798-1877 *BioIn 17, Expl 93 [port], HarEnMi, IntDcAn*
Wilkes, Clem Cabell, Jr. 1953- *WhoSSW 93*
Wilkes, Corbin Mccue 1946- *St&PR 93*
Wilkes, David R. 1922- *St&PR 93*
Wilkes, George 1817-1885 *JrnUS*
Wilkes, Hilbert Garrison 1937- *WhoE 93*
Wilkes, Jackson Keith *BiDAMSp 1989*
Wilkes, Jamaal 1953- *BiDAMSp 1989*
Wilkes, James C. 1949- *St&PR 93*
Wilkes, John 1727-1797 *BioIn 17*
Wilkes, John David 1944- *St&PR 93*
Wilkes, Joseph Allen 1919- *WhoAm 92*
Wilkes, Josue Teofilo 1883-1968 *Baker 92*
Wilkes, Marilyn Z. *ScF&FL 92*
Wilkes, Penny F. 1946- *WhoWrEP 92*
Wilkes, R. Mitchell 1951- *WhoSSW 93*
Wilkes, Robert Edmond 1933- *St&PR 93*
Wilkes, Shar 1951- *WhoAmW 93*
Wilkes, Wilhemen *AmWomPl*
Wilkeson, Leon 195-?- *See* Lynyrd Skynyrd *ConMus 9*
Wilkey, David Homer 1947- *WhoSSW 93*
Wilkey, Jeffrey R. 1942- *St&PR 93*
Wilkey, Malcolm Richard *BioIn 17*
Wilkey, Malcolm Richard 1918- *WhoAm 92, WhoWor 93*
Wilkey, Mary 1940- *WhoAmW 93*
Wilkie, Christine *ScF&FL 92*
Wilkie, Donald Walter 1931- *WhoAm 92*
Wilkie, Franc Bangs 1832-1892 *JrnUS*
Wilkie, John 1904-1991 *BioIn 17*
Wilkie, Jonathan Paul 1947- *St&PR 93*
Wilkie, Kevin S. 1963- *St&PR 93*
Wilkie, Leighton A. 1900- *St&PR 93*
Wilkie, Leighton Allyn 1900- *WhoAm 92*
Wilkie, Ross Conway 1942- *WhoWor 93*
Wilkie, Valleau, Jr. 1923- *WhoAm 92, WhoWor 93*
Wilkin, Charles M. *St&PR 93*
Wilkin, Colin *WhoScE 91-1*
Wilkin, Eloise (Burns) 1904-1987 *MajAI [port]*
Wilkin, Eugene Welch 1923- *WhoAm 92*
Wilkin, James Whitney 1762-1845 *BioIn 17*
Wilkin, Richard Edwin 1930- *WhoAm 92*
Wilkins, Barratt 1943- *WhoAm 92*
Wilkins, Burleigh Taylor 1932- *WhoAm 92*
Wilkins, C. Howard, Jr. 1938- *WhoAm 92, WhoWor 93*
Wilkins, Caroline Hanke 1937- *WhoAm 92*
Wilkins, Cary 1954- *ScF&FL 92*
Wilkins, Charles L. 1938- *WhoAm 92*
Wilkins, Charles S. 1950- *St&PR 93*
Wilkins, Christina L. 1950- *St&PR 93, WhoAmW 93*
Wilkins, Christine Catherine 1930- *WhoAmW 93*
Wilkins, Christopher Putnam 1957- *WhoAm 92*
Wilkins, Daniel *BioIn 17*
Wilkins, Daniel J. *Law&B 92*
Wilkins, David George 1939- *WhoAm 92*
Wilkins, David J. 1934- *WhoScE 91-2*
Wilkins, Dominique *BioIn 17*
Wilkins, Dominique 1960- *WhoAm 92*
Wilkins, Earle Wayne, Jr. 1919- *WhoAm 92*
Wilkins, Elmer V. *AfrAmBi [port]*
Wilkins, Esther Mae 1916- *WhoAmW 93*
Wilkins, Eva *AmWomPl*
Wilkins, Floyd, Jr. 1925- *WhoAm 92*
Wilkins, Frank J. 1931- *St&PR 93*
Wilkins, Frederick C. 1935- *WhoWrEP 92*
Wilkins, Gary Lynn 1944- *WhoSSW 93*
Wilkins, Gary Lynn 1958- *WhoSSW 93*
Wilkins, Graham John 1924- *WhoWor 93*
Wilkins, Gregory Charles 1956- *St&PR 93*
Wilkins, H. Andrew 1950- *WhoSSW 93*
Wilkins, Herbert Putnam 1930- *WhoAm 92*
Wilkins, (George) Hubert 1888-1958 *Expl 93 [port]*
Wilkins, J. Ernest, Jr. 1923- *WhoAm 92*
Wilkins, Jacques Dominique 1960- *BiDAMSp 1989*
Wilkins, Jerry Lynn 1936- *WhoSSW 93*
Wilkins, John Antoine 1943- *WhoSSW 93*
Wilkins, John Warren 1936- *WhoAm 92*
Wilkins, Josetta Edwards 1932- *WhoSSW 93*
Wilkins, Kent Myrup 1935- *St&PR 93*
Wilkins, Linda Ann 1951- *WhoAmW 93*
Wilkins, Martha Huddleston 1940- *WhoSSW 93*
Wilkins, Mary Eleanor 1852-1930 *BioIn 17*
Wilkins, Maurice Gray, Jr. 1931- *St&PR 93*
Wilkins, Maurice Hugh Frederick 1916- *WhoWor 93*
Wilkins, Michael Compton Lockwood 1933- *WhoWor 93*
Wilkins, Michael D. *Law&B 92*
Wilkins, Noel P. 1939- *WhoScE 91-3*
Wilkins, Ormsby *WhoAm 92*
Wilkins, R.J. *WhoScE 91-1*
Wilkins, Ray, Jr. 1937- *WhoAm 92*
Wilkins, Richard Michael 1942- *WhoWor 93*
Wilkins, Richard W. 1947- *St&PR 93*
Wilkins, Rita Denise 1951- *WhoAmW 93*
Wilkins, Robert Eugene 1944- *WhoE 93*
Wilkins, Robert H. 1934- *WhoAm 92*
Wilkins, Robert L. 1925- *St&PR 93*
Wilkins, Robert Pearce 1933- *WhoAm 92*
Wilkins, Roger Carson 1906- *WhoAm 92*
Wilkins, Roger W. 1932- *BioIn 17*
Wilkins, Roy 1901-1981 *ConBlB 4 [port], DcTwHis, EncAACR [port]*
Wilkins, Sheila Scanlon 1936- *WhoAmW 93*
Wilkins, Stephen L. 1943- *St&PR 93*
Wilkins, T.D. *WhoScE 91-1*
Wilkins, Tracy Dale 1943- *WhoAm 92*
Wilkins, Warren W. *Law&B 92*
Wilkins, Wendy Karen 1949- *WhoAmW 93*
Wilkins, William S. 1942- *WhoWor 93*
Wilkins, William Walter, Jr. 1942- *WhoAm 92, WhoSSW 93*
Wilkinson, Albert Mims, Jr. 1925- *WhoAm 92*
Wilkinson, Andrew M. *BioIn 17*
Wilkinson, Anthony *MiSFD 9*
Wilkinson, B. Andrew 1944- *St&PR 93*
Wilkinson, Ben 1932- *WhoSSW 93*
Wilkinson, Brenda 1946- *BlkAuII 92, DcAmChF 1960*
Wilkinson, Brian *BioIn 17*
Wilkinson, Bruce W. 1944- *BioIn 17, St&PR 93*
Wilkinson, Charles F. *Law&B 92*
Wilkinson, Christine Mary *WhoScE 91-1*
Wilkinson, Christopher David Wicks *WhoScE 91-1*
Wilkinson, Christopher Foster 1938- *WhoAm 92, WhoE 93*
Wilkinson, Colin D. 1936- *St&PR 93*
Wilkinson, Colm 1944- *ConTFT 10*
Wilkinson, Connie Marie 1965- *WhoAmW 93*
Wilkinson, D.A. *WhoScE 91-1*
Wilkinson, David Anthony 1951- *St&PR 93*
Wilkinson, David J. *Law&B 92*
Wilkinson, David Todd 1935- *WhoAm 92*
Wilkinson, Donald C. 1934- *St&PR 93*
Wilkinson, Donald McLean, Jr. 1938- *WhoWor 93*
Wilkinson, Doris Yvonne 1936- *WhoAm 92, WhoAmW 93*
Wilkinson, E. G., Jr. *WhoAm 92*
Wilkinson, Earl W. *St&PR 93*
Wilkinson, Edward Anderson, Jr. 1933- *WhoAm 92*
Wilkinson, Ella Crane *AmWomPl*
Wilkinson, Eugene Parks 1918- *WhoAm 92*
Wilkinson, Frances Catherine 1955- *WhoAmW 93*
Wilkinson, Francis *WhoScE 91-1*
Wilkinson, Frank Smith, Jr. 1939- *WhoIns 93*
Wilkinson, Geoffrey *WhoScE 91-1*
Wilkinson, Geoffrey 1921- *WhoAm 92, WhoWor 93*
Wilkinson, George W. 1935- *WhoSSW 93*
Wilkinson, Glenda Burgin 1952- *WhoAmW 93, WhoSSW 93*
Wilkinson, Gregg Stuart 1942- *WhoSSW 93*
Wilkinson, Harold Arthur 1935- *WhoAm 92*
Wilkinson, Harry Edward 1930- *WhoSSW 93*
Wilkinson, Harry John 1937- *St&PR 93*
Wilkinson, Harry Matthews 1922- *WhoSSW 93*
Wilkinson, Harry R. 1942- *St&PR 93*
Wilkinson, Hei Sook 1947- *WhoAmW 93*
Wilkinson, Howard Neal 1930- *WhoSSW 93*
Wilkinson, Ian Peter 1949- *WhoWor 93*
Wilkinson, Ivan Eugene 1941- *St&PR 93*
Wilkinson, J. Jay 1950- *St&PR 93*
Wilkinson, James 1757?-1825 *CmdGen 1991 [port], HarEnMi*
Wilkinson, James E. 1948- *St&PR 93*
Wilkinson, James Harvie, III 1944- *WhoAm 92, WhoSSW 93*
Wilkinson, James Howland 1942- *WhoE 93*
Wilkinson, Janet Worman 1944- *WhoAmW 93*
Wilkinson, John 1940- *St&PR 93*
Wilkinson, John B. *Law&B 92*
Wilkinson, John Burke 1913- *WhoAm 92*
Wilkinson, John H. *St&PR 93*
Wilkinson, John Hart 1940- *WhoAm 92*
Wilkinson, John M. 1948- *St&PR 93*
Wilkinson, Kenneth Herbert 1928- *WhoAm 92*
Wilkinson, Linda Cornelia Painton 1927- *WhoAmW 93*
Wilkinson, Louise Cherry 1948- *WhoAm 92*
Wilkinson, Lynn 1951- *St&PR 93*
Wilkinson, Marguerite Ogden Bigelow 1883-1928 *AmWomPl*
Wilkinson, Mary Ellen 1947- *WhoAmW 93*
Wilkinson, Mary Emily 1940- *WhoAm 92*
Wilkinson, Michael Douglas 1949- *St&PR 93*
Wilkinson, Michael Ian *WhoScE 91-1*
Wilkinson, Michael Kennerly 1921- *WhoAm 92*
Wilkinson, Milton James 1937- *WhoAm 92*
Wilkinson, Norman Edward *WhoScE 91-1*
Wilkinson, Owen Inglis 1944- *St&PR 93*
Wilkinson, Peter Charles *WhoScE 91-1*
Wilkinson, Peter Maurice 1941- *WhoWor 93*
Wilkinson, Richard W. 1932- *St&PR 93*
Wilkinson, Robert Bawden 1933- *WhoWor 93*

Wilkinson, Robert Eugene 1926- *WhoSSW 93*
Wilkinson, Robert F. *Law&B 92*
Wilkinson, Ronald Sterne 1934- *WhoWor 93*
Wilkinson, Rosemary 1924- *WhoWrEP 92*
Wilkinson, Roy Keith *WhoScE 91-1*
Wilkinson, Roy Keith 1933- *WhoWor 93*
Wilkinson, Sandra *ScF&FL 92*
Wilkinson, Senora Mae *AmWomPl*
Wilkinson, Signe *WhoAmW 93*
Wilkinson, Stanley Ralph 1931- *WhoSSW 93*
Wilkinson, Theodore Stark 1888-1946 *HarEnMi*
Wilkinson, Thomas Lloyd, Jr. 1939- *WhoSSW 93*
Wilkinson, Vernon 1916- *ScF&FL 92*
Wilkinson, Wallace G. 1941- *WhoSSW 93*
Wilkinson, Warren S. 1920- *St&PR 93*
Wilkinson, Warren Scripps 1920- *WhoAm 92*
Wilkinson, William R. 1942- *St&PR 93*
Wilkinson, William Sherwood *Law&B 92*
Wilkinson, William Sherwood 1933- *St&PR 93, WhoAm 92*
Wilkof, Robert E. 1949- *St&PR 93*
Wilkomirska, Maria 1904- *Baker 92*
Wilkomirska, Wanda 1929- *Baker 92, PolBiDi*
Wilkomirski, Alfred 1873-1950 *Baker 92*
Wilkomirski, Kazimierz 1900- *Baker 92*
Wilkomirski, Kazimierz 1901- *PolBiDi*
Wilkon, Jozef 1930- *MajAI [port], SmATA 71 [port]*
Wilkoski, Joseph S. 1952- *St&PR 93*
Wilkoszewski, Edward 1904- *WhoWor 93*
Wilkov, Marcy E. *Law&B 92*
Wilks, Alan Delbert 1943- *WhoAm 92*
Wilks, David M. 1946- *St&PR 93*
Wilks, Graham *WhoScE 91-1*
Wilks, Ivor Gordon Hughes 1928- *WhoAm 92*
Wilks, Joseph Wayne 1956- *St&PR 93*
Wilks, Kevin Lamar 1961- *WhoSSW 93*
Wilks, Peter Goodwin *WhoScE 91-1*
Wilks, Phillip 1934- *St&PR 93*
Wilks, Rich *BioIn 17*
Wilks, William Lee 1931- *WhoAm 92*
Will, Allen Sinclair 1868-1934 *JrnUS*
Will, Bruno E. 1942- *WhoScE 91-2*
Will, Clifford M(artin) 1946- *ConAu 136*
Will, Clifford Martin 1946- *WhoAm 92*
Will, Georg 1930- *WhoScE 91-3*
Will, George 1941- *JrnUS*
Will, George F. *BioIn 17*
Will, George F. 1941- *WhoWrEP 92*
Will, George Frederick 1941- *WhoAm 92*
Will, Hubert Louis 1914- *WhoAm 92*
Will, James Fredrick 1938- *WhoAm 92, WhoE 93*
Will, James M. 1942- *St&PR 93*
Will, Joanne Marie 1937- *WhoAm 92*
Will, Joanne P. *Law&B 92*
Will, John 1917- *WhoAm 92*
Will, Mari Maseng 1954- *WhoAm 92*
Will, Montford S. 1943- *St&PR 93*
Will, Peter 1935- *St&PR 93*
Will, Robert Erwin 1928- *WhoAm 92*
Will, Thomas Joseph 1939- *St&PR 93, WhoAm 92*
Willaert, Adrian c. 1490-1562 *Baker 92*
Willaime, Christian 1940- *WhoScE 91-2*
Willam, Kaspar Jodok 1940- *WhoAm 92*
Willaman, Rogert Glenn 1951- *WhoE 93*
Willan, Elizabeth Anne 1938- *WhoWor 93*
Willan, Healey 1880-1968 *Baker 92, OxDcOp*
Willand, Lois Carlson 1935- *WhoWrEP 92*
Willander, Lars Magnus 1948- *WhoWor 93*
Willans, Jean Stone 1924- *WhoWor 93*
Willard, Barbara (Mary) 1909- *MajAI [port]*
Willard, C. Lawson *Law&B 92*
Willard, Carolyn Ann 1962- *WhoAmW 93*
Willard, Charles d1991 *BioIn 17*
Willard, Charles Grayson 1924- *St&PR 93*
Willard, Charles H. d1990 *BioIn 17*
Willard, Daniel 1928- *WhoScE 91-2*
Willard, Dean Marvin 1946- *St&PR 93, WhoAm 92*
Willard, Donald Smith 1924- *WhoAm 92*
Willard, Ellen Melville 1853- *AmWomPl*
Willard, Elmo R. *BioIn 17*
Willard, Frances Elizabeth Caroline 1839-1898 *GayN*
Willard, Gail M. 1949- *WhoAmW 93*
Willard, Ivor Neal 1945-1991 *BioIn 17*
Willard, James Douglas 1945- *WhoAm 92*
Willard, John Gerard 1952- *WhoEmL 93*
Willard, Mildred Wilds 1911-1978 *ScF&FL 92*
Willard, Nancy *BioIn 17*
Willard, Nancy 1936- *ConAu 39NR, DcAmChF 1960, MajAI [port], ScF&FL 92, SmATA 71 [port]*
Willard, Nancy Margaret *WhoAm 92, WhoAmW 93*
Willard, Norman, Jr. 1924- *St&PR 93*
Willard, Ralph Lawrence 1922- *WhoAm 92, WhoWor 93*
Willard, Richard Kennon 1948- *WhoAm 92*
Willard, Robert Edgar 1929- *WhoAm 92*
Willard, Samuel 1640-1707 *BioIn 17*
Willard, Sherwood S. *Law&B 92*
Willard, Sherwood Skelton 1941- *St&PR 93*
Willard, Theodore Elwood 1924- *WhoE 93*
Willard, Thomas Maxwell 1937- *WhoSSW 93*
Willard, Timothy Holmes 1951- *WhoWrEP 92*
Willard, Tom *ScF&FL 92*
Willard, Walter V. 1934- *St&PR 93*
Willard, Wanda Ann 1962- *WhoE 93*
Willardson, Kimberly Ann Carey 1959- *WhoAmW 93*
Willardson, Niel D. *Law&B 92*
Willauer, George Jacob 1935- *WhoE 93*
Willauer, Whiting Russell 1931- *WhoAm 92*
Willbrandt, Barry William 1947- *WhoSSW 93*
Willcocks, David (Valentine) 1919- *Baker 92*
Willcocks, Theo J. 1941- *WhoScE 91-1*
Willcox, Breckinridge Long 1944- *WhoAm 92*
Willcox, Frederick Preston 1910- *WhoE 93, WhoWor 93*
Willcox, Georgie Bain 1930- *WhoSSW 93*
Willcox, Helen Lida 1883- *AmWomPl*
Willcox, Hugh L. 1905- *St&PR 93*
Willcox, Peter *BioIn 17*
Willcox, William R. 1863-1940 *PolPar*
Willcox, William Russell 1863-1940 *BioIn 17*
Willcoxson, Mary Frances 1944- *WhoAmW 93*
Wille, Friedrich 1935- *WhoWor 93*
Wille, Gunnar Edvard 1937- *WhoWor 93*
Wille, Lois Jean 1932- *WhoAm 92, WhoAmW 93*
Wille, Louis J. *Law&B 92*
Wille, Vicki Lynn 1948- *WhoAmW 93*
Wille, Volker 1941- *WhoWor 93*
Wille, Wayne Martin 1930- *WhoAm 92*
Willeberg, Preben W. 1942- *WhoScE 91-2*
Willebrands, Johannes Gerardus Maria Cardinal 1909- *WhoWor 93*
Willeford, Charles 1919-1988 *ScF&FL 92*
Willeitner, Hubert *WhoScE 91-4*
Willem, Michel Georges Jules 1953- *WhoWor 93*
Willems, Emilio 1905- *IntDcAn*
Willems, Gerard 1938- *WhoScE 91-2*
Willems, Jos L.H. 1939- *WhoScE 91-2*
Willems, Richard 1944- *WhoWor 93*
Willemsen, Alan Mitchell 1933- *WhoIns 93*
Willemstyn, Willem 1927- *St&PR 93*
Willen, Arnold N.V. 1931- *WhoUN 92*
Willenbecher, James Frederic 1943- *WhoE 93*
Willenbecher, John 1936- *WhoAm 92*
Willenberg, Harvey Jack 1945- *WhoSSW 93*
Willenbockel, Ulrich 1930- *WhoScE 91-3, WhoWor 93*
Willenbrink, Johannes 1930- *WhoScE 91-3*
Willenbrink, Rose Ann *Law&B 92*
Willenbrink, Rose Ann 1950- *St&PR 93, WhoAmW 93*
Willenbrock, Frederick Karl 1920- *WhoAm 92*
Willenbucher, Peggy C. *Law&B 92*
Willens, Howard Penney 1931- *WhoAm 92*
Willens, Rita Jacobs d1990 *BioIn 17*
Willens, Tina Kirkwood 1962- *WhoAmW 93*
Willensky, Elliot 1933-1990 *BioIn 17*
Willenson, Kim Jeremy 1937- *WhoAm 92*
Willent-Bordogni, Jean-Baptiste-Joseph 1809-1852 *Baker 92*
Willenz, June Adele *WhoAmW 93*
Willer, Edward Herman 1941- *WhoSSW 93*
Willer, Hanne *WhoScE 91-2*
Willerding, Margaret Frances 1919- *WhoAm 92*
Willerman, Lee 1939- *WhoAm 92*
Willert, August W. 1910- *St&PR 93*
Willert, John A. 1930- *St&PR 93, WhoIns 93*
Willes, Mark Hinckley 1941- *St&PR 93*
Willet, E. Crosby 1929- *St&PR 93*
Willet, Richard A. *WhoSSW 93*
Willets, Jeffrey *BioIn 17*
Willets, Kathy *BioIn 17*
Willett, A. L. Thompson 1909- *WhoWor 93*
Willett, Albert James, Jr. 1944- *WhoSSW 93*
Willett, David A. 1935- *St&PR 93*
Willett, Edith Morgan *AmWomPl*
Willett, Edward Farrand, Jr. 1933- *WhoAm 92*
Willett, Fehrunissa Maureen 1953- *WhoSSW 93*
Willett, Hurd C. d1992 *NewYTBS 92 [port]*
Willett, Hurd C. 1903-1992 *BioIn 17*
Willett, John 1932- *ScF&FL 92*
Willett, John E. 1930- *St&PR 93*
Willett, Kenneth B. 1901- *St&PR 93*
Willett, Michael Scott 1958- *WhoSSW 93*
Willett, Robert Bynum 1939- *St&PR 93*
Willett, Walter Churchill 1945- *WhoE 93*
Willette, Edward David 1935- *St&PR 93*
Willette, Leslie Ray 1927- *St&PR 93*
Willetts, Brian B. *WhoScE 91-1*
Willey, C.S. *St&PR 93*
Willey, Calvert Livingston 1920- *WhoAm 92*
Willey, Frank Patrick *Law&B 92*
Willey, Gordon Randolph 1913- *IntDcAn, WhoAm 92*
Willey, Grafton H., III 1923- *St&PR 93*
Willey, James Lee 1953- *WhoEmL 93*
Willey, John C. 1914-1990 *BioIn 17*
Willey, John Douglas 1917- *WhoAm 92*
Willey, Lawrence A. *Law&B 92*
Willey, Margaret 1950- *ConAu 40NR*
Willey, Paul Wayne 1938- *WhoAm 92*
Willey, Phyllis D. 1945- *St&PR 93*
Willey, Roger James *WhoScE 91-1*
Willging, Paul Raymond 1942- *WhoAm 92*
Willham, Richard Lewis 1932- *WhoAm 92*
Willhite, Donald H. 1936- *St&PR 93*
Willhite-Wright, Jeanne Elmore 1946- *WhoAmW 93*
Willhoite, Michael A. 1946- *SmATA 71 [port]*
Willhoit-Rudt, Marilyn Jean 1947- *WhoEmL 93*
Willi, Edward John 1903-1991 *BioIn 17*
William, Prince of Great Britain 1982- *BioIn 17*
William, I 1120-1166 *OxDcByz*
William, II 1153-1189 *HarEnMi*
William, II 1154-1189 *OxDcByz*
William, II 1859-1941 *DcTwHis*
William, II, German Emperor 1859-1941 *BioIn 17*
William, IV, King of Great Britain 1765-1837 *BioIn 17*
William, Barry *ScF&FL 92*
William, David *BioIn 17*
William, Gordon L. *St&PR 93*
William, Kathlyn 188-?-1960 *SweetSg A [port]*
William, Wayne 1942- *St&PR 93*
William, de Wadington 13th cent.- *BioIn 17*
William Morris Society *ScF&FL 92*
William of Apulia fl. 11th cent.- *OxDcByz*
William of Champlitte, I d1208? *OxDcByz*
William of England and the House of Orange, III 1650-1702 *HarEnMi*
William of Moerbeke c. 1220-c. 1286 *OxDcByz*
William of Rubruck 1215?-1270? *Expl 93*
William of Tyre c. 1130-1186 *OxDcByz*
William Rufus, II 1056-1100 *HarEnMi*
Williams, A. Ben, Jr. 1919- *WhoIns 93*
Williams, A.E.H. 1929- *WhoScE 91-1*
Williams, Adrian Gerard *WhoScE 91-1*
Williams, Alan *WhoScE 91-1*
Williams, Alan 1952- *WhoSSW 93*
Williams, Alan Davison 1925- *WhoAm 92*
Williams, Alan Frederick *WhoScE 91-1*
Williams, Alan Gentry 1951- *St&PR 93*
Williams, Alan L(arson) 1947- *ConAu 139*
Williams, Alan Ray 1953- *St&PR 93*
Williams, Alan Woodward *WhoScE 91-1*
Williams, Albert E. 1940- *St&PR 93*
Williams, Albert Paine 1935- *WhoAm 92*
Williams, Albert Theophilus Wadi 1922- *WhoSSW 93*
Williams, Alberta Norine 1908- *WhoWrEP 92*
Williams, Alberto 1862-1952 *Baker 92*
Williams, Alexander George 1952- *WhoE 93*
Williams, Alexander Stephens, III 1936- *WhoAm 92, WhoIns 93*
Williams, Alice Noel Tuckerman 1918- *WhoAmW 93, WhoE 93*
Williams, Alice Stevens *AmWomPl*
Williams, Alice Trump 1940- *WhoSSW 93*
Williams, Allan Nathaniel 1946- *WhoWor 93*
Williams, Allan Thomas *WhoScE 91-1*
Williams, Amanda Kyle 1957- *ConAu 138*
Williams, Amy Greaves *Law&B 92*
Williams, Andrew *WhoScE 91-1*
Williams, Andrew Carter *Law&B 92*
Williams, Andy 1930- *Baker 92, WhoAm 92*
Williams, Angie C. 1927- *St&PR 93*
Williams, Ann C. 1949- *WhoAm 92, WhoAmW 93*
Williams, Ann Meagher 1929- *WhoAmW 93*
Williams, Anne *WhoScE 91-1*
Williams, Anne D. *BioIn 17*
Williams, Anne Kinlaw 1949- *WhoAmW 93*
Williams, Anne M. *Law&B 92*
Williams, Anne Wall 1934- *WhoAmW 93*
Williams, Annette *BioIn 17*
Williams, Annie John 1913- *WhoAmW 93, WhoSSW 93, WhoWor 93*
Williams, Anson *MiSFD 9*
Williams, Anthony Gordon 1955- *WhoSSW 93*
Williams, Anthony R. 1958- *St&PR 93*
Williams, Arthur 1904- *WhoAm 92*
Williams, Arthur Cozad 1926- *WhoAm 92*
Williams, Arthur J. *ScF&FL 92*
Williams, Aubrey 1890-1965 *EncAACR*
Williams, Aubrey Willis 1924- *WhoAm 92*
Williams, Austin Beatty 1919- *WhoE 93*
Williams, Averill M. *Law&B 92*
Williams, Avon N., Jr. 1921- *AfrAmBi*
Williams, Avon Nyanza, Jr. 1921- *WhoSSW 93*
Williams, Babette Deanna 1960- *WhoE 93*
Williams, Barbara *Law&B 92*
Williams, Barbara 1925- *SmATA 16AS [port]*
Williams, Barbara 1937- *BioIn 17*
Williams, Barbara Bruce *Law&B 92*
Williams, Barbara Elaine 1952- *WhoWor 93*
Williams, Barbara Ivory 1936- *WhoE 93*
Williams, Barbara Jean 1946- *WhoAmW 93*
Williams, Barbara Jean May 1927- *WhoAm 92*
Williams, Barbara Joann 1933- *WhoWrEP 92*
Williams, Barbara Lou 1927- *WhoAmW 93*
Williams, Barbara R. 1933- *St&PR 93*
Williams, Barry *BioIn 17*
Williams, Bea Stoffel 1951- *WhoSSW 93*
Williams, Ben Ames 1889-1953 *BioIn 17*
Williams, Ben Franklin, Jr. 1929- *WhoAm 92*
Williams, Ben Wayne 1932- *St&PR 93*
Williams, Benjamin Buford 1923- *WhoSSW 93*
Williams, Benjamin Tallifaro 1931- *WhoAm 92*
Williams, Bernard J.S. 1931- *WhoScE 91-1*
Williams, Bert 1875-1922 *BioIn 17*
Williams, Bertha *AmWomPl*
Williams, Beryl *ConAu 39NR*
Williams, Betty 1943- *WhoWor 93*
Williams, Betty Joan 1928- *WhoAmW 93*
Williams, Beverly Jean 1945- *St&PR 93*
Williams, Big Boy 1900-1962 *BioIn 17*
Williams, Bill d1992 *NewYTBS 92 [port]*
Williams, Bill 1787-1849 *BioIn 17*
Williams, Bill 1939- *WhoWrEP 92*
Williams, Billy *BioIn 17*
Williams, Billy Brinn 1941- *St&PR 93*
Williams, Billy Dee *BioIn 17*
Williams, Billy Dee 1937- *AfrAmBi, WhoAm 92*
Williams, Billy Leo 1938- *WhoAm 92*
Williams, Brandt Hugh 1950- *WhoSSW 93*
Williams, Brenda E. *Law&B 92*
Williams, Brenda Joan 1965- *WhoAmW 93*
Williams, Brian Edward *Law&B 92*
Williams, Brian K. *Law&B 92*
Williams, Brian Patrick John *WhoScE 91-1*
Williams, Brian Thomas 1948- *St&PR 93*
Williams, Bronwyn *ScF&FL 92*
Williams, Brown F. 1940- *WhoAm 92*
Williams, Bruce David 1932- *St&PR 93, WhoE 93*
Williams, Bruce Edward 1931- *WhoE 93*
Williams, Bruce K. 1948- *St&PR 93*
Williams, Bruce Livingston 1945- *WhoSSW 93*
Williams, Bruce S. 1918- *St&PR 93*
Williams, Buck 1960- *BioIn 17, WhoAm 92*
Williams, Bunny *BioIn 17*
Williams, Buster *BioIn 17*
Williams, Byrd 1945- *St&PR 93*
Williams, C. Terry 1944- *St&PR 93*
Williams, Calvin *Law&B 92*
Williams, Camilla *WhoAm 92*

Williams, Camilla 1922- *Baker 92*
Williams, Carl Chanson 1937- *St&PR 93, WhoAm 92, WhoE 93*
Williams, Carl Harwell 1915- *WhoAm 92*
Williams, Carlton Hinkle 1914- *WhoAm 92*
Williams, Carol A. *Law&B 92*
Williams, Carol Cavan *Law&B 92*
Williams, Carol Jorgensen 1944- *WhoAmW 93, WhoE 93, WhoWor 93*
Williams, Carol Kennedy 1956- *WhoSSW 93*
Williams, Carolyn Antonides 1939- *WhoAmW 93*
Williams, Carolyn Elizabeth 1943- *St&PR 93, WhoAmW 93*
Williams, Carolyn Ruth Armstrong 1944- *WhoAmW 93*
Williams, Carroll M. 1916-1991 *BioIn 17*
Williams, Charlene *BioIn 17*
Williams, Charles *MajAI, SmATA 70*
Williams, Charles 1886-1945 *BioIn 17*
Williams, Charles David 1935- *WhoAm 92*
Williams, Charles David 1960- *WhoSSW 93*
Williams, Charles Dudley 1933- *St&PR 93*
Williams, Charles E. 1928- *St&PR 93*
Williams, Charles Finn 1954- *St&PR 93*
Williams, Charles Finn, II 1954- *WhoWor 93*
Williams, Charles G. 1933- *St&PR 93*
Williams, Charles Herbert 1935- *WhoSSW 93*
Williams, Charles Kenneth 1936- *WhoAm 92, WhoWrEP 92*
Williams, Charles Laval, Jr. 1916- *WhoAm 92*
Williams, Charles Lee 1947- *WhoEmL 93*
Williams, Charles Linwood 1960- *WhoAm 92*
Williams, Charles M. *ScF&FL 92*
Williams, Charles M. 1912- *St&PR 93*
Williams, Charles Marvin 1917- *WhoAm 92*
Williams, Charles Murray 1931- *WhoSSW 93, WhoWor 93*
Williams, Charles Pickens 1926- *WhoAm 92*
Williams, Charles R. 1947- *St&PR 93*
Williams, Charles S. 1926- *WhoIns 93*
Williams, Charles Wesley *WhoAm 92*
Williams, Charlotte Bell 1944- *WhoSSW 93*
Williams, Charlotte Evelyn Forrester 1905- *WhoAmW 93, WhoWor 93*
Williams, Charlotte L. 1928- *AfrAmBi [port]*
Williams, Chester Arthur, Jr. 1924- *WhoAm 92*
Williams, Christopher *Law&B 92*
Williams, Christopher Brian 1950- *St&PR 93*
Williams, Christopher Hodder- *ScF&FL 92*
Williams, Claire *AmWomPl*
Williams, Clara 1891-1928 *SweetSg A*
Williams, Clarence Leon 1937- *WhoE 93*
Williams, Clarke McRae 1922- *St&PR 93*
Williams, Claudine E. 1937- *WhoScE 91-2*
Williams, Clayton Wheat, Jr. *BioIn 17*
Williams, Clifford 1885-1971 *BioIn 17*
Williams, Clifford T. 1955- *St&PR 93*
Williams, Clifton 1923-1976 *Baker 92*
Williams, Clive Shearer *WhoScE 91-1*
Williams, Clyde *WhoScE 91-1*
Williams, Clyde E., Jr. 1919- *St&PR 93, WhoAm 92*
Williams, Colette Copeland 1966- *WhoAmW 93*
Williams, Collen Marie 1924- *WhoAm 92*
Williams, Collin Peter 1941- *St&PR 93*
Williams, Connie Keenum 1949- *WhoAmW 93*
Williams, "Cootie" (Charles Melvin) 1908-1985 *Baker 92*
Williams, Craig Lamar 1952- *WhoSSW 93*
Williams, Curt Alan 1953- *WhoSSW 93*
Williams, Curtis Alvin, Jr. 1927- *WhoE 93*
Williams, Cynda *BioIn 17*
Williams, Cynthia 1952- *WhoAmW 93*
Williams, Cynthia Ann 1958- *WhoAmW 93*
Williams, D. Kenyon, Jr. *Law&B 92*
Williams, Dale 1908- *WhoAmW 93*
Williams, Dale C. 1955- *St&PR 93*
Williams, Dale Philip 1928- *St&PR 93*
Williams, Dan Edward 1950- *WhoEmL 93*
Williams, Daniel Hale 1856-1931 *BioIn 17*
Williams, Daniel V. *BioIn 17*
Williams, Darlene *BioIn 17*
Williams, Darryl Marlowe 1938- *WhoAm 92*
Williams, Daryl Robert 1942- *WhoWor 93*
Williams, Dauna R. *Law&B 92*
Williams, Dave Harrell 1932- *WhoAm 92, WhoWor 93*
Williams, Davey 1927- *BioIn 17*
Williams, David *WhoScE 91-1*
Williams, David 1939- *ScF&FL 92*
Williams, David 1945- *WhoCanL 92*
Williams, David Allan 1949- *WhoEmL 93*
Williams, David Arnold *WhoScE 91-1*
Williams, David Benton 1920- *WhoAm 92*
Williams, David Francis 1938- *WhoSSW 93*
Williams, David Franklyn *WhoScE 91-1*
Williams, David Fulton 1926- *St&PR 93, WhoAm 92*
Williams, David Henry, Jr. 1931- *St&PR 93, WhoAm 92*
Williams, David Irvin 1942- *WhoAm 92*
Williams, David Islwyn *WhoScE 91-1*
Williams, David J. 1951- *St&PR 93*
Williams, David John *Law&B 92, WhoScE 91-1*
Williams, David John Alfred *WhoScE 91-1*
Williams, David Keith 1965- *WhoE 93*
Williams, David L. *Law&B 92*
Williams, David Lloyd 1935- *WhoE 93*
Williams, David Michael *Law&B 92*
Williams, David Owen 1937- *WhoAm 92*
Williams, David Perry 1934- *St&PR 93, WhoAm 92*
Williams, David R. *Law&B 92*
Williams, David R. 1943- *St&PR 93*
Williams, David R., Jr. 1921- *St&PR 93*
Williams, David Randolph 1955- *WhoSSW 93*
Williams, David Raymond *WhoScE 91-1*
Williams, David Rogerson, Jr. 1921- *WhoAm 92*
Williams, David Royal 1937- *WhoE 93*
Williams, David Russell 1932- *WhoAm 92*
Williams, David Vandergrift 1943- *WhoE 93*
Williams, David Welford 1910- *WhoAm 92*
Williams, Dean Elvin 1925- *WhoAm 92*
Williams, Debbie Kaye 1960- *WhoSSW 93*
Williams, Deborah Spiceland 1958- *WhoSSW 93*
Williams, Deborah White 1954- *St&PR 93*
Williams, Debra W. 1959- *St&PR 93*
Williams, Delwyn Charles 1936- *WhoAm 92*
Williams, Deniece 1951- *SoulM*
Williams, Denis (Joseph Ivan) 1923- *DcLB 117 [port]*
Williams, Denise 1950- *WhoAmW 93*
Williams, Dennis *BioIn 17*
Williams, Dennis A. *BioIn 17, Law&B 92*
Williams, Dennis B. 1943- *WhoIns 93*
Williams, Dennis K. 1946- *St&PR 93*
Williams, Dennis R. *Law&B 92*
Williams, Dennis Thomas 1925- *WhoWor 93*
Williams, Dennis Vaughn 1946- *WhoE 93, WhoEmL 93, WhoWor 93*
Williams, Derek R. 1963- *St&PR 93*
Williams, Dewey Gene 1925- *WhoAm 92*
Williams, Dexter Bradford 1950- *WhoE 93*
Williams, Di *ScF&FL 92*
Williams, Diane *WhoWrEP 92*
Williams, Diane Anita 1961- *WhoAmW 93*
Williams, Diane Denise 1959- *WhoSSW 93*
Williams, Diane Marie 1954- *WhoSSW 93*
Williams, Diane Theresa 1955- *WhoE 93*
Williams, Dianne *BlkAmWO*
Williams, Dianne Barber 1964- *WhoSSW 93*
Williams, Dick 1928- *BioIn 17*
Williams, Don E. 1923- *St&PR 93*
Williams, Donald Clyde 1939- *WhoAm 92*
Williams, Donald Elmer 1930- *WhoSSW 93*
Williams, Donald Herbert 1936- *WhoAm 92*
Williams, Donald John 1933- *WhoAm 92, WhoE 93*
Williams, Donald Lloyd, Jr. 1938- *WhoSSW 93*
Williams, Donald Maxey 1959- *WhoAm 92*
Williams, Donald R. 1946- *St&PR 93*
Williams, Donald R., Jr. *Law&B 92*
Williams, Donald Rosa 1934- *WhoWrEP 92*
Williams, Donald Shand 1930- *WhoAm 92*
Williams, Donna Jean 1941- *WhoAmW 93*
Williams, Doris Terry 1951- *WhoEmL 93*
Williams, Dorothy Jean O'Neal 1955- *WhoAmW 93*
Williams, (Marcia) Dorothy 1945- *SmATA 71 [port]*
Williams, Doug *BioIn 17*
Williams, Douglas Eric *Law&B 92*
Williams, Douglas Lee 1955- *AfrAmBi*
Williams, Doyle Z. 1939- *WhoAm 92*
Williams, Drew Davis 1935- *WhoAm 92, WhoWor 93*
Williams, Duane Edward 1944- *WhoE 93*
Williams, Earl Duane 1929- *WhoWor 93*
Williams, Earl Patrick, Jr. 1950- *WhoE 93*
Williams, Earle Carter 1929- *St&PR 93, WhoAm 92, WhoSSW 93*
Williams, Eda Dunstan *WhoAmW 93*
Williams, Eddie N. *AfrAmBi*
Williams, Eddie Nathan 1932- *WhoAm 92*
Williams, Edgar Gene 1922- *WhoAm 92*
Williams, Edith Clifford 1885-1971 *BioIn 17*
Williams, Edna Aleta Theadora Johnston 1923- *WhoAmW 93*
Williams, Edna Doris 1908- *WhoAmW 93*
Williams, Edson Poe 1923- *WhoAm 92*
Williams, Edward Bennett *BioIn 17*
Williams, Edward David 1932- *WhoE 93*
Williams, Edward Earl, Jr. 1945- *WhoAm 92*
Williams, Edward F., III 1935- *WhoWrEP 92*
Williams, Edward Foster, III 1935- *WhoSSW 93, WhoWor 93*
Williams, Edward G. 1929- *WhoWrEP 92*
Williams, Edward Gilman 1926- *WhoAm 92*
Williams, Edward Idris *WhoScE 91-1*
Williams, Edward J. d1990 *BioIn 17*
Williams, Edward Joseph 1942- *WhoAm 92*
Williams, Edward Lee, Jr. *Law&B 92*
Williams, Edward Vinson 1935- *WhoAm 92*
Williams, Edwin William 1912- *WhoAm 92*
Williams, Eira *WhoScE 91-1*
Williams, Elaine *Law&B 92*
Williams, Eleanor Joyce 1936- *WhoAmW 93*
Williams, Elizabeth Evenson 1940- *WhoAmW 93*
Williams, Elizabeth Gertner 1927- *WhoAmW 93*
Williams, Elizabeth Rosario 1968- *WhoAmW 93*
Williams, Ella D. *BioIn 17*
Williams, Ellen Claire 1966- *WhoAmW 93*
Williams, Elliot Joseph 1939- *St&PR 93*
Williams, Ellis Keith 1927- *WhoSSW 93*
Williams, Ellwood Elijah 1937- *WhoE 93*
Williams, Elynor A. *AfrAmBi [port], St&PR 93*
Williams, Elynor Alberta 1946- *WhoAmW 93*
Williams, Emily Coddington 1876- *AmWomPl*
Williams, Emily Jean 1928- *WhoAmW 93*
Williams, Emlyn 1905-1987 *BioIn 17*
Williams, Emory 1911- *St&PR 93, WhoAm 92*
Williams, Eric *WhoScE 91-1*
Williams, Eric 1911-1981 *DcCPCAm*
Williams, Eric C. 1918- *ScF&FL 92*
Williams, Eric Eustace 1911-1981 *BioIn 17, DcTwHis*
Williams, Eric Stanton 1958- *WhoSSW 93, WhoWor 93*
Williams, Erika 1947- *St&PR 93, WhoAmW 93*
Williams, Ernest Edward 1914- *WhoAm 92*
Williams, Ernest Franklin 1917- *WhoSSW 93*
Williams, Ernest Going 1915- *St&PR 93, WhoAm 92*
Williams, Ernest William, Jr. 1916- *WhoAm 92*
Williams, Ernest Y. 1900-1990 *BioIn 17*
Williams, Esther 1923- *IntDcF 2-3 [port]*
Williams, Ethel Laverna 1920- *WhoSSW 93*
Williams, Eugene D. 1921- *St&PR 93*
Williams, Eugene F., Jr. 1923- *St&PR 93*
Williams, Eva *AmWomPl*
Williams, Everard 1962- *BioIn 17*
Williams, Fannie Barrier 1855-1944 *BioIn 17*
Williams, Florian 1879-1973 *See* Williams, Joseph 1819-1883 *Baker 92*
Williams, Forman Arthur 1934- *WhoAm 92*
Williams, Francis Michael 1941- *St&PR 93*
Williams, Frank D. d1991 *BioIn 17*
Williams, Frank J. 1940- *WhoE 93, WhoWor 93*
Williams, Frank James, Jr. *Law&B 92*
Williams, Frank James, Jr. 1938- *St&PR 93, WhoAm 92*
Williams, Frank R. 1948- *St&PR 93*
Williams, Franklin Cadmus, Jr. 1941- *WhoSSW 93*
Williams, Franklin H. *BioIn 17*
Williams, Franklin P. *St&PR 93*
Williams, Fred A. 1938- *St&PR 93, WhoIns 93*
Williams, Fred Alton, Jr. 1923- *WhoSSW 93*
Williams, Fred B. *St&PR 93*
Williams, Frederic Ward *WhoScE 91-1*
Williams, Frederick Boyd 1939- *WhoE 93*
Williams, Frederick DeForrest 1918- *WhoAm 92*
Williams, Frederick (Dowell) 1933- *ConAu 136*
Williams, Frederick M. *Law&B 92*
Williams, Frederick R. 1947- *St&PR 93*
Williams, Fredrick Elbert 1939- *WhoSSW 93*
Williams, Freeman, Jr. 1956- *BiDAMSp 1989*
Williams, G. Bretnell 1929- *St&PR 93*
Williams, G.H. 1957- *WhoScE 91-1*
Williams, G. Mennen 1911-1989 *PolPar*
Williams, Gail *BioIn 17*
Williams, Garth 1912- *BioIn 17*
Williams, Garth (Montgomery) 1912- *MajAI [port], WhoAm 92*
Williams, Gary Michael 1964- *WhoE 93*
Williams, Gary Murray 1940- *WhoAm 92, WhoE 93*
Williams, Gene Troy 1940- *St&PR 93*
Williams, Genevieve Macdonald *AmWomPl*
Williams, Geoffrey John 1942- *WhoScE 91-1*
Williams, Geoffrey Reginald John 1945- *WhoWor 93*
Williams, George Cabell 1926- *St&PR 93*
Williams, George Christopher 1926- *WhoAm 92*
Williams, George Connor 1929- *St&PR 93*
Williams, George David 1951- *WhoSSW 93*
Williams, George Earnest 1923- *WhoAm 92*
Williams, George H. 1932- *St&PR 93*
Williams, George Henry 1820-1910 *OxCSupC*
Williams, George Howard 1918- *WhoAm 92*
Williams, George Huntston 1914- *WhoAm 92*
Williams, George Leo 1931- *WhoE 93, WhoWor 93*
Williams, George Masayasu 1930- *WhoAm 92*
Williams, George Melville 1930- *WhoAm 92*
Williams, George Rainey 1926- *WhoAm 92*
Williams, George T. *Law&B 92*
Williams, George W., III 1930- *St&PR 93*
Williams, George Walton 1922- *WhoAm 92, WhoSSW 93*
Williams, George Washington 1849-1891 *BioIn 17, EncAACR*
Williams, George Zur 1907- *WhoAm 92*
Williams, Gerald L. *Law&B 92*
Williams, Gerard John Paul 1949- *WhoWor 93*
Williams, Geroy D. *St&PR 93*
Williams, Gilbert 1913-1990 *BioIn 17*
Williams, Glen Morgan 1920- *WhoAm 92, WhoSSW 93*
Williams, Gordon 1939- *ScF&FL 92*
Williams, Gordon Bretnell 1929- *WhoAm 92*
Williams, Gordon Roland 1914- *WhoAm 92*
Williams, Grace 1906-1977 *BioIn 17, OxDcOp*
Williams, Grace (Mary) 1906-1977 *Baker 92*
Williams, Grace P. *AmWomPl*
Williams, Graham *ScF&FL 92, WhoScE 91-1*
Williams, Gregory Graham *Law&B 92*
Williams, Gregory Howard 1943- *WhoAm 92*
Williams, Gretchen Minyard 1956- *WhoAmW 93*
Williams, Guinn 1900-1962 *BioIn 17*
Williams, Gunther Gebel- *BioIn 17*
Williams, Gurney 1941- *BioIn 17*
Williams, Guy Thomas 1944- *WhoSSW 93*
Williams, H. Hunter d1991 *BioIn 17*
Williams, H. Kirk, III 1924- *St&PR 93*
Williams, Hamilton Wayne 1942- *St&PR 93*
Williams, Hank 1923-1953 *Baker 92, BioIn 17*
Williams, Hank, Jr. 1949- *WhoAm 92*

See Also Williams, Hank 1923-1953 *Baker 92*
Williams, Harold 1934- *WhoAm 92*
Williams, Harold Anthony 1916- *WhoAm 92*
Williams, Harold David 1952- *WhoSSW 93*
Williams, Harold David 1959- *WhoSSW 93*
Williams, Harold Duane 1942- *St&PR 93*
Williams, Harold Marvin 1928- *WhoAm 92*
Williams, Harold Milton 1907- *WhoAm 92*
Williams, Harold Roger 1935- *WhoAm 92*
Williams, Harriet Clarke 1922- *WhoAmW 93, WhoE 93, WhoWor 93*
Williams, Harriet E. *AmWomPl*
Williams, Harriet Elizabeth 1918- *WhoAmW 93*
Williams, Harry Alston, Mrs. *AmWomPl*
Williams, Harry Leverne 1916- *WhoAm 92*
Williams, Hattie Plum 1878-1963 *BioIn 17*
Williams, Heather Niles 1962- *WhoAmW 93, WhoE 93*
Williams, Heidi Lee 1962- *WhoAmW 93*
Williams, Helen Margaret 1947- *WhoAmW 93*
Williams, Helen Morgan 1933- *WhoWrEP 92*
Williams, Helena Ann Ditko 1962- *WhoAmW 93*
Williams, Helena V. *AmWomPl*
Williams, Henry Rudolph 1919- *WhoSSW 93*
Williams, Henry Thomas 1932- *WhoAm 92*
Williams, Henry Ward, Jr. 1930- *St&PR 93, WhoE 93*
Williams, Herbert B. 1933- *St&PR 93*
Williams, Hibbard Earl 1932- *WhoAm 92*
Williams, Hilary Paul *WhoScE 91-1*
Williams, Hilary Paul 1943- *WhoWor 93*
Williams, Hiram Draper 1917- *WhoAm 92*
Williams, Holly Thomas 1931- *WhoAmW 93*
Williams, Hope 1897-1990 *BioIn 17*
Williams, Hosea 1926- *PolPar*
Williams, Hosea Lorenzo 1926- *EncAACR*
Williams, Howard Russell 1915- *WhoAm 92*
Williams, Hugh Aldersey *ConAu 138*
Williams, Hugh Alexander, Jr. 1926- *WhoAm 92*
Williams, Hugh C. 1930- *St&PR 93*
Williams, Hulen Brown 1920- *WhoAm 92*
Williams, Ian *ScF&FL 92*
Williams, Ingrid Helvi *WhoScE 91-1*
Williams, Irene E.G. 1951- *WhoWrEP 92*
Williams, Irene Mae 1943- *WhoWrEP 92*
Williams, Irving Laurence 1935- *WhoE 93, WhoWor 93*
Williams, Iwan Prys *WhoScE 91-1*
Williams, J. Clare *Law&B 92*
Williams, J. D. 1937- *WhoAm 92*
Williams, J.E. Ffowcs *WhoScE 91-1*
Williams, J. Hulon, III 1952- *St&PR 93*
Williams, J. Lynn 1948- *St&PR 93*
Williams, J. Maxwell *Law&B 92*
Williams, J. Robert 1955-1992 *NewYTBS 92 [port]*
Williams, J.T., Jr. 1933- *St&PR 93*
Williams, J. Trevor 1938- *WhoScE 91-3*
Williams, J. Vernon 1921- *WhoAm 92*
Williams, J.W., Jr. 1925- *St&PR 93*
Williams, Jack Marvin 1938- *WhoAm 92*
Williams, Jack R. 1929- *St&PR 93*
Williams, Jack Raymond 1923- *WhoWor 93*
Williams, James Alexander 1929- *WhoAm 92*
Williams, James Arthur 1932- *WhoAm 92*
Williams, James B. 1945- *WhoAm 92, WhoE 93*
Williams, James Barry 1946- *WhoSSW 93*
Williams, James Bryan 1933- *St&PR 93, WhoAm 92, WhoSSW 93*
Williams, James Case 1938- *WhoAm 92, WhoE 93, WhoWor 93*
Williams, James D. 1957- *St&PR 93*
Williams, James Dale 1935- *WhoAm 92*
Williams, James E. *Law&B 92*
Williams, James Edgar 1924- *St&PR 93*
Williams, James Eugene 1953- *WhoE 93*
Williams, James Eugene, Jr. 1927- *WhoAm 92*
Williams, James Francis 1935- *WhoWor 93*
Williams, James Franklin, II 1944- *WhoAm 92*
Williams, James Gordon *WhoScE 91-1*
Williams, James Howard 1920- *WhoSSW 93*
Williams, James J. *Law&B 92*
Williams, James Joseph 1954- *WhoWor 93*
Williams, James Kay 1931- *WhoE 93*
Williams, James Kelley 1934- *St&PR 93, WhoAm 92, WhoSSW 93*
Williams, James Kendrick *WhoAm 92, WhoSSW 93*
Williams, James Lee 1941- *WhoAm 92*
Williams, James Lloyd 1940- *St&PR 93*
Williams, James Lynn 1943- *St&PR 93*
Williams, James M. *Law&B 92*
Williams, James O. 1931- *St&PR 93*
Williams, James Orrin 1937- *WhoAm 92, WhoSSW 93*
Williams, James P., Jr. 1944- *WhoAm 92*
Williams, James Peter Jerome 1940- *WhoWor 93*
Williams, James R. *AfrAmBi [port]*
Williams, James Richard 1932- *WhoE 93*
Williams, James Robert 1947- *St&PR 93*
Williams, James Stanley 1934- *St&PR 93*
Williams, James Thomas 1933- *WhoE 93*
Williams, Jane 1947- *WhoAmW 93*
Williams, Janelle Evon 1959- *WhoAmW 93*
Williams, Janet Lyda 1960- *WhoSSW 93*
Williams, Janet Page 1952- *WhoSSW 93*
Williams, Janice Denise 1951- *WhoAmW 93*
Williams, Janice Elaine *Law&B 92*
Williams, Janis Adaire 1933- *WhoAmW 93*
Williams, Jay *BioIn 17*
Williams, Jay 1914-1978 *ConAu 39NR, MajAI [port], ScF&FL 92*
Williams, Jay 1924-1978 *DcAmChF 1960*
Williams, Jean Person 1947- *WhoSSW 93*
Williams, Jeanne *DcAmChF 1960*
Williams, Jeanne 1930- *ScF&FL 92*
Williams, Jeanne Douglas 1962- *WhoAmW 93*
Williams, Jeanne L. 1953- *St&PR 93*
Williams, Jeanne Rea 1955- *WhoAmW 93*
Williams, Jeffrey Gerard *Law&B 92*
Williams, Jeffrey Scott 1952- *WhoSSW 93*
Williams, Jeffrey T. *Law&B 92*
Williams, Jennifer 1962- *WhoAmW 93*
Williams, Jenny 1939- *BioIn 17*
Williams, Jeremy N. *Law&B 92*
Williams, Jerre Stockton 1916- *WhoAm 92, WhoSSW 93*
Williams, Jerry 1932- *St&PR 93*
Williams, Jerry Arthur 1925- *St&PR 93*
Williams, Jerry David 1930- *WhoSSW 93*
Williams, Jerry O. 1938- *St&PR 93*
Williams, Jett *BioIn 17*
Williams, Jim *BioIn 17*
Williams, Jo Watts 1929- *WhoAmW 93*
Williams, Joan 1928- *WhoWrEP 92*
Williams, Joanne Molitor 1935- *WhoAmW 93*
Williams, JoBeth *BioIn 17*
Williams, Jody L. *Law&B 92*
Williams, Joe *BioIn 17*
Williams, Joe 1918- *WhoAm 92*
Williams, Joe Ed 1945- *St&PR 93*
Williams, Joel *Law&B 92*
Williams, John *Law&B 92*
Williams, John 1664-1729 *BioIn 17*
Williams, John 1932- *ConMus 9 [port], ConTFT 10*
Williams, John 1941- *WhoWor 93*
Williams, John A. 1925- *ScF&FL 92, WhoAm 92, WhoWrEP 92*
Williams, John A. 1955- *St&PR 93*
Williams, John Alfred 1925- *BioIn 17*
Williams, John Andrew 1941- *WhoAm 92*
Williams, John Brock 1958- *WhoSSW 93*
Williams, John Brooks 1921- *St&PR 93*
Williams, John Byrd 1945- *St&PR 93*
Williams, John Chamberlin 1919- *WhoE 93*
Williams, John (Christopher) 1941- *Baker 92*
Williams, John Cornelius 1903- *WhoAm 92*
Williams, John David *WhoScE 91-1*
Williams, John Dickinson 1923- *St&PR 93*
Williams, John Dickinson, Jr. 1952- *St&PR 93*
Williams, John Edwin 1928- *WhoAm 92*
Williams, John Frederick 1923- *WhoSSW 93*
Williams, John Gerrard 1888-1947 *Baker 92*
Williams, John H. 1918- *St&PR 93*
Williams, John Horter 1918- *WhoAm 92*
Williams, John Howard 1942- *St&PR 93*
Williams, John Irven 1933- *WhoUN 92*
Williams, John Kelvin 1932- *St&PR 93*
Williams, John Lee 1942- *WhoSSW 93*
Williams, John Leonard *WhoScE 91-1*
Williams, John M. 1884-1974 *Baker 92*
Williams, John M. 1944- *WhoSSW 93*
Williams, John Owen *WhoScE 91-1*
Williams, John Pattison, Jr. 1941- *WhoAm 92*
Williams, John S. *Law&B 92*
Williams, John T. *ConTFT 10*
Williams, John Taylor 1938- *WhoAm 92*
Williams, John Tilman 1925- *WhoAm 92*
Williams, John Tolliver 1944- *WhoSSW 93*
Williams, John (Towner) 1932- *Baker 92, WhoAm 92, WhoWor 93*
Williams, John Trent 1952- *WhoSSW 93*
Williams, John Wesley 1928- *WhoAm 92*
Williams, Johnny *ConTFT 10*
Williams, Johnny 1942- *BioIn 17*
Williams, Jojo Macasaet 1948- *WhoAmW 93*
Williams, Jon Edward 1937- *WhoE 93*
Williams, Joseph 1819-1883 *Baker 92*
Williams, Joseph B. d1992 *NewYTBS 92 [port]*
Williams, Joseph B. 1921-1992 *BioIn 17*
Williams, Joseph Benjamin 1847-1923 *See* Williams, Joseph 1819-1883 *Baker 92*
Williams, Joseph Dalton 1926- *St&PR 93, WhoAm 92, WhoE 93*
Williams, Joseph Donald 1936- *WhoIns 93*
Williams, Joseph G., Jr. *Law&B 92*
Williams, Joseph H. 1933- *St&PR 93*
Williams, Joseph Hill 1933- *WhoAm 92, WhoSSW 93*
Williams, Joseph R. 1931- *WhoAm 92, WhoSSW 93*
Williams, Joseph Richard 1955- *WhoE 93*
Williams, Joseph Theodore 1937- *WhoAm 92, WhoSSW 93*
Williams, Joshua 1952- *WhoSSW 93*
Williams, Josie R. 1941- *WhoSSW 93*
Williams, Joy 1944- *WhoWrEP 92*
Williams, Joy Anne 1961- *WhoAmW 93*
Williams, Joy Rhonda 1945- *WhoWor 93*
Williams, Joyce Bernice 1958- *WhoAmW 93*
Williams, Juan *BioIn 17*
Williams, Judith Ann 1954- *WhoAmW 93*
Williams, Judson F. 1913- *St&PR 93*
Williams, Julie Belle 1950- *WhoAmW 93*
Williams, Julie F. 1948- *St&PR 93*
Williams, Julie Ford 1948- *WhoAm 92*
Williams, Justin 1906- *WhoSSW 93*
Williams, Justin W. 1942- *WhoAm 92*
Williams, Karen Hastie 1944- *WhoAm 92*
Williams, Karen Lynn *BioIn 17*
Williams, Kathryn Blake 1923- *WhoAmW 93*
Williams, Kenneth 1926-1988 *QDrFCA 92 [port]*
Williams, Kenneth Charles *Law&B 92*
Williams, Kenneth Lee 1934- *WhoSSW 93*
Williams, Kenneth Ogden 1924- *WhoSSW 93*
Williams, Kenneth Scott 1955- *WhoAm 92*
Williams, Kenneth Scott 1961- *WhoSSW 93*
Williams, Kenneth Timothy 1949- *WhoSSW 93*
Williams, Kent Alan 1946- *WhoSSW 93*
Williams, Kevin Turner *Law&B 92*
Williams, Kimberly *BioIn 17*
Williams, Kimmika Lyvette Hawes 1959- *WhoWrEP 92*
Williams, Kirby Elmore 1940- *WhoUN 92*
Williams, Kit 1946?- *ScF&FL 92*
Williams, Kitty *St&PR 93*
Williams, La Ronnia Vernon Dobson 1934- *WhoAmW 93*
Williams, Langbourne Meade 1903- *WhoAm 92*
Williams, Larry 1935-1980 *SoulM*
Williams, Larry Bill 1945- *WhoAm 92*
Williams, Larry D. 1941- *WhoIns 93*
Williams, Larry Dale 1955- *WhoSSW 93*
Williams, Larry E. 1936- *St&PR 93*
Williams, Larry Emmett 1936- *WhoAm 92*
Williams, Laura A. *Law&B 92*
Williams, Laura M. *AmWomPl*
Williams, Lavinia *BioIn 17*
Williams, Lawrence Carroll 1934- *WhoSSW 93*
Williams, Lawrence Eugene 1949- *WhoAm 92*
Williams, Lawrence Soper 1917- *WhoE 93*
Williams, Lea Esther 1947- *WhoAmW 93*
Williams, Lea Everard 1924- *WhoAm 92*
Williams, Leamon D. 1935- *WhoAm 92*
Williams, Lee 1938- *BioIn 17*
Williams, Lee Dwain 1950- *WhoEmL 93*
Williams, Lee Erskine, II 1946- *WhoSSW 93*
Williams, Leland Hendry 1930- *WhoE 93*
Williams, Leslie A. *BioIn 17*
Williams, Leslie Howard, Jr. 1942- *WhoAm 92*
Williams, Leslie Pearce 1927- *WhoAm 92*
Williams, Lewis *Law&B 92*
Williams, Lewis C. 1912-1990 *BioIn 17*
Williams, Lewis Edmund 1939- *WhoE 93*
Williams, Lewis Lanier 1929- *St&PR 93*
Williams, Lillian D. *Law&B 92*
Williams, Lillie B. 1945- *WhoAmW 93*
Williams, Linda Joan 1960- *WhoAmW 93*
Williams, Linda Jones 1955- *WhoAmW 93*
Williams, Linda Mangham 1945- *WhoAmW 93*
Williams, Linda Turner 1941- *WhoAmW 93, WhoWor 93*
Williams, Lon Rayburn, Jr. *Law&B 92*
Williams, Loraine Plant 1929- *WhoSSW 93*
Williams, Lori Elizabeth 1957- *WhoAmW 93*
Williams, Lorie Ann 1965- *WhoAmW 93*
Williams, Lorraine Link 1952- *St&PR 93*
Williams, Louis A. *BioIn 17*
Williams, Louis Clair, Jr. 1940- *WhoAm 92*
Williams, Louis Gressett 1913- *WhoAm 92*
Williams, Louis Otho 1908-1991 *BioIn 17*
Williams, Louis Stanton 1919- *WhoAm 92*
Williams, Louise Taylor 1921- *WhoAmW 93*
Williams, Lowell *Law&B 92*
Williams, Lowell Craig 1947- *WhoAm 92*
Williams, Lowell Eugene *Law&B 92*
Williams, Lucinda *BioIn 17, BlkAmWO*
Williams, Lucious Lawrence 1932- *WhoSSW 93*
Williams, Luke G. 1923- *St&PR 93*
Williams, Lula Agnes 1904- *WhoAmW 93*
Williams, Luther Steward 1940- *WhoAm 92*
Williams, Lyman Neil, Jr. 1936- *WhoAm 92*
Williams, Lynn Russell 1924- *WhoAm 92*
Williams, M. Jane 1955- *WhoAmW 93*
Williams, M. Wright 1949- *WhoSSW 93*
Williams, Madonna Jo 1945- *WhoAmW 93*
Williams, Margaret Helen 1926- *WhoAmW 93*
Williams, Margaret Lu Wertha Hiett 1938- *WhoAmW 93, WhoSSW 93, WhoWor 93*
Williams, Margaret Ruth 1957- *WhoSSW 93*
Williams, Margery *AmWomPl, MajAI*
Williams, Mariann Sue 1953- *WhoAmW 93*
Williams, Marilyn 1950- *WhoAmW 93*
Williams, Marion Lester 1933- *WhoWor 93*
Williams, Marion Vernese 1946- *WhoWor 93*
Williams, Mark 1951- *ConAu 138*
Williams, Mark Carmichael 1963- *WhoSSW 93*
Williams, Mark Travis 1952- *WhoE 93*
Williams, Marsha Kay 1963- *WhoAmW 93*
Williams, Marsha Rhea 1948- *WhoEmL 93, WhoWor 93*
Williams, Marshall Henry, Jr. 1924- *WhoAm 92, WhoE 93*
Williams, Marshall MacKenzie 1923- *St&PR 93*
Williams, Martha Ethelyn 1934- *WhoAm 92, WhoAmW 93*
Williams, Martha G. 1942- *St&PR 93*
Williams, Martha Garrison *Law&B 92*
Williams, Martha Jane Shipe 1935- *WhoAm 92*
Williams, Martha Spring 1951- *WhoAm 92, WhoAmW 93, WhoSSW 93*
Williams, Martha Toedt *Law&B 92*
Williams, Martin d1992 *NewYTBS 92*
Williams, Martin 1924-1992 *ConAu 137*
Williams, Martin Berry 1956- *WhoE 93*
Williams, Martin T. *BioIn 17*
Williams, Martyn D. *St&PR 93*
Williams, Marvin 1944- *WhoSSW 93*
Williams, Mary 1925?- *ScF&FL 92*
Williams, Mary 1943- *WhoIns 93*
Williams, Mary Alice *WhoAm 92, WhoAmW 93*
Williams, Mary Bearden 1936- *WhoE 93*
Williams, Mary Elmore 1931- *WhoAmW 93, WhoSSW 93, WhoWor 93*
Williams, Mary Lou 1910-1981 *Baker 92, BioIn 17*
Williams, Mary Lou Newman 1918- *WhoAm 92*
Williams, Mary Lowe 1944- *WhoAmW 93*
Williams, Mary Macaulay 1959- *St&PR 93*
Williams, Mary Pearl 1928- *WhoAm 92*
Williams, Mary R. d1991 *BioIn 17*
Williams, Matthew Derrick Matt 1965- *WhoAm 92*
Williams, Maurice 1932- *WhoScE 91-1*
Williams, Maurice 1938-

See Williams, Maurice, & the Zodiacs *SoulM*
Williams, Maurice, & the Zodiacs *SoulM*
Williams, Maurice Jacoutot 1920- *WhoAm 92*
Williams, Maurice Leander *Law&B 92*
Williams, Max Lea, Jr. 1922- *WhoAm 92*
Williams, Maxine Eleanor 1940- *WhoAmW 93*
Williams, Melvin Donald 1933- *WhoWor 93*
Williams, Melvin John 1915- *WhoAm 92*
Williams, Michael 1952- *ScF&FL 92*
Williams, Michael Alan 1948- *WhoEmL 93*
Williams, Michael Anthony 1932- *WhoAm 92*
Williams, Michael Arnold *WhoScE 91-1*
Williams, Michael Dale 1947- *WhoIns 93*
Williams, Michael David 1947- *WhoSSW 93*
Williams, Michael E. *Law&B 92*
Williams, Michael Edward 1954- *WhoWrEP 92*
Williams, Michael J. *Law&B 92*
Williams, Michael Judson 1937- *St&PR 93*
Williams, Michael Keith *Law&B 92*
Williams, Michael L. *BioIn 17, Law&B 92*
Williams, Michael Lindsay 1940- *ScF&FL 92*
Williams, Mildred Jane 1944- *WhoSSW 93*
Williams, Miller *BioIn 17*
Williams, Miller 1930- *WhoAm 92, WhoSSW 93, WhoWor 93, WhoWrEP 92*
Williams, Milton Lawrence 1932- *WhoAm 92*
Williams, Molly Snyder *Law&B 92*
Williams, Mona 1916- *ScF&FL 92*
Williams, Monica B. *Law&B 92*
Williams, Montel 1956?- *ConBlB 4 [port]*
Williams, Morgan Howard *WhoScE 91-1*
Williams, Morgan Lewis 1948- *WhoSSW 93*
Williams, Morgan Lloyd 1935- *St&PR 93, WhoAm 92*
Williams, Murat Willis 1914- *WhoAm 92*
Williams, Myra Nicol 1941- *WhoAm 92*
Williams, Myrtle Helena 1944- *WhoAmW 93*
Williams, Nan Parker 1930- *WhoAmW 93*
Williams, Nancy Ann 1962- *WhoAmW 93*
Williams, Nancy Ellen-Webb *WhoWor 93, WhoWrEP 92*
Williams, Natalie *BioIn 17*
Williams, Nathan *BioIn 17*
Williams, Neville 1943- *WhoE 93*
Williams, Nick B. d1992 *NewYTBS 92*
Williams, Nick Boddie 1906-1992 *ScF&FL 92*
Williams, Nigel 1948- *ScF&FL 92*
Williams, Norman 1915- *WhoE 93*
Williams, Norman Dale 1924- *WhoAm 92*
Williams, Norman F. 1916- *WhoSSW 93*
Williams, Numan Arthur 1928- *WhoIns 93*
Williams, O. Jean *Law&B 92*
Williams, Omer S. J. 1940- *WhoAm 92*
Williams, Oni 1943- *WhoWrEP 92*
Williams, Oscar 1944- *MiSFD 9*
Williams, Otis *SoulM*
Williams, Otis Wise, Jr. 1948- *WhoSSW 93*
Williams, P.O. *WhoScE 91-1*
Williams, Pamela Bernice 1948- *WhoAmW 93*
Williams, Parham Henry, Jr. 1931- *WhoAm 92*
Williams, Parham Wilson 1938- *St&PR 93*
Williams, Parker 1929- *WhoSSW 93*
Williams, Pat 1937- *BioIn 17, CngDr 91, WhoAm 92*
Williams, Pat 1940- *WhoAm 92*
Williams, Pat Ward *BioIn 17*
Williams, Patrice Dale 1952- *WhoSSW 93*
Williams, Patricia A. 1942- *WhoSSW 93*
Williams, Patricia Ann 1950- *St&PR 93, WhoSSW 93*
Williams, Patricia Anne Johnson 1944- *WhoAmW 93*
Williams, Patricia Bell 1945- *WhoAmW 93*
Williams, Patricia R. *Law&B 92*
Williams, Patrick *BioIn 17*
Williams, Patrick J. *ConAu 40NR*
Williams, Patrick Moody 1939- *WhoAm 92*
Williams, Paul *BioIn 17*
Williams, Paul 1896-1980 *BioIn 17*
Williams, Paul 1943- *MiSFD 9*
Williams, Paul 1948- *ScF&FL 92*
Williams, Paul A., II 1946- *St&PR 93*
Williams, Paul Alan 1934- *WhoE 93*
Williams, Paul Chester 1926- *St&PR 93*
Williams, Paul Hamilton 1940- *WhoAm 92*
Williams, Paul L. *AfrAmBi [port]*
Williams, Paul O. 1935- *ScF&FL 92*
Williams, Paul Randall 1934- *WhoScE 91-1*
Williams, Paul Stratton *Law&B 92*
Williams, Paul T. 1934- *St&PR 93*
Williams, Paul Thomas 1934- *WhoSSW 93*
Williams, Paul W. 1957- *St&PR 93*
Williams, Paul X. *St&PR 93*
Williams, Peggy Ryan 1947- *WhoAmW 93*
Williams, Penny 1937- *WhoAmW 93*
Williams, Percy Don 1922- *WhoAm 92, WhoSSW 93*
Williams, Perdexter Hogue 1961- *WhoAmW 93*
Williams, Pete *BioIn 17*
Williams, Peter *WhoScE 91-1*
Williams, Peter 1937- *ConAu 138*
Williams, Peter Anthony *WhoScE 91-1*
Williams, Peter C. 1946- *St&PR 93*
Williams, Peter Charles 1933- *WhoE 93*
Williams, Peter James 1952- *WhoWor 93*
Williams, Peter James Le Breton *WhoScE 91-1*
Williams, Peter Maclellan 1931- *WhoE 93, WhoWor 93*
Williams, Peter Richard *WhoScE 91-1*
Williams, Petra Schatz 1913- *WhoAmW 93*
Williams, Philip Copelain 1917- *WhoWor 93*
Williams, Philip H. 1953- *St&PR 93*
Williams, Philip Laurence 1949- *WhoWor 93*
Williams, Philip Mitchell 1933- *St&PR 93*
Williams, Philip Needles 1953- *WhoE 93*
Williams, Phillip L. 1922- *St&PR 93*
Williams, Phillip Stephen 1949- *WhoAm 92*
Williams, Phillip Wayne 1939- *WhoSSW 93*
Williams, Phyllis Cutforth 1917- *WhoAmW 93*
Williams, Polly *BioIn 17*
Williams, Preston C., Jr. 1925- *St&PR 93*
Williams, Preston Noah 1926- *WhoAm 92*
Williams, Quinn Patrick 1949- *St&PR 93*
Williams, R.G. *Law&B 92*
Williams, R.J. *BioIn 17*
Williams, R. Jon *St&PR 93*
Williams, R. Leon 1909- *St&PR 93*
Williams, Ralph B. *Law&B 92*
Williams, Ralph Chester, Jr. 1928- *WhoAm 92*
Williams, Ralph J. 1954- *WhoE 93*
Williams, Ralph Vaughan *Baker 92*
Williams, Ralph Watson, Jr. 1933- *WhoAm 92*
Williams, Raymond 1921-1988 *BioIn 17, ScF&FL 92*
Williams, Raymond A., Jr. *St&PR 93*
Williams, Raymond F. *St&PR 93*
Williams, Redford Brown 1940- *WhoAm 92*
Williams, Reggie *BioIn 17*
Williams, Rex D. 1955- *St&PR 93*
Williams, Rhys 1929- *WhoAm 92, WhoWor 93*
Williams, Richard 1890-1980 *BioIn 17*
Williams, Richard 1933- *MiSFD 9*
Williams, Richard A., Jr. *Law&B 92*
Williams, Richard Clarence 1923- *WhoAm 92*
Williams, Richard D. *Law&B 92*
Williams, Richard Donald 1926- *WhoAm 92*
Williams, Richard Dwayne 1944- *WhoAm 92*
Williams, Richard F. 1941- *WhoIns 93*
Williams, Richard J. 1936- *St&PR 93*
Williams, Richard J. 1947- *WhoSSW 93*
Williams, Richard James 1942- *WhoSSW 93*
Williams, Richard Leroy 1923- *WhoSSW 93*
Williams, Richard Lloyd 1934- *St&PR 93*
Williams, Richard Lucas, III 1940- *WhoAm 92*
Williams, Richard N. 1957- *WhoSSW 93*
Williams, Richard Thomas Glyndwr 1924- *WhoWor 93*
Williams, Richard Walter 1945- *WhoSSW 93*
Williams, Richmond Dean 1925- *WhoAm 92*
Williams, Richmond Lyttleton *Law&B 92*
Williams, Robert B. 1921- *WhoIns 93*
Williams, Robert Bruce *BioIn 17*
Williams, Robert C. 1930- *WhoAm 92, WhoSSW 93*
Williams, Robert Carlton 1948- *WhoSSW 93, WhoWor 93*
Williams, Robert Carson 1944- *WhoSSW 93*
Williams, Robert Chadwell 1938- *WhoAm 92*
Williams, Robert Cody 1948- *WhoIns 93*
Williams, Robert D. 1961- *WhoSSW 93*
Williams, Robert E. 1934- *WhoIns 93*
Williams, Robert F. 1925- *EncAACR*
Williams, Robert Henry 1946- *WhoSSW 93, WhoWor 93*
Williams, Robert Hughes *WhoScE 91-1*
Williams, Robert Hughes 1941- *WhoWor 93*
Williams, Robert Jene 1931- *St&PR 93, WhoAm 92*
Williams, Robert Joseph 1926- *WhoAm 92*
Williams, Robert Joseph 1944- *WhoE 93*
Williams, Robert Joseph 1953- *St&PR 93*
Williams, Robert Joseph Paton *WhoScE 91-1*
Williams, Robert Leon 1922- *WhoAm 92*
Williams, Robert Lewis *Law&B 92*
Williams, Robert Luther 1923- *WhoAm 92*
Williams, Robert Lyle 1942- *WhoAm 92*
Williams, Robert M. 1941- *St&PR 93*
Williams, Robert Martin 1913- *WhoAm 92*
Williams, Robert Nowell 1930- *St&PR 93*
Williams, Robert O. 1948- *St&PR 93*
Williams, Robert P. *ScF&FL 92*
Williams, Robert R.V. 1922- *St&PR 93*
Williams, Robert Thomas, Jr. 1946- *St&PR 93*
Williams, Robert W. *Law&B 92*
Williams, Robert Walter 1920- *WhoAm 92*
Williams, Robin *NewYTBS 92 [port]*
Williams, Robin 1951- *ConTFT 10, WhoAm 92*
Williams, Robin 1952- *BioIn 17, HolBB [port], IntDcF 2-3, QDrFCA 92 [port]*
Williams, Robin Joy 1964- *WhoAmW 93*
Williams, Robin Murphy, Jr. 1914- *WhoAm 92*
Williams, Rogelio L. 1947- *St&PR 93*
Williams, Roger *WhoScE 91-1*
Williams, Roger 1604?-1683 *BioIn 17*
Williams, Roger 1924- *WhoAm 92*
Williams, Roger 1939- *St&PR 93*
Williams, Roger 1947- *ScF&FL 92*
Williams, Roger A. *Law&B 92*
Williams, Roger Allen 1955- *WhoSSW 93*
Williams, Roger Lawrence 1923- *WhoAm 92*
Williams, Roger M. *BioIn 17*
Williams, Roger Stanley 1931- *WhoWor 93*
Williams, Roger Stewart 1941- *WhoAm 92*
Williams, Roger T. 1903-1991 *BioIn 17*
Williams, Roger W. 1932- *St&PR 93*
Williams, Roger Wright 1918- *WhoAm 92*
Williams, Roland Charles 1928- *St&PR 93*
Williams, Ron 1945- *WhoIns 93*
Williams, Ronald A. *Law&B 92*
Williams, Ronald Doherty 1927- *WhoE 93*
Williams, Ronald John 1927- *WhoSSW 93, WhoWor 93*
Williams, Ronald L. 1935- *WhoAm 92*
Williams, Ronald N. 1951- *WhoE 93*
Williams, Ronald Oscar 1940- *WhoWor 93*
Williams, Rosalind Dodie 1947- *WhoSSW 93*
Williams, Ross Neil 1962- *WhoWor 93*
Williams, Rowland Wyn *WhoScE 91-1*
Williams, Roy Henry 1936- *WhoE 93*
Williams, Roy L. 1943- *St&PR 93*
Williams, Russ *ScF&FL 92*
Williams, Russell *BioIn 17*
Williams, Russell, II 1952- *WhoAm 92*
Williams, Russell Eugene 1951- *WhoE 93*
Williams, Russell F.V. 1944- *WhoScE 91-1*
Williams, Ruth *Law&B 92*
Williams, Ruth Arlene 1956- *WhoWrEP 92*
Williams, Ruth C. *DcChlFi*
Williams, S. Bradford, Jr. 1944- *WhoWrEP 92*
Williams, S. Lloyd 1948- *WhoE 93*
Williams, Sally Mae 1954- *WhoAmW 93*
Williams, Sam Kelly 1939- *WhoSSW 93*
Williams, Sammy 1948- *ConTFT 10*
Williams, Samuel Dunstan 1936- *St&PR 93*
Williams, Sandra *Law&B 92*
Williams, Sandra Anne *Law&B 92*
Williams, Sandra Keller 1944- *WhoAmW 93*
Williams, Sandra Wheeler 1957- *WhoAmW 93*
Williams, Sara M. *AmWomPl*
Williams, Sarette Briggs *Law&B 92*
Williams, Scott C. *Law&B 92*
Williams, Scott R. *Law&B 92*
Williams, Sheila *ScF&FL 92*
Williams, Sherry Lynne 1952- *WhoAm 92*
Williams, Shirley Jean Oostenbroek 1931- *WhoWor 93*
Williams, Shirley Vivian Teresa Brittain 1930- *WhoWor 93*
Williams, Sidney *ScF&FL 92*
Williams, Sidney B., Jr. *Law&B 92*
Williams, Smallwood E. 1907-1991 *BioIn 17*
Williams, Spencer 1889-1965 *Baker 92*
Williams, Spencer M. 1922- *WhoAm 92*
Williams, Stanley 1925- *WhoAm 92*
Williams, Stanley Thomas *WhoScE 91-1*
Williams, Stephen 1693-1782 *BioIn 17*
Williams, Stephen 1926- *WhoAm 92*
Williams, Stephen Arthur 1952- *WhoWrEP 92*
Williams, Stephen Edward *Law&B 92*
Williams, Stephen F. 1936- *CngDr 91*
Williams, Stephen Fain 1936- *WhoAm 92, WhoE 93*
Williams, Stephen M. *Law&B 92*
Williams, Sterling Lee 1943- *WhoAm 92*
Williams, Steve *ScF&FL 92*
Williams, Steve 1952- *WhoIns 93*
Williams, Steven Paul *Law&B 92*
Williams, Steven Randell 1954- *WhoSSW 93*
Williams, Steven Roger 1951- *St&PR 93*
Williams, Steven Wilson 1955- *WhoSSW 93*
Williams, Stirling Bacot, Jr. 1943- *WhoSSW 93*
Williams, Sue Darden 1943- *WhoSSW 93*
Williams, Susan Eileen 1952- *WhoAmW 93*
Williams, Suzanne (Bullock) 1953- *SmATA 71 [port]*
Williams, Sylvia Hill 1936- *WhoAm 92, WhoAmW 93*
Williams, Tad 1957- *ScF&FL 92*
Williams, Talcott 1849-1928 *JrnUS*
Williams, Talmage Theodore, Jr. 1933- *WhoSSW 93*
Williams, Ted 1918- *BioIn 17, WhoAm 92*
Williams, Temple Weatherly, Jr. 1934- *WhoAm 92*
Williams, Tennessee 1911-1983 *BioIn 17, ConLC 71 [port], MagSAmL [port], ScF&FL 92, WorLitC [port]*
Williams, Terrie *BioIn 17*
Williams, Terry M. 1948- *BioIn 17*
Williams, Terry Tempest *BioIn 17*
Williams, Terry Wesley 1952- *St&PR 93*
Williams, Theodore E. 1943- *WhoAm 92*
Williams, Theodore Earle 1920- *St&PR 93, WhoAm 92*
Williams, Theodore Joseph 1923- *WhoAm 92*
Williams, Thom Albert 1941- *WhoWor 93*
Williams, Thomas 1926-1990 *BioIn 17, ScF&FL 92*
Williams, Thomas 1950- *WhoAm 92*
Williams, Thomas A. 1939-1992 *BioIn 17*
Williams, Thomas Allan 1936- *WhoAm 92*
Williams, Thomas Allison 1936- *WhoAm 92, WhoE 93*
Williams, Thomas C. 1939- *St&PR 93*
Williams, Thomas Carl 1940- *St&PR 93*
Williams, Thomas D. 1957- *St&PR 93*
Williams, Thomas Donald 1950- *WhoSSW 93*
Williams, Thomas E. 1948- *St&PR 93*
Williams, Thomas E., III *Law&B 92*
Williams, Thomas Eifion Hopkins *WhoScE 91-1*
Williams, Thomas Eugene 1936- *WhoSSW 93, WhoWor 93*
Williams, Thomas Eugene 1961- *WhoSSW 93*
Williams, Thomas Ffrancon 1928- *WhoAm 92*
Williams, Thomas Franklin 1921- *WhoAm 92*
Williams, Thomas Henry Lee 1951- *WhoSSW 93*
Williams, Thomas J. *Law&B 92*
Williams, Thomas J. 1948- *WhoIns 93*
Williams, Thomas L. *Law&B 92, ScF&FL 92*
Williams, Thomas Lanier 1911-1983 *BioIn 17*
Williams, Thomas Lee 1945- *St&PR 93*
Williams, Thomas Owen, III 1937- *WhoSSW 93*
Williams, Thomas Rice 1928- *St&PR 93*
Williams, Thomas Stafford Cardinal 1930- *WhoWor 93*
Williams, Thomas Thackery 1925- *WhoSSW 93*
Williams, Timothy C. 1958- *St&PR 93*
Williams, Timothy John 1945- *WhoScE 91-1*
Williams, Timothy John 1966- *WhoSSW 93*
Williams, Timothy Shaler 1928- *WhoAm 92*

Willingham, Mary Maxine 1928- WhoAmW 93
Willingham, T.K. 1945- St&PR 93
Willingham, Thomas W. 1945- WhoIns 93
Willingham, Thomas Wasson 1945- St&PR 93
Willingham, Warren Willcox 1930- WhoAm 92
Willingham, Welborn Kiefer 1928- WhoSSW 93
Williquette, Gerald F. 1940- St&PR 93, WhoIns 93
Willis, Albert L. Law&B 92
Willis, Allen B. 1948- St&PR 93
Willis, B.J. WhoScE 91-1, -91-3
Willis, Barbara Cummings 1949- WhoSSW 93
Willis, Barbara Florence 1932- WhoE 93
Willis, Betty Jo 1942- WhoWrEP 92
Willis, Bill 1921- BioIn 17
Willis, Bobby J. 1936- St&PR 93
Willis, Bruce BioIn 17
Willis, Bruce 1955- HolBB [port]
Willis, Bruce Donald 1941- WhoAm 92
Willis, Bruce Donald 1954- WhoSSW 93
Willis, Bruce Walter 1955- WhoAm 92
Willis, Charles MajAI, SmATA 70
Willis, Charles L. Law&B 92
Willis, Chuck 1928-1958 SoulM
Willis, Clayton 1933- WhoAm 92
Willis, Clifford Leon 1913- WhoWor 93
Willis, Clyde Arnold 1922- St&PR 93
Willis, Connie 1945- ScF&FL 92
Willis, Constance E. ScF&FL 92
Willis, Craig Dean 1935- WhoAm 92, WhoE 93
Willis, Cynthia Elaine 1955- WhoAmW 93
Willis, D.R. WhoScE 91-1
Willis, Dave BioIn 17
Willis, David Arthur 1940- WhoAm 92
Willis, David Edwin 1926- WhoAm 92
Willis, David Lee 1927- WhoAm 92
Willis, Dawn Louise 1959- WhoAmW 93
Willis, Dennis Daryl 1948- WhoEmL 93
Willis, Diana May 1943- WhoAmW 93
Willis, Donald C. 1947- ScF&FL 92
Willis, Douglas Garrett 1961- WhoSSW 93
Willis, Earl William, Jr. 1948- WhoSSW 93
Willis, Eleanor Lawson 1936- WhoAmW 93
Willis, Ernest W. 1934- St&PR 93
Willis, Everett Irving 1908- WhoAm 92
Willis, Frank Edward 1939- WhoAm 92
Willis, Frank Roy 1930- WhoAm 92
Willis, Franklin Knight 1942- WhoAm 92
Willis, Gary K. 1946- WhoAm 92
Willis, Gary R. 1951- St&PR 93
Willis, George ScF&FL 92
Willis, George E. 1944- St&PR 93
Willis, Gerald 1938- St&PR 93
Willis, Gladys January 1944- WhoAmW 93
Willis, Gordon MiSFD 9, WhoAm 92
Willis, Gordon A. 1938- St&PR 93, WhoAm 92
Willis, Gordon C. 1920- St&PR 93
Willis, Hal L. Law&B 92
Willis, Harold Wendt, Sr. 1927- WhoWor 93
Willis, Helen BioIn 17
Willis, Henry 1821-1901 Baker 92
Willis, Isaac 1940- WhoSSW 93, WhoWor 93
Willis, Jakie Arleta WhoE 93
Willis, James Edward 1953- WhoSSW 93
Willis, Jan Burt 1951- St&PR 93
Willis, Jeanne BioIn 17
Willis, Jerry Weldon 1943- WhoSSW 93, WhoWor 93
Willis, Jill Michelle Law&B 92
Willis, JoAnn 1944- WhoAmW 93
Willis, Joe St&PR 93
Willis, John Alvin 1916- WhoAm 92, WhoWrEP 92
Willis, John Fristoe 1910- WhoAm 92
Willis, John Randolph ScF&FL 92
Willis, John Raymond WhoScE 91-1
Willis, John W. Law&B 92
Willis, Judith J. St&PR 93
Willis, Judith Laura Levine 1941- WhoWrEP 92
Willis, Judy Ann Law&B 92
Willis, Kathi Grant Law&B 92
Willis, Kenneth R. 1932- St&PR 93, WhoIns 93
Willis, Kevin BioIn 17
Willis, Kirby Roger 1951- St&PR 93
Willis, L.E. BioIn 17
Willis, Laura Smith 1934- WhoAmW 93
Willis, Linda Lorraine Everett 1957- WhoAmW 93
Willis, Lisle ScF&FL 92
Willis, Louise McKinney 1924- WhoAmW 93
Willis, Lynn ScF&FL 92
Willis, Martha Summers 1949- WhoAmW 93
Willis, Mary Catherine 1940- WhoAmW 93
Willis, Mary S. Law&B 92
Willis, Maud ScF&FL 92
Willis, Maxine Cooper 1944- WhoAmW 93
Willis, Meredith Sue 1946- WhoWrEP 92
Willis, Michael 1942- St&PR 93
Willis, Michael S. 1956- WhoSSW 93
Willis, Millie WhoAm 92
Willis, Nathaniel Parker 1806-1867 JrnUS
Willis, Patricia Cannon 1938- WhoE 93
Willis, Paul Allen 1941- WhoAm 92
Willis, Paul J. 1955- ScF&FL 92
Willis, Peter D. Law&B 92
Willis, Philip John WhoScE 91-1
Willis, Ralph 1938- WhoAsAP 91
Willis, Ralph Houston 1942- WhoSSW 93, WhoWor 93
Willis, Raymond Edson 1930- WhoAm 92
Willis, Raymond Smith 1906-1991 BioIn 17
Willis, Resa 1949- ConAu 138
Willis, Richard Elston 1934- WhoAm 92
Willis, Richard Hutchinson 1933- St&PR 93
Willis, Richard Storrs 1819-1900 Baker 92
Willis, Rick WhoSSW 93
Willis, Robert D. 1936- St&PR 93
Willis, Robert James 1940- WhoAm 92
Willis, Robert T. 1927- St&PR 93
Willis, Sharon White 1964- WhoSSW 93
Willis, Shirley Ann 1938- WhoAmW 93
Willis, Sid Frank 1930- WhoE 93
Willis, Susan Lockie 1947- WhoSSW 93
Willis, Ted d1992 NewYTBS 92
Willis, Thomas Delena 1955- WhoSSW 93
Willis, Thornton Wilson 1936- WhoAm 92
Willis, Wesley Robert 1941- WhoAm 92
Willis, William A. 1934- St&PR 93
Willis, William Darrell, Jr. 1934- WhoAm 92
Willis, William Ervin 1926- WhoAm 92
Willis, William F. WhoAm 92
Willis, William H., Jr. 1927- St&PR 93
Willis, William Harold, Jr. 1927- WhoAm 92
Willis, William Henry 1951- WhoAm 92
Willis, William Scott 1921- WhoAm 92
Williscroft, Beverly Ruth 1945- WhoAmW 93
Willison, Bruce G. 1948- St&PR 93
Willison, Bruce Gray 1948- WhoAm 92
Willison, Charles 1935- St&PR 93
Willison, Keith R. 1953- WhoScE 91-1
Willison, Robert Swithin 1898-1988 BioIn 17
Willke, Thomas Aloys 1932- WhoAm 92
Willkie, Wendell L. 1892-1944 PolPar
Willkie, Wendell Lewis 1892-1944 BioIn 17
Willkie, Wendell Lewis, II 1951- WhoAm 92, WhoE 93
Willman, Allan (Arthur) 1909- Baker 92
Willman, Hubert Law&B 92
Willman, John Norman 1915- WhoAm 92
Willman, Lee A. WhoIns 93
Willman, Sue K. Law&B 92
Willman, Vallee L. 1925- WhoAm 92
Willmann, Donnie Glenn 1955- WhoSSW 93
Willmann, Neal O. Law&B 92
Willmarth, William Walter 1924- WhoAm 92
Willmers, Rudolf 1821-1878 Baker 92
Willmes, Francis Edwin 1929- St&PR 93
Willmore, Albert Peter WhoScE 91-1
Willmore, Robert Louis 1955- WhoAm 92
Willmore, Thomas James 1919- WhoWor 93
Willmot, Donald G. 1916- St&PR 93
Willmot, Donald Gilpin 1916- WhoAm 92
Willmot, William Clarence 1925- WhoSSW 93, WhoWrEP 92
Willmott, David J. 1938- St&PR 93
Willmott, Frank 1948- DcChlFi
Willmott, John Charles WhoScE 91-1
Willmott, Paul Kenneth 1939- WhoAm 92
Willmott, Peter Sherman 1937- St&PR 93, WhoAm 92
Willmott, Phyllis ConAu 40NR
Willms, Arthur Henry 1939- WhoAm 92
Willmschen, Robert W. 1947- St&PR 93
Willner, Ann Ruth 1924- WhoAm 92
Willner, Arthur 1881-1959 Baker 92
Willner, Dina S. Law&B 92
Willner, Dorothy 1927- WhoAm 92
Willner, Eugene Burton 1934- WhoSSW 93
Willner, Hal BioIn 17
Willner, Larry Elliott 1932- WhoSSW 93
Willoch, Bjorn-Erik 1961- WhoWor 93
Willoch, Kare 1928- WhoWor 93
Willoch, Raymond 1933- St&PR 93
Willoch, Raymond S. Law&B 92
Willock, Marcelle Monica 1938- WhoAm 92
Willock, Roland D. 1936- St&PR 93
Willock, William Charles, Jr. 1952- WhoSSW 93
Willocks, Robert Max 1924- WhoAm 92
Willoughby, Arthur Frank Wesley WhoScE 91-1
Willoughby, Carroll Vernon 1913- WhoAm 92
Willoughby, Cass ConAu 39NR
Willoughby, Christopher Ronald 1938- WhoAm 92
Willoughby, Doris Mellott 1936- WhoWrEP 92
Willoughby, Edward 1926- St&PR 93
Willoughby, George Vernon, Jr. 1933- St&PR 93
Willoughby, Harvey William 1946- WhoAm 92
Willoughby, John Wallace 1932- WhoAm 92
Willoughby, Lee Davis ConAu 38NR, -39NR
Willoughby, Mark Law&B 92
Willoughby, Michael James 1945- WhoE 93
Willoughby, R.J. 1927- St&PR 93
Willoughby, Rodney Erwin 1925- WhoAm 92
Willoughby, Stephen Schuyler 1932- WhoAm 92, WhoWor 93
Willoughby, William E. 1920- St&PR 93
Willoughby, William Franklin, II 1936- WhoAm 92, WhoSSW 93
Willour, Byron J. 1936- St&PR 93
Willow, Judith Ann Loye 1939- WhoE 93
Willoxson, Terry D. 1952- St&PR 93
Willrich, Mason 1933- St&PR 93
Wills, Alma Jean 1947- St&PR 93
Wills, Arthur 1926- Baker 92
Wills, Barbara Y. 1940- WhoSSW 93
Wills, Bob 1905-1975 Baker 92
Wills, Bonnie 1945- St&PR 93
Wills, Charles Francis 1914- WhoAm 92
Wills, Clyde BioIn 17
Wills, Cornelia WhoAmW 93
Wills, Craig R. 1948- St&PR 93
Wills, David Arthur 1952- WhoWrEP 92
Wills, David Crawford 1872-1925 BioIn 17
Wills, David Wood 1942- WhoAm 92
Wills, Duane Arthur 1939- WhoAm 92
Wills, E. William 1943- St&PR 93
Wills, Garry 1934- WhoAm 92, WhoWrEP 92
Wills, Georgia Deacon 1944- WhoSSW 93
Wills, Helen 1905- BioIn 17
Wills, Isabel H. 1917- WhoSSW 93
Wills, J. Robert 1940- WhoAm 92
Wills, James Donald 1940- WhoSSW 93
Wills, Jean Marie 1939- WhoE 93
Wills, Joerg Michael 1937- WhoWor 93
Wills, John Arthur 1946- WhoWor 93
Wills, John Gordon 1931- WhoAm 92
Wills, Katherine Vasilios 1957- WhoAmW 93
Wills, Lawrence I. St&PR 93
Wills, Lisa Christine Illing 1962- WhoSSW 93
Wills, Maury BioIn 17
Wills, Michael Ralph 1931- WhoAm 92
Wills, Reid Nash 1933- St&PR 93
Wills, Ritchie Jean 1928- WhoAmW 93
Wills, Robert Hamilton 1926- St&PR 93, WhoAm 92
Wills, Robert Roy 1950- WhoSSW 93
Wills, Roger E., Jr. Law&B 92
Wills, Sylvia Lucy 1964- WhoAmW 93
Wills, Thomas Barling 1937- St&PR 93
Wills, Thomas Daniel 1961- St&PR 93
Wills, William John 1834-1861 See Burke, Robert O'Hara 1820-1861 & Wills, William John 1834-1861 Expl 93
Wills, William Ridley, II 1934- WhoAm 92
Willse, James P. NewYTBS 92 [port]
Willse, James Patrick 1944- St&PR 93
Willse, Jim BioIn 17
Willsey, Alice Rachel 1940- WhoAmW 93
Willsey, Lynn Willcox 1933- St&PR 93
Willson, Alan Neil, Jr. 1939- WhoAm 92
Willson, Carlette M. Law&B 92
Willson, David Russell Law&B 92
Willson, Dennis Frederick 1951- St&PR 93
Willson, Harry ScF&FL 92
Willson, James Douglas 1915- WhoAm 92
Willson, John M. 1940- WhoAm 92
Willson, L.H. 1935- St&PR 93
Willson, Linda Stout 1951- WhoAmW 93
Willson, Mary F. 1938- WhoAm 92, WhoAmW 93
Willson, (Robert Reiniger) Meredith 1902-1984 Baker 92
Willson, Richard C., Jr. Law&B 92
Willson, Robert 1912- WhoWrEP 92
Willson, Robert Alan 1918- WhoAm 92
Willson, Robert Frank 1939- WhoWrEP 92
Willson, Robin Linhope WhoScE 91-1
Willson, Steven R. 1949- WhoAm 92
Willson, William Harry 1920- St&PR 93
Will-Sparber, Elaine Ingeborg 1954- WhoWrEP 92
Wills-Raftery, Dorothy 1959- WhoWrEP 92
Willuhn, Gunter 1934- WhoScE 91-3
Willumsen, Jens 1942- WhoScE 91-2
Willvonseder, Robert 1939- WhoScE 91-4
Willy Baker 92
Willy, Warren B. 1943- St&PR 93
Willyoung, David Mac Cleggan 1924- WhoAm 92
Wilm, (Peter) Nicolai von 1834-1911 Baker 92
Wilmanns, Ottilie 1928- WhoScE 91-3
Wilmer, Charlotte M. 1946- WhoAmW 93
Wilmer, Cindy Jean 1965- WhoAmW 93
Wilmer, Harry Aron 1917- WhoSSW 93
Wilmer, Harry Aron 1945- St&PR 93
Wilmer, Mary Charles 1930- WhoAmW 93, WhoWor 93
Wilmerding, Harold Pratt 1937- St&PR 93, WhoAm 92
Wilmerding, John 1938- WhoAm 92
Wilmers, Robert G. 1934- St&PR 93
Wilmers, Robert George 1934- WhoAm 92
Wilmeth, Harvey Delbert 1918- St&PR 93
Wilmink, Jan T. 1943- WhoScE 91-3
Wilmoski, Scott Emery 1953- St&PR 93
Wilmot, David 1814-1868 PolPar
Wilmot, Dorothy AmWomPl
Wilmot, Fred Woodfin 1924- St&PR 93
Wilmot, Gretchen Kathryn 1939- St&PR 93
Wilmot, Irvin Gorsage 1922- WhoAm 92
Wilmot, Louise C. 1942- WhoAmW 93
Wilmot, Magali Law&B 92
Wilmot, Paul George 1946- WhoEmL 93
Wilmot, Renee Maree Law&B 92
Wilmoth, Gregory Hicks 1947- WhoE 93
Wilmoth, Patricia Baranowski 1950- WhoAmW 93, WhoSSW 93
Wilmoth, Ralph Eugene 1927- St&PR 93
Wilmoth, Robert Earnest Law&B 92
Wilmoth, Sharon Kay 1958- WhoAmW 93
Wilmotte, Raymond M. 1901- WhoAm 92
Wilmouth, Robert K. 1928- WhoAm 92
Wilmouth, Robert Kearney 1928- St&PR 93
Wilms, Jan Willem 1772-1847 Baker 92
Wilner, Alvin G. 1940- St&PR 93
Wilner, Alvin Gustav 1940- WhoAm 92
Wilner, Eleanor 1937- ConAu 37NR
Wilner, Lois Annette 1935- WhoAmW 93
Wilner, Milton 1924- WhoE 93
Wilner, Morton Harrison 1908- WhoAm 92
Wilner, Peter Jon 1945- WhoE 93
Wiloch, Thomas 1953- WhoWrEP 92
Wilroy, Thomas Jefferson 1907- WhoSSW 93
Wilsey, H. Lawrence 1923- WhoSSW 93
Wilsey, Stephen J. Law&B 92
Wilshire, Brian WhoScE 91-1
Wilshire, Everett S. 1946- St&PR 93
Wilshire, Rich 1949- WhoSSW 93
Wilshire, Susannah B. Law&B 92
Wilshire, Thomas E. 1931- WhoAm 92
Wilsie, Ronald Thomas 1951- St&PR 93
Wilsie, Russell W. 1953- St&PR 93
Wilsing, Daniel Friedrich Eduard 1809-1893 Baker 92
Wilske, Kenneth Ray 1935- WhoAm 92
Wilsker, Jay M. 1929- St&PR 93
Wilski, Krzysztof Marek 1941- WhoUN 92
Wilsman, Larry W. d1991 BioIn 17
Wilson, A.B. WhoScE 91-1
Wilson, A.N. 1950- BioIn 17, NewYTBS 92 [port], ScF&FL 92
Wilson, Abbott E. 1931- St&PR 93
Wilson, Abraham 1922- WhoE 93
Wilson, Addison Graves 1947- WhoSSW 93
Wilson, Adrian N. Law&B 92
Wilson, Alan Geoffrey WhoScE 91-1
Wilson, Albert Eugene 1927- WhoAm 92
Wilson, Albert J. 1932- St&PR 93
Wilson, Albert John Endsley, III 1934- WhoSSW 93
Wilson, Aleda Jean 1943- WhoAmW 93
Wilson, Alexander Erwin, Jr. 1910- WhoAm 92
Wilson, Alexander Erwin, III 1937- WhoAm 92
Wilson, Alexander Murray 1922- WhoAm 92
Wilson, Alice Bland 1938- WhoAmW 93, WhoE 93, WhoWor 93
Wilson, Alice Hornbuckle 1909- WhoAmW 93
Wilson, Alison M. 1932- ScF&FL 92
Wilson, Allan 1934-1991 AnObit 1991

Wilson, Allan Byron 1948- *St&PR 93, WhoAm 92, WhoSSW 93*
Wilson, Allan C. 1934-1991 *BioIn 17*
Wilson, Allison 1953- *WhoSSW 93, WhoWrEP 92*
Wilson, Alma *WhoAm 92*
Wilson, Alma D. *WhoAmW 93, WhoSSW 93*
Wilson, Almon Chapman 1924- *WhoAm 92*
Wilson, Andrew Norman 1950- *BioIn 17*
Wilson, Andrew R. 1941- *St&PR 93*
Wilson, Angela Dawn Lingerfelt 1964- *WhoSSW 93*
Wilson, Angus *BioIn 17*
Wilson, Angus 1913-1991 *AnObit 1991, ScF&FL 92*
Wilson, Ann Allbritton 1943- *WhoAmW 93*
Wilson, Ann Dustin 1950- *WhoAm 92, WhoAmW 93, WhoWor 93*
Wilson, Anna *ScF&FL 92*
Wilson, Anne Deirdre 1934- *ScF&FL 92*
Wilson, Anthony Aaron 1966- *WhoWrEP 92*
Wilson, Anthony Vincent 1936- *WhoAm 92*
Wilson, Arthur William 1961- *WhoE 93*
Wilson, August *BioIn 17, NewYTBS 92 [port]*
Wilson, August 1945- *ConTFT 10, WhoAm 92*
Wilson, Augusta Jane Evans 1835-1909 *BioIn 17*
Wilson, B.L.H. *WhoScE 91-1*
Wilson, Barbara H. 1959- *St&PR 93*
Wilson, Barbara Jan 1957- *WhoAmW 93*
Wilson, Barbara Ker *SmATA 70*
Wilson, Barbara Ker 1929- *ScF&FL 92*
Wilson, Barbara Louise 1952- *WhoAmW 93*
Wilson, Basil Wrigley 1909- *WhoAm 92*
Wilson, Berkeley B. 1926- *St&PR 93*
Wilson, Bernard J. 1949- *St&PR 93*
Wilson, Bertha 1923- *WhoAm 92, WhoAmW 93*
Wilson, Bertha M. *AmWomPl*
Wilson, Bertina Iolia 1938- *WhoAmW 93*
Wilson, Beth *BlkAuII 92*
Wilson, Betty M. 1947- *St&PR 93, WhoIns 93*
Wilson, Betty May 1947- *WhoAm 92*
Wilson, Billy 1859-1935 *BioIn 17*
Wilson, Blakely 1923- *St&PR 93*
Wilson, Blenda Jacqueline 1941- *WhoAm 92, WhoAmW 93*
Wilson, Boyd Cecil, Jr. 1952- *St&PR 93*
Wilson, Brad Marshall 1951- *St&PR 93*
Wilson, Bradley, Jr. 1928- *St&PR 93*
Wilson, Brian *BioIn 17*
Wilson, Brian 1942- *Baker 92*
Wilson, Brian Douglas 1942- *WhoAm 92*
Wilson, Bruce 1942- *MiSFD 9*
Wilson, Bruce Allan 1957- *WhoE 93*
Wilson, Bruce B. *Law&B 92*
Wilson, Bruce Brighton 1936- *St&PR 93, WhoAm 92*
Wilson, Budge 1927- *WhoCanL 92*
Wilson, Butler Roland 1860-1939 *EncAACR*
Wilson, Byron 1918- *BioIn 17*
Wilson, C. Daniel, Jr. 1941- *WhoAm 92, WhoSSW 93*
Wilson, C. Dexter, Jr. *St&PR 93*
Wilson, C. Edwin 1947- *St&PR 93*
Wilson, C.I. *WhoScE 91-1*
Wilson, C. Ivan *St&PR 93*
Wilson, Camilla Mary 1948- *WhoAmW 93*
Wilson, Carina Lord 1959- *WhoAmW 93*
Wilson, Carl 1946-
See Wilson, Brian 1942- *Baker 92*
Wilson, Carl W., Jr. 1933- *St&PR 93*
Wilson, Carl Weldon, Jr. 1933- *WhoSSW 93, WhoWor 93*
Wilson, Carnie *BioIn 17*
Wilson, Carolyn *AmWomPl*
Wilson, Carolyn Alice 1946- *WhoSSW 93*
Wilson, Carolyn Taylor 1936- *WhoAmW 93*
Wilson, Cassandra *WhoAm 92*
Wilson, Catherine Cooper 1955- *WhoAmW 93, WhoWrEP 92*
Wilson, Cecilia Rosezetta 1955- *WhoAmW 93*
Wilson, Charlene Willa 1943- *WhoAmW 93*
Wilson, Charles 1933- *CngDr 91, WhoAm 92*
Wilson, Charles Alden 1943- *WhoE 93*
Wilson, Charles Banks 1918- *BioIn 17, WhoAm 92*
Wilson, Charles Charlie 1933- *WhoSSW 93*
Wilson, Charles Edward 1943- *WhoSSW 93*
Wilson, Charles Elmer 1931- *WhoE 93*
Wilson, Charles G. 1949- *St&PR 93*
Wilson, Charles Glen 1948- *WhoAm 92, WhoSSW 93*
Wilson, Charles H. d1991 *BioIn 17*
Wilson, Charles Lee 1915- *WhoSSW 93*
Wilson, Charles M. 1931- *Baker 92*
Wilson, Charles Maye 1916-1989 *BioIn 17*
Wilson, Charles Reginald 1904- *WhoAm 92*
Wilson, Charles T., Jr. 1942- *St&PR 93*
Wilson, Charles Thomas 1907- *St&PR 93*
Wilson, Charles Zachary, Jr. 1929- *WhoAm 92*
Wilson, Cheryl Lee 1956- *WhoWrEP 92*
Wilson, Chris *BioIn 17*
Wilson, Christine Dalphin 1946- *WhoE 93*
Wilson, Christine Shearer *WhoAmW 93*
Wilson, Chuck W. 1939- *St&PR 93*
Wilson, Clara *AmWomPl*
Wilson, Clarence Ivan 1927- *WhoAm 92*
Wilson, Claude Raymond, Jr. 1933- *WhoAm 92, WhoWor 93*
Wilson, Claudia Lisa 1957- *WhoAmW 93*
Wilson, Clifford D., Jr. 1928- *St&PR 93*
Wilson, Clyde N(orman, Jr.) 1941- *ConAu 40NR*
Wilson, Colin 1931- *BioIn 17, ScF&FL 92*
Wilson, Colin Henry 1931- *WhoAm 92, WhoWor 93*
Wilson, Craig *Law&B 92*
Wilson, Curtis Wayne 1941- *WhoSSW 93*
Wilson, Cynthia Lindsay 1945- *WhoE 93*
Wilson, D. *WhoScE 91-1*
Wilson, D. James 1939- *St&PR 93*
Wilson, Dana Lynn Bartlett *WhoE 93*
Wilson, Daniel Donald 1958- *WhoE 93*
Wilson, Darla Sharon 1943- *WhoAmW 93*
Wilson, David 1935- *BioIn 17, WhoAsAP 91*
Wilson, David 1942- *ConAu 38NR*
Wilson, David Buckingham 1940- *WhoE 93*
Wilson, David Clive 1935- *WhoWor 93*
Wilson, David D. *Law&B 92*
Wilson, David Eugene 1939- *WhoUN 92*
Wilson, David H. *St&PR 93*
Wilson, David Henry 1937- *ChlFicS, ScF&FL 92, WhoAm 92*
Wilson, David Lown 1930- *WhoSSW 93*
Wilson, David Mackenzie 1931- *WhoWor 93*
Wilson, David Merl 1941- *WhoSSW 93*
Wilson, David Randall 1933- *St&PR 93*
Wilson, David Richard 1948- *WhoE 93*
Wilson, Dawn Karen 1960- *WhoAmW 93*
Wilson, Dawn L. *Law&B 92*
Wilson, Dean G. 1929- *St&PR 93*
Wilson, Debby Allyson 1955- *WhoAmW 93*
Wilson, Delano Dee 1934- *WhoAm 92*
Wilson, Delbert Ray 1926- *WhoAm 92, WhoWrEP 92*
Wilson, Denise Jane 1958- *WhoWrEP 92*
Wilson, Dennis *BioIn 17*
Wilson, Dennis 1944-1983
See Wilson, Brian 1942- *Baker 92*
Wilson, Dennis Oliver *Law&B 92*
Wilson, Dennis Robert 1949- *St&PR 93*
Wilson, Dennis W. *Law&B 92*
Wilson, Dewey Errol 1950- *WhoSSW 93*
Wilson, Dianne Carol 1951- *WhoAmW 93*
Wilson, Dierdre Lynn 1945- *WhoWor 93*
Wilson, Dirk *ConAu 37NR*
Wilson, Domingo Santa Cruz *Baker 92*
Wilson, Don 1900-1982 *BioIn 17*
Wilson, Don Whitman 1942- *WhoAm 92, WhoE 93, WhoWor 93*
Wilson, Donald 1926- *WhoWor 93*
Wilson, Donald Alfred 1941- *WhoE 93*
Wilson, Donald Andrew *WhoScE 91-1*
Wilson, Donald Douglas 1930- *WhoWrEP 92*
Wilson, Donald Edward 1936- *WhoAm 92*
Wilson, Donald Grey 1917- *WhoAm 92*
Wilson, Donald K., Jr. 1935- *WhoIns 93*
Wilson, Donald King, Jr. 1935- *St&PR 93*
Wilson, Donald Malcolm 1925- *WhoAm 92*
Wilson, Donald Richard 1936- *WhoE 93*
Wilson, Donald Wallin 1938- *WhoAm 92*
Wilson, Donn H. *Law&B 92*
Wilson, Doris Fanuzzi 1935- *WhoAmW 93, WhoE 93, WhoWor 93*
Wilson, Dorothy Clarke 1904- *AmWomPl, WhoAm 92*
Wilson, Douglas D. 1943- *St&PR 93*
Wilson, Douglas Edwin 1917- *WhoWor 93*
Wilson, Douglas J. 1939- *St&PR 93*
Wilson, Douglas Lawson 1935- *WhoAm 92*
Wilson, Douglas Roy 1935- *WhoAm 92*
Wilson, Dwight Liston 1931- *WhoAm 92*
Wilson, E. Bright d1992 *NewYTBS 92*
Wilson, Earle Frederick, Jr. 1932- *St&PR 93*
Wilson, Edith Bolling Galt 1872-1961 *BioIn 17*
Wilson, Edmund 1895-1972 *BioIn 17, JrnUS*
Wilson, Edna Erle *AmWomPl*
Wilson, Edward Converse, Jr. 1928- *WhoAm 92*
Wilson, Edward Nathan 1941- *WhoAm 92*
Wilson, Edward O. 1929- *BioIn 17, ConAu 16AS [port]*
Wilson, Edward Osborne 1929- *WhoAm 92, WhoE 93*
Wilson, Edwin Graves *WhoAm 92*
Wilson, Edwina Allison *Law&B 92*
Wilson, Elizabeth 1867- *AmWomPl*
Wilson, Elizabeth A. *Law&B 92*
Wilson, Elizabeth M. *Law&B 92*
Wilson, Elizabeth Weisenbacher 1938- *WhoE 93*
Wilson, Ellen Axson *BioIn 17*
Wilson, Elta M. *Law&B 92*
Wilson, Ephraim King 1771-1834 *BioIn 17*
Wilson, Eric 1938- *WhoWrEP 92*
Wilson, Eric 1940- *ScF&FL 92, WhoCanL 92*
Wilson, Eric Montgomery *WhoScE 91-1*
Wilson, Ernest I. 1957- *St&PR 93*
Wilson, Ethel 1888-1980 *BioIn 17*
Wilson, Eugene Rolland 1938- *WhoAm 92*
Wilson, Evan *BioIn 17*
Wilson, Evelyn Olga 1915- *WhoSSW 93*
Wilson, Evelyn Sue 1951- *WhoSSW 93*
Wilson, Ewen Maclellan 1944- *WhoAm 92, WhoE 93*
Wilson, F.G. *WhoScE 91-1*
Wilson, F. Paul 1946- *ScF&FL 92*
Wilson, F(rancis) Paul 1946- *ConAu 138*
Wilson, Flip 1933- *WhoAm 92*
Wilson, Francis Paul 1946- *WhoAm 92*
Wilson, Frank Elmore 1909- *WhoAm 92*
Wilson, Frank G. 1919- *St&PR 93*
Wilson, Frank J. 1926- *St&PR 93*
Wilson, Frank L. *Law&B 92*
Wilson, Frank Lyndall 1926- *WhoSSW 93*
Wilson, Franklin Leondus, III 1941- *WhoAm 92*
Wilson, Fred 1954- *BioIn 17*
Wilson, Fred Lee 1938- *WhoE 93*
Wilson, Frederic Rowland 1947- *WhoEmL 93*
Wilson, Frederick 1941- *WhoE 93*
Wilson, Frederick Allen 1937- *WhoAm 92*
Wilson, Frederick Calvin 1932- *St&PR 93*
Wilson, Frederick J., III *Law&B 92*
Wilson, G.L. *ScF&FL 92*
Wilson, G. Larry 1946- *St&PR 93*
Wilson, Gahan 1930- *ScF&FL 92, WhoAm 92*
Wilson, Gail *AmWomPl*
Wilson, Gary Charles 1949- *St&PR 93*
Wilson, Gary D. *Law&B 92*
Wilson, Gary D. 1942- *WhoSSW 93*
Wilson, Gary E. 1939- *St&PR 93*
Wilson, Gary Lee 1940- *BioIn 17, St&PR 93*
Wilson, George Andrew 1925- *WhoAm 92*
Wilson, George Hugh 1932- *WhoSSW 93*
Wilson, George Larry 1946- *WhoAm 92*
Wilson, George Peter 1935- *WhoAm 92*
Wilson, George Wharton 1923- *WhoAm 92*
Wilson, George Wilton 1928- *WhoAm 92*
Wilson, Gerald Einar 1922- *WhoAm 92*
Wilson, Gina 1947- *WhoAmW 93*
Wilson, Gladys Marie 1913- *WhoWrEP 92*
Wilson, Glen Parten 1922- *WhoE 93*
Wilson, Glen Wesley 1930- *St&PR 93*
Wilson, Glenn 1929- *WhoAm 92*
Wilson, Glenn Shaw 1932- *WhoE 93*
Wilson, Graham MacGregor 1944- *St&PR 93*
Wilson, Graham McGregor 1944- *WhoAm 92*
Wilson, Granville 1912- *ScF&FL 92*
Wilson, Gregory K. 1952- *St&PR 93*
Wilson, Grenville Dean 1833-1897 *Baker 92*
Wilson, H. Brian 1928- *St&PR 93*
Wilson, H.K. 1947- *WhoScE 91-1*
Wilson, Hack 1900-1948 *BioIn 17*
Wilson, Halford M. 1940- *WhoAm 92*
Wilson, Hamline C. 1937- *St&PR 93*
Wilson, Harold 1916- *ColdWar 1 [port]*
Wilson, Harold Charles 1931- *WhoWrEP 92*
Wilson, Harold Frederick 1922- *WhoAm 92*
Wilson, Harold Graham 1931- *WhoAm 92*
Wilson, Harold Hiller, Jr. 1930- *St&PR 93*
Wilson, Harold Kermit 1940- *St&PR 93*
Wilson, Harriet E. 1828?-1870? *AmWomWr 92*
Wilson, Harriet Smirle *AmWomPl*
Wilson, Harrison B. 1928- *WhoSSW 93*
Wilson, Harry B. 1917- *WhoAm 92*
Wilson, Harry Cochrane 1945- *WhoAm 92*
Wilson, Hazel (Hutchins) 1898-1992 *ConAu 139, SmATA 73*
Wilson, Helen A. d1992 *NewYTBS 92*
Wilson, Helen Marie 1930- *WhoAmW 93*
Wilson, Henry 1812-1875 *PolPar*
Wilson, Henry Hughes 1864-1922 *HarEnMi*
Wilson, Henry Maitland 1881-1964 *HarEnMi*
Wilson, Henry Rene 1957- *WhoSSW 93*
Wilson, Herbert Bendel 1950- *WhoSSW 93*
Wilson, Herbert Rees *WhoScE 91-1*
Wilson, Herman d1990 *BioIn 17*
Wilson, Herman T., Jr. 1941- *St&PR 93*
Wilson, Hillsman Vaughan 1928- *WhoAm 92*
Wilson, Hugh 1943- *MiSFD 9*
Wilson, Hugh Shannon 1926- *WhoAm 92*
Wilson, Hugh Steven 1947- *WhoAm 92*
Wilson, Ian Bonython Cameron 1932- *WhoAsAP 91*
Wilson, Ian Robert 1929- *WhoAm 92*
Wilson, Ira Lee 1927- *WhoWor 93*
Wilson, Irene K. 1955- *WhoWrEP 92*
Wilson, Iva *BioIn 17*
Wilson, J. Lawrence 1936- *St&PR 93*
Wilson, J. Robert 1927- *St&PR 93*
Wilson, J. Steven *St&PR 93*
Wilson, J. Tylee 1931- *St&PR 93, WhoAm 92*
Wilson, Jack c. 1858-1932 *BioIn 17*
Wilson, Jack Fredrick 1920- *WhoAm 92*
Wilson, Jack Harold Jay 1943- *St&PR 93*
Wilson, Jack Martin 1945- *WhoAm 92*
Wilson, Jackie *BioIn 17*
Wilson, Jackie 1934-1984 *Baker 92, SoulM*
Wilson, Jacqueline *BioIn 17*
Wilson, Jacqueline 1945- *ConAu 38NR*
Wilson, James 1742-1798 *OxCSupC [port]*
Wilson, James 1835-1920 *BioIn 17*
Wilson, James Adams 1913- *WhoSSW 93*
Wilson, James Arthur 1944- *WhoWor 93*
Wilson, James Blyth *WhoScE 91-1*
Wilson, James Carl 1933- *WhoSSW 93*
Wilson, James Charles, Jr. 1947- *WhoSSW 93, WhoWor 93*
Wilson, James Edward 1935- *St&PR 93*
Wilson, James Ernest 1915- *WhoAm 92*
Wilson, James Hargrove, Jr. 1920- *WhoAm 92*
Wilson, James Harold 1916- *DcTwHis*
Wilson, James Harris 1945- *WhoSSW 93*
Wilson, James Harrison 1837-1925 *HarEnMi*
Wilson, James John 1951- *WhoSSW 93*
Wilson, James K. *Law&B 92*
Wilson, James Lawrence 1936- *WhoAm 92*
Wilson, James Lee 1920- *WhoAm 92*
Wilson, James Leslie, Jr. 1948- *WhoSSW 93*
Wilson, James Loyd 1949- *WhoSSW 93*
Wilson, James M. *BioIn 17*
Wilson, James Madison 1916- *St&PR 93*
Wilson, James Milton, III 1934- *St&PR 93, WhoAm 92*
Wilson, James Murray 1931- *WhoSSW 93*
Wilson, James Newman 1927- *WhoAm 92*
Wilson, James Noble Ross 1935- *WhoAm 92*
Wilson, James Oliver 1926- *St&PR 93*
Wilson, James Quinn *WhoAm 92*
Wilson, James Ray 1930- *WhoWor 93*
Wilson, James Rigg 1941- *WhoAm 92*
Wilson, James Robert 1927- *WhoAm 92*
Wilson, James Rodney 1937- *WhoWor 93*
Wilson, James V. *St&PR 93*
Wilson, James W. *BioIn 17, Law&B 92*
Wilson, James William 1928- *St&PR 93, WhoAm 92*
Wilson, James William 1936- *WhoSSW 93*
Wilson, Jane *BioIn 17*
Wilson, Jane 1924- *WhoAm 92*
Wilson, Jane E. *Law&B 92*
Wilson, Janie Menchaca 1936- *WhoAm 92, WhoAmW 93, WhoSSW 93*
Wilson, Jean Avis 1924- *WhoWrEP 92*
Wilson, Jean Donald 1932- *WhoAm 92*
Wilson, Jean Gaddy 1944- *WhoAmW 93*
Wilson, Jean L. 1928- *WhoAmW 93*
Wilson, Jean Marie Haley 1921- *WhoAmW 93*
Wilson, Jeanette Kurtz 1929- *WhoAmW 93*
Wilson, Jeannette Solomon 1915- *WhoAmW 93*
Wilson, Jeff *St&PR 93*
Wilson, Jeffrey A. 1946- *St&PR 93*
Wilson, Jennifer Joy 1953- *WhoAm 92, WhoAmW 93*
Wilson, Jennifer Lee 1963- *WhoSSW 93*

Wilson, Jerome Martin 1916- *St&PR 93*
Wilson, Jim *BioIn 17, MiSFD 9*
Wilson, Joan M. 1956- *St&PR 93*
Wilson, Jodi Granda *Law&B 92*
Wilson, John *BioIn 17, WhoScE 91-1*
Wilson, John d1992 *NewYTBS 92*
Wilson, John 1595-1674 *Baker 92*
Wilson, John 1785-1854 *BioIn 17*
Wilson, John 1922- *WhoAm 92*
Wilson, John 1924- *WhoWor 93*
Wilson, John A. 1900-1991 *BioIn 17*
Wilson, John Anthony 1938- *WhoWor 93*
Wilson, John Anthony Burgess *ScF&FL 92*
Wilson, John Anthony Burgess 1917- *BioIn 17*
Wilson, John Anthony Clark 1918- *WhoWor 93*
Wilson, John B. 1959- *St&PR 93*
Wilson, John Cowles 1921- *WhoAm 92*
Wilson, John D. 1931- *WhoAm 92, WhoSSW 93*
Wilson, John David *WhoScE 91-1*
Wilson, John Donald 1913- *WhoAm 92*
Wilson, John Eric 1919- *WhoAm 92, WhoWor 93*
Wilson, John F. *Law&B 92*
Wilson, John Fletcher 1923- *WhoE 93*
Wilson, John Fletcher 1923-1991 *BioIn 17*
Wilson, John Foster 1919- *WhoWor 93*
Wilson, John G. 1947- *St&PR 93*
Wilson, John George 1925- *WhoWor 93*
Wilson, John Hill Tucker 1934- *WhoAm 92*
Wilson, John Leo *WhoE 93*
Wilson, John Louis 1899-1989 *BioIn 17*
Wilson, John Malcolm *Law&B 92*
Wilson, John Michael 1946- *WhoIns 93*
Wilson, John Morgan 1942- *WhoSSW 93*
Wilson, John Oliver 1938- *St&PR 93*
Wilson, John Page 1922- *St&PR 93*
Wilson, John Patrick 1923- *WhoWor 93*
Wilson, John Randolph 1948- *WhoE 93*
Wilson, John Ross 1920- *WhoAm 92*
Wilson, John S., Jr. *Law&B 92*
Wilson, John S., Jr. 1942- *St&PR 93*
Wilson, John Samuel 1916- *WhoAm 92*
Wilson, John T. 1914-1990 *BioIn 17*
Wilson, John T. 1938- *WhoSSW 93*
Wilson, John W. 1938- *St&PR 93*
Wilson, John William 1940- *WhoSSW 93*
Wilson, Johnnie Edward 1944- *AfrAmBi*
Wilson, Johnniece Marshall 1944- *BlkAull 92*
Wilson, Joseph Dennis 1949- *WhoE 93*
Wilson, Joseph Lopez 1960- *WhoWor 93*
Wilson, Joseph V., III 1949- *St&PR 93*
Wilson, Joy Ann 1941- *WhoAmW 93*
Wilson, Judy Vantrease 1939- *WhoAm 92, WhoAmW 93*
Wilson, Karen Lee 1949- *WhoAm 92, WhoAmW 93*
Wilson, Karen Lerohl *Law&B 92*
Wilson, Karl A. 1947- *WhoE 93*
Wilson, Kathleen Ann 1957- *WhoAmW 93*
Wilson, Keith *BioIn 17*
Wilson, Keith Charles 1927- *WhoWrEP 92*
Wilson, Keith N. *Law&B 92*
Wilson, Kemmons *BioIn 17*
Wilson, Kemmons 1913- *St&PR 93*
Wilson, Kendrick R., III 1947- *St&PR 93*
Wilson, Kenneth Geddes 1936- *WhoAm 92, WhoWor 93*
Wilson, Kenneth George 1923- *WhoE 93*
Wilson, Kenneth Jay 1944- *WhoAm 92*
Wilson, Kermit H. 1916- *St&PR 93*
Wilson, Lana Yvonne 1969- *WhoAmW 93*
Wilson, Lanford 1937- *WhoAm 92*
Wilson, Larry 1938- *BioIn 17*
Wilson, Larry Joseph 1948- *WhoSSW 93*
Wilson, Larry Michael 1951- *WhoSSW 93*
Wilson, Lauren Ross 1936- *WhoAm 92, WhoSSW 93*
Wilson, Lawrence Alan 1949- *WhoAm 92*
Wilson, Lawrence Alexander 1935- *St&PR 93, WhoAm 92*
Wilson, Lawrence Edward *Law&B 92*
Wilson, Lawrence Frank 1938- *WhoAm 92*
Wilson, Lawrence R. 1935- *St&PR 93*
Wilson, Leila Weekes *AmWomPl*
Wilson, Leisa Greame *AmWomPl*
Wilson, Lennox Norwood 1932- *WhoAm 92*
Wilson, Leonard Gilchrist 1928- *WhoAm 92*
Wilson, Leonard M. 1926- *WhoAm 92*
Wilson, Leonard Richard 1906- *WhoWor 93*
Wilson, Leroy 1928- *WhoAm 92*
Wilson, Leslie 1941- *WhoAm 92*
Wilson, Leslie Blackett *WhoScE 91-1*
Wilson, Leslie N. 1923-1988 *BioIn 17*
Wilson, LeVon Edward 1954- *WhoEmL 93, WhoSSW 93, WhoWor 93*
Wilson, Lewis Lansing 1932- *WhoE 93*
Wilson, Lillian P. *AmWomPl*
Wilson, Linda *ScF&FL 92*
Wilson, Linda 1945- *WhoAmW 93*
Wilson, Linda Lee 1943- *WhoAmW 93*
Wilson, Linda S. *BioIn 17*
Wilson, Linda Smith 1936- *WhoAm 92, WhoAmW 93, WhoE 93*
Wilson, Lindsay Edward 1949- *WhoSSW 93*
Wilson, Lionel *WhoScE 91-1*
Wilson, Lisa 1959- *WhoE 93*
Wilson, Lisa Kristine 1963- *WhoWrEP 92*
Wilson, Lloyd Lee 1947- *WhoAm 92*
Wilson, Logan 1907-1990 *BioIn 17*
Wilson, Lois 1896?-1990 *SweetSg B [port]*
Wilson, Lois Fair 1924- *WhoAmW 93*
Wilson, Lois M. 1927- *WhoAm 92*
Wilson, Lonnie Edward 1930- *St&PR 93*
Wilson, Louie Cecil 1937- *WhoSSW 93*
Wilson, Louis H. 1920- *St&PR 93*
Wilson, Louis Hugh 1920- *BioIn 17*
Wilson, Louis Round 1876-1979 *BioIn 17*
Wilson, Louise Astell Morse 1937- *WhoE 93*
Wilson, Louise Latham *AmWomPl*
Wilson, Lowell Lewis 1936- *WhoE 93*
Wilson, Lucius Roy, Jr. 1926- *WhoSSW 93*
Wilson, Luther 1944- *WhoWrEP 92*
Wilson, Luzena Stanley 1821?- *BioIn 17*
Wilson, Lyle L. 1928- *St&PR 93*
Wilson, Lynn Howard 1954- *WhoSSW 93*
Wilson, Lynn R. 1913- *St&PR 93*
Wilson, Lynton Ronald 1940- *WhoAm 92, WhoWor 93*
Wilson, M. *WhoScE 91-1*
Wilson, Malcolm *BioIn 17*
Wilson, Malcolm 1914- *St&PR 93, WhoAm 92*
Wilson, Malcolm Campbell 1942- *WhoAm 92, WhoE 93*
Wilson, Malcolm E., Jr. 1925- *St&PR 93*
Wilson, Marc Fraser 1941- *WhoAm 92*
Wilson, Margaret Bush 1919- *WhoAm 92*
Wilson, Margaret Dauler 1939- *WhoAm 92, WhoAmW 93*
Wilson, Margaret Elizabeth 1935- *WhoE 93*
Wilson, Margery Lauren 1951- *WhoAmW 93*
Wilson, Margot Lois 1957- *WhoSSW 93*
Wilson, Marian *AmWomPl*
Wilson, Marily Sharronn 1942- *WhoAmW 93*
Wilson, Marjorie M. 1960- *WhoAmW 93*
Wilson, Marjorie Price *WhoAm 92, WhoAmW 93*
Wilson, Mark D. *Law&B 92*
Wilson, Mark D. 1960- *St&PR 93*
Wilson, Marolyn Caldwell 1934- *WhoWrEP 92*
Wilson, Martha 1947- *BioIn 17*
Wilson, Martin N. 1939- *WhoScE 91-1*
Wilson, Mary *ScF&FL 92*
Wilson, Mary 1944- *BioIn 17*
Wilson, Mary A. *Law&B 92*
Wilson, Mary Anne 1922- *WhoAmW 93*
Wilson, Mary Catherine 1962- *WhoAmW 93*
Wilson, Mary Elizabeth 1942- *WhoAmW 93, WhoWor 93*
Wilson, Mary Louise 1940- *WhoAm 92*
Wilson, Mary P. *Law&B 92*
Wilson, Mathew Kent 1920- *WhoAm 92*
Wilson, Melinda Jean 1956- *WhoAmW 93*
Wilson, Melissa Anne 1968- *WhoE 93*
Wilson, Melvin Harry *Law&B 92*
Wilson, Melvin Nathaniel 1948- *WhoSSW 93*
Wilson, Meretle Hampton 1940- *WhoSSW 93*
Wilson, Merzie *ScF&FL 92*
Wilson, Michael 1928- *WhoUN 92*
Wilson, Michael B. *Law&B 92*
Wilson, Michael D. *Law&B 92*
Wilson, Michael Dudley 1955- *WhoSSW 93*
Wilson, Michael G. *Law&B 92*
Wilson, Michael Gerald 1942- *WhoWor 93*
Wilson, Michael H. *BioIn 17*
Wilson, Michael Holcombe 1937- *WhoAm 92, WhoE 93, WhoWor 93*
Wilson, Michael John *Law&B 92*
Wilson, Michael Joseph 1953- *WhoWor 93*
Wilson, Michelle L. *Law&B 92*
Wilson, Mike 1958- *BioIn 17*
Wilson, Mike L. 1940- *St&PR 93*
Wilson, Miles Scott 1943- *WhoWrEP 92*
Wilson, Miles (Scott, Jr.) 1943- *ConAu 139*
Wilson, Milner Bradley, III 1933- *WhoAm 92*
Wilson, Minter Lowther, Jr. 1925- *WhoAm 92*
Wilson, Miriam *AmWomPl*
Wilson, Miriam Geisendorfer 1922- *WhoAm 92, WhoAmW 93*
Wilson, Miriam Janet Williams 1939- *WhoAmW 93*
Wilson, Myron Robert, Jr. 1932- *WhoWor 93*
Wilson, Nairn Hutchison Fulton *WhoScE 91-1*
Wilson, Nancy 1937- *WhoAm 92*
Wilson, Nancy Keeler 1937- *WhoSSW 93*
Wilson, Nancy (Sue) 1937- *Baker 92*
Wilson, Neal Clayton 1920- *WhoAm 92*
Wilson, Neil Ernest 1955- *WhoE 93*
Wilson, Newton W., III *Law&B 92*
Wilson, Newton W., III 1950- *St&PR 93*
Wilson, Nicholas 1947- *BioIn 17*
Wilson, Norman Ward 1948- *WhoIns 93*
Wilson, Olin Chaddock 1909- *WhoAm 92*
Wilson, Olivia Lovell *AmWomPl*
Wilson, Olly (Woodrow) 1937- *Baker 92*
Wilson, Orrin A. 1940- *St&PR 93*
Wilson, Pamela L. *Law&B 92*
Wilson, Pat Leighton 1939- *St&PR 93*
Wilson, Patricia Ann *Law&B 92*
Wilson, Patricia Ann 1937- *WhoWrEP 92*
Wilson, Patricia Jane 1946- *WhoAmW 93, WhoWor 93*
Wilson, Patricia Marie 1942- *WhoAmW 93*
Wilson, Patrick C. *Law&B 92*
Wilson, Patrick Elliott 1934- *St&PR 93, WhoE 93, WhoIns 93*
Wilson, Paul 1935- See Flamingos *SoulM*
Wilson, Paul Edwin 1913- *WhoAm 92*
Wilson, Paul Lowell 1951- *WhoSSW 93*
Wilson, Perkins 1929- *WhoSSW 93, WhoWor 93*
Wilson, Pete *BioIn 17, NewYTBS 92 [port]*
Wilson, Pete 1933- *News 92 [port], -92-3 [port], WhoAm 92*
Wilson, Peter F. *Law&B 92*
Wilson, Peter Lamborn 1945- *ScF&FL 92*
Wilson, Peter Richard 1935- *WhoWor 93*
Wilson, Peter Robert 1929- *WhoWor 93*
Wilson, Philip 1886-1924 *Baker 92*
Wilson, Philip Duncan, Jr. 1920- *WhoAm 92*
Wilson, Phillip R. 1945- *St&PR 93*
Wilson, Ralph Cookerly, Jr. 1918- *WhoAm 92*
Wilson, Ralph Edwin 1921- *WhoAm 92*
Wilson, Ralph Martin *Law&B 92*
Wilson, Ramon B. 1922- *WhoAm 92*
Wilson, Randal D. 1950- *WhoSSW 93*
Wilson, Ransom 1951- *Baker 92*
Wilson, Ransom Carlos *Law&B 92*
Wilson, Ray C. 1929- *St&PR 93*
Wilson, Raymond 1938- *WhoScE 91-1*
Wilson, Raymond Clark 1915- *WhoAm 92*
Wilson, Rebecca Sue 1950- *WhoAmW 93*
Wilson, Rhea 1946- *WhoAm 92*
Wilson, Rhys Thaddeus 1955- *WhoEmL 93*
Wilson, Richard *BioIn 17, St&PR 93*
Wilson, Richard d1990 *BioIn 17*
Wilson, Richard 1915-1991 *BioIn 17, MiSFD 9N*
Wilson, Richard 1920-1987 *ScF&FL 92*
Wilson, Richard Allan 1927- *WhoAm 92*
Wilson, Richard Christian 1921- *WhoAm 92*
Wilson, Richard (Edward) 1941- *Baker 92*
Wilson, Richard Ferrol 1947- *WhoAm 92*
Wilson, Richard Harold 1930- *WhoAm 92*
Wilson, Richard Lee 1944- *WhoSSW 93*
Wilson, Richard M. 1932- *St&PR 93*
Wilson, Richard Philip 1947- *WhoE 93*
Wilson, Rick D. 1948- *WhoWrEP 92*
Wilson, Riley 1954- *St&PR 93*
Wilson, Rita P. 1946- *St&PR 93*
Wilson, Robert *NewYTBS 92 [port], ScF&FL 92, WhoScE 91-1*
Wilson, Robert 1941- *BioIn 17, IntDcOp*
Wilson, Robert Alan *WhoScE 91-1*
Wilson, Robert Albert 1936- *WhoE 93*
Wilson, Robert Anton 1932- *ScF&FL 92, WhoWrEP 92*
Wilson, Robert Arthur 1937- *WhoE 93*
Wilson, Robert B. 1936- *St&PR 93*
Wilson, Robert Burton 1936- *WhoAm 92*
Wilson, Robert Bynum 1943- *WhoSSW 93*
Wilson, Robert C. d1991 *BioIn 17*
Wilson, Robert C. 1951- *ScF&FL 92*
Wilson, Robert C. 1953- *ScF&FL 92*
Wilson, Robert Charles *WhoScE 91-1*
Wilson, Robert Craig 1941- *WhoE 93*
Wilson, Robert Dean *Law&B 92*
Wilson, Robert Edward 1951- *WhoWrEP 92*
Wilson, Robert Eugene 1932- *WhoSSW 93*
Wilson, Robert F. *Law&B 92*
Wilson, Robert Foster 1926- *WhoWor 93*
Wilson, Robert G. *Law&B 92*
Wilson, Robert Gordon 1933- *WhoSSW 93*
Wilson, Robert Hendrie *ScF&FL 92*
Wilson, Robert Henry 1909- *WhoAm 92*
Wilson, Robert Henry 1945- *WhoE 93*
Wilson, Robert Howell 1928- *WhoE 93*
Wilson, Robert J. 1928- *St&PR 93*
Wilson, Robert James Montgomery 1920- *WhoAm 92*
Wilson, Robert Leroy 1925-1991 *BioIn 17*
Wilson, Robert M. 1941- *WhoAm 92*
Wilson, Robert Neal 1924- *WhoAm 92*
Wilson, Robert Oliver 1927- *WhoSSW 93, WhoWor 93*
Wilson, Robert P. 1942- *St&PR 93*
Wilson, Robert Rathbun 1914- *WhoAm 92*
Wilson, Robert Sidney 1947- *WhoEmL 93, WhoWor 93*
Wilson, Robert Spencer 1951- *WhoAm 92*
Wilson, Robert Storey 1949- *WhoSSW 93*
Wilson, Robert Walter 1936- *St&PR 93*
Wilson, Robert William 1935- *St&PR 93, WhoAm 92*
Wilson, Robert Woodrow 1936- *WhoAm 92, WhoE 93, WhoWor 93*
Wilson, Roberta May 1943- *WhoAmW 93*
Wilson, Robin J. *BioIn 17*
Wilson, Robin Scott 1928- *WhoAm 92*
Wilson, Robley Conant, Jr. 1930- *WhoAm 92, WhoWrEP 92*
Wilson, Rodney James 1946- *WhoWor 93*
Wilson, Rodney James Alexander *WhoScE 91-1*
Wilson, Roger Charles 1949- *St&PR 93*
Wilson, Roger Goodwin 1950- *WhoAm 92*
Wilson, Ron *BioIn 17*
Wilson, Ronald Franklin *Law&B 92*
Wilson, Ronald J. 1934- *St&PR 93*
Wilson, Ronnie *SoulM*
Wilson, Rose S. *Law&B 92*
Wilson, Roy Gardiner 1932- *WhoAm 92*
Wilson, Roy Kenneth 1913- *WhoAm 92*
Wilson, Ruby Leila 1931- *WhoAm 92, WhoAmW 93*
Wilson, Rudy *ScF&FL 92*
Wilson, Rudy 1950- *ConAu 136*
Wilson, Samuel *BioIn 17*
Wilson, Samuel, Jr. 1911- *WhoAm 92*
Wilson, Samuel Grayson *WhoSSW 93*
Wilson, Samuel J. *Law&B 92*
Wilson, Samuel Mack 1921- *WhoAm 92*
Wilson, Samuel R. 1948- *St&PR 93*
Wilson, Sandra 1947- *MiSFD 9*
Wilson, Sara Redding *Law&B 92*
Wilson, Selma M. *St&PR 93*
Wilson, Selma Pierce 1956- *WhoAmW 93*
Wilson, Sheryl A. 1957- *WhoSSW 93*
Wilson, Sidney Maurice 1963- *WhoSSW 93*
Wilson, Skeeter J.H. 1952- *WhoAmW 93*
Wilson, Sloan 1920- *WhoAm 92*
Wilson, Sloan Jacob 1910- *WhoAm 92*
Wilson, Snoo 1948- *ScF&FL 92*
Wilson, Stanley P. 1922- *WhoAm 92*
Wilson, Stephanie Y. 1952- *St&PR 93*
Wilson, Stephen Douglas 1952- *WhoSSW 93*
Wilson, Stephen Edward 1945- *WhoSSW 93*
Wilson, Stephen L. *Law&B 92*
Wilson, Stephen L. 1953- *St&PR 93*
Wilson, Stephen Ray 1948- *St&PR 93*
Wilson, Stephen Rip 1948- *WhoEmL 93*
Wilson, Stephen Roy 1946- *St&PR 93, WhoAm 92*
Wilson, Stephen Victor 1941- *WhoAm 92*
Wilson, Steve 1943- *ScF&FL 92*
Wilson, Steven B. 1941- *St&PR 93*
Wilson, Steven Dale 1952- *WhoSSW 93*
Wilson, Steven Eugene 1948- *St&PR 93*
Wilson, Steven Nevin *Law&B 92*
Wilson, Sue Ann *AmWomPl*
Wilson, Sule Greg C. 1957- *WhoE 93*
Wilson, Susan Bernadette 1954- *WhoAmW 93*
Wilson, Sylvia d1991 *BioIn 17*
Wilson, T. Patrick *Law&B 92*
Wilson, Teddy 1912-1986 *Baker 92*
Wilson, Terrence Raymond 1943- *WhoAm 92*
Wilson, Terry Wayne 1934- *St&PR 93*
Wilson, Theda Morris 1922- *WhoAmW 93*
Wilson, Theodore 1943-1991 *BioIn 17*
Wilson, Theodore Alexander 1935- *WhoAm 92*
Wilson, Theodore Henry 1940- *WhoAm 92*
Wilson, Thomas Arthur 1935- *WhoAm 92*
Wilson, Thomas Daniel *WhoScE 91-1*
Wilson, Thomas Daniel 1935- *WhoWor 93*
Wilson, Thomas Daniel 1953- *St&PR 93*
Wilson, Thomas E. *Law&B 92*
Wilson, Thomas H. 1938- *St&PR 93*
Wilson, Thomas Hastings 1925- *WhoAm 92*

Wilson, Thomas Leon 1942- WhoWor 93
Wilson, Thomas Matthew, III 1936- WhoE 93, WhoWor 93
Wilson, Thomas Raiford, Jr. 1930- WhoSSW 93
Wilson, Thomas William 1935- WhoAm 92, WhoWor 93
Wilson, Thomas Woodrow 1856-1924 DcTwHis
Wilson, Thornton Arnold 1921- WhoAm 92
Wilson, Timothy Kenneth 1960- WhoE 93
Wilson, Todd Dorian 1953- WhoWrEP 92
Wilson, Tom BioIn 17
Wilson, Tom 1931- WhoAm 92
Wilson, Valerie WhoE 93
Wilson, Vincent Joseph, Jr. 1921- WhoE 93, WhoWor 93
Wilson, Virginia A. 1932- St&PR 93
Wilson, W. Michael Law&B 92
Wilson, Wallace 1947- WhoAm 92
Wilson, Wallace S. 1929- St&PR 93, WhoAm 92
Wilson, Wanda Lee 1950- WhoAmW 93, WhoE 93, WhoWor 93
Wilson, Warner Rushing 1935- WhoAm 92
Wilson, Wayne 1946- ConAu 136
Wilson, Wayne Jerome 1932- WhoSSW 93
Wilson, Wayne R. 1943- St&PR 93
Wilson, Wendy BioIn 17
Wilson, Wilburn Leroy 1913- WhoAm 92
Wilson, Wilburn Martin 1930- WhoWrEP 92
Wilson, Wilfred 1922-1990 BioIn 17
Wilson, William A. 1933- St&PR 93
Wilson, William Allen Law&B 92
Wilson, William Arthur 1949- WhoSSW 93
Wilson, William Craig 1951- St&PR 93
Wilson, William George 1935- WhoAm 92
Wilson, William Glenn, Jr. 1955- WhoSSW 93
Wilson, William Griffith 1895-1971 BioIn 17, ConHero 2 [port]
Wilson, William Howard 1924- WhoAm 92
Wilson, William J. 1932- WhoSSW 93
Wilson, William James 1936- St&PR 93
Wilson, William Julius 1935- WhoAm 92
Wilson, William L. 1910-1990 BioIn 17
Wilson, William M. 1937- WhoIns 93
Wilson, William Maxwell 1927- St&PR 93
Wilson, William Monroe, Jr. Law&B 92
Wilson, William Preston 1922- WhoAm 92
Wilson, William R. 1954- WhoSSW 93
Wilson, William Robert 1927- WhoAm 92
Wilson, William S. 1932- BioIn 17, WhoWrEP 92
Wilson, William Stanley 1938- WhoE 93
Wilson, William Thomas Law&B 92
Wilson, Woodrow 1856-1924 BioIn 17, PolPar
Wilson, Woodrow, Mrs. 1872-1961 BioIn 17
Wilson, Woodrow S. 1915- St&PR 93
Wilson, Worth B., Jr. 1952- St&PR 93
Wilson, Yvonne Montgomery BioIn 17
Wilson-Barnett, Jenifer WhoScE 91-1
Wilson-Deloje, Molly Law&B 92
Wilson Family BioIn 17
Wilson-Hopkins, Deborah Dana 1955- WhoAmW 93
Wilson Jones, Edward WhoScE 91-1
Wilson-Simpson, Dorothy Andrea 1945- WhoAmW 93
Wilson-Webb, Nancy Lou 1932- WhoSSW 93
Wilsz, Karol WhoScE 91-4
Wilt, Alan Freese 1937- WhoAm 92
Wilt, Catherine Chesser 1954- WhoAmW 93
Wilt, David (Edward) 1955- ConAu 137
Wilt, Dennis Michael Law&B 92
Wilt, Frederick Loren 1920- BiDAMSp 1989
Wilt, Katherine Hodges 1919- WhoAmW 93
Wilt, Marie 1833-1891 OxDcOp
Wilt, Steven J. 1945- St&PR 93
Wiltenburg, Robert 1947- ConAu 139
Wilton, Douglas H. St&PR 93
Wilton, Douglas Hughes 1941- WhoAm 92
Wilton, Frank Putnam 1930- St&PR 93
Wilton, Michael c. 1965- See Queensryche ConMus 8
Wilton, Robert Frederick 1953- WhoE 93
Wiltrakis, John N. Law&B 92
Wiltraut, Douglas Scott 1951- WhoE 93
Wiltrout, Ann Elizabeth 1939- WhoSSW 93
Wilts, Merle David 1938- St&PR 93
Wiltschko, Wolfgang 1938- WhoScE 91-3
Wiltse, George LeRoy 1880-1959 BiDAMSp 1989
Wiltse, James Clark 1927- WhoAm 92
Wiltse, Jon Frederick 1950- WhoE 93
Wiltsek, Kenneth M. 1942- St&PR 93
Wiltsek, Linda Rones 1947- St&PR 93
Wiltshire, David 1935- ScF&FL 92
Wiltshire, James Merrill, Jr. 1925- St&PR 93
Wiltshire, Richard W. 1921- St&PR 93
Wiltshire, Richard Watkins, Sr. 1921- WhoAm 92
Wiltshire, Richard Watkins, Jr. 1945- St&PR 93
Wiltshire, Stephen BioIn 17
Wiltshire, Suzanne Kathryn Law&B 92
Wiltshire, William E. BioIn 17
Wiltz, James Wesley 1945- St&PR 93
Wiltz, Robert E. 1936- St&PR 93
Wiltz, Teresa Y. BioIn 17
Wiltzer, Jack 1943- St&PR 93
Wilver, Wayne Riegel 1933- St&PR 93
Wilzack, Adele WhoAm 92
Wilzig, Siggi Bert 1926- WhoAm 92
Wimalaratne, Kelaniyage Don Garvin 1942- WhoWor 93
Wimberger, Gerhard 1923- Baker 92
Wimberley, Geraldine Joubert 1943- WhoSSW 93
Wimberly, Beadie Reneau 1937- WhoAmW 93, WhoWor 93
Wimberly, Elliott 1954- WhoWor 93
Wimberly, George James 1915- WhoAm 92
Wimberly, Sharon L. 1944- WhoAmW 93
Wimbish, Richard S. 1934- St&PR 93
Wimbish, Robert Allan Law&B 92
Wimbish, Shack Burke, Jr. 1935- St&PR 93
Wimble, Edward ScF&FL 92
Wimbly, Carolyn A. Law&B 92
Wimbrow, Peter Ayers, III 1947- WhoEmL 93
Wimbush, F. Blair Law&B 92
Wimbush, J.P. WhoScE 91-1
Wimer, Sarah Joyce 1951- WhoEmL 93, WhoSSW 93
Wimer, William John 1934- St&PR 93, WhoAm 92
Wimmel, Walter Erwin 1922- WhoWor 93
Wimmer, Brian BioIn 17
Wimmer, Brian 1960?- ConTFT 10
Wimmer, Carl Thomas 1952- WhoSSW 93
Wimmer, Dorn C. 1946- St&PR 93
Wimmer, Josef 1947- WhoScE 91-4
Wimmer, Mike 1961- SmATA 70 [port]
Wimmer, Rene W. 1955- St&PR 93
Wimmer, Ruth M. BioIn 17
Wimpee, Andy C. 1946- St&PR 93
Wimpfheimer, Jacques D. 1918- St&PR 93
Wimpfheimer, Michael Clark 1944- WhoWor 93
Wimpress, Gordon Duncan, Jr. 1922- WhoAm 92, WhoSSW 93
Wims, Lois Ann 1956- WhoAmW 93
Wims, Mary 1952- St&PR 93
Wims, Thomas Roberts 1953- WhoSSW 93
Winafeld, James M. 1946- St&PR 93
Winahradsky, Michael F. 1948- St&PR 93
Winahradsky, Michael Francis 1948- WhoAm 92
Winand, Rene F.P. 1932- WhoScE 91-2
Winans SoulM
Winans, Allan Davis 1936- WhoWrEP 92
Winans, Anna Jane 1939- WhoAmW 93
Winans, Cece WhoAmW 93
Winans, Gary L. 1949- St&PR 93
Winans, Thomas J. Law&B 92
Winant, William 1953- Baker 92
Winants, Ona AmWomPl
Winarsky, Lewis I. Law&B 92
Winawer, Gail Triffleman 1939- WhoE 93
Winawer, Sidney Jerome 1931- WhoAm 92
Winay, Nora Law&B 92
Winbeck, Heinz 1946- Baker 92
Winberg, Jan 1923- WhoScE 91-4
Winbigler, Leon Francis 1926- St&PR 93, WhoE 93
Winblad, Bengt 1943- WhoScE 91-4
Winbow, Graham Arthur 1943- WhoSSW 93
Winburn, Hardy L., Jr. 1932- St&PR 93
Winbush, Angela BioIn 17
Winbush, Wanda Gail 1958- WhoE 93
Winby, Mary Bernadette 1958- WhoAmW 93
Wincel, Henryk 1934- WhoScE 91-4
Wincenc, Carol 1949- Baker 92
Wincentz, Peer 1944- WhoWor 93
Wincer, Simon MiSFD 9
Wince-Smith, Deborah L. WhoAm 92, WhoAmW 93, WhoE 93
Winch, David Monk 1933- WhoAm 92
Winch, Peter Guy 1926- WhoAm 92
Winchell, Constance Mabel 1896-1983 BioIn 17
Winchell, Margaret Webster St. Clair 1923- WhoAmW 93
Winchell, Michael George 1949- WhoWor 93
Winchell, Patricia Anne Law&B 92
Winchell, Paul 1922- WhoAm 92
Winchell, Richard W. Law&B 92
Winchell, Walter 1897-1972 BioIn 17, JrnUS
Winchester, A. Richard Law&B 92
Winchester, Albert McCombs 1908- WhoAm 92
Winchester, Alice 1907- WhoE 93
Winchester, Bonnie Posick 1960- WhoE 93
Winchester, Jacqueline Canton 1930- WhoSSW 93
Winchester, James E. 1946- St&PR 93
Winchester, James Frank 1944- WhoE 93
Winchester, Jeanette M. 1953- WhoAmW 93
Winchester, John G. d1991 BioIn 17
Winchester, Kirk Handley 1952- St&PR 93
Winchester, Robert Joseph 1937- WhoAm 92
Winchester, Robert M. 1956- St&PR 93
Winchester, Rush B. 1924- St&PR 93
Winchester, Sandra Evadene 1960- WhoAmW 93
Winchester, Simon 1944- WhoWor 93
Winchilsea, Anne Finch, Countess of 1661-1720 BioIn 17
Winckelmann, Johann Joachim 1717-1768 BioIn 17
Winckler, Kathrine 1898-1976 BioIn 17
Winckler, Robert E. 1934- St&PR 93
Wincor, Michael Z. 1946- WhoEmL 93, WhoWor 93
Wincor, Richard 1921- WhoE 93
Wincott, Gerald Jay 1935- St&PR 93
Wincup, G. Kim 1944- WhoAm 92
Wind, David ScF&FL 92
Wind, Herbert Warren 1916- WhoAm 92
Wind, Marlise Wabun 1945- WhoWrEP 92
Wind, Moe 1924- St&PR 93
Wind, William Joseph 1934- St&PR 93
Windahl, Sven R. 1942- WhoScE 91-4
Windelev, Claus 1943- WhoE 93
Windels, Paul, Jr. 1921- St&PR 93, WhoAm 92
Winder, Anthony F. 1938- WhoScE 91-1
Winder, Barbara Dietz 1927- WhoWrEP 92
Winder, Bayly Philip 1951- WhoWor 93
Winder, Clarence Leland 1921- WhoAm 92
Winder, David Kent 1932- WhoAm 92
Winder, David William 1947- WhoSSW 93
Winder, Francis G.A. 1928- WhoScE 91-3
Winder, John H. 1800-1865 BioIn 17
Winder, Robert Owen 1934- WhoAm 92
Winder, William Henry 1775-1824 HarEnMi
Winderman, Alan J. Law&B 92
Winders, William Rudolph, Jr. Law&B 92
Winder-Thomas, Rosalind Ann 1957- WhoWor 93
Windfeldt, Thomas A. 1949- St&PR 93
Windgassen, Fritz 1883-1963 Baker 92, OxDcOp
Windgassen, Wolfgang 1914-1974 IntDcOp, OxDcOp
Windgassen, Wolfgang (Fritz Hermann) 1914-1974 Baker 92
Windhager, Erich Ernst 1928- WhoAm 92, WhoE 93
Windham, Bernard Moore 1942- WhoSSW 93
Windham, Danny L. Law&B 92
Windham, Donald 1920- BioIn 17, ConGAN
Windham, Kathryn Tucker BioIn 17
Windham, Patricia Wood 1946- WhoSSW 93
Windham, Revish 1949- WhoWrEP 92
Windham, Ronald H. BioIn 17
Windham, Wanda Hope 1953- WhoWrEP 92
Windham-Bannister, Susan R. 1951- St&PR 93
Windham-Bannister, Susan Richards 1951- WhoE 93
Windhausen, John Daniel WhoE 93
Windhauser, John William 1943- WhoSSW 93
Windheim, Daniel Robert 1930- St&PR 93
Windholz, Francis Leo 1932- WhoAm 92
Windhorst, Dave Alan 1953- St&PR 93
Windhorst, Hans-Wilhelm 1944- WhoWor 93
Winding, August (Henrik) 1835-1899 Baker 92
Winding, Charles A. 1907- St&PR 93
Winding, Kai (Chresten) 1922-1983 Baker 92
Winding, Ole 1932- WhoScE 91-2
Winding, Walter G. 1941- St&PR 93
Windingstad, Ole 1886-1959 Baker 92
Windisch, Cheryl Lee 1946- WhoAmW 93
Windisch, E.C. 1927- St&PR 93
Windle, Timothy J. Law&B 92
Windler, Larry St&PR 93
Windley, Brian Frederick WhoScE 91-1
Windling, Terri 1958- ScF&FL 92
Windman, Arnold Lewis 1926- St&PR 93, WhoAm 92
Windmuller, Jan P. 1943- WhoScE 91-2
Windmuller, John Philip 1923- WhoAm 92
Windolph, Gary R. 1942- WhoUN 92
Windolph, Gary Robert 1942- St&PR 93
Windom, William 1923- WhoAm 92
Windover, Fred A. Law&B 92
Windram, A. WhoScE 91-1
Windram-Brown, Kay Law&B 92
Windross, Gene R. BioIn 17
Windrow, Martin BioIn 17
Windsor, Barbara 1937- QDrFCA 92 [port]
Windsor, Colin George WhoScE 91-1
Windsor, Edward, Duke of 1894-1972 BioIn 17
Windsor, James Thomas, Jr. 1924- WhoSSW 93
Windsor, John Golay, Jr. 1947- WhoSSW 93
Windsor, Laurence Charles, Jr. 1935- WhoAm 92
Windsor, Marie SweetSg D [port]
Windsor, Oliver Duane 1947- WhoSSW 93
Windsor, Patricia 1938- DcAmChF 1985, ScF&FL 92, WhoAm 92
Windsor, Robert Kennedy 1933- WhoAm 92
Windsor, Wallis Warfield, Duchess of 1896-1986 BioIn 17
Windsor-Cothias, Micheline Josette WhoScE 91-1
Windsor, House of BioIn 17
Windt, Herbert 1894-1965 Baker 92
Wine, Donald Arthur 1922- WhoAm 92, WhoWor 93
Wine, James W. 1918-1990 BioIn 17
Wine, Sherwin Theodore 1928- WhoAm 92
Winearls, Joan 1937- ConAu 139
Wine-Banks, Jill Susan 1943- WhoAm 92, WhoAmW 93
Winebarger, Estel C. 1946- St&PR 93
Winebarger, Joe P. 1948- St&PR 93
Winebrenner, Douglas Joseph 1942- St&PR 93
Winebrenner, Janis L. 1949- WhoWrEP 92
Wineburgh, Joel 1941- St&PR 93
Winegar, Albert Lee 1931- St&PR 93, WhoAm 92
Winegar, Deborah Ann 1961- WhoAmW 93
Winegard, Deborah Jane Law&B 92
Winegard, William Charles 1924- WhoAm 92, WhoE 93
Winegarden, Joel I. 1938- St&PR 93
Winegrad, Gerald William 1944- WhoE 93
Wineinger, Barbara Ann 1941- WhoAmW 93
Wineland, Robert L. 1955- St&PR 93
Wineman, Alan Stuart 1937- WhoAm 92
Wineman, Clarence Edward 1961- WhoSSW 93
Wineman, James Martin 1949- St&PR 93
Wineman, William Richard Law&B 92
Winer, Deborah Grace 1961- ConAu 136
Winer, Harold 1910- WhoAm 92
Winer, Harry 1947- MiSFD 9
Winer, Jonathan H. 1951- St&PR 93
Winer, Michael Raymond 1957- St&PR 93
Winer, Morton J. 1914- St&PR 93
Winer, Robert Harry 1933- St&PR 93
Winer, Stephen J. 1954- St&PR 93
Winer, Ward Otis 1936- WhoAm 92, WhoSSW 93
Wines, Fred James 1931- St&PR 93
Wines, James BioIn 17
Wines, Richard A. 1946- St&PR 93
Winett, Heather C. Law&B 92
Winett, Joel M. 1938- WhoE 93
Winett, Samuel Joseph 1934- WhoAm 92
Winfield, Arthur M. MajAI
Winfield, Arthur M. 1862-1930 BioIn 17
Winfield, Bruce W. D. 1947- St&PR 93
Winfield, Dave 1951- BioIn 17
Winfield, David Mark 1951- WhoAm 92
Winfield, Donald H. 1942- St&PR 93
Winfield, Edna MajAI
Winfield, Elizabeth Virginia 1965- WhoAmW 93
Winfield, Helmsley 1907?-1934 BioIn 17
Winfield, Joe A. Law&B 92
Winfield, John Buckner 1942- WhoAm 92, WhoSSW 93
Winfield, Michael David 1939- St&PR 93
Winfield, Michael James WhoScE 91-1

Winfield, Novalyn L. 1950- *WhoAmW 93*
Winfield, Paul *BioIn 17*
Winfield, Paul Edward 1941- *WhoAm 92*
Winfield, Richard Neill 1933- *WhoAm 92*
Winford, Donald C. 1945- *ConAu 137*
Winford, Maria 1945- *WhoWor 93*
Winfree, Arthur Taylor 1942- *WhoAm 92*
Winfrey, Carey Wells 1941- *WhoAm 92*
Winfrey, Diana Lee 1955- *WhoAmW 93*
Winfrey, Frances Holton 1961- *WhoSSW 93*
Winfrey, John Crawford 1935- *WhoAm 92*
Winfrey, Jonathan Allen *MiSFD 9*
Winfrey, Marion Lee 1932- *WhoAm 92*
Winfrey, Oprah *BioIn 17*
Winfrey, Oprah 1954- *ConHero 2 [port], HolBB [port], WhoAm 92, WhoAmW 93*
Winfrey, Oprah Gail 1954- *AfrAmBi*
Wing, Antony John 1933- *WhoWor 93*
Wing, Christopher D. 1954- *St&PR 93*
Wing, Elizabeth Schwarz 1932- *WhoAm 92, WhoAmW 93*
Wing, Jasper *WhoWrEP 92*
Wing, Jeannette Marie 1956- *WhoAmW 93*
Wing, John Adams 1935- *St&PR 93*
Wing, John F. 1934- *St&PR 93*
Wing, John Faxon 1934- *WhoWor 93*
Wing, John Kenneth *WhoScE 91-1*
Wing, Lauren Lee 1957- *WhoAmW 93*
Wing, Martin Richard 1954- *WhoSSW 93*
Wing, Robert L. 1929- *St&PR 93*
Wing, Roger C. 1932- *St&PR 93*
Wing, Sandra Mei 1951- *WhoAmW 93*
Wing, Sidney E. *St&PR 93*
Wingad, Keith *BioIn 17*
Wingard, Anita Rae 1960- *WhoAmW 93*
Wingard, Deborah Lee 1952- *WhoAmW 93*
Wingard, George Clifton 1963- *WhoSSW 93*
Wingart, Cleland J. 1921- *St&PR 93*
Wingate, Anne Lynch 1938- *WhoAmW 93*
Wingate, Barbara Ann 1955- *WhoAmW 93*
Wingate, Catharine Louise *WhoE 93*
Wingate, David A. 1921- *St&PR 93*
Wingate, David Aaron 1921- *WhoAm 92*
Wingate, Edwin Henry 1932- *WhoAm 92*
Wingate, George Bradbury 1941- *WhoE 93*
Wingate, Henry Taylor, Jr. 1929- *WhoAm 92*
Wingate, Henry Travillion 1947- *WhoAm 92, WhoSSW 93*
Wingate, John Barnum 1937- *WhoE 93*
Wingate, John Williams 1899-1990 *BioIn 17*
Wingate, Lydia *WhoAmW 93*
Wingate, Mark Wade 1963- *WhoSSW 93*
Wingate, Orde Charles 1903-1944 *DcTwHis, HarEnMi*
Wingate, P.S. *WhoScE 91-1*
Wingate, Paul D. 1921- *St&PR 93*
Wingate, Robert Lee, Jr. 1936- *WhoSSW 93, WhoWor 93*
Wingate, Rosalee Martin 1944- *WhoAmW 93*
Wingate, Tessa Elizabeth 1947- *WhoAmW 93*
Wingate, Viva Louise 1940- *WhoAmW 93, WhoE 93*
Wingate, William Peter 1944- *WhoAm 92*
Winge, Charles Edwin 1945- *WhoAm 92*
Wingenfeld, Sabine Andrea 1959- *WhoAmW 93*
Winger, Charles Joseph 1945- *St&PR 93*
Winger, Debra *BioIn 17*
Winger, Debra 1955- *HolBB [port], WhoAm 92, WhoAmW 93*
Winger, Dennis Lawrence 1947- *WhoAm 92*
Winger, Eric R. 1941- *St&PR 93*
Winger, Howard Woodrow 1914- *WhoAm 92*
Winger, Kenneth Wayne 1938- *St&PR 93*
Winger, Kip *BioIn 17*
Winger, Kristine A. *Law&B 92*
Winger, Ralph O. 1919- *WhoAm 92*
Wingert, Friedrich 1939- *WhoScE 91-3*
Wingert, Hannelore Christiane *WhoE 93, WhoWor 93*
Wingerter, John Parker 1940- *WhoE 93*
Wingerter, Laurence Adrian 1942- *St&PR 93*
Wingfield, Sheila (Claude) 1906-1992 *ConAu 136*
Wingfield, Susan 1952- *WhoAmW 93*
Wingfield, William Terrell, Jr. *Law&B 92*
Winglass, Robert Joseph 1935- *WhoAm 92*
Wingler, Lucille Kay Thompson 1941- *WhoAmW 93*
Wingo, Charles William 1931- *St&PR 93*
Wingo, Effiegene Locke 1883-1962 *BioIn 17*
Wingo, Harthorne *BioIn 17*
Wingo, Paul Gene 1945- *WhoSSW 93*
Wingo, Phyllis Anne 1947- *WhoAmW 93*
Wingrove, David 1954- *ScF&FL 92*
Wingrove, Robert C. 1932- *St&PR 93*
Wingstrand, Hans Anders 1949- *WhoWor 93*
Wingti, Paias *WhoWor 93*
Wingti, Paias 1951- *WhoAsAP 91*
Winham, Gilbert Rathbone 1938- *WhoAm 92*
Winham, Godfrey 1934-1975 *Baker 92*
Winiarski, Mark Gregory 1950- *WhoE 93*
Winiarski, Wojciech Juliusz 1921- *WhoScE 91-4*
Winick, Alfred Zell 1941- *St&PR 93*
Winick, Calvin P. 1931- *WhoIns 93*
Winick, Calvin Phillip 1931- *WhoE 93*
Winick, Charles 1922- *WhoAm 92*
Winick, Darvin M. 1929- *St&PR 93*
Winick, Gary *MiSFD 9*
Winick, Myron 1929- *WhoAm 92*
Winick, Theodore 1935- *St&PR 93*
Winicour, Sheldon B. *Law&B 92*
Winicov, Ilga Butelis 1935- *WhoAmW 93*
Winiecki, Jan 1938- *WhoWor 93*
Winik, Jay B. 1957- *WhoAm 92*
Winikoff, Beverly 1945- *WhoAmW 93*
Wininger, Deborah Kay 1950- *WhoWrEP 92*
Winings, Michael Harry 1952- *St&PR 93*
Winings, Ronald D. 1954- *St&PR 93*
Wink, Douglas G. 1958- *St&PR 93*
Wink, Michael 1951- *WhoWor 93*
Winkel, Judy K. 1947- *St&PR 93*
Winkel, Judy Kay 1947- *WhoAm 92*
Winkel, Michael W. 1945- *St&PR 93*
Winkel, Nina 1905-1990 *BioIn 17*
Winkel, P. 1935- *WhoScE 91-3*
Winkel, Raymond Norman 1928- *WhoAm 92*
Winkel, Wolfgang 1941- *WhoScE 91-3*
Winkelhaus, John William 1950- *St&PR 93*
Winkeljohann, Rosemary Josephine 1929- *WhoE 93*
Winkelman, Benjamin Earl 1958- *WhoSSW 93*
Winkelman, Earl L. 1927- *St&PR 93*
Winkelman, Earl Leroy *Law&B 92*
Winkelman, Edward E. 1938- *St&PR 93*
Winkelman, James Warren 1935- *WhoAm 92*
Winkelman, John 1953- *WhoE 93*
Winkelman, John D. *Law&B 92*
Winkelman, Stanley J. 1922- *St&PR 93*
Winkelmann, Hermann 1849-1912 *Baker 92, OxDcOp*
Winkelmann, John Paul 1933- *WhoWrEP 92*
Winkelmann, Paul 1933- *St&PR 93*
Winkelstein, Jerry Allen 1940- *WhoE 93*
Winkelstein, Warren 1922- *WhoAm 92*
Winkelstern, Philip Norman 1930- *St&PR 93, WhoAm 92*
Winker, James Anthony 1928- *St&PR 93*
Winkfield, Trevor *BioIn 17*
Winkin, Justin Philip 1922- *St&PR 93, WhoAm 92*
Winkle, Charles Wayne 1948- *WhoSSW 93*
Winkle, Joseph Van *ScF&FL 92*
Winkle, Monica F. Van *ScF&FL 92*
Winkle, Sharon L. 1950- *WhoAmW 93*
Winkle, William Allan 1940- *WhoWor 93*
Winkleblack, Jack Dean 1928- *WhoSSW 93*
Winkleman, Bradley Carl 1954- *WhoSSW 93*
Winkleman, Henry W. 1945- *St&PR 93*
Winkleman, Henry Wainer *Law&B 92*
Winkler, Agnieszka M. 1946- *WhoAmW 93*
Winkler, Alexander (Gustav Adolfovich) 1865-1935 *Baker 92*
Winkler, Angelika *IntDcF 2-3*
Winkler, Arthur 1944- *St&PR 93*
Winkler, Charles *MiSFD 9*
Winkler, Cuno 1919- *WhoWor 93*
Winkler, Cuno G. 1919- *WhoScE 91-3*
Winkler, Edward D. 1942- *St&PR 93*
Winkler, Ernst W. 1934- *St&PR 93*
Winkler, Franz 1955- *WhoWor 93*
Winkler, Hans 1939- *WhoScE 91-4*
Winkler, Hans Wolfgang 1933- *WhoWor 93*
Winkler, Henry 1945- *BioIn 17*
Winkler, Henry 1946- *MiSFD 9*
Winkler, Henry Franklin 1945- *WhoAm 92*
Winkler, Henry Ralph 1916- *WhoAm 92*
Winkler, Herbert M. 1933- *St&PR 93*
Winkler, Howard Leslie 1950- *WhoWor 93*
Winkler, Hugo 1954- *St&PR 93*
Winkler, Irwin 1931- *ConTFT 10, MiSFD 9, WhoAm 92*
Winkler, Joseph Conrad 1916- *WhoAm 92, WhoWor 93*
Winkler, Juergen Fritz Hermann *WhoWor 93*
Winkler, Katherine Maurine 1940- *WhoE 93*
Winkler, Kenneth M. 1928- *St&PR 93*
Winkler, Lee B. 1925- *WhoAm 92, WhoWor 93*
Winkler, Leonard P. 1944- *WhoE 93*
Winkler, Lyle D. 1939- *St&PR 93*
Winkler, Martin Kenneth 1943- *WhoAm 92*
Winkler, Martin M. 1952- *WhoSSW 93*
Winkler, Peter K(enton) 1943- *Baker 92*
Winkler, Richard *Law&B 92*
Winkler, Richard G. *Law&B 92*
Winkler, Robert Charles 1927- *St&PR 93*
Winkler, Robert Lewis 1943- *WhoAm 92*
Winkler, Sheldon 1932- *WhoAm 92*
Winkler, Siegfried Reinhard 1932- *WhoWor 93*
Winkler, Steven Robert 1953- *WhoSSW 93*
Winkler, Thomas Edward *Law&B 92*
Winkler, William F. 1956- *St&PR 93*
Winkler Prins, Cor F. 1939- *WhoScE 91-3*
Winkles, Bobby Brooks 1930- *BiDAMSp 1989*
Winkles, Stuart *WhoWrEP 92*
Winkless, Terence H. *MiSFD 9*
Winklevoss, Carl R. 1919- *St&PR 93*
Winks, Robin W. 1930- *BioIn 17*
Winks, Robin William 1930- *WhoAm 92*
Winkworth, W.W. 1897-1991 *BioIn 17*
Winkworth, William Wilberforce 1897-1991 *BioIn 17*
Winland, Denise Lynn 1951- *WhoAmW 93*
Winley, Barry Jones 1959- *WhoWrEP 92*
Winmill, Bassett S. 1930- *St&PR 93*
Winmill, Mark C. 1957- *St&PR 93*
Winmill, Thomas B. *St&PR 93*
Winn, Alan Randolph *Law&B 92*
Winn, Albert Curry 1921- *WhoAm 92*
Winn, Alison *BioIn 17*
Winn, David B. 1937- *WhoAm 92, WhoIns 93*
Winn, David Baker 1937- *St&PR 93*
Winn, Edward Barriere 1922- *WhoWor 93*
Winn, Edward Burton 1920- *WhoAm 92*
Winn, Evelyn Dawson d1990 *BioIn 17*
Winn, George Michael 1944- *St&PR 93, WhoAm 92*
Winn, Herschel C. 1931- *St&PR 93*
Winn, Herschel Clyde 1931- *WhoAm 92, WhoSSW 93*
Winn, Jacquelyn Mary 1949- *WhoAmW 93*
Winn, Janice Gail 1954- *WhoAmW 93*
Winn, Jerry Ray 1939- *St&PR 93*
Winn, John A. 1946- *St&PR 93*
Winn, Judith Katz 1938- *WhoAmW 93*
Winn, Kevin *BioIn 17*
Winn, Patrick J. *Law&B 92*
Winn, Paul J. 1940- *St&PR 93*
Winn, Paul T. 1944- *St&PR 93*
Winn, Paula Diane 1947- *WhoAmW 93*
Winn, Rowland 1916-1984 *ScF&FL 92*
Winn, Ruth Helms 1932- *WhoAmW 93*
Winn, Sara Elizabeth 1961- *WhoEmL 93*
Winn, Stewart Dowse, Jr. 1936- *WhoE 93*
Winn, Thomas James, Jr. 1944- *WhoSSW 93*
Winn, Walter Garnett, Jr. 1941- *WhoSSW 93*
Winn, Walter Vincent 1963- *WhoSSW 93*
Winnacker, Albrecht 1942- *WhoScE 91-3*
Winnacker, Ernst-Ludwig 1941- *WhoScE 91-3*
Winne, Mark T. 1950- *St&PR 93*
Winnefeld, James Alexander 1929- *WhoAm 92*
Winnegrad, Mark Harris 1948- *WhoE 93*
Winnek, Marian F. *AmWomPl*
Winnemucca, Sarah 1844?-1891 *BioIn 17, GayN*
Winner, Christian O.G. 1927- *WhoScE 91-3*
Winner, Ellen Plucknett 1943- *WhoAmW 93*
Winner, Larry J. 1947- *St&PR 93*
Winner, Michael 1935- *MiSFD 9*
Winner, Michael Robert 1935- *ConAu 137, WhoAm 92, WhoWor 93*
Winner, Septimus 1827-1902 *Baker 92*
Winner, Thomas G. 1917- *WhoAm 92*
Winnerman, Robert H. 1921- *St&PR 93*
Winnerman, Robert Henry 1921- *WhoAm 92*
Winnett, Franklin Roy 1932- *WhoAm 92*
Winnett, Frederick Victor 1903-1989 *BioIn 17*
Winnett, Michael David 1955- *WhoE 93*
Winney, Ronald Dean 1942- *St&PR 93*
Winnick, Andrew Jay 1939- *WhoWor 93*
Winnick, Stephen 1939- *WhoAm 92*
Winnicki, Aleksander K. 1929- *WhoScE 91-4*
Winnicki, Tomasz 1934- *WhoScE 91-4*
Winnie, Alon Palm 1932- *WhoAm 92*
Winnie, Dayle David 1935- *WhoSSW 93*
Winnifrith, Thomas John 1938- *WhoWor 93*
Winning, David 1961- *MiSFD 9*
Winning, Joseph S. 1930- *St&PR 93*
Winningstad, C. Norman 1925- *St&PR 93*
Winningstad, Chester Norman 1925- *WhoAm 92*
Winnowski, T.R. 1942- *St&PR 93*
Winnowski, Thaddeus Richard 1942- *WhoAm 92*
Winograd, Arthur 1920- *Baker 92*
Winograd, Audrey Lesser 1933- *WhoAmW 93, WhoE 93*
Winograd, Eugene 1933- *WhoSSW 93*
Winograd, Florence L. 1923- *St&PR 93*
Winograd, Harold S. 1921- *St&PR 93*
Winograd, Nicholas 1945- *WhoAm 92*
Winograd, Shmuel 1936- *WhoAm 92*
Winoker, Diana Lee 1953- *WhoSSW 93*
Winokur, George 1925- *WhoAm 92*
Winokur, Harvey Jay 1950- *WhoSSW 93*
Winokur, James L. 1922- *St&PR 93*
Winokur, Jon 1947- *WhoWrEP 92*
Winokur, Melvin *Law&B 92*
Winokur, Robert M. 1924- *WhoAm 92*
Winpisinger, William 1924- *WhoAm 92*
Winquist, Vernon Nathaniel 1921- *WhoSSW 93*
Winsby, Roger Merritt 1951- *St&PR 93*
Winschel, Diane Perron *BioIn 17*
Winsett, Anna Pawlik *Law&B 92*
Winship, Blanton C. 1959- *St&PR 93*
Winship, Frederick Moery 1924- *WhoAm 92*
Winship, Gary M. 1945- *St&PR 93*
Winship, Glen B. 1887-1966 *ScF&FL 92*
Winship, James D. 1948- *St&PR 93*
Winship, M. Douglas 1949- *WhoE 93*
Winship, Neil *WhoScE 91-1*
Winship, Wadleigh Chichester 1940- *WhoAm 92*
Winski, Louise Florence 1950- *WhoE 93*
Winski, Norman *ScF&FL 92*
Winsky, Gregory J. 1949- *St&PR 93*
Winsky, Gregory John *Law&B 92*
Winslade, Thomas E. *Law&B 92*
Winslade, Thomas Edwin 1952- *WhoE 93*
Winsloe, Christa 1888-1944 *DcLB 124 [port]*
Winslow, Anne Branan 1920- *WhoAmW 93*
Winslow, Betty J. 1945- *WhoAmW 93*
Winslow, David Allen 1944- *WhoWor 93*
Winslow, Debra L. 1954- *St&PR 93*
Winslow, Don O. *Law&B 92*
Winslow, Frances Edwards 1948- *WhoAmW 93, WhoEmL 93, WhoWor 93*
Winslow, Francis Dana 1939- *WhoWor 93*
Winslow, Gail H. 1929- *St&PR 93*
Winslow, Henry Nichols 1938- *St&PR 93*
Winslow, James E. 1954- *St&PR 93*
Winslow, Johanna Marie 1953- *WhoAmW 93*
Winslow, John 1938- *BioIn 17*
Winslow, Julian Dallas 1914- *WhoE 93*
Winslow, Karen *BioIn 17*
Winslow, Michael T. *Law&B 92*
Winslow, Pauline Glen 1934?- *ScF&FL 92*
Winslow, Philip D. *St&PR 93*
Winslow, Robert Albert 1922- *WhoAm 92*
Winslow, Walter William 1925- *WhoAm 92*
Winsor, Eleanor Webster 1941- *WhoE 93*
Winsor, Jackie 1941- *BioIn 17, WhoAm 92*
Winsor, Kathleen *WhoAm 92, WhoAmW 93, WhoWrEP 92*
Winsor, Mary *AmWomPl*
Winsor, Terry *MiSFD 9*
Winsor, Travis Walter 1914- *WhoWor 93*
Winsor, V. Jacqueline 1941- *BioIn 17*
Winstanley, Gerrard 1609-1676 *BioIn 17*
Winstanley, Peter F. 1944- *St&PR 93*
Winstanley, Raymond Bates *WhoScE 91-1*
Winstead, Carol Jackson 1947- *WhoE 93*
Winstead, Elisabeth Weaver 1926- *WhoAmW 93, WhoWrEP 92*
Winstead, George Alvis 1916- *WhoWor 93*
Winstead, Marsha Deriene 1958- *WhoAmW 93*
Winstead, Nash Nicks 1925- *WhoAm 92*
Winstead, Ray L. 1909- *St&PR 93*
Winstead, Rebecca Noyes *ScF&FL 92*
Winstel, Gunter H. 1929- *WhoScE 91-3*
Winsten, Archer 1904- *WhoAm 92*
Winsten, Royce L. 1957- *WhoE 93*
Winston, Annie Steger *AmWomPl*
Winston, Brian Norman 1941- *WhoE 93*
Winston, Bruce H. 1948- *St&PR 93*
Winston, Chriss Hurst 1948- *WhoAmW 93*
Winston, Daoma 1922- *ScF&FL 92*
Winston, George 1949- *ConMus 9 [port]*
Winston, Gordon Chester 1929- *WhoAm 92*
Winston, Hollies M. *Law&B 92*

Winston, Jacqueline Berrier *Law&B 92*
Winston, Janet Margaret 1937- *WhoAmW 93*
Winston, Joan *ScF&FL 92*
Winston, John Clark, Jr. 1923- *WhoWor 93*
Winston, Joseph Mosby, Jr. 1916- *WhoSSW 93*
Winston, Judith Ann 1943- *WhoAmW 93*
Winston, Krishna Ricarda 1944- *WhoE 93*
Winston, Lena *WhoWrEP 92*
Winston, Marshall G. 1941- *St&PR 93*
Winston, Michael D. 1942- *WhoIns 93*
Winston, Michael G. 1951- *WhoEmL 93*
Winston, Michael Russell 1941- *WhoAm 92, WhoWor 93*
Winston, Patrick Henry, Jr. 1935- *St&PR 93*
Winston, Peter R. 1967- *St&PR 93*
Winston, Robert T. 1937- *WhoE 93*
Winston, Robert Ward, Jr. 1942- *WhoSSW 93*
Winston, Roland 1936- *WhoAm 92*
Winston, Ronald *St&PR 93*
Winston, Sarah 1912- *WhoWrEP 92*
Winston, Stacey *BioIn 17*
Winston, Stan *MiSFD 9*
Winston, Stephen Edward 1949- *WhoWrEP 92*
Winston, Susan Amy 1961- *WhoEmL 93*
Winstone, C.A. *ScF&FL 92*
Winstone, Reece 1909-1991 *BioIn 17*
Wint, Arthur d1992 *NewYTBS 92*
Wint, Dennis Michael 1943- *WhoAm 92*
Winter, Alan 1937- *WhoAm 92*
Winter, Alex *BioIn 17*
Winter, Alison A. 1946- *St&PR 93*
Winter, Arch Reese 1913- *WhoAm 92*
Winter, Bernadette Grace 1925- *WhoAmW 93*
Winter, Calvin Arnold, Jr. 1955- *WhoSSW 93*
Winter, Carl d1991 *BioIn 17*
Winter, Carl-Jochen 1934- *WhoScE 91-3*
Winter, Caryl 1944- *WhoWrEP 92*
Winter, Chester Caldwell 1922- *WhoAm 92*
Winter, Chester Norman 1931- *St&PR 93*
Winter, Colin Q. *Law&B 92*
Winter, Daryl Bentley *Law&B 92*
Winter, David Ferdinand 1920- *WhoAm 92*
Winter, Dennis W. 1937- *St&PR 93*
Winter, Donald Francis 1941- *WhoAm 92*
Winter, Donovan *MiSFD 9*
Winter, Douglas E. 1950- *ScF&FL 92*
Winter, Edward H. d1990 *BioIn 17*
Winter, Edwin Thomas 1936- *St&PR 93*
Winter, Eleanor Anna *WhoAmW 93*
Winter, Elizabeth H. 1950- *WhoAmW 93*
Winter, Ellen Irwin *AmWomPl*
Winter, Fred David 1921- *St&PR 93*
Winter, Fred Joseph 1950- *WhoE 93*
Winter, Frederick Elliot 1922- *WhoAm 92*
Winter, G. *WhoScE 91-2*
Winter, G.B. 1928- *WhoScE 91-1*
Winter, Harvey John 1915- *WhoAm 92*
Winter, Heinz 1935- *WhoScE 91-3*
Winter, J. Burgess 1933- *St&PR 93*
Winter, J.W. 1953- *St&PR 93*
Winter, Jack A. 1908-1991 *BioIn 17*
Winter, Joan Elizabeth 1947- *WhoAmW 93*
Winter, John Dawson, III 1944- *WhoAm 92*
Winter, John Sam *Law&B 92*
Winter, Johnny *BioIn 17*
Winter, Kari J. 1960- *ConAu 137*
Winter, Knut Rochus Roland 1927- *WhoWor 93*
Winter, Larry Eugene 1950- *WhoEmL 93, WhoSSW 93*
Winter, Lewis S., III 1945- *WhoIns 93*
Winter, Mark Lee 1950- *WhoEmL 93, WhoSSW 93*
Winter, Mary *AmWomPl*
Winter, Nicholas Radford 1966- *WhoE 93*
Winter, Pat *ScF&FL 92*
Winter, Paul d1992 *NewYTBS 92*
Winter, Paul 1939- *Baker 92, BioIn 17*
Winter, Paul Theodore 1939- *WhoAm 92*
Winter, Peter Michael 1934- *WhoAm 92, WhoWor 93*
Winter, Peter (von) 1754?-1825 *Baker 92, OxDcOp*
Winter, Phillip Emil 1935- *WhoSSW 93*
Winter, Ralph Karl, Jr. 1935- *WhoAm 92, WhoE 93*
Winter, Renee C. *Law&B 92*
Winter, Richard Lawrence 1945- *WhoWor 93*
Winter, Robert 1938- *WhoE 93*
Winter, Robert Bruce 1932- *WhoAm 92*
Winter, Robert R. *Law&B 92*
Winter, Robin Michael 1950- *WhoWor 93*
Winter, Roger C. 1946- *St&PR 93*
Winter, Roger Paul 1942- *WhoAm 92*
Winter, Rolf Gerhard 1928- *WhoAm 92*
Winter, Ronald E. 1926- *St&PR 93*
Winter, Ruth Grosman 1930- *WhoAm 92*
Winter, Sidney Graham, Jr. 1935- *WhoAm 92*
Winter, Steve 1955- *ScF&FL 92*
Winter, Susan *Law&B 92*
Winter, Terry Marie 1946- *WhoAmW 93*
Winter, Thomas Swanson 1937- *WhoAm 92*
Winter, Wallace E. 1930- *WhoIns 93*
Winter, Warren H. *Law&B 92*
Winter, Will *BioIn 17*
Winter, William Bergford 1928- *WhoAm 92*
Winter, William E. 1920- *St&PR 93*
Winter, William Earl 1920- *WhoAm 92*
Winter, William Edward 1952- *WhoSSW 93*
Winter, William Forrest 1923- *WhoAm 92*
Winter, William J. *Law&B 92*
Winter, William R., Jr. 1942- *St&PR 93*
Winterbauer, John E. 1938- *St&PR 93*
Winterbauer, Richard Hill 1936- *WhoAm 92*
Winterberger, Alexander 1834-1914 *Baker 92*
Winterbone, Desmond Edward *WhoScE 91-1*
Winterbotham, F.W. 1897-1990 *BioIn 17*
Winterbotham, Frederick William 1897-1990 *BioIn 17*
Winterbottom, Nancy 1948- *WhoAmW 93*
Winterer, Heinrich *WhoScE 91-4*
Winterer, Philip Steele 1931- *WhoAm 92*
Winterer, William G. 1934- *WhoE 93*
Winterfeld, Carl (Georg Vivigens) von 1784-1852 *Baker 92*
Winterfeld, Henry 1901-1990 *ScF&FL 92*
Winterfeldt, Ekkehard 1932- *WhoWor 93*
Winterfeldt, Esther A. 1926- *WhoAmW 93*
Winterhalter, Dolores August 1928- *WhoAmW 93*
Winterhalter, Kaspar 1934- *WhoScE 91-4*
Winterhalter, Kaspar Heinrich 1934- *WhoWor 93*
Winter-Hjelm, Otto 1837-1931 *Baker 92*
Winterling, Mary Ann 1943- *WhoE 93*
Wintermans, Jos 1946- *St&PR 93*
Wintermans, Joseph J. G. F. 1946- *WhoAm 92*
Wintermans, Joseph Jack Gerard Francis 1946- *WhoE 93*
Wintermantel, Erich 1956- *WhoWor 93*
Wintermute, Jack R. 1939- *WhoIns 93*
Wintermute, Marjorie McLean 1919- *WhoAm 92*
Winternitz, Emanuel 1898-1983 *Baker 92*
Winterowd, Walter Ross 1930- *WhoAm 92, WhoWrEP 92*
Winterrowd, Shirley Lawrence 1935- *WhoAmW 93*
Winters, Alice Graham Butler 1907- *WhoAmW 93*
Winters, Allen S. 1940- *St&PR 93*
Winters, Anne K. 1937- *WhoWrEP 92*
Winters, Arthur Yvor 1900-1968 *BioIn 17*
Winters, Barbara Jo *WhoAm 92, WhoAmW 93*
Winters, Bernie 1932-1991 *AnObit 1991*
Winters, Burt *BioIn 17*
Winters, Cheryl Louise 1947- *WhoEmL 93*
Winters, David 1939- *MiSFD 9*
Winters, Donald Wayne 1949- *WhoWrEP 92*
Winters, Douglas E. *Law&B 92*
Winters, Edward William 1947- *WhoWor 93*
Winters, Elizabeth *AmWomPl, BioIn 17*
Winters, Ernest Cope, II 1944- *WhoSSW 93*
Winters, Frederick Peter 1929- *St&PR 93*
Winters, Herbert A. 1904- *WhoIns 93*
Winters, J. Otis 1932- *WhoAm 92*
Winters, James Robert 1947- *St&PR 93*
Winters, Janet Lewis 1899- *WhoWrEP 92*
Winters, Jesse 1899-1971 *BiDAMSp 1989*
Winters, Jonathan 1925- *BioIn 17, WhoAm 92*
Winters, Kent D. 1943- *St&PR 93*
Winters, Laurence Howard 1947- *WhoE 93*
Winters, Logan *ScF&FL 92*
Winters, Mary Ann 1937- *WhoAmW 93*
Winters, Matthew Littleton 1926- *WhoE 93*
Winters, Mel 1936- *WhoAm 92*
Winters, Melinda Schmill 1943- *WhoAmW 93*
Winters, Mick *ScF&FL 92*
Winters, Nina 1944- *BioIn 17*
Winters, Nola Frances 1925- *WhoAm 92*
Winters, Paul E. 1944- *St&PR 93*
Winters, Ralph E. *WhoAm 92*
Winters, Richard Carl 1929- *St&PR 93*
Winters, Robert C. 1931- *St&PR 93*
Winters, Robert Charles 1946- *WhoAm 92*
Winters, Robert Cushing 1931- *WhoAm 92, WhoE 93, WhoIns 93*
Winters, Shelley 1922- *IntDcF 2-3 [port], WhoAm 92*
Winters, Shirley Royce 1922- *WhoWrEP 92*
Winters, Sidney A. 1921- *St&PR 93*
Winters, Stephen Robert *Law&B 92*
Winters, William d1862? *BioIn 17*
Winters, Yvor 1900-1968 *BioIn 17*
Winterscheidt, Mary 1930- *WhoAmW 93*
Wintersheimer, Donald Carl 1932- *WhoAm 92, WhoSSW 93*
Winterson, Jeanette 1959- *ConAu 136, ScF&FL 92*
Winter-Switz, Cheryl Donna 1947- *WhoAmW 93*
Winterton, Joseph Henry 1948- *WhoE 93*
Winther, Aage F.R. 1926- *WhoScE 91-2*
Winther, Eva 1946- *WhoWor 93*
Winther, Finn O. 1932- *WhoScE 91-4*
Winther, Hans Thoger 1786-1851 *BioIn 17*
Winther, William Paul 1944- *St&PR 93*
Winthrop, Debra F. *Law&B 92*
Winthrop, Edith 1932- *WhoAmW 93*
Winthrop, Elizabeth *BioIn 17*
Winthrop, Elizabeth 1948- *ScF&FL 92*
Winthrop, Elizabeth Amory 1931- *WhoE 93*
Winthrop, John 1588-1649 *BioIn 17*
Winthrop, John 1936- *WhoAm 92*
Winthrop, John 1947- *WhoAm 92, WhoWor 93*
Winthrop, Kathryn E. *Law&B 92*
Winthrop, Robert C. 1809-1894 *PolPar*
Winthrop, Sherman 1931- *WhoWor 93*
Wintle, Elizabeth *ScF&FL 92*
Wintle, Francis Edward 1948- *ConAu 139*
Winton, Calhoun 1927- *WhoE 93, WhoWrEP 92*
Winton, Craig Brewster 1951- *WhoE 93*
Winton, David Michael 1928- *WhoAm 92*
Winton, Ed 1931- *WhoAm 92*
Winton, Stanley J. 1923- *St&PR 93*
Wintour, Anna *BioIn 17*
Wintour, Anna 1949- *WhoAm 92, WhoAmW 93*
Wintringham, Margaret 1879-1955 *BioIn 17*
Wintrob, Jay S. *Law&B 92*
Wintrob, Jay S. 1957- *St&PR 93*
Wintroub, Bruce Urich 1943- *WhoAm 92*
Wintsch, H. Frederick 1940- *St&PR 93*
Wintz, Cary D. 1943- *ConAu 137*
Wintz, Cary Decordova 1943- *WhoSSW 93*
Wintz, Lester Merrill 1927- *St&PR 93*
Wintzer, Hanns-Juergen 1926- *WhoScE 91-3*
Wintzer, Richard 1866-1952 *Baker 92*
Winwood, Graham *WhoScE 91-1*
Winwood, Stephen Lawrence 1948- *WhoAm 92*
Winwood, Steve *BioIn 17*
Winwood, Stevie 1948- *Baker 92*
Winzeler, John H., Jr. 1943- *St&PR 93*
Winzeler, Robert Cameron 1931- *St&PR 93*
Winzeler, Ted J. 1948- *WhoSSW 93*
Winzenreid, James Ernest 1951- *WhoEmL 93, WhoWor 93*
Winzenried, Barbara E. 1935- *St&PR 93*
Winzenried, Jesse David 1922- *WhoAm 92*
Winzenried, Ora A. 1933- *St&PR 93*
Winzerling, Joy Johnson *WhoAmW 93*
Winzler, John R. 1930- *St&PR 93*
Wio, Horacio Sergio 1946- *WhoWor 93*
Wiora, Walter 1906- *Baker 92*
Wiorkowski, John James 1943- *WhoSSW 93*
Wiot, Jerome Francis 1927- *WhoAm 92*
Wipf, Helmut Heinrich 1941- *WhoScE 91-3*
Wipior, Kurt Victor 1960- *WhoWor 93*
Wipke, W. Todd 1940- *WhoAm 92*
Wippel, John Francis 1933- *WhoE 93*
Wippern, Ronald Frank 1933- *WhoE 93, WhoWor 93*
Wippersberg, W.J.M. 1945- *ScF&FL 92*
Wippler, Constant 1927- *WhoScE 91-2*
Wiqvist, Nils E. 1923- *WhoScE 91-4*
Wirathmulana, Jayalath Priyantha 1954- *WhoWor 93*
Wire, Donald Richard, II 1940- *WhoSSW 93*
Wire, Janel 1954- *WhoWor 93*
Wire, Marguerite Helene 1949- *WhoAmW 93*
Wire, Teddy Kermit 1936- *WhoSSW 93*
Wire, William Shidaker, II 1932- *St&PR 93, WhoAm 92*
Wiren, Dag (Ivar) 1905-1986 *Baker 92*
Wire'n, Myra Page *AmWomPl*
Wirges, Manford Frank 1925- *WhoAm 92*
Wirick, Weldon J., III 1951- *St&PR 93*
Wirken, James Charles 1944- *WhoAm 92*
Wirkkala, Brian M. 1941- *St&PR 93*
Wirkler, Norman Edward 1937- *WhoAm 92*
Wironen, Robert Alan 1955- *WhoE 93*
Wirowski, Zbigniew 1927- *WhoScE 91-4*
Wirsching, Charles Philipp, Jr. 1935- *WhoWor 93*
Wirsig, Woodrow 1916- *WhoAm 92, WhoWor 93*
Wirsing, Martin Hermann Friedrich 1948- *WhoWor 93*
Wirsing, Sabine 1954- *BioIn 17*
Wirszup, Izaak 1915- *WhoAm 92, WhoWor 93*
Wirt, Ann *MajAI*
Wirt, David B. 1940- *WhoAm 92*
Wirt, Frederick Marshall 1924- *WhoAm 92*
Wirt, Gary Lauck 1948- *WhoE 93*
Wirt, George H. 1943- *St&PR 93*
Wirt, Michael James 1947- *WhoAm 92*
Wirt, Mildred A. *MajAI*
Wirt, William 1772-1834 *BioIn 17, OxCSupC, PolPar*
Wirta, Ray *St&PR 93*
Wirtanen, P.L. 1944- *St&PR 93*
Wirtanen, Philip Laurie 1944- *WhoIns 93*
Wirth, Alfred G. 1941- *WhoIns 93*
Wirth, Arthur George 1919- *WhoAm 92*
Wirth, Barry Dennis 1953- *St&PR 93*
Wirth, Beverly 1938- *BioIn 17*
Wirth, Donna Lynn 1947- *WhoAmW 93*
Wirth, Emanuel 1842-1923 *Baker 92*
Wirth, Endre 1933- *WhoScE 91-4*
Wirth, Franz Peter *MiSFD 9*
Wirth, Fritz *WhoScE 91-3*
Wirth, Harold Edward 1905- *WhoE 93*
Wirth, Helmut 1912- *Baker 92*
Wirth, John Francis 1929- *St&PR 93*
Wirth, Niklaus *BioIn 17*
Wirth, Otto Howard 1935- *St&PR 93*
Wirth, Peter Theodor 1934- *WhoWor 93*
Wirth, Tim *NewYTBS 92 [port]*
Wirth, Timothy E. *BioIn 17*
Wirth, Timothy E. 1939- *CngDr 91*
Wirth, Timothy Endicott 1939- *WhoAm 92*
Wirthlin, Richard B. 1931- *PolPar*
Wirthlin, Richard Bitner 1931- *WhoAm 92*
Wirths, Claudine G. *BioIn 17*
Wirths, Claudine Gibson 1926- *WhoWrEP 92*
Wirths, Theodore William 1924- *WhoAm 92*
Wirtschafter, Jonathan Dine 1935- *WhoAm 92*
Wirtz, Arthur Michael, Jr. *WhoAm 92*
Wirtz, John W. 1925- *St&PR 93*
Wirtz, Norman Richard 1944- *WhoAm 92*
Wirtz, Richard Stanley 1940- *WhoSSW 93*
Wirtz, Wayne A. *Law&B 92*
Wirtz, Willem Kindler 1912- *WhoAm 92*
Wirtz, William Wadsworth 1929- *WhoAm 92*
Wirtz, William Willard 1912- *WhoAm 92*
Wirz, George O. 1929- *WhoAm 92*
Wirz, Jakob 1942- *WhoWor 93*
Wirz, Jost 1941- *WhoWor 93*
Wirz, Pascal F. 1943- *St&PR 93*
Wirz, Pascal Francois 1943- *WhoAm 92*
Wirzhbitski, Yan 1952- *WhoWor 93*
Wisan, Joseph E. 1901-1990 *BioIn 17*
Wisbaum, Wayne David 1935- *WhoAm 92*
Wisberg, Aubrey 1909-1990 *BioIn 17*
Wisberg, Folke Bernadotte 1895-1948 *BioIn 17*
Wisch, Bill 1947- *WhoE 93*
Wischer, Irene Stimson *WhoAm 92*
Wischermann, Roderick H. 1947- *St&PR 93*
Wischers, Gerd *WhoScE 91-3*
Wischnitzer, Rachel Bernstein 1885-1989 *BioIn 17*
Wisdom, Daniel W. 1952- *St&PR 93*
Wisdom, Graham John 1949- *WhoE 93*
Wisdom, Guyrena Knight 1923- *WhoAmW 93, WhoWor 93*
Wisdom, John Minor 1905- *EncAACR, WhoAm 92, WhoSSW 93*
Wisdom, Linda Randall *ScF&FL 92*
Wisdom, Norman 1915- *QDrFCA 92 [port]*
Wisdom, Norman 1920?- *IntDcF 2-3 [port]*
Wise, A. Walter *Law&B 92*
Wise, Arthur E. *BioIn 17*
Wise, Barbara Ann Gordon- *ScF&FL 92*
Wise, Beverly Denise 1954- *WhoE 93*
Wise, Bob G. 1930- *St&PR 93*
Wise, Carl L. *Law&B 92*
Wise, Carol 1951- *WhoAmW 93*
Wise, Charles Conrad, Jr. 1913- *WhoAm 92*
Wise, Charles Michael 1958- *WhoSSW 93*
Wise, David 1930- *ScF&FL 92, WhoAm 92, WhoWrEP 92*
Wise, David M. *Law&B 92*
Wise, Dennis 1954- *BioIn 17*

Wise, Dewey D. 1926- St&PR 93
Wise, Dewey Dennis 1926- St&PR 93
Wise, Douglas 1945- St&PR 93
Wise, Edmund Allen, Jr. 1967- WhoWrEP 92
Wise, Edwina Morris 1928- WhoSSW 93
Wise, Erbon Wilbur 1920- WhoAm 92, WhoWrEP 92
Wise, Ernie 1925-
See Morecambe, Eric 1926-1984 & Wise, Ernie 1925- QDrFCA 92
Wise, Ferdinand Andre 1926- St&PR 93
Wise, George Edward 1924- WhoAm 92
Wise, George Urban 1945- WhoAm 92
Wise, Harold Lake, Jr. Law&B 92
Wise, Harry H. 1938- WhoE 93, WhoWor 93
Wise, Helena Sunny 1954- WhoEmL 93, WhoWor 93
Wise, Herbert 1924- MiSFD 9
Wise, Howard 1903-1989 BioIn 17
Wise, Isaac Mayer 1819-1900 BioIn 17, JeAmHC
Wise, J. David Law&B 92
Wise, James Tough WhoScE 91-1
Wise, Jamie Martin BioIn 17
Wise, Janet Eugenia Wherry 1942- WhoAmW 93
Wise, Jeremy Lambert 1942- St&PR 93
Wise, Jerry Edmond 1929- WhoSSW 93
Wise, Jim P. 1943- St&PR 93
Wise, Jim Price 1943- WhoAm 92
Wise, Joe Robert, Jr. 1939- WhoE 93
Wise, Joel A. 1942- St&PR 93
Wise, John 1652-1725 BioIn 17
Wise, John Augustus 1938- WhoAm 92
Wise, John James 1932- WhoAm 92
Wise, John Perry 1924- WhoE 93
Wise, John Richard 1946- WhoSSW 93
Wise, Jonathon Keith 1945- St&PR 93
Wise, K. Kelly 1932- WhoWrEP 92
Wise, Kenneth Kelly 1932- WhoAm 92, WhoE 93
Wise, Kirk MiSFD 9
Wise, L.E. Law&B 92
Wise, L. Gene Law&B 92
Wise, Lauren Ann Law&B 92
Wise, Lawrence Charles 1942- St&PR 93
Wise, Lawrence George 1946- WhoSSW 93
Wise, Marion J. d1991 BioIn 17
Wise, Marvin Jay 1926- WhoAm 92
Wise, Meghan F. Law&B 92
Wise, Michael c. 1647-1687 Baker 92
Wise, Michael Joseph 1954- WhoWor 93
Wise, Miguel David 1960- WhoSSW 93, WhoWor 93
Wise, Milton B. 1929- WhoAm 92
Wise, Pamela Kay 1967- WhoAmW 93
Wise, Patricia Ann 1944- WhoAm 92
Wise, Patricia C. Law&B 92
Wise, Paul Schuyler 1920- WhoAm 92
Wise, Richard Evans 1947- WhoE 93, WhoWor 93
Wise, Richard W. Law&B 92
Wise, Robert 1914- BioIn 17, MiSFD 9, WhoAm 92, WhoWor 93
Wise, Robert E., Jr. 1948- CngDr 91
Wise, Robert Edward 1918- WhoAm 92
Wise, Robert Ellsworth, Jr. 1948- WhoAm 92, WhoSSW 93
Wise, Robert L. 1943- St&PR 93
Wise, Robert Lester 1943- WhoAm 92
Wise, Robert Philip 1949- WhoE 93
Wise, Robert Powell 1951- WhoEmL 93
Wise, Ronald Lee 1936- St&PR 93
Wise, S. ScF&FL 92
Wise, S.H. 1955- St&PR 93
Wise, Sally Ann 1947- WhoAmW 93
Wise, Samuel Paul, III 1921- WhoE 93
Wise, Scott 1958- BioIn 17
Wise, Sherwood Willing 1910- WhoAm 92, WhoWor 93
Wise, Stephen 1874-1949 JeAmHC
Wise, Stephen Carl 1954- St&PR 93
Wise, Stephen Samuel 1874-1949 BioIn 17
Wise, Susan Tamsberg 1945- WhoAmW 93, WhoSSW 93, WhoWor 93
Wise, Sybil Zulalian 1935- WhoE 93
Wise, Urban Gregg 1941- St&PR 93
Wise, Vernon Laing, Jr. 1929- St&PR 93
Wise, Walter L., Jr. 1912- St&PR 93
Wise, Warren R. Law&B 92
Wise, Warren R. 1929- St&PR 93
Wise, Warren Roberts 1929- WhoAm 92
Wise, William A. Law&B 92
Wise, William Allan 1945- St&PR 93, WhoAm 92, WhoSSW 93
Wise, William Dean 1931- St&PR 93
Wise, William Harvey, IV 1948- WhoE 93
Wise, William Jerrard 1934- WhoAm 92
Wiseall, Stephen Samuel 1957- WhoWor 93
Wisecarver, Keith Douglas 1957- WhoSSW 93
Wisecarver, William D. St&PR 93
Wisehart, Arthur McKee 1928- WhoAm 92
Wisekal, Frank William 1934- St&PR 93, WhoAm 92
Wiseman, Adele 1928- WhoCanL 92
Wiseman, Billy Ray 1937- WhoSSW 93
Wiseman, Carl Donald 1925- WhoAm 92
Wiseman, Carol MiSFD 9
Wiseman, Christopher 1936- WhoCanL 92
Wiseman, Clare Teal AmWomPl
Wiseman, David 1916- ScF&FL 92
Wiseman, David Brian Law&B 92
Wiseman, Dennis Gene 1947- WhoSSW 93
Wiseman, Donald F. Law&B 92
Wiseman, Douglas Carl 1935- WhoE 93
Wiseman, Frederick BioIn 17
Wiseman, Frederick 1930- MiSFD 9, WhoAm 92
Wiseman, James Richard 1934- WhoAm 92
Wiseman, Jay Donald 1952- WhoEmL 93
Wiseman, John A. 1945- ConAu 139
Wiseman, Laurence D. 1947- St&PR 93
Wiseman, Laurence Donald 1947- WhoAm 92
Wiseman, Michael L. 1952- St&PR 93
Wiseman, Paul Vincent BioIn 17
Wiseman, Rex ScF&FL 92
Wiseman, T(imothy) P(eter) 1940- ConAu 40NR
Wiseman, Thomas Anderton, Jr. 1930- WhoSSW 93
Wiseman, Thomas Lynn 1944- WhoWrEP 92
Wiseman, Troy D. St&PR 93
Wiseman, Walter S. 1945- St&PR 93
Wiseman, William Fenton 1939- WhoE 93
Wisener, Robert A. 1927- St&PR 93
Wiser, George L. 1925- St&PR 93
Wiser, James Louis 1945- WhoAm 92
Wiser, Richard Calvin 1945- St&PR 93, WhoAm 92
Wiser, Robert Law&B 92
Wiser, Roxane C. Law&B 92
Wisgerhof, Jerry G. 1938- WhoIns 93
Wish, Jay Barry 1950- WhoWor 93
Wish, Linda H. Law&B 92
Wish, Paul E. 1937- St&PR 93
Wisham, Lawrence Herman 1918- WhoAm 92
Wishard, Gordon Davis 1945- WhoAm 92
Wishart, Leonard Plumer, III 1934- WhoAm 92
Wishart, Peter (Charles Arthur) 1921-1984 Baker 92
Wishart, Ronald Sinclair 1925- WhoAm 92
Wishart, Steven William 1943- St&PR 93
Wisher, W.H. ScF&FL 92
Wishert, Jo Ann Chappell 1951- WhoAmW 93
Wishik, Laura Law&B 92
Wishinsky, Frieda 1948- ConAu 138, SmATA 70 [port]
Wishlade, Fiona Grace WhoScE 91-1
Wishner, Maynard Ira 1923- WhoAm 92
Wishner, Steven R. 1950- St&PR 93, WhoAm 92, WhoE 93
Wishnick, Marcia Margolis 1938- WhoAmW 93
Wishnie, Peter Allan 1960- WhoE 93
Wishnietsky, Dan Harvey 1950- WhoSSW 93
Wishnoff, Stanley 1935- St&PR 93
Wisinger, John E. Law&B 92
Wisker, Jennifer BioIn 17
Wiskich, Joseph Tony 1935- WhoWor 93
Wiskind, Milton Ira 1925- St&PR 93
Wiskowski, John P. 1938- St&PR 93
Wisla, Marek 1955- WhoWor 93
Wisler, Charles Clifton, Jr. 1926- WhoAm 92
Wisler, G. Clifton 1950- ScF&FL 92
Wisler, G(ary) Clifton DcAmChF 1960
Wislocki, Peter Gregory 1947- WhoE 93
Wislocki, Stanislaw 1921- Baker 92
Wismer, David Joseph 1950- St&PR 93
Wismer, Don 1946- ScF&FL 92
Wismer, Harvey G. 1916- St&PR 93
Wismer, Patricia Ann 1936- WhoAmW 93
Wismer, Stephen Hanawalt 1946- St&PR 93
Wisne, Pamela Jeanne Law&B 92
Wisnefsky, Walter 1944- WhoE 93
Wisner, Benjamin Goodwin 1943- WhoE 93
Wisner, Diana Law&B 92
Wisner, E. James 1942- St&PR 93
Wisner, Frank George 1938- WhoAm 92, WhoWor 93
Wisner, George 1812-1849 JrnUS
Wisner, Jay D. 1923- St&PR 93
Wisner, Linda Ann 1951- WhoAmW 93
Wisner, Lucille Green 1958- WhoAmW 93
Wisner, Roscoe William, Jr. 1926- WhoE 93
Wisner, W.E. Law&B 92
Wisneski, Mary Jo Elizabeth 1938- WhoAmW 93
Wisneski, William John 1946- St&PR 93
Wisnieswki, Konstanty 1935- WhoWor 93
Wisniewski, David Earl, Sr. 1947- WhoSSW 93
Wisniewski, Henryk Miroslaw 1931- WhoAm 92
Wisniewski, Janusz Zdzislaw 1923- WhoScE 91-4
Wisniewski, John William 1932- WhoAm 92
Wisniewski, Joseph Michael 1954- WhoWor 93
Wisniewski, Leszek 1939- WhoScE 91-4
Wisniewski, Richard J. 1950- WhoIns 93
Wisniewski, Robert Jude 1950- WhoAm 92
Wisniewski, Roland 1929- WhoWor 93
Wisniewski, Sewer Mieczyslaw 1926- WhoScE 91-4
Wisniewski, Stainslaw 1927- WhoScE 91-4
Wisniewski, Stefan 1923- WhoScE 91-4
Wisniewski, Thomas Joseph 1926- WhoAm 92
Wisnioski, Stanley Walter, Jr. 1926- WhoSSW 93
Wisniowiecki, Michal Korybut 1640-1673 PolBiDi
Wisniowski, Sigurd 1841-1892 PolBiDi
Wisot, Richard Alan 1946- St&PR 93
Wisott, Richard L. 1933- St&PR 93
Wisse, Eddie 1938- WhoScE 91-2
Wisse, Frederik 1947- WhoWor 93
Wissel, Christian 1943- WhoScE 91-3
Wissemann-Widrig, Nancy 1929- WhoE 93
Wisser, Lawrence 1922- WhoE 93
Wisser, William P. St&PR 93
Wissing, Neil Phillip 1931- St&PR 93, WhoAm 92
Wissler, Clark 1870-1947 IntDcAn
Wissler, Eugene Harley 1927- WhoAm 92
Wissler-Thomas, Carrie 1946- WhoAmW 93
Wissmann, Carol Renee 1946- WhoAmW 93
Wissmer, Pierre 1915- Baker 92
Wissner, Robert C. 1924- St&PR 93
Wissner, Seth Ernst 1922- WhoAm 92
Wist, Abund Ottokar 1926- WhoSSW 93
Wist, Eugene Raymond 1932- WhoScE 91-3
Wist, Gregory John 1947- WhoE 93
Wist, Paul Gabriel 1929- WhoE 93
Wister, Fanny Kemble d1992 BioIn 17, NewYTBS 92
Wister, Owen 1860-1938 BioIn 17, GayN
Wister, William David 1938- St&PR 93
Wistert, Alvin L. 1916- BiDAMSp 1989
Wistisen, Martin J. 1938- St&PR 93, WhoAm 92
Wistrand, Edwin M. Law&B 92
Wistreich, Hugo E. 1930- St&PR 93
Wiswall, Frank Lawrence, Jr. 1939- WhoAm 92, WhoWor 93
Wiswall, Maureen LeRae 1942- WhoAmW 93
Wiszniewski, Wojciech 1946-1981 PolBiDi
Wiszniewski, Zbigniew 1922- Baker 92
Wit, Antoni 1944- Baker 92
Wit, Daniel 1923- WhoAm 92
Wit, David Edmund 1962- WhoE 93
Wit, Harold Maurice 1928- WhoAm 92
Wit, Paul de 1852-1925 Baker 92
Witajewski, Robert M. 1946- WhoSSW 93
Witalis, Lawrence C. Law&B 92
Witanowski, Michal 1934- WhoScE 91-4
Witaschek, Fred V. Law&B 92
Witaszek, Linda Strobel 1957- WhoSSW 93
Witbeck, Norman C. 1925- St&PR 93
Witbeck, Robert William, Sr. 1952- WhoE 93
Witbooi, Hendrik 1934- WhoAfr
Witchel, Alex BioIn 17
Witcher, Daniel Dougherty 1924- WhoAm 92
Witcher, David L. 1939- St&PR 93
Witcher, Mark Law&B 92
Witcher, Phyllis Herrmann 1938- WhoAmW 93
Witcher, Robert Campbell 1926- WhoAm 92, WhoE 93
Witcher, Rodney Fernell 1953- WhoSSW 93
Witcoff, Sheldon William 1925- St&PR 93, WhoAm 92
Witcop, Rose 1890-1932 BioIn 17
Witcover, Jules Joseph 1927- WhoAm 92
Witczak, Franciszek 1921- WhoScE 91-4, WhoWor 93
Witek, James Eugene 1932- WhoAm 92
Witelo, Erazm c. 1230-1280 PolBiDi
Witenberg, Earl George 1917- WhoWor 93
Witfeld, Hartmut 1936- WhoScE 91-3
Withaeger, Rosemary Anne WhoAmW 93
Withagen, L.M. 1936- WhoScE 91-3
Withall, Gary A. 1949- St&PR 93
Withalm, Claudio Immanuel 1943- WhoWor 93
Witham, Peter Hugh 1948- WhoUN 92
Witham, Richard Nicholas 1938- St&PR 93
Witham, Robert G. St&PR 93
Witham, Rodney Arthur 1924- St&PR 93
Wither, George 1588-1667 DcLB 121 [port]
Witherell, James Leston 1953- WhoE 93
Witherell, Peter Charles 1943- WhoE 93
Witherington, A. Thomas Law&B 92
Witherite, Richard L. 1940- WhoIns 93
Withers, Alton M. 1926- St&PR 93
Withers, Arlene Falk 1951- St&PR 93
Withers, Barbara Ann 1939- WhoE 93
Withers, Bill 1938- SoulM
Withers, Christopher Stroude 1943- WhoWor 93
Withers, Debra Manning 1961- WhoSSW 93
Withers, Googie 1917- IntDcF 2-3 [port]
Withers, Jane 1926- BioIn 17
Withers, Mark Vernon Law&B 92
Withers, Marshall Scott 1954- St&PR 93
Withers, Michael J. 1938- WhoScE 91-1
Withers, Ramsey Muir 1930- WhoAm 92
Withers, Robert Wayne 1932- St&PR 93
Withers, Simon John 1958- WhoWor 93
Withers, W. Mark Law&B 92
Withers, W. Russell, Jr. 1936- WhoAm 92
Withers, W. Wayne Law&B 92
Withers, W. Wayne 1940- WhoAm 92
Withers, Walter 1854-1914 BioIn 17
Withers, Welty Kenney 1927- WhoAm 92
Withers, William, Jr. BioIn 17
Withers, William Marlin 1954- St&PR 93
Witherspoon, Frances AmWomPl
Witherspoon, Fredda Lilly WhoAmW 93
Witherspoon, Gregory J. St&PR 93
Witherspoon, Herbert 1873-1935 Baker 92
Witherspoon, Jere Wathen 1932- WhoAm 92
Witherspoon, John Knox, Jr. 1928- WhoAm 92, WhoIns 93
Witherspoon, John Marshall 1945- WhoSSW 93
Witherspoon, Jonathan H. 1942- St&PR 93
Witherspoon, Lynn Ralph 1942- WhoSSW 93
Witherspoon, Richard Wayne 1943- St&PR 93
Witherspoon, Sharon 1955- WhoAm 92
Witherspoon, Walter Pennington, Jr. 1938- WhoSSW 93
Witherspoon, William 1909- WhoWor 93
Witherup, Mary Beth 1957- WhoAmW 93
Witherup, William Allen 1935- WhoWrEP 92
Withey, Carole Anne 1946- WhoWor 93
Withey, Katherine Hobbs 1962- WhoAmW 93
Withey, Stephen Bassett 1918-1983 BioIn 17
Withgott, James William 1945- St&PR 93
Withington, Antoinette AmWomPl
Withington, Arthur, Mrs. AmWomPl
Withington, Georgiana Bowen AmWomPl
Withrow, James L. 1937- St&PR 93
Withrow, Kimberly Finch Law&B 92
Withrow, Lillian C. 1947- WhoAmW 93
Withrow, Lucille Monnot 1923- WhoAmW 93, WhoSSW 93, WhoWor 93
Withrow, Mary Ellen 1930- WhoAm 92, WhoAmW 93
Withrow, Michael V. Law&B 92
Withrow, Stephen MiSFD 9
Withrow, Tommy Austin 1949- St&PR 93
Withrow, William Henry 1839-1908 BioIn 17
Withrow-Gallanter, Sherrie Anne 1960- WhoAmW 93
Withuhn, William Lawrence 1941- WhoE 93
Withycombe, Thomas E. Law&B 92
Witiak, Donald Theodore 1935- WhoAm 92
Witkay, Paul Richard 1954- St&PR 93
Witke, David Rodney 1937- WhoAm 92
Witkiewicz, Jan 1809-1839 PolBiDi
Witkiewicz, Stanislaw Ignacy 1885-1939 PolBiDi, ScF&FL 92
Witkin, Arthur Aaron 1921- WhoE 93
Witkin, Beatrice 1916-1990 BioIn 17
Witkin, Evelyn Maisel 1921- WhoAm 92, WhoAmW 93
Witkin, Georgia Hope WhoAmW 93
Witkin, Jerome 1939- BioIn 17
Witkin, Joel-Peter 1939- WhoAm 92
Witkin, Mildred Hope Fisher WhoE 93, WhoWor 93

Witkin, Nathan d1990 *BioIn 17*
Witkin, Zara 1900-1940 *BioIn 17*
Witko, Frank P. *St&PR 93*
Witko, Linda Lee 1948- *WhoAmW 93*
Witkop, Bernhard 1917- *WhoAm 92*
Witkop, Carl Jacob 1920- *WhoAm 92*
Witkop, Robert 1948- *St&PR 93*
Witkow, Stanley P. 1948- *St&PR 93*
Witkowski, Andrzej 1934- *WhoScE 91-4*
Witkowski, Andrzej 1947- *WhoScE 91-4*
Witkowski, Andrzej S. 1930- *WhoScE 91-4*
Witkowski, Audrey J. *Law&B 92*
Witkowski, Georges-Martin 1867-1943 *Baker 92*
Witkowski, Romuld Kamil 1876-1950 *PolBiDi*
Witkowski, Ronald Joseph 1944- *St&PR 93*
Witkowski, Siegbert 1927- *WhoScE 91-3*
Witkowsky, Gizella *WhoAm 92*
Witman, George Bodo, III 1945- *WhoE 93*
Witmer, George Robert, Jr. 1937- *WhoAm 92*
Witmer, Harriette F. 1921- *St&PR 93*
Witmer, John Albert 1920- *WhoAm 92*
Witmer, John E., Jr. 1935- *WhoE 93*
Witmer, John H., Jr. *Law&B 92*
Witmer, John H., Jr. 1940- *St&PR 93*
Witmer, John Harper, Jr. 1940- *WhoAm 92*
Witmer, John Light 1908- *St&PR 93*
Witmer, Melvin P., Sr. 1940- *St&PR 93*
Witmeyer, John Jacob, III 1946- *WhoE 93*
Witmeyer, Richard James 1948- *WhoSSW 93*
Witmeyer, Stanley Herbert 1913- *WhoE 93*
Witnauer, Ericka *WhoAm 92, WhoAmW 93*
Witnauer, Ericka Anne *St&PR 93*
Witney, Brian D. 1938- *WhoScE 91-1*
Witney, Brian David *WhoScE 91-1*
Witney, William 1910- *MiSFD 9*
Witomski, Theodore Raymond 1953- *WhoWrEP 92*
Witonsky, Carl *St&PR 93*
Witort, Stephen F. *Law&B 92*
Witos, Wincenty 1875-1945 *PolBiDi*
Witowski, Patrick A. 1946- *St&PR 93*
Witrick, Joseph J. 1937- *St&PR 93*
Witry, Bernard J. 1925- *St&PR 93*
Witsen Elias, Jan Willem 1930- *WhoWor 93*
Witsken, Clarence H. 1933- *St&PR 93*
Witsman, Karl Robert 1959- *WhoWrEP 92*
Witt, Charles E. 1917- *WhoAm 92*
Witt, Christopher John 1931- *WhoE 93*
Witt, Currie B. 1908-1990 *ScF&FL 92*
Witt, David L. 1951- *WhoAm 92*
Witt, Debora Esensee 1956- *WhoSSW 93*
Witt, Doreen Marie 1960- *WhoAmW 93*
Witt, Evan Robert *Law&B 92*
Witt, Franz Xaver 1834-1888 *Baker 92*
Witt, Friedrich 1770-1836 *Baker 92*
Witt, Gary B. *Law&B 92*
Witt, Georg *WhoScE 91-4*
Witt, Georgia Strong 1923- *WhoAmW 93*
Witt, Harold (Vernon) 1923- *ConAu 39NR, WhoWrEP 92*
Witt, Hazel Bond *AmWomPl*
Witt, Horst-Herbert 1943- *WhoScE 91-3*
Witt, Hugh Ernest 1921- *WhoAm 92*
Witt, Katarina *BioIn 17, NewYTBS 92 [port]*
Witt, Kathryn Lisa 1963- *WhoAmW 93*
Witt, Mike *BioIn 17*
Witt, Norbert A. 1908-1990 *BioIn 17*
Witt, Paul Junger 1941- *WhoAm 92*
Witt, Paul M. 1943- *St&PR 93*
Witt, Raymond Buckner, Jr. 1915- *WhoAm 92*
Witt, Richard Allen 1951- *St&PR 93*
Witt, Richard Michael 1948- *WhoSSW 93*
Witt, Robert Charles 1941- *WhoAm 92*
Witt, Robert Edward 1909- *St&PR 93*
Witt, Robert Louis 1940- *St&PR 93*
Witt, Robert Wayne 1937- *WhoSSW 93*
Witt, Ronald J. 1949- *St&PR 93*
Witt, Ruth Elizabeth 1922- *WhoAm 92*
Witt, Sally Eleanor *WhoAmW 93*
Witt, Samuel Brown, III 1935- *St&PR 93*
Witt, Sandra Lea 1949- *WhoWrEP 92*
Witt, Sandra Smith 1944- *WhoAmW 93*
Witt, Stephen Frank *WhoScE 91-1*
Witt, Stephen S. 1937- *WhoIns 93*
Witt, Susan Carol 1951- *St&PR 93*
Witt, Thomas A. *Law&B 92*
Witt, Thomas A. 1950- *St&PR 93*
Witt, Tom 1944- *WhoSSW 93*
Witta, George Thermes 1947- *St&PR 93*
Wittaker, Teri L. *Law&B 92*
Wittassek, Johann Nepomuk August 1770-1839 *Baker 92*
Wittbold, Patricia Elaine 1929- *WhoSSW 93*
Wittbrodt, Edmund 1947- *WhoScE 91-4*
Wittbrodt, Edwin Stanley 1918- *WhoAm 92*
Wittcoff, Harold Aaron 1918- *WhoAm 92*
Witte, Alan C. *Law&B 92*
Witte, Bertold Ulrich 1937- *WhoScE 91-3*
Witte, Carlton Royal Vincent 1946- *WhoE 93*
Witte, Dale Frederick 1951- *St&PR 93*
Witte, David Lynn 1942- *St&PR 93*
Witte, David William 1942- *St&PR 93*
Witte, Derek Paul *Law&B 92*
Witte, Hartmut 1937- *WhoWor 93*
Witte, James R. 1955- *St&PR 93*
Witte, Laura Hicks *Law&B 92*
Witte, Leslie 1911-1973 *BiDAMSp 1989*
Witte, Linda R. *Law&B 92*
Witte, Louise W. 1915- *WhoAmW 93*
Witte, M.D. *Law&B 92*
Witte, Margaret *BioIn 17*
Witte, Margaret K. 1953- *St&PR 93*
Witte, Marvin Edwin 1929- *WhoE 93*
Witte, Merlin Michael 1926- *WhoAm 92*
Witte, Michael 1911- *WhoSSW 93*
Witte, Randall Erwyn 1948- *WhoAm 92*
Witte, Richard C. *Law&B 92*
Witte, Sergei IUl'evich 1849-1915 *BioIn 17*
Wittebort, Nancy H. *Law&B 92*
Wittek, Gerhard Rudolf 1939- *WhoWor 93*
Wittekind, Raymond Richard *Law&B 92*
Wittels, Howard Bernard 1950- *St&PR 93*
Witten, David Melvin 1926- *WhoAm 92*
Witten, E. *BioIn 17*
Witten, Edward *WhoAm 92*
Witten, Lillian L. *St&PR 93*
Witten, Louis 1921- *WhoAm 92*
Witten, Matthew 1951- *WhoSSW 93*
Witten, Randall Stewart *Law&B 92*
Wittenauer, Bill 1944- *St&PR 93*
Wittenberg, Elizabeth L. *Law&B 92*
Wittenberg, Ernest 1920- *WhoAm 92*
Wittenberg, Hans 1925- *WhoScE 91-3*
Wittenberg, Howard Ira 1930- *St&PR 93*
Wittenberg, Joseph D. *St&PR 93*
Wittenberg, Ruth d1990 *BioIn 17*
Wittenborg, Alfred 1940- *WhoWor 93*
Wittenborn, August F. 1923- *St&PR 93*
Wittenmark, Bjorn E.T. 1943- *WhoScE 91-4*
Wittenmeyer, Charles E. 1903- *WhoAm 92*
Wittenstein, Michael David 1958- *WhoSSW 93*
Wittenwyler, Ronald P. 1947- *WhoIns 93*
Wittenwyler, Ronald Paul 1947- *St&PR 93*
Witter, Gerd Karl 1944- *St&PR 93*
Witter, Jill *Law&B 92*
Witter, Jill 1954- *St&PR 93*
Witter, Ray Cowden 1942- *WhoAm 92*
Witter, Richard Lawrence 1936- *WhoAm 92*
Witter, Robert Nelson, Jr. 1932- *St&PR 93*
Witter, Thomas W. 1928- *St&PR 93*
Witter, Thomas Winship 1928- *WhoAm 92*
Witter, William D. 1929- *St&PR 93*
Witterholt, Vincent Gerard 1932- *WhoE 93*
Witterschein, Judith A. *Law&B 92*
Wittersheim, Gerard 1930- *WhoScE 91-2*
Witteveen, Jelle 1933- *WhoScE 91-3*
Witteveen, Sibble Jozef 1956- *WhoWor 93*
Wittgen, Mary Carol *Law&B 92*
Wittgenstein, Carolyne de Sayn- 1819-1887 *BioIn 17*
Wittgenstein, Friedrich Ernst *Baker 92*
Wittgenstein, Ludwig 1889-1951 *BioIn 17*
Wittgenstein, Ludwig Adolf Peter 1769-1843 *HarEnMi*
Wittgenstein, Ludwig Josef Johann 1889-1951 *DcTwHis*
Wittgenstein, Paul 1887-1961 *Baker 92*
Wittgenstein-Sayn, Marianne Sayn- *BioIn 17*
Witthuhn, Burton Orrin 1934- *WhoAm 92*
Witthuhn, Kay Lynn 1957- *WhoAmW 93*
Wittich, Guenter *WhoUN 92*
Wittich, Hugh Meade 1925- *WhoSSW 93*
Wittich, John Jacob 1921- *WhoAm 92*
Wittich, Marie 1868-1931 *Baker 92, OxDcOp*
Wittig, Edith A. *Law&B 92*
Wittig, Edward c. 1880-1941 *PolBiDi*
Wittig, Monique 1935- *BioIn 17, ScF&FL 92*
Wittig, Philip Martin 1934- *St&PR 93*
Wittig, Raymond Shaffer 1944- *WhoE 93*
Wittig, Richard E. 1934- *St&PR 93*
Wittig, Siegmar Winfried 1939- *WhoWor 93*
Wittinbel, Gregory A. 1953- *St&PR 93*
Witting, Chris J. 1915- *St&PR 93, WhoWor 93*
Witting, Lloyd Allen 1930- *WhoE 93*
Witting, Philip Anthony *WhoScE 91-1*
Wittinger, Robert 1945- *Baker 92*
Wittke, Dayton D. 1932- *St&PR 93*
Wittkemper, Gerd 1943- *St&PR 93*
Wittkower, Rudolf 1901-1971 *BioIn 17*
Wittler, Manfred 1940- *St&PR 93*
Wittler, Shirley Joyce 1927- *WhoAm 92*
Wittlich, Gary Eugene 1934- *WhoAm 92*
Wittlich, Jae L. 1942- *St&PR 93*
Wittliff, William D. *MiSFD 9*
Wittlin, Jozef 1896-1976 *PolBiDi*
Wittlinger, Timothy David 1940- *WhoAm 92*
Wittlock, Mary Lenore 1932- *WhoAmW 93*
Wittman, Folker H. 1936- *WhoScE 91-4*
Wittman, Laura Elizabeth 1963- *WhoAmW 93*
Wittman, Peter *MiSFD 9*
Wittman, Robert Emil 1940- *St&PR 93*
Wittman, Sandra Marie 1943- *WhoAmW 93*
Wittmann, G. *WhoScE 91-3*
Wittmann, Heinz-Gunter *WhoScE 91-3*
Wittmann, Horst Richard 1936- *WhoE 93*
Wittmann, Mihaly 1939- *WhoScE 91-4*
Wittmann, Otto *WhoScE 91-3*
Wittmann, Otto 1911- *WhoAm 92*
Wittmer, Giovanni 1925- *WhoScE 91-3*
Wittmer, James F. 1932- *St&PR 93*
Wittmer, James Frederick 1932- *WhoAm 92*
Wittmer, Pierre (Jean) 1942- *ConAu 139*
Wittmer, Robert Howard 1926- *St&PR 93*
Wittmer, Wilmer William 1940- *WhoWor 93*
Wittmeyer, Kenneth E. 1929- *St&PR 93*
Wittner, Loren Antonow 1938- *WhoAm 92*
Wittner, Nicholas J. *Law&B 92*
Wittner, Ted Philip 1928- *WhoAm 92*
Wittreich, Joseph Anthony, Jr. 1939- *WhoAm 92, WhoWrEP 92*
Wittrisch, Marcel 1901-1955 *Baker 92*
Wittrock, Gregory D. *Law&B 92*
Wittrock, Merlin Carl 1931- *WhoAm 92, WhoWor 93*
Wittry, David Beryle 1929- *WhoAm 92*
Wittstadt, Klaus 1936- *WhoWor 93*
Wittstein, Edwin Frank 1929- *WhoAm 92*
Wittwer, Chester Allen, Jr. 1937- *St&PR 93*
Wittwer, John W. 1945- *St&PR 93*
Wittwer, Reto 1948- *WhoAm 92*
Witty, John Barber 1946- *WhoSSW 93*
Witty, Lela Dawn 1943- *St&PR 93*
Witty, Robert William 1949- *WhoWor 93*
Witus, David G. *Law&B 92*
Witwer, Andrew S. d1990 *BioIn 17*
Witwer, Samuel Weiler, Sr. 1908- *WhoAm 92*
Witzel, Carla Stone 1948- *WhoAmW 93*
Witzel, Frederick Chase 1923- *St&PR 93*
Witzel, Herbert 1924- *WhoScE 91-3*
Witzel, Lothar Gustav 1939- *WhoWor 93*
Witzeman, Amy Lynn 1957- *WhoAmW 93*
Witzeman, Frank Charles 1926- *St&PR 93*
Witzig, Gene R. 1929- *St&PR 93*
Witzig, Harold L. 1927- *St&PR 93*
Witzig, John J. *Law&B 92*
Witzig, Scott A. 1959- *St&PR 93*
Witzig, Warren Frank 1921- *WhoAm 92*
Witzleb, Erich 1924- *WhoScE 91-3*
Witzleben, Erwin Job von 1881-1944 *BioIn 17*
Witzleben, Erwin von 1881-1944 *HarEnMi*
Wiweger, Antoni Witold 1931- *WhoWor 93*
Wiwi, Robert P. 1941- *St&PR 93*
Wiwi, Robert Paul 1941- *WhoAm 92*
Wix, Emma Lou 1924- *St&PR 93*
Wixell, Ingvar 1931- *Baker 92, OxDcOp*
Wixom, G.R. *St&PR 93*
Wixom, William David 1929- *WhoAm 92, WhoE 93*
Wixon, Clarence Manter d1990 *BioIn 17*
Wixon, Rufus 1911- *WhoAm 92*
Wixon, William N. 1930- *St&PR 93*
Wixson, Douglas Charles 1933- *WhoWrEP 92*
Wixted, John G. *Law&B 92*
Wizner, William Wolfgang 1928- *WhoSSW 93*
Wiznitzer, Jane T. *Law&B 92*
Wiznitzer, Stephen B. *Law&B 92*
Wladimiroff, Juriy W. 1939- *WhoScE 91-3*
Wladyslaw, I 1260-1333 *PolBiDi*
Wladyslaw, III 1424-1444 *PolBiDi*
Wladyslaw, IV 1595-1648 *PolBiDi*
Wlaschin, Ken 1934- *WhoWor 93*
Wlazelek, Brian Gene 1957- *WhoE 93*
Wleugel, Johan Peter 1929- *WhoAm 92*
Wleugel, John P. 1929- *St&PR 93*
Wlochowicz, Andrzej 1931- *WhoScE 91-4*
Wlodarski, Jan Kazimierz 1931- *WhoScE 91-4*
Wlodarski, Marek 1903-1960 *PolBiDi*
Wlodek, Jan-Marian 1924- *WhoScE 91-4*
Wlodkowic, Pawel 1370-1435 *PolBiDi*
Wlosowicz, Zbigniew 1955- *WhoUN 92*
Wludyka, Peter *ScF&FL 92*
Wluka, David 1946- *WhoE 93*
Wnek, Richard S. 1954- *WhoIns 93*
Wnuk, Wade Joseph 1944- *St&PR 93, WhoSSW 93*
Wobbeking, Ronald Lee 1943- *St&PR 93*
Wobig, Ellen 1911-1989 *ScF&FL 92*
Wobig, Marybeth 1960- *WhoAmW 93*
Wobrauschek, Peter 1939- *WhoScE 91-4*
Wobst, Frank 1933- *St&PR 93*
Wobst, Frank Georg 1933- *WhoAm 92*
Wobus, Reinhard Arthur 1941- *WhoAm 92*
Wodehouse, Lawrence Michael 1934- *WhoSSW 93*
Wodehouse, P.G. 1881-1975 *BioIn 17, MagSWL [port]*
Wodehouse, Pelham Grenville 1881-1975 *BioIn 17*
Wodell, Judith Juanita 1952- *WhoSSW 93*
Wodhams, Jack 1931- *ScF&FL 92*
Wodkiewicz, Krzysztof 1949- *WhoWor 93*
Wodlinger, Mark Louis 1922- *WhoAm 92*
Wodzina, Maria 1819-1896 *PolBiDi*
Wodzislawska, Maia 1942- *WhoWor 93*
Wodzisz, Janet Marie 1969- *WhoAmW 93*
Woehl, Waldemar 1902- *Baker 92*
Woehling, Mary-Patrice 1959- *WhoE 93*
Woehning, Huberta Marianne Plum *AmWomPl*
Woehr, Mindell Small 1927- *WhoAmW 93*
Woehrel, Joseph A. *Law&B 92*
Woehrlen, Arthur Edward, Jr. 1947- *WhoEmL 93*
Woehrmyer, Robert L. 1938- *St&PR 93*
Woelfel, James Warren 1937- *WhoAm 92*
Woelfel, Martha Jane 1948- *WhoSSW 93*
Woelffer, Emerson Seville 1914- *WhoAm 92*
Woelffer, Gale 1955- *St&PR 93*
Woelfle, Peter Klaus 1942- *WhoWor 93*
Woelfle, Walter Thomas *Law&B 92*
Woelflein, Ann Buckley 1933- *WhoE 93*
Woelflein, Kevin Gerard 1933- *WhoAm 92*
Woelk, Guy G. 1944- *St&PR 93*
Woelke, O'Neil L. *Law&B 92*
Woerdehoff, Valorie Anne 1954- *WhoWrEP 92*
Woermann, Dietrich B. 1931- *WhoScE 91-3*
Woerner, Barbara H. 1965- *WhoSSW 93*
Woerner, Markus Hilmar 1945- *WhoWor 93*
Woerner, Paul S. d1992 *NewYTBS 92*
Woerner, Robert Lester 1925- *WhoAm 92*
Woernie, Hans-Theo 1927- *WhoScE 91-3*
Woessner, Frederick T. 1935- *WhoWor 93*
Woessner, Mark Matthias 1938- *WhoAm 92*
Woeste, John Theodore 1934- *WhoAm 92*
Woeste, William Franklin 1920- *WhoIns 93*
Woestenburg, Laurent Cornelius 1932- *WhoWor 93*
Woestendiek, John, Jr. 1953- *WhoAm 92*
Woets, Jacob 1940- *WhoScE 91-3*
Woetzel, Damian *BioIn 17*
Woetzel, Damian Abdo 1967- *WhoAm 92*
Woetzel, Robert Kurt 1930-1991 *BioIn 17*
Woffington, Margaret 1714?-1760 *BioIn 17*
Wofford, Drew 1954- *St&PR 93*
Wofford, Harris 1926- *BioIn 17, CngDr 91, CurBio 92 [port]*
Wofford, Harris Llewellyn 1926- *WhoAm 92, WhoE 93*
Wofford, Michael Charles *Law&B 92*
Woford, Henry Sanford 1940- *WhoSSW 93*
Wofsey, Carol Miller *Law&B 92*
Wofsy, Steven Charles 1946- *WhoE 93*
Wogaman, Ronald d1991 *BioIn 17*
Wogan, Amelie 1947- *St&PR 93*
Wogan, Gerald Norman 1930- *WhoAm 92*
Wogan, Gordon Lee *Law&B 92*
Wogan, Robert 1925- *WhoAm 92*
Wogderes, Fikre Selassie *WhoAfr*
Wogen, Warren Ronald 1943- *WhoAm 92*
Wogrin, Conrad Anthony 1924- *WhoE 93*
Wogsland, James Willard 1931- *St&PR 93, WhoAm 92*
Woh, Edgar Augusto 1955- *WhoE 93*
Wohl, Armand Jeffrey 1946- *WhoWor 93*
Wohl, David 1950- *WhoSSW 93*
Wohl, Faith A. *BioIn 17*
Wohl, Ira *MiSFD 9*
Wohl, Linda Susan *Law&B 92*
Wohl, Patricia Jeanne 1959- *WhoSSW 93*
Wohl, Robert Allen 1931- *WhoAm 92*
Wohl, Ronald Gene 1934- *WhoE 93*
Wohl, Sheila Beth 1965- *WhoAmW 93*
Wohl, Yehuda 1904-1988 *Baker 92*
Wohlberg, Meg 1905-1990 *BioIn 17*
Wohleber, Robert Michael 1951- *WhoAm 92*

Wolfberg, Melvin Donald 1926- *WhoAm 92*
Wolfberg, Steven S. 1946- *St&PR 93*
Wolfcale, Arthur D., Jr. *Law&B 92*
Wolfe, Aaron *ScF&FL 92*
Wolfe, Al 1932- *WhoAm 92*
Wolfe, Albert Blakeslee 1909- *WhoAm 92*
Wolfe, Allan 1942- *WhoE 93*
Wolfe, Barbara A. 1943- *St&PR 93*
Wolfe, Barbara Ahmajan 1943- *WhoAm 92*
Wolfe, Barbara Blair 1940- *WhoAmW 93*
Wolfe, Bari Jane *Law&B 92*
Wolfe, Bernard 1915-1985 *ScF&FL 92*
Wolfe, Bertram 1927- *WhoAm 92*
Wolfe, Bertram D(avid) 1896-1977 *ConAu 40NR*
Wolfe, Bertram David 1896-1977 *BioIn 17*
Wolfe, Bruce G. 1942- *St&PR 93*
Wolfe, Charles Keith 1943- *WhoSSW 93*
Wolfe, Charles Morgan 1935- *WhoAm 92*
Wolfe, Charles Wren *Law&B 92*
Wolfe, Chris Anne *ScF&FL 92*
Wolfe, Christopher 1971- *BioIn 17*
Wolfe, Christopher D. *Law&B 92*
Wolfe, Corinne Howell 1912- *WhoWor 93*
Wolfe, Dale E. *St&PR 93*
Wolfe, David Joe 1938- *WhoSSW 93*
Wolfe, David Louis 1951- *WhoEmL 93*
Wolfe, Deborah Cannon Patridge *WhoAm 92, WhoAmW 93, WhoWor 93*
Wolfe, Deborah Marie 1964- *WhoAmW 93*
Wolfe, Donald H. 1926- *St&PR 93*
Wolfe, Donald P. 1943- *St&PR 93*
Wolfe, Douglas P. 1925- *St&PR 93*
Wolfe, Edward C. *Law&B 92*
Wolfe, Elsie de 1865-1950 *BioIn 17*
Wolfe, Ethyle Renee 1919- *WhoAm 92*
Wolfe, Frederic D. 1929- *St&PR 93*
Wolfe, Gail Sommers 1947- *WhoAmW 93*
Wolfe, Gary K. 1946- *ScF&FL 92*
Wolfe, Gene *BioIn 17*
Wolfe, Gene 1931- *ScF&FL 92*
Wolfe, George *BioIn 17*
Wolfe, George C. *BioIn 17*
Wolfe, Gerald Alfred 1948- *WhoIns 93*
Wolfe, Gregory Baker 1922- *WhoAm 92*
Wolfe, Harold Joel 1940- *St&PR 93, WhoAm 92*
Wolfe, Harry F., Jr. 1931- *St&PR 93*
Wolfe, Harry Kirke 1858-1918 *BioIn 17*
Wolfe, Harvey Edward 1924- *WhoE 93*
Wolfe, Ian d1992 *NewYTBS 92*
Wolfe, Ian 1896-1992 *BioIn 17, ConTFT 10*
Wolfe, J. Matthew 1956- *WhoE 93, WhoWor 93*
Wolfe, Jacob Merle 1924- *St&PR 93*
Wolfe, Jacques (Leon) 1896-1973 *Baker 92*
Wolfe, James 1727-1759 *BioIn 17, HarEnMi*
Wolfe, James Franklin 1936- *WhoAm 92*
Wolfe, James Ronald 1932- *WhoAm 92, WhoE 93, WhoWor 93*
Wolfe, James Willard 1955- *WhoE 93*
Wolfe, Jean Elizabeth 1925- *WhoAmW 93, WhoE 93, WhoWor 93*
Wolfe, Joel William 1960- *WhoE 93*
Wolfe, John J. *Law&B 92*
Wolfe, John T., Jr. 1942- *AfrAmBi [port]*
Wolfe, John Thomas, Jr. 1942- *WhoAm 92, WhoSSW 93*
Wolfe, John Walton 1928- *WhoAm 92*
Wolfe, Jonathan Scott 1950- *WhoEmL 93, WhoWor 93*
Wolfe, Joseph H. 1945- *St&PR 93*
Wolfe, Joseph H., Jr. *Law&B 92*
Wolfe, Kenneth Gilbert 1920- *WhoAm 92*
Wolfe, L. Stephen *ScF&FL 92*
Wolfe, Larry T. 1948- *St&PR 93*
Wolfe, Leigh Ann 1956- *St&PR 93*
Wolfe, Leonhard Scott 1926- *WhoAm 92*
Wolfe, Linda 1935- *ConAu 138*
Wolfe, Lisa Ann 1962- *WhoAmW 93*
Wolfe, Lisa Helene 1959- *WhoAmW 93*
Wolfe, Louis 1905-1985 *ScF&FL 92*
Wolfe, Louise Dahl- *BioIn 17*
Wolfe, Margaret Ripley 1947- *WhoAmW 93*
Wolfe, Martha Campbell 1938- *WhoAmW 93*
Wolfe, Martin *BioIn 17*
Wolfe, Matthew *St&PR 93*
Wolfe, Melba Reynolds 1941- *WhoAmW 93*
Wolfe, Michael David 1950- *WhoSSW 93*
Wolfe, Mildred Burke Younker 1915-1989 *BiDAMSp 1989*
Wolfe, Mitchell S. *Law&B 92*
Wolfe, Morris 1938- *WhoCanL 92*
Wolfe, Norman 1926- *St&PR 93*
Wolfe, Norman Lawrence 1926- *WhoAm 92*
Wolfe, Norman N. 1940- *St&PR 93*
Wolfe, Phyllis Jean 1958- *WhoAmW 93*
Wolfe, Ralph Stoner 1921- *WhoAm 92*
Wolfe, Ray 1931- *St&PR 93*
Wolfe, Raymond 1927- *WhoE 93*
Wolfe, Robert H. *Law&B 92*
Wolfe, Robert Richard 1937- *WhoAm 92*
Wolfe, Ron 1945- *ScF&FL 92*
Wolfe, Russell Marshall 1925- *St&PR 93*
Wolfe, Russell Simmons, Jr. 1952- *WhoE 93*
Wolfe, Sandra Jean 1951- *WhoAmW 93*
Wolfe, Sheila *WhoAm 92*
Wolfe, Sidney Manuel 1937- *WhoAm 92*
Wolfe, Stanley 1924- *Baker 92*
Wolfe, Terry C. 1946- *St&PR 93*
Wolfe, Theodore Ernest, III 1945- *WhoSSW 93*
Wolfe, Theodore Joseph 1935- *St&PR 93, WhoAm 92*
Wolfe, Thomas 1900-1938 *BioIn 17, MagSAmL [port], WorLitC [port]*
Wolfe, Thomas Kennerly, Jr. 1931- *JrnUS, WhoAm 92, WhoE 93, WhoWrEP 92*
Wolfe, Tom *BioIn 17*
Wolfe, Tom 1931- *AmWrS3, MagSAmL [port]*
Wolfe, Tom J. 1958- *St&PR 93*
Wolfe, Townsend Durant, III 1935- *WhoAm 92, WhoSSW 93*
Wolfe, Tracey Dianne 1951- *WhoEmL 93*
Wolfe, Walter Brewster 1925-1991 *BioIn 17*
Wolfe, Warren Dwight 1926- *WhoAm 92*
Wolfe, William Downing 1947- *WhoEmL 93*
Wolfe, William Louis 1931- *WhoAm 92*
Wolfe, William S. *Law&B 92*
Wolfel, Dominik Josef 1888-1963 *IntDcAn*
Wolfen, Werner F. 1930- *WhoAm 92*
Wolfendale, Arnold Whittaker *WhoScE 91-1*
Wolfendale, Arnold Whittaker 1927- *WhoWor 93*
Wolfendale, P.C.F. *WhoScE 91-1*
Wolfenden, James Douglas 1938- *St&PR 93, WhoIns 93*
Wolfenden, Richard Vance 1935- *WhoAm 92*
Wolfensberger, Wolf Peregrine Joachim 1934- *WhoE 93*
Wolfensohn, James David 1933- *BioIn 17, St&PR 93, WhoAm 92, WhoE 93*
Wolfenson, Azi U. 1933- *WhoWor 93*
Wolfenson, Marv *WhoAm 92*
Wolfenstein, Lincoln 1923- *WhoAm 92*
Wolfer, Alan B. *Law&B 92*
Wolfers, Alan M. 1961- *St&PR 93*
Wolfers, Michael 1938- *ConAu 136*
Wolfert, Alan R. *Law&B 92*
Wolfert, Frederick E. 1954- *St&PR 93*
Wolfert, Frederick Paul 1937- *WhoAm 92*
Wolfert, Hubert H. 1916- *St&PR 93*
Wolfert, Laurence Mark 1947- *St&PR 93*
Wolfert, Paula *BioIn 17*
Wolfert, Ruth 1933- *WhoAmW 93, WhoE 93, WhoWor 93*
Wolfes, Felix 1892-1971 *Baker 92*
Wolff, Aaron Sidney 1930- *WhoAm 92*
Wolff, Albert 1884-1970 *IntDcOp, OxDcOp*
Wolff, Albert (Louis) 1884-1970 *Baker 92*
Wolff, Alexander *BioIn 17*
Wolff, Arthur Samuels 1907- *BioIn 17*
Wolff, Ashley *ChlBIID [port]*
Wolff, Auguste (Desire Bernard) 1821-1887 *Baker 92*
Wolff, Beverly 1928- *Baker 92*
Wolff, Brian Richard 1955- *WhoEmL 93*
Wolff, Charles Godfrey 1934- *St&PR 93*
Wolff, Christian 1934- *Baker 92*
Wolff, Christian Cornelius Petrus 1959- *WhoWor 93*
Wolff, Christoph (Johannes) 1940- *Baker 92, WhoAm 92*
Wolff, Christopher 1949- *WhoAm 92*
Wolff, Claude 1935- *WhoScE 91-2*
Wolff, Cynthia Griffin 1936- *WhoAm 92*
Wolff, Cyril M. 1944- *St&PR 93*
Wolff, Daniel J. *WhoWrEP 92*
Wolff, Derish Michael 1935- *WhoAm 92*
Wolff, Diana Elaine 1937- *WhoAmW 93*
Wolff, Donald Edward 1922- *WhoIns 93*
Wolff, Donald J. 1943- *St&PR 93*
Wolff, Edouard 1816-1880 *Baker 92, PolBiDi*
Wolff, Edward A. 1929- *WhoAm 92*
Wolff, Edward Nathan 1946- *WhoE 93*
Wolff, Elroy Harris 1935- *WhoAm 92*
Wolff, Erich 1874-1913 *Baker 92*
Wolff, Frank Pierce, Jr. 1946- *WhoAm 92*
Wolff, Fritz 1894-1957 *Baker 92*
Wolff, G.M. 1957- *St&PR 93*
Wolff, Geoffrey 1937- *BioIn 17*
Wolff, Geoffrey Ansell 1937- *WhoAm 92, WhoWrEP 92*
Wolff, Georgetta Ann *Law&B 92*
Wolff, Gregory Steven 1951- *WhoE 93, WhoWor 93*
Wolff, Gunther Arthur 1918- *WhoAm 92*
Wolff, H.S. *WhoScE 91-1*
Wolff, Hellmuth Christian 1906-1988 *Baker 92*
Wolff, Herbert Eric 1925- *WhoAm 92, WhoWor 93*
Wolff, Hugh *BioIn 17*
Wolff, Hugh (MacPherson) 1953- *Baker 92*
Wolff, Ivan A. 1917- *WhoE 93*
Wolff, Ivan Lawrence 1944- *WhoAm 92*
Wolff, Jay L. *BioIn 17*
Wolff, Jesse David 1913- *WhoAm 92*
Wolff, Joel C. 1929- *St&PR 93*
Wolff, Joel Henry 1966- *WhoWor 93*
Wolff, Julian 1905-1990 *BioIn 17*
Wolff, Kay *BioIn 17*
Wolff, Kenneth John 1956- *WhoE 93*
Wolff, Kurt 1887-1963 *BioIn 17*
Wolff, Kurt H(einrich) 1912- *ConAu 39NR*
Wolff, Kurt Jakob 1936- *WhoE 93, WhoWor 93*
Wolff, Lester Bruce 1945- *WhoSSW 93*
Wolff, Manfred Ernst 1930- *WhoAm 92*
Wolff, Martha Anne Wood 1949- *WhoAm 92*
Wolff, Max 1840-1886 *Baker 92*
Wolff, Michael *BioIn 17*
Wolff, Nelson W. 1940- *WhoAm 92, WhoSSW 93*
Wolff, Paul Davis 1954- *St&PR 93*
Wolff, Paul R. *Law&B 92*
Wolff, Per 1936- *WhoScE 91-2*
Wolff, Peter Adalbert 1923- *WhoAm 92*
Wolff, Peter H.E. 1933- *WhoScE 91-3*
Wolff, Randall P. 1950- *St&PR 93*
Wolff, Regina
See Wolff, Edouard 1816-1880 *Baker 92*
Wolff, Reinhold 1941- *WhoWor 93*
Wolff, Richard A. 1933- *WhoIns 93*
Wolff, Richard Carl 1933- *WhoE 93*
Wolff, Richard H. *Law&B 92*
Wolff, Robert J. *Law&B 92*
Wolff, Robert Lee 1915-1980 *ScF&FL 92*
Wolff, Robert Paul 1933- *WhoAm 92*
Wolff, Robert S. 1925- *St&PR 93*
Wolff, Robert Sherman *ScF&FL 92*
Wolff, Russell B., Jr. 1953- *St&PR 93*
Wolff, Sanford Irving 1915- *WhoAm 92*
Wolff, Sara *AmWomPl*
Wolff, Sheldon 1928- *WhoAm 92*
Wolff, Sheldon Malcolm 1930- *WhoAm 92*
Wolff, Sidney Carne 1941- *WhoAm 92, WhoAmW 93*
Wolff, Sonia *MajAI*
Wolff, Stanley B. 1919- *WhoE 93*
Wolff, Stephane 1904-1980 *OxDcOp*
Wolff, Steven Alexander 1957- *WhoE 93*
Wolff, Steven Noel 1964- *WhoSSW 93*
Wolff, Stuart Ira 1940- *WhoE 93*
Wolff, Susan L. *Law&B 92*
Wolff, Thomas J. 1928- *WhoIns 93*
Wolff, Thomas John 1928- *WhoAm 92*
Wolff, Tobias 1945- *BioIn 17, WhoWrEP 92*
Wolff, Torben Lunn 1919- *WhoWor 93*
Wolff, Virginia Euwer 1937- *DcAmChF 1985*
Wolff, Werner 1929- *St&PR 93*
Wolff, Willem J. 1940- *WhoScE 91-3*
Wolff, William F., III 1945- *WhoAm 92*
Wolff, William H. 1906-1991 *BioIn 17*
Wolf-Ferrari, Ermanno 1876-1948 *Baker 92, IntDcOp, OxDcOp*
Wolffl, Joseph 1773-1812 *Baker 92*
Wolff-Salin, Mary Rietta Helen 1932- *WhoE 93*
Wolfgang, Bonnie Arlene 1944- *WhoAm 92*
Wolfgang, Jerald Ira 1938- *WhoE 93*
Wolfgang, Marvin E. 1924- *BioIn 17*
Wolfgang, Marvin Eugene 1924- *WhoAm 92*
Wolfin, Louis 1931- *St&PR 93*
Wolfinbarger, Lloyd, Jr. 1943- *WhoSSW 93*
Wolfinger, Bernd E. 1951- *WhoScE 91-3*
Wolfinger, Bernd Emil 1951- *WhoWor 93*
Wolfinger, Raymond Edwin 1931- *WhoAm 92*
Wolfinger, Robert C. 1950- *St&PR 93*
Wolfkill, Ronald V. 1938- *St&PR 93*
Wolfl, Joseph 1773-1812 *Baker 92*
Wolfle, Dael Lee 1906- *WhoAm 92*
Wolfley, Alan 1923- *WhoAm 92*
Wolfley, Ron *BioIn 17*
Wolfley, Scott *Law&B 92*
Wolfli, Adolf 1864-1930 *BioIn 17*
Wolfman, Bernard 1924- *WhoAm 92*
Wolfman, Brunetta Reid 1931- *WhoAmW 93, WhoE 93*
Wolfman, Burton I. 1930- *WhoE 93*
Wolfman, Earl Frank, Jr. 1926- *WhoAm 92*
Wolfman, Ira Joel 1950- *WhoAm 92*
Wolfman, Judith Barbara 1933- *WhoAmW 93*
Wolfman, Marv 1946- *ScF&FL 92*
Wolfman Jack 1938- *WhoAm 92*
Wolford, Clyde Richard 1951- *WhoE 93*
Wolford, Kathryn Frances 1957- *WhoAmW 93*
Wolford, Larry Eugene 1952- *WhoE 93*
Wolford, Patricia Weber 1940- *WhoAmW 93*
Wolford, Roy, Jr. 1946- *WhoEmL 93*
Wolford-Barnard, Eileen Joyce 1938- *WhoWrEP 92*
Wolfort, Louis Philip 1916- *St&PR 93*
Wolfowitz, Paul D. *BioIn 17*
Wolfowitz, Paul Dundes 1943- *WhoAm 92*
Wolfram, Charles William 1937- *WhoAm 92*
Wolfram, Gunther 1936- *WhoScE 91-3*
Wolfram, Joseph Maria 1789-1839 *Baker 92*
Wolfram, Julian *WhoScE 91-1*
Wolfram, Stephen 1959- *WhoAm 92*
Wolfram, Thomas 1936- *WhoAm 92*
Wolfram von Eschenbach fl. c. 1170-1220 *OxDcOp*
Wolfrom, Anna *AmWomPl*
Wolfrom, Howard E. 1948- *St&PR 93*
Wolfrum, Juergen M. 1939- *WhoScE 91-3*
Wolfrum, Karl 1856-1937
See Wolfrum, Philipp 1854-1919 *Baker 92*
Wolfrum, Otfried 1935- *WhoScE 91-3*
Wolfrum, Philipp 1854-1919 *Baker 92*
Wolfrum, William Harvey 1926- *WhoAm 92*
Wolfs, Denise Y. *Law&B 92*
Wolfs, Hans 1944- *WhoWor 93*
Wolfsberg, Max 1928- *WhoAm 92*
Wolfsheimer, Ronald M. 1952- *St&PR 93*
Wolfson, Alan William 1951- *WhoWor 93*
Wolfson, Bernard Terry 1919- *WhoSSW 93*
Wolfson, Edward Albert 1926-1990 *BioIn 17*
Wolfson, Evelyn *BioIn 17*
Wolfson, Harold K. d1991 *BioIn 17*
Wolfson, Harry 1887-1974 *JeAmHC*
Wolfson, Harry Austryn 1887-1974 *BioIn 17*
Wolfson, Isaac 1897-1991 *AnObit 1991, BioIn 17*
Wolfson, Jay 1952- *WhoSSW 93*
Wolfson, Lawrence Scott 1960- *WhoSSW 93*
Wolfson, Mark Alan 1952- *WhoAm 92*
Wolfson, Martin 1936- *St&PR 93*
Wolfson, Michael George 1938- *WhoAm 92*
Wolfson, Milton Jay 1942- *St&PR 93*
Wolfson, Miriam *AmWomPl*
Wolfson, Paulette S. *Law&B 92*
Wolfson, Philip Jay 1920- *WhoWor 93*
Wolfson, Richard F. 1923- *St&PR 93*
Wolfson, Richard Frederick 1923- *WhoAm 92*
Wolfson, Robert Joseph 1925- *WhoE 93*
Wolfson, Robert L. *St&PR 93*
Wolfson, Robert Pred 1926- *WhoWor 93*
Wolfson, Samuel *Law&B 92*
Wolfson, Sherry Lynn 1944- *WhoSSW 93*
Wolfson, Victor 1910-1990 *BioIn 17*
Wolfson, Warren D. *Law&B 92*
Wolfson, Warren David 1949- *St&PR 93, WhoAm 92*
Wolfurt, Kurt von 1880-1957 *Baker 92*
Wolfzahn, Annabelle Forsmith 1932- *WhoAmW 93*
Wolicki, Eligius Anthony 1927- *WhoAm 92*
Wolicki, Nancy Frieda 1953- *WhoAmW 93*
Wolin, Alfred M. 1932- *WhoAm 92, WhoE 93*
Wolin, Deborah Ellen *Law&B 92*
Wolin, Doris Diamond 1929- *WhoE 93*
Wolin, James Michael 1955- *WhoE 93*
Wolin, Meyer Jerome 1930- *WhoE 93*
Wolin, Michael Stuart 1953- *WhoE 93*
Wolin, Ron d1990 *BioIn 17*
Wolins, Joseph 1915- *WhoAm 92, WhoE 93*
Wolinski, Wieslaw 1929- *WhoScE 91-4*
Wolinsky, Cary Sol 1947- *WhoE 93*
Wolinsky, David *Law&B 92*
Wolinsky, Emanuel 1917- *WhoAm 92*
Wolinsky, Ira 1938- *WhoSSW 93*
Wolintz, Arthur Harry 1937- *WhoAm 92*
Wolis, Steven Evan *Law&B 92*
Wolis, Steven Evan 1960- *St&PR 93*
Wolitarsky, Bruce W. *Law&B 92*
Wolitarsky, James William 1946- *WhoAm 92*
Wolitzer, Hilma 1930- *ConAu 40NR, WhoWrEP 92*
Wolitzer, Meg 1959- *ScF&FL 92*
Wolitzer, Steven B. 1953- *WhoAm 92*
Wolk, Andy *MiSFD 9*
Wolk, Asher d1991 *BioIn 17*
Wolk, Beryl J. 1929- *St&PR 93*

Wolk, David B. 1956- *St&PR 93*
Wolk, Elliot K. 1935- *St&PR 93*
Wolk, George *ScF&FL 92*
Wolk, Herbert 1932- *St&PR 93*
Wolk, Howard Marvin 1920- *WhoWrEP 92*
Wolk, Howard William 1938- *St&PR 93*
Wolk, Jerome 1916-1990 *BioIn 17*
Wolk, Kenneth Ira *St&PR 93*
Wolk, Mike Joseph 1949- *St&PR 93*
Wolke, Milton S., Jr. *Law&B 92*
Wolken, Jerome Jay 1917- *WhoAm 92*
Wolkenstein, Oswald von c. 1377-1445 *Baker 92*
Wolkin, Douglas A. *Law&B 92*
Wolkin, Paul Alexander 1917- *WhoAm 92*
Wolking, Joseph Anthony 1934- *St&PR 93, WhoAm 92*
Wolkinger, Franz 1936- *WhoScE 91-4*
Wolko, Howard Stephen 1925- *WhoE 93*
Wolkoff, Eugene Arnold 1932- *WhoAm 92*
Wolkomir, Joyce Rogers 1942- *WhoWrEP 92*
Wolkomir, Richard 1943- *WhoWrEP 92*
Wolkonsky, Catherine d1992 *BioIn 17*
Wolkow, Alan Edward 1946- *WhoSSW 93*
Wolkstein, Diane *WhoWrEP 92*
Wolkstein, Diane 1942- *WhoE 93*
Woll, Harry J. 1920- *WhoAm 92*
Woll, Michael G. 1944- *WhoIns 93*
Woll, S. Raymond 1919- *St&PR 93*
Wollaeger, Timothy John 1943- *St&PR 93*
Wollan, Curtis Noel 1951- *WhoWor 93*
Wollanck, (Johann Ernst) Friedrich 1781-1831 *Baker 92*
Wollast, Roland 1932- *WhoScE 91-2*
Wollaston, Scott Edward *Law&B 92*
Wolle, Charles Robert 1935- *WhoAm 92*
Wolle, John Frederick 1863-1933 *Baker 92*
Wolle, June Rose Bush 1941- *WhoAmW 93*
Wolle, Peter 1792-1871 *Baker 92*
Wolle, William Down 1928- *WhoAm 92*
Wollemborg, Leo Joseph 1912- *WhoWor 93*
Wollen, A. Ross *Law&B 92*
Wollen, Nalla 1942- *St&PR 93*
Wollen, Peter *MiSFD 9*
Wollenberg, Bruce Frederick 1942- *WhoAm 92*
Wollenberg, J. Roger 1919- *WhoAm 92*
Wollenberg, Richard Peter 1915- *St&PR 93, WhoAm 92*
Wollenberger, Heinrich J. 1931- *WhoScE 91-3*
Wollenhaupt, Hermann Adolf 1827-1863 *Baker 92*
Wollensak, Richard John 1930- *St&PR 93*
Wollenweber, Eckhard 1941- *WhoScE 91-3*
Woller, Richard Lee 1957- *WhoE 93*
Wollersheim, Janet Puccinelli 1936- *WhoAmW 93*
Wollert, Gerald Dale 1935- *St&PR 93, WhoAm 92*
Wollett, Jan *BioIn 17*
Wollheim, Claes Benedict 1943- *WhoWor 93*
Wollheim, Donald A. 1914-1990 *BioIn 17, ScF&FL 92*
Wollheim, Donald A(llen) 1914-1990 *SmATA 69*
Wollheim, Donald Allen 1914- *WhoWrEP 92*
Wollheim, Frank A. 1932- *WhoScE 91-4*
Wollin, Richard Anderson 1952- *St&PR 93*
Wollman, Eric 1951- *WhoE 93*
Wollman, Harry 1932- *WhoAm 92, WhoE 93*
Wollman, June Rose 1929- *WhoE 93*
Wollman, Leo 1914- *WhoAm 92, WhoE 93*
Wollman, Nathaniel 1915- *WhoAm 92*
Wollman, Roger Leland 1934- *WhoAm 92*
Wollmer, H.H. Axel 1935- *WhoScE 91-3*
Wollmer, R.J. 1920- *St&PR 93*
Wollner, Barry Stuart 1953- *WhoE 93*
Wollner, Thomas Edward 1936- *WhoAm 92*
Wolloch, Richard *Law&B 92*
Wollstonecraft, Mary 1759-1797 *BioIn 17*
Wollum, Arthur George, II 1937- *WhoAm 92*
Wollum, Raymond M. *St&PR 93*
Wolman, Dan 1941- *MiSFD 9*
Wolman, J. Martin 1919- *St&PR 93, WhoAm 92*
Wolman, M. Gordon 1924- *WhoAm 92, WhoE 93*
Wolman, Roger L. 1947- *St&PR 93*
Wolman, Stephen Robert 1943- *WhoE 93*
Wolman, Tara Sophia 1948- *WhoAmW 93*
Wolman, William *WhoAm 92, WhoE 93*
Wolnek, Stephen S. 1938- *St&PR 93*
Wolner, Ernst 1939- *WhoScE 91-4*
Wolner, Rena Meryl 1945- *WhoAm 92*
Wolniewicz, Lutoslaw 1930- *WhoScE 91-4*
Wolo, Elaine Ruth Armour 1935- *WhoSSW 93*
Woloch, Anthony Nicholas *Law&B 92*
Wolohan, James L. 1951- *St&PR 93*
Wolohan, Richard Vincent 1915- *St&PR 93*
Woloshin, Marvin 1934- *St&PR 93*
Wolosky, Joel Martin 1942- *WhoAm 92*
Woloszyk, Holly Arlene 1960- *WhoAmW 93*
Woloszyn, Stanislaw 1920- *WhoScE 91-4*
Wolotkiewicz, Marian Margaret 1954- *WhoWrEP 92*
Wolotsky, Hyman 1918- *WhoE 93*
Wolowitz, Steven 1952- *WhoAm 92, WhoE 93, WhoWor 93*
Wolownik, Stephen Michael 1946- *WhoE 93*
Wolpe, Howard 1939- *CngDr 91*
Wolpe, Howard Eliot 1939- *WhoAm 92*
Wolpe, Stefan 1902-1972 *Baker 92*
Wolper, Allan L. *WhoE 93*
Wolper, Barry *BioIn 17*
Wolper, Barry Mark 1955- *St&PR 93*
Wolper, David Lloyd 1928- *WhoAm 92, WhoWor 93*
Wolper, Jacques T. 1934- *WhoScE 91-2*
Wolper, Marjorie Wright 1941- *WhoAmW 93*
Wolper, Marshall 1922- *WhoAm 92, WhoWor 93*
Wolper, Pierre 1955- *WhoScE 91-2*
Wolpert, Edward Alan 1930- *WhoAm 92*
Wolpert, Etta 1930- *WhoE 93*
Wolpert, Franz Alfons 1917-1978 *Baker 92*
Wolpert, Julian 1932- *WhoAm 92*
Wolpert, Richard W. 1926- *St&PR 93*
Wolpin, Alan David 1940- *WhoE 93*
Wolpoff, Alvin S. 1926- *St&PR 93*
Wolpoff, Milford Howell 1942- *WhoAm 92*
Wolschon, Peg Ann 1951- *WhoSSW 93*
Wolseley, Garnet Joseph 1833-1913 *HarEnMi*
Wolseley, Roland E. 1904- *ConAu 39NR*
Wolsey, Laurence A. 1945- *WhoScE 91-2*
Wolsey, Thomas 1475?-1530 *BioIn 17*
Wolshaw, Dorene Lee *WhoWrEP 92*
Wolsiffer, Patricia Rae 1933- *WhoAm 92*
Wolski, Antoni 1946- *WhoWor 93*
Wolski, Donna Catherine *WhoE 93*
Wolski, Kalikst 1816-1885 *PolBiDi*
Wolski, Lawrence George 1944- *St&PR 93*
Wolski, Patrick Edward 1939- *WhoAm 92*
Wolski, Tadeusz 1932- *WhoWor 93*
Wolsky, Murray 1931- *St&PR 93, WhoAm 92*
Wolslayer, Valerie Ann 1966- *WhoE 93*
Wolson, Craig Alan *Law&B 92*
Wolson, Craig Alan 1949- *WhoAm 92, WhoE 93*
Wolson, Morton *ScF&FL 92*
Wolstencroft, Ramon David 1936- *WhoScE 91-1, WhoWor 93*
Wolstenholm, Verne L. 1941- *St&PR 93*
Wolstenholme, William 1865-1931 *Baker 92*
Wolter, Anne Margaret 1937- *WhoAmW 93*
Wolter, Duane Roland 1948- *WhoAm 92*
Wolter, Frank 1943- *WhoUN 92*
Wolter, Gary Joseph *Law&B 92*
Wolter, John Amadeus *BioIn 17*
Wolter, John Amadeus 1925- *WhoAm 92*
Wolter, Roger 1935- *WhoScE 91-2*
Woltering, David F. 1946- *St&PR 93*
Woltering, Margaret Mae 1913- *WhoAmW 93*
Wolterink, Lester Floyd 1915- *WhoAm 92*
Wolters, Curt Cornelis Frederik 1938- *WhoE 93*
Wolters, Mannes 1948- *WhoScE 91-3*
Wolters, Oliver William 1915- *WhoAm 92*
Wolters, Raymond 1938- *WhoAm 92*
Woltersdorf, Hans Werner *BioIn 17*
Woltersdorf, Otto William, Jr. 1935- *WhoE 93*
Wolterstorff, Walter S. 1944- *St&PR 93*
Wolthausen, Reed C. 1947- *St&PR 93*
Woltmann, Jon Leith *Law&B 92*
Woltz, Alan E. 1932- *St&PR 93*
Woltz, H.O., III 1956- *St&PR 93*
Woltz, Howard Osler 1925- *St&PR 93*
Woltz, Howard Osler, Jr. 1925- *WhoAm 92, WhoSSW 93*
Woltz, Howard Osler, III 1956- *WhoAm 92*
Woltz, Mary Lynn Monaco 1951- *WhoAmW 93*
Wolverton, Dave 1957- *ScF&FL 92*
Wolverton, David 1940- *St&PR 93*
Wolverton, John D. *ScF&FL 92*
Wolverton, Robert Earl 1925- *WhoAm 92*
Wolverton, Susan 1960- *WhoAmW 93*
Wolverton, William T. 1937- *St&PR 93*
Wolverton, William Thomas, Jr. 1937- *WhoAm 92*
Wolwowicz, Ryszard 1921- *WhoScE 91-4*
Wolynes, Peter Guy 1953- *WhoAm 92*
Wolynic, Edward Thomas 1948- *St&PR 93, WhoAm 92*
Wolz, Henry George 1905- *WhoAm 92*
Wolzogen, Alfred, Freiherr von 1823-1883 *Baker 92*
Wolzogen, Ernst, Freiherr von 1855-1934 *Baker 92*
Wolzogen, Hans (Paul), Freiherr von 1848-1938 *Baker 92*
Womach, Emily Hitch 1927- *WhoAm 92*
Womach, Merrill P. 1927- *St&PR 93*
Womack, Bobby 1944- *SoulM*
Womack, C. Michael 1943- *St&PR 93*
Womack, Carter Devon 1951- *WhoSSW 93*
Womack, Craig Paul 1950- *St&PR 93*
Womack, Doug C. 1950- *WhoEmL 93*
Womack, Edgar Allen, Jr. 1942- *WhoAm 92*
Womack, Eric 1959- *WhoWrEP 92*
Womack, George W. *Law&B 92*
Womack, Idalah Demina 1943- *WhoE 93*
Womack, J. *Law&B 92*
Womack, Jack 1956- *ScF&FL 92*
Womack, James Scott 1928- *St&PR 93*
Womack, John Calvin 1950- *WhoSSW 93*
Womack, Joseph Donald, Sr. 1926- *WhoSSW 93*
Womack, Lowell Asher 1938- *St&PR 93*
Womack, Pamela *WhoAm 92, WhoAmW 93, WhoSSW 93*
Womack, Richard Muse 1928- *St&PR 93*
Womack, Richard R. 1936- *St&PR 93*
Womack, Robert Duncan 1942- *WhoAm 92*
Womack, Russell O. 1951- *St&PR 93*
Womack, Sharon Gennelle *WhoAm 92, WhoAmW 93*
Womack, Steven James 1952- *WhoWrEP 92*
Womack, Terry Dean 1953- *WhoWor 93*
Womack, Walter Charles 1947- *St&PR 93*
Womack & Womack *SoulM*
Wombacher, Gerald Thomas 1929- *St&PR 93*
Womble, Carol Merriwether 1946- *WhoAmW 93*
Womble, George Morgan 1926- *WhoSSW 93*
Womble, William Fletcher 1916- *WhoAm 92*
Womeldorf, Donald W. 1933- *St&PR 93*
Womeldorff, Porter John 1933- *St&PR 93, WhoAm 92*
Womer, Charles Berry 1926- *WhoAm 92*
Womersley, J. Lewis 1910-1990 *BioIn 17*
Wommack, William Walton 1922- *WhoAm 92*
Won, Hayon 1960- *WhoWor 93*
Wonder, David Royden 1958- *WhoSSW 93*
Wonder, Stevie *BioIn 17*
Wonder, Stevie 1950- *AfrAmBi, Baker 92, ConHero 2 [port], SoulM, WhoAm 92, WhoWor 93*
Wonders, William Clare 1924- *WhoAm 92*
Wondra, Janet C. 1952- *WhoWrEP 92*
Wondratschek, Hans 1925- *WhoScE 91-3*
Wong, Alfred Chun-Yin *Law&B 92*
Wong, Amy AnMei 1941- *WhoE 93*
Wong, Andrew Wang-fat 1943- *WhoAsAP 91*
Wong, Anna May 1907-1961 *IntDcF 2-3 [port]*
Wong, B. D. 1962- *ConTFT 10, WhoAm 92*
Wong, Bernard K. 1947- *St&PR 93*
Wong, Bing Kuen 1938- *WhoE 93*
Wong, Calvin Robert 1958- *St&PR 93*
Wong, Chak-Kuen 1938- *WhoAm 92*
Wong, Chi-ming *BioIn 17*
Wong, Chin Wah 1954- *WhoWor 93*
Wong, Ching-Ping 1947- *WhoAm 92*
Wong, Chong Fatt 1954- *WhoWor 93*
Wong, Daniel Choong Yun 1952- *WhoWor 93*
Wong, David *Law&B 92*
Wong, David T. 1935- *WhoWor 93*
Wong, David Tat-Kee 1952- *WhoWor 93*
Wong, David Yue 1934- *WhoAm 92*
Wong, Dennis Ka-Cheong 1954- *WhoE 93*
Wong, Derek D. *Law&B 92*
Wong, Donald 1957- *St&PR 93*
Wong, Doris S.W. *Law&B 92*
Wong, Edward Y. *Law&B 92*
Wong, Edwin Sau Nin 1929- *St&PR 93*
Wong, Elaine Dang 1936- *WhoAmW 93*
Wong, Elizabeth Ann 1958- *WhoE 93*
Wong, Gene 1922- *St&PR 93*
Wong, George Chi-Hung 1961- *WhoSSW 93*
Wong, Gordon 1965- *WhoWor 93*
Wong, Grace H. 1926- *St&PR 93*
Wong, Harry 1933- *St&PR 93*
Wong, Henry L. *St&PR 93*
Wong, Henry Li-Nan 1940- *WhoWor 93*
Wong, Ho Sang 1943- *WhoWor 93*
Wong, How Kin 1941- *WhoScE 91-3*
Wong, Howard Joseph 1940- *St&PR 93*
Wong, Iu Ming 1955- *WhoWor 93*
Wong, J., Jr. *Law&B 92*
Wong, James *Law&B 92*
Wong, Jim 1931- *St&PR 93*
Wong, John L. 1951- *WhoAm 92*
Wong, John Wing-Chung 1934- *WhoWor 93*
Wong, Kau-Fui Vincent 1949- *WhoSSW 93*
Wong, Kellogg H. 1928- *WhoAm 92*
Wong, Kenneth T. *Law&B 92*
Wong, Kim-pok *Law&B 92*
Wong, Kin-Ping 1941- *WhoAm 92*
Wong, Kok Siew 1946- *WhoWor 93*
Wong, Kuang Chung 1936- *WhoAm 92*
Wong, Kwok Chi 1942- *WhoSSW 93*
Wong, Kwok Lai 1935- *WhoAsAP 91*
Wong, Lan Kan 1950- *WhoE 93*
Wong, Lenny *MiSFD 9*
Wong, Ling 1946- *WhoWor 93*
Wong, Maria Mei 1959- *St&PR 93*
Wong, Marie Lisa 1965- *WhoE 93*
Wong, Martha Jee 1939- *WhoAmW 93*
Wong, Martin J. *Law&B 92*
Wong, Mary Ann 1953- *WhoWor 93*
Wong, Nancy 1949- *WhoWrEP 92*
Wong, Nellie 1934- *WhoWrEP 92*
Wong, Ngai Ying 1956- *WhoWor 93*
Wong, Patricia Kay *Law&B 92*
Wong, Patricia Uyehara *Law&B 92*
Wong, Peggy B. 1959- *St&PR 93*
Wong, Peter d1991 *BioIn 17*
Wong, Peter Hong-Yuen 1944- *WhoAsAP 91*
Wong, Po Kee 1934- *WhoAm 92*
Wong, Richard S. H. 1933- *WhoAm 92*
Wong, Richard Yue-Chim 1952- *WhoWor 93*
Wong, Shirley Y. *Law&B 92*
Wong, Steven Ho-Chong 1961- *WhoSSW 93*
Wong, Tak Yam Audie 1952- *WhoWor 93*
Wong, Victor Kenneth 1938- *WhoAm 92*
Wong, Vincent *St&PR 93*
Wong, Wai Ming 1966- *WhoE 93*
Wong, Wallace 1941- *WhoWor 93*
Wong, Wayne D. 1950- *WhoWor 93*
Wong, Weng Khing *Law&B 92*
Wong, William G. 1941- *WhoIns 93*
Wong, William Wai-Lun 1948- *WhoSSW 93*
Wong, Wing-Chun Godwin 1959- *WhoWor 93*
Wong, Wing Keung 1933- *WhoWor 93*
Wong, Wing-Wah Mary *Law&B 92*
Wong, Winston P. 1946- *St&PR 93*
Wong, Ying Wood 1950- *WhoWor 93*
Wong, Yiu Chu 1947- *WhoWor 93*
Wong, Yong-Chuan 1942- *WhoWor 93*
Wongar, B. 1938?- *ScF&FL 92*
Wong Chien Chi-Lien, Elizabeth 1937- *WhoAsAP 91*
Wongchuking, Caesar Dy 1965- *WhoWor 93*
Wong Kan Seng 1946- *WhoWor 93*
Wong Kan Seng, Hon. 1946- *WhoAsAP 91*
Wong Kie Yik 1942- *WhoAsAP 91*
Wong Mark, Kin Heng 1950- *WhoWor 93*
Wong Pun Sze, Wong Kwee Siong 1939- *WhoUN 92*
Wong-Staal, Flossie *BioIn 17*
Wongwantanee, Lucksmee Ongkasuwan 1940- *WhoWor 93*
Wonham, Frederick Stapley 1931- *WhoAm 92*
Wonham, Jon 1938- *WhoUN 92*
Wonham, Walter Murray 1934- *WhoAm 92*
Wonke-Hirko, Beatrix 1939- *WhoWor 93*
Wonnacott, James Brian 1945- *WhoSSW 93*
Wonnacott, Paul 1933- *WhoAm 92*
Wonnacott, Ronald Johnston 1930- *WhoAm 92*
Wonnell, Donn T. *Law&B 92*
Wonnell, Donn T. 1947- *St&PR 93*
Wonson-Liukkonen, Barbara Boyce 1953- *WhoAmW 93*
Wontner, Hugh Walter Kingwell d1992 *NewYTBS 92*
Woo, Carolina *BioIn 17*
Woo, David Charles 1956- *St&PR 93*
Woo, Frances Mei Soo 1949- *WhoAmW 93*
Woo, James Tsuan-wen 1936- *WhoE 93*
Woo, John 1948- *MiSFD 9*
Woo, Jung Woo 1933- *WhoSSW 93, WhoWor 93*
Woo, Nelson 1961- *BioIn 17*
Woo, Patricia *WhoScE 91-1*
Woo, Peggy 1949- *St&PR 93*

Woo, R.E. *Law&B 92*
Woo, S. B. 1937- *WhoAm 92*
Woo, Savio Lau-Yuen 1942- *WhoAm 92*
Woo, Shirley A. *Law&B 92*
Woo, Terry Kuo *Law&B 92*
Woo, Walter 1948- *WhoSSW 93*
Woo, Wilbert Yuk Cheong 1942- *WhoWor 93*
Woo, William Franklin 1936- *WhoAm 92*
Woo, Young Sik 1953- *WhoWor 93*
Wood, A(rthur) Skevington 1916- *ConAu 40NR*
Wood, Albert Douglas 1930- *WhoSSW 93*
Wood, Alexander Wallace 1944- *WhoE 93*
Wood, Allen John 1925- *WhoAm 92*
Wood, Allen W(illiam) 1942- *ConAu 37NR*
Wood, Amy Katheryn 1955- *WhoAmW 93*
Wood, Andrew Sinclair 1923- *WhoSSW 93*
Wood, Anne 1937- *BioIn 17*
Wood, Arthur MacDougall 1913- *WhoAm 92*
Wood, Arthur Thomson 1944- *WhoSSW 93*
Wood, Audrey *ConAu 137, MajAI [port]*
Wood, Barbara 1947- *ScF&FL 92, WhoAmW 93*
Wood, Barbara Louise Champion 1924- *WhoAmW 93*
Wood, Bari 1936- *ScF&FL 92*
Wood, Barrie Ross 1934- *St&PR 93*
Wood, Beatrice *BioIn 17*
Wood, Benjamin O. 1936- *St&PR 93*
Wood, Berenice Howland 1910- *WhoE 93*
Wood, Bernard Anthony *WhoScE 91-1*
Wood, Billie Augustine 1924- *WhoAmW 93, WhoSSW 93, WhoWor 93*
Wood, Brenda Sue 1961- *WhoE 93*
Wood, Brian 1932-1991 *BioIn 17*
Wood, Bridget *ScF&FL 92*
Wood, Brison Robert 1931- *WhoE 93*
Wood, Bruce *BioIn 17*
Wood, C.V. d1992 *BioIn 17*
Wood, C. V., Jr. d1992 *NewYTBS 92 [port]*
Wood, Carol Mae 1927- *WhoAmW 93*
Wood, Catherine Theresa 1961- *WhoE 93*
Wood, Cathy Lynn 1951- *WhoAmW 93*
Wood, Chalmers Benedict 1917-1991 *BioIn 17*
Wood, Charles 1866-1926 *Baker 92*
Wood, Charles Erskine Scott 1852-1944 *BioIn 17*
Wood, Charles Evans 1952- *WhoSSW 93*
Wood, Charles Martin, III 1943- *St&PR 93, WhoAm 92*
Wood, Charles Norman 1938- *WhoAm 92*
Wood, Charles R. 1933- *St&PR 93*
Wood, Charles Tuttle 1933- *WhoAm 92*
Wood, Cheryl *BioIn 17*
Wood, Christie Ann 1955- *WhoAmW 93*
Wood, Christopher 1935- *ScF&FL 92*
Wood, Christopher Bryan Somerset *WhoScE 91-1*
Wood, Clinton Wayne 1954- *WhoSSW 93*
Wood, Cora Antoinette 1867- *AmWomPl*
Wood, Craig Breckinridge 1943- *WhoWor 93*
Wood, Curtis L. *WhoWrEP 92*
Wood, Curtis William, Jr. 1941- *WhoSSW 93*
Wood, Cynthia Cooley *Law&B 92*
Wood, D. Joseph 1941- *WhoUN 92*
Wood, Daniel 1943- *WhoCanL 92*
Wood, Daniel Gordon 1937- *St&PR 93*
Wood, Danny 1969- *BioIn 17*
Wood, Darlene Sprinkle 1954- *WhoAmW 93*
Wood, Darrell Wayne 1939- *WhoSSW 93*
Wood, David Charles 1943- *St&PR 93, WhoAm 92*
Wood, David Duffle 1838-1910 *Baker 92*
Wood, David Kennedy Cornell 1925- *WhoAm 92*
Wood, David Muir *WhoScE 91-1*
Wood, David R. 1943- *St&PR 93*
Wood, David Robert 1952- *St&PR 93*
Wood, David Wayne 1952- *WhoSSW 93*
Wood, Debra Lynn 1961- *WhoAmW 93*
Wood, Delmas Byrom 1938- *St&PR 93*
Wood, Dennis *Law&B 92*
Wood, Derek Edward *Law&B 92*
Wood, Derek L. 1939- *St&PR 93*
Wood, Desmond P. 1930- *St&PR 93*
Wood, Diana 1961- *WhoAmW 93*
Wood, Diane Pamela 1950- *WhoAm 92*
Wood, Diane Sharp 1946- *WhoE 93*
Wood, Diane Tomlinson 1962- *WhoAmW 93*
Wood, Dolores Funai 1931- *WhoSSW 93*
Wood, Dolores Idel 1938- *WhoSSW 93*
Wood, Don *ChlBIID [port]*
Wood, Don 1945- *ConAu 136, MajAI [port]*
Wood, Donald C. 1937- *St&PR 93*
Wood, Donald Euriah 1935- *WhoAm 92*
Wood, Dorothy *SweetSg B [port]*
Wood, Douglass G. 1938- *St&PR 93*
Wood, Duncan Wilson 1948- *St&PR 93*
Wood, Edward D. *BioIn 17*
Wood, Edward D. 1933- *WhoAm 92*
Wood, Edward D., Jr. 1924-1978 *MiSFD 9N, ScF&FL 92*
Wood, Edwin Carlyle 1929- *WhoWor 93*
Wood, Elwood Steven, III 1934- *WhoAm 92*
Wood, Eric *St&PR 93*
Wood, Eric Franklin 1947- *WhoAm 92*
Wood, Erskine Biddle 1911- *WhoAm 92*
Wood, Evelyn Nielsen 1909- *WhoAm 92, WhoAmW 93*
Wood, Everett *BioIn 17*
Wood, Fay S. *WhoAmW 93*
Wood, Fernando 1812-1881 *BioIn 17, PolPar*
Wood, Frances Gilchrist *AmWomPl*
Wood, Francis C. 1901-1990 *BioIn 17*
Wood, Frank Bradshaw 1915- *WhoAm 92*
Wood, Frank M. 1935- *St&PR 93*
Wood, Frank Preuit 1916- *WhoAm 92*
Wood, Frederick Harrison 1936- *WhoSSW 93*
Wood, G. Pierce 1927- *St&PR 93*
Wood, Gail Graves *Law&B 92*
Wood, Geoffrey C. *WhoScE 91-1*
Wood, Geoffrey Edward *WhoScE 91-1*
Wood, George H. 1946- *WhoAm 92*
Wood, Gerald David 1947- *WhoEmL 93, WhoSSW 93, WhoWor 93*
Wood, Gordon Stewart 1933- *WhoAm 92*
Wood, Graham Charles *WhoScE 91-1*
Wood, Grant 1892-1942 *BioIn 17*
Wood, Gregory Burton, Jr. 1943- *WhoSSW 93*
Wood, Hap 1941- *St&PR 93*
Wood, Harland G. 1907-1991 *BioIn 17*
Wood, Harleston Read 1913- *WhoAm 92*
Wood, Harlington, Jr. 1920- *WhoAm 92*
Wood, Harrison F. 1919-1991 *BioIn 17*
Wood, Harvey Joseph 1919- *WhoWrEP 92*
Wood, Haydn 1882-1959 *Baker 92*
Wood, Henry 1869-1944 *OxDcOp*
Wood, Henry Evelyn 1838-1919 *HarEnMi*
Wood, Henry J(oseph) 1869-1944 *Baker 92*
Wood, Howard Eugene 1932- *St&PR 93*
Wood, Howard Graham 1910- *WhoAm 92*
Wood, Hugh (Bradshaw) 1932- *Baker 92*
Wood, J.A. *ScF&FL 92*
Wood, J. Kenneth 1935- *St&PR 93*
Wood, J. Kenneth, Jr. 1935- *WhoIns 93*
Wood, Jacalyn Kay 1949- *WhoAmW 93, WhoEmL 93*
Wood, Jack Calvin 1933- *WhoAm 92*
Wood, Jack W. 1925- *St&PR 93*
Wood, James 1927- *WhoAm 92*
Wood, James 1930- *St&PR 93, WhoAm 92, WhoE 93*
Wood, James Allen 1906- *WhoAm 92*
Wood, James Claude 1939- *WhoSSW 93*
Wood, James E., Jr. 1922- *WhoAm 92, WhoWor 93*
Wood, James Nowell 1941- *WhoAm 92*
Wood, James Robert Gardham *WhoScE 91-1*
Wood, Jane Semple 1940- *WhoAmW 93*
Wood, Janet Ann 1950- *WhoAmW 93*
Wood, Jeanne Clarke 1916- *WhoAm 92, WhoSSW 93, WhoWor 93*
Wood, Jeannette Griffin 1928- *WhoAmW 93*
Wood, Jeannine Guillevin *BioIn 17*
Wood, Jeff J. 1932- *St&PR 93*
Wood, Jeffrey B. *Law&B 92*
Wood, Jeremy Scott 1941- *WhoE 93, WhoWor 93*
Wood, Joanna E. 1867-1927 *BioIn 17*
Wood, John 1942- *ScF&FL 92*
Wood, John 1947- *ConAu 136*
Wood, John A. 1937- *St&PR 93*
Wood, John Armstead 1932- *WhoAm 92*
Wood, John Daniel *Law&B 92*
Wood, John Denison 1931- *WhoAm 92, WhoWor 93*
Wood, John F. 1940- *St&PR 93*
Wood, John Herbert 1936- *St&PR 93*
Wood, John Thurston 1928- *WhoSSW 93*
Wood, John V. *WhoScE 91-1*
Wood, John Walter, Jr. 1941- *WhoWor 93*
Wood, Joseph 1915- *Baker 92*
Wood, Joseph George 1928- *WhoAm 92*
Wood, Joshua Warren, III 1941- *WhoAm 92*
Wood, Karen Ann *BioIn 17*
Wood, Karen Sue 1950- *WhoAm 92*
Wood, Kathleen Marie 1962- *WhoAmW 93*
Wood, Keith S. 1917- *St&PR 93*
Wood, Kenneth Arthur 1926- *WhoAm 92, WhoWor 93*
Wood, Kenneth Laverne 1936- *WhoSSW 93*
Wood, Kenneth Stanley 1941- *WhoWor 93*
Wood, Kerry 1907- *DcChlFi*
Wood, Kevin *BioIn 17*
Wood, Kimba M. 1944- *WhoAm 92, WhoAmW 93*
Wood, Kimberly Janelle 1968- *WhoAmW 93*
Wood, Lana 1946- *ConAu 139*
Wood, Larry *BioIn 17, WhoAm 92, WhoAmW 93, WhoWor 93*
Wood, Laura Gale *St&PR 93*
Wood, Laurence Arthur *WhoScE 91-1*
Wood, Leonard 1860-1927 *CmdGen 1991 [port], GayN, HarEnMi, PolPar*
Wood, Leslie Carol 1955- *WhoWrEP 92*
Wood, Letitia W. *AmWomPl*
Wood, Linda May 1942- *WhoAm 92, WhoAmW 93*
Wood, Lisa Fortlouis 1954- *WhoAmW 93*
Wood, Lisa Gaye 1957- *WhoAmW 93*
Wood, Lockett 1939- *St&PR 93*
Wood, Loren Edwin 1927- *WhoSSW 93*
Wood, Loren Morris 1930- *St&PR 93*
Wood, Lyman Phillips 1910- *St&PR 93*
Wood, Lysle A. 1904-1991 *BioIn 17*
Wood, Margaret Gray 1918- *WhoAmW 93*
Wood, Marian Starr 1938- *WhoAm 92, WhoAmW 93*
Wood, Martha Swain 1943- *WhoAm 92, WhoAmW 93, WhoSSW 93*
Wood, Mary Catherine 1957- *WhoSSW 93*
Wood, Mary Juanita *Law&B 92*
Wood, Mary Knight 1857-1944 *Baker 92*
Wood, Maurice 1922- *WhoAm 92*
Wood, Mel H. *WhoScE 91-1*
Wood, Merle W., II *Law&B 92*
Wood, Michael Allen 1956- *WhoWor 93*
Wood, Michael B. *Law&B 92*
Wood, Michael B. 1936- *WhoScE 91-1*
Wood, Nancy Elizabeth *WhoAm 92, WhoAmW 93*
Wood, Nancy K. 1955- *WhoAmW 93*
Wood, Nancy Virginia 1934- *WhoSSW 93*
Wood, Nara Sue 1949- *WhoSSW 93*
Wood, Natalie *BioIn 17*
Wood, Natalie 1938-1981 *IntDcF 2-3 [port]*
Wood, Neil Roderick 1931- *St&PR 93, WhoAm 92, WhoWor 93*
Wood, Norman Dwight 1941- *WhoE 93*
Wood, Norman S. 1928- *St&PR 93*
Wood, Oliver Gillan, Jr. 1937- *WhoSSW 93*
Wood, Owen 1929- *BioIn 17*
Wood, Patricia Knowles 1942- *WhoAmW 93*
Wood, Paul Donald 1945- *WhoSSW 93*
Wood, Paul R. 1929- *St&PR 93*
Wood, Paul Roy 1936- *WhoSSW 93*
Wood, Paul W. 1944- *St&PR 93*
Wood, Peggy 1892-1978 *AmWomPl*
Wood, Peter 1927?- *ConTFT 10*
Wood, Peter John 1953- *WhoE 93*
Wood, Presnall Hansel 1932- *WhoAm 92*
Wood, Quentin Eugene 1923- *WhoAm 92*
Wood, Quentin Howard *Law&B 92*
Wood, R.A. 1893-1991 *BioIn 17*
Wood, R. Lyman 1937- *St&PR 93*
Wood, R. Ray 1942- *St&PR 93*
Wood, Ralph B. 1940- *St&PR 93*
Wood, Reba Maxine 1919- *WhoAmW 93*
Wood, Rebecca Buckner 1943- *WhoAmW 93*
Wood, Renate 1938- *WhoWrEP 92*
Wood, Rex B. 1942- *St&PR 93*
Wood, Richard Albert 1893-1991 *BioIn 17*
Wood, Richard Courtney 1943- *WhoSSW 93*
Wood, Richard Donald 1926- *St&PR 93, WhoAm 92*
Wood, Richard Eugene 1943- *WhoSSW 93*
Wood, Richard J. *WhoAm 92*
Wood, Richard P. 1945- *St&PR 93*
Wood, Richard R. 1950- *WhoIns 93*
Wood, Richard Robert 1950- *St&PR 93*
Wood, Richard W. 1943- *St&PR 93*
Wood, Robert 1949- *WhoAsAP 91*
Wood, Robert 1953- *ScF&FL 92*
Wood, Robert C. *WhoIns 93*
Wood, Robert Chapman 1949- *ConAu 139*
Wood, Robert Charles 1939- *St&PR 93*
Wood, Robert Charles 1956- *WhoEmL 93, WhoSSW 93, WhoWor 93*
Wood, Robert Coldwell 1923- *WhoAm 92*
Wood, Robert Edward 1941- *WhoAm 92*
Wood, Robert Elkington, II 1938- *WhoAm 92*
Wood, Robert H., Jr. *Law&B 92*
Wood, Robert Hart 1910- *WhoAm 92*
Wood, Robert J. 1918-1990 *BioIn 17*
Wood, Robert L. 1939- *St&PR 93*
Wood, Robert Lee 1940- *WhoSSW 93*
Wood, Robert P. *ScF&FL 92*
Wood, Robert S. *BioIn 17*
Wood, Robert S. 1928- *St&PR 93*
Wood, Robert Warren 1955- *WhoEmL 93*
Wood, Robert William 1926- *St&PR 93*
Wood, Roberta Susan 1948- *WhoAmW 93*
Wood, Robin 1931- *ScF&FL 92*
Wood, Roderick M. *St&PR 93*
Wood, Roger S. 1927- *St&PR 93*
Wood, Ronald 1947- *WhoAm 92*
Wood, Ronald Brian *WhoScE 91-1*
Wood, Ronald Karslake Starr *WhoScE 91-1*
Wood, Ruby Fern 1922- *WhoAmW 93*
Wood, Ruth Lundgren Williamson *WhoAmW 93, WhoWor 93*
Wood, S. Andrew 1890- *ScF&FL 92*
Wood, Sally Ann 1949- *WhoWrEP 92*
Wood, Sam 1883-1949 *MiSFD 9N*
Wood, Samuel Eugene 1934- *WhoWor 93*
Wood, Sandra Kay 1956- *St&PR 93*
Wood, Sharon 1957- *WhoAmW 93*
Wood, Shelton Eugene 1938- *WhoWor 93*
Wood, Silas 1769-1847 *BioIn 17*
Wood, Stephen V. 1936- *St&PR 93*
Wood, Susan 1948-1980 *ScF&FL 92*
Wood, Susan Elliott 1951- *WhoAmW 93*
Wood, Susan T. *ScF&FL 92*
Wood, Susan Yardley 1957- *WhoE 93*
Wood, T.G. 1937- *WhoScE 91-1*
Wood, Teresa Melvin 1953- *WhoAmW 93*
Wood, Teri Wilford *Law&B 92*
Wood, Thomas 1892-1950 *Baker 92*
Wood, Thomas A. 1926- *St&PR 93*
Wood, Thomas Kemble 1919- *WhoAm 92*
Wood, Thomas Marion 1952- *St&PR 93*
Wood, Thomas W. 1944- *St&PR 93*
Wood, Timothy McDonald 1947- *St&PR 93, WhoAm 92*
Wood, Tyrus Cobb, Jr. 1945- *WhoWrEP 92*
Wood, Vivian Elliott *AmWomPl*
Wood, Vivian Poates 1923- *WhoAmW 93*
Wood, Vonnie Ellen 1927- *WhoSSW 93*
Wood, W. Carlton 1939- *St&PR 93*
Wood, W.F., Jr. *Law&B 92*
Wood, Wallace 1927-1981 *ScF&FL 92*
Wood, Walter Samuel *Law&B 92*
Wood, Wayne Barry 1958- *WhoEmL 93, WhoWor 93*
Wood, Wendy Deborah 1940- *WhoE 93*
Wood, Wendy Lloyd 1944- *WhoE 93*
Wood, Wilbur Forrester, Jr. 1941- *BiDAMSp 1989*
Wood, Will C. 1939- *WhoAm 92*
Wood, William A. d1992 *NewYTBS 92*
Wood, William A., Jr. *Law&B 92*
Wood, William Andrew, Jr. 1919- *St&PR 93*
Wood, William Barry, Jr. 1910-1971 *BiDAMSp 1989*
Wood, William Clarke 1952- *WhoSSW 93*
Wood, William G. 1859-1895 *Baker 92*
Wood, William J. *Law&B 92, WhoSSW 93*
Wood, William J. 1943- *WhoSSW 93*
Wood, William Jerome 1928- *WhoAm 92*
Wood, William Lawrence 1927- *WhoSSW 93*
Wood, William McBrayer 1942- *WhoWor 93*
Wood, William Philler 1927- *WhoAm 92*
Wood, William Ransom 1907- *WhoAm 92, WhoWor 93*
Wood, Willie *BioIn 17*
Wood, Willis B., Jr. 1934- *St&PR 93*
Wood, Willis Bowne, Jr. 1934- *WhoAm 92*
Woodall, Arthur Ray 1943- *WhoSSW 93*
Woodall, Hubert C., Jr. 1918- *St&PR 93*
Woodall, Jack David 1936- *WhoAm 92*
Woodall, John Payne 1935- *WhoUN 92*
Woodall, Lowery A. 1929- *WhoSSW 93*
Woodall, Margaret Carol 1942- *WhoAmW 93*
Woodall, Natalie Joy 1946- *WhoAmW 93*
Woodall, Norman Eugene 1916- *WhoAm 92*
Woodall, Robert E. 1926- *St&PR 93*
Woodall, S. Roy, Jr. 1936- *WhoIns 93*
Woodall, Samuel Roy, Jr. 1936- *WhoAm 92, WhoE 93*
Woodall, Timothy M. 1945- *St&PR 93*
Woodall, William L. 1923- *St&PR 93*
Woodall, William Leon 1923- *WhoAm 92*
Woodard, Alfre *BioIn 17*
Woodard, Alfre 1953- *WhoAm 92*
Woodard, Alva Abe 1928- *WhoWor 93*
Woodard, Bobby Louis 1930- *WhoSSW 93*
Woodard, Carol Jane 1929- *WhoAm 92, WhoAmW 93*
Woodard, Clarence J. 1923- *St&PR 93*
Woodard, Clarence James 1923- *WhoAm 92*
Woodard, Dorothy Marie 1932- *WhoAmW 93*
Woodard, Edwin *ScF&FL 92*
Woodard, Elizabeth Barbara *Law&B 92*
Woodard, G. Daniel *Law&B 92*
Woodard, George 1939- *WhoWor 93*
Woodard, George Sawyer, Jr. 1924- *WhoAm 92*
Woodard, Gerald Walter 1932- *WhoAm 92*

Woodard, Harold Raymond 1911- *WhoAm 92*
Woodard, Jennifer Lee *Law&B 92*
Woodard, John Bennett 1953- *WhoSSW 93*
Woodard, John Roger 1932- *WhoAm 92*
Woodard, Larry Charles 1943- *WhoSSW 93*
Woodard, Lynette *BioIn 17*
Woodard, Nina Elizabeth 1947- *WhoAmW 93*
Woodard, Ralph Frank 1937- *St&PR 93*
Woodard, Richard Charles 1939- *WhoE 93*
Woodard, Ronald B. 1913- *St&PR 93*
Woodard, Wallace William, III 1950- *WhoSSW 93*
Woodard, Wayne *ScF&FL 92*
Woodbeck, Milford E. 1911- *St&PR 93*
Woodberry, George E. 1855-1930 *BioIn 17, ScF&FL 92*
Woodberry, Isaac Baker 1819-1858 *Baker 92*
Woodberry, Joan (Merle) 1921- *DcChlFi*
Woodberry, Paul 1927- *St&PR 93*
Woodbrey, Edward F., Jr. 1955- *St&PR 93*
Woodbridge, Benjamin M. 1884-1969 *ScF&FL 92*
Woodbridge, Elizabeth *AmWomPl*
Woodbridge, Henry S. 1906- *St&PR 93*
Woodbridge, Henry Sewall 1906- *WhoAm 92*
Woodbridge, Hensley Charles 1923- *WhoAm 92*
Woodbridge, John Marshall 1929- *WhoAm 92*
Woodbridge, John Sylvester 1897-1991 *BioIn 17*
Woodbridge, Joseph Eliot 1921- *WhoE 93*
Woodbridge, Linda 1945- *WhoAm 92*
Woodburn, David Marshall, Jr. 1946- *WhoAm 92*
Woodburn, E.T. *WhoScE 91-1*
Woodburn, Elisabeth d1990 *BioIn 17*
Woodburn, Frank Craig 1959- *WhoE 93*
Woodburn, Robert James 1929- *WhoSSW 93*
Woodburn, Scott Edward 1958- *WhoE 93*
Woodbury, Alan Tenney 1943- *WhoAm 92*
Woodbury, Arthur N(eum) 1930- *Baker 92*
Woodbury, C. Troy, Jr. 1947- *St&PR 93*
Woodbury, Charles Putnam 1919- *WhoIns 93*
Woodbury, David B. 1940- *St&PR 93*
Woodbury, David O. 1896-1981 *ScF&FL 92*
Woodbury, David Oakes 1896-1981 *BioIn 17*
Woodbury, Edwina D. 1951- *St&PR 93*
Woodbury, Franklin Bennett Wessler 1937- *WhoE 93, WhoWor 93*
Woodbury, Isaac Baker 1819-1858 *Baker 92*
Woodbury, Joan 1915-1989 *SweetSg C [port]*
Woodbury, Lael Jay 1927- *WhoAm 92*
Woodbury, Levi 1789-1851 *OxCSupC [port]*
Woodbury, Louie E., Jr. 1914- *WhoIns 93*
Woodbury, Marion A. 1923- *WhoAm 92*
Woodbury, Max Atkin 1917- *WhoAm 92*
Woodbury, Mitchell R. *Law&B 92*
Woodbury, Nathalie F.S. 1918- *IntDcAn*
Woodbury, Peter 1951- *St&PR 93*
Woodbury, Richard B. 1917- *IntDcAn*
Woodbury, Richard Benjamin 1917- *WhoAm 92*
Woodbury, Robert Louis 1938- *WhoAm 92, WhoE 93*
Woodbury, Robert William 1956- *St&PR 93*
Woodbury, Rollin Edwin 1913- *WhoAm 92*
Woodbury, Ronald Glen 1943- *WhoE 93*
Woodbury, T. Bowring, II *Law&B 92*
Woodbury, Thomas Bowring, II 1937- *WhoAm 92*
Woodbury, Thomas M. *Law&B 92*
Woodbury, Thomas W. *Law&B 92*
Woodcock, D. John 1945- *WhoE 93*
Woodcock, David Geoffrey 1937- *WhoSSW 93*
Woodcock, Eugene Floyd 1957- *WhoSSW 93*
Woodcock, George 1912- *ScF&FL 92, WhoAm 92, WhoCanL 92, WhoWor 93, WhoWrEP 92*
Woodcock, Herman H. 1935- *St&PR 93*
Woodcock, Janet Lynn 1957- *WhoAmW 93*
Woodcock, John Richard 1927- *St&PR 93*
Woodcock, Leonard 1911- *WhoAm 92*
Woodcock, Leonard F. 1911- *PolPar*
Woodcock, Les 1927- *WhoE 93*
Woodcock, Ray Chester 1946- *WhoSSW 93*
Woodcock, Robert C. *Law&B 92*
Wood-Collins, John Charles 1942- *St&PR 93*
Woodcott, Keith *ConAu 37NR*
Wooden, Charles Ronald 1943- *St&PR 93*
Wooden, Douglas L. 1956- *St&PR 93*
Wooden, Howard Edmund 1919- *WhoAm 92*
Wooden, John R. *BioIn 17*
Wooden, John Robert 1910- *WhoAm 92*
Wooden, Ruth A. 1946- *WhoAm 92, WhoAmW 93*
Wood Family *BioIn 17*
Woodfield, Graeme 1935- *WhoWor 93*
Woodfield, Grant M. 1930- *St&PR 93*
Woodfill, John F. 1947- *St&PR 93*
Woodfin, Beulah M. 1936- *WhoAmW 93*
Woodfin, George W. 1930- *St&PR 93*
Woodfin, Ira John 1910- *St&PR 93*
Woodfin, Paul Beverly, II 1928- *WhoE 93*
Woodfine, B.C. *WhoScE 91-1*
Woodford, Bruce Powers 1919- *WhoWrEP 92*
Woodford, Charles 1931- *St&PR 93*
Woodford, Clive Edward 1946- *WhoUN 92*
Woodford, Duane H. 1939- *St&PR 93*
Woodford, G. Clark *St&PR 93*
Woodford, Harvey *Law&B 92*
Woodfork, Nancy Ann 1948- *WhoAmW 93*
Woodger, Walter James, Jr. 1913- *WhoWor 93*
Woodhall, John Alexander, Jr. 1929- *WhoWor 93*
Woodhams, Frank William David *WhoScE 91-1*
Woodhams, Stephen Vance 1955- *WhoWrEP 92*
Woodhatch, Maynard Maurice 1925- *St&PR 93*
Woodhead, Leslie *BioIn 17, MiSFD 9*
Woodhead, Robert Kenneth 1925- *WhoAm 92*
Woodhouse, Barbara *BioIn 17*
Woodhouse, Charles F. *St&PR 93*
Woodhouse, Chase Going 1890-1984 *BioIn 17*
Woodhouse, Derrick Fergus 1927- *WhoWor 93*
Woodhouse, Edward James, Jr. *Law&B 92*
Woodhouse, John C. 1898-1991 *BioIn 17*
Woodhouse, John F. *BioIn 17*
Woodhouse, John F. 1930- *St&PR 93*
Woodhouse, John Frederick 1930- *WhoAm 92, WhoSSW 93, WhoWor 93*
Woodhouse, Martin 1932- *ScF&FL 92*
Woodhouse, Stephen James 1948- *WhoUN 92*
Woodhull, George Spafford 1773-1834 *BioIn 17*
Woodhull, John Richard 1933- *St&PR 93*
Woodhull, Nancy Jane 1945- *WhoAmW 93*
Woodhull, Victoria 1838-1927 *PolPar*
Woodin, Martin Dwight 1915- *WhoAm 92*
Wooding, Lucille Rogers 1936- *WhoAmW 93*
Wooding, Peter Holden 1940- *WhoAm 92*
Wooding, Sam 1895-1985 *BioIn 17*
Wooding, Sharon *ConAu 136*
Wooding, Sharon 1943- *BioIn 17*
Wooding, Sharon L(ouise) 1943- *ConAu 136*
Woodiwiss, Kathleen E. *BioIn 17*
Woodiwiss, Kathleen Erin 1939- *WhoWrEP 92*
Woodland, Hugh Robert *WhoScE 91-1*
Woodland, Leon L. 1925- *St&PR 93*
Woodlawn, Holly *BioIn 17*
Woodle, Roy V. 1935- *St&PR 93*
Woodley, D.B. 1951- *St&PR 93*
Woodley, John Paul 1926- *WhoSSW 93*
Woodley, Michael Raymond 1950- *WhoSSW 93*
Woodley, Richard *ScF&FL 92*
Woodley, Robert Denis 1946- *WhoWrEP 92*
Woodlief, Annette Matthews 1940- *WhoSSW 93*
Woodlief, Joseph B. 1920 *St&PR 93*
Woodlock, David Jerome 1947- *WhoE 93*
Woodlock, Douglas Preston 1947- *WhoAm 92, WhoE 93*
Woodman, Allen 1954- *WhoWrEP 92*
Woodman, Chandler S. 1935- *St&PR 93*
Woodman, Chester Leroy, Jr. 1935- *St&PR 93*
Woodman, Hannah Rea 1870- *AmWomPl*
Woodman, Harold David 1928- *WhoAm 92*
Woodman, Harry Andrews 1928- *WhoAm 92*
Woodman, Herbert B. 1904-1991 *BioIn 17*
Woodman, (Raymond) Huntington 1861-1943 *Baker 92*
Woodman, Jean Wilson 1949- *WhoE 93*
Woodman, Wayne L. 1934- *St&PR 93*
Woodman, William E. *WhoAm 92*
Woodmansee, Bruce James 1946- *WhoAm 92*
Woodner, Ian *BioIn 17*
Wood Prince, William Norman 1942- *St&PR 93*
Woodress, James Leslie *BioIn 17*
Woodress, James Leslie, Jr. 1916- *WhoAm 92*
Woodrich, Richard H. 1945- *St&PR 93*
Woodring, Beryl F. *WhoAmW 93*
Woodring, Carole Lyn 1945- *WhoAmW 93*
Woodring, DeWayne Stanley 1931- *WhoAm 92*
Woodring, Harry Hines 1887-1967 *BioIn 17*
Woodring, John Olmer, Jr. 1947- *WhoE 93*
Woodring, Thomas Joseph 1953- *WhoE 93*
Woodroffe, Enrique Antonio 1950- *WhoSSW 93*
Woodroffe, Patrick 1940- *ScF&FL 92*
Woodrow, Bill *BioIn 17*
Woodrow, Hal Brent *Law&B 92*
Woodrow, James Richard 1933- *St&PR 93*
Woodrow, Murray 1925-1991 *BioIn 17*
Woodrow, Nancy Mann Waddel 1866?-1935 *AmWomPl*
Woodrow, Robert Elliot 1941- *St&PR 93*
Woodrow, Susan M. *Law&B 92*
Woodrow, Terry *ScF&FL 92*
Woodruff, Abner 1767-1842 *BioIn 17*
Woodruff, Anne Marie 1966- *WhoSSW 93*
Woodruff, Asahel D. 1904- *BioIn 17*
Woodruff, Chivers Richard, Jr. 1944- *WhoSSW 93*
Woodruff, Dan *MiSFD 9*
Woodruff, David H. 1930- *St&PR 93*
Woodruff, David Philip *WhoScE 91-1*
Woodruff, David Phillip 1944- *WhoWor 93*
Woodruff, Elvira *ScF&FL 92*
Woodruff, Elvira 1951- *ConAu 138, SmATA 70 [port]*
Woodruff, Eugene Sidney 1931- *St&PR 93*
Woodruff, Flora Campbell *AmWomPl*
Woodruff, Gene Lowry 1934- *WhoAm 92*
Woodruff, George Washington 1864-1934 *BiDAMSp 1989*
Woodruff, Georgia Delores 1926- *WhoAmW 93*
Woodruff, Helen S. *AmWomPl*
Woodruff, Howard Thomas 1961- *WhoWor 93*
Woodruff, J. Knox 1910- *St&PR 93*
Woodruff, James Arthur 1943- *St&PR 93*
Woodruff, James Thurman 1920- *St&PR 93*
Woodruff, Jeff Robert 1943- *WhoWor 93*
Woodruff, John, Mrs. *AmWomPl*
Woodruff, John David, Jr. *Law&B 92*
Woodruff, Judith Marie 1953- *WhoAmW 93*
Woodruff, Judson Sage 1925- *WhoAm 92*
Woodruff, Judy 1946- *JrnUS*
Woodruff, Judy Carline 1946- *WhoAm 92*
Woodruff, Juliette Baldwin 1943- *WhoSSW 93*
Woodruff, K. Brent d1991 *BioIn 17*
Woodruff, Kathryn Elaine 1940- *WhoAmW 93, WhoWor 93*
Woodruff, Lawrence Theodore 1945- *St&PR 93*
Woodruff, Martha Joyce 1941- *WhoSSW 93*
Woodruff, Michael Lester 1947- *WhoSSW 93*
Woodruff, Myra de Haven d1992 *NewYTBS 92*
Woodruff, Myra deHaven 1896-1992 *BioIn 17*
Woodruff, Neil Parker 1919- *WhoAm 92*
Woodruff, Patricia 1945- *WhoAm 92*
Woodruff, Paul Bestor 1943- *WhoAm 92, WhoSSW 93*
Woodruff, Paul H. 1937- *St&PR 93*
Woodruff, Paul Harrison 1937- *WhoAm 92, WhoE 93*
Woodruff, Samuel M. *Law&B 92*
Woodruff, Sandra Lorraine *WhoAmW 93*
Woodruff, Stuart C. *ScF&FL 92*
Woodruff, Thomas Ellis 1921- *WhoAm 92*
Woodruff, Truman Owen 1925- *WhoAm 92*
Woodruff, Virginia *WhoAm 92, WhoAmW 93*
Woodruff, Wilford 1807-1898 *BioIn 17*
Woodruff, William 1916- *WhoSSW 93*
Woodrum, Douglas N. 1957- *St&PR 93*
Woodrum, Patricia Ann 1941- *WhoAm 92, WhoAmW 93, WhoSSW 93*
Woodrum, Robert L. 1945- *St&PR 93*
Woodrum, Robert Lee 1945- *WhoAm 92*
Woods, Alfred David Braine 1932- *WhoWor 93*
Woods, Alfred Lloyd 1944- *WhoWrEP 92*
Woods, Alice *AmWomPl*
Woods, Barbara Ann 1943- *WhoAmW 93*
Woods, Barry Alan 1942- *WhoWor 93*
Woods, Bernadette *Law&B 92*
Woods, Bill 1947- *St&PR 93*
Woods, Bruce Walter 1947- *WhoAm 92*
Woods, Bryan Tighe 1936- *WhoAm 92*
Woods, Carol G. 1958- *WhoSSW 93*
Woods, Charles G. 1953- *WhoE 93*
Woods, Charlotte O. 1942- *St&PR 93*
Woods, Chris F. 1924- *St&PR 93*
Woods, Christopher Lee 1950- *WhoWrEP 92*
Woods, Daniel d1992 *NewYTBS 92*
Woods, Daniel E. d1992 *BioIn 17*
Woods, David John 1946- *WhoUN 92*
Woods, David M. *Law&B 92*
Woods, Dick H., Jr. *Law&B 92*
Woods, Donald 1933- *BioIn 17*
Woods, Donald Peter 1911- *WhoWor 93*
Woods, Donald W. d1992 *NewYTBS 92*
Woods, Dorothy Jane 1921- *WhoAmW 93*
Woods, Edward Richard 1943- *St&PR 93*
Woods, Edward V. *WhoAm 92*
Woods, Eldrick *BioIn 17*
Woods, Elizabeth 1940- *WhoCanL 92*
Woods, Ellen Louise 1960- *WhoAmW 93*
Woods, Frances *AmWomPl*
Woods, Frank A. 1940- *St&PR 93*
Woods, Frederick Conrad 1916- *WhoSSW 93*
Woods, George A(llan) 1926- *DcAmChF 1960*
Woods, Gerald Marion Irwin 1947- *WhoEmL 93*
Woods, Gerald Ray *Law&B 92*
Woods, Gerald Wayne 1946- *WhoAm 92*
Woods, Geraldine 1966- *WhoAmW 93*
Woods, Geraldine Pittman *WhoAm 92*
Woods, Grant *WhoAm 92*
Woods, Granville 1856-1910 *BioIn 17*
Woods, Gurdon Grant 1915- *WhoAm 92*
Woods, Harriett Ruth 1927- *WhoAm 92, WhoAmW 93*
Woods, Henry 1918- *WhoAm 92, WhoSSW 93*
Woods, Isa Lou *WhoWrEP 92*
Woods, J. Michael 1949- *St&PR 93*
Woods, J. P. 1950- *WhoE 93, WhoEmL 93, WhoSSW 93, WhoWor 93*
Woods, Jack *ScF&FL 92*
Woods, James *BioIn 17*
Woods, James 1947- *HolBB [port]*
Woods, James D. 1931- *St&PR 93*
Woods, James Dudley 1931- *WhoAm 92, WhoSSW 93*
Woods, James E. 1939- *St&PR 93*
Woods, James Howard 1947- *WhoAm 92*
Woods, James L. *Law&B 92*
Woods, James Watson, Jr. 1918- *WhoAm 92*
Woods, Jane Haycock 1946- *WhoAmW 93*
Woods, Janet Lee 1949- *WhoAmW 93*
Woods, Janis Hamrick 1945- *WhoAmW 93*
Woods, Joel Grant 1954- *WhoAm 92*
Woods, John *WhoScE 91-1*
Woods, John Cahal 1955- *WhoSSW 93*
Woods, John D. 1939- *WhoScE 91-1*
Woods, John Elmer 1929- *WhoAm 92*
Woods, John Joseph 1937- *St&PR 93*
Woods, John L. *Law&B 92*
Woods, John Lucius 1912- *WhoAm 92*
Woods, John Merle 1943- *WhoSSW 93, WhoWor 93*
Woods, John Odin Wentworth 1937- *WhoAsAP 91*
Woods, John W. 1931- *St&PR 93*
Woods, John William 1912- *WhoAm 92*
Woods, John William 1943- *WhoAm 92, WhoE 93*
Woods, John William, Jr. 1963- *WhoE 93*
Woods, John Witherspoon 1931- *WhoAm 92, WhoSSW 93*
Woods, Judith Fell 1946- *WhoE 93*
Woods, Julie Chenault- *BioIn 17*
Woods, K.G. *WhoScE 91-1*
Woods, Karen Marguerite 1945- *WhoAmW 93*
Woods, Kathleen Mary 1946- *WhoAmW 93*
Woods, Kay *Law&B 92*
Woods, Keith F. *Law&B 92*
Woods, Kenneth 1954- *WhoWrEP 92*
Woods, Kenneth M. 1935- *St&PR 93*
Woods, Kristina M. *Law&B 92*
Woods, Laurie 1947- *WhoAmW 93*
Woods, Lawrence Milton 1932- *St&PR 93, WhoAm 92*
Woods, Leonard 1774-1854 *BioIn 17*
Woods, Leslie Colin *WhoScE 91-1*
Woods, M. Malloy 1951- *St&PR 93*
Woods, Marcus E. *Law&B 92*
Woods, Marcus E. 1930- *St&PR 93*
Woods, Marcus Eugene 1930- *WhoAm 92*
Woods, Marjorie *AmWomPl*
Woods, Mary Kay 1960- *WhoE 93*

Woods, Merilyn Baron 1927- *WhoAmW 93, WhoE 93*
Woods, Michael 1952- *ConAu 137*
Woods, Millicent Wasell 1946- *WhoAm 92, WhoAmW 93*
Woods, Nat *MajAI*
Woods, Norman E., Jr. 1943- *St&PR 93*
Woods, Pendleton 1923- *WhoSSW 93, WhoWor 93*
Woods, Peter T. 1942- *WhoScE 91-1*
Woods, Phil *BioIn 17*
Woods, Philip Wells 1931- *WhoAm 92*
Woods, R. Glen *Law&B 92*
Woods, Raymond George, Jr. 1958- *WhoE 93*
Woods, Raymond Lynn 1931- *WhoSSW 93*
Woods, Reginald Foster 1939- *WhoAm 92*
Woods, Richard James 1939- *WhoAm 92*
Woods, Richard S. *Law&B 92*
Woods, Richard Seavey 1919- *WhoAm 92*
Woods, Robert Archer 1920- *WhoAm 92*
Woods, Robert Lawrence 1911- *WhoWor 93*
Woods, Robert Leslie 1947- *WhoAsAP 91*
Woods, Roberta Everett 1949- *WhoAmW 93*
Woods, Robin R. *Law&B 92*
Woods, Rodney Ian 1941- *WhoAm 92*
Woods, Rose Mary 1917- *WhoAm 92*
Woods, Sam 1892-1953 *BioIn 17*
Woods, Samuel Hubert, Jr. 1926- *WhoSSW 93*
Woods, Sandra Kay 1944- *St&PR 93, WhoAmW 93*
Woods, Stephanie *BioIn 17*
Woods, Stephanie Elise Ellison 1962- *WhoAmW 93, WhoEmL 93*
Woods, Steven Alan 1952- *St&PR 93*
Woods, Stuart 1938- *ScF&FL 92*
Woods, Susanne 1943- *WhoAm 92, WhoAmW 93*
Woods, Thomas Brian 1938- *WhoWor 93*
Woods, Tiger *BioIn 17*
Woods, Virna 1864-1903 *AmWomPl*
Woods, W.A. *WhoScE 91-1*
Woods, Walter Earl 1944- *WhoE 93*
Woods, Walter Ralph 1931- *WhoAm 92*
Woods, Ward Wilson, Jr. 1942- *WhoAm 92*
Woods, Wendell David 1932- *WhoSSW 93*
Woods, William A. 1945- *St&PR 93*
Woods, William Burnham 1824-1887 *OxCSupC [port]*
Woods, William Ellis 1917- *WhoAm 92*
Woodside, Howard Bush 1921- *St&PR 93*
Woodside, John Archibald 1781-1852 *BioIn 17*
Woodside, Kenneth Hall 1938- *WhoSSW 93*
Woodside, Lisa Nicole 1944- *WhoAmW 93, WhoE 93*
Woodside, Robert Elmer 1904- *WhoAm 92*
Woodside, Samuel Talgart 1953- *St&PR 93*
Woodside, Sharon Clark *Law&B 92*
Woodside, William S. 1922- *St&PR 93*
Woodside, William Stewart 1922- *WhoAm 92*
Wood-Smith, Donald 1931- *WhoWor 93*
Woodson, Alfred F. 1952- *St&PR 93*
Woodson, Benjamin N. 1908- *St&PR 93, WhoIns 93*
Woodson, Benjamin Nelson, III 1908- *WhoAm 92*
Woodson, Brenda G. *Law&B 92*
Woodson, Carter Godwin 1875-1950 *BioIn 17, EncAACR*
Woodson, Carter Goodwin 1875-1950 *BlkAuII 92*
Woodson, Daniel 1824-1894 *BioIn 17*
Woodson, David 1934- *St&PR 93*
Woodson, Dennis Marshall, II 1949- *WhoSSW 93*
Woodson, Ernie *BioIn 17*
Woodson, Herbert Horace 1925- *WhoAm 92*
Woodson, Jacqueline 1964- *BlkAuII 92*
Woodson, James Charles 1942- *St&PR 93*
Woodson, Jane Holt 1937- *WhoAmW 93*
Woodson, Meg *BioIn 17*
Woodson, Melinda Beth 1952- *St&PR 93*
Woodson, Oscar *BioIn 17*
Woodson, Peggie *BioIn 17*
Woodson, Richard Peyton, III 1923- *St&PR 93, WhoAm 92*
Woodson, Robert Ray 1932- *St&PR 93*
Woodson, Thomas 1931- *ScF&FL 92*
Woodson-Corley, Shelley Cecile 1961- *WhoE 93*
Woodson-Howard, Marlene Erdley 1937- *WhoAmW 93*
Woods-Smith, Sybil 1954- *WhoWrEP 92*
Woodsworth, Anne 1941- *WhoAm 92, WhoAmW 93, WhoE 93*
Woodsworth, James Shaver 1874-1942 *DcTwHis*
Woodul, Carolyn Pauline 1942- *WhoAmW 93*
Woodward, Aaron Alphonso, III 1947- *WhoE 93, WhoWor 93*
Woodward, Amy Lois *WhoAmW 93*
Woodward, Anne Spivey 1949- *WhoAm 92*
Woodward, Bob 1943- *BioIn 17, JrnUS*
Woodward, Brian *BioIn 17*
Woodward, C. Vann 1908- *BioIn 17, WhoAm 92*
Woodward, C(omer) Vann 1908- *WhoWrEP 92*
Woodward, Charles C. M. 1929- *St&PR 93*
Woodward, Comer Vann 1908- *BioIn 17*
Woodward, Daniel Holt 1931- *WhoAm 92*
Woodward, David Luther 1942- *WhoSSW 93*
Woodward, Diana d1989 *BioIn 17*
Woodward, Edward 1930- *WhoAm 92*
Woodward, Edwin Geoffrey *WhoScE 91-1*
Woodward, Eugenie *AmWomPl*
Woodward, F. Robert, Jr. 1936- *St&PR 93*
Woodward, Forrest J., II 1942- *St&PR 93*
Woodward, Fred *BioIn 17*
Woodward, Frederick Miller 1943- *WhoAm 92*
Woodward, George W. 1809-1875 *OxCSupC*
Woodward, Gilbert Leavitt 1917- *WhoE 93*
Woodward, Halbert Owen 1918- *WhoAm 92*
Woodward, Helen De Long 1896- *WhoWrEP 92*
Woodward, Herbert Norton 1911- *St&PR 93*
Woodward, Isabel Avila 1906- *WhoAmW 93, WhoWor 93*
Woodward, J.C. *WhoScE 91-1*
Woodward, J. Taylor, III *Law&B 92*
Woodward, J. Taylor, III 1940- *St&PR 93*
Woodward, James Arthur 1934- *St&PR 93*
Woodward, James Hoyt 1939- *WhoAm 92*
Woodward, James Hoyt, Jr. 1939- *WhoSSW 93*
Woodward, Jen Simone 1960- *WhoWor 93*
Woodward, Joanne 1930- *BioIn 17, IntDcF 2-3, MiSFD 9*
Woodward, Joanne Gignilliat 1930- *WhoAm 92, WhoAmW 93*
Woodward, John F. *WhoScE 91-1*
Woodward, John Forster 1932- *BioIn 17*
Woodward, John Robert *WhoScE 91-1*
Woodward, John Taylor, III 1940- *WhoAm 92, WhoE 93*
Woodward, Kirk 1947- *WhoE 93*
Woodward, Lester Ray 1932- *WhoAm 92*
Woodward, Linda L. 1949- *St&PR 93*
Woodward, M. Cabell, Jr. 1929- *St&PR 93, WhoAm 92*
Woodward, Madison Truman, Jr. 1908- *WhoAm 92, WhoWor 93*
Woodward, Mary Dodge 1826-1890 *BioIn 17*
Woodward, Michael Clifford 1955- *WhoWor 93*
Woodward, Michael Dean 1958- *WhoWor 93*
Woodward, Michael R. 1946- *St&PR 93*
Woodward, Patricia Beal 1949- *WhoWrEP 92*
Woodward, Ralph Lee, Jr. 1934- *WhoAm 92, WhoWrEP 92*
Woodward, Richard B. *St&PR 93*
Woodward, Richard H., Jr. 1947- *St&PR 93*
Woodward, Richard Hollis, Jr. 1947- *WhoAm 92*
Woodward, Richard Joseph, Jr. 1907- *WhoAm 92, WhoWor 93*
Woodward, Robert A. 1947- *WhoE 93*
Woodward, Robert D. 1920- *St&PR 93*
Woodward, Robert Forbes 1908- *WhoAm 92*
Woodward, Robert J., Jr. 1941- *WhoAm 92*
Woodward, Robert Upshur 1943- *NewYTBS 92 [port], WhoAm 92, WhoE 93, WhoWrEP 92*
Woodward, Roger (Robert) 1942- *Baker 92*
Woodward, Ruth M. *AmWomPl*
Woodward, Sandy 1932- *BioIn 17*
Woodward, Stanley 1899-1992 *CurBio 92N*
Woodward, Stanley, Sr. d1992 *NewYTBS 92*
Woodward, Susan Ellen 1949- *WhoAm 92, WhoAmW 93*
Woodward, Theodore Englar 1914- *WhoAm 92*
Woodward, Thomas Aiken 1933- *WhoAm 92*
Woodward, Thomas Morgan 1925- *WhoAm 92, WhoWor 93*
Woodward, Wayne William 1930- *WhoSSW 93*
Woodward, William P. 1939- *St&PR 93*
Woodwell, George Masters 1928- *WhoAm 92*
Woodwell, Joseph David 1938- *St&PR 93*
Woodwell, Margot Bell 1936- *WhoE 93*
Woodworth, Donald Duryea 1935- *WhoE 93, WhoWor 93*
Woodworth, G(eorge) Wallace 1902-1969 *Baker 92*
Woodworth, Mary L. d1986 *BioIn 17*
Woodworth, Peter Walker 1946- *St&PR 93*
Woodworth, Ralph Leon 1933- *WhoWrEP 92*
Woodworth, Robert Hugo 1902-1990 *BioIn 17*
Woodworth, Samuel 1784-1842 *JrnUS*
Woody, C.O. *St&PR 93*
Woody, Carol Clayman 1949- *WhoAmW 93*
Woody, Claudia LaVergne 1955- *WhoSSW 93*
Woody, Clyde Woodrow 1920- *WhoSSW 93, WhoWor 93*
Woody, Craig L. 1951- *WhoE 93*
Woody, Jacquelyn Kay 1955- *WhoAmW 93*
Woody, John Frederick 1941- *WhoWor 93*
Woody, Julie 1939- *WhoAmW 93*
Woody, Leroy William 1938- *WhoSSW 93*
Woody, Ronnie *BioIn 17*
Woody, Victor Morton, III 1943- *WhoSSW 93*
Woody, Walter Ruffin, Jr. 1933- *St&PR 93*
Woodyard, Carolyn Beatrice 1954- *WhoAmW 93*
Woodyard, Jeffrey Lynn 1957- *WhoE 93*
Woodyard, Thomas William 1956- *WhoSSW 93*
Woodyshek, J. Daniel 1948- *WhoE 93*
Woofter, R.D. 1923- *St&PR 93, WhoAm 92*
Wool, Abbe *MiSFD 9*
Wool, Harlene E. 1930- *St&PR 93*
Wool, John Ellis 1784-1869 *HarEnMi*
Wool, Marvin S. 1928- *St&PR 93*
Woolam, Gerald Lynn 1937- *WhoAm 92*
Woolard, Beulah Bailey *AmWomPl*
Woolard, Edgar S., Jr. 1934- *WhoAm 92, WhoE 93, WhoWor 93*
Woolard, Edgar Smith, Jr. 1934- *St&PR 93*
Woolard, Roderick Staton 1950- *St&PR 93*
Woolard, William Leon 1931- *WhoAm 92, WhoSSW 93*
Woolbert, Richard E. 1933- *St&PR 93*
Woolcock, Alan R. 1944- *St&PR 93*
Wooldredge, William Dunbar 1937- *WhoAm 92*
Wooldridge, Bruce Alan 1939- *St&PR 93*
Wooldridge, David (Humphry Michael) 1927- *Baker 92*
Wooldridge, Dean Everett 1913- *WhoAm 92*
Wooldridge, H(arry) E(llis) 1845-1917 *Baker 92*
Wooldridge, Helene 1913- *WhoAmW 93*
Wooldridge, Jerry Evan 1937- *WhoIns 93*
Wooldridge, John R. 1939- *St&PR 93*
Wooldridge, Michael Richard Lewis 1956- *WhoAsAP 91*
Wooldridge, Raymond E. *St&PR 93*
Wooldridge, Tim L. 1960- *WhoSSW 93*
Wooldridge, William C. *Law&B 92*
Wooldridge, William Charles 1943- *WhoSSW 93*
Woolery, Chuck *BioIn 17*
Woolery, Donald Ray 1933- *WhoSSW 93*
Woolery, George William 1931- *WhoWrEP 92*
Woolery, Tim Lynn 1956- *WhoSSW 93*
Woolever, Naomi Louise 1922- *WhoAm 92, WhoWrEP 92*
Woolever, Patricia 1938- *WhoAmW 93*
Wooley, Allan Delmas 1936- *WhoE 93*
Wooley, Bruce Allen 1943- *WhoAm 92*
Wooley, Donald Alan 1926- *WhoAm 92*
Wooley, John 1949- *ScF&FL 92*
Wooley, John P. 1928- *St&PR 93*
Wooley, Olive F. *AmWomPl*
Wooley, R. Randall, II *Law&B 92*
Wooley, Richard Earl 1965- *WhoE 93*
Woolf, Benjamin Edward 1836-1901 *Baker 92*
Woolf, Cecil *ScF&FL 92*
Woolf, Harry 1923- *WhoAm 92, WhoE 93*
Woolf, Howard 1947- *WhoE 93*
Woolf, Jack 1936- *St&PR 93*
Woolf, Jack J. 1933- *St&PR 93*
Woolf, John 1908-1980 *BioIn 17*
Woolf, Leonard 1880-1969 *BioIn 17, DcLB DS10*
Woolf, Leonard S(idney) 1880-1969 *ConAu 39NR*
Woolf, Nancy C. *Law&B 92*
Woolf, Neville *WhoScE 91-1*
Woolf, Paul Daniel 1942- *WhoE 93*
Woolf, Robert Leslie, Jr. 1929- *St&PR 93*
Woolf, Robert W. 1942- *St&PR 93*
Woolf, Ronald Alan *WhoSSW 93*
Woolf, Sheldon M. 1932- *St&PR 93*
Woolf, Virginia 1882-1941 *BioIn 17, DcLB DS10, MagSWL [port], WorLitC [port]*
Woolf, William B. 1927- *St&PR 93*
Woolf, William Blauvelt 1932- *WhoAm 92*
Woolfe, Terence J. *Law&B 92*
Woolfenden, Milton, Jr. 1925- *WhoAm 92*
Woolfenden, William Edward 1918- *WhoAm 92*
Woolfolk, Anita Elizabeth 1947- *WhoAmW 93*
Woolfolk, Joanne *ScF&FL 92*
Woolfolk, Robert M. 1923- *St&PR 93*
Woolfolk, Robert William 1937- *WhoSSW 93*
Woolfolk, William 1917- *ScF&FL 92*
Woolford, John R. 1934- *St&PR 93*
Woolford, John Riddick, Jr. 1934- *WhoAm 92*
Woolfson, Michael Mark *WhoScE 91-1*
Woolheater, Robert Leroy 1930- *St&PR 93, WhoAm 92*
Woolhiser, David Arthur 1932- *WhoAm 92*
Woolhouse, H. *WhoScE 91-1*
Woollacott, Angela Mary 1955- *WhoAmW 93*
Woollacott, Robert A. 1949- *St&PR 93*
Woollaston, Alan Keith 1932- *WhoScE 91-1*
Woollaston, Philip T.E. 1944- *WhoUN 92*
Woollaston, Philip Tosswill Edmond 1944- *WhoAsAP 91*
Woollcott, Alexander 1887-1943 *BioIn 17, JrnUS*
Woollen, Evans 1927- *WhoAm 92*
Woollen, (Charles) Russell 1923- *Baker 92*
Woollett, Henri Edouard 1864-1936 *Baker 92*
Woolley, Catherine 1904- *WhoAm 92, WhoAmW 93, WhoWor 93*
Woolley, Catherine An 1952- *WhoSSW 93*
Woolley, Celia Parker 1848-1918 *AmWomPl*
Woolley, Clara Virginia 1938- *WhoAmW 93*
Woolley, Donna P. 1926- *St&PR 93*
Woolley, Donna Pearl 1926- *WhoAmW 93*
Woolley, George Walter 1904- *WhoAm 92*
Woolley, John Edward 1935- *WhoE 93*
Woolley, Kenneth Frank 1933- *WhoWor 93*
Woolley, Margaret Anne 1946- *WhoAmW 93*
Woolley, Mary Elizabeth 1947- *WhoAm 92*
Woolley, Michael W. 1947- *St&PR 93*
Woolley, Persia 1935- *ScF&FL 92*
Woolley, Richard Guy *WhoScE 91-1*
Woolley, Robert Carleton 1944- *WhoAm 92*
Woolley, Samuel H. 1909- *St&PR 93*
Woolley, Steven E. 1943- *WhoE 93*
Woolley, Victor H. 1942- *St&PR 93*
Woolley, W.D. *WhoScE 91-1*
Woollons, David John *WhoScE 91-1*
Woolls, (Esther) Blanche 1935- *ConAu 39NR*
Woolls, Esther Blanche 1935- *WhoAm 92*
Woolls, Patricia *Law&B 92*
Woolman, C. E. 1889-1966 *EncABHB 8 [port]*
Woolman, Maurice John 1953- *WhoEmL 93*
Woolman, Michael Louis 1944- *St&PR 93*
Woolman, Patricia Gail 1950- *WhoAmW 93*
Woolner, James L., Jr. *Law&B 92*
Woolpert, Laura Diane 1960- *WhoAmW 93, WhoWor 93*
Woolpert, Mary Elizabeth 1926- *St&PR 93*
Woolrich, Cornell 1903-1968 *ScF&FL 92*
Woolsey, David Arthur 1941- *WhoAm 92*
Woolsey, Frederick William 1919- *WhoAm 92*
Woolsey, James C. 1949- *St&PR 93*
Woolsey, Janette 1904-1989 *ScF&FL 92*
Woolsey, John Munro, Jr. 1916- *WhoAm 92*
Woolsey, Lynn *NewYTBS 92*
Woolsey, R. James 1941- *BioIn 17*
Woolsey, R. James, Jr. 1941- *WhoAm 92*
Woolsey, Robert 1889-1938 *See* Wheeler, Bert 1895-1968 & Woolsey, Robert 1889-1938 *QDrFCA 92*
Woolsey, Robert Eugene Donald 1936- *WhoAm 92*
Woolsey, Sarah Chauncey 1835-1905 *AmWomPl*
Woolson, Constance Fenimore 1840-1894 *AmWomWr 92*
Woolson, Lawrence B. 1929- *St&PR 93*

Woolston, James R. *Law&B 92*
Woolston-Catlin, Marian 1931- *WhoE 93*
Woolums, James, Jr. 1959- *WhoSSW 93*
Woolums, Margaret Carmichael 1935- *WhoSSW 93*
Woolverton, Dalton L. 1938- *St&PR 93*
Woolverton, John J., Jr. 1905- *St&PR 93*
Woolverton, Linda *ScF&FL 92*
Woolverton, Paul 1930- *WhoE 93*
Woolverton, William H. *Law&B 92*
Woolwich, Elliott William 1939- *WhoE 93*
Woolwine, George M. 1947- *St&PR 93*
Woolwine, Richard *St&PR 93*
Woon, Paul Sam 1942- *WhoSSW 93*
Woon See Chin 1944- *WhoAsAP 91*
Woontner, Marc Oliver 1946- *St&PR 93*
Woosley, Clarence Edgar, Jr. 1936- *WhoSSW 93*
Woosley, Patrick G. *Law&B 92*
Woosnam, Ian Harold 1958- *WhoAm 92, WhoWor 93*
Woosnam, Richard Edward 1942- *WhoE 93*
Wooster, Ann-Sargent *WhoE 93*
Wooster, Doris Irene Christensen 1937- *WhoSSW 93*
Wooster, Robert 1956- *WhoAm 92*
Wooster, Warren Scriver 1921- *WhoAm 92*
Wootan, Gerald Don 1944- *WhoSSW 93*
Wooten, Arthur Lee 1922-1990 *BioIn 17*
Wooten, Brenda Southard 1952- *WhoAmW 93*
Wooten, Cecil Aaron 1924- *WhoAm 92*
Wooten, Frank Thomas 1935- *St&PR 93, WhoAm 92*
Wooten, Frederick Oliver 1928- *WhoAm 92*
Wooten, James H., Jr. *Law&B 92*
Wooten, James Mccormick 1920- *St&PR 93*
Wooten, William D. 1951- *St&PR 93*
Wooten, William James 1924- *St&PR 93*
Wooten-Bryant, Helen Catherine 1940- *WhoWor 93*
Wooten-Rhines, Maryann 1951- *WhoSSW 93*
Wooters, J.M. *St&PR 93*
Wooton, E.J. 1953- *St&PR 93*
Wooton, Elmer Ottis 1865-1945 *BioIn 17*
Wooton, John R. *Law&B 92*
Wooton, Turner 1770?-1797 *BioIn 17*
Wootten, Henry Alwyn 1948- *WhoSSW 93*
Wootten, John Robert 1929- *WhoSSW 93*
Wootten, Rike Ditzler 1932- *St&PR 93*
Wootton, Alan James *WhoScE 91-1*
Wootton, Barbara 1897-1988 *ScF&FL 92*
Wootton, Brookii E. 1965- *WhoAmW 93, WhoWor 93*
Wootton, Charles Greenwood 1924- *WhoAm 92*
Wootton, Clyde Archer *Law&B 92*
Wootton, L.R. *WhoScE 91-1*
Wootton, Mack Edward 1937- *WhoAm 92*
Wootton, Richard *WhoScE 91-1*
Wootton, Thomas Alexander *Law&B 92*
Worbs, Hans Christoph 1927- *Baker 92*
Worcel, Abraham 1938-1989 *BioIn 17*
Worcester, Dean Conant 1866-1924 *IntDcAn*
Worcester, Donald Emmet 1915- *WhoAm 92, WhoSSW 93*
Worcester, Gurdon S(altonstall) 1897- *DcAmChF 1960*
Worcester, Harris Eugene 1950- *WhoSSW 93*
Worcester, Maude Lavon *AmWomPl*
Worcester, Theodore E. *Law&B 92*
Worchel, Stephen 1946- *ConAu 37NR*
Word, Kathryn Mary Coe 1951- *WhoAmW 93*
Word, Reuben Mabry 1922- *WhoSSW 93*
Word, Thomas S., Jr. 1938- *WhoAm 92*
Word, Virginia Steele 1951- *WhoAmW 93*
Word, Weldon *BioIn 17*
Wordeman, Ann Marie 1947- *WhoE 93*
Worden, Alfred Merrill 1932- *WhoAm 92*
Worden, Barbara Standley 1942- *WhoSSW 93*
Worden, Hank d1992 *NewYTBS 92*
Worden, John Robert 1947- *St&PR 93*
Worden, Joseph R. *Law&B 92*
Worden, Katharine Cole 1925- *WhoAmW 93, WhoE 93, WhoWor 93*
Worden, Robert W. 1943- *St&PR 93*
Worden, Rolfe Allan 1939- *WhoAm 92*
Worden, Ronald Dean 1938- *WhoSSW 93*
Worden, Roxane F. 1954- *WhoAmW 93*
Worden, William C. *Law&B 92*
Wordsworth, Dorothy 1771-1855 *BioIn 17*
Wordsworth, Elizabeth 1840-1932 *BioIn 17*
Wordsworth, Iris B. 1944- *St&PR 93*
Wordsworth, William 1770-1850 *BioIn 17, MagSWL [port], NinCLC 38 [port], WorLitC [port]*
Wordsworth, William (Brocklesby) 1908-1988 *Baker 92*
Worell, Judith P. *WhoAm 92*
Worenklein, Jacob Joshua 1948- *WhoAm 92, WhoEmL 93*
Wores, Theodore 1859?-1939 *BioIn 17*
Work, Alvin R. 1948- *St&PR 93*
Work, Bruce Van Syoc 1942- *WhoAm 92*
Work, Chris Herbert *WhoAsAP 91*
Work, Clyde Everette 1924- *WhoE 93*
Work, Henry Clay 1832-1884 *Baker 92*
Work, Henry Harcus 1911- *WhoAm 92*
Work, Hubert 1860-1942 *BioIn 17, PolPar*
Work, Jane Allen 1916- *WhoE 93*
Work, Jane Magruder 1927- *WhoAmW 93*
Work, John David 1933- *St&PR 93*
Work, Monroe Nathan 1866-1945 *EncAACR*
Work, Phillip L. 1933- *St&PR 93*
Work, William 1923- *WhoAm 92*
Work, William Henry 1948- *WhoE 93*
Workeneh, Debra H. *Law&B 92*
Workinger, Paul Edward 1929- *St&PR 93*
Workley, Ida 1934- *WhoE 93*
Workman, Chuck *MiSFD 9*
Workman, Douglas Alex 1963- *WhoE 93*
Workman, Fanny Bullock 1859-1925 *Expl 93*
Workman, Gale Ann 1954- *WhoWrEP 92*
Workman, George Henry 1939- *WhoSSW 93, WhoWor 93*
Workman, Helen Chaffee 1868- *AmWomPl*
Workman, Jerome James, Jr. 1952- *WhoWor 93*
Workman, John Mitchell 1949- *WhoWor 93*
Workman, Kenneth T. 1941- *St&PR 93*
Workman, Larry Eugene 1943- *St&PR 93*
Workman, Margaret Lee 1947- *WhoAm 92, WhoAmW 93, WhoSSW 93*
Workman, Mary J. *Law&B 92*
Workman, Melvin C., Jr. 1947- *St&PR 93*
Workman, Paul *WhoScE 91-1*
Workman, William 1940- *Baker 92*
Workman, William Douglas, III 1940- *WhoSSW 93*
Works, George A. 1877-1957 *BioIn 17*
Works, John Hamilton, Jr. *Law&B 92*
Works, John Hamilton, Jr. 1954- *WhoE 93, WhoWor 93*
Works, Robert Jefferson 1952- *St&PR 93*
Workstus, John Paul, Jr. 1954- *St&PR 93*
Worku, Tsagga Amlak 1936- *WhoUN 92*
Worley, Bland Wallace 1917- *St&PR 93, WhoAm 92, WhoSSW 93*
Worley, Charlotte Coker 1925- *WhoWor 93*
Worley, David Clark *Law&B 92*
Worley, Elaine *BioIn 17*
Worley, Floyd Leonard 1937- *St&PR 93*
Worley, Gordon Roger 1919- *WhoAm 92*
Worley, Jeff Robert 1947- *WhoWrEP 92*
Worley, Karen Boyd 1952- *WhoAmW 93, WhoSSW 93*
Worley, Letitia W. *Law&B 92*
Worley, M. Keate *Law&B 92*
Worley, Merry Penelope 1949- *WhoAmW 93*
Worley, Ray Edward 1932- *WhoSSW 93*
Worley, Robert W., Jr. *Law&B 92*
Worley, Robert William, Jr. 1935- *WhoE 93, WhoWor 93*
Worman, Howard Jay 1959- *WhoE 93*
Wormann, Horst 1948- *WhoScE 91-3*
Wormet, H. Arthur 1921- *St&PR 93*
Wormhoudt, Arthur Louis 1917- *WhoWrEP 92*
Wormhoudt, Pearl Shinn 1915- *WhoAmW 93*
Wormington, Robert Joseph 1926- *St&PR 93*
Wormley, Lillian Delores 1951- *WhoAmW 93*
Wormser, Andre (Alphonse-Toussaint) 1851-1926 *Baker 92*
Wormser, Eric M. 1921- *St&PR 93*
Wormser, Eric Max 1921- *WhoE 93*
Wormser, Florine R. *AmWomPl*
Wormser, Richard 1908-1977 *ScF&FL 92*
Wormser, Richard (Edward) 1908- *DcAmChF 1960*
Wormwood, Dale *St&PR 93*
Wormwood, Edyth M. *AmWomPl*
Wormwood, Richard Naughton 1936- *WhoWor 93*
Worner, Karl(heinz) H(einrich) 1910-1969 *Baker 92*
Worner, Lloyd Edson 1918- *WhoAm 92*
Worner, Manfred 1934- *WhoWor 93*
Worner, Ruby Kathryn 1900- *WhoAmW 93*
Worning, Ib 1922- *WhoScE 91-2*
Wornom, Samuel J. 1942- *St&PR 93*
Worona, Mikolaj 1937- *WhoScE 91-4*
Woroniak, Alexander 1922- *WhoAm 92*
Woronick, Charles Louis 1930- *WhoE 93*
Woroniecki, Jan 1944- *WhoWor 93*
Woronoff, Wladimir 1903-1980 *Baker 92*
Worowski, Krzysztof 1936- *WhoScE 91-4*
Worowski, Steven 1952- *WhoWrEP 92*
Worp, Johannes 1821-1891 *Baker 92*
Worrall, Bruce K. 1951- *St&PR 93*
Worrall, Denis John 1935- *WhoAfr*
Worrall, Margaret Howard 1942- *WhoWrEP 92*
Worrell, Albert Cadwallader 1913- *WhoAm 92*
Worrell, Audrey Martiny 1935- *WhoAmW 93*
Worrell, Bernie *BioIn 17*
Worrell, Bill *BioIn 17*
Worrell, Billy Frank 1939- *WhoSSW 93*
Worrell, Cynthia Lee 1957- *WhoAmW 93*
Worrell, David W. *Law&B 92*
Worrell, Edna Randolph *AmWomPl*
Worrell, Jane Carson 1934- *WhoAmW 93*
Worrell, John, Sr. 1947- *St&PR 93*
Worrell, John R. 1951- *St&PR 93*
Worrell, Judy S. 1949- *WhoAmW 93*
Worrell, Richard Vernon 1931- *WhoWor 93*
Worrell, Rupert Delisle 1945- *WhoWor 93*
Worrell, Ruth Mougey *AmWomPl*
Worrell, Thomas E., Jr. *Law&B 92*
Worsdell, Jacoba Marlene 1943- *WhoAmW 93*
Worseck, Raymond Adams 1937- *WhoAm 92*
Worsfold, Paul John *WhoScE 91-1*
Worsham, Arch Douglas 1933- *WhoSSW 93*
Worsham, Betty 1923- *St&PR 93*
Worsham, Elizabeth Penry 1960- *WhoSSW 93*
Worsham, Fabian 1952- *WhoWrEP 92*
Worsham, James Everett *WhoAm 92*
Worsham, Jerry Doyle, II *Law&B 92*
Worsham, John Gibson, Jr. 1953- *WhoSSW 93*
Worsham, Lesa Marie Spacek 1950- *WhoAmW 93*
Worsham, Lew 1917-1990 *BioIn 17*
Worsham, Lewis Elmer, Jr. 1917-1990 *BiDAMSp 1989*
Worsham, Macklynn D. 1923- *St&PR 93*
Worsham, Shirley Barnes 1959- *WhoSSW 93*
Worsick, Andrew Colin *WhoScE 91-1*
Worsley, C. Dale 1948- *WhoWrEP 92*
Worsley, David E. *Law&B 92*
Worsley, John Clayton 1919- *WhoAm 92*
Worsley, Peter *WhoScE 91-1*
Worsoe-Schmidt, Peder M. 1926- *WhoScE 91-2*
Worst, Susan Gail 1964- *WhoE 93*
Worstell, Brenton Richard 1955- *St&PR 93*
Worstell, Michael R. 1938- *St&PR 93*
Worster, Merle C. d1990 *BioIn 17*
Worswick, Lisa *Law&B 92*
Worswick, Richard David 1946- *WhoScE 91-1*
Worswick, Todd *Law&B 92*
Worth, Aaron *MiSFD 9*
Worth, David *MiSFD 9*
Worth, Dorothy Janis 1939- *WhoWrEP 92*
Worth, Dorothy Williamson 1930- *WhoSSW 93*
Worth, Douglas Grey 1940- *WhoWrEP 92*
Worth, Gary J. *St&PR 93*
Worth, Gary James 1940- *WhoAm 92, WhoWor 93*
Worth, George John 1929- *WhoAm 92, WhoWrEP 92*
Worth, Irene 1916- *ConTFT 10, WhoAm 92, WhoAmW 93, WhoE 93*
Worth, Joseph C. 1949- *St&PR 93*
Worth, Mary Page 1924- *WhoAmW 93, WhoE 93*
Worth, Michael John 1946- *WhoE 93*
Worth, Nicholas 1855-1918 *BioIn 17*
Worth, Nicholas Edwin 1943- *St&PR 93*
Worth, Richard S. *BioIn 17*
Worth, Sidney Victor 1920- *St&PR 93*
Worth, Suzanne 1959- *WhoSSW 93*
Worth, Valerie *BioIn 17*
Worth, Valerie 1933- *MajAI [port], ScF&FL 92, SmATA 70 [port]*
Worth, Walter Fritz 1939- *St&PR 93*
Worth, William Jenkins 1794-1849 *HarEnMi*
Wortham, Claude Harry 1937- *WhoSSW 93, WhoWor 93*
Wortham, Lisa K. *Law&B 92*
Wortham, Robert John 1947- *WhoAm 92*
Worthan, Russell Lee 1937- *St&PR 93*
Worthen, Frederick P., Jr. 1946- *St&PR 93*
Worthen, John Edward 1933- *WhoAm 92*
Worthen, Thomas 1920- *St&PR 93*
Worthing, Carol Marie 1934- *WhoAmW 93*
Worthing, Ford B. *St&PR 93*
Worthing, Marcia Lynn 1943- *WhoAmW 93*
Worthing, Richard Westlake 1941- *WhoIns 93*
Worthington, Barbara Cavedo 1942- *WhoSSW 93*
Worthington, Barry K. 1954- *WhoE 93*
Worthington, Brian Stewart *WhoScE 91-1*
Worthington, Bruce R. *Law&B 92*
Worthington, C. Wayne 1923- *WhoAm 92*
Worthington, Charles Roy 1925- *WhoAm 92, WhoE 93*
Worthington, Donald R. 1946- *St&PR 93*
Worthington, George Marshall 1953- *WhoE 93*
Worthington, George Rhodes 1937- *WhoAm 92*
Worthington, James L. d1990 *BioIn 17*
Worthington, Janet Evans 1942- *WhoAmW 93*
Worthington, John R. *Law&B 92*
Worthington, John R. 1930- *St&PR 93*
Worthington, Kathy Ann *Law&B 92*
Worthington, Lorne R. 1938- *St&PR 93*
Worthington, Melvin Leroy 1937- *WhoAm 92, WhoSSW 93*
Worthington, Michael Hugh *WhoScE 91-1*
Worthington, O. Douglas 1949- *St&PR 93*
Worthington, Paul F. 1945- *WhoScE 91-1*
Worthington, Robert Melvin 1922- *WhoE 93*
Worthington, Stephen Alexander 1935- *St&PR 93*
Worthington, William Albert, III 1950- *WhoEmL 93, WhoSSW 93*
Worthington, William D. 1947- *WhoIns 93*
Worthley, Warren William 1935- *WhoAm 92*
Worthman, Moses 1911- *WhoE 93*
Worthy, Bill 1945- *WhoSSW 93*
Worthy, Dianne Hudson 1943- *WhoAmW 93*
Worthy, James *BioIn 17*
Worthy, James 1961- *WhoAm 92*
Worthy, James Ager 1961- *BiDAMSp 1989*
Worthy, James Carson 1910- *WhoAm 92*
Worthy, Jasper Fredrick 1928- *St&PR 93*
Worthy, Kenneth Martin 1920- *WhoAm 92*
Worthy, Patricia Morris 1944- *WhoAm 92*
Worthylake, Mary Moore 1904- *WhoWrEP 92*
Wortis, Avi 1937- *MajAI [port], WhoAm 92*
Wortis, Edward *ScF&FL 92*
Wortis, Joseph 1906- *WhoE 93*
Wortkoetter, Judith Freeman 1960- *WhoAmW 93*
Wortley, George C. *St&PR 93*
Wortley, George Cornelius 1926- *WhoAm 92*
Wortley, Neil C. 1921- *WhoAm 92*
Wortley, Thomas C. 1931- *St&PR 93*
Wortman, Beth *Law&B 92*
Wortman, J. John *St&PR 93*
Wortman, Joseph John 1940- *WhoIns 93*
Wortman, Margaret J. 1960- *St&PR 93*
Wortman, Richard S. 1938- *WhoAm 92, WhoE 93*
Wortman, Thomas Ildephonse 1965- *WhoE 93*
Worton, Ronald Gibert 1942- *WhoAm 92*
Worton, Stanley Ivan 1932- *WhoSSW 93*
Worts, George F. 1892-1967 *ScF&FL 92*
Worts, Richard Charles 1954- *WhoWor 93*
Wortsman, Peter 1952- *ConAu 137*
Wortzel, Lawrence Herbert 1932- *WhoAm 92, WhoE 93*
Wortzel, Murray N. 1923- *WhoE 93*
Worz-Busekros, Angelika 1946- *WhoWor 93*
Worzbyt, John Charles 1943- *WhoE 93*
Worzel, John Lamar 1919- *WhoAm 92*
Worzischek, Johann Hugo 1791-1825 *Baker 92*
Wos, Alojzy 1939- *WhoWor 93*
Wos, Augustyn 1932- *WhoScE 91-4*
Wos, Carol Elaine 1957- *WhoAmW 93*
Wosczyna-Birch, Karen Lee 1954- *WhoAmW 93*
Wosko, Ignacy 1925- *WhoScE 91-4*
Wosmek, Frances 1917- *DcAmChF 1960*
Wosnitzer, Morey 1929- *WhoE 93*
Woss, Josef Venantius von 1863-1943 *Baker 92*
Woss, Kurt 1914-1987 *Baker 92*
Wossner, Mark Matthias 1938- *WhoWor 93*
Woszczyk, Andrzej S. 1935- *WhoScE 91-4*
Wotava, Richard 1933- *WhoUN 92*
Wotherspoon, William A. *Law&B 92*
Wotherspoon, William W. 1850-1921 *CmdGen 1991 [port]*
Wotiz, John Henry 1919- *WhoAm 92*
Wotman, Stephen 1931- *WhoAm 92*
Wotquenne (-Plattel), Alfred (Camille) 1867-1939 *Baker 92*

Wotton, Henry 1568-1639 DcLB 121 [port]
Wou, Leo S. 1927- WhoAm 92
Woudstra, Frank Robert 1945- St&PR 93
Wouk, Herman 1915- BioIn 17, JeAmFiW, JeAmHC, WhoAm 92, WhoWor 93, WhoWrEP 92
Woundy, Douglas Stanley 1939- WhoSSW 93
Woung, Marguerite Natalie Law&B 92
Wourms, John Peter Barton 1937- WhoSSW 93
Woutat, Donald 1944- ConAu 136
Wouters, (Francois) Adolphe 1849-1924 Baker 92
Wouters, Jan T.M. 1936- WhoScE 91-3
Wouters, Joyce Biegler 1937- WhoAmW 93
Wovoka 1854-1932 GayN
Wovoka c. 1858-1932 BioIn 17
Wowchuk, Rosann 1945- WhoAmW 93
Wowtschuk, Walter 1924- St&PR 93
Woyar Gekas, Canella Law&B 92
Woycehoski, Thomas L. St&PR 93
Woychuk, Denis 1953- SmATA 71 [port]
Woyczynski, Wojbor Andrzej 1943- WhoAm 92
Woyke, Jerzy 1926- WhoScE 91-4
Woyner, Lynn 1951- WhoIns 93
Woyrsch, Felix von 1860-1944 Baker 92
Woyski, Margaret Skillman 1921- WhoAmW 93
Woytek, Mary Elizabeth Law&B 92
Woytowicz, Boleslaw 1899-1980 Baker 92
Woywod, Pamelia Campbell-Clark 1931- WhoAmW 93
Wozar, Alese Danielle Law&B 92
Wozencraft, Kim BioIn 17
Wozniak, Albert James 1938- St&PR 93
Wozniak, Debra G. Law&B 92
Wozniak, Debra Gail 1954- WhoAmW 93, WhoEmL 93
Wozniak, Edward F. 1941- St&PR 93
Wozniak, Edward Joseph 1955- WhoE 93
Wozniak, Joyce Marie 1955- WhoAmW 93
Wozniak, Leszek Wlodzimierz 1925- WhoScE 91-4
Wozniak, Marian 1936- WhoScE 91-4
Wozniak, Robert Howard 1944- WhoE 93
Wozniak, Stephen BioIn 17
Woznicki-Likavec, Marie Elaine 1952- WhoWrEP 92
Wozniuk, Vladimir 1950- WhoE 93
Woznowski, Jan 1944- WhoUN 92
Wozny, Joseph Edward 1951- St&PR 93
Wozny, Thaddeus G. Law&B 92
Wraase, Dennis Richard 1944- St&PR 93, WhoAm 92
Wrabel, Joseph John 1939- St&PR 93
Wragg, Joanna DiCarlo 1941- WhoAmW 93
Wragg, Laishley Palmer, Jr. 1933- WhoAm 92, WhoE 93, WhoWor 93
Wramstedt, Svante WhoScE 91-4
Wrancher, Elizabeth Ann 1930- WhoSSW 93
Wrangel, Karl Gustav von 1613-1676 HarEnMi
Wrangel, Piotr Nikolayevich 1878-1928 DcTwHis
Wrangel, Pyotr Nikolaevich 1878-1928 HarEnMi
Wrangel, Vasili 1862-1901 Baker 92
Wrangham, Richard Walter 1948- WhoAm 92
Wranglen, Karl Gustaf Gosta 1923- WhoWor 93
Wranitzky, Anna Katherina 1801-1851 OxDcOp
Wranitzky, Anton 1761-1820 Baker 92, OxDcOp
Wranitzky, Karoline 1794-1872 OxDcOp
Wranitzky, Paul 1756-1808 Baker 92, OxDcOp
Wrasman, Cynthia Christine 1961- WhoAmW 93
Wratislaw, A.C. 1862- ScF&FL 92
Wratten, Richard W. 1938- St&PR 93
Wray, Charles Williamson, Jr. 1933- WhoAm 92
Wray, Dennis WhoScE 91-1
Wray, Fay SweetSg B [port]
Wray, Fay 1907- BioIn 17, IntDcF 2-3 [port]
Wray, Gilbert Andrew 1940- WhoE 93
Wray, Gordon Richard WhoScE 91-1
Wray, Karl 1913- WhoAm 92, WhoWor 93
Wray, Marc Frederick 1932- St&PR 93
Wray, Mark S. 1953- WhoIns 93
Wray, Richard W. Law&B 92
Wray, Robert L. 1925- St&PR 93
Wray, Ronald Edmonds 1949- WhoWrEP 92
Wrba, Heinrich 1922- WhoScE 91-4, WhoWor 93
Wrean, William Hamilton 1935- WhoE 93
Wrebiak, Andrzej 1954- WhoWor 93
Wredberg, Lars Olof 1931- WhoUN 92
Wredden, Margaret ScF&FL 92
Wrede, Barbara 1931- WhoWrEP 92
Wrede, Casper MiSFD 9
Wrede, Harold Franz 1939- St&PR 93
Wrede, Karl Philipp von 1767-1838 HarEnMi
Wrede, Patrica Collins 1953- WhoWrEP 92
Wrede, Patricia C. 1953- BioIn 17, ScF&FL 92
Wrede, Patricia Collins 1953- WhoAmW 93
Wrede, Paul 1948- WhoWor 93
Wrede, Stuart Henrik 1944- WhoAm 92
Wreford, David Mathews 1943- WhoAm 92
Wreford, Debra Renee 1955- WhoAmW 93
Wrege, Beth Marie 1954- WhoWrEP 92
Wrege, Charles Deck 1924- WhoE 93
Wrege, Julia Bouchelle 1944- WhoAmW 93
Wreggitt, Andrew 1955- ConAu 138
Wrembel, Henryk Zbigniew 1930- WhoWor 93
Wren, Christopher 1632-1723 BioIn 17
Wren, Colin Ward 1943- St&PR 93
Wren, Harold Gwyn 1921- WhoAm 92
Wren, James 1825- BioIn 17
Wren, Jenny AmWomPl
Wren, Jill Robinson 1954- WhoWrEP 92
Wren, John Josiah 1933- WhoWor 93
Wren, M.K. 1938- ScF&FL 92
Wren, Robert James 1935- WhoSSW 93
Wren, Robert M. d1989 BioIn 17
Wren, T.W. St&PR 93
Wren, Thomas ScF&FL 92
Wren, Thomas Wayne 1922- WhoAm 92
Wren, William C. St&PR 93
Wren, William Marcel 1906- WhoSSW 93
Wren, William R. BioIn 17
Wrench, Carl Francis Law&B 92
Wrenick, Rudy E., Jr. 1944- St&PR 93
Wrenn, James Joseph 1926- WhoAm 92
Wrenn, Mary Jane 1951- WhoAmW 93
Wrenn, P. Christopher Law&B 92
Wrenn, Richard Barry 1944- St&PR 93
Wrenn, Thomas G. 1944- St&PR 93
Wresche, James W. 1935- St&PR 93
Wretlind, Bengt Magnus 1940- WhoWor 93
Wrey, Caroline BioIn 17
Wreyford, Donald M. 1928- St&PR 93
Wrice, Herman BioIn 17
Wright, A(mos) J(asper), III 1952- WhoWrEP 92
Wright, Adrian Carl 1944- WhoWor 93
Wright, Alan Carl 1939- WhoE 93
Wright, Albert Jay, III 1927- WhoE 93
Wright, Alfred George James 1916- WhoAm 92, WhoWor 93
Wright, Alice Morgan AmWomPl
Wright, Ami 1956- WhoAmW 93
Wright, Andrew 1923- WhoAm 92
Wright, Anita Dorene 1951- WhoAmW 93
Wright, Arthur Dotson 1944- WhoSSW 93
Wright, Arthur J. Law&B 92
Wright, Arthur M. 1930- St&PR 93
Wright, Arthur McIntosh 1930- WhoAm 92
Wright, Arthur W. WhoIns 93
Wright, Austin M. 1922- WhoWrEP 92
Wright, B. Ann WhoAmW 93, WhoE 93
Wright, Barbara Clare 1943- WhoAmW 93
Wright, Barbara Evelyn 1926- WhoAmW 93
Wright, Benjamin Drake 1926- WhoAm 92
Wright, Beryl J. BioIn 17
Wright, Betsey NewYTBS 92 [port]
Wright, Betty 1953- SoulM
Wright, Betty Ren BioIn 17, DcAmChF 1960
Wright, Betty Ren 1927- ScF&FL 92
Wright, Beverly L. St&PR 93
Wright, Bill Acton 1923- WhoAm 92
Wright, Blandin J. Law&B 92
Wright, Blandin James 1947- WhoWor 93
Wright, Bobbie Jean 1933- WhoSSW 93
Wright, Brenda Carol 1952- WhoSSW 93
Wright, Brian 1937- WhoWor 93
Wright, Bruce 1918- BioIn 17
Wright, Bruce McMarion 1918- ConBlB 3 [port]
Wright, C. D. 1949- DcLB 120 [port], WhoWrEP 92
Wright, C. Lamar 1940- St&PR 93
Wright, Caleb Merrill 1908- WhoAm 92, WhoE 93
Wright, Calvin Persinger 1928- WhoSSW 93
Wright, Calvin Ray, Jr. 1958- WhoSSW 93
Wright, Carole Dean 1943- WhoAmW 93
Wright, Carole Yvonne 1932- WhoAmW 93
Wright, Caroline AmWomPl, BioIn 17
Wright, Carolyn 1949- WhoWrEP 92
Wright, Cecelia Marie 1944- WhoAmW 93
Wright, Cecil M. 1942- St&PR 93
Wright, Celeste Turner 1906- WhoWrEP 92
Wright, Charles 1935- BioIn 17
Wright, Charles Alan 1927- ConAu 37NR, WhoAm 92, WhoWor 93
Wright, Charles Edward 1906- WhoAm 92
Wright, Charles Joseph 1938- WhoE 93
Wright, Charles Leslie 1945- WhoWor 93
Wright, Charles Penzel, Jr. 1935- WhoAm 92, WhoWrEP 92
Wright, Charles Richard 1941- WhoAm 92
Wright, Charlotte Hughes 1939- WhoWrEP 92
Wright, Chatt Grandison 1941- WhoAm 92
Wright, Christine Allen 1921- WhoAmW 93
Wright, Clark Phillips 1942- WhoSSW 93
Wright, Claude Holtman 1946- St&PR 93
Wright, Colin 1936- WhoAm 92
Wright, Craig BioIn 17
Wright, Craig 1929- WhoAm 92
Wright, Craig N. Law&B 92
Wright, Daniel 1931- WhoSSW 93
Wright, Darcy BioIn 17
Wright, David A. 1933- St&PR 93
Wright, David B. 1933- St&PR 93
Wright, David Burton 1933- WhoAm 92
Wright, David C. Law&B 92
Wright, David George 1931- WhoAm 92
Wright, David H. d1991 BioIn 17
Wright, David J. Law&B 92
Wright, David John 1944- WhoWor 93
Wright, David John 1947- WhoWor 93
Wright, David K. 1943- SmATA 73
Wright, David L. 1949- WhoAm 92
Wright, David Lee 1949- St&PR 93
Wright, Deborah Law&B 92
Wright, Deil Spencer 1930- WhoAm 92
Wright, Denise Yvonne 1964- WhoAmW 93
Wright, Denney L. Law&B 92
Wright, Dennis Earl 1951- WhoE 93
Wright, Dennis Howard WhoScE 91-1
Wright, Diane Montllor Law&B 92
Wright, Don C. 1934- WhoAm 92
Wright, Don G. 1942- St&PR 93
Wright, Donald Eugene 1930- WhoAm 92
Wright, Donald Franklin 1934- WhoAm 92
Wright, Donald Gene 1950- WhoSSW 93
Wright, Donald William, Jr. 1947- WhoE 93
Wright, Douglas Tyndall 1927- WhoAm 92
Wright, Douglass Brownell 1912- WhoAm 92
Wright, Edward Benton, Jr. 1938- WhoWrEP 92
Wright, Edward G. 1948- WhoIns 93
Wright, Edward Galbraith 1948- St&PR 93
Wright, Edward Hennen 1959- WhoSSW 93
Wright, Eldon Edward 1930- St&PR 93
Wright, Ellen Hayes 1939- WhoAmW 93
Wright, Ellen Marie 1953- WhoWrEP 92
Wright, Emily Powers 1953- WhoSSW 93
Wright, Eric 1929- WhoCanL 92
Wright, Eric 1959- BioIn 17
Wright, Erik Olin 1947- WhoAm 92
Wright, Ernest James Law&B 92
Wright, Ernest Marshall 1940- WhoAm 92
Wright, Eugene A. ScF&FL 92
Wright, Eugene Allen 1913- WhoAm 92
Wright, Eugene Patrick 1936- WhoSSW 93
Wright, Evan ScF&FL 92
Wright, Faith-Dorian 1934- WhoAmW 93, WhoE 93
Wright, Ferdinand von 1822-1906 BioIn 17
Wright, Fielding L. 1895-1956 PolPar
Wright, Flavel Allen 1913- WhoAm 92
Wright, Frank Gardner 1931- ConAu 136, WhoAm 92
Wright, Frank Leon 1916- WhoSSW 93
Wright, Frank Lloyd 1867-1959 BioIn 17, NewYTBS 92 [port]
Wright, Frank Lloyd 1869-1959 GayN
Wright, Franklin L. 1945- St&PR 93
Wright, Franklin Leatherbury, Jr. 1945- WhoAm 92
Wright, Franz 1953- ConAu 139
Wright, Frederick Arthur, Jr. 1936- St&PR 93
Wright, Gabriela Maria 1952- WhoAmW 93
Wright, Gail Blake 1943- WhoSSW 93
Wright, Garland 1946- WhoAm 92
Wright, Gary 1930- ScF&FL 92
Wright, Gary C. 1950- St&PR 93
Wright, Gene 1939- ScF&FL 92
Wright, George C., Jr. AfrAmBi [port]
Wright, George Frederick 1838-1921 BioIn 17
Wright, George J. Law&B 92
Wright, Gladys Stone 1925- WhoAmW 93
Wright, Glenn C. 1943- St&PR 93
Wright, Glenn S. 1946- St&PR 93
Wright, Glover 1940- ScF&FL 92
Wright, Gordon Brooks 1934- WhoAm 92
Wright, Gordon Kennedy 1920- WhoAm 92
Wright, Gordon Lee 1942- St&PR 93
Wright, Gordon Pribyl 1938- WhoAm 92
Wright, Grace Latimer AmWomPl
Wright, Graham P. 1944- WhoAm 92
Wright, Grahame 1947-1977 ScF&FL 92
Wright, Gregory Scott, Jr. ScF&FL 92
Wright, Guier S., III ScF&FL 92
Wright, Gwen Sloas 1960- WhoAmW 93
Wright, Gwendolyn 1946- WhoAm 92
Wright, H. LeArthur, II Law&B 92
Wright, Hardy WhoWrEP 92
Wright, Harlan Tonie 1941- WhoSSW 93
Wright, Harold Madison WhoAm 92
Wright, Harriet Sabra AmWomPl
Wright, Harrison Morris 1928- WhoAm 92
Wright, Harrold Eugene 1924- WhoSSW 93
Wright, Harry, III 1925- WhoAm 92
Wright, Harry Bowden Law&B 92
Wright, Harry D. 1932- St&PR 93
Wright, Harry Forrest, Jr. 1931- WhoAm 92
Wright, Harry Hercules 1948- WhoEmL 93, WhoSSW 93
Wright, Hastings Kemper 1928- WhoAm 92
Wright, Helen ScF&FL 92
Wright, Helen Kennedy 1927- WhoAmW 93, WhoWor 93
Wright, Helen Patton 1919- WhoAm 92, WhoWor 93
Wright, Helen Renee 1948- WhoAmW 93
Wright, Helene Segal 1955- WhoAmW 93
Wright, Herbert Edgar, Jr. 1917- WhoAm 92
Wright, Horatio Gouverneur 1820-1899 HarEnMi
Wright, Howard W(ilson) 1915-1992 ConAu 136
Wright, Howard Walter, Jr. 1922- St&PR 93
Wright, Hugh Elliott, Jr. 1937- WhoAm 92, WhoWrEP 92
Wright, Ian Kenneth 1953- WhoWor 93
Wright, Irving Sherwood 1901- WhoAm 92
Wright, J.A., Jr. 1916- St&PR 93
Wright, J. Skelly 1911-1988 EncAACR
Wright, James 1927-1980 AmWr S3
Wright, James Arlington 1927-1980 BioIn 17
Wright, James B. Law&B 92
Wright, James Bowers 1950- WhoWrEP 92
Wright, James C. 1922- PolPar
Wright, James Carter 1924- WhoSSW 93
Wright, James David 1947- WhoAm 92
Wright, James Edward 1921- WhoAm 92
Wright, James Foley 1943- WhoSSW 93
Wright, James H. Law&B 92
Wright, James O. 1921- St&PR 93
Wright, James Philip 1934- WhoE 93
Wright, James Roscoe 1922- WhoAm 92
Wright, Jane Brooks 1935- WhoSSW 93
Wright, Jane Cooke 1919- WhoAm 92
Wright, Janet Poe 1959- WhoSSW 93
Wright, Jay Brown 1940- WhoE 93
Wright, Jeanette Tornow 1927- WhoAm 92, WhoAmW 93
Wright, Jeanne Elizabeth Jason 1934- WhoAm 92, WhoE 93, WhoWrEP 92
Wright, Jefferson Chandler, Jr. 1958- WhoWor 93
Wright, Jeffrey Joseph 1951- WhoSSW 93
Wright, Jerry Raymond 1935- WhoAm 92, WhoWor 93
Wright, Jerry S. Law&B 92
Wright, Jim DcCPCAm
Wright, Joe d1990 BioIn 17
Wright, Joe Carrol 1933- WhoSSW 93
Wright, Joe F. Law&B 92
Wright, John BioIn 17
Wright, John 1934- WhoUN 92
Wright, John 1941- WhoAm 92
Wright, John B. St&PR 93
Wright, John C. 1925- St&PR 93
Wright, John C., II 1927- WhoSSW 93
Wright, John Charles 1951- St&PR 93
Wright, John Charles Young 1925- WhoAm 92, WhoSSW 93
Wright, John Collins 1927- WhoAm 92
Wright, John Cushing 1947- WhoSSW 93
Wright, John David Law&B 92

Wright, John David Maitland *WhoScE 91-1*
Wright, John Don 1935- *WhoSSW 93*
Wright, John Emerson 1937- *WhoAm 92*
Wright, John G. 1928- *BioIn 17*
Wright, John George, Jr. 1947- *WhoWor 93*
Wright, John King 1947- *WhoIns 93*
Wright, John M. 1930- *St&PR 93*
Wright, John MacNair, Jr. 1916- *WhoAm 92*
Wright, John Pardee 1957- *WhoE 93*
Wright, John Peale 1924- *WhoAm 92*
Wright, John Robert 1935- *WhoAm 92*
Wright, John Winthrop 1912- *St&PR 93*
Wright, Jonathan Alan *Law&B 92*
Wright, Jonathan Clifford 1949- *WhoIns 93*
Wright, Jordan M. 1958- *WhoAm 92*
Wright, Joseph 1734-1797 *BioIn 17*
Wright, Joseph Robert, Jr. 1938- *WhoAm 92*
Wright, Josephine Page *AmWomPl*
Wright, Judith *Law&B 92*
Wright, Judith 1915- *BioIn 17, IntLitE*
Wright, Judith 1959- *WhoAmW 93*
Wright, Judith Rae 1929- *WhoAmW 93*
Wright, Kara-Lyn Annette 1963- *WhoAmW 93*
Wright, Katharine Miranda 1945- *WhoWrEP 92*
Wright, Katie Harper 1923- *WhoAmW 93, WhoWor 93*
Wright, Keith 1963- *ConAu 136*
Wright, Keith Robert 1925- *St&PR 93*
Wright, Keith Webb 1942- *WhoAsAP 91*
Wright, Kenneth 1948- *WhoScE 91-1*
Wright, Kenneth Brooks 1934- *WhoAm 92*
Wright, Kenneth Lyle 1926- *WhoWor 93*
Wright, Kenneth Osborne 1911 *WhoAm 92*
Wright, Kevin Neil 1951- *WhoE 93*
Wright, Kevin W. 1952- *WhoE 93*
Wright, Kieth Carter 1933- *WhoAm 92*
Wright, L(aurali) R. 1939- *ConAu 138*
Wright, Larry *BioIn 17*
Wright, Laurali R. 1939- *WhoAm 92, WhoAmW 93, WhoCanL 92*
Wright, Laurence Sedgwick, II 1935- *St&PR 93*
Wright, Lawrence A. 1927- *CngDr 91, WhoAm 92*
Wright, Lee 1904?-1986 *ScF&FL 92*
Wright, Lewis Jones 1927- *St&PR 93, WhoAm 92*
Wright, Leyton L. 1937- *St&PR 93*
Wright, Lilyan Boyd 1920- *WhoAmW 93*
Wright, Linda Diane 1948- *WhoAmW 93*
Wright, Linda Elizabeth 1948- *WhoAmW 93*
Wright, Linda Jean 1949- *WhoAmW 93, WhoSSW 93, WhoWor 93*
Wright, Linda K. 1953- *WhoAmW 93*
Wright, Linsey Hardy 1928- *WhoWrEP 92*
Wright, Linus Douglas 1927- *WhoAm 92*
Wright, Lisa Ann 1965- *WhoAmW 93*
Wright, Lloyd George 1922- *St&PR 93*
Wright, Lois Lilyan 1962- *WhoSSW 93*
Wright, Lois Maxine 1923- *WhoWrEP 92*
Wright, Louis Tompkins 1891-1952 *ConBlB 4 [port]*
Wright, Louise Leonard d1992 *NewYTBS 92*
Wright, Louise Leonard 1896-1992 *BioIn 17*
Wright, Lucy *AmWomPl*
Wright, Mabel Osgood 1859-1934 *ScF&FL 92*
Wright, Marcellus Eugene, Jr. 1907- *WhoAm 92*
Wright, Marie Anne 1953- *WhoAmW 93*
Wright, Mark Joseph 1956- *WhoWor 93*
Wright, Mark R. *Law&B 92*
Wright, Marshall 1926- *St&PR 93, WhoAm 92*
Wright, Martha B. *Law&B 92*
Wright, Mary Beth 1952- *WhoAmW 93*
Wright, Mary Dombrowski *Law&B 92*
Wright, Mary James 1946- *WhoSSW 93*
Wright, Mary M. *ScF&FL 92*
Wright, Mary M. 1894-1967 *BioIn 17*
Wright, Mary McKenzie 1945- *WhoAmW 93*
Wright, Marye Louise *Law&B 92*
Wright, Maureen Elizabeth 1954- *WhoAmW 93*
Wright, Max 1954- *WhoE 93*
Wright, Meg *ScF&FL 92*
Wright, Melanie Louise 1958- *WhoAmW 93*
Wright, Merle Levine 1928- *WhoSSW 93*
Wright, Michael *BioIn 17*
Wright, Michael Frank 1947- *WhoE 93*
Wright, Michael Gordon 1935- *WhoAm 92*
Wright, Michael John *WhoScE 91-1*
Wright, Michael Kearney 1928- *WhoE 93*
Wright, Michael W. 1938- *St&PR 93*
Wright, Mickey 1935- *BioIn 17*
Wright, Mildred Anne 1939- *WhoAmW 93*
Wright, Milton 1920- *WhoE 93*
Wright, Minturn Tatum, III 1925- *WhoAm 92*
Wright, Myron Arnold 1911- *WhoAm 92*
Wright, Nancy Jean 1929- *WhoAmW 93*
Wright, Nancy Means *WhoWrEP 92*
Wright, Nathalia 1913- *WhoWrEP 92*
Wright, Neil Richard 1946- *St&PR 93*
Wright, Nicholas Alcwyn *WhoScE 91-1*
Wright, Nicholas Rodney Molyneux 1945- *WhoWor 93*
Wright, Norman Gray *WhoScE 91-1*
Wright, O.V. 1939-1980 *SoulM*
Wright, Oliver 1921- *WhoAm 92*
Wright, Orville 1871-1948 *BioIn 17*
Wright, Otis Clarence, Jr. 1940- *WhoE 93*
Wright, Patricia 1931- *WhoAmW 93*
Wright, Patricia Ann 1934- *St&PR 93*
Wright, Patricia Dillin 1951- *WhoE 93*
Wright, Patrick 1939- *MiSFD 9*
Wright, Paul, Jr. 1911- *WhoAm 92*
Wright, Paul Combe 1954- *WhoE 93*
Wright, Paul Michael 1939- *WhoE 93*
Wright, Paul William *Law&B 92*
Wright, Peggy Ann 1947- *WhoAmW 93*
Wright, Peter 1935- *BioIn 17*
Wright, Peter Christian *Law&B 92*
Wright, Princa McManus 1931- *WhoSSW 93*
Wright, R. Stephen *Law&B 92*
Wright, Raleigh Lewis 1931- *WhoSSW 93*
Wright, Randolph Earle 1920- *WhoAm 92*
Wright, Rayburn 1922-1990 *BioIn 17*
Wright, Raymond S. *Law&B 92*
Wright, Richard 1908-1960 *BioIn 17, ConLC 74 [port], EncAACR, MagSAmL [port], WorLitC [port]*
Wright, Richard B. 1937- *WhoCanL 92*
Wright, Richard Donald 1936- *St&PR 93, WhoE 93*
Wright, Richard E., III *Law&B 92*
Wright, Richard Harrell 1950- *WhoSSW 93*
Wright, Richard John 1951- *WhoAm 92*
Wright, Richard L. 1932- *St&PR 93*
Wright, Richard Newport, III 1932- *WhoAm 92*
Wright, Richard Robert, Sr. 1855?-1947 *EncAACR*
Wright, Richard Robert, Jr. 1878-1967 *EncAACR*
Wright, Robert Burroughs 1916- *WhoAm 92*
Wright, Robert C. 1943- *ConTFT 10, WhoAm 92, WhoE 93*
Wright, Robert Charles *BioIn 17*
Wright, Robert E. 1914- *St&PR 93*
Wright, Robert F. 1925- *St&PR 93*
Wright, Robert G. 1937- *ScF&FL 92*
Wright, Robert Joseph 1949- *WhoAm 92, WhoEmL 93*
Wright, Robert Lee 1919- *WhoAm 92*
Wright, Robert Marlow 1956- *WhoSSW 93*
Wright, Robert Michael *Law&B 92*
Wright, Robert Morley 1939- *WhoAm 92*
Wright, Robert N. 1932- *St&PR 93*
Wright, Robert Stephen 1946- *WhoAm 92*
Wright, Robin *BioIn 17*
Wright, Rodger Lee 1944- *St&PR 93*
Wright, Rodney H. 1931- *WhoAm 92*
Wright, Roger Ellerton 1946- *St&PR 93*
Wright, Roger Lane 1936- *WhoAm 92*
Wright, Ronald 1948- *ConAu 139*
Wright, Ronald A. 1932- *WhoAm 92*
Wright, Ronald A. 1935- *St&PR 93*
Wright, Rosalie Muller 1942- *WhoAm 92, WhoAmW 93*
Wright, Russel 1905-1976 *BioIn 17*
Wright, Russell D. 1946- *St&PR 93*
Wright, S. Fowler 1874-1967 *ScF&FL 92*
Wright, S. Wayne *Law&B 92*
Wright, Sam *BioIn 17*
Wright, Samuel H. *Law&B 92*
Wright, Samuel H. 1946- *St&PR 93*
Wright, Sara-Alyce Parson 1918- *WhoAm 92*
Wright, Sarah Bird 1933- *WhoAmW 93, WhoSSW 93*
Wright, Scott A. *Law&B 92*
Wright, Sewall 1889-1988 *BioIn 17*
Wright, Shannon 1956- *WhoAmW 93*
Wright, Sharon L. 1945- *St&PR 93*
Wright, Sherryl Leigh 1950- *WhoAmW 93*
Wright, Sonya Selby- d1990 *BioIn 17*
Wright, Stephen *BioIn 17*
Wright, Stephen 1922- *WhoWrEP 92*
Wright, Stephen 1946- *ScF&FL 92*
Wright, Stephen Gailord 1943- *WhoAm 92*
Wright, Stephen Lee 1957- *WhoE 93*
Wright, Stephen W. 1935- *St&PR 93*
Wright, Susan J. *Law&B 92*
Wright, Susan Webber 1948- *WhoAm 92, WhoAmW 93, WhoSSW 93*
Wright, T. Lucien 1947- *ScF&FL 92*
Wright, T.M. 1947- *ScF&FL 92*
Wright, Ted Whitaker, Sr. 1935- *WhoSSW 93*
Wright, Terence R. *WhoScE 91-1*
Wright, Teresa 1918- *BioIn 17, ConTFT 10, IntDcF 2-3*
Wright, Terry Alan 1952- *WhoWrEP 92*
Wright, Theodore Otis 1921- *WhoWor 93*
Wright, Theodore Paul, Jr. 1926- *WhoAm 92*
Wright, Theodore Robert Fairbank 1928- *WhoAm 92*
Wright, Thomas David 1937- *WhoAm 92*
Wright, Thomas H., Jr. 1918- *St&PR 93*
Wright, Thomas Henry 1904- *WhoAm 92*
Wright, Thomas J. *MiSFD 9*
Wright, Thomas James 1932- *St&PR 93*
Wright, Thomas Joe 1946- *WhoAm 92*
Wright, Thomas L. *Law&B 92*
Wright, Thomas William 1941- *WhoAm 92*
Wright, Thomas William Dunstan 1919- *WhoAm 92*
Wright, Timothy C. *Law&B 92*
Wright, Timothy T. *St&PR 93*
Wright, Tina A. *Law&B 92*
Wright, Tom Z. 1908- *WhoAm 92*
Wright, Toni Lynn 1962- *WhoAmW 93*
Wright, Trevor John 1940- *WhoWor 93*
Wright, Verna *WhoScE 91-1*
Wright, Vernon Orville 1920- *St&PR 93, WhoAm 92*
Wright, Vickie Jan 1951- *WhoAmW 93*
Wright, Victor R. 1945- *St&PR 93*
Wright, Virginia B. *AmWomPl*
Wright, W. Kevin *Law&B 92*
Wright, Wallace Mathias 1928- *WhoAm 92*
Wright, Wayne Kenneth 1944- *WhoSSW 93*
Wright, Wilbur 1867-1912 *BioIn 17*
Wright, Wiley Reed, Jr. 1932- *WhoAm 92*
Wright, Willard Jurey 1914- *WhoAm 92*
Wright, William 1829-1898 *BioIn 17*
Wright, William Bigelow 1924- *St&PR 93, WhoAm 92*
Wright, William Charles 1921- *St&PR 93*
Wright, William Cook 1939- *WhoE 93*
Wright, William E. 1938- *St&PR 93*
Wright, William M. 1947- *St&PR 93*
Wright, William Michael 1955- *WhoSSW 93*
Wright, William Pelton d1990 *BioIn 17*
Wright, William Wynn 1923- *WhoE 93*
Wright, Wyllis Eaton 1903-1979 *BioIn 17*
Wright, Yvonne Gibson 1921- *WhoAmW 93*
Wright de Kleinhans, Laureana 1846-1896 *DcMexL*
Wright-Lloyd, Joset *Law&B 92*
Wright Miller, Gill Elizabeth 1952- *WhoAmW 93*
Wright of Derby 1734-1797 *BioIn 17*
Wrighton, Mark Stephen 1949- *WhoAm 92, WhoE 93*
Wright-Simpson, Janet Ann *Law&B 92*
Wrightson, Berni 1948- *ScF&FL 92*
Wrightson, Herbert James 1869-1949 *Baker 92*
Wrightson, John Chaffe 1923- *St&PR 93*
Wrightson, John Chaffe 1923-1991 *BioIn 17*
Wrightson, Patricia 1921- *BioIn 17, ScF&FL 92*
Wrightson, (Alice) Patricia 1921- *ChlFicS, DcChlFi, MajAI [port]*
Wright-Stevenson, Linda Mae 1948- *WhoE 93*
Wright-Tatum, Patricia 1953- *WhoAmW 93*
Wrigley, Elizabeth Springer 1915- *WhoAmW 93, WhoWor 93*
Wrigley, Gladys M. 1885-1975 *BioIn 17*
Wrigley, Robert Alan 1951- *WhoWrEP 92*
Wrigley, William 1933- *St&PR 93, WhoAm 92*
Wrigley, William, Jr. 1861-1932 *GayN*
Wrinkle, John Newton 1929- *WhoSSW 93*
Wrischer, Mercedes 1929- *WhoScE 91-4*
Wrist, Peter Ellis 1927- *St&PR 93, WhoAm 92*
Wriston, Kathryn Dineen *WhoAmW 93*
Wriston, Walter Bigelow 1919- *WhoAm 92*
Wrixon, Gerard T. 1940- *WhoScE 91-3*
Wrobbel, Patricia Ann 1959- *WhoAmW 93*
Wrobel, Brian E. *Law&B 92*
Wrobel, David M. 1964- *ConAu 139*
Wrobel, Elizabeth Anne 1965- *WhoAmW 93*
Wrobel, Patrick Joseph 1952- *WhoSSW 93*
Wrobel, Robert F. *Law&B 92*
Wrobel, Robert F. 1944- *St&PR 93*
Wrobel, Robert Franklin 1944- *WhoAm 92*
Wroblewski, Andrzej K. 1933- *WhoScE 91-4*
Wroblewski, Celeste Judine *WhoAm 92*
Wroblewski, Edward C. 1941- *St&PR 93*
Wroblewski, Kenneth J. 1958- *St&PR 93*
Wroblewski, Sandra Susan 1953- *WhoAmW 93*
Wroblewski, Zygmunt 1845-1888 *PolBiDi*
Wrobley, Ralph Gene 1935- *WhoAm 92*
Wrolsen, Jean Losee 1920- *WhoWrEP 92*
Wrong, Colin B. 1927- *St&PR 93*
Wrong, Dennis Hume 1923- *WhoAm 92*
Wronkowski, Zbigniew L. 1935- *WhoScE 91-4*
Wronska, Maria 1919- *WhoScE 91-4*
Wronski, Mieczyslaw 1926- *WhoScE 91-4*
Wronski, Stanislaw K. 1929- *WhoScE 91-4*
Wroth, Elizabeth Cameron 1941- *St&PR 93*
Wroth, James Melvin 1929- *WhoAm 92*
Wroth, Lawrence Kinvin 1932- *WhoAm 92, WhoE 93*
Wroth, Mary 1587-c. 1653 *DcLB 121 [port]*
Wrotniak, Chester Michael 1956- *WhoE 93*
Wrtjak, Sandra M. *St&PR 93*
Wruble, Brian F. 1943- *St&PR 93*
Wruble, Brian Frederick 1943- *WhoAm 92*
Wruck, Erich-Oskar 1928- *WhoSSW 93*
Wrucke, Lowell Thomas 1936- *WhoE 93*
Wryde, Dogear *MajAI, SmATA 70*
Wrye, Donald *MiSFD 9*
Wrzesinski, Elizabeth Jane 1938- *WhoAmW 93*
Wrzyszcz, Jozef Karol 1932- *WhoScE 91-4*
Wschebor, Mario 1939- *WhoWor 93*
Wu, Albert M. 1940- *WhoWor 93*
Wu, Andrew H.T. *Law&B 92*
Wu, Annie *BioIn 17*
Wu, Boxi 1926- *WhoWor 93*
Wu, Carl Cherng-Miin 1938- *WhoE 93*
Wu, Chang-Chuan 1937- *WhoUN 92*
Wu, Chang-chun 1946- *WhoWor 93*
Wu, Changhui 1963- *WhoWor 93*
Wu, Cheng Yi 1938- *WhoWor 93*
Wu, Ching-Mai 1947- *WhoWor 93*
Wu, Daisy Yen 1902- *WhoE 93*
Wu, Delon 1941- *WhoWor 93*
Wu, Deyan 1936- *WhoUN 92*
Wu, Dingbo *ScF&FL 92*
Wu, Gordon *BioIn 17*
Wu, Hansheng 1956- *WhoWor 93*
Wu, Harry *BioIn 17*
Wu, Hsiu Kwang 1935- *WhoAm 92*
Wu, Hung-tak 1911-1990 *BioIn 17*
Wu, Jack H. *Law&B 92*
Wu, James Chen-Yuan 1931- *WhoAm 92*
Wu, James Kwan Min 1949- *WhoWor 93*
Wu, Jin 1934- *WhoAm 92*
Wu, Jin Zhong 1945- *WhoAmW 93*
Wu, Jingbo 1935- *WhoWor 93*
Wu, John Baptist 1925- *WhoWor 93*
Wu, Kathleen Johnson 1940- *WhoSSW 93*
Wu, Kung Chao 1922- *WhoWor 93*
Wu, L.P. 1934- *St&PR 93*
Wu, Li-Pei 1934- *WhoAm 92*
Wu, Michael *Law&B 92*
Wu, Ming-Chieh d1990 *BioIn 17*
Wu, Ming-yen 1939- *WhoWor 93*
Wu, Miranda Lai-Yeung 1954- *WhoWor 93*
Wu, Nelson Ikon 1919- *WhoAm 92, WhoWor 93*
Wu, Ping Chih 1945- *WhoAm 92*
Wu, Ray Jui 1928- *WhoAm 92*
Wu, Shi Tsan 1933- *WhoAm 92*
Wu, Shien-Ming d1992 *NewYTBS 92 [port]*
Wu, Shien-Ming 1924- *WhoAm 92*
Wu, Shuo-Xian 1947- *WhoWor 93*
Wu, Stephen S. 1922- *WhoE 93*
Wu, Tai Te 1935- *WhoAm 92*
Wu, Tai Tsun 1933- *WhoAm 92*
Wu, Theodore Wai 1936- *WhoAm 92*
Wu, Theodore Yao-Tsu 1924- *WhoAm 92*
Wu, Tianming *MiSFD 9*
Wu, Tung 1940- *WhoAm 92*
Wu, Wen Chuan 1931- *WhoWor 93*
Wu, William F. 1951- *ScF&FL 92*
Wu, William Lung-Shen 1921- *WhoWor 93, WhoWrEP 92*
Wu, Xi-jun 1933- *WhoWor 93*
Wu, Ying Chu Lin Susan 1932- *WhoAmW 93, WhoSSW 93*
Wu, Yongshi 1927- *WhoWor 93*
Wu, Zhengsheng 1935- *WhoWor 93*
Wu, Zhenshan 1939- *WhoWor 93*
Wu, Zongmin 1957- *WhoWor 93*
Wu Bangguo 1942- *WhoAsAP 91*
Wubbel, Richard H. *Law&B 92*
Wubbenhorst, Jeannette Louise 1951- *WhoAmW 93*
Wuchenich, Allen Samuel *Law&B 92*
Wucherer, Ruth Marie 1948- *WhoWrEP 92*
Wucherpfennig, Karl 1925- *WhoScE 91-3*

Wu Ch'i c. 430BC-381BC *HarEnMi*
Wuchinich, Susan Alexandra 1948- *WhoAmW 93*
Wuchiski, Walter A. 1945- *St&PR 93*
Wuckel, Dieter *ScF&FL 92*
WuDunn, Sheryl 1959- *WhoAmW 93*
Wuebbling, Donald J. *Law&B 92*
Wuensch, Bernhardt John 1933- *WhoAm 92*
Wuensch, Gerhard 1925- *Baker 92*
Wuensch, Marc Courtney 1952- *WhoE 93*
Wuensche, Vernon Edgar 1945- *WhoSSW 93*
Wuenscher, David E. 1936- *St&PR 93*
Wuerkaixi *BioIn 17*
Wuerl, Donald W. 1940- *WhoAm 92, WhoE 93*
Wuerst, Richard (Ferdinand) 1824-1881 *Baker 92*
Wuerthner, J.J., Jr. 1924- *St&PR 93*
Wuerthner, William 1954- *St&PR 93*
Wuest, George W. 1925- *WhoAm 92*
Wuest, Karen M. *Law&B 92*
Wuest, Mark *WhoAm 92*
Wueste, Ward W., Jr. *Law&B 92*
Wueste, Ward William, Jr. 1937- *WhoAm 92*
Wuestman, Tony 1933- *St&PR 93*
Wuetig, Joyce Linda 1938- *WhoAmW 93*
Wu Guanzhem 1938- *WhoAsAP 91*
Wuhl, Charles Michael 1943- *WhoE 93, WhoWor 93*
Wuhrer, Friedrich (Anton Franz) 1900-1975 *Baker 92*
Wuhrman, Elsa H. 1959- *WhoAmW 93*
Wuidart, Willy 1943- *WhoScE 91-2*
Wujciak, Sandra Criscuolo 1949- *WhoAmW 93, WhoE 93*
Wu Jinghua 1931- *WhoAsAP 91*
Wulbert, Daniel Eliot 1941- *WhoAm 92*
Wuletich-Brinberg, Sybil 1921- *ScF&FL 92*
Wulf, Christoph 1944- *WhoWor 93*
Wulf, Jerold W. 1931- *St&PR 93*
Wulf, Melvin Lawrence 1927- *WhoAm 92*
Wulf, Ronald James 1928- *WhoE 93*
Wulf, Sharon Ann 1954- *WhoAmW 93*
Wulf, Stanley 1947- *WhoWor 93*
Wulf, William Allan 1939- *WhoAm 92*
Wulfe, Carl E. 1932- *St&PR 93*
Wulfe, Heidi 1954- *St&PR 93*
Wulfe, Jesse E. 1924- *St&PR 93*
Wulff, Geraldine Schepker 1947- *WhoAmW 93*
Wulff, Guenter 1935- *WhoWor 93*
Wulff, Gunter 1935- *WhoScE 91-3*
Wulff, Henrik Ramsing 1932- *WhoWor 93*
Wulff, Jochen *BioIn 17*
Wulff, John K. 1948- *St&PR 93*
Wulff, John Kenneth 1948- *WhoAm 92*
Wulff, Lee 1905-1991 *AnObit 1991, BioIn 17*
Wulff, Robert King *Law&B 92*
Wulff, Robert King 1938- *St&PR 93*
Wulff, Roger LaVern 1940- *WhoE 93, WhoWor 93*
Wulffraat, Robert A. *Law&B 92*
Wulfing, George A. 1925- *St&PR 93*
Wulfing, Sulamith 1901- *ScF&FL 92*
Wulfsberg, Rolf M. 1947- *St&PR 93*
Wulfstan, Saint c. 1008-1095 *BioIn 17*
Wuliger, Ernest M. d1992 *NewYTBS 92 [port]*
Wullenweber, Michael 1947- *WhoScE 91-3*
Wullkopf, Uwe Erich Walter 1940- *WhoWor 93*
Wullner, Franz 1832-1902 *Baker 92, OxDcOp*
Wullner, Ludwig 1858-1938 *Baker 92, OxDcOp*
Wumpelmann, Knud 1922- *WhoAm 92*
Wunch, James W. 1948- *St&PR 93*
Wunder, Charles Cooper 1928- *WhoAm 92*
Wunder, Gene Carroll 1939- *WhoSSW 93*
Wunder, Gustave Frederick 1926- *WhoAm 92*
Wunder, Haroldene Fowler 1944- *WhoAmW 93*
Wunder, John Remley 1945- *ConAu 37NR*
Wunder, Stephen Joseph 1955- *WhoSSW 93*
Wunderer, Alexander 1877-1955 *Baker 92*
Wunderle, James A. 1952- *St&PR 93*
Wunderli, Earl M. *Law&B 92*
Wunderli, Werner Hans Karl 1942- *WhoWor 93*
Wunderlich, Alfred Leon 1939- *WhoAm 92*
Wunderlich, Bernhard 1931- *WhoAm 92, WhoSSW 93*
Wunderlich, Fritz 1930-1966 *Baker 92, IntDcOp [port], OxDcOp*
Wunderlich, Heinz 1919- *Baker 92*
Wunderlich, Hermann *WhoAm 92, WhoE 93*
Wunderlich, P.K. *St&PR 93*
Wunderlich, Peggy Duke 1951- *St&PR 93*
Wunderlich, Ray C(harles), Jr. 1929- *WhoWrEP 92*
Wunderman, Lester 1920- *WhoAm 92*
Wundt, Wilhelm 1832-1920 *IntDcAn*
Wunnicke, Brooke 1918- *WhoAmW 93*
Wunsch, Carl Isaac 1941- *WhoAm 92*
Wunsch, Charles Robert *Law&B 92*
Wunsch, Erich 1923- *WhoScE 91-3*
Wunsch, Hermann 1884-1954 *Baker 92*
Wunsch, James S(tevenson) 1946- *ConAu 136*
Wunsch, James Stevenson 1946- *WhoAm 92*
Wunsch, Josephine 1914- *BioIn 17*
Wunsch, Kathryn Sutherland 1935- *WhoAmW 93*
Wunsch, Roy Christopher 1965- *WhoSSW 93*
Wunsch, Volkmar Norbert 1941- *WhoWor 93*
Wunsch, Walther 1908- *Baker 92*
Wunschel, Ronald Louis 1946- *St&PR 93*
Wuori, Matti Ossian 1945- *WhoWor 93*
Wuori, Paul 1933- *WhoScE 91-4*
Wuori, Paul Adolf 1933- *WhoWor 93*
Wuorinen, Charles *BioIn 17*
Wuorinen, Charles 1938- *Baker 92, WhoAm 92*
Wuorio, Eva-Lis 1918- *ConAu 40NR, DcChlFi, ScF&FL 92*
Wuornos, Aileen *BioIn 17*
Wu P'ei-fu 1873-1939 *HarEnMi*
Wu Poh-Hsiung 1939- *WhoAsAP 91*
Wurdeman, Lew Edward 1949- *WhoEmL 93*
Wurdinger, Victoria 1957- *WhoAm 92*
Wurfel, Clifford 1927- *ScF&FL 92*
Wurfel, Wenzel Wilhelm 1790-1832 *Baker 92*
Wurgler, Friedrich 1936- *WhoScE 91-4*
Wurlitzer *Baker 92*
Wurlitzer, Farny Reginald 1883-1972 *Baker 92*
Wurlitzer, Howard Eugene 1871-1928 *Baker 92*
Wurlitzer, Rembert 1904-1963 *Baker 92*
Wurlitzer, Rudolph *MiSFD 9*
Wurlitzer, Rudolph 1831-1914 *Baker 92*
Wurlitzer, Rudolph 1937- *ScF&FL 92*
Wurlitzer, Rudolph Henry 1873-1948 *Baker 92*
Wurm, Adela
See Wurm, Marie 1860-1938 *Baker 92*
Wurm, Marie 1860-1938 *Baker 92*
Wurm, Mark Alfred *Law&B 92*
Wurm, Mathilda
See Wurm, Marie 1860-1938 *Baker 92*
Wurman, Richard Saul 1935- *WhoAm 92*
Wurmbrand, Harry George 1938- *WhoAm 92*
Wurmser, Dagobert Sigismond 1724-1797 *HarEnMi*
Wurmser, Jeanne Hahn 1932- *WhoE 93*
Wursig, Bernd Gerhard 1948- *WhoAm 92, WhoSSW 93*
Wursta, John M. *Law&B 92*
Wurster, Charles Frederick 1930- *WhoAm 92*
Wurster, Dale Eric 1951- *WhoWor 93*
Wurster, Dale Erwin 1918- *WhoWor 93*
Wurster, Donald F. 1953- *St&PR 93*
Wurster, James C. 1947- *St&PR 93*
Wurster, Lisa A. *Law&B 92*
Wurster, Michael 1940- *WhoWrEP 92*
Wurster, Ralph 1930- *WhoWrEP 92*
Wurster, Stephen Harry 1941- *WhoAm 92*
Wurster-Hill, Doris Hadley 1932- *WhoAmW 93*
Wurtele, C. Angus 1934- *St&PR 93*
Wurtele, Christopher Angus 1934- *WhoAm 92*
Wurtele, Morton Gaither 1919- *WhoAm 92*
Wurth, Bernard J. 1953- *St&PR 93*
Wurtman, Judith Joy 1937- *WhoAmW 93*
Wurtman, Richard Jay 1938- *WhoAm 92*
Wurts, Janny 1953- *ScF&FL 92*
Wurts, John S. *BioIn 17*
Wurts, John S. 1948- *St&PR 93*
Wurttemberg, Albrecht Maria Alexander Philipp Joseph, Duke of 1865-1939 *HarEnMi*
Wurtz, James 1934- *St&PR 93*
Wurtz, James L. *Law&B 92*
Wurtz, Lyle Dean 1931- *St&PR 93*
Wurtz, Merryrose 1936- *St&PR 93, WhoAm 92*
Wurtz, Robert Henry 1936- *WhoAm 92, WhoE 93*
Wurtzel, Alan Henry 1947- *St&PR 93*
Wurtzel, Alan Leon 1933- *St&PR 93, WhoAm 92*
Wurtzel, Elizabeth *BioIn 17*
Wurtzel, Franklin R. *Law&B 92*
Wurtzel, Stuart 1940- *WhoAm 92*
Wurtzler, Aristid von 1930- *Baker 92*
Wurtzler, Stephen D. 1947- *St&PR 93*
Wurz, James J. 1957- *St&PR 93*
Wurzbacher, Terrie 1948- *WhoAmW 93*
Wurzberger, Bezalel 1945- *WhoE 93*
Wurzburg, Reginald 1901- *St&PR 93*
Wurzburg, Warren Seymour 1926- *St&PR 93*
Wurzburger, John 1945- *St&PR 93*
Wurzburger, Walter Samuel 1920- *WhoAm 92, WhoE 93, WhoWor 93*
Wurzel, Leonard 1918- *WhoAm 92*
Wurzel, Stephen Berke 1947- *St&PR 93*
Wurzer, Henry Kahl 1936- *WhoAm 92*
Wurzner, Hans-Peter 1934- *WhoScE 91-4*
Wu San-kuei 1612-1678 *HarEnMi*
Wu Shaozu 1939- *WhoAsAP 91*
Wussler, Robert Joseph 1936- *WhoAm 92*
Wust, Carl John 1928- *WhoSSW 93*
Wustenhagen, Karl *WhoScE 91-3*
Wustrack, Paul Karl, Jr. 1943- *St&PR 93*
Wuthrich, Kurt 1938- *WhoScE 91-4, WhoWor 93*
Wu Ti dc. 87BC *HarEnMi*
Wu Ti d290 *HarEnMi*
Wuttke, Dieter 1929- *WhoWor 93*
Wuttke, Ruth Ellen 1928- *WhoAmW 93*
Wuttke, Stephen A. *Law&B 92*
Wutzler, Jerry A. 1937- *St&PR 93*
Wu Weiran 1921- *WhoAsAP 91*
Wu Wenying 1932- *WhoAsAP 91*
Wu Wenzao 1901-1985 *IntDcAn*
Wu Xueqian 1921- *WhoAsAP 91*
Wu Xueqian 1922- *WhoWor 93*
Wu Yi 1939- *WhoAsAP 91*
W.W. 1948- *ScF&FL 92*
Wyandt, Steven P. 1944- *St&PR 93*
Wyant, Clyde 1938- *St&PR 93*
Wyant, Clyde W., Jr. 1938- *WhoAm 92*
Wyant, Jeffrey C. *Law&B 92*
Wyatt, Adrian Frederick George *WhoScE 91-1*
Wyatt, Barry Keith *WhoScE 91-1*
Wyatt, Bruce H. *Law&B 92*
Wyatt, Bruce H. 1946- *St&PR 93*
Wyatt, Clarence Ray 1956- *WhoSSW 93*
Wyatt, David Kent 1937- *WhoAm 92*
Wyatt, Doris Fay Chapman 1935- *WhoAmW 93*
Wyatt, Douglas *BioIn 17*
Wyatt, Edith Elizabeth 1914- *WhoAmW 93*
Wyatt, Euphemia Van Rensselaer *AmWomPl*
Wyatt, Forest Kent 1934- *WhoAm 92*
Wyatt, Geoffrey James *WhoScE 91-1*
Wyatt, George Millard 1929- *WhoSSW 93*
Wyatt, Gerard Robert 1925- *WhoAm 92*
Wyatt, Glenn Thomas 1939- *WhoAm 92*
Wyatt, Gloria Maxine 1953- *WhoAmW 93*
Wyatt, Greg Alan 1949- *WhoE 93*
Wyatt, Harold Edmund 1921- *WhoAm 92*
Wyatt, Harry Joel 1942- *WhoE 93*
Wyatt, J. Allen 1945- *St&PR 93*
Wyatt, Jack D. *Law&B 92*
Wyatt, James A., Jr. 1945- *St&PR 93*
Wyatt, James Frank, Jr. 1922- *WhoAm 92*
Wyatt, James Franklin 1934- *WhoAm 92*
Wyatt, James L. 1924- *St&PR 93*
Wyatt, James Luther 1924- *WhoAm 92*
Wyatt, Jane *ConAu 37NR, MajAI*
Wyatt, Janice Barber 1947- *WhoAm 92*
Wyatt, Joan 1934?- *ScF&FL 92*
Wyatt, Joe Billy 1935- *WhoAm 92, WhoSSW 93*
Wyatt, Joe Bob *Law&B 92*
Wyatt, Joseph Lucian, Jr. 1924- *WhoAm 92*
Wyatt, Julie 1939- *WhoAmW 93*
Wyatt, Kathryn Elizabeth Benton 1928- *WhoAmW 93, WhoWor 93*
Wyatt, Lee *ScF&FL 92*
Wyatt, Leland Wayne 1942- *St&PR 93*
Wyatt, Loretta Sharon 1940- *WhoE 93*
Wyatt, Lynn *BioIn 17*
Wyatt, Marsha Kapnicky 1956- *WhoAmW 93*
Wyatt, Mary Ann 1960- *WhoAmW 93*
Wyatt, Michael A. *Law&B 92*
Wyatt, Michael A. 1932- *St&PR 93*
Wyatt, Mona Gordon 1954- *WhoAmW 93, WhoSSW 93*
Wyatt, Monica *BioIn 17*
Wyatt, Nancy Virginia 1943- *WhoAmW 93*
Wyatt, Nathaniel Ellsworth 1863-1895 *BioIn 17*
Wyatt, Oscar Sherman, Jr. *BioIn 17*
Wyatt, Oscar Sherman, Jr. 1924- *St&PR 93, WhoAm 92, WhoSSW 93*
Wyatt, Patrick *ScF&FL 92*
Wyatt, Phillipa Kathleen *WhoAmW 93, WhoWor 93*
Wyatt, Rachel 1929- *WhoCanL 92*
Wyatt, Raymond Michael 1946- *WhoWor 93*
Wyatt, Richard Jed 1939- *WhoAm 92*
Wyatt, Robert Odell 1946- *WhoSSW 93*
Wyatt, Rose Marie 1937- *WhoWor 93*
Wyatt, Sandra Mitchell 1945- *St&PR 93*
Wyatt, Stephen 1948- *ScF&FL 92*
Wyatt, Steve *BioIn 17*
Wyatt, Teddy R. 1961- *WhoSSW 93*
Wyatt, Thomas c. 1519-1554 *HarEnMi*
Wyatt, Thomas C. *Law&B 92*
Wyatt, W. Whitlow 1948- *St&PR 93*
Wyatt, Walter 1893-1978 *OxCSupC*
Wyatt, William Frank, Jr. 1932- *WhoAm 92*
Wyatt, Wilson Watkins 1905- *WhoAm 92*
Wyatt, Wilson Watkins, Jr. 1943- *WhoAm 92, WhoE 93*
Wyatt, Woodrow Lyle 1918- *ConAu 40NR*
Wyatt-Brown, Anne M(arbury) 1939- *ConAu 139*
Wyatt-Brown, Bertram 1932- *WhoAm 92, WhoWrEP 92*
Wyatt-Cummings, Thelma Lavern 1945- *AfrAmBi*
Wybicki, Jozef Rufin 1747-1822 *PolBiDi*
Wybierala, Alice Sophie 1939- *St&PR 93*
Wybierala, Richard Anthony 1932- *St&PR 93*
Wybieralski, Jerzy 1939- *WhoScE 91-4*
Wyble, George F. 1931- *St&PR 93*
Wybo, Luc Rene 1952- *WhoWor 93*
Wybran, Joseph 1940- *WhoScE 91-2*
Wyche, Alex T. *Law&B 92*
Wyche, Paul Byron, Jr. *Law&B 92*
Wyche, Samuel David 1945- *WhoAm 92, WhoSSW 93*
Wycherley, William 1640?-1716 *LitC 21 [port]*
Wychulis, Adam Robert 1935- *WhoWor 93*
Wyckoff, Alexander 1898- *WhoWor 93*
Wyckoff, Edward Lisk, Jr. 1934- *WhoAm 92*
Wyckoff, James M. 1918- *ConAu 39NR*
Wyckoff, James Marshal 1924- *WhoE 93*
Wyckoff, Jean Bratton 1932- *WhoAm 92*
Wyckoff, Julie Ann 1952- *WhoWrEP 92*
Wyckoff, Linda S. *Law&B 92*
Wyckoff, Linda Sue 1948- *St&PR 93*
Wyckoff, Margo Gail 1941- *WhoAmW 93, WhoWor 93*
Wyckoff, Priscilla G. 1945- *WhoAmW 93*
Wyckoff, Raymond W. 1923- *St&PR 93, WhoAm 92, WhoSSW 93*
Wyckoff, Richard D. *Law&B 92*
Wyckoff, Richard Darrel, Sr. 1944- *WhoE 93*
Wyckoff, Richard Hunt 1933- *St&PR 93*
Wyckoff, Sara Louise *Law&B 92*
Wyckoff, Susan 1941- *WhoAmW 93*
Wyckoff, Walter A. 1865-1908 *GayN*
Wycliff, Noel Don 1946- *WhoAm 92*
Wycliffe, John d1384 *BioIn 17*
Wycoff, Charles Coleman 1918- *WhoWor 93*
Wycoff, Kathleen F. 1952- *WhoAm 92, WhoAmW 93*
Wycoff, Minnie E. *AmWomPl*
Wycoff, Robert E. 1930- *WhoAm 92, WhoSSW 93*
Wycoff, Robert Elmer 1930- *St&PR 93*
Wycoff, W.A. 1947- *St&PR 93*
Wyczanski, Pawel Tadeusz 1951- *WhoWor 93*
Wyczolkowska, Janina 1935- *WhoScE 91-4*
Wyczolkowski, Leon 1852-1936 *PolBiDi*
Wyden, Ron *BioIn 17*
Wyden, Ron 1949- *CngDr 91*
Wyden, Ronald Lee 1949- *WhoAm 92*
Wyder, Peter 1934- *WhoScE 91-2*
Wyder, Peter R. 1934- *WhoScE 91-2*
Wydick, Richard Crews 1937- *WhoAm 92*
Wydler, Hans Ulrich 1923- *WhoE 93, WhoWor 93*
Wydman, Marcy R. 1958- *St&PR 93*
Wydman, Mary Witt 1925- *St&PR 93*
Wydra, Clement John 1935- *WhoSSW 93*
Wydra, Frank Thomas 1939- *WhoWrEP 92*
Wydra, Jan 1902-1937 *PolBiDi*
Wyer, James Ingersoll 1923- *WhoAm 92*
Wyer, Jean Conover 1950- *WhoE 93*
Wyer, William Clarke 1946- *WhoAm 92*
Wyers, Charles H. *St&PR 93*
Wyers, Monique 1941- *WhoScE 91-2*
Wyeth, Adelaide H. *AmWomPl*
Wyeth, Andrew 1917- *BioIn 17, WhoAm 92*
Wyeth, Ann *BioIn 17*
Wyeth, Carolyn 1909- *BioIn 17*
Wyeth, Henriette 1907- *BioIn 17*
Wyeth, James Browning 1946- *WhoAm 92*
Wyeth, N.C. 1882-1945 *BioIn 17*
Wyeth, N(ewell) C(onvers) 1882-1945 *MajAI [port]*
Wyeth, Nathaniel C. 1911-1990 *BioIn 17*
Wyeth, Newell Convers 1882-1945 *BioIn 17*
Wygant, Alice Chambers 1948- *WhoAmW 93*

Wygant, Foster Laurance 1920- *WhoAm 92*
Wygle, Peter R. *BioIn 17*
Wygle, Robert Howard 1897-1961 *BioIn 17*
Wygnanski, Israel Jerzy 1935- *WhoAm 92*
Wygod, Martin J. *WhoAm 92*
Wygod, Martin J. 1940- *St&PR 93*
Wyk, Arnold(us Christian Vlok) van 1916-1983 *Baker 92*
Wyka, Kenneth Andrew 1948- *WhoE 93*
Wyke, Charles Lennox 1815-1897 *BioIn 17*
Wyke, Robert James 1933- *St&PR 93, WhoIns 93*
Wyker, Kenneth E. *Law&B 92*
Wyker, Robert 1935- *St&PR 93*
Wykes, Alan 1914- *ScF&FL 92*
Wykes, E. Harold *Law&B 92*
Wykes, Edmund Harold 1928- *St&PR 93, WhoAm 92*
Wykes, Robert (Arthur) 1926- *Baker 92*
Wykle, Peggy Carpenter 1950- *WhoSSW 93*
Wykoff, Frank Champion 1942- *WhoAm 92*
Wyland, Dwight W. 1950- *St&PR 93*
Wyland, Harold E. 1936- *St&PR 93*
Wyland, Jim *BioIn 17*
Wyld, Jean Anne 1951- *WhoAmW 93*
Wyld, Lionel Darcy 1925- *WhoE 93*
Wylde, Henry 1822-1890 *Baker 92*
Wylde, Sam M. 1914- *St&PR 93*
Wylde, Sam Mayo, III 1951- *St&PR 93*
Wylde, Thomas 1946- *ScF&FL 92*
Wyle, Clement J. 1908-1991 *BioIn 17*
Wyle, Frank S. 1919- *St&PR 93*
Wyle, Frederick S. 1928- *WhoAm 92*
Wyler, David John 1944- *WhoE 93*
Wyler, Margaret Tallichet d1991 *BioIn 17*
Wyler, Robert 1924- *WhoScE 91-4*
Wyler, Stephen Marc Wohlfeiler 1945- *WhoE 93*
Wyler, William 1902-1981 *MiSFD 9N*
Wylie, B.M. *St&PR 93*
Wylie, Betty Jane *WhoCanL 92*
Wylie, Cathy Lynn 1964- *WhoAmW 93*
Wylie, Chalmers P. 1920- *CngDr 91*
Wylie, Chalmers Pangburn 1920- *WhoAm 92*
Wylie, Christopher Craig *WhoScE 91-1*
Wylie, Clarence Raymond, Jr. 1911- *WhoAm 92*
Wylie, Evan Benjamin 1931- *WhoAm 92*
Wylie, Faith Lubben 1953- *WhoSSW 93*
Wylie, Francis E(rnest) 1905- *ConAu 37NR*
Wylie, Henry Kenneth 1943- *WhoScE 91-3*
Wylie, J. Kenneth 1927- *WhoIns 93*
Wylie, Jeff *ConAu 37NR*
Wylie, John Angus *WhoScE 91-1*
Wylie, John M., II 1953- *WhoSSW 93*
Wylie, Jonathan *ScF&FL 92*
Wylie, Kenneth Millar, Jr. 1927- *WhoWrEP 92*
Wylie, Laura *ScF&FL 92*
Wylie, Martin E. *St&PR 93*
Wylie, Mary Evelyn 1947- *WhoAmW 93*
Wylie, Neta Evangeline 1921- *WhoSSW 93*
Wylie, Roger L. *St&PR 93*
Wylie, Ted David 1945- *WhoSSW 93*
Wylie, William T. 1940- *St&PR 93*
Wyller, Egil Anders 1925- *WhoWor 93*
Wyllie, Alfred Linn 1949- *WhoSSW 93*
Wyllie, John *WhoScE 91-1*
Wyllie, Loring A., Jr. 1938- *WhoAm 92*
Wyllie, Michael Eugene 1953- *WhoE 93*
Wyllie, Peter John 1930- *WhoAm 92*
Wyllie, Stuart Sloan 1954- *St&PR 93*
Wylly, Barbara Bentley 1924- *WhoSSW 93*
Wylly, L. Ralston 1932- *St&PR 93*
Wyllys, Ronald Eugene 1930- *WhoAm 92*
Wyly, Charles J., Jr. 1933- *St&PR 93*
Wyly, Charles Joseph, Jr. 1933- *WhoAm 92*
Wyly, Michael 1949- *WhoSSW 93*
Wyly, Sam E. 1934- *St&PR 93*
Wyma, John K. *Law&B 92*
Wyman, Alan Duane 1949- *St&PR 93*
Wyman, Anne F. 1926- *St&PR 93*
Wyman, Bill *BioIn 17*
Wyman, Bruce C. 1947- *ConAu 139*
Wyman, Bruce Charles 1947- *WhoSSW 93*
Wyman, David Sword 1929- *WhoAm 92*
Wyman, Debra Jean 1952- *WhoWrEP 92*
Wyman, Donald 1903- *WhoAm 92*
Wyman, Donald Paul 1931- *St&PR 93*
Wyman, Elizabeth Heywood *AmWomPl*
Wyman, Franklin, Jr. 1921- *St&PR 93*
Wyman, George Martin 1921- *WhoSSW 93*
Wyman, Henry W. 1919- *St&PR 93*
Wyman, Henry Walter 1919- *WhoAm 92*
Wyman, James T. 1920- *St&PR 93*
Wyman, James Thomas 1920- *WhoAm 92*
Wyman, James V. 1923- *St&PR 93*
Wyman, James Vernon 1923- *WhoAm 92, WhoE 93*
Wyman, Jane 1914- *WhoAm 92, WhoAmW 93*
Wyman, Jane 1916- *IntDcF 2-3*
Wyman, Jeffries 1814-1874 *IntDcAn*
Wyman, Joel Wentworth, Jr. 1943- *WhoE 93*
Wyman, Louis Crosby 1917- *WhoAm 92*
Wyman, Morton 1922- *St&PR 93*
Wyman, Nancy S. 1946- *WhoAmW 93*
Wyman, Ralph M. 1926- *St&PR 93*
Wyman, Ralph Mark 1926- *WhoAm 92*
Wyman, Richard Thomas 1951- *WhoSSW 93*
Wyman, Richard Vaughn 1927- *St&PR 93, WhoAm 92*
Wyman, Robert H. *Law&B 92*
Wyman, Stanley Moore 1913- *WhoAm 92*
Wyman, William George 1941- *WhoAm 92*
Wymann, Peter 1946- *WhoWor 93*
Wymbs, Norman Elwood 1923- *WhoSSW 93*
Wymer, Martin T. *Law&B 92*
Wymer, Robert Ernest 1947- *WhoEmL 93*
Wymer, Thomas L. 1938- *ScF&FL 92*
Wymor, Larry L. 1936- *St&PR 93, WhoWor 93*
Wymore, Bill D. 1940- *WhoIns 93*
Wynand, Derk 1944- *WhoCanL 92*
Wynar, Bohdan Stephen 1926- *WhoAm 92, WhoWrEP 92*
Wynberg, Hans 1922- *WhoScE 91-3*
Wynblatt, Paul Pinhas 1935- *WhoAm 92*
Wynd, Oswald Morris 1913- *ConAu 39NR*
Wynder, Ernst Ludwig 1922- *WhoAm 92*
Wyndham, Harald P. 1946- *WhoWrEP 92*
Wyndham, John 1903-1969 *BioIn 17, ScF&FL 92*
Wyndham, John S. 1915- *St&PR 93*
Wyndrum, Ralph W., Jr. 1937- *WhoAm 92*
Wyne, Margaret Mary 1965- *WhoAmW 93*
Wyner, Aaron Daniel 1939- *WhoAm 92*
Wyner, Genevieve G. 1930- *St&PR 93*
Wyner, Justin L. 1925- *St&PR 93*
Wyner, Susan Davenny 1943- *Baker 92*
Wyner, Yehudi 1929- *Baker 92, WhoAm 92*
Wynette, Tammy *BioIn 17*
Wynette, Tammy 1942- *Baker 92, WhoAm 92*
Wyngaarden, James Barnes 1924- *WhoAm 92*
Wyn-Jones, Evan *WhoScE 91-1*
Wyn Jones, Richard Gareth *WhoScE 91-1*
Wynkoop, Mildred Bangs 1905- *ConAu 40NR*
Wynkoop, Randall L. *Law&B 92*
Wynkoop, Roger D. 1948- *St&PR 93*
Wynn, Charles Martin, Sr. 1939- *WhoE 93*
Wynn, Coy Wilton 1920- *WhoAm 92*
Wynn, Dale Richard 1918- *WhoWrEP 92*
Wynn, Early 1920- *BioIn 17*
Wynn, Ed 1886-1966 *QDrFCA 92 [port]*
Wynn, Francis J. *WhoIns 93*
Wynn, H. Edward *Law&B 92*
Wynn, J(ohn) (Charles) 1920- *WhoWrEP 92*
Wynn, James Sherman 1942- *BiDAMSp 1989*
Wynn, Jean Marie 1954- *WhoAmW 93*
Wynn, Joe Allen 1953- *WhoWrEP 92*
Wynn, John Charles 1920- *WhoAm 92*
Wynn, John Thomas *Law&B 92*
Wynn, John Thomas 1938- *WhoSSW 93, WhoWor 93*
Wynn, Keenan 1916-1986 *BioIn 17*
Wynn, Kenneth Richard 1952- *St&PR 93, WhoAm 92*
Wynn, Matthew David 1964- *WhoE 93*
Wynn, Ned *BioIn 17*
Wynn, Robert L. *Law&B 92*
Wynn, Robert Lipscomb, III *Law&B 92*
Wynn, Sarah Woodfin *Law&B 92*
Wynn, Si Richard 1923- *St&PR 93*
Wynn, Stephen A. *BioIn 17*
Wynn, Stephen A. 1941- *WhoAm 92*
Wynn, Stephen A. 1942- *St&PR 93*
Wynn, Susan Rudd *WhoSSW 93*
Wynn, Thomas Joseph 1918- *WhoAm 92*
Wynn, Tracy Keenan 1945- *MiSFD 9*
Wynn, Willard Kendall 1932-1989 *BioIn 17*
Wynne, Anna *AmWomPl*
Wynne, Brian James 1950- *WhoAm 92*
Wynne, Carey Howard, Jr. 1950- *WhoWor 93*
Wynne, David Michael 1952- *WhoSSW 93*
Wynne, Diana S. 1955- *St&PR 93*
Wynne, Donald Everett 1952- *St&PR 93*
Wynne, Donna Elizabeth *Law&B 92*
Wynne, Elise Marcia *WhoWrEP 92*
Wynne, Frank *WhoWrEP 92*
Wynne, George C. 1949- *WhoIns 93*
Wynne, Greville Maynard 1919-1990 *BioIn 17*
Wynne, James Riley, Jr. 1961- *WhoSSW 93*
Wynne, Jim *BioIn 17*
Wynne, John *ScF&FL 92*
Wynne, John B. 1930- *St&PR 93*
Wynne, John Benedict 1930- *WhoAm 92*
Wynne, John Boyce 1945- *WhoE 93*
Wynne, John Oliver 1945- *St&PR 93, WhoAm 92, WhoSSW 93*
Wynne, John Watterson 1933- *St&PR 93*
Wynne, Joseph J. 1936- *St&PR 93*
Wynne, Lyman Carroll 1923- *WhoAm 92*
Wynne, Michael Walter 1944- *WhoAm 92*
Wynne, Paul *BioIn 17*
Wynne, Paul Emmett 1940- *St&PR 93*
Wynne, Wreno S. *Law&B 92*
Wynne-Edwards, Hugh Robert 1934- *WhoAm 92*
Wynne-Jones, Tim *BioIn 17*
Wynne-Jones, Tim 1948- *ScF&FL 92*
Wynne-Jones, Tim(othy) 1948- *ConAu 39NR*
Wynne-Jones, Timothy 1948- *WhoCanL 92*
Wynne-Willson, William Salisbury 1932- *WhoWor 93*
Wynns, Theresia 1947- *WhoAmW 93*
Wynorski, Jim 1950- *MiSFD 9, ScF&FL 92*
Wynsma, James Burton 1936- *St&PR 93*
Wynstra, Nancy Ann 1941- *WhoAmW 93, WhoWor 93*
Wynter, Dana 1930- *WhoAm 92*
Wynter, Hector Lincoln 1926- *WhoWor 93*
Wyon, John Benjamin 1918- *WhoE 93*
Wyrick, Charles Lloyd, Jr. 1939- *WhoAm 92*
Wyrick, Jack Boyd 1937- *WhoSSW 93*
Wyrick, Jesse Eugene 1928- *St&PR 93*
Wyrick, Priscilla Blakeney 1940- *WhoAmW 93*
Wyrsch, Dieter 1942- *WhoScE 91-4*
Wyrsch, James Robert 1942- *WhoWor 93*
Wyrsch, Martha Brown *Law&B 92*
Wyrtki, Klaus 1925- *WhoAm 92*
Wyrwas, Margaret E. *St&PR 93*
Wysack, Roy L. *ScF&FL 92*
Wyschnegradsky, Ivan (Alexandrovich) 1893-1979 *Baker 92*
Wyschogrod, Michael 1928- *WhoAm 92*
Wyse, Bonita Wensink 1945- *WhoAmW 93*
Wyse, Bonnie L. 1953- *WhoE 93*
Wyse, Lois *BioIn 17, WhoAm 92, WhoAmW 93*
Wyse, Sheila Ruth 1950- *St&PR 93*
Wyse, Sheryl King 1946- *WhoAmW 93*
Wyse, William Walker 1919- *WhoAm 92*
Wyser-Pratte, Eugene J. d1990 *BioIn 17*
Wysiecki, Mieczyslaw 1935- *WhoScE 91-4*
Wysinski, Robert M. 1948- *St&PR 93*
Wysling, Paulo 1925- *WhoWor 93*
Wyslocki, Boleslaw 1933- *WhoScE 91-4*
Wysocki, Ann M. 1956- *St&PR 93*
Wysocki, Boleslaw Antoni 1912- *WhoE 93*
Wysocki, Conrad E. 1927- *St&PR 93*
Wysocki, Henry Victor *Law&B 92*
Wysocki, Jerzy 1930- *WhoScE 91-4*
Wysocki, Jo Ann 1935- *WhoAmW 93*
Wysocki, Miroslaw J. 1941- *WhoScE 91-4, WhoUN 92*
Wysocki, Nancy 1940- *WhoWrEP 92*
Wysocki, R.J. *ScF&FL 92*
Wysocki, Sharon Ann 1955- *WhoWrEP 92*
Wysong, Ronald Eugene 1943- *St&PR 93*
Wysor, Bettie *WhoWrEP 92*
Wyspianski, Stanislaw 1869-1907 *PolBiDi*
Wyss, David A. 1944- *St&PR 93*
Wyss, David Alen 1944- *WhoAm 92*
Wyss, Dianne Dunlop 1950- *WhoAmW 93*
Wyss, James Michael 1948- *WhoSSW 93*
Wyss, Johann David Von 1743-1818 *MajAI*
Wyss, Kurt 1943- *WhoWor 93*
Wyss, Loren Lee 1934- *WhoAm 92*
Wyss, Niklaus 1936- *Baker 92*
Wyss, Orville 1912- *WhoAm 92*
Wyss, Roland 1944- *WhoWor 93*
Wyszkowski, Jeffrey Paul 1953- *WhoE 93*
Wyszkowski, Stanislaw Wladyslaw Paul 1934- *WhoE 93*
Wyszomirski, Margaret Jane 1949- *WhoAmW 93*
Wyszynski, Casimir 1700-1755 *PolBiDi*
Wyszynski, Stefan 1901-1981 *PolBiDi*
Wyszynski, Stefan, Cardinal 1901-1981 *ColdWar 2 [port]*
Wythe, George 1893-1990 *BioIn 17*
Wythes, Paul M. 1933- *St&PR 93*
Wytmar, Richard J. 1924- *St&PR 93*
Wytock, Dale Harrison 1952- *WhoE 93*
Wyton, Alec 1921- *WhoAm 92*
Wyttenbach, Charles Richard 1933- *WhoAm 92*
Wyttenbach, Jurg 1935- *Baker 92*
Wyzanski, Charles Max 1944- *WhoE 93*
Wyzanski, Gisela Warburg 1912-1991 *BioIn 17*
Wyzard, John Wiley, III 1952- *WhoSSW 93*
Wyzewa, Theodore de 1862-1917 *Baker 92*
Wyzewski, Teodor de 1862-1917 *Baker 92*
Wyzner, Eugeniusz 1931- *WhoUN 92*
Wzorek, Lawrence E. *Law&B 92*

X-Y

X, Madeleine *ScF&FL 92*
X, Malcolm 1925-1965 *AfrAmBi, ConHero 2 [port]*
Xagas, Steven George James 1951- *WhoEmL 93*
Xalabarder, Eudaldo *WhoScE 91-3*
Xander, Al 1921- *St&PR 93*
Xanrof, Leon 1867-1953 *Baker 92*
Xanthakis, John *WhoScE 91-3*
Xanthaky, Nicholas 1911- *St&PR 93*
Xanthopoulos, Nikephoros Kallistos c. 1256-1335? *OxDcByz*
Xanthopoulos, Philip, Sr. 1944- *WhoSSW 93*
Xavier, Francis 1916- *WhoE 93*
Xavier, Francis 1964- *WhoWor 93*
Xavier, Isaac De Melo 1954- *WhoWor 93*
Xavier, St. Francis 1506-1552 *Expl 93 [port]*
Xenakis, Constantin 1931- *BioIn 17*
Xenakis, Iannis 1922- *Baker 92*
Xenakis, Stephen Nicholas 1948- *WhoAm 92*
Xenophon c. 430BC-c. 355BC *HarEnMi*
Xenophon 435?BC-355?BC *Expl 93*
Xenos, John 970?-c. 1027 *OxDcByz*
Xenos, Philippos John 1949- *WhoWor 93*
Xenoulis, Alexander 1940- *WhoScE 91-3*
Xeros *OxDcByz*
Xesspe, M. Toribio Mejia *IntDcAn*
Xia, Guang 1944- *WhoWor 93*
Xia, Ning-Mao 1944- *WhoWor 93*
Xia Nai 1910-1985 *IntDcAn*
Xiao, Dingquan 1946- *WhoWor 93*
Xiao, Jia-xin 1936- *WhoWor 93*
Xiao Youmei d1940 *BioIn 17*
Xiarhos, Louis G. *Law&B 92*
Xie, Jin *MiSFD 9*
Xie, Nan-Zhu 1925- *WhoWor 93*
Xie, Wendou 1935- *WhoWor 93*
Xie, Xiang Sheng 1957- *WhoWor 93*
Xie Fei 1932- *WhoAsAP 91*
Xieting, You 1930- *WhoUN 92*
Xie Xide *BioIn 17*
Xie Xide 1920- *WhoAsAP 91*
Xin, Ding Jian 1931- *WhoWor 93*
Xing Chongzhi 1928- *WhoAsAP 91*
Xing Jun *BioIn 17*
Xing Zhikang 1930- *WhoAsAP 91*
Xiong Qingquan 1928- *WhoAsAP 91*
Xiphilinos *OxDcByz*
Xiphilinos, John the Younger dc. 1081 *OxDcByz*
Xippo, Lea *WhoScE 91-4*
Xistris, Victor D. *Law&B 92*
Xi Zhongxun 1913- *WhoAsAP 91*
Xolocotzi, Efraim Hernandez *BioIn 17*
Xu, Bo-Wei 1934- *WhoWor 93*
Xu, Daoyi 1947- *WhoWor 93*
Xu, Gang 1961- *WhoWor 93*
Xu, Hong-Kun 1960- *WhoWor 93*
Xu, Ji Hua 1952- *WhoWor 93*
Xu, Jianlin 1965- *WhoWor 93*
Xu, Jing-hua 1922- *WhoWor 93*
Xu, Kezun 1940- *WhoWor 93*
Xu, Luo-shan 1932- *WhoWor 93*
Xu, Ronglie 1931- *WhoWor 93*
Xu, Sengen 1941- *WhoWor 93*
Xu, Shanda 1947- *WhoWor 93*
Xu, Shaohong 1921- *WhoWor 93*
Xu, Shu-Rong 1936- *WhoWor 93*
Xu, Shu Yun 1943- *WhoUN 92*
Xu, Xiao-Quan 1961- *WhoWor 93*
Xu, Yonghua 1932- *WhoWor 93*
Xu, Yuantong 1945- *WhoWor 93*
Xu, Zeng Kun 1944- *WhoWor 93*
Xu, Zhizhan 1938- *WhoWor 93*
Xu, Zong-Ben 1955- *WhoWor 93*
Xuan, Ti Zuo 1937- *WhoWor 93*
Xuan Tong 1906-1967 *BioIn 17*
Xue, Bin 1938- *WhoWor 93*
Xue, Miao 1929- *WhoWor 93*
Xue, Zi Ping 1932- *WhoUN 92*
Xue Ju 1922- *WhoAsAP 91*
Xu Meihong *BioIn 17*
Xu Shijie 1920- *WhoAsAP 91*
Xu Shiqun 1941- *WhoAsAP 91*
Xuxa *BioIn 17*
Xu Xiake 1587-1641? *BioIn 17*
Xu Xiangqian 1902-1990 *BioIn 17*
Xyndas, Spyridon 1812-1896 *Baker 92*
Xyndas, Spyridon 1814-1896 *OxDcOp*
Yaacob, Mohamed Bin 1926- *WhoAsAP 91*
Yabh Allaha, III 1245-1317 *OxDcByz*
Yablans, Frank 1935- *WhoAm 92*
Yablecki, Edward J. 1940- *St&PR 93, WhoIns 93*
Yablon, Jeffery Lee 1948- *WhoE 93*
Yablon, Leonard H. 1929- *St&PR 93*
Yablon, Leonard Harold 1929- *WhoAm 92*
Yablonowitz, Scott R. *Law&B 92*
Yablonskaya, Oxana *BioIn 17*
Yablonski, Joseph John 1944- *WhoE 93*
Yablonski, Stephen C. *Law&B 92*
Yabsley, James 1934- *St&PR 93*
Yabuki, Susumu 1938- *WhoWor 93*
Yabunaka, Yoshihiko *WhoAsAP 91*
Yabuuchi, Takao 1950- *WhoWor 93*
Yacavone, David William 1945- *WhoSSW 93*
Yace, Philippe 1920- *WhoAfr*
Yacher, Leon Isaac 1950- *WhoE 93*
Yachmetz, Philip K. *Law&B 92*
Yackel, James William 1936- *WhoAm 92*
Yackel, Kenneth Raymond 1946- *St&PR 93*
Yackell, Harriet Elaine 1958- *WhoAmW 93*
Yackira, Michael W. 1951- *St&PR 93*
Yackira, Michael William 1951- *WhoAm 92*
Yacktman, Donald Arthur 1941- *St&PR 93, WhoAm 92*
Yacobi, Stephen 1955- *WhoSSW 93*
Yacobian, Sonia Simone 1943- *WhoAmW 93*
Yaconetti, Dianne M. 1946- *St&PR 93*
Yaconetti, Dianne Mary 1946- *WhoAm 92, WhoAmW 93*
Yacoub, Ignatius I. 1937- *WhoAm 92*
Yacoub, Salah Musleh 1936- *WhoUN 92*
Yacovone, Ellen Elaine 1951- *WhoAmW 93*
Yacowitz, Harold 1922- *WhoAm 92*
Yacyshyn, Paul Michael *Law&B 92*
Yadalam, Kashinath Gangadhara 1954- *WhoSSW 93*
Yadav, Ish Dutt 1936- *WhoAsAP 91*
Yadav, Kailash Nath 1944- *WhoAsAP 91*
Yadav, Ram Naresh 1928- *WhoAsAP 91*
Yadav, Sharad 1945- *WhoAsAP 91*
Yadigaroglu, George 1939- *WhoScE 91-4*
Yadov, Vladimir *BioIn 17*
Yaecker, Scott A. 1952- *St&PR 93*
Yaeger, Alan Martin 1946- *St&PR 93*
Yaeger, Billie Patricia 1949- *WhoEmL 93, WhoWor 93*
Yaeger, Dewey R. 1940- *St&PR 93*
Yaeger, Thomas A. *St&PR 93*
Yafaev, Dimitrij Raueljevich 1948- *WhoWor 93*
Yaffa, R.A. *St&PR 93*
Yaffe, Alan *ConAu 38NR, MajAI*
Yaffe, Harold J. 1947- *St&PR 93*
Yaffe, Harvey Morton 1931- *St&PR 93*
Yaffe, James 1927- *WhoAm 92, WhoWrEP 92*
Yaffe, Robert Norton 1933- *St&PR 93*
Yaffe, Sumner Jason 1923- *WhoAm 92*
Yagasaki, Kazuyuki 1960- *WhoWor 93*
Yager, Barry E. 1944- *St&PR 93*
Yager, Cinda 1954- *WhoWrEP 92*
Yager, Deborah L. *St&PR 93*
Yager, Earl L. 1946- *St&PR 93*
Yager, Faye *BioIn 17*
Yager, Hunter 1929- *WhoAm 92*
Yager, James Donald, Jr. 1943- *WhoE 93*
Yager, James Leo 1961- *WhoSSW 93*
Yager, Jay Jerome 1947- *St&PR 93*
Yager, John Warren 1920- *WhoAm 92*
Yager, Joseph Arthur, Jr. 1916- *WhoAm 92*
Yager, Pamela Hall 1953- *St&PR 93*
Yager, Robert Henry 1913- *WhoSSW 93*
Yager, Vincent Cook 1928- *St&PR 93, WhoAm 92*
Yaghi, Husam M. 1961- *WhoEmL 93, WhoSSW 93*
Yaghjian, Arthur David 1943- *WhoE 93*
Yagi, Hiroshi 1928- *WhoWor 93*
Yagi, Mikio 1939- *WhoWor 93*
Yagi, Robert S. 1946- *St&PR 93*
Yagi, Takashi 1951- *WhoWor 93*
Yagi, Tatsuhiko 1933- *WhoWor 93*
Yagi Siyan d1098 *HarEnMi*
Yagjian, Anita P. *Law&B 92*
Yagjian, Michael Arthur *Law&B 92*
Yago, Bernard Cardinal 1916- *WhoWor 93*
Yago, C.E. 1934- *St&PR 93*
Yago, Glenn Harvey 1950- *WhoE 93*
Yagoda, Louis 1909-1990 *BioIn 17*
Yagoda, Richard 1941- *St&PR 93*
Yagyu, Yasuko 1959- *WhoWor 93*
Yahara, Hideo 1930- *WhoAsAP 91*
Yahi, Ismail Ould 1944- *WhoWor 93*
Yahia, Laurence H.S. *Law&B 92*
Yahne, Kenneth R. *Law&B 92*
Yahr, Melvin David 1917- *WhoAm 92, WhoE 93*
Yahweh Ben Yahweh *BioIn 17*
Yahya d1948 *BioIn 17*
Yahya Khan, Agha Mohammed 1917-1980 *DcTwHis*
Yahya of Antioch dc. 1066 *OxDcByz*
Yaist, Ronald Patrick *Law&B 92*
Yaji, Shigeru *BioIn 17*
Yakatan, Stan 1942- *St&PR 93*
Yaker, Bernard *Law&B 92*
Yaker, Lynda E. 1945- *WhoAmW 93, WhoWor 93*
Yakes, Helen Z. *Law&B 92*
Yaki, Roy 1951- *WhoAsAP 91*
Yakimovicz, Ann Denise 1950- *WhoAmW 93*
Yakinthos, John K. 1937- *WhoScE 91-3*
Yakip, James 1949- *WhoAsAP 91*
Yakob, Adrian F. *Law&B 92*
Yakos, Barbara Verlee 1912- *WhoWrEP 92*
Yakovlev, Aleksander *BioIn 17*
Yakovlev, Aleksandr Nikolayevich 1923- *WhoWor 93*
Yaku, Takeo Kawagoe Chichibu Taira 1947- *WhoWor 93*
Yakubov, Ashab Yakubovich 1938- *WhoWor 93*
Yakubov, Sasun Yakubovich 1935- *WhoWor 93*
Yakubovich, Dmitry Vladimirovich 1961- *WhoWor 93*
Yakubovich, Semen Borisovich 1961- *WhoWor 93*
Yakura, Hidetaka 1947- *WhoWor 93*
Yakymiv, Arsen Lubomir 1955- *WhoWor 93*
Yalcin, Burhan Cahit 1933- *WhoScE 91-4*
Yale, Elsie Duncan *AmWomPl*
Yale, Jeffrey Franklin 1943- *WhoE 93*
Yale, Seymour Hershel 1920- *WhoAm 92, WhoWor 93*
Yalen, Gary N. 1942- *WhoAm 92*
Yaley, Carole Jean *Law&B 92*
Yalkovsky, Rafael 1917- *WhoE 93, WhoWrEP 92*
Yalkut, Arlen Spencer 1945- *WhoAmW 93*
Yalman, Ann 1948- *WhoAmW 93*
Yalom, Marilyn K. 1932- *ConAu 40NR*
Yalow, Rosalyn S. 1921- *BioIn 17*
Yalow, Rosalyn Sussman 1921- *WhoAm 92, WhoAmW 93, WhoWor 93*
Yam, Chi Ming Stephen 1954- *WhoWor 93*
Yamabe, Shigeru 1923- *WhoWor 93*
Yamabe, Tokio 1936- *WhoWor 93*
Yamada, Chikashi 1945- *WhoWor 93*
Yamada, Eisuke 1945- *WhoAsAP 91*
Yamada, Fukiko 1924- *WhoWor 93*
Yamada, Haruki 1947- *WhoWor 93*
Yamada, Hidenori 1947- *WhoWor 93*
Yamada, Hirofumi 1956- *WhoWor 93*
Yamada, Hisatoshi 1932- *WhoWor 93*
Yamada, Isamu 1932- *WhoAsAP 91*
Yamada, Isuzu 1917- *IntDcF 2-3*
Yamada, Keiichi 1931- *WhoWor 93*
Yamada, Kenichi 1946- *WhoAsAP 91*
Yamada, Kenji 1943- *WhoWor 93*
Yamada, Kosaku 1886-1965 *Baker 92, OxDcOp*
Yamada, Kozaburo 1917- *WhoAsAP 91*
Yamada, Makiko 1938- *WhoWor 93*
Yamada, Mitsuye *BioIn 17*
Yamada, Mitsuye May 1923- *WhoWrEP 92*
Yamada, Noboru 1935- *WhoWor 93*
Yamada, Otozo 1881-1965 *HarEnMi*
Yamada, Ryoji 1928- *WhoWor 93*
Yamada, Sachiko 1939- *WhoWor 93*
Yamada, Satoshi 1934- *WhoWor 93*
Yamada, Shinichi 1937- *WhoWor 93*
Yamada, Shoichiro 1922- *WhoWor 93*
Yamada, Taro 1934- *WhoAm 92*
Yamada, Tomohiko Albert 1938- *WhoE 93*
Yamada, William Yukio 1951- *WhoAm 92*
Yamada, Yastel 1939- *WhoWor 93*
Yamada, Yasuyuki 1931- *WhoWor 93*

Yarbro, Chelsea Quinn 1942- DcAmChF 1985, ScF&FL 92
Yarbro, James Wesley 1920- WhoAm 92
Yarbrough, Billy A. 1939- St&PR 93
Yarbrough, Brenda Kay 1952- WhoAmW 93
Yarbrough, C. Richard 1937- St&PR 93
Yarbrough, Camille 1938- ChlLR 29 [port]
Yarbrough, Camille 1948- BlkAuII 92
Yarbrough, Charles A. 1935- St&PR 93
Yarbrough, David Wylie 1937- WhoSSW 93
Yarbrough, Dena Cox 1933- WhoAmW 93
Yarbrough, Henry 1948- BioIn 17
Yarbrough, James Wayne 1948- WhoSSW 93
Yarbrough, Jerry A. 1938- St&PR 93
Yarbrough, Karen Marguerite 1938- WhoAmW 93, WhoSSW 93
Yarbrough, Marilyn Virginia 1945- WhoAm 92, WhoSSW 93
Yarbrough, Martha Cornelia 1940- WhoAmW 93
Yarbrough, Richard R. 1945- St&PR 93
Yarbrough, Sonja Dianne 1948- WhoAmW 93
Yarbrough, Stephen R. 1950- ConAu 138
Yarchun, Hyman Joshua 1946- WhoWor 93
Yard, Molly WhoAmW 93
Yard, Rix Nelson 1917- WhoAm 92
Yard, Theresa Irene 1962- WhoAmW 93
Yarden, Abraham L. 1930- St&PR 93
Yarden, Linda Law&B 92
Yardis, Pamela Hintz 1944- WhoE 93
Yardley, Edna Ramsaier d1990 BioIn 17
Yardley, John Finley 1925- WhoAm 92
Yardley, John Howard 1926- WhoAm 92
Yardley, Jonathan 1939- WhoAm 92, WhoE 93
Yardley, Rosemary Roberts 1938- WhoAmW 93
Yardumian, Richard 1917-1985 Baker 92
Yared, Paul D. Law&B 92
Yared, Paul David 1949- St&PR 93
Yaremko-Jarvis, Helene Law&B 92
Yarger, Sam Jacob 1937- WhoAm 92
Yarhi, Nassin 1929- St&PR 93
Yari, Bob MiSFD 9
Yarin, Veniamin BioIn 17
Yarington, Charles Thomas, Jr. 1934- WhoAm 92
Yariv, Amnon 1930- WhoAm 92
Yariv, Fran Pokras ScF&FL 92
Yarlagadda, Rambabu Venkata 1959- WhoWor 93
Yarlow, Loretta 1948- WhoAm 92
Yarmolinsky, Adam 1922- WhoAm 92
Yarmolinsky, Michael Bezalel 1929- WhoE 93
Yarmon, Betty WhoAm 92
Yarmus, James J. 1941- WhoE 93
Yarnall, D. Robert, Jr. 1925- WhoAm 92
Yarnell, Ann Elizabeth 1938- WhoAmW 93
Yarnell, Michael Allan 1944- WhoAm 92
Yarnell, Richard Asa 1929- WhoAm 92
Yaro, John Michael Law&B 92
Yaros, Constance Lenore Greenberg WhoE 93
Yarosewick, Stanley J. 1939- WhoAm 92
Yaross, Wendy Ann 1952- WhoAmW 93
Yarra, Nirmala Karnam 1944- WhoE 93
Yarrigle, Charlene Sandra Shuey 1940- WhoWor 93
Yarrington, Alfred R. Law&B 92
Yarrington, Hollis Roger 1931- St&PR 93
Yarrington, Hugh J. 1942- St&PR 93
Yarrington, William H. 1918- St&PR 93
Yarrow, Christopher 1942- WhoWor 93
Yarrow, Peter 1938- Baker 92, WhoAm 92
Yarrow, Vera 1903-1991 BioIn 17
Yarsinske, Amy Melissa 1963- WhoSSW 93
Yarus, Donna G. 1956- WhoAmW 93
Yarus, Mike St&PR 93
Yarustovsky, Boris (Mikhailovich) 1911-1978 Baker 92
Yarwood, Dean Lesley 1935- WhoAm 92
Yarwood, Jack WhoScE 91-1
Yarzabal, Bartolomeu Robert y 1842-1902 BioIn 17
Yasar, Tug 1941- St&PR 93
Yasbeck, Amy BioIn 17
YaShad 1965- WhoE 93
Yashima, Eiji 1958- WhoWor 93
Yashima, Taro MajAI
Yashiro, Akio 1929-1976 Baker 92
Yashiro, Eita 1937- WhoAsAP 91
Yashiro, Rokuro 1860-1930 HarEnMi
Yashnikov, Victor Petrovitch 1944- WhoWor 93
Yashon, David 1935- WhoAm 92
Yasinsky, John Bernard 1939- WhoAm 92
Yaskulka, Louise Katherine 1966- WhoE 93
Yaslowitz, Lawrence Philip 1945- WhoE 93
Yasnyi, Allan David 1942- WhoWor 93
Yass, Robert K. Law&B 92
Yassa, Guirguis Fahmy 1930- WhoE 93
Yassen, Thomas Alexander Law&B 92
Yasser, Joseph 1893-1981 Baker 92
Yassin, Robert Alan 1941- WhoAm 92
Yassky, Harold 1930- WhoSSW 93, WhoWor 93
Yassky, James L. d1992 BioIn 17, NewYTBS 92
Yassky, Lester 1941- WhoAm 92
Yastremsky, Alexander Ivanovich 1951- WhoWor 93
Yastrow, Shelby Law&B 92
Yastrow, Shelby 1935- St&PR 93
Yastrzemski, Carl Michael 1939- WhoAm 92
Yastrzemski, J. Richard 1943- St&PR 93
Yasuda, Hajime 1941- WhoWor 93
Yasuda, Han 1927- WhoAsAP 91
Yasuda, Hirotsugu Koge 1930- WhoAm 92
Yasuda, Kenji 1952- WhoWor 93
Yasuda, Mineo 1937- WhoWor 93
Yasuda, Shuzo 1927- WhoAsAP 91
Yasue, Hideyuki Law&B 92
Yasue, Kunio 1951- WhoWor 93
Yasugi, Mariko 1937- WhoWor 93
Yasui, Ikuro 1937- St&PR 93
Yasui, Koji 1959- WhoWor 93
Yasui, Nobuo 1930- WhoWor 93
Yasuki, Hirohiko 1940- WhoWor 93
Yasumatsu, Katsuharu 1931- WhoWor 93
Yasumoto, Kyoden 1934- WhoWor 93
Yasumoto, Takeshi 1935- WhoWor 93
Yasumura, Michiaki 1947- WhoWor 93
Yasunaga, Hideo 1920- WhoAsAP 91
Yasuoka, Shotaro 1920- BioIn 17
Yasutsune, Ryoichi 1924- WhoAsAP 91
Yasuyoshi, Sekiguchi 1935- WhoWor 93
Yasuyuki, Ohta 1929- WhoWor 93
Yasuyuki, Watai 1952- WhoWor 93
Yata, Noboru 1933- WhoWor 93
Yatabe, Osamu 1932- WhoAsAP 91
Yatagai, Mitsuyoshi 1943- WhoWor 93
Yates, Alan 1923-1985 ScF&FL 92
Yates, Albert Carl 1941- WhoAm 92
Yates, Barbara 1950- WhoSSW 93
Yates, Bernard WhoScE 91-1
Yates, Charles Richardson 1913- WhoAm 92
Yates, Danny Dewain 1954- WhoSSW 93
Yates, David John C. 1927- WhoAm 92
Yates, Donald BioIn 17
Yates, Donald Glen 1939- St&PR 93, WhoSSW 93
Yates, Douglas Martin 1943- St&PR 93
Yates, Edward Carson, Jr. 1926- WhoSSW 93
Yates, Elizabeth 1905- BioIn 17, MajAI [port]
Yates, Elizabeth Hall AmWomPl
Yates, Ella Gaines 1927- WhoAm 92, WhoSSW 93
Yates, Elton G. 1935- St&PR 93, WhoAm 92
Yates, Frances R. 1935- St&PR 93
Yates, G. Neil 1950- WhoSSW 93
Yates, Harry Robert, Jr. 1926- WhoSSW 93
Yates, Hazel A. 1925- St&PR 93
Yates, Helen Louise 1941- WhoSSW 93
Yates, Herbert Spencer 1942- St&PR 93
Yates, J. Michael 1938- WhoCanL 92
Yates, James D. 1911- St&PR 93
Yates, Jeffrey M. 1948- WhoIns 93
Yates, Jeffrey McKee 1948- WhoAm 92
Yates, Jeffrey W. 1941- St&PR 93
Yates, Jessica ScF&FL 92
Yates, Joe Elton 1938- WhoSSW 93
Yates, John Gordon WhoScE 91-1
Yates, John Robert, Jr. 1930- WhoE 93
Yates, John Thomas, Jr. 1935- WhoAm 92
Yates, Juanita 1924- WhoWrEP 92
Yates, Kathleen Barrett 1954- WhoAmW 93
Yates, Keith 1928- WhoAm 92
Yates, Lenore Easley 1945- WhoAmW 93
Yates, Linda Snow 1938- WhoAmW 93
Yates, M. Geoffrey WhoScE 91-1
Yates, Margery Gordon 1910- WhoAmW 93
Yates, Mark L. Law&B 92
Yates, Marvin L. WhoSSW 93
Yates, Marypaul 1957- WhoE 93
Yates, Maurice Marvin, III 1954- WhoEmL 93, WhoSSW 93
Yates, Michael Francis 1946- WhoE 93
Yates, Nancy G. Law&B 92
Yates, Patricia England 1958- WhoAmW 93
Yates, Patty M. AmWomPl
Yates, Peter 1924- WhoAm 92
Yates, Peter 1929- MiSFD 9, WhoAm 92, WhoWor 93
Yates, Peter B. 1909-1976 Baker 92
Yates, Peter O. WhoScE 91-1
Yates, Rebecca 1950- MiSFD 9
Yates, Renee Harris 1950- WhoAmW 93
Yates, Richard d1992 NewYTBS 92 [port]
Yates, Richard 1926-1992 ConAu 139, DcLB Y92N [port]
Yates, Richard L. 1950- St&PR 93
Yates, Robert Doyle 1931- WhoAm 92
Yates, Robert Duane 1946- WhoAm 92
Yates, Robert Lynn 1947- WhoAm 92
Yates, Ronald Eugene 1941- WhoAm 92
Yates, Ronald Wilburn 1938- WhoAm 92
Yates, Samuel 1919- WhoWrEP 92
Yates, Sandra Kay 1946- WhoAmW 93, WhoSSW 93
Yates, Sidney R. 1909- CngDr 91
Yates, Sidney Richard 1909- WhoAm 92
Yates, Stephanie Law&B 92
Yates, Thomas H. 1938- St&PR 93
Yates, Victoria A. Law&B 92
Yates, W.R. 1950- ScF&FL 92
Yates, William Albert 1929- WhoE 93
Yates, William Harrison, Jr. 1930- St&PR 93
Yates-Buckles, Jeannette Keber 1942- WhoE 93, WhoWor 93
Yatiman Yusof 1946- WhoAsAP 91
Yatron, Gus 1927- CngDr 91, WhoAm 92, WhoE 93
Yatron, Stratton D. 1966- St&PR 93
Yatsevitch, Gratian Michael 1911- WhoE 93
Yatsko, Michael Samuel Law&B 92
Yatsu, Frank d1992 NewYTBS 92
Yatsu, Kiyoshi 1939- WhoWor 93
Yatsuzuka, Mashio 1943- WhoWor 93
Yatvin, Joanne Ina 1931- WhoAmW 93
Yau, Edward Tintai 1944- WhoWor 93
Yau, Stephen Sik-sang 1935- WhoAm 92
Yauch, Adam c. 1965- See Beastie Boys, The ConMus 8
Yavitz, Boris 1923- St&PR 93, WhoAm 92
Yavneh, Raphael d1990 BioIn 17
Yavner, Louis E. 1910-1991 BioIn 17
Yavorsky, Boleslav (Leopoldovich) 1877-1942 Baker 92
Yaw, Elbert M. 1940- St&PR 93
Yawkey, Jean R. 1909-1992 BioIn 17, NewYTBS 92 [port]
Yawman, James Gregory Law&B 92
Yawn, David McDonald 1956- WhoSSW 93
Yawo, Wap 1951- WhoAsAP 91
Yaworski, JoAnn 1956- WhoE 93
Yaworsky, George Myroslaw 1940- WhoWor 93
Yaws, Cynthia Sue 1965- WhoAmW 93
Yax, Emile Marcel 1937- WhoScE 91-2
Yaxley, Jack Thomas 1943- WhoSSW 93
Yaygin, Hasan 1939- WhoScE 91-4
Yaz, Engin 1954- WhoSSW 93
Yazan, Gulden 1951- WhoScE 91-4
Yazbak, Eugene Paul 1960- WhoE 93
Yazdani, Golam 1917- WhoAsAP 91
Yazdgird, III c. 617-651? OxDcByz
Yazici, Ali 1950- WhoScE 91-4
Yazici, Yuksel 1934- WhoScE 91-4
Yazid, II c. 685-724 OxDcByz
Yazov, Dmitry BioIn 17
Yazulla, Stephen 1945- WhoE 93
Yazzie, Larry 1958- BioIn 17
Ybarnegaray, Jean 1883-1956 BioIn 17
Ybarra, Raymond 1946- WhoUN 92
Ybarra, Shirley J. 1945- St&PR 93
Ydigoras Fuentes, Miguel DcCPCAm
Ye, Jia Chen 1944- WhoWor 93
Ye, Ling 1938- WhoWor 93
Ye, Mao-Dong 1945- WhoWor 93
Ye, Shangchun 1937- WhoUN 92
Ye, Yiying 1939- WhoWor 93
Yeager, Anson Anders 1919- WhoWor 93
Yeager, C. Clayton 1942- St&PR 93
Yeager, Carl W. 1926- St&PR 93
Yeager, Charles E. 1923- Expl 93 [port]
Yeager, Charles Elwood Chuck 1923- WhoAm 92
Yeager, Charles William 1921- WhoSSW 93
Yeager, David Clark ScF&FL 92
Yeager, Dennis Randall 1941- WhoE 93
Yeager, Ernest Bill 1924- WhoAm 92
Yeager, Glenn Allen Law&B 92
Yeager, Jacques Stalder 1921- St&PR 93
Yeager, Jacques Stalder, Sr. 1921- WhoAm 92
Yeager, James L. 1952- St&PR 93
Yeager, Jancie Skinner 1945- WhoAmW 93
Yeager, Jeana 1952- See Rutan, Dick 1939- & Yeager, Jeana 1952- Expl 93
Yeager, John N. 1938- St&PR 93
Yeager, John S. 1940- St&PR 93
Yeager, John Spencer 1940- WhoAm 92
Yeager, John T. 1959- St&PR 93
Yeager, Joseph Cornelius 1940- WhoE 93
Yeager, Joseph Harold 1950- St&PR 93
Yeager, Paul David 1938- St&PR 93, WhoAm 92
Yeager, Phyllis Diane 1949- WhoWrEP 92
Yeager, Ronald Kent 1935- St&PR 93
Yeager, Sally Law&B 92
Yeager, Waldo E. 1936- St&PR 93
Yeager, William W. St&PR 93
Yeagle, Beverly Joanne 1947- WhoAmW 93
Yeagle, Gary M. Law&B 92
Yeagle, Paul Harry 1939- St&PR 93
Yeago, R.S. 1925- St&PR 93
Yeakel, Steven B. Law&B 92
Yealy, Dana A. 1959- St&PR 93
Yeargain, Dallas G. 1922- St&PR 93
Yeargan, Michael 1945- BioIn 17
Yeargin, Robert Harper 1926- St&PR 93, WhoAm 92
Yeargin-Allsopp, Marshalyn 1948- WhoAmW 93
Yearick, Ralph Wood 1952- St&PR 93
Yearley, Douglas Cain BioIn 17
Yearley, Douglas Cain 1936- St&PR 93, WhoAm 92
Yearsley, Ann Cromartie 1752-1806 BioIn 17
Yearwood, Donald R. 1939- St&PR 93
Yearwood, Donald Robert 1939- WhoAm 92
Yeary, Jo Ellen Diehl Law&B 92
Yeary, Pamela S. Law&B 92
Yeary, Wilma 1931- St&PR 93
Yeary, Wilma Joyce 1931- WhoSSW 93
Yeater, David Allan 1947- St&PR 93
Yeates, Brenda L. Law&B 92
Yeates, J. Lorin Law&B 92
Yeates, James R. 1949- WhoAm 92
Yeates, Zeno Lanier 1915- WhoAm 92
Yeatman, C. James St&PR 93
Yeatman, Harry Clay 1916- WhoAm 92
Yeatman, Hoyt WhoAm 92
Yeatman, Trezevant Player, III 1951- WhoWrEP 92
Yeats, Audrey M. 1940- St&PR 93
Yeats, Jack Butler 1871-1957 BioIn 17
Yeats, Richard W. 1936- St&PR 93
Yeats, Robert Sheppard 1931- WhoAm 92
Yeats, W.B. 1865-1939 BioIn 17
Yeats, William Butler 1865-1939 BioIn 17, MagSWL [port], OxDcOp, WorLitC [port]
Yeatts, Guillermo M. 1937- WhoWor 93
Yeazel, Nicholas John 1948- WhoE 93
Yeazell, Ruth Bernard 1947- WhoAmW 93
Yeboa, Emmanuel Kwame 1960- WhoWor 93
Yecies, Laura Susan 1964- WhoAmW 93
Yecies, Paul Richard 1945- St&PR 93
Yedlicka, William George 1922- WhoWor 93
Yedlik, Edwon G. 1945- WhoWor 93
Yee, Albert Hoy 1929- WhoAm 92, WhoE 93
Yee, Alfred Alphonse 1925- WhoAm 92
Yee, Darlene 1958- WhoAmW 93
Yee, Kim Law&B 92
Yee, Mabel WhoAmW 93
Yee, Mable BioIn 17
Yee, Paul BioIn 17
Yee, Paul 1956- DcChlFi
Yee, Paul Yeun Po Law&B 92
Yee, Yen S. Law&B 92
Ye Fei, Col.-Gen. 1914- WhoAsAP 91
Yefimov, Igor ScF&FL 92
Yefimov, Igor 1937- WhoWrEP 92
Yefimov, Igor Markovich 1937- WhoE 93
Yegge, Robert Bernard 1934- WhoAm 92, WhoWor 93
Yeh, Benjamin H. 1931- St&PR 93
Yeh, Chai 1911- WhoAm 92
Yeh, George Hon Cheng 1948- WhoSSW 93
Yeh, Grace C. Law&B 92
Yeh, James Kuen-Jann 1942- WhoE 93
Yeh, Jesse 1955- WhoSSW 93
Yeh, K. H. 1932- WhoWor 93
Yeh, Kung Chie 1930- WhoAm 92
Yeh, Raymond Wei-Hwa 1942- WhoAm 92
Yeh, Rui Zong 1930- WhoWor 93
Yeh, William Wen-Gong 1938- WhoAm 92
Yehoshua, Abraham B. BioIn 17
Yeh T'ing d1946 HarEnMi
Yehuda, Eliezer Ben- 1858-1922 BioIn 17
Yehuda, Levy 1935- WhoWor 93
Yehuda, Nachman Ben- ScF&FL 92
Yehudah Halevi 12th cent.- BioIn 17
Yeiri, Akira BioIn 17
Yeiser, Patti Kissel 1954- WhoSSW 93
Yeisley, Rexford A. 1947- St&PR 93
Ye Jianying 1899- HarEnMi
Yekpe, Vitrice 1963- WhoWor 93
Yektai, Manoucher 1922- WhoAm 92
Yeldell, Eric B. Law&B 92
Yeldell, James Willis, Jr. 1936- St&PR 93
Yeldezian, Gary Law&B 92
Ye Liansong 1935- WhoAsAP 91
Yelin, Max I. BioIn 17
Yeliseyev, Alexei 1934- BioIn 17

Yelity, Stephen C. 1949- *WhoAm 92*
Yell, Ralph W. 1938- *WhoScE 91-1*
Yelle, George Francis 1913- *St&PR 93*
Yelle, Richard J. 1936- *St&PR 93*
Yelle, Richard Wilfred 1951- *WhoAm 92*
Yellen, Jack 1892-1991 *BioIn 17*
Yellen, Linda *MiSFD 9*
Yellen, Linda Beverly *WhoAmW 93*
Yellen, Maurice 1943- *St&PR 93*
Yellen, Richard D. *St&PR 93*
Yellen, Steven L. *St&PR 93*
Yellin, Judith *WhoAmW 93*
Yellin, Melvin A. *Law&B 92*
Yellin, Stephen Louis 1943- *St&PR 93*
Yellin, Thomas Gilmer 1953- *WhoAm 92*
Yellin, Victor Fell 1924- *WhoAm 92*
Yellott, Mary *AmWomPl*
Yellow Robe, William *BioIn 17*
Yellowtail, Bill *BioIn 17*
Yellowtail, Thomas *BioIn 17*
Yelnick, Louis *BioIn 17*
Yeltsin, Boris *BioIn 17*
Yel'tsin, Boris Nikolayevich 1931- *WhoWor 93*
Yelverton, Shirley Ann Shane 1948- *WhoAmW 93*
Yemin, Edward 1936- *WhoUN 92*
Yen, David Chi-Chung 1953- *WhoEmL 93*
Yen, Dominic Francis *Law&B 92*
Yen, Douglas Ernest 1924- *WhoWor 93*
Yen, Duen Hsi 1949- *WhoWor 93*
Yen, Jing Gwo 1937- *WhoSSW 93*
Yen, Samuel Show-Chih 1927- *WhoAm 92*
Yen, Teh Fu 1927- *WhoAm 92*
Yen, William Mao-Shung 1935- *WhoSSW 93*
Yen, Y.C. James 1893-1990 *BioIn 17*
Yena, John A. *BioIn 17*
Yen Ching-hwang 1937- *ConAu 136*
Yencik, Robert John 1960- *WhoE 93*
Yendell, Robert William 1927- *St&PR 93*
Yendo, Masayoshi 1920- *WhoWor 93*
Yener, Gungor 1942- *WhoScE 91-4*
Yener, K. Aslihan *BioIn 17*
Yen Hsi-shan 1883-1960 *HarEnMi*
Yeniscavich, William 1934- *WhoE 93*
Yenkin, Bernard K. 1930- *St&PR 93*
Yenkin, Fred 1911- *St&PR 93*
Yenne, Allen Wayne 1906- *St&PR 93*
Yenne, Charles Richard 1930- *St&PR 93*
Yensen, Arthur 1898- *WhoWrEP 92*
Yeo, Edwin Harley, III 1934- *WhoAm 92*
Yeo, Ning-Hong 1943- *WhoWor 93*
Yeo, Ron 1933- *WhoAm 92*
Yeo, Ronald Frederick 1923- *WhoAm 92*
Yeo Chew Tong 1947- *WhoAsAP 91*
Yeoh, Rosemary H. *Law&B 92*
Yeoman, Lynn Chalmers 1943- *WhoSSW 93*
Yeoman, S. Jackson *Law&B 92*
Yeomans, Donald Ralph 1925- *WhoAm 92*
Yeo Ning Hong, Hon. Dr. 1943- *WhoAsAP 91*
Yeosock, John J. *BioIn 17*
Yeosock, John John 1937- *WhoAm 92*
Yeovil, Jack *ScF&FL 92*
Yep, Laurence *BioIn 17*
Yep, Laurence 1948- *ScF&FL 92*
Yep, Laurence M(ichael) 1948- *DcAmChF 1960*
Yep, Laurence Michael 1948- *MajAI [port], SmATA 69 [port], WhoAm 92*
Yepes, Narciso 1927- *Baker 92*
Yeracaris, Bernice Levenfeld 1920- *WhoE 93*
Yerant, Gene S. 1947- *WhoIns 93*
Yerant, Gene Stephen 1947- *St&PR 93*
Yerby, Alonzo Smythe 1921- *WhoAm 92*
Yerby, Frank d1991 *NewYTBS 92 [port]*
Yerby, Frank 1916- *WhoWrEP 92*
Yerby, Frank 1916-1991 *BioIn 17, ConLC 70, ScF&FL 92*
Yerby, Frank G(arvin) 1916-1991 *ConAu 136*
Yerby, Frank (Garvin) 1916-1991 *CurBio 92N*
Yerby, Karen 1953- *WhoSSW 93*
Yergan, Max 1892- *BioIn 17*
Yerganian, George 1923- *WhoE 93*
Yergeau, Edgar J. *Law&B 92*
Yerger, John R. 1946- *St&PR 93*
Yergin, Daniel *BioIn 17*
Yergin, Daniel Howard 1947- *WhoAm 92, WhoE 93, WhoWor 93*
Yerkes, David Norton 1911- *WhoAm 92*
Yerkes, Robert H. 1962- *St&PR 93*
Yerkes, Susan Gamble 1951- *WhoAmW 93*
Yerkes, Wendy V. *Law&B 92*
Yermakov, Nicholas *ScF&FL 92*
Yerman, James P. *St&PR 93*
Yernault, J.-C. 1943- *WhoScE 91-2*
Yerow, Mara H. 1951- *WhoE 93*
Yerrill, Victor Malcolm 1941- *WhoIns 93*
Yershov, Peter 1895-1965 *ScF&FL 92*
Yerushalmi, Joseph 1938- *WhoAm 92*
Yerushalmi, Yosef Hayim 1932- *WhoAm 92*
Yerxa, Donald A(llan) 1950- *ConAu 139*
Yeryar, Betty Gwen 1942- *WhoAmW 93*
Yes *ConMus 8 [port]*
Yesawich, Peter Charles 1950- *WhoAm 92*
Yeshion, Theodore Elliot 1951- *WhoSSW 93*
Yeshurun, Avot d1992 *BioIn 17, NewYTBS 92*
Yeshurun, Avot 1904-1992 *ConAu 136*
Yesilsoy, M. Sefik 1932- *WhoScE 91-4*
Yeslow, Rose Marie *WhoAmW 93*
Yeslow, Todd David *Law&B 92*
Yesner, A. Glenn 1958- *St&PR 93*
Yesner, Raymond 1914- *WhoE 93*
Yessa, John M. 1939- *St&PR 93*
Yesselman, Robert Alan 1944- *WhoAm 92*
Yessian, James J. 1931- *St&PR 93*
Yessian-Smith, Suzanne Marie 1962- *WhoAmW 93*
Yessman, Timothy Michael *Law&B 92*
Yeston, Maury 1945- *Baker 92, ConTFT 10, WhoAm 92*
Yetnikoff, Walter R. *BioIn 17*
Yetter, David G. *Law&B 92*
Yetter, J.J. *Law&B 92*
Yetter, Karolyn Kaye 1943- *WhoAmW 93*
Yetter, Larry L. *Law&B 92*
Yetter, Thomas G. 1952- *St&PR 93*
Yettram, Alan Leonard *WhoScE 91-1*
Yeung, Chap-Yung 1936- *WhoWor 93*
Yeung, Edward Szeshing 1948- *WhoAm 92*
Yeung, Lawrence C. 1946- *WhoUN 92*
Yeung, Peter C. 1958- *St&PR 93*
Yeung, William 1947- *St&PR 93*
Yeung, Wing-Kay David 1955- *WhoWor 93*
Yeung Kai-Yin, Hon 1941- *WhoAsAP 91*
Yeutter, Clayton Keith 1930- *WhoAm 92, WhoE 93, WhoWor 93*
Yevcak, Jeffrey Karl 1965- *WhoSSW 93*
Yevtushenko, Yevgeniy Aleksandrovich 1933- *WhoWor 93*
Yevtushenko, Yevgeny *MiSFD 9*
Yevtushenko, Yevgeny 1933- *MagSWL [port]*
Yevtushenko, Yevgeny Aleksandrovich 1933- *BioIn 17*
Yewaisis, Joseph Stephen 1939- *St&PR 93*
Ye Xuanping 1924- *WhoAsAP 91*
Ye Yongqing *BioIn 17*
Yezierska, Anzia 1880?-1970 *AmWomWr 92*
Yezierska, Anzia 1885-1970 *BioIn 17, JeAmFiW*
Yezzo, Dominick 1947- *WhoE 93*
Yglesias, Helen *BioIn 17*
Yglesias, Helen Bassine 1915- *WhoAm 92*
Yglesias, Ricardo Andres, Jr. 1968- *WhoE 93*
Yhouse, Paul A. 1949- *St&PR 93*
Yi, Arthur C. 1946- *St&PR 93*
Yi, Gyoseob 1952- *WhoE 93*
Yi, Hongxun 1944- *WhoWor 93*
Yiannes 1943- *WhoE 93*
Yiannopoulos, Athanassios Nicholas 1928- *WhoAm 92*
Yieizah, Nishima 1945- *WhoAsAP 91*
Yielding, K. Lemone 1931- *WhoAm 92*
Yiengpruksawan, Anusak *WhoE 93*
Yih, Chia-Shun 1918- *WhoAm 92*
Yih, Mae Dunn 1928- *WhoAmW 93*
Yildirim, Aykut 1939- *WhoScE 91-4*
Yildiz, Mehmet Can 1932- *WhoScE 91-4*
Yilmaz, Baydur *WhoScE 91-4*
Yilmaz, Mehmet Asil 1938- *WhoScE 91-4*
Yilmaz, Nevzat 1945- *WhoScE 91-4*
Yilmaz, Tuncay 1945- *WhoScE 91-4*
Yilmazcetin, Muriel Jean 1946- *WhoAmW 93*
Yim, Charlie 1959- *WhoE 93*
Yim, George W.Y. *Law&B 92*
Yim, Ho *MiSFD 9*
Yim, Suck-Soon 1937- *WhoUN 92*
Yim, Vera S.W. 1950- *WhoWrEP 92*
Yimou, Zhang 1950- *MiSFD 9*
Yin, Frank Chi-Pong 1943- *WhoE 93*
Yin, Gerald Zheyao 1944- *WhoWor 93*
Yin, Leslie *ScF&FL 92*
Yin, Wan-Lee 1941- *WhoSSW 93*
Yin Changmin 1923- *WhoAsAP 91*
Ying, John L. 1948- *WhoEmL 93, WhoWor 93*
Ying, Leong 1961- *WhoWor 93*
Yinger, Carl Lawrence *Law&B 92*
Yingling, Adrienne Elizabeth 1959- *WhoEmL 93*
Yingling, William E., III 1944- *WhoAm 92*
Ying Ruocheng 1929- *WhoWor 93*
Yingst, Thomas E. 1950- *St&PR 93*
Yin Jun 1932- *WhoAsAP 91*
Yin Kesheng 1932- *WhoAsAP 91*
Yip, Cecil Cheung-Ching 1937- *WhoAm 92*
Yirku, Marilyn 1939- *WhoAmW 93*
Yi Sun Shin d1598 *HarEnMi*
Yi Tok Ho 1942- *WhoAsAP 91*
Yitts, Rose Marie 1942- *WhoAmW 93*
Yizar, Donald 1956- *St&PR 93*
Yizar, Jeanette 1959- *St&PR 93*
Yizar, Marvin 1950- *St&PR 93*
Yizar, Raymond 1952- *St&PR 93*
Yliheljo, Pentti Olavi 1945- *WhoWor 93*
Yli-Jokipii, Pentti Olavi 1941- *WhoScE 91-4*
Yliniemi, Hazel Alice 1941- *WhoAmW 93*
Ylitalo, Pauli 1944- *WhoScE 91-4*
Ylvisaker, Barbara Ewing d1991 *BioIn 17*
Ylvisaker, James William 1938- *WhoWor 93*
Ylvisaker, Paul 1921-1992 *ConAu 137*
Ylvisaker, Paul N. *BioIn 17*
Ylvisaker, Paul N. d1992 *NewYTBS 92*
Ylvisaker, William T. 1924- *St&PR 93*
Ylvisaker, William Townend 1924- *WhoAm 92*
Yngve, John Anton 1924- *St&PR 93*
Yntema, Mary Katherine 1928- *WhoAmW 93*
Yntema, Sharon *ScF&FL 92*
Yoakam, Dwight 1956- *News 92 [port], WhoAm 92*
Yoakum, James A. *Law&B 92*
Yoakum, Joseph E. 1886?-1972 *BioIn 17*
Yob, Iris Mae 1944- *WhoAmW 93*
Yoburn, Byron Crocker 1950- *WhoE 93*
Yocam, Delbert Wayne 1943- *WhoAm 92*
Yochelson, Bonnie Ellen 1952- *WhoAm 92*
Yochelson, Ellis Leon 1928- *WhoAm 92*
Yochelson, John 1944- *WhoAm 92*
Yochelson, Kathryn Mersey 1910- *WhoE 93*
Yochem, Barbara June 1945- *WhoAmW 93, WhoWor 93*
Yocher, Margaret C. 1951- *St&PR 93*
Yochim, Marie Hirst *WhoAm 92, WhoAmW 93*
Yochim, Susan Laurel 1952- *WhoAmW 93*
Yochum, Cynthia Ruth 1959- *WhoAmW 93*
Yochum, Dory *BioIn 17*
Yochum, Leo William 1927- *WhoAm 92*
Yochum, Philip Theodore 1924- *WhoAm 92*
Yochum, Sharon Kay 1950- *WhoAmW 93*
Yock, Robert J. 1938- *CngDr 91*
Yockey, Donald Jay 1921- *WhoAm 92*
Yocom, John E. 1922- *St&PR 93*
Yoculan, Mary Clotilda 1949- *WhoAmW 93*
Yocum, Arlene M. *Law&B 92*
Yocum, Charles Edmund *Law&B 92*
Yocum, Ronald H. 1939- *St&PR 93*
Yocum, Ronald Harris 1939- *WhoAm 92, WhoE 93*
Yoda, Hidemi 1956- *WhoWor 93*
Yoda, Yoshikata 1909- *WhoWor 93*
Yoder, Allen 1927- *St&PR 93*
Yoder, Amos 1921- *WhoAm 92*
Yoder, Anna A. 1934- *WhoAmW 93*
Yoder, Bruce Alan 1962- *WhoWor 93*
Yoder, Carl W. 1937- *WhoAm 92*
Yoder, Carolyn Patricia 1953- *WhoWrEP 92*
Yoder, Daniel W. 1952- *WhoWor 93*
Yoder, Edith Lee 1936- *WhoAmW 93*
Yoder, Edwin Milton 1934- *WhoAm 92, WhoWrEP 92*
Yoder, Eileen Rhude 1946- *WhoWrEP 92*
Yoder, Frederick Floyd 1935- *WhoAm 92*
Yoder, Hatten Schuyler, Jr. 1921- *WhoAm 92*
Yoder, Janice Dana 1952- *WhoAmW 93*
Yoder, Kent Allen 1955- *St&PR 93*
Yoder, Mary Jane Warwick 1933- *WhoAmW 93*
Yoder, Myron Eugene 1953- *WhoE 93*
Yoder, Nelson Brent 1944- *WhoSSW 93*
Yoder, Norman Wayne 1943- *WhoSSW 93*
Yoder, Patricia Doherty 1942- *WhoAm 92*
Yoder, Richard Franklin 1930- *WhoAm 92*
Yoder, Ronnie A. 1937- *WhoAm 92*
Yoder, Stephen A. *Law&B 92*
Yoder Wise, Patricia Snyder 1941- *WhoAmW 93*
Yodhes, David J. *Law&B 92*
Yodhes, David John *Law&B 92*
Yoe, Harry Warner 1912- *WhoAm 92*
Yoelson, Asa d1950 *BioIn 17*
Yoerg, Norman *Law&B 92*
Yoerger, Roger Raymond 1929- *WhoAm 92*
Yoes, Janice 1942- *WhoAmW 93*
Yoffe, Shlomo 1909- *Baker 92*
Yoffe, Stuart A. *Law&B 92*
Yoffe, Stuart Alan 1936- *St&PR 93*
Yoffie, Alan Steven *Law&B 92*
Yogev, Sara 1946- *WhoAmW 93*
Yogi, Mahesh, Maharishi *BioIn 17*
Yogmour, Gus, Jr. *Law&B 92*
Yoh, Harold L., Jr. 1936- *St&PR 93*
Yoh, Harold Lionel, Jr. 1936- *WhoAm 92*
Yoh, Harold Lionel, III 1960- *St&PR 93*
Yohalem, Alan Daniel 1940- *St&PR 93*
Yohannan, Kohle *BioIn 17*
Yohay, Steven Jacob 1950- *WhoE 93*
Yohe, D. Scott 1952- *St&PR 93*
Yohe, Gary W. 1948- *WhoE 93*
Yohe, John Christopher 1943- *St&PR 93*
Yohe, Merrill A. 1934- *St&PR 93*
Yohe, Robert L. 1936- *WhoAm 92*
Yohman, Edward J. 1932- *St&PR 93*
Yohn, David Stewart 1929- *WhoAm 92*
Yohn, Sharon A. 1952- *WhoAmW 93, WhoEmL 93, WhoWor 93*
Yoichi, Kodera 1960- *WhoWor 93*
Yok, Thomas Hock Choon 1940- *WhoWor 93*
Yoke, Carl B. 1937- *ScF&FL 92*
Yokell, Michael David 1946- *St&PR 93, WhoAm 92*
Yokem, James William 1929- *St&PR 93*
Yoken, Mel B. 1939- *WhoE 93, WhoWor 93*
Yoken, Stephen B. *Law&B 92*
Yokley, Arlen G. 1937- *St&PR 93*
Yokley, Richard Clarence 1942- *WhoWor 93*
Yokogawa, Akira 1934- *WhoWor 93*
Yokoi, Mitsuru 1927- *WhoWor 93*
Yokoi, Myodo 1761-1832 *BioIn 17*
Yokomitsu Riichi 1898-1947 *TwCLC 47 [port]*
Yokomizo, Yoichi 1955- *WhoWor 93*
Yokota, Hideshi 1936- *WhoWor 93*
Yokota, Shin-ichi 1962- *WhoWor 93*
Yokota, Yozo 1940- *WhoWor 93*
Yokoyama, Akira 1927- *WhoWor 93*
Yokoyama, Kenji 1959- *WhoWor 93*
Yokoyama, Masahiro 1927- *WhoWor 93*
Yokoyama, N. *Law&B 92*
Yokoyama, Shizuo 1890-1961 *HarEnMi*
Yokoyama, Toshio 1947- *ConAu 136*
Yokozeki, Shunsuke 1940- *WhoWor 93*
Yoksh, R.M. 1947- *St&PR 93*
Yolanda of Montferrat *OxDcByz*
Yolande d1219 *OxDcByz*
Yolen, Jane 1939- *ScF&FL 92*
Yolen, Jane (Hyatt) 1939- *DcAmChF 1985, MajAI [port], WhoAm 92, WhoWrEP 92*
Yoli, Lupe Victoria d1992 *BioIn 17*
Yolton, John William 1921- *WhoAm 92*
Yomantas, Gary Charles 1949- *St&PR 93*
Yomazzo, Michael Joseph 1942- *St&PR 93*
Yon, Charles E. *Law&B 92*
Yon, Eugene T. 1936- *St&PR 93*
Yon, Pietro Alessandro 1886-1943 *Baker 92*
Yon, R.B. 1942- *St&PR 93*
Yon, Robert James *WhoScE 91-1*
Yonadi, Albert Joseph 1929- *St&PR 93*
Yonai, Mitsumasa 1880-1948 *HarEnMi*
Yonas, Martin I. 1938- *St&PR 93*
Yonath, Ada E. *WhoScE 91-3*
Yonce, Samuel Mcclay 1931- *St&PR 93*
Yonchak, Robert Francis *Law&B 92*
Yonchev, Elia *WhoAm 92*
Yonda, Alfred William 1919- *WhoE 93, WhoWor 93*
Yoneda, Elaine 1906-1988 *BioIn 17*
Yoneda, Kaoru 1941- *WhoWor 93*
Yoneda, Kimimaru 1931- *WhoWor 93*
Yoneda, Norihiko 1938- *WhoWor 93*
Yonetani, Kaoru 1938- *WhoWor 93*
Yonezawa, Akinori 1947- *WhoWor 93*
Yonezawa, Shigeru 1911- *WhoWor 93*
Yonezawa, Takashi 1940- *WhoAsAP 91*
Yong, James C. *Law&B 92*
Yong, Jiongmin 1958- *WhoWor 93*
Yong, Paul H. *Law&B 92*
Yong, Raymond Nen-Yiu 1929- *WhoAm 92*
Yong, Yan 1955- *WhoSSW 93*
Yong, Yook-Kong *WhoE 93*
Yonge, Charlotte 1823-1901 *TwCLC 48 [port]*
Yonge, Nicholas dc. 1619 *Baker 92*
Yong Kuet Tze, Amar Stephen 1921- *WhoAsAP 91*
Yongue, Jean Turner 1926- *WhoSSW 93*
Yon Hyong Muk *WhoAsAP 91*
Yon Hyong-muk 1925- *WhoWor 93*
Yonis, Robin *Law&B 92*
Yon Je Wong 1928- *WhoAsAP 91*
Yonkers, Winifred Frances 1939- *WhoE 93*
Yonkman, Fredrick Albers 1930- *WhoAm 92*
Yonkman, Mark W. *Law&B 92*
Yon Sosa, Marco Antonio *DcCPCAm*
Yonto, Anthony J. 1921- *St&PR 93*
Yontz, Donald Wayne 1950- *WhoSSW 93*
Yontz, Kenneth Frederic 1944- *St&PR 93*
Yontz, Kenneth Fredric 1944- *WhoAm 92*
Yoo 1942- *WhoAsAP 91*
Yoo, Hyeong Seon *WhoWor 93*
Yoo, Ji Sung 1945- *WhoWor 93*

Yoo, Paul J. 1939- St&PR 93
Yoo, Tae-Ho 1936- WhoUN 92
Yoobamrung, Chalerm WhoAsAP 91
Yood, Harold Stanley 1920- WhoWor 93
Yood-Moore, Wendy Elizabeth 1964- WhoAmW 93
Yoo Hak Seong 1928- WhoAsAP 91
Yoo Han Yul 1938- WhoAsAP 91
Yoo In Hak 1940- WhoAsAP 91
Yoo Joon Sang 1943- WhoAsAP 91
Yoo Ki Jun 1925- WhoAsAP 91
Yoon, Hoil 1943- WhoWor 93
Yoon, Ji-Won 1939- WhoWor 93
Yoon, Leah BioIn 17
Yoon Giel-Joong 1917- WhoAsAP 91
Yoon Jae Ki 1945- WhoAsAP 91
Yoo Su-Ho 1932- WhoAsAP 91
Yopp, H. John Law&B 92
Yopps, Fredric Robert 1945- St&PR 93
Yorburg, Betty 1926- WhoAmW 93
Yorck von Wartenburg, Johann David Ludwig 1759-1830 HarEnMi
Yordan, Carlos Manuel 1925- WhoAm 92
Yordan, Philip BioIn 17
Yorganci, Ulku 1941- WhoScE 91-4
Yori, Lawrence George 1950- St&PR 93
Yorinks, Arthur 1953- BioIn 17, ConAu 38NR, MajAI [port]
Yorio, Edward 1947-1992 BioIn 17
Yorio, Frank A. 1947- St&PR 93
York BioIn 17
York, Duchess of 1959- BioIn 17
York, Andrew J. St&PR 93
York, Anthony James 1948- St&PR 93
York, Arnold G. BioIn 17
York, Carol Beach 1928- ScF&FL 92
York, David H. St&PR 93
York, Dennis J. 1945- St&PR 93
York, Dick BioIn 17
York, Dick 1923-1992 News 92
York, Dick 1928-1992 NewYTBS 92 [port]
York, Donald Gilbert 1944- WhoAm 92
York, E. Malcolm 1936- St&PR 93
York, E. Travis, Jr. 1922- WhoAm 92
York, Elinor Janice 1939- WhoAmW 93
York, Elizabeth 1927- ScF&FL 92
York, Glen D. 1950- St&PR 93
York, Harry Lawrence 1944- WhoAm 92
York, Harvey Leffert 1946- WhoE 93
York, Henry Edward 1929- WhoSSW 93
York, Herbert Frank 1921- WhoAm 92
York, Howard WhoIns 93
York, James Lester 1942- WhoE 93
York, James Orison 1927- WhoAm 92
York, James Wesley 1912- St&PR 93
York, James Wesley, Jr. 1939- WhoAm 92
York, Janet Brewster 1941- WhoE 93
York, Jerome B. 1938- St&PR 93
York, John
See Byrds, The ConMus 8
York, John C. St&PR 93
York, John Christopher 1946- WhoEmL 93
York, John Thomas 1953- WhoWrEP 92
York, Linda 1959- WhoAmW 93
York, Michael 1942- WhoAm 92
York, Nancy Ann 1947- WhoAmW 93
York, Pat 1949- WhoWrEP 92
York, Preston Rudolph 1913-1970 BiDAMSp 1989
York, Rebecca ScF&FL 92
York, Richard, Duke of 1411-1460 HarEnMi
York, Richard Travis 1950- WhoAm 92
York, Simon MajAI, SmATA 69
York, Stephen M. Law&B 92
York, Stephen R. Law&B 92
York, Susannah 1939- IntDcF 2-3
York, Susannah 1942- WhoAm 92, WhoWor 93
York, Theodore C. 1942- St&PR 93
York, Thomas Lee 1940-1989 WhoCanL 92
York, Tina 1951- WhoEmL 93
York, William E. St&PR 93
York and Albany, Frederick Augustus, Duke of 1763-1827 HarEnMi
Yorke, Amanda 1954- ConAu 139
Yorke, Erin ScF&FL 92
Yorke, Harold W. 1948- WhoWor 93
Yorke, Henry ScF&FL 92
Yorke, John Bundy Law&B 92
Yorke, Marianne 1948- WhoAmW 93
Yorke, Preston ScF&FL 92
Yorkin, Bud 1926- MiSFD 9, WhoAm 92
York-Johnson, Michael 1942- WhoAm 92
Yorks, W. Brinton, Jr. Law&B 92
Yorra, David Ian 1923- St&PR 93
Yorston, Robert Scott 1942- St&PR 93
Yorty, Samuel 1909- WhoAm 92
Yosano, Akiko 1878-1942 BioIn 17
Yosano, Kaoru 1938- WhoAsAP 91
Yoseloff, Julien David 1941- WhoAm 92
Yoseloff, Martin 1919- WhoWrEP 92
Yoseloff, Thomas 1913- WhoAm 92, WhoWrEP 92
Yosha, Yaky MiSFD 9
Yoshi, Hidekatsu 1942- WhoAsAP 91

Yoshida, Akito 1919- WhoWor 93
Yoshida, Hiroaki MiSFD 9
Yoshida, Hiroshi 1938- WhoWor 93
Yoshida, Kazuko 1949- WhoAsAP 91
Yoshida, Kenji 1938- WhoWor 93
Yoshida, Masao 1923- WhoAsAP 91
Yoshida, Roland Kiyoshi 1948- WhoE 93
Yoshida, Tatsuo 1935- WhoAsAP 91
Yoshida, Tohru 1924- WhoWor 93
Yoshida, Tsunezo 1872-1957 Baker 92
Yoshida, Zen-Ichi 1925- WhoWor 93
Yoshida, Zensho 1958- WhoWor 93
Yoshida Shigeru 1878-1967 DcTwHis
Yoshie, Makoto 1935- WhoWor 93
Yoshifuji, Masaaki 1941- WhoWor 93
Yoshihara, Ken-ichi 1932- WhoWor 93
Yoshihara, Ronald T. 1955- St&PR 93
Yoshiharu, Shimizu 1929- WhoWor 93
Yoshihiko, Kubouchi 1920- WhoWor 93
Yoshihiko, Miki 1928- WhoWor 93
Yoshihisa, Suzuki 1929- WhoWor 93
Yoshii, Mitsuteru 1931- WhoAsAP 91
Yoshikawa, Haruko 1940- WhoAsAP 91
Yoshikawa, Hiroshi 1923- WhoAsAP 91
Yoshikawa, Kenichi 1948- WhoWor 93
Yoshikawa, Masakazu 1953- WhoWor 93
Yoshikawa, Takeo BioIn 17
Yoshikawa, Viveca Ruth 1944- WhoAmW 93
Yoshikawa, Yoshio 1931- WhoAsAP 91
Yoshimine-Webster, Carol 1955- WhoAmW 93
Yoshimizou, Minoru 1939- St&PR 93
Yoshimoto, Shinji 1909- WhoWor 93
Yoshimura, Emogene Kazue 1946- WhoAmW 93
Yoshimura, Junzo 1908- WhoWor 93
Yoshimura, Masaharu Shoji 1925- WhoWor 93
Yoshinaga, Ben K. 1922- St&PR 93
Yoshinaga, Hiroshi BioIn 17
Yoshinaga, Terry N. 1950- St&PR 93
Yoshinaga, Terry Nui Law&B 92
Yoshino, Masafumi 1954- WhoWor 93
Yoshino, Naoyuki 1950- WhoWor 93
Yoshinobu, Susumu 1927- WhoWor 93
Yoshioka, Hirosuke 1933- WhoWor 93
Yoshioka, Kaoru David 1936- St&PR 93
Yoshioka, Kenji 1938- WhoAsAP 91
Yoshioka, Masanori 1941- WhoWor 93
Yoshioka, Morimasa 1921- WhoWor 93
Yoshioka, Yoshinori 1928- WhoAsAP 91
Yoshitake, Akira 1937- WhoWor 93
Yoshiuchi, Ellen Haven 1949- WhoE 93
Yoshiyuki, Junnosuke 1924- BioIn 17
Yoshiyuki, Mitsui 1940- WhoWor 93
Yoshizaki, Shiro 1944- WhoWor 93
Yoshizaki, Yasuhiro 1943- WhoWor 93
Yoshizumi, Kenneth K. St&PR 93
Yosikazu, Eda WhoWor 93
Yoskowitz, Irving B. Law&B 92
Yoskowitz, Irving B. 1945- St&PR 93
Yoskowitz, Irving Benjamin 1945- WhoAm 92
Yosowitz, Sanford Law&B 92
Yosowitz, Sanford 1939- St&PR 93, WhoAm 92
Yossif, George 1939- WhoSSW 93, WhoWor 93
Yossifov, Alexander 1940- Baker 92
Yost, Bernice WhoAmW 93
Yost, Byron Lee 1939- St&PR 93
Yost, David John 1938- WhoE 93
Yost, Deborah Spillane 1953- WhoE 93
Yost, Donald H. 1927- St&PR 93
Yost, Edward Fred Joseph 1926- BiDAMSp 1989
Yost, Ellen Ginsberg 1945- WhoAmW 93
Yost, Francis BioIn 17
Yost, Frank A. 1902- St&PR 93
Yost, Frederick Maurice 1914- St&PR 93
Yost, James Everett 1925- WhoAm 92
Yost, Jean Marie 1928- WhoAmW 93
Yost, John A. Law&B 92
Yost, Kelly Lou 1940- WhoAmW 93
Yost, L. Morgan 1908- WhoAm 92
Yost, Lyle Edgar 1913- WhoAm 92
Yost, Marlene J. 1934- WhoAmW 93
Yost, Mary Marcella 1947- WhoAmW 93
Yost, Michel 1754-1786 Baker 92
Yost, Nancy Runyon 1933- WhoAmW 93, WhoWor 93
Yost, Nellie Snyder 1905-1992 BioIn 17
Yost, Paul Alexander, Jr. 1929- WhoAm 92
Yost, Pauline Chambers 1916- St&PR 93
Yost, R. David 1947- St&PR 93
Yost, Richard Alan 1953- WhoSSW 93
Yost, William A., III Law&B 92
Yost, William Albert 1944- WhoAm 92
Yost, William Arthur, III 1935- St&PR 93, WhoAm 92, WhoWor 93
Yoste, Charles Todd 1948- WhoEmL 93, WhoSSW 93
Yother, Michele 1965- WhoAmW 93
Youcha, Geraldine BioIn 17
Youd, Christopher ScF&FL 92
Youd, (Christopher) Samuel 1922- ConAu 37NR, MajAI [port]

Youde, Judith Dianne Atwood 1940- WhoAmW 93
Youdelman, Robert A. Law&B 92
Youdelman, Robert Arthur 1942- WhoAm 92
Youden, James D. Law&B 92
Youdi, Robert Vesituluta 1935- WhoUN 92
Youdin, Mikhail 1893-1948 Baker 92
Youel, Kenneth 1901-1990 BioIn 17
Youkalov, Youri Alexeevich 1932- WhoWor 93
Youker, James E. 1928- WhoAm 92
You Key Chun 1928- WhoAsAP 91
Youkharibache, Philippe Bijin 1955- WhoWor 93
Youlio, Anne Marie Rose Danchak 1964- WhoAmW 93
Youll, Henry fl. c. 1600- Baker 92
Youman, Lillian Hobson Lincoln 1940- WhoAmW 93
Youman, Robert Inis 1928- St&PR 93
Youman, Roger Jacob 1932- WhoAm 92, WhoE 93
Youmans, Claire WhoWrEP 92
Youmans, James BioIn 17
Youmans, Julian Ray 1928- WhoAm 92
Youmans, Rich 1960- WhoWrEP 92
Youmans, Scott BioIn 17
Youmans, Valerie BioIn 17
Youmans, Vincent (Millie) 1898-1946 Baker 92
Younce, Huston Howard 1936- St&PR 93
Younce, Leonard 1917- BiDAMSp 1989
Younes, Talal WhoScE 91-2
Younes, Talal 1944- WhoScE 91-2
Young, A. Thomas 1938- WhoAm 92, WhoE 93, WhoWor 93
Young, Alan Wayne 1950- WhoSSW 93
Young, Albert James 1939- WhoWrEP 92
Young, Alec David WhoScE 91-1
Young, (Basil) Alexander 1920- Baker 92
Young, Alexander Renfrew WhoScE 91-1
Young, Alice 1950- WhoAmW 93
Young, Alistair WhoScE 91-1
Young, Allen 1941- ConAu 39NR, WhoE 93, WhoWrEP 92
Young, Allen I. Law&B 92
Young, Anderson Briggs 1949- WhoE 93
Young, Andrew 1932- BioIn 17, ConBlB 3 [port], EncAACR, WhoAm 92, WhoWor 93
Young, Andrew B. 1907- St&PR 93
Young, Andrew Brodbeck 1907- WhoAm 92
Young, Andrew J., Jr. 1932- PolPar
Young, Andrew Jackson, Jr. 1932- AfrAmBi [port]
Young, Andrew Sturgeon Nash 1924- BlkAull 92
Young, Andrew William WhoScE 91-1
Young, Anita AmWomPl
Young, Anita Hattie WhoAmW 93
Young, Ann Elizabeth O'Quinn WhoAmW 93
Young, Anthony L. AfrAmBi [port]
Young, Archie WhoScE 91-1
Young, Archie 1946- WhoScE 91-1
Young, Ardell Moody 1911- WhoAm 92
Young, Arnold L. 1932- St&PR 93
Young, Arthur Gordon 1921- WhoAm 92
Young, Arthur Price 1940- WhoAm 92, WhoSSW 93
Young, Austin Prentiss 1940- St&PR 93
Young, Austin Prentiss, III 1940- WhoAm 92
Young, B.A. 1912- ScF&FL 92
Young, Babette Spero 1918- St&PR 93
Young, Barbara 1920- WhoAm 92
Young, Barbara Aldie 1964- WhoAmW 93
Young, Barbara Pisaro 1939- WhoAmW 93
Young, Barney Thornton 1934- WhoAm 92, WhoWor 93
Young, Barry N. Law&B 92
Young, Bernice Elizabeth 1931- BlkAull 92
Young, Betty 1933- WhoAmW 93
Young, Betty Lou 1930- WhoAmW 93
Young, Betty Read 1953- WhoAmW 93
Young, Beverly J. 1934- St&PR 93
Young, Billie 1933- WhoSSW 93
Young, Billie Jean BioIn 17
Young, Billy Devon 1947- WhoSSW 93
Young, Bing Edward Law&B 92
Young, Bracebridge Hemyng 1956- WhoAm 92, WhoWor 93
Young, Bradley 1955- St&PR 93
Young, Brian W. 1939- St&PR 93
Young, Brigham 1801-1877 BioIn 17
Young, Bryant Llewellyn 1948- WhoAm 92
Young, Buddy BioIn 17
Young, Burt 1940- WhoAm 92
Young, C. B. Fehrler 1908- WhoSSW 93
Young, C. Clifton 1922- WhoAm 92
Young, C. W. 1930- WhoSSW 93
Young, C. W. Bill 1930- CngDr 91, WhoAm 92

Young, Carlton Raymond 1926- WhoSSW 93
Young, Carol Ann Morizot 1944- WhoWrEP 92
Young, Carole 1943- St&PR 93
Young, Catherine Alicia 1963- ConAu 136
Young, Catherine Marie Law&B 92
Young, Cathy ConAu 136
Young, Cecilia 1711-1789 Baker 92, OxDcOp
Young, Cecilia Mary AmWomPl
Young, Cedric BioIn 17
Young, Charles ScF&FL 92
Young, Charles 1864-1922 EncAACR [port]
Young, Charles Edward 1931- WhoAm 92, WhoWor 93
Young, Charles W. 1916- St&PR 93
Young, Chester George 1944- St&PR 93
Young, Chris BioIn 17
Young, Christine Dorothea 1952- WhoAmW 93
Young, Christine H. 1948- St&PR 93
Young, Clarence MajAI
Young, Clarence M. 1889-1973 EncABHB 8 [port]
Young, Coleman BioIn 17
Young, Coleman A. 1918- AfrAmBi [port], PolPar
Young, Coleman Alexander 1918- WhoAm 92
Young, Cornelius Bryant, Jr. 1926- WhoE 93
Young, Cy 1867-1955 BioIn 17
Young, Cynthia W. Law&B 92
Young, D. Michael Law&B 92
Young, D.W. Law&B 92
Young, D. W. 1929- WhoIns 93
Young, Daisy Almeda 1932- WhoSSW 93
Young, Dale L. 1928- St&PR 93
Young, Dale Lee 1928- WhoAm 92
Young, Damson 1936- WhoWor 93
Young, Darlene 1954- WhoAmW 93
Young, Darlene Ann WhoSSW 93
Young, Daryl Alan 1955- WhoSSW 93
Young, David 1936- ScF&FL 92
Young, David 1946- WhoCanL 92
Young, David A. Law&B 92
Young, David Harold Law&B 92
Young, David Maynard 1928- WhoE 93
Young, David Michael 1935- WhoAm 92
Young, David Pollock 1936- WhoAm 92, WhoWrEP 92
Young, David Thad 1943- WhoSSW 93
Young, David William 1942- WhoE 93, WhoWor 93
Young, Debbie L. Law&B 92
Young, Deborah Nelson 1961- WhoE 93
Young, Deborah S. Law&B 92
Young, Deborah Schultz 1954- WhoSSW 93
Young, Delano Victor 1945- WhoE 93
Young, Dennis Charles 1936- WhoAsAP 91
Young, Dennis Eugene 1943- St&PR 93, WhoAm 92
Young, Dennis M. Law&B 92
Young, Dick 1918-1987 BiDAMSp 1989
Young, Don 1933- CngDr 91
Young, Don J. 1910- WhoAm 92
Young, Dona D. 1954- St&PR 93
Young, Dona Davis Law&B 92
Young, Dona Davis Gagliano 1954- WhoAm 92, WhoAmW 93
Young, Donald Alan 1939- WhoAm 92
Young, Donald Arthur 1958- WhoSSW 93
Young, Donald E. 1933- WhoAm 92
Young, Donald F. d1991 BioIn 17
Young, Donald Francis 1944- WhoSSW 93
Young, Donald Fredrick 1928- WhoAm 92
Young, Donald Richard 1933- WhoE 93
Young, Donald Roy 1935- WhoE 93
Young, Donald Stirling 1933- WhoAm 92
Young, Donna BiDAMSp 1989
Young, Donna J. ScF&FL 92
Young, Dorothy Theressa 1929- WhoWor 93
Young, Douglas 1947- Baker 92
Young, Douglas Alan 1955- WhoE 93
Young, Douglas E. 1949- St&PR 93
Young, Douglas Earle 1957- WhoE 93
Young, Douglas Hamilton 1938- WhoSSW 93
Young, Douglas Logan 1938- St&PR 93
Young, Douglas Wilson WhoScE 91-1
Young, Dwight Wayne 1925- WhoAm 92
Young, Ed BioIn 17, ChlBIID [port]
Young, Ed 1931- ChlLR 27 [port]
Young, Ed (Tse-chun) 1931- MajAI
Young, Edmond Grove 1917- WhoE 93
Young, Edward 1683-1765 BioIn 17
Young, Edward D., III Law&B 92
Young, Edward S. 1926- St&PR 93
Young, Edwin Harold 1918- WhoAm 92
Young, Edwin Reynolds, Jr. 1926- WhoSSW 93
Young, Elaine BioIn 17

Young, Elaine Claire 1931- WhoE 93
Young, Elisabeth Larsh 1910- WhoWrEP 92
Young, Elizabeth fl. 1756-1765 OxDcOp
Young, Elizabeth Bell 1929- WhoE 93
Young, Ella 1867-1956 ScF&FL 92
Young, Emily AmWomPl
Young, Eric 1962- St&PR 93
Young, Eric A. 1958- St&PR 93
Young, Eric Alan 1958- WhoSSW 93
Young, Erma AmWomPl
Young, Ernestine Jones 1930- WhoSSW 93
Young, Esther fl. 1739-1762 OxDcOp
Young, Eve Alexander 1947- WhoAmW 93
Young, Faron 1932- Baker 92
Young, Florence H. 1923- St&PR 93
Young, Francine B. 1956- WhoAmW 93
Young, Francis Allan 1918- WhoAm 92
Young, Frank, Jr. 1925- WhoWrEP 92
Young, Frank Edward 1931- WhoAm 92
Young, Frank Nelson, Jr. 1915- WhoAm 92
Young, Franklin 1928- WhoE 93
Young, Fredda Florine 1937- WhoSSW 93
Young, Freddie 1902- MiSFD 9
Young, Frederic Hisgin 1936- WhoWor 93
Young, Frederick John 1931- WhoE 93
Young, Gail Adaline 1948- WhoEmL 93
Young, Gary 1951- ConAu 40NR
Young, Gary Eugene 1951- WhoWrEP 92
Young, Gary M. d1990 BioIn 17
Young, Gary Thomas 1946- WhoSSW 93
Young, Gary W. St&PR 93
Young, Genevieve Leman 1930- St&PR 93, WhoAm 92
Young, Genevieve Marie 1963- WhoE 93
Young, Geoffrey P. Law&B 92
Young, George Bernard, Jr. 1930- WhoAm 92
Young, George Cressler 1916- WhoAm 92
Young, George Hansen 1962- WhoWor 93
Young, George James 1932- WhoUN 92
Young, George M. 1949- St&PR 93
Young, Gig 1917-1978 BioIn 17
Young, Gladys I. AmWomPl
Young, Glenn 1953- WhoE 93
Young, Glenn Reid 1951- WhoSSW 93
Young, Glennda Sue 1965- WhoAmW 93
Young, Gordon Ellsworth 1919- WhoAm 92
Young, Gregory B. St&PR 93
Young, Gregory E. Law&B 92
Young, H.R. 1918- St&PR 93
Young, Harold H., Jr. Law&B 92
Young, Harold William, Jr. 1946- WhoSSW 93
Young, Harrison BioIn 17
Young, Harrison Hurst, III 1944- WhoAm 92
Young, Harvey Michael 1937- St&PR 93
Young, Heidi R. Law&B 92
Young, Henry Ben 1913- WhoAm 92
Young, Henry C. Law&B 92
Young, Herbert Floyd 1929- St&PR 93
Young, Herrick B. 1904-1990 BioIn 17
Young, Hobart Peyton 1945- WhoE 93
Young, Holly Peacock 1949- WhoAmW 93
Young, Howard 1932- WhoIns 93
Young, Howard Seth 1924- WhoAm 92
Young, Howard Thomas 1926- WhoAm 92
Young, Hubert Howell, Jr. 1945- WhoSSW 93
Young, Hugh David 1930- WhoAm 92
Young, Ian Musgrave 1941- WhoAm 92
Young, Irving Gustav 1919- WhoE 93
Young, Isabella d1791 OxDcOp
Young, Isabella fl. 1730-1753 OxDcOp
Young, J. Anthony WhoAm 92
Young, J. Givens 1921- St&PR 93
Young, J. Will 1906- St&PR 93
Young, Jacqueline 1934- WhoAmW 93
Young, James Bernard Law&B 92
Young, James E. 1941- WhoWor 93
Young, James Earl 1922- WhoAm 92
Young, James Fred 1934- WhoAm 92
Young, James H. 1932- St&PR 93
Young, James Harry 1936- WhoAm 92, WhoSSW 93
Young, James Harvey 1915- WhoAm 92
Young, James Hilliard 1946- WhoAm 92
Young, James Houston 1945- WhoSSW 93
Young, James Julius 1926- WhoAm 92
Young, James L. Law&B 92
Young, James M. ScF&FL 92
Young, James Morningstar 1929- WhoAm 92
Young, James Oliver 1945- WhoSSW 93
Young, James R. Law&B 92
Young, James Richard 1960- St&PR 93
Young, James Scott 1956- WhoWrEP 92
Young, Janet Cheryl 1960- WhoAmW 93
Young, Janet Nevins d1990 BioIn 17
Young, Janice Roberts 1947- WhoAmW 93, WhoSSW 93
Young, Jeffrey MiSFD 9
Young, Jeffrey 1942- St&PR 93
Young, Jeffrey A. Law&B 92
Young, Jeffrey Thomas 1948- WhoE 93
Young, Jere Arnold 1936- WhoAm 92
Young, Jerry Lee 1951- WhoSSW 93
Young, Jess R. 1928- WhoAm 92
Young, Jess Wollett 1926- WhoSSW 93, WhoWor 93
Young, Jesse Robert 1938- St&PR 93
Young, Jewell 1913- BiDAMSp 1989
Young, Jim 1951- ScF&FL 92
Young, Joan Carol 1928- WhoSSW 93
Young, Joan Crawford 1931- WhoAmW 93
Young, Joan E. Law&B 92
Young, Joan Patricia 1956- WhoAm 92, WhoAmW 93
Young, Joe, Sr. 1927- AfrAmBi [port]
Young, John WhoScE 91-1
Young, John 1930- BioIn 17
Young, John A. St&PR 93
Young, John Alan 1932- WhoAm 92
Young, John C. Law&B 92
Young, John Ding-E 1958- WhoE 93
Young, John Edward 1935- WhoAm 92, WhoWor 93
Young, John F. 1957- St&PR 93
Young, John Hardin 1948- WhoAm 92, WhoEmL 93
Young, John Hendricks 1912- WhoAm 92
Young, John Karl 1951- WhoE 93
Young, John L. Law&B 92
Young, John Lane 1930- WhoE 93
Young, John Leonard 1943- WhoE 93
Young, John Marvin 1941- St&PR 93
Young, John Michael 1944- WhoAm 92
Young, John Morgan 1941- St&PR 93, WhoAm 92
Young, John Paul 1952- WhoSSW 93
Young, John Paul, II 1945- St&PR 93
Young, John Peter Wakeham WhoScE 91-1
Young, John Russell 1840-1899 JrnUS
Young, John Watts 1930- WhoAm 92
Young, John Wesley 1951- ConAu 138
Young, John William 1912- WhoSSW 93
Young, Johnny 1940- WhoAm 92, WhoWor 93
Young, Jordan R. 1950- WhoWrEP 92
Young, Joseph A. Law&B 92
Young, Joseph Beverly 1934- St&PR 93
Young, Joseph H. 1922- WhoAm 92, WhoE 93
Young, Joseph Laurie 1924- WhoAm 92
Young, Joseph Leslie 1940- WhoE 93
Young, Joseph Louis 1919- WhoAm 92
Young, Joseph Lum-Jip 1935- St&PR 93
Young, Joseph Paul d1991 BioIn 17
Young, Joseph Samuel, Jr. 1932- WhoWrEP 92
Young, Joseph W. Law&B 92
Young, Judith Lynne Law&B 92
Young, Judy (Elaine) Dockrey 1949- SmATA 72 [port]
Young, Karen M. 1942- ConAu 138
Young, Kathleen 1961- WhoAmW 93
Young, Kay Lynn 1955- WhoAmW 93
Young, Kenneth WhoScE 91-1
Young, Kenneth 1927- WhoAm 92
Young, Kenneth Evans 1922- WhoAm 92
Young, Kevin C. Law&B 92
Young, Kevin E. Law&B 92
Young, La Monte 1935- BioIn 17
Young, La Monte (Thornton) 1935- Baker 92
Young, Larry D. 1941- St&PR 93
Young, Larry Dale 1948- WhoSSW 93
Young, Laura 1947- WhoAm 92
Young, Laura Frances 1926- WhoAmW 93
Young, Laura S. BioIn 17
Young, Laurence Byron 1932- St&PR 93, WhoWor 93
Young, Laurence Retman 1935- WhoAm 92
Young, Lawrence 1925- WhoAm 92
Young, Lawrence Eugene 1913- WhoSSW 93
Young, Lawrence Evan Law&B 92
Young, Lawrence J. 1944- St&PR 93
Young, LeGrande L. Law&B 92
Young, Legrande L. 1936- St&PR 93
Young, Leo 1926- WhoAm 92
Young, Leo J. Law&B 92
Young, Leonard Joseph, Sr. 1920- WhoE 93
Young, Lester (Willis) 1909-1959 Baker 92
Young, Lias Carl Law&B 92
Young, Lillian AmWomPl, BlkAmWO
Young, Linda Joan Law&B 92
Young, Linda Wilcox 1954- WhoE 93
Young, Llewellyn P., Jr. Law&B 92
Young, Lois Catherine 1930- WhoAmW 93
Young, Lois Moran 1909-1990 BioIn 17
Young, Loretta 1913- WhoAm 92, WhoAmW 93
Young, Loretta 1914- IntDcF 2-3 [port]
Young, Loretta Ann 1962- WhoAmW 93
Young, Lorraine K. 1935- St&PR 93
Young, Lorraine Kelly 1935- WhoAmW 93
Young, Louise A. BioIn 17
Young, Louise B. BioIn 17
Young, Louise Merwin 1903-1992 ConAu 139
Young, Lucy Cleaver 1943- WhoAmW 93
Young, M. Clemewell 1925- WhoWrEP 92
Young, Malcolm Black 1940- St&PR 93
Young, Margaret Aletha McMullen 1916- WhoAmW 93, WhoSSW 93, WhoWor 93
Young, Margaret B. 1922- BlkAuII 92
Young, Margaret Buckner WhoAm 92, WhoAmW 93, WhoE 93
Young, Margaret Condren 1934- St&PR 93
Young, Margaret Hays 1954- WhoAmW 93
Young, Margaret Ruth 1953- WhoEmL 93
Young, Marilyn Ann Law&B 92
Young, Marjorie Ann 1945- WhoAmW 93
Young, Marjorie H. 1946- WhoAmW 93
Young, Marjorie Willis WhoAm 92
Young, Mark BioIn 17, NewYTBS 92 [port]
Young, Mark 1960- ConAu 139
Young, Mark E. 1957- St&PR 93
Young, Martin BioIn 17
Young, Marvin BioIn 17
Young, Marvin O. 1929- St&PR 93
Young, Marvin Oscar 1929- WhoAm 92
Young, Mary Eleanor 1940- WhoAmW 93
Young, Mary Elizabeth 1929- WhoAm 92, WhoAmW 93
Young, Mary Ellen 1949- WhoWrEP 92
Young, Mary Jane Law&B 92
Young, Mary Louise 1920- WhoWrEP 92
Young, Matt Norvel, Jr. 1915- WhoAm 92
Young, Maurice Alan 1914- St&PR 93
Young, Maurice Isaac 1927- WhoAm 92
Young, Melinda Moorman 1964- WhoAmW 93
Young, Melville Curtis 1935- St&PR 93
Young, Meredith Anne 1952- WhoAmW 93
Young, Meredith Lady ScF&FL 92
Young, Merwin Crawford 1931- WhoAm 92
Young, Michael Arthur 1956- WhoAm 92
Young, Michael Frank 1949- WhoSSW 93
Young, Michael James Law&B 92
Young, Michael Jerome 1936- WhoAsAP 91
Young, Michael Richard 1956- WhoEmL 93
Young, Michael Warren 1947- St&PR 93
Young, Michael Warren 1949- WhoAm 92
Young, Milton Earl 1929- WhoAm 92
Young, Myron D. 1943- St&PR 93
Young, Nancy 1954- WhoAm 92, WhoE 93
Young, Nancy Carol 1948- WhoAmW 93
Young, Naomi Berry 1936- WhoAmW 93
Young, Nathan B. 1862- BioIn 17
Young, Neal E. 1943- St&PR 93
Young, Neil BioIn 17
Young, Neil 1945- Baker 92, NewYTBS 92 [port], WhoAm 92
Young, Neil Thomas 1962- WhoWor 93
Young, Nicholas John WhoScE 91-1
Young, Nick 1948- WhoE 93
Young, Noel B. 1922- WhoWrEP 92
Young, Olivia Knowles 1922- WhoAm 92
Young, Oran Reed 1941- WhoAm 92
Young, P.(lummer) B.(ernard) 1884-1962 EncAACR
Young, Parry 1943- St&PR 93
Young, Patricia Jones 1947- WhoAmW 93
Young, Patrick 1937- WhoAm 92
Young, Patrick 1946- WhoCanL 92
Young, Paul Andrew 1926- WhoAm 92
Young, Paul D. Law&B 92
Young, Paul Francis 1921- WhoE 93
Young, Paul R. 1932- WhoAm 92
Young, Paul Ruel 1936- WhoAm 92
Young, Pauline Rodgers AmWomPl
Young, Percy M(arshall) 1912- Baker 92
Young, Peter A. 1962- St&PR 93
Young, Peter Colin WhoScE 91-1
Young, Peter R. BioIn 17
Young, Peter V. 1936- St&PR 93
Young, Philip 1918-1991 BioIn 17
Young, Philip Stuart 1947- St&PR 93
Young, Phyllis Casselman 1925- WhoAm 92
Young, Polly c. 1749-1799 OxDcOp
Young, Polly Ann 1908- SweetSg C [port]
Young, Polly (Mary) c. 1745-1799 Baker 92
Young, Quentin BioIn 17
Young, Quentin Hayes 1944- St&PR 93
Young, R.M. 1945- WhoScE 91-1
Young, Rachel Cashion 1954- WhoAmW 93
Young, Rachel D. Law&B 92
Young, Ralph Alden 1920- WhoAm 92
Young, Ralph O. 1931- St&PR 93
Young, Randel R. 1956- WhoWor 93
Young, Raymond A. d1991 BioIn 17
Young, Raymond Henry 1927- WhoAm 92
Young, Raymond Holmes 1928- St&PR 93
Young, Raymond N. 1938- St&PR 93
Young, Rebecca Mary Conrad 1934- WhoAmW 93
Young, Revel Paul 1944- St&PR 93
Young, Richard 1919- WhoAm 92
Young, Richard Alan 1935- WhoAm 92
Young, Richard Alan 1946- SmATA 72 [port]
Young, Richard Allen 1915- WhoAm 92
Young, Richard Benjamin d1991 BioIn 17
Young, Richard Robert 1946- WhoE 93
Young, Richard Stuart 1927- WhoAm 92
Young, Richard W. 1929- St&PR 93
Young, Richard William 1926- St&PR 93, WhoAm 92
Young, Rida Johnson 1875?-1926 AmWomPl
Young, Robert 1907- IntDcF 2-3, WhoAm 92
Young, Robert 1945- WhoSSW 93
Young, Robert A. 1952- St&PR 93
Young, Robert A., III 1940- St&PR 93, WhoAm 92, WhoSSW 93
Young, Robert Alan 1921- WhoAm 92
Young, Robert B. 1929- St&PR 93
Young, Robert Bunnell 1928- WhoIns 93
Young, Robert Craig 1960- WhoE 93
Young, Robert F. 1915-1986 ScF&FL 92
Young, Robert Francis 1919- WhoAm 92
Young, Robert Harris 1947- St&PR 93
Young, Robert Joseph WhoScE 91-1
Young, Robert Joseph 1947- WhoIns 93
Young, Robert Lerton 1936- St&PR 93
Young, Robert M. 1924- MiSFD 9
Young, Robert N. 1926- St&PR 93
Young, Robert Thomas 1945- WhoE 93
Young, Robert William MiSFD 9
Young, Robin Ray 1952- St&PR 93
Young, Roderick A. 1943- St&PR 93
Young, Rodger 1918?-1943 BioIn 17
Young, Roger 1942- MiSFD 9
Young, Roger Austin 1946- St&PR 93, WhoAm 92
Young, Roland 1887-1953 QDrFCA 92 [port]
Young, Ronald A. 1928- St&PR 93
Young, Ronald D. Law&B 92
Young, Ronald Faris 1939- WhoAm 92
Young, Ronnie Lee 1943- St&PR 93
Young, Roy Alton 1921- WhoAm 92
Young, Roy Archibald 1882-1960 BioIn 17
Young, Roy Robert 1917- St&PR 93
Young, Ruby Jean 1923- WhoWrEP 92
Young, Russell Dawson 1923- WhoE 93
Young, Ruth BioIn 17
Young, Ruth 1946- ConAu 136
Young, S. June 1937- WhoAmW 93, WhoSSW 93
Young, Sally Burton 1944- WhoSSW 93
Young, Samuel A. 1940- St&PR 93
Young, Samuel B. M. 1840-1924 CmdGen 1991 [port]
Young, Sarah Moskowitz 1947- WhoAmW 93
Young, Scott 1918- WhoCanL 92
Young, Scott 1946- St&PR 93
Young, Scott Alexander 1918- WhoAm 92
Young, Sean BioIn 17
Young, Selina Gaye 1963- WhoAmW 93
Young, Shawna Malloy 1966- WhoAmW 93
Young, Sheila 1950- BioIn 17
Young, Sheila Jane 1952- WhoAmW 93
Young, Sheri Law&B 92
Young, Shirley BioIn 17
Young, Shirley 1935- WhoAmW 93
Young, Shirley Jean 1944- WhoAmW 93
Young, Stanton Alan Law&B 92
Young, Stark 1881-1963 BioIn 17, JrnUS
Young, Stephanie Clark 1940- WhoE 93
Young, Stephen WhoScE 91-1
Young, Stephen A. Law&B 92
Young, Stephen Blase 1949- WhoE 93
Young, Stephen C. St&PR 93
Young, Stephen N. Law&B 92
Young, Steve St&PR 93
Young, Steven Dale 1948- St&PR 93
Young, Steven George 1960- WhoE 93
Young, Stuart F., Jr. 1950- St&PR 93
Young, Susan BioIn 17
Young, Susan D. 1957- WhoIns 93
Young, Susan Frances WhoAmW 93
Young, Sylvia Snider 1961- WhoAmW 93
Young, T. Michael St&PR 93
Young, Terence 1915- MiSFD 9, WhoAm 92
Young, Teri Ann Butler 1958- WhoAmW 93
Young, Terry Alan 1954- WhoSSW 93
Young, Thomas d1804 BioIn 17
Young, Thomas 1773-1829 BioIn 17

Young, Thomas Andrew Law&B 92
Young, Thomas Daniel 1919- WhoAm 92
Young, Thomas Ganley WhoAm 92
Young, Thomas L. Law&B 92
Young, Thomas L. 1944- St&PR 93
Young, Thomas Lee 1944- WhoAm 92
Young, Thomas Richard 1959- WhoSSW 93
Young, Timothy J. Law&B 92
Young, Tommie Morton WhoAmW 93
Young, Trevor James 1925- WhoAsAP 91
Young, Tyler F. 1959- St&PR 93
Young, Tyler Jennings 1912- WhoSSW 93
Young, Tzay Y. 1933- WhoAm 92
Young, Venus DeMilo 1959- WhoE 93
Young, Vera Lee Hall 1944- WhoAmW 93
Young, Vera M. 1927- St&PR 93
Young, Vera Miller 1927- WhoAmW 93, WhoSSW 93
Young, Victor 1889-1968 Baker 92
Young, Victor 1900-1956 Baker 92
Young, Vincent E. Law&B 92
Young, Virginia Brady 1918- WhoWrEP 92
Young, Virginia K. Law&B 92
Young, Virginia S. 1944- St&PR 93
Young, Wallace C. 1928- St&PR 93
Young, Walter C. 1927- St&PR 93
Young, Walter Martin 1922- St&PR 93
Young, Walter O. 1937- St&PR 93
Young, Walter Richard 1947- WhoAm 92, WhoSSW 93
Young, Walter Russell, Jr. 1944- St&PR 93
Young, Whitney M., Jr. 1921-1971 ConBlB 4
Young, Whitney Moore, Jr. 1921-1971 EncAACR [port]
Young, Wilhelmina G. 1938- WhoWrEP 92
Young, William d1662 Baker 92
Young, William Charles 1940- St&PR 93
Young, William Dean 1946- WhoSSW 93
Young, William Edgar 1930- WhoSSW 93
Young, William Edmund 1916- WhoE 93
Young, William Glover 1940- WhoAm 92
Young, William Hurlburt, Jr. 1920- WhoSSW 93
Young, William John 1925- WhoAm 92
Young, William Lee 1954- WhoWor 93
Young, William Lewis 1929- WhoE 93
Young, William Maurice 1924- St&PR 93
Young, William P. Law&B 92
Young, William P. 1943- St&PR 93
Young, William T. 1918- St&PR 93
Young, William Thomas 1924- WhoSSW 93
Young, William Victor 1937- WhoAm 92
Young, Wills Morrison 1935- St&PR 93
Young Adult Reviewers Of California ScF&FL 92
Youngbauer, Steven R. Law&B 92
Youngberg, David Arthur 1955- St&PR 93
Youngberg, Robert Alan Law&B 92
Youngblood, Betty WhoAmW 93
Youngblood, Denise J. 1952- ConAu 139
Youngblood, Eddie 1956- BioIn 17
Youngblood, G.R. 1930- St&PR 93
Youngblood, Herbert Jackson, III 1950- BiDAMSp 1989
Youngblood, J. Craig 1947- WhoAm 92
Youngblood, John C. 1926- St&PR 93
Youngblood, John Curtis, Jr. 1949- St&PR 93
Youngblood, John L. 1941- St&PR 93
Youngblood, Michelle Karen Wolstein 1958- WhoAmW 93
Youngblood, Nat 1916- BioIn 17
Youngblood, Peggy Joyce 1943- St&PR 93
Youngblood, Ray W. 1931- St&PR 93
Youngblood, Samuel C. 1955- St&PR 93
Youngblood, William Randolph 1957- WhoSSW 93
Young-Cummings, Mary AfrAmBi
Youngdahl, James Edward 1926- WhoAm 92
Youngdahl, Patricia Lucy 1927- WhoSSW 93
Youngdahl, Russell Charles 1924- WhoAm 92
Younge, Samuel, Jr. 1944-1966 EncAACR
Youngelman, David Roy 1959- WhoE 93
Younger, Bob 1853-1889 BioIn 17
Younger, Cathy D. Law&B 92
Younger, Cole 1844-1916 BioIn 17
Younger, Derell Joseph 1939- St&PR 93
Younger, Doris Anne 1924- WhoAm 92
Younger, Gary J. Law&B 92
Younger, Gary Paul 1947- St&PR 93
Younger, George Kenneth Hotson 1931- WhoWor 93
Younger, Gordon Myles 1938- St&PR 93
Younger, Henry St&PR 93
Younger, J.C. WhoWrEP 92
Younger, J. Michael 1930- St&PR 93
Younger, Jack 1927?- ScF&FL 92
Younger, James Michael WhoWor 93
Younger, Jim 1848-1902 BioIn 17
Younger, John 1851-1874 BioIn 17
Younger, John M. D. 1946- St&PR 93
Younger, Judith Tess 1933- WhoAm 92, WhoAmW 93
Younger, Kenneth Maurice 1952- WhoSSW 93
Younger, Thomas Carlton, Jr. Law&B 92
Younger, William Carl 1919- WhoAm 92, WhoSSW 93, WhoWor 93
Youngerman, Jack 1926- WhoAm 92
Youngers, Marion A. Law&B 92
Youngers, Marion Anthony 1930- St&PR 93
Youngert, Barbara Ann 1938- WhoWrEP 92
Youngfellow, Michael Law&B 92
Younghusband, Francis 1863-1942 Expl 93 [port]
Youngken, Heber Wilkinson, Jr. 1913- WhoAm 92
Young Lively, Sandra Lee 1943- WhoAmW 93, WhoWor 93
Young-Mallin, Judith 1937- WhoE 93
Youngman, Henny BioIn 17, WhoAm 92
Youngman, John Crawford 1903- WhoWor 93
Youngman, Kirk E. Law&B 92
Youngman, Melissa Ann 1949- WhoAmW 93
Youngman, Michael Warren 1962- WhoWor 93
Youngman, William Sterling Law&B 92
Youngman, William Sterling 1907- WhoAm 92
Young M.C. BioIn 17
Youngner, Julius Stuart 1920- WhoAm 92
Youngquist, Alvin Menvid, Jr. 1925- WhoAm 92, WhoWrEP 92
Youngquist, Andrew L. 1940- WhoAm 92
Youngren, Ralph Park 1924- St&PR 93, WhoAm 92
Youngs, Bettie Burres 1948- WhoAmW 93
Youngs, Christopher Jay 1956- WhoEmL 93
Youngs, John Robert 1950- St&PR 93
Youngs, Joseph 1930- WhoIns 93
Youngs, Joseph Harry 1930- St&PR 93
Youngs, Maynard L. Law&B 92
Youngs, Shirley Cean 1939- WhoAmW 93
Youngs-Andersen, Marie Alice 1958- WhoAmW 93, WhoE 93
Youngson, Jeanne 1924- ScF&FL 92
Youngstrom, Steve P. 1961- WhoSSW 93
Youngstrum, David Mansfield 1942- WhoSSW 93
Young-Tatum, Susan Lynn 1959- WhoAmW 93
Young-Uck Kim Baker 92
Youngwood, Alfred Donald 1938- WhoAm 92
Younie, William John 1932- WhoE 93
Younis, Mahmoud Rachid 1948- WhoWor 93
Younis, Tal WhoScE 91-1
Younk, James L. 1942- St&PR 93
Younker, Donald Keith 1939- St&PR 93
Younker, Fred D. 1949- St&PR 93
Younker, Mildred Burke BiDAMSp 1989
Younkin, Richard Ambrose 1949- WhoWor 93
Yount, Bradley A. St&PR 93
Yount, David Eugene 1935- WhoAm 92
Yount, George Stuart 1949- St&PR 93, WhoEmL 93, WhoWor 93
Yount, George W. 1929- St&PR 93
Yount, James L. 1936- St&PR 93
Yount, John Alonzo 1935- WhoWrEP 92
Yount, Robin BioIn 17
Yount, Stuart 1949- St&PR 93
Yount, William Jay 1936- WhoSSW 93
Younts, Elizabeth Mendenhall 1919- WhoSSW 93
Younts, Melvin K. 1929- St&PR 93
Younts, Sanford Eugene 1930- WhoAm 92
Youpa, Jennifer Ashmos Law&B 92
Youra, Daniel George 1944- WhoWrEP 92
Yourassowsky, Eugene 1929- WhoScE 91-2
Yourcenar, Marguerite BioIn 17
Yourcenar, Marguerite 1903-1987 ScF&FL 92
Yourdon, Patricia 1944- WhoUN 92
Youree, William F. St&PR 93
Yourell, Agnes Bond ScF&FL 92
Yourgrau, Barry ScF&FL 92
Yourish, Ghulam Sarwar 1944- WhoUN 92
Youron, Michael Robert 1955- WhoE 93
Yousef, Fathi Salaama 1934- WhoWor 93
Youssef, Edwar Kolta Faltas ConAu 136
Youssef, Magdy Anis 1935- WhoUN 92
Youssef, Michael ScF&FL 92
Youssef, Nasr H. 1945- St&PR 93
Youssoupoff, Nikolai Borisovich 1827-1891 Baker 92
Youssri, Ibrahim 1935- WhoWor 93
Yousten, Allan Arthur 1936- WhoSSW 93
Youtan, Norman 1938- WhoAm 92
Youtcheff, John Sheldon 1925- WhoWor 93
Youtt, Stanley Addison 1946- St&PR 93
Yova, Steven P. Law&B 92
Yovanovic, Nicholas Stevphen Law&B 92
Yovanovich, Deborah Theresa 1953- WhoAmW 93, WhoEmL 93
Yovev, Yovi Kirilov 1942- WhoScE 91-4
Yovich, Daniel John 1930- WhoAm 92
Yovicich, George Steven Jones 1929- WhoAm 92
Yovits, Marshall Clinton 1923- WhoAm 92
Yovos, John George 1947- WhoWor 93
Yovovich, Paul G. 1953- St&PR 93
Yow, John Stuart, Jr. 1926- WhoSSW 93
Yow, Raymond Murray 1924- St&PR 93
Yowell, Linda Miriam 1951- WhoE 93
Yowell, Ronald Lee 1951- WhoIns 93
Yowell, William C., Jr. 1926- St&PR 93
Yoxall, G. Patrick 1934- St&PR 93
YoYo BioIn 17
Yo Yo 1971- ConMus 9 [port]
Yo-Yo Ma Baker 92
Yphantis, David Andrew 1930- WhoE 93
Ypres, Earl of 1852-1925 BioIn 17
Yradier, Sebastian de 1809-1865 Baker 92
Yriarte, Tomas de 1750-1791 Baker 92
Yrjanheikki, Erkki Juhani 1944- WhoScE 91-4
Yrjola, Erkki Olavi 1922- WhoScE 91-4
Yrjola, Erkki Pentti Juhani 1941- WhoWor 93
Yrjola, Timo 1941- WhoScE 91-4
Ysaye, Eugene 1858-1931 OxDcOp
Ysaye, Eugene (-Auguste) 1858-1931 Baker 92
Ysaye, Theophile 1865-1918 Baker 92
Ysern y Alie, Pere 1875?-1946 BioIn 17
Yslas, Stephen Daniel Law&B 92
Ysseldyke, James Edward 1944- WhoAm 92
Ystaas, Jonas 1929- WhoScE 91-4
Ytterberg, Donald Victor 1926- St&PR 93
Ytterberg, Ralph Warren 1927- St&PR 93, WhoAm 92
Ytterbo, Greta Law&B 92
Yttrehus, Rolv (Berger) 1926- Baker 92
Yturry, Julio 1959- WhoWor 93
Yu, Aiting Tobey 1921- WhoAm 92
Yu, Albert Y. C. 1941- St&PR 93
Yu, Anne Ramona Wing-mui 1948- WhoEmL 93
Yu, Anthony C. 1938- WhoAm 92
Yu, Bernice Law&B 92
Yu, Chi-chung 1911- WhoWor 93
Yu, Chien-Chih 1953- WhoWor 93
Yu, Chih-chen 1915- BioIn 17
Yu, Chul Soo 1937- WhoWor 93
Yu, Dajing 1941- WhoUN 92
Yu, Francis T. S. 1932- WhoAm 92
Yu, Frederick Sak Kwong 1934- WhoWor 93
Yu, Geoffrey S.K. 1948- WhoUN 92
Yu, George Tzuchiao 1931- WhoAm 92
Yu, Hoi Hong 1953- St&PR 93
Yu, Jen 1943- WhoAm 92
Yu, Jia-rong 1920- WhoWor 93
Yu, Ju-Hyun 1934- WhoWor 93
Yu, Julie Hung-Hsua 1954- WhoAmW 93, WhoEmL 93, WhoWor 93
Yu, Ka Fai Joseph 1953- WhoWor 93
Yu, Kai-cheng 1932- WhoWor 93
Yu, Kitson Szewai 1950- WhoEmL 93
Yu, Kwang-chung BioIn 17
Yu, Leslie Law&B 92
Yu, Li 1956- WhoWor 93
Yu, Lily 1950- St&PR 93
Yu, Linda 1946- WhoAmW 93
Yu, Paul N. 1915-1991 BioIn 17
Yu, Pingen 1932- WhoWor 93
Yu, Pufan 1923- WhoWor 93
Yu, Quingyu 1941- WhoWor 93
Yu, Robert Kuan-jen 1938- WhoSSW 93
Yu, Rong-jin 1935- WhoWor 93
Yu, Shu-Cheng 1942- WhoWor 93
Yu, Simon Shyi-Jian 1935- WhoSSW 93
Yu, Tan BioIn 17
Yu, Tian-yi 1927- WhoWor 93
Yu, Timothy Pan 1974- WhoWrEP 92
Yu, Victor Lin-Kai 1943- WhoE 93
Yu, Wenhuan 1940- WhoWor 93
Yu, Xiaotong 1929- WhoWor 93
Yu, Xin 1941- WhoWor 93
Yu, Yanlin 1939- WhoWor 93
Yu, Yeun-Chung 1935- WhoUN 92
Yu, Yi-Yuan 1923- WhoAm 92
Yu, Yong Ming 1945- WhoE 93
Yu, Zhanji 1939- WhoWor 93
Yuan, Cheng-Ye 1924- WhoWor 93
Yuan, Heh-Hsiang 1933- WhoWor 93
Yuan, James C.M. 1943- WhoWor 93
Yuan, Shao Wen 1914- WhoAm 92, WhoWor 93
Yuan, Sidney Wei Kwun 1957- WhoAm 92
Yuan Jun 1939- WhoAsAP 91
Yuan Longping BioIn 17
Yuan Shih-k'ai c. 1859-1916 HarEnMi
Yuan Shikai 1859-1916 DcTwHis
Yuan Weimin 1939- WhoAsAP 91
Yuan Xiaoyuan BioIn 17
Yuasa, Joji 1929- Baker 92
Yucel, Ayhan 1933- WhoScE 91-4
Yucel, Edgar K. Law&B 92
Yucel, Ercan 1944- WhoScE 91-4
Yucel, M. Nadir 1930- WhoScE 91-4
Yucel, Mehmet WhoScE 91-4
Yucelt, Ugur 1937- WhoE 93
Yucer, Onder 1945- WhoUN 92
Yu Chien-Min 1924- WhoAsAP 91
Yudain, Carole Gewirtz WhoE 93
Yudell, Linda 1952- WhoSSW 93
Yudelson, Joseph Samuel 1925- WhoE 93
Yudenich, Nikolai Nikolaevich 1862-1933 HarEnMi
Yudilevich, David Levy WhoScE 91-1
Yudina, Maria 1899-1970 Baker 92
Yudis, Melvin 1937- WhoE 93
Yudkin, Joshua Peter 1957- WhoE 93
Yudkin, Marcia BioIn 17
Yudkin, Marcia 1952- WhoAmW 93
Yudkin, Mark 1959- WhoWor 93
Yudof, Mark G. 1944- WhoAm 92
Yue, Alfred Shui-choh 1920- WhoAm 92
Yue, Edward 1928- WhoSSW 93
Yuechiming, Roger Yue Yuen Shing 1937- WhoWor 93
Yueh, Norma N. 1928- WhoE 93
Yueh Fei 1104-1142 HarEnMi
Yuelys, Alexander 1926- WhoAm 92
Yuen, Corey MiSFD 9
Yuen, Darrel 1951- St&PR 93
Yuen, Henry C. BioIn 17
Yuen, Janet 1958- WhoAmW 93
Yuen, Thomas C.K. 1952- See Qureshey, Safi U. 1951- & Yuen, Thomas C.K. 1952- ConEn
Yuen, Thomas Chi Kwan 1951- WhoAm 92
Yuen, William 1929- St&PR 93
Yuen, Yu Tai 1955- WhoWor 93
Yuenger, James Laury 1939- WhoAm 92
Yuenger, Stephen J. WhoIns 93
Yu-Fai, Antonio Choi 1952- St&PR 93
Yufe, Ona Rita 1932- WhoAmW 93
Yu-Hallada, Lorraine Ching-Fong 1964- WhoAmW 93
Yuhas, Alan Thomas 1948- WhoAm 92
Yuhi, Mitsue 1860-1940 HarEnMi
Yu Hongen 1928- WhoAsAP 91
Yuill, Douglas MacDonald WhoScE 91-1
Yuill, Thomas MacKay 1937- WhoAm 92
Yuki, Yoji 1942- St&PR 93
Yukio, Takeda 1927- WhoWor 93
Yule, Andrew 1936- ScF&FL 92
Yule, Joe 1888-1950 & Riano, Renie 1899-1971 QDrFCA 92 [port]
Yule, Roger Law&B 92
Yulek, Gurcu Gurcan 1942- WhoScE 91-4
Yulin, Vladimir Alekseyevich 1931- WhoUN 92
Yulish, Charles Barry 1936- WhoAm 92, WhoWor 93
Yulo, Mariano M. 1933- WhoAsAP 91
Yulsman, Jerry ScF&FL 92
Yumino, Masahiko 1940- St&PR 93
Yun, Caroline J. Law&B 92
Yun, Daniel Duwhan 1933- WhoE 93, WhoWor 93
Yun, David D. 1948- WhoSSW 93
Yun, Isang 1917- Baker 92, OxDcOp
Yun, James Myung Ju 1938- WhoE 93, WhoWor 93
Yun, Judy Law&B 92
Yun, Peter Subueng 1936- WhoAm 92
Yun, Po Sun d1990 BioIn 17
Yunck, Donald A. 1927- St&PR 93
Yuncker, Barbara WhoAm 92
Yund, Theodore Joseph 1947- WhoWrEP 92
Yundt, Delbert G. St&PR 93
Yundt, Jeffrey W. 1945- St&PR 93
Yune, Johnny MiSFD 9
Yunes, Hank 1957- St&PR 93
Yung, Chung Se 1928- WhoWor 93
Yung, Gerald E. Law&B 92
Yungbluth, Thomas Alan 1934- WhoSSW 93
Yunger, Libby Marie 1944- WhoAmW 93
Yung-Lo 1356-1424 HarEnMi
Yungman, Bruce A. 1944- St&PR 93
Yunich, David L. 1917- St&PR 93
Yunich, David Lawrence 1917- WhoAm 92
Yunick, Robert Peter 1935- St&PR 93
Yunick, Smokey BioIn 17
Yunis, Jorge Jose WhoAm 92, WhoWor 93
Yunker, Philip L. 1944- WhoE 93
Yunker, Ronald Charles 1927- St&PR 93
Yunker, Todd Elliott 1960- WhoWrEP 92
Yun Sung Hun 1937- WhoAsAP 91
Yunus Emre d1320? BioIn 17
Yuokila, Yrjo Ilmari 1924- WhoScE 91-4
Yuon, Paul Baker 92
Yuori, Trenchard Domegure 1944- WhoWor 93
Yup, Paula Anne 1957- WhoWrEP 92
Yupanqui, Atahualpa 1908-1992 BioIn 17, NewYTBS 92

Yu Qiwei 1911?-1958 *BioIn 17*
Yura, Joseph Andrew 1938- *WhoAm 92*
Yuracko, Ellen B. 1939- *St&PR 93*
Yurchak, Metro 1928- *WhoE 93*
Yurchenco, Henrietta Weiss 1916- *WhoAm 92*
Yurchenko, Vitaly *BioIn 17*
Yurchuck, Elizabeth Ruth 1935- *WhoAmW 93*
Yurchuck, Roger Alexander 1938- *WhoAm 92*
Yurchyshyn, George Bohdan 1940- *St&PR 93*
Yurcon, G. Edward *Law&B 92*
Yurcon, George Edward 1929- *St&PR 93*
Yure, Bilman *WhoScE 91-4*
Yurecko, Claudia Joy 1957- *WhoAmW 93*
Yuregir, Gunes T. 1930- *WhoScE 91-4*
Yurgenson, Peter *Baker 92*
Yurick, Sol 1925- *JeAmFiW, WhoWrEP 92*
Yurinich, Debra Lea *Law&B 92*
Yurinsky, Vadim Vladimirovich 1945- *WhoWor 93*
Yurko, Mike 1924- *St&PR 93*
Yurko, Vjacheslav Anatoljevich 1949- *WhoWor 93*
Yurkovic, Leonard Stephen 1937- *St&PR 93*
Yurkoviitch, Jennie Lynne 1960- *WhoAmW 93*
Yurow, John Jesse 1931- *WhoAm 92*
Yurowski, G. Edmund 1931- *St&PR 93*
Yurut, Avni 1935- *WhoScE 91-4*
Yus, Miguel 1947- *WhoScE 91-3*
Yuschak, William 1925- *St&PR 93*
Yusk, Janice Woods 1942- *WhoSSW 93*
Yusko, David Paul *Law&B 92*
Yusko, Gary John 1955- *St&PR 93*
Yusko, Rose *BioIn 17*
Yuspeh, Alan Ralph 1949- *WhoAm 92, WhoE 93*
Yuspeh, Sonia 1928-1990 *BioIn 17*
Yussupov, Nikolai Borisovich *Baker 92*
Yust, Larry *MiSFD 9*
Yuster, Jane Margaret 1955- *WhoAmW 93*
Yuster, Leigh Carol 1949- *WhoE 93*
Yusuf, Yusuf bin Umayer al *WhoWor 93*
Yutalo, Rodney W. 1943- *St&PR 93*
Yutani, Hiroshi *WhoWor 93*
Yuthasastrkosol, Charin 1930- *WhoAmW 93*
Yutkevich, Sergei 1904-1985 *MiSFD 9N*
Yutkin, Gerald David 1943- *WhoWor 93*
Yuval, Peter *MiSFD 9*
Yuwono, Johnlin Hy 1947- *WhoWor 93*
Yu Yongbo 1931- *WhoAsAP 91*
Yu Yu-Hsien 1934- *WhoAsAP 91*
Yu Zhan *BioIn 17*
Yu Zhensan *BioIn 17*
Yu Zhenwu 1931- *WhoAsAP 91*
Yu Zhizhen 1915- *BioIn 17*
Yuzna, Brian *MiSFD 9*
Yvain, Maurice 1891-1965 *Baker 92*
Yves, J.S. 1938- *WhoScE 91-2*
Yves, Martin 1929- *WhoAm 92*
Yvon, Bernard Rene 1935- *WhoE 93*
Yvon, Klaus 1943- *WhoScE 91-4*
Yzac, Heinrich *Baker 92*
Yzaguirre, Leslie Killinger *Law&B 92*
Yzerman, Steve *BioIn 17*
Yzerman, Steve 1965- *WhoAm 92*

Z

Z, Bobby *BioIn 17*
Zaanen, Jan 1957- *WhoWor 93*
Zaback, Robert C. 1931- *St&PR 93*
Zabala, Ana Marie *Law&B 92*
Zabaldo, Joel T. 1947- *St&PR 93*
Zabaleta, Nicanor 1907- *Baker 92*
Zabalza y Olaso, Damaso 1833-1894 *Baker 92*
Zaban, Erwin 1921- *WhoSSW 93*
Zabar, Kahil El' *BioIn 17*
Zabara, Jacob 1932- *WhoE 93*
Zabaronick, R.W. 1946- *St&PR 93*
Zabawa, Robert Thomas 1941- *St&PR 93*
Zabecki, David Tadeusz 1947- *WhoWor 93*
Zabel, Albert Heinrich 1834-1910 *Baker 92*
Zabel, Catherine Lueck *Law&B 92*
Zabel, Edward 1927- *WhoAm 92*
Zabel, Jeffrey D. 1954- *St&PR 93*
Zabel, Sheldon Alter 1941- *WhoAm 92*
Zabel, Sue 1944- *WhoAmW 93*
Zabel, William David 1936- *WhoAm 92, WhoE 93, WhoWor 93*
Zabelsky, Robert *St&PR 93*
Zabergan fl. 6th cent.- *OxDcByz*
Zabielski, Kazimierz 1932- *WhoWor 93*
Zabierowski, Kazimierz Ignacy 1926- *WhoScE 91-4*
Zabin, Helen 1935- *WhoAmW 93*
Zable, David 1936- *St&PR 93*
Zable, Marian Magdelen 1933- *WhoAmW 93*
Zable, Walter Joseph 1915- *St&PR 93, WhoAm 92*
Zablocki, Franciszek 1754-1821 *PolBiDi*
Zablocki, Jozef Antoni 1924- *WhoScE 91-4*
Zaborsky, Daniel John 1945- *WhoIns 93*
Zabrack, Harold 1928- *Baker 92*
Zabriskie, Virginia M. *WhoAm 92*
Zabrodsky, Thomas Oleg 1952- *WhoWor 93*
Zabron, Floyd Stanley 1940- *St&PR 93*
Zabza, Andrzej S. 1932- *WhoScE 91-4*
Zacapa, Jackal of *DcCPCAm*
Zacarias, Abilo Pires 1957- *WhoWor 93*
Zacarias, David James 1949- *St&PR 93*
Zaccaglin, Victor 1921- *St&PR 93*
Zaccaglini, Lisa 1961- *BioIn 17*
Zaccagnini, Benigno 1912-1989 *BioIn 17*
Zaccardo, Daniel A. *Law&B 92*
Zaccarello, Michael D. 1947- *St&PR 93*
Zaccari, Joseph M., Jr. 1955- *St&PR 93*
Zaccaria *OxDcByz*
Zaccaria, Nicola (Angelo) 1923 *Baker 92*
Zaccaro, John, Jr. *BioIn 17*
Zaccone, Robert Michael 1946- *WhoE 93*
Zaccone, Suzanne Maria 1957- *WhoAmW 93, WhoEmL 93, WhoWor 93*
Zaccone-Tzannetakis, Paula Rose 1946- *WhoE 93*
Zacconi, Lodovico (Giulio Cesare) 1555-1627 *Baker 92*
Zacek, Hubert 1924- *WhoScE 91-4*
Zacek, Joseph Frederick 1930- *WhoAm 92*
Zach, George O. 1942- *St&PR 93*
Zach, Jan 1699-1773 *Baker 92*
Zach, Max (Wilhelm) 1864-1921 *Baker 92*
Zachar, Joel Stephen 1948- *St&PR 93*
Zachar, Jozef 1925- *WhoScE 91-4*
Zacharewitsch, Michael 1879-1953 *Baker 92*
Zacharia, Friedrich Wilhelm 1726-1777 *BioIn 17*
Zacharia, Irwin *ScF&FL 92*
Zacharia, Joseph 1867-1965 *BioIn 17*
Zacharia, Sebastian K. 1936- *WhoUN 92*
Zachariae, Hugh 1925- *WhoScE 91-2*
Zacharias 679- *OxDcByz*
Zacharias, Christian 1950- *Baker 92*
Zacharias, Donald Wayne 1935- *WhoAm 92, WhoSSW 93*
Zacharias, Edwin H., Sr. 1910- *St&PR 93*
Zacharias, Helmut W. 1942- *St&PR 93*
Zacharias, John *OxDcByz*
Zacharias, John Spero 1932- *St&PR 93*
Zacharias, Lela Ann 1944- *WhoWrEP 92*
Zacharias, Thomas Elling 1954- *WhoE 93*
Zacharias, Veronika 1939- *BioIn 17*
Zacharias of Mytilene c. 465-c. 536 *OxDcByz*
Zachariasse, Levinus C. 1942- *WhoScE 91-3*
Zacharius, Walter 1923- *WhoAm 92*
Zacharski, Marian *BioIn 17*
Zachary, Fay N. 1931- *WhoWrEP 92*
Zachary, Fay Nedra 1931- *ScF&FL 92*
Zachary, Hugh *ScF&FL 92*
Zachary, Judy *ScF&FL 92*
Zachary, Norman 1926- *St&PR 93*
Zachary, Phillip Eugene 1934- *St&PR 93*
Zachary, Ronald F. 1938- *St&PR 93, WhoAm 92*
Zachau, Friedrich Wilhelm 1663-1712 *Baker 92*
Zachau, Hans G. 1930- *WhoScE 91-3*
Zachau, Reinhard Konrad 1948- *WhoSSW 93*
Zachau-Christiansen, Bengt Niels 1927- *WhoScE 91-2*
Zachcial, Manfred *WhoScE 91-3*
Zacheis, Carleton F. 1933- *St&PR 93*
Zacher, Allan Norman, Jr. 1928- *WhoWor 93*
Zacher, Giovanni Giorgio 1926- *WhoWor 93*
Zacher, Robert P. *Law&B 92*
Zachert, Martha Jane 1920- *WhoAm 92*
Zachert, Virginia 1920- *WhoAm 92, WhoAmW 93*
Zachery-Hopkins, Donna S. 1952- *WhoAmW 93*
Zachmann, Jeffrey Thomas *Law&B 92*
Zachmann, Virginia Joyce 1933- *WhoWrEP 92*
Zachos, Kimon Stephen 1930- *St&PR 93, WhoAm 92*
Zachow, Friedrich Wilhelm 1663-1712 *Baker 92*
Zachow, William A. 1942- *St&PR 93*
Zachreson, Nick Bernard 1952- *WhoWrEP 92*
Zachrich, James Martin 1921- *St&PR 93*
Zachrison, Mats Jacob 1957- *WhoWor 93*
Zachry, Henry Bartell, Jr. 1933- *St&PR 93, WhoAm 92*
Zachry, William Marvin 1954- *St&PR 93*
Zachry, Woodie M. 1938- *St&PR 93*
Zack, Arnold Marshall 1931- *WhoAm 92*
Zack, David 1917- *St&PR 93*
Zack, Earl R. 1913-1990 *BioIn 17*
Zack, George J. 1936- *WhoSSW 93*
Zack, Samuel Alan 1951- *WhoE 93*
Zack, Timothy Edwin 1959- *WhoE 93*
Zackaroff, Peter T. 1955- *St&PR 93*
Zackheim, Adrian Walter 1951- *WhoAm 92*
Zackheim, Marc Allen 1950- *WhoEmL 93*
Zacklin, Ralph 1937- *WhoUN 92*
Zackrisson, Olle 1945- *WhoScE 91-4*
Zacks, Gordon 1933- *St&PR 93*
Zacks, Gordon Benjamin 1933- *WhoAm 92*
Zacks, Philip H. 1948- *St&PR 93*
Zacks, Sumner Irwin 1929- *WhoAm 92*
Zackula, Michael Leroy 1947- *WhoWor 93*
Zacny, R.J. 1937- *St&PR 93*
Zaczek, Zbigniew 1925- *WhoScE 91-4*
Zadeck, Donald J. 1937- *St&PR 93*
Zadeck, Julie *St&PR 93*
Zadeh, Lotfi A. 1921- *WhoAm 92*
Zadek, Robert L. 1940- *St&PR 93*
Zadikow, Victor H. 1943- *St&PR 93*
Zadjeika, Dolores Marie 1934- *WhoE 93*
Zadkine, Ossip 1890-1967 *BioIn 17*
Zadoks, Jan C. 1929- *WhoScE 91-3*
Zadonick, Larry Allen 1941- *St&PR 93*
Zador, Dezso 1873-1931 *Baker 92*
Zador, Eugene 1894-1977 *Baker 92*
Zadora, Michael 1882-1946 *Baker 92*
Zadorozhnij, Vladimir 1943- *WhoWor 93*
Zadra, Joseph James 1922- *St&PR 93*
Zadra, Larry 1961- *St&PR 93*
Zadra, Nolan H. *Law&B 92*
Zadrazil, Stanislav 1935- *WhoScE 91-4*
Zadrozny, Arthur John 1954- *WhoE 93*
Zadrozny, W.T. 1945- *St&PR 93*
Zadunaisky, Jose Atilio 1932- *WhoE 93*
Zaengl, Walter S. 1931- *WhoScE 91-4*
Zaenglein, William G., Jr. *Law&B 92*
Zaenglein, William George, Jr. 1929- *St&PR 93, WhoAm 92*
Zaentz, Saul *WhoAm 92*
Zaepfel, Glenn Peter 1951- *WhoEmL 93, WhoSSW 93*
Zafar, Iftikhar Ali 1919- *WhoWor 93*
Zaferiou, Paul John 1934- *WhoE 93*
Zaffaroni, Alejandro C. 1923- *St&PR 93, WhoAm 92*
Zaffe, Gwen 1949- *St&PR 93*
Zaffino, Frank D. *St&PR 93*
Zaffirini, Judith 1946- *NotHsAW 93, WhoAmW 93*
Zaffos, Gerald 1950- *WhoEmL 93*
Zafiris, Nicos *WhoScE 91-1*
Zafranovic, Lordan 1944- *DrEEuF*
Zafred, Mario 1922-1987 *Baker 92, OxDcOp*
Zafren, Herbert Cecil 1925- *WhoAm 92*
Zagaja, S. *WhoScE 91-4*
Zagaja, Stanislaw W. 1925- *WhoScE 91-4*
Zagame, Susan Koerber 1951- *WhoAmW 93*
Zagano, Phyllis 1947- *WhoE 93*
Zagar, Carol Eversull 1958- *WhoAmW 93*
Zagar, Zivojin 1925- *WhoWor 93*
Zagara, Maurizio 1946- *WhoWor 93*
Zagare, Frank Cosmo 1947- *WhoE 93*
Zagarella, Eugene *Law&B 92*
Zagaroli, Mark *Law&B 92*
Zagat, Nina *BioIn 17*
Zagat, Tim *BioIn 17*
Zagel, James Block 1941- *WhoAm 92*
Zagel, Margaret Maxwell *Law&B 92*
Zager, Jan G. *Law&B 92*
Zager, Lynne Donna 1954- *WhoAmW 93*
Zager, Ronald I. 1934- *WhoE 93*
Zaghloul, Mona Elwakkad 1944- *WhoAmW 93*
Zagiba, Franz 1912-1977 *Baker 92*
Zagnoli, M. Andre *WhoScE 91-4*
Zagnoli, Roland Candiano 1931- *WhoSSW 93, WhoWor 93*
Zagon, Ian Stuart 1943- *WhoE 93*
Zagorac, Michael, Jr. 1941- *St&PR 93*
Zagoren, Allen Jeffrey 1947- *WhoEmL 93*
Zagoren, Joy Carroll 1933- *WhoE 93*
Zagoria, Sam David 1919- *WhoAm 92*
Zagorin, Bernard 1921- *WhoUN 92*
Zagorin, Perez 1920- *WhoAm 92*
Zagorski, Michael Gerard 1955- *WhoWor 93*
Zagorski, Stanislaw *BioIn 17*
Zagorsky, Carol Lacci 1942- *WhoAmW 93, WhoE 93*
Zagortsev, Vladimir 1944- *Baker 92*
Zagoruiko, Nikolay 1931- *WhoWor 93*
Zagrans, Eric Hyman *Law&B 92*
Zagrebnov, Valentine Anatole 1946- *WhoWor 93*
Zagrodnik, Diane Jeanne 1950- *WhoWrEP 92*
Zagrodny, Dariusz Grzegorz 1958- *WhoWor 93*
Zagrosek, Lothar 1942- *Baker 92*
Zagursky, George Palmer 1943- *WhoSSW 93*
Zagwijn, Henri 1878-1954 *Baker 92*
Zagwijn, Waldo H. 1928- *WhoScE 91-3*
Zah, Peterson 1937- *WhoAm 92*
Zahaczewski, Roman Marian 1921- *WhoScE 91-4*
Zahajkiewicz, Szczesny 1861-1917 *PolBiDi*
Zahalak, George Ireneus 1939- *WhoAm 92*
Zaharia, Eric Stafford 1948- *WhoAm 92*
Zaharias, Babe Didrikson 1911-1956 *BioIn 17, ConHero 2 [port]*
Zahariev, Eduard 1938- *DrEEuF*
Zahariev, George Kostadinov 1941- *WhoWor 93*
Zahariev, Georgi K. 1941- *WhoScE 91-4*
Zaharis, Janis Lynn 1946- *WhoAmW 93*
Zaharoff, Basil 1850-1936 *DcTwHis*
Zahav, Sharon Brophy 1948- *WhoSSW 93*
Zahava, Irene 1951- *ScF&FL 92*
Zahavy, Reuvain 1953- *WhoE 93, WhoWor 93*
Zahed, Ismail 1956- *WhoE 93*
Zaheer, Neyamat 1937- *WhoWor 93*
Zaher, Celia Ribeiro 1931- *WhoUN 92, WhoWor 93*
Zaher, Mouafak Arif 1944- *WhoWor 93*
Zahir Bin Haji Ismail, Dato Mohamed 1924- *WhoAsAP 91*
Zahir Shah 1914- *BioIn 17*
Zahler, Robert A. *St&PR 93*
Zahler, Stanley Arnold 1926- *WhoE 93*
Zahn, Anton James 1941- *St&PR 93*
Zahn, Carl Frederick 1928- *WhoAm 92*
Zahn, Curtis Langalier 1912- *WhoWrEP 92*
Zahn, Donald Jack 1941- *WhoAm 92*
Zahn, Fritz-Georg 1934- *WhoScE 91-3*
Zahn, Jean-Paul 1935- *WhoScE 91-2*
Zahn, Johannes 1817-1895 *Baker 92*
Zahn, Louis Jennings 1922- *WhoSSW 93*

Zahn, Margaret Ann 1941- *WhoSSW 93*
Zahn, Markus 1946- *WhoE 93*
Zahn, Paula *BioIn 17*
Zahn, Paula c. 1956- *News 92 [port], -92-3 [port]*
Zahn, Peter E. *Law&B 92*
Zahn, R.K. *WhoScE 91-3*
Zahn, Rudolf Karl 1920- *WhoWor 93*
Zahn, Timothy 1951- *ScF&FL 92*
Zahnd, Richard Hugo 1946- *WhoAm 92*
Zahner, Harold E. *Law&B 92*
Zahner, Horst 1941- *WhoScE 91-3*
Zahner, Lilly *ScF&FL 92*
Zahner, Roland 1961- *WhoWor 93*
Zahorchak, Michael 1929- *WhoWrEP 92*
Zahorian, Stephen Glen 1938- *St&PR 93, WhoAm 92*
Zahorski, Kenneth J. 1939- *ScF&FL 92*
Zahorski, Stefan 1933- *WhoScE 91-4*
Zahra, Susan Gore 1950- *WhoWrEP 92*
Zahran, Mohamed Juma 1948- *WhoWor 93*
Zahreddine, Ziad Nassib 1952- *WhoWor 93*
Zahrn, Catherine Denise 1952- *WhoEmL 93*
Zahrn, James Frederick 1950- *St&PR 93, WhoAm 92*
Zahrt, Merton Stroebel 1910- *WhoSSW 93*
Zaia, Mary Teresa 1965- *WhoAmW 93*
Zaid bin Sultan al-Nahayan, Sheik 1918- *BioIn 17*
Zaidel, Michael J. *Law&B 92*
Zaidenberg, Arthur 1908-1990 *BioIn 17*
Zaidens, Sadie H. 1910-1991 *BioIn 17*
Zaidi, Iqbal Mehdi 1954- *WhoUN 92*
Zaidi, Mahmood A. 1930- *WhoAm 92*
Zaidi, Saiyed Abidali 1936- *WhoWor 93*
Zaidi, Shuja Haider 1952- *WhoEmL 93*
Zaidlewicz, Marek Jan 1939- *WhoScE 91-4*
Zaik, Carol Ford 1955- *WhoE 93*
Zaikov, Raiko Paunov 1935- *WhoWor 93*
Zaim, Semih 1926- *St&PR 93*
Zaiman, Joel Hirsh 1938- *WhoAm 92*
Zainal Abidin Bin Zin, Dato' 1940- *WhoAsAP 91*
Zaininger, Karl Heinz 1929- *WhoAm 92*
Zaino, Russell B. 1948- *St&PR 93*
Zaino, William J. *Law&B 92*
Zais, Bernard H. 1916- *WhoIns 93*
Zaitlin, Michael A. 1956- *St&PR 93*
Zaitsoff, I.M. 1943- *St&PR 93*
Zaitzeff, Roger Michael 1940- *WhoWor 93*
Zajac, Jack 1929- *WhoAm 92*
Zajac, John 1946- *WhoEmL 93*
Zajac, Michael T. *Law&B 92*
Zajaczkowski, Kazimierz 1940- *WhoScE 91-4*
Zajc, Andrej 1938- *WhoScE 91-4*
Zajc, Ivan *Baker 92*
Zajc, Ivan 1832-1914 *OxDcOp*
Zajczyk, Szymon c. 1895-1943 *PolBiDi*
Zajic, Elisabeth C. *Law&B 92*
Zajic, Keith C. *Law&B 92*
Zajicek, Iva Marie 1925- *WhoAmW 93*
Zajicek, Jeronym 1926- *Baker 92*
Zajicek, Lynn Engelbrecht 1950- *WhoAmW 93*
Zajicek-Coleman, Eva Maria 1951- *WhoWor 93*
Zajick, Kenneth 1926- *St&PR 93*
Zajkas, Gabor 1935- *WhoScE 91-4*
Zajlich, Piotr 1884-1948 *PolBiDi*
Zajonc, Arthur Guy 1949- *WhoE 93*
Zajonc, Robert Boleslaw 1923- *WhoAm 92*
Zak, A. Jeanne 1932- *St&PR 93*
Zak, Dorothy Zerykier 1950- *WhoE 93*
Zak, Fyodor Lazarus 1949- *WhoWor 93*
Zak, Miroslaw 1936- *WhoScE 91-4*
Zak, Steven Allen 1947- *WhoE 93*
Zak, Thomas C. 1938- *St&PR 93*
Zak, Victoria Jo *WhoE 93*
Zak, Vladimir Ivan Pavel 1937- *WhoWor 93*
Zak, Yakov (Izrailevich) 1913-1976 *Baker 92*
Zak, Zdzislaw 1930- *WhoScE 91-4*
Zakaib, Lorne 1932- *WhoE 93*
Zakanitch, Robert S. 1935- *WhoAm 92*
Zakaria, Haji Ahmad 1947- *ConAu 138*
Zakaria Bin Datu Mahawangsa Haji Awang, Dato Haji Laila Jasa Awang *WhoAsAP 91*
Zakarian, Albert 1940- *WhoAm 92*
Zaken, Kenneth Allen 1958- *WhoSSW 93*
Zakens, Judith A. *Law&B 92*
Zakharevich, Yuri *BioIn 17*
Zakharov, Olive 1929- *WhoAsAP 91*
Zakharov, Valerij Konstantinovich 1947- *WhoWor 93*
Zakharov, Vladimir 1901-1956 *Baker 92*
Zakheim, Barbara Jane 1953- *WhoAmW 93, WhoE 93*
Zakheim, Dov Solomon 1948- *WhoAm 92*
Zakheim, Joshua H. *Law&B 92*
Zakhem, Sam Hanna 1935- *WhoAm 92*
Zaki, Hoda M. 1950- *ScF&FL 92*
Zaki, N. 1942- *St&PR 93*
Zaki, Saleh Abbas 1935- *WhoSSW 93*
Zakibe, Thomas Anthony 1947- *St&PR 93*
Zakic, Borislav 1926- *WhoScE 91-4*
Zakim, David 1935- *WhoAm 92*
Zakin, Alexander d1990 *BioIn 17*
Zakin, Jacques Louis 1927- *WhoAm 92*
Zakin, Jonathan N. *St&PR 93*
Zakka, Afafe 1950- *WhoWor 93*
Zakkay, Victor 1927- *WhoAm 92*
Zaklan, Mary Frances 1964- *WhoAmW 93*
Zaklan-Kavic, Dragica 1934- *WhoScE 91-4*
Zaknic, Ivan 1938- *ConAu 138*
Zakowski, Wojciech Mscislaw 1929- *WhoScE 91-4*
Zakrajsheck, James Daniel *Law&B 92*
Zakreski, Randall James *Law&B 92*
Zakrzewska, Marie Elizabeth 1829-1912 *PolBiDi*
Zakrzewski, Janusz A. 1932- *WhoScE 91-4*
Zakrzewski, Kazimierz 1938- *WhoScE 91-4*
Zakrzewski, Stephanie Diane 1963- *WhoAmW 93*
Zakrzewski, Thomas M. 1943- *St&PR 93*
Zakrzewski, Vladimir Jan 1946- *WhoE 93*
Zaks, Jerry *BioIn 17*
Zaks, Jerry 1946- *WhoAm 92, WhoE 93*
Zakusilo, Oleg Kalenikovich 1947- *WhoWor 93*
Zala, Nancy *MiSFD 9*
Zalacain, Daniel 1948- *WhoE 93*
Zalaha, John Charles 1916- *St&PR 93*
Zalai, Karoly 1921- *WhoScE 91-4*
Zalakevicius, Vytautas 1930- *DrEEuF*
Zalanyi, Samuel 1923- *WhoScE 91-4*
Zalar, Anthony J. *St&PR 93*
Zalaznick, Sheldon 1928- *WhoAm 92, WhoWrEP 92*
Zalben, Jane Breskin 1950- *WhoWrEP 92*
Zalben, Simon 1917- *St&PR 93*
Zaldastani, Guivy 1919- *WhoE 93, WhoWor 93*
Zaldastani, Othar 1922- *WhoE 93*
Zaldin, Arthur H. 1916- *St&PR 93*
Zaldivar-Bunt, Juan Carlos *Law&B 92*
Zale, Lawrence P. *Law&B 92*
Zalecki, Paul Henry 1931- *WhoAm 92*
Zaleha Bt Ismail, Datin Paduka Hajjah 1936- *WhoAsAP 91*
Zalenski, Cathy Ann 1952- *WhoSSW 93*
Zalenski, Thaddeus Arthur *Law&B 92*
Zaleski, Andrew B. 1938- *St&PR 93*
Zaleski, August 1883-1972 *BioIn 17, PolBiDi*
Zaleski, James Vincent 1943- *WhoWor 93*
Zaleski, Jean *WhoAmW 93*
Zaleski, Krystyn S. 1935- *WhoUN 92*
Zaleski, Marcin 1796-1877 *PolBiDi*
Zaleski, Marek Bohdan 1936- *WhoAm 92*
Zaleski, Margaret E. *Law&B 92*
Zaleski, Philip *BioIn 17*
Zaleski, Ronald Joseph 1954- *WhoIns 93*
Zalesskii, Alexandre Efimovich 1939- *WhoWor 93*
Zalewa, Donald Andrew 1950- *WhoEmL 93*
Zalewski, C.V. 1937- *St&PR 93*
Zalewski, Jozef 1926- *WhoScE 91-4*
Zalewski, S. Maciej 1932- *WhoScE 91-4*
Zaleznik, Abraham 1924- *ConAu 37NR, WhoAm 92*
Zalieckas, Joseph John 1943- *St&PR 93*
Zalinski, Edmund L. G. 1915- *St&PR 93*
Zalinski, Edmund Louis Gray 1915- *WhoAm 92*
Zaliouk, Yuval Nathan 1939- *WhoAm 92*
Zalis, Paul 1952- *ConAu 138*
Zalk, Charles Leonard 1923- *St&PR 93*
Zalka, Saul 1934- *St&PR 93*
Zalkin, Kenneth G. 1943-1990 *BioIn 17*
Zalkin, Larry 1942- *St&PR 93*
Zall, Jayne C. *Law&B 92*
Zall, Paul Maxwell 1922- *WhoAm 92, WhoWrEP 92*
Zall, Robert J. 1923- *St&PR 93*
Zall, Robert Rouben 1925- *WhoAm 92*
Zallen, Harold 1926- *WhoAm 92*
Zaller, Robert Michael 1940- *WhoWrEP 92*
Zallie, James Paul 1961- *WhoE 93*
Zallinger, Meinhard von 1897-1990 *Baker 92*
Zallinger, Rudolph Franz 1919- *WhoE 93*
Zalokar, Robert H. 1927- *St&PR 93, WhoAm 92, WhoSSW 93*
Zalonis, John William 1949- *St&PR 93*
Zalonski, Susan F. 1963- *WhoAmW 93*
Zaloom, Ernest F. d1991 *BioIn 17*
Zaloom, John B. 1941- *St&PR 93*
Zaloum, Rosemarie 1962- *WhoWrEP 92*
Zalta, Edward 1930- *WhoAm 92*
Zalta, J.P. *WhoScE 91-2*
Zalucha, Peggy Flora *BioIn 17*
Zalucki, Robert J. *Law&B 92*
Zaluk, Ellen Louise 1948- *St&PR 93*
Zaluska, Stanislaw 1924- *WhoWor 93*
Zaluski, Jozef Andrzej 1702-1774 *PolBiDi*
Zaluski, Roman 1936- *DrEEuF*
Zalusky, Lawrence 1926- *St&PR 93*
Zalusky, Sharon 1951- *WhoAmW 93*
Zalutsky, Morton Herman 1935- *WhoAm 92*
Zalygin, Sergei 1913- *BioIn 17*
Zamacois, Niceto de 1820-1885 *DcMexL*
Zaman, Fiazud Din 1950- *WhoWor 93*
Zaman, Mohammad Badiuz 1939- *WhoWor 93*
Zamara, Antonio 1829-1901 *Baker 92*
Zamarlik, Henri 1939- *WhoScE 91-2*
Zamarripa, Sam J. 1952- *WhoSSW 93*
Zambarano, William J. 1944- *St&PR 93*
Zambardino, Rodolfo Alfredo 1930- *WhoWor 93*
Zambetti, Frank X. d1992 *NewYTBS 92*
Zambie, Allan J. *Law&B 92*
Zambie, Allan John 1935- *WhoAm 92*
Zambito, Steven Anthony 1953- *St&PR 93*
Zamble, Allan J. 1935- *St&PR 93*
Zamboldi, Robert Joseph 1940- *St&PR 93*
Zamboni, Frank Joseph 1921- *WhoAm 92*
Zamboni, Helen Attena *Law&B 92*
Zamboni, Luigi 1767-1837 *Baker 92, OxDcOp*
Zambonini, Giuseppe 1942-1990 *BioIn 17*
Zambreno, John *Law&B 92*
Zambreno, Mary Frances 1954- *ScF&FL 92*
Zambreno, Pasquale A. *Law&B 92*
Zambrini, Jean-Claude 1951- *WhoWor 93*
Zamecnik, Paul Charles 1912- *WhoAm 92*
Zameenzad, Adam *ScF&FL 92*
Zamenhof, Ludwik Lazarus 1859-1917 *PolBiDi*
Zames, George David 1934- *WhoAm 92*
Zamiatin, Evgenii Ivanovich 1884-1937 *BioIn 17*
Zamir, Alisa 1940- *St&PR 93*
Zamiska, E.J. 1937- *St&PR 93*
Zamlowski, Peter Steven 1958- *WhoE 93*
Zammataro, Jeanne *Law&B 92*
Zammit, Joseph Paul 1948- *WhoAm 92*
Zammitt, Norman 1931- *WhoAm 92*
Zammuto, Carmela T. *Law&B 92*
Zamojski, Aleksander W. 1929- *WhoScE 91-4*
Zamojski, Jan 1541-1605 *HarEnMi*
Zamora, Antonio 1942- *WhoE 93*
Zamora, Bernice 1938- *NotHsAW 93*
Zamora, Elvira Abao 1955- *WhoWor 93*
Zamora, Maria Helena Paluch 1906- *WhoWrEP 92*
Zamora, Mario *DcCPCAm*
Zamora, Mario Dimarucut 1935- *WhoAm 92*
Zamora, Marjorie Dixon 1933- *WhoAmW 93*
Zamora, Ricardo Mesinas 1963- *WhoE 93*
Zamora, Ronaldo B. 1944- *WhoAsAP 91*
Zamora, Ruben *BioIn 17, DcCPCAm*
Zamoyski, Andrzej 1716-1792 *PolBiDi*
Zamoyski, Jan 1542-1605 *PolBiDi*
Zamoyski, Stanislaw Kostka 1775-1856 *PolBiDi*
Zampa, Luigi 1905-1991 *AnObit 1991, BioIn 17*
Zampella, Arthur Dante Louis 1917- *WhoE 93*
Zampetis, Theodore K. 1945- *St&PR 93*
Zampiello, Richard Sidney 1933- *WhoAm 92, WhoE 93, WhoWor 93*
Zampol, W. Paul *Law&B 92*
Zamski, Ronald John 1939- *St&PR 93*
Zamudio Collado, Luis Manuel 1945- *WhoUN 92*
Zan *BioIn 17*
Zana, Donald Dominick 1942- *WhoSSW 93*
Zanakis, Steve H. 1940- *WhoSSW 93*
Zanardelli, John Joseph 1950- *WhoE 93*
Zanca, Minerva Martinez *WhoWrEP 92*
Zancanaro, Giorgio 1939- *OxDcOp*
Zanchetti, Alberto 1926- *WhoScE 91-3*
Zanchuk, Walter Andrew 1950- *St&PR 93*
Zand, Charlene Rooth 1930- *WhoAmW 93*
Zand, Dale Ezra 1926- *WhoAm 92*
Zand, Lloyd Craig 1942- *WhoSSW 93*
Zand, Roxanne 1952- *ConAu 138*
Zandberg, Jeff 1944- *BioIn 17*
Zande, Michael Dominic 1960- *WhoSSW 93*
Zander, Alvin Frederick 1913- *WhoAm 92*
Zander, Janet Adele 1950- *WhoAmW 93*
Zanders, Pattie Baldwin 1951- *WhoAmW 93*
Zandi, Bahram 1957- *WhoSSW 93*
Zandi, Giampado *WhoScE 91-3*
Zandin, Kjell Bertil 1937- *St&PR 93*
Zandman, Felix *BioIn 17*
Zandman, Felix 1928- *St&PR 93*
Zando, Peter Anthony 1941- *WhoSSW 93*
Zandonai, Riccardo 1883-1944 *Baker 92, IntDcOp, OxDcOp*
Zandov, Zahari 1911- *DrEEuF*
Zandt, Marie Van *Baker 92*
Zandvoort, Reinard Willem 1894-1990 *BioIn 17*
Zane, Arnie *BioIn 17*
Zane, James Orville 1933- *St&PR 93*
Zane, Raymond J. 1939- *WhoE 93*
Zanella, Amilcare 1873-1949 *Baker 92*
Zanella, P. *WhoScE 91-3*
Zanella, Paolo 1933- *WhoScE 91-4*
Zanelli (Morales), Renato 1892-1935 *Baker 92*
Zanelli, Renato 1892-1935 *OxDcOp*
Zanen, Jacqueline 1938- *WhoScE 91-2*
Zaner, Eileen 1947- *WhoAmW 93*
Zanes, George William 1926- *WhoSSW 93*
Zanesco, Luigi 1935- *WhoScE 91-3*
Zaneski, Anne Marla 1960- *WhoAmW 93*
Zanetos, Joseph C. 1947- *St&PR 93*
Zanetta Hurtado, Sergio M. 1942- *WhoWor 93*
Zanetti, Joseph Maurice, Jr. 1928- *St&PR 93*
Zanetti, Richard Joseph 1939- *WhoE 93*
Zanettin, Bruno 1923- *WhoScE 91-3*
Zanettini, Antonio *Baker 92*
Zanev, Vladimir 1946- *WhoScE 91-4*
Zanfi, Aldo 1960- *WhoScE 91-3*
Zang, Allen 1927- *St&PR 93*
Zang, Johann Heinrich 1733-1811 *Baker 92*
Zang, Joseph Paul, III *Law&B 92*
Zang, William L. 1953- *St&PR 93*
Zangaglia, Sergio 1958- *WhoWor 93*
Zange, Nikolaus c. 1570-c. 1618 *Baker 92*
Zangen, Miriam Griina 1929- *WhoWor 93*
Zangeneh, Fereydoun 1937- *WhoSSW 93, WhoWor 93*
Zanger, Allene C. *Law&B 92*
Zanger, Allene C. 1955- *St&PR 93*
Zanger, Jan F. de 1932-1991 *BioIn 17*
Zanger, Johannes 1517-1587 *Baker 92*
Zangerle, Gaston Andre 1958- *WhoWor 93*
Zangerus, Johannes 1517-1587 *Baker 92*
Zangger, Eberhard 1958- *ConAu 138*
Zangheri, Sergio 1926- *WhoScE 91-3, WhoWor 93*
Zanghi, Santo Anthony 1955- *St&PR 93*
Zangi c. 1084-1146 *OxDcByz*
Zangius, Nikolaus c. 1570-c. 1618 *Baker 92*
Zangr, Allene C. *St&PR 93*
Zangrilli, John Anthony 1939- *WhoE 93*
Zangwill, Israel 1864-1926 *BioIn 17*
Zangwio, Akwo-opi Harrison 1953- *WhoWor 93*
Zani, Frederick Caesar 1929- *WhoWor 93*
Zani, Gerald Andrew 1934- *St&PR 93*
Zaniewski, Christine F. *Law&B 92*
Zanine Caldas, Jose 1919- *BioIn 17*
Zaninetti, Louisette Angeline 1940- *WhoScE 91-4*
Zankel, Arthur 1932- *St&PR 93*
Zankel, Franz 1941- *WhoScE 91-4*
Zankel, Nathan 1928- *St&PR 93*
Zankl, Heinrich 1941- *WhoScE 91-3*
Zankowska-Jasinska, Wanda 1921- *WhoScE 91-4*
Zankowski, Doreen M. 1959- *WhoE 93*
Zankteler, Maciej 1931- *WhoWor 93*
Zanlongo, Alejandro Raul 1955- *WhoSSW 93*
Zann, Nicholas T. 1943- *WhoE 93*
Zannad, Faiez 1951- *WhoScE 91-2*
Zannoni, Peter J. 1921- *St&PR 93*
Zanobetti, Dino 1919- *WhoScE 91-3*
Zanoni, Mickey G. 1945- *St&PR 93*
Zanoni, Ronald Albert 1942- *St&PR 93, WhoAm 92*
Zanot, Craig Allen 1955- *WhoEmL 93*
Zanotti, Luciano 1932- *WhoWor 93*
Zanotti, Lucio 1944- *WhoScE 91-3*
Zanotti, Martin P. 1932- *St&PR 93, WhoAm 92*
Zanow, Lois A. 1933- *WhoAmW 93*
Zanowiak, Paul 1933- *WhoE 93*
Zant, John L. 1948- *WhoScE 91-3*
Zant, Robert Franklin 1943- *WhoAm 92*
Zanten, Cornelie Van *Baker 92*
Zanuck, Lili *BioIn 17*
Zanuck, Lili Fini *MiSFD 9*
Zanuck, Richard D. 1934- *BioIn 17, St&PR 93*
Zanuck, Richard Darryl 1934- *WhoAm 92*
Zanussi, Krzysztof 1939- *DrEEuF, MiSFD 9, PolBiDi, WhoWor 93*
Zanuttini, Francesco Luciano 1937- *WhoUN 92*
Zanuy Doste, Silvia 1947- *WhoScE 91-3*
Zanzi, James Michael 1940- *WhoAm 92*
Zanzotto, Andrea 1921- *DcLB 128 [port]*

Zaorska, Helena 1930- *WhoScE 91-4*
Zaorski, Janusz 1947- *DrEEuF*
Zaoui, Andre *WhoScE 91-2*
Zaoutzes, Stylianos d899 *OxDcByz*
Zapala, Robin Miller 1952- *WhoE 93*
Zapapas, James Richard 1926- *WhoAm 92*
Zapata, Carmen 1927- *HispAmA [port], NotHsAW 93 [port]*
Zapata, Elssy-Fedora 1950- *WhoEmL 93*
Zapata, Emiliano *DcCPCAm*
Zapata, Emiliano 1877?-1919 *HarEnMi*
Zapata, Emiliano 1879-1919 *BioIn 17, DcTwHis*
Zapata, Marcos *BioIn 17*
Zapata, Mario *DcCPCAm*
Zapatochny, Rebecca Jo 1963- *WhoAmW 93*
Zapel, Scott Owen *Law&B 92*
Zapf, Hermann 1918- *WhoAm 92, WhoWor 93*
Zapf, John G. 1915- *St&PR 93*
Zapf, Matthew A.C. *Law&B 92*
Zaphiriou, James Alexander *Law&B 92*
Zapisek, John R. 1938- *St&PR 93*
Zapletal, Vladimir *WhoScE 91-4*
Zapletulek, Miroslav 1926- *WhoScE 91-4*
Zapolska, Gabriela 1860-1921 *PolBiDi*
Zaporowski, Mark Paul 1957- *WhoE 93*
Zappa, Charles R. 1943- *WhoE 93*
Zappa, Frank *BioIn 17*
Zappa, Frank 1940- *Baker 92, MiSFD 9, WhoAm 92*
Zappa, Lala *BioIn 17*
Zappa, Vincent E. *Law&B 92*
Zappacosta, Serafino 1935- *WhoWor 93*
Zappala, Joseph *WhoAm 92, WhoWor 93*
Zappala, Stephen A. 1932- *WhoAm 92*
Zappe, Ronald *BioIn 17*
Zappetti, Thomas A. 1942- *St&PR 93*
Zappia, Dominic Carmen 1929- *WhoSSW 93*
Zappia, Vincenzo 1939- *WhoScE 91-3*
Zaprzalek, Piotr Janusz 1951- *WhoScE 91-4*
Zar, Jerrold Howard 1941- *WhoAm 92*
Zara, Gerard Joseph 1939- *WhoE 93*
Zara, Louis 1910- *WhoAm 92, WhoWrEP 92*
Zarabet, Joseph 1932- *St&PR 93*
Zarada, Nancy J. *Law&B 92*
Zarada, Nancy J. 1945- *St&PR 93*
Zarafonetis, Chris John Dimiter 1914- *WhoAm 92*
Zarafu, Gheorghe 1933- *WhoWor 93*
Zaragoza, Federico Mayor *BioIn 17*
Zaragoza, Solis, III 1946- *St&PR 93*
Zarakas, Peter 1928- *St&PR 93*
Zarandona, Joseph L. 1953- *WhoIns 93*
Zarangas, Leonidas Pantelis 1949- *WhoWor 93*
Zaranka, Albert J. 1949- *WhoSSW 93, WhoWor 93*
Zaranka, William F. 1944- *WhoAm 92*
Zarate, Eliodoro Ortiz de 1865-1953 *Baker 92*
Zarate, Manuel *BioIn 17*
Zarate Martinez, Alberto 1948- *WhoWor 93*
Zarb, Frank Gustave 1935- *St&PR 93, WhoAm 92, WhoE 93*
Zarb, Haj Muhammad Hassan Amin al- d1898 *BioIn 17*
Zarchan, Paul 1944- *WhoE 93*
Zarco Mateos, Francisco 1829-1869 *DcMexL*
Zarcone, Vincent Peter, Jr. 1937- *WhoAm 92*
Zardiackas, Lyle Dean 1944- *WhoSSW 93*
Zardis, Chester 1900-1990 *BioIn 17*
Zare, Richard N. *BioIn 17*
Zare, Richard Neil 1939- *WhoAm 92*
Zarebski, Juliusz 1854-1885 *Baker 92*
Zarefsky, David Harris 1946- *WhoAm 92*
Zareh, Mo 1943- *WhoSSW 93*
Zarelli, Michael R. 1923- *St&PR 93*
Zarem, Abe Mordecai 1917- *WhoAm 92*
Zaremba, Alan Jay 1949- *WhoE 93*
Zaremba, Carolyn Weis 1953- *WhoAmW 93*
Zaremba, Jerome Francis *Law&B 92*
Zaremba, Nikolai (Ivanovich) 1821-1879 *Baker 92*
Zaremba, Peter Andrew 1948- *WhoWor 93*
Zaremba, Stanislaw 1942- *WhoScE 91-4*
Zaremba, Thomas Edmund Michael Barry *WhoWor 93*
Zaremba, Wincenty 1921- *WhoScE 91-4*
Zaremba-Tymieniecka, Anna-Teresa *WhoE 93*
Zarembski, Julius 1854-1885 *PolBiDi*
Zarembski, Juliusz 1854-1885 *Baker 92*
Zaremski, Miles Jay 1948- *WhoAm 92*
Zarenko, Ronald P. 1946- *St&PR 93*
Zaret, Barry Lewis 1940- *WhoAm 92, WhoE 93*
Zaret, Martin 1948- *St&PR 93*
Zaretsky, Alan *St&PR 93*
Zaretsky, Eli 1940- *ConAu 37NR*
Zargaj, Tomislav 1933- *WhoE 93*
Zarges, H. *WhoScE 91-3*
Zarges, Thomas Henry 1948- *St&PR 93*
Zarghamee, Mehdi S. 1941- *St&PR 93*
Zarhi, Aleksandr 1908- *DrEEuF*
Zarif, M. Javad 1960- *WhoUN 92*
Zarifopol-Johnston, Ilinca Marina *ConAu 139*
Zarifopoulos, Deppie-Tinny Soter 1960- *WhoWor 93*
Zarins, Bertram 1942- *WhoAm 92*
Zarins, Christopher Kristaps 1943- *WhoAm 92*
Zarins, Edgar Alexander *Law&B 92*
Zarins, Joyce Audy *ConAu 136*
Zarins, Margeris 1910- *Baker 92*
Zariski, Oscar 1899-1986 *BioIn 17*
Zaritsky, John 1943- *MiSFD 9*
Zaritsky, Max *BioIn 17*
Zarka, Joseph 1942- *WhoScE 91-2*
Zarkovich, Slobodan S. 1913-1991 *BioIn 17*
Zarky, Karen Jane 1948- *WhoAmW 93*
Zarlenga, Carol A. *St&PR 93*
Zarling, Robert Stanley 1931- *St&PR 93*
Zarlino, Gioseffo 1517-1590 *Baker 92*
Zarnecka-Bialy, Ewa 1930- *WhoWor 93*
Zarnick, Bernard F. 1936- *St&PR 93*
Zarnick, Genny R. 1939- *St&PR 93*
Zarnick, Laura Lynn 1968- *St&PR 93*
Zarnow, William Robert, Jr. 1934- *St&PR 93*
Zarnowiecki, Krzysztof 1925- *WhoScE 91-4*
Zarnowitz, Victor 1919- *WhoAm 92*
Zarnowski, James David 1950- *WhoEmL 93*
Zaroff, Carolyn Rein 1936- *WhoAmW 93*
Zarojanu, Horia 1928- *WhoScE 91-4*
Zarotti, G. Luca *WhoScE 91-3*
Zarotus, Antonio *Baker 92*
Zaroulis, N.L. *ScF&FL 92*
Zarr, Melvyn 1936- *WhoAm 92*
Zarraga, Isidro Clarin 1925- *WhoAsAP 91*
Zarraga, Jose Cruz 1935- *WhoUN 92*
Zarrella, Ronald L. 1949- *St&PR 93*
Zarrella, Vincent Joseph 1925- *St&PR 93*
Zarrett, Linda Pauline 1956- *WhoEmL 93, WhoWor 93*
Zarrilli, Gary Anthony 1947- *St&PR 93*
Zarro, Janice Anne 1947- *WhoAm 92*
Zarrow, Herbert Daniel 1933- *St&PR 93*
Zarrow, Joshua David *Law&B 92*
Zarski, David E. *Law&B 92*
Zarth, Georg 1708-c. 1778 *Baker 92*
Zartler, R.A. 1940- *St&PR 93*
Zartman, David Lester 1940- *WhoAm 92*
Zartman, Joann M. 1938- *St&PR 93*
Zartman, Richard E. 1946- *WhoSSW 93*
Zaruba, Karel L. *Law&B 92*
Zaruby, Walter Stephen 1930- *WhoAm 92*
Zarucchi, Jeanne Morgan 1955- *ConAu 138*
Zarur, Pedro 1947- *St&PR 93*
Zarutskie, Paul Walter 1951- *WhoEmL 93, WhoWor 93*
Zarwyn, Berthold 1921- *WhoAm 92*
Zarzycki, Alexander 1834-1895 *Baker 92, PolBiDi*
Zarzycki, Jan 1921- *WhoScE 91-4*
Zarzycki, Jerzy 1911-1971 *DrEEuF*
Zarzycki, Piotr Mieczyslaw 1954- *WhoWor 93*
Zasadil, Jeanne 1940- *WhoAmW 93*
Zaskurski, J. *WhoScE 91-4*
Zaslav, Barry A. *Law&B 92*
Zaslavskaya, T. I. *ConAu 138*
Zaslavskaya, Tatyana (Ivanovna) 1924- *ConAu 138*
Zaslavsky, Boris Gregory 1944- *WhoWor 93*
Zaslaw, Neal (Alexander) 1939- *Baker 92*
Zasloff, Etta Lee Orr 1947- *WhoAmW 93*
Zaslonka, Janusz-Romuald 1936- *WhoScE 91-4*
Zaslow, Burton 1946- *St&PR 93*
Zaslow, Edmund Morris 1917- *WhoWrEP 92*
Zaslow, Jeffrey *BioIn 17*
Zaslow, Jeffrey Lloyd 1958- *WhoAm 92*
Zaslowsky, David Paul 1960- *WhoWor 93*
Zassenhaus, Hiltgunt Margret 1916- *WhoAm 92*
Zastawny, Jan 1940- *WhoScE 91-4*
Zastrow, Colleen Elizabeth 1956- *WhoAmW 93*
Zastrow, John Thurman 1937- *WhoWor 93*
Zastrow, Klaus D. 1929- *St&PR 93*
Zastrow, William Lee 1937- *WhoIns 93*
Zatina, Elizabeth A. *Law&B 92*
Zatkins, Karen Marie 1950- *WhoE 93*
Zatkoff, Lawrence P. *WhoAm 92*
Zatkovic, Thomas N. 1948- *St&PR 93*
Zatlin, Linda Gertner 1938- *WhoAmW 93, WhoSSW 93*
Zatonski, Witold Antoni 1942- *WhoScE 91-4*
Zatopek, Emil *BioIn 17*
Zatopkova, Dana *BioIn 17*
Zatti, Mario 1931- *WhoWor 93*
Zatuchni, Gerald Irving 1933- *WhoAm 92*
Zatuchni, Jacob 1920- *WhoE 93*
Zaturenska, Marya 1902-1982 *BioIn 17*
Zatz, Arline 1937- *WhoAmW 93, WhoWrEP 92*
Zatz, Glen M. *Law&B 92*
Zatz, Irving J. 1953- *WhoE 93, WhoEmL 93*
Zatz, Marvin 1932- *WhoE 93*
Zatzkis, Henry 1915- *WhoE 93*
Zaubler, Norman W. d1990 *BioIn 17*
Zauder, Fred *St&PR 93*
Zauder, Helene *St&PR 93*
Zauderer, Mark Carl 1946- *WhoEmL 93*
Zaugg, Robert *St&PR 93*
Zauli, Carlo 1931- *WhoScE 91-3*
Zaun, Anne Marie 1949- *WhoAmW 93*
Zaun, Bruce G. 1930- *St&PR 93*
Zaun, Jeffrey *BioIn 17*
Zaun, P.S. 1954- *St&PR 93*
Zauner, Christian Walter 1930- *WhoAm 92*
Zausner, Hy d1992 *BioIn 17, NewYTBS 92*
Zausner, L. Andrew 1949- *WhoAm 92*
Zausner, Martin 1929- *WhoE 93*
Zausner, Teddy R. d1991 *BioIn 17*
Zauzich, Karl-Theodor 1939- *WhoWor 93*
Zavada, Michael Stephan 1952- *WhoSSW 93*
Zavala, Iris M. 1936- *NotHsAW 93*
Zavala, Paul *Law&B 92*
Zavatsky, Kathleen Hanson *Law&B 92*
Zavelberg, Heinz Gunter *WhoUN 92*
Zavella, Patricia 1949- *NotHsAW 93*
Zavertal, Ladislaw 1849-1942 *Baker 92*
Zaveruha, Alexander 1917- *St&PR 93*
Zavik, Jeffrey Scott 1948- *WhoSSW 93*
Zavis, Michael William 1937- *WhoAm 92*
Zavisa, Christopher *ScF&FL 92*
Zavitsas, Andreas Athanasios 1937- *WhoE 93*
Zavitz, Gerald William 1949- *WhoSSW 93*
Zavoina, Andrew M. 1958- *St&PR 93*
Zavon, N.H. 1918- *St&PR 93*
Zavracky, Paul 1948- *WhoE 93*
Zavrian, Suzanne Ostro *WhoWrEP 92*
Zavrtal, Josef Rudolf 1819-1893 *Baker 92*
Zavrtal, Wenceslaw Hugo 1821-1899 *Baker 92*
Zawacki, John Edward 1949- *St&PR 93*
Zawada, Edward Thaddeus, Jr. 1947- *WhoEmL 93, WhoWor 93*
Zawada, John Henry 1941- *St&PR 93*
Zawadowski, Alfred 1936- *WhoScE 91-4*
Zawadzki, Jerzy Romuald 1941- *WhoScE 91-4*
Zawadzki, Joseph Nathan 1949- *St&PR 93*
Zaweski, Richard Stanley 1954- *St&PR 93*
Zawidoski, Gregory *ScF&FL 92*
Zawieyski, Jerzy 1902-1969 *PolBiDi*
Zawinul, Josef 1932- *WhoAm 92, WhoWor 93*
Zawirska, Bozenna Stanislawa 1923- *WhoWor 93*
Zawisha, Richard Garry 1956- *St&PR 93*
Zawistowicz-Adamska, Kazimiera 1897-1984 *IntDcAn*
Zawistowski, Stephen Louis 1955- *WhoE 93*
Zawisza, Czarny c. 1375-1428 *PolBiDi*
Zawoyski, Denise M. 1965- *WhoAmW 93*
Zax, Kenneth Charles 1924- *St&PR 93*
Zax, Leonard A. 1950- *WhoAm 92*
Zax, Melvin 1928- *WhoAm 92, WhoE 93*
Zax, Stanley R. 1937- *St&PR 93*
Zay, Jean 1904-1944 *BioIn 17*
Zay, Thomas Charles 1932- *WhoSSW 93*
Zayadi, Hani Joseph 1948- *WhoAm 92*
Zayak, Elaine 1965- *BiDAMSp 1989*
Zayas-Bazan, Eduardo 1935- *ConAu 37NR, WhoAm 92*
Zayas Enriquez, Rafael de 1848-1932 *DcMexL*
Zayed, Georges 1916- *ScF&FL 92*
Zayed, I.E.D. *WhoScE 91-3*
Zayed bin Sultan Al-Nahayan, Sheikh 1918- *WhoWor 93*
Zaytoun, Joseph Ellis 1920- *WhoIns 93*
Zaytz, Giovanni von 1831-1914 *Baker 92*
Zazik, Jesse 1938- *St&PR 93*
Zazzali, George Peter 1939- *St&PR 93*
Zbar, Michel 1942- *Baker 92*
Zbarsky, John Jacob 1946- *St&PR 93*
Zbiek, Paul John 1952- *WhoE 93*
Zbik, Edward Marian 1953- *WhoWor 93*
Zbinden, Gerhard 1924- *WhoScE 91-4*
Zbinden, Julien-Francois 1917- *Baker 92*
Zborowski, R.W. 1951- *St&PR 93*
Zborzil, Jozef 1924- *WhoScE 91-4*
Zbozen, Susan Michelle 1964- *WhoAmW 93*
Zbytkower, Joseph Samuel 1730-1801 *PolBiDi*
Zdaniewicz, Witold 1928- *WhoWor 93*
Zdanis, Richard Albert 1935- *WhoAm 92*
Zdanowicz, Lidia 1925- *WhoScE 91-4*
Zdanowicz, W. *WhoScE 91-4*
Zdanowicz, Witold 1923- *WhoScE 91-4*
Zdansky, K. 1934- *WhoScE 91-4*
Zdeb, Lorraine Marie Louise 1954- *WhoE 93*
Zdellar, R.C. 1944- *St&PR 93*
Zdobnov, Nikolai Vasil'evich 1888-1942 *BioIn 17*
Zdon, Joseph Paul, Jr. 1941- *St&PR 93*
Zdun, Marek Cezary 1948- *WhoWor 93*
Zdunkiewicz, Lech 1932- *WhoScE 91-4*
Zdybiewska, Maria Wanda 1924- *WhoScE 91-4*
Zdychnec, John S. 1929- *St&PR 93*
Zea, Betty J. *Law&B 92*
Zea, Kristi *BioIn 17*
Zea, Kristi 1948- *ConTFT 10, MiSFD 9*
Zea, Leopoldo 1912- *BioIn 17*
Zea Aguilar, Leopoldo 1912- *WhoWor 93*
Zeager, Samuel A. 1950- *St&PR 93*
Zealand, Hilary Anne *Law&B 92*
Zeanah, Frances McCurry 1951- *WhoSSW 93*
Zeanah, Robert Clyde 1951- *WhoSSW 93*
Zeani, Virginia 1928- *Baker 92*
See Also Rossi-Lemeni, Nicola 1920-1991 *OxDcOp*
Zearfoss, Herbert K. *Law&B 92*
Zearfoss, Herbert Keyser 1929- *WhoWor 93*
Zeavin, Edna A. 1930- *ConAu 138*
Zeavin, Edna Arlone 1930- *WhoAmW 93*
Zebauers, Vladimirs Valdis 1903- *WhoWrEP 92*
Zebedee, William Arthur 1937- *St&PR 93*
Zebley, Arthur 1923- *St&PR 93*
Zebley, Joseph Wildman, Jr. 1914- *WhoE 93, WhoWor 93*
Zebra, A. *SmATA 72*
Zebrak, Ira Lee *Law&B 92*
Zebriunas, Arunas 1930- *DrEEuF*
Zebroski, Edwin Leopold 1921- *WhoAm 92*
Zebrovious, David *St&PR 93*
Zebrowitz, Leslie Ann 1944- *WhoAm 92, WhoE 93*
Zebrowski, Edward A. 1931- *St&PR 93*
Zebrowski, Ernest, Jr. 1944- *WhoE 93, WhoWrEP 92*
Zebrowski, George 1945- *BioIn 17, ScF&FL 92*
Zebrowski, Gerald R. 1942- *St&PR 93*
Zebrowski, Jerzy *ScF&FL 92*
Zebrowski, Marilyn Frances *WhoAmW 93, WhoE 93*
Zebrowski, Mary Theodorette 1916- *WhoE 93*
Zebrowski, Zenon 1890-1981 *PolBiDi*
Zecca, John Andrew 1914- *WhoAm 92*
Zecchi, Adone 1904- *Baker 92*
Zecchi, Carlo 1903-1984 *Baker 92*
Zecevic, Miodrag Dj. 1930- *WhoWor 93*
Zech, Frederick, Jr. 1858-1926 *Baker 92*
Zech, Paul Y. 1932- *WhoScE 91-2*
Zech, Ronald H. 1943- *St&PR 93*
Zech, William Albert 1918- *WhoAm 92*
Zecha, Austen Victor Lauw 1940- *WhoWor 93*
Zechberger, Gunther 1951- *Baker 92*
Zechella, Alexander Philip 1920- *WhoAm 92*
Zecher, J. Richard 1940- *St&PR 93*
Zechiel, William A. 1951- *St&PR 93*
Zechlin, Ruth 1926- *Baker 92*
Zechman, Fred William, Jr. 1928- *WhoAm 92*
Zechner, Frank J.E. *Law&B 92*
Zechner, Rudolf 1954- *WhoWor 93*
Zechter, Sol 1926- *St&PR 93*
Zeckendorf, William, Jr. 1929- *WhoAm 92*
Zeckwer, Camille 1875-1924 *Baker 92*
Zeckwer, Richard 1850-1922 *Baker 92*
Zedda, Alberto 1928- *Baker 92*
Zeddies, Ann Tonsor 1951- *ScF&FL 92*
Zedeck, Morris Samuel 1940- *WhoE 93*
Zedeker, Daniel Lee 1956- *WhoE 93*
Zeder, Fred *BioIn 17*
Zeder, Fred Monroe, II 1921- *WhoAm 92*
Zederfeldt, Bengt H. 1929- *WhoScE 91-4*
Zedler, Empress Young 1908- *WhoSSW 93*
Zednik, Heinz 1940- *Baker 92*
Zedrosser, Joseph John 1938- *WhoAm 92, WhoE 93*
Zee, A. *ConAu 138*
Zee, Elizabeth W. *Law&B 92*
Zeeble, Bill T. 1957- *WhoSSW 93*
Zeeck, Erich Hans Christan 1932- *WhoScE 91-3*
Zeegers, Jacques 1946- *WhoWor 93*
Zeelen, Filippus J. 1928- *WhoScE 91-3*
Zeeman, Joan Javits 1928- *WhoAmW 93*
Zeerleder, Niklaus 1628-1691 *Baker 92*
Zeferino, Augusto Cesar 1947- *WhoWor 93*

Zeff, Mark BioIn 17
Zeff, Stephen Addam 1933- WhoAm 92
Zeff, Susan Leah 1945- WhoAmW 93
Zeffer, Alan E. 1952- St&PR 93
Zeffirelli, Franco BioIn 17
Zeffirelli, Franco 1923- Baker 92, IntDcOp, MiSFD 9, OxDcOp, WhoAm 92, WhoWor 93
Zeffren, Eugene 1941- St&PR 93, WhoAm 92
Zegar, Frank Anthony 1938- St&PR 93
Zegarelli, Edward Victor 1912- WhoAm 92
Zegarlinski, Boguslaw Joseph 1955- WhoWor 93
Zeger, Steven A. 1954- WhoE 93
Zeger, Warren Yale Law&B 92
Zegers, Kip 1943- WhoWrEP 92
Zegler, Chester J. 1936- St&PR 93
Zeglis, John D. Law&B 92, WhoAm 92
Zegveld, W.C.L. WhoScE 91-3
Zeh, Geoffrey N. BioIn 17
Zeh, Heinz-Dieter 1932- WhoWor 93
Zeh, Herbert J., Jr. Law&B 92
ZeHagen, Bonnie Lee 1947- WhoAmW 93
Zehe, Alfred Fritz Karl 1939- WhoWor 93
Zehe, Theresa Marie 1963- WhoE 93
Zehendner, Horst H.J. 1935- WhoScE 91-3
Zeheralis, Louis C. Law&B 92
Zehler, Edward Joseph 1940- WhoE 93
Zehler, Mark R. Law&B 92
Zehnder, Alexander J.B. 1946- WhoScE 91-3
Zehnder, Max 1901-1972 Baker 92
Zehner, Lee R. 1947- St&PR 93
Zehner, Lee Randall 1947- WhoE 93
Zehner, Marsha Louise 1951- WhoE 93
Zehner, Richard N. 1953- St&PR 93
Zehner, Richard Norman 1953- WhoWor 93
Zehner, Thomas Henry 1944- WhoE 93
Zehnwirth, Ben Zion 1947- WhoWor 93
Zehr, Dale R. 1934- St&PR 93
Zehr, Eldon Irvin 1935- WhoSSW 93
Zehr, Robert F. 1950- St&PR 93
Zehring, John William 1947- WhoE 93, WhoWrEP 92
Zehring, Karen 1945- WhoAmW 93, WhoE 93
Zeiber, Linda Marie 1948- WhoE 93
Zeichner, Mark 1949- WhoE 93
Zeichner, Oscar 1916- WhoAm 92
Zeichner, Saul 1935- WhoE 93
Zeid, Fahrelnissa, Princess of Iraq 1901?-1991 BioIn 17
Zeidenberg, Leonard 1925-1990 BioIn 17
Zeidenfeld, David 1909- St&PR 93
Zeidenstein, George 1929- WhoAm 92
Zeiderman, Abraham Moshe 1952- St&PR 93
Zeidler, Eberhard Heinrich 1926- WhoWor 93
Zeidler, Frank P. 1912- WhoAm 92
Zeidler, Manfred D. 1935- WhoScE 91-3
Zeidman, Boris 1908-1981 Baker 92
Zeidner, Lisa 1955- DcLB 120 [port]
Zeidner, Lisa A. 1955- WhoWrEP 92
Zeien, Alfred M. 1930- WhoAm 92, WhoE 93
Zeien, Alfred Michael 1930- St&PR 93
Zeig, Sande ScF&FL 92
Zeiger, Diane Mary 1956- WhoE 93
Zeiger, Larry ConAu 139
Zeiger, Lila L. 1927- WhoWrEP 92
Zeiger, Martin 1937- St&PR 93
Zeiger, Richard G. Law&B 92
Zeigfried, Karl ScF&FL 92
Zeigler, Alan 1951- St&PR 93
Zeigler, Bernard Phillip 1940- WhoAm 92
Zeigler, Bloise Alan 1951- WhoSSW 93
Zeigler, Charles E., Jr. St&PR 93
Zeigler, Donald Jay 1951- WhoSSW 93
Zeigler, Earle F. BioIn 17
Zeigler, Earle Frederick 1919- WhoAm 92
Zeigler, Eugene Noel 1921- WhoSSW 93
Zeigler, George M. 1934- St&PR 93
Zeigler, Jeanine Bahram Patton 1928- WhoAmW 93
Zeigler, Joseph Wesley 1938- WhoE 93
Zeigler, Judy Rose 1946- WhoAmW 93, WhoEmL 93
Zeigler, Kenneth Baron 1948- St&PR 93
Zeigler, Linda Kilgore 1939- WhoAmW 93
Zeigler, Luther Harmon 1936- WhoAm 92
Zeigler, Michael C. 1946- St&PR 93
Zeigler, Nancy Kay 1963- WhoAmW 93
Zeigler, Stephen F. 1951- St&PR 93
Zeihen, Lester Gregory 1913- WhoWor 93
Zeijlemaker, Wim P. 1939- WhoScE 91-3
Zeikel, Arthur 1932- WhoAm 92
Zeikowitz, Benson J. 1926- St&PR 93
Zeile, Todd BioIn 17
Zeiler, Michael Donald 1933- WhoAm 92
Zeilig, Nancy Meeks 1943- WhoAmW 93, WhoWrEP 92
Zeilinger, Jimmy MiSFD 9
Zeiller, Warren 1929- WhoAm 92
Zeilmaker, G.H. 1936- WhoScE 91-3
Zeilman, William Whitney 1939- St&PR 93
Zeinally, Assaf 1909-1932 Baker 92
Zeiner, Ann Oreski 1939- WhoAmW 93
Zeiner, Joseph A. 1928- St&PR 93
Zeiner, W.A. 1950- WhoScE 91-4
Zeinert, Karen Kay 1942- WhoWrEP 92
Zeipi, Parry 1947- WhoAsAP 91
Zeis, John Francis 1950- WhoE 93
Zeis, Paul M. Law&B 92
Zeisberger, David 1721-1808 BioIn 17
Zeise, Ingo 1932- WhoE 93
Zeisel, Hans BioIn 17
Zeisel, Hans 1905- WhoAm 92
Zeisel, Hans 1905-1992 ConAu 137, NewYTBS 92 [port]
Zeiser, Daniel G. Law&B 92
Zeisl, Eric(h) 1905-1959 Baker 92
Zeisler, Claire 1903-1991 BioIn 17
Zeisler, Fannie Bloomfield 1863-1927 Baker 92, BioIn 17
Zeisler, Richard Spiro 1916- WhoAm 92
Zeiss, Clifford John 1920- WhoE 93
Zeiss, Michael G. Law&B 92
Zeissig, Hilmar Richard 1938- WhoSSW 93
Zeit, Ruth Mae 1945- WhoAmW 93
Zeiter, William Emmet 1934- WhoAm 92
Zeitler, Elmar H. 1927- WhoScE 91-3
Zeitlin, Bruce Allen 1943- St&PR 93, WhoAm 92
Zeitlin, Eugenia Pawlik WhoAmW 93
Zeitlin, Herbert Zakary WhoAm 92
Zeitlin, Ida 1885?-1984? ScF&FL 92
Zeitlin, Irving M. 1928- ConAu 37NR
Zeitlin, Jacob 1883-1937 BioIn 17
Zeitlin, Jacob 1902-1987 ScF&FL 92
Zeitlin, Jide James WhoE 93
Zeitlin, Michelle BioIn 17
Zeitlin, Robert Norman 1935- WhoE 93
Zeitlin, Zvi 1923- Baker 92
Zeitlin-Siegel, Rhonda D. Law&B 92
Zeitman, Lea S. Law&B 92
Zeitman, Lea S. 1947- St&PR 93
Zeitner, June Culp WhoWrEP 92
Zeitnitz, Bernhard 1932- WhoScE 91-3
Zeitz, Baila 1943- WhoAmW 93, WhoE 93
Zejc, Alfred 1929- WhoScE 91-4
Zekind, Diane Marie 1961- WhoAmW 93
Zekman, Pamela Lois 1944- WhoAm 92
Zekman, Terri Margaret 1950- WhoAm 92, WhoAmW 93
Zekowski, Arlene 1922- WhoWrEP 92
Zelander, Tor 1925- WhoScE 91-2
Zelaya, Gianna Annette 1963- WhoAmW 93, WhoWor 93
Zelaya, Lorenzo DcCPCAm
Zelazko, Wieslaw Tadeusz 1933- WhoWor 93
Zelazny, Roger BioIn 17
Zelazny, Roger 1937- ScF&FL 92
Zelazny, Roger Joseph 1937- WhoAm 92, WhoWrEP 92
Zelazny, Roman S. 1926- WhoScE 91-4
Zelazo, Helene 1920- St&PR 93
Zelazo, Nathaniel K. 1918- St&PR 93, WhoAm 92
Zelazo, Ronald Elliott 1946- St&PR 93
Zelby, Rachel 1930- WhoAmW 93
Zelda 1915?- BioIn 17
Zeldes, Ilya Michael 1933- WhoWor 93
Zeldin, Jeanette Strack Law&B 92
Zeldin, Jesse 1923-1988 BioIn 17
Zeldin, Richard Packer 1918- WhoAm 92
Zeldin, Theodore 1933- ScF&FL 92
Zeldis, Stephen Martin 1946- WhoE 93
Zel'dovich, IAkov Borisovich BioIn 17
Zeledon, Benjamin DcCPCAm
Zelen, Herbert Jack 1931- WhoE 93
Zelen, Marvin 1927- WhoE 93
Zelencik, Stephen J. 1935- WhoAm 92
Zelenin, D.K. 1878-1954 IntDcAn
Zelenka, Istvan 1936- Baker 92
Zelenka, Jan Dismas (Lukas) 1679-1745 Baker 92
Zelenka, Jiri 1938- WhoScE 91-4
Zelen-Neier, Melissa Law&B 92
Zelenski, Wladislaw 1837-1921 Baker 92
Zelenski, Wladyslaw 1837-1921 OxDcOp, PolBiDi
Zelenski-Boy, Tadeusz 1874-1941 PolBiDi
Zeleny, Ann Douglas 1955- WhoE 93
Zeleny, Charles 1923- WhoSSW 93
Zeleny, Marjorie Pfeiffer 1924- WhoAmW 93, WhoSSW 93
Zeleny, Robert Owen 1930- St&PR 93, WhoAm 92
Zelevansky, Paul 1946- WhoWrEP 92
Zelezny, Lubomir 1925-1979 Baker 92
Zeliff, Bill, Jr. 1936- CngDr 91
Zeliff, William 1936- WhoE 93
Zeligson, Laurie Law&B 92
Zelikow, Howard Monroe 1934- WhoAm 92
Zelin, Jerome 1930- St&PR 93, WhoAm 92
Zelin, Robert Alan 1948- St&PR 93
Zelinka, Jan Evangelista 1893-1969 Baker 92
Zelinski, Joseph John 1922- WhoWor 93
Zelinskij, Yurij Borisovich 1947- WhoWor 93
Zelinsky, Paul O. BioIn 17, ChlBIID [port]
Zelinsky, Paul O. 1953- ConAu 38NR, MajAI [port]
Zelis, Robert Felix 1939- WhoAm 92
Zelisko, Mark 1951- St&PR 93
Zelisko, Sandra Pearl 1950- WhoSSW 93
Zelitch, David S. 1924- WhoIns 93
Zeljazkova, Binka 1923- DrEEuF
Zeljenka, Ilja 1932- Baker 92
Zell, Bonnie Dee 1951- WhoAmW 93
Zell, Cheryl Ann 1955- WhoSSW 93
Zell, Donald David 1928- WhoSSW 93
Zell, Howard Charles 1922- WhoE 93
Zell, Mary Alice 1948- St&PR 93
Zell, Ronald A. 1939- St&PR 93
Zell, Samuel BioIn 17
Zell, Samuel 1941- St&PR 93, WhoAm 92
Zell, Steven Peter 1946- WhoAm 92
Zelle, Charles A. 1955- St&PR 93
Zelle, Friedrich 1845-1927 Baker 92
Zeller, Belle 1903- BioIn 17
Zeller, C. Nick 1949- St&PR 93
Zeller, Carl 1842-1898 OxDcOp
Zeller, Carl (Johann Adam) 1842-1898 Baker 92
Zeller, Charles J. Law&B 92
Zeller, Claude van ScF&FL 92
Zeller, Edward Jacob 1925- WhoAm 92
Zeller, Francis Joseph 1943- WhoWor 93
Zeller, Harvey Law&B 92
Zeller, Helmut 1918- WhoScE 91-3
Zeller, John 1950- St&PR 93
Zeller, Mark C. 1948- St&PR 93
Zeller, Michael Edward 1939- WhoAm 92
Zeller, Noel E. BioIn 17
Zeller, Paul W. Law&B 92
Zeller, Paul William 1948- St&PR 93, WhoAm 92
Zeller, Randi E. Law&B 92
Zeller, Richard A. 1948- St&PR 93
Zeller, Robert Lee, Jr. 1951- St&PR 93
Zeller, Steven L. Law&B 92
Zeller, Thomas Law&B 92
Zellerbach, William Joseph 1920- WhoAm 92
Zellers, C.F., Jr. 1932- St&PR 93
Zellers, Carl Fredrick, Jr. 1932- WhoAm 92
Zellers, George, III 1925- WhoE 93
Zellers, Harold George 1948- WhoSSW 93
Zellers, Larry 1922- BioIn 17
Zellers, Roger William 1945- St&PR 93
Zelles, Tivadar 1937- WhoScE 91-4
Zellick, Graham John 1948- WhoWor 93
Zellinger, James A. Law&B 92
Zelliot, Eleanor Mae 1926- WhoAmW 93
Zellner, Julius 1832-1900 Baker 92
Zellner, Leopold Alexander 1823-1894 Baker 92
Zelmanowitz, Julius Martin 1941- WhoAm 92
Zelmer, Amy Elliott 1935- WhoAm 92
Zelmon, David Norman 1945- WhoWor 93
Zelner, Lawrence 1941- WhoE 93
Zelnick, Carl Robert 1940- WhoAm 92
Zelnick, David R. 1929- St&PR 93
Zelnick, Peter 1957- St&PR 93
Zelnick, Strauss 1957- WhoAm 92
Zelnio, Robert Norman 1950- WhoE 93
Zelon, Laurie Dee 1952- WhoAmW 93
Zelov, Randolph Dickinson 1925- St&PR 93
Zelov, V.H. 1923- St&PR 93
Zelov, V. Scott 1957- St&PR 93
Zelter, Carl Friedrich 1758-1832 Baker 92
Zeltins, Teodors 1914- WhoWrEP 92
Zeltser, Mark 1947- Baker 92
Zeltser, Yuri MiSFD 9
Zeluck, Roy S. 1952- St&PR 93
Zelver, Patricia 1923- WhoWrEP 92
Zelvin, Elizabeth 1944- WhoWrEP 92
Zelvin, Robert 1923- St&PR 93
Zemach, Beth BioIn 17
Zemach, Margot BioIn 17
Zemach, Margot 1931-1989 ChlBIID [port], ConAu 38NR, MajAI [port], SmATA 70 [port]
Zemaitis, Algirdas Jonas Alexis WhoWor 93
Zemaitis, Thomas E. Law&B 92
Zeman, Anton Leonard 1930- St&PR 93
Zeman, Edward L. 1955- St&PR 93
Zeman, Jarold Knox 1926- WhoAm 92, WhoWrEP 92
Zeman, John Robert 1940- St&PR 93, WhoAm 92
Zeman, Karel 1910-1989 DrEEuF
Zemanian, Armen Humpartsoum 1925- WhoAm 92, WhoE 93
Zemans, Joyce Pearl 1940- WhoAm 92
Zemanski, Kevin M. 1958- St&PR 93
Zemarchos OxDcByz
Zembala, Marek Andrzej 1940- WhoScE 91-4
Zembriski, Walter BioIn 17
Zemeckis, Robert 1952- MiSFD 9
Zemeckis, Robert L. 1952- WhoAm 92
Zemel, Jay Norman 1928- WhoAm 92
Zemelman, David 1948- St&PR 93
Zemelman, James L. Law&B 92
Zemelman, James L. 1931- St&PR 93
Zemelman, James Louis 1931- WhoAm 92, WhoWor 93
Zemenick, James Michael 1947- St&PR 93
Zemetis, Joseph C. Law&B 92
Zeminski, Joseph J., Jr. 1943- St&PR 93
Zemke, Hub 1914- BioIn 17
Zemlinsky, Alexander 1871-1942 OxDcOp
Zemlinsky, Alexander von 1871-1942 Baker 92, IntDcOp [port]
Zemlock, Barbara Ann 1966- WhoAmW 93
Zemmer, Joseph Lawrence, Jr. 1922- WhoAm 92
Zemmin, Richard William 1941- St&PR 93
Zemmol, Allen Law&B 92
Zemojtel, Alexander Michael 1952- WhoE 93
Zemon, Vance Marc 1951- WhoE 93
Zemp, G.R. Law&B 92
Zempel, Clare W. 1946- St&PR 93
Zemplenyi, Tibor Karol 1916- WhoAm 92
Zemtsov, Alexander 1959- WhoSSW 93
Zemzare, Lauma BioIn 17
Zen, E-an 1928- WhoAm 92
Zenatello, Giovanni 1876-1949 Baker 92, IntDcOp, OxDcOp
Zenawi, Legesse (Meles) 1955- WhoAfr
Zenawi, Meles BioIn 17
Zenck, Hermann 1898-1950 Baker 92
Zend, Robert 1929-1985 WhoCanL 92
Zendejas, Francisco 1917- DcMexL
Zendel, Patricia Kern 1946- WhoAmW 93
Zender, David B. Law&B 92
Zender, (Johannes Wolfgang) Hans 1936- Baker 92
Zender, Karl Francis 1937- WhoAm 92
Zendle, Howard Mark 1949- WhoE 93
Zenere, R.P. 1929- St&PR 93
Zeng, Guangxing 1947- WhoWor 93
Zeng, Zhaopan 1939- WhoWor 93
Zengel, Hans G. 1935- WhoScE 91-3
Zenger, Andre Luc 1942- WhoUN 92
Zenger, Christoph 1940- WhoScE 91-3
Zenger, John Peter 1697-1746 JrnUS
Zenger, Joseph 1962- St&PR 93
Zenger, Max 1837-1911 Baker 92
Zengerle, Marylouise 1953- WhoAmW 93
Zeng-fan, Zhang 1924- WhoWor 93
Zengilowski, Margaret Edna 1953- WhoAmW 93
Zengo, George Victor 1934- St&PR 93
Zeng Qingcun 1935- WhoAsAP 91
Zengulis, Sherry Lee 1952- WhoE 93
Zeng Xianlin 1929- WhoAsAP 91
Zeni, Jane Elizabeth 1945- WhoAmW 93
Zeni, Thomas Guy 1948- WhoWor 93
Zenick, Gerald 1946- St&PR 93
Zenith, Richard 1956- ConAu 139
Zenk, Ann Marie Law&B 92
Zenk, M.H. 1933- BioIn 17
Zenk, Patti Lynn Law&B 92
Zenke, Larry WhoAm 92, WhoSSW 93
Zenkel, Elliott L. Law&B 92
Zenker, Gary 1962- WhoE 93
Zenker, Richard C. 1954- St&PR 93
Zenker, Stefan 1940- WhoScE 91-4
Zenkovich, Brian 1956- St&PR 93
Zenkovich, Victor 1925- St&PR 93
Zenkovsky, Serge A. 1907-1990 BioIn 17
Zenner, Hans Peter 1947- WhoScE 91-3, WhoWor 93
Zenner, Ronald Peter 1938- St&PR 93
Zenny, Frederick Bancroft 1937- WhoUN 92
Zeno d491 OxDcByz
Zeno, Apostolo 1668-1750 Baker 92, IntDcOp, OxDcOp
Zeno, Jo Ann 1952- WhoAmW 93
Zeno, Phyllis Wolfe WhoAm 92, WhoAmW 93
Zenone, John Mark 1958- WhoSSW 93
Zenov, Eugene St&PR 93
Zenowitz, Allan Ralph 1928- WhoAm 92
Zentella, Yoly Gabriela 1949- WhoWrEP 92
Zentes, Joachim 1947- WhoWor 93
Zentgraf, A.J. 1925- St&PR 93
Zentmeyer, Donald W. Law&B 92
Zentmyer, George Aubrey 1913- WhoAm 92
Zentz, Gregory L. ScF&FL 92
Zentz, Robert W. Law&B 92
Zenzie, Henry 1929- St&PR 93
Zenzipper, Menachem St&PR 93

Zenzola, Edward V. 1943- *St&PR 93*
Zeo, Frank James 1910- *WhoE 93, WhoWor 93*
Zepeda, Eraclio 1937- *DcMexL, SpAmA*
Zepernick, Mary Weiland 1939- *WhoAm 92*
Zepf, Edward Charles 1938- *St&PR 93*
Zepf, Joseph J. *Law&B 92*
Zepf, Thomas Herman 1935- *WhoAm 92, WhoWor 93*
Zepht, Fritz H. 1923- *St&PR 93*
Zepht, Peter 1963- *St&PR 93*
Zepke, Brent Eric *Law&B 92*
Zepler, Bogumil 1858-1918 *Baker 92*
Zeplowitz, Franklin 1933- *WhoE 93*
Zeppa, Robert 1924- *WhoAm 92*
Zeppelin, Ferdinand 1838-1917 *DcTwHis*
Zeppetella, Anthony John 1949- *WhoE 93*
Zera, Carol Joyce 1943- *WhoAmW 93*
Zeratsky, John Gibbons 1939- *St&PR 93*
Zerbe, Anthony *WhoAm 92*
Zerbe, D.G. 1946- *St&PR 93*
Zerbe, Jerome (B.) 1904-1988 *ConAu 37NR*
Zerbe, John B. 1929- *St&PR 93*
Zerbey, Joseph Henry, IV 1942- *St&PR 93*
Zerbini, Euryclides de Jesus 1912- *WhoWor 93*
Zerbo, Saye 1932- *WhoAfr*
Zerbst, Ekkehard W. 1926- *WhoScE 91-3*
Zerby, Judy Ann 1941- *WhoAmW 93*
Zerby, Kim William *Law&B 92*
Zerby, Sandra Lois 1947- *WhoE 93*
Zerella, Joseph T. 1941- *WhoAm 92*
Zerella, William Robert 1956- *St&PR 93*
Zerezghi, Kidane M. 1931- *WhoUN 92*
Zerfoss, David B. 1948- *St&PR 93*
Zerfoss, Lester Frank 1903- *WhoSSW 93, WhoWor 93*
Zergollern-Cupak, Ljilana 1926- *WhoScE 91-4*
Zeri, Federico 1921- *BioIn 17*
Zeribi, Taoufik 1938- *WhoUN 92*
Zerin, Steven David 1953- *WhoAm 92*
Zerkel, Fred H. 1940- *St&PR 93*
Zerkel, Jacqulyn Wade 1961- *WhoEmL 93*
Zerkin, E(dmund) Leif 1949- *WhoWrEP 92*
Zerman, Melvyn Bernard 1930- *WhoE 93*
Zerman, William Sheridan 1924- *WhoSSW 93*
Zermani, John Thomas 1947- *St&PR 93*
Zern, John R. *Law&B 92*
Zerna, Wolfgang 1916- *WhoWor 93*
Zerner, Michael Charles 1940- *WhoSSW 93*
Zernhelt, Francis L. 1938- *St&PR 93*
Zernhelt, Francis Leo 1938- *WhoAm 92*
Zernial, Gus Edward 1923- *BiDAMSp 1989*
Zernicki, Boguslaw 1931- *WhoScE 91-4*
Zerobin, Konrad 1931- *WhoScE 91-4*
Zeroka, Daniel 1941- *WhoE 93*
Zeromski, Jan Olgierd 1938- *WhoWor 93*
Zeromski, Stefan 1864-1925 *PolBiDi*
Zerong, He 1939- *WhoWor 93*
Zerrahn, Carl 1826-1909 *Baker 92*
Zerres, Klaus 1949- *WhoScE 91-3*
Zertal, Adam *BioIn 17*
Zervas, Nicholas Themistocles 1929- *WhoAm 92*
Zerwas, P.M. 1942- *WhoScE 91-3*
Zerweck, Charles W. 1908- *St&PR 93*
Zerwekh, Robert Paul 1939- *WhoAm 92*
Zerwekh-Lee, Zoe 1957- *WhoE 93*
Zespedes, Vicente Manuel de *BioIn 17*
Zessar, William L. *Law&B 92*
Zetelaki-Horvath, Kornelia 1931- *WhoScE 91-4*
Zetes, Maria J. *Law&B 92*
Zetford, Tully *ScF&FL 92*
Zetler, James William 1939- *WhoSSW 93*
Zetlin, Lev d1992 *NewYTBS 92*
Zetlin, Lev 1918- *WhoAm 92*
Zetsche, Klaus 1930- *WhoScE 91-3*
Zettek, Chris R. 1960- *St&PR 93*
Zetterberg, Alan Cowles *Law&B 92*
Zetterholm, Tore 1915- *ScF&FL 92*
Zetterling, Mai 1925- *MiSFD 9*
Zetterling, Mai Elisabeth 1925- *WhoWor 93*
Zetterstroem, Olle O.E. 1940- *WhoScE 91-4*
Zetterstrom, Rolf O.F. 1920- *WhoScE 91-4*
Zettlemoyer, Albert C. 1915-1991 *BioIn 17*
Zettlemoyer, Ave Jeanne 1953- *WhoWrEP 92*
Zettlemoyer, Christine M. *Law&B 92*
Zettner, Pat *ScF&FL 92*
Zettner, Pat 1940- *ConAu 138, SmATA 70*
Zetzer, Robert S. 1930- *WhoIns 93*
Zetzmann, Robert E. 1929- *St&PR 93*
Zeughauser, Peter D. *Law&B 92*
Zeugner, John Finn 1938- *WhoAm 92*
Zeuner, Charles 1795-1857 *Baker 92*
Zeuner, Karl Traugott 1775-1841 *Baker 92*
Zeuschner, Erwin Arnold 1935- *WhoAm 92*
Zeuthen, Jesper 1947- *WhoScE 91-2*
Zeuthen, Vibeke Q. 1941- *WhoScE 91-2*
Zevi, Bruno 1918- *WhoWor 93*
Zevin, Robert B. 1936- *St&PR 93*
Zevon, Renee S. *Law&B 92*
Zevon, Susan Jane 1944- *WhoAmW 93*
Zevon, Warren 1947- *ConMus 9 [port], WhoAm 92*
Zevon Tschacbasov, Irene Ann 1918- *WhoE 93*
Zewail, Ahmed Hassan 1946- *WhoAm 92*
Zewe, Judith Lynn 1947- *WhoAmW 93*
Zewiey, Mark Anthony 1961- *WhoE 93*
Zeytounian, Radyadour Khatchik 1928- *WhoScE 91-2*
Zezulak, Jiri 1937- *WhoScE 91-4*
Zezza, Carlo 1936- *ScF&FL 92*
Zganec, Vinko 1890-1976 *Baker 92*
Zgonc, Janice Ann 1956- *WhoAmW 93*
Zgorski, Robert Francis 1952- *WhoIns 93*
Zgrodnik, Kimberly Ann 1967- *WhoE 93*
Zhabjaku, Ismail 1932- *DrEEuF*
Zhabotinskii, Vladimir Evgen'evich 1880-1940 *BioIn 17*
Zhang, Ben 1933- *WhoUN 92*
Zhang, Binggen 1934- *WhoWor 93*
Zhang, Binglin 1937- *WhoWor 93*
Zhang, Cheng-Yue 1945- *WhoWor 93*
Zhang, Chi 1963- *WhoE 93*
Zhang, Fu-Xue 1939- *WhoWor 93*
Zhang, Guo-xi 1952- *WhoWor 93*
Zhang, Jian 1958- *WhoWor 93*
Zhang, Jian-Wu 1954- *WhoWor 93*
Zhang, Jingshang 1941- *WhoWor 93*
Zhang, Jingzhong 1936- *WhoWor 93*
Zhang, Jiping 1958- *WhoWor 93*
Zhang, Ke Min 1935- *WhoWor 93*
Zhang, Kewei 1957- *WhoWor 93*
Zhang, Li-Xing 1934- *WhoWor 93*
Zhang, Pei-Lin 1933- *WhoWor 93*
Zhang, Qing 1933- *WhoWor 93*
Zhang, Ruiyao 1935- *WhoWor 93*
Zhang, Shi-Chang 1945- *WhoWor 93*
Zhang, Shu Jing 1933- *WhoWor 93*
Zhang, Shunian 1940- *WhoWor 93*
Zhang, Shuying 1938- *WhoWor 93*
Zhang, Tao 1942- *WhoWor 93*
Zhang, Wen Xian 1938- *WhoWor 93*
Zhang, Wen Xun 1937- *WhoWor 93*
Zhang, Xian 1946- *WhoUN 92*
Zhang, Yimou *MiSFD 9*
Zhang, Yuan Fu 1940- *WhoWor 93*
Zhang, Yuanduan 1940- *WhoWor 93*
Zhang, Zhi Rang 1946- *WhoWor 93*
Zhang Baochi 1956- *BioIn 17*
Zhang Bo *BioIn 17*
Zhang Boxing 1930- *WhoAsAP 91*
Zhang Guoying 1935- *WhoAsAP 91*
Zhang Jie 1937- *BioIn 17*
Zhang Lianzhong 1931- *WhoAsAP 91*
Zhang Lichang 1939- *WhoAsAP 91*
Zhang Ming *WhoAsAP 91*
Zhang Shenfu d1986 *BioIn 17*
Zhang Shou 1930- *WhoAsAP 91*
Zhang Siqing 1932- *WhoAsAP 91*
Zhang Wannian 1928- *WhoAsAP 91*
Zhang Wanxin 1930- *WhoAsAP 91*
Zhang Wenjin 1914-1991 *BioIn 17*
Zhang Xianliang 1936- *BioIn 17*
Zhang Yanzhong 1930- *WhoAsAP 91*
Zhang Yimou *BioIn 17, NewYTBS 92 [port]*
Zhang Yimou 1951- *CurBio 92 [port]*
Zhang Zhongxian 1926- *WhoAsAP 91*
Zhao, Cui-Kui 1936- *WhoWor 93*
Zhao, Guanghua 1954- *WhoSSW 93*
Zhao, Hua-ming 1918- *WhoWor 93*
Zhao, Hui-Yang 1931- *WhoWor 93*
Zhao, Lincheng 1942- *WhoWor 93*
Zhao, Mae 1965- *WhoAmW 93*
Zhao, Yan Da 1935- *WhoWor 93*
Zhao, Zijun 1962- *WhoE 93, WhoWor 93*
Zhao Bai, Feng 1927- *WhoWor 93*
Zhao Dan 1914-1980 *IntDcF 2-3 [port]*
Zhao Di 1939- *WhoAsAP 91*
Zhao Dongwan 1925- *WhoAsAP 91*
Zhao Fulin 1932- *WhoAsAP 91*
Zhao Nanqi 1935- *WhoAsAP 91*
Zhao Xianshun 1925- *WhoAsAP 91*
Zhao Yannian 1929- *WhoAsAP 91*
Zhao Ziyang 1919- *ColdWar 2 [port], WhoAsAP 91, WhoWor 93*
Zhao Zongnai 1929- *WhoAsAP 91*
Zhdanko, T.A. 1909- *IntDcAn*
Zhdanov, Andrei A. 1896-1948 *ColdWar 2 [port]*
Zhdanov, Andrey 1896-1948 *DcTwHis*
Zhelev, Zhelyu Mitev 1935- *WhoWor 93*
Zheljazkov, Ivan *WhoScE 91-4*
Zheljazkov, Ljubomir *WhoScE 91-4*
Zhelobinsky, Valeri (Viktorovich) 1913-1946 *Baker 92*
Zheltov, Lev M. 1935- *WhoUN 92*
Zhelyaskova-Panayotova, Maria 1928- *WhoScE 91-4*
Zhemaitis, Sergei 1908- *ScF&FL 92*
Zheng, Jiaju 1925- *WhoWor 93*
Zheng, Maggie Xiaoci 1949- *WhoAmW 93*
Zheng, Rong 1947- *WhoWor 93*
Zheng, Sining 1946- *WhoWor 93*
Zheng, Weixing 1932- *WhoWor 93*
Zheng, Youlu 1942- *WhoWor 93*
Zheng, Zhong-Zhi 1914- *WhoWor 93*
Zheng Hua 1930- *WhoAsAP 91*
Zheng Tuobin 1924- *WhoAsAP 91*
Zhevandrov, Peter Nikolaevitch 1959- *WhoWor 93*
Zhezhko, Irina Vitalievna 1945- *WhoAmW 93*
Zhiganov, Nazib 1911- *OxDcOp*
Zhiganov, Nazib 1911-1988 *Baker 92*
Zhilinsky, Yakov Gregorievich 1853-c. 1920 *HarEnMi*
Zhitomirsky, Alexander 1881-1937 *Baker 92*
Zhivkov, Todor 1911- *ColdWar 2 [port], DcTwHis*
Zhivotov, Alexei 1904-1964 *Baker 92*
Zhong, Renbao 1937- *WhoWor 93*
Zhou, Chiping 1957- *WhoWor 93*
Zhou, Guang-Fu 1939- *WhoWor 93*
Zhou, Jianying 1936- *WhoWor 93*
Zhou, Jiazu 1954- *WhoE 93*
Zhou, Shuzi 1940- *WhoWor 93*
Zhou, Tian Xiao 1938- *WhoWor 93*
Zhou, Wei 1934- *WhoUN 92*
Zhou, Yongping 1936- *WhoWor 93*
Zhou Enlai 1898-1976 *ColdWar 2 [port], DcTwHis*
Zhou Erfu 1914- *BioIn 17*
Zhou Guangzhao 1929- *WhoAsAP 91*
Zhou Keqin 1936-1990 *BioIn 17*
Zhou Keyu 1929- *WhoAsAP 91*
Zhou Wenyuan 1940?- *WhoAsAP 91*
Zhou Yibing 1922- *WhoAsAP 91*
Zhou Yushu *WhoAsAP 91*
Zhu, Ai-Lan 1956- *WhoAm 92*
Zhu, Bu-Yao 1936- *WhoWor 93*
Zhu, Deming 1947- *WhoWor 93*
Zhu, Jianchao 1952- *WhoEmL 93, WhoSSW 93, WhoWor 93*
Zhu, Jun 1959- *WhoWor 93*
Zhu, Kehe 1961- *WhoE 93*
Zhu, Rong 1953- *WhoWor 93*
Zhu, Xiaoyuan 1961- *WhoWor 93*
Zhu, Zuhua 1939- *WhoWor 93*
Zhuang, Nan 1959- *WhoWor 93*
Zhuang, Wan 1936- *WhoWor 93*
Zhu De 1886-1976 *DcTwHis*
Zhu Gaofeng 1935- *WhoAsAP 91*
Zhu Guang 1922- *WhoAsAP 91*
Zhu Guangya 1924- *WhoAsAP 91*
Zhu Hong 1933- *ConAu 139*
Zhuk, Isaak 1902-1973 *Baker 92*
Zhuk, Valentin 1934- *Baker 92*
Zhu Kaixuan 1932- *WhoAsAP 91*
Zhukov, Georgi K. 1896-1974 *ColdWar 2 [port]*
Zhukov, Georgi Konstantinovich 1896-1974 *DcTwHis, HarEnMi*
Zhukov, Georgii Konstantinovich 1896-1974 *BioIn 17*
Zhukov, Leonid 1892-1951 *BioIn 17*
Zhukovsky, Herman 1913-1976 *Baker 92*
Zhukovsky, Vasily 1783-1852 *NinCLC 35 [port]*
Zhu Liang 1924- *WhoAsAP 91*
Zhu Qizhen *BioIn 17*
Zhuravlev, Vladimir Georgievich 1948- *WhoWor 93*
Zhuravleva, Valentina *ScF&FL 92*
Zhu Rongji 1928- *WhoAsAP 91, WhoWor 93*
Zhu Senlin 1930- *WhoAsAP 91*
Zhu Senyuan *BioIn 17*
Zhu Xuefan 1905- *WhoAsAP 91*
Zhu Xun 1930- *WhoAsAP 91*
Zia, Begum Khaleda *WhoAsAP 91*
Zia, Begum Khaleda 1945- *WhoWor 93*
Zia, Fereydoon Bob 1945- *St&PR 93*
Zia, Hoyt E. *Law&B 92*
Zia, Khaleda *BioIn 17*
Ziadeh, Farhat J. 1917- *WhoAm 92*
Ziance, James P. 1947- *St&PR 93*
Ziani, Marc'Antonio c. 1653-1715 *OxDcOp*
Ziani, Marco Antonio c. 1653-1715 *Baker 92*
Ziani, Pietro Andrea c. 1616-1684 *Baker 92, OxDcOp*
Zia ul-Haq, Mohammad 1924-1988 *ColdWar 2 [port]*
Zia ul-Haq, Mohammed 1924-1988 *DcTwHis*
Ziavras, Charles Efthemios (Jarvis) 1921- *WhoWrEP 92*
Zibart, Michael Alan 1947- *WhoAm 92*
Zibbell, David R. 1939- *St&PR 93*
Zibelli, Ronald *Law&B 92*
Zibelman, Audrey A. *Law&B 92*
Zibolsky, Kay *BioIn 17*
Ziccarelli, Paul D. *Law&B 92*
Zich, Jaroslav 1912- *Baker 92*
Zich, Otakar 1879-1934 *Baker 92*
Zicha, Elizabeth Ann 1958- *WhoAmW 93*
Zichek, Melvin Eddie 1918- *WhoWor 93*
Zichlin, Sidney 1923- *St&PR 93*
Zichy, Geza 1849-1924 *Baker 92*
Zick, Janice Lee 1958- *WhoAmW 93*
Zick, John Walter 1925- *WhoAm 92*
Zick, Leonard Otto 1905- *WhoWor 93*
Zickau, William E. 1936- *St&PR 93*
Zickel, John 1919- *WhoAm 92*
Zickler, Leo E. 1936- *St&PR 93*
Zicklin, Lawrence 1936- *St&PR 93*
Zicree, Marc Scott 1955- *ScF&FL 92*
Zide, Donna Comeaux *ScF&FL 92*
Zide-Booth, Rochelle Deena 1938- *WhoAmW 93*
Zidek, James Victor 1939- *WhoAm 92*
Zider, Robert Warren 1950- *St&PR 93*
Ziebarth, E. William 1910- *WhoAm 92*
Ziebarth, Karl Rex 1938- *WhoAm 92*
Ziebarth, Robert Charles 1936- *WhoAm 92*
Ziebell, R.P. 1946- *St&PR 93*
Zieff, Howard 1943- *ConTFT 10, MiSFD 9*
Zieg, Lynda Kaye 1946- *WhoAmW 93*
Ziegaus, Alan James 1948- *WhoAm 92*
Ziegele, William John 1940- *St&PR 93*
Ziegelman, Robert Lee 1936- *WhoAm 92, WhoWor 93*
Ziegelmeier, Robert E. 1954- *St&PR 93*
Ziegenfuss, Alan *ScF&FL 92*
Ziegenmeyer, Nancy *BioIn 17*
Ziegfeld, Richard E. 1948- *ScF&FL 92*
Ziegfield, Kay *AmWomPl*
Ziegler, Alan Stephen *Law&B 92*
Ziegler, Arthur B. 1930- *WhoAm 92*
Ziegler, Bette J. 1940- *WhoWrEP 92*
Ziegler, Bradley Jay *Law&B 92*
Ziegler, Christine B. 1951- *WhoAmW 93*
Ziegler, Daniel Martin 1927- *WhoAm 92*
Ziegler, Delores *BioIn 17, WhoAm 92*
Ziegler, Dewey Kiper 1920- *WhoAm 92*
Ziegler, Dhyana 1949- *WhoAmW 93, WhoEmL 93*
Ziegler, Donald E. 1949- *St&PR 93*
Ziegler, Donald Emil 1936- *WhoE 93*
Ziegler, Donald Robert 1932- *WhoAm 92*
Ziegler, Edward Paul 1951- *St&PR 93*
Ziegler, Ekhard Erich 1940- *WhoAm 92*
Ziegler, Eldon A. 1939- *WhoIns 93*
Ziegler, Eldon Arthur 1939- *St&PR 93*
Ziegler, Evarts d1990 *BioIn 17*
Ziegler, Frank J. *Law&B 92*
Ziegler, George Herbert 1951- *St&PR 93*
Ziegler, Hans Konrad 1911- *WhoE 93*
Ziegler, Henry Steinway 1933- *WhoAm 92*
Ziegler, Hubert 1924- *WhoScE 91-3*
Ziegler, Jack 1942- *BioIn 17*
Ziegler, Jack Denmore 1942- *WhoAm 92*
Ziegler, James Russell 1922- *WhoWor 93*
Ziegler, Jan 1953- *WhoAmW 93*
Ziegler, Jesse H. 1913- *WhoAm 92*
Ziegler, John Alan 1933- *WhoSSW 93, WhoWor 93*
Ziegler, John Augustus, Jr. 1934- *WhoAm 92*
Ziegler, John Benjamin 1917- *WhoE 93*
Ziegler, John K. 1937- *St&PR 93*
Ziegler, John R. *WhoIns 93*
Ziegler, Joseph d1882 *BioIn 17*
Ziegler, Kurt 1942- *St&PR 93*
Ziegler, Kurt A.E. 1931- *WhoScE 91-3*
Ziegler, Laurene Louise 1951- *WhoE 93*
Ziegler, Leonard Charles 1931- *St&PR 93*
Ziegler, Linda Kay 1969- *WhoAmW 93*
Ziegler, Linda Sue 1963- *WhoAmW 93*
Ziegler, Mandell Stanley 1921- *WhoAm 92, WhoE 93*
Ziegler, Miriam Mary 1945- *WhoAmW 93*
Ziegler, R.D. 1927- *St&PR 93*
Ziegler, Raymond Stewart 1919- *WhoAm 92*
Ziegler, Reinhard 1935- *WhoScE 91-3*
Ziegler, Renatus Johannes M. 1955- *WhoWor 93*
Ziegler, Robert Baldwin 1932- *St&PR 93*
Ziegler, Robert George 1924- *WhoSSW 93*
Ziegler, Ronald Louis 1939- *WhoAm 92, WhoWor 93*
Ziegler, Russell A. 1907-1991 *BioIn 17*
Ziegler, Sheila Gerber 1949- *WhoAmW 93*
Ziegler, Stephen R. 1959- *St&PR 93*
Ziegler, T.C. 1954- *St&PR 93*
Ziegler, Theresa W. 1935- *St&PR 93*
Ziegler, William, III 1928- *St&PR 93, WhoAm 92*
Ziegler, William Alexander 1924- *WhoAm 92*
Ziegler, William John, Jr. 1922- *WhoE 93*
Ziegler, William Paul 1922- *St&PR 93*
Ziegner, Edward Henry 1920- *WhoAm 92*
Ziehm, Eugene Carl *Law&B 92*
Ziehm, Howard *MiSFD 9*
Ziehm, Richard W. 1948- *St&PR 93*

Ziehn, Bernhard 1845-1912 *Baker 92*
Ziehrer, Carl Michael 1843-1922 *Baker 92*
Ziel, Charles D. 1923- *St&PR 93*
Zieleniewski, Jerzy 1929- *WhoScE 91-4*
Zielenkiewicz, Wojciech *WhoScE 91-4*
Zielenski, Mikolaj c. 1530-1615 *PolBiDi*
Zielinksi, Beth Babich 1947- *WhoAmW 93*
Zielinski, Andrzej Franciszek 1938- *WhoScE 91-4*
Zielinski, Charles Anthony 1944- *WhoAm 92*
Zielinski, Christopher Thomas 1950- *WhoUN 92*
Zielinski, David 1953- *ScF&FL 92*
Zielinski, Frank D. *Law&B 92*
Zielinski, H. *WhoScE 91-4*
Zielinski, Henryk 1925- *WhoScE 91-4*
Zielinski, Jan 1930- *WhoScE 91-4*
Zielinski, Jan 1933- *WhoScE 91-4*
Zielinski, Jaroslaw 1847-1922 *PolBiDi*
Zielinski, Jaroslaw de 1844-1922 *Baker 92*
Zielinski, Jerzy 1914- *WhoWor 93*
Zielinski, Jerzy Stanislaw 1933- *WhoWor 93*
Zielinski, Kathryn Manfredi 1959- *St&PR 93*
Zielinski, Kazimierz 1929- *WhoScE 91-4*
Zielinski, Leszek 1948- *WhoWrEP 92*
Zielinski, Mieczyslaw 1933- *WhoWor 93*
Zielinski, Paul Bernard 1932- *WhoE 93*
Zielinski, Peter A. 1929- *St&PR 93*
Zielinski, Rafal 1954- *MiSFD 9*
Zielinski, Scott *BioIn 17*
Zielinski, Tadeusz 1918-1977 *PolBiDi*
Zielinski, Walt Thomas *Law&B 92*
Zielinski, Wojciech 1957- *WhoWor 93*
Zielinski, Zbigniew 1929- *WhoScE 91-4*
Zielke, William A. 1946- *St&PR 93*
Ziemann, Edward F. 1944- *St&PR 93*
Ziemann, F. Joseph 1939- *St&PR 93*
Ziemba, Boleslaw 1929- *WhoScE 91-4*
Ziemba, Eugene Stanley 1946- *St&PR 93*
Ziemba, Mark Vincent 1950- *WhoE 93*
Ziemba, Ronald S. 1943- *St&PR 93*
Ziemba, Thomas M. *Law&B 92*
Ziembo, Zbigniew 1928- *WhoScE 91-4*
Ziemer, Charles O. *Law&B 92*
Ziemer, James L. 1950- *St&PR 93*
Ziemer, Marlyn E. 1936- *WhoIns 93*
Ziemer, Rodger Edmund 1937- *WhoAm 92*
Zientara, James Edward 1943- *WhoSSW 93*
Zientara, Jeffrey Raymond 1967- *WhoE 93*
Zients, Steven Jeffrey 1954- *WhoE 93*
Zienty, Jerome A. *Law&B 92*
Zier, Alex Richard 1949- *St&PR 93*
Zier, Ronald Edward 1931- *St&PR 93*
Zierau, Harold K. 1922- *St&PR 93*
Zierden, William Ernest 1938- *St&PR 93*
Zierdt, Charles Henry 1922- *WhoE 93, WhoWor 93*
Zierhut, Ingried *ScF&FL 92*
Ziering, Ian *BioIn 17*
Ziering, Sigi 1928- *St&PR 93*
Ziering, William Mark 1931- *WhoAm 92*
Zierler, Kenneth 1917- *WhoE 93*
Zierler, Neal 1926- *WhoAm 92*
Ziermaier, Klaus Michael *Law&B 92*
Ziermann, Arnold L.E. 1932- *WhoScE 91-3*
Zieroth, Dale 1946- *WhoCanL 92*
Ziesenis, Randy Theodore 1948- *WhoSSW 93*
Zieserl, Robert M. *St&PR 93*
Ziesing, Mark V. 1953- *ScF&FL 92*
Ziessow, Dieter 1940- *WhoScE 91-3*
Zieten, Hans Ernst Karl von 1770-1848 *HarEnMi*
Zieten, Hans Joachim von 1698-1786 *HarEnMi*
Ziety, James P. *Law&B 92*
Zietz, Joachim 1953- *WhoSSW 93*
Zietz, Karyl Lynn Kopelman 1943- *WhoE 93*
Zietz, Susan Margaret 1950- *WhoAmW 93*
Zietzschmann, Ernst 1907-1991 *BioIn 17*
Zieve, Leonard S. 1920- *St&PR 93*
Zieve, Morton I. 1927- *St&PR 93*
Zieve, Morton L. 1932- *St&PR 93*
Zieverink, Sara Elizabeth 1943- *WhoAmW 93*
Ziewiec, Andrzej 1955- *WhoScE 91-4*
Ziferstein, Isidore 1909- *WhoWor 93*
Ziff, Charles E. d1992 *NewYTBS 92*
Ziff, Gil *ScF&FL 92*
Ziff, Howard G. *Law&B 92*
Ziff, Joel David 1947- *WhoE 93*
Ziff, Larzer 1927- *WhoAm 92*
Ziff, Lloyd *BioIn 17*
Ziff, Lloyd Richard 1942- *WhoAm 92, WhoWor 93*
Ziff, Matthew Dionysius 1952- *WhoSSW 93*
Ziff, Morris 1913- *WhoAm 92, WhoSSW 93*
Ziff, Paul 1922- *WhoAm 92*
Ziff, Robert Alan 1952- *WhoWor 93*
Ziff, Ruth 1924- *St&PR 93*
Ziff, William B. *BioIn 17*
Ziff, William Bernard, Jr. 1930- *WhoAm 92*
Zifferero, Maurizio 1930- *WhoScE 91-4, WhoUN 92*
Ziffren, Lester 1925- *WhoAm 92*
Ziffren, Paul 1913-1991 *BioIn 17*
Ziga, Mary Jane 1953- *St&PR 93*
Ziga, Victor San Andres 1945- *WhoAsAP 91*
Zigabenos, Euthymios fl. c. 1100- *OxDcByz*
Zigal, Thomas 1948- *WhoWrEP 92*
Zigarlick, John 1937- *St&PR 93*
Zigeuner Muller 1874-1930 *BioIn 17*
Ziglar, James W. 1945- *WhoAm 92*
Zigler, Edward Frank 1930- *BioIn 17, WhoAm 92*
Zigler, M.R. 1891-1985 *BioIn 17*
Zigler, Michael Robert 1891-1985 *BioIn 17*
Zigman, Barbara Deanne 1956- *WhoAmW 93*
Zigman, Robert S. 1919- *WhoAm 92*
Zigmanth, Robert E. 1947- *St&PR 93*
Zigment, Robert A. 1956- *St&PR 93*
Zigmunt, Ted John 1951- *WhoEmL 93*
Zigterman, Kent Alan *Law&B 92*
Zigterman, Paul *Law&B 92*
Zigun, Stuart Bruce *Law&B 92*
Zigun, Sylvia Helene 1934- *WhoE 93*
Zihlman, Adrienne L. *BioIn 17*
Ziino, Joseph J., Jr. *Law&B 92*
Zijlstra, J.J. *WhoScE 91-3*
Zijlstra, Willem G. 1925- *WhoScE 91-3*
Zikakis, John P. 1933- *WhoAm 92, WhoWor 93*
Zikmund, Barbara Brown 1939- *WhoAm 92, WhoAmW 93*
Zikolov, Peter Slavov 1937- *WhoScE 91-4*
Zil, John Stephen 1947- *WhoWor 93*
Zilahi-Szabo, Miklos Geza 1936- *WhoScE 91-3*
Zilai, Janos *WhoScE 91-4*
Zilber, Maurice Leonard 1938- *St&PR 93*
Zilber, Suzanne M. 1963- *WhoAmW 93*
Zil'bershtein, Il'ia Samoilovich 1905-1988 *BioIn 17*
Zilboorg, Caroline (Crawford) 1948- *ConAu 137*
Zilcher, Hermann (Karl Josef) 1881-1948 *Baker 92*
Zilczer, Judith Katy 1948- *WhoE 93*
Zile, Ronald L. 1933- *St&PR 93*
Zile, Ronald Leo 1933- *WhoAm 92*
Zilenovski, Judith Ryan 1952- *WhoWor 93*
Zilenziger, Rodman J. 1928- *St&PR 93*
Zilg, Robert John 1954- *WhoE 93*
Zilinskas, Antanas 1946- *WhoWor 93*
Zilinskas, Barbara Ann 1947- *WhoAmW 93*
Zilke, Timothy A. 1957- *St&PR 93*
Zilkha, Donald Elias 1951- *WhoE 93*
Zilkha, Ezra Khedouri 1925- *St&PR 93, WhoAm 92*
Zill, Arthur C. 1927- *St&PR 93*
Zillbauer, J. *WhoScE 91-4*
Ziller, Richard Patrick 1941- *St&PR 93*
Zilles, J.P. 1936- *St&PR 93*
Zilli, Harry A., Jr. 1930- *St&PR 93*
Zilli, Harry Angelo, Jr. 1930- *WhoAm 92*
Zillig, Winfried (Petrus Ignatius) 1905-1963 *Baker 92*
Zillig, Wolfram *WhoScE 91-3*
Zilligen, Joseph H. 1941- *St&PR 93*
Zilly, Thomas Samuel 1935- *WhoAm 92*
Zilnik, Zelimir 1942- *DrEEuF*
Ziloti, Alexander *Baker 92*
Zils, Joseph C. *Law&B 92*
Zilversmit, Donald Berthold 1919- *WhoAm 92*
Zilz, David Arthur 1937- *WhoAm 92*
Zim, Herbert S(pencer) 1909- *MajAI [port]*
Zim, Herbert Spencer 1909- *WhoAm 92*
Zima, Vaclav *WhoScE 91-4*
Zima, Vladimir Grigorijevich 1946- *WhoWor 93*
Ziman, Harry John 1963- *WhoWor 93*
Zimand, Harvey Folks 1928- *WhoAm 92*
Zimanyi, Magdolna 1934- *WhoScE 91-4*
Zimbalist, Efrem (Alexandrovich) 1889-1985 *Baker 92*
Zimbardo, Philip George 1933- *WhoAm 92*
Zimbardo, Rose A. 1932- *ScF&FL 92*
Zimbeck, David L. *Law&B 92*
Zimbelman, Darrell Frank 1963- *WhoE 93*
Zimbert, Jonathan A. *ScF&FL 92*
Zimbert, Richard *Law&B 92*
Zimble, James Allen 1933- *WhoAm 92*
Zimcosky, James 1948- *St&PR 93*
Zimdras-Orthman, Marjorie A. 1949- *St&PR 93*
Zimelman, Nathan *BioIn 17*
Zimerman, Krystian 1956- *Baker 92*
Zimet, Carl Norman 1925- *WhoAm 92*
Zimet, Irvin M. 1925- *St&PR 93*
Zimet, Robert D. *Law&B 92*
Zimin, Sergey 1875-1942 *OxDcOp*
Zimm, Bruno Hasbrouck 1920- *WhoAm 92*
Zimm, Louise Seymour Hasbrouck *AmWomPl*
Zimmar, George Peter 1937- *WhoAm 92, WhoE 93*
Zimmer, Alan Mark 1959- *St&PR 93*
Zimmer, Albert Arthur 1918- *WhoAm 92*
Zimmer, Alf Conrad 1943- *WhoWor 93*
Zimmer, Anne Fern Young 1920- *WhoAmW 93*
Zimmer, Charles Edward 1924- *St&PR 93*
Zimmer, Daryl L. *Law&B 92*
Zimmer, David Arthur 1956- *WhoE 93*
Zimmer, David J. 1943- *St&PR 93*
Zimmer, Dick 1944- *CngDr 91*
Zimmer, Dirk *BioIn 17*
Zimmer, Don 1931- *BioIn 17*
Zimmer, Donald William 1931- *WhoAm 92*
Zimmer, E. *WhoScE 91-3*
Zimmer, Edward Michael 1937- *St&PR 93*
Zimmer, Edward Paul *Law&B 92*
Zimmer, Edward Paul 1949- *St&PR 93*
Zimmer, Elizabeth Ann 1940- *WhoWrEP 92*
Zimmer, Friedrich 1855-1919 *Baker 92*
Zimmer, Friedrich August 1826-1899 *Baker 92*
Zimmer, G. *WhoScE 91-3*
Zimmer, Gregory F. 1944- *St&PR 93*
Zimmer, Gyorgy J. 1939- *WhoScE 91-4*
Zimmer, Hans 1958?- *ConTFT 10*
Zimmer, Hans M. *Law&B 92*
Zimmer, Horst Gunter 1937- *WhoWor 93*
Zimmer, Jack Anthony 1932- *St&PR 93*
Zimmer, Jan 1926- *Baker 92*
Zimmer, Jay Alan 1952- *WhoE 93*
Zimmer, John Herman 1922- *WhoWor 93*
Zimmer, Karl R. 1926- *St&PR 93*
Zimmer, Norman Cunningham 1924- *WhoAm 92*
Zimmer, Paul *BioIn 17*
Zimmer, Paul Edwin 1943- *ScF&FL 92*
Zimmer, Paul H. 1929- *St&PR 93*
Zimmer, Paul J. 1934- *WhoWrEP 92*
Zimmer, Richard Alan 1944- *WhoAm 92, WhoE 93*
Zimmer, Richard P. 1945- *St&PR 93*
Zimmer, Robert James 1942- *St&PR 93*
Zimmer, Robert W. 1951- *St&PR 93*
Zimmer, Roberta G. 1924- *St&PR 93*
Zimmer, Thomas R. 1931- *St&PR 93*
Zimmer, Walter C. 1935- *St&PR 93, WhoIns 93*
Zimmer, William H. 1953- *St&PR 93*
Zimmer, William H., Jr. 1930- *St&PR 93*
Zimmer, William R. *St&PR 93*
Zimmerer, Anna Morgan 1923- *WhoAm 92*
Zimmerer, Joseph J. *Law&B 92*
Zimmerer, Vincent Hugh 1926- *St&PR 93*
Zimmererman, M.A. *St&PR 93*
Zimmerli, Alice 1906- *St&PR 93*
Zimmerli, Louis E. 1919- *St&PR 93*
Zimmerli, Traugott 1935- *WhoScE 91-4*
Zimmer-Long, Janie Louise 1943- *WhoE 93*
Zimmerly, John 1933- *St&PR 93*
Zimmerma, David R. 1946- *St&PR 93*
Zimmerman, Aaron Mark 1953- *WhoEmL 93*
Zimmerman, Adam *BioIn 17*
Zimmerman, Alan K. 1925- *St&PR 93*
Zimmerman, Anne E. 1942- *WhoAmW 93*
Zimmerman, B.J. *Law&B 92*
Zimmerman, Barry 1938- *St&PR 93*
Zimmerman, Barry Joseph 1942- *WhoE 93*
Zimmerman, Ben, Jr. 1916- *St&PR 93*
Zimmerman, Bernard 1932- *WhoE 93*
Zimmerman, Bill J. 1932- *St&PR 93, WhoAm 92*
Zimmerman, Billy Raymond 1941- *WhoWrEP 92*
Zimmerman, Carole Ellen Young 1960- *WhoAmW 93*
Zimmerman, Carole Lee 1948- *WhoAmW 93, WhoE 93*
Zimmerman, Charles Hinckley 1905- *WhoAm 92*
Zimmerman, Clarence D. 1936- *St&PR 93*
Zimmerman, Clearence Daniel, III 1941- *St&PR 93*
Zimmerman, Daniel John 1930- *St&PR 93*
Zimmerman, David R. 1946- *St&PR 93*
Zimmerman, David Radoff 1934- *WhoWrEP 92*
Zimmerman, Dean McIntosh 1951- *WhoAm 92*
Zimmerman, Deborah Hill 1950- *WhoIns 93*
Zimmerman, Diane Leenheer 1941- *WhoAmW 93*
Zimmerman, Diane Marie 1957- *WhoAmW 93*
Zimmerman, Don *WhoAm 92*
Zimmerman, Don G. 1940- *St&PR 93*
Zimmerman, Don S. *Law&B 92*
Zimmerman, Donald J. *Law&B 92*
Zimmerman, Donald Joseph 1937- *St&PR 93*
Zimmerman, Donald Patrick 1942- *WhoE 93*
Zimmerman, Doris Lucile 1942- *WhoAmW 93*
Zimmerman, Dorothy Wynne 1925- *WhoAmW 93*
Zimmerman, Doug *BioIn 17*
Zimmerman, Edwin Morton 1924- *WhoAm 92*
Zimmerman, Ellen Dinah 1944- *WhoAmW 93*
Zimmerman, Elyn 1945- *BioIn 17*
Zimmerman, Everett Lee 1936- *WhoAm 92*
Zimmerman, Florence Arline 1924- *WhoAmW 93, WhoE 93*
Zimmerman, Franklin B(ershir) 1923- *Baker 92*
Zimmerman, Gail Marie 1945- *WhoAm 92*
Zimmerman, Gary Alan 1938- *WhoAm 92*
Zimmerman, Gary M. *Law&B 92*
Zimmerman, George *St&PR 93*
Zimmerman, George Ogurek 1935- *WhoAm 92*
Zimmerman, Gideon K. 1920- *WhoAm 92*
Zimmerman, Gifford *Law&B 92*
Zimmerman, Helene Loretta 1933- *WhoAmW 93*
Zimmerman, Henry 1887-1969 *BiDAMSp 1989*
Zimmerman, Howard *ScF&FL 92*
Zimmerman, Howard Elliot 1926- *WhoAm 92*
Zimmerman, Howard Eric 1932- *St&PR 93*
Zimmerman, Howard Jay 1946- *St&PR 93*
Zimmerman, Hyman Joseph 1914- *WhoAm 92*
Zimmerman, James A. 1928- *St&PR 93*
Zimmerman, James Kenneth 1943- *WhoSSW 93*
Zimmerman, James Louis 1936- *WhoE 93*
Zimmerman, James Winfield 1919- *WhoAm 92*
Zimmerman, Jamie *WhoAm 92*
Zimmerman, Janice Lee 1947- *WhoAmW 93*
Zimmerman, Jay James 1954- *WhoE 93*
Zimmerman, Jean *Law&B 92*
Zimmerman, Jean 1947- *WhoAmW 93, WhoE 93, WhoEmL 93, WhoWor 93*
Zimmerman, Jean Hoehn *BioIn 17*
Zimmerman, Jeffrey 1954- *WhoE 93*
Zimmerman, Jo Ann 1936- *WhoAm 92, WhoAmW 93, WhoWor 93*
Zimmerman, John *BioIn 17*
Zimmerman, John H. 1932- *St&PR 93, WhoAm 92*
Zimmerman, John W. 1945- *St&PR 93*
Zimmerman, John William 1945- *WhoSSW 93*
Zimmerman, Joseph Dale 1934- *St&PR 93, WhoAm 92*
Zimmerman, Joseph Francis 1928- *ConAu 37NR, WhoAm 92*
Zimmerman, Judith Elin 1939- *WhoE 93*
Zimmerman, Jules 1934- *St&PR 93*
Zimmerman, Justin Fred 1912- *St&PR 93*
Zimmerman, Karen Michelle 1957- *WhoEmL 93*
Zimmerman, Kathleen Marie 1923- *WhoAmW 93*
Zimmerman, Keith W. 1947- *St&PR 93*
Zimmerman, Keith Wayne 1947- *WhoIns 93*
Zimmerman, Kenneth B. *St&PR 93*
Zimmerman, Leonard Norman 1923- *WhoE 93*
Zimmerman, LeRoy S. 1934- *WhoAm 92*
Zimmerman, Levi B. 1943- *St&PR 93*
Zimmerman, Lorraine 1936- *WhoAmW 93*
Zimmerman, M. Paul 1934- *WhoAm 92*
Zimmerman, Margaret Catherine 1915- *WhoWrEP 92*
Zimmerman, Mari Sperry 1942- *WhoAmW 93*
Zimmerman, Marlene Mae 1936- *WhoAmW 93*
Zimmerman, Martin E. 1938- *St&PR 93*
Zimmerman, Mary Ganson *WhoSSW 93*
Zimmerman, Matthew Augustus 1941- *AfrAmBi*
Zimmerman, Matthew Augustus, Jr. 1941- *WhoAm 92*
Zimmerman, Maurice Jacob 1932- *WhoE 93*
Zimmerman, Michael David 1943- *WhoAm 92*
Zimmerman, Michael E. *Law&B 92*

Zimmerman, Milton J. *St&PR 93*
Zimmerman, Muriel Cecile 1920- *WhoAmW 93*
Zimmerman, Nancy Ann 1958- *WhoSSW 93*
Zimmerman, Paul *Law&B 92*
Zimmerman, Paul Albert 1918- *WhoAm 92*
Zimmerman, Peter C. 1946- *St&PR 93*
Zimmerman, Philip Louis 1943- *St&PR 93*
Zimmerman, Pierre-Joseph-Guillaume 1785-1853 *Baker 92*
Zimmerman, R.D. 1952- *ScF&FL 92*
Zimmerman, Raymond *BioIn 17, WhoAm 92*
Zimmerman, Raymond 1933- *WhoSSW 93*
Zimmerman, Richard *Law&B 92*
Zimmerman, Richard Albert 1930- *WhoWor 93*
Zimmerman, Richard Anson 1932- *St&PR 93, WhoAm 92*
Zimmerman, Richard E. 1940- *St&PR 93*
Zimmerman, Richard Gayford 1934- *WhoAm 92*
Zimmerman, Rina E. *Law&B 92*
Zimmerman, Robert A. 1930- *St&PR 93*
Zimmerman, Robert Allen 1941- *BioIn 17*
Zimmerman, Robert Dingwall 1952- *WhoWrEP 92*
Zimmerman, Robert E. 1928- *St&PR 93*
Zimmerman, Robert Raymond 1919- *St&PR 93*
Zimmerman, Robert S. 1951- *St&PR 93*
Zimmerman, Roger William 1945- *St&PR 93*
Zimmerman, Ronald 1940- *St&PR 93*
Zimmerman, S. LaNette 1944- *St&PR 93*
Zimmerman, S Mort 1927- *St&PR 93*
Zimmerman, Samuel Morton 1927- *WhoSSW 93, WhoWor 93*
Zimmerman, Scott Franklin 1935- *WhoAm 92*
Zimmerman, Sheldon 1942- *WhoSSW 93*
Zimmerman, Solomon 1948- *WhoSSW 93*
Zimmerman, Stanley Allen 1948- *WhoSSW 93*
Zimmerman, Stanley Elliot, Jr. 1947- *St&PR 93*
Zimmerman, Stephen D. 1942- *St&PR 93*
Zimmerman, Thom Jay 1942- *WhoAm 92*
Zimmerman, Thomas A. 1953- *St&PR 93*
Zimmerman, Thomas F. 1912-1991 *BioIn 17*
Zimmerman, Thomas Paul 1946- *St&PR 93*
Zimmerman, Todd Jones-Foster Volney 1946- *WhoE 93*
Zimmerman, Vernon *MiSFD 9*
Zimmerman, Vicky T. *Law&B 92*
Zimmerman, Walter *Law&B 92*
Zimmerman, Warren 1934- *WhoAm 92*
Zimmerman, Werner *ScF&FL 92*
Zimmerman, William Edwin 1941- *WhoAm 92, WhoWrEP 92*
Zimmerman, William Frederick 1938- *WhoAm 92*
Zimmerman, William R. 1927- *St&PR 93*
Zimmerman, William Robert 1927- *WhoAm 92*
Zimmerman, Winona Estelle 1941- *WhoWrEP 92*
Zimmerman, Yale 1945- *St&PR 93*
Zimmerman Joseph Francis 1928- *WhoWrEP 92*
Zimmermann, Agnes (Marie Jacobina) 1845-1925 *Baker 92*
Zimmermann, Alan Lewis 1950- *WhoAm 92*
Zimmermann, Anton 1741-1781 *Baker 92*
Zimmermann, B.A. *Law&B 92*
Zimmermann, Bernd Alois 1918-1970 *Baker 92, IntDcOp, OxDcOp*
Zimmermann, Claus 1940- *WhoScE 91-3*
Zimmermann, David Scott 1955- *WhoEmL 93*
Zimmermann, Eleonore M. 1931- *WhoAm 92*
Zimmermann, Felicia *BioIn 17*
Zimmermann, Frank Peter 1965- *Baker 92*
Zimmermann, Frederick Karl 1952- *St&PR 93*
Zimmermann, Friedrich Karl 1934- *WhoScE 91-3*
Zimmermann, G. Floyd, III 1944- *WhoSSW 93*
Zimmermann, Gail *St&PR 93*
Zimmermann, Gerald *St&PR 93*
Zimmermann, Gerhard 1930- *WhoWor 93*
Zimmermann, Gerhardt 1945- *WhoAm 92*
Zimmermann, Herbert 1944- *WhoScE 91-3*
Zimmermann, Herbert Werner 1928- *WhoScE 91-3*
Zimmermann, Horst Ernst Friedrich 1934- *WhoWor 93*
Zimmermann, John 1937- *St&PR 93, WhoAm 92*
Zimmermann, John Joseph 1939- *WhoWor 93*
Zimmermann, Louis 1873-1954 *Baker 92*
Zimmermann, Manfred 1933- *WhoScE 91-3*
Zimmermann, R. Peter 1940- *WhoAm 92*
Zimmermann, Steven G. 1950- *St&PR 93*
Zimmermann, T. C. Price 1934- *WhoAm 92*
Zimmermann, Theodore Andrew *Law&B 92*
Zimmermann, Udo 1943- *Baker 92, OxDcOp*
Zimmermann, Uwe Toni 1947- *WhoWor 93*
Zimmermann, Walter 1949- *Baker 92*
Zimmermann, Warren 1934- *WhoAm 92*
Zimmermann, Wolfgang K.E. 1927- *WhoScE 91-3*
Zimmermann, Wolfgang Karl 1953- *WhoWor 93*
Zimmet, Arthur Laurence 1936- *St&PR 93*
Zimmett, Mark Paul 1950- *WhoAm 92, WhoWor 93*
Zimmon, David Samuel 1933- *WhoE 93*
Zimmy *MajAI*
Zimny, Marilyn Lucile 1927- *WhoAm 92*
Zimolo, Armando 1938- *WhoWor 93*
Zimolong, Bernhard Michael 1944- *WhoWor 93*
Zimonick, Frank Edward 1928- *St&PR 93*
Zimpelmann, Uwe Jorg 1943- *WhoWor 93*
Zimpfer, Kenneth G. 1946- *St&PR 93*
Zimring, Franklin E. 1942- *WhoAm 92*
Zimroth, Evan 1943- *WhoWrEP 92*
Zinaman, Helaine Madeleine 1951- *WhoAmW 93*
Zinatelli, Frank *Law&B 92*
Zinbarg, Benson *BioIn 17*
Zinbarg, Edward Donald 1934- *St&PR 93, WhoAm 92*
Zinberg, Dorothy Shore 1928- *WhoAm 92*
Zinberg, Michael *MiSFD 9*
Zinberg, Norman Earl 1921-1989 *BioIn 17*
Zinberg, Stanley 1934- *WhoE 93*
Zinchenko, Alexei Alexeyevich 1947- *WhoUN 92*
Zinchuk, Aleksander Ivanovich 1920- *WhoWor 93*
Zinck, Bendix Friedrich 1743?-1801 *Baker 92*
Zinck, Hardenack Otto Conrad 1746-1832 *Baker 92*
Zinda, Craig James *Law&B 92*
Zinda, Robert Stephen 1949- *St&PR 93*
Zindel, Paul *BioIn 17*
Zindel, Paul 1936- *DcAmChF 1960, MagSAmL [port], MajAI [port], WhoAm 92, WhoWrEP 92*
Zindel, William 1934- *St&PR 93*
Zindell, David 1952- *ScF&FL 92*
Zindell, Paul J. 1948- *St&PR 93, WhoE 93*
Zinder, Newton Donald 1927- *WhoAm 92*
Zinder, Norton David 1928- *WhoAm 92*
Zine, Larry Joseph 1954- *St&PR 93, WhoAm 92*
Zines, Leslie 1930- *ConAu 137*
Zingale, Salvatore Anthony 1950- *WhoSSW 93*
Zingales, Giuseppe 1927- *WhoScE 91-3*
Zingarelli, Niccolo Antonio 1752-1837 *OxDcOp*
Zingarelli, Nicola Antonio 1752-1837 *Baker 92*
Zingel, Rudolf Ewald 1876-1944 *Baker 92*
Zingerline, Arthur William 1950- *WhoE 93*
Zingher, Edy B. 1944- *St&PR 93*
Zingle, Mark R. 1952- *St&PR 93*
Zingmark, Richard Gregory 1941- *WhoSSW 93*
Zingraff, Michael, Jr. 1920- *WhoAm 92*
Zinik, Zinovy 1945- *ConAu 139*
Zink, Charles Talbott 1937- *WhoAm 92*
Zink, Dolph Warren 1922- *WhoWor 93*
Zink, John H., Jr. 1918- *St&PR 93*
Zink, Joseph Paul, III 1945- *WhoWrEP 92*
Zink, Lubor Jan 1920- *WhoE 93*
Zink, Maria 1751-1821
See Neefe, Christian Gottlob 1748-1798 *OxDcOp*
Zink, Michelle Lyrae 1965- *WhoAmW 93*
Zink, Philip Ripley 1947- *St&PR 93*
Zink, Robert L. *Law&B 92*
Zink, Robert Lee 1935- *St&PR 93*
Zink, William Pirotte 1951- *WhoSSW 93*
Zinkan, K. James 1938- *St&PR 93*
Zinkan, Lisa Ann *Law&B 92*
Zinkann, Peter Christian 1928- *WhoWor 93*
Zinke, Michael Duane 1954- *WhoSSW 93*
Zinkeisen, Doris 1898-1991 *AnObit 1991*
Zinkeisen, Konrad Ludwig Dietrich 1779-1838 *Baker 92*
Zinkil, George A., Jr. 1944- *St&PR 93*
Zinky, Richard Bruce 1949- *St&PR 93*
Zinman, David (Joel) 1936- *Baker 92, WhoAm 92, WhoE 93*
Zinman, Jacques 1922- *WhoWor 93*
Zinman, Jacques S. 1922- *WhoIns 93*
Zinman, Philip 1904- *St&PR 93*
Zinman, Roberta S. *Law&B 92*
Zinman, Zoe *MiSFD 9*
Zinn, Ben T. 1937- *WhoAm 92*
Zinn, Chester A., Jr. 1934- *St&PR 93*
Zinn, Chester Allen, Jr. *Law&B 92*
Zinn, David Benjamin 1953- *WhoE 93*
Zinn, Dennis Bradley 1957- *WhoWor 93*
Zinn, Donald J. 1954- *St&PR 93*
Zinn, Elias Paul 1954- *St&PR 93*
Zinn, Frank Kleman 1934- *WhoAm 92*
Zinn, Fredric M. 1951- *St&PR 93*
Zinn, Grover Alfonso, Jr. 1937- *WhoAm 92*
Zinn, Herbert Irwin *Law&B 92*
Zinn, Keith A. 1955- *St&PR 93*
Zinn, Keith Marshall 1940- *WhoAm 92*
Zinn, Maxine Baca *NotHsAW 93*
Zinn, Maxine Baca 1942- *HispAmA*
Zinn, Raymond D. 1937- *St&PR 93*
Zinn, Stanley 1929- *St&PR 93*
Zinn, Terry Leigh 1951- *WhoSSW 93*
Zinn, Thomas Roger 1949- *St&PR 93*
Zinn, William 1924- *WhoAm 92*
Zinna, Eduardo *WhoUN 92*
Zinnemann, Fred 1907- *BioIn 17, MiSFD 9, WhoAm 92*
Zinnemann, Tim *ConTFT 10*
Zinnen, Jean-Antoine 1827-1898 *Baker 92*
Zinnen, Robert Oliver 1929- *WhoAm 92*
Zinner, Gilbert Paul 1935- *WhoSSW 93*
Zinner, Peter 1919- *MiSFD 9*
Zinnes, Harriet F. *WhoWrEP 92*
Zinni, Anthony Charles 1943- *WhoAm 92*
Zinni, Eugene J. 1915- *St&PR 93*
Zinober, Joan Wagner 1944- *WhoAmW 93, WhoSSW 93*
Zinovich, Jordan Samuel 1955- *WhoWrEP 92*
Zinoviev, Alexander 1922- *ScF&FL 92*
Zinoviev, Grigori Yevseyevich 1883-1936 *DcTwHis*
Zinoviev, Viktor Aleksandrovich 1941- *WhoWor 93*
Zinovjev, Valery Ivanovich 1937- *WhoWor 93*
Zinram, Stephen Joseph 1963- *WhoE 93*
Zins, Martha Lee 1945- *WhoAmW 93*
Zinser, Armin Josef 1956- *WhoWor 93*
Zinser, Elisabeth Ann 1940- *WhoAm 92, WhoAmW 93*
Zinser, Hartmut 1944- *WhoWor 93*
Zinski, Lawrence W. 1940- *St&PR 93*
Zinsser, August 1941- *St&PR 93*
Zinsser, William Knowlton 1922- *WhoAm 92*
Zinterhof, Peter 1944- *WhoScE 91-4*
Zintl, Robert T. d1991 *BioIn 17*
Zinzow, Lee Alan 1947- *St&PR 93*
Ziobron, Wladyslaw 1928- *WhoScE 91-4*
Ziock, Klaus Otto Heinrich 1925- *WhoAm 92*
Ziol, Gwen G. *Law&B 92*
Ziolecka, Aleksandra Zofia 1924- *WhoScE 91-4*
Ziolko, Jerzy 1934- *WhoScE 91-4*
Ziolkowski, Bruno E. 1939- *St&PR 93*
Ziolkowski, Eric J(ozef) 1958- *ConAu 139*
Ziolkowski, Janusz 1934- *WhoScE 91-4*
Ziolkowski, Jozef Julian 1934- *WhoScE 91-4*
Ziolkowski, Theodore Joseph 1932- *WhoAm 92, WhoWrEP 92*
Ziolkowski, Thomas A. *Law&B 92*
Ziomek, Henryk 1922- *WhoSSW 93*
Ziomek, Patricia Ann 1932- *WhoAmW 93*
Zion, Glen J. 1936- *St&PR 93*
Zion, Roger H. 1921- *WhoAm 92*
Zipay, Daniel *St&PR 93*
Ziperski, James R. *Law&B 92*
Ziperski, James R. 1932- *St&PR 93*
Ziperski, James Richard 1932- *WhoAm 92*
Zipes, Douglas Peter 1939- *WhoAm 92*
Zipes, Jack 1937- *ScF&FL 92*
Zipfinger, Frank Peter 1953- *WhoEmL 93*
Zipkin, Janis Lynn 1956- *WhoAmW 93*
Zipko, Raymond Edward 1946- *St&PR 93, WhoAm 92*
Zipoli, Domenico 1688-1726 *Baker 92*
Zipp, Arden Peter 1938- *WhoAm 92*
Zipp, Brian Roger 1953- *WhoAm 92*
Zipp, Friedrich 1914- *Baker 92*
Zipp, Joel Frederick 1948- *WhoAm 92, WhoEmL 93*
Zipp, Ronald Duane 1946- *WhoEmL 93*
Zipper, Herbert 1904- *WhoAm 92*
Zipperer, Kathleen Anne 1940- *WhoSSW 93*
Zipperman, Louis 1915- *St&PR 93*
Zippin, Calvin 1926- *WhoAm 92*
Zippin, Lawrence M. 1942- *WhoIns 93*
Zipprodt, Patricia *BioIn 17, WhoAm 92, WhoAmW 93*
Zipser, Geraldine M. *Law&B 92*
Zipser, Tadeusz Maria 1930- *WhoScE 91-4*
Zirbel, Ronald DuWayne 1937- *St&PR 93*
Zirin, Harold 1929- *WhoAm 92*
Zirin, James David 1940- *WhoAm 92*
Zirinsky, Lawrence d1990 *BioIn 17*
Zirkelbach, Werner Karl 1929- *St&PR 93*
Zirkind, Ralph 1918- *WhoAm 92*
Zirkle, John William 1945- *WhoSSW 93*
Zirkle, L.G. 1946- *St&PR 93*
Zirkle, Lewis Greer 1940- *WhoAm 92*
Zirnkilton, Frank C., Jr. 1955- *St&PR 93*
Ziros, Christos Konstantinos *WhoWrEP 92*
Zirpoli, Alfonso Joseph 1905- *WhoAm 92*
Zirpolo, Richard A. 1946- *WhoE 93*
Zirpolo, Walter d1991 *BioIn 17*
Zirps, Fotena Anatolia 1958- *WhoSSW 93*
Zirra, Alexandru 1883-1946 *OxDcOp*
Zirschky, Stephen Lee 1949- *WhoWor 93*
Zischke, Douglas Arthur 1929- *WhoAm 92*
Ziska, David Lee 1931- *WhoSSW 93*
Ziska, Jan c. 1376-1424 *HarEnMi*
Ziskin, Barry 1952- *St&PR 93*
Ziskin, Laura *BioIn 17*
Ziskind, Martha Andes *Law&B 92*
Zisman, Barry Stuart 1937- *WhoSSW 93, WhoWor 93*
Zissimos, Maria M. *Law&B 92*
Zissman, Lorin 1930- *St&PR 93*
Zisson, James Stern 1952- *WhoSSW 93*
Zissu, Frederick 1913- *St&PR 93*
Zissu, Leonard d1992 *NewYTBS 92*
Zistler, Betty A. 1930- *St&PR 93*
Ziswiler, Vincent 1935- *WhoScE 91-4*
Zitek, Otakar 1892-1955 *Baker 92*
Zitkala-Sa 1876-1938 *AmWomWr 92*
Zitko, Peg 1950- *WhoAmW 93*
Zito, Allison Ann 1960- *WhoE 93*
Zito, James Anthony 1931- *WhoAm 92*
Zito, Joseph 1946- *MiSFD 9*
Zito, Michael 1953- *St&PR 93*
Zito, Michael Anthony 1957- *WhoWor 93*
Zito, Ross Alan 1952- *WhoE 93*
Zito, Thomas W. d1991 *BioIn 17*
Zitomer, Bernard B. 1942- *St&PR 93*
Zitomer, Sheldon Barry 1948- *WhoE 93*
Zitrin, Anthony Michael *Law&B 92*
Zitrin, Arthur 1918- *WhoAm 92*
Zittel, John David 1953- *WhoE 93*
Zitter, Herbert 1929- *WhoScE 91-4*
Zitterkopf, Irvin Leroy 1933- *St&PR 93, WhoAm 92*
Zitting, Brent Reed 1964- *WhoSSW 93*
Zittoun, Robert 1932- *WhoScE 91-2*
Zitz, Kathinka 1801-1877 *BioIn 17*
Zitzmann, Michael Georg 1947- *St&PR 93*
Ziukovic, Milan *MiSFD 9*
Ziulek, Richard Stanley, Jr. 1949- *St&PR 93*
Ziv, Mikhail 1921- *Baker 92*
Zivanovic, Branislav M. 1937- *WhoScE 91-4*
Zivanovic, Jovan 1924- *DrEEuF*
Zivanovic, Zarko 1925- *WhoScE 91-4*
Zivian, Charles H. 1944- *St&PR 93*
Zivich, Norma Gase 1947- *WhoAmW 93*
Ziviello, Alfred Gerald 1930- *WhoE 93*
Zivkovic, Milenko 1901-1964 *Baker 92*
Zivkovic, Zivan 1949- *WhoScE 91-4*
Zivley, Gloria June 1949- *WhoAmW 93*
Zivojinov, Jovanka 1919- *WhoScE 91-4*
Ziza, Oksana 1930- *WhoWor 93*
Zizic, Bogdan 1934- *DrEEuF*
Zizza, Salvatore J. 1945- *St&PR 93, WhoAm 92*
Zizzo, Alicia 1945- *WhoAm 92*
Zjawin, Dorothy Arlene 1945- *WhoWrEP 92*
Zlatev, Zahari 1939- *WhoWor 93*
Zlatic, Hrvoje 1923- *WhoScE 91-4*
Zlatkis, Albert 1924- *WhoAm 92*
Zlatkov, Nikola Botev 1928- *WhoScE 91-4*
Zlatoff-Mirsky, Everett Igor 1937- *WhoAm 92, WhoWor 93*
Zlatoper, Ronald Joseph 1942- *WhoAm 92*
Zlenko, Anatoliy *WhoWor 93*
Zlevor, William L. 1930- *St&PR 93*
Zlobec, Paolo 1939- *WhoScE 91-3*
Zloch, William J. 1944- *WhoAm 92*
Zlotchew, Clark Michael 1932- *WhoE 93*
WhoWrEP 92
Zlotin, Patricia A. 1946- *St&PR 93*
Zlotnik, Jack V. *Law&B 92*
Zlotnitsky, Michael Jacob 1945- *WhoE 93*
Zlotoff, Lee David *MiSFD 9*
Zlotolow-Stambler, Ernest 1943- *WhoE 93*
Zlotorzycka, Jadwiga 1926- *WhoScE 91-4*
Zlotowski, Martin 1934- *WhoE 93*
Zlowe, Florence Markowitz *WhoAm 92*
Zmarlicki, Stanislaw 1936- *WhoScE 91-4*
Zmeskal, Kim *BioIn 17*
Zmeskal, Kim 1976- *WhoAmW 93*
Zmeskall, Nikolaus Paul 1759-1833 *Baker 92*
Zmijewski, Chester Michael 1932- *WhoE 93*

Zminda, Margaret Barton 1958- *St&PR 93*
Zmora, Ohad 1933- *WhoWor 93*
Zmudzki, Jan 1947- *WhoWor 93*
Zmudzki, Stefan Czeslaw 1939- *WhoScE 91-4*
Zmyslowski, Wojciech 1938- *WhoScE 91-4*
Znaimer, Moses *BioIn 17*
Znamierowski, Donald J. 1934- *WhoIns 93*
Znaniecki, Florian 1882-1958 *PolBiDi*
Znosko, Jerzy Tadeusz 1922- *WhoScE 91-4*
Znosko-Borovsky, Alexander 1908-1983 *Baker 92*
Zobel, Enrique *BioIn 17*
Zobel, Enrique J. 1927- *WhoIns 93*
Zobel, Gerald 1929- *St&PR 93*
Zobel, Hiller Bellin 1932- *WhoAm 92*
Zobel, Jan Arleen 1947- *WhoAmW 93*
Zobel, Louise Purwin 1922- *WhoAmW 93*
Zobel, Robert Edward 1948- *WhoSSW 93*
Zobel, Rya W. 1931- *WhoAm 92, WhoAmW 93, WhoE 93*
ZoBell, Karl 1932- *WhoAm 92*
Zobkiw, David J. *Law&B 92*
Zoble, Adrienne Kaplan 1940- *WhoAmW 93*
Zobrist, Benedict Karl 1921- *WhoAm 92*
Zobrist, Charles 1928- *St&PR 93*
Zobrist, George Winston 1934- *WhoAm 92*
Zobrist, Gerald J. 1943- *St&PR 93*
Zoby, Ernest Vincent 1939- *WhoSSW 93*
Zocca, Robert Lewis *Law&B 92*
Zocchi, Louis Joseph 1935- *WhoSSW 93*
Zocchi, Rodolfo 1922- *WhoScE 91-3*
Zocco, Joy Marie 1942- *WhoE 93*
Zocco, Roseanne Marie 1955- *WhoAmW 93, WhoEmL 93*
Zoch, Carl Robert, Jr. 1953- *St&PR 93*
Zoch, Richmond Tucker 1903- *WhoSSW 93*
Zocholl, Stanley Ernest 1929- *WhoAm 92*
Zock, George J. 1950- *St&PR 93*
Zodhiates, Spiros George 1922- *WhoAm 92*
Zodiacs *SoulM*
Zodikoff, David Hyman 1933- *WhoE 93*
Zodikoff, Howard Paul 1941- *WhoAm 92*
Zodrow, Christopher Noel *Law&B 92*
Zodrow, John 1944- *ScF&FL 92*
Zoe c. 978-1050 *OxDcByz*
Zoe Karbonopsina dc. 920 *OxDcByz*
Zoeller, Betty Ann 1931- *WhoE 93*
Zoeller, Carl Joseph 1920- *St&PR 93*
Zoeller, Carli 1840-1889 *Baker 92*
Zoeller, David *Law&B 92*
Zoeller, David L. 1949- *St&PR 93*
Zoeller, Donald J. 1930- *WhoAm 92*
Zoeller, Frank Urban, Jr. 1951- *BiDAMSp 1989*
Zoeller, Henry 1928- *St&PR 93*
Zoeller, Jack Carl 1949- *WhoAm 92, WhoE 93, WhoWor 93*
Zoellick, Robert *BioIn 17*
Zoellick, Robert Bruce 1953- *WhoAm 92*
Zoellner, James W. 1941- *St&PR 93*
Zoellner, Joseph, Sr. 1862-1950 *Baker 92*
Zoellner, Michael 1953- *WhoSSW 93*
Zoellner, Sandra Ann 1964- *WhoAmW 93*
Zoffer, David B. *Law&B 92*
Zoffer, David B. 1947- *WhoIns 93*
Zoffer, H. Jerome 1930- *WhoAm 92, WhoE 93*
Zoffmann, Henrik *WhoScE 91-2*
Zofka, Jan 1943- *WhoScE 91-4*
Zofkie, Michael J. 1942- *St&PR 93*
Zofnass, Paul Jesse 1947- *WhoAm 92*
Zog 1895-1961 *DcTwHis*
Zogby, James Edward 1948- *St&PR 93*
Zogby, James Joseph 1945- *WhoE 93*
Zogby, Joann Helen 1943- *WhoE 93*
Zogg, Chris J. *Law&B 92*
Zogg, Chris John 1929- *St&PR 93*
Zogg, Hans 1946- *WhoWor 93*
Zoghbi, Habib George 1955- *WhoE 93*
Zoghby, Guy A. *Law&B 92*
Zoghby, Guy A. 1934- *St&PR 93*
Zoghby, Guy Anthony 1934- *WhoAm 92*
Zoghby, Linda 1949- *Baker 92*
Zoghi, Behbood 1960- *WhoSSW 93*
Zografos, Michael J. 1957- *St&PR 93*
Zografos, Nota K. 1958- *St&PR 93*
Zohn, Fred *St&PR 93*
Zohn, Harry 1923- *WhoAm 92*
Zohrob, Lee M. *Law&B 92*
Zoidis, Marilyn Amelia 1949- *WhoE 93*
Zoilo, Annibale c. 1537-1592 *Baker 92*
Zois, Constantine Nicholas Athanasios 1938- *WhoWor 93*
Zojer, H. 1945- *WhoScE 91-4*
Zola, Emile 1840-1902 *BioIn 17, DcLB 123 [port], MagSWL [port], OxDcOp, ScF&FL 92, WorLitC [port]*
Zola, Emile (Edouard Charles Antoine) 1840-1902 *ConAu 138*
Zola, Lisa 1958- *WhoAm 92, WhoAmW 93*
Zola, Meguido 1939- *WhoCanL 92*
Zola, Nazzi Cameo 1952- *St&PR 93*
Zoladek, Henryk 1953- *WhoWor 93*
Zolan, Robert Edward 1936- *St&PR 93*
Zolber, Kathleen Keen 1916- *WhoAmW 93*
Zolberg, Aristide Rodolphe 1931- *WhoAm 92, WhoE 93*
Zolberg, Vera L. 1932- *ConAu 139*
Zolberg, Vera Lenchner 1932- *WhoE 93*
Zolbert, William Arnold *Law&B 92*
Zoldak, Susan 1965- *WhoAmW 93*
Zoley, George C. 1950- *St&PR 93*
Zolides, William H. 1930- *St&PR 93*
Zoline, Pamela 1941- *ScF&FL 92*
Zolkiewski, Stanislaw 1547-1620 *PolBiDi*
Zolkower, Daniel 1933- *WhoIns 93*
Zoll, Lawrence J. 1933- *St&PR 93*
Zoll, Paul Maurice 1911- *WhoAm 92*
Zoll, Steven Daniel 1963- *St&PR 93*
Zolla, Elemire 1926- *WhoWor 93*
Zollar, Carolyn Catherine 1947- *WhoSSW 93*
Zollar, Michael Edward 1944- *St&PR 93*
Zollars, Thomas Earl 1947- *St&PR 93*
Zoller, Gale *Law&B 92*
Zoller, George G. 1951- *St&PR 93*
Zoller, Gerhard H. 1939- *St&PR 93*
Zoller, Karlheinz 1928- *Baker 92*
Zoller, Margot 1943- *WhoScE 91-3*
Zoller, Michael 1947- *WhoSSW 93*
Zoller, Richard Bernard 1929- *WhoAm 92*
Zoller, Richard Eugene 1931- *WhoE 93*
Zoller, Robert 1946- *St&PR 93*
Zollicoffer, Felix Kirk 1812-1862 *BioIn 17, HarEnMi*
Zollinger, Gary 1948- *St&PR 93*
Zollinger, Heinrich 1919- *WhoScE 91-4*
Zollinger, Jack J. 1937- *St&PR 93*
Zollinger, John J., Jr. 1911- *St&PR 93*
Zollinger, Philip I. 1952- *St&PR 93*
Zollinger, William Daniel 1940- *St&PR 93*
Zollner, Carl Friedrich 1800-1860 *Baker 92*
Zollner, Heinrich 1792-1836 *Baker 92*
Zollner, Heinrich 1854-1941 *Baker 92*
Zollner, Herbert F.K. 1942- *WhoUN 92*
Zollner, Stephen R. *Law&B 92*
Zollner de Medeiros, Maxime Leopold 1934- *WhoUN 92*
Zolomy, Jack 1948- *St&PR 93*
Zolotarev, A.M. 1907-1943 *IntDcAn*
Zolotarev, D.A. 1885-1935 *IntDcAn*
Zolotarev, Vasili (Andreievich) 1872-1964 *Baker 92*
Zolotow, Charlotte 1915- *BioIn 17, St&PR 93*
Zolotow, Charlotte S(hapiro) 1915- *ConAu 38NR, MajAI [port]*
Zolotow, Charlotte Shapiro 1915- *WhoAm 92, WhoAmW 93, WhoWrEP 92*
Zolotow, Maurice 1913- *WhoAm 92*
Zolotow, Maurice 1913-1991 *BioIn 17*
Zoltan, Aladar 1929-1978 *Baker 92*
Zoltok-Seltzer, Harriet *WhoWrEP 92*
Zolton, Gregory Michael 1948- *WhoE 93*
Zoltowski, Andrzej 1933- *WhoScE 91-4*
Zolyneak, Corneliu Constantin 1928- *WhoScE 91-4*
Zombanakis, Minos 1926- *St&PR 93*
Zombory, Laszlo 1942- *WhoScE 91-4*
Zomick, David Alan 1941- *WhoAm 92*
Zomorrodian, David Jose 1960- *St&PR 93*
Zompanis, Thomas Anastasios 1942- *WhoE 93*
Zona, Louis Albert 1944- *WhoAm 92*
Zona, Richard A. 1944- *St&PR 93*
Zonailo, Carolyn 1947- *WhoCanL 92*
Zonaras, John dc. 1159 *OxDcByz*
Zonarich, Frank J. 1945- *St&PR 93*
Zonco, Alain Jean Yves 1940- *WhoUN 92*
Zondag, Sharon Jones 1954- *St&PR 93*
Zondervan, Peter J. 1909- *St&PR 93*
Zone, Joseph Pacter 1903-1990 *BioIn 17*
Zong Shunliu 1941- *WhoAsAP 91*
Zonis, Marvin 1936- *WhoAm 92*
Zonneveld, Isack S. 1924- *WhoScE 91-3*
Zonta, Roberto 1958- *WhoScE 91-3*
Zoobkoff, Anthony A. *Law&B 92*
Zoobkoff, Anthony A. 1949- *St&PR 93*
Zook, Amy Jo Schoonover 1937- *WhoWrEP 92*
Zook, Bernard Charles 1935- *WhoE 93*
Zook, Elvin Glenn 1937- *WhoAm 92*
Zook, Merlin Wayne 1937- *WhoWor 93*
Zook, Michael R. 1943- *St&PR 93*
Zook, Royce Duane 1940- *St&PR 93*
Zook, Woodrow J. 1915- *St&PR 93*
Zool, M.H. *ScF&FL 92*
Zoon, Kathryn Egloff 1948- *WhoAm 92*
Zoon, William Kenneth 1943- *St&PR 93*
Zopf, Paul Edward 1931- *WhoAm 92*
Zopff, Hermann 1826-1883 *Baker 92*
Zopfi, E. *WhoScE 91-4*
Zophy, Angela Howard 1945- *WhoAmW 93*
Zophy, Jonathan Walter 1945- *WhoSSW 93*
Zopp, E. Frederick 1932- *St&PR 93*
Zorab, George 1898-1990 *BioIn 17*
Zorach, Marguerite Thompson 1887-1968 *BioIn 17*
Zorach, William 1887-1966 *BioIn 17*
Zoraian, John Paul 1955- *WhoE 93*
Zoras, Leonidas 1905-1987 *Baker 92*
Zorawski, Cezariusz 1927- *WhoScE 91-4*
Zorc, Davor 1954- *WhoWor 93*
Zore, Edward John 1945- *St&PR 93, WhoAm 92*
Zore-Armanda, Mira 1930- *WhoScE 91-4*
Zorek, John d1991 *BioIn 17*
Zorich, Chris *BioIn 17*
Zorich, Zorka *BioIn 17*
Zorie, Stephanie Marie 1951- *WhoEmL 93, WhoSSW 93*
Zorio, John W. 1946- *St&PR 93*
Zorio, John William 1946- *WhoAm 92*
Zorn, Donald *St&PR 93*
Zorn, Edward 1926- *St&PR 93*
Zorn, Gunther Joseph 1932- *WhoUN 92*
Zorn, Gus Tom 1924- *WhoE 93*
Zorn, John *BioIn 17*
Zorn, John 1953- *Baker 92*
Zorn, Richard Laurence 1940- *St&PR 93*
Zorner, Karl-Heinz 1936- *WhoWor 93*
Zornes, Milford 1908- *WhoAm 92*
Zornman, Jeannette Rousseau 1945- *WhoSSW 93*
Zornow, David M. 1955- *WhoE 93*
Zornow, Edith d1991 *BioIn 17*
Zornow, Martha Malkin *Law&B 92*
Zornow, Peter L. 1955- *St&PR 93*
Zornow, William Frank 1920- *WhoAm 92, WhoWor 93*
Zorns, Bruce C. 1913- *BioIn 17*
Zorowski, Carl Frank 1930- *WhoAm 92*
Zorrilla, Jose Ruben 1952- *WhoWor 93*
Zorrilla-Vazquez, Emilio Manuel 1933- *WhoWor 93*
Zorro *ScF&FL 92*
Zorski, Henryk 1927- *WhoScE 91-4*
Zorthian, Barry 1920- *WhoAm 92*
Zorthian, Gregory *BioIn 17*
Zorzor, Stefan 1932- *Baker 92*
Zoser, H. *WhoScE 91-4*
Zosima *OxDcByz*
Zosima 1767-1833 *BioIn 17*
Zosimos fl. 5th cent.-6th cent. *OxDcByz*
Zoss, Abraham Oscar 1917- *WhoE 93*
Zoss, Dean L. 1939- *St&PR 93, WhoIns 93*
Zoss, Joel 1944- *ScF&FL 92*
Zotter, DonnaMarie *Law&B 92*
Zotter, Jeffrey Lee 1954- *WhoE 93*
Zottmayr, Georg 1869-1941 *Baker 92*
Zottoli, Danny 1946- *WhoAm 92*
Zottoli, Danny A. 1946- *St&PR 93*
Zottoli, Robert A. 1939- *WhoAm 92*
Zou, Yong Xian 1924- *WhoWor 93*
Zou, Yun 1962- *WhoWor 93*
Zouary, Maurice H. 1921- *WhoE 93*
Zoubareff, Olga Vladimir *WhoAmW 93*
Zouhar, Zdenek 1927- *Baker 92*
Zou Jiahua 1927- *WhoAsAP 91, WhoWor 93*
Zou Jingmeng 1929- *WhoAsAP 91*
Zoumas, Barry Lee 1942- *WhoAm 92*
Zoungrana, Paul Cardinal 1917- *WhoWor 93*
Zoupanos, Theodore S. 1935- *WhoUN 92, WhoWor 93*
Zox, Larry 1936- *WhoAm 92*
Zpevak, Michael J. *Law&B 92*
Zraket, Charles Anthony 1924- *WhoAm 92, WhoWor 93*
Zralek, Marek Zdzislaw 1947- *WhoWor 93*
Zraly, Kevin *BioIn 17*
Zrebiec, Louis, Jr. 1936- *WhoE 93*
Zrinsky, Christine Marie 1964- *WhoAmW 93*
Zriny, Jeffrey L. 1948- *WhoIns 93*
Zrinyi, Miklos 1508-1566 *HarEnMi*
Zrubek, Henryk Walerian 1929- *WhoScE 91-4*
Zrupko, Maria Mann 1938- *WhoAmW 93*
Zsamboki, Sandor 1935- *WhoScE 91-4*
Zschau, Marilyn 1944- *WhoAm 92*
Zschoche, Herrmann 1934- *DrEEuF*
Zschocher, Johann 1821-1897 *Baker 92*
Zschokke, Heinrich 1771-1848 *BioIn 17*
Zschunke, Willmut Rolf 1940- *WhoScE 91-3*
Zsevc, Linda Marie 1951- *WhoAmW 93*
Zsigmond, Vilmos 1930- *BioIn 17, MiSFD 9, WhoAm 92*
Zsilak, Gyorgy Laszlo 1935- *WhoScE 91-4*
Zsinka, Laszlo 1935- *WhoScE 91-4*
Zsoldos, Ferenc 1927- *WhoScE 91-4*
Zsoldos, Lehel 1931- *WhoScE 91-4*
Zsolt, Nandor 1887-1936 *Baker 92*
Zsombolyai, Janos 1939- *DrEEuF*
Zuanelli, Carl 1938- *WhoIns 93*
Zuanich, Anthony J. 1943- *St&PR 93*
Zubak, Cheryl Lockett 1961- *WhoAmW 93*
Zubaydi, Muhammad Hamza al *WhoWor 93*
Zubayr Ibn Al-Awwam d656 *HarEnMi*
Zube, Ervin Herbert 1931- *WhoAm 92*
Zubeir, Mohamed Salih 1944- *WhoAfr*
Zuber, Bernie *ScF&FL 92*
Zuber, Norma Keen 1934- *WhoAmW 93*
Zuber, Richard Arthur 1951- *WhoE 93*
Zuberbier, Lee A. 1942- *St&PR 93*
Zubi, Mahmoud 1938- *WhoWor 93*
Zubiaurre (y Urionabarrenechea), Valenti 1837-1914 *Baker 92*
Zubillaga, Jose Gustavo 1945- *WhoSSW 93*
Zubin, Joseph 1900-1990 *BioIn 17*
Zubir Bin Embong *WhoAsAP 91*
Zubiri, Jose R., Jr. 1940- *WhoAsAP 91*
Zubitur, Inaki Aizpuru 1946- *WhoWor 93*
Zubizarreta, Teresa 1938- *NotHsAW 93*
Zubkoff, Michael 1944- *WhoAm 92*
Zubly, John Joachim 1724-1781 *BioIn 17*
Zuboff, Shoshana 1951- *BioIn 17*
Zubov, Vladimir Ivanovich 1930- *WhoWor 93*
Zubowicz, Vincent Nicholas 1951- *WhoSSW 93*
Zubroff, Leonard Saul 1925- *WhoWor 93*
Zubrow, Barry L. 1953- *St&PR 93*
Zubrow, Sidney N. 1913- *WhoE 93*
Zucaro, Aldo Charles 1939- *St&PR 93, WhoAm 92, WhoIns 93*
Zucca *BioIn 17*
Zucca, Mana *Baker 92*
Zuccalmaglio, Anton Wilhelm Florentin von 1803-1869 *Baker 92*
Zuccari, Federico c. 1540-1609 *BioIn 17*
Zuccaro, Louis J. *Law&B 92*
Zuccaro, Robert S. 1957- *St&PR 93*
Zucchero, Lucille A. 1943- *WhoAmW 93*
Zucchi, John E. 1955- *ConAu 138*
Zucco, Bill *Law&B 92*
Zucco, Cathleen Maria 1954- *WhoE 93*
Zucco, George 1886-1960 *BioIn 17*
Zuccotti, John Eugene 1937- *WhoAm 92*
Zuccotti, Susan 1940- *ConAu 139*
Zuck, Alfred Christian 1924- *WhoAm 92*
Zuck, Alfred Miller 1934- *WhoE 93*
Zuck, Roy Ben 1932- *WhoSSW 93*
Zuck, Wynona Colleen 1939- *WhoAmW 93*
Zucker, Alexander 1924- *WhoAm 92*
Zucker, Barbara S. 1929- *St&PR 93*
Zucker, Bernard *Law&B 92*
Zucker, David *BioIn 17*
Zucker, David 1947- *ConAu 138, MiSFD 9, WhoAm 92*
Zucker, Herbert 1928- *WhoE 93, WhoWor 93*
Zucker, Jack S. 1935- *WhoWrEP 92*
Zucker, Jean Maxson 1925- *WhoAmW 93*
Zucker, Jeff *BioIn 17*
Zucker, Jerry *BioIn 17*
Zucker, Jerry 1940- *WhoAm 92*
Zucker, Jerry 1949- *WhoAm 92*
Zucker, Jerry 1950- *ConAu 138, MiSFD 9*
Zucker, Jerry M. 1960- *WhoE 93*
Zucker, John W. *Law&B 92*
Zucker, Karen Lee *Law&B 92*
Zucker, Malcolm 1914- *St&PR 93*
Zucker, Marjorie Bass 1919- *WhoAmW 93*
Zucker, Martin Paul *Law&B 92*
Zucker, Miriam S. *ScF&FL 92*
Zucker, Naomi Flink 1938- *WhoWrEP 92*
Zucker, Norman Livingston 1933- *WhoAm 92, WhoWrEP 92*
Zucker, Othmar 1959- *WhoWor 93*
Zucker, Rick Edward *Law&B 92*
Zucker, Robert Alpert 1935- *WhoAm 92*
Zucker, Robert Lewis 1928- *St&PR 93*
Zucker, Rudolph 1896- *St&PR 93*
Zucker, Stefan *WhoE 93, WhoWor 93*
Zucker, William 1917- *WhoAm 92*
Zuckerberg, David Alan 1946- *St&PR 93, WhoAm 92*
Zuckerberg, Roy J. 1936- *WhoAm 92*
Zuckerbrod, Todd Alan *Law&B 92*
Zucker-Franklin, Dorothea 1930- *WhoAmW 93, WhoE 93*
Zuckerkandl, Emile 1922- *WhoAm 92*
Zuckerkandl, Victor 1896-1965 *Baker 92*
Zucker-Maltese, Cher R. 1949- *St&PR 93*
Zuckerman, Abraham 1922- *BioIn 17*
Zuckerman, Adrian *Law&B 92*
Zuckerman, Anna Elaine 1958- *WhoWrEP 92*
Zuckerman, Arie Jeremy 1932- *WhoScE 91-1*
Zuckerman, Burt M. 1933- *St&PR 93*
Zuckerman, Edward Paul 1942- *WhoE 93*
Zuckerman, Emily J. *Law&B 92*
Zuckerman, Frederick William 1934- *St&PR 93, WhoAm 92*
Zuckerman, George D. *Law&B 92*
Zuckerman, Gilbert George 1932- *St&PR 93*

Zuckerman, Harriet 1937- *ConAu 136, WhoAm 92*
Zuckerman, Jeffrey Ira 1950- *WhoAm 92, WhoE 93*
Zuckerman, John Vitto 1918- *WhoSSW 93*
Zuckerman, Kenneth Stuart 1946- *WhoSSW 93*
Zuckerman, Leo 1930- *St&PR 93*
Zuckerman, Linda Dix 1956- *WhoE 93*
Zuckerman, M. Michael *BioIn 17*
Zuckerman, Marc A. 1951- *St&PR 93*
Zuckerman, Marilyn 1925- *WhoWrEP 92*
Zuckerman, Martin H. 1942- *St&PR 93*
Zuckerman, Martin Harvey 1942- *WhoAm 92*
Zuckerman, Marvin 1928- *WhoAm 92*
Zuckerman, Mary Ellen 1954- *ConAu 137*
Zuckerman, Mary Ellen Waller 1954- *WhoE 93*
Zuckerman, Mitchell 1946- *St&PR 93, WhoAm 92*
Zuckerman, Mortimer B. *BioIn 17*
Zuckerman, Mortimer Benjamin 1937- *WhoAm 92*
Zuckerman, Nancy Ann 1962- *WhoAmW 93*
Zuckerman, Philip Warren 1951- *WhoE 93*
Zuckerman, Richard M. *Law&B 92*
Zuckerman, Robert S. *Law&B 92*
Zuckerman, Ronald K. 1942- *St&PR 93*
Zuckerman, Stuart 1933- *WhoAm 92*
Zuckermann, Doron Peter 1952- *WhoWor 93*
Zuckermann, Lydia 1919- *DcMexL*
Zuckermann, Rudolf 1910- *WhoWor 93*
Zuckermann, Wolfgang (Joachim) 1922- *ConAu 139*
Zuckernik, Burton 1925- *St&PR 93*
Zucker Seeman, Helene *WhoE 93*
Zuckert, Donald Mack 1934- *St&PR 93, WhoAm 92*
Zuckert, Leon 1904- *Baker 92*
Zuckert, Michael Steven *Law&B 92*
Zuckerwar, Richard J. 1944- *St&PR 93*
Zuckman, Harvey Lyle 1934- *WhoAm 92*
Zuckmayer, Carl 1896-1977 *BioIn 17, DcLB 124 [port]*
Zuckrow, Edward 1941- *WhoWrEP 92*
Zudeck, Darryl S. 1961- *BioIn 17*
Zudov, Igor Alexeyevich 1942- *WhoWor 93*
Zuege, David A. 1941- *St&PR 93*
Zuehlke, Carl William 1916- *WhoE 93*
Zuehlke, Gus A. 1921- *St&PR 93*
Zuehlke, Richard William 1933- *WhoAm 92*
Zuelli, Guglielmo 1859-1941 *Baker 92*
Zuendt, William F. 1946- *WhoAm 92*
Zuercher, Joseph Clement 1956- *St&PR 93*
Zuern, David E. 1949- *St&PR 93*
Zuern, David Ernest 1949- *WhoAm 92*
Zuev, Yuri Anatolievich 1949- *WhoWor 93*
Zuffa, Gian Gaspare 1943- *WhoScE 91-3*
Zufryden, Fred S. 1943- *WhoAm 92*
Zugby, Robert Coury 1941- *WhoE 93*
Zugravescu, Alexandra *BioIn 17*
Zugsmith, Albert 1910- *MiSFD 9*
Zuhdi, Nazih 1925- *WhoSSW 93, WhoWor 93*
Zuhrt, Rainer Werner Christian 1932- *WhoWor 93*
Zuidema, George Dale 1928- *WhoAm 92*
Zuidema, Onno T. *Law&B 92*
zu Irmelshausen, Charles Henneberg *ScF&FL 92*
Zuk, Beverly C. *ScF&FL 92*
Zuk, Georges *WhoCanL 92*
Zuk, Nicholas W. *Law&B 92*
Zuk, Tomasz 1921- *WhoScE 91-4, WhoWor 93*
Zukauckas, Anthony Victor 1937- *St&PR 93*
Zuker, Howard *MiSFD 9*
Zuker, Michael 1949- *WhoAm 92*
Zukerman, Allan Benjamin 1938- *St&PR 93*
Zukerman, Eugenia *BioIn 17*
Zukerman, Eugenia 1944- *Baker 92*
Zukerman, Jay 1938- *St&PR 93*
Zukerman, Michael 1940- *WhoE 93, WhoWor 93*
Zukerman, Morris E. 1944- *WhoAm 92*
Zukerman, Pinchas 1948- *Baker 92, WhoAm 92, WhoWor 93*
Zukerman, Sidney 1929- *St&PR 93*
Zukin, Jane 1948- *WhoWrEP 92*
Zukin, Jane Shetzer 1948- *WhoAmW 93*
Zukin, Stephen Randolph 1948- *WhoE 93*
Zukof, Debra Leigh 1957- *WhoAmW 93*
Zukofsky, Louis 1904-1978 *AmWrS3, BioIn 17, ConAu 39NR*
Zukofsky, Paul 1943- *Baker 92*
Zukotynski, Thaddeus 1855-1912 *PolBiDi*
Zukowski, Janet M. *Law&B 92*
Zukowski, Kazimierz 1928- *WhoScE 91-4*
Zukowski, Kimberly Joan 1962- *WhoE 93*
Zukowski, Leszek Stanislaw 1929- *WhoScE 91-4*
Zukowski, Virginia A. 1950- *WhoAmW 93*
Zukowski, Walter Henry 1914- *WhoAm 92, WhoE 93*
Zukowsky, John Robert 1948- *WhoAm 92*
Zukrigl, Kurt 1931- *WhoWor 93*
Zukrowski, Wojciech 1916- *WhoWor 93*
Zulaika, Joseba 1948- *ConAu 137*
Zulawski, Andrzej 1940- *DrEEuF*
Zulch, Joan Carolyn 1931- *WhoAm 92*
Zulch, Johnstephen 1951- *St&PR 93*
Zulficar, Said Ibrahim 1935- *WhoUN 92*
Zulfikar Ghose 1935- *BioIn 17*
Zulim, Thomas M. *Law&B 92*
Zulker, Charles Bates 1926- *WhoAm 92*
Zullah, Mohammad Afzal 1928- *WhoWor 93*
Zulli, Joseph Dennis *Law&B 92*
Zullig, Greg Peter 1959- *WhoSSW 93*
Zullig, Irwin P. 1927- *St&PR 93*
Zullig, Walter E., Jr. *Law&B 92*
Zulliger, Hans W. 1945- *WhoScE 91-4*
zu Loewenstein-Wertheim-Freudenberg, Rupert Louis Ferdinand 1933- *WhoWor 93*
Zultowski, Walter Henry 1951- *WhoIns 93*
Zulu, Alexander Grey 1924- *WhoAfr, WhoWor 93*
Zulu, Itibari Masekela 1953- *WhoWrEP 92*
Zulueta, Leopoldo Pastelero 1945- *WhoWor 93*
Zumba, Charles F. 1931- *St&PR 93*
Zumbano, Anthony Ralph 1947- *WhoSSW 93*
Zumbe, Albert 1953- *WhoWor 93*
Zumberge, James H. d1992 *NewYTBS 92 [port]*
Zumberge, James Herbert 1923-1992 *BioIn 17*
Zumbiel, Robert W. 1932- *St&PR 93*
Zumbiel, Thomas James 1933- *St&PR 93*
Zumbo, Thomas Duffy d1991 *BioIn 17*
Zumeta, Bertram William 1919- *WhoAm 92*
Zumino, Bruno 1923- *WhoAm 92*
Zumo, Billie Thomas 1936- *WhoAmW 93*
Zumoff, Barnett 1926- *WhoE 93*
Zumpano, Giuseppe 1929- *WhoScE 91-3*
Zumpe, Doris 1940- *WhoAmW 93*
Zumpe, Herman 1850-1903 *Baker 92*
Zumpe, Hermann 1850-1903 *OxDcOp*
Zumsteeg, Johann Rudolf 1760-1802 *Baker 92, OxDcOp*
Zumsteg, Stephen William 1946- *St&PR 93*
Zumthor, Paul 1915- *WhoCanL 92*
Zumwalt, Elmo, Jr. 1920- *ColdWar 1 [port]*
Zumwalt, Elmo Russell 1920- *HarEnMi*
Zumwalt, Elmo Russell, Jr. 1920- *St&PR 93, WhoAm 92*
Zumwalt, Judith Ann Atkins 1939- *WhoWrEP 92*
Zumwalt, Kenneth D. d1992 *NewYTBS 92*
Zumwalt, Richard Dowling 1912- *WhoAm 92*
Zumwalt, Roger Carl 1943- *WhoAm 92*
Zuna, William Frank 1943- *WhoSSW 93*
Zunde, Steven 1955- *St&PR 93*
Zundel, Carolyn Steidley 1940- *WhoAmW 93*
Zundel, Georg 1931- *WhoWor 93*
Zundel, John 1815-1882 *Baker 92*
Zundel, Rolf 1929- *WhoScE 91-3*
Zunenshine, David *St&PR 93*
Zung, William Wen-Kwai 1929- *WhoWor 93*
Zunick, Franklin Harvey 1939- *WhoE 93*
Zuniga, Frank 1936- *MiSFD 9*
Zuniga, Olivia 1916- *DcMexL*
Zunino, Frank Joseph 1933- *St&PR 93*
Zunino, Natalia 1937- *WhoE 93*
Zunkel, Darrell *BioIn 17*
Zunker, Sharon Jienell 1943- *WhoAmW 93, WhoSSW 93, WhoWor 93*
Zunz, Lyonel E. 1921- *St&PR 93*
Zunz, Olivier Jean 1946- *WhoAm 92*
Zupanic, Richard Louis 1944- *St&PR 93*
Zupko, Arthur George 1916- *WhoAm 92*
Zupko, Ramon 1932- *Baker 92*
Zupkus, Ellen Ciccone 1954- *WhoAmW 93*
Zupnick, Elliot 1923- *WhoAm 92*
Zupnik, David A. 1940- *St&PR 93*
Zupon, Mark 1956- *St&PR 93*
Zupringer, Jeremy *ScF&FL 92*
Zupsic, Matthew Michael 1950- *WhoE 93, WhoEmL 93, WhoWor 93*
Zu Putlitz, Gisbert 1931- *WhoScE 91-3*
Zur, Tadeusz Waclaw 1925- *WhoScE 91-4*
Zurav, Edward H. 1956- *WhoE 93*
Zuraw, Kathleen Ann 1960- *WhoAmW 93, WhoEmL 93, WhoWor 93*
Zurawicz, Edward 1947- *WhoScE 91-4*
Zurawski, Vincent R., Jr. 1946- *St&PR 93*
Zurawski, Vincent Richard, Jr. 1946- *WhoAm 92*
Zurawski, Wladyslaw 1901-1989 *PolBiDi*
Zurbaran, Francisco de 1598-1664 *BioIn 17*
Zurcher, Ulrich 1931- *WhoScE 91-4*
Zurdo, Jean Paul *WhoScE 91-3*
Zureick, Abdul-Hamid 1956- *WhoSSW 93*
Zurek, Janusz *WhoScE 91-4*
Zurek, Richard R. 1956- *St&PR 93*
Zurek, Wojciech Hubert 1951- *WhoAm 92*
Zurfluh, Charles Victor 1942- *St&PR 93*
Zur Hausen, Harald *BioIn 17*
Zur Hausen, Harald 1936- *WhoScE 91-3*
Zurheide, Charles Henry 1923- *WhoAm 92*
Zurhellen, Joseph Owen 1920-1990 *BioIn 17*
Zurich, John C. 1951- *St&PR 93*
Zurick, Jack 1952- *WhoE 93*
Zurier, Robert Burton 1934- *WhoAm 92, WhoE 93*
Zurilla, William A. 1952- *St&PR 93*
Zurinaga, Marcos *MiSFD 9*
Zurkowski, Paul George 1932- *WhoAm 92*
Zurliene, Donald H., Jr. 1955- *St&PR 93*
zur Loye, Dieter 1928- *WhoAm 92*
Zurmuhle, Robert Walter 1933- *WhoAm 92*
Zur Muhlen, Raimund von 1854-1931 *Baker 92*
Zurna, Carol Ann 1942- *WhoAmW 93*
Zur Nieden, Albrecht 1819-1873 *Baker 92*
Zurowski, Adam 1929- *WhoScE 91-4*
Zurro, Bernardo 1948- *WhoWor 93*
Zurschmiede, W. Tom, Jr. 1926- *St&PR 93*
Zuschek, Mark A. *Law&B 92*
Zuschlag, Harold 1944- *St&PR 93*
Zuschlag, Richard Emery 1948- *WhoSSW 93*
Zuschneid, Karl 1854-1926 *Baker 92*
Zusman, Lee *St&PR 93*
Zuspan, Frederick Paul 1922- *WhoAm 92*
Zuspan, William Harris 1939- *St&PR 93, WhoSSW 93*
Zussman, Jack *WhoScE 91-1*
Zussy, Nancy Louise 1947- *WhoAm 92, WhoAmW 93*
Zutaut, Tom *BioIn 17*
Zuth, Josef 1879-1932 *Baker 92*
Zutshi, Balkrishan 1938- *WhoUN 92*
Zutter, John D., Jr. 1948- *St&PR 93*
Zutter, John Daniel, Jr. 1948- *WhoAm 92*
Zuzelo, Edward A. 1924- *St&PR 93*
Zuzov, Janice Claire 1963- *WhoE 93*
Zuzzio, Elizabeth Ann 1946- *WhoE 93*
Zverev, Nikolai 1832-1893 *Baker 92*
Zvetina, James Raymond 1913- *WhoWor 93*
Zvezdotchetov, Konstantin 1958- *BioIn 17*
Zvobgo, Eddison Jonas 1935- *WhoAfr*
Zvolensky, John, Jr. 1941- *WhoAm 92*
Zvonar, Joseph Leopold 1824-1865 *Baker 92*
Zvonimir, Demetrios d1089 *OxDcByz*
Zwaal, Pete 1935- *WhoWor 93*
Zwaan, C. *WhoScE 91-3*
Zwaan, Pieter C. 1928- *WhoScE 91-3*
Zwach, John M. 1907-1990 *BioIn 17*
Zwack, Henry Francis 1952- *WhoEmL 93*
Zwack, Peter *BioIn 17*
Zwagemaker, Abraham Cornelis 1946- *WhoWor 93*
Zwahlen, Fred Casper, Jr. 1924- *WhoWor 93*
Zwahlen, Jean 1931- *WhoWor 93*
Zwain, Laurence Michael 1952- *St&PR 93*
Zwakenberg, Larry W. 1947- *St&PR 93*
Zwane, Ambrose Phesheya 1924- *WhoAfr*
Zwanzig, Robert Walter 1928- *WhoAm 92*
Zwanziger, Daniel 1935- *WhoE 93*
Zwart, D. 1930- *WhoScE 91-3*
Zwart, H.J. *WhoScE 91-3*
Zwart, Peernel 1930- *WhoScE 91-3*
Zwass, Vladimir 1946- *WhoAm 92, WhoWor 93*
Zwaveling, A. 1927- *WhoScE 91-3*
Zwecker, Irving 1927- *St&PR 93*
Zweers, Bernard 1854-1924 *Baker 92*
Zweiback, A. Martin *WhoWor 93*
Zweibaum, Alain *WhoScE 91-2*
Zweibel, Joel Burton 1935- *WhoAm 92*
Zweier, Richard Joseph, Jr. 1951- *WhoE 93*
Zweifel, Richard George 1926- *WhoAm 92*
Zweig, Ellen 1947- *WhoWrEP 92*
Zweig, Fritz 1893-1984 *Baker 92*
Zweig, George 1937- *WhoAm 92*
Zweig, M.E. *St&PR 93*
Zweig, Philip Leon 1946- *WhoWrEP 92*
Zweig, Stanley 1929- *St&PR 93*
Zweig, Stefan 1881-1942 *BioIn 17, DcLB 118 [port], OxDcOp*
Zweigart, Jacqueline 1934- *St&PR 93*
Zweigart, Pierre Max 1925- *St&PR 93*
Zweigenthal, Gail 1944- *WhoAmW 93*
Zweiman, Beverly Heafitz 1944- *WhoAmW 93*
Zweiman, Burton 1931- *WhoAm 92*
Zweizig, Lawrence C. d1991 *BioIn 17*
Zwenk, Hugo 1938- *WhoScE 91-3*
Zwerdling, Alex 1932- *ScF&FL 92, WhoAm 92*
Zwerg, Charles Alvin 1936- *St&PR 93*
Zwerger, Lisbeth *BioIn 17*
Zwerger, Lisbeth 1954- *MajAI [port]*
Zwerin, Charlotte *MiSFD 9*
Zwerling, Frederick 1931- *St&PR 93*
Zwerling, Gary L. 1949- *St&PR 93*
Zwerling, Gary Leslie 1949- *WhoAm 92*
Zwern, Linda Gail 1945- *WhoAm 92*
Zwetsloot, H.J.C. *WhoScE 91-3*
Zwick, Charles J. *BioIn 17*
Zwick, Charles J. 1926- *St&PR 93*
Zwick, Deborah Sue 1955- *WhoAmW 93*
Zwick, Edward *BioIn 17*
Zwick, Edward 1952- *MiSFD 9*
Zwick, Joel *MiSFD 9*
Zwick, Peter 1941- *WhoScE 91-3*
Zwicke, Dianne Lynn 1952- *WhoAmW 93*
Zwicker, Ralph W. 1903-1991 *BioIn 17*
Zwickler, Phil 1955-1991 *BioIn 17*
Zwicky, Kathleen M. 1946- *St&PR 93*
Zwicky, Peter Ernst 1953- *WhoWor 93*
Zwiebe, Sherman 1942- *St&PR 93*
Zwiebel, Alan Howard 1938- *WhoAm 92*
Zwiebel, Malvina Dee 1943- *St&PR 93*
Zwiebel, Marie Bee 1934- *WhoAmW 93*
Zwiebel, Sherman 1942- *St&PR 93*
Zwiener, David K. 1954- *St&PR 93*
Zwiep, Donald Nelson 1924- *WhoAm 92, WhoE 93*
Zwiercan, Gary A. 1942- *St&PR 93*
Zwierzak, Andrzej K. 1931- *WhoScE 91-4*
Zwierzchowski, Henryk 1926- *WhoScE 91-4*
Zwiesler, Hans-Joachim Hermann 1957- *WhoWor 93*
Zwilich, Ellen Taaffe 1939- *Baker 92, BioIn 17, WhoAm 92, WhoAmW 93*
Zwinge, Randall James Hamilton 1928- *WhoAm 92*
Zwingli, John C. 1956- *St&PR 93*
Zwink, Timothy Ashley 1949- *WhoWrEP 92*
Zwintscher, Bruno 1838-1905 *Baker 92*
Zwiren, Jan Marie 1944- *WhoAm 92, WhoAmW 93*
Zwirko, Franciszek 1895-1932 *PolBiDi*
Zwislocki, Jozef John 1922- *WhoAm 92*
Zwit, Joan Zaworski *Law&B 92*
Zwoyer, Eugene Milton 1926- *WhoAm 92*
Zwygart, Kathy Ann 1954- *WhoAmW 93*
Zwyssig, Alberich 1808-1854 *Baker 92*
Zyberk, Elizabeth Plater- 1950- *BioIn 17*
Zyborski, Jacek 1929- *WhoScE 91-4*
Zych, Leonard A. 1948- *St&PR 93*
Zychowicz, Ralph Charles 1948- *WhoEmL 93*
Zyczkowski, Michal J. 1930- *WhoScE 91-4*
Zygadenos, Euthymios *OxDcByz*
Zygadlo, Tomasz 1947- *DrEEuF*
Zygmund, Antoni d1992 *NewYTBS 92*
Zygmund, Antoni 1900-1992 *BioIn 17*
Zygmunt, I 1467-1548 *PolBiDi*
Zygmunt, II 1520-1572 *PolBiDi*
Zygmunt, III 1566-1632 *PolBiDi*
Zygmunt, W. John 1945- *St&PR 93*
Zygmunt, Zielinski 1939- *WhoWor 93*
Zygourakis, Themistocles Nicos 1957- *WhoWor 93*
Zygulska-Mach, Helena 1926- *WhoScE 91-4*
Zykan, Otto M. 1935- *Baker 92*
Zyl, Robert Van *St&PR 93*
Zyla, Gregory Joseph 1949- *WhoWrEP 92*
Zyla, Mark Lawrence 1960- *WhoSSW 93*
Zylicz, Jan 1932- *WhoScE 91-4*
Zylicz, Maciej 1953- *WhoScE 91-4*
Zylis-Gara, Teresa 1935- *Baker 92*
Zylis-Gara, Teresa Gerarda 1935- *WhoAm 92*
Zylstra, Stanley James 1943- *WhoAm 92*
Zyne, Yasmine Beatrice *Law&B 92*
Zyroff, Ellen Slotoroff 1946- *WhoAmW 93, WhoEmL 93, WhoWor 93*
Zyromski, Jean 1890-1975 *BioIn 17*
Zysblat, William Larry 1950- *WhoE 93*
Zyskowski, James C. *Law&B 92*
Zyskowski, Kathleen Anne 1953- *WhoAmW 93*
Zywicki, Robert Albert 1930- *WhoAm 92*
Zywny, Wojciech 1756-1840 *PolBiDi*